Profiles
of
Pennsylvania

2013
Third Edition

Profiles
of
Pennsylvania

A UNIVERSAL REFERENCE BOOK

Grey House
Publishing

PUBLISHER: Leslie Mackenzie
EDITORIAL DIRECTOR: Laura Mars
EDITOR: David Garoogian
MARKETING DIRECTOR: Jessica Moody

Grey House Publishing, Inc.
4919 Route 22
Amenia, NY 12501
518.789.8700
FAX 845.373.6390
www.greyhouse.com
e-mail: books @greyhouse.com

While every effort has been made to ensure the reliability of the information presented in this publication, Grey House Publishing neither guarantees the accuracy of the data contained herein nor assumes any responsibility for errors, omissions or discrepancies. Grey House accepts no payment for listing; inclusion in the publication of any organization, agency, institution, publication, service or individual does not imply endorsement of the editors or publisher.

Errors brought to the attention of the publisher and verified to the satisfaction of the publisher will be corrected in future editions.

First edition published 2006
Printed in Canada

ISBN: 978-1-59237-926-2

Table of Contents

Introduction

This is the third edition of *Profiles of Pennsylvania—Facts, Figures & Statistics for 3,787 Populated Places in Pennsylvania.* As with the other titles in our *State Profiles* series, it was built with content from Grey House Publishing's award-winning *Profiles of America*—a 4-volume compilation of data on more than 42,000 places in the United States. We have updated and included the Pennsylvania chapter from *Profiles of America,* and added several new chapters of demographic information and ranking sections, so that *Profiles of Pennsylvania* is the most comprehensive portrait of the state of Pennsylvania ever published.

Profiles of Pennsylvania provides data on all populated communities and counties in the state of Pennsylvania for which the US Census provides individual statistics. This edition also includes profiles of 477 unincorporated places based on US Census data by zip code and, for the first time, includes communities that span multiple zip codes.

This premier reference work includes five major sections that cover everything from **Education** to **Ethnic Backgrounds** to **Climate**. All sections include **Comparative Statistics** or **Rankings**. New to this edtion is a section called **About Pennsylvania** at the front of the book, comprised of detailed narrative and colorful photos and maps. Here is an overview of each section:

1. About Pennsylvania
This NEW 4-color section gives the researcher a real sense of the state and its history. It includes a Photo Gallery, and comprehensive sections on Pennsylvania's Government, Land and Natural Resources, and Demographic Maps. With charts and maps, these 67 pages help to anchor the researcher to the state, both physically and politically.

2. Profiles
This section, organized by county, gives detailed profiles of 3,787 places plus 67 counties, based on Census 2010 and data from the American Community Survey. In addition, we have added current government statistics and original research, so that these profiles pull together statistical and descriptive information on every Census-recognized place in the state. Major fields of information include:

Geography	*Housing*	*Education*	*Religion*
Ancestry	*Transportation*	*Population*	*Climate*
Economy	*Industry*	*Health*	

In addition to place profiles, this section includes an **Alphabetical Place Index** and **Comparative Statistics** that compare Pennsylvania's 100 largest communities by dozens of data points.

3. Education
This section begins with an **Educational State Profile,** summarizing number of schools, students, diplomas granted and educational dollars spent. Following the state profile are **School District Rankings** on 16 topics ranging from *Teacher/Student Ratios* to *High School Drop-Out Rates.* Following these rankings are statewide *National Assessment of Educational Progress (NAEP)* results and data from the *Pennsylvania System of School Assessment (PSSA)*—an overview of student performance by subject, including easy-to-read charts and graphs.

4. Ancestry and Ethnicity
This section provides a detailed look at the ancestral, Hispanic and racial makeup of Pennsylvania's 200+ ethnic categories. Profiles are included for the state, for all 67 counties, and for all places with 50,000 or more residents. In the ranking section, data is displayed three ways: 1) by number, based on all places regardless of population; 2) by percent, based on all places regardless of population; 3) by percent, based on places with populations of 50,000 or more. You will discover, for example, that Hampden Township has the greatest number of *Egyptians* in the state (600), and that 29.2% of the population of Lancaster are of *Puerto Rican* ancestry.

5. Climate

Each state chapter includes a State Summary, three colorful maps and profiles of both National and Cooperative Weather Stations. In addition, you'll find Weather Station Rankings with hundreds of interesting details, such as Erie International Airport reporting the highest annual snowfall with 99.6 inches.

This section also includes Significant Storm Event data from January 2000 through December 2009. Here you will learn that a flash flood caused $100 million in property damage in Luzerne County in September 2004 and that excessive heat was responsible for 24 deaths in Southeastern Pennsylvania in August 2006.

Note: The extensive **User's Guide** that follows this Introduction is segmented into four sections and examines, in some detail, each data field in the individual profiles and comparative sections for all chapters. It provides sources for all data points and statistical definitions as necessary.

User's Guide: Profiles

Places Covered

All 67 counties.

2,561 incorporated municipalities and minor civil divisions. Includes 1,544 townships, 956 boroughs, 57 cities, three municipalities, and one town.

749 census designated places (CDP). The U.S. Bureau of the Census defines a CDP as "a statistical entity, defined for each decennial census according to Census Bureau guidelines, comprising a densely settled concentration of population that is not within an incorporated place, but is locally identified by a name. CDPs are delineated cooperatively by state and local officials and the Census Bureau, following Census Bureau guidelines.

477 unincorporated communities. The communities included have statistics for their ZIP Code Tabulation Area (ZCTA) available from the Census Bureau. They are referred to as "postal areas." A ZCTA is a statistical entity developed by the Census Bureau to approximate the delivery area for a US Postal Service 5-digit or 3-digit ZIP Code in the US and Puerto Rico. A ZCTA is an aggregation of census blocks that have the same predominant ZIP Code associated with the mailing addresses in the Census Bureau's Master Address File. Thus, the Postal Service's delivery areas have been adjusted to encompass whole census blocks so that the Census Bureau can tabulate census data for the ZCTAs. ZCTAs do not include all ZIP Codes used for mail delivery and therefore do not precisely depict the area within which mail deliveries associated with that ZIP Code occur. Additionally, some areas that are known by a unique name, although they are part of a larger incorporated place, are also included as "postal areas."

For a more in-depth discussion of geographic areas, please refer to the Census Bureau's Geographic Areas Reference Manual at http://www.census.gov/geo/www/garm.html.

Important Notes

- *Profiles of Pennsylvania* uses the term "community" to refer to all places except counties. The term "county" is used to refer to counties and county-equivalents. All places are defined as of the 2010 Census.

- Several states, including Pennsylvania, have incorporated municipalities and minor civil divisions in the same county with the same name. Those communities are given separate entries (e.g. Addison, Pennsylvania, in Somerset County will be listed under both the borough and township of Addison).

- In each community profile, only school districts that have schools that are physically located within the community are shown. In addition, statistics for each school district cover the entire district, regardless of the physical location of the schools within the district.

- Special care should be taken when interpreting certain statistics for communities containing large colleges or universities. College students were counted as residents of the area in which they were living while attending college (as they have been since the 1950 census). One effect this may have is skewing the figures for population, income, housing, and educational attainment.

- Some information (e.g. unemployment rates) is available for both counties and individual communities. Other information is available for just counties (e.g. election results), or just individual communities (e.g. local newspapers).

- Some statistical information is available only for larger communities. In addition, the larger places are more apt to have services such as newspapers, airports, school districts, etc.

- For the most complete information on any community, you should also check the entry for the county in which the community is located. In addition, more information and services will be listed under the larger places in the county.

Information for Incorporated Communities and Census Designated Places

PHYSICAL CHARACTERISTICS

Place Type: Lists the type of place (city, town, village, borough, special city, CDP, township, plantation, gore, district, grant, location, reservation, or postal area). *Source: U.S. Census Bureau, Census 2010 and U.S. Postal Service, City State File.*

Land and Water Area: Land and water area in square miles. *Source: U.S. Census Bureau, Census 2010.*

Latitude and Longitude: Latitude and longitude in degrees. *Source: U.S. Census Bureau, Census 2010.*

Elevation: Elevation in feet. *Source: U.S. Geological Survey, Geographic Names Information System (GNIS).*

HISTORY

History: Historical information. *Source: Columbia University Press, The Columbia Gazetteer of North America; Original research.*

POPULATION

Population: 1990, 2000 and 2010 figures are a 100% count of population. *Source: U.S. Census Bureau, Census 1990, 2000 and 2010.*

Race/Hispanic Origin: Figures are from Census 2010 and include the U.S. Census Bureau categories of White alone; Black alone; Asian alone; American Indian/Alaska Native alone; Native Hawaiian/Other Pacific Islander alone; Hispanic of any race. Alone refers to the fact that these figures are not in combination with any other race.

The concept of race, as used by the Census Bureau, reflects self-identification by people according to the race or races with which they most closely identify. These categories are socio-political constructs and should not be interpreted as being scientific or anthropological in nature. Furthermore, the race categories include both racial and national-origin groups.

- **African American or Black:** A person having origins in any of the Black racial groups of Africa. It includes people who indicated their race(s) as "Black, African Am., or Negro" or reported entries such as African American, Kenyan, Nigerian, or Haitian.
- **American Indian or Alaska Native:** A person having origins in any of the original peoples of North and South America (including Central America) and who maintains tribal affiliation or community attachment. This category includes people who indicated their race(s) as "American Indian or Alaska Native" or reported their enrolled or principal tribe, such as Navajo, Blackfeet, Inupiat, Yup'ik, or Central American Indian groups or South American Indian groups.
- **Asian:** A person having origins in any of the original peoples of the Far East, Southeast Asia, or the Indian subcontinent, including, for example, Cambodia, China, India, Japan, Korea, Malaysia, Pakistan, the Philippine Islands, Thailand, and Vietnam. It includes people who indicated their race(s) as "Asian" or reported entries such as "Asian Indian," "Chinese," "Filipino," "Korean," "Japanese," "Vietnamese," and "Other Asian" or provided other detailed Asian responses.
- **Native Hawaiian or Other Pacific Islander:** A person having origins in any of the original peoples of Hawaii, Guam, Samoa, or other Pacific Islands. It includes people who indicated their race(s) as "Pacific Islander" or reported entries such as "Native Hawaiian," "Guamanian or Chamorro," "Samoan," and "Other Pacific Islander" or provided other detailed Pacific Islander responses.
- **White:** A person having origins in any of the original peoples of Europe, the Middle East, or North Africa. It includes people who indicated their race(s) as "White" or reported entries such as Irish, German, Italian, Lebanese, Arab, Moroccan, or Caucasian.
- **Hispanic:** The data on the Hispanic or Latino population were derived from answers to a question that was asked of all people. The terms "Spanish," "Hispanic origin," and "Latino" are used interchangeably. Some respondents identify with all three terms while others may identify with only one of these three specific terms. Hispanics or Latinos who identify with the terms "Spanish," "Hispanic," or "Latino" are those who classify themselves in one of the specific Spanish, Hispanic, or Latino categories listed on the questionnaire ("Mexican," "Puerto Rican," or "Cuban") as well as those who indicate that they are "other Spanish/Hispanic/Latino." People who do not identify with one of the specific origins listed on the

questionnaire but indicate that they are "other Spanish/Hispanic/Latino" are those whose origins are from Spain, the Spanish-speaking countries of Central or South America, the Dominican Republic, or people identifying themselves generally as Spanish, Spanish-American, Hispanic, Hispano, Latino, and so on. All write-in responses to the "other Spanish/Hispanic/Latino" category were coded. Origin can be viewed as the heritage, nationality group, lineage, or country of birth of the person or the person's parents or ancestors before their arrival in the United States. People who identify their origin as Spanish, Hispanic, or Latino may be of any race.

Population Density: Total population divided by the land area in square miles. *Source: U.S. Census Bureau, Census 2010.*

Average Household Size: Number of persons in the average household. *Source: U.S. Census Bureau, Census 2010.*

Median Age: Median age of the population. *Source: U.S. Census Bureau, Census 2010.*

Male/Female Ratio: Number of males per 100 females. *Source: U.S. Census Bureau, Census 2010.*

Marital Status: Percentage of population never married, now married, widowed, or divorced. *Source: U.S. Census Bureau, American Community Survey, 2006-2010 Five-Year Estimates.*

The marital status classification refers to the status at the time of enumeration. Data on marital status are tabulated only for the population 15 years old and over. Each person was asked whether they were "Now married," "Widowed," "Divorced," or "Never married." Couples who live together (for example, people in common-law marriages) were able to report the marital status they considered to be the most appropriate.

- **Never married.** Never married includes all people who have never been married, including people whose only marriage(s) was annulled.
- **Now married.** All people whose current marriage has not ended by widowhood or divorce. This category includes people defined as "separated."
- **Widowed.** This category includes widows and widowers who have not remarried.
- **Divorced.** This category includes people who are legally divorced and who have not remarried.

Foreign Born: Percentage of population who were not U.S. citizens at birth. Foreign-born people are those who indicated they were either a U.S. citizen by naturalization or they were not a citizen of the United States. *Source: U.S. Census Bureau, American Community Survey, 2006-2010 Five-Year Estimates.*

Ancestry: Largest ancestry groups reported (up to five). The data includes persons who report multiple ancestries. For example, if a person reported being Irish and Italian, they would be included in both categories. Thus, the sum of the percentages may be greater than 100%. *Source: U.S. Census Bureau, American Community Survey, 2006-2010 Five-Year Estimates.*

The data represent self-classification by people according to the ancestry group or groups with which they most closely identify. Ancestry refers to a person's ethnic origin or descent, "roots," heritage, or the place of birth of the person, the person's parents, or their ancestors before their arrival in the United States. Some ethnic identities, such as Egyptian or Polish, can be traced to geographic areas outside the United States, while other ethnicities such as Pennsylvania German or Cajun evolved in the United States.

The ancestry question was intended to provide data for groups that were not included in the Hispanic origin and race questions. Therefore, although data on all groups are collected, the ancestry data shown in these tabulations are for non-Hispanic and non-race groups. *See Race/Hispanic Origin for information on Hispanic and race groups.*

ECONOMY

Unemployment Rate: Unemployment rate as of August 2012. Includes all civilians age 16 or over who were unemployed and looking for work. *Source: U.S. Department of Labor, Bureau of Labor Statistics, Local Area Unemployment Statistics.*

Total Civilian Labor Force: Total civilian labor force as of August 2012. Includes all civilians age 16 or over who were either employed, or unemployed and looking for work. *Source: U.S. Department of Labor, Bureau of Labor Statistics, Local Area Unemployment Statistics.*

Single-Family Building Permits Issued: Building permits issued for new single-family housing units in 2011. *Source: U.S. Census Bureau, Manufacturing and Construction Division.*

Multi-Family Building Permits Issued: Building permits issued for new multi-family housing units in 2011. *Source: U.S. Census Bureau, Manufacturing and Construction Division.*

Statistics on housing units authorized by building permits include housing units issued in local permit-issuing jurisdictions by a building or zoning permit. Not all areas of the country require a building or zoning permit. The statistics only represent those areas that do require a permit. Current surveys indicate that construction is undertaken for all but a very small percentage of housing units authorized by building permits. A major portion typically get under way during the month of permit issuance and most of the remainder begin within the three following months. Because of this lag, the housing unit authorization statistics do not represent the number of units actually put into construction for the period shown, and should therefore not be directly interpreted as "housing starts."

Statistics are based upon reports submitted by local building permit officials in response to a mail survey. They are obtained using Form C-404 const/www/c404.pdf, "Report of New Privately-Owned Residential Building or Zoning Permits Issued." When a report is not received, missing data are either (1) obtained from the Survey of Use of Permits (SUP) which is used to collect information on housing starts, or (2) imputed based on the assumption that the ratio of current month authorizations to those of a year ago should be the same for reporting and non-reporting places.

Employment by Occupation: Percentage of the employed civilian population 16 years and over in management, professional, service, sales, farming, construction, and production occupations. *Source: U.S. Census Bureau, American Community Survey, 2006-2010 Five-Year Estimates.*

- **Management** includes management, business, and financial operations occupations:
    Management occupations, except farmers and farm managers
    Farmers and farm managers
    Business and financial operations occupations:
        Business operations specialists
        Financial specialists

- **Professional** includes professional and related occupations:
    Computer and mathematical occupations
    Architecture and engineering occupations:
        Architects, surveyors, cartographers, and engineers
        Drafters, engineering, and mapping technicians
    Life, physical, and social science occupations
    Community and social services occupations
    Legal occupations
    Education, training, and library occupations
    Arts, design, entertainment, sports, and media occupations
    Healthcare practitioners and technical occupations:
        Health diagnosing and treating practitioners and technical occupations
        Health technologists and technicians

- **Service** occupations include:
    Healthcare support occupations
    Protective service occupations:
        Fire fighting, prevention, and law enforcement workers, including supervisors
        Other protective service workers, including supervisors
    Food preparation and serving related occupations
    Building and grounds cleaning and maintenance occupations
    Personal care and service occupations

- **Sales** and office occupations include:
    Sales and related occupations
    Office and administrative support occupations

- **Farming,** fishing, and forestry occupations

- **Construction,** extraction, and maintenance occupations include:

Construction and extraction occupations:
    Supervisors, construction, and extraction workers
    Construction trades workers
    Extraction workers
Installation, maintenance, and repair occupations

- **Production,** transportation, and material moving occupations include:
Production occupations
Transportation and material moving occupations:
    Supervisors, transportation, and material moving workers
    Aircraft and traffic control occupations
    Motor vehicle operators
    Rail, water, and other transportation occupations
    Material moving workers

INCOME

Per Capita Income: Per capita income is the mean income computed for every man, woman, and child in a particular group. It is derived by dividing the total income of a particular group by the total population in that group. Per capita income is rounded to the nearest whole dollar. *Source: U.S. Census Bureau, American Community Survey, 2006-2010 Five-Year Estimates.*

Median Household Income: Includes the income of the householder and all other individuals 15 years old and over in the household, whether they are related to the householder or not. The median divides the income distribution into two equal parts: one-half of the cases falling below the median income and one-half above the median. For households, the median income is based on the distribution of the total number of households including those with no income. Median income for households is computed on the basis of a standard distribution and is rounded to the nearest whole dollar. *Source: U.S. Census Bureau, American Community Survey, 2006-2010 Five-Year Estimates.*

Average Household Income: Average household income is obtained by dividing total household income by the total number of households. *Source: U.S. Census Bureau, American Community Survey, 2006-2010 Five-Year Estimates.*

Percent of Households with Income of $100,000 or more: Percent of households with income of $100,000 or more. *Source: U.S. Census Bureau, American Community Survey, 2006-2010 Five-Year Estimates.*

Poverty Rate: Percentage of population with income below the poverty level. Based on individuals for whom poverty status is determined. Poverty status was determined for all people except institutionalized people, people in military group quarters, people in college dormitories, and unrelated individuals under 15 years old. *Source: U.S. Census Bureau, American Community Survey, 2006-2010 Five-Year Estimates.*

TAXES

Total City Taxes Per Capita: Total city taxes collected divided by the population of the city. *Source: U.S. Census Bureau, State and Local Government Finances, 2009.*

Taxes include:

- Property Taxes
- Sales and Gross Receipts Taxes
- Federal Customs Duties
- General Sales and Gross Receipts Taxes
- Selective Sales Taxes (alcoholic beverages; amusements; insurance premiums; motor fuels; pari-mutuels; public utilities; tobacco products; other)
- License Taxes (alcoholic beverages; amusements; corporations in general; hunting and fishing; motor vehicles motor vehicle operators; public utilities; occupation and business, NEC; other)
- Income Taxes (individual income; corporation net income; other)
- Death and Gift
- Documentary & Stock Transfer
- Severance
- Taxes, NEC

Total City Property Taxes Per Capita: Total city property taxes collected divided by the population of the city. *Source: U.S. Census Bureau, State and Local Government Finances, 2009.*

Property Taxes include general property taxes, relating to property as a whole, taxed at a single rate or at classified rates according to the class of property. Property refers to real property (e.g. land and structures) as well as personal property; personal property can be either tangible (e.g. automobiles and boats) or intangible (e.g. bank accounts and stocks and bonds). Special property taxes, levied on selected types of property (e.g. oil and gas properties, house trailers, motor vehicles, and intangibles) and subject to rates not directly related to general property tax rates. Taxes based on income produced by property as a measure of its value on the assessment date.

EDUCATION

Educational Attainment: Figures show the percent of population age 25 and over with:

- **High school diploma (including GED) or higher:** Includes people whose highest degree is a high school diploma or its equivalent, people who attended college but did not receive a degree, and people who received a college, university, or professional degree.
- **Bachelor's degree or higher:** Includes people who received a bachelor's, master's, doctorate, or professional degree.
- **Master's degree or higher:** Includes people who received a master's, doctorate, or professional degree. *Source: U.S. Census Bureau, American Community Survey, 2006-2010 Five-Year Estimates.*

School Districts: Lists the name of each school district, the grade range (PK=pre-kindergarten; KG=kindergarten), the student enrollment, and the district headquarters' phone number. In each community profile, only school districts that have schools that are physically located within the community are shown. In addition, statistics for each school district cover the entire district, regardless of the physical location of the schools within the district. *Source: U.S. Department of Education, National Center for Educational Statistics, Directory of Public Elementary and Secondary Education Agencies, 2010-11.*

Four-year Colleges: Lists the name of each four-year college, the type of institution (private or public; for-profit or non-profit; religious affiliation; historically black), the total student enrollment (Fall 2010), the general telephone number, and the annual tuition and fees for full-time, first-time undergraduate students (in-state and out-of-state). *Source: U.S. Department of Education, National Center for Educational Statistics, IPEDS College Data, 2011-12.*

Two-year Colleges: Lists the name of each two-year college, the type of institution (private or public; for-profit or non-profit; religious affiliation; historically black), the total student enrollment (Fall 2010), the general telephone number, and the annual tuition and fees for full-time, first-time undergraduate students (in-state and out-of-state). *Source: U.S. Department of Education, National Center for Educational Statistics, IPEDS College Data, 2011-12.*

Vocational/Technical Schools: Lists the name of each vocational/technical school, the type of institution (private or public; for-profit or non-profit; religious affiliation; historically black), the total student enrollment (Fall 2010), the general telephone number, and the annual tuition and fees for full-time students. *Source: U.S. Department of Education, National Center for Educational Statistics, IPEDS College Data, 2011-12.*

HOUSING

Homeownership Rate: Percentage of housing units that are owner-occupied. *Source: U.S. Census Bureau, Census 2010.*

Median Home Value: Median value of all owner-occupied housing units as reported by the owner. Figures shown are 2010 estimates. *Source: U.S. Census Bureau, American Community Survey, 2006-2010 Five-Year Estimates.*

Median Rent: Median monthly contract rent on specified renter-occupied and specified vacant-for-rent units. Specified renter-occupied and specified vacant-for-rent units exclude 1-family houses on 10 acres or more. Contract rent is the monthly rent agreed to or contracted for, regardless of any furnishings, utilities, fees, meals, or services that may be included. For vacant units, it is the monthly rent asked for the rental unit at the time of enumeration. *Source: U.S. Census Bureau, American Community Survey, 2006-2010 Five-Year Estimates.*

Median Year Structure Built: Year structure built refers to when the building was first constructed, not when it was remodeled, added to, or converted. For mobile homes, houseboats, RVs, etc, the manufacturer's model year was assumed to be the year built. The data relate to the number of units built during the specified periods that were still in

existence at the time of enumeration. *Source: U.S. Census Bureau, American Community Survey, 2006-2010 Five-Year Estimates.*

HOSPITALS

Lists the hospital name and the number of licensed beds. *Source: Grey House Publishing, Directory of Hospital Personnel, 2010.*

SAFETY

Violent Crime Rate: Number of violent crimes reported per 10,000 population. Violent crimes include murder, forcible rape, robbery, and aggravated assault. *Source: Federal Bureau of Investigation, Uniform Crime Reports 2011*

Property Crime Rate: Number of property crimes reported per 10,000 population. Property crimes include burglary, larceny-theft, and motor vehicle theft. *Source: Federal Bureau of Investigation, Uniform Crime Reports 2011*

NEWSPAPERS

Lists the name, circulation and news focus of daily and weekly newspapers. Includes newspapers with offices located in the community profiled. *Source: MediaContactsPro 2010*

TRANSPORTATION

Commute to Work: Percentage of workers 16 years old and over that use the following means of transportation to commute to work: car; public transportation; walk; work from home. *Source: U.S. Census Bureau, American Community Survey, 2006-2010 Five-Year Estimates.*

The means of transportation data for some areas may show workers using modes of public transportation that are not available in those areas (e.g. subway or elevated riders in a metropolitan area where there actually is no subway or elevated service). This result is largely due to people who worked during the reference week at a location that was different from their usual place of work (such as people away from home on business in an area where subway service was available) and people who used more than one means of transportation each day but whose principal means was unavailable where they lived (e.g. residents of non-metropolitan areas who drove to the fringe of a metropolitan area and took the commuter railroad most of the distance to work).

Travel Time to Work: Travel time to work for workers 16 years old and over. Reported for the following intervals: less than 15 minutes; 15 to 30 minutes; 30 to 45 minutes; 45 to 60 minutes; 60 minutes or more. *Source: U.S. Census Bureau, American Community Survey, 2006-2010 Five-Year Estimates.*

Travel time to work refers to the total number of minutes that it usually took the person to get from home to work each day during the reference week. The elapsed time includes time spent waiting for public transportation, picking up passengers in carpools, and time spent in other activities related to getting to work.

Amtrak: Indicates if Amtrak rail or bus service is available. Please note that the cities being served continually change. *Source: National Railroad Passenger Corporation, Amtrak National Timetable, 2012*

AIRPORTS

Lists the local airport(s) along with type of service and hub size. *Source: U.S. Department of Transportation, Bureau of Transportation Statistics*

ADDITIONAL INFORMATION CONTACTS

The following phone numbers are provided as sources of additional information: Chambers of Commerce; Economic Development Agencies; and Convention & Visitors Bureaus. Efforts have been made to provide the most recent area codes. However, area code changes may have occurred in listed numbers. *Source: Original research.*

Information for Unincorporated Communities (Postal Areas)

PHYSICAL CHARACTERISTICS

Zip Code: The statistics that follow cover the corresponding ZIP Code Tabulation Area (ZCTA). A ZCTA is a statistical entity developed by the Census Bureau to approximate the delivery area for a US Postal Service 5-digit or 3-digit ZIP Code in the US and Puerto Rico. A ZCTA is an aggregation of census blocks that have the same predominant ZIP Code associated with the mailing addresses in the Census Bureau's Master Address File. Thus, the Postal Service's delivery areas have been adjusted to encompass whole census blocks so that the Census Bureau can tabulate census data for the ZCTAs. ZCTAs do not include all ZIP Codes used for mail delivery and therefore do not precisely depict the area within which mail deliveries associated with that ZIP Code occur. Additionally, some areas that are known by a unique name, although they are part of a larger incorporated place, are also included as "postal areas." *Source: U.S. Census Bureau, Census 2010 and U.S. Postal Service, City State File.*

Land and Water Area: Land and water area in square miles. *Source: U.S. Census Bureau, Census 2010.*

Latitude and Longitude: Latitude and longitude in degrees. *Source: U.S. Census Bureau, Census 2010.*

Elevation: Elevation in feet. *Source: U.S. Geological Survey, Geographic Names Information System (GNIS).*

POPULATION

Population: Figures are a 100% count of population. *Source: U.S. Census Bureau, Census 2010.*

Population Density: Total population divided by the land area in square miles. *Source: U.S. Census Bureau, Census 2010.*

Race/Hispanic Origin: Figures are from Census 2010 and include the U.S. Census Bureau categories of White alone; Black alone; Asian alone; American Indian/Alaska Native alone; Native Hawaiian/Other Pacific Islander alone; Hispanic of any race. Alone refers to the fact that these figures are not in combination with any other race.

The concept of race, as used by the Census Bureau, reflects self-identification by people according to the race or races with which they most closely identify. These categories are socio-political constructs and should not be interpreted as being scientific or anthropological in nature. Furthermore, the race categories include both racial and national-origin groups.

- **African American or Black:** A person having origins in any of the Black racial groups of Africa. It includes people who indicated their race(s) as "Black, African Am., or Negro" or reported entries such as African American, Kenyan, Nigerian, or Haitian.
- **American Indian or Alaska Native:** A person having origins in any of the original peoples of North and South America (including Central America) and who maintains tribal affiliation or community attachment. This category includes people who indicated their race(s) as "American Indian or Alaska Native" or reported their enrolled or principal tribe, such as Navajo, Blackfeet, Inupiat, Yup'ik, or Central American Indian groups or South American Indian groups.
- **Asian:** A person having origins in any of the original peoples of the Far East, Southeast Asia, or the Indian subcontinent, including, for example, Cambodia, China, India, Japan, Korea, Malaysia, Pakistan, the Philippine Islands, Thailand, and Vietnam. It includes people who indicated their race(s) as "Asian" or reported entries such as "Asian Indian," "Chinese," "Filipino," "Korean," "Japanese," "Vietnamese," and "Other Asian" or provided other detailed Asian responses.
- **Native Hawaiian or Other Pacific Islander:** A person having origins in any of the original peoples of Hawaii, Guam, Samoa, or other Pacific Islands. It includes people who indicated their race(s) as "Pacific Islander" or reported entries such as "Native Hawaiian," "Guamanian or Chamorro," "Samoan," and "Other Pacific Islander" or provided other detailed Pacific Islander responses.
- **White:** A person having origins in any of the original peoples of Europe, the Middle East, or North Africa. It includes people who indicated their race(s) as "White" or reported entries such as Irish, German, Italian, Lebanese, Arab, Moroccan, or Caucasian.
- **Hispanic:** The data on the Hispanic or Latino population were derived from answers to a question that was asked of all people. The terms "Spanish," "Hispanic origin," and "Latino" are used interchangeably. Some respondents identify with all three terms while others may identify with only one of these three specific terms. Hispanics or Latinos who identify with the terms "Spanish," "Hispanic," or "Latino" are those who classify themselves in one of the specific Spanish, Hispanic, or Latino categories listed on the questionnaire ("Mexican," "Puerto Rican," or "Cuban") as well as those who indicate that they are "other

Spanish/Hispanic/Latino." People who do not identify with one of the specific origins listed on the questionnaire but indicate that they are "other Spanish/Hispanic/Latino" are those whose origins are from Spain, the Spanish-speaking countries of Central or South America, the Dominican Republic, or people identifying themselves generally as Spanish, Spanish-American, Hispanic, Hispano, Latino, and so on. All write-in responses to the "other Spanish/Hispanic/Latino" category were coded. Origin can be viewed as the heritage, nationality group, lineage, or country of birth of the person or the person's parents or ancestors before their arrival in the United States. People who identify their origin as Spanish, Hispanic, or Latino may be of any race.

Average Household Size: Number of persons in the average household. *Source: U.S. Census Bureau, Census 2010.*

Median Age: Median age of the population. *Source: U.S. Census Bureau, Census 2010.*

Male/Female Ratio: Number of males per 100 females. *Source: U.S. Census Bureau, Census 2010.*

Homeownership Rate: Percentage of housing units that are owner-occupied. *Source: U.S. Census Bureau, Census 2010.*

Information for Counties

PHYSICAL CHARACTERISTICS

Physical Location: Describes the physical location of the county. *Source: Columbia University Press, The Columbia Gazetteer of North America and original research.*

Land and Water Area: Land and water area in square miles. *Source: U.S. Census Bureau, Census 2010.*

Time Zone: Lists the time zone. *Source: Original research.*

Year Organized: Year the county government was organized. *Source: National Association of Counties*

County Seat: Lists the county seat. If a county has more than one seat, then both are listed. *Source: National Association of Counties*

Metropolitan Area: Indicates the metropolitan area the county is located in. Also lists all the component counties of that metropolitan area. The Office of Management and Budget (OMB) defines metropolitan and micropolitan statistical areas. The most current definitions are as of December 2009. *Source: U.S. Census Bureau.*

Climate: Includes all weather stations located within the county. Indicates the station name and elevation as well as the monthly average high and low temperatures, average precipitation, and average snowfall. The period of record is generally 1980-2009, however, certain weather stations contain averages going back as far as 1900. *Source: Grey House Publishing, Weather America: A Thirty-Year Summary of Statistical Weather Data and Rankings, 2010.*

POPULATION

Population: 1990, 2000 and 2010 figures are a 100% count of population. *Source: U.S. Census Bureau, Census 1990, 2000 and 2010.*

Race/Hispanic Origin: Figures are from Census 2010 and include the U.S. Census Bureau categories of White alone; Black alone; Asian alone; American Indian/Alaska Native alone; Native Hawaiian/Other Pacific Islander alone; Hispanic of any race. Alone refers to the fact that these figures are not in combination with any other race.

The concept of race, as used by the Census Bureau, reflects self-identification by people according to the race or races with which they most closely identify. These categories are socio-political constructs and should not be interpreted as being scientific or anthropological in nature. Furthermore, the race categories include both racial and national-origin groups.

- **African American or Black:** A person having origins in any of the Black racial groups of Africa. It includes people who indicated their race(s) as "Black, African Am., or Negro" or reported entries such as African American, Kenyan, Nigerian, or Haitian.
- **American Indian or Alaska Native:** A person having origins in any of the original peoples of North and South America (including Central America) and who maintains tribal affiliation or community attachment. This category includes people who indicated their race(s) as "American Indian or Alaska Native" or reported their enrolled or principal tribe, such as Navajo, Blackfeet, Inupiat, Yup'ik, or Central American Indian groups or South American Indian groups.
- **Asian:** A person having origins in any of the original peoples of the Far East, Southeast Asia, or the Indian subcontinent, including, for example, Cambodia, China, India, Japan, Korea, Malaysia, Pakistan, the Philippine Islands, Thailand, and Vietnam. It includes people who indicated their race(s) as "Asian" or reported entries such as "Asian Indian," "Chinese," "Filipino," "Korean," "Japanese," "Vietnamese," and "Other Asian" or provided other detailed Asian responses.
- **Native Hawaiian or Other Pacific Islander:** A person having origins in any of the original peoples of Hawaii, Guam, Samoa, or other Pacific Islands. It includes people who indicated their race(s) as "Pacific Islander" or reported entries such as "Native Hawaiian," "Guamanian or Chamorro," "Samoan," and "Other Pacific Islander" or provided other detailed Pacific Islander responses.
- **White:** A person having origins in any of the original peoples of Europe, the Middle East, or North Africa. It includes people who indicated their race(s) as "White" or reported entries such as Irish, German, Italian, Lebanese, Arab, Moroccan, or Caucasian.
- **Hispanic:** The data on the Hispanic or Latino population were derived from answers to a question that was asked of all people. The terms "Spanish," "Hispanic origin," and "Latino" are used interchangeably. Some respondents identify with all three terms while others may identify with only one of these three

specific terms. Hispanics or Latinos who identify with the terms "Spanish," "Hispanic," or "Latino" are those who classify themselves in one of the specific Spanish, Hispanic, or Latino categories listed on the questionnaire ("Mexican," "Puerto Rican," or "Cuban") as well as those who indicate that they are "other Spanish/Hispanic/Latino." People who do not identify with one of the specific origins listed on the questionnaire but indicate that they are "other Spanish/Hispanic/Latino" are those whose origins are from Spain, the Spanish-speaking countries of Central or South America, the Dominican Republic, or people identifying themselves generally as Spanish, Spanish-American, Hispanic, Hispano, Latino, and so on. All write-in responses to the "other Spanish/Hispanic/Latino" category were coded. Origin can be viewed as the heritage, nationality group, lineage, or country of birth of the person or the person's parents or ancestors before their arrival in the United States. People who identify their origin as Spanish, Hispanic, or Latino may be of any race.

Population Density: Total population divided by the land area in square miles. *Source: U.S. Census Bureau, Census 2010.*

Average Household Size: Number of persons in the average household. *Source: U.S. Census Bureau, Census 2010.*

Median Age: Median age of the population. *Source: U.S. Census Bureau, Census 2010.*

Male/Female Ratio: Number of males per 100 females. *Source: U.S. Census Bureau, Census 2010.*

RELIGION

Religion: Lists the largest religious groups (up to six) based on the number of adherents divided by the population of the county. Adherents are defined as "all members, including full members, their children and the estimated number of other regular participants who are not considered as communicant, confirmed or full members." *Source: American Religious Bodies, 2010 U.S. Religion Census: Religious Congregations & Membership Study*

ECONOMY

Unemployment Rate: Unemployment rate as of August 2012. Includes all civilians age 16 or over who were unemployed and looking for work. *Source: U.S. Department of Labor, Bureau of Labor Statistics, Local Area Unemployment Statistics.*

Total Civilian Labor Force: Total civilian labor force as of August 2012. Includes all civilians age 16 or over who were either employed, or unemployed and looking for work. *Source: U.S. Department of Labor, Bureau of Labor Statistics, Local Area Unemployment Statistics.*

Leading Industries: Lists the three largest industries (excluding government) based on the number of employees. *Source: U.S. Census Bureau, County Business Patterns 2010 (http://www.census.gov/epcd/cbp/view/cbpview.html).*

Farms: The total number of farms and the total acreage they occupy. *Source: U.S. Department of Agriculture, National Agricultural Statistics Service, 2007 Census of Agriculture (http://www.agcensus.usda.gov).*

Companies that Employ 500 or more persons: The numbers of companies that employ 500 or more persons. Includes private employers only. *Source: U.S. Census Bureau, County Business Patterns 2010*

Companies that Employ 100–499 persons: The numbers of companies that employ 100–499 persons. Includes private employers only. *Source: U.S. Census Bureau, County Business Patterns 2010*

Companies that Employ 1–99 persons: The numbers of companies that employ 1–99 persons. Includes private employers only. *Source: U.S. Census Bureau, County Business Patterns 2010*

Black-Owned Businesses: Number of businesses that are majority-owned by a Black or African-American person(s). Majority ownership is defined as having 51 percent or more of the stock or equity in the business. Black or African American is defined as a person having origins in any of the black racial groups of Africa, including those who consider themselves to be "Haitian." *Source: U.S. Census Bureau, 2007 Economic Census, Survey of Business Owners: Black-Owned Firms, 2007*

Asian-Owned Businesses: Number of businesses that are majority-owned by an Asian person(s). Majority ownership is defined as having 51 percent or more of the stock or equity in the business. *Source: U.S. Census Bureau, 2007 Economic Census, Survey of Business Owners: Asian-Owned Firms, 2007*

Hispanic-Owned Businesses: Number of businesses that are majority-owned by a person(s) of Hispanic or Latino origin. Majority ownership is defined as having 51 percent or more of the stock or equity in the business. Hispanic or Latino origin is defined as a person of Cuban, Mexican, Puerto Rican, South or Central American, or other Spanish culture or origin, regardless of race. *Source: U.S. Census Bureau, 2007 Economic Census, Survey of Business Owners: Hispanic-Owned Firms, 2007*

Women-Owned Businesses: Number of businesses that are majority-owned by a woman. Majority ownership is defined as having 51 percent or more of the stock or equity in the business. *Source: U.S. Census Bureau, 2007 Economic Census, Survey of Business Owners: Women-Owned Firms, 2007*

Retail Sales per Capita: Total dollar amount of estimated retail sales divided by the estimated population of the county in 2010. *Source: Editor & Publisher Market Guide 2010*

Single-Family Building Permits Issued: Building permits issued for new, single-family housing units in 2011. *Source: U.S. Census Bureau, Manufacturing and Construction Division*

Multi-Family Building Permits Issued: Building permits issued for new, multi-family housing units in 2011. *Source: U.S. Census Bureau, Manufacturing and Construction Division*

Statistics on housing units authorized by building permits include housing units issued in local permit-issuing jurisdictions by a building or zoning permit. Not all areas of the country require a building or zoning permit. The statistics only represent those areas that do require a permit. Current surveys indicate that construction is undertaken for all but a very small percentage of housing units authorized by building permits. A major portion typically get under way during the month of permit issuance and most of the remainder begin within the three following months. Because of this lag, the housing unit authorization statistics do not represent the number of units actually put into construction for the period shown, and should therefore not be directly interpreted as "housing starts."

Statistics are based upon reports submitted by local building permit officials in response to a mail survey. They are obtained using Form C-404 const/www/c404.pdf, "Report of New Privately-Owned Residential Building or Zoning Permits Issued." When a report is not received, missing data are either (1) obtained from the Survey of Use of Permits (SUP) which is used to collect information on housing starts, or (2) imputed based on the assumption that the ratio of current month authorizations to those of a year ago should be the same for reporting and non-reporting places.

INCOME

Per Capita Income: Per capita income is the mean income computed for every man, woman, and child in a particular group. It is derived by dividing the total income of a particular group by the total population in that group. Per capita income is rounded to the nearest whole dollar. *Source: U.S. Census Bureau, American Community Survey, 2006-2010 Five-Year Estimates.*

Median Household Income: Includes the income of the householder and all other individuals 15 years old and over in the household, whether they are related to the householder or not. The median divides the income distribution into two equal parts: one-half of the cases falling below the median income and one-half above the median. For households, the median income is based on the distribution of the total number of households including those with no income. Median income for households is computed on the basis of a standard distribution and is rounded to the nearest whole dollar. *Source: U.S. Census Bureau, American Community Survey, 2006-2010 Five-Year Estimates.*

Average Household Income: Average household income is obtained by dividing total household income by the total number of households. *Source: U.S. Census Bureau, American Community Survey, 2006-2010 Five-Year Estimates.*

Percent of Households with Income of $100,000 or more: Percent of households with income of $100,000 or more. *Source: U.S. Census Bureau, American Community Survey, 2006-2010 Five-Year Estimates.*

Poverty Rate: Percentage of population with income below the poverty level. Based on individuals for whom poverty status is determined. Poverty status was determined for all people except institutionalized people, people in military group quarters, people in college dormitories, and unrelated individuals under 15 years old. *Source: U.S. Census Bureau, American Community Survey, 2006-2010 Five-Year Estimates.*

Bankruptcy Rate: The personal bankruptcy filing rate is the number of bankruptcies per thousand residents in 2011. Personal bankruptcy filings include both Chapter 7 (liquidations) and Chapter 13 (reorganizations) based on the county of residence of the filer. *Source: Federal Deposit Insurance Corporation, Regional Economic Conditions*

TAXES

Total County Taxes Per Capita: Total county taxes collected divided by the population of the county. *Source: U.S. Census Bureau, State and Local Government Finances, 2009*

Taxes include:

- Property Taxes
- Sales and Gross Receipts Taxes
- Federal Customs Duties
- General Sales and Gross Receipts Taxes
- Selective Sales Taxes (alcoholic beverages; amusements; insurance premiums; motor fuels; pari-mutuels; public utilities; tobacco products; other)
- License Taxes (alcoholic beverages; amusements; corporations in general; hunting and fishing; motor vehicles motor vehicle operators; public utilities; occupation and business, NEC; other)
- Income Taxes (individual income; corporation net income; other)
- Death and Gift
- Documentary & Stock Transfer
- Severance
- Taxes, NEC

Total County Property Taxes Per Capita: Total county property taxes collected divided by the population of the county. *Source: U.S. Census Bureau, State and Local Government Finances, 2009*

Property Taxes include general property taxes, relating to property as a whole, taxed at a single rate or at classified rates according to the class of property. Property refers to real property (e.g. land and structures) as well as personal property; personal property can be either tangible (e.g. automobiles and boats) or intangible (e.g. bank accounts and stocks and bonds). Special property taxes, levied on selected types of property (e.g. oil and gas properties, house trailers, motor vehicles, and intangibles) and subject to rates not directly related to general property tax rates. Taxes based on income produced by property as a measure of its value on the assessment date.

EDUCATION

Educational Attainment: Figures show the percent of population age 25 and over with:

- **High school diploma (including GED) or higher:** Includes people whose highest degree is a high school diploma or its equivalent, people who attended college but did not receive a degree, and people who received a college, university, or professional degree.
- **Bachelor's degree or higher:** Includes people who received a bachelor's, master's, doctorate, or professional degree.
- **Master's degree or higher:** Includes people who received a master's, doctorate, or professional degree. *Source: U.S. Census Bureau, American Community Survey, 2006-2010 Five-Year Estimates.*

HOUSING

Homeownership Rate: Percentage of housing units that are owner-occupied. *Source: U.S. Census Bureau, Census 2010.*

Median Home Value: Median value of all owner-occupied housing units as reported by the owner. Figures shown are 2010 estimates. *Source: U.S. Census Bureau, American Community Survey, 2006-2010 Five-Year Estimates.*

Median Rent: Median monthly contract rent on specified renter-occupied and specified vacant-for-rent units. Specified renter-occupied and specified vacant-for-rent units exclude 1-family houses on 10 acres or more. Contract rent is the monthly rent agreed to or contracted for, regardless of any furnishings, utilities, fees, meals, or services that may be included. For vacant units, it is the monthly rent asked for the rental unit at the time of enumeration. *Source: U.S. Census Bureau, American Community Survey, 2006-2010 Five-Year Estimates.*

Median Year Structure Built: Year structure built refers to when the building was first constructed, not when it was remodeled, added to, or converted. For mobile homes, houseboats, RVs, etc, the manufacturer's model year was assumed to be the year built. The data relate to the number of units built during the specified periods that were still in

existence at the time of enumeration. *Source: U.S. Census Bureau, American Community Survey, 2006-2010 Five-Year Estimates.*

HEALTH AND VITAL STATISTICS

Birth Rate: Estimated number of births per 10,000 population in 2011. *Source: U.S. Census Bureau, Annual Components of Population Change, July 1, 2010 – July 1, 2011*

Death Rate: Estimated number of deaths per 10,000 population in 2011. *Source: U.S. Census Bureau, Annual Components of Population Change, July 1, 2010 – July 1, 2011*

Age-adjusted Cancer Mortality Rate: Number of age-adjusted deaths from cancer per 100,000 population in 2009. Cancer is defined as International Classification of Disease (ICD) codes C00 – D48.9 Neoplasms. *Source: Centers for Disease Control, CDC Wonder*

Age-adjusted death rates are weighted averages of the age-specific death rates, where the weights represent a fixed population by age. They are used because the rates of almost all causes of death vary by age. Age adjustment is a technique for "removing" the effects of age from crude rates, so as to allow meaningful comparisons across populations with different underlying age structures. For example, comparing the crude rate of heart disease in New York to that of California is misleading, because the relatively older population in New York will lead to a higher crude death rate, even if the age-specific rates of heart disease in New York and California are the same. For such a comparison, age-adjusted rates would be preferable. Age-adjusted rates should be viewed as relative indexes rather than as direct or actual measures of mortality risk.

Death rates based on counts of twenty or less (≤ 20) are flagged as "Unreliable". Death rates based on fewer than three years of data for counties with populations of less than 100,000 in the 2000 Census counts, are also flagged as "Unreliable" if the number of deaths is five or less (≤ 5).

Air Quality Index: The percentage of days in 2011 the AQI fell into the Good (0-50), Moderate (51-100), Unhealthy for Sensitive Groups (101-150), Unhealthy (151-199), and Very Unhealthy (200-299) ranges. Data covers January 2011 through December 2011. *Source: AirData: Access to Air Pollution Data, U.S. Environmental Protection Agency, Office of Air and Radiation*

The AQI is an index for reporting daily air quality. It tells you how clean or polluted your air is, and what associated health concerns you should be aware of. The AQI focuses on health effects that can happen within a few hours or days after breathing polluted air. EPA uses the AQI for five major air pollutants regulated by the Clean Air Act: ground-level ozone, particulate matter, carbon monoxide, sulfur dioxide, and nitrogen dioxide. For each of these pollutants, EPA has established national air quality standards to protect against harmful health effects.

The AQI runs from 0 to 500. The higher the AQI value, the greater the level of air pollution and the greater the health danger. For example, an AQI value of 50 represents good air quality and little potential to affect public health, while an AQI value over 300 represents hazardous air quality. An AQI value of 100 generally corresponds to the national air quality standard for the pollutant, which is the level EPA has set to protect public health. So, AQI values below 100 are generally thought of as satisfactory. When AQI values are above 100, air quality is considered to be unhealthy— at first for certain sensitive groups of people, then for everyone as AQI values get higher. Each category corresponds to a different level of health concern. For example, when the AQI for a pollutant is between 51 and 100, the health concern is "Moderate." Here are the six levels of health concern and what they mean:

- "Good" The AQI value for your community is between 0 and 50. Air quality is considered satisfactory and air pollution poses little or no risk.
- "Moderate" The AQI for your community is between 51 and 100. Air quality is acceptable; however, for some pollutants there may be a moderate health concern for a very small number of individuals. For example, people who are unusually sensitive to ozone may experience respiratory symptoms.
- "Unhealthy for Sensitive Groups" Certain groups of people are particularly sensitive to the harmful effects of certain air pollutants. This means they are likely to be affected at lower levels than the general public. For example, children and adults who are active outdoors and people with respiratory disease are at greater risk from exposure to ozone, while people with heart disease are at greater risk from carbon monoxide. Some people may be sensitive to more than one pollutant. When AQI values are between 101 and 150, members of sensitive groups may experience health effects. The general public is not likely to be affected when the AQI is in this range.
- "Unhealthy" AQI values are between 151 and 200. Everyone may begin to experience health effects. Members of sensitive groups may experience more serious health effects.

- "Very Unhealthy" AQI values between 201 and 300 trigger a health alert, meaning everyone may experience more serious health effects.
- "Hazardous" AQI values over 300 trigger health warnings of emergency conditions. The entire population is more likely to be affected.

Number of Physicians: The number of active, non-federal physicians per 10,000 population in 2010.
Source: Area Resource File (ARF) 2011-2012. U.S. Department of Health and Human Services, Health Resources and Services Administration, Bureau of Health Professions, Rockville, MD.

Number of Hospital Beds: The number of hospital beds per 10,000 population in 2008.
Source: Area Resource File (ARF) 2011-2012. U.S. Department of Health and Human Services, Health Resources and Services Administration, Bureau of Health Professions, Rockville, MD.

Number of Hospital Admissions: The number of hospital admissions per 10,000 population in 2008.
Source: Area Resource File (ARF) 2011-2012. U.S. Department of Health and Human Services, Health Resources and Services Administration, Bureau of Health Professions, Rockville, MD.

ELECTIONS

Elections: 2008 Presidential election results. *Source: Dave Leip's Atlas of U.S. Presidential Elections (http://www.uselectionatlas.org).*

NATIONAL AND STATE PARKS

Lists National and State parks located in the area. *Source: U.S. Geological Survey, Geographic Names Information System.*

ADDITIONAL INFORMATION CONTACTS

The following phone numbers are provided as sources of additional information: Chambers of Commerce; Economic Development Agencies; and Convention & Visitors Bureaus. Efforts have been made to provide the most recent area codes. However, area code changes may have occurred in listed numbers. *Source: Original research.*

User's Guide: Education

School District Rankings

Number of Schools: Total number of schools in the district. *Source: U.S. Department of Education, National Center for Education Statistics, Common Core of Data, Public Elementary/Secondary School Universe Survey: School Year 2009-2010.*

Number of Teachers: Teachers are defined as individuals who provide instruction to pre-kindergarten, kindergarten, grades 1 through 12, or ungraded classes, or individuals who teach in an environment other than a classroom setting, and who maintain daily student attendance records. Numbers reported are full-time equivalents (FTE). *Source: U.S. Department of Education, National Center for Education Statistics, Common Core of Data, Local Education Agency (School District) Universe Survey: School Year 2009-2010.*

Number of Students: A student is an individual for whom instruction is provided in an elementary or secondary education program that is not an adult education program and is under the jurisdiction of a school, school system, or other education institution. *Sources: U.S. Department of Education, National Center for Education Statistics, Common Core of Data, Local Education Agency (School District) Universe Survey: School Year 2009-2010 and Public Elementary/Secondary School Universe Survey: School Year 2009-2010*

Individual Education Program (IEP) Students: A written instructional plan for students with disabilities designated as special education students under IDEA-Part B. The written instructional plan includes a statement of present levels of educational performance of a child; statement of annual goals, including short-term instructional objectives; statement of specific educational services to be provided and the extent to which the child will be able to participate in regular educational programs; the projected date for initiation and anticipated duration of services; the appropriate objectives, criteria and evaluation procedures; and the schedules for determining, on at least an annual basis, whether instructional objectives are being achieved. *Source: U.S. Department of Education, National Center for Education Statistics, Common Core of Data, Local Education Agency (School District) Universe Survey: School Year 2009-2010*

English Language Learner (ELL) Students: Formerly referred to as Limited English Proficient (LEP). Students being served in appropriate programs of language assistance (e.g., English as a Second Language, High Intensity Language Training, bilingual education). Does not include pupils enrolled in a class to learn a language other than English. Also Limited-English-Proficient students are individuals who were not born in the United States or whose native language is a language other than English; or individuals who come from environments where a language other than English is dominant; or individuals who are American Indians and Alaskan Natives and who come from environments where a language other than English has had a significant impact on their level of English language proficiency; and who, by reason thereof, have sufficient difficulty speaking, reading, writing, or understanding the English language, to deny such individuals the opportunity to learn successfully in classrooms where the language of instruction is English or to participate fully in our society. *Source: U.S. Department of Education, National Center for Education Statistics, Common Core of Data, Local Education Agency (School District) Universe Survey: School Year 2009-2010*

Students Eligible for Free Lunch Program: The free lunch program is defined as a program under the National School Lunch Act that provides cash subsidies for free lunches to students based on family size and income criteria. *Source: U.S. Department of Education, National Center for Education Statistics, Common Core of Data, Public Elementary/Secondary School Universe Survey: School Year 2009-2010*

Students Eligible for Reduced-Price Lunch Program: A student who is eligible to participate in the Reduced-Price Lunch Program under the National School Lunch Act. *Source: U.S. Department of Education, National Center for Education Statistics, Common Core of Data, Public Elementary/Secondary School Universe Survey: School Year 2009-2010*

Student/Teacher Ratio: The number of students divided by the number of teachers (FTE). See Number of Students and Number of Teachers above for for information.

Student/Librarian Ratio: The number of students divided by the number of library and media support staff. Library and media support staff are defined as staff members who render other professional library and media services; also includes library aides and those involved in library/media support. Their duties include selecting, preparing, caring for, and making available to instructional staff, equipment, films, filmstrips, transparencies, tapes, TV programs, and similar materials maintained separately or as part of an instructional materials center. Also included are activities in the audio-visual center, TV studio, related-work-study areas, and services provided by audio-visual personnel.

Numbers are based on full-time equivalents. *Source: U.S. Department of Education, National Center for Education Statistics, Common Core of Data, Local Education Agency (School District) Universe Survey: School Year 2009-2010.*

Student/Counselor Ratio: The number of students divided by the number of guidance counselors. Guidance counselors are professional staff assigned specific duties and school time for any of the following activities in an elementary or secondary setting: counseling with students and parents; consulting with other staff members on learning problems; evaluating student abilities; assisting students in making educational and career choices; assisting students in personal and social development; providing referral assistance; and/or working with other staff members in planning and conducting guidance programs for students. The state applies its own standards in apportioning the aggregate of guidance counselors/directors into the elementary and secondary level components. Numbers reported are full-time equivalents. *Source: U.S. Department of Education, National Center for Education Statistics, Common Core of Data, Local Education Agency (School District) Universe Survey: School Year 2009-2010.*

Current Spending per Student: Expenditure for Instruction, Support Services, and Other Elementary/Secondary Programs. Includes salaries, employee benefits, purchased services, and supplies, as well as payments made by states on behalf of school districts. Also includes transfers made by school districts into their own retirement system. Excludes expenditure for Non-Elementary/Secondary Programs, debt service, capital outlay, and transfers to other governments or school districts. This item is formally called "Current Expenditures for Public Elementary/Secondary Education."

Instruction: Includes payments from all funds for salaries, employee benefits, supplies, materials, and contractual services for elementary/secondary instruction. It excludes capital outlay, debt service, and interfund transfers for elementary/secondary instruction. Instruction covers regular, special, and vocational programs offered in both the regular school year and summer school. It excludes instructional support activities as well as adult education and community services. Instruction salaries includes salaries for teachers and teacher aides and assistants.

Support Services: Relates to support services functions (series 2000) defined in Financial Accounting for Local and State School Systems (National Center for Education Statistics 2000). Includes payments from all funds for salaries, employee benefits, supplies, materials, and contractual services. It excludes capital outlay, debt service, and interfund transfers. It includes expenditure for the following functions:

- Business/Central/Other Support Services
- General Administration
- Instructional Staff Support
- Operation and Maintenance
- Pupil Support Services
- Pupil Transportation Services
- School Administration
- Nonspecified Support Services

Values shown are dollars per pupil per year. They were calculated by dividing the total dollar amounts by the fall membership. Fall membership is comprised of the total student enrollment on October 1 (or the closest school day to October 1) for all grade levels (including prekindergarten and kindergarten) and ungraded pupils. Membership includes students both present and absent on the measurement day. *Source: U.S. Department of Education, National Center for Education Statistics, Common Core of Data, School District Finance Survey (F-33), Fiscal Year 2007-2008.*

Drop-out Rate: A dropout is a student who was enrolled in school at some time during the previous school year; was not enrolled at the beginning of the current school year; has not graduated from high school or completed a state or district approved educational program; and does not meet any of the following exclusionary conditions: has transferred to another public school district, private school, or state- or district-approved educational program; is temporarily absent due to suspension or school-approved illness; or has died. The values shown cover grades 9 through 12. *Note: Drop-out rates are no longer available to the general public disaggregated by grade, race/ethnicity, and gender at the school district level. Beginning with the 2005–06 school year the CCD is reporting dropout data aggregated from the local education agency (district) level to the state level. This allows data users to compare event dropout rates across states, regions, and other jurisdictions. Source: U.S. Department of Education, National Center for Education Statistics, Common Core of Data, Local Education Agency (School District) Universe Survey Dropout and Completion Data, 2005-2006; U.S. Department of Education, National Center for Education Statistics, Common Core of Data, State Dropout and Completion Data File, 2008-2009*

Average Freshman Graduation Rate (AFGR): The AFGR is the number of regular diploma recipients in a given year divided by the average of the membership in grades 8, 9, and 10, reported 5, 4, and 3 years earlier, respectively. For example, the denominator of the 2008–09 AFGR is the average of the 8th-grade membership in 2004–05, 9th-grade membership in 2005–06, and 10th-grade membership in 2006–07. Ungraded students are prorated into

these grades. Averaging these three grades provides an estimate of the number of first-time freshmen in the class of 2005–06 freshmen in order to estimate the on-time graduation rate for 2008–09.

Caution in interpreting the AFGR. Although the AFGR was selected as the best of the available alternatives, several factors make it fall short of a true on-time graduation rate. First, the AFGR does not take into account any imbalances in the number of students moving in and out of the nation or individual states over the high school years. As a result, the averaged freshman class is at best an approximation of the actual number of freshmen, where differences in the rates of transfers, retention, and dropping out in the three grades affect the average. Second, by including all graduates in a specific year, the graduates may include students who repeated a grade in high school or completed high school early and thus are not on-time graduates in that year. *Source: U.S. Department of Education, National Center for Education Statistics, Common Core of Data, Local Education Agency (School District) Universe Survey Dropout and Completion Data, 2008-2009; U.S. Department of Education, National Center for Education Statistics, Common Core of Data, State Dropout and Completion Data File, 2008-2009*

Number of Diploma Recipients: A student who has received a diploma during the previous school year or subsequent summer school. This category includes regular diploma recipients and other diploma recipients. A High School Diploma is a formal document certifying the successful completion of a secondary school program prescribed by the state education agency or other appropriate body. *Note: Diploma counts are no longer available to the general public disaggregated by grade, race/ethnicity, and gender at the school district level. Source: U.S. Department of Education, National Center for Education Statistics, Common Core of Data, Local Education Agency (School District) Universe Survey Dropout and Completion Data, 2008-2009; U.S. Department of Education, National Center for Education Statistics, Common Core of Data, State Dropout and Completion Data File, 2008-2009*

Note: n/a indicates data not available.

State Educational Profile

Please refer to the District Rankings section in the front of this User's Guide for an explanation of data for all items except for the following:

Average Salary: The average salary for classroom teachers in 2011-2012. *Source: National Education Association, Rankings & Estimates: Rankings of the States 2011 and Estimates of School Statistics 2012*

College Entrance Exam Scores:

Scholastic Aptitude Test (SAT). *Note: Data covers the 2011 school year. The College Board strongly discourages the comparison or ranking of states on the basis of SAT scores alone. Source: The College Board, SAT Trends*

American College Testing Program (ACT). *ACT, 2011 ACT National and State Scores*

National Assessment of Educational Progress (NAEP)

The National Assessment of Educational Progress (NAEP), also known as "the Nation's Report Card," is the only nationally representative and continuing assessment of what America's students know and can do in various subject areas. As a result of the "No Child Left Behind" legislation, all states are required to participate in NAEP.

For more information, visit the U.S. Department of Education, National Center for Education Statistics at http://nces.ed.gov/nationsreportcard.

User's Guide: Ancestry and Ethnicity

Places Covered

The ancestry and ethnicity profile section of this book covers the state, all counties, and all places with populations of 50,000 or more. Places included fall into one of the following categories:

Incorporated Places. Depending on the state, places are incorporated as either cities, towns, villages, boroughs, municipalities, independent cities, or corporations. A few municipalities have a form of government combined with another entity (e.g. county) and are listed as special cities or consolidated, unified, or metropolitan governments.

Census Designated Places (CDP). The U.S. Census Bureau defines a CDP as "a statistical entity," defined for each decennial census according to Census Bureau guidelines, comprising a densely settled concentration of population that is not within an incorporated place, but is locally identified by a name. CDPs are delineated cooperatively by state and local officials and the Census Bureau, following Census Bureau guidelines.

Minor Civil Divisions (called charter townships, districts, gores, grants, locations, plantations, purchases, reservations, towns, townships, and unorganized territories) for the states where the Census Bureau has determined that they serve as general-purpose governments. Those states are Connecticut, Maine, Massachusetts, Michigan, Minnesota, New Hampshire, New Jersey, New York, Pennsylvania, Rhode Island, Vermont, and Wisconsin. In some states incorporated municipalities are part of minor civil divisions and in some states they are independent of them.

Note: Several states have incorporated municipalities and minor civil divisions in the same county with the same name. Those communities are given separate entries (e.g. Burlington, New Jersey, in Burlington County will be listed under both the city and township of Burlington). A few states have Census Designated Places and minor civil divisions in the same county with the same name. Those communities are given separate entries (e.g. Bridgewater, Massachusetts, in Plymouth County will be listed under both the CDP and town of Bridgewater).

Source of Data

The ethnicities shown in this book were compiled from two different sources. Data for Race and Hispanic Origin was taken from Census 2010 Summary File 1 (SF1) while Ancestry data was taken from the American Community Survey (ACS) 2006-2010 Five-Year Estimate. The distinction is important because SF1 contains 100-percent data, which is the information compiled from the questions asked of all people and about every housing unit. ACS estimates are compiled from a sampling of households. The 2006-2010 Five-Year Estimate is based on data collected from January 1, 2006 to December 31, 2010.

The American Community Survey (ACS) is a relatively new survey conducted by the U.S. Census Bureau. It uses a series of monthly samples to produce annually updated data for the same small areas (census tracts and block groups) formerly surveyed via the decennial census long-form sample. While some version of this survey has been in the field since 1999, it was not fully implemented in terms of coverage until 2006. In 2005 it was expanded to cover all counties in the country and the 1-in-40 households sampling rate was first applied. The full implementation of the (household) sampling strategy for ACS entails having the survey mailed to about 250,000 households nationwide every month of every year and was begun in January 2005. In January 2006 sampling of group quarters was added to complete the sample as planned. In any given year about 2.5% (1 in 40) of U.S. households will receive the survey. Over any 5-year period about 1 in 8 households should receive the survey (as compared to about 1 in 6 that received the census long form in the 2000 census). Since receiving the survey is not the same as responding to it, the Bureau has adopted a strategy of sampling for non-response, resulting in something closer to 1 in 11 households actually participating in the survey over any 5-year period. For more information about the American Community Survey visit http://www.census.gov/acs/www.

Ancestry

Ancestry refers to a person's ethnic origin, heritage, descent, or "roots," which may reflect their place of birth or that of previous generations of their family. Some ethnic identities, such as "Egyptian" or "Polish" can be traced to geographic areas outside the United States, while other ethnicities such as "Pennsylvania German" or "Cajun" evolved in the United States.

The intent of the ancestry question in the ACS was not to measure the degree of attachment the respondent had to a particular ethnicity, but simply to establish that the respondent had a connection to and self-identified with a particular

ethnic group. For example, a response of "Irish" might reflect total involvement in an Irish community or only a memory of ancestors several generations removed from the respondent.

The Census Bureau coded the responses into a numeric representation of over 1,000 categories. Responses initially were processed through an automated coding system; then, those that were not automatically assigned a code were coded by individuals trained in coding ancestry responses. The code list reflects the results of the Census Bureau's own research and consultations with many ethnic experts. Many decisions were made to determine the classification of responses. These decisions affected the grouping of the tabulated data. For example, the "Indonesian" category includes the responses of "Indonesian," "Celebesian," "Moluccan," and a number of other responses.

Ancestries Covered

Afghan	Palestinian	French, ex. Basque	Scottish
African, Sub-Saharan	Syrian	French Canadian	Serbian
African	Other Arab	German	Slavic
Cape Verdean	Armenian	German Russian	Slovak
Ethiopian	Assyrian/Chaldean/Syriac	Greek	Slovene
Ghanaian	Australian	Guyanese	Soviet Union
Kenyan	Austrian	Hungarian	Swedish
Liberian	Basque	Icelander	Swiss
Nigerian	Belgian	Iranian	Turkish
Senegalese	Brazilian	Irish	Ukrainian
Sierra Leonean	British	Israeli	Welsh
Somalian	Bulgarian	Italian	West Indian, ex.
South African	Cajun	Latvian	Hispanic
Sudanese	Canadian	Lithuanian	Bahamian
Ugandan	Carpatho Rusyn	Luxemburger	Barbadian
Zimbabwean	Celtic	Macedonian	Belizean
Other Sub-Saharan African	Croatian	Maltese	Bermudan
Albanian	Cypriot	New Zealander	British West Indian
Alsatian	Czech	Northern European	Dutch West Indian
American	Czechoslovakian	Norwegian	Haitian
Arab	Danish	Pennsylvania German	Jamaican
Arab	Dutch	Polish	Trinidadian/
Egyptian	Eastern European	Portuguese	Tobagonian
Iraqi	English	Romanian	U.S. Virgin Islander
Jordanian	Estonian	Russian	West Indian
Lebanese	European	Scandinavian	Other West Indian
Moroccan	Finnish	Scotch-Irish	Yugoslavian

The ancestry question allowed respondents to report one or more ancestry groups. Generally, only the first two responses reported were coded. If a response was in terms of a dual ancestry, for example, "Irish English," the person was assigned two codes, in this case one for Irish and another for English. However, in certain cases, multiple responses such as "French Canadian," "Scotch-Irish," "Greek Cypriot," and "Black Dutch" were assigned a single code reflecting their status as unique groups. If a person reported one of these unique groups in addition to another group, for example, "Scotch-Irish English," resulting in three terms, that person received one code for the unique group (Scotch-Irish) and another one for the remaining group (English). If a person reported "English Irish French," only English and Irish were coded. If there were more than two ancestries listed and one of the ancestries was a part of another, such as "German Bavarian Hawaiian," the responses were coded using the more detailed groups (Bavarian and Hawaiian).

The Census Bureau accepted "American" as a unique ethnicity if it was given alone or with one other ancestry. There were some groups such as "American Indian," "Mexican American," and "African American" that were coded and identified separately.

The ancestry question is asked for every person in the American Community Survey, regardless of age, place of birth, Hispanic origin, or race.

Although some people consider religious affiliation a component of ethnic identity, the ancestry question was not designed to collect any information concerning religion. Thus, if a religion was given as an answer to the ancestry question, it was listed in the "Other groups" category which is not shown in this book.

Ancestry should not be confused with a person's place of birth, although a person's place of birth and ancestry may be the same.

Hispanic Origin

The data on the Hispanic or Latino population were derived from answers to a Census 2010 question that was asked of all people. The terms "Spanish," "Hispanic origin," and "Latino" are used interchangeably. Some respondents identify with all three terms while others may identify with only one of these three specific terms. Hispanics or Latinos who identify with the terms "Spanish," "Hispanic," or "Latino" are those who classify themselves in one of the specific Spanish, Hispanic, or Latino categories listed on the questionnaire ("Mexican," "Puerto Rican," or "Cuban") as well as those who indicate that they are "other Spanish/Hispanic/Latino." People who do not identify with one of the specific origins listed on the questionnaire but indicate that they are "other Spanish/Hispanic/Latino" are those whose origins are from Spain, the Spanish-speaking countries of Central or South America, the Dominican Republic, or people identifying themselves generally as Spanish, Spanish-American, Hispanic, Hispano, Latino, and so on. All write-in responses to the "other Spanish/Hispanic/Latino" category were coded.

Hispanic Origins Covered

Hispanic or Latino	Salvadoran	Argentinean	Uruguayan
Central American, ex. Mexican	Other Central American	Bolivian	Venezuelan
Costa Rican	Cuban	Chilean	Other South American
Guatemalan	Dominican Republic	Colombian	Other Hispanic or Latino
Honduran	Mexican	Ecuadorian	
Nicaraguan	Puerto Rican	Paraguayan	
Panamanian	South American	Peruvian	

Origin can be viewed as the heritage, nationality group, lineage, or country of birth of the person or the person's parents or ancestors before their arrival in the United States. People who identify their origin as Hispanic, Latino, or Spanish may be of any race.

Ethnicities Based on Race

The data on race were derived from answers to the Census 2010 question on race that was asked of individuals in the United States. The Census Bureau collects racial data in accordance with guidelines provided by the U.S. Office of Management and Budget (OMB), and these data are based on self-identification.

The racial categories included in the census questionnaire generally reflect a social definition of race recognized in this country and not an attempt to define race biologically, anthropologically, or genetically. In addition, it is recognized that the categories of the race item include racial and national origin or sociocultural groups. People may choose to report more than one race to indicate their racial mixture, such as "American Indian" and "White." People who identify their origin as Hispanic, Latino, or Spanish may be of any race.

Racial Groups Covered

African-American/Black	Crow	Spanish American Indian	Korean
Not Hispanic	Delaware	Tlingit-Haida *(Alaska Native)*	Laotian
Hispanic	Hopi	Tohono O'Odham	Malaysian
American Indian/Alaska Native	Houma	Tsimshian *(Alaska Native)*	Nepalese
Not Hispanic	Inupiat *(Alaska Native)*	Ute	Pakistani
Hispanic	Iroquois	Yakama	Sri Lankan
Alaska Athabascan *(Ala. Nat.)*	Kiowa	Yaqui	Taiwanese
Aleut *(Alaska Native)*	Lumbee	Yuman	Thai
Apache	Menominee	Yup'ik *(Alaska Native)*	Vietnamese
Arapaho	Mexican American Indian	**Asian**	**Hawaii Native/Pacific Islander**
Blackfeet	Navajo	*Not Hispanic*	*Not Hispanic*
Canadian/French Am. Indian	Osage	*Hispanic*	*Hispanic*
Central American Indian	Ottawa	Bangladeshi	Fijian
Cherokee	Paiute	Bhutanese	Guamanian/Chamorro
Cheyenne	Pima	Burmese	Marshallese
Chickasaw	Potawatomi	Cambodian	Native Hawaiian
Chippewa	Pueblo	Chinese, ex. Taiwanese	Samoan
Choctaw	Puget Sound Salish	Filipino	Tongan
Colville	Seminole	Hmong	**White**
Comanche	Shoshone	Indian	*Not Hispanic*
Cree	Sioux	Indonesian	*Hispanic*
Creek	South American Indian	Japanese	

African American or Black: A person having origins in any of the Black racial groups of Africa. It includes people who indicated their race(s) as "Black, African Am., or Negro" or reported entries such as African American, Kenyan, Nigerian, or Haitian.

American Indian or Alaska Native: A person having origins in any of the original peoples of North and South America (including Central America) and who maintains tribal affiliation or community attachment. This category includes people who indicated their race(s) as "American Indian or Alaska Native" or reported their enrolled or principal tribe, such as Navajo, Blackfeet, Inupiat, Yup'ik, or Central American Indian groups or South American Indian groups.

Asian: A person having origins in any of the original peoples of the Far East, Southeast Asia, or the Indian subcontinent, including, for example, Cambodia, China, India, Japan, Korea, Malaysia, Pakistan, the Philippine Islands, Thailand, and Vietnam. It includes people who indicated their race(s) as "Asian" or reported entries such as "Asian Indian," "Chinese," "Filipino," "Korean," "Japanese," "Vietnamese," and "Other Asian" or provided other detailed Asian responses.

Native Hawaiian or Other Pacific Islander: A person having origins in any of the original peoples of Hawaii, Guam, Samoa, or other Pacific Islands. It includes people who indicated their race(s) as "Pacific Islander" or reported entries such as "Native Hawaiian," "Guamanian or Chamorro," "Samoan," and "Other Pacific Islander" or provided other detailed Pacific Islander responses.

White: A person having origins in any of the original peoples of Europe, the Middle East, or North Africa. It includes people who indicated their race(s) as "White" or reported entries such as Irish, German, Italian, Lebanese, Arab, Moroccan, or Caucasian.

Profiles

Each profile shows the name of the place, the county (if a place spans more than one county, the county that holds the majority of the population is shown), and the 2010 population (based on 100-percent data from Census 2010 Summary File 1). The rest of each profile is comprised of all 218 ethnicities grouped into three sections: ancestry; Hispanic origin; and race.

Column one displays the ancestry/Hispanic origin/race name, column two displays the number of people reporting each ancestry/Hispanic origin/race, and column three is the percent of the total population reporting each ancestry/Hispanic origin/race. The population figure shown is used to calculate the value in the "%" column for ethnicities based on race and Hispanic origin. The 2006-2010 estimated population figure from the American Community Survey (not shown) is used to calculate the value in the "%" column for all other ancestries.

For ethnicities in the ancestries group, the value in the "Number" column includes multiple ancestries reported. For example, if a person reported a multiple ancestry such as "French Danish," that response was counted twice in the tabulations, once in the French category and again in the Danish category. Thus, the sum of the counts is not the total population but the total of all responses. Numbers in parentheses indicate the number of people reporting a single ancestry. People reporting a single ancestry includes all people who reported only one ethnic group such as "German." Also included in this category are people with only a multiple-term response such as "Scotch-Irish" who are assigned a single code because they represent one distinct group. For example, the count for German would be interpreted as "The number of people who reported that German was their only ancestry."

For ethnicities based on Hispanic origin, the value in the "Number" column represents the number of people who reported being Mexican, Puerto Rican, Cuban or other Spanish/Hispanic/ Latino (all written-in responses were coded). All ethnicities based on Hispanic origin can be of any race.

For ethnicities based on race data the value in the "Number" column represents the total number of people who reported each category alone or in combination with one or more other race categories. This number represents the maximum number of people reporting and therefore the individual race categories may add up to more than the total population because people may be included in more than one category. The figures in parentheses show the number of people that reported that particular ethnicity alone, not in combination with any other race. For example, in Alabama, the entry for Korean shows 8,320 in parentheses and 10,624 in the "Number" column. This means that 8,320 people reported being Korean alone and 10,624 people reported being Korean alone or in combination with one or more other races.

Rankings

In the rankings section, each ethnicity has three tables. The first table shows the top 10 places sorted by ethnic population (based on all places, regardless of total population), the second table shows the top 10 places sorted by percent of the total population (based on all places, regardless of total population), the third table shows the top 10 places sorted by percent of the total population (based on places with total population of 50,000 or more).

Within each table, column one displays the place name, the state, and the county (if a place spans more than one county, the county that holds the majority of the population is shown). Column one in the first table displays the state only. Column two displays the number of people reporting each ancestry (includes people reporting multiple ancestries), Hispanic origin, or race (alone or in combination with any other race). Column three is the percent of the total population reporting each ancestry, Hispanic origin or race. For tables representing ethnicities based on race or Hispanic origin, the 100-percent population figure from SF1 is used to calculate the value in the "%" column. For all other ancestries, the 2006-2010 five-year estimated population figure from the American Community Survey is used to calculate the value in the "%" column.

Alphabetical Ethnicity Cross-Reference Guide

Afghan see Ancestry–Afghan
African see Ancestry–African, Sub-Saharan: African
African-American see Race–African-American/Black
African-American: Hispanic see Race–African-American/Black: Hispanic
African-American: Not Hispanic see Race–African-American/Black: Not Hispanic
Alaska Athabascan see Race–Alaska Native: Alaska Athabascan
Alaska Native see Race–American Indian/Alaska Native
Alaska Native: Hispanic see Race–American Indian/Alaska Native: Hispanic
Alaska Native: Not Hispanic see Race–American Indian/Alaska Native: Not Hispanic
Albanian see Ancestry–Albanian
Aleut see Race–Alaska Native: Aleut
Alsatian see Ancestry–Alsatian
American see Ancestry–American
American Indian see Race–American Indian/Alaska Native
American Indian: Hispanic see Race–American Indian/Alaska Native: Hispanic
American Indian: Not Hispanic see Race–American Indian/Alaska Native: Not Hispanic
Apache see Race–American Indian: Apache
Arab see Ancestry–Arab: Arab
Arab: Other see Ancestry–Arab: Other
Arapaho see Race–American Indian: Arapaho
Argentinean see Hispanic Origin–South American: Argentinean
Armenian see Ancestry–Armenian
Asian see Race–Asian
Asian Indian see Race–Asian: Indian
Asian: Hispanic see Race–Asian: Hispanic
Asian: Not Hispanic see Race–Asian: Not Hispanic
Assyrian see Ancestry–Assyrian/Chaldean/Syriac
Australian see Ancestry–Australian
Austrian see Ancestry–Austrian
Bahamian see Ancestry–West Indian: Bahamian, except Hispanic
Bangladeshi see Race–Asian: Bangladeshi
Barbadian see Ancestry–West Indian: Barbadian, except Hispanic
Basque see Ancestry–Basque
Belgian see Ancestry–Belgian
Belizean see Ancestry–West Indian: Belizean, except Hispanic
Bermudan see Ancestry–West Indian: Bermudan, except Hispanic
Bhutanese see Race–Asian: Bhutanese
Black see Race–African-American/Black
Black: Hispanic see Race–African-American/Black: Hispanic
Black: Not Hispanic see Race–African-American/Black: Not Hispanic
Blackfeet see Race–American Indian: Blackfeet
Bolivian see Hispanic Origin–South American: Bolivian
Brazilian see Ancestry–Brazilian
British see Ancestry–British

British West Indian *see* Ancestry–West Indian: British West Indian, except Hispanic
Bulgarian *see* Ancestry–Bulgarian
Burmese *see* Race–Asian: Burmese
Cajun *see* Ancestry–Cajun
Cambodian *see* Race–Asian: Cambodian
Canadian *see* Ancestry–Canadian
Canadian/French American Indian *see* Race–American Indian: Canadian/French American Indian
Cape Verdean *see* Ancestry–African, Sub-Saharan: Cape Verdean
Carpatho Rusyn *see* Ancestry–Carpatho Rusyn
Celtic *see* Ancestry–Celtic
Central American *see* Hispanic Origin–Central American, except Mexican
Central American Indian *see* Race–American Indian: Central American Indian
Central American: Other *see* Hispanic Origin–Central American: Other Central American
Chaldean *see* Ancestry–Assyrian/Chaldean/Syriac
Chamorro *see* Race–Hawaii Native/Pacific Islander: Guamanian or Chamorro
Cherokee *see* Race–American Indian: Cherokee
Cheyenne *see* Race–American Indian: Cheyenne
Chickasaw *see* Race–American Indian: Chickasaw
Chilean *see* Hispanic Origin–South American: Chilean
Chinese (except Taiwanese) *see* Race–Asian: Chinese, except Taiwanese
Chippewa *see* Race–American Indian: Chippewa
Choctaw *see* Race–American Indian: Choctaw
Colombian *see* Hispanic Origin–South American: Colombian
Colville *see* Race–American Indian: Colville
Comanche *see* Race–American Indian: Comanche
Costa Rican *see* Hispanic Origin–Central American: Costa Rican
Cree *see* Race–American Indian: Cree
Creek *see* Race–American Indian: Creek
Croatian *see* Ancestry–Croatian
Crow *see* Race–American Indian: Crow
Cuban *see* Hispanic Origin–Cuban
Cypriot *see* Ancestry–Cypriot
Czech *see* Ancestry–Czech
Czechoslovakian *see* Ancestry–Czechoslovakian
Danish *see* Ancestry–Danish
Delaware *see* Race–American Indian: Delaware
Dominican Republic *see* Hispanic Origin–Dominican Republic
Dutch *see* Ancestry–Dutch
Dutch West Indian *see* Ancestry–West Indian: Dutch West Indian, except Hispanic
Eastern European *see* Ancestry–Eastern European
Ecuadorian *see* Hispanic Origin–South American: Ecuadorian
Egyptian *see* Ancestry–Arab: Egyptian
English *see* Ancestry–English
Eskimo *see* Race–Alaska Native: Inupiat
Estonian *see* Ancestry–Estonian
Ethiopian *see* Ancestry–African, Sub-Saharan: Ethiopian
European *see* Ancestry–European
Fijian *see* Race–Hawaii Native/Pacific Islander: Fijian
Filipino *see* Race–Asian: Filipino
Finnish *see* Ancestry–Finnish
French (except Basque) *see* Ancestry–French, except Basque
French Canadian *see* Ancestry–French Canadian
German *see* Ancestry–German
German Russian *see* Ancestry–German Russian
Ghanaian *see* Ancestry–African, Sub-Saharan: Ghanaian
Greek *see* Ancestry–Greek
Guamanian *see* Race–Hawaii Native/Pacific Islander: Guamanian or Chamorro
Guatemalan *see* Hispanic Origin–Central American: Guatemalan
Guyanese *see* Ancestry–Guyanese
Haitian *see* Ancestry–West Indian: Haitian, except Hispanic
Hawaii Native *see* Race–Hawaii Native/Pacific Islander
Hawaii Native: Hispanic *see* Race–Hawaii Native/Pacific Islander: Hispanic

Hawaii Native: Not Hispanic *see* Race–Hawaii Native/Pacific Islander: Not Hispanic
Hispanic or Latino: *see* Hispanic Origin–Hispanic or Latino (of any race)
Hispanic or Latino: Other *see* Hispanic Origin–Other Hispanic or Latino
Hmong *see* Race–Asian: Hmong
Honduran *see* Hispanic Origin–Central American: Honduran
Hopi *see* Race–American Indian: Hopi
Houma *see* Race–American Indian: Houma
Hungarian *see* Ancestry–Hungarian
Icelander *see* Ancestry–Icelander
Indonesian *see* Race–Asian: Indonesian
Inupiat *see* Race–Alaska Native: Inupiat
Iranian *see* Ancestry–Iranian
Iraqi *see* Ancestry–Arab: Iraqi
Irish *see* Ancestry–Irish
Iroquois *see* Race–American Indian: Iroquois
Israeli *see* Ancestry–Israeli
Italian *see* Ancestry–Italian
Jamaican *see* Ancestry–West Indian: Jamaican, except Hispanic
Japanese *see* Race–Asian: Japanese
Jordanian *see* Ancestry–Arab: Jordanian
Kenyan *see* Ancestry–African, Sub-Saharan: Kenyan
Kiowa *see* Race–American Indian: Kiowa
Korean *see* Race–Asian: Korean
Laotian *see* Race–Asian: Laotian
Latvian *see* Ancestry–Latvian
Lebanese *see* Ancestry–Arab: Lebanese
Liberian *see* Ancestry–African, Sub-Saharan: Liberian
Lithuanian *see* Ancestry–Lithuanian
Lumbee *see* Race–American Indian: Lumbee
Luxemburger *see* Ancestry–Luxemburger
Macedonian *see* Ancestry–Macedonian
Malaysian *see* Race–Asian: Malaysian
Maltese *see* Ancestry–Maltese
Marshallese *see* Race–Hawaii Native/Pacific Islander: Marshallese
Menominee *see* Race–American Indian: Menominee
Mexican *see* Hispanic Origin–Mexican
Mexican American Indian *see* Race–American Indian: Mexican American Indian
Moroccan *see* Ancestry–Arab: Moroccan
Native Hawaiian *see* Race–Hawaii Native/Pacific Islander: Native Hawaiian
Navajo *see* Race–American Indian: Navajo
Nepalese *see* Race–Asian: Nepalese
New Zealander *see* Ancestry–New Zealander
Nicaraguan *see* Hispanic Origin–Central American: Nicaraguan
Nigerian *see* Ancestry–African, Sub-Saharan: Nigerian
Northern European *see* Ancestry–Northern European
Norwegian *see* Ancestry–Norwegian
Osage *see* Race–American Indian: Osage
Ottawa *see* Race–American Indian: Ottawa
Pacific Islander *see* Race–Hawaii Native/Pacific Islander
Pacific Islander: Hispanic *see* Race–Hawaii Native/Pacific Islander: Hispanic
Pacific Islander: Not Hispanic *see* Race–Hawaii Native/Pacific Islander: Not Hispanic
Paiute *see* Race–American Indian: Paiute
Pakistani *see* Race–Asian: Pakistani
Palestinian *see* Ancestry–Arab: Palestinian
Panamanian *see* Hispanic Origin–Central American: Panamanian
Paraguayan *see* Hispanic Origin–South American: Paraguayan
Pennsylvania German *see* Ancestry–Pennsylvania German
Peruvian *see* Hispanic Origin–South American: Peruvian
Pima *see* Race–American Indian: Pima
Polish *see* Ancestry–Polish
Portuguese *see* Ancestry–Portuguese
Potawatomi *see* Race–American Indian: Potawatomi

Pueblo *see* Race–American Indian: Pueblo
Puerto Rican *see* Hispanic Origin–Puerto Rican
Puget Sound Salish *see* Race–American Indian: Puget Sound Salish
Romanian *see* Ancestry–Romanian
Russian *see* Ancestry–Russian
Salvadoran *see* Hispanic Origin–Central American: Salvadoran
Samoan *see* Race–Hawaii Native/Pacific Islander: Samoan
Scandinavian *see* Ancestry–Scandinavian
Scotch-Irish *see* Ancestry–Scotch-Irish
Scottish *see* Ancestry–Scottish
Seminole *see* Race–American Indian: Seminole
Senegalese *see* Ancestry–African, Sub-Saharan: Senegalese
Serbian *see* Ancestry–Serbian
Shoshone *see* Race–American Indian: Shoshone
Sierra Leonean *see* Ancestry–African, Sub-Saharan: Sierra Leonean
Sioux *see* Race–American Indian: Sioux
Slavic *see* Ancestry–Slavic
Slovak *see* Ancestry–Slovak
Slovene *see* Ancestry–Slovene
Somalian *see* Ancestry–African, Sub-Saharan: Somalian
South African *see* Ancestry–African, Sub-Saharan: South African
South American *see* Hispanic Origin–South American
South American Indian *see* Race–American Indian: South American Indian
South American: Other *see* Hispanic Origin–South American: Other South American
Soviet Union *see* Ancestry–Soviet Union
Spanish American Indian *see* Race–American Indian: Spanish American Indian
Sri Lankan *see* Race–Asian: Sri Lankan
Sub-Saharan African *see* Ancestry–African, Sub-Saharan
Sub-Saharan African: Other *see* Ancestry–African, Sub-Saharan: Other
Sudanese *see* Ancestry–African, Sub-Saharan: Sudanese
Swedish *see* Ancestry–Swedish
Swiss *see* Ancestry–Swiss
Syriac *see* Ancestry–Assyrian/Chaldean/Syriac
Syrian *see* Ancestry–Arab: Syrian
Taiwanese *see* Race–Asian: Taiwanese
Thai *see* Race–Asian: Thai
Tlingit-Haida *see* Race–Alaska Native: Tlingit-Haida
Tohono O'Odham *see* Race–American Indian: Tohono O'Odham
Tongan *see* Race–Hawaii Native/Pacific Islander: Tongan
Trinidadian and Tobagonian *see* Ancestry–West Indian: Trinidadian and Tobagonian, except Hispanic
Tsimshian *see* Race–Alaska Native: Tsimshian
Turkish *see* Ancestry–Turkish
U.S. Virgin Islander *see* Ancestry–West Indian: U.S. Virgin Islander, except Hispanic
Ugandan *see* Ancestry–African, Sub-Saharan: Ugandan
Ukrainian *see* Ancestry–Ukrainian
Uruguayan *see* Hispanic Origin–South American: Uruguayan
Ute *see* Race–American Indian: Ute
Venezuelan *see* Hispanic Origin–South American: Venezuelan
Vietnamese *see* Race–Asian: Vietnamese
Welsh *see* Ancestry–Welsh
West Indian *see* Ancestry–West Indian: West Indian, except Hispanic
West Indian (except Hispanic) *see* Ancestry–West Indian, except Hispanic
West Indian: Other *see* Ancestry–West Indian: Other, except Hispanic
White *see* Race–White
White: Hispanic *see* Race–White: Hispanic
White: Not Hispanic *see* Race–White: Not Hispanic
Yakama *see* Race–American Indian: Yakama
Yaqui *see* Race–American Indian: Yaqui
Yugoslavian *see* Ancestry–Yugoslavian
Yuman *see* Race–American Indian: Yuman
Yup'ik *see* Race–Alaska Native: Yup'ik
Zimbabwean *see* Ancestry–African, Sub-Saharan: Zimbabwean

User's Guide: Climate

Sources of the Data

The National Climactic Data Center (NCDC) has two main classes or types of weather stations; first-order stations which are staffed by professional meteorologists and cooperative stations which are staffed by volunteers. All National Weather Service (NWS) stations included in this book are first-order stations.

The data in the climate section of *Profiles of Pennsylvania* is compiled from several sources. The majority comes from the original NCDC computer tapes (DSI-3220 Summary of Month Cooperative). This data was used to create the entire table for each cooperative station and part of each National Weather Service station. The remainder of the data for each NWS station comes from the International Station Meteorological Climate Summary, Version 4.0, September 1996, which is also available from the NCDC.

Storm events come from the NCDC Storm Events Database which is accessible over the Internet at http://www4.ncdc.noaa.gov/ cgi-win/wwcgi.dll?wwevent~storms.

Weather Station Tables

The weather station tables are grouped by type (National Weather Service and Cooperative) and then arranged alphabetically. The station name is almost always a place name, and is shown here just as it appears in NCDC data. The station name is followed by the county in which the station is located (or by county equivalent name), the elevation of the station (at the time beginning of the thirty year period) and the latitude and longitude.

The National Weather Service Station tables contain 32 data elements which were compiled from two different sources, the International Station Meteorological Climate Summary (ISMCS) and NCDC DSI-3220 data tapes. The following 13 elements are from the ISMCS: maximum precipitation, minimum precipitation, maximum snowfall, maximum 24-hour snowfall, thunderstorm days, foggy days, predominant sky cover, relative humidity (morning and afternoon), dewpoint, wind speed and direction, and maximum wind gust. The remaining 19 elements come from the DSI-3220 data tapes. The period of record (POR) for data from the DSI-3220 data tapes is 1980-2009. The POR for ISMCS data varies from station to station and appears in a note below each station.

The Cooperative Station tables contain 19 data elements which were all compiled from the DSI-3220 data tapes with a POR of 1980-2009.

Weather Elements (NWS and Cooperative Stations)

The following elements were compiled by the editor from the NCDC DSI-3220 data tapes using a period of record of 1980-2009.

The average temperatures (maximum, minimum, and mean) are the average (see Methodology below) of those temperatures for all available values for a given month. For example, for a given station the average maximum temperature for July is the arithmetic average of all available maximum July temperatures for that station. (Maximum means the highest recorded temperature, minimum means the lowest recorded temperature, and mean means an arithmetic average temperature.)

The extreme maximum temperature is the highest temperature recorded in each month over the period 1980-2009. The extreme minimum temperature is the lowest temperature recorded in each month over the same time period. The extreme maximum daily precipitation is the largest amount of precipitation recorded over a 24-hour period in each month from 1980-2009. The maximum snow depth is the maximum snow depth recorded in each month over the period 1980-2009.

The days for maximum temperature and minimum temperature are the average number of days those criteria were met for all available instances. The symbol ≥ means greater than or equal to, the symbol ≤ means less than or equal to. For example, for a given station, the number of days the maximum temperature was greater than or equal to 90°F in July, is just an arithmetic average of the number of days in all the available Julys for that station.

Heating and cooling degree days are based on the median temperature for a given day and its variance from 65°F. For example, for a given station if the day's high temperature was 50°F and the day's low temperature was 30°F, the median (midpoint) temperature was 40°F. 40°F is 25 degrees below 65°F, hence on this day there would be 25 heating degree days. This also applies for cooling degree days. For example, for a given station if the day's high temperature was 80°F and the day's low temperature was 70°F, the median (midpoint) temperature was 75°F. 75°F is 10 degrees above 65°F, hence on this day there would be 10 cooling degree days. All heating and/or cooling degree

days in a month are summed for the month giving respective totals for each element for that month. These sums for a given month for a given station over the past thirty years are again summed and then arithmetically averaged. It should be noted that the heating and cooling degree days do not cancel each other out. It is possible to have both for a given station in the same month.

Precipitation data is computed the same as heating and cooling degree days. Mean precipitation and mean snowfall are arithmetic averages of cumulative totals for the month. All available values for the thirty year period for a given month for a given station are summed and then divided by the number of values. The same is true for days of greater than or equal to 0.1", 0.5",and 1.0" of precipitation, and days of greater than or equal to 1.0" of snow depth on the ground. The word trace appears for precipitation and snowfall amounts that are too small to measure.

Finally, remember that all values presented in the tables and the rankings are averages, maximums, or minimums of available data (see Methodology below) for that specific data element for the last thirty years (1980-2009).

Weather Elements (NWS Stations Only)

The following elements were taken directly from the International Station Meteorological Climate Summary. The periods of records vary per station and are noted at the bottom of each table.

Maximum precipitation, minimum precipitation, maximum snowfall, maximum snow depth, maximum 24-hour snowfall, thunderstorm days, foggy days, relative humidity (morning and afternoon), dewpoint, prevailing wind speed and direction, and maximum wind gust are all self-explanatory.

The word trace appears for precipitation and snowfall amounts that are too small to measure.

Predominant sky cover contains four possible entries: CLR (clear); SCT (scattered); BRK (broken); and OVR (overcast).

Inclusion Criteria—How Stations Were Selected

The basic criteria is that a station must have data for temperature, precipitation, heating and cooling degree days of sufficient quantity in order to create a meaningful average. More specifically, the definition of sufficiency here has two parts. First, there must be 22 values for a given data element, and second, ten of the nineteen elements included in the table must pass this sufficiency test. For example, in regard to mean maximum temperature (the first element on every data table), a given station needs to have a value for every month of at least 22 of the last thirty years in order to meet the criteria, and, in addition, every station included must have at least ten of the nineteen elements with at least this minimal level of completeness in order to fulfill the criteria. We then removed stations that were geographically close together, giving preference to stations with better data quality.

Methodology

The following discussion applies only to data compiled from the NCDC DSI-3220 data tapes and excludes weather elements that are extreme maximums or minimums.

The data in *Profiles of Pennsylvania* is based on an arithmetic average of all available data for a specific data element at a given station. For example, the average maximum daily high temperature during July for Rochester, New York, was abstracted from NCDC source tapes for the thirty Julys, starting in July, 1980 and ending in July, 2009. These thirty figures were then summed and divided by thirty to produce an arithmetic average. As might be expected, there were not thirty values for every data element on every table. For a variety of reasons, NCDC data is sometimes incomplete. Thus the following standards were established.

For those data elements where there were 26-30 values, the data was taken to be essentially complete and an average was computed. For data elements where there were 22-25 values, the data was taken as being partly complete but still valid enough to use to compute an average. Such averages are shown in **bold italic** type to indicate that there was less than 26 values. For the few data elements where there were not even 22 values, no average was computed and 'na' appears in the space. If any of the twelve months for a given data element reported a value of 'na', no annual average was computed and the annual average was reported as 'na' as well.

Thus the basic computational methodology used in *Profiles of Pennsylvania* is designed to provide an arithmetic average. Because of this, such a pure arithmetic average is somewhat different from the special type of average (called a "normal") which NCDC procedures produces and appears in federal publications.

Perhaps the best outline of the contrasting normalization methodology is found in the following paragraph (which appears as part of an NCDC technical document titled, CLIM81 1961-1990 NORMALS TD-9641 prepared by Lewis France of NCDC in May, 1992):

Normals have been defined as the arithmetic mean of a climatological element computed over a long time period. International agreements eventually led to the decision that the appropriate time period would be three consecutive decades (Guttman, 1989). The data record should be consistent (have no changes in location, instruments, observation practices, etc.; these are identified here as "exposure changes") and have no missing values so a normal will reflect the actual average climatic conditions. If any significant exposure changes have occurred, the data record is said to be "inhomogeneous," and the normal may not reflect a true climatic average. Such data need to be adjusted to remove the nonclimatic inhomogeneities. The resulting (adjusted) record is then said to be "homogeneous." If no exposure changes have occurred at a station, the normal is calculated simply by averaging the appropriate 30 values from the 1961-1990 record.

In the main, there are two "inhomogeneities" that NCDC is correcting for with normalization: adjusting for variances in time of day of observation (at the so-called First Order stations data is based on midnight to midnight observation times and this practice is not necessarily followed at cooperative stations which are staffed by volunteers), and second, estimating data that is either missing or incongruent.

The editors had some concerns regarding the comparative results of the two methodologies. Would our methodology produce strikingly different results than NCDC's? To allay concerns, results of the two processes were compared for the time period normalized results are available (1971-2000). In short, what was found was that the answer to this question is no. Never the less, users should be aware that because of both the time period covered (1980-2009) and the methodology used, data in *Profiles of Pennsylvania* is not compatible with data from other sources.

Potential Cautions

First, as with any statistical reference work of this type, users need to be aware of the source of the data. The information here comes from NOAA, and it is the most comprehensive and reliable core data available. Although it is the best, it is not perfect. Most weather stations are staffed by volunteers, times of observation sometimes vary, stations occasionally are moved (especially over a thirty year period), equipment is changed or upgraded, and all of these factors affect the uniformity of the data. The editors do not attempt to correct for these factors, and this data is not intended for either climatologists or atmospheric scientists. Users with concerns about data collection and reporting protocols are both referred to NCDC technical documentation.

Second, users need to be aware of the methodology here which is described above. Although this methodology has produced fully satisfactory results, it is not directly compatible with other methodologies, hence variances in the results published here and those which appear in other publications will doubtlessly arise.

Third, is the trap of that informal logical fallacy known as "hasty generalization," and its corollaries. This may involve presuming the future will be like the past (specifically, next year will be an average year), or it may involve misunderstanding the limitations of an arithmetic average, but more interestingly, it may involve those mistakes made most innocently by generalizing informally on too broad a basis. As weather is highly localized, the data should be taken in that context. A weather station collects data about climatic conditions at that spot, and that spot may or may not be an effective paradigm for an entire town or area.

About Pennsylvania

Governor . . . . **Tom Corbett (R)**
Lieutenant Governor . . . . **Jim Cawley (R)**
717-787-2500

State Capital . . . . Harrisburg
Largest City . . . . Philadelphia
Highest Point . . . . Mount Davis (3,213 feet)
State Animal . . . . White-tailed Deer
State Beverage . . . . Milk
State Dog . . . . Great Dane
State Fish . . . . Brook Trout
State Flower . . . . Mountain Laurel
State Fossil . . . . Phacops Rana
State Game Bird . . . . Ruffed Grouse
State Insect . . . . Pennsylvania Firefly
State Motto . . . . Virtue, Liberty and Independence
State Nickname . . . . Keystone State
State Song . . . . Pennsylvania
State Tree . . . . Eastern Hemlock

CONTENTS

Philadelphia, top, is the largest city in Pennsylvania, and the fifth most populous city in the United States. It is the economic and cultural center of Delaware County. The bottom photo shows a strip mine in the anthracite coal region in northeastern Pennsylvania. The region is home to the largest known deposits of anthracite coal in the Americas, and the mining industry is vital to the state's economy.

The top photo shows a row of Amish buggies in the Amish/Dutch Country of southeastern Pennsylvania, which has grown in the last 50 years as a tourist destination. The Eastern State Penitentiary, bottom, built in 1829, was the largest, most expensive public structure ever constructed. It refined the revolutionary system of separate incarceration, and housed notorious criminals such as Willie Sutton and Al Capone. The building is currently a U.S. National Historic Landmark, open to the public as a museum for tours.

The Cathedral of Learning is on the National Register of Historic Places and the centerpiece of the University of Pittsburgh's main campus. At 535 feet, the 42-story structure is the tallest educational building in the western hemisphere. It held its first class in 1931.

The Liberty Bell is the iconic symbol of American independence and is located in Independence Hall, formerly the Pennsylvania State House, in Philadelphia. The bell has been featured on coins and stamps, and its name and image have been widely used by American corporations.

History of Pennsylvania

PENNSYLVANIA ON THE EVE OF COLONIZATION

Indians: The First Inhabitants

When first discovered by Europeans, Pennsylvania, like the rest of the continent, was inhabited by groups of American Indians, people of Mongoloid ancestry unaware of European culture. The life of the Indians reflected Stone Age backgrounds, especially in material arts and crafts. Tools, weapons and household equipment were made from stone, wood, and bark. Transportation was on foot or by canoe. Houses were made of bark, clothing from the skins of animals. The rudiments of a more complex civilization were at hand in the arts of weaving, pottery, and agriculture, although hunting and food gathering prevailed. Some Indians formed confederacies such as the League of the Five Nations, which was made up of certain New York-Pennsylvania groups of Iroquoian speech. The other large linguistic group in Pennsylvania was the Algonkian, represented by the Delawares, Shawnees, and other tribes.

The Delawares, calling themselves Leni-Lenape or "real men," originally occupied the basin of the Delaware River and were the most important of several tribes that spoke an Algonkian language. Under the pressure of white settlement, they began to drift westward to the Wyoming Valley, to the Allegheny and, finally, to eastern Ohio. Many of them took the French side in the French and Indian War, joined in Pontiac's War, and fought on the British side in the Revolutionary War. Afterward, some fled to Ontario and the rest wandered west. Their descendants now live on reservations in Oklahoma and Ontario. The Munsees were a division of the Delawares, who lived on the upper Delaware River, above the Lehigh River.

The Susquehannocks were a powerful Iroquoian-speaking tribe who lived along the Susquehanna in Pennsylvania and Maryland. An energetic people living in Algonkian-speaking tribes' territory, they engaged in many wars. In the end, they fell victim to new diseases brought by European settlers, and to attacks by Marylanders and by the Iroquois, which destroyed them as a nation by 1675. A few descendants were among the Conestoga Indians who were massacred in 1763 in Lancaster County.

The Shawnees were an important Algonkian-speaking tribe who came to Pennsylvania from the west in the 1690s, some groups settling on the lower Susquehanna and others with the Munsees near Easton. In the course of time they moved to the Wyoming Valley and the Ohio Valley, where they joined other Shawnees who had gone there directly. They were allies of the French in the French and Indian War and of the British in the Revolution, being almost constantly at war with settlers for forty years preceding the Treaty of Greenville in 1795. After Wayne's victory at Fallen Timbers (1794), they settled near the Delawares in Indiana, and their descendants now live in Oklahoma.

The Iroquois Confederacy of Iroquoian-speaking tribes, at first known as the Five Nations, included the Mohawks, Oneidas, Onondagas, Cayugas, and Senecas. After about 1723 when the Tuscaroras from the South were admitted to the confederacy, it was called the Six Nations. The five original tribes, when first known to Europeans, held much of New York State from Lake Champlain to the Genesee River. From this central position they gradually extended their power. As middlemen in the fur trade with the western Indians, as intermediaries skilled in dealing with the whites, and as the largest single group of Indians in northeastern America, they gained influence over Indian tribes from Illinois and Lake Michigan to the eastern seaboard. During the colonial wars their alliance or their neutrality was eagerly sought by both the French and the British. The Senecas, the westernmost tribe, established villages on the upper Allegheny in the 1730s. Small groups of Iroquois also scattered westward into Ohio and became known as Mingoes. During the Revolution, most of the Six Nations took the British side, but the Oneidas and many Tuscaroras were pro-American. Gen. John Sullivan's expedition up the Susquehanna River and Gen. Daniel Brodhead's expedition up the Allegheny River laid waste to their villages and cornfields in 1779 and disrupted their society. Many who had fought for the British moved to Canada alter the Revolution, but the rest worked out peaceful relations with the United States under the leadership of such chiefs as Cornplanter. The General Assembly recognized this noted chief by granting him a tract of land on the upper Allegheny in 1791.

Other Tribes, which cannot be identified with certainty, occupied western Pennsylvania before the Europeans arrived, but were eliminated by wars and diseases in the 17th century, long before the Delawares, Shawnees and Senecas began to move there. The Eries, a great Iroquoian-speaking tribe, lived along the south shore of Lake Erie, but were wiped out by the Iroquois about 1654. The Mahicans, an Algonkian-speaking tribe related to the Mohegans of Connecticut, lived in the upper Hudson Valley of New York but were driven out by pressure from the Iroquois and from the white settlers, some joining the Delawares in the Wyoming Valley about 1730 and some settling at Stockbridge, Massachusetts. Two Algonkian-speaking tribes, the Conoys and the Nanticokes, moved northward from Maryland early in the 18th century, settling in southern New York, and eventually moved west with the Delawares, with whom they merged. The Saponis, Siouan-speaking tribes from Virginia and North Carolina, moved northward to seek Iroquois protection and were eventually absorbed into the Cayugas. In the latter part of the 18th century there were temporary villages of Wyandots, Chippewas, Missisaugas, and Ottawas in western Pennsylvania.

European Background and Early Settlements

The rise of nation-states in Europe coincided with the age of discovery and brought a desire for territorial gains beyond the seas, first by Spain and Portugal and later by England, France, the Netherlands, and Sweden. Wars in southern Germany caused many Germans to migrate eventually to Pennsylvania. The struggle in England between the Crown and Parliament also had a pronounced effect on migration to America. The Reformation led to religious ferment and division, and minorities of various faiths sought refuge in America. Such an impulse brought Quakers, Puritans, and Catholics from England, German Pietists from the Rhineland, Scotch Calvinists via Ireland, and Huguenots from France. Also, great economic changes took place in Europe in the 17th century. The old manorial system was breaking down, creating a large class of landless men ready to seek new homes. An increase in commerce and trade led to an accumulation of capital available for colonial ventures. The Swedish and Dutch colonies were financed in this way, and William Penn's colony was also a business enterprise.

Exploration

The English based their claims in North America on the discoveries of the Cabots (1497), while the French pointed to the voyage of Verrazano in 1524. The Spanish claim was founded on Columbus' discovery of the West Indies, but there is evidence that Spanish ships sailed up the coast of North America as early as 1520. It is uncertain, however, that any of these explorers touched land that became Pennsylvania. Captain John Smith journeyed from Virginia up the Susquehanna River in 1608, visiting the Susquehannock Indians. In 1609 Henry Hudson, an Englishman in the Dutch service, sailed the *Half Moon* into Delaware Bay, thus giving the Dutch a claim to the area. In 1610 Captain Samuel Argall of Virginia visited the bay and named it for Lord de la Warr, governor of Virginia. After Hudson's time, the Dutch navigators Cornelis Hendricksenm (1616) and Cornelis Jacobsen (1623) explored the Delaware region more thoroughly, and trading posts were established in 1623 and in later years, though not on Pennsylvania soil until 1647.

The Colony of New Sweden, 1638-1655

The Swedes were the first to make permanent settlement, beginning with the expedition of 1637-1638, which occupied the site of Wilmington, Delaware. In 1643 Governor Johan Printz of New Sweden established his capital at Tinicum Island within the present limits of Pennsylvania, where there is now a state park bearing his name.

Dutch Dominion on the Delaware, 1655-1664, and the Duke of York's Rule, 1664-1681

Trouble broke out between the Swedes and the Dutch, who had trading posts in the region. In 1655 Governor Peter Stuyvesant of New Netherlands seized New Sweden and made it part of the Dutch colony. In 1664 the English seized the Dutch possessions in the name of the Duke of York, the king's brother. Except when it was recaptured by the Dutch in 1673-1674, the Delaware region remained under his jurisdiction until 1681. English laws and civil government were introduced by The Duke of Yorke's Laws in 1676.

THE QUAKER PROVINCE: 1681-1776

THE FOUNDING OF PENNSYLVANIA

William Penn and the Quakers

Penn was born in London on October 24, 1644, the son of Admiral Sir William Penn. Despite high social position and an excellent education, he shocked his upper-class associates by his conversion to the beliefs of the Society of Friends, or Quakers, then a persecuted sect. He used his inherited wealth and rank to benefit and protect his fellow believers. Despite the unpopularity of his religion, he was socially acceptable in the king's court because he was trusted by the Duke of York, later King James II. The origins of the Society of Friends lie in the intense religious ferment of 17th century England. George Fox, the son of a Leicestershire weaver, is credited with founding it in 1647, though there was no definite organization before 1668. The Society's rejections of rituals and oaths, its opposition to war, and its simplicity of speech and dress soon attracted attention, usually hostile.

The Charter

King Charles II owed William Penn £16,000, money which Admiral Penn had lent him. Seeking a haven in the New World for persecuted Friends, Penn asked the King to grant him land in the territory between Lord Baltimore's province of Maryland and the Duke of York's province of New York. With the Duke's support, Penn's petition was granted. The King signed the Charter of Pennsylvania on March 4, 1681, and it was officially proclaimed on April 2. The King named the new colony in honor of William Penn's father. It was to include the land between the 39th and 42nd degrees of north latitude and from the Delaware River westward for five degrees of longitude. Other provisions assured its people the protection of English laws and, to a certain degree, kept it subject to the government in England. Provincial laws could be annulled by the King. In 1682 the Duke of York deeded to Penn his claim to the three lower counties on the Delaware, which are now the state of Delaware.

The New Colony

In April 1681, Penn made his cousin William Markham deputy governor of the province and sent him to take control. In England, Penn drew up the *First Frame of Government*, his proposed constitution for Pennsylvania. Penn's preface to *First Frame of Government* has become famous as a summation of his governmental ideals. Later, in October 1682, the Proprietor arrived in Pennsylvania on the ship *Welcome*. He visited Philadelphia, just laid out as the capital city, created the three original counties, and summoned a General Assembly to Chester on December 4. This first Assembly united the Delaware counties with Pennsylvania, adopted a naturalization act and, on December 7, adopted the *Great Law*, a humanitarian code that became the fundamental basis of Pennsylvania law and which guaranteed liberty of conscience. The second Assembly, in 1683, reviewed and amended Penn's *First Frame* with his cooperation and created the *Second Frame of Government*. By the time of Penn's return to England late in 1684, the foundations of the Quaker Province were well established.

In 1984, William Penn and his wife Hannah Callowhill Penn were made the third and fourth honorary citizens of the United States, by act of Congress. On May 8, 1985, the Penns were granted honorary citizenship of the Commonwealth of Pennsylvania.

POPULATION AND IMMIGRATION

Indians

Although William Penn was granted all the land in Pennsylvania by the King, he and his heirs chose not to grant or settle any part of it without first buying the claims of Indians who lived there. In this manner, all of Pennsylvania except the northwestern third was purchased by 1768. The Commonwealth bought the Six Nations' claims to the remainder of the land in 1784 and 1789, and the claims of the Delawares and Wyandots in 1785. The defeat of the French and Indian war alliance by 1760, the withdrawal of the French, the crushing of Chief Pontiac's Indian alliance in 1764, and the failure of all attempts by Indians and colonists to live side by side led the Indians to migrate westward, gradually leaving Pennsylvania.

English

English Quakers were the dominant element, although many English settlers were Anglican. The English settled heavily in the southeastern counties, which soon lost frontier characteristics and became the center of a thriving agricultural and commercial society. Philadelphia became the metropolis of the British colonies and a center of intellectual and commercial life.

Germans

Thousands of Germans were also attracted to the colony and, by the time of the Revolution, comprised a third of the population. The volume of German immigration increased after 1727, coming largely from the Rhineland. The Pennsylvania Germans settled most heavily in the interior counties of Northampton, Berks, Lancaster and Lehigh, and neighboring areas. Their skill and industry transformed this region into a rich farming country, contributing greatly to the expanding prosperity of the province.

Scotch-Irish

Another important immigrant group was the Scotch-Irish, who migrated from about 1717 until the Revolution in a series of waves caused by hardships in Ireland. They were primarily frontiersmen, pushing first into the Cumberland Valley region and then farther into central and western Pennsylvania. They, with immigrants from old Scotland, numbered about one-fourth of the population by 1776.

African Americans

Despite Quaker opposition to slavery, about 4,000 slaves were brought to Pennsylvania by 1730, most of them owned by English, Welsh, and Scotch-Irish colonists. The census of 1790 showed that the number of African-Americans had increased to about 10,000, of whom about 6,300 had received their freedom. The Pennsylvania Gradual Abolition Act of 1780 was the first emancipation statute in the United States.

Others

Many Quakers were Irish and Welsh, and they settled in the area immediately outside of Philadelphia. French Huguenot and Jewish settlers, together with Dutch, Swedes, and other groups, contributed in smaller numbers to the development of colonial Pennsylvania. The mixture of various national groups in the Quaker Province helped to create its broad-minded tolerance and cosmopolitan outlook.

Politics

Pennsylvania's political history ran a rocky course during the provincial era. There was a natural conflict between the proprietary and popular elements in the government which began under Penn and grew stronger under his successors. As a result of the English Revolution of 1688 which overthrew King James II, Penn was deprived of his province from 1692 until 1694. A popular party led by David Lloyd demanded greater powers for the Assembly, and in 1696 *Markham's Frame of Government* granted some of these. In December 1699, the Proprietor again visited Pennsylvania and, just before his return to England in 1701, agreed with the Assembly on a revised constitution, the *Charter of Privileges*, which remained in effect until 1776. This gave the Assembly full legislative powers and permitted the three Delaware counties to have a separate legislature.

Deputy or lieutenant governors (addressed as "governor") resided in Pennsylvania and represented the Penn family proprietors who themselves remained in England until 1773. After 1763, these governors were members of the Penn family. From 1773 until independence, John Penn was both a proprietor and the governor.

William Penn's heirs, who eventually abandoned Quakerism, were often in conflict with the Assembly, which was usually dominated by the Quakers until 1756. One after another, governors defending the proprietors' prerogatives battered themselves against the rock of an Assembly vigilant in the defense of its own rights. The people of the frontier areas contended with the people of the older, southeastern region for more adequate representation in the Assembly and better protection in time of war. Such controversies prepared the people for their part in the Revolution.

The Colonial Wars

As part of the British Empire, Pennsylvania was involved in the wars between Great Britain and France for dominance in North America. These wars ended the long period when Pennsylvania was virtually without

defense. The government built forts and furnished men and supplies to help defend the empire to which it belonged. The territory claimed for New France included western Pennsylvania. The Longueuil and Celoron expeditions of the French in 1739 and 1749 traversed this region, and French traders competed with Pennsylvanians for Indian trade. The French efforts in 1753 and 1754 to establish control over the upper Ohio Valley led to the last and conclusive colonial war, the French and Indian War (1754-1763). French forts at Erie (Fort Presque Isle), Waterford (Fort LeBoeuf), Pittsburgh (Fort Duquesne) and Franklin (Fort Machault) threatened all the middle colonies. In 1753 Washington failed to persuade the French to leave. In the ensuing war, Gen. Braddock's British and colonial army was slaughtered on the Monongahela in 1755, but Gen. John Forbes recaptured the site of Pittsburgh in 1758. After the war, the Indians rose up against the British colonies in Pontiac's War, but in August 1763, Colonel Henry Bouquet defeated them at Bushy Run, interrupting the threat to the frontier in this region.

ECONOMICS

Agriculture
From its beginning, Pennsylvania ranked as a leading agricultural area and produced surpluses for export, adding to its wealth. By the 1750s an exceptionally prosperous farming area had developed in southeastern Pennsylvania. Wheat and corn were the leading crops, though rye, hemp, and flax were also important.

Manufacturing
The abundant natural resources of the colony made for early development of industries. Arts and crafts, as well as home manufactures, grew rapidly. Sawmills and gristmills were usually the first to appear, using the power of the numerous streams. Textile products were spun and woven mainly in the home, though factory production was not unknown. Shipbuilding became important on the Delaware. The province early gained importance in iron manufacture, producing pig iron as well as finished products. Printing, publishing, and the related industry of papermaking, as well as tanning, were significant industries. The Pennsylvania long rifle was an adaptation of a German hunting rifle developed in Lancaster County. Its superiority was so well recognized that by 1776 gunsmiths were duplicating it in Virginia, Georgia, North Carolina, and Maryland. The Conestoga wagon was also developed in Lancaster County. Capable of carrying as much as four tons, it was the prototype for the principal vehicle for American westward migration, the prairie schooner.

Commerce and Transportation
The rivers were important as early arteries of commerce and were soon supplemented by roads in the southeastern area. Stagecoach lines by 1776 reached from Philadelphia into the southcentral region. Trade with the Indians for furs was important in the colonial period. Later, the transport and sale of farm products to Philadelphia and Baltimore, by water and road, formed an important business. Philadelphia became one of the most important centers in the colonies for the conduct of foreign trade and the commercial metropolis of an expanding hinterland. By 1776, the province's imports and exports were worth several million dollars.

SOCIETY AND CULTURE

The Arts and Learning
Philadelphia was known in colonial times as the "Athens of America" because of its rich cultural life. Because of the liberality of Penn's principles and the freedom of expression that prevailed, the province was noted for the variety and strength of its intellectual and educational institutions and interests. An academy that held its first classes in 1740 became the College of Philadelphia in 1755, and ultimately grew into the University of Pennsylvania. It was the only nondenominational college of the colonial period. The arts and sciences flourished, and the public buildings of Philadelphia were the marvel of the colonies. Many fine old buildings in the Philadelphia area still bear witness to the richness of Pennsylvania's civilization in the 18th century. Such men of intellect as Benjamin Franklin, David Rittenhouse, John Bartram, and Benjamin West achieved international renown. Newspapers and magazines flourished, as did law and medicine. Pennsylvania can claim America's first hospital, first library, and first insurance company.

Religion
Quakers held their first meeting at Upland (now Chester) in 1675, and came to Pennsylvania in great numbers

after William Penn received his Charter. Most numerous in the southeastern counties, the Quakers gradually declined in number but retained considerable influence. The Pennsylvania Germans belonged largely to the Lutheran and Reformed churches, but there were also several smaller sects: Mennonites, Amish, German Baptist Brethren or "Dunkers," Schwenkfelders and Moravians. Although the Lutheran Church was established by the Swedes on Tinicum Island in 1643, it only began its growth to become the largest of the Protestant denominations in Pennsylvania upon the arrival of Henry Metchior Muhlenberg in 1742. The Reformed Church owed its expansion to Michael Schlatter, who arrived in 1746. The Moravians did notable missionary work among the Indians. The Church of England held services in Philadelphia as early as 1695. The first Catholic congregation was organized in Philadelphia in 1720, and the first chapel was erected in 1733; Pennsylvania had the second largest Catholic population among the colonies. The Scotch brought Presbyterianism; its first congregation was organized in Philadelphia in 1698. Scotch-Irish immigrants swelled its numbers. Methodism began late in the colonial period. St. George's Church, built in Philadelphia in 1769, is the oldest Methodist building in America. There was a significant Jewish population in colonial Pennsylvania. Its Mikveh Israel Congregation was established in Philadelphia in 1740.

Pennsylvania on the Eve of the Revolution
By 1776, the Province of Pennsylvania had become the third largest English colony in America, though next to the last to be founded, Philadelphia had become the largest English-speaking city in the world next to London. There were originally only three counties: Philadelphia, Chester, and Bucks. By 1773 there were eleven. Westmoreland, the last new county created before the Revolution, was the first county located entirely west of the Allegheny Mountains. The American Revolution had urban origins, and Philadelphia was a center of ferment. Groups of artisans and mechanics, many loyal to Benjamin Franklin, formed grassroots leadership. Philadelphia was a center of resistance to the Stamp Act (1765) and moved quickly to support Boston in opposition to the Intolerable Acts, in 1774.

INDEPENDENCE TO THE CIVIL WAR: 1776-1861

Pennsylvania in the Revolution
Pennsylvanians may well take pride in the dominant role played by their state in the early development of the national government. At the same time that Pennsylvania was molding its own statehood, it was providing leadership and a meeting place for the men concerned with building a nation.

Philadelphia was the nation's capital during the Revolution, except when the British threat caused the capital to be moved, respectively, to Baltimore, Lancaster, and York. While Congress was sitting in York (October 1777 - June 1778), it approved the Articles of Confederation, the first step toward a national government. After the war, the capital was moved to New York, but from 1790 until the opening of the District of Columbia in 1800, Philadelphia was again the capital. In 1787, the U.S. Constitutional Convention met in Philadelphia.

The Declaration of Independence
The movement to defend American rights grew into the movement for independence in the meetings of the Continental Congress at Carpenters' Hall and the State House (Independence Hall) in Philadelphia. The spirit of independence ran high, as shown by spontaneous declarations of frontiersmen in the western areas and by the political events that displaced the old provincial government.

The War for Independence
Pennsylvania troops took part in almost all the campaigns of the Revolution. A rifle battalion joined in the siege of Boston in August 1775. Others fought bravely in the ill-fated Canadian campaign of 1776 and in the New York and New Jersey campaigns. The British naturally considered Philadelphia of key importance and, in the summer of 1777, invaded the state and captured the capital. The battles of Brandywine, Germantown, and Whitemarsh were important engagements of this period. Following these battles, Washington went into winter quarters at Valley Forge from December 1777 to June 1778. News of the French alliance, which Benjamin Franklin had helped to negotiate, and the adoption of new strategy caused the British to leave Philadelphia in the spring of 1778. Frontier Pennsylvania suffered heavily from British and Indian raids until they were answered in 1779 by John Sullivan's and Daniel Brodhead's expeditions against the Six Nations Indians.

Pennsylvania soldiers formed a major portion of Washington's army, and such military leaders as Arthur St. Clair, Anthony Wayne, Thomas Mifflin, and Peter Muhlenberg gave valuable service. Pennsylvania also aided in the creation of the Continental navy, many ships being built or purchased in Philadelphia and manned by Pennsylvania sailors. The Irish-born John Barry became first in a long list of Pennsylvania's naval heroes.

The Arsenal of Independence

The products of Pennsylvania farms, factories, and mines were essential to the success of the Revolutionary armies. At Carlisle a Continental ordnance arsenal turned out cannons, swords, pikes, and muskets. The state actively encouraged the manufacture of gunpowder. Pennsylvania's financial support, both from its government and from individuals, was of great importance. By 1780, the state had contributed more than $6 million to the Congress and, when the American states had reached financial exhaustion, ninety Philadelphians subscribed a loan of £300,000 to supply the army. Later, in 1782, the Bank of North America was chartered to support government fiscal needs. Robert Morris and Haym Salomon were important financial supporters of the Revolution.

FOUNDING A COMMONWEALTH

A Pennsylvania Revolution

Pennsylvania's part in the American Revolution was complicated by political changes within the state, constituting a Pennsylvania revolution of which not all patriots approved. The temper of the people outran the conservatism of the Provincial Assembly. Extralegal committees gradually took over the reins of government, and in June 1776 these committees called a state convention to meet on July 15,1776.

The Constitution of 1776

The convention superseded the old government completely, established a Council of Safety to rule in the interim, and drew up the first state constitution, adopted on September 28, 1776. This provided an assembly of one house and a supreme executive council instead of a governor. The Declaration of Rights section has been copied in subsequent constitutions without significant change.

Many patriot leaders were bitterly opposed to the new Pennsylvania constitution. Led by such men as John Dickinson, James Wilson, Robert Morris, and Frederick Muhlenberg, they carried on a long fight with the Constitutional party, a radical group. Joseph Reed, George Bryan, William Findley, and other radicals governed Pennsylvania until 1790. Their most noteworthy accomplishments were the act for the gradual abolition of slavery (1780) and an act of 1779 which took over the public lands owned by the Penn family (but allowed them some compensation in recognition of the services of the founder). The conservatives gradually gained more strength, helped by the Constitutionalists' poor financial administration.

The Constitution of 1790

By 1789 the conservatives felt strong enough to rewrite the state constitution, and the Assembly called a convention to meet in November. In the convention, both the conservative majority and the radical minority showed a tendency to compromise and to settle their differences along moderate lines. As a result, the new constitution embodied the best ideas of both parties and was adopted with little objection. It provided for a second legislative house, the State Senate, and for a strong governor with extensive appointing powers.

FOUNDING A NATION

Pennsylvania and the United States Constitution

Because of a lack of central power, as well as financial difficulties, the Articles of Confederation could no longer bind together the newly independent states. As a result, the Federal Constitutional Convention met in Philadelphia in 1787. The structure that evolved remains the basis of our government today.

The Pennsylvania Assembly sent eight delegates to the Federal Convention. Four of these had been signers of the Declaration of Independence. The delegation included the venerable Benjamin Franklin, whose counsels of moderation on several occasions kept the convention from dissolving; the brilliant Gouverneur Morris, who spoke more often than any other member; and the able lawyer James Wilson, who, next to Madison of Virginia,

was the principal architect of the Constitution. Pennsylvania's delegation supported every move to strengthen the national government and signed the finished Constitution on September 17. The conservatives in the Pennsylvania Assembly took swift action to call a ratifying convention, which met in Philadelphia on November 21. The Federalists, favoring ratification, elected a majority of delegates and, led by Wilson, made Pennsylvania the second state to ratify, on December 12,1787.

Population and Immigration

Large areas of the northern and western parts of the state were undistributed or undeveloped in 1790, and many other sections were thinly populated. The state adopted generous land policies, distributed free "Donation Lands" to Revolutionary veterans and offered other lands at reasonable prices to actual settlers. Conflicting methods of land distribution and the activities of land companies and of unduly optimistic speculators caused much legal confusion. By 1860, with the possible exception of the northern tier counties, population was scattered throughout the state. There was increased urbanization, although rural life remained strong and agriculture involved large numbers of people. The immigrant tide swelled because of large numbers of Irish fleeing the potato famine of the late 1840s and Germans fleeing the political turbulence of their homeland about the same time. As a result of the Gradual Emancipation Act of 1780, the 3,737 African American slave population of 1790 dropped to 64 by 1840, and by 1850 all Pennsylvania African Americans were free unless they were fugitives from the South. The African American community had 6,500 free people in 1790, rising to 57,000 in 1860. Philadelphia was their population and cultural center.

POLITICAL DEVELOPMENTS

Reaction Against the Federalist Party

From 1790 to 1800, Philadelphia was the capital of the United States. While Washington was president, the state supported the Federalist Party, but grew gradually suspicious of its aristocratic goals. From the beginning, Senator William Maclay of Pennsylvania was an outspoken critic of the party. When Thomas Jefferson organized the Democrat-Republican Party, he had many supporters in Pennsylvania. Thomas Mifflin, Pennsylvania's first governor under the Constitution of 1790, was a moderate who avoided commitment to any party but leaned toward the Jeffersonians. The Whiskey Rebellion in Western Pennsylvania in 1794 hastened the reaction against the Federalists and provided a test of national unity. The insurrection was suppressed by an army assembled at Carlisle and Fort Cumberland and headed by President Washington. Partly as a result, Jefferson drew more votes than Adams in Pennsylvania in the presidential election in 1796. It was a foreboding sign for the Federalists, who were defeated in the national election of 1800.

Jeffersonian and Jacksonian Democratic Dominance

In 1799 Mifflin was succeeded by Thomas McKean, a conservative Jeffersonian Democrat-Republican, who governed until 1808. McKean's opposition to measures advocated by the liberal element in his party led to a split in its ranks and an unsuccessful attempt to impeach him. His successor, Simon Snyder of Selinsgrove, represented the liberal wing. Snyder, who served three terms until 1817, was the first governor to come from common, nonaristocratic origins. In this period, the capital was transferred from Philadelphia to Lancaster in 1799 and finally to Harrisburg in 1812. During the War of 1812, Pennsylvanians General Jacob Brown and Commodore Stephen Decatur were major military leaders. Stephen Girard, Albert Gallatin, and Alexander James Dallas helped organize national war finances, and Gallatin served as peace commissioner at Ghent. Oliver Hazard Perry's fleet, which won the Battle of Lake Erie in 1813, was built at Erie by Daniel Dobbins, a native Pennsylvanian. Today, the Historical and Museum Commission has extensively restored Perry's flagship, the U.S.S. Niagara, which may be appreciated by the public when visiting Erie. In 1820, a coalition of Federalists and conservative Democrats elected Joseph Hiester, whose non-partisan approach reformed government but destroyed his own coalition. The election of 1820 marked the end of the use of caucuses to select candidates and the triumph of the open conventions system. The Family Party Democrats elected the two succeeding governors, John Andrew Shulze and George Wolf (1823-1834), who launched the progressive but very costly Public Works system of state built canals. Attitudes toward President Andrew Jackson and his policies, especially that concerning the Second Bank of the United States, altered political alignments in Pennsylvania during this period. In 1834, Gov. Wolf signed the Free School Act which alienated many, including Pennsylvania Germans, so that the Democrats lost the next governorship to the Anti-Masonic Joseph Ritner who was supported by the

Whig Party. In a dramatic speech, Thaddeus Stevens persuaded the Assembly not to repeal the Free School Law. But the Masonic investigations in the Assembly which followed were ludicrous, and the Democrat David R. Porter received five thousand more votes than Ritner in the 1838 election. Ritner's followers claimed fraud, and violence nearly erupted in the "Buckshot War," until several of Ritner's legislative followers bolted and placed Porter in office.

The Constitution of 1838
In 1837, a convention was called to revise the state's laws and draft a new constitution. The resulting constitution, in 1838, reduced the governor's appointive power, increased the number of elective offices, and shortened terms of office. The voters were given a greater voice in government and were better protected from abuses of power. However, free African Americans were disenfranchised. The burning of Pennsylvania Hall in Philadelphia, a center for many reform activities, in the same year, showed that the new constitution coincided with an awakened hostility toward abolition and racial equality.

Shifting Tides
Following the adoption of the new constitution in 1838, six governors followed in succession prior to the Civil War, two of whom were Whigs. State debts incurred for internal improvements, such as the canal system, almost bankrupted the state, until the Public Works were finally sold. The search for a sound banking and currency policy and the rising political career of James Buchanan dominated this period. It was marred by the tragic religious riots of the Native American Association at Kensington in 1844.

The annexation of Texas and the war with Mexico which ensued in 1846 were generally supported in Pennsylvania. More men enlisted than could be accepted by the armed forces, but many Pennsylvanians were opposed to any expansion of slavery into the territory taken from Mexico. David Wilmot of Bradford County became a national figure in 1846 by his presentation in Congress of the Wilmot Proviso opposing slavery's extension, and his action was supported almost unanimously by the Pennsylvania Assembly.

Pennsylvania and the Antislavery Movement
The Quakers were the first group to express organized opposition to slavery. Slavery slowly disappeared in Pennsylvania under the Gradual Emancipation Act of 1780, but nationally the issue of slavery became acute after 1820. Many Pennsylvanians were averse to the return of fugitive slaves to their masters. Under an act of 1826, which was passed to restrain this, a Maryland agent was convicted of kidnapping in 1837, but the United States Supreme Court declared the act unconstitutional in 1842. The state forbade the use of its jails to detain fugitive African Americans in 1847. The Compromise of 1850, a national program intended to quiet the agitation over slavery, imposed a new Federal Fugitive Slave Law, but citizens in Christiana, Lancaster County, rioted in 1851 to prevent the law from being implemented. Opposition to slavery and the desire for a high tariff led to the rise of the new Republican Party in Pennsylvania. Pennsylvania Democrat James Buchanan was elected President because of a deadlock over the slavery issue among the other major politicians, and he then announced a policy of noninterference with slavery in the states and popular sovereignty in the federal territories. Because of controversy over the admission of Kansas as a state, Buchanan lost support of most Northern Democrats, and disruption within the Democratic Party made possible Abraham Lincoln's election to the Presidency in 1860. The Civil War followed. The expression "underground railroad" may have originated in Pennsylvania, where numerous citizens aided the escape of slaves to freedom in Canada. Anna Dickinson, Lucretia Mott, Ann Preston, and Jane Swisshelm were among Pennsylvania women who led the antislavery cause. Thaddeus Stevens was an uncompromising foe of slavery in Congress after he was reelected to the House of Representatives in 1859. Pennsylvania abolitionist leaders were both African American and white. African American leaders included those who made political appeals, like James Forten and Robert Purvis, underground railroad workers Robert Porter and William Still; publication activist John B. Vashon and his son George; and the organizer of the Christiana Riot of 1851 against fugitive slave hunters, William Parker.

African Americans made some cultural advances during this period. William Whipper organized reading rooms in Philadelphia. In 1794, Rev. Absolam Jones founded St. Thomas African Episcopal Church, and Rev. Richard Allen opened the Mother Bethel African Methodist Episcopal Church, both in Philadelphia. The first African American church in Pittsburgh (A.M.E.) was founded in 1822.

Women

Courageous individual women worked not only for their own cause but also for other reforms, although the status of the whole female population changed little during this period. Catherine Smith, for example, manufactured musket barrels for the Revolutionary Army, and the mythical battle heroine Molly Pitcher was probably also a Pennsylvanian. Sara Franklin Bache and Ester De Berdt Reed organized a group of 2,200 Pennsylvania women to collect money, buy cloth, and sew clothing for Revolutionary soldiers. Lucretia Mott, a Quaker preacher and teacher, was one of four women to participate at the formation of the American Anti-Slavery Society in Philadelphia in 1833, and became president of the Female Anti-Slavery Society. With Elizabeth Cady Stanton she launched the campaign for women's rights at Seneca Falls, New York, in 1848. Jane Grey Swisshelm, abolitionist and advocate of women's rights, used newspapers and lectures. In 1848, she launched her abolitionist paper, *The Saturday Visiter*, which featured antislavery propaganda and women's rights. Her essays influenced the state legislature to grant married women the right to own property, in 1848.

Disruption of the Democracy

The political winds began to shift due to the Southern domination of the Democratic Party, rising abolition sentiment and a desire to promote Pennsylvania's growing industries by raising tariffs. In 1856, Pennsylvania took the lead in the organization of the new Republican Party, with former Democratic leader Simon Cameron throwing his support to the new party. Congressmen David Wilmot and Galusha Grow typified the national statesmanship of Pennsylvania in this period. In 1860 the Republicans emerged as the dominant party in the state and nation with the elections of Governor Andrew Gregg Curtin and President Abraham Lincoln.

Industry

By 1861, the factory system had largely replaced the domestic system of home manufacture, and the foundation of the state's industrial greatness was established. The change was most noticeable after 1840 because of a shift to machinery and factories in the textile industry. By 1860, there were more than two hundred textile mills. Leathermaking, lumbering, shipbuilding, publishing, and tobacco and paper manufacture also prospered in the 1800s.

Pennsylvania's outstanding industrial achievements were in iron and steel. Its production of iron was notable even in colonial times, and the charcoal furnaces of the state spread into the Juniata and western regions during the mid-1800s. Foundries, rolling mills, and machine shops became numerous and, by the Civil War, the state rolled about half the nation's iron, aiding the development of railroads. The Baldwin Works were established in Philadelphia in 1842, and the Bethlehem Company was organized in 1862. The Cambria Works at Johnstown were established in 1854 and, by the end of the Civil War, were the largest mills in the country. William Kelly, a native of Pittsburgh, is regarded as the inventor of the Bessemer process of making steel.

Although much importance is given to the discovery of gold in California, the discovery and development of Pennsylvania's mineral and energy resources far overshadowed that event. Cornwall, in Lebanon County, provided iron ore from colonial times, and ore was also found in many other sections of Pennsylvania in which the charcoal iron industry flourished. The use of anthracite coal began on a large scale after 1820 with the organization of important mining companies.

Labor

After the Revolution, the use of indentured servants sharply declined. The growth of industrial factories up to 1860, however, enlarged the gulf between skilled and unskilled labor, and immigrants were as much subordinated by this as they had been under indenture. Local, specialized labor unions had brief successes, especially in Philadelphia where in 1845 a city ordinance placed a ten-hour limit on the laborer's day. The state's mechanics' lien law of 1854 was another victory for the rights of labor.

TRANSPORTATION

Roads

The settlement of new regions of the state was accompanied by provisions for new roads. The original Lancaster Pike connecting Philadelphia with Lancaster was completed in 1794. By 1832, the state led the nation in improved roads, having more than three thousand miles. The National or Cumberland Road was a major route

for western movement before 1850. Between 1811 and 1818 the section of this road in Pennsylvania was built through Somerset, Fayette, and Washington Counties. It is now Route 40.

Waterways

Most of the state's major cities were built along important river routes. In the 1790s, the state made extensive studies for improving the navigation of all major streams, and canals began to supplement natural waterways. Canals extending the use of the Delaware and Schuylkill rivers were chartered before 1815, and the Lehigh Canal was completed in 1838. The vast system named the State Works of Pennsylvania soon overshadowed privately constructed canals. The system linked the east and the west by 1834, but the expense nearly made the state financially insolvent. The benefits to the economic progress of distant regions, however, provided ample justification for the high cost.

Although canals declined rapidly with the advent of the railroad, Pennsylvania's ports and waterways remained active. The steamboat originated with experiments by John Fitch of Philadelphia from 1787 to 1790, and Lancaster County native Robert Fulton established it as a practical medium of transportation on the Ohio, Allegheny and Monongahela Rivers.

Railroads

Rail transport began in 1827, operated at first by horse power or cables. The tracks connected anthracite fields with canals or rivers. The Columbia and Philadelphia Railroad, completed in 1834 as part of the State Works, was the first ever built by a government. Pennsylvania's first railroad built as a common carrier was the Philadelphia, Germantown and Norristown Railroad, completed in 1835.

Major railroads chartered in the state included the Philadelphia and Reading (1833) and the Lehigh Valley (1846, reincorporated 1853). However, the most important of all was the Pennsylvania Railroad, chartered April 13, 1846, and completed to Pittsburgh by 1852. It absorbed so many short railroad lines by 1860 that it had nearly a monopoly on rail traffic from Chicago through Pennsylvania. And whereas Pennsylvania had reached its maximum of 954 canal miles by 1840, total railroad trackage grew by 1860 to 2,598 miles. In miles of rail and in total capital invested in railroads, Pennsylvania led all other states on the eve of the Civil War.

CULTURE

Education

The Constitution of 1790 provided the basis for a public system of education, and several acts were passed for that purpose. It was not until the Free School Act of 1834, however, that a genuinely democratic system of public schools was initiated. By 1865 the number of public schools had quadrupled. In 1852 a state association of teachers was organized. Five years later the Normal School Act was passed, and a separate government department was created for the supervision of schools. These were significant advances in social organization. Numerous private schools supplemented the public system. There also was a rapid development of academies, corresponding to modern high schools. Many academies received public aid.

Science

The traditions of scientific inquiry established in Pennsylvania by Benjamin Franklin, David Rittenhouse, and the Bartrams continued. The American Philosophical Society was the first of many organizations founded in Philadelphia to encourage scientific work. The Academy of Natural Sciences was founded in 1812 and the Franklin Institute in 1824. The American Association of Geologists, formed in Philadelphia in 1840, later grew into the American Association for the Advancement of Science. The scientific leadership of Pennsylvania was represented by many individuals, of whom only a few can be named. James Woodhouse (1770-1809) pioneered in chemical analysis, plant chemistry, and the scientific study of industrial processes. Isaac Hayes (1796-1879) of Philadelphia pioneered in the study of astigmatism and color blindness. The Moravian clergyman Lewis David von Schweinitz (1780-1834) made great contributions to botany, discovering more than twelve hundred species of fungi.

Literature and the Arts

Charles Brockden Brown of Philadelphia was the first American novelist of distinction and the first to follow a

purely literary career. Hugh Henry Brackenridge of Pittsburgh gave the American West its first literary work in his satire *Modern Chivalry*. Philadelphia continued as an important center for printing with J. B. Lippincott taking the lead and, for magazines, with the publication of the *Saturday Evening Post*. Bayard Taylor, who began his literary career before the Civil War, published his most notable work in 1870-71-the famous translation of Goethe's *Faust*.

In architecture, the red brick construction of southeastern Pennsylvania was supplemented by buildings in the Greek Revival style. The New England influence was strong in the domestic architecture of the northern tier counties. Thomas U. Walter and William Strickland gave Pennsylvania an important place in the architectural history of the early 1800s. Walter designed the Treasury Building and the Capitol dome in Washington. The nation's first institution of art-the Pennsylvania Academy of the Fine Arts-was founded in Philadelphia in 1805, although by then, such painters as Gilbert Stuart, Benjamin West, and the Peale family had already made Philadelphia famous.

Philadelphia was the theatrical center of America until 1830, a leader in music publishing and piano manufacture, and the birthplace of American opera. William Henry Fry's *Lenora* (1845) was probably the first publicly performed opera by an American composer. Stephen Foster became the songwriter for the nation.

Religion
In the years between independence and the Civil War, religion flourished in the Commonwealth. In addition to the growth of worship, religion led the way to enlargement of the educational system. In this period, churches threw off European ties and established governing bodies in the United States. In 1789 John Carroll of Maryland became the first Catholic bishop in America. In 1820 the establishment of a national Lutheran synod was the last of the breaks from Europe by a major Protestant denomination. Some new churches were formed: Jacob Albright formed the Evangelical Association, a Pennsylvania German parallel to Methodism; Richard Alien formed the African Methodist Episcopal Church in 1816; and John Winebrenner founded the Church of God in Harrisburg in 1830. Isaac Leeser, who founded Conservative Judaism in America, did most of his important writing in Philadelphia in this period. Presbyterianism, which was the largest Protestant denomination before 1860, drifted westward and had its stronghold in western Pennsylvania. Quakers, although decreasing in number, led many humanitarian and reform movements. Although anti-Catholic riots occurred at Kensington in 1844, German and Irish immigrants enlarged the number of Catholics in the state.

THE ERA OF INDUSTRIAL ASCENDANCY: 1861-1945

After 1861 Pennsylvania's influence on national politics diminished gradually, but its industrial complex grew rapidly.

The Civil War
During the Civil War, Pennsylvania played an important role in preserving the Union. Southern forces invaded Pennsylvania three times by way of the Cumberland Valley, a natural highway from Virginia to the North. Pennsylvania shielded the other northeastern states.

Pennsylvania's industrial enterprise and natural resources were essential factors in the economic strength of the northern cause. Its railroad system, iron and steel industry, and agricultural wealth were vital to the war effort. The shipbuilders of Pennsylvania, led by the famous Cramp Yards, contributed to the strength of the navy and merchant marine. Thomas Scott, as Assistant Secretary of War, directed telegraph and railway services. Engineer Herman Haupt directed railroad movement of troops and was personally commended by President Lincoln. Jay Cooke helped finance the Union cause, and Thaddeus Stevens was an important congressional leader. Simon Cameron was the Secretary of War until January 1862.

No man made a greater impression as a state governor during the Civil War than Pennsylvania's Andrew Curtin. At his first inaugural he denied the right of the South to secede and throughout the war was active in support of the national draft. In September 1862, he was the host at Altoona to a conference of northern governors which pledged support to Lincoln's policies.

Nearly 350,000 Pennsylvanians served in the Union forces, including 8,600 African American volunteers. At the beginning, Lincoln's call for 14 regiments of volunteers was answered by 25 regiments. In May 1861, the Assembly, at Curtin's suggestion, created the Pennsylvania Reserve Corps of 15 regiments enlisted for three years' service. They were mustered into the Army of the Potomac after the first Battle of Bull Run, and thousands of other Pennsylvanians followed them. Camp Curtin at Harrisburg was one of the major troop concentration centers of the war. Admiral David D. Porter opened the Mississippi and Rear Admiral John A. Dahlgren made innovations in ordnance which greatly improved naval fire power. Army leaders from Pennsylvania were numerous and able, including such outstanding officers as George B. McClellan, George G. Meade, John F. Reynolds, Winfield S. Hancock, John W. Geary, and John F. Hartranft.

After the Battle of Antietam, General J.E.B. Stewart's cavalry rode around General George McClellan's army and reached Chambersburg on October 10, 1862. There they seized supplies and horses, burned a large storehouse, and then withdrew as rapidly as they had come.

In June 1863, General Robert E. Lee turned his 75,000 men northward on a major invasion of Pennsylvania. The state called up reserves and volunteers for emergency duty. At Pittsburgh the citizens fortified the surrounding hills, and at Harrisburg fortifications were thrown up on both sides of the Susquehanna. Confederate forces captured Carlisle and advanced to within three miles of Harrisburg; the bridge at Wrightsville had to be burned to prevent their crossing. These outlying forces were recalled when the Union army under General George G. Meade met Lee's army at Gettysburg. In a bitterly fought engagement on the first three days of July, the Union army threw back the Confederate forces, a major turning point in the struggle to save the Union. Not only was the battle fought on Pennsylvania soil, but nearly a third of General Meade's army were Pennsylvania troops. Governor Curtin led the movement to establish the battlefield as a memorial park.

In 1864, in retaliation for Union raids on Virginia, a Confederate force under General John McCausland advanced to Chambersburg and threatened to burn the town unless a large ransom was paid. The citizens refused, and Chambersburg was burned on July 20, leaving two-thirds of its people homeless and causing damage of almost two million dollars.

Republican Dominance

After the Civil War the Republican Party was dominant. The war was viewed as a victory for its principles. Conflicts between conservatives and liberals took place within the party. A series of political managers or bosses-Simon and J. Donald Cameron, Matthew Quay, and Boies Penrose-assured Republican control of the state, although reformers were shocked by their methods. These bosses sat in Congress. Other Republican leaders prevailed in most cities. From 1861 to 1883 Republicans held the governorship. Then, a factional split within the Republicans led to the election of Democrat Robert E. Pattison, and his reelection in 1891. After that, Republicans held the governor's office until 1935. The death of Senator Penrose in 1921 ended the era of Republican state bosses in Congress. Joseph R. Grundy of the Pennsylvania Manufacturers Association and Andrew W. Mellon, U.S. Secretary of the Treasury (1921-1932), were typical of Republican leadership after Penrose. While Pennsylvania's government was closely allied to industry and big business, it also spawned progressive programs. Governor Gifford Pinchot was a remarkable reformer. On balance, the Republican system's justification was that in assisting industry it fostered prosperity for all-"the full dinner pail." The enormous adjustments necessary for dealing with the unemployment and economic chaos of the 1930s led to the revival of the Democratic Party. Democrats captured Pittsburgh in 1933, and the administration of Governor George H. Earle (1935-1939) was modeled on the New Deal of President Roosevelt. But the state returned to Republican administration in 1940 and remained so until 1954.

The Constitution of 1874

The fourth constitution of the Commonwealth was partly a result of a nationwide reform movement in the 1870s and partly a result of specific corrections to the previous constitution. It provided for the popular election of judges, the State Treasurer, and the Auditor General. It created an office of Lieutenant Governor and a Department of Internal Affairs which combined several offices under an elected secretary. The head of the public school system received the title of Superintendent of Public Instruction. The General Assembly was

required to provide efficient public education for no less than one million dollars per year. The Governor's term was lengthened from three to four years, but he could no longer succeed himself. He was empowered to veto individual items within appropriations bills. The membership of the General Assembly was increased, but its powers were limited by a prohibition of special or local legislation about certain specified subjects, a constitutional debt limit, and other restrictions. Sessions of the General Assembly became biennial.

New State Agencies

Although the new constitution was detailed, it provided flexibility in the creation of new agencies. Thus in 1873, even while the new constitution was being discussed, the Insurance Department was created to supervise and regulate insurance companies. In the following years many other agencies were created, sometimes as full-fledged departments and sometimes as boards, bureaus, or commissions, while existing agencies were often changed or abolished. For example, the Factory Inspectorship of 1889 became the Department of Labor and Industry in 1913. The Board of Public Charities (1869), the Committee on Lunacy (1883), the Mothers' Assistance Fund (1913), and the Prison Labor Commission (1915) were consolidated into the Department of Welfare in 1921. By 1922 there were 139 separate state agencies, demonstrating the need for simplification, consolidation and reorganization. The Administrative Codes of 1923 and 1929 accomplished these goals. The judicial branch of government was also changed by the creation of the Superior Court in 1895 to relieve the mounting caseload of the Supreme Court.

The Spanish-American War

By 1895 the island of Cuba was in a state of revolution, its people desiring to break away from Spanish rule. News of harsh methods used to suppress Cuban outbreaks aroused anger in the United States. When the battleship *Maine* blew up in Havana harbor, war became inevitable in 1898. Congressman Robert Adams of Philadelphia wrote the resolutions declaring war on Spain and recognizing the independence of Cuba. President McKinley's call for volunteers was answered with enthusiasm throughout the Commonwealth. Pennsylvania military leaders included Brigadier General Abraham K. Arnold and Brigadier General James M. Bell. Major General John R. Brooks, a native of Pottsville, served as military governor in Cuba and Puerto Rico. Although no Pennsylvania troops fought in Cuba, units from the Commonwealth saw action in Puerto Rico. A Pennsylvania regiment was the first American organization to engage in land combat in the Philippine Islands. It remained there for the Filipino Insurrection.

The First World War

Pennsylvania's resources and manpower were of great value to the war effort of 1917-1918. The shipyards of Philadelphia and Chester were decisive in maintaining maritime transport. Pennsylvania's mills and factories provided a large part of the war materials for the nation. Nearly three thousand separate firms held contracts for war supplies of various types. Pennsylvanians subscribed to nearly three billion dollars worth of Liberty and Victory Bonds, and paid well over a billion dollars in federal taxes during the war. Civilian resources were organized through a State Defense Council with local affiliates. Pennsylvania furnished more than three hundred thousand men for the armed forces, and the 28th Division won special distinction. The Saint Mihiel drive and the Argonne offensive were among the famous campaigns of the war in which Pennsylvania troops took part. General Tasker H. Bliss, a native of Lewisburg, was appointed chief of staff in 1917, and later was made a member of the Supreme War Council and the American Peace Commission. He was succeeded as chief of staff by another Pennsylvania West Point graduate, General Peyton C. March, originally from Easton. Admiral William S. Sims, a Pennsylvania graduate of the Naval Academy, was in charge of American naval operations.

Population

Large areas of the northern and western parts of the state were unsettled or thinly populated in 1800. By the time of the Civil War, with the exception of the northern tier counties, population was scattered throughout the state. There was increased urbanization, although rural life remained strong and agriculture involved large numbers of people. The immigrant tide continued alter the Civil War and brought about a remarkable change in the composition of the population. While most of the state's pre-1861 population was composed of ethnic groups from northern Europe such as the English, Irish, Scotch-Irish and Germans, the later period brought increased numbers of Slavic, Italian, Finn, Scandinavian, and Jewish immigrants. At the height of this "new

immigration," between 1900 and 1910, the Commonwealth witnessed the largest population increase of any decade in its history. African American migration from the South intensified after 1917, when World War I curtailed European immigration, and again during World War II. By World War II almost five percent of the state's population was African American. In 1940 the Commonwealth was the second largest state in the nation with a population two-thirds that of New York.

Women

The status of women began to improve by the 1860s. In 1861, the first school for nurses in America opened in Pennsylvania. Pennsylvania played a prominent part in the suffrage movement. Philadelphia was a hotbed of feminist agitation. In 1868 women in Philadelphia organized a Pennsylvania Women's Suffrage Association. On July 4, 1876, Susan B. Anthony read her famous "Declaration of Rights for Women" at the Washington statue in front of Independence Hall. Well-known Pennsylvania feminists such as Lucretia Mott, Ann Davies, Florence Kelley, Ann Preston, and Emma Guffey Miller were all active in the long battle which culminated in women receiving the vote.

The General Assembly approved a women's suffrage amendment to the state's Constitution in 1913 and again in 1915, but Pennsylvania's male voters rejected the amendment by fifty-five thousand votes. On June 4, 1919, the Nineteenth Amendment to the U.S. Constitution was approved by Congress. Just ten days later, Pennsylvania became the seventh state to ratify it. By August 1920, the amendment became law and women could vote.

Florence Kelley was a Philadelphia-born lawyer and social worker who championed the fight for better working conditions for women and children. For thirty-two years she was the leader of the National Consumers League, which demanded consumer protection as well as improved working conditions. Isabel Darlington was the first female lawyer admitted to practice before the Pennsylvania Supreme and Superior Courts.

Sarah C. F. Hallowell was active in the work of the Philadelphia Centennial Exposition and in charge of a newspaper, the *New Century*, published by the Women's Executive Committee and staffed entirely by women who worked as editors, reporters, correspondents, and compositors.

When the ten greatest American painters of all time were exhibited in a special section of the Chicago Century of Progress Art Exhibition, Mary Cassatt was the only woman represented. Born in Allegheny City, she received her only formal training at the Pennsylvania Academy of the Fine Arts. This institution has always regarded her as one of its most important alumnae, granting her its gold medal of honor in 1914.

From 1893 to 1906, Ida Tarbell, from Erie, worked for the publisher S.S. McClure as a feature writer and editor of *McClure's Magazine*. It was during this time that she published her *History of the Standard Oil Company*, a muckraking account which brought her to the forefront of her profession.

Because of the Quakers' traditional high view of women's capabilities, Philadelphia had long been a center for female education. The founding of Women's Medical College there in 1850 led to the entrance of women into the medical profession. Hannah E. Myers Longshore was the first female with a medical degree to establish a successful private practice. Beaver College in Jenkintown was the first women's college of higher education in the state. Women were very successful in the teaching profession. Mollie Woods Hare pioneered in teaching the mentally retarded before World War 1. In 1887, Ella M. Boyce was made school superintendent of Bradford, the first woman to hold such a position in the United States.

Labor

Pennsylvanians played an important role in the development of the labor movement, and the Commonwealth was the site of some of the largest strikes in the history of American labor. William H. Sylvis, from Indiana County, was a founder of the Iron-Molders' International Union, and he later led the National Labor Union in 1868-69. Uriah Stephens of Philadelphia and Terence V. Powderly of Scranton were leaders of the Knights of Labor, the most important national union between 1871 and 1886. At their peak in the mid-1880s, the Knights had about seven hundred thousand members. Pennsylvanians played an important role in the formation of the

Amalgamated Association of Iron and Steel Workers in 1876. Pennsylvania's anthracite miners in Schuylkill, Carbon and Northumberland Counties organized the Workingmen's Benevolent Association in 1868.

From the Civil War until 1877 a secret group named the Molly Maguires was powerful in the anthracite region, working for miners of Irish descent and sympathetic to a miners' union. In 1877 private resources led by railroad executive Franklin B. Gowen smashed the Mollies using a private force and the coal and iron police. But continued problems in the anthracite area gave rise to the United Mine Workers union. At first a union for skilled miners opposed to immigrant mine laborers, under the leadership of John Mitchell it grew to encompass all coal mine workers. The anthracite strike of 1902, in which President Theodore Roosevelt intervened, set the pattern for non-violent arbitration in labor relations. Alter Mitchell, John L. Lewis led the union for many years and membership spread throughout the bituminous areas. Intervention in the anthracite strikes of the 1920s by Governor Gifford Pinchot brought the 8-hour day but no permanent end to labor discontent; many customers began to shift to other heating sources at that time. In 1929 the coal and iron police were subjected to higher standards of conduct.

Pittsburgh was the scene of major violence and property destruction during the Great Railroad Strike of 1877. Historically significant and violent strikes in the steel industry occurred at Homestead, Pennsylvania, in 1892 and throughout the greater Pittsburgh district and Monongahela River Valley in 1919. During the late 1930s, western Pennsylvania was a major center of strength in the formation of the Steel Workers Organization Committee (S.W.O.C.), which in 1942 became the United Steelworkers of America. Since the labor legislation of President Franklin D. Roosevelt's New Deal, unions have flourished and workers have received fairer treatment. It was a dispute over the right of S.W.O.C. to organize workers at the Aliquippa plant of Jones and Laughlin Steel Corporation that led, in 1936, to the U.S. Supreme Court's decision upholding the constitutionality of the Wagner Labor Relations Act and its agency, the National Labor Relations Board. This was a major advance for the cause of labor.

INDUSTRY

Manufacturing

The manufacture of steel and iron products was the largest single industry. The lives of Andrew Carnegie, Henry C. Frick, Charles M. Schwab, Eugene Grace and other "iron men" of Pennsylvania in large measure tell the story of modern American business. Concentrated for the most part in western Pennsylvania, but with important centers also at Bethlehem, Harrisburg, Lewistown, Carlisle, and Morrisville, Pennsylvania's steel industry furnished the rails for the nation's railway empire, the structural steel for its modern cities, and the armament for national defense.

The career of Andrew Carnegie, a Scotch immigrant, coincided with the rise of Pennsylvania's steel industry. Starting as a telegrapher for the Pennsylvania Railroad, he handled messages for the Army during the Civil War and entered railroad management thereafter. In 1873 he began to build new steel mills. His success in steel went on and on. Carnegie balanced his own success and ability by pledging to pay the world back through benevolent distribution of his wealth. In 1901 he sold Carnegie Steel Corporation to J. P. Morgan's new giant corporation, U.S. Steel, and spent the rest of his life managing his enormous charitable foundation.

Charles M. Schwab was born in Williamsburg in Blair County and attended St. Francis College. He taught himself metallurgy in a chemistry lab in his own basement and rose to be Carnegie's managing president. Schwab decided that he preferred to invest his own savings, so he bought Bethlehem Steel Company. He successfully advanced its interests until his death in 1939, making sure that the giant he had helped spawn, U.S. Steel, always had strong competition.

U.S. Steel Corporation was concentrated within a 100-mile radius around Pittsburgh. By sheer size it set industry standards, its ownership spilling over into the coal, coke, limestone and iron ore industries. By 1900, the steel industry had begun its inevitable migration west of Pennsylvania, but 60 percent of the nation's production still came from our state. This slipped below 50 percent by 1916, but our steel industry received new life as a result of World War 1. In the 1920s the growth of the auto industry gave steel renewed vigor, and

World War II revived the industry once again. By that time, the aluminum industry was also growing in western Pennsylvania, where Andrew W. Mellon was the main financier of the giant Alcoa Corporation.

In the 19th century, textiles and clothing manufacturing, especially worsteds and silk, grew from a base in Philadelphia, so that the state led the nation in production by 1900. Willingness to invest in new technology and new styles was largely responsible. By the 1920s, competition from the South and overseas made inroads into textile production. In 1900 the state also led the nation in tanning leather.

Food processing grew into a major industry. 1905 was the year of the Hershey Chocolate factory and the incorporation of the H. J. Heinz Co. Henry J. Heinz, known as "The Good Provider," led a movement for model factories based on the principle that workers deserve clean, pleasant work conditions with some chance for sell-improvement. Also, he fought for federal legislation outlawing commercially processed foods that had false labels and harmful chemical adulterations. This culminated in the passage of federal legislation in 1906.

During this period, Pennsylvania dominated the manufacture of railroad equipment. In the 20th century, electrical equipment manufacture also became prominent. George Westinghouse was a leader in both these fields. His air brake, patented in 1869, revolutionized railroading and was followed by his numerous inventions of signals, switches, and other safety features for trains. His Union Switch and Signal Company was formed in Pittsburgh in 1882, and about that time he turned to improving natural gas transmission and control. Then he turned to improving the nation's utilization of electricity by perfecting a means for generating large amounts of power in a more practical form, alternating current. Eventually all his laboratory and manufacturing plants were moved out of Pittsburgh to nearby Turtle Creek Valley.

Representative of America's "Management Revolution" was the Philadelphia genius Frederick Winslow Taylor, who abandoned a law career because of poor eyesight and worked as a laboring mechanic. He excelled at organizing work shops. Soon he advanced to making improvements in the organization of major corporations like Bethlehem Steel, for which he worked from 1898 to 1901. While there he developed a revolutionary method for producing fine tool steel. He set up his own management consulting company in Philadelphia, becoming America's first efficiency engineer. His crowning achievement was the publication, in 1911, of *Scientific Management*.

Lumber, Petroleum, Natural Gas, and Coal

Pennsylvania has exercised leadership in the extractive industries of lumber, petroleum, natural gas, and coal. Many of the natural stands of timber were exhausted before conservation concepts were recognized. In the 1860s the state led the nation in lumber production, but by 1900 it had dropped to fourth. During that period, Williamsport's log boom on the Susquehanna had been the world's largest lumber pile. Twentieth-century timber conservation planning owes much to Gifford Pinchot, the nation's first professional forester.

Following the discovery of oil near Titusville in 1859, the production and marketing of Pennsylvania oil grew. The oil-producing counties extended from Tioga west to Crawford and south to the West Virginia line. By 1891 Warren, Venango and McKean Counties established leadership in production. Once practical methods of transmitting and burning natural gas were developed, Pennsylvania became a leading producer in that area, also. John D. Rockefeller's Standard Oil Company was always foremost in the refining and marketing of petroleum. The early lead Pennsylvania had achieved in oil made the Keystone State the natural battleground for competing investors. Rockefeller founded Standard Oil in 1868 and, as a result of a freight price rebate deal with the New York Central Railroad, it grew to be the world's largest refinery by 1870. To overwhelm Pennsylvania's small, independent refiners, he engaged in secret agreements with such powerful interests as the Pennsylvania Railroad. He allowed the independent refiners to survive-they finally merged into the Pure Oil Company just before 1900-as long as they did not undersell Standard Oil. The corporate organization of refiners in Pennsylvania before 1900 is one reason why the state has continued to be a leading refining area even though the raw petroleum is now almost entirely imported.

Anthracite coal was the main fuel used to smelt iron until the 1880s, when the manufacture of coke from bituminous coal was developed to a degree that it replaced anthracite. Coke was used both to smelt iron and to make steel from iron. But production of anthracite continued to increase because it was used for heating and

other purposes. The bituminous and coke industries were responsible for the late 19th century industrial growth of western Pennsylvania; the iron ore deposits there would not alone have merited such growth. World War I caused two years (1917-1918) of the largest production of both types of coal the state has ever seen. In the 1920s a new coke-making process produced valuable by-products, making the old beehive coke ovens obsolete. The new coke plants were built, in many cases, outside of Pennsylvania. A declining market for coal in the 1920s caused business and labor problems. These increased in the 1930s during the nation's economic depression. Production demands in World War II revived the coal industry for those few years. In its heyday the industry was notorious for its dangers. Between 1902 and 1920 mine accident deaths occurred on an average of 525 per year.

Agriculture

The prosperous farms of the Pennsylvania Germans have always been a bulwark of our agricultural economy. The settlement and development of western and northern Pennsylvania initially occurred because of agriculture. Cereals and livestock continued to be the mainstays of the farmer. The rise of agricultural societies such as the Grange and of county fairs led to improvements in farm methods and machinery. Pennsylvania turned toward a market-oriented approach in the mid-1800s. While the number of farms has declined since 1900, farm production has increased dramatically to meet consumer demands.

After 1880, the pattern of increasing total area farmed in Pennsylvania, which began in the colonial period, ended. Total farm acreage has declined ever since, but this trend has been outweighed by improved farming methods. In 1874 a dairymen's association was formed; in 1876 a State Board of Agriculture was created which was made a department in 1895. In 1887 the federal government established an agricultural experiment station at the Agricultural College of Pennsylvania, in Centre County (the predecessor of the Pennsylvania State University), and cooperation between the college's faculty and working farmers, so important for improving production, began. In 1895 a State Veterinarian was appointed, who eventually eliminated bovine tuberculosis. The nature of farm products changed because of competition from expanding agriculture in the West, distances from markets, and changing patterns of the American diet. The first statewide farm products show was held in Harrisburg in January 1907. The State Farm Show became an annual event beginning in 1917, and the present Farm Show Building was completed in 1931.

TRANSPORTATION

Railways

Pennsylvania pioneered in early rail development. By 1860 railroad mileage had increased to 2,598, and the Reading, Lehigh and Pennsylvania systems were developing. The Pennsylvania Railroad, chartered in 1846, reached Pittsburgh in 1852. Alexander Cassatt, Thomas Scott, and John A. Roebling, who was the surveyor of the Pennsylvania's route, were leaders in its development. After 1865 Pennsylvania extended its lines to New York, Washington, Buffalo, Chicago, and St. Louis, becoming one of the great trunk-line railroads of the nation, and developed a network of subsidiary lines within the state. The Reading and Lehigh Valley systems also expanded to become great carriers of freight and important links in the industrial economy of the Middle Atlantic region. Numerous smaller lines were built to serve districts or special purposes. For example, the Bessemer and Lake Erie carried Lake Superior ore to the steel mills of Pittsburgh. All the important trunk lines of the eastern United States passed through Pennsylvania and had subsidiary feeders within the state. At its peak, the Commonwealth had more than 10,000 miles of railroad track. By 1915 the state's railroads had ceased to expand, and after World War I both passenger and freight service were reduced.

Urban Transit

Pennsylvania has a long tradition of urban public transport, beginning with horsecars in Pittsburgh and Philadelphia in the 1850s. The first of many Pittsburgh inclines-two of which operate today-opened in 1870. Philadelphia's first streetcar system began in 1892, and the Market Street Elevated train began operation in 1907. The Market Street subway, which is still in operation, was one of the first in the nation. Transit use increased steadily in Pennsylvania until the end of World War II.

Roads

Although 1,700 state-owned bridges were built before 1900, road building activity had lapsed during the canal and railroad era. It sprang anew with the advent of the automobile. Charles and Frank Duryea experimented with automobiles in Reading, and on March 24, 1898, Robert Allison of Port Carbon became the first purchaser of an automobile. Between 1903 and 1911 Pennsylvania took the lead in creating a modern road system, establishing a department of highways, requiring automobile licenses and taking over more than 8,000 miles of highway for maintenance and improvement. Operators' license fees, fines for violation of driving regulations, and a gasoline tax swelled the Motor Fund, making the motoring public the chief funder of the system. Most highway construction consisted of improvements to existing routes, including widening, laying hard surfaces, and relocating routes to eliminate sharp curves and grades. Repair garages and filling stations became numerous. The world's first "drive-in gas station" opened in Pittsburgh in 1913. An outstanding road was the Lincoln Highway. Designated in 1913, it connected the state's two largest cities and stretched from New York City to San Francisco. In 1916 the federal government instituted grants to states for highway construction, beginning a great primary highway construction effort which peaked in the 1930s. By 1928 the transcontinental system of U.S.-numbered, through highways was in use in Pennsylvania, and at about the same time an expanded state-numbered system came into being. Governor Gifford Pinchot promised in his 1930 campaign to "get the farmers out of the mud." The following year, the state took over 20,156 miles of township roads and began paving them, using light construction costing less than $7,000 a mile. As the economic depression deepened, this road-building program became an important means of providing relief work. Special federal programs also benefited the state's highways during the depression. In 1940 Pennsylvania opened the first high-speed, multi-lane highway in the country, the Pennsylvania Turnpike, which set the pattern for modern super-highways throughout the nation. The Turnpike initially connected Pittsburgh and Harrisburg, and was later expanded from the western boundary to the Delaware River, as well as northward into the anthracite region.

Aviation

In 1925 Philadelphia Congressman Clyde Kelly introduced the Airmail Act which set the American aviation industry on the road to progress. In 1927 Governor Pinchot created a State Bureau of Aeronautics. In 1939 All American Aviation, a Pennsylvania company, was licensed to carry mail to 54 communities in Pennsylvania, Ohio, Delaware, and West Virginia. All American entered a period of rapid expansion and became Allegheny Airlines. By the beginning of World War II passenger service was still in its infancy, although the very reliable DC-3 plane had been developed. Hog Island was developed in the late 1930s, with city and federal WPA assistance, and became the Philadelphia International Airport.

Society and Culture

Pennsylvania made rapid progress in social and cultural fields by expanding educational and cultural opportunities. Although Philadelphia lost the preeminent position it had earlier enjoyed as a center for new enterprises, the wealth and position of the state as a whole exerted a powerful influence in almost every phase of the nation's social and cultural development.

Communication, Performing Arts and the Media

Philadelphia was the birthplace of many publications and served as the center of publishing in the early national period. By 1840 Pennsylvania was the home of more newspapers than any other state. In the 1900s economic pressures forced many newspapers and magazines into bankruptcy, failure, or consolidation. Today most cities have only one newspaper, although Philadelphia and Pittsburgh continue to support several dailies.

Telegraph and telephone spread rapidly after the Civil War. Following Samuel Morse's development of the telegraph in the 1840s, the state was interlaced by a network of telegraph lines. Alexander Graham Bell's telephone was first demonstrated publicly at the Philadelphia Centennial Exhibition in 1876. By the end of the century, the telephone had become universal. Pennsylvanian Daniel Drawbaugh claimed to have invented a working telephone ten years before Bell, but his claim did not hold up in patent litigation. The Commonwealth now has thousands of miles of telegraph and telephone lines and almost 10 million telephones.

Pennsylvania played a key role in the development of a major 20th-century contribution to the dissemination of ideas and information-the radio. The first commercial broadcast station in the world was KDKA in Pittsburgh, which started daily schedule broadcasting on November 2, 1920. The first church service broadcast by radio occurred on KDKA a year later, and the first public address by radio was made by Herbert Hoover at the Duquesne Club in Pittsburgh in 1921. Radio quickly became a fixture in most homes, but lost its dominance in the broadcasting market with the advent of television in the 1950s.

Philadelphia, which had been the theatrical capital of America before 1830, continued to be a leader in music publishing and piano manufacture and was the birthplace of American opera. Edwin Forest, Joseph Jefferson, the Drews, and the Barrymores were important stage actors in the late 1800s and the early 1900s. The first all-motion-picture theater in the world was opened on Smithfield Street in Pittsburgh on June 19, 1905, by John P. Harris and Harry Davis. The term "nickelodeon" was coined there. The Warner brothers began their careers in western Pennsylvania.

Education

In 1857 The Normal School Act was passed, and a separate department was created for the supervision of public schools. In 1860 there were only six public high schools in the state. Beginning in 1887 the Assembly passed general laws authorizing the establishment of high schools. They had enrolled only 2 percent of the public school population when the state began to appropriate money for high schools in 1895. Ten years later the system was firmly established. By 1895 every school district was authorized to establish a high school. Initially high schools offered only two-year courses. Between 1913 and 1920 the state assumed control of all the normal schools, which were given college status in 1927. Probably the most important school legislation since 1834 was the Edmonds Act in 1921, which established minimum salary standards and qualifications for teachers and county superintendents, centralized teacher certification, set up a state Council of Education, provided for consolidation of rural schools, increased state aid to education, and made other improvements.

In 1790 there were only three institutions of university or college rank. Today there are almost two hundred institutions of higher education, a majority of which were founded after 1865. Most higher education before 1900 was sponsored by churches. The development of higher education for women, the broadening of the curriculum, and the decline of purely denominational control were important trends of the 20th century.

Science and Invention

Scientific leadership in Pennsylvania was exhibited by many individuals. Isaac Hayes (1796-1879) of Philadelphia pioneered in the study of astigmatism and color blindness. The four Rogers brothers of Philadelphia were a remarkable scientific family. James (1802-1852) and Robert (1813-1884) were noted chemists; William (1804-1882) was the state geologist of Virginia and later president of the Massachusetts Institute of Technology; and Henry (1808-1866) directed the first geological survey of Pennsylvania (1836-1847). Spencer Baird (1823-1887) of Reading was a leader in the natural sciences and the secretary of the Smithsonian Institution. Joseph Saxton (1799-1873) of Huntingdon was the father of photography in America.

Pennsylvanians also led in invention and the application of science in industry and daily life. John A. Roebling, who came to America in 1839 and spent most of his active life in Pennsylvania, led in the development of steel wire rope and steel bridges, and his engineering work was carried forward by his son Washington. William Kelly (1811-1888) exhibited leadership in invention. Edward G. Acheson (1856-1931), chemist and inventor, contributed to the development of carborundum as an abrasive and graphite as a lubricant. Henry P. Armsby (1853-1921), director of the Pennsylvania State University Agricultural Experiment Station, was internationally known for his contributions to nutritional science. Edgar Fahs Smith (1854-1928) of the University of Pennsylvania was a leading American chemist and helped to found the American Chemical Society. In the field of medicine, the Hahnemann Medical College, Jefferson Medical College, and the University of Pennsylvania Medical School made Philadelphia one of the outstanding medical centers of the nation. Medical colleges were established at the University of Pittsburgh in 1885 and at Temple University in 1901. These institutions made noteworthy contributions to medical science.

John A. Brashear (1840-1920) of Pittsburgh was important in the development of astronomical precision instruments, which made great contributions to knowledge. The inventor George Westinghouse (1846-1914), while not a native of the state, spent the greater portion of his life here. The earliest successful experiment of Thomas A. Edison with electric lighting was made in Sunbury. John R. Carson (1887-1940) and Dr. Harry Davis (1868-1931), of Pittsburgh, were notable for contributions to the development of radio. Elihu Thomson (1853-1937), one of the founders of General Electric, continued the Franklin tradition in electrical science. The world's first computer was developed at the University of Pennsylvania, in recent times, the engineering schools of the state's universities and such institutions as the Franklin Institute and the Mellon Institute have placed Pennsylvania in the forefront of modern industrial research and invention.

The Second World War

In World War II, 1.25 million Pennsylvanians served in the armed forces, or about one-eighth of the population. Also, one out of every seven members of the armed forces in World War II was a Pennsylvanian. The chief of staff, General of the Army George C. Marshall, was a native of Uniontown, and the commander of the Army Air Forces was General of the Army Henry H. Arnold, born in Gladwyne. Pennsylvania also had three full generals: Jacob L. Devers, from York, commander of the Sixth Army Group; Joseph T. McNarney, from Emporium, Deputy Allied Commander in the Mediterranean; and Carl Spaatz, from Boyertown, commander of the American Strategic Air Forces in Europe. Lieutenant General Lewis H. Brereton, from Pittsburgh, commanded the First Allied Airborne Army, and Lieutenant General Alexander M. Patch, from Lebanon, commanded the Seventh Army. The Chief of Naval Operations at the outbreak of hostilities was Admiral Harold R. Stark, from Wilkes-Barre, who later became commander of American naval forces in European waters. Admiral Richard S. Edwards, from Philadelphia, was deputy chief of naval operations, and an adopted Philadelphian, Admiral Thomas C. Kinkaid, commanded the Seventh Fleet in the South Pacific.

Altogether, there were 130 generals and admirals from Pennsylvania. More Medals of Honor were awarded to Pennsylvanians than to citizens of any other state. There were 40 military and naval installations in Pennsylvania, including two large camps, Indiantown Gap and Camp Reynolds. All the Army's doctors received training at Carlisle Barracks, and the Navy's photographic reconnaissance pilots were instructed at the Harrisburg Airport. The Philadelphia Navy Yard built two of the world's largest battleships and many lesser vessels. Among a dozen military depots in the state were Mechanicsburg Naval Supply Depot, Middletown Air Depot, Letterkenny Ordnance Depot, Frankford Arsenal, and the Philadelphia Quartermaster Depot.

Pennsylvania's industrial resources made it the "Arsenal of America." Planes, tanks, armored cars, guns and shells poured out of its factories. Ships were launched in the Delaware and Ohio rivers and on Lake Erie. Steady streams of war goods flowed over its railroads and highways. Pennsylvania oil lubricated the machines of war, and its coal kept the steel mills going. Food from its fields fed war workers and soldiers. In total war production Pennsylvania ranked sixth among the states, in shipbuilding fifth, and in ordnance fourth. It furnished almost one-third of the nation's steel. More money was spent to expand production capacity in Pennsylvania than in any other state. Three hundred Pennsylvania firms were honored with production awards.

Pennsylvanians paid over two billion dollars a year in taxes and were second only to New Yorkers in the purchase of war bonds. Under the leadership of the State Council of Defense, more than a million and a half people were organized to protect the state against enemy attack and to aid in the war effort.

MATURITY: 1945-1997

Population

Pennsylvania's population was estimated by the U.S. Census Bureau as 12,071,842 in mid-1995. Pennsylvania had long been the second most populous state, behind New York, but in 1950 it fell to third due to the growth of California. In 1980 Texas also exceeded our population, as did Florida in 1987. Thus, the present national rank is fifth. In terms of the U.S. Census Bureau's current standard for urbanization, Pennsylvania is 68.9 percent urbanized and 31.1 percent rural. Philadelphia has the fifth largest city population in the country. Pittsburgh has the 45th, but it ranks 29th under the Census Bureau's system of measuring Metropolitan Statistical Areas. Pennsylvania is the 25th most urbanized state, below such traditional farm states as Kansas.

The median age has risen more in the years since 1980 than ever before and is now thirty-six years, higher than any other states except Florida and West Virginia. Women outnumber men by about one-half million.

The 1990 Census showed 9.17 percent of the population to be African American, including 40 percent of the population of Philadelphia, 15 percent of Dauphin County, and 11 percent of both Allegheny and Delaware Counties. People of Hispanic origin (regardless of race) comprised 1.95 percent of Pennsylvania's population. There are about 16,000 Native Americans.

The population growth pattern since 1980 has been one of increases in the eastern border counties other than Philadelphia and Delaware, in the southern tier counties as far west as Somerset, along the Susquehanna Valley, and in the other southeastern counties up to the line bordering the traditional anthracite producing counties. The only western Pennsylvania county to grow in population was Butler. Monroe and Pike Counties, formerly sparsely populated, grew at astonishing rates. Seven other counties increased by 10 percent or more between 1980 and 1990: Adams, Bucks, Chester, Lancaster, Perry, Union, and Wayne. Since 1980, remarkably high population growth has occurred in the eastern, non-industrial border areas, stimulated by improved interstate highways. Young workers with children and retired workers from New York, New Jersey, and Maryland have been attracted by lower living costs and a cleaner environment.

Health

Health is a major concern of this population. Although the birth rate in Pennsylvania has gradually increased since 1980, the rate in 1994, 13 live births per thousand residents, was 15 percent below the national average. The birth pattern has changed since 1980 because of a marked decline in births to women under twenty-five and an increase in births to women age thirty-five to forty-four. Since 1960 the general fertility rate has declined by 43 percent. In comparing Pennsylvania birth and fertility rates with the United States rates back to 1950, Pennsylvania rates have been consistently lower, even during the "babyboom" years of 1950 through 1964.

In 1988 Pennsylvania finally dropped below the national average in infant mortality. It then shared with New Jersey the ranking of 22nd highest rate in the nation, 9.9 deaths in the first year of life per one thousand births. Although this achievement was eradicated by reverse trends in 1989, Pennsylvania again equaled the national average in 1990 when the state's lowest annual rate, 9.5, occurred. Statistics exist from 1975 for induced abortions to Pennsylvania residents occurring within the state. The peak rate was 23.1 per thousand women of childbearing age in 1980. The rate then declined, reaching 17 in 1988, rose in 1990, and fell to 15 in 1994.

Although it had long been higher than the national average, Pennsylvania's rate of deaths per thousand residents gradually declined to 10.0 in 1982. In 1994 it was 10.5, fifth highest in the nation (behind Missouri, Arkansas, Florida, and West Virginia). When adjusted for our aging population, however, our death rate almost exactly matches the national rate.

The state's ranking for the three most frequent causes of death in America - 1: heart disease, 2: cancer, 3: stroke - has remained the same since 1945. Together they account for two-thirds of deaths in Pennsylvania. However, cancer's share of deaths has consistently increased since 1950, while the other two have declined. All three have been higher than the U.S. average since 1950, as is appropriate for our older aged population. But death rates for external causes including accidental injury, homicide, pneumonia, and influenza have been lower than the nation's. In the 1980s Pennsylvania's suicide rate had risen to nearly match the U.S. rate, but is now significantly lower. A new category, chronic obstructive pulmonary disease, has risen to supplant accidental injuries as the fourth greatest killer. Deaths from syphilis and tuberculosis have decreased markedly in every decade since 1940, to the extent that they are now rare.

Pennsylvania is fortunate to have the sixth lowest state rate for persons not covered by health insurance. Our state is the ninth highest in the proportion of physicians to the general population, but in 1991 it had the ninth highest percentage of adult smokers.

Labor

The entire decade following World War II was a period of frequent labor strife. Fringe benefits for wage earners were points of heated dispute; they had scarcely been dreamt of before 1941. The steel strikes of 1952 and

1959-1960 required the intervention of Presidents Truman and Eisenhower. The outcome in 1960 was a triumph for the Taft-Hartley Labor Relations Act which was less favorable to labor's power to bargain than the preceding Wagner Labor Act. Although the merger of the AFL and the CIO in 1955 gave organized labor more strength, the recessions of the 1970s prevented expansion of unionization into many manufacturing areas and may have diminished membership in traditional factory forces. Unionization of office workers, however, has gone on, in line with the increasing involvement of workers in the service sector of the economy. Pennsylvania is not considered to be among the right-to-work states. In 1970 the Public Employees Relations Act established collective bargaining for teachers and other public workers. Both state and federal programs have retrained workers who were laid off due to technological change. Today Pennsylvania has the sixth largest labor pool force in the nation, 5.89 million people. From 1976 through 1985 Pennsylvania's unemployment rate ran above the national rate, but from 1986 through 1990 it was below the national average. The state unemployment rate was 4.8% in November 1996, compared to a national rate of 5.0%.

Minorities
In the post-World War II period, African American leaders in government have included State Budget Secretary Andrew W. Bradley, Pennsylvania Secretary of State C. Dolores Tucker, Speaker of the State House of Representatives K. Leroy Irvis, U.S. District Court Justice A. Leon Higginbotham Jr., and Chief Justice Robert N. C. Nix Jr. of the Pennsylvania Supreme Court. Many African Americans in the performing arts, such as Bill Cosby and Ernest "Chubby" Checker, were born in Pennsylvania and have pursued their careers here. David H. Bradley Jr. and John E. Wideman are forefront writers whose works touch on deeper themes of African American development.

The total sales receipts of the state's businesses owned by African Americans was the eighth largest in the nation. Pennsylvania was ninth among the states in the number of businesses owned by people of Hispanic origin.

Women
After World War II, Pennsylvania women continued to add to their record of achievement. Rachel Carson, whose *Silent Spring* (1962) did much to awaken the nation to environmental dangers, was born in Springdale and educated at Chatham College. The theories of anthropologist Margaret Mead continue to provoke discussion and research in that field of science. Catherine Drinker Bowen's historical and biographical works have received general acclaim. Jean Collins Kerr, dramatist, and drama critic, has influenced a generation of cinema and television audiences. Actresses Lizabeth Scott and Grace Kelly were national idols in the 1950s. Hulda Magalhaes of Bucknell University has had a remarkable career in biological research and teaching. Kathryn O'Hay Granahan was the first female member of Congress from Philadelphia and the Treasurer of the United States from 1962 to 1966. Marianne Moore (1887-1972), who was educated at Bryn Mawr College and taught at the United States Indian School in Carlisle, was a famous poet and the winner of many international awards. Hilda Doolittle from Bethlehem, a renowned imagist poet, wrote many of her works between World War II and 1961.

Elizabeth Nath Marshall, four times mayor of York, was largely responsible for urban renewal there. The remarkable career of Genevieve Blatt included twelve years as Secretary of Internal Affairs and judgeship on the Commonwealth Court in 1972. In February 1975, the state's Commission for Women was created.

In 1987, Pennsylvania was sixth among the states in the number of business firms owned by women, and these generated over 29 billion dollars in sales and receipts. Our state in 1994 had the sixth largest number of women in the work force but rated 47th among the states in the ratio of women workers to total workers.

Industry and Commerce
Diversity came to Pennsylvania as the coal, steel, and railroad industries declined. Ironically, Pennsylvania's early preeminence in industrial development poses a major liability in plants and equipment. Its enormous capital investment, past and present, is in plants and equipment now less efficient than that of newer industrial areas. In steel, Pennsylvania's integrated mills are less efficient than the South's minimills and the new steel complexes abroad, especially since nature has placed western Pennsylvania at a geographic disadvantage to the

Great Lakes-Midwest steel area in terms of iron ore deposits and water transportation. The proximity of steel plants to sources of ore and coal is not, however, as important a cost factor in corporate competition as it was forty years ago. Our steel industry began to contract in 1963, although we still lead the nation in specialty steel production. In 1995 Pennsylvania produced 9,092,986 short tons of raw steel, which was 8.66 percent of the nation's total production.

In value added from all manufacturing, an important economic indicator, Pennsylvania in 1992 was seventh among the states, with a figure of nearly 70 billion dollars, an increase of 21 percent since 1987. We were also seventh in value of shipped manufactured merchandise.

The tremendous consumer power of Pennsylvania is reflected in statistics for 1992. Our state is fifth in total retail sales receipts, over the last three decades gradually exceeding Illinois. It is fifth in the number of food retail stores and supermarkets and seventh in total sales receipts from shopping centers.

Among the fifty states, Pennsylvania in 1993 had the fourth largest state general revenue, although we were only 26th in the amount spent per capita (to each Pennsylvanian). In the amount of state indebtedness outstanding per capita we were 32nd. Statistics for 1992 show that Pennsylvania was sixth among the states in expenditures for research and development. In the breakdown of R&D spending, it was seventh in the total amount derived from industrial corporations and seventh in the amount derived from the federal government. The financial stability of the state is attested to by 1993 statistics. Pennsylvania was fifth among the states in insured commercial bank deposits and fourth in total assets of insured commercial banks. It was 14th in the number of bankruptcies in 1994.

The production and distribution of chemicals, food, and electrical machinery and equipment are important elements of Pennsylvania's industrial life. The state is also a leader in the cement industry, providing more than 10 percent of the nation's supply. Pennsylvania also produces quantities of clay products-brick, tile and fire clay-as well as glass, limestone and slate. However, by 1980 the apparels industry showed marked decline. Electronic data processing has increased tremendously, and computerization has improved many basic manufacturing and service processes.

Energy Resources

The market for Pennsylvania's coal began to decline at the end of World War II. Oil and natural gas were regarded as so much more convenient that they replaced anthracite coal as a heating fuel. The 1959 Knox Mine flood disaster in Luzerne County foretold the end of deep mining in the anthracite region. In the 1960s the market revived because large amounts of coal were used to produce electric power. Mining methods became much more efficient during this period, but in 1969 the Coal Mine Health and Safety Act was passed, followed in 1971 by the Federal Clean Air Act. Safety measures required so much additional labor that productivity per worker fell dramatically. Pennsylvania's coal was at a disadvantage by cleanliness standards because of its high sulfur content. Although the two world oil crises of the 1970s revived the market for coal again, by 1980 cheap oil was once again available. Anthracite production is now so low that it is not a major industry, although production by reclamation methods has risen since 1989.

The past two decades have not been favorable to the Pennsylvania coal industry, with the state's share of national output shrinking from nearly 15 percent to under 6 percent. The decline illustrates both a slip in competitive position and the rising output nationwide, especially in the West. Indeed, as U.S. production has risen 71 percent since 1970, Pennsylvania output dropped by over 17 percent. West Virginia and Kentucky lead the Commonwealth by substantial production margins, and Wyoming, in first place, mined more than four times as much coal as Pennsylvania in 1995. A disconcerting proportion of this production decline has been felt by the surface mining portion of the industry since 1977, the year that the U.S. Congress passed the Surface Mining Control and Reclamation Act. Production from the state's surface operations has fallen over 60 percent since its peak that year.

Reasons for the decline in Pennsylvania's bituminous coal output are many. They include loss of coking coal markets brought on by the steel industry's decline; less use of higher sulfur coals; and competitive disadvantages relative to neighboring coal-producing states caused by Pennsylvania's more stringent-and

costly-environmental regulations. More loss of market share is expected as electric utilities struggle to comply with new emissions requirements stipulated by the 1990 Federal Clean Air Act's acid rain amendments. It is widely hoped, however, that emerging clean coal technologies, such as advanced flue gas scrubbers and fluidized bed combustion, will ultimately brighten the market horizon for higher sulfur Pennsylvania coals in the twenty-first century.

In 1994, Pennsylvania's nine nuclear plants produced over one-third of our electricity, placing us second to Illinois in total nuclear produced electricity. Many object to it as a health hazard and point to the nuclear plant accident on Three Mile Island in March 1979.

Although one of John D. Rockefeller's associates once joked that he could drink all the oil that was not produced in Pennsylvania, Pennsylvania now barely produces one-thousandth of the nation's crude oil. Natural gas, however, is still a major product.

Agriculture

While the number of farms and the acreage farmed have generally declined over the past fifty years, farm production has increased dramatically due to technical improvements. The state government has fostered many agricultural developments. Pennsylvania's over 51,000 farms are the backbone of the state's economy. Pennsylvania is an important food distribution center, supplying farm and food products to markets from New England to the Mississippi River. Pennsylvania agriculture continues to grow stronger through the statewide efforts of farm and commodity organizations, agricultural extension services, strong vocational agricultural programs, and the Pennsylvania Department of Agriculture, all of which keep farmers informed of new developments and assist them in promoting and marketing farm products. Today, Pennsylvania farmers sell more than $3.6 billion in crop and livestock products annually, and agribusiness and food-related industries account for $39 billion in economic activity annually. Over four million acres of land are harvested crop land, and another four million acres are in farm woodlands and pastures. This is nearly one-third of the state's total land area. Agricultural diversity in the Commonwealth is demonstrated by the fact that Pennsylvania ranks among the top ten states in such varied products as milk, poultry, eggs, ice cream, pears, apples, grapes, cherries, sweet corn, potatoes, mushrooms, tomatoes, cheese, maple syrup, cabbage, snap beans, Christmas trees and floriculture crops, pretzels, potato chips, sausage, wheat flour, and bakery products. The state is nineteenth in the nation in total farm income, although in total farm acreage it is thirty-seventh. In livestock Pennsylvania is ranked fifth in milk cows, seventeenth in total cattle, fifteenth in hogs, and twenty-fourth in sheep. It ranks seventh in noncitrus fruits.

TRANSPORTATION

Highways

The Pennsylvania Turnpike, which set the pattern for modern super-highways throughout the nation, was expanded from the western boundary to the Delaware River, as well as northward into the anthracite region. A far-reaching federal highway act was passed in 1956, authorizing the federal government to pay 90 percent of the costs of new roads connecting the nation's principal urban centers. More turnpike miles would probably have been built had it not been for the toll-free interstate highway system established by the Federal Highway Act of 1956. Pennsylvania took advantage of these funds to build an interstate system that today stretches along 1,588 miles. The most outstanding example of the system is Interstate 80, known as the Keystone Shortway, which is 313 miles long and transverses 15 northern Pennsylvania counties.

In 1993, Pennsylvania was eighth in total highway mileage, a mere 621 miles behind seventh ranked Michigan. Our state is also seventh in number of cars, sixth in number of all vehicles, and sixth in total vehicle miles driven. Pennsylvania is third in highway funds disbursed by the state, behind only Texas and California. We rank eighth in total number of gasoline service stations. In the ratio of highway fatalities to the number of motor vehicle miles traveled, Pennsylvania is sixth highest among the 50 states.

Waterways

Waterways have always been of major importance to Pennsylvania. The state has three major ports: Philadelphia, Pittsburgh, and Erie. The Port of Philadelphia complex, encompassing Philadelphia proper and

four other cities along the Delaware River, is the largest freshwater port in the world and has the second largest volume of international tonnage in the United States. Located at the confluence of the Ohio, Monongahela, and Allegheny Rivers, Pittsburgh has long been a center for barge transportation, especially of coal and limestone. Erie has been a major center for Great Lakes transportation, especially of steel and zinc, and is connected to the St. Lawrence Seaway.

Aviation
Constant expansion of passenger service has been the story of aviation in Pennsylvania since World War II. Today there are sixteen major airports, five of which have been granted international status. Instrument landing systems became standard at airports in all the smaller cities following the Bradford Regional Airport accidents of 1968-1969. In the 1970s, automated radar terminal systems were installed at all the major airports, to handle the increased volume of traffic with safety. The international airports of Pittsburgh and Philadelphia are among the nation's twenty-nine major aviation terminals, and compete favorably with the others in total numbers of scheduled flights.

The expansion of All American Aviation to Allegheny Airlines, and then to U.S. Air, is typical of progress in the industry. The energy crises beginning in the late 1970s caused reorganization involving commuter lines, using smaller craft, operating as feeders from smaller cities to the major airports. Deregulation and the trend toward corporate mergers in the 1980s have caused further reorganization of the industry.

Two aircraft manufacturers prospered during this period. Piper Aircraft Corporation of Lock Haven outdistanced its competitors and produced America's most popular light airplane until the 1970s. Vertol Division of Boeing Corporation, successor to Piasecki Helicopter Corporation, located in Delaware County, was a major manufacturer of helicopters.

Railroads
Because of its extensive service during World War II, the railroad industry in 1946 was financially more sound than it had been since 1920, but by the end of the 1950s it was losing ground rapidly to the enlarging trucking industry. Diesel engines and a few electrified systems replaced the coal-burning locomotives which had been the railroads' pulling units for a century. In 1962 the Pennsylvania Railroad and the New York Central merged as the Penn Central Railroad, but it did not receive federal ICC approval until 1968, after having made extensive reductions in services and divestiture of assets. The new giant was bankrupt in 1970, the same year the federal government created Amtrak, a service system subsidizing passenger service on the major rail lines of the northeastern states. The federal government took control of the major freight lines in 1974 by the formation of Conrail, which subsidized 80 percent of the freight lines in Pennsylvania. Rail mileage was reduced by eliminating obsolete and unnecessary lines, typically those to now non-productive coal mines. The work force was reduced by a quarter and commuter service trains which were at first the responsibility of Conrail were gradually eliminated. In 1981 Conrail finally began to operate profitably, and in 1987 the federal government sold it to private stockholders. Although passenger service to smaller municipalities has been eliminated, faster travel is possible on the remaining routes. Seamless rails, cement ties, and the elimination of grade crossings have made this possible.

CULTURE

Literature
A major figure in the American literary scene, Pearl S. Buck (1872-1973), won both a Nobel Prize and a Pulitzer Prize. She made her home in Perkasie. Christopher Morley (1890-1957) and John O'Hara (1905-1970) were other famous 20th century Pennsylvania novelists. Marguerite de Angelis (1889-1987) wrote and illustrated books that thrilled generations of children, such as *Thee, Hannah!* and *Yonie Wondernose.*

Among living writers associated with Pennsylvania are L. Sprague deCamp, science fiction author, and John Updike, who won the Pulitzer Prize for fiction in 1982 for *Rabbit Is Rich* and received the 1983 Governor's Distinguished Pennsylvania Artist Award. James A. Michener, recipient of the 1981 Governor's Distinguished Pennsylvania Artist Award, is the author of forty books including the Pulitzer Prize winning *Tales of the South Pacific*. Poet Gerald Stern, born in Pittsburgh and now living in Easton, received the prestigious Lamont Poetry

Prize for "Lucky Leaf", as well as a 1980 Hazlett Memorial Award for Excellence in the Arts. In 1981, David Bradley's novel *The Chaneysville Incident* won acclaim as a profound and sensitive analysis of the African American male in American life. Jerry Spinelli, of Radnor and Melrose Park, has preserved adventure and imagination in his children's books with stories taking place in our contemporary culture.

Performing Arts and Media

Among the famous Pennsylvanians who starred in the movies were W. C. Fields, Gene Kelly, Joe E. Brown, Richard Gere, Tom Mix, Jack Palance, and James Stewart, who received the first Governor's Distinguished Pennsylvania Artist Award in 1980. In 1984 Bill Cosby received this award. From the 1930s until the late 1950s, audiences throughout the country thrilled to the romantic musical drama of two native Pennsylvanians, singers Jeannette MacDonald and Nelson Eddy.

In 1977, Pennsylvania began to be the site of the filming of an ever increasing number of major motion pictures. *Slapshot* and *The Deer Hunter* were among the first of these productions.

In the field of dance the Pennsylvania Ballet, founded by Barbara Weisberger in 1964, has an international reputation, and the Pittsburgh Ballet is also widely known. Band leaders Fred Waring and Les Brown distinguished themselves in the 1940s and 1950s.

The Curtis Institute in Philadelphia has a worldwide reputation for the advanced study of music. Distinguished singers who are Pennsylvanians by birth or association include Louis Homer, Paul Athouse, Dusolina Giannini, Mario Lanza, Helen Jepson, Perry Como, Bobby Vinton, and Marian Anderson (who received the 1982 Governor's Distinguished Pennsylvania Artist Award). Leopold Stowkowski rose to fame as the conductor of the Philadelphia Orchestra. Victor Herbert was conductor of the Pittsburgh Symphony during part of his career. Eugene Ormandy, conductor of the world-renowned Philadelphia Orchestra for forty-four years, received the 1980 Hazlett Memorial Award for Excellence in the Arts in the field of music. For twenty-five years the Philadelphia Orchestra has been chosen for extended summer performances at the Saratoga Springs, NY, Performing Arts Festival. The Pittsburgh Symphony is proud to have had Andre Previn (recipient of the 1983 Hazlett Memorial Award for Excellence in the Arts) as its conductor. Samuel Barber, Peter Mennin, and Charles Wakefield Cadman are among the better-known Pennsylvania symphonic composers.

Television grew rapidly, and today Philadelphia is the fourth largest television market in the country and Pittsburgh is the 11th. Each city has three major network stations, a public broadcasting station, and smaller independent stations. WQED in Pittsburgh pioneered community-sponsored educational television when it began broadcasting in 1954.

In 1993, Pennsylvania was behind only Texas and California in the total number of daily newspapers and was fifth among the states in paid circulation of dailies and Sunday newspapers.

Religion

Pennsylvanians are typically religious. Although standards for enumerating followers differ greatly among the various religious bodies, confusing the statistics, it is estimated that 64.4 percent of the population adheres to some recognized religious faith. This places Pennsylvania among the top ten states in percentage of worshippers.

The Roman Catholic Church is by far the largest religious body. It has 3.88 million adherents, which is about 32 percent of the population. There are three Catholic archdiocese in Pennsylvania cities: one Latin Rite and one Byzantine Rite in Philadelphia and one Byzantine Rite in Pittsburgh.

The Lutherans and United Methodists are the two largest Protestant denominations, each having more than three-quarters of a million adherents. There are slightly less than a half million Presbyterian adherents. Three other denominations have over one hundred thousand: The United Church of Christ, the Episcopal Church, and the American Baptists. The Quakers, so important in colonial times, had only 13,174 adherents in 1980. Significant smaller Protestant denominations are: Christian Scientists, Mormons, Seventh-Day Adventists,

Jehovah's Witnesses, Assembly of God, Disciples of Christ, Church of the Brethren, Nazarene Church, Evangelical Congregational, and Church of God.

Philadelphia was the home of Bishop Richard Allen, who founded the African Methodist Episcopal (A.M.E.) Church in 1816; today this is a leading Protestant denomination with churches around the world. African Americans in Pennsylvania have belonged to many of the same churches (both Protestant and Catholic) as whites. Nonetheless, predominantly African-American denominations include the African Methodist Episcopal and A.M.E. Zion Churches, and two National Baptist Conventions.

The Jewish religious population is divided among Orthodox, Reconstructionist, Conservative, and Reform Judaism. These four bodies have about 63,000 adherents in Pennsylvania, over half of them in Philadelphia. The secular Jewish population is much larger, being estimated as 347,000.

Reliable counts of the adherents to the twenty-one Eastern Orthodox churches do not exist. The largest of these denominations are the Greek Orthodox, Russian Orthodox, American Carpatho-Russian Orthodox, Ukrainian Orthodox, Antiochian Orthodox, Syrian Orthodox, Serbian Eastern Orthodox, and the Orthodox Church in America. In July 1990, His All Holiness Dimitrios I, Patriarch of 250 million Orthodox Christians around the world, visited the United States and participated in services at St. Mary's Ukrainian Orthodox Church in Allentown, and in the Carpatho-Russian Orthodox See in Johnstown. In addition to his efforts to unite all Orthodox Christians, his mission here emphasized the ongoing effort to reach an accord between his Church and Roman Catholics.

The German sects-the Mennonites and the Amish, for example-brought distinction to the Commonwealth through the appellation "Pennsylvania Dutch," but there are today more Plain People in Ohio and Indiana than there are in Pennsylvania. They are struggling to preserve their culture and religion in the face of technological change, popular fads and attitudes of the general American public.

Education

School consolidation became a major goal after World War II. By 1968 the number of school districts had been compressed from over 2,000 to 742; today there are only 500. Centralization and improved spending had the desired effects. In the 1970s programs for exceptional and for disadvantaged students were becoming available, and the vocational-technical secondary school option assisted many youths in finding career areas. In 1974, Pennsylvania's Human Relations Commission ordered that racial imbalance in public schools be eliminated by the end of the year.

Today, education is one of the Commonwealth's most treasured assets. Total enrollment in its schools and learning institutions is declining, although not as much as it had in the mid-1980s. Because many adolescents drop out of school, there is a crisis in school attendance in children from age 5 through 17. Enrollment in institutions of higher education within the state, which is not as closely linked to the Pennsylvania population as the primary and secondary school student bodies, is growing, and the state ranks sixth in the country in this category. Adult, post-secondary education, much of which is technical education, is also increasing, whereas the vo-tech high schools, so popular in the 1970s, are experiencing more rapid enrollment decline than the standard high schools. The state's executive administration is striving to upgrade the quality of teaching and the students' level of learning, both of which are considered critical to the future of emerging generations. Outcome based education was adopted as a guiding principle in 1993.

Based on U.S. Census data, about 88 percent of the rising generation of Pennsylvanians can expect to complete four years of high school, and 22 percent to complete four years of college. Of the total population over twenty-four years of age, 65 percent have completed four years of high school and 14 percent have completed four years of college.

POLITICAL DEVELOPMENTS

Two-Party State

The New Deal, the rising influence of labor, and the growing urbanization of the state ended a long period of

Republican dominance. In stride with the New Deal, the Democrats fielded a successful gubernatorial candidate in 1934, but the Republicans dominated the next four gubernatorial elections. The Democrats, however, took control of the two major cities, Pittsburgh in 1933 and Philadelphia in 1951, and achieved electoral majorities in seven of the eleven presidential elections from 1936 to 1976. In 1954 and 1958 the Democrats elected George M. Leader and David L. Lawrence successively as governors. They were followed in 1962 by Republican William Warren Scranton, and in 1966 by Republican Raymond P. Shafer. In 1970 the Democrats elected Milton Shapp and regained firm control of the legislature for the first time since 1936. Shapp became the first governor eligible to succeed himself under the 1968 Constitution, and he was reelected in 1974. In 1978 Republican Dick Thornburgh was elected governor. Within two years, the Republicans became the majority party when, in addition to the govemorship, they held both U.S. Senate seats, supported President Ronald Reagan's candidacy in 1980, and won majorities in both houses of the state legislature. In 1982 Thornburgh was reelected to a second term; President Ronald Reagan was reelected in 1984. In 1985 the Democrats became the majority party in the House of Representatives. In 1986 the Democrat Robert P. Casey of Scranton, a former State Auditor General, defeated Lieutenant Governor William W. Scranton III for the govemorship, becoming the 42nd person to hold that office. In 1990, Governor Casey was reelected by an overwhelming majority over the Republican candidate, Auditor General Barbara Hafer.

The accidental death of U.S. Senator John Heinz led to the appointment and then overwhelming election victory for the vacant seat by Democrat Harris Wofford, who raised the issue of reform of the nation's health care system. He defeated former Governor Thornburgh. In 1992 Democratic majorities were returned in both houses of the General Assembly for the first time since 1978. On June 14, 1993, Gov. Robert P. Casey underwent a heart-and-liver transplant operation necessitated by a rare disease, familial amyloidosis. He was the first American for whom this operation was performed as a cure for the condition. Lieutenant Governor Mark S. Singel exercised the powers and performed the duties of Governor until Governor Casey returned to work on December 21.

In November 1994, U.S. Representative Tom Ridge defeated Lieutenant Governor Singel and third-party candidate Peg Luksic of Johnstown in the gubernatorial election. In 1995 and 1996 the majority in the House of Representatives switched from Democratic to Republican by the shift of one seat, but the November 1996 elections gave Republicans a five member House majority and they maintained their majority in the State Senate.

The Cold War, Korean Conflict, Vietnam Involvement, and Persian Gulf War

Alter the end of World War II, the United Nations was established as a parliament of governments in which disputes between nations could be settled peacefully. Nevertheless, the United States and Communist countries started an arms race that led to a "cold war," resulting in several undeclared limited wars. From 1950 to 1953, individual Pennsylvanians were among the many Americans who fought with the South Koreans against the North Koreans and their Red Chinese allies. Pennsylvania's 28th Infantry Division was one of four National Guard divisions called to active duty during the crisis, being deployed to Germany to help deflect any aggression from Russia or its allies.

Pennsylvanians served their country faithfully during the Korean and Vietnam conflicts. In Korea, Pfc. Melvin L. Brown of Mahaffey, Sfc. William S. Sitman of Bellwood, and Cpl. Clifton T. Speicher of Gray gave their lives in self-sacrificing combat deeds for which they were awarded the Congressional Medal of Honor. Major General John Huston Church (1892-1953) commanded the 24th Infantry Division in the first year of fighting. Lieutenant General Henry Aurand commanded the U.S. Army-Pacific (which included the Korean operation) from 1949 to 1952. General Lyman L. Lemnitzer, a native of Honesdale, was Chairman of the Joint Chiefs of Staff during the Cuban Missile Crisis of 1962, which brought the Cold War to an end.

In 1964 a conflict developed in Vietnam. American troops fought beside the South Vietnamese against the North Vietnamese and their supporters until 1973, and many Pennsylvanians served and died there. Cpl. Michael J. Crescenz of Philadelphia and Sgt. Glenn H. English Jr., a native of Altoona, were mortally wounded white performing courageous acts for which they were both awarded the Congressional Medal of Honor. Pfc. William D. Port of Harrisburg, Spec. David C. Dolby of Norristown, and Lt. Walter J. Marm Jr. of Pittsburgh

received the Medal of Honor for conspicuous acts of leadership and personal valor. Major General Charles W. Eifler, a native of Altoona, directed the First Logistical Command in South Vietnam until May 1967. The Vietnam War Memorial in Washington, D.C., includes 1,449 Pennsylvanians among the 58,715 who died as a result of combat.

In 1995, Pennsylvania's 1,363,000 veterans population still included 600 veterans of World War 1; 446,490 veterans of World War II; 229,930 veterans of the Korean Conflict, 376,240 veterans of the Vietnam era, and 67,320 veterans of the Persian Gulf War.

In 1990 and 1991 Pennsylvania units sent to Saudi Arabia, as part of the international force confronting Iraqi aggression, included the 121st and 131st Transportation Companies of the Pennsylvania National Guard, the 193rd Squadron of the Air National Guard and the 316th Strategic Hospital Reserve. On February 25, 1992, 13 members of the 14th Quartermaster Detachment, U.S. Army Reserves, a Greensburg unit, were killed by an Iraqi scud missile attack.

Government Modernization

After the Second World War there was a renewed emphasis on reorganizing state government. In 1945 the State Museum and State Archives were placed under the Historical and Museum Commission. In 1947 the Tax Equalization Board was created to review school tax assessments so that the burden of public education would fall evenly on all districts. In 1951 the Council on Civil Defense was created, and in 1978 it became the Emergency Management Agency. In 1955, during the administration of Governor Leader, an Office of Administration was set up within the executive branch. A government reorganization act permitted any governor to transfer functions from one department to another, subject to the approval of the General Assembly. The Human Relations Commission was established in 1955 to prevent discrimination in employment. In 1966 the Department of Community Affairs was created to deal with matters concerning local governments. The termination, in 1968, of the Department of Internal Affairs resulted in four of its bureaus being placed in other agencies. In 1970 the creating of a Department of Transportation and a Department of Environmental Resources were results of an enlarged concept of the role of state government. Both had broader functions than the departments they replaced, the Highways Department and Forest and Waters. The consolidation of two agencies into the Department of General Services in 1975 was another step in the direction of efficiency.The creation of a Commission for Women by executive order in 1975, and the replacement of the Council on Aging with a Department of Aging in 1978, both followed the trend toward serving population segments that have special needs. As a result of a constitutional amendment, the Attorney General became an elected official in 1980, and that office became an independent department. The designation Department of Justice was discontinued. Within the executive branch an Office of General Counsel was formed to continue the old function of an attorney appointed and subordinate to the Governor. A further result of the amendment was the eventual creation, in 1984, of a separate Department of Corrections. The establishment of an Ethics Commission in 1978 and an Independent Regulatory Review Commission in 1982 were two of the many measures dealing with particular problems that have surfaced in the governmental process. The augmentation of the Department of Commerce, in 1987, by the Economic Development Partnership, anticipated a more powerful economic policy. In June 1996 the Departments of Commerce and Community Affairs were merged to form the Department of Economic and Community Development.

A series of important constitutional amendments culminated in the calling of a Constitutional Convention in 1967-1968, which revised the 1874 Constitution. A significant provision prohibits the denial to any person of his or her civil rights. The General Assembly now meets annually and is a continuing body. The governor and other elective state officers are eligible to succeed themselves for one additional term. A unified judicial system has been established under the Supreme Court, a Commonwealth Court has been created and the inferior courts have been modernized. Broad extensions of county and local home rule are possible. In 1971 the voters amended the state constitution to guarantee that equal rights could not be denied because of sex. By an act of Dec. 6, 1972, the State Constitution so amended was declared to be henceforth known and cited as the Constitution of 1968.

A Guide To Pennsylvania State Government

GENERAL INFORMATION

What is a commonwealth?
In reference to Pennsylvania, the word "commonwealth" is synonymous with "state." The term is of English derivation and implies a special devotion of the government to the common "weal," or the welfare of its citizens.

The colony of William Penn was known as the Quaker Commonwealth, and records show that those who framed the Pennsylvania constitutions from 1776 through 1878 continued this terminology. Interestingly, the state seal of Pennsylvania does not use the term, but as a matter of tradition it is the legal designation used in referring to the state.

How many commonwealths are there in the United States?
Four. In addition to Pennsylvania, Kentucky, Massachusetts, and Virginia are also considered commonwealths.

Why is Pennsylvania called the "Keystone State"?
This nickname for Pennsylvania first appeared shortly after the American Revolution and was in common usage by the early 1800s. It is believed that the original attribution referred to Pennsylvania's central geographic location among the Atlantic seaboard states. Modern use of the designation is justified in view of Pennsylvania's key position in the economic, social, and political development of the United States.

Has Harrisburg always been the capital of Pennsylvania?
No. The Pennsylvania Colony established its first capital in 1643 at Tinicum Island in the Delaware River.

William Penn arrived in 1682 and convened the first General Assembly in Chester, which remained the capital until the following year. Philadelphia became the state capital when the Provincial Government was established there in 1683.

Lancaster became the capital on the first Monday of November 1799 and remained so until Harrisburg was designated as the seat of state government in 1812.

What Pennsylvania cities were once the capital of this country?
Philadelphia, Lancaster, and York. During the Revolutionary War, when General Washington was defeated by General Howe at Brandywine, it was decided to move the capital from Philadelphia because of the fear of attack. Congress adjourned and met in Lancaster for one day before moving to York. York remained the capital during the British occupation of Philadelphia from 1777 until 1778. The seat of government was transferred briefly to New York City and then returned to Philadelphia until 1800, when it moved to Washington, D.C.

Who was the only native Pennsylvanian to be elected President of the United States?
James Buchanan, born in Cove Cap, Franklin County, in 1791, was elected President of the United States in 1856.

PENNSYLVANIA CONSTITUTION

The Pennsylvania Constitution is the foundation of our state government-the well from which liberty and justice spring forth. Our first Constitution was adopted in 1776 and was a framework for the U.S. Constitution, which did not take effect until 1789.

The articles and amendments of the Pennsylvania Constitution compose the fundamental law of the Commonwealth. It ensures basic rights to our citizens, outlines the structure of our government, and provides the rules by which our representatives are elected and how they conduct the business of the state.

DECLARATION OF RIGHTS

What are the rights set forth in the declaration of rights of the Pennsylvania Constitution?
The Declaration of Rights of the Pennsylvania Constitution predates and was a model for the Bill of Rights of the United States Constitution. It is primarily a list of "don'ts" for the General Assembly in that it prohibits the enactment of laws that would infringe on certain rights.

Those rights and prohibitions are set forth in the 28 sections of the declaration.

CONSTITUTIONAL CONVENTIONS

How many constitutions has Pennsylvania had?
Four. The first Constitution was created in 1776 by a convention presided over by Benjamin Franklin. It was drafted when the great experiment of launching a free government in America was being undertaken and marked the passing of the old proprietary government and the transition from a colonial commonwealth. The second Constitution, in 1790, eliminated features of the original document found to be unwise or unworkable. It gave the Commonwealth a body of law that served as a model for future state constitutions in Pennsylvania and many other states as well. The convention that framed the Constitution of 1838 merely amended the previous version, keeping its main features intact. The fourth Constitution, that of 1874, was largely a result of public demand to address the issue of special legislation. It was drafted and adopted to meet new conditions and problems that resulted from the rapid growth and development of the state during and following the Civil War.

GENERAL ASSEMBLY

The heart of Pennsylvania government is the General Assembly. These are the men and women elected by the people of the Commonwealth to serve as our state Senators and Representatives. As voters, we give them the right and responsibility to act on our behalf, expect them to be knowledgeable of the issues facing our citizens, and to do their best to lead us into the future.

The Pennsylvania Constitution, the laws of the state, and the customs of our government form an often stormy ocean across which our 253 legislators must navigate the ship of state.

The General Assembly is the branch of Pennsylvania government closest to the people. Each elected legislator represents, serves, and is responsible to a specific portion of the Commonwealth. It is up to the voters to determine how well they reflect the wants and needs of their constituencies and, through the election electoral process, whether or not they will be allowed to continue to serve.

STATE LEGISLATURES

What is the General Assembly?
Pennsylvania's General Assembly is the legislative branch of government. Commonly called the state Legislature, it consists of two bodies-the Senate and the House of Representatives. The General Assembly's existence, authority, and limitations are provided by Article II of the Constitution.

How many members are there in the Pennsylvania Legislature?
There are 253-50 Senators and 203 members of the House of Representatives.

DISTRICT APPORTIONMENT

How are the senatorial and representative districts apportioned?

The Constitution provides for the state to be divided into 50 senatorial districts and 203 representative districts. Each is to be composed of compact and contiguous territory as nearly equal in population as is practical. One Senator and one Representative are elected from each of the respective districts. No county, city, town, borough, township, or ward is to be divided in forming these districts unless absolutely necessary (see Article II, Section 16).

LEGISLATORS—Qualifications and Terms of Office

What is a legislator?

A legislator is a member of the General Assembly. However, a member of the Senate is usually referred to as a Senator, and a member of the House of Representatives is referred to as a Representative.

How long are their terms?

Senators are elected for a term of four years and Representatives for a term of two years. All 203 members of the House and half of the Senate (25 members) are elected every two years (see Article II, Section 3).

Who presides over the senate?

The Lieutenant Governor is President of the Senate by authority of the Constitution (see Article IV, Section 4).

The Senate elects from its members a President Pro Tempore to preside in the absence of the President. If both the President and the President Pro Tempore are absent, then the Majority Leader, or someone designated by the Majority Leader, presides. When this happens, the Majority Leader is vested with all the powers of the President (except as specifically prohibited by the Constitution or laws). This authority, however, does not extend beyond the day's adjournment.

Has a president of the Senate ever resigned?

Yes. John C. Bell resigned on January 2, 1947, 20 days before the expiration of his term, in order to become Governor. He replaced Governor Edward Martin, who was elected to the United States Senate.

The seven-member committee includes the President Pro Tempore and the Majority and Minority Leaders, Whips, and Appropriations Committee chairmen.

COMMITTEES—Standing Committees

Why are standing committees necessary?

Standing committees, as permanent units of the General Assembly, serve as the workshops of the Legislature. It is their duty to carefully study all bills referred to them and to prepare bills to be reported with a favorable recommendation to each house.

The Constitution requires that "no bill shall be considered unless referred to a committee" (see Article III, Section 2).

During an average session, more than 4,000 bills, representing a wide range of subjects, are introduced in both houses. Many of these bills are controversial and require long debate and consideration of many amendments. Without an effective committee system, it would be impossible for the General Assembly to attend to its business of enacting new laws, amending present ones, appropriating money, investigating governmental operations, and seeing to other duties.

Are committee meetings open to the public?
Yes. The "Sunshine Act" (Act 84 of 1986) makes all committee meetings in which bills are considered or testimony taken open to the public. This does not apply to party caucuses or any Senate or House Ethics Committee.

LEGISLATIVE PROCESS—Rules of Procedure

How are the rules of procedure in the General Assembly determined?
The Constitution provides that "each house shall have power to determine the rules of its proceedings" (see Article II, Section 11).

The parliamentary practices of the Senate and House come from six sources:
- the Pennsylvania Constitution,
- statutory law,
- rules adopted by the Senate and House,
- precedents established by the presiding officers of each house,
- Jefferson's Manual, which lists the rules and precedents of the U.S. House of Representatives, and
- Mason's Manual, containing the rules of procedure for legislative bodies.

What happens when a bill is presented to the Governor for signing?
When a bill is sent to the Governor, one of four things can happen:
- The Governor can sign it, whereupon it becomes a law.
- The Governor can veto the bill. In this case, the General Assembly can choose to vote on it again. A two-thirds vote of all members in both houses will override the veto.
- The Governor can hold it for a time without taking action-either signature or veto-(10 days while the General Assembly is in session or 30 days after final adjournment), after which it will automatically become law. The Governor's refusal to sign a bill may indicate disapproval of the measure but with an acknowledgement that a veto is either useless or politically unwise. It may also indicate that the Governor is undecided about the bill's constitutionality.
- The Governor can employ a line-item veto. This means that any portion of a bill that appropriates money for a particular use can be disapproved while allowing for remaining parts of the bill to become law. Those items vetoed by the Governor can still be restored by a legislative override.

What is the history of impeachment in the Pennsylvania General Assembly?
Pennsylvania has not often used the impeachment process, probably because citizens are wary of political trials. The House of Representatives demands very clear and serious evidence before it will begin the impeachment process.

The first impeachment was in 1685, barely three years after the founding of the unicameral Colonial House. Nicholas More, a physician and the second Speaker of the House, was expelled from the body and removed by the Governor as judge of the Provincial Court.

In 1803, the House impeached three Pennsylvania Supreme Court judges, but the Senate acquitted them.

On three different occasions in 1816, the House voted to impeach Judge Walter Franklin. But his attorney, James Buchanan, (only 25 and just completing two years as a Representative) argued brilliantly to convince the General Assembly that it should undertake impeachment only in the most dire circumstances. Buchanan later became the 15th President of the United States.

Efforts were made to impeach Governor George H. Earle during the Great Depression of the 1930s for failing to send the state police to arrest unemployed bootleg coal miners in northeastern Pennsylvania. The House, however, did not consider the charge serious enough.

On May 24, 1994, Rolf Larsen, Justice of the Supreme Court of Pennsylvania, was impeached by the House.

EXECUTIVE BRANCH

The executive branch of Pennsylvania government, consisting of both elected and appointed officials, is headed by the Governor, who holds the state's highest office. Citizens look to the Governor as a leader who will set the agenda for state government, see that current problems are dealt with effectively and that plans for the future are put into place.

The Attorney General, Auditor General, and State Treasurer, all of whom are elected to administer agencies independent of the Governor, are also executive-branch officials. The Lieutenant Governor, an elected official, and the appointed members of the Governor's cabinet constitute the rest of the executive branch of government. Cabinet members manage the operations of state government agencies and provide their expertise as advisors to the Governor.

What is the executive department?
The Pennsylvania Constitution defines the executive department as consisting of the Governor, Lieutenant Governor, Attorney General, Auditor General, State Treasurer, and Secretary of Education (see Article IV, Section 1). The executive department, however, has grown to include all state government agencies under the jurisdiction of the Governor.

Who has executive power?
The Constitution grants supreme executive power to the Governor (see Article IV, Section 2).

The Constitution of 1776 gave executive power to a Supreme Executive Council composed of 12 members elected by the House every three years. The Governor has had supreme executive power in Pennsylvania since the Constitution of 1790.

What is the oath of office taken by the Governor?
The Governor takes the same oath of office as do all members of the General Assembly and all judicial, state, and county officers. The wording of that oath is as follows:

"I do solemnly swear (or affirm*) that I will support, obey and defend the Constitution of the United States and the Constitution of this Commonwealth and that I will discharge the duties of my office with fidelity."

*NOTE: If the individual taking the oath objects to the term "swear," which is a declaration that implies an appeal to God, that individual may substitute the word "affirm."

Who was the youngest Governor of Pennsylvania? the oldest?
Robert Pattison was the youngest Governor. He was 32 years old at the time he was elected. Governor Pattison served two terms, 1883-87 and 1891-95.

At 69, David Lawrence was Pennsylvania's oldest Governor. He took the oath of office in 1959 and served until his term expired in January 1963.

Who are the elected officers of the commonwealth?
The Governor, Lieutenant Governor, Treasurer, Auditor General, and Attorney General are Pennsylvania's elected officers.

What are the terms of office of the Attorney General, Auditor General, and State Treasurer?
Their terms are four years, beginning on the third Tuesday of January following their election.

Who are members of the Governor's cabinet?
The Governor's cabinet includes, in the order of creation: the Secretary of the Commonwealth (established in 1777); Adjutant General (1793); Secretary of Education (1837); Insurance Commissioner (1873); Secretary of Banking (1891); Secretary of Agriculture (1895); Secretary of Health (1905); State Police Commissioner (1905); Secretary of Labor and Industry (1913); Secretary of Public Welfare (1921); Secretary of Revenue (1927); Secretary of Commerce (1939); Secretary of Community Affairs (1966); Secretary of Transportation (1970); Secretary of Environmental Resources (1970); Secretary of General Services (1975); Secretary of Aging (1978); and Corrections Commissioner (1984).

The formation of additional cabinet-level agencies can come as a result of a request from the Governor or through the initiative of the General Assembly. In either case, any proposed additions to the cabinet must be approved by the General Assembly.

The reverse is true also. The elimination of a cabinet- level agency must be approved by the General Assembly, whether the action is proposed by the Governor or the General Assembly.

JUDICIAL BRANCH

Pennsylvania's unified judicial system means that every court in the Commonwealth is under the supervision of the state Supreme Court. The judicial system may be thought of as a pyramid, with the Supreme Court at the apex. Below it are the two appellate courts, Superior Court and Commonwealth Court, followed by the Courts of Common Pleas. The base of the pyramid is the minor judiciary of the community courts, district justices, the municipal and traffic courts of Philadelphia, and Pittsburgh's police magistrate courts.

The citizens of Pennsylvania depend on the judicial system to interpret and apply the laws of our Commonwealth. It is a great responsibility and a very important one in terms of maintaining order and justice in our state.

How does the Constitution provide for judicial power?
The fifth article of the Constitution vests judicial power of the Commonwealth in a "unified judicial system consisting of the Supreme Court, the Superior Court, the Commonwealth Court, Courts of Common Pleas, community courts, municipal and traffic courts in the City of Philadelphia" and other courts as provided by law and justices of the peace.

How is the unified judicial system administered?
The Administrative Office of Pennsylvania Courts oversees the unified judicial system and is responsible for the prompt and proper disposition of the business of all courts. A court administrator heads the office and is appointed by the Supreme Court.

What is the difference between Supreme, Superior, and Commonwealth Courts?
Aside from differences in jurisdiction, the primary distinction is that the Supreme Court is part of the constitutional framework of Pennsylvania's state government. Both the Superior and Commonwealth Courts were established by an act of the General Assembly.

The Supreme Court is Pennsylvania's highest court and holds the Commonwealth's supreme judicial power. It makes the final judgment on interpreting the Constitution in regard to statutes enacted by the General Assembly.

THE SUPREME COURT

What is the jurisdiction of the Supreme Court?
The Supreme Court has original but not exclusive jurisdiction over:
   a) all cases of habeas corpus (any of several common law writs issued to bring a party before a court or judge);

b) all cases of mandamus (a command by a superior court for the performance of a specified official act or duty) or prohibition to courts of inferior jurisdiction; and

c) all cases of quo warranto as to any officer of statewide jurisdiction (requiring demonstration of the authority by which an individual exercises a public office).

The Supreme Court has exclusive jurisdiction of appeals from final orders of the Courts of Common Pleas in cases of:

a) felony murder;

b) the right to public office;

c) matters decided in the orphans' court division;

d) certain actions or proceedings in equity;

e) direct criminal contempt in the Courts of Common Pleas and other contempt proceedings relating to orders appealable directly to the Court;

f) suspension or disbarment from the practice of law and other related disciplinary orders or sanctions;

g) supersession of a District Attorney by an Attorney General or a court;

h) matters in which the right or power of the Commonwealth or any political subdivision to create or issue indebtedness is in question; and

i) rulings of unconstitutionality by a Court of Common Pleas.

The Supreme Court has exclusive jurisdiction of appeals from all final orders of the Commonwealth Court, provided the matter was originally commenced in that court and not as an appeal from another court, an administrative agency, or justice of the peace. (One exception is an appeal to a final order of the Commonwealth Court that was made on an appeal from the Board of Finance and Revenue.)

The Supreme Court can review certain final orders of the Superior and Commonwealth Courts if any party to the matter petitions the court and an appeal is granted by any two justices.

In addition, the Court can assume full jurisdiction over any matter involving an issue of immediate public importance pending before any court or justice of the peace in the Commonwealth, either on its own motion or upon petition of any party.

Does the Pennsylvania Supreme Court sit in any city other than Harrisburg?
Yes, it also sits in Philadelphia and Pittsburgh. In order to expedite the business of the court, the Commonwealth is divided into three districts.

The Eastern District, with a prothonotary's office in Philadelphia, includes the counties of Bedford, Berks, Bradford, Bucks, Cameron, Carbon, Centre, Chester, Clinton, Columbia, Cumberland, Delaware, Elk, Huntingdon, Juniata, Lackawanna, Lancaster, Lebanon, Lehigh, Luzerne, Lycoming, Monroe, Montgomery, Montour, Northampton, Northumberland, Philadelphia, Pike, Potter, Schuyikill, Snyder, Sullivan, Susquehanna, Tioga, Union, Wayne, and Wyoming.

The Middle District, with a prothonotary's office in Harrisburg, includes Adams, Dauphin, Franklin, Fulton, Mifflin, Perry, and York counties.

The Western District, with a prothonotary's office in Pittsburgh, includes the remaining counties of Allegheny, Armstrong, Beaver, Blair, Butler, Cambria, Clarion, Clearfield, Crawford, Erie, Fayette, Forest, Greene, Indiana, Jefferson, Lawrence, McKean, Mercer, Somerset, Venango, Warren, Washington, and Westmoreland.

Who was the first chief justice of the Pennsylvania Supreme Court?
William Penn appointed Captain William Crispin as the first Chief Justice in a letter dated August 18, 1681. Crispin died at sea on his way to Pennsylvania.

The first Chief Justice to fulfill his duties was Dr. Nicholas Moore, who undertook the position on June 4, 1684.

SUPERIOR COURT

What is the jurisdiction of the Superior Court?
The Superior Court has exclusive jurisdiction over appeals from the Courts of Common Pleas, except for those types of appeals under exclusive jurisdiction of the Supreme or Commonwealth Courts. The Superior Court has original jurisdiction to entertain, hold hearings on, and decide applications for wiretapping and electronic surveillance.

When was the Superior Court established?
The Superior Court was established by legislation approved by the Governor in June 1895. The 1968 Constitutional Convention made it a constitutional court.

How many judges are on the Superior Court?
There are 15, with one serving as President Judge, who in addition to judicial duties, is responsible for assigning cases.

Does the Pennsylvania Superior Court sit in any city other than Harrisburg?
Yes, in Philadelphia and Pittsburgh. The state is divided into the Philadelphia District, the Harrisburg District, and the Pittsburgh District. These districts have the same composition as the Eastern, Middle, and Western Districts of the Supreme Court.

Who was the first President Judge of the Superior Court?
Charles E. Rice of Wilkes-Barre, Luzerne County, became the first President Judge on June 28, 1895.

COMMONWEALTH COURT

What is the jurisdiction of the Commonwealth Court?
The Commonwealth Court is primarily an appellate court, but it does have some original jurisdiction.

It has exclusive appellate jurisdiction of:
   a) final orders of the Courts of Common Pleas in certain specific cases;
   b) final orders of Commonwealth agencies including appeals from the Environmental Hearing Board, Public Utility Commission, Unemployment Compensation Board of Review, and any other Commonwealth agency having statewide authority, with certain specific exceptions;
   c) awards of arbitrators in disputes between the Commonwealth and a state employee; and
   d) any other matter as set by statute.

The Commonwealth Court also has original jurisdiction of:
   a) all civil actions or proceedings against state government, including, with some exceptions, any state officer acting in an official capacity;
   b) all civil actions by state government or an officer of it except eminent domain;
   c) all civil actions under certain provisions of the Insurance Department Act of 1921;
   d) election matters relating to statewide offices; and
   e) any other matter as determined by statute.

How many judges are on the Commonwealth Court?
Nine, with one serving as President Judge. The Supreme Court also designates six senior judges to sit with the Commonwealth Court.

Does the commonwealth court sit in any city other than Harrisburg?
Yes. The court holds regular sessions in Philadelphia and Pittsburgh in addition to Harrisburg. Special sessions may be held in any judicial district of the state when deemed to be in the interest of justice, for the convenience of parties and/or witnesses, or for any other reason.

PHILADELPHIA MUNICIPAL AND TRAFFIC COURTS

What is the jurisdiction of the municipal court of Philadelphia?
The criminal jurisdiction of the Municipal Court of Philadelphia includes:
- summary offenses except those under motor vehicle law;
- all criminal offenses in which no prison term can be imposed or which are punishable by imprisonment of no more than five years; and
- certain more serious offenses under motor vehicle law.
- In civil cases, the court has jurisdiction in:
- landlord and tenant matters;
- damage from breach of agreement, recovering damages for breach of contract or promise;
- trespass claims involving no more than $5,000; and
- actions for fines and penalties by a governmental agency involving $5,000 or less (exclusive of interest and costs) or in matters concerning local taxes, up to $15,000.

In any of these criminal or civil cases, the defendant has no right of trial by jury in this court but can appeal to the Court of Common Pleas for a new trial and does have the right to trial by jury there.

When was the traffic court of Philadelphia established?
The Traffic Court of Philadelphia, established by Act 106, was approved by the Governor on October 17, 1969.

How many judges are assigned to the traffic court of Philadelphia?
Six judges are appointed by the Governor, who also names one of the six to be President Judge.

What is the jurisdiction of the traffic court of Philadelphia?
It has exclusive jurisdiction of all summary offenses under Title 75 of the state motor vehicle laws and the violation of any motor vehicle ordinance committed within Philadelphia County.

DISTRICT JUSTICES

When were the justices of the peace established and how have they evolved?
The Constitution of 1776 provided for justices of the peace-now called district justices-to be elected by the freeholders of each city and county respectively. Two or more could be elected for a seven-year term, but the General Assembly could remove them for misconduct.

The Constitution of 1874 called for the election of justices of the peace when constables were elected, and the Governor was now to commission them for a five-year term. No ward, district, borough, or township could elect more than two justices without the electors' consent. This Constitution also established a residency requirement of one year preceding the election.

In 1909, a constitutional amendment required the election of justices of the peace through a municipal election and changed the term of office from five to six years.

A 1968 constitutional amendment abolished all this, except for the residency requirement. The amendment provided that in any judicial district-other than the City of Philadelphia-where no community court exists, there shall be one justice of the peace in each magisterial district (see Article V, Section 7(a)).

Since the adoption of this amendment and the passage of subsequent legislation, justices of the peace are now referred to as district justices.

What is the jurisdiction of district justices?
In general, district justices have jurisdiction over the following matters:
1) summary offenses, except those within the jurisdiction of a traffic court;

2) certain matters arising under the Landlord and Tenant Act of 1951;

3) certain civil claims (except by or against a Commonwealth party) in which the sum demanded does not exceed $4,000;

4) as commissioners to preside at arraignments, fix and accept bail, issue warrants, and perform duties of a similar nature;

5) offenses relating to driving under the influence of alcohol or controlled substance, within specific criteria;

6) misdemeanors of the third degree, within specific criteria and with certain exceptions, under Title 18 (crimes and offenses) and Title 30 (fish);

7) all offenses under Title 34 (game); and

8) any other matter for which district justices have jurisdiction by statute.

COURTS OF COMMON PLEAS

What is the jurisdiction of the courts of common pleas?

Except where an exclusive original jurisdiction is vested in another court, the Courts of Common Pleas have unlimited original jurisdiction of all civil and criminal actions and proceedings.

Their jurisdiction includes:

* appeals from final orders of the district's minor judiciary (also called justice of the peace);
* appeals from state agencies, such as matters relating to motor vehicle violations, liquor code violations, birth and death records, inheritance and estate taxes, occupational disease, and public employee disputes; and
* petitions for review of awards by arbitrators in disputes between local government agencies and their employees.

There must be at least one Court of Common Pleas in each judicial district, and each judicial district has a President Judge. Courts with eight or more judges elect a President Judge for a non-successive, five-year term. In courts with fewer judges, the judge with the longest continuous service is appointed President Judge.

All districts have a trial division within the Court of Common Pleas, and larger counties have other divisions as well. The divisions are administrative units composed of judges who are responsible for specific types of court business. Each division is presided over by an administrative judge who assists the President Judge.

What is the jurisdiction of the court of common pleas of Philadelphia County?

The Court of Common Pleas of Philadelphia County has three divisions.

The Trial Division has jurisdiction over criminal and civil matters.

The Orphans' Court Division has jurisdiction over all adoptions, custody of minors, and numerous other matters.

The Family Court Division has exclusive jurisdiction in adoptions and delayed birth certificates. It also has jurisdiction in domestic relations matters such as desertion or non-payment of support, child custody, divorce, and delinquent children.

What is the jurisdiction of the court of common pleas of Allegheny County?

The Court of Common Pleas of Allegheny County consists of four divisions: the Civil Division, the Criminal Division, Orphans' Court, and Family Court.

The jurisdiction of these divisions is very similar to the divisions of the Philadelphia court, except that Philadelphia's Trial Division handles all the matters included in Allegheny County's separate Civil and Criminal Divisions.

What other courts are there in Allegheny County?
Pittsburgh's police magistrate courts are a unique part of the unified judicial system and are the only city courts in the state. Six judges are appointed by the Mayor of Pittsburgh to serve during the same term of office. These are the only Pennsylvania judges not elected to office.

What is the jurisdiction of Pittsburgh's police magistrate courts?
Jurisdiction of these courts roughly parallels that of the district justices except that its functions are limited within the boundaries of the City of Pittsburgh. Judges of these courts also serve in the city's traffic and housing courts.

What courts are known as the "minor judiciary"?
The minor judiciary includes community courts, district justices, Philadelphia Municipal Court, Pittsburgh police magistrate courts, and the Philadelphia Traffic Court.

Source: Excerpted from Creating a Commonwealth: A Guide to Your State Government. Produced by the Pennsylvania House of Representatives under the direction of the Office of the Parliamentarian.

PENNSYLVANIA

nationalatlas.gov™
Where We Are

CONGRESSIONAL DISTRICTS
112th Congress (January 2011–January 2013)

The Constitution prescribes Congressional apportionment based on decennial census population data. Each state has at least one Representative, no matter how small its population. Since 1941, distribution of Representatives has been based on total U.S. population, so that the average population per Representative has the least possible variation between one state and any other. Congress fixes the number of voting Representatives at each apportionment. States delineate the district boundaries. The first House of Representatives in 1789 had 65 members; currently there are 435. There are non-voting delegates from American Samoa, the District of Columbia, Guam, Puerto Rico, and the Virgin Islands.

CANADA

Lake Erie

NEW YORK

OHIO

NEW JERSEY

DE

MARYLAND

WEST VIRGINIA

VA

The National Atlas of the United States of America®

MILES

Albers equal area projection

U.S. Department of the Interior
U.S. Geological Survey

Percent of Population Who Voted for Barack Obama in 2012

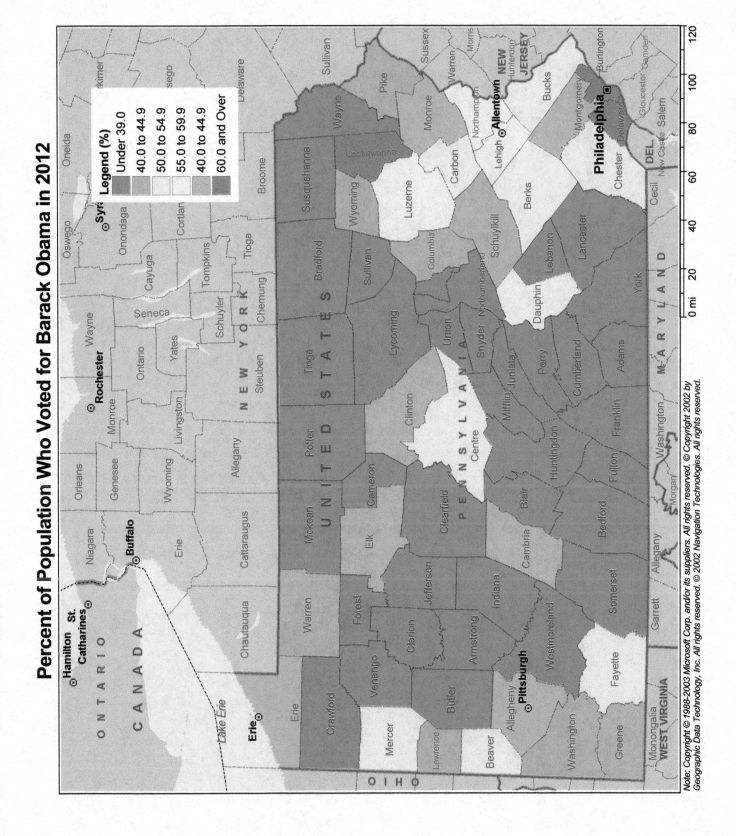

Legend (%)

- Under 39.0
- 40.0 to 44.9
- 50.0 to 54.9
- 55.0 to 59.9
- 40.0 to 44.9
- 60.0 and Over

Land and Natural Resources

Pennsylvania

Topic	Value	Time Period
Total Surface Area (acres)	28,995,200	2007
Land	28,514,400	2007
Federal Land	724,300	2007
Owned	156,380	FY 2009
Leased	35,659	FY 2009
Otherwise Managed	1,423	FY 2009
National Forest	513,000	September 2006
National Wilderness	9,002	October 2011
Non-Federal Land, Developed	4,360,700	2007
Non-Federal Land, Rural	23,429,400	2007
Water	480,800	2007
National Natural Landmarks	27	December 2010
National Historic Landmarks	161	December 2010
National Register of Historic Places	3,268	December 2010
National Parks	18	December 2010
Visitors to National Parks	8,970,475	2010
Historic Places Documented by the National Park Service	3,724	December 2010
Archeological Sites in National Parks	1,000	December 2010
Threatened and Endangered Species in National Parks	4	December 2010
Economic Benefit from National Park Tourism (dollars)	295,605,000	2009
Conservation Reserve Program (acres)	203,656	October 2011
Land and Water Conservation Fund Grants (dollars)	162,163,928	Since 1965
Historic Preservation Grants (dollars)	52,341,882	2010
Community Conservation and Recreation Projects	136	Since 1987
Federal Acres Transferred for Local Parks and Recreation	9,683	Since 1948
Crude Petroleum Production (millions of barrels)	3	2010
Crude Oil Proved Reserves (millions of barrels)	10	2009
Natural Gas Reserves (billions of cubic feet)	6,985	2009
Natural Gas Liquid Reserves (millions of barrels)	Not Available	2008
Natural Gas Marketed Production (billions of cubic feet)	274	2009
Coal Reserves (millions of short tons)	26,998	2009

Sources: U.S. Department of the Interior, National Park Service, State Profiles, December 2010; United States Department of Agriculture, Natural Resources Conservation Service, 2007 National Resources Inventory; U.S. General Services Administration, Federal Real Property Council, FY 2009 Federal Real Property Report, September 2010; University of Montana, www.wilderness.net; U.S. Department of Agriculture, Farm Services Agency, Conservation Reserve Program, October 2011; U.S Census Bureau, 2012 Statistical Abstract of the United States

Pennsylvania Energy Overview and Analysis

Quick Facts

- The first commercial U.S. nuclear power plant came online in 1957 in Shippingport; today, Pennsylvania ranks second in the Nation in nuclear power generating capacity.
- Pennsylvania is a major coal-producing State and sells about one-half of its coal output to other States throughout the East Coast and Midwest.
- Pennsylvania is the leading petroleum-refining State in the Northeast.
- The Drake Well in Titusville, Pennsylvania, was the world's first commercial oil well, and western Pennsylvania was the site of the world's first oil boom.

Analysis

Resources and Consumption

Pennsylvania is rich in fossil fuels. The Appalachian Basin, which covers most of the State, holds substantial reserves of coal and minor reserves of conventional natural gas. The Basin's Marcellus shale region, an area of increased activity in recent years, is estimated to contain potentially large reserves of unconventional shale gas.

Renewable energy resources are also abundant. The Susquehanna River and several smaller river basins offer considerable hydropower resources, and the Appalachian and Allegheny mountain ranges are areas of high wind power potential, as are areas both onshore and offshore along Pennsylvania's short Lake Erie shoreline.

The industrial sector is Pennsylvania's leading energy-consuming sector, due in part to energy-intensive industries including aluminum production, chemical manufacturing, glass making, petroleum refining, forest product manufacturing, and steel production.

Petroleum

Pennsylvania is the leading petroleum-refining State in the Northeast. Although Pennsylvania is credited with drilling the first commercial oil well in 1859, the State's current production is minimal, with output derived primarily from stripper wells that produce less than 10 barrels per day. Pennsylvania's large-scale petroleum refineries are located along the Delaware River near Philadelphia and process primarily foreign crude oil shipped from overseas. These refineries supply regional Northeast markets. In addition to local Pennsylvania and New Jersey refineries, Pennsylvania receives propane via the TEPPCO pipeline from the Gulf Coast and by rail from other States and Canada. To reduce emissions of smog-forming pollutants, motorists in the heavily populated areas of southeastern Pennsylvania, including Philadelphia, are required to use reformulated motor gasoline blended with ethanol. The Pittsburgh area requires 7.8 RVP gasoline, a fuel specially blended to reduce emissions that contribute to ozone formation.

Pennsylvania, along with much of the U.S. Northeast, is vulnerable to distillate fuel oil shortages and price spikes during winter months, due to high demand for home heating. More than one-fifth of Pennsylvania households rely on fuel oil as their primary energy source for home heating. In January and February 2000, distillate fuel oil prices rose sharply when extreme winter weather increased demand unexpectedly and hindered the arrival of new supply, as frozen rivers

and high winds slowed the docking and unloading of barges and tankers. In July 2000, in order to reduce the risk of future shortages, the President directed the U.S. Department of Energy to establish the Northeast Heating Oil Reserve. The Reserve gives Northeast consumers adequate supplies for about 10 days, the time required for ships to carry heating oil from the Gulf of Mexico to New York Harbor. The Reserve's storage terminals are located in Perth Amboy, New Jersey, and Groton and New Haven, Connecticut.

Natural Gas

Although minor, Pennsylvania's natural gas production has grown in recent years. The State's Marcellus shale region, in particular, has experienced markedly increased new development over the past few years. However, compared to Pennsylvania's total natural gas production, shale gas production remains minimal.

Pennsylvania remains dependent on several major interstate pipelines, most of which originate in the Gulf Coast region, to meet the majority of State demand. Two proposed projects could increase natural gas supply to Pennsylvania: an eastern expansion of the Rockies Express Pipeline system, which is expected to be completed in 2009 and a liquefied natural gas (LNG) terminal in Logan Township, New Jersey, just across the Delaware River from Philadelphia, that has been approved by the Federal Energy Regulatory Commission (FERC) but for which construction has not begun. Pennsylvania delivers over three-fifths of its natural gas receipts to New Jersey.

Pennsylvania's natural gas storage capacity is among the highest in the Nation, which allows the State to store the fuel during the summer when national demand is typically low, and quickly ramp up delivery during the winter months when markets across the Nation require greater volumes of natural gas to meet their home heating needs. Natural gas is used in Pennsylvania primarily for residential and industrial use, although its use for electricity generation has grown rapidly in recent years.

Coal, Electricity, and Renewables

Pennsylvania is a major coal-producing State. Northeastern Pennsylvania's coal region holds the Nation's largest remaining reserves of anthracite coal, a type of coal that burns cleanly with little soot. It is used primarily as a domestic fuel in either hand-fired stoves or automatic stoker furnaces. Although Pennsylvania supplies virtually all of the Nation's anthracite, most of the State's coal production consists of bituminous coal mined in the western part of the State, where several of the Nation's largest underground coal mines are located. Enlow Fork Mine is the largest underground coal mine in the United States.

Large volumes of coal are moved both into and out of Pennsylvania, mostly by railcar, river barge, and truck. Pennsylvania transports close to one-half of its coal production to other States throughout the East Coast and Midwest. Pennsylvania coal demand is high, and it is one of the top coal-consuming States in the Nation. Pennsylvania's coal dominates the State's power generation market, typically accounting for more than one-half of net electricity production.

Pennsylvania's electricity markets also rely substantially on nuclear power, and the State ranks second in the Nation after Illinois in nuclear generating capacity. Pennsylvania's five operating nuclear plants have supplied slightly more than one-third of State electricity generation in recent

years. Nuclear power has been an important fuel for electricity generation in Pennsylvania since 1957, when the first commercial U.S. nuclear power plant came online in Shippingport. The Shippingport plant was shut down and decommissioned in 1982 after 25 years of service. Pennsylvania's nuclear power industry has experienced problems in the past. In 1979, an accident led to a partial meltdown at the Three Mile Island nuclear plant and became the most serious accident in U.S. nuclear power plant operating history, changing the U.S. nuclear industry and leading to sweeping changes at the Nuclear Regulatory Commission.

Pennsylvania is one of the top electricity-producing States in the Nation and electricity production exceeds State demand. Pennsylvania is among the largest users of municipal solid waste and landfill gas for electricity generation and produces substantial hydroelectric power. The State also produces a small amount of energy from wind. In December 2004, Pennsylvania adopted an alternative energy portfolio standard that requires electric distribution companies and generators in the State to supply 18.5 percent of Pennsylvania's electricity from alternative energy sources by 2020.

Source: *U.S. Energy Information Administration, October 2009*

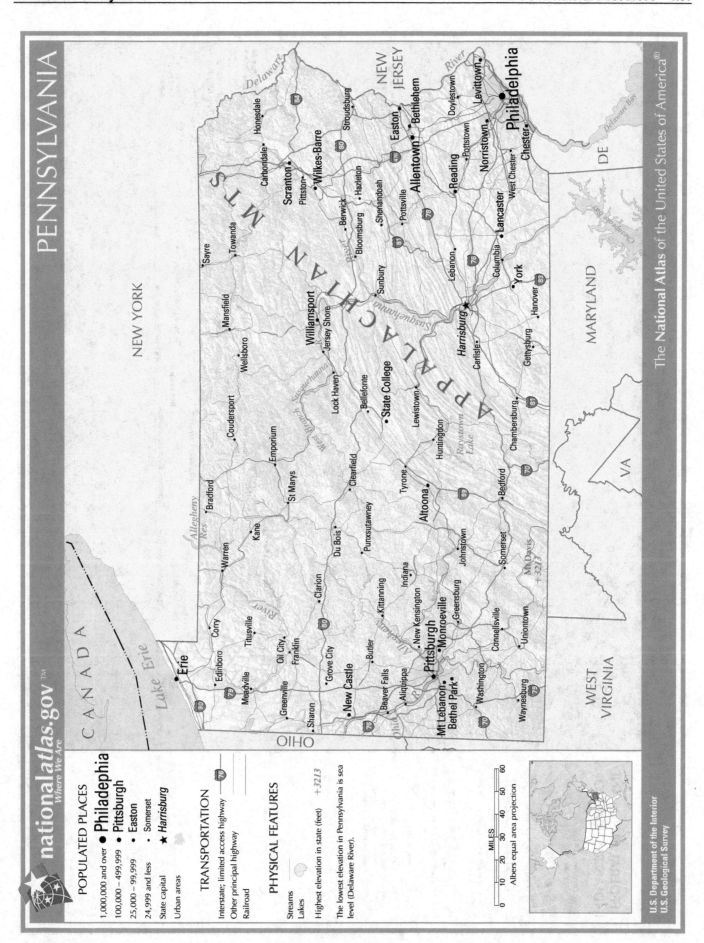

PENNSYLVANIA

nationalatlas.gov™
Where We Are

POPULATED PLACES

● **Philadelphia**   1,000,000 and over
● **Pittsburgh**   100,000 – 499,999
● **Easton**   25,000 – 99,999
· Somerset   24,999 and less
★ *Harrisburg*   State capital
    Urban areas

TRANSPORTATION

Interstate; limited access highway
Other principal highway
Railroad

PHYSICAL FEATURES

Streams
Lakes
+3213   Highest elevation in state (feet)

The lowest elevation in Pennsylvania is sea level (Delaware River).

MILES
0   10   20   30   40   50   60
Albers equal area projection

U.S. Department of the Interior
U.S. Geological Survey

The National Atlas of the United States of America®

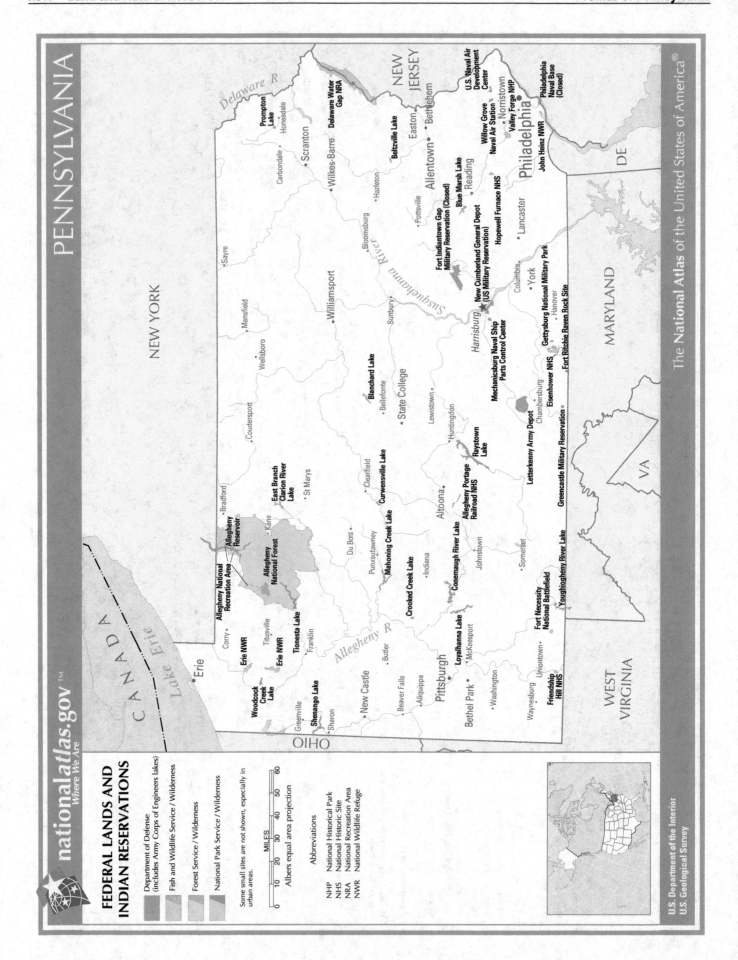

PENNSYLVANIA

nationalatlas.gov ™
Where We Are

FEDERAL LANDS AND INDIAN RESERVATIONS

Department of Defense
(includes Army Corps of Engineers lakes)

Fish and Wildlife Service / Wilderness

Forest Service / Wilderness

National Park Service / Wilderness

Some small sites are not shown, especially in urban areas.

MILES
0   10   20   30   40   50   60

Albers equal area projection

Abbreviations

NHP   National Historical Park
NHS   National Historic Site
NRA   National Recreation Area
NWR   National Wildlife Refuge

The National Atlas of the United States of America®

U.S. Department of the Interior
U.S. Geological Survey

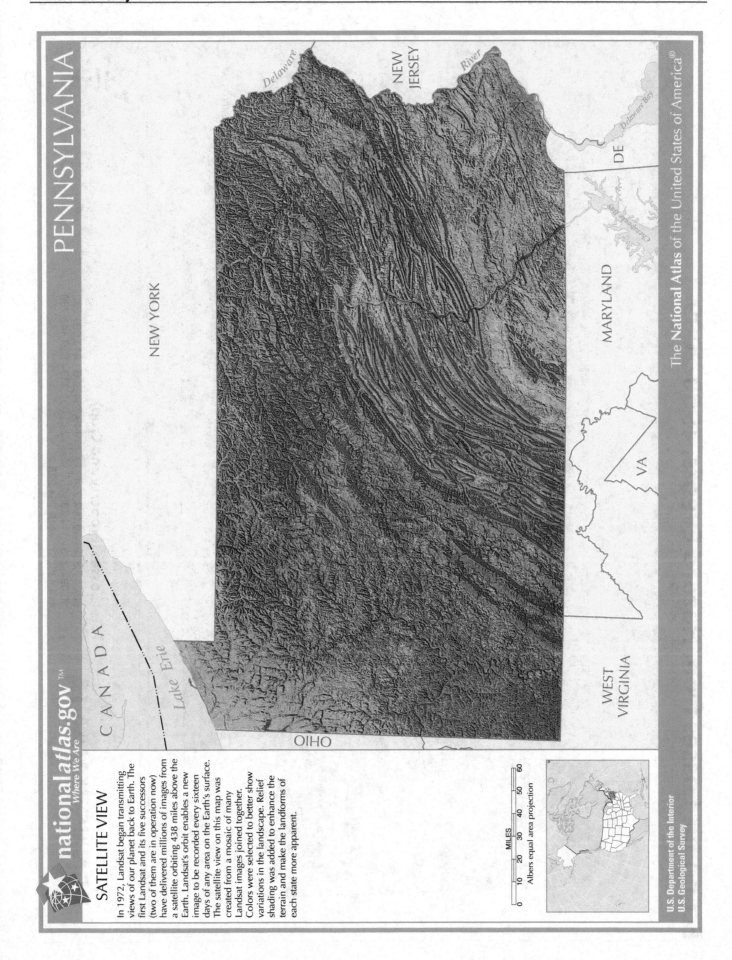

PENNSYLVANIA

nationalatlas.gov™
Where We Are

SATELLITE VIEW

In 1972, Landsat began transmitting views of our planet back to Earth. The first Landsat and its five successors (two of them are in operation now) have delivered millions of images from a satellite orbiting 438 miles above the Earth. Landsat's orbit enables a new image to be recorded every sixteen days of any area on the Earth's surface. The satellite view on this map was created from a mosaic of many Landsat images joined together. Colors were selected to better show variations in the landscape. Relief shading was added to enhance the terrain and make the landforms of each state more apparent.

CANADA

Lake Erie

NEW YORK

Delaware

NEW JERSEY

River

OHIO

WEST VIRGINIA

MARYLAND

DE

Delaware Bay

Chesapeake Bay

VA

The **National Atlas** of the United States of America®

MILES

0   10   20   30   40   50   60

Albers equal area projection

U.S. Department of the Interior
U.S. Geological Survey

Economic Losses from Hazard Events, 1960-2009

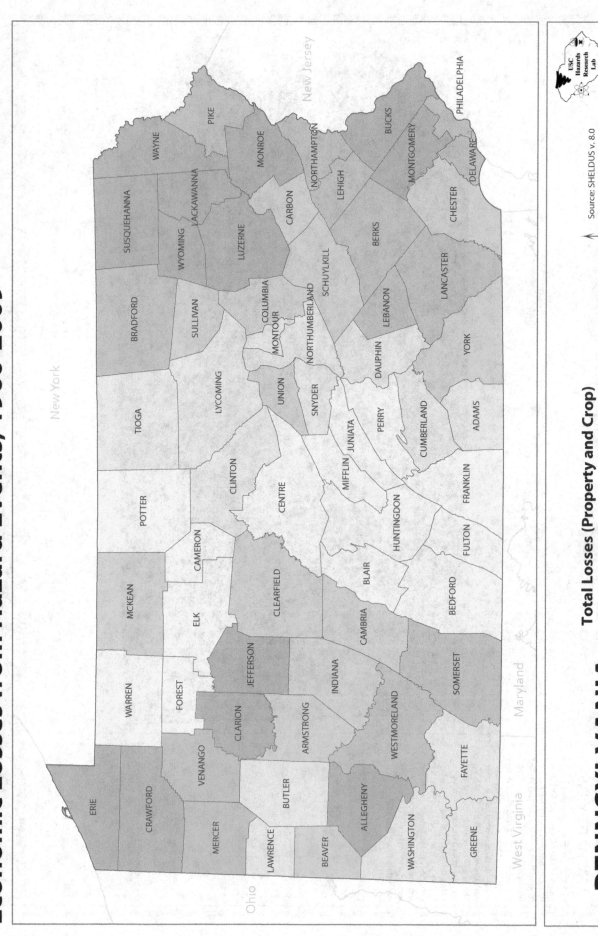

PENNSYLVANIA

Source: SHELDUS v. 8.0
Classification: Quantiles
Losses adjusted to 2009 Dollars

Total Losses (Property and Crop)

53,387,387 - 80,092,224	149,754,226 - 213,001,232
80,092,225 - 114,438,200	213,001,233 - 529,143,739
114,438,201 - 149,754,225	

PENNSYLVANIA

Hazard Losses
1960-2009

Distribution of Losses by Hazard Type
(in 2009 USD million)

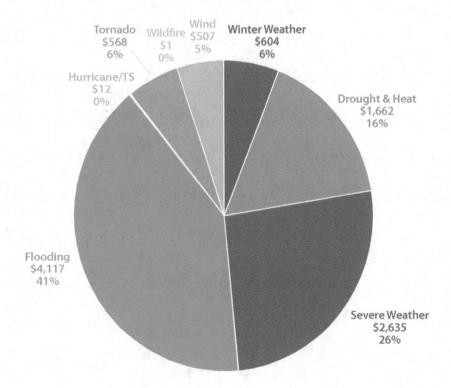

Tornado
$568
6%

Wildfire
$1
0%

Wind
$507
5%

Winter Weather
$604
6%

Hurricane/TS
$12
0%

Drought & Heat
$1,662
16%

Flooding
$4,117
41%

Severe Weather
$2,635
26%

Distribution of Hazard Events
(number of events)

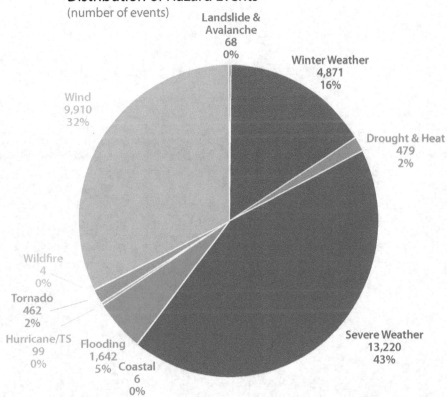

Landslide &
Avalanche
68
0%

Winter Weather
4,871
16%

Wind
9,910
32%

Drought & Heat
479
2%

Wildfire
4
0%

Tornado
462
2%

Severe Weather
13,220
43%

Hurricane/TS
99
0%

Flooding
1,642
5%

Coastal
6
0%

Demographic Maps

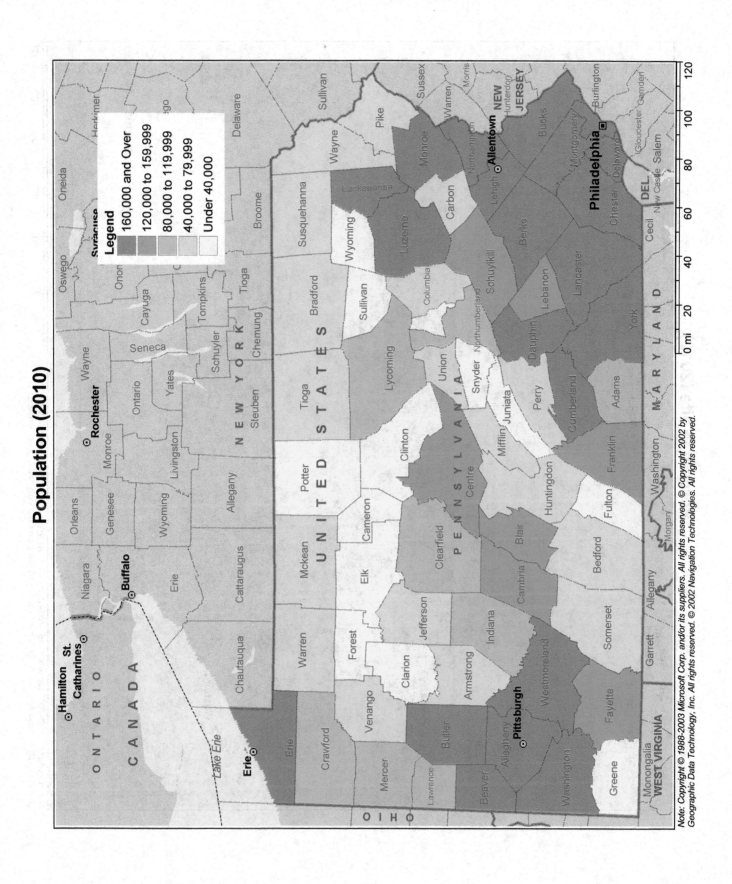

Population (2010)

Legend
- 160,000 and Over
- 120,000 to 159,999
- 80,000 to 119,999
- 40,000 to 79,999
- Under 40,000

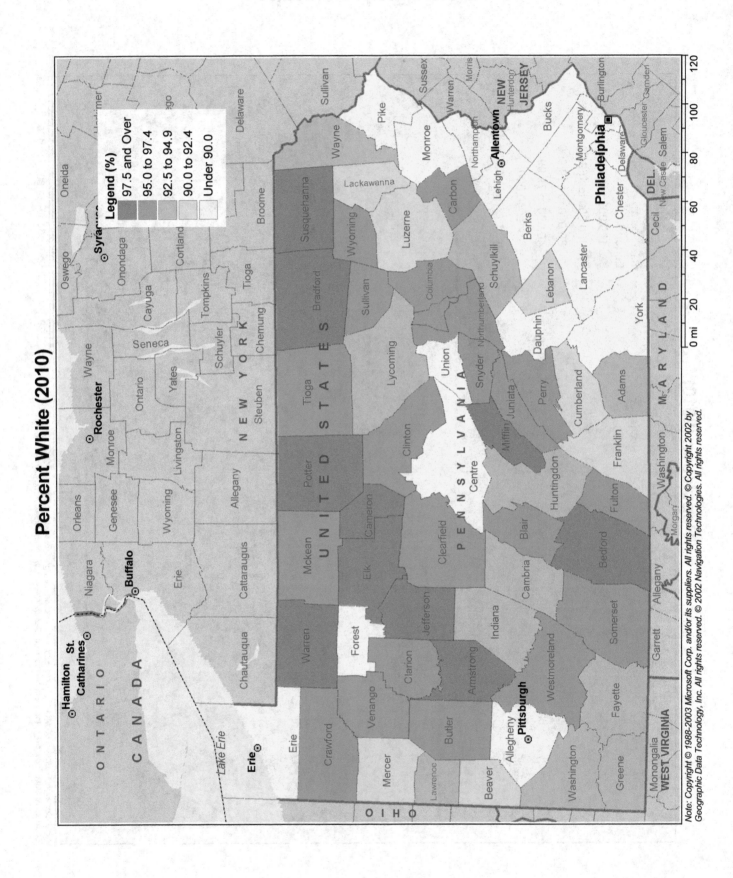

Percent White (2010)

Legend (%)

97.5 and Over
95.0 to 97.4
92.5 to 94.9
90.0 to 92.4
Under 90.0

Percent Black (2010)

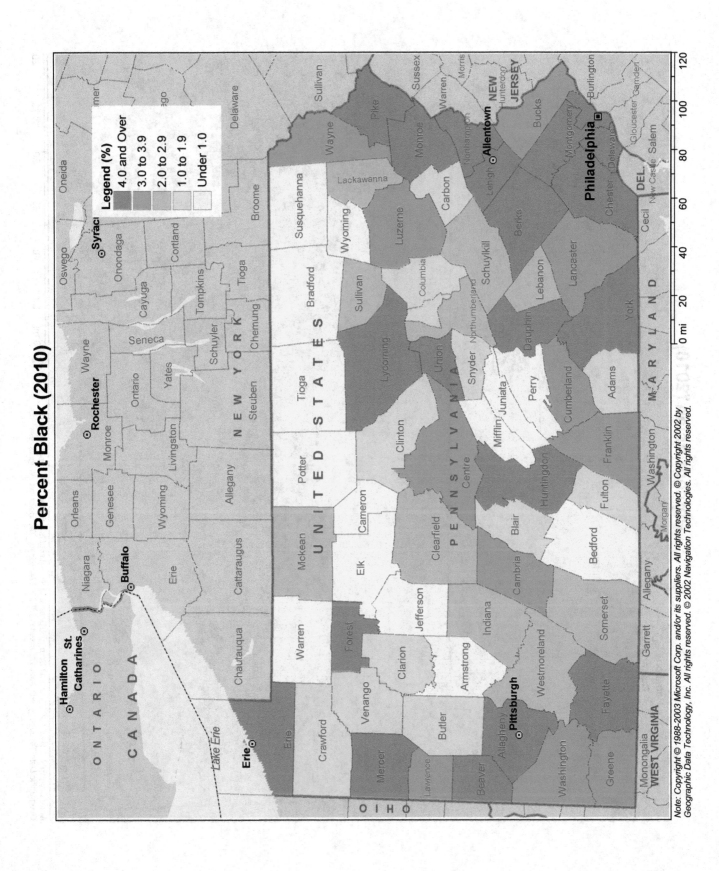

Legend (%)

- 4.0 and Over
- 3.0 to 3.9
- 2.0 to 2.9
- 1.0 to 1.9
- Under 1.0

Percent Asian (2010)

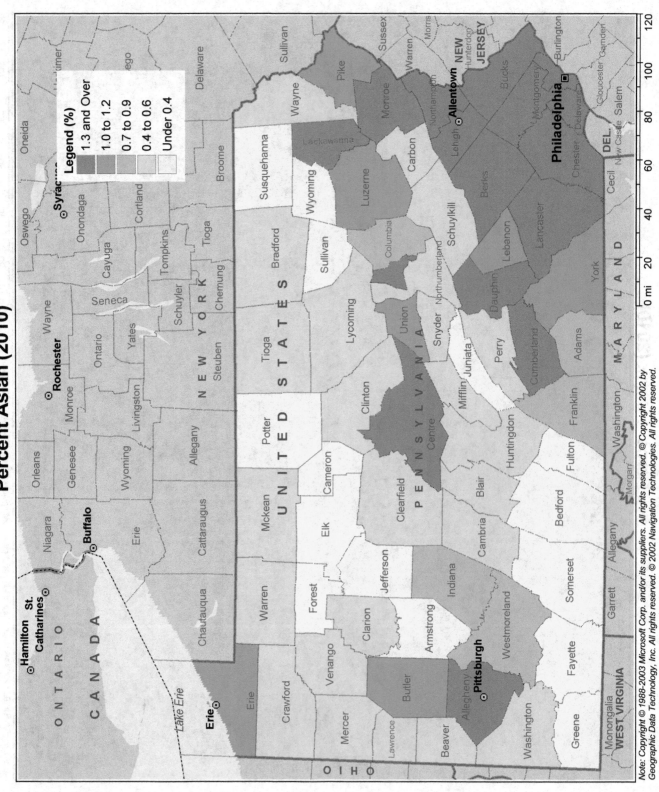

Legend (%)

- 1.3 and Over
- 1.0 to 1.2
- 0.7 to 0.9
- 0.4 to 0.6
- Under 0.4

Percent Hispanic (2010)

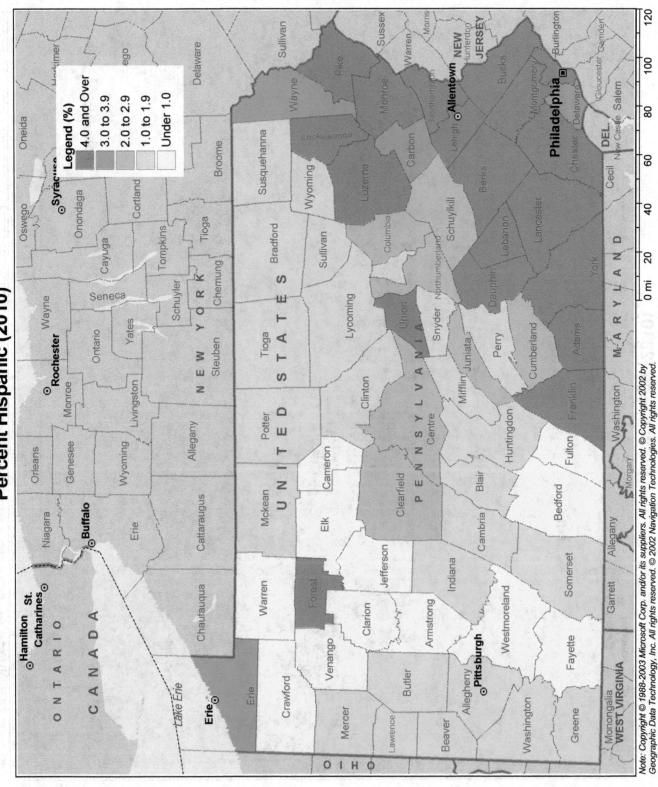

Legend (%)

- 4.0 and Over
- 3.0 to 3.9
- 2.0 to 2.9
- 1.0 to 1.9
- Under 1.0

Median Age (2010)

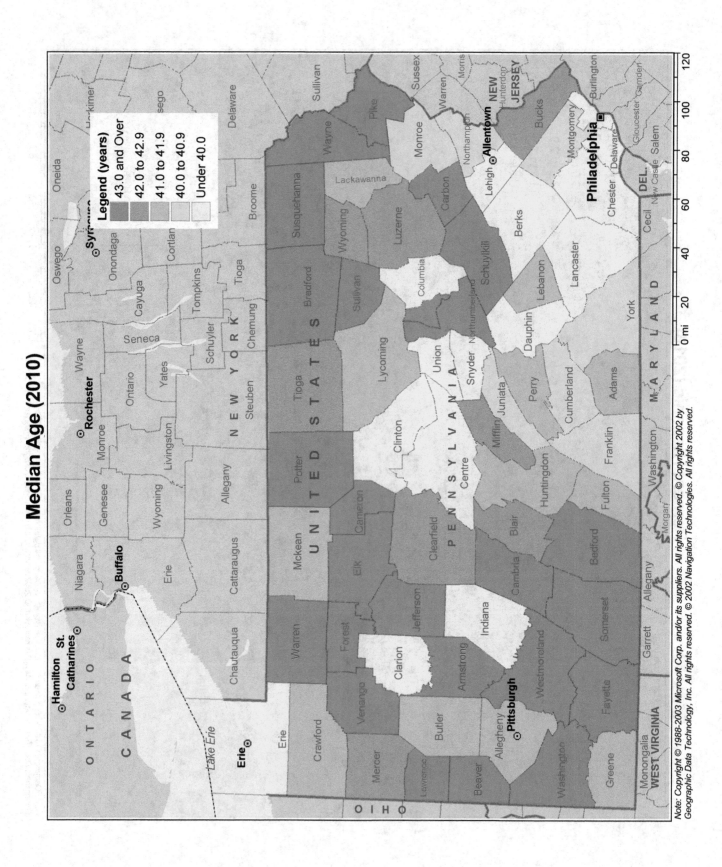

Legend (years)

- 43.0 and Over
- 42.0 to 42.9
- 41.0 to 41.9
- 40.0 to 40.9
- Under 40.0

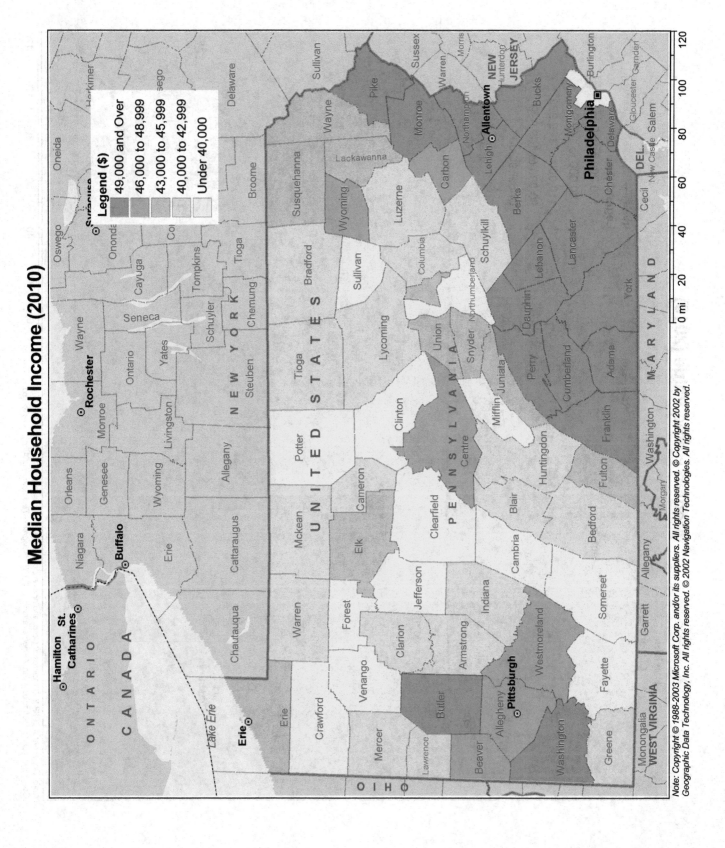

Median Household Income (2010)

Legend ($)

49,000 and Over
46,000 to 48,999
43,000 to 45,999
40,000 to 42,999
Under 40,000

Median Home Value (2010)

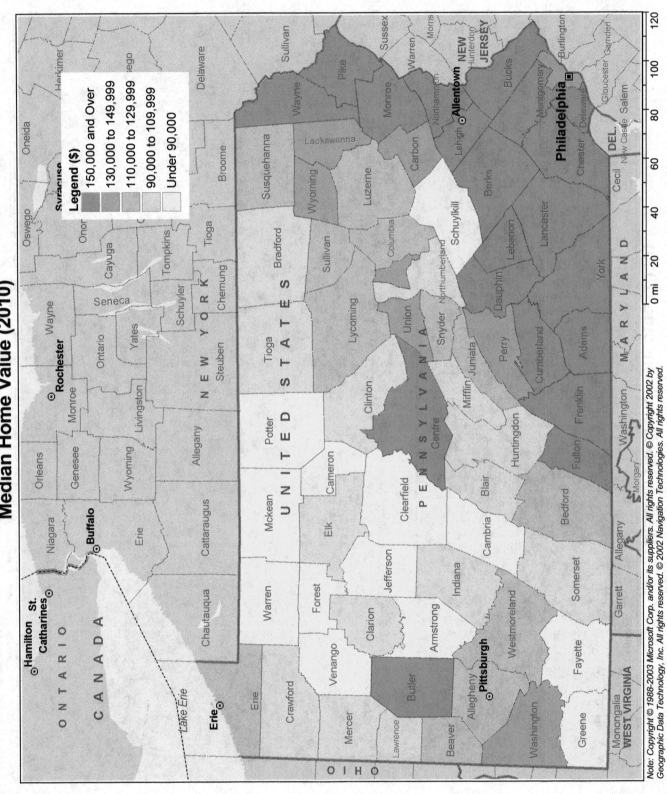

Legend ($)

- 150,000 and Over
- 130,000 to 149,999
- 110,000 to 129,999
- 90,000 to 109,999
- Under 90,000

High School Graduates* (2010)

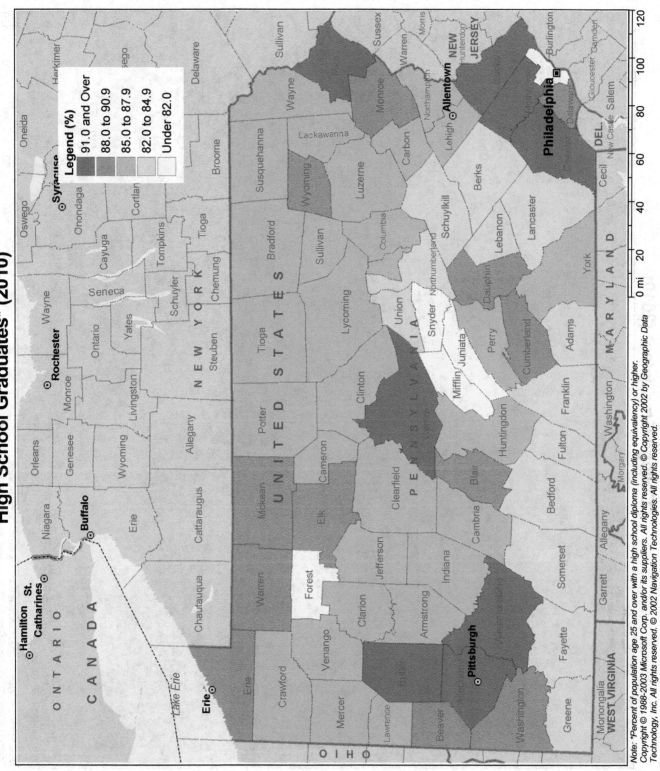

Legend (%)
- 91.0 and Over
- 88.0 to 90.9
- 85.0 to 87.9
- 82.0 to 84.9
- Under 82.0

Note: *Percent of population age 25 and over with a high school diploma (including equivalency) or higher.
Copyright © 1988-2003 Microsoft Corp. and/or its suppliers. All rights reserved. © Copyright 2002 by Geographic Data
Technology, Inc. All rights reserved. © 2002 Navigation Technologies. All rights reserved.

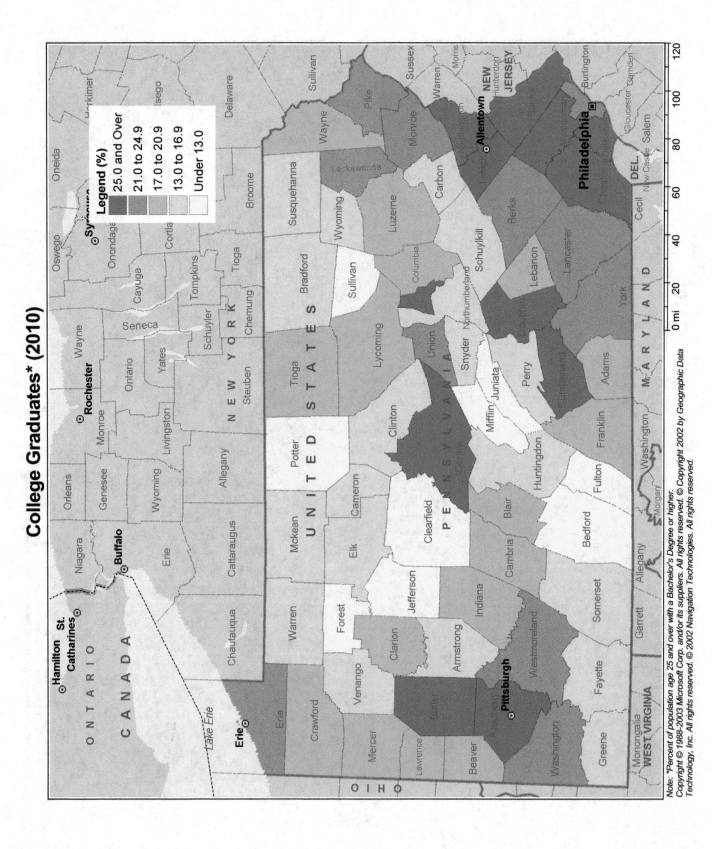

College Graduates* (2010)

Legend (%)
- 25.0 and Over
- 21.0 to 24.9
- 17.0 to 20.9
- 13.0 to 16.9
- Under 13.0

PENNSYLVANIA - Core Based Statistical Areas and Counties

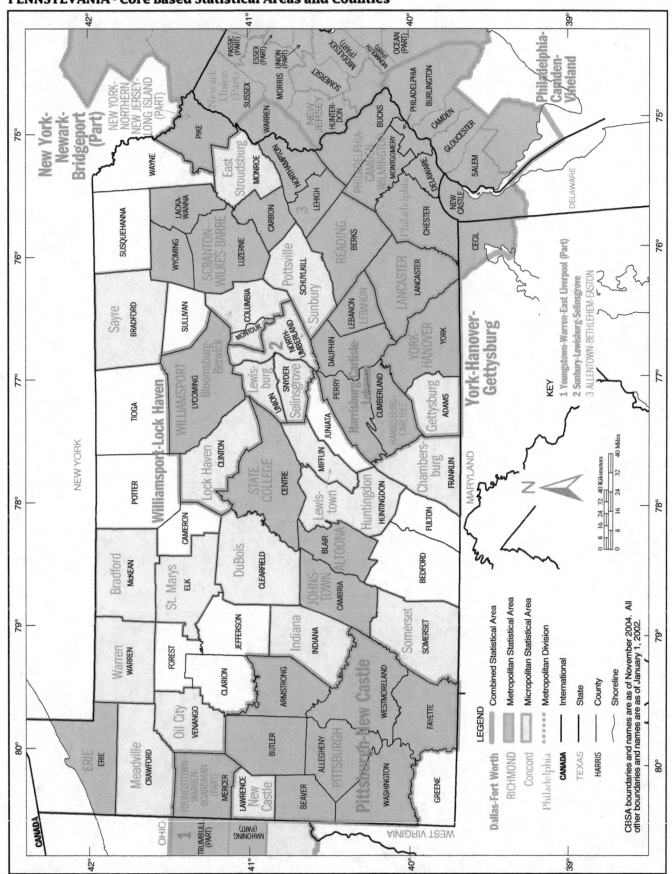

Adams County

Located in southern Pennsylvania; bounded on the south by Maryland, and on the west and northwest by the South Mountains. Covers a land area of 518.668 square miles, a water area of 3.120 square miles, and is located in the Eastern Time Zone at 39.87° N. Lat., 77.22° W. Long. The county was founded in 1800. County seat is Gettysburg.

Adams County is part of the Gettysburg, PA Micropolitan Statistical Area. The entire metro area includes: Adams County, PA

Weather Station: Biglerville   Elevation: 720 feet

	Jan	Feb	Mar	Apr	May	Jun	Jul	Aug	Sep	Oct	Nov	Dec
High	38	41	49	62	72	81	85	83	76	64	53	42
Low	20	22	29	39	49	58	63	61	53	42	33	24
Precip	3.0	2.7	3.7	3.7	4.4	4.0	3.5	3.5	4.3	3.4	3.6	3.2
Snow	8.9	8.0	3.9	0.6	0.0	0.0	0.0	0.0	0.0	0.0	0.6	4.4

High and Low temperatures in degrees Fahrenheit; Precipitation and Snow in inches

Weather Station: Eisenhower Natl Hist Site   Elevation: 540 feet

	Jan	Feb	Mar	Apr	May	Jun	Jul	Aug	Sep	Oct	Nov	Dec
High	40	44	52	64	73	82	86	85	77	67	55	44
Low	21	23	30	40	49	58	63	61	53	42	33	25
Precip	3.0	2.7	3.6	3.6	4.3	4.3	3.4	3.6	4.3	3.2	3.6	3.3
Snow	6.3	5.8	2.7	0.1	tr	0.0	0.0	0.0	0.0	0.0	0.5	3.6

High and Low temperatures in degrees Fahrenheit; Precipitation and Snow in inches

Population: 78,274 (1990); 91,292 (2000); 101,407 (2010); Race: 93.7% White, 1.5% Black, 0.7% Asian, 0.2% American Indian/Alaska Native, 0.0% Native Hawaiian/Other Pacific Islander, 3.9% Other, 6.0% Hispanic of any race (2010); Density: 195.5 persons per square mile (2010); Average household size: 2.56 (2010); Median age: 41.3 (2010); Males per 100 females: 96.7 (2010).

Religion: Six largest groups: 14.8% Catholicism, 10.8% Lutheran, 5.5% Pentecostal, 4.5% Presbyterian-Reformed, 2.9% Methodist/Pietist, 2.5% Baptist (2010)

Economy: Unemployment rate: 6.8% (August 2012); Total civilian labor force: 54,616 (August 2012); Leading industries: 20.0% manufacturing; 15.7% health care and social assistance; 14.9% accommodation & food services (2010); Farms: 1,289 totaling 174,595 acres (2007); Companies that employ 500 or more persons: 4 (2010); Companies that employ 100 to 499 persons: 43 (2010); Companies that employ less than 100 persons: 1,866 (2010); Black-owned businesses: n/a (2007); Hispanic-owned businesses: 55 (2007); Asian-owned businesses: n/a (2007); Women-owned businesses: n/a (2007); Retail sales per capita: $8,437 (2010). Single-family building permits issued: 146 (2011); Multi-family building permits issued: 2 (2011).

Income: Per capita income: $25,606 (2006-2010 5-year est.); Median household income: $56,529 (2006-2010 5-year est.); Average household income: $66,483 (2006-2010 5-year est.); Percent of households with income of $100,000 or more: 18.6% (2006-2010 5-year est.); Poverty rate: 7.6% (2006-2010 5-year est.); Bankruptcy rate: 3.10% (2011).

Taxes: Total county taxes per capita: $299 (2009); County property taxes per capita: $287 (2009).

Education: Percent of population age 25 and over with: High school diploma (including GED) or higher: 84.7% (2006-2010 5-year est.); Bachelor's degree or higher: 18.5% (2006-2010 5-year est.); Master's degree or higher: 7.3% (2006-2010 5-year est.).

Housing: Homeownership rate: 77.3% (2010); Median home value: $200,700 (2006-2010 5-year est.); Median contract rent: $578 per month (2006-2010 5-year est.); Median year structure built: 1976 (2006-2010 5-year est.)

Health: Birth rate: 102.6 per 10,000 population (2011); Death rate: 87.2 per 10,000 population (2011); Age-adjusted cancer mortality rate: 170.8 deaths per 100,000 population (2009); Number of physicians: 12.2 per 10,000 population (2010); Hospital beds: 9.3 per 10,000 population (2008); Hospital admissions: 432.4 per 10,000 population (2008).

Environment: Air Quality Index: 74.7% good, 24.8% moderate, 0.6% unhealthy for sensitive individuals, 0.0% unhealthy (percent of days in 2011)

Elections: 2012 Presidential election results: 35.5% Obama, 63.1% Romney

National and State Parks: Eisenhower National Historic Site; Gettysburg National Military Park; Michaux State Forest

Additional Information Contacts

Adams County Government . . . . (717) 334-6781
  http://www.adamscounty.us

Adams County Communities

ABBOTTSTOWN (borough). Covers a land area of 0.547 square miles and a water area of 0.007 square miles. Located at 39.88° N. Lat; 76.99° W. Long. Elevation is 541 feet.

Population: 539 (1990); 905 (2000); 1,011 (2010); Density: 1,847.9 persons per square mile (2010); Race: 92.7% White, 1.4% Black, 1.0% Asian, 0.1% American Indian/Alaska Native, 0.0% Native Hawaiian/Other Pacific Islander, 4.8% Other, 9.4% Hispanic of any race (2010); Average household size: 2.73 (2010); Median age: 37.1 (2010); Males per 100 females: 97.5 (2010); Marriage status: 27.4% never married, 54.7% now married, 4.9% widowed, 13.1% divorced (2006-2010 5-year est.); Foreign born: 3.1% (2006-2010 5-year est.); Ancestry (includes multiple ancestries): 37.8% German, 14.1% American, 10.3% Irish, 5.6% English, 4.3% Italian (2006-2010 5-year est.).

Economy: Employment by occupation: 3.6% management, 4.6% professional, 5.8% services, 18.8% sales, 6.6% farming, 16.8% construction, 13.4% production (2006-2010 5-year est.).

Income: Per capita income: $21,659 (2006-2010 5-year est.); Median household income: $58,009 (2006-2010 5-year est.); Average household income: $58,311 (2006-2010 5-year est.); Percent of households with income of $100,000 or more: 9.5% (2006-2010 5-year est.); Poverty rate: 7.2% (2006-2010 5-year est.).

Education: Percent of population age 25 and over with: High school diploma (including GED) or higher: 81.0% (2006-2010 5-year est.); Bachelor's degree or higher: 7.2% (2006-2010 5-year est.); Master's degree or higher: 1.7% (2006-2010 5-year est.).

Housing: Homeownership rate: 75.8% (2010); Median home value: $150,900 (2006-2010 5-year est.); Median contract rent: $540 per month (2006-2010 5-year est.); Median year structure built: 1959 (2006-2010 5-year est.).

Transportation: Commute to work: 97.4% car, 0.0% public transportation, 0.6% walk, 0.6% work from home (2006-2010 5-year est.); Travel time to work: 25.7% less than 15 minutes, 43.0% 15 to 30 minutes, 13.3% 30 to 45 minutes, 6.3% 45 to 60 minutes, 11.7% 60 minutes or more (2006-2010 5-year est.)

Additional Information Contacts

Gettysburg Adams Chamber of Commerce . . . . (717) 334-8151
  http://www.gettysburg-chamber.org

ARENDTSVILLE (borough). Covers a land area of 0.818 square miles and a water area of 0 square miles. Located at 39.92° N. Lat; 77.30° W. Long. Elevation is 705 feet.

Population: 693 (1990); 848 (2000); 952 (2010); Density: 1,163.3 persons per square mile (2010); Race: 83.0% White, 2.8% Black, 0.5% Asian, 0.5% American Indian/Alaska Native, 0.0% Native Hawaiian/Other Pacific Islander, 13.2% Other, 16.4% Hispanic of any race (2010); Average household size: 2.66 (2010); Median age: 34.5 (2010); Males per 100 females: 101.7 (2010); Marriage status: 26.8% never married, 65.4% now married, 5.4% widowed, 2.5% divorced (2006-2010 5-year est.); Foreign born: 10.3% (2006-2010 5-year est.); Ancestry (includes multiple ancestries): 46.3% German, 20.4% Irish, 11.9% English, 7.0% Polish, 2.0% American (2006-2010 5-year est.).

Economy: Employment by occupation: 9.8% management, 0.8% professional, 11.9% services, 13.5% sales, 3.2% farming, 12.4% construction, 15.6% production (2006-2010 5-year est.).

Income: Per capita income: $29,143 (2006-2010 5-year est.); Median household income: $54,583 (2006-2010 5-year est.); Average household income: $74,812 (2006-2010 5-year est.); Percent of households with income of $100,000 or more: 23.8% (2006-2010 5-year est.); Poverty rate: 7.4% (2006-2010 5-year est.).

Education: Percent of population age 25 and over with: High school diploma (including GED) or higher: 81.7% (2006-2010 5-year est.); Bachelor's degree or higher: 30.6% (2006-2010 5-year est.); Master's degree or higher: 14.0% (2006-2010 5-year est.).

School District(s)

Upper Adams SD (KG-12)
  2010-11 Enrollment: 1,705 . . . . (717) 677-7191

Housing: Homeownership rate: 68.1% (2010); Median home value: $200,000 (2006-2010 5-year est.); Median contract rent: $521 per month

(2006-2010 5-year est.); Median year structure built: 1965 (2006-2010 5-year est.).

Transportation: Commute to work: 84.1% car, 0.0% public transportation, 14.5% walk, 1.4% work from home (2006-2010 5-year est.); Travel time to work: 51.1% less than 15 minutes, 15.3% 15 to 30 minutes, 11.6% 30 to 45 minutes, 11.3% 45 to 60 minutes, 10.7% 60 minutes or more (2006-2010 5-year est.)

ASPERS (CDP).
Covers a land area of 0.524 square miles and a water area of 0.024 square miles. Located at 39.98° N. Lat; 77.23° W. Long. Elevation is 705 feet.

Population: n/a (1990); n/a (2000); 350 (2010); Density: 668.3 persons per square mile (2010); Race: 82.6% White, 1.7% Black, 0.0% Asian, 0.0% American Indian/Alaska Native, 0.0% Native Hawaiian/Other Pacific Islander, 15.7% Other, 25.4% Hispanic of any race (2010); Average household size: 2.94 (2010); Median age: 31.4 (2010); Males per 100 females: 104.7 (2010); Marriage status: 27.5% never married, 50.4% now married, 0.0% widowed, 22.1% divorced (2006-2010 5-year est.); Foreign born: 25.8% (2006-2010 5-year est.); Ancestry (includes multiple ancestries): 26.4% German, 13.6% English, 10.3% Irish, 6.7% Scottish, 4.8% Dutch (2006-2010 5-year est.).

Economy: Employment by occupation: 5.3% management, 0.0% professional, 14.2% services, 12.1% sales, 0.0% farming, 17.9% construction, 17.4% production (2006-2010 5-year est.).

Income: Per capita income: $21,983 (2006-2010 5-year est.); Median household income: $48,047 (2006-2010 5-year est.); Average household income: $54,042 (2006-2010 5-year est.); Percent of households with income of $100,000 or more: 8.8% (2006-2010 5-year est.); Poverty rate: 0.0% (2006-2010 5-year est.).

Education: Percent of population age 25 and over with: High school diploma (including GED) or higher: 83.2% (2006-2010 5-year est.); Bachelor's degree or higher: 10.6% (2006-2010 5-year est.); Master's degree or higher: 4.9% (2006-2010 5-year est.).

Housing: Homeownership rate: 68.1% (2010); Median home value: $152,600 (2006-2010 5-year est.); Median contract rent: $535 per month (2006-2010 5-year est.); Median year structure built: 1951 (2006-2010 5-year est.).

Transportation: Commute to work: 91.6% car, 0.0% public transportation, 0.0% walk, 8.4% work from home (2006-2010 5-year est.); Travel time to work: 32.2% less than 15 minutes, 32.8% 15 to 30 minutes, 19.5% 30 to 45 minutes, 15.5% 45 to 60 minutes, 0.0% 60 minutes or more (2006-2010 5-year est.)

BENDERSVILLE (borough).
Covers a land area of 0.452 square miles and a water area of 0 square miles. Located at 39.98° N. Lat; 77.25° W. Long. Elevation is 741 feet.

Population: 560 (1990); 576 (2000); 641 (2010); Density: 1,419.2 persons per square mile (2010); Race: 84.4% White, 1.7% Black, 0.5% Asian, 1.1% American Indian/Alaska Native, 0.0% Native Hawaiian/Other Pacific Islander, 12.3% Other, 21.1% Hispanic of any race (2010); Average household size: 2.85 (2010); Median age: 34.7 (2010); Males per 100 females: 105.4 (2010); Marriage status: 20.4% never married, 67.8% now married, 9.2% widowed, 2.5% divorced (2006-2010 5-year est.); Foreign born: 4.6% (2006-2010 5-year est.); Ancestry (includes multiple ancestries): 50.9% German, 13.6% English, 8.0% Irish, 5.2% Italian, 3.1% Scotch-Irish (2006-2010 5-year est.).

Economy: Employment by occupation: 14.5% management, 1.1% professional, 17.2% services, 8.8% sales, 0.0% farming, 8.4% construction, 15.6% production (2006-2010 5-year est.).

Income: Per capita income: $23,614 (2006-2010 5-year est.); Median household income: $46,731 (2006-2010 5-year est.); Average household income: $53,774 (2006-2010 5-year est.); Percent of households with income of $100,000 or more: 8.2% (2006-2010 5-year est.); Poverty rate: 1.5% (2006-2010 5-year est.).

Education: Percent of population age 25 and over with: High school diploma (including GED) or higher: 84.2% (2006-2010 5-year est.); Bachelor's degree or higher: 12.6% (2006-2010 5-year est.); Master's degree or higher: 3.4% (2006-2010 5-year est.).

School District(s)
Upper Adams SD (KG-12)
   2010-11 Enrollment: 1,705 . . . . (717) 677-7191
Housing: Homeownership rate: 69.8% (2010); Median home value: $160,500 (2006-2010 5-year est.); Median contract rent: $582 per month (2006-2010 5-year est.); Median year structure built: 1951 (2006-2010 5-year est.).

Safety: Violent crime rate: 0.0 per 10,000 population; Property crime rate: 31.1 per 10,000 population (2011).

Transportation: Commute to work: 94.4% car, 0.0% public transportation, 4.0% walk, 0.0% work from home (2006-2010 5-year est.); Travel time to work: 26.9% less than 15 minutes, 45.4% 15 to 30 minutes, 17.3% 30 to 45 minutes, 9.2% 45 to 60 minutes, 1.2% 60 minutes or more (2006-2010 5-year est.)

BERWICK (township).
Covers a land area of 7.724 square miles and a water area of 0.020 square miles. Located at 39.86° N. Lat; 77.00° W. Long.

Population: 1,831 (1990); 1,818 (2000); 2,389 (2010); Density: 309.3 persons per square mile (2010); Race: 92.4% White, 2.5% Black, 1.0% Asian, 0.1% American Indian/Alaska Native, 0.0% Native Hawaiian/Other Pacific Islander, 4.0% Other, 5.0% Hispanic of any race (2010); Average household size: 2.60 (2010); Median age: 45.3 (2010); Males per 100 females: 98.9 (2010); Marriage status: 24.9% never married, 58.5% now married, 7.2% widowed, 9.4% divorced (2006-2010 5-year est.); Foreign born: 9.3% (2006-2010 5-year est.); Ancestry (includes multiple ancestries): 40.4% German, 12.5% American, 10.6% Irish, 6.2% English, 3.3% Italian (2006-2010 5-year est.).

Economy: Employment by occupation: 7.7% management, 0.8% professional, 13.4% services, 18.8% sales, 2.8% farming, 9.3% construction, 12.7% production (2006-2010 5-year est.).

Income: Per capita income: $27,528 (2006-2010 5-year est.); Median household income: $55,917 (2006-2010 5-year est.); Average household income: $66,769 (2006-2010 5-year est.); Percent of households with income of $100,000 or more: 15.6% (2006-2010 5-year est.); Poverty rate: 6.6% (2006-2010 5-year est.).

Education: Percent of population age 25 and over with: High school diploma (including GED) or higher: 81.6% (2006-2010 5-year est.); Bachelor's degree or higher: 12.3% (2006-2010 5-year est.); Master's degree or higher: 5.1% (2006-2010 5-year est.).

Housing: Homeownership rate: 90.1% (2010); Median home value: $185,700 (2006-2010 5-year est.); Median contract rent: $563 per month (2006-2010 5-year est.); Median year structure built: 1985 (2006-2010 5-year est.).

Transportation: Commute to work: 91.3% car, 1.8% public transportation, 0.9% walk, 4.3% work from home (2006-2010 5-year est.); Travel time to work: 44.3% less than 15 minutes, 22.8% 15 to 30 minutes, 13.6% 30 to 45 minutes, 7.6% 45 to 60 minutes, 11.6% 60 minutes or more (2006-2010 5-year est.)

Additional Information Contacts
Hanover Area Chamber of Commerce . . . . (717) 637-6130
  http://www.hanoverchamber.com

BIGLERVILLE (borough).
Covers a land area of 0.653 square miles and a water area of 0 square miles. Located at 39.93° N. Lat; 77.25° W. Long. Elevation is 646 feet.

History: North terminus of Gettysburg Railroad, scenic Railroad. National Apple Museum.

Population: 993 (1990); 1,101 (2000); 1,200 (2010); Density: 1,837.8 persons per square mile (2010); Race: 91.7% White, 0.8% Black, 0.3% Asian, 0.1% American Indian/Alaska Native, 0.0% Native Hawaiian/Other Pacific Islander, 7.1% Other, 19.1% Hispanic of any race (2010); Average household size: 2.51 (2010); Median age: 38.8 (2010); Males per 100 females: 95.4 (2010); Marriage status: 30.4% never married, 50.2% now married, 8.3% widowed, 11.1% divorced (2006-2010 5-year est.); Foreign born: 8.0% (2006-2010 5-year est.); Ancestry (includes multiple ancestries): 44.6% German, 19.0% Irish, 10.5% English, 4.4% American, 3.5% Italian (2006-2010 5-year est.).

Economy: Employment by occupation: 9.6% management, 3.6% professional, 5.4% services, 12.3% sales, 4.3% farming, 15.0% construction, 12.8% production (2006-2010 5-year est.).

Income: Per capita income: $25,616 (2006-2010 5-year est.); Median household income: $44,087 (2006-2010 5-year est.); Average household income: $56,472 (2006-2010 5-year est.); Percent of households with income of $100,000 or more: 13.9% (2006-2010 5-year est.); Poverty rate: 7.4% (2006-2010 5-year est.).

Education: Percent of population age 25 and over with: High school diploma (including GED) or higher: 79.7% (2006-2010 5-year est.); Bachelor's degree or higher: 19.0% (2006-2010 5-year est.); Master's degree or higher: 11.1% (2006-2010 5-year est.).

School District(s)

Upper Adams SD (KG-12)

  2010-11 Enrollment: 1,705 . . . . (717) 677-7191

Housing: Homeownership rate: 59.5% (2010); Median home value: $177,500 (2006-2010 5-year est.); Median contract rent: $523 per month (2006-2010 5-year est.); Median year structure built: 1948 (2006-2010 5-year est.).

Safety: Violent crime rate: 0.0 per 10,000 population; Property crime rate: 240.9 per 10,000 population (2011).

Transportation: Commute to work: 91.1% car, 0.0% public transportation, 6.0% walk, 1.1% work from home (2006-2010 5-year est.); Travel time to work: 31.9% less than 15 minutes, 32.8% 15 to 30 minutes, 21.2% 30 to 45 minutes, 8.1% 45 to 60 minutes, 6.0% 60 minutes or more (2006-2010 5-year est.)

Additional Information Contacts

Gettysburg Adams Chamber of Commerce . . . . (717) 334-8151

  http://www.gettysburg-chamber.org

BONNEAUVILLE (borough). Covers a land area of 0.966 square miles and a water area of 0 square miles. Located at 39.81° N. Lat; 77.14° W. Long. Elevation is 558 feet.

Population: 1,282 (1990); 1,378 (2000); 1,800 (2010); Density: 1,862.9 persons per square mile (2010); Race: 93.4% White, 1.9% Black, 0.9% Asian, 0.1% American Indian/Alaska Native, 0.0% Native Hawaiian/Other Pacific Islander, 3.7% Other, 4.6% Hispanic of any race (2010); Average household size: 2.74 (2010); Median age: 35.1 (2010); Males per 100 females: 91.9 (2010); Marriage status: 21.3% never married, 61.3% now married, 7.0% widowed, 10.4% divorced (2006-2010 5-year est.); Foreign born: 4.3% (2006-2010 5-year est.); Ancestry (includes multiple ancestries): 36.9% German, 17.2% Irish, 11.5% Italian, 10.0% American, 8.1% English (2006-2010 5-year est.).

Economy: Employment by occupation: 8.4% management, 1.5% professional, 12.0% services, 15.6% sales, 2.1% farming, 17.9% construction, 9.7% production (2006-2010 5-year est.).

Income: Per capita income: $19,662 (2006-2010 5-year est.); Median household income: $45,957 (2006-2010 5-year est.); Average household income: $53,776 (2006-2010 5-year est.); Percent of households with income of $100,000 or more: 13.7% (2006-2010 5-year est.); Poverty rate: 10.4% (2006-2010 5-year est.).

Education: Percent of population age 25 and over with: High school diploma (including GED) or higher: 77.0% (2006-2010 5-year est.); Bachelor's degree or higher: 9.9% (2006-2010 5-year est.); Master's degree or higher: 4.6% (2006-2010 5-year est.).

Housing: Homeownership rate: 73.0% (2010); Median home value: $184,400 (2006-2010 5-year est.); Median contract rent: $622 per month (2006-2010 5-year est.); Median year structure built: 1982 (2006-2010 5-year est.).

Transportation: Commute to work: 96.2% car, 0.6% public transportation, 1.6% walk, 0.8% work from home (2006-2010 5-year est.); Travel time to work: 22.9% less than 15 minutes, 39.9% 15 to 30 minutes, 16.8% 30 to 45 minutes, 8.4% 45 to 60 minutes, 12.1% 60 minutes or more (2006-2010 5-year est.)

Additional Information Contacts

Gettysburg Adams Chamber of Commerce . . . . (717) 334-8151

  http://www.gettysburg-chamber.org

BUTLER (township). Covers a land area of 23.962 square miles and a water area of 0.098 square miles. Located at 39.92° N. Lat; 77.24° W. Long.

Population: 2,566 (1990); 2,678 (2000); 2,567 (2010); Density: 107.1 persons per square mile (2010); Race: 95.6% White, 0.6% Black, 0.2% Asian, 0.2% American Indian/Alaska Native, 0.0% Native Hawaiian/Other Pacific Islander, 3.4% Other, 7.1% Hispanic of any race (2010); Average household size: 2.56 (2010); Median age: 46.5 (2010); Males per 100 females: 100.1 (2010); Marriage status: 20.3% never married, 61.3% now married, 6.6% widowed, 11.9% divorced (2006-2010 5-year est.); Foreign born: 5.7% (2006-2010 5-year est.); Ancestry (includes multiple ancestries): 34.4% German, 12.9% Irish, 11.2% American, 11.1% English, 3.7% French (2006-2010 5-year est.).

Economy: Employment by occupation: 7.7% management, 2.4% professional, 8.4% services, 17.6% sales, 2.3% farming, 10.1% construction, 13.5% production (2006-2010 5-year est.).

Income: Per capita income: $28,368 (2006-2010 5-year est.); Median household income: $56,346 (2006-2010 5-year est.); Average household income: $70,469 (2006-2010 5-year est.); Percent of households with

income of $100,000 or more: 20.1% (2006-2010 5-year est.); Poverty rate: 6.4% (2006-2010 5-year est.).

Education: Percent of population age 25 and over with: High school diploma (including GED) or higher: 82.6% (2006-2010 5-year est.); Bachelor's degree or higher: 17.1% (2006-2010 5-year est.); Master's degree or higher: 7.9% (2006-2010 5-year est.).

Housing: Homeownership rate: 83.0% (2010); Median home value: $180,600 (2006-2010 5-year est.); Median contract rent: $559 per month (2006-2010 5-year est.); Median year structure built: 1969 (2006-2010 5-year est.).

Transportation: Commute to work: 93.8% car, 0.4% public transportation, 0.4% walk, 3.0% work from home (2006-2010 5-year est.); Travel time to work: 30.9% less than 15 minutes, 36.1% 15 to 30 minutes, 14.1% 30 to 45 minutes, 8.5% 45 to 60 minutes, 10.3% 60 minutes or more (2006-2010 5-year est.)

Additional Information Contacts

Gettysburg Adams Chamber of Commerce . . . . (717) 334-8151

  http://www.gettysburg-chamber.org

CARROLL VALLEY (borough). Covers a land area of 5.393 square miles and a water area of 0.072 square miles. Located at 39.75° N. Lat; 77.38° W. Long. Elevation is 607 feet.

History: Covered bridges. Appalachian Trail to West.

Population: 1,508 (1990); 3,291 (2000); 3,876 (2010); Density: 718.7 persons per square mile (2010); Race: 97.3% White, 0.6% Black, 0.5% Asian, 0.2% American Indian/Alaska Native, 0.0% Native Hawaiian/Other Pacific Islander, 1.4% Other, 1.4% Hispanic of any race (2010); Average household size: 2.73 (2010); Median age: 40.7 (2010); Males per 100 females: 96.3 (2010); Marriage status: 23.8% never married, 62.6% now married, 3.5% widowed, 10.1% divorced (2006-2010 5-year est.); Foreign born: 0.6% (2006-2010 5-year est.); Ancestry (includes multiple ancestries): 39.2% German, 26.8% Irish, 13.4% English, 11.6% American, 7.7% Italian (2006-2010 5-year est.).

Economy: Employment by occupation: 12.4% management, 8.4% professional, 9.8% services, 14.8% sales, 2.9% farming, 11.8% construction, 3.6% production (2006-2010 5-year est.).

Income: Per capita income: $30,518 (2006-2010 5-year est.); Median household income: $76,875 (2006-2010 5-year est.); Average household income: $89,681 (2006-2010 5-year est.); Percent of households with income of $100,000 or more: 37.1% (2006-2010 5-year est.); Poverty rate: 0.7% (2006-2010 5-year est.).

Education: Percent of population age 25 and over with: High school diploma (including GED) or higher: 90.7% (2006-2010 5-year est.); Bachelor's degree or higher: 21.6% (2006-2010 5-year est.); Master's degree or higher: 5.8% (2006-2010 5-year est.).

Housing: Homeownership rate: 92.9% (2010); Median home value: $241,500 (2006-2010 5-year est.); Median contract rent: $819 per month (2006-2010 5-year est.); Median year structure built: 1992 (2006-2010 5-year est.).

Transportation: Commute to work: 95.5% car, 0.0% public transportation, 0.5% walk, 3.4% work from home (2006-2010 5-year est.); Travel time to work: 17.8% less than 15 minutes, 25.0% 15 to 30 minutes, 31.0% 30 to 45 minutes, 9.9% 45 to 60 minutes, 16.3% 60 minutes or more (2006-2010 5-year est.)

Additional Information Contacts

Borough of Carroll Valley . . . . (717) 642-8269

  http://www.carrollvalley.org

Gettysburg Adams Chamber of Commerce . . . . (717) 334-8151

  http://www.gettysburg-chamber.org

CASHTOWN (CDP). Covers a land area of 1.504 square miles and a water area of 0.010 square miles. Located at 39.88° N. Lat; 77.35° W. Long. Elevation is 755 feet.

Population: n/a (1990); n/a (2000); 459 (2010); Density: 305.3 persons per square mile (2010); Race: 97.6% White, 0.2% Black, 0.0% Asian, 0.2% American Indian/Alaska Native, 0.0% Native Hawaiian/Other Pacific Islander, 2.0% Other, 5.9% Hispanic of any race (2010); Average household size: 2.58 (2010); Median age: 43.0 (2010); Males per 100 females: 95.3 (2010); Marriage status: 25.4% never married, 42.5% now married, 4.9% widowed, 27.2% divorced (2006-2010 5-year est.); Foreign born: 0.0% (2006-2010 5-year est.); Ancestry (includes multiple ancestries): 72.9% German, 15.2% Scottish, 5.4% English, 4.4% Dutch, 4.2% Irish (2006-2010 5-year est.).

Economy: Employment by occupation: 21.0% management, 0.0% professional, 37.1% services, 13.7% sales, 3.2% farming, 0.0% construction, 0.0% production (2006-2010 5-year est.).
Income: Per capita income: $18,264 (2006-2010 5-year est.); Median household income: $57,825 (2006-2010 5-year est.); Average household income: $57,911 (2006-2010 5-year est.); Percent of households with income of $100,000 or more: 4.4% (2006-2010 5-year est.); Poverty rate: 17.8% (2006-2010 5-year est.).
Education: Percent of population age 25 and over with: High school diploma (including GED) or higher: 84.1% (2006-2010 5-year est.); Bachelor's degree or higher: 21.7% (2006-2010 5-year est.); Master's degree or higher: 14.2% (2006-2010 5-year est.).

School District(s)
Gettysburg Area SD (KG-12)
   2010-11 Enrollment: 3,141 . . . . (717) 334-6254
Housing: Homeownership rate: 86.1% (2010); Median home value: $230,200 (2006-2010 5-year est.); Median contract rent: $668 per month (2006-2010 5-year est.); Median year structure built: 1965 (2006-2010 5-year est.).
Transportation: Commute to work: 97.2% car, 0.0% public transportation, 2.8% walk, 0.0% work from home (2006-2010 5-year est.); Travel time to work: 21.0% less than 15 minutes, 65.5% 15 to 30 minutes, 2.8% 30 to 45 minutes, 10.7% 45 to 60 minutes, 0.0% 60 minutes or more (2006-2010 5-year est.)

CONEWAGO (township).
Covers a land area of 10.419 square miles and a water area of 0.065 square miles. Located at 39.80° N. Lat; 77.02° W. Long.
Population: 4,532 (1990); 5,709 (2000); 7,085 (2010); Density: 680.0 persons per square mile (2010); Race: 96.1% White, 0.8% Black, 0.8% Asian, 0.1% American Indian/Alaska Native, 0.0% Native Hawaiian/Other Pacific Islander, 2.2% Other, 2.3% Hispanic of any race (2010); Average household size: 2.65 (2010); Median age: 40.9 (2010); Males per 100 females: 93.2 (2010); Marriage status: 22.4% never married, 62.1% now married, 5.3% widowed, 10.2% divorced (2006-2010 5-year est.); Foreign born: 1.0% (2006-2010 5-year est.); Ancestry (includes multiple ancestries): 40.6% German, 15.4% American, 13.3% Irish, 6.0% English, 4.8% Italian (2006-2010 5-year est.).
Economy: Employment by occupation: 8.9% management, 2.7% professional, 8.1% services, 16.7% sales, 1.8% farming, 13.1% construction, 11.0% production (2006-2010 5-year est.).
Income: Per capita income: $25,518 (2006-2010 5-year est.); Median household income: $61,933 (2006-2010 5-year est.); Average household income: $65,384 (2006-2010 5-year est.); Percent of households with income of $100,000 or more: 16.9% (2006-2010 5-year est.); Poverty rate: 4.0% (2006-2010 5-year est.).
Education: Percent of population age 25 and over with: High school diploma (including GED) or higher: 86.3% (2006-2010 5-year est.); Bachelor's degree or higher: 11.4% (2006-2010 5-year est.); Master's degree or higher: 3.3% (2006-2010 5-year est.).
Housing: Homeownership rate: 83.7% (2010); Median home value: $190,100 (2006-2010 5-year est.); Median contract rent: $642 per month (2006-2010 5-year est.); Median year structure built: 1983 (2006-2010 5-year est.).
Safety: Violent crime rate: 1.4 per 10,000 population; Property crime rate: 126.6 per 10,000 population (2011).
Transportation: Commute to work: 95.0% car, 0.5% public transportation, 2.5% walk, 1.3% work from home (2006-2010 5-year est.); Travel time to work: 34.2% less than 15 minutes, 28.9% 15 to 30 minutes, 10.8% 30 to 45 minutes, 11.1% 45 to 60 minutes, 15.0% 60 minutes or more (2006-2010 5-year est.)
Additional Information Contacts
Conewago Township. . . . . (717) 637-0411
Hanover Area Chamber of Commerce . . . . (717) 637-6130
  http://www.hanoverchamber.com

CUMBERLAND (township).
Covers a land area of 33.428 square miles and a water area of 0.176 square miles. Located at 39.80° N. Lat; 77.25° W. Long.
Population: 5,432 (1990); 5,718 (2000); 6,162 (2010); Density: 184.3 persons per square mile (2010); Race: 92.4% White, 3.1% Black, 1.6% Asian, 0.3% American Indian/Alaska Native, 0.0% Native Hawaiian/Other Pacific Islander, 2.6% Other, 3.6% Hispanic of any race (2010); Average household size: 2.30 (2010); Median age: 50.6 (2010); Males per 100 females: 91.4 (2010); Marriage status: 20.9% never married, 59.4% now

married, 10.3% widowed, 9.4% divorced (2006-2010 5-year est.); Foreign born: 2.3% (2006-2010 5-year est.); Ancestry (includes multiple ancestries): 39.5% German, 17.0% Irish, 10.8% English, 5.7% American, 3.6% Italian (2006-2010 5-year est.).
Economy: Employment by occupation: 14.2% management, 3.9% professional, 9.6% services, 14.7% sales, 2.7% farming, 11.3% construction, 5.9% production (2006-2010 5-year est.).
Income: Per capita income: $29,877 (2006-2010 5-year est.); Median household income: $56,513 (2006-2010 5-year est.); Average household income: $69,712 (2006-2010 5-year est.); Percent of households with income of $100,000 or more: 20.2% (2006-2010 5-year est.); Poverty rate: 9.6% (2006-2010 5-year est.).
Education: Percent of population age 25 and over with: High school diploma (including GED) or higher: 85.7% (2006-2010 5-year est.); Bachelor's degree or higher: 33.1% (2006-2010 5-year est.); Master's degree or higher: 13.9% (2006-2010 5-year est.).
Housing: Homeownership rate: 81.5% (2010); Median home value: $227,300 (2006-2010 5-year est.); Median contract rent: $607 per month (2006-2010 5-year est.); Median year structure built: 1975 (2006-2010 5-year est.).
Safety: Violent crime rate: 1.6 per 10,000 population; Property crime rate: 89.0 per 10,000 population (2011).
Transportation: Commute to work: 93.3% car, 1.0% public transportation, 0.8% walk, 3.5% work from home (2006-2010 5-year est.); Travel time to work: 43.6% less than 15 minutes, 25.7% 15 to 30 minutes, 13.5% 30 to 45 minutes, 6.5% 45 to 60 minutes, 10.8% 60 minutes or more (2006-2010 5-year est.)
Additional Information Contacts
Cumberland Township . . . . (717) 334-6485
  http://www.cumberlandtownship.com
Gettysburg Adams Chamber of Commerce . . . . (717) 334-8151
  http://www.gettysburg-chamber.org

EAST BERLIN (borough).
Covers a land area of 0.700 square miles and a water area of 0.026 square miles. Located at 39.94° N. Lat; 76.98° W. Long. Elevation is 430 feet.
Population: 1,175 (1990); 1,365 (2000); 1,521 (2010); Density: 2,172.2 persons per square mile (2010); Race: 96.2% White, 0.7% Black, 0.7% Asian, 0.1% American Indian/Alaska Native, 0.2% Native Hawaiian/Other Pacific Islander, 2.1% Other, 2.6% Hispanic of any race (2010); Average household size: 2.36 (2010); Median age: 41.4 (2010); Males per 100 females: 91.3 (2010); Marriage status: 23.4% never married, 60.9% now married, 7.2% widowed, 8.5% divorced (2006-2010 5-year est.); Foreign born: 1.1% (2006-2010 5-year est.); Ancestry (includes multiple ancestries): 50.3% German, 11.3% Irish, 9.7% American, 7.7% English, 3.5% Dutch (2006-2010 5-year est.).
Economy: Employment by occupation: 6.6% management, 2.0% professional, 10.9% services, 19.5% sales, 3.1% farming, 8.3% construction, 9.5% production (2006-2010 5-year est.).
Income: Per capita income: $24,846 (2006-2010 5-year est.); Median household income: $46,932 (2006-2010 5-year est.); Average household income: $57,657 (2006-2010 5-year est.); Percent of households with income of $100,000 or more: 14.1% (2006-2010 5-year est.); Poverty rate: 6.2% (2006-2010 5-year est.).
Education: Percent of population age 25 and over with: High school diploma (including GED) or higher: 83.8% (2006-2010 5-year est.); Bachelor's degree or higher: 16.0% (2006-2010 5-year est.); Master's degree or higher: 7.6% (2006-2010 5-year est.).

School District(s)
Dover Area SD (KG-12)
   2010-11 Enrollment: 3,613 . . . . (717) 292-3671
Housing: Homeownership rate: 65.5% (2010); Median home value: $183,100 (2006-2010 5-year est.); Median contract rent: $519 per month (2006-2010 5-year est.); Median year structure built: 1954 (2006-2010 5-year est.).
Transportation: Commute to work: 93.4% car, 0.0% public transportation, 2.9% walk, 1.7% work from home (2006-2010 5-year est.); Travel time to work: 20.1% less than 15 minutes, 44.0% 15 to 30 minutes, 20.0% 30 to 45 minutes, 10.0% 45 to 60 minutes, 5.8% 60 minutes or more (2006-2010 5-year est.)
Additional Information Contacts
Hanover Area Chamber of Commerce . . . . (717) 637-6130
  http://www.hanoverchamber.com

FAIRFIELD (borough). Covers a land area of 0.671 square miles and a water area of 0 square miles. Located at 39.79° N. Lat; 77.37° W. Long. Elevation is 600 feet.

Population: 491 (1990); 486 (2000); 507 (2010); Density: 755.7 persons per square mile (2010); Race: 95.5% White, 2.4% Black, 0.2% Asian, 0.0% American Indian/Alaska Native, 0.0% Native Hawaiian/Other Pacific Islander, 1.9% Other, 2.4% Hispanic of any race (2010); Average household size: 2.11 (2010); Median age: 47.4 (2010); Males per 100 females: 79.2 (2010); Marriage status: 24.6% never married, 51.8% now married, 13.6% widowed, 10.0% divorced (2006-2010 5-year est.); Foreign born: 1.1% (2006-2010 5-year est.); Ancestry (includes multiple ancestries): 44.6% German, 30.2% Irish, 11.4% English, 8.2% French, 7.4% American (2006-2010 5-year est.).

Economy: Employment by occupation: 8.1% management, 6.3% professional, 9.2% services, 23.2% sales, 2.1% farming, 17.3% construction, 9.5% production (2006-2010 5-year est.).

Income: Per capita income: $28,003 (2006-2010 5-year est.); Median household income: $53,393 (2006-2010 5-year est.); Average household income: $66,207 (2006-2010 5-year est.); Percent of households with income of $100,000 or more: 17.5% (2006-2010 5-year est.); Poverty rate: 8.2% (2006-2010 5-year est.).

Education: Percent of population age 25 and over with: High school diploma (including GED) or higher: 86.5% (2006-2010 5-year est.); Bachelor's degree or higher: 23.2% (2006-2010 5-year est.); Master's degree or higher: 6.4% (2006-2010 5-year est.).

School District(s)

Fairfield Area SD (KG-12)

    2010-11 Enrollment: 1,208 . . . . (717) 642-8228

Housing: Homeownership rate: 69.6% (2010); Median home value: $206,900 (2006-2010 5-year est.); Median contract rent: $543 per month (2006-2010 5-year est.); Median year structure built: 1958 (2006-2010 5-year est.).

Transportation: Commute to work: 86.1% car, 0.0% public transportation, 3.9% walk, 6.0% work from home (2006-2010 5-year est.); Travel time to work: 32.2% less than 15 minutes, 44.3% 15 to 30 minutes, 13.3% 30 to 45 minutes, 7.2% 45 to 60 minutes, 3.0% 60 minutes or more (2006-2010 5-year est.)

FLORA DALE (CDP). Covers a land area of 0.060 square miles and a water area of 0 square miles. Located at 39.96° N. Lat; 77.25° W. Long. Elevation is 640 feet.

Population: n/a (1990); n/a (2000); 38 (2010); Density: 634.8 persons per square mile (2010); Race: 94.7% White, 0.0% Black, 0.0% Asian, 0.0% American Indian/Alaska Native, 0.0% Native Hawaiian/Other Pacific Islander, 5.3% Other, 18.4% Hispanic of any race (2010); Average household size: 2.27 (2010); Median age: 34.0 (2010); Males per 100 females: 137.5 (2010); Marriage status: n/a never married, n/a now married, n/a widowed, n/a divorced (2006-2010 5-year est.); Foreign born: n/a (2006-2010 5-year est.); Ancestry (includes multiple ancestries): n/a (2006-2010 5-year est.).

Economy: Employment by occupation: n/a management, n/a professional, n/a services, n/a sales, n/a farming, n/a construction, n/a production (2006-2010 5-year est.).

Income: Per capita income: n/a (2006-2010 5-year est.); Median household income: n/a (2006-2010 5-year est.); Average household income: n/a (2006-2010 5-year est.); Percent of households with income of $100,000 or more: n/a (2006-2010 5-year est.); Poverty rate: n/a (2006-2010 5-year est.).

Education: Percent of population age 25 and over with: High school diploma (including GED) or higher: n/a (2006-2010 5-year est.); Bachelor's degree or higher: n/a (2006-2010 5-year est.); Master's degree or higher: n/a (2006-2010 5-year est.).

Housing: Homeownership rate: 53.4% (2010); Median home value: n/a (2006-2010 5-year est.); Median contract rent: n/a per month (2006-2010 5-year est.); Median year structure built: n/a (2006-2010 5-year est.).

Transportation: Commute to work: n/a car, n/a public transportation, n/a walk, n/a work from home (2006-2010 5-year est.); Travel time to work: n/a less than 15 minutes, n/a 15 to 30 minutes, n/a 30 to 45 minutes, n/a 45 to 60 minutes, n/a 60 minutes or more (2006-2010 5-year est.)

FRANKLIN (township). Covers a land area of 68.076 square miles and a water area of 0.397 square miles. Located at 39.90° N. Lat; 77.37° W. Long.

Population: 4,045 (1990); 4,590 (2000); 4,877 (2010); Density: 71.6 persons per square mile (2010); Race: 95.1% White, 1.5% Black, 0.3%

Asian, 0.1% American Indian/Alaska Native, 0.1% Native Hawaiian/Other Pacific Islander, 2.9% Other, 6.0% Hispanic of any race (2010); Average household size: 2.56 (2010); Median age: 45.2 (2010); Males per 100 females: 98.0 (2010); Marriage status: 21.2% never married, 60.6% now married, 7.2% widowed, 11.0% divorced (2006-2010 5-year est.); Foreign born: 5.4% (2006-2010 5-year est.); Ancestry (includes multiple ancestries): 41.4% German, 12.4% American, 11.6% Irish, 4.5% English, 4.1% Scottish (2006-2010 5-year est.).

Economy: Employment by occupation: 14.0% management, 3.1% professional, 19.8% services, 16.8% sales, 3.2% farming, 8.8% construction, 7.0% production (2006-2010 5-year est.).

Income: Per capita income: $25,566 (2006-2010 5-year est.); Median household income: $58,261 (2006-2010 5-year est.); Average household income: $65,320 (2006-2010 5-year est.); Percent of households with income of $100,000 or more: 19.4% (2006-2010 5-year est.); Poverty rate: 7.7% (2006-2010 5-year est.).

Education: Percent of population age 25 and over with: High school diploma (including GED) or higher: 87.4% (2006-2010 5-year est.); Bachelor's degree or higher: 16.3% (2006-2010 5-year est.); Master's degree or higher: 8.4% (2006-2010 5-year est.).

Housing: Homeownership rate: 80.2% (2010); Median home value: $196,300 (2006-2010 5-year est.); Median contract rent: $535 per month (2006-2010 5-year est.); Median year structure built: 1969 (2006-2010 5-year est.).

Transportation: Commute to work: 94.6% car, 0.7% public transportation, 1.3% walk, 3.3% work from home (2006-2010 5-year est.); Travel time to work: 19.8% less than 15 minutes, 36.3% 15 to 30 minutes, 21.1% 30 to 45 minutes, 10.4% 45 to 60 minutes, 12.4% 60 minutes or more (2006-2010 5-year est.)

Additional Information Contacts

Gettysburg Adams Chamber of Commerce . . . . (717) 334-8151
    http://www.gettysburg-chamber.org

FREEDOM (township). Covers a land area of 13.951 square miles and a water area of 0.066 square miles. Located at 39.76° N. Lat; 77.29° W. Long.

Population: 692 (1990); 844 (2000); 831 (2010); Density: 59.6 persons per square mile (2010); Race: 97.1% White, 1.0% Black, 0.6% Asian, 0.0% American Indian/Alaska Native, 0.0% Native Hawaiian/Other Pacific Islander, 1.3% Other, 1.2% Hispanic of any race (2010); Average household size: 2.44 (2010); Median age: 49.9 (2010); Males per 100 females: 99.3 (2010); Marriage status: 17.1% never married, 69.8% now married, 3.9% widowed, 9.1% divorced (2006-2010 5-year est.); Foreign born: 1.8% (2006-2010 5-year est.); Ancestry (includes multiple ancestries): 43.7% German, 15.7% English, 14.0% Irish, 11.6% Italian, 11.5% American (2006-2010 5-year est.).

Economy: Employment by occupation: 14.4% management, 3.6% professional, 5.9% services, 24.1% sales, 3.8% farming, 10.0% construction, 4.8% production (2006-2010 5-year est.).

Income: Per capita income: $43,391 (2006-2010 5-year est.); Median household income: $76,176 (2006-2010 5-year est.); Average household income: $113,711 (2006-2010 5-year est.); Percent of households with income of $100,000 or more: 35.8% (2006-2010 5-year est.); Poverty rate: 5.5% (2006-2010 5-year est.).

Education: Percent of population age 25 and over with: High school diploma (including GED) or higher: 89.6% (2006-2010 5-year est.); Bachelor's degree or higher: 26.5% (2006-2010 5-year est.); Master's degree or higher: 11.7% (2006-2010 5-year est.).

Housing: Homeownership rate: 85.3% (2010); Median home value: $256,300 (2006-2010 5-year est.); Median contract rent: $1,125 per month (2006-2010 5-year est.); Median year structure built: 1969 (2006-2010 5-year est.).

Transportation: Commute to work: 90.1% car, 0.0% public transportation, 1.1% walk, 7.3% work from home (2006-2010 5-year est.); Travel time to work: 17.7% less than 15 minutes, 43.0% 15 to 30 minutes, 23.5% 30 to 45 minutes, 7.0% 45 to 60 minutes, 8.8% 60 minutes or more (2006-2010 5-year est.)

Additional Information Contacts

Gettysburg Adams Chamber of Commerce . . . . (717) 334-8151
    http://www.gettysburg-chamber.org

GARDNERS (CDP). Covers a land area of 0.462 square miles and a water area of 0 square miles. Located at 40.01° N. Lat; 77.21° W. Long. Elevation is 866 feet.

Population: n/a (1990); n/a (2000); 150 (2010); Density: 324.7 persons per square mile (2010); Race: 86.0% White, 2.7% Black, 0.0% Asian, 0.7% American Indian/Alaska Native, 0.0% Native Hawaiian/Other Pacific Islander, 10.6% Other, 8.7% Hispanic of any race (2010); Average household size: 2.68 (2010); Median age: 33.8 (2010); Males per 100 females: 102.7 (2010); Marriage status: 17.5% never married, 68.4% now married, 6.1% widowed, 7.9% divorced (2006-2010 5-year est.); Foreign born: 0.0% (2006-2010 5-year est.); Ancestry (includes multiple ancestries): 32.8% English, 14.3% American, 5.9% German, 5.9% Irish, 5.9% Italian (2006-2010 5-year est.).

Economy: Employment by occupation: 0.0% management, 0.0% professional, 8.0% services, 0.0% sales, 8.0% farming, 18.2% construction, 10.2% production (2006-2010 5-year est.).

Income: Per capita income: $30,220 (2006-2010 5-year est.); Median household income: $90,833 (2006-2010 5-year est.); Average household income: $77,674 (2006-2010 5-year est.); Percent of households with income of $100,000 or more: 41.3% (2006-2010 5-year est.); Poverty rate: 0.0% (2006-2010 5-year est.).

Education: Percent of population age 25 and over with: High school diploma (including GED) or higher: 73.4% (2006-2010 5-year est.); Bachelor's degree or higher: 14.9% (2006-2010 5-year est.); Master's degree or higher: 7.4% (2006-2010 5-year est.).

Housing: Homeownership rate: 67.8% (2010); Median home value: $89,300 (2006-2010 5-year est.); Median contract rent: n/a per month (2006-2010 5-year est.); Median year structure built: 1955 (2006-2010 5-year est.).

Transportation: Commute to work: 68.2% car, 0.0% public transportation, 31.8% walk, 0.0% work from home (2006-2010 5-year est.); Travel time to work: 31.8% less than 15 minutes, 8.0% 15 to 30 minutes, 38.6% 30 to 45 minutes, 21.6% 45 to 60 minutes, 0.0% 60 minutes or more (2006-2010 5-year est.)

GERMANY (township). Covers a land area of 10.900 square miles and a water area of 0.014 square miles. Located at 39.73° N. Lat; 77.11° W. Long.

Population: 1,949 (1990); 2,269 (2000); 2,700 (2010); Density: 247.7 persons per square mile (2010); Race: 97.2% White, 0.3% Black, 0.9% Asian, 0.1% American Indian/Alaska Native, 0.0% Native Hawaiian/Other Pacific Islander, 1.5% Other, 1.4% Hispanic of any race (2010); Average household size: 2.78 (2010); Median age: 42.8 (2010); Males per 100 females: 101.6 (2010); Marriage status: 15.2% never married, 68.4% now married, 7.0% widowed, 9.4% divorced (2006-2010 5-year est.); Foreign born: 1.1% (2006-2010 5-year est.); Ancestry (includes multiple ancestries): 41.4% German, 15.5% Irish, 11.6% English, 9.6% American, 6.0% Polish (2006-2010 5-year est.).

Economy: Employment by occupation: 10.4% management, 4.6% professional, 8.0% services, 18.6% sales, 2.5% farming, 10.0% construction, 11.8% production (2006-2010 5-year est.).

Income: Per capita income: $27,962 (2006-2010 5-year est.); Median household income: $72,667 (2006-2010 5-year est.); Average household income: $76,310 (2006-2010 5-year est.); Percent of households with income of $100,000 or more: 19.8% (2006-2010 5-year est.); Poverty rate: 7.0% (2006-2010 5-year est.).

Education: Percent of population age 25 and over with: High school diploma (including GED) or higher: 83.9% (2006-2010 5-year est.); Bachelor's degree or higher: 17.4% (2006-2010 5-year est.); Master's degree or higher: 4.9% (2006-2010 5-year est.).

Housing: Homeownership rate: 87.8% (2010); Median home value: $260,700 (2006-2010 5-year est.); Median contract rent: $475 per month (2006-2010 5-year est.); Median year structure built: 1979 (2006-2010 5-year est.).

Transportation: Commute to work: 95.0% car, 0.0% public transportation, 1.6% walk, 2.9% work from home (2006-2010 5-year est.); Travel time to work: 19.6% less than 15 minutes, 33.4% 15 to 30 minutes, 16.8% 30 to 45 minutes, 8.4% 45 to 60 minutes, 21.8% 60 minutes or more (2006-2010 5-year est.)

Additional Information Contacts

Hanover Area Chamber of Commerce . . . . (717) 637-6130
  http://www.hanoverchamber.com

GETTYSBURG (borough). Aka Granite Hill. County seat. Covers a land area of 1.661 square miles and a water area of 0.005 square miles. Located at 39.83° N. Lat; 77.23° W. Long. Elevation is 531 feet.

History: Gettysburg was laid out in the 1780's and named for the family of General James Gettys, who presided over the first court in 1800 when the town became a county seat. The first settlers were Scots-Irish and English, followed by Germans and Swiss. Gettysburg is most noted as the scene of one of the Civil War's most decisive conflicts, where Confederate forces were defeated and thousands were killed or injured. After the war, the United States government set aside part of the battlefield as a soldiers' national cemetery. For the dedicatory services in 1863, Abraham Lincoln gave his now-famous Gettysburg Address.

Population: 7,025 (1990); 7,490 (2000); 7,620 (2010); Density: 4,586.7 persons per square mile (2010); Race: 84.5% White, 5.8% Black, 1.9% Asian, 0.3% American Indian/Alaska Native, 0.0% Native Hawaiian/Other Pacific Islander, 7.5% Other, 10.9% Hispanic of any race (2010); Average household size: 2.15 (2010); Median age: 23.0 (2010); Males per 100 females: 92.9 (2010); Marriage status: 57.7% never married, 31.3% now married, 5.7% widowed, 5.3% divorced (2006-2010 5-year est.); Foreign born: 4.0% (2006-2010 5-year est.); Ancestry (includes multiple ancestries): 30.1% German, 19.9% Irish, 13.7% English, 8.5% Italian, 4.0% French (2006-2010 5-year est.).

Economy: Employment by occupation: 12.7% management, 2.6% professional, 17.0% services, 18.9% sales, 3.0% farming, 3.9% construction, 2.4% production (2006-2010 5-year est.).

Income: Per capita income: $17,856 (2006-2010 5-year est.); Median household income: $41,314 (2006-2010 5-year est.); Average household income: $55,898 (2006-2010 5-year est.); Percent of households with income of $100,000 or more: 19.0% (2006-2010 5-year est.); Poverty rate: 20.1% (2006-2010 5-year est.).

Education: Percent of population age 25 and over with: High school diploma (including GED) or higher: 88.3% (2006-2010 5-year est.); Bachelor's degree or higher: 35.8% (2006-2010 5-year est.); Master's degree or higher: 15.4% (2006-2010 5-year est.).

School District(s)

Gettysburg Area SD (KG-12)
  2010-11 Enrollment: 3,141 . . . . (717) 334-6254
Gettysburg Montessori Charter School (KG-09)
  2010-11 Enrollment: 44 . . . . (717) 321-4795
Vida Charter School (KG-06)
  2010-11 Enrollment: 88 . . . . (717) 339-8224

Four-year College(s)

Gettysburg College (Private, Not-for-profit, Evangelical Lutheran Church)
  Fall 2010 Enrollment: 2,662 . . . . (717) 337-6000
    2011-12 Tuition: In-state $42,610; Out-of-state $42,610
Lutheran Theological Seminary at Gettysburg (Private, Not-for-profit, Evangelical Lutheran Church)
  Fall 2010 Enrollment: 170 . . . . (717) 334-6286

Housing: Homeownership rate: 37.2% (2010); Median home value: $187,900 (2006-2010 5-year est.); Median contract rent: $577 per month (2006-2010 5-year est.); Median year structure built: 1942 (2006-2010 5-year est.).

Hospitals: Gettysburg Hospital (76 beds)

Safety: Violent crime rate: 47.1 per 10,000 population; Property crime rate: 251.2 per 10,000 population (2011).

Newspapers: Gettysburg Times (Local news; Circulation 9,906)

Transportation: Commute to work: 62.9% car, 0.0% public transportation, 30.6% walk, 5.6% work from home (2006-2010 5-year est.); Travel time to work: 63.0% less than 15 minutes, 23.1% 15 to 30 minutes, 8.3% 30 to 45 minutes, 3.4% 45 to 60 minutes, 2.1% 60 minutes or more (2006-2010 5-year est.)

Additional Information Contacts

Borough of Gettysburg . . . . (717) 334-1160
  http://www.gettysburg-pa.gov
Gettysburg Adams Chamber of Commerce . . . . (717) 334-8151
  http://www.gettysburg-chamber.org

HAMILTON (township). Covers a land area of 13.506 square miles and a water area of 0.145 square miles. Located at 39.90° N. Lat; 77.02° W. Long.

Population: 1,760 (1990); 2,044 (2000); 2,530 (2010); Density: 187.3 persons per square mile (2010); Race: 97.1% White, 0.4% Black, 0.4% Asian, 0.0% American Indian/Alaska Native, 0.0% Native Hawaiian/Other Pacific Islander, 2.1% Other, 2.6% Hispanic of any race (2010); Average household size: 2.71 (2010); Median age: 42.5 (2010); Males per 100

females: 105.7 (2010); Marriage status: 19.4% never married, 66.0% now married, 6.3% widowed, 8.3% divorced (2006-2010 5-year est.); Foreign born: 1.6% (2006-2010 5-year est.); Ancestry (includes multiple ancestries): 45.4% German, 14.9% English, 14.7% Irish, 11.6% American, 4.5% Italian (2006-2010 5-year est.).

Economy: Employment by occupation: 12.4% management, 5.0% professional, 11.8% services, 14.0% sales, 1.3% farming, 11.9% construction, 9.7% production (2006-2010 5-year est.).

Income: Per capita income: $27,179 (2006-2010 5-year est.); Median household income: $63,333 (2006-2010 5-year est.); Average household income: $73,828 (2006-2010 5-year est.); Percent of households with income of $100,000 or more: 23.6% (2006-2010 5-year est.); Poverty rate: 4.8% (2006-2010 5-year est.).

Education: Percent of population age 25 and over with: High school diploma (including GED) or higher: 87.0% (2006-2010 5-year est.); Bachelor's degree or higher: 15.7% (2006-2010 5-year est.); Master's degree or higher: 5.9% (2006-2010 5-year est.).

Housing: Homeownership rate: 90.0% (2010); Median home value: $219,200 (2006-2010 5-year est.); Median contract rent: $540 per month (2006-2010 5-year est.); Median year structure built: 1988 (2006-2010 5-year est.).

Transportation: Commute to work: 93.6% car, 2.3% public transportation, 0.4% walk, 3.7% work from home (2006-2010 5-year est.); Travel time to work: 24.3% less than 15 minutes, 41.0% 15 to 30 minutes, 17.2% 30 to 45 minutes, 9.2% 45 to 60 minutes, 8.4% 60 minutes or more (2006-2010 5-year est.)

Additional Information Contacts

Gettysburg Adams Chamber of Commerce . . . . (717) 334-8151
  http://www.gettysburg-chamber.org

HAMILTONBAN (township). Covers a land area of 39.170 square miles and a water area of 0.114 square miles. Located at 39.80° N. Lat; 77.41° W. Long.

Population: 1,882 (1990); 2,216 (2000); 2,372 (2010); Density: 60.6 persons per square mile (2010); Race: 96.1% White, 0.9% Black, 0.7% Asian, 0.3% American Indian/Alaska Native, 0.0% Native Hawaiian/Other Pacific Islander, 2.0% Other, 2.0% Hispanic of any race (2010); Average household size: 2.47 (2010); Median age: 44.3 (2010); Males per 100 females: 102.0 (2010); Marriage status: 24.7% never married, 63.1% now married, 5.1% widowed, 7.1% divorced (2006-2010 5-year est.); Foreign born: 1.7% (2006-2010 5-year est.); Ancestry (includes multiple ancestries): 28.5% German, 17.3% Irish, 13.9% English, 8.8% American, 6.1% Scotch-Irish (2006-2010 5-year est.).

Economy: Employment by occupation: 10.4% management, 3.0% professional, 16.7% services, 13.3% sales, 3.0% farming, 17.6% construction, 8.6% production (2006-2010 5-year est.).

Income: Per capita income: $23,726 (2006-2010 5-year est.); Median household income: $54,696 (2006-2010 5-year est.); Average household income: $58,939 (2006-2010 5-year est.); Percent of households with income of $100,000 or more: 9.9% (2006-2010 5-year est.); Poverty rate: 7.0% (2006-2010 5-year est.).

Education: Percent of population age 25 and over with: High school diploma (including GED) or higher: 87.0% (2006-2010 5-year est.); Bachelor's degree or higher: 20.2% (2006-2010 5-year est.); Master's degree or higher: 7.7% (2006-2010 5-year est.).

Housing: Homeownership rate: 83.3% (2010); Median home value: $212,800 (2006-2010 5-year est.); Median contract rent: $631 per month (2006-2010 5-year est.); Median year structure built: 1967 (2006-2010 5-year est.).

Safety: Violent crime rate: 4.2 per 10,000 population; Property crime rate: 33.6 per 10,000 population (2011).

Transportation: Commute to work: 96.6% car, 0.0% public transportation, 0.6% walk, 1.1% work from home (2006-2010 5-year est.); Travel time to work: 22.1% less than 15 minutes, 29.0% 15 to 30 minutes, 23.1% 30 to 45 minutes, 13.1% 45 to 60 minutes, 12.6% 60 minutes or more (2006-2010 5-year est.)

Additional Information Contacts

Gettysburg Adams Chamber of Commerce . . . . (717) 334-8151
  http://www.gettysburg-chamber.org

HAMPTON (CDP). Covers a land area of 0.615 square miles and a water area of 0.001 square miles. Located at 39.93° N. Lat; 77.06° W. Long. Elevation is 541 feet.

Population: 542 (1990); 633 (2000); 632 (2010); Density: 1,028.3 persons per square mile (2010); Race: 92.2% White, 0.0% Black, 1.4% Asian,

0.3% American Indian/Alaska Native, 0.0% Native Hawaiian/Other Pacific Islander, 6.1% Other, 7.4% Hispanic of any race (2010); Average household size: 2.74 (2010); Median age: 34.8 (2010); Males per 100 females: 94.5 (2010); Marriage status: 26.3% never married, 35.5% now married, 4.3% widowed, 34.0% divorced (2006-2010 5-year est.); Foreign born: 0.0% (2006-2010 5-year est.); Ancestry (includes multiple ancestries): 28.0% German, 12.9% American, 9.2% Italian, 8.1% English, 7.9% Dutch (2006-2010 5-year est.).

Economy: Employment by occupation: 0.0% management, 0.0% professional, 15.1% services, 27.1% sales, 0.0% farming, 5.4% construction, 12.7% production (2006-2010 5-year est.).

Income: Per capita income: $17,199 (2006-2010 5-year est.); Median household income: $34,018 (2006-2010 5-year est.); Average household income: $34,724 (2006-2010 5-year est.); Percent of households with income of $100,000 or more: n/a (2006-2010 5-year est.); Poverty rate: 31.5% (2006-2010 5-year est.).

Education: Percent of population age 25 and over with: High school diploma (including GED) or higher: 79.4% (2006-2010 5-year est.); Bachelor's degree or higher: 2.0% (2006-2010 5-year est.); Master's degree or higher: 0.0% (2006-2010 5-year est.).

Housing: Homeownership rate: 68.8% (2010); Median home value: $120,700 (2006-2010 5-year est.); Median contract rent: $519 per month (2006-2010 5-year est.); Median year structure built: 1985 (2006-2010 5-year est.).

Transportation: Commute to work: 81.9% car, 0.0% public transportation, 0.0% walk, 0.0% work from home (2006-2010 5-year est.); Travel time to work: 21.7% less than 15 minutes, 35.5% 15 to 30 minutes, 0.0% 30 to 45 minutes, 7.8% 45 to 60 minutes, 34.9% 60 minutes or more (2006-2010 5-year est.)

HEIDLERSBURG (CDP). Covers a land area of 1.082 square miles and a water area of 0 square miles. Located at 39.95° N. Lat; 77.15° W. Long. Elevation is 571 feet.

Population: n/a (1990); n/a (2000); 707 (2010); Density: 653.3 persons per square mile (2010); Race: 91.5% White, 0.3% Black, 0.3% Asian, 0.4% American Indian/Alaska Native, 0.0% Native Hawaiian/Other Pacific Islander, 7.5% Other, 12.2% Hispanic of any race (2010); Average household size: 2.84 (2010); Median age: 36.8 (2010); Males per 100 females: 94.8 (2010); Marriage status: 34.0% never married, 45.8% now married, 7.0% widowed, 13.2% divorced (2006-2010 5-year est.); Foreign born: 4.6% (2006-2010 5-year est.); Ancestry (includes multiple ancestries): 41.7% German, 18.7% Irish, 8.6% American, 4.9% Italian, 2.0% English (2006-2010 5-year est.).

Economy: Employment by occupation: 4.7% management, 2.2% professional, 23.9% services, 10.0% sales, 2.5% farming, 25.1% construction, 19.2% production (2006-2010 5-year est.).

Income: Per capita income: $22,860 (2006-2010 5-year est.); Median household income: $69,000 (2006-2010 5-year est.); Average household income: $65,639 (2006-2010 5-year est.); Percent of households with income of $100,000 or more: 17.2% (2006-2010 5-year est.); Poverty rate: 3.0% (2006-2010 5-year est.).

Education: Percent of population age 25 and over with: High school diploma (including GED) or higher: 81.7% (2006-2010 5-year est.); Bachelor's degree or higher: 4.0% (2006-2010 5-year est.); Master's degree or higher: 0.0% (2006-2010 5-year est.).

Housing: Homeownership rate: 88.4% (2010); Median home value: $54,100 (2006-2010 5-year est.); Median contract rent: $803 per month (2006-2010 5-year est.); Median year structure built: 1995 (2006-2010 5-year est.).

Transportation: Commute to work: 100.0% car, 0.0% public transportation, 0.0% walk, 0.0% work from home (2006-2010 5-year est.); Travel time to work: 24.9% less than 15 minutes, 36.5% 15 to 30 minutes, 29.0% 30 to 45 minutes, 2.5% 45 to 60 minutes, 7.1% 60 minutes or more (2006-2010 5-year est.)

HIGHLAND (township). Covers a land area of 12.136 square miles and a water area of 0.036 square miles. Located at 39.82° N. Lat; 77.33° W. Long.

Population: 832 (1990); 825 (2000); 943 (2010); Density: 77.7 persons per square mile (2010); Race: 95.5% White, 0.7% Black, 0.2% Asian, 0.4% American Indian/Alaska Native, 0.0% Native Hawaiian/Other Pacific Islander, 3.2% Other, 2.7% Hispanic of any race (2010); Average household size: 2.53 (2010); Median age: 45.7 (2010); Males per 100 females: 90.5 (2010); Marriage status: 18.0% never married, 68.8% now married, 4.0% widowed, 9.2% divorced (2006-2010 5-year est.); Foreign

born: 0.8% (2006-2010 5-year est.); Ancestry (includes multiple ancestries): 50.3% German, 15.4% Irish, 12.2% English, 9.4% American, 4.7% Italian (2006-2010 5-year est.).

Economy: Employment by occupation: 8.7% management, 3.3% professional, 12.0% services, 19.5% sales, 3.3% farming, 20.7% construction, 14.1% production (2006-2010 5-year est.).

Income: Per capita income: $32,929 (2006-2010 5-year est.); Median household income: $65,833 (2006-2010 5-year est.); Average household income: $84,064 (2006-2010 5-year est.); Percent of households with income of $100,000 or more: 24.6% (2006-2010 5-year est.); Poverty rate: 6.4% (2006-2010 5-year est.).

Education: Percent of population age 25 and over with: High school diploma (including GED) or higher: 85.2% (2006-2010 5-year est.); Bachelor's degree or higher: 17.3% (2006-2010 5-year est.); Master's degree or higher: 8.6% (2006-2010 5-year est.).

Housing: Homeownership rate: 86.4% (2010); Median home value: $235,300 (2006-2010 5-year est.); Median contract rent: $731 per month (2006-2010 5-year est.); Median year structure built: 1976 (2006-2010 5-year est.).

Transportation: Commute to work: 85.9% car, 0.6% public transportation, 5.0% walk, 6.5% work from home (2006-2010 5-year est.); Travel time to work: 36.4% less than 15 minutes, 39.6% 15 to 30 minutes, 14.2% 30 to 45 minutes, 3.1% 45 to 60 minutes, 6.7% 60 minutes or more (2006-2010 5-year est.)

HUNTERSTOWN (CDP).

Covers a land area of 1.724 square miles and a water area of 0.005 square miles. Located at 39.88° N. Lat; 77.15° W. Long. Elevation is 554 feet.

Population: n/a (1990); n/a (2000); 547 (2010); Density: 317.3 persons per square mile (2010); Race: 90.3% White, 1.5% Black, 0.4% Asian, 0.2% American Indian/Alaska Native, 0.0% Native Hawaiian/Other Pacific Islander, 7.6% Other, 13.0% Hispanic of any race (2010); Average household size: 2.58 (2010); Median age: 39.3 (2010); Males per 100 females: 107.2 (2010); Marriage status: 32.2% never married, 48.1% now married, 9.8% widowed, 10.0% divorced (2006-2010 5-year est.); Foreign born: 23.1% (2006-2010 5-year est.); Ancestry (includes multiple ancestries): 24.4% English, 13.5% American, 11.8% Dutch, 9.6% German, 4.2% Irish (2006-2010 5-year est.).

Economy: Employment by occupation: 0.0% management, 2.7% professional, 20.7% services, 26.4% sales, 2.2% farming, 0.0% construction, 0.0% production (2006-2010 5-year est.).

Income: Per capita income: $17,104 (2006-2010 5-year est.); Median household income: $61,000 (2006-2010 5-year est.); Average household income: $58,013 (2006-2010 5-year est.); Percent of households with income of $100,000 or more: 3.7% (2006-2010 5-year est.); Poverty rate: 18.2% (2006-2010 5-year est.).

Education: Percent of population age 25 and over with: High school diploma (including GED) or higher: 68.7% (2006-2010 5-year est.); Bachelor's degree or higher: 7.2% (2006-2010 5-year est.); Master's degree or higher: 0.0% (2006-2010 5-year est.).

Housing: Homeownership rate: 77.3% (2010); Median home value: $65,500 (2006-2010 5-year est.); Median contract rent: $617 per month (2006-2010 5-year est.); Median year structure built: 1980 (2006-2010 5-year est.).

Transportation: Commute to work: 100.0% car, 0.0% public transportation, 0.0% walk, 0.0% work from home (2006-2010 5-year est.); Travel time to work: 11.0% less than 15 minutes, 74.1% 15 to 30 minutes, 2.2% 30 to 45 minutes, 9.7% 45 to 60 minutes, 3.0% 60 minutes or more (2006-2010 5-year est.)

HUNTINGTON (township).

Covers a land area of 25.089 square miles and a water area of 0.051 square miles. Located at 40.00° N. Lat; 77.14° W. Long.

Population: 1,969 (1990); 2,233 (2000); 2,369 (2010); Density: 94.4 persons per square mile (2010); Race: 95.4% White, 0.5% Black, 0.8% Asian, 0.4% American Indian/Alaska Native, 0.0% Native Hawaiian/Other Pacific Islander, 2.9% Other, 5.7% Hispanic of any race (2010); Average household size: 2.65 (2010); Median age: 41.3 (2010); Males per 100 females: 101.3 (2010); Marriage status: 22.5% never married, 63.9% now married, 5.6% widowed, 8.0% divorced (2006-2010 5-year est.); Foreign born: 4.6% (2006-2010 5-year est.); Ancestry (includes multiple ancestries): 40.7% German, 9.6% American, 8.9% English, 8.8% Irish, 2.9% Italian (2006-2010 5-year est.).

Economy: Employment by occupation: 13.2% management, 4.7% professional, 10.9% services, 9.1% sales, 3.8% farming, 15.0% construction, 10.3% production (2006-2010 5-year est.).

Income: Per capita income: $23,128 (2006-2010 5-year est.); Median household income: $52,043 (2006-2010 5-year est.); Average household income: $58,655 (2006-2010 5-year est.); Percent of households with income of $100,000 or more: 10.1% (2006-2010 5-year est.); Poverty rate: 4.8% (2006-2010 5-year est.).

Education: Percent of population age 25 and over with: High school diploma (including GED) or higher: 79.7% (2006-2010 5-year est.); Bachelor's degree or higher: 14.0% (2006-2010 5-year est.); Master's degree or higher: 4.8% (2006-2010 5-year est.).

Housing: Homeownership rate: 81.2% (2010); Median home value: $203,200 (2006-2010 5-year est.); Median contract rent: $505 per month (2006-2010 5-year est.); Median year structure built: 1979 (2006-2010 5-year est.).

Transportation: Commute to work: 90.0% car, 0.0% public transportation, 0.6% walk, 9.4% work from home (2006-2010 5-year est.); Travel time to work: 17.5% less than 15 minutes, 29.1% 15 to 30 minutes, 34.2% 30 to 45 minutes, 13.4% 45 to 60 minutes, 5.8% 60 minutes or more (2006-2010 5-year est.)

Additional Information Contacts

Gettysburg Adams Chamber of Commerce . . . . (717) 334-8151
   http://www.gettysburg-chamber.org

IDAVILLE (CDP).

Covers a land area of 0.695 square miles and a water area of 0.003 square miles. Located at 40.02° N. Lat; 77.20° W. Long. Elevation is 804 feet.

Population: n/a (1990); n/a (2000); 177 (2010); Density: 254.8 persons per square mile (2010); Race: 96.6% White, 2.3% Black, 0.6% Asian, 0.0% American Indian/Alaska Native, 0.0% Native Hawaiian/Other Pacific Islander, 0.5% Other, 2.3% Hispanic of any race (2010); Average household size: 2.57 (2010); Median age: 43.5 (2010); Males per 100 females: 103.4 (2010); Marriage status: 16.2% never married, 71.1% now married, 8.1% widowed, 4.6% divorced (2006-2010 5-year est.); Foreign born: 8.6% (2006-2010 5-year est.); Ancestry (includes multiple ancestries): 18.8% German, 17.3% Pennsylvania German, 8.1% English, 7.1% American, 2.0% Dutch (2006-2010 5-year est.).

Economy: Employment by occupation: 18.4% management, 0.0% professional, 4.4% services, 20.2% sales, 4.4% farming, 19.3% construction, 0.0% production (2006-2010 5-year est.).

Income: Per capita income: $21,113 (2006-2010 5-year est.); Median household income: $41,484 (2006-2010 5-year est.); Average household income: $53,120 (2006-2010 5-year est.); Percent of households with income of $100,000 or more: 6.2% (2006-2010 5-year est.); Poverty rate: 0.0% (2006-2010 5-year est.).

Education: Percent of population age 25 and over with: High school diploma (including GED) or higher: 74.1% (2006-2010 5-year est.); Bachelor's degree or higher: 14.0% (2006-2010 5-year est.); Master's degree or higher: 9.8% (2006-2010 5-year est.).

Housing: Homeownership rate: 85.5% (2010); Median home value: $113,500 (2006-2010 5-year est.); Median contract rent: n/a per month (2006-2010 5-year est.); Median year structure built: 1945 (2006-2010 5-year est.).

Transportation: Commute to work: 100.0% car, 0.0% public transportation, 0.0% walk, 0.0% work from home (2006-2010 5-year est.); Travel time to work: 23.7% less than 15 minutes, 43.0% 15 to 30 minutes, 26.3% 30 to 45 minutes, 7.0% 45 to 60 minutes, 0.0% 60 minutes or more (2006-2010 5-year est.)

LAKE HERITAGE (CDP).

Covers a land area of 0.687 square miles and a water area of 0.226 square miles. Located at 39.81° N. Lat; 77.19° W. Long. Elevation is 486 feet.

Population: 1,039 (1990); 1,136 (2000); 1,333 (2010); Density: 1,939.3 persons per square mile (2010); Race: 96.0% White, 0.9% Black, 1.2% Asian, 0.5% American Indian/Alaska Native, 0.0% Native Hawaiian/Other Pacific Islander, 1.4% Other, 2.6% Hispanic of any race (2010); Average household size: 2.53 (2010); Median age: 47.1 (2010); Males per 100 females: 105.4 (2010); Marriage status: 19.5% never married, 67.8% now married, 9.5% widowed, 3.2% divorced (2006-2010 5-year est.); Foreign born: 3.3% (2006-2010 5-year est.); Ancestry (includes multiple ancestries): 38.4% German, 16.6% American, 10.4% English, 9.5% Irish, 6.8% Polish (2006-2010 5-year est.).

Economy: Employment by occupation: 15.0% management, 4.5% professional, 12.7% services, 10.9% sales, 3.0% farming, 7.7% construction, 5.1% production (2006-2010 5-year est.).

Income: Per capita income: $33,702 (2006-2010 5-year est.); Median household income: $95,172 (2006-2010 5-year est.); Average household income: $97,177 (2006-2010 5-year est.); Percent of households with income of $100,000 or more: 45.4% (2006-2010 5-year est.); Poverty rate: 0.5% (2006-2010 5-year est.).

Education: Percent of population age 25 and over with: High school diploma (including GED) or higher: 97.4% (2006-2010 5-year est.); Bachelor's degree or higher: 36.4% (2006-2010 5-year est.); Master's degree or higher: 13.1% (2006-2010 5-year est.).

Housing: Homeownership rate: 94.6% (2010); Median home value: $300,900 (2006-2010 5-year est.); Median contract rent: $1,115 per month (2006-2010 5-year est.); Median year structure built: 1985 (2006-2010 5-year est.).

Transportation: Commute to work: 96.8% car, 0.0% public transportation, 0.0% walk, 3.2% work from home (2006-2010 5-year est.); Travel time to work: 23.9% less than 15 minutes, 40.8% 15 to 30 minutes, 17.0% 30 to 45 minutes, 8.1% 45 to 60 minutes, 10.1% 60 minutes or more (2006-2010 5-year est.)

Additional Information Contacts

Gettysburg Adams Chamber of Commerce . . . . (717) 334-8151
  http://www.gettysburg-chamber.org

LAKE MEADE (CDP). Covers a land area of 1.323 square miles and a water area of 0.424 square miles. Located at 39.98° N. Lat; 77.04° W. Long. Elevation is 518 feet.

Population: 1,344 (1990); 1,832 (2000); 2,563 (2010); Density: 1,937.9 persons per square mile (2010); Race: 98.3% White, 0.2% Black, 0.4% Asian, 0.1% American Indian/Alaska Native, 0.0% Native Hawaiian/Other Pacific Islander, 1.0% Other, 1.8% Hispanic of any race (2010); Average household size: 2.80 (2010); Median age: 40.8 (2010); Males per 100 females: 101.5 (2010); Marriage status: 15.6% never married, 71.3% now married, 4.2% widowed, 9.0% divorced (2006-2010 5-year est.); Foreign born: 0.1% (2006-2010 5-year est.); Ancestry (includes multiple ancestries): 42.8% German, 18.1% Irish, 11.5% Italian, 9.4% English, 8.1% Polish (2006-2010 5-year est.).

Economy: Employment by occupation: 15.7% management, 9.3% professional, 6.5% services, 14.4% sales, 4.9% farming, 3.6% construction, 7.4% production (2006-2010 5-year est.).

Income: Per capita income: $29,954 (2006-2010 5-year est.); Median household income: $74,075 (2006-2010 5-year est.); Average household income: $79,432 (2006-2010 5-year est.); Percent of households with income of $100,000 or more: 30.0% (2006-2010 5-year est.); Poverty rate: 2.1% (2006-2010 5-year est.).

Education: Percent of population age 25 and over with: High school diploma (including GED) or higher: 95.0% (2006-2010 5-year est.); Bachelor's degree or higher: 22.5% (2006-2010 5-year est.); Master's degree or higher: 6.7% (2006-2010 5-year est.).

Housing: Homeownership rate: 96.3% (2010); Median home value: $220,900 (2006-2010 5-year est.); Median contract rent: n/a per month (2006-2010 5-year est.); Median year structure built: 1986 (2006-2010 5-year est.).

Transportation: Commute to work: 93.2% car, 1.9% public transportation, 0.0% walk, 2.7% work from home (2006-2010 5-year est.); Travel time to work: 3.6% less than 15 minutes, 25.9% 15 to 30 minutes, 49.4% 30 to 45 minutes, 9.6% 45 to 60 minutes, 11.5% 60 minutes or more (2006-2010 5-year est.)

Additional Information Contacts

New Oxford Area Chamber of Commerce. . . . . (717) 624-2800
  http://newoxford.org

LATIMORE (township). Covers a land area of 21.140 square miles and a water area of 0.349 square miles. Located at 40.01° N. Lat; 77.09° W. Long. Elevation is 640 feet.

Population: 2,262 (1990); 2,528 (2000); 2,580 (2010); Density: 122.0 persons per square mile (2010); Race: 97.3% White, 0.3% Black, 0.3% Asian, 0.1% American Indian/Alaska Native, 0.0% Native Hawaiian/Other Pacific Islander, 2.0% Other, 2.9% Hispanic of any race (2010); Average household size: 2.74 (2010); Median age: 42.6 (2010); Males per 100 females: 100.6 (2010); Marriage status: 16.4% never married, 72.5% now married, 5.1% widowed, 6.0% divorced (2006-2010 5-year est.); Foreign born: 1.5% (2006-2010 5-year est.); Ancestry (includes multiple

ancestries): 39.9% German, 16.4% Irish, 10.7% English, 10.5% Italian, 9.4% American (2006-2010 5-year est.).

Economy: Employment by occupation: 9.0% management, 7.8% professional, 5.0% services, 18.5% sales, 5.9% farming, 14.7% construction, 8.9% production (2006-2010 5-year est.).

Income: Per capita income: $27,030 (2006-2010 5-year est.); Median household income: $70,729 (2006-2010 5-year est.); Average household income: $76,988 (2006-2010 5-year est.); Percent of households with income of $100,000 or more: 23.4% (2006-2010 5-year est.); Poverty rate: 3.5% (2006-2010 5-year est.).

Education: Percent of population age 25 and over with: High school diploma (including GED) or higher: 89.6% (2006-2010 5-year est.); Bachelor's degree or higher: 18.8% (2006-2010 5-year est.); Master's degree or higher: 6.3% (2006-2010 5-year est.).

Housing: Homeownership rate: 89.7% (2010); Median home value: $207,700 (2006-2010 5-year est.); Median contract rent: $604 per month (2006-2010 5-year est.); Median year structure built: 1981 (2006-2010 5-year est.).

Safety: Violent crime rate: 3.9 per 10,000 population; Property crime rate: 88.9 per 10,000 population (2011).

Transportation: Commute to work: 95.8% car, 0.0% public transportation, 0.4% walk, 3.1% work from home (2006-2010 5-year est.); Travel time to work: 14.1% less than 15 minutes, 32.5% 15 to 30 minutes, 38.5% 30 to 45 minutes, 4.5% 45 to 60 minutes, 10.4% 60 minutes or more (2006-2010 5-year est.)

Additional Information Contacts

Greater Carlisle Area Chamber of Commerce . . . . (717) 243-4515
  http://carlislechamber.org
Latimore Township . . . . (717) 528-4614
  http://www.latimore.org

LIBERTY (township). Covers a land area of 16.230 square miles and a water area of 0.006 square miles. Located at 39.74° N. Lat; 77.36° W. Long.

Population: 921 (1990); 1,063 (2000); 1,237 (2010); Density: 76.2 persons per square mile (2010); Race: 96.7% White, 1.3% Black, 0.6% Asian, 0.2% American Indian/Alaska Native, 0.0% Native Hawaiian/Other Pacific Islander, 1.2% Other, 1.6% Hispanic of any race (2010); Average household size: 2.53 (2010); Median age: 45.3 (2010); Males per 100 females: 103.1 (2010); Marriage status: 24.3% never married, 63.2% now married, 3.4% widowed, 9.1% divorced (2006-2010 5-year est.); Foreign born: 4.4% (2006-2010 5-year est.); Ancestry (includes multiple ancestries): 42.5% German, 15.3% English, 11.4% American, 8.1% Irish, 4.0% Scottish (2006-2010 5-year est.).

Economy: Employment by occupation: 8.3% management, 2.8% professional, 13.1% services, 17.8% sales, 4.1% farming, 21.7% construction, 9.6% production (2006-2010 5-year est.).

Income: Per capita income: $27,189 (2006-2010 5-year est.); Median household income: $53,587 (2006-2010 5-year est.); Average household income: $73,147 (2006-2010 5-year est.); Percent of households with income of $100,000 or more: 21.1% (2006-2010 5-year est.); Poverty rate: 7.4% (2006-2010 5-year est.).

Education: Percent of population age 25 and over with: High school diploma (including GED) or higher: 81.5% (2006-2010 5-year est.); Bachelor's degree or higher: 17.5% (2006-2010 5-year est.); Master's degree or higher: 6.8% (2006-2010 5-year est.).

Housing: Homeownership rate: 85.7% (2010); Median home value: $256,400 (2006-2010 5-year est.); Median contract rent: $586 per month (2006-2010 5-year est.); Median year structure built: 1981 (2006-2010 5-year est.).

Safety: Violent crime rate: 8.1 per 10,000 population; Property crime rate: 120.9 per 10,000 population (2011).

Transportation: Commute to work: 94.3% car, 0.0% public transportation, 0.7% walk, 4.4% work from home (2006-2010 5-year est.); Travel time to work: 27.3% less than 15 minutes, 29.5% 15 to 30 minutes, 22.2% 30 to 45 minutes, 10.5% 45 to 60 minutes, 10.5% 60 minutes or more (2006-2010 5-year est.)

Additional Information Contacts

Gettysburg Adams Chamber of Commerce . . . . (717) 334-8151
  http://www.gettysburg-chamber.org

LITTLESTOWN (borough). Covers a land area of 1.503 square miles and a water area of 0 square miles. Located at 39.75° N. Lat; 77.09° W. Long. Elevation is 630 feet.

History: Laid out 1765, incorporated 1864.

Population: 2,974 (1990); 3,947 (2000); 4,434 (2010); Density: 2,950.7 persons per square mile (2010); Race: 96.0% White, 0.9% Black, 0.4% Asian, 0.2% American Indian/Alaska Native, 0.0% Native Hawaiian/Other Pacific Islander, 2.5% Other, 2.5% Hispanic of any race (2010); Average household size: 2.46 (2010); Median age: 37.6 (2010); Males per 100 females: 95.3 (2010); Marriage status: 24.5% never married, 57.1% now married, 6.3% widowed, 12.1% divorced (2006-2010 5-year est.); Foreign born: 1.1% (2006-2010 5-year est.); Ancestry (includes multiple ancestries): 42.1% German, 16.2% Irish, 10.6% English, 9.5% American, 6.8% Italian (2006-2010 5-year est.).
Economy: Employment by occupation: 5.2% management, 4.5% professional, 10.6% services, 15.9% sales, 5.6% farming, 14.4% construction, 9.4% production (2006-2010 5-year est.).
Income: Per capita income: $23,575 (2006-2010 5-year est.); Median household income: $50,568 (2006-2010 5-year est.); Average household income: $59,941 (2006-2010 5-year est.); Percent of households with income of $100,000 or more: 14.6% (2006-2010 5-year est.); Poverty rate: 10.6% (2006-2010 5-year est.).
Education: Percent of population age 25 and over with: High school diploma (including GED) or higher: 87.7% (2006-2010 5-year est.); Bachelor's degree or higher: 14.5% (2006-2010 5-year est.); Master's degree or higher: 5.2% (2006-2010 5-year est.).

School District(s)

Littlestown Area SD (KG-12)
   2010-11 Enrollment: 2,134 . . . . (717) 359-4146
Housing: Homeownership rate: 69.2% (2010); Median home value: $181,000 (2006-2010 5-year est.); Median contract rent: $569 per month (2006-2010 5-year est.); Median year structure built: 1964 (2006-2010 5-year est.).
Transportation: Commute to work: 94.7% car, 0.0% public transportation, 3.2% walk, 0.8% work from home (2006-2010 5-year est.); Travel time to work: 19.7% less than 15 minutes, 30.9% 15 to 30 minutes, 17.4% 30 to 45 minutes, 12.0% 45 to 60 minutes, 20.0% 60 minutes or more (2006-2010 5-year est.)

Additional Information Contacts
Littlestown Area Chamber of Commerce . . . . (717) 359-7006
   http://www.littlestownchamber.org

MCKNIGHTSTOWN (CDP). Covers a land area of 0.892 square miles and a water area of 0 square miles. Located at 39.87° N. Lat; 77.33° W. Long. Elevation is 640 feet.
Population: n/a (1990); n/a (2000); 226 (2010); Density: 253.4 persons per square mile (2010); Race: 96.5% White, 0.0% Black, 2.2% Asian, 0.0% American Indian/Alaska Native, 0.0% Native Hawaiian/Other Pacific Islander, 1.3% Other, 1.8% Hispanic of any race (2010); Average household size: 2.48 (2010); Median age: 44.4 (2010); Males per 100 females: 101.8 (2010); Marriage status: 7.8% never married, 85.6% now married, 0.0% widowed, 6.7% divorced (2006-2010 5-year est.); Foreign born: 0.0% (2006-2010 5-year est.); Ancestry (includes multiple ancestries): 51.6% German, 34.5% Irish, 10.1% American, 7.0% Welsh, 4.7% Scandinavian (2006-2010 5-year est.).
Economy: Employment by occupation: 14.4% management, 0.0% professional, 13.3% services, 27.8% sales, 0.0% farming, 12.2% construction, 0.0% production (2006-2010 5-year est.).
Income: Per capita income: $16,567 (2006-2010 5-year est.); Median household income: $34,340 (2006-2010 5-year est.); Average household income: $47,521 (2006-2010 5-year est.); Percent of households with income of $100,000 or more: 14.3% (2006-2010 5-year est.); Poverty rate: 0.0% (2006-2010 5-year est.).
Education: Percent of population age 25 and over with: High school diploma (including GED) or higher: 78.9% (2006-2010 5-year est.); Bachelor's degree or higher: 15.1% (2006-2010 5-year est.); Master's degree or higher: 7.2% (2006-2010 5-year est.).
Housing: Homeownership rate: 86.8% (2010); Median home value: $211,800 (2006-2010 5-year est.); Median contract rent: n/a per month (2006-2010 5-year est.); Median year structure built: before 1940 (2006-2010 5-year est.).
Transportation: Commute to work: 100.0% car, 0.0% public transportation, 0.0% walk, 0.0% work from home (2006-2010 5-year est.); Travel time to work: 0.0% less than 15 minutes, 38.9% 15 to 30 minutes, 15.6% 30 to 45 minutes, 18.9% 45 to 60 minutes, 26.7% 60 minutes or more (2006-2010 5-year est.)

MCSHERRYSTOWN (borough). Covers a land area of 0.512 square miles and a water area of 0 square miles. Located at 39.80° N. Lat; 77.02° W. Long. Elevation is 584 feet.
History: Conewago Chapel (1787) to Northwest. Incorporated 1882.
Population: 2,769 (1990); 2,691 (2000); 3,038 (2010); Density: 5,936.6 persons per square mile (2010); Race: 94.6% White, 1.2% Black, 0.8% Asian, 0.2% American Indian/Alaska Native, 0.0% Native Hawaiian/Other Pacific Islander, 3.2% Other, 5.3% Hispanic of any race (2010); Average household size: 2.36 (2010); Median age: 36.1 (2010); Males per 100 females: 82.4 (2010); Marriage status: 16.4% never married, 60.4% now married, 12.4% widowed, 10.8% divorced (2006-2010 5-year est.); Foreign born: 2.6% (2006-2010 5-year est.); Ancestry (includes multiple ancestries): 54.8% German, 17.5% American, 9.3% Irish, 5.0% French, 4.0% Italian (2006-2010 5-year est.).
Economy: Employment by occupation: 3.2% management, 2.8% professional, 9.3% services, 16.0% sales, 2.3% farming, 5.6% construction, 7.6% production (2006-2010 5-year est.).
Income: Per capita income: $18,416 (2006-2010 5-year est.); Median household income: $42,147 (2006-2010 5-year est.); Average household income: $43,161 (2006-2010 5-year est.); Percent of households with income of $100,000 or more: 1.6% (2006-2010 5-year est.); Poverty rate: 4.3% (2006-2010 5-year est.).
Education: Percent of population age 25 and over with: High school diploma (including GED) or higher: 85.3% (2006-2010 5-year est.); Bachelor's degree or higher: 13.8% (2006-2010 5-year est.); Master's degree or higher: 9.3% (2006-2010 5-year est.).
Housing: Homeownership rate: 52.1% (2010); Median home value: $156,600 (2006-2010 5-year est.); Median contract rent: $608 per month (2006-2010 5-year est.); Median year structure built: 1955 (2006-2010 5-year est.).
Safety: Violent crime rate: 13.1 per 10,000 population; Property crime rate: 150.9 per 10,000 population (2011).
Transportation: Commute to work: 95.9% car, 0.0% public transportation, 0.0% walk, 1.7% work from home (2006-2010 5-year est.); Travel time to work: 46.9% less than 15 minutes, 26.4% 15 to 30 minutes, 15.3% 30 to 45 minutes, 6.2% 45 to 60 minutes, 5.2% 60 minutes or more (2006-2010 5-year est.)

Additional Information Contacts
Hanover Area Chamber of Commerce . . . . (717) 637-6130
   http://www.hanoverchamber.com

MENALLEN (township). Covers a land area of 42.698 square miles and a water area of 0.124 square miles. Located at 39.98° N. Lat; 77.30° W. Long.
Population: 2,700 (1990); 2,974 (2000); 3,515 (2010); Density: 82.3 persons per square mile (2010); Race: 92.2% White, 1.1% Black, 0.2% Asian, 0.3% American Indian/Alaska Native, 0.0% Native Hawaiian/Other Pacific Islander, 6.2% Other, 12.8% Hispanic of any race (2010); Average household size: 2.75 (2010); Median age: 39.4 (2010); Males per 100 females: 106.8 (2010); Marriage status: 23.5% never married, 63.8% now married, 3.3% widowed, 9.4% divorced (2006-2010 5-year est.); Foreign born: 11.3% (2006-2010 5-year est.); Ancestry (includes multiple ancestries): 35.4% German, 14.2% Irish, 7.8% English, 6.5% American, 6.3% Dutch (2006-2010 5-year est.).
Economy: Employment by occupation: 8.8% management, 0.6% professional, 11.7% services, 12.1% sales, 3.2% farming, 16.7% construction, 13.2% production (2006-2010 5-year est.).
Income: Per capita income: $22,619 (2006-2010 5-year est.); Median household income: $53,287 (2006-2010 5-year est.); Average household income: $63,206 (2006-2010 5-year est.); Percent of households with income of $100,000 or more: 18.7% (2006-2010 5-year est.); Poverty rate: 4.2% (2006-2010 5-year est.).
Education: Percent of population age 25 and over with: High school diploma (including GED) or higher: 82.0% (2006-2010 5-year est.); Bachelor's degree or higher: 18.1% (2006-2010 5-year est.); Master's degree or higher: 6.9% (2006-2010 5-year est.).
Housing: Homeownership rate: 79.3% (2010); Median home value: $188,000 (2006-2010 5-year est.); Median contract rent: $577 per month (2006-2010 5-year est.); Median year structure built: 1975 (2006-2010 5-year est.).
Transportation: Commute to work: 91.3% car, 0.0% public transportation, 1.8% walk, 3.9% work from home (2006-2010 5-year est.); Travel time to work: 25.9% less than 15 minutes, 36.4% 15 to 30 minutes, 23.0% 30 to 45 minutes, 8.0% 45 to 60 minutes, 6.7% 60 minutes or more (2006-2010 5-year est.)

Additional Information Contacts
Gettysburg Adams Chamber of Commerce . . . . (717) 334-8151
  http://www.gettysburg-chamber.org

MIDWAY (CDP).
Covers a land area of 0.650 square miles and a water area of 0.002 square miles. Located at 39.80° N. Lat; 77.00° W. Long. Elevation is 574 feet.
Population: 2,254 (1990); 2,323 (2000); 2,125 (2010); Density: 3,271.5 persons per square mile (2010); Race: 96.9% White, 0.3% Black, 0.2% Asian, 0.1% American Indian/Alaska Native, 0.0% Native Hawaiian/Other Pacific Islander, 2.5% Other, 3.3% Hispanic of any race (2010); Average household size: 2.43 (2010); Median age: 41.6 (2010); Males per 100 females: 93.2 (2010); Marriage status: 21.1% never married, 55.7% now married, 6.9% widowed, 16.4% divorced (2006-2010 5-year est.); Foreign born: 0.7% (2006-2010 5-year est.); Ancestry (includes multiple ancestries): 43.2% German, 17.6% American, 11.3% Irish, 6.0% English, 3.5% Scottish (2006-2010 5-year est.).
Economy: Employment by occupation: 3.3% management, 2.9% professional, 2.7% services, 15.8% sales, 2.6% farming, 17.3% construction, 14.5% production (2006-2010 5-year est.).
Income: Per capita income: $24,888 (2006-2010 5-year est.); Median household income: $55,109 (2006-2010 5-year est.); Average household income: $57,565 (2006-2010 5-year est.); Percent of households with income of $100,000 or more: 11.8% (2006-2010 5-year est.); Poverty rate: 5.7% (2006-2010 5-year est.).
Education: Percent of population age 25 and over with: High school diploma (including GED) or higher: 84.0% (2006-2010 5-year est.); Bachelor's degree or higher: 8.9% (2006-2010 5-year est.); Master's degree or higher: 3.2% (2006-2010 5-year est.).
Housing: Homeownership rate: 74.8% (2010); Median home value: $157,200 (2006-2010 5-year est.); Median contract rent: $629 per month (2006-2010 5-year est.); Median year structure built: 1969 (2006-2010 5-year est.).
Transportation: Commute to work: 92.8% car, 0.0% public transportation, 7.2% walk, 0.0% work from home (2006-2010 5-year est.); Travel time to work: 29.9% less than 15 minutes, 32.4% 15 to 30 minutes, 13.5% 30 to 45 minutes, 13.0% 45 to 60 minutes, 11.3% 60 minutes or more (2006-2010 5-year est.)
Additional Information Contacts
Gettysburg Adams Chamber of Commerce . . . . (717) 334-8151
  http://www.gettysburg-chamber.org

MOUNT JOY (township).
Covers a land area of 26.002 square miles and a water area of 0.226 square miles. Located at 39.77° N. Lat; 77.18° W. Long.
Population: 2,888 (1990); 3,232 (2000); 3,670 (2010); Density: 141.1 persons per square mile (2010); Race: 94.9% White, 2.0% Black, 0.9% Asian, 0.3% American Indian/Alaska Native, 0.0% Native Hawaiian/Other Pacific Islander, 1.9% Other, 2.0% Hispanic of any race (2010); Average household size: 2.53 (2010); Median age: 46.9 (2010); Males per 100 females: 99.2 (2010); Marriage status: 17.8% never married, 66.9% now married, 8.3% widowed, 7.0% divorced (2006-2010 5-year est.); Foreign born: 1.7% (2006-2010 5-year est.); Ancestry (includes multiple ancestries): 41.7% German, 11.2% American, 9.3% Irish, 9.0% English, 4.5% Welsh (2006-2010 5-year est.).
Economy: Employment by occupation: 18.3% management, 7.1% professional, 7.4% services, 11.1% sales, 4.8% farming, 5.7% construction, 5.8% production (2006-2010 5-year est.).
Income: Per capita income: $31,016 (2006-2010 5-year est.); Median household income: $61,630 (2006-2010 5-year est.); Average household income: $75,426 (2006-2010 5-year est.); Percent of households with income of $100,000 or more: 27.9% (2006-2010 5-year est.); Poverty rate: 6.7% (2006-2010 5-year est.).
Education: Percent of population age 25 and over with: High school diploma (including GED) or higher: 90.5% (2006-2010 5-year est.); Bachelor's degree or higher: 28.7% (2006-2010 5-year est.); Master's degree or higher: 12.2% (2006-2010 5-year est.).
Housing: Homeownership rate: 87.5% (2010); Median home value: $249,400 (2006-2010 5-year est.); Median contract rent: $572 per month (2006-2010 5-year est.); Median year structure built: 1979 (2006-2010 5-year est.).
Transportation: Commute to work: 87.1% car, 0.0% public transportation, 4.7% walk, 8.3% work from home (2006-2010 5-year est.); Travel time to work: 25.7% less than 15 minutes, 35.2% 15 to 30 minutes, 14.5% 30 to

45 minutes, 14.1% 45 to 60 minutes, 10.5% 60 minutes or more (2006-2010 5-year est.)
Additional Information Contacts
Gettysburg Adams Chamber of Commerce . . . . (717) 334-8151
  http://www.gettysburg-chamber.org

MOUNT PLEASANT (township).
Covers a land area of 30.412 square miles and a water area of 0.169 square miles. Located at 39.83° N. Lat; 77.11° W. Long. Elevation is 673 feet.
Population: 4,041 (1990); 4,420 (2000); 4,693 (2010); Density: 154.3 persons per square mile (2010); Race: 94.4% White, 0.8% Black, 0.6% Asian, 0.1% American Indian/Alaska Native, 0.0% Native Hawaiian/Other Pacific Islander, 4.1% Other, 6.5% Hispanic of any race (2010); Average household size: 2.62 (2010); Median age: 42.6 (2010); Males per 100 females: 96.9 (2010); Marriage status: 20.5% never married, 60.2% now married, 5.7% widowed, 13.5% divorced (2006-2010 5-year est.); Foreign born: 5.3% (2006-2010 5-year est.); Ancestry (includes multiple ancestries): 38.0% German, 13.2% American, 12.0% Irish, 6.5% English, 4.7% French (2006-2010 5-year est.).
Economy: Employment by occupation: 9.3% management, 1.4% professional, 7.8% services, 17.5% sales, 1.2% farming, 10.0% construction, 12.7% production (2006-2010 5-year est.).
Income: Per capita income: $23,529 (2006-2010 5-year est.); Median household income: $51,020 (2006-2010 5-year est.); Average household income: $59,734 (2006-2010 5-year est.); Percent of households with income of $100,000 or more: 18.1% (2006-2010 5-year est.); Poverty rate: 11.6% (2006-2010 5-year est.).
Education: Percent of population age 25 and over with: High school diploma (including GED) or higher: 81.7% (2006-2010 5-year est.); Bachelor's degree or higher: 15.5% (2006-2010 5-year est.); Master's degree or higher: 3.1% (2006-2010 5-year est.).
Housing: Homeownership rate: 85.5% (2010); Median home value: $167,800 (2006-2010 5-year est.); Median contract rent: $623 per month (2006-2010 5-year est.); Median year structure built: 1986 (2006-2010 5-year est.).
Transportation: Commute to work: 95.5% car, 0.0% public transportation, 2.3% walk, 2.2% work from home (2006-2010 5-year est.); Travel time to work: 25.0% less than 15 minutes, 50.9% 15 to 30 minutes, 10.3% 30 to 45 minutes, 4.3% 45 to 60 minutes, 9.5% 60 minutes or more (2006-2010 5-year est.)
Additional Information Contacts
Gettysburg Adams Chamber of Commerce . . . . (717) 334-8151
  http://www.gettysburg-chamber.org

NEW OXFORD (borough).
Covers a land area of 0.619 square miles and a water area of 0 square miles. Located at 39.86° N. Lat; 77.06° W. Long. Elevation is 558 feet.
Population: 1,617 (1990); 1,696 (2000); 1,783 (2010); Density: 2,880.4 persons per square mile (2010); Race: 90.7% White, 1.8% Black, 0.4% Asian, 0.7% American Indian/Alaska Native, 0.1% Native Hawaiian/Other Pacific Islander, 6.3% Other, 15.4% Hispanic of any race (2010); Average household size: 2.42 (2010); Median age: 37.1 (2010); Males per 100 females: 86.5 (2010); Marriage status: 32.7% never married, 45.2% now married, 8.1% widowed, 14.0% divorced (2006-2010 5-year est.); Foreign born: 8.0% (2006-2010 5-year est.); Ancestry (includes multiple ancestries): 37.0% German, 12.8% Irish, 10.2% American, 4.3% English, 3.5% Italian (2006-2010 5-year est.).
Economy: Employment by occupation: 7.0% management, 1.0% professional, 7.8% services, 17.9% sales, 4.9% farming, 21.3% construction, 12.7% production (2006-2010 5-year est.).
Income: Per capita income: $22,472 (2006-2010 5-year est.); Median household income: $39,565 (2006-2010 5-year est.); Average household income: $47,496 (2006-2010 5-year est.); Percent of households with income of $100,000 or more: 5.6% (2006-2010 5-year est.); Poverty rate: 13.6% (2006-2010 5-year est.).
Education: Percent of population age 25 and over with: High school diploma (including GED) or higher: 77.9% (2006-2010 5-year est.); Bachelor's degree or higher: 10.2% (2006-2010 5-year est.); Master's degree or higher: 4.5% (2006-2010 5-year est.).
School District(s)
Conewago Valley SD (KG-12)
  2010-11 Enrollment: 3,941 . . . . (717) 624-2157
Housing: Homeownership rate: 47.2% (2010); Median home value: $155,300 (2006-2010 5-year est.); Median contract rent: $530 per month

(2006-2010 5-year est.); Median year structure built: 1954 (2006-2010 5-year est.).

Transportation: Commute to work: 89.3% car, 0.0% public transportation, 7.6% walk, 2.8% work from home (2006-2010 5-year est.); Travel time to work: 27.2% less than 15 minutes, 36.6% 15 to 30 minutes, 20.8% 30 to 45 minutes, 5.6% 45 to 60 minutes, 9.8% 60 minutes or more (2006-2010 5-year est.)

Additional Information Contacts

New Oxford Area Chamber of Commerce. . . . . (717) 624-2800
    http://newoxford.org

ORRTANNA (CDP). Covers a land area of 0.192 square miles and a water area of 0.002 square miles. Located at 39.85° N. Lat; 77.36° W. Long. Elevation is 673 feet.

Population: 160 (1990); 169 (2000); 173 (2010); Density: 899.5 persons per square mile (2010); Race: 99.4% White, 0.0% Black, 0.0% Asian, 0.0% American Indian/Alaska Native, 0.0% Native Hawaiian/Other Pacific Islander, 0.6% Other, 1.2% Hispanic of any race (2010); Average household size: 2.40 (2010); Median age: 42.3 (2010); Males per 100 females: 88.0 (2010); Marriage status: 9.1% never married, 61.8% now married, 20.9% widowed, 8.2% divorced (2006-2010 5-year est.); Foreign born: 2.5% (2006-2010 5-year est.); Ancestry (includes multiple ancestries): 24.1% German, 23.5% Italian, 15.4% Irish, 10.5% European, 6.2% Barbadian (2006-2010 5-year est.).

Economy: Employment by occupation: 17.1% management, 10.0% professional, 15.7% services, 8.6% sales, 12.9% farming, 0.0% construction, 0.0% production (2006-2010 5-year est.).

Income: Per capita income: $28,904 (2006-2010 5-year est.); Median household income: $59,583 (2006-2010 5-year est.); Average household income: $77,612 (2006-2010 5-year est.); Percent of households with income of $100,000 or more: 32.2% (2006-2010 5-year est.); Poverty rate: 4.9% (2006-2010 5-year est.).

Education: Percent of population age 25 and over with: High school diploma (including GED) or higher: 93.3% (2006-2010 5-year est.); Bachelor's degree or higher: 40.4% (2006-2010 5-year est.); Master's degree or higher: 26.0% (2006-2010 5-year est.).

Housing: Homeownership rate: 84.7% (2010); Median home value: $186,500 (2006-2010 5-year est.); Median contract rent: n/a per month (2006-2010 5-year est.); Median year structure built: before 1940 (2006-2010 5-year est.).

Transportation: Commute to work: 100.0% car, 0.0% public transportation, 0.0% walk, 0.0% work from home (2006-2010 5-year est.); Travel time to work: 17.1% less than 15 minutes, 32.9% 15 to 30 minutes, 14.3% 30 to 45 minutes, 18.6% 45 to 60 minutes, 17.1% 60 minutes or more (2006-2010 5-year est.)

OXFORD (township). Covers a land area of 9.483 square miles and a water area of 0.249 square miles. Located at 39.85° N. Lat; 77.04° W. Long.

History: Laid out 1792, incorporated 1874.

Population: 3,437 (1990); 4,876 (2000); 5,517 (2010); Density: 581.8 persons per square mile (2010); Race: 93.6% White, 1.3% Black, 0.4% Asian, 0.2% American Indian/Alaska Native, 0.0% Native Hawaiian/Other Pacific Islander, 4.5% Other, 7.7% Hispanic of any race (2010); Average household size: 2.58 (2010); Median age: 44.8 (2010); Males per 100 females: 87.0 (2010); Marriage status: 20.4% never married, 56.9% now married, 15.1% widowed, 7.6% divorced (2006-2010 5-year est.); Foreign born: 1.5% (2006-2010 5-year est.); Ancestry (includes multiple ancestries): 40.9% German, 12.7% Irish, 10.8% English, 9.8% American, 4.8% Italian (2006-2010 5-year est.).

Economy: Employment by occupation: 6.0% management, 2.9% professional, 5.9% services, 18.7% sales, 4.4% farming, 13.0% construction, 10.2% production (2006-2010 5-year est.).

Income: Per capita income: $23,725 (2006-2010 5-year est.); Median household income: $51,661 (2006-2010 5-year est.); Average household income: $57,803 (2006-2010 5-year est.); Percent of households with income of $100,000 or more: 14.0% (2006-2010 5-year est.); Poverty rate: 6.6% (2006-2010 5-year est.).

Education: Percent of population age 25 and over with: High school diploma (including GED) or higher: 84.1% (2006-2010 5-year est.); Bachelor's degree or higher: 14.2% (2006-2010 5-year est.); Master's degree or higher: 5.4% (2006-2010 5-year est.).

Housing: Homeownership rate: 76.3% (2010); Median home value: $180,100 (2006-2010 5-year est.); Median contract rent: $575 per month

(2006-2010 5-year est.); Median year structure built: 1988 (2006-2010 5-year est.).

Transportation: Commute to work: 95.8% car, 0.0% public transportation, 2.7% walk, 1.5% work from home (2006-2010 5-year est.); Travel time to work: 42.7% less than 15 minutes, 35.5% 15 to 30 minutes, 10.6% 30 to 45 minutes, 5.6% 45 to 60 minutes, 5.6% 60 minutes or more (2006-2010 5-year est.)

Additional Information Contacts

Gettysburg Adams Chamber of Commerce . . . . (717) 334-8151
    http://www.gettysburg-chamber.org

READING (township). Covers a land area of 26.314 square miles and a water area of 0.428 square miles. Located at 39.95° N. Lat; 77.04° W. Long.

Population: 3,828 (1990); 5,106 (2000); 5,780 (2010); Density: 219.7 persons per square mile (2010); Race: 95.4% White, 0.3% Black, 0.6% Asian, 0.1% American Indian/Alaska Native, 0.1% Native Hawaiian/Other Pacific Islander, 3.5% Other, 5.3% Hispanic of any race (2010); Average household size: 2.79 (2010); Median age: 39.1 (2010); Males per 100 females: 106.0 (2010); Marriage status: 19.8% never married, 64.6% now married, 4.8% widowed, 10.8% divorced (2006-2010 5-year est.); Foreign born: 5.9% (2006-2010 5-year est.); Ancestry (includes multiple ancestries): 40.1% German, 13.4% American, 10.1% Irish, 8.2% English, 6.3% Polish (2006-2010 5-year est.).

Economy: Employment by occupation: 10.8% management, 3.4% professional, 9.9% services, 13.5% sales, 3.8% farming, 10.1% construction, 7.9% production (2006-2010 5-year est.).

Income: Per capita income: $31,156 (2006-2010 5-year est.); Median household income: $62,372 (2006-2010 5-year est.); Average household income: $80,112 (2006-2010 5-year est.); Percent of households with income of $100,000 or more: 24.6% (2006-2010 5-year est.); Poverty rate: 7.2% (2006-2010 5-year est.).

Education: Percent of population age 25 and over with: High school diploma (including GED) or higher: 83.8% (2006-2010 5-year est.); Bachelor's degree or higher: 15.7% (2006-2010 5-year est.); Master's degree or higher: 4.3% (2006-2010 5-year est.).

Housing: Homeownership rate: 88.8% (2010); Median home value: $207,400 (2006-2010 5-year est.); Median contract rent: $564 per month (2006-2010 5-year est.); Median year structure built: 1984 (2006-2010 5-year est.).

Transportation: Commute to work: 87.0% car, 0.9% public transportation, 4.8% walk, 4.6% work from home (2006-2010 5-year est.); Travel time to work: 15.8% less than 15 minutes, 35.3% 15 to 30 minutes, 25.8% 30 to 45 minutes, 11.0% 45 to 60 minutes, 12.1% 60 minutes or more (2006-2010 5-year est.)

Additional Information Contacts

Gettysburg Adams Chamber of Commerce . . . . (717) 334-8151
    http://www.gettysburg-chamber.org
Reading Township. . . . . (717) 624-4222
    http://dsf.pacounties.org/adams/cwp/view.asp?a=1669&q=488414

STRABAN (township). Covers a land area of 34.297 square miles and a water area of 0.159 square miles. Located at 39.88° N. Lat; 77.17° W. Long.

Population: 4,565 (1990); 4,539 (2000); 4,928 (2010); Density: 143.7 persons per square mile (2010); Race: 92.8% White, 2.1% Black, 1.0% Asian, 0.1% American Indian/Alaska Native, 0.1% Native Hawaiian/Other Pacific Islander, 3.9% Other, 6.2% Hispanic of any race (2010); Average household size: 2.53 (2010); Median age: 44.8 (2010); Males per 100 females: 100.5 (2010); Marriage status: 23.7% never married, 56.4% now married, 8.5% widowed, 11.4% divorced (2006-2010 5-year est.); Foreign born: 8.7% (2006-2010 5-year est.); Ancestry (includes multiple ancestries): 30.1% German, 17.8% English, 10.8% Irish, 7.1% American, 5.3% Dutch (2006-2010 5-year est.).

Economy: Employment by occupation: 8.5% management, 0.7% professional, 12.1% services, 18.8% sales, 4.1% farming, 15.5% construction, 8.0% production (2006-2010 5-year est.).

Income: Per capita income: $26,018 (2006-2010 5-year est.); Median household income: $60,964 (2006-2010 5-year est.); Average household income: $73,494 (2006-2010 5-year est.); Percent of households with income of $100,000 or more: 18.5% (2006-2010 5-year est.); Poverty rate: 10.3% (2006-2010 5-year est.).

Education: Percent of population age 25 and over with: High school diploma (including GED) or higher: 79.8% (2006-2010 5-year est.);

Bachelor's degree or higher: 20.7% (2006-2010 5-year est.); Master's degree or higher: 10.3% (2006-2010 5-year est.).
Housing: Homeownership rate: 77.4% (2010); Median home value: $219,500 (2006-2010 5-year est.); Median contract rent: $602 per month (2006-2010 5-year est.); Median year structure built: 1975 (2006-2010 5-year est.).
Transportation: Commute to work: 93.0% car, 0.6% public transportation, 1.8% walk, 4.1% work from home (2006-2010 5-year est.); Travel time to work: 30.3% less than 15 minutes, 41.3% 15 to 30 minutes, 10.0% 30 to 45 minutes, 7.1% 45 to 60 minutes, 11.3% 60 minutes or more (2006-2010 5-year est.)
Additional Information Contacts
Gettysburg Adams Chamber of Commerce . . . . (717) 334-8151
    http://www.gettysburg-chamber.org

TABLE ROCK (CDP).
Covers a land area of 0.076 square miles and a water area of 0 square miles. Located at 39.91° N. Lat; 77.22° W. Long. Elevation is 564 feet.
Population: n/a (1990); n/a (2000); 62 (2010); Density: 819.2 persons per square mile (2010); Race: 93.5% White, 0.0% Black, 0.0% Asian, 0.0% American Indian/Alaska Native, 0.0% Native Hawaiian/Other Pacific Islander, 6.5% Other, 6.5% Hispanic of any race (2010); Average household size: 2.48 (2010); Median age: 41.5 (2010); Males per 100 females: 87.9 (2010); Marriage status: 18.8% never married, 40.6% now married, 40.6% widowed, 0.0% divorced (2006-2010 5-year est.); Foreign born: 0.0% (2006-2010 5-year est.); Ancestry (includes multiple ancestries): 78.1% German, 40.6% Irish (2006-2010 5-year est.).
Economy: Employment by occupation: 0.0% management, 0.0% professional, 100.0% services, 0.0% sales, 0.0% farming, 0.0% construction, 0.0% production (2006-2010 5-year est.).
Income: Per capita income: $14,281 (2006-2010 5-year est.); Median household income: $19,286 (2006-2010 5-year est.); Average household income: $23,890 (2006-2010 5-year est.); Percent of households with income of $100,000 or more: n/a (2006-2010 5-year est.); Poverty rate: 0.0% (2006-2010 5-year est.).
Education: Percent of population age 25 and over with: High school diploma (including GED) or higher: 59.4% (2006-2010 5-year est.); Bachelor's degree or higher: 0.0% (2006-2010 5-year est.); Master's degree or higher: 0.0% (2006-2010 5-year est.).
Housing: Homeownership rate: 72.0% (2010); Median home value: $114,300 (2006-2010 5-year est.); Median contract rent: n/a per month (2006-2010 5-year est.); Median year structure built: 1966 (2006-2010 5-year est.).
Transportation: Commute to work: 100.0% car, 0.0% public transportation, 0.0% walk, 0.0% work from home (2006-2010 5-year est.); Travel time to work: 0.0% less than 15 minutes, 50.0% 15 to 30 minutes, 0.0% 30 to 45 minutes, 0.0% 45 to 60 minutes, 50.0% 60 minutes or more (2006-2010 5-year est.)

TYRONE (township).
Covers a land area of 21.476 square miles and a water area of 0.088 square miles. Located at 39.95° N. Lat; 77.16° W. Long.
Population: 1,829 (1990); 2,273 (2000); 2,298 (2010); Density: 107.0 persons per square mile (2010); Race: 93.3% White, 1.0% Black, 0.1% Asian, 0.2% American Indian/Alaska Native, 0.0% Native Hawaiian/Other Pacific Islander, 5.4% Other, 9.2% Hispanic of any race (2010); Average household size: 2.76 (2010); Median age: 40.7 (2010); Males per 100 females: 102.8 (2010); Marriage status: 26.2% never married, 59.0% now married, 4.0% widowed, 10.7% divorced (2006-2010 5-year est.); Foreign born: 2.5% (2006-2010 5-year est.); Ancestry (includes multiple ancestries): 37.2% German, 14.3% Irish, 11.0% American, 9.1% English, 6.1% Italian (2006-2010 5-year est.).
Economy: Employment by occupation: 7.9% management, 0.8% professional, 16.9% services, 12.1% sales, 2.1% farming, 16.8% construction, 13.7% production (2006-2010 5-year est.).
Income: Per capita income: $25,560 (2006-2010 5-year est.); Median household income: $57,955 (2006-2010 5-year est.); Average household income: $69,355 (2006-2010 5-year est.); Percent of households with income of $100,000 or more: 21.3% (2006-2010 5-year est.); Poverty rate: 5.6% (2006-2010 5-year est.).
Education: Percent of population age 25 and over with: High school diploma (including GED) or higher: 83.3% (2006-2010 5-year est.); Bachelor's degree or higher: 9.9% (2006-2010 5-year est.); Master's degree or higher: 2.9% (2006-2010 5-year est.).

Housing: Homeownership rate: 84.5% (2010); Median home value: $144,000 (2006-2010 5-year est.); Median contract rent: $722 per month (2006-2010 5-year est.); Median year structure built: 1982 (2006-2010 5-year est.).
Transportation: Commute to work: 93.0% car, 0.0% public transportation, 3.2% walk, 3.0% work from home (2006-2010 5-year est.); Travel time to work: 28.9% less than 15 minutes, 37.8% 15 to 30 minutes, 18.6% 30 to 45 minutes, 6.9% 45 to 60 minutes, 7.9% 60 minutes or more (2006-2010 5-year est.)
Additional Information Contacts
Gettysburg Adams Chamber of Commerce . . . . (717) 334-8151
    http://www.gettysburg-chamber.org

UNION (township).
Covers a land area of 17.544 square miles and a water area of 0.032 square miles. Located at 39.76° N. Lat; 77.05° W. Long.
Population: 2,173 (1990); 2,989 (2000); 3,148 (2010); Density: 179.4 persons per square mile (2010); Race: 97.0% White, 0.6% Black, 0.7% Asian, 0.1% American Indian/Alaska Native, 0.0% Native Hawaiian/Other Pacific Islander, 1.6% Other, 2.1% Hispanic of any race (2010); Average household size: 2.75 (2010); Median age: 43.7 (2010); Males per 100 females: 99.4 (2010); Marriage status: 21.2% never married, 68.8% now married, 5.9% widowed, 4.2% divorced (2006-2010 5-year est.); Foreign born: 1.5% (2006-2010 5-year est.); Ancestry (includes multiple ancestries): 49.3% German, 20.1% Irish, 10.0% English, 8.0% American, 7.7% Italian (2006-2010 5-year est.).
Economy: Employment by occupation: 12.6% management, 2.5% professional, 10.0% services, 16.8% sales, 1.6% farming, 16.0% construction, 9.9% production (2006-2010 5-year est.).
Income: Per capita income: $29,219 (2006-2010 5-year est.); Median household income: $66,563 (2006-2010 5-year est.); Average household income: $79,426 (2006-2010 5-year est.); Percent of households with income of $100,000 or more: 26.2% (2006-2010 5-year est.); Poverty rate: 2.7% (2006-2010 5-year est.).
Education: Percent of population age 25 and over with: High school diploma (including GED) or higher: 86.5% (2006-2010 5-year est.); Bachelor's degree or higher: 16.7% (2006-2010 5-year est.); Master's degree or higher: 7.0% (2006-2010 5-year est.).
Housing: Homeownership rate: 88.3% (2010); Median home value: $244,900 (2006-2010 5-year est.); Median contract rent: $654 per month (2006-2010 5-year est.); Median year structure built: 1979 (2006-2010 5-year est.).
Transportation: Commute to work: 93.2% car, 0.0% public transportation, 1.8% walk, 3.3% work from home (2006-2010 5-year est.); Travel time to work: 24.5% less than 15 minutes, 35.1% 15 to 30 minutes, 14.0% 30 to 45 minutes, 8.5% 45 to 60 minutes, 17.9% 60 minutes or more (2006-2010 5-year est.)
Additional Information Contacts
Gettysburg Adams Chamber of Commerce . . . . (717) 334-8151
    http://www.gettysburg-chamber.org

YORK SPRINGS (borough).
Covers a land area of 0.215 square miles and a water area of 0 square miles. Located at 40.01° N. Lat; 77.12° W. Long. Elevation is 614 feet.
Population: 514 (1990); 574 (2000); 833 (2010); Density: 3,873.6 persons per square mile (2010); Race: 70.1% White, 0.5% Black, 0.2% Asian, 1.1% American Indian/Alaska Native, 0.0% Native Hawaiian/Other Pacific Islander, 28.1% Other, 46.1% Hispanic of any race (2010); Average household size: 3.10 (2010); Median age: 29.4 (2010); Males per 100 females: 115.2 (2010); Marriage status: 41.6% never married, 47.6% now married, 2.5% widowed, 8.2% divorced (2006-2010 5-year est.); Foreign born: 29.4% (2006-2010 5-year est.); Ancestry (includes multiple ancestries): 33.5% German, 8.9% English, 7.8% Irish, 6.5% Italian, 4.5% Polish (2006-2010 5-year est.).
Economy: Employment by occupation: 2.8% management, 1.7% professional, 5.8% services, 19.4% sales, 5.8% farming, 15.5% construction, 16.0% production (2006-2010 5-year est.).
Income: Per capita income: $16,862 (2006-2010 5-year est.); Median household income: $42,778 (2006-2010 5-year est.); Average household income: $51,207 (2006-2010 5-year est.); Percent of households with income of $100,000 or more: 6.1% (2006-2010 5-year est.); Poverty rate: 17.8% (2006-2010 5-year est.).
Education: Percent of population age 25 and over with: High school diploma (including GED) or higher: 68.7% (2006-2010 5-year est.);

Bachelor's degree or higher: 10.5% (2006-2010 5-year est.); Master's degree or higher: 1.3% (2006-2010 5-year est.).

School District(s)

Bermudian Springs SD (KG-12)

2010-11 Enrollment: 2,084 . . . . (717) 528-4113

Housing: Homeownership rate: 46.4% (2010); Median home value: $119,000 (2006-2010 5-year est.); Median contract rent: $564 per month (2006-2010 5-year est.); Median year structure built: 1943 (2006-2010 5-year est.).

Transportation: Commute to work: 97.2% car, 0.0% public transportation, 0.6% walk, 1.7% work from home (2006-2010 5-year est.); Travel time to work: 13.5% less than 15 minutes, 48.6% 15 to 30 minutes, 17.3% 30 to 45 minutes, 11.9% 45 to 60 minutes, 8.7% 60 minutes or more (2006-2010 5-year est.)

Allegheny County

Located in western Pennsylvania; drained by the Allegheny and Monongahela Rivers. Covers a land area of 730.074 square miles, a water area of 14.448 square miles, and is located in the Eastern Time Zone at 40.47° N. Lat., 79.98° W. Long. The county was founded in 1788. County seat is Pittsburgh.

Allegheny County is part of the Pittsburgh, PA Metropolitan Statistical Area. The entire metro area includes: Allegheny County, PA; Armstrong County, PA; Beaver County, PA; Butler County, PA; Fayette County, PA; Washington County, PA; Westmoreland County, PA

Weather Station: Pittsburgh Intl Arpt   Elevation: 1,149 feet

	Jan	Feb	Mar	Apr	May	Jun	Jul	Aug	Sep	Oct	Nov	Dec
High	36	40	49	62	71	79	83	82	75	63	51	40
Low	21	23	30	40	49	58	63	62	54	43	35	25
Precip	2.7	2.3	3.1	3.2	3.9	4.3	4.0	3.6	3.0	2.3	3.1	2.8
Snow	11.4	8.8	7.8	1.5	tr	tr	tr	tr	tr	0.4	2.4	8.1

High and Low temperatures in degrees Fahrenheit; Precipitation and Snow in inches

Population: 1,336,449 (1990); 1,281,666 (2000); 1,223,348 (2010); Race: 81.5% White, 13.2% Black, 2.8% Asian, 0.1% American Indian/Alaska Native, 0.0% Native Hawaiian/Other Pacific Islander, 2.4% Other, 1.6% Hispanic of any race (2010); Density: 1,675.6 persons per square mile (2010); Average household size: 2.23 (2010); Median age: 41.3 (2010); Males per 100 females: 91.8 (2010).

Religion: Six largest groups: 37.7% Catholicism, 4.4% Methodist/Pietist, 4.1% Presbyterian-Reformed, 2.7% Non-Denominational, 2.4% Lutheran, 2.3% Baptist (2010)

Economy: Unemployment rate: 7.3% (August 2012); Total civilian labor force: 668,223 (August 2012); Leading industries: 18.3% health care and social assistance; 11.2% retail trade; 8.8% professional, scientific & technical services (2010); Farms: 534 totaling 38,023 acres (2007); Companies that employ 500 or more persons: 117 (2010); Companies that employ 100 to 499 persons: 870 (2010); Companies that employ less than 100 persons: 32,360 (2010); Black-owned businesses: 5,005 (2007); Hispanic-owned businesses: 928 (2007); Asian-owned businesses: 3,002 (2007); Women-owned businesses: 26,420 (2007); Retail sales per capita: $15,274 (2010). Single-family building permits issued: 1,196 (2011); Multi-family building permits issued: 104 (2011).

Income: Per capita income: $29,549 (2006-2010 5-year est.); Median household income: $47,961 (2006-2010 5-year est.); Average household income: $67,485 (2006-2010 5-year est.); Percent of households with income of $100,000 or more: 18.5% (2006-2010 5-year est.); Poverty rate: 12.3% (2006-2010 5-year est.); Bankruptcy rate: 3.18% (2011).

Taxes: Total county taxes per capita: $346 (2009); County property taxes per capita: $211 (2009).

Education: Percent of population age 25 and over with: High school diploma (including GED) or higher: 91.6% (2006-2010 5-year est.); Bachelor's degree or higher: 34.1% (2006-2010 5-year est.); Master's degree or higher: 13.6% (2006-2010 5-year est.).

Housing: Homeownership rate: 64.7% (2010); Median home value: $115,200 (2006-2010 5-year est.); Median contract rent: $555 per month (2006-2010 5-year est.); Median year structure built: 1954 (2006-2010 5-year est.)

Health: Birth rate: 105.2 per 10,000 population (2011); Death rate: 110.8 per 10,000 population (2011); Age-adjusted cancer mortality rate: 194.3 deaths per 100,000 population (2009); Number of physicians: 62.2 per 10,000 population (2010); Hospital beds: 65.4 per 10,000 population (2008); Hospital admissions: 2,593.1 per 10,000 population (2008).

Environment: Air Quality Index: 48.2% good, 42.7% moderate, 8.2% unhealthy for sensitive individuals, 0.8% unhealthy (percent of days in 2011)

Elections: 2012 Presidential election results: 56.6% Obama, 42.2% Romney

National and State Parks: Point State Park

Additional Information Contacts

Allegheny County Government . . . . (412) 350-6500
http://www.county.allegheny.pa.us

Allegheny County Communities

ALEPPO (township). Covers a land area of 1.772 square miles and a water area of 0 square miles. Located at 40.53° N. Lat; 80.14° W. Long.

Population: 1,246 (1990); 1,039 (2000); 1,916 (2010); Density: 1,081.4 persons per square mile (2010); Race: 96.9% White, 1.5% Black, 0.8% Asian, 0.0% American Indian/Alaska Native, 0.0% Native Hawaiian/Other Pacific Islander, 0.8% Other, 0.7% Hispanic of any race (2010); Average household size: 1.65 (2010); Median age: 69.9 (2010); Males per 100 females: 71.2 (2010); Marriage status: 15.5% never married, 58.5% now married, 16.4% widowed, 9.6% divorced (2006-2010 5-year est.); Foreign born: 3.8% (2006-2010 5-year est.); Ancestry (includes multiple ancestries): 29.0% German, 16.8% Irish, 16.8% English, 15.7% Italian, 5.8% Scottish (2006-2010 5-year est.).

Economy: Single-family building permits issued: 0 (2011); Multi-family building permits issued: 0 (2011); Employment by occupation: 24.3% management, 5.3% professional, 5.2% services, 10.5% sales, 3.1% farming, 2.7% construction, 2.7% production (2006-2010 5-year est.).

Income: Per capita income: $40,293 (2006-2010 5-year est.); Median household income: $65,250 (2006-2010 5-year est.); Average household income: $82,277 (2006-2010 5-year est.); Percent of households with income of $100,000 or more: 30.3% (2006-2010 5-year est.); Poverty rate: 2.4% (2006-2010 5-year est.).

Education: Percent of population age 25 and over with: High school diploma (including GED) or higher: 93.2% (2006-2010 5-year est.); Bachelor's degree or higher: 49.2% (2006-2010 5-year est.); Master's degree or higher: 21.0% (2006-2010 5-year est.).

Housing: Homeownership rate: 50.3% (2010); Median home value: $170,600 (2006-2010 5-year est.); Median contract rent: $1,716 per month (2006-2010 5-year est.); Median year structure built: 1984 (2006-2010 5-year est.).

Safety: Violent crime rate: 0.0 per 10,000 population; Property crime rate: 119.7 per 10,000 population (2011).

Transportation: Commute to work: 86.9% car, 2.7% public transportation, 3.2% walk, 5.5% work from home (2006-2010 5-year est.); Travel time to work: 18.8% less than 15 minutes, 36.8% 15 to 30 minutes, 34.4% 30 to 45 minutes, 5.3% 45 to 60 minutes, 4.8% 60 minutes or more (2006-2010 5-year est.)

Additional Information Contacts

Waynesburg Area Chamber of Commerce . . . . (724) 627-5926
http://www.waynesburgchamber.com

ALLISON PARK (CDP). Covers a land area of 13.839 square miles and a water area of 0 square miles. Located at 40.57° N. Lat; 79.96° W. Long. Elevation is 860 feet.

Population: n/a (1990); n/a (2000); 21,552 (2010); Density: 1,557.4 persons per square mile (2010); Race: 94.4% White, 1.5% Black, 3.1% Asian, 0.1% American Indian/Alaska Native, 0.0% Native Hawaiian/Other Pacific Islander, 0.9% Other, 0.9% Hispanic of any race (2010); Average household size: 2.42 (2010); Median age: 44.8 (2010); Males per 100 females: 91.3 (2010); Marriage status: 28.2% never married, 59.4% now married, 8.1% widowed, 4.3% divorced (2006-2010 5-year est.); Foreign born: 4.9% (2006-2010 5-year est.); Ancestry (includes multiple ancestries): 41.2% German, 21.8% Irish, 17.0% Italian, 10.9% Polish, 7.7% English (2006-2010 5-year est.).

Economy: Employment by occupation: 17.1% management, 5.5% professional, 6.6% services, 17.0% sales, 4.8% farming, 4.7% construction, 3.0% production (2006-2010 5-year est.).

Income: Per capita income: $37,297 (2006-2010 5-year est.); Median household income: $74,034 (2006-2010 5-year est.); Average household income: $95,529 (2006-2010 5-year est.); Percent of households with income of $100,000 or more: 30.7% (2006-2010 5-year est.); Poverty rate: 7.4% (2006-2010 5-year est.).

Education: Percent of population age 25 and over with: High school diploma (including GED) or higher: 96.3% (2006-2010 5-year est.);

Bachelor's degree or higher: 48.8% (2006-2010 5-year est.); Master's degree or higher: 20.2% (2006-2010 5-year est.).

School District(s)

A W Beattie Career Center (10-12)
    2010-11 Enrollment: n/a . . . . (412) 847-1900
Hampton Township SD (PK-12)
    2010-11 Enrollment: 3,111 . . . . (412) 492-6302
North Allegheny SD (KG-12)
    2010-11 Enrollment: 8,105 . . . . (412) 366-2100
Shaler Area SD (KG-12)
    2010-11 Enrollment: 4,968 . . . . (412) 492-1200

Housing: Homeownership rate: 77.7% (2010); Median home value: $181,300 (2006-2010 5-year est.); Median contract rent: $753 per month (2006-2010 5-year est.); Median year structure built: 1970 (2006-2010 5-year est.).

Transportation: Commute to work: 89.7% car, 2.9% public transportation, 1.3% walk, 5.4% work from home (2006-2010 5-year est.); Travel time to work: 21.2% less than 15 minutes, 34.4% 15 to 30 minutes, 28.4% 30 to 45 minutes, 10.4% 45 to 60 minutes, 5.6% 60 minutes or more (2006-2010 5-year est.)

ASPINWALL (borough). Covers a land area of 0.350 square miles and a water area of 0.034 square miles. Located at 40.49° N. Lat; 79.90° W. Long. Elevation is 751 feet.

History: Settled 1796; incorporated 1893.

Population: 2,880 (1990); 2,960 (2000); 2,801 (2010); Density: 7,997.9 persons per square mile (2010); Race: 91.7% White, 1.4% Black, 5.4% Asian, 0.0% American Indian/Alaska Native, 0.0% Native Hawaiian/Other Pacific Islander, 1.5% Other, 1.9% Hispanic of any race (2010); Average household size: 2.04 (2010); Median age: 39.6 (2010); Males per 100 females: 81.9 (2010); Marriage status: 38.7% never married, 41.6% now married, 7.9% widowed, 11.8% divorced (2006-2010 5-year est.); Foreign born: 7.1% (2006-2010 5-year est.); Ancestry (includes multiple ancestries): 24.8% German, 23.5% Irish, 18.0% Italian, 12.6% English, 5.4% Polish (2006-2010 5-year est.).

Economy: Single-family building permits issued: 1 (2011); Multi-family building permits issued: 0 (2011); Employment by occupation: 19.5% management, 5.0% professional, 5.8% services, 14.4% sales, 1.3% farming, 7.3% construction, 4.5% production (2006-2010 5-year est.).

Income: Per capita income: $41,890 (2006-2010 5-year est.); Median household income: $55,395 (2006-2010 5-year est.); Average household income: $86,559 (2006-2010 5-year est.); Percent of households with income of $100,000 or more: 29.4% (2006-2010 5-year est.); Poverty rate: 8.7% (2006-2010 5-year est.).

Education: Percent of population age 25 and over with: High school diploma (including GED) or higher: 95.8% (2006-2010 5-year est.); Bachelor's degree or higher: 51.2% (2006-2010 5-year est.); Master's degree or higher: 25.4% (2006-2010 5-year est.).

Housing: Homeownership rate: 51.1% (2010); Median home value: $192,400 (2006-2010 5-year est.); Median contract rent: $693 per month (2006-2010 5-year est.); Median year structure built: 1944 (2006-2010 5-year est.).

Safety: Violent crime rate: 7.1 per 10,000 population; Property crime rate: 142.3 per 10,000 population (2011).

Newspapers: Herald (Local news; Circulation 4,500); The Herald (Local news; Circulation 4,500)

Transportation: Commute to work: 80.5% car, 7.6% public transportation, 5.0% walk, 4.6% work from home (2006-2010 5-year est.); Travel time to work: 19.9% less than 15 minutes, 41.1% 15 to 30 minutes, 32.5% 30 to 45 minutes, 4.3% 45 to 60 minutes, 2.2% 60 minutes or more (2006-2010 5-year est.)

Additional Information Contacts
Aspinwall Chamber of Commerce . . . . (412) 781-0213
    http://www.aspinwallpa.com/chamber.aspx

AVALON (borough). Covers a land area of 0.617 square miles and a water area of 0.074 square miles. Located at 40.50° N. Lat; 80.07° W. Long. Elevation is 935 feet.

History: Settled 1802, incorporated 1874.

Population: 5,817 (1990); 5,294 (2000); 4,705 (2010); Density: 7,629.8 persons per square mile (2010); Race: 87.5% White, 8.7% Black, 0.5% Asian, 0.4% American Indian/Alaska Native, 0.0% Native Hawaiian/Other Pacific Islander, 2.9% Other, 1.2% Hispanic of any race (2010); Average household size: 1.92 (2010); Median age: 43.1 (2010); Males per 100 females: 87.3 (2010); Marriage status: 34.2% never married, 39.3% now married, 14.7% widowed, 11.8% divorced (2006-2010 5-year est.); Foreign born: 6.0% (2006-2010 5-year est.); Ancestry (includes multiple ancestries): 33.5% German, 26.8% Irish, 12.4% Polish, 8.8% Italian, 8.5% English (2006-2010 5-year est.).

Economy: Single-family building permits issued: 0 (2011); Multi-family building permits issued: 0 (2011); Employment by occupation: 8.2% management, 4.3% professional, 14.7% services, 21.6% sales, 4.8% farming, 2.9% construction, 3.6% production (2006-2010 5-year est.).

Income: Per capita income: $21,068 (2006-2010 5-year est.); Median household income: $33,669 (2006-2010 5-year est.); Average household income: $40,013 (2006-2010 5-year est.); Percent of households with income of $100,000 or more: 5.5% (2006-2010 5-year est.); Poverty rate: 17.5% (2006-2010 5-year est.).

Education: Percent of population age 25 and over with: High school diploma (including GED) or higher: 91.4% (2006-2010 5-year est.); Bachelor's degree or higher: 22.6% (2006-2010 5-year est.); Master's degree or higher: 9.4% (2006-2010 5-year est.).

Housing: Homeownership rate: 48.5% (2010); Median home value: $80,100 (2006-2010 5-year est.); Median contract rent: $513 per month (2006-2010 5-year est.); Median year structure built: 1947 (2006-2010 5-year est.).

Safety: Violent crime rate: 36.0 per 10,000 population; Property crime rate: 178.0 per 10,000 population (2011).

Transportation: Commute to work: 84.1% car, 8.8% public transportation, 4.7% walk, 1.9% work from home (2006-2010 5-year est.); Travel time to work: 21.2% less than 15 minutes, 47.0% 15 to 30 minutes, 22.2% 30 to 45 minutes, 6.8% 45 to 60 minutes, 2.9% 60 minutes or more (2006-2010 5-year est.)

Additional Information Contacts
Borough of Avalon . . . . (412) 761-5820
    http://www.boroughofavalon.org
North Suburban Chamber of Commerce . . . . (412) 761-2113
    http://www.northsuburbancoc.org

BAIRDFORD (CDP). Covers a land area of 1.514 square miles and a water area of 0 square miles. Located at 40.63° N. Lat; 79.88° W. Long. Elevation is 1,099 feet.

Population: n/a (1990); n/a (2000); 698 (2010); Density: 461.1 persons per square mile (2010); Race: 99.1% White, 0.4% Black, 0.0% Asian, 0.0% American Indian/Alaska Native, 0.0% Native Hawaiian/Other Pacific Islander, 0.5% Other, 1.1% Hispanic of any race (2010); Average household size: 2.28 (2010); Median age: 44.9 (2010); Males per 100 females: 91.8 (2010); Marriage status: 20.9% never married, 61.1% now married, 7.5% widowed, 10.4% divorced (2006-2010 5-year est.); Foreign born: 0.0% (2006-2010 5-year est.); Ancestry (includes multiple ancestries): 32.3% German, 30.4% Polish, 27.4% Irish, 14.8% Italian, 11.1% Hungarian (2006-2010 5-year est.).

Economy: Employment by occupation: 6.6% management, 0.0% professional, 18.4% services, 23.4% sales, 0.0% farming, 13.9% construction, 9.5% production (2006-2010 5-year est.).

Income: Per capita income: $20,723 (2006-2010 5-year est.); Median household income: $48,750 (2006-2010 5-year est.); Average household income: $52,184 (2006-2010 5-year est.); Percent of households with income of $100,000 or more: 5.2% (2006-2010 5-year est.); Poverty rate: 5.0% (2006-2010 5-year est.).

Education: Percent of population age 25 and over with: High school diploma (including GED) or higher: 88.4% (2006-2010 5-year est.); Bachelor's degree or higher: 14.8% (2006-2010 5-year est.); Master's degree or higher: 0.0% (2006-2010 5-year est.).

Housing: Homeownership rate: 85.2% (2010); Median home value: $109,600 (2006-2010 5-year est.); Median contract rent: $548 per month (2006-2010 5-year est.); Median year structure built: 1965 (2006-2010 5-year est.).

Transportation: Commute to work: 100.0% car, 0.0% public transportation, 0.0% walk, 0.0% work from home (2006-2010 5-year est.); Travel time to work: 29.1% less than 15 minutes, 53.6% 15 to 30 minutes, 13.8% 30 to 45 minutes, 3.5% 45 to 60 minutes, 0.0% 60 minutes or more (2006-2010 5-year est.)

BAKERSTOWN (CDP). Covers a land area of 2.181 square miles and a water area of 0 square miles. Located at 40.65° N. Lat; 79.94° W. Long. Elevation is 1,083 feet.

Population: n/a (1990); n/a (2000); 1,761 (2010); Density: 807.3 persons per square mile (2010); Race: 97.3% White, 0.6% Black, 1.0% Asian, 0.3% American Indian/Alaska Native, 0.0% Native Hawaiian/Other Pacific

Islander, 0.8% Other, 1.8% Hispanic of any race (2010); Average household size: 2.40 (2010); Median age: 47.4 (2010); Males per 100 females: 84.0 (2010); Marriage status: 24.6% never married, 54.3% now married, 16.5% widowed, 4.5% divorced (2006-2010 5-year est.); Foreign born: 0.3% (2006-2010 5-year est.); Ancestry (includes multiple ancestries): 35.1% German, 31.6% Irish, 23.8% Italian, 10.6% English, 7.4% Polish (2006-2010 5-year est.).

Economy: Employment by occupation: 9.9% management, 3.4% professional, 12.6% services, 21.2% sales, 1.2% farming, 3.8% construction, 0.0% production (2006-2010 5-year est.).

Income: Per capita income: $38,067 (2006-2010 5-year est.); Median household income: $69,500 (2006-2010 5-year est.); Average household income: $104,077 (2006-2010 5-year est.); Percent of households with income of $100,000 or more: 33.7% (2006-2010 5-year est.); Poverty rate: 2.0% (2006-2010 5-year est.).

Education: Percent of population age 25 and over with: High school diploma (including GED) or higher: 97.4% (2006-2010 5-year est.); Bachelor's degree or higher: 39.6% (2006-2010 5-year est.); Master's degree or higher: 12.7% (2006-2010 5-year est.).

Housing: Homeownership rate: 66.6% (2010); Median home value: $230,200 (2006-2010 5-year est.); Median contract rent: $1,996 per month (2006-2010 5-year est.); Median year structure built: 1978 (2006-2010 5-year est.).

Transportation: Commute to work: 80.1% car, 1.1% public transportation, 1.3% walk, 17.6% work from home (2006-2010 5-year est.); Travel time to work: 19.1% less than 15 minutes, 45.6% 15 to 30 minutes, 23.8% 30 to 45 minutes, 8.2% 45 to 60 minutes, 3.3% 60 minutes or more (2006-2010 5-year est.)

BALDWIN (borough). Covers a land area of 5.783 square miles and a water area of 0.106 square miles. Located at 40.38° N. Lat; 79.95° W. Long. Elevation is 1,145 feet.

Population: 21,923 (1990); 19,999 (2000); 19,767 (2010); Density: 3,418.1 persons per square mile (2010); Race: 91.6% White, 5.3% Black, 1.2% Asian, 0.1% American Indian/Alaska Native, 0.0% Native Hawaiian/Other Pacific Islander, 1.8% Other, 1.1% Hispanic of any race (2010); Average household size: 2.28 (2010); Median age: 44.7 (2010); Males per 100 females: 90.8 (2010); Marriage status: 25.4% never married, 57.5% now married, 9.6% widowed, 7.5% divorced (2006-2010 5-year est.); Foreign born: 2.1% (2006-2010 5-year est.); Ancestry (includes multiple ancestries): 40.1% German, 25.6% Irish, 19.5% Italian, 14.9% Polish, 7.1% English (2006-2010 5-year est.).

Economy: Single-family building permits issued: 13 (2011); Multi-family building permits issued: 0 (2011); Employment by occupation: 11.4% management, 6.5% professional, 10.1% services, 22.6% sales, 5.1% farming, 8.5% construction, 5.3% production (2006-2010 5-year est.).

Income: Per capita income: $24,917 (2006-2010 5-year est.); Median household income: $48,514 (2006-2010 5-year est.); Average household income: $56,590 (2006-2010 5-year est.); Percent of households with income of $100,000 or more: 12.9% (2006-2010 5-year est.); Poverty rate: 10.5% (2006-2010 5-year est.).

Taxes: Total city taxes per capita: $388 (2009); City property taxes per capita: $263 (2009).

Education: Percent of population age 25 and over with: High school diploma (including GED) or higher: 92.4% (2006-2010 5-year est.); Bachelor's degree or higher: 22.1% (2006-2010 5-year est.); Master's degree or higher: 7.4% (2006-2010 5-year est.).

Housing: Homeownership rate: 76.3% (2010); Median home value: $106,900 (2006-2010 5-year est.); Median contract rent: $583 per month (2006-2010 5-year est.); Median year structure built: 1956 (2006-2010 5-year est.).

Safety: Violent crime rate: 9.6 per 10,000 population; Property crime rate: 79.2 per 10,000 population (2011).

Transportation: Commute to work: 87.4% car, 7.1% public transportation, 2.2% walk, 2.8% work from home (2006-2010 5-year est.); Travel time to work: 21.1% less than 15 minutes, 34.1% 15 to 30 minutes, 25.5% 30 to 45 minutes, 11.2% 45 to 60 minutes, 8.0% 60 minutes or more (2006-2010 5-year est.)

Additional Information Contacts
Borough of Baldwin . . . . (412) 882-9600
   http://www.baldwinborough.org
Brentwood Baldwin Whitehall Chamber of Commerce . . . . (412) 884-1233
   http://www.bbwchamber.com

BALDWIN (township). Covers a land area of 0.506 square miles and a water area of 0 square miles. Located at 40.38° N. Lat; 80.01° W. Long. Elevation is 1,145 feet.

History: Incorporated 1952.

Population: 2,479 (1990); 2,244 (2000); 1,992 (2010); Density: 3,935.1 persons per square mile (2010); Race: 96.5% White, 0.3% Black, 1.7% Asian, 0.0% American Indian/Alaska Native, 0.0% Native Hawaiian/Other Pacific Islander, 1.5% Other, 0.6% Hispanic of any race (2010); Average household size: 2.35 (2010); Median age: 44.4 (2010); Males per 100 females: 95.1 (2010); Marriage status: 24.0% never married, 59.2% now married, 6.1% widowed, 10.8% divorced (2006-2010 5-year est.); Foreign born: 2.8% (2006-2010 5-year est.); Ancestry (includes multiple ancestries): 44.0% German, 31.0% Irish, 21.1% Italian, 16.2% Polish, 8.1% English (2006-2010 5-year est.).

Economy: Single-family building permits issued: 0 (2011); Multi-family building permits issued: 0 (2011); Employment by occupation: 13.0% management, 5.8% professional, 11.2% services, 15.3% sales, 4.8% farming, 4.9% construction, 4.3% production (2006-2010 5-year est.).

Income: Per capita income: $29,916 (2006-2010 5-year est.); Median household income: $62,500 (2006-2010 5-year est.); Average household income: $68,046 (2006-2010 5-year est.); Percent of households with income of $100,000 or more: 18.7% (2006-2010 5-year est.); Poverty rate: 2.6% (2006-2010 5-year est.).

Education: Percent of population age 25 and over with: High school diploma (including GED) or higher: 94.2% (2006-2010 5-year est.); Bachelor's degree or higher: 26.6% (2006-2010 5-year est.); Master's degree or higher: 11.7% (2006-2010 5-year est.).

Housing: Homeownership rate: 94.2% (2010); Median home value: $103,900 (2006-2010 5-year est.); Median contract rent: $536 per month (2006-2010 5-year est.); Median year structure built: 1951 (2006-2010 5-year est.).

Transportation: Commute to work: 89.6% car, 6.5% public transportation, 2.7% walk, 0.5% work from home (2006-2010 5-year est.); Travel time to work: 18.9% less than 15 minutes, 43.3% 15 to 30 minutes, 31.0% 30 to 45 minutes, 5.7% 45 to 60 minutes, 1.1% 60 minutes or more (2006-2010 5-year est.)

Additional Information Contacts
Brentwood Baldwin Whitehall Chamber of Commerce . . . . (412) 884-1233
   http://www.bbwchamber.com

BELL ACRES (borough). Covers a land area of 5.367 square miles and a water area of 0 square miles. Located at 40.59° N. Lat; 80.17° W. Long. Elevation is 1,178 feet.

Population: 1,436 (1990); 1,382 (2000); 1,388 (2010); Density: 258.6 persons per square mile (2010); Race: 94.2% White, 2.7% Black, 1.3% Asian, 0.1% American Indian/Alaska Native, 0.1% Native Hawaiian/Other Pacific Islander, 1.6% Other, 1.3% Hispanic of any race (2010); Average household size: 2.61 (2010); Median age: 47.0 (2010); Males per 100 females: 97.4 (2010); Marriage status: 23.7% never married, 66.0% now married, 5.1% widowed, 5.2% divorced (2006-2010 5-year est.); Foreign born: 1.3% (2006-2010 5-year est.); Ancestry (includes multiple ancestries): 40.6% German, 15.5% Irish, 15.3% Italian, 11.6% English, 7.8% Polish (2006-2010 5-year est.).

Economy: Single-family building permits issued: 3 (2011); Multi-family building permits issued: 0 (2011); Employment by occupation: 20.1% management, 6.7% professional, 7.3% services, 10.7% sales, 2.5% farming, 8.8% construction, 6.5% production (2006-2010 5-year est.).

Income: Per capita income: $56,297 (2006-2010 5-year est.); Median household income: $68,571 (2006-2010 5-year est.); Average household income: $146,317 (2006-2010 5-year est.); Percent of households with income of $100,000 or more: 40.1% (2006-2010 5-year est.); Poverty rate: 2.2% (2006-2010 5-year est.).

Education: Percent of population age 25 and over with: High school diploma (including GED) or higher: 94.4% (2006-2010 5-year est.); Bachelor's degree or higher: 46.5% (2006-2010 5-year est.); Master's degree or higher: 25.0% (2006-2010 5-year est.).

Housing: Homeownership rate: 91.4% (2010); Median home value: $214,600 (2006-2010 5-year est.); Median contract rent: $613 per month (2006-2010 5-year est.); Median year structure built: 1959 (2006-2010 5-year est.).

Safety: Violent crime rate: 0.0 per 10,000 population; Property crime rate: 7.2 per 10,000 population (2011).

Transportation: Commute to work: 84.3% car, 0.0% public pennsportation, 1.5% walk, 9.1% work from home (2006-2010 5-year est.); Travel time to work: 19.8% less than 15 minutes, 43.4% 15 to 30 minutes, 22.4% 30 to

45 minutes, 9.4% 45 to 60 minutes, 5.0% 60 minutes or more (2006-2010 5-year est.)

Additional Information Contacts
Ambridge Area Chamber of Commerce . . . . (724) 266-3040
   http://www.ambridgechamberofcommerce.com

BELLEVUE (borough). Covers a land area of 1.009 square miles and a water area of 0.114 square miles. Located at 40.49° N. Lat; 80.06° W. Long. Elevation is 981 feet.

History: Settled 1802, incorporated 1867.
Population: 9,093 (1990); 8,770 (2000); 8,370 (2010); Density: 8,295.7 persons per square mile (2010); Race: 86.8% White, 8.9% Black, 1.1% Asian, 0.1% American Indian/Alaska Native, 0.0% Native Hawaiian/Other Pacific Islander, 3.1% Other, 1.9% Hispanic of any race (2010); Average household size: 1.96 (2010); Median age: 37.3 (2010); Males per 100 females: 90.9 (2010); Marriage status: 42.9% never married, 38.2% now married, 8.1% widowed, 10.8% divorced (2006-2010 5-year est.); Foreign born: 4.3% (2006-2010 5-year est.); Ancestry (includes multiple ancestries): 36.5% German, 23.7% Irish, 15.0% Italian, 10.8% Polish, 7.5% English (2006-2010 5-year est.).
Economy: Single-family building permits issued: 0 (2011); Multi-family building permits issued: 0 (2011); Employment by occupation: 11.9% management, 4.3% professional, 12.0% services, 17.7% sales, 4.0% farming, 6.4% construction, 5.8% production (2006-2010 5-year est.).
Income: Per capita income: $25,508 (2006-2010 5-year est.); Median household income: $39,586 (2006-2010 5-year est.); Average household income: $50,080 (2006-2010 5-year est.); Percent of households with income of $100,000 or more: 9.5% (2006-2010 5-year est.); Poverty rate: 11.7% (2006-2010 5-year est.).
Education: Percent of population age 25 and over with: High school diploma (including GED) or higher: 93.0% (2006-2010 5-year est.); Bachelor's degree or higher: 25.9% (2006-2010 5-year est.); Master's degree or higher: 7.5% (2006-2010 5-year est.).
Housing: Homeownership rate: 36.8% (2010); Median home value: $99,700 (2006-2010 5-year est.); Median contract rent: $510 per month (2006-2010 5-year est.); Median year structure built: before 1940 (2006-2010 5-year est.).
Safety: Violent crime rate: 21.4 per 10,000 population; Property crime rate: 270.3 per 10,000 population (2011).
Newspapers: Citizen (Community news; Circulation 4,000)
Transportation: Commute to work: 78.0% car, 12.9% public transportation, 6.2% walk, 2.3% work from home (2006-2010 5-year est.); Travel time to work: 17.6% less than 15 minutes, 46.3% 15 to 30 minutes, 27.6% 30 to 45 minutes, 5.2% 45 to 60 minutes, 3.4% 60 minutes or more (2006-2010 5-year est.)

Additional Information Contacts
Borough of Bellevue . . . . (412) 766-6164
   http://borough.bellevue.pa.us
North Suburban Chamber of Commerce. . . . . (412) 761-2113
   http://www.northsuburbancoc.org

BEN AVON (borough). Covers a land area of 0.379 square miles and a water area of 0.079 square miles. Located at 40.51° N. Lat; 80.08° W. Long. Elevation is 837 feet.

History: Incorporated 1891.
Population: 2,081 (1990); 1,917 (2000); 1,781 (2010); Density: 4,700.0 persons per square mile (2010); Race: 93.7% White, 3.6% Black, 0.8% Asian, 0.1% American Indian/Alaska Native, 0.0% Native Hawaiian/Other Pacific Islander, 1.8% Other, 1.1% Hispanic of any race (2010); Average household size: 2.40 (2010); Median age: 39.2 (2010); Males per 100 females: 92.1 (2010); Marriage status: 23.5% never married, 64.8% now married, 3.9% widowed, 7.8% divorced (2006-2010 5-year est.); Foreign born: 1.2% (2006-2010 5-year est.); Ancestry (includes multiple ancestries): 36.8% German, 24.1% Irish, 16.4% English, 14.0% Italian, 6.4% Polish (2006-2010 5-year est.).
Economy: Single-family building permits issued: 0 (2011); Multi-family building permits issued: 0 (2011); Employment by occupation: 21.9% management, 4.3% professional, 5.2% services, 17.2% sales, 4.4% farming, 4.4% construction, 1.9% production (2006-2010 5-year est.).
Income: Per capita income: $43,281 (2006-2010 5-year est.); Median household income: $78,843 (2006-2010 5-year est.); Average household income: $112,142 (2006-2010 5-year est.); Percent of households with income of $100,000 or more: 39.7% (2006-2010 5-year est.); Poverty rate: 3.3% (2006-2010 5-year est.).

Education: Percent of population age 25 and over with: High school diploma (including GED) or higher: 95.3% (2006-2010 5-year est.); Bachelor's degree or higher: 60.0% (2006-2010 5-year est.); Master's degree or higher: 27.7% (2006-2010 5-year est.).
Housing: Homeownership rate: 72.0% (2010); Median home value: $181,700 (2006-2010 5-year est.); Median contract rent: $628 per month (2006-2010 5-year est.); Median year structure built: before 1940 (2006-2010 5-year est.).
Safety: Violent crime rate: 0.0 per 10,000 population; Property crime rate: 156.7 per 10,000 population (2011).
Transportation: Commute to work: 84.8% car, 4.8% public transportation, 4.6% walk, 4.9% work from home (2006-2010 5-year est.); Travel time to work: 13.9% less than 15 minutes, 53.9% 15 to 30 minutes, 25.5% 30 to 45 minutes, 3.6% 45 to 60 minutes, 3.1% 60 minutes or more (2006-2010 5-year est.)

Additional Information Contacts
North Suburban Chamber of Commerce. . . . . (412) 761-2113
   http://www.northsuburbancoc.org

BEN AVON HEIGHTS (borough). Covers a land area of 0.173 square miles and a water area of 0 square miles. Located at 40.51° N. Lat; 80.07° W. Long. Elevation is 1,155 feet.

Population: 373 (1990); 392 (2000); 371 (2010); Density: 2,140.0 persons per square mile (2010); Race: 97.8% White, 0.3% Black, 0.3% Asian, 0.0% American Indian/Alaska Native, 0.0% Native Hawaiian/Other Pacific Islander, 1.6% Other, 0.8% Hispanic of any race (2010); Average household size: 2.81 (2010); Median age: 43.8 (2010); Males per 100 females: 89.3 (2010); Marriage status: 20.4% never married, 71.2% now married, 1.3% widowed, 7.1% divorced (2006-2010 5-year est.); Foreign born: 4.5% (2006-2010 5-year est.); Ancestry (includes multiple ancestries): 27.0% German, 21.2% Irish, 20.5% Italian, 19.9% English, 6.3% Scotch-Irish (2006-2010 5-year est.).
Economy: Single-family building permits issued: 0 (2011); Multi-family building permits issued: 0 (2011); Employment by occupation: 35.7% management, 0.0% professional, 0.0% services, 11.0% sales, 1.1% farming, 2.2% construction, 1.1% production (2006-2010 5-year est.).
Income: Per capita income: $55,524 (2006-2010 5-year est.); Median household income: $116,250 (2006-2010 5-year est.); Average household income: $153,631 (2006-2010 5-year est.); Percent of households with income of $100,000 or more: 60.0% (2006-2010 5-year est.); Poverty rate: 0.5% (2006-2010 5-year est.).
Education: Percent of population age 25 and over with: High school diploma (including GED) or higher: 99.3% (2006-2010 5-year est.); Bachelor's degree or higher: 71.5% (2006-2010 5-year est.); Master's degree or higher: 41.2% (2006-2010 5-year est.).
Housing: Homeownership rate: 99.2% (2010); Median home value: $321,100 (2006-2010 5-year est.); Median contract rent: n/a per month (2006-2010 5-year est.); Median year structure built: before 1940 (2006-2010 5-year est.).
Safety: Violent crime rate: 0.0 per 10,000 population; Property crime rate: 80.6 per 10,000 population (2011).
Transportation: Commute to work: 84.1% car, 4.0% public transportation, 0.0% walk, 11.9% work from home (2006-2010 5-year est.); Travel time to work: 22.6% less than 15 minutes, 56.1% 15 to 30 minutes, 16.8% 30 to 45 minutes, 3.2% 45 to 60 minutes, 1.3% 60 minutes or more (2006-2010 5-year est.)

BETHEL PARK (municipality). Covers a land area of 11.671 square miles and a water area of 0 square miles. Located at 40.32° N. Lat; 80.04° W. Long. Elevation is 1,198 feet.

History: Incorporated 1949.
Population: 33,823 (1990); 33,556 (2000); 32,313 (2010); Density: 2,768.7 persons per square mile (2010); Race: 96.1% White, 1.3% Black, 1.4% Asian, 0.1% American Indian/Alaska Native, 0.0% Native Hawaiian/Other Pacific Islander, 1.1% Other, 1.0% Hispanic of any race (2010); Average household size: 2.35 (2010); Median age: 46.1 (2010); Males per 100 females: 91.3 (2010); Marriage status: 23.3% never married, 61.1% now married, 8.0% widowed, 7.5% divorced (2006-2010 5-year est.); Foreign born: 3.1% (2006-2010 5-year est.); Ancestry (includes multiple ancestries): 37.7% German, 24.7% Irish, 21.5% Italian, 11.1% English, 11.0% Polish (2006-2010 5-year est.).
Economy: Unemployment rate: 5.9% (August 2012); Total civilian labor force: 18,269 (August 2012); Single-family building permits issued: 8 (2011); Multi-family building permits issued: 0 (2011); Employment by occupation: 16.1% management, 7.1% professional, 6.4% services, 16.9%

sales, 5.4% farming, 6.5% construction, 3.6% production (2006-2010 5-year est.).

Income: Per capita income: $31,642 (2006-2010 5-year est.); Median household income: $61,074 (2006-2010 5-year est.); Average household income: $77,084 (2006-2010 5-year est.); Percent of households with income of $100,000 or more: 25.5% (2006-2010 5-year est.); Poverty rate: 3.2% (2006-2010 5-year est.).

Education: Percent of population age 25 and over with: High school diploma (including GED) or higher: 94.9% (2006-2010 5-year est.); Bachelor's degree or higher: 40.8% (2006-2010 5-year est.); Master's degree or higher: 13.2% (2006-2010 5-year est.).

School District(s)
Bethel Park SD (KG-12)
    2010-11 Enrollment: 4,696 . . . . (412) 833-5000

Housing: Homeownership rate: 79.2% (2010); Median home value: $147,100 (2006-2010 5-year est.); Median contract rent: $730 per month (2006-2010 5-year est.); Median year structure built: 1964 (2006-2010 5-year est.).

Safety: Violent crime rate: 8.0 per 10,000 population; Property crime rate: 100.9 per 10,000 population (2011).

Newspapers: Pittsburgh Post-Gazette - South Bureau (Community news)

Transportation: Commute to work: 84.2% car, 9.2% public transportation, 1.6% walk, 4.2% work from home (2006-2010 5-year est.); Travel time to work: 25.2% less than 15 minutes, 25.6% 15 to 30 minutes, 26.0% 30 to 45 minutes, 15.4% 45 to 60 minutes, 7.7% 60 minutes or more (2006-2010 5-year est.)

Additional Information Contacts
Borough of Bethel Park . . . . (412) 831-6398
    http://www.bethelpark.net
North Suburban Chamber of Commerce . . . . (412) 761-2113
    http://www.northsuburbancoc.org

BLAWNOX (borough). Covers a land area of 0.297 square miles and a water area of 0.144 square miles. Located at 40.49° N. Lat; 79.86° W. Long. Elevation is 814 feet.

History: Settled 1867.

Population: 1,626 (1990); 1,550 (2000); 1,432 (2010); Density: 4,829.3 persons per square mile (2010); Race: 92.9% White, 1.9% Black, 4.0% Asian, 0.1% American Indian/Alaska Native, 0.0% Native Hawaiian/Other Pacific Islander, 1.1% Other, 0.8% Hispanic of any race (2010); Average household size: 1.73 (2010); Median age: 46.9 (2010); Males per 100 females: 93.0 (2010); Marriage status: 27.2% never married, 51.4% now married, 9.3% widowed, 12.1% divorced (2006-2010 5-year est.); Foreign born: 4.0% (2006-2010 5-year est.); Ancestry (includes multiple ancestries): 40.8% German, 24.1% Italian, 20.9% Irish, 10.5% Polish, 7.8% English (2006-2010 5-year est.).

Economy: Single-family building permits issued: 0 (2011); Multi-family building permits issued: 0 (2011); Employment by occupation: 12.2% management, 3.1% professional, 13.1% services, 15.0% sales, 5.6% farming, 5.1% construction, 5.5% production (2006-2010 5-year est.).

Income: Per capita income: $29,150 (2006-2010 5-year est.); Median household income: $40,313 (2006-2010 5-year est.); Average household income: $49,112 (2006-2010 5-year est.); Percent of households with income of $100,000 or more: 8.9% (2006-2010 5-year est.); Poverty rate: 8.4% (2006-2010 5-year est.).

Education: Percent of population age 25 and over with: High school diploma (including GED) or higher: 89.8% (2006-2010 5-year est.); Bachelor's degree or higher: 31.1% (2006-2010 5-year est.); Master's degree or higher: 6.3% (2006-2010 5-year est.).

Housing: Homeownership rate: 42.7% (2010); Median home value: $98,800 (2006-2010 5-year est.); Median contract rent: $518 per month (2006-2010 5-year est.); Median year structure built: 1957 (2006-2010 5-year est.).

Safety: Violent crime rate: 48.7 per 10,000 population; Property crime rate: 48.7 per 10,000 population (2011).

Transportation: Commute to work: 90.3% car, 4.6% public transportation, 3.2% walk, 1.6% work from home (2006-2010 5-year est.); Travel time to work: 44.0% less than 15 minutes, 22.7% 15 to 30 minutes, 24.5% 30 to 45 minutes, 2.8% 45 to 60 minutes, 6.0% 60 minutes or more (2006-2010 5-year est.)

Additional Information Contacts
Allegheny Valley Chamber of Commerce . . . . (724) 224-3400

    http://alleghenyvalleychamber.com/community/community-profiles/blawnox

BOSTON (CDP). Covers a land area of 0.326 square miles and a water area of 0.039 square miles. Located at 40.31° N. Lat; 79.82° W. Long. Elevation is 761 feet.

Population: n/a (1990); n/a (2000); 545 (2010); Density: 1,671.1 persons per square mile (2010); Race: 95.8% White, 1.1% Black, 0.0% Asian, 0.0% American Indian/Alaska Native, 0.0% Native Hawaiian/Other Pacific Islander, 3.1% Other, 1.8% Hispanic of any race (2010); Average household size: 2.25 (2010); Median age: 46.3 (2010); Males per 100 females: 91.2 (2010); Marriage status: 19.3% never married, 48.3% now married, 0.0% widowed, 32.4% divorced (2006-2010 5-year est.); Foreign born: 0.0% (2006-2010 5-year est.); Ancestry (includes multiple ancestries): 33.1% German, 24.5% Irish, 16.4% English, 14.8% Italian, 13.3% Scotch-Irish (2006-2010 5-year est.).

Economy: Employment by occupation: 0.0% management, 0.0% professional, 23.0% services, 12.8% sales, 6.1% farming, 6.1% construction, 12.8% production (2006-2010 5-year est.).

Income: Per capita income: $18,186 (2006-2010 5-year est.); Median household income: $33,165 (2006-2010 5-year est.); Average household income: $37,330 (2006-2010 5-year est.); Percent of households with income of $100,000 or more: n/a (2006-2010 5-year est.); Poverty rate: 3.1% (2006-2010 5-year est.).

Education: Percent of population age 25 and over with: High school diploma (including GED) or higher: 94.5% (2006-2010 5-year est.); Bachelor's degree or higher: 10.0% (2006-2010 5-year est.); Master's degree or higher: 5.2% (2006-2010 5-year est.).

Housing: Homeownership rate: 67.8% (2010); Median home value: $73,800 (2006-2010 5-year est.); Median contract rent: $620 per month (2006-2010 5-year est.); Median year structure built: before 1940 (2006-2010 5-year est.).

Transportation: Commute to work: 76.5% car, 8.7% public transportation, 8.7% walk, 6.1% work from home (2006-2010 5-year est.); Travel time to work: 47.3% less than 15 minutes, 9.2% 15 to 30 minutes, 34.2% 30 to 45 minutes, 0.0% 45 to 60 minutes, 9.2% 60 minutes or more (2006-2010 5-year est.)

BRACKENRIDGE (borough). Covers a land area of 0.511 square miles and a water area of 0.045 square miles. Located at 40.61° N. Lat; 79.74° W. Long. Elevation is 827 feet.

History: Incorporated 1901.

Population: 3,784 (1990); 3,543 (2000); 3,260 (2010); Density: 6,373.4 persons per square mile (2010); Race: 93.3% White, 4.3% Black, 0.3% Asian, 0.1% American Indian/Alaska Native, 0.0% Native Hawaiian/Other Pacific Islander, 2.0% Other, 0.7% Hispanic of any race (2010); Average household size: 2.12 (2010); Median age: 43.4 (2010); Males per 100 females: 83.9 (2010); Marriage status: 32.0% never married, 43.6% now married, 10.1% widowed, 14.3% divorced (2006-2010 5-year est.); Foreign born: 1.6% (2006-2010 5-year est.); Ancestry (includes multiple ancestries): 43.2% German, 19.7% Irish, 19.1% Polish, 12.8% Slovak, 11.8% Italian (2006-2010 5-year est.).

Economy: Single-family building permits issued: 0 (2011); Multi-family building permits issued: 0 (2011); Employment by occupation: 5.0% management, 0.8% professional, 10.2% services, 20.5% sales, 3.2% farming, 11.3% construction, 10.2% production (2006-2010 5-year est.).

Income: Per capita income: $18,935 (2006-2010 5-year est.); Median household income: $39,949 (2006-2010 5-year est.); Average household income: $46,237 (2006-2010 5-year est.); Percent of households with income of $100,000 or more: 4.6% (2006-2010 5-year est.); Poverty rate: 13.2% (2006-2010 5-year est.).

Education: Percent of population age 25 and over with: High school diploma (including GED) or higher: 88.3% (2006-2010 5-year est.); Bachelor's degree or higher: 13.5% (2006-2010 5-year est.); Master's degree or higher: 2.9% (2006-2010 5-year est.).

School District(s)
Highlands SD (PK-12)
    2010-11 Enrollment: 2,742 . . . . (724) 226-2400

Housing: Homeownership rate: 61.9% (2010); Median home value: $60,600 (2006-2010 5-year est.); Median contract rent: $505 per month (2006-2010 5-year est.); Median year structure built: 1941 (2006-2010 5-year est.).

Safety: Violent crime rate: 9.2 per 10,000 population; Property crime rate: 232.4 per 10,000 population (2011).

Transportation: Commute to work: 92.4% car, 1.5% public transportation, 1.7% walk, 2.2% work from home (2006-2010 5-year est.); Travel time to work: 29.0% less than 15 minutes, 32.3% 15 to 30 minutes, 26.3% 30 to

45 minutes, 5.8% 45 to 60 minutes, 6.5% 60 minutes or more (2006-2010 5-year est.)

Additional Information Contacts

Allegheny Valley Chamber of Commerce . . . . (724) 224-3400
http://alleghenyvalleychamber.com

BRADDOCK (borough). Covers a land area of 0.563 square miles and a water area of 0.083 square miles. Located at 40.40° N. Lat; 79.87° W. Long. Elevation is 764 feet.

History: Once a steel-manufacturing center, the population has decreased with the decline of the industry. In 1755, Gen. Edward Braddock was defeated here by French and Native American forces. Settled 1742, incorporated 1867.

Population: 4,682 (1990); 2,912 (2000); 2,159 (2010); Density: 3,833.5 persons per square mile (2010); Race: 22.9% White, 72.7% Black, 0.1% Asian, 0.7% American Indian/Alaska Native, 0.2% Native Hawaiian/Other Pacific Islander, 3.4% Other, 1.9% Hispanic of any race (2010); Average household size: 2.40 (2010); Median age: 34.9 (2010); Males per 100 females: 93.8 (2010); Marriage status: 57.2% never married, 18.9% now married, 11.3% widowed, 12.7% divorced (2006-2010 5-year est.); Foreign born: 0.0% (2006-2010 5-year est.); Ancestry (includes multiple ancestries): 6.1% Slovak, 5.5% Polish, 4.2% Italian, 4.1% African, 2.9% German (2006-2010 5-year est.).

Economy: Single-family building permits issued: 0 (2011); Multi-family building permits issued: 0 (2011); Employment by occupation: 4.9% management, 1.7% professional, 25.7% services, 11.7% sales, 3.1% farming, 0.0% construction, 0.8% production (2006-2010 5-year est.).

Income: Per capita income: $13,825 (2006-2010 5-year est.); Median household income: $21,667 (2006-2010 5-year est.); Average household income: $30,113 (2006-2010 5-year est.); Percent of households with income of $100,000 or more: 6.3% (2006-2010 5-year est.); Poverty rate: 37.4% (2006-2010 5-year est.).

Taxes: Total city taxes per capita: $323 (2009); City property taxes per capita: $161 (2009).

Education: Percent of population age 25 and over with: High school diploma (including GED) or higher: 83.1% (2006-2010 5-year est.); Bachelor's degree or higher: 17.3% (2006-2010 5-year est.); Master's degree or higher: 5.1% (2006-2010 5-year est.).

School District(s)

Woodland Hills SD (PK-12)

    2010-11 Enrollment: 4,050 . . . . (412) 731-1300

Housing: Homeownership rate: 44.1% (2010); Median home value: $33,600 (2006-2010 5-year est.); Median contract rent: $304 per month (2006-2010 5-year est.); Median year structure built: before 1940 (2006-2010 5-year est.).

Transportation: Commute to work: 45.9% car, 33.7% public transportation, 7.6% walk, 11.9% work from home (2006-2010 5-year est.); Travel time to work: 21.6% less than 15 minutes, 31.4% 15 to 30 minutes, 19.0% 30 to 45 minutes, 7.1% 45 to 60 minutes, 20.8% 60 minutes or more (2006-2010 5-year est.)

Additional Information Contacts

South Side Chamber of Commerce . . . . (412) 431-3360
http://www.southsidechamber.org

BRADDOCK HILLS (borough). Covers a land area of 0.948 square miles and a water area of 0.008 square miles. Located at 40.41° N. Lat; 79.86° W. Long. Elevation is 1,024 feet.

History: Incorporated 1946.

Population: 2,026 (1990); 1,998 (2000); 1,880 (2010); Density: 1,983.9 persons per square mile (2010); Race: 68.9% White, 27.9% Black, 0.3% Asian, 0.3% American Indian/Alaska Native, 0.0% Native Hawaiian/Other Pacific Islander, 2.6% Other, 1.4% Hispanic of any race (2010); Average household size: 1.85 (2010); Median age: 48.0 (2010); Males per 100 females: 79.7 (2010); Marriage status: 32.1% never married, 43.0% now married, 13.0% widowed, 11.8% divorced (2006-2010 5-year est.); Foreign born: 4.2% (2006-2010 5-year est.); Ancestry (includes multiple ancestries): 18.1% German, 17.9% Irish, 15.8% Italian, 7.8% American, 7.0% Slovak (2006-2010 5-year est.).

Economy: Single-family building permits issued: 0 (2011); Multi-family building permits issued: 0 (2011); Employment by occupation: 10.1% management, 3.3% professional, 13.8% services, 22.8% sales, 4.0% farming, 1.4% construction, 0.0% production (2006-2010 5-year est.).

Income: Per capita income: $24,585 (2006-2010 5-year est.); Median household income: $30,735 (2006-2010 5-year est.); Average household income: $45,136 (2006-2010 5-year est.); Percent of households with

income of $100,000 or more: 9.4% (2006-2010 5-year est.); Poverty rate: 24.6% (2006-2010 5-year est.).

Education: Percent of population age 25 and over with: High school diploma (including GED) or higher: 90.4% (2006-2010 5-year est.); Bachelor's degree or higher: 25.8% (2006-2010 5-year est.); Master's degree or higher: 4.6% (2006-2010 5-year est.).

Housing: Homeownership rate: 50.3% (2010); Median home value: $78,300 (2006-2010 5-year est.); Median contract rent: $276 per month (2006-2010 5-year est.); Median year structure built: 1959 (2006-2010 5-year est.).

Safety: Violent crime rate: 5.3 per 10,000 population; Property crime rate: 15.9 per 10,000 population (2011).

Transportation: Commute to work: 80.8% car, 17.1% public transportation, 1.3% walk, 0.7% work from home (2006-2010 5-year est.); Travel time to work: 34.6% less than 15 minutes, 39.3% 15 to 30 minutes, 18.5% 30 to 45 minutes, 6.0% 45 to 60 minutes, 1.6% 60 minutes or more (2006-2010 5-year est.)

Additional Information Contacts

Brentwood Baldwin Whitehall Chamber of Commerce . . . . (412) 884-1233
http://www.bbwchamber.com

BRADFORD WOODS (borough). Covers a land area of 0.890 square miles and a water area of 0 square miles. Located at 40.64° N. Lat; 80.08° W. Long. Elevation is 1,204 feet.

Population: 1,249 (1990); 1,149 (2000); 1,171 (2010); Density: 1,316.1 persons per square mile (2010); Race: 97.4% White, 0.6% Black, 0.9% Asian, 0.0% American Indian/Alaska Native, 0.2% Native Hawaiian/Other Pacific Islander, 0.9% Other, 0.5% Hispanic of any race (2010); Average household size: 2.47 (2010); Median age: 49.0 (2010); Males per 100 females: 91.3 (2010); Marriage status: 17.8% never married, 71.9% now married, 6.1% widowed, 4.3% divorced (2006-2010 5-year est.); Foreign born: 5.4% (2006-2010 5-year est.); Ancestry (includes multiple ancestries): 31.6% German, 19.4% Irish, 15.9% English, 9.8% Italian, 8.4% Polish (2006-2010 5-year est.).

Economy: Single-family building permits issued: 1 (2011); Multi-family building permits issued: 0 (2011); Employment by occupation: 19.4% management, 6.1% professional, 8.2% services, 16.0% sales, 2.6% farming, 2.8% construction, 0.7% production (2006-2010 5-year est.).

Income: Per capita income: $64,073 (2006-2010 5-year est.); Median household income: $111,591 (2006-2010 5-year est.); Average household income: $177,722 (2006-2010 5-year est.); Percent of households with income of $100,000 or more: 54.2% (2006-2010 5-year est.); Poverty rate: 3.1% (2006-2010 5-year est.).

Education: Percent of population age 25 and over with: High school diploma (including GED) or higher: 99.6% (2006-2010 5-year est.); Bachelor's degree or higher: 63.0% (2006-2010 5-year est.); Master's degree or higher: 24.7% (2006-2010 5-year est.).

School District(s)

North Allegheny SD (KG-12)

    2010-11 Enrollment: 8,105 . . . . (412) 366-2100

Housing: Homeownership rate: 95.2% (2010); Median home value: $260,100 (2006-2010 5-year est.); Median contract rent: $1,250 per month (2006-2010 5-year est.); Median year structure built: 1962 (2006-2010 5-year est.).

Transportation: Commute to work: 82.0% car, 1.9% public transportation, 1.3% walk, 14.4% work from home (2006-2010 5-year est.); Travel time to work: 22.6% less than 15 minutes, 37.1% 15 to 30 minutes, 30.4% 30 to 45 minutes, 7.2% 45 to 60 minutes, 2.7% 60 minutes or more (2006-2010 5-year est.)

BRADFORDWOODS (unincorporated postal area)

Zip Code: 15015

    Covers a land area of 0.935 square miles and a water area of 0 square miles. Located at 40.63° N. Lat; 80.08° W. Long. Population: 1,175 (2010); Density: 1,255.7 persons per square mile (2010); Race: 97.4% White, 0.6% Black, 0.9% Asian, 0.0% American Indian/Alaska Native, 0.2% Native Hawaiian/Other Pacific Islander, 0.9% Other, 0.5% Hispanic of any race (2010); Average household size: 2.47 (2010); Median age: 49.0 (2010); Males per 100 females: 91.4 (2010); Homeownership rate: 95.1% (2010)

BRENTWOOD (borough). Covers a land area of 1.448 square miles and a water area of 0 square miles. Located at 40.37° N. Lat; 79.98° W. Long. Elevation is 1,181 feet.

History: Incorporated 1915.

Population: 10,823 (1990); 10,466 (2000); 9,643 (2010); Density: 6,660.8 persons per square mile (2010); Race: 95.2% White, 2.0% Black, 0.8% Asian, 0.2% American Indian/Alaska Native, 0.0% Native Hawaiian/Other Pacific Islander, 1.8% Other, 1.8% Hispanic of any race (2010); Average household size: 2.20 (2010); Median age: 39.4 (2010); Males per 100 females: 95.7 (2010); Marriage status: 33.5% never married, 50.3% now married, 6.7% widowed, 9.6% divorced (2006-2010 5-year est.); Foreign born: 2.3% (2006-2010 5-year est.); Ancestry (includes multiple ancestries): 39.7% German, 26.3% Irish, 19.3% Italian, 12.8% Polish, 6.5% English (2006-2010 5-year est.).

Economy: Single-family building permits issued: 0 (2011); Multi-family building permits issued: 0 (2011); Employment by occupation: 14.4% management, 6.2% professional, 9.2% services, 15.3% sales, 6.2% farming, 9.2% construction, 5.8% production (2006-2010 5-year est.).

Income: Per capita income: $23,966 (2006-2010 5-year est.); Median household income: $45,285 (2006-2010 5-year est.); Average household income: $53,276 (2006-2010 5-year est.); Percent of households with income of $100,000 or more: 9.8% (2006-2010 5-year est.); Poverty rate: 14.8% (2006-2010 5-year est.).

Education: Percent of population age 25 and over with: High school diploma (including GED) or higher: 93.4% (2006-2010 5-year est.); Bachelor's degree or higher: 23.0% (2006-2010 5-year est.); Master's degree or higher: 5.4% (2006-2010 5-year est.).

Housing: Homeownership rate: 62.4% (2010); Median home value: $91,300 (2006-2010 5-year est.); Median contract rent: $495 per month (2006-2010 5-year est.); Median year structure built: 1945 (2006-2010 5-year est.).

Safety: Violent crime rate: 13.4 per 10,000 population; Property crime rate: 196.4 per 10,000 population (2011).

Transportation: Commute to work: 81.5% car, 10.7% public transportation, 3.7% walk, 3.9% work from home (2006-2010 5-year est.); Travel time to work: 18.1% less than 15 minutes, 33.0% 15 to 30 minutes, 30.0% 30 to 45 minutes, 11.1% 45 to 60 minutes, 7.9% 60 minutes or more (2006-2010 5-year est.)

Additional Information Contacts
Borough of Brentwood. . . . . (412) 884-1500
    http://www.brentwoodborough.com
Brentwood Baldwin Whitehall Chamber of Commerce . . . . (412) 884-1233
    http://www.bbwchamber.com

BRIDGEVILLE (borough). Covers a land area of 1.096 square miles and a water area of 0.001 square miles. Located at 40.36° N. Lat; 80.11° W. Long. Elevation is 866 feet.

History: Incorporated 1901.

Population: 5,445 (1990); 5,341 (2000); 5,148 (2010); Density: 4,697.4 persons per square mile (2010); Race: 92.2% White, 4.2% Black, 1.2% Asian, 0.1% American Indian/Alaska Native, 0.0% Native Hawaiian/Other Pacific Islander, 2.3% Other, 1.1% Hispanic of any race (2010); Average household size: 2.05 (2010); Median age: 45.4 (2010); Males per 100 females: 87.7 (2010); Marriage status: 31.0% never married, 42.2% now married, 14.2% widowed, 12.5% divorced (2006-2010 5-year est.); Foreign born: 1.3% (2006-2010 5-year est.); Ancestry (includes multiple ancestries): 35.9% German, 28.1% Irish, 23.2% Italian, 15.0% Polish, 10.4% English (2006-2010 5-year est.).

Economy: Single-family building permits issued: 0 (2011); Multi-family building permits issued: 0 (2011); Employment by occupation: 12.1% management, 0.9% professional, 9.2% services, 24.9% sales, 7.0% farming, 6.0% construction, 6.0% production (2006-2010 5-year est.).

Income: Per capita income: $26,726 (2006-2010 5-year est.); Median household income: $36,839 (2006-2010 5-year est.); Average household income: $51,676 (2006-2010 5-year est.); Percent of households with income of $100,000 or more: 11.3% (2006-2010 5-year est.); Poverty rate: 8.9% (2006-2010 5-year est.).

Education: Percent of population age 25 and over with: High school diploma (including GED) or higher: 91.0% (2006-2010 5-year est.); Bachelor's degree or higher: 24.5% (2006-2010 5-year est.); Master's degree or higher: 5.4% (2006-2010 5-year est.).

School District(s)
Chartiers Valley SD (KG-12)
    2010-11 Enrollment: 3,489 . . . . (412) 429-2201
Housing: Homeownership rate: 61.8% (2010); Median home value: $100,800 (2006-2010 5-year est.); Median contract rent: $474 per month (2006-2010 5-year est.); Median year structure built: 1955 (2006-2010 5-year est.).
Hospitals: Mayview State Hospital (354 beds)

Safety: Violent crime rate: 7.7 per 10,000 population; Property crime rate: 174.3 per 10,000 population (2011).

Transportation: Commute to work: 82.4% car, 7.6% public transportation, 3.9% walk, 2.4% work from home (2006-2010 5-year est.); Travel time to work: 41.2% less than 15 minutes, 29.5% 15 to 30 minutes, 16.1% 30 to 45 minutes, 6.8% 45 to 60 minutes, 6.4% 60 minutes or more (2006-2010 5-year est.)

Additional Information Contacts
Borough of Bridgeville . . . . (412) 221-6012
    http://www.bridgevilleboro.com
South West Communities Chamber of Commerce . . . . (412) 221-4100
    http://www.swccoc.org

BUENA VISTA (unincorporated postal area)
Zip Code: 15018
    Covers a land area of 1.883 square miles and a water area of 0.159 square miles. Located at 40.26° N. Lat; 79.79° W. Long. Elevation is 771 feet. Population: 821 (2010); Density: 435.9 persons per square mile (2010); Race: 94.8% White, 2.6% Black, 0.6% Asian, 0.5% American Indian/Alaska Native, 0.0% Native Hawaiian/Other Pacific Islander, 1.5% Other, 0.5% Hispanic of any race (2010); Average household size: 2.41 (2010); Median age: 42.3 (2010); Males per 100 females: 105.3 (2010); Homeownership rate: 81.4% (2010)

BUNOLA (unincorporated postal area)
Zip Code: 15020
    Covers a land area of 1.319 square miles and a water area of 0.457 square miles. Located at 40.23° N. Lat; 79.95° W. Long. Elevation is 791 feet. Population: 231 (2010); Density: 175.0 persons per square mile (2010); Race: 99.1% White, 0.0% Black, 0.0% Asian, 0.0% American Indian/Alaska Native, 0.0% Native Hawaiian/Other Pacific Islander, 0.9% Other, 0.0% Hispanic of any race (2010); Average household size: 2.18 (2010); Median age: 47.2 (2010); Males per 100 females: 83.3 (2010); Homeownership rate: 76.4% (2010)

CARNEGIE (borough). Covers a land area of 1.617 square miles and a water area of 0 square miles. Located at 40.41° N. Lat; 80.09° W. Long. Elevation is 774 feet.

History: The Neville House was the home of Gen. John Neville, an officer in the French and Indian Wars and the American Revolution. The borough was named for Andrew Carnegie. Incorporated 1894.

Population: 9,228 (1990); 8,389 (2000); 7,972 (2010); Density: 4,928.7 persons per square mile (2010); Race: 87.7% White, 7.4% Black, 1.6% Asian, 0.2% American Indian/Alaska Native, 0.1% Native Hawaiian/Other Pacific Islander, 3.0% Other, 1.6% Hispanic of any race (2010); Average household size: 2.04 (2010); Median age: 40.9 (2010); Males per 100 females: 90.8 (2010); Marriage status: 33.1% never married, 46.6% now married, 8.0% widowed, 12.3% divorced (2006-2010 5-year est.); Foreign born: 2.7% (2006-2010 5-year est.); Ancestry (includes multiple ancestries): 31.5% German, 23.2% Italian, 21.1% Irish, 14.7% Polish, 7.0% English (2006-2010 5-year est.).

Economy: Single-family building permits issued: 0 (2011); Multi-family building permits issued: 0 (2011); Employment by occupation: 11.7% management, 4.0% professional, 8.8% services, 19.2% sales, 9.4% farming, 6.2% construction, 4.0% production (2006-2010 5-year est.).

Income: Per capita income: $28,420 (2006-2010 5-year est.); Median household income: $45,038 (2006-2010 5-year est.); Average household income: $59,236 (2006-2010 5-year est.); Percent of households with income of $100,000 or more: 14.6% (2006-2010 5-year est.); Poverty rate: 13.9% (2006-2010 5-year est.).

Education: Percent of population age 25 and over with: High school diploma (including GED) or higher: 91.1% (2006-2010 5-year est.); Bachelor's degree or higher: 25.1% (2006-2010 5-year est.); Master's degree or higher: 7.3% (2006-2010 5-year est.).

School District(s)
Carlynton SD (KG-12)
    2010-11 Enrollment: 1,424 . . . . (412) 429-8400
Housing: Homeownership rate: 52.0% (2010); Median home value: $113,400 (2006-2010 5-year est.); Median contract rent: $491 per month (2006-2010 5-year est.); Median year structure built: 1948 (2006-2010 5-year est.).
Safety: Violent crime rate: 12.5 per 10,000 population; Property crime rate: 262.6 per 10,000 population (2011).
Transportation: Commute to work: 85.6% car, 7.3% public transportation, 3.1% walk, 2.3% work from home (2006-2010 5-year est.); Travel time to

work: 26.6% less than 15 minutes, 42.4% 15 to 30 minutes, 19.6% 30 to 45 minutes, 6.7% 45 to 60 minutes, 4.7% 60 minutes or more (2006-2010 5-year est.)

Additional Information Contacts

Borough of Carnegie . . . . (412) 276-1414
    http://carnegieborough.com

Pittsburgh Airport Area Chamber of Commerce . . . . (412) 264-6270
    http://www.paacc.com

CARNOT-MOON (CDP). Covers a land area of 5.979 square miles and a water area of 0 square miles. Located at 40.52° N. Lat; 80.22° W. Long.

Population: 10,579 (1990); 10,637 (2000); 11,372 (2010); Density: 1,902.0 persons per square mile (2010); Race: 86.8% White, 6.4% Black, 3.5% Asian, 0.1% American Indian/Alaska Native, 0.0% Native Hawaiian/Other Pacific Islander, 3.2% Other, 2.5% Hispanic of any race (2010); Average household size: 2.11 (2010); Median age: 34.5 (2010); Males per 100 females: 102.5 (2010); Marriage status: 46.6% never married, 40.0% now married, 6.3% widowed, 7.1% divorced (2006-2010 5-year est.); Foreign born: 6.4% (2006-2010 5-year est.); Ancestry (includes multiple ancestries): 33.7% German, 24.1% Irish, 17.3% Italian, 9.9% Polish, 7.9% English (2006-2010 5-year est.).

Economy: Employment by occupation: 13.4% management, 6.7% professional, 7.2% services, 20.8% sales, 7.3% farming, 5.1% construction, 4.5% production (2006-2010 5-year est.).

Income: Per capita income: $26,438 (2006-2010 5-year est.); Median household income: $55,511 (2006-2010 5-year est.); Average household income: $68,608 (2006-2010 5-year est.); Percent of households with income of $100,000 or more: 19.5% (2006-2010 5-year est.); Poverty rate: 7.8% (2006-2010 5-year est.).

Education: Percent of population age 25 and over with: High school diploma (including GED) or higher: 96.8% (2006-2010 5-year est.); Bachelor's degree or higher: 34.4% (2006-2010 5-year est.); Master's degree or higher: 9.6% (2006-2010 5-year est.).

Housing: Homeownership rate: 53.9% (2010); Median home value: $152,400 (2006-2010 5-year est.); Median contract rent: $662 per month (2006-2010 5-year est.); Median year structure built: 1969 (2006-2010 5-year est.).

Transportation: Commute to work: 84.8% car, 2.8% public transportation, 8.0% walk, 2.3% work from home (2006-2010 5-year est.); Travel time to work: 39.6% less than 15 minutes, 31.8% 15 to 30 minutes, 14.2% 30 to 45 minutes, 7.4% 45 to 60 minutes, 7.0% 60 minutes or more (2006-2010 5-year est.).

Additional Information Contacts

Pittsburgh Airport Area Chamber of Commerce . . . . (412) 264-6270
    http://www.paacc.com

CASTLE SHANNON (borough). Covers a land area of 1.597 square miles and a water area of 0 square miles. Located at 40.37° N. Lat; 80.02° W. Long. Elevation is 1,027 feet.

History: Incorporated 1919.

Population: 9,135 (1990); 8,556 (2000); 8,316 (2010); Density: 5,207.8 persons per square mile (2010); Race: 93.9% White, 2.0% Black, 2.4% Asian, 0.0% American Indian/Alaska Native, 0.0% Native Hawaiian/Other Pacific Islander, 1.7% Other, 1.1% Hispanic of any race (2010); Average household size: 2.13 (2010); Median age: 42.2 (2010); Males per 100 females: 95.4 (2010); Marriage status: 37.8% never married, 47.4% now married, 7.0% widowed, 7.9% divorced (2006-2010 5-year est.); Foreign born: 5.4% (2006-2010 5-year est.); Ancestry (includes multiple ancestries): 39.9% German, 25.5% Irish, 16.1% Italian, 13.0% Polish, 9.1% English (2006-2010 5-year est.).

Economy: Single-family building permits issued: 0 (2011); Multi-family building permits issued: 0 (2011); Employment by occupation: 12.5% management, 3.2% professional, 13.4% services, 18.9% sales, 3.2% farming, 5.4% construction, 3.2% production (2006-2010 5-year est.).

Income: Per capita income: $25,883 (2006-2010 5-year est.); Median household income: $44,795 (2006-2010 5-year est.); Average household income: $54,927 (2006-2010 5-year est.); Percent of households with income of $100,000 or more: 11.4% (2006-2010 5-year est.); Poverty rate: 9.5% (2006-2010 5-year est.).

Taxes: Total city taxes per capita: $422 (2009); City property taxes per capita: $297 (2009).

Education: Percent of population age 25 and over with: High school diploma (including GED) or higher: 91.9% (2006-2010 5-year est.);

Bachelor's degree or higher: 24.5% (2006-2010 5-year est.); Master's degree or higher: 6.0% (2006-2010 5-year est.).

Housing: Homeownership rate: 60.6% (2010); Median home value: $99,900 (2006-2010 5-year est.); Median contract rent: $599 per month (2006-2010 5-year est.); Median year structure built: 1956 (2006-2010 5-year est.).

Safety: Violent crime rate: 15.6 per 10,000 population; Property crime rate: 105.5 per 10,000 population (2011).

Transportation: Commute to work: 82.4% car, 9.8% public transportation, 4.2% walk, 2.4% work from home (2006-2010 5-year est.); Travel time to work: 18.3% less than 15 minutes, 41.3% 15 to 30 minutes, 23.8% 30 to 45 minutes, 9.9% 45 to 60 minutes, 6.6% 60 minutes or more (2006-2010 5-year est.).

Additional Information Contacts

Borough of Castle Shannon . . . . (412) 885-9200
    http://borough.castle-shannon.pa.us

Brentwood Baldwin Whitehall Chamber of Commerce . . . . (412) 884-1233
    http://www.bbwchamber.com

CHALFANT (borough). Covers a land area of 0.159 square miles and a water area of 0 square miles. Located at 40.41° N. Lat; 79.84° W. Long. Elevation is 1,043 feet.

Population: 959 (1990); 870 (2000); 800 (2010); Density: 5,039.6 persons per square mile (2010); Race: 85.9% White, 8.1% Black, 0.5% Asian, 0.8% American Indian/Alaska Native, 0.0% Native Hawaiian/Other Pacific Islander, 4.7% Other, 0.4% Hispanic of any race (2010); Average household size: 1.98 (2010); Median age: 43.9 (2010); Males per 100 females: 101.0 (2010); Marriage status: 36.6% never married, 51.4% now married, 5.2% widowed, 6.9% divorced (2006-2010 5-year est.); Foreign born: 0.3% (2006-2010 5-year est.); Ancestry (includes multiple ancestries): 32.6% Irish, 22.1% Italian, 21.9% German, 9.5% Polish, 8.3% Slovak (2006-2010 5-year est.).

Economy: Single-family building permits issued: 0 (2011); Multi-family building permits issued: 0 (2011); Employment by occupation: 8.3% management, 5.6% professional, 8.8% services, 15.5% sales, 6.7% farming, 6.5% construction, 7.7% production (2006-2010 5-year est.).

Income: Per capita income: $25,660 (2006-2010 5-year est.); Median household income: $51,331 (2006-2010 5-year est.); Average household income: $56,744 (2006-2010 5-year est.); Percent of households with income of $100,000 or more: 12.8% (2006-2010 5-year est.); Poverty rate: 8.0% (2006-2010 5-year est.).

Education: Percent of population age 25 and over with: High school diploma (including GED) or higher: 95.2% (2006-2010 5-year est.); Bachelor's degree or higher: 31.1% (2006-2010 5-year est.); Master's degree or higher: 6.6% (2006-2010 5-year est.).

Housing: Homeownership rate: 68.8% (2010); Median home value: $80,600 (2006-2010 5-year est.); Median contract rent: $478 per month (2006-2010 5-year est.); Median year structure built: 1946 (2006-2010 5-year est.).

Transportation: Commute to work: 89.6% car, 5.7% public transportation, 0.0% walk, 3.8% work from home (2006-2010 5-year est.); Travel time to work: 19.7% less than 15 minutes, 47.4% 15 to 30 minutes, 16.5% 30 to 45 minutes, 15.6% 45 to 60 minutes, 0.8% 60 minutes or more (2006-2010 5-year est.)

CHESWICK (borough). Covers a land area of 0.463 square miles and a water area of 0.086 square miles. Located at 40.54° N. Lat; 79.80° W. Long. Elevation is 771 feet.

History: Incorporated 1902.

Population: 1,971 (1990); 1,899 (2000); 1,746 (2010); Density: 3,773.5 persons per square mile (2010); Race: 98.8% White, 0.2% Black, 0.4% Asian, 0.1% American Indian/Alaska Native, 0.0% Native Hawaiian/Other Pacific Islander, 0.5% Other, 0.6% Hispanic of any race (2010); Average household size: 2.12 (2010); Median age: 50.5 (2010); Males per 100 females: 88.1 (2010); Marriage status: 20.1% never married, 58.6% now married, 11.8% widowed, 9.5% divorced (2006-2010 5-year est.); Foreign born: 1.5% (2006-2010 5-year est.); Ancestry (includes multiple ancestries): 32.4% German, 20.0% Irish, 17.5% Italian, 15.6% Polish, 9.4% English (2006-2010 5-year est.).

Economy: Single-family building permits issued: 0 (2011); Multi-family building permits issued: 0 (2011); Employment by occupation: 5.1% management, 4.3% professional, 6.2% services, 18.6% sales, 5.7% farming, 8.7% construction, 6.2% production (2006-2010 5-year est.).

Income: Per capita income: $30,602 (2006-2010 5-year est.); Median household income: $56,563 (2006-2010 5-year est.); Average household

income: $63,461 (2006-2010 5-year est.); Percent of households with income of $100,000 or more: 13.1% (2006-2010 5-year est.); Poverty rate: 0.4% (2006-2010 5-year est.).

Education: Percent of population age 25 and over with: High school diploma (including GED) or higher: 93.3% (2006-2010 5-year est.); Bachelor's degree or higher: 27.3% (2006-2010 5-year est.); Master's degree or higher: 8.1% (2006-2010 5-year est.).

School District(s)

Allegheny Valley SD (KG-12)

   2010-11 Enrollment: 1,075 . . . . (724) 274-5300

Housing: Homeownership rate: 85.5% (2010); Median home value: $102,100 (2006-2010 5-year est.); Median contract rent: $554 per month (2006-2010 5-year est.); Median year structure built: 1952 (2006-2010 5-year est.).

Safety: Violent crime rate: 0.0 per 10,000 population; Property crime rate: 45.7 per 10,000 population (2011).

Transportation: Commute to work: 85.6% car, 8.2% public transportation, 5.5% walk, 0.7% work from home (2006-2010 5-year est.); Travel time to work: 27.9% less than 15 minutes, 38.5% 15 to 30 minutes, 23.8% 30 to 45 minutes, 7.0% 45 to 60 minutes, 2.9% 60 minutes or more (2006-2010 5-year est.)

Additional Information Contacts

Allegheny Valley Chamber of Commerce . . . . (724) 224-3400

http://alleghenyvalleychamber.com/community/community-profiles/blawnox

---

CHURCHILL (borough). Covers a land area of 2.187 square miles and a water area of 0 square miles. Located at 40.44° N. Lat; 79.84° W. Long. Elevation is 1,083 feet.

Population: 3,883 (1990); 3,566 (2000); 3,011 (2010); Density: 1,376.6 persons per square mile (2010); Race: 81.9% White, 13.8% Black, 2.7% Asian, 0.0% American Indian/Alaska Native, 0.0% Native Hawaiian/Other Pacific Islander, 1.6% Other, 1.8% Hispanic of any race (2010); Average household size: 2.21 (2010); Median age: 52.7 (2010); Males per 100 females: 90.1 (2010); Marriage status: 21.4% never married, 64.5% now married, 5.8% widowed, 8.3% divorced (2006-2010 5-year est.); Foreign born: 5.3% (2006-2010 5-year est.); Ancestry (includes multiple ancestries): 18.2% German, 14.5% Italian, 13.1% English, 12.6% Polish, 12.2% Irish (2006-2010 5-year est.).

Economy: Single-family building permits issued: 0 (2011); Multi-family building permits issued: 0 (2011); Employment by occupation: 21.9% management, 4.7% professional, 4.3% services, 16.1% sales, 2.4% farming, 6.3% construction, 4.1% production (2006-2010 5-year est.).

Income: Per capita income: $39,271 (2006-2010 5-year est.); Median household income: $79,100 (2006-2010 5-year est.); Average household income: $90,386 (2006-2010 5-year est.); Percent of households with income of $100,000 or more: 30.5% (2006-2010 5-year est.); Poverty rate: 3.0% (2006-2010 5-year est.).

Education: Percent of population age 25 and over with: High school diploma (including GED) or higher: 96.3% (2006-2010 5-year est.); Bachelor's degree or higher: 54.2% (2006-2010 5-year est.); Master's degree or higher: 23.6% (2006-2010 5-year est.).

Housing: Homeownership rate: 96.1% (2010); Median home value: $158,100 (2006-2010 5-year est.); Median contract rent: $813 per month (2006-2010 5-year est.); Median year structure built: 1958 (2006-2010 5-year est.).

Safety: Violent crime rate: 82.8 per 10,000 population; Property crime rate: 92.7 per 10,000 population (2011).

Transportation: Commute to work: 86.7% car, 5.6% public transportation, 0.0% walk, 6.4% work from home (2006-2010 5-year est.); Travel time to work: 21.0% less than 15 minutes, 29.7% 15 to 30 minutes, 30.4% 30 to 45 minutes, 15.4% 45 to 60 minutes, 3.5% 60 minutes or more (2006-2010 5-year est.)

Additional Information Contacts

Borough of Churchill . . . . (412) 241-7113
   http://churchillborough.com
Penn Hills Chamber of Commerce . . . . (412) 795-8741
   http://www.pennhillschamber.org

CLAIRTON (city). Covers a land area of 2.788 square miles and a water area of 0.233 square miles. Located at 40.30° N. Lat; 79.89° W. Long. Elevation is 906 feet.

History: Settled 1770, incorporated 1903.

Population: 9,656 (1990); 8,491 (2000); 6,796 (2010); Density: 2,437.4 persons per square mile (2010); Race: 58.5% White, 37.6% Black, 0.3%

Asian, 0.1% American Indian/Alaska Native, 0.0% Native Hawaiian/Other Pacific Islander, 3.5% Other, 1.6% Hispanic of any race (2010); Average household size: 2.16 (2010); Median age: 42.6 (2010); Males per 100 females: 83.5 (2010); Marriage status: 39.8% never married, 36.2% now married, 11.9% widowed, 12.1% divorced (2006-2010 5-year est.); Foreign born: 1.7% (2006-2010 5-year est.); Ancestry (includes multiple ancestries): 19.9% German, 16.6% Irish, 13.9% Italian, 9.4% English, 8.2% Slovak (2006-2010 5-year est.).

Economy: Single-family building permits issued: 0 (2011); Multi-family building permits issued: 0 (2011); Employment by occupation: 7.5% management, 0.8% professional, 15.7% services, 18.3% sales, 3.5% farming, 4.4% construction, 3.3% production (2006-2010 5-year est.).

Income: Per capita income: $20,293 (2006-2010 5-year est.); Median household income: $28,816 (2006-2010 5-year est.); Average household income: $41,538 (2006-2010 5-year est.); Percent of households with income of $100,000 or more: 8.0% (2006-2010 5-year est.); Poverty rate: 23.7% (2006-2010 5-year est.).

Education: Percent of population age 25 and over with: High school diploma (including GED) or higher: 87.5% (2006-2010 5-year est.); Bachelor's degree or higher: 14.6% (2006-2010 5-year est.); Master's degree or higher: 3.3% (2006-2010 5-year est.).

School District(s)

Clairton City SD (KG-12)

   2010-11 Enrollment: 766. . . . . (412) 233-7090

Housing: Homeownership rate: 60.1% (2010); Median home value: $47,600 (2006-2010 5-year est.); Median contract rent: $435 per month (2006-2010 5-year est.); Median year structure built: 1943 (2006-2010 5-year est.).

Transportation: Commute to work: 82.2% car, 8.3% public transportation, 2.7% walk, 5.3% work from home (2006-2010 5-year est.); Travel time to work: 25.5% less than 15 minutes, 29.5% 15 to 30 minutes, 17.4% 30 to 45 minutes, 14.0% 45 to 60 minutes, 13.7% 60 minutes or more (2006-2010 5-year est.)

Additional Information Contacts

Brentwood Baldwin Whitehall Chamber of Commerce . . . . (412) 884-1233
   http://www.bbwchamber.com
City of Clairton. . . . . (412) 233-8113
   http://www.cityofclairton.com

CLINTON (CDP). Covers a land area of 0.824 square miles and a water area of 0.006 square miles. Located at 40.50° N. Lat; 80.29° W. Long. Elevation is 1,214 feet.

Population: n/a (1990); n/a (2000); 434 (2010); Density: 526.4 persons per square mile (2010); Race: 99.3% White, 0.5% Black, 0.0% Asian, 0.2% American Indian/Alaska Native, 0.0% Native Hawaiian/Other Pacific Islander, 0.0% Other, 0.7% Hispanic of any race (2010); Average household size: 2.15 (2010); Median age: 47.6 (2010); Males per 100 females: 101.9 (2010); Marriage status: 14.9% never married, 62.0% now married, 14.1% widowed, 9.1% divorced (2006-2010 5-year est.); Foreign born: 6.7% (2006-2010 5-year est.); Ancestry (includes multiple ancestries): 43.6% German, 24.2% Italian, 15.1% Scotch-Irish, 11.9% English, 10.2% Russian (2006-2010 5-year est.).

Economy: Employment by occupation: 0.0% management, 6.9% professional, 11.7% services, 23.4% sales, 0.0% farming, 25.5% construction, 5.2% production (2006-2010 5-year est.).

Income: Per capita income: $27,036 (2006-2010 5-year est.); Median household income: $50,556 (2006-2010 5-year est.); Average household income: $63,313 (2006-2010 5-year est.); Percent of households with income of $100,000 or more: 29.9% (2006-2010 5-year est.); Poverty rate: 0.0% (2006-2010 5-year est.).

Education: Percent of population age 25 and over with: High school diploma (including GED) or higher: 74.5% (2006-2010 5-year est.); Bachelor's degree or higher: 17.8% (2006-2010 5-year est.); Master's degree or higher: 9.3% (2006-2010 5-year est.).

Housing: Homeownership rate: 75.7% (2010); Median home value: $81,300 (2006-2010 5-year est.); Median contract rent: n/a per month (2006-2010 5-year est.); Median year structure built: 1957 (2006-2010 5-year est.).

Transportation: Commute to work: 100.0% car, 0.0% public transportation, 0.0% walk, 0.0% work from home (2006-2010 5-year est.); Travel time to work: 28.6% less than 15 minutes, 51.5% 15 to 30 minutes, 0.0% 30 to 45 minutes, 12.6% 45 to 60 minutes, 7.4% 60 minutes or more (2006-2010 5-year est.)

COLLIER (township). Covers a land area of 13.879 square miles and a water area of 0.049 square miles. Located at 40.40° N. Lat; 80.13° W. Long.

Population: 4,834 (1990); 5,265 (2000); 7,080 (2010); Density: 510.1 persons per square mile (2010); Race: 94.3% White, 1.3% Black, 3.3% Asian, 0.0% American Indian/Alaska Native, 0.1% Native Hawaiian/Other Pacific Islander, 1.0% Other, 1.0% Hispanic of any race (2010); Average household size: 2.28 (2010); Median age: 47.0 (2010); Males per 100 females: 95.4 (2010); Marriage status: 26.8% never married, 57.9% now married, 8.8% widowed, 6.5% divorced (2006-2010 5-year est.); Foreign born: 3.7% (2006-2010 5-year est.); Ancestry (includes multiple ancestries): 33.2% German, 27.9% Irish, 21.8% Italian, 11.8% Polish, 9.2% English (2006-2010 5-year est.).

Economy: Single-family building permits issued: 83 (2011); Multi-family building permits issued: 0 (2011); Employment by occupation: 15.2% management, 2.2% professional, 8.3% services, 18.4% sales, 3.9% farming, 9.1% construction, 5.0% production (2006-2010 5-year est.).

Income: Per capita income: $43,754 (2006-2010 5-year est.); Median household income: $62,487 (2006-2010 5-year est.); Average household income: $99,095 (2006-2010 5-year est.); Percent of households with income of $100,000 or more: 28.6% (2006-2010 5-year est.); Poverty rate: 5.0% (2006-2010 5-year est.).

Education: Percent of population age 25 and over with: High school diploma (including GED) or higher: 94.9% (2006-2010 5-year est.); Bachelor's degree or higher: 32.7% (2006-2010 5-year est.); Master's degree or higher: 12.1% (2006-2010 5-year est.).

Housing: Homeownership rate: 81.8% (2010); Median home value: $155,600 (2006-2010 5-year est.); Median contract rent: $784 per month (2006-2010 5-year est.); Median year structure built: 1984 (2006-2010 5-year est.).

Safety: Violent crime rate: 12.7 per 10,000 population; Property crime rate: 264.7 per 10,000 population (2011).

Transportation: Commute to work: 86.4% car, 4.0% public transportation, 2.3% walk, 7.2% work from home (2006-2010 5-year est.); Travel time to work: 20.2% less than 15 minutes, 49.9% 15 to 30 minutes, 20.0% 30 to 45 minutes, 6.1% 45 to 60 minutes, 3.9% 60 minutes or more (2006-2010 5-year est.)

Additional Information Contacts

Collier Township . . . . (412) 276-5277
    http://www.colliertownship.net
South West Communities Chamber of Commerce . . . . (412) 221-4100
    http://www.swccoc.org

CORAOPOLIS (borough). Covers a land area of 1.328 square miles and a water area of 0.133 square miles. Located at 40.51° N. Lat; 80.16° W. Long. Elevation is 719 feet.

History: Robert Morris College to West. Settled c.1760, incorporated 1886.

Population: 6,747 (1990); 6,131 (2000); 5,677 (2010); Density: 4,273.3 persons per square mile (2010); Race: 83.1% White, 12.0% Black, 0.4% Asian, 0.2% American Indian/Alaska Native, 0.1% Native Hawaiian/Other Pacific Islander, 4.2% Other, 1.8% Hispanic of any race (2010); Average household size: 2.05 (2010); Median age: 42.2 (2010); Males per 100 females: 90.8 (2010); Marriage status: 36.0% never married, 36.6% now married, 10.5% widowed, 16.9% divorced (2006-2010 5-year est.); Foreign born: 4.7% (2006-2010 5-year est.); Ancestry (includes multiple ancestries): 26.9% German, 21.7% Irish, 19.7% Italian, 6.8% Polish, 5.2% English (2006-2010 5-year est.).

Economy: Single-family building permits issued: 0 (2011); Multi-family building permits issued: 0 (2011); Employment by occupation: 10.3% management, 5.3% professional, 18.8% services, 20.6% sales, 4.3% farming, 4.7% construction, 5.4% production (2006-2010 5-year est.).

Income: Per capita income: $21,032 (2006-2010 5-year est.); Median household income: $32,087 (2006-2010 5-year est.); Average household income: $43,637 (2006-2010 5-year est.); Percent of households with income of $100,000 or more: 6.5% (2006-2010 5-year est.); Poverty rate: 20.6% (2006-2010 5-year est.).

Education: Percent of population age 25 and over with: High school diploma (including GED) or higher: 84.3% (2006-2010 5-year est.); Bachelor's degree or higher: 14.7% (2006-2010 5-year est.); Master's degree or higher: 4.0% (2006-2010 5-year est.).

School District(s)

Cornell SD (KG-12)
    2010-11 Enrollment: 672 . . . . (412) 264-5010

Montour SD (KG-12)
    2010-11 Enrollment: 2,946 . . . . (412) 490-6500

Housing: Homeownership rate: 52.0% (2010); Median home value: $81,900 (2006-2010 5-year est.); Median contract rent: $431 per month (2006-2010 5-year est.); Median year structure built: before 1940 (2006-2010 5-year est.).

Safety: Violent crime rate: 80.8 per 10,000 population; Property crime rate: 193.2 per 10,000 population (2011).

Newspapers: The Allegheny Times (Regional news; Circulation 10,000); Pittsburgh Post-Gazette - West Bureau (Community news)

Transportation: Commute to work: 81.8% car, 5.7% public transportation, 8.2% walk, 3.0% work from home (2006-2010 5-year est.); Travel time to work: 30.9% less than 15 minutes, 42.0% 15 to 30 minutes, 16.4% 30 to 45 minutes, 3.9% 45 to 60 minutes, 6.8% 60 minutes or more (2006-2010 5-year est.)

Additional Information Contacts

Borough of Coraopolis . . . . (412) 264-3002
    http://www.coraopolispa.com
Pittsburgh Airport Area Chamber of Commerce . . . . (412) 264-6270
    http://www.paacc.com

COULTERS (unincorporated postal area)

Zip Code: 15028

Covers a land area of 0.199 square miles and a water area of 0.090 square miles. Located at 40.31° N. Lat; 79.78° W. Long. Population: 142 (2010); Density: 710.7 persons per square mile (2010); Race: 100.0% White, 0.0% Black, 0.0% Asian, 0.0% American Indian/Alaska Native, 0.0% Native Hawaiian/Other Pacific Islander, 0.0% Other, 0.7% Hispanic of any race (2010); Average household size: 2.25 (2010); Median age: 48.5 (2010); Males per 100 females: 91.9 (2010); Homeownership rate: 82.6% (2010)

CRAFTON (borough). Covers a land area of 1.143 square miles and a water area of 0 square miles. Located at 40.43° N. Lat; 80.07° W. Long. Elevation is 876 feet.

History: Incorporated 1894.

Population: 7,188 (1990); 6,706 (2000); 5,951 (2010); Density: 5,206.9 persons per square mile (2010); Race: 91.7% White, 4.6% Black, 0.8% Asian, 0.1% American Indian/Alaska Native, 0.0% Native Hawaiian/Other Pacific Islander, 2.8% Other, 1.4% Hispanic of any race (2010); Average household size: 2.13 (2010); Median age: 40.7 (2010); Males per 100 females: 90.5 (2010); Marriage status: 35.3% never married, 47.8% now married, 7.5% widowed, 9.4% divorced (2006-2010 5-year est.); Foreign born: 1.6% (2006-2010 5-year est.); Ancestry (includes multiple ancestries): 39.3% German, 30.9% Irish, 23.0% Italian, 13.0% Polish, 10.5% English (2006-2010 5-year est.).

Economy: Single-family building permits issued: 1 (2011); Multi-family building permits issued: 0 (2011); Employment by occupation: 11.9% management, 6.5% professional, 9.2% services, 17.5% sales, 6.6% farming, 4.5% construction, 3.5% production (2006-2010 5-year est.).

Income: Per capita income: $28,092 (2006-2010 5-year est.); Median household income: $45,124 (2006-2010 5-year est.); Average household income: $59,081 (2006-2010 5-year est.); Percent of households with income of $100,000 or more: 17.1% (2006-2010 5-year est.); Poverty rate: 7.1% (2006-2010 5-year est.).

Education: Percent of population age 25 and over with: High school diploma (including GED) or higher: 93.1% (2006-2010 5-year est.); Bachelor's degree or higher: 31.2% (2006-2010 5-year est.); Master's degree or higher: 8.4% (2006-2010 5-year est.).

Housing: Homeownership rate: 51.7% (2010); Median home value: $111,400 (2006-2010 5-year est.); Median contract rent: $517 per month (2006-2010 5-year est.); Median year structure built: before 1940 (2006-2010 5-year est.).

Safety: Violent crime rate: 42.0 per 10,000 population; Property crime rate: 228.8 per 10,000 population (2011).

Transportation: Commute to work: 77.5% car, 13.8% public transportation, 1.9% walk, 5.3% work from home (2006-2010 5-year est.); Travel time to work: 13.6% less than 15 minutes, 47.6% 15 to 30 minutes, 28.6% 30 to 45 minutes, 6.6% 45 to 60 minutes, 3.6% 60 minutes or more (2006-2010 5-year est.)

Additional Information Contacts

Borough of Crafton . . . . (412) 921-0752
    http://www.crafton.org
South Hills Chamber of Commerce . . . . (412) 306-8090
    http://www.shchamber.org

CREIGHTON (unincorporated postal area)
Zip Code: 15030

Covers a land area of 1.879 square miles and a water area of 0.252 square miles. Located at 40.59° N. Lat; 79.78° W. Long. Elevation is 863 feet. Population: 1,128 (2010); Density: 600.1 persons per square mile (2010); Race: 95.2% White, 2.0% Black, 0.5% Asian, 0.0% American Indian/Alaska Native, 0.0% Native Hawaiian/Other Pacific Islander, 2.3% Other, 0.1% Hispanic of any race (2010); Average household size: 2.11 (2010); Median age: 43.1 (2010); Males per 100 females: 95.5 (2010); Homeownership rate: 56.8% (2010)

CRESCENT (township).
Covers a land area of 2.097 square miles and a water area of 0.211 square miles. Located at 40.56° N. Lat; 80.23° W. Long.

Population: 2,490 (1990); 2,314 (2000); 2,640 (2010); Density: 1,258.7 persons per square mile (2010); Race: 94.8% White, 2.2% Black, 1.4% Asian, 0.2% American Indian/Alaska Native, 0.0% Native Hawaiian/Other Pacific Islander, 1.4% Other, 1.4% Hispanic of any race (2010); Average household size: 2.47 (2010); Median age: 42.9 (2010); Males per 100 females: 95.6 (2010); Marriage status: 28.5% never married, 54.3% now married, 10.3% widowed, 7.0% divorced (2006-2010 5-year est.); Foreign born: 2.1% (2006-2010 5-year est.); Ancestry (includes multiple ancestries): 37.2% German, 17.3% Irish, 17.1% Italian, 13.4% English, 7.0% Slovak (2006-2010 5-year est.).

Economy: Single-family building permits issued: 2 (2011); Multi-family building permits issued: 0 (2011); Employment by occupation: 13.9% management, 4.4% professional, 11.6% services, 17.5% sales, 3.5% farming, 7.3% construction, 5.6% production (2006-2010 5-year est.).

Income: Per capita income: $30,596 (2006-2010 5-year est.); Median household income: $56,133 (2006-2010 5-year est.); Average household income: $74,044 (2006-2010 5-year est.); Percent of households with income of $100,000 or more: 21.1% (2006-2010 5-year est.); Poverty rate: 10.0% (2006-2010 5-year est.).

Education: Percent of population age 25 and over with: High school diploma (including GED) or higher: 92.2% (2006-2010 5-year est.); Bachelor's degree or higher: 29.1% (2006-2010 5-year est.); Master's degree or higher: 11.0% (2006-2010 5-year est.).

Housing: Homeownership rate: 83.6% (2010); Median home value: $129,100 (2006-2010 5-year est.); Median contract rent: $574 per month (2006-2010 5-year est.); Median year structure built: 1962 (2006-2010 5-year est.).

Safety: Violent crime rate: 37.8 per 10,000 population; Property crime rate: 166.2 per 10,000 population (2011).

Transportation: Commute to work: 91.2% car, 2.0% public transportation, 1.5% walk, 4.7% work from home (2006-2010 5-year est.); Travel time to work: 25.3% less than 15 minutes, 38.4% 15 to 30 minutes, 20.4% 30 to 45 minutes, 6.3% 45 to 60 minutes, 9.5% 60 minutes or more (2006-2010 5-year est.)

Additional Information Contacts
Crescent Township . . . . (724) 457-8100
  http://www.crescenttownship.com
Pittsburgh Airport Area Chamber of Commerce . . . . (412) 264-6270
  http://www.paacc.com

CUDDY (unincorporated postal area)
Zip Code: 15031

Covers a land area of 0.466 square miles and a water area of 0 square miles. Located at 40.34° N. Lat; 80.16° W. Long. Population: 513 (2010); Density: 1,100.7 persons per square mile (2010); Race: 92.6% White, 3.1% Black, 0.4% Asian, 0.0% American Indian/Alaska Native, 0.4% Native Hawaiian/Other Pacific Islander, 3.5% Other, 2.5% Hispanic of any race (2010); Average household size: 2.30 (2010); Median age: 38.3 (2010); Males per 100 females: 107.7 (2010); Homeownership rate: 60.1% (2010)

CURTISVILLE (CDP).
Covers a land area of 1.424 square miles and a water area of 0 square miles. Located at 40.65° N. Lat; 79.85° W. Long. Elevation is 1,070 feet.

Population: 1,285 (1990); 1,173 (2000); 1,064 (2010); Density: 747.4 persons per square mile (2010); Race: 97.9% White, 0.4% Black, 0.2% Asian, 0.6% American Indian/Alaska Native, 0.0% Native Hawaiian/Other Pacific Islander, 0.9% Other, 0.7% Hispanic of any race (2010); Average household size: 2.24 (2010); Median age: 42.8 (2010); Males per 100 females: 98.1 (2010); Marriage status: 39.2% never married, 33.9% now married, 5.4% widowed, 21.4% divorced (2006-2010 5-year est.); Foreign

born: 0.0% (2006-2010 5-year est.); Ancestry (includes multiple ancestries): 33.7% German, 22.4% Irish, 19.8% Italian, 19.5% Polish, 6.3% Slovak (2006-2010 5-year est.).

Economy: Employment by occupation: 3.4% management, 6.9% professional, 20.8% services, 8.7% sales, 3.5% farming, 12.2% construction, 8.9% production (2006-2010 5-year est.).

Income: Per capita income: $21,485 (2006-2010 5-year est.); Median household income: $34,089 (2006-2010 5-year est.); Average household income: $44,360 (2006-2010 5-year est.); Percent of households with income of $100,000 or more: 12.7% (2006-2010 5-year est.); Poverty rate: 7.3% (2006-2010 5-year est.).

Education: Percent of population age 25 and over with: High school diploma (including GED) or higher: 92.3% (2006-2010 5-year est.); Bachelor's degree or higher: 15.8% (2006-2010 5-year est.); Master's degree or higher: 2.5% (2006-2010 5-year est.).

Housing: Homeownership rate: 77.4% (2010); Median home value: $74,500 (2006-2010 5-year est.); Median contract rent: $393 per month (2006-2010 5-year est.); Median year structure built: before 1940 (2006-2010 5-year est.).

Transportation: Commute to work: 95.9% car, 0.0% public transportation, 4.1% walk, 0.0% work from home (2006-2010 5-year est.); Travel time to work: 24.8% less than 15 minutes, 37.5% 15 to 30 minutes, 25.9% 30 to 45 minutes, 9.4% 45 to 60 minutes, 2.4% 60 minutes or more (2006-2010 5-year est.)

Additional Information Contacts
Allegheny Valley Chamber of Commerce . . . . (724) 224-3400
  http://alleghenyvalleychamber.com

DORMONT (borough).
Covers a land area of 0.760 square miles and a water area of 0 square miles. Located at 40.39° N. Lat; 80.04° W. Long. Elevation is 1,191 feet.

History: Settled c.1790, incorporated 1909.

Population: 9,774 (1990); 9,305 (2000); 8,593 (2010); Density: 11,301.6 persons per square mile (2010); Race: 94.2% White, 2.1% Black, 1.5% Asian, 0.1% American Indian/Alaska Native, 0.0% Native Hawaiian/Other Pacific Islander, 2.1% Other, 2.5% Hispanic of any race (2010); Average household size: 2.12 (2010); Median age: 36.4 (2010); Males per 100 females: 95.9 (2010); Marriage status: 38.7% never married, 44.9% now married, 8.8% widowed, 7.6% divorced (2006-2010 5-year est.); Foreign born: 4.5% (2006-2010 5-year est.); Ancestry (includes multiple ancestries): 33.9% German, 26.8% Irish, 21.9% Italian, 10.1% Polish, 8.0% English (2006-2010 5-year est.).

Economy: Single-family building permits issued: 0 (2011); Multi-family building permits issued: 0 (2011); Employment by occupation: 14.4% management, 4.0% professional, 8.8% services, 18.5% sales, 4.2% farming, 7.6% construction, 3.5% production (2006-2010 5-year est.).

Income: Per capita income: $26,968 (2006-2010 5-year est.); Median household income: $46,780 (2006-2010 5-year est.); Average household income: $56,011 (2006-2010 5-year est.); Percent of households with income of $100,000 or more: 9.9% (2006-2010 5-year est.); Poverty rate: 8.5% (2006-2010 5-year est.).

Taxes: Total city taxes per capita: $568 (2009); City property taxes per capita: $440 (2009).

Education: Percent of population age 25 and over with: High school diploma (including GED) or higher: 92.4% (2006-2010 5-year est.); Bachelor's degree or higher: 33.7% (2006-2010 5-year est.); Master's degree or higher: 9.2% (2006-2010 5-year est.).

Housing: Homeownership rate: 55.5% (2010); Median home value: $101,100 (2006-2010 5-year est.); Median contract rent: $574 per month (2006-2010 5-year est.); Median year structure built: before 1940 (2006-2010 5-year est.).

Safety: Violent crime rate: 38.3 per 10,000 population; Property crime rate: 100.9 per 10,000 population (2011).

Transportation: Commute to work: 70.7% car, 19.8% public transportation, 7.2% walk, 1.7% work from home (2006-2010 5-year est.); Travel time to work: 19.4% less than 15 minutes, 41.0% 15 to 30 minutes, 25.8% 30 to 45 minutes, 8.6% 45 to 60 minutes, 5.3% 60 minutes or more (2006-2010 5-year est.)

Additional Information Contacts
Borough of Dormont . . . . (412) 561-8900
  http://boro.dormont.pa.us
South Hills Chamber of Commerce . . . . (412) 306-8090
  http://www.shchamber.org

DRAVOSBURG (borough). Covers a land area of 0.968 square miles and a water area of 0.095 square miles. Located at 40.35° N. Lat; 79.89° W. Long. Elevation is 722 feet.

History: Incorporated 1903.

Population: 2,377 (1990); 2,015 (2000); 1,792 (2010); Density: 1,850.9 persons per square mile (2010); Race: 94.4% White, 3.0% Black, 0.3% Asian, 0.7% American Indian/Alaska Native, 0.0% Native Hawaiian/Other Pacific Islander, 1.6% Other, 1.1% Hispanic of any race (2010); Average household size: 2.01 (2010); Median age: 48.5 (2010); Males per 100 females: 91.9 (2010); Marriage status: 24.2% never married, 54.5% now married, 9.9% widowed, 11.4% divorced (2006-2010 5-year est.); Foreign born: 0.1% (2006-2010 5-year est.); Ancestry (includes multiple ancestries): 31.5% German, 25.2% Irish, 13.4% Italian, 11.3% Slovak, 8.3% English (2006-2010 5-year est.).

Economy: Single-family building permits issued: 0 (2011); Multi-family building permits issued: 0 (2011); Employment by occupation: 5.4% management, 2.0% professional, 13.3% services, 17.1% sales, 14.4% farming, 9.1% construction, 5.4% production (2006-2010 5-year est.).

Income: Per capita income: $22,701 (2006-2010 5-year est.); Median household income: $45,362 (2006-2010 5-year est.); Average household income: $48,084 (2006-2010 5-year est.); Percent of households with income of $100,000 or more: 7.1% (2006-2010 5-year est.); Poverty rate: 7.3% (2006-2010 5-year est.).

Education: Percent of population age 25 and over with: High school diploma (including GED) or higher: 89.4% (2006-2010 5-year est.); Bachelor's degree or higher: 16.8% (2006-2010 5-year est.); Master's degree or higher: 1.8% (2006-2010 5-year est.).

Housing: Homeownership rate: 60.6% (2010); Median home value: $73,600 (2006-2010 5-year est.); Median contract rent: $268 per month (2006-2010 5-year est.); Median year structure built: 1944 (2006-2010 5-year est.).

Transportation: Commute to work: 92.2% car, 3.6% public transportation, 0.8% walk, 3.0% work from home (2006-2010 5-year est.); Travel time to work: 19.2% less than 15 minutes, 35.6% 15 to 30 minutes, 25.7% 30 to 45 minutes, 16.3% 45 to 60 minutes, 3.2% 60 minutes or more (2006-2010 5-year est.).

Additional Information Contacts
Brentwood Baldwin Whitehall Chamber of Commerce . . . . (412) 884-1233
  http://www.bbwchamber.com

DUQUESNE (city). Covers a land area of 1.818 square miles and a water area of 0.218 square miles. Located at 40.37° N. Lat; 79.85° W. Long. Elevation is 909 feet.

History: Settled 1789, laid out by the Duquesne Steel Co. in 1885, incorporated as a city 1917.

Population: 8,525 (1990); 7,332 (2000); 5,565 (2010); Density: 3,061.0 persons per square mile (2010); Race: 39.6% White, 55.3% Black, 0.4% Asian, 0.2% American Indian/Alaska Native, 0.0% Native Hawaiian/Other Pacific Islander, 4.5% Other, 2.3% Hispanic of any race (2010); Average household size: 2.22 (2010); Median age: 36.4 (2010); Males per 100 females: 80.2 (2010); Marriage status: 39.8% never married, 33.2% now married, 14.6% widowed, 12.4% divorced (2006-2010 5-year est.); Foreign born: 1.5% (2006-2010 5-year est.); Ancestry (includes multiple ancestries): 11.9% African, 8.7% Irish, 8.7% Italian, 8.6% German, 8.1% Slovak (2006-2010 5-year est.).

Economy: Single-family building permits issued: 0 (2011); Multi-family building permits issued: 0 (2011); Employment by occupation: 2.8% management, 2.4% professional, 18.0% services, 21.6% sales, 6.7% farming, 10.7% construction, 2.3% production (2006-2010 5-year est.).

Income: Per capita income: $14,513 (2006-2010 5-year est.); Median household income: $21,909 (2006-2010 5-year est.); Average household income: $29,903 (2006-2010 5-year est.); Percent of households with income of $100,000 or more: 1.5% (2006-2010 5-year est.); Poverty rate: 34.3% (2006-2010 5-year est.).

Education: Percent of population age 25 and over with: High school diploma (including GED) or higher: 84.8% (2006-2010 5-year est.); Bachelor's degree or higher: 8.8% (2006-2010 5-year est.); Master's degree or higher: 3.1% (2006-2010 5-year est.).

School District(s)
Duquesne City SD (KG-12)
  2010-11 Enrollment: 411 . . . . (412) 466-5300

Housing: Homeownership rate: 45.0% (2010); Median home value: $38,000 (2006-2010 5-year est.); Median contract rent: $452 per month (2006-2010 5-year est.); Median year structure built: 1946 (2006-2010 5-year est.).

Safety: Violent crime rate: 155.8 per 10,000 population; Property crime rate: 566.0 per 10,000 population (2011).

Transportation: Commute to work: 66.6% car, 28.5% public transportation, 3.4% walk, 1.4% work from home (2006-2010 5-year est.); Travel time to work: 17.4% less than 15 minutes, 27.8% 15 to 30 minutes, 24.1% 30 to 45 minutes, 17.1% 45 to 60 minutes, 13.6% 60 minutes or more (2006-2010 5-year est.).

Additional Information Contacts
Brentwood Baldwin Whitehall Chamber of Commerce . . . . (412) 884-1233
  http://www.bbwchamber.com
City of Duquesne . . . . (412) 466-4746
  http://www.cityofduquesne.com

EAST DEER (township). Covers a land area of 2.273 square miles and a water area of 0.253 square miles. Located at 40.59° N. Lat; 79.78° W. Long.

Population: 1,558 (1990); 1,362 (2000); 1,500 (2010); Density: 659.9 persons per square mile (2010); Race: 95.6% White, 1.9% Black, 0.6% Asian, 0.0% American Indian/Alaska Native, 0.0% Native Hawaiian/Other Pacific Islander, 1.9% Other, 0.1% Hispanic of any race (2010); Average household size: 2.13 (2010); Median age: 42.8 (2010); Males per 100 females: 93.8 (2010); Marriage status: 29.6% never married, 50.3% now married, 9.0% widowed, 11.1% divorced (2006-2010 5-year est.); Foreign born: 1.9% (2006-2010 5-year est.); Ancestry (includes multiple ancestries): 30.4% German, 20.3% Polish, 20.0% Italian, 15.8% Irish, 12.5% Slovak (2006-2010 5-year est.).

Economy: Single-family building permits issued: 0 (2011); Multi-family building permits issued: 0 (2011); Employment by occupation: 8.1% management, 5.3% professional, 9.0% services, 17.3% sales, 2.5% farming, 6.9% construction, 3.5% production (2006-2010 5-year est.).

Income: Per capita income: $22,808 (2006-2010 5-year est.); Median household income: $43,092 (2006-2010 5-year est.); Average household income: $48,527 (2006-2010 5-year est.); Percent of households with income of $100,000 or more: 10.4% (2006-2010 5-year est.); Poverty rate: 17.1% (2006-2010 5-year est.).

Education: Percent of population age 25 and over with: High school diploma (including GED) or higher: 93.7% (2006-2010 5-year est.); Bachelor's degree or higher: 26.4% (2006-2010 5-year est.); Master's degree or higher: 3.5% (2006-2010 5-year est.).

Housing: Homeownership rate: 65.0% (2010); Median home value: $74,800 (2006-2010 5-year est.); Median contract rent: $464 per month (2006-2010 5-year est.); Median year structure built: 1942 (2006-2010 5-year est.).

Transportation: Commute to work: 91.6% car, 4.5% public transportation, 2.3% walk, 1.1% work from home (2006-2010 5-year est.); Travel time to work: 26.9% less than 15 minutes, 32.7% 15 to 30 minutes, 26.0% 30 to 45 minutes, 8.7% 45 to 60 minutes, 5.8% 60 minutes or more (2006-2010 5-year est.).

Additional Information Contacts
Allegheny Valley Chamber of Commerce . . . . (724) 224-3400
  http://alleghenyvalleychamber.com

EAST MCKEESPORT (borough). Covers a land area of 0.413 square miles and a water area of 0 square miles. Located at 40.38° N. Lat; 79.81° W. Long. Elevation is 1,142 feet.

Population: 2,678 (1990); 2,343 (2000); 2,126 (2010); Density: 5,147.9 persons per square mile (2010); Race: 89.1% White, 7.0% Black, 0.3% Asian, 0.0% American Indian/Alaska Native, 0.0% Native Hawaiian/Other Pacific Islander, 3.6% Other, 1.8% Hispanic of any race (2010); Average household size: 2.12 (2010); Median age: 43.0 (2010); Males per 100 females: 93.3 (2010); Marriage status: 30.8% never married, 46.4% now married, 12.8% widowed, 10.0% divorced (2006-2010 5-year est.); Foreign born: 0.9% (2006-2010 5-year est.); Ancestry (includes multiple ancestries): 29.5% Irish, 27.8% German, 14.1% Slovak, 13.6% Italian, 11.1% Polish (2006-2010 5-year est.).

Economy: Single-family building permits issued: 0 (2011); Multi-family building permits issued: 0 (2011); Employment by occupation: 8.0% management, 4.5% professional, 17.0% services, 19.4% sales, 3.4% farming, 12.1% construction, 2.6% production (2006-2010 5-year est.).

Income: Per capita income: $21,565 (2006-2010 5-year est.); Median household income: $41,271 (2006-2010 5-year est.); Average household income: $46,799 (2006-2010 5-year est.); Percent of households with income of $100,000 or more: 3.0% (2006-2010 5-year est.); Poverty rate: 9.0% (2006-2010 5-year est.).

Education: Percent of population age 25 and over with: High school diploma (including GED) or higher: 90.3% (2006-2010 5-year est.); Bachelor's degree or higher: 17.6% (2006-2010 5-year est.); Master's degree or higher: 7.6% (2006-2010 5-year est.).

Housing: Homeownership rate: 61.6% (2010); Median home value: $72,300 (2006-2010 5-year est.); Median contract rent: $468 per month (2006-2010 5-year est.); Median year structure built: 1952 (2006-2010 5-year est.).

Safety: Violent crime rate: 70.0 per 10,000 population; Property crime rate: 165.7 per 10,000 population (2011).

Transportation: Commute to work: 90.9% car, 6.9% public transportation, 1.7% walk, 0.5% work from home (2006-2010 5-year est.); Travel time to work: 23.8% less than 15 minutes, 39.6% 15 to 30 minutes, 19.5% 30 to 45 minutes, 9.9% 45 to 60 minutes, 7.2% 60 minutes or more (2006-2010 5-year est.).

Additional Information Contacts

Penn Hills Chamber of Commerce . . . . (412) 795-8741
  http://www.pennhillschamber.org

EAST PITTSBURGH (borough). Covers a land area of 0.388 square miles and a water area of 0 square miles. Located at 40.40° N. Lat; 79.84° W. Long. Elevation is 892 feet.

Population: 2,160 (1990); 2,017 (2000); 1,822 (2010); Density: 4,699.1 persons per square mile (2010); Race: 48.8% White, 45.4% Black, 0.2% Asian, 0.1% American Indian/Alaska Native, 0.0% Native Hawaiian/Other Pacific Islander, 5.5% Other, 2.5% Hispanic of any race (2010); Average household size: 2.21 (2010); Median age: 35.6 (2010); Males per 100 females: 80.6 (2010); Marriage status: 51.9% never married, 29.8% now married, 11.6% widowed, 6.7% divorced (2006-2010 5-year est.); Foreign born: 0.4% (2006-2010 5-year est.); Ancestry (includes multiple ancestries): 14.4% Irish, 13.9% German, 7.6% Slovak, 5.3% Italian, 3.9% Polish (2006-2010 5-year est.).

Economy: Single-family building permits issued: 0 (2011); Multi-family building permits issued: 0 (2011); Employment by occupation: 12.4% management, 1.6% professional, 19.0% services, 17.3% sales, 6.4% farming, 2.1% construction, 5.7% production (2006-2010 5-year est.).

Income: Per capita income: $14,798 (2006-2010 5-year est.); Median household income: $22,800 (2006-2010 5-year est.); Average household income: $34,223 (2006-2010 5-year est.); Percent of households with income of $100,000 or more: 3.0% (2006-2010 5-year est.); Poverty rate: 31.6% (2006-2010 5-year est.).

Education: Percent of population age 25 and over with: High school diploma (including GED) or higher: 90.3% (2006-2010 5-year est.); Bachelor's degree or higher: 12.7% (2006-2010 5-year est.); Master's degree or higher: 5.7% (2006-2010 5-year est.).

Housing: Homeownership rate: 38.5% (2010); Median home value: $54,900 (2006-2010 5-year est.); Median contract rent: $391 per month (2006-2010 5-year est.); Median year structure built: before 1940 (2006-2010 5-year est.).

Transportation: Commute to work: 65.7% car, 27.6% public transportation, 5.7% walk, 0.7% work from home (2006-2010 5-year est.); Travel time to work: 26.6% less than 15 minutes, 21.7% 15 to 30 minutes, 22.0% 30 to 45 minutes, 15.7% 45 to 60 minutes, 14.1% 60 minutes or more (2006-2010 5-year est.).

Additional Information Contacts

Penn Hills Chamber of Commerce . . . . (412) 795-8741
  http://www.pennhillschamber.org

EDGEWOOD (borough). Covers a land area of 0.587 square miles and a water area of 0 square miles. Located at 40.43° N. Lat; 79.88° W. Long. Elevation is 978 feet.

History: Incorporated 1888.

Population: 3,581 (1990); 3,311 (2000); 3,118 (2010); Density: 5,307.6 persons per square mile (2010); Race: 85.1% White, 9.3% Black, 2.6% Asian, 0.3% American Indian/Alaska Native, 0.1% Native Hawaiian/Other Pacific Islander, 2.6% Other, 2.7% Hispanic of any race (2010); Average household size: 1.97 (2010); Median age: 40.8 (2010); Males per 100 females: 89.3 (2010); Marriage status: 36.4% never married, 49.6% now married, 6.0% widowed, 8.0% divorced (2006-2010 5-year est.); Foreign born: 4.7% (2006-2010 5-year est.); Ancestry (includes multiple ancestries): 19.4% German, 14.4% Italian, 14.4% Irish, 10.0% American, 9.2% English (2006-2010 5-year est.).

Economy: Single-family building permits issued: 0 (2011); Multi-family building permits issued: 0 (2011); Employment by occupation: 18.6%

management, 6.5% professional, 2.9% services, 15.3% sales, 1.6% farming, 3.9% construction, 3.4% production (2006-2010 5-year est.).

Income: Per capita income: $39,022 (2006-2010 5-year est.); Median household income: $58,400 (2006-2010 5-year est.); Average household income: $84,602 (2006-2010 5-year est.); Percent of households with income of $100,000 or more: 30.1% (2006-2010 5-year est.); Poverty rate: 9.5% (2006-2010 5-year est.).

Education: Percent of population age 25 and over with: High school diploma (including GED) or higher: 94.1% (2006-2010 5-year est.); Bachelor's degree or higher: 60.0% (2006-2010 5-year est.); Master's degree or higher: 32.6% (2006-2010 5-year est.).

Housing: Homeownership rate: 65.4% (2010); Median home value: $156,900 (2006-2010 5-year est.); Median contract rent: $589 per month (2006-2010 5-year est.); Median year structure built: before 1940 (2006-2010 5-year est.).

Transportation: Commute to work: 77.9% car, 12.8% public transportation, 2.9% walk, 3.7% work from home (2006-2010 5-year est.); Travel time to work: 13.1% less than 15 minutes, 53.5% 15 to 30 minutes, 20.9% 30 to 45 minutes, 10.9% 45 to 60 minutes, 1.6% 60 minutes or more (2006-2010 5-year est.)

Additional Information Contacts

Borough of Edgewood. . . . . (412) 242-4824
  http://www.edgewood.pgh.pa.us
Wilkinsburg Chamber of Commerce . . . . (412) 242-0234
  http://wilkinsburgchamber.com/wilkinsburginfo.html

EDGEWORTH (borough). Covers a land area of 1.496 square miles and a water area of 0.180 square miles. Located at 40.55° N. Lat; 80.19° W. Long. Elevation is 738 feet.

History: First municipality in Pennsylvania to adopt borough-manager government. Incorporated 1904.

Population: 1,670 (1990); 1,730 (2000); 1,680 (2010); Density: 1,122.7 persons per square mile (2010); Race: 97.1% White, 1.0% Black, 0.7% Asian, 0.0% American Indian/Alaska Native, 0.0% Native Hawaiian/Other Pacific Islander, 1.2% Other, 1.6% Hispanic of any race (2010); Average household size: 2.76 (2010); Median age: 45.9 (2010); Males per 100 females: 84.6 (2010); Marriage status: 17.0% never married, 71.0% now married, 6.1% widowed, 5.9% divorced (2006-2010 5-year est.); Foreign born: 6.3% (2006-2010 5-year est.); Ancestry (includes multiple ancestries): 31.0% German, 21.1% Irish, 18.8% English, 14.0% Italian, 4.5% Scottish (2006-2010 5-year est.).

Economy: Single-family building permits issued: 2 (2011); Multi-family building permits issued: 0 (2011); Employment by occupation: 30.1% management, 1.8% professional, 5.2% services, 10.6% sales, 0.9% farming, 1.2% construction, 1.5% production (2006-2010 5-year est.).

Income: Per capita income: $75,540 (2006-2010 5-year est.); Median household income: $135,781 (2006-2010 5-year est.); Average household income: $205,779 (2006-2010 5-year est.); Percent of households with income of $100,000 or more: 65.2% (2006-2010 5-year est.); Poverty rate: 1.3% (2006-2010 5-year est.).

Education: Percent of population age 25 and over with: High school diploma (including GED) or higher: 99.1% (2006-2010 5-year est.); Bachelor's degree or higher: 77.2% (2006-2010 5-year est.); Master's degree or higher: 41.6% (2006-2010 5-year est.).

Housing: Homeownership rate: 90.8% (2010); Median home value: $488,600 (2006-2010 5-year est.); Median contract rent: $2,000 per month (2006-2010 5-year est.); Median year structure built: before 1940 (2006-2010 5-year est.).

Safety: Violent crime rate: 0.0 per 10,000 population; Property crime rate: 0.0 per 10,000 population (2011).

Transportation: Commute to work: 81.8% car, 2.3% public transportation, 2.7% walk, 10.2% work from home (2006-2010 5-year est.); Travel time to work: 26.2% less than 15 minutes, 31.1% 15 to 30 minutes, 31.3% 30 to 45 minutes, 5.1% 45 to 60 minutes, 6.3% 60 minutes or more (2006-2010 5-year est.)

Additional Information Contacts

Pittsburgh Airport Area Chamber of Commerce . . . . (412) 264-6270
  http://www.paacc.com

ELIZABETH (borough). Covers a land area of 0.342 square miles and a water area of 0.072 square miles. Located at 40.27° N. Lat; 79.89° W. Long. Elevation is 771 feet.

Population: 1,610 (1990); 1,609 (2000); 1,493 (2010); Density: 4,359.3 persons per square mile (2010); Race: 92.0% White, 4.9% Black, 0.2% Asian, 0.3% American Indian/Alaska Native, 0.0% Native Hawaiian/Other

Pacific Islander, 2.6% Other, 1.3% Hispanic of any race (2010); Average household size: 2.38 (2010); Median age: 39.7 (2010); Males per 100 females: 85.7 (2010); Marriage status: 30.1% never married, 45.0% now married, 12.6% widowed, 12.3% divorced (2006-2010 5-year est.); Foreign born: 3.1% (2006-2010 5-year est.); Ancestry (includes multiple ancestries): 23.4% German, 21.8% English, 17.9% Irish, 12.2% Italian, 7.7% Polish (2006-2010 5-year est.).

Economy: Single-family building permits issued: 0 (2011); Multi-family building permits issued: 0 (2011); Employment by occupation: 5.4% management, 3.1% professional, 15.1% services, 17.5% sales, 3.9% farming, 12.0% construction, 4.2% production (2006-2010 5-year est.).

Income: Per capita income: $20,543 (2006-2010 5-year est.); Median household income: $38,333 (2006-2010 5-year est.); Average household income: $45,650 (2006-2010 5-year est.); Percent of households with income of $100,000 or more: 6.3% (2006-2010 5-year est.); Poverty rate: 11.9% (2006-2010 5-year est.).

Education: Percent of population age 25 and over with: High school diploma (including GED) or higher: 90.3% (2006-2010 5-year est.); Bachelor's degree or higher: 13.5% (2006-2010 5-year est.); Master's degree or higher: 4.9% (2006-2010 5-year est.).

School District(s)
Elizabeth Forward SD (KG-12)
　　2010-11 Enrollment: 2,491 . . . . (412) 896-2300

Housing: Homeownership rate: 58.7% (2010); Median home value: $75,800 (2006-2010 5-year est.); Median contract rent: $429 per month (2006-2010 5-year est.); Median year structure built: before 1940 (2006-2010 5-year est.).

Transportation: Commute to work: 77.1% car, 9.3% public transportation, 10.4% walk, 2.0% work from home (2006-2010 5-year est.); Travel time to work: 31.4% less than 15 minutes, 35.2% 15 to 30 minutes, 14.9% 30 to 45 minutes, 7.6% 45 to 60 minutes, 10.8% 60 minutes or more (2006-2010 5-year est.)

Additional Information Contacts
Mon Valley Regional Chamber of Commerce . . . . (724) 483-3507
　　http://www.mvrchamber.org

ELIZABETH (township). Covers a land area of 22.834 square miles and a water area of 0.431 square miles. Located at 40.27° N. Lat; 79.82° W. Long. Elevation is 771 feet.

History: Pioneer boat construction center after 1778. Settled 1769, incorporated 1834.

Population: 14,747 (1990); 13,839 (2000); 13,271 (2010); Density: 581.2 persons per square mile (2010); Race: 97.1% White, 1.5% Black, 0.3% Asian, 0.1% American Indian/Alaska Native, 0.0% Native Hawaiian/Other Pacific Islander, 1.0% Other, 0.6% Hispanic of any race (2010); Average household size: 2.37 (2010); Median age: 46.8 (2010); Males per 100 females: 93.7 (2010); Marriage status: 22.4% never married, 59.3% now married, 7.9% widowed, 10.4% divorced (2006-2010 5-year est.); Foreign born: 1.3% (2006-2010 5-year est.); Ancestry (includes multiple ancestries): 29.5% German, 22.7% Irish, 16.5% Italian, 13.7% English, 10.4% Polish (2006-2010 5-year est.).

Economy: Single-family building permits issued: 7 (2011); Multi-family building permits issued: 0 (2011); Employment by occupation: 8.2% management, 3.9% professional, 11.3% services, 16.4% sales, 2.9% farming, 8.0% construction, 4.9% production (2006-2010 5-year est.).

Income: Per capita income: $26,739 (2006-2010 5-year est.); Median household income: $50,941 (2006-2010 5-year est.); Average household income: $62,395 (2006-2010 5-year est.); Percent of households with income of $100,000 or more: 15.1% (2006-2010 5-year est.); Poverty rate: 6.3% (2006-2010 5-year est.).

Taxes: Total city taxes per capita: $303 (2009); City property taxes per capita: $179 (2009).

Education: Percent of population age 25 and over with: High school diploma (including GED) or higher: 93.4% (2006-2010 5-year est.); Bachelor's degree or higher: 24.2% (2006-2010 5-year est.); Master's degree or higher: 8.1% (2006-2010 5-year est.).

Housing: Homeownership rate: 83.1% (2010); Median home value: $100,400 (2006-2010 5-year est.); Median contract rent: $539 per month (2006-2010 5-year est.); Median year structure built: 1958 (2006-2010 5-year est.).

Safety: Violent crime rate: 2.3 per 10,000 population; Property crime rate: 72.1 per 10,000 population (2011).

Transportation: Commute to work: 92.2% car, 2.9% public transportation, 2.2% walk, 1.4% work from home (2006-2010 5-year est.); Travel time to work: 25.7% less than 15 minutes, 31.4% 15 to 30 minutes, 21.0% 30 to

45 minutes, 8.8% 45 to 60 minutes, 13.2% 60 minutes or more (2006-2010 5-year est.)

Additional Information Contacts
Elizabeth Township . . . . (412) 751-2880
　　http://www.elizabethtwp.com
Mon Valley Regional Chamber of Commerce . . . . (724) 483-3507
　　http://www.mvrchamber.org

EMSWORTH (borough). Covers a land area of 0.569 square miles and a water area of 0.123 square miles. Located at 40.51° N. Lat; 80.10° W. Long. Elevation is 732 feet.

History: Settled 1803; incorporated 1897.

Population: 2,892 (1990); 2,598 (2000); 2,449 (2010); Density: 4,306.8 persons per square mile (2010); Race: 91.8% White, 4.4% Black, 1.7% Asian, 0.0% American Indian/Alaska Native, 0.0% Native Hawaiian/Other Pacific Islander, 2.1% Other, 1.0% Hispanic of any race (2010); Average household size: 2.12 (2010); Median age: 38.7 (2010); Males per 100 females: 104.1 (2010); Marriage status: 42.8% never married, 44.0% now married, 5.6% widowed, 7.5% divorced (2006-2010 5-year est.); Foreign born: 7.1% (2006-2010 5-year est.); Ancestry (includes multiple ancestries): 31.4% German, 24.5% Irish, 12.2% Italian, 8.0% English, 6.6% Polish (2006-2010 5-year est.).

Economy: Single-family building permits issued: 0 (2011); Multi-family building permits issued: 0 (2011); Employment by occupation: 11.1% management, 5.2% professional, 8.1% services, 19.4% sales, 8.8% farming, 10.0% construction, 5.8% production (2006-2010 5-year est.).

Income: Per capita income: $24,931 (2006-2010 5-year est.); Median household income: $51,595 (2006-2010 5-year est.); Average household income: $57,996 (2006-2010 5-year est.); Percent of households with income of $100,000 or more: 11.2% (2006-2010 5-year est.); Poverty rate: 7.9% (2006-2010 5-year est.).

Education: Percent of population age 25 and over with: High school diploma (including GED) or higher: 87.9% (2006-2010 5-year est.); Bachelor's degree or higher: 27.3% (2006-2010 5-year est.); Master's degree or higher: 5.8% (2006-2010 5-year est.).

Housing: Homeownership rate: 62.5% (2010); Median home value: $108,300 (2006-2010 5-year est.); Median contract rent: $565 per month (2006-2010 5-year est.); Median year structure built: 1947 (2006-2010 5-year est.).

Safety: Violent crime rate: 4.1 per 10,000 population; Property crime rate: 105.8 per 10,000 population (2011).

Transportation: Commute to work: 82.4% car, 9.3% public transportation, 3.9% walk, 4.4% work from home (2006-2010 5-year est.); Travel time to work: 22.0% less than 15 minutes, 37.4% 15 to 30 minutes, 17.9% 30 to 45 minutes, 17.8% 45 to 60 minutes, 5.0% 60 minutes or more (2006-2010 5-year est.)

Additional Information Contacts
North Suburban Chamber of Commerce . . . . (412) 761-2113
　　http://www.northsuburbancoc.org

ENLOW (CDP). Covers a land area of 0.674 square miles and a water area of 0 square miles. Located at 40.45° N. Lat; 80.23° W. Long. Elevation is 965 feet.

Population: n/a (1990); n/a (2000); 1,013 (2010); Density: 1,502.0 persons per square mile (2010); Race: 96.2% White, 1.1% Black, 1.2% Asian, 0.0% American Indian/Alaska Native, 0.3% Native Hawaiian/Other Pacific Islander, 1.2% Other, 0.9% Hispanic of any race (2010); Average household size: 2.17 (2010); Median age: 45.2 (2010); Males per 100 females: 96.3 (2010); Marriage status: 22.2% never married, 43.0% now married, 11.8% widowed, 23.0% divorced (2006-2010 5-year est.); Foreign born: 3.0% (2006-2010 5-year est.); Ancestry (includes multiple ancestries): 48.0% German, 24.5% Italian, 13.7% Irish, 11.5% English, 8.7% Welsh (2006-2010 5-year est.).

Economy: Employment by occupation: 11.7% management, 9.9% professional, 19.1% services, 14.1% sales, 11.0% farming, 9.1% construction, 6.3% production (2006-2010 5-year est.).

Income: Per capita income: $34,065 (2006-2010 5-year est.); Median household income: $38,542 (2006-2010 5-year est.); Average household income: $62,730 (2006-2010 5-year est.); Percent of households with income of $100,000 or more: 10.9% (2006-2010 5-year est.); Poverty rate: 4.0% (2006-2010 5-year est.).

Education: Percent of population age 25 and over with: High school diploma (including GED) or higher: 88.8% (2006-2010 5-year est.); Bachelor's degree or higher: 34.8% (2006-2010 5-year est.); Master's degree or higher: 9.6% (2006-2010 5-year est.).

Housing: Homeownership rate: 90.6% (2010); Median home value: $16,800 (2006-2010 5-year est.); Median contract rent: $313 per month (2006-2010 5-year est.); Median year structure built: 1977 (2006-2010 5-year est.).

Transportation: Commute to work: 79.4% car, 6.0% public transportation, 2.1% walk, 5.7% work from home (2006-2010 5-year est.); Travel time to work: 31.3% less than 15 minutes, 41.6% 15 to 30 minutes, 15.2% 30 to 45 minutes, 8.6% 45 to 60 minutes, 3.3% 60 minutes or more (2006-2010 5-year est.)

ETNA (borough). Covers a land area of 0.731 square miles and a water area of 0.064 square miles. Located at 40.50° N. Lat; 79.95° W. Long. Elevation is 745 feet.

History: Ironmaking began here 1832. Incorporated 1868.

Population: 4,200 (1990); 3,924 (2000); 3,451 (2010); Density: 4,723.4 persons per square mile (2010); Race: 95.7% White, 1.4% Black, 0.7% Asian, 0.1% American Indian/Alaska Native, 0.0% Native Hawaiian/Other Pacific Islander, 2.1% Other, 1.9% Hispanic of any race (2010); Average household size: 2.14 (2010); Median age: 39.5 (2010); Males per 100 females: 97.2 (2010); Marriage status: 32.3% never married, 45.4% now married, 7.3% widowed, 15.0% divorced (2006-2010 5-year est.); Foreign born: 1.3% (2006-2010 5-year est.); Ancestry (includes multiple ancestries): 37.5% German, 24.9% Irish, 23.2% Italian, 11.2% Polish, 6.8% Croatian (2006-2010 5-year est.).

Economy: Single-family building permits issued: 0 (2011); Multi-family building permits issued: 0 (2011); Employment by occupation: 3.8% management, 1.0% professional, 11.2% services, 17.4% sales, 5.3% farming, 11.1% construction, 6.8% production (2006-2010 5-year est.).

Income: Per capita income: $22,154 (2006-2010 5-year est.); Median household income: $34,434 (2006-2010 5-year est.); Average household income: $45,784 (2006-2010 5-year est.); Percent of households with income of $100,000 or more: 7.6% (2006-2010 5-year est.); Poverty rate: 16.6% (2006-2010 5-year est.).

Education: Percent of population age 25 and over with: High school diploma (including GED) or higher: 86.1% (2006-2010 5-year est.); Bachelor's degree or higher: 16.3% (2006-2010 5-year est.); Master's degree or higher: 7.9% (2006-2010 5-year est.).

Housing: Homeownership rate: 56.5% (2010); Median home value: $82,800 (2006-2010 5-year est.); Median contract rent: $439 per month (2006-2010 5-year est.); Median year structure built: before 1940 (2006-2010 5-year est.).

Safety: Violent crime rate: 63.5 per 10,000 population; Property crime rate: 335.1 per 10,000 population (2011).

Transportation: Commute to work: 84.4% car, 6.3% public transportation, 6.9% walk, 1.8% work from home (2006-2010 5-year est.); Travel time to work: 25.6% less than 15 minutes, 47.2% 15 to 30 minutes, 20.3% 30 to 45 minutes, 0.7% 45 to 60 minutes, 6.2% 60 minutes or more (2006-2010 5-year est.)

Additional Information Contacts
Northside Northshore Chamber of Commerce . . . . (412) 231-6500
  http://www.northsidechamberofcommerce.com

FAWN (township). Covers a land area of 12.947 square miles and a water area of 0 square miles. Located at 40.65° N. Lat; 79.77° W. Long.

Population: 2,712 (1990); 2,504 (2000); 2,376 (2010); Density: 183.5 persons per square mile (2010); Race: 97.9% White, 0.4% Black, 0.7% Asian, 0.1% American Indian/Alaska Native, 0.0% Native Hawaiian/Other Pacific Islander, 0.9% Other, 0.4% Hispanic of any race (2010); Average household size: 2.47 (2010); Median age: 46.8 (2010); Males per 100 females: 107.0 (2010); Marriage status: 18.6% never married, 67.3% now married, 6.4% widowed, 7.6% divorced (2006-2010 5-year est.); Foreign born: 1.1% (2006-2010 5-year est.); Ancestry (includes multiple ancestries): 46.1% German, 25.2% Irish, 15.2% Polish, 15.0% Italian, 12.0% English (2006-2010 5-year est.).

Economy: Single-family building permits issued: 1 (2011); Multi-family building permits issued: 0 (2011); Employment by occupation: 13.2% management, 7.3% professional, 9.7% services, 16.9% sales, 3.2% farming, 9.2% construction, 3.6% production (2006-2010 5-year est.).

Income: Per capita income: $26,773 (2006-2010 5-year est.); Median household income: $53,750 (2006-2010 5-year est.); Average household income: $66,376 (2006-2010 5-year est.); Percent of households with income of $100,000 or more: 17.3% (2006-2010 5-year est.); Poverty rate: 5.8% (2006-2010 5-year est.).

Education: Percent of population age 25 and over with: High school diploma (including GED) or higher: 91.3% (2006-2010 5-year est.);

Bachelor's degree or higher: 16.2% (2006-2010 5-year est.); Master's degree or higher: 5.9% (2006-2010 5-year est.).

Housing: Homeownership rate: 83.6% (2010); Median home value: $116,400 (2006-2010 5-year est.); Median contract rent: $450 per month (2006-2010 5-year est.); Median year structure built: 1957 (2006-2010 5-year est.).

Safety: Violent crime rate: 16.8 per 10,000 population; Property crime rate: 109.1 per 10,000 population (2011).

Transportation: Commute to work: 94.9% car, 0.9% public transportation, 1.6% walk, 1.7% work from home (2006-2010 5-year est.); Travel time to work: 28.5% less than 15 minutes, 37.8% 15 to 30 minutes, 22.2% 30 to 45 minutes, 8.3% 45 to 60 minutes, 3.2% 60 minutes or more (2006-2010 5-year est.)

Additional Information Contacts
Allegheny Valley Chamber of Commerce . . . . (724) 224-3400
  http://alleghenyvalleychamber.com

FINDLAY (township). Covers a land area of 32.285 square miles and a water area of 0.006 square miles. Located at 40.48° N. Lat; 80.28° W. Long.

Population: 4,493 (1990); 5,145 (2000); 5,060 (2010); Density: 156.7 persons per square mile (2010); Race: 96.1% White, 1.9% Black, 0.7% Asian, 0.1% American Indian/Alaska Native, 0.0% Native Hawaiian/Other Pacific Islander, 1.2% Other, 0.8% Hispanic of any race (2010); Average household size: 2.41 (2010); Median age: 42.1 (2010); Males per 100 females: 96.4 (2010); Marriage status: 21.7% never married, 62.8% now married, 8.2% widowed, 7.4% divorced (2006-2010 5-year est.); Foreign born: 4.8% (2006-2010 5-year est.); Ancestry (includes multiple ancestries): 32.6% German, 21.5% Italian, 19.5% Irish, 11.7% English, 11.6% Polish (2006-2010 5-year est.).

Economy: Single-family building permits issued: 20 (2011); Multi-family building permits issued: 10 (2011); Employment by occupation: 15.1% management, 5.1% professional, 10.1% services, 17.4% sales, 4.6% farming, 7.7% construction, 4.9% production (2006-2010 5-year est.).

Income: Per capita income: $32,275 (2006-2010 5-year est.); Median household income: $64,031 (2006-2010 5-year est.); Average household income: $77,699 (2006-2010 5-year est.); Percent of households with income of $100,000 or more: 24.9% (2006-2010 5-year est.); Poverty rate: 5.9% (2006-2010 5-year est.).

Education: Percent of population age 25 and over with: High school diploma (including GED) or higher: 89.0% (2006-2010 5-year est.); Bachelor's degree or higher: 31.3% (2006-2010 5-year est.); Master's degree or higher: 10.4% (2006-2010 5-year est.).

Housing: Homeownership rate: 78.7% (2010); Median home value: $144,800 (2006-2010 5-year est.); Median contract rent: $559 per month (2006-2010 5-year est.); Median year structure built: 1976 (2006-2010 5-year est.).

Transportation: Commute to work: 92.0% car, 1.5% public transportation, 1.3% walk, 5.2% work from home (2006-2010 5-year est.); Travel time to work: 36.6% less than 15 minutes, 39.1% 15 to 30 minutes, 15.7% 30 to 45 minutes, 6.4% 45 to 60 minutes, 2.2% 60 minutes or more (2006-2010 5-year est.)

Additional Information Contacts
Findlay Township . . . . (724) 695-0500
  http://www.findlay.pa.us
Pittsburgh Airport Area Chamber of Commerce . . . . (412) 264-6270
  http://www.paacc.com

FOREST HILLS (borough). Covers a land area of 1.564 square miles and a water area of 0 square miles. Located at 40.43° N. Lat; 79.85° W. Long. Elevation is 981 feet.

History: Incorporated 1920.

Population: 7,335 (1990); 6,831 (2000); 6,518 (2010); Density: 4,168.1 persons per square mile (2010); Race: 87.7% White, 9.1% Black, 1.2% Asian, 0.1% American Indian/Alaska Native, 0.0% Native Hawaiian/Other Pacific Islander, 1.9% Other, 1.3% Hispanic of any race (2010); Average household size: 2.10 (2010); Median age: 47.5 (2010); Males per 100 females: 87.3 (2010); Marriage status: 28.2% never married, 52.8% now married, 8.8% widowed, 10.2% divorced (2006-2010 5-year est.); Foreign born: 3.0% (2006-2010 5-year est.); Ancestry (includes multiple ancestries): 24.6% German, 21.4% Irish, 18.0% Italian, 9.4% English, 7.5% Slovak (2006-2010 5-year est.).

Economy: Single-family building permits issued: 0 (2011); Multi-family building permits issued: 0 (2011); Employment by occupation: 15.7%

management, 9.2% professional, 8.5% services, 14.2% sales, 2.1% farming, 2.3% construction, 1.5% production (2006-2010 5-year est.).
Income: Per capita income: $30,842 (2006-2010 5-year est.); Median household income: $55,188 (2006-2010 5-year est.); Average household income: $65,207 (2006-2010 5-year est.); Percent of households with income of $100,000 or more: 18.5% (2006-2010 5-year est.); Poverty rate: 7.9% (2006-2010 5-year est.).
Education: Percent of population age 25 and over with: High school diploma (including GED) or higher: 97.2% (2006-2010 5-year est.); Bachelor's degree or higher: 49.5% (2006-2010 5-year est.); Master's degree or higher: 26.9% (2006-2010 5-year est.).
Housing: Homeownership rate: 78.0% (2010); Median home value: $112,200 (2006-2010 5-year est.); Median contract rent: $645 per month (2006-2010 5-year est.); Median year structure built: 1950 (2006-2010 5-year est.).
Safety: Violent crime rate: 4.6 per 10,000 population; Property crime rate: 136.1 per 10,000 population (2011).
Transportation: Commute to work: 81.6% car, 12.3% public transportation, 1.5% walk, 4.6% work from home (2006-2010 5-year est.); Travel time to work: 17.2% less than 15 minutes, 36.7% 15 to 30 minutes, 35.2% 30 to 45 minutes, 7.3% 45 to 60 minutes, 3.6% 60 minutes or more (2006-2010 5-year est.)
Additional Information Contacts
Borough of Forest Hills . . . . (412) 351-7330
    http://www.foresthillspa.org
Wilkinsburg Chamber of Commerce . . . . (412) 242-0234
    http://wilkinsburgchamber.com

FORWARD (township).
Covers a land area of 18.947 square miles and a water area of 0.871 square miles. Located at 40.23° N. Lat; 79.91° W. Long.
Population: 3,877 (1990); 3,771 (2000); 3,376 (2010); Density: 178.2 persons per square mile (2010); Race: 97.5% White, 1.4% Black, 0.1% Asian, 0.1% American Indian/Alaska Native, 0.0% Native Hawaiian/Other Pacific Islander, 0.9% Other, 0.6% Hispanic of any race (2010); Average household size: 2.40 (2010); Median age: 47.3 (2010); Males per 100 females: 92.9 (2010); Marriage status: 21.9% never married, 56.6% now married, 11.2% widowed, 10.3% divorced (2006-2010 5-year est.); Foreign born: 0.8% (2006-2010 5-year est.); Ancestry (includes multiple ancestries): 29.7% German, 25.1% Irish, 17.3% English, 11.2% Polish, 11.1% Italian (2006-2010 5-year est.).
Economy: Single-family building permits issued: 1 (2011); Multi-family building permits issued: 0 (2011); Employment by occupation: 6.0% management, 1.9% professional, 12.4% services, 14.5% sales, 6.4% farming, 8.6% construction, 9.3% production (2006-2010 5-year est.).
Income: Per capita income: $21,476 (2006-2010 5-year est.); Median household income: $44,201 (2006-2010 5-year est.); Average household income: $55,264 (2006-2010 5-year est.); Percent of households with income of $100,000 or more: 12.4% (2006-2010 5-year est.); Poverty rate: 9.8% (2006-2010 5-year est.).
Education: Percent of population age 25 and over with: High school diploma (including GED) or higher: 87.1% (2006-2010 5-year est.); Bachelor's degree or higher: 7.5% (2006-2010 5-year est.); Master's degree or higher: 2.9% (2006-2010 5-year est.).
Housing: Homeownership rate: 86.0% (2010); Median home value: $91,500 (2006-2010 5-year est.); Median contract rent: $470 per month (2006-2010 5-year est.); Median year structure built: 1956 (2006-2010 5-year est.).
Safety: Violent crime rate: 3.0 per 10,000 population; Property crime rate: 85.6 per 10,000 population (2011).
Transportation: Commute to work: 98.0% car, 1.2% public transportation, 0.0% walk, 0.8% work from home (2006-2010 5-year est.); Travel time to work: 24.6% less than 15 minutes, 29.2% 15 to 30 minutes, 16.2% 30 to 45 minutes, 15.1% 45 to 60 minutes, 14.9% 60 minutes or more (2006-2010 5-year est.)
Additional Information Contacts
Mon Valley Regional Chamber of Commerce . . . . (724) 483-3507
    http://www.mvrchamber.org

FOX CHAPEL (borough).
Covers a land area of 7.866 square miles and a water area of 0.008 square miles. Located at 40.53° N. Lat; 79.89° W. Long. Elevation is 981 feet.
History: Incorporated 1934.
Population: 5,241 (1990); 5,436 (2000); 5,388 (2010); Density: 685.0 persons per square mile (2010); Race: 91.9% White, 0.9% Black, 5.7% Asian, 0.1% American Indian/Alaska Native, 0.1% Native Hawaiian/Other Pacific Islander, 1.3% Other, 1.4% Hispanic of any race (2010); Average household size: 2.61 (2010); Median age: 48.1 (2010); Males per 100 females: 107.4 (2010); Marriage status: 21.7% never married, 69.6% now married, 2.8% widowed, 5.9% divorced (2006-2010 5-year est.); Foreign born: 9.3% (2006-2010 5-year est.); Ancestry (includes multiple ancestries): 22.0% German, 18.0% Irish, 17.5% English, 15.0% Italian, 7.1% Polish (2006-2010 5-year est.).
Economy: Single-family building permits issued: 2 (2011); Multi-family building permits issued: 0 (2011); Employment by occupation: 22.0% management, 5.0% professional, 1.9% services, 10.3% sales, 1.7% farming, 0.8% construction, 0.0% production (2006-2010 5-year est.).
Income: Per capita income: $88,208 (2006-2010 5-year est.); Median household income: $178,542 (2006-2010 5-year est.); Average household income: $263,292 (2006-2010 5-year est.); Percent of households with income of $100,000 or more: 74.4% (2006-2010 5-year est.); Poverty rate: 6.2% (2006-2010 5-year est.).
Education: Percent of population age 25 and over with: High school diploma (including GED) or higher: 97.2% (2006-2010 5-year est.); Bachelor's degree or higher: 75.9% (2006-2010 5-year est.); Master's degree or higher: 43.6% (2006-2010 5-year est.).
Housing: Homeownership rate: 84.9% (2010); Median home value: $515,000 (2006-2010 5-year est.); Median contract rent: $1,434 per month (2006-2010 5-year est.); Median year structure built: 1961 (2006-2010 5-year est.).
Safety: Violent crime rate: 0.0 per 10,000 population; Property crime rate: 40.7 per 10,000 population (2011).
Transportation: Commute to work: 92.7% car, 1.6% public transportation, 0.9% walk, 4.8% work from home (2006-2010 5-year est.); Travel time to work: 18.5% less than 15 minutes, 45.7% 15 to 30 minutes, 28.0% 30 to 45 minutes, 5.8% 45 to 60 minutes, 2.0% 60 minutes or more (2006-2010 5-year est.)
Additional Information Contacts
Borough of Fox Chapel . . . . (412) 963-1100
    http://www.fox-chapel.pa.us
Northside Northshore Chamber of Commerce . . . . (412) 231-6500
    http://www.northsidechamberofcommerce.com

FRANKLIN PARK (borough).
Covers a land area of 13.523 square miles and a water area of 0.004 square miles. Located at 40.59° N. Lat; 80.10° W. Long. Elevation is 1,230 feet.
History: Named in Honor of ben Franklin, the borough was established in 1823.
Population: 10,111 (1990); 11,364 (2000); 13,470 (2010); Density: 996.1 persons per square mile (2010); Race: 86.8% White, 1.2% Black, 10.4% Asian, 0.1% American Indian/Alaska Native, 0.1% Native Hawaiian/Other Pacific Islander, 1.4% Other, 1.5% Hispanic of any race (2010); Average household size: 2.85 (2010); Median age: 40.9 (2010); Males per 100 females: 97.0 (2010); Marriage status: 22.2% never married, 70.3% now married, 2.0% widowed, 5.4% divorced (2006-2010 5-year est.); Foreign born: 8.7% (2006-2010 5-year est.); Ancestry (includes multiple ancestries): 33.0% German, 24.6% Irish, 14.7% English, 14.2% Italian, 6.2% Polish (2006-2010 5-year est.).
Economy: Single-family building permits issued: 55 (2011); Multi-family building permits issued: 30 (2011); Employment by occupation: 24.7% management, 8.4% professional, 4.3% services, 12.8% sales, 3.0% farming, 3.9% construction, 1.5% production (2006-2010 5-year est.).
Income: Per capita income: $51,570 (2006-2010 5-year est.); Median household income: $114,981 (2006-2010 5-year est.); Average household income: $152,092 (2006-2010 5-year est.); Percent of households with income of $100,000 or more: 59.1% (2006-2010 5-year est.); Poverty rate: 1.2% (2006-2010 5-year est.).
Education: Percent of population age 25 and over with: High school diploma (including GED) or higher: 97.9% (2006-2010 5-year est.); Bachelor's degree or higher: 69.6% (2006-2010 5-year est.); Master's degree or higher: 34.9% (2006-2010 5-year est.).
Housing: Homeownership rate: 93.8% (2010); Median home value: $285,700 (2006-2010 5-year est.); Median contract rent: $955 per month (2006-2010 5-year est.); Median year structure built: 1984 (2006-2010 5-year est.).
Safety: Violent crime rate: 5.9 per 10,000 population; Property crime rate: 34.8 per 10,000 population (2011).
Transportation: Commute to work: 88.4% car, 4.4% public transportation, 0.5% walk, 6.0% work from home (2006-2010 5-year est.); Travel time to work: 15.4% less than 15 minutes, 41.8% 15 to 30 minutes, 29.6% 30 to

45 minutes, 8.4% 45 to 60 minutes, 4.8% 60 minutes or more (2006-2010 5-year est.)

Additional Information Contacts

Borough of Franklin Park . . . . (412) 364-4115
  http://www.franklinparkborough.us

Franklin Area Chamber of Commerce. . . . . (814) 432-5823
  http://www.franklinareachamber.org

FRAZER (township). Covers a land area of 9.344 square miles and a water area of 0 square miles. Located at 40.61° N. Lat; 79.80° W. Long.
Population: 1,388 (1990); 1,286 (2000); 1,157 (2010); Density: 123.8 persons per square mile (2010); Race: 97.6% White, 0.1% Black, 0.5% Asian, 0.0% American Indian/Alaska Native, 0.0% Native Hawaiian/Other Pacific Islander, 1.8% Other, 0.3% Hispanic of any race (2010); Average household size: 2.32 (2010); Median age: 48.7 (2010); Males per 100 females: 99.5 (2010); Marriage status: 22.4% never married, 62.5% now married, 6.5% widowed, 8.6% divorced (2006-2010 5-year est.); Foreign born: 0.8% (2006-2010 5-year est.); Ancestry (includes multiple ancestries): 38.4% German, 16.9% Irish, 15.7% Polish, 13.1% Slovak, 13.0% Italian (2006-2010 5-year est.).
Economy: Single-family building permits issued: 1 (2011); Multi-family building permits issued: 0 (2011); Employment by occupation: 7.2% management, 8.8% professional, 7.6% services, 11.8% sales, 2.2% farming, 15.3% construction, 9.2% production (2006-2010 5-year est.).
Income: Per capita income: $26,398 (2006-2010 5-year est.); Median household income: $49,934 (2006-2010 5-year est.); Average household income: $60,278 (2006-2010 5-year est.); Percent of households with income of $100,000 or more: 13.3% (2006-2010 5-year est.); Poverty rate: 8.7% (2006-2010 5-year est.).
Education: Percent of population age 25 and over with: High school diploma (including GED) or higher: 86.9% (2006-2010 5-year est.); Bachelor's degree or higher: 18.8% (2006-2010 5-year est.); Master's degree or higher: 4.8% (2006-2010 5-year est.).
Housing: Homeownership rate: 85.4% (2010); Median home value: $105,200 (2006-2010 5-year est.); Median contract rent: $407 per month (2006-2010 5-year est.); Median year structure built: 1956 (2006-2010 5-year est.).
Safety: Violent crime rate: 0.0 per 10,000 population; Property crime rate: 542.6 per 10,000 population (2011).
Transportation: Commute to work: 95.1% car, 0.0% public transportation, 2.9% walk, 2.0% work from home (2006-2010 5-year est.); Travel time to work: 20.0% less than 15 minutes, 41.5% 15 to 30 minutes, 25.3% 30 to 45 minutes, 6.1% 45 to 60 minutes, 7.1% 60 minutes or more (2006-2010 5-year est.)

Additional Information Contacts

Great Valley Regional Chamber of Commerce . . . . (610) 889-2069
  http://www.greatvalleyonline.com

GIBSONIA (CDP). Covers a land area of 3.846 square miles and a water area of 0 square miles. Located at 40.63° N. Lat; 79.97° W. Long. Elevation is 1,037 feet.
Population: n/a (1990); n/a (2000); 2,733 (2010); Density: 710.6 persons per square mile (2010); Race: 97.3% White, 0.7% Black, 0.9% Asian, 0.2% American Indian/Alaska Native, 0.0% Native Hawaiian/Other Pacific Islander, 0.9% Other, 1.3% Hispanic of any race (2010); Average household size: 2.66 (2010); Median age: 43.4 (2010); Males per 100 females: 96.8 (2010); Marriage status: 20.9% never married, 61.7% now married, 6.7% widowed, 10.7% divorced (2006-2010 5-year est.); Foreign born: 2.9% (2006-2010 5-year est.); Ancestry (includes multiple ancestries): 45.6% German, 18.8% Irish, 12.0% English, 11.4% Polish, 11.2% Italian (2006-2010 5-year est.).
Economy: Employment by occupation: 15.0% management, 7.6% professional, 9.1% services, 15.4% sales, 2.3% farming, 11.4% construction, 7.1% production (2006-2010 5-year est.).
Income: Per capita income: $33,249 (2006-2010 5-year est.); Median household income: $74,970 (2006-2010 5-year est.); Average household income: $87,021 (2006-2010 5-year est.); Percent of households with income of $100,000 or more: 36.4% (2006-2010 5-year est.); Poverty rate: 5.2% (2006-2010 5-year est.).
Education: Percent of population age 25 and over with: High school diploma (including GED) or higher: 97.1% (2006-2010 5-year est.); Bachelor's degree or higher: 33.4% (2006-2010 5-year est.); Master's degree or higher: 10.1% (2006-2010 5-year est.).

School District(s)

Hampton Township SD (PK-12)
  2010-11 Enrollment: 3,111 . . . . (412) 492-6302
Pine-Richland SD (KG-12)
  2010-11 Enrollment: 4,604 . . . . (724) 625-7773
Pine-Richland SD (KG-12)
  2010-11 Enrollment: 4,604 . . . . (724) 625-7773
Housing: Homeownership rate: 93.0% (2010); Median home value: $181,000 (2006-2010 5-year est.); Median contract rent: $444 per month (2006-2010 5-year est.); Median year structure built: 1959 (2006-2010 5-year est.).
Transportation: Commute to work: 95.9% car, 1.4% public transportation, 0.4% walk, 2.3% work from home (2006-2010 5-year est.); Travel time to work: 18.3% less than 15 minutes, 35.5% 15 to 30 minutes, 30.8% 30 to 45 minutes, 11.3% 45 to 60 minutes, 4.1% 60 minutes or more (2006-2010 5-year est.)

GLASSPORT (borough). Covers a land area of 1.582 square miles and a water area of 0.205 square miles. Located at 40.33° N. Lat; 79.89° W. Long. Elevation is 764 feet.
History: Incorporated 1902.
Population: 5,582 (1990); 4,993 (2000); 4,483 (2010); Density: 2,834.5 persons per square mile (2010); Race: 96.2% White, 1.7% Black, 0.2% Asian, 0.2% American Indian/Alaska Native, 0.0% Native Hawaiian/Other Pacific Islander, 1.7% Other, 1.3% Hispanic of any race (2010); Average household size: 2.27 (2010); Median age: 43.2 (2010); Males per 100 females: 93.9 (2010); Marriage status: 36.8% never married, 40.9% now married, 10.0% widowed, 12.3% divorced (2006-2010 5-year est.); Foreign born: 1.5% (2006-2010 5-year est.); Ancestry (includes multiple ancestries): 26.1% German, 22.2% Irish, 21.3% Polish, 19.1% Italian, 9.8% Slovak (2006-2010 5-year est.).
Economy: Single-family building permits issued: 0 (2011); Multi-family building permits issued: 0 (2011); Employment by occupation: 6.0% management, 1.3% professional, 13.4% services, 17.2% sales, 2.7% farming, 11.8% construction, 7.4% production (2006-2010 5-year est.).
Income: Per capita income: $18,572 (2006-2010 5-year est.); Median household income: $33,017 (2006-2010 5-year est.); Average household income: $41,133 (2006-2010 5-year est.); Percent of households with income of $100,000 or more: 3.8% (2006-2010 5-year est.); Poverty rate: 15.0% (2006-2010 5-year est.).
Education: Percent of population age 25 and over with: High school diploma (including GED) or higher: 84.2% (2006-2010 5-year est.); Bachelor's degree or higher: 12.8% (2006-2010 5-year est.); Master's degree or higher: 2.1% (2006-2010 5-year est.).
Housing: Homeownership rate: 64.2% (2010); Median home value: $60,000 (2006-2010 5-year est.); Median contract rent: $370 per month (2006-2010 5-year est.); Median year structure built: 1942 (2006-2010 5-year est.).
Safety: Violent crime rate: 28.9 per 10,000 population; Property crime rate: 284.6 per 10,000 population (2011).
Transportation: Commute to work: 87.8% car, 5.0% public transportation, 4.0% walk, 2.2% work from home (2006-2010 5-year est.); Travel time to work: 31.2% less than 15 minutes, 38.1% 15 to 30 minutes, 15.2% 30 to 45 minutes, 8.9% 45 to 60 minutes, 6.5% 60 minutes or more (2006-2010 5-year est.)

Additional Information Contacts

Brentwood Baldwin Whitehall Chamber of Commerce . . . . (412) 884-1233
  http://www.bbwchamber.com

GLEN OSBORNE (borough). Covers a land area of 0.428 square miles and a water area of 0.135 square miles. Located at 40.53° N. Lat; 80.17° W. Long.
Population: n/a (1990); n/a (2000); 547 (2010); Density: 1,276.8 persons per square mile (2010); Race: 95.6% White, 1.6% Black, 1.8% Asian, 0.0% American Indian/Alaska Native, 0.0% Native Hawaiian/Other Pacific Islander, 1.0% Other, 0.5% Hispanic of any race (2010); Average household size: 2.65 (2010); Median age: 44.7 (2010); Males per 100 females: 93.3 (2010); Marriage status: 19.5% never married, 66.4% now married, 7.6% widowed, 6.5% divorced (2006-2010 5-year est.); Foreign born: 7.6% (2006-2010 5-year est.); Ancestry (includes multiple ancestries): 33.5% Irish, 26.3% German, 17.4% English, 14.8% Italian, 5.4% Scotch-Irish (2006-2010 5-year est.).
Economy: Single-family building permits issued: 0 (2011); Multi-family building permits issued: 0 (2011); Employment by occupation: 22.2%

management, 4.3% professional, 9.2% services, 12.6% sales, 5.3% farming, 6.8% construction, 2.9% production (2006-2010 5-year est.).
Income: Per capita income: $61,823 (2006-2010 5-year est.); Median household income: $113,571 (2006-2010 5-year est.); Average household income: $160,802 (2006-2010 5-year est.); Percent of households with income of $100,000 or more: 55.1% (2006-2010 5-year est.); Poverty rate: 2.8% (2006-2010 5-year est.).
Education: Percent of population age 25 and over with: High school diploma (including GED) or higher: 96.5% (2006-2010 5-year est.); Bachelor's degree or higher: 63.7% (2006-2010 5-year est.); Master's degree or higher: 26.7% (2006-2010 5-year est.).
Housing: Homeownership rate: 90.6% (2010); Median home value: $385,200 (2006-2010 5-year est.); Median contract rent: $717 per month (2006-2010 5-year est.); Median year structure built: before 1940 (2006-2010 5-year est.).
Transportation: Commute to work: 80.7% car, 2.9% public transportation, 1.4% walk, 9.2% work from home (2006-2010 5-year est.); Travel time to work: 30.3% less than 15 minutes, 33.0% 15 to 30 minutes, 27.7% 30 to 45 minutes, 5.9% 45 to 60 minutes, 3.2% 60 minutes or more (2006-2010 5-year est.)

GLENFIELD (borough). Covers a land area of 0.820 square miles and a water area of 0.168 square miles. Located at 40.52° N. Lat; 80.14° W. Long. Elevation is 768 feet.
Population: 201 (1990); 236 (2000); 205 (2010); Density: 250.0 persons per square mile (2010); Race: 94.6% White, 0.0% Black, 2.4% Asian, 1.0% American Indian/Alaska Native, 0.0% Native Hawaiian/Other Pacific Islander, 2.0% Other, 0.5% Hispanic of any race (2010); Average household size: 2.28 (2010); Median age: 46.1 (2010); Males per 100 females: 91.6 (2010); Marriage status: 15.8% never married, 62.7% now married, 6.3% widowed, 15.2% divorced (2006-2010 5-year est.); Foreign born: 2.3% (2006-2010 5-year est.); Ancestry (includes multiple ancestries): 33.1% German, 22.9% Irish, 13.7% Italian, 9.7% Slovak, 7.4% Lebanese (2006-2010 5-year est.).
Economy: Single-family building permits issued: 4 (2011); Multi-family building permits issued: 0 (2011); Employment by occupation: 2.8% management, 4.7% professional, 8.5% services, 19.8% sales, 6.6% farming, 21.7% construction, 13.2% production (2006-2010 5-year est.).
Income: Per capita income: $34,017 (2006-2010 5-year est.); Median household income: $39,063 (2006-2010 5-year est.); Average household income: $64,515 (2006-2010 5-year est.); Percent of households with income of $100,000 or more: 18.3% (2006-2010 5-year est.); Poverty rate: 9.1% (2006-2010 5-year est.).
Education: Percent of population age 25 and over with: High school diploma (including GED) or higher: 93.9% (2006-2010 5-year est.); Bachelor's degree or higher: 15.6% (2006-2010 5-year est.); Master's degree or higher: 5.4% (2006-2010 5-year est.).
Housing: Homeownership rate: 80.0% (2010); Median home value: $105,000 (2006-2010 5-year est.); Median contract rent: $319 per month (2006-2010 5-year est.); Median year structure built: 1949 (2006-2010 5-year est.).
Transportation: Commute to work: 94.1% car, 2.0% public transportation, 0.0% walk, 3.9% work from home (2006-2010 5-year est.); Travel time to work: 26.5% less than 15 minutes, 46.9% 15 to 30 minutes, 26.5% 30 to 45 minutes, 0.0% 45 to 60 minutes, 0.0% 60 minutes or more (2006-2010 5-year est.)

GLENSHAW (CDP). Covers a land area of 3.101 square miles and a water area of 0 square miles. Located at 40.54° N. Lat; 79.97° W. Long. Elevation is 1,089 feet.
Population: n/a (1990); n/a (2000); 8,981 (2010); Density: 2,895.8 persons per square mile (2010); Race: 97.7% White, 0.7% Black, 0.7% Asian, 0.0% American Indian/Alaska Native, 0.0% Native Hawaiian/Other Pacific Islander, 0.9% Other, 0.7% Hispanic of any race (2010); Average household size: 2.44 (2010); Median age: 46.2 (2010); Males per 100 females: 94.4 (2010); Marriage status: 22.8% never married, 65.3% now married, 6.9% widowed, 5.0% divorced (2006-2010 5-year est.); Foreign born: 1.7% (2006-2010 5-year est.); Ancestry (includes multiple ancestries): 43.1% German, 23.7% Irish, 18.5% Italian, 12.0% Polish, 9.3% English (2006-2010 5-year est.).
Economy: Employment by occupation: 13.2% management, 6.2% professional, 6.3% services, 21.7% sales, 3.7% farming, 4.9% construction, 3.5% production (2006-2010 5-year est.).
Income: Per capita income: $37,877 (2006-2010 5-year est.); Median household income: $67,500 (2006-2010 5-year est.); Average household

income: $90,554 (2006-2010 5-year est.); Percent of households with income of $100,000 or more: 22.8% (2006-2010 5-year est.); Poverty rate: 0.7% (2006-2010 5-year est.).
Education: Percent of population age 25 and over with: High school diploma (including GED) or higher: 92.8% (2006-2010 5-year est.); Bachelor's degree or higher: 35.0% (2006-2010 5-year est.); Master's degree or higher: 10.5% (2006-2010 5-year est.).

School District(s)

Shaler Area SD (KG-12)
   2010-11 Enrollment: 4,968 . . . . (412) 492-1200
Housing: Homeownership rate: 93.0% (2010); Median home value: $143,800 (2006-2010 5-year est.); Median contract rent: $528 per month (2006-2010 5-year est.); Median year structure built: 1955 (2006-2010 5-year est.).
Transportation: Commute to work: 91.9% car, 3.9% public transportation, 1.3% walk, 2.2% work from home (2006-2010 5-year est.); Travel time to work: 21.1% less than 15 minutes, 42.2% 15 to 30 minutes, 26.8% 30 to 45 minutes, 6.7% 45 to 60 minutes, 3.3% 60 minutes or more (2006-2010 5-year est.)

GREEN TREE (borough). Covers a land area of 2.075 square miles and a water area of 0 square miles. Located at 40.42° N. Lat; 80.05° W. Long. Elevation is 1,207 feet.
History: Incorporated 1885.
Population: 4,903 (1990); 4,719 (2000); 4,432 (2010); Density: 2,135.5 persons per square mile (2010); Race: 94.7% White, 1.8% Black, 2.5% Asian, 0.1% American Indian/Alaska Native, 0.0% Native Hawaiian/Other Pacific Islander, 0.9% Other, 1.2% Hispanic of any race (2010); Average household size: 2.26 (2010); Median age: 47.4 (2010); Males per 100 females: 92.1 (2010); Marriage status: 26.3% never married, 62.1% now married, 6.4% widowed, 5.3% divorced (2006-2010 5-year est.); Foreign born: 3.0% (2006-2010 5-year est.); Ancestry (includes multiple ancestries): 29.0% Irish, 27.5% German, 26.0% Italian, 14.2% Polish, 4.8% English (2006-2010 5-year est.).
Economy: Single-family building permits issued: 1 (2011); Multi-family building permits issued: 0 (2011); Employment by occupation: 24.0% management, 4.9% professional, 4.7% services, 17.8% sales, 4.5% farming, 4.9% construction, 2.3% production (2006-2010 5-year est.).
Income: Per capita income: $38,844 (2006-2010 5-year est.); Median household income: $70,398 (2006-2010 5-year est.); Average household income: $89,239 (2006-2010 5-year est.); Percent of households with income of $100,000 or more: 25.2% (2006-2010 5-year est.); Poverty rate: 3.0% (2006-2010 5-year est.).
Education: Percent of population age 25 and over with: High school diploma (including GED) or higher: 96.1% (2006-2010 5-year est.); Bachelor's degree or higher: 37.6% (2006-2010 5-year est.); Master's degree or higher: 13.1% (2006-2010 5-year est.).
Housing: Homeownership rate: 88.1% (2010); Median home value: $143,300 (2006-2010 5-year est.); Median contract rent: $572 per month (2006-2010 5-year est.); Median year structure built: 1957 (2006-2010 5-year est.).
Transportation: Commute to work: 83.1% car, 9.9% public transportation, 2.6% walk, 4.4% work from home (2006-2010 5-year est.); Travel time to work: 22.2% less than 15 minutes, 50.9% 15 to 30 minutes, 18.5% 30 to 45 minutes, 3.5% 45 to 60 minutes, 4.9% 60 minutes or more (2006-2010 5-year est.)
Additional Information Contacts
Borough of Green Tree . . . . (412) 921-1110
   http://www.greentreeboro.com
Northside Northshore Chamber of Commerce . . . . (412) 231-6500
   http://www.northsidechamberofcommerce.com

GREENOCK (CDP). Covers a land area of 1.066 square miles and a water area of 0.100 square miles. Located at 40.31° N. Lat; 79.80° W. Long. Elevation is 971 feet.
Population: n/a (1990); n/a (2000); 2,195 (2010); Density: 2,059.7 persons per square mile (2010); Race: 97.9% White, 0.3% Black, 0.4% Asian, 0.0% American Indian/Alaska Native, 0.0% Native Hawaiian/Other Pacific Islander, 1.4% Other, 0.5% Hispanic of any race (2010); Average household size: 2.28 (2010); Median age: 45.0 (2010); Males per 100 females: 94.8 (2010); Marriage status: 22.1% never married, 53.8% now married, 9.4% widowed, 14.6% divorced (2006-2010 5-year est.); Foreign born: 2.2% (2006-2010 5-year est.); Ancestry (includes multiple ancestries): 18.9% German, 16.9% Irish, 16.2% English, 13.8% Slovak, 13.2% Italian (2006-2010 5-year est.).

Economy: Employment by occupation: 7.5% management, 1.4% professional, 18.8% services, 20.2% sales, 3.2% farming, 8.4% construction, 3.3% production (2006-2010 5-year est.).

Income: Per capita income: $24,163 (2006-2010 5-year est.); Median household income: $44,083 (2006-2010 5-year est.); Average household income: $49,206 (2006-2010 5-year est.); Percent of households with income of $100,000 or more: 6.2% (2006-2010 5-year est.); Poverty rate: 2.7% (2006-2010 5-year est.).

Education: Percent of population age 25 and over with: High school diploma (including GED) or higher: 91.4% (2006-2010 5-year est.); Bachelor's degree or higher: 14.4% (2006-2010 5-year est.); Master's degree or higher: 5.6% (2006-2010 5-year est.).

Housing: Homeownership rate: 76.8% (2010); Median home value: $87,900 (2006-2010 5-year est.); Median contract rent: $511 per month (2006-2010 5-year est.); Median year structure built: 1955 (2006-2010 5-year est.).

Transportation: Commute to work: 94.4% car, 1.3% public transportation, 1.6% walk, 2.7% work from home (2006-2010 5-year est.); Travel time to work: 20.2% less than 15 minutes, 34.8% 15 to 30 minutes, 23.6% 30 to 45 minutes, 10.0% 45 to 60 minutes, 11.4% 60 minutes or more (2006-2010 5-year est.)

HAMPTON (township). Covers a land area of 16.198 square miles and a water area of 0.007 square miles. Located at 40.59° N. Lat; 79.95° W. Long.

Population: 15,588 (1990); 17,526 (2000); 18,363 (2010); Density: 1,133.7 persons per square mile (2010); Race: 96.0% White, 0.9% Black, 2.1% Asian, 0.0% American Indian/Alaska Native, 0.0% Native Hawaiian/Other Pacific Islander, 1.0% Other, 0.8% Hispanic of any race (2010); Average household size: 2.54 (2010); Median age: 44.7 (2010); Males per 100 females: 93.8 (2010); Marriage status: 21.6% never married, 65.0% now married, 7.0% widowed, 6.4% divorced (2006-2010 5-year est.); Foreign born: 4.6% (2006-2010 5-year est.); Ancestry (includes multiple ancestries): 38.1% German, 22.9% Irish, 19.3% Italian, 10.2% Polish, 9.0% English (2006-2010 5-year est.).

Economy: Single-family building permits issued: 8 (2011); Multi-family building permits issued: 0 (2011); Employment by occupation: 17.9% management, 6.3% professional, 5.7% services, 17.4% sales, 5.1% farming, 5.3% construction, 3.0% production (2006-2010 5-year est.).

Income: Per capita income: $40,720 (2006-2010 5-year est.); Median household income: $76,230 (2006-2010 5-year est.); Average household income: $103,083 (2006-2010 5-year est.); Percent of households with income of $100,000 or more: 32.7% (2006-2010 5-year est.); Poverty rate: 4.1% (2006-2010 5-year est.).

Taxes: Total city taxes per capita: $424 (2009); City property taxes per capita: $165 (2009).

Education: Percent of population age 25 and over with: High school diploma (including GED) or higher: 95.5% (2006-2010 5-year est.); Bachelor's degree or higher: 45.6% (2006-2010 5-year est.); Master's degree or higher: 15.9% (2006-2010 5-year est.).

Housing: Homeownership rate: 83.5% (2010); Median home value: $192,300 (2006-2010 5-year est.); Median contract rent: $801 per month (2006-2010 5-year est.); Median year structure built: 1974 (2006-2010 5-year est.).

Safety: Violent crime rate: 10.3 per 10,000 population; Property crime rate: 66.2 per 10,000 population (2011).

Transportation: Commute to work: 90.0% car, 2.6% public transportation, 1.1% walk, 5.3% work from home (2006-2010 5-year est.); Travel time to work: 20.7% less than 15 minutes, 34.6% 15 to 30 minutes, 25.2% 30 to 45 minutes, 13.0% 45 to 60 minutes, 6.6% 60 minutes or more (2006-2010 5-year est.)

Additional Information Contacts
Hampton Township . . . . (412) 486-0400
  http://www.hampton-pa.org
The Chamber of Commerce, Inc. (724) 934-9700
  http://www.thechamberinc.com

HARMAR (township). Covers a land area of 5.881 square miles and a water area of 0.450 square miles. Located at 40.55° N. Lat; 79.85° W. Long.

Population: 3,144 (1990); 3,242 (2000); 2,921 (2010); Density: 496.7 persons per square mile (2010); Race: 97.7% White, 0.6% Black, 0.7% Asian, 0.0% American Indian/Alaska Native, 0.0% Native Hawaiian/Other Pacific Islander, 1.0% Other, 1.1% Hispanic of any race (2010); Average household size: 1.93 (2010); Median age: 53.6 (2010); Males per 100

females: 86.6 (2010); Marriage status: 26.3% never married, 39.2% now married, 17.2% widowed, 17.2% divorced (2006-2010 5-year est.); Foreign born: 2.2% (2006-2010 5-year est.); Ancestry (includes multiple ancestries): 31.1% German, 20.4% Irish, 17.6% Italian, 17.0% Polish, 12.8% English (2006-2010 5-year est.).

Economy: Single-family building permits issued: 40 (2011); Multi-family building permits issued: 0 (2011); Employment by occupation: 16.6% management, 5.0% professional, 6.6% services, 13.2% sales, 4.1% farming, 4.9% construction, 5.4% production (2006-2010 5-year est.).

Income: Per capita income: $39,792 (2006-2010 5-year est.); Median household income: $38,779 (2006-2010 5-year est.); Average household income: $71,907 (2006-2010 5-year est.); Percent of households with income of $100,000 or more: 19.8% (2006-2010 5-year est.); Poverty rate: 12.4% (2006-2010 5-year est.).

Education: Percent of population age 25 and over with: High school diploma (including GED) or higher: 89.9% (2006-2010 5-year est.); Bachelor's degree or higher: 28.7% (2006-2010 5-year est.); Master's degree or higher: 12.8% (2006-2010 5-year est.).

Housing: Homeownership rate: 72.0% (2010); Median home value: $97,400 (2006-2010 5-year est.); Median contract rent: $441 per month (2006-2010 5-year est.); Median year structure built: 1965 (2006-2010 5-year est.).

Safety: Violent crime rate: 37.5 per 10,000 population; Property crime rate: 198.0 per 10,000 population (2011).

Transportation: Commute to work: 87.0% car, 2.6% public transportation, 4.8% walk, 4.5% work from home (2006-2010 5-year est.); Travel time to work: 32.6% less than 15 minutes, 35.9% 15 to 30 minutes, 20.7% 30 to 45 minutes, 4.6% 45 to 60 minutes, 6.2% 60 minutes or more (2006-2010 5-year est.)

Additional Information Contacts
Allegheny Valley Chamber of Commerce . . . . (724) 224-3400
  http://alleghenyvalleychamber.com

HARRISON (township). Covers a land area of 7.360 square miles and a water area of 0.525 square miles. Located at 40.64° N. Lat; 79.72° W. Long.

Population: 11,763 (1990); 10,934 (2000); 10,461 (2010); Density: 1,421.3 persons per square mile (2010); Race: 93.8% White, 3.5% Black, 0.6% Asian, 0.1% American Indian/Alaska Native, 0.0% Native Hawaiian/Other Pacific Islander, 2.0% Other, 0.9% Hispanic of any race (2010); Average household size: 2.22 (2010); Median age: 44.5 (2010); Males per 100 females: 89.0 (2010); Marriage status: 30.5% never married, 46.5% now married, 10.4% widowed, 12.6% divorced (2006-2010 5-year est.); Foreign born: 1.4% (2006-2010 5-year est.); Ancestry (includes multiple ancestries): 32.0% German, 19.0% Polish, 16.6% Irish, 14.8% Italian, 14.1% Slovak (2006-2010 5-year est.).

Economy: Single-family building permits issued: 3 (2011); Multi-family building permits issued: 0 (2011); Employment by occupation: 8.7% management, 4.7% professional, 9.9% services, 19.1% sales, 4.4% farming, 9.8% construction, 5.1% production (2006-2010 5-year est.).

Income: Per capita income: $22,538 (2006-2010 5-year est.); Median household income: $40,452 (2006-2010 5-year est.); Average household income: $51,649 (2006-2010 5-year est.); Percent of households with income of $100,000 or more: 12.7% (2006-2010 5-year est.); Poverty rate: 14.7% (2006-2010 5-year est.).

Education: Percent of population age 25 and over with: High school diploma (including GED) or higher: 90.5% (2006-2010 5-year est.); Bachelor's degree or higher: 19.7% (2006-2010 5-year est.); Master's degree or higher: 6.6% (2006-2010 5-year est.).

Housing: Homeownership rate: 68.8% (2010); Median home value: $90,300 (2006-2010 5-year est.); Median contract rent: $491 per month (2006-2010 5-year est.); Median year structure built: 1952 (2006-2010 5-year est.).

Transportation: Commute to work: 92.0% car, 2.1% public transportation, 4.2% walk, 1.3% work from home (2006-2010 5-year est.); Travel time to work: 36.3% less than 15 minutes, 31.5% 15 to 30 minutes, 22.0% 30 to 45 minutes, 5.5% 45 to 60 minutes, 4.6% 60 minutes or more (2006-2010 5-year est.)

Additional Information Contacts
Allegheny Valley Chamber of Commerce . . . . (724) 224-3400
  http://alleghenyvalleychamber.com
Harrison Township . . . . (724) 226-1393

HARWICK (CDP). Covers a land area of 0.442 square miles and a water area of 0 square miles. Located at 40.56° N. Lat; 79.81° W. Long. Elevation is 955 feet.

Population: n/a (1990); n/a (2000); 899 (2010); Density: 2,034.3 persons per square mile (2010); Race: 99.4% White, 0.2% Black, 0.1% Asian, 0.2% American Indian/Alaska Native, 0.0% Native Hawaiian/Other Pacific Islander, 0.1% Other, 0.8% Hispanic of any race (2010); Average household size: 1.90 (2010); Median age: 50.6 (2010); Males per 100 females: 84.2 (2010); Marriage status: 23.3% never married, 49.0% now married, 15.9% widowed, 11.8% divorced (2006-2010 5-year est.); Foreign born: 1.0% (2006-2010 5-year est.); Ancestry (includes multiple ancestries): 38.2% German, 20.3% Italian, 19.9% Polish, 19.3% Irish, 7.2% Slovak (2006-2010 5-year est.).

Economy: Employment by occupation: 6.4% management, 5.1% professional, 6.1% services, 24.3% sales, 0.7% farming, 6.9% construction, 6.9% production (2006-2010 5-year est.).

Income: Per capita income: $24,967 (2006-2010 5-year est.); Median household income: $37,240 (2006-2010 5-year est.); Average household income: $47,001 (2006-2010 5-year est.); Percent of households with income of $100,000 or more: 9.9% (2006-2010 5-year est.); Poverty rate: 6.5% (2006-2010 5-year est.).

Education: Percent of population age 25 and over with: High school diploma (including GED) or higher: 84.3% (2006-2010 5-year est.); Bachelor's degree or higher: 24.9% (2006-2010 5-year est.); Master's degree or higher: 7.9% (2006-2010 5-year est.).

Housing: Homeownership rate: 77.2% (2010); Median home value: $91,700 (2006-2010 5-year est.); Median contract rent: $429 per month (2006-2010 5-year est.); Median year structure built: 1960 (2006-2010 5-year est.).

Transportation: Commute to work: 93.5% car, 0.0% public transportation, 2.7% walk, 3.0% work from home (2006-2010 5-year est.); Travel time to work: 42.1% less than 15 minutes, 27.9% 15 to 30 minutes, 15.4% 30 to 45 minutes, 11.8% 45 to 60 minutes, 2.8% 60 minutes or more (2006-2010 5-year est.)

HAYSVILLE (borough). Covers a land area of 0.172 square miles and a water area of 0.061 square miles. Located at 40.53° N. Lat; 80.15° W. Long. Elevation is 725 feet.

Population: 114 (1990); 78 (2000); 70 (2010); Density: 405.9 persons per square mile (2010); Race: 94.3% White, 0.0% Black, 1.4% Asian, 0.0% American Indian/Alaska Native, 0.0% Native Hawaiian/Other Pacific Islander, 4.3% Other, 2.9% Hispanic of any race (2010); Average household size: 2.06 (2010); Median age: 49.5 (2010); Males per 100 females: 94.4 (2010); Marriage status: 20.5% never married, 46.6% now married, 15.1% widowed, 17.8% divorced (2006-2010 5-year est.); Foreign born: 0.0% (2006-2010 5-year est.); Ancestry (includes multiple ancestries): 45.3% German, 32.0% Irish, 16.0% English, 9.3% Italian, 6.7% Polish (2006-2010 5-year est.).

Economy: Single-family building permits issued: 0 (2011); Multi-family building permits issued: 0 (2011); Employment by occupation: 16.7% management, 0.0% professional, 13.3% services, 33.3% sales, 0.0% farming, 0.0% construction, 0.0% production (2006-2010 5-year est.).

Income: Per capita income: $23,049 (2006-2010 5-year est.); Median household income: $48,750 (2006-2010 5-year est.); Average household income: $44,938 (2006-2010 5-year est.); Percent of households with income of $100,000 or more: 5.4% (2006-2010 5-year est.); Poverty rate: 2.7% (2006-2010 5-year est.).

Education: Percent of population age 25 and over with: High school diploma (including GED) or higher: 92.6% (2006-2010 5-year est.); Bachelor's degree or higher: 4.4% (2006-2010 5-year est.); Master's degree or higher: 0.0% (2006-2010 5-year est.).

Housing: Homeownership rate: 79.4% (2010); Median home value: $82,900 (2006-2010 5-year est.); Median contract rent: n/a per month (2006-2010 5-year est.); Median year structure built: before 1940 (2006-2010 5-year est.).

Transportation: Commute to work: 100.0% car, 0.0% public transportation, 0.0% walk, 0.0% work from home (2006-2010 5-year est.); Travel time to work: 0.0% less than 15 minutes, 80.0% 15 to 30 minutes, 13.3% 30 to 45 minutes, 6.7% 45 to 60 minutes, 0.0% 60 minutes or more (2006-2010 5-year est.)

HEIDELBERG (borough). Covers a land area of 0.283 square miles and a water area of 0 square miles. Located at 40.39° N. Lat; 80.09° W. Long. Elevation is 827 feet.

Population: 1,238 (1990); 1,225 (2000); 1,244 (2010); Density: 4,390.2 persons per square mile (2010); Race: 95.9% White, 2.3% Black, 0.4% Asian, 0.0% American Indian/Alaska Native, 0.0% Native Hawaiian/Other Pacific Islander, 1.4% Other, 1.5% Hispanic of any race (2010); Average household size: 2.02 (2010); Median age: 43.9 (2010); Males per 100 females: 98.4 (2010); Marriage status: 36.1% never married, 43.9% now married, 8.1% widowed, 11.9% divorced (2006-2010 5-year est.); Foreign born: 1.4% (2006-2010 5-year est.); Ancestry (includes multiple ancestries): 37.7% German, 26.4% Irish, 24.9% Polish, 13.9% Italian, 8.6% English (2006-2010 5-year est.).

Economy: Single-family building permits issued: 0 (2011); Multi-family building permits issued: 0 (2011); Employment by occupation: 12.7% management, 3.2% professional, 11.0% services, 16.7% sales, 6.3% farming, 7.9% construction, 5.5% production (2006-2010 5-year est.).

Income: Per capita income: $22,512 (2006-2010 5-year est.); Median household income: $34,559 (2006-2010 5-year est.); Average household income: $47,053 (2006-2010 5-year est.); Percent of households with income of $100,000 or more: 8.8% (2006-2010 5-year est.); Poverty rate: 9.3% (2006-2010 5-year est.).

Education: Percent of population age 25 and over with: High school diploma (including GED) or higher: 92.7% (2006-2010 5-year est.); Bachelor's degree or higher: 19.0% (2006-2010 5-year est.); Master's degree or higher: 4.2% (2006-2010 5-year est.).

Housing: Homeownership rate: 67.4% (2010); Median home value: $87,400 (2006-2010 5-year est.); Median contract rent: $518 per month (2006-2010 5-year est.); Median year structure built: 1945 (2006-2010 5-year est.).

Transportation: Commute to work: 90.1% car, 7.0% public transportation, 1.0% walk, 1.9% work from home (2006-2010 5-year est.); Travel time to work: 30.8% less than 15 minutes, 37.1% 15 to 30 minutes, 18.6% 30 to 45 minutes, 7.2% 45 to 60 minutes, 6.2% 60 minutes or more (2006-2010 5-year est.)

Additional Information Contacts

South Hills Chamber of Commerce . . . . (412) 306-8090
http://www.shchamber.org

HOMESTEAD (borough). Covers a land area of 0.575 square miles and a water area of 0.069 square miles. Located at 40.41° N. Lat; 79.91° W. Long. Elevation is 787 feet.

History: Once a foremost U.S. steel producer. In 1892 the famous outbreak of the Homestead Strike, one of the most bitterly fought industrial disputes in U.S. labor history, occurred here. Incorporated 1880.

Population: 4,179 (1990); 3,569 (2000); 3,165 (2010); Density: 5,499.7 persons per square mile (2010); Race: 32.8% White, 59.1% Black, 3.0% Asian, 0.2% American Indian/Alaska Native, 0.0% Native Hawaiian/Other Pacific Islander, 4.9% Other, 1.8% Hispanic of any race (2010); Average household size: 2.11 (2010); Median age: 40.3 (2010); Males per 100 females: 85.7 (2010); Marriage status: 43.1% never married, 37.3% now married, 7.3% widowed, 12.3% divorced (2006-2010 5-year est.); Foreign born: 5.4% (2006-2010 5-year est.); Ancestry (includes multiple ancestries): 16.2% American, 9.7% Irish, 6.3% French, 4.6% German, 3.3% Russian (2006-2010 5-year est.).

Economy: Single-family building permits issued: 0 (2011); Multi-family building permits issued: 0 (2011); Employment by occupation: 6.0% management, 3.4% professional, 13.5% services, 26.3% sales, 2.0% farming, 0.0% construction, 5.1% production (2006-2010 5-year est.).

Income: Per capita income: $15,494 (2006-2010 5-year est.); Median household income: $25,063 (2006-2010 5-year est.); Average household income: $38,017 (2006-2010 5-year est.); Percent of households with income of $100,000 or more: 5.5% (2006-2010 5-year est.); Poverty rate: 38.0% (2006-2010 5-year est.).

Education: Percent of population age 25 and over with: High school diploma (including GED) or higher: 86.3% (2006-2010 5-year est.); Bachelor's degree or higher: 17.9% (2006-2010 5-year est.); Master's degree or higher: 9.2% (2006-2010 5-year est.).

School District(s)

Pa Learners Online Regional Cyber CS (KG-12)
    2010-11 Enrollment: 467 . . . . (412) 394-5733
Propel CS-Homestead (KG-12)
    2010-11 Enrollment: 555 . . . . (412) 464-2604
Steel Valley SD (KG-12)
    2010-11 Enrollment: 1,846 . . . . (412) 464-3600

Housing: Homeownership rate: 34.9% (2010); Median home value: $39,600 (2006-2010 5-year est.); Median contract rent: $385 per month (2006-2010 5-year est.); Median year structure built: before 1940 (2006-2010 5-year est.).
Safety: Violent crime rate: 122.8 per 10,000 population; Property crime rate: 869.3 per 10,000 population (2011).
Transportation: Commute to work: 52.8% car, 20.8% public transportation, 20.7% walk, 5.6% work from home (2006-2010 5-year est.); Travel time to work: 22.8% less than 15 minutes, 37.7% 15 to 30 minutes, 29.3% 30 to 45 minutes, 5.5% 45 to 60 minutes, 4.6% 60 minutes or more (2006-2010 5-year est.)
Additional Information Contacts
South Side Chamber of Commerce . . . . (412) 431-3360
  http://www.southsidechamber.org

IMPERIAL (CDP). Covers a land area of 3.131 square miles and a water area of 0 square miles. Located at 40.45° N. Lat; 80.25° W. Long. Elevation is 971 feet.
Population: n/a (1990); n/a (2000); 2,541 (2010); Density: 811.5 persons per square mile (2010); Race: 95.6% White, 2.1% Black, 0.8% Asian, 0.2% American Indian/Alaska Native, 0.0% Native Hawaiian/Other Pacific Islander, 1.3% Other, 0.9% Hispanic of any race (2010); Average household size: 2.31 (2010); Median age: 40.9 (2010); Males per 100 females: 98.5 (2010); Marriage status: 21.3% never married, 60.0% now married, 7.7% widowed, 11.0% divorced (2006-2010 5-year est.); Foreign born: 6.0% (2006-2010 5-year est.); Ancestry (includes multiple ancestries): 38.0% German, 24.1% Italian, 14.4% Irish, 11.7% English, 9.2% Polish (2006-2010 5-year est.).
Economy: Employment by occupation: 10.3% management, 4.3% professional, 5.1% services, 20.1% sales, 3.5% farming, 7.6% construction, 7.6% production (2006-2010 5-year est.).
Income: Per capita income: $21,136 (2006-2010 5-year est.); Median household income: $44,091 (2006-2010 5-year est.); Average household income: $51,484 (2006-2010 5-year est.); Percent of households with income of $100,000 or more: 11.4% (2006-2010 5-year est.); Poverty rate: 11.1% (2006-2010 5-year est.).
Education: Percent of population age 25 and over with: High school diploma (including GED) or higher: 85.8% (2006-2010 5-year est.); Bachelor's degree or higher: 22.5% (2006-2010 5-year est.); Master's degree or higher: 12.2% (2006-2010 5-year est.).
School District(s)
West Allegheny SD (KG-12)
  2010-11 Enrollment: 3,262 . . . . (724) 695-3422
Housing: Homeownership rate: 64.7% (2010); Median home value: $121,700 (2006-2010 5-year est.); Median contract rent: $428 per month (2006-2010 5-year est.); Median year structure built: 1957 (2006-2010 5-year est.).
Transportation: Commute to work: 93.8% car, 1.3% public transportation, 0.0% walk, 4.9% work from home (2006-2010 5-year est.); Travel time to work: 34.5% less than 15 minutes, 37.7% 15 to 30 minutes, 15.3% 30 to 45 minutes, 9.8% 45 to 60 minutes, 2.7% 60 minutes or more (2006-2010 5-year est.)

INDIANA (township). Covers a land area of 17.568 square miles and a water area of 0 square miles. Located at 40.57° N. Lat; 79.87° W. Long.
Population: 6,308 (1990); 6,809 (2000); 7,253 (2010); Density: 412.8 persons per square mile (2010); Race: 91.6% White, 1.4% Black, 5.6% Asian, 0.1% American Indian/Alaska Native, 0.0% Native Hawaiian/Other Pacific Islander, 1.3% Other, 1.6% Hispanic of any race (2010); Average household size: 2.63 (2010); Median age: 43.7 (2010); Males per 100 females: 95.0 (2010); Marriage status: 22.7% never married, 62.9% now married, 6.6% widowed, 7.9% divorced (2006-2010 5-year est.); Foreign born: 6.4% (2006-2010 5-year est.); Ancestry (includes multiple ancestries): 32.0% German, 25.7% Irish, 19.6% Italian, 12.7% Polish, 8.4% English (2006-2010 5-year est.).
Economy: Single-family building permits issued: 12 (2011); Multi-family building permits issued: 0 (2011); Employment by occupation: 17.5% management, 5.7% professional, 6.2% services, 12.5% sales, 2.4% farming, 6.9% construction, 5.9% production (2006-2010 5-year est.).
Income: Per capita income: $38,766 (2006-2010 5-year est.); Median household income: $73,242 (2006-2010 5-year est.); Average household income: $110,412 (2006-2010 5-year est.); Percent of households with income of $100,000 or more: 35.0% (2006-2010 5-year est.); Poverty rate: 4.8% (2006-2010 5-year est.).

Education: Percent of population age 25 and over with: High school diploma (including GED) or higher: 91.7% (2006-2010 5-year est.); Bachelor's degree or higher: 43.9% (2006-2010 5-year est.); Master's degree or higher: 18.1% (2006-2010 5-year est.).
Housing: Homeownership rate: 84.2% (2010); Median home value: $193,300 (2006-2010 5-year est.); Median contract rent: $622 per month (2006-2010 5-year est.); Median year structure built: 1958 (2006-2010 5-year est.).
Safety: Violent crime rate: 11.0 per 10,000 population; Property crime rate: 82.5 per 10,000 population (2011).
Transportation: Commute to work: 91.7% car, 2.5% public transportation, 0.0% walk, 4.6% work from home (2006-2010 5-year est.); Travel time to work: 19.5% less than 15 minutes, 40.9% 15 to 30 minutes, 24.3% 30 to 45 minutes, 8.2% 45 to 60 minutes, 7.1% 60 minutes or more (2006-2010 5-year est.)
Additional Information Contacts
Allegheny Valley Chamber of Commerce . . . . (724) 224-3400
  http://alleghenyvalleychamber.com
Indiana Township . . . . (412) 767-5333
  http://www.indianatownship.com

INDIANOLA (unincorporated postal area)
Zip Code: 15051
  Covers a land area of 0.827 square miles and a water area of 0 square miles. Located at 40.56° N. Lat; 79.86° W. Long. Elevation is 922 feet. Population: 461 (2010); Density: 556.8 persons per square mile (2010); Race: 97.6% White, 2.0% Black, 0.0% Asian, 0.2% American Indian/Alaska Native, 0.0% Native Hawaiian/Other Pacific Islander, 0.2% Other, 1.3% Hispanic of any race (2010); Average household size: 2.06 (2010); Median age: 45.8 (2010); Males per 100 females: 92.9 (2010); Homeownership rate: 71.9% (2010)

INGRAM (borough). Covers a land area of 0.434 square miles and a water area of 0 square miles. Located at 40.44° N. Lat; 80.07° W. Long. Elevation is 925 feet.
History: Incorporated 1902.
Population: 3,901 (1990); 3,712 (2000); 3,330 (2010); Density: 7,672.2 persons per square mile (2010); Race: 91.7% White, 5.7% Black, 0.7% Asian, 0.2% American Indian/Alaska Native, 0.0% Native Hawaiian/Other Pacific Islander, 1.7% Other, 1.1% Hispanic of any race (2010); Average household size: 2.20 (2010); Median age: 41.8 (2010); Males per 100 females: 91.0 (2010); Marriage status: 26.3% never married, 50.5% now married, 10.7% widowed, 12.4% divorced (2006-2010 5-year est.); Foreign born: 0.7% (2006-2010 5-year est.); Ancestry (includes multiple ancestries): 41.0% German, 35.3% Irish, 20.4% Italian, 8.7% Polish, 5.5% English (2006-2010 5-year est.).
Economy: Single-family building permits issued: 0 (2011); Multi-family building permits issued: 0 (2011); Employment by occupation: 6.3% management, 1.0% professional, 9.3% services, 20.6% sales, 8.8% farming, 9.2% construction, 5.7% production (2006-2010 5-year est.).
Income: Per capita income: $21,447 (2006-2010 5-year est.); Median household income: $44,564 (2006-2010 5-year est.); Average household income: $49,309 (2006-2010 5-year est.); Percent of households with income of $100,000 or more: 11.9% (2006-2010 5-year est.); Poverty rate: 9.3% (2006-2010 5-year est.).
Education: Percent of population age 25 and over with: High school diploma (including GED) or higher: 91.8% (2006-2010 5-year est.); Bachelor's degree or higher: 20.8% (2006-2010 5-year est.); Master's degree or higher: 2.3% (2006-2010 5-year est.).
Housing: Homeownership rate: 63.9% (2010); Median home value: $89,500 (2006-2010 5-year est.); Median contract rent: $529 per month (2006-2010 5-year est.); Median year structure built: 1942 (2006-2010 5-year est.).
Safety: Violent crime rate: 12.0 per 10,000 population; Property crime rate: 56.9 per 10,000 population (2011).
Transportation: Commute to work: 83.9% car, 11.6% public transportation, 2.4% walk, 2.1% work from home (2006-2010 5-year est.); Travel time to work: 33.3% less than 15 minutes, 45.8% 15 to 30 minutes, 13.7% 30 to 45 minutes, 6.0% 45 to 60 minutes, 1.2% 60 minutes or more (2006-2010 5-year est.)
Additional Information Contacts
South Hills Chamber of Commerce . . . . (412) 306-8090
  http://www.shchamber.org

JEFFERSON HILLS (borough). Covers a land area of 16.516 square miles and a water area of 0.166 square miles. Located at 40.29° N. Lat; 79.94° W. Long.

Population: 9,533 (1990); 9,666 (2000); 10,619 (2010); Density: 642.9 persons per square mile (2010); Race: 95.9% White, 1.8% Black, 1.3% Asian, 0.1% American Indian/Alaska Native, 0.0% Native Hawaiian/Other Pacific Islander, 0.9% Other, 0.9% Hispanic of any race (2010); Average household size: 2.45 (2010); Median age: 43.9 (2010); Males per 100 females: 94.6 (2010); Marriage status: 25.0% never married, 60.6% now married, 6.8% widowed, 7.6% divorced (2006-2010 5-year est.); Foreign born: 3.9% (2006-2010 5-year est.); Ancestry (includes multiple ancestries): 32.2% German, 20.7% Irish, 18.3% Italian, 10.0% English, 8.6% Polish (2006-2010 5-year est.).

Economy: Single-family building permits issued: 57 (2011); Multi-family building permits issued: 0 (2011); Employment by occupation: 9.7% management, 7.1% professional, 9.3% services, 16.6% sales, 6.0% farming, 9.9% construction, 4.1% production (2006-2010 5-year est.).

Income: Per capita income: $37,161 (2006-2010 5-year est.); Median household income: $70,293 (2006-2010 5-year est.); Average household income: $89,036 (2006-2010 5-year est.); Percent of households with income of $100,000 or more: 30.6% (2006-2010 5-year est.); Poverty rate: 5.4% (2006-2010 5-year est.).

Education: Percent of population age 25 and over with: High school diploma (including GED) or higher: 93.9% (2006-2010 5-year est.); Bachelor's degree or higher: 38.0% (2006-2010 5-year est.); Master's degree or higher: 16.2% (2006-2010 5-year est.).

School District(s)

Steel Center Avts (10-12)
    2010-11 Enrollment: n/a . . . . (412) 469-3200
West Jefferson Hills SD (KG-12)
    2010-11 Enrollment: 2,820 . . . . (412) 655-8450

Housing: Homeownership rate: 78.8% (2010); Median home value: $167,600 (2006-2010 5-year est.); Median contract rent: $672 per month (2006-2010 5-year est.); Median year structure built: 1973 (2006-2010 5-year est.).

Hospitals: Jefferson Regional Medical Center (370 beds)

Safety: Violent crime rate: 5.6 per 10,000 population; Property crime rate: 79.8 per 10,000 population (2011).

Transportation: Commute to work: 92.3% car, 3.6% public transportation, 1.1% walk, 2.3% work from home (2006-2010 5-year est.); Travel time to work: 27.9% less than 15 minutes, 29.0% 15 to 30 minutes, 19.7% 30 to 45 minutes, 14.1% 45 to 60 minutes, 9.4% 60 minutes or more (2006-2010 5-year est.)

Additional Information Contacts

Borough of Jefferson Hills . . . . (412) 655-2222
    http://www.jeffersonhills.boroughs.org
Brentwood Baldwin Whitehall Chamber of Commerce . . . . (412) 884-1233
    http://www.bbwchamber.com

KENNEDY (township). Covers a land area of 5.483 square miles and a water area of 0.047 square miles. Located at 40.48° N. Lat; 80.10° W. Long.

Population: 7,265 (1990); 7,504 (2000); 7,672 (2010); Density: 1,399.3 persons per square mile (2010); Race: 96.9% White, 1.3% Black, 0.8% Asian, 0.1% American Indian/Alaska Native, 0.0% Native Hawaiian/Other Pacific Islander, 0.9% Other, 0.6% Hispanic of any race (2010); Average household size: 2.32 (2010); Median age: 47.8 (2010); Males per 100 females: 91.5 (2010); Marriage status: 27.0% never married, 54.0% now married, 13.3% widowed, 5.7% divorced (2006-2010 5-year est.); Foreign born: 3.4% (2006-2010 5-year est.); Ancestry (includes multiple ancestries): 33.8% German, 25.8% Italian, 20.0% Irish, 11.9% Polish, 6.8% Slovak (2006-2010 5-year est.).

Economy: Single-family building permits issued: 32 (2011); Multi-family building permits issued: 0 (2011); Employment by occupation: 13.2% management, 5.0% professional, 5.3% services, 22.6% sales, 5.2% farming, 9.4% construction, 4.3% production (2006-2010 5-year est.).

Income: Per capita income: $31,699 (2006-2010 5-year est.); Median household income: $63,468 (2006-2010 5-year est.); Average household income: $78,650 (2006-2010 5-year est.); Percent of households with income of $100,000 or more: 25.4% (2006-2010 5-year est.); Poverty rate: 7.6% (2006-2010 5-year est.).

Education: Percent of population age 25 and over with: High school diploma (including GED) or higher: 90.1% (2006-2010 5-year est.); Bachelor's degree or higher: 28.4% (2006-2010 5-year est.); Master's degree or higher: 6.2% (2006-2010 5-year est.).

Housing: Homeownership rate: 85.2% (2010); Median home value: $152,200 (2006-2010 5-year est.); Median contract rent: $720 per month (2006-2010 5-year est.); Median year structure built: 1967 (2006-2010 5-year est.).

Transportation: Commute to work: 92.4% car, 4.5% public transportation, 0.3% walk, 1.8% work from home (2006-2010 5-year est.); Travel time to work: 27.9% less than 15 minutes, 41.8% 15 to 30 minutes, 20.5% 30 to 45 minutes, 4.6% 45 to 60 minutes, 5.1% 60 minutes or more (2006-2010 5-year est.)

Additional Information Contacts

Kennedy Township . . . . (412) 771-2321
South Hills Chamber of Commerce . . . . (412) 306-8090
    http://www.shchamber.org

KILBUCK (township). Covers a land area of 2.534 square miles and a water area of 0.062 square miles. Located at 40.52° N. Lat; 80.10° W. Long.

Population: 905 (1990); 723 (2000); 697 (2010); Density: 275.1 persons per square mile (2010); Race: 97.8% White, 0.7% Black, 0.1% Asian, 0.0% American Indian/Alaska Native, 0.0% Native Hawaiian/Other Pacific Islander, 1.4% Other, 0.6% Hispanic of any race (2010); Average household size: 2.45 (2010); Median age: 46.9 (2010); Males per 100 females: 94.2 (2010); Marriage status: 17.9% never married, 67.3% now married, 7.3% widowed, 7.5% divorced (2006-2010 5-year est.); Foreign born: 0.4% (2006-2010 5-year est.); Ancestry (includes multiple ancestries): 39.7% German, 30.7% Irish, 13.6% Italian, 12.7% English, 7.5% Polish (2006-2010 5-year est.).

Economy: Single-family building permits issued: 1 (2011); Multi-family building permits issued: 0 (2011); Employment by occupation: 10.6% management, 8.5% professional, 1.8% services, 14.3% sales, 4.6% farming, 10.3% construction, 5.5% production (2006-2010 5-year est.).

Income: Per capita income: $35,515 (2006-2010 5-year est.); Median household income: $82,500 (2006-2010 5-year est.); Average household income: $87,693 (2006-2010 5-year est.); Percent of households with income of $100,000 or more: 32.2% (2006-2010 5-year est.); Poverty rate: 4.5% (2006-2010 5-year est.).

Education: Percent of population age 25 and over with: High school diploma (including GED) or higher: 93.6% (2006-2010 5-year est.); Bachelor's degree or higher: 45.5% (2006-2010 5-year est.); Master's degree or higher: 16.8% (2006-2010 5-year est.).

Housing: Homeownership rate: 92.2% (2010); Median home value: $162,300 (2006-2010 5-year est.); Median contract rent: $338 per month (2006-2010 5-year est.); Median year structure built: 1954 (2006-2010 5-year est.).

Safety: Violent crime rate: 0.0 per 10,000 population; Property crime rate: 100.1 per 10,000 population (2011).

Transportation: Commute to work: 91.7% car, 2.1% public transportation, 0.9% walk, 5.2% work from home (2006-2010 5-year est.); Travel time to work: 12.3% less than 15 minutes, 58.4% 15 to 30 minutes, 15.8% 30 to 45 minutes, 2.3% 45 to 60 minutes, 11.3% 60 minutes or more (2006-2010 5-year est.)

LEET (township). Covers a land area of 1.501 square miles and a water area of 0 square miles. Located at 40.57° N. Lat; 80.20° W. Long.

History: Settled 1796, incorporated 1904.

Population: 1,731 (1990); 1,568 (2000); 1,634 (2010); Density: 1,088.3 persons per square mile (2010); Race: 91.6% White, 3.5% Black, 2.6% Asian, 0.2% American Indian/Alaska Native, 0.0% Native Hawaiian/Other Pacific Islander, 2.1% Other, 2.1% Hispanic of any race (2010); Average household size: 2.72 (2010); Median age: 41.3 (2010); Males per 100 females: 91.6 (2010); Marriage status: 22.1% never married, 62.2% now married, 5.6% widowed, 10.0% divorced (2006-2010 5-year est.); Foreign born: 5.0% (2006-2010 5-year est.); Ancestry (includes multiple ancestries): 26.4% German, 23.9% Irish, 17.1% English, 16.2% Italian, 9.1% Polish (2006-2010 5-year est.).

Economy: Single-family building permits issued: 0 (2011); Multi-family building permits issued: 0 (2011); Employment by occupation: 19.8% management, 8.3% professional, 4.2% services, 18.0% sales, 2.0% farming, 6.4% construction, 6.8% production (2006-2010 5-year est.).

Income: Per capita income: $34,581 (2006-2010 5-year est.); Median household income: $64,792 (2006-2010 5-year est.); Average household income: $90,063 (2006-2010 5-year est.); Percent of households with income of $100,000 or more: 29.6% (2006-2010 5-year est.); Poverty rate: 6.2% (2006-2010 5-year est.).

Education: Percent of population age 25 and over with: High school diploma (including GED) or higher: 94.0% (2006-2010 5-year est.); Bachelor's degree or higher: 43.2% (2006-2010 5-year est.); Master's degree or higher: 18.8% (2006-2010 5-year est.).

Housing: Homeownership rate: 87.4% (2010); Median home value: $151,900 (2006-2010 5-year est.); Median contract rent: $621 per month (2006-2010 5-year est.); Median year structure built: 1961 (2006-2010 5-year est.).

Safety: Violent crime rate: 0.0 per 10,000 population; Property crime rate: 0.0 per 10,000 population (2011).

Transportation: Commute to work: 95.2% car, 0.5% public transportation, 0.0% walk, 2.9% work from home (2006-2010 5-year est.); Travel time to work: 15.1% less than 15 minutes, 35.6% 15 to 30 minutes, 32.4% 30 to 45 minutes, 9.3% 45 to 60 minutes, 7.5% 60 minutes or more (2006-2010 5-year est.)

Additional Information Contacts

Ambridge Area Chamber of Commerce . . . . (724) 266-3040
  http://www.ambridgechamberofcommerce.com

LEETSDALE (borough). Covers a land area of 1.000 square miles and a water area of 0.176 square miles. Located at 40.57° N. Lat; 80.22° W. Long. Elevation is 715 feet.

Population: 1,387 (1990); 1,232 (2000); 1,218 (2010); Density: 1,217.6 persons per square mile (2010); Race: 86.0% White, 7.6% Black, 1.5% Asian, 0.1% American Indian/Alaska Native, 0.0% Native Hawaiian/Other Pacific Islander, 4.8% Other, 2.3% Hispanic of any race (2010); Average household size: 2.16 (2010); Median age: 44.5 (2010); Males per 100 females: 89.4 (2010); Marriage status: 31.5% never married, 45.8% now married, 10.3% widowed, 12.4% divorced (2006-2010 5-year est.); Foreign born: 1.3% (2006-2010 5-year est.); Ancestry (includes multiple ancestries): 26.0% German, 21.7% Irish, 20.5% Italian, 16.3% English, 5.5% Scotch-Irish (2006-2010 5-year est.).

Economy: Single-family building permits issued: 0 (2011); Multi-family building permits issued: 0 (2011); Employment by occupation: 12.6% management, 1.9% professional, 13.3% services, 17.8% sales, 3.3% farming, 9.8% construction, 7.2% production (2006-2010 5-year est.).

Income: Per capita income: $24,834 (2006-2010 5-year est.); Median household income: $37,132 (2006-2010 5-year est.); Average household income: $51,619 (2006-2010 5-year est.); Percent of households with income of $100,000 or more: 11.3% (2006-2010 5-year est.); Poverty rate: 5.8% (2006-2010 5-year est.).

Education: Percent of population age 25 and over with: High school diploma (including GED) or higher: 90.8% (2006-2010 5-year est.); Bachelor's degree or higher: 21.0% (2006-2010 5-year est.); Master's degree or higher: 6.5% (2006-2010 5-year est.).

School District(s)

Quaker Valley SD (KG-12)
  2010-11 Enrollment: 1,983 . . . . (412) 749-3600

Housing: Homeownership rate: 60.7% (2010); Median home value: $80,200 (2006-2010 5-year est.); Median contract rent: $517 per month (2006-2010 5-year est.); Median year structure built: before 1940 (2006-2010 5-year est.).

Safety: Violent crime rate: 40.9 per 10,000 population; Property crime rate: 319.1 per 10,000 population (2011).

Transportation: Commute to work: 85.2% car, 3.9% public transportation, 6.7% walk, 1.6% work from home (2006-2010 5-year est.); Travel time to work: 29.1% less than 15 minutes, 44.3% 15 to 30 minutes, 13.9% 30 to 45 minutes, 9.1% 45 to 60 minutes, 3.6% 60 minutes or more (2006-2010 5-year est.)

Additional Information Contacts

The Chamber of Commerce, Inc. (724) 776-4949
  http://www.thechamberinc.com

LIBERTY (borough). Covers a land area of 1.430 square miles and a water area of 0.056 square miles. Located at 40.32° N. Lat; 79.86° W. Long. Elevation is 912 feet.

History: Incorporated c.1912.

Population: 2,744 (1990); 2,670 (2000); 2,551 (2010); Density: 1,783.4 persons per square mile (2010); Race: 97.5% White, 1.4% Black, 0.2% Asian, 0.1% American Indian/Alaska Native, 0.0% Native Hawaiian/Other Pacific Islander, 0.8% Other, 0.4% Hispanic of any race (2010); Average household size: 2.31 (2010); Median age: 45.3 (2010); Males per 100 females: 93.0 (2010); Marriage status: 28.3% never married, 49.0% now married, 10.3% widowed, 12.4% divorced (2006-2010 5-year est.); Foreign born: 1.6% (2006-2010 5-year est.); Ancestry (includes multiple

ancestries): 28.4% German, 21.7% Irish, 14.1% Polish, 13.1% English, 13.0% Italian (2006-2010 5-year est.).

Economy: Single-family building permits issued: 0 (2011); Multi-family building permits issued: 0 (2011); Employment by occupation: 4.5% management, 3.1% professional, 8.9% services, 22.3% sales, 4.5% farming, 12.0% construction, 5.4% production (2006-2010 5-year est.).

Income: Per capita income: $22,613 (2006-2010 5-year est.); Median household income: $47,891 (2006-2010 5-year est.); Average household income: $54,619 (2006-2010 5-year est.); Percent of households with income of $100,000 or more: 7.8% (2006-2010 5-year est.); Poverty rate: 6.7% (2006-2010 5-year est.).

Education: Percent of population age 25 and over with: High school diploma (including GED) or higher: 92.0% (2006-2010 5-year est.); Bachelor's degree or higher: 14.2% (2006-2010 5-year est.); Master's degree or higher: 3.9% (2006-2010 5-year est.).

Housing: Homeownership rate: 84.9% (2010); Median home value: $75,400 (2006-2010 5-year est.); Median contract rent: $474 per month (2006-2010 5-year est.); Median year structure built: 1953 (2006-2010 5-year est.).

Transportation: Commute to work: 89.5% car, 4.8% public transportation, 1.4% walk, 2.9% work from home (2006-2010 5-year est.); Travel time to work: 29.8% less than 15 minutes, 36.3% 15 to 30 minutes, 11.6% 30 to 45 minutes, 8.2% 45 to 60 minutes, 14.1% 60 minutes or more (2006-2010 5-year est.)

Additional Information Contacts

Norwin Chamber of Commerce. . . . . (724) 863-0888
  http://www.norwinchamber.com/index.php

LINCOLN (borough). Covers a land area of 4.798 square miles and a water area of 0.211 square miles. Located at 40.29° N. Lat; 79.86° W. Long. Elevation is 1,086 feet.

Population: 1,152 (1990); 1,218 (2000); 1,072 (2010); Density: 223.4 persons per square mile (2010); Race: 98.3% White, 0.7% Black, 0.4% Asian, 0.1% American Indian/Alaska Native, 0.0% Native Hawaiian/Other Pacific Islander, 0.5% Other, 0.2% Hispanic of any race (2010); Average household size: 2.45 (2010); Median age: 47.0 (2010); Males per 100 females: 100.7 (2010); Marriage status: 23.1% never married, 55.9% now married, 11.8% widowed, 9.2% divorced (2006-2010 5-year est.); Foreign born: 2.5% (2006-2010 5-year est.); Ancestry (includes multiple ancestries): 36.7% German, 21.2% Italian, 18.7% Irish, 11.9% Slovak, 11.6% English (2006-2010 5-year est.).

Economy: Single-family building permits issued: 0 (2011); Multi-family building permits issued: 0 (2011); Employment by occupation: 11.6% management, 1.0% professional, 16.0% services, 14.9% sales, 0.8% farming, 11.6% construction, 9.1% production (2006-2010 5-year est.).

Income: Per capita income: $22,715 (2006-2010 5-year est.); Median household income: $49,875 (2006-2010 5-year est.); Average household income: $52,976 (2006-2010 5-year est.); Percent of households with income of $100,000 or more: 7.8% (2006-2010 5-year est.); Poverty rate: 4.9% (2006-2010 5-year est.).

Education: Percent of population age 25 and over with: High school diploma (including GED) or higher: 89.2% (2006-2010 5-year est.); Bachelor's degree or higher: 12.8% (2006-2010 5-year est.); Master's degree or higher: 4.3% (2006-2010 5-year est.).

Housing: Homeownership rate: 87.0% (2010); Median home value: $86,800 (2006-2010 5-year est.); Median contract rent: $496 per month (2006-2010 5-year est.); Median year structure built: 1954 (2006-2010 5-year est.).

Safety: Violent crime rate: 0.0 per 10,000 population; Property crime rate: 158.1 per 10,000 population (2011).

Transportation: Commute to work: 94.3% car, 1.3% public transportation, 0.8% walk, 3.0% work from home (2006-2010 5-year est.); Travel time to work: 15.1% less than 15 minutes, 31.3% 15 to 30 minutes, 20.1% 30 to 45 minutes, 23.4% 45 to 60 minutes, 10.1% 60 minutes or more (2006-2010 5-year est.)

Additional Information Contacts

Borough of Lincoln . . . . (412) 751-2655
  http://lincolnboro.tripod.com
Norwin Chamber of Commerce. . . . . (724) 863-0888
  http://www.norwinchamber.com/index.php

MARSHALL (township).

MARSHALL (township). Covers a land area of 15.455 square miles and a water area of 0 square miles. Located at 40.65° N. Lat; 80.11° W. Long.

History: Incorporated June 3, 1863, it was named for Thomas Mercer Marshall, a famous trial lawyer who practiced law in Allegheny County.

Population: 4,090 (1990); 5,996 (2000); 6,915 (2010); Density: 447.4 persons per square mile (2010); Race: 90.4% White, 1.2% Black, 6.6% Asian, 0.1% American Indian/Alaska Native, 0.0% Native Hawaiian/Other Pacific Islander, 1.7% Other, 2.2% Hispanic of any race (2010); Average household size: 2.86 (2010); Median age: 41.4 (2010); Males per 100 females: 99.1 (2010); Marriage status: 24.9% never married, 66.9% now married, 4.7% widowed, 3.5% divorced (2006-2010 5-year est.); Foreign born: 10.4% (2006-2010 5-year est.); Ancestry (includes multiple ancestries): 34.2% German, 17.8% Italian, 16.8% Irish, 12.7% English, 5.8% Polish (2006-2010 5-year est.).

Economy: Single-family building permits issued: 38 (2011); Multi-family building permits issued: 0 (2011); Employment by occupation: 23.1% management, 6.4% professional, 5.0% services, 13.4% sales, 1.3% farming, 3.1% construction, 3.3% production (2006-2010 5-year est.).

Income: Per capita income: $60,113 (2006-2010 5-year est.); Median household income: $124,740 (2006-2010 5-year est.); Average household income: $183,822 (2006-2010 5-year est.); Percent of households with income of $100,000 or more: 59.1% (2006-2010 5-year est.); Poverty rate: 1.1% (2006-2010 5-year est.).

Education: Percent of population age 25 and over with: High school diploma (including GED) or higher: 98.1% (2006-2010 5-year est.); Bachelor's degree or higher: 67.9% (2006-2010 5-year est.); Master's degree or higher: 35.7% (2006-2010 5-year est.).

Housing: Homeownership rate: 91.7% (2010); Median home value: $290,500 (2006-2010 5-year est.); Median contract rent: $900 per month (2006-2010 5-year est.); Median year structure built: 1989 (2006-2010 5-year est.).

Transportation: Commute to work: 88.8% car, 1.3% public transportation, 0.8% walk, 8.3% work from home (2006-2010 5-year est.); Travel time to work: 23.7% less than 15 minutes, 32.3% 15 to 30 minutes, 29.2% 30 to 45 minutes, 5.3% 45 to 60 minutes, 9.5% 60 minutes or more (2006-2010 5-year est.)

Additional Information Contacts
Marshall Township . . . . (724) 935-3090
    http://www.twp.marshall.pa.us
The Chamber of Commerce, Inc. (724) 934-9700
    http://www.thechamberinc.com

MCCANDLESS (township).

MCCANDLESS (township). Covers a land area of 16.499 square miles and a water area of 0.104 square miles. Located at 40.58° N. Lat; 80.03° W. Long.

Population: 28,781 (1990); 29,022 (2000); 28,457 (2010); Density: 1,724.8 persons per square mile (2010); Race: 91.9% White, 1.7% Black, 5.0% Asian, 0.1% American Indian/Alaska Native, 0.0% Native Hawaiian/Other Pacific Islander, 1.3% Other, 1.1% Hispanic of any race (2010); Average household size: 2.36 (2010); Median age: 44.0 (2010); Males per 100 females: 90.2 (2010); Marriage status: 27.3% never married, 59.2% now married, 6.9% widowed, 6.7% divorced (2006-2010 5-year est.); Foreign born: 5.6% (2006-2010 5-year est.); Ancestry (includes multiple ancestries): 39.0% German, 22.8% Irish, 16.1% Italian, 10.0% Polish, 7.9% English (2006-2010 5-year est.).

Economy: Unemployment rate: 5.4% (August 2012); Total civilian labor force: 16,302 (August 2012); Single-family building permits issued: 27 (2011); Multi-family building permits issued: 0 (2011); Employment by occupation: 17.6% management, 6.8% professional, 6.7% services, 15.9% sales, 4.2% farming, 5.1% construction, 3.2% production (2006-2010 5-year est.).

Income: Per capita income: $38,491 (2006-2010 5-year est.); Median household income: $75,132 (2006-2010 5-year est.); Average household income: $95,623 (2006-2010 5-year est.); Percent of households with income of $100,000 or more: 34.6% (2006-2010 5-year est.); Poverty rate: 5.4% (2006-2010 5-year est.).

Education: Percent of population age 25 and over with: High school diploma (including GED) or higher: 96.2% (2006-2010 5-year est.); Bachelor's degree or higher: 54.5% (2006-2010 5-year est.); Master's degree or higher: 24.0% (2006-2010 5-year est.).

Housing: Homeownership rate: 76.5% (2010); Median home value: $187,700 (2006-2010 5-year est.); Median contract rent: $727 per month (2006-2010 5-year est.); Median year structure built: 1971 (2006-2010 5-year est.).

Safety: Violent crime rate: 1.8 per 10,000 population; Property crime rate: 86.2 per 10,000 population (2011).

Transportation: Commute to work: 90.1% car, 3.5% public transportation, 0.8% walk, 4.9% work from home (2006-2010 5-year est.); Travel time to work: 20.7% less than 15 minutes, 34.7% 15 to 30 minutes, 31.5% 30 to 45 minutes, 10.2% 45 to 60 minutes, 2.9% 60 minutes or more (2006-2010 5-year est.)

Additional Information Contacts
McCandless Township . . . . (724) 369-7905
    http://www.townofmccandless.org
The Chamber of Commerce, Inc. (724) 934-9700
    http://www.thechamberinc.com

MCKEES ROCKS (borough).

MCKEES ROCKS (borough). Covers a land area of 1.057 square miles and a water area of 0.063 square miles. Located at 40.47° N. Lat; 80.06° W. Long. Elevation is 751 feet.

History: Settled c.1764, incorporated 1892.

Population: 7,691 (1990); 6,622 (2000); 6,104 (2010); Density: 5,777.5 persons per square mile (2010); Race: 63.8% White, 30.8% Black, 0.4% Asian, 0.2% American Indian/Alaska Native, 0.0% Native Hawaiian/Other Pacific Islander, 4.8% Other, 1.7% Hispanic of any race (2010); Average household size: 2.17 (2010); Median age: 38.9 (2010); Males per 100 females: 88.6 (2010); Marriage status: 51.2% never married, 26.8% now married, 9.4% widowed, 12.7% divorced (2006-2010 5-year est.); Foreign born: 1.6% (2006-2010 5-year est.); Ancestry (includes multiple ancestries): 28.2% German, 18.4% Irish, 13.8% Italian, 8.3% English, 8.2% Polish (2006-2010 5-year est.).

Economy: Single-family building permits issued: 0 (2011); Multi-family building permits issued: 0 (2011); Employment by occupation: 3.4% management, 4.7% professional, 22.0% services, 19.0% sales, 1.2% farming, 9.0% construction, 5.1% production (2006-2010 5-year est.).

Income: Per capita income: $15,879 (2006-2010 5-year est.); Median household income: $20,767 (2006-2010 5-year est.); Average household income: $33,478 (2006-2010 5-year est.); Percent of households with income of $100,000 or more: 6.5% (2006-2010 5-year est.); Poverty rate: 36.6% (2006-2010 5-year est.).

Education: Percent of population age 25 and over with: High school diploma (including GED) or higher: 83.2% (2006-2010 5-year est.); Bachelor's degree or higher: 9.4% (2006-2010 5-year est.); Master's degree or higher: 3.8% (2006-2010 5-year est.).

School District(s)
Montour SD (KG-12)
    2010-11 Enrollment: 2,946 . . . . (412) 490-6500
Sto-Rox SD (KG-12)
    2010-11 Enrollment: 1,432 . . . . (412) 771-3213
Vocational/Technical School(s)
Pittsburgh's Ohio Valley Hospital School of Nursing (Private, Not-for-profit)
    Fall 2010 Enrollment: 36 . . . . (412) 777-6204
    2011-12 Tuition: In-state $13,229; Out-of-state $13,229

Housing: Homeownership rate: 40.8% (2010); Median home value: $57,500 (2006-2010 5-year est.); Median contract rent: $399 per month (2006-2010 5-year est.); Median year structure built: 1941 (2006-2010 5-year est.).

Hospitals: Ohio Valley General Hospital (103 beds)

Newspapers: Suburban Gazette (Local news; Circulation 8,300)

Transportation: Commute to work: 64.6% car, 21.1% public transportation, 9.1% walk, 2.4% work from home (2006-2010 5-year est.); Travel time to work: 35.0% less than 15 minutes, 37.4% 15 to 30 minutes, 18.9% 30 to 45 minutes, 4.4% 45 to 60 minutes, 4.2% 60 minutes or more (2006-2010 5-year est.)

Additional Information Contacts
Borough of McKees Rocks . . . . (412) 331-2498
    http://www.mckeesrocks.com
South Hills Chamber of Commerce . . . . (412) 306-8090
    http://www.shchamber.org

MCKEESPORT (city).

MCKEESPORT (city). Covers a land area of 5.044 square miles and a water area of 0.368 square miles. Located at 40.34° N. Lat; 79.85° W. Long. Elevation is 764 feet.

History: Named for David McKee, an Irishman who settled on the Youghiogheny River. Has undergone decline since the collapse of the U.S. steel industry in the 1980s. Pennsylvania State University—McKeesport Campus is here. Settled 1755. Incorporated as a city 1890.

Population: 26,016 (1990); 24,040 (2000); 19,731 (2010); Density: 3,911.5 persons per square mile (2010); Race: 62.3% White, 31.9% Black,

0.3% Asian, 0.3% American Indian/Alaska Native, 0.0% Native Hawaiian/Other Pacific Islander, 5.2% Other, 2.3% Hispanic of any race (2010); Average household size: 2.25 (2010); Median age: 41.5 (2010); Males per 100 females: 86.7 (2010); Marriage status: 41.6% never married, 33.1% now married, 12.1% widowed, 13.2% divorced (2006-2010 5-year est.); Foreign born: 1.8% (2006-2010 5-year est.); Ancestry (includes multiple ancestries): 16.8% German, 13.2% Irish, 11.9% Italian, 9.0% Polish, 7.2% English (2006-2010 5-year est.).
Economy: Unemployment rate: 10.9% (August 2012); Total civilian labor force: 8,571 (August 2012); Single-family building permits issued: 0 (2011); Multi-family building permits issued: 0 (2011); Employment by occupation: 7.6% management, 1.1% professional, 14.2% services, 19.1% sales, 6.1% farming, 8.0% construction, 5.2% production (2006-2010 5-year est.).
Income: Per capita income: $15,992 (2006-2010 5-year est.); Median household income: $25,943 (2006-2010 5-year est.); Average household income: $34,483 (2006-2010 5-year est.); Percent of households with income of $100,000 or more: 3.7% (2006-2010 5-year est.); Poverty rate: 29.1% (2006-2010 5-year est.).
Taxes: Total city taxes per capita: $274 (2009); City property taxes per capita: $101 (2009).
Education: Percent of population age 25 and over with: High school diploma (including GED) or higher: 82.7% (2006-2010 5-year est.); Bachelor's degree or higher: 9.6% (2006-2010 5-year est.); Master's degree or higher: 3.5% (2006-2010 5-year est.).

School District(s)

Elizabeth Forward SD (KG-12)
   2010-11 Enrollment: 2,491 . . . . (412) 896-2300
Elizabeth Forward SD (KG-12)
   2010-11 Enrollment: 2,491 . . . . (412) 896-2300
Mckeesport Area SD (KG-12)
   2010-11 Enrollment: 3,823 . . . . (412) 664-3610
Mckeesport Area Tech Ctr (10-12)
   2010-11 Enrollment: n/a . . . . (412) 948-3664
Propel CS-Mckeesport (KG-08)
   2010-11 Enrollment: 381 . . . . (412) 678-7215
South Allegheny SD (KG-12)
   2010-11 Enrollment: 1,572 . . . . (412) 675-3070
South Allegheny SD (KG-12)
   2010-11 Enrollment: 1,572 . . . . (412) 675-3070

Four-year College(s)

Pennsylvania State University-Penn State Greater Allegheny (Public)
   Fall 2010 Enrollment: 742 . . . . (412) 675-9000
   2011-12 Tuition: In-state $13,102; Out-of-state $19,542
Housing: Homeownership rate: 53.7% (2010); Median home value: $47,100 (2006-2010 5-year est.); Median contract rent: $388 per month (2006-2010 5-year est.); Median year structure built: 1941 (2006-2010 5-year est.).
Hospitals: Select Specialty Hospital of McKeesport (30 beds)
Safety: Violent crime rate: 169.7 per 10,000 population; Property crime rate: 385.5 per 10,000 population (2011).
Newspapers: The Daily News (Local news; Circulation 21,929)
Transportation: Commute to work: 81.4% car, 8.1% public transportation, 7.0% walk, 3.0% work from home (2006-2010 5-year est.); Travel time to work: 34.8% less than 15 minutes, 28.0% 15 to 30 minutes, 19.9% 30 to 45 minutes, 11.4% 45 to 60 minutes, 5.9% 60 minutes or more (2006-2010 5-year est.)
Additional Information Contacts
City of McKeesport . . . . (412) 675-5020
   http://www.mckeesport.org
Shadyside Chamber of Commerce . . . . (412) 682-1298
   http://www.thinkshadyside.com

MILLVALE (borough).
Covers a land area of 0.619 square miles and a water area of 0.059 square miles. Located at 40.48° N. Lat; 79.97° W. Long. Elevation is 794 feet.
History: Settled c.1844, incorporated 1868.
Population: 4,164 (1990); 4,028 (2000); 3,744 (2010); Density: 6,044.3 persons per square mile (2010); Race: 93.1% White, 3.8% Black, 0.2% Asian, 0.3% American Indian/Alaska Native, 0.0% Native Hawaiian/Other Pacific Islander, 2.6% Other, 1.4% Hispanic of any race (2010); Average household size: 2.09 (2010); Median age: 37.5 (2010); Males per 100 females: 95.5 (2010); Marriage status: 32.5% never married, 48.4% now married, 8.5% widowed, 10.5% divorced (2006-2010 5-year est.); Foreign born: 2.5% (2006-2010 5-year est.); Ancestry (includes multiple

ancestries): 38.5% German, 20.5% Italian, 19.5% Irish, 14.3% Polish, 6.1% English (2006-2010 5-year est.).
Economy: Single-family building permits issued: 0 (2011); Multi-family building permits issued: 0 (2011); Employment by occupation: 7.3% management, 3.1% professional, 15.7% services, 17.6% sales, 5.8% farming, 11.1% construction, 9.0% production (2006-2010 5-year est.).
Income: Per capita income: $22,733 (2006-2010 5-year est.); Median household income: $35,754 (2006-2010 5-year est.); Average household income: $46,582 (2006-2010 5-year est.); Percent of households with income of $100,000 or more: 4.1% (2006-2010 5-year est.); Poverty rate: 13.9% (2006-2010 5-year est.).
Education: Percent of population age 25 and over with: High school diploma (including GED) or higher: 82.6% (2006-2010 5-year est.); Bachelor's degree or higher: 14.8% (2006-2010 5-year est.); Master's degree or higher: 2.5% (2006-2010 5-year est.).
Housing: Homeownership rate: 42.5% (2010); Median home value: $55,900 (2006-2010 5-year est.); Median contract rent: $455 per month (2006-2010 5-year est.); Median year structure built: before 1940 (2006-2010 5-year est.).
Safety: Violent crime rate: 18.6 per 10,000 population; Property crime rate: 127.8 per 10,000 population (2011).
Transportation: Commute to work: 81.4% car, 10.0% public transportation, 5.5% walk, 2.8% work from home (2006-2010 5-year est.); Travel time to work: 28.6% less than 15 minutes, 49.9% 15 to 30 minutes, 10.9% 30 to 45 minutes, 3.3% 45 to 60 minutes, 7.3% 60 minutes or more (2006-2010 5-year est.)
Additional Information Contacts
Northside Northshore Chamber of Commerce . . . . (412) 231-6500
   http://www.northsidechamberofcommerce.com

MONROEVILLE (municipality).
Covers a land area of 19.739 square miles and a water area of 0.006 square miles. Located at 40.43° N. Lat; 79.76° W. Long. Elevation is 1,230 feet.
History: Settled 1810, Incorporated 1952.
Population: 29,304 (1990); 29,349 (2000); 28,386 (2010); Density: 1,438.1 persons per square mile (2010); Race: 79.5% White, 11.7% Black, 5.9% Asian, 0.2% American Indian/Alaska Native, 0.0% Native Hawaiian/Other Pacific Islander, 2.7% Other, 1.5% Hispanic of any race (2010); Average household size: 2.21 (2010); Median age: 45.9 (2010); Males per 100 females: 89.5 (2010); Marriage status: 29.0% never married, 55.9% now married, 8.3% widowed, 6.7% divorced (2006-2010 5-year est.); Foreign born: 7.8% (2006-2010 5-year est.); Ancestry (includes multiple ancestries): 24.2% German, 19.8% Irish, 15.0% Italian, 7.3% Polish, 7.1% English (2006-2010 5-year est.).
Economy: Unemployment rate: 7.3% (August 2012); Total civilian labor force: 16,295 (August 2012); Single-family building permits issued: 8 (2011); Multi-family building permits issued: 0 (2011); Employment by occupation: 15.0% management, 8.6% professional, 8.6% services, 14.1% sales, 5.1% farming, 5.2% construction, 3.8% production (2006-2010 5-year est.).
Income: Per capita income: $30,813 (2006-2010 5-year est.); Median household income: $57,254 (2006-2010 5-year est.); Average household income: $69,255 (2006-2010 5-year est.); Percent of households with income of $100,000 or more: 19.6% (2006-2010 5-year est.); Poverty rate: 6.3% (2006-2010 5-year est.).
Taxes: Total city taxes per capita: $753 (2009); City property taxes per capita: $154 (2009).
Education: Percent of population age 25 and over with: High school diploma (including GED) or higher: 94.5% (2006-2010 5-year est.); Bachelor's degree or higher: 40.7% (2006-2010 5-year est.); Master's degree or higher: 14.2% (2006-2010 5-year est.).

School District(s)

Forbes Road CTC (09-12)
   2010-11 Enrollment: n/a . . . . (412) 373-8100
Gateway SD (KG-12)
   2010-11 Enrollment: 3,800 . . . . (412) 372-5300
Spectrum CS (07-12)
   2010-11 Enrollment: 31 . . . . (412) 374-8130

Two-year College(s)

Career Training Academy-Monroeville (Private, For-profit)
   Fall 2010 Enrollment: 62 . . . . (412) 372-3900
ITT Technical Institute-Tarentum (Private, For-profit)
   Fall 2010 Enrollment: 297 . . . . (724) 274-1400
   2011-12 Tuition: In-state $18,048; Out-of-state $18,048

Vocational/Technical School(s)

Bella Capelli Academy (Private, For-profit)
Fall 2010 Enrollment: 74 . . . . (412) 373-3402
2011-12 Tuition: $14,400

Empire Beauty School-Monroeville (Private, For-profit)
Fall 2010 Enrollment: 265 . . . . (800) 223-3271
2011-12 Tuition: $14,490

Forbes Road Career and Technology Center (Public)
Fall 2010 Enrollment: 9 . . . . (412) 373-8100
2011-12 Tuition: $8,319

Housing: Homeownership rate: 67.4% (2010); Median home value: $122,200 (2006-2010 5-year est.); Median contract rent: $712 per month (2006-2010 5-year est.); Median year structure built: 1964 (2006-2010 5-year est.).

Hospitals: HealthSouth Rehabilitation Hospital of Greater Pittsburgh (89 beds); Western Pennsylvania Hospital - Forbes Regional Campus (340 beds)

Safety: Violent crime rate: 19.0 per 10,000 population; Property crime rate: 120.1 per 10,000 population (2011).

Newspapers: The Advance Leader (Community news; Circulation 6,030); Monroeville Times Express (Community news; Circulation 6,225); Murrysville Star (Community news; Circulation 5,000); Norwin Star (Community news; Circulation 5,000); Oakmont-Verona Advance Leader Star (Community news; Circulation 5,000); Penn-Trafford Star (Local news; Circulation 5,000); Plum Advance Leader (Community news; Circulation 3,200); Woodland Progress (Community news; Circulation 1,900)

Transportation: Commute to work: 88.2% car, 5.5% public transportation, 2.1% walk, 3.3% work from home (2006-2010 5-year est.); Travel time to work: 27.9% less than 15 minutes, 31.1% 15 to 30 minutes, 23.4% 30 to 45 minutes, 11.9% 45 to 60 minutes, 5.7% 60 minutes or more (2006-2010 5-year est.)

Additional Information Contacts

Municipality of Monroeville . . . . (412) 856-1000
http://www.monroeville.pa.us

Penn Hills Chamber of Commerce . . . . (412) 795-8741
http://www.pennhillschamber.org

MOON (township). Covers a land area of 23.924 square miles and a water area of 0.292 square miles. Located at 40.51° N. Lat; 80.21° W. Long. Elevation is 1,171 feet.

Population: 19,638 (1990); 22,290 (2000); 24,185 (2010); Density: 1,010.9 persons per square mile (2010); Race: 89.8% White, 4.5% Black, 3.1% Asian, 0.1% American Indian/Alaska Native, 0.0% Native Hawaiian/Other Pacific Islander, 2.5% Other, 2.0% Hispanic of any race (2010); Average household size: 2.37 (2010); Median age: 39.0 (2010); Males per 100 females: 99.0 (2010); Marriage status: 36.3% never married, 51.4% now married, 6.1% widowed, 6.2% divorced (2006-2010 5-year est.); Foreign born: 5.3% (2006-2010 5-year est.); Ancestry (includes multiple ancestries): 32.3% German, 22.7% Irish, 21.2% Italian, 11.9% Polish, 10.4% English (2006-2010 5-year est.).

Economy: Single-family building permits issued: 66 (2011); Multi-family building permits issued: 0 (2011); Employment by occupation: 16.3% management, 7.2% professional, 6.2% services, 20.2% sales, 5.2% farming, 4.5% construction, 4.2% production (2006-2010 5-year est.).

Income: Per capita income: $32,451 (2006-2010 5-year est.); Median household income: $70,387 (2006-2010 5-year est.); Average household income: $86,639 (2006-2010 5-year est.); Percent of households with income of $100,000 or more: 31.0% (2006-2010 5-year est.); Poverty rate: 8.0% (2006-2010 5-year est.).

Education: Percent of population age 25 and over with: High school diploma (including GED) or higher: 97.0% (2006-2010 5-year est.); Bachelor's degree or higher: 44.6% (2006-2010 5-year est.); Master's degree or higher: 15.0% (2006-2010 5-year est.).

School District(s)

Moon Area SD (KG-12)
2010-11 Enrollment: 3,705 . . . . (412) 264-9440

Four-year College(s)

Robert Morris University (Private, Not-for-profit)
Fall 2010 Enrollment: 4,560 . . . . (800) 762-0097
2011-12 Tuition: In-state $23,038; Out-of-state $23,038

Two-year College(s)

Heritage Valley Sewickley School of Nursing (Private, Not-for-profit)
Fall 2010 Enrollment: 95 . . . . (412) 269-7520
2011-12 Tuition: In-state $10,995; Out-of-state $10,995

Housing: Homeownership rate: 71.6% (2010); Median home value: $169,800 (2006-2010 5-year est.); Median contract rent: $688 per month (2006-2010 5-year est.); Median year structure built: 1972 (2006-2010 5-year est.).

Safety: Violent crime rate: 6.6 per 10,000 population; Property crime rate: 108.4 per 10,000 population (2011).

Transportation: Commute to work: 88.5% car, 2.5% public transportation, 4.1% walk, 2.9% work from home (2006-2010 5-year est.); Travel time to work: 35.9% less than 15 minutes, 33.7% 15 to 30 minutes, 17.9% 30 to 45 minutes, 7.0% 45 to 60 minutes, 5.5% 60 minutes or more (2006-2010 5-year est.)

Additional Information Contacts

Moon Township . . . . (412) 262-1700
http://www.moontwp.com

Pittsburgh Airport Area Chamber of Commerce . . . . (412) 264-6270
http://www.paacc.com

MOUNT LEBANON (township). Covers a land area of 6.078 square miles and a water area of 0.003 square miles. Located at 40.38° N. Lat; 80.05° W. Long. Elevation is 1,060 feet.

Population: 33,655 (1990); 33,017 (2000); 33,137 (2010); Density: 5,451.9 persons per square mile (2010); Race: 93.6% White, 1.1% Black, 3.7% Asian, 0.0% American Indian/Alaska Native, 0.0% Native Hawaiian/Other Pacific Islander, 1.6% Other, 1.8% Hispanic of any race (2010); Average household size: 2.30 (2010); Median age: 43.8 (2010); Males per 100 females: 87.7 (2010); Marriage status: 22.4% never married, 61.0% now married, 8.1% widowed, 8.5% divorced (2006-2010 5-year est.); Foreign born: 6.7% (2006-2010 5-year est.); Ancestry (includes multiple ancestries): 30.2% German, 24.8% Irish, 19.8% Italian, 12.4% English, 8.5% Polish (2006-2010 5-year est.).

Economy: Unemployment rate: 4.9% (August 2012); Total civilian labor force: 18,152 (August 2012); Single-family building permits issued: 6 (2011); Multi-family building permits issued: 0 (2011); Employment by occupation: 19.0% management, 6.6% professional, 5.7% services, 14.5% sales, 3.3% farming, 2.8% construction, 1.8% production (2006-2010 5-year est.).

Income: Per capita income: $44,561 (2006-2010 5-year est.); Median household income: $77,742 (2006-2010 5-year est.); Average household income: $104,460 (2006-2010 5-year est.); Percent of households with income of $100,000 or more: 39.8% (2006-2010 5-year est.); Poverty rate: 3.9% (2006-2010 5-year est.).

Taxes: Total city taxes per capita: $747 (2009); City property taxes per capita: $357 (2009).

Education: Percent of population age 25 and over with: High school diploma (including GED) or higher: 97.9% (2006-2010 5-year est.); Bachelor's degree or higher: 63.4% (2006-2010 5-year est.); Master's degree or higher: 28.7% (2006-2010 5-year est.).

Housing: Homeownership rate: 71.4% (2010); Median home value: $192,800 (2006-2010 5-year est.); Median contract rent: $661 per month (2006-2010 5-year est.); Median year structure built: 1950 (2006-2010 5-year est.).

Safety: Violent crime rate: 5.4 per 10,000 population; Property crime rate: 63.2 per 10,000 population (2011).

Transportation: Commute to work: 79.2% car, 12.0% public transportation, 2.9% walk, 5.1% work from home (2006-2010 5-year est.); Travel time to work: 23.3% less than 15 minutes, 31.4% 15 to 30 minutes, 30.4% 30 to 45 minutes, 8.0% 45 to 60 minutes, 6.8% 60 minutes or more (2006-2010 5-year est.)

Additional Information Contacts

Municipality of Mount Lebanon . . . . (412) 343-3400
http://mtlebanon.org

South Hills Chamber of Commerce . . . . (412) 306-8090
http://www.shchamber.org

MOUNT OLIVER (borough). Covers a land area of 0.340 square miles and a water area of 0 square miles. Located at 40.41° N. Long; 79.99° W. Long. Elevation is 1,148 feet.

History: Incorporated 1892.

Population: 4,160 (1990); 3,970 (2000); 3,403 (2010); Density: 10,022.6 persons per square mile (2010); Race: 61.4% White, 32.9% Black, 1.1% Asian, 0.3% American Indian/Alaska Native, 0.0% Native Hawaiian/Other Pacific Islander, 4.3% Other, 1.9% Hispanic of any race (2010); Average household size: 2.32 (2010); Median age: 36.2 (2010); Males per 100 females: 88.1 (2010); Marriage status: 39.1% never married, 37.5% now married, 6.2% widowed, 17.2% divorced (2006-2010 5-year est.); Foreign

born: 7.0% (2006-2010 5-year est.); Ancestry (includes multiple ancestries): 32.0% German, 19.2% Irish, 14.6% Polish, 9.0% Italian, 4.2% English (2006-2010 5-year est.).

Economy: Single-family building permits issued: 0 (2011); Multi-family building permits issued: 0 (2011); Employment by occupation: 2.9% management, 1.5% professional, 11.5% services, 21.9% sales, 2.5% farming, 9.3% construction, 13.7% production (2006-2010 5-year est.).

Income: Per capita income: $16,101 (2006-2010 5-year est.); Median household income: $31,663 (2006-2010 5-year est.); Average household income: $36,306 (2006-2010 5-year est.); Percent of households with income of $100,000 or more: 3.1% (2006-2010 5-year est.); Poverty rate: 24.1% (2006-2010 5-year est.).

Education: Percent of population age 25 and over with: High school diploma (including GED) or higher: 78.7% (2006-2010 5-year est.); Bachelor's degree or higher: 12.4% (2006-2010 5-year est.); Master's degree or higher: 8.1% (2006-2010 5-year est.).

Housing: Homeownership rate: 45.9% (2010); Median home value: $52,300 (2006-2010 5-year est.); Median contract rent: $513 per month (2006-2010 5-year est.); Median year structure built: before 1940 (2006-2010 5-year est.).

Safety: Violent crime rate: 105.4 per 10,000 population; Property crime rate: 489.2 per 10,000 population (2011).

Transportation: Commute to work: 71.6% car, 23.8% public transportation, 2.2% walk, 2.4% work from home (2006-2010 5-year est.); Travel time to work: 18.9% less than 15 minutes, 40.7% 15 to 30 minutes, 18.8% 30 to 45 minutes, 6.0% 45 to 60 minutes, 15.7% 60 minutes or more (2006-2010 5-year est.)

Additional Information Contacts

South Side Chamber of Commerce . . . . (412) 431-3360
http://www.southsidechamber.org

MUNHALL (borough). Covers a land area of 2.298 square miles and a water area of 0.089 square miles. Located at 40.39° N. Lat; 79.90° W. Long. Elevation is 1,043 feet.

History: Named for Captain John Munhall, who owned the land for the railway right-of-way. The once-large steel and iron works here have declined significantly along with the national steel industry. Munhall was a site of the Homestead Strike in 1892. Incorporated 1901.

Population: 13,158 (1990); 12,264 (2000); 11,406 (2010); Density: 4,964.2 persons per square mile (2010); Race: 87.5% White, 9.5% Black, 1.0% Asian, 0.1% American Indian/Alaska Native, 0.0% Native Hawaiian/Other Pacific Islander, 1.9% Other, 1.5% Hispanic of any race (2010); Average household size: 2.17 (2010); Median age: 43.4 (2010); Males per 100 females: 88.0 (2010); Marriage status: 34.0% never married, 44.1% now married, 12.0% widowed, 9.9% divorced (2006-2010 5-year est.); Foreign born: 2.6% (2006-2010 5-year est.); Ancestry (includes multiple ancestries): 24.1% German, 23.5% Irish, 15.9% Italian, 14.6% Slovak, 9.2% Hungarian (2006-2010 5-year est.).

Economy: Single-family building permits issued: 0 (2011); Multi-family building permits issued: 0 (2011); Employment by occupation: 9.1% management, 2.4% professional, 16.5% services, 21.7% sales, 5.2% farming, 9.1% construction, 4.2% production (2006-2010 5-year est.).

Income: Per capita income: $23,415 (2006-2010 5-year est.); Median household income: $38,515 (2006-2010 5-year est.); Average household income: $49,095 (2006-2010 5-year est.); Percent of households with income of $100,000 or more: 9.3% (2006-2010 5-year est.); Poverty rate: 9.4% (2006-2010 5-year est.).

Education: Percent of population age 25 and over with: High school diploma (including GED) or higher: 91.9% (2006-2010 5-year est.); Bachelor's degree or higher: 23.4% (2006-2010 5-year est.); Master's degree or higher: 7.3% (2006-2010 5-year est.).

School District(s)

Steel Valley SD (KG-12)

2010-11 Enrollment: 1,846 . . . . (412) 464-3600

Housing: Homeownership rate: 63.0% (2010); Median home value: $77,600 (2006-2010 5-year est.); Median contract rent: $447 per month (2006-2010 5-year est.); Median year structure built: 1949 (2006-2010 5-year est.).

Safety: Violent crime rate: 18.4 per 10,000 population; Property crime rate: 187.9 per 10,000 population (2011).

Newspapers: Valley Mirror (Local news; Circulation 6,000)

Transportation: Commute to work: 84.0% car, 10.7% public transportation, 2.2% walk, 1.3% work from home (2006-2010 5-year est.); Travel time to work: 26.1% less than 15 minutes, 30.4% 15 to 30 minutes,

25.7% 30 to 45 minutes, 11.9% 45 to 60 minutes, 5.8% 60 minutes or more (2006-2010 5-year est.)

Additional Information Contacts

Borough of Munhall . . . . (412) 464-7310
http://www.munhallpa.us
Shadyside Chamber of Commerce . . . . (412) 682-1298
http://www.thinkshadyside.com

NATRONA HEIGHTS (unincorporated postal area)

Zip Code: 15065

Covers a land area of 12.381 square miles and a water area of 0.524 square miles. Located at 40.64° N. Lat; 79.72° W. Long. Elevation is 994 feet. Population: 11,588 (2010); Density: 935.9 persons per square mile (2010); Race: 94.2% White, 3.2% Black, 0.6% Asian, 0.1% American Indian/Alaska Native, 0.0% Native Hawaiian/Other Pacific Islander, 1.9% Other, 0.9% Hispanic of any race (2010); Average household size: 2.25 (2010); Median age: 44.8 (2010); Males per 100 females: 90.9 (2010); Homeownership rate: 70.5% (2010)

NEVILLE (township). Covers a land area of 1.531 square miles and a water area of 0.814 square miles. Located at 40.51° N. Lat; 80.11° W. Long.

Population: 1,273 (1990); 1,232 (2000); 1,084 (2010); Density: 708.0 persons per square mile (2010); Race: 88.4% White, 3.3% Black, 0.1% Asian, 0.3% American Indian/Alaska Native, 0.0% Native Hawaiian/Other Pacific Islander, 7.9% Other, 6.5% Hispanic of any race (2010); Average household size: 2.01 (2010); Median age: 46.0 (2010); Males per 100 females: 103.4 (2010); Marriage status: 30.0% never married, 39.3% now married, 11.9% widowed, 18.8% divorced (2006-2010 5-year est.); Foreign born: 0.8% (2006-2010 5-year est.); Ancestry (includes multiple ancestries): 37.5% German, 20.8% Irish, 11.2% American, 11.1% Italian, 10.9% English (2006-2010 5-year est.).

Economy: Single-family building permits issued: 0 (2011); Multi-family building permits issued: 0 (2011); Employment by occupation: 3.1% management, 5.8% professional, 11.2% services, 19.1% sales, 2.6% farming, 21.3% construction, 12.9% production (2006-2010 5-year est.).

Income: Per capita income: $24,673 (2006-2010 5-year est.); Median household income: $40,759 (2006-2010 5-year est.); Average household income: $48,045 (2006-2010 5-year est.); Percent of households with income of $100,000 or more: 6.2% (2006-2010 5-year est.); Poverty rate: 12.1% (2006-2010 5-year est.).

Education: Percent of population age 25 and over with: High school diploma (including GED) or higher: 88.4% (2006-2010 5-year est.); Bachelor's degree or higher: 12.2% (2006-2010 5-year est.); Master's degree or higher: 2.6% (2006-2010 5-year est.).

Housing: Homeownership rate: 52.4% (2010); Median home value: $83,900 (2006-2010 5-year est.); Median contract rent: $466 per month (2006-2010 5-year est.); Median year structure built: 1947 (2006-2010 5-year est.).

Safety: Violent crime rate: 0.0 per 10,000 population; Property crime rate: 542.8 per 10,000 population (2011).

Transportation: Commute to work: 88.3% car, 5.5% public transportation, 4.1% walk, 2.1% work from home (2006-2010 5-year est.); Travel time to work: 21.8% less than 15 minutes, 56.2% 15 to 30 minutes, 13.4% 30 to 45 minutes, 5.8% 45 to 60 minutes, 2.8% 60 minutes or more (2006-2010 5-year est.)

Additional Information Contacts

Pittsburgh Airport Area Chamber of Commerce . . . . (412) 264-6270
http://www.paacc.com

NOBLESTOWN (CDP). Covers a land area of 1.208 square miles and a water area of 0 square miles. Located at 40.40° N. Lat; 80.20° W. Long. Elevation is 925 feet.

Population: n/a (1990); n/a (2000); 575 (2010); Density: 476.0 persons per square mile (2010); Race: 97.4% White, 1.2% Black, 0.3% Asian, 0.0% American Indian/Alaska Native, 0.0% Native Hawaiian/Other Pacific Islander, 1.1% Other, 0.9% Hispanic of any race (2010); Average household size: 2.67 (2010); Median age: 36.5 (2010); Males per 100 females: 103.2 (2010); Marriage status: 17.8% never married, 61.6% now married, 3.6% widowed, 17.0% divorced (2006-2010 5-year est.); Foreign born: 0.0% (2006-2010 5-year est.); Ancestry (includes multiple ancestries): 39.9% German, 33.8% Italian, 25.3% Polish, 18.5% Scottish, 15.3% English (2006-2010 5-year est.).

Economy: Employment by occupation: 6.5% management, 13.6% professional, 0.0% services, 13.6% sales, 5.9% farming, 2.4% construction, 7.7% production (2006-2010 5-year est.).

Income: Per capita income: $25,391 (2006-2010 5-year est.); Median household income: $52,917 (2006-2010 5-year est.); Average household income: $69,834 (2006-2010 5-year est.); Percent of households with income of $100,000 or more: 23.0% (2006-2010 5-year est.); Poverty rate: 0.0% (2006-2010 5-year est.).

Education: Percent of population age 25 and over with: High school diploma (including GED) or higher: 95.5% (2006-2010 5-year est.); Bachelor's degree or higher: 13.1% (2006-2010 5-year est.); Master's degree or higher: 4.1% (2006-2010 5-year est.).

Housing: Homeownership rate: 82.3% (2010); Median home value: $125,600 (2006-2010 5-year est.); Median contract rent: $507 per month (2006-2010 5-year est.); Median year structure built: 1954 (2006-2010 5-year est.).

Transportation: Commute to work: 91.7% car, 0.0% public transportation, 0.0% walk, 8.3% work from home (2006-2010 5-year est.); Travel time to work: 23.2% less than 15 minutes, 27.7% 15 to 30 minutes, 31.0% 30 to 45 minutes, 12.3% 45 to 60 minutes, 5.8% 60 minutes or more (2006-2010 5-year est.)

NORTH BRADDOCK (borough). Covers a land area of 1.492 square miles and a water area of 0.061 square miles. Located at 40.40° N. Lat; 79.85° W. Long. Elevation is 1,004 feet.

History: Andrew Carnegie's first steel plant was built here in 1875. The borough was the site of Gen. Edward Braddock's defeat in the last conflict of the French and Indian wars and of a mass meeting of farmers instituting the Whiskey Rebellion. Incorporated 1897.

Population: 7,036 (1990); 6,410 (2000); 4,857 (2010); Density: 3,254.7 persons per square mile (2010); Race: 51.2% White, 44.9% Black, 0.2% Asian, 0.1% American Indian/Alaska Native, 0.0% Native Hawaiian/Other Pacific Islander, 3.6% Other, 1.3% Hispanic of any race (2010); Average household size: 2.22 (2010); Median age: 41.7 (2010); Males per 100 females: 88.6 (2010); Marriage status: 46.2% never married, 32.3% now married, 10.0% widowed, 11.5% divorced (2006-2010 5-year est.); Foreign born: 1.6% (2006-2010 5-year est.); Ancestry (includes multiple ancestries): 16.9% Irish, 14.9% German, 10.2% Italian, 6.8% Slovak, 5.9% Polish (2006-2010 5-year est.).

Economy: Single-family building permits issued: 0 (2011); Multi-family building permits issued: 0 (2011); Employment by occupation: 5.0% management, 4.1% professional, 18.8% services, 13.0% sales, 10.4% farming, 4.7% construction, 6.5% production (2006-2010 5-year est.).

Income: Per capita income: $16,803 (2006-2010 5-year est.); Median household income: $25,217 (2006-2010 5-year est.); Average household income: $38,697 (2006-2010 5-year est.); Percent of households with income of $100,000 or more: 6.5% (2006-2010 5-year est.); Poverty rate: 23.8% (2006-2010 5-year est.).

Education: Percent of population age 25 and over with: High school diploma (including GED) or higher: 82.2% (2006-2010 5-year est.); Bachelor's degree or higher: 5.9% (2006-2010 5-year est.); Master's degree or higher: 1.1% (2006-2010 5-year est.).

Housing: Homeownership rate: 51.5% (2010); Median home value: $45,100 (2006-2010 5-year est.); Median contract rent: $370 per month (2006-2010 5-year est.); Median year structure built: before 1940 (2006-2010 5-year est.).

Transportation: Commute to work: 78.0% car, 13.5% public transportation, 2.9% walk, 5.5% work from home (2006-2010 5-year est.); Travel time to work: 17.6% less than 15 minutes, 40.1% 15 to 30 minutes, 28.8% 30 to 45 minutes, 5.0% 45 to 60 minutes, 8.5% 60 minutes or more (2006-2010 5-year est.)

Additional Information Contacts
Borough of North Braddock. . . . . (412) 824-0447
Shadyside Chamber of Commerce . . . . (412) 682-1298
   http://www.thinkshadyside.com

NORTH FAYETTE (township). Covers a land area of 25.184 square miles and a water area of 0 square miles. Located at 40.42° N. Lat; 80.22° W. Long.

Population: 9,537 (1990); 12,254 (2000); 13,934 (2010); Density: 553.3 persons per square mile (2010); Race: 92.9% White, 2.8% Black, 2.5% Asian, 0.1% American Indian/Alaska Native, 0.0% Native Hawaiian/Other Pacific Islander, 1.7% Other, 1.4% Hispanic of any race (2010); Average household size: 2.40 (2010); Median age: 38.2 (2010); Males per 100 females: 98.7 (2010); Marriage status: 25.7% never married, 59.2% now

married, 5.1% widowed, 10.1% divorced (2006-2010 5-year est.); Foreign born: 3.8% (2006-2010 5-year est.); Ancestry (includes multiple ancestries): 36.5% German, 22.8% Irish, 22.3% Italian, 10.2% English, 10.0% Polish (2006-2010 5-year est.).

Economy: Single-family building permits issued: 10 (2011); Multi-family building permits issued: 0 (2011); Employment by occupation: 16.1% management, 6.9% professional, 7.3% services, 15.1% sales, 5.3% farming, 5.0% construction, 4.1% production (2006-2010 5-year est.).

Income: Per capita income: $35,560 (2006-2010 5-year est.); Median household income: $65,647 (2006-2010 5-year est.); Average household income: $82,029 (2006-2010 5-year est.); Percent of households with income of $100,000 or more: 25.6% (2006-2010 5-year est.); Poverty rate: 3.9% (2006-2010 5-year est.).

Education: Percent of population age 25 and over with: High school diploma (including GED) or higher: 95.8% (2006-2010 5-year est.); Bachelor's degree or higher: 39.0% (2006-2010 5-year est.); Master's degree or higher: 13.8% (2006-2010 5-year est.).

Housing: Homeownership rate: 76.5% (2010); Median home value: $137,300 (2006-2010 5-year est.); Median contract rent: $821 per month (2006-2010 5-year est.); Median year structure built: 1985 (2006-2010 5-year est.).

Transportation: Commute to work: 92.0% car, 1.9% public transportation, 0.3% walk, 4.2% work from home (2006-2010 5-year est.); Travel time to work: 28.3% less than 15 minutes, 34.9% 15 to 30 minutes, 18.8% 30 to 45 minutes, 9.7% 45 to 60 minutes, 8.3% 60 minutes or more (2006-2010 5-year est.)

Additional Information Contacts
North Fayette Township . . . . (412) 788-4888
   http://www.north-fayette.com
Pittsburgh Airport Area Chamber of Commerce . . . . (412) 264-6270
   http://www.paacc.com

NORTH VERSAILLES (township). Covers a land area of 8.022 square miles and a water area of 0.166 square miles. Located at 40.38° N. Lat; 79.81° W. Long. Elevation is 1,171 feet.

Population: 12,301 (1990); 11,125 (2000); 10,229 (2010); Density: 1,275.1 persons per square mile (2010); Race: 82.9% White, 13.8% Black, 0.7% Asian, 0.1% American Indian/Alaska Native, 0.0% Native Hawaiian/Other Pacific Islander, 2.5% Other, 0.9% Hispanic of any race (2010); Average household size: 2.13 (2010); Median age: 44.8 (2010); Males per 100 females: 89.7 (2010); Marriage status: 29.1% never married, 48.1% now married, 9.3% widowed, 13.6% divorced (2006-2010 5-year est.); Foreign born: 1.2% (2006-2010 5-year est.); Ancestry (includes multiple ancestries): 22.7% German, 20.1% Irish, 18.9% Italian, 11.7% Polish, 11.0% English (2006-2010 5-year est.).

Economy: Single-family building permits issued: 0 (2011); Multi-family building permits issued: 0 (2011); Employment by occupation: 9.9% management, 6.5% professional, 8.8% services, 20.0% sales, 5.8% farming, 6.5% construction, 5.8% production (2006-2010 5-year est.).

Income: Per capita income: $23,349 (2006-2010 5-year est.); Median household income: $41,291 (2006-2010 5-year est.); Average household income: $49,390 (2006-2010 5-year est.); Percent of households with income of $100,000 or more: 10.1% (2006-2010 5-year est.); Poverty rate: 13.6% (2006-2010 5-year est.).

Taxes: Total city taxes per capita: $362 (2009); City property taxes per capita: $214 (2009).

Education: Percent of population age 25 and over with: High school diploma (including GED) or higher: 90.3% (2006-2010 5-year est.); Bachelor's degree or higher: 17.9% (2006-2010 5-year est.); Master's degree or higher: 4.1% (2006-2010 5-year est.).

School District(s)
East Allegheny SD (PK-12)
   2010-11 Enrollment: 1,875 . . . . (412) 824-8012
Vocational/Technical School(s)
All-State Career School-Pittsburgh (Private, For-profit)
   Fall 2010 Enrollment: 198 . . . . (412) 823-1818
Housing: Homeownership rate: 68.0% (2010); Median home value: $78,000 (2006-2010 5-year est.); Median contract rent: $532 per month (2006-2010 5-year est.); Median year structure built: 1956 (2006-2010 5-year est.).

Safety: Violent crime rate: 61.8 per 10,000 population; Property crime rate: 224.7 per 10,000 population (2011).

Transportation: Commute to work: 89.6% car, 6.0% public transportation, 2.5% walk, 1.2% work from home (2006-2010 5-year est.); Travel time to work: 16.4% less than 15 minutes, 34.3% 15 to 30 minutes, 31.5% 30 to

45 minutes, 10.3% 45 to 60 minutes, 7.4% 60 minutes or more (2006-2010 5-year est.)

Additional Information Contacts

North Versailles Township. . . . . (412) 823-6602
  http://www.tcvcog.com/North%20Versailles%20Township%20Page.htm

Norwin Chamber of Commerce. (724) 863-0888
  http://www.norwinchamber.com/index.php

O'HARA (township). Covers a land area of 7.015 square miles and a water area of 0.356 square miles. Located at 40.50° N. Lat; 79.87° W. Long.

History: O'Hara Township is a township in Allegheny County, Pennsylvania, USA six miles northeast of downtown Pittsburgh. It is named for James O'Hara (1752?-1819), an early American industrialist in Western Pennsylvania.

Population: 9,198 (1990); 8,856 (2000); 8,407 (2010); Density: 1,198.4 persons per square mile (2010); Race: 93.1% White, 0.6% Black, 5.0% Asian, 0.1% American Indian/Alaska Native, 0.0% Native Hawaiian/Other Pacific Islander, 1.2% Other, 1.5% Hispanic of any race (2010); Average household size: 2.45 (2010); Median age: 47.9 (2010); Males per 100 females: 95.1 (2010); Marriage status: 17.7% never married, 67.6% now married, 7.4% widowed, 7.4% divorced (2006-2010 5-year est.); Foreign born: 7.4% (2006-2010 5-year est.); Ancestry (includes multiple ancestries): 24.7% German, 19.9% Italian, 19.5% Irish, 10.2% English, 7.9% Polish (2006-2010 5-year est.).

Economy: Single-family building permits issued: 4 (2011); Multi-family building permits issued: 0 (2011); Employment by occupation: 22.4% management, 7.4% professional, 6.4% services, 16.9% sales, 1.9% farming, 3.9% construction, 2.7% production (2006-2010 5-year est.).

Income: Per capita income: $49,579 (2006-2010 5-year est.); Median household income: $81,319 (2006-2010 5-year est.); Average household income: $119,949 (2006-2010 5-year est.); Percent of households with income of $100,000 or more: 42.3% (2006-2010 5-year est.); Poverty rate: 3.5% (2006-2010 5-year est.).

Education: Percent of population age 25 and over with: High school diploma (including GED) or higher: 95.1% (2006-2010 5-year est.); Bachelor's degree or higher: 55.8% (2006-2010 5-year est.); Master's degree or higher: 31.1% (2006-2010 5-year est.).

Housing: Homeownership rate: 87.3% (2010); Median home value: $222,500 (2006-2010 5-year est.); Median contract rent: $757 per month (2006-2010 5-year est.); Median year structure built: 1963 (2006-2010 5-year est.).

Safety: Violent crime rate: 0.0 per 10,000 population; Property crime rate: 83.0 per 10,000 population (2011).

Transportation: Commute to work: 92.5% car, 2.2% public transportation, 0.9% walk, 3.7% work from home (2006-2010 5-year est.); Travel time to work: 25.4% less than 15 minutes, 38.1% 15 to 30 minutes, 31.0% 30 to 45 minutes, 4.0% 45 to 60 minutes, 1.5% 60 minutes or more (2006-2010 5-year est.)

Additional Information Contacts

O'Hara Township. . . . . (412) 782-1400
  http://www.ohara.pa.us

Shadyside Chamber of Commerce . . . . (412) 682-1298
  http://www.thinkshadyside.com

OAKDALE (borough). Covers a land area of 0.469 square miles and a water area of 0 square miles. Located at 40.40° N. Lat; 80.19° W. Long. Elevation is 896 feet.

History: Incorporated 1872.

Population: 1,752 (1990); 1,551 (2000); 1,459 (2010); Density: 3,108.1 persons per square mile (2010); Race: 96.7% White, 1.6% Black, 0.3% Asian, 0.1% American Indian/Alaska Native, 0.0% Native Hawaiian/Other Pacific Islander, 1.3% Other, 0.7% Hispanic of any race (2010); Average household size: 2.35 (2010); Median age: 47.4 (2010); Males per 100 females: 93.2 (2010); Marriage status: 23.6% never married, 61.0% now married, 5.9% widowed, 9.5% divorced (2006-2010 5-year est.); Foreign born: 1.7% (2006-2010 5-year est.); Ancestry (includes multiple ancestries): 32.4% German, 21.8% Irish, 17.9% Italian, 12.3% Polish, 12.2% English (2006-2010 5-year est.).

Economy: Single-family building permits issued: 0 (2011); Multi-family building permits issued: 0 (2011); Employment by occupation: 8.1% management, 3.7% professional, 10.2% services, 25.1% sales, 2.1% farming, 10.3% construction, 4.2% production (2006-2010 5-year est.).

Income: Per capita income: $27,010 (2006-2010 5-year est.); Median household income: $57,014 (2006-2010 5-year est.); Average household

income: $64,645 (2006-2010 5-year est.); Percent of households with income of $100,000 or more: 16.7% (2006-2010 5-year est.); Poverty rate: 6.7% (2006-2010 5-year est.).

Education: Percent of population age 25 and over with: High school diploma (including GED) or higher: 95.8% (2006-2010 5-year est.); Bachelor's degree or higher: 18.3% (2006-2010 5-year est.); Master's degree or higher: 3.8% (2006-2010 5-year est.).

School District(s)

Parkway West CTC (09-12)
  2010-11 Enrollment: n/a . . . . (412) 923-1772

West Allegheny SD (KG-12)
  2010-11 Enrollment: 3,262 . . . . (724) 695-3422

Two-year College(s)

Pittsburgh Technical Institute (Private, For-profit)
  Fall 2010 Enrollment: 3,226 . . . . (412) 809-5100
  2011-12 Tuition: In-state $15,055; Out-of-state $15,055

Housing: Homeownership rate: 79.7% (2010); Median home value: $114,100 (2006-2010 5-year est.); Median contract rent: $494 per month (2006-2010 5-year est.); Median year structure built: 1961 (2006-2010 5-year est.).

Transportation: Commute to work: 91.0% car, 1.6% public transportation, 1.9% walk, 3.7% work from home (2006-2010 5-year est.); Travel time to work: 29.4% less than 15 minutes, 38.9% 15 to 30 minutes, 18.8% 30 to 45 minutes, 5.3% 45 to 60 minutes, 7.6% 60 minutes or more (2006-2010 5-year est.).

Additional Information Contacts

Pittsburgh Airport Area Chamber of Commerce . . . . (412) 264-6270
  http://www.paacc.com

OAKMONT (borough). Covers a land area of 1.589 square miles and a water area of 0.182 square miles. Located at 40.52° N. Lat; 79.84° W. Long. Elevation is 774 feet.

History: Incorporated 1889.

Population: 6,961 (1990); 6,911 (2000); 6,303 (2010); Density: 3,965.9 persons per square mile (2010); Race: 97.1% White, 1.0% Black, 0.7% Asian, 0.1% American Indian/Alaska Native, 0.0% Native Hawaiian/Other Pacific Islander, 1.1% Other, 1.5% Hispanic of any race (2010); Average household size: 2.05 (2010); Median age: 46.9 (2010); Males per 100 females: 84.6 (2010); Marriage status: 30.3% never married, 50.1% now married, 9.5% widowed, 10.1% divorced (2006-2010 5-year est.); Foreign born: 1.0% (2006-2010 5-year est.); Ancestry (includes multiple ancestries): 27.8% German, 21.6% Irish, 21.3% Italian, 11.1% English, 8.6% Polish (2006-2010 5-year est.).

Economy: Single-family building permits issued: 35 (2011); Multi-family building permits issued: 10 (2011); Employment by occupation: 9.2% management, 6.3% professional, 9.9% services, 14.7% sales, 2.1% farming, 4.6% construction, 4.6% production (2006-2010 5-year est.).

Income: Per capita income: $36,605 (2006-2010 5-year est.); Median household income: $51,420 (2006-2010 5-year est.); Average household income: $76,087 (2006-2010 5-year est.); Percent of households with income of $100,000 or more: 23.8% (2006-2010 5-year est.); Poverty rate: 6.7% (2006-2010 5-year est.).

Taxes: Total city taxes per capita: $367 (2009); City property taxes per capita: $206 (2009).

Education: Percent of population age 25 and over with: High school diploma (including GED) or higher: 93.6% (2006-2010 5-year est.); Bachelor's degree or higher: 44.0% (2006-2010 5-year est.); Master's degree or higher: 16.2% (2006-2010 5-year est.).

School District(s)

Riverview SD (KG-12)
  2010-11 Enrollment: 1,091 . . . . (412) 828-1800

Housing: Homeownership rate: 58.1% (2010); Median home value: $159,100 (2006-2010 5-year est.); Median contract rent: $603 per month (2006-2010 5-year est.); Median year structure built: 1955 (2006-2010 5-year est.).

Safety: Violent crime rate: 26.9 per 10,000 population; Property crime rate: 159.7 per 10,000 population (2011).

Transportation: Commute to work: 86.2% car, 4.3% public transportation, 4.4% walk, 3.5% work from home (2006-2010 5-year est.); Travel time to work: 27.1% less than 15 minutes, 29.8% 15 to 30 minutes, 23.8% 30 to 45 minutes, 12.5% 45 to 60 minutes, 6.8% 60 minutes or more (2006-2010 5-year est.)

Additional Information Contacts

Borough of Oakmont. . . . . (412) 828-3232
  http://www.borough.oakmont.pa.us

Oakmont Chamber of Commerce . . . . (412) 828-3238
  http://www.oakmont-pa.com

OHIO (township). Covers a land area of 6.858 square miles and a water area of 0 square miles. Located at 40.54° N. Lat; 80.09° W. Long.

History: Ohio Township was the third township to be formed in Allegheny County in September, 1803. Ohio Township is a Township of the Second Class.

Population: 2,454 (1990); 3,086 (2000); 4,757 (2010); Density: 693.6 persons per square mile (2010); Race: 93.8% White, 1.8% Black, 3.1% Asian, 0.0% American Indian/Alaska Native, 0.0% Native Hawaiian/Other Pacific Islander, 1.3% Other, 1.7% Hispanic of any race (2010); Average household size: 2.55 (2010); Median age: 38.2 (2010); Males per 100 females: 98.5 (2010); Marriage status: 34.6% never married, 51.8% now married, 6.0% widowed, 7.6% divorced (2006-2010 5-year est.); Foreign born: 2.4% (2006-2010 5-year est.); Ancestry (includes multiple ancestries): 39.2% German, 22.6% Irish, 14.5% Italian, 10.6% Polish, 7.3% Slovak (2006-2010 5-year est.).

Economy: Single-family building permits issued: 27 (2011); Multi-family building permits issued: 29 (2011); Employment by occupation: 19.0% management, 5.7% professional, 10.0% services, 13.6% sales, 2.6% farming, 3.7% construction, 4.3% production (2006-2010 5-year est.).

Income: Per capita income: $47,974 (2006-2010 5-year est.); Median household income: $81,875 (2006-2010 5-year est.); Average household income: $129,994 (2006-2010 5-year est.); Percent of households with income of $100,000 or more: 43.9% (2006-2010 5-year est.); Poverty rate: 11.1% (2006-2010 5-year est.).

Taxes: Total city taxes per capita: $592 (2009); City property taxes per capita: $258 (2009).

Education: Percent of population age 25 and over with: High school diploma (including GED) or higher: 96.5% (2006-2010 5-year est.); Bachelor's degree or higher: 49.0% (2006-2010 5-year est.); Master's degree or higher: 22.3% (2006-2010 5-year est.).

Housing: Homeownership rate: 75.9% (2010); Median home value: $235,400 (2006-2010 5-year est.); Median contract rent: $890 per month (2006-2010 5-year est.); Median year structure built: 1993 (2006-2010 5-year est.).

Safety: Violent crime rate: 0.0 per 10,000 population; Property crime rate: 121.5 per 10,000 population (2011).

Transportation: Commute to work: 89.7% car, 3.1% public transportation, 1.0% walk, 5.7% work from home (2006-2010 5-year est.); Travel time to work: 15.2% less than 15 minutes, 55.4% 15 to 30 minutes, 23.3% 30 to 45 minutes, 4.3% 45 to 60 minutes, 1.9% 60 minutes or more (2006-2010 5-year est.)

Additional Information Contacts

North Suburban Chamber of Commerce . . . . (412) 761-2113
  http://www.northsuburbancoc.org

PENN HILLS (township). Aka Milltown. Covers a land area of 19.118 square miles and a water area of 0.239 square miles. Located at 40.48° N. Lat; 79.83° W. Long. Elevation is 942 feet.

Population: 51,479 (1990); 46,809 (2000); 42,329 (2010); Density: 2,214.1 persons per square mile (2010); Race: 61.4% White, 34.6% Black, 0.8% Asian, 0.2% American Indian/Alaska Native, 0.0% Native Hawaiian/Other Pacific Islander, 3.0% Other, 1.4% Hispanic of any race (2010); Average household size: 2.24 (2010); Median age: 45.3 (2010); Males per 100 females: 86.6 (2010); Marriage status: 30.1% never married, 50.9% now married, 9.8% widowed, 9.2% divorced (2006-2010 5-year est.); Foreign born: 2.8% (2006-2010 5-year est.); Ancestry (includes multiple ancestries): 20.0% German, 16.8% Italian, 15.1% Irish, 6.6% English, 5.9% Polish (2006-2010 5-year est.).

Economy: Unemployment rate: 8.1% (August 2012); Total civilian labor force: 23,737 (August 2012); Single-family building permits issued: 1 (2011); Multi-family building permits issued: 0 (2011); Employment by occupation: 9.7% management, 3.9% professional, 11.4% services, 17.5% sales, 5.3% farming, 8.3% construction, 6.8% production (2006-2010 5-year est.).

Income: Per capita income: $24,336 (2006-2010 5-year est.); Median household income: $45,893 (2006-2010 5-year est.); Average household income: $55,370 (2006-2010 5-year est.); Percent of households with income of $100,000 or more: 10.8% (2006-2010 5-year est.); Poverty rate: 9.2% (2006-2010 5-year est.).

Taxes: Total city taxes per capita: $398 (2009); City property taxes per capita: $156 (2009).

Education: Percent of population age 25 and over with: High school diploma (including GED) or higher: 91.2% (2006-2010 5-year est.); Bachelor's degree or higher: 22.6% (2006-2010 5-year est.); Master's degree or higher: 7.6% (2006-2010 5-year est.).

Housing: Homeownership rate: 76.8% (2010); Median home value: $86,200 (2006-2010 5-year est.); Median contract rent: $538 per month (2006-2010 5-year est.); Median year structure built: 1956 (2006-2010 5-year est.).

Safety: Violent crime rate: 33.2 per 10,000 population; Property crime rate: 200.2 per 10,000 population (2011).

Transportation: Commute to work: 88.1% car, 7.3% public transportation, 1.4% walk, 2.6% work from home (2006-2010 5-year est.); Travel time to work: 21.9% less than 15 minutes, 34.3% 15 to 30 minutes, 26.1% 30 to 45 minutes, 9.6% 45 to 60 minutes, 8.0% 60 minutes or more (2006-2010 5-year est.)

Additional Information Contacts

Penn Hills Chamber of Commerce . . . . (412) 795-8741
  http://www.pennhillschamber.org
Penn Hills Township . . . . (412) 795-3500
  http://www.pennhills.org

PENNSBURY VILLAGE (borough). Covers a land area of 0.076 square miles and a water area of 0 square miles. Located at 40.43° N. Lat; 80.10° W. Long. Elevation is 1,109 feet.

Population: 774 (1990); 738 (2000); 661 (2010); Density: 8,753.1 persons per square mile (2010); Race: 97.0% White, 1.5% Black, 0.6% Asian, 0.0% American Indian/Alaska Native, 0.0% Native Hawaiian/Other Pacific Islander, 0.9% Other, 1.2% Hispanic of any race (2010); Average household size: 1.40 (2010); Median age: 38.7 (2010); Males per 100 females: 71.7 (2010); Marriage status: 48.2% never married, 24.0% now married, 7.5% widowed, 20.3% divorced (2006-2010 5-year est.); Foreign born: 2.5% (2006-2010 5-year est.); Ancestry (includes multiple ancestries): 37.5% German, 31.3% Irish, 24.6% Italian, 12.7% Polish, 6.7% English (2006-2010 5-year est.).

Economy: Employment by occupation: 16.8% management, 8.2% professional, 3.9% services, 12.5% sales, 4.1% farming, 4.1% construction, 3.3% production (2006-2010 5-year est.).

Income: Per capita income: $38,085 (2006-2010 5-year est.); Median household income: $53,365 (2006-2010 5-year est.); Average household income: $54,002 (2006-2010 5-year est.); Percent of households with income of $100,000 or more: 4.4% (2006-2010 5-year est.); Poverty rate: 4.2% (2006-2010 5-year est.).

Education: Percent of population age 25 and over with: High school diploma (including GED) or higher: 99.7% (2006-2010 5-year est.); Bachelor's degree or higher: 58.2% (2006-2010 5-year est.); Master's degree or higher: 16.1% (2006-2010 5-year est.).

Housing: Homeownership rate: 80.1% (2010); Median home value: $95,100 (2006-2010 5-year est.); Median contract rent: $824 per month (2006-2010 5-year est.); Median year structure built: 1972 (2006-2010 5-year est.).

Transportation: Commute to work: 84.4% car, 11.4% public transportation, 3.0% walk, 0.4% work from home (2006-2010 5-year est.); Travel time to work: 16.6% less than 15 minutes, 48.4% 15 to 30 minutes, 22.3% 30 to 45 minutes, 8.5% 45 to 60 minutes, 4.2% 60 minutes or more (2006-2010 5-year est.)

PINE (township). Covers a land area of 16.963 square miles and a water area of 0.013 square miles. Located at 40.64° N. Lat; 80.04° W. Long.

History: The Township of Pine was established in 1796. At that time it included that part of Allegheny County north of the Ohio and Allegheny rivers and west of the boundary between Jones' and Cunningham's districts. Its original limits comprised the whole of eleven current townships and parts of three others.

Population: 4,048 (1990); 7,683 (2000); 11,497 (2010); Density: 677.8 persons per square mile (2010); Race: 93.1% White, 1.2% Black, 4.0% Asian, 0.1% American Indian/Alaska Native, 0.0% Native Hawaiian/Other Pacific Islander, 1.6% Other, 1.9% Hispanic of any race (2010); Average household size: 2.92 (2010); Median age: 38.8 (2010); Males per 100 females: 100.5 (2010); Marriage status: 22.1% never married, 68.5% now married, 5.9% widowed, 3.5% divorced (2006-2010 5-year est.); Foreign born: 5.5% (2006-2010 5-year est.); Ancestry (includes multiple ancestries): 34.4% German, 24.0% Irish, 17.9% Italian, 8.6% English, 8.4% Polish (2006-2010 5-year est.).

Economy: Single-family building permits issued: 64 (2011); Multi-family building permits issued: 13 (2011); Employment by occupation: 27.7%

management, 4.2% professional, 6.8% services, 10.7% sales, 2.1% farming, 4.9% construction, 1.9% production (2006-2010 5-year est.).
Income: Per capita income: $56,705 (2006-2010 5-year est.); Median household income: $130,194 (2006-2010 5-year est.); Average household income: $176,049 (2006-2010 5-year est.); Percent of households with income of $100,000 or more: 62.3% (2006-2010 5-year est.); Poverty rate: 3.6% (2006-2010 5-year est.).
Education: Percent of population age 25 and over with: High school diploma (including GED) or higher: 95.6% (2006-2010 5-year est.); Bachelor's degree or higher: 66.6% (2006-2010 5-year est.); Master's degree or higher: 27.5% (2006-2010 5-year est.).
Housing: Homeownership rate: 81.9% (2010); Median home value: $345,400 (2006-2010 5-year est.); Median contract rent: $1,067 per month (2006-2010 5-year est.); Median year structure built: 1994 (2006-2010 5-year est.).
Transportation: Commute to work: 89.2% car, 1.1% public transportation, 2.1% walk, 6.8% work from home (2006-2010 5-year est.); Travel time to work: 20.7% less than 15 minutes, 33.5% 15 to 30 minutes, 31.4% 30 to 45 minutes, 9.0% 45 to 60 minutes, 5.4% 60 minutes or more (2006-2010 5-year est.)

Additional Information Contacts
Pine Township. . . . . (724) 625-1591
   http://twp.pine.pa.us
The Chamber of Commerce, Inc. . . . . (724) 934-9700
   http://www.thechamberinc.com

PITCAIRN (borough). Covers a land area of 0.505 square miles and a water area of 0 square miles. Located at 40.41° N. Lat; 79.78° W. Long. Elevation is 784 feet.
History: Laid out c.1890, incorporated 1891.
Population: 4,087 (1990); 3,689 (2000); 3,294 (2010); Density: 6,521.5 persons per square mile (2010); Race: 86.4% White, 10.0% Black, 0.3% Asian, 0.1% American Indian/Alaska Native, 0.0% Native Hawaiian/Other Pacific Islander, 3.2% Other, 2.0% Hispanic of any race (2010); Average household size: 2.12 (2010); Median age: 40.4 (2010); Males per 100 females: 87.9 (2010); Marriage status: 45.2% never married, 35.1% now married, 6.9% widowed, 12.8% divorced (2006-2010 5-year est.); Foreign born: 1.5% (2006-2010 5-year est.); Ancestry (includes multiple ancestries): 31.3% German, 18.5% Irish, 15.2% Italian, 14.9% English, 9.9% American (2006-2010 5-year est.).
Economy: Single-family building permits issued: 0 (2011); Multi-family building permits issued: 0 (2011); Employment by occupation: 6.9% management, 2.9% professional, 10.3% services, 24.5% sales, 8.9% farming, 3.4% construction, 1.1% production (2006-2010 5-year est.).
Income: Per capita income: $19,469 (2006-2010 5-year est.); Median household income: $36,563 (2006-2010 5-year est.); Average household income: $42,132 (2006-2010 5-year est.); Percent of households with income of $100,000 or more: 5.0% (2006-2010 5-year est.); Poverty rate: 12.3% (2006-2010 5-year est.).
Education: Percent of population age 25 and over with: High school diploma (including GED) or higher: 90.8% (2006-2010 5-year est.); Bachelor's degree or higher: 20.2% (2006-2010 5-year est.); Master's degree or higher: 5.5% (2006-2010 5-year est.).
School District(s)
Gateway SD (KG-12)
   2010-11 Enrollment: 3,800 . . . . (412) 372-5300
Housing: Homeownership rate: 44.3% (2010); Median home value: $58,800 (2006-2010 5-year est.); Median contract rent: $427 per month (2006-2010 5-year est.); Median year structure built: before 1940 (2006-2010 5-year est.).
Safety: Violent crime rate: 124.1 per 10,000 population; Property crime rate: 496.2 per 10,000 population (2011).
Transportation: Commute to work: 91.0% car, 3.6% public transportation, 3.6% walk, 1.8% work from home (2006-2010 5-year est.); Travel time to work: 24.5% less than 15 minutes, 41.0% 15 to 30 minutes, 18.6% 30 to 45 minutes, 8.9% 45 to 60 minutes, 7.0% 60 minutes or more (2006-2010 5-year est.)
Additional Information Contacts
Chamber of Commerce. . . . . (724) 863-0888
   http://www.norwinchamber.com/index.php

PITTSBURGH (city). County seat. Covers a land area of 55.367 square miles and a water area of 2.971 square miles. Located at 40.44° N. Lat; 79.98° W. Long. Elevation is 764 feet.
History: Pittsburgh began in 1748 when George II of England granted land to the Ohio Land Company. French claims to the area resulted in both French and English forts being built here. In 1758, General John Forbes secured the land for England. He named the settlement Pittsburgh for William Pitt, the British statesman. Beginning in 1763, large numbers of settlers from the colonies and from Europe came to Pittsburgh, most of them artisans and farmers. The settlement was incorporated as a borough in 1794. One of the earliest industries was boatbuilding, which had begun in the 1760's. By the early 1800's, Pittsburgh had many cotton-weaving plants, a glass works, a brewery, and several tanneries. When the western division of the Pennsylvania Canal was completed in 1829, Pittsburgh became a busy river port. The arrival of several railroads in the 1850's further spurred industrial development, particularly in the iron and coal industries.
Population: 369,785 (1990); 334,563 (2000); 305,704 (2010); Density: 5,521.4 persons per square mile (2010); Race: 66.0% White, 26.1% Black, 4.4% Asian, 0.2% American Indian/Alaska Native, 0.0% Native Hawaiian/Other Pacific Islander, 3.3% Other, 2.3% Hispanic of any race (2010); Average household size: 2.07 (2010); Median age: 33.2 (2010); Males per 100 females: 94.0 (2010); Marriage status: 48.4% never married, 34.2% now married, 7.9% widowed, 9.6% divorced (2006-2010 5-year est.); Foreign born: 6.9% (2006-2010 5-year est.); Ancestry (includes multiple ancestries): 21.4% German, 16.7% Irish, 13.4% Italian, 8.0% Polish, 5.4% English (2006-2010 5-year est.).
Economy: Unemployment rate: 8.2% (August 2012); Total civilian labor force: 157,701 (August 2012); Single-family building permits issued: 284 (2011); Multi-family building permits issued: 0 (2011); Employment by occupation: 9.5% management, 5.3% professional, 12.4% services, 16.5% sales, 5.0% farming, 5.0% construction, 3.2% production (2006-2010 5-year est.).
Income: Per capita income: $24,833 (2006-2010 5-year est.); Median household income: $36,019 (2006-2010 5-year est.); Average household income: $54,453 (2006-2010 5-year est.); Percent of households with income of $100,000 or more: 12.5% (2006-2010 5-year est.); Poverty rate: 21.9% (2006-2010 5-year est.).
Taxes: Total city taxes per capita: $1,116 (2009); City property taxes per capita: $413 (2009).
Education: Percent of population age 25 and over with: High school diploma (including GED) or higher: 88.3% (2006-2010 5-year est.); Bachelor's degree or higher: 33.8% (2006-2010 5-year est.); Master's degree or higher: 16.2% (2006-2010 5-year est.).
School District(s)
Academy CS (09-12)
   2010-11 Enrollment: 175. . . . . (412) 885-5200
Avonworth SD (KG-12)
   2010-11 Enrollment: 1,450 . . . . (412) 369-8738
Baldwin-Whitehall SD (KG-12)
   2010-11 Enrollment: 4,227 . . . . (412) 885-7810
Bethel Park SD (KG-12)
   2010-11 Enrollment: 4,696 . . . . (412) 833-5000
Brentwood Borough SD (KG-12)
   2010-11 Enrollment: 1,255 . . . . (412) 881-2227
Career Connections CHS (09-12)
   2010-11 Enrollment: 263. . . . . (412) 682-1816
Carlynton SD (KG-12)
   2010-11 Enrollment: 1,424 . . . . (412) 429-8400
Chartiers Valley SD (KG-12)
   2010-11 Enrollment: 3,489 . . . . (412) 429-2201
City CHS (09-12)
   2010-11 Enrollment: 574. . . . . (412) 690-2489
Environmental Charter School at Frick Park (KG-05)
   2010-11 Enrollment: 380. . . . . (412) 247-7970
Fox Chapel Area SD (KG-12)
   2010-11 Enrollment: 4,340 . . . . (412) 963-9600
Keystone Oaks SD (KG-12)
   2010-11 Enrollment: 2,111 . . . . (412) 571-6000
Manchester Academic CS (KG-08)
   2010-11 Enrollment: 218. . . . . (412) 322-0585
Montour SD (KG-12)
   2010-11 Enrollment: 2,946 . . . . (412) 490-6500
Mt Lebanon SD (KG-12)
   2010-11 Enrollment: 5,259 . . . . (412) 344-2077

North Allegheny SD (KG-12)
   2010-11 Enrollment: 8,105 . . . . (412) 366-2100
North Hills SD (KG-12)
   2010-11 Enrollment: 4,251 . . . . (412) 318-1000
Northgate SD (KG-12)
   2010-11 Enrollment: 1,242 . . . . (412) 732-3300
Northside Urban Pathways CS (06-12)
   2010-11 Enrollment: 364 . . . . (412) 392-4601
Penn Hills SD (PK-12)
   2010-11 Enrollment: 4,284 . . . . (412) 793-7000
Pittsburgh SD (PK-12)
   2010-11 Enrollment: 27,982 . . . . (412) 622-3500
Plum Borough SD (KG-12)
   2010-11 Enrollment: 4,110 . . . . (412) 795-0100
Propel CS-Montour (KG-08)
   2010-11 Enrollment: 388 . . . . (412) 539-0100
Propel Charter School-Sunrise (KG-10)
   2010-11 Enrollment: 290 . . . . (412) 325-7305
Shaler Area SD (KG-12)
   2010-11 Enrollment: 4,968 . . . . (412) 492-1200
Upper Saint Clair SD (KG-12)
   2010-11 Enrollment: 4,089 . . . . (412) 833-1600
Urban League of Greater Pittsburgh CS (KG-05)
   2010-11 Enrollment: 229 . . . . (412) 361-1008
West Jefferson Hills SD (KG-12)
   2010-11 Enrollment: 2,820 . . . . (412) 655-8450
Wilkinsburg Borough SD (PK-12)
   2010-11 Enrollment: 1,228 . . . . (412) 371-9667
Woodland Hills SD (PK-12)
   2010-11 Enrollment: 4,050 . . . . (412) 731-1300

Four-year College(s)

Byzantine Catholic Seminary of Saints Cyril and Methodius (Private, Not-for-profit, Other (none of the above))
   Fall 2010 Enrollment: 10 . . . . (412) 321-7550
Carlow University (Private, Not-for-profit, Roman Catholic)
   Fall 2010 Enrollment: 2,051 . . . . (412) 578-6000
   2011-12 Tuition: In-state $23,504; Out-of-state $23,504
Carnegie Mellon University (Private, Not-for-profit)
   Fall 2010 Enrollment: 10,609 . . . . (412) 268-2000
   2011-12 Tuition: In-state $44,010; Out-of-state $44,010
Chatham University (Private, Not-for-profit)
   Fall 2010 Enrollment: 2,180 . . . . (412) 365-1100
   2011-12 Tuition: In-state $30,312; Out-of-state $30,312
Duquesne University (Private, Not-for-profit, Roman Catholic)
   Fall 2010 Enrollment: 9,788 . . . . (412) 396-6000
   2011-12 Tuition: In-state $28,671; Out-of-state $28,671
La Roche College (Private, Not-for-profit, Roman Catholic)
   Fall 2010 Enrollment: 1,229 . . . . (412) 367-9300
   2011-12 Tuition: In-state $23,160; Out-of-state $23,160
Pittsburgh Theological Seminary (Private, Not-for-profit, Presbyterian Church (USA))
   Fall 2010 Enrollment: 230 . . . . (412) 362-5610
Point Park University (Private, Not-for-profit)
   Fall 2010 Enrollment: 3,572 . . . . (412) 391-4100
   2011-12 Tuition: In-state $23,720; Out-of-state $23,720
Reformed Presbyterian Theological Seminary (Private, Not-for-profit, Reformed Presbyterian Church)
   Fall 2010 Enrollment: 60 . . . . (412) 731-8690
The Art Institute of Pittsburgh (Private, For-profit)
   Fall 2010 Enrollment: 2,584 . . . . (412) 291-6200
   2011-12 Tuition: In-state $17,832; Out-of-state $17,832
The Art Institute of Pittsburgh-Online Division (Private, For-profit)
   Fall 2010 Enrollment: 6,599 . . . . (412) 291-6200
   2011-12 Tuition: In-state $18,520; Out-of-state $18,520
University of Phoenix-Pittsburgh Campus (Private, For-profit)
   Fall 2010 Enrollment: 107 . . . . (412) 747-9000
   2011-12 Tuition: In-state $9,859; Out-of-state $9,859
University of Pittsburgh-Pittsburgh Campus (Public)
   Fall 2010 Enrollment: 29,140 . . . . (412) 624-4141
   2011-12 Tuition: In-state $16,132; Out-of-state $25,540

Two-year College(s)

Academy of Court Reporting and Technology-Pittsburgh (Private, For-profit)
   Fall 2010 Enrollment: 71 . . . . (412) 535-0560
   2011-12 Tuition: In-state $9,087; Out-of-state $9,087

Bidwell Training Center Inc (Private, Not-for-profit)
   Fall 2010 Enrollment: 200 . . . . (412) 323-4000
Bradford School (Private, For-profit)
   Fall 2010 Enrollment: 696 . . . . (412) 391-6710
   2011-12 Tuition: In-state $14,820; Out-of-state $14,820
Career Training Academy-Pittsburgh (Private, For-profit)
   Fall 2010 Enrollment: 64 . . . . (412) 367-4000
Community College of Allegheny County (Public)
   Fall 2010 Enrollment: 14,935 . . . . (412) 323-2323
   2011-12 Tuition: In-state $5,854; Out-of-state $8,564
Dean Institute of Technology (Private, For-profit)
   Fall 2010 Enrollment: 153 . . . . (412) 531-4433
   2011-12 Tuition: In-state $11,600; Out-of-state $11,600
Everest Institute-Pittsburgh (Private, For-profit)
   Fall 2010 Enrollment: 861 . . . . (412) 261-4520
   2011-12 Tuition: In-state $12,996; Out-of-state $12,996
ITT Technical Institute-Pittsburgh (Private, For-profit)
   Fall 2010 Enrollment: 340 . . . . (412) 937-9150
   2011-12 Tuition: In-state $18,048; Out-of-state $18,048
Kaplan Career Institute-Pittsburgh (Private, For-profit)
   Fall 2010 Enrollment: 1,651 . . . . (412) 261-2647
Le Cordon Bleu Institute of Culinary Arts-Pittsburgh (Private, For-profit)
   Fall 2010 Enrollment: 1,391 . . . . (412) 566-2433
   2011-12 Tuition: In-state $15,550; Out-of-state $15,550
Mercy Hospital School of Nursing (Private, Not-for-profit, Roman Catholic)
   Fall 2010 Enrollment: 51 . . . . (412) 232-8171
   2011-12 Tuition: In-state $12,645; Out-of-state $12,645
Pennsylvania Gunsmith School (Private, For-profit)
   Fall 2010 Enrollment: 99 . . . . (412) 766-1812
Pittsburgh Institute of Mortuary Science Inc (Private, Not-for-profit)
   Fall 2010 Enrollment: 279 . . . . (412) 362-8500
Rosedale Technical Institute (Private, Not-for-profit)
   Fall 2010 Enrollment: 1,124 . . . . (412) 521-6200
   2011-12 Tuition: In-state $12,230; Out-of-state $12,230
Sanford-Brown Institute-Monroeville (Private, For-profit)
   Fall 2010 Enrollment: 1,028 . . . . (412) 373-6400
   2011-12 Tuition: In-state $12,319; Out-of-state $12,319
Sanford-Brown Institute-Pittsburgh (Private, For-profit)
   Fall 2010 Enrollment: 1,547 . . . . (412) 281-2600
   2011-12 Tuition: In-state $13,121; Out-of-state $13,121
St Margaret School of Nursing (Private, Not-for-profit)
   Fall 2010 Enrollment: 278 . . . . (412) 784-4980
   2011-12 Tuition: In-state $8,905; Out-of-state $8,905
Triangle Tech Inc-Pittsburgh (Private, For-profit)
   Fall 2010 Enrollment: 448 . . . . (412) 359-1000
   2011-12 Tuition: In-state $15,651; Out-of-state $15,651
University of Pittsburgh Medical Center-Shadyside School of Nursing (Private, Not-for-profit)
   Fall 2010 Enrollment: 443 . . . . (412) 623-2950
   2011-12 Tuition: In-state $16,368; Out-of-state $16,368
Vet Tech Institute (Private, For-profit)
   Fall 2010 Enrollment: 441 . . . . (412) 391-7021
   2011-12 Tuition: In-state $14,080; Out-of-state $14,080
Western Pennsylvania Hospital School of Nursing (Private, Not-for-profit)
   Fall 2010 Enrollment: 112 . . . . (412) 578-5531
   2011-12 Tuition: In-state $6,530; Out-of-state $6,530

Vocational/Technical School(s)

Empire Beauty School-North Hills (Private, For-profit)
   Fall 2010 Enrollment: 286 . . . . (412) 367-1765
   2011-12 Tuition: $14,490
Institute of Medical Careers (Private, For-profit)
   Fall 2010 Enrollment: 3 . . . . (412) 244-3240
South Hills Beauty Academy Inc (Private, For-profit)
   Fall 2010 Enrollment: 93 . . . . (412) 561-3381
   2011-12 Tuition: $13,974

Housing: Homeownership rate: 47.6% (2010); Median home value: $85,200 (2006-2010 5-year est.); Median contract rent: $572 per month (2006-2010 5-year est.); Median year structure built: before 1940 (2006-2010 5-year est.).
Hospitals: Allegheny General Hospital (829 beds); Children's Hospital of Pittsburgh of UPMC (260 beds); Healthsouth-Harmarville Rehabilitation Center (202 beds); Magee-Womens Hospital of UPMC (287 beds); Mercy Providence Hospital (146 beds); Passavant Hospital (272 beds); Shadyside Hospital (486 beds); Southwood Psychiatric Hospital (63 beds); St. Clair Hospital (314 beds); Suburban General Hospital (154 beds); The

Western Pennsylvania Hospital (542 beds); UPMC South Side Outpatient Center; University of Pittsburgh Medical Center & Health System (1227 beds); University of Pittsburgh Medical Center - St. Margaret (250 beds); VA Pittsburgh Healthcare System - H.J Heinz Campus (262 beds); VA Pittsburgh Healthcare System - Highland Drive Campus (79 beds); VA Pittsburgh Healthcare System - University Drive Campus (146 beds); Western Psychiatric Institute & Clinic (279 beds)

Safety: Violent crime rate: 80.2 per 10,000 population; Property crime rate: 326.1 per 10,000 population (2011).

Newspapers: The Byzantine Catholic World (Local news; Circulation 7,000); Green Tree Times (Local news; Circulation 9,000); Here's to Your Health - WHJB-AM (Local news); Jewish Chronicle (Local news; Circulation 5,000); The Jewish Chronicle (Regional news; Circulation 5,000); New Pittsburgh Courier (Local news; Circulation 31,923); Northside Chronicle (Local news; Circulation 7,000); Pittsburgh Catholic (Regional news; Circulation 110,443); Pittsburgh Legal Journal (Daily) (Local news; Circulation 1,600); Pittsburgh Post-Gazette (Local news; Circulation 332,617); Pittsburgh Post-Gazette - East Bureau (Community news); Pittsburgh Tribune-Review (Local news; Circulation 185,331); Pittsburgh Tribune-Review - East Bureau (Local news); Pulp (Local news); Sewickley Herald Star (Local news; Circulation 4,300); South Pittsburgh Reporter (Community news; Circulation 12,000); Unione (Local news; Circulation 13,000); The Wall Street Journal - Pittsburgh Bureau (Regional news)

Transportation: Commute to work: 63.8% car, 19.5% public transportation, 11.8% walk, 3.1% work from home (2006-2010 5-year est.); Travel time to work: 27.1% less than 15 minutes, 44.4% 15 to 30 minutes, 18.4% 30 to 45 minutes, 5.5% 45 to 60 minutes, 4.5% 60 minutes or more (2006-2010 5-year est.); Amtrak: train service available.

Airports: Allegheny County (general aviation); Pittsburgh International (primary service/medium hub)

Additional Information Contacts
City of Pittsburgh . . . . (412) 255-2138
    http://pittsburghpa.gov
Greater Pittsburgh Chamber of Commerce . . . . (412) 281-1890
    http://www.alleghenyconference.org/chamber

PLEASANT HILLS (borough). Covers a land area of 2.777 square miles and a water area of 0 square miles. Located at 40.33° N. Lat; 79.96° W. Long. Elevation is 1,227 feet.

History: Incorporated 1947.

Population: 8,884 (1990); 8,397 (2000); 8,268 (2010); Density: 2,977.5 persons per square mile (2010); Race: 94.8% White, 2.7% Black, 1.3% Asian, 0.0% American Indian/Alaska Native, 0.0% Native Hawaiian/Other Pacific Islander, 1.2% Other, 1.0% Hispanic of any race (2010); Average household size: 2.29 (2010); Median age: 46.8 (2010); Males per 100 females: 89.9 (2010); Marriage status: 24.7% never married, 59.1% now married, 10.2% widowed, 6.0% divorced (2006-2010 5-year est.); Foreign born: 3.5% (2006-2010 5-year est.); Ancestry (includes multiple ancestries): 32.4% German, 23.4% Irish, 15.0% Italian, 13.1% English, 10.7% Polish (2006-2010 5-year est.).

Economy: Single-family building permits issued: 7 (2011); Multi-family building permits issued: 0 (2011); Employment by occupation: 12.7% management, 5.9% professional, 5.0% services, 18.8% sales, 3.2% farming, 8.0% construction, 3.0% production (2006-2010 5-year est.).

Income: Per capita income: $31,984 (2006-2010 5-year est.); Median household income: $64,272 (2006-2010 5-year est.); Average household income: $76,029 (2006-2010 5-year est.); Percent of households with income of $100,000 or more: 22.8% (2006-2010 5-year est.); Poverty rate: 4.5% (2006-2010 5-year est.).

Education: Percent of population age 25 and over with: High school diploma (including GED) or higher: 94.0% (2006-2010 5-year est.); Bachelor's degree or higher: 40.8% (2006-2010 5-year est.); Master's degree or higher: 13.2% (2006-2010 5-year est.).

Housing: Homeownership rate: 76.7% (2010); Median home value: $137,300 (2006-2010 5-year est.); Median contract rent: $769 per month (2006-2010 5-year est.); Median year structure built: 1957 (2006-2010 5-year est.).

Safety: Violent crime rate: 0.0 per 10,000 population; Property crime rate: 108.5 per 10,000 population (2011).

Transportation: Commute to work: 92.2% car, 4.7% public transportation, 1.1% walk, 1.6% work from home (2006-2010 5-year est.); Travel time to work: 27.8% less than 15 minutes, 28.7% 15 to 30 minutes, 25.9% 30 to 45 minutes, 12.7% 45 to 60 minutes, 5.0% 60 minutes or more (2006-2010 5-year est.)

Additional Information Contacts
Borough of Pleasant Hills . . . . (412) 655-3300
    http://www.pleasanthillspa.com
Brentwood Baldwin Whitehall Chamber of Commerce . . . . (412) 884-1233
    http://www.bbwchamber.com

PLUM (borough). Covers a land area of 28.582 square miles and a water area of 0.378 square miles. Located at 40.50° N. Lat; 79.75° W. Long. Elevation is 1,138 feet.

History: Named for its native wild plum trees. Founded 1788. Incorporated 1956.

Population: 25,609 (1990); 26,940 (2000); 27,126 (2010); Density: 949.1 persons per square mile (2010); Race: 93.9% White, 3.6% Black, 1.1% Asian, 0.1% American Indian/Alaska Native, 0.0% Native Hawaiian/Other Pacific Islander, 1.3% Other, 0.9% Hispanic of any race (2010); Average household size: 2.48 (2010); Median age: 42.6 (2010); Males per 100 females: 95.3 (2010); Marriage status: 25.1% never married, 61.5% now married, 7.0% widowed, 6.4% divorced (2006-2010 5-year est.); Foreign born: 3.2% (2006-2010 5-year est.); Ancestry (includes multiple ancestries): 32.1% German, 24.7% Italian, 21.9% Irish, 10.0% English, 9.0% Polish (2006-2010 5-year est.).

Economy: Unemployment rate: 6.7% (August 2012); Total civilian labor force: 15,726 (August 2012); Single-family building permits issued: 40 (2011); Multi-family building permits issued: 0 (2011); Employment by occupation: 11.9% management, 6.0% professional, 10.0% services, 18.7% sales, 3.4% farming, 7.6% construction, 5.9% production (2006-2010 5-year est.).

Income: Per capita income: $29,637 (2006-2010 5-year est.); Median household income: $66,700 (2006-2010 5-year est.); Average household income: $75,725 (2006-2010 5-year est.); Percent of households with income of $100,000 or more: 22.2% (2006-2010 5-year est.); Poverty rate: 4.3% (2006-2010 5-year est.).

Taxes: Total city taxes per capita: $346 (2009); City property taxes per capita: $192 (2009).

Education: Percent of population age 25 and over with: High school diploma (including GED) or higher: 94.7% (2006-2010 5-year est.); Bachelor's degree or higher: 32.6% (2006-2010 5-year est.); Master's degree or higher: 10.4% (2006-2010 5-year est.).

Housing: Homeownership rate: 79.0% (2010); Median home value: $132,100 (2006-2010 5-year est.); Median contract rent: $638 per month (2006-2010 5-year est.); Median year structure built: 1970 (2006-2010 5-year est.).

Transportation: Commute to work: 92.0% car, 3.8% public transportation, 0.9% walk, 2.5% work from home (2006-2010 5-year est.); Travel time to work: 20.0% less than 15 minutes, 35.0% 15 to 30 minutes, 20.4% 30 to 45 minutes, 15.3% 45 to 60 minutes, 9.3% 60 minutes or more (2006-2010 5-year est.)

Additional Information Contacts
Borough of Plum . . . . (412) 795-6800
    http://www.plumboro.com
Oakmont Chamber of Commerce . . . . (412) 828-3238
    http://www.oakmont-pa.com

PORT VUE (borough). Covers a land area of 1.136 square miles and a water area of 0.039 square miles. Located at 40.34° N. Lat; 79.87° W. Long. Elevation is 1,076 feet.

History: Incorporated 1892.

Population: 4,641 (1990); 4,228 (2000); 3,798 (2010); Density: 3,343.5 persons per square mile (2010); Race: 96.8% White, 1.4% Black, 0.2% Asian, 0.3% American Indian/Alaska Native, 0.1% Native Hawaiian/Other Pacific Islander, 1.2% Other, 0.7% Hispanic of any race (2010); Average household size: 2.24 (2010); Median age: 44.6 (2010); Males per 100 females: 89.2 (2010); Marriage status: 20.2% never married, 52.9% now married, 9.0% widowed, 17.9% divorced (2006-2010 5-year est.); Foreign born: 0.8% (2006-2010 5-year est.); Ancestry (includes multiple ancestries): 20.3% Italian, 17.5% Irish, 17.5% English, 16.4% Slovak, 15.7% German (2006-2010 5-year est.).

Economy: Single-family building permits issued: 0 (2011); Multi-family building permits issued: 0 (2011); Employment by occupation: 6.7% management, 0.5% professional, 5.6% services, 23.7% sales, 5.7% farming, 16.3% construction, 9.4% production (2006-2010 5-year est.).

Income: Per capita income: $22,774 (2006-2010 5-year est.); Median household income: $36,719 (2006-2010 5-year est.); Average household income: $47,899 (2006-2010 5-year est.); Percent of households with

income of $100,000 or more: 8.0% (2006-2010 5-year est.); Poverty rate: 8.2% (2006-2010 5-year est.).

Education: Percent of population age 25 and over with: High school diploma (including GED) or higher: 92.6% (2006-2010 5-year est.); Bachelor's degree or higher: 10.5% (2006-2010 5-year est.); Master's degree or higher: 2.0% (2006-2010 5-year est.).

School District(s)

South Allegheny SD (KG-12)

    2010-11 Enrollment: 1,572 . . . . (412) 675-3070

Housing: Homeownership rate: 78.9% (2010); Median home value: $64,200 (2006-2010 5-year est.); Median contract rent: $444 per month (2006-2010 5-year est.); Median year structure built: 1951 (2006-2010 5-year est.).

Safety: Violent crime rate: 18.4 per 10,000 population; Property crime rate: 126.0 per 10,000 population (2011).

Transportation: Commute to work: 94.7% car, 1.1% public transportation, 2.0% walk, 2.3% work from home (2006-2010 5-year est.); Travel time to work: 28.7% less than 15 minutes, 31.2% 15 to 30 minutes, 18.0% 30 to 45 minutes, 10.7% 45 to 60 minutes, 11.4% 60 minutes or more (2006-2010 5-year est.)

Additional Information Contacts

Norwin Chamber of Commerce . . . . (724) 863-0888
    http://www.norwinchamber.com/index.php

PRESTO (unincorporated postal area)

Zip Code: 15142

    Covers a land area of 1.465 square miles and a water area of 0.015 square miles. Located at 40.38° N. Lat; 80.11° W. Long. Elevation is 823 feet. Population: 1,163 (2010); Density: 793.5 persons per square mile (2010); Race: 90.9% White, 0.9% Black, 6.4% Asian, 0.0% American Indian/Alaska Native, 0.0% Native Hawaiian/Other Pacific Islander, 1.8% Other, 2.0% Hispanic of any race (2010); Average household size: 2.57 (2010); Median age: 46.5 (2010); Males per 100 females: 98.1 (2010); Homeownership rate: 90.7% (2010)

RANKIN (borough). Covers a land area of 0.437 square miles and a water area of 0.066 square miles. Located at 40.41° N. Lat; 79.88° W. Long. Elevation is 879 feet.

History: Incorporated 1892.

Population: 2,503 (1990); 2,315 (2000); 2,122 (2010); Density: 4,855.8 persons per square mile (2010); Race: 18.0% White, 77.4% Black, 0.1% Asian, 0.3% American Indian/Alaska Native, 0.0% Native Hawaiian/Other Pacific Islander, 4.2% Other, 1.0% Hispanic of any race (2010); Average household size: 2.32 (2010); Median age: 30.9 (2010); Males per 100 females: 68.5 (2010); Marriage status: 46.1% never married, 28.3% now married, 8.1% widowed, 17.6% divorced (2006-2010 5-year est.); Foreign born: 0.5% (2006-2010 5-year est.); Ancestry (includes multiple ancestries): 9.1% African, 9.1% German, 6.8% Italian, 4.8% Irish, 2.9% Hungarian (2006-2010 5-year est.).

Economy: Single-family building permits issued: 0 (2011); Multi-family building permits issued: 0 (2011); Employment by occupation: 1.4% management, 0.0% professional, 11.3% services, 20.9% sales, 8.4% farming, 9.3% construction, 6.3% production (2006-2010 5-year est.).

Income: Per capita income: $14,134 (2006-2010 5-year est.); Median household income: $19,336 (2006-2010 5-year est.); Average household income: $30,918 (2006-2010 5-year est.); Percent of households with income of $100,000 or more: 2.7% (2006-2010 5-year est.); Poverty rate: 39.6% (2006-2010 5-year est.).

Education: Percent of population age 25 and over with: High school diploma (including GED) or higher: 88.2% (2006-2010 5-year est.); Bachelor's degree or higher: 11.7% (2006-2010 5-year est.); Master's degree or higher: 3.6% (2006-2010 5-year est.).

Housing: Homeownership rate: 34.3% (2010); Median home value: $34,300 (2006-2010 5-year est.); Median contract rent: $336 per month (2006-2010 5-year est.); Median year structure built: before 1940 (2006-2010 5-year est.).

Transportation: Commute to work: 63.9% car, 30.3% public transportation, 5.8% walk, 0.0% work from home (2006-2010 5-year est.); Travel time to work: 11.9% less than 15 minutes, 33.8% 15 to 30 minutes, 35.1% 30 to 45 minutes, 14.8% 45 to 60 minutes, 4.4% 60 minutes or more (2006-2010 5-year est.)

Additional Information Contacts

Shadyside Chamber of Commerce . . . . (412) 682-1298
    http://www.thinkshadyside.com

RENNERDALE (CDP). Covers a land area of 0.791 square miles and a water area of 0 square miles. Located at 40.40° N. Lat; 80.14° W. Long. Elevation is 971 feet.

Population: n/a (1990); n/a (2000); 1,150 (2010); Density: 1,453.2 persons per square mile (2010); Race: 98.3% White, 0.7% Black, 0.4% Asian, 0.0% American Indian/Alaska Native, 0.0% Native Hawaiian/Other Pacific Islander, 0.6% Other, 0.3% Hispanic of any race (2010); Average household size: 2.54 (2010); Median age: 46.9 (2010); Males per 100 females: 93.0 (2010); Marriage status: 22.4% never married, 69.8% now married, 2.9% widowed, 4.9% divorced (2006-2010 5-year est.); Foreign born: 0.0% (2006-2010 5-year est.); Ancestry (includes multiple ancestries): 43.6% Irish, 22.4% German, 22.2% Italian, 18.4% Polish, 12.0% Greek (2006-2010 5-year est.).

Economy: Employment by occupation: 14.9% management, 1.9% professional, 8.0% services, 22.6% sales, 5.7% farming, 10.8% construction, 4.4% production (2006-2010 5-year est.).

Income: Per capita income: $43,971 (2006-2010 5-year est.); Median household income: $74,583 (2006-2010 5-year est.); Average household income: $128,197 (2006-2010 5-year est.); Percent of households with income of $100,000 or more: 41.6% (2006-2010 5-year est.); Poverty rate: 5.3% (2006-2010 5-year est.).

Education: Percent of population age 25 and over with: High school diploma (including GED) or higher: 100.0% (2006-2010 5-year est.); Bachelor's degree or higher: 30.2% (2006-2010 5-year est.); Master's degree or higher: 6.7% (2006-2010 5-year est.).

Housing: Homeownership rate: 93.3% (2010); Median home value: $166,300 (2006-2010 5-year est.); Median contract rent: n/a per month (2006-2010 5-year est.); Median year structure built: 1963 (2006-2010 5-year est.).

Transportation: Commute to work: 95.9% car, 1.7% public transportation, 0.0% walk, 2.4% work from home (2006-2010 5-year est.); Travel time to work: 36.2% less than 15 minutes, 40.1% 15 to 30 minutes, 18.5% 30 to 45 minutes, 5.2% 45 to 60 minutes, 0.0% 60 minutes or more (2006-2010 5-year est.)

RESERVE (township). Covers a land area of 2.061 square miles and a water area of 0 square miles. Located at 40.49° N. Lat; 79.99° W. Long.

Population: 3,958 (1990); 3,856 (2000); 3,333 (2010); Density: 1,617.2 persons per square mile (2010); Race: 97.7% White, 1.1% Black, 0.3% Asian, 0.3% American Indian/Alaska Native, 0.0% Native Hawaiian/Other Pacific Islander, 0.6% Other, 0.4% Hispanic of any race (2010); Average household size: 2.31 (2010); Median age: 46.8 (2010); Males per 100 females: 97.7 (2010); Marriage status: 34.0% never married, 52.4% now married, 7.9% widowed, 5.8% divorced (2006-2010 5-year est.); Foreign born: 1.1% (2006-2010 5-year est.); Ancestry (includes multiple ancestries): 57.9% German, 24.3% Irish, 11.9% Polish, 9.6% Italian, 6.4% English (2006-2010 5-year est.).

Economy: Single-family building permits issued: 0 (2011); Multi-family building permits issued: 0 (2011); Employment by occupation: 7.4% management, 7.5% professional, 11.7% services, 21.5% sales, 2.9% farming, 9.9% construction, 2.7% production (2006-2010 5-year est.).

Income: Per capita income: $24,668 (2006-2010 5-year est.); Median household income: $51,378 (2006-2010 5-year est.); Average household income: $60,889 (2006-2010 5-year est.); Percent of households with income of $100,000 or more: 12.7% (2006-2010 5-year est.); Poverty rate: 12.4% (2006-2010 5-year est.).

Education: Percent of population age 25 and over with: High school diploma (including GED) or higher: 90.6% (2006-2010 5-year est.); Bachelor's degree or higher: 17.8% (2006-2010 5-year est.); Master's degree or higher: 7.1% (2006-2010 5-year est.).

Housing: Homeownership rate: 87.5% (2010); Median home value: $99,300 (2006-2010 5-year est.); Median contract rent: $485 per month (2006-2010 5-year est.); Median year structure built: 1953 (2006-2010 5-year est.).

Safety: Violent crime rate: 3.0 per 10,000 population; Property crime rate: 101.7 per 10,000 population (2011).

Transportation: Commute to work: 93.9% car, 2.7% public transportation, 1.2% walk, 0.7% work from home (2006-2010 5-year est.); Travel time to work: 25.6% less than 15 minutes, 54.6% 15 to 30 minutes, 13.5% 30 to 45 minutes, 4.8% 45 to 60 minutes, 1.5% 60 minutes or more (2006-2010 5-year est.)

Additional Information Contacts

South Side Chamber of Commerce . . . . (412) 431-3360
    http://www.southsidechamber.org

RICHLAND (township). Covers a land area of 14.630 square miles and a water area of 0 square miles. Located at 40.64° N. Lat; 79.96° W. Long.

Population: 8,600 (1990); 9,231 (2000); 11,100 (2010); Density: 758.7 persons per square mile (2010); Race: 96.7% White, 0.5% Black, 1.7% Asian, 0.1% American Indian/Alaska Native, 0.0% Native Hawaiian/Other Pacific Islander, 1.0% Other, 1.1% Hispanic of any race (2010); Average household size: 2.60 (2010); Median age: 42.3 (2010); Males per 100 females: 91.9 (2010); Marriage status: 19.7% never married, 63.6% now married, 9.7% widowed, 7.0% divorced (2006-2010 5-year est.); Foreign born: 2.8% (2006-2010 5-year est.); Ancestry (includes multiple ancestries): 40.3% German, 23.2% Irish, 16.3% Italian, 10.9% Polish, 9.6% English (2006-2010 5-year est.).

Economy: Single-family building permits issued: 40 (2011); Multi-family building permits issued: 0 (2011); Employment by occupation: 16.4% management, 6.2% professional, 7.8% services, 16.3% sales, 1.8% farming, 6.4% construction, 4.5% production (2006-2010 5-year est.).

Income: Per capita income: $35,782 (2006-2010 5-year est.); Median household income: $84,135 (2006-2010 5-year est.); Average household income: $97,133 (2006-2010 5-year est.); Percent of households with income of $100,000 or more: 40.6% (2006-2010 5-year est.); Poverty rate: 3.1% (2006-2010 5-year est.).

Education: Percent of population age 25 and over with: High school diploma (including GED) or higher: 96.6% (2006-2010 5-year est.); Bachelor's degree or higher: 45.2% (2006-2010 5-year est.); Master's degree or higher: 16.1% (2006-2010 5-year est.).

Housing: Homeownership rate: 82.9% (2010); Median home value: $188,400 (2006-2010 5-year est.); Median contract rent: $794 per month (2006-2010 5-year est.); Median year structure built: 1972 (2006-2010 5-year est.).

Transportation: Commute to work: 91.3% car, 0.7% public transportation, 1.1% walk, 6.5% work from home (2006-2010 5-year est.); Travel time to work: 21.2% less than 15 minutes, 33.3% 15 to 30 minutes, 26.2% 30 to 45 minutes, 16.4% 45 to 60 minutes, 2.9% 60 minutes or more (2006-2010 5-year est.)

Additional Information Contacts
Richland Township . . . . (724) 443-5921
  http://richland.pa.us
The Chamber of Commerce, Inc. (724) 776-4949
  http://www.thechamberinc.com

ROBINSON (township). Covers a land area of 14.909 square miles and a water area of 0.118 square miles. Located at 40.46° N. Lat; 80.13° W. Long.

Population: 10,856 (1990); 12,289 (2000); 13,354 (2010); Density: 895.7 persons per square mile (2010); Race: 91.4% White, 3.3% Black, 3.6% Asian, 0.1% American Indian/Alaska Native, 0.0% Native Hawaiian/Other Pacific Islander, 1.6% Other, 1.5% Hispanic of any race (2010); Average household size: 2.31 (2010); Median age: 42.4 (2010); Males per 100 females: 98.8 (2010); Marriage status: 31.7% never married, 54.4% now married, 6.5% widowed, 7.4% divorced (2006-2010 5-year est.); Foreign born: 5.5% (2006-2010 5-year est.); Ancestry (includes multiple ancestries): 29.4% German, 22.2% Italian, 21.3% Irish, 12.6% Polish, 11.6% English (2006-2010 5-year est.).

Economy: Single-family building permits issued: 17 (2011); Multi-family building permits issued: 6 (2011); Employment by occupation: 16.2% management, 7.5% professional, 6.0% services, 17.7% sales, 3.6% farming, 6.3% construction, 3.9% production (2006-2010 5-year est.).

Income: Per capita income: $34,194 (2006-2010 5-year est.); Median household income: $65,445 (2006-2010 5-year est.); Average household income: $80,990 (2006-2010 5-year est.); Percent of households with income of $100,000 or more: 28.5% (2006-2010 5-year est.); Poverty rate: 6.2% (2006-2010 5-year est.).

Education: Percent of population age 25 and over with: High school diploma (including GED) or higher: 92.9% (2006-2010 5-year est.); Bachelor's degree or higher: 37.6% (2006-2010 5-year est.); Master's degree or higher: 11.8% (2006-2010 5-year est.).

Housing: Homeownership rate: 73.3% (2010); Median home value: $159,200 (2006-2010 5-year est.); Median contract rent: $726 per month (2006-2010 5-year est.); Median year structure built: 1982 (2006-2010 5-year est.).

Safety: Violent crime rate: 21.6 per 10,000 population; Property crime rate: 288.9 per 10,000 population (2011).

Transportation: Commute to work: 92.9% car, 2.6% public transportation, 0.8% walk, 3.3% work from home (2006-2010 5-year est.); Travel time to work: 30.6% less than 15 minutes, 39.3% 15 to 30 minutes, 19.7% 30 to 45 minutes, 5.3% 45 to 60 minutes, 5.1% 60 minutes or more (2006-2010 5-year est.)

Additional Information Contacts
Pittsburgh Airport Area Chamber of Commerce . . . . (412) 264-6270
  http://www.paacc.com
Robinson Township. . . . . (412) 788-8120
  http://www.townshipofrobinson.com

ROSS (township). Covers a land area of 14.475 square miles and a water area of 0 square miles. Located at 40.53° N. Lat; 80.02° W. Long.

Population: 33,496 (1990); 32,551 (2000); 31,105 (2010); Density: 2,148.9 persons per square mile (2010); Race: 94.0% White, 2.1% Black, 2.5% Asian, 0.1% American Indian/Alaska Native, 0.0% Native Hawaiian/Other Pacific Islander, 1.3% Other, 1.1% Hispanic of any race (2010); Average household size: 2.15 (2010); Median age: 45.4 (2010); Males per 100 females: 88.5 (2010); Marriage status: 28.2% never married, 54.1% now married, 8.8% widowed, 9.0% divorced (2006-2010 5-year est.); Foreign born: 3.8% (2006-2010 5-year est.); Ancestry (includes multiple ancestries): 40.1% German, 24.8% Irish, 16.5% Italian, 10.1% Polish, 8.8% English (2006-2010 5-year est.).

Economy: Unemployment rate: 6.1% (August 2012); Total civilian labor force: 18,414 (August 2012); Single-family building permits issued: 3 (2011); Multi-family building permits issued: 0 (2011); Employment by occupation: 14.8% management, 5.3% professional, 7.4% services, 16.4% sales, 4.0% farming, 6.5% construction, 2.7% production (2006-2010 5-year est.).

Income: Per capita income: $33,121 (2006-2010 5-year est.); Median household income: $57,354 (2006-2010 5-year est.); Average household income: $72,686 (2006-2010 5-year est.); Percent of households with income of $100,000 or more: 21.3% (2006-2010 5-year est.); Poverty rate: 6.8% (2006-2010 5-year est.).

Education: Percent of population age 25 and over with: High school diploma (including GED) or higher: 93.9% (2006-2010 5-year est.); Bachelor's degree or higher: 38.4% (2006-2010 5-year est.); Master's degree or higher: 13.5% (2006-2010 5-year est.).

Housing: Homeownership rate: 74.7% (2010); Median home value: $139,300 (2006-2010 5-year est.); Median contract rent: $621 per month (2006-2010 5-year est.); Median year structure built: 1962 (2006-2010 5-year est.).

Safety: Violent crime rate: 9.6 per 10,000 population; Property crime rate: 214.1 per 10,000 population (2011).

Transportation: Commute to work: 90.3% car, 4.1% public transportation, 2.0% walk, 3.3% work from home (2006-2010 5-year est.); Travel time to work: 20.5% less than 15 minutes, 46.5% 15 to 30 minutes, 24.9% 30 to 45 minutes, 4.2% 45 to 60 minutes, 3.9% 60 minutes or more (2006-2010 5-year est.)

Additional Information Contacts
Ross Township . . . . (412) 931-7055
  http://www.ross.pa.us
The Chamber of Commerce, Inc. (724) 934-9700
  http://www.thechamberinc.com

ROSSLYN FARMS (borough). Aka Rosslyn. Covers a land area of 0.561 square miles and a water area of 0 square miles. Located at 40.42° N. Lat; 80.09° W. Long. Elevation is 1,089 feet.

Population: 483 (1990); 464 (2000); 427 (2010); Density: 761.4 persons per square mile (2010); Race: 97.0% White, 0.9% Black, 1.4% Asian, 0.0% American Indian/Alaska Native, 0.0% Native Hawaiian/Other Pacific Islander, 0.7% Other, 2.3% Hispanic of any race (2010); Average household size: 2.47 (2010); Median age: 46.6 (2010); Males per 100 females: 102.4 (2010); Marriage status: 17.1% never married, 74.5% now married, 2.9% widowed, 5.5% divorced (2006-2010 5-year est.); Foreign born: 1.6% (2006-2010 5-year est.); Ancestry (includes multiple ancestries): 27.5% German, 25.1% Italian, 16.7% Irish, 16.1% English, 8.2% Polish (2006-2010 5-year est.).

Economy: Single-family building permits issued: 0 (2011); Multi-family building permits issued: 0 (2011); Employment by occupation: 27.5% management, 6.8% professional, 2.9% services, 16.4% sales, 0.0% farming, 3.2% construction, 2.5% production (2006-2010 5-year est.).

Income: Per capita income: $51,126 (2006-2010 5-year est.); Median household income: $106,750 (2006-2010 5-year est.); Average household income: $130,052 (2006-2010 5-year est.); Percent of households with income of $100,000 or more: 54.4% (2006-2010 5-year est.); Poverty rate: 0.0% (2006-2010 5-year est.).

Education: Percent of population age 25 and over with: High school diploma (including GED) or higher: 99.4% (2006-2010 5-year est.); Bachelor's degree or higher: 72.2% (2006-2010 5-year est.); Master's degree or higher: 30.1% (2006-2010 5-year est.).

Housing: Homeownership rate: 97.1% (2010); Median home value: $251,700 (2006-2010 5-year est.); Median contract rent: $1,750 per month (2006-2010 5-year est.); Median year structure built: before 1940 (2006-2010 5-year est.).

Safety: Violent crime rate: 0.0 per 10,000 population; Property crime rate: 0.0 per 10,000 population (2011).

Transportation: Commute to work: 87.5% car, 3.7% public transportation, 1.5% walk, 6.3% work from home (2006-2010 5-year est.); Travel time to work: 18.9% less than 15 minutes, 57.1% 15 to 30 minutes, 16.9% 30 to 45 minutes, 3.5% 45 to 60 minutes, 3.5% 60 minutes or more (2006-2010 5-year est.)

RURAL RIDGE (unincorporated postal area)
Zip Code: 15075

Covers a land area of 0.023 square miles and a water area of 0 square miles. Located at 40.58° N. Lat; 79.82° W. Long. Elevation is 850 feet. Population: 128 (2010); Density: 5,396.7 persons per square mile (2010); Race: 100.0% White, 0.0% Black, 0.0% Asian, 0.0% American Indian/Alaska Native, 0.0% Native Hawaiian/Other Pacific Islander, 0.0% Other, 0.0% Hispanic of any race (2010); Average household size: 2.78 (2010); Median age: 33.5 (2010); Males per 100 females: 68.4 (2010); Homeownership rate: 69.5% (2010)

RUSSELLTON (CDP). Covers a land area of 1.429 square miles and a water area of 0 square miles. Located at 40.61° N. Lat; 79.84° W. Long. Elevation is 955 feet.
Population: 1,691 (1990); 1,530 (2000); 1,440 (2010); Density: 1,007.7 persons per square mile (2010); Race: 97.9% White, 0.9% Black, 0.4% Asian, 0.1% American Indian/Alaska Native, 0.0% Native Hawaiian/Other Pacific Islander, 0.7% Other, 0.7% Hispanic of any race (2010); Average household size: 2.34 (2010); Median age: 45.5 (2010); Males per 100 females: 101.1 (2010); Marriage status: 25.9% never married, 46.9% now married, 8.3% widowed, 18.9% divorced (2006-2010 5-year est.); Foreign born: 0.0% (2006-2010 5-year est.); Ancestry (includes multiple ancestries): 28.2% German, 24.0% Italian, 23.9% Polish, 10.7% Slovak, 10.5% Croatian (2006-2010 5-year est.).

Economy: Employment by occupation: 8.1% management, 0.0% professional, 4.4% services, 22.1% sales, 1.2% farming, 20.5% construction, 15.3% production (2006-2010 5-year est.).

Income: Per capita income: $23,346 (2006-2010 5-year est.); Median household income: $50,625 (2006-2010 5-year est.); Average household income: $51,567 (2006-2010 5-year est.); Percent of households with income of $100,000 or more: 10.7% (2006-2010 5-year est.); Poverty rate: 9.5% (2006-2010 5-year est.).

Education: Percent of population age 25 and over with: High school diploma (including GED) or higher: 91.7% (2006-2010 5-year est.); Bachelor's degree or higher: 10.2% (2006-2010 5-year est.); Master's degree or higher: 6.3% (2006-2010 5-year est.).

School District(s)
Deer Lakes SD (KG-12)
    2010-11 Enrollment: 1,953 . . . . (724) 265-5300

Housing: Homeownership rate: 72.9% (2010); Median home value: $89,700 (2006-2010 5-year est.); Median contract rent: $449 per month (2006-2010 5-year est.); Median year structure built: 1953 (2006-2010 5-year est.).

Transportation: Commute to work: 79.3% car, 7.8% public transportation, 0.0% walk, 10.9% work from home (2006-2010 5-year est.); Travel time to work: 22.1% less than 15 minutes, 22.1% 15 to 30 minutes, 40.5% 30 to 45 minutes, 1.8% 45 to 60 minutes, 13.4% 60 minutes or more (2006-2010 5-year est.)

Additional Information Contacts
Oakmont Chamber of Commerce . . . . (412) 828-3238
    http://www.oakmont-pa.com

SCOTT (township). Covers a land area of 3.912 square miles and a water area of 0 square miles. Located at 40.39° N. Lat; 80.08° W. Long.
Population: 16,969 (1990); 17,288 (2000); 17,024 (2010); Density: 4,351.7 persons per square mile (2010); Race: 85.6% White, 1.9% Black, 10.7% Asian, 0.1% American Indian/Alaska Native, 0.0% Native Hawaiian/Other Pacific Islander, 1.7% Other, 0.9% Hispanic of any race (2010); Average household size: 2.10 (2010); Median age: 43.6 (2010);

Males per 100 females: 88.3 (2010); Marriage status: 27.5% never married, 51.8% now married, 11.9% widowed, 8.8% divorced (2006-2010 5-year est.); Foreign born: 12.9% (2006-2010 5-year est.); Ancestry (includes multiple ancestries): 29.8% German, 20.2% Irish, 19.4% Italian, 14.6% Polish, 7.1% English (2006-2010 5-year est.).

Economy: Single-family building permits issued: 1 (2011); Multi-family building permits issued: 0 (2011); Employment by occupation: 11.4% management, 12.6% professional, 6.2% services, 17.8% sales, 4.6% farming, 4.0% construction, 1.6% production (2006-2010 5-year est.).

Income: Per capita income: $30,777 (2006-2010 5-year est.); Median household income: $52,240 (2006-2010 5-year est.); Average household income: $63,701 (2006-2010 5-year est.); Percent of households with income of $100,000 or more: 17.6% (2006-2010 5-year est.); Poverty rate: 8.3% (2006-2010 5-year est.).

Education: Percent of population age 25 and over with: High school diploma (including GED) or higher: 91.1% (2006-2010 5-year est.); Bachelor's degree or higher: 38.8% (2006-2010 5-year est.); Master's degree or higher: 13.7% (2006-2010 5-year est.).

Housing: Homeownership rate: 65.2% (2010); Median home value: $122,500 (2006-2010 5-year est.); Median contract rent: $666 per month (2006-2010 5-year est.); Median year structure built: 1958 (2006-2010 5-year est.).

Safety: Violent crime rate: 9.4 per 10,000 population; Property crime rate: 130.0 per 10,000 population (2011).

Transportation: Commute to work: 81.8% car, 10.8% public transportation, 2.6% walk, 1.2% work from home (2006-2010 5-year est.); Travel time to work: 25.2% less than 15 minutes, 41.7% 15 to 30 minutes, 22.3% 30 to 45 minutes, 5.9% 45 to 60 minutes, 5.0% 60 minutes or more (2006-2010 5-year est.)

Additional Information Contacts
Brentwood Baldwin Whitehall Chamber of Commerce . . . . (412) 884-1233
    http://www.bbwchamber.com
Scott Township . . . . (412) 276-5300
    http://www.scott-twp.com

SEWICKLEY (borough). Covers a land area of 0.999 square miles and a water area of 0.137 square miles. Located at 40.54° N. Lat; 80.18° W. Long. Elevation is 741 feet.
History: Incorporated 1853.

Population: 4,134 (1990); 3,902 (2000); 3,827 (2010); Density: 3,829.4 persons per square mile (2010); Race: 88.8% White, 7.3% Black, 1.3% Asian, 0.1% American Indian/Alaska Native, 0.1% Native Hawaiian/Other Pacific Islander, 2.4% Other, 1.8% Hispanic of any race (2010); Average household size: 2.17 (2010); Median age: 42.3 (2010); Males per 100 females: 82.5 (2010); Marriage status: 23.6% never married, 51.8% now married, 11.7% widowed, 12.9% divorced (2006-2010 5-year est.); Foreign born: 6.2% (2006-2010 5-year est.); Ancestry (includes multiple ancestries): 34.7% German, 21.0% Irish, 20.1% Italian, 11.6% English, 9.3% Polish (2006-2010 5-year est.).

Economy: Single-family building permits issued: 1 (2011); Multi-family building permits issued: 0 (2011); Employment by occupation: 15.0% management, 5.1% professional, 7.2% services, 19.7% sales, 2.2% farming, 3.4% construction, 1.1% production (2006-2010 5-year est.).

Income: Per capita income: $41,468 (2006-2010 5-year est.); Median household income: $54,021 (2006-2010 5-year est.); Average household income: $88,959 (2006-2010 5-year est.); Percent of households with income of $100,000 or more: 27.9% (2006-2010 5-year est.); Poverty rate: 5.8% (2006-2010 5-year est.).

Education: Percent of population age 25 and over with: High school diploma (including GED) or higher: 92.9% (2006-2010 5-year est.); Bachelor's degree or higher: 56.5% (2006-2010 5-year est.); Master's degree or higher: 22.2% (2006-2010 5-year est.).

School District(s)
North Allegheny SD (KG-12)
    2010-11 Enrollment: 8,105 . . . . (412) 366-2100
Pennsylvania Distance Learning CS (KG-12)
    2010-11 Enrollment: 327 . . . . (724) 933-7300
Quaker Valley SD (KG-12)
    2010-11 Enrollment: 1,983 . . . . (412) 749-3600

Housing: Homeownership rate: 61.3% (2010); Median home value: $222,400 (2006-2010 5-year est.); Median contract rent: $586 per month (2006-2010 5-year est.); Median year structure built: before 1940 (2006-2010 5-year est.).

Hospitals: Health South Rehabilitation Hospital (44 beds); Sewickley Valley Hospital (221 beds)

Safety: Violent crime rate: 22.8 per 10,000 population; Property crime rate: 139.0 per 10,000 population (2011).

Transportation: Commute to work: 73.9% car, 6.4% public transportation, 15.0% walk, 3.9% work from home (2006-2010 5-year est.); Travel time to work: 40.2% less than 15 minutes, 21.8% 15 to 30 minutes, 19.2% 30 to 45 minutes, 12.8% 45 to 60 minutes, 6.0% 60 minutes or more (2006-2010 5-year est.)

Additional Information Contacts

The Chamber of Commerce, Inc. . . . . (724) 776-4949
http://www.thechamberinc.com

SEWICKLEY HEIGHTS (borough). Covers a land area of 7.263 square miles and a water area of 0 square miles. Located at 40.56° N. Lat; 80.15° W. Long. Elevation is 1,191 feet.

Population: 984 (1990); 981 (2000); 810 (2010); Density: 111.5 persons per square mile (2010); Race: 97.2% White, 0.6% Black, 0.9% Asian, 0.4% American Indian/Alaska Native, 0.0% Native Hawaiian/Other Pacific Islander, 0.9% Other, 1.6% Hispanic of any race (2010); Average household size: 2.61 (2010); Median age: 48.8 (2010); Males per 100 females: 103.5 (2010); Marriage status: 21.1% never married, 68.3% now married, 7.8% widowed, 2.8% divorced (2006-2010 5-year est.); Foreign born: 5.9% (2006-2010 5-year est.); Ancestry (includes multiple ancestries): 19.4% German, 17.1% English, 16.0% Irish, 14.6% Italian, 12.0% Scottish (2006-2010 5-year est.).

Economy: Single-family building permits issued: 0 (2011); Multi-family building permits issued: 0 (2011); Employment by occupation: 30.2% management, 1.5% professional, 1.8% services, 6.9% sales, 3.9% farming, 3.0% construction, 3.0% production (2006-2010 5-year est.).

Income: Per capita income: $114,879 (2006-2010 5-year est.); Median household income: $118,438 (2006-2010 5-year est.); Average household income: $288,091 (2006-2010 5-year est.); Percent of households with income of $100,000 or more: 61.4% (2006-2010 5-year est.); Poverty rate: 2.2% (2006-2010 5-year est.).

Education: Percent of population age 25 and over with: High school diploma (including GED) or higher: 98.2% (2006-2010 5-year est.); Bachelor's degree or higher: 71.7% (2006-2010 5-year est.); Master's degree or higher: 38.2% (2006-2010 5-year est.).

Housing: Homeownership rate: 87.4% (2010); Median home value: $954,900 (2006-2010 5-year est.); Median contract rent: $642 per month (2006-2010 5-year est.); Median year structure built: 1954 (2006-2010 5-year est.).

Safety: Violent crime rate: 0.0 per 10,000 population; Property crime rate: 36.9 per 10,000 population (2011).

Transportation: Commute to work: 88.6% car, 0.0% public transportation, 2.4% walk, 7.2% work from home (2006-2010 5-year est.); Travel time to work: 23.5% less than 15 minutes, 34.8% 15 to 30 minutes, 25.8% 30 to 45 minutes, 10.0% 45 to 60 minutes, 5.8% 60 minutes or more (2006-2010 5-year est.)

SEWICKLEY HILLS (borough). Covers a land area of 2.528 square miles and a water area of 0 square miles. Located at 40.57° N. Lat; 80.13° W. Long. Elevation is 1,135 feet.

Population: 625 (1990); 652 (2000); 639 (2010); Density: 252.7 persons per square mile (2010); Race: 95.5% White, 2.3% Black, 1.4% Asian, 0.0% American Indian/Alaska Native, 0.0% Native Hawaiian/Other Pacific Islander, 0.8% Other, 1.9% Hispanic of any race (2010); Average household size: 2.66 (2010); Median age: 47.6 (2010); Males per 100 females: 100.9 (2010); Marriage status: 35.2% never married, 56.7% now married, 3.9% widowed, 4.2% divorced (2006-2010 5-year est.); Foreign born: 2.6% (2006-2010 5-year est.); Ancestry (includes multiple ancestries): 31.6% German, 27.2% Irish, 11.4% English, 11.2% Italian, 6.3% French (2006-2010 5-year est.).

Economy: Single-family building permits issued: 10 (2011); Multi-family building permits issued: 0 (2011); Employment by occupation: 11.2% management, 5.9% professional, 3.1% services, 22.5% sales, 5.5% farming, 5.1% construction, 3.5% production (2006-2010 5-year est.).

Income: Per capita income: $44,370 (2006-2010 5-year est.); Median household income: $88,571 (2006-2010 5-year est.); Average household income: $116,394 (2006-2010 5-year est.); Percent of households with income of $100,000 or more: 44.8% (2006-2010 5-year est.); Poverty rate: 2.3% (2006-2010 5-year est.).

Education: Percent of population age 25 and over with: High school diploma (including GED) or higher: 95.1% (2006-2010 5-year est.); Bachelor's degree or higher: 48.6% (2006-2010 5-year est.); Master's degree or higher: 27.8% (2006-2010 5-year est.).

Housing: Homeownership rate: 90.0% (2010); Median home value: $271,000 (2006-2010 5-year est.); Median contract rent: n/a per month (2006-2010 5-year est.); Median year structure built: 1986 (2006-2010 5-year est.).

Transportation: Commute to work: 84.9% car, 0.0% public transportation, 0.0% walk, 10.8% work from home (2006-2010 5-year est.); Travel time to work: 19.9% less than 15 minutes, 43.3% 15 to 30 minutes, 27.5% 30 to 45 minutes, 2.5% 45 to 60 minutes, 6.8% 60 minutes or more (2006-2010 5-year est.)

SHALER (township). Covers a land area of 11.075 square miles and a water area of 0.095 square miles. Located at 40.52° N. Lat; 79.96° W. Long.

Population: 30,276 (1990); 29,757 (2000); 28,757 (2010); Density: 2,596.5 persons per square mile (2010); Race: 97.4% White, 0.7% Black, 0.9% Asian, 0.1% American Indian/Alaska Native, 0.0% Native Hawaiian/Other Pacific Islander, 0.9% Other, 0.8% Hispanic of any race (2010); Average household size: 2.38 (2010); Median age: 45.2 (2010); Males per 100 females: 92.5 (2010); Marriage status: 25.1% never married, 60.6% now married, 7.3% widowed, 7.0% divorced (2006-2010 5-year est.); Foreign born: 2.2% (2006-2010 5-year est.); Ancestry (includes multiple ancestries): 44.8% German, 22.7% Irish, 20.5% Italian, 17.0% Polish, 7.8% English (2006-2010 5-year est.).

Economy: Unemployment rate: 7.1% (August 2012); Total civilian labor force: 16,744 (August 2012); Single-family building permits issued: 8 (2011); Multi-family building permits issued: 0 (2011); Employment by occupation: 14.2% management, 4.2% professional, 8.7% services, 20.2% sales, 3.3% farming, 6.8% construction, 3.6% production (2006-2010 5-year est.).

Income: Per capita income: $29,576 (2006-2010 5-year est.); Median household income: $62,416 (2006-2010 5-year est.); Average household income: $70,371 (2006-2010 5-year est.); Percent of households with income of $100,000 or more: 19.4% (2006-2010 5-year est.); Poverty rate: 3.8% (2006-2010 5-year est.).

Taxes: Total city taxes per capita: $280 (2009); City property taxes per capita: $131 (2009).

Education: Percent of population age 25 and over with: High school diploma (including GED) or higher: 91.7% (2006-2010 5-year est.); Bachelor's degree or higher: 32.8% (2006-2010 5-year est.); Master's degree or higher: 10.7% (2006-2010 5-year est.).

Housing: Homeownership rate: 86.4% (2010); Median home value: $135,700 (2006-2010 5-year est.); Median contract rent: $571 per month (2006-2010 5-year est.); Median year structure built: 1959 (2006-2010 5-year est.).

Safety: Violent crime rate: 4.5 per 10,000 population; Property crime rate: 112.0 per 10,000 population (2011).

Transportation: Commute to work: 91.7% car, 3.0% public transportation, 1.1% walk, 3.0% work from home (2006-2010 5-year est.); Travel time to work: 18.6% less than 15 minutes, 45.0% 15 to 30 minutes, 25.3% 30 to 45 minutes, 6.8% 45 to 60 minutes, 4.4% 60 minutes or more (2006-2010 5-year est.)

Additional Information Contacts

Northside Northshore Chamber of Commerce . . . . (412) 231-6500
http://www.northsidechamberofcommerce.com
Shaler Township . . . . (412) 486-9700
http://www.shaler.org

SHARPSBURG (borough). Covers a land area of 0.487 square miles and a water area of 0.152 square miles. Located at 40.49° N. Lat; 79.92° W. Long. Elevation is 738 feet.

History: Incorporated 1842.

Population: 3,781 (1990); 3,594 (2000); 3,446 (2010); Density: 7,078.3 persons per square mile (2010); Race: 86.9% White, 6.7% Black, 1.7% Asian, 0.2% American Indian/Alaska Native, 0.0% Native Hawaiian/Other Pacific Islander, 4.5% Other, 3.3% Hispanic of any race (2010); Average household size: 2.09 (2010); Median age: 40.2 (2010); Males per 100 females: 90.6 (2010); Marriage status: 43.5% never married, 28.9% now married, 7.9% widowed, 19.7% divorced (2006-2010 5-year est.); Foreign born: 1.2% (2006-2010 5-year est.); Ancestry (includes multiple ancestries): 35.6% German, 35.3% Italian, 28.5% Irish, 12.3% Polish, 3.7% American (2006-2010 5-year est.).

Economy: Single-family building permits issued: 0 (2011); Multi-family building permits issued: 0 (2011); Employment by occupation: 5.8% management, 0.6% professional, 11.0% services, 23.2% sales, 5.9% farming, 15.1% construction, 8.2% production (2006-2010 5-year est.).

Income: Per capita income: $17,985 (2006-2010 5-year est.); Median household income: $30,089 (2006-2010 5-year est.); Average household income: $36,625 (2006-2010 5-year est.); Percent of households with income of $100,000 or more: 3.9% (2006-2010 5-year est.); Poverty rate: 22.2% (2006-2010 5-year est.).

Education: Percent of population age 25 and over with: High school diploma (including GED) or higher: 86.1% (2006-2010 5-year est.); Bachelor's degree or higher: 11.7% (2006-2010 5-year est.); Master's degree or higher: 3.0% (2006-2010 5-year est.).

Housing: Homeownership rate: 40.9% (2010); Median home value: $67,700 (2006-2010 5-year est.); Median contract rent: $445 per month (2006-2010 5-year est.); Median year structure built: before 1940 (2006-2010 5-year est.).

Safety: Violent crime rate: 49.2 per 10,000 population; Property crime rate: 217.0 per 10,000 population (2011).

Transportation: Commute to work: 62.2% car, 14.4% public transportation, 15.0% walk, 0.8% work from home (2006-2010 5-year est.); Travel time to work: 28.1% less than 15 minutes, 36.0% 15 to 30 minutes, 25.0% 30 to 45 minutes, 4.4% 45 to 60 minutes, 6.5% 60 minutes or more (2006-2010 5-year est.)

Additional Information Contacts
Northside Northshore Chamber of Commerce . . . . (412) 231-6500
  http://www.northsidechamberofcommerce.com

SOUTH FAYETTE (township).
Covers a land area of 20.384 square miles and a water area of 0.004 square miles. Located at 40.37° N. Lat; 80.18° W. Long.

Population: 10,329 (1990); 12,271 (2000); 14,416 (2010); Density: 707.2 persons per square mile (2010); Race: 91.7% White, 2.2% Black, 4.6% Asian, 0.1% American Indian/Alaska Native, 0.0% Native Hawaiian/Other Pacific Islander, 1.4% Other, 1.0% Hispanic of any race (2010); Average household size: 2.41 (2010); Median age: 41.0 (2010); Males per 100 females: 91.0 (2010); Marriage status: 25.3% never married, 59.5% now married, 6.5% widowed, 8.8% divorced (2006-2010 5-year est.); Foreign born: 4.3% (2006-2010 5-year est.); Ancestry (includes multiple ancestries): 27.4% German, 25.1% Italian, 20.4% Irish, 12.0% Polish, 10.8% English (2006-2010 5-year est.).

Economy: Single-family building permits issued: 102 (2011); Multi-family building permits issued: 0 (2011); Employment by occupation: 15.6% management, 6.9% professional, 8.7% services, 13.5% sales, 3.5% farming, 6.6% construction, 4.7% production (2006-2010 5-year est.).

Income: Per capita income: $34,411 (2006-2010 5-year est.); Median household income: $68,034 (2006-2010 5-year est.); Average household income: $86,258 (2006-2010 5-year est.); Percent of households with income of $100,000 or more: 32.8% (2006-2010 5-year est.); Poverty rate: 2.9% (2006-2010 5-year est.).

Education: Percent of population age 25 and over with: High school diploma (including GED) or higher: 94.7% (2006-2010 5-year est.); Bachelor's degree or higher: 43.4% (2006-2010 5-year est.); Master's degree or higher: 16.6% (2006-2010 5-year est.).

Housing: Homeownership rate: 76.9% (2010); Median home value: $169,000 (2006-2010 5-year est.); Median contract rent: $715 per month (2006-2010 5-year est.); Median year structure built: 1983 (2006-2010 5-year est.).

Safety: Violent crime rate: 7.6 per 10,000 population; Property crime rate: 63.6 per 10,000 population (2011).

Transportation: Commute to work: 88.0% car, 5.3% public transportation, 0.8% walk, 5.6% work from home (2006-2010 5-year est.); Travel time to work: 21.6% less than 15 minutes, 39.1% 15 to 30 minutes, 21.0% 30 to 45 minutes, 11.4% 45 to 60 minutes, 7.0% 60 minutes or more (2006-2010 5-year est.)

Additional Information Contacts
South Fayette Township . . . . (412) 221-8700
  http://www.south-fayette.pa.us
South West Communities Chamber of Commerce . . . . (412) 221-4100
  http://www.swccoc.org

SOUTH PARK (township).
Covers a land area of 9.270 square miles and a water area of 0 square miles. Located at 40.30° N. Lat; 79.99° W. Long.

Population: 14,292 (1990); 14,340 (2000); 13,416 (2010); Density: 1,447.2 persons per square mile (2010); Race: 94.9% White, 2.8% Black, 0.8% Asian, 0.1% American Indian/Alaska Native, 0.0% Native Hawaiian/Other Pacific Islander, 1.4% Other, 0.8% Hispanic of any race (2010); Average household size: 2.46 (2010); Median age: 42.8 (2010);

Males per 100 females: 97.5 (2010); Marriage status: 26.1% never married, 58.1% now married, 6.4% widowed, 9.4% divorced (2006-2010 5-year est.); Foreign born: 2.7% (2006-2010 5-year est.); Ancestry (includes multiple ancestries): 38.3% German, 23.6% Irish, 22.4% Italian, 12.5% Polish, 7.8% English (2006-2010 5-year est.).

Economy: Single-family building permits issued: 10 (2011); Multi-family building permits issued: 0 (2011); Employment by occupation: 12.7% management, 6.5% professional, 9.5% services, 15.2% sales, 4.6% farming, 6.7% construction, 3.3% production (2006-2010 5-year est.).

Income: Per capita income: $29,468 (2006-2010 5-year est.); Median household income: $65,492 (2006-2010 5-year est.); Average household income: $72,307 (2006-2010 5-year est.); Percent of households with income of $100,000 or more: 26.5% (2006-2010 5-year est.); Poverty rate: 5.8% (2006-2010 5-year est.).

Education: Percent of population age 25 and over with: High school diploma (including GED) or higher: 92.1% (2006-2010 5-year est.); Bachelor's degree or higher: 31.3% (2006-2010 5-year est.); Master's degree or higher: 10.4% (2006-2010 5-year est.).

School District(s)
South Park SD (KG-12)
  2010-11 Enrollment: 2,145 . . . . (412) 655-3111

Housing: Homeownership rate: 78.7% (2010); Median home value: $136,900 (2006-2010 5-year est.); Median contract rent: $628 per month (2006-2010 5-year est.); Median year structure built: 1972 (2006-2010 5-year est.).

Safety: Violent crime rate: 2.2 per 10,000 population; Property crime rate: 39.4 per 10,000 population (2011).

Transportation: Commute to work: 91.5% car, 4.9% public transportation, 0.6% walk, 2.3% work from home (2006-2010 5-year est.); Travel time to work: 19.7% less than 15 minutes, 30.7% 15 to 30 minutes, 23.4% 30 to 45 minutes, 15.9% 45 to 60 minutes, 10.2% 60 minutes or more (2006-2010 5-year est.)

Additional Information Contacts
South Hills Chamber of Commerce . . . . (412) 306-8090
  http://www.shchamber.org
South Park Township . . . . (412) 831-7000
  http://www.southparktwp.com

SOUTH PARK TOWNSHIP (CDP).
Covers a land area of 9.270 square miles and a water area of 0 square miles. Located at 40.30° N. Lat; 79.99° W. Long.

Population: 14,292 (1990); 14,340 (2000); 13,416 (2010); Density: 1,447.2 persons per square mile (2010); Race: 94.9% White, 2.8% Black, 0.8% Asian, 0.1% American Indian/Alaska Native, 0.0% Native Hawaiian/Other Pacific Islander, 1.4% Other, 0.8% Hispanic of any race (2010); Average household size: 2.46 (2010); Median age: 42.8 (2010); Males per 100 females: 97.5 (2010); Marriage status: 26.1% never married, 58.1% now married, 6.4% widowed, 9.4% divorced (2006-2010 5-year est.); Foreign born: 2.7% (2006-2010 5-year est.); Ancestry (includes multiple ancestries): 38.3% German, 23.6% Irish, 22.4% Italian, 12.5% Polish, 7.8% English (2006-2010 5-year est.).

Economy: Employment by occupation: 12.7% management, 6.5% professional, 9.5% services, 15.2% sales, 4.6% farming, 6.7% construction, 3.3% production (2006-2010 5-year est.).

Income: Per capita income: $29,468 (2006-2010 5-year est.); Median household income: $65,492 (2006-2010 5-year est.); Average household income: $72,307 (2006-2010 5-year est.); Percent of households with income of $100,000 or more: 26.5% (2006-2010 5-year est.); Poverty rate: 5.8% (2006-2010 5-year est.).

Education: Percent of population age 25 and over with: High school diploma (including GED) or higher: 92.1% (2006-2010 5-year est.); Bachelor's degree or higher: 31.3% (2006-2010 5-year est.); Master's degree or higher: 10.4% (2006-2010 5-year est.).

Housing: Homeownership rate: 78.7% (2010); Median home value: $136,900 (2006-2010 5-year est.); Median contract rent: $628 per month (2006-2010 5-year est.); Median year structure built: 1972 (2006-2010 5-year est.).

Transportation: Commute to work: 91.5% car, 4.9% public transportation, 0.6% walk, 2.3% work from home (2006-2010 5-year est.); Travel time to work: 19.7% less than 15 minutes, 30.7% 15 to 30 minutes, 23.4% 30 to 45 minutes, 15.9% 45 to 60 minutes, 10.2% 60 minutes or more (2006-2010 5-year est.)

SOUTH VERSAILLES (township). Covers a land area of 0.879 square miles and a water area of 0.091 square miles. Located at 40.30° N. Lat; 79.80° W. Long.

Population: 515 (1990); 351 (2000); 351 (2010); Density: 399.3 persons per square mile (2010); Race: 97.4% White, 1.4% Black, 0.9% Asian, 0.0% American Indian/Alaska Native, 0.0% Native Hawaiian/Other Pacific Islander, 0.3% Other, 0.3% Hispanic of any race (2010); Average household size: 2.29 (2010); Median age: 49.6 (2010); Males per 100 females: 97.2 (2010); Marriage status: 27.6% never married, 58.7% now married, 10.5% widowed, 3.2% divorced (2006-2010 5-year est.); Foreign born: 0.0% (2006-2010 5-year est.); Ancestry (includes multiple ancestries): 30.9% German, 19.1% Slovak, 15.2% Irish, 11.0% Italian, 10.7% American (2006-2010 5-year est.).

Economy: Single-family building permits issued: 0 (2011); Multi-family building permits issued: 0 (2011); Employment by occupation: 4.5% management, 2.3% professional, 15.0% services, 17.3% sales, 6.0% farming, 14.3% construction, 8.3% production (2006-2010 5-year est.).

Income: Per capita income: $22,282 (2006-2010 5-year est.); Median household income: $44,643 (2006-2010 5-year est.); Average household income: $54,256 (2006-2010 5-year est.); Percent of households with income of $100,000 or more: 9.3% (2006-2010 5-year est.); Poverty rate: 3.4% (2006-2010 5-year est.).

Education: Percent of population age 25 and over with: High school diploma (including GED) or higher: 93.4% (2006-2010 5-year est.); Bachelor's degree or higher: 13.6% (2006-2010 5-year est.); Master's degree or higher: 1.7% (2006-2010 5-year est.).

Housing: Homeownership rate: 89.5% (2010); Median home value: $83,800 (2006-2010 5-year est.); Median contract rent: $875 per month (2006-2010 5-year est.); Median year structure built: 1953 (2006-2010 5-year est.).

Transportation: Commute to work: 94.6% car, 4.7% public transportation, 0.0% walk, 0.8% work from home (2006-2010 5-year est.); Travel time to work: 30.5% less than 15 minutes, 24.2% 15 to 30 minutes, 24.2% 30 to 45 minutes, 7.8% 45 to 60 minutes, 13.3% 60 minutes or more (2006-2010 5-year est.)

SPRINGDALE (borough). Covers a land area of 0.934 square miles and a water area of 0.160 square miles. Located at 40.54° N. Lat; 79.78° W. Long. Elevation is 807 feet.

Population: 3,992 (1990); 3,828 (2000); 3,405 (2010); Density: 3,647.1 persons per square mile (2010); Race: 98.2% White, 0.6% Black, 0.1% Asian, 0.1% American Indian/Alaska Native, 0.0% Native Hawaiian/Other Pacific Islander, 1.0% Other, 0.6% Hispanic of any race (2010); Average household size: 2.12 (2010); Median age: 44.9 (2010); Males per 100 females: 88.2 (2010); Marriage status: 22.2% never married, 54.9% now married, 13.0% widowed, 9.9% divorced (2006-2010 5-year est.); Foreign born: 1.2% (2006-2010 5-year est.); Ancestry (includes multiple ancestries): 26.2% German, 23.4% Irish, 22.1% Italian, 15.7% Polish, 5.8% Scotch-Irish (2006-2010 5-year est.).

Economy: Single-family building permits issued: 1 (2011); Multi-family building permits issued: 0 (2011); Employment by occupation: 6.9% management, 6.5% professional, 15.0% services, 12.7% sales, 6.5% farming, 8.2% construction, 8.9% production (2006-2010 5-year est.).

Income: Per capita income: $22,084 (2006-2010 5-year est.); Median household income: $43,038 (2006-2010 5-year est.); Average household income: $49,815 (2006-2010 5-year est.); Percent of households with income of $100,000 or more: 8.0% (2006-2010 5-year est.); Poverty rate: 7.5% (2006-2010 5-year est.).

Education: Percent of population age 25 and over with: High school diploma (including GED) or higher: 89.9% (2006-2010 5-year est.); Bachelor's degree or higher: 14.5% (2006-2010 5-year est.); Master's degree or higher: 5.5% (2006-2010 5-year est.).

School District(s)

Allegheny Valley SD (KG-12)

   2010-11 Enrollment: 1,075 . . . . (724) 274-5300

Housing: Homeownership rate: 64.5% (2010); Median home value: $88,500 (2006-2010 5-year est.); Median contract rent: $478 per month (2006-2010 5-year est.); Median year structure built: 1947 (2006-2010 5-year est.).

Safety: Violent crime rate: 17.6 per 10,000 population; Property crime rate: 61.5 per 10,000 population (2011).

Transportation: Commute to work: 85.0% car, 6.1% public transportation, 5.3% walk, 1.3% work from home (2006-2010 5-year est.); Travel time to work: 28.0% less than 15 minutes, 35.2% 15 to 30 minutes, 22.1% 30 to 45 minutes, 10.5% 45 to 60 minutes, 4.2% 60 minutes or more (2006-2010 5-year est.)

Additional Information Contacts

Allegheny Valley Chamber of Commerce . . . . (724) 224-3400

   http://alleghenyvalleychamber.com

SPRINGDALE (township). Covers a land area of 2.253 square miles and a water area of 0.151 square miles. Located at 40.55° N. Lat; 79.79° W. Long. Elevation is 807 feet.

History: Incorporated 1906.

Population: 1,777 (1990); 1,802 (2000); 1,636 (2010); Density: 726.2 persons per square mile (2010); Race: 99.6% White, 0.2% Black, 0.1% Asian, 0.1% American Indian/Alaska Native, 0.0% Native Hawaiian/Other Pacific Islander, 0.0% Other, 0.6% Hispanic of any race (2010); Average household size: 2.06 (2010); Median age: 50.5 (2010); Males per 100 females: 92.0 (2010); Marriage status: 22.9% never married, 55.9% now married, 11.1% widowed, 10.1% divorced (2006-2010 5-year est.); Foreign born: 0.8% (2006-2010 5-year est.); Ancestry (includes multiple ancestries): 34.2% German, 20.1% Irish, 19.2% Polish, 18.8% Italian, 11.0% Slovak (2006-2010 5-year est.).

Economy: Single-family building permits issued: 0 (2011); Multi-family building permits issued: 0 (2011); Employment by occupation: 10.3% management, 7.0% professional, 6.6% services, 24.9% sales, 0.4% farming, 8.9% construction, 8.2% production (2006-2010 5-year est.).

Income: Per capita income: $26,079 (2006-2010 5-year est.); Median household income: $42,132 (2006-2010 5-year est.); Average household income: $52,752 (2006-2010 5-year est.); Percent of households with income of $100,000 or more: 11.2% (2006-2010 5-year est.); Poverty rate: 6.7% (2006-2010 5-year est.).

Education: Percent of population age 25 and over with: High school diploma (including GED) or higher: 88.2% (2006-2010 5-year est.); Bachelor's degree or higher: 22.8% (2006-2010 5-year est.); Master's degree or higher: 7.9% (2006-2010 5-year est.).

Housing: Homeownership rate: 82.6% (2010); Median home value: $98,800 (2006-2010 5-year est.); Median contract rent: $417 per month (2006-2010 5-year est.); Median year structure built: 1960 (2006-2010 5-year est.).

Transportation: Commute to work: 93.5% car, 2.0% public transportation, 1.5% walk, 2.5% work from home (2006-2010 5-year est.); Travel time to work: 34.4% less than 15 minutes, 32.5% 15 to 30 minutes, 17.0% 30 to 45 minutes, 10.8% 45 to 60 minutes, 5.3% 60 minutes or more (2006-2010 5-year est.)

Additional Information Contacts

Allegheny Valley Chamber of Commerce . . . . (724) 224-3400

   http://alleghenyvalleychamber.com

STOWE (township). Covers a land area of 1.982 square miles and a water area of 0.315 square miles. Located at 40.48° N. Lat; 80.07° W. Long.

Population: 7,681 (1990); 6,706 (2000); 6,362 (2010); Density: 3,209.4 persons per square mile (2010); Race: 77.9% White, 17.5% Black, 0.4% Asian, 0.1% American Indian/Alaska Native, 0.0% Native Hawaiian/Other Pacific Islander, 4.1% Other, 1.4% Hispanic of any race (2010); Average household size: 2.19 (2010); Median age: 40.8 (2010); Males per 100 females: 89.5 (2010); Marriage status: 39.1% never married, 42.2% now married, 10.8% widowed, 7.9% divorced (2006-2010 5-year est.); Foreign born: 1.8% (2006-2010 5-year est.); Ancestry (includes multiple ancestries): 28.7% German, 23.5% Irish, 17.6% Italian, 10.9% Polish, 5.7% English (2006-2010 5-year est.).

Economy: Single-family building permits issued: 0 (2011); Multi-family building permits issued: 0 (2011); Employment by occupation: 7.4% management, 3.3% professional, 18.6% services, 21.7% sales, 3.1% farming, 11.9% construction, 7.0% production (2006-2010 5-year est.).

Income: Per capita income: $19,583 (2006-2010 5-year est.); Median household income: $33,209 (2006-2010 5-year est.); Average household income: $42,388 (2006-2010 5-year est.); Percent of households with income of $100,000 or more: 7.3% (2006-2010 5-year est.); Poverty rate: 21.8% (2006-2010 5-year est.).

Taxes: Total city taxes per capita: $300 (2009); City property taxes per capita: $200 (2009).

Education: Percent of population age 25 and over with: High school diploma (including GED) or higher: 84.5% (2006-2010 5-year est.); Bachelor's degree or higher: 17.9% (2006-2010 5-year est.); Master's degree or higher: 4.6% (2006-2010 5-year est.).

Housing: Homeownership rate: 56.8% (2010); Median home value: $72,900 (2006-2010 5-year est.); Median contract rent: $444 per month (2006-2010 5-year est.); Median year structure built: 1940 (2006-2010 5-year est.).

Safety: Violent crime rate: 34.5 per 10,000 population; Property crime rate: 377.6 per 10,000 population (2011).

Transportation: Commute to work: 85.1% car, 9.3% public transportation, 1.9% walk, 1.7% work from home (2006-2010 5-year est.); Travel time to work: 31.5% less than 15 minutes, 36.7% 15 to 30 minutes, 22.1% 30 to 45 minutes, 2.4% 45 to 60 minutes, 7.3% 60 minutes or more (2006-2010 5-year est.)

Additional Information Contacts

Pittsburgh Airport Area Chamber of Commerce . . . . (412) 264-6270
    http://www.paacc.com

STURGEON (CDP).

Covers a land area of 1.120 square miles and a water area of 0 square miles. Located at 40.38° N. Lat; 80.22° W. Long. Elevation is 945 feet.

Population: n/a (1990); n/a (2000); 1,710 (2010); Density: 1,526.6 persons per square mile (2010); Race: 96.8% White, 1.1% Black, 0.3% Asian, 0.2% American Indian/Alaska Native, 0.0% Native Hawaiian/Other Pacific Islander, 1.6% Other, 0.4% Hispanic of any race (2010); Average household size: 2.60 (2010); Median age: 40.6 (2010); Males per 100 females: 91.9 (2010); Marriage status: 23.8% never married, 59.1% now married, 7.2% widowed, 9.8% divorced (2006-2010 5-year est.); Foreign born: 0.0% (2006-2010 5-year est.); Ancestry (includes multiple ancestries): 39.5% German, 26.7% Italian, 22.2% Irish, 15.9% English, 12.9% Polish (2006-2010 5-year est.).

Economy: Employment by occupation: 22.2% management, 5.3% professional, 11.0% services, 16.3% sales, 3.4% farming, 4.3% construction, 2.5% production (2006-2010 5-year est.).

Income: Per capita income: $27,439 (2006-2010 5-year est.); Median household income: $54,393 (2006-2010 5-year est.); Average household income: $65,501 (2006-2010 5-year est.); Percent of households with income of $100,000 or more: 13.3% (2006-2010 5-year est.); Poverty rate: 6.2% (2006-2010 5-year est.).

Education: Percent of population age 25 and over with: High school diploma (including GED) or higher: 91.4% (2006-2010 5-year est.); Bachelor's degree or higher: 31.5% (2006-2010 5-year est.); Master's degree or higher: 12.5% (2006-2010 5-year est.).

Housing: Homeownership rate: 88.4% (2010); Median home value: $119,400 (2006-2010 5-year est.); Median contract rent: $479 per month (2006-2010 5-year est.); Median year structure built: 1978 (2006-2010 5-year est.).

Transportation: Commute to work: 89.4% car, 5.9% public transportation, 0.0% walk, 1.6% work from home (2006-2010 5-year est.); Travel time to work: 20.8% less than 15 minutes, 36.6% 15 to 30 minutes, 20.3% 30 to 45 minutes, 4.6% 45 to 60 minutes, 17.7% 60 minutes or more (2006-2010 5-year est.)

SWISSVALE (borough).

Covers a land area of 1.201 square miles and a water area of 0.042 square miles. Located at 40.42° N. Lat; 79.89° W. Long. Elevation is 1,024 feet.

History: Settled c.1760, incorporated 1898.

Population: 10,637 (1990); 9,653 (2000); 8,983 (2010); Density: 7,480.2 persons per square mile (2010); Race: 59.1% White, 35.0% Black, 1.7% Asian, 0.2% American Indian/Alaska Native, 0.0% Native Hawaiian/Other Pacific Islander, 4.0% Other, 2.2% Hispanic of any race (2010); Average household size: 2.02 (2010); Median age: 39.0 (2010); Males per 100 females: 80.8 (2010); Marriage status: 45.9% never married, 33.0% now married, 9.5% widowed, 11.6% divorced (2006-2010 5-year est.); Foreign born: 3.0% (2006-2010 5-year est.); Ancestry (includes multiple ancestries): 15.2% German, 14.2% Irish, 13.9% Italian, 7.8% English, 4.5% Slovak (2006-2010 5-year est.).

Economy: Single-family building permits issued: 0 (2011); Multi-family building permits issued: 0 (2011); Employment by occupation: 11.7% management, 9.9% professional, 10.4% services, 16.2% sales, 5.6% farming, 3.8% construction, 2.6% production (2006-2010 5-year est.).

Income: Per capita income: $25,614 (2006-2010 5-year est.); Median household income: $39,938 (2006-2010 5-year est.); Average household income: $50,297 (2006-2010 5-year est.); Percent of households with income of $100,000 or more: 8.8% (2006-2010 5-year est.); Poverty rate: 16.1% (2006-2010 5-year est.).

Education: Percent of population age 25 and over with: High school diploma (including GED) or higher: 92.6% (2006-2010 5-year est.);

Bachelor's degree or higher: 32.6% (2006-2010 5-year est.); Master's degree or higher: 14.7% (2006-2010 5-year est.).

Housing: Homeownership rate: 50.1% (2010); Median home value: $73,500 (2006-2010 5-year est.); Median contract rent: $554 per month (2006-2010 5-year est.); Median year structure built: 1941 (2006-2010 5-year est.).

Safety: Violent crime rate: 85.4 per 10,000 population; Property crime rate: 241.9 per 10,000 population (2011).

Transportation: Commute to work: 69.8% car, 20.8% public transportation, 3.5% walk, 4.4% work from home (2006-2010 5-year est.); Travel time to work: 17.3% less than 15 minutes, 46.0% 15 to 30 minutes, 24.3% 30 to 45 minutes, 5.6% 45 to 60 minutes, 6.8% 60 minutes or more (2006-2010 5-year est.)

Additional Information Contacts

Borough of Swissvale . . . . (412) 271-7101
    http://boroughofswissvale.com
Wilkinsburg Chamber of Commerce . . . . (412) 242-0234
    http://wilkinsburgchamber.com

TARENTUM (borough).

Covers a land area of 1.225 square miles and a water area of 0.167 square miles. Located at 40.60° N. Lat; 79.76° W. Long. Elevation is 794 feet.

History: On site of Indian village, laid out 1829, incorporated 1842.

Population: 5,674 (1990); 4,993 (2000); 4,530 (2010); Density: 3,698.3 persons per square mile (2010); Race: 91.9% White, 5.1% Black, 0.5% Asian, 0.3% American Indian/Alaska Native, 0.0% Native Hawaiian/Other Pacific Islander, 2.2% Other, 1.0% Hispanic of any race (2010); Average household size: 2.22 (2010); Median age: 39.4 (2010); Males per 100 females: 92.0 (2010); Marriage status: 39.1% never married, 47.6% now married, 5.8% widowed, 7.5% divorced (2006-2010 5-year est.); Foreign born: 0.0% (2006-2010 5-year est.); Ancestry (includes multiple ancestries): 41.4% German, 27.3% Irish, 15.1% Italian, 9.0% Hungarian, 8.8% Polish (2006-2010 5-year est.).

Economy: Single-family building permits issued: 1 (2011); Multi-family building permits issued: 0 (2011); Employment by occupation: 4.5% management, 1.6% professional, 14.5% services, 12.4% sales, 2.8% farming, 12.1% construction, 8.5% production (2006-2010 5-year est.).

Income: Per capita income: $17,242 (2006-2010 5-year est.); Median household income: $31,681 (2006-2010 5-year est.); Average household income: $43,581 (2006-2010 5-year est.); Percent of households with income of $100,000 or more: 11.1% (2006-2010 5-year est.); Poverty rate: 23.2% (2006-2010 5-year est.).

Education: Percent of population age 25 and over with: High school diploma (including GED) or higher: 88.1% (2006-2010 5-year est.); Bachelor's degree or higher: 12.4% (2006-2010 5-year est.); Master's degree or higher: 5.0% (2006-2010 5-year est.).

School District(s)

Deer Lakes SD (KG-12)
    2010-11 Enrollment: 1,953 . . . . (724) 265-5300
Highlands SD (PK-12)
    2010-11 Enrollment: 2,742 . . . . (724) 226-2400

Housing: Homeownership rate: 51.9% (2010); Median home value: $62,800 (2006-2010 5-year est.); Median contract rent: $397 per month (2006-2010 5-year est.); Median year structure built: before 1940 (2006-2010 5-year est.).

Safety: Violent crime rate: 52.8 per 10,000 population; Property crime rate: 283.9 per 10,000 population (2011).

Newspapers: Valley News Dispatch (Local news; Circulation 29,376)

Transportation: Commute to work: 91.3% car, 0.0% public transportation, 5.8% walk, 1.1% work from home (2006-2010 5-year est.); Travel time to work: 40.4% less than 15 minutes, 33.5% 15 to 30 minutes, 15.3% 30 to 45 minutes, 7.4% 45 to 60 minutes, 3.3% 60 minutes or more (2006-2010 5-year est.)

Additional Information Contacts

Allegheny Valley Chamber of Commerce . . . . (724) 224-3400
    http://alleghenyvalleychamber.com

THORNBURG (borough).

Covers a land area of 0.434 square miles and a water area of 0 square miles. Located at 40.43° N. Lat; 80.08° W. Long. Elevation is 869 feet.

Population: 442 (1990); 468 (2000); 455 (2010); Density: 1,048.6 persons per square mile (2010); Race: 98.0% White, 0.0% Black, 0.9% Asian, 0.0% American Indian/Alaska Native, 0.0% Native Hawaiian/Other Pacific Islander, 1.1% Other, 1.1% Hispanic of any race (2010); Average household size: 2.49 (2010); Median age: 48.7 (2010); Males per 100

females: 89.6 (2010); Marriage status: 24.0% never married, 60.9% now married, 6.8% widowed, 8.3% divorced (2006-2010 5-year est.); Foreign born: 2.2% (2006-2010 5-year est.); Ancestry (includes multiple ancestries): 34.2% Irish, 33.8% German, 19.3% Italian, 17.1% English, 16.7% Polish (2006-2010 5-year est.).

Economy: Single-family building permits issued: 0 (2011); Multi-family building permits issued: 0 (2011); Employment by occupation: 21.6% management, 8.8% professional, 3.5% services, 17.2% sales, 3.5% farming, 2.6% construction, 0.4% production (2006-2010 5-year est.).

Income: Per capita income: $61,466 (2006-2010 5-year est.); Median household income: $106,250 (2006-2010 5-year est.); Average household income: $161,747 (2006-2010 5-year est.); Percent of households with income of $100,000 or more: 51.9% (2006-2010 5-year est.); Poverty rate: 5.0% (2006-2010 5-year est.).

Education: Percent of population age 25 and over with: High school diploma (including GED) or higher: 98.8% (2006-2010 5-year est.); Bachelor's degree or higher: 66.9% (2006-2010 5-year est.); Master's degree or higher: 33.7% (2006-2010 5-year est.).

Housing: Homeownership rate: 97.8% (2010); Median home value: $263,000 (2006-2010 5-year est.); Median contract rent: $646 per month (2006-2010 5-year est.); Median year structure built: 1955 (2006-2010 5-year est.).

Transportation: Commute to work: 81.2% car, 5.4% public transportation, 0.9% walk, 9.4% work from home (2006-2010 5-year est.); Travel time to work: 11.4% less than 15 minutes, 47.5% 15 to 30 minutes, 29.2% 30 to 45 minutes, 5.0% 45 to 60 minutes, 6.9% 60 minutes or more (2006-2010 5-year est.)

TURTLE CREEK (borough). Aka Westinghouse. Covers a land area of 0.970 square miles and a water area of 0 square miles. Located at 40.41° N. Lat; 79.82° W. Long. Elevation is 738 feet.

History: Trading post near here c.1750. Settled c.1765, incorporated 1892.

Population: 6,556 (1990); 6,076 (2000); 5,349 (2010); Density: 5,516.8 persons per square mile (2010); Race: 78.4% White, 17.3% Black, 0.6% Asian, 0.3% American Indian/Alaska Native, 0.0% Native Hawaiian/Other Pacific Islander, 3.4% Other, 1.3% Hispanic of any race (2010); Average household size: 2.12 (2010); Median age: 41.2 (2010); Males per 100 females: 84.3 (2010); Marriage status: 33.0% never married, 41.3% now married, 12.8% widowed, 12.8% divorced (2006-2010 5-year est.); Foreign born: 0.8% (2006-2010 5-year est.); Ancestry (includes multiple ancestries): 29.0% German, 26.4% Irish, 16.5% Italian, 9.7% Scotch-Irish, 8.3% Slovak (2006-2010 5-year est.).

Economy: Single-family building permits issued: 0 (2011); Multi-family building permits issued: 0 (2011); Employment by occupation: 10.0% management, 3.1% professional, 20.8% services, 27.5% sales, 2.4% farming, 10.8% construction, 5.5% production (2006-2010 5-year est.).

Income: Per capita income: $21,801 (2006-2010 5-year est.); Median household income: $34,653 (2006-2010 5-year est.); Average household income: $44,294 (2006-2010 5-year est.); Percent of households with income of $100,000 or more: 8.0% (2006-2010 5-year est.); Poverty rate: 16.5% (2006-2010 5-year est.).

Education: Percent of population age 25 and over with: High school diploma (including GED) or higher: 88.3% (2006-2010 5-year est.); Bachelor's degree or higher: 14.6% (2006-2010 5-year est.); Master's degree or higher: 1.9% (2006-2010 5-year est.).

School District(s)

Propel CS-East (KG-08)
    2010-11 Enrollment: 396. . . . . (412) 823-0347
Woodland Hills SD (PK-12)
    2010-11 Enrollment: 4,050 . . . . (412) 731-1300

Housing: Homeownership rate: 41.3% (2010); Median home value: $56,100 (2006-2010 5-year est.); Median contract rent: $336 per month (2006-2010 5-year est.); Median year structure built: 1943 (2006-2010 5-year est.).

Safety: Violent crime rate: 44.7 per 10,000 population; Property crime rate: 20.5 per 10,000 population (2011).

Transportation: Commute to work: 85.4% car, 6.8% public transportation, 2.5% walk, 4.9% work from home (2006-2010 5-year est.); Travel time to work: 24.9% less than 15 minutes, 35.3% 15 to 30 minutes, 25.0% 30 to 45 minutes, 8.4% 45 to 60 minutes, 6.3% 60 minutes or more (2006-2010 5-year est.)

Additional Information Contacts
Borough of Turtle Creek . . . . (412) 824-2500
    http://www.tcvcog.com/Turtle%20Creek%20%20Borough%20Page.htm

Shadyside Chamber of Commerce . . . . (412) 682-1298
    http://www.thinkshadyside.com

UPPER SAINT CLAIR (cdp/township). Covers a land area of 9.818 square miles and a water area of 0.008 square miles. Located at 40.33° N. Lat; 80.08° W. Long. Elevation is 1,099 feet.

Population: 19,692 (1990); 20,053 (2000); 19,229 (2010); Density: 1,958.5 persons per square mile (2010); Race: 92.1% White, 0.8% Black, 5.7% Asian, 0.0% American Indian/Alaska Native, 0.0% Native Hawaiian/Other Pacific Islander, 1.4% Other, 1.3% Hispanic of any race (2010); Average household size: 2.75 (2010); Median age: 44.3 (2010); Males per 100 females: 96.5 (2010); Marriage status: 21.1% never married, 68.0% now married, 6.2% widowed, 4.7% divorced (2006-2010 5-year est.); Foreign born: 7.9% (2006-2010 5-year est.); Ancestry (includes multiple ancestries): 31.1% German, 25.4% Irish, 18.3% Italian, 10.8% English, 7.9% Polish (2006-2010 5-year est.).

Economy: Single-family building permits issued: 9 (2011); Multi-family building permits issued: 0 (2011); Employment by occupation: 22.2% management, 7.3% professional, 3.7% services, 15.9% sales, 2.4% farming, 3.2% construction, 2.2% production (2006-2010 5-year est.).

Income: Per capita income: $51,589 (2006-2010 5-year est.); Median household income: $112,828 (2006-2010 5-year est.); Average household income: $143,037 (2006-2010 5-year est.); Percent of households with income of $100,000 or more: 55.1% (2006-2010 5-year est.); Poverty rate: 2.2% (2006-2010 5-year est.).

Taxes: Total city taxes per capita: $701 (2009); City property taxes per capita: $228 (2009).

Education: Percent of population age 25 and over with: High school diploma (including GED) or higher: 98.3% (2006-2010 5-year est.); Bachelor's degree or higher: 66.9% (2006-2010 5-year est.); Master's degree or higher: 28.5% (2006-2010 5-year est.).

Housing: Homeownership rate: 92.0% (2010); Median home value: $236,400 (2006-2010 5-year est.); Median contract rent: $1,394 per month (2006-2010 5-year est.); Median year structure built: 1969 (2006-2010 5-year est.).

Safety: Violent crime rate: 2.1 per 10,000 population; Property crime rate: 49.2 per 10,000 population (2011).

Transportation: Commute to work: 86.0% car, 6.5% public transportation, 0.6% walk, 5.7% work from home (2006-2010 5-year est.); Travel time to work: 21.3% less than 15 minutes, 31.6% 15 to 30 minutes, 24.7% 30 to 45 minutes, 12.5% 45 to 60 minutes, 9.9% 60 minutes or more (2006-2010 5-year est.)

VERONA (borough). Covers a land area of 0.505 square miles and a water area of 0.091 square miles. Located at 40.51° N. Lat; 79.84° W. Long. Elevation is 761 feet.

History: Incorporated 1871.

Population: 3,260 (1990); 3,124 (2000); 2,474 (2010); Density: 4,899.0 persons per square mile (2010); Race: 89.9% White, 7.8% Black, 0.2% Asian, 0.1% American Indian/Alaska Native, 0.0% Native Hawaiian/Other Pacific Islander, 2.0% Other, 2.2% Hispanic of any race (2010); Average household size: 2.20 (2010); Median age: 40.1 (2010); Males per 100 females: 96.0 (2010); Marriage status: 40.8% never married, 30.9% now married, 11.8% widowed, 16.4% divorced (2006-2010 5-year est.); Foreign born: 0.0% (2006-2010 5-year est.); Ancestry (includes multiple ancestries): 31.6% German, 29.6% Italian, 17.1% Irish, 7.9% Polish, 7.6% English (2006-2010 5-year est.).

Economy: Single-family building permits issued: 0 (2011); Multi-family building permits issued: 0 (2011); Employment by occupation: 11.2% management, 0.8% professional, 9.8% services, 21.6% sales, 3.1% farming, 8.3% construction, 4.2% production (2006-2010 5-year est.).

Income: Per capita income: $17,814 (2006-2010 5-year est.); Median household income: $30,758 (2006-2010 5-year est.); Average household income: $39,494 (2006-2010 5-year est.); Percent of households with income of $100,000 or more: 6.1% (2006-2010 5-year est.); Poverty rate: 25.5% (2006-2010 5-year est.).

Education: Percent of population age 25 and over with: High school diploma (including GED) or higher: 84.8% (2006-2010 5-year est.); Bachelor's degree or higher: 14.0% (2006-2010 5-year est.); Master's degree or higher: 4.2% (2006-2010 5-year est.).

School District(s)

Penn Hills SD (PK-12)
    2010-11 Enrollment: 4,284 . . . . (412) 793-7000
Riverview SD (KG-12)
    2010-11 Enrollment: 1,091 . . . . (412) 828-1800

Housing: Homeownership rate: 48.5% (2010); Median home value: $78,500 (2006-2010 5-year est.); Median contract rent: $454 per month (2006-2010 5-year est.); Median year structure built: 1946 (2006-2010 5-year est.).

Safety: Violent crime rate: 24.2 per 10,000 population; Property crime rate: 382.8 per 10,000 population (2011).

Transportation: Commute to work: 82.8% car, 6.9% public transportation, 9.2% walk, 0.0% work from home (2006-2010 5-year est.); Travel time to work: 30.8% less than 15 minutes, 27.7% 15 to 30 minutes, 24.5% 30 to 45 minutes, 10.8% 45 to 60 minutes, 6.2% 60 minutes or more (2006-2010 5-year est.)

Additional Information Contacts

Penn Hills Chamber of Commerce . . . . (412) 795-8741
   http://www.pennhillschamber.org

VERSAILLES (borough). Covers a land area of 0.486 square miles and a water area of 0.051 square miles. Located at 40.32° N. Lat; 79.83° W. Long. Elevation is 833 feet.

History: Incorporated 1892.

Population: 1,821 (1990); 1,724 (2000); 1,515 (2010); Density: 3,118.4 persons per square mile (2010); Race: 90.8% White, 6.2% Black, 0.7% Asian, 0.1% American Indian/Alaska Native, 0.0% Native Hawaiian/Other Pacific Islander, 2.2% Other, 1.0% Hispanic of any race (2010); Average household size: 1.97 (2010); Median age: 47.9 (2010); Males per 100 females: 84.5 (2010); Marriage status: 25.9% never married, 49.7% now married, 11.3% widowed, 13.2% divorced (2006-2010 5-year est.); Foreign born: 0.9% (2006-2010 5-year est.); Ancestry (includes multiple ancestries): 25.5% German, 17.7% English, 16.6% Irish, 15.2% Italian, 10.2% Slovak (2006-2010 5-year est.).

Economy: Single-family building permits issued: 0 (2011); Multi-family building permits issued: 0 (2011); Employment by occupation: 6.3% management, 1.7% professional, 15.6% services, 15.6% sales, 8.6% farming, 6.4% construction, 9.3% production (2006-2010 5-year est.).

Income: Per capita income: $20,704 (2006-2010 5-year est.); Median household income: $32,625 (2006-2010 5-year est.); Average household income: $40,876 (2006-2010 5-year est.); Percent of households with income of $100,000 or more: 6.0% (2006-2010 5-year est.); Poverty rate: 12.2% (2006-2010 5-year est.).

Education: Percent of population age 25 and over with: High school diploma (including GED) or higher: 88.9% (2006-2010 5-year est.); Bachelor's degree or higher: 11.7% (2006-2010 5-year est.); Master's degree or higher: 2.9% (2006-2010 5-year est.).

Housing: Homeownership rate: 48.1% (2010); Median home value: $55,700 (2006-2010 5-year est.); Median contract rent: $506 per month (2006-2010 5-year est.); Median year structure built: 1952 (2006-2010 5-year est.).

Safety: Violent crime rate: 52.6 per 10,000 population; Property crime rate: 184.2 per 10,000 population (2011).

Transportation: Commute to work: 91.4% car, 4.7% public transportation, 1.5% walk, 2.4% work from home (2006-2010 5-year est.); Travel time to work: 22.1% less than 15 minutes, 40.1% 15 to 30 minutes, 21.5% 30 to 45 minutes, 6.9% 45 to 60 minutes, 9.4% 60 minutes or more (2006-2010 5-year est.)

Additional Information Contacts

Norwin Chamber of Commerce . . . . (724) 863-0888
   http://www.norwinchamber.com/index.php

WALL (borough). Covers a land area of 0.438 square miles and a water area of 0 square miles. Located at 40.39° N. Lat; 79.79° W. Long. Elevation is 814 feet.

History: Incorporated 1904.

Population: 853 (1990); 727 (2000); 580 (2010); Density: 1,325.3 persons per square mile (2010); Race: 89.8% White, 7.1% Black, 0.5% Asian, 0.0% American Indian/Alaska Native, 0.0% Native Hawaiian/Other Pacific Islander, 2.6% Other, 1.0% Hispanic of any race (2010); Average household size: 2.24 (2010); Median age: 40.9 (2010); Males per 100 females: 93.3 (2010); Marriage status: 29.5% never married, 44.9% now married, 13.3% widowed, 12.3% divorced (2006-2010 5-year est.); Foreign born: 3.3% (2006-2010 5-year est.); Ancestry (includes multiple ancestries): 31.5% German, 20.7% Irish, 19.4% Italian, 9.2% Polish, 7.5% Serbian (2006-2010 5-year est.).

Economy: Single-family building permits issued: 0 (2011); Multi-family building permits issued: 0 (2011); Employment by occupation: 10.5% management, 0.0% professional, 17.7% services, 17.7% sales, 7.9% farming, 10.5% construction, 14.7% production (2006-2010 5-year est.).

Income: Per capita income: $18,777 (2006-2010 5-year est.); Median household income: $40,865 (2006-2010 5-year est.); Average household income: $41,984 (2006-2010 5-year est.); Percent of households with income of $100,000 or more: 6.3% (2006-2010 5-year est.); Poverty rate: 18.5% (2006-2010 5-year est.).

Education: Percent of population age 25 and over with: High school diploma (including GED) or higher: 89.4% (2006-2010 5-year est.); Bachelor's degree or higher: 8.9% (2006-2010 5-year est.); Master's degree or higher: 2.8% (2006-2010 5-year est.).

Housing: Homeownership rate: 59.8% (2010); Median home value: $43,600 (2006-2010 5-year est.); Median contract rent: $414 per month (2006-2010 5-year est.); Median year structure built: before 1940 (2006-2010 5-year est.).

Transportation: Commute to work: 90.8% car, 2.7% public transportation, 1.5% walk, 3.1% work from home (2006-2010 5-year est.); Travel time to work: 35.3% less than 15 minutes, 32.1% 15 to 30 minutes, 14.7% 30 to 45 minutes, 9.9% 45 to 60 minutes, 7.9% 60 minutes or more (2006-2010 5-year est.)

WARRENDALE (unincorporated postal area)

Zip Code: 15086

Covers a land area of 1.640 square miles and a water area of 0 square miles. Located at 40.67° N. Lat; 80.10° W. Long. Elevation is 1,050 feet. Population: 300 (2010); Density: 182.8 persons per square mile (2010); Race: 98.3% White, 0.0% Black, 1.3% Asian, 0.0% American Indian/Alaska Native, 0.0% Native Hawaiian/Other Pacific Islander, 0.4% Other, 5.7% Hispanic of any race (2010); Average household size: 2.40 (2010); Median age: 41.5 (2010); Males per 100 females: 108.3 (2010); Homeownership rate: 65.6% (2010)

WEST DEER (township). Covers a land area of 28.869 square miles and a water area of 0.005 square miles. Located at 40.63° N. Lat; 79.87° W. Long.

Population: 11,371 (1990); 11,563 (2000); 11,771 (2010); Density: 407.7 persons per square mile (2010); Race: 98.3% White, 0.5% Black, 0.4% Asian, 0.1% American Indian/Alaska Native, 0.0% Native Hawaiian/Other Pacific Islander, 0.7% Other, 0.8% Hispanic of any race (2010); Average household size: 2.43 (2010); Median age: 44.7 (2010); Males per 100 females: 97.3 (2010); Marriage status: 23.4% never married, 60.1% now married, 7.3% widowed, 9.1% divorced (2006-2010 5-year est.); Foreign born: 0.5% (2006-2010 5-year est.); Ancestry (includes multiple ancestries): 35.1% German, 21.5% Irish, 18.6% Italian, 13.5% Polish, 7.7% English (2006-2010 5-year est.).

Economy: Single-family building permits issued: 6 (2011); Multi-family building permits issued: 6 (2011); Employment by occupation: 9.1% management, 5.4% professional, 10.2% services, 17.2% sales, 3.7% farming, 12.4% construction, 8.2% production (2006-2010 5-year est.).

Income: Per capita income: $27,684 (2006-2010 5-year est.); Median household income: $60,533 (2006-2010 5-year est.); Average household income: $68,442 (2006-2010 5-year est.); Percent of households with income of $100,000 or more: 21.0% (2006-2010 5-year est.); Poverty rate: 5.7% (2006-2010 5-year est.).

Education: Percent of population age 25 and over with: High school diploma (including GED) or higher: 92.0% (2006-2010 5-year est.); Bachelor's degree or higher: 26.1% (2006-2010 5-year est.); Master's degree or higher: 8.2% (2006-2010 5-year est.).

Housing: Homeownership rate: 86.2% (2010); Median home value: $142,800 (2006-2010 5-year est.); Median contract rent: $437 per month (2006-2010 5-year est.); Median year structure built: 1972 (2006-2010 5-year est.).

Safety: Violent crime rate: 4.2 per 10,000 population; Property crime rate: 108.4 per 10,000 population (2011).

Transportation: Commute to work: 94.3% car, 1.6% public transportation, 0.8% walk, 2.6% work from home (2006-2010 5-year est.); Travel time to work: 20.7% less than 15 minutes, 33.8% 15 to 30 minutes, 28.8% 30 to 45 minutes, 11.8% 45 to 60 minutes, 4.9% 60 minutes or more (2006-2010 5-year est.)

Additional Information Contacts

Allegheny Valley Chamber of Commerce . . . . (724) 224-3400
   http://alleghenyvalleychamber.com

West Deer Township . . . . (724) 265-3680
   http://www.westdeertownship.com

WEST ELIZABETH (borough). Covers a land area of 0.182 square miles and a water area of 0.065 square miles. Located at 40.27° N. Lat; 79.90° W. Long. Elevation is 748 feet.

History: Laid out 1833, incorporated 1848.

Population: 634 (1990); 565 (2000); 518 (2010); Density: 2,853.2 persons per square mile (2010); Race: 96.7% White, 2.9% Black, 0.0% Asian, 0.0% American Indian/Alaska Native, 0.0% Native Hawaiian/Other Pacific Islander, 0.4% Other, 0.0% Hispanic of any race (2010); Average household size: 2.47 (2010); Median age: 40.4 (2010); Males per 100 females: 96.2 (2010); Marriage status: 32.3% never married, 42.4% now married, 5.3% widowed, 20.0% divorced (2006-2010 5-year est.); Foreign born: 0.6% (2006-2010 5-year est.); Ancestry (includes multiple ancestries): 45.2% German, 21.6% Irish, 18.5% English, 8.9% Polish, 8.1% Italian (2006-2010 5-year est.).

Economy: Single-family building permits issued: 0 (2011); Multi-family building permits issued: 0 (2011); Employment by occupation: 12.4% management, 1.9% professional, 22.8% services, 20.6% sales, 4.9% farming, 7.5% construction, 4.1% production (2006-2010 5-year est.).

Income: Per capita income: $14,702 (2006-2010 5-year est.); Median household income: $37,569 (2006-2010 5-year est.); Average household income: $44,121 (2006-2010 5-year est.); Percent of households with income of $100,000 or more: 7.3% (2006-2010 5-year est.); Poverty rate: 20.8% (2006-2010 5-year est.).

Education: Percent of population age 25 and over with: High school diploma (including GED) or higher: 78.7% (2006-2010 5-year est.); Bachelor's degree or higher: 8.0% (2006-2010 5-year est.); Master's degree or higher: 1.0% (2006-2010 5-year est.).

Housing: Homeownership rate: 69.0% (2010); Median home value: $62,300 (2006-2010 5-year est.); Median contract rent: $463 per month (2006-2010 5-year est.); Median year structure built: 1947 (2006-2010 5-year est.).

Transportation: Commute to work: 82.2% car, 3.0% public transportation, 7.2% walk, 7.6% work from home (2006-2010 5-year est.); Travel time to work: 23.8% less than 15 minutes, 43.9% 15 to 30 minutes, 15.6% 30 to 45 minutes, 11.1% 45 to 60 minutes, 5.7% 60 minutes or more (2006-2010 5-year est.)

WEST HOMESTEAD (borough). Covers a land area of 0.922 square miles and a water area of 0.091 square miles. Located at 40.39° N. Lat; 79.91° W. Long. Elevation is 1,040 feet.

History: Incorporated 1900.

Population: 2,495 (1990); 2,197 (2000); 1,929 (2010); Density: 2,092.4 persons per square mile (2010); Race: 84.0% White, 12.9% Black, 0.4% Asian, 0.1% American Indian/Alaska Native, 0.0% Native Hawaiian/Other Pacific Islander, 2.6% Other, 0.9% Hispanic of any race (2010); Average household size: 2.23 (2010); Median age: 49.1 (2010); Males per 100 females: 93.9 (2010); Marriage status: 37.4% never married, 49.7% now married, 6.3% widowed, 6.6% divorced (2006-2010 5-year est.); Foreign born: 0.0% (2006-2010 5-year est.); Ancestry (includes multiple ancestries): 20.2% Irish, 16.0% Slovak, 15.9% Italian, 15.9% German, 12.3% English (2006-2010 5-year est.).

Economy: Single-family building permits issued: 0 (2011); Multi-family building permits issued: 0 (2011); Employment by occupation: 11.0% management, 4.6% professional, 11.9% services, 22.1% sales, 5.6% farming, 8.5% construction, 4.4% production (2006-2010 5-year est.).

Income: Per capita income: $22,082 (2006-2010 5-year est.); Median household income: $48,750 (2006-2010 5-year est.); Average household income: $53,766 (2006-2010 5-year est.); Percent of households with income of $100,000 or more: 12.0% (2006-2010 5-year est.); Poverty rate: 13.9% (2006-2010 5-year est.).

Education: Percent of population age 25 and over with: High school diploma (including GED) or higher: 87.7% (2006-2010 5-year est.); Bachelor's degree or higher: 20.2% (2006-2010 5-year est.); Master's degree or higher: 7.0% (2006-2010 5-year est.).

Housing: Homeownership rate: 75.1% (2010); Median home value: $94,100 (2006-2010 5-year est.); Median contract rent: $414 per month (2006-2010 5-year est.); Median year structure built: 1952 (2006-2010 5-year est.).

Safety: Violent crime rate: 87.9 per 10,000 population; Property crime rate: 273.9 per 10,000 population (2011).

Transportation: Commute to work: 90.2% car, 4.8% public transportation, 1.6% walk, 1.1% work from home (2006-2010 5-year est.); Travel time to work: 15.1% less than 15 minutes, 45.4% 15 to 30 minutes, 28.7% 30 to 45 minutes, 2.3% 45 to 60 minutes, 8.6% 60 minutes or more (2006-2010 5-year est.)

Additional Information Contacts
Brentwood Baldwin Whitehall Chamber of Commerce . . . . (412) 884-1233
   http://www.bbwchamber.com

WEST MIFFLIN (borough). Covers a land area of 14.214 square miles and a water area of 0.294 square miles. Located at 40.36° N. Lat; 79.91° W. Long. Elevation is 1,096 feet.

Population: 23,644 (1990); 22,464 (2000); 20,313 (2010); Density: 1,429.1 persons per square mile (2010); Race: 86.5% White, 11.0% Black, 0.4% Asian, 0.1% American Indian/Alaska Native, 0.0% Native Hawaiian/Other Pacific Islander, 2.0% Other, 1.2% Hispanic of any race (2010); Average household size: 2.30 (2010); Median age: 44.8 (2010); Males per 100 females: 89.8 (2010); Marriage status: 30.1% never married, 52.4% now married, 9.7% widowed, 7.8% divorced (2006-2010 5-year est.); Foreign born: 1.1% (2006-2010 5-year est.); Ancestry (includes multiple ancestries): 26.4% German, 21.4% Irish, 14.3% Slovak, 13.3% Italian, 10.6% Polish (2006-2010 5-year est.).

Economy: Unemployment rate: 8.5% (August 2012); Total civilian labor force: 10,775 (August 2012); Single-family building permits issued: 1 (2011); Multi-family building permits issued: 0 (2011); Employment by occupation: 8.4% management, 3.8% professional, 10.1% services, 21.5% sales, 4.3% farming, 10.2% construction, 5.6% production (2006-2010 5-year est.).

Income: Per capita income: $23,201 (2006-2010 5-year est.); Median household income: $44,190 (2006-2010 5-year est.); Average household income: $53,099 (2006-2010 5-year est.); Percent of households with income of $100,000 or more: 11.0% (2006-2010 5-year est.); Poverty rate: 11.3% (2006-2010 5-year est.).

Education: Percent of population age 25 and over with: High school diploma (including GED) or higher: 92.5% (2006-2010 5-year est.); Bachelor's degree or higher: 17.7% (2006-2010 5-year est.); Master's degree or higher: 5.8% (2006-2010 5-year est.).

School District(s)
West Mifflin Area SD (PK-12)
   2010-11 Enrollment: 3,084 . . . . (412) 466-9131

Two-year College(s)
Pittsburgh Institute of Aeronautics (Private, Not-for-profit)
   Fall 2010 Enrollment: 375 . . . . (412) 346-2100
   2011-12 Tuition: In-state $14,865; Out-of-state $14,865

Vocational/Technical School(s)
Empire Beauty School-West Mifflin (Private, For-profit)
   Fall 2010 Enrollment: 217 . . . . (800) 223-3271
   2011-12 Tuition: $14,490

Housing: Homeownership rate: 78.0% (2010); Median home value: $85,500 (2006-2010 5-year est.); Median contract rent: $380 per month (2006-2010 5-year est.); Median year structure built: 1955 (2006-2010 5-year est.).

Safety: Violent crime rate: 22.1 per 10,000 population; Property crime rate: 294.9 per 10,000 population (2011).

Transportation: Commute to work: 86.4% car, 8.0% public transportation, 2.5% walk, 2.9% work from home (2006-2010 5-year est.); Travel time to work: 26.9% less than 15 minutes, 35.6% 15 to 30 minutes, 22.8% 30 to 45 minutes, 8.4% 45 to 60 minutes, 6.3% 60 minutes or more (2006-2010 5-year est.)

Additional Information Contacts
Borough of West Mifflin . . . . (412) 466-8174
   http://www.westmifflinborough.com
Shadyside Chamber of Commerce . . . . (412) 682-1298
   http://www.thinkshadyside.com

WEST VIEW (borough). Covers a land area of 1.010 square miles and a water area of 0 square miles. Located at 40.52° N. Lat; 80.03° W. Long. Elevation is 1,132 feet.

History: Incorporated 1905.

Population: 7,734 (1990); 7,277 (2000); 6,771 (2010); Density: 6,705.9 persons per square mile (2010); Race: 96.0% White, 1.7% Black, 0.5% Asian, 0.0% American Indian/Alaska Native, 0.0% Native Hawaiian/Other Pacific Islander, 1.8% Other, 1.0% Hispanic of any race (2010); Average household size: 2.25 (2010); Median age: 38.9 (2010); Males per 100 females: 90.8 (2010); Marriage status: 32.0% never married, 47.9% now married, 8.2% widowed, 11.9% divorced (2006-2010 5-year est.); Foreign born: 1.3% (2006-2010 5-year est.); Ancestry (includes multiple ancestries): 50.3% German, 30.5% Irish, 18.8% Italian, 13.3% Polish, 7.5% English (2006-2010 5-year est.).

Economy: Single-family building permits issued: 0 (2011); Multi-family building permits issued: 0 (2011); Employment by occupation: 12.2% management, 4.4% professional, 11.7% services, 16.1% sales, 4.0% farming, 11.8% construction, 4.0% production (2006-2010 5-year est.).
Income: Per capita income: $29,087 (2006-2010 5-year est.); Median household income: $50,258 (2006-2010 5-year est.); Average household income: $63,874 (2006-2010 5-year est.); Percent of households with income of $100,000 or more: 15.3% (2006-2010 5-year est.); Poverty rate: 5.2% (2006-2010 5-year est.).
Education: Percent of population age 25 and over with: High school diploma (including GED) or higher: 92.7% (2006-2010 5-year est.); Bachelor's degree or higher: 30.8% (2006-2010 5-year est.); Master's degree or higher: 7.8% (2006-2010 5-year est.).
Housing: Homeownership rate: 67.3% (2010); Median home value: $107,500 (2006-2010 5-year est.); Median contract rent: $545 per month (2006-2010 5-year est.); Median year structure built: 1947 (2006-2010 5-year est.).
Safety: Violent crime rate: 22.1 per 10,000 population; Property crime rate: 248.8 per 10,000 population (2011).
Transportation: Commute to work: 84.5% car, 8.3% public transportation, 3.7% walk, 3.5% work from home (2006-2010 5-year est.); Travel time to work: 23.2% less than 15 minutes, 42.8% 15 to 30 minutes, 20.0% 30 to 45 minutes, 7.0% 45 to 60 minutes, 7.1% 60 minutes or more (2006-2010 5-year est.)
Additional Information Contacts
Borough of West View . . . . (412) 931-2800
    http://www.westviewborough.com
The Chamber of Commerce, Inc. . . . . (724) 934-9700
    http://www.thechamberinc.com

WEXFORD (unincorporated postal area)
Zip Code: 15090
Covers a land area of 21.119 square miles and a water area of 0.013 square miles. Located at 40.62° N. Lat; 80.06° W. Long. Elevation is 1,204 feet. Population: 21,202 (2010); Density: 1,003.9 persons per square mile (2010); Race: 90.2% White, 1.6% Black, 6.3% Asian, 0.2% American Indian/Alaska Native, 0.1% Native Hawaiian/Other Pacific Islander, 1.6% Other, 2.0% Hispanic of any race (2010); Average household size: 2.67 (2010); Median age: 40.8 (2010); Males per 100 females: 95.5 (2010); Homeownership rate: 80.8% (2010)

WHITAKER (borough). Covers a land area of 0.296 square miles and a water area of 0.033 square miles. Located at 40.40° N. Lat; 79.89° W. Long. Elevation is 994 feet.
History: Incorporated 1906.
Population: 1,416 (1990); 1,338 (2000); 1,271 (2010); Density: 4,298.7 persons per square mile (2010); Race: 85.8% White, 12.0% Black, 0.0% Asian, 0.0% American Indian/Alaska Native, 0.0% Native Hawaiian/Other Pacific Islander, 2.2% Other, 1.4% Hispanic of any race (2010); Average household size: 2.35 (2010); Median age: 41.6 (2010); Males per 100 females: 92.3 (2010); Marriage status: 29.1% never married, 49.3% now married, 10.0% widowed, 11.5% divorced (2006-2010 5-year est.); Foreign born: 1.2% (2006-2010 5-year est.); Ancestry (includes multiple ancestries): 23.4% German, 23.3% Irish, 20.9% Slovak, 12.3% Italian, 11.2% Polish (2006-2010 5-year est.).
Economy: Single-family building permits issued: 1 (2011); Multi-family building permits issued: 0 (2011); Employment by occupation: 5.1% management, 0.8% professional, 9.5% services, 22.0% sales, 2.5% farming, 15.0% construction, 7.1% production (2006-2010 5-year est.).
Income: Per capita income: $18,664 (2006-2010 5-year est.); Median household income: $37,898 (2006-2010 5-year est.); Average household income: $43,893 (2006-2010 5-year est.); Percent of households with income of $100,000 or more: 6.5% (2006-2010 5-year est.); Poverty rate: 8.8% (2006-2010 5-year est.).
Education: Percent of population age 25 and over with: High school diploma (including GED) or higher: 86.5% (2006-2010 5-year est.); Bachelor's degree or higher: 8.8% (2006-2010 5-year est.); Master's degree or higher: 4.0% (2006-2010 5-year est.).
Housing: Homeownership rate: 68.9% (2010); Median home value: $57,900 (2006-2010 5-year est.); Median contract rent: $433 per month (2006-2010 5-year est.); Median year structure built: before 1940 (2006-2010 5-year est.).
Safety: Violent crime rate: 15.7 per 10,000 population; Property crime rate: 258.8 per 10,000 population (2011).

Transportation: Commute to work: 84.7% car, 11.6% public transportation, 1.9% walk, 1.4% work from home (2006-2010 5-year est.); Travel time to work: 25.5% less than 15 minutes, 42.9% 15 to 30 minutes, 18.7% 30 to 45 minutes, 4.1% 45 to 60 minutes, 8.7% 60 minutes or more (2006-2010 5-year est.)
Additional Information Contacts
Shadyside Chamber of Commerce . . . . (412) 682-1298
    http://www.thinkshadyside.com

WHITE OAK (borough). Covers a land area of 6.621 square miles and a water area of 0.048 square miles. Located at 40.34° N. Lat; 79.80° W. Long. Elevation is 817 feet.
History: Incorporated 1948.
Population: 8,762 (1990); 8,437 (2000); 7,862 (2010); Density: 1,187.4 persons per square mile (2010); Race: 93.7% White, 3.6% Black, 0.9% Asian, 0.1% American Indian/Alaska Native, 0.1% Native Hawaiian/Other Pacific Islander, 1.6% Other, 0.9% Hispanic of any race (2010); Average household size: 2.12 (2010); Median age: 49.9 (2010); Males per 100 females: 87.9 (2010); Marriage status: 26.1% never married, 52.6% now married, 12.6% widowed, 8.7% divorced (2006-2010 5-year est.); Foreign born: 1.7% (2006-2010 5-year est.); Ancestry (includes multiple ancestries): 27.6% German, 15.7% Irish, 13.2% English, 11.7% Polish, 11.6% Italian (2006-2010 5-year est.).
Economy: Single-family building permits issued: 1 (2011); Multi-family building permits issued: 0 (2011); Employment by occupation: 11.9% management, 3.1% professional, 6.2% services, 21.0% sales, 4.0% farming, 8.3% construction, 6.6% production (2006-2010 5-year est.).
Income: Per capita income: $26,668 (2006-2010 5-year est.); Median household income: $45,430 (2006-2010 5-year est.); Average household income: $57,090 (2006-2010 5-year est.); Percent of households with income of $100,000 or more: 14.5% (2006-2010 5-year est.); Poverty rate: 7.9% (2006-2010 5-year est.).
Education: Percent of population age 25 and over with: High school diploma (including GED) or higher: 94.5% (2006-2010 5-year est.); Bachelor's degree or higher: 24.4% (2006-2010 5-year est.); Master's degree or higher: 6.8% (2006-2010 5-year est.).
Housing: Homeownership rate: 74.1% (2010); Median home value: $95,500 (2006-2010 5-year est.); Median contract rent: $615 per month (2006-2010 5-year est.); Median year structure built: 1957 (2006-2010 5-year est.).
Safety: Violent crime rate: 3.8 per 10,000 population; Property crime rate: 96.4 per 10,000 population (2011).
Transportation: Commute to work: 93.6% car, 3.1% public transportation, 1.0% walk, 1.6% work from home (2006-2010 5-year est.); Travel time to work: 33.5% less than 15 minutes, 29.1% 15 to 30 minutes, 18.2% 30 to 45 minutes, 11.5% 45 to 60 minutes, 7.6% 60 minutes or more (2006-2010 5-year est.)
Additional Information Contacts
Borough of White Oak . . . . (412) 672-9727
    http://www.woboro.com
Norwin Chamber of Commerce . . . . (724) 863-0888
    http://www.norwinchamber.com/index.php

WHITEHALL (borough). Covers a land area of 3.325 square miles and a water area of 0 square miles. Located at 40.36° N. Lat; 79.99° W. Long. Elevation is 1,253 feet.
History: Named for Whitehall, site of government offices in London, England. Incorporated 1948.
Population: 14,451 (1990); 14,444 (2000); 13,944 (2010); Density: 4,193.1 persons per square mile (2010); Race: 91.1% White, 3.7% Black, 3.8% Asian, 0.1% American Indian/Alaska Native, 0.0% Native Hawaiian/Other Pacific Islander, 1.3% Other, 0.9% Hispanic of any race (2010); Average household size: 2.20 (2010); Median age: 47.0 (2010); Males per 100 females: 89.1 (2010); Marriage status: 26.4% never married, 56.8% now married, 10.8% widowed, 5.9% divorced (2006-2010 5-year est.); Foreign born: 8.6% (2006-2010 5-year est.); Ancestry (includes multiple ancestries): 35.0% German, 25.1% Irish, 21.9% Italian, 11.3% Polish, 6.6% English (2006-2010 5-year est.).
Economy: Single-family building permits issued: 3 (2011); Multi-family building permits issued: 0 (2011); Employment by occupation: 16.6% management, 3.4% professional, 8.1% services, 16.7% sales, 3.4% farming, 7.1% construction, 4.2% production (2006-2010 5-year est.).
Income: Per capita income: $27,783 (2006-2010 5-year est.); Median household income: $50,301 (2006-2010 5-year est.); Average household income: $62,261 (2006-2010 5-year est.); Percent of households with

income of $100,000 or more: 17.3% (2006-2010 5-year est.); Poverty rate: 9.0% (2006-2010 5-year est.).

Education: Percent of population age 25 and over with: High school diploma (including GED) or higher: 91.8% (2006-2010 5-year est.); Bachelor's degree or higher: 30.3% (2006-2010 5-year est.); Master's degree or higher: 11.7% (2006-2010 5-year est.).

Housing: Homeownership rate: 73.7% (2010); Median home value: $129,500 (2006-2010 5-year est.); Median contract rent: $566 per month (2006-2010 5-year est.); Median year structure built: 1956 (2006-2010 5-year est.).

Safety: Violent crime rate: 9.3 per 10,000 population; Property crime rate: 45.8 per 10,000 population (2011).

Transportation: Commute to work: 82.5% car, 12.5% public transportation, 1.9% walk, 2.2% work from home (2006-2010 5-year est.); Travel time to work: 18.7% less than 15 minutes, 28.4% 15 to 30 minutes, 33.5% 30 to 45 minutes, 14.4% 45 to 60 minutes, 5.0% 60 minutes or more (2006-2010 5-year est.).

Additional Information Contacts

Borough of Whitehall . . . . (412) 884-0505
http://www.whitehallboro.org

Brentwood Baldwin Whitehall Chamber of Commerce . . . . (412) 884-1233
http://www.bbwchamber.com

WILKINS (township). Covers a land area of 2.745 square miles and a water area of 0 square miles. Located at 40.43° N. Lat; 79.82° W. Long.

Population: 7,585 (1990); 6,917 (2000); 6,357 (2010); Density: 2,316.0 persons per square mile (2010); Race: 83.7% White, 11.8% Black, 2.1% Asian, 0.3% American Indian/Alaska Native, 0.0% Native Hawaiian/Other Pacific Islander, 2.1% Other, 1.3% Hispanic of any race (2010); Average household size: 2.02 (2010); Median age: 48.0 (2010); Males per 100 females: 87.0 (2010); Marriage status: 31.9% never married, 47.8% now married, 10.5% widowed, 9.8% divorced (2006-2010 5-year est.); Foreign born: 2.9% (2006-2010 5-year est.); Ancestry (includes multiple ancestries): 25.3% German, 18.2% Italian, 17.6% Irish, 11.3% English, 8.2% Polish (2006-2010 5-year est.).

Economy: Single-family building permits issued: 2 (2011); Multi-family building permits issued: 0 (2011); Employment by occupation: 10.5% management, 5.0% professional, 13.0% services, 24.8% sales, 2.0% farming, 7.2% construction, 3.3% production (2006-2010 5-year est.).

Income: Per capita income: $27,335 (2006-2010 5-year est.); Median household income: $43,398 (2006-2010 5-year est.); Average household income: $55,158 (2006-2010 5-year est.); Percent of households with income of $100,000 or more: 12.5% (2006-2010 5-year est.); Poverty rate: 10.7% (2006-2010 5-year est.).

Education: Percent of population age 25 and over with: High school diploma (including GED) or higher: 94.8% (2006-2010 5-year est.); Bachelor's degree or higher: 32.7% (2006-2010 5-year est.); Master's degree or higher: 12.4% (2006-2010 5-year est.).

Housing: Homeownership rate: 66.2% (2010); Median home value: $88,400 (2006-2010 5-year est.); Median contract rent: $708 per month (2006-2010 5-year est.); Median year structure built: 1956 (2006-2010 5-year est.).

Transportation: Commute to work: 87.7% car, 6.2% public transportation, 2.5% walk, 3.1% work from home (2006-2010 5-year est.); Travel time to work: 25.7% less than 15 minutes, 32.3% 15 to 30 minutes, 32.0% 30 to 45 minutes, 6.2% 45 to 60 minutes, 3.7% 60 minutes or more (2006-2010 5-year est.)

Additional Information Contacts

Oakmont Chamber of Commerce . . . . (412) 828-3238
http://www.oakmont-pa.com

Wilkins Township . . . . (412) 824-6650
http://www.wilkinstownship.com

WILKINSBURG (borough). Covers a land area of 2.251 square miles and a water area of 0 square miles. Located at 40.44° N. Lat; 79.87° W. Long. Elevation is 942 feet.

History: Named for William Wilkins (1779-1865), Pennsylvania statesman. Settled c.1800. Incorporated 1887.

Population: 21,080 (1990); 19,196 (2000); 15,930 (2010); Density: 7,076.4 persons per square mile (2010); Race: 28.3% White, 66.6% Black, 1.0% Asian, 0.4% American Indian/Alaska Native, 0.0% Native Hawaiian/Other Pacific Islander, 3.7% Other, 1.8% Hispanic of any race (2010); Average household size: 1.92 (2010); Median age: 41.2 (2010); Males per 100 females: 79.7 (2010); Marriage status: 44.6% never married, 32.2% now married, 8.8% widowed, 14.4% divorced (2006-2010

5-year est.); Foreign born: 5.1% (2006-2010 5-year est.); Ancestry (includes multiple ancestries): 6.5% German, 5.0% Irish, 4.9% Italian, 4.0% African, 2.3% English (2006-2010 5-year est.).

Economy: Single-family building permits issued: 3 (2011); Multi-family building permits issued: 0 (2011); Employment by occupation: 7.0% management, 3.4% professional, 13.1% services, 18.4% sales, 4.8% farming, 4.9% construction, 4.6% production (2006-2010 5-year est.).

Income: Per capita income: $20,426 (2006-2010 5-year est.); Median household income: $29,620 (2006-2010 5-year est.); Average household income: $39,685 (2006-2010 5-year est.); Percent of households with income of $100,000 or more: 6.0% (2006-2010 5-year est.); Poverty rate: 21.8% (2006-2010 5-year est.).

Education: Percent of population age 25 and over with: High school diploma (including GED) or higher: 89.2% (2006-2010 5-year est.); Bachelor's degree or higher: 27.0% (2006-2010 5-year est.); Master's degree or higher: 11.2% (2006-2010 5-year est.).

School District(s)

Wilkinsburg Borough SD (PK-12)
    2010-11 Enrollment: 1,228 . . . . (412) 371-9667

Housing: Homeownership rate: 37.7% (2010); Median home value: $67,000 (2006-2010 5-year est.); Median contract rent: $536 per month (2006-2010 5-year est.); Median year structure built: 1944 (2006-2010 5-year est.).

Transportation: Commute to work: 65.1% car, 23.9% public transportation, 4.2% walk, 4.7% work from home (2006-2010 5-year est.); Travel time to work: 15.1% less than 15 minutes, 43.9% 15 to 30 minutes, 24.8% 30 to 45 minutes, 6.8% 45 to 60 minutes, 9.4% 60 minutes or more (2006-2010 5-year est.)

Additional Information Contacts

Borough of Wilkinsburg . . . . (412) 244-2920
http://www.wilkinsburg.pgh.pa.us

Wilkinsburg Chamber of Commerce . . . . (412) 242-0234
http://wilkinsburgchamber.com

WILMERDING (borough). Covers a land area of 0.428 square miles and a water area of 0 square miles. Located at 40.39° N. Lat; 79.81° W. Long. Elevation is 794 feet.

History: Incorporated 1890.

Population: 2,087 (1990); 2,145 (2000); 2,190 (2010); Density: 5,116.7 persons per square mile (2010); Race: 75.2% White, 18.0% Black, 0.3% Asian, 0.5% American Indian/Alaska Native, 0.0% Native Hawaiian/Other Pacific Islander, 6.0% Other, 2.3% Hispanic of any race (2010); Average household size: 2.14 (2010); Median age: 36.9 (2010); Males per 100 females: 81.3 (2010); Marriage status: 37.9% never married, 35.2% now married, 11.7% widowed, 15.3% divorced (2006-2010 5-year est.); Foreign born: 0.3% (2006-2010 5-year est.); Ancestry (includes multiple ancestries): 22.6% Italian, 18.5% German, 18.2% Irish, 10.3% Polish, 7.2% English (2006-2010 5-year est.).

Economy: Single-family building permits issued: 0 (2011); Multi-family building permits issued: 0 (2011); Employment by occupation: 7.7% management, 2.0% professional, 20.7% services, 13.3% sales, 1.8% farming, 10.6% construction, 10.6% production (2006-2010 5-year est.).

Income: Per capita income: $15,047 (2006-2010 5-year est.); Median household income: $21,682 (2006-2010 5-year est.); Average household income: $29,673 (2006-2010 5-year est.); Percent of households with income of $100,000 or more: 2.1% (2006-2010 5-year est.); Poverty rate: 31.5% (2006-2010 5-year est.).

Education: Percent of population age 25 and over with: High school diploma (including GED) or higher: 87.0% (2006-2010 5-year est.); Bachelor's degree or higher: 14.1% (2006-2010 5-year est.); Master's degree or higher: 4.3% (2006-2010 5-year est.).

Housing: Homeownership rate: 33.5% (2010); Median home value: $47,900 (2006-2010 5-year est.); Median contract rent: $428 per month (2006-2010 5-year est.); Median year structure built: before 1940 (2006-2010 5-year est.).

Transportation: Commute to work: 87.7% car, 7.3% public transportation, 4.0% walk, 0.9% work from home (2006-2010 5-year est.); Travel time to work: 26.6% less than 15 minutes, 38.2% 15 to 30 minutes, 21.1% 30 to 45 minutes, 8.3% 45 to 60 minutes, 5.7% 60 minutes or more (2006-2010 5-year est.)

Additional Information Contacts

Norwin Chamber of Commerce . . . . (724) 863-0888
http://www.norwinchamber.com/index.php

Armstrong County

Located in western Pennsylvania; bounded on the southwest by the Kiskiminetas River. Covers a land area of 653.203 square miles, a water area of 10.640 square miles, and is located in the Eastern Time Zone at 40.81° N. Lat., 79.46° W. Long. The county was founded in 1800. County seat is Kittanning.

Armstrong County is part of the Pittsburgh, PA Metropolitan Statistical Area. The entire metro area includes: Allegheny County, PA; Armstrong County, PA; Beaver County, PA; Butler County, PA; Fayette County, PA; Washington County, PA; Westmoreland County, PA

Weather Station: Ford City 4 S Dam										Elevation: 930 feet		
	Jan	Feb	Mar	Apr	May	Jun	Jul	Aug	Sep	Oct	Nov	Dec
High	36	40	49	63	72	80	84	83	76	64	52	40
Low	18	19	26	36	46	55	60	58	51	39	31	22
Precip	2.8	2.3	3.1	3.2	3.9	4.3	4.1	4.0	3.5	2.7	3.6	3.0
Snow	8.9	5.6	4.9	0.6	0.0	0.0	0.0	0.0	0.0	tr	0.9	5.0

High and Low temperatures in degrees Fahrenheit; Precipitation and Snow in inches

Weather Station: Putneyville 2 SE Dam										Elevation: 1,279 feet		
	Jan	Feb	Mar	Apr	May	Jun	Jul	Aug	Sep	Oct	Nov	Dec
High	34	37	46	60	70	78	82	81	74	62	50	38
Low	17	18	24	34	44	53	57	56	49	38	31	21
Precip	3.1	2.6	3.5	3.6	4.1	4.5	4.5	4.0	3.7	3.0	3.9	3.3
Snow	10.1	6.9	5.8	0.6	0.0	0.0	0.0	0.0	0.0	tr	1.6	6.1

High and Low temperatures in degrees Fahrenheit; Precipitation and Snow in inches

Population: 73,478 (1990); 72,392 (2000); 68,941 (2010); Race: 98.0% White, 0.8% Black, 0.2% Asian, 0.1% American Indian/Alaska Native, 0.0% Native Hawaiian/Other Pacific Islander, 0.9% Other, 0.5% Hispanic of any race (2010); Density: 105.5 persons per square mile (2010); Average household size: 2.38 (2010); Median age: 44.5 (2010); Males per 100 females: 97.4 (2010).
Religion: Six largest groups: 17.3% Catholicism, 10.2% Presbyterian-Reformed, 8.2% Lutheran, 6.9% Methodist/Pietist, 3.1% Holiness, 2.6% Non-Denominational (2010)
Economy: Unemployment rate: 8.5% (August 2012); Total civilian labor force: 34,585 (August 2012); Leading industries: 23.5% health care and social assistance; 16.3% retail trade; 11.0% manufacturing (2010); Farms: 794 totaling 122,275 acres (2007); Companies that employ 500 or more persons: 1 (2010); Companies that employ 100 to 499 persons: 11 (2010); Companies that employ less than 100 persons: 1,261 (2010); Black-owned businesses: n/a (2007); Hispanic-owned businesses: n/a (2007); Asian-owned businesses: n/a (2007); Women-owned businesses: 1,250 (2007); Retail sales per capita: $10,907 (2010). Single-family building permits issued: 41 (2011); Multi-family building permits issued: 2 (2011).
Income: Per capita income: $21,828 (2006-2010 5-year est.); Median household income: $42,752 (2006-2010 5-year est.); Average household income: $52,054 (2006-2010 5-year est.); Percent of households with income of $100,000 or more: 10.1% (2006-2010 5-year est.); Poverty rate: 11.7% (2006-2010 5-year est.); Bankruptcy rate: 2.94% (2011).
Education: Percent of population age 25 and over with: High school diploma (including GED) or higher: 87.7% (2006-2010 5-year est.); Bachelor's degree or higher: 13.9% (2006-2010 5-year est.); Master's degree or higher: 4.0% (2006-2010 5-year est.).
Housing: Homeownership rate: 75.5% (2010); Median home value: $89,100 (2006-2010 5-year est.); Median contract rent: $395 per month (2006-2010 5-year est.); Median year structure built: 1954 (2006-2010 5-year est.)
Health: Birth rate: 99.0 per 10,000 population (2011); Death rate: 128.5 per 10,000 population (2011); Age-adjusted cancer mortality rate: 203.8 deaths per 100,000 population (2009); Number of physicians: 9.4 per 10,000 population (2010); Hospital beds: 24.8 per 10,000 population (2008); Hospital admissions: 1,082.6 per 10,000 population (2008).
Environment: Air Quality Index: 76.2% good, 23.8% moderate, 0.0% unhealthy for sensitive individuals, 0.0% unhealthy (percent of days in 2011)
Elections: 2012 Presidential election results: 30.6% Obama, 68.0% Romney
National and State Parks: Crooked Creek State Park
Additional Information Contacts
Armstrong County Government . . . . (724) 543-2500
  http://www.co.armstrong.pa.us

Armstrong County Communities

ADRIAN (unincorporated postal area)
Zip Code: 16210
  Covers a land area of 19.748 square miles and a water area of 1.090 square miles. Located at 40.89° N. Lat; 79.51° W. Long. Elevation is 1,047 feet. Population: 1,014 (2010); Density: 51.3 persons per square mile (2010); Race: 98.5% White, 0.2% Black, 0.1% Asian, 0.1% American Indian/Alaska Native, 0.0% Native Hawaiian/Other Pacific Islander, 1.1% Other, 1.1% Hispanic of any race (2010); Average household size: 2.54 (2010); Median age: 41.7 (2010); Males per 100 females: 103.2 (2010); Homeownership rate: 81.2% (2010)

APOLLO (borough). Covers a land area of 0.305 square miles and a water area of 0.043 square miles. Located at 40.59° N. Lat; 79.56° W. Long. Elevation is 817 feet.
History: Laid out 1815, incorporated 1848.
Population: 1,895 (1990); 1,765 (2000); 1,647 (2010); Density: 5,394.9 persons per square mile (2010); Race: 94.4% White, 2.3% Black, 0.5% Asian, 0.2% American Indian/Alaska Native, 0.0% Native Hawaiian/Other Pacific Islander, 2.6% Other, 0.9% Hispanic of any race (2010); Average household size: 2.36 (2010); Median age: 37.6 (2010); Males per 100 females: 87.2 (2010); Marriage status: 32.3% never married, 45.1% now married, 8.2% widowed, 14.3% divorced (2006-2010 5-year est.); Foreign born: 0.4% (2006-2010 5-year est.); Ancestry (includes multiple ancestries): 34.4% German, 21.4% Irish, 14.1% Italian, 9.6% English, 8.8% Polish (2006-2010 5-year est.).
Economy: Single-family building permits issued: 0 (2011); Multi-family building permits issued: 0 (2011); Employment by occupation: 7.4% management, 5.3% professional, 19.3% services, 13.5% sales, 3.3% farming, 12.1% construction, 10.6% production (2006-2010 5-year est.).
Income: Per capita income: $18,283 (2006-2010 5-year est.); Median household income: $33,681 (2006-2010 5-year est.); Average household income: $43,395 (2006-2010 5-year est.); Percent of households with income of $100,000 or more: 4.2% (2006-2010 5-year est.); Poverty rate: 10.1% (2006-2010 5-year est.).
Education: Percent of population age 25 and over with: High school diploma (including GED) or higher: 85.8% (2006-2010 5-year est.); Bachelor's degree or higher: 16.6% (2006-2010 5-year est.); Master's degree or higher: 6.6% (2006-2010 5-year est.).
School District(s)
Kiski Area SD (KG-12)
  2010-11 Enrollment: 3,967 . . . . (724) 845-2022
Housing: Homeownership rate: 55.0% (2010); Median home value: $60,700 (2006-2010 5-year est.); Median contract rent: $412 per month (2006-2010 5-year est.); Median year structure built: before 1940 (2006-2010 5-year est.).
Transportation: Commute to work: 90.1% car, 0.0% public transportation, 4.4% walk, 2.0% work from home (2006-2010 5-year est.); Travel time to work: 29.6% less than 15 minutes, 27.2% 15 to 30 minutes, 15.5% 30 to 45 minutes, 15.4% 45 to 60 minutes, 12.2% 60 minutes or more (2006-2010 5-year est.)
Additional Information Contacts
Strongland Chamber of Commerce . . . . (724) 845-5426
  http://www.strongland.org

APPLEWOLD (borough). Covers a land area of 0.047 square miles and a water area of 0 square miles. Located at 40.81° N. Lat; 79.52° W. Long. Elevation is 787 feet.
Population: 392 (1990); 356 (2000); 310 (2010); Density: 6,601.1 persons per square mile (2010); Race: 98.1% White, 0.3% Black, 0.0% Asian, 0.0% American Indian/Alaska Native, 0.0% Native Hawaiian/Other Pacific Islander, 1.6% Other, 1.0% Hispanic of any race (2010); Average household size: 1.90 (2010); Median age: 46.6 (2010); Males per 100 females: 86.7 (2010); Marriage status: 30.6% never married, 53.7% now married, 8.2% widowed, 7.5% divorced (2006-2010 5-year est.); Foreign born: 0.0% (2006-2010 5-year est.); Ancestry (includes multiple ancestries): 47.3% German, 16.7% Irish, 13.0% English, 12.3% Polish, 8.3% Slovak (2006-2010 5-year est.).
Economy: Single-family building permits issued: 0 (2011); Multi-family building permits issued: 0 (2011); Employment by occupation: 3.1% management, 11.2% professional, 18.6% services, 12.4% sales, 0.0% farming, 4.3% construction, 1.2% production (2006-2010 5-year est.).

Income: Per capita income: $25,888 (2006-2010 5-year est.); Median household income: $40,865 (2006-2010 5-year est.); Average household income: $52,888 (2006-2010 5-year est.); Percent of households with income of $100,000 or more: 14.4% (2006-2010 5-year est.); Poverty rate: 7.7% (2006-2010 5-year est.).

Education: Percent of population age 25 and over with: High school diploma (including GED) or higher: 95.3% (2006-2010 5-year est.); Bachelor's degree or higher: 25.9% (2006-2010 5-year est.); Master's degree or higher: 11.8% (2006-2010 5-year est.).

Housing: Homeownership rate: 55.2% (2010); Median home value: $89,100 (2006-2010 5-year est.); Median contract rent: $438 per month (2006-2010 5-year est.); Median year structure built: before 1940 (2006-2010 5-year est.).

Transportation: Commute to work: 91.6% car, 0.0% public transportation, 5.8% walk, 2.6% work from home (2006-2010 5-year est.); Travel time to work: 50.7% less than 15 minutes, 16.0% 15 to 30 minutes, 24.7% 30 to 45 minutes, 4.0% 45 to 60 minutes, 4.7% 60 minutes or more (2006-2010 5-year est.)

ATWOOD (borough). Covers a land area of 2.092 square miles and a water area of 0.021 square miles. Located at 40.75° N. Lat; 79.25° W. Long. Elevation is 1,237 feet.

Population: 118 (1990); 112 (2000); 107 (2010); Density: 51.1 persons per square mile (2010); Race: 100.0% White, 0.0% Black, 0.0% Asian, 0.0% American Indian/Alaska Native, 0.0% Native Hawaiian/Other Pacific Islander, 0.0% Other, 0.0% Hispanic of any race (2010); Average household size: 2.43 (2010); Median age: 44.2 (2010); Males per 100 females: 105.8 (2010); Marriage status: 9.5% never married, 81.0% now married, 3.4% widowed, 6.0% divorced (2006-2010 5-year est.); Foreign born: 1.4% (2006-2010 5-year est.); Ancestry (includes multiple ancestries): 45.3% German, 23.0% Slovak, 15.8% Irish, 6.5% Scotch-Irish, 4.3% Dutch (2006-2010 5-year est.).

Economy: Employment by occupation: 8.6% management, 0.0% professional, 12.3% services, 30.9% sales, 0.0% farming, 11.1% construction, 2.5% production (2006-2010 5-year est.).

Income: Per capita income: $26,344 (2006-2010 5-year est.); Median household income: $55,938 (2006-2010 5-year est.); Average household income: $60,181 (2006-2010 5-year est.); Percent of households with income of $100,000 or more: 4.8% (2006-2010 5-year est.); Poverty rate: 3.6% (2006-2010 5-year est.).

Education: Percent of population age 25 and over with: High school diploma (including GED) or higher: 85.2% (2006-2010 5-year est.); Bachelor's degree or higher: 0.0% (2006-2010 5-year est.); Master's degree or higher: 0.0% (2006-2010 5-year est.).

Housing: Homeownership rate: 84.1% (2010); Median home value: $154,200 (2006-2010 5-year est.); Median contract rent: $400 per month (2006-2010 5-year est.); Median year structure built: 1968 (2006-2010 5-year est.).

Transportation: Commute to work: 85.2% car, 2.5% public transportation, 0.0% walk, 12.3% work from home (2006-2010 5-year est.); Travel time to work: 2.8% less than 15 minutes, 66.2% 15 to 30 minutes, 12.7% 30 to 45 minutes, 5.6% 45 to 60 minutes, 12.7% 60 minutes or more (2006-2010 5-year est.)

BETHEL (township). Covers a land area of 15.271 square miles and a water area of 0.591 square miles. Located at 40.70° N. Lat; 79.55° W. Long.

Population: 1,261 (1990); 1,290 (2000); 1,183 (2010); Density: 77.5 persons per square mile (2010); Race: 98.4% White, 0.2% Black, 0.2% Asian, 0.6% American Indian/Alaska Native, 0.0% Native Hawaiian/Other Pacific Islander, 0.6% Other, 0.5% Hispanic of any race (2010); Average household size: 2.44 (2010); Median age: 45.9 (2010); Males per 100 females: 111.3 (2010); Marriage status: 21.1% never married, 64.9% now married, 5.2% widowed, 8.9% divorced (2006-2010 5-year est.); Foreign born: 0.5% (2006-2010 5-year est.); Ancestry (includes multiple ancestries): 53.6% German, 15.0% Polish, 14.3% English, 10.8% Irish, 9.1% Italian (2006-2010 5-year est.).

Economy: Employment by occupation: 10.9% management, 1.5% professional, 8.2% services, 12.6% sales, 4.6% farming, 21.1% construction, 7.3% production (2006-2010 5-year est.).

Income: Per capita income: $19,126 (2006-2010 5-year est.); Median household income: $44,135 (2006-2010 5-year est.); Average household income: $49,616 (2006-2010 5-year est.); Percent of households with income of $100,000 or more: 5.8% (2006-2010 5-year est.); Poverty rate: 14.0% (2006-2010 5-year est.).

Education: Percent of population age 25 and over with: High school diploma (including GED) or higher: 89.8% (2006-2010 5-year est.); Bachelor's degree or higher: 11.2% (2006-2010 5-year est.); Master's degree or higher: 0.6% (2006-2010 5-year est.).

Housing: Homeownership rate: 89.9% (2010); Median home value: $104,100 (2006-2010 5-year est.); Median contract rent: $285 per month (2006-2010 5-year est.); Median year structure built: 1962 (2006-2010 5-year est.).

Safety: Violent crime rate: 0.0 per 10,000 population; Property crime rate: 0.0 per 10,000 population (2011).

Transportation: Commute to work: 95.4% car, 0.0% public transportation, 1.2% walk, 2.8% work from home (2006-2010 5-year est.); Travel time to work: 7.2% less than 15 minutes, 27.2% 15 to 30 minutes, 37.7% 30 to 45 minutes, 17.3% 45 to 60 minutes, 10.7% 60 minutes or more (2006-2010 5-year est.)

Additional Information Contacts

Armstrong County Chamber of Commerce . . . . (724) 543-1305
http://www.armstrongchamber.org

BOGGS (township). Covers a land area of 24.582 square miles and a water area of 0.326 square miles. Located at 40.89° N. Lat; 79.41° W. Long.

Population: 981 (1990); 979 (2000); 936 (2010); Density: 38.1 persons per square mile (2010); Race: 97.9% White, 1.4% Black, 0.2% Asian, 0.0% American Indian/Alaska Native, 0.0% Native Hawaiian/Other Pacific Islander, 0.5% Other, 0.3% Hispanic of any race (2010); Average household size: 2.70 (2010); Median age: 43.1 (2010); Males per 100 females: 98.7 (2010); Marriage status: 23.0% never married, 68.5% now married, 2.4% widowed, 6.1% divorced (2006-2010 5-year est.); Foreign born: 0.6% (2006-2010 5-year est.); Ancestry (includes multiple ancestries): 40.4% German, 17.2% Irish, 13.8% English, 9.1% Polish, 7.6% Italian (2006-2010 5-year est.).

Economy: Single-family building permits issued: 2 (2011); Multi-family building permits issued: 0 (2011); Employment by occupation: 5.8% management, 6.0% professional, 11.8% services, 11.0% sales, 8.2% farming, 18.4% construction, 13.2% production (2006-2010 5-year est.).

Income: Per capita income: $18,541 (2006-2010 5-year est.); Median household income: $42,396 (2006-2010 5-year est.); Average household income: $49,721 (2006-2010 5-year est.); Percent of households with income of $100,000 or more: 4.7% (2006-2010 5-year est.); Poverty rate: 9.1% (2006-2010 5-year est.).

Education: Percent of population age 25 and over with: High school diploma (including GED) or higher: 93.4% (2006-2010 5-year est.); Bachelor's degree or higher: 10.9% (2006-2010 5-year est.); Master's degree or higher: 1.8% (2006-2010 5-year est.).

Housing: Homeownership rate: 86.8% (2010); Median home value: $74,600 (2006-2010 5-year est.); Median contract rent: $369 per month (2006-2010 5-year est.); Median year structure built: 1958 (2006-2010 5-year est.).

Transportation: Commute to work: 97.2% car, 0.0% public transportation, 0.0% walk, 2.8% work from home (2006-2010 5-year est.); Travel time to work: 10.4% less than 15 minutes, 45.8% 15 to 30 minutes, 16.8% 30 to 45 minutes, 12.5% 45 to 60 minutes, 14.5% 60 minutes or more (2006-2010 5-year est.)

BRADYS BEND (township). Covers a land area of 12.613 square miles and a water area of 0 square miles. Located at 40.98° N. Lat; 79.65° W. Long. Elevation is 935 feet.

Population: 963 (1990); 939 (2000); 773 (2010); Density: 61.3 persons per square mile (2010); Race: 99.5% White, 0.0% Black, 0.1% Asian, 0.0% American Indian/Alaska Native, 0.0% Native Hawaiian/Other Pacific Islander, 0.4% Other, 0.3% Hispanic of any race (2010); Average household size: 2.39 (2010); Median age: 43.6 (2010); Males per 100 females: 114.1 (2010); Marriage status: 22.6% never married, 64.8% now married, 4.9% widowed, 7.8% divorced (2006-2010 5-year est.); Foreign born: 0.0% (2006-2010 5-year est.); Ancestry (includes multiple ancestries): 54.0% German, 34.9% Irish, 21.0% Italian, 7.8% English, 6.9% Polish (2006-2010 5-year est.).

Economy: Single-family building permits issued: 1 (2011); Multi-family building permits issued: 0 (2011); Employment by occupation: 4.4% management, 2.8% professional, 4.4% services, 12.9% sales, 11.6% farming, 13.8% construction, 16.0% production (2006-2010 5-year est.).

Income: Per capita income: $18,868 (2006-2010 5-year est.); Median household income: $52,875 (2006-2010 5-year est.); Average household income: $53,857 (2006-2010 5-year est.); Percent of households with

income of $100,000 or more: 8.9% (2006-2010 5-year est.); Poverty rate: 15.8% (2006-2010 5-year est.).

Education: Percent of population age 25 and over with: High school diploma (including GED) or higher: 86.2% (2006-2010 5-year est.); Bachelor's degree or higher: 12.0% (2006-2010 5-year est.); Master's degree or higher: 1.6% (2006-2010 5-year est.).

Housing: Homeownership rate: 83.6% (2010); Median home value: $94,400 (2006-2010 5-year est.); Median contract rent: $339 per month (2006-2010 5-year est.); Median year structure built: 1962 (2006-2010 5-year est.).

Transportation: Commute to work: 94.4% car, 0.0% public transportation, 3.6% walk, 2.0% work from home (2006-2010 5-year est.); Travel time to work: 28.0% less than 15 minutes, 20.7% 15 to 30 minutes, 32.3% 30 to 45 minutes, 9.3% 45 to 60 minutes, 9.7% 60 minutes or more (2006-2010 5-year est.)

BURRELL (township). Covers a land area of 21.465 square miles and a water area of 0.515 square miles. Located at 40.67° N. Lat; 79.47° W. Long.

Population: 728 (1990); 749 (2000); 689 (2010); Density: 32.1 persons per square mile (2010); Race: 98.4% White, 1.2% Black, 0.0% Asian, 0.1% American Indian/Alaska Native, 0.0% Native Hawaiian/Other Pacific Islander, 0.3% Other, 0.4% Hispanic of any race (2010); Average household size: 2.43 (2010); Median age: 44.4 (2010); Males per 100 females: 108.2 (2010); Marriage status: 25.4% never married, 56.3% now married, 8.7% widowed, 9.6% divorced (2006-2010 5-year est.); Foreign born: 3.0% (2006-2010 5-year est.); Ancestry (includes multiple ancestries): 50.3% German, 18.4% Irish, 8.3% Scotch-Irish, 7.8% Polish, 6.7% Italian (2006-2010 5-year est.).

Economy: Single-family building permits issued: 2 (2011); Multi-family building permits issued: 0 (2011); Employment by occupation: 6.6% management, 4.7% professional, 9.4% services, 17.8% sales, 6.1% farming, 22.1% construction, 12.7% production (2006-2010 5-year est.).

Income: Per capita income: $19,818 (2006-2010 5-year est.); Median household income: $38,750 (2006-2010 5-year est.); Average household income: $50,537 (2006-2010 5-year est.); Percent of households with income of $100,000 or more: 12.3% (2006-2010 5-year est.); Poverty rate: 17.6% (2006-2010 5-year est.).

Education: Percent of population age 25 and over with: High school diploma (including GED) or higher: 80.1% (2006-2010 5-year est.); Bachelor's degree or higher: 12.2% (2006-2010 5-year est.); Master's degree or higher: 4.8% (2006-2010 5-year est.).

Housing: Homeownership rate: 81.2% (2010); Median home value: $104,200 (2006-2010 5-year est.); Median contract rent: $359 per month (2006-2010 5-year est.); Median year structure built: 1961 (2006-2010 5-year est.).

Transportation: Commute to work: 90.1% car, 1.5% public transportation, 0.0% walk, 6.4% work from home (2006-2010 5-year est.); Travel time to work: 11.1% less than 15 minutes, 26.8% 15 to 30 minutes, 35.8% 30 to 45 minutes, 15.8% 45 to 60 minutes, 10.5% 60 minutes or more (2006-2010 5-year est.)

CADOGAN (township). Covers a land area of 0.986 square miles and a water area of 0.121 square miles. Located at 40.76° N. Lat; 79.58° W. Long. Elevation is 892 feet.

Population: 427 (1990); 390 (2000); 344 (2010); Density: 348.9 persons per square mile (2010); Race: 99.7% White, 0.0% Black, 0.0% Asian, 0.0% American Indian/Alaska Native, 0.0% Native Hawaiian/Other Pacific Islander, 0.3% Other, 0.3% Hispanic of any race (2010); Average household size: 2.23 (2010); Median age: 46.2 (2010); Males per 100 females: 94.4 (2010); Marriage status: 19.1% never married, 64.6% now married, 10.2% widowed, 6.1% divorced (2006-2010 5-year est.); Foreign born: 0.0% (2006-2010 5-year est.); Ancestry (includes multiple ancestries): 44.1% German, 30.0% Italian, 13.0% Polish, 11.0% Irish, 8.6% English (2006-2010 5-year est.).

Economy: Single-family building permits issued: 0 (2011); Multi-family building permits issued: 0 (2011); Employment by occupation: 5.4% management, 3.0% professional, 11.4% services, 22.8% sales, 0.0% farming, 8.4% construction, 6.0% production (2006-2010 5-year est.).

Income: Per capita income: $20,059 (2006-2010 5-year est.); Median household income: $35,000 (2006-2010 5-year est.); Average household income: $43,207 (2006-2010 5-year est.); Percent of households with income of $100,000 or more: 2.5% (2006-2010 5-year est.); Poverty rate: 4.3% (2006-2010 5-year est.).

Education: Percent of population age 25 and over with: High school diploma (including GED) or higher: 79.0% (2006-2010 5-year est.); Bachelor's degree or higher: 4.7% (2006-2010 5-year est.); Master's degree or higher: 0.0% (2006-2010 5-year est.).

Housing: Homeownership rate: 81.9% (2010); Median home value: $74,100 (2006-2010 5-year est.); Median contract rent: $291 per month (2006-2010 5-year est.); Median year structure built: 1945 (2006-2010 5-year est.).

Transportation: Commute to work: 83.2% car, 0.0% public transportation, 11.4% walk, 0.0% work from home (2006-2010 5-year est.); Travel time to work: 35.3% less than 15 minutes, 27.5% 15 to 30 minutes, 26.9% 30 to 45 minutes, 5.4% 45 to 60 minutes, 4.8% 60 minutes or more (2006-2010 5-year est.)

COWANSHANNOCK (township). Covers a land area of 45.665 square miles and a water area of 0.689 square miles. Located at 40.80° N. Lat; 79.30° W. Long.

Population: 2,809 (1990); 3,006 (2000); 2,899 (2010); Density: 63.5 persons per square mile (2010); Race: 98.9% White, 0.2% Black, 0.0% Asian, 0.0% American Indian/Alaska Native, 0.0% Native Hawaiian/Other Pacific Islander, 0.9% Other, 0.4% Hispanic of any race (2010); Average household size: 2.57 (2010); Median age: 41.5 (2010); Males per 100 females: 106.0 (2010); Marriage status: 19.9% never married, 63.0% now married, 10.0% widowed, 7.1% divorced (2006-2010 5-year est.); Foreign born: 0.7% (2006-2010 5-year est.); Ancestry (includes multiple ancestries): 36.8% German, 28.1% Irish, 11.9% Italian, 7.6% Polish, 5.8% Dutch (2006-2010 5-year est.).

Economy: Single-family building permits issued: 5 (2011); Multi-family building permits issued: 0 (2011); Employment by occupation: 10.5% management, 1.6% professional, 15.8% services, 13.0% sales, 0.0% farming, 22.8% construction, 5.8% production (2006-2010 5-year est.).

Income: Per capita income: $20,520 (2006-2010 5-year est.); Median household income: $39,931 (2006-2010 5-year est.); Average household income: $49,558 (2006-2010 5-year est.); Percent of households with income of $100,000 or more: 12.4% (2006-2010 5-year est.); Poverty rate: 9.1% (2006-2010 5-year est.).

Education: Percent of population age 25 and over with: High school diploma (including GED) or higher: 82.8% (2006-2010 5-year est.); Bachelor's degree or higher: 15.5% (2006-2010 5-year est.); Master's degree or higher: 4.8% (2006-2010 5-year est.).

Housing: Homeownership rate: 83.6% (2010); Median home value: $73,500 (2006-2010 5-year est.); Median contract rent: $373 per month (2006-2010 5-year est.); Median year structure built: before 1940 (2006-2010 5-year est.).

Transportation: Commute to work: 97.7% car, 0.0% public transportation, 0.0% walk, 1.7% work from home (2006-2010 5-year est.); Travel time to work: 20.9% less than 15 minutes, 28.1% 15 to 30 minutes, 31.3% 30 to 45 minutes, 4.5% 45 to 60 minutes, 15.1% 60 minutes or more (2006-2010 5-year est.)

Additional Information Contacts

Indiana County Chamber of Commerce . . . . (724) 465-2511
   http://www.indianapa.com/chamber

COWANSVILLE (unincorporated postal area)

Zip Code: 16218

   Covers a land area of 28.363 square miles and a water area of 0.237 square miles. Located at 40.93° N. Lat; 79.59° W. Long. Elevation is 1,365 feet. Population: 1,195 (2010); Density: 42.1 persons per square mile (2010); Race: 97.4% White, 1.9% Black, 0.3% Asian, 0.1% American Indian/Alaska Native, 0.0% Native Hawaiian/Other Pacific Islander, 0.3% Other, 0.2% Hispanic of any race (2010); Average household size: 2.57 (2010); Median age: 46.5 (2010); Males per 100 females: 109.3 (2010); Homeownership rate: 82.6% (2010)

DAYTON (borough). Covers a land area of 0.376 square miles and a water area of 0 square miles. Located at 40.88° N. Lat; 79.24° W. Long. Elevation is 1,342 feet.

Population: 572 (1990); 543 (2000); 553 (2010); Density: 1,469.5 persons per square mile (2010); Race: 97.6% White, 0.0% Black, 0.4% Asian, 0.0% American Indian/Alaska Native, 0.0% Native Hawaiian/Other Pacific Islander, 2.0% Other, 0.0% Hispanic of any race (2010); Average household size: 2.45 (2010); Median age: 42.3 (2010); Males per 100 females: 104.1 (2010); Marriage status: 18.5% never married, 64.0% now married, 6.8% widowed, 10.6% divorced (2006-2010 5-year est.); Foreign born: 1.3% (2006-2010 5-year est.); Ancestry (includes multiple

ancestries): 45.5% German, 34.2% Irish, 9.7% Polish, 7.0% English, 3.4% Scotch-Irish (2006-2010 5-year est.).

Economy: Single-family building permits issued: 0 (2011); Multi-family building permits issued: 0 (2011); Employment by occupation: 7.1% management, 1.8% professional, 18.4% services, 8.9% sales, 3.9% farming, 22.0% construction, 8.2% production (2006-2010 5-year est.).

Income: Per capita income: $18,574 (2006-2010 5-year est.); Median household income: $50,278 (2006-2010 5-year est.); Average household income: $53,433 (2006-2010 5-year est.); Percent of households with income of $100,000 or more: 6.5% (2006-2010 5-year est.); Poverty rate: 14.9% (2006-2010 5-year est.).

Education: Percent of population age 25 and over with: High school diploma (including GED) or higher: 94.3% (2006-2010 5-year est.); Bachelor's degree or higher: 17.5% (2006-2010 5-year est.); Master's degree or higher: 1.0% (2006-2010 5-year est.).

School District(s)

Armstrong SD (KG-12)
   2010-11 Enrollment: 5,544 . . . . (724) 763-7151

Housing: Homeownership rate: 81.9% (2010); Median home value: $57,000 (2006-2010 5-year est.); Median contract rent: $454 per month (2006-2010 5-year est.); Median year structure built: before 1940 (2006-2010 5-year est.).

Transportation: Commute to work: 92.2% car, 0.0% public transportation, 2.1% walk, 3.2% work from home (2006-2010 5-year est.); Travel time to work: 39.6% less than 15 minutes, 18.3% 15 to 30 minutes, 12.5% 30 to 45 minutes, 4.4% 45 to 60 minutes, 25.3% 60 minutes or more (2006-2010 5-year est.)

DISTANT (unincorporated postal area)
Zip Code: 16223
   Covers a land area of 1.082 square miles and a water area of 0 square miles. Located at 40.97° N. Lat; 79.36° W. Long. Elevation is 1,401 feet. Population: 154 (2010); Density: 142.3 persons per square mile (2010); Race: 100.0% White, 0.0% Black, 0.0% Asian, 0.0% American Indian/Alaska Native, 0.0% Native Hawaiian/Other Pacific Islander, 0.0% Other, 0.0% Hispanic of any race (2010); Average household size: 2.48 (2010); Median age: 41.0 (2010); Males per 100 females: 85.5 (2010); Homeownership rate: 82.3% (2010)

EAST FRANKLIN (township). Covers a land area of 30.885 square miles and a water area of 0.669 square miles. Located at 40.87° N. Lat; 79.56° W. Long.

Population: 3,919 (1990); 3,900 (2000); 4,082 (2010); Density: 132.2 persons per square mile (2010); Race: 99.0% White, 0.2% Black, 0.2% Asian, 0.0% American Indian/Alaska Native, 0.0% Native Hawaiian/Other Pacific Islander, 0.6% Other, 0.8% Hispanic of any race (2010); Average household size: 2.46 (2010); Median age: 45.4 (2010); Males per 100 females: 100.4 (2010); Marriage status: 21.5% never married, 63.6% now married, 7.8% widowed, 7.0% divorced (2006-2010 5-year est.); Foreign born: 0.5% (2006-2010 5-year est.); Ancestry (includes multiple ancestries): 48.2% German, 15.6% Irish, 11.6% English, 8.1% Polish, 7.0% Italian (2006-2010 5-year est.).

Economy: Single-family building permits issued: 0 (2011); Multi-family building permits issued: 0 (2011); Employment by occupation: 10.7% management, 6.7% professional, 11.4% services, 23.3% sales, 3.9% farming, 5.6% construction, 4.4% production (2006-2010 5-year est.).

Income: Per capita income: $26,857 (2006-2010 5-year est.); Median household income: $50,188 (2006-2010 5-year est.); Average household income: $59,157 (2006-2010 5-year est.); Percent of households with income of $100,000 or more: 13.9% (2006-2010 5-year est.); Poverty rate: 5.8% (2006-2010 5-year est.).

Education: Percent of population age 25 and over with: High school diploma (including GED) or higher: 89.9% (2006-2010 5-year est.); Bachelor's degree or higher: 25.8% (2006-2010 5-year est.); Master's degree or higher: 7.7% (2006-2010 5-year est.).

Housing: Homeownership rate: 83.8% (2010); Median home value: $129,100 (2006-2010 5-year est.); Median contract rent: $494 per month (2006-2010 5-year est.); Median year structure built: 1973 (2006-2010 5-year est.).

Transportation: Commute to work: 91.0% car, 0.0% public transportation, 3.7% walk, 5.3% work from home (2006-2010 5-year est.); Travel time to work: 31.4% less than 15 minutes, 25.0% 15 to 30 minutes, 20.7% 30 to 45 minutes, 6.5% 45 to 60 minutes, 16.3% 60 minutes or more (2006-2010 5-year est.)

Additional Information Contacts
Armstrong County Chamber of Commerce . . . . (724) 543-1305
   http://www.armstrongchamber.org

ELDERTON (borough). Covers a land area of 0.323 square miles and a water area of 0 square miles. Located at 40.69° N. Lat; 79.34° W. Long. Elevation is 1,270 feet.

Population: 371 (1990); 358 (2000); 356 (2010); Density: 1,100.7 persons per square mile (2010); Race: 95.2% White, 0.0% Black, 0.0% Asian, 0.0% American Indian/Alaska Native, 0.0% Native Hawaiian/Other Pacific Islander, 4.8% Other, 1.7% Hispanic of any race (2010); Average household size: 2.26 (2010); Median age: 48.3 (2010); Males per 100 females: 86.4 (2010); Marriage status: 26.5% never married, 56.1% now married, 9.0% widowed, 8.4% divorced (2006-2010 5-year est.); Foreign born: 0.0% (2006-2010 5-year est.); Ancestry (includes multiple ancestries): 67.3% German, 32.0% Irish, 8.4% Italian, 6.1% Dutch, 3.8% French (2006-2010 5-year est.).

Economy: Employment by occupation: 0.0% management, 8.7% professional, 15.5% services, 13.0% sales, 1.4% farming, 22.2% construction, 13.0% production (2006-2010 5-year est.).

Income: Per capita income: $23,748 (2006-2010 5-year est.); Median household income: $41,736 (2006-2010 5-year est.); Average household income: $55,490 (2006-2010 5-year est.); Percent of households with income of $100,000 or more: 14.5% (2006-2010 5-year est.); Poverty rate: 5.8% (2006-2010 5-year est.).

Education: Percent of population age 25 and over with: High school diploma (including GED) or higher: 91.6% (2006-2010 5-year est.); Bachelor's degree or higher: 14.5% (2006-2010 5-year est.); Master's degree or higher: 3.3% (2006-2010 5-year est.).

School District(s)

Armstrong SD (KG-12)
   2010-11 Enrollment: 5,544 . . . . (724) 763-7151

Housing: Homeownership rate: 63.5% (2010); Median home value: $103,400 (2006-2010 5-year est.); Median contract rent: $346 per month (2006-2010 5-year est.); Median year structure built: 1971 (2006-2010 5-year est.).

Transportation: Commute to work: 89.9% car, 0.0% public transportation, 1.5% walk, 8.5% work from home (2006-2010 5-year est.); Travel time to work: 40.7% less than 15 minutes, 31.9% 15 to 30 minutes, 9.9% 30 to 45 minutes, 3.8% 45 to 60 minutes, 13.7% 60 minutes or more (2006-2010 5-year est.)

FORD CITY (borough). Aka Kelley. Covers a land area of 0.645 square miles and a water area of 0.116 square miles. Located at 40.77° N. Lat; 79.53° W. Long. Elevation is 787 feet.

History: Laid out 1871, incorporated 1889.

Population: 3,499 (1990); 3,451 (2000); 2,991 (2010); Density: 4,640.1 persons per square mile (2010); Race: 95.6% White, 2.9% Black, 0.1% Asian, 0.1% American Indian/Alaska Native, 0.0% Native Hawaiian/Other Pacific Islander, 1.3% Other, 1.1% Hispanic of any race (2010); Average household size: 2.13 (2010); Median age: 42.0 (2010); Males per 100 females: 86.6 (2010); Marriage status: 29.7% never married, 49.5% now married, 10.7% widowed, 10.1% divorced (2006-2010 5-year est.); Foreign born: 0.4% (2006-2010 5-year est.); Ancestry (includes multiple ancestries): 34.5% German, 18.4% Polish, 10.8% Irish, 10.5% Slovak, 6.2% American (2006-2010 5-year est.).

Economy: Single-family building permits issued: 0 (2011); Multi-family building permits issued: 0 (2011); Employment by occupation: 4.4% management, 2.5% professional, 25.1% services, 12.3% sales, 5.3% farming, 3.7% construction, 1.5% production (2006-2010 5-year est.).

Income: Per capita income: $19,337 (2006-2010 5-year est.); Median household income: $29,239 (2006-2010 5-year est.); Average household income: $39,594 (2006-2010 5-year est.); Percent of households with income of $100,000 or more: 3.7% (2006-2010 5-year est.); Poverty rate: 17.9% (2006-2010 5-year est.).

Education: Percent of population age 25 and over with: High school diploma (including GED) or higher: 89.3% (2006-2010 5-year est.); Bachelor's degree or higher: 14.6% (2006-2010 5-year est.); Master's degree or higher: 2.6% (2006-2010 5-year est.).

School District(s)

Armstrong SD (KG-12)
   2010-11 Enrollment: 5,544 . . . . (724) 763-7151
Lenape Tech (11-12)
   2010-11 Enrollment: 435 . . . . (724) 763-7116

Housing: Homeownership rate: 59.0% (2010); Median home value: $61,500 (2006-2010 5-year est.); Median contract rent: $363 per month (2006-2010 5-year est.); Median year structure built: before 1940 (2006-2010 5-year est.).
Safety: Violent crime rate: 23.3 per 10,000 population; Property crime rate: 153.3 per 10,000 population (2011).
Transportation: Commute to work: 92.4% car, 0.0% public transportation, 5.2% walk, 1.5% work from home (2006-2010 5-year est.); Travel time to work: 50.0% less than 15 minutes, 24.4% 15 to 30 minutes, 14.8% 30 to 45 minutes, 6.7% 45 to 60 minutes, 4.0% 60 minutes or more (2006-2010 5-year est.)

Additional Information Contacts
Armstrong County Chamber of Commerce . . . . (724) 543-1305
    http://www.armstrongchamber.org

FORD CLIFF (borough). Covers a land area of 0.076 square miles and a water area of 0 square miles. Located at 40.76° N. Lat; 79.54° W. Long. Elevation is 955 feet.
Population: 450 (1990); 412 (2000); 371 (2010); Density: 4,881.6 persons per square mile (2010); Race: 96.5% White, 0.8% Black, 1.9% Asian, 0.0% American Indian/Alaska Native, 0.0% Native Hawaiian/Other Pacific Islander, 0.8% Other, 0.5% Hispanic of any race (2010); Average household size: 2.21 (2010); Median age: 45.3 (2010); Males per 100 females: 88.3 (2010); Marriage status: 22.6% never married, 65.4% now married, 6.1% widowed, 5.9% divorced (2006-2010 5-year est.); Foreign born: 0.2% (2006-2010 5-year est.); Ancestry (includes multiple ancestries): 32.4% German, 17.0% Irish, 13.0% Slovak, 11.3% Italian, 11.1% Polish (2006-2010 5-year est.).
Economy: Single-family building permits issued: 2 (2011); Multi-family building permits issued: 2 (2011); Employment by occupation: 7.3% management, 1.7% professional, 27.5% services, 11.2% sales, 5.6% farming, 8.6% construction, 4.3% production (2006-2010 5-year est.).
Income: Per capita income: $19,729 (2006-2010 5-year est.); Median household income: $46,146 (2006-2010 5-year est.); Average household income: $49,342 (2006-2010 5-year est.); Percent of households with income of $100,000 or more: 5.6% (2006-2010 5-year est.); Poverty rate: 7.2% (2006-2010 5-year est.).
Education: Percent of population age 25 and over with: High school diploma (including GED) or higher: 84.6% (2006-2010 5-year est.); Bachelor's degree or higher: 13.8% (2006-2010 5-year est.); Master's degree or higher: 2.6% (2006-2010 5-year est.).
Housing: Homeownership rate: 85.1% (2010); Median home value: $71,300 (2006-2010 5-year est.); Median contract rent: $411 per month (2006-2010 5-year est.); Median year structure built: 1942 (2006-2010 5-year est.).
Transportation: Commute to work: 96.0% car, 0.0% public transportation, 0.0% walk, 0.9% work from home (2006-2010 5-year est.); Travel time to work: 38.6% less than 15 minutes, 32.3% 15 to 30 minutes, 18.8% 30 to 45 minutes, 2.2% 45 to 60 minutes, 8.1% 60 minutes or more (2006-2010 5-year est.)

FREEPORT (borough). Aka Laneville. Covers a land area of 1.270 square miles and a water area of 0.029 square miles. Located at 40.69° N. Lat; 79.68° W. Long. Elevation is 791 feet.
History: Canal town in mid-19th century. Settled c.1792, laid out c.1800.
Population: 1,983 (1990); 1,962 (2000); 1,813 (2010); Density: 1,427.7 persons per square mile (2010); Race: 96.8% White, 0.6% Black, 0.2% Asian, 0.1% American Indian/Alaska Native, 0.2% Native Hawaiian/Other Pacific Islander, 2.1% Other, 1.1% Hispanic of any race (2010); Average household size: 2.23 (2010); Median age: 40.4 (2010); Males per 100 females: 92.5 (2010); Marriage status: 21.4% never married, 57.8% now married, 9.3% widowed, 11.4% divorced (2006-2010 5-year est.); Foreign born: 0.6% (2006-2010 5-year est.); Ancestry (includes multiple ancestries): 45.5% German, 27.7% Irish, 20.4% Italian, 11.3% Polish, 7.3% English (2006-2010 5-year est.).
Economy: Single-family building permits issued: 1 (2011); Multi-family building permits issued: 0 (2011); Employment by occupation: 11.0% management, 1.7% professional, 15.5% services, 14.0% sales, 5.4% farming, 8.0% construction, 5.6% production (2006-2010 5-year est.).
Income: Per capita income: $21,696 (2006-2010 5-year est.); Median household income: $48,802 (2006-2010 5-year est.); Average household income: $48,754 (2006-2010 5-year est.); Percent of households with income of $100,000 or more: 3.8% (2006-2010 5-year est.); Poverty rate: 8.2% (2006-2010 5-year est.).

Education: Percent of population age 25 and over with: High school diploma (including GED) or higher: 91.5% (2006-2010 5-year est.); Bachelor's degree or higher: 17.4% (2006-2010 5-year est.); Master's degree or higher: 5.6% (2006-2010 5-year est.).
School District(s)
Freeport Area SD (KG-12)
    2010-11 Enrollment: 2,007 . . . . (724) 295-5141
Freeport Area SD (KG-12)
    2010-11 Enrollment: 2,007 . . . . (724) 295-5141
Housing: Homeownership rate: 56.4% (2010); Median home value: $78,100 (2006-2010 5-year est.); Median contract rent: $417 per month (2006-2010 5-year est.); Median year structure built: before 1940 (2006-2010 5-year est.).
Safety: Violent crime rate: 16.5 per 10,000 population; Property crime rate: 16.5 per 10,000 population (2011).
Transportation: Commute to work: 88.5% car, 1.1% public transportation, 7.8% walk, 2.1% work from home (2006-2010 5-year est.); Travel time to work: 32.6% less than 15 minutes, 32.1% 15 to 30 minutes, 16.4% 30 to 45 minutes, 13.5% 45 to 60 minutes, 5.5% 60 minutes or more (2006-2010 5-year est.)

Additional Information Contacts
Allegheny Valley Chamber of Commerce . . . . (724) 224-3400
    http://alleghenyvalleychamber.com

GILPIN (township). Covers a land area of 16.449 square miles and a water area of 0.694 square miles. Located at 40.67° N. Lat; 79.60° W. Long.
Population: 2,795 (1990); 2,587 (2000); 2,496 (2010); Density: 151.7 persons per square mile (2010); Race: 97.4% White, 0.9% Black, 0.8% Asian, 0.1% American Indian/Alaska Native, 0.0% Native Hawaiian/Other Pacific Islander, 0.8% Other, 0.4% Hispanic of any race (2010); Average household size: 2.37 (2010); Median age: 48.5 (2010); Males per 100 females: 98.7 (2010); Marriage status: 22.3% never married, 67.2% now married, 5.3% widowed, 5.2% divorced (2006-2010 5-year est.); Foreign born: 2.4% (2006-2010 5-year est.); Ancestry (includes multiple ancestries): 41.7% German, 14.7% Irish, 14.7% Italian, 11.7% Polish, 7.2% Slovak (2006-2010 5-year est.).
Economy: Single-family building permits issued: 1 (2011); Multi-family building permits issued: 0 (2011); Employment by occupation: 5.2% management, 3.3% professional, 11.4% services, 11.8% sales, 3.9% farming, 16.7% construction, 10.5% production (2006-2010 5-year est.).
Income: Per capita income: $25,873 (2006-2010 5-year est.); Median household income: $60,982 (2006-2010 5-year est.); Average household income: $63,333 (2006-2010 5-year est.); Percent of households with income of $100,000 or more: 13.4% (2006-2010 5-year est.); Poverty rate: 7.3% (2006-2010 5-year est.).
Education: Percent of population age 25 and over with: High school diploma (including GED) or higher: 90.3% (2006-2010 5-year est.); Bachelor's degree or higher: 17.8% (2006-2010 5-year est.); Master's degree or higher: 5.7% (2006-2010 5-year est.).
Housing: Homeownership rate: 87.8% (2010); Median home value: $105,200 (2006-2010 5-year est.); Median contract rent: $482 per month (2006-2010 5-year est.); Median year structure built: 1956 (2006-2010 5-year est.).
Safety: Violent crime rate: 0.0 per 10,000 population; Property crime rate: 0.0 per 10,000 population (2011).
Transportation: Commute to work: 96.7% car, 2.1% public transportation, 0.0% walk, 1.2% work from home (2006-2010 5-year est.); Travel time to work: 28.4% less than 15 minutes, 29.4% 15 to 30 minutes, 24.0% 30 to 45 minutes, 10.2% 45 to 60 minutes, 8.0% 60 minutes or more (2006-2010 5-year est.)

Additional Information Contacts
Allegheny Valley Chamber of Commerce . . . . (724) 224-3400
    http://alleghenyvalleychamber.com

HOVEY (township). Covers a land area of 2.153 square miles and a water area of 0 square miles. Located at 41.13° N. Lat; 79.69° W. Long.
Population: 99 (1990); 93 (2000); 97 (2010); Density: 45.1 persons per square mile (2010); Race: 95.9% White, 1.0% Black, 0.0% Asian, 0.0% American Indian/Alaska Native, 0.0% Native Hawaiian/Other Pacific Islander, 3.1% Other, 0.0% Hispanic of any race (2010); Average household size: 2.31 (2010); Median age: 51.9 (2010); Males per 100 females: 125.6 (2010); Marriage status: 25.7% never married, 67.6% now married, 1.9% widowed, 4.8% divorced (2006-2010 5-year est.); Foreign born: 0.0% (2006-2010 5-year est.); Ancestry (includes multiple

ancestries): 28.4% German, 10.1% American, 9.2% Irish, 5.5% French, 2.8% Scandinavian (2006-2010 5-year est.).
Economy: Single-family building permits issued: 0 (2011); Multi-family building permits issued: 0 (2011); Employment by occupation: 10.0% management, 10.0% professional, 15.0% services, 0.0% sales, 0.0% farming, 10.0% construction, 10.0% production (2006-2010 5-year est.).
Income: Per capita income: $19,826 (2006-2010 5-year est.); Median household income: $37,045 (2006-2010 5-year est.); Average household income: $41,810 (2006-2010 5-year est.); Percent of households with income of $100,000 or more: 3.8% (2006-2010 5-year est.); Poverty rate: 0.0% (2006-2010 5-year est.).
Education: Percent of population age 25 and over with: High school diploma (including GED) or higher: 93.9% (2006-2010 5-year est.); Bachelor's degree or higher: 7.1% (2006-2010 5-year est.); Master's degree or higher: 2.0% (2006-2010 5-year est.).
Housing: Homeownership rate: 76.2% (2010); Median home value: $90,000 (2006-2010 5-year est.); Median contract rent: $431 per month (2006-2010 5-year est.); Median year structure built: 1961 (2006-2010 5-year est.).
Transportation: Commute to work: 85.0% car, 0.0% public transportation, 0.0% walk, 15.0% work from home (2006-2010 5-year est.); Travel time to work: 11.8% less than 15 minutes, 41.2% 15 to 30 minutes, 17.6% 30 to 45 minutes, 17.6% 45 to 60 minutes, 11.8% 60 minutes or more (2006-2010 5-year est.)

KISKIMERE (CDP). Covers a land area of 0.319 square miles and a water area of 0.050 square miles. Located at 40.62° N. Lat; 79.59° W. Long. Elevation is 912 feet.
Population: n/a (1990); n/a (2000); 136 (2010); Density: 426.8 persons per square mile (2010); Race: 87.5% White, 11.0% Black, 0.0% Asian, 0.0% American Indian/Alaska Native, 0.0% Native Hawaiian/Other Pacific Islander, 1.5% Other, 0.0% Hispanic of any race (2010); Average household size: 2.34 (2010); Median age: 42.0 (2010); Males per 100 females: 94.3 (2010); Marriage status: 0.0% never married, 82.5% now married, 0.0% widowed, 17.5% divorced (2006-2010 5-year est.); Foreign born: 0.0% (2006-2010 5-year est.); Ancestry (includes multiple ancestries): 17.5% German, 17.5% Italian, 15.0% French, 12.5% Dutch (2006-2010 5-year est.).
Economy: Income: Per capita income: $32,395 (2006-2010 5-year est.); Median household income: $37,250 (2006-2010 5-year est.); Average household income: $56,122 (2006-2010 5-year est.); Percent of households with income of $100,000 or more: n/a (2006-2010 5-year est.); Poverty rate: 0.0% (2006-2010 5-year est.).
Education: Percent of population age 25 and over with: High school diploma (including GED) or higher: 72.5% (2006-2010 5-year est.); Bachelor's degree or higher: 0.0% (2006-2010 5-year est.); Master's degree or higher: 0.0% (2006-2010 5-year est.).
Housing: Homeownership rate: 79.3% (2010); Median home value: $65,900 (2006-2010 5-year est.); Median contract rent: n/a per month (2006-2010 5-year est.); Median year structure built: 1969 (2006-2010 5-year est.).
Transportation: Commute to work: 100.0% car, 0.0% public transportation, 0.0% walk, 0.0% work from home (2006-2010 5-year est.); Travel time to work: 0.0% less than 15 minutes, 0.0% 15 to 30 minutes, 100.0% 30 to 45 minutes, 0.0% 45 to 60 minutes, 0.0% 60 minutes or more (2006-2010 5-year est.)

KISKIMINETAS (township). Covers a land area of 40.674 square miles and a water area of 0.367 square miles. Located at 40.58° N. Lat; 79.48° W. Long.
Population: 5,456 (1990); 4,950 (2000); 4,800 (2010); Density: 118.0 persons per square mile (2010); Race: 98.8% White, 0.5% Black, 0.1% Asian, 0.0% American Indian/Alaska Native, 0.0% Native Hawaiian/Other Pacific Islander, 0.6% Other, 0.4% Hispanic of any race (2010); Average household size: 2.46 (2010); Median age: 46.2 (2010); Males per 100 females: 100.3 (2010); Marriage status: 19.2% never married, 61.8% now married, 8.3% widowed, 10.7% divorced (2006-2010 5-year est.); Foreign born: 0.0% (2006-2010 5-year est.); Ancestry (includes multiple ancestries): 41.3% German, 21.3% Irish, 10.7% Italian, 7.4% Polish, 6.2% Dutch (2006-2010 5-year est.).
Economy: Single-family building permits issued: 2 (2011); Multi-family building permits issued: 0 (2011); Employment by occupation: 7.9% management, 1.4% professional, 18.8% services, 15.8% sales, 2.8% farming, 14.7% construction, 10.1% production (2006-2010 5-year est.).

Income: Per capita income: $23,732 (2006-2010 5-year est.); Median household income: $41,890 (2006-2010 5-year est.); Average household income: $52,633 (2006-2010 5-year est.); Percent of households with income of $100,000 or more: 8.3% (2006-2010 5-year est.); Poverty rate: 12.2% (2006-2010 5-year est.).
Education: Percent of population age 25 and over with: High school diploma (including GED) or higher: 85.5% (2006-2010 5-year est.); Bachelor's degree or higher: 9.8% (2006-2010 5-year est.); Master's degree or higher: 1.8% (2006-2010 5-year est.).
Housing: Homeownership rate: 84.0% (2010); Median home value: $93,800 (2006-2010 5-year est.); Median contract rent: $489 per month (2006-2010 5-year est.); Median year structure built: 1970 (2006-2010 5-year est.).
Safety: Violent crime rate: 2.1 per 10,000 population; Property crime rate: 116.3 per 10,000 population (2011).
Transportation: Commute to work: 97.0% car, 0.0% public transportation, 0.7% walk, 1.4% work from home (2006-2010 5-year est.); Travel time to work: 17.3% less than 15 minutes, 31.7% 15 to 30 minutes, 32.3% 30 to 45 minutes, 6.8% 45 to 60 minutes, 11.9% 60 minutes or more (2006-2010 5-year est.)
Additional Information Contacts
Allegheny Valley Chamber of Commerce . . . . (724) 224-3400
  http://alleghenyvalleychamber.com

KITTANNING (borough). County seat. Covers a land area of 0.996 square miles and a water area of 0.254 square miles. Located at 40.83° N. Lat; 79.52° W. Long. Elevation is 791 feet.
History: The town of Kittanning occupies the site of a Native American town of the same name, the largest in western Pennsylvania. Homesteaders arrived here in 1791, and by 1796 a permanent settlement had been established. Many of the early settlers were of German and Scots-Irish heritage.
Population: 5,120 (1990); 4,787 (2000); 4,044 (2010); Density: 4,058.8 persons per square mile (2010); Race: 97.0% White, 0.9% Black, 0.4% Asian, 0.1% American Indian/Alaska Native, 0.0% Native Hawaiian/Other Pacific Islander, 1.6% Other, 0.9% Hispanic of any race (2010); Average household size: 2.12 (2010); Median age: 40.9 (2010); Males per 100 females: 82.0 (2010); Marriage status: 28.5% never married, 43.4% now married, 12.0% widowed, 16.1% divorced (2006-2010 5-year est.); Foreign born: 0.7% (2006-2010 5-year est.); Ancestry (includes multiple ancestries): 27.5% German, 16.7% Irish, 13.7% Italian, 9.6% American, 7.5% English (2006-2010 5-year est.).
Economy: Single-family building permits issued: 0 (2011); Multi-family building permits issued: 0 (2011); Employment by occupation: 6.4% management, 2.4% professional, 9.1% services, 20.9% sales, 2.4% farming, 15.8% construction, 9.4% production (2006-2010 5-year est.).
Income: Per capita income: $18,104 (2006-2010 5-year est.); Median household income: $33,135 (2006-2010 5-year est.); Average household income: $41,081 (2006-2010 5-year est.); Percent of households with income of $100,000 or more: 5.4% (2006-2010 5-year est.); Poverty rate: 21.5% (2006-2010 5-year est.).
Education: Percent of population age 25 and over with: High school diploma (including GED) or higher: 85.5% (2006-2010 5-year est.); Bachelor's degree or higher: 14.1% (2006-2010 5-year est.); Master's degree or higher: 5.4% (2006-2010 5-year est.).
School District(s)
Armstrong SD (KG-12)
  2010-11 Enrollment: 5,544 . . . . (724) 763-7151
Vocational/Technical School(s)
Kittanning Beauty School (Private, For-profit)
  Fall 2010 Enrollment: 62 . . . . (724) 287-0708
  2011-12 Tuition: $13,800
Lenape Area Vocational Technical School Practical Nursing Program (Public)
  Fall 2010 Enrollment: 138 . . . . (724) 545-7311
  2011-12 Tuition: $12,000
Housing: Homeownership rate: 39.0% (2010); Median home value: $61,200 (2006-2010 5-year est.); Median contract rent: $388 per month (2006-2010 5-year est.); Median year structure built: before 1940 (2006-2010 5-year est.).
Hospitals: Armstrong County Memorial Hospital
Safety: Violent crime rate: 12.3 per 10,000 population; Property crime rate: 61.6 per 10,000 population (2011).
Newspapers: Leader Times (Local news; Circulation 8,181)

Transportation: Commute to work: 88.8% car, 0.9% public transportation, 6.0% walk, 3.6% work from home (2006-2010 5-year est.); Travel time to work: 44.5% less than 15 minutes, 29.3% 15 to 30 minutes, 14.1% 30 to 45 minutes, 5.3% 45 to 60 minutes, 6.9% 60 minutes or more (2006-2010 5-year est.)

Additional Information Contacts
Armstrong County Chamber of Commerce . . . . (724) 543-1305
http://www.armstrongchamber.org

KITTANNING (township).
Covers a land area of 30.712 square miles and a water area of 0.083 square miles. Located at 40.76° N. Lat; 79.44° W. Long.

History: Original site was an Indian village. Settled 1796; laid out 1804; incorporated 1821.

Population: 2,322 (1990); 2,359 (2000); 2,265 (2010); Density: 73.7 persons per square mile (2010); Race: 99.0% White, 0.3% Black, 0.2% Asian, 0.0% American Indian/Alaska Native, 0.0% Native Hawaiian/Other Pacific Islander, 0.5% Other, 0.3% Hispanic of any race (2010); Average household size: 2.46 (2010); Median age: 47.4 (2010); Males per 100 females: 95.8 (2010); Marriage status: 25.4% never married, 57.6% now married, 10.3% widowed, 6.8% divorced (2006-2010 5-year est.); Foreign born: 0.4% (2006-2010 5-year est.); Ancestry (includes multiple ancestries): 52.4% German, 17.1% Irish, 13.8% English, 6.7% Italian, 4.3% American (2006-2010 5-year est.).

Economy: Employment by occupation: 6.3% management, 0.9% professional, 10.7% services, 16.4% sales, 3.0% farming, 17.9% construction, 8.6% production (2006-2010 5-year est.).

Income: Per capita income: $22,406 (2006-2010 5-year est.); Median household income: $46,151 (2006-2010 5-year est.); Average household income: $55,680 (2006-2010 5-year est.); Percent of households with income of $100,000 or more: 12.5% (2006-2010 5-year est.); Poverty rate: 11.3% (2006-2010 5-year est.).

Education: Percent of population age 25 and over with: High school diploma (including GED) or higher: 92.6% (2006-2010 5-year est.); Bachelor's degree or higher: 9.9% (2006-2010 5-year est.); Master's degree or higher: 2.4% (2006-2010 5-year est.).

Vocational/Technical School(s)
Kittanning Beauty School (Private, For-profit)
    Fall 2010 Enrollment: 62 . . . . (724) 287-0708
    2011-12 Tuition: $13,800
Lenape Area Vocational Technical School Practical Nursing Program (Public)
    Fall 2010 Enrollment: 138 . . . . (724) 545-7311
    2011-12 Tuition: $12,000

Housing: Homeownership rate: 82.3% (2010); Median home value: $106,600 (2006-2010 5-year est.); Median contract rent: $477 per month (2006-2010 5-year est.); Median year structure built: 1969 (2006-2010 5-year est.).

Hospitals: Armstrong County Memorial Hospital

Newspapers: Leader Times (Local news; Circulation 8,181)

Transportation: Commute to work: 91.5% car, 0.0% public transportation, 1.4% walk, 4.2% work from home (2006-2010 5-year est.); Travel time to work: 30.8% less than 15 minutes, 32.9% 15 to 30 minutes, 16.0% 30 to 45 minutes, 10.1% 45 to 60 minutes, 10.2% 60 minutes or more (2006-2010 5-year est.)

Additional Information Contacts
Armstrong County Chamber of Commerce . . . . (724) 543-1305
http://www.armstrongchamber.org

LEECHBURG (borough).
Covers a land area of 0.439 square miles and a water area of 0.041 square miles. Located at 40.63° N. Lat; 79.60° W. Long. Elevation is 794 feet.

History: Laid out 1828, incorporated 1850.

Population: 2,504 (1990); 2,386 (2000); 2,156 (2010); Density: 4,907.5 persons per square mile (2010); Race: 96.6% White, 1.3% Black, 0.2% Asian, 0.0% American Indian/Alaska Native, 0.0% Native Hawaiian/Other Pacific Islander, 1.9% Other, 1.1% Hispanic of any race (2010); Average household size: 2.13 (2010); Median age: 41.8 (2010); Males per 100 females: 88.5 (2010); Marriage status: 24.1% never married, 50.4% now married, 13.5% widowed, 12.0% divorced (2006-2010 5-year est.); Foreign born: 1.2% (2006-2010 5-year est.); Ancestry (includes multiple ancestries): 39.5% German, 21.0% Irish, 19.3% Italian, 8.0% Polish, 7.7% English (2006-2010 5-year est.).

Economy: Single-family building permits issued: 0 (2011); Multi-family building permits issued: 0 (2011); Employment by occupation: 4.4% management, 3.1% professional, 16.0% services, 22.2% sales, 1.0% farming, 16.1% construction, 11.1% production (2006-2010 5-year est.).

Income: Per capita income: $22,159 (2006-2010 5-year est.); Median household income: $38,466 (2006-2010 5-year est.); Average household income: $47,904 (2006-2010 5-year est.); Percent of households with income of $100,000 or more: 9.4% (2006-2010 5-year est.); Poverty rate: 17.0% (2006-2010 5-year est.).

Education: Percent of population age 25 and over with: High school diploma (including GED) or higher: 87.2% (2006-2010 5-year est.); Bachelor's degree or higher: 12.5% (2006-2010 5-year est.); Master's degree or higher: 2.7% (2006-2010 5-year est.).

School District(s)
Kiski Area SD (KG-12)
    2010-11 Enrollment: 3,967 . . . . (724) 845-2022
Leechburg Area SD (KG-12)
    2010-11 Enrollment: 815 . . . . (724) 845-7701

Housing: Homeownership rate: 59.9% (2010); Median home value: $69,500 (2006-2010 5-year est.); Median contract rent: $419 per month (2006-2010 5-year est.); Median year structure built: before 1940 (2006-2010 5-year est.).

Transportation: Commute to work: 89.8% car, 1.4% public transportation, 4.9% walk, 3.3% work from home (2006-2010 5-year est.); Travel time to work: 24.5% less than 15 minutes, 22.6% 15 to 30 minutes, 16.5% 30 to 45 minutes, 23.9% 45 to 60 minutes, 12.6% 60 minutes or more (2006-2010 5-year est.)

Additional Information Contacts
Allegheny Valley Chamber of Commerce . . . . (724) 224-3400
http://alleghenyvalleychamber.com

LENAPE HEIGHTS (CDP).
Covers a land area of 0.737 square miles and a water area of 0 square miles. Located at 40.76° N. Lat; 79.52° W. Long. Elevation is 971 feet.

Population: 1,230 (1990); 1,212 (2000); 1,167 (2010); Density: 1,583.0 persons per square mile (2010); Race: 99.0% White, 0.5% Black, 0.3% Asian, 0.0% American Indian/Alaska Native, 0.0% Native Hawaiian/Other Pacific Islander, 0.2% Other, 0.1% Hispanic of any race (2010); Average household size: 2.24 (2010); Median age: 50.3 (2010); Males per 100 females: 92.9 (2010); Marriage status: 14.5% never married, 56.8% now married, 7.6% widowed, 21.0% divorced (2006-2010 5-year est.); Foreign born: 0.0% (2006-2010 5-year est.); Ancestry (includes multiple ancestries): 41.5% German, 21.1% Irish, 16.8% American, 13.1% English, 7.2% Slovak (2006-2010 5-year est.).

Economy: Employment by occupation: 2.5% management, 2.9% professional, 18.0% services, 24.5% sales, 0.0% farming, 6.5% construction, 10.1% production (2006-2010 5-year est.).

Income: Per capita income: $20,026 (2006-2010 5-year est.); Median household income: $41,316 (2006-2010 5-year est.); Average household income: $45,997 (2006-2010 5-year est.); Percent of households with income of $100,000 or more: 5.4% (2006-2010 5-year est.); Poverty rate: 15.7% (2006-2010 5-year est.).

Education: Percent of population age 25 and over with: High school diploma (including GED) or higher: 85.4% (2006-2010 5-year est.); Bachelor's degree or higher: 16.0% (2006-2010 5-year est.); Master's degree or higher: 7.5% (2006-2010 5-year est.).

Housing: Homeownership rate: 85.4% (2010); Median home value: $94,700 (2006-2010 5-year est.); Median contract rent: $442 per month (2006-2010 5-year est.); Median year structure built: 1956 (2006-2010 5-year est.).

Transportation: Commute to work: 93.9% car, 0.0% public transportation, 6.1% walk, 0.0% work from home (2006-2010 5-year est.); Travel time to work: 69.3% less than 15 minutes, 15.8% 15 to 30 minutes, 14.9% 30 to 45 minutes, 0.0% 45 to 60 minutes, 0.0% 60 minutes or more (2006-2010 5-year est.)

Additional Information Contacts
Armstrong County Chamber of Commerce . . . . (724) 543-1305
http://www.armstrongchamber.org

MADISON (township).
Covers a land area of 30.030 square miles and a water area of 0.887 square miles. Located at 40.96° N. Lat; 79.45° W. Long.

Population: 941 (1990); 943 (2000); 820 (2010); Density: 27.3 persons per square mile (2010); Race: 98.8% White, 0.5% Black, 0.0% Asian, 0.0% American Indian/Alaska Native, 0.0% Native Hawaiian/Other Pacific Islander, 0.7% Other, 0.1% Hispanic of any race (2010); Average household size: 2.32 (2010); Median age: 47.1 (2010); Males per 100

females: 104.5 (2010); Marriage status: 23.4% never married, 66.7% now married, 4.3% widowed, 5.6% divorced (2006-2010 5-year est.); Foreign born: 0.0% (2006-2010 5-year est.); Ancestry (includes multiple ancestries): 52.3% German, 14.3% Irish, 8.3% Italian, 4.8% English, 4.3% Dutch (2006-2010 5-year est.).

Economy: Single-family building permits issued: 0 (2011); Multi-family building permits issued: 0 (2011); Employment by occupation: 5.2% management, 1.1% professional, 12.5% services, 12.3% sales, 3.8% farming, 29.2% construction, 20.4% production (2006-2010 5-year est.).

Income: Per capita income: $22,907 (2006-2010 5-year est.); Median household income: $48,750 (2006-2010 5-year est.); Average household income: $51,326 (2006-2010 5-year est.); Percent of households with income of $100,000 or more: 10.4% (2006-2010 5-year est.); Poverty rate: 6.7% (2006-2010 5-year est.).

Education: Percent of population age 25 and over with: High school diploma (including GED) or higher: 85.1% (2006-2010 5-year est.); Bachelor's degree or higher: 9.7% (2006-2010 5-year est.); Master's degree or higher: 2.5% (2006-2010 5-year est.).

Housing: Homeownership rate: 82.7% (2010); Median home value: $101,200 (2006-2010 5-year est.); Median contract rent: $246 per month (2006-2010 5-year est.); Median year structure built: before 1940 (2006-2010 5-year est.).

Transportation: Commute to work: 94.0% car, 0.0% public transportation, 2.3% walk, 3.7% work from home (2006-2010 5-year est.); Travel time to work: 9.5% less than 15 minutes, 31.2% 15 to 30 minutes, 24.9% 30 to 45 minutes, 20.8% 45 to 60 minutes, 13.6% 60 minutes or more (2006-2010 5-year est.)

MAHONING (township). Covers a land area of 24.782 square miles and a water area of 0.437 square miles. Located at 40.96° N. Lat; 79.34° W. Long. Elevation is 833 feet.

Population: 1,504 (1990); 1,502 (2000); 1,425 (2010); Density: 57.5 persons per square mile (2010); Race: 99.4% White, 0.1% Black, 0.1% Asian, 0.1% American Indian/Alaska Native, 0.0% Native Hawaiian/Other Pacific Islander, 0.3% Other, 0.3% Hispanic of any race (2010); Average household size: 2.44 (2010); Median age: 44.7 (2010); Males per 100 females: 95.2 (2010); Marriage status: 20.6% never married, 63.0% now married, 10.6% widowed, 5.8% divorced (2006-2010 5-year est.); Foreign born: 0.2% (2006-2010 5-year est.); Ancestry (includes multiple ancestries): 53.4% German, 21.3% Irish, 9.4% Italian, 5.2% American, 4.8% Dutch (2006-2010 5-year est.).

Economy: Single-family building permits issued: 0 (2011); Multi-family building permits issued: 0 (2011); Employment by occupation: 9.8% management, 1.4% professional, 14.6% services, 14.2% sales, 1.2% farming, 17.8% construction, 12.8% production (2006-2010 5-year est.).

Income: Per capita income: $21,201 (2006-2010 5-year est.); Median household income: $42,361 (2006-2010 5-year est.); Average household income: $50,120 (2006-2010 5-year est.); Percent of households with income of $100,000 or more: 6.7% (2006-2010 5-year est.); Poverty rate: 6.8% (2006-2010 5-year est.).

Education: Percent of population age 25 and over with: High school diploma (including GED) or higher: 86.3% (2006-2010 5-year est.); Bachelor's degree or higher: 9.2% (2006-2010 5-year est.); Master's degree or higher: 3.4% (2006-2010 5-year est.).

Housing: Homeownership rate: 80.5% (2010); Median home value: $69,900 (2006-2010 5-year est.); Median contract rent: $319 per month (2006-2010 5-year est.); Median year structure built: 1950 (2006-2010 5-year est.).

Transportation: Commute to work: 92.1% car, 0.4% public transportation, 4.4% walk, 3.1% work from home (2006-2010 5-year est.); Travel time to work: 31.9% less than 15 minutes, 13.4% 15 to 30 minutes, 25.5% 30 to 45 minutes, 13.2% 45 to 60 minutes, 16.0% 60 minutes or more (2006-2010 5-year est.)

Additional Information Contacts
Armstrong County Chamber of Commerce . . . . (724) 543-1305
http://www.armstrongchamber.org

MANOR (township). Covers a land area of 16.585 square miles and a water area of 0.554 square miles. Located at 40.77° N. Lat; 79.51° W. Long.

Population: 4,384 (1990); 4,231 (2000); 4,227 (2010); Density: 254.9 persons per square mile (2010); Race: 98.6% White, 0.5% Black, 0.1% Asian, 0.0% American Indian/Alaska Native, 0.0% Native Hawaiian/Other Pacific Islander, 0.8% Other, 0.4% Hispanic of any race (2010); Average household size: 2.27 (2010); Median age: 48.4 (2010); Males per 100

females: 95.9 (2010); Marriage status: 24.9% never married, 53.3% now married, 8.8% widowed, 13.0% divorced (2006-2010 5-year est.); Foreign born: 3.9% (2006-2010 5-year est.); Ancestry (includes multiple ancestries): 38.0% German, 17.5% Irish, 12.6% English, 11.5% Polish, 8.8% Italian (2006-2010 5-year est.).

Economy: Employment by occupation: 8.6% management, 1.2% professional, 16.8% services, 21.9% sales, 2.9% farming, 5.0% construction, 3.6% production (2006-2010 5-year est.).

Income: Per capita income: $21,723 (2006-2010 5-year est.); Median household income: $37,304 (2006-2010 5-year est.); Average household income: $49,638 (2006-2010 5-year est.); Percent of households with income of $100,000 or more: 12.4% (2006-2010 5-year est.); Poverty rate: 12.4% (2006-2010 5-year est.).

Education: Percent of population age 25 and over with: High school diploma (including GED) or higher: 87.3% (2006-2010 5-year est.); Bachelor's degree or higher: 12.9% (2006-2010 5-year est.); Master's degree or higher: 4.8% (2006-2010 5-year est.).

Housing: Homeownership rate: 78.9% (2010); Median home value: $98,300 (2006-2010 5-year est.); Median contract rent: $422 per month (2006-2010 5-year est.); Median year structure built: 1959 (2006-2010 5-year est.).

Safety: Violent crime rate: 0.0 per 10,000 population; Property crime rate: 0.0 per 10,000 population (2011).

Transportation: Commute to work: 94.5% car, 0.0% public transportation, 3.0% walk, 2.5% work from home (2006-2010 5-year est.); Travel time to work: 52.0% less than 15 minutes, 15.8% 15 to 30 minutes, 19.9% 30 to 45 minutes, 5.1% 45 to 60 minutes, 7.1% 60 minutes or more (2006-2010 5-year est.)

Additional Information Contacts
Armstrong County Chamber of Commerce . . . . (724) 543-1305
http://www.armstrongchamber.org

MANORVILLE (borough). Covers a land area of 0.101 square miles and a water area of 0.019 square miles. Located at 40.79° N. Lat; 79.52° W. Long. Elevation is 797 feet.

Population: 418 (1990); 401 (2000); 410 (2010); Density: 4,069.6 persons per square mile (2010); Race: 98.8% White, 0.5% Black, 0.5% Asian, 0.0% American Indian/Alaska Native, 0.0% Native Hawaiian/Other Pacific Islander, 0.2% Other, 0.2% Hispanic of any race (2010); Average household size: 2.46 (2010); Median age: 40.1 (2010); Males per 100 females: 91.6 (2010); Marriage status: 33.7% never married, 49.4% now married, 8.4% widowed, 8.4% divorced (2006-2010 5-year est.); Foreign born: 0.5% (2006-2010 5-year est.); Ancestry (includes multiple ancestries): 43.3% German, 16.4% Polish, 15.0% Irish, 13.7% Slovak, 13.5% English (2006-2010 5-year est.).

Economy: Single-family building permits issued: 0 (2011); Multi-family building permits issued: 0 (2011); Employment by occupation: 0.0% management, 1.8% professional, 17.0% services, 14.8% sales, 2.2% farming, 10.8% construction, 8.5% production (2006-2010 5-year est.).

Income: Per capita income: $25,918 (2006-2010 5-year est.); Median household income: $49,792 (2006-2010 5-year est.); Average household income: $56,457 (2006-2010 5-year est.); Percent of households with income of $100,000 or more: 7.6% (2006-2010 5-year est.); Poverty rate: 8.2% (2006-2010 5-year est.).

Education: Percent of population age 25 and over with: High school diploma (including GED) or higher: 93.4% (2006-2010 5-year est.); Bachelor's degree or higher: 22.1% (2006-2010 5-year est.); Master's degree or higher: 8.5% (2006-2010 5-year est.).

Housing: Homeownership rate: 70.0% (2010); Median home value: $94,400 (2006-2010 5-year est.); Median contract rent: $445 per month (2006-2010 5-year est.); Median year structure built: before 1940 (2006-2010 5-year est.).

Transportation: Commute to work: 96.3% car, 0.9% public transportation, 2.8% walk, 0.0% work from home (2006-2010 5-year est.); Travel time to work: 36.9% less than 15 minutes, 9.7% 15 to 30 minutes, 33.2% 30 to 45 minutes, 9.7% 45 to 60 minutes, 10.6% 60 minutes or more (2006-2010 5-year est.)

MCGRANN (unincorporated postal area)
Zip Code: 16236

Covers a land area of 0.065 square miles and a water area of 0.080 square miles. Located at 40.78° N. Lat; 79.52° W. Long. Elevation is 804 feet. Population: 262 (2010); Density: 3,987.0 persons per square mile (2010); Race: 98.9% White, 0.0% Black, 0.0% Asian, 0.0% American Indian/Alaska Native, 0.0% Native Hawaiian/Other Pacific

Islander, 1.1% Other, 1.1% Hispanic of any race (2010); Average household size: 2.26 (2010); Median age: 40.3 (2010); Males per 100 females: 92.6 (2010); Homeownership rate: 62.9% (2010)

NORTH APOLLO (borough). Covers a land area of 0.543 square miles and a water area of 0.055 square miles. Located at 40.59° N. Lat; 79.56° W. Long. Elevation is 817 feet.

History: Incorporated 1930.

Population: 1,391 (1990); 1,426 (2000); 1,297 (2010); Density: 2,386.8 persons per square mile (2010); Race: 96.1% White, 1.6% Black, 0.3% Asian, 0.0% American Indian/Alaska Native, 0.0% Native Hawaiian/Other Pacific Islander, 2.0% Other, 0.8% Hispanic of any race (2010); Average household size: 2.38 (2010); Median age: 44.5 (2010); Males per 100 females: 95.9 (2010); Marriage status: 23.7% never married, 59.0% now married, 6.5% widowed, 10.7% divorced (2006-2010 5-year est.); Foreign born: 0.3% (2006-2010 5-year est.); Ancestry (includes multiple ancestries): 35.2% German, 29.2% Irish, 13.1% Italian, 11.5% English, 8.7% Slovak (2006-2010 5-year est.).

Economy: Single-family building permits issued: 0 (2011); Multi-family building permits issued: 0 (2011); Employment by occupation: 8.8% management, 8.0% professional, 12.6% services, 16.4% sales, 1.8% farming, 10.7% construction, 6.5% production (2006-2010 5-year est.).

Income: Per capita income: $22,346 (2006-2010 5-year est.); Median household income: $42,083 (2006-2010 5-year est.); Average household income: $50,007 (2006-2010 5-year est.); Percent of households with income of $100,000 or more: 11.0% (2006-2010 5-year est.); Poverty rate: 11.4% (2006-2010 5-year est.).

Education: Percent of population age 25 and over with: High school diploma (including GED) or higher: 94.0% (2006-2010 5-year est.); Bachelor's degree or higher: 16.5% (2006-2010 5-year est.); Master's degree or higher: 3.2% (2006-2010 5-year est.).

Housing: Homeownership rate: 78.3% (2010); Median home value: $90,700 (2006-2010 5-year est.); Median contract rent: $431 per month (2006-2010 5-year est.); Median year structure built: 1953 (2006-2010 5-year est.).

Transportation: Commute to work: 92.1% car, 0.0% public transportation, 6.4% walk, 1.5% work from home (2006-2010 5-year est.); Travel time to work: 29.5% less than 15 minutes, 31.8% 15 to 30 minutes, 15.0% 30 to 45 minutes, 9.1% 45 to 60 minutes, 14.7% 60 minutes or more (2006-2010 5-year est.)

Additional Information Contacts

Strongland Chamber of Commerce................... (724) 845-5426
    http://www.strongland.org

NORTH BUFFALO (township). Covers a land area of 24.713 square miles and a water area of 0.426 square miles. Located at 40.78° N. Lat; 79.61° W. Long. Elevation is 1,073 feet.

Population: 2,897 (1990); 2,942 (2000); 3,011 (2010); Density: 121.8 persons per square mile (2010); Race: 98.8% White, 0.3% Black, 0.4% Asian, 0.0% American Indian/Alaska Native, 0.0% Native Hawaiian/Other Pacific Islander, 0.5% Other, 0.2% Hispanic of any race (2010); Average household size: 2.44 (2010); Median age: 46.8 (2010); Males per 100 females: 103.0 (2010); Marriage status: 21.0% never married, 65.8% now married, 5.0% widowed, 8.3% divorced (2006-2010 5-year est.); Foreign born: 0.8% (2006-2010 5-year est.); Ancestry (includes multiple ancestries): 38.1% German, 21.6% Irish, 16.6% Italian, 10.0% English, 8.4% American (2006-2010 5-year est.).

Economy: Single-family building permits issued: 6 (2011); Multi-family building permits issued: 0 (2011); Employment by occupation: 12.7% management, 1.2% professional, 12.5% services, 14.5% sales, 4.0% farming, 8.4% construction, 7.1% production (2006-2010 5-year est.).

Income: Per capita income: $23,733 (2006-2010 5-year est.); Median household income: $52,713 (2006-2010 5-year est.); Average household income: $61,303 (2006-2010 5-year est.); Percent of households with income of $100,000 or more: 14.7% (2006-2010 5-year est.); Poverty rate: 5.4% (2006-2010 5-year est.).

Education: Percent of population age 25 and over with: High school diploma (including GED) or higher: 90.7% (2006-2010 5-year est.); Bachelor's degree or higher: 17.2% (2006-2010 5-year est.); Master's degree or higher: 5.6% (2006-2010 5-year est.).

Housing: Homeownership rate: 83.8% (2010); Median home value: $110,100 (2006-2010 5-year est.); Median contract rent: $434 per month (2006-2010 5-year est.); Median year structure built: 1965 (2006-2010 5-year est.).

Transportation: Commute to work: 96.5% car, 0.0% public transportation, 0.0% walk, 2.9% work from home (2006-2010 5-year est.); Travel time to work: 41.0% less than 15 minutes, 24.3% 15 to 30 minutes, 13.1% 30 to 45 minutes, 10.8% 45 to 60 minutes, 10.7% 60 minutes or more (2006-2010 5-year est.)

Additional Information Contacts

Allegheny Valley Chamber of Commerce.............. (724) 224-3400
    http://alleghenyvalleychamber.com

NORTH VANDERGRIFT (CDP). Covers a land area of 0.606 square miles and a water area of 0.038 square miles. Located at 40.61° N. Lat; 79.55° W. Long. Elevation is 787 feet.

Population: n/a (1990); n/a (2000); 447 (2010); Density: 738.0 persons per square mile (2010); Race: 88.6% White, 8.5% Black, 0.0% Asian, 0.0% American Indian/Alaska Native, 0.0% Native Hawaiian/Other Pacific Islander, 2.9% Other, 0.4% Hispanic of any race (2010); Average household size: 2.39 (2010); Median age: 40.5 (2010); Males per 100 females: 111.8 (2010); Marriage status: 29.8% never married, 51.7% now married, 9.4% widowed, 9.1% divorced (2006-2010 5-year est.); Foreign born: 0.0% (2006-2010 5-year est.); Ancestry (includes multiple ancestries): 41.6% German, 32.8% Irish, 11.9% Italian, 3.4% Slovak, 3.4% Pennsylvania German (2006-2010 5-year est.).

Economy: Employment by occupation: 0.0% management, 0.0% professional, 7.3% services, 0.0% sales, 0.0% farming, 19.2% construction, 32.5% production (2006-2010 5-year est.).

Income: Per capita income: $18,279 (2006-2010 5-year est.); Median household income: $26,719 (2006-2010 5-year est.); Average household income: $37,877 (2006-2010 5-year est.); Percent of households with income of $100,000 or more: n/a (2006-2010 5-year est.); Poverty rate: 28.0% (2006-2010 5-year est.).

Education: Percent of population age 25 and over with: High school diploma (including GED) or higher: 78.4% (2006-2010 5-year est.); Bachelor's degree or higher: 5.2% (2006-2010 5-year est.); Master's degree or higher: 2.1% (2006-2010 5-year est.).

Housing: Homeownership rate: 56.1% (2010); Median home value: $35,600 (2006-2010 5-year est.); Median contract rent: $433 per month (2006-2010 5-year est.); Median year structure built: before 1940 (2006-2010 5-year est.).

Transportation: Commute to work: 98.7% car, 0.0% public transportation, 1.3% walk, 0.0% work from home (2006-2010 5-year est.); Travel time to work: 56.4% less than 15 minutes, 28.6% 15 to 30 minutes, 12.8% 30 to 45 minutes, 2.2% 45 to 60 minutes, 0.0% 60 minutes or more (2006-2010 5-year est.)

NU MINE (unincorporated postal area)

Zip Code: 16244

Covers a land area of 1.205 square miles and a water area of 0 square miles. Located at 40.79° N. Lat; 79.27° W. Long. Population: 265 (2010); Density: 219.8 persons per square mile (2010); Race: 98.5% White, 0.8% Black, 0.0% Asian, 0.0% American Indian/Alaska Native, 0.0% Native Hawaiian/Other Pacific Islander, 0.7% Other, 0.4% Hispanic of any race (2010); Average household size: 2.62 (2010); Median age: 40.4 (2010); Males per 100 females: 87.9 (2010); Homeownership rate: 86.2% (2010)

OAK RIDGE (unincorporated postal area)

Zip Code: 16245

Covers a land area of 0.593 square miles and a water area of 0 square miles. Located at 41.00° N. Lat; 79.29° W. Long. Elevation is 1,076 feet. Population: 207 (2010); Density: 348.9 persons per square mile (2010); Race: 98.1% White, 0.0% Black, 0.0% Asian, 0.0% American Indian/Alaska Native, 0.0% Native Hawaiian/Other Pacific Islander, 1.9% Other, 1.0% Hispanic of any race (2010); Average household size: 2.33 (2010); Median age: 41.9 (2010); Males per 100 females: 88.2 (2010); Homeownership rate: 74.1% (2010)

ORCHARD HILLS (CDP). Covers a land area of 3.946 square miles and a water area of 0.026 square miles. Located at 40.58° N. Lat; 79.55° W. Long. Elevation is 1,142 feet.

Population: 2,271 (1990); 2,152 (2000); 1,952 (2010); Density: 494.6 persons per square mile (2010); Race: 98.8% White, 0.8% Black, 0.2% Asian, 0.0% American Indian/Alaska Native, 0.0% Native Hawaiian/Other Pacific Islander, 0.2% Other, 0.4% Hispanic of any race (2010); Average household size: 2.42 (2010); Median age: 46.6 (2010); Males per 100 females: 96.8 (2010); Marriage status: 16.6% never married, 57.3% now

married, 9.4% widowed, 16.7% divorced (2006-2010 5-year est.); Foreign born: 0.0% (2006-2010 5-year est.); Ancestry (includes multiple ancestries): 30.7% German, 16.2% Italian, 12.4% Irish, 9.4% Polish, 9.0% American (2006-2010 5-year est.).

Economy: Employment by occupation: 8.9% management, 1.1% professional, 22.5% services, 16.4% sales, 1.7% farming, 11.8% construction, 9.8% production (2006-2010 5-year est.).

Income: Per capita income: $16,779 (2006-2010 5-year est.); Median household income: $27,179 (2006-2010 5-year est.); Average household income: $36,352 (2006-2010 5-year est.); Percent of households with income of $100,000 or more: 1.2% (2006-2010 5-year est.); Poverty rate: 17.4% (2006-2010 5-year est.).

Education: Percent of population age 25 and over with: High school diploma (including GED) or higher: 83.2% (2006-2010 5-year est.); Bachelor's degree or higher: 6.3% (2006-2010 5-year est.); Master's degree or higher: 0.7% (2006-2010 5-year est.).

Housing: Homeownership rate: 78.5% (2010); Median home value: $77,600 (2006-2010 5-year est.); Median contract rent: $343 per month (2006-2010 5-year est.); Median year structure built: 1963 (2006-2010 5-year est.).

Transportation: Commute to work: 98.6% car, 0.0% public transportation, 0.0% walk, 1.4% work from home (2006-2010 5-year est.); Travel time to work: 24.2% less than 15 minutes, 26.8% 15 to 30 minutes, 31.7% 30 to 45 minutes, 7.6% 45 to 60 minutes, 9.7% 60 minutes or more (2006-2010 5-year est.)

Additional Information Contacts
Strongland Chamber of Commerce . . . . (724) 845-5426
  http://www.strongland.org

PARKER (city). Aka Parker City. Covers a land area of 0.956 square miles and a water area of 0 square miles. Located at 41.09° N. Lat; 79.68° W. Long. Elevation is 1,020 feet.

Population: 853 (1990); 799 (2000); 840 (2010); Density: 878.3 persons per square mile (2010); Race: 98.8% White, 0.4% Black, 0.0% Asian, 0.0% American Indian/Alaska Native, 0.0% Native Hawaiian/Other Pacific Islander, 0.8% Other, 0.5% Hispanic of any race (2010); Average household size: 2.37 (2010); Median age: 38.9 (2010); Males per 100 females: 88.8 (2010); Marriage status: 19.0% never married, 62.5% now married, 10.7% widowed, 7.8% divorced (2006-2010 5-year est.); Foreign born: 0.0% (2006-2010 5-year est.); Ancestry (includes multiple ancestries): 38.0% German, 22.6% Irish, 12.9% English, 9.0% Scotch-Irish, 6.3% American (2006-2010 5-year est.).

Economy: Employment by occupation: 7.9% management, 2.8% professional, 9.0% services, 15.5% sales, 1.7% farming, 16.7% construction, 5.4% production (2006-2010 5-year est.).

Income: Per capita income: $18,661 (2006-2010 5-year est.); Median household income: $33,750 (2006-2010 5-year est.); Average household income: $42,723 (2006-2010 5-year est.); Percent of households with income of $100,000 or more: 5.9% (2006-2010 5-year est.); Poverty rate: 10.4% (2006-2010 5-year est.).

Education: Percent of population age 25 and over with: High school diploma (including GED) or higher: 83.3% (2006-2010 5-year est.); Bachelor's degree or higher: 11.7% (2006-2010 5-year est.); Master's degree or higher: 1.5% (2006-2010 5-year est.).

Housing: Homeownership rate: 59.7% (2010); Median home value: $77,400 (2006-2010 5-year est.); Median contract rent: $370 per month (2006-2010 5-year est.); Median year structure built: 1947 (2006-2010 5-year est.).

Transportation: Commute to work: 95.7% car, 3.1% public transportation, 0.0% walk, 1.2% work from home (2006-2010 5-year est.); Travel time to work: 23.5% less than 15 minutes, 28.8% 15 to 30 minutes, 15.5% 30 to 45 minutes, 15.8% 45 to 60 minutes, 16.4% 60 minutes or more (2006-2010 5-year est.)

PARKS (township). Covers a land area of 14.037 square miles and a water area of 0.165 square miles. Located at 40.64° N. Lat; 79.55° W. Long.

Population: 2,739 (1990); 2,754 (2000); 2,744 (2010); Density: 195.5 persons per square mile (2010); Race: 95.5% White, 3.2% Black, 0.1% Asian, 0.0% American Indian/Alaska Native, 0.0% Native Hawaiian/Other Pacific Islander, 1.2% Other, 0.5% Hispanic of any race (2010); Average household size: 2.38 (2010); Median age: 45.0 (2010); Males per 100 females: 103.4 (2010); Marriage status: 18.9% never married, 67.1% now married, 5.1% widowed, 8.9% divorced (2006-2010 5-year est.); Foreign born: 1.1% (2006-2010 5-year est.); Ancestry (includes multiple

ancestries): 41.3% German, 28.3% Irish, 12.4% Italian, 9.3% Slovak, 6.0% English (2006-2010 5-year est.).

Economy: Single-family building permits issued: 0 (2011); Multi-family building permits issued: 0 (2011); Employment by occupation: 5.9% management, 5.1% professional, 4.9% services, 11.8% sales, 3.4% farming, 14.5% construction, 16.2% production (2006-2010 5-year est.).

Income: Per capita income: $22,709 (2006-2010 5-year est.); Median household income: $46,574 (2006-2010 5-year est.); Average household income: $53,518 (2006-2010 5-year est.); Percent of households with income of $100,000 or more: 14.1% (2006-2010 5-year est.); Poverty rate: 16.8% (2006-2010 5-year est.).

Education: Percent of population age 25 and over with: High school diploma (including GED) or higher: 89.2% (2006-2010 5-year est.); Bachelor's degree or higher: 12.7% (2006-2010 5-year est.); Master's degree or higher: 4.1% (2006-2010 5-year est.).

Housing: Homeownership rate: 78.9% (2010); Median home value: $97,700 (2006-2010 5-year est.); Median contract rent: $392 per month (2006-2010 5-year est.); Median year structure built: 1953 (2006-2010 5-year est.).

Transportation: Commute to work: 98.7% car, 0.0% public transportation, 0.2% walk, 0.0% work from home (2006-2010 5-year est.); Travel time to work: 38.3% less than 15 minutes, 23.9% 15 to 30 minutes, 14.7% 30 to 45 minutes, 14.6% 45 to 60 minutes, 8.5% 60 minutes or more (2006-2010 5-year est.)

Additional Information Contacts
Strongland Chamber of Commerce . . . . (724) 845-5426
  http://www.strongland.org

PERRY (township). Covers a land area of 15.023 square miles and a water area of 0 square miles. Located at 41.03° N. Lat; 79.66° W. Long.

Population: 322 (1990); 404 (2000); 352 (2010); Density: 23.4 persons per square mile (2010); Race: 97.2% White, 2.3% Black, 0.0% Asian, 0.0% American Indian/Alaska Native, 0.0% Native Hawaiian/Other Pacific Islander, 0.5% Other, 0.0% Hispanic of any race (2010); Average household size: 2.55 (2010); Median age: 48.4 (2010); Males per 100 females: 109.5 (2010); Marriage status: 27.3% never married, 59.1% now married, 3.6% widowed, 10.0% divorced (2006-2010 5-year est.); Foreign born: 0.0% (2006-2010 5-year est.); Ancestry (includes multiple ancestries): 50.5% German, 25.0% Irish, 16.3% Italian, 11.7% English, 5.1% Croatian (2006-2010 5-year est.).

Economy: Single-family building permits issued: 0 (2011); Multi-family building permits issued: 0 (2011); Employment by occupation: 3.7% management, 2.2% professional, 18.7% services, 12.7% sales, 1.5% farming, 19.4% construction, 8.2% production (2006-2010 5-year est.).

Income: Per capita income: $17,571 (2006-2010 5-year est.); Median household income: $46,375 (2006-2010 5-year est.); Average household income: $51,242 (2006-2010 5-year est.); Percent of households with income of $100,000 or more: 7.9% (2006-2010 5-year est.); Poverty rate: 17.0% (2006-2010 5-year est.).

Education: Percent of population age 25 and over with: High school diploma (including GED) or higher: 92.5% (2006-2010 5-year est.); Bachelor's degree or higher: 8.6% (2006-2010 5-year est.); Master's degree or higher: 4.3% (2006-2010 5-year est.).

Housing: Homeownership rate: 91.3% (2010); Median home value: $112,200 (2006-2010 5-year est.); Median contract rent: $413 per month (2006-2010 5-year est.); Median year structure built: 1964 (2006-2010 5-year est.).

Transportation: Commute to work: 97.7% car, 0.0% public transportation, 0.0% walk, 2.3% work from home (2006-2010 5-year est.); Travel time to work: 19.2% less than 15 minutes, 15.2% 15 to 30 minutes, 37.6% 30 to 45 minutes, 17.6% 45 to 60 minutes, 10.4% 60 minutes or more (2006-2010 5-year est.)

PINE (township). Covers a land area of 4.344 square miles and a water area of 0.252 square miles. Located at 40.92° N. Lat; 79.43° W. Long.

Population: 534 (1990); 499 (2000); 412 (2010); Density: 94.8 persons per square mile (2010); Race: 98.8% White, 0.5% Black, 0.0% Asian, 0.0% American Indian/Alaska Native, 0.0% Native Hawaiian/Other Pacific Islander, 0.7% Other, 0.0% Hispanic of any race (2010); Average household size: 2.45 (2010); Median age: 42.2 (2010); Males per 100 females: 106.0 (2010); Marriage status: 21.0% never married, 53.3% now married, 8.4% widowed, 17.3% divorced (2006-2010 5-year est.); Foreign born: 0.0% (2006-2010 5-year est.); Ancestry (includes multiple ancestries): 44.4% German, 25.8% Irish, 12.3% American, 6.5% English, 2.7% Dutch (2006-2010 5-year est.).

Economy: Single-family building permits issued: 0 (2011); Multi-family building permits issued: 0 (2011); Employment by occupation: 0.0% management, 2.8% professional, 7.7% services, 24.6% sales, 7.0% farming, 11.3% construction, 16.2% production (2006-2010 5-year est.).
Income: Per capita income: $16,741 (2006-2010 5-year est.); Median household income: $39,265 (2006-2010 5-year est.); Average household income: $38,151 (2006-2010 5-year est.); Percent of households with income of $100,000 or more: 1.1% (2006-2010 5-year est.); Poverty rate: 12.7% (2006-2010 5-year est.).
Education: Percent of population age 25 and over with: High school diploma (including GED) or higher: 91.9% (2006-2010 5-year est.); Bachelor's degree or higher: 5.5% (2006-2010 5-year est.); Master's degree or higher: 1.8% (2006-2010 5-year est.).
Housing: Homeownership rate: 75.0% (2010); Median home value: $41,800 (2006-2010 5-year est.); Median contract rent: $289 per month (2006-2010 5-year est.); Median year structure built: before 1940 (2006-2010 5-year est.).
Transportation: Commute to work: 95.1% car, 0.0% public transportation, 1.4% walk, 0.0% work from home (2006-2010 5-year est.); Travel time to work: 12.5% less than 15 minutes, 41.0% 15 to 30 minutes, 12.5% 30 to 45 minutes, 13.9% 45 to 60 minutes, 20.1% 60 minutes or more (2006-2010 5-year est.)

PLEASANT VIEW (CDP). Covers a land area of 0.978 square miles and a water area of 0.055 square miles. Located at 40.61° N. Lat; 79.57° W. Long. Elevation is 968 feet.
Population: n/a (1990); n/a (2000); 780 (2010); Density: 797.2 persons per square mile (2010); Race: 98.6% White, 0.5% Black, 0.3% Asian, 0.0% American Indian/Alaska Native, 0.0% Native Hawaiian/Other Pacific Islander, 0.6% Other, 0.3% Hispanic of any race (2010); Average household size: 2.21 (2010); Median age: 47.2 (2010); Males per 100 females: 92.6 (2010); Marriage status: 16.4% never married, 71.7% now married, 6.1% widowed, 5.8% divorced (2006-2010 5-year est.); Foreign born: 1.7% (2006-2010 5-year est.); Ancestry (includes multiple ancestries): 42.2% Irish, 41.1% German, 14.1% Italian, 11.6% English, 10.9% Slovak (2006-2010 5-year est.).
Economy: Employment by occupation: 3.3% management, 5.0% professional, 2.5% services, 22.2% sales, 1.9% farming, 19.5% construction, 16.8% production (2006-2010 5-year est.).
Income: Per capita income: $20,664 (2006-2010 5-year est.); Median household income: $45,625 (2006-2010 5-year est.); Average household income: $50,103 (2006-2010 5-year est.); Percent of households with income of $100,000 or more: 9.7% (2006-2010 5-year est.); Poverty rate: 20.4% (2006-2010 5-year est.).
Education: Percent of population age 25 and over with: High school diploma (including GED) or higher: 92.6% (2006-2010 5-year est.); Bachelor's degree or higher: 15.6% (2006-2010 5-year est.); Master's degree or higher: 7.4% (2006-2010 5-year est.).
Housing: Homeownership rate: 81.0% (2010); Median home value: $85,200 (2006-2010 5-year est.); Median contract rent: $617 per month (2006-2010 5-year est.); Median year structure built: 1950 (2006-2010 5-year est.).
Transportation: Commute to work: 97.0% car, 0.0% public transportation, 0.0% walk, 0.0% work from home (2006-2010 5-year est.); Travel time to work: 36.1% less than 15 minutes, 21.2% 15 to 30 minutes, 19.5% 30 to 45 minutes, 21.2% 45 to 60 minutes, 1.9% 60 minutes or more (2006-2010 5-year est.)

PLUMCREEK (township). Covers a land area of 42.377 square miles and a water area of 0.668 square miles. Located at 40.71° N. Lat; 79.34° W. Long.
Population: 2,414 (1990); 2,304 (2000); 2,375 (2010); Density: 56.0 persons per square mile (2010); Race: 99.3% White, 0.2% Black, 0.2% Asian, 0.0% American Indian/Alaska Native, 0.0% Native Hawaiian/Other Pacific Islander, 0.3% Other, 0.2% Hispanic of any race (2010); Average household size: 2.48 (2010); Median age: 44.5 (2010); Males per 100 females: 99.2 (2010); Marriage status: 22.2% never married, 56.9% now married, 11.8% widowed, 9.1% divorced (2006-2010 5-year est.); Foreign born: 0.6% (2006-2010 5-year est.); Ancestry (includes multiple ancestries): 46.1% German, 12.2% Irish, 10.4% English, 9.2% American, 6.6% Italian (2006-2010 5-year est.).
Economy: Single-family building permits issued: 1 (2011); Multi-family building permits issued: 0 (2011); Employment by occupation: 4.8% management, 4.4% professional, 14.4% services, 14.8% sales, 5.8% farming, 12.7% construction, 6.5% production (2006-2010 5-year est.).

Income: Per capita income: $22,642 (2006-2010 5-year est.); Median household income: $40,175 (2006-2010 5-year est.); Average household income: $53,928 (2006-2010 5-year est.); Percent of households with income of $100,000 or more: 8.5% (2006-2010 5-year est.); Poverty rate: 6.6% (2006-2010 5-year est.).
Education: Percent of population age 25 and over with: High school diploma (including GED) or higher: 83.9% (2006-2010 5-year est.); Bachelor's degree or higher: 12.1% (2006-2010 5-year est.); Master's degree or higher: 4.2% (2006-2010 5-year est.).
Housing: Homeownership rate: 80.9% (2010); Median home value: $86,300 (2006-2010 5-year est.); Median contract rent: $488 per month (2006-2010 5-year est.); Median year structure built: 1973 (2006-2010 5-year est.).
Transportation: Commute to work: 97.6% car, 0.0% public transportation, 1.2% walk, 1.2% work from home (2006-2010 5-year est.); Travel time to work: 18.7% less than 15 minutes, 38.3% 15 to 30 minutes, 27.9% 30 to 45 minutes, 8.8% 45 to 60 minutes, 6.3% 60 minutes or more (2006-2010 5-year est.)
Additional Information Contacts
Armstrong County Chamber of Commerce . . . . (724) 543-1305
   http://www.armstrongchamber.org

RAYBURN (township). Covers a land area of 11.848 square miles and a water area of 0.247 square miles. Located at 40.83° N. Lat; 79.49° W. Long.
Population: 1,823 (1990); 1,811 (2000); 1,907 (2010); Density: 161.0 persons per square mile (2010); Race: 97.0% White, 1.5% Black, 0.1% Asian, 0.1% American Indian/Alaska Native, 0.1% Native Hawaiian/Other Pacific Islander, 1.2% Other, 0.8% Hispanic of any race (2010); Average household size: 2.44 (2010); Median age: 41.9 (2010); Males per 100 females: 113.1 (2010); Marriage status: 25.5% never married, 58.2% now married, 7.5% widowed, 8.9% divorced (2006-2010 5-year est.); Foreign born: 0.4% (2006-2010 5-year est.); Ancestry (includes multiple ancestries): 42.6% German, 21.7% Irish, 11.2% English, 6.7% Dutch, 6.7% Italian (2006-2010 5-year est.).
Economy: Single-family building permits issued: 0 (2011); Multi-family building permits issued: 0 (2011); Employment by occupation: 7.8% management, 1.5% professional, 12.4% services, 15.7% sales, 6.3% farming, 12.9% construction, 7.5% production (2006-2010 5-year est.).
Income: Per capita income: $18,867 (2006-2010 5-year est.); Median household income: $40,551 (2006-2010 5-year est.); Average household income: $47,500 (2006-2010 5-year est.); Percent of households with income of $100,000 or more: 7.7% (2006-2010 5-year est.); Poverty rate: 16.5% (2006-2010 5-year est.).
Education: Percent of population age 25 and over with: High school diploma (including GED) or higher: 84.2% (2006-2010 5-year est.); Bachelor's degree or higher: 7.7% (2006-2010 5-year est.); Master's degree or higher: 0.9% (2006-2010 5-year est.).
Housing: Homeownership rate: 78.3% (2010); Median home value: $72,000 (2006-2010 5-year est.); Median contract rent: $329 per month (2006-2010 5-year est.); Median year structure built: 1953 (2006-2010 5-year est.).
Transportation: Commute to work: 91.1% car, 0.0% public transportation, 6.9% walk, 1.3% work from home (2006-2010 5-year est.); Travel time to work: 36.8% less than 15 minutes, 28.1% 15 to 30 minutes, 18.8% 30 to 45 minutes, 6.8% 45 to 60 minutes, 9.5% 60 minutes or more (2006-2010 5-year est.)
Additional Information Contacts
Armstrong County Chamber of Commerce . . . . (724) 543-1305
   http://www.armstrongchamber.org

REDBANK (township). Covers a land area of 32.302 square miles and a water area of 0.289 square miles. Located at 40.98° N. Lat; 79.26° W. Long.
Population: 1,058 (1990); 1,296 (2000); 1,064 (2010); Density: 32.9 persons per square mile (2010); Race: 99.0% White, 0.2% Black, 0.0% Asian, 0.2% American Indian/Alaska Native, 0.0% Native Hawaiian/Other Pacific Islander, 0.6% Other, 0.2% Hispanic of any race (2010); Average household size: 2.42 (2010); Median age: 42.5 (2010); Males per 100 females: 94.2 (2010); Marriage status: 27.0% never married, 62.3% now married, 5.6% widowed, 5.1% divorced (2006-2010 5-year est.); Foreign born: 0.0% (2006-2010 5-year est.); Ancestry (includes multiple ancestries): 53.4% German, 11.9% Irish, 10.4% Dutch, 8.0% French, 4.5% Italian (2006-2010 5-year est.).

Economy: Single-family building permits issued: 0 (2011); Multi-family building permits issued: 0 (2011); Employment by occupation: 2.5% management, 0.2% professional, 9.7% services, 20.3% sales, 0.8% farming, 16.7% construction, 10.3% production (2006-2010 5-year est.).
Income: Per capita income: $20,470 (2006-2010 5-year est.); Median household income: $51,250 (2006-2010 5-year est.); Average household income: $56,166 (2006-2010 5-year est.); Percent of households with income of $100,000 or more: 7.1% (2006-2010 5-year est.); Poverty rate: 8.7% (2006-2010 5-year est.).
Education: Percent of population age 25 and over with: High school diploma (including GED) or higher: 83.7% (2006-2010 5-year est.); Bachelor's degree or higher: 6.7% (2006-2010 5-year est.); Master's degree or higher: 0.7% (2006-2010 5-year est.).
Housing: Homeownership rate: 78.4% (2010); Median home value: $75,000 (2006-2010 5-year est.); Median contract rent: $314 per month (2006-2010 5-year est.); Median year structure built: 1946 (2006-2010 5-year est.).
Transportation: Commute to work: 98.1% car, 0.0% public transportation, 0.0% walk, 0.8% work from home (2006-2010 5-year est.); Travel time to work: 17.2% less than 15 minutes, 23.4% 15 to 30 minutes, 28.4% 30 to 45 minutes, 19.3% 45 to 60 minutes, 11.8% 60 minutes or more (2006-2010 5-year est.)
Additional Information Contacts
Armstrong County Chamber of Commerce . . . . (724) 543-1305
   http://www.armstrongchamber.org

RURAL VALLEY (borough). Covers a land area of 2.111 square miles and a water area of 0 square miles. Located at 40.80° N. Lat; 79.31° W. Long. Elevation is 1,122 feet.
Population: 957 (1990); 922 (2000); 876 (2010); Density: 414.9 persons per square mile (2010); Race: 99.2% White, 0.2% Black, 0.0% Asian, 0.2% American Indian/Alaska Native, 0.0% Native Hawaiian/Other Pacific Islander, 0.4% Other, 0.5% Hispanic of any race (2010); Average household size: 2.28 (2010); Median age: 43.8 (2010); Males per 100 females: 88.4 (2010); Marriage status: 21.5% never married, 58.7% now married, 11.9% widowed, 7.9% divorced (2006-2010 5-year est.); Foreign born: 0.0% (2006-2010 5-year est.); Ancestry (includes multiple ancestries): 36.0% German, 25.2% Italian, 18.6% Irish, 10.1% Dutch, 6.7% English (2006-2010 5-year est.).
Economy: Single-family building permits issued: 0 (2011); Multi-family building permits issued: 0 (2011); Employment by occupation: 5.2% management, 4.7% professional, 17.9% services, 13.9% sales, 2.7% farming, 11.9% construction, 5.2% production (2006-2010 5-year est.).
Income: Per capita income: $22,513 (2006-2010 5-year est.); Median household income: $42,542 (2006-2010 5-year est.); Average household income: $52,524 (2006-2010 5-year est.); Percent of households with income of $100,000 or more: 12.1% (2006-2010 5-year est.); Poverty rate: 14.6% (2006-2010 5-year est.).
Education: Percent of population age 25 and over with: High school diploma (including GED) or higher: 87.0% (2006-2010 5-year est.); Bachelor's degree or higher: 11.5% (2006-2010 5-year est.); Master's degree or higher: 3.4% (2006-2010 5-year est.).
School District(s)
Armstrong SD (KG-12)
   2010-11 Enrollment: 5,544 . . . . (724) 763-7151
Housing: Homeownership rate: 67.5% (2010); Median home value: $88,800 (2006-2010 5-year est.); Median contract rent: $322 per month (2006-2010 5-year est.); Median year structure built: 1945 (2006-2010 5-year est.).
Safety: Violent crime rate: 0.0 per 10,000 population; Property crime rate: 11.4 per 10,000 population (2011).
Transportation: Commute to work: 97.5% car, 0.0% public transportation, 0.9% walk, 1.6% work from home (2006-2010 5-year est.); Travel time to work: 29.3% less than 15 minutes, 26.0% 15 to 30 minutes, 16.7% 30 to 45 minutes, 14.2% 45 to 60 minutes, 13.7% 60 minutes or more (2006-2010 5-year est.)

SAGAMORE (unincorporated postal area)
Zip Code: 16250
   Covers a land area of 2.755 square miles and a water area of 0.309 square miles. Located at 40.76° N. Lat; 79.23° W. Long. Elevation is 1,125 feet. Population: 315 (2010); Density: 114.3 persons per square mile (2010); Race: 97.8% White, 1.0% Black, 0.0% Asian, 0.0% American Indian/Alaska Native, 0.0% Native Hawaiian/Other Pacific Islander, 1.2% Other, 0.0% Hispanic of any race (2010); Average

household size: 2.56 (2010); Median age: 41.6 (2010); Males per 100 females: 112.8 (2010); Homeownership rate: 87.8% (2010)

SEMINOLE (unincorporated postal area)
Zip Code: 16253
   Covers a land area of 0.211 square miles and a water area of 0 square miles. Located at 40.95° N. Lat; 79.34° W. Long. Elevation is 1,381 feet. Population: 91 (2010); Density: 430.8 persons per square mile (2010); Race: 97.8% White, 2.2% Black, 0.0% Asian, 0.0% American Indian/Alaska Native, 0.0% Native Hawaiian/Other Pacific Islander, 0.0% Other, 0.0% Hispanic of any race (2010); Average household size: 2.39 (2010); Median age: 46.8 (2010); Males per 100 females: 89.6 (2010); Homeownership rate: 76.3% (2010)

SOUTH BEND (township). Covers a land area of 22.535 square miles and a water area of 0.070 square miles. Located at 40.63° N. Lat; 79.39° W. Long. Elevation is 961 feet.
Population: 1,304 (1990); 1,259 (2000); 1,167 (2010); Density: 51.8 persons per square mile (2010); Race: 98.7% White, 0.1% Black, 0.3% Asian, 0.1% American Indian/Alaska Native, 0.1% Native Hawaiian/Other Pacific Islander, 0.7% Other, 0.1% Hispanic of any race (2010); Average household size: 2.52 (2010); Median age: 44.1 (2010); Males per 100 females: 104.4 (2010); Marriage status: 20.8% never married, 67.8% now married, 5.1% widowed, 6.4% divorced (2006-2010 5-year est.); Foreign born: 0.0% (2006-2010 5-year est.); Ancestry (includes multiple ancestries): 47.5% German, 21.8% Irish, 10.1% English, 6.4% Italian, 5.6% Polish (2006-2010 5-year est.).
Economy: Single-family building permits issued: 4 (2011); Multi-family building permits issued: 0 (2011); Employment by occupation: 8.4% management, 0.0% professional, 9.6% services, 17.0% sales, 2.1% farming, 20.1% construction, 16.6% production (2006-2010 5-year est.).
Income: Per capita income: $20,444 (2006-2010 5-year est.); Median household income: $46,488 (2006-2010 5-year est.); Average household income: $54,416 (2006-2010 5-year est.); Percent of households with income of $100,000 or more: 11.1% (2006-2010 5-year est.); Poverty rate: 9.8% (2006-2010 5-year est.).
Education: Percent of population age 25 and over with: High school diploma (including GED) or higher: 89.7% (2006-2010 5-year est.); Bachelor's degree or higher: 14.9% (2006-2010 5-year est.); Master's degree or higher: 6.1% (2006-2010 5-year est.).
Housing: Homeownership rate: 86.8% (2010); Median home value: $85,300 (2006-2010 5-year est.); Median contract rent: $426 per month (2006-2010 5-year est.); Median year structure built: 1972 (2006-2010 5-year est.).
Transportation: Commute to work: 89.9% car, 0.3% public transportation, 2.5% walk, 7.3% work from home (2006-2010 5-year est.); Travel time to work: 13.7% less than 15 minutes, 38.3% 15 to 30 minutes, 36.6% 30 to 45 minutes, 5.3% 45 to 60 minutes, 6.2% 60 minutes or more (2006-2010 5-year est.)
Additional Information Contacts
Indiana County Chamber of Commerce . . . . (724) 465-2511
   http://www.indianapa.com/chamber

SOUTH BETHLEHEM (borough). Covers a land area of 0.152 square miles and a water area of 0 square miles. Located at 41.00° N. Lat; 79.34° W. Long. Elevation is 1,086 feet.
Population: 479 (1990); 444 (2000); 481 (2010); Density: 3,163.0 persons per square mile (2010); Race: 96.9% White, 0.4% Black, 1.2% Asian, 0.0% American Indian/Alaska Native, 0.0% Native Hawaiian/Other Pacific Islander, 1.5% Other, 0.4% Hispanic of any race (2010); Average household size: 2.33 (2010); Median age: 39.3 (2010); Males per 100 females: 85.0 (2010); Marriage status: 17.0% never married, 57.7% now married, 10.2% widowed, 15.0% divorced (2006-2010 5-year est.); Foreign born: 0.0% (2006-2010 5-year est.); Ancestry (includes multiple ancestries): 45.0% German, 15.1% Irish, 10.5% American, 9.8% English, 8.1% Italian (2006-2010 5-year est.).
Economy: Single-family building permits issued: 0 (2011); Multi-family building permits issued: 0 (2011); Employment by occupation: 6.3% management, 0.9% professional, 13.9% services, 12.6% sales, 4.9% farming, 16.1% construction, 4.9% production (2006-2010 5-year est.).
Income: Per capita income: $21,707 (2006-2010 5-year est.); Median household income: $41,750 (2006-2010 5-year est.); Average household income: $52,671 (2006-2010 5-year est.); Percent of households with income of $100,000 or more: 9.2% (2006-2010 5-year est.); Poverty rate: 10.7% (2006-2010 5-year est.).

Education: Percent of population age 25 and over with: High school diploma (including GED) or higher: 81.8% (2006-2010 5-year est.); Bachelor's degree or higher: 13.3% (2006-2010 5-year est.); Master's degree or higher: 7.4% (2006-2010 5-year est.).

Housing: Homeownership rate: 64.5% (2010); Median home value: $75,300 (2006-2010 5-year est.); Median contract rent: $336 per month (2006-2010 5-year est.); Median year structure built: 1943 (2006-2010 5-year est.).

Transportation: Commute to work: 91.8% car, 0.0% public transportation, 1.8% walk, 6.4% work from home (2006-2010 5-year est.); Travel time to work: 29.3% less than 15 minutes, 24.9% 15 to 30 minutes, 37.6% 30 to 45 minutes, 4.4% 45 to 60 minutes, 3.9% 60 minutes or more (2006-2010 5-year est.)

SOUTH BUFFALO (township). Covers a land area of 26.957 square miles and a water area of 0.823 square miles. Located at 40.73° N. Lat; 79.64° W. Long.

Population: 2,696 (1990); 2,785 (2000); 2,636 (2010); Density: 97.8 persons per square mile (2010); Race: 99.2% White, 0.2% Black, 0.1% Asian, 0.1% American Indian/Alaska Native, 0.0% Native Hawaiian/Other Pacific Islander, 0.4% Other, 0.6% Hispanic of any race (2010); Average household size: 2.61 (2010); Median age: 44.3 (2010); Males per 100 females: 99.8 (2010); Marriage status: 23.0% never married, 67.0% now married, 5.0% widowed, 5.0% divorced (2006-2010 5-year est.); Foreign born: 0.0% (2006-2010 5-year est.); Ancestry (includes multiple ancestries): 43.8% German, 19.6% Irish, 17.2% Italian, 13.0% English, 12.5% Polish (2006-2010 5-year est.).

Economy: Single-family building permits issued: 6 (2011); Multi-family building permits issued: 0 (2011); Employment by occupation: 11.3% management, 2.6% professional, 12.5% services, 9.6% sales, 7.6% farming, 12.7% construction, 8.1% production (2006-2010 5-year est.).

Income: Per capita income: $27,440 (2006-2010 5-year est.); Median household income: $63,304 (2006-2010 5-year est.); Average household income: $71,042 (2006-2010 5-year est.); Percent of households with income of $100,000 or more: 21.1% (2006-2010 5-year est.); Poverty rate: 4.7% (2006-2010 5-year est.).

Education: Percent of population age 25 and over with: High school diploma (including GED) or higher: 96.0% (2006-2010 5-year est.); Bachelor's degree or higher: 21.2% (2006-2010 5-year est.); Master's degree or higher: 5.6% (2006-2010 5-year est.).

Housing: Homeownership rate: 91.0% (2010); Median home value: $148,400 (2006-2010 5-year est.); Median contract rent: $464 per month (2006-2010 5-year est.); Median year structure built: 1966 (2006-2010 5-year est.).

Transportation: Commute to work: 94.0% car, 0.0% public transportation, 1.4% walk, 4.3% work from home (2006-2010 5-year est.); Travel time to work: 18.7% less than 15 minutes, 39.5% 15 to 30 minutes, 21.3% 30 to 45 minutes, 7.7% 45 to 60 minutes, 12.8% 60 minutes or more (2006-2010 5-year est.)

Additional Information Contacts
Strongland Chamber of Commerce.................. (724) 845-5426
  http://www.strongland.org

SPRING CHURCH (unincorporated postal area)
Zip Code: 15686
  Covers a land area of 10.158 square miles and a water area of 0.082 square miles. Located at 40.62° N. Lat; 79.43° W. Long. Population: 972 (2010); Density: 95.7 persons per square mile (2010); Race: 98.8% White, 0.6% Black, 0.0% Asian, 0.1% American Indian/Alaska Native, 0.0% Native Hawaiian/Other Pacific Islander, 0.5% Other, 0.9% Hispanic of any race (2010); Average household size: 2.51 (2010); Median age: 46.4 (2010); Males per 100 females: 102.5 (2010); Homeownership rate: 88.8% (2010)

SUGARCREEK (township). Covers a land area of 26.667 square miles and a water area of 0 square miles. Located at 40.93° N. Lat; 79.64° W. Long.

Population: 1,496 (1990); 1,557 (2000); 1,539 (2010); Density: 57.7 persons per square mile (2010); Race: 97.9% White, 1.8% Black, 0.1% Asian, 0.1% American Indian/Alaska Native, 0.0% Native Hawaiian/Other Pacific Islander, 0.1% Other, 0.3% Hispanic of any race (2010); Average household size: 2.47 (2010); Median age: 49.3 (2010); Males per 100 females: 101.7 (2010); Marriage status: 14.4% never married, 50.3% now married, 21.9% widowed, 13.4% divorced (2006-2010 5-year est.); Foreign born: 2.3% (2006-2010 5-year est.); Ancestry (includes multiple

ancestries): 38.2% German, 14.7% Irish, 7.9% Italian, 7.2% English, 7.1% American (2006-2010 5-year est.).

Economy: Single-family building permits issued: 0 (2011); Multi-family building permits issued: 0 (2011); Employment by occupation: 4.0% management, 2.5% professional, 15.2% services, 15.0% sales, 0.0% farming, 17.9% construction, 12.9% production (2006-2010 5-year est.).

Income: Per capita income: $18,806 (2006-2010 5-year est.); Median household income: $41,167 (2006-2010 5-year est.); Average household income: $57,188 (2006-2010 5-year est.); Percent of households with income of $100,000 or more: 11.9% (2006-2010 5-year est.); Poverty rate: 21.3% (2006-2010 5-year est.).

Education: Percent of population age 25 and over with: High school diploma (including GED) or higher: 74.8% (2006-2010 5-year est.); Bachelor's degree or higher: 6.7% (2006-2010 5-year est.); Master's degree or higher: 1.5% (2006-2010 5-year est.).

Housing: Homeownership rate: 83.1% (2010); Median home value: $94,600 (2006-2010 5-year est.); Median contract rent: $272 per month (2006-2010 5-year est.); Median year structure built: 1970 (2006-2010 5-year est.).

Transportation: Commute to work: 94.2% car, 0.0% public transportation, 1.3% walk, 2.8% work from home (2006-2010 5-year est.); Travel time to work: 28.4% less than 15 minutes, 28.4% 15 to 30 minutes, 25.5% 30 to 45 minutes, 10.4% 45 to 60 minutes, 7.3% 60 minutes or more (2006-2010 5-year est.)

Additional Information Contacts
Armstrong County Chamber of Commerce .... (724) 543-1305
  http://www.armstrongchamber.org

TEMPLETON (CDP). Covers a land area of 0.462 square miles and a water area of 0.122 square miles. Located at 40.92° N. Lat; 79.46° W. Long. Elevation is 860 feet.

Population: n/a (1990); n/a (2000); 325 (2010); Density: 702.9 persons per square mile (2010); Race: 98.5% White, 0.6% Black, 0.0% Asian, 0.0% American Indian/Alaska Native, 0.0% Native Hawaiian/Other Pacific Islander, 0.9% Other, 0.0% Hispanic of any race (2010); Average household size: 2.44 (2010); Median age: 39.9 (2010); Males per 100 females: 94.6 (2010); Marriage status: 18.4% never married, 55.4% now married, 8.2% widowed, 18.0% divorced (2006-2010 5-year est.); Foreign born: 0.0% (2006-2010 5-year est.); Ancestry (includes multiple ancestries): 47.3% German, 28.6% Irish, 13.6% American, 7.2% English, 2.9% Scotch-Irish (2006-2010 5-year est.).

Economy: Employment by occupation: 0.0% management, 2.9% professional, 8.1% services, 23.5% sales, 7.4% farming, 9.6% construction, 14.7% production (2006-2010 5-year est.).

Income: Per capita income: $17,205 (2006-2010 5-year est.); Median household income: $40,163 (2006-2010 5-year est.); Average household income: $39,555 (2006-2010 5-year est.); Percent of households with income of $100,000 or more: 1.2% (2006-2010 5-year est.); Poverty rate: 8.6% (2006-2010 5-year est.).

Education: Percent of population age 25 and over with: High school diploma (including GED) or higher: 92.9% (2006-2010 5-year est.); Bachelor's degree or higher: 6.0% (2006-2010 5-year est.); Master's degree or higher: 2.0% (2006-2010 5-year est.).

Housing: Homeownership rate: 70.7% (2010); Median home value: $43,200 (2006-2010 5-year est.); Median contract rent: $289 per month (2006-2010 5-year est.); Median year structure built: before 1940 (2006-2010 5-year est.).

Transportation: Commute to work: 94.9% car, 0.0% public transportation, 1.4% walk, 0.0% work from home (2006-2010 5-year est.); Travel time to work: 13.0% less than 15 minutes, 40.6% 15 to 30 minutes, 13.0% 30 to 45 minutes, 14.5% 45 to 60 minutes, 18.8% 60 minutes or more (2006-2010 5-year est.)

VALLEY (township). Covers a land area of 14.745 square miles and a water area of 0 square miles. Located at 40.83° N. Lat; 79.41° W. Long.

Population: 709 (1990); 681 (2000); 656 (2010); Density: 44.5 persons per square mile (2010); Race: 97.6% White, 1.1% Black, 0.8% Asian, 0.2% American Indian/Alaska Native, 0.0% Native Hawaiian/Other Pacific Islander, 0.3% Other, 0.2% Hispanic of any race (2010); Average household size: 2.55 (2010); Median age: 42.9 (2010); Males per 100 females: 108.3 (2010); Marriage status: 20.6% never married, 70.5% now married, 1.1% widowed, 7.7% divorced (2006-2010 5-year est.); Foreign born: 0.0% (2006-2010 5-year est.); Ancestry (includes multiple ancestries): 46.3% German, 17.9% English, 17.6% Irish, 7.4% Polish, 5.0% Swedish (2006-2010 5-year est.).

Economy: Single-family building permits issued: 2 (2011); Multi-family building permits issued: 0 (2011); Employment by occupation: 17.1% management, 8.2% professional, 10.6% services, 9.9% sales, 2.6% farming, 25.5% construction, 10.1% production (2006-2010 5-year est.).
Income: Per capita income: $21,813 (2006-2010 5-year est.); Median household income: $60,169 (2006-2010 5-year est.); Average household income: $61,480 (2006-2010 5-year est.); Percent of households with income of $100,000 or more: 10.4% (2006-2010 5-year est.); Poverty rate: 7.0% (2006-2010 5-year est.).
Education: Percent of population age 25 and over with: High school diploma (including GED) or higher: 88.1% (2006-2010 5-year est.); Bachelor's degree or higher: 13.4% (2006-2010 5-year est.); Master's degree or higher: 4.1% (2006-2010 5-year est.).
Housing: Homeownership rate: 82.8% (2010); Median home value: $102,800 (2006-2010 5-year est.); Median contract rent: $275 per month (2006-2010 5-year est.); Median year structure built: 1976 (2006-2010 5-year est.).
Transportation: Commute to work: 91.3% car, 0.0% public transportation, 0.7% walk, 8.0% work from home (2006-2010 5-year est.); Travel time to work: 16.6% less than 15 minutes, 46.3% 15 to 30 minutes, 15.0% 30 to 45 minutes, 8.7% 45 to 60 minutes, 13.4% 60 minutes or more (2006-2010 5-year est.)

WASHINGTON (township). Covers a land area of 22.455 square miles and a water area of 0.894 square miles. Located at 40.93° N. Lat; 79.53° W. Long.
Population: 984 (1990); 1,029 (2000); 923 (2010); Density: 41.1 persons per square mile (2010); Race: 98.5% White, 0.2% Black, 0.3% Asian, 0.1% American Indian/Alaska Native, 0.0% Native Hawaiian/Other Pacific Islander, 0.9% Other, 0.1% Hispanic of any race (2010); Average household size: 2.57 (2010); Median age: 44.4 (2010); Males per 100 females: 98.9 (2010); Marriage status: 37.3% never married, 55.1% now married, 3.7% widowed, 4.0% divorced (2006-2010 5-year est.); Foreign born: 2.0% (2006-2010 5-year est.); Ancestry (includes multiple ancestries): 34.0% German, 23.2% Irish, 12.1% English, 9.8% American, 5.4% Polish (2006-2010 5-year est.).
Economy: Single-family building permits issued: 6 (2011); Multi-family building permits issued: 0 (2011); Employment by occupation: 1.6% management, 1.8% professional, 16.4% services, 9.9% sales, 2.0% farming, 26.7% construction, 12.3% production (2006-2010 5-year est.).
Income: Per capita income: $16,599 (2006-2010 5-year est.); Median household income: $33,750 (2006-2010 5-year est.); Average household income: $46,240 (2006-2010 5-year est.); Percent of households with income of $100,000 or more: 12.7% (2006-2010 5-year est.); Poverty rate: 22.9% (2006-2010 5-year est.).
Education: Percent of population age 25 and over with: High school diploma (including GED) or higher: 79.4% (2006-2010 5-year est.); Bachelor's degree or higher: 7.7% (2006-2010 5-year est.); Master's degree or higher: 2.1% (2006-2010 5-year est.).
Housing: Homeownership rate: 85.7% (2010); Median home value: $81,400 (2006-2010 5-year est.); Median contract rent: $406 per month (2006-2010 5-year est.); Median year structure built: 1967 (2006-2010 5-year est.).
Transportation: Commute to work: 94.3% car, 0.0% public transportation, 0.0% walk, 1.8% work from home (2006-2010 5-year est.); Travel time to work: 8.6% less than 15 minutes, 36.8% 15 to 30 minutes, 13.8% 30 to 45 minutes, 21.4% 45 to 60 minutes, 19.3% 60 minutes or more (2006-2010 5-year est.)

WAYNE (township). Covers a land area of 44.717 square miles and a water area of 0.293 square miles. Located at 40.89° N. Lat; 79.29° W. Long.
Population: 937 (1990); 1,117 (2000); 1,200 (2010); Density: 26.8 persons per square mile (2010); Race: 98.5% White, 0.5% Black, 0.1% Asian, 0.2% American Indian/Alaska Native, 0.1% Native Hawaiian/Other Pacific Islander, 0.6% Other, 1.2% Hispanic of any race (2010); Average household size: 2.73 (2010); Median age: 39.6 (2010); Males per 100 females: 102.4 (2010); Marriage status: 18.5% never married, 68.7% now married, 7.5% widowed, 5.3% divorced (2006-2010 5-year est.); Foreign born: 0.0% (2006-2010 5-year est.); Ancestry (includes multiple ancestries): 45.5% German, 15.5% Irish, 9.8% English, 6.6% Dutch, 6.4% Pennsylvania German (2006-2010 5-year est.).
Economy: Single-family building permits issued: 0 (2011); Multi-family building permits issued: 0 (2011); Employment by occupation: 12.9%

management, 0.0% professional, 9.5% services, 16.5% sales, 3.0% farming, 23.5% construction, 9.7% production (2006-2010 5-year est.).
Income: Per capita income: $21,340 (2006-2010 5-year est.); Median household income: $44,000 (2006-2010 5-year est.); Average household income: $51,843 (2006-2010 5-year est.); Percent of households with income of $100,000 or more: 13.1% (2006-2010 5-year est.); Poverty rate: 10.4% (2006-2010 5-year est.).
Education: Percent of population age 25 and over with: High school diploma (including GED) or higher: 84.0% (2006-2010 5-year est.); Bachelor's degree or higher: 11.2% (2006-2010 5-year est.); Master's degree or higher: 3.4% (2006-2010 5-year est.).
Housing: Homeownership rate: 85.2% (2010); Median home value: $120,400 (2006-2010 5-year est.); Median contract rent: $348 per month (2006-2010 5-year est.); Median year structure built: 1974 (2006-2010 5-year est.).
Transportation: Commute to work: 72.8% car, 0.0% public transportation, 6.7% walk, 15.1% work from home (2006-2010 5-year est.); Travel time to work: 25.7% less than 15 minutes, 16.3% 15 to 30 minutes, 30.3% 30 to 45 minutes, 6.6% 45 to 60 minutes, 21.1% 60 minutes or more (2006-2010 5-year est.)
Additional Information Contacts
Armstrong County Chamber of Commerce . . . . (724) 543-1305
    http://www.armstrongchamber.org

WEST FRANKLIN (township). Covers a land area of 26.081 square miles and a water area of 0 square miles. Located at 40.85° N. Lat; 79.65° W. Long.
Population: 2,008 (1990); 1,935 (2000); 1,853 (2010); Density: 71.0 persons per square mile (2010); Race: 99.2% White, 0.0% Black, 0.2% Asian, 0.0% American Indian/Alaska Native, 0.0% Native Hawaiian/Other Pacific Islander, 0.6% Other, 0.3% Hispanic of any race (2010); Average household size: 2.48 (2010); Median age: 45.3 (2010); Males per 100 females: 103.2 (2010); Marriage status: 22.4% never married, 61.1% now married, 6.6% widowed, 9.8% divorced (2006-2010 5-year est.); Foreign born: 1.0% (2006-2010 5-year est.); Ancestry (includes multiple ancestries): 35.6% German, 16.9% Irish, 8.6% English, 6.5% American, 5.4% Italian (2006-2010 5-year est.).
Economy: Single-family building permits issued: 0 (2011); Multi-family building permits issued: 0 (2011); Employment by occupation: 5.7% management, 3.1% professional, 10.1% services, 15.7% sales, 3.4% farming, 13.1% construction, 4.9% production (2006-2010 5-year est.).
Income: Per capita income: $22,327 (2006-2010 5-year est.); Median household income: $46,600 (2006-2010 5-year est.); Average household income: $56,361 (2006-2010 5-year est.); Percent of households with income of $100,000 or more: 14.6% (2006-2010 5-year est.); Poverty rate: 9.4% (2006-2010 5-year est.).
Education: Percent of population age 25 and over with: High school diploma (including GED) or higher: 88.1% (2006-2010 5-year est.); Bachelor's degree or higher: 14.4% (2006-2010 5-year est.); Master's degree or higher: 4.5% (2006-2010 5-year est.).
Housing: Homeownership rate: 80.3% (2010); Median home value: $103,300 (2006-2010 5-year est.); Median contract rent: $410 per month (2006-2010 5-year est.); Median year structure built: 1971 (2006-2010 5-year est.).
Transportation: Commute to work: 93.2% car, 0.5% public transportation, 1.8% walk, 4.1% work from home (2006-2010 5-year est.); Travel time to work: 20.9% less than 15 minutes, 53.0% 15 to 30 minutes, 11.9% 30 to 45 minutes, 7.1% 45 to 60 minutes, 7.1% 60 minutes or more (2006-2010 5-year est.)
Additional Information Contacts
Armstrong County Chamber of Commerce . . . . (724) 543-1305
    http://www.armstrongchamber.org

WEST HILLS (CDP). Covers a land area of 3.250 square miles and a water area of 0.199 square miles. Located at 40.83° N. Lat; 79.54° W. Long. Elevation is 1,138 feet.
Population: 1,242 (1990); 1,229 (2000); 1,263 (2010); Density: 388.6 persons per square mile (2010); Race: 98.8% White, 0.3% Black, 0.2% Asian, 0.1% American Indian/Alaska Native, 0.0% Native Hawaiian/Other Pacific Islander, 0.6% Other, 0.1% Hispanic of any race (2010); Average household size: 2.47 (2010); Median age: 45.6 (2010); Males per 100 females: 99.5 (2010); Marriage status: 18.1% never married, 72.4% now married, 3.6% widowed, 5.8% divorced (2006-2010 5-year est.); Foreign born: 1.3% (2006-2010 5-year est.); Ancestry (includes multiple

ancestries): 47.9% German, 20.5% Irish, 11.2% Hungarian, 10.1% English, 9.9% Italian (2006-2010 5-year est.).
Economy: Employment by occupation: 14.6% management, 9.7% professional, 7.2% services, 24.5% sales, 4.1% farming, 5.8% construction, 2.7% production (2006-2010 5-year est.).
Income: Per capita income: $26,272 (2006-2010 5-year est.); Median household income: $59,096 (2006-2010 5-year est.); Average household income: $59,937 (2006-2010 5-year est.); Percent of households with income of $100,000 or more: 13.1% (2006-2010 5-year est.); Poverty rate: 7.5% (2006-2010 5-year est.).
Education: Percent of population age 25 and over with: High school diploma (including GED) or higher: 94.0% (2006-2010 5-year est.); Bachelor's degree or higher: 40.7% (2006-2010 5-year est.); Master's degree or higher: 3.4% (2006-2010 5-year est.).
Housing: Homeownership rate: 83.3% (2010); Median home value: $140,100 (2006-2010 5-year est.); Median contract rent: $245 per month (2006-2010 5-year est.); Median year structure built: 1978 (2006-2010 5-year est.).
Transportation: Commute to work: 85.2% car, 0.0% public transportation, 9.2% walk, 5.5% work from home (2006-2010 5-year est.); Travel time to work: 25.2% less than 15 minutes, 20.3% 15 to 30 minutes, 26.3% 30 to 45 minutes, 8.5% 45 to 60 minutes, 19.7% 60 minutes or more (2006-2010 5-year est.)
Additional Information Contacts
Armstrong County Chamber of Commerce . . . . (724) 543-1305
   http://www.armstrongchamber.org

WEST KITTANNING (borough).
Covers a land area of 0.429 square miles and a water area of 0 square miles. Located at 40.81° N. Lat; 79.53° W. Long. Elevation is 1,024 feet.
Population: 1,253 (1990); 1,199 (2000); 1,175 (2010); Density: 2,742.0 persons per square mile (2010); Race: 99.1% White, 0.3% Black, 0.3% Asian, 0.0% American Indian/Alaska Native, 0.0% Native Hawaiian/Other Pacific Islander, 0.3% Other, 0.3% Hispanic of any race (2010); Average household size: 2.09 (2010); Median age: 47.4 (2010); Males per 100 females: 85.3 (2010); Marriage status: 23.3% never married, 51.8% now married, 11.5% widowed, 13.4% divorced (2006-2010 5-year est.); Foreign born: 0.4% (2006-2010 5-year est.); Ancestry (includes multiple ancestries): 43.2% German, 16.7% Irish, 14.3% Italian, 11.9% English, 7.9% Dutch (2006-2010 5-year est.).
Economy: Single-family building permits issued: 0 (2011); Multi-family building permits issued: 0 (2011); Employment by occupation: 6.0% management, 4.5% professional, 7.5% services, 17.7% sales, 7.8% farming, 11.5% construction, 6.8% production (2006-2010 5-year est.).
Income: Per capita income: $25,710 (2006-2010 5-year est.); Median household income: $43,963 (2006-2010 5-year est.); Average household income: $56,532 (2006-2010 5-year est.); Percent of households with income of $100,000 or more: 14.5% (2006-2010 5-year est.); Poverty rate: 4.6% (2006-2010 5-year est.).
Education: Percent of population age 25 and over with: High school diploma (including GED) or higher: 93.4% (2006-2010 5-year est.); Bachelor's degree or higher: 18.0% (2006-2010 5-year est.); Master's degree or higher: 3.8% (2006-2010 5-year est.).
Housing: Homeownership rate: 71.3% (2010); Median home value: $97,000 (2006-2010 5-year est.); Median contract rent: $461 per month (2006-2010 5-year est.); Median year structure built: 1949 (2006-2010 5-year est.).
Transportation: Commute to work: 94.2% car, 0.5% public transportation, 3.4% walk, 1.9% work from home (2006-2010 5-year est.); Travel time to work: 42.6% less than 15 minutes, 17.4% 15 to 30 minutes, 17.7% 30 to 45 minutes, 12.3% 45 to 60 minutes, 9.9% 60 minutes or more (2006-2010 5-year est.)
Additional Information Contacts
Armstrong County Chamber of Commerce . . . . (724) 543-1305
   http://www.armstrongchamber.org

WORTHINGTON (borough).
Covers a land area of 0.688 square miles and a water area of 0 square miles. Located at 40.84° N. Lat; 79.64° W. Long. Elevation is 1,112 feet.
Population: 713 (1990); 778 (2000); 639 (2010); Density: 929.2 persons per square mile (2010); Race: 99.1% White, 0.3% Black, 0.2% Asian, 0.0% American Indian/Alaska Native, 0.0% Native Hawaiian/Other Pacific Islander, 0.4% Other, 0.6% Hispanic of any race (2010); Average household size: 2.51 (2010); Median age: 42.1 (2010); Males per 100 females: 97.8 (2010); Marriage status: 26.6% never married, 50.6% now

married, 4.6% widowed, 18.2% divorced (2006-2010 5-year est.); Foreign born: 0.0% (2006-2010 5-year est.); Ancestry (includes multiple ancestries): 48.0% German, 19.2% Irish, 10.4% Swedish, 10.3% American, 7.6% Scotch-Irish (2006-2010 5-year est.).
Economy: Single-family building permits issued: 0 (2011); Multi-family building permits issued: 0 (2011); Employment by occupation: 1.2% management, 6.9% professional, 6.9% services, 24.2% sales, 1.2% farming, 9.9% construction, 6.9% production (2006-2010 5-year est.).
Income: Per capita income: $19,014 (2006-2010 5-year est.); Median household income: $44,821 (2006-2010 5-year est.); Average household income: $49,546 (2006-2010 5-year est.); Percent of households with income of $100,000 or more: 4.6% (2006-2010 5-year est.); Poverty rate: 18.0% (2006-2010 5-year est.).
Education: Percent of population age 25 and over with: High school diploma (including GED) or higher: 96.4% (2006-2010 5-year est.); Bachelor's degree or higher: 10.9% (2006-2010 5-year est.); Master's degree or higher: 1.3% (2006-2010 5-year est.).
Housing: Homeownership rate: 77.7% (2010); Median home value: $90,400 (2006-2010 5-year est.); Median contract rent: $368 per month (2006-2010 5-year est.); Median year structure built: 1943 (2006-2010 5-year est.).
Transportation: Commute to work: 94.3% car, 1.8% public transportation, 2.4% walk, 1.5% work from home (2006-2010 5-year est.); Travel time to work: 41.9% less than 15 minutes, 27.5% 15 to 30 minutes, 14.4% 30 to 45 minutes, 3.1% 45 to 60 minutes, 13.1% 60 minutes or more (2006-2010 5-year est.)

YATESBORO (unincorporated postal area)
Zip Code: 16263
   Covers a land area of 1.570 square miles and a water area of 0 square miles. Located at 40.80° N. Lat; 79.33° W. Long. Elevation is 1,119 feet.
   Population: 317 (2010); Density: 201.9 persons per square mile (2010); Race: 99.7% White, 0.0% Black, 0.0% Asian, 0.0% American Indian/Alaska Native, 0.0% Native Hawaiian/Other Pacific Islander, 0.3% Other, 0.3% Hispanic of any race (2010); Average household size: 2.54 (2010); Median age: 38.8 (2010); Males per 100 females: 87.6 (2010); Homeownership rate: 75.2% (2010)

Beaver County

Located in western Pennsylvania; bounded on the west by Ohio. Covers a land area of 434.712 square miles, a water area of 9.331 square miles, and is located in the Eastern Time Zone at 40.68° N. Lat., 80.35° W. Long. The county was founded in 1800. County seat is Beaver.

Beaver County is part of the Pittsburgh, PA Metropolitan Statistical Area. The entire metro area includes: Allegheny County, PA; Armstrong County, PA; Beaver County, PA; Butler County, PA; Fayette County, PA; Washington County, PA; Westmoreland County, PA

Weather Station: Montgomery Lock & Dam									Elevation: 689 feet		
	Jan	Feb	Mar	Apr	May	Jun	Jul	Aug	Sep	Oct	Nov	Dec
High	37	41	50	64	73	80	84	82	76	64	53	41
Low	22	24	30	40	49	58	63	62	55	44	35	27
Precip	2.5	2.1	2.9	3.2	3.8	3.7	4.4	3.4	3.6	2.4	3.1	2.7
Snow	4.0	2.9	2.4	0.2	0.0	0.0	0.0	0.0	0.0	tr	0.2	2.4

High and Low temperatures in degrees Fahrenheit; Precipitation and Snow in inches

Population: 186,093 (1990); 181,412 (2000); 170,539 (2010); Race: 91.2% White, 6.3% Black, 0.4% Asian, 0.1% American Indian/Alaska Native, 0.0% Native Hawaiian/Other Pacific Islander, 2.0% Other, 1.2% Hispanic of any race (2010); Density: 392.3 persons per square mile (2010); Average household size: 2.34 (2010); Median age: 44.4 (2010); Males per 100 females: 93.2 (2010).
Religion: Six largest groups: 27.0% Catholicism, 7.5% Methodist/Pietist, 4.8% Presbyterian-Reformed, 4.3% Lutheran, 1.9% Baptist, 1.9% Holiness (2010)
Economy: Unemployment rate: 8.1% (August 2012); Total civilian labor force: 92,451 (August 2012); Leading industries: 20.2% health care and social assistance; 15.9% retail trade; 14.1% manufacturing (2010); Farms: 824 totaling 67,075 acres (2007); Companies that employ 500 or more persons: 7 (2010); Companies that employ 100 to 499 persons: 68 (2010); Companies that employ less than 100 persons: 3,383 (2010); Black-owned businesses: 352 (2007); Hispanic-owned businesses: n/a (2007); Asian-owned businesses: n/a (2007); Women-owned businesses: 3,095

(2007); Retail sales per capita: $10,907 (2010). Single-family building permits issued: 169 (2011); Multi-family building permits issued: 6 (2011).

Income: Per capita income: $24,168 (2006-2010 5-year est.); Median household income: $46,190 (2006-2010 5-year est.); Average household income: $57,839 (2006-2010 5-year est.); Percent of households with income of $100,000 or more: 13.8% (2006-2010 5-year est.); Poverty rate: 11.1% (2006-2010 5-year est.); Bankruptcy rate: 3.49% (2011).

Taxes: Total county taxes per capita: $264 (2009); County property taxes per capita: $262 (2009).

Education: Percent of population age 25 and over with: High school diploma (including GED) or higher: 89.6% (2006-2010 5-year est.); Bachelor's degree or higher: 19.2% (2006-2010 5-year est.); Master's degree or higher: 6.2% (2006-2010 5-year est.).

Housing: Homeownership rate: 73.3% (2010); Median home value: $112,400 (2006-2010 5-year est.); Median contract rent: $430 per month (2006-2010 5-year est.); Median year structure built: 1956 (2006-2010 5-year est.)

Health: Birth rate: 101.2 per 10,000 population (2011); Death rate: 121.1 per 10,000 population (2011); Age-adjusted cancer mortality rate: 192.7 deaths per 100,000 population (2009); Number of physicians: 14.7 per 10,000 population (2010); Hospital beds: 31.5 per 10,000 population (2008); Hospital admissions: 1,275.9 per 10,000 population (2008).

Environment: Air Quality Index: 63.3% good, 32.3% moderate, 4.4% unhealthy for sensitive individuals, 0.0% unhealthy (percent of days in 2011)

Elections: 2012 Presidential election results: 46.0% Obama, 52.6% Romney

National and State Parks: Raccoon Creek State Park

Additional Information Contacts
Beaver County Government . . . . (724) 728-5700
    http://www.beavercountypa.gov
Beaver County Chamber of Commerce . . . . (724) 775-3944
    http://beavercountychamber.com
Beaver County Chamber of Commerce . . . . (724) 775-3944
    http://www.beavercountychamber.com

Beaver County Communities

ALIQUIPPA (city). Covers a land area of 4.194 square miles and a water area of 0.402 square miles. Located at 40.62° N. Lat; 80.26° W. Long. Elevation is 741 feet.

History: Aliquippa was named for "Queen" Aliquippa, an Iriquois woman.

Population: 13,374 (1990); 11,734 (2000); 9,438 (2010); Density: 2,250.6 persons per square mile (2010); Race: 57.6% White, 38.6% Black, 0.4% Asian, 0.1% American Indian/Alaska Native, 0.0% Native Hawaiian/Other Pacific Islander, 3.3% Other, 1.3% Hispanic of any race (2010); Average household size: 2.15 (2010); Median age: 42.2 (2010); Males per 100 females: 85.3 (2010); Marriage status: 41.0% never married, 36.0% now married, 10.4% widowed, 12.6% divorced (2006-2010 5-year est.); Foreign born: 5.3% (2006-2010 5-year est.); Ancestry (includes multiple ancestries): 19.1% Italian, 12.3% German, 11.9% Irish, 4.6% Polish, 2.7% Slovak (2006-2010 5-year est.).

Economy: Single-family building permits issued: 0 (2011); Multi-family building permits issued: 0 (2011); Employment by occupation: 6.5% management, 2.1% professional, 19.9% services, 19.5% sales, 5.0% farming, 4.5% construction, 6.2% production (2006-2010 5-year est.).

Income: Per capita income: $18,732 (2006-2010 5-year est.); Median household income: $31,023 (2006-2010 5-year est.); Average household income: $41,580 (2006-2010 5-year est.); Percent of households with income of $100,000 or more: 5.9% (2006-2010 5-year est.); Poverty rate: 21.3% (2006-2010 5-year est.).

Education: Percent of population age 25 and over with: High school diploma (including GED) or higher: 86.7% (2006-2010 5-year est.); Bachelor's degree or higher: 13.2% (2006-2010 5-year est.); Master's degree or higher: 2.8% (2006-2010 5-year est.).

School District(s)
Aliquippa SD (KG-12)
    2010-11 Enrollment: 1,199 . . . . (724) 857-7500
Central Valley SD (KG-12)
    2010-11 Enrollment: 2,405 . . . . (724) 775-5600
Hopewell Area SD (KG-12)
    2010-11 Enrollment: 2,503 . . . . (724) 375-6691

Housing: Homeownership rate: 57.4% (2010); Median home value: $71,100 (2006-2010 5-year est.); Median contract rent: $357 per month

(2006-2010 5-year est.); Median year structure built: 1945 (2006-2010 5-year est.).

Hospitals: Aliquippa Community Hospital (104 beds); Gateway Rehabilitation Center (360 beds)

Safety: Violent crime rate: 43.3 per 10,000 population; Property crime rate: 198.6 per 10,000 population (2011).

Transportation: Commute to work: 86.6% car, 4.8% public transportation, 4.4% walk, 2.1% work from home (2006-2010 5-year est.); Travel time to work: 22.3% less than 15 minutes, 48.2% 15 to 30 minutes, 15.5% 30 to 45 minutes, 4.5% 45 to 60 minutes, 9.5% 60 minutes or more (2006-2010 5-year est.)

Additional Information Contacts
Beaver County Chamber of Commerce . . . . (724) 775-3944
    http://beavercountychamber.com
City of Aliquippa . . . . (724) 375-5188
    http://www.aliquippapa.gov

AMBRIDGE (borough). Covers a land area of 1.486 square miles and a water area of 0.206 square miles. Located at 40.59° N. Lat; 80.23° W. Long. Elevation is 771 feet.

History: Founded by and named for the American Bridge Company in 1901. Near Old Economy Village, 17 restored buildings of German communal group (1824-1906). Incorporated 1905.

Population: 8,133 (1990); 7,769 (2000); 7,050 (2010); Density: 4,743.5 persons per square mile (2010); Race: 77.5% White, 17.0% Black, 0.4% Asian, 0.1% American Indian/Alaska Native, 0.0% Native Hawaiian/Other Pacific Islander, 5.0% Other, 2.5% Hispanic of any race (2010); Average household size: 2.14 (2010); Median age: 39.6 (2010); Males per 100 females: 93.3 (2010); Marriage status: 36.9% never married, 43.3% now married, 7.3% widowed, 12.5% divorced (2006-2010 5-year est.); Foreign born: 2.4% (2006-2010 5-year est.); Ancestry (includes multiple ancestries): 21.4% German, 20.8% Irish, 15.2% Italian, 7.7% Polish, 5.3% English (2006-2010 5-year est.).

Economy: Single-family building permits issued: 0 (2011); Multi-family building permits issued: 0 (2011); Employment by occupation: 4.5% management, 0.9% professional, 15.9% services, 12.3% sales, 5.0% farming, 6.2% construction, 7.6% production (2006-2010 5-year est.).

Income: Per capita income: $17,685 (2006-2010 5-year est.); Median household income: $30,266 (2006-2010 5-year est.); Average household income: $37,329 (2006-2010 5-year est.); Percent of households with income of $100,000 or more: 5.1% (2006-2010 5-year est.); Poverty rate: 25.0% (2006-2010 5-year est.).

Education: Percent of population age 25 and over with: High school diploma (including GED) or higher: 84.5% (2006-2010 5-year est.); Bachelor's degree or higher: 12.6% (2006-2010 5-year est.); Master's degree or higher: 5.5% (2006-2010 5-year est.).

School District(s)
Ambridge Area SD (KG-12)
    2010-11 Enrollment: 2,785 . . . . (724) 266-2833

Four-year College(s)
Trinity Episcopal School for Ministry (Private, Not-for-profit, Protestant Episcopal)
    Fall 2010 Enrollment: 130 . . . . (724) 266-3838

Housing: Homeownership rate: 46.9% (2010); Median home value: $70,400 (2006-2010 5-year est.); Median contract rent: $435 per month (2006-2010 5-year est.); Median year structure built: before 1940 (2006-2010 5-year est.).

Safety: Violent crime rate: 173.9 per 10,000 population; Property crime rate: 435.5 per 10,000 population (2011).

Transportation: Commute to work: 82.3% car, 5.0% public transportation, 10.6% walk, 1.3% work from home (2006-2010 5-year est.); Travel time to work: 31.9% less than 15 minutes, 37.1% 15 to 30 minutes, 19.8% 30 to 45 minutes, 8.3% 45 to 60 minutes, 3.0% 60 minutes or more (2006-2010 5-year est.)

Additional Information Contacts
Ambridge Area Chamber of Commerce . . . . (724) 266-3040
    http://www.ambridgechamberofcommerce.com
Borough of Ambridge . . . . (724) 266-4070
    http://www.ambridgeboro.org

BADEN (borough). Covers a land area of 2.261 square miles and a water area of 0.223 square miles. Located at 40.64° N. Lat; 80.22° W. Long. Elevation is 787 feet.

History: Laid out c.1839, incorporated 1868.

Population: 5,074 (1990); 4,377 (2000); 4,135 (2010); Density: 1,829.1 persons per square mile (2010); Race: 96.9% White, 1.5% Black, 0.3% Asian, 0.1% American Indian/Alaska Native, 0.0% Native Hawaiian/Other Pacific Islander, 1.2% Other, 0.9% Hispanic of any race (2010); Average household size: 2.08 (2010); Median age: 47.3 (2010); Males per 100 females: 87.3 (2010); Marriage status: 23.1% never married, 53.2% now married, 11.9% widowed, 11.7% divorced (2006-2010 5-year est.); Foreign born: 0.8% (2006-2010 5-year est.); Ancestry (includes multiple ancestries): 31.4% German, 23.4% Irish, 19.1% Italian, 11.6% Polish, 9.8% English (2006-2010 5-year est.).
Economy: Single-family building permits issued: 0 (2011); Multi-family building permits issued: 0 (2011); Employment by occupation: 6.9% management, 1.9% professional, 14.0% services, 19.5% sales, 6.0% farming, 11.4% construction, 7.5% production (2006-2010 5-year est.).
Income: Per capita income: $26,431 (2006-2010 5-year est.); Median household income: $38,585 (2006-2010 5-year est.); Average household income: $55,910 (2006-2010 5-year est.); Percent of households with income of $100,000 or more: 10.7% (2006-2010 5-year est.); Poverty rate: 12.1% (2006-2010 5-year est.).
Taxes: Total city taxes per capita: $304 (2009); City property taxes per capita: $201 (2009).
Education: Percent of population age 25 and over with: High school diploma (including GED) or higher: 89.7% (2006-2010 5-year est.); Bachelor's degree or higher: 17.4% (2006-2010 5-year est.); Master's degree or higher: 4.2% (2006-2010 5-year est.).

School District(s)
Ambridge Area SD (KG-12)
    2010-11 Enrollment: 2,785 . . . . (724) 266-2833
Housing: Homeownership rate: 68.2% (2010); Median home value: $91,600 (2006-2010 5-year est.); Median contract rent: $388 per month (2006-2010 5-year est.); Median year structure built: 1953 (2006-2010 5-year est.).
Safety: Violent crime rate: 2.4 per 10,000 population; Property crime rate: 106.1 per 10,000 population (2011).
Transportation: Commute to work: 94.8% car, 1.8% public transportation, 2.5% walk, 0.5% work from home (2006-2010 5-year est.); Travel time to work: 22.9% less than 15 minutes, 48.2% 15 to 30 minutes, 18.3% 30 to 45 minutes, 8.6% 45 to 60 minutes, 2.1% 60 minutes or more (2006-2010 5-year est.)
Additional Information Contacts
Beaver County Chamber of Commerce . . . . (724) 775-3944
    http://beavercountychamber.com

BEAVER (borough). County seat. Covers a land area of 0.916 square miles and a water area of 0.207 square miles. Located at 40.69° N. Lat; 80.31° W. Long. Elevation is 791 feet.
History: Site of Fort McIntosh (1778); Laid out 1791, incorporated 1802.
Population: 5,028 (1990); 4,775 (2000); 4,531 (2010); Density: 4,947.3 persons per square mile (2010); Race: 95.9% White, 1.4% Black, 0.9% Asian, 0.1% American Indian/Alaska Native, 0.0% Native Hawaiian/Other Pacific Islander, 1.7% Other, 1.7% Hispanic of any race (2010); Average household size: 2.13 (2010); Median age: 46.4 (2010); Males per 100 females: 85.0 (2010); Marriage status: 23.4% never married, 56.5% now married, 10.6% widowed, 9.4% divorced (2006-2010 5-year est.); Foreign born: 2.3% (2006-2010 5-year est.); Ancestry (includes multiple ancestries): 37.6% German, 18.0% English, 17.4% Irish, 10.0% Italian, 9.0% Polish (2006-2010 5-year est.).
Economy: Single-family building permits issued: 0 (2011); Multi-family building permits issued: 0 (2011); Employment by occupation: 16.4% management, 3.3% professional, 7.9% services, 24.9% sales, 2.1% farming, 6.6% construction, 2.5% production (2006-2010 5-year est.).
Income: Per capita income: $32,986 (2006-2010 5-year est.); Median household income: $54,185 (2006-2010 5-year est.); Average household income: $72,955 (2006-2010 5-year est.); Percent of households with income of $100,000 or more: 20.5% (2006-2010 5-year est.); Poverty rate: 3.8% (2006-2010 5-year est.).
Education: Percent of population age 25 and over with: High school diploma (including GED) or higher: 95.5% (2006-2010 5-year est.); Bachelor's degree or higher: 39.9% (2006-2010 5-year est.); Master's degree or higher: 15.3% (2006-2010 5-year est.).

School District(s)
Beaver Area Academic CS (09-12)
    2010-11 Enrollment: 80 . . . . (724) 774-4022
Beaver Area SD (KG-12)
    2010-11 Enrollment: 1,984 . . . . (724) 774-4010

Housing: Homeownership rate: 61.1% (2010); Median home value: $164,700 (2006-2010 5-year est.); Median contract rent: $508 per month (2006-2010 5-year est.); Median year structure built: before 1940 (2006-2010 5-year est.).
Hospitals: Medical Center of Beaver (358 beds)
Safety: Violent crime rate: 4.4 per 10,000 population; Property crime rate: 211.2 per 10,000 population (2011).
Newspapers: Beaver County Times (Regional news; Circulation 45,568)
Transportation: Commute to work: 91.1% car, 2.5% public transportation, 4.1% walk, 1.9% work from home (2006-2010 5-year est.); Travel time to work: 37.0% less than 15 minutes, 34.3% 15 to 30 minutes, 14.4% 30 to 45 minutes, 3.5% 45 to 60 minutes, 10.8% 60 minutes or more (2006-2010 5-year est.)
Additional Information Contacts
Beaver County Chamber of Commerce . . . . (724) 775-3944
    http://beavercountychamber.com
Borough of Beaver . . . . (800) 342-8192
    http://www.beaverpa.us

BEAVER FALLS (city). Covers a land area of 2.128 square miles and a water area of 0.223 square miles. Located at 40.76° N. Lat; 80.32° W. Long. Elevation is 801 feet.
History: The city was founded on a Native American trail that later became a pioneer road. Beaver Falls Historical Society Museum. Settled c.1793, Incorporated 1868.
Population: 10,687 (1990); 9,920 (2000); 8,987 (2010); Density: 4,223.6 persons per square mile (2010); Race: 75.3% White, 19.3% Black, 0.4% Asian, 0.2% American Indian/Alaska Native, 0.0% Native Hawaiian/Other Pacific Islander, 4.8% Other, 1.2% Hispanic of any race (2010); Average household size: 2.28 (2010); Median age: 34.1 (2010); Males per 100 females: 89.1 (2010); Marriage status: 45.5% never married, 36.0% now married, 8.0% widowed, 10.5% divorced (2006-2010 5-year est.); Foreign born: 1.5% (2006-2010 5-year est.); Ancestry (includes multiple ancestries): 28.5% German, 17.5% Irish, 11.5% Italian, 9.3% English, 6.0% Scotch-Irish (2006-2010 5-year est.).
Economy: Single-family building permits issued: 0 (2011); Multi-family building permits issued: 0 (2011); Employment by occupation: 5.7% management, 2.4% professional, 17.1% services, 18.1% sales, 5.9% farming, 7.3% construction, 5.2% production (2006-2010 5-year est.).
Income: Per capita income: $14,935 (2006-2010 5-year est.); Median household income: $30,655 (2006-2010 5-year est.); Average household income: $37,601 (2006-2010 5-year est.); Percent of households with income of $100,000 or more: 3.7% (2006-2010 5-year est.); Poverty rate: 24.9% (2006-2010 5-year est.).
Education: Percent of population age 25 and over with: High school diploma (including GED) or higher: 85.9% (2006-2010 5-year est.); Bachelor's degree or higher: 13.0% (2006-2010 5-year est.); Master's degree or higher: 4.6% (2006-2010 5-year est.).

School District(s)
Big Beaver Falls Area SD (PK-12)
    2010-11 Enrollment: 1,721 . . . . (724) 843-3470
Blackhawk SD (KG-12)
    2010-11 Enrollment: 2,535 . . . . (724) 846-6600

Four-year College(s)
Geneva College (Private, Not-for-profit, Reformed Presbyterian Church)
    Fall 2010 Enrollment: 2,141 . . . . (724) 846-5100
    2011-12 Tuition: In-state $23,330; Out-of-state $23,330

Vocational/Technical School(s)
Beaver Falls Beauty Academy (Private, For-profit)
    Fall 2010 Enrollment: 78 . . . . (724) 724-0708
    2011-12 Tuition: $13,800

Housing: Homeownership rate: 48.6% (2010); Median home value: $66,400 (2006-2010 5-year est.); Median contract rent: $404 per month (2006-2010 5-year est.); Median year structure built: before 1940 (2006-2010 5-year est.).
Safety: Violent crime rate: 59.9 per 10,000 population; Property crime rate: 329.4 per 10,000 population (2011).
Transportation: Commute to work: 78.7% car, 3.0% public transportation, 16.8% walk, 1.1% work from home (2006-2010 5-year est.); Travel time to work: 41.7% less than 15 minutes, 29.1% 15 to 30 minutes, 18.0% 30 to 45 minutes, 7.1% 45 to 60 minutes, 4.1% 60 minutes or more (2006-2010 5-year est.)
Airports: Zelienople Municipal (general aviation)

Additional Information Contacts
Beaver County Chamber of Commerce . . . . (724) 775-3944
   http://beavercountychamber.com
City of Beaver Falls . . . . (724) 847-2900
   http://www.co.beaver.pa.us

BIG BEAVER (borough). Covers a land area of 17.794 square miles
and a water area of 0.232 square miles. Located at 40.82° N. Lat; 80.36°
W. Long. Elevation is 1,089 feet.
Population: 2,298 (1990); 2,186 (2000); 1,970 (2010); Density: 110.7
persons per square mile (2010); Race: 97.4% White, 1.5% Black, 0.2%
Asian, 0.0% American Indian/Alaska Native, 0.0% Native Hawaiian/Other
Pacific Islander, 0.9% Other, 0.7% Hispanic of any race (2010); Average
household size: 2.34 (2010); Median age: 48.9 (2010); Males per 100
females: 99.8 (2010); Marriage status: 22.9% never married, 64.5% now
married, 7.2% widowed, 5.3% divorced (2006-2010 5-year est.); Foreign
born: 1.7% (2006-2010 5-year est.); Ancestry (includes multiple
ancestries): 25.5% Irish, 23.8% German, 15.5% English, 14.0% Italian,
11.9% Polish (2006-2010 5-year est.).
Economy: Single-family building permits issued: 1 (2011); Multi-family
building permits issued: 0 (2011); Employment by occupation: 4.2%
management, 3.7% professional, 14.3% services, 12.1% sales, 3.6%
farming, 12.0% construction, 7.9% production (2006-2010 5-year est.).
Income: Per capita income: $23,495 (2006-2010 5-year est.); Median
household income: $45,700 (2006-2010 5-year est.); Average household
income: $55,818 (2006-2010 5-year est.); Percent of households with
income of $100,000 or more: 10.7% (2006-2010 5-year est.); Poverty rate:
7.1% (2006-2010 5-year est.).
Education: Percent of population age 25 and over with: High school
diploma (including GED) or higher: 86.5% (2006-2010 5-year est.);
Bachelor's degree or higher: 16.5% (2006-2010 5-year est.); Master's
degree or higher: 6.0% (2006-2010 5-year est.).
Housing: Homeownership rate: 87.7% (2010); Median home value:
$102,500 (2006-2010 5-year est.); Median contract rent: $610 per month
(2006-2010 5-year est.); Median year structure built: 1961 (2006-2010
5-year est.).
Transportation: Commute to work: 93.8% car, 0.7% public transportation,
0.0% walk, 3.6% work from home (2006-2010 5-year est.); Travel time to
work: 19.4% less than 15 minutes, 38.3% 15 to 30 minutes, 25.7% 30 to
45 minutes, 11.1% 45 to 60 minutes, 5.5% 60 minutes or more (2006-2010
5-year est.)
Additional Information Contacts
Beaver County Chamber of Commerce . . . . (724) 775-3944
   http://beavercountychamber.com

BRIDGEWATER (borough). Aka West Bridgewater. Covers a land
area of 0.623 square miles and a water area of 0.105 square miles.
Located at 40.71° N. Lat; 80.30° W. Long. Elevation is 797 feet.
History: Was 19th-century river port. Incorporated 1835.
Population: 751 (1990); 739 (2000); 704 (2010); Density: 1,130.5 persons
per square mile (2010); Race: 92.8% White, 5.3% Black, 0.4% Asian,
0.0% American Indian/Alaska Native, 0.0% Native Hawaiian/Other Pacific
Islander, 1.5% Other, 1.0% Hispanic of any race (2010); Average
household size: 2.01 (2010); Median age: 47.7 (2010); Males per 100
females: 88.7 (2010); Marriage status: 14.6% never married, 58.0% now
married, 11.8% widowed, 15.7% divorced (2006-2010 5-year est.); Foreign
born: 0.7% (2006-2010 5-year est.); Ancestry (includes multiple
ancestries): 34.5% German, 25.7% Irish, 14.7% Italian, 9.5% English,
9.2% Polish (2006-2010 5-year est.).
Economy: Single-family building permits issued: 0 (2011); Multi-family
building permits issued: 0 (2011); Employment by occupation: 9.5%
management, 1.9% professional, 16.1% services, 17.0% sales, 0.6%
farming, 13.2% construction, 14.8% production (2006-2010 5-year est.).
Income: Per capita income: $21,171 (2006-2010 5-year est.); Median
household income: $32,031 (2006-2010 5-year est.); Average household
income: $43,584 (2006-2010 5-year est.); Percent of households with
income of $100,000 or more: 8.2% (2006-2010 5-year est.); Poverty rate:
13.5% (2006-2010 5-year est.).
Education: Percent of population age 25 and over with: High school
diploma (including GED) or higher: 91.8% (2006-2010 5-year est.);
Bachelor's degree or higher: 16.2% (2006-2010 5-year est.); Master's
degree or higher: 4.5% (2006-2010 5-year est.).
Housing: Homeownership rate: 62.6% (2010); Median home value:
$98,800 (2006-2010 5-year est.); Median contract rent: $430 per month

(2006-2010 5-year est.); Median year structure built: 1954 (2006-2010
5-year est.).
Transportation: Commute to work: 88.8% car, 1.3% public transportation,
4.8% walk, 1.0% work from home (2006-2010 5-year est.); Travel time to
work: 46.8% less than 15 minutes, 37.7% 15 to 30 minutes, 8.4% 30 to 45
minutes, 1.3% 45 to 60 minutes, 5.8% 60 minutes or more (2006-2010
5-year est.)

BRIGHTON (township). Covers a land area of 19.404 square miles
and a water area of 0.040 square miles. Located at 40.70° N. Lat; 80.38°
W. Long.
History: Blockhouse erected here 1789. Settled c.1801, incorporated
1838.
Population: 7,412 (1990); 8,024 (2000); 8,227 (2010); Density: 424.0
persons per square mile (2010); Race: 97.1% White, 1.1% Black, 0.7%
Asian, 0.1% American Indian/Alaska Native, 0.1% Native Hawaiian/Other
Pacific Islander, 0.9% Other, 1.1% Hispanic of any race (2010); Average
household size: 2.52 (2010); Median age: 47.8 (2010); Males per 100
females: 91.8 (2010); Marriage status: 21.6% never married, 61.7% now
married, 11.5% widowed, 5.1% divorced (2006-2010 5-year est.); Foreign
born: 2.5% (2006-2010 5-year est.); Ancestry (includes multiple
ancestries): 34.1% German, 18.8% Irish, 15.9% Italian, 11.6% English,
5.7% Polish (2006-2010 5-year est.).
Economy: Single-family building permits issued: 10 (2011); Multi-family
building permits issued: 0 (2011); Employment by occupation: 15.9%
management, 4.5% professional, 6.6% services, 17.7% sales, 2.0%
farming, 7.2% construction, 5.2% production (2006-2010 5-year est.).
Income: Per capita income: $31,024 (2006-2010 5-year est.); Median
household income: $61,094 (2006-2010 5-year est.); Average household
income: $84,420 (2006-2010 5-year est.); Percent of households with
income of $100,000 or more: 24.8% (2006-2010 5-year est.); Poverty rate:
2.1% (2006-2010 5-year est.).
Education: Percent of population age 25 and over with: High school
diploma (including GED) or higher: 90.3% (2006-2010 5-year est.);
Bachelor's degree or higher: 29.1% (2006-2010 5-year est.); Master's
degree or higher: 11.3% (2006-2010 5-year est.).
Housing: Homeownership rate: 86.2% (2010); Median home value:
$164,800 (2006-2010 5-year est.); Median contract rent: $498 per month
(2006-2010 5-year est.); Median year structure built: 1960 (2006-2010
5-year est.).
Safety: Violent crime rate: 4.8 per 10,000 population; Property crime rate:
53.3 per 10,000 population (2011).
Transportation: Commute to work: 91.8% car, 1.5% public transportation,
1.9% walk, 3.7% work from home (2006-2010 5-year est.); Travel time to
work: 33.9% less than 15 minutes, 32.9% 15 to 30 minutes, 15.9% 30 to
45 minutes, 5.9% 45 to 60 minutes, 11.2% 60 minutes or more (2006-2010
5-year est.)
Additional Information Contacts
Beaver County Chamber of Commerce . . . . (724) 775-3944
   http://beavercountychamber.com
Brighton Township . . . . (724) 774-4803
   http://www.brightontwp.org

CENTER (township). Covers a land area of 15.049 square miles and a
water area of 0.300 square miles. Located at 40.65° N. Lat; 80.30° W.
Long.
Population: 10,742 (1990); 11,492 (2000); 11,795 (2010); Density: 783.8
persons per square mile (2010); Race: 94.2% White, 3.5% Black, 0.9%
Asian, 0.0% American Indian/Alaska Native, 0.0% Native Hawaiian/Other
Pacific Islander, 1.4% Other, 1.3% Hispanic of any race (2010); Average
household size: 2.47 (2010); Median age: 43.8 (2010); Males per 100
females: 94.7 (2010); Marriage status: 22.4% never married, 64.5% now
married, 5.9% widowed, 7.2% divorced (2006-2010 5-year est.); Foreign
born: 1.1% (2006-2010 5-year est.); Ancestry (includes multiple
ancestries): 29.2% German, 28.3% Italian, 19.3% Irish, 9.8% English,
6.0% Slovak (2006-2010 5-year est.).
Economy: Single-family building permits issued: 12 (2011); Multi-family
building permits issued: 0 (2011); Employment by occupation: 9.2%
management, 4.5% professional, 7.9% services, 20.7% sales, 3.1%
farming, 7.3% construction, 6.5% production (2006-2010 5-year est.).
Income: Per capita income: $28,826 (2006-2010 5-year est.); Median
household income: $58,705 (2006-2010 5-year est.); Average household
income: $73,544 (2006-2010 5-year est.); Percent of households with
income of $100,000 or more: 23.2% (2006-2010 5-year est.); Poverty rate:
4.9% (2006-2010 5-year est.).

Taxes: Total city taxes per capita: $307 (2009); City property taxes per capita: $134 (2009).

Education: Percent of population age 25 and over with: High school diploma (including GED) or higher: 92.7% (2006-2010 5-year est.); Bachelor's degree or higher: 27.4% (2006-2010 5-year est.); Master's degree or higher: 11.1% (2006-2010 5-year est.).

Housing: Homeownership rate: 82.0% (2010); Median home value: $165,600 (2006-2010 5-year est.); Median contract rent: $662 per month (2006-2010 5-year est.); Median year structure built: 1973 (2006-2010 5-year est.).

Transportation: Commute to work: 92.5% car, 1.1% public transportation, 1.4% walk, 3.4% work from home (2006-2010 5-year est.); Travel time to work: 32.4% less than 15 minutes, 36.9% 15 to 30 minutes, 17.1% 30 to 45 minutes, 6.2% 45 to 60 minutes, 7.4% 60 minutes or more (2006-2010 5-year est.).

Additional Information Contacts

Beaver County Chamber of Commerce . . . . (724) 775-3944
   http://beavercountychamber.com
Center Township . . . . (724) 774-0271
   http://www.ctbos.com

CHIPPEWA (township). Covers a land area of 15.690 square miles and a water area of 0 square miles. Located at 40.76° N. Lat; 80.38° W. Long.

Population: 6,972 (1990); 7,021 (2000); 7,620 (2010); Density: 485.7 persons per square mile (2010); Race: 97.1% White, 0.8% Black, 0.8% Asian, 0.0% American Indian/Alaska Native, 0.1% Native Hawaiian/Other Pacific Islander, 1.2% Other, 0.6% Hispanic of any race (2010); Average household size: 2.42 (2010); Median age: 46.1 (2010); Males per 100 females: 93.0 (2010); Marriage status: 17.6% never married, 66.3% now married, 8.9% widowed, 7.2% divorced (2006-2010 5-year est.); Foreign born: 1.5% (2006-2010 5-year est.); Ancestry (includes multiple ancestries): 43.5% German, 21.9% Irish, 17.6% Italian, 14.0% English, 10.7% Polish (2006-2010 5-year est.).

Economy: Single-family building permits issued: 32 (2011); Multi-family building permits issued: 0 (2011); Employment by occupation: 13.6% management, 5.3% professional, 6.6% services, 18.8% sales, 4.4% farming, 8.1% construction, 5.3% production (2006-2010 5-year est.).

Income: Per capita income: $29,210 (2006-2010 5-year est.); Median household income: $55,289 (2006-2010 5-year est.); Average household income: $71,504 (2006-2010 5-year est.); Percent of households with income of $100,000 or more: 25.2% (2006-2010 5-year est.); Poverty rate: 5.7% (2006-2010 5-year est.).

Taxes: Total city taxes per capita: $408 (2009); City property taxes per capita: $246 (2009).

Education: Percent of population age 25 and over with: High school diploma (including GED) or higher: 95.9% (2006-2010 5-year est.); Bachelor's degree or higher: 29.7% (2006-2010 5-year est.); Master's degree or higher: 10.1% (2006-2010 5-year est.).

Housing: Homeownership rate: 80.6% (2010); Median home value: $158,900 (2006-2010 5-year est.); Median contract rent: $616 per month (2006-2010 5-year est.); Median year structure built: 1962 (2006-2010 5-year est.).

Safety: Violent crime rate: 1.2 per 10,000 population; Property crime rate: 312.8 per 10,000 population (2011).

Transportation: Commute to work: 97.7% car, 0.0% public transportation, 0.0% walk, 2.1% work from home (2006-2010 5-year est.); Travel time to work: 32.5% less than 15 minutes, 37.5% 15 to 30 minutes, 20.3% 30 to 45 minutes, 5.0% 45 to 60 minutes, 4.7% 60 minutes or more (2006-2010 5-year est.)

Additional Information Contacts

Beaver County Chamber of Commerce . . . . (724) 775-3944
   http://beavercountychamber.com
Chippewa Township . . . . (724) 843-8177
   http://www.chippewa-twp.org

CONWAY (borough). Covers a land area of 1.276 square miles and a water area of 0.183 square miles. Located at 40.67° N. Lat; 80.24° W. Long. Elevation is 745 feet.

Population: 2,424 (1990); 2,290 (2000); 2,176 (2010); Density: 1,704.9 persons per square mile (2010); Race: 96.7% White, 1.1% Black, 0.3% Asian, 0.1% American Indian/Alaska Native, 0.0% Native Hawaiian/Other Pacific Islander, 1.8% Other, 1.0% Hispanic of any race (2010); Average household size: 2.23 (2010); Median age: 46.1 (2010); Males per 100 females: 87.6 (2010); Marriage status: 25.2% never married, 51.2% now

married, 12.4% widowed, 11.3% divorced (2006-2010 5-year est.); Foreign born: 1.6% (2006-2010 5-year est.); Ancestry (includes multiple ancestries): 39.9% German, 25.0% Italian, 20.8% Irish, 10.3% Polish, 7.3% English (2006-2010 5-year est.).

Economy: Single-family building permits issued: 2 (2011); Multi-family building permits issued: 0 (2011); Employment by occupation: 7.1% management, 0.5% professional, 13.3% services, 22.3% sales, 6.6% farming, 11.6% construction, 10.9% production (2006-2010 5-year est.).

Income: Per capita income: $21,263 (2006-2010 5-year est.); Median household income: $42,308 (2006-2010 5-year est.); Average household income: $48,146 (2006-2010 5-year est.); Percent of households with income of $100,000 or more: 7.1% (2006-2010 5-year est.); Poverty rate: 7.4% (2006-2010 5-year est.).

Education: Percent of population age 25 and over with: High school diploma (including GED) or higher: 91.1% (2006-2010 5-year est.); Bachelor's degree or higher: 11.9% (2006-2010 5-year est.); Master's degree or higher: 4.2% (2006-2010 5-year est.).

School District(s)

Freedom Area SD (KG-12)
   2010-11 Enrollment: 1,573 . . . . (724) 775-5464

Housing: Homeownership rate: 74.4% (2010); Median home value: $112,500 (2006-2010 5-year est.); Median contract rent: $346 per month (2006-2010 5-year est.); Median year structure built: 1959 (2006-2010 5-year est.).

Safety: Violent crime rate: 0.0 per 10,000 population; Property crime rate: 82.5 per 10,000 population (2011).

Transportation: Commute to work: 91.3% car, 1.4% public transportation, 4.5% walk, 2.2% work from home (2006-2010 5-year est.); Travel time to work: 27.1% less than 15 minutes, 48.2% 15 to 30 minutes, 12.5% 30 to 45 minutes, 7.9% 45 to 60 minutes, 4.3% 60 minutes or more (2006-2010 5-year est.).

Additional Information Contacts

Beaver County Chamber of Commerce . . . . (724) 775-3944
   http://beavercountychamber.com

DARLINGTON (borough). Covers a land area of 0.082 square miles and a water area of 0 square miles. Located at 40.81° N. Lat; 80.42° W. Long. Elevation is 906 feet.

Population: 311 (1990); 299 (2000); 254 (2010); Density: 3,090.4 persons per square mile (2010); Race: 98.8% White, 0.0% Black, 1.2% Asian, 0.0% American Indian/Alaska Native, 0.0% Native Hawaiian/Other Pacific Islander, 0.0% Other, 0.4% Hispanic of any race (2010); Average household size: 2.65 (2010); Median age: 35.0 (2010); Males per 100 females: 95.4 (2010); Marriage status: 26.9% never married, 61.4% now married, 5.8% widowed, 5.8% divorced (2006-2010 5-year est.); Foreign born: 0.0% (2006-2010 5-year est.); Ancestry (includes multiple ancestries): 50.5% German, 25.8% English, 20.6% Irish, 12.9% Italian, 7.2% Polish (2006-2010 5-year est.).

Economy: Single-family building permits issued: 0 (2011); Multi-family building permits issued: 0 (2011); Employment by occupation: 2.3% management, 0.0% professional, 3.4% services, 23.0% sales, 6.9% farming, 20.7% construction, 8.0% production (2006-2010 5-year est.).

Income: Per capita income: $18,074 (2006-2010 5-year est.); Median household income: $30,833 (2006-2010 5-year est.); Average household income: $40,677 (2006-2010 5-year est.); Percent of households with income of $100,000 or more: 4.7% (2006-2010 5-year est.); Poverty rate: 12.5% (2006-2010 5-year est.).

Education: Percent of population age 25 and over with: High school diploma (including GED) or higher: 95.2% (2006-2010 5-year est.); Bachelor's degree or higher: 8.2% (2006-2010 5-year est.); Master's degree or higher: 5.4% (2006-2010 5-year est.).

School District(s)

Big Beaver Falls Area SD (PK-12)
   2010-11 Enrollment: 1,721 . . . . (724) 843-3470
Blackhawk SD (KG-12)
   2010-11 Enrollment: 2,535 . . . . (724) 846-6600

Housing: Homeownership rate: 71.9% (2010); Median home value: $95,700 (2006-2010 5-year est.); Median contract rent: $483 per month (2006-2010 5-year est.); Median year structure built: before 1940 (2006-2010 5-year est.).

Transportation: Commute to work: 87.4% car, 0.0% public transportation, 6.9% walk, 5.7% work from home (2006-2010 5-year est.); Travel time to work: 30.5% less than 15 minutes, 24.4% 15 to 30 minutes, 15.9% 30 to 45 minutes, 19.5% 45 to 60 minutes, 9.8% 60 minutes or more (2006-2010 5-year est.)

DARLINGTON (township). Covers a land area of 21.972 square miles and a water area of 0.073 square miles. Located at 40.82° N. Lat; 80.45° W. Long. Elevation is 906 feet.

Population: 2,040 (1990); 1,974 (2000); 1,962 (2010); Density: 89.3 persons per square mile (2010); Race: 98.1% White, 0.1% Black, 0.5% Asian, 0.2% American Indian/Alaska Native, 0.2% Native Hawaiian/Other Pacific Islander, 0.9% Other, 0.4% Hispanic of any race (2010); Average household size: 2.47 (2010); Median age: 46.1 (2010); Males per 100 females: 97.8 (2010); Marriage status: 28.6% never married, 54.5% now married, 8.8% widowed, 8.2% divorced (2006-2010 5-year est.); Foreign born: 0.0% (2006-2010 5-year est.); Ancestry (includes multiple ancestries): 45.5% German, 30.4% Irish, 12.6% Italian, 8.6% English, 7.1% Scotch-Irish (2006-2010 5-year est.).

Economy: Single-family building permits issued: 3 (2011); Multi-family building permits issued: 0 (2011); Employment by occupation: 1.3% management, 0.4% professional, 13.7% services, 15.7% sales, 3.9% farming, 11.9% construction, 10.9% production (2006-2010 5-year est.).

Income: Per capita income: $19,125 (2006-2010 5-year est.); Median household income: $39,063 (2006-2010 5-year est.); Average household income: $46,994 (2006-2010 5-year est.); Percent of households with income of $100,000 or more: 4.8% (2006-2010 5-year est.); Poverty rate: 9.0% (2006-2010 5-year est.).

Education: Percent of population age 25 and over with: High school diploma (including GED) or higher: 90.8% (2006-2010 5-year est.); Bachelor's degree or higher: 12.6% (2006-2010 5-year est.); Master's degree or higher: 3.1% (2006-2010 5-year est.).

Housing: Homeownership rate: 84.3% (2010); Median home value: $96,300 (2006-2010 5-year est.); Median contract rent: $405 per month (2006-2010 5-year est.); Median year structure built: 1957 (2006-2010 5-year est.).

Transportation: Commute to work: 95.6% car, 0.7% public transportation, 1.8% walk, 1.9% work from home (2006-2010 5-year est.); Travel time to work: 21.8% less than 15 minutes, 41.5% 15 to 30 minutes, 23.3% 30 to 45 minutes, 11.5% 45 to 60 minutes, 1.8% 60 minutes or more (2006-2010 5-year est.)

Additional Information Contacts
Beaver County Chamber of Commerce . . . . (724) 775-3944
    http://beavercountychamber.com

DAUGHERTY (township). Covers a land area of 9.886 square miles and a water area of 0.035 square miles. Located at 40.75° N. Lat; 80.27° W. Long.

Population: 3,433 (1990); 3,441 (2000); 3,187 (2010); Density: 322.4 persons per square mile (2010); Race: 96.2% White, 2.1% Black, 0.3% Asian, 0.1% American Indian/Alaska Native, 0.0% Native Hawaiian/Other Pacific Islander, 1.3% Other, 0.8% Hispanic of any race (2010); Average household size: 2.47 (2010); Median age: 46.2 (2010); Males per 100 females: 100.6 (2010); Marriage status: 27.1% never married, 54.8% now married, 11.0% widowed, 7.2% divorced (2006-2010 5-year est.); Foreign born: 1.1% (2006-2010 5-year est.); Ancestry (includes multiple ancestries): 29.2% German, 19.7% English, 16.7% Italian, 14.0% Irish, 8.4% Polish (2006-2010 5-year est.).

Economy: Single-family building permits issued: 1 (2011); Multi-family building permits issued: 0 (2011); Employment by occupation: 11.9% management, 1.8% professional, 5.4% services, 23.2% sales, 5.2% farming, 10.1% construction, 10.8% production (2006-2010 5-year est.).

Income: Per capita income: $21,986 (2006-2010 5-year est.); Median household income: $55,250 (2006-2010 5-year est.); Average household income: $58,104 (2006-2010 5-year est.); Percent of households with income of $100,000 or more: 13.1% (2006-2010 5-year est.); Poverty rate: 11.9% (2006-2010 5-year est.).

Education: Percent of population age 25 and over with: High school diploma (including GED) or higher: 91.0% (2006-2010 5-year est.); Bachelor's degree or higher: 17.3% (2006-2010 5-year est.); Master's degree or higher: 6.7% (2006-2010 5-year est.).

Housing: Homeownership rate: 90.6% (2010); Median home value: $125,500 (2006-2010 5-year est.); Median contract rent: $557 per month (2006-2010 5-year est.); Median year structure built: 1959 (2006-2010 5-year est.).

Transportation: Commute to work: 93.0% car, 1.5% public transportation, 0.8% walk, 3.2% work from home (2006-2010 5-year est.); Travel time to work: 35.2% less than 15 minutes, 35.6% 15 to 30 minutes, 12.6% 30 to 45 minutes, 11.6% 45 to 60 minutes, 5.0% 60 minutes or more (2006-2010 5-year est.)

Additional Information Contacts
Beaver County Chamber of Commerce . . . . (724) 775-3944
    http://beavercountychamber.com
Daugherty Township . . . . (724) 846-5337
    http://www.daughertytownship-pa.gov

EAST ROCHESTER (borough). Covers a land area of 0.366 square miles and a water area of 0.091 square miles. Located at 40.70° N. Lat; 80.27° W. Long. Elevation is 860 feet.

Population: 672 (1990); 623 (2000); 567 (2010); Density: 1,549.9 persons per square mile (2010); Race: 94.5% White, 3.2% Black, 0.0% Asian, 0.2% American Indian/Alaska Native, 0.0% Native Hawaiian/Other Pacific Islander, 2.1% Other, 1.4% Hispanic of any race (2010); Average household size: 2.26 (2010); Median age: 41.9 (2010); Males per 100 females: 84.1 (2010); Marriage status: 22.9% never married, 52.6% now married, 10.4% widowed, 14.1% divorced (2006-2010 5-year est.); Foreign born: 2.0% (2006-2010 5-year est.); Ancestry (includes multiple ancestries): 27.0% Italian, 26.0% German, 16.7% Irish, 15.4% Polish, 11.1% English (2006-2010 5-year est.).

Economy: Single-family building permits issued: 0 (2011); Multi-family building permits issued: 0 (2011); Employment by occupation: 12.7% management, 6.2% professional, 21.6% services, 17.2% sales, 5.6% farming, 5.9% construction, 2.7% production (2006-2010 5-year est.).

Income: Per capita income: $20,273 (2006-2010 5-year est.); Median household income: $33,333 (2006-2010 5-year est.); Average household income: $45,189 (2006-2010 5-year est.); Percent of households with income of $100,000 or more: 7.4% (2006-2010 5-year est.); Poverty rate: 6.4% (2006-2010 5-year est.).

Education: Percent of population age 25 and over with: High school diploma (including GED) or higher: 88.4% (2006-2010 5-year est.); Bachelor's degree or higher: 13.8% (2006-2010 5-year est.); Master's degree or higher: 5.1% (2006-2010 5-year est.).

Housing: Homeownership rate: 57.8% (2010); Median home value: $85,500 (2006-2010 5-year est.); Median contract rent: $374 per month (2006-2010 5-year est.); Median year structure built: 1949 (2006-2010 5-year est.).

Transportation: Commute to work: 95.5% car, 1.2% public transportation, 0.9% walk, 2.4% work from home (2006-2010 5-year est.); Travel time to work: 39.6% less than 15 minutes, 38.0% 15 to 30 minutes, 17.8% 30 to 45 minutes, 2.1% 45 to 60 minutes, 2.5% 60 minutes or more (2006-2010 5-year est.)

EASTVALE (borough). Covers a land area of 0.090 square miles and a water area of 0.027 square miles. Located at 40.77° N. Lat; 80.31° W. Long. Elevation is 791 feet.

Population: 328 (1990); 293 (2000); 225 (2010); Density: 2,487.8 persons per square mile (2010); Race: 97.3% White, 1.8% Black, 0.0% Asian, 0.0% American Indian/Alaska Native, 0.0% Native Hawaiian/Other Pacific Islander, 0.9% Other, 0.4% Hispanic of any race (2010); Average household size: 2.39 (2010); Median age: 39.5 (2010); Males per 100 females: 106.4 (2010); Marriage status: 26.8% never married, 42.7% now married, 9.6% widowed, 21.0% divorced (2006-2010 5-year est.); Foreign born: 1.2% (2006-2010 5-year est.); Ancestry (includes multiple ancestries): 29.7% German, 20.9% Irish, 12.2% Italian, 8.7% Polish, 7.0% American (2006-2010 5-year est.).

Economy: Single-family building permits issued: 0 (2011); Multi-family building permits issued: 0 (2011); Employment by occupation: 7.2% management, 2.1% professional, 23.7% services, 20.6% sales, 5.2% farming, 10.3% construction, 8.2% production (2006-2010 5-year est.).

Income: Per capita income: $21,256 (2006-2010 5-year est.); Median household income: $35,833 (2006-2010 5-year est.); Average household income: $40,631 (2006-2010 5-year est.); Percent of households with income of $100,000 or more: 2.2% (2006-2010 5-year est.); Poverty rate: 14.5% (2006-2010 5-year est.).

Education: Percent of population age 25 and over with: High school diploma (including GED) or higher: 71.6% (2006-2010 5-year est.); Bachelor's degree or higher: 5.0% (2006-2010 5-year est.); Master's degree or higher: 2.8% (2006-2010 5-year est.).

Housing: Homeownership rate: 69.2% (2010); Median home value: $61,600 (2006-2010 5-year est.); Median contract rent: $396 per month (2006-2010 5-year est.); Median year structure built: before 1940 (2006-2010 5-year est.).

Transportation: Commute to work: 92.0% car, 0.0% public pennsylvania, 8.0% walk, 0.0% work from home (2006-2010 5-year est.); Travel time to work: 38.6% less than 15 minutes, 36.4% 15 to 30 minutes, 15.9% 30 to

45 minutes, 2.3% 45 to 60 minutes, 6.8% 60 minutes or more (2006-2010 5-year est.)

ECONOMY (borough). Covers a land area of 17.884 square miles and a water area of 0.048 square miles. Located at 40.64° N. Lat; 80.19° W. Long. Elevation is 791 feet.

Population: 9,519 (1990); 9,363 (2000); 8,970 (2010); Density: 501.6 persons per square mile (2010); Race: 98.2% White, 0.6% Black, 0.4% Asian, 0.1% American Indian/Alaska Native, 0.0% Native Hawaiian/Other Pacific Islander, 0.7% Other, 0.8% Hispanic of any race (2010); Average household size: 2.48 (2010); Median age: 47.1 (2010); Males per 100 females: 98.3 (2010); Marriage status: 22.2% never married, 66.5% now married, 5.5% widowed, 5.8% divorced (2006-2010 5-year est.); Foreign born: 1.1% (2006-2010 5-year est.); Ancestry (includes multiple ancestries): 32.9% German, 20.2% Irish, 15.4% Polish, 14.2% Italian, 6.4% English (2006-2010 5-year est.).
Economy: Single-family building permits issued: 32 (2011); Multi-family building permits issued: 0 (2011); Employment by occupation: 13.2% management, 6.7% professional, 7.6% services, 14.1% sales, 5.6% farming, 9.7% construction, 8.5% production (2006-2010 5-year est.).
Income: Per capita income: $30,156 (2006-2010 5-year est.); Median household income: $69,882 (2006-2010 5-year est.); Average household income: $79,054 (2006-2010 5-year est.); Percent of households with income of $100,000 or more: 27.3% (2006-2010 5-year est.); Poverty rate: 6.4% (2006-2010 5-year est.).
Education: Percent of population age 25 and over with: High school diploma (including GED) or higher: 92.7% (2006-2010 5-year est.); Bachelor's degree or higher: 26.3% (2006-2010 5-year est.); Master's degree or higher: 10.0% (2006-2010 5-year est.).
Housing: Homeownership rate: 93.7% (2010); Median home value: $154,100 (2006-2010 5-year est.); Median contract rent: $522 per month (2006-2010 5-year est.); Median year structure built: 1972 (2006-2010 5-year est.).
Safety: Violent crime rate: 3.3 per 10,000 population; Property crime rate: 51.1 per 10,000 population (2011).
Transportation: Commute to work: 94.3% car, 1.3% public transportation, 0.8% walk, 3.0% work from home (2006-2010 5-year est.); Travel time to work: 15.4% less than 15 minutes, 39.6% 15 to 30 minutes, 25.5% 30 to 45 minutes, 12.3% 45 to 60 minutes, 7.2% 60 minutes or more (2006-2010 5-year est.)
Additional Information Contacts
Ambridge Area Chamber of Commerce . . . . (724) 266-3040
   http://www.ambridgechamberofcommerce.com
Borough of Economy. . . . . (724) 869-4779
   http://www.economyborough.org

FALLSTON (borough). Covers a land area of 0.477 square miles and a water area of 0.038 square miles. Located at 40.73° N. Lat; 80.31° W. Long. Elevation is 997 feet.

Population: 392 (1990); 307 (2000); 266 (2010); Density: 557.2 persons per square mile (2010); Race: 94.7% White, 2.6% Black, 0.0% Asian, 0.0% American Indian/Alaska Native, 0.0% Native Hawaiian/Other Pacific Islander, 2.7% Other, 0.8% Hispanic of any race (2010); Average household size: 2.38 (2010); Median age: 45.4 (2010); Males per 100 females: 97.0 (2010); Marriage status: 23.9% never married, 56.9% now married, 8.2% widowed, 11.0% divorced (2006-2010 5-year est.); Foreign born: 1.2% (2006-2010 5-year est.); Ancestry (includes multiple ancestries): 32.6% German, 25.6% Italian, 18.3% Irish, 9.5% English, 7.0% Scotch-Irish (2006-2010 5-year est.).
Economy: Single-family building permits issued: 0 (2011); Multi-family building permits issued: 0 (2011); Employment by occupation: 9.1% management, 1.8% professional, 18.2% services, 17.0% sales, 3.0% farming, 16.4% construction, 2.4% production (2006-2010 5-year est.).
Income: Per capita income: $23,917 (2006-2010 5-year est.); Median household income: $48,542 (2006-2010 5-year est.); Average household income: $56,291 (2006-2010 5-year est.); Percent of households with income of $100,000 or more: 9.1% (2006-2010 5-year est.); Poverty rate: 10.4% (2006-2010 5-year est.).
Education: Percent of population age 25 and over with: High school diploma (including GED) or higher: 95.9% (2006-2010 5-year est.); Bachelor's degree or higher: 23.5% (2006-2010 5-year est.); Master's degree or higher: 6.8% (2006-2010 5-year est.).
Housing: Homeownership rate: 77.7% (2010); Median home value: $104,200 (2006-2010 5-year est.); Median contract rent: $531 per month

(2006-2010 5-year est.); Median year structure built: before 1940 (2006-2010 5-year est.).
Transportation: Commute to work: 90.9% car, 0.0% public transportation, 3.6% walk, 5.5% work from home (2006-2010 5-year est.); Travel time to work: 51.3% less than 15 minutes, 23.1% 15 to 30 minutes, 9.6% 30 to 45 minutes, 9.6% 45 to 60 minutes, 6.4% 60 minutes or more (2006-2010 5-year est.)

FOMBELL (unincorporated postal area)
Zip Code: 16123

Covers a land area of 20.240 square miles and a water area of 0.240 square miles. Located at 40.82° N. Lat; 80.19° W. Long. Elevation is 879 feet. Population: 2,237 (2010); Density: 110.5 persons per square mile (2010); Race: 98.7% White, 0.3% Black, 0.2% Asian, 0.1% American Indian/Alaska Native, 0.2% Native Hawaiian/Other Pacific Islander, 0.5% Other, 0.8% Hispanic of any race (2010); Average household size: 2.54 (2010); Median age: 44.6 (2010); Males per 100 females: 106.4 (2010); Homeownership rate: 83.6% (2010)

FRANKFORT SPRINGS (borough). Covers a land area of 0.260 square miles and a water area of 0 square miles. Located at 40.48° N. Lat; 80.44° W. Long. Elevation is 1,152 feet.

Population: 134 (1990); 130 (2000); 130 (2010); Density: 499.7 persons per square mile (2010); Race: 98.5% White, 0.8% Black, 0.0% Asian, 0.0% American Indian/Alaska Native, 0.0% Native Hawaiian/Other Pacific Islander, 0.7% Other, 0.0% Hispanic of any race (2010); Average household size: 2.71 (2010); Median age: 46.3 (2010); Males per 100 females: 109.7 (2010); Marriage status: 20.4% never married, 55.8% now married, 13.3% widowed, 10.6% divorced (2006-2010 5-year est.); Foreign born: 1.2% (2006-2010 5-year est.); Ancestry (includes multiple ancestries): 27.7% Irish, 22.9% English, 12.7% German, 4.8% Italian, 3.6% Dutch (2006-2010 5-year est.).
Economy: Single-family building permits issued: 0 (2011); Multi-family building permits issued: 0 (2011); Employment by occupation: 5.9% management, 2.9% professional, 7.4% services, 17.6% sales, 4.4% farming, 13.2% construction, 8.8% production (2006-2010 5-year est.).
Income: Per capita income: $38,430 (2006-2010 5-year est.); Median household income: $58,750 (2006-2010 5-year est.); Average household income: $120,865 (2006-2010 5-year est.); Percent of households with income of $100,000 or more: 19.2% (2006-2010 5-year est.); Poverty rate: 32.5% (2006-2010 5-year est.).
Education: Percent of population age 25 and over with: High school diploma (including GED) or higher: 96.3% (2006-2010 5-year est.); Bachelor's degree or higher: 4.7% (2006-2010 5-year est.); Master's degree or higher: 1.9% (2006-2010 5-year est.).
Housing: Homeownership rate: 81.2% (2010); Median home value: $107,500 (2006-2010 5-year est.); Median contract rent: $833 per month (2006-2010 5-year est.); Median year structure built: 1950 (2006-2010 5-year est.).
Transportation: Commute to work: 97.1% car, 0.0% public transportation, 0.0% walk, 2.9% work from home (2006-2010 5-year est.); Travel time to work: 24.2% less than 15 minutes, 51.5% 15 to 30 minutes, 12.1% 30 to 45 minutes, 12.1% 45 to 60 minutes, 0.0% 60 minutes or more (2006-2010 5-year est.)

FRANKLIN (township). Covers a land area of 17.691 square miles and a water area of 0.162 square miles. Located at 40.82° N. Lat; 80.20° W. Long.

Population: 3,821 (1990); 4,307 (2000); 4,052 (2010); Density: 229.0 persons per square mile (2010); Race: 98.6% White, 0.2% Black, 0.1% Asian, 0.1% American Indian/Alaska Native, 0.1% Native Hawaiian/Other Pacific Islander, 0.9% Other, 0.8% Hispanic of any race (2010); Average household size: 2.45 (2010); Median age: 44.3 (2010); Males per 100 females: 97.8 (2010); Marriage status: 24.3% never married, 62.8% now married, 6.5% widowed, 6.4% divorced (2006-2010 5-year est.); Foreign born: 0.8% (2006-2010 5-year est.); Ancestry (includes multiple ancestries): 42.3% German, 22.2% Irish, 11.4% Italian, 10.6% Polish, 7.8% American (2006-2010 5-year est.).
Economy: Single-family building permits issued: 1 (2011); Multi-family building permits issued: 0 (2011); Employment by occupation: 11.4% management, 1.9% professional, 13.4% services, 18.5% sales, 2.9% farming, 13.6% construction, 8.0% production (2006-2010 5-year est.).
Income: Per capita income: $24,365 (2006-2010 5-year est.); Median household income: $51,591 (2006-2010 5-year est.); Average household income: $63,131 (2006-2010 5-year est.); Percent of households with

income of $100,000 or more: 17.5% (2006-2010 5-year est.); Poverty rate: 7.8% (2006-2010 5-year est.).

Education: Percent of population age 25 and over with: High school diploma (including GED) or higher: 89.2% (2006-2010 5-year est.); Bachelor's degree or higher: 17.2% (2006-2010 5-year est.); Master's degree or higher: 5.3% (2006-2010 5-year est.).

Housing: Homeownership rate: 80.4% (2010); Median home value: $131,900 (2006-2010 5-year est.); Median contract rent: $463 per month (2006-2010 5-year est.); Median year structure built: 1970 (2006-2010 5-year est.).

Transportation: Commute to work: 94.3% car, 1.1% public transportation, 1.0% walk, 2.2% work from home (2006-2010 5-year est.); Travel time to work: 25.3% less than 15 minutes, 32.4% 15 to 30 minutes, 22.2% 30 to 45 minutes, 11.0% 45 to 60 minutes, 9.0% 60 minutes or more (2006-2010 5-year est.)

Additional Information Contacts

Beaver County Chamber of Commerce . . . . (724) 775-3944
  http://beavercountychamber.com

FREEDOM (borough). Covers a land area of 0.604 square miles and a water area of 0.133 square miles. Located at 40.69° N. Lat; 80.25° W. Long. Elevation is 781 feet.

History: Settled 1832, incorporated 1838.

Population: 1,897 (1990); 1,763 (2000); 1,569 (2010); Density: 2,598.4 persons per square mile (2010); Race: 91.8% White, 4.1% Black, 0.6% Asian, 0.0% American Indian/Alaska Native, 0.0% Native Hawaiian/Other Pacific Islander, 3.5% Other, 1.6% Hispanic of any race (2010); Average household size: 2.51 (2010); Median age: 37.5 (2010); Males per 100 females: 96.6 (2010); Marriage status: 30.0% never married, 43.8% now married, 10.1% widowed, 16.0% divorced (2006-2010 5-year est.); Foreign born: 1.0% (2006-2010 5-year est.); Ancestry (includes multiple ancestries): 36.1% German, 19.3% Irish, 15.5% Italian, 10.4% English, 5.6% Polish (2006-2010 5-year est.).

Economy: Single-family building permits issued: 0 (2011); Multi-family building permits issued: 0 (2011); Employment by occupation: 4.5% management, 0.0% professional, 11.4% services, 22.1% sales, 8.0% farming, 8.0% construction, 9.9% production (2006-2010 5-year est.).

Income: Per capita income: $16,462 (2006-2010 5-year est.); Median household income: $29,265 (2006-2010 5-year est.); Average household income: $37,628 (2006-2010 5-year est.); Percent of households with income of $100,000 or more: 5.4% (2006-2010 5-year est.); Poverty rate: 28.0% (2006-2010 5-year est.).

Education: Percent of population age 25 and over with: High school diploma (including GED) or higher: 78.9% (2006-2010 5-year est.); Bachelor's degree or higher: 9.4% (2006-2010 5-year est.); Master's degree or higher: 1.8% (2006-2010 5-year est.).

School District(s)

Ambridge Area SD (KG-12)

  2010-11 Enrollment: 2,785 . . . . (724) 266-2833

Freedom Area SD (KG-12)

  2010-11 Enrollment: 1,573 . . . . (724) 775-5464

Housing: Homeownership rate: 65.5% (2010); Median home value: $59,200 (2006-2010 5-year est.); Median contract rent: $401 per month (2006-2010 5-year est.); Median year structure built: before 1940 (2006-2010 5-year est.).

Safety: Violent crime rate: 50.8 per 10,000 population; Property crime rate: 235.1 per 10,000 population (2011).

Transportation: Commute to work: 96.4% car, 1.8% public transportation, 1.0% walk, 0.8% work from home (2006-2010 5-year est.); Travel time to work: 21.0% less than 15 minutes, 50.1% 15 to 30 minutes, 19.7% 30 to 45 minutes, 5.3% 45 to 60 minutes, 4.0% 60 minutes or more (2006-2010 5-year est.)

Additional Information Contacts

Beaver County Chamber of Commerce . . . . (724) 775-3944
  http://beavercountychamber.com

GEORGETOWN (borough). Covers a land area of 0.175 square miles and a water area of 0.076 square miles. Located at 40.64° N. Lat; 80.50° W. Long. Elevation is 755 feet.

Population: 181 (1990); 182 (2000); 174 (2010); Density: 994.6 persons per square mile (2010); Race: 99.4% White, 0.0% Black, 0.0% Asian, 0.0% American Indian/Alaska Native, 0.0% Native Hawaiian/Other Pacific Islander, 0.6% Other, 0.0% Hispanic of any race (2010); Average household size: 2.85 (2010); Median age: 38.4 (2010); Males per 100 females: 83.2 (2010); Marriage status: 13.8% never married, 76.1% now

married, 1.8% widowed, 8.3% divorced (2006-2010 5-year est.); Foreign born: 0.0% (2006-2010 5-year est.); Ancestry (includes multiple ancestries): 31.7% Irish, 25.2% German, 10.8% English, 9.4% Italian, 7.9% Scotch-Irish (2006-2010 5-year est.).

Economy: Single-family building permits issued: 0 (2011); Multi-family building permits issued: 0 (2011); Employment by occupation: 3.8% management, 0.0% professional, 7.7% services, 28.8% sales, 3.8% farming, 7.7% construction, 3.8% production (2006-2010 5-year est.).

Income: Per capita income: $20,913 (2006-2010 5-year est.); Median household income: $62,750 (2006-2010 5-year est.); Average household income: $60,702 (2006-2010 5-year est.); Percent of households with income of $100,000 or more: 4.3% (2006-2010 5-year est.); Poverty rate: 0.0% (2006-2010 5-year est.).

Education: Percent of population age 25 and over with: High school diploma (including GED) or higher: 92.9% (2006-2010 5-year est.); Bachelor's degree or higher: 0.0% (2006-2010 5-year est.); Master's degree or higher: 0.0% (2006-2010 5-year est.).

Housing: Homeownership rate: 90.2% (2010); Median home value: $131,800 (2006-2010 5-year est.); Median contract rent: $400 per month (2006-2010 5-year est.); Median year structure built: before 1940 (2006-2010 5-year est.).

Transportation: Commute to work: 96.2% car, 0.0% public transportation, 0.0% walk, 3.8% work from home (2006-2010 5-year est.); Travel time to work: 8.0% less than 15 minutes, 28.0% 15 to 30 minutes, 52.0% 30 to 45 minutes, 4.0% 45 to 60 minutes, 8.0% 60 minutes or more (2006-2010 5-year est.)

GLASGOW (borough). Covers a land area of 0.060 square miles and a water area of 0.050 square miles. Located at 40.64° N. Lat; 80.51° W. Long. Elevation is 682 feet.

Population: 74 (1990); 63 (2000); 60 (2010); Density: 1,002.6 persons per square mile (2010); Race: 100.0% White, 0.0% Black, 0.0% Asian, 0.0% American Indian/Alaska Native, 0.0% Native Hawaiian/Other Pacific Islander, 0.0% Other, 5.0% Hispanic of any race (2010); Average household size: 2.07 (2010); Median age: 47.3 (2010); Males per 100 females: 122.2 (2010); Marriage status: 37.2% never married, 27.9% now married, 14.0% widowed, 20.9% divorced (2006-2010 5-year est.); Foreign born: 0.0% (2006-2010 5-year est.); Ancestry (includes multiple ancestries): 28.8% English, 21.2% Irish, 19.2% Italian, 15.4% Serbian, 7.7% American (2006-2010 5-year est.).

Economy: Employment by occupation: 12.5% management, 0.0% professional, 16.7% services, 12.5% sales, 16.7% farming, 0.0% construction, 8.3% production (2006-2010 5-year est.).

Income: Per capita income: $13,808 (2006-2010 5-year est.); Median household income: $26,667 (2006-2010 5-year est.); Average household income: $31,092 (2006-2010 5-year est.); Percent of households with income of $100,000 or more: n/a (2006-2010 5-year est.); Poverty rate: 13.5% (2006-2010 5-year est.).

Education: Percent of population age 25 and over with: High school diploma (including GED) or higher: 89.5% (2006-2010 5-year est.); Bachelor's degree or higher: 0.0% (2006-2010 5-year est.); Master's degree or higher: 0.0% (2006-2010 5-year est.).

Housing: Homeownership rate: 62.1% (2010); Median home value: $32,500 (2006-2010 5-year est.); Median contract rent: $563 per month (2006-2010 5-year est.); Median year structure built: 1946 (2006-2010 5-year est.).

Transportation: Commute to work: 100.0% car, 0.0% public transportation, 0.0% walk, 0.0% work from home (2006-2010 5-year est.); Travel time to work: 29.2% less than 15 minutes, 50.0% 15 to 30 minutes, 8.3% 30 to 45 minutes, 4.2% 45 to 60 minutes, 8.3% 60 minutes or more (2006-2010 5-year est.)

GREENE (township). Covers a land area of 25.021 square miles and a water area of 1.196 square miles. Located at 40.59° N. Lat; 80.47° W. Long.

Population: 2,603 (1990); 2,705 (2000); 2,356 (2010); Density: 94.2 persons per square mile (2010); Race: 98.7% White, 0.4% Black, 0.2% Asian, 0.2% American Indian/Alaska Native, 0.1% Native Hawaiian/Other Pacific Islander, 0.4% Other, 0.8% Hispanic of any race (2010); Average household size: 2.77 (2010); Median age: 41.5 (2010); Males per 100 females: 102.8 (2010); Marriage status: 23.0% never married, 64.2% now married, 7.5% widowed, 5.4% divorced (2006-2010 5-year est.); Foreign born: 2.5% (2006-2010 5-year est.); Ancestry (includes multiple ancestries): 27.4% German, 22.0% Irish, 12.3% Italian, 10.7% English, 8.1% Polish (2006-2010 5-year est.).

Economy: Single-family building permits issued: 9 (2011); Multi-family building permits issued: 0 (2011); Employment by occupation: 7.6% management, 7.5% professional, 8.8% services, 20.5% sales, 2.5% farming, 17.6% construction, 9.0% production (2006-2010 5-year est.).
Income: Per capita income: $26,153 (2006-2010 5-year est.); Median household income: $65,119 (2006-2010 5-year est.); Average household income: $73,231 (2006-2010 5-year est.); Percent of households with income of $100,000 or more: 22.0% (2006-2010 5-year est.); Poverty rate: 8.5% (2006-2010 5-year est.).
Education: Percent of population age 25 and over with: High school diploma (including GED) or higher: 93.0% (2006-2010 5-year est.); Bachelor's degree or higher: 17.5% (2006-2010 5-year est.); Master's degree or higher: 2.1% (2006-2010 5-year est.).
Housing: Homeownership rate: 92.0% (2010); Median home value: $154,400 (2006-2010 5-year est.); Median contract rent: $333 per month (2006-2010 5-year est.); Median year structure built: 1977 (2006-2010 5-year est.).
Transportation: Commute to work: 93.9% car, 1.1% public transportation, 2.9% walk, 0.4% work from home (2006-2010 5-year est.); Travel time to work: 22.1% less than 15 minutes, 27.9% 15 to 30 minutes, 31.2% 30 to 45 minutes, 11.3% 45 to 60 minutes, 7.4% 60 minutes or more (2006-2010 5-year est.)
Additional Information Contacts
Beaver County Chamber of Commerce . . . . (724) 775-3944
http://beavercountychamber.com

HANOVER (township). Covers a land area of 44.879 square miles and a water area of 0.153 square miles. Located at 40.52° N. Lat; 80.44° W. Long.
Population: 3,448 (1990); 3,529 (2000); 3,690 (2010); Density: 82.2 persons per square mile (2010); Race: 98.3% White, 0.7% Black, 0.2% Asian, 0.1% American Indian/Alaska Native, 0.0% Native Hawaiian/Other Pacific Islander, 0.7% Other, 0.7% Hispanic of any race (2010); Average household size: 2.66 (2010); Median age: 43.0 (2010); Males per 100 females: 104.0 (2010); Marriage status: 21.4% never married, 69.6% now married, 3.9% widowed, 5.2% divorced (2006-2010 5-year est.); Foreign born: 1.7% (2006-2010 5-year est.); Ancestry (includes multiple ancestries): 25.4% German, 23.8% Irish, 15.9% English, 11.0% Polish, 10.8% Italian (2006-2010 5-year est.).
Economy: Single-family building permits issued: 2 (2011); Multi-family building permits issued: 0 (2011); Employment by occupation: 8.2% management, 2.6% professional, 6.6% services, 25.3% sales, 5.8% farming, 18.7% construction, 7.7% production (2006-2010 5-year est.).
Income: Per capita income: $25,033 (2006-2010 5-year est.); Median household income: $58,339 (2006-2010 5-year est.); Average household income: $63,595 (2006-2010 5-year est.); Percent of households with income of $100,000 or more: 18.4% (2006-2010 5-year est.); Poverty rate: 8.9% (2006-2010 5-year est.).
Education: Percent of population age 25 and over with: High school diploma (including GED) or higher: 93.1% (2006-2010 5-year est.); Bachelor's degree or higher: 16.4% (2006-2010 5-year est.); Master's degree or higher: 3.3% (2006-2010 5-year est.).
Housing: Homeownership rate: 88.2% (2010); Median home value: $151,100 (2006-2010 5-year est.); Median contract rent: $473 per month (2006-2010 5-year est.); Median year structure built: 1976 (2006-2010 5-year est.).
Transportation: Commute to work: 90.3% car, 0.0% public transportation, 3.6% walk, 5.3% work from home (2006-2010 5-year est.); Travel time to work: 13.8% less than 15 minutes, 38.3% 15 to 30 minutes, 28.5% 30 to 45 minutes, 11.2% 45 to 60 minutes, 8.1% 60 minutes or more (2006-2010 5-year est.)
Additional Information Contacts
Beaver County Chamber of Commerce . . . . (724) 775-3944
http://beavercountychamber.com

HARMONY (township). Aka Harmony Township CDP. Covers a land area of 2.909 square miles and a water area of 0.160 square miles. Located at 40.61° N. Lat; 80.21° W. Long.
Population: 3,694 (1990); 3,373 (2000); 3,197 (2010); Density: 1,098.9 persons per square mile (2010); Race: 95.5% White, 2.4% Black, 0.7% Asian, 0.0% American Indian/Alaska Native, 0.1% Native Hawaiian/Other Pacific Islander, 1.3% Other, 1.3% Hispanic of any race (2010); Average household size: 2.33 (2010); Median age: 44.2 (2010); Males per 100 females: 95.4 (2010); Marriage status: 24.5% never married, 55.5% now married, 13.8% widowed, 6.2% divorced (2006-2010 5-year est.); Foreign

born: 4.5% (2006-2010 5-year est.); Ancestry (includes multiple ancestries): 28.0% Italian, 24.4% German, 15.7% Polish, 11.7% Irish, 7.2% Ukrainian (2006-2010 5-year est.).
Economy: Single-family building permits issued: 0 (2011); Multi-family building permits issued: 0 (2011); Employment by occupation: 5.8% management, 2.0% professional, 9.6% services, 20.2% sales, 4.7% farming, 10.0% construction, 3.5% production (2006-2010 5-year est.).
Income: Per capita income: $26,317 (2006-2010 5-year est.); Median household income: $45,172 (2006-2010 5-year est.); Average household income: $59,134 (2006-2010 5-year est.); Percent of households with income of $100,000 or more: 14.3% (2006-2010 5-year est.); Poverty rate: 6.8% (2006-2010 5-year est.).
Education: Percent of population age 25 and over with: High school diploma (including GED) or higher: 89.5% (2006-2010 5-year est.); Bachelor's degree or higher: 18.0% (2006-2010 5-year est.); Master's degree or higher: 8.0% (2006-2010 5-year est.).
Housing: Homeownership rate: 87.8% (2010); Median home value: $93,700 (2006-2010 5-year est.); Median contract rent: $442 per month (2006-2010 5-year est.); Median year structure built: 1950 (2006-2010 5-year est.).
Safety: Violent crime rate: 9.4 per 10,000 population; Property crime rate: 274.4 per 10,000 population (2011).
Transportation: Commute to work: 90.6% car, 0.9% public transportation, 1.0% walk, 5.5% work from home (2006-2010 5-year est.); Travel time to work: 27.3% less than 15 minutes, 38.6% 15 to 30 minutes, 25.1% 30 to 45 minutes, 6.9% 45 to 60 minutes, 2.1% 60 minutes or more (2006-2010 5-year est.)
Additional Information Contacts
Zelienople-Harmony Area Chamber of Commerce . . . . (724) 452-5232
http://www.zhchamber.com

HOMEWOOD (borough). Aka Racine. Covers a land area of 0.169 square miles and a water area of 0 square miles. Located at 40.81° N. Lat; 80.33° W. Long. Elevation is 971 feet.
Population: 162 (1990); 147 (2000); 109 (2010); Density: 644.0 persons per square mile (2010); Race: 98.2% White, 0.9% Black, 0.0% Asian, 0.0% American Indian/Alaska Native, 0.0% Native Hawaiian/Other Pacific Islander, 0.9% Other, 0.0% Hispanic of any race (2010); Average household size: 1.98 (2010); Median age: 51.5 (2010); Males per 100 females: 105.7 (2010); Marriage status: 31.4% never married, 41.5% now married, 11.9% widowed, 15.3% divorced (2006-2010 5-year est.); Foreign born: 0.0% (2006-2010 5-year est.); Ancestry (includes multiple ancestries): 30.4% German, 22.4% Italian, 16.8% Irish, 11.2% English, 7.2% Croatian (2006-2010 5-year est.).
Economy: Single-family building permits issued: 0 (2011); Multi-family building permits issued: 0 (2011); Employment by occupation: 0.0% management, 0.0% professional, 2.6% services, 19.2% sales, 0.0% farming, 11.5% construction, 10.3% production (2006-2010 5-year est.).
Income: Per capita income: $24,122 (2006-2010 5-year est.); Median household income: $33,750 (2006-2010 5-year est.); Average household income: $43,716 (2006-2010 5-year est.); Percent of households with income of $100,000 or more: 2.9% (2006-2010 5-year est.); Poverty rate: 18.4% (2006-2010 5-year est.).
Education: Percent of population age 25 and over with: High school diploma (including GED) or higher: 91.1% (2006-2010 5-year est.); Bachelor's degree or higher: 7.1% (2006-2010 5-year est.); Master's degree or higher: 0.0% (2006-2010 5-year est.).
Housing: Homeownership rate: 76.4% (2010); Median home value: $63,100 (2006-2010 5-year est.); Median contract rent: n/a per month (2006-2010 5-year est.); Median year structure built: before 1940 (2006-2010 5-year est.).
Transportation: Commute to work: 97.2% car, 0.0% public transportation, 0.0% walk, 2.8% work from home (2006-2010 5-year est.); Travel time to work: 18.6% less than 15 minutes, 15.7% 15 to 30 minutes, 21.4% 30 to 45 minutes, 30.0% 45 to 60 minutes, 14.3% 60 minutes or more (2006-2010 5-year est.)

HOOKSTOWN (borough). Covers a land area of 0.135 square miles and a water area of 0 square miles. Located at 40.60° N. Lat; 80.47° W. Long. Elevation is 1,010 feet.
Population: 169 (1990); 152 (2000); 147 (2010); Density: 1,086.0 persons per square mile (2010); Race: 95.9% White, 0.7% Black, 0.0% Asian, 0.0% American Indian/Alaska Native, 0.0% Native Hawaiian/Other Pacific Islander, 3.4% Other, 1.4% Hispanic of any race (2010); Average household size: 2.37 (2010); Median age: 42.6 (2010); Males per 100

females: 119.4 (2010); Marriage status: 20.6% never married, 62.4% now married, 9.4% widowed, 7.6% divorced (2006-2010 5-year est.); Foreign born: 0.0% (2006-2010 5-year est.); Ancestry (includes multiple ancestries): 42.9% German, 18.9% Russian, 14.3% Scotch-Irish, 11.2% French, 10.2% Italian (2006-2010 5-year est.).

Economy: Single-family building permits issued: 0 (2011); Multi-family building permits issued: 0 (2011); Employment by occupation: 4.6% management, 0.0% professional, 10.3% services, 5.7% sales, 11.5% farming, 0.0% construction, 2.3% production (2006-2010 5-year est.).

Income: Per capita income: $18,347 (2006-2010 5-year est.); Median household income: $52,961 (2006-2010 5-year est.); Average household income: $45,709 (2006-2010 5-year est.); Percent of households with income of $100,000 or more: 3.9% (2006-2010 5-year est.); Poverty rate: 2.0% (2006-2010 5-year est.).

Education: Percent of population age 25 and over with: High school diploma (including GED) or higher: 83.4% (2006-2010 5-year est.); Bachelor's degree or higher: 17.9% (2006-2010 5-year est.); Master's degree or higher: 2.6% (2006-2010 5-year est.).

School District(s)

South Side Area SD (KG-12)
   2010-11 Enrollment: 1,235 . . . . (724) 573-9581

Housing: Homeownership rate: 87.1% (2010); Median home value: $66,800 (2006-2010 5-year est.); Median contract rent: n/a per month (2006-2010 5-year est.); Median year structure built: 1955 (2006-2010 5-year est.).

Transportation: Commute to work: 100.0% car, 0.0% public transportation, 0.0% walk, 0.0% work from home (2006-2010 5-year est.); Travel time to work: 34.5% less than 15 minutes, 13.8% 15 to 30 minutes, 32.2% 30 to 45 minutes, 17.2% 45 to 60 minutes, 2.3% 60 minutes or more (2006-2010 5-year est.)

HOPEWELL (township).
Covers a land area of 16.757 square miles and a water area of 0.238 square miles. Located at 40.59° N. Lat; 80.27° W. Long.

Population: 13,274 (1990); 13,254 (2000); 12,593 (2010); Density: 751.5 persons per square mile (2010); Race: 94.6% White, 3.7% Black, 0.4% Asian, 0.1% American Indian/Alaska Native, 0.0% Native Hawaiian/Other Pacific Islander, 1.2% Other, 1.2% Hispanic of any race (2010); Average household size: 2.33 (2010); Median age: 45.1 (2010); Males per 100 females: 94.0 (2010); Marriage status: 21.8% never married, 63.1% now married, 8.8% widowed, 6.3% divorced (2006-2010 5-year est.); Foreign born: 3.0% (2006-2010 5-year est.); Ancestry (includes multiple ancestries): 25.6% German, 22.0% Italian, 20.0% Irish, 8.7% Slovak, 8.2% English (2006-2010 5-year est.).

Economy: Single-family building permits issued: 15 (2011); Multi-family building permits issued: 3 (2011); Employment by occupation: 9.5% management, 5.6% professional, 7.8% services, 22.6% sales, 5.4% farming, 6.7% construction, 6.0% production (2006-2010 5-year est.).

Income: Per capita income: $26,481 (2006-2010 5-year est.); Median household income: $54,493 (2006-2010 5-year est.); Average household income: $63,249 (2006-2010 5-year est.); Percent of households with income of $100,000 or more: 17.3% (2006-2010 5-year est.); Poverty rate: 4.0% (2006-2010 5-year est.).

Taxes: Total city taxes per capita: $280 (2009); City property taxes per capita: $140 (2009).

Education: Percent of population age 25 and over with: High school diploma (including GED) or higher: 90.6% (2006-2010 5-year est.); Bachelor's degree or higher: 23.8% (2006-2010 5-year est.); Master's degree or higher: 5.8% (2006-2010 5-year est.).

Housing: Homeownership rate: 84.2% (2010); Median home value: $113,600 (2006-2010 5-year est.); Median contract rent: $555 per month (2006-2010 5-year est.); Median year structure built: 1959 (2006-2010 5-year est.).

Transportation: Commute to work: 93.0% car, 0.7% public transportation, 1.6% walk, 3.4% work from home (2006-2010 5-year est.); Travel time to work: 26.6% less than 15 minutes, 41.3% 15 to 30 minutes, 18.8% 30 to 45 minutes, 7.6% 45 to 60 minutes, 5.8% 60 minutes or more (2006-2010 5-year est.)

Additional Information Contacts
Beaver County Chamber of Commerce . . . . (724) 775-3944
   http://beavercountychamber.com
Hopewell Township. . . . . (724) 378-1460
   http://www.hopewelltwp.com

INDEPENDENCE (township).
Covers a land area of 23.179 square miles and a water area of 0.237 square miles. Located at 40.54° N. Lat; 80.33° W. Long. Elevation is 797 feet.

Population: 2,585 (1990); 2,802 (2000); 2,503 (2010); Density: 108.0 persons per square mile (2010); Race: 98.2% White, 0.4% Black, 0.2% Asian, 0.4% American Indian/Alaska Native, 0.0% Native Hawaiian/Other Pacific Islander, 0.8% Other, 0.5% Hispanic of any race (2010); Average household size: 2.56 (2010); Median age: 44.6 (2010); Males per 100 females: 106.2 (2010); Marriage status: 29.4% never married, 58.6% now married, 3.3% widowed, 8.8% divorced (2006-2010 5-year est.); Foreign born: 2.5% (2006-2010 5-year est.); Ancestry (includes multiple ancestries): 31.8% German, 24.9% Irish, 18.8% Italian, 12.2% English, 9.5% Polish (2006-2010 5-year est.).

Economy: Single-family building permits issued: 1 (2011); Multi-family building permits issued: 0 (2011); Employment by occupation: 10.2% management, 4.6% professional, 7.4% services, 15.2% sales, 5.1% farming, 17.9% construction, 12.5% production (2006-2010 5-year est.).

Income: Per capita income: $29,770 (2006-2010 5-year est.); Median household income: $63,938 (2006-2010 5-year est.); Average household income: $79,572 (2006-2010 5-year est.); Percent of households with income of $100,000 or more: 24.3% (2006-2010 5-year est.); Poverty rate: 1.8% (2006-2010 5-year est.).

Education: Percent of population age 25 and over with: High school diploma (including GED) or higher: 93.3% (2006-2010 5-year est.); Bachelor's degree or higher: 24.4% (2006-2010 5-year est.); Master's degree or higher: 8.6% (2006-2010 5-year est.).

Housing: Homeownership rate: 89.1% (2010); Median home value: $147,300 (2006-2010 5-year est.); Median contract rent: $363 per month (2006-2010 5-year est.); Median year structure built: 1976 (2006-2010 5-year est.).

Safety: Violent crime rate: 0.0 per 10,000 population; Property crime rate: 55.8 per 10,000 population (2011).

Transportation: Commute to work: 93.1% car, 1.6% public transportation, 2.8% walk, 2.0% work from home (2006-2010 5-year est.); Travel time to work: 16.0% less than 15 minutes, 54.0% 15 to 30 minutes, 15.8% 30 to 45 minutes, 9.0% 45 to 60 minutes, 5.2% 60 minutes or more (2006-2010 5-year est.)

Additional Information Contacts
Beaver County Chamber of Commerce . . . . (724) 775-3944
   http://beavercountychamber.com

INDUSTRY (borough).
Covers a land area of 10.135 square miles and a water area of 0.843 square miles. Located at 40.66° N. Lat; 80.41° W. Long. Elevation is 699 feet.

Population: 2,221 (1990); 1,921 (2000); 1,835 (2010); Density: 181.1 persons per square mile (2010); Race: 96.7% White, 1.5% Black, 0.5% Asian, 0.1% American Indian/Alaska Native, 0.1% Native Hawaiian/Other Pacific Islander, 1.1% Other, 1.4% Hispanic of any race (2010); Average household size: 2.39 (2010); Median age: 45.4 (2010); Males per 100 females: 95.6 (2010); Marriage status: 23.5% never married, 59.0% now married, 7.2% widowed, 10.3% divorced (2006-2010 5-year est.); Foreign born: 1.7% (2006-2010 5-year est.); Ancestry (includes multiple ancestries): 29.2% German, 20.9% Italian, 18.4% Irish, 13.3% English, 7.8% Polish (2006-2010 5-year est.).

Economy: Single-family building permits issued: 0 (2011); Multi-family building permits issued: 0 (2011); Employment by occupation: 6.2% management, 6.2% professional, 14.8% services, 18.6% sales, 3.4% farming, 8.0% construction, 4.8% production (2006-2010 5-year est.).

Income: Per capita income: $24,949 (2006-2010 5-year est.); Median household income: $49,643 (2006-2010 5-year est.); Average household income: $60,280 (2006-2010 5-year est.); Percent of households with income of $100,000 or more: 17.7% (2006-2010 5-year est.); Poverty rate: 6.0% (2006-2010 5-year est.).

Education: Percent of population age 25 and over with: High school diploma (including GED) or higher: 91.3% (2006-2010 5-year est.); Bachelor's degree or higher: 18.8% (2006-2010 5-year est.); Master's degree or higher: 3.8% (2006-2010 5-year est.).

School District(s)

Western Beaver County SD (PK-12)
   2010-11 Enrollment: 789 . . . . (724) 643-9310

Housing: Homeownership rate: 85.9% (2010); Median home value: $108,100 (2006-2010 5-year est.); Median contract rent: $555 per month (2006-2010 5-year est.); Median year structure built: 1956 (2006-2010 5-year est.).

Safety: Violent crime rate: 16.3 per 10,000 population; Property crime rate: 124.9 per 10,000 population (2011).
Transportation: Commute to work: 93.8% car, 0.7% public transportation, 1.0% walk, 2.6% work from home (2006-2010 5-year est.); Travel time to work: 21.9% less than 15 minutes, 41.2% 15 to 30 minutes, 18.9% 30 to 45 minutes, 8.2% 45 to 60 minutes, 9.8% 60 minutes or more (2006-2010 5-year est.)
Additional Information Contacts
Beaver County Chamber of Commerce . . . . (724) 775-3944
http://www.beavercountychamber.com

KOPPEL (borough). Covers a land area of 0.537 square miles and a water area of 0.035 square miles. Located at 40.84° N. Lat; 80.32° W. Long. Elevation is 899 feet.
Population: 1,024 (1990); 856 (2000); 762 (2010); Density: 1,418.1 persons per square mile (2010); Race: 96.1% White, 2.1% Black, 0.3% Asian, 0.0% American Indian/Alaska Native, 0.0% Native Hawaiian/Other Pacific Islander, 1.5% Other, 1.7% Hispanic of any race (2010); Average household size: 2.16 (2010); Median age: 43.3 (2010); Males per 100 females: 91.5 (2010); Marriage status: 21.4% never married, 47.8% now married, 13.5% widowed, 17.3% divorced (2006-2010 5-year est.); Foreign born: 1.3% (2006-2010 5-year est.); Ancestry (includes multiple ancestries): 35.4% German, 22.9% Italian, 18.9% Irish, 14.7% English, 11.9% Scotch-Irish (2006-2010 5-year est.).
Economy: Single-family building permits issued: 0 (2011); Multi-family building permits issued: 0 (2011); Employment by occupation: 6.4% management, 0.0% professional, 12.8% services, 20.7% sales, 0.8% farming, 17.3% construction, 7.8% production (2006-2010 5-year est.).
Income: Per capita income: $23,264 (2006-2010 5-year est.); Median household income: $39,167 (2006-2010 5-year est.); Average household income: $47,985 (2006-2010 5-year est.); Percent of households with income of $100,000 or more: 7.2% (2006-2010 5-year est.); Poverty rate: 6.7% (2006-2010 5-year est.).
Education: Percent of population age 25 and over with: High school diploma (including GED) or higher: 83.6% (2006-2010 5-year est.); Bachelor's degree or higher: 13.5% (2006-2010 5-year est.); Master's degree or higher: 1.3% (2006-2010 5-year est.).
Housing: Homeownership rate: 66.7% (2010); Median home value: $75,400 (2006-2010 5-year est.); Median contract rent: $434 per month (2006-2010 5-year est.); Median year structure built: before 1940 (2006-2010 5-year est.).
Safety: Violent crime rate: 65.4 per 10,000 population; Property crime rate: 353.4 per 10,000 population (2011).
Transportation: Commute to work: 95.7% car, 0.0% public transportation, 4.3% walk, 0.0% work from home (2006-2010 5-year est.); Travel time to work: 40.7% less than 15 minutes, 31.1% 15 to 30 minutes, 22.2% 30 to 45 minutes, 1.7% 45 to 60 minutes, 4.3% 60 minutes or more (2006-2010 5-year est.)

MARION (township). Covers a land area of 10.247 square miles and a water area of 0.237 square miles. Located at 40.79° N. Lat; 80.21° W. Long.
Population: 909 (1990); 940 (2000); 913 (2010); Density: 89.1 persons per square mile (2010); Race: 99.3% White, 0.1% Black, 0.1% Asian, 0.0% American Indian/Alaska Native, 0.0% Native Hawaiian/Other Pacific Islander, 0.5% Other, 1.0% Hispanic of any race (2010); Average household size: 2.47 (2010); Median age: 44.6 (2010); Males per 100 females: 105.2 (2010); Marriage status: 15.9% never married, 63.2% now married, 7.9% widowed, 13.0% divorced (2006-2010 5-year est.); Foreign born: 1.5% (2006-2010 5-year est.); Ancestry (includes multiple ancestries): 55.8% German, 18.4% Italian, 15.1% English, 13.2% Irish, 4.6% Polish (2006-2010 5-year est.).
Economy: Single-family building permits issued: 1 (2011); Multi-family building permits issued: 0 (2011); Employment by occupation: 11.2% management, 2.9% professional, 8.8% services, 16.1% sales, 6.1% farming, 13.9% construction, 7.5% production (2006-2010 5-year est.).
Income: Per capita income: $26,353 (2006-2010 5-year est.); Median household income: $44,213 (2006-2010 5-year est.); Average household income: $57,078 (2006-2010 5-year est.); Percent of households with income of $100,000 or more: 14.1% (2006-2010 5-year est.); Poverty rate: 14.3% (2006-2010 5-year est.).
Education: Percent of population age 25 and over with: High school diploma (including GED) or higher: 96.8% (2006-2010 5-year est.); Bachelor's degree or higher: 24.0% (2006-2010 5-year est.); Master's degree or higher: 4.9% (2006-2010 5-year est.).

Housing: Homeownership rate: 74.0% (2010); Median home value: $138,600 (2006-2010 5-year est.); Median contract rent: $589 per month (2006-2010 5-year est.); Median year structure built: 1967 (2006-2010 5-year est.).
Safety: Violent crime rate: 0.0 per 10,000 population; Property crime rate: 43.7 per 10,000 population (2011).
Transportation: Commute to work: 94.4% car, 0.0% public transportation, 4.2% walk, 1.4% work from home (2006-2010 5-year est.); Travel time to work: 38.3% less than 15 minutes, 38.5% 15 to 30 minutes, 10.4% 30 to 45 minutes, 8.4% 45 to 60 minutes, 4.5% 60 minutes or more (2006-2010 5-year est.)

MIDLAND (borough). Covers a land area of 1.809 square miles and a water area of 0.182 square miles. Located at 40.63° N. Lat; 80.46° W. Long. Elevation is 784 feet.
History: Settled c.1820.
Population: 3,312 (1990); 3,137 (2000); 2,635 (2010); Density: 1,456.6 persons per square mile (2010); Race: 74.4% White, 20.3% Black, 0.3% Asian, 0.3% American Indian/Alaska Native, 0.0% Native Hawaiian/Other Pacific Islander, 4.7% Other, 4.3% Hispanic of any race (2010); Average household size: 2.19 (2010); Median age: 41.3 (2010); Males per 100 females: 80.4 (2010); Marriage status: 28.6% never married, 41.0% now married, 11.2% widowed, 19.2% divorced (2006-2010 5-year est.); Foreign born: 3.4% (2006-2010 5-year est.); Ancestry (includes multiple ancestries): 18.1% Italian, 17.6% German, 12.0% Irish, 10.6% English, 8.9% Serbian (2006-2010 5-year est.).
Economy: Single-family building permits issued: 0 (2011); Multi-family building permits issued: 0 (2011); Employment by occupation: 3.8% management, 6.2% professional, 16.5% services, 14.7% sales, 9.0% farming, 6.2% construction, 5.5% production (2006-2010 5-year est.).
Income: Per capita income: $19,722 (2006-2010 5-year est.); Median household income: $29,684 (2006-2010 5-year est.); Average household income: $42,134 (2006-2010 5-year est.); Percent of households with income of $100,000 or more: 5.9% (2006-2010 5-year est.); Poverty rate: 27.0% (2006-2010 5-year est.).
Education: Percent of population age 25 and over with: High school diploma (including GED) or higher: 84.1% (2006-2010 5-year est.); Bachelor's degree or higher: 11.6% (2006-2010 5-year est.); Master's degree or higher: 3.0% (2006-2010 5-year est.).

School District(s)
Lincoln Park Performing Arts CS (08-12)
   2010-11 Enrollment: 545. . . . . (724) 643-9004
Midland Borough SD (PK-12)
   2010-11 Enrollment: 358. . . . . (724) 643-8650
Pennsylvania Cyber CS (KG-12)
   2010-11 Enrollment: 9,651 . . . . (724) 643-1180
Western Beaver County SD (PK-12)
   2010-11 Enrollment: 789. . . . . (724) 643-9310
Housing: Homeownership rate: 45.2% (2010); Median home value: $54,100 (2006-2010 5-year est.); Median contract rent: $339 per month (2006-2010 5-year est.); Median year structure built: 1944 (2006-2010 5-year est.).
Safety: Violent crime rate: 34.1 per 10,000 population; Property crime rate: 1,486.9 per 10,000 population (2011).
Transportation: Commute to work: 86.0% car, 0.8% public transportation, 9.0% walk, 1.7% work from home (2006-2010 5-year est.); Travel time to work: 37.3% less than 15 minutes, 31.5% 15 to 30 minutes, 19.1% 30 to 45 minutes, 3.2% 45 to 60 minutes, 8.9% 60 minutes or more (2006-2010 5-year est.)
Additional Information Contacts
Beaver County Chamber of Commerce . . . . (724) 775-3944
http://beavercountychamber.com

MONACA (borough). Covers a land area of 2.027 square miles and a water area of 0.355 square miles. Located at 40.68° N. Lat; 80.27° W. Long. Elevation is 738 feet.
History: Penn State University Beaver Campus to West. Settled 1813, incorporated 1839.
Population: 6,739 (1990); 6,286 (2000); 5,737 (2010); Density: 2,830.2 persons per square mile (2010); Race: 95.4% White, 2.1% Black, 0.4% Asian, 0.1% American Indian/Alaska Native, 0.0% Native Hawaiian/Other Pacific Islander, 2.0% Other, 1.2% Hispanic of any race (2010); Average household size: 2.20 (2010); Median age: 43.1 (2010); Males per 100 females: 88.6 (2010); Marriage status: 24.2% never married, 56.8% now married, 8.8% widowed, 10.2% divorced (2006-2010 5-year est.); Foreign

born: 2.8% (2006-2010 5-year est.); Ancestry (includes multiple ancestries): 30.2% German, 21.3% Italian, 20.4% Irish, 8.5% Polish, 8.0% English (2006-2010 5-year est.).

Economy: Single-family building permits issued: 1 (2011); Multi-family building permits issued: 0 (2011); Employment by occupation: 8.0% management, 3.5% professional, 13.6% services, 19.7% sales, 3.2% farming, 7.1% construction, 3.8% production (2006-2010 5-year est.).

Income: Per capita income: $21,726 (2006-2010 5-year est.); Median household income: $40,370 (2006-2010 5-year est.); Average household income: $45,912 (2006-2010 5-year est.); Percent of households with income of $100,000 or more: 9.1% (2006-2010 5-year est.); Poverty rate: 14.2% (2006-2010 5-year est.).

Education: Percent of population age 25 and over with: High school diploma (including GED) or higher: 86.4% (2006-2010 5-year est.); Bachelor's degree or higher: 13.7% (2006-2010 5-year est.); Master's degree or higher: 3.0% (2006-2010 5-year est.).

School District(s)

Beaver County CTC (10-12)
   2010-11 Enrollment: n/a . . . . (724) 728-5800
Central Valley SD (KG-12)
   2010-11 Enrollment: 2,405 . . . . (724) 775-5600

Four-year College(s)

Pennsylvania State University-Penn State Beaver (Public)
   Fall 2010 Enrollment: 808 . . . . (724) 773-3800
   2011-12 Tuition: In-state $13,102; Out-of-state $19,542

Two-year College(s)

Community College of Beaver County (Public)
   Fall 2010 Enrollment: 2,171 . . . . (724) 480-2222
   2011-12 Tuition: In-state $6,828; Out-of-state $10,158

Vocational/Technical School(s)

DCI Career Institute (Private, For-profit)
   Fall 2010 Enrollment: 142 . . . . (724) 728-0260
   2011-12 Tuition: $11,545

Housing: Homeownership rate: 61.9% (2010); Median home value: $95,500 (2006-2010 5-year est.); Median contract rent: $400 per month (2006-2010 5-year est.); Median year structure built: 1950 (2006-2010 5-year est.).

Safety: Violent crime rate: 22.6 per 10,000 population; Property crime rate: 225.9 per 10,000 population (2011).

Transportation: Commute to work: 89.0% car, 2.9% public transportation, 6.2% walk, 0.3% work from home (2006-2010 5-year est.); Travel time to work: 44.2% less than 15 minutes, 27.7% 15 to 30 minutes, 12.9% 30 to 45 minutes, 7.9% 45 to 60 minutes, 7.3% 60 minutes or more (2006-2010 5-year est.).

Additional Information Contacts
Beaver County Chamber of Commerce . . . . (724) 775-3944
   http://www.beavercountychamber.com
Borough of Monaca . . . . (724) 728-5700
   http://monacapa.net

NEW BRIGHTON (borough). Covers a land area of 1.032 square miles and a water area of 0.089 square miles. Located at 40.74° N. Lat; 80.31° W. Long. Elevation is 738 feet.

Population: 6,854 (1990); 6,641 (2000); 6,025 (2010); Density: 5,835.7 persons per square mile (2010); Race: 84.0% White, 10.7% Black, 0.1% Asian, 0.3% American Indian/Alaska Native, 0.0% Native Hawaiian/Other Pacific Islander, 4.9% Other, 1.5% Hispanic of any race (2010); Average household size: 2.27 (2010); Median age: 38.1 (2010); Males per 100 females: 88.3 (2010); Marriage status: 35.7% never married, 43.4% now married, 9.3% widowed, 11.5% divorced (2006-2010 5-year est.); Foreign born: 0.2% (2006-2010 5-year est.); Ancestry (includes multiple ancestries): 37.5% German, 22.2% Irish, 10.7% Italian, 10.2% English, 5.6% Polish (2006-2010 5-year est.).

Economy: Single-family building permits issued: 4 (2011); Multi-family building permits issued: 3 (2011); Employment by occupation: 5.9% management, 2.0% professional, 18.3% services, 14.0% sales, 4.5% farming, 6.8% construction, 4.5% production (2006-2010 5-year est.).

Income: Per capita income: $17,785 (2006-2010 5-year est.); Median household income: $33,203 (2006-2010 5-year est.); Average household income: $43,878 (2006-2010 5-year est.); Percent of households with income of $100,000 or more: 7.7% (2006-2010 5-year est.); Poverty rate: 22.7% (2006-2010 5-year est.).

Education: Percent of population age 25 and over with: High school diploma (including GED) or higher: 84.9% (2006-2010 5-year est.);

Bachelor's degree or higher: 11.9% (2006-2010 5-year est.); Master's degree or higher: 4.0% (2006-2010 5-year est.).

School District(s)

New Brighton Area SD (KG-12)
   2010-11 Enrollment: 1,705 . . . . (724) 843-1795

Housing: Homeownership rate: 49.0% (2010); Median home value: $74,900 (2006-2010 5-year est.); Median contract rent: $372 per month (2006-2010 5-year est.); Median year structure built: before 1940 (2006-2010 5-year est.).

Safety: Violent crime rate: 67.1 per 10,000 population; Property crime rate: 445.8 per 10,000 population (2011).

Transportation: Commute to work: 91.6% car, 1.1% public transportation, 5.1% walk, 0.7% work from home (2006-2010 5-year est.); Travel time to work: 28.1% less than 15 minutes, 38.1% 15 to 30 minutes, 21.6% 30 to 45 minutes, 5.0% 45 to 60 minutes, 7.1% 60 minutes or more (2006-2010 5-year est.)

Additional Information Contacts
Beaver County Chamber of Commerce . . . . (724) 775-3944
   http://www.beavercountychamber.com
Borough of New Brighton . . . . (724) 846-1870
   http://www.newbrightonborough.org

NEW GALILEE (borough). Covers a land area of 0.277 square miles and a water area of 0 square miles. Located at 40.83° N. Lat; 80.40° W. Long. Elevation is 978 feet.

Population: 500 (1990); 424 (2000); 379 (2010); Density: 1,370.1 persons per square mile (2010); Race: 95.8% White, 2.4% Black, 0.0% Asian, 0.0% American Indian/Alaska Native, 0.0% Native Hawaiian/Other Pacific Islander, 1.8% Other, 2.1% Hispanic of any race (2010); Average household size: 2.40 (2010); Median age: 44.6 (2010); Males per 100 females: 99.5 (2010); Marriage status: 28.4% never married, 53.6% now married, 11.8% widowed, 6.2% divorced (2006-2010 5-year est.); Foreign born: 0.0% (2006-2010 5-year est.); Ancestry (includes multiple ancestries): 33.5% German, 24.3% Irish, 17.2% Italian, 10.4% Polish, 9.0% English (2006-2010 5-year est.).

Economy: Single-family building permits issued: 0 (2011); Multi-family building permits issued: 0 (2011); Employment by occupation: 5.5% management, 9.4% professional, 18.7% services, 10.6% sales, 1.3% farming, 12.3% construction, 5.1% production (2006-2010 5-year est.).

Income: Per capita income: $23,904 (2006-2010 5-year est.); Median household income: $60,268 (2006-2010 5-year est.); Average household income: $59,759 (2006-2010 5-year est.); Percent of households with income of $100,000 or more: 16.5% (2006-2010 5-year est.); Poverty rate: 12.7% (2006-2010 5-year est.).

Education: Percent of population age 25 and over with: High school diploma (including GED) or higher: 87.9% (2006-2010 5-year est.); Bachelor's degree or higher: 21.2% (2006-2010 5-year est.); Master's degree or higher: 7.1% (2006-2010 5-year est.).

Housing: Homeownership rate: 74.0% (2010); Median home value: $77,100 (2006-2010 5-year est.); Median contract rent: $339 per month (2006-2010 5-year est.); Median year structure built: before 1940 (2006-2010 5-year est.).

Transportation: Commute to work: 92.2% car, 0.0% public transportation, 0.9% walk, 1.7% work from home (2006-2010 5-year est.); Travel time to work: 16.7% less than 15 minutes, 55.5% 15 to 30 minutes, 19.8% 30 to 45 minutes, 6.2% 45 to 60 minutes, 1.8% 60 minutes or more (2006-2010 5-year est.)

NEW SEWICKLEY (township). Covers a land area of 32.692 square miles and a water area of 0 square miles. Located at 40.72° N. Lat; 80.20° W. Long.

Population: 6,861 (1990); 7,076 (2000); 7,360 (2010); Density: 225.1 persons per square mile (2010); Race: 98.3% White, 0.3% Black, 0.5% Asian, 0.0% American Indian/Alaska Native, 0.0% Native Hawaiian/Other Pacific Islander, 0.9% Other, 0.4% Hispanic of any race (2010); Average household size: 2.35 (2010); Median age: 47.6 (2010); Males per 100 females: 95.1 (2010); Marriage status: 22.0% never married, 63.4% now married, 8.1% widowed, 6.5% divorced (2006-2010 5-year est.); Foreign born: 2.1% (2006-2010 5-year est.); Ancestry (includes multiple ancestries): 47.3% German, 19.4% Irish, 18.1% Italian, 9.5% English, 4.5% Polish (2006-2010 5-year est.).

Economy: Single-family building permits issued: 26 (2011); Multi-family building permits issued: 0 (2011); Employment by occupation: 10.0% management, 3.3% professional, 11.1% services, 20.8% sales, 4.9% farming, 9.1% construction, 6.2% production (2006-2010 5-year est.).

Income: Per capita income: $25,687 (2006-2010 5-year est.); Median household income: $53,911 (2006-2010 5-year est.); Average household income: $60,941 (2006-2010 5-year est.); Percent of households with income of $100,000 or more: 13.7% (2006-2010 5-year est.); Poverty rate: 9.8% (2006-2010 5-year est.).

Education: Percent of population age 25 and over with: High school diploma (including GED) or higher: 90.8% (2006-2010 5-year est.); Bachelor's degree or higher: 15.2% (2006-2010 5-year est.); Master's degree or higher: 5.5% (2006-2010 5-year est.).

Housing: Homeownership rate: 84.2% (2010); Median home value: $121,000 (2006-2010 5-year est.); Median contract rent: $919 per month (2006-2010 5-year est.); Median year structure built: 1979 (2006-2010 5-year est.).

Safety: Violent crime rate: 21.7 per 10,000 population; Property crime rate: 140.9 per 10,000 population (2011).

Transportation: Commute to work: 93.0% car, 2.3% public transportation, 0.6% walk, 3.6% work from home (2006-2010 5-year est.); Travel time to work: 20.2% less than 15 minutes, 49.6% 15 to 30 minutes, 16.0% 30 to 45 minutes, 8.0% 45 to 60 minutes, 6.2% 60 minutes or more (2006-2010 5-year est.)

Additional Information Contacts

New Sewickley Township . . . . (724) 774-2473
  http://www.newsewickley.com
Zelienople-Harmony Area Chamber of Commerce . . . . (724) 452-5232
  http://www.zhchamber.com

NORTH SEWICKLEY (township). Covers a land area of 20.768 square miles and a water area of 0.303 square miles. Located at 40.81° N. Lat; 80.27° W. Long. Elevation is 896 feet.

Population: 6,409 (1990); 6,120 (2000); 5,488 (2010); Density: 264.2 persons per square mile (2010); Race: 97.9% White, 0.7% Black, 0.2% Asian, 0.1% American Indian/Alaska Native, 0.0% Native Hawaiian/Other Pacific Islander, 1.1% Other, 0.9% Hispanic of any race (2010); Average household size: 2.54 (2010); Median age: 45.8 (2010); Males per 100 females: 96.7 (2010); Marriage status: 24.0% never married, 61.7% now married, 5.4% widowed, 9.0% divorced (2006-2010 5-year est.); Foreign born: 0.8% (2006-2010 5-year est.); Ancestry (includes multiple ancestries): 42.9% German, 17.2% Irish, 15.5% Italian, 14.2% English, 8.4% Polish (2006-2010 5-year est.).

Economy: Single-family building permits issued: 3 (2011); Multi-family building permits issued: 0 (2011); Employment by occupation: 7.5% management, 2.8% professional, 11.7% services, 16.3% sales, 4.6% farming, 14.9% construction, 10.1% production (2006-2010 5-year est.).

Income: Per capita income: $21,941 (2006-2010 5-year est.); Median household income: $46,845 (2006-2010 5-year est.); Average household income: $54,682 (2006-2010 5-year est.); Percent of households with income of $100,000 or more: 10.0% (2006-2010 5-year est.); Poverty rate: 9.0% (2006-2010 5-year est.).

Education: Percent of population age 25 and over with: High school diploma (including GED) or higher: 87.7% (2006-2010 5-year est.); Bachelor's degree or higher: 14.0% (2006-2010 5-year est.); Master's degree or higher: 4.8% (2006-2010 5-year est.).

Housing: Homeownership rate: 86.3% (2010); Median home value: $124,700 (2006-2010 5-year est.); Median contract rent: $427 per month (2006-2010 5-year est.); Median year structure built: 1960 (2006-2010 5-year est.).

Safety: Violent crime rate: 10.9 per 10,000 population; Property crime rate: 343.3 per 10,000 population (2011).

Transportation: Commute to work: 97.8% car, 0.0% public transportation, 0.0% walk, 1.8% work from home (2006-2010 5-year est.); Travel time to work: 19.1% less than 15 minutes, 39.5% 15 to 30 minutes, 28.1% 30 to 45 minutes, 7.2% 45 to 60 minutes, 6.1% 60 minutes or more (2006-2010 5-year est.)

Additional Information Contacts

Beaver County Chamber of Commerce . . . . (724) 775-3944
  http://www.beavercountychamber.com
North Sewickley Township . . . . (724) 843-5826

OHIOVILLE (borough). Covers a land area of 23.336 square miles and a water area of 0.355 square miles. Located at 40.68° N. Lat; 80.48° W. Long. Elevation is 1,115 feet.

Population: 3,885 (1990); 3,759 (2000); 3,533 (2010); Density: 151.4 persons per square mile (2010); Race: 97.5% White, 1.1% Black, 0.2% Asian, 0.3% American Indian/Alaska Native, 0.0% Native Hawaiian/Other Pacific Islander, 0.9% Other, 1.0% Hispanic of any race (2010); Average

household size: 2.50 (2010); Median age: 46.1 (2010); Males per 100 females: 98.6 (2010); Marriage status: 30.7% never married, 49.9% now married, 8.2% widowed, 11.2% divorced (2006-2010 5-year est.); Foreign born: 1.1% (2006-2010 5-year est.); Ancestry (includes multiple ancestries): 27.6% German, 17.0% Irish, 14.4% English, 10.9% Italian, 10.2% Polish (2006-2010 5-year est.).

Economy: Single-family building permits issued: 0 (2011); Multi-family building permits issued: 0 (2011); Employment by occupation: 6.5% management, 2.7% professional, 12.1% services, 15.6% sales, 2.9% farming, 11.9% construction, 8.8% production (2006-2010 5-year est.).

Income: Per capita income: $22,183 (2006-2010 5-year est.); Median household income: $50,786 (2006-2010 5-year est.); Average household income: $58,718 (2006-2010 5-year est.); Percent of households with income of $100,000 or more: 11.7% (2006-2010 5-year est.); Poverty rate: 11.1% (2006-2010 5-year est.).

Education: Percent of population age 25 and over with: High school diploma (including GED) or higher: 89.1% (2006-2010 5-year est.); Bachelor's degree or higher: 13.8% (2006-2010 5-year est.); Master's degree or higher: 5.0% (2006-2010 5-year est.).

Housing: Homeownership rate: 86.5% (2010); Median home value: $115,400 (2006-2010 5-year est.); Median contract rent: $446 per month (2006-2010 5-year est.); Median year structure built: 1958 (2006-2010 5-year est.).

Safety: Violent crime rate: 25.4 per 10,000 population; Property crime rate: 107.2 per 10,000 population (2011).

Transportation: Commute to work: 94.1% car, 2.5% public transportation, 1.4% walk, 1.9% work from home (2006-2010 5-year est.); Travel time to work: 14.7% less than 15 minutes, 43.9% 15 to 30 minutes, 23.5% 30 to 45 minutes, 10.8% 45 to 60 minutes, 7.1% 60 minutes or more (2006-2010 5-year est.)

Additional Information Contacts

Beaver County Chamber of Commerce . . . . (724) 775-3944
  http://www.beavercountychamber.com

PATTERSON (township). Covers a land area of 1.636 square miles and a water area of 0.006 square miles. Located at 40.74° N. Lat; 80.33° W. Long.

Population: 3,074 (1990); 3,197 (2000); 3,029 (2010); Density: 1,851.5 persons per square mile (2010); Race: 95.9% White, 2.1% Black, 0.5% Asian, 0.1% American Indian/Alaska Native, 0.0% Native Hawaiian/Other Pacific Islander, 1.4% Other, 1.6% Hispanic of any race (2010); Average household size: 2.16 (2010); Median age: 47.9 (2010); Males per 100 females: 90.6 (2010); Marriage status: 20.5% never married, 54.1% now married, 10.8% widowed, 14.6% divorced (2006-2010 5-year est.); Foreign born: 1.7% (2006-2010 5-year est.); Ancestry (includes multiple ancestries): 28.8% German, 22.4% Italian, 15.9% English, 15.1% Irish, 4.4% Polish (2006-2010 5-year est.).

Economy: Single-family building permits issued: 1 (2011); Multi-family building permits issued: 0 (2011); Employment by occupation: 12.4% management, 2.6% professional, 11.5% services, 19.6% sales, 4.9% farming, 7.7% construction, 6.1% production (2006-2010 5-year est.).

Income: Per capita income: $26,984 (2006-2010 5-year est.); Median household income: $51,250 (2006-2010 5-year est.); Average household income: $61,166 (2006-2010 5-year est.); Percent of households with income of $100,000 or more: 14.3% (2006-2010 5-year est.); Poverty rate: 3.0% (2006-2010 5-year est.).

Education: Percent of population age 25 and over with: High school diploma (including GED) or higher: 96.6% (2006-2010 5-year est.); Bachelor's degree or higher: 23.1% (2006-2010 5-year est.); Master's degree or higher: 8.0% (2006-2010 5-year est.).

Housing: Homeownership rate: 69.5% (2010); Median home value: $113,500 (2006-2010 5-year est.); Median contract rent: $420 per month (2006-2010 5-year est.); Median year structure built: 1954 (2006-2010 5-year est.).

Safety: Violent crime rate: 16.5 per 10,000 population; Property crime rate: 227.0 per 10,000 population (2011).

Transportation: Commute to work: 95.0% car, 2.9% public transportation, 0.2% walk, 1.0% work from home (2006-2010 5-year est.); Travel time to work: 29.2% less than 15 minutes, 32.7% 15 to 30 minutes, 21.2% 30 to 45 minutes, 8.7% 45 to 60 minutes, 8.1% 60 minutes or more (2006-2010 5-year est.)

Additional Information Contacts

Beaver County Chamber of Commerce . . . . (724) 775-3944
  http://www.beavercountychamber.com

PATTERSON HEIGHTS (borough). Covers a land area of 0.230 square miles and a water area of 0.006 square miles. Located at 40.74° N. Lat; 80.33° W. Long. Elevation is 1,066 feet.
Population: 576 (1990); 670 (2000); 636 (2010); Density: 2,766.7 persons per square mile (2010); Race: 96.9% White, 0.8% Black, 0.2% Asian, 0.0% American Indian/Alaska Native, 0.0% Native Hawaiian/Other Pacific Islander, 2.1% Other, 2.5% Hispanic of any race (2010); Average household size: 2.46 (2010); Median age: 46.1 (2010); Males per 100 females: 83.8 (2010); Marriage status: 25.5% never married, 59.2% now married, 4.3% widowed, 10.9% divorced (2006-2010 5-year est.); Foreign born: 0.7% (2006-2010 5-year est.); Ancestry (includes multiple ancestries): 35.7% German, 25.2% Italian, 14.8% English, 10.7% Irish, 8.7% Dutch (2006-2010 5-year est.).
Economy: Single-family building permits issued: 0 (2011); Multi-family building permits issued: 0 (2011); Employment by occupation: 19.3% management, 1.6% professional, 5.6% services, 15.3% sales, 2.4% farming, 6.3% construction, 3.4% production (2006-2010 5-year est.).
Income: Per capita income: $28,491 (2006-2010 5-year est.); Median household income: $61,875 (2006-2010 5-year est.); Average household income: $70,867 (2006-2010 5-year est.); Percent of households with income of $100,000 or more: 26.0% (2006-2010 5-year est.); Poverty rate: 10.7% (2006-2010 5-year est.).
Education: Percent of population age 25 and over with: High school diploma (including GED) or higher: 95.5% (2006-2010 5-year est.); Bachelor's degree or higher: 40.3% (2006-2010 5-year est.); Master's degree or higher: 8.5% (2006-2010 5-year est.).
Housing: Homeownership rate: 90.0% (2010); Median home value: $143,100 (2006-2010 5-year est.); Median contract rent: $510 per month (2006-2010 5-year est.); Median year structure built: before 1940 (2006-2010 5-year est.).
Transportation: Commute to work: 91.5% car, 2.9% public transportation, 0.8% walk, 4.0% work from home (2006-2010 5-year est.); Travel time to work: 40.2% less than 15 minutes, 38.3% 15 to 30 minutes, 13.2% 30 to 45 minutes, 4.1% 45 to 60 minutes, 4.1% 60 minutes or more (2006-2010 5-year est.)

POTTER (township). Covers a land area of 6.462 square miles and a water area of 0.468 square miles. Located at 40.65° N. Lat; 80.36° W. Long.
Population: 546 (1990); 580 (2000); 548 (2010); Density: 84.8 persons per square mile (2010); Race: 98.7% White, 0.5% Black, 0.2% Asian, 0.0% American Indian/Alaska Native, 0.0% Native Hawaiian/Other Pacific Islander, 0.6% Other, 0.7% Hispanic of any race (2010); Average household size: 2.49 (2010); Median age: 47.2 (2010); Males per 100 females: 100.7 (2010); Marriage status: 20.6% never married, 52.8% now married, 9.2% widowed, 17.3% divorced (2006-2010 5-year est.); Foreign born: 0.9% (2006-2010 5-year est.); Ancestry (includes multiple ancestries): 40.7% German, 22.6% Irish, 14.1% English, 12.9% American, 8.9% Italian (2006-2010 5-year est.).
Economy: Single-family building permits issued: 2 (2011); Multi-family building permits issued: 0 (2011); Employment by occupation: 8.3% management, 4.0% professional, 13.2% services, 16.2% sales, 5.9% farming, 15.5% construction, 10.2% production (2006-2010 5-year est.).
Income: Per capita income: $28,269 (2006-2010 5-year est.); Median household income: $50,859 (2006-2010 5-year est.); Average household income: $59,365 (2006-2010 5-year est.); Percent of households with income of $100,000 or more: 14.1% (2006-2010 5-year est.); Poverty rate: 8.2% (2006-2010 5-year est.).
Education: Percent of population age 25 and over with: High school diploma (including GED) or higher: 90.0% (2006-2010 5-year est.); Bachelor's degree or higher: 14.6% (2006-2010 5-year est.); Master's degree or higher: 4.4% (2006-2010 5-year est.).
Housing: Homeownership rate: 85.0% (2010); Median home value: $134,700 (2006-2010 5-year est.); Median contract rent: $542 per month (2006-2010 5-year est.); Median year structure built: 1959 (2006-2010 5-year est.).
Transportation: Commute to work: 92.3% car, 0.0% public transportation, 1.3% walk, 5.0% work from home (2006-2010 5-year est.); Travel time to work: 35.0% less than 15 minutes, 43.1% 15 to 30 minutes, 10.6% 30 to 45 minutes, 3.2% 45 to 60 minutes, 8.1% 60 minutes or more (2006-2010 5-year est.)

PULASKI (township). Covers a land area of 0.726 square miles and a water area of 0 square miles. Located at 40.73° N. Lat; 80.30° W. Long. Elevation is 1,076 feet.
Population: 1,697 (1990); 1,674 (2000); 1,500 (2010); Density: 2,064.8 persons per square mile (2010); Race: 92.3% White, 4.2% Black, 0.1% Asian, 0.0% American Indian/Alaska Native, 0.0% Native Hawaiian/Other Pacific Islander, 3.4% Other, 1.5% Hispanic of any race (2010); Average household size: 2.26 (2010); Median age: 43.3 (2010); Males per 100 females: 90.1 (2010); Marriage status: 26.1% never married, 53.6% now married, 9.9% widowed, 10.5% divorced (2006-2010 5-year est.); Foreign born: 1.8% (2006-2010 5-year est.); Ancestry (includes multiple ancestries): 31.0% German, 19.7% Italian, 15.8% Irish, 9.2% English, 6.9% Polish (2006-2010 5-year est.).
Economy: Single-family building permits issued: 0 (2011); Multi-family building permits issued: 0 (2011); Employment by occupation: 6.0% management, 4.6% professional, 17.5% services, 18.3% sales, 4.9% farming, 10.7% construction, 9.1% production (2006-2010 5-year est.).
Income: Per capita income: $19,297 (2006-2010 5-year est.); Median household income: $32,500 (2006-2010 5-year est.); Average household income: $43,025 (2006-2010 5-year est.); Percent of households with income of $100,000 or more: 6.3% (2006-2010 5-year est.); Poverty rate: 18.2% (2006-2010 5-year est.).
Education: Percent of population age 25 and over with: High school diploma (including GED) or higher: 83.2% (2006-2010 5-year est.); Bachelor's degree or higher: 6.9% (2006-2010 5-year est.); Master's degree or higher: 2.1% (2006-2010 5-year est.).
Housing: Homeownership rate: 66.0% (2010); Median home value: $71,700 (2006-2010 5-year est.); Median contract rent: $426 per month (2006-2010 5-year est.); Median year structure built: 1948 (2006-2010 5-year est.).
Transportation: Commute to work: 95.8% car, 0.8% public transportation, 1.8% walk, 0.6% work from home (2006-2010 5-year est.); Travel time to work: 33.6% less than 15 minutes, 34.7% 15 to 30 minutes, 20.5% 30 to 45 minutes, 6.1% 45 to 60 minutes, 5.0% 60 minutes or more (2006-2010 5-year est.)
Additional Information Contacts
Beaver County Chamber of Commerce . . . . (724) 775-3944
    http://www.beavercountychamber.com

RACCOON (township). Covers a land area of 18.836 square miles and a water area of 0.602 square miles. Located at 40.60° N. Lat; 80.38° W. Long.
Population: 3,426 (1990); 3,397 (2000); 3,064 (2010); Density: 162.7 persons per square mile (2010); Race: 98.1% White, 0.6% Black, 0.2% Asian, 0.2% American Indian/Alaska Native, 0.0% Native Hawaiian/Other Pacific Islander, 0.9% Other, 1.1% Hispanic of any race (2010); Average household size: 2.59 (2010); Median age: 45.9 (2010); Males per 100 females: 102.9 (2010); Marriage status: 29.2% never married, 61.1% now married, 6.0% widowed, 3.7% divorced (2006-2010 5-year est.); Foreign born: 1.0% (2006-2010 5-year est.); Ancestry (includes multiple ancestries): 34.2% German, 21.7% Irish, 9.8% Italian, 8.8% Polish, 8.1% English (2006-2010 5-year est.).
Economy: Single-family building permits issued: 1 (2011); Multi-family building permits issued: 0 (2011); Employment by occupation: 5.6% management, 6.6% professional, 10.6% services, 18.2% sales, 1.5% farming, 14.4% construction, 9.5% production (2006-2010 5-year est.).
Income: Per capita income: $27,916 (2006-2010 5-year est.); Median household income: $57,045 (2006-2010 5-year est.); Average household income: $72,938 (2006-2010 5-year est.); Percent of households with income of $100,000 or more: 15.4% (2006-2010 5-year est.); Poverty rate: 8.9% (2006-2010 5-year est.).
Education: Percent of population age 25 and over with: High school diploma (including GED) or higher: 87.6% (2006-2010 5-year est.); Bachelor's degree or higher: 19.3% (2006-2010 5-year est.); Master's degree or higher: 2.3% (2006-2010 5-year est.).
Housing: Homeownership rate: 89.5% (2010); Median home value: $130,600 (2006-2010 5-year est.); Median contract rent: $1,279 per month (2006-2010 5-year est.); Median year structure built: 1981 (2006-2010 5-year est.).
Transportation: Commute to work: 91.6% car, 3.4% public transportation, 1.7% walk, 1.9% work from home (2006-2010 5-year est.); Travel time to work: 18.5% less than 15 minutes, 39.6% 15 to 30 minutes, 25.0% 30 to 45 minutes, 11.8% 45 to 60 minutes, 5.1% 60 minutes or more (2006-2010 5-year est.)

ROCHESTER (borough). Covers a land area of 0.588 square miles and a water area of 0.141 square miles. Located at 40.70° N. Lat; 80.28° W. Long. Elevation is 797 feet.

Population: 4,156 (1990); 4,014 (2000); 3,657 (2010); Density: 6,218.5 persons per square mile (2010); Race: 78.3% White, 16.1% Black, 0.1% Asian, 0.2% American Indian/Alaska Native, 0.0% Native Hawaiian/Other Pacific Islander, 5.3% Other, 1.8% Hispanic of any race (2010); Average household size: 2.22 (2010); Median age: 39.9 (2010); Males per 100 females: 88.4 (2010); Marriage status: 26.8% never married, 51.3% now married, 6.9% widowed, 15.1% divorced (2006-2010 5-year est.); Foreign born: 0.6% (2006-2010 5-year est.); Ancestry (includes multiple ancestries): 26.3% German, 21.1% Italian, 17.1% Irish, 5.6% English, 5.1% Polish (2006-2010 5-year est.).

Economy: Single-family building permits issued: 0 (2011); Multi-family building permits issued: 0 (2011); Employment by occupation: 3.0% management, 4.8% professional, 16.6% services, 20.1% sales, 3.3% farming, 7.6% construction, 8.9% production (2006-2010 5-year est.).

Income: Per capita income: $18,184 (2006-2010 5-year est.); Median household income: $33,561 (2006-2010 5-year est.); Average household income: $40,079 (2006-2010 5-year est.); Percent of households with income of $100,000 or more: 5.2% (2006-2010 5-year est.); Poverty rate: 20.1% (2006-2010 5-year est.).

Education: Percent of population age 25 and over with: High school diploma (including GED) or higher: 86.4% (2006-2010 5-year est.); Bachelor's degree or higher: 13.2% (2006-2010 5-year est.); Master's degree or higher: 4.1% (2006-2010 5-year est.).

School District(s)

Rochester Area SD (KG-12)
    2010-11 Enrollment: 880. . . . . (724) 775-7500

Housing: Homeownership rate: 49.0% (2010); Median home value: $75,400 (2006-2010 5-year est.); Median contract rent: $460 per month (2006-2010 5-year est.); Median year structure built: before 1940 (2006-2010 5-year est.).

Hospitals: WPIC-Beaver Valley Mental Health Services (26 beds)

Safety: Violent crime rate: 87.2 per 10,000 population; Property crime rate: 831.3 per 10,000 population (2011).

Transportation: Commute to work: 84.4% car, 6.6% public transportation, 4.8% walk, 2.6% work from home (2006-2010 5-year est.); Travel time to work: 42.1% less than 15 minutes, 34.9% 15 to 30 minutes, 11.8% 30 to 45 minutes, 2.6% 45 to 60 minutes, 8.6% 60 minutes or more (2006-2010 5-year est.)

Additional Information Contacts

Beaver County Chamber of Commerce . . . . (724) 775-3944
    http://www.beavercountychamber.com
Borough of Rochester . . . . (724) 728-4998

ROCHESTER (township). Covers a land area of 3.885 square miles and a water area of 0.066 square miles. Located at 40.71° N. Lat; 80.27° W. Long. Elevation is 797 feet.

Population: 3,247 (1990); 3,129 (2000); 2,802 (2010); Density: 721.2 persons per square mile (2010); Race: 95.1% White, 3.0% Black, 0.1% Asian, 0.1% American Indian/Alaska Native, 0.0% Native Hawaiian/Other Pacific Islander, 1.7% Other, 0.7% Hispanic of any race (2010); Average household size: 2.38 (2010); Median age: 46.8 (2010); Males per 100 females: 101.6 (2010); Marriage status: 21.1% never married, 57.5% now married, 8.6% widowed, 12.8% divorced (2006-2010 5-year est.); Foreign born: 1.3% (2006-2010 5-year est.); Ancestry (includes multiple ancestries): 43.0% German, 27.6% Italian, 21.0% Irish, 4.5% American, 4.1% English (2006-2010 5-year est.).

Economy: Single-family building permits issued: 2 (2011); Multi-family building permits issued: 0 (2011); Employment by occupation: 8.1% management, 3.4% professional, 9.3% services, 18.2% sales, 2.4% farming, 9.0% construction, 4.8% production (2006-2010 5-year est.).

Income: Per capita income: $24,512 (2006-2010 5-year est.); Median household income: $48,497 (2006-2010 5-year est.); Average household income: $57,404 (2006-2010 5-year est.); Percent of households with income of $100,000 or more: 14.3% (2006-2010 5-year est.); Poverty rate: 7.9% (2006-2010 5-year est.).

Education: Percent of population age 25 and over with: High school diploma (including GED) or higher: 85.3% (2006-2010 5-year est.);

Bachelor's degree or higher: 12.1% (2006-2010 5-year est.); Master's degree or higher: 2.7% (2006-2010 5-year est.).

Housing: Homeownership rate: 81.5% (2010); Median home value: $105,100 (2006-2010 5-year est.); Median contract rent: $433 per month (2006-2010 5-year est.); Median year structure built: 1951 (2006-2010 5-year est.).

Hospitals: WPIC-Beaver Valley Mental Health Services (26 beds)

Safety: Violent crime rate: 3.6 per 10,000 population; Property crime rate: 213.4 per 10,000 population (2011).

Transportation: Commute to work: 99.0% car, 0.1% public transportation, 0.0% walk, 0.8% work from home (2006-2010 5-year est.); Travel time to work: 31.8% less than 15 minutes, 40.8% 15 to 30 minutes, 19.6% 30 to 45 minutes, 2.9% 45 to 60 minutes, 4.9% 60 minutes or more (2006-2010 5-year est.)

Additional Information Contacts

Beaver County Chamber of Commerce . . . . (724) 775-3944
    http://www.beavercountychamber.com

SHIPPINGPORT (borough). Covers a land area of 3.327 square miles and a water area of 0.355 square miles. Located at 40.62° N. Lat; 80.42° W. Long. Elevation is 781 feet.

Population: 210 (1990); 237 (2000); 214 (2010); Density: 64.3 persons per square mile (2010); Race: 94.4% White, 1.4% Black, 0.0% Asian, 0.0% American Indian/Alaska Native, 0.0% Native Hawaiian/Other Pacific Islander, 4.2% Other, 0.0% Hispanic of any race (2010); Average household size: 2.55 (2010); Median age: 38.5 (2010); Males per 100 females: 98.1 (2010); Marriage status: 28.4% never married, 40.7% now married, 15.4% widowed, 15.4% divorced (2006-2010 5-year est.); Foreign born: 0.0% (2006-2010 5-year est.); Ancestry (includes multiple ancestries): 31.3% Irish, 26.7% German, 15.9% American, 11.8% Slovak, 10.8% Polish (2006-2010 5-year est.).

Economy: Single-family building permits issued: 0 (2011); Multi-family building permits issued: 0 (2011); Employment by occupation: 8.9% management, 1.3% professional, 25.3% services, 24.1% sales, 2.5% farming, 0.0% construction, 2.5% production (2006-2010 5-year est.).

Income: Per capita income: $15,955 (2006-2010 5-year est.); Median household income: $31,083 (2006-2010 5-year est.); Average household income: $35,907 (2006-2010 5-year est.); Percent of households with income of $100,000 or more: n/a (2006-2010 5-year est.); Poverty rate: 11.3% (2006-2010 5-year est.).

Education: Percent of population age 25 and over with: High school diploma (including GED) or higher: 84.9% (2006-2010 5-year est.); Bachelor's degree or higher: 5.0% (2006-2010 5-year est.); Master's degree or higher: 0.0% (2006-2010 5-year est.).

Housing: Homeownership rate: 64.3% (2010); Median home value: $88,100 (2006-2010 5-year est.); Median contract rent: $585 per month (2006-2010 5-year est.); Median year structure built: before 1940 (2006-2010 5-year est.).

Transportation: Commute to work: 88.7% car, 0.0% public transportation, 11.3% walk, 0.0% work from home (2006-2010 5-year est.); Travel time to work: 21.1% less than 15 minutes, 39.4% 15 to 30 minutes, 29.6% 30 to 45 minutes, 7.0% 45 to 60 minutes, 2.8% 60 minutes or more (2006-2010 5-year est.)

SOUTH BEAVER (township). Covers a land area of 29.689 square miles and a water area of 0.081 square miles. Located at 40.76° N. Lat; 80.46° W. Long.

Population: 2,927 (1990); 2,974 (2000); 2,717 (2010); Density: 91.5 persons per square mile (2010); Race: 97.9% White, 0.9% Black, 0.2% Asian, 0.2% American Indian/Alaska Native, 0.0% Native Hawaiian/Other Pacific Islander, 0.8% Other, 0.6% Hispanic of any race (2010); Average household size: 2.42 (2010); Median age: 49.3 (2010); Males per 100 females: 93.8 (2010); Marriage status: 16.4% never married, 62.1% now married, 13.9% widowed, 7.6% divorced (2006-2010 5-year est.); Foreign born: 0.4% (2006-2010 5-year est.); Ancestry (includes multiple ancestries): 36.3% German, 17.6% Irish, 11.4% Italian, 10.8% English, 7.1% Polish (2006-2010 5-year est.).

Economy: Single-family building permits issued: 4 (2011); Multi-family building permits issued: 0 (2011); Employment by occupation: 10.3% management, 5.3% professional, 5.4% services, 15.1% sales, 3.1% farming, 14.4% construction, 11.6% production (2006-2010 5-year est.).

Income: Per capita income: $26,260 (2006-2010 5-year est.); Median household income: $56,310 (2006-2010 5-year est.); Average household income: $63,467 (2006-2010 5-year est.); Percent of households with

income of $100,000 or more: 14.2% (2006-2010 5-year est.); Poverty rate: 4.2% (2006-2010 5-year est.).

Education: Percent of population age 25 and over with: High school diploma (including GED) or higher: 91.6% (2006-2010 5-year est.); Bachelor's degree or higher: 17.9% (2006-2010 5-year est.); Master's degree or higher: 6.3% (2006-2010 5-year est.).

Housing: Homeownership rate: 89.2% (2010); Median home value: $142,200 (2006-2010 5-year est.); Median contract rent: $375 per month (2006-2010 5-year est.); Median year structure built: 1969 (2006-2010 5-year est.).

Transportation: Commute to work: 95.3% car, 0.0% public transportation, 1.1% walk, 2.5% work from home (2006-2010 5-year est.); Travel time to work: 24.6% less than 15 minutes, 34.8% 15 to 30 minutes, 26.3% 30 to 45 minutes, 7.7% 45 to 60 minutes, 6.6% 60 minutes or more (2006-2010 5-year est.)

Additional Information Contacts

Beaver County Chamber of Commerce . . . . (724) 775-3944
  http://www.beavercountychamber.com

SOUTH HEIGHTS (borough).
Covers a land area of 0.327 square miles and a water area of 0.085 square miles. Located at 40.57° N. Lat; 80.24° W. Long. Elevation is 774 feet.

Population: 647 (1990); 542 (2000); 475 (2010); Density: 1,453.5 persons per square mile (2010); Race: 97.1% White, 1.9% Black, 0.0% Asian, 0.0% American Indian/Alaska Native, 0.0% Native Hawaiian/Other Pacific Islander, 1.0% Other, 1.3% Hispanic of any race (2010); Average household size: 2.20 (2010); Median age: 46.3 (2010); Males per 100 females: 103.0 (2010); Marriage status: 26.3% never married, 51.3% now married, 6.6% widowed, 15.8% divorced (2006-2010 5-year est.); Foreign born: 1.2% (2006-2010 5-year est.); Ancestry (includes multiple ancestries): 48.6% German, 25.4% Irish, 16.5% Italian, 9.2% Slovak, 9.2% Scotch-Irish (2006-2010 5-year est.).

Economy: Single-family building permits issued: 0 (2011); Multi-family building permits issued: 0 (2011); Employment by occupation: 5.8% management, 4.1% professional, 8.2% services, 22.2% sales, 0.0% farming, 21.1% construction, 20.5% production (2006-2010 5-year est.).

Income: Per capita income: $19,321 (2006-2010 5-year est.); Median household income: $43,214 (2006-2010 5-year est.); Average household income: $44,653 (2006-2010 5-year est.); Percent of households with income of $100,000 or more: 2.9% (2006-2010 5-year est.); Poverty rate: 14.1% (2006-2010 5-year est.).

Education: Percent of population age 25 and over with: High school diploma (including GED) or higher: 81.7% (2006-2010 5-year est.); Bachelor's degree or higher: 20.0% (2006-2010 5-year est.); Master's degree or higher: 0.7% (2006-2010 5-year est.).

Housing: Homeownership rate: 80.1% (2010); Median home value: $95,200 (2006-2010 5-year est.); Median contract rent: $425 per month (2006-2010 5-year est.); Median year structure built: 1946 (2006-2010 5-year est.).

Safety: Violent crime rate: 0.0 per 10,000 population; Property crime rate: 0.0 per 10,000 population (2011).

Transportation: Commute to work: 95.8% car, 0.0% public transportation, 4.2% walk, 0.0% work from home (2006-2010 5-year est.); Travel time to work: 25.6% less than 15 minutes, 50.6% 15 to 30 minutes, 19.6% 30 to 45 minutes, 0.0% 45 to 60 minutes, 4.2% 60 minutes or more (2006-2010 5-year est.)

VANPORT (township).
Aka Borough. Covers a land area of 0.915 square miles and a water area of 0.280 square miles. Located at 40.68° N. Lat; 80.33° W. Long. Elevation is 751 feet.

Population: 1,700 (1990); 1,451 (2000); 1,321 (2010); Density: 1,444.2 persons per square mile (2010); Race: 96.7% White, 1.6% Black, 0.5% Asian, 0.1% American Indian/Alaska Native, 0.0% Native Hawaiian/Other Pacific Islander, 1.1% Other, 0.8% Hispanic of any race (2010); Average household size: 1.82 (2010); Median age: 57.3 (2010); Males per 100 females: 75.4 (2010); Marriage status: 20.9% never married, 49.7% now married, 14.3% widowed, 15.1% divorced (2006-2010 5-year est.); Foreign born: 1.3% (2006-2010 5-year est.); Ancestry (includes multiple ancestries): 32.1% German, 17.6% Irish, 14.1% Italian, 13.4% English, 7.0% Scotch-Irish (2006-2010 5-year est.).

Economy: Single-family building permits issued: 3 (2011); Multi-family building permits issued: 0 (2011); Employment by occupation: 4.3% management, 4.8% professional, 13.6% services, 19.6% sales, 4.0% farming, 6.2% construction, 7.0% production (2006-2010 5-year est.).

Income: Per capita income: $21,526 (2006-2010 5-year est.); Median household income: $33,462 (2006-2010 5-year est.); Average household income: $40,200 (2006-2010 5-year est.); Percent of households with income of $100,000 or more: 3.5% (2006-2010 5-year est.); Poverty rate: 7.4% (2006-2010 5-year est.).

Education: Percent of population age 25 and over with: High school diploma (including GED) or higher: 89.0% (2006-2010 5-year est.); Bachelor's degree or higher: 17.2% (2006-2010 5-year est.); Master's degree or higher: 3.8% (2006-2010 5-year est.).

Housing: Homeownership rate: 40.6% (2010); Median home value: $98,300 (2006-2010 5-year est.); Median contract rent: $326 per month (2006-2010 5-year est.); Median year structure built: 1946 (2006-2010 5-year est.).

Transportation: Commute to work: 93.8% car, 2.4% public transportation, 1.9% walk, 1.9% work from home (2006-2010 5-year est.); Travel time to work: 43.2% less than 15 minutes, 34.3% 15 to 30 minutes, 15.0% 30 to 45 minutes, 4.9% 45 to 60 minutes, 2.6% 60 minutes or more (2006-2010 5-year est.)

Additional Information Contacts

Beaver County Chamber of Commerce . . . . (724) 775-3944
  http://www.beavercountychamber.com

WEST MAYFIELD (borough).
Covers a land area of 0.795 square miles and a water area of 0 square miles. Located at 40.78° N. Lat; 80.34° W. Long. Elevation is 1,096 feet.

Population: 1,312 (1990); 1,187 (2000); 1,239 (2010); Density: 1,558.5 persons per square mile (2010); Race: 94.2% White, 2.7% Black, 0.7% Asian, 0.0% American Indian/Alaska Native, 0.0% Native Hawaiian/Other Pacific Islander, 2.4% Other, 1.4% Hispanic of any race (2010); Average household size: 2.43 (2010); Median age: 39.9 (2010); Males per 100 females: 93.6 (2010); Marriage status: 23.6% never married, 60.9% now married, 6.2% widowed, 9.2% divorced (2006-2010 5-year est.); Foreign born: 0.5% (2006-2010 5-year est.); Ancestry (includes multiple ancestries): 38.5% German, 23.1% Irish, 14.9% Italian, 7.8% Polish, 5.5% English (2006-2010 5-year est.).

Economy: Single-family building permits issued: 0 (2011); Multi-family building permits issued: 0 (2011); Employment by occupation: 11.5% management, 1.8% professional, 13.5% services, 20.5% sales, 4.0% farming, 4.5% construction, 5.2% production (2006-2010 5-year est.).

Income: Per capita income: $19,069 (2006-2010 5-year est.); Median household income: $44,083 (2006-2010 5-year est.); Average household income: $48,389 (2006-2010 5-year est.); Percent of households with income of $100,000 or more: 2.6% (2006-2010 5-year est.); Poverty rate: 10.1% (2006-2010 5-year est.).

Education: Percent of population age 25 and over with: High school diploma (including GED) or higher: 86.1% (2006-2010 5-year est.); Bachelor's degree or higher: 11.0% (2006-2010 5-year est.); Master's degree or higher: 2.3% (2006-2010 5-year est.).

Housing: Homeownership rate: 67.2% (2010); Median home value: $88,400 (2006-2010 5-year est.); Median contract rent: $455 per month (2006-2010 5-year est.); Median year structure built: 1955 (2006-2010 5-year est.).

Safety: Violent crime rate: 16.1 per 10,000 population; Property crime rate: 120.7 per 10,000 population (2011).

Transportation: Commute to work: 94.8% car, 0.0% public transportation, 3.3% walk, 0.4% work from home (2006-2010 5-year est.); Travel time to work: 33.3% less than 15 minutes, 36.1% 15 to 30 minutes, 21.0% 30 to 45 minutes, 5.0% 45 to 60 minutes, 4.6% 60 minutes or more (2006-2010 5-year est.)

Additional Information Contacts

Beaver County Chamber of Commerce . . . . (724) 775-3944
  http://www.beavercountychamber.com

WHITE (township).
Covers a land area of 0.697 square miles and a water area of 0 square miles. Located at 40.77° N. Lat; 80.34° W. Long.

Population: 1,610 (1990); 1,434 (2000); 1,394 (2010); Density: 1,999.2 persons per square mile (2010); Race: 86.7% White, 8.8% Black, 0.8% Asian, 0.1% American Indian/Alaska Native, 0.0% Native Hawaiian/Other Pacific Islander, 3.6% Other, 1.2% Hispanic of any race (2010); Average household size: 2.23 (2010); Median age: 39.0 (2010); Males per 100 females: 93.6 (2010); Marriage status: 33.3% never married, 43.4% now married, 7.6% widowed, 15.7% divorced (2006-2010 5-year est.); Foreign born: 2.1% (2006-2010 5-year est.); Ancestry (includes multiple ancestries): 37.7% German, 15.0% Irish, 12.1% English, 11.7% Italian, 7.4% Polish (2006-2010 5-year est.).

Economy: Single-family building permits issued: 0 (2011); Multi-family building permits issued: 0 (2011); Employment by occupation: 6.3% management, 2.0% professional, 17.7% services, 21.0% sales, 3.7% farming, 7.3% construction, 5.0% production (2006-2010 5-year est.).
Income: Per capita income: $20,734 (2006-2010 5-year est.); Median household income: $37,037 (2006-2010 5-year est.); Average household income: $44,671 (2006-2010 5-year est.); Percent of households with income of $100,000 or more: 5.3% (2006-2010 5-year est.); Poverty rate: 16.6% (2006-2010 5-year est.).
Education: Percent of population age 25 and over with: High school diploma (including GED) or higher: 84.6% (2006-2010 5-year est.); Bachelor's degree or higher: 15.6% (2006-2010 5-year est.); Master's degree or higher: 4.4% (2006-2010 5-year est.).
Housing: Homeownership rate: 53.3% (2010); Median home value: $89,400 (2006-2010 5-year est.); Median contract rent: $482 per month (2006-2010 5-year est.); Median year structure built: 1965 (2006-2010 5-year est.).
Safety: Violent crime rate: 21.5 per 10,000 population; Property crime rate: 243.2 per 10,000 population (2011).
Transportation: Commute to work: 95.5% car, 1.7% public transportation, 1.4% walk, 1.4% work from home (2006-2010 5-year est.); Travel time to work: 27.9% less than 15 minutes, 38.4% 15 to 30 minutes, 24.8% 30 to 45 minutes, 5.1% 45 to 60 minutes, 3.7% 60 minutes or more (2006-2010 5-year est.)
Additional Information Contacts
Beaver County Chamber of Commerce . . . . (724) 775-3944
  http://www.beavercountychamber.com

Bedford County

Located in southern Pennsylvania; mountainous area, bounded on the south by Maryland, and on the east by Sideling Hill; includes the Allegheny Mountains along the northwest border, and the Wills Mountains in the southwest. Covers a land area of 1,012.296 square miles, a water area of 4.609 square miles, and is located in the Eastern Time Zone at 40.00° N. Lat., 78.49° W. Long. The county was founded in 1771. County seat is Bedford.

Weather Station: Everett   Elevation: 1,000 feet

	Jan	Feb	Mar	Apr	May	Jun	Jul	Aug	Sep	Oct	Nov	Dec
High	37	40	48	61	70	79	83	82	75	63	52	40
Low	19	21	27	36	45	54	59	58	50	38	31	23
Precip	2.1	2.2	3.1	4.0	4.1	3.7	3.4	3.3	3.6	2.9	3.1	2.6
Snow	7.7	6.6	3.8	tr	0.0	0.0	0.0	0.0	0.0	tr	0.6	4.6

High and Low temperatures in degrees Fahrenheit; Precipitation and Snow in inches

Population: 47,919 (1990); 49,984 (2000); 49,762 (2010); Race: 98.0% White, 0.5% Black, 0.2% Asian, 0.2% American Indian/Alaska Native, 0.0% Native Hawaiian/Other Pacific Islander, 1.1% Other, 0.9% Hispanic of any race (2010); Density: 49.2 persons per square mile (2010); Average household size: 2.43 (2010); Median age: 43.9 (2010); Males per 100 females: 98.6 (2010).
Religion: Six largest groups: 9.9% Methodist/Pietist, 7.2% Non-Denominational, 7.0% European Free-Church, 5.5% Presbyterian-Reformed, 5.2% Lutheran, 4.5% Pentecostal (2010)
Economy: Unemployment rate: 8.5% (August 2012); Total civilian labor force: 24,717 (August 2012); Leading industries: 16.6% retail trade; 15.8% manufacturing; 14.4% health care and social assistance (2010); Farms: 1,173 totaling 210,990 acres (2007); Companies that employ 500 or more persons: 1 (2010); Companies that employ 100 to 499 persons: 15 (2010); Companies that employ less than 100 persons: 1,078 (2010); Black-owned businesses: n/a (2007); Hispanic-owned businesses: n/a (2007); Asian-owned businesses: n/a (2007); Women-owned businesses: n/a (2007); Retail sales per capita: $14,745 (2010). Single-family building permits issued: 54 (2011); Multi-family building permits issued: 64 (2011).
Income: Per capita income: $20,545 (2006-2010 5-year est.); Median household income: $40,249 (2006-2010 5-year est.); Average household income: $49,801 (2006-2010 5-year est.); Percent of households with income of $100,000 or more: 8.8% (2006-2010 5-year est.); Poverty rate: 13.5% (2006-2010 5-year est.); Bankruptcy rate: 2.15% (2011).
Education: Percent of population age 25 and over with: High school diploma (including GED) or higher: 83.9% (2006-2010 5-year est.); Bachelor's degree or higher: 12.5% (2006-2010 5-year est.); Master's degree or higher: 3.8% (2006-2010 5-year est.).
Housing: Homeownership rate: 78.5% (2010); Median home value: $112,800 (2006-2010 5-year est.); Median contract rent: $413 per month

(2006-2010 5-year est.); Median year structure built: 1968 (2006-2010 5-year est.)
Health: Birth rate: 99.1 per 10,000 population (2011); Death rate: 101.5 per 10,000 population (2011); Age-adjusted cancer mortality rate: 144.1 deaths per 100,000 population (2009); Number of physicians: 7.4 per 10,000 population (2010); Hospital beds: 5.4 per 10,000 population (2008); Hospital admissions: 470.7 per 10,000 population (2008).
Elections: 2012 Presidential election results: 22.1% Obama, 77.0% Romney
National and State Parks: Blue Knob State Park; Buchanan State Forest; Shawnee State Park; Warriors Path State Park
Additional Information Contacts
Bedford County Government . . . . (814) 623-4807
  http://www.bedfordcountypa.org
Bedford County Chamber of Commerce . . . . (814) 623-2233
  http://www.bedfordcountychamber.com
Huntingdon County Chamber of Commerce . . . . (814) 643-1110
  http://www.huntingdonchamber.com

Bedford County Communities

ALUM BANK (unincorporated postal area)
Zip Code: 15521
  Covers a land area of 35.585 square miles and a water area of 0.004 square miles. Located at 40.20° N. Lat; 78.63° W. Long. Elevation is 1,247 feet. Population: 1,872 (2010); Density: 52.6 persons per square mile (2010); Race: 97.8% White, 0.2% Black, 0.1% Asian, 0.1% American Indian/Alaska Native, 0.0% Native Hawaiian/Other Pacific Islander, 1.8% Other, 0.2% Hispanic of any race (2010); Average household size: 2.68 (2010); Median age: 41.0 (2010); Males per 100 females: 104.4 (2010); Homeownership rate: 82.8% (2010)

ARTEMAS (unincorporated postal area)
Zip Code: 17211
  Covers a land area of 25.027 square miles and a water area of 0.017 square miles. Located at 39.75° N. Lat; 78.40° W. Long. Population: 368 (2010); Density: 14.7 persons per square mile (2010); Race: 98.4% White, 0.0% Black, 0.3% Asian, 0.8% American Indian/Alaska Native, 0.0% Native Hawaiian/Other Pacific Islander, 0.5% Other, 0.0% Hispanic of any race (2010); Average household size: 2.15 (2010); Median age: 47.8 (2010); Males per 100 females: 103.3 (2010); Homeownership rate: 80.7% (2010)

BEDFORD (borough). County seat. Covers a land area of 1.085 square miles and a water area of 0.028 square miles. Located at 40.02° N. Lat; 78.50° W. Long. Elevation is 1,119 feet.
History: Bedford was settled about 1750 and first named Raystown for a Scottish trader who had a post here. A British fort was erected on the site, first known as Fort Raystown and later renamed Fort Bedford for the Duke of Bedford. The fort was destroyed by the colonists in 1769, before the Revolution really began.
Population: 3,080 (1990); 3,141 (2000); 2,841 (2010); Density: 2,618.2 persons per square mile (2010); Race: 96.1% White, 1.2% Black, 0.5% Asian, 0.1% American Indian/Alaska Native, 0.0% Native Hawaiian/Other Pacific Islander, 2.1% Other, 2.0% Hispanic of any race (2010); Average household size: 1.90 (2010); Median age: 48.8 (2010); Males per 100 females: 85.1 (2010); Marriage status: 26.9% never married, 45.1% now married, 11.3% widowed, 16.7% divorced (2006-2010 5-year est.); Foreign born: 1.4% (2006-2010 5-year est.); Ancestry (includes multiple ancestries): 47.3% German, 13.0% American, 11.5% Irish, 8.6% English, 4.3% Italian (2006-2010 5-year est.).
Economy: Single-family building permits issued: 0 (2011); Multi-family building permits issued: 0 (2011); Employment by occupation: 5.9% management, 0.6% professional, 7.7% services, 23.0% sales, 4.7% farming, 6.7% construction, 3.4% production (2006-2010 5-year est.).
Income: Per capita income: $18,711 (2006-2010 5-year est.); Median household income: $28,988 (2006-2010 5-year est.); Average household income: $36,359 (2006-2010 5-year est.); Percent of households with income of $100,000 or more: 4.4% (2006-2010 5-year est.); Poverty rate: 19.7% (2006-2010 5-year est.).
Education: Percent of population age 25 and over with: High school diploma (including GED) or higher: 79.6% (2006-2010 5-year est.); Bachelor's degree or higher: 17.6% (2006-2010 5-year est.); Master's degree or higher: 6.5% (2006-2010 5-year est.).

School District(s)

Bedford Area SD (KG-12)

   2010-11 Enrollment: 2,240 . . . . (814) 623-4290

Housing: Homeownership rate: 50.8% (2010); Median home value: $135,800 (2006-2010 5-year est.); Median contract rent: $425 per month (2006-2010 5-year est.); Median year structure built: 1947 (2006-2010 5-year est.).

Safety: Violent crime rate: 14.0 per 10,000 population; Property crime rate: 84.2 per 10,000 population (2011).

Newspapers: Bedford Gazette (Local news; Circulation 10,500)

Transportation: Commute to work: 92.0% car, 0.0% public transportation, 5.0% walk, 3.0% work from home (2006-2010 5-year est.); Travel time to work: 62.3% less than 15 minutes, 26.0% 15 to 30 minutes, 2.3% 30 to 45 minutes, 4.2% 45 to 60 minutes, 5.1% 60 minutes or more (2006-2010 5-year est.)

Airports: Bedford County (general aviation)

Additional Information Contacts

Bedford County Chamber of Commerce . . . . (814) 623-2233

   http://www.bedfordcountychamber.com

BEDFORD (township). Covers a land area of 68.075 square miles and a water area of 0.230 square miles. Located at 40.06° N. Lat; 78.50° W. Long. Elevation is 1,119 feet.

History: Old Bedford Village period restoration, to north. Fort Bedford Park and Museum, scale model of Old Fort Bedford. Settled c.1750, laid out 1766, Incorporated 1795.

Population: 5,002 (1990); 5,417 (2000); 5,395 (2010); Density: 79.3 persons per square mile (2010); Race: 95.9% White, 1.6% Black, 0.6% Asian, 0.2% American Indian/Alaska Native, 0.0% Native Hawaiian/Other Pacific Islander, 1.7% Other, 1.5% Hispanic of any race (2010); Average household size: 2.28 (2010); Median age: 47.8 (2010); Males per 100 females: 101.4 (2010); Marriage status: 22.1% never married, 60.0% now married, 6.8% widowed, 11.1% divorced (2006-2010 5-year est.); Foreign born: 0.4% (2006-2010 5-year est.); Ancestry (includes multiple ancestries): 43.8% German, 12.6% Irish, 8.7% English, 6.7% American, 4.9% Italian (2006-2010 5-year est.).

Economy: Single-family building permits issued: 4 (2011); Multi-family building permits issued: 0 (2011); Employment by occupation: 9.8% management, 1.7% professional, 9.0% services, 15.0% sales, 3.0% farming, 6.9% construction, 8.7% production (2006-2010 5-year est.).

Income: Per capita income: $22,761 (2006-2010 5-year est.); Median household income: $40,711 (2006-2010 5-year est.); Average household income: $53,743 (2006-2010 5-year est.); Percent of households with income of $100,000 or more: 11.4% (2006-2010 5-year est.); Poverty rate: 18.3% (2006-2010 5-year est.).

Education: Percent of population age 25 and over with: High school diploma (including GED) or higher: 83.6% (2006-2010 5-year est.); Bachelor's degree or higher: 13.9% (2006-2010 5-year est.); Master's degree or higher: 3.0% (2006-2010 5-year est.).

Housing: Homeownership rate: 79.7% (2010); Median home value: $120,000 (2006-2010 5-year est.); Median contract rent: $457 per month (2006-2010 5-year est.); Median year structure built: 1971 (2006-2010 5-year est.).

Newspapers: Bedford Gazette (Local news; Circulation 10,500)

Transportation: Commute to work: 93.5% car, 0.0% public transportation, 2.6% walk, 3.9% work from home (2006-2010 5-year est.); Travel time to work: 53.5% less than 15 minutes, 22.6% 15 to 30 minutes, 10.1% 30 to 45 minutes, 4.5% 45 to 60 minutes, 9.3% 60 minutes or more (2006-2010 5-year est.)

Airports: Bedford County (general aviation)

Additional Information Contacts

Bedford County Chamber of Commerce . . . . (814) 623-2233

   http://www.bedfordcountychamber.com

Bedford Township . . . . (814) 623-4811

   http://bedfordtwppagov.com

BLOOMFIELD (township). Covers a land area of 19.392 square miles and a water area of 0.005 square miles. Located at 40.25° N. Lat; 78.42° W. Long.

Population: 766 (1990); 973 (2000); 1,016 (2010); Density: 52.4 persons per square mile (2010); Race: 98.8% White, 0.0% Black, 0.0% Asian, 0.1% American Indian/Alaska Native, 0.0% Native Hawaiian/Other Pacific Islander, 1.1% Other, 0.4% Hispanic of any race (2010); Average household size: 2.90 (2010); Median age: 40.7 (2010); Males per 100 females: 103.2 (2010); Marriage status: 23.6% never married, 65.9% now

married, 6.7% widowed, 3.8% divorced (2006-2010 5-year est.); Foreign born: 0.0% (2006-2010 5-year est.); Ancestry (includes multiple ancestries): 52.1% German, 14.5% Irish, 7.3% Dutch, 7.1% American, 5.7% English (2006-2010 5-year est.).

Economy: Single-family building permits issued: 1 (2011); Multi-family building permits issued: 0 (2011); Employment by occupation: 3.1% management, 3.7% professional, 8.9% services, 19.8% sales, 0.6% farming, 25.7% construction, 12.9% production (2006-2010 5-year est.).

Income: Per capita income: $19,325 (2006-2010 5-year est.); Median household income: $48,512 (2006-2010 5-year est.); Average household income: $55,301 (2006-2010 5-year est.); Percent of households with income of $100,000 or more: 12.0% (2006-2010 5-year est.); Poverty rate: 7.9% (2006-2010 5-year est.).

Education: Percent of population age 25 and over with: High school diploma (including GED) or higher: 88.2% (2006-2010 5-year est.); Bachelor's degree or higher: 12.4% (2006-2010 5-year est.); Master's degree or higher: 4.3% (2006-2010 5-year est.).

Housing: Homeownership rate: 90.3% (2010); Median home value: $131,300 (2006-2010 5-year est.); Median contract rent: $500 per month (2006-2010 5-year est.); Median year structure built: 1980 (2006-2010 5-year est.).

Transportation: Commute to work: 86.1% car, 0.0% public transportation, 3.2% walk, 9.0% work from home (2006-2010 5-year est.); Travel time to work: 26.7% less than 15 minutes, 42.9% 15 to 30 minutes, 14.7% 30 to 45 minutes, 4.1% 45 to 60 minutes, 11.6% 60 minutes or more (2006-2010 5-year est.)

Additional Information Contacts

Bedford County Chamber of Commerce . . . . (814) 623-2233

   http://www.bedfordcountychamber.com

BREEZEWOOD (unincorporated postal area)

Zip Code: 15533

   Covers a land area of 37.248 square miles and a water area of 0.280 square miles. Located at 39.99° N. Lat; 78.22° W. Long. Elevation is 1,286 feet. Population: 1,370 (2010); Density: 36.8 persons per square mile (2010); Race: 98.5% White, 0.7% Black, 0.0% Asian, 0.1% American Indian/Alaska Native, 0.0% Native Hawaiian/Other Pacific Islander, 0.7% Other, 0.5% Hispanic of any race (2010); Average household size: 2.34 (2010); Median age: 43.0 (2010); Males per 100 females: 95.7 (2010); Homeownership rate: 80.7% (2010)

BROAD TOP (township). Covers a land area of 48.176 square miles and a water area of 0.305 square miles. Located at 40.13° N. Lat; 78.21° W. Long.

Population: 1,918 (1990); 1,827 (2000); 1,687 (2010); Density: 35.0 persons per square mile (2010); Race: 98.6% White, 0.2% Black, 0.1% Asian, 0.1% American Indian/Alaska Native, 0.0% Native Hawaiian/Other Pacific Islander, 1.0% Other, 0.5% Hispanic of any race (2010); Average household size: 2.46 (2010); Median age: 43.6 (2010); Males per 100 females: 102.5 (2010); Marriage status: 25.4% never married, 58.6% now married, 6.0% widowed, 10.0% divorced (2006-2010 5-year est.); Foreign born: 0.0% (2006-2010 5-year est.); Ancestry (includes multiple ancestries): 30.0% German, 11.0% Irish, 10.3% English, 7.9% American, 4.5% Dutch (2006-2010 5-year est.).

Economy: Single-family building permits issued: 3 (2011); Multi-family building permits issued: 0 (2011); Employment by occupation: 5.8% management, 1.2% professional, 11.7% services, 12.9% sales, 2.7% farming, 12.0% construction, 11.9% production (2006-2010 5-year est.).

Income: Per capita income: $17,055 (2006-2010 5-year est.); Median household income: $35,363 (2006-2010 5-year est.); Average household income: $42,674 (2006-2010 5-year est.); Percent of households with income of $100,000 or more: 5.0% (2006-2010 5-year est.); Poverty rate: 18.8% (2006-2010 5-year est.).

Education: Percent of population age 25 and over with: High school diploma (including GED) or higher: 79.5% (2006-2010 5-year est.); Bachelor's degree or higher: 3.5% (2006-2010 5-year est.); Master's degree or higher: 0.7% (2006-2010 5-year est.).

Housing: Homeownership rate: 79.9% (2010); Median home value: $75,400 (2006-2010 5-year est.); Median contract rent: $365 per month (2006-2010 5-year est.); Median year structure built: 1942 (2006-2010 5-year est.).

Transportation: Commute to work: 92.0% car, 0.0% public transportation, 4.2% walk, 3.3% work from home (2006-2010 5-year est.); Travel time to work: 25.4% less than 15 minutes, 22.0% 15 to 30 minutes, 15.4% 30 to

45 minutes, 22.6% 45 to 60 minutes, 14.5% 60 minutes or more (2006-2010 5-year est.)
Additional Information Contacts
Huntingdon County Chamber of Commerce . . . . (814) 643-1110
   http://www.huntingdonchamber.com

BUFFALO MILLS (unincorporated postal area)
Zip Code: 15534
   Covers a land area of 48.515 square miles and a water area of 0.013 square miles. Located at 39.89° N. Lat; 78.69° W. Long. Population: 932 (2010); Density: 19.2 persons per square mile (2010); Race: 97.2% White, 0.4% Black, 0.0% Asian, 0.6% American Indian/Alaska Native, 0.1% Native Hawaiian/Other Pacific Islander, 1.7% Other, 0.5% Hispanic of any race (2010); Average household size: 2.60 (2010); Median age: 44.5 (2010); Males per 100 females: 100.9 (2010); Homeownership rate: 85.3% (2010)

CLEARVILLE (unincorporated postal area)
Zip Code: 15535
   Covers a land area of 157.763 square miles and a water area of 0.114 square miles. Located at 39.82° N. Lat; 78.44° W. Long. Population: 2,203 (2010); Density: 14.0 persons per square mile (2010); Race: 98.4% White, 0.3% Black, 0.0% Asian, 0.0% American Indian/Alaska Native, 0.0% Native Hawaiian/Other Pacific Islander, 1.3% Other, 1.1% Hispanic of any race (2010); Average household size: 2.46 (2010); Median age: 46.2 (2010); Males per 100 females: 105.5 (2010); Homeownership rate: 89.2% (2010)

COALDALE (borough). Aka Six Mile Run. Covers a land area of 0.034 square miles and a water area of 0 square miles. Located at 40.17° N. Lat; 78.22° W. Long. Elevation is 1,129 feet.
Population: 143 (1990); 146 (2000); 161 (2010); Density: 4,772.5 persons per square mile (2010); Race: 95.0% White, 2.5% Black, 0.0% Asian, 0.0% American Indian/Alaska Native, 0.0% Native Hawaiian/Other Pacific Islander, 2.5% Other, 0.0% Hispanic of any race (2010); Average household size: 3.04 (2010); Median age: 39.5 (2010); Males per 100 females: 89.4 (2010); Marriage status: 34.2% never married, 55.9% now married, 7.2% widowed, 2.7% divorced (2006-2010 5-year est.); Foreign born: 0.0% (2006-2010 5-year est.); Ancestry (includes multiple ancestries): 19.3% German, 14.3% Irish, 9.3% English, 6.4% Italian, 4.3% Welsh (2006-2010 5-year est.).
Economy: Single-family building permits issued: 0 (2011); Multi-family building permits issued: 0 (2011); Employment by occupation: 0.0% management, 0.0% professional, 9.5% services, 7.9% sales, 7.9% farming, 27.0% construction, 7.9% production (2006-2010 5-year est.).
Income: Per capita income: $16,973 (2006-2010 5-year est.); Median household income: $41,250 (2006-2010 5-year est.); Average household income: $44,843 (2006-2010 5-year est.); Percent of households with income of $100,000 or more: n/a (2006-2010 5-year est.); Poverty rate: 5.0% (2006-2010 5-year est.).
Education: Percent of population age 25 and over with: High school diploma (including GED) or higher: 72.6% (2006-2010 5-year est.); Bachelor's degree or higher: 0.0% (2006-2010 5-year est.); Master's degree or higher: 0.0% (2006-2010 5-year est.).
Housing: Homeownership rate: 66.1% (2010); Median home value: $47,100 (2006-2010 5-year est.); Median contract rent: $363 per month (2006-2010 5-year est.); Median year structure built: before 1940 (2006-2010 5-year est.).
Transportation: Commute to work: 96.8% car, 0.0% public transportation, 0.0% walk, 3.2% work from home (2006-2010 5-year est.); Travel time to work: 49.2% less than 15 minutes, 14.8% 15 to 30 minutes, 4.9% 30 to 45 minutes, 23.0% 45 to 60 minutes, 8.2% 60 minutes or more (2006-2010 5-year est.)

COLERAIN (township). Covers a land area of 41.927 square miles and a water area of 0.072 square miles. Located at 39.93° N. Lat; 78.51° W. Long.
Population: 1,058 (1990); 1,147 (2000); 1,195 (2010); Density: 28.5 persons per square mile (2010); Race: 99.0% White, 0.2% Black, 0.1% Asian, 0.3% American Indian/Alaska Native, 0.0% Native Hawaiian/Other Pacific Islander, 0.4% Other, 0.0% Hispanic of any race (2010); Average household size: 2.61 (2010); Median age: 45.2 (2010); Males per 100 females: 101.9 (2010); Marriage status: 20.7% never married, 62.9% now married, 6.3% widowed, 10.1% divorced (2006-2010 5-year est.); Foreign born: 0.0% (2006-2010 5-year est.); Ancestry (includes multiple

ancestries): 53.4% German, 11.8% American, 9.1% Irish, 8.1% English, 3.6% Italian (2006-2010 5-year est.).
Economy: Single-family building permits issued: 1 (2011); Multi-family building permits issued: 0 (2011); Employment by occupation: 9.4% management, 1.0% professional, 11.7% services, 20.1% sales, 4.5% farming, 16.0% construction, 10.1% production (2006-2010 5-year est.).
Income: Per capita income: $19,994 (2006-2010 5-year est.); Median household income: $41,042 (2006-2010 5-year est.); Average household income: $51,456 (2006-2010 5-year est.); Percent of households with income of $100,000 or more: 7.3% (2006-2010 5-year est.); Poverty rate: 12.4% (2006-2010 5-year est.).
Education: Percent of population age 25 and over with: High school diploma (including GED) or higher: 85.5% (2006-2010 5-year est.); Bachelor's degree or higher: 9.2% (2006-2010 5-year est.); Master's degree or higher: 1.5% (2006-2010 5-year est.).
Housing: Homeownership rate: 86.5% (2010); Median home value: $162,300 (2006-2010 5-year est.); Median contract rent: $325 per month (2006-2010 5-year est.); Median year structure built: 1973 (2006-2010 5-year est.).
Transportation: Commute to work: 84.6% car, 0.0% public transportation, 4.4% walk, 8.8% work from home (2006-2010 5-year est.); Travel time to work: 36.3% less than 15 minutes, 38.5% 15 to 30 minutes, 10.7% 30 to 45 minutes, 3.3% 45 to 60 minutes, 11.2% 60 minutes or more (2006-2010 5-year est.)
Additional Information Contacts
Bedford County Chamber of Commerce . . . . (814) 623-2233
   http://www.bedfordcountychamber.com

CUMBERLAND VALLEY (township). Covers a land area of 59.658 square miles and a water area of 0.588 square miles. Located at 39.81° N. Lat; 78.64° W. Long.
Population: 1,473 (1990); 1,494 (2000); 1,597 (2010); Density: 26.8 persons per square mile (2010); Race: 98.6% White, 0.1% Black, 0.2% Asian, 0.1% American Indian/Alaska Native, 0.0% Native Hawaiian/Other Pacific Islander, 1.0% Other, 0.9% Hispanic of any race (2010); Average household size: 2.59 (2010); Median age: 44.3 (2010); Males per 100 females: 104.5 (2010); Marriage status: 17.9% never married, 61.9% now married, 5.0% widowed, 15.2% divorced (2006-2010 5-year est.); Foreign born: 0.2% (2006-2010 5-year est.); Ancestry (includes multiple ancestries): 39.7% German, 17.7% Irish, 11.8% American, 10.7% English, 4.2% Dutch (2006-2010 5-year est.).
Economy: Single-family building permits issued: 3 (2011); Multi-family building permits issued: 0 (2011); Employment by occupation: 9.9% management, 5.1% professional, 14.5% services, 11.0% sales, 0.5% farming, 16.6% construction, 8.3% production (2006-2010 5-year est.).
Income: Per capita income: $21,798 (2006-2010 5-year est.); Median household income: $43,056 (2006-2010 5-year est.); Average household income: $52,770 (2006-2010 5-year est.); Percent of households with income of $100,000 or more: 10.8% (2006-2010 5-year est.); Poverty rate: 9.7% (2006-2010 5-year est.).
Taxes: Total city taxes per capita: $89 (2009); City property taxes per capita: $9 (2009).
Education: Percent of population age 25 and over with: High school diploma (including GED) or higher: 87.9% (2006-2010 5-year est.); Bachelor's degree or higher: 13.2% (2006-2010 5-year est.); Master's degree or higher: 3.8% (2006-2010 5-year est.).
Housing: Homeownership rate: 86.2% (2010); Median home value: $132,200 (2006-2010 5-year est.); Median contract rent: $440 per month (2006-2010 5-year est.); Median year structure built: 1965 (2006-2010 5-year est.).
Transportation: Commute to work: 94.1% car, 0.0% public transportation, 1.3% walk, 3.3% work from home (2006-2010 5-year est.); Travel time to work: 13.0% less than 15 minutes, 48.7% 15 to 30 minutes, 19.1% 30 to 45 minutes, 7.3% 45 to 60 minutes, 12.0% 60 minutes or more (2006-2010 5-year est.)
Additional Information Contacts
Greater Carlisle Area Chamber of Commerce . . . . (717) 243-4515
   http://carlislechamber.org

DEFIANCE (CDP). Covers a land area of 0.169 square miles and a water area of 0 square miles. Located at 40.16° N. Lat; 78.23° W. Long. Elevation is 1,024 feet.
Population: n/a (1990); n/a (2000); 239 (2010); Density: 1,414.2 persons per square mile (2010); Race: 98.7% White, 0.4% Black, 0.0% Asian, 0.0% American Indian/Alaska Native, 0.0% Native Hawaiian/Other Pacific

Islander, 0.9% Other, 0.4% Hispanic of any race (2010); Average household size: 2.63 (2010); Median age: 31.5 (2010); Males per 100 females: 94.3 (2010); Marriage status: 27.6% never married, 52.4% now married, 8.1% widowed, 11.9% divorced (2006-2010 5-year est.); Foreign born: 0.0% (2006-2010 5-year est.); Ancestry (includes multiple ancestries): 29.5% German, 11.8% Irish, 10.5% English, 6.6% Russian, 6.6% Lithuanian (2006-2010 5-year est.).
Economy: Employment by occupation: 0.0% management, 0.0% professional, 15.5% services, 9.1% sales, 7.3% farming, 14.5% construction, 17.3% production (2006-2010 5-year est.).
Income: Per capita income: $11,660 (2006-2010 5-year est.); Median household income: $26,625 (2006-2010 5-year est.); Average household income: $36,018 (2006-2010 5-year est.); Percent of households with income of $100,000 or more: 4.3% (2006-2010 5-year est.); Poverty rate: 32.3% (2006-2010 5-year est.).
Education: Percent of population age 25 and over with: High school diploma (including GED) or higher: 95.7% (2006-2010 5-year est.); Bachelor's degree or higher: 2.2% (2006-2010 5-year est.); Master's degree or higher: 0.0% (2006-2010 5-year est.).

School District(s)

Tussey Mountain SD (PK-12)
    2010-11 Enrollment: 1,110 . . . . (814) 635-3670
Housing: Homeownership rate: 74.8% (2010); Median home value: $84,400 (2006-2010 5-year est.); Median contract rent: $355 per month (2006-2010 5-year est.); Median year structure built: 1945 (2006-2010 5-year est.).
Transportation: Commute to work: 95.5% car, 0.0% public transportation, 4.5% walk, 0.0% work from home (2006-2010 5-year est.); Travel time to work: 24.5% less than 15 minutes, 30.0% 15 to 30 minutes, 21.8% 30 to 45 minutes, 15.5% 45 to 60 minutes, 8.2% 60 minutes or more (2006-2010 5-year est.)

EARLSTON (CDP). Covers a land area of 1.080 square miles and a water area of 0.001 square miles. Located at 40.00° N. Lat; 78.37° W. Long. Elevation is 1,086 feet.
Population: n/a (1990); n/a (2000); 1,122 (2010); Density: 1,039.2 persons per square mile (2010); Race: 99.3% White, 0.4% Black, 0.1% Asian, 0.0% American Indian/Alaska Native, 0.0% Native Hawaiian/Other Pacific Islander, 0.2% Other, 0.3% Hispanic of any race (2010); Average household size: 2.31 (2010); Median age: 44.1 (2010); Males per 100 females: 94.1 (2010); Marriage status: 6.3% never married, 77.5% now married, 13.0% widowed, 3.2% divorced (2006-2010 5-year est.); Foreign born: 0.0% (2006-2010 5-year est.); Ancestry (includes multiple ancestries): 54.6% German, 7.2% Irish, 5.4% English, 3.7% American, 2.2% Lithuanian (2006-2010 5-year est.).
Economy: Employment by occupation: 6.7% management, 0.0% professional, 7.2% services, 34.6% sales, 2.1% farming, 9.4% construction, 0.0% production (2006-2010 5-year est.).
Income: Per capita income: $19,324 (2006-2010 5-year est.); Median household income: $35,625 (2006-2010 5-year est.); Average household income: $41,825 (2006-2010 5-year est.); Percent of households with income of $100,000 or more: 4.7% (2006-2010 5-year est.); Poverty rate: 13.1% (2006-2010 5-year est.).
Education: Percent of population age 25 and over with: High school diploma (including GED) or higher: 81.3% (2006-2010 5-year est.); Bachelor's degree or higher: 9.1% (2006-2010 5-year est.); Master's degree or higher: 3.0% (2006-2010 5-year est.).
Housing: Homeownership rate: 75.9% (2010); Median home value: $98,200 (2006-2010 5-year est.); Median contract rent: $452 per month (2006-2010 5-year est.); Median year structure built: 1970 (2006-2010 5-year est.).
Transportation: Commute to work: 90.6% car, 0.0% public transportation, 7.2% walk, 2.2% work from home (2006-2010 5-year est.); Travel time to work: 52.8% less than 15 minutes, 26.4% 15 to 30 minutes, 13.0% 30 to 45 minutes, 2.1% 45 to 60 minutes, 5.7% 60 minutes or more (2006-2010 5-year est.)

EAST PROVIDENCE (township). Covers a land area of 50.373 square miles and a water area of 0.384 square miles. Located at 40.00° N. Lat; 78.26° W. Long.
Population: 1,785 (1990); 1,858 (2000); 1,854 (2010); Density: 36.8 persons per square mile (2010); Race: 98.6% White, 0.7% Black, 0.0% Asian, 0.1% American Indian/Alaska Native, 0.0% Native Hawaiian/Other Pacific Islander, 0.6% Other, 0.5% Hispanic of any race (2010); Average household size: 2.38 (2010); Median age: 43.3 (2010); Males per 100

females: 95.8 (2010); Marriage status: 19.6% never married, 60.4% now married, 6.7% widowed, 13.4% divorced (2006-2010 5-year est.); Foreign born: 0.4% (2006-2010 5-year est.); Ancestry (includes multiple ancestries): 36.0% German, 12.8% Irish, 11.0% American, 5.3% English, 4.9% Dutch (2006-2010 5-year est.).
Economy: Single-family building permits issued: 8 (2011); Multi-family building permits issued: 0 (2011); Employment by occupation: 6.9% management, 0.9% professional, 13.3% services, 20.2% sales, 1.7% farming, 12.3% construction, 4.8% production (2006-2010 5-year est.).
Income: Per capita income: $17,652 (2006-2010 5-year est.); Median household income: $39,750 (2006-2010 5-year est.); Average household income: $44,440 (2006-2010 5-year est.); Percent of households with income of $100,000 or more: 3.9% (2006-2010 5-year est.); Poverty rate: 16.8% (2006-2010 5-year est.).
Education: Percent of population age 25 and over with: High school diploma (including GED) or higher: 75.2% (2006-2010 5-year est.); Bachelor's degree or higher: 7.3% (2006-2010 5-year est.); Master's degree or higher: 3.0% (2006-2010 5-year est.).
Housing: Homeownership rate: 80.9% (2010); Median home value: $98,400 (2006-2010 5-year est.); Median contract rent: $436 per month (2006-2010 5-year est.); Median year structure built: 1976 (2006-2010 5-year est.).
Transportation: Commute to work: 93.2% car, 0.0% public transportation, 3.1% walk, 2.3% work from home (2006-2010 5-year est.); Travel time to work: 24.0% less than 15 minutes, 33.3% 15 to 30 minutes, 22.8% 30 to 45 minutes, 8.0% 45 to 60 minutes, 11.9% 60 minutes or more (2006-2010 5-year est.)
Additional Information Contacts
Bedford County Chamber of Commerce . . . . (814) 623-2233
  http://www.bedfordcountychamber.com

EAST SAINT CLAIR (township). Covers a land area of 33.892 square miles and a water area of 0.154 square miles. Located at 40.13° N. Lat; 78.56° W. Long.
Population: 2,765 (1990); 3,123 (2000); 3,048 (2010); Density: 89.9 persons per square mile (2010); Race: 98.0% White, 0.3% Black, 0.2% Asian, 0.3% American Indian/Alaska Native, 0.0% Native Hawaiian/Other Pacific Islander, 1.2% Other, 0.8% Hispanic of any race (2010); Average household size: 2.52 (2010); Median age: 42.5 (2010); Males per 100 females: 99.9 (2010); Marriage status: 24.3% never married, 60.0% now married, 7.7% widowed, 8.1% divorced (2006-2010 5-year est.); Foreign born: 0.0% (2006-2010 5-year est.); Ancestry (includes multiple ancestries): 42.7% German, 16.2% American, 13.5% Irish, 8.7% English, 6.0% Dutch (2006-2010 5-year est.).
Economy: Single-family building permits issued: 2 (2011); Multi-family building permits issued: 0 (2011); Employment by occupation: 7.8% management, 4.2% professional, 10.9% services, 18.6% sales, 4.0% farming, 6.6% construction, 7.5% production (2006-2010 5-year est.).
Income: Per capita income: $21,316 (2006-2010 5-year est.); Median household income: $45,000 (2006-2010 5-year est.); Average household income: $53,023 (2006-2010 5-year est.); Percent of households with income of $100,000 or more: 11.4% (2006-2010 5-year est.); Poverty rate: 6.8% (2006-2010 5-year est.).
Education: Percent of population age 25 and over with: High school diploma (including GED) or higher: 91.2% (2006-2010 5-year est.); Bachelor's degree or higher: 12.0% (2006-2010 5-year est.); Master's degree or higher: 4.6% (2006-2010 5-year est.).
Housing: Homeownership rate: 84.8% (2010); Median home value: $116,500 (2006-2010 5-year est.); Median contract rent: $450 per month (2006-2010 5-year est.); Median year structure built: 1976 (2006-2010 5-year est.).
Transportation: Commute to work: 96.9% car, 1.1% public transportation, 0.0% walk, 1.1% work from home (2006-2010 5-year est.); Travel time to work: 37.0% less than 15 minutes, 42.8% 15 to 30 minutes, 17.7% 30 to 45 minutes, 1.9% 45 to 60 minutes, 0.7% 60 minutes or more (2006-2010 5-year est.)

EVERETT (borough). Covers a land area of 0.980 square miles and a water area of 0.079 square miles. Located at 40.01° N. Lat; 78.35° W. Long. Elevation is 1,010 feet.
History: Laid out 1795, incorporated 1873.
Population: 1,777 (1990); 1,905 (2000); 1,834 (2010); Density: 1,871.1 persons per square mile (2010); Race: 96.9% White, 1.3% Black, 0.1% Asian, 0.1% American Indian/Alaska Native, 0.0% Native Hawaiian/Other Pacific Islander, 1.6% Other, 1.4% Hispanic of any race (2010); Average

household size: 2.16 (2010); Median age: 39.9 (2010); Males per 100 females: 84.5 (2010); Marriage status: 23.5% never married, 52.8% now married, 7.0% widowed, 16.7% divorced (2006-2010 5-year est.); Foreign born: 1.7% (2006-2010 5-year est.); Ancestry (includes multiple ancestries): 35.2% German, 16.0% Irish, 11.7% Dutch, 11.3% American, 10.2% French (2006-2010 5-year est.).

Economy: Single-family building permits issued: 0 (2011); Multi-family building permits issued: 0 (2011); Employment by occupation: 7.0% management, 3.5% professional, 19.0% services, 12.2% sales, 5.0% farming, 5.9% construction, 6.1% production (2006-2010 5-year est.).

Income: Per capita income: $19,673 (2006-2010 5-year est.); Median household income: $35,216 (2006-2010 5-year est.); Average household income: $44,186 (2006-2010 5-year est.); Percent of households with income of $100,000 or more: 5.7% (2006-2010 5-year est.); Poverty rate: 25.0% (2006-2010 5-year est.).

Education: Percent of population age 25 and over with: High school diploma (including GED) or higher: 88.2% (2006-2010 5-year est.); Bachelor's degree or higher: 13.2% (2006-2010 5-year est.); Master's degree or higher: 5.7% (2006-2010 5-year est.).

School District(s)

Bedford County Technical Center (09-12)
    2010-11 Enrollment: n/a . . . . (814) 623-2760
Everett Area SD (KG-12)
    2010-11 Enrollment: 1,422 . . . . (814) 652-9114

Housing: Homeownership rate: 48.4% (2010); Median home value: $83,000 (2006-2010 5-year est.); Median contract rent: $396 per month (2006-2010 5-year est.); Median year structure built: 1944 (2006-2010 5-year est.).

Hospitals: UPMC Bedford Memorial (49 beds)

Safety: Violent crime rate: 10.9 per 10,000 population; Property crime rate: 195.7 per 10,000 population (2011).

Newspapers: The Shopper's Guide (Local news; Circulation 29,153)

Transportation: Commute to work: 91.5% car, 0.0% public transportation, 6.2% walk, 2.3% work from home (2006-2010 5-year est.); Travel time to work: 43.6% less than 15 minutes, 22.6% 15 to 30 minutes, 11.2% 30 to 45 minutes, 10.7% 45 to 60 minutes, 12.0% 60 minutes or more (2006-2010 5-year est.)

Additional Information Contacts
Bedford County Chamber of Commerce . . . . (814) 623-2233
    http://www.bedfordcountychamber.com

FISHERTOWN (unincorporated postal area)

Zip Code: 15539
    Covers a land area of 1.377 square miles and a water area of 0 square miles. Located at 40.12° N. Lat; 78.59° W. Long. Elevation is 1,175 feet.
    Population: 498 (2010); Density: 361.5 persons per square mile (2010); Race: 97.8% White, 0.4% Black, 0.0% Asian, 0.2% American Indian/Alaska Native, 0.0% Native Hawaiian/Other Pacific Islander, 1.6% Other, 0.6% Hispanic of any race (2010); Average household size: 2.59 (2010); Median age: 38.8 (2010); Males per 100 females: 104.9 (2010); Homeownership rate: 84.9% (2010)

HARRISON (township).

Covers a land area of 37.057 square miles and a water area of 0.034 square miles. Located at 39.96° N. Lat; 78.63° W. Long.

Population: 968 (1990); 1,007 (2000); 972 (2010); Density: 26.2 persons per square mile (2010); Race: 97.1% White, 0.2% Black, 0.1% Asian, 0.4% American Indian/Alaska Native, 0.8% Native Hawaiian/Other Pacific Islander, 1.4% Other, 1.4% Hispanic of any race (2010); Average household size: 2.51 (2010); Median age: 44.7 (2010); Males per 100 females: 103.3 (2010); Marriage status: 12.9% never married, 75.3% now married, 6.8% widowed, 5.0% divorced (2006-2010 5-year est.); Foreign born: 0.2% (2006-2010 5-year est.); Ancestry (includes multiple ancestries): 51.1% German, 10.3% Irish, 9.7% English, 7.6% American, 2.8% Polish (2006-2010 5-year est.).

Economy: Single-family building permits issued: 0 (2011); Multi-family building permits issued: 0 (2011); Employment by occupation: 9.9% management, 0.0% professional, 12.9% services, 9.1% sales, 1.3% farming, 11.6% construction, 9.4% production (2006-2010 5-year est.).

Income: Per capita income: $19,066 (2006-2010 5-year est.); Median household income: $45,500 (2006-2010 5-year est.); Average household income: $48,048 (2006-2010 5-year est.); Percent of households with income of $100,000 or more: 7.6% (2006-2010 5-year est.); Poverty rate: 4.5% (2006-2010 5-year est.).

Education: Percent of population age 25 and over with: High school diploma (including GED) or higher: 88.9% (2006-2010 5-year est.); Bachelor's degree or higher: 10.3% (2006-2010 5-year est.); Master's degree or higher: 3.2% (2006-2010 5-year est.).

Housing: Homeownership rate: 83.2% (2010); Median home value: $122,900 (2006-2010 5-year est.); Median contract rent: $291 per month (2006-2010 5-year est.); Median year structure built: 1966 (2006-2010 5-year est.).

Transportation: Commute to work: 88.2% car, 0.0% public transportation, 2.2% walk, 8.8% work from home (2006-2010 5-year est.); Travel time to work: 17.5% less than 15 minutes, 49.5% 15 to 30 minutes, 18.1% 30 to 45 minutes, 2.7% 45 to 60 minutes, 12.1% 60 minutes or more (2006-2010 5-year est.)

HOPEWELL (borough).

Covers a land area of 0.114 square miles and a water area of 0.002 square miles. Located at 40.13° N. Lat; 78.27° W. Long. Elevation is 896 feet.

Population: 194 (1990); 222 (2000); 230 (2010); Density: 2,023.7 persons per square mile (2010); Race: 97.8% White, 0.4% Black, 0.0% Asian, 0.4% American Indian/Alaska Native, 0.0% Native Hawaiian/Other Pacific Islander, 1.4% Other, 3.0% Hispanic of any race (2010); Average household size: 2.50 (2010); Median age: 37.6 (2010); Males per 100 females: 84.0 (2010); Marriage status: 15.9% never married, 62.5% now married, 9.1% widowed, 12.5% divorced (2006-2010 5-year est.); Foreign born: 0.0% (2006-2010 5-year est.); Ancestry (includes multiple ancestries): 46.1% German, 23.0% English, 8.7% Irish, 7.0% Dutch, 6.5% American (2006-2010 5-year est.).

Economy: Single-family building permits issued: 1 (2011); Multi-family building permits issued: 0 (2011); Employment by occupation: 6.3% management, 8.9% professional, 11.4% services, 10.1% sales, 3.8% farming, 13.9% construction, 10.1% production (2006-2010 5-year est.).

Income: Per capita income: $15,156 (2006-2010 5-year est.); Median household income: $37,679 (2006-2010 5-year est.); Average household income: $37,340 (2006-2010 5-year est.); Percent of households with income of $100,000 or more: n/a (2006-2010 5-year est.); Poverty rate: 16.1% (2006-2010 5-year est.).

Education: Percent of population age 25 and over with: High school diploma (including GED) or higher: 80.5% (2006-2010 5-year est.); Bachelor's degree or higher: 10.7% (2006-2010 5-year est.); Master's degree or higher: 1.3% (2006-2010 5-year est.).

Housing: Homeownership rate: 69.6% (2010); Median home value: $77,100 (2006-2010 5-year est.); Median contract rent: $133 per month (2006-2010 5-year est.); Median year structure built: before 1940 (2006-2010 5-year est.).

Transportation: Commute to work: 93.7% car, 0.0% public transportation, 0.0% walk, 6.3% work from home (2006-2010 5-year est.); Travel time to work: 16.2% less than 15 minutes, 10.8% 15 to 30 minutes, 29.7% 30 to 45 minutes, 24.3% 45 to 60 minutes, 18.9% 60 minutes or more (2006-2010 5-year est.)

HOPEWELL (township).

Covers a land area of 34.202 square miles and a water area of 0.267 square miles. Located at 40.13° N. Lat; 78.33° W. Long. Elevation is 896 feet.

Population: 1,928 (1990); 1,894 (2000); 2,010 (2010); Density: 58.8 persons per square mile (2010); Race: 98.4% White, 0.0% Black, 0.1% Asian, 0.1% American Indian/Alaska Native, 0.0% Native Hawaiian/Other Pacific Islander, 1.4% Other, 0.3% Hispanic of any race (2010); Average household size: 2.58 (2010); Median age: 42.1 (2010); Males per 100 females: 99.2 (2010); Marriage status: 23.1% never married, 62.9% now married, 6.1% widowed, 7.9% divorced (2006-2010 5-year est.); Foreign born: 0.0% (2006-2010 5-year est.); Ancestry (includes multiple ancestries): 44.1% German, 12.9% Irish, 10.6% American, 6.4% English, 5.8% Dutch (2006-2010 5-year est.).

Economy: Single-family building permits issued: 5 (2011); Multi-family building permits issued: 0 (2011); Employment by occupation: 5.9% management, 1.5% professional, 10.9% services, 14.3% sales, 2.9% farming, 20.9% construction, 6.4% production (2006-2010 5-year est.).

Income: Per capita income: $19,418 (2006-2010 5-year est.); Median household income: $41,761 (2006-2010 5-year est.); Average household income: $47,938 (2006-2010 5-year est.); Percent of households with income of $100,000 or more: 6.2% (2006-2010 5-year est.); Poverty rate: 13.7% (2006-2010 5-year est.).

Education: Percent of population age 25 and over with: High school diploma (including GED) or higher: 84.6% (2006-2010 5-year est.);

Bachelor's degree or higher: 12.9% (2006-2010 5-year est.); Master's degree or higher: 4.7% (2006-2010 5-year est.).

Housing: Homeownership rate: 83.6% (2010); Median home value: $108,600 (2006-2010 5-year est.); Median contract rent: $414 per month (2006-2010 5-year est.); Median year structure built: 1975 (2006-2010 5-year est.).

Transportation: Commute to work: 91.1% car, 1.5% public transportation, 1.9% walk, 4.3% work from home (2006-2010 5-year est.); Travel time to work: 18.3% less than 15 minutes, 41.5% 15 to 30 minutes, 20.0% 30 to 45 minutes, 7.3% 45 to 60 minutes, 13.0% 60 minutes or more (2006-2010 5-year est.)

Additional Information Contacts
Bedford County Chamber of Commerce . . . . (814) 623-2233
    http://www.bedfordcountychamber.com

HYNDMAN (borough). Covers a land area of 0.512 square miles and a water area of 0.016 square miles. Located at 39.82° N. Lat; 78.72° W. Long. Elevation is 938 feet.

History: Severely damaged by fire, 1949. Laid out 1840, incorporated 1877.

Population: 1,066 (1990); 1,005 (2000); 910 (2010); Density: 1,779.0 persons per square mile (2010); Race: 98.6% White, 0.3% Black, 0.0% Asian, 0.4% American Indian/Alaska Native, 0.0% Native Hawaiian/Other Pacific Islander, 0.7% Other, 0.8% Hispanic of any race (2010); Average household size: 2.37 (2010); Median age: 42.5 (2010); Males per 100 females: 93.6 (2010); Marriage status: 19.3% never married, 56.4% now married, 10.5% widowed, 13.9% divorced (2006-2010 5-year est.); Foreign born: 0.2% (2006-2010 5-year est.); Ancestry (includes multiple ancestries): 54.2% German, 22.1% Irish, 10.2% English, 4.1% Dutch, 3.5% American (2006-2010 5-year est.).

Economy: Single-family building permits issued: 1 (2011); Multi-family building permits issued: 0 (2011); Employment by occupation: 3.4% management, 2.8% professional, 16.3% services, 14.0% sales, 0.8% farming, 12.9% construction, 11.5% production (2006-2010 5-year est.).

Income: Per capita income: $18,099 (2006-2010 5-year est.); Median household income: $36,250 (2006-2010 5-year est.); Average household income: $40,235 (2006-2010 5-year est.); Percent of households with income of $100,000 or more: 5.4% (2006-2010 5-year est.); Poverty rate: 20.0% (2006-2010 5-year est.).

Education: Percent of population age 25 and over with: High school diploma (including GED) or higher: 80.6% (2006-2010 5-year est.); Bachelor's degree or higher: 11.6% (2006-2010 5-year est.); Master's degree or higher: 1.9% (2006-2010 5-year est.).

School District(s)
Bedford Area SD (KG-12)
    2010-11 Enrollment: 2,240 . . . . (814) 623-4290

Housing: Homeownership rate: 72.4% (2010); Median home value: $78,200 (2006-2010 5-year est.); Median contract rent: $321 per month (2006-2010 5-year est.); Median year structure built: before 1940 (2006-2010 5-year est.).

Transportation: Commute to work: 93.6% car, 0.0% public transportation, 3.5% walk, 2.9% work from home (2006-2010 5-year est.); Travel time to work: 18.8% less than 15 minutes, 20.6% 15 to 30 minutes, 36.4% 30 to 45 minutes, 10.4% 45 to 60 minutes, 13.7% 60 minutes or more (2006-2010 5-year est.)

IMLER (unincorporated postal area)
Zip Code: 16655
    Covers a land area of 34.903 square miles and a water area of 0.027 square miles. Located at 40.22° N. Lat; 78.50° W. Long. Elevation is 1,184 feet. Population: 1,601 (2010); Density: 45.9 persons per square mile (2010); Race: 98.9% White, 0.1% Black, 0.1% Asian, 0.0% American Indian/Alaska Native, 0.0% Native Hawaiian/Other Pacific Islander, 0.9% Other, 0.2% Hispanic of any race (2010); Average household size: 2.54 (2010); Median age: 40.9 (2010); Males per 100 females: 97.7 (2010); Homeownership rate: 83.8% (2010)

JUNIATA (township). Covers a land area of 47.427 square miles and a water area of 0.083 square miles. Located at 39.99° N. Lat; 78.72° W. Long.

Population: 865 (1990); 1,016 (2000); 954 (2010); Density: 20.1 persons per square mile (2010); Race: 98.7% White, 0.1% Black, 0.1% Asian, 0.1% American Indian/Alaska Native, 0.0% Native Hawaiian/Other Pacific Islander, 1.0% Other, 1.0% Hispanic of any race (2010); Average household size: 2.38 (2010); Median age: 46.8 (2010); Males per 100

females: 95.1 (2010); Marriage status: 18.9% never married, 53.0% now married, 11.3% widowed, 16.8% divorced (2006-2010 5-year est.); Foreign born: 0.0% (2006-2010 5-year est.); Ancestry (includes multiple ancestries): 42.4% German, 14.2% American, 11.6% Irish, 7.4% English, 4.8% Dutch (2006-2010 5-year est.).

Economy: Single-family building permits issued: 1 (2011); Multi-family building permits issued: 0 (2011); Employment by occupation: 5.8% management, 4.4% professional, 11.9% services, 15.1% sales, 1.5% farming, 18.0% construction, 8.3% production (2006-2010 5-year est.).

Income: Per capita income: $19,948 (2006-2010 5-year est.); Median household income: $36,591 (2006-2010 5-year est.); Average household income: $43,322 (2006-2010 5-year est.); Percent of households with income of $100,000 or more: 5.4% (2006-2010 5-year est.); Poverty rate: 19.1% (2006-2010 5-year est.).

Education: Percent of population age 25 and over with: High school diploma (including GED) or higher: 85.3% (2006-2010 5-year est.); Bachelor's degree or higher: 12.8% (2006-2010 5-year est.); Master's degree or higher: 4.1% (2006-2010 5-year est.).

Housing: Homeownership rate: 85.5% (2010); Median home value: $129,900 (2006-2010 5-year est.); Median contract rent: $338 per month (2006-2010 5-year est.); Median year structure built: 1970 (2006-2010 5-year est.).

Transportation: Commute to work: 90.0% car, 0.0% public transportation, 0.5% walk, 6.0% work from home (2006-2010 5-year est.); Travel time to work: 7.2% less than 15 minutes, 38.0% 15 to 30 minutes, 26.6% 30 to 45 minutes, 13.8% 45 to 60 minutes, 14.4% 60 minutes or more (2006-2010 5-year est.)

Additional Information Contacts
Bedford County Chamber of Commerce . . . . (814) 623-2233
    http://www.bedfordcountychamber.com

KIMMEL (township). Covers a land area of 20.177 square miles and a water area of 0.009 square miles. Located at 40.24° N. Lat; 78.51° W. Long.

Population: 1,605 (1990); 1,609 (2000); 1,616 (2010); Density: 80.1 persons per square mile (2010); Race: 98.5% White, 0.3% Black, 0.2% Asian, 0.0% American Indian/Alaska Native, 0.0% Native Hawaiian/Other Pacific Islander, 1.0% Other, 0.1% Hispanic of any race (2010); Average household size: 2.49 (2010); Median age: 42.4 (2010); Males per 100 females: 98.8 (2010); Marriage status: 19.4% never married, 65.8% now married, 6.9% widowed, 7.9% divorced (2006-2010 5-year est.); Foreign born: 0.2% (2006-2010 5-year est.); Ancestry (includes multiple ancestries): 41.5% German, 14.3% American, 12.3% Irish, 5.1% English, 2.1% Pennsylvania German (2006-2010 5-year est.).

Economy: Single-family building permits issued: 1 (2011); Multi-family building permits issued: 0 (2011); Employment by occupation: 5.0% management, 2.4% professional, 13.3% services, 23.1% sales, 3.0% farming, 16.0% construction, 7.6% production (2006-2010 5-year est.).

Income: Per capita income: $20,206 (2006-2010 5-year est.); Median household income: $40,774 (2006-2010 5-year est.); Average household income: $48,787 (2006-2010 5-year est.); Percent of households with income of $100,000 or more: 6.1% (2006-2010 5-year est.); Poverty rate: 10.3% (2006-2010 5-year est.).

Education: Percent of population age 25 and over with: High school diploma (including GED) or higher: 81.6% (2006-2010 5-year est.); Bachelor's degree or higher: 8.3% (2006-2010 5-year est.); Master's degree or higher: 1.6% (2006-2010 5-year est.).

Housing: Homeownership rate: 83.5% (2010); Median home value: $100,400 (2006-2010 5-year est.); Median contract rent: $367 per month (2006-2010 5-year est.); Median year structure built: 1969 (2006-2010 5-year est.).

Transportation: Commute to work: 97.2% car, 0.0% public transportation, 0.6% walk, 1.0% work from home (2006-2010 5-year est.); Travel time to work: 28.4% less than 15 minutes, 33.1% 15 to 30 minutes, 26.2% 30 to 45 minutes, 2.8% 45 to 60 minutes, 9.6% 60 minutes or more (2006-2010 5-year est.)

Additional Information Contacts
Blair County Chamber of Commerce . . . . (814) 943-8151
    http://www.blairchamber.com

KING (township). Covers a land area of 15.696 square miles and a water area of 0.035 square miles. Located at 40.20° N. Lat; 78.51° W. Long. Elevation is 1,335 feet.

Population: 1,226 (1990); 1,264 (2000); 1,238 (2010); Density: 78.9 persons per square mile (2010); Race: 99.4% White, 0.2% Black, 0.1%

Asian, 0.0% American Indian/Alaska Native, 0.0% Native Hawaiian/Other Pacific Islander, 0.3% Other, 0.3% Hispanic of any race (2010); Average household size: 2.52 (2010); Median age: 41.0 (2010); Males per 100 females: 98.4 (2010); Marriage status: 23.3% never married, 63.5% now married, 6.1% widowed, 7.2% divorced (2006-2010 5-year est.); Foreign born: 0.8% (2006-2010 5-year est.); Ancestry (includes multiple ancestries): 47.9% German, 9.8% Irish, 7.3% American, 6.0% English, 5.3% Italian (2006-2010 5-year est.).

Economy: Single-family building permits issued: 1 (2011); Multi-family building permits issued: 0 (2011); Employment by occupation: 7.5% management, 2.0% professional, 11.2% services, 8.3% sales, 2.9% farming, 14.9% construction, 10.9% production (2006-2010 5-year est.).

Income: Per capita income: $20,048 (2006-2010 5-year est.); Median household income: $41,169 (2006-2010 5-year est.); Average household income: $50,990 (2006-2010 5-year est.); Percent of households with income of $100,000 or more: 8.4% (2006-2010 5-year est.); Poverty rate: 11.8% (2006-2010 5-year est.).

Education: Percent of population age 25 and over with: High school diploma (including GED) or higher: 88.0% (2006-2010 5-year est.); Bachelor's degree or higher: 12.1% (2006-2010 5-year est.); Master's degree or higher: 3.5% (2006-2010 5-year est.).

Housing: Homeownership rate: 81.2% (2010); Median home value: $101,000 (2006-2010 5-year est.); Median contract rent: $365 per month (2006-2010 5-year est.); Median year structure built: 1973 (2006-2010 5-year est.).

Transportation: Commute to work: 93.4% car, 0.6% public transportation, 4.1% walk, 0.8% work from home (2006-2010 5-year est.); Travel time to work: 22.3% less than 15 minutes, 41.0% 15 to 30 minutes, 22.6% 30 to 45 minutes, 6.1% 45 to 60 minutes, 8.0% 60 minutes or more (2006-2010 5-year est.).

Additional Information Contacts
Greater Philadelphia Chamber of Commerce . . . . (215) 545-1234
   http://www.greaterphilachamber.com/about

LIBERTY (township). Covers a land area of 26.187 square miles and a water area of 0.348 square miles. Located at 40.21° N. Lat; 78.28° W. Long.

Population: 1,492 (1990); 1,477 (2000); 1,368 (2010); Density: 52.2 persons per square mile (2010); Race: 98.9% White, 0.0% Black, 0.1% Asian, 0.1% American Indian/Alaska Native, 0.0% Native Hawaiian/Other Pacific Islander, 0.9% Other, 1.2% Hispanic of any race (2010); Average household size: 2.39 (2010); Median age: 44.8 (2010); Males per 100 females: 97.7 (2010); Marriage status: 20.0% never married, 61.3% now married, 10.9% widowed, 7.9% divorced (2006-2010 5-year est.); Foreign born: 0.6% (2006-2010 5-year est.); Ancestry (includes multiple ancestries): 36.5% German, 15.1% Irish, 10.4% English, 9.0% American, 4.0% Polish (2006-2010 5-year est.).

Economy: Single-family building permits issued: 0 (2011); Multi-family building permits issued: 0 (2011); Employment by occupation: 10.4% management, 1.0% professional, 10.6% services, 11.9% sales, 0.5% farming, 13.7% construction, 14.0% production (2006-2010 5-year est.).

Income: Per capita income: $22,166 (2006-2010 5-year est.); Median household income: $38,882 (2006-2010 5-year est.); Average household income: $51,490 (2006-2010 5-year est.); Percent of households with income of $100,000 or more: 12.6% (2006-2010 5-year est.); Poverty rate: 17.5% (2006-2010 5-year est.).

Education: Percent of population age 25 and over with: High school diploma (including GED) or higher: 83.7% (2006-2010 5-year est.); Bachelor's degree or higher: 15.3% (2006-2010 5-year est.); Master's degree or higher: 3.5% (2006-2010 5-year est.).

Housing: Homeownership rate: 83.2% (2010); Median home value: $92,800 (2006-2010 5-year est.); Median contract rent: $458 per month (2006-2010 5-year est.); Median year structure built: 1970 (2006-2010 5-year est.).

Transportation: Commute to work: 90.0% car, 0.3% public transportation, 2.1% walk, 5.3% work from home (2006-2010 5-year est.); Travel time to work: 36.5% less than 15 minutes, 20.2% 15 to 30 minutes, 23.0% 30 to 45 minutes, 6.1% 45 to 60 minutes, 14.3% 60 minutes or more (2006-2010 5-year est.)

Additional Information Contacts
Bedford County Chamber of Commerce . . . . (814) 623-2233
   http://www.bedfordcountychamber.com

LINCOLN (township). Covers a land area of 16.280 square miles and a water area of 0.014 square miles. Located at 40.24° N. Lat; 78.60° W. Long.

Population: 394 (1990); 380 (2000); 425 (2010); Density: 26.1 persons per square mile (2010); Race: 96.5% White, 0.2% Black, 0.0% Asian, 0.0% American Indian/Alaska Native, 0.0% Native Hawaiian/Other Pacific Islander, 3.3% Other, 0.2% Hispanic of any race (2010); Average household size: 2.83 (2010); Median age: 40.2 (2010); Males per 100 females: 119.1 (2010); Marriage status: 18.8% never married, 66.6% now married, 7.8% widowed, 6.9% divorced (2006-2010 5-year est.); Foreign born: 0.0% (2006-2010 5-year est.); Ancestry (includes multiple ancestries): 34.4% German, 12.3% American, 7.3% Irish, 4.0% Welsh, 3.5% English (2006-2010 5-year est.).

Economy: Single-family building permits issued: 0 (2011); Multi-family building permits issued: 0 (2011); Employment by occupation: 10.9% management, 1.0% professional, 11.5% services, 15.1% sales, 2.6% farming, 15.6% construction, 10.9% production (2006-2010 5-year est.).

Income: Per capita income: $20,125 (2006-2010 5-year est.); Median household income: $41,250 (2006-2010 5-year est.); Average household income: $51,745 (2006-2010 5-year est.); Percent of households with income of $100,000 or more: 15.8% (2006-2010 5-year est.); Poverty rate: 10.3% (2006-2010 5-year est.).

Education: Percent of population age 25 and over with: High school diploma (including GED) or higher: 78.9% (2006-2010 5-year est.); Bachelor's degree or higher: 8.2% (2006-2010 5-year est.); Master's degree or higher: 1.1% (2006-2010 5-year est.).

Housing: Homeownership rate: 88.0% (2010); Median home value: $100,000 (2006-2010 5-year est.); Median contract rent: $763 per month (2006-2010 5-year est.); Median year structure built: 1968 (2006-2010 5-year est.).

Transportation: Commute to work: 88.9% car, 0.0% public transportation, 2.8% walk, 6.7% work from home (2006-2010 5-year est.); Travel time to work: 14.3% less than 15 minutes, 36.9% 15 to 30 minutes, 31.0% 30 to 45 minutes, 9.5% 45 to 60 minutes, 8.3% 60 minutes or more (2006-2010 5-year est.)

LONDONDERRY (township). Covers a land area of 54.791 square miles and a water area of 0.173 square miles. Located at 39.83° N. Lat; 78.73° W. Long.

Population: 1,846 (1990); 1,760 (2000); 1,856 (2010); Density: 33.9 persons per square mile (2010); Race: 98.5% White, 0.2% Black, 0.1% Asian, 0.2% American Indian/Alaska Native, 0.1% Native Hawaiian/Other Pacific Islander, 0.9% Other, 0.2% Hispanic of any race (2010); Average household size: 2.55 (2010); Median age: 43.0 (2010); Males per 100 females: 104.9 (2010); Marriage status: 20.9% never married, 62.7% now married, 9.5% widowed, 6.9% divorced (2006-2010 5-year est.); Foreign born: 0.9% (2006-2010 5-year est.); Ancestry (includes multiple ancestries): 37.7% German, 10.5% American, 10.3% Irish, 7.7% English, 3.2% Scottish (2006-2010 5-year est.).

Economy: Single-family building permits issued: 4 (2011); Multi-family building permits issued: 0 (2011); Employment by occupation: 7.9% management, 2.2% professional, 12.6% services, 18.3% sales, 2.3% farming, 16.8% construction, 7.2% production (2006-2010 5-year est.).

Income: Per capita income: $19,318 (2006-2010 5-year est.); Median household income: $37,938 (2006-2010 5-year est.); Average household income: $43,439 (2006-2010 5-year est.); Percent of households with income of $100,000 or more: 6.1% (2006-2010 5-year est.); Poverty rate: 9.2% (2006-2010 5-year est.).

Education: Percent of population age 25 and over with: High school diploma (including GED) or higher: 83.1% (2006-2010 5-year est.); Bachelor's degree or higher: 7.2% (2006-2010 5-year est.); Master's degree or higher: 1.8% (2006-2010 5-year est.).

Housing: Homeownership rate: 83.4% (2010); Median home value: $103,300 (2006-2010 5-year est.); Median contract rent: $288 per month (2006-2010 5-year est.); Median year structure built: 1969 (2006-2010 5-year est.).

Transportation: Commute to work: 93.3% car, 0.0% public transportation, 0.8% walk, 5.9% work from home (2006-2010 5-year est.); Travel time to work: 22.2% less than 15 minutes, 25.4% 15 to 30 minutes, 32.5% 30 to 45 minutes, 9.2% 45 to 60 minutes, 10.7% 60 minutes or more (2006-2010 5-year est.)

Additional Information Contacts
Bedford County Chamber of Commerce . . . . (814) 623-2233
   http://www.bedfordcountychamber.com

LOYSBURG (unincorporated postal area)

Zip Code: 16659

Covers a land area of 1.818 square miles and a water area of 0 square miles. Located at 40.16° N. Lat; 78.38° W. Long. Elevation is 1,112 feet. Population: 303 (2010); Density: 166.6 persons per square mile (2010); Race: 98.7% White, 0.7% Black, 0.0% Asian, 0.0% American Indian/Alaska Native, 0.0% Native Hawaiian/Other Pacific Islander, 0.6% Other, 0.0% Hispanic of any race (2010); Average household size: 2.46 (2010); Median age: 41.9 (2010); Males per 100 females: 93.0 (2010); Homeownership rate: 69.9% (2010)

MANN (township).

Covers a land area of 35.684 square miles and a water area of 0.021 square miles. Located at 39.77° N. Lat; 78.41° W. Long.

Population: 481 (1990); 481 (2000); 500 (2010); Density: 14.0 persons per square mile (2010); Race: 99.0% White, 0.0% Black, 0.0% Asian, 0.6% American Indian/Alaska Native, 0.0% Native Hawaiian/Other Pacific Islander, 0.4% Other, 0.0% Hispanic of any race (2010); Average household size: 2.23 (2010); Median age: 49.0 (2010); Males per 100 females: 107.5 (2010); Marriage status: 24.6% never married, 58.1% now married, 5.1% widowed, 12.1% divorced (2006-2010 5-year est.); Foreign born: 0.5% (2006-2010 5-year est.); Ancestry (includes multiple ancestries): 32.3% German, 6.6% Irish, 5.4% American, 5.2% English, 4.0% Italian (2006-2010 5-year est.).
Economy: Single-family building permits issued: 0 (2011); Multi-family building permits issued: 0 (2011); Employment by occupation: 7.1% management, 2.6% professional, 11.3% services, 9.4% sales, 10.9% farming, 21.1% construction, 13.9% production (2006-2010 5-year est.).
Income: Per capita income: $20,600 (2006-2010 5-year est.); Median household income: $34,740 (2006-2010 5-year est.); Average household income: $54,622 (2006-2010 5-year est.); Percent of households with income of $100,000 or more: 16.7% (2006-2010 5-year est.); Poverty rate: 9.7% (2006-2010 5-year est.).
Education: Percent of population age 25 and over with: High school diploma (including GED) or higher: 82.6% (2006-2010 5-year est.); Bachelor's degree or higher: 13.0% (2006-2010 5-year est.); Master's degree or higher: 4.9% (2006-2010 5-year est.).
Housing: Homeownership rate: 83.9% (2010); Median home value: $127,900 (2006-2010 5-year est.); Median contract rent: $325 per month (2006-2010 5-year est.); Median year structure built: 1977 (2006-2010 5-year est.).
Transportation: Commute to work: 93.6% car, 0.8% public transportation, 1.9% walk, 2.6% work from home (2006-2010 5-year est.); Travel time to work: 10.0% less than 15 minutes, 13.9% 15 to 30 minutes, 34.4% 30 to 45 minutes, 27.4% 45 to 60 minutes, 14.3% 60 minutes or more (2006-2010 5-year est.)

MANNS CHOICE (borough).

Covers a land area of 0.501 square miles and a water area of 0.005 square miles. Located at 40.00° N. Lat; 78.59° W. Long. Elevation is 1,198 feet.

Population: 248 (1990); 291 (2000); 300 (2010); Density: 599.2 persons per square mile (2010); Race: 98.7% White, 0.0% Black, 0.0% Asian, 0.0% American Indian/Alaska Native, 0.0% Native Hawaiian/Other Pacific Islander, 1.3% Other, 1.3% Hispanic of any race (2010); Average household size: 2.34 (2010); Median age: 38.0 (2010); Males per 100 females: 91.1 (2010); Marriage status: 23.8% never married, 50.3% now married, 12.7% widowed, 13.3% divorced (2006-2010 5-year est.); Foreign born: 2.1% (2006-2010 5-year est.); Ancestry (includes multiple ancestries): 45.1% German, 13.2% Irish, 8.5% English, 5.5% American, 3.8% Scottish (2006-2010 5-year est.).
Economy: Single-family building permits issued: 0 (2011); Multi-family building permits issued: 0 (2011); Employment by occupation: 5.8% management, 0.0% professional, 8.7% services, 18.8% sales, 2.9% farming, 36.2% construction, 7.2% production (2006-2010 5-year est.).
Income: Per capita income: $16,351 (2006-2010 5-year est.); Median household income: $27,273 (2006-2010 5-year est.); Average household income: $36,367 (2006-2010 5-year est.); Percent of households with income of $100,000 or more: 1.9% (2006-2010 5-year est.); Poverty rate: 15.3% (2006-2010 5-year est.).
Education: Percent of population age 25 and over with: High school diploma (including GED) or higher: 74.5% (2006-2010 5-year est.); Bachelor's degree or higher: 7.0% (2006-2010 5-year est.); Master's degree or higher: 4.5% (2006-2010 5-year est.).
Housing: Homeownership rate: 72.6% (2010); Median home value: $80,400 (2006-2010 5-year est.); Median contract rent: $423 per month

(2006-2010 5-year est.); Median year structure built: before 1940 (2006-2010 5-year est.).
Transportation: Commute to work: 97.1% car, 0.0% public transportation, 2.9% walk, 0.0% work from home (2006-2010 5-year est.); Travel time to work: 29.0% less than 15 minutes, 44.9% 15 to 30 minutes, 13.0% 30 to 45 minutes, 5.8% 45 to 60 minutes, 7.2% 60 minutes or more (2006-2010 5-year est.)

MONROE (township).

Covers a land area of 87.586 square miles and a water area of 0.096 square miles. Located at 39.88° N. Lat; 78.38° W. Long.

Population: 1,305 (1990); 1,372 (2000); 1,336 (2010); Density: 15.3 persons per square mile (2010); Race: 98.4% White, 0.5% Black, 0.0% Asian, 0.1% American Indian/Alaska Native, 0.0% Native Hawaiian/Other Pacific Islander, 1.0% Other, 1.3% Hispanic of any race (2010); Average household size: 2.51 (2010); Median age: 44.8 (2010); Males per 100 females: 104.6 (2010); Marriage status: 18.7% never married, 67.9% now married, 6.4% widowed, 7.0% divorced (2006-2010 5-year est.); Foreign born: 0.6% (2006-2010 5-year est.); Ancestry (includes multiple ancestries): 40.1% German, 12.1% American, 10.9% Irish, 5.8% English, 2.9% Italian (2006-2010 5-year est.).
Economy: Single-family building permits issued: 0 (2011); Multi-family building permits issued: 0 (2011); Employment by occupation: 8.4% management, 0.0% professional, 4.5% services, 15.8% sales, 4.9% farming, 16.0% construction, 9.9% production (2006-2010 5-year est.).
Income: Per capita income: $21,155 (2006-2010 5-year est.); Median household income: $43,922 (2006-2010 5-year est.); Average household income: $50,243 (2006-2010 5-year est.); Percent of households with income of $100,000 or more: 9.4% (2006-2010 5-year est.); Poverty rate: 9.0% (2006-2010 5-year est.).
Education: Percent of population age 25 and over with: High school diploma (including GED) or higher: 73.5% (2006-2010 5-year est.); Bachelor's degree or higher: 10.9% (2006-2010 5-year est.); Master's degree or higher: 4.9% (2006-2010 5-year est.).
Housing: Homeownership rate: 86.2% (2010); Median home value: $126,800 (2006-2010 5-year est.); Median contract rent: $341 per month (2006-2010 5-year est.); Median year structure built: 1977 (2006-2010 5-year est.).
Transportation: Commute to work: 94.1% car, 0.0% public transportation, 0.0% walk, 4.3% work from home (2006-2010 5-year est.); Travel time to work: 12.8% less than 15 minutes, 31.6% 15 to 30 minutes, 26.7% 30 to 45 minutes, 12.6% 45 to 60 minutes, 16.2% 60 minutes or more (2006-2010 5-year est.)
Additional Information Contacts
Bedford County Chamber of Commerce . . . . (814) 623-2233
http://www.bedfordcountychamber.com

NAPIER (township).

Covers a land area of 57.784 square miles and a water area of 0.865 square miles. Located at 40.07° N. Lat; 78.65° W. Long. Elevation is 1,112 feet.

Population: 2,054 (1990); 2,145 (2000); 2,198 (2010); Density: 38.0 persons per square mile (2010); Race: 99.0% White, 0.1% Black, 0.2% Asian, 0.1% American Indian/Alaska Native, 0.0% Native Hawaiian/Other Pacific Islander, 0.6% Other, 1.7% Hispanic of any race (2010); Average household size: 2.47 (2010); Median age: 46.8 (2010); Males per 100 females: 109.1 (2010); Marriage status: 18.9% never married, 69.2% now married, 5.7% widowed, 6.2% divorced (2006-2010 5-year est.); Foreign born: 2.1% (2006-2010 5-year est.); Ancestry (includes multiple ancestries): 42.1% German, 11.7% English, 9.4% Irish, 7.7% American, 5.7% Italian (2006-2010 5-year est.).
Economy: Single-family building permits issued: 2 (2011); Multi-family building permits issued: 0 (2011); Employment by occupation: 11.1% management, 1.4% professional, 6.0% services, 13.4% sales, 2.5% farming, 19.4% construction, 10.8% production (2006-2010 5-year est.).
Income: Per capita income: $24,548 (2006-2010 5-year est.); Median household income: $43,528 (2006-2010 5-year est.); Average household income: $59,229 (2006-2010 5-year est.); Percent of households with income of $100,000 or more: 11.9% (2006-2010 5-year est.); Poverty rate: 15.1% (2006-2010 5-year est.).
Education: Percent of population age 25 and over with: High school diploma (including GED) or higher: 85.4% (2006-2010 5-year est.); Bachelor's degree or higher: 15.7% (2006-2010 5-year est.); Master's degree or higher: 3.3% (2006-2010 5-year est.).
Housing: Homeownership rate: 87.1% (2010); Median home value: $130,200 (2006-2010 5-year est.); Median contract rent: $379 per month

(2006-2010 5-year est.); Median year structure built: 1968 (2006-2010 5-year est.).

Transportation: Commute to work: 94.0% car, 0.0% public transportation, 1.5% walk, 3.2% work from home (2006-2010 5-year est.); Travel time to work: 12.1% less than 15 minutes, 51.0% 15 to 30 minutes, 18.8% 30 to 45 minutes, 13.7% 45 to 60 minutes, 4.3% 60 minutes or more (2006-2010 5-year est.)

Additional Information Contacts

Bedford County Chamber of Commerce . . . . (814) 623-2233
    http://www.bedfordcountychamber.com

NEW ENTERPRISE (unincorporated postal area)

Zip Code: 16664

Covers a land area of 40.861 square miles and a water area of 0.035 square miles. Located at 40.18° N. Lat; 78.42° W. Long. Elevation is 1,260 feet. Population: 2,104 (2010); Density: 51.5 persons per square mile (2010); Race: 98.8% White, 0.3% Black, 0.2% Asian, 0.1% American Indian/Alaska Native, 0.0% Native Hawaiian/Other Pacific Islander, 0.6% Other, 0.1% Hispanic of any race (2010); Average household size: 2.93 (2010); Median age: 37.0 (2010); Males per 100 females: 101.3 (2010); Homeownership rate: 88.3% (2010)

NEW PARIS (borough). Covers a land area of 0.058 square miles and a water area of 0 square miles. Located at 40.11° N. Lat; 78.64° W. Long. Elevation is 1,273 feet.

History: Several covered bridges to Northeast.

Population: 223 (1990); 214 (2000); 186 (2010); Density: 3,223.7 persons per square mile (2010); Race: 97.3% White, 0.0% Black, 0.5% Asian, 0.5% American Indian/Alaska Native, 0.0% Native Hawaiian/Other Pacific Islander, 1.7% Other, 0.0% Hispanic of any race (2010); Average household size: 2.55 (2010); Median age: 34.5 (2010); Males per 100 females: 97.9 (2010); Marriage status: 28.7% never married, 50.4% now married, 9.6% widowed, 11.3% divorced (2006-2010 5-year est.); Foreign born: 0.0% (2006-2010 5-year est.); Ancestry (includes multiple ancestries): 43.6% German, 22.9% Irish, 12.9% English, 10.7% Dutch, 10.0% American (2006-2010 5-year est.).

Economy: Single-family building permits issued: 0 (2011); Multi-family building permits issued: 0 (2011); Employment by occupation: 4.3% management, 5.8% professional, 17.4% services, 11.6% sales, 2.9% farming, 20.3% construction, 8.7% production (2006-2010 5-year est.).

Income: Per capita income: $19,899 (2006-2010 5-year est.); Median household income: $41,250 (2006-2010 5-year est.); Average household income: $43,652 (2006-2010 5-year est.); Percent of households with income of $100,000 or more: 4.8% (2006-2010 5-year est.); Poverty rate: 18.6% (2006-2010 5-year est.).

Education: Percent of population age 25 and over with: High school diploma (including GED) or higher: 85.4% (2006-2010 5-year est.); Bachelor's degree or higher: 8.3% (2006-2010 5-year est.); Master's degree or higher: 0.0% (2006-2010 5-year est.).

School District(s)

Chestnut Ridge SD (PK-12)
    2010-11 Enrollment: 1,690 . . . . (814) 839-4195

Housing: Homeownership rate: 69.8% (2010); Median home value: $83,800 (2006-2010 5-year est.); Median contract rent: $504 per month (2006-2010 5-year est.); Median year structure built: before 1940 (2006-2010 5-year est.).

Transportation: Commute to work: 94.2% car, 0.0% public transportation, 0.0% walk, 5.8% work from home (2006-2010 5-year est.); Travel time to work: 20.0% less than 15 minutes, 30.8% 15 to 30 minutes, 26.2% 30 to 45 minutes, 10.8% 45 to 60 minutes, 12.3% 60 minutes or more (2006-2010 5-year est.)

OSTERBURG (unincorporated postal area)

Zip Code: 16667

Covers a land area of 16.955 square miles and a water area of 0.068 square miles. Located at 40.17° N. Lat; 78.53° W. Long. Elevation is 1,152 feet. Population: 1,392 (2010); Density: 82.1 persons per square mile (2010); Race: 99.1% White, 0.3% Black, 0.1% Asian, 0.1% American Indian/Alaska Native, 0.0% Native Hawaiian/Other Pacific Islander, 0.4% Other, 0.1% Hispanic of any race (2010); Average household size: 2.56 (2010); Median age: 41.4 (2010); Males per 100 females: 100.3 (2010); Homeownership rate: 81.6% (2010)

PAVIA (township). Covers a land area of 22.142 square miles and a water area of 0.005 square miles. Located at 40.28° N. Lat; 78.59° W. Long. Elevation is 1,424 feet.

Population: 296 (1990); 325 (2000); 295 (2010); Density: 13.3 persons per square mile (2010); Race: 98.3% White, 0.7% Black, 0.0% Asian, 0.0% American Indian/Alaska Native, 0.0% Native Hawaiian/Other Pacific Islander, 1.0% Other, 0.0% Hispanic of any race (2010); Average household size: 2.46 (2010); Median age: 41.5 (2010); Males per 100 females: 100.7 (2010); Marriage status: 26.3% never married, 54.7% now married, 5.2% widowed, 13.8% divorced (2006-2010 5-year est.); Foreign born: 0.0% (2006-2010 5-year est.); Ancestry (includes multiple ancestries): 38.9% German, 7.4% Irish, 5.3% American, 3.9% Polish, 3.9% Dutch (2006-2010 5-year est.).

Economy: Single-family building permits issued: 0 (2011); Multi-family building permits issued: 0 (2011); Employment by occupation: 10.4% management, 0.0% professional, 13.9% services, 17.4% sales, 3.5% farming, 18.8% construction, 13.9% production (2006-2010 5-year est.).

Income: Per capita income: $23,448 (2006-2010 5-year est.); Median household income: $44,028 (2006-2010 5-year est.); Average household income: $51,922 (2006-2010 5-year est.); Percent of households with income of $100,000 or more: 8.2% (2006-2010 5-year est.); Poverty rate: 8.4% (2006-2010 5-year est.).

Education: Percent of population age 25 and over with: High school diploma (including GED) or higher: 84.3% (2006-2010 5-year est.); Bachelor's degree or higher: 6.9% (2006-2010 5-year est.); Master's degree or higher: 2.8% (2006-2010 5-year est.).

Housing: Homeownership rate: 89.2% (2010); Median home value: $105,800 (2006-2010 5-year est.); Median contract rent: $375 per month (2006-2010 5-year est.); Median year structure built: 1977 (2006-2010 5-year est.).

Transportation: Commute to work: 86.1% car, 0.0% public transportation, 0.0% walk, 13.9% work from home (2006-2010 5-year est.); Travel time to work: 4.0% less than 15 minutes, 33.9% 15 to 30 minutes, 41.9% 30 to 45 minutes, 17.7% 45 to 60 minutes, 2.4% 60 minutes or more (2006-2010 5-year est.)

PLEASANTVILLE (borough). Aka Alum Bank. Covers a land area of 0.074 square miles and a water area of 0 square miles. Located at 40.18° N. Lat; 78.61° W. Long.

History: Covered bridge in area.

Population: 215 (1990); 211 (2000); 198 (2010); Density: 2,670.0 persons per square mile (2010); Race: 99.0% White, 0.0% Black, 0.0% Asian, 0.0% American Indian/Alaska Native, 0.0% Native Hawaiian/Other Pacific Islander, 1.0% Other, 0.0% Hispanic of any race (2010); Average household size: 2.51 (2010); Median age: 40.3 (2010); Males per 100 females: 70.7 (2010); Marriage status: 18.1% never married, 61.9% now married, 6.2% widowed, 13.8% divorced (2006-2010 5-year est.); Foreign born: 0.0% (2006-2010 5-year est.); Ancestry (includes multiple ancestries): 43.6% German, 16.8% Irish, 10.2% English, 7.9% American, 7.9% Italian (2006-2010 5-year est.).

Economy: Employment by occupation: 5.9% management, 2.5% professional, 11.9% services, 11.9% sales, 0.0% farming, 3.4% construction, 5.1% production (2006-2010 5-year est.).

Income: Per capita income: $17,922 (2006-2010 5-year est.); Median household income: $36,750 (2006-2010 5-year est.); Average household income: $52,930 (2006-2010 5-year est.); Percent of households with income of $100,000 or more: 13.0% (2006-2010 5-year est.); Poverty rate: 18.8% (2006-2010 5-year est.).

Education: Percent of population age 25 and over with: High school diploma (including GED) or higher: 84.1% (2006-2010 5-year est.); Bachelor's degree or higher: 6.8% (2006-2010 5-year est.); Master's degree or higher: 1.1% (2006-2010 5-year est.).

Housing: Homeownership rate: 62.0% (2010); Median home value: $85,800 (2006-2010 5-year est.); Median contract rent: $473 per month (2006-2010 5-year est.); Median year structure built: before 1940 (2006-2010 5-year est.).

Transportation: Commute to work: 86.4% car, 0.0% public transportation, 5.1% walk, 0.0% work from home (2006-2010 5-year est.); Travel time to work: 28.8% less than 15 minutes, 47.5% 15 to 30 minutes, 17.8% 30 to 45 minutes, 3.4% 45 to 60 minutes, 2.5% 60 minutes or more (2006-2010 5-year est.)

QUEEN (unincorporated postal area)

Zip Code: 16670

Covers a land area of 0.159 square miles and a water area of 0 square miles. Located at 40.26° N. Lat; 78.50° W. Long. Elevation is 1,283 feet. Population: 47 (2010); Density: 295.1 persons per square mile (2010); Race: 100.0% White, 0.0% Black, 0.0% Asian, 0.0% American Indian/Alaska Native, 0.0% Native Hawaiian/Other Pacific Islander, 0.0% Other, 0.0% Hispanic of any race (2010); Average household size: 1.96 (2010); Median age: 48.5 (2010); Males per 100 females: 104.3 (2010); Homeownership rate: 66.6% (2010)

RAINSBURG (borough). Covers a land area of 0.163 square miles and a water area of 0 square miles. Located at 39.90° N. Lat; 78.52° W. Long. Elevation is 1,407 feet.
Population: 175 (1990); 146 (2000); 133 (2010); Density: 818.3 persons per square mile (2010); Race: 96.2% White, 0.0% Black, 0.0% Asian, 0.8% American Indian/Alaska Native, 0.0% Native Hawaiian/Other Pacific Islander, 3.0% Other, 3.0% Hispanic of any race (2010); Average household size: 2.51 (2010); Median age: 39.5 (2010); Males per 100 females: 107.8 (2010); Marriage status: 11.0% never married, 70.7% now married, 15.9% widowed, 2.4% divorced (2006-2010 5-year est.); Foreign born: 0.0% (2006-2010 5-year est.); Ancestry (includes multiple ancestries): 53.6% German, 16.5% English, 15.5% Irish, 11.3% Scotch-Irish, 10.3% Italian (2006-2010 5-year est.).
Economy: Single-family building permits issued: 0 (2011); Multi-family building permits issued: 0 (2011); Employment by occupation: 28.6% management, 7.1% professional, 7.1% services, 0.0% sales, 0.0% farming, 0.0% construction, 7.1% production (2006-2010 5-year est.).
Income: Per capita income: $17,921 (2006-2010 5-year est.); Median household income: $36,250 (2006-2010 5-year est.); Average household income: $37,130 (2006-2010 5-year est.); Percent of households with income of $100,000 or more: 5.0% (2006-2010 5-year est.); Poverty rate: 7.2% (2006-2010 5-year est.).
Education: Percent of population age 25 and over with: High school diploma (including GED) or higher: 73.8% (2006-2010 5-year est.); Bachelor's degree or higher: 10.0% (2006-2010 5-year est.); Master's degree or higher: 0.0% (2006-2010 5-year est.).
Housing: Homeownership rate: 81.1% (2010); Median home value: $101,600 (2006-2010 5-year est.); Median contract rent: $408 per month (2006-2010 5-year est.); Median year structure built: before 1940 (2006-2010 5-year est.).
Transportation: Commute to work: 82.6% car, 0.0% public transportation, 0.0% walk, 8.7% work from home (2006-2010 5-year est.); Travel time to work: 0.0% less than 15 minutes, 61.9% 15 to 30 minutes, 38.1% 30 to 45 minutes, 0.0% 45 to 60 minutes, 0.0% 60 minutes or more (2006-2010 5-year est.)

RIDDLESBURG (unincorporated postal area)
Zip Code: 16672
Covers a land area of 4.332 square miles and a water area of 0.043 square miles. Located at 40.17° N. Lat; 78.24° W. Long. Population: 187 (2010); Density: 43.2 persons per square mile (2010); Race: 97.9% White, 0.0% Black, 0.0% Asian, 0.0% American Indian/Alaska Native, 0.0% Native Hawaiian/Other Pacific Islander, 2.1% Other, 0.0% Hispanic of any race (2010); Average household size: 2.37 (2010); Median age: 39.7 (2010); Males per 100 females: 101.1 (2010); Homeownership rate: 83.5% (2010)

SAINT CLAIRSVILLE (borough). Covers a land area of 0.030 square miles and a water area of 0 square miles. Located at 40.16° N. Lat; 78.51° W. Long. Elevation is 1,230 feet.
Population: 88 (1990); 86 (2000); 78 (2010); Density: 2,580.9 persons per square mile (2010); Race: 93.6% White, 1.3% Black, 0.0% Asian, 0.0% American Indian/Alaska Native, 0.0% Native Hawaiian/Other Pacific Islander, 5.1% Other, 1.3% Hispanic of any race (2010); Average household size: 2.52 (2010); Median age: 37.3 (2010); Males per 100 females: 110.8 (2010); Marriage status: 32.8% never married, 50.8% now married, 9.8% widowed, 6.6% divorced (2006-2010 5-year est.); Foreign born: 0.0% (2006-2010 5-year est.); Ancestry (includes multiple ancestries): 59.5% German, 20.3% Irish, 6.8% American, 2.7% Hungarian, 2.7% Ukrainian (2006-2010 5-year est.).
Economy: Single-family building permits issued: 0 (2011); Multi-family building permits issued: 0 (2011); Employment by occupation: 0.0% management, 0.0% professional, 11.8% services, 29.4% sales, 0.0% farming, 17.6% construction, 17.6% production (2006-2010 5-year est.).
Income: Per capita income: $19,431 (2006-2010 5-year est.); Median household income: $27,188 (2006-2010 5-year est.); Average household

income: $42,633 (2006-2010 5-year est.); Percent of households with income of $100,000 or more: 6.1% (2006-2010 5-year est.); Poverty rate: 2.7% (2006-2010 5-year est.).
Education: Percent of population age 25 and over with: High school diploma (including GED) or higher: 83.0% (2006-2010 5-year est.); Bachelor's degree or higher: 7.5% (2006-2010 5-year est.); Master's degree or higher: 3.8% (2006-2010 5-year est.).
Housing: Homeownership rate: 67.8% (2010); Median home value: $90,800 (2006-2010 5-year est.); Median contract rent: $375 per month (2006-2010 5-year est.); Median year structure built: before 1940 (2006-2010 5-year est.).
Transportation: Commute to work: 94.1% car, 0.0% public transportation, 0.0% walk, 0.0% work from home (2006-2010 5-year est.); Travel time to work: 0.0% less than 15 minutes, 67.6% 15 to 30 minutes, 23.5% 30 to 45 minutes, 5.9% 45 to 60 minutes, 2.9% 60 minutes or more (2006-2010 5-year est.)

SAXTON (borough). Covers a land area of 0.406 square miles and a water area of 0 square miles. Located at 40.21° N. Lat; 78.25° W. Long. Elevation is 896 feet.
History: Incorporated 1867.
Population: 824 (1990); 803 (2000); 736 (2010); Density: 1,810.9 persons per square mile (2010); Race: 98.4% White, 0.4% Black, 0.0% Asian, 0.3% American Indian/Alaska Native, 0.0% Native Hawaiian/Other Pacific Islander, 0.9% Other, 1.1% Hispanic of any race (2010); Average household size: 2.13 (2010); Median age: 39.1 (2010); Males per 100 females: 78.6 (2010); Marriage status: 30.1% never married, 35.8% now married, 16.3% widowed, 17.8% divorced (2006-2010 5-year est.); Foreign born: 0.5% (2006-2010 5-year est.); Ancestry (includes multiple ancestries): 28.3% German, 14.3% English, 14.0% Irish, 9.3% American, 7.9% Welsh (2006-2010 5-year est.).
Economy: Single-family building permits issued: 0 (2011); Multi-family building permits issued: 0 (2011); Employment by occupation: 5.0% management, 1.0% professional, 14.0% services, 15.7% sales, 2.3% farming, 5.7% construction, 6.4% production (2006-2010 5-year est.).
Income: Per capita income: $17,498 (2006-2010 5-year est.); Median household income: $28,906 (2006-2010 5-year est.); Average household income: $37,967 (2006-2010 5-year est.); Percent of households with income of $100,000 or more: 6.8% (2006-2010 5-year est.); Poverty rate: 20.5% (2006-2010 5-year est.).
Education: Percent of population age 25 and over with: High school diploma (including GED) or higher: 75.9% (2006-2010 5-year est.); Bachelor's degree or higher: 11.6% (2006-2010 5-year est.); Master's degree or higher: 2.1% (2006-2010 5-year est.).
School District(s)
Tussey Mountain SD (PK-12)
    2010-11 Enrollment: 1,110 . . . . (814) 635-3670
Housing: Homeownership rate: 50.9% (2010); Median home value: $75,200 (2006-2010 5-year est.); Median contract rent: $358 per month (2006-2010 5-year est.); Median year structure built: before 1940 (2006-2010 5-year est.).
Safety: Violent crime rate: 0.0 per 10,000 population; Property crime rate: 0.0 per 10,000 population (2011).
Newspapers: Broad Top Bulletin (Local news; Circulation 3,250)
Transportation: Commute to work: 89.9% car, 2.4% public transportation, 4.5% walk, 3.1% work from home (2006-2010 5-year est.); Travel time to work: 36.9% less than 15 minutes, 25.4% 15 to 30 minutes, 11.5% 30 to 45 minutes, 15.4% 45 to 60 minutes, 10.8% 60 minutes or more (2006-2010 5-year est.)

SCHELLSBURG (borough). Covers a land area of 0.254 square miles and a water area of 0 square miles. Located at 40.05° N. Lat; 78.64° W. Long. Elevation is 1,253 feet.
Population: 245 (1990); 316 (2000); 338 (2010); Density: 1,332.1 persons per square mile (2010); Race: 99.4% White, 0.0% Black, 0.0% Asian, 0.6% American Indian/Alaska Native, 0.0% Native Hawaiian/Other Pacific Islander, 0.0% Other, 1.2% Hispanic of any race (2010); Average household size: 2.40 (2010); Median age: 40.3 (2010); Males per 100 females: 103.6 (2010); Marriage status: 25.4% never married, 59.7% now married, 5.2% widowed, 9.7% divorced (2006-2010 5-year est.); Foreign born: 0.0% (2006-2010 5-year est.); Ancestry (includes multiple ancestries): 48.3% German, 11.6% Irish, 9.2% American, 8.0% English, 6.1% Italian (2006-2010 5-year est.).
Economy: Single-family building permits issued: 1 (2011); Multi-family building permits issued: 0 (2011); Employment by occupation: 1.8%

management, 1.2% professional, 13.3% services, 26.1% sales, 7.9% farming, 11.5% construction, 17.0% production (2006-2010 5-year est.).

Income: Per capita income: $19,746 (2006-2010 5-year est.); Median household income: $41,932 (2006-2010 5-year est.); Average household income: $48,468 (2006-2010 5-year est.); Percent of households with income of $100,000 or more: 6.1% (2006-2010 5-year est.); Poverty rate: 4.3% (2006-2010 5-year est.).

Education: Percent of population age 25 and over with: High school diploma (including GED) or higher: 93.1% (2006-2010 5-year est.); Bachelor's degree or higher: 11.6% (2006-2010 5-year est.); Master's degree or higher: 3.4% (2006-2010 5-year est.).

Housing: Homeownership rate: 67.7% (2010); Median home value: $112,000 (2006-2010 5-year est.); Median contract rent: $468 per month (2006-2010 5-year est.); Median year structure built: before 1940 (2006-2010 5-year est.).

Transportation: Commute to work: 87.6% car, 0.0% public transportation, 3.9% walk, 8.5% work from home (2006-2010 5-year est.); Travel time to work: 24.3% less than 15 minutes, 46.4% 15 to 30 minutes, 9.3% 30 to 45 minutes, 9.3% 45 to 60 minutes, 10.7% 60 minutes or more (2006-2010 5-year est.)

SIX MILE RUN (unincorporated postal area)
Zip Code: 16679

Covers a land area of 21.037 square miles and a water area of <.001 square miles. Located at 40.15° N. Lat; 78.19° W. Long. Population: 844 (2010); Density: 40.1 persons per square mile (2010); Race: 97.9% White, 0.5% Black, 0.1% Asian, 0.0% American Indian/Alaska Native, 0.0% Native Hawaiian/Other Pacific Islander, 1.5% Other, 0.4% Hispanic of any race (2010); Average household size: 2.50 (2010); Median age: 45.5 (2010); Males per 100 females: 102.4 (2010); Homeownership rate: 81.9% (2010)

SNAKE SPRING (township). Covers a land area of 26.074 square miles and a water area of 0.187 square miles. Located at 40.04° N. Lat; 78.42° W. Long.

Population: 1,511 (1990); 1,482 (2000); 1,639 (2010); Density: 62.9 persons per square mile (2010); Race: 98.0% White, 0.2% Black, 0.4% Asian, 0.1% American Indian/Alaska Native, 0.1% Native Hawaiian/Other Pacific Islander, 1.2% Other, 1.0% Hispanic of any race (2010); Average household size: 2.42 (2010); Median age: 50.7 (2010); Males per 100 females: 88.0 (2010); Marriage status: 19.5% never married, 62.2% now married, 10.6% widowed, 7.7% divorced (2006-2010 5-year est.); Foreign born: 2.1% (2006-2010 5-year est.); Ancestry (includes multiple ancestries): 43.5% German, 13.2% American, 12.1% English, 10.8% Irish, 3.9% Polish (2006-2010 5-year est.).

Economy: Single-family building permits issued: 3 (2011); Multi-family building permits issued: 64 (2011); Employment by occupation: 10.6% management, 1.4% professional, 13.7% services, 14.9% sales, 3.4% farming, 11.4% construction, 7.6% production (2006-2010 5-year est.).

Income: Per capita income: $23,211 (2006-2010 5-year est.); Median household income: $49,531 (2006-2010 5-year est.); Average household income: $57,874 (2006-2010 5-year est.); Percent of households with income of $100,000 or more: 14.9% (2006-2010 5-year est.); Poverty rate: 7.5% (2006-2010 5-year est.).

Education: Percent of population age 25 and over with: High school diploma (including GED) or higher: 81.4% (2006-2010 5-year est.); Bachelor's degree or higher: 15.5% (2006-2010 5-year est.); Master's degree or higher: 6.1% (2006-2010 5-year est.).

Housing: Homeownership rate: 80.9% (2010); Median home value: $145,700 (2006-2010 5-year est.); Median contract rent: $480 per month (2006-2010 5-year est.); Median year structure built: 1973 (2006-2010 5-year est.).

Transportation: Commute to work: 94.1% car, 0.0% public transportation, 0.4% walk, 4.6% work from home (2006-2010 5-year est.); Travel time to work: 38.9% less than 15 minutes, 41.3% 15 to 30 minutes, 6.6% 30 to 45 minutes, 7.7% 45 to 60 minutes, 5.5% 60 minutes or more (2006-2010 5-year est.)

Additional Information Contacts
Bedford County Chamber of Commerce . . . . (814) 623-2233
http://www.bedfordcountychamber.com

SOUTH WOODBURY (township). Covers a land area of 33.718 square miles and a water area of 0.035 square miles. Located at 40.16° N. Lat; 78.41° W. Long.

Population: 1,839 (1990); 2,000 (2000); 2,155 (2010); Density: 63.9 persons per square mile (2010); Race: 98.9% White, 0.4% Black, 0.2% Asian, 0.0% American Indian/Alaska Native, 0.0% Native Hawaiian/Other Pacific Islander, 0.5% Other, 0.0% Hispanic of any race (2010); Average household size: 2.82 (2010); Median age: 37.6 (2010); Males per 100 females: 99.7 (2010); Marriage status: 22.9% never married, 64.5% now married, 6.0% widowed, 6.6% divorced (2006-2010 5-year est.); Foreign born: 0.0% (2006-2010 5-year est.); Ancestry (includes multiple ancestries): 51.3% German, 11.2% Irish, 10.4% American, 6.0% English, 5.1% Swiss (2006-2010 5-year est.).

Economy: Single-family building permits issued: 5 (2011); Multi-family building permits issued: 0 (2011); Employment by occupation: 8.0% management, 2.0% professional, 12.3% services, 16.6% sales, 3.1% farming, 14.5% construction, 7.8% production (2006-2010 5-year est.).

Income: Per capita income: $19,758 (2006-2010 5-year est.); Median household income: $47,882 (2006-2010 5-year est.); Average household income: $56,084 (2006-2010 5-year est.); Percent of households with income of $100,000 or more: 11.8% (2006-2010 5-year est.); Poverty rate: 12.5% (2006-2010 5-year est.).

Education: Percent of population age 25 and over with: High school diploma (including GED) or higher: 86.3% (2006-2010 5-year est.); Bachelor's degree or higher: 14.3% (2006-2010 5-year est.); Master's degree or higher: 4.0% (2006-2010 5-year est.).

Housing: Homeownership rate: 85.1% (2010); Median home value: $117,900 (2006-2010 5-year est.); Median contract rent: $395 per month (2006-2010 5-year est.); Median year structure built: 1974 (2006-2010 5-year est.).

Transportation: Commute to work: 88.4% car, 0.0% public transportation, 5.2% walk, 5.3% work from home (2006-2010 5-year est.); Travel time to work: 26.7% less than 15 minutes, 35.1% 15 to 30 minutes, 19.4% 30 to 45 minutes, 7.1% 45 to 60 minutes, 11.8% 60 minutes or more (2006-2010 5-year est.)

Additional Information Contacts
Bedford County Chamber of Commerce . . . . (814) 623-2233
http://www.bedfordcountychamber.com

SOUTHAMPTON (township). Covers a land area of 80.153 square miles and a water area of 0.038 square miles. Located at 39.78° N. Lat; 78.53° W. Long.

Population: 920 (1990); 1,010 (2000); 976 (2010); Density: 12.2 persons per square mile (2010); Race: 98.3% White, 0.1% Black, 0.1% Asian, 0.1% American Indian/Alaska Native, 0.0% Native Hawaiian/Other Pacific Islander, 1.4% Other, 0.7% Hispanic of any race (2010); Average household size: 2.44 (2010); Median age: 46.4 (2010); Males per 100 females: 105.0 (2010); Marriage status: 18.2% never married, 64.2% now married, 8.9% widowed, 8.6% divorced (2006-2010 5-year est.); Foreign born: 1.1% (2006-2010 5-year est.); Ancestry (includes multiple ancestries): 29.1% German, 16.1% American, 10.9% Irish, 5.5% English, 4.2% Italian (2006-2010 5-year est.).

Economy: Single-family building permits issued: 2 (2011); Multi-family building permits issued: 0 (2011); Employment by occupation: 7.1% management, 2.0% professional, 6.3% services, 19.6% sales, 5.7% farming, 18.2% construction, 8.0% production (2006-2010 5-year est.).

Income: Per capita income: $24,856 (2006-2010 5-year est.); Median household income: $34,722 (2006-2010 5-year est.); Average household income: $56,403 (2006-2010 5-year est.); Percent of households with income of $100,000 or more: 7.5% (2006-2010 5-year est.); Poverty rate: 3.9% (2006-2010 5-year est.).

Education: Percent of population age 25 and over with: High school diploma (including GED) or higher: 82.2% (2006-2010 5-year est.); Bachelor's degree or higher: 12.7% (2006-2010 5-year est.); Master's degree or higher: 4.6% (2006-2010 5-year est.).

Housing: Homeownership rate: 90.8% (2010); Median home value: $117,800 (2006-2010 5-year est.); Median contract rent: $375 per month (2006-2010 5-year est.); Median year structure built: 1975 (2006-2010 5-year est.).

Transportation: Commute to work: 97.4% car, 0.0% public transportation, 0.0% walk, 2.6% work from home (2006-2010 5-year est.); Travel time to work: 10.1% less than 15 minutes, 41.4% 15 to 30 minutes, 26.5% 30 to 45 minutes, 10.4% 45 to 60 minutes, 11.6% 60 minutes or more (2006-2010 5-year est.)

Additional Information Contacts
Bedford County Chamber of Commerce . . . . (814) 623-2233
http://www.bedfordcountychamber.com

STONERSTOWN (CDP).

Covers a land area of 0.356 square miles and a water area of 0 square miles. Located at 40.22° N. Lat; 78.26° W. Long. Elevation is 837 feet.

Population: n/a (1990); n/a (2000); 376 (2010); Density: 1,056.8 persons per square mile (2010); Race: 99.5% White, 0.0% Black, 0.0% Asian, 0.3% American Indian/Alaska Native, 0.0% Native Hawaiian/Other Pacific Islander, 0.2% Other, 2.1% Hispanic of any race (2010); Average household size: 2.28 (2010); Median age: 43.8 (2010); Males per 100 females: 103.2 (2010); Marriage status: 21.6% never married, 57.1% now married, 13.0% widowed, 8.3% divorced (2006-2010 5-year est.); Foreign born: 0.0% (2006-2010 5-year est.); Ancestry (includes multiple ancestries): 32.6% German, 10.2% Irish, 7.8% American, 6.7% English, 6.1% Italian (2006-2010 5-year est.).

Economy: Employment by occupation: 8.0% management, 0.0% professional, 10.8% services, 14.8% sales, 0.0% farming, 13.6% construction, 13.1% production (2006-2010 5-year est.).

Income: Per capita income: $22,068 (2006-2010 5-year est.); Median household income: $34,583 (2006-2010 5-year est.); Average household income: $47,194 (2006-2010 5-year est.); Percent of households with income of $100,000 or more: 7.7% (2006-2010 5-year est.); Poverty rate: 14.7% (2006-2010 5-year est.).

Education: Percent of population age 25 and over with: High school diploma (including GED) or higher: 78.9% (2006-2010 5-year est.); Bachelor's degree or higher: 19.7% (2006-2010 5-year est.); Master's degree or higher: 3.8% (2006-2010 5-year est.).

Housing: Homeownership rate: 82.4% (2010); Median home value: $84,200 (2006-2010 5-year est.); Median contract rent: $519 per month (2006-2010 5-year est.); Median year structure built: 1955 (2006-2010 5-year est.).

Transportation: Commute to work: 86.8% car, 1.1% public transportation, 2.3% walk, 3.4% work from home (2006-2010 5-year est.); Travel time to work: 38.1% less than 15 minutes, 10.1% 15 to 30 minutes, 29.8% 30 to 45 minutes, 8.9% 45 to 60 minutes, 13.1% 60 minutes or more (2006-2010 5-year est.)

WEST PROVIDENCE (township).

Covers a land area of 38.237 square miles and a water area of 0.499 square miles. Located at 39.99° N. Lat; 78.35° W. Long.

Population: 3,233 (1990); 3,323 (2000); 3,210 (2010); Density: 83.9 persons per square mile (2010); Race: 99.1% White, 0.2% Black, 0.2% Asian, 0.0% American Indian/Alaska Native, 0.0% Native Hawaiian/Other Pacific Islander, 0.5% Other, 0.4% Hispanic of any race (2010); Average household size: 2.40 (2010); Median age: 45.5 (2010); Males per 100 females: 99.9 (2010); Marriage status: 14.1% never married, 70.9% now married, 7.5% widowed, 7.5% divorced (2006-2010 5-year est.); Foreign born: 0.6% (2006-2010 5-year est.); Ancestry (includes multiple ancestries): 44.4% German, 10.8% English, 10.7% Irish, 9.6% American, 3.3% Dutch (2006-2010 5-year est.).

Economy: Single-family building permits issued: 3 (2011); Multi-family building permits issued: 0 (2011); Employment by occupation: 9.6% management, 0.0% professional, 14.6% services, 18.5% sales, 1.7% farming, 11.1% construction, 3.5% production (2006-2010 5-year est.).

Income: Per capita income: $21,607 (2006-2010 5-year est.); Median household income: $47,729 (2006-2010 5-year est.); Average household income: $52,649 (2006-2010 5-year est.); Percent of households with income of $100,000 or more: 9.0% (2006-2010 5-year est.); Poverty rate: 6.2% (2006-2010 5-year est.).

Education: Percent of population age 25 and over with: High school diploma (including GED) or higher: 85.3% (2006-2010 5-year est.); Bachelor's degree or higher: 17.2% (2006-2010 5-year est.); Master's degree or higher: 5.9% (2006-2010 5-year est.).

Housing: Homeownership rate: 82.6% (2010); Median home value: $125,400 (2006-2010 5-year est.); Median contract rent: $452 per month (2006-2010 5-year est.); Median year structure built: 1967 (2006-2010 5-year est.).

Transportation: Commute to work: 91.3% car, 0.0% public transportation, 5.7% walk, 3.0% work from home (2006-2010 5-year est.); Travel time to work: 41.8% less than 15 minutes, 36.4% 15 to 30 minutes, 8.5% 30 to 45 minutes, 5.2% 45 to 60 minutes, 8.0% 60 minutes or more (2006-2010 5-year est.)

Additional Information Contacts
Bedford County Chamber of Commerce . . . . (814) 623-2233
http://www.bedfordcountychamber.com

WEST SAINT CLAIR (township).

Covers a land area of 29.847 square miles and a water area of 0.003 square miles. Located at 40.18° N. Lat; 78.63° W. Long.

Population: 1,543 (1990); 1,647 (2000); 1,730 (2010); Density: 58.0 persons per square mile (2010); Race: 98.0% White, 0.2% Black, 0.2% Asian, 0.6% American Indian/Alaska Native, 0.0% Native Hawaiian/Other Pacific Islander, 1.0% Other, 0.8% Hispanic of any race (2010); Average household size: 2.69 (2010); Median age: 40.9 (2010); Males per 100 females: 105.7 (2010); Marriage status: 21.6% never married, 65.2% now married, 5.8% widowed, 7.4% divorced (2006-2010 5-year est.); Foreign born: 0.8% (2006-2010 5-year est.); Ancestry (includes multiple ancestries): 42.8% German, 10.7% American, 6.4% Irish, 5.4% English, 4.2% French (2006-2010 5-year est.).

Economy: Single-family building permits issued: 2 (2011); Multi-family building permits issued: 0 (2011); Employment by occupation: 2.9% management, 3.6% professional, 15.0% services, 11.1% sales, 0.9% farming, 17.2% construction, 12.8% production (2006-2010 5-year est.).

Income: Per capita income: $19,040 (2006-2010 5-year est.); Median household income: $43,603 (2006-2010 5-year est.); Average household income: $53,207 (2006-2010 5-year est.); Percent of households with income of $100,000 or more: 7.4% (2006-2010 5-year est.); Poverty rate: 14.1% (2006-2010 5-year est.).

Education: Percent of population age 25 and over with: High school diploma (including GED) or higher: 92.3% (2006-2010 5-year est.); Bachelor's degree or higher: 10.4% (2006-2010 5-year est.); Master's degree or higher: 3.6% (2006-2010 5-year est.).

Housing: Homeownership rate: 86.6% (2010); Median home value: $111,400 (2006-2010 5-year est.); Median contract rent: $367 per month (2006-2010 5-year est.); Median year structure built: 1973 (2006-2010 5-year est.).

Transportation: Commute to work: 93.2% car, 0.0% public transportation, 2.5% walk, 3.8% work from home (2006-2010 5-year est.); Travel time to work: 21.5% less than 15 minutes, 39.5% 15 to 30 minutes, 21.5% 30 to 45 minutes, 9.3% 45 to 60 minutes, 8.3% 60 minutes or more (2006-2010 5-year est.)

Additional Information Contacts
Bedford County Chamber of Commerce . . . . (814) 623-2233
http://www.bedfordcountychamber.com

WOODBURY (borough).

Covers a land area of 0.128 square miles and a water area of 0.006 square miles. Located at 40.23° N. Lat; 78.37° W. Long. Elevation is 1,280 feet.

Population: 239 (1990); 269 (2000); 284 (2010); Density: 2,223.6 persons per square mile (2010); Race: 98.6% White, 0.0% Black, 0.0% Asian, 0.7% American Indian/Alaska Native, 0.0% Native Hawaiian/Other Pacific Islander, 0.7% Other, 2.5% Hispanic of any race (2010); Average household size: 2.49 (2010); Median age: 40.3 (2010); Males per 100 females: 91.9 (2010); Marriage status: 20.8% never married, 55.8% now married, 10.2% widowed, 13.2% divorced (2006-2010 5-year est.); Foreign born: 1.1% (2006-2010 5-year est.); Ancestry (includes multiple ancestries): 56.2% German, 12.5% American, 7.2% Irish, 3.4% English, 2.6% Pennsylvania German (2006-2010 5-year est.).

Economy: Single-family building permits issued: 0 (2011); Multi-family building permits issued: 0 (2011); Employment by occupation: 6.9% management, 0.0% professional, 12.9% services, 14.7% sales, 1.7% farming, 6.0% construction, 8.6% production (2006-2010 5-year est.).

Income: Per capita income: $16,081 (2006-2010 5-year est.); Median household income: $36,346 (2006-2010 5-year est.); Average household income: $44,755 (2006-2010 5-year est.); Percent of households with income of $100,000 or more: 6.4% (2006-2010 5-year est.); Poverty rate: 12.1% (2006-2010 5-year est.).

Education: Percent of population age 25 and over with: High school diploma (including GED) or higher: 94.6% (2006-2010 5-year est.); Bachelor's degree or higher: 6.5% (2006-2010 5-year est.); Master's degree or higher: 1.8% (2006-2010 5-year est.).

Housing: Homeownership rate: 77.2% (2010); Median home value: $98,300 (2006-2010 5-year est.); Median contract rent: $518 per month (2006-2010 5-year est.); Median year structure built: 1956 (2006-2010 5-year est.).

Transportation: Commute to work: 85.3% car, 0.0% public transportation, 12.1% walk, 2.6% work from home (2006-2010 5-year est.); Travel time to

work: 36.3% less than 15 minutes, 29.2% 15 to 30 minutes, 30.1% 30 to 45 minutes, 2.7% 45 to 60 minutes, 1.8% 60 minutes or more (2006-2010 5-year est.)

WOODBURY (township). Covers a land area of 23.424 square miles and a water area of 0.022 square miles. Located at 40.23° N. Lat; 78.35° W. Long. Elevation is 1,280 feet.
Population: 1,129 (1990); 1,198 (2000); 1,263 (2010); Density: 53.9 persons per square mile (2010); Race: 98.7% White, 0.5% Black, 0.0% Asian, 0.0% American Indian/Alaska Native, 0.0% Native Hawaiian/Other Pacific Islander, 0.8% Other, 1.7% Hispanic of any race (2010); Average household size: 3.04 (2010); Median age: 36.3 (2010); Males per 100 females: 101.8 (2010); Marriage status: 24.7% never married, 66.4% now married, 4.8% widowed, 4.0% divorced (2006-2010 5-year est.); Foreign born: 1.3% (2006-2010 5-year est.); Ancestry (includes multiple ancestries): 50.7% German, 10.7% Pennsylvania German, 5.9% American, 5.9% Irish, 5.0% English (2006-2010 5-year est.).
Economy: Single-family building permits issued: 1 (2011); Multi-family building permits issued: 0 (2011); Employment by occupation: 18.2% management, 1.8% professional, 9.3% services, 9.3% sales, 5.5% farming, 12.4% construction, 8.5% production (2006-2010 5-year est.).
Income: Per capita income: $21,776 (2006-2010 5-year est.); Median household income: $47,634 (2006-2010 5-year est.); Average household income: $68,595 (2006-2010 5-year est.); Percent of households with income of $100,000 or more: 17.0% (2006-2010 5-year est.); Poverty rate: 15.5% (2006-2010 5-year est.).
Education: Percent of population age 25 and over with: High school diploma (including GED) or higher: 80.3% (2006-2010 5-year est.); Bachelor's degree or higher: 14.2% (2006-2010 5-year est.); Master's degree or higher: 3.6% (2006-2010 5-year est.).
Housing: Homeownership rate: 81.7% (2010); Median home value: $122,900 (2006-2010 5-year est.); Median contract rent: $473 per month (2006-2010 5-year est.); Median year structure built: 1976 (2006-2010 5-year est.).
Transportation: Commute to work: 74.0% car, 0.9% public transportation, 5.8% walk, 11.2% work from home (2006-2010 5-year est.); Travel time to work: 25.7% less than 15 minutes, 47.2% 15 to 30 minutes, 15.4% 30 to 45 minutes, 1.7% 45 to 60 minutes, 10.1% 60 minutes or more (2006-2010 5-year est.)
Additional Information Contacts
Bedford County Chamber of Commerce . . . . (814) 623-2233
http://www.bedfordcountychamber.com

Berks County

Located in southeast central Pennsylvania; bounded on the northwest by the Blue Mountains. Covers a land area of 856.506 square miles, a water area of 9.249 square miles, and is located in the Eastern Time Zone at 40.41° N. Lat., 75.93° W. Long. The county was founded in 1751. County seat is Reading.

Berks County is part of the Reading, PA Metropolitan Statistical Area. The entire metro area includes: Berks County, PA

Weather Station: Blue Marsh Lake										Elevation: 350 feet		
	Jan	Feb	Mar	Apr	May	Jun	Jul	Aug	Sep	Oct	Nov	Dec
High	36	39	48	60	71	80	84	83	75	64	52	41
Low	19	21	29	38	48	58	63	62	53	41	33	25
Precip	3.0	2.5	3.6	3.9	4.1	4.5	4.5	3.8	4.4	3.7	3.7	3.7
Snow	7.0	6.2	3.6	0.5	0.0	0.0	0.0	0.0	0.0	0.0	0.5	3.3

High and Low temperatures in degrees Fahrenheit; Precipitation and Snow in inches

Weather Station: Hamburg										Elevation: 350 feet		
	Jan	Feb	Mar	Apr	May	Jun	Jul	Aug	Sep	Oct	Nov	Dec
High	37	40	49	62	72	81	85	83	75	64	52	41
Low	20	22	30	40	49	59	63	62	54	41	34	24
Precip	3.0	2.6	3.5	3.7	4.4	4.8	4.5	4.0	4.5	3.8	3.8	3.6
Snow	6.6	5.7	3.1	0.5	0.0	0.0	0.0	0.0	0.0	0.0	0.4	3.0

High and Low temperatures in degrees Fahrenheit; Precipitation and Snow in inches

Weather Station: Reading 4 NNW										Elevation: 359 feet		
	Jan	Feb	Mar	Apr	May	Jun	Jul	Aug	Sep	Oct	Nov	Dec
High	38	41	50	62	73	81	85	84	77	65	54	42
Low	21	23	30	40	50	60	64	63	55	43	35	26
Precip	3.0	2.7	3.4	3.7	4.0	4.3	4.5	3.5	4.4	3.6	3.5	3.1
Snow	na	6.8	3.6	0.2	0.0	0.0	0.0	0.0	0.0	0.0	0.6	3.8

High and Low temperatures in degrees Fahrenheit; Precipitation and Snow in inches

Weather Station: Rodale Research Center										Elevation: 549 feet		
	Jan	Feb	Mar	Apr	May	Jun	Jul	Aug	Sep	Oct	Nov	Dec
High	38	41	50	62	72	80	84	83	76	65	53	41
Low	20	22	28	38	47	57	60	59	51	40	32	23
Precip	3.1	2.6	3.4	3.6	4.3	4.3	5.3	4.0	5.3	4.1	3.8	3.7
Snow	na	1.6	na	0.0	0.0	0.0	0.0	0.0	0.0	0.0	tr	na

High and Low temperatures in degrees Fahrenheit; Precipitation and Snow in inches

Population: 336,524 (1990); 373,638 (2000); 411,442 (2010); Race: 83.2% White, 4.9% Black, 1.3% Asian, 0.3% American Indian/Alaska Native, 0.0% Native Hawaiian/Other Pacific Islander, 10.3% Other, 16.4% Hispanic of any race (2010); Density: 480.4 persons per square mile (2010); Average household size: 2.59 (2010); Median age: 39.1 (2010); Males per 100 females: 96.3 (2010).
Religion: Six largest groups: 18.4% Catholicism, 10.3% Lutheran, 6.9% Presbyterian-Reformed, 3.1% Methodist/Pietist, 2.4% Pentecostal, 2.1% Non-Denominational (2010)
Economy: Unemployment rate: 8.2% (August 2012); Total civilian labor force: 209,314 (August 2012); Leading industries: 19.3% manufacturing; 16.7% health care and social assistance; 14.1% retail trade (2010); Farms: 1,980 totaling 222,119 acres (2007); Companies that employ 500 or more persons: 18 (2010); Companies that employ 100 to 499 persons: 206 (2010); Companies that employ less than 100 persons: 8,061 (2010); Black-owned businesses: 1,036 (2007); Hispanic-owned businesses: 1,655 (2007); Asian-owned businesses: 512 (2007); Women-owned businesses: 8,290 (2007); Retail sales per capita: $12,957 (2010). Single-family building permits issued: 267 (2011); Multi-family building permits issued: 39 (2011).
Income: Per capita income: $25,518 (2006-2010 5-year est.); Median household income: $53,470 (2006-2010 5-year est.); Average household income: $66,356 (2006-2010 5-year est.); Percent of households with income of $100,000 or more: 18.3% (2006-2010 5-year est.); Poverty rate: 12.4% (2006-2010 5-year est.); Bankruptcy rate: 3.02% (2011).
Taxes: Total county taxes per capita: $315 (2009); County property taxes per capita: $311 (2009).
Education: Percent of population age 25 and over with: High school diploma (including GED) or higher: 83.1% (2006-2010 5-year est.); Bachelor's degree or higher: 21.7% (2006-2010 5-year est.); Master's degree or higher: 7.3% (2006-2010 5-year est.).
Housing: Homeownership rate: 71.7% (2010); Median home value: $170,400 (2006-2010 5-year est.); Median contract rent: $607 per month (2006-2010 5-year est.); Median year structure built: 1963 (2006-2010 5-year est.)
Health: Birth rate: 120.8 per 10,000 population (2011); Death rate: 85.7 per 10,000 population (2011); Age-adjusted cancer mortality rate: 177.5 deaths per 100,000 population (2009); Number of physicians: 20.7 per 10,000 population (2010); Hospital beds: 29.4 per 10,000 population (2008); Hospital admissions: 1,010.7 per 10,000 population (2008).
Environment: Air Quality Index: 69.9% good, 29.3% moderate, 0.8% unhealthy for sensitive individuals, 0.0% unhealthy (percent of days in 2011)
Elections: 2012 Presidential election results: 48.9% Obama, 49.5% Romney
National and State Parks: French Creek State Park; Hopewell Village National Historic Site; Nolde Forest State Park
Additional Information Contacts
Berks County Government . . . . (610) 478-6100
http://www.co.berks.pa.us
TriCounty Area Chamber of Commerce . . . . (610) 326-2900
http://tricountyareachamber.com

Berks County Communities

ALBANY (township). Covers a land area of 39.764 square miles and a water area of 0.062 square miles. Located at 40.64° N. Lat; 75.92° W. Long. Elevation is 407 feet.
Population: 1,547 (1990); 1,662 (2000); 1,724 (2010); Density: 43.4 persons per square mile (2010); Race: 98.6% White, 0.5% Black, 0.1% Asian, 0.1% American Indian/Alaska Native, 0.0% Native Hawaiian/Other Pacific Islander, 0.7% Other, 1.4% Hispanic of any race (2010); Average household size: 2.58 (2010); Median age: 44.8 (2010); Males per 100 females: 107.0 (2010); Marriage status: 21.8% never married, 66.8% now married, 4.8% widowed, 6.6% divorced (2006-2010 5-year est.); Foreign born: 2.2% (2006-2010 5-year est.); Ancestry (includes multiple

ancestries): 47.7% German, 13.4% Irish, 11.8% Pennsylvania German, 6.4% English, 5.0% American (2006-2010 5-year est.).

Economy: Single-family building permits issued: 1 (2011); Multi-family building permits issued: 0 (2011); Employment by occupation: 13.2% management, 4.1% professional, 9.7% services, 16.9% sales, 1.1% farming, 10.5% construction, 8.9% production (2006-2010 5-year est.).

Income: Per capita income: $32,829 (2006-2010 5-year est.); Median household income: $63,542 (2006-2010 5-year est.); Average household income: $82,319 (2006-2010 5-year est.); Percent of households with income of $100,000 or more: 26.4% (2006-2010 5-year est.); Poverty rate: 2.0% (2006-2010 5-year est.).

Education: Percent of population age 25 and over with: High school diploma (including GED) or higher: 91.0% (2006-2010 5-year est.); Bachelor's degree or higher: 31.1% (2006-2010 5-year est.); Master's degree or higher: 10.9% (2006-2010 5-year est.).

Housing: Homeownership rate: 82.3% (2010); Median home value: $222,000 (2006-2010 5-year est.); Median contract rent: $708 per month (2006-2010 5-year est.); Median year structure built: 1952 (2006-2010 5-year est.).

Transportation: Commute to work: 86.7% car, 0.0% public transportation, 2.3% walk, 8.7% work from home (2006-2010 5-year est.); Travel time to work: 13.4% less than 15 minutes, 42.1% 15 to 30 minutes, 24.4% 30 to 45 minutes, 10.3% 45 to 60 minutes, 9.8% 60 minutes or more (2006-2010 5-year est.)

Additional Information Contacts
Northeast Berks Chamber of Commerce . . . . (610) 683-8860
　http://www.northeastberkschamber.com

ALLEGHENYVILLE (CDP). Covers a land area of 2.679 square miles and a water area of 0.008 square miles. Located at 40.23° N. Lat; 75.98° W. Long. Elevation is 561 feet.

Population: n/a (1990); n/a (2000); 1,134 (2010); Density: 423.3 persons per square mile (2010); Race: 98.2% White, 0.4% Black, 1.0% Asian, 0.0% American Indian/Alaska Native, 0.0% Native Hawaiian/Other Pacific Islander, 0.4% Other, 1.6% Hispanic of any race (2010); Average household size: 3.02 (2010); Median age: 41.7 (2010); Males per 100 females: 108.8 (2010); Marriage status: 17.7% never married, 71.7% now married, 2.8% widowed, 7.8% divorced (2006-2010 5-year est.); Foreign born: 0.0% (2006-2010 5-year est.); Ancestry (includes multiple ancestries): 54.6% German, 18.0% Polish, 12.1% Irish, 10.3% Welsh, 9.4% Italian (2006-2010 5-year est.).

Economy: Employment by occupation: 24.9% management, 8.1% professional, 7.7% services, 4.3% sales, 0.0% farming, 15.3% construction, 4.8% production (2006-2010 5-year est.).

Income: Per capita income: $39,710 (2006-2010 5-year est.); Median household income: $102,143 (2006-2010 5-year est.); Average household income: $110,389 (2006-2010 5-year est.); Percent of households with income of $100,000 or more: 60.1% (2006-2010 5-year est.); Poverty rate: 0.0% (2006-2010 5-year est.).

Education: Percent of population age 25 and over with: High school diploma (including GED) or higher: 100.0% (2006-2010 5-year est.); Bachelor's degree or higher: 39.2% (2006-2010 5-year est.); Master's degree or higher: 8.6% (2006-2010 5-year est.).

Housing: Homeownership rate: 94.7% (2010); Median home value: $293,600 (2006-2010 5-year est.); Median contract rent: n/a per month (2006-2010 5-year est.); Median year structure built: 1982 (2006-2010 5-year est.).

Transportation: Commute to work: 91.6% car, 0.0% public transportation, 0.0% walk, 8.4% work from home (2006-2010 5-year est.); Travel time to work: 6.5% less than 15 minutes, 54.0% 15 to 30 minutes, 17.0% 30 to 45 minutes, 4.2% 45 to 60 minutes, 18.3% 60 minutes or more (2006-2010 5-year est.)

ALSACE (township). Covers a land area of 12.156 square miles and a water area of 0.023 square miles. Located at 40.39° N. Lat; 75.86° W. Long.

Population: 3,543 (1990); 3,689 (2000); 3,751 (2010); Density: 308.6 persons per square mile (2010); Race: 97.1% White, 0.5% Black, 0.6% Asian, 0.2% American Indian/Alaska Native, 0.0% Native Hawaiian/Other Pacific Islander, 1.6% Other, 2.1% Hispanic of any race (2010); Average household size: 2.52 (2010); Median age: 46.3 (2010); Males per 100 females: 104.7 (2010); Marriage status: 21.9% never married, 65.0% now married, 3.5% widowed, 9.7% divorced (2006-2010 5-year est.); Foreign born: 0.7% (2006-2010 5-year est.); Ancestry (includes multiple

ancestries): 40.9% German, 15.4% Irish, 12.2% American, 9.6% Italian, 9.6% English (2006-2010 5-year est.).

Economy: Single-family building permits issued: 1 (2011); Multi-family building permits issued: 0 (2011); Employment by occupation: 11.3% management, 4.0% professional, 8.8% services, 19.0% sales, 1.5% farming, 14.3% construction, 5.7% production (2006-2010 5-year est.).

Income: Per capita income: $27,315 (2006-2010 5-year est.); Median household income: $58,370 (2006-2010 5-year est.); Average household income: $63,147 (2006-2010 5-year est.); Percent of households with income of $100,000 or more: 18.0% (2006-2010 5-year est.); Poverty rate: 4.9% (2006-2010 5-year est.).

Education: Percent of population age 25 and over with: High school diploma (including GED) or higher: 87.7% (2006-2010 5-year est.); Bachelor's degree or higher: 12.4% (2006-2010 5-year est.); Master's degree or higher: 4.2% (2006-2010 5-year est.).

Housing: Homeownership rate: 89.1% (2010); Median home value: $162,000 (2006-2010 5-year est.); Median contract rent: $531 per month (2006-2010 5-year est.); Median year structure built: 1969 (2006-2010 5-year est.).

Transportation: Commute to work: 96.1% car, 0.0% public transportation, 0.7% walk, 2.3% work from home (2006-2010 5-year est.); Travel time to work: 31.8% less than 15 minutes, 47.2% 15 to 30 minutes, 9.5% 30 to 45 minutes, 4.1% 45 to 60 minutes, 7.3% 60 minutes or more (2006-2010 5-year est.)

Additional Information Contacts
Alsace Township. . . . . (610) 929-5324
　http://www.alsacetownship.org
Greater Reading Chamber of Commerce & Industry . . . . . (610) 376-6766
　http://www.greaterreadingchamber.org

ALSACE MANOR (CDP). Covers a land area of 0.340 square miles and a water area of 0.001 square miles. Located at 40.40° N. Lat; 75.86° W. Long. Elevation is 912 feet.

Population: n/a (1990); n/a (2000); 478 (2010); Density: 1,407.2 persons per square mile (2010); Race: 98.7% White, 0.2% Black, 0.0% Asian, 0.2% American Indian/Alaska Native, 0.0% Native Hawaiian/Other Pacific Islander, 0.9% Other, 0.6% Hispanic of any race (2010); Average household size: 2.64 (2010); Median age: 38.7 (2010); Males per 100 females: 108.7 (2010); Marriage status: 18.9% never married, 70.3% now married, 4.1% widowed, 6.7% divorced (2006-2010 5-year est.); Foreign born: 0.0% (2006-2010 5-year est.); Ancestry (includes multiple ancestries): 43.3% German, 13.8% English, 13.0% Irish, 12.1% American, 8.3% Dutch (2006-2010 5-year est.).

Economy: Employment by occupation: 0.0% management, 13.6% professional, 16.8% services, 17.6% sales, 0.0% farming, 12.8% construction, 16.4% production (2006-2010 5-year est.).

Income: Per capita income: $24,847 (2006-2010 5-year est.); Median household income: $65,125 (2006-2010 5-year est.); Average household income: $59,367 (2006-2010 5-year est.); Percent of households with income of $100,000 or more: 6.2% (2006-2010 5-year est.); Poverty rate: 4.0% (2006-2010 5-year est.).

Education: Percent of population age 25 and over with: High school diploma (including GED) or higher: 85.3% (2006-2010 5-year est.); Bachelor's degree or higher: 3.4% (2006-2010 5-year est.); Master's degree or higher: 3.4% (2006-2010 5-year est.).

Housing: Homeownership rate: 90.6% (2010); Median home value: $122,900 (2006-2010 5-year est.); Median contract rent: n/a per month (2006-2010 5-year est.); Median year structure built: 1953 (2006-2010 5-year est.).

Transportation: Commute to work: 100.0% car, 0.0% public transportation, 0.0% walk, 0.0% work from home (2006-2010 5-year est.); Travel time to work: 49.6% less than 15 minutes, 25.2% 15 to 30 minutes, 3.8% 30 to 45 minutes, 14.3% 45 to 60 minutes, 7.1% 60 minutes or more (2006-2010 5-year est.)

AMITY (township). Covers a land area of 18.166 square miles and a water area of 0.317 square miles. Located at 40.29° N. Lat; 75.75° W. Long.

Population: 6,434 (1990); 8,867 (2000); 12,583 (2010); Density: 692.7 persons per square mile (2010); Race: 91.9% White, 3.7% Black, 2.0% Asian, 0.1% American Indian/Alaska Native, 0.0% Native Hawaiian/Other Pacific Islander, 2.3% Other, 2.4% Hispanic of any race (2010); Average household size: 2.93 (2010); Median age: 38.5 (2010); Males per 100 females: 97.5 (2010); Marriage status: 20.4% never married, 66.3% now married, 5.7% widowed, 7.6% divorced (2006-2010 5-year est.); Foreign

born: 2.7% (2006-2010 5-year est.); Ancestry (includes multiple ancestries): 35.2% German, 20.0% Irish, 16.8% Italian, 12.0% English, 9.2% American (2006-2010 5-year est.).

Economy: Single-family building permits issued: 21 (2011); Multi-family building permits issued: 0 (2011); Employment by occupation: 17.0% management, 5.6% professional, 7.7% services, 17.2% sales, 3.6% farming, 10.0% construction, 6.6% production (2006-2010 5-year est.).

Income: Per capita income: $29,691 (2006-2010 5-year est.); Median household income: $79,424 (2006-2010 5-year est.); Average household income: $87,896 (2006-2010 5-year est.); Percent of households with income of $100,000 or more: 38.6% (2006-2010 5-year est.); Poverty rate: 4.6% (2006-2010 5-year est.).

Education: Percent of population age 25 and over with: High school diploma (including GED) or higher: 91.1% (2006-2010 5-year est.); Bachelor's degree or higher: 30.0% (2006-2010 5-year est.); Master's degree or higher: 9.6% (2006-2010 5-year est.).

Housing: Homeownership rate: 84.4% (2010); Median home value: $266,900 (2006-2010 5-year est.); Median contract rent: $846 per month (2006-2010 5-year est.); Median year structure built: 1992 (2006-2010 5-year est.).

Safety: Violent crime rate: 0.8 per 10,000 population; Property crime rate: 100.6 per 10,000 population (2011).

Transportation: Commute to work: 92.1% car, 0.2% public transportation, 1.6% walk, 5.7% work from home (2006-2010 5-year est.); Travel time to work: 22.5% less than 15 minutes, 34.3% 15 to 30 minutes, 17.0% 30 to 45 minutes, 13.7% 45 to 60 minutes, 12.5% 60 minutes or more (2006-2010 5-year est.)

Additional Information Contacts
Amity Township . . . . (610) 689-6000
  http://www.amitytownshippa.com
TriCounty Area Chamber of Commerce . . . . (610) 326-2900
  http://tricountyareachamber.com

AMITY GARDENS (CDP). Covers a land area of 1.187 square miles and a water area of 0.002 square miles. Located at 40.27° N. Lat; 75.73° W. Long. Elevation is 243 feet.

Population: 2,714 (1990); 3,370 (2000); 3,402 (2010); Density: 2,865.9 persons per square mile (2010); Race: 93.3% White, 2.8% Black, 1.3% Asian, 0.0% American Indian/Alaska Native, 0.0% Native Hawaiian/Other Pacific Islander, 2.6% Other, 2.9% Hispanic of any race (2010); Average household size: 2.77 (2010); Median age: 40.6 (2010); Males per 100 females: 96.5 (2010); Marriage status: 23.8% never married, 62.5% now married, 6.9% widowed, 6.8% divorced (2006-2010 5-year est.); Foreign born: 1.2% (2006-2010 5-year est.); Ancestry (includes multiple ancestries): 39.1% German, 20.1% Irish, 14.8% Italian, 10.5% American, 9.6% English (2006-2010 5-year est.).

Economy: Employment by occupation: 11.9% management, 6.7% professional, 11.4% services, 17.5% sales, 3.2% farming, 13.2% construction, 7.3% production (2006-2010 5-year est.).

Income: Per capita income: $28,063 (2006-2010 5-year est.); Median household income: $67,411 (2006-2010 5-year est.); Average household income: $78,120 (2006-2010 5-year est.); Percent of households with income of $100,000 or more: 36.2% (2006-2010 5-year est.); Poverty rate: 8.7% (2006-2010 5-year est.).

Education: Percent of population age 25 and over with: High school diploma (including GED) or higher: 91.3% (2006-2010 5-year est.); Bachelor's degree or higher: 26.4% (2006-2010 5-year est.); Master's degree or higher: 8.0% (2006-2010 5-year est.).

Housing: Homeownership rate: 81.5% (2010); Median home value: $230,900 (2006-2010 5-year est.); Median contract rent: $853 per month (2006-2010 5-year est.); Median year structure built: 1977 (2006-2010 5-year est.).

Transportation: Commute to work: 94.9% car, 0.0% public transportation, 0.9% walk, 2.8% work from home (2006-2010 5-year est.); Travel time to work: 23.8% less than 15 minutes, 33.3% 15 to 30 minutes, 15.1% 30 to 45 minutes, 12.3% 45 to 60 minutes, 15.5% 60 minutes or more (2006-2010 5-year est.)

Additional Information Contacts
TriCounty Area Chamber of Commerce . . . . (610) 326-2900
  http://tricountyareachamber.com

BALLY (borough). Covers a land area of 0.518 square miles and a water area of 0 square miles. Located at 40.40° N. Lat; 75.59° W. Long. Elevation is 482 feet.

Population: 1,024 (1990); 1,062 (2000); 1,090 (2010); Density: 2,103.9 persons per square mile (2010); Race: 97.5% White, 0.6% Black, 0.6% Asian, 0.1% American Indian/Alaska Native, 0.0% Native Hawaiian/Other Pacific Islander, 1.2% Other, 1.4% Hispanic of any race (2010); Average household size: 2.47 (2010); Median age: 41.9 (2010); Males per 100 females: 98.5 (2010); Marriage status: 19.7% never married, 65.6% now married, 5.9% widowed, 8.8% divorced (2006-2010 5-year est.); Foreign born: 0.5% (2006-2010 5-year est.); Ancestry (includes multiple ancestries): 39.1% German, 15.4% Pennsylvania German, 13.2% Irish, 12.7% English, 8.6% Italian (2006-2010 5-year est.).

Economy: Single-family building permits issued: 1 (2011); Multi-family building permits issued: 0 (2011); Employment by occupation: 4.8% management, 4.0% professional, 4.8% services, 18.9% sales, 2.5% farming, 10.3% construction, 19.2% production (2006-2010 5-year est.).

Income: Per capita income: $24,273 (2006-2010 5-year est.); Median household income: $55,039 (2006-2010 5-year est.); Average household income: $58,002 (2006-2010 5-year est.); Percent of households with income of $100,000 or more: 12.2% (2006-2010 5-year est.); Poverty rate: 11.0% (2006-2010 5-year est.).

Education: Percent of population age 25 and over with: High school diploma (including GED) or higher: 78.9% (2006-2010 5-year est.); Bachelor's degree or higher: 17.3% (2006-2010 5-year est.); Master's degree or higher: 4.9% (2006-2010 5-year est.).

Housing: Homeownership rate: 81.9% (2010); Median home value: $184,800 (2006-2010 5-year est.); Median contract rent: $730 per month (2006-2010 5-year est.); Median year structure built: 1961 (2006-2010 5-year est.).

Safety: Violent crime rate: 18.3 per 10,000 population; Property crime rate: 0.0 per 10,000 population (2011).

Transportation: Commute to work: 85.9% car, 0.0% public transportation, 9.0% walk, 5.1% work from home (2006-2010 5-year est.); Travel time to work: 34.7% less than 15 minutes, 24.5% 15 to 30 minutes, 25.0% 30 to 45 minutes, 10.1% 45 to 60 minutes, 5.6% 60 minutes or more (2006-2010 5-year est.)

Additional Information Contacts
Borough of Bally . . . . (610) 845-2351
  http://www.co.berks.pa.us/Muni/Bally/Pages/Home.aspx

BARTO (unincorporated postal area)
Zip Code: 19504

Covers a land area of 22.525 square miles and a water area of 0.047 square miles. Located at 40.41° N. Lat; 75.58° W. Long. Elevation is 456 feet. Population: 4,998 (2010); Density: 221.9 persons per square mile (2010); Race: 97.9% White, 0.3% Black, 0.6% Asian, 0.1% American Indian/Alaska Native, 0.0% Native Hawaiian/Other Pacific Islander, 1.1% Other, 1.1% Hispanic of any race (2010); Average household size: 2.72 (2010); Median age: 43.9 (2010); Males per 100 females: 101.3 (2010); Homeownership rate: 88.0% (2010)

BAUMSTOWN (CDP). Covers a land area of 0.999 square miles and a water area of 0.002 square miles. Located at 40.28° N. Lat; 75.81° W. Long. Elevation is 279 feet.

Population: n/a (1990); n/a (2000); 422 (2010); Density: 422.5 persons per square mile (2010); Race: 95.0% White, 3.6% Black, 0.7% Asian, 0.0% American Indian/Alaska Native, 0.0% Native Hawaiian/Other Pacific Islander, 0.7% Other, 1.4% Hispanic of any race (2010); Average household size: 2.57 (2010); Median age: 42.1 (2010); Males per 100 females: 107.9 (2010); Marriage status: 24.3% never married, 65.5% now married, 4.3% widowed, 6.0% divorced (2006-2010 5-year est.); Foreign born: 0.0% (2006-2010 5-year est.); Ancestry (includes multiple ancestries): 33.0% German, 26.3% English, 23.5% Dutch, 15.4% Slovak, 11.1% Irish (2006-2010 5-year est.).

Economy: Employment by occupation: 8.5% management, 11.5% professional, 5.2% services, 3.9% sales, 14.4% farming, 12.5% construction, 1.6% production (2006-2010 5-year est.).

Income: Per capita income: $39,494 (2006-2010 5-year est.); Median household income: $54,068 (2006-2010 5-year est.); Average household income: $81,367 (2006-2010 5-year est.); Percent of households with income of $100,000 or more: 11.3% (2006-2010 5-year est.); Poverty rate: 0.0% (2006-2010 5-year est.).

Education: Percent of population age 25 and over with: High school diploma (including GED) or higher: 50.3% (2006-2010 5-year est.);

Bachelor's degree or higher: 9.3% (2006-2010 5-year est.); Master's degree or higher: 6.1% (2006-2010 5-year est.).

Housing: Homeownership rate: 61.6% (2010); Median home value: $117,700 (2006-2010 5-year est.); Median contract rent: $660 per month (2006-2010 5-year est.); Median year structure built: 1953 (2006-2010 5-year est.).

Transportation: Commute to work: 100.0% car, 0.0% public transportation, 0.0% walk, 0.0% work from home (2006-2010 5-year est.); Travel time to work: 38.4% less than 15 minutes, 25.6% 15 to 30 minutes, 23.0% 30 to 45 minutes, 5.9% 45 to 60 minutes, 7.2% 60 minutes or more (2006-2010 5-year est.)

BECHTELSVILLE (borough). Covers a land area of 0.504 square miles and a water area of 0.002 square miles. Located at 40.37° N. Lat; 75.63° W. Long. Elevation is 417 feet.

History: Founded 1852, incorporated 1890.

Population: 884 (1990); 931 (2000); 942 (2010); Density: 1,867.9 persons per square mile (2010); Race: 98.3% White, 0.2% Black, 0.1% Asian, 0.1% American Indian/Alaska Native, 0.0% Native Hawaiian/Other Pacific Islander, 1.3% Other, 1.3% Hispanic of any race (2010); Average household size: 2.60 (2010); Median age: 39.6 (2010); Males per 100 females: 96.3 (2010); Marriage status: 27.1% never married, 59.0% now married, 4.0% widowed, 9.9% divorced (2006-2010 5-year est.); Foreign born: 0.5% (2006-2010 5-year est.); Ancestry (includes multiple ancestries): 45.8% German, 8.6% Irish, 8.6% American, 7.6% Pennsylvania German, 6.3% Northern European (2006-2010 5-year est.).

Economy: Single-family building permits issued: 0 (2011); Multi-family building permits issued: 0 (2011); Employment by occupation: 5.8% management, 2.1% professional, 10.6% services, 27.0% sales, 8.9% farming, 8.1% construction, 6.4% production (2006-2010 5-year est.).

Income: Per capita income: $35,284 (2006-2010 5-year est.); Median household income: $53,750 (2006-2010 5-year est.); Average household income: $81,441 (2006-2010 5-year est.); Percent of households with income of $100,000 or more: 10.9% (2006-2010 5-year est.); Poverty rate: 5.9% (2006-2010 5-year est.).

Taxes: Total city taxes per capita: $266 (2009); City property taxes per capita: $132 (2009).

Education: Percent of population age 25 and over with: High school diploma (including GED) or higher: 74.4% (2006-2010 5-year est.); Bachelor's degree or higher: 16.6% (2006-2010 5-year est.); Master's degree or higher: 5.1% (2006-2010 5-year est.).

Housing: Homeownership rate: 72.9% (2010); Median home value: $150,900 (2006-2010 5-year est.); Median contract rent: $696 per month (2006-2010 5-year est.); Median year structure built: 1958 (2006-2010 5-year est.).

Transportation: Commute to work: 91.5% car, 0.0% public transportation, 1.3% walk, 7.3% work from home (2006-2010 5-year est.); Travel time to work: 29.7% less than 15 minutes, 27.6% 15 to 30 minutes, 20.7% 30 to 45 minutes, 12.4% 45 to 60 minutes, 9.4% 60 minutes or more (2006-2010 5-year est.)

Additional Information Contacts
TriCounty Area Chamber of Commerce . . . . (610) 326-2900
    http://tricountyareachamber.com

BERN (township). Covers a land area of 19.346 square miles and a water area of 0.809 square miles. Located at 40.40° N. Lat; 76.00° W. Long.

History: Founded 1819, incorporated 1851.

Population: 6,303 (1990); 6,758 (2000); 6,797 (2010); Density: 351.3 persons per square mile (2010); Race: 91.0% White, 5.8% Black, 0.7% Asian, 0.1% American Indian/Alaska Native, 0.0% Native Hawaiian/Other Pacific Islander, 2.4% Other, 9.3% Hispanic of any race (2010); Average household size: 2.51 (2010); Median age: 45.3 (2010); Males per 100 females: 117.6 (2010); Marriage status: 34.3% never married, 45.0% now married, 11.6% widowed, 9.2% divorced (2006-2010 5-year est.); Foreign born: 2.9% (2006-2010 5-year est.); Ancestry (includes multiple ancestries): 35.2% German, 15.5% Irish, 8.4% Italian, 6.8% American, 5.8% Pennsylvania German (2006-2010 5-year est.).

Economy: Single-family building permits issued: 9 (2011); Multi-family building permits issued: 0 (2011); Employment by occupation: 12.3% management, 5.7% professional, 7.5% services, 20.8% sales, 2.9% farming, 8.9% construction, 6.2% production (2006-2010 5-year est.).

Income: Per capita income: $23,890 (2006-2010 5-year est.); Median household income: $73,620 (2006-2010 5-year est.); Average household income: $77,816 (2006-2010 5-year est.); Percent of households with

income of $100,000 or more: 28.3% (2006-2010 5-year est.); Poverty rate: 4.4% (2006-2010 5-year est.).

Education: Percent of population age 25 and over with: High school diploma (including GED) or higher: 77.8% (2006-2010 5-year est.); Bachelor's degree or higher: 17.0% (2006-2010 5-year est.); Master's degree or higher: 5.0% (2006-2010 5-year est.).

Housing: Homeownership rate: 88.1% (2010); Median home value: $216,400 (2006-2010 5-year est.); Median contract rent: $545 per month (2006-2010 5-year est.); Median year structure built: 1969 (2006-2010 5-year est.).

Safety: Violent crime rate: 32.3 per 10,000 population; Property crime rate: 107.1 per 10,000 population (2011).

Transportation: Commute to work: 92.3% car, 0.0% public transportation, 2.2% walk, 4.1% work from home (2006-2010 5-year est.); Travel time to work: 36.9% less than 15 minutes, 42.4% 15 to 30 minutes, 7.5% 30 to 45 minutes, 6.1% 45 to 60 minutes, 7.1% 60 minutes or more (2006-2010 5-year est.)

Additional Information Contacts
Bern Township . . . . (610) 926-2267
    http://www.co.berks.pa.us/bern
Greater Reading Chamber of Commerce & Industry . . . . . (610) 376-6766
    http://www.greaterreadingchamber.org

BERNVILLE (borough). Covers a land area of 0.432 square miles and a water area of 0.007 square miles. Located at 40.43° N. Lat; 76.11° W. Long. Elevation is 328 feet.

Population: 789 (1990); 865 (2000); 955 (2010); Density: 2,209.7 persons per square mile (2010); Race: 94.1% White, 1.4% Black, 0.1% Asian, 0.3% American Indian/Alaska Native, 0.2% Native Hawaiian/Other Pacific Islander, 3.9% Other, 7.6% Hispanic of any race (2010); Average household size: 2.68 (2010); Median age: 37.1 (2010); Males per 100 females: 90.6 (2010); Marriage status: 27.4% never married, 51.3% now married, 4.0% widowed, 17.4% divorced (2006-2010 5-year est.); Foreign born: 0.7% (2006-2010 5-year est.); Ancestry (includes multiple ancestries): 56.3% German, 12.4% Irish, 8.5% Pennsylvania German, 4.8% Finnish, 4.5% American (2006-2010 5-year est.).

Economy: Single-family building permits issued: 0 (2011); Multi-family building permits issued: 0 (2011); Employment by occupation: 1.6% management, 4.4% professional, 13.7% services, 18.3% sales, 1.4% farming, 14.3% construction, 6.9% production (2006-2010 5-year est.).

Income: Per capita income: $23,696 (2006-2010 5-year est.); Median household income: $52,868 (2006-2010 5-year est.); Average household income: $60,869 (2006-2010 5-year est.); Percent of households with income of $100,000 or more: 14.0% (2006-2010 5-year est.); Poverty rate: 6.8% (2006-2010 5-year est.).

Education: Percent of population age 25 and over with: High school diploma (including GED) or higher: 79.2% (2006-2010 5-year est.); Bachelor's degree or higher: 9.9% (2006-2010 5-year est.); Master's degree or higher: 2.4% (2006-2010 5-year est.).

School District(s)
Tulpehocken Area SD (KG-12)
    2010-11 Enrollment: 1,537 . . . . (717) 933-4611

Housing: Homeownership rate: 66.8% (2010); Median home value: $151,500 (2006-2010 5-year est.); Median contract rent: $712 per month (2006-2010 5-year est.); Median year structure built: 1946 (2006-2010 5-year est.).

Transportation: Commute to work: 93.9% car, 0.6% public transportation, 0.8% walk, 4.6% work from home (2006-2010 5-year est.); Travel time to work: 14.9% less than 15 minutes, 59.6% 15 to 30 minutes, 16.4% 30 to 45 minutes, 5.9% 45 to 60 minutes, 3.1% 60 minutes or more (2006-2010 5-year est.)

BETHEL (CDP). Covers a land area of 0.876 square miles and a water area of <.001 square miles. Located at 40.48° N. Lat; 76.29° W. Long. Elevation is 561 feet.

Population: n/a (1990); n/a (2000); 499 (2010); Density: 569.7 persons per square mile (2010); Race: 94.0% White, 0.2% Black, 1.8% Asian, 0.0% American Indian/Alaska Native, 0.0% Native Hawaiian/Other Pacific Islander, 4.0% Other, 6.2% Hispanic of any race (2010); Average household size: 2.59 (2010); Median age: 39.4 (2010); Males per 100 females: 109.7 (2010); Marriage status: 21.3% never married, 56.3% now married, 9.6% widowed, 12.9% divorced (2006-2010 5-year est.); Foreign born: 0.0% (2006-2010 5-year est.); Ancestry (includes multiple ancestries): 69.9% German, 12.9% Pennsylvania German, 7.2% Dutch, 6.8% English, 3.5% American (2006-2010 5-year est.).

Economy: Employment by occupation: 0.0% management, 14.2% professional, 0.0% services, 17.4% sales, 6.8% farming, 5.7% construction, 10.3% production (2006-2010 5-year est.).
Income: Per capita income: $31,158 (2006-2010 5-year est.); Median household income: $59,135 (2006-2010 5-year est.); Average household income: $60,781 (2006-2010 5-year est.); Percent of households with income of $100,000 or more: 6.5% (2006-2010 5-year est.); Poverty rate: 3.7% (2006-2010 5-year est.).
Education: Percent of population age 25 and over with: High school diploma (including GED) or higher: 89.1% (2006-2010 5-year est.); Bachelor's degree or higher: 0.0% (2006-2010 5-year est.); Master's degree or higher: 0.0% (2006-2010 5-year est.).

School District(s)
Tulpehocken Area SD (KG-12)
   2010-11 Enrollment: 1,537 . . . . (717) 933-4611
Housing: Homeownership rate: 71.0% (2010); Median home value: $110,700 (2006-2010 5-year est.); Median contract rent: n/a per month (2006-2010 5-year est.); Median year structure built: 1957 (2006-2010 5-year est.).
Transportation: Commute to work: 100.0% car, 0.0% public transportation, 0.0% walk, 0.0% work from home (2006-2010 5-year est.); Travel time to work: 18.9% less than 15 minutes, 20.3% 15 to 30 minutes, 40.2% 30 to 45 minutes, 10.7% 45 to 60 minutes, 10.0% 60 minutes or more (2006-2010 5-year est.)

BETHEL (township). Covers a land area of 42.220 square miles and a water area of 0.113 square miles. Located at 40.48° N. Lat; 76.32° W. Long. Elevation is 561 feet.
Population: 3,676 (1990); 4,166 (2000); 4,112 (2010); Density: 97.4 persons per square mile (2010); Race: 95.4% White, 0.8% Black, 0.9% Asian, 0.1% American Indian/Alaska Native, 0.0% Native Hawaiian/Other Pacific Islander, 2.8% Other, 4.0% Hispanic of any race (2010); Average household size: 2.87 (2010); Median age: 38.8 (2010); Males per 100 females: 102.3 (2010); Marriage status: 26.3% never married, 60.4% now married, 4.5% widowed, 8.8% divorced (2006-2010 5-year est.); Foreign born: 0.0% (2006-2010 5-year est.); Ancestry (includes multiple ancestries): 53.0% German, 11.4% American, 9.8% English, 7.8% Irish, 6.5% Swiss (2006-2010 5-year est.).
Economy: Single-family building permits issued: 4 (2011); Multi-family building permits issued: 0 (2011); Employment by occupation: 12.5% management, 3.7% professional, 3.9% services, 14.3% sales, 2.4% farming, 18.2% construction, 15.1% production (2006-2010 5-year est.).
Income: Per capita income: $23,450 (2006-2010 5-year est.); Median household income: $55,580 (2006-2010 5-year est.); Average household income: $64,419 (2006-2010 5-year est.); Percent of households with income of $100,000 or more: 15.5% (2006-2010 5-year est.); Poverty rate: 11.5% (2006-2010 5-year est.).
Education: Percent of population age 25 and over with: High school diploma (including GED) or higher: 82.5% (2006-2010 5-year est.); Bachelor's degree or higher: 9.2% (2006-2010 5-year est.); Master's degree or higher: 2.8% (2006-2010 5-year est.).
Housing: Homeownership rate: 79.9% (2010); Median home value: $183,800 (2006-2010 5-year est.); Median contract rent: $398 per month (2006-2010 5-year est.); Median year structure built: 1970 (2006-2010 5-year est.).
Safety: Violent crime rate: 7.3 per 10,000 population; Property crime rate: 84.8 per 10,000 population (2011).
Transportation: Commute to work: 88.2% car, 0.0% public transportation, 4.0% walk, 6.9% work from home (2006-2010 5-year est.); Travel time to work: 17.4% less than 15 minutes, 38.3% 15 to 30 minutes, 30.4% 30 to 45 minutes, 8.6% 45 to 60 minutes, 5.4% 60 minutes or more (2006-2010 5-year est.)
Additional Information Contacts
Bethel Township . . . . (717) 933-8813
   http://www.bethel-pa.com
Greater Reading Chamber of Commerce & Industry . . . . . (610) 376-6766
   http://www.greaterreadingchamber.org

BIRDSBORO (borough). Aka Naomi. Covers a land area of 1.334 square miles and a water area of 0.031 square miles. Located at 40.26° N. Lat; 75.81° W. Long. Elevation is 167 feet.
History: Hopewell Furnace National Historic Site is here. Daniel Boone Homestead, 18th-century farmhouse built on foundation of Daniel Boone's birthplace. Settled 1740, Incorporated 1872.

Population: 4,222 (1990); 5,064 (2000); 5,163 (2010); Density: 3,870.0 persons per square mile (2010); Race: 95.5% White, 1.4% Black, 0.3% Asian, 0.2% American Indian/Alaska Native, 0.0% Native Hawaiian/Other Pacific Islander, 2.6% Other, 3.2% Hispanic of any race (2010); Average household size: 2.68 (2010); Median age: 36.8 (2010); Males per 100 females: 98.3 (2010); Marriage status: 27.7% never married, 55.2% now married, 6.0% widowed, 11.1% divorced (2006-2010 5-year est.); Foreign born: 2.7% (2006-2010 5-year est.); Ancestry (includes multiple ancestries): 41.0% German, 20.0% Irish, 18.1% Italian, 10.1% English, 7.6% Polish (2006-2010 5-year est.).
Economy: Single-family building permits issued: 0 (2011); Multi-family building permits issued: 0 (2011); Employment by occupation: 9.1% management, 2.6% professional, 9.6% services, 20.4% sales, 3.7% farming, 12.2% construction, 7.8% production (2006-2010 5-year est.).
Income: Per capita income: $25,555 (2006-2010 5-year est.); Median household income: $61,679 (2006-2010 5-year est.); Average household income: $69,945 (2006-2010 5-year est.); Percent of households with income of $100,000 or more: 21.1% (2006-2010 5-year est.); Poverty rate: 5.4% (2006-2010 5-year est.).
Education: Percent of population age 25 and over with: High school diploma (including GED) or higher: 91.7% (2006-2010 5-year est.); Bachelor's degree or higher: 19.8% (2006-2010 5-year est.); Master's degree or higher: 4.6% (2006-2010 5-year est.).

School District(s)
Daniel Boone Area SD (KG-12)
   2010-11 Enrollment: 3,928 . . . . (610) 582-6140
Twin Valley SD (KG-12)
   2010-11 Enrollment: 3,390 . . . . (610) 286-8600
Housing: Homeownership rate: 74.4% (2010); Median home value: $174,600 (2006-2010 5-year est.); Median contract rent: $585 per month (2006-2010 5-year est.); Median year structure built: 1962 (2006-2010 5-year est.).
Safety: Violent crime rate: 11.6 per 10,000 population; Property crime rate: 196.9 per 10,000 population (2011).
Transportation: Commute to work: 92.9% car, 0.5% public transportation, 3.0% walk, 1.8% work from home (2006-2010 5-year est.); Travel time to work: 15.2% less than 15 minutes, 47.0% 15 to 30 minutes, 13.8% 30 to 45 minutes, 9.4% 45 to 60 minutes, 14.6% 60 minutes or more (2006-2010 5-year est.)
Additional Information Contacts
Borough of Birdsboro . . . . (610) 582-6030
   http://www.co.berks.pa.us/birdsboro/site/default.asp
TriCounty Area Chamber of Commerce . . . . (610) 326-2900
   http://tricountyareachamber.com

BLANDON (CDP). Covers a land area of 4.438 square miles and a water area of 0.007 square miles. Located at 40.45° N. Lat; 75.88° W. Long. Elevation is 377 feet.
Population: n/a (1990); n/a (2000); 7,152 (2010); Density: 1,611.6 persons per square mile (2010); Race: 91.1% White, 3.6% Black, 1.5% Asian, 0.1% American Indian/Alaska Native, 0.0% Native Hawaiian/Other Pacific Islander, 3.7% Other, 5.9% Hispanic of any race (2010); Average household size: 2.89 (2010); Median age: 37.7 (2010); Males per 100 females: 96.3 (2010); Marriage status: 18.9% never married, 68.2% now married, 4.1% widowed, 8.7% divorced (2006-2010 5-year est.); Foreign born: 5.7% (2006-2010 5-year est.); Ancestry (includes multiple ancestries): 41.2% German, 17.3% Irish, 15.5% Italian, 8.9% Polish, 6.2% Pennsylvania German (2006-2010 5-year est.).
Economy: Employment by occupation: 11.7% management, 5.6% professional, 7.1% services, 20.1% sales, 3.5% farming, 8.2% construction, 8.5% production (2006-2010 5-year est.).
Income: Per capita income: $27,554 (2006-2010 5-year est.); Median household income: $69,894 (2006-2010 5-year est.); Average household income: $78,446 (2006-2010 5-year est.); Percent of households with income of $100,000 or more: 28.0% (2006-2010 5-year est.); Poverty rate: 5.6% (2006-2010 5-year est.).
Education: Percent of population age 25 and over with: High school diploma (including GED) or higher: 93.0% (2006-2010 5-year est.); Bachelor's degree or higher: 28.9% (2006-2010 5-year est.); Master's degree or higher: 10.3% (2006-2010 5-year est.).

School District(s)
Fleetwood Area SD (KG-12)
   2010-11 Enrollment: 2,716 . . . . (610) 944-9598
Housing: Homeownership rate: 88.8% (2010); Median home value: $202,600 (2006-2010 5-year est.); Median contract rent: $806 per month

(2006-2010 5-year est.); Median year structure built: 1996 (2006-2010 5-year est.).
Transportation: Commute to work: 94.8% car, 0.6% public transportation, 0.5% walk, 2.5% work from home (2006-2010 5-year est.); Travel time to work: 27.6% less than 15 minutes, 41.9% 15 to 30 minutes, 15.7% 30 to 45 minutes, 7.5% 45 to 60 minutes, 7.4% 60 minutes or more (2006-2010 5-year est.)

BOWERS (CDP).
Covers a land area of 0.610 square miles and a water area of 0.002 square miles. Located at 40.49° N. Lat; 75.74° W. Long. Elevation is 443 feet.
Population: n/a (1990); n/a (2000); 326 (2010); Density: 534.6 persons per square mile (2010); Race: 97.9% White, 0.6% Black, 0.3% Asian, 0.9% American Indian/Alaska Native, 0.0% Native Hawaiian/Other Pacific Islander, 0.3% Other, 2.1% Hispanic of any race (2010); Average household size: 2.51 (2010); Median age: 45.8 (2010); Males per 100 females: 103.8 (2010); Marriage status: 33.5% never married, 56.2% now married, 10.3% widowed, 0.0% divorced (2006-2010 5-year est.); Foreign born: 0.0% (2006-2010 5-year est.); Ancestry (includes multiple ancestries): 68.8% German, 22.7% English, 21.6% Italian, 9.3% French, 8.9% Irish (2006-2010 5-year est.).
Economy: Employment by occupation: 12.2% management, 0.0% professional, 0.0% services, 43.9% sales, 16.4% farming, 0.0% construction, 0.0% production (2006-2010 5-year est.).
Income: Per capita income: $21,040 (2006-2010 5-year est.); Median household income: $42,788 (2006-2010 5-year est.); Average household income: $50,655 (2006-2010 5-year est.); Percent of households with income of $100,000 or more: 11.0% (2006-2010 5-year est.); Poverty rate: 22.7% (2006-2010 5-year est.).
Education: Percent of population age 25 and over with: High school diploma (including GED) or higher: 89.2% (2006-2010 5-year est.); Bachelor's degree or higher: 26.3% (2006-2010 5-year est.); Master's degree or higher: 3.1% (2006-2010 5-year est.).
Housing: Homeownership rate: 82.4% (2010); Median home value: $219,500 (2006-2010 5-year est.); Median contract rent: $582 per month (2006-2010 5-year est.); Median year structure built: 1970 (2006-2010 5-year est.).
Transportation: Commute to work: 89.2% car, 0.0% public transportation, 0.0% walk, 5.2% work from home (2006-2010 5-year est.); Travel time to work: 44.5% less than 15 minutes, 33.5% 15 to 30 minutes, 22.1% 30 to 45 minutes, 0.0% 45 to 60 minutes, 0.0% 60 minutes or more (2006-2010 5-year est.)

BOYERTOWN (borough).
Covers a land area of 0.778 square miles and a water area of 0 square miles. Located at 40.33° N. Lat; 75.64° W. Long. Elevation is 420 feet.
History: Boyertown Area Historical Society; Boyertown Museum of Historic Vehicles. Founded c.1835, incorporated 1866.
Population: 3,759 (1990); 3,940 (2000); 4,055 (2010); Density: 5,209.6 persons per square mile (2010); Race: 97.5% White, 0.5% Black, 0.6% Asian, 0.0% American Indian/Alaska Native, 0.0% Native Hawaiian/Other Pacific Islander, 1.4% Other, 1.1% Hispanic of any race (2010); Average household size: 2.10 (2010); Median age: 41.7 (2010); Males per 100 females: 90.0 (2010); Marriage status: 22.3% never married, 50.2% now married, 13.7% widowed, 13.8% divorced (2006-2010 5-year est.); Foreign born: 0.6% (2006-2010 5-year est.); Ancestry (includes multiple ancestries): 45.7% German, 18.9% Irish, 9.7% Italian, 8.3% Pennsylvania German, 6.1% American (2006-2010 5-year est.).
Economy: Single-family building permits issued: 0 (2011); Multi-family building permits issued: 0 (2011); Employment by occupation: 4.6% management, 1.7% professional, 11.6% services, 16.4% sales, 1.7% farming, 11.1% construction, 12.8% production (2006-2010 5-year est.).
Income: Per capita income: $23,835 (2006-2010 5-year est.); Median household income: $39,647 (2006-2010 5-year est.); Average household income: $50,558 (2006-2010 5-year est.); Percent of households with income of $100,000 or more: 7.7% (2006-2010 5-year est.); Poverty rate: 7.2% (2006-2010 5-year est.).
Education: Percent of population age 25 and over with: High school diploma (including GED) or higher: 83.7% (2006-2010 5-year est.); Bachelor's degree or higher: 12.3% (2006-2010 5-year est.); Master's degree or higher: 5.3% (2006-2010 5-year est.).
School District(s)
Boyertown Area SD (KG-12)
    2010-11 Enrollment: 7,099 . . . . (610) 367-6031

Housing: Homeownership rate: 48.6% (2010); Median home value: $157,700 (2006-2010 5-year est.); Median contract rent: $626 per month (2006-2010 5-year est.); Median year structure built: 1944 (2006-2010 5-year est.).
Newspapers: Boyertown Area Times (Community news; Circulation 6,500); The Southern Berks News (Community news; Circulation 5,200)
Transportation: Commute to work: 93.6% car, 0.0% public transportation, 5.5% walk, 0.6% work from home (2006-2010 5-year est.); Travel time to work: 41.2% less than 15 minutes, 33.9% 15 to 30 minutes, 11.5% 30 to 45 minutes, 7.0% 45 to 60 minutes, 6.4% 60 minutes or more (2006-2010 5-year est.)
Additional Information Contacts
Borough of Boyertown . . . . (610) 369-3028
    http://www.boyertownborough.org
TriCounty Area Chamber of Commerce . . . . (610) 326-2900
    http://tricountyareachamber.com

BRECKNOCK (township).
Covers a land area of 17.671 square miles and a water area of 0.086 square miles. Located at 40.23° N. Lat; 75.97° W. Long.
Population: 3,770 (1990); 4,459 (2000); 4,585 (2010); Density: 259.5 persons per square mile (2010); Race: 95.6% White, 1.2% Black, 1.7% Asian, 0.1% American Indian/Alaska Native, 0.0% Native Hawaiian/Other Pacific Islander, 1.4% Other, 2.1% Hispanic of any race (2010); Average household size: 2.76 (2010); Median age: 44.4 (2010); Males per 100 females: 106.9 (2010); Marriage status: 19.7% never married, 67.2% now married, 2.9% widowed, 10.2% divorced (2006-2010 5-year est.); Foreign born: 3.4% (2006-2010 5-year est.); Ancestry (includes multiple ancestries): 53.8% German, 14.0% Irish, 11.4% Polish, 9.9% Italian, 5.4% English (2006-2010 5-year est.).
Economy: Single-family building permits issued: 1 (2011); Multi-family building permits issued: 0 (2011); Employment by occupation: 11.6% management, 7.7% professional, 7.6% services, 13.5% sales, 4.1% farming, 12.8% construction, 10.6% production (2006-2010 5-year est.).
Income: Per capita income: $33,774 (2006-2010 5-year est.); Median household income: $88,622 (2006-2010 5-year est.); Average household income: $95,918 (2006-2010 5-year est.); Percent of households with income of $100,000 or more: 41.1% (2006-2010 5-year est.); Poverty rate: 1.3% (2006-2010 5-year est.).
Education: Percent of population age 25 and over with: High school diploma (including GED) or higher: 91.7% (2006-2010 5-year est.); Bachelor's degree or higher: 27.9% (2006-2010 5-year est.); Master's degree or higher: 6.4% (2006-2010 5-year est.).
Housing: Homeownership rate: 91.4% (2010); Median home value: $264,600 (2006-2010 5-year est.); Median contract rent: $488 per month (2006-2010 5-year est.); Median year structure built: 1982 (2006-2010 5-year est.).
Safety: Violent crime rate: 0.0 per 10,000 population; Property crime rate: 56.5 per 10,000 population (2011).
Transportation: Commute to work: 92.5% car, 2.1% public transportation, 0.0% walk, 4.6% work from home (2006-2010 5-year est.); Travel time to work: 18.3% less than 15 minutes, 52.0% 15 to 30 minutes, 16.8% 30 to 45 minutes, 7.0% 45 to 60 minutes, 5.8% 60 minutes or more (2006-2010 5-year est.)
Additional Information Contacts
Brecknock Township . . . . (717) 445-6683
    http://www.co.berks.pa.us/Muni/Brecknock/Pages/default.aspx
Greater Reading Chamber of Commerce & Industry . . . . . (610) 376-6766
    http://www.greaterreadingchamber.org

CAERNARVON (township).
Covers a land area of 8.885 square miles and a water area of 0.023 square miles. Located at 40.16° N. Lat; 75.88° W. Long.
Population: 1,924 (1990); 2,312 (2000); 4,006 (2010); Density: 450.9 persons per square mile (2010); Race: 93.8% White, 1.6% Black, 2.3% Asian, 0.0% American Indian/Alaska Native, 0.0% Native Hawaiian/Other Pacific Islander, 2.3% Other, 1.6% Hispanic of any race (2010); Average household size: 2.78 (2010); Median age: 36.7 (2010); Males per 100 females: 96.5 (2010); Marriage status: 22.3% never married, 61.6% now married, 6.9% widowed, 9.1% divorced (2006-2010 5-year est.); Foreign born: 3.8% (2006-2010 5-year est.); Ancestry (includes multiple ancestries): 39.2% German, 24.7% Irish, 15.5% Italian, 11.9% English, 7.2% Polish (2006-2010 5-year est.).
Economy: Single-family building permits issued: 2 (2011); Multi-family building permits issued: 0 (2011); Employment by occupation: 17.2%

management, 9.7% professional, 7.7% services, 17.3% sales, 3.1% farming, 10.4% construction, 7.5% production (2006-2010 5-year est.).

Income: Per capita income: $31,767 (2006-2010 5-year est.); Median household income: $71,715 (2006-2010 5-year est.); Average household income: $83,825 (2006-2010 5-year est.); Percent of households with income of $100,000 or more: 31.5% (2006-2010 5-year est.); Poverty rate: 2.9% (2006-2010 5-year est.).

Education: Percent of population age 25 and over with: High school diploma (including GED) or higher: 95.8% (2006-2010 5-year est.); Bachelor's degree or higher: 34.5% (2006-2010 5-year est.); Master's degree or higher: 8.0% (2006-2010 5-year est.).

Housing: Homeownership rate: 83.7% (2010); Median home value: $246,500 (2006-2010 5-year est.); Median contract rent: $674 per month (2006-2010 5-year est.); Median year structure built: 1984 (2006-2010 5-year est.).

Safety: Violent crime rate: 22.4 per 10,000 population; Property crime rate: 246.3 per 10,000 population (2011).

Transportation: Commute to work: 93.0% car, 1.3% public transportation, 1.0% walk, 4.5% work from home (2006-2010 5-year est.); Travel time to work: 22.7% less than 15 minutes, 24.9% 15 to 30 minutes, 25.5% 30 to 45 minutes, 15.9% 45 to 60 minutes, 11.1% 60 minutes or more (2006-2010 5-year est.)

Additional Information Contacts

Caernarvon Township . . . . (610) 286-1010
    http://www.caernarvon.org
Greater Reading Chamber of Commerce & Industry . . . . . (610) 376-6766
    http://www.greaterreadingchamber.org

CENTERPORT (borough). Covers a land area of 0.189 square miles and a water area of 0.002 square miles. Located at 40.49° N. Lat; 76.00° W. Long. Elevation is 331 feet.

Population: 284 (1990); 327 (2000); 387 (2010); Density: 2,049.1 persons per square mile (2010); Race: 96.4% White, 0.5% Black, 0.0% Asian, 0.5% American Indian/Alaska Native, 0.0% Native Hawaiian/Other Pacific Islander, 2.6% Other, 3.6% Hispanic of any race (2010); Average household size: 2.60 (2010); Median age: 37.9 (2010); Males per 100 females: 96.4 (2010); Marriage status: 31.7% never married, 57.8% now married, 1.0% widowed, 9.6% divorced (2006-2010 5-year est.); Foreign born: 0.0% (2006-2010 5-year est.); Ancestry (includes multiple ancestries): 46.5% German, 19.3% Italian, 18.7% Irish, 14.7% Polish, 12.5% Pennsylvania German (2006-2010 5-year est.).

Economy: Employment by occupation: 3.0% management, 1.0% professional, 9.4% services, 21.5% sales, 1.3% farming, 14.1% construction, 6.4% production (2006-2010 5-year est.).

Income: Per capita income: $22,301 (2006-2010 5-year est.); Median household income: $49,107 (2006-2010 5-year est.); Average household income: $63,489 (2006-2010 5-year est.); Percent of households with income of $100,000 or more: 16.4% (2006-2010 5-year est.); Poverty rate: 15.3% (2006-2010 5-year est.).

Education: Percent of population age 25 and over with: High school diploma (including GED) or higher: 84.3% (2006-2010 5-year est.); Bachelor's degree or higher: 11.8% (2006-2010 5-year est.); Master's degree or higher: 5.3% (2006-2010 5-year est.).

Housing: Homeownership rate: 61.0% (2010); Median home value: $173,400 (2006-2010 5-year est.); Median contract rent: $584 per month (2006-2010 5-year est.); Median year structure built: before 1940 (2006-2010 5-year est.).

Transportation: Commute to work: 98.0% car, 0.7% public transportation, 0.0% walk, 1.3% work from home (2006-2010 5-year est.); Travel time to work: 15.0% less than 15 minutes, 37.9% 15 to 30 minutes, 29.0% 30 to 45 minutes, 2.4% 45 to 60 minutes, 15.7% 60 minutes or more (2006-2010 5-year est.)

CENTRE (township). Covers a land area of 21.361 square miles and a water area of 0.184 square miles. Located at 40.48° N. Lat; 76.02° W. Long.

Population: 3,154 (1990); 3,631 (2000); 4,036 (2010); Density: 188.9 persons per square mile (2010); Race: 97.4% White, 0.8% Black, 0.5% Asian, 0.1% American Indian/Alaska Native, 0.0% Native Hawaiian/Other Pacific Islander, 1.2% Other, 2.5% Hispanic of any race (2010); Average household size: 2.67 (2010); Median age: 43.0 (2010); Males per 100 females: 105.9 (2010); Marriage status: 18.6% never married, 68.3% now married, 5.6% widowed, 7.5% divorced (2006-2010 5-year est.); Foreign born: 1.9% (2006-2010 5-year est.); Ancestry (includes multiple

ancestries): 50.4% German, 14.0% Irish, 9.8% Italian, 7.4% Polish, 6.6% Pennsylvania German (2006-2010 5-year est.).

Economy: Single-family building permits issued: 2 (2011); Multi-family building permits issued: 0 (2011); Employment by occupation: 6.7% management, 3.8% professional, 8.5% services, 16.4% sales, 5.4% farming, 8.5% construction, 6.3% production (2006-2010 5-year est.).

Income: Per capita income: $27,525 (2006-2010 5-year est.); Median household income: $68,206 (2006-2010 5-year est.); Average household income: $75,129 (2006-2010 5-year est.); Percent of households with income of $100,000 or more: 27.3% (2006-2010 5-year est.); Poverty rate: 7.9% (2006-2010 5-year est.).

Education: Percent of population age 25 and over with: High school diploma (including GED) or higher: 83.4% (2006-2010 5-year est.); Bachelor's degree or higher: 14.9% (2006-2010 5-year est.); Master's degree or higher: 3.5% (2006-2010 5-year est.).

Housing: Homeownership rate: 90.5% (2010); Median home value: $173,200 (2006-2010 5-year est.); Median contract rent: $665 per month (2006-2010 5-year est.); Median year structure built: 1983 (2006-2010 5-year est.).

Transportation: Commute to work: 93.8% car, 0.0% public transportation, 0.3% walk, 4.1% work from home (2006-2010 5-year est.); Travel time to work: 12.0% less than 15 minutes, 54.7% 15 to 30 minutes, 22.5% 30 to 45 minutes, 1.8% 45 to 60 minutes, 9.1% 60 minutes or more (2006-2010 5-year est.)

Additional Information Contacts

Greater Reading Chamber of Commerce & Industry . . . . . (610) 376-6766
    http://www.greaterreadingchamber.org

COLEBROOKDALE (township). Covers a land area of 8.437 square miles and a water area of 0.024 square miles. Located at 40.34° N. Lat; 75.65° W. Long. Elevation is 318 feet.

Population: 5,469 (1990); 5,270 (2000); 5,078 (2010); Density: 601.8 persons per square mile (2010); Race: 97.8% White, 0.1% Black, 0.5% Asian, 0.2% American Indian/Alaska Native, 0.0% Native Hawaiian/Other Pacific Islander, 1.4% Other, 1.4% Hispanic of any race (2010); Average household size: 2.54 (2010); Median age: 44.0 (2010); Males per 100 females: 95.5 (2010); Marriage status: 27.0% never married, 60.2% now married, 6.0% widowed, 6.7% divorced (2006-2010 5-year est.); Foreign born: 0.4% (2006-2010 5-year est.); Ancestry (includes multiple ancestries): 44.0% German, 15.4% Irish, 11.2% Italian, 7.9% Polish, 7.6% Pennsylvania German (2006-2010 5-year est.).

Economy: Single-family building permits issued: 1 (2011); Multi-family building permits issued: 0 (2011); Employment by occupation: 12.7% management, 4.1% professional, 9.4% services, 19.8% sales, 3.3% farming, 10.4% construction, 8.8% production (2006-2010 5-year est.).

Income: Per capita income: $28,666 (2006-2010 5-year est.); Median household income: $64,905 (2006-2010 5-year est.); Average household income: $74,730 (2006-2010 5-year est.); Percent of households with income of $100,000 or more: 25.6% (2006-2010 5-year est.); Poverty rate: 0.7% (2006-2010 5-year est.).

Education: Percent of population age 25 and over with: High school diploma (including GED) or higher: 83.6% (2006-2010 5-year est.); Bachelor's degree or higher: 15.0% (2006-2010 5-year est.); Master's degree or higher: 3.3% (2006-2010 5-year est.).

Housing: Homeownership rate: 85.6% (2010); Median home value: $196,500 (2006-2010 5-year est.); Median contract rent: $684 per month (2006-2010 5-year est.); Median year structure built: 1972 (2006-2010 5-year est.).

Safety: Violent crime rate: 8.3 per 10,000 population; Property crime rate: 160.6 per 10,000 population (2011).

Transportation: Commute to work: 95.4% car, 0.3% public transportation, 0.5% walk, 3.3% work from home (2006-2010 5-year est.); Travel time to work: 33.9% less than 15 minutes, 25.1% 15 to 30 minutes, 24.3% 30 to 45 minutes, 5.7% 45 to 60 minutes, 11.0% 60 minutes or more (2006-2010 5-year est.)

Additional Information Contacts

Colebrookdale Township . . . . (610) 369-1362
    http://colebrookdale.org
TriCounty Area Chamber of Commerce . . . . (610) 326-2900
    http://tricountyareachamber.com

COLONY PARK (CDP). Covers a land area of 0.382 square miles and a water area of 0 square miles. Located at 40.35° N. Lat; 75.98° W. Long.

Population: n/a (1990); n/a (2000); 1,076 (2010); Density: 2,817.9 persons per square mile (2010); Race: 82.4% White, 4.1% Black, 10.6% Asian, 0.0% American Indian/Alaska Native, 0.0% Native Hawaiian/Other Pacific Islander, 2.9% Other, 5.4% Hispanic of any race (2010); Average household size: 2.75 (2010); Median age: 45.6 (2010); Males per 100 females: 98.9 (2010); Marriage status: 14.1% never married, 79.6% now married, 3.8% widowed, 2.5% divorced (2006-2010 5-year est.); Foreign born: 10.4% (2006-2010 5-year est.); Ancestry (includes multiple ancestries): 38.7% German, 25.9% Italian, 10.5% Polish, 8.7% Irish, 5.9% English (2006-2010 5-year est.).

Economy: Employment by occupation: 18.5% management, 11.4% professional, 1.8% services, 21.1% sales, 1.7% farming, 0.0% construction, 0.0% production (2006-2010 5-year est.).

Income: Per capita income: $35,883 (2006-2010 5-year est.); Median household income: $77,313 (2006-2010 5-year est.); Average household income: $95,452 (2006-2010 5-year est.); Percent of households with income of $100,000 or more: 40.1% (2006-2010 5-year est.); Poverty rate: 0.0% (2006-2010 5-year est.).

Education: Percent of population age 25 and over with: High school diploma (including GED) or higher: 95.7% (2006-2010 5-year est.); Bachelor's degree or higher: 37.8% (2006-2010 5-year est.); Master's degree or higher: 10.2% (2006-2010 5-year est.).

Housing: Homeownership rate: 95.7% (2010); Median home value: $217,400 (2006-2010 5-year est.); Median contract rent: n/a per month (2006-2010 5-year est.); Median year structure built: 1976 (2006-2010 5-year est.).

Transportation: Commute to work: 86.4% car, 0.0% public transportation, 0.0% walk, 13.6% work from home (2006-2010 5-year est.); Travel time to work: 46.5% less than 15 minutes, 37.9% 15 to 30 minutes, 6.5% 30 to 45 minutes, 4.3% 45 to 60 minutes, 4.8% 60 minutes or more (2006-2010 5-year est.)

CUMRU (township). Covers a land area of 20.901 square miles and a water area of 0.282 square miles. Located at 40.27° N. Lat; 75.96° W. Long.

Population: 13,339 (1990); 13,816 (2000); 15,147 (2010); Density: 724.7 persons per square mile (2010); Race: 90.8% White, 3.4% Black, 1.8% Asian, 0.1% American Indian/Alaska Native, 0.0% Native Hawaiian/Other Pacific Islander, 3.9% Other, 6.5% Hispanic of any race (2010); Average household size: 2.25 (2010); Median age: 45.5 (2010); Males per 100 females: 93.0 (2010); Marriage status: 23.6% never married, 55.3% now married, 9.3% widowed, 11.9% divorced (2006-2010 5-year est.); Foreign born: 5.6% (2006-2010 5-year est.); Ancestry (includes multiple ancestries): 43.6% German, 13.4% Irish, 12.4% Italian, 11.0% Polish, 7.6% English (2006-2010 5-year est.).

Economy: Single-family building permits issued: 2 (2011); Multi-family building permits issued: 0 (2011); Employment by occupation: 12.4% management, 5.4% professional, 9.5% services, 15.2% sales, 2.7% farming, 8.3% construction, 6.6% production (2006-2010 5-year est.).

Income: Per capita income: $32,662 (2006-2010 5-year est.); Median household income: $60,404 (2006-2010 5-year est.); Average household income: $74,225 (2006-2010 5-year est.); Percent of households with income of $100,000 or more: 23.1% (2006-2010 5-year est.); Poverty rate: 5.5% (2006-2010 5-year est.).

Education: Percent of population age 25 and over with: High school diploma (including GED) or higher: 86.8% (2006-2010 5-year est.); Bachelor's degree or higher: 31.6% (2006-2010 5-year est.); Master's degree or higher: 11.2% (2006-2010 5-year est.).

Housing: Homeownership rate: 68.2% (2010); Median home value: $179,600 (2006-2010 5-year est.); Median contract rent: $780 per month (2006-2010 5-year est.); Median year structure built: 1974 (2006-2010 5-year est.).

Safety: Violent crime rate: 6.6 per 10,000 population; Property crime rate: 235.6 per 10,000 population (2011).

Transportation: Commute to work: 94.0% car, 0.7% public transportation, 1.2% walk, 3.4% work from home (2006-2010 5-year est.); Travel time to work: 35.3% less than 15 minutes, 41.4% 15 to 30 minutes, 10.8% 30 to 45 minutes, 5.6% 45 to 60 minutes, 7.0% 60 minutes or more (2006-2010 5-year est.)

Additional Information Contacts

Cumru Township . . . . (610) 777-1343
  http://www.cumrutownship.com

Greater Reading Chamber of Commerce & Industry . . . . . (610) 376-6766
  http://www.greaterreadingchamber.org

DAUBERVILLE (CDP). Covers a land area of 2.095 square miles and a water area of 0.017 square miles. Located at 40.46° N. Lat; 75.99° W. Long. Elevation is 331 feet.

Population: n/a (1990); n/a (2000); 848 (2010); Density: 404.8 persons per square mile (2010); Race: 97.4% White, 1.7% Black, 0.0% Asian, 0.0% American Indian/Alaska Native, 0.0% Native Hawaiian/Other Pacific Islander, 0.9% Other, 2.4% Hispanic of any race (2010); Average household size: 2.71 (2010); Median age: 42.9 (2010); Males per 100 females: 109.4 (2010); Marriage status: 19.9% never married, 77.8% now married, 0.0% widowed, 2.3% divorced (2006-2010 5-year est.); Foreign born: 0.0% (2006-2010 5-year est.); Ancestry (includes multiple ancestries): 63.1% German, 19.3% Irish, 16.6% Italian, 8.7% Polish, 7.3% American (2006-2010 5-year est.).

Economy: Employment by occupation: 14.7% management, 0.0% professional, 11.5% services, 11.7% sales, 7.6% farming, 0.0% construction, 0.0% production (2006-2010 5-year est.).

Income: Per capita income: $22,645 (2006-2010 5-year est.); Median household income: $62,083 (2006-2010 5-year est.); Average household income: $71,796 (2006-2010 5-year est.); Percent of households with income of $100,000 or more: 17.3% (2006-2010 5-year est.); Poverty rate: 0.0% (2006-2010 5-year est.).

Education: Percent of population age 25 and over with: High school diploma (including GED) or higher: 79.9% (2006-2010 5-year est.); Bachelor's degree or higher: 13.3% (2006-2010 5-year est.); Master's degree or higher: 2.6% (2006-2010 5-year est.).

Housing: Homeownership rate: 87.6% (2010); Median home value: $153,400 (2006-2010 5-year est.); Median contract rent: n/a per month (2006-2010 5-year est.); Median year structure built: 1991 (2006-2010 5-year est.).

Transportation: Commute to work: 93.7% car, 0.0% public transportation, 0.0% walk, 3.3% work from home (2006-2010 5-year est.); Travel time to work: 19.7% less than 15 minutes, 59.1% 15 to 30 minutes, 21.2% 30 to 45 minutes, 0.0% 45 to 60 minutes, 0.0% 60 minutes or more (2006-2010 5-year est.)

DISTRICT (township). Covers a land area of 11.510 square miles and a water area of 0.030 square miles. Located at 40.43° N. Lat; 75.66° W. Long.

Population: 1,211 (1990); 1,449 (2000); 1,337 (2010); Density: 116.2 persons per square mile (2010); Race: 97.8% White, 0.6% Black, 0.1% Asian, 0.5% American Indian/Alaska Native, 0.0% Native Hawaiian/Other Pacific Islander, 1.0% Other, 0.5% Hispanic of any race (2010); Average household size: 2.49 (2010); Median age: 46.7 (2010); Males per 100 females: 106.0 (2010); Marriage status: 25.9% never married, 58.0% now married, 6.9% widowed, 9.1% divorced (2006-2010 5-year est.); Foreign born: 0.9% (2006-2010 5-year est.); Ancestry (includes multiple ancestries): 52.0% German, 10.3% English, 10.3% Irish, 9.8% Italian, 6.0% Pennsylvania German (2006-2010 5-year est.).

Economy: Single-family building permits issued: 3 (2011); Multi-family building permits issued: 0 (2011); Employment by occupation: 9.3% management, 4.0% professional, 9.2% services, 19.1% sales, 4.3% farming, 10.6% construction, 11.7% production (2006-2010 5-year est.).

Income: Per capita income: $27,075 (2006-2010 5-year est.); Median household income: $54,615 (2006-2010 5-year est.); Average household income: $69,741 (2006-2010 5-year est.); Percent of households with income of $100,000 or more: 19.1% (2006-2010 5-year est.); Poverty rate: 6.7% (2006-2010 5-year est.).

Education: Percent of population age 25 and over with: High school diploma (including GED) or higher: 84.3% (2006-2010 5-year est.); Bachelor's degree or higher: 17.8% (2006-2010 5-year est.); Master's degree or higher: 5.2% (2006-2010 5-year est.).

Housing: Homeownership rate: 86.0% (2010); Median home value: $247,400 (2006-2010 5-year est.); Median contract rent: $574 per month (2006-2010 5-year est.); Median year structure built: 1977 (2006-2010 5-year est.).

Transportation: Commute to work: 94.3% car, 0.4% public transportation, 0.0% walk, 4.8% work from home (2006-2010 5-year est.); Travel time to work: 10.3% less than 15 minutes, 51.4% 15 to 30 minutes, 21.1% 30 to 45 minutes, 7.6% 45 to 60 minutes, 9.7% 60 minutes or more (2006-2010 5-year est.)

Northeast Berks Chamber of Commerce . . . . (610) 683-8860
  http://www.northeastberkschamber.com

DOUGLASS (township). Covers a land area of 12.536 square miles and a water area of 0.114 square miles. Located at 40.29° N. Lat; 75.68° W. Long.
Population: 3,570 (1990); 3,327 (2000); 3,306 (2010); Density: 263.7 persons per square mile (2010); Race: 93.4% White, 4.9% Black, 0.4% Asian, 0.2% American Indian/Alaska Native, 0.0% Native Hawaiian/Other Pacific Islander, 1.1% Other, 1.1% Hispanic of any race (2010); Average household size: 2.46 (2010); Median age: 47.7 (2010); Males per 100 females: 103.9 (2010); Marriage status: 22.7% never married, 59.8% now married, 6.3% widowed, 11.2% divorced (2006-2010 5-year est.); Foreign born: 1.4% (2006-2010 5-year est.); Ancestry (includes multiple ancestries): 37.1% German, 13.5% English, 12.3% Irish, 11.1% Pennsylvania German, 6.9% Italian (2006-2010 5-year est.).
Economy: Single-family building permits issued: 8 (2011); Multi-family building permits issued: 0 (2011); Employment by occupation: 11.3% management, 5.3% professional, 5.2% services, 17.7% sales, 3.7% farming, 11.8% construction, 6.5% production (2006-2010 5-year est.).
Income: Per capita income: $27,967 (2006-2010 5-year est.); Median household income: $64,357 (2006-2010 5-year est.); Average household income: $74,604 (2006-2010 5-year est.); Percent of households with income of $100,000 or more: 18.2% (2006-2010 5-year est.); Poverty rate: 1.8% (2006-2010 5-year est.).
Education: Percent of population age 25 and over with: High school diploma (including GED) or higher: 83.6% (2006-2010 5-year est.); Bachelor's degree or higher: 22.9% (2006-2010 5-year est.); Master's degree or higher: 3.2% (2006-2010 5-year est.).
Housing: Homeownership rate: 85.3% (2010); Median home value: $219,100 (2006-2010 5-year est.); Median contract rent: $684 per month (2006-2010 5-year est.); Median year structure built: 1964 (2006-2010 5-year est.).
Safety: Violent crime rate: 24.1 per 10,000 population; Property crime rate: 111.5 per 10,000 population (2011).
Transportation: Commute to work: 93.8% car, 1.0% public transportation, 1.6% walk, 2.4% work from home (2006-2010 5-year est.); Travel time to work: 36.6% less than 15 minutes, 29.8% 15 to 30 minutes, 12.1% 30 to 45 minutes, 8.9% 45 to 60 minutes, 12.6% 60 minutes or more (2006-2010 5-year est.)

TriCounty Area Chamber of Commerce . . . . (610) 326-2900
  http://tricountyareachamber.com

DOUGLASSVILLE (CDP). Covers a land area of 0.648 square miles and a water area of 0.052 square miles. Located at 40.26° N. Lat; 75.72° W. Long. Elevation is 203 feet.
Population: n/a (1990); n/a (2000); 448 (2010); Density: 691.6 persons per square mile (2010); Race: 93.1% White, 1.3% Black, 2.0% Asian, 0.0% American Indian/Alaska Native, 0.0% Native Hawaiian/Other Pacific Islander, 3.6% Other, 5.1% Hispanic of any race (2010); Average household size: 1.81 (2010); Median age: 67.5 (2010); Males per 100 females: 77.8 (2010); Marriage status: 7.5% never married, 65.9% now married, 26.6% widowed, 0.0% divorced (2006-2010 5-year est.); Foreign born: 3.7% (2006-2010 5-year est.); Ancestry (includes multiple ancestries): 26.6% German, 24.5% Italian, 11.6% Welsh, 11.6% Polish, 6.6% Irish (2006-2010 5-year est.).
Economy: Employment by occupation: 0.0% management, 0.0% professional, 0.0% services, 23.4% sales, 0.0% farming, 18.8% construction, 0.0% production (2006-2010 5-year est.).
Income: Per capita income: $47,725 (2006-2010 5-year est.); Median household income: $39,531 (2006-2010 5-year est.); Average household income: $86,283 (2006-2010 5-year est.); Percent of households with income of $100,000 or more: 18.7% (2006-2010 5-year est.); Poverty rate: 4.1% (2006-2010 5-year est.).
Education: Percent of population age 25 and over with: High school diploma (including GED) or higher: 74.7% (2006-2010 5-year est.); Bachelor's degree or higher: 30.6% (2006-2010 5-year est.); Master's degree or higher: 4.8% (2006-2010 5-year est.).
School District(s)
Daniel Boone Area SD (KG-12)
    2010-11 Enrollment: 3,928 . . . . (610) 582-6140
Housing: Homeownership rate: 19.0% (2010); Median home value: $208,000 (2006-2010 5-year est.); Median contract rent: $1,565 per month

(2006-2010 5-year est.); Median year structure built: 2005 (2006-2010 5-year est.).
Transportation: Commute to work: 100.0% car, 0.0% public transportation, 0.0% walk, 0.0% work from home (2006-2010 5-year est.); Travel time to work: 23.4% less than 15 minutes, 57.8% 15 to 30 minutes, 0.0% 30 to 45 minutes, 0.0% 45 to 60 minutes, 18.8% 60 minutes or more (2006-2010 5-year est.)

DRYVILLE (CDP). Covers a land area of 1.390 square miles and a water area of 0.004 square miles. Located at 40.46° N. Lat; 75.75° W. Long. Elevation is 745 feet.
Population: n/a (1990); n/a (2000); 398 (2010); Density: 286.2 persons per square mile (2010); Race: 97.7% White, 0.0% Black, 0.0% Asian, 0.3% American Indian/Alaska Native, 0.0% Native Hawaiian/Other Pacific Islander, 2.0% Other, 2.5% Hispanic of any race (2010); Average household size: 2.64 (2010); Median age: 43.5 (2010); Males per 100 females: 105.2 (2010); Marriage status: 17.0% never married, 61.0% now married, 7.6% widowed, 14.4% divorced (2006-2010 5-year est.); Foreign born: 0.0% (2006-2010 5-year est.); Ancestry (includes multiple ancestries): 55.8% German, 18.6% Irish, 13.0% American, 10.7% Polish, 5.9% Austrian (2006-2010 5-year est.).
Economy: Employment by occupation: 0.0% management, 3.4% professional, 9.7% services, 17.0% sales, 0.0% farming, 8.9% construction, 12.3% production (2006-2010 5-year est.).
Income: Per capita income: $24,055 (2006-2010 5-year est.); Median household income: $80,000 (2006-2010 5-year est.); Average household income: $78,931 (2006-2010 5-year est.); Percent of households with income of $100,000 or more: 19.0% (2006-2010 5-year est.); Poverty rate: 1.8% (2006-2010 5-year est.).
Education: Percent of population age 25 and over with: High school diploma (including GED) or higher: 90.7% (2006-2010 5-year est.); Bachelor's degree or higher: 16.8% (2006-2010 5-year est.); Master's degree or higher: 13.6% (2006-2010 5-year est.).
Housing: Homeownership rate: 84.8% (2010); Median home value: $190,200 (2006-2010 5-year est.); Median contract rent: n/a per month (2006-2010 5-year est.); Median year structure built: 1980 (2006-2010 5-year est.).
Transportation: Commute to work: 97.2% car, 2.8% public transportation, 0.0% walk, 0.0% work from home (2006-2010 5-year est.); Travel time to work: 33.6% less than 15 minutes, 35.3% 15 to 30 minutes, 20.4% 30 to 45 minutes, 7.3% 45 to 60 minutes, 3.4% 60 minutes or more (2006-2010 5-year est.)

EARL (township). Covers a land area of 13.741 square miles and a water area of 0.081 square miles. Located at 40.35° N. Lat; 75.70° W. Long.
Population: 3,016 (1990); 3,050 (2000); 3,195 (2010); Density: 232.5 persons per square mile (2010); Race: 97.9% White, 0.7% Black, 0.2% Asian, 0.2% American Indian/Alaska Native, 0.0% Native Hawaiian/Other Pacific Islander, 1.0% Other, 1.1% Hispanic of any race (2010); Average household size: 2.60 (2010); Median age: 43.9 (2010); Males per 100 females: 105.6 (2010); Marriage status: 21.0% never married, 63.7% now married, 6.7% widowed, 8.5% divorced (2006-2010 5-year est.); Foreign born: 1.5% (2006-2010 5-year est.); Ancestry (includes multiple ancestries): 43.3% German, 20.8% Irish, 10.7% English, 10.0% Pennsylvania German, 9.3% Italian (2006-2010 5-year est.).
Economy: Single-family building permits issued: 3 (2011); Multi-family building permits issued: 0 (2011); Employment by occupation: 8.8% management, 4.9% professional, 7.4% services, 7.6% sales, 5.5% farming, 23.9% construction, 13.5% production (2006-2010 5-year est.).
Income: Per capita income: $34,509 (2006-2010 5-year est.); Median household income: $60,192 (2006-2010 5-year est.); Average household income: $83,613 (2006-2010 5-year est.); Percent of households with income of $100,000 or more: 32.4% (2006-2010 5-year est.); Poverty rate: 2.7% (2006-2010 5-year est.).
Education: Percent of population age 25 and over with: High school diploma (including GED) or higher: 83.9% (2006-2010 5-year est.); Bachelor's degree or higher: 29.9% (2006-2010 5-year est.); Master's degree or higher: 10.4% (2006-2010 5-year est.).
Housing: Homeownership rate: 87.7% (2010); Median home value: $220,200 (2006-2010 5-year est.); Median contract rent: $559 per month (2006-2010 5-year est.); Median year structure built: 1973 (2006-2010 5-year est.).
Transportation: Commute to work: 94.2% car, 1.0% public transportation, 0.0% walk, 4.8% work from home (2006-2010 5-year est.); Travel time to

work: 21.0% less than 15 minutes, 34.1% 15 to 30 minutes, 19.3% 30 to 45 minutes, 12.3% 45 to 60 minutes, 13.3% 60 minutes or more (2006-2010 5-year est.)

Additional Information Contacts

TriCounty Area Chamber of Commerce . . . . (610) 326-2900
http://tricountyareachamber.com

EARLVILLE (unincorporated postal area)

Zip Code: 19519

Covers a land area of 0.116 square miles and a water area of 0.004 square miles. Located at 40.32° N. Lat; 75.73° W. Long. Elevation is 259 feet. Population: 101 (2010); Density: 870.4 persons per square mile (2010); Race: 96.0% White, 0.0% Black, 0.0% Asian, 1.0% American Indian/Alaska Native, 0.0% Native Hawaiian/Other Pacific Islander, 3.0% Other, 3.0% Hispanic of any race (2010); Average household size: 2.46 (2010); Median age: 45.3 (2010); Males per 100 females: 102.0 (2010); Homeownership rate: 65.8% (2010)

EDENBURG (CDP).

Covers a land area of 0.580 square miles and a water area of 0.038 square miles. Located at 40.57° N. Lat; 75.96° W. Long.

Population: n/a (1990); n/a (2000); 681 (2010); Density: 1,173.5 persons per square mile (2010); Race: 95.9% White, 1.2% Black, 0.6% Asian, 0.0% American Indian/Alaska Native, 0.0% Native Hawaiian/Other Pacific Islander, 2.3% Other, 1.2% Hispanic of any race (2010); Average household size: 2.49 (2010); Median age: 43.8 (2010); Males per 100 females: 91.3 (2010); Marriage status: 18.9% never married, 63.6% now married, 7.1% widowed, 10.5% divorced (2006-2010 5-year est.); Foreign born: 0.0% (2006-2010 5-year est.); Ancestry (includes multiple ancestries): 39.4% German, 18.2% American, 10.7% Hungarian, 9.6% Pennsylvania German, 9.1% Scottish (2006-2010 5-year est.).

Economy: Employment by occupation: 3.8% management, 4.0% professional, 10.7% services, 20.7% sales, 2.9% farming, 14.9% construction, 11.8% production (2006-2010 5-year est.).

Income: Per capita income: $31,099 (2006-2010 5-year est.); Median household income: $69,821 (2006-2010 5-year est.); Average household income: $78,348 (2006-2010 5-year est.); Percent of households with income of $100,000 or more: 28.3% (2006-2010 5-year est.); Poverty rate: 3.9% (2006-2010 5-year est.).

Education: Percent of population age 25 and over with: High school diploma (including GED) or higher: 82.2% (2006-2010 5-year est.); Bachelor's degree or higher: 24.7% (2006-2010 5-year est.); Master's degree or higher: 5.3% (2006-2010 5-year est.).

Housing: Homeownership rate: 89.1% (2010); Median home value: $165,000 (2006-2010 5-year est.); Median contract rent: $620 per month (2006-2010 5-year est.); Median year structure built: 1967 (2006-2010 5-year est.).

Transportation: Commute to work: 95.3% car, 0.0% public transportation, 0.0% walk, 4.7% work from home (2006-2010 5-year est.); Travel time to work: 31.2% less than 15 minutes, 31.5% 15 to 30 minutes, 21.9% 30 to 45 minutes, 9.1% 45 to 60 minutes, 6.3% 60 minutes or more (2006-2010 5-year est.)

EXETER (township).

Covers a land area of 24.232 square miles and a water area of 0.345 square miles. Located at 40.31° N. Lat; 75.84° W. Long.

Population: 17,252 (1990); 21,161 (2000); 25,550 (2010); Density: 1,054.4 persons per square mile (2010); Race: 91.9% White, 3.3% Black, 1.9% Asian, 0.1% American Indian/Alaska Native, 0.0% Native Hawaiian/Other Pacific Islander, 2.8% Other, 3.6% Hispanic of any race (2010); Average household size: 2.61 (2010); Median age: 41.4 (2010); Males per 100 females: 95.0 (2010); Marriage status: 21.7% never married, 63.4% now married, 5.5% widowed, 9.4% divorced (2006-2010 5-year est.); Foreign born: 3.2% (2006-2010 5-year est.); Ancestry (includes multiple ancestries): 40.5% German, 17.5% Irish, 15.1% Italian, 10.0% Polish, 9.3% English (2006-2010 5-year est.).

Economy: Unemployment rate: 6.9% (August 2012); Total civilian labor force: 13,873 (August 2012); Single-family building permits issued: 16 (2011); Multi-family building permits issued: 4 (2011); Employment by occupation: 13.3% management, 5.5% professional, 8.2% services, 18.4% sales, 4.5% farming, 7.8% construction, 5.9% production (2006-2010 5-year est.).

Income: Per capita income: $32,883 (2006-2010 5-year est.); Median household income: $69,093 (2006-2010 5-year est.); Average household income: $83,896 (2006-2010 5-year est.); Percent of households with

income of $100,000 or more: 28.1% (2006-2010 5-year est.); Poverty rate: 4.5% (2006-2010 5-year est.).

Taxes: Total city taxes per capita: $291 (2009); City property taxes per capita: $111 (2009).

Education: Percent of population age 25 and over with: High school diploma (including GED) or higher: 90.8% (2006-2010 5-year est.); Bachelor's degree or higher: 30.5% (2006-2010 5-year est.); Master's degree or higher: 10.0% (2006-2010 5-year est.).

Housing: Homeownership rate: 86.2% (2010); Median home value: $189,900 (2006-2010 5-year est.); Median contract rent: $787 per month (2006-2010 5-year est.); Median year structure built: 1981 (2006-2010 5-year est.).

Safety: Violent crime rate: 5.1 per 10,000 population; Property crime rate: 151.4 per 10,000 population (2011).

Transportation: Commute to work: 94.1% car, 0.9% public transportation, 0.8% walk, 3.6% work from home (2006-2010 5-year est.); Travel time to work: 26.1% less than 15 minutes, 41.1% 15 to 30 minutes, 14.0% 30 to 45 minutes, 8.6% 45 to 60 minutes, 10.2% 60 minutes or more (2006-2010 5-year est.)

Additional Information Contacts

Exeter Township . . . . (610) 779-5660
http://www.co.berks.pa.us/exeter
Greater Reading Chamber of Commerce & Industry . . . . . (610) 376-6766
http://greaterreadingchamber.org

FLEETWOOD (borough).

Covers a land area of 1.030 square miles and a water area of 0.005 square miles. Located at 40.46° N. Lat; 75.82° W. Long. Elevation is 440 feet.

History: Founded 1800, incorporated 1873.

Population: 3,478 (1990); 4,018 (2000); 4,085 (2010); Density: 3,965.5 persons per square mile (2010); Race: 95.8% White, 0.9% Black, 0.8% Asian, 0.1% American Indian/Alaska Native, 0.0% Native Hawaiian/Other Pacific Islander, 2.4% Other, 3.4% Hispanic of any race (2010); Average household size: 2.44 (2010); Median age: 39.9 (2010); Males per 100 females: 95.5 (2010); Marriage status: 26.5% never married, 53.1% now married, 9.4% widowed, 11.0% divorced (2006-2010 5-year est.); Foreign born: 0.3% (2006-2010 5-year est.); Ancestry (includes multiple ancestries): 50.9% German, 12.0% Irish, 10.5% Italian, 7.8% American, 6.1% Pennsylvania German (2006-2010 5-year est.).

Economy: Single-family building permits issued: 0 (2011); Multi-family building permits issued: 0 (2011); Employment by occupation: 6.9% management, 5.3% professional, 11.6% services, 16.7% sales, 4.9% farming, 7.6% construction, 5.1% production (2006-2010 5-year est.).

Income: Per capita income: $28,493 (2006-2010 5-year est.); Median household income: $63,480 (2006-2010 5-year est.); Average household income: $64,919 (2006-2010 5-year est.); Percent of households with income of $100,000 or more: 16.4% (2006-2010 5-year est.); Poverty rate: 4.2% (2006-2010 5-year est.).

Education: Percent of population age 25 and over with: High school diploma (including GED) or higher: 95.3% (2006-2010 5-year est.); Bachelor's degree or higher: 23.6% (2006-2010 5-year est.); Master's degree or higher: 7.7% (2006-2010 5-year est.).

School District(s)

Fleetwood Area SD (KG-12)
2010-11 Enrollment: 2,716 . . . . (610) 944-9598

Housing: Homeownership rate: 76.4% (2010); Median home value: $158,200 (2006-2010 5-year est.); Median contract rent: $598 per month (2006-2010 5-year est.); Median year structure built: 1965 (2006-2010 5-year est.).

Safety: Violent crime rate: 7.3 per 10,000 population; Property crime rate: 195.2 per 10,000 population (2011).

Transportation: Commute to work: 95.0% car, 0.0% public transportation, 1.7% walk, 2.3% work from home (2006-2010 5-year est.); Travel time to work: 37.5% less than 15 minutes, 35.1% 15 to 30 minutes, 18.0% 30 to 45 minutes, 5.4% 45 to 60 minutes, 4.1% 60 minutes or more (2006-2010 5-year est.)

Additional Information Contacts

Northeast Berks Chamber of Commerce . . . . (610) 683-8860
http://www.northeastberkschamber.com

FLYING HILLS (CDP).

Covers a land area of 0.584 square miles and a water area of 0.005 square miles. Located at 40.28° N. Lat; 75.91° W. Long. Elevation is 410 feet.

Population: 1,337 (1990); 1,191 (2000); 2,568 (2010); Density: 4,398.8 persons per square mile (2010); Race: 93.6% White, 2.8% Black, 2.1%

Asian, 0.2% American Indian/Alaska Native, 0.0% Native Hawaiian/Other Pacific Islander, 1.3% Other, 3.7% Hispanic of any race (2010); Average household size: 1.81 (2010); Median age: 46.8 (2010); Males per 100 females: 92.8 (2010); Marriage status: 28.6% never married, 39.9% now married, 12.4% widowed, 19.1% divorced (2006-2010 5-year est.); Foreign born: 8.3% (2006-2010 5-year est.); Ancestry (includes multiple ancestries): 37.8% German, 18.3% Irish, 12.8% Italian, 8.8% English, 5.6% Lithuanian (2006-2010 5-year est.).
Economy: Employment by occupation: 8.1% management, 14.1% professional, 8.7% services, 13.3% sales, 2.4% farming, 3.2% construction, 1.0% production (2006-2010 5-year est.).
Income: Per capita income: $39,181 (2006-2010 5-year est.); Median household income: $54,550 (2006-2010 5-year est.); Average household income: $66,663 (2006-2010 5-year est.); Percent of households with income of $100,000 or more: 14.9% (2006-2010 5-year est.); Poverty rate: 8.3% (2006-2010 5-year est.).
Education: Percent of population age 25 and over with: High school diploma (including GED) or higher: 92.7% (2006-2010 5-year est.); Bachelor's degree or higher: 44.1% (2006-2010 5-year est.); Master's degree or higher: 16.6% (2006-2010 5-year est.).
Housing: Homeownership rate: 47.2% (2010); Median home value: $169,400 (2006-2010 5-year est.); Median contract rent: $799 per month (2006-2010 5-year est.); Median year structure built: 1977 (2006-2010 5-year est.).
Transportation: Commute to work: 94.0% car, 0.7% public transportation, 0.0% walk, 5.3% work from home (2006-2010 5-year est.); Travel time to work: 25.8% less than 15 minutes, 51.2% 15 to 30 minutes, 5.6% 30 to 45 minutes, 11.3% 45 to 60 minutes, 6.1% 60 minutes or more (2006-2010 5-year est.)
Additional Information Contacts
Greater Reading Chamber of Commerce & Industry . . . . . (610) 376-6766
   http://www.greaterreadingchamber.org

FOX CHASE (CDP). Covers a land area of 0.345 square miles and a water area of 0.013 square miles. Located at 40.39° N. Lat; 75.96° W. Long.

Population: n/a (1990); n/a (2000); 1,622 (2010); Density: 4,704.4 persons per square mile (2010); Race: 91.1% White, 3.6% Black, 1.7% Asian, 0.1% American Indian/Alaska Native, 0.1% Native Hawaiian/Other Pacific Islander, 3.4% Other, 5.3% Hispanic of any race (2010); Average household size: 2.79 (2010); Median age: 45.6 (2010); Males per 100 females: 97.3 (2010); Marriage status: 23.6% never married, 67.9% now married, 4.3% widowed, 4.1% divorced (2006-2010 5-year est.); Foreign born: 5.7% (2006-2010 5-year est.); Ancestry (includes multiple ancestries): 43.6% German, 19.2% Italian, 16.4% Irish, 13.0% English, 6.0% Scottish (2006-2010 5-year est.).
Economy: Employment by occupation: 14.1% management, 2.6% professional, 5.5% services, 11.0% sales, 4.4% farming, 8.1% construction, 9.1% production (2006-2010 5-year est.).
Income: Per capita income: $42,308 (2006-2010 5-year est.); Median household income: $83,295 (2006-2010 5-year est.); Average household income: $105,350 (2006-2010 5-year est.); Percent of households with income of $100,000 or more: 31.4% (2006-2010 5-year est.); Poverty rate: 3.1% (2006-2010 5-year est.).
Education: Percent of population age 25 and over with: High school diploma (including GED) or higher: 95.9% (2006-2010 5-year est.); Bachelor's degree or higher: 24.8% (2006-2010 5-year est.); Master's degree or higher: 12.9% (2006-2010 5-year est.).
Housing: Homeownership rate: 98.3% (2010); Median home value: $211,300 (2006-2010 5-year est.); Median contract rent: n/a per month (2006-2010 5-year est.); Median year structure built: 1992 (2006-2010 5-year est.).
Transportation: Commute to work: 95.3% car, 1.4% public transportation, 0.0% walk, 3.3% work from home (2006-2010 5-year est.); Travel time to work: 43.5% less than 15 minutes, 44.3% 15 to 30 minutes, 6.9% 30 to 45 minutes, 1.3% 45 to 60 minutes, 4.0% 60 minutes or more (2006-2010 5-year est.)

FRYSTOWN (CDP). Covers a land area of 1.214 square miles and a water area of 0.011 square miles. Located at 40.46° N. Lat; 76.33° W. Long. Elevation is 469 feet.

Population: n/a (1990); n/a (2000); 380 (2010); Density: 313.1 persons per square mile (2010); Race: 93.4% White, 0.8% Black, 1.6% Asian, 0.0% American Indian/Alaska Native, 0.0% Native Hawaiian/Other Pacific Islander, 4.2% Other, 6.3% Hispanic of any race (2010); Average

household size: 2.90 (2010); Median age: 36.3 (2010); Males per 100 females: 103.2 (2010); Marriage status: 56.8% never married, 35.6% now married, 0.0% widowed, 7.7% divorced (2006-2010 5-year est.); Foreign born: 0.0% (2006-2010 5-year est.); Ancestry (includes multiple ancestries): 86.5% German, 9.8% Irish (2006-2010 5-year est.).
Economy: Employment by occupation: 5.9% management, 0.0% professional, 6.5% services, 22.8% sales, 0.0% farming, 21.9% construction, 15.1% production (2006-2010 5-year est.).
Income: Per capita income: $20,096 (2006-2010 5-year est.); Median household income: $47,981 (2006-2010 5-year est.); Average household income: $68,042 (2006-2010 5-year est.); Percent of households with income of $100,000 or more: 33.8% (2006-2010 5-year est.); Poverty rate: 13.7% (2006-2010 5-year est.).
Education: Percent of population age 25 and over with: High school diploma (including GED) or higher: 72.1% (2006-2010 5-year est.); Bachelor's degree or higher: 5.2% (2006-2010 5-year est.); Master's degree or higher: 5.2% (2006-2010 5-year est.).
Housing: Homeownership rate: 73.3% (2010); Median home value: $166,800 (2006-2010 5-year est.); Median contract rent: n/a per month (2006-2010 5-year est.); Median year structure built: before 1940 (2006-2010 5-year est.).
Transportation: Commute to work: 87.9% car, 0.0% public transportation, 12.1% walk, 0.0% work from home (2006-2010 5-year est.); Travel time to work: 22.8% less than 15 minutes, 44.1% 15 to 30 minutes, 28.1% 30 to 45 minutes, 0.0% 45 to 60 minutes, 5.0% 60 minutes or more (2006-2010 5-year est.)

GEIGERTOWN (unincorporated postal area)
Zip Code: 19523
   Covers a land area of 1.418 square miles and a water area of 0.020 square miles. Located at 40.20° N. Lat; 75.85° W. Long. Population: 250 (2010); Density: 176.3 persons per square mile (2010); Race: 96.4% White, 1.6% Black, 0.0% Asian, 0.0% American Indian/Alaska Native, 0.0% Native Hawaiian/Other Pacific Islander, 2.0% Other, 0.0% Hispanic of any race (2010); Average household size: 2.60 (2010); Median age: 37.0 (2010); Males per 100 females: 98.4 (2010); Homeownership rate: 67.7% (2010)

GIBRALTAR (CDP). Covers a land area of 1.236 square miles and a water area of 0.064 square miles. Located at 40.28° N. Lat; 75.87° W. Long. Elevation is 187 feet.

Population: n/a (1990); n/a (2000); 680 (2010); Density: 550.1 persons per square mile (2010); Race: 96.8% White, 0.1% Black, 0.9% Asian, 0.6% American Indian/Alaska Native, 0.0% Native Hawaiian/Other Pacific Islander, 1.6% Other, 2.6% Hispanic of any race (2010); Average household size: 2.59 (2010); Median age: 40.7 (2010); Males per 100 females: 103.0 (2010); Marriage status: 21.2% never married, 52.0% now married, 13.3% widowed, 13.5% divorced (2006-2010 5-year est.); Foreign born: 0.0% (2006-2010 5-year est.); Ancestry (includes multiple ancestries): 59.3% Irish, 41.4% German, 27.7% English, 12.8% Pennsylvania German, 5.7% Welsh (2006-2010 5-year est.).
Economy: Employment by occupation: 4.5% management, 0.0% professional, 24.5% services, 8.3% sales, 0.0% farming, 18.2% construction, 10.2% production (2006-2010 5-year est.).
Income: Per capita income: $22,843 (2006-2010 5-year est.); Median household income: $69,167 (2006-2010 5-year est.); Average household income: $62,230 (2006-2010 5-year est.); Percent of households with income of $100,000 or more: 23.4% (2006-2010 5-year est.); Poverty rate: 18.4% (2006-2010 5-year est.).
Education: Percent of population age 25 and over with: High school diploma (including GED) or higher: 87.7% (2006-2010 5-year est.); Bachelor's degree or higher: 30.4% (2006-2010 5-year est.); Master's degree or higher: 6.3% (2006-2010 5-year est.).
Housing: Homeownership rate: 80.2% (2010); Median home value: $157,600 (2006-2010 5-year est.); Median contract rent: n/a per month (2006-2010 5-year est.); Median year structure built: before 1940 (2006-2010 5-year est.).
Transportation: Commute to work: 100.0% car, 0.0% public transportation, 0.0% walk, 0.0% work from home (2006-2010 5-year est.); Travel time to work: 10.0% less than 15 minutes, 47.5% 15 to 30 minutes, 23.9% 30 to 45 minutes, 13.6% 45 to 60 minutes, 5.0% 60 minutes or more (2006-2010 5-year est.)

GOUGLERSVILLE (CDP). Covers a land area of 1.375 square miles and a water area of <.001 square miles. Located at 40.27° N. Lat; 76.02° W. Long. Elevation is 738 feet.
Population: n/a (1990); n/a (2000); 548 (2010); Density: 398.6 persons per square mile (2010); Race: 96.2% White, 0.9% Black, 0.2% Asian, 0.0% American Indian/Alaska Native, 0.0% Native Hawaiian/Other Pacific Islander, 2.7% Other, 3.1% Hispanic of any race (2010); Average household size: 2.44 (2010); Median age: 46.7 (2010); Males per 100 females: 97.1 (2010); Marriage status: 9.5% never married, 52.7% now married, 13.3% widowed, 24.5% divorced (2006-2010 5-year est.); Foreign born: 20.1% (2006-2010 5-year est.); Ancestry (includes multiple ancestries): 62.6% German, 17.3% English, 12.6% Italian, 9.4% Irish, 9.1% Polish (2006-2010 5-year est.).
Economy: Employment by occupation: 0.0% management, 8.5% professional, 29.5% services, 14.7% sales, 17.8% farming, 14.7% construction, 0.0% production (2006-2010 5-year est.).
Income: Per capita income: $33,946 (2006-2010 5-year est.); Median household income: $33,021 (2006-2010 5-year est.); Average household income: $53,551 (2006-2010 5-year est.); Percent of households with income of $100,000 or more: 25.7% (2006-2010 5-year est.); Poverty rate: 16.9% (2006-2010 5-year est.).
Education: Percent of population age 25 and over with: High school diploma (including GED) or higher: 80.7% (2006-2010 5-year est.); Bachelor's degree or higher: 13.8% (2006-2010 5-year est.); Master's degree or higher: 9.2% (2006-2010 5-year est.).
Housing: Homeownership rate: 79.1% (2010); Median home value: $161,500 (2006-2010 5-year est.); Median contract rent: n/a per month (2006-2010 5-year est.); Median year structure built: 1964 (2006-2010 5-year est.).
Transportation: Commute to work: 90.7% car, 0.0% public transportation, 0.0% walk, 9.3% work from home (2006-2010 5-year est.); Travel time to work: 47.9% less than 15 minutes, 33.3% 15 to 30 minutes, 0.0% 30 to 45 minutes, 9.4% 45 to 60 minutes, 9.4% 60 minutes or more (2006-2010 5-year est.)

GREENFIELDS (CDP). Covers a land area of 0.734 square miles and a water area of 0.028 square miles. Located at 40.36° N. Lat; 75.96° W. Long.
Population: n/a (1990); n/a (2000); 1,170 (2010); Density: 1,594.4 persons per square mile (2010); Race: 90.0% White, 3.2% Black, 1.4% Asian, 0.0% American Indian/Alaska Native, 0.0% Native Hawaiian/Other Pacific Islander, 5.4% Other, 7.8% Hispanic of any race (2010); Average household size: 2.29 (2010); Median age: 51.4 (2010); Males per 100 females: 91.5 (2010); Marriage status: 18.8% never married, 60.8% now married, 12.6% widowed, 7.8% divorced (2006-2010 5-year est.); Foreign born: 1.5% (2006-2010 5-year est.); Ancestry (includes multiple ancestries): 44.0% German, 16.0% American, 12.2% English, 11.8% Irish, 8.4% Polish (2006-2010 5-year est.).
Economy: Employment by occupation: 12.5% management, 5.0% professional, 10.6% services, 20.1% sales, 5.9% farming, 5.2% construction, 6.1% production (2006-2010 5-year est.).
Income: Per capita income: $27,101 (2006-2010 5-year est.); Median household income: $59,792 (2006-2010 5-year est.); Average household income: $65,973 (2006-2010 5-year est.); Percent of households with income of $100,000 or more: 18.1% (2006-2010 5-year est.); Poverty rate: 0.0% (2006-2010 5-year est.).
Education: Percent of population age 25 and over with: High school diploma (including GED) or higher: 88.9% (2006-2010 5-year est.); Bachelor's degree or higher: 26.4% (2006-2010 5-year est.); Master's degree or higher: 6.9% (2006-2010 5-year est.).
Housing: Homeownership rate: 87.1% (2010); Median home value: $173,900 (2006-2010 5-year est.); Median contract rent: $752 per month (2006-2010 5-year est.); Median year structure built: 1957 (2006-2010 5-year est.).
Transportation: Commute to work: 91.2% car, 0.0% public transportation, 0.0% walk, 4.8% work from home (2006-2010 5-year est.); Travel time to work: 42.1% less than 15 minutes, 36.5% 15 to 30 minutes, 11.9% 30 to 45 minutes, 9.5% 45 to 60 minutes, 0.0% 60 minutes or more (2006-2010 5-year est.)

GREENWICH (township). Covers a land area of 31.000 square miles and a water area of 0.096 square miles. Located at 40.56° N. Lat; 75.83° W. Long.
Population: 2,977 (1990); 3,386 (2000); 3,725 (2010); Density: 120.2 persons per square mile (2010); Race: 96.9% White, 1.0% Black, 0.5%

Asian, 0.2% American Indian/Alaska Native, 0.0% Native Hawaiian/Other Pacific Islander, 1.4% Other, 2.6% Hispanic of any race (2010); Average household size: 2.59 (2010); Median age: 44.9 (2010); Males per 100 females: 102.0 (2010); Marriage status: 16.3% never married, 72.7% now married, 3.9% widowed, 7.1% divorced (2006-2010 5-year est.); Foreign born: 1.7% (2006-2010 5-year est.); Ancestry (includes multiple ancestries): 48.5% German, 10.5% Irish, 7.9% English, 6.1% Italian, 5.4% Dutch (2006-2010 5-year est.).
Economy: Single-family building permits issued: 2 (2011); Multi-family building permits issued: 0 (2011); Employment by occupation: 23.6% management, 2.5% professional, 5.6% services, 19.2% sales, 6.0% farming, 5.8% construction, 5.8% production (2006-2010 5-year est.).
Income: Per capita income: $32,296 (2006-2010 5-year est.); Median household income: $68,790 (2006-2010 5-year est.); Average household income: $78,784 (2006-2010 5-year est.); Percent of households with income of $100,000 or more: 27.9% (2006-2010 5-year est.); Poverty rate: 8.6% (2006-2010 5-year est.).
Education: Percent of population age 25 and over with: High school diploma (including GED) or higher: 87.0% (2006-2010 5-year est.); Bachelor's degree or higher: 28.2% (2006-2010 5-year est.); Master's degree or higher: 8.2% (2006-2010 5-year est.).
Housing: Homeownership rate: 84.7% (2010); Median home value: $220,400 (2006-2010 5-year est.); Median contract rent: $675 per month (2006-2010 5-year est.); Median year structure built: 1978 (2006-2010 5-year est.).
Transportation: Commute to work: 93.7% car, 0.0% public transportation, 0.6% walk, 4.9% work from home (2006-2010 5-year est.); Travel time to work: 21.1% less than 15 minutes, 43.5% 15 to 30 minutes, 18.7% 30 to 45 minutes, 4.7% 45 to 60 minutes, 12.0% 60 minutes or more (2006-2010 5-year est.)
Additional Information Contacts
Northeast Berks Chamber of Commerce . . . . (610) 683-8860
  http://www.northeastberkschamber.com

GRILL (CDP). Covers a land area of 0.766 square miles and a water area of 0.008 square miles. Located at 40.30° N. Lat; 75.93° W. Long. Elevation is 338 feet.
Population: n/a (1990); n/a (2000); 1,468 (2010); Density: 1,916.9 persons per square mile (2010); Race: 94.0% White, 1.4% Black, 1.8% Asian, 0.3% American Indian/Alaska Native, 0.0% Native Hawaiian/Other Pacific Islander, 2.5% Other, 4.9% Hispanic of any race (2010); Average household size: 2.54 (2010); Median age: 40.6 (2010); Males per 100 females: 97.6 (2010); Marriage status: 28.5% never married, 52.5% now married, 4.5% widowed, 14.6% divorced (2006-2010 5-year est.); Foreign born: 2.4% (2006-2010 5-year est.); Ancestry (includes multiple ancestries): 44.3% German, 19.4% Irish, 17.1% English, 11.3% Italian, 11.2% Polish (2006-2010 5-year est.).
Economy: Employment by occupation: 12.8% management, 5.0% professional, 7.2% services, 19.2% sales, 3.5% farming, 4.9% construction, 2.8% production (2006-2010 5-year est.).
Income: Per capita income: $39,473 (2006-2010 5-year est.); Median household income: $61,354 (2006-2010 5-year est.); Average household income: $85,355 (2006-2010 5-year est.); Percent of households with income of $100,000 or more: 25.7% (2006-2010 5-year est.); Poverty rate: 3.3% (2006-2010 5-year est.).
Education: Percent of population age 25 and over with: High school diploma (including GED) or higher: 85.3% (2006-2010 5-year est.); Bachelor's degree or higher: 37.5% (2006-2010 5-year est.); Master's degree or higher: 17.3% (2006-2010 5-year est.).
Housing: Homeownership rate: 86.3% (2010); Median home value: $181,600 (2006-2010 5-year est.); Median contract rent: n/a per month (2006-2010 5-year est.); Median year structure built: 1987 (2006-2010 5-year est.).
Transportation: Commute to work: 94.1% car, 0.0% public transportation, 1.8% walk, 0.0% work from home (2006-2010 5-year est.); Travel time to work: 35.1% less than 15 minutes, 33.4% 15 to 30 minutes, 12.6% 30 to 45 minutes, 4.9% 45 to 60 minutes, 14.0% 60 minutes or more (2006-2010 5-year est.)

HAMBURG (borough). Covers a land area of 1.878 square miles and a water area of 0.069 square miles. Located at 40.56° N. Lat; 75.98° W. Long. Elevation is 400 feet.
History: Pennsylvania Dutch Folk Culture Center to East at Lenhartsville. Appalachian Trail, in Blue Mt. ridge to North. Founded 1779, incorporated 1837.

Population: 3,987 (1990); 4,114 (2000); 4,289 (2010); Density: 2,283.3 persons per square mile (2010); Race: 96.3% White, 1.2% Black, 0.4% Asian, 0.2% American Indian/Alaska Native, 0.0% Native Hawaiian/Other Pacific Islander, 1.9% Other, 3.0% Hispanic of any race (2010); Average household size: 2.23 (2010); Median age: 42.8 (2010); Males per 100 females: 88.0 (2010); Marriage status: 25.6% never married, 54.2% now married, 7.1% widowed, 13.1% divorced (2006-2010 5-year est.); Foreign born: 1.3% (2006-2010 5-year est.); Ancestry (includes multiple ancestries): 46.5% German, 10.8% Irish, 8.6% Pennsylvania German, 7.2% American, 6.3% Italian (2006-2010 5-year est.).
Economy: Single-family building permits issued: 0 (2011); Multi-family building permits issued: 0 (2011); Employment by occupation: 8.0% management, 3.5% professional, 13.5% services, 16.9% sales, 5.0% farming, 9.4% construction, 11.6% production (2006-2010 5-year est.).
Income: Per capita income: $22,435 (2006-2010 5-year est.); Median household income: $39,815 (2006-2010 5-year est.); Average household income: $52,269 (2006-2010 5-year est.); Percent of households with income of $100,000 or more: 11.5% (2006-2010 5-year est.); Poverty rate: 11.1% (2006-2010 5-year est.).
Education: Percent of population age 25 and over with: High school diploma (including GED) or higher: 81.3% (2006-2010 5-year est.); Bachelor's degree or higher: 10.5% (2006-2010 5-year est.); Master's degree or higher: 3.1% (2006-2010 5-year est.).

School District(s)
Hamburg Area SD (KG-12)
    2010-11 Enrollment: 2,445 . . . . (610) 562-2241
Housing: Homeownership rate: 61.3% (2010); Median home value: $118,200 (2006-2010 5-year est.); Median contract rent: $527 per month (2006-2010 5-year est.); Median year structure built: 1947 (2006-2010 5-year est.).
Safety: Violent crime rate: 23.2 per 10,000 population; Property crime rate: 167.3 per 10,000 population (2011).
Newspapers: East Penn Valley Merchandiser (Community news; Circulation 35,000); The Hamburg Area Item (Community news; Circulation 3,960); The Kutztown Area Patriot (Community news; Circulation 6,000); Northern Berks Merchandiser (Community news; Circulation 30,000)
Transportation: Commute to work: 86.7% car, 0.5% public transportation, 12.2% walk, 0.0% work from home (2006-2010 5-year est.); Travel time to work: 39.5% less than 15 minutes, 25.3% 15 to 30 minutes, 24.4% 30 to 45 minutes, 7.0% 45 to 60 minutes, 3.8% 60 minutes or more (2006-2010 5-year est.).
Additional Information Contacts
Borough of Hamburg . . . . (610) 562-7821
    http://hamburgboro.com
Northeast Berks Chamber of Commerce . . . . (610) 683-8860
    http://www.northeastberkschamber.com

HEIDELBERG (township). Covers a land area of 14.236 square miles and a water area of 0.076 square miles. Located at 40.37° N. Lat; 76.17° W. Long.
Population: 1,513 (1990); 1,636 (2000); 1,724 (2010); Density: 121.1 persons per square mile (2010); Race: 94.5% White, 3.2% Black, 0.6% Asian, 0.0% American Indian/Alaska Native, 0.1% Native Hawaiian/Other Pacific Islander, 1.6% Other, 2.3% Hispanic of any race (2010); Average household size: 2.66 (2010); Median age: 41.9 (2010); Males per 100 females: 103.3 (2010); Marriage status: 24.3% never married, 65.0% now married, 5.6% widowed, 5.1% divorced (2006-2010 5-year est.); Foreign born: 1.5% (2006-2010 5-year est.); Ancestry (includes multiple ancestries): 46.6% German, 10.8% English, 9.7% Irish, 7.3% American, 5.7% Pennsylvania German (2006-2010 5-year est.).
Economy: Single-family building permits issued: 1 (2011); Multi-family building permits issued: 0 (2011); Employment by occupation: 13.6% management, 3.2% professional, 11.2% services, 12.8% sales, 4.9% farming, 7.0% construction, 5.3% production (2006-2010 5-year est.).
Income: Per capita income: $28,559 (2006-2010 5-year est.); Median household income: $60,875 (2006-2010 5-year est.); Average household income: $75,186 (2006-2010 5-year est.); Percent of households with income of $100,000 or more: 25.4% (2006-2010 5-year est.); Poverty rate: 8.0% (2006-2010 5-year est.).
Education: Percent of population age 25 and over with: High school diploma (including GED) or higher: 85.7% (2006-2010 5-year est.); Bachelor's degree or higher: 26.5% (2006-2010 5-year est.); Master's degree or higher: 9.2% (2006-2010 5-year est.).

Housing: Homeownership rate: 85.8% (2010); Median home value: $187,500 (2006-2010 5-year est.); Median contract rent: $581 per month (2006-2010 5-year est.); Median year structure built: 1975 (2006-2010 5-year est.).
Safety: Violent crime rate: 5.8 per 10,000 population; Property crime rate: 28.9 per 10,000 population (2011).
Transportation: Commute to work: 92.4% car, 0.0% public transportation, 2.0% walk, 5.2% work from home (2006-2010 5-year est.); Travel time to work: 29.0% less than 15 minutes, 38.1% 15 to 30 minutes, 23.4% 30 to 45 minutes, 6.4% 45 to 60 minutes, 3.1% 60 minutes or more (2006-2010 5-year est.)
Additional Information Contacts
Greater Reading Chamber of Commerce & Industry . . . . . (610) 376-6766
    http://www.greaterreadingchamber.org

HEREFORD (CDP). Covers a land area of 1.015 square miles and a water area of 0.003 square miles. Located at 40.45° N. Lat; 75.55° W. Long. Elevation is 449 feet.
Population: n/a (1990); n/a (2000); 930 (2010); Density: 916.3 persons per square mile (2010); Race: 92.0% White, 0.4% Black, 0.6% Asian, 0.1% American Indian/Alaska Native, 0.0% Native Hawaiian/Other Pacific Islander, 6.9% Other, 4.5% Hispanic of any race (2010); Average household size: 2.27 (2010); Median age: 47.9 (2010); Males per 100 females: 98.3 (2010); Marriage status: 20.1% never married, 66.5% now married, 5.8% widowed, 7.6% divorced (2006-2010 5-year est.); Foreign born: 8.3% (2006-2010 5-year est.); Ancestry (includes multiple ancestries): 35.2% German, 14.9% American, 12.5% Irish, 9.2% English, 6.4% French Canadian (2006-2010 5-year est.).
Economy: Employment by occupation: 2.4% management, 13.3% professional, 3.0% services, 10.9% sales, 6.3% farming, 21.2% construction, 14.3% production (2006-2010 5-year est.).
Income: Per capita income: $27,883 (2006-2010 5-year est.); Median household income: $44,942 (2006-2010 5-year est.); Average household income: $62,707 (2006-2010 5-year est.); Percent of households with income of $100,000 or more: 14.5% (2006-2010 5-year est.); Poverty rate: 2.0% (2006-2010 5-year est.).
Education: Percent of population age 25 and over with: High school diploma (including GED) or higher: 84.1% (2006-2010 5-year est.); Bachelor's degree or higher: 3.7% (2006-2010 5-year est.); Master's degree or higher: 1.8% (2006-2010 5-year est.).

School District(s)
Upper Perkiomen SD (KG-12)
    2010-11 Enrollment: 3,187 . . . . (215) 679-7961
Housing: Homeownership rate: 93.9% (2010); Median home value: $23,100 (2006-2010 5-year est.); Median contract rent: n/a per month (2006-2010 5-year est.); Median year structure built: 1984 (2006-2010 5-year est.).
Transportation: Commute to work: 83.7% car, 0.0% public transportation, 0.0% walk, 9.8% work from home (2006-2010 5-year est.); Travel time to work: 13.1% less than 15 minutes, 26.2% 15 to 30 minutes, 19.7% 30 to 45 minutes, 14.7% 45 to 60 minutes, 26.2% 60 minutes or more (2006-2010 5-year est.)

HEREFORD (township). Covers a land area of 15.358 square miles and a water area of 0.053 square miles. Located at 40.44° N. Lat; 75.58° W. Long. Elevation is 449 feet.
Population: 3,026 (1990); 3,174 (2000); 2,997 (2010); Density: 195.1 persons per square mile (2010); Race: 96.8% White, 0.2% Black, 0.5% Asian, 0.1% American Indian/Alaska Native, 0.0% Native Hawaiian/Other Pacific Islander, 2.4% Other, 2.1% Hispanic of any race (2010); Average household size: 2.50 (2010); Median age: 46.7 (2010); Males per 100 females: 101.0 (2010); Marriage status: 18.7% never married, 69.4% now married, 6.1% widowed, 5.8% divorced (2006-2010 5-year est.); Foreign born: 3.1% (2006-2010 5-year est.); Ancestry (includes multiple ancestries): 38.2% German, 12.0% Pennsylvania German, 10.5% English, 10.3% Irish, 9.7% American (2006-2010 5-year est.).
Economy: Single-family building permits issued: 0 (2011); Multi-family building permits issued: 0 (2011); Employment by occupation: 8.9% management, 8.9% professional, 13.0% services, 10.5% sales, 3.5% farming, 13.8% construction, 13.4% production (2006-2010 5-year est.).
Income: Per capita income: $33,883 (2006-2010 5-year est.); Median household income: $67,273 (2006-2010 5-year est.); Average household income: $81,898 (2006-2010 5-year est.); Percent of households with income of $100,000 or more: 23.0% (2006-2010 5-year est.); Poverty rate: 1.6% (2006-2010 5-year est.).

Education: Percent of population age 25 and over with: High school diploma (including GED) or higher: 88.0% (2006-2010 5-year est.); Bachelor's degree or higher: 16.1% (2006-2010 5-year est.); Master's degree or higher: 8.0% (2006-2010 5-year est.).
Housing: Homeownership rate: 89.1% (2010); Median home value: $211,800 (2006-2010 5-year est.); Median contract rent: $851 per month (2006-2010 5-year est.); Median year structure built: 1976 (2006-2010 5-year est.).
Transportation: Commute to work: 84.3% car, 0.0% public transportation, 3.4% walk, 9.3% work from home (2006-2010 5-year est.); Travel time to work: 26.8% less than 15 minutes, 26.6% 15 to 30 minutes, 18.5% 30 to 45 minutes, 17.5% 45 to 60 minutes, 10.6% 60 minutes or more (2006-2010 5-year est.)
Additional Information Contacts
Upper Bucks Chamber of Commerce . . . . (215) 536-3211
  http://www.ubcc.org

HYDE PARK (CDP). Covers a land area of 0.502 square miles and a water area of <.001 square miles. Located at 40.38° N. Lat; 75.92° W. Long. Elevation is 318 feet.
Population: n/a (1990); n/a (2000); 2,528 (2010); Density: 5,036.4 persons per square mile (2010); Race: 81.0% White, 3.4% Black, 0.9% Asian, 0.2% American Indian/Alaska Native, 0.0% Native Hawaiian/Other Pacific Islander, 14.5% Other, 23.2% Hispanic of any race (2010); Average household size: 2.46 (2010); Median age: 39.1 (2010); Males per 100 females: 97.7 (2010); Marriage status: 31.7% never married, 48.7% now married, 6.9% widowed, 12.8% divorced (2006-2010 5-year est.); Foreign born: 5.6% (2006-2010 5-year est.); Ancestry (includes multiple ancestries): 44.7% German, 20.8% Italian, 13.4% Irish, 8.3% American, 6.1% Polish (2006-2010 5-year est.).
Economy: Employment by occupation: 9.3% management, 1.9% professional, 12.4% services, 17.3% sales, 4.4% farming, 2.1% construction, 2.0% production (2006-2010 5-year est.).
Income: Per capita income: $18,668 (2006-2010 5-year est.); Median household income: $41,849 (2006-2010 5-year est.); Average household income: $50,067 (2006-2010 5-year est.); Percent of households with income of $100,000 or more: 8.7% (2006-2010 5-year est.); Poverty rate: 19.5% (2006-2010 5-year est.).
Education: Percent of population age 25 and over with: High school diploma (including GED) or higher: 80.8% (2006-2010 5-year est.); Bachelor's degree or higher: 20.6% (2006-2010 5-year est.); Master's degree or higher: 9.0% (2006-2010 5-year est.).
Housing: Homeownership rate: 65.6% (2010); Median home value: $115,800 (2006-2010 5-year est.); Median contract rent: $531 per month (2006-2010 5-year est.); Median year structure built: 1944 (2006-2010 5-year est.).
Transportation: Commute to work: 85.0% car, 2.0% public transportation, 8.1% walk, 3.2% work from home (2006-2010 5-year est.); Travel time to work: 47.8% less than 15 minutes, 28.4% 15 to 30 minutes, 12.7% 30 to 45 minutes, 0.0% 45 to 60 minutes, 11.1% 60 minutes or more (2006-2010 5-year est.)

JACKSONWALD (CDP). Covers a land area of 1.785 square miles and a water area of 0.002 square miles. Located at 40.33° N. Lat; 75.84° W. Long. Elevation is 351 feet.
Population: n/a (1990); n/a (2000); 3,393 (2010); Density: 1,901.3 persons per square mile (2010); Race: 94.0% White, 2.8% Black, 1.0% Asian, 0.1% American Indian/Alaska Native, 0.0% Native Hawaiian/Other Pacific Islander, 2.1% Other, 2.4% Hispanic of any race (2010); Average household size: 2.89 (2010); Median age: 41.9 (2010); Males per 100 females: 97.3 (2010); Marriage status: 19.7% never married, 72.3% now married, 3.0% widowed, 5.0% divorced (2006-2010 5-year est.); Foreign born: 2.7% (2006-2010 5-year est.); Ancestry (includes multiple ancestries): 49.6% German, 18.2% Irish, 13.3% Italian, 12.6% English, 8.5% Polish (2006-2010 5-year est.).
Economy: Employment by occupation: 8.5% management, 10.8% professional, 6.3% services, 13.5% sales, 1.1% farming, 8.6% construction, 7.3% production (2006-2010 5-year est.).
Income: Per capita income: $34,377 (2006-2010 5-year est.); Median household income: $87,879 (2006-2010 5-year est.); Average household income: $98,772 (2006-2010 5-year est.); Percent of households with income of $100,000 or more: 34.0% (2006-2010 5-year est.); Poverty rate: 5.3% (2006-2010 5-year est.).
Education: Percent of population age 25 and over with: High school diploma (including GED) or higher: 97.0% (2006-2010 5-year est.);

Bachelor's degree or higher: 42.6% (2006-2010 5-year est.); Master's degree or higher: 12.1% (2006-2010 5-year est.).
Housing: Homeownership rate: 96.4% (2010); Median home value: $222,900 (2006-2010 5-year est.); Median contract rent: n/a per month (2006-2010 5-year est.); Median year structure built: 1984 (2006-2010 5-year est.).
Transportation: Commute to work: 96.3% car, 0.0% public transportation, 0.9% walk, 2.8% work from home (2006-2010 5-year est.); Travel time to work: 20.9% less than 15 minutes, 52.8% 15 to 30 minutes, 12.6% 30 to 45 minutes, 7.4% 45 to 60 minutes, 6.2% 60 minutes or more (2006-2010 5-year est.)

JEFFERSON (township). Covers a land area of 15.912 square miles and a water area of 0.112 square miles. Located at 40.44° N. Lat; 76.16° W. Long.
Population: 1,370 (1990); 1,604 (2000); 1,977 (2010); Density: 124.2 persons per square mile (2010); Race: 93.9% White, 2.0% Black, 1.0% Asian, 0.3% American Indian/Alaska Native, 0.0% Native Hawaiian/Other Pacific Islander, 2.8% Other, 3.6% Hispanic of any race (2010); Average household size: 2.78 (2010); Median age: 41.6 (2010); Males per 100 females: 101.3 (2010); Marriage status: 21.5% never married, 65.5% now married, 4.8% widowed, 8.3% divorced (2006-2010 5-year est.); Foreign born: 4.1% (2006-2010 5-year est.); Ancestry (includes multiple ancestries): 56.3% German, 7.8% Italian, 7.2% English, 6.5% Irish, 4.9% Haitian (2006-2010 5-year est.).
Economy: Single-family building permits issued: 0 (2011); Multi-family building permits issued: 0 (2011); Employment by occupation: 12.6% management, 4.7% professional, 12.0% services, 14.7% sales, 3.3% farming, 15.6% construction, 14.3% production (2006-2010 5-year est.).
Income: Per capita income: $25,717 (2006-2010 5-year est.); Median household income: $63,487 (2006-2010 5-year est.); Average household income: $73,205 (2006-2010 5-year est.); Percent of households with income of $100,000 or more: 19.3% (2006-2010 5-year est.); Poverty rate: 4.3% (2006-2010 5-year est.).
Education: Percent of population age 25 and over with: High school diploma (including GED) or higher: 86.8% (2006-2010 5-year est.); Bachelor's degree or higher: 19.1% (2006-2010 5-year est.); Master's degree or higher: 6.6% (2006-2010 5-year est.).
Housing: Homeownership rate: 90.6% (2010); Median home value: $224,200 (2006-2010 5-year est.); Median contract rent: $581 per month (2006-2010 5-year est.); Median year structure built: 1979 (2006-2010 5-year est.).
Transportation: Commute to work: 90.6% car, 0.0% public transportation, 2.8% walk, 6.3% work from home (2006-2010 5-year est.); Travel time to work: 18.6% less than 15 minutes, 40.2% 15 to 30 minutes, 28.0% 30 to 45 minutes, 8.5% 45 to 60 minutes, 4.8% 60 minutes or more (2006-2010 5-year est.)
Additional Information Contacts
Greater Reading Chamber of Commerce & Industry . . . . . (610) 376-6766
  http://www.greaterreadingchamber.org

KEMPTON (CDP). Covers a land area of 0.793 square miles and a water area of 0.008 square miles. Located at 40.63° N. Lat; 75.86° W. Long. Elevation is 430 feet.
Population: n/a (1990); n/a (2000); 169 (2010); Density: 213.0 persons per square mile (2010); Race: 96.4% White, 0.6% Black, 0.0% Asian, 0.0% American Indian/Alaska Native, 0.0% Native Hawaiian/Other Pacific Islander, 3.0% Other, 3.0% Hispanic of any race (2010); Average household size: 2.82 (2010); Median age: 39.9 (2010); Males per 100 females: 98.8 (2010); Marriage status: 14.9% never married, 76.3% now married, 8.8% widowed, 0.0% divorced (2006-2010 5-year est.); Foreign born: 2.0% (2006-2010 5-year est.); Ancestry (includes multiple ancestries): 47.4% German, 11.2% American, 11.2% Welsh, 9.2% European, 6.6% Irish (2006-2010 5-year est.).
Economy: Employment by occupation: 8.9% management, 7.6% professional, 0.0% services, 29.1% sales, 2.5% farming, 12.7% construction, 12.7% production (2006-2010 5-year est.).
Income: Per capita income: $26,045 (2006-2010 5-year est.); Median household income: $64,167 (2006-2010 5-year est.); Average household income: $75,011 (2006-2010 5-year est.); Percent of households with income of $100,000 or more: 18.6% (2006-2010 5-year est.); Poverty rate: 1.3% (2006-2010 5-year est.).
Education: Percent of population age 25 and over with: High school diploma (including GED) or higher: 95.0% (2006-2010 5-year est.);

Bachelor's degree or higher: 22.0% (2006-2010 5-year est.); Master's degree or higher: 13.0% (2006-2010 5-year est.).

School District(s)

Kutztown Area SD (KG-12)

    2010-11 Enrollment: 1,552 . . . . (610) 683-7361

Housing: Homeownership rate: 85.0% (2010); Median home value: $150,000 (2006-2010 5-year est.); Median contract rent: n/a per month (2006-2010 5-year est.); Median year structure built: before 1940 (2006-2010 5-year est.).

Transportation: Commute to work: 72.2% car, 0.0% public transportation, 11.4% walk, 11.4% work from home (2006-2010 5-year est.); Travel time to work: 27.1% less than 15 minutes, 24.3% 15 to 30 minutes, 32.9% 30 to 45 minutes, 10.0% 45 to 60 minutes, 5.7% 60 minutes or more (2006-2010 5-year est.)

KENHORST (borough).

KENHORST (borough). Covers a land area of 0.587 square miles and a water area of 0 square miles. Located at 40.31° N. Lat; 75.94° W. Long. Elevation is 348 feet.

History: Incorporated 1931.

Population: 2,918 (1990); 2,679 (2000); 2,877 (2010); Density: 4,897.2 persons per square mile (2010); Race: 89.0% White, 4.3% Black, 1.4% Asian, 0.0% American Indian/Alaska Native, 0.0% Native Hawaiian/Other Pacific Islander, 5.3% Other, 9.6% Hispanic of any race (2010); Average household size: 2.36 (2010); Median age: 42.4 (2010); Males per 100 females: 93.9 (2010); Marriage status: 34.5% never married, 44.1% now married, 7.8% widowed, 13.5% divorced (2006-2010 5-year est.); Foreign born: 2.6% (2006-2010 5-year est.); Ancestry (includes multiple ancestries): 41.4% German, 21.0% Italian, 12.9% Polish, 12.4% Irish, 7.2% Pennsylvania German (2006-2010 5-year est.).

Economy: Single-family building permits issued: 0 (2011); Multi-family building permits issued: 0 (2011); Employment by occupation: 10.3% management, 2.4% professional, 14.6% services, 17.9% sales, 7.3% farming, 5.1% construction, 6.1% production (2006-2010 5-year est.).

Income: Per capita income: $22,745 (2006-2010 5-year est.); Median household income: $52,481 (2006-2010 5-year est.); Average household income: $57,400 (2006-2010 5-year est.); Percent of households with income of $100,000 or more: 9.3% (2006-2010 5-year est.); Poverty rate: 7.9% (2006-2010 5-year est.).

Education: Percent of population age 25 and over with: High school diploma (including GED) or higher: 84.9% (2006-2010 5-year est.); Bachelor's degree or higher: 17.8% (2006-2010 5-year est.); Master's degree or higher: 6.8% (2006-2010 5-year est.).

Housing: Homeownership rate: 86.3% (2010); Median home value: $135,900 (2006-2010 5-year est.); Median contract rent: $695 per month (2006-2010 5-year est.); Median year structure built: 1952 (2006-2010 5-year est.).

Transportation: Commute to work: 91.7% car, 1.9% public transportation, 2.7% walk, 3.0% work from home (2006-2010 5-year est.); Travel time to work: 35.7% less than 15 minutes, 47.3% 15 to 30 minutes, 7.7% 30 to 45 minutes, 5.6% 45 to 60 minutes, 3.6% 60 minutes or more (2006-2010 5-year est.).

Additional Information Contacts

Greater Reading Chamber of Commerce & Industry . . . . . (610) 376-6766

    http://www.greaterreadingchamber.org

KUTZTOWN (borough).

KUTZTOWN (borough). Covers a land area of 1.636 square miles and a water area of 0.005 square miles. Located at 40.52° N. Lat; 75.78° W. Long. Elevation is 420 feet.

History: Seat of Kutztown University of Pennsylvania. Two covered bridges to Northwest. Settled 1733 by Germans, incorporated 1815.

Population: 4,677 (1990); 5,067 (2000); 5,012 (2010); Density: 3,062.9 persons per square mile (2010); Race: 95.8% White, 1.4% Black, 1.0% Asian, 0.0% American Indian/Alaska Native, 0.0% Native Hawaiian/Other Pacific Islander, 1.8% Other, 2.6% Hispanic of any race (2010); Average household size: 2.33 (2010); Median age: 28.3 (2010); Males per 100 females: 93.0 (2010); Marriage status: 55.6% never married, 35.0% now married, 5.2% widowed, 4.2% divorced (2006-2010 5-year est.); Foreign born: 1.5% (2006-2010 5-year est.); Ancestry (includes multiple ancestries): 41.5% German, 16.2% Irish, 8.7% Italian, 6.6% Polish, 6.3% Pennsylvania German (2006-2010 5-year est.).

Economy: Single-family building permits issued: 0 (2011); Multi-family building permits issued: 0 (2011); Employment by occupation: 5.8% management, 3.7% professional, 16.2% services, 19.1% sales, 1.5% farming, 5.3% construction, 5.5% production (2006-2010 5-year est.).

Income: Per capita income: $20,795 (2006-2010 5-year est.); Median household income: $40,448 (2006-2010 5-year est.); Average household income: $54,037 (2006-2010 5-year est.); Percent of households with income of $100,000 or more: 13.0% (2006-2010 5-year est.); Poverty rate: 29.1% (2006-2010 5-year est.).

Education: Percent of population age 25 and over with: High school diploma (including GED) or higher: 90.9% (2006-2010 5-year est.); Bachelor's degree or higher: 40.5% (2006-2010 5-year est.); Master's degree or higher: 21.6% (2006-2010 5-year est.).

School District(s)

Kutztown Area SD (KG-12)

    2010-11 Enrollment: 1,552 . . . . (610) 683-7361

Northwestern Lehigh SD (KG-12)

    2010-11 Enrollment: 2,337 . . . . (610) 298-8661

Four-year College(s)

Kutztown University of Pennsylvania (Public)

    Fall 2010 Enrollment: 9,794 . . . . (610) 683-4000

    2011-12 Tuition: In-state $8,359; Out-of-state $17,897

Housing: Homeownership rate: 46.5% (2010); Median home value: $179,200 (2006-2010 5-year est.); Median contract rent: $705 per month (2006-2010 5-year est.); Median year structure built: 1957 (2006-2010 5-year est.).

Safety: Violent crime rate: 19.9 per 10,000 population; Property crime rate: 274.5 per 10,000 population (2011).

Transportation: Commute to work: 85.4% car, 1.2% public transportation, 9.4% walk, 3.7% work from home (2006-2010 5-year est.); Travel time to work: 46.3% less than 15 minutes, 25.5% 15 to 30 minutes, 19.4% 30 to 45 minutes, 4.6% 45 to 60 minutes, 4.2% 60 minutes or more (2006-2010 5-year est.).

Additional Information Contacts

Borough of Kutztown . . . . (610) 683-6131

    http://www.kutztownboro.org

Northeast Berks Chamber of Commerce . . . . (610) 683-8860

    http://www.northeastberkschamber.com

KUTZTOWN UNIVERSITY (CDP).

KUTZTOWN UNIVERSITY (CDP). Covers a land area of 0.366 square miles and a water area of 0.003 square miles. Located at 40.51° N. Lat; 75.79° W. Long.

Population: n/a (1990); n/a (2000); 2,918 (2010); Density: 7,970.7 persons per square mile (2010); Race: 88.2% White, 7.3% Black, 0.5% Asian, 0.4% American Indian/Alaska Native, 0.2% Native Hawaiian/Other Pacific Islander, 3.4% Other, 4.5% Hispanic of any race (2010); Average household size: 0.00 (2010); Median age: 19.6 (2010); Males per 100 females: 75.6 (2010); Marriage status: 100.0% never married, 0.0% now married, 0.0% widowed, 0.0% divorced (2006-2010 5-year est.); Foreign born: 2.5% (2006-2010 5-year est.); Ancestry (includes multiple ancestries): 39.4% German, 32.1% Irish, 19.6% Italian, 10.5% Polish, 5.1% English (2006-2010 5-year est.).

Economy: Employment by occupation: 3.8% management, 0.0% professional, 11.4% services, 35.8% sales, 18.7% farming, 0.0% construction, 0.0% production (2006-2010 5-year est.).

Income: Per capita income: $4,755 (2006-2010 5-year est.); Median household income: n/a (2006-2010 5-year est.); Average household income: n/a (2006-2010 5-year est.); Percent of households with income of $100,000 or more: n/a (2006-2010 5-year est.); Poverty rate: n/a (2006-2010 5-year est.).

Education: Percent of population age 25 and over with: High school diploma (including GED) or higher: n/a (2006-2010 5-year est.); Bachelor's degree or higher: n/a (2006-2010 5-year est.); Master's degree or higher: n/a (2006-2010 5-year est.).

Housing: Homeownership rate: 0.0% (2010); Median home value: n/a (2006-2010 5-year est.); Median contract rent: n/a per month (2006-2010 5-year est.); Median year structure built: n/a (2006-2010 5-year est.).

Transportation: Commute to work: 59.2% car, 0.0% public transportation, 33.8% walk, 7.1% work from home (2006-2010 5-year est.); Travel time to work: 53.5% less than 15 minutes, 24.9% 15 to 30 minutes, 11.9% 30 to 45 minutes, 3.3% 45 to 60 minutes, 6.4% 60 minutes or more (2006-2010 5-year est.).

LAURELDALE (borough).

LAURELDALE (borough). Covers a land area of 0.795 square miles and a water area of 0 square miles. Located at 40.39° N. Lat; 75.91° W. Long. Elevation is 384 feet.

History: Settled 1902, incorporated 1930.

Population: 3,726 (1990); 3,759 (2000); 3,911 (2010); Density: 4,918.7 persons per square mile (2010); Race: 86.8% White, 2.5% Black, 0.9%

Asian, 0.4% American Indian/Alaska Native, 0.0% Native Hawaiian/Other Pacific Islander, 9.4% Other, 16.1% Hispanic of any race (2010); Average household size: 2.43 (2010); Median age: 42.1 (2010); Males per 100 females: 92.4 (2010); Marriage status: 22.9% never married, 59.2% now married, 7.4% widowed, 10.4% divorced (2006-2010 5-year est.); Foreign born: 4.2% (2006-2010 5-year est.); Ancestry (includes multiple ancestries): 42.9% German, 10.3% Irish, 8.4% Italian, 6.1% English, 5.5% Polish (2006-2010 5-year est.).

Economy: Single-family building permits issued: 0 (2011); Multi-family building permits issued: 0 (2011); Employment by occupation: 5.9% management, 0.8% professional, 8.9% services, 15.5% sales, 3.9% farming, 9.2% construction, 15.6% production (2006-2010 5-year est.).

Income: Per capita income: $25,389 (2006-2010 5-year est.); Median household income: $50,951 (2006-2010 5-year est.); Average household income: $56,895 (2006-2010 5-year est.); Percent of households with income of $100,000 or more: 7.0% (2006-2010 5-year est.); Poverty rate: 5.8% (2006-2010 5-year est.).

Education: Percent of population age 25 and over with: High school diploma (including GED) or higher: 81.3% (2006-2010 5-year est.); Bachelor's degree or higher: 11.9% (2006-2010 5-year est.); Master's degree or higher: 3.4% (2006-2010 5-year est.).

School District(s)
Muhlenberg SD (KG-12)
  2010-11 Enrollment: 3,551 . . . . (610) 921-8000

Housing: Homeownership rate: 81.7% (2010); Median home value: $127,700 (2006-2010 5-year est.); Median contract rent: $635 per month (2006-2010 5-year est.); Median year structure built: 1951 (2006-2010 5-year est.).

Safety: Violent crime rate: 10.2 per 10,000 population; Property crime rate: 58.6 per 10,000 population (2011).

Transportation: Commute to work: 95.0% car, 0.6% public transportation, 2.5% walk, 0.0% work from home (2006-2010 5-year est.); Travel time to work: 37.3% less than 15 minutes, 43.1% 15 to 30 minutes, 12.7% 30 to 45 minutes, 3.5% 45 to 60 minutes, 3.3% 60 minutes or more (2006-2010 5-year est.)

Additional Information Contacts
Greater Reading Chamber of Commerce & Industry . . . . . (610) 376-6766
  http://www.greaterreadingchamber.org

LEESPORT (borough). Aka West Leesport. Covers a land area of 0.703 square miles and a water area of 0.028 square miles. Located at 40.44° N. Lat; 75.97° W. Long. Elevation is 302 feet.

Population: 1,270 (1990); 1,805 (2000); 1,918 (2010); Density: 2,727.6 persons per square mile (2010); Race: 94.8% White, 1.5% Black, 0.6% Asian, 0.3% American Indian/Alaska Native, 0.1% Native Hawaiian/Other Pacific Islander, 2.7% Other, 4.2% Hispanic of any race (2010); Average household size: 2.57 (2010); Median age: 37.7 (2010); Males per 100 females: 98.6 (2010); Marriage status: 25.3% never married, 56.7% now married, 5.9% widowed, 12.2% divorced (2006-2010 5-year est.); Foreign born: 2.1% (2006-2010 5-year est.); Ancestry (includes multiple ancestries): 48.1% German, 11.9% Italian, 10.8% Irish, 6.3% Polish, 6.2% English (2006-2010 5-year est.).

Economy: Single-family building permits issued: 0 (2011); Multi-family building permits issued: 0 (2011); Employment by occupation: 9.4% management, 5.0% professional, 12.3% services, 12.0% sales, 3.6% farming, 8.0% construction, 8.8% production (2006-2010 5-year est.).

Income: Per capita income: $22,555 (2006-2010 5-year est.); Median household income: $53,092 (2006-2010 5-year est.); Average household income: $64,041 (2006-2010 5-year est.); Percent of households with income of $100,000 or more: 21.7% (2006-2010 5-year est.); Poverty rate: 3.9% (2006-2010 5-year est.).

Education: Percent of population age 25 and over with: High school diploma (including GED) or higher: 89.2% (2006-2010 5-year est.); Bachelor's degree or higher: 16.1% (2006-2010 5-year est.); Master's degree or higher: 4.1% (2006-2010 5-year est.).

School District(s)
Berks CTC (09-12)
  2010-11 Enrollment: n/a . . . . (610) 374-4073
Schuylkill Valley SD (KG-12)
  2010-11 Enrollment: 1,949 . . . . (610) 916-0957

Housing: Homeownership rate: 79.8% (2010); Median home value: $144,900 (2006-2010 5-year est.); Median contract rent: $619 per month (2006-2010 5-year est.); Median year structure built: 1972 (2006-2010 5-year est.).

Transportation: Commute to work: 94.9% car, 0.0% public transportation, 2.6% walk, 0.9% work from home (2006-2010 5-year est.); Travel time to work: 25.5% less than 15 minutes, 49.3% 15 to 30 minutes, 15.5% 30 to 45 minutes, 3.9% 45 to 60 minutes, 5.7% 60 minutes or more (2006-2010 5-year est.)

Additional Information Contacts
Greater Reading Chamber of Commerce & Industry . . . . . (610) 376-6766
  http://www.greaterreadingchamber.org

LENHARTSVILLE (borough). Covers a land area of 0.132 square miles and a water area of 0.004 square miles. Located at 40.57° N. Lat; 75.89° W. Long. Elevation is 390 feet.

History: Pennsylvania Dutch Folk Culture Center is here.

Population: 195 (1990); 173 (2000); 165 (2010); Density: 1,248.4 persons per square mile (2010); Race: 95.8% White, 0.0% Black, 1.2% Asian, 0.0% American Indian/Alaska Native, 0.0% Native Hawaiian/Other Pacific Islander, 3.0% Other, 3.0% Hispanic of any race (2010); Average household size: 2.32 (2010); Median age: 37.5 (2010); Males per 100 females: 108.9 (2010); Marriage status: 28.2% never married, 61.1% now married, 6.1% widowed, 4.6% divorced (2006-2010 5-year est.); Foreign born: 4.5% (2006-2010 5-year est.); Ancestry (includes multiple ancestries): 53.7% German, 12.4% Austrian, 11.9% English, 9.6% Czech, 7.9% Italian (2006-2010 5-year est.).

Economy: Single-family building permits issued: 0 (2011); Multi-family building permits issued: 0 (2011); Employment by occupation: 8.8% management, 2.2% professional, 2.2% services, 17.6% sales, 0.0% farming, 2.2% construction, 17.6% production (2006-2010 5-year est.).

Income: Per capita income: $22,529 (2006-2010 5-year est.); Median household income: $50,313 (2006-2010 5-year est.); Average household income: $54,962 (2006-2010 5-year est.); Percent of households with income of $100,000 or more: 8.2% (2006-2010 5-year est.); Poverty rate: 19.2% (2006-2010 5-year est.).

Education: Percent of population age 25 and over with: High school diploma (including GED) or higher: 86.6% (2006-2010 5-year est.); Bachelor's degree or higher: 22.3% (2006-2010 5-year est.); Master's degree or higher: 1.8% (2006-2010 5-year est.).

School District(s)
Kutztown Area SD (KG-12)
  2010-11 Enrollment: 1,552 . . . . (610) 683-7361

Housing: Homeownership rate: 60.6% (2010); Median home value: $116,700 (2006-2010 5-year est.); Median contract rent: $650 per month (2006-2010 5-year est.); Median year structure built: before 1940 (2006-2010 5-year est.).

Transportation: Commute to work: 80.2% car, 0.0% public transportation, 11.0% walk, 8.8% work from home (2006-2010 5-year est.); Travel time to work: 39.8% less than 15 minutes, 32.5% 15 to 30 minutes, 25.3% 30 to 45 minutes, 0.0% 45 to 60 minutes, 2.4% 60 minutes or more (2006-2010 5-year est.)

LIMEKILN (unincorporated postal area)
Zip Code: 19535
  Covers a land area of 0.045 square miles and a water area of 0.002 square miles. Located at 40.33° N. Lat; 75.80° W. Long. Population: 23 (2010); Density: 502.9 persons per square mile (2010); Race: 100.0% White, 0.0% Black, 0.0% Asian, 0.0% American Indian/Alaska Native, 0.0% Native Hawaiian/Other Pacific Islander, 0.0% Other, 0.0% Hispanic of any race (2010); Average household size: 2.56 (2010); Median age: 57.8 (2010); Males per 100 females: 130.0 (2010); Homeownership rate: 77.7% (2010)

LINCOLN PARK (CDP). Covers a land area of 0.314 square miles and a water area of 0 square miles. Located at 40.31° N. Lat; 75.99° W. Long. Elevation is 305 feet.

Population: n/a (1990); n/a (2000); 1,615 (2010); Density: 5,144.2 persons per square mile (2010); Race: 90.3% White, 3.0% Black, 1.9% Asian, 0.0% American Indian/Alaska Native, 0.1% Native Hawaiian/Other Pacific Islander, 4.7% Other, 7.4% Hispanic of any race (2010); Average household size: 2.20 (2010); Median age: 39.7 (2010); Males per 100 females: 91.6 (2010); Marriage status: 37.2% never married, 38.1% now married, 13.7% widowed, 11.0% divorced (2006-2010 5-year est.); Foreign born: 5.4% (2006-2010 5-year est.); Ancestry (includes multiple ancestries): 33.4% German, 17.2% Italian, 12.7% Irish, 10.3% Polish, 8.4% English (2006-2010 5-year est.).

Economy: Employment by occupation: 8.5% management, 8.1% professional, 7.4% services, 13.6% sales, 9.4% farming, 9.2% construction, 3.3% production (2006-2010 5-year est.).
Income: Per capita income: $26,058 (2006-2010 5-year est.); Median household income: $49,420 (2006-2010 5-year est.); Average household income: $55,335 (2006-2010 5-year est.); Percent of households with income of $100,000 or more: 9.7% (2006-2010 5-year est.); Poverty rate: 5.8% (2006-2010 5-year est.).
Education: Percent of population age 25 and over with: High school diploma (including GED) or higher: 88.9% (2006-2010 5-year est.); Bachelor's degree or higher: 25.1% (2006-2010 5-year est.); Master's degree or higher: 8.7% (2006-2010 5-year est.).
Housing: Homeownership rate: 68.6% (2010); Median home value: $148,000 (2006-2010 5-year est.); Median contract rent: $680 per month (2006-2010 5-year est.); Median year structure built: 1958 (2006-2010 5-year est.).
Transportation: Commute to work: 95.0% car, 0.0% public transportation, 3.4% walk, 0.0% work from home (2006-2010 5-year est.); Travel time to work: 36.4% less than 15 minutes, 51.1% 15 to 30 minutes, 6.5% 30 to 45 minutes, 2.6% 45 to 60 minutes, 3.4% 60 minutes or more (2006-2010 5-year est.)

LONGSWAMP (township). Covers a land area of 22.845 square miles and a water area of 0.069 square miles. Located at 40.49° N. Lat; 75.66° W. Long. Elevation is 505 feet.
Population: 5,388 (1990); 5,608 (2000); 5,679 (2010); Density: 248.6 persons per square mile (2010); Race: 97.7% White, 0.5% Black, 0.4% Asian, 0.1% American Indian/Alaska Native, 0.0% Native Hawaiian/Other Pacific Islander, 1.3% Other, 1.5% Hispanic of any race (2010); Average household size: 2.36 (2010); Median age: 46.7 (2010); Males per 100 females: 94.0 (2010); Marriage status: 24.8% never married, 57.2% now married, 7.6% widowed, 10.4% divorced (2006-2010 5-year est.); Foreign born: 0.5% (2006-2010 5-year est.); Ancestry (includes multiple ancestries): 49.8% German, 13.1% Pennsylvania German, 11.1% Irish, 8.2% Dutch, 7.0% American (2006-2010 5-year est.).
Economy: Single-family building permits issued: 2 (2011); Multi-family building permits issued: 0 (2011); Employment by occupation: 5.2% management, 4.1% professional, 7.1% services, 19.9% sales, 5.3% farming, 11.0% construction, 5.4% production (2006-2010 5-year est.).
Income: Per capita income: $29,652 (2006-2010 5-year est.); Median household income: $62,393 (2006-2010 5-year est.); Average household income: $73,514 (2006-2010 5-year est.); Percent of households with income of $100,000 or more: 21.9% (2006-2010 5-year est.); Poverty rate: 3.9% (2006-2010 5-year est.).
Education: Percent of population age 25 and over with: High school diploma (including GED) or higher: 81.6% (2006-2010 5-year est.); Bachelor's degree or higher: 18.2% (2006-2010 5-year est.); Master's degree or higher: 6.9% (2006-2010 5-year est.).
Housing: Homeownership rate: 78.0% (2010); Median home value: $181,600 (2006-2010 5-year est.); Median contract rent: $647 per month (2006-2010 5-year est.); Median year structure built: 1973 (2006-2010 5-year est.).
Transportation: Commute to work: 96.1% car, 0.0% public transportation, 1.0% walk, 3.0% work from home (2006-2010 5-year est.); Travel time to work: 26.9% less than 15 minutes, 40.9% 15 to 30 minutes, 18.3% 30 to 45 minutes, 8.2% 45 to 60 minutes, 5.7% 60 minutes or more (2006-2010 5-year est.).
Additional Information Contacts
Longswamp Township . . . . (610) 682-7388
  http://www.co.berks.pa.us/longswamp
Northeast Berks Chamber of Commerce . . . . (610) 683-8860
  http://www.northeastberkschamber.com

LORANE (CDP). Covers a land area of 1.779 square miles and a water area of 0.006 square miles. Located at 40.29° N. Lat; 75.85° W. Long. Elevation is 203 feet.
History: Daniel Boone Homestead State Historical Site to East.
Population: 2,387 (1990); 2,994 (2000); 4,236 (2010); Density: 2,381.3 persons per square mile (2010); Race: 93.6% White, 2.3% Black, 1.7% Asian, 0.0% American Indian/Alaska Native, 0.0% Native Hawaiian/Other Pacific Islander, 2.4% Other, 3.7% Hispanic of any race (2010); Average household size: 2.41 (2010); Median age: 44.8 (2010); Males per 100 females: 93.4 (2010); Marriage status: 19.1% never married, 61.7% now married, 10.0% widowed, 9.1% divorced (2006-2010 5-year est.); Foreign born: 2.2% (2006-2010 5-year est.); Ancestry (includes multiple

ancestries): 36.5% German, 17.6% Irish, 15.2% Polish, 12.7% Italian, 7.1% English (2006-2010 5-year est.).
Economy: Employment by occupation: 8.2% management, 4.7% professional, 9.8% services, 26.8% sales, 4.1% farming, 8.0% construction, 4.5% production (2006-2010 5-year est.).
Income: Per capita income: $26,880 (2006-2010 5-year est.); Median household income: $61,622 (2006-2010 5-year est.); Average household income: $62,974 (2006-2010 5-year est.); Percent of households with income of $100,000 or more: 17.5% (2006-2010 5-year est.); Poverty rate: 5.2% (2006-2010 5-year est.).
Education: Percent of population age 25 and over with: High school diploma (including GED) or higher: 86.3% (2006-2010 5-year est.); Bachelor's degree or higher: 20.0% (2006-2010 5-year est.); Master's degree or higher: 3.9% (2006-2010 5-year est.).
Housing: Homeownership rate: 79.7% (2010); Median home value: $160,500 (2006-2010 5-year est.); Median contract rent: $981 per month (2006-2010 5-year est.); Median year structure built: 1983 (2006-2010 5-year est.).
Transportation: Commute to work: 93.6% car, 1.7% public transportation, 0.5% walk, 4.1% work from home (2006-2010 5-year est.); Travel time to work: 29.0% less than 15 minutes, 45.9% 15 to 30 minutes, 9.2% 30 to 45 minutes, 8.0% 45 to 60 minutes, 7.9% 60 minutes or more (2006-2010 5-year est.)
Additional Information Contacts
Greater Reading Chamber of Commerce & Industry . . . . . (610) 376-6766
  http://www.greaterreadingchamber.org

LOWER ALSACE (township). Covers a land area of 4.740 square miles and a water area of 0.042 square miles. Located at 40.35° N. Lat; 75.89° W. Long.
Population: 4,635 (1990); 4,478 (2000); 4,475 (2010); Density: 944.1 persons per square mile (2010); Race: 92.2% White, 2.3% Black, 0.6% Asian, 0.2% American Indian/Alaska Native, 0.0% Native Hawaiian/Other Pacific Islander, 4.7% Other, 7.8% Hispanic of any race (2010); Average household size: 2.44 (2010); Median age: 41.2 (2010); Males per 100 females: 93.0 (2010); Marriage status: 30.8% never married, 53.1% now married, 8.5% widowed, 7.6% divorced (2006-2010 5-year est.); Foreign born: 1.6% (2006-2010 5-year est.); Ancestry (includes multiple ancestries): 44.8% German, 17.5% Irish, 11.0% Polish, 9.4% English, 8.9% Italian (2006-2010 5-year est.).
Economy: Single-family building permits issued: 2 (2011); Multi-family building permits issued: 0 (2011); Employment by occupation: 7.4% management, 3.4% professional, 10.8% services, 18.0% sales, 3.4% farming, 9.3% construction, 7.6% production (2006-2010 5-year est.).
Income: Per capita income: $25,069 (2006-2010 5-year est.); Median household income: $50,458 (2006-2010 5-year est.); Average household income: $58,891 (2006-2010 5-year est.); Percent of households with income of $100,000 or more: 11.1% (2006-2010 5-year est.); Poverty rate: 6.2% (2006-2010 5-year est.).
Education: Percent of population age 25 and over with: High school diploma (including GED) or higher: 88.4% (2006-2010 5-year est.); Bachelor's degree or higher: 22.4% (2006-2010 5-year est.); Master's degree or higher: 8.7% (2006-2010 5-year est.).
Housing: Homeownership rate: 76.7% (2010); Median home value: $141,700 (2006-2010 5-year est.); Median contract rent: $754 per month (2006-2010 5-year est.); Median year structure built: 1954 (2006-2010 5-year est.).
Transportation: Commute to work: 96.3% car, 0.5% public transportation, 1.2% walk, 1.5% work from home (2006-2010 5-year est.); Travel time to work: 34.3% less than 15 minutes, 48.0% 15 to 30 minutes, 9.6% 30 to 45 minutes, 2.8% 45 to 60 minutes, 5.4% 60 minutes or more (2006-2010 5-year est.)
Additional Information Contacts
Greater Reading Chamber of Commerce & Industry . . . . . (610) 376-6766
  http://www.greaterreadingchamber.org

LOWER HEIDELBERG (township). Covers a land area of 14.862 square miles and a water area of 0.575 square miles. Located at 40.35° N. Lat; 76.05° W. Long.
Population: 2,209 (1990); 4,150 (2000); 5,513 (2010); Density: 370.9 persons per square mile (2010); Race: 92.7% White, 2.5% Black, 2.2% Asian, 0.1% American Indian/Alaska Native, 0.0% Native Hawaiian/Other Pacific Islander, 2.5% Other, 4.0% Hispanic of any race (2010); Average household size: 2.75 (2010); Median age: 42.8 (2010); Males per 100 females: 97.5 (2010); Marriage status: 18.6% never married, 62.5% now

married, 13.6% widowed, 5.4% divorced (2006-2010 5-year est.); Foreign born: 7.2% (2006-2010 5-year est.); Ancestry (includes multiple ancestries): 45.8% German, 19.0% Irish, 16.2% Italian, 7.7% English, 6.9% Polish (2006-2010 5-year est.).

Economy: Single-family building permits issued: 12 (2011); Multi-family building permits issued: 0 (2011); Employment by occupation: 24.4% management, 3.4% professional, 5.1% services, 13.8% sales, 2.3% farming, 4.6% construction, 4.7% production (2006-2010 5-year est.).

Income: Per capita income: $36,633 (2006-2010 5-year est.); Median household income: $79,402 (2006-2010 5-year est.); Average household income: $101,469 (2006-2010 5-year est.); Percent of households with income of $100,000 or more: 41.6% (2006-2010 5-year est.); Poverty rate: 4.6% (2006-2010 5-year est.).

Education: Percent of population age 25 and over with: High school diploma (including GED) or higher: 88.1% (2006-2010 5-year est.); Bachelor's degree or higher: 42.7% (2006-2010 5-year est.); Master's degree or higher: 16.7% (2006-2010 5-year est.).

Housing: Homeownership rate: 84.8% (2010); Median home value: $296,100 (2006-2010 5-year est.); Median contract rent: $978 per month (2006-2010 5-year est.); Median year structure built: 1993 (2006-2010 5-year est.).

Safety: Violent crime rate: 3.6 per 10,000 population; Property crime rate: 54.2 per 10,000 population (2011).

Transportation: Commute to work: 91.5% car, 0.0% public transportation, 1.9% walk, 5.7% work from home (2006-2010 5-year est.); Travel time to work: 30.4% less than 15 minutes, 45.9% 15 to 30 minutes, 12.8% 30 to 45 minutes, 4.3% 45 to 60 minutes, 6.7% 60 minutes or more (2006-2010 5-year est.).

Additional Information Contacts

Greater Reading Chamber of Commerce & Industry . . . . . (610) 376-6766
http://www.greaterreadingchamber.org

LYON STATION (unincorporated postal area)

Zip Code: 19536

Covers a land area of 0.386 square miles and a water area of <.001 square miles. Located at 40.48° N. Lat; 75.75° W. Long. Population: 490 (2010); Density: 1,268.5 persons per square mile (2010); Race: 97.3% White, 0.8% Black, 0.8% Asian, 0.0% American Indian/Alaska Native, 0.0% Native Hawaiian/Other Pacific Islander, 1.1% Other, 1.8% Hispanic of any race (2010); Average household size: 2.40 (2010); Median age: 34.3 (2010); Males per 100 females: 93.7 (2010); Homeownership rate: 60.2% (2010)

LYONS (borough). Aka Lyon Station. Covers a land area of 0.356 square miles and a water area of <.001 square miles. Located at 40.48° N. Lat; 75.76° W. Long. Elevation is 463 feet.

Population: 499 (1990); 504 (2000); 478 (2010); Density: 1,343.6 persons per square mile (2010); Race: 97.3% White, 0.8% Black, 0.8% Asian, 0.0% American Indian/Alaska Native, 0.0% Native Hawaiian/Other Pacific Islander, 1.1% Other, 1.9% Hispanic of any race (2010); Average household size: 2.38 (2010); Median age: 34.0 (2010); Males per 100 females: 95.1 (2010); Marriage status: 39.7% never married, 49.3% now married, 3.0% widowed, 8.1% divorced (2006-2010 5-year est.); Foreign born: 2.9% (2006-2010 5-year est.); Ancestry (includes multiple ancestries): 39.0% German, 13.4% Pennsylvania German, 12.6% English, 11.9% Irish, 6.6% Dutch (2006-2010 5-year est.).

Economy: Single-family building permits issued: 0 (2011); Multi-family building permits issued: 0 (2011); Employment by occupation: 5.4% management, 2.7% professional, 18.8% services, 11.4% sales, 6.7% farming, 13.8% construction, 17.4% production (2006-2010 5-year est.).

Income: Per capita income: $20,598 (2006-2010 5-year est.); Median household income: $55,000 (2006-2010 5-year est.); Average household income: $54,134 (2006-2010 5-year est.); Percent of households with income of $100,000 or more: 5.7% (2006-2010 5-year est.); Poverty rate: 14.8% (2006-2010 5-year est.).

Education: Percent of population age 25 and over with: High school diploma (including GED) or higher: 81.5% (2006-2010 5-year est.); Bachelor's degree or higher: 11.7% (2006-2010 5-year est.); Master's degree or higher: 2.7% (2006-2010 5-year est.).

Housing: Homeownership rate: 60.2% (2010); Median home value: $133,300 (2006-2010 5-year est.); Median contract rent: $538 per month (2006-2010 5-year est.); Median year structure built: 1953 (2006-2010 5-year est.).

Transportation: Commute to work: 94.6% car, 0.0% public transportation, 2.0% walk, 3.4% work from home (2006-2010 5-year est.); Travel time to

work: 61.4% less than 15 minutes, 11.2% 15 to 30 minutes, 24.2% 30 to 45 minutes, 3.2% 45 to 60 minutes, 0.0% 60 minutes or more (2006-2010 5-year est.)

MAIDENCREEK (township). Covers a land area of 13.659 square miles and a water area of 1.167 square miles. Located at 40.47° N. Lat; 75.89° W. Long.

Population: 3,457 (1990); 6,553 (2000); 9,126 (2010); Density: 668.1 persons per square mile (2010); Race: 91.8% White, 3.1% Black, 1.6% Asian, 0.1% American Indian/Alaska Native, 0.0% Native Hawaiian/Other Pacific Islander, 3.4% Other, 5.7% Hispanic of any race (2010); Average household size: 2.85 (2010); Median age: 38.0 (2010); Males per 100 females: 96.4 (2010); Marriage status: 20.5% never married, 67.0% now married, 3.8% widowed, 8.6% divorced (2006-2010 5-year est.); Foreign born: 5.4% (2006-2010 5-year est.); Ancestry (includes multiple ancestries): 39.0% German, 18.1% Irish, 14.7% Italian, 8.0% Polish, 7.0% English (2006-2010 5-year est.).

Economy: Single-family building permits issued: 23 (2011); Multi-family building permits issued: 0 (2011); Employment by occupation: 12.2% management, 4.9% professional, 7.1% services, 19.5% sales, 3.2% farming, 7.7% construction, 8.5% production (2006-2010 5-year est.).

Income: Per capita income: $27,062 (2006-2010 5-year est.); Median household income: $65,802 (2006-2010 5-year est.); Average household income: $75,353 (2006-2010 5-year est.); Percent of households with income of $100,000 or more: 25.0% (2006-2010 5-year est.); Poverty rate: 5.5% (2006-2010 5-year est.).

Education: Percent of population age 25 and over with: High school diploma (including GED) or higher: 92.1% (2006-2010 5-year est.); Bachelor's degree or higher: 28.0% (2006-2010 5-year est.); Master's degree or higher: 8.8% (2006-2010 5-year est.).

Housing: Homeownership rate: 87.9% (2010); Median home value: $193,700 (2006-2010 5-year est.); Median contract rent: $715 per month (2006-2010 5-year est.); Median year structure built: 1995 (2006-2010 5-year est.).

Transportation: Commute to work: 94.0% car, 0.5% public transportation, 0.4% walk, 3.5% work from home (2006-2010 5-year est.); Travel time to work: 25.3% less than 15 minutes, 44.2% 15 to 30 minutes, 15.3% 30 to 45 minutes, 7.5% 45 to 60 minutes, 7.7% 60 minutes or more (2006-2010 5-year est.)

Additional Information Contacts

Greater Reading Chamber of Commerce & Industry . . . . . (610) 376-6766
http://www.greaterreadingchamber.org
Maidencreek Township . . . . (610) 926-4920
http://www.maidencreek.net

MARION (township). Covers a land area of 15.077 square miles and a water area of 0.051 square miles. Located at 40.39° N. Lat; 76.23° W. Long.

Population: 1,415 (1990); 1,573 (2000); 1,688 (2010); Density: 112.0 persons per square mile (2010); Race: 97.5% White, 0.5% Black, 0.2% Asian, 0.0% American Indian/Alaska Native, 0.0% Native Hawaiian/Other Pacific Islander, 1.8% Other, 2.0% Hispanic of any race (2010); Average household size: 2.58 (2010); Median age: 45.5 (2010); Males per 100 females: 107.4 (2010); Marriage status: 23.9% never married, 64.7% now married, 6.1% widowed, 5.4% divorced (2006-2010 5-year est.); Foreign born: 0.7% (2006-2010 5-year est.); Ancestry (includes multiple ancestries): 53.4% German, 13.0% Irish, 11.3% American, 6.1% Pennsylvania German, 5.6% Italian (2006-2010 5-year est.).

Economy: Single-family building permits issued: 6 (2011); Multi-family building permits issued: 0 (2011); Employment by occupation: 17.7% management, 4.3% professional, 13.1% services, 10.1% sales, 3.6% farming, 13.1% construction, 10.6% production (2006-2010 5-year est.).

Income: Per capita income: $24,345 (2006-2010 5-year est.); Median household income: $61,136 (2006-2010 5-year est.); Average household income: $67,064 (2006-2010 5-year est.); Percent of households with income of $100,000 or more: 17.4% (2006-2010 5-year est.); Poverty rate: 4.9% (2006-2010 5-year est.).

Education: Percent of population age 25 and over with: High school diploma (including GED) or higher: 76.2% (2006-2010 5-year est.); Bachelor's degree or higher: 15.0% (2006-2010 5-year est.); Master's degree or higher: 6.8% (2006-2010 5-year est.).

Housing: Homeownership rate: 76.6% (2010); Median home value: $170,400 (2006-2010 5-year est.); Median contract rent: $621 per month (2006-2010 5-year est.); Median year structure built: 1957 (2006-2010 5-year est.).

Safety: Violent crime rate: 0.0 per 10,000 population; Property crime rate: 59.1 per 10,000 population (2011).
Transportation: Commute to work: 88.4% car, 0.0% public transportation, 1.0% walk, 9.7% work from home (2006-2010 5-year est.); Travel time to work: 29.7% less than 15 minutes, 32.1% 15 to 30 minutes, 28.3% 30 to 45 minutes, 5.3% 45 to 60 minutes, 4.7% 60 minutes or more (2006-2010 5-year est.)
Additional Information Contacts
Lebanon Valley Chamber of Commerce . . . . (717) 273-3727
　　http://www.lvchamber.org

MAXATAWNY (township). Covers a land area of 25.880 square miles and a water area of 0.072 square miles. Located at 40.53° N. Lat; 75.75° W. Long. Elevation is 479 feet.
Population: 5,751 (1990); 5,982 (2000); 7,906 (2010); Density: 305.5 persons per square mile (2010); Race: 92.1% White, 4.8% Black, 0.7% Asian, 0.3% American Indian/Alaska Native, 0.1% Native Hawaiian/Other Pacific Islander, 2.0% Other, 2.8% Hispanic of any race (2010); Average household size: 2.60 (2010); Median age: 20.9 (2010); Males per 100 females: 81.5 (2010); Marriage status: 59.2% never married, 34.3% now married, 3.6% widowed, 2.8% divorced (2006-2010 5-year est.); Foreign born: 1.8% (2006-2010 5-year est.); Ancestry (includes multiple ancestries): 41.0% German, 17.1% Irish, 16.3% Italian, 7.4% Pennsylvania German, 6.7% Polish (2006-2010 5-year est.).
Economy: Single-family building permits issued: 1 (2011); Multi-family building permits issued: 0 (2011); Employment by occupation: 12.2% management, 2.4% professional, 9.1% services, 24.3% sales, 6.4% farming, 9.7% construction, 10.5% production (2006-2010 5-year est.).
Income: Per capita income: $17,735 (2006-2010 5-year est.); Median household income: $44,221 (2006-2010 5-year est.); Average household income: $62,806 (2006-2010 5-year est.); Percent of households with income of $100,000 or more: 19.4% (2006-2010 5-year est.); Poverty rate: 13.5% (2006-2010 5-year est.).
Education: Percent of population age 25 and over with: High school diploma (including GED) or higher: 86.3% (2006-2010 5-year est.); Bachelor's degree or higher: 24.9% (2006-2010 5-year est.); Master's degree or higher: 7.0% (2006-2010 5-year est.).
Housing: Homeownership rate: 70.5% (2010); Median home value: $203,100 (2006-2010 5-year est.); Median contract rent: $483 per month (2006-2010 5-year est.); Median year structure built: 1973 (2006-2010 5-year est.).
Transportation: Commute to work: 76.8% car, 0.0% public transportation, 14.2% walk, 8.0% work from home (2006-2010 5-year est.); Travel time to work: 40.1% less than 15 minutes, 32.9% 15 to 30 minutes, 17.6% 30 to 45 minutes, 4.5% 45 to 60 minutes, 5.0% 60 minutes or more (2006-2010 5-year est.)
Additional Information Contacts
Maxatawny Township . . . . (610) 683-6518
　　http://www.maxatawny.net
Northeast Berks Chamber of Commerce . . . . (610) 683-8860
　　http://www.northeastberkschamber.com

MERTZTOWN (CDP). Covers a land area of 1.057 square miles and a water area of 0.004 square miles. Located at 40.50° N. Lat; 75.67° W. Long. Elevation is 469 feet.
Population: n/a (1990); n/a (2000); 664 (2010); Density: 628.0 persons per square mile (2010); Race: 97.4% White, 0.2% Black, 0.6% Asian, 0.3% American Indian/Alaska Native, 0.0% Native Hawaiian/Other Pacific Islander, 1.5% Other, 2.3% Hispanic of any race (2010); Average household size: 2.47 (2010); Median age: 40.3 (2010); Males per 100 females: 99.4 (2010); Marriage status: 20.3% never married, 57.5% now married, 4.9% widowed, 17.3% divorced (2006-2010 5-year est.); Foreign born: 0.0% (2006-2010 5-year est.); Ancestry (includes multiple ancestries): 46.5% German, 13.8% Dutch, 11.7% Irish, 10.8% Pennsylvania German, 8.8% Italian (2006-2010 5-year est.).
Economy: Employment by occupation: 2.4% management, 0.0% professional, 0.0% services, 32.1% sales, 0.0% farming, 13.3% construction, 15.6% production (2006-2010 5-year est.).
Income: Per capita income: $31,368 (2006-2010 5-year est.); Median household income: $62,143 (2006-2010 5-year est.); Average household income: $69,300 (2006-2010 5-year est.); Percent of households with income of $100,000 or more: 28.8% (2006-2010 5-year est.); Poverty rate: 1.7% (2006-2010 5-year est.).
Education: Percent of population age 25 and over with: High school diploma (including GED) or higher: 92.1% (2006-2010 5-year est.);

Bachelor's degree or higher: 11.3% (2006-2010 5-year est.); Master's degree or higher: 0.0% (2006-2010 5-year est.).
School District(s)
Brandywine Heights Area SD (KG-12)
　　2010-11 Enrollment: 1,776 . . . . (610) 682-5100
Housing: Homeownership rate: 71.4% (2010); Median home value: $147,300 (2006-2010 5-year est.); Median contract rent: $638 per month (2006-2010 5-year est.); Median year structure built: before 1940 (2006-2010 5-year est.).
Transportation: Commute to work: 96.7% car, 0.0% public transportation, 3.3% walk, 0.0% work from home (2006-2010 5-year est.); Travel time to work: 41.0% less than 15 minutes, 41.8% 15 to 30 minutes, 6.5% 30 to 45 minutes, 10.7% 45 to 60 minutes, 0.0% 60 minutes or more (2006-2010 5-year est.)

MOHNTON (borough). Covers a land area of 0.764 square miles and a water area of 0.005 square miles. Located at 40.29° N. Lat; 75.99° W. Long. Elevation is 495 feet.
History: Founded 1850, incorporated 1907.
Population: 2,431 (1990); 2,963 (2000); 3,043 (2010); Density: 3,981.7 persons per square mile (2010); Race: 94.5% White, 1.7% Black, 0.7% Asian, 0.2% American Indian/Alaska Native, 0.0% Native Hawaiian/Other Pacific Islander, 2.9% Other, 4.9% Hispanic of any race (2010); Average household size: 2.42 (2010); Median age: 40.0 (2010); Males per 100 females: 91.9 (2010); Marriage status: 26.1% never married, 55.4% now married, 6.6% widowed, 11.9% divorced (2006-2010 5-year est.); Foreign born: 2.4% (2006-2010 5-year est.); Ancestry (includes multiple ancestries): 43.8% German, 16.7% Italian, 16.1% Irish, 6.1% English, 5.6% Polish (2006-2010 5-year est.).
Economy: Single-family building permits issued: 1 (2011); Multi-family building permits issued: 0 (2011); Employment by occupation: 11.0% management, 2.7% professional, 8.4% services, 20.1% sales, 1.5% farming, 10.3% construction, 3.1% production (2006-2010 5-year est.).
Income: Per capita income: $30,278 (2006-2010 5-year est.); Median household income: $48,555 (2006-2010 5-year est.); Average household income: $66,881 (2006-2010 5-year est.); Percent of households with income of $100,000 or more: 20.5% (2006-2010 5-year est.); Poverty rate: 5.3% (2006-2010 5-year est.).
Education: Percent of population age 25 and over with: High school diploma (including GED) or higher: 87.8% (2006-2010 5-year est.); Bachelor's degree or higher: 28.6% (2006-2010 5-year est.); Master's degree or higher: 11.8% (2006-2010 5-year est.).
School District(s)
Governor Mifflin SD (KG-12)
　　2010-11 Enrollment: 4,249 . . . . (610) 775-1461
Housing: Homeownership rate: 73.7% (2010); Median home value: $148,800 (2006-2010 5-year est.); Median contract rent: $551 per month (2006-2010 5-year est.); Median year structure built: 1971 (2006-2010 5-year est.).
Transportation: Commute to work: 96.7% car, 0.0% public transportation, 0.8% walk, 1.9% work from home (2006-2010 5-year est.); Travel time to work: 31.0% less than 15 minutes, 50.9% 15 to 30 minutes, 9.0% 30 to 45 minutes, 3.4% 45 to 60 minutes, 5.7% 60 minutes or more (2006-2010 5-year est.)
Additional Information Contacts
Greater Reading Chamber of Commerce & Industry . . . . . (610) 376-6766
　　http://www.greaterreadingchamber.org

MOHRSVILLE (CDP). Covers a land area of 1.165 square miles and a water area of 0 square miles. Located at 40.48° N. Lat; 75.98° W. Long. Elevation is 351 feet.
Population: n/a (1990); n/a (2000); 383 (2010); Density: 328.7 persons per square mile (2010); Race: 92.7% White, 1.3% Black, 3.7% Asian, 0.3% American Indian/Alaska Native, 0.0% Native Hawaiian/Other Pacific Islander, 2.0% Other, 2.3% Hispanic of any race (2010); Average household size: 2.50 (2010); Median age: 40.9 (2010); Males per 100 females: 101.6 (2010); Marriage status: 10.2% never married, 34.0% now married, 4.2% widowed, 51.6% divorced (2006-2010 5-year est.); Foreign born: 5.5% (2006-2010 5-year est.); Ancestry (includes multiple ancestries): 33.3% German, 22.3% Pennsylvania German, 11.6% English, 6.4% Polish, 6.1% Irish (2006-2010 5-year est.).
Economy: Employment by occupation: 0.0% management, 11.0% professional, 15.0% services, 11.9% sales, 0.0% farming, 0.0% construction, 6.6% production (2006-2010 5-year est.).

Income: Per capita income: $34,167 (2006-2010 5-year est.); Median household income: $103,529 (2006-2010 5-year est.); Average household income: $79,778 (2006-2010 5-year est.); Percent of households with income of $100,000 or more: 55.1% (2006-2010 5-year est.); Poverty rate: 35.2% (2006-2010 5-year est.).

Education: Percent of population age 25 and over with: High school diploma (including GED) or higher: 75.6% (2006-2010 5-year est.); Bachelor's degree or higher: 12.2% (2006-2010 5-year est.); Master's degree or higher: 4.4% (2006-2010 5-year est.).

Housing: Homeownership rate: 81.7% (2010); Median home value: $160,100 (2006-2010 5-year est.); Median contract rent: n/a per month (2006-2010 5-year est.); Median year structure built: 1970 (2006-2010 5-year est.).

Transportation: Commute to work: 100.0% car, 0.0% public transportation, 0.0% walk, 0.0% work from home (2006-2010 5-year est.); Travel time to work: 14.1% less than 15 minutes, 79.8% 15 to 30 minutes, 6.1% 30 to 45 minutes, 0.0% 45 to 60 minutes, 0.0% 60 minutes or more (2006-2010 5-year est.)

MONOCACY STATION (unincorporated postal area)

Zip Code: 19542

Covers a land area of 0.046 square miles and a water area of 0 square miles. Located at 40.26° N. Lat; 75.76° W. Long. Population: 67 (2010); Density: 1,442.3 persons per square mile (2010); Race: 97.0% White, 0.0% Black, 0.0% Asian, 0.0% American Indian/Alaska Native, 0.0% Native Hawaiian/Other Pacific Islander, 3.0% Other, 1.5% Hispanic of any race (2010); Average household size: 2.31 (2010); Median age: 39.3 (2010); Males per 100 females: 97.1 (2010); Homeownership rate: 55.2% (2010)

MONTROSE MANOR (CDP). Covers a land area of 0.231 square miles and a water area of 0 square miles. Located at 40.31° N. Lat; 75.99° W. Long.

Population: n/a (1990); n/a (2000); 604 (2010); Density: 2,613.5 persons per square mile (2010); Race: 94.2% White, 1.8% Black, 1.5% Asian, 0.0% American Indian/Alaska Native, 0.0% Native Hawaiian/Other Pacific Islander, 2.5% Other, 7.5% Hispanic of any race (2010); Average household size: 2.22 (2010); Median age: 47.4 (2010); Males per 100 females: 100.0 (2010); Marriage status: 28.1% never married, 55.9% now married, 5.5% widowed, 10.6% divorced (2006-2010 5-year est.); Foreign born: 3.7% (2006-2010 5-year est.); Ancestry (includes multiple ancestries): 52.6% German, 13.5% Italian, 11.5% Irish, 11.3% Dutch, 10.4% American (2006-2010 5-year est.).

Economy: Employment by occupation: 12.3% management, 0.0% professional, 18.2% services, 10.0% sales, 4.1% farming, 18.6% construction, 8.6% production (2006-2010 5-year est.).

Income: Per capita income: $33,583 (2006-2010 5-year est.); Median household income: $70,104 (2006-2010 5-year est.); Average household income: $68,549 (2006-2010 5-year est.); Percent of households with income of $100,000 or more: 12.8% (2006-2010 5-year est.); Poverty rate: 5.5% (2006-2010 5-year est.).

Education: Percent of population age 25 and over with: High school diploma (including GED) or higher: 82.4% (2006-2010 5-year est.); Bachelor's degree or higher: 30.3% (2006-2010 5-year est.); Master's degree or higher: 5.7% (2006-2010 5-year est.).

Housing: Homeownership rate: 87.1% (2010); Median home value: $139,800 (2006-2010 5-year est.); Median contract rent: $740 per month (2006-2010 5-year est.); Median year structure built: 1953 (2006-2010 5-year est.).

Transportation: Commute to work: 91.5% car, 0.0% public transportation, 4.2% walk, 0.0% work from home (2006-2010 5-year est.); Travel time to work: 59.6% less than 15 minutes, 17.7% 15 to 30 minutes, 14.6% 30 to 45 minutes, 3.8% 45 to 60 minutes, 4.2% 60 minutes or more (2006-2010 5-year est.)

MORGANTOWN (CDP). Covers a land area of 0.940 square miles and a water area of <.001 square miles. Located at 40.15° N. Lat; 75.89° W. Long. Elevation is 600 feet.

Population: n/a (1990); n/a (2000); 826 (2010); Density: 878.3 persons per square mile (2010); Race: 94.4% White, 0.2% Black, 2.3% Asian, 0.1% American Indian/Alaska Native, 0.0% Native Hawaiian/Other Pacific Islander, 3.0% Other, 2.5% Hispanic of any race (2010); Average household size: 2.41 (2010); Median age: 40.1 (2010); Males per 100 females: 100.5 (2010); Marriage status: 18.7% never married, 56.5% now married, 12.4% widowed, 12.4% divorced (2006-2010 5-year est.); Foreign

born: 3.9% (2006-2010 5-year est.); Ancestry (includes multiple ancestries): 51.3% German, 22.9% Irish, 20.2% English, 12.6% Italian, 6.3% Welsh (2006-2010 5-year est.).

Economy: Employment by occupation: 3.7% management, 4.3% professional, 10.0% services, 27.6% sales, 6.5% farming, 9.2% construction, 4.5% production (2006-2010 5-year est.).

Income: Per capita income: $25,421 (2006-2010 5-year est.); Median household income: $55,625 (2006-2010 5-year est.); Average household income: $56,386 (2006-2010 5-year est.); Percent of households with income of $100,000 or more: 8.3% (2006-2010 5-year est.); Poverty rate: 3.6% (2006-2010 5-year est.).

Education: Percent of population age 25 and over with: High school diploma (including GED) or higher: 90.4% (2006-2010 5-year est.); Bachelor's degree or higher: 32.3% (2006-2010 5-year est.); Master's degree or higher: 5.6% (2006-2010 5-year est.).

Housing: Homeownership rate: 61.5% (2010); Median home value: $218,200 (2006-2010 5-year est.); Median contract rent: $638 per month (2006-2010 5-year est.); Median year structure built: 1959 (2006-2010 5-year est.).

Transportation: Commute to work: 92.0% car, 0.0% public transportation, 2.7% walk, 5.3% work from home (2006-2010 5-year est.); Travel time to work: 42.2% less than 15 minutes, 31.5% 15 to 30 minutes, 15.9% 30 to 45 minutes, 4.7% 45 to 60 minutes, 5.6% 60 minutes or more (2006-2010 5-year est.)

MOUNT AETNA (CDP). Covers a land area of 0.439 square miles and a water area of 0.001 square miles. Located at 40.42° N. Lat; 76.30° W. Long. Elevation is 623 feet.

Population: n/a (1990); n/a (2000); 354 (2010); Density: 805.7 persons per square mile (2010); Race: 94.1% White, 1.1% Black, 0.0% Asian, 1.1% American Indian/Alaska Native, 0.0% Native Hawaiian/Other Pacific Islander, 3.7% Other, 3.4% Hispanic of any race (2010); Average household size: 2.55 (2010); Median age: 40.7 (2010); Males per 100 females: 114.5 (2010); Marriage status: 31.4% never married, 60.4% now married, 3.3% widowed, 4.9% divorced (2006-2010 5-year est.); Foreign born: 0.0% (2006-2010 5-year est.); Ancestry (includes multiple ancestries): 58.7% German, 12.7% Scotch-Irish, 6.3% Swiss, 4.6% Ukrainian, 2.2% Swedish (2006-2010 5-year est.).

Economy: Employment by occupation: 2.9% management, 4.3% professional, 27.4% services, 26.9% sales, 2.9% farming, 6.3% construction, 3.4% production (2006-2010 5-year est.).

Income: Per capita income: $20,533 (2006-2010 5-year est.); Median household income: $48,158 (2006-2010 5-year est.); Average household income: $47,786 (2006-2010 5-year est.); Percent of households with income of $100,000 or more: 3.4% (2006-2010 5-year est.); Poverty rate: 4.6% (2006-2010 5-year est.).

Education: Percent of population age 25 and over with: High school diploma (including GED) or higher: 90.7% (2006-2010 5-year est.); Bachelor's degree or higher: 0.0% (2006-2010 5-year est.); Master's degree or higher: 0.0% (2006-2010 5-year est.).

Housing: Homeownership rate: 77.7% (2010); Median home value: $164,100 (2006-2010 5-year est.); Median contract rent: $622 per month (2006-2010 5-year est.); Median year structure built: before 1940 (2006-2010 5-year est.).

Transportation: Commute to work: 85.9% car, 0.0% public transportation, 8.0% walk, 6.0% work from home (2006-2010 5-year est.); Travel time to work: 53.5% less than 15 minutes, 32.1% 15 to 30 minutes, 0.0% 30 to 45 minutes, 4.3% 45 to 60 minutes, 10.2% 60 minutes or more (2006-2010 5-year est.)

MOUNT PENN (borough). Covers a land area of 0.430 square miles and a water area of 0 square miles. Located at 40.33° N. Lat; 75.89° W. Long. Elevation is 522 feet.

Population: 2,883 (1990); 3,016 (2000); 3,106 (2010); Density: 7,225.8 persons per square mile (2010); Race: 84.3% White, 4.3% Black, 1.3% Asian, 0.5% American Indian/Alaska Native, 0.0% Native Hawaiian/Other Pacific Islander, 9.6% Other, 14.1% Hispanic of any race (2010); Average household size: 2.47 (2010); Median age: 35.9 (2010); Males per 100 females: 92.3 (2010); Marriage status: 32.1% never married, 49.3% now married, 3.6% widowed, 15.0% divorced (2006-2010 5-year est.); Foreign born: 4.4% (2006-2010 5-year est.); Ancestry (includes multiple ancestries): 35.5% German, 13.0% Irish, 10.7% Polish, 8.9% Italian, 7.5% English (2006-2010 5-year est.).

Economy: Single-family building permits issued: 0 (2011); Multi-family building permits issued: 35 (2011); Employment by occupation: 8.7%

management, 3.0% professional, 11.2% services, 17.7% sales, 4.7% farming, 5.6% construction, 8.1% production (2006-2010 5-year est.).
Income: Per capita income: $23,512 (2006-2010 5-year est.); Median household income: $57,696 (2006-2010 5-year est.); Average household income: $57,744 (2006-2010 5-year est.); Percent of households with income of $100,000 or more: 13.5% (2006-2010 5-year est.); Poverty rate: 14.6% (2006-2010 5-year est.).
Education: Percent of population age 25 and over with: High school diploma (including GED) or higher: 91.6% (2006-2010 5-year est.); Bachelor's degree or higher: 27.2% (2006-2010 5-year est.); Master's degree or higher: 6.3% (2006-2010 5-year est.).

School District(s)
Antietam SD (KG-12)
  2010-11 Enrollment: 1,046 . . . . (610) 779-0554
Housing: Homeownership rate: 70.6% (2010); Median home value: $130,800 (2006-2010 5-year est.); Median contract rent: $572 per month (2006-2010 5-year est.); Median year structure built: before 1940 (2006-2010 5-year est.).
Transportation: Commute to work: 95.9% car, 1.3% public transportation, 0.4% walk, 2.4% work from home (2006-2010 5-year est.); Travel time to work: 37.3% less than 15 minutes, 37.6% 15 to 30 minutes, 11.5% 30 to 45 minutes, 4.9% 45 to 60 minutes, 8.7% 60 minutes or more (2006-2010 5-year est.)
Additional Information Contacts
Greater Reading Chamber of Commerce & Industry . . . . . (610) 376-6766
  http://www.greaterreadingchamber.org

MUHLENBERG (township). Covers a land area of 11.775 square miles and a water area of 0.228 square miles. Located at 40.40° N. Lat; 75.92° W. Long. Elevation is 331 feet.
Population: 14,043 (1990); 16,305 (2000); 19,628 (2010); Density: 1,666.9 persons per square mile (2010); Race: 85.9% White, 4.3% Black, 1.5% Asian, 0.3% American Indian/Alaska Native, 0.0% Native Hawaiian/Other Pacific Islander, 8.0% Other, 13.8% Hispanic of any race (2010); Average household size: 2.49 (2010); Median age: 42.9 (2010); Males per 100 females: 93.3 (2010); Marriage status: 26.5% never married, 53.6% now married, 9.1% widowed, 10.7% divorced (2006-2010 5-year est.); Foreign born: 6.0% (2006-2010 5-year est.); Ancestry (includes multiple ancestries): 40.0% German, 14.2% Italian, 12.9% Irish, 6.8% English, 6.0% Pennsylvania German (2006-2010 5-year est.).
Economy: Single-family building permits issued: 28 (2011); Multi-family building permits issued: 0 (2011); Employment by occupation: 9.3% management, 1.8% professional, 9.5% services, 19.3% sales, 5.0% farming, 8.3% construction, 6.8% production (2006-2010 5-year est.).
Income: Per capita income: $26,635 (2006-2010 5-year est.); Median household income: $55,132 (2006-2010 5-year est.); Average household income: $65,834 (2006-2010 5-year est.); Percent of households with income of $100,000 or more: 16.3% (2006-2010 5-year est.); Poverty rate: 9.1% (2006-2010 5-year est.).
Education: Percent of population age 25 and over with: High school diploma (including GED) or higher: 84.4% (2006-2010 5-year est.); Bachelor's degree or higher: 17.1% (2006-2010 5-year est.); Master's degree or higher: 7.0% (2006-2010 5-year est.).
Housing: Homeownership rate: 79.4% (2010); Median home value: $156,200 (2006-2010 5-year est.); Median contract rent: $598 per month (2006-2010 5-year est.); Median year structure built: 1964 (2006-2010 5-year est.).
Safety: Violent crime rate: 14.2 per 10,000 population; Property crime rate: 379.9 per 10,000 population (2011).
Transportation: Commute to work: 92.5% car, 1.6% public transportation, 2.1% walk, 2.4% work from home (2006-2010 5-year est.); Travel time to work: 39.9% less than 15 minutes, 45.4% 15 to 30 minutes, 7.1% 30 to 45 minutes, 2.5% 45 to 60 minutes, 5.1% 60 minutes or more (2006-2010 5-year est.)
Additional Information Contacts
Greater Reading Chamber of Commerce & Industry . . . . . (610) 376-6766
  http://www.greaterreadingchamber.org
Muhlenberg Township. . . . . (610) 929-4727
  http://www.muhlenbergtwp.com

MUHLENBERG PARK (CDP). Covers a land area of 0.592 square miles and a water area of 0 square miles. Located at 40.39° N. Lat; 75.94° W. Long. Elevation is 272 feet.
Population: n/a (1990); n/a (2000); 1,420 (2010); Density: 2,400.6 persons per square mile (2010); Race: 93.3% White, 2.6% Black, 0.1%

Asian, 0.1% American Indian/Alaska Native, 0.0% Native Hawaiian/Other Pacific Islander, 3.9% Other, 8.7% Hispanic of any race (2010); Average household size: 2.31 (2010); Median age: 51.6 (2010); Males per 100 females: 94.0 (2010); Marriage status: 21.0% never married, 64.9% now married, 6.8% widowed, 7.3% divorced (2006-2010 5-year est.); Foreign born: 1.8% (2006-2010 5-year est.); Ancestry (includes multiple ancestries): 52.8% German, 14.1% Italian, 9.5% English, 8.7% Polish, 7.8% Dutch (2006-2010 5-year est.).
Economy: Employment by occupation: 6.7% management, 0.0% professional, 3.6% services, 12.8% sales, 4.6% farming, 11.2% construction, 6.7% production (2006-2010 5-year est.).
Income: Per capita income: $25,430 (2006-2010 5-year est.); Median household income: $57,206 (2006-2010 5-year est.); Average household income: $66,548 (2006-2010 5-year est.); Percent of households with income of $100,000 or more: 22.9% (2006-2010 5-year est.); Poverty rate: 12.1% (2006-2010 5-year est.).
Education: Percent of population age 25 and over with: High school diploma (including GED) or higher: 90.2% (2006-2010 5-year est.); Bachelor's degree or higher: 10.9% (2006-2010 5-year est.); Master's degree or higher: 6.5% (2006-2010 5-year est.).
Housing: Homeownership rate: 94.7% (2010); Median home value: $166,000 (2006-2010 5-year est.); Median contract rent: n/a per month (2006-2010 5-year est.); Median year structure built: 1962 (2006-2010 5-year est.).
Transportation: Commute to work: 91.7% car, 2.1% public transportation, 0.0% walk, 4.3% work from home (2006-2010 5-year est.); Travel time to work: 36.8% less than 15 minutes, 54.6% 15 to 30 minutes, 6.4% 30 to 45 minutes, 2.2% 45 to 60 minutes, 0.0% 60 minutes or more (2006-2010 5-year est.)

NEW BERLINVILLE (CDP). Covers a land area of 1.510 square miles and a water area of 0.003 square miles. Located at 40.35° N. Lat; 75.63° W. Long. Elevation is 400 feet.
Population: n/a (1990); n/a (2000); 1,368 (2010); Density: 905.8 persons per square mile (2010); Race: 96.9% White, 0.1% Black, 0.3% Asian, 0.1% American Indian/Alaska Native, 0.0% Native Hawaiian/Other Pacific Islander, 2.6% Other, 0.9% Hispanic of any race (2010); Average household size: 2.48 (2010); Median age: 43.4 (2010); Males per 100 females: 93.5 (2010); Marriage status: 28.3% never married, 61.0% now married, 4.2% widowed, 6.5% divorced (2006-2010 5-year est.); Foreign born: 0.8% (2006-2010 5-year est.); Ancestry (includes multiple ancestries): 48.8% German, 15.1% Irish, 7.7% Polish, 7.7% Pennsylvania German, 5.9% American (2006-2010 5-year est.).
Economy: Employment by occupation: 4.4% management, 1.9% professional, 3.1% services, 19.4% sales, 10.2% farming, 12.0% construction, 11.7% production (2006-2010 5-year est.).
Income: Per capita income: $24,783 (2006-2010 5-year est.); Median household income: $61,395 (2006-2010 5-year est.); Average household income: $62,940 (2006-2010 5-year est.); Percent of households with income of $100,000 or more: 9.8% (2006-2010 5-year est.); Poverty rate: 0.0% (2006-2010 5-year est.).
Education: Percent of population age 25 and over with: High school diploma (including GED) or higher: 81.3% (2006-2010 5-year est.); Bachelor's degree or higher: 13.7% (2006-2010 5-year est.); Master's degree or higher: 2.8% (2006-2010 5-year est.).
Housing: Homeownership rate: 79.7% (2010); Median home value: $177,200 (2006-2010 5-year est.); Median contract rent: $669 per month (2006-2010 5-year est.); Median year structure built: 1946 (2006-2010 5-year est.).
Transportation: Commute to work: 98.1% car, 0.0% public transportation, 1.9% walk, 0.0% work from home (2006-2010 5-year est.); Travel time to work: 36.9% less than 15 minutes, 17.2% 15 to 30 minutes, 30.1% 30 to 45 minutes, 4.4% 45 to 60 minutes, 11.4% 60 minutes or more (2006-2010 5-year est.)

NEW JERUSALEM (CDP). Covers a land area of 1.817 square miles and a water area of 0.003 square miles. Located at 40.44° N. Lat; 75.76° W. Long. Elevation is 899 feet.
Population: n/a (1990); n/a (2000); 649 (2010); Density: 357.1 persons per square mile (2010); Race: 97.5% White, 0.8% Black, 0.3% Asian, 0.0% American Indian/Alaska Native, 0.0% Native Hawaiian/Other Pacific Islander, 1.4% Other, 3.5% Hispanic of any race (2010); Average household size: 2.81 (2010); Median age: 38.2 (2010); Males per 100 females: 105.4 (2010); Marriage status: 20.8% never married, 71.3% now married, 5.4% widowed, 2.4% divorced (2006-2010 5-year est.); Foreign

born: 0.0% (2006-2010 5-year est.); Ancestry (includes multiple ancestries): 58.2% German, 20.7% Italian, 13.1% Irish, 11.9% Dutch, 10.0% Pennsylvania German (2006-2010 5-year est.).

Economy: Employment by occupation: 20.3% management, 3.4% professional, 21.7% services, 8.3% sales, 0.0% farming, 13.7% construction, 0.0% production (2006-2010 5-year est.).

Income: Per capita income: $31,277 (2006-2010 5-year est.); Median household income: $65,114 (2006-2010 5-year est.); Average household income: $75,538 (2006-2010 5-year est.); Percent of households with income of $100,000 or more: 28.3% (2006-2010 5-year est.); Poverty rate: 5.9% (2006-2010 5-year est.).

Education: Percent of population age 25 and over with: High school diploma (including GED) or higher: 92.7% (2006-2010 5-year est.); Bachelor's degree or higher: 37.3% (2006-2010 5-year est.); Master's degree or higher: 16.7% (2006-2010 5-year est.).

Housing: Homeownership rate: 93.1% (2010); Median home value: $263,200 (2006-2010 5-year est.); Median contract rent: n/a per month (2006-2010 5-year est.); Median year structure built: 1991 (2006-2010 5-year est.).

Transportation: Commute to work: 88.9% car, 0.0% public transportation, 0.0% walk, 0.0% work from home (2006-2010 5-year est.); Travel time to work: 26.0% less than 15 minutes, 19.7% 15 to 30 minutes, 30.6% 30 to 45 minutes, 6.6% 45 to 60 minutes, 17.1% 60 minutes or more (2006-2010 5-year est.)

NEW MORGAN (borough). Covers a land area of 5.483 square miles and a water area of 0.263 square miles. Located at 40.19° N. Lat; 75.90° W. Long. Elevation is 630 feet.

Population: 30 (1990); 35 (2000); 71 (2010); Density: 12.9 persons per square mile (2010); Race: 35.2% White, 45.1% Black, 1.4% Asian, 0.0% American Indian/Alaska Native, 0.0% Native Hawaiian/Other Pacific Islander, 18.3% Other, 19.7% Hispanic of any race (2010); Average household size: 2.50 (2010); Median age: 17.5 (2010); Males per 100 females: ***.* (2010); Marriage status: 9.1% never married, 63.6% now married, 0.0% widowed, 27.3% divorced (2006-2010 5-year est.); Foreign born: 0.0% (2006-2010 5-year est.); Ancestry (includes multiple ancestries): 58.8% German, 47.1% Irish, 41.2% Italian, 11.8% Portuguese, 11.8% Dutch (2006-2010 5-year est.).

Economy: Single-family building permits issued: 0 (2011); Multi-family building permits issued: 0 (2011); Employment by occupation: 20.0% management, 0.0% professional, 0.0% services, 0.0% sales, 0.0% farming, 20.0% construction, 20.0% production (2006-2010 5-year est.).

Income: Per capita income: $34,935 (2006-2010 5-year est.); Median household income: $83,125 (2006-2010 5-year est.); Average household income: $90,714 (2006-2010 5-year est.); Percent of households with income of $100,000 or more: 28.6% (2006-2010 5-year est.); Poverty rate: 6.3% (2006-2010 5-year est.).

Education: Percent of population age 25 and over with: High school diploma (including GED) or higher: 60.0% (2006-2010 5-year est.); Bachelor's degree or higher: 0.0% (2006-2010 5-year est.); Master's degree or higher: 0.0% (2006-2010 5-year est.).

Housing: Homeownership rate: 0.0% (2010); Median home value: n/a (2006-2010 5-year est.); Median contract rent: $775 per month (2006-2010 5-year est.); Median year structure built: 1953 (2006-2010 5-year est.).

Transportation: Commute to work: 100.0% car, 0.0% public transportation, 0.0% walk, 0.0% work from home (2006-2010 5-year est.); Travel time to work: 40.0% less than 15 minutes, 20.0% 15 to 30 minutes, 30.0% 30 to 45 minutes, 0.0% 45 to 60 minutes, 10.0% 60 minutes or more (2006-2010 5-year est.)

NEW SCHAEFFERSTOWN (CDP). Covers a land area of 1.037 square miles and a water area of <.001 square miles. Located at 40.45° N. Lat; 76.17° W. Long.

Population: n/a (1990); n/a (2000); 223 (2010); Density: 215.1 persons per square mile (2010); Race: 97.8% White, 1.8% Black, 0.0% Asian, 0.0% American Indian/Alaska Native, 0.0% Native Hawaiian/Other Pacific Islander, 0.4% Other, 3.1% Hispanic of any race (2010); Average household size: 2.82 (2010); Median age: 42.4 (2010); Males per 100 females: 108.4 (2010); Marriage status: 21.6% never married, 61.9% now married, 3.1% widowed, 13.4% divorced (2006-2010 5-year est.); Foreign born: 0.0% (2006-2010 5-year est.); Ancestry (includes multiple ancestries): 53.7% German, 15.6% Hungarian, 15.6% Ukrainian, 8.2% Italian, 6.1% Pennsylvania German (2006-2010 5-year est.).

Economy: Employment by occupation: 8.6% management, 5.2% professional, 32.8% services, 12.1% sales, 0.0% farming, 17.2% construction, 6.9% production (2006-2010 5-year est.).

Income: Per capita income: $26,136 (2006-2010 5-year est.); Median household income: $68,750 (2006-2010 5-year est.); Average household income: $77,171 (2006-2010 5-year est.); Percent of households with income of $100,000 or more: 39.6% (2006-2010 5-year est.); Poverty rate: 0.0% (2006-2010 5-year est.).

Education: Percent of population age 25 and over with: High school diploma (including GED) or higher: 79.1% (2006-2010 5-year est.); Bachelor's degree or higher: 8.8% (2006-2010 5-year est.); Master's degree or higher: 5.5% (2006-2010 5-year est.).

Housing: Homeownership rate: 89.8% (2010); Median home value: $134,400 (2006-2010 5-year est.); Median contract rent: n/a per month (2006-2010 5-year est.); Median year structure built: 1965 (2006-2010 5-year est.).

Transportation: Commute to work: 85.7% car, 0.0% public transportation, 8.9% walk, 5.4% work from home (2006-2010 5-year est.); Travel time to work: 30.2% less than 15 minutes, 22.6% 15 to 30 minutes, 35.8% 30 to 45 minutes, 5.7% 45 to 60 minutes, 5.7% 60 minutes or more (2006-2010 5-year est.)

NORTH HEIDELBERG (township). Covers a land area of 13.467 square miles and a water area of 0.372 square miles. Located at 40.40° N. Lat; 76.12° W. Long. Elevation is 446 feet.

Population: 1,288 (1990); 1,325 (2000); 1,214 (2010); Density: 90.1 persons per square mile (2010); Race: 97.2% White, 0.3% Black, 0.4% Asian, 0.2% American Indian/Alaska Native, 0.0% Native Hawaiian/Other Pacific Islander, 1.9% Other, 2.0% Hispanic of any race (2010); Average household size: 2.56 (2010); Median age: 49.6 (2010); Males per 100 females: 101.0 (2010); Marriage status: 16.7% never married, 72.0% now married, 5.4% widowed, 5.9% divorced (2006-2010 5-year est.); Foreign born: 2.3% (2006-2010 5-year est.); Ancestry (includes multiple ancestries): 62.3% German, 15.2% Italian, 9.0% Irish, 6.0% American, 5.9% Polish (2006-2010 5-year est.).

Economy: Single-family building permits issued: 0 (2011); Multi-family building permits issued: 0 (2011); Employment by occupation: 19.8% management, 4.4% professional, 7.5% services, 12.8% sales, 3.1% farming, 11.4% construction, 8.2% production (2006-2010 5-year est.).

Income: Per capita income: $31,128 (2006-2010 5-year est.); Median household income: $67,885 (2006-2010 5-year est.); Average household income: $80,035 (2006-2010 5-year est.); Percent of households with income of $100,000 or more: 29.4% (2006-2010 5-year est.); Poverty rate: 1.5% (2006-2010 5-year est.).

Education: Percent of population age 25 and over with: High school diploma (including GED) or higher: 91.7% (2006-2010 5-year est.); Bachelor's degree or higher: 19.4% (2006-2010 5-year est.); Master's degree or higher: 6.5% (2006-2010 5-year est.).

Housing: Homeownership rate: 91.2% (2010); Median home value: $235,500 (2006-2010 5-year est.); Median contract rent: $375 per month (2006-2010 5-year est.); Median year structure built: 1974 (2006-2010 5-year est.).

Transportation: Commute to work: 85.0% car, 0.0% public transportation, 12.0% walk, 2.9% work from home (2006-2010 5-year est.); Travel time to work: 25.4% less than 15 minutes, 43.8% 15 to 30 minutes, 21.8% 30 to 45 minutes, 3.4% 45 to 60 minutes, 5.7% 60 minutes or more (2006-2010 5-year est.)

Additional Information Contacts
Greater Reading Chamber of Commerce & Industry . . . . . (610) 376-6766
http://www.greaterreadingchamber.org

OLEY (CDP). Covers a land area of 1.227 square miles and a water area of 0.016 square miles. Located at 40.39° N. Lat; 75.79° W. Long. Elevation is 440 feet.

Population: n/a (1990); n/a (2000); 1,282 (2010); Density: 1,044.5 persons per square mile (2010); Race: 97.8% White, 0.4% Black, 0.6% Asian, 0.0% American Indian/Alaska Native, 0.0% Native Hawaiian/Other Pacific Islander, 1.2% Other, 3.0% Hispanic of any race (2010); Average household size: 2.42 (2010); Median age: 42.6 (2010); Males per 100 females: 96.3 (2010); Marriage status: 26.2% never married, 66.0% now married, 4.0% widowed, 3.8% divorced (2006-2010 5-year est.); Foreign born: 0.6% (2006-2010 5-year est.); Ancestry (includes multiple ancestries): 39.0% German, 14.8% Pennsylvania German, 14.4% American, 11.1% Irish, 11.0% Polish (2006-2010 5-year est.).

Economy: Employment by occupation: 2.8% management, 2.2% professional, 11.7% services, 14.0% sales, 1.4% farming, 15.9% construction, 9.9% production (2006-2010 5-year est.).
Income: Per capita income: $23,279 (2006-2010 5-year est.); Median household income: $64,038 (2006-2010 5-year est.); Average household income: $63,854 (2006-2010 5-year est.); Percent of households with income of $100,000 or more: 12.7% (2006-2010 5-year est.); Poverty rate: 1.0% (2006-2010 5-year est.).
Education: Percent of population age 25 and over with: High school diploma (including GED) or higher: 92.0% (2006-2010 5-year est.); Bachelor's degree or higher: 21.6% (2006-2010 5-year est.); Master's degree or higher: 4.8% (2006-2010 5-year est.).

School District(s)

Berks CTC (09-12)
    2010-11 Enrollment: n/a . . . . (610) 374-4073
Oley Valley SD (KG-12)
    2010-11 Enrollment: 1,873 . . . . (610) 987-4100
Housing: Homeownership rate: 72.9% (2010); Median home value: $191,000 (2006-2010 5-year est.); Median contract rent: $762 per month (2006-2010 5-year est.); Median year structure built: 1971 (2006-2010 5-year est.).
Transportation: Commute to work: 87.4% car, 1.2% public transportation, 9.5% walk, 1.8% work from home (2006-2010 5-year est.); Travel time to work: 25.4% less than 15 minutes, 49.9% 15 to 30 minutes, 16.9% 30 to 45 minutes, 6.2% 45 to 60 minutes, 1.5% 60 minutes or more (2006-2010 5-year est.)

OLEY (township). Covers a land area of 23.896 square miles and a water area of 0.192 square miles. Located at 40.37° N. Lat; 75.77° W. Long. Elevation is 440 feet.
Population: 3,362 (1990); 3,583 (2000); 3,620 (2010); Density: 151.5 persons per square mile (2010); Race: 97.9% White, 0.4% Black, 0.4% Asian, 0.1% American Indian/Alaska Native, 0.0% Native Hawaiian/Other Pacific Islander, 1.2% Other, 1.9% Hispanic of any race (2010); Average household size: 2.48 (2010); Median age: 43.8 (2010); Males per 100 females: 99.8 (2010); Marriage status: 24.0% never married, 65.7% now married, 4.9% widowed, 5.4% divorced (2006-2010 5-year est.); Foreign born: 0.2% (2006-2010 5-year est.); Ancestry (includes multiple ancestries): 46.7% German, 13.5% Pennsylvania German, 12.6% Irish, 9.1% Polish, 7.9% English (2006-2010 5-year est.).
Economy: Single-family building permits issued: 5 (2011); Multi-family building permits issued: 0 (2011); Employment by occupation: 11.1% management, 0.9% professional, 9.3% services, 13.3% sales, 3.3% farming, 15.0% construction, 12.9% production (2006-2010 5-year est.).
Income: Per capita income: $26,792 (2006-2010 5-year est.); Median household income: $58,390 (2006-2010 5-year est.); Average household income: $69,982 (2006-2010 5-year est.); Percent of households with income of $100,000 or more: 18.2% (2006-2010 5-year est.); Poverty rate: 3.0% (2006-2010 5-year est.).
Education: Percent of population age 25 and over with: High school diploma (including GED) or higher: 88.9% (2006-2010 5-year est.); Bachelor's degree or higher: 20.7% (2006-2010 5-year est.); Master's degree or higher: 7.8% (2006-2010 5-year est.).
Housing: Homeownership rate: 75.2% (2010); Median home value: $214,600 (2006-2010 5-year est.); Median contract rent: $639 per month (2006-2010 5-year est.); Median year structure built: 1960 (2006-2010 5-year est.).
Transportation: Commute to work: 84.7% car, 0.5% public transportation, 9.4% walk, 5.3% work from home (2006-2010 5-year est.); Travel time to work: 28.5% less than 15 minutes, 41.8% 15 to 30 minutes, 15.9% 30 to 45 minutes, 8.0% 45 to 60 minutes, 5.7% 60 minutes or more (2006-2010 5-year est.)

Additional Information Contacts
Greater Reading Chamber of Commerce & Industry . . . . . (610) 376-6766
  http://www.greaterreadingchamber.org

ONTELAUNEE (township). Covers a land area of 8.723 square miles and a water area of 0.638 square miles. Located at 40.45° N. Lat; 75.94° W. Long. Elevation is 259 feet.
Population: 1,299 (1990); 1,217 (2000); 1,646 (2010); Density: 188.7 persons per square mile (2010); Race: 86.2% White, 5.2% Black, 2.6% Asian, 0.2% American Indian/Alaska Native, 0.0% Native Hawaiian/Other Pacific Islander, 5.8% Other, 8.4% Hispanic of any race (2010); Average household size: 2.58 (2010); Median age: 40.6 (2010); Males per 100 females: 106.3 (2010); Marriage status: 27.7% never married, 61.8% now

married, 4.3% widowed, 6.3% divorced (2006-2010 5-year est.); Foreign born: 3.3% (2006-2010 5-year est.); Ancestry (includes multiple ancestries): 39.4% German, 16.2% Irish, 9.4% Pennsylvania German, 6.4% Italian, 5.7% Swiss (2006-2010 5-year est.).
Economy: Single-family building permits issued: 4 (2011); Multi-family building permits issued: 0 (2011); Employment by occupation: 5.6% management, 5.5% professional, 5.2% services, 21.9% sales, 4.1% farming, 4.3% construction, 12.6% production (2006-2010 5-year est.).
Income: Per capita income: $23,808 (2006-2010 5-year est.); Median household income: $50,903 (2006-2010 5-year est.); Average household income: $60,257 (2006-2010 5-year est.); Percent of households with income of $100,000 or more: 17.9% (2006-2010 5-year est.); Poverty rate: 12.5% (2006-2010 5-year est.).
Education: Percent of population age 25 and over with: High school diploma (including GED) or higher: 86.4% (2006-2010 5-year est.); Bachelor's degree or higher: 18.4% (2006-2010 5-year est.); Master's degree or higher: 7.1% (2006-2010 5-year est.).
Housing: Homeownership rate: 82.5% (2010); Median home value: $191,100 (2006-2010 5-year est.); Median contract rent: $700 per month (2006-2010 5-year est.); Median year structure built: 1967 (2006-2010 5-year est.).
Transportation: Commute to work: 94.9% car, 0.0% public transportation, 0.4% walk, 4.7% work from home (2006-2010 5-year est.); Travel time to work: 28.9% less than 15 minutes, 43.5% 15 to 30 minutes, 18.3% 30 to 45 minutes, 6.6% 45 to 60 minutes, 2.7% 60 minutes or more (2006-2010 5-year est.)

Additional Information Contacts
Greater Reading Chamber of Commerce & Industry . . . . . (610) 376-6766
  http://www.greaterreadingchamber.org

PENN (township). Covers a land area of 18.490 square miles and a water area of 0.486 square miles. Located at 40.43° N. Lat; 76.08° W. Long.
History: Mt. Penn, with observation tower and the Pagoda, to Northwest. Laid out 1884, incorporated 1902.
Population: 1,831 (1990); 1,993 (2000); 1,949 (2010); Density: 105.4 persons per square mile (2010); Race: 95.9% White, 1.2% Black, 0.4% Asian, 0.3% American Indian/Alaska Native, 0.0% Native Hawaiian/Other Pacific Islander, 2.2% Other, 4.9% Hispanic of any race (2010); Average household size: 2.62 (2010); Median age: 47.2 (2010); Males per 100 females: 107.3 (2010); Marriage status: 19.0% never married, 65.1% now married, 5.9% widowed, 10.0% divorced (2006-2010 5-year est.); Foreign born: 2.0% (2006-2010 5-year est.); Ancestry (includes multiple ancestries): 58.8% German, 10.3% Irish, 6.8% Pennsylvania German, 6.3% Italian, 5.9% American (2006-2010 5-year est.).
Economy: Single-family building permits issued: 7 (2011); Multi-family building permits issued: 0 (2011); Employment by occupation: 14.0% management, 3.1% professional, 6.6% services, 14.4% sales, 2.2% farming, 14.0% construction, 9.7% production (2006-2010 5-year est.).
Income: Per capita income: $31,151 (2006-2010 5-year est.); Median household income: $73,250 (2006-2010 5-year est.); Average household income: $78,239 (2006-2010 5-year est.); Percent of households with income of $100,000 or more: 26.0% (2006-2010 5-year est.); Poverty rate: 4.9% (2006-2010 5-year est.).
Education: Percent of population age 25 and over with: High school diploma (including GED) or higher: 89.8% (2006-2010 5-year est.); Bachelor's degree or higher: 24.3% (2006-2010 5-year est.); Master's degree or higher: 8.7% (2006-2010 5-year est.).
Housing: Homeownership rate: 91.9% (2010); Median home value: $214,100 (2006-2010 5-year est.); Median contract rent: $575 per month (2006-2010 5-year est.); Median year structure built: 1979 (2006-2010 5-year est.).
Transportation: Commute to work: 91.7% car, 0.0% public transportation, 2.4% walk, 4.5% work from home (2006-2010 5-year est.); Travel time to work: 17.4% less than 15 minutes, 51.3% 15 to 30 minutes, 19.0% 30 to 45 minutes, 6.7% 45 to 60 minutes, 5.6% 60 minutes or more (2006-2010 5-year est.)

Additional Information Contacts
Greater Reading Chamber of Commerce & Industry . . . . . (610) 376-6766
  http://www.greaterreadingchamber.org

PENNSIDE (CDP). Covers a land area of 0.919 square miles and a water area of 0.010 square miles. Located at 40.34° N. Lat; 75.88° W. Long. Elevation is 338 feet.
Population: n/a (1990); n/a (2000); 4,215 (2010); Density: 4,584.0 persons per square mile (2010); Race: 91.7% White, 2.7% Black, 0.5% Asian, 0.2% American Indian/Alaska Native, 0.0% Native Hawaiian/Other Pacific Islander, 4.9% Other, 8.5% Hispanic of any race (2010); Average household size: 2.39 (2010); Median age: 41.1 (2010); Males per 100 females: 92.6 (2010); Marriage status: 28.0% never married, 53.6% now married, 9.4% widowed, 9.0% divorced (2006-2010 5-year est.); Foreign born: 3.2% (2006-2010 5-year est.); Ancestry (includes multiple ancestries): 44.4% German, 18.6% Irish, 13.7% Polish, 8.8% Italian, 8.3% English (2006-2010 5-year est.).
Economy: Employment by occupation: 6.8% management, 2.3% professional, 10.6% services, 17.1% sales, 4.1% farming, 10.2% construction, 10.7% production (2006-2010 5-year est.).
Income: Per capita income: $23,885 (2006-2010 5-year est.); Median household income: $49,725 (2006-2010 5-year est.); Average household income: $57,984 (2006-2010 5-year est.); Percent of households with income of $100,000 or more: 13.2% (2006-2010 5-year est.); Poverty rate: 6.0% (2006-2010 5-year est.).
Education: Percent of population age 25 and over with: High school diploma (including GED) or higher: 86.1% (2006-2010 5-year est.); Bachelor's degree or higher: 18.1% (2006-2010 5-year est.); Master's degree or higher: 7.6% (2006-2010 5-year est.).
Housing: Homeownership rate: 76.2% (2010); Median home value: $139,800 (2006-2010 5-year est.); Median contract rent: $752 per month (2006-2010 5-year est.); Median year structure built: 1955 (2006-2010 5-year est.).
Transportation: Commute to work: 95.8% car, 2.2% public transportation, 1.2% walk, 0.9% work from home (2006-2010 5-year est.); Travel time to work: 28.7% less than 15 minutes, 49.4% 15 to 30 minutes, 10.0% 30 to 45 minutes, 4.9% 45 to 60 minutes, 7.0% 60 minutes or more (2006-2010 5-year est.)

PENNWYN (CDP). Covers a land area of 0.526 square miles and a water area of 0.005 square miles. Located at 40.29° N. Lat; 75.97° W. Long. Elevation is 374 feet.
Population: n/a (1990); n/a (2000); 780 (2010); Density: 1,482.0 persons per square mile (2010); Race: 93.1% White, 2.4% Black, 1.4% Asian, 0.1% American Indian/Alaska Native, 0.0% Native Hawaiian/Other Pacific Islander, 3.0% Other, 5.4% Hispanic of any race (2010); Average household size: 2.38 (2010); Median age: 46.4 (2010); Males per 100 females: 102.6 (2010); Marriage status: 25.6% never married, 61.7% now married, 6.4% widowed, 6.3% divorced (2006-2010 5-year est.); Foreign born: 2.7% (2006-2010 5-year est.); Ancestry (includes multiple ancestries): 47.4% German, 22.0% Italian, 12.4% American, 9.6% Pennsylvania German, 9.6% Polish (2006-2010 5-year est.).
Economy: Employment by occupation: 18.9% management, 0.0% professional, 7.4% services, 8.6% sales, 3.9% farming, 17.9% construction, 16.0% production (2006-2010 5-year est.).
Income: Per capita income: $28,096 (2006-2010 5-year est.); Median household income: $51,250 (2006-2010 5-year est.); Average household income: $57,094 (2006-2010 5-year est.); Percent of households with income of $100,000 or more: 13.8% (2006-2010 5-year est.); Poverty rate: 13.9% (2006-2010 5-year est.).
Education: Percent of population age 25 and over with: High school diploma (including GED) or higher: 89.2% (2006-2010 5-year est.); Bachelor's degree or higher: 16.9% (2006-2010 5-year est.); Master's degree or higher: 0.0% (2006-2010 5-year est.).
Housing: Homeownership rate: 87.8% (2010); Median home value: $142,400 (2006-2010 5-year est.); Median contract rent: $348 per month (2006-2010 5-year est.); Median year structure built: 1950 (2006-2010 5-year est.).
Transportation: Commute to work: 79.6% car, 3.0% public transportation, 17.4% walk, 0.0% work from home (2006-2010 5-year est.); Travel time to work: 51.1% less than 15 minutes, 35.0% 15 to 30 minutes, 7.6% 30 to 45 minutes, 2.5% 45 to 60 minutes, 3.8% 60 minutes or more (2006-2010 5-year est.)

PERRY (township). Covers a land area of 18.009 square miles and a water area of 0.166 square miles. Located at 40.51° N. Lat; 75.94° W. Long.
Population: 2,516 (1990); 2,517 (2000); 2,417 (2010); Density: 134.2 persons per square mile (2010); Race: 95.4% White, 0.7% Black, 0.5%

Asian, 0.0% American Indian/Alaska Native, 0.0% Native Hawaiian/Other Pacific Islander, 3.4% Other, 3.8% Hispanic of any race (2010); Average household size: 2.45 (2010); Median age: 46.9 (2010); Males per 100 females: 107.8 (2010); Marriage status: 22.8% never married, 57.7% now married, 5.9% widowed, 13.6% divorced (2006-2010 5-year est.); Foreign born: 2.0% (2006-2010 5-year est.); Ancestry (includes multiple ancestries): 50.9% German, 10.6% Dutch, 10.2% Italian, 7.5% American, 7.2% Irish (2006-2010 5-year est.).
Economy: Single-family building permits issued: 1 (2011); Multi-family building permits issued: 0 (2011); Employment by occupation: 10.3% management, 3.4% professional, 10.9% services, 17.7% sales, 7.4% farming, 7.6% construction, 7.1% production (2006-2010 5-year est.).
Income: Per capita income: $28,053 (2006-2010 5-year est.); Median household income: $55,655 (2006-2010 5-year est.); Average household income: $64,573 (2006-2010 5-year est.); Percent of households with income of $100,000 or more: 12.7% (2006-2010 5-year est.); Poverty rate: 6.9% (2006-2010 5-year est.).
Education: Percent of population age 25 and over with: High school diploma (including GED) or higher: 78.7% (2006-2010 5-year est.); Bachelor's degree or higher: 15.5% (2006-2010 5-year est.); Master's degree or higher: 4.1% (2006-2010 5-year est.).
Housing: Homeownership rate: 82.0% (2010); Median home value: $150,100 (2006-2010 5-year est.); Median contract rent: $482 per month (2006-2010 5-year est.); Median year structure built: 1967 (2006-2010 5-year est.).
Transportation: Commute to work: 89.5% car, 0.0% public transportation, 3.3% walk, 5.7% work from home (2006-2010 5-year est.); Travel time to work: 29.7% less than 15 minutes, 42.0% 15 to 30 minutes, 15.2% 30 to 45 minutes, 10.2% 45 to 60 minutes, 2.8% 60 minutes or more (2006-2010 5-year est.).
Additional Information Contacts
Greater Reading Chamber of Commerce & Industry . . . . . (610) 376-6766
  http://www.greaterreadingchamber.org

PIKE (township). Covers a land area of 13.990 square miles and a water area of 0.034 square miles. Located at 40.40° N. Lat; 75.68° W. Long.
Population: 1,359 (1990); 1,677 (2000); 1,723 (2010); Density: 123.2 persons per square mile (2010); Race: 97.8% White, 0.2% Black, 0.7% Asian, 0.0% American Indian/Alaska Native, 0.0% Native Hawaiian/Other Pacific Islander, 1.3% Other, 0.8% Hispanic of any race (2010); Average household size: 2.67 (2010); Median age: 45.9 (2010); Males per 100 females: 106.8 (2010); Marriage status: 24.9% never married, 61.8% now married, 4.1% widowed, 9.2% divorced (2006-2010 5-year est.); Foreign born: 1.1% (2006-2010 5-year est.); Ancestry (includes multiple ancestries): 56.2% German, 13.5% Irish, 12.5% Polish, 10.8% English, 6.6% Pennsylvania German (2006-2010 5-year est.).
Economy: Single-family building permits issued: 4 (2011); Multi-family building permits issued: 0 (2011); Employment by occupation: 11.0% management, 4.2% professional, 9.0% services, 11.7% sales, 1.4% farming, 13.9% construction, 8.0% production (2006-2010 5-year est.).
Income: Per capita income: $29,276 (2006-2010 5-year est.); Median household income: $76,731 (2006-2010 5-year est.); Average household income: $83,648 (2006-2010 5-year est.); Percent of households with income of $100,000 or more: 32.3% (2006-2010 5-year est.); Poverty rate: 5.2% (2006-2010 5-year est.).
Education: Percent of population age 25 and over with: High school diploma (including GED) or higher: 90.2% (2006-2010 5-year est.); Bachelor's degree or higher: 24.6% (2006-2010 5-year est.); Master's degree or higher: 6.9% (2006-2010 5-year est.).
Housing: Homeownership rate: 90.9% (2010); Median home value: $249,400 (2006-2010 5-year est.); Median contract rent: $738 per month (2006-2010 5-year est.); Median year structure built: 1976 (2006-2010 5-year est.).
Transportation: Commute to work: 95.1% car, 0.0% public transportation, 2.3% walk, 2.2% work from home (2006-2010 5-year est.); Travel time to work: 27.0% less than 15 minutes, 27.8% 15 to 30 minutes, 27.8% 30 to 45 minutes, 5.7% 45 to 60 minutes, 11.7% 60 minutes or more (2006-2010 5-year est.).
Additional Information Contacts
TriCounty Area Chamber of Commerce . . . . (610) 326-2900
  http://tricountyareachamber.com

READING

READING (city). County seat. Covers a land area of 9.884 square miles and a water area of 0.255 square miles. Located at 40.34° N. Lat; 75.93° W. Long. Elevation is 305 feet.

History: Two of William Penn's relatives began the settlement of Reading in 1733. In 1748, the town was laid out under the supervision of Thomas Penn. Penn named it for the seat of Berkshire, England, the name of which was derived from the Saxon words "rhedin" (a fern) and "ing" (a meadow). Four years later, when Berks County was established, Reading became the county seat. By 1783, Reading was incorporated as a borough. Industry was developing, due in part to the hundreds of skilled German craftsmen who were making creative use of the raw materials at hand.

Population: 78,441 (1990); 81,207 (2000); 88,082 (2010); Density: 8,911.9 persons per square mile (2010); Race: 48.4% White, 13.2% Black, 1.2% Asian, 0.9% American Indian/Alaska Native, 0.1% Native Hawaiian/Other Pacific Islander, 36.2% Other, 58.2% Hispanic of any race (2010); Average household size: 2.85 (2010); Median age: 28.9 (2010); Males per 100 females: 94.3 (2010); Marriage status: 45.3% never married, 38.4% now married, 5.6% widowed, 10.7% divorced (2006-2010 5-year est.); Foreign born: 17.4% (2006-2010 5-year est.); Ancestry (includes multiple ancestries): 12.0% German, 6.0% Irish, 5.1% Italian, 4.1% Polish, 2.4% Pennsylvania German (2006-2010 5-year est.).

Economy: Unemployment rate: 11.5% (August 2012); Total civilian labor force: 36,976 (August 2012); Single-family building permits issued: 0 (2011); Multi-family building permits issued: 0 (2011); Employment by occupation: 4.7% management, 0.9% professional, 13.8% services, 16.2% sales, 5.3% farming, 9.2% construction, 12.5% production (2006-2010 5-year est.).

Income: Per capita income: $13,135 (2006-2010 5-year est.); Median household income: $28,197 (2006-2010 5-year est.); Average household income: $35,916 (2006-2010 5-year est.); Percent of households with income of $100,000 or more: 3.7% (2006-2010 5-year est.); Poverty rate: 35.0% (2006-2010 5-year est.).

Taxes: Total city taxes per capita: $469 (2009); City property taxes per capita: $190 (2009).

Education: Percent of population age 25 and over with: High school diploma (including GED) or higher: 64.7% (2006-2010 5-year est.); Bachelor's degree or higher: 9.8% (2006-2010 5-year est.); Master's degree or higher: 3.2% (2006-2010 5-year est.).

School District(s)
Antietam SD (KG-12)
    2010-11 Enrollment: 1,046 . . . . (610) 779-0554
Exeter Township SD (KG-12)
    2010-11 Enrollment: 4,378 . . . . (610) 779-0700
Reading Muhlenberg CTC (09-12)
    2010-11 Enrollment: n/a . . . . (610) 921-7300
Reading SD (PK-12)
    2010-11 Enrollment: 18,194 . . . . (610) 371-5611

Four-year College(s)
Albright College (Private, Not-for-profit, United Methodist)
    Fall 2010 Enrollment: 2,316 . . . . (610) 921-2381
    2011-12 Tuition: In-state $33,990; Out-of-state $33,990
Alvernia University (Private, Not-for-profit, Roman Catholic)
    Fall 2010 Enrollment: 2,555 . . . . (610) 796-8200
    2011-12 Tuition: In-state $26,630; Out-of-state $26,630
Pennsylvania State University-Penn State Berks (Public)
    Fall 2010 Enrollment: 2,770 . . . . (610) 396-6000
    2011-12 Tuition: In-state $13,636; Out-of-state $20,408

Two-year College(s)
Pace Institute (Private, For-profit)
    Fall 2010 Enrollment: 358 . . . . (610) 375-1212
    2011-12 Tuition: In-state $7,464; Out-of-state $7,464
Reading Area Community College (Public)
    Fall 2010 Enrollment: 3,567 . . . . (610) 372-4721
    2011-12 Tuition: In-state $6,900; Out-of-state $9,630

Vocational/Technical School(s)
Empire Beauty School-Reading (Private, For-profit)
    Fall 2010 Enrollment: 255 . . . . (800) 223-3271
    2011-12 Tuition: $14,490

Housing: Homeownership rate: 42.4% (2010); Median home value: $65,500 (2006-2010 5-year est.); Median contract rent: $529 per month (2006-2010 5-year est.); Median year structure built: before 1940 (2006-2010 5-year est.).

Hospitals: HealthSouth Reading Rehabilitation Center (95 beds); Reading Hospital and Medical Center (804 beds); St. Joseph Medical Center (220 beds)

Safety: Violent crime rate: 85.8 per 10,000 population; Property crime rate: 373.6 per 10,000 population (2011).

Newspapers: Reading Eagle (Local news; Circulation 83,340); Shalom Newspaper (Local news; Circulation 1,200)

Transportation: Commute to work: 78.6% car, 7.3% public transportation, 8.4% walk, 3.0% work from home (2006-2010 5-year est.); Travel time to work: 31.9% less than 15 minutes, 40.1% 15 to 30 minutes, 14.3% 30 to 45 minutes, 6.5% 45 to 60 minutes, 7.1% 60 minutes or more (2006-2010 5-year est.)

Airports: Reading Regional/Carl A Spaatz Field (general aviation)

Additional Information Contacts
City of Reading . . . . (877) 727-3234
    http://www.readingpa.gov
Greater Reading Chamber of Commerce & Industry . . . . . (610) 376-6766
    http://www.greaterreadingchamber.org

REHRERSBURG

REHRERSBURG (CDP). Covers a land area of 0.536 square miles and a water area of 0 square miles. Located at 40.46° N. Lat; 76.25° W. Long. Elevation is 584 feet.

Population: n/a (1990); n/a (2000); 319 (2010); Density: 595.3 persons per square mile (2010); Race: 89.0% White, 1.9% Black, 0.0% Asian, 0.0% American Indian/Alaska Native, 0.0% Native Hawaiian/Other Pacific Islander, 9.1% Other, 8.8% Hispanic of any race (2010); Average household size: 2.68 (2010); Median age: 36.5 (2010); Males per 100 females: 111.3 (2010); Marriage status: 45.6% never married, 39.0% now married, 0.0% widowed, 15.4% divorced (2006-2010 5-year est.); Foreign born: 2.8% (2006-2010 5-year est.); Ancestry (includes multiple ancestries): 32.1% German, 18.3% American, 4.8% Irish, 2.5% Portuguese, 2.5% Scotch-Irish (2006-2010 5-year est.).

Economy: Employment by occupation: 0.0% management, 0.0% professional, 12.7% services, 10.8% sales, 0.0% farming, 16.6% construction, 10.2% production (2006-2010 5-year est.).

Income: Per capita income: $11,407 (2006-2010 5-year est.); Median household income: $38,750 (2006-2010 5-year est.); Average household income: $44,828 (2006-2010 5-year est.); Percent of households with income of $100,000 or more: 15.2% (2006-2010 5-year est.); Poverty rate: 47.2% (2006-2010 5-year est.).

Education: Percent of population age 25 and over with: High school diploma (including GED) or higher: 73.7% (2006-2010 5-year est.); Bachelor's degree or higher: 4.4% (2006-2010 5-year est.); Master's degree or higher: 4.4% (2006-2010 5-year est.).

Housing: Homeownership rate: 65.6% (2010); Median home value: $117,000 (2006-2010 5-year est.); Median contract rent: $405 per month (2006-2010 5-year est.); Median year structure built: before 1940 (2006-2010 5-year est.).

Transportation: Commute to work: 75.2% car, 0.0% public transportation, 16.5% walk, 8.3% work from home (2006-2010 5-year est.); Travel time to work: 27.0% less than 15 minutes, 63.1% 15 to 30 minutes, 4.9% 30 to 45 minutes, 4.9% 45 to 60 minutes, 0.0% 60 minutes or more (2006-2010 5-year est.)

REIFFTON

REIFFTON (CDP). Covers a land area of 1.887 square miles and a water area of 0.001 square miles. Located at 40.31° N. Lat; 75.86° W. Long. Elevation is 397 feet.

Population: 2,643 (1990); 2,888 (2000); 4,178 (2010); Density: 2,214.2 persons per square mile (2010); Race: 90.3% White, 4.0% Black, 2.8% Asian, 0.2% American Indian/Alaska Native, 0.0% Native Hawaiian/Other Pacific Islander, 2.7% Other, 2.6% Hispanic of any race (2010); Average household size: 2.63 (2010); Median age: 44.0 (2010); Males per 100 females: 92.6 (2010); Marriage status: 24.2% never married, 60.5% now married, 6.1% widowed, 9.2% divorced (2006-2010 5-year est.); Foreign born: 4.3% (2006-2010 5-year est.); Ancestry (includes multiple ancestries): 43.2% German, 21.5% Irish, 16.4% Italian, 11.7% English, 5.2% Haitian (2006-2010 5-year est.).

Economy: Employment by occupation: 14.1% management, 5.8% professional, 10.0% services, 18.6% sales, 6.6% farming, 5.6% construction, 1.5% production (2006-2010 5-year est.).

Income: Per capita income: $31,274 (2006-2010 5-year est.); Median household income: $65,737 (2006-2010 5-year est.); Average household income: $81,124 (2006-2010 5-year est.); Percent of households with income of $100,000 or more: 31.0% (2006-2010 5-year est.); Poverty rate: 7.4% (2006-2010 5-year est.).

Education: Percent of population age 25 and over with: High school diploma (including GED) or higher: 92.8% (2006-2010 5-year est.);

Bachelor's degree or higher: 35.3% (2006-2010 5-year est.); Master's degree or higher: 12.6% (2006-2010 5-year est.).
Housing: Homeownership rate: 91.5% (2010); Median home value: $211,400 (2006-2010 5-year est.); Median contract rent: $880 per month (2006-2010 5-year est.); Median year structure built: 1972 (2006-2010 5-year est.).
Transportation: Commute to work: 93.6% car, 1.9% public transportation, 0.0% walk, 4.5% work from home (2006-2010 5-year est.); Travel time to work: 34.0% less than 15 minutes, 36.6% 15 to 30 minutes, 5.2% 30 to 45 minutes, 9.3% 45 to 60 minutes, 15.0% 60 minutes or more (2006-2010 5-year est.)
Additional Information Contacts
Greater Reading Chamber of Commerce & Industry . . . . . (610) 376-6766
    http://www.greaterreadingchamber.org

RICHMOND (township). Covers a land area of 23.525 square miles and a water area of 0.052 square miles. Located at 40.49° N. Lat; 75.84° W. Long.
Population: 3,439 (1990); 3,500 (2000); 3,397 (2010); Density: 144.4 persons per square mile (2010); Race: 97.7% White, 0.6% Black, 0.4% Asian, 0.1% American Indian/Alaska Native, 0.0% Native Hawaiian/Other Pacific Islander, 1.2% Other, 1.8% Hispanic of any race (2010); Average household size: 2.48 (2010); Median age: 44.4 (2010); Males per 100 females: 103.3 (2010); Marriage status: 19.8% never married, 64.8% now married, 7.5% widowed, 7.9% divorced (2006-2010 5-year est.); Foreign born: 0.4% (2006-2010 5-year est.); Ancestry (includes multiple ancestries): 49.3% German, 10.7% Italian, 10.4% Swiss, 9.2% Pennsylvania German, 8.3% Dutch (2006-2010 5-year est.).
Economy: Single-family building permits issued: 0 (2011); Multi-family building permits issued: 0 (2011); Employment by occupation: 15.7% management, 1.7% professional, 10.4% services, 14.9% sales, 4.9% farming, 10.6% construction, 12.7% production (2006-2010 5-year est.).
Income: Per capita income: $22,868 (2006-2010 5-year est.); Median household income: $42,500 (2006-2010 5-year est.); Average household income: $55,373 (2006-2010 5-year est.); Percent of households with income of $100,000 or more: 11.5% (2006-2010 5-year est.); Poverty rate: 3.0% (2006-2010 5-year est.).
Education: Percent of population age 25 and over with: High school diploma (including GED) or higher: 74.3% (2006-2010 5-year est.); Bachelor's degree or higher: 14.5% (2006-2010 5-year est.); Master's degree or higher: 1.3% (2006-2010 5-year est.).
Housing: Homeownership rate: 75.6% (2010); Median home value: $182,400 (2006-2010 5-year est.); Median contract rent: $607 per month (2006-2010 5-year est.); Median year structure built: 1972 (2006-2010 5-year est.).
Transportation: Commute to work: 81.1% car, 0.0% public transportation, 3.4% walk, 7.3% work from home (2006-2010 5-year est.); Travel time to work: 22.0% less than 15 minutes, 46.9% 15 to 30 minutes, 23.6% 30 to 45 minutes, 5.9% 45 to 60 minutes, 1.5% 60 minutes or more (2006-2010 5-year est.)
Additional Information Contacts
Greater Reading Chamber of Commerce & Industry . . . . . (610) 376-6766
    http://www.greaterreadingchamber.org

RIVERVIEW PARK (CDP). Covers a land area of 0.992 square miles and a water area of 0.033 square miles. Located at 40.39° N. Lat; 75.95° W. Long. Elevation is 318 feet.
Population: n/a (1990); n/a (2000); 3,380 (2010); Density: 3,408.5 persons per square mile (2010); Race: 87.8% White, 3.8% Black, 3.3% Asian, 0.1% American Indian/Alaska Native, 0.0% Native Hawaiian/Other Pacific Islander, 5.0% Other, 8.0% Hispanic of any race (2010); Average household size: 2.46 (2010); Median age: 47.1 (2010); Males per 100 females: 94.4 (2010); Marriage status: 20.2% never married, 62.5% now married, 9.4% widowed, 7.9% divorced (2006-2010 5-year est.); Foreign born: 4.9% (2006-2010 5-year est.); Ancestry (includes multiple ancestries): 36.1% German, 11.8% Italian, 9.5% English, 6.6% American, 6.6% Pennsylvania German (2006-2010 5-year est.).
Economy: Employment by occupation: 15.3% management, 1.0% professional, 5.2% services, 24.8% sales, 3.6% farming, 9.0% construction, 5.2% production (2006-2010 5-year est.).
Income: Per capita income: $30,036 (2006-2010 5-year est.); Median household income: $61,625 (2006-2010 5-year est.); Average household income: $76,958 (2006-2010 5-year est.); Percent of households with income of $100,000 or more: 20.7% (2006-2010 5-year est.); Poverty rate: 9.6% (2006-2010 5-year est.).

Education: Percent of population age 25 and over with: High school diploma (including GED) or higher: 86.6% (2006-2010 5-year est.); Bachelor's degree or higher: 20.7% (2006-2010 5-year est.); Master's degree or higher: 9.9% (2006-2010 5-year est.).
Housing: Homeownership rate: 79.2% (2010); Median home value: $191,200 (2006-2010 5-year est.); Median contract rent: $974 per month (2006-2010 5-year est.); Median year structure built: 1969 (2006-2010 5-year est.).
Transportation: Commute to work: 95.9% car, 1.2% public transportation, 0.0% walk, 2.9% work from home (2006-2010 5-year est.); Travel time to work: 27.8% less than 15 minutes, 58.3% 15 to 30 minutes, 6.8% 30 to 45 minutes, 1.8% 45 to 60 minutes, 5.4% 60 minutes or more (2006-2010 5-year est.)

ROBESON (township). Covers a land area of 33.917 square miles and a water area of 0.305 square miles. Located at 40.24° N. Lat; 75.87° W. Long.
History: Founded 1855.
Population: 5,969 (1990); 6,869 (2000); 7,216 (2010); Density: 212.8 persons per square mile (2010); Race: 97.8% White, 0.5% Black, 0.4% Asian, 0.1% American Indian/Alaska Native, 0.0% Native Hawaiian/Other Pacific Islander, 1.2% Other, 1.3% Hispanic of any race (2010); Average household size: 2.72 (2010); Median age: 42.7 (2010); Males per 100 females: 103.5 (2010); Marriage status: 21.8% never married, 67.3% now married, 5.0% widowed, 5.9% divorced (2006-2010 5-year est.); Foreign born: 1.6% (2006-2010 5-year est.); Ancestry (includes multiple ancestries): 45.3% German, 21.0% Irish, 12.8% English, 7.8% Italian, 7.5% Polish (2006-2010 5-year est.).
Economy: Single-family building permits issued: 14 (2011); Multi-family building permits issued: 0 (2011); Employment by occupation: 14.3% management, 4.5% professional, 15.1% services, 13.6% sales, 3.3% farming, 12.4% construction, 6.9% production (2006-2010 5-year est.).
Income: Per capita income: $33,870 (2006-2010 5-year est.); Median household income: $75,763 (2006-2010 5-year est.); Average household income: $94,244 (2006-2010 5-year est.); Percent of households with income of $100,000 or more: 33.0% (2006-2010 5-year est.); Poverty rate: 6.2% (2006-2010 5-year est.).
Education: Percent of population age 25 and over with: High school diploma (including GED) or higher: 92.5% (2006-2010 5-year est.); Bachelor's degree or higher: 29.0% (2006-2010 5-year est.); Master's degree or higher: 8.7% (2006-2010 5-year est.).
Housing: Homeownership rate: 87.9% (2010); Median home value: $235,500 (2006-2010 5-year est.); Median contract rent: $625 per month (2006-2010 5-year est.); Median year structure built: 1977 (2006-2010 5-year est.).
Safety: Violent crime rate: 5.5 per 10,000 population; Property crime rate: 118.8 per 10,000 population (2011).
Transportation: Commute to work: 91.0% car, 0.0% public transportation, 1.3% walk, 7.3% work from home (2006-2010 5-year est.); Travel time to work: 27.9% less than 15 minutes, 37.7% 15 to 30 minutes, 16.8% 30 to 45 minutes, 9.7% 45 to 60 minutes, 7.9% 60 minutes or more (2006-2010 5-year est.)
Additional Information Contacts
Greater Reading Chamber of Commerce & Industry . . . . . (610) 376-6766
    http://www.greaterreadingchamber.org
Robeson Township . . . . (610) 582-4636

ROBESONIA (borough). Covers a land area of 0.891 square miles and a water area of 0.003 square miles. Located at 40.35° N. Lat; 76.14° W. Long. Elevation is 427 feet.
Population: 1,944 (1990); 2,036 (2000); 2,061 (2010); Density: 2,313.5 persons per square mile (2010); Race: 94.3% White, 1.1% Black, 1.2% Asian, 0.1% American Indian/Alaska Native, 0.0% Native Hawaiian/Other Pacific Islander, 3.3% Other, 4.4% Hispanic of any race (2010); Average household size: 2.39 (2010); Median age: 40.9 (2010); Males per 100 females: 92.6 (2010); Marriage status: 28.3% never married, 49.0% now married, 10.6% widowed, 12.1% divorced (2006-2010 5-year est.); Foreign born: 1.1% (2006-2010 5-year est.); Ancestry (includes multiple ancestries): 52.6% German, 18.2% Irish, 10.3% Italian, 7.8% Dutch, 5.9% Polish (2006-2010 5-year est.).
Economy: Single-family building permits issued: 0 (2011); Multi-family building permits issued: 0 (2011); Employment by occupation: 11.0% management, 3.2% professional, 13.3% services, 14.3% sales, 3.2% farming, 12.1% construction, 9.9% production (2006-2010 5-year est.).

Income: Per capita income: $23,100 (2006-2010 5-year est.); Median household income: $52,386 (2006-2010 5-year est.); Average household income: $55,961 (2006-2010 5-year est.); Percent of households with income of $100,000 or more: 5.3% (2006-2010 5-year est.); Poverty rate: 1.7% (2006-2010 5-year est.).

Education: Percent of population age 25 and over with: High school diploma (including GED) or higher: 87.9% (2006-2010 5-year est.); Bachelor's degree or higher: 9.4% (2006-2010 5-year est.); Master's degree or higher: 1.7% (2006-2010 5-year est.).

School District(s)

Conrad Weiser Area SD (KG-12)

 2010-11 Enrollment: 2,851 . . . . (610) 693-8545

Housing: Homeownership rate: 72.6% (2010); Median home value: $131,500 (2006-2010 5-year est.); Median contract rent: $541 per month (2006-2010 5-year est.); Median year structure built: 1950 (2006-2010 5-year est.).

Newspapers: West Berks Crier (Local news; Circulation 2,000)

Transportation: Commute to work: 96.6% car, 0.0% public transportation, 1.6% walk, 1.8% work from home (2006-2010 5-year est.); Travel time to work: 29.3% less than 15 minutes, 31.7% 15 to 30 minutes, 24.7% 30 to 45 minutes, 7.4% 45 to 60 minutes, 6.9% 60 minutes or more (2006-2010 5-year est.)

Additional Information Contacts

Greater Reading Chamber of Commerce & Industry . . . . . (610) 376-6766
 http://www.greaterreadingchamber.org

ROCKLAND (township). Covers a land area of 16.953 square miles and a water area of 0.065 square miles. Located at 40.45° N. Lat; 75.74° W. Long.

Population: 2,675 (1990); 3,765 (2000); 3,778 (2010); Density: 222.8 persons per square mile (2010); Race: 97.7% White, 0.3% Black, 0.4% Asian, 0.1% American Indian/Alaska Native, 0.0% Native Hawaiian/Other Pacific Islander, 1.5% Other, 1.8% Hispanic of any race (2010); Average household size: 2.67 (2010); Median age: 44.4 (2010); Males per 100 females: 102.8 (2010); Marriage status: 14.5% never married, 73.9% now married, 4.6% widowed, 7.1% divorced (2006-2010 5-year est.); Foreign born: 0.0% (2006-2010 5-year est.); Ancestry (includes multiple ancestries): 57.9% German, 11.2% Irish, 8.2% Pennsylvania German, 7.9% English, 7.6% Polish (2006-2010 5-year est.).

Economy: Single-family building permits issued: 4 (2011); Multi-family building permits issued: 0 (2011); Employment by occupation: 10.8% management, 6.7% professional, 8.7% services, 10.8% sales, 2.1% farming, 10.9% construction, 11.3% production (2006-2010 5-year est.).

Income: Per capita income: $31,516 (2006-2010 5-year est.); Median household income: $77,500 (2006-2010 5-year est.); Average household income: $84,924 (2006-2010 5-year est.); Percent of households with income of $100,000 or more: 34.1% (2006-2010 5-year est.); Poverty rate: 4.6% (2006-2010 5-year est.).

Education: Percent of population age 25 and over with: High school diploma (including GED) or higher: 90.0% (2006-2010 5-year est.); Bachelor's degree or higher: 28.4% (2006-2010 5-year est.); Master's degree or higher: 10.7% (2006-2010 5-year est.).

Housing: Homeownership rate: 92.6% (2010); Median home value: $216,600 (2006-2010 5-year est.); Median contract rent: $242 per month (2006-2010 5-year est.); Median year structure built: 1984 (2006-2010 5-year est.).

Transportation: Commute to work: 92.9% car, 1.1% public transportation, 0.7% walk, 2.3% work from home (2006-2010 5-year est.); Travel time to work: 26.2% less than 15 minutes, 35.9% 15 to 30 minutes, 25.2% 30 to 45 minutes, 6.1% 45 to 60 minutes, 6.6% 60 minutes or more (2006-2010 5-year est.)

Additional Information Contacts

Greater Reading Chamber of Commerce & Industry . . . . . (610) 376-6766
 http://www.greaterreadingchamber.org

RUSCOMBMANOR (township). Covers a land area of 13.684 square miles and a water area of 0.058 square miles. Located at 40.42° N. Lat; 75.83° W. Long.

Population: 3,129 (1990); 3,776 (2000); 4,112 (2010); Density: 300.5 persons per square mile (2010); Race: 98.1% White, 0.5% Black, 0.5% Asian, 0.1% American Indian/Alaska Native, 0.1% Native Hawaiian/Other Pacific Islander, 0.7% Other, 1.1% Hispanic of any race (2010); Average household size: 2.64 (2010); Median age: 46.5 (2010); Males per 100 females: 104.3 (2010); Marriage status: 19.3% never married, 70.3% now married, 1.3% widowed, 9.1% divorced (2006-2010 5-year est.); Foreign

born: 3.2% (2006-2010 5-year est.); Ancestry (includes multiple ancestries): 49.3% German, 14.9% Irish, 12.4% Italian, 6.6% Pennsylvania German, 6.6% English (2006-2010 5-year est.).

Economy: Single-family building permits issued: 4 (2011); Multi-family building permits issued: 0 (2011); Employment by occupation: 13.4% management, 6.4% professional, 2.8% services, 16.3% sales, 2.3% farming, 9.1% construction, 7.2% production (2006-2010 5-year est.).

Income: Per capita income: $37,679 (2006-2010 5-year est.); Median household income: $81,964 (2006-2010 5-year est.); Average household income: $97,968 (2006-2010 5-year est.); Percent of households with income of $100,000 or more: 34.0% (2006-2010 5-year est.); Poverty rate: 1.9% (2006-2010 5-year est.).

Education: Percent of population age 25 and over with: High school diploma (including GED) or higher: 91.4% (2006-2010 5-year est.); Bachelor's degree or higher: 32.1% (2006-2010 5-year est.); Master's degree or higher: 10.2% (2006-2010 5-year est.).

Housing: Homeownership rate: 91.1% (2010); Median home value: $232,100 (2006-2010 5-year est.); Median contract rent: $537 per month (2006-2010 5-year est.); Median year structure built: 1981 (2006-2010 5-year est.).

Transportation: Commute to work: 88.0% car, 0.0% public transportation, 2.2% walk, 7.1% work from home (2006-2010 5-year est.); Travel time to work: 19.0% less than 15 minutes, 50.7% 15 to 30 minutes, 13.0% 30 to 45 minutes, 6.8% 45 to 60 minutes, 10.5% 60 minutes or more (2006-2010 5-year est.)

Additional Information Contacts

Greater Reading Chamber of Commerce & Industry . . . . . (610) 376-6766
 http://www.greaterreadingchamber.org

SAINT LAWRENCE (borough). Covers a land area of 0.881 square miles and a water area of <.001 square miles. Located at 40.33° N. Lat; 75.87° W. Long. Elevation is 295 feet.

Population: 1,542 (1990); 1,812 (2000); 1,809 (2010); Density: 2,052.2 persons per square mile (2010); Race: 91.7% White, 2.3% Black, 0.8% Asian, 0.4% American Indian/Alaska Native, 0.0% Native Hawaiian/Other Pacific Islander, 4.8% Other, 7.5% Hispanic of any race (2010); Average household size: 2.44 (2010); Median age: 38.9 (2010); Males per 100 females: 91.2 (2010); Marriage status: 24.9% never married, 56.7% now married, 7.8% widowed, 10.6% divorced (2006-2010 5-year est.); Foreign born: 4.0% (2006-2010 5-year est.); Ancestry (includes multiple ancestries): 40.7% German, 12.0% Irish, 11.1% Polish, 10.7% Italian, 7.6% American (2006-2010 5-year est.).

Economy: Single-family building permits issued: 0 (2011); Multi-family building permits issued: 0 (2011); Employment by occupation: 8.9% management, 3.5% professional, 10.7% services, 14.3% sales, 2.4% farming, 9.3% construction, 6.8% production (2006-2010 5-year est.).

Income: Per capita income: $26,074 (2006-2010 5-year est.); Median household income: $54,000 (2006-2010 5-year est.); Average household income: $60,719 (2006-2010 5-year est.); Percent of households with income of $100,000 or more: 15.6% (2006-2010 5-year est.); Poverty rate: 8.2% (2006-2010 5-year est.).

Taxes: Total city taxes per capita: $267 (2009); City property taxes per capita: $157 (2009).

Education: Percent of population age 25 and over with: High school diploma (including GED) or higher: 85.5% (2006-2010 5-year est.); Bachelor's degree or higher: 21.9% (2006-2010 5-year est.); Master's degree or higher: 6.8% (2006-2010 5-year est.).

Housing: Homeownership rate: 70.3% (2010); Median home value: $155,900 (2006-2010 5-year est.); Median contract rent: $689 per month (2006-2010 5-year est.); Median year structure built: 1961 (2006-2010 5-year est.).

Transportation: Commute to work: 94.9% car, 0.7% public transportation, 2.4% walk, 2.0% work from home (2006-2010 5-year est.); Travel time to work: 23.4% less than 15 minutes, 51.1% 15 to 30 minutes, 12.9% 30 to 45 minutes, 7.0% 45 to 60 minutes, 5.6% 60 minutes or more (2006-2010 5-year est.)

Additional Information Contacts

Lawrence County Chamber of Commerce . . . . (724) 654-5593
 http://www.lawrencecountychamber.org

SCHUBERT (CDP). Covers a land area of 0.609 square miles and a water area of <.001 square miles. Located at 40.50° N. Lat; 76.22° W. Long. Elevation is 636 feet.

Population: n/a (1990); n/a (2000); 249 (2010); Density: 408.8 persons per square mile (2010); Race: 94.0% White, 1.2% Black, 0.4% Asian,

0.4% American Indian/Alaska Native, 0.0% Native Hawaiian/Other Pacific Islander, 4.0% Other, 5.2% Hispanic of any race (2010); Average household size: 2.59 (2010); Median age: 44.7 (2010); Males per 100 females: 96.1 (2010); Marriage status: 8.6% never married, 81.4% now married, 0.0% widowed, 10.0% divorced (2006-2010 5-year est.); Foreign born: 0.0% (2006-2010 5-year est.); Ancestry (includes multiple ancestries): 63.4% German, 14.2% Irish, 6.6% Dutch (2006-2010 5-year est.).

Economy: Employment by occupation: 13.9% management, 22.8% professional, 0.0% services, 0.0% sales, 0.0% farming, 13.9% construction, 42.6% production (2006-2010 5-year est.).

Income: Per capita income: $23,205 (2006-2010 5-year est.); Median household income: $56,196 (2006-2010 5-year est.); Average household income: $54,503 (2006-2010 5-year est.); Percent of households with income of $100,000 or more: n/a (2006-2010 5-year est.); Poverty rate: 0.0% (2006-2010 5-year est.).

Education: Percent of population age 25 and over with: High school diploma (including GED) or higher: 59.4% (2006-2010 5-year est.); Bachelor's degree or higher: 0.0% (2006-2010 5-year est.); Master's degree or higher: 0.0% (2006-2010 5-year est.).

Housing: Homeownership rate: 81.3% (2010); Median home value: $205,600 (2006-2010 5-year est.); Median contract rent: n/a per month (2006-2010 5-year est.); Median year structure built: 1978 (2006-2010 5-year est.).

Transportation: Commute to work: 100.0% car, 0.0% public transportation, 0.0% walk, 0.0% work from home (2006-2010 5-year est.); Travel time to work: 20.8% less than 15 minutes, 56.4% 15 to 30 minutes, 22.8% 30 to 45 minutes, 0.0% 45 to 60 minutes, 0.0% 60 minutes or more (2006-2010 5-year est.)

SHARTLESVILLE (CDP). Covers a land area of 0.902 square miles and a water area of 0.009 square miles. Located at 40.52° N. Lat; 76.10° W. Long. Elevation is 561 feet.

Population: n/a (1990); n/a (2000); 455 (2010); Density: 504.4 persons per square mile (2010); Race: 96.5% White, 0.0% Black, 0.2% Asian, 0.0% American Indian/Alaska Native, 0.0% Native Hawaiian/Other Pacific Islander, 3.3% Other, 5.1% Hispanic of any race (2010); Average household size: 2.51 (2010); Median age: 37.5 (2010); Males per 100 females: 117.7 (2010); Marriage status: 30.3% never married, 55.9% now married, 4.5% widowed, 9.3% divorced (2006-2010 5-year est.); Foreign born: 5.5% (2006-2010 5-year est.); Ancestry (includes multiple ancestries): 55.8% German, 19.8% Pennsylvania German, 16.6% Irish, 6.3% Italian, 3.0% English (2006-2010 5-year est.).

Economy: Employment by occupation: 10.0% management, 2.9% professional, 13.6% services, 13.9% sales, 8.2% farming, 8.6% construction, 2.1% production (2006-2010 5-year est.).

Income: Per capita income: $22,304 (2006-2010 5-year est.); Median household income: $51,250 (2006-2010 5-year est.); Average household income: $58,174 (2006-2010 5-year est.); Percent of households with income of $100,000 or more: 11.0% (2006-2010 5-year est.); Poverty rate: 10.1% (2006-2010 5-year est.).

Education: Percent of population age 25 and over with: High school diploma (including GED) or higher: 75.4% (2006-2010 5-year est.); Bachelor's degree or higher: 9.0% (2006-2010 5-year est.); Master's degree or higher: 3.7% (2006-2010 5-year est.).

Housing: Homeownership rate: 66.8% (2010); Median home value: $133,300 (2006-2010 5-year est.); Median contract rent: $438 per month (2006-2010 5-year est.); Median year structure built: 1951 (2006-2010 5-year est.).

Transportation: Commute to work: 87.8% car, 0.0% public transportation, 10.3% walk, 1.8% work from home (2006-2010 5-year est.); Travel time to work: 28.9% less than 15 minutes, 24.8% 15 to 30 minutes, 33.8% 30 to 45 minutes, 6.8% 45 to 60 minutes, 5.6% 60 minutes or more (2006-2010 5-year est.)

SHILLINGTON (borough). Covers a land area of 0.960 square miles and a water area of 0.005 square miles. Located at 40.30° N. Lat; 75.97° W. Long. Elevation is 351 feet.

History: Founded 1860, incorporated 1908.

Population: 5,015 (1990); 5,059 (2000); 5,273 (2010); Density: 5,490.6 persons per square mile (2010); Race: 89.9% White, 3.4% Black, 1.2% Asian, 0.2% American Indian/Alaska Native, 0.0% Native Hawaiian/Other Pacific Islander, 5.3% Other, 8.5% Hispanic of any race (2010); Average household size: 2.34 (2010); Median age: 39.3 (2010); Males per 100 females: 93.4 (2010); Marriage status: 28.7% never married, 52.4% now

married, 5.5% widowed, 13.4% divorced (2006-2010 5-year est.); Foreign born: 2.4% (2006-2010 5-year est.); Ancestry (includes multiple ancestries): 50.0% German, 13.5% Irish, 10.3% English, 9.2% Polish, 7.2% Italian (2006-2010 5-year est.).

Economy: Single-family building permits issued: 0 (2011); Multi-family building permits issued: 0 (2011); Employment by occupation: 9.8% management, 4.2% professional, 11.9% services, 14.2% sales, 4.3% farming, 7.6% construction, 6.5% production (2006-2010 5-year est.).

Income: Per capita income: $27,915 (2006-2010 5-year est.); Median household income: $55,775 (2006-2010 5-year est.); Average household income: $65,637 (2006-2010 5-year est.); Percent of households with income of $100,000 or more: 12.6% (2006-2010 5-year est.); Poverty rate: 8.6% (2006-2010 5-year est.).

Education: Percent of population age 25 and over with: High school diploma (including GED) or higher: 94.1% (2006-2010 5-year est.); Bachelor's degree or higher: 23.7% (2006-2010 5-year est.); Master's degree or higher: 9.2% (2006-2010 5-year est.).

School District(s)

Governor Mifflin SD (KG-12)

   2010-11 Enrollment: 4,249 . . . . (610) 775-1461

Housing: Homeownership rate: 74.9% (2010); Median home value: $136,200 (2006-2010 5-year est.); Median contract rent: $681 per month (2006-2010 5-year est.); Median year structure built: 1942 (2006-2010 5-year est.).

Safety: Violent crime rate: 3.8 per 10,000 population; Property crime rate: 173.9 per 10,000 population (2011).

Transportation: Commute to work: 91.2% car, 0.0% public transportation, 2.4% walk, 6.5% work from home (2006-2010 5-year est.); Travel time to work: 39.6% less than 15 minutes, 38.1% 15 to 30 minutes, 10.7% 30 to 45 minutes, 4.9% 45 to 60 minutes, 6.7% 60 minutes or more (2006-2010 5-year est.)

Additional Information Contacts

Borough of Shillington . . . . (610) 777-1338

   http://www.co.berks.pa.us/shillington/site/default.asp

Greater Reading Chamber of Commerce & Industry . . . . . (610) 376-6766

   http://www.greaterreadingchamber.org

SHOEMAKERSVILLE (borough). Covers a land area of 0.557 square miles and a water area of 0.023 square miles. Located at 40.50° N. Lat; 75.97° W. Long. Elevation is 361 feet.

History: Founded 1833.

Population: 1,443 (1990); 2,124 (2000); 1,378 (2010); Density: 2,474.2 persons per square mile (2010); Race: 98.4% White, 0.1% Black, 0.1% Asian, 0.0% American Indian/Alaska Native, 0.1% Native Hawaiian/Other Pacific Islander, 1.3% Other, 2.7% Hispanic of any race (2010); Average household size: 2.30 (2010); Median age: 40.4 (2010); Males per 100 females: 97.7 (2010); Marriage status: 27.7% never married, 52.0% now married, 9.5% widowed, 10.8% divorced (2006-2010 5-year est.); Foreign born: 3.8% (2006-2010 5-year est.); Ancestry (includes multiple ancestries): 45.9% German, 17.4% Pennsylvania German, 10.4% Irish, 6.7% Italian, 5.2% American (2006-2010 5-year est.).

Economy: Single-family building permits issued: 0 (2011); Multi-family building permits issued: 0 (2011); Employment by occupation: 6.1% management, 3.4% professional, 11.7% services, 19.7% sales, 5.5% farming, 6.8% construction, 10.5% production (2006-2010 5-year est.).

Income: Per capita income: $24,258 (2006-2010 5-year est.); Median household income: $45,720 (2006-2010 5-year est.); Average household income: $58,218 (2006-2010 5-year est.); Percent of households with income of $100,000 or more: 8.2% (2006-2010 5-year est.); Poverty rate: 8.3% (2006-2010 5-year est.).

Education: Percent of population age 25 and over with: High school diploma (including GED) or higher: 71.5% (2006-2010 5-year est.); Bachelor's degree or higher: 9.1% (2006-2010 5-year est.); Master's degree or higher: 2.0% (2006-2010 5-year est.).

School District(s)

Hamburg Area SD (KG-12)

   2010-11 Enrollment: 2,445 . . . . (610) 562-2241

Housing: Homeownership rate: 67.2% (2010); Median home value: $125,900 (2006-2010 5-year est.); Median contract rent: $593 per month (2006-2010 5-year est.); Median year structure built: 1945 (2006-2010 5-year est.).

Transportation: Commute to work: 82.2% car, 7.2% public transportation, 3.2% walk, 1.4% work from home (2006-2010 5-year est.); Travel time to work: 25.7% less than 15 minutes, 46.8% 15 to 30 minutes, 20.6% 30 to

45 minutes, 4.5% 45 to 60 minutes, 2.3% 60 minutes or more (2006-2010 5-year est.)

Additional Information Contacts

Greater Reading Chamber of Commerce & Industry . . . . . (610) 376-6766
    http://www.greaterreadingchamber.org

SINKING SPRING (borough). Covers a land area of 1.257 square miles and a water area of 0.003 square miles. Located at 40.32° N. Lat; 76.02° W. Long. Elevation is 404 feet.

Population: 2,467 (1990); 2,639 (2000); 4,008 (2010); Density: 3,188.8 persons per square mile (2010); Race: 84.9% White, 6.4% Black, 2.4% Asian, 0.1% American Indian/Alaska Native, 0.0% Native Hawaiian/Other Pacific Islander, 6.2% Other, 8.9% Hispanic of any race (2010); Average household size: 2.40 (2010); Median age: 36.8 (2010); Males per 100 females: 92.2 (2010); Marriage status: 30.4% never married, 51.2% now married, 9.7% widowed, 8.7% divorced (2006-2010 5-year est.); Foreign born: 5.5% (2006-2010 5-year est.); Ancestry (includes multiple ancestries): 41.1% German, 13.4% Irish, 12.9% Polish, 10.1% Italian, 5.4% English (2006-2010 5-year est.).

Economy: Single-family building permits issued: 0 (2011); Multi-family building permits issued: 0 (2011); Employment by occupation: 10.8% management, 4.1% professional, 15.7% services, 17.9% sales, 2.2% farming, 7.3% construction, 4.6% production (2006-2010 5-year est.).

Income: Per capita income: $29,156 (2006-2010 5-year est.); Median household income: $56,422 (2006-2010 5-year est.); Average household income: $67,750 (2006-2010 5-year est.); Percent of households with income of $100,000 or more: 15.9% (2006-2010 5-year est.); Poverty rate: 5.8% (2006-2010 5-year est.).

Education: Percent of population age 25 and over with: High school diploma (including GED) or higher: 88.4% (2006-2010 5-year est.); Bachelor's degree or higher: 25.5% (2006-2010 5-year est.); Master's degree or higher: 5.4% (2006-2010 5-year est.).

School District(s)

Wilson SD (KG-12)

    2010-11 Enrollment: 5,828 . . . . (610) 670-0180

Housing: Homeownership rate: 60.6% (2010); Median home value: $187,700 (2006-2010 5-year est.); Median contract rent: $701 per month (2006-2010 5-year est.); Median year structure built: 1967 (2006-2010 5-year est.).

Safety: Violent crime rate: 2.5 per 10,000 population; Property crime rate: 186.5 per 10,000 population (2011).

Transportation: Commute to work: 90.0% car, 3.2% public transportation, 2.3% walk, 3.5% work from home (2006-2010 5-year est.); Travel time to work: 39.3% less than 15 minutes, 43.6% 15 to 30 minutes, 9.1% 30 to 45 minutes, 4.2% 45 to 60 minutes, 3.7% 60 minutes or more (2006-2010 5-year est.)

Additional Information Contacts

Borough of Sinking Spring . . . . (610) 678-4903
    http://www.borough.sinking-spring.pa.us

Greater Reading Chamber of Commerce & Industry . . . . . (610) 376-6766
    http://www.greaterreadingchamber.org

SOUTH HEIDELBERG (township). Covers a land area of 13.810 square miles and a water area of 0.036 square miles. Located at 40.31° N. Lat; 76.10° W. Long.

Population: 4,331 (1990); 5,491 (2000); 7,271 (2010); Density: 526.5 persons per square mile (2010); Race: 91.9% White, 3.7% Black, 1.4% Asian, 0.1% American Indian/Alaska Native, 0.0% Native Hawaiian/Other Pacific Islander, 2.9% Other, 4.9% Hispanic of any race (2010); Average household size: 2.66 (2010); Median age: 42.1 (2010); Males per 100 females: 99.5 (2010); Marriage status: 29.2% never married, 59.6% married, 4.7% widowed, 6.5% divorced (2006-2010 5-year est.); Foreign born: 3.0% (2006-2010 5-year est.); Ancestry (includes multiple ancestries): 39.7% German, 14.0% Italian, 13.0% Irish, 7.8% Polish, 5.5% English (2006-2010 5-year est.).

Economy: Single-family building permits issued: 5 (2011); Multi-family building permits issued: 0 (2011); Employment by occupation: 10.1% management, 5.3% professional, 9.7% services, 14.8% sales, 5.0% farming, 11.9% construction, 8.4% production (2006-2010 5-year est.).

Income: Per capita income: $25,404 (2006-2010 5-year est.); Median household income: $64,558 (2006-2010 5-year est.); Average household income: $72,603 (2006-2010 5-year est.); Percent of households with income of $100,000 or more: 24.4% (2006-2010 5-year est.); Poverty rate: 8.4% (2006-2010 5-year est.).

Education: Percent of population age 25 and over with: High school diploma (including GED) or higher: 84.4% (2006-2010 5-year est.); Bachelor's degree or higher: 19.8% (2006-2010 5-year est.); Master's degree or higher: 5.4% (2006-2010 5-year est.).

Housing: Homeownership rate: 88.3% (2010); Median home value: $208,200 (2006-2010 5-year est.); Median contract rent: $864 per month (2006-2010 5-year est.); Median year structure built: 1991 (2006-2010 5-year est.).

Safety: Violent crime rate: 12.3 per 10,000 population; Property crime rate: 82.3 per 10,000 population (2011).

Transportation: Commute to work: 95.9% car, 0.7% public transportation, 1.0% walk, 2.3% work from home (2006-2010 5-year est.); Travel time to work: 26.6% less than 15 minutes, 39.9% 15 to 30 minutes, 20.7% 30 to 45 minutes, 6.0% 45 to 60 minutes, 6.8% 60 minutes or more (2006-2010 5-year est.)

Additional Information Contacts

Greater Reading Chamber of Commerce & Industry . . . . . (610) 376-6766
    http://www.greaterreadingchamber.org

South Heidelberg Township . . . . (610) 678-9652

SOUTH TEMPLE (CDP). Covers a land area of 0.331 square miles and a water area of <.001 square miles. Located at 40.40° N. Lat; 75.92° W. Long. Elevation is 344 feet.

Population: n/a (1990); n/a (2000); 1,424 (2010); Density: 4,302.1 persons per square mile (2010); Race: 89.0% White, 2.9% Black, 0.8% Asian, 0.5% American Indian/Alaska Native, 0.0% Native Hawaiian/Other Pacific Islander, 6.8% Other, 14.8% Hispanic of any race (2010); Average household size: 2.38 (2010); Median age: 45.3 (2010); Males per 100 females: 91.4 (2010); Marriage status: 25.2% never married, 54.2% now married, 14.5% widowed, 6.1% divorced (2006-2010 5-year est.); Foreign born: 6.0% (2006-2010 5-year est.); Ancestry (includes multiple ancestries): 41.4% German, 21.3% Irish, 19.2% Italian, 5.7% Pennsylvania German, 5.1% Dutch (2006-2010 5-year est.).

Economy: Employment by occupation: 1.2% management, 2.6% professional, 5.5% services, 25.0% sales, 8.2% farming, 1.6% construction, 9.6% production (2006-2010 5-year est.).

Income: Per capita income: $28,285 (2006-2010 5-year est.); Median household income: $53,194 (2006-2010 5-year est.); Average household income: $61,056 (2006-2010 5-year est.); Percent of households with income of $100,000 or more: 16.4% (2006-2010 5-year est.); Poverty rate: 2.7% (2006-2010 5-year est.).

Education: Percent of population age 25 and over with: High school diploma (including GED) or higher: 85.0% (2006-2010 5-year est.); Bachelor's degree or higher: 22.4% (2006-2010 5-year est.); Master's degree or higher: 2.1% (2006-2010 5-year est.).

Housing: Homeownership rate: 87.1% (2010); Median home value: $155,200 (2006-2010 5-year est.); Median contract rent: $559 per month (2006-2010 5-year est.); Median year structure built: 1954 (2006-2010 5-year est.).

Transportation: Commute to work: 83.0% car, 1.5% public transportation, 8.4% walk, 0.9% work from home (2006-2010 5-year est.); Travel time to work: 40.6% less than 15 minutes, 47.3% 15 to 30 minutes, 3.7% 30 to 45 minutes, 1.6% 45 to 60 minutes, 6.8% 60 minutes or more (2006-2010 5-year est.)

SPRING (township). Covers a land area of 18.480 square miles and a water area of 0.064 square miles. Located at 40.31° N. Lat; 76.03° W. Long.

History: Settled 1793, laid out 1831, incorporated 1913.

Population: 18,840 (1990); 21,805 (2000); 27,119 (2010); Density: 1,467.5 persons per square mile (2010); Race: 87.9% White, 4.8% Black, 3.2% Asian, 0.2% American Indian/Alaska Native, 0.0% Native Hawaiian/Other Pacific Islander, 3.9% Other, 6.1% Hispanic of any race (2010); Average household size: 2.46 (2010); Median age: 41.4 (2010); Males per 100 females: 94.3 (2010); Marriage status: 29.8% never married, 55.4% now married, 6.4% widowed, 8.4% divorced (2006-2010 5-year est.); Foreign born: 7.7% (2006-2010 5-year est.); Ancestry (includes multiple ancestries): 40.1% German, 15.1% Italian, 14.7% Irish, 8.7% Polish, 7.8% English (2006-2010 5-year est.).

Economy: Unemployment rate: 6.7% (August 2012); Total civilian labor force: 14,500 (August 2012); Single-family building permits issued: 31 (2011); Multi-family building permits issued: 0 (2011); Employment by occupation: 11.1% management, 4.2% professional, 8.5% services, 15.7% sales, 5.6% farming, 5.0% construction, 5.1% production (2006-2010 5-year est.).

Income: Per capita income: $29,364 (2006-2010 5-year est.); Median household income: $62,471 (2006-2010 5-year est.); Average household income: $74,098 (2006-2010 5-year est.); Percent of households with income of $100,000 or more: 21.6% (2006-2010 5-year est.); Poverty rate: 6.3% (2006-2010 5-year est.).

Education: Percent of population age 25 and over with: High school diploma (including GED) or higher: 91.9% (2006-2010 5-year est.); Bachelor's degree or higher: 33.3% (2006-2010 5-year est.); Master's degree or higher: 12.0% (2006-2010 5-year est.).

Housing: Homeownership rate: 78.3% (2010); Median home value: $185,400 (2006-2010 5-year est.); Median contract rent: $801 per month (2006-2010 5-year est.); Median year structure built: 1975 (2006-2010 5-year est.).

Safety: Violent crime rate: 2.2 per 10,000 population; Property crime rate: 104.0 per 10,000 population (2011).

Transportation: Commute to work: 92.4% car, 0.8% public transportation, 2.6% walk, 3.1% work from home (2006-2010 5-year est.); Travel time to work: 41.5% less than 15 minutes, 41.0% 15 to 30 minutes, 8.1% 30 to 45 minutes, 3.0% 45 to 60 minutes, 6.4% 60 minutes or more (2006-2010 5-year est.)

Additional Information Contacts

Greater Reading Chamber of Commerce & Industry . . . . . (610) 376-6766
http://www.greaterreadingchamber.org
Spring Township . . . . (610) 678-5393
http://www.springtwpberks.org

SPRING RIDGE (CDP). Covers a land area of 0.900 square miles and a water area of 0 square miles. Located at 40.35° N. Lat; 75.99° W. Long. Elevation is 436 feet.

Population: 244 (1990); 786 (2000); 1,003 (2010); Density: 1,114.7 persons per square mile (2010); Race: 89.5% White, 2.4% Black, 6.8% Asian, 0.0% American Indian/Alaska Native, 0.0% Native Hawaiian/Other Pacific Islander, 1.3% Other, 3.3% Hispanic of any race (2010); Average household size: 1.94 (2010); Median age: 59.8 (2010); Males per 100 females: 84.4 (2010); Marriage status: 7.6% never married, 67.3% now married, 14.2% widowed, 11.0% divorced (2006-2010 5-year est.); Foreign born: 2.9% (2006-2010 5-year est.); Ancestry (includes multiple ancestries): 39.4% German, 16.2% English, 15.2% Irish, 14.9% Italian, 5.7% Polish (2006-2010 5-year est.).

Economy: Employment by occupation: 23.8% management, 4.7% professional, 0.0% services, 13.0% sales, 10.3% farming, 0.0% construction, 3.7% production (2006-2010 5-year est.).

Income: Per capita income: $53,496 (2006-2010 5-year est.); Median household income: $76,786 (2006-2010 5-year est.); Average household income: $100,970 (2006-2010 5-year est.); Percent of households with income of $100,000 or more: 26.1% (2006-2010 5-year est.); Poverty rate: 1.0% (2006-2010 5-year est.).

Education: Percent of population age 25 and over with: High school diploma (including GED) or higher: 94.3% (2006-2010 5-year est.); Bachelor's degree or higher: 43.1% (2006-2010 5-year est.); Master's degree or higher: 27.2% (2006-2010 5-year est.).

Housing: Homeownership rate: 90.4% (2010); Median home value: $258,200 (2006-2010 5-year est.); Median contract rent: $1,260 per month (2006-2010 5-year est.); Median year structure built: 1998 (2006-2010 5-year est.).

Transportation: Commute to work: 90.7% car, 0.0% public transportation, 0.0% walk, 9.3% work from home (2006-2010 5-year est.); Travel time to work: 54.5% less than 15 minutes, 24.4% 15 to 30 minutes, 7.0% 30 to 45 minutes, 0.0% 45 to 60 minutes, 14.1% 60 minutes or more (2006-2010 5-year est.)

Additional Information Contacts

Greater Reading Chamber of Commerce & Industry . . . . . (610) 376-6766
http://www.greaterreadingchamber.org

SPRINGMONT (CDP). Covers a land area of 0.169 square miles and a water area of 0 square miles. Located at 40.33° N. Lat; 76.00° W. Long. Elevation is 364 feet.

Population: n/a (1990); n/a (2000); 724 (2010); Density: 4,286.5 persons per square mile (2010); Race: 93.5% White, 3.5% Black, 0.4% Asian, 0.7% American Indian/Alaska Native, 0.0% Native Hawaiian/Other Pacific Islander, 1.9% Other, 6.4% Hispanic of any race (2010); Average household size: 2.41 (2010); Median age: 41.4 (2010); Males per 100 females: 93.1 (2010); Marriage status: 10.2% never married, 70.5% now married, 8.7% widowed, 10.7% divorced (2006-2010 5-year est.); Foreign born: 7.6% (2006-2010 5-year est.); Ancestry (includes multiple

ancestries): 36.7% German, 21.8% Polish, 15.1% Italian, 13.9% Scottish, 10.4% Irish (2006-2010 5-year est.).

Economy: Employment by occupation: 13.8% management, 0.0% professional, 8.2% services, 4.3% sales, 19.1% farming, 8.2% construction, 18.8% production (2006-2010 5-year est.).

Income: Per capita income: $26,233 (2006-2010 5-year est.); Median household income: $53,274 (2006-2010 5-year est.); Average household income: $60,350 (2006-2010 5-year est.); Percent of households with income of $100,000 or more: 17.5% (2006-2010 5-year est.); Poverty rate: 2.9% (2006-2010 5-year est.).

Education: Percent of population age 25 and over with: High school diploma (including GED) or higher: 92.3% (2006-2010 5-year est.); Bachelor's degree or higher: 26.6% (2006-2010 5-year est.); Master's degree or higher: 8.4% (2006-2010 5-year est.).

Housing: Homeownership rate: 88.3% (2010); Median home value: $123,000 (2006-2010 5-year est.); Median contract rent: n/a per month (2006-2010 5-year est.); Median year structure built: 1953 (2006-2010 5-year est.).

Transportation: Commute to work: 100.0% car, 0.0% public transportation, 0.0% walk, 0.0% work from home (2006-2010 5-year est.); Travel time to work: 35.8% less than 15 minutes, 54.6% 15 to 30 minutes, 0.0% 30 to 45 minutes, 0.0% 45 to 60 minutes, 9.6% 60 minutes or more (2006-2010 5-year est.)

STONY CREEK MILLS (CDP). Covers a land area of 0.588 square miles and a water area of 0 square miles. Located at 40.35° N. Lat; 75.86° W. Long. Elevation is 381 feet.

Population: n/a (1990); n/a (2000); 1,045 (2010); Density: 1,777.9 persons per square mile (2010); Race: 93.0% White, 1.1% Black, 0.0% Asian, 0.4% American Indian/Alaska Native, 0.0% Native Hawaiian/Other Pacific Islander, 5.5% Other, 9.5% Hispanic of any race (2010); Average household size: 2.59 (2010); Median age: 40.1 (2010); Males per 100 females: 95.7 (2010); Marriage status: 25.3% never married, 58.0% now married, 4.2% widowed, 12.5% divorced (2006-2010 5-year est.); Foreign born: 0.0% (2006-2010 5-year est.); Ancestry (includes multiple ancestries): 38.9% German, 23.5% American, 13.2% English, 8.9% Irish, 8.2% Italian (2006-2010 5-year est.).

Economy: Employment by occupation: 11.8% management, 0.0% professional, 11.5% services, 16.0% sales, 6.8% farming, 7.0% construction, 8.5% production (2006-2010 5-year est.).

Income: Per capita income: $23,757 (2006-2010 5-year est.); Median household income: $50,602 (2006-2010 5-year est.); Average household income: $60,339 (2006-2010 5-year est.); Percent of households with income of $100,000 or more: 4.8% (2006-2010 5-year est.); Poverty rate: 2.2% (2006-2010 5-year est.).

Education: Percent of population age 25 and over with: High school diploma (including GED) or higher: 89.3% (2006-2010 5-year est.); Bachelor's degree or higher: 22.3% (2006-2010 5-year est.); Master's degree or higher: 8.6% (2006-2010 5-year est.).

Housing: Homeownership rate: 81.2% (2010); Median home value: $138,100 (2006-2010 5-year est.); Median contract rent: n/a per month (2006-2010 5-year est.); Median year structure built: 1961 (2006-2010 5-year est.).

Transportation: Commute to work: 93.4% car, 3.3% public transportation, 0.0% walk, 3.3% work from home (2006-2010 5-year est.); Travel time to work: 41.1% less than 15 minutes, 53.1% 15 to 30 minutes, 3.7% 30 to 45 minutes, 2.1% 45 to 60 minutes, 0.0% 60 minutes or more (2006-2010 5-year est.)

STOUCHSBURG (CDP). Covers a land area of 1.346 square miles and a water area of 0.003 square miles. Located at 40.38° N. Lat; 76.23° W. Long. Elevation is 440 feet.

Population: n/a (1990); n/a (2000); 600 (2010); Density: 445.9 persons per square mile (2010); Race: 97.5% White, 0.5% Black, 0.3% Asian, 0.0% American Indian/Alaska Native, 0.0% Native Hawaiian/Other Pacific Islander, 1.7% Other, 2.0% Hispanic of any race (2010); Average household size: 2.42 (2010); Median age: 44.0 (2010); Males per 100 females: 120.6 (2010); Marriage status: 21.6% never married, 62.8% now married, 6.3% widowed, 9.3% divorced (2006-2010 5-year est.); Foreign born: 1.5% (2006-2010 5-year est.); Ancestry (includes multiple ancestries): 55.6% German, 16.6% Irish, 11.6% Pennsylvania German, 9.9% American, 7.5% Italian (2006-2010 5-year est.).

Economy: Employment by occupation: 9.3% management, 4.5% professional, 15.6% services, 6.3% sales, 4.8% farming, 19.8% construction, 11.7% production (2006-2010 5-year est.).

Income: Per capita income: $27,626 (2006-2010 5-year est.); Median household income: $60,417 (2006-2010 5-year est.); Average household income: $68,694 (2006-2010 5-year est.); Percent of households with income of $100,000 or more: 16.9% (2006-2010 5-year est.); Poverty rate: 4.5% (2006-2010 5-year est.).
Education: Percent of population age 25 and over with: High school diploma (including GED) or higher: 81.1% (2006-2010 5-year est.); Bachelor's degree or higher: 13.1% (2006-2010 5-year est.); Master's degree or higher: 5.3% (2006-2010 5-year est.).
Housing: Homeownership rate: 66.9% (2010); Median home value: $161,100 (2006-2010 5-year est.); Median contract rent: $617 per month (2006-2010 5-year est.); Median year structure built: before 1940 (2006-2010 5-year est.).
Transportation: Commute to work: 94.9% car, 0.0% public transportation, 1.6% walk, 0.9% work from home (2006-2010 5-year est.); Travel time to work: 29.4% less than 15 minutes, 26.2% 15 to 30 minutes, 33.9% 30 to 45 minutes, 4.8% 45 to 60 minutes, 5.8% 60 minutes or more (2006-2010 5-year est.)

STRAUSSTOWN (borough). Covers a land area of 0.164 square miles and a water area of <.001 square miles. Located at 40.49° N. Lat; 76.18° W. Long. Elevation is 581 feet.
Population: 353 (1990); 339 (2000); 342 (2010); Density: 2,083.4 persons per square mile (2010); Race: 98.2% White, 0.9% Black, 0.0% Asian, 0.0% American Indian/Alaska Native, 0.0% Native Hawaiian/Other Pacific Islander, 0.9% Other, 2.3% Hispanic of any race (2010); Average household size: 2.43 (2010); Median age: 37.4 (2010); Males per 100 females: 97.7 (2010); Marriage status: 22.9% never married, 57.9% now married, 7.2% widowed, 12.0% divorced (2006-2010 5-year est.); Foreign born: 0.6% (2006-2010 5-year est.); Ancestry (includes multiple ancestries): 58.5% German, 16.9% Pennsylvania German, 12.1% Irish, 6.8% Italian, 5.9% Dutch (2006-2010 5-year est.).
Economy: Single-family building permits issued: 0 (2011); Multi-family building permits issued: 0 (2011); Employment by occupation: 13.3% management, 1.0% professional, 11.7% services, 12.2% sales, 2.0% farming, 7.1% construction, 8.2% production (2006-2010 5-year est.).
Income: Per capita income: $22,850 (2006-2010 5-year est.); Median household income: $56,375 (2006-2010 5-year est.); Average household income: $57,512 (2006-2010 5-year est.); Percent of households with income of $100,000 or more: 8.6% (2006-2010 5-year est.); Poverty rate: 5.9% (2006-2010 5-year est.).
Education: Percent of population age 25 and over with: High school diploma (including GED) or higher: 83.3% (2006-2010 5-year est.); Bachelor's degree or higher: 11.9% (2006-2010 5-year est.); Master's degree or higher: 3.2% (2006-2010 5-year est.).
Housing: Homeownership rate: 69.5% (2010); Median home value: $110,600 (2006-2010 5-year est.); Median contract rent: $469 per month (2006-2010 5-year est.); Median year structure built: before 1940 (2006-2010 5-year est.).
Transportation: Commute to work: 92.3% car, 0.0% public transportation, 7.7% walk, 0.0% work from home (2006-2010 5-year est.); Travel time to work: 20.4% less than 15 minutes, 26.0% 15 to 30 minutes, 36.7% 30 to 45 minutes, 10.7% 45 to 60 minutes, 6.1% 60 minutes or more (2006-2010 5-year est.)

TEMPLE (CDP). Covers a land area of 0.336 square miles and a water area of 0.003 square miles. Located at 40.41° N. Lat; 75.92° W. Long. Elevation is 361 feet.
Population: n/a (1990); n/a (2000); 1,877 (2010); Density: 5,580.6 persons per square mile (2010); Race: 84.5% White, 4.2% Black, 1.0% Asian, 0.4% American Indian/Alaska Native, 0.2% Native Hawaiian/Other Pacific Islander, 9.7% Other, 16.8% Hispanic of any race (2010); Average household size: 2.36 (2010); Median age: 39.3 (2010); Males per 100 females: 97.6 (2010); Marriage status: 35.6% never married, 40.9% now married, 7.3% widowed, 16.1% divorced (2006-2010 5-year est.); Foreign born: 6.8% (2006-2010 5-year est.); Ancestry (includes multiple ancestries): 38.4% German, 12.4% Irish, 11.7% Italian, 11.3% Dutch, 5.9% English (2006-2010 5-year est.).
Economy: Employment by occupation: 7.0% management, 0.0% professional, 7.3% services, 33.5% sales, 9.4% farming, 15.5% construction, 5.6% production (2006-2010 5-year est.).
Income: Per capita income: $27,535 (2006-2010 5-year est.); Median household income: $54,879 (2006-2010 5-year est.); Average household income: $64,551 (2006-2010 5-year est.); Percent of households with

income of $100,000 or more: 13.7% (2006-2010 5-year est.); Poverty rate: 7.6% (2006-2010 5-year est.).
Education: Percent of population age 25 and over with: High school diploma (including GED) or higher: 80.6% (2006-2010 5-year est.); Bachelor's degree or higher: 9.1% (2006-2010 5-year est.); Master's degree or higher: 3.8% (2006-2010 5-year est.).
Housing: Homeownership rate: 59.6% (2010); Median home value: $123,300 (2006-2010 5-year est.); Median contract rent: $587 per month (2006-2010 5-year est.); Median year structure built: 1950 (2006-2010 5-year est.).
Transportation: Commute to work: 93.4% car, 1.4% public transportation, 2.2% walk, 2.3% work from home (2006-2010 5-year est.); Travel time to work: 47.8% less than 15 minutes, 43.6% 15 to 30 minutes, 3.5% 30 to 45 minutes, 4.4% 45 to 60 minutes, 0.7% 60 minutes or more (2006-2010 5-year est.)

TILDEN (township). Covers a land area of 18.982 square miles and a water area of 0.227 square miles. Located at 40.54° N. Lat; 76.03° W. Long.
Population: 2,622 (1990); 3,553 (2000); 3,597 (2010); Density: 189.5 persons per square mile (2010); Race: 96.7% White, 0.8% Black, 0.3% Asian, 0.1% American Indian/Alaska Native, 0.3% Native Hawaiian/Other Pacific Islander, 1.8% Other, 4.0% Hispanic of any race (2010); Average household size: 2.60 (2010); Median age: 44.5 (2010); Males per 100 females: 96.8 (2010); Marriage status: 28.7% never married, 56.2% now married, 6.4% widowed, 8.7% divorced (2006-2010 5-year est.); Foreign born: 3.2% (2006-2010 5-year est.); Ancestry (includes multiple ancestries): 56.3% German, 17.1% Irish, 8.2% Pennsylvania German, 4.8% English, 3.6% American (2006-2010 5-year est.).
Economy: Single-family building permits issued: 0 (2011); Multi-family building permits issued: 0 (2011); Employment by occupation: 6.1% management, 1.1% professional, 9.0% services, 12.9% sales, 3.5% farming, 8.0% construction, 12.0% production (2006-2010 5-year est.).
Income: Per capita income: $22,487 (2006-2010 5-year est.); Median household income: $57,054 (2006-2010 5-year est.); Average household income: $62,973 (2006-2010 5-year est.); Percent of households with income of $100,000 or more: 11.0% (2006-2010 5-year est.); Poverty rate: 4.7% (2006-2010 5-year est.).
Education: Percent of population age 25 and over with: High school diploma (including GED) or higher: 84.4% (2006-2010 5-year est.); Bachelor's degree or higher: 8.8% (2006-2010 5-year est.); Master's degree or higher: 3.8% (2006-2010 5-year est.).
Housing: Homeownership rate: 84.5% (2010); Median home value: $127,300 (2006-2010 5-year est.); Median contract rent: $546 per month (2006-2010 5-year est.); Median year structure built: 1982 (2006-2010 5-year est.).
Transportation: Commute to work: 92.4% car, 1.8% public transportation, 2.7% walk, 2.1% work from home (2006-2010 5-year est.); Travel time to work: 28.4% less than 15 minutes, 25.8% 15 to 30 minutes, 27.0% 30 to 45 minutes, 12.6% 45 to 60 minutes, 6.2% 60 minutes or more (2006-2010 5-year est.)
Additional Information Contacts
Schuylkill Chamber of Commerce . . . . (570) 622-1942
   http://www.schuylkillchamber.com

TOPTON (borough). Covers a land area of 0.692 square miles and a water area of 0.001 square miles. Located at 40.50° N. Lat; 75.70° W. Long. Elevation is 482 feet.
History: Founded 1859; incorporated 1875.
Population: 1,987 (1990); 1,948 (2000); 2,069 (2010); Density: 2,991.6 persons per square mile (2010); Race: 97.4% White, 0.6% Black, 0.0% Asian, 0.2% American Indian/Alaska Native, 0.0% Native Hawaiian/Other Pacific Islander, 1.8% Other, 2.8% Hispanic of any race (2010); Average household size: 2.48 (2010); Median age: 39.3 (2010); Males per 100 females: 92.3 (2010); Marriage status: 24.7% never married, 43.4% now married, 20.6% widowed, 11.2% divorced (2006-2010 5-year est.); Foreign born: 3.2% (2006-2010 5-year est.); Ancestry (includes multiple ancestries): 42.5% German, 15.3% Pennsylvania German, 10.8% English, 10.4% Italian, 10.1% Irish (2006-2010 5-year est.).
Economy: Single-family building permits issued: 0 (2011); Multi-family building permits issued: 0 (2011); Employment by occupation: 6.9% management, 2.4% professional, 12.7% services, 18.0% sales, 7.0% farming, 2.5% construction, 11.5% production (2006-2010 5-year est.).
Income: Per capita income: $24,954 (2006-2010 5-year est.); Median household income: $55,464 (2006-2010 5-year est.); Average household

income: $63,796 (2006-2010 5-year est.); Percent of households with income of $100,000 or more: 14.6% (2006-2010 5-year est.); Poverty rate: 2.4% (2006-2010 5-year est.).

Taxes: Total city taxes per capita: $374 (2009); City property taxes per capita: $198 (2009).

Education: Percent of population age 25 and over with: High school diploma (including GED) or higher: 76.8% (2006-2010 5-year est.); Bachelor's degree or higher: 17.7% (2006-2010 5-year est.); Master's degree or higher: 5.9% (2006-2010 5-year est.).

School District(s)

Brandywine Heights Area SD (KG-12)

   2010-11 Enrollment: 1,776 . . . . (610) 682-5100

Housing: Homeownership rate: 68.9% (2010); Median home value: $162,200 (2006-2010 5-year est.); Median contract rent: $654 per month (2006-2010 5-year est.); Median year structure built: 1949 (2006-2010 5-year est.).

Transportation: Commute to work: 92.5% car, 0.0% public transportation, 3.1% walk, 2.7% work from home (2006-2010 5-year est.); Travel time to work: 37.5% less than 15 minutes, 34.6% 15 to 30 minutes, 16.9% 30 to 45 minutes, 5.8% 45 to 60 minutes, 5.2% 60 minutes or more (2006-2010 5-year est.)

Additional Information Contacts

Northeast Berks Chamber of Commerce . . . . (610) 683-8860
  http://www.northeastberkschamber.com

TULPEHOCKEN (township). Aka New Schaefferstown. Covers a land area of 23.496 square miles and a water area of 0.048 square miles. Located at 40.44° N. Lat; 76.25° W. Long.

Population: 2,843 (1990); 3,290 (2000); 3,274 (2010); Density: 139.3 persons per square mile (2010); Race: 93.8% White, 1.8% Black, 0.1% Asian, 0.5% American Indian/Alaska Native, 0.0% Native Hawaiian/Other Pacific Islander, 3.8% Other, 4.6% Hispanic of any race (2010); Average household size: 2.94 (2010); Median age: 35.4 (2010); Males per 100 females: 122.4 (2010); Marriage status: 26.4% never married, 64.6% now married, 1.1% widowed, 7.9% divorced (2006-2010 5-year est.); Foreign born: 1.6% (2006-2010 5-year est.); Ancestry (includes multiple ancestries): 49.3% German, 12.7% Irish, 7.7% American, 5.5% English, 4.0% Pennsylvania German (2006-2010 5-year est.).

Economy: Single-family building permits issued: 0 (2011); Multi-family building permits issued: 0 (2011); Employment by occupation: 11.1% management, 2.1% professional, 14.1% services, 12.3% sales, 4.3% farming, 14.9% construction, 9.1% production (2006-2010 5-year est.).

Income: Per capita income: $21,923 (2006-2010 5-year est.); Median household income: $55,882 (2006-2010 5-year est.); Average household income: $64,602 (2006-2010 5-year est.); Percent of households with income of $100,000 or more: 19.3% (2006-2010 5-year est.); Poverty rate: 8.9% (2006-2010 5-year est.).

Education: Percent of population age 25 and over with: High school diploma (including GED) or higher: 77.7% (2006-2010 5-year est.); Bachelor's degree or higher: 9.8% (2006-2010 5-year est.); Master's degree or higher: 2.8% (2006-2010 5-year est.).

Housing: Homeownership rate: 80.3% (2010); Median home value: $185,500 (2006-2010 5-year est.); Median contract rent: $522 per month (2006-2010 5-year est.); Median year structure built: 1975 (2006-2010 5-year est.).

Safety: Violent crime rate: 0.0 per 10,000 population; Property crime rate: 48.7 per 10,000 population (2011).

Transportation: Commute to work: 86.6% car, 0.0% public transportation, 5.7% walk, 4.9% work from home (2006-2010 5-year est.); Travel time to work: 34.7% less than 15 minutes, 41.7% 15 to 30 minutes, 9.6% 30 to 45 minutes, 5.7% 45 to 60 minutes, 8.3% 60 minutes or more (2006-2010 5-year est.)

Additional Information Contacts

Lebanon Valley Chamber of Commerce . . . . (717) 273-3727
  http://www.lvchamber.org

UNION (township). Covers a land area of 23.413 square miles and a water area of 0.386 square miles. Located at 40.22° N. Lat; 75.78° W. Long.

Population: 3,440 (1990); 3,453 (2000); 3,503 (2010); Density: 149.6 persons per square mile (2010); Race: 97.1% White, 1.1% Black, 0.5% Asian, 0.0% American Indian/Alaska Native, 0.0% Native Hawaiian/Other Pacific Islander, 1.3% Other, 1.2% Hispanic of any race (2010); Average household size: 2.57 (2010); Median age: 45.6 (2010); Males per 100 females: 104.0 (2010); Marriage status: 20.4% never married, 65.1% now

married, 6.7% widowed, 7.7% divorced (2006-2010 5-year est.); Foreign born: 1.8% (2006-2010 5-year est.); Ancestry (includes multiple ancestries): 38.2% German, 18.1% Irish, 14.3% Italian, 7.9% Polish, 7.7% American (2006-2010 5-year est.).

Economy: Single-family building permits issued: 1 (2011); Multi-family building permits issued: 0 (2011); Employment by occupation: 5.9% management, 4.5% professional, 15.7% services, 13.4% sales, 0.4% farming, 16.2% construction, 9.4% production (2006-2010 5-year est.).

Income: Per capita income: $30,824 (2006-2010 5-year est.); Median household income: $64,655 (2006-2010 5-year est.); Average household income: $77,872 (2006-2010 5-year est.); Percent of households with income of $100,000 or more: 22.1% (2006-2010 5-year est.); Poverty rate: 2.9% (2006-2010 5-year est.).

Education: Percent of population age 25 and over with: High school diploma (including GED) or higher: 91.4% (2006-2010 5-year est.); Bachelor's degree or higher: 17.1% (2006-2010 5-year est.); Master's degree or higher: 4.7% (2006-2010 5-year est.).

Housing: Homeownership rate: 86.8% (2010); Median home value: $212,700 (2006-2010 5-year est.); Median contract rent: $681 per month (2006-2010 5-year est.); Median year structure built: 1968 (2006-2010 5-year est.).

Transportation: Commute to work: 93.5% car, 0.6% public transportation, 1.6% walk, 3.9% work from home (2006-2010 5-year est.); Travel time to work: 19.2% less than 15 minutes, 39.6% 15 to 30 minutes, 22.6% 30 to 45 minutes, 8.2% 45 to 60 minutes, 10.4% 60 minutes or more (2006-2010 5-year est.)

Additional Information Contacts

Greater Reading Chamber of Commerce & Industry . . . . . (610) 376-6766
  http://www.greaterreadingchamber.org

UPPER BERN (township). Covers a land area of 17.663 square miles and a water area of 0.068 square miles. Located at 40.52° N. Lat; 76.09° W. Long.

Population: 1,458 (1990); 1,479 (2000); 1,734 (2010); Density: 98.2 persons per square mile (2010); Race: 96.5% White, 0.9% Black, 0.5% Asian, 0.1% American Indian/Alaska Native, 0.0% Native Hawaiian/Other Pacific Islander, 2.0% Other, 2.7% Hispanic of any race (2010); Average household size: 2.50 (2010); Median age: 43.5 (2010); Males per 100 females: 109.7 (2010); Marriage status: 23.3% never married, 63.1% now married, 3.8% widowed, 9.7% divorced (2006-2010 5-year est.); Foreign born: 2.2% (2006-2010 5-year est.); Ancestry (includes multiple ancestries): 55.2% German, 13.8% Irish, 12.3% Pennsylvania German, 6.5% Italian, 5.9% English (2006-2010 5-year est.).

Economy: Single-family building permits issued: 1 (2011); Multi-family building permits issued: 0 (2011); Employment by occupation: 9.2% management, 3.6% professional, 10.1% services, 13.8% sales, 5.5% farming, 13.1% construction, 7.6% production (2006-2010 5-year est.).

Income: Per capita income: $26,019 (2006-2010 5-year est.); Median household income: $59,345 (2006-2010 5-year est.); Average household income: $66,938 (2006-2010 5-year est.); Percent of households with income of $100,000 or more: 19.6% (2006-2010 5-year est.); Poverty rate: 7.6% (2006-2010 5-year est.).

Education: Percent of population age 25 and over with: High school diploma (including GED) or higher: 84.0% (2006-2010 5-year est.); Bachelor's degree or higher: 10.8% (2006-2010 5-year est.); Master's degree or higher: 4.0% (2006-2010 5-year est.).

Housing: Homeownership rate: 81.7% (2010); Median home value: $170,900 (2006-2010 5-year est.); Median contract rent: $460 per month (2006-2010 5-year est.); Median year structure built: 1974 (2006-2010 5-year est.).

Transportation: Commute to work: 92.1% car, 0.0% public transportation, 4.5% walk, 3.2% work from home (2006-2010 5-year est.); Travel time to work: 21.5% less than 15 minutes, 30.3% 15 to 30 minutes, 35.8% 30 to 45 minutes, 5.8% 45 to 60 minutes, 6.6% 60 minutes or more (2006-2010 5-year est.)

Additional Information Contacts

Schuylkill Chamber of Commerce . . . . (570) 622-1942
  http://www.schuylkillchamber.com

UPPER TULPEHOCKEN (township). Covers a land area of 23.049 square miles and a water area of 0.074 square miles. Located at 40.50° N. Lat; 76.17° W. Long.

Population: 1,329 (1990); 1,495 (2000); 1,575 (2010); Density: 68.3 persons per square mile (2010); Race: 96.6% White, 0.7% Black, 0.2% Asian, 0.4% American Indian/Alaska Native, 0.0% Native Hawaiian/Other

Pacific Islander, 2.1% Other, 3.3% Hispanic of any race (2010); Average household size: 2.71 (2010); Median age: 42.4 (2010); Males per 100 females: 110.0 (2010); Marriage status: 23.1% never married, 63.0% now married, 4.2% widowed, 9.8% divorced (2006-2010 5-year est.); Foreign born: 3.7% (2006-2010 5-year est.); Ancestry (includes multiple ancestries): 56.6% German, 13.4% Irish, 6.3% English, 5.1% American, 3.8% Pennsylvania German (2006-2010 5-year est.).

Economy: Single-family building permits issued: 0 (2011); Multi-family building permits issued: 0 (2011); Employment by occupation: 6.6% management, 2.3% professional, 12.3% services, 11.6% sales, 1.8% farming, 23.7% construction, 12.6% production (2006-2010 5-year est.).

Income: Per capita income: $23,985 (2006-2010 5-year est.); Median household income: $58,710 (2006-2010 5-year est.); Average household income: $67,240 (2006-2010 5-year est.); Percent of households with income of $100,000 or more: 13.0% (2006-2010 5-year est.); Poverty rate: 10.0% (2006-2010 5-year est.).

Education: Percent of population age 25 and over with: High school diploma (including GED) or higher: 78.9% (2006-2010 5-year est.); Bachelor's degree or higher: 12.8% (2006-2010 5-year est.); Master's degree or higher: 4.3% (2006-2010 5-year est.).

Housing: Homeownership rate: 81.2% (2010); Median home value: $198,300 (2006-2010 5-year est.); Median contract rent: $618 per month (2006-2010 5-year est.); Median year structure built: 1978 (2006-2010 5-year est.).

Transportation: Commute to work: 89.9% car, 0.0% public transportation, 4.8% walk, 5.3% work from home (2006-2010 5-year est.); Travel time to work: 25.4% less than 15 minutes, 28.0% 15 to 30 minutes, 25.9% 30 to 45 minutes, 13.1% 45 to 60 minutes, 7.6% 60 minutes or more (2006-2010 5-year est.)

Additional Information Contacts

Schuylkill Chamber of Commerce . . . . (570) 622-1942
   http://www.schuylkillchamber.com

VIRGINVILLE (CDP). Covers a land area of 1.136 square miles and a water area of 0.004 square miles. Located at 40.52° N. Lat; 75.86° W. Long. Elevation is 335 feet.

Population: n/a (1990); n/a (2000); 309 (2010); Density: 272.0 persons per square mile (2010); Race: 98.7% White, 0.3% Black, 0.0% Asian, 0.0% American Indian/Alaska Native, 0.0% Native Hawaiian/Other Pacific Islander, 1.0% Other, 1.3% Hispanic of any race (2010); Average household size: 2.34 (2010); Median age: 48.3 (2010); Males per 100 females: 106.0 (2010); Marriage status: 4.9% never married, 78.4% now married, 0.0% widowed, 16.8% divorced (2006-2010 5-year est.); Foreign born: 0.0% (2006-2010 5-year est.); Ancestry (includes multiple ancestries): 56.9% German, 21.4% Pennsylvania German, 13.9% Swiss, 11.0% French, 10.7% Irish (2006-2010 5-year est.).

Economy: Employment by occupation: 0.0% management, 0.0% professional, 17.3% services, 11.3% sales, 0.0% farming, 0.0% construction, 11.3% production (2006-2010 5-year est.).

Income: Per capita income: $32,807 (2006-2010 5-year est.); Median household income: $82,955 (2006-2010 5-year est.); Average household income: $72,810 (2006-2010 5-year est.); Percent of households with income of $100,000 or more: 35.7% (2006-2010 5-year est.); Poverty rate: 0.0% (2006-2010 5-year est.).

Education: Percent of population age 25 and over with: High school diploma (including GED) or higher: 93.7% (2006-2010 5-year est.); Bachelor's degree or higher: 28.6% (2006-2010 5-year est.); Master's degree or higher: 6.3% (2006-2010 5-year est.).

Housing: Homeownership rate: 90.9% (2010); Median home value: $168,500 (2006-2010 5-year est.); Median contract rent: n/a per month (2006-2010 5-year est.); Median year structure built: 1953 (2006-2010 5-year est.).

Transportation: Commute to work: 82.7% car, 0.0% public transportation, 0.0% walk, 17.3% work from home (2006-2010 5-year est.); Travel time to work: 0.0% less than 15 minutes, 62.7% 15 to 30 minutes, 37.3% 30 to 45 minutes, 0.0% 45 to 60 minutes, 0.0% 60 minutes or more (2006-2010 5-year est.)

WALNUTTOWN (CDP). Covers a land area of 0.537 square miles and a water area of 0 square miles. Located at 40.45° N. Lat; 75.84° W. Long. Elevation is 394 feet.

Population: n/a (1990); n/a (2000); 484 (2010); Density: 900.8 persons per square mile (2010); Race: 99.8% White, 0.0% Black, 0.0% Asian, 0.0% American Indian/Alaska Native, 0.0% Native Hawaiian/Other Pacific Islander, 0.2% Other, 1.4% Hispanic of any race (2010); Average

household size: 2.37 (2010); Median age: 45.6 (2010); Males per 100 females: 98.4 (2010); Marriage status: 11.9% never married, 82.2% now married, 5.9% widowed, 0.0% divorced (2006-2010 5-year est.); Foreign born: 0.0% (2006-2010 5-year est.); Ancestry (includes multiple ancestries): 55.7% German, 17.9% Dutch, 10.0% Italian, 4.7% Russian, 4.4% Irish (2006-2010 5-year est.).

Economy: Employment by occupation: 48.5% management, 0.0% professional, 0.0% services, 13.6% sales, 8.6% farming, 14.6% construction, 16.7% production (2006-2010 5-year est.).

Income: Per capita income: $18,249 (2006-2010 5-year est.); Median household income: $36,691 (2006-2010 5-year est.); Average household income: $40,415 (2006-2010 5-year est.); Percent of households with income of $100,000 or more: n/a (2006-2010 5-year est.); Poverty rate: 0.0% (2006-2010 5-year est.).

Education: Percent of population age 25 and over with: High school diploma (including GED) or higher: 82.2% (2006-2010 5-year est.); Bachelor's degree or higher: 45.2% (2006-2010 5-year est.); Master's degree or higher: 0.0% (2006-2010 5-year est.).

Housing: Homeownership rate: 83.3% (2010); Median home value: $193,800 (2006-2010 5-year est.); Median contract rent: n/a per month (2006-2010 5-year est.); Median year structure built: 1977 (2006-2010 5-year est.).

Transportation: Commute to work: 51.5% car, 0.0% public transportation, 0.0% walk, 0.0% work from home (2006-2010 5-year est.); Travel time to work: 23.2% less than 15 minutes, 55.1% 15 to 30 minutes, 13.6% 30 to 45 minutes, 8.1% 45 to 60 minutes, 0.0% 60 minutes or more (2006-2010 5-year est.)

WASHINGTON (township). Covers a land area of 14.102 square miles and a water area of 0.033 square miles. Located at 40.39° N. Lat; 75.61° W. Long.

Population: 2,748 (1990); 3,354 (2000); 3,810 (2010); Density: 270.2 persons per square mile (2010); Race: 97.9% White, 0.4% Black, 0.7% Asian, 0.0% American Indian/Alaska Native, 0.0% Native Hawaiian/Other Pacific Islander, 1.0% Other, 1.2% Hispanic of any race (2010); Average household size: 2.65 (2010); Median age: 44.5 (2010); Males per 100 females: 97.3 (2010); Marriage status: 20.2% never married, 67.8% now married, 5.7% widowed, 6.2% divorced (2006-2010 5-year est.); Foreign born: 4.2% (2006-2010 5-year est.); Ancestry (includes multiple ancestries): 49.0% German, 14.8% Italian, 12.3% Irish, 9.9% Polish, 9.9% English (2006-2010 5-year est.).

Economy: Single-family building permits issued: 27 (2011); Multi-family building permits issued: 0 (2011); Employment by occupation: 17.2% management, 2.2% professional, 8.8% services, 19.0% sales, 2.5% farming, 11.9% construction, 10.8% production (2006-2010 5-year est.).

Income: Per capita income: $30,933 (2006-2010 5-year est.); Median household income: $72,674 (2006-2010 5-year est.); Average household income: $87,495 (2006-2010 5-year est.); Percent of households with income of $100,000 or more: 30.7% (2006-2010 5-year est.); Poverty rate: 5.1% (2006-2010 5-year est.).

Education: Percent of population age 25 and over with: High school diploma (including GED) or higher: 89.7% (2006-2010 5-year est.); Bachelor's degree or higher: 22.9% (2006-2010 5-year est.); Master's degree or higher: 9.7% (2006-2010 5-year est.).

Housing: Homeownership rate: 87.4% (2010); Median home value: $260,500 (2006-2010 5-year est.); Median contract rent: $988 per month (2006-2010 5-year est.); Median year structure built: 1970 (2006-2010 5-year est.).

Transportation: Commute to work: 89.1% car, 0.0% public transportation, 0.8% walk, 7.4% work from home (2006-2010 5-year est.); Travel time to work: 32.6% less than 15 minutes, 20.2% 15 to 30 minutes, 25.5% 30 to 45 minutes, 10.2% 45 to 60 minutes, 11.6% 60 minutes or more (2006-2010 5-year est.)

Additional Information Contacts

Greater Reading Chamber of Commerce & Industry . . . . . (610) 376-6766
   http://www.greaterreadingchamber.org
Washington Township . . . . (610) 845-7760
   http://www.washtwpberks.org

WERNERSVILLE (borough). Covers a land area of 0.763 square miles and a water area of 0.001 square miles. Located at 40.33° N. Lat; 76.08° W. Long. Elevation is 374 feet.

History: Founded c.1855.

Population: 1,934 (1990); 2,150 (2000); 2,494 (2010); Density: 3,269.3 persons per square mile (2010); Race: 92.9% White, 2.6% Black, 1.1%

Asian, 0.2% American Indian/Alaska Native, 0.0% Native Hawaiian/Other Pacific Islander, 3.2% Other, 4.0% Hispanic of any race (2010); Average household size: 2.44 (2010); Median age: 43.4 (2010); Males per 100 females: 93.0 (2010); Marriage status: 30.3% never married, 55.7% now married, 6.4% widowed, 7.7% divorced (2006-2010 5-year est.); Foreign born: 2.1% (2006-2010 5-year est.); Ancestry (includes multiple ancestries): 55.0% German, 13.6% Irish, 7.0% Italian, 6.1% English, 5.3% Polish (2006-2010 5-year est.).

Economy: Single-family building permits issued: 0 (2011); Multi-family building permits issued: 0 (2011); Employment by occupation: 11.4% management, 0.7% professional, 10.2% services, 22.6% sales, 3.5% farming, 10.7% construction, 7.2% production (2006-2010 5-year est.).

Income: Per capita income: $22,590 (2006-2010 5-year est.); Median household income: $51,007 (2006-2010 5-year est.); Average household income: $56,686 (2006-2010 5-year est.); Percent of households with income of $100,000 or more: 10.8% (2006-2010 5-year est.); Poverty rate: 6.4% (2006-2010 5-year est.).

Education: Percent of population age 25 and over with: High school diploma (including GED) or higher: 89.4% (2006-2010 5-year est.); Bachelor's degree or higher: 14.4% (2006-2010 5-year est.); Master's degree or higher: 4.5% (2006-2010 5-year est.).

School District(s)

Conrad Weiser Area SD (KG-12)
  2010-11 Enrollment: 2,851 . . . . (610) 693-8545

Housing: Homeownership rate: 75.8% (2010); Median home value: $157,900 (2006-2010 5-year est.); Median contract rent: $647 per month (2006-2010 5-year est.); Median year structure built: 1958 (2006-2010 5-year est.).

Hospitals: Caron Treatment Centers (250 beds); Wernersville State Hospital (240 beds)

Transportation: Commute to work: 93.7% car, 0.0% public transportation, 2.4% walk, 3.9% work from home (2006-2010 5-year est.); Travel time to work: 29.4% less than 15 minutes, 47.3% 15 to 30 minutes, 13.7% 30 to 45 minutes, 1.1% 45 to 60 minutes, 8.6% 60 minutes or more (2006-2010 5-year est.)

Additional Information Contacts

Greater Reading Chamber of Commerce & Industry . . . . . (610) 376-6766
  http://www.greaterreadingchamber.org

WEST HAMBURG (CDP).

Covers a land area of 3.361 square miles and a water area of 0.036 square miles. Located at 40.55° N. Lat; 76.00° W. Long. Elevation is 456 feet.

Population: n/a (1990); n/a (2000); 1,979 (2010); Density: 588.8 persons per square mile (2010); Race: 97.3% White, 1.1% Black, 0.2% Asian, 0.1% American Indian/Alaska Native, 0.0% Native Hawaiian/Other Pacific Islander, 1.3% Other, 3.4% Hispanic of any race (2010); Average household size: 2.46 (2010); Median age: 46.1 (2010); Males per 100 females: 90.7 (2010); Marriage status: 21.5% never married, 57.4% now married, 8.0% widowed, 13.0% divorced (2006-2010 5-year est.); Foreign born: 1.0% (2006-2010 5-year est.); Ancestry (includes multiple ancestries): 48.1% German, 13.8% Irish, 11.2% Pennsylvania German, 4.8% American, 4.7% Scotch-Irish (2006-2010 5-year est.).

Economy: Employment by occupation: 1.9% management, 1.3% professional, 4.9% services, 15.0% sales, 3.4% farming, 3.2% construction, 13.1% production (2006-2010 5-year est.).

Income: Per capita income: $19,265 (2006-2010 5-year est.); Median household income: $46,971 (2006-2010 5-year est.); Average household income: $51,302 (2006-2010 5-year est.); Percent of households with income of $100,000 or more: 4.4% (2006-2010 5-year est.); Poverty rate: 7.4% (2006-2010 5-year est.).

Education: Percent of population age 25 and over with: High school diploma (including GED) or higher: 83.7% (2006-2010 5-year est.); Bachelor's degree or higher: 7.4% (2006-2010 5-year est.); Master's degree or higher: 2.1% (2006-2010 5-year est.).

Housing: Homeownership rate: 86.0% (2010); Median home value: $99,100 (2006-2010 5-year est.); Median contract rent: $579 per month (2006-2010 5-year est.); Median year structure built: 1977 (2006-2010 5-year est.).

Transportation: Commute to work: 92.8% car, 3.5% public transportation, 0.8% walk, 0.9% work from home (2006-2010 5-year est.); Travel time to work: 31.1% less than 15 minutes, 19.8% 15 to 30 minutes, 22.1% 30 to 45 minutes, 16.0% 45 to 60 minutes, 11.0% 60 minutes or more (2006-2010 5-year est.)

WEST LAWN (CDP).

Covers a land area of 0.211 square miles and a water area of 0 square miles. Located at 40.33° N. Lat; 75.99° W. Long. Elevation is 384 feet.

History: Incorporated 1920.

Population: 1,606 (1990); 1,597 (2000); 1,715 (2010); Density: 8,137.2 persons per square mile (2010); Race: 86.8% White, 6.2% Black, 0.9% Asian, 0.1% American Indian/Alaska Native, 0.0% Native Hawaiian/Other Pacific Islander, 6.0% Other, 9.6% Hispanic of any race (2010); Average household size: 2.49 (2010); Median age: 36.2 (2010); Males per 100 females: 97.8 (2010); Marriage status: 20.0% never married, 67.9% now married, 3.7% widowed, 8.4% divorced (2006-2010 5-year est.); Foreign born: 2.8% (2006-2010 5-year est.); Ancestry (includes multiple ancestries): 49.7% German, 16.5% Irish, 14.0% Italian, 9.1% Polish, 6.0% English (2006-2010 5-year est.).

Economy: Single-family building permits issued: 0 (2011); Multi-family building permits issued: 0 (2011); Employment by occupation: 5.3% management, 1.9% professional, 10.1% services, 17.1% sales, 6.2% farming, 11.1% construction, 10.1% production (2006-2010 5-year est.).

Income: Per capita income: $25,630 (2006-2010 5-year est.); Median household income: $53,872 (2006-2010 5-year est.); Average household income: $55,364 (2006-2010 5-year est.); Percent of households with income of $100,000 or more: 5.9% (2006-2010 5-year est.); Poverty rate: 4.5% (2006-2010 5-year est.).

Education: Percent of population age 25 and over with: High school diploma (including GED) or higher: 95.4% (2006-2010 5-year est.); Bachelor's degree or higher: 16.9% (2006-2010 5-year est.); Master's degree or higher: 5.4% (2006-2010 5-year est.).

School District(s)

Wilson SD (KG-12)
  2010-11 Enrollment: 5,828 . . . . (610) 670-0180

Housing: Homeownership rate: 71.6% (2010); Median home value: $129,800 (2006-2010 5-year est.); Median contract rent: $643 per month (2006-2010 5-year est.); Median year structure built: before 1940 (2006-2010 5-year est.).

Transportation: Commute to work: 92.9% car, 4.4% public transportation, 1.0% walk, 1.5% work from home (2006-2010 5-year est.); Travel time to work: 52.3% less than 15 minutes, 23.7% 15 to 30 minutes, 13.2% 30 to 45 minutes, 2.9% 45 to 60 minutes, 8.0% 60 minutes or more (2006-2010 5-year est.)

Additional Information Contacts

Greater Reading Chamber of Commerce & Industry . . . . . (610) 376-6766
  http://www.greaterreadingchamber.org

WEST READING (borough).

Covers a land area of 0.592 square miles and a water area of 0.004 square miles. Located at 40.33° N. Lat; 75.95° W. Long. Elevation is 322 feet.

History: Founded 1873, incorporated 1907.

Population: 4,142 (1990); 4,049 (2000); 4,212 (2010); Density: 7,119.5 persons per square mile (2010); Race: 77.6% White, 8.6% Black, 2.1% Asian, 0.3% American Indian/Alaska Native, 0.0% Native Hawaiian/Other Pacific Islander, 11.4% Other, 18.3% Hispanic of any race (2010); Average household size: 2.34 (2010); Median age: 36.5 (2010); Males per 100 females: 90.2 (2010); Marriage status: 22.8% never married, 52.4% now married, 11.2% widowed, 13.6% divorced (2006-2010 5-year est.); Foreign born: 9.7% (2006-2010 5-year est.); Ancestry (includes multiple ancestries): 28.3% German, 17.4% Irish, 14.3% Italian, 6.7% English, 4.9% Polish (2006-2010 5-year est.).

Economy: Single-family building permits issued: 0 (2011); Multi-family building permits issued: 0 (2011); Employment by occupation: 7.3% management, 3.2% professional, 10.7% services, 24.6% sales, 3.3% farming, 7.8% construction, 7.4% production (2006-2010 5-year est.).

Income: Per capita income: $22,345 (2006-2010 5-year est.); Median household income: $45,867 (2006-2010 5-year est.); Average household income: $53,163 (2006-2010 5-year est.); Percent of households with income of $100,000 or more: 10.4% (2006-2010 5-year est.); Poverty rate: 12.1% (2006-2010 5-year est.).

Taxes: Total city taxes per capita: $620 (2009); City property taxes per capita: $245 (2009).

Education: Percent of population age 25 and over with: High school diploma (including GED) or higher: 73.5% (2006-2010 5-year est.); Bachelor's degree or higher: 20.7% (2006-2010 5-year est.); Master's degree or higher: 5.5% (2006-2010 5-year est.).

School District(s)

Wyomissing Area SD (KG-12)
  2010-11 Enrollment: 1,858 . . . . (610) 374-0739

The Reading Hospital School of Health Sciences (Private, Not-for-profit)
Fall 2010 Enrollment: 274 . . . . (610) 741-0105
2011-12 Tuition: In-state $14,895; Out-of-state $14,895
Housing: Homeownership rate: 57.0% (2010); Median home value:
$116,600 (2006-2010 5-year est.); Median contract rent: $654 per month
(2006-2010 5-year est.); Median year structure built: before 1940
(2006-2010 5-year est.).
Safety: Violent crime rate: 45.0 per 10,000 population; Property crime rate:
516.0 per 10,000 population (2011).
Transportation: Commute to work: 84.6% car, 2.7% public transportation,
8.1% walk, 2.5% work from home (2006-2010 5-year est.); Travel time to
work: 57.3% less than 15 minutes, 28.8% 15 to 30 minutes, 8.7% 30 to 45
minutes, 3.3% 45 to 60 minutes, 1.9% 60 minutes or more (2006-2010
5-year est.)
Additional Information Contacts
Borough of West Reading . . . . (610) 374-8273
http://www.westreadingborough.com
Greater Reading Chamber of Commerce & Industry . . . . . (610) 376-6766
http://www.greaterreadingchamber.org

WEST WYOMISSING (CDP). Covers a land area of 0.834 square
miles and a water area of 0 square miles. Located at 40.32° N. Lat; 75.99°
W. Long. Elevation is 361 feet.
Population: 3,222 (1990); 3,016 (2000); 3,407 (2010); Density: 4,083.1
persons per square mile (2010); Race: 88.5% White, 4.0% Black, 1.2%
Asian, 0.1% American Indian/Alaska Native, 0.0% Native Hawaiian/Other
Pacific Islander, 6.2% Other, 8.9% Hispanic of any race (2010); Average
household size: 2.30 (2010); Median age: 41.3 (2010); Males per 100
females: 89.0 (2010); Marriage status: 30.1% never married, 47.8% now
married, 7.7% widowed, 14.4% divorced (2006-2010 5-year est.); Foreign
born: 3.6% (2006-2010 5-year est.); Ancestry (includes multiple
ancestries): 41.1% German, 19.7% Italian, 16.7% Irish, 8.0% Polish, 6.5%
English (2006-2010 5-year est.).
Economy: Employment by occupation: 8.7% management, 3.2%
professional, 9.2% services, 20.8% sales, 4.6% farming, 3.3%
construction, 1.8% production (2006-2010 5-year est.).
Income: Per capita income: $21,937 (2006-2010 5-year est.); Median
household income: $48,457 (2006-2010 5-year est.); Average household
income: $53,625 (2006-2010 5-year est.); Percent of households with
income of $100,000 or more: 8.7% (2006-2010 5-year est.); Poverty rate:
7.9% (2006-2010 5-year est.).
Education: Percent of population age 25 and over with: High school
diploma (including GED) or higher: 89.5% (2006-2010 5-year est.);
Bachelor's degree or higher: 16.8% (2006-2010 5-year est.); Master's
degree or higher: 4.9% (2006-2010 5-year est.).
Housing: Homeownership rate: 82.2% (2010); Median home value:
$127,100 (2006-2010 5-year est.); Median contract rent: $776 per month
(2006-2010 5-year est.); Median year structure built: 1955 (2006-2010
5-year est.).
Transportation: Commute to work: 94.4% car, 0.4% public transportation,
2.2% walk, 2.5% work from home (2006-2010 5-year est.); Travel time to
work: 43.6% less than 15 minutes, 35.3% 15 to 30 minutes, 9.4% 30 to 45
minutes, 5.8% 45 to 60 minutes, 5.9% 60 minutes or more (2006-2010
5-year est.)
Additional Information Contacts
Greater Reading Chamber of Commerce & Industry . . . . . (610) 376-6766
http://www.greaterreadingchamber.org

WHITFIELD (CDP). Covers a land area of 1.055 square miles and a
water area of <.001 square miles. Located at 40.34° N. Lat; 76.01° W.
Long. Elevation is 341 feet.
Population: 2,755 (1990); 2,952 (2000); 4,733 (2010); Density: 4,484.4
persons per square mile (2010); Race: 90.0% White, 3.0% Black, 2.9%
Asian, 0.3% American Indian/Alaska Native, 0.0% Native Hawaiian/Other
Pacific Islander, 3.8% Other, 5.9% Hispanic of any race (2010); Average
household size: 2.49 (2010); Median age: 47.6 (2010); Males per 100
females: 95.0 (2010); Marriage status: 22.8% never married, 66.0% now
married, 6.5% widowed, 4.7% divorced (2006-2010 5-year est.); Foreign
born: 6.7% (2006-2010 5-year est.); Ancestry (includes multiple
ancestries): 39.7% German, 16.0% Irish, 12.6% Italian, 8.6% English,
8.5% American (2006-2010 5-year est.).
Economy: Employment by occupation: 11.6% management, 4.7%
professional, 6.5% services, 12.3% sales, 2.9% farming, 4.8%
construction, 5.2% production (2006-2010 5-year est.).

Income: Per capita income: $32,790 (2006-2010 5-year est.); Median
household income: $74,680 (2006-2010 5-year est.); Average household
income: $82,121 (2006-2010 5-year est.); Percent of households with
income of $100,000 or more: 30.2% (2006-2010 5-year est.); Poverty rate:
6.7% (2006-2010 5-year est.).
Education: Percent of population age 25 and over with: High school
diploma (including GED) or higher: 95.9% (2006-2010 5-year est.); Master's
Bachelor's degree or higher: 50.7% (2006-2010 5-year est.); Master's
degree or higher: 20.6% (2006-2010 5-year est.).
Housing: Homeownership rate: 87.5% (2010); Median home value:
$197,200 (2006-2010 5-year est.); Median contract rent: $1,068 per month
(2006-2010 5-year est.); Median year structure built: 1973 (2006-2010
5-year est.).
Transportation: Commute to work: 95.0% car, 2.0% public transportation,
1.0% walk, 1.6% work from home (2006-2010 5-year est.); Travel time to
work: 42.4% less than 15 minutes, 36.6% 15 to 30 minutes, 8.2% 30 to 45
minutes, 3.1% 45 to 60 minutes, 9.6% 60 minutes or more (2006-2010
5-year est.)
Additional Information Contacts
Greater Scranton Chamber of Commerce . . . . (570) 342-7711
http://www.scrantonchamber.com

WINDSOR (township). Covers a land area of 22.995 square miles and
a water area of 0.167 square miles. Located at 40.57° N. Lat; 75.95° W.
Long.
Population: 2,101 (1990); 2,392 (2000); 2,279 (2010); Density: 99.1
persons per square mile (2010); Race: 96.8% White, 0.6% Black, 0.5%
Asian, 0.1% American Indian/Alaska Native, 0.0% Native Hawaiian/Other
Pacific Islander, 2.0% Other, 1.3% Hispanic of any race (2010); Average
household size: 2.47 (2010); Median age: 44.8 (2010); Males per 100
females: 101.0 (2010); Marriage status: 28.8% never married, 58.5% now
married, 4.8% widowed, 8.0% divorced (2006-2010 5-year est.); Foreign
born: 0.2% (2006-2010 5-year est.); Ancestry (includes multiple
ancestries): 46.8% German, 10.2% Pennsylvania German, 8.9%
American, 8.7% Irish, 8.5% Dutch (2006-2010 5-year est.).
Economy: Single-family building permits issued: 6 (2011); Multi-family
building permits issued: 0 (2011); Employment by occupation: 5.6%
management, 2.3% professional, 9.9% services, 19.2% sales, 5.9%
farming, 15.8% construction, 12.7% production (2006-2010 5-year est.).
Income: Per capita income: $29,352 (2006-2010 5-year est.); Median
household income: $65,750 (2006-2010 5-year est.); Average household
income: $76,049 (2006-2010 5-year est.); Percent of households with
income of $100,000 or more: 20.8% (2006-2010 5-year est.); Poverty rate:
4.4% (2006-2010 5-year est.).
Education: Percent of population age 25 and over with: High school
diploma (including GED) or higher: 77.3% (2006-2010 5-year est.);
Bachelor's degree or higher: 17.2% (2006-2010 5-year est.); Master's
degree or higher: 3.7% (2006-2010 5-year est.).
Housing: Homeownership rate: 82.2% (2010); Median home value:
$185,400 (2006-2010 5-year est.); Median contract rent: $579 per month
(2006-2010 5-year est.); Median year structure built: 1975 (2006-2010
5-year est.).
Transportation: Commute to work: 93.0% car, 1.3% public transportation,
1.5% walk, 4.2% work from home (2006-2010 5-year est.); Travel time to
work: 32.2% less than 15 minutes, 28.8% 15 to 30 minutes, 25.6% 30 to
45 minutes, 6.5% 45 to 60 minutes, 6.9% 60 minutes or more (2006-2010
5-year est.)
Additional Information Contacts
Northeast Berks Chamber of Commerce . . . . (610) 683-8860
http://www.northeastberkschamber.com

WOMELSDORF (borough). Covers a land area of 0.901 square
miles and a water area of 0.002 square miles. Located at 40.37° N. Lat;
76.18° W. Long. Elevation is 413 feet.
History: Conrad Weisel Homestead to West. Settled 1723, laid out 1762,
incorporated 1833.
Population: 2,270 (1990); 2,599 (2000); 2,810 (2010); Density: 3,120.1
persons per square mile (2010); Race: 92.5% White, 2.8% Black, 2.0%
Asian, 0.0% American Indian/Alaska Native, 0.0% Native Hawaiian/Other
Pacific Islander, 2.7% Other, 4.2% Hispanic of any race (2010); Average
household size: 2.37 (2010); Median age: 39.5 (2010); Males per 100
females: 92.7 (2010); Marriage status: 23.7% never married, 61.7% now
married, 5.3% widowed, 9.4% divorced (2006-2010 5-year est.); Foreign
born: 5.7% (2006-2010 5-year est.); Ancestry (includes multiple

ancestries): 48.2% German, 11.1% Irish, 7.8% Italian, 6.3% English, 4.8% Pennsylvania German (2006-2010 5-year est.).
Economy: Single-family building permits issued: 0 (2011); Multi-family building permits issued: 0 (2011); Employment by occupation: 3.6% management, 3.8% professional, 13.7% services, 17.7% sales, 3.8% farming, 10.0% construction, 8.0% production (2006-2010 5-year est.).
Income: Per capita income: $24,192 (2006-2010 5-year est.); Median household income: $56,094 (2006-2010 5-year est.); Average household income: $58,669 (2006-2010 5-year est.); Percent of households with income of $100,000 or more: 11.5% (2006-2010 5-year est.); Poverty rate: 6.3% (2006-2010 5-year est.).
Education: Percent of population age 25 and over with: High school diploma (including GED) or higher: 87.4% (2006-2010 5-year est.); Bachelor's degree or higher: 16.5% (2006-2010 5-year est.); Master's degree or higher: 4.0% (2006-2010 5-year est.).

School District(s)
Conrad Weiser Area SD (KG-12)
    2010-11 Enrollment: 2,851 . . . . (610) 693-8545
Housing: Homeownership rate: 69.5% (2010); Median home value: $128,100 (2006-2010 5-year est.); Median contract rent: $524 per month (2006-2010 5-year est.); Median year structure built: 1978 (2006-2010 5-year est.).
Safety: Violent crime rate: 31.9 per 10,000 population; Property crime rate: 113.5 per 10,000 population (2011).
Transportation: Commute to work: 93.8% car, 0.0% public transportation, 0.2% walk, 3.4% work from home (2006-2010 5-year est.); Travel time to work: 23.5% less than 15 minutes, 30.7% 15 to 30 minutes, 30.7% 30 to 45 minutes, 9.1% 45 to 60 minutes, 6.0% 60 minutes or more (2006-2010 5-year est.)
Additional Information Contacts
Greater Reading Chamber of Commerce & Industry . . . . . (610) 376-6766
    http://www.greaterreadingchamber.org

WYOMISSING (borough). Covers a land area of 4.478 square miles and a water area of 0.021 square miles. Located at 40.34° N. Lat; 75.97° W. Long. Elevation is 315 feet.
History: Berks County Heritage Center. Founded 1896, incorporated 1906.
Population: 7,284 (1990); 8,587 (2000); 10,461 (2010); Density: 2,336.3 persons per square mile (2010); Race: 91.0% White, 2.4% Black, 3.3% Asian, 0.1% American Indian/Alaska Native, 0.0% Native Hawaiian/Other Pacific Islander, 3.2% Other, 5.4% Hispanic of any race (2010); Average household size: 2.24 (2010); Median age: 48.8 (2010); Males per 100 females: 86.6 (2010); Marriage status: 17.1% never married, 66.3% now married, 10.2% widowed, 6.3% divorced (2006-2010 5-year est.); Foreign born: 6.0% (2006-2010 5-year est.); Ancestry (includes multiple ancestries): 35.3% German, 14.8% Irish, 14.2% Italian, 10.0% English, 8.2% Polish (2006-2010 5-year est.).
Economy: Single-family building permits issued: 0 (2011); Multi-family building permits issued: 0 (2011); Employment by occupation: 16.6% management, 4.2% professional, 7.7% services, 16.3% sales, 5.2% farming, 4.7% construction, 2.2% production (2006-2010 5-year est.).
Income: Per capita income: $51,103 (2006-2010 5-year est.); Median household income: $65,010 (2006-2010 5-year est.); Average household income: $112,540 (2006-2010 5-year est.); Percent of households with income of $100,000 or more: 30.4% (2006-2010 5-year est.); Poverty rate: 2.2% (2006-2010 5-year est.).
Education: Percent of population age 25 and over with: High school diploma (including GED) or higher: 92.9% (2006-2010 5-year est.); Bachelor's degree or higher: 48.8% (2006-2010 5-year est.); Master's degree or higher: 20.1% (2006-2010 5-year est.).

School District(s)
Wilson SD (KG-12)
    2010-11 Enrollment: 5,828 . . . . (610) 670-0180
Wyomissing Area SD (KG-12)
    2010-11 Enrollment: 1,858 . . . . (610) 374-0739

Two-year College(s)
Berks Technical Institute (Private, For-profit)
    Fall 2010 Enrollment: 1,325 . . . . (610) 372-1722
    2011-12 Tuition: In-state $10,120; Out-of-state $10,120
Housing: Homeownership rate: 68.3% (2010); Median home value: $199,800 (2006-2010 5-year est.); Median contract rent: $903 per month (2006-2010 5-year est.); Median year structure built: 1965 (2006-2010 5-year est.).

Safety: Violent crime rate: 11.4 per 10,000 population; Property crime rate: 511.7 per 10,000 population (2011).
Transportation: Commute to work: 89.1% car, 0.5% public transportation, 2.5% walk, 7.3% work from home (2006-2010 5-year est.); Travel time to work: 53.8% less than 15 minutes, 30.4% 15 to 30 minutes, 6.4% 30 to 45 minutes, 3.7% 45 to 60 minutes, 5.8% 60 minutes or more (2006-2010 5-year est.)
Additional Information Contacts
Borough of Wyomissing . . . . (610) 376-7481
    http://www.co.berks.pa.us/wyomissing/site/default.asp
Greater Reading Chamber of Commerce & Industry . . . . . (610) 376-6766
    http://www.greaterreadingchamber.org

Blair County

Located in central Pennsylvania; bounded on the west by the Allegheny Mountains, and on the east by the Tussey Mountains. Covers a land area of 525.800 square miles, a water area of 1.269 square miles, and is located in the Eastern Time Zone at 40.50° N. Lat., 78.31° W. Long. The county was founded in 1846. County seat is Hollidaysburg.

Blair County is part of the Altoona, PA Metropolitan Statistical Area. The entire metro area includes: Blair County, PA

Weather Station: Altoona 3 W   Elevation: 1,319 feet

	Jan	Feb	Mar	Apr	May	Jun	Jul	Aug	Sep	Oct	Nov	Dec
High	33	36	45	58	68	77	81	80	72	61	49	37
Low	18	20	27	38	47	56	61	59	52	41	33	23
Precip	2.6	2.5	3.6	3.6	4.5	4.0	3.9	3.6	3.8	3.5	4.0	3.1
Snow	10.6	8.3	6.9	0.9	tr	0.0	0.0	0.0	0.0	tr	1.4	6.9

High and Low temperatures in degrees Fahrenheit; Precipitation and Snow in inches

Weather Station: Altoona Blair Co Arpt   Elevation: 1,479 feet

	Jan	Feb	Mar	Apr	May	Jun	Jul	Aug	Sep	Oct	Nov	Dec
High	34	38	46	60	69	78	82	80	73	61	50	38
Low	21	23	29	39	48	57	61	60	52	42	34	24
Precip	2.2	2.1	3.1	3.3	3.7	3.4	3.3	2.9	3.4	2.5	3.3	2.2
Snow	na	na	na	na	na	na	na	na	na	na	na	na

High and Low temperatures in degrees Fahrenheit; Precipitation and Snow in inches

Population: 130,542 (1990); 129,144 (2000); 127,089 (2010); Race: 96.2% White, 1.7% Black, 0.6% Asian, 0.1% American Indian/Alaska Native, 0.0% Native Hawaiian/Other Pacific Islander, 1.4% Other, 1.0% Hispanic of any race (2010); Density: 241.7 persons per square mile (2010); Average household size: 2.37 (2010); Median age: 42.0 (2010); Males per 100 females: 94.4 (2010).
Religion: Six largest groups: 21.7% Catholicism, 7.3% Methodist/Pietist, 6.5% Lutheran, 3.8% Non-Denominational, 3.3% European Free-Church, 2.7% Pentecostal (2010)
Economy: Unemployment rate: 7.5% (August 2012); Total civilian labor force: 66,073 (August 2012); Leading industries: 22.9% health care and social assistance; 18.0% retail trade; 13.3% manufacturing (2010); Farms: 523 totaling 87,434 acres (2007); Companies that employ 500 or more persons: 3 (2010); Companies that employ 100 to 499 persons: 83 (2010); Companies that employ less than 100 persons: 3,131 (2010); Black-owned businesses: n/a (2007); Hispanic-owned businesses: n/a (2007); Asian-owned businesses: n/a (2007); Women-owned businesses: 2,382 (2007); Retail sales per capita: $13,734 (2010). Single-family building permits issued: 69 (2011); Multi-family building permits issued: 6 (2011).
Income: Per capita income: $22,880 (2006-2010 5-year est.); Median household income: $42,363 (2006-2010 5-year est.); Average household income: $54,872 (2006-2010 5-year est.); Percent of households with income of $100,000 or more: 10.7% (2006-2010 5-year est.); Poverty rate: 12.9% (2006-2010 5-year est.); Bankruptcy rate: 2.47% (2011).
Taxes: Total county taxes per capita: $160 (2009); County property taxes per capita: $160 (2009).
Education: Percent of population age 25 and over with: High school diploma (including GED) or higher: 89.7% (2006-2010 5-year est.); Bachelor's degree or higher: 17.3% (2006-2010 5-year est.); Master's degree or higher: 5.1% (2006-2010 5-year est.).
Housing: Homeownership rate: 70.3% (2010); Median home value: $97,400 (2006-2010 5-year est.); Median contract rent: $432 per month (2006-2010 5-year est.); Median year structure built: 1954 (2006-2010 5-year est.)
Health: Birth rate: 110.9 per 10,000 population (2011); Death rate: 126.9 per 10,000 population (2011); Age-adjusted cancer mortality rate: 207.8

deaths per 100,000 population (2009); Number of physicians: 26.0 per 10,000 population (2010); Hospital beds: 69.8 per 10,000 population (2008); Hospital admissions: 2,258.9 per 10,000 population (2008).

Environment: Air Quality Index: 76.2% good, 23.0% moderate, 0.8% unhealthy for sensitive individuals, 0.0% unhealthy (percent of days in 2011)

Elections: 2012 Presidential election results: 32.4% Obama, 66.3% Romney

National and State Parks: Canoe Creek State Park

Additional Information Contacts
Blair County Government . . . . (814) 693-3000
    http://blair.pacounties.org/Pages/default.aspx
Blair County Chamber of Commerce . . . . (814) 943-8151
    http://www.blairchamber.com

Blair County Communities

ALLEGHENY (township). Covers a land area of 29.615 square miles and a water area of 0.005 square miles. Located at 40.45° N. Lat; 78.48° W. Long.

Population: 7,064 (1990); 6,965 (2000); 6,738 (2010); Density: 227.5 persons per square mile (2010); Race: 96.8% White, 1.4% Black, 0.5% Asian, 0.0% American Indian/Alaska Native, 0.0% Native Hawaiian/Other Pacific Islander, 1.3% Other, 0.8% Hispanic of any race (2010); Average household size: 2.28 (2010); Median age: 48.3 (2010); Males per 100 females: 105.1 (2010); Marriage status: 21.9% never married, 57.0% now married, 9.7% widowed, 11.4% divorced (2006-2010 5-year est.); Foreign born: 0.8% (2006-2010 5-year est.); Ancestry (includes multiple ancestries): 45.3% German, 21.1% Irish, 8.9% Italian, 8.8% English, 5.9% American (2006-2010 5-year est.).

Economy: Single-family building permits issued: 5 (2011); Multi-family building permits issued: 0 (2011); Employment by occupation: 11.5% management, 1.3% professional, 15.4% services, 16.4% sales, 5.6% farming, 9.8% construction, 6.5% production (2006-2010 5-year est.).

Income: Per capita income: $28,360 (2006-2010 5-year est.); Median household income: $39,292 (2006-2010 5-year est.); Average household income: $66,996 (2006-2010 5-year est.); Percent of households with income of $100,000 or more: 12.3% (2006-2010 5-year est.); Poverty rate: 8.1% (2006-2010 5-year est.).

Education: Percent of population age 25 and over with: High school diploma (including GED) or higher: 90.2% (2006-2010 5-year est.); Bachelor's degree or higher: 16.9% (2006-2010 5-year est.); Master's degree or higher: 3.8% (2006-2010 5-year est.).

Housing: Homeownership rate: 78.7% (2010); Median home value: $97,900 (2006-2010 5-year est.); Median contract rent: $427 per month (2006-2010 5-year est.); Median year structure built: 1973 (2006-2010 5-year est.).

Transportation: Commute to work: 95.8% car, 0.0% public transportation, 1.7% walk, 1.9% work from home (2006-2010 5-year est.); Travel time to work: 41.0% less than 15 minutes, 40.8% 15 to 30 minutes, 8.6% 30 to 45 minutes, 3.9% 45 to 60 minutes, 5.8% 60 minutes or more (2006-2010 5-year est.)

Additional Information Contacts
Allegheny Township . . . . (814) 695-9563
    http://blair.pacounties.org/alleghenytwp
Blair County Chamber of Commerce . . . . (814) 943-8151
    http://www.blairchamber.com

ALTOONA (city). Covers a land area of 9.907 square miles and a water area of 0.002 square miles. Located at 40.51° N. Lat; 78.40° W. Long. Elevation is 1,165 feet.

History: Altoona was named for Altona, an important river port in Schleswig-Holstein, Germany. Modern history began in 1849 with the purchase of a farm by Archibald Wright, who laid out a town. German, Scottish, and Irish immigrants soon appeared, and in 1854, when railroad lines were extended, more settlers arrived. Wright sold 35 acres to the Pennsylvania Railroad Company for depot, offices, and shops, and the railroad became Altoona's main industry.

Population: 52,151 (1990); 49,523 (2000); 46,320 (2010); Density: 4,675.3 persons per square mile (2010); Race: 93.8% White, 3.3% Black, 0.4% Asian, 0.1% American Indian/Alaska Native, 0.0% Native Hawaiian/Other Pacific Islander, 2.4% Other, 1.3% Hispanic of any race (2010); Average household size: 2.34 (2010); Median age: 38.9 (2010); Males per 100 females: 92.4 (2010); Marriage status: 32.8% never married, 47.7% now married, 8.7% widowed, 10.8% divorced (2006-2010

5-year est.); Foreign born: 1.2% (2006-2010 5-year est.); Ancestry (includes multiple ancestries): 42.3% German, 21.8% Irish, 15.1% Italian, 7.5% English, 5.2% Polish (2006-2010 5-year est.).

Economy: Unemployment rate: 8.8% (August 2012); Total civilian labor force: 23,367 (August 2012); Single-family building permits issued: 4 (2011); Multi-family building permits issued: 0 (2011); Employment by occupation: 6.6% management, 2.0% professional, 12.0% services, 21.0% sales, 5.2% farming, 7.3% construction, 5.4% production (2006-2010 5-year est.).

Income: Per capita income: $19,245 (2006-2010 5-year est.); Median household income: $35,629 (2006-2010 5-year est.); Average household income: $46,245 (2006-2010 5-year est.); Percent of households with income of $100,000 or more: 7.6% (2006-2010 5-year est.); Poverty rate: 17.8% (2006-2010 5-year est.).

Taxes: Total city taxes per capita: $375 (2009); City property taxes per capita: $235 (2009).

Education: Percent of population age 25 and over with: High school diploma (including GED) or higher: 88.5% (2006-2010 5-year est.); Bachelor's degree or higher: 15.8% (2006-2010 5-year est.); Master's degree or higher: 4.2% (2006-2010 5-year est.).

School District(s)
Altoona Area SD (KG-12)
    2010-11 Enrollment: 7,984 . . . . (814) 946-8211
Central PA Digital Learning Foundation CS (KG-12)
    2010-11 Enrollment: 127. . . . . (814) 940-6989
Greater Altoona CTC (10-12)
    2010-11 Enrollment: n/a . . . . (814) 946-8450
Four-year College(s)
Pennsylvania State University-Penn State Altoona (Public)
    Fall 2010 Enrollment: 4,256 . . . . (814) 949-5000
    2011-12 Tuition: In-state $13,636; Out-of-state $20,408
Two-year College(s)
YTI Career Institute-Altoona (Private, For-profit)
    Fall 2010 Enrollment: 536 . . . . (814) 944-5643
Vocational/Technical School(s)
Altoona Beauty School Inc (Private, For-profit)
    Fall 2010 Enrollment: 196 . . . . (814) 942-3141
    2011-12 Tuition: $10,250
Greater Altoona Career & Technology Center (Public)
    Fall 2010 Enrollment: 243 . . . . (814) 946-8450
    2011-12 Tuition: $11,480
The Salon Professional Academy (Private, For-profit)
    Fall 2010 Enrollment: 45 . . . . (814) 944-4494
    2011-12 Tuition: $9,400

Housing: Homeownership rate: 64.5% (2010); Median home value: $79,800 (2006-2010 5-year est.); Median contract rent: $405 per month (2006-2010 5-year est.); Median year structure built: before 1940 (2006-2010 5-year est.).

Hospitals: Altoona Hospital (470 beds); Bon Secours Holy Family Hospital (150 beds); HealthSouth Rehabilitation Hospital of Altoona (70 beds); James E. Van Zandt VA Medical Center (68 beds)

Safety: Violent crime rate: 30.8 per 10,000 population; Property crime rate: 234.6 per 10,000 population (2011).

Newspapers: Altoona Mirror (Local news; Circulation 38,023)

Transportation: Commute to work: 91.3% car, 0.9% public transportation, 3.8% walk, 2.2% work from home (2006-2010 5-year est.); Travel time to work: 54.7% less than 15 minutes, 30.3% 15 to 30 minutes, 7.6% 30 to 45 minutes, 3.5% 45 to 60 minutes, 4.0% 60 minutes or more (2006-2010 5-year est.); Amtrak: train service available.

Airports: Altoona-Blair County (commercial service)

Additional Information Contacts
Blair County Chamber of Commerce . . . . (814) 943-8151
    http://www.blairchamber.com
City of Altoona. . . . . (814) 949-2486
    http://www.altoonapa.gov

ANTIS (township). Covers a land area of 60.828 square miles and a water area of 0.241 square miles. Located at 40.64° N. Lat; 78.36° W. Long.

Population: 6,176 (1990); 6,328 (2000); 6,499 (2010); Density: 106.8 persons per square mile (2010); Race: 98.9% White, 0.3% Black, 0.2% Asian, 0.1% American Indian/Alaska Native, 0.0% Native Hawaiian/Other Pacific Islander, 0.5% Other, 0.5% Hispanic of any race (2010); Average household size: 2.36 (2010); Median age: 46.8 (2010); Males per 100 females: 94.4 (2010); Marriage status: 26.0% never married, 55.5% now

married, 8.8% widowed, 9.6% divorced (2006-2010 5-year est.); Foreign born: 0.8% (2006-2010 5-year est.); Ancestry (includes multiple ancestries): 36.3% German, 17.8% Irish, 11.0% American, 10.6% English, 7.3% Dutch (2006-2010 5-year est.).

Economy: Single-family building permits issued: 3 (2011); Multi-family building permits issued: 0 (2011); Employment by occupation: 11.4% management, 2.7% professional, 6.4% services, 19.8% sales, 3.4% farming, 11.6% construction, 11.3% production (2006-2010 5-year est.).

Income: Per capita income: $22,302 (2006-2010 5-year est.); Median household income: $49,018 (2006-2010 5-year est.); Average household income: $53,255 (2006-2010 5-year est.); Percent of households with income of $100,000 or more: 9.1% (2006-2010 5-year est.); Poverty rate: 7.9% (2006-2010 5-year est.).

Education: Percent of population age 25 and over with: High school diploma (including GED) or higher: 91.8% (2006-2010 5-year est.); Bachelor's degree or higher: 16.4% (2006-2010 5-year est.); Master's degree or higher: 3.3% (2006-2010 5-year est.).

Housing: Homeownership rate: 77.8% (2010); Median home value: $123,900 (2006-2010 5-year est.); Median contract rent: $423 per month (2006-2010 5-year est.); Median year structure built: 1968 (2006-2010 5-year est.).

Transportation: Commute to work: 95.7% car, 0.0% public transportation, 0.0% walk, 2.3% work from home (2006-2010 5-year est.); Travel time to work: 37.0% less than 15 minutes, 46.6% 15 to 30 minutes, 10.0% 30 to 45 minutes, 3.8% 45 to 60 minutes, 2.7% 60 minutes or more (2006-2010 5-year est.)

Additional Information Contacts

Antis Township . . . . (814) 742-7361
    http://blair.pacounties.org/AntisTwp
Tyron Area Chamber of Commerce . . . . (814) 684-0736
    http://www.tyronechamber.com

BELLWOOD (borough). Covers a land area of 0.423 square miles and a water area of 0 square miles. Located at 40.60° N. Lat; 78.33° W. Long. Elevation is 1,053 feet.

Population: 1,976 (1990); 2,016 (2000); 1,828 (2010); Density: 4,325.9 persons per square mile (2010); Race: 98.2% White, 0.3% Black, 0.1% Asian, 0.2% American Indian/Alaska Native, 0.0% Native Hawaiian/Other Pacific Islander, 1.2% Other, 1.0% Hispanic of any race (2010); Average household size: 2.52 (2010); Median age: 36.8 (2010); Males per 100 females: 94.1 (2010); Marriage status: 25.0% never married, 59.9% now married, 9.4% widowed, 5.7% divorced (2006-2010 5-year est.); Foreign born: 0.0% (2006-2010 5-year est.); Ancestry (includes multiple ancestries): 47.0% German, 20.2% Irish, 9.0% English, 6.2% Italian, 5.7% American (2006-2010 5-year est.).

Economy: Single-family building permits issued: 0 (2011); Multi-family building permits issued: 0 (2011); Employment by occupation: 5.8% management, 3.8% professional, 14.0% services, 22.1% sales, 1.6% farming, 6.4% construction, 7.0% production (2006-2010 5-year est.).

Income: Per capita income: $19,221 (2006-2010 5-year est.); Median household income: $46,354 (2006-2010 5-year est.); Average household income: $49,287 (2006-2010 5-year est.); Percent of households with income of $100,000 or more: 3.5% (2006-2010 5-year est.); Poverty rate: 13.0% (2006-2010 5-year est.).

Education: Percent of population age 25 and over with: High school diploma (including GED) or higher: 91.6% (2006-2010 5-year est.); Bachelor's degree or higher: 8.2% (2006-2010 5-year est.); Master's degree or higher: 2.1% (2006-2010 5-year est.).

School District(s)

Bellwood-Antis SD (KG-12)
    2010-11 Enrollment: 1,258 . . . . (814) 742-2271

Housing: Homeownership rate: 71.8% (2010); Median home value: $92,200 (2006-2010 5-year est.); Median contract rent: $406 per month (2006-2010 5-year est.); Median year structure built: before 1940 (2006-2010 5-year est.).

Safety: Violent crime rate: 0.0 per 10,000 population; Property crime rate: 98.1 per 10,000 population (2011).

Transportation: Commute to work: 97.4% car, 0.0% public transportation, 2.1% walk, 0.5% work from home (2006-2010 5-year est.); Travel time to work: 33.6% less than 15 minutes, 41.8% 15 to 30 minutes, 15.1% 30 to 45 minutes, 6.0% 45 to 60 minutes, 3.5% 60 minutes or more (2006-2010 5-year est.)

Additional Information Contacts

Blair County Chamber of Commerce . . . . (814) 943-8151
    http://www.blairchamber.com

BLAIR (township). Covers a land area of 13.610 square miles and a water area of 0.083 square miles. Located at 40.40° N. Lat; 78.41° W. Long.

Population: 4,012 (1990); 4,587 (2000); 4,494 (2010); Density: 330.2 persons per square mile (2010); Race: 97.3% White, 0.4% Black, 1.2% Asian, 0.1% American Indian/Alaska Native, 0.0% Native Hawaiian/Other Pacific Islander, 1.0% Other, 1.0% Hispanic of any race (2010); Average household size: 2.45 (2010); Median age: 43.4 (2010); Males per 100 females: 96.1 (2010); Marriage status: 25.8% never married, 60.1% now married, 5.4% widowed, 8.6% divorced (2006-2010 5-year est.); Foreign born: 1.1% (2006-2010 5-year est.); Ancestry (includes multiple ancestries): 44.0% German, 25.0% Irish, 11.9% Italian, 7.1% English, 4.0% Polish (2006-2010 5-year est.).

Economy: Single-family building permits issued: 12 (2011); Multi-family building permits issued: 0 (2011); Employment by occupation: 11.4% management, 6.0% professional, 7.4% services, 14.6% sales, 1.3% farming, 11.6% construction, 8.0% production (2006-2010 5-year est.).

Income: Per capita income: $35,297 (2006-2010 5-year est.); Median household income: $54,207 (2006-2010 5-year est.); Average household income: $82,718 (2006-2010 5-year est.); Percent of households with income of $100,000 or more: 20.0% (2006-2010 5-year est.); Poverty rate: 7.2% (2006-2010 5-year est.).

Education: Percent of population age 25 and over with: High school diploma (including GED) or higher: 92.4% (2006-2010 5-year est.); Bachelor's degree or higher: 35.5% (2006-2010 5-year est.); Master's degree or higher: 13.6% (2006-2010 5-year est.).

Housing: Homeownership rate: 84.1% (2010); Median home value: $150,800 (2006-2010 5-year est.); Median contract rent: $482 per month (2006-2010 5-year est.); Median year structure built: 1979 (2006-2010 5-year est.).

Transportation: Commute to work: 94.0% car, 0.0% public transportation, 0.6% walk, 2.6% work from home (2006-2010 5-year est.); Travel time to work: 39.3% less than 15 minutes, 41.7% 15 to 30 minutes, 10.8% 30 to 45 minutes, 3.6% 45 to 60 minutes, 4.5% 60 minutes or more (2006-2010 5-year est.)

Additional Information Contacts

Blair County Chamber of Commerce . . . . (814) 943-8151
    http://www.blairchamber.com
Blair Township . . . . (814) 693-3000
    http://blair.pacounties.org/blair/site

CATHARINE (township). Covers a land area of 30.821 square miles and a water area of 0.010 square miles. Located at 40.53° N. Lat; 78.22° W. Long.

Population: 748 (1990); 758 (2000); 724 (2010); Density: 23.5 persons per square mile (2010); Race: 98.2% White, 0.3% Black, 0.6% Asian, 0.1% American Indian/Alaska Native, 0.0% Native Hawaiian/Other Pacific Islander, 0.8% Other, 1.1% Hispanic of any race (2010); Average household size: 2.51 (2010); Median age: 44.8 (2010); Males per 100 females: 110.5 (2010); Marriage status: 19.8% never married, 67.6% now married, 7.4% widowed, 5.2% divorced (2006-2010 5-year est.); Foreign born: 0.5% (2006-2010 5-year est.); Ancestry (includes multiple ancestries): 52.2% German, 15.6% Irish, 13.8% English, 6.5% American, 5.2% Italian (2006-2010 5-year est.).

Economy: Single-family building permits issued: 1 (2011); Multi-family building permits issued: 0 (2011); Employment by occupation: 12.1% management, 0.0% professional, 11.8% services, 9.2% sales, 6.4% farming, 22.3% construction, 11.5% production (2006-2010 5-year est.).

Income: Per capita income: $22,997 (2006-2010 5-year est.); Median household income: $50,125 (2006-2010 5-year est.); Average household income: $63,763 (2006-2010 5-year est.); Percent of households with income of $100,000 or more: 13.0% (2006-2010 5-year est.); Poverty rate: 6.8% (2006-2010 5-year est.).

Education: Percent of population age 25 and over with: High school diploma (including GED) or higher: 88.1% (2006-2010 5-year est.); Bachelor's degree or higher: 8.7% (2006-2010 5-year est.); Master's degree or higher: 0.7% (2006-2010 5-year est.).

Housing: Homeownership rate: 84.8% (2010); Median home value: $118,400 (2006-2010 5-year est.); Median contract rent: $346 per month (2006-2010 5-year est.); Median year structure built: 1961 (2006-2010 5-year est.).

Transportation: Commute to work: 91.0% car, 0.0% public transportation, 2.4% walk, 6.6% work from home (2006-2010 5-year est.); Travel time to work: 31.4% less than 15 minutes, 34.3% 15 to 30 minutes, 16.1% 30 to

45 minutes, 4.0% 45 to 60 minutes, 14.2% 60 minutes or more (2006-2010 5-year est.)

CLAYSBURG (CDP).
Covers a land area of 2.572 square miles and a water area of 0 square miles. Located at 40.29° N. Lat; 78.45° W. Long. Elevation is 1,145 feet.

Population: 1,447 (1990); 1,503 (2000); 1,625 (2010); Density: 631.9 persons per square mile (2010); Race: 98.2% White, 0.4% Black, 0.1% Asian, 0.0% American Indian/Alaska Native, 0.0% Native Hawaiian/Other Pacific Islander, 1.3% Other, 0.9% Hispanic of any race (2010); Average household size: 2.44 (2010); Median age: 36.2 (2010); Males per 100 females: 89.6 (2010); Marriage status: 27.7% never married, 47.6% now married, 11.0% widowed, 13.8% divorced (2006-2010 5-year est.); Foreign born: 0.4% (2006-2010 5-year est.); Ancestry (includes multiple ancestries): 39.2% German, 18.6% Irish, 7.1% English, 6.6% American, 6.3% Italian (2006-2010 5-year est.).

Economy: Employment by occupation: 12.2% management, 0.0% professional, 11.1% services, 17.7% sales, 0.0% farming, 17.5% construction, 10.1% production (2006-2010 5-year est.).

Income: Per capita income: $21,924 (2006-2010 5-year est.); Median household income: $45,536 (2006-2010 5-year est.); Average household income: $54,407 (2006-2010 5-year est.); Percent of households with income of $100,000 or more: 10.8% (2006-2010 5-year est.); Poverty rate: 13.1% (2006-2010 5-year est.).

Education: Percent of population age 25 and over with: High school diploma (including GED) or higher: 91.6% (2006-2010 5-year est.); Bachelor's degree or higher: 12.7% (2006-2010 5-year est.); Master's degree or higher: 5.4% (2006-2010 5-year est.).

School District(s)
Claysburg-Kimmel SD (KG-12)
   2010-11 Enrollment: 872 . . . . (814) 239-5141

Housing: Homeownership rate: 63.4% (2010); Median home value: $83,500 (2006-2010 5-year est.); Median contract rent: $229 per month (2006-2010 5-year est.); Median year structure built: 1949 (2006-2010 5-year est.).

Transportation: Commute to work: 92.9% car, 0.0% public transportation, 4.2% walk, 1.2% work from home (2006-2010 5-year est.); Travel time to work: 24.7% less than 15 minutes, 50.2% 15 to 30 minutes, 16.3% 30 to 45 minutes, 1.7% 45 to 60 minutes, 7.0% 60 minutes or more (2006-2010 5-year est.)

Additional Information Contacts
Blair County Chamber of Commerce . . . . (814) 943-8151
   http://www.blairchamber.com

CURRYVILLE (unincorporated postal area)
Zip Code: 16631
   Covers a land area of 0.601 square miles and a water area of 0 square miles. Located at 40.27° N. Lat; 78.34° W. Long. Elevation is 1,434 feet. Population: 90 (2010); Density: 149.6 persons per square mile (2010); Race: 98.9% White, 0.0% Black, 1.1% Asian, 0.0% American Indian/Alaska Native, 0.0% Native Hawaiian/Other Pacific Islander, 0.0% Other, 0.0% Hispanic of any race (2010); Average household size: 2.81 (2010); Median age: 36.0 (2010); Males per 100 females: 91.5 (2010); Homeownership rate: 87.6% (2010)

DUNCANSVILLE (borough).
Covers a land area of 0.532 square miles and a water area of 0 square miles. Located at 40.43° N. Lat; 78.43° W. Long. Elevation is 1,037 feet.

History: Allegheny Portage Railroad National Historic Site to West. Laid out 1831.

Population: 1,309 (1990); 1,238 (2000); 1,233 (2010); Density: 2,316.0 persons per square mile (2010); Race: 97.9% White, 0.2% Black, 1.0% Asian, 0.0% American Indian/Alaska Native, 0.0% Native Hawaiian/Other Pacific Islander, 0.9% Other, 0.4% Hispanic of any race (2010); Average household size: 2.07 (2010); Median age: 46.0 (2010); Males per 100 females: 74.4 (2010); Marriage status: 21.3% never married, 47.2% now married, 16.4% widowed, 15.0% divorced (2006-2010 5-year est.); Foreign born: 1.0% (2006-2010 5-year est.); Ancestry (includes multiple ancestries): 43.8% German, 21.0% Irish, 13.7% Italian, 11.0% English, 6.3% American (2006-2010 5-year est.).

Economy: Single-family building permits issued: 0 (2011); Multi-family building permits issued: 0 (2011); Employment by occupation: 3.3% management, 2.0% professional, 13.8% services, 23.5% sales, 6.9% farming, 10.4% construction, 11.8% production (2006-2010 5-year est.).

Income: Per capita income: $22,519 (2006-2010 5-year est.); Median household income: $36,830 (2006-2010 5-year est.); Average household income: $45,442 (2006-2010 5-year est.); Percent of households with income of $100,000 or more: 7.3% (2006-2010 5-year est.); Poverty rate: 12.2% (2006-2010 5-year est.).

Education: Percent of population age 25 and over with: High school diploma (including GED) or higher: 84.8% (2006-2010 5-year est.); Bachelor's degree or higher: 13.8% (2006-2010 5-year est.); Master's degree or higher: 4.6% (2006-2010 5-year est.).

School District(s)
Hollidaysburg Area SD (KG-12)
   2010-11 Enrollment: 3,471 . . . . (814) 695-8702

Housing: Homeownership rate: 56.8% (2010); Median home value: $92,900 (2006-2010 5-year est.); Median contract rent: $531 per month (2006-2010 5-year est.); Median year structure built: 1959 (2006-2010 5-year est.).

Transportation: Commute to work: 93.1% car, 1.0% public transportation, 3.5% walk, 1.6% work from home (2006-2010 5-year est.); Travel time to work: 40.2% less than 15 minutes, 44.4% 15 to 30 minutes, 7.0% 30 to 45 minutes, 5.2% 45 to 60 minutes, 3.2% 60 minutes or more (2006-2010 5-year est.)

Additional Information Contacts
Blair County Chamber of Commerce . . . . (814) 943-8151
   http://www.blairchamber.com

EAST FREEDOM (CDP).
Covers a land area of 1.678 square miles and a water area of 0 square miles. Located at 40.36° N. Lat; 78.44° W. Long. Elevation is 1,010 feet.

Population: n/a (1990); n/a (2000); 972 (2010); Density: 579.3 persons per square mile (2010); Race: 96.1% White, 1.6% Black, 0.3% Asian, 0.0% American Indian/Alaska Native, 0.0% Native Hawaiian/Other Pacific Islander, 2.0% Other, 0.6% Hispanic of any race (2010); Average household size: 2.35 (2010); Median age: 39.0 (2010); Males per 100 females: 94.4 (2010); Marriage status: 23.4% never married, 55.7% now married, 9.3% widowed, 11.7% divorced (2006-2010 5-year est.); Foreign born: 0.0% (2006-2010 5-year est.); Ancestry (includes multiple ancestries): 29.4% German, 18.4% French, 5.6% American, 5.5% Polish, 5.3% English (2006-2010 5-year est.).

Economy: Employment by occupation: 0.0% management, 0.0% professional, 14.5% services, 25.0% sales, 0.0% farming, 44.6% construction, 22.8% production (2006-2010 5-year est.).

Income: Per capita income: $17,382 (2006-2010 5-year est.); Median household income: $32,847 (2006-2010 5-year est.); Average household income: $37,889 (2006-2010 5-year est.); Percent of households with income of $100,000 or more: n/a (2006-2010 5-year est.); Poverty rate: 29.0% (2006-2010 5-year est.).

Education: Percent of population age 25 and over with: High school diploma (including GED) or higher: 100.0% (2006-2010 5-year est.); Bachelor's degree or higher: 4.3% (2006-2010 5-year est.); Master's degree or higher: 0.0% (2006-2010 5-year est.).

Housing: Homeownership rate: 75.8% (2010); Median home value: $132,400 (2006-2010 5-year est.); Median contract rent: $418 per month (2006-2010 5-year est.); Median year structure built: 1956 (2006-2010 5-year est.).

Transportation: Commute to work: 100.0% car, 0.0% public transportation, 0.0% walk, 0.0% work from home (2006-2010 5-year est.); Travel time to work: 14.5% less than 15 minutes, 56.5% 15 to 30 minutes, 7.2% 30 to 45 minutes, 0.0% 45 to 60 minutes, 21.7% 60 minutes or more (2006-2010 5-year est.)

FOOT OF TEN (CDP).
Covers a land area of 0.585 square miles and a water area of 0 square miles. Located at 40.42° N. Lat; 78.46° W. Long. Elevation is 1,102 feet.

Population: n/a (1990); n/a (2000); 672 (2010); Density: 1,148.6 persons per square mile (2010); Race: 98.2% White, 0.4% Black, 0.1% Asian, 0.0% American Indian/Alaska Native, 0.0% Native Hawaiian/Other Pacific Islander, 1.3% Other, 0.4% Hispanic of any race (2010); Average household size: 2.35 (2010); Median age: 45.3 (2010); Males per 100 females: 105.5 (2010); Marriage status: 19.5% never married, 66.2% now married, 11.1% widowed, 3.2% divorced (2006-2010 5-year est.); Foreign born: 0.0% (2006-2010 5-year est.); Ancestry (includes multiple ancestries): 55.8% German, 27.3% Irish, 13.3% French, 8.4% English, 6.9% Polish (2006-2010 5-year est.).

Economy: Employment by occupation: 7.1% management, 0.0% professional, 8.6% services, 15.9% sales, 3.3% farming, 9.1% construction, 2.5% production (2006-2010 5-year est.).
Income: Per capita income: $21,783 (2006-2010 5-year est.); Median household income: $37,202 (2006-2010 5-year est.); Average household income: $53,148 (2006-2010 5-year est.); Percent of households with income of $100,000 or more: 19.8% (2006-2010 5-year est.); Poverty rate: 6.4% (2006-2010 5-year est.).
Education: Percent of population age 25 and over with: High school diploma (including GED) or higher: 88.4% (2006-2010 5-year est.); Bachelor's degree or higher: 17.9% (2006-2010 5-year est.); Master's degree or higher: 1.0% (2006-2010 5-year est.).
Housing: Homeownership rate: 84.9% (2010); Median home value: $107,800 (2006-2010 5-year est.); Median contract rent: $286 per month (2006-2010 5-year est.); Median year structure built: 1960 (2006-2010 5-year est.).
Transportation: Commute to work: 98.2% car, 0.0% public transportation, 0.0% walk, 1.8% work from home (2006-2010 5-year est.); Travel time to work: 42.3% less than 15 minutes, 44.0% 15 to 30 minutes, 8.6% 30 to 45 minutes, 3.6% 45 to 60 minutes, 1.5% 60 minutes or more (2006-2010 5-year est.)

FRANKSTOWN (township). Covers a land area of 48.827 square miles and a water area of 0.430 square miles. Located at 40.45° N. Lat; 78.31° W. Long. Elevation is 925 feet.
Population: 7,175 (1990); 7,694 (2000); 7,381 (2010); Density: 151.2 persons per square mile (2010); Race: 96.5% White, 0.5% Black, 1.9% Asian, 0.0% American Indian/Alaska Native, 0.1% Native Hawaiian/Other Pacific Islander, 1.0% Other, 0.6% Hispanic of any race (2010); Average household size: 2.45 (2010); Median age: 48.2 (2010); Males per 100 females: 93.1 (2010); Marriage status: 20.2% never married, 66.9% now married, 6.9% widowed, 6.1% divorced (2006-2010 5-year est.); Foreign born: 1.3% (2006-2010 5-year est.); Ancestry (includes multiple ancestries): 44.9% German, 23.5% Irish, 9.7% English, 9.2% Italian, 5.8% Dutch (2006-2010 5-year est.).
Economy: Single-family building permits issued: 8 (2011); Multi-family building permits issued: 0 (2011); Employment by occupation: 14.5% management, 4.8% professional, 6.8% services, 16.0% sales, 4.7% farming, 7.4% construction, 3.0% production (2006-2010 5-year est.).
Income: Per capita income: $35,927 (2006-2010 5-year est.); Median household income: $65,255 (2006-2010 5-year est.); Average household income: $87,524 (2006-2010 5-year est.); Percent of households with income of $100,000 or more: 30.1% (2006-2010 5-year est.); Poverty rate: 6.5% (2006-2010 5-year est.).
Education: Percent of population age 25 and over with: High school diploma (including GED) or higher: 91.8% (2006-2010 5-year est.); Bachelor's degree or higher: 31.5% (2006-2010 5-year est.); Master's degree or higher: 11.2% (2006-2010 5-year est.).
Housing: Homeownership rate: 82.4% (2010); Median home value: $170,400 (2006-2010 5-year est.); Median contract rent: $635 per month (2006-2010 5-year est.); Median year structure built: 1976 (2006-2010 5-year est.).
Transportation: Commute to work: 96.1% car, 0.0% public transportation, 1.2% walk, 2.3% work from home (2006-2010 5-year est.); Travel time to work: 39.1% less than 15 minutes, 43.5% 15 to 30 minutes, 6.9% 30 to 45 minutes, 4.5% 45 to 60 minutes, 5.9% 60 minutes or more (2006-2010 5-year est.)
Additional Information Contacts
Blair County Chamber of Commerce . . . . (814) 943-8151
    http://www.blairchamber.com
Frankstown Township . . . . (814) 695-7151
    http://blair.pacounties.org/frankstown/site/default.asp

FREEDOM (township). Covers a land area of 17.374 square miles and a water area of 0.007 square miles. Located at 40.36° N. Lat; 78.46° W. Long.
Population: 2,959 (1990); 3,261 (2000); 3,458 (2010); Density: 199.0 persons per square mile (2010); Race: 98.1% White, 0.8% Black, 0.2% Asian, 0.0% American Indian/Alaska Native, 0.0% Native Hawaiian/Other Pacific Islander, 0.9% Other, 0.2% Hispanic of any race (2010); Average household size: 2.46 (2010); Median age: 42.2 (2010); Males per 100 females: 94.2 (2010); Marriage status: 24.5% never married, 59.2% now married, 6.8% widowed, 9.6% divorced (2006-2010 5-year est.); Foreign born: 0.1% (2006-2010 5-year est.); Ancestry (includes multiple

ancestries): 45.2% German, 23.0% Irish, 7.2% Polish, 7.1% American, 5.2% French (2006-2010 5-year est.).
Economy: Single-family building permits issued: 8 (2011); Multi-family building permits issued: 0 (2011); Employment by occupation: 12.0% management, 0.4% professional, 18.0% services, 14.3% sales, 4.1% farming, 19.6% construction, 13.3% production (2006-2010 5-year est.).
Income: Per capita income: $20,834 (2006-2010 5-year est.); Median household income: $44,524 (2006-2010 5-year est.); Average household income: $49,138 (2006-2010 5-year est.); Percent of households with income of $100,000 or more: 3.0% (2006-2010 5-year est.); Poverty rate: 11.0% (2006-2010 5-year est.).
Education: Percent of population age 25 and over with: High school diploma (including GED) or higher: 94.1% (2006-2010 5-year est.); Bachelor's degree or higher: 12.3% (2006-2010 5-year est.); Master's degree or higher: 1.8% (2006-2010 5-year est.).
Housing: Homeownership rate: 80.6% (2010); Median home value: $108,800 (2006-2010 5-year est.); Median contract rent: $407 per month (2006-2010 5-year est.); Median year structure built: 1976 (2006-2010 5-year est.).
Safety: Violent crime rate: 8.6 per 10,000 population; Property crime rate: 198.9 per 10,000 population (2011).
Transportation: Commute to work: 99.5% car, 0.0% public transportation, 0.5% walk, 0.0% work from home (2006-2010 5-year est.); Travel time to work: 27.7% less than 15 minutes, 55.5% 15 to 30 minutes, 9.6% 30 to 45 minutes, 0.4% 45 to 60 minutes, 6.7% 60 minutes or more (2006-2010 5-year est.)
Additional Information Contacts
Blair County Chamber of Commerce . . . . (814) 943-8151
    http://www.blairchamber.com

GRAZIERVILLE (CDP). Covers a land area of 1.100 square miles and a water area of 0 square miles. Located at 40.66° N. Lat; 78.27° W. Long. Elevation is 942 feet.
Population: n/a (1990); n/a (2000); 665 (2010); Density: 604.7 persons per square mile (2010); Race: 96.4% White, 2.9% Black, 0.3% Asian, 0.2% American Indian/Alaska Native, 0.0% Native Hawaiian/Other Pacific Islander, 0.2% Other, 0.0% Hispanic of any race (2010); Average household size: 2.48 (2010); Median age: 37.6 (2010); Males per 100 females: 97.9 (2010); Marriage status: 26.4% never married, 32.4% now married, 19.1% widowed, 22.2% divorced (2006-2010 5-year est.); Foreign born: 0.0% (2006-2010 5-year est.); Ancestry (includes multiple ancestries): 25.0% German, 23.0% Pennsylvania German, 22.1% English, 8.6% Irish, 5.8% Welsh (2006-2010 5-year est.).
Economy: Employment by occupation: 14.6% management, 0.0% professional, 0.0% services, 9.6% sales, 0.0% farming, 12.9% construction, 3.8% production (2006-2010 5-year est.).
Income: Per capita income: $22,062 (2006-2010 5-year est.); Median household income: $34,968 (2006-2010 5-year est.); Average household income: $50,572 (2006-2010 5-year est.); Percent of households with income of $100,000 or more: 14.3% (2006-2010 5-year est.); Poverty rate: 1.6% (2006-2010 5-year est.).
Education: Percent of population age 25 and over with: High school diploma (including GED) or higher: 95.6% (2006-2010 5-year est.); Bachelor's degree or higher: 17.9% (2006-2010 5-year est.); Master's degree or higher: 9.0% (2006-2010 5-year est.).
Housing: Homeownership rate: 63.8% (2010); Median home value: $83,600 (2006-2010 5-year est.); Median contract rent: $490 per month (2006-2010 5-year est.); Median year structure built: 1943 (2006-2010 5-year est.).
Transportation: Commute to work: 86.8% car, 0.0% public transportation, 0.0% walk, 0.0% work from home (2006-2010 5-year est.); Travel time to work: 39.0% less than 15 minutes, 38.2% 15 to 30 minutes, 18.4% 30 to 45 minutes, 0.0% 45 to 60 minutes, 4.4% 60 minutes or more (2006-2010 5-year est.)

GREENFIELD (township). Covers a land area of 36.250 square miles and a water area of 0 square miles. Located at 40.31° N. Lat; 78.51° W. Long.
Population: 3,802 (1990); 3,904 (2000); 4,173 (2010); Density: 115.1 persons per square mile (2010); Race: 98.6% White, 0.2% Black, 0.1% Asian, 0.0% American Indian/Alaska Native, 0.0% Native Hawaiian/Other Pacific Islander, 1.1% Other, 0.6% Hispanic of any race (2010); Average household size: 2.45 (2010); Median age: 40.6 (2010); Males per 100 females: 97.7 (2010); Marriage status: 27.3% never married, 55.3% now married, 9.0% widowed, 8.4% divorced (2006-2010 5-year est.); Foreign

born: 0.1% (2006-2010 5-year est.); Ancestry (includes multiple ancestries): 44.6% German, 15.2% Irish, 6.6% American, 6.1% Italian, 4.5% English (2006-2010 5-year est.).

Economy: Single-family building permits issued: 9 (2011); Multi-family building permits issued: 0 (2011); Employment by occupation: 6.9% management, 0.0% professional, 8.3% services, 19.4% sales, 6.6% farming, 16.1% construction, 12.5% production (2006-2010 5-year est.).

Income: Per capita income: $23,347 (2006-2010 5-year est.); Median household income: $37,667 (2006-2010 5-year est.); Average household income: $58,125 (2006-2010 5-year est.); Percent of households with income of $100,000 or more: 7.7% (2006-2010 5-year est.); Poverty rate: 14.6% (2006-2010 5-year est.).

Taxes: Total city taxes per capita: $136 (2009); City property taxes per capita: $37 (2009).

Education: Percent of population age 25 and over with: High school diploma (including GED) or higher: 85.0% (2006-2010 5-year est.); Bachelor's degree or higher: 9.7% (2006-2010 5-year est.); Master's degree or higher: 3.0% (2006-2010 5-year est.).

Housing: Homeownership rate: 70.3% (2010); Median home value: $87,500 (2006-2010 5-year est.); Median contract rent: $373 per month (2006-2010 5-year est.); Median year structure built: 1963 (2006-2010 5-year est.).

Safety: Violent crime rate: 19.1 per 10,000 population; Property crime rate: 293.8 per 10,000 population (2011).

Transportation: Commute to work: 94.6% car, 0.0% public transportation, 1.8% walk, 1.9% work from home (2006-2010 5-year est.); Travel time to work: 26.8% less than 15 minutes, 43.1% 15 to 30 minutes, 21.2% 30 to 45 minutes, 4.7% 45 to 60 minutes, 4.2% 60 minutes or more (2006-2010 5-year est.).

Additional Information Contacts
Blair County Chamber of Commerce . . . . (814) 943-8151
   http://www.blairchamber.com

GREENWOOD (CDP). Covers a land area of 1.029 square miles and a water area of 0 square miles. Located at 40.53° N. Lat; 78.36° W. Long. Elevation is 1,181 feet.

Population: n/a (1990); n/a (2000); 2,458 (2010); Density: 2,388.4 persons per square mile (2010); Race: 97.6% White, 1.2% Black, 0.6% Asian, 0.0% American Indian/Alaska Native, 0.0% Native Hawaiian/Other Pacific Islander, 0.6% Other, 0.6% Hispanic of any race (2010); Average household size: 2.23 (2010); Median age: 45.0 (2010); Males per 100 females: 86.9 (2010); Marriage status: 36.9% never married, 45.0% now married, 4.8% widowed, 13.3% divorced (2006-2010 5-year est.); Foreign born: 1.6% (2006-2010 5-year est.); Ancestry (includes multiple ancestries): 36.4% German, 19.0% Italian, 15.3% Irish, 8.3% Pennsylvania German, 4.6% English (2006-2010 5-year est.).

Economy: Employment by occupation: 7.2% management, 2.7% professional, 12.1% services, 16.8% sales, 10.7% farming, 5.6% construction, 6.8% production (2006-2010 5-year est.).

Income: Per capita income: $26,306 (2006-2010 5-year est.); Median household income: $56,029 (2006-2010 5-year est.); Average household income: $65,318 (2006-2010 5-year est.); Percent of households with income of $100,000 or more: 18.8% (2006-2010 5-year est.); Poverty rate: 14.4% (2006-2010 5-year est.).

Education: Percent of population age 25 and over with: High school diploma (including GED) or higher: 91.7% (2006-2010 5-year est.); Bachelor's degree or higher: 13.3% (2006-2010 5-year est.); Master's degree or higher: 7.8% (2006-2010 5-year est.).

Housing: Homeownership rate: 63.1% (2010); Median home value: $113,200 (2006-2010 5-year est.); Median contract rent: $508 per month (2006-2010 5-year est.); Median year structure built: 1975 (2006-2010 5-year est.).

Transportation: Commute to work: 97.2% car, 0.0% public transportation, 0.0% walk, 2.8% work from home (2006-2010 5-year est.); Travel time to work: 42.2% less than 15 minutes, 43.9% 15 to 30 minutes, 3.3% 30 to 45 minutes, 3.5% 45 to 60 minutes, 7.1% 60 minutes or more (2006-2010 5-year est.).

HOLLIDAYSBURG (borough). Aka Loop. County seat. Covers a land area of 2.348 square miles and a water area of 0 square miles. Located at 40.43° N. Lat; 78.39° W. Long. Elevation is 955 feet.

History: Allegheny Portage Railroad National Historic Site to West, carried canal boats over Allegheny Mts. to Johnstown in mid-19th century. Settled 1768, laid out 1820.

Population: 5,606 (1990); 5,368 (2000); 5,791 (2010); Density: 2,466.3 persons per square mile (2010); Race: 96.3% White, 1.7% Black, 1.0% Asian, 0.1% American Indian/Alaska Native, 0.0% Native Hawaiian/Other Pacific Islander, 0.9% Other, 0.9% Hispanic of any race (2010); Average household size: 2.09 (2010); Median age: 44.2 (2010); Males per 100 females: 90.1 (2010); Marriage status: 27.7% never married, 44.6% now married, 16.0% widowed, 11.7% divorced (2006-2010 5-year est.); Foreign born: 0.3% (2006-2010 5-year est.); Ancestry (includes multiple ancestries): 44.7% German, 18.1% Irish, 12.6% Italian, 10.8% English, 3.9% American (2006-2010 5-year est.).

Economy: Single-family building permits issued: 1 (2011); Multi-family building permits issued: 4 (2011); Employment by occupation: 10.0% management, 2.5% professional, 8.8% services, 20.3% sales, 3.4% farming, 5.7% construction, 5.5% production (2006-2010 5-year est.).

Income: Per capita income: $24,034 (2006-2010 5-year est.); Median household income: $40,257 (2006-2010 5-year est.); Average household income: $48,656 (2006-2010 5-year est.); Percent of households with income of $100,000 or more: 9.1% (2006-2010 5-year est.); Poverty rate: 8.7% (2006-2010 5-year est.).

Education: Percent of population age 25 and over with: High school diploma (including GED) or higher: 91.0% (2006-2010 5-year est.); Bachelor's degree or higher: 26.0% (2006-2010 5-year est.); Master's degree or higher: 5.9% (2006-2010 5-year est.).

School District(s)
Hollidaysburg Area SD (KG-12)
   2010-11 Enrollment: 3,471 . . . . (814) 695-8702

Housing: Homeownership rate: 54.5% (2010); Median home value: $113,000 (2006-2010 5-year est.); Median contract rent: $508 per month (2006-2010 5-year est.); Median year structure built: 1945 (2006-2010 5-year est.).

Newspapers: The Catholic Register (Regional news; Circulation 36,000)

Transportation: Commute to work: 90.9% car, 0.0% public transportation, 3.9% walk, 3.5% work from home (2006-2010 5-year est.); Travel time to work: 48.6% less than 15 minutes, 35.2% 15 to 30 minutes, 10.7% 30 to 45 minutes, 1.1% 45 to 60 minutes, 4.4% 60 minutes or more (2006-2010 5-year est.)

Additional Information Contacts
Blair County Chamber of Commerce . . . . (814) 943-8151
   http://www.blairchamber.com
Borough of Hollidaysburg . . . . (814) 695-7543
   http://hollidaysburgpa.org

HUSTON (township). Covers a land area of 34.891 square miles and a water area of 0.012 square miles. Located at 40.36° N. Lat; 78.26° W. Long.

Population: 1,189 (1990); 1,262 (2000); 1,336 (2010); Density: 38.3 persons per square mile (2010); Race: 98.1% White, 0.1% Black, 0.1% Asian, 0.1% American Indian/Alaska Native, 0.0% Native Hawaiian/Other Pacific Islander, 1.6% Other, 1.8% Hispanic of any race (2010); Average household size: 2.78 (2010); Median age: 38.7 (2010); Males per 100 females: 101.8 (2010); Marriage status: 29.2% never married, 59.1% now married, 7.0% widowed, 4.8% divorced (2006-2010 5-year est.); Foreign born: 0.2% (2006-2010 5-year est.); Ancestry (includes multiple ancestries): 46.6% German, 12.6% American, 9.6% English, 7.9% Irish, 3.3% Italian (2006-2010 5-year est.).

Economy: Single-family building permits issued: 2 (2011); Multi-family building permits issued: 0 (2011); Employment by occupation: 14.5% management, 2.1% professional, 10.5% services, 11.3% sales, 6.2% farming, 18.9% construction, 10.5% production (2006-2010 5-year est.).

Income: Per capita income: $19,691 (2006-2010 5-year est.); Median household income: $50,083 (2006-2010 5-year est.); Average household income: $56,707 (2006-2010 5-year est.); Percent of households with income of $100,000 or more: 11.1% (2006-2010 5-year est.); Poverty rate: 5.9% (2006-2010 5-year est.).

Education: Percent of population age 25 and over with: High school diploma (including GED) or higher: 84.2% (2006-2010 5-year est.); Bachelor's degree or higher: 12.5% (2006-2010 5-year est.); Master's degree or higher: 5.3% (2006-2010 5-year est.).

Housing: Homeownership rate: 81.1% (2010); Median home value: $137,500 (2006-2010 5-year est.); Median contract rent: $409 per month (2006-2010 5-year est.); Median year structure built: 1972 (2006-2010 5-year est.).

Transportation: Commute to work: 82.1% car, 0.0% public transportation, 5.2% walk, 10.2% work from home (2006-2010 5-year est.); Travel time to work: 42.4% less than 15 minutes, 36.6% 15 to 30 minutes, 12.9% 30 to

45 minutes, 4.5% 45 to 60 minutes, 3.6% 60 minutes or more (2006-2010 5-year est.)

Additional Information Contacts

Blair County Chamber of Commerce . . . . (814) 943-8151
    http://www.blairchamber.com

JUNIATA (township). Covers a land area of 26.070 square miles and a water area of 0.056 square miles. Located at 40.40° N. Lat; 78.53° W. Long.

Population: 1,116 (1990); 1,115 (2000); 1,112 (2010); Density: 42.7 persons per square mile (2010); Race: 98.2% White, 0.4% Black, 0.3% Asian, 0.0% American Indian/Alaska Native, 0.0% Native Hawaiian/Other Pacific Islander, 1.1% Other, 0.5% Hispanic of any race (2010); Average household size: 2.61 (2010); Median age: 42.9 (2010); Males per 100 females: 104.0 (2010); Marriage status: 17.4% never married, 66.6% now married, 7.4% widowed, 8.6% divorced (2006-2010 5-year est.); Foreign born: 0.0% (2006-2010 5-year est.); Ancestry (includes multiple ancestries): 48.4% German, 28.9% Irish, 8.9% English, 8.5% American, 4.8% Pennsylvania German (2006-2010 5-year est.).

Economy: Single-family building permits issued: 1 (2011); Multi-family building permits issued: 0 (2011); Employment by occupation: 10.7% management, 0.7% professional, 13.3% services, 13.1% sales, 2.3% farming, 13.5% construction, 8.1% production (2006-2010 5-year est.).

Income: Per capita income: $22,567 (2006-2010 5-year est.); Median household income: $47,069 (2006-2010 5-year est.); Average household income: $55,343 (2006-2010 5-year est.); Percent of households with income of $100,000 or more: 10.2% (2006-2010 5-year est.); Poverty rate: 4.1% (2006-2010 5-year est.).

Education: Percent of population age 25 and over with: High school diploma (including GED) or higher: 90.2% (2006-2010 5-year est.); Bachelor's degree or higher: 11.9% (2006-2010 5-year est.); Master's degree or higher: 4.1% (2006-2010 5-year est.).

Housing: Homeownership rate: 88.8% (2010); Median home value: $117,700 (2006-2010 5-year est.); Median contract rent: $417 per month (2006-2010 5-year est.); Median year structure built: 1976 (2006-2010 5-year est.).

Transportation: Commute to work: 92.1% car, 0.0% public transportation, 1.1% walk, 6.5% work from home (2006-2010 5-year est.); Travel time to work: 26.1% less than 15 minutes, 45.6% 15 to 30 minutes, 14.2% 30 to 45 minutes, 8.4% 45 to 60 minutes, 5.7% 60 minutes or more (2006-2010 5-year est.)

Additional Information Contacts

Blair County Chamber of Commerce . . . . (814) 943-8151
    http://www.blairchamber.com

LAKEMONT (CDP). Covers a land area of 1.646 square miles and a water area of 0.023 square miles. Located at 40.47° N. Lat; 78.39° W. Long. Elevation is 1,175 feet.

Population: n/a (1990); n/a (2000); 1,868 (2010); Density: 1,135.0 persons per square mile (2010); Race: 97.9% White, 0.8% Black, 0.9% Asian, 0.1% American Indian/Alaska Native, 0.0% Native Hawaiian/Other Pacific Islander, 0.3% Other, 0.5% Hispanic of any race (2010); Average household size: 2.19 (2010); Median age: 46.7 (2010); Males per 100 females: 94.6 (2010); Marriage status: 18.5% never married, 67.8% now married, 4.8% widowed, 9.0% divorced (2006-2010 5-year est.); Foreign born: 0.0% (2006-2010 5-year est.); Ancestry (includes multiple ancestries): 50.8% German, 27.1% Irish, 7.6% English, 4.3% Italian, 3.7% Polish (2006-2010 5-year est.).

Economy: Employment by occupation: 8.2% management, 2.2% professional, 11.8% services, 17.3% sales, 1.6% farming, 5.7% construction, 4.8% production (2006-2010 5-year est.).

Income: Per capita income: $26,793 (2006-2010 5-year est.); Median household income: $47,071 (2006-2010 5-year est.); Average household income: $65,728 (2006-2010 5-year est.); Percent of households with income of $100,000 or more: 11.1% (2006-2010 5-year est.); Poverty rate: 4.1% (2006-2010 5-year est.).

Education: Percent of population age 25 and over with: High school diploma (including GED) or higher: 93.5% (2006-2010 5-year est.); Bachelor's degree or higher: 15.4% (2006-2010 5-year est.); Master's degree or higher: 5.0% (2006-2010 5-year est.).

Housing: Homeownership rate: 75.5% (2010); Median home value: $95,200 (2006-2010 5-year est.); Median contract rent: $637 per month (2006-2010 5-year est.); Median year structure built: 1957 (2006-2010 5-year est.).

Transportation: Commute to work: 91.2% car, 0.0% public transportation, 5.8% walk, 0.9% work from home (2006-2010 5-year est.); Travel time to work: 60.5% less than 15 minutes, 25.9% 15 to 30 minutes, 4.4% 30 to 45 minutes, 5.2% 45 to 60 minutes, 4.0% 60 minutes or more (2006-2010 5-year est.)

LOGAN (township). Covers a land area of 46.394 square miles and a water area of 0.328 square miles. Located at 40.53° N. Lat; 78.43° W. Long.

Population: 12,111 (1990); 11,925 (2000); 12,289 (2010); Density: 264.9 persons per square mile (2010); Race: 96.6% White, 1.2% Black, 0.9% Asian, 0.2% American Indian/Alaska Native, 0.0% Native Hawaiian/Other Pacific Islander, 1.1% Other, 0.9% Hispanic of any race (2010); Average household size: 2.42 (2010); Median age: 41.5 (2010); Males per 100 females: 96.8 (2010); Marriage status: 31.3% never married, 51.8% now married, 6.8% widowed, 10.1% divorced (2006-2010 5-year est.); Foreign born: 1.9% (2006-2010 5-year est.); Ancestry (includes multiple ancestries): 43.9% German, 20.1% Irish, 13.9% Italian, 9.3% English, 5.9% American (2006-2010 5-year est.).

Economy: Single-family building permits issued: 10 (2011); Multi-family building permits issued: 0 (2011); Employment by occupation: 12.0% management, 2.0% professional, 11.9% services, 17.7% sales, 7.0% farming, 7.6% construction, 5.6% production (2006-2010 5-year est.).

Income: Per capita income: $26,033 (2006-2010 5-year est.); Median household income: $48,943 (2006-2010 5-year est.); Average household income: $65,593 (2006-2010 5-year est.); Percent of households with income of $100,000 or more: 17.6% (2006-2010 5-year est.); Poverty rate: 14.1% (2006-2010 5-year est.).

Taxes: Total city taxes per capita: $342 (2009); City property taxes per capita: $108 (2009).

Education: Percent of population age 25 and over with: High school diploma (including GED) or higher: 90.1% (2006-2010 5-year est.); Bachelor's degree or higher: 18.0% (2006-2010 5-year est.); Master's degree or higher: 6.9% (2006-2010 5-year est.).

Housing: Homeownership rate: 73.3% (2010); Median home value: $114,700 (2006-2010 5-year est.); Median contract rent: $516 per month (2006-2010 5-year est.); Median year structure built: 1973 (2006-2010 5-year est.).

Transportation: Commute to work: 95.2% car, 0.0% public transportation, 2.5% walk, 2.1% work from home (2006-2010 5-year est.); Travel time to work: 48.8% less than 15 minutes, 36.1% 15 to 30 minutes, 5.2% 30 to 45 minutes, 4.3% 45 to 60 minutes, 5.5% 60 minutes or more (2006-2010 5-year est.)

Additional Information Contacts

Greater Philadelphia Chamber of Commerce . . . . (215) 545-1234
    http://www.greaterphilachamber.com
Logan Township . . . . (814) 944-5349
    http://logantownship-pa.gov

MARTINSBURG (borough). Covers a land area of 0.632 square miles and a water area of 0 square miles. Located at 40.31° N. Lat; 78.32° W. Long. Elevation is 1,407 feet.

History: Settled c.1793, laid out 1815, incorporated 1832.

Population: 2,101 (1990); 2,236 (2000); 1,958 (2010); Density: 3,096.0 persons per square mile (2010); Race: 98.6% White, 0.6% Black, 0.1% Asian, 0.1% American Indian/Alaska Native, 0.1% Native Hawaiian/Other Pacific Islander, 0.5% Other, 0.7% Hispanic of any race (2010); Average household size: 2.16 (2010); Median age: 48.6 (2010); Males per 100 females: 86.5 (2010); Marriage status: 17.5% never married, 59.4% now married, 13.6% widowed, 9.5% divorced (2006-2010 5-year est.); Foreign born: 1.9% (2006-2010 5-year est.); Ancestry (includes multiple ancestries): 44.5% German, 9.9% American, 8.9% English, 6.9% Irish, 5.8% Italian (2006-2010 5-year est.).

Economy: Single-family building permits issued: 0 (2011); Multi-family building permits issued: 0 (2011); Employment by occupation: 8.1% management, 3.8% professional, 15.0% services, 12.3% sales, 2.4% farming, 12.0% construction, 9.2% production (2006-2010 5-year est.).

Income: Per capita income: $20,309 (2006-2010 5-year est.); Median household income: $37,716 (2006-2010 5-year est.); Average household income: $44,456 (2006-2010 5-year est.); Percent of households with income of $100,000 or more: 3.6% (2006-2010 5-year est.); Poverty rate: 6.6% (2006-2010 5-year est.).

Education: Percent of population age 25 and over with: High school diploma (including GED) or higher: 93.8% (2006-2010 5-year est.);

Bachelor's degree or higher: 19.7% (2006-2010 5-year est.); Master's degree or higher: 9.8% (2006-2010 5-year est.).

School District(s)

Spring Cove SD (KG-12)

   2010-11 Enrollment: 1,825 . . . . (814) 224-5124

Housing: Homeownership rate: 68.4% (2010); Median home value: $104,300 (2006-2010 5-year est.); Median contract rent: $487 per month (2006-2010 5-year est.); Median year structure built: 1962 (2006-2010 5-year est.).

Safety: Violent crime rate: 0.0 per 10,000 population; Property crime rate: 208.8 per 10,000 population (2011).

Newspapers: Morrisons Cove Herald (Community news; Circulation 6,360)

Transportation: Commute to work: 94.0% car, 0.0% public transportation, 5.3% walk, 0.7% work from home (2006-2010 5-year est.); Travel time to work: 38.4% less than 15 minutes, 31.5% 15 to 30 minutes, 20.9% 30 to 45 minutes, 6.2% 45 to 60 minutes, 3.0% 60 minutes or more (2006-2010 5-year est.)

Additional Information Contacts

Blair County Chamber of Commerce . . . . (814) 943-8151
   http://www.blairchamber.com

NEWRY (borough). Covers a land area of 0.098 square miles and a water area of 0 square miles. Located at 40.39° N. Lat; 78.44° W. Long. Elevation is 1,050 feet.

Population: 288 (1990); 245 (2000); 270 (2010); Density: 2,752.7 persons per square mile (2010); Race: 96.7% White, 0.4% Black, 0.0% Asian, 0.0% American Indian/Alaska Native, 0.4% Native Hawaiian/Other Pacific Islander, 2.5% Other, 1.1% Hispanic of any race (2010); Average household size: 2.27 (2010); Median age: 37.2 (2010); Males per 100 females: 92.9 (2010); Marriage status: 21.7% never married, 53.9% now married, 9.4% widowed, 15.0% divorced (2006-2010 5-year est.); Foreign born: 2.8% (2006-2010 5-year est.); Ancestry (includes multiple ancestries): 63.6% German, 35.5% Irish, 12.0% Italian, 9.2% English, 3.2% Pennsylvania German (2006-2010 5-year est.).

Economy: Single-family building permits issued: 0 (2011); Multi-family building permits issued: 0 (2011); Employment by occupation: 0.0% management, 3.3% professional, 8.3% services, 27.5% sales, 10.8% farming, 14.2% construction, 9.2% production (2006-2010 5-year est.).

Income: Per capita income: $20,787 (2006-2010 5-year est.); Median household income: $30,375 (2006-2010 5-year est.); Average household income: $40,007 (2006-2010 5-year est.); Percent of households with income of $100,000 or more: 8.0% (2006-2010 5-year est.); Poverty rate: 10.1% (2006-2010 5-year est.).

Education: Percent of population age 25 and over with: High school diploma (including GED) or higher: 86.4% (2006-2010 5-year est.); Bachelor's degree or higher: 21.0% (2006-2010 5-year est.); Master's degree or higher: 3.1% (2006-2010 5-year est.).

Housing: Homeownership rate: 59.3% (2010); Median home value: $78,800 (2006-2010 5-year est.); Median contract rent: $421 per month (2006-2010 5-year est.); Median year structure built: 1943 (2006-2010 5-year est.).

Transportation: Commute to work: 95.6% car, 0.0% public transportation, 2.6% walk, 1.8% work from home (2006-2010 5-year est.); Travel time to work: 37.5% less than 15 minutes, 48.2% 15 to 30 minutes, 11.6% 30 to 45 minutes, 2.7% 45 to 60 minutes, 0.0% 60 minutes or more (2006-2010 5-year est.)

NORTH WOODBURY (township). Covers a land area of 21.074 square miles and a water area of 0 square miles. Located at 40.29° N. Lat; 78.31° W. Long.

Population: 2,237 (1990); 2,276 (2000); 2,644 (2010); Density: 125.5 persons per square mile (2010); Race: 98.0% White, 0.3% Black, 0.1% Asian, 0.1% American Indian/Alaska Native, 0.0% Native Hawaiian/Other Pacific Islander, 1.5% Other, 1.6% Hispanic of any race (2010); Average household size: 2.38 (2010); Median age: 47.3 (2010); Males per 100 females: 89.7 (2010); Marriage status: 19.4% never married, 57.8% now married, 13.1% widowed, 9.6% divorced (2006-2010 5-year est.); Foreign born: 0.0% (2006-2010 5-year est.); Ancestry (includes multiple ancestries): 37.7% German, 11.9% Irish, 10.6% English, 8.9% American, 4.9% Scotch-Irish (2006-2010 5-year est.).

Economy: Single-family building permits issued: 1 (2011); Multi-family building permits issued: 2 (2011); Employment by occupation: 19.4% management, 2.4% professional, 8.7% services, 13.8% sales, 2.7% farming, 13.3% construction, 8.7% production (2006-2010 5-year est.).

Income: Per capita income: $25,316 (2006-2010 5-year est.); Median household income: $46,202 (2006-2010 5-year est.); Average household income: $57,519 (2006-2010 5-year est.); Percent of households with income of $100,000 or more: 12.4% (2006-2010 5-year est.); Poverty rate: 9.1% (2006-2010 5-year est.).

Education: Percent of population age 25 and over with: High school diploma (including GED) or higher: 87.2% (2006-2010 5-year est.); Bachelor's degree or higher: 18.7% (2006-2010 5-year est.); Master's degree or higher: 4.8% (2006-2010 5-year est.).

Housing: Homeownership rate: 72.5% (2010); Median home value: $130,100 (2006-2010 5-year est.); Median contract rent: $629 per month (2006-2010 5-year est.); Median year structure built: 1979 (2006-2010 5-year est.).

Transportation: Commute to work: 94.3% car, 0.0% public transportation, 1.4% walk, 3.8% work from home (2006-2010 5-year est.); Travel time to work: 28.9% less than 15 minutes, 37.3% 15 to 30 minutes, 27.2% 30 to 45 minutes, 2.4% 45 to 60 minutes, 4.3% 60 minutes or more (2006-2010 5-year est.).

Additional Information Contacts

Blair County Chamber of Commerce . . . . (814) 943-8151
   http://www.blairchamber.com

NORTHWOOD (CDP). Covers a land area of 0.528 square miles and a water area of 0 square miles. Located at 40.69° N. Lat; 78.23° W. Long. Elevation is 997 feet.

Population: n/a (1990); n/a (2000); 296 (2010); Density: 560.2 persons per square mile (2010); Race: 98.3% White, 0.0% Black, 0.0% Asian, 1.0% American Indian/Alaska Native, 0.0% Native Hawaiian/Other Pacific Islander, 0.7% Other, 0.0% Hispanic of any race (2010); Average household size: 2.41 (2010); Median age: 41.4 (2010); Males per 100 females: 104.1 (2010); Marriage status: 33.8% never married, 57.7% now married, 5.0% widowed, 3.5% divorced (2006-2010 5-year est.); Foreign born: 0.0% (2006-2010 5-year est.); Ancestry (includes multiple ancestries): 11.9% Pennsylvania German, 11.3% German, 9.9% Polish, 6.6% Dutch, 3.9% Hungarian (2006-2010 5-year est.).

Economy: Employment by occupation: 0.0% management, 0.0% professional, 11.2% services, 33.6% sales, 21.6% farming, 14.4% construction, 23.2% production (2006-2010 5-year est.).

Income: Per capita income: $15,283 (2006-2010 5-year est.); Median household income: $37,500 (2006-2010 5-year est.); Average household income: $45,466 (2006-2010 5-year est.); Percent of households with income of $100,000 or more: 9.8% (2006-2010 5-year est.); Poverty rate: 7.2% (2006-2010 5-year est.).

Education: Percent of population age 25 and over with: High school diploma (including GED) or higher: 68.8% (2006-2010 5-year est.); Bachelor's degree or higher: 5.6% (2006-2010 5-year est.); Master's degree or higher: 0.0% (2006-2010 5-year est.).

Housing: Homeownership rate: 84.6% (2010); Median home value: $75,000 (2006-2010 5-year est.); Median contract rent: n/a per month (2006-2010 5-year est.); Median year structure built: before 1940 (2006-2010 5-year est.).

Transportation: Commute to work: 100.0% car, 0.0% public transportation, 0.0% walk, 0.0% work from home (2006-2010 5-year est.); Travel time to work: 60.8% less than 15 minutes, 32.0% 15 to 30 minutes, 7.2% 30 to 45 minutes, 0.0% 45 to 60 minutes, 0.0% 60 minutes or more (2006-2010 5-year est.)

ROARING SPRING (borough). Covers a land area of 0.805 square miles and a water area of 0 square miles. Located at 40.33° N. Lat; 78.40° W. Long. Elevation is 1,306 feet.

History: Incorporated 1888.

Population: 2,627 (1990); 2,418 (2000); 2,585 (2010); Density: 3,210.6 persons per square mile (2010); Race: 98.1% White, 0.5% Black, 0.6% Asian, 0.0% American Indian/Alaska Native, 0.0% Native Hawaiian/Other Pacific Islander, 0.8% Other, 0.6% Hispanic of any race (2010); Average household size: 2.35 (2010); Median age: 37.5 (2010); Males per 100 females: 92.1 (2010); Marriage status: 23.1% never married, 57.0% now married, 10.7% widowed, 9.2% divorced (2006-2010 5-year est.); Foreign born: 1.6% (2006-2010 5-year est.); Ancestry (includes multiple ancestries): 48.9% German, 15.8% Irish, 6.7% English, 5.9% Italian, 5.2% Polish (2006-2010 5-year est.).

Economy: Single-family building permits issued: 0 (2011); Multi-family building permits issued: 0 (2011); Employment by occupation: 6.1% management, 1.3% professional, 10.7% services, 18.1% sales, 6.7% farming, 7.4% construction, 5.3% production (2006-2010 5-year est.).

Income: Per capita income: $19,934 (2006-2010 5-year est.); Median household income: $43,056 (2006-2010 5-year est.); Average household income: $48,742 (2006-2010 5-year est.); Percent of households with income of $100,000 or more: 8.6% (2006-2010 5-year est.); Poverty rate: 10.3% (2006-2010 5-year est.).

Education: Percent of population age 25 and over with: High school diploma (including GED) or higher: 91.6% (2006-2010 5-year est.); Bachelor's degree or higher: 14.0% (2006-2010 5-year est.); Master's degree or higher: 4.6% (2006-2010 5-year est.).

School District(s)

Spring Cove SD (KG-12)

    2010-11 Enrollment: 1,825 . . . . (814) 224-5124

Housing: Homeownership rate: 66.2% (2010); Median home value: $89,100 (2006-2010 5-year est.); Median contract rent: $407 per month (2006-2010 5-year est.); Median year structure built: 1948 (2006-2010 5-year est.).

Hospitals: Nason Hospital (40 beds)

Safety: Violent crime rate: 3.9 per 10,000 population; Property crime rate: 250.7 per 10,000 population (2011).

Transportation: Commute to work: 96.2% car, 0.0% public transportation, 1.8% walk, 1.3% work from home (2006-2010 5-year est.); Travel time to work: 41.5% less than 15 minutes, 34.8% 15 to 30 minutes, 15.0% 30 to 45 minutes, 3.0% 45 to 60 minutes, 5.8% 60 minutes or more (2006-2010 5-year est.)

Additional Information Contacts

Blair County Chamber of Commerce . . . . (814) 943-8151
    http://www.blairchamber.com

SNYDER (township). Covers a land area of 45.096 square miles and a water area of 0.050 square miles. Located at 40.71° N. Lat; 78.25° W. Long.

Population: 3,163 (1990); 3,358 (2000); 3,364 (2010); Density: 74.6 persons per square mile (2010); Race: 98.5% White, 0.8% Black, 0.2% Asian, 0.1% American Indian/Alaska Native, 0.0% Native Hawaiian/Other Pacific Islander, 0.4% Other, 0.2% Hispanic of any race (2010); Average household size: 2.41 (2010); Median age: 43.9 (2010); Males per 100 females: 100.7 (2010); Marriage status: 22.8% never married, 60.8% now married, 8.1% widowed, 8.3% divorced (2006-2010 5-year est.); Foreign born: 0.0% (2006-2010 5-year est.); Ancestry (includes multiple ancestries): 35.8% German, 14.7% English, 11.6% Irish, 10.7% Italian, 8.4% American (2006-2010 5-year est.).

Economy: Single-family building permits issued: 0 (2011); Multi-family building permits issued: 0 (2011); Employment by occupation: 9.8% management, 3.3% professional, 13.5% services, 17.2% sales, 5.2% farming, 11.0% construction, 6.0% production (2006-2010 5-year est.).

Income: Per capita income: $21,049 (2006-2010 5-year est.); Median household income: $43,404 (2006-2010 5-year est.); Average household income: $52,513 (2006-2010 5-year est.); Percent of households with income of $100,000 or more: 12.3% (2006-2010 5-year est.); Poverty rate: 9.3% (2006-2010 5-year est.).

Education: Percent of population age 25 and over with: High school diploma (including GED) or higher: 87.1% (2006-2010 5-year est.); Bachelor's degree or higher: 8.7% (2006-2010 5-year est.); Master's degree or higher: 2.9% (2006-2010 5-year est.).

Housing: Homeownership rate: 81.4% (2010); Median home value: $90,500 (2006-2010 5-year est.); Median contract rent: $476 per month (2006-2010 5-year est.); Median year structure built: 1957 (2006-2010 5-year est.).

Transportation: Commute to work: 93.7% car, 0.0% public transportation, 2.0% walk, 2.2% work from home (2006-2010 5-year est.); Travel time to work: 38.6% less than 15 minutes, 35.2% 15 to 30 minutes, 22.2% 30 to 45 minutes, 1.7% 45 to 60 minutes, 2.3% 60 minutes or more (2006-2010 5-year est.)

Additional Information Contacts

Blair County Chamber of Commerce . . . . (814) 943-8151
    http://www.blairchamber.com

SPROUL (unincorporated postal area)

Zip Code: 16682

    Covers a land area of 0.214 square miles and a water area of 0 square miles. Located at 40.26° N. Lat; 78.45° W. Long. Elevation is 1,227 feet. Population: 117 (2010); Density: 545.4 persons per square mile (2010); Race: 99.1% White, 0.0% Black, 0.0% Asian, 0.0% American Indian/Alaska Native, 0.0% Native Hawaiian/Other Pacific Islander, 0.9% Other, 0.9% Hispanic of any race (2010); Average household size:

2.49 (2010); Median age: 43.8 (2010); Males per 100 females: 105.3 (2010); Homeownership rate: 85.1% (2010)

TAYLOR (township). Covers a land area of 23.345 square miles and a water area of 0 square miles. Located at 40.33° N. Lat; 78.38° W. Long.

Population: 2,315 (1990); 2,239 (2000); 2,465 (2010); Density: 105.6 persons per square mile (2010); Race: 99.2% White, 0.0% Black, 0.1% Asian, 0.0% American Indian/Alaska Native, 0.0% Native Hawaiian/Other Pacific Islander, 0.7% Other, 0.4% Hispanic of any race (2010); Average household size: 2.43 (2010); Median age: 46.5 (2010); Males per 100 females: 98.3 (2010); Marriage status: 21.9% never married, 63.5% now married, 8.5% widowed, 6.1% divorced (2006-2010 5-year est.); Foreign born: 0.0% (2006-2010 5-year est.); Ancestry (includes multiple ancestries): 53.1% German, 16.9% Irish, 9.5% American, 8.1% English, 5.0% Dutch (2006-2010 5-year est.).

Economy: Single-family building permits issued: 2 (2011); Multi-family building permits issued: 0 (2011); Employment by occupation: 8.3% management, 1.8% professional, 6.9% services, 15.5% sales, 6.0% farming, 12.4% construction, 14.8% production (2006-2010 5-year est.).

Income: Per capita income: $23,956 (2006-2010 5-year est.); Median household income: $45,000 (2006-2010 5-year est.); Average household income: $56,128 (2006-2010 5-year est.); Percent of households with income of $100,000 or more: 9.6% (2006-2010 5-year est.); Poverty rate: 6.5% (2006-2010 5-year est.).

Education: Percent of population age 25 and over with: High school diploma (including GED) or higher: 88.0% (2006-2010 5-year est.); Bachelor's degree or higher: 10.6% (2006-2010 5-year est.); Master's degree or higher: 2.3% (2006-2010 5-year est.).

Housing: Homeownership rate: 74.7% (2010); Median home value: $135,200 (2006-2010 5-year est.); Median contract rent: $690 per month (2006-2010 5-year est.); Median year structure built: 1971 (2006-2010 5-year est.).

Transportation: Commute to work: 97.2% car, 0.0% public transportation, 0.7% walk, 1.2% work from home (2006-2010 5-year est.); Travel time to work: 44.1% less than 15 minutes, 40.8% 15 to 30 minutes, 11.5% 30 to 45 minutes, 1.4% 45 to 60 minutes, 2.1% 60 minutes or more (2006-2010 5-year est.)

Additional Information Contacts

Blair County Chamber of Commerce . . . . (814) 943-8151
    http://www.blairchamber.com

TIPTON (CDP). Covers a land area of 1.823 square miles and a water area of 0 square miles. Located at 40.64° N. Lat; 78.30° W. Long. Elevation is 997 feet.

Population: 1,158 (1990); 1,225 (2000); 1,083 (2010); Density: 594.1 persons per square mile (2010); Race: 99.2% White, 0.5% Black, 0.1% Asian, 0.1% American Indian/Alaska Native, 0.0% Native Hawaiian/Other Pacific Islander, 0.1% Other, 0.4% Hispanic of any race (2010); Average household size: 2.35 (2010); Median age: 46.3 (2010); Males per 100 females: 95.8 (2010); Marriage status: 38.1% never married, 42.9% now married, 6.9% widowed, 12.1% divorced (2006-2010 5-year est.); Foreign born: 0.0% (2006-2010 5-year est.); Ancestry (includes multiple ancestries): 43.3% German, 40.9% Dutch, 26.9% Irish, 12.1% English, 10.6% American (2006-2010 5-year est.).

Economy: Employment by occupation: 7.9% management, 0.0% professional, 10.0% services, 19.1% sales, 0.0% farming, 14.5% construction, 10.6% production (2006-2010 5-year est.).

Income: Per capita income: $22,373 (2006-2010 5-year est.); Median household income: $44,817 (2006-2010 5-year est.); Average household income: $53,480 (2006-2010 5-year est.); Percent of households with income of $100,000 or more: 9.0% (2006-2010 5-year est.); Poverty rate: 7.8% (2006-2010 5-year est.).

Education: Percent of population age 25 and over with: High school diploma (including GED) or higher: 96.1% (2006-2010 5-year est.); Bachelor's degree or higher: 15.1% (2006-2010 5-year est.); Master's degree or higher: 0.0% (2006-2010 5-year est.).

Housing: Homeownership rate: 75.2% (2010); Median home value: $153,900 (2006-2010 5-year est.); Median contract rent: $429 per month (2006-2010 5-year est.); Median year structure built: 1949 (2006-2010 5-year est.).

Transportation: Commute to work: 100.0% car, 0.0% public transportation, 0.0% walk, 0.0% work from home (2006-2010 5-year est.); Travel time to work: 42.0% less than 15 minutes, 46.2% 15 to 30 minutes, 11.8% 30 to 45 minutes, 0.0% 45 to 60 minutes, 0.0% 60 minutes or more (2006-2010 5-year est.)

Additional Information Contacts

Tyrone Area Chamber of Commerce . . . . (814) 684-0736
http://www.tyronechamber.com

TYRONE (borough).

Covers a land area of 2.035 square miles and a water area of 0 square miles. Located at 40.68° N. Lat; 78.25° W. Long. Elevation is 892 feet.

Population: 5,743 (1990); 5,528 (2000); 5,477 (2010); Density: 2,691.4 persons per square mile (2010); Race: 97.3% White, 0.7% Black, 0.3% Asian, 0.3% American Indian/Alaska Native, 0.0% Native Hawaiian/Other Pacific Islander, 1.4% Other, 1.0% Hispanic of any race (2010); Average household size: 2.34 (2010); Median age: 40.1 (2010); Males per 100 females: 88.8 (2010); Marriage status: 27.3% never married, 54.7% now married, 7.0% widowed, 11.0% divorced (2006-2010 5-year est.); Foreign born: 0.3% (2006-2010 5-year est.); Ancestry (includes multiple ancestries): 39.0% German, 23.5% Irish, 10.0% Italian, 6.8% American, 6.2% English (2006-2010 5-year est.).

Economy: Single-family building permits issued: 0 (2011); Multi-family building permits issued: 0 (2011); Employment by occupation: 10.1% management, 4.1% professional, 10.7% services, 13.8% sales, 5.7% farming, 7.3% construction, 7.2% production (2006-2010 5-year est.).

Income: Per capita income: $18,664 (2006-2010 5-year est.); Median household income: $34,850 (2006-2010 5-year est.); Average household income: $45,608 (2006-2010 5-year est.); Percent of households with income of $100,000 or more: 6.1% (2006-2010 5-year est.); Poverty rate: 14.0% (2006-2010 5-year est.).

Education: Percent of population age 25 and over with: High school diploma (including GED) or higher: 92.2% (2006-2010 5-year est.); Bachelor's degree or higher: 12.2% (2006-2010 5-year est.); Master's degree or higher: 4.1% (2006-2010 5-year est.).

School District(s)

Tyrone Area SD (PK-12)

2010-11 Enrollment: 1,939 . . . . (814) 684-0710

Housing: Homeownership rate: 60.7% (2010); Median home value: $92,400 (2006-2010 5-year est.); Median contract rent: $355 per month (2006-2010 5-year est.); Median year structure built: before 1940 (2006-2010 5-year est.).

Hospitals: Tyrone Hospital (59 beds)

Safety: Violent crime rate: 45.5 per 10,000 population; Property crime rate: 294.9 per 10,000 population (2011).

Newspapers: The Daily Herald (Local news; Circulation 1,900)

Transportation: Commute to work: 88.9% car, 0.0% public transportation, 6.4% walk, 3.4% work from home (2006-2010 5-year est.); Travel time to work: 44.5% less than 15 minutes, 21.5% 15 to 30 minutes, 26.8% 30 to 45 minutes, 4.5% 45 to 60 minutes, 2.6% 60 minutes or more (2006-2010 5-year est.); Amtrak: train service available.

Additional Information Contacts

Blair County Chamber of Commerce . . . . (814) 943-8151
http://www.blairchamber.com

Borough of Tyrone. . . . . (814) 684-1337
http://www.tyroneboropa.com

TYRONE (township).

Covers a land area of 41.819 square miles and a water area of 0.046 square miles. Located at 40.58° N. Lat; 78.25° W. Long. Elevation is 892 feet.

History: Laid out c.1850, incorporated 1857.

Population: 1,677 (1990); 1,800 (2000); 1,885 (2010); Density: 45.1 persons per square mile (2010); Race: 98.8% White, 0.2% Black, 0.4% Asian, 0.0% American Indian/Alaska Native, 0.0% Native Hawaiian/Other Pacific Islander, 0.6% Other, 0.6% Hispanic of any race (2010); Average household size: 2.72 (2010); Median age: 44.1 (2010); Males per 100 females: 107.1 (2010); Marriage status: 25.8% never married, 59.4% now married, 6.5% widowed, 8.3% divorced (2006-2010 5-year est.); Foreign born: 0.3% (2006-2010 5-year est.); Ancestry (includes multiple ancestries): 49.6% German, 13.4% Irish, 11.2% Italian, 9.4% English, 7.7% American (2006-2010 5-year est.).

Economy: Single-family building permits issued: 2 (2011); Multi-family building permits issued: 0 (2011); Employment by occupation: 21.7% management, 2.0% professional, 4.6% services, 17.6% sales, 4.3% farming, 12.0% construction, 6.5% production (2006-2010 5-year est.).

Income: Per capita income: $26,595 (2006-2010 5-year est.); Median household income: $57,422 (2006-2010 5-year est.); Average household income: $71,586 (2006-2010 5-year est.); Percent of households with income of $100,000 or more: 20.1% (2006-2010 5-year est.); Poverty rate: 4.9% (2006-2010 5-year est.).

Education: Percent of population age 25 and over with: High school diploma (including GED) or higher: 92.3% (2006-2010 5-year est.); Bachelor's degree or higher: 17.2% (2006-2010 5-year est.); Master's degree or higher: 4.8% (2006-2010 5-year est.).

Housing: Homeownership rate: 86.2% (2010); Median home value: $157,600 (2006-2010 5-year est.); Median contract rent: $383 per month (2006-2010 5-year est.); Median year structure built: 1962 (2006-2010 5-year est.).

Hospitals: Tyrone Hospital (59 beds)

Newspapers: The Daily Herald (Local news; Circulation 1,900)

Transportation: Commute to work: 84.1% car, 0.0% public transportation, 9.2% walk, 4.0% work from home (2006-2010 5-year est.); Travel time to work: 30.7% less than 15 minutes, 46.0% 15 to 30 minutes, 11.9% 30 to 45 minutes, 6.2% 45 to 60 minutes, 5.3% 60 minutes or more (2006-2010 5-year est.); Amtrak: train service available.

Additional Information Contacts

Blair County Chamber of Commerce . . . . (814) 943-8151
http://www.blairchamber.com

WILLIAMSBURG (borough).

Covers a land area of 0.366 square miles and a water area of 0 square miles. Located at 40.46° N. Lat; 78.20° W. Long. Elevation is 843 feet.

History: Settled 1790, laid out 1795, incorporated 1827.

Population: 1,456 (1990); 1,345 (2000); 1,254 (2010); Density: 3,430.0 persons per square mile (2010); Race: 98.4% White, 0.6% Black, 0.2% Asian, 0.1% American Indian/Alaska Native, 0.0% Native Hawaiian/Other Pacific Islander, 0.7% Other, 1.0% Hispanic of any race (2010); Average household size: 2.33 (2010); Median age: 39.4 (2010); Males per 100 females: 87.7 (2010); Marriage status: 29.9% never married, 43.9% now married, 14.1% widowed, 12.1% divorced (2006-2010 5-year est.); Foreign born: 0.1% (2006-2010 5-year est.); Ancestry (includes multiple ancestries): 47.6% German, 19.7% Irish, 6.8% American, 5.4% English, 5.2% Dutch (2006-2010 5-year est.).

Economy: Single-family building permits issued: 0 (2011); Multi-family building permits issued: 0 (2011); Employment by occupation: 3.7% management, 2.0% professional, 9.1% services, 14.1% sales, 3.5% farming, 10.8% construction, 17.8% production (2006-2010 5-year est.).

Income: Per capita income: $17,139 (2006-2010 5-year est.); Median household income: $29,545 (2006-2010 5-year est.); Average household income: $39,916 (2006-2010 5-year est.); Percent of households with income of $100,000 or more: 6.4% (2006-2010 5-year est.); Poverty rate: 17.8% (2006-2010 5-year est.).

Education: Percent of population age 25 and over with: High school diploma (including GED) or higher: 89.5% (2006-2010 5-year est.); Bachelor's degree or higher: 7.8% (2006-2010 5-year est.); Master's degree or higher: 3.2% (2006-2010 5-year est.).

School District(s)

Williamsburg Community SD (KG-12)

2010-11 Enrollment: 535 . . . . (814) 832-2125

Housing: Homeownership rate: 59.6% (2010); Median home value: $78,000 (2006-2010 5-year est.); Median contract rent: $373 per month (2006-2010 5-year est.); Median year structure built: before 1940 (2006-2010 5-year est.).

Hospitals: White Deer Run (260 beds)

Safety: Violent crime rate: 0.0 per 10,000 population; Property crime rate: 111.3 per 10,000 population (2011).

Transportation: Commute to work: 87.1% car, 0.0% public transportation, 9.8% walk, 0.7% work from home (2006-2010 5-year est.); Travel time to work: 31.7% less than 15 minutes, 38.3% 15 to 30 minutes, 18.2% 30 to 45 minutes, 7.7% 45 to 60 minutes, 4.1% 60 minutes or more (2006-2010 5-year est.)

Additional Information Contacts

Huntingdon County Chamber of Commerce . . . . (814) 643-1110
http://www.huntingdonchamber.com

WOODBURY (township).

Covers a land area of 32.376 square miles and a water area of 0 square miles. Located at 40.44° N. Lat; 78.21° W. Long.

Population: 1,418 (1990); 1,637 (2000); 1,693 (2010); Density: 52.3 persons per square mile (2010); Race: 97.9% White, 0.6% Black, 0.2% Asian, 0.1% American Indian/Alaska Native, 0.0% Native Hawaiian/Other Pacific Islander, 1.2% Other, 1.2% Hispanic of any race (2010); Average household size: 2.67 (2010); Median age: 40.0 (2010); Males per 100 females: 113.8 (2010); Marriage status: 25.8% never married, 60.4% now married, 6.0% widowed, 7.8% divorced (2006-2010 5-year est.); Foreign

born: 3.7% (2006-2010 5-year est.); Ancestry (includes multiple ancestries): 38.5% German, 16.5% Irish, 8.5% American, 6.8% Polish, 5.3% English (2006-2010 5-year est.).

Economy: Single-family building permits issued: 0 (2011); Multi-family building permits issued: 0 (2011); Employment by occupation: 12.5% management, 1.7% professional, 10.6% services, 12.2% sales, 2.2% farming, 26.6% construction, 16.2% production (2006-2010 5-year est.).

Income: Per capita income: $18,216 (2006-2010 5-year est.); Median household income: $45,913 (2006-2010 5-year est.); Average household income: $47,801 (2006-2010 5-year est.); Percent of households with income of $100,000 or more: 5.5% (2006-2010 5-year est.); Poverty rate: 15.9% (2006-2010 5-year est.).

Education: Percent of population age 25 and over with: High school diploma (including GED) or higher: 86.4% (2006-2010 5-year est.); Bachelor's degree or higher: 9.5% (2006-2010 5-year est.); Master's degree or higher: 3.0% (2006-2010 5-year est.).

Housing: Homeownership rate: 82.7% (2010); Median home value: $109,800 (2006-2010 5-year est.); Median contract rent: $319 per month (2006-2010 5-year est.); Median year structure built: 1967 (2006-2010 5-year est.).

Transportation: Commute to work: 83.8% car, 0.0% public transportation, 11.1% walk, 3.9% work from home (2006-2010 5-year est.); Travel time to work: 37.2% less than 15 minutes, 28.4% 15 to 30 minutes, 16.7% 30 to 45 minutes, 11.1% 45 to 60 minutes, 6.6% 60 minutes or more (2006-2010 5-year est.)

Additional Information Contacts

Blair County Chamber of Commerce . . . . (814) 943-8151
    http://www.blairchamber.com

Bradford County

Located in northeast Pennsylvania; bounded on the north by New York; drained by the Susquehanna River. Covers a land area of 1,147.399 square miles, a water area of 13.620 square miles, and is located in the Eastern Time Zone at 41.79° N. Lat., 76.50° W. Long. The county was founded in 1810. County seat is Towanda.

Bradford County is part of the Sayre, PA Micropolitan Statistical Area. The entire metro area includes: Bradford County, PA

Weather Station: Canton   Elevation: 1,160 feet

	Jan	Feb	Mar	Apr	May	Jun	Jul	Aug	Sep	Oct	Nov	Dec
High	33	36	45	58	69	77	81	80	72	60	48	37
Low	14	15	23	33	42	52	56	54	47	35	29	19
Precip	2.5	2.2	3.0	3.7	3.4	4.1	3.7	3.5	3.9	3.3	3.4	2.7
Snow	10.0	6.7	8.1	1.5	tr	0.0	0.0	0.0	0.0	0.2	2.3	6.4

High and Low temperatures in degrees Fahrenheit; Precipitation and Snow in inches

Weather Station: Towanda 1 ESE   Elevation: 750 feet

	Jan	Feb	Mar	Apr	May	Jun	Jul	Aug	Sep	Oct	Nov	Dec
High	34	37	46	59	70	79	83	81	74	62	50	38
Low	16	18	25	35	45	55	59	58	50	39	31	22
Precip	2.0	1.9	2.8	3.3	3.1	3.7	3.5	3.1	3.4	3.0	2.9	2.4
Snow	10.2	7.5	7.7	1.5	0.0	0.0	0.0	0.0	0.0	0.2	2.2	6.5

High and Low temperatures in degrees Fahrenheit; Precipitation and Snow in inches

Population: 60,967 (1990); 62,761 (2000); 62,622 (2010); Race: 97.5% White, 0.5% Black, 0.5% Asian, 0.2% American Indian/Alaska Native, 0.0% Native Hawaiian/Other Pacific Islander, 1.3% Other, 1.1% Hispanic of any race (2010); Density: 54.6 persons per square mile (2010); Average household size: 2.45 (2010); Median age: 43.4 (2010); Males per 100 females: 97.0 (2010).

Religion: Six largest groups: 10.5% Catholicism, 7.8% Methodist/Pietist, 5.8% Baptist, 4.0% Non-Denominational, 2.5% Presbyterian-Reformed, 2.4% Holiness (2010)

Economy: Unemployment rate: 6.7% (August 2012); Total civilian labor force: 35,627 (August 2012); Leading industries: 24.5% health care and social assistance; 23.9% manufacturing; 16.9% retail trade (2010); Farms: 1,457 totaling 266,635 acres (2007); Companies that employ 500 or more persons: 5 (2010); Companies that employ 100 to 499 persons: 17 (2010); Companies that employ less than 100 persons: 1,357 (2010); Black-owned businesses: n/a (2007); Hispanic-owned businesses: n/a (2007); Asian-owned businesses: n/a (2007); Women-owned businesses: 1,171 (2007); Retail sales per capita: $12,922 (2010). Single-family building permits issued: 87 (2011); Multi-family building permits issued: 0 (2011).

Income: Per capita income: $20,979 (2006-2010 5-year est.); Median household income: $40,543 (2006-2010 5-year est.); Average household income: $51,372 (2006-2010 5-year est.); Percent of households with income of $100,000 or more: 9.9% (2006-2010 5-year est.); Poverty rate: 13.6% (2006-2010 5-year est.); Bankruptcy rate: 1.43% (2011).

Taxes: Total county taxes per capita: $183 (2009); County property taxes per capita: $179 (2009).

Education: Percent of population age 25 and over with: High school diploma (including GED) or higher: 85.4% (2006-2010 5-year est.); Bachelor's degree or higher: 15.7% (2006-2010 5-year est.); Master's degree or higher: 5.1% (2006-2010 5-year est.).

Housing: Homeownership rate: 74.2% (2010); Median home value: $101,700 (2006-2010 5-year est.); Median contract rent: $412 per month (2006-2010 5-year est.); Median year structure built: 1963 (2006-2010 5-year est.)

Health: Birth rate: 114.4 per 10,000 population (2011); Death rate: 110.3 per 10,000 population (2011); Age-adjusted cancer mortality rate: 198.8 deaths per 100,000 population (2009); Number of physicians: 39.8 per 10,000 population (2010); Hospital beds: 70.9 per 10,000 population (2008); Hospital admissions: 2,391.0 per 10,000 population (2008).

Elections: 2012 Presidential election results: 36.9% Obama, 61.4% Romney

National and State Parks: Mount Pisgah State Park

Additional Information Contacts

Bradford County Government . . . . (570) 265-1727
    http://bradford-pa.com/gov
Central Bradford County Chamber of Commerce . . . . (570) 268-2732
    http://cbradchamber.org
Central Bradford County Chamber of Commerce . . . . (570) 268-2732
    http://cbradchamber.org/community

Bradford County Communities

ALBA (borough). Covers a land area of 0.671 square miles and a water area of 0 square miles. Located at 41.71° N. Lat; 76.83° W. Long. Elevation is 1,339 feet.

Population: 170 (1990); 186 (2000); 157 (2010); Density: 233.8 persons per square mile (2010); Race: 97.5% White, 1.9% Black, 0.0% Asian, 0.0% American Indian/Alaska Native, 0.0% Native Hawaiian/Other Pacific Islander, 0.6% Other, 2.5% Hispanic of any race (2010); Average household size: 2.42 (2010); Median age: 42.9 (2010); Males per 100 females: 93.8 (2010); Marriage status: 35.4% never married, 55.1% now married, 1.9% widowed, 7.6% divorced (2006-2010 5-year est.); Foreign born: 0.0% (2006-2010 5-year est.); Ancestry (includes multiple ancestries): 20.5% German, 9.9% English, 7.0% Irish, 6.4% Scottish, 6.4% American (2006-2010 5-year est.).

Economy: Single-family building permits issued: 0 (2011); Multi-family building permits issued: 0 (2011); Employment by occupation: 6.1% management, 0.0% professional, 20.4% services, 16.3% sales, 7.1% farming, 6.1% construction, 14.3% production (2006-2010 5-year est.).

Income: Per capita income: $17,504 (2006-2010 5-year est.); Median household income: $38,250 (2006-2010 5-year est.); Average household income: $41,844 (2006-2010 5-year est.); Percent of households with income of $100,000 or more: n/a (2006-2010 5-year est.); Poverty rate: 3.5% (2006-2010 5-year est.).

Education: Percent of population age 25 and over with: High school diploma (including GED) or higher: 89.6% (2006-2010 5-year est.); Bachelor's degree or higher: 2.6% (2006-2010 5-year est.); Master's degree or higher: 0.0% (2006-2010 5-year est.).

Housing: Homeownership rate: 81.5% (2010); Median home value: $72,500 (2006-2010 5-year est.); Median contract rent: n/a per month (2006-2010 5-year est.); Median year structure built: 1959 (2006-2010 5-year est.).

Transportation: Commute to work: 93.9% car, 0.0% public transportation, 0.0% walk, 6.1% work from home (2006-2010 5-year est.); Travel time to work: 30.4% less than 15 minutes, 40.2% 15 to 30 minutes, 14.1% 30 to 45 minutes, 9.8% 45 to 60 minutes, 5.4% 60 minutes or more (2006-2010 5-year est.)

ALBANY (township). Covers a land area of 32.758 square miles and a water area of 0.103 square miles. Located at 41.60° N. Lat; 76.42° W. Long.

Population: 927 (1990); 927 (2000); 911 (2010); Density: 27.8 persons per square mile (2010); Race: 97.9% White, 0.4% Black, 0.1% Asian, 0.1% American Indian/Alaska Native, 0.0% Native Hawaiian/Other Pacific

Islander, 1.5% Other, 0.7% Hispanic of any race (2010); Average household size: 2.45 (2010); Median age: 46.8 (2010); Males per 100 females: 104.7 (2010); Marriage status: 17.6% never married, 56.2% now married, 5.5% widowed, 20.6% divorced (2006-2010 5-year est.); Foreign born: 0.4% (2006-2010 5-year est.); Ancestry (includes multiple ancestries): 25.8% German, 13.6% Irish, 12.2% English, 10.1% Pennsylvania German, 8.4% Italian (2006-2010 5-year est.).
Economy: Single-family building permits issued: 3 (2011); Multi-family building permits issued: 0 (2011); Employment by occupation: 7.4% management, 4.0% professional, 13.1% services, 15.4% sales, 2.0% farming, 16.0% construction, 17.4% production (2006-2010 5-year est.).
Income: Per capita income: $19,873 (2006-2010 5-year est.); Median household income: $40,000 (2006-2010 5-year est.); Average household income: $45,760 (2006-2010 5-year est.); Percent of households with income of $100,000 or more: 2.7% (2006-2010 5-year est.); Poverty rate: 12.7% (2006-2010 5-year est.).
Education: Percent of population age 25 and over with: High school diploma (including GED) or higher: 81.3% (2006-2010 5-year est.); Bachelor's degree or higher: 6.1% (2006-2010 5-year est.); Master's degree or higher: 1.5% (2006-2010 5-year est.).
Housing: Homeownership rate: 85.7% (2010); Median home value: $117,400 (2006-2010 5-year est.); Median contract rent: $392 per month (2006-2010 5-year est.); Median year structure built: 1972 (2006-2010 5-year est.).
Transportation: Commute to work: 83.9% car, 0.0% public transportation, 5.8% walk, 10.4% work from home (2006-2010 5-year est.); Travel time to work: 20.3% less than 15 minutes, 47.3% 15 to 30 minutes, 14.8% 30 to 45 minutes, 7.1% 45 to 60 minutes, 10.6% 60 minutes or more (2006-2010 5-year est.)

ARMENIA (township). Covers a land area of 18.288 square miles and a water area of 0.123 square miles. Located at 41.73° N. Lat; 76.88° W. Long.
Population: 134 (1990); 166 (2000); 180 (2010); Density: 9.8 persons per square mile (2010); Race: 100.0% White, 0.0% Black, 0.0% Asian, 0.0% American Indian/Alaska Native, 0.0% Native Hawaiian/Other Pacific Islander, 0.0% Other, 0.0% Hispanic of any race (2010); Average household size: 2.37 (2010); Median age: 49.3 (2010); Males per 100 females: 119.5 (2010); Marriage status: 20.9% never married, 64.7% now married, 3.6% widowed, 10.8% divorced (2006-2010 5-year est.); Foreign born: 0.0% (2006-2010 5-year est.); Ancestry (includes multiple ancestries): 17.8% German, 10.6% French, 10.6% Irish, 6.7% Polish, 6.7% English (2006-2010 5-year est.).
Economy: Single-family building permits issued: 2 (2011); Multi-family building permits issued: 0 (2011); Employment by occupation: 4.8% management, 3.6% professional, 8.4% services, 8.4% sales, 0.0% farming, 26.5% construction, 12.0% production (2006-2010 5-year est.).
Income: Per capita income: $21,029 (2006-2010 5-year est.); Median household income: $54,688 (2006-2010 5-year est.); Average household income: $54,701 (2006-2010 5-year est.); Percent of households with income of $100,000 or more: 7.0% (2006-2010 5-year est.); Poverty rate: 8.9% (2006-2010 5-year est.).
Education: Percent of population age 25 and over with: High school diploma (including GED) or higher: 73.2% (2006-2010 5-year est.); Bachelor's degree or higher: 24.4% (2006-2010 5-year est.); Master's degree or higher: 2.4% (2006-2010 5-year est.).
Housing: Homeownership rate: 92.1% (2010); Median home value: $116,700 (2006-2010 5-year est.); Median contract rent: $438 per month (2006-2010 5-year est.); Median year structure built: 1978 (2006-2010 5-year est.).
Transportation: Commute to work: 91.4% car, 0.0% public transportation, 0.0% walk, 8.6% work from home (2006-2010 5-year est.); Travel time to work: 14.9% less than 15 minutes, 36.5% 15 to 30 minutes, 16.2% 30 to 45 minutes, 23.0% 45 to 60 minutes, 9.5% 60 minutes or more (2006-2010 5-year est.)

ASYLUM (township). Covers a land area of 25.330 square miles and a water area of 1.087 square miles. Located at 41.70° N. Lat; 76.37° W. Long. Elevation is 745 feet.
Population: 981 (1990); 1,097 (2000); 1,058 (2010); Density: 41.8 persons per square mile (2010); Race: 99.1% White, 0.4% Black, 0.0% Asian, 0.3% American Indian/Alaska Native, 0.0% Native Hawaiian/Other Pacific Islander, 0.2% Other, 0.5% Hispanic of any race (2010); Average household size: 2.42 (2010); Median age: 46.4 (2010); Males per 100 females: 101.9 (2010); Marriage status: 21.3% never married, 58.0% now

married, 8.6% widowed, 12.1% divorced (2006-2010 5-year est.); Foreign born: 3.2% (2006-2010 5-year est.); Ancestry (includes multiple ancestries): 19.4% German, 18.8% English, 15.1% Irish, 11.9% American, 5.2% Italian (2006-2010 5-year est.).
Economy: Single-family building permits issued: 1 (2011); Multi-family building permits issued: 0 (2011); Employment by occupation: 10.1% management, 2.4% professional, 10.1% services, 11.7% sales, 2.4% farming, 11.7% construction, 10.5% production (2006-2010 5-year est.).
Income: Per capita income: $20,980 (2006-2010 5-year est.); Median household income: $43,021 (2006-2010 5-year est.); Average household income: $49,696 (2006-2010 5-year est.); Percent of households with income of $100,000 or more: 5.7% (2006-2010 5-year est.); Poverty rate: 12.4% (2006-2010 5-year est.).
Education: Percent of population age 25 and over with: High school diploma (including GED) or higher: 85.4% (2006-2010 5-year est.); Bachelor's degree or higher: 10.6% (2006-2010 5-year est.); Master's degree or higher: 1.4% (2006-2010 5-year est.).
Housing: Homeownership rate: 88.1% (2010); Median home value: $113,000 (2006-2010 5-year est.); Median contract rent: $348 per month (2006-2010 5-year est.); Median year structure built: 1976 (2006-2010 5-year est.).
Transportation: Commute to work: 95.6% car, 0.8% public transportation, 0.0% walk, 3.0% work from home (2006-2010 5-year est.); Travel time to work: 25.6% less than 15 minutes, 47.8% 15 to 30 minutes, 14.4% 30 to 45 minutes, 6.0% 45 to 60 minutes, 6.2% 60 minutes or more (2006-2010 5-year est.)
Additional Information Contacts
Greater Wyalusing Chamber of Commerce . . . . (570) 746-4922
　　http://www.wyalusing.net

ATHENS (borough). Covers a land area of 1.797 square miles and a water area of 0.028 square miles. Located at 41.93° N. Lat; 76.52° W. Long. Elevation is 764 feet.
Population: 3,468 (1990); 3,415 (2000); 3,367 (2010); Density: 1,874.0 persons per square mile (2010); Race: 97.1% White, 0.9% Black, 0.5% Asian, 0.1% American Indian/Alaska Native, 0.0% Native Hawaiian/Other Pacific Islander, 1.4% Other, 1.4% Hispanic of any race (2010); Average household size: 2.28 (2010); Median age: 41.4 (2010); Males per 100 females: 83.2 (2010); Marriage status: 34.2% never married, 39.0% now married, 14.8% widowed, 12.0% divorced (2006-2010 5-year est.); Foreign born: 0.0% (2006-2010 5-year est.); Ancestry (includes multiple ancestries): 21.6% Irish, 16.8% Italian, 15.5% German, 15.1% English, 4.3% Dutch (2006-2010 5-year est.).
Economy: Single-family building permits issued: 1 (2011); Multi-family building permits issued: 0 (2011); Employment by occupation: 7.5% management, 1.6% professional, 10.5% services, 15.4% sales, 4.1% farming, 6.3% construction, 6.3% production (2006-2010 5-year est.).
Income: Per capita income: $19,453 (2006-2010 5-year est.); Median household income: $31,146 (2006-2010 5-year est.); Average household income: $48,842 (2006-2010 5-year est.); Percent of households with income of $100,000 or more: 8.2% (2006-2010 5-year est.); Poverty rate: 14.5% (2006-2010 5-year est.).
Education: Percent of population age 25 and over with: High school diploma (including GED) or higher: 79.8% (2006-2010 5-year est.); Bachelor's degree or higher: 16.9% (2006-2010 5-year est.); Master's degree or higher: 5.3% (2006-2010 5-year est.).
School District(s)
Athens Area SD (KG-12)
　　2010-11 Enrollment: 2,271 . . . . (570) 888-7766
Housing: Homeownership rate: 58.1% (2010); Median home value: $84,200 (2006-2010 5-year est.); Median contract rent: $363 per month (2006-2010 5-year est.); Median year structure built: before 1940 (2006-2010 5-year est.).
Safety: Violent crime rate: 32.6 per 10,000 population; Property crime rate: 245.7 per 10,000 population (2011).
Transportation: Commute to work: 76.6% car, 3.7% public transportation, 8.8% walk, 7.8% work from home (2006-2010 5-year est.); Travel time to work: 62.7% less than 15 minutes, 15.7% 15 to 30 minutes, 12.8% 30 to 45 minutes, 4.9% 45 to 60 minutes, 4.0% 60 minutes or more (2006-2010 5-year est.)
Additional Information Contacts
Greater Wyalusing Chamber of Commerce . . . . (570) 746-4922
　　http://www.wyalusing.net

ATHENS (township). Covers a land area of 43.576 square miles and a water area of 1.445 square miles. Located at 41.96° N. Lat; 76.56° W. Long. Elevation is 764 feet.

History: Yioga Point Museum. Originally the site of a Native American village. Settled c.1778, incorporated 1831.

Population: 4,755 (1990); 5,058 (2000); 5,251 (2010); Density: 120.5 persons per square mile (2010); Race: 96.3% White, 0.3% Black, 1.8% Asian, 0.2% American Indian/Alaska Native, 0.0% Native Hawaiian/Other Pacific Islander, 1.4% Other, 1.0% Hispanic of any race (2010); Average household size: 2.41 (2010); Median age: 45.7 (2010); Males per 100 females: 97.0 (2010); Marriage status: 22.6% never married, 57.1% now married, 6.3% widowed, 14.0% divorced (2006-2010 5-year est.); Foreign born: 2.8% (2006-2010 5-year est.); Ancestry (includes multiple ancestries): 21.5% German, 17.2% English, 14.5% Irish, 7.4% Italian, 4.4% French (2006-2010 5-year est.).

Economy: Single-family building permits issued: 3 (2011); Multi-family building permits issued: 0 (2011); Employment by occupation: 9.2% management, 5.3% professional, 13.6% services, 14.8% sales, 3.1% farming, 7.1% construction, 8.4% production (2006-2010 5-year est.).

Income: Per capita income: $24,244 (2006-2010 5-year est.); Median household income: $43,494 (2006-2010 5-year est.); Average household income: $59,113 (2006-2010 5-year est.); Percent of households with income of $100,000 or more: 14.7% (2006-2010 5-year est.); Poverty rate: 14.3% (2006-2010 5-year est.).

Education: Percent of population age 25 and over with: High school diploma (including GED) or higher: 88.3% (2006-2010 5-year est.); Bachelor's degree or higher: 20.9% (2006-2010 5-year est.); Master's degree or higher: 8.9% (2006-2010 5-year est.).

Housing: Homeownership rate: 82.4% (2010); Median home value: $106,000 (2006-2010 5-year est.); Median contract rent: $481 per month (2006-2010 5-year est.); Median year structure built: 1974 (2006-2010 5-year est.).

Transportation: Commute to work: 93.1% car, 0.0% public transportation, 3.4% walk, 2.5% work from home (2006-2010 5-year est.); Travel time to work: 55.5% less than 15 minutes, 26.3% 15 to 30 minutes, 10.0% 30 to 45 minutes, 3.9% 45 to 60 minutes, 4.3% 60 minutes or more (2006-2010 5-year est.)

Additional Information Contacts

Athens Township..................................... (570) 888-2325
   http://www.athenstownship.org
Greater Wyalusing Chamber of Commerce .... (570) 746-4922
   http://www.wyalusing.net

BURLINGTON (borough). Covers a land area of 0.585 square miles and a water area of 0.014 square miles. Located at 41.78° N. Lat; 76.61° W. Long. Elevation is 892 feet.

Population: 479 (1990); 182 (2000); 156 (2010); Density: 266.7 persons per square mile (2010); Race: 97.4% White, 0.0% Black, 0.0% Asian, 0.0% American Indian/Alaska Native, 0.0% Native Hawaiian/Other Pacific Islander, 2.6% Other, 1.3% Hispanic of any race (2010); Average household size: 2.48 (2010); Median age: 39.0 (2010); Males per 100 females: 105.3 (2010); Marriage status: 25.9% never married, 57.4% now married, 1.2% widowed, 15.4% divorced (2006-2010 5-year est.); Foreign born: 0.0% (2006-2010 5-year est.); Ancestry (includes multiple ancestries): 32.9% German, 11.0% Irish, 7.6% English, 3.8% Welsh, 3.3% Scottish (2006-2010 5-year est.).

Economy: Single-family building permits issued: 0 (2011); Multi-family building permits issued: 0 (2011); Employment by occupation: 2.5% management, 6.7% professional, 5.0% services, 10.1% sales, 11.8% farming, 11.8% construction, 12.6% production (2006-2010 5-year est.).

Income: Per capita income: $23,578 (2006-2010 5-year est.); Median household income: $47,813 (2006-2010 5-year est.); Average household income: $56,918 (2006-2010 5-year est.); Percent of households with income of $100,000 or more: 3.4% (2006-2010 5-year est.); Poverty rate: 2.9% (2006-2010 5-year est.).

Education: Percent of population age 25 and over with: High school diploma (including GED) or higher: 77.4% (2006-2010 5-year est.); Bachelor's degree or higher: 2.2% (2006-2010 5-year est.); Master's degree or higher: 0.0% (2006-2010 5-year est.).

Housing: Homeownership rate: 68.3% (2010); Median home value: $76,900 (2006-2010 5-year est.); Median contract rent: $367 per month (2006-2010 5-year est.); Median year structure built: before 1940 (2006-2010 5-year est.).

Transportation: Commute to work: 85.7% car, 2.5% public transportation, 0.0% walk, 8.4% work from home (2006-2010 5-year est.); Travel time to work: 37.6% less than 15 minutes, 31.2% 15 to 30 minutes, 12.8% 30 to 45 minutes, 0.0% 45 to 60 minutes, 18.3% 60 minutes or more (2006-2010 5-year est.)

BURLINGTON (township). Covers a land area of 25.068 square miles and a water area of 0.213 square miles. Located at 41.76° N. Lat; 76.57° W. Long. Elevation is 892 feet.

Population: 705 (1990); 799 (2000); 791 (2010); Density: 31.6 persons per square mile (2010); Race: 96.3% White, 1.0% Black, 0.3% Asian, 0.0% American Indian/Alaska Native, 0.0% Native Hawaiian/Other Pacific Islander, 2.4% Other, 1.0% Hispanic of any race (2010); Average household size: 2.58 (2010); Median age: 45.2 (2010); Males per 100 females: 108.2 (2010); Marriage status: 25.3% never married, 58.1% now married, 6.6% widowed, 10.0% divorced (2006-2010 5-year est.); Foreign born: 0.0% (2006-2010 5-year est.); Ancestry (includes multiple ancestries): 18.1% German, 14.3% English, 14.1% Irish, 12.9% American, 5.9% Polish (2006-2010 5-year est.).

Economy: Single-family building permits issued: 4 (2011); Multi-family building permits issued: 0 (2011); Employment by occupation: 5.4% management, 1.3% professional, 14.8% services, 13.8% sales, 5.4% farming, 12.5% construction, 12.0% production (2006-2010 5-year est.).

Income: Per capita income: $19,432 (2006-2010 5-year est.); Median household income: $49,750 (2006-2010 5-year est.); Average household income: $49,634 (2006-2010 5-year est.); Percent of households with income of $100,000 or more: 3.3% (2006-2010 5-year est.); Poverty rate: 5.5% (2006-2010 5-year est.).

Education: Percent of population age 25 and over with: High school diploma (including GED) or higher: 88.2% (2006-2010 5-year est.); Bachelor's degree or higher: 12.0% (2006-2010 5-year est.); Master's degree or higher: 3.1% (2006-2010 5-year est.).

Housing: Homeownership rate: 84.0% (2010); Median home value: $112,100 (2006-2010 5-year est.); Median contract rent: $409 per month (2006-2010 5-year est.); Median year structure built: 1971 (2006-2010 5-year est.).

Transportation: Commute to work: 87.8% car, 0.0% public transportation, 5.3% walk, 5.0% work from home (2006-2010 5-year est.); Travel time to work: 22.1% less than 15 minutes, 40.8% 15 to 30 minutes, 14.0% 30 to 45 minutes, 1.1% 45 to 60 minutes, 22.1% 60 minutes or more (2006-2010 5-year est.)

CANTON (borough). Covers a land area of 1.149 square miles and a water area of 0.005 square miles. Located at 41.66° N. Lat; 76.85° W. Long. Elevation is 1,227 feet.

Population: 1,822 (1990); 1,807 (2000); 1,976 (2010); Density: 1,719.7 persons per square mile (2010); Race: 97.4% White, 0.1% Black, 0.1% Asian, 0.3% American Indian/Alaska Native, 0.0% Native Hawaiian/Other Pacific Islander, 2.1% Other, 1.4% Hispanic of any race (2010); Average household size: 2.31 (2010); Median age: 40.4 (2010); Males per 100 females: 87.1 (2010); Marriage status: 29.1% never married, 41.0% now married, 13.3% widowed, 16.6% divorced (2006-2010 5-year est.); Foreign born: 0.5% (2006-2010 5-year est.); Ancestry (includes multiple ancestries): 22.1% German, 19.8% Irish, 14.1% English, 11.2% American, 5.7% Polish (2006-2010 5-year est.).

Economy: Single-family building permits issued: 1 (2011); Multi-family building permits issued: 0 (2011); Employment by occupation: 6.7% management, 2.1% professional, 13.7% services, 13.7% sales, 0.0% farming, 14.3% construction, 11.1% production (2006-2010 5-year est.).

Income: Per capita income: $16,824 (2006-2010 5-year est.); Median household income: $28,382 (2006-2010 5-year est.); Average household income: $37,152 (2006-2010 5-year est.); Percent of households with income of $100,000 or more: 2.7% (2006-2010 5-year est.); Poverty rate: 29.7% (2006-2010 5-year est.).

Education: Percent of population age 25 and over with: High school diploma (including GED) or higher: 77.4% (2006-2010 5-year est.); Bachelor's degree or higher: 14.2% (2006-2010 5-year est.); Master's degree or higher: 4.3% (2006-2010 5-year est.).

School District(s)

Canton Area SD (KG-12)
   2010-11 Enrollment: 1,024 .... (570) 673-3191

Housing: Homeownership rate: 49.2% (2010); Median home value: $82,000 (2006-2010 5-year est.); Median contract rent: $327 per month (2006-2010 5-year est.); Median year structure built: before 1940 (2006-2010 5-year est.).

Safety: Violent crime rate: 15.1 per 10,000 population; Property crime rate: 171.5 per 10,000 population (2011).

Newspapers: Independent-Sentinel (Local news; Circulation 2,000)
Transportation: Commute to work: 88.4% car, 1.2% public transportation, 5.6% walk, 4.4% work from home (2006-2010 5-year est.); Travel time to work: 42.7% less than 15 minutes, 18.1% 15 to 30 minutes, 14.9% 30 to 45 minutes, 15.1% 45 to 60 minutes, 9.1% 60 minutes or more (2006-2010 5-year est.)
Additional Information Contacts
Canton Area Chamber of Commerce . . . . (570) 364-2600
  http://cantonareachamberofcommerce.com

CANTON (township). Covers a land area of 37.143 square miles and a water area of 0.160 square miles. Located at 41.65° N. Lat; 76.83° W. Long. Elevation is 1,227 feet.
History: Settled c.1796, incorporated 1864.
Population: 2,243 (1990); 2,084 (2000); 2,143 (2010); Density: 57.7 persons per square mile (2010); Race: 98.7% White, 0.7% Black, 0.1% Asian, 0.0% American Indian/Alaska Native, 0.0% Native Hawaiian/Other Pacific Islander, 0.5% Other, 0.2% Hispanic of any race (2010); Average household size: 2.73 (2010); Median age: 41.0 (2010); Males per 100 females: 102.9 (2010); Marriage status: 20.3% never married, 62.2% now married, 4.5% widowed, 13.0% divorced (2006-2010 5-year est.); Foreign born: 0.3% (2006-2010 5-year est.); Ancestry (includes multiple ancestries): 26.3% German, 12.3% Irish, 10.8% English, 7.1% American, 5.9% Dutch (2006-2010 5-year est.).
Economy: Single-family building permits issued: 8 (2011); Multi-family building permits issued: 0 (2011); Employment by occupation: 9.8% management, 2.0% professional, 13.7% services, 13.4% sales, 3.2% farming, 17.5% construction, 12.9% production (2006-2010 5-year est.).
Income: Per capita income: $16,727 (2006-2010 5-year est.); Median household income: $38,472 (2006-2010 5-year est.); Average household income: $45,012 (2006-2010 5-year est.); Percent of households with income of $100,000 or more: 5.2% (2006-2010 5-year est.); Poverty rate: 10.1% (2006-2010 5-year est.).
Education: Percent of population age 25 and over with: High school diploma (including GED) or higher: 86.1% (2006-2010 5-year est.); Bachelor's degree or higher: 6.0% (2006-2010 5-year est.); Master's degree or higher: 2.5% (2006-2010 5-year est.).
Housing: Homeownership rate: 79.9% (2010); Median home value: $94,900 (2006-2010 5-year est.); Median contract rent: $409 per month (2006-2010 5-year est.); Median year structure built: 1971 (2006-2010 5-year est.).
Newspapers: Independent-Sentinel (Local news; Circulation 2,000)
Transportation: Commute to work: 81.5% car, 0.0% public transportation, 5.7% walk, 10.3% work from home (2006-2010 5-year est.); Travel time to work: 48.3% less than 15 minutes, 20.0% 15 to 30 minutes, 13.8% 30 to 45 minutes, 8.9% 45 to 60 minutes, 8.9% 60 minutes or more (2006-2010 5-year est.)
Additional Information Contacts
Canton Area Chamber of Commerce . . . . (570) 364-2600
  http://cantonareachamberofcommerce.com

COLUMBIA (township). Covers a land area of 40.863 square miles and a water area of 0.085 square miles. Located at 41.85° N. Lat; 76.86° W. Long.
Population: 1,077 (1990); 1,162 (2000); 1,196 (2010); Density: 29.3 persons per square mile (2010); Race: 96.1% White, 1.5% Black, 0.3% Asian, 0.3% American Indian/Alaska Native, 0.1% Native Hawaiian/Other Pacific Islander, 1.7% Other, 1.0% Hispanic of any race (2010); Average household size: 2.66 (2010); Median age: 42.1 (2010); Males per 100 females: 98.3 (2010); Marriage status: 25.6% never married, 59.8% now married, 6.4% widowed, 8.2% divorced (2006-2010 5-year est.); Foreign born: 0.2% (2006-2010 5-year est.); Ancestry (includes multiple ancestries): 21.5% German, 14.6% English, 11.9% American, 11.6% Irish, 6.7% Italian (2006-2010 5-year est.).
Economy: Single-family building permits issued: 1 (2011); Multi-family building permits issued: 0 (2011); Employment by occupation: 12.3% management, 4.0% professional, 15.8% services, 13.8% sales, 2.0% farming, 10.5% construction, 12.9% production (2006-2010 5-year est.).
Income: Per capita income: $16,557 (2006-2010 5-year est.); Median household income: $35,956 (2006-2010 5-year est.); Average household income: $45,400 (2006-2010 5-year est.); Percent of households with income of $100,000 or more: 8.9% (2006-2010 5-year est.); Poverty rate: 23.6% (2006-2010 5-year est.).
Education: Percent of population age 25 and over with: High school diploma (including GED) or higher: 87.2% (2006-2010 5-year est.);

Bachelor's degree or higher: 11.5% (2006-2010 5-year est.); Master's degree or higher: 5.5% (2006-2010 5-year est.).
Housing: Homeownership rate: 77.3% (2010); Median home value: $89,900 (2006-2010 5-year est.); Median contract rent: $403 per month (2006-2010 5-year est.); Median year structure built: 1965 (2006-2010 5-year est.).
Transportation: Commute to work: 87.6% car, 0.4% public transportation, 1.9% walk, 9.6% work from home (2006-2010 5-year est.); Travel time to work: 32.6% less than 15 minutes, 30.1% 15 to 30 minutes, 20.6% 30 to 45 minutes, 6.7% 45 to 60 minutes, 10.0% 60 minutes or more (2006-2010 5-year est.)
Additional Information Contacts
Mansfield Chamber of Commerce, Inc. . . . . (570) 662-3442
  http://www.mansfield.org

COLUMBIA CROSS ROADS (unincorporated postal area)
Zip Code: 16914
  Covers a land area of 75.627 square miles and a water area of 0.373 square miles. Located at 41.85° N. Lat; 76.78° W. Long. Population: 2,347 (2010); Density: 31.0 persons per square mile (2010); Race: 96.9% White, 0.8% Black, 0.2% Asian, 0.2% American Indian/Alaska Native, 0.0% Native Hawaiian/Other Pacific Islander, 1.9% Other, 1.2% Hispanic of any race (2010); Average household size: 2.67 (2010); Median age: 42.0 (2010); Males per 100 females: 97.2 (2010); Homeownership rate: 82.0% (2010)

EAST SMITHFIELD (unincorporated postal area)
Zip Code: 18817
  Covers a land area of 1.841 square miles and a water area of 0.005 square miles. Located at 41.87° N. Lat; 76.63° W. Long. Elevation is 1,293 feet. Population: 306 (2010); Density: 166.2 persons per square mile (2010); Race: 98.4% White, 0.3% Black, 0.7% Asian, 0.0% American Indian/Alaska Native, 0.0% Native Hawaiian/Other Pacific Islander, 0.6% Other, 0.0% Hispanic of any race (2010); Average household size: 2.59 (2010); Median age: 42.0 (2010); Males per 100 females: 106.8 (2010); Homeownership rate: 78.0% (2010)

FRANKLIN (township). Covers a land area of 33.406 square miles and a water area of 0.309 square miles. Located at 41.68° N. Lat; 76.57° W. Long.
Population: 557 (1990); 698 (2000); 723 (2010); Density: 21.6 persons per square mile (2010); Race: 99.4% White, 0.1% Black, 0.0% Asian, 0.0% American Indian/Alaska Native, 0.0% Native Hawaiian/Other Pacific Islander, 0.5% Other, 0.0% Hispanic of any race (2010); Average household size: 2.66 (2010); Median age: 40.2 (2010); Males per 100 females: 104.2 (2010); Marriage status: 36.0% never married, 42.1% now married, 7.3% widowed, 14.6% divorced (2006-2010 5-year est.); Foreign born: 0.0% (2006-2010 5-year est.); Ancestry (includes multiple ancestries): 19.7% German, 16.0% Dutch, 14.3% Irish, 6.3% English, 3.0% Polish (2006-2010 5-year est.).
Economy: Single-family building permits issued: 1 (2011); Multi-family building permits issued: 0 (2011); Employment by occupation: 6.7% management, 0.0% professional, 5.8% services, 17.9% sales, 1.6% farming, 19.9% construction, 14.4% production (2006-2010 5-year est.).
Income: Per capita income: $14,819 (2006-2010 5-year est.); Median household income: $32,500 (2006-2010 5-year est.); Average household income: $39,042 (2006-2010 5-year est.); Percent of households with income of $100,000 or more: 4.4% (2006-2010 5-year est.); Poverty rate: 24.5% (2006-2010 5-year est.).
Education: Percent of population age 25 and over with: High school diploma (including GED) or higher: 78.5% (2006-2010 5-year est.); Bachelor's degree or higher: 0.7% (2006-2010 5-year est.); Master's degree or higher: 0.7% (2006-2010 5-year est.).
Housing: Homeownership rate: 76.8% (2010); Median home value: $118,200 (2006-2010 5-year est.); Median contract rent: $335 per month (2006-2010 5-year est.); Median year structure built: 1984 (2006-2010 5-year est.).
Transportation: Commute to work: 84.9% car, 0.0% public transportation, 5.8% walk, 7.1% work from home (2006-2010 5-year est.); Travel time to work: 21.4% less than 15 minutes, 42.4% 15 to 30 minutes, 21.7% 30 to 45 minutes, 10.7% 45 to 60 minutes, 3.8% 60 minutes or more (2006-2010 5-year est.)

GILLETT (unincorporated postal area)
Zip Code: 16925

Covers a land area of 77.150 square miles and a water area of 0.235 square miles. Located at 41.94° N. Lat; 76.78° W. Long. Population: 3,186 (2010); Density: 41.3 persons per square mile (2010); Race: 97.8% White, 0.4% Black, 0.1% Asian, 0.5% American Indian/Alaska Native, 0.0% Native Hawaiian/Other Pacific Islander, 1.2% Other, 1.1% Hispanic of any race (2010); Average household size: 2.55 (2010); Median age: 44.5 (2010); Males per 100 females: 104.4 (2010); Homeownership rate: 84.0% (2010)

GRANVILLE (township). Covers a land area of 24.641 square miles and a water area of 0.055 square miles. Located at 41.71° N. Lat; 76.71° W. Long.
Population: 837 (1990); 873 (2000); 950 (2010); Density: 38.6 persons per square mile (2010); Race: 98.9% White, 0.3% Black, 0.1% Asian, 0.1% American Indian/Alaska Native, 0.0% Native Hawaiian/Other Pacific Islander, 0.6% Other, 0.2% Hispanic of any race (2010); Average household size: 2.72 (2010); Median age: 40.7 (2010); Males per 100 females: 101.3 (2010); Marriage status: 20.5% never married, 63.4% now married, 9.3% widowed, 6.7% divorced (2006-2010 5-year est.); Foreign born: 0.8% (2006-2010 5-year est.); Ancestry (includes multiple ancestries): 19.3% American, 14.1% German, 11.5% Irish, 11.5% English, 6.6% Italian (2006-2010 5-year est.).
Economy: Single-family building permits issued: 1 (2011); Multi-family building permits issued: 0 (2011); Employment by occupation: 12.5% management, 0.0% professional, 6.8% services, 20.6% sales, 1.3% farming, 11.4% construction, 2.4% production (2006-2010 5-year est.).
Income: Per capita income: $19,842 (2006-2010 5-year est.); Median household income: $45,000 (2006-2010 5-year est.); Average household income: $54,901 (2006-2010 5-year est.); Percent of households with income of $100,000 or more: 7.7% (2006-2010 5-year est.); Poverty rate: 15.0% (2006-2010 5-year est.).
Education: Percent of population age 25 and over with: High school diploma (including GED) or higher: 83.9% (2006-2010 5-year est.); Bachelor's degree or higher: 15.2% (2006-2010 5-year est.); Master's degree or higher: 7.6% (2006-2010 5-year est.).
Housing: Homeownership rate: 80.2% (2010); Median home value: $111,100 (2006-2010 5-year est.); Median contract rent: $325 per month (2006-2010 5-year est.); Median year structure built: 1967 (2006-2010 5-year est.).
Transportation: Commute to work: 89.4% car, 0.0% public transportation, 1.6% walk, 7.9% work from home (2006-2010 5-year est.); Travel time to work: 28.3% less than 15 minutes, 42.4% 15 to 30 minutes, 6.1% 30 to 45 minutes, 8.0% 45 to 60 minutes, 15.1% 60 minutes or more (2006-2010 5-year est.)

GRANVILLE SUMMIT (unincorporated postal area)
Zip Code: 16926
Covers a land area of 24.228 square miles and a water area of 0.081 square miles. Located at 41.72° N. Lat; 76.70° W. Long. Population: 872 (2010); Density: 36.0 persons per square mile (2010); Race: 99.1% White, 0.3% Black, 0.0% Asian, 0.1% American Indian/Alaska Native, 0.0% Native Hawaiian/Other Pacific Islander, 0.5% Other, 0.3% Hispanic of any race (2010); Average household size: 2.79 (2010); Median age: 39.5 (2010); Males per 100 females: 99.1 (2010); Homeownership rate: 81.8% (2010)

GREENS LANDING (CDP). Covers a land area of 2.678 square miles and a water area of 0.061 square miles. Located at 41.94° N. Lat; 76.55° W. Long.
Population: n/a (1990); n/a (2000); 894 (2010); Density: 333.8 persons per square mile (2010); Race: 94.7% White, 0.0% Black, 2.0% Asian, 0.3% American Indian/Alaska Native, 0.0% Native Hawaiian/Other Pacific Islander, 3.0% Other, 1.5% Hispanic of any race (2010); Average household size: 2.72 (2010); Median age: 36.5 (2010); Males per 100 females: 98.2 (2010); Marriage status: 9.8% never married, 51.3% now married, 18.9% widowed, 20.0% divorced (2006-2010 5-year est.); Foreign born: 9.1% (2006-2010 5-year est.); Ancestry (includes multiple ancestries): 14.3% English, 13.6% Dutch, 11.8% American, 10.9% Italian, 10.8% German (2006-2010 5-year est.).
Economy: Employment by occupation: 18.2% management, 0.0% professional, 3.6% services, 13.1% sales, 0.0% farming, 18.6% construction, 23.7% production (2006-2010 5-year est.).
Income: Per capita income: $21,676 (2006-2010 5-year est.); Median household income: $39,038 (2006-2010 5-year est.); Average household income: $51,680 (2006-2010 5-year est.); Percent of households with

income of $100,000 or more: 11.4% (2006-2010 5-year est.); Poverty rate: 0.0% (2006-2010 5-year est.).
Education: Percent of population age 25 and over with: High school diploma (including GED) or higher: 80.6% (2006-2010 5-year est.); Bachelor's degree or higher: 14.8% (2006-2010 5-year est.); Master's degree or higher: 13.2% (2006-2010 5-year est.).
Housing: Homeownership rate: 77.5% (2010); Median home value: $65,300 (2006-2010 5-year est.); Median contract rent: $426 per month (2006-2010 5-year est.); Median year structure built: 1978 (2006-2010 5-year est.).
Transportation: Commute to work: 75.9% car, 0.0% public transportation, 24.1% walk, 0.0% work from home (2006-2010 5-year est.); Travel time to work: 55.5% less than 15 minutes, 37.6% 15 to 30 minutes, 0.0% 30 to 45 minutes, 2.6% 45 to 60 minutes, 4.4% 60 minutes or more (2006-2010 5-year est.)

HERRICK (township). Covers a land area of 22.481 square miles and a water area of 0.212 square miles. Located at 41.79° N. Lat; 76.25° W. Long.
Population: 647 (1990); 676 (2000); 754 (2010); Density: 33.5 persons per square mile (2010); Race: 98.7% White, 0.5% Black, 0.1% Asian, 0.0% American Indian/Alaska Native, 0.0% Native Hawaiian/Other Pacific Islander, 0.7% Other, 1.5% Hispanic of any race (2010); Average household size: 2.65 (2010); Median age: 40.3 (2010); Males per 100 females: 101.6 (2010); Marriage status: 22.0% never married, 59.9% now married, 5.9% widowed, 12.2% divorced (2006-2010 5-year est.); Foreign born: 1.1% (2006-2010 5-year est.); Ancestry (includes multiple ancestries): 33.0% German, 23.7% English, 15.1% Irish, 9.4% American, 9.0% Italian (2006-2010 5-year est.).
Economy: Single-family building permits issued: 2 (2011); Multi-family building permits issued: 0 (2011); Employment by occupation: 8.6% management, 3.8% professional, 8.1% services, 24.1% sales, 4.6% farming, 11.6% construction, 8.1% production (2006-2010 5-year est.).
Income: Per capita income: $23,177 (2006-2010 5-year est.); Median household income: $47,083 (2006-2010 5-year est.); Average household income: $60,867 (2006-2010 5-year est.); Percent of households with income of $100,000 or more: 10.8% (2006-2010 5-year est.); Poverty rate: 12.4% (2006-2010 5-year est.).
Education: Percent of population age 25 and over with: High school diploma (including GED) or higher: 90.1% (2006-2010 5-year est.); Bachelor's degree or higher: 15.5% (2006-2010 5-year est.); Master's degree or higher: 2.2% (2006-2010 5-year est.).
Housing: Homeownership rate: 85.2% (2010); Median home value: $145,800 (2006-2010 5-year est.); Median contract rent: $359 per month (2006-2010 5-year est.); Median year structure built: 1956 (2006-2010 5-year est.).
Transportation: Commute to work: 85.7% car, 1.1% public transportation, 5.7% walk, 5.9% work from home (2006-2010 5-year est.); Travel time to work: 18.7% less than 15 minutes, 39.7% 15 to 30 minutes, 30.5% 30 to 45 minutes, 6.0% 45 to 60 minutes, 5.2% 60 minutes or more (2006-2010 5-year est.)

LE RAYSVILLE (borough). Covers a land area of 1.042 square miles and a water area of 0.003 square miles. Located at 41.84° N. Lat; 76.17° W. Long. Elevation is 1,394 feet.
Population: 336 (1990); 318 (2000); 290 (2010); Density: 278.3 persons per square mile (2010); Race: 99.3% White, 0.0% Black, 0.0% Asian, 0.0% American Indian/Alaska Native, 0.0% Native Hawaiian/Other Pacific Islander, 0.7% Other, 0.0% Hispanic of any race (2010); Average household size: 2.59 (2010); Median age: 33.0 (2010); Males per 100 females: 95.9 (2010); Marriage status: 18.1% never married, 61.5% now married, 2.7% widowed, 17.7% divorced (2006-2010 5-year est.); Foreign born: 1.0% (2006-2010 5-year est.); Ancestry (includes multiple ancestries): 23.3% German, 15.8% English, 11.3% Irish, 5.5% American, 4.8% Italian (2006-2010 5-year est.).
Economy: Single-family building permits issued: 0 (2011); Multi-family building permits issued: 0 (2011); Employment by occupation: 8.8% management, 5.6% professional, 13.6% services, 12.8% sales, 0.0% farming, 11.2% construction, 14.4% production (2006-2010 5-year est.).
Income: Per capita income: $17,279 (2006-2010 5-year est.); Median household income: $36,875 (2006-2010 5-year est.); Average household income: $41,787 (2006-2010 5-year est.); Percent of households with income of $100,000 or more: 6.6% (2006-2010 5-year est.); Poverty rate: 4.5% (2006-2010 5-year est.).

Education: Percent of population age 25 and over with: High school diploma (including GED) or higher: 89.5% (2006-2010 5-year est.); Bachelor's degree or higher: 13.1% (2006-2010 5-year est.); Master's degree or higher: 5.8% (2006-2010 5-year est.).

Housing: Homeownership rate: 78.6% (2010); Median home value: $85,500 (2006-2010 5-year est.); Median contract rent: $438 per month (2006-2010 5-year est.); Median year structure built: before 1940 (2006-2010 5-year est.).

Transportation: Commute to work: 93.6% car, 0.0% public transportation, 1.6% walk, 2.4% work from home (2006-2010 5-year est.); Travel time to work: 21.3% less than 15 minutes, 30.3% 15 to 30 minutes, 26.2% 30 to 45 minutes, 14.8% 45 to 60 minutes, 7.4% 60 minutes or more (2006-2010 5-year est.)

LEROY (township). Covers a land area of 44.246 square miles and a water area of 0.301 square miles. Located at 41.65° N. Lat; 76.72° W. Long. Elevation is 1,024 feet.

Population: 610 (1990); 627 (2000); 718 (2010); Density: 16.2 persons per square mile (2010); Race: 98.5% White, 0.4% Black, 0.0% Asian, 0.0% American Indian/Alaska Native, 0.0% Native Hawaiian/Other Pacific Islander, 1.1% Other, 0.7% Hispanic of any race (2010); Average household size: 2.69 (2010); Median age: 40.1 (2010); Males per 100 females: 105.1 (2010); Marriage status: 18.7% never married, 71.2% now married, 6.0% widowed, 4.0% divorced (2006-2010 5-year est.); Foreign born: 0.6% (2006-2010 5-year est.); Ancestry (includes multiple ancestries): 17.9% German, 16.5% English, 11.9% American, 9.0% Irish, 7.2% Italian (2006-2010 5-year est.).

Economy: Single-family building permits issued: 1 (2011); Multi-family building permits issued: 0 (2011); Employment by occupation: 8.1% management, 0.0% professional, 12.9% services, 20.7% sales, 3.7% farming, 17.0% construction, 12.2% production (2006-2010 5-year est.).

Income: Per capita income: $15,395 (2006-2010 5-year est.); Median household income: $37,917 (2006-2010 5-year est.); Average household income: $42,667 (2006-2010 5-year est.); Percent of households with income of $100,000 or more: 3.4% (2006-2010 5-year est.); Poverty rate: 16.8% (2006-2010 5-year est.).

Education: Percent of population age 25 and over with: High school diploma (including GED) or higher: 93.4% (2006-2010 5-year est.); Bachelor's degree or higher: 6.9% (2006-2010 5-year est.); Master's degree or higher: 1.4% (2006-2010 5-year est.).

Housing: Homeownership rate: 80.6% (2010); Median home value: $87,300 (2006-2010 5-year est.); Median contract rent: $404 per month (2006-2010 5-year est.); Median year structure built: 1971 (2006-2010 5-year est.).

Transportation: Commute to work: 81.8% car, 0.0% public transportation, 5.6% walk, 10.0% work from home (2006-2010 5-year est.); Travel time to work: 31.8% less than 15 minutes, 34.3% 15 to 30 minutes, 16.9% 30 to 45 minutes, 7.4% 45 to 60 minutes, 9.5% 60 minutes or more (2006-2010 5-year est.)

LITCHFIELD (township). Covers a land area of 30.166 square miles and a water area of 0.234 square miles. Located at 41.96° N. Lat; 76.44° W. Long. Elevation is 1,526 feet.

Population: 1,296 (1990); 1,307 (2000); 1,320 (2010); Density: 43.8 persons per square mile (2010); Race: 96.8% White, 0.8% Black, 0.2% Asian, 0.3% American Indian/Alaska Native, 0.0% Native Hawaiian/Other Pacific Islander, 1.9% Other, 1.4% Hispanic of any race (2010); Average household size: 2.55 (2010); Median age: 45.5 (2010); Males per 100 females: 106.6 (2010); Marriage status: 24.1% never married, 59.5% now married, 5.4% widowed, 11.0% divorced (2006-2010 5-year est.); Foreign born: 1.0% (2006-2010 5-year est.); Ancestry (includes multiple ancestries): 26.4% German, 21.2% Irish, 12.2% English, 11.8% American, 10.9% Italian (2006-2010 5-year est.).

Economy: Single-family building permits issued: 2 (2011); Multi-family building permits issued: 0 (2011); Employment by occupation: 7.0% management, 0.7% professional, 8.3% services, 17.3% sales, 6.3% farming, 11.7% construction, 5.9% production (2006-2010 5-year est.).

Income: Per capita income: $22,201 (2006-2010 5-year est.); Median household income: $47,500 (2006-2010 5-year est.); Average household income: $56,115 (2006-2010 5-year est.); Percent of households with income of $100,000 or more: 13.1% (2006-2010 5-year est.); Poverty rate: 8.5% (2006-2010 5-year est.).

Education: Percent of population age 25 and over with: High school diploma (including GED) or higher: 89.2% (2006-2010 5-year est.);

Bachelor's degree or higher: 16.8% (2006-2010 5-year est.); Master's degree or higher: 5.5% (2006-2010 5-year est.).

Housing: Homeownership rate: 88.0% (2010); Median home value: $128,900 (2006-2010 5-year est.); Median contract rent: $463 per month (2006-2010 5-year est.); Median year structure built: 1974 (2006-2010 5-year est.).

Transportation: Commute to work: 93.3% car, 0.0% public transportation, 4.5% walk, 2.2% work from home (2006-2010 5-year est.); Travel time to work: 36.0% less than 15 minutes, 36.9% 15 to 30 minutes, 20.7% 30 to 45 minutes, 2.3% 45 to 60 minutes, 4.0% 60 minutes or more (2006-2010 5-year est.)

Additional Information Contacts

Greater Wyalusing Chamber of Commerce . . . . (570) 746-4922
http://www.wyalusing.net

MILAN (unincorporated postal area)
Zip Code: 18831

Covers a land area of 29.173 square miles and a water area of 0.277 square miles. Located at 41.89° N. Lat; 76.59° W. Long. Population: 1,039 (2010); Density: 35.6 persons per square mile (2010); Race: 98.9% White, 0.1% Black, 0.1% Asian, 0.2% American Indian/Alaska Native, 0.0% Native Hawaiian/Other Pacific Islander, 0.7% Other, 1.7% Hispanic of any race (2010); Average household size: 2.34 (2010); Median age: 47.3 (2010); Males per 100 females: 98.7 (2010); Homeownership rate: 78.8% (2010)

MONROE (borough). Aka Monroeton. Covers a land area of 0.494 square miles and a water area of 0.005 square miles. Located at 41.71° N. Lat; 76.48° W. Long.

Population: 540 (1990); 514 (2000); 554 (2010); Density: 1,122.1 persons per square mile (2010); Race: 98.0% White, 0.9% Black, 0.2% Asian, 0.5% American Indian/Alaska Native, 0.0% Native Hawaiian/Other Pacific Islander, 0.4% Other, 2.2% Hispanic of any race (2010); Average household size: 2.52 (2010); Median age: 40.7 (2010); Males per 100 females: 98.6 (2010); Marriage status: 24.8% never married, 52.5% now married, 11.7% widowed, 11.0% divorced (2006-2010 5-year est.); Foreign born: 0.0% (2006-2010 5-year est.); Ancestry (includes multiple ancestries): 41.6% German, 26.7% Irish, 13.3% English, 6.9% Welsh, 6.5% Scottish (2006-2010 5-year est.).

Economy: Single-family building permits issued: 0 (2011); Multi-family building permits issued: 0 (2011); Employment by occupation: 5.9% management, 2.2% professional, 7.3% services, 10.6% sales, 1.7% farming, 7.3% construction, 6.7% production (2006-2010 5-year est.).

Income: Per capita income: $24,664 (2006-2010 5-year est.); Median household income: $53,750 (2006-2010 5-year est.); Average household income: $65,030 (2006-2010 5-year est.); Percent of households with income of $100,000 or more: 16.4% (2006-2010 5-year est.); Poverty rate: 8.7% (2006-2010 5-year est.).

Education: Percent of population age 25 and over with: High school diploma (including GED) or higher: 90.8% (2006-2010 5-year est.); Bachelor's degree or higher: 23.4% (2006-2010 5-year est.); Master's degree or higher: 5.2% (2006-2010 5-year est.).

Housing: Homeownership rate: 74.1% (2010); Median home value: $95,900 (2006-2010 5-year est.); Median contract rent: $396 per month (2006-2010 5-year est.); Median year structure built: before 1940 (2006-2010 5-year est.).

Transportation: Commute to work: 97.1% car, 0.0% public transportation, 0.9% walk, 2.1% work from home (2006-2010 5-year est.); Travel time to work: 38.4% less than 15 minutes, 44.1% 15 to 30 minutes, 8.4% 30 to 45 minutes, 7.2% 45 to 60 minutes, 1.8% 60 minutes or more (2006-2010 5-year est.)

MONROE (township). Aka Monroeton. Covers a land area of 36.515 square miles and a water area of 0.152 square miles. Located at 41.67° N. Lat; 76.49° W. Long.

Population: 1,235 (1990); 1,271 (2000); 1,250 (2010); Density: 34.2 persons per square mile (2010); Race: 98.8% White, 0.2% Black, 0.0% Asian, 0.2% American Indian/Alaska Native, 0.0% Native Hawaiian/Other Pacific Islander, 0.8% Other, 1.2% Hispanic of any race (2010); Average household size: 2.60 (2010); Median age: 43.5 (2010); Males per 100 females: 95.9 (2010); Marriage status: 24.9% never married, 52.5% now married, 8.7% widowed, 14.0% divorced (2006-2010 5-year est.); Foreign born: 0.2% (2006-2010 5-year est.); Ancestry (includes multiple ancestries): 22.4% German, 17.6% Irish, 11.5% English, 9.8% American, 7.4% Dutch (2006-2010 5-year est.).

Economy: Single-family building permits issued: 6 (2011); Multi-family building permits issued: 0 (2011); Employment by occupation: 13.5% management, 1.0% professional, 8.4% services, 14.1% sales, 5.5% farming, 19.4% construction, 24.5% production (2006-2010 5-year est.).
Income: Per capita income: $18,889 (2006-2010 5-year est.); Median household income: $44,667 (2006-2010 5-year est.); Average household income: $46,687 (2006-2010 5-year est.); Percent of households with income of $100,000 or more: 4.3% (2006-2010 5-year est.); Poverty rate: 11.7% (2006-2010 5-year est.).
Education: Percent of population age 25 and over with: High school diploma (including GED) or higher: 79.2% (2006-2010 5-year est.); Bachelor's degree or higher: 6.3% (2006-2010 5-year est.); Master's degree or higher: 0.8% (2006-2010 5-year est.).
Housing: Homeownership rate: 79.6% (2010); Median home value: $95,700 (2006-2010 5-year est.); Median contract rent: $441 per month (2006-2010 5-year est.); Median year structure built: 1957 (2006-2010 5-year est.).
Transportation: Commute to work: 92.9% car, 0.0% public transportation, 2.2% walk, 5.0% work from home (2006-2010 5-year est.); Travel time to work: 39.0% less than 15 minutes, 37.5% 15 to 30 minutes, 14.4% 30 to 45 minutes, 5.4% 45 to 60 minutes, 3.8% 60 minutes or more (2006-2010 5-year est.)
Additional Information Contacts
Central Bradford County Chamber of Commerce . . . . (570) 268-2732
  http://cbradchamber.org

MONROETON (unincorporated postal area)
Zip Code: 18832
  Covers a land area of 59.596 square miles and a water area of 0.402 square miles. Located at 41.67° N. Lat; 76.56° W. Long. Population: 1,874 (2010); Density: 31.4 persons per square mile (2010); Race: 98.8% White, 0.3% Black, 0.1% Asian, 0.2% American Indian/Alaska Native, 0.0% Native Hawaiian/Other Pacific Islander, 0.6% Other, 0.8% Hispanic of any race (2010); Average household size: 2.60 (2010); Median age: 41.2 (2010); Males per 100 females: 99.6 (2010); Homeownership rate: 77.3% (2010)

NEW ALBANY (borough). Covers a land area of 0.463 square miles and a water area of <.001 square miles. Located at 41.60° N. Lat; 76.45° W. Long. Elevation is 1,214 feet.
Population: 306 (1990); 306 (2000); 356 (2010); Density: 769.0 persons per square mile (2010); Race: 98.3% White, 0.6% Black, 0.0% Asian, 0.0% American Indian/Alaska Native, 0.0% Native Hawaiian/Other Pacific Islander, 1.1% Other, 2.8% Hispanic of any race (2010); Average household size: 2.70 (2010); Median age: 30.3 (2010); Males per 100 females: 94.5 (2010); Marriage status: 36.1% never married, 43.1% now married, 5.3% widowed, 15.5% divorced (2006-2010 5-year est.); Foreign born: 0.0% (2006-2010 5-year est.); Ancestry (includes multiple ancestries): 53.2% German, 17.3% Irish, 7.7% English, 7.7% Pennsylvania German, 7.2% Italian (2006-2010 5-year est.).
Economy: Single-family building permits issued: 0 (2011); Multi-family building permits issued: 0 (2011); Employment by occupation: 7.1% management, 1.9% professional, 11.0% services, 12.3% sales, 2.6% farming, 9.7% construction, 12.9% production (2006-2010 5-year est.).
Income: Per capita income: $16,130 (2006-2010 5-year est.); Median household income: $33,906 (2006-2010 5-year est.); Average household income: $43,966 (2006-2010 5-year est.); Percent of households with income of $100,000 or more: 6.4% (2006-2010 5-year est.); Poverty rate: 24.5% (2006-2010 5-year est.).
Education: Percent of population age 25 and over with: High school diploma (including GED) or higher: 75.3% (2006-2010 5-year est.); Bachelor's degree or higher: 6.5% (2006-2010 5-year est.); Master's degree or higher: 1.9% (2006-2010 5-year est.).
School District(s)
Wyalusing Area SD (KG-12)
  2010-11 Enrollment: 1,435 . . . . (570) 746-1605
Housing: Homeownership rate: 62.8% (2010); Median home value: $69,700 (2006-2010 5-year est.); Median contract rent: $420 per month (2006-2010 5-year est.); Median year structure built: before 1940 (2006-2010 5-year est.).
Transportation: Commute to work: 86.5% car, 0.0% public transportation, 11.0% walk, 2.6% work from home (2006-2010 5-year est.); Travel time to work: 39.1% less than 15 minutes, 30.5% 15 to 30 minutes, 18.5% 30 to 45 minutes, 0.0% 45 to 60 minutes, 11.9% 60 minutes or more (2006-2010 5-year est.)

NORTH TOWANDA (township). Covers a land area of 8.737 square miles and a water area of 0.226 square miles. Located at 41.79° N. Lat; 76.48° W. Long. Elevation is 771 feet.
Population: 909 (1990); 927 (2000); 1,132 (2010); Density: 129.6 persons per square mile (2010); Race: 98.5% White, 0.1% Black, 0.4% Asian, 0.3% American Indian/Alaska Native, 0.0% Native Hawaiian/Other Pacific Islander, 0.7% Other, 1.0% Hispanic of any race (2010); Average household size: 1.95 (2010); Median age: 55.2 (2010); Males per 100 females: 73.6 (2010); Marriage status: 20.7% never married, 55.6% now married, 12.2% widowed, 11.6% divorced (2006-2010 5-year est.); Foreign born: 0.7% (2006-2010 5-year est.); Ancestry (includes multiple ancestries): 30.5% German, 20.4% English, 14.9% Irish, 9.3% Dutch, 6.0% Polish (2006-2010 5-year est.).
Economy: Single-family building permits issued: 1 (2011); Multi-family building permits issued: 0 (2011); Employment by occupation: 8.0% management, 1.1% professional, 9.2% services, 15.7% sales, 4.2% farming, 7.7% construction, 19.9% production (2006-2010 5-year est.).
Income: Per capita income: $25,481 (2006-2010 5-year est.); Median household income: $30,573 (2006-2010 5-year est.); Average household income: $47,400 (2006-2010 5-year est.); Percent of households with income of $100,000 or more: 12.9% (2006-2010 5-year est.); Poverty rate: 18.8% (2006-2010 5-year est.).
Education: Percent of population age 25 and over with: High school diploma (including GED) or higher: 82.3% (2006-2010 5-year est.); Bachelor's degree or higher: 15.6% (2006-2010 5-year est.); Master's degree or higher: 4.3% (2006-2010 5-year est.).
Housing: Homeownership rate: 49.7% (2010); Median home value: $130,200 (2006-2010 5-year est.); Median contract rent: $293 per month (2006-2010 5-year est.); Median year structure built: 1966 (2006-2010 5-year est.).
Transportation: Commute to work: 93.0% car, 1.6% public transportation, 2.3% walk, 0.0% work from home (2006-2010 5-year est.); Travel time to work: 52.5% less than 15 minutes, 21.8% 15 to 30 minutes, 9.7% 30 to 45 minutes, 9.3% 45 to 60 minutes, 6.6% 60 minutes or more (2006-2010 5-year est.)

ORWELL (township). Covers a land area of 32.161 square miles and a water area of 0.268 square miles. Located at 41.87° N. Lat; 76.27° W. Long. Elevation is 1,496 feet.
Population: 1,107 (1990); 1,097 (2000); 1,159 (2010); Density: 36.0 persons per square mile (2010); Race: 98.5% White, 0.0% Black, 0.0% Asian, 0.0% American Indian/Alaska Native, 0.0% Native Hawaiian/Other Pacific Islander, 1.5% Other, 1.0% Hispanic of any race (2010); Average household size: 2.67 (2010); Median age: 41.6 (2010); Males per 100 females: 100.2 (2010); Marriage status: 24.9% never married, 63.2% now married, 1.9% widowed, 10.0% divorced (2006-2010 5-year est.); Foreign born: 0.6% (2006-2010 5-year est.); Ancestry (includes multiple ancestries): 22.2% English, 20.9% German, 14.9% Irish, 9.3% Polish, 6.1% American (2006-2010 5-year est.).
Economy: Single-family building permits issued: 0 (2011); Multi-family building permits issued: 0 (2011); Employment by occupation: 14.2% management, 2.7% professional, 12.6% services, 15.2% sales, 3.0% farming, 12.7% construction, 8.1% production (2006-2010 5-year est.).
Income: Per capita income: $20,354 (2006-2010 5-year est.); Median household income: $50,625 (2006-2010 5-year est.); Average household income: $59,746 (2006-2010 5-year est.); Percent of households with income of $100,000 or more: 16.9% (2006-2010 5-year est.); Poverty rate: 13.2% (2006-2010 5-year est.).
Education: Percent of population age 25 and over with: High school diploma (including GED) or higher: 84.6% (2006-2010 5-year est.); Bachelor's degree or higher: 19.0% (2006-2010 5-year est.); Master's degree or higher: 6.5% (2006-2010 5-year est.).
Housing: Homeownership rate: 85.0% (2010); Median home value: $129,300 (2006-2010 5-year est.); Median contract rent: $441 per month (2006-2010 5-year est.); Median year structure built: 1975 (2006-2010 5-year est.).
Transportation: Commute to work: 78.4% car, 0.6% public transportation, 10.4% walk, 9.6% work from home (2006-2010 5-year est.); Travel time to work: 29.0% less than 15 minutes, 34.9% 15 to 30 minutes, 20.9% 30 to 45 minutes, 12.8% 45 to 60 minutes, 2.4% 60 minutes or more (2006-2010 5-year est.)
Additional Information Contacts
Greater Wyalusing Chamber of Commerce . . . . (570) 746-4922
  http://www.wyalusing.net

OVERTON (township).
Covers a land area of 46.738 square miles and a water area of 0.234 square miles. Located at 41.62° N. Lat; 76.58° W. Long. Elevation is 1,640 feet.

Population: 157 (1990); 187 (2000); 247 (2010); Density: 5.3 persons per square mile (2010); Race: 97.2% White, 0.4% Black, 0.0% Asian, 0.8% American Indian/Alaska Native, 0.0% Native Hawaiian/Other Pacific Islander, 1.6% Other, 0.0% Hispanic of any race (2010); Average household size: 2.35 (2010); Median age: 47.5 (2010); Males per 100 females: 107.6 (2010); Marriage status: 25.3% never married, 60.5% now married, 6.8% widowed, 7.4% divorced (2006-2010 5-year est.); Foreign born: 1.2% (2006-2010 5-year est.); Ancestry (includes multiple ancestries): 24.0% German, 18.6% American, 16.1% Irish, 10.7% English, 5.4% Dutch (2006-2010 5-year est.).

Economy: Single-family building permits issued: 0 (2011); Multi-family building permits issued: 0 (2011); Employment by occupation: 4.3% management, 6.5% professional, 14.1% services, 9.8% sales, 3.3% farming, 10.9% construction, 15.2% production (2006-2010 5-year est.).

Income: Per capita income: $22,900 (2006-2010 5-year est.); Median household income: $50,417 (2006-2010 5-year est.); Average household income: $56,515 (2006-2010 5-year est.); Percent of households with income of $100,000 or more: 9.7% (2006-2010 5-year est.); Poverty rate: 12.1% (2006-2010 5-year est.).

Education: Percent of population age 25 and over with: High school diploma (including GED) or higher: 82.5% (2006-2010 5-year est.); Bachelor's degree or higher: 4.9% (2006-2010 5-year est.); Master's degree or higher: 0.0% (2006-2010 5-year est.).

Housing: Homeownership rate: 86.7% (2010); Median home value: $99,000 (2006-2010 5-year est.); Median contract rent: n/a per month (2006-2010 5-year est.); Median year structure built: 1982 (2006-2010 5-year est.).

Transportation: Commute to work: 97.8% car, 0.0% public transportation, 2.2% walk, 0.0% work from home (2006-2010 5-year est.); Travel time to work: 10.9% less than 15 minutes, 29.3% 15 to 30 minutes, 38.0% 30 to 45 minutes, 9.8% 45 to 60 minutes, 12.0% 60 minutes or more (2006-2010 5-year est.)

PIKE (township).
Covers a land area of 27.492 square miles and a water area of 0.180 square miles. Located at 41.85° N. Lat; 76.18° W. Long.

Population: 684 (1990); 657 (2000); 671 (2010); Density: 24.4 persons per square mile (2010); Race: 98.5% White, 0.1% Black, 0.7% Asian, 0.1% American Indian/Alaska Native, 0.0% Native Hawaiian/Other Pacific Islander, 0.6% Other, 0.7% Hispanic of any race (2010); Average household size: 2.77 (2010); Median age: 39.7 (2010); Males per 100 females: 115.1 (2010); Marriage status: 20.2% never married, 70.1% now married, 7.1% widowed, 2.7% divorced (2006-2010 5-year est.); Foreign born: 0.7% (2006-2010 5-year est.); Ancestry (includes multiple ancestries): 15.7% German, 14.5% Irish, 14.1% English, 11.8% American, 9.0% Pennsylvania German (2006-2010 5-year est.).

Economy: Single-family building permits issued: 4 (2011); Multi-family building permits issued: 0 (2011); Employment by occupation: 37.2% management, 1.3% professional, 4.2% services, 5.0% sales, 1.7% farming, 14.2% construction, 4.2% production (2006-2010 5-year est.).

Income: Per capita income: $20,271 (2006-2010 5-year est.); Median household income: $38,491 (2006-2010 5-year est.); Average household income: $47,192 (2006-2010 5-year est.); Percent of households with income of $100,000 or more: 7.2% (2006-2010 5-year est.); Poverty rate: 8.3% (2006-2010 5-year est.).

Education: Percent of population age 25 and over with: High school diploma (including GED) or higher: 80.3% (2006-2010 5-year est.); Bachelor's degree or higher: 11.5% (2006-2010 5-year est.); Master's degree or higher: 3.7% (2006-2010 5-year est.).

Housing: Homeownership rate: 82.7% (2010); Median home value: $121,100 (2006-2010 5-year est.); Median contract rent: n/a per month (2006-2010 5-year est.); Median year structure built: 1975 (2006-2010 5-year est.).

Transportation: Commute to work: 72.0% car, 1.3% public transportation, 16.9% walk, 6.4% work from home (2006-2010 5-year est.); Travel time to work: 29.9% less than 15 minutes, 29.4% 15 to 30 minutes, 22.6% 30 to 45 minutes, 11.8% 45 to 60 minutes, 6.3% 60 minutes or more (2006-2010 5-year est.)

RIDGEBURY (township).
Aka Centerville. Covers a land area of 38.300 square miles and a water area of 0.199 square miles. Located at 41.94° N. Lat; 76.70° W. Long. Elevation is 961 feet.

Population: 2,026 (1990); 1,982 (2000); 1,978 (2010); Density: 51.6 persons per square mile (2010); Race: 98.7% White, 0.4% Black, 0.2% Asian, 0.0% American Indian/Alaska Native, 0.1% Native Hawaiian/Other Pacific Islander, 0.6% Other, 0.7% Hispanic of any race (2010); Average household size: 2.58 (2010); Median age: 43.4 (2010); Males per 100 females: 104.8 (2010); Marriage status: 19.7% never married, 68.9% now married, 3.6% widowed, 7.7% divorced (2006-2010 5-year est.); Foreign born: 0.7% (2006-2010 5-year est.); Ancestry (includes multiple ancestries): 26.7% German, 18.7% Irish, 10.6% English, 9.8% American, 6.2% Polish (2006-2010 5-year est.).

Economy: Single-family building permits issued: 7 (2011); Multi-family building permits issued: 0 (2011); Employment by occupation: 4.8% management, 0.5% professional, 8.2% services, 22.8% sales, 2.1% farming, 16.4% construction, 19.0% production (2006-2010 5-year est.).

Income: Per capita income: $20,459 (2006-2010 5-year est.); Median household income: $41,000 (2006-2010 5-year est.); Average household income: $56,061 (2006-2010 5-year est.); Percent of households with income of $100,000 or more: 14.0% (2006-2010 5-year est.); Poverty rate: 16.6% (2006-2010 5-year est.).

Education: Percent of population age 25 and over with: High school diploma (including GED) or higher: 87.6% (2006-2010 5-year est.); Bachelor's degree or higher: 11.0% (2006-2010 5-year est.); Master's degree or higher: 3.6% (2006-2010 5-year est.).

Housing: Homeownership rate: 83.9% (2010); Median home value: $89,700 (2006-2010 5-year est.); Median contract rent: $358 per month (2006-2010 5-year est.); Median year structure built: 1978 (2006-2010 5-year est.).

Transportation: Commute to work: 92.3% car, 0.5% public transportation, 1.5% walk, 3.0% work from home (2006-2010 5-year est.); Travel time to work: 12.9% less than 15 minutes, 49.0% 15 to 30 minutes, 26.9% 30 to 45 minutes, 3.3% 45 to 60 minutes, 8.0% 60 minutes or more (2006-2010 5-year est.)

Additional Information Contacts

Mansfield Chamber of Commerce, Inc. . . . . (570) 662-3442
   http://www.mansfield.org

ROME (borough).
Covers a land area of 0.520 square miles and a water area of 0.008 square miles. Located at 41.86° N. Lat; 76.34° W. Long. Elevation is 817 feet.

Population: 475 (1990); 382 (2000); 441 (2010); Density: 847.7 persons per square mile (2010); Race: 98.9% White, 0.0% Black, 0.2% Asian, 0.0% American Indian/Alaska Native, 0.0% Native Hawaiian/Other Pacific Islander, 0.9% Other, 0.0% Hispanic of any race (2010); Average household size: 2.56 (2010); Median age: 34.6 (2010); Males per 100 females: 96.9 (2010); Marriage status: 19.8% never married, 58.1% now married, 3.6% widowed, 18.5% divorced (2006-2010 5-year est.); Foreign born: 1.6% (2006-2010 5-year est.); Ancestry (includes multiple ancestries): 18.7% German, 14.1% Irish, 9.8% Italian, 7.7% English, 5.9% Dutch (2006-2010 5-year est.).

Economy: Single-family building permits issued: 0 (2011); Multi-family building permits issued: 0 (2011); Employment by occupation: 3.1% management, 0.0% professional, 11.0% services, 9.8% sales, 0.0% farming, 9.2% construction, 8.0% production (2006-2010 5-year est.).

Income: Per capita income: $19,842 (2006-2010 5-year est.); Median household income: $35,750 (2006-2010 5-year est.); Average household income: $49,584 (2006-2010 5-year est.); Percent of households with income of $100,000 or more: 6.5% (2006-2010 5-year est.); Poverty rate: 19.6% (2006-2010 5-year est.).

Education: Percent of population age 25 and over with: High school diploma (including GED) or higher: 84.3% (2006-2010 5-year est.); Bachelor's degree or higher: 7.3% (2006-2010 5-year est.); Master's degree or higher: 2.4% (2006-2010 5-year est.).

School District(s)
Northeast Bradford SD (KG-12)
   2010-11 Enrollment: 803 . . . . (570) 744-2521

Housing: Homeownership rate: 67.4% (2010); Median home value: $86,300 (2006-2010 5-year est.); Median contract rent: $377 per month (2006-2010 5-year est.); Median year structure built: 1964 (2006-2010 5-year est.).

Transportation: Commute to work: 95.7% car, 0.0% public transportation, 2.5% walk, 1.8% work from home (2006-2010 5-year est.); Travel time to work: 9.4% less than 15 minutes, 53.8% 15 to 30 minutes, 15.6% 30 to 45

minutes, 13.1% 45 to 60 minutes, 8.1% 60 minutes or more (2006-2010 5-year est.)

ROME (township).
Covers a land area of 29.912 square miles and a water area of 0.172 square miles. Located at 41.87° N. Lat; 76.36° W. Long. Elevation is 817 feet.

Population: 1,043 (1990); 1,221 (2000); 1,191 (2010); Density: 39.8 persons per square mile (2010); Race: 98.4% White, 0.8% Black, 0.1% Asian, 0.3% American Indian/Alaska Native, 0.0% Native Hawaiian/Other Pacific Islander, 0.4% Other, 0.9% Hispanic of any race (2010); Average household size: 2.61 (2010); Median age: 41.4 (2010); Males per 100 females: 96.5 (2010); Marriage status: 23.9% never married, 59.1% now married, 12.0% widowed, 5.0% divorced (2006-2010 5-year est.); Foreign born: 0.5% (2006-2010 5-year est.); Ancestry (includes multiple ancestries): 24.3% German, 12.4% Irish, 10.9% English, 4.3% American, 4.2% French (2006-2010 5-year est.).

Economy: Single-family building permits issued: 15 (2011); Multi-family building permits issued: 0 (2011); Employment by occupation: 14.1% management, 1.0% professional, 17.3% services, 10.9% sales, 1.0% farming, 16.7% construction, 8.1% production (2006-2010 5-year est.).

Income: Per capita income: $20,078 (2006-2010 5-year est.); Median household income: $39,798 (2006-2010 5-year est.); Average household income: $54,895 (2006-2010 5-year est.); Percent of households with income of $100,000 or more: 9.5% (2006-2010 5-year est.); Poverty rate: 12.7% (2006-2010 5-year est.).

Education: Percent of population age 25 and over with: High school diploma (including GED) or higher: 79.8% (2006-2010 5-year est.); Bachelor's degree or higher: 17.1% (2006-2010 5-year est.); Master's degree or higher: 5.8% (2006-2010 5-year est.).

Housing: Homeownership rate: 83.6% (2010); Median home value: $108,400 (2006-2010 5-year est.); Median contract rent: $368 per month (2006-2010 5-year est.); Median year structure built: 1977 (2006-2010 5-year est.).

Transportation: Commute to work: 90.8% car, 0.7% public transportation, 4.2% walk, 3.0% work from home (2006-2010 5-year est.); Travel time to work: 18.0% less than 15 minutes, 38.6% 15 to 30 minutes, 22.1% 30 to 45 minutes, 8.6% 45 to 60 minutes, 12.7% 60 minutes or more (2006-2010 5-year est.).

Additional Information Contacts
Greater Wyalusing Chamber of Commerce . . . . (570) 746-4922
   http://www.wyalusing.net

SAYRE (borough).
Covers a land area of 2.022 square miles and a water area of 0.014 square miles. Located at 41.99° N. Lat; 76.52° W. Long. Elevation is 771 feet.

History: Sayre was a small railway settlement until the Lehigh Valley Railroad constructed a roundhouse and shops here in 1871 and named the place for Robert H. Sayre, superintendent of the road.

Population: 5,791 (1990); 5,813 (2000); 5,587 (2010); Density: 2,763.4 persons per square mile (2010); Race: 96.0% White, 0.8% Black, 1.7% Asian, 0.3% American Indian/Alaska Native, 0.0% Native Hawaiian/Other Pacific Islander, 1.2% Other, 1.1% Hispanic of any race (2010); Average household size: 2.23 (2010); Median age: 40.7 (2010); Males per 100 females: 88.4 (2010); Marriage status: 23.1% never married, 50.2% now married, 10.8% widowed, 15.9% divorced (2006-2010 5-year est.); Foreign born: 0.6% (2006-2010 5-year est.); Ancestry (includes multiple ancestries): 21.5% Irish, 18.8% German, 17.3% Italian, 11.3% English, 7.6% American (2006-2010 5-year est.).

Economy: Single-family building permits issued: 5 (2011); Multi-family building permits issued: 0 (2011); Employment by occupation: 8.6% management, 2.8% professional, 12.1% services, 21.0% sales, 4.7% farming, 3.9% construction, 4.6% production (2006-2010 5-year est.).

Income: Per capita income: $20,956 (2006-2010 5-year est.); Median household income: $34,221 (2006-2010 5-year est.); Average household income: $46,709 (2006-2010 5-year est.); Percent of households with income of $100,000 or more: 8.0% (2006-2010 5-year est.); Poverty rate: 11.7% (2006-2010 5-year est.).

Education: Percent of population age 25 and over with: High school diploma (including GED) or higher: 84.8% (2006-2010 5-year est.); Bachelor's degree or higher: 22.8% (2006-2010 5-year est.); Master's degree or higher: 6.7% (2006-2010 5-year est.).

School District(s)
Sayre Area SD (KG-12)
   2010-11 Enrollment: 1,154 . . . . (570) 888-7615

Housing: Homeownership rate: 58.1% (2010); Median home value: $92,400 (2006-2010 5-year est.); Median contract rent: $450 per month (2006-2010 5-year est.); Median year structure built: before 1940 (2006-2010 5-year est.).

Hospitals: Robert Packer Hospital (238 beds)

Safety: Violent crime rate: 8.9 per 10,000 population; Property crime rate: 335.4 per 10,000 population (2011).

Newspapers: Morning Times (Local news; Circulation 8,200)

Transportation: Commute to work: 86.2% car, 0.0% public transportation, 8.5% walk, 2.1% work from home (2006-2010 5-year est.); Travel time to work: 59.8% less than 15 minutes, 17.4% 15 to 30 minutes, 15.2% 30 to 45 minutes, 5.6% 45 to 60 minutes, 2.1% 60 minutes or more (2006-2010 5-year est.).

Additional Information Contacts
Borough of Sayre . . . . (570) 888-7730
   http://home.cqservices.com/sayre
Greater Valley Chamber of Commerce . . . . (570) 888-2217
   http://www.greatervalleychamberofcommerce.com

SHESHEQUIN (township).
Covers a land area of 35.350 square miles and a water area of 0.730 square miles. Located at 41.86° N. Lat; 76.47° W. Long. Elevation is 755 feet.

Population: 1,211 (1990); 1,300 (2000); 1,348 (2010); Density: 38.1 persons per square mile (2010); Race: 97.5% White, 0.1% Black, 0.1% Asian, 0.9% American Indian/Alaska Native, 0.0% Native Hawaiian/Other Pacific Islander, 1.4% Other, 1.4% Hispanic of any race (2010); Average household size: 2.51 (2010); Median age: 43.5 (2010); Males per 100 females: 101.5 (2010); Marriage status: 21.4% never married, 60.0% now married, 6.3% widowed, 12.3% divorced (2006-2010 5-year est.); Foreign born: 0.0% (2006-2010 5-year est.); Ancestry (includes multiple ancestries): 21.5% Irish, 19.6% German, 13.9% English, 10.1% Italian, 8.5% American (2006-2010 5-year est.).

Economy: Single-family building permits issued: 0 (2011); Multi-family building permits issued: 0 (2011); Employment by occupation: 7.0% management, 1.3% professional, 6.8% services, 17.4% sales, 1.1% farming, 16.5% construction, 10.8% production (2006-2010 5-year est.).

Income: Per capita income: $20,684 (2006-2010 5-year est.); Median household income: $44,750 (2006-2010 5-year est.); Average household income: $51,588 (2006-2010 5-year est.); Percent of households with income of $100,000 or more: 11.0% (2006-2010 5-year est.); Poverty rate: 8.7% (2006-2010 5-year est.).

Education: Percent of population age 25 and over with: High school diploma (including GED) or higher: 85.2% (2006-2010 5-year est.); Bachelor's degree or higher: 11.3% (2006-2010 5-year est.); Master's degree or higher: 2.9% (2006-2010 5-year est.).

Housing: Homeownership rate: 83.8% (2010); Median home value: $108,400 (2006-2010 5-year est.); Median contract rent: $431 per month (2006-2010 5-year est.); Median year structure built: 1968 (2006-2010 5-year est.).

Transportation: Commute to work: 92.0% car, 0.0% public transportation, 3.7% walk, 4.3% work from home (2006-2010 5-year est.); Travel time to work: 36.1% less than 15 minutes, 36.1% 15 to 30 minutes, 19.1% 30 to 45 minutes, 6.4% 45 to 60 minutes, 2.1% 60 minutes or more (2006-2010 5-year est.).

Additional Information Contacts
Greater Wyalusing Chamber of Commerce . . . . (570) 746-4922
   http://www.wyalusing.net

SMITHFIELD (township).
Covers a land area of 41.881 square miles and a water area of 0.165 square miles. Located at 41.85° N. Lat; 76.61° W. Long.

Population: 1,520 (1990); 1,538 (2000); 1,498 (2010); Density: 35.8 persons per square mile (2010); Race: 98.3% White, 0.3% Black, 0.2% Asian, 0.1% American Indian/Alaska Native, 0.0% Native Hawaiian/Other Pacific Islander, 1.1% Other, 1.0% Hispanic of any race (2010); Average household size: 2.53 (2010); Median age: 45.0 (2010); Males per 100 females: 99.5 (2010); Marriage status: 20.1% never married, 64.8% now married, 6.7% widowed, 8.3% divorced (2006-2010 5-year est.); Foreign born: 0.5% (2006-2010 5-year est.); Ancestry (includes multiple ancestries): 25.7% German, 21.6% Irish, 19.6% English, 10.0% American, 7.4% Dutch (2006-2010 5-year est.).

Economy: Single-family building permits issued: 0 (2011); Multi-family building permits issued: 0 (2011); Employment by occupation: 12.8% management, 2.8% professional, 13.5% services, 12.0% sales, 4.3% farming, 13.3% construction, 9.9% production (2006-2010 5-year est.).

Income: Per capita income: $23,591 (2006-2010 5-year est.); Median household income: $46,023 (2006-2010 5-year est.); Average household income: $59,622 (2006-2010 5-year est.); Percent of households with income of $100,000 or more: 14.0% (2006-2010 5-year est.); Poverty rate: 4.9% (2006-2010 5-year est.).

Education: Percent of population age 25 and over with: High school diploma (including GED) or higher: 88.5% (2006-2010 5-year est.); Bachelor's degree or higher: 18.8% (2006-2010 5-year est.); Master's degree or higher: 4.6% (2006-2010 5-year est.).

Housing: Homeownership rate: 85.0% (2010); Median home value: $123,200 (2006-2010 5-year est.); Median contract rent: $406 per month (2006-2010 5-year est.); Median year structure built: 1970 (2006-2010 5-year est.).

Transportation: Commute to work: 90.4% car, 0.0% public transportation, 1.5% walk, 7.3% work from home (2006-2010 5-year est.); Travel time to work: 16.8% less than 15 minutes, 40.6% 15 to 30 minutes, 21.4% 30 to 45 minutes, 12.1% 45 to 60 minutes, 9.1% 60 minutes or more (2006-2010 5-year est.)

Additional Information Contacts

Central Bradford County Chamber of Commerce . . . . (570) 268-2732
  http://cbradchamber.org

SOUTH CREEK (township).
Covers a land area of 27.906 square miles and a water area of 0.034 square miles. Located at 41.95° N. Lat; 76.78° W. Long.

Population: 1,229 (1990); 1,261 (2000); 1,128 (2010); Density: 40.4 persons per square mile (2010); Race: 97.1% White, 0.4% Black, 0.1% Asian, 1.2% American Indian/Alaska Native, 0.0% Native Hawaiian/Other Pacific Islander, 1.2% Other, 1.0% Hispanic of any race (2010); Average household size: 2.47 (2010); Median age: 45.5 (2010); Males per 100 females: 95.2 (2010); Marriage status: 23.7% never married, 61.3% now married, 7.7% widowed, 7.2% divorced (2006-2010 5-year est.); Foreign born: 0.5% (2006-2010 5-year est.); Ancestry (includes multiple ancestries): 23.9% English, 22.6% German, 12.1% Irish, 10.2% Polish, 9.1% American (2006-2010 5-year est.).

Economy: Single-family building permits issued: 0 (2011); Multi-family building permits issued: 0 (2011); Employment by occupation: 11.2% management, 6.1% professional, 12.0% services, 8.7% sales, 1.5% farming, 15.7% construction, 16.6% production (2006-2010 5-year est.).

Income: Per capita income: $22,899 (2006-2010 5-year est.); Median household income: $40,625 (2006-2010 5-year est.); Average household income: $48,097 (2006-2010 5-year est.); Percent of households with income of $100,000 or more: 8.6% (2006-2010 5-year est.); Poverty rate: 6.1% (2006-2010 5-year est.).

Education: Percent of population age 25 and over with: High school diploma (including GED) or higher: 80.9% (2006-2010 5-year est.); Bachelor's degree or higher: 13.1% (2006-2010 5-year est.); Master's degree or higher: 5.0% (2006-2010 5-year est.).

Housing: Homeownership rate: 81.2% (2010); Median home value: $112,500 (2006-2010 5-year est.); Median contract rent: $463 per month (2006-2010 5-year est.); Median year structure built: 1971 (2006-2010 5-year est.).

Transportation: Commute to work: 91.9% car, 0.0% public transportation, 5.1% walk, 0.0% work from home (2006-2010 5-year est.); Travel time to work: 19.8% less than 15 minutes, 41.8% 15 to 30 minutes, 26.8% 30 to 45 minutes, 4.0% 45 to 60 minutes, 7.6% 60 minutes or more (2006-2010 5-year est.)

Additional Information Contacts

Mansfield Chamber of Commerce, Inc. . . . . (570) 662-3442
  http://www.mansfield.org

SOUTH WAVERLY (borough).
Covers a land area of 0.882 square miles and a water area of 0.004 square miles. Located at 41.99° N. Lat; 76.54° W. Long. Elevation is 823 feet.

History: Incorporated 1878.

Population: 1,049 (1990); 987 (2000); 1,027 (2010); Density: 1,164.2 persons per square mile (2010); Race: 98.0% White, 0.3% Black, 0.2% Asian, 0.6% American Indian/Alaska Native, 0.0% Native Hawaiian/Other Pacific Islander, 0.9% Other, 1.8% Hispanic of any race (2010); Average household size: 2.43 (2010); Median age: 46.1 (2010); Males per 100 females: 87.8 (2010); Marriage status: 28.0% never married, 52.3% now married, 8.4% widowed, 11.3% divorced (2006-2010 5-year est.); Foreign born: 2.8% (2006-2010 5-year est.); Ancestry (includes multiple ancestries): 18.3% German, 17.6% Italian, 15.0% Irish, 14.8% English, 8.7% American (2006-2010 5-year est.).

Economy: Single-family building permits issued: 1 (2011); Multi-family building permits issued: 0 (2011); Employment by occupation: 6.8% management, 1.3% professional, 13.3% services, 7.9% sales, 4.8% farming, 8.7% construction, 14.4% production (2006-2010 5-year est.).

Income: Per capita income: $22,402 (2006-2010 5-year est.); Median household income: $42,222 (2006-2010 5-year est.); Average household income: $56,809 (2006-2010 5-year est.); Percent of households with income of $100,000 or more: 12.1% (2006-2010 5-year est.); Poverty rate: 13.7% (2006-2010 5-year est.).

Education: Percent of population age 25 and over with: High school diploma (including GED) or higher: 91.1% (2006-2010 5-year est.); Bachelor's degree or higher: 19.7% (2006-2010 5-year est.); Master's degree or higher: 10.1% (2006-2010 5-year est.).

Housing: Homeownership rate: 85.0% (2010); Median home value: $89,100 (2006-2010 5-year est.); Median contract rent: $480 per month (2006-2010 5-year est.); Median year structure built: 1951 (2006-2010 5-year est.).

Transportation: Commute to work: 88.7% car, 0.0% public transportation, 4.3% walk, 4.7% work from home (2006-2010 5-year est.); Travel time to work: 62.6% less than 15 minutes, 21.5% 15 to 30 minutes, 10.7% 30 to 45 minutes, 3.4% 45 to 60 minutes, 1.8% 60 minutes or more (2006-2010 5-year est.)

SPRINGFIELD (township).
Covers a land area of 41.593 square miles and a water area of 0.240 square miles. Located at 41.86° N. Lat; 76.73° W. Long. Elevation is 1,414 feet.

Population: 1,118 (1990); 1,167 (2000); 1,124 (2010); Density: 27.0 persons per square mile (2010); Race: 97.2% White, 0.7% Black, 0.1% Asian, 0.3% American Indian/Alaska Native, 0.0% Native Hawaiian/Other Pacific Islander, 1.7% Other, 1.6% Hispanic of any race (2010); Average household size: 2.63 (2010); Median age: 44.3 (2010); Males per 100 females: 100.7 (2010); Marriage status: 21.0% never married, 66.4% now married, 5.0% widowed, 7.5% divorced (2006-2010 5-year est.); Foreign born: 2.2% (2006-2010 5-year est.); Ancestry (includes multiple ancestries): 32.8% German, 17.8% English, 12.7% Irish, 6.1% American, 5.0% French (2006-2010 5-year est.).

Economy: Single-family building permits issued: 0 (2011); Multi-family building permits issued: 0 (2011); Employment by occupation: 15.1% management, 0.5% professional, 15.0% services, 11.7% sales, 4.9% farming, 20.2% construction, 7.0% production (2006-2010 5-year est.).

Income: Per capita income: $19,681 (2006-2010 5-year est.); Median household income: $46,167 (2006-2010 5-year est.); Average household income: $55,942 (2006-2010 5-year est.); Percent of households with income of $100,000 or more: 12.3% (2006-2010 5-year est.); Poverty rate: 10.5% (2006-2010 5-year est.).

Education: Percent of population age 25 and over with: High school diploma (including GED) or higher: 89.1% (2006-2010 5-year est.); Bachelor's degree or higher: 14.0% (2006-2010 5-year est.); Master's degree or higher: 6.4% (2006-2010 5-year est.).

Housing: Homeownership rate: 82.6% (2010); Median home value: $119,300 (2006-2010 5-year est.); Median contract rent: $414 per month (2006-2010 5-year est.); Median year structure built: 1972 (2006-2010 5-year est.).

Transportation: Commute to work: 79.6% car, 0.0% public transportation, 9.5% walk, 5.6% work from home (2006-2010 5-year est.); Travel time to work: 36.6% less than 15 minutes, 21.5% 15 to 30 minutes, 23.6% 30 to 45 minutes, 10.0% 45 to 60 minutes, 8.3% 60 minutes or more (2006-2010 5-year est.)

Additional Information Contacts

Central Bradford County Chamber of Commerce . . . . (570) 268-2732
  http://cbradchamber.org

STANDING STONE (township).
Covers a land area of 15.681 square miles and a water area of 0.549 square miles. Located at 41.77° N. Lat; 76.33° W. Long. Elevation is 705 feet.

Population: 436 (1990); 596 (2000); 642 (2010); Density: 40.9 persons per square mile (2010); Race: 97.7% White, 0.0% Black, 0.3% Asian, 0.0% American Indian/Alaska Native, 0.0% Native Hawaiian/Other Pacific Islander, 2.0% Other, 0.3% Hispanic of any race (2010); Average household size: 2.53 (2010); Median age: 44.6 (2010); Males per 100 females: 100.6 (2010); Marriage status: 30.9% never married, 56.4% now married, 3.5% widowed, 9.2% divorced (2006-2010 5-year est.); Foreign born: 1.5% (2006-2010 5-year est.); Ancestry (includes multiple ancestries): 23.6% German, 23.4% Irish, 14.3% English, 9.5% American, 6.8% Italian (2006-2010 5-year est.).

Economy: Single-family building permits issued: 7 (2011); Multi-family building permits issued: 0 (2011); Employment by occupation: 7.9% management, 2.3% professional, 22.4% services, 6.6% sales, 5.3% farming, 13.2% construction, 11.8% production (2006-2010 5-year est.).
Income: Per capita income: $23,564 (2006-2010 5-year est.); Median household income: $52,500 (2006-2010 5-year est.); Average household income: $56,959 (2006-2010 5-year est.); Percent of households with income of $100,000 or more: 9.6% (2006-2010 5-year est.); Poverty rate: 5.1% (2006-2010 5-year est.).
Education: Percent of population age 25 and over with: High school diploma (including GED) or higher: 91.4% (2006-2010 5-year est.); Bachelor's degree or higher: 7.6% (2006-2010 5-year est.); Master's degree or higher: 2.5% (2006-2010 5-year est.).
Housing: Homeownership rate: 85.1% (2010); Median home value: $123,400 (2006-2010 5-year est.); Median contract rent: $484 per month (2006-2010 5-year est.); Median year structure built: 1981 (2006-2010 5-year est.).
Transportation: Commute to work: 93.1% car, 0.0% public transportation, 5.5% walk, 0.7% work from home (2006-2010 5-year est.); Travel time to work: 15.3% less than 15 minutes, 63.2% 15 to 30 minutes, 10.1% 30 to 45 minutes, 5.2% 45 to 60 minutes, 6.3% 60 minutes or more (2006-2010 5-year est.)

STEVENS (township). Covers a land area of 15.523 square miles and a water area of 0.177 square miles. Located at 41.77° N. Lat; 76.17° W. Long.
Population: 401 (1990); 414 (2000); 437 (2010); Density: 28.2 persons per square mile (2010); Race: 97.7% White, 0.9% Black, 0.7% Asian, 0.2% American Indian/Alaska Native, 0.0% Native Hawaiian/Other Pacific Islander, 0.5% Other, 1.1% Hispanic of any race (2010); Average household size: 2.38 (2010); Median age: 47.4 (2010); Males per 100 females: 103.3 (2010); Marriage status: 18.8% never married, 64.3% now married, 11.3% widowed, 5.5% divorced (2006-2010 5-year est.); Foreign born: 2.3% (2006-2010 5-year est.); Ancestry (includes multiple ancestries): 33.2% German, 13.6% English, 12.6% Italian, 10.7% Irish, 6.1% Dutch (2006-2010 5-year est.).
Economy: Single-family building permits issued: 1 (2011); Multi-family building permits issued: 0 (2011); Employment by occupation: 10.4% management, 0.0% professional, 13.6% services, 12.3% sales, 3.9% farming, 16.9% construction, 11.0% production (2006-2010 5-year est.).
Income: Per capita income: $21,991 (2006-2010 5-year est.); Median household income: $43,250 (2006-2010 5-year est.); Average household income: $56,055 (2006-2010 5-year est.); Percent of households with income of $100,000 or more: 12.5% (2006-2010 5-year est.); Poverty rate: 15.2% (2006-2010 5-year est.).
Education: Percent of population age 25 and over with: High school diploma (including GED) or higher: 77.3% (2006-2010 5-year est.); Bachelor's degree or higher: 18.0% (2006-2010 5-year est.); Master's degree or higher: 5.3% (2006-2010 5-year est.).
Housing: Homeownership rate: 85.4% (2010); Median home value: $138,900 (2006-2010 5-year est.); Median contract rent: $488 per month (2006-2010 5-year est.); Median year structure built: 1972 (2006-2010 5-year est.).
Transportation: Commute to work: 93.8% car, 0.0% public transportation, 0.0% walk, 4.8% work from home (2006-2010 5-year est.); Travel time to work: 24.5% less than 15 minutes, 33.1% 15 to 30 minutes, 40.3% 30 to 45 minutes, 0.0% 45 to 60 minutes, 2.2% 60 minutes or more (2006-2010 5-year est.)

STEVENSVILLE (unincorporated postal area)
Zip Code: 18845
Covers a land area of 9.671 square miles and a water area of 0.123 square miles. Located at 41.78° N. Lat; 76.18° W. Long. Elevation is 860 feet. Population: 297 (2010); Density: 30.7 persons per square mile (2010); Race: 98.0% White, 0.7% Black, 0.7% Asian, 0.3% American Indian/Alaska Native, 0.0% Native Hawaiian/Other Pacific Islander, 0.3% Other, 1.0% Hispanic of any race (2010); Average household size: 2.20 (2010); Median age: 50.8 (2010); Males per 100 females: 112.1 (2010); Homeownership rate: 86.7% (2010)

SUGAR RUN (unincorporated postal area)
Zip Code: 18846
Covers a land area of 26.941 square miles and a water area of 0.671 square miles. Located at 41.62° N. Lat; 76.22° W. Long. Elevation is 722 feet. Population: 847 (2010); Density: 31.4 persons per square mile

(2010); Race: 96.6% White, 0.8% Black, 0.5% Asian, 0.1% American Indian/Alaska Native, 0.0% Native Hawaiian/Other Pacific Islander, 2.0% Other, 1.1% Hispanic of any race (2010); Average household size: 2.54 (2010); Median age: 44.6 (2010); Males per 100 females: 107.1 (2010); Homeownership rate: 88.6% (2010)

SYLVANIA (borough). Covers a land area of 1.115 square miles and a water area of <.001 square miles. Located at 41.80° N. Lat; 76.86° W. Long. Elevation is 1,280 feet.
Population: 203 (1990); 200 (2000); 219 (2010); Density: 196.4 persons per square mile (2010); Race: 96.3% White, 0.0% Black, 0.9% Asian, 0.5% American Indian/Alaska Native, 0.0% Native Hawaiian/Other Pacific Islander, 2.3% Other, 0.0% Hispanic of any race (2010); Average household size: 2.67 (2010); Median age: 39.6 (2010); Males per 100 females: 110.6 (2010); Marriage status: 24.9% never married, 58.5% now married, 4.4% widowed, 12.2% divorced (2006-2010 5-year est.); Foreign born: 0.7% (2006-2010 5-year est.); Ancestry (includes multiple ancestries): 22.4% English, 18.7% German, 17.5% Irish, 13.1% Italian, 5.2% French (2006-2010 5-year est.).
Economy: Single-family building permits issued: 0 (2011); Multi-family building permits issued: 0 (2011); Employment by occupation: 2.4% management, 0.0% professional, 23.2% services, 22.4% sales, 4.0% farming, 18.4% construction, 0.0% production (2006-2010 5-year est.).
Income: Per capita income: $22,699 (2006-2010 5-year est.); Median household income: $42,813 (2006-2010 5-year est.); Average household income: $56,221 (2006-2010 5-year est.); Percent of households with income of $100,000 or more: 5.0% (2006-2010 5-year est.); Poverty rate: 18.3% (2006-2010 5-year est.).
Education: Percent of population age 25 and over with: High school diploma (including GED) or higher: 83.9% (2006-2010 5-year est.); Bachelor's degree or higher: 12.4% (2006-2010 5-year est.); Master's degree or higher: 4.8% (2006-2010 5-year est.).
Housing: Homeownership rate: 75.6% (2010); Median home value: $90,000 (2006-2010 5-year est.); Median contract rent: $275 per month (2006-2010 5-year est.); Median year structure built: before 1940 (2006-2010 5-year est.).
Transportation: Commute to work: 95.4% car, 0.0% public transportation, 0.0% walk, 1.5% work from home (2006-2010 5-year est.); Travel time to work: 40.6% less than 15 minutes, 25.8% 15 to 30 minutes, 7.8% 30 to 45 minutes, 9.4% 45 to 60 minutes, 16.4% 60 minutes or more (2006-2010 5-year est.)

TERRY (township). Covers a land area of 32.568 square miles and a water area of 0.801 square miles. Located at 41.65° N. Lat; 76.33° W. Long.
Population: 878 (1990); 942 (2000); 992 (2010); Density: 30.5 persons per square mile (2010); Race: 98.2% White, 0.0% Black, 0.8% Asian, 0.4% American Indian/Alaska Native, 0.3% Native Hawaiian/Other Pacific Islander, 0.3% Other, 1.6% Hispanic of any race (2010); Average household size: 2.47 (2010); Median age: 44.3 (2010); Males per 100 females: 110.6 (2010); Marriage status: 20.0% never married, 67.5% now married, 6.2% widowed, 6.3% divorced (2006-2010 5-year est.); Foreign born: 2.6% (2006-2010 5-year est.); Ancestry (includes multiple ancestries): 28.2% German, 25.3% Irish, 12.9% English, 10.2% American, 8.5% Swiss (2006-2010 5-year est.).
Economy: Single-family building permits issued: 0 (2011); Multi-family building permits issued: 0 (2011); Employment by occupation: 10.3% management, 0.0% professional, 10.0% services, 5.7% sales, 0.0% farming, 19.4% construction, 13.4% production (2006-2010 5-year est.).
Income: Per capita income: $20,852 (2006-2010 5-year est.); Median household income: $46,964 (2006-2010 5-year est.); Average household income: $56,247 (2006-2010 5-year est.); Percent of households with income of $100,000 or more: 11.0% (2006-2010 5-year est.); Poverty rate: 14.1% (2006-2010 5-year est.).
Education: Percent of population age 25 and over with: High school diploma (including GED) or higher: 74.4% (2006-2010 5-year est.); Bachelor's degree or higher: 15.5% (2006-2010 5-year est.); Master's degree or higher: 3.5% (2006-2010 5-year est.).
Housing: Homeownership rate: 85.3% (2010); Median home value: $134,700 (2006-2010 5-year est.); Median contract rent: $379 per month (2006-2010 5-year est.); Median year structure built: 1968 (2006-2010 5-year est.).
Transportation: Commute to work: 88.5% car, 0.0% public transportation, 0.6% walk, 6.9% work from home (2006-2010 5-year est.); Travel time to work: 31.6% less than 15 minutes, 38.1% 15 to 30 minutes, 20.7% 30 to

45 minutes, 1.9% 45 to 60 minutes, 7.7% 60 minutes or more (2006-2010 5-year est.)

Additional Information Contacts
Greater Wyalusing Chamber of Commerce . . . . (570) 746-4922
   http://www.wyalusing.net

TOWANDA (borough). County seat. Covers a land area of 1.138 square miles and a water area of 0.030 square miles. Located at 41.77° N. Lat; 76.45° W. Long. Elevation is 732 feet.
Population: 3,242 (1990); 3,024 (2000); 2,919 (2010); Density: 2,564.4 persons per square mile (2010); Race: 96.6% White, 0.6% Black, 0.4% Asian, 0.1% American Indian/Alaska Native, 0.0% Native Hawaiian/Other Pacific Islander, 2.3% Other, 2.4% Hispanic of any race (2010); Average household size: 2.35 (2010); Median age: 38.7 (2010); Males per 100 females: 103.1 (2010); Marriage status: 36.0% never married, 43.1% now married, 4.7% widowed, 16.2% divorced (2006-2010 5-year est.); Foreign born: 3.3% (2006-2010 5-year est.); Ancestry (includes multiple ancestries): 25.5% German, 15.5% English, 11.0% Irish, 4.5% Italian, 4.4% Swedish (2006-2010 5-year est.).
Economy: Single-family building permits issued: 3 (2011); Multi-family building permits issued: 0 (2011); Employment by occupation: 5.4% management, 2.1% professional, 14.6% services, 10.6% sales, 1.6% farming, 18.5% construction, 8.9% production (2006-2010 5-year est.).
Income: Per capita income: $20,785 (2006-2010 5-year est.); Median household income: $36,799 (2006-2010 5-year est.); Average household income: $48,569 (2006-2010 5-year est.); Percent of households with income of $100,000 or more: 12.3% (2006-2010 5-year est.); Poverty rate: 23.4% (2006-2010 5-year est.).
Education: Percent of population age 25 and over with: High school diploma (including GED) or higher: 86.4% (2006-2010 5-year est.); Bachelor's degree or higher: 20.7% (2006-2010 5-year est.); Master's degree or higher: 6.3% (2006-2010 5-year est.).

School District(s)
Northern Tier Career Center (10-12)
   2010-11 Enrollment: n/a . . . . (570) 265-8111
Towanda Area SD (KG-12)
   2010-11 Enrollment: 1,653 . . . . (570) 265-9894

Vocational/Technical School(s)
Northern Tier Career Center (Public)
   Fall 2010 Enrollment: 60. . . . . (570) 265-8113
   2011-12 Tuition: $10,782
Housing: Homeownership rate: 58.2% (2010); Median home value: $87,800 (2006-2010 5-year est.); Median contract rent: $486 per month (2006-2010 5-year est.); Median year structure built: before 1940 (2006-2010 5-year est.).
Hospitals: Memorial Hospital (94 beds)
Safety: Violent crime rate: 17.1 per 10,000 population; Property crime rate: 280.1 per 10,000 population (2011).
Newspapers: The Bradford/Sullivan Pennysaver (Community news; Circulation 10,500); The Daily Review (Local news; Circulation 10,000); The Farmer's Friend (National news; Circulation 9,850)
Transportation: Commute to work: 92.5% car, 1.2% public transportation, 4.9% walk, 1.4% work from home (2006-2010 5-year est.); Travel time to work: 53.2% less than 15 minutes, 20.7% 15 to 30 minutes, 13.8% 30 to 45 minutes, 8.1% 45 to 60 minutes, 4.1% 60 minutes or more (2006-2010 5-year est.)
Airports: Bradford County (general aviation)
Additional Information Contacts
Central Bradford County Chamber of Commerce . . . . (570) 268-2732
   http://cbradchamber.org/community

TOWANDA (township). Covers a land area of 15.227 square miles and a water area of 0.281 square miles. Located at 41.75° N. Lat; 76.48° W. Long. Elevation is 732 feet.
History: Settled 1794, laid out 1812 as Meansville, incorporated and renamed 1828.
Population: 1,133 (1990); 1,131 (2000); 1,149 (2010); Density: 75.5 persons per square mile (2010); Race: 97.5% White, 0.5% Black, 0.5% Asian, 0.0% American Indian/Alaska Native, 0.0% Native Hawaiian/Other Pacific Islander, 1.5% Other, 1.4% Hispanic of any race (2010); Average household size: 2.55 (2010); Median age: 45.5 (2010); Males per 100 females: 104.1 (2010); Marriage status: 20.7% never married, 54.5% now married, 11.9% widowed, 13.0% divorced (2006-2010 5-year est.); Foreign born: 1.2% (2006-2010 5-year est.); Ancestry (includes multiple

ancestries): 19.2% German, 14.3% English, 12.0% Irish, 9.9% Dutch, 9.4% American (2006-2010 5-year est.).
Economy: Single-family building permits issued: 0 (2011); Multi-family building permits issued: 0 (2011); Employment by occupation: 13.6% management, 5.9% professional, 13.6% services, 9.0% sales, 3.1% farming, 12.4% construction, 9.6% production (2006-2010 5-year est.).
Income: Per capita income: $20,273 (2006-2010 5-year est.); Median household income: $33,828 (2006-2010 5-year est.); Average household income: $45,198 (2006-2010 5-year est.); Percent of households with income of $100,000 or more: 7.3% (2006-2010 5-year est.); Poverty rate: 18.1% (2006-2010 5-year est.).
Education: Percent of population age 25 and over with: High school diploma (including GED) or higher: 78.6% (2006-2010 5-year est.); Bachelor's degree or higher: 15.4% (2006-2010 5-year est.); Master's degree or higher: 4.9% (2006-2010 5-year est.).

Vocational/Technical School(s)
Northern Tier Career Center (Public)
   Fall 2010 Enrollment: 60 . . . . (570) 265-8113
   2011-12 Tuition: $10,782
Housing: Homeownership rate: 70.5% (2010); Median home value: $97,700 (2006-2010 5-year est.); Median contract rent: $360 per month (2006-2010 5-year est.); Median year structure built: 1973 (2006-2010 5-year est.).
Hospitals: Memorial Hospital (94 beds)
Newspapers: The Bradford/Sullivan Pennysaver (Community news; Circulation 10,500); The Daily Review (Local news; Circulation 10,000); The Farmer's Friend (National news; Circulation 9,850)
Transportation: Commute to work: 94.7% car, 0.0% public transportation, 1.2% walk, 4.1% work from home (2006-2010 5-year est.); Travel time to work: 55.2% less than 15 minutes, 26.2% 15 to 30 minutes, 12.8% 30 to 45 minutes, 4.0% 45 to 60 minutes, 1.8% 60 minutes or more (2006-2010 5-year est.)
Airports: Bradford County (general aviation)
Additional Information Contacts
Central Bradford County Chamber of Commerce . . . . (570) 268-2732
   http://cbradchamber.org/community

TROY (borough). Covers a land area of 0.766 square miles and a water area of 0.003 square miles. Located at 41.78° N. Lat; 76.79° W. Long. Elevation is 1,099 feet.
Population: 1,276 (1990); 1,508 (2000); 1,354 (2010); Density: 1,766.7 persons per square mile (2010); Race: 97.1% White, 0.9% Black, 0.7% Asian, 0.2% American Indian/Alaska Native, 0.0% Native Hawaiian/Other Pacific Islander, 1.1% Other, 0.5% Hispanic of any race (2010); Average household size: 2.24 (2010); Median age: 44.7 (2010); Males per 100 females: 74.7 (2010); Marriage status: 27.9% never married, 51.3% now married, 8.4% widowed, 12.4% divorced (2006-2010 5-year est.); Foreign born: 0.9% (2006-2010 5-year est.); Ancestry (includes multiple ancestries): 25.8% German, 17.7% Irish, 15.9% English, 7.1% American, 6.0% Polish (2006-2010 5-year est.).
Economy: Single-family building permits issued: 0 (2011); Multi-family building permits issued: 0 (2011); Employment by occupation: 5.5% management, 1.3% professional, 15.3% services, 15.7% sales, 2.3% farming, 10.8% construction, 7.4% production (2006-2010 5-year est.).
Income: Per capita income: $18,446 (2006-2010 5-year est.); Median household income: $33,750 (2006-2010 5-year est.); Average household income: $42,452 (2006-2010 5-year est.); Percent of households with income of $100,000 or more: 6.8% (2006-2010 5-year est.); Poverty rate: 17.3% (2006-2010 5-year est.).
Education: Percent of population age 25 and over with: High school diploma (including GED) or higher: 85.8% (2006-2010 5-year est.); Bachelor's degree or higher: 15.8% (2006-2010 5-year est.); Master's degree or higher: 6.3% (2006-2010 5-year est.).

School District(s)
Troy Area SD (KG-12)
   2010-11 Enrollment: 1,564 . . . . (570) 297-2750
Housing: Homeownership rate: 51.7% (2010); Median home value: $95,300 (2006-2010 5-year est.); Median contract rent: $332 per month (2006-2010 5-year est.); Median year structure built: 1946 (2006-2010 5-year est.).
Hospitals: Troy Community Hospital (32 beds)
Newspapers: Gazette-Register (Local news; Circulation 1,000); The Troy Pennysaver (Community news; Circulation 12,851)
Transportation: Commute to work: 80.7% car, 0.0% public transportation, 13.0% walk, 4.5% work from home (2006-2010 5-year est.); Travel time to

work: 49.5% less than 15 minutes, 17.7% 15 to 30 minutes, 15.7% 30 to 45 minutes, 6.0% 45 to 60 minutes, 11.0% 60 minutes or more (2006-2010 5-year est.)

Additional Information Contacts
Mansfield Chamber of Commerce, Inc. . . . . (570) 662-3442
http://www.mansfield.org

TROY (township). Covers a land area of 36.041 square miles and a water area of 0.146 square miles. Located at 41.76° N. Lat; 76.78° W. Long. Elevation is 1,099 feet.
History: Farm Museum. Settled 1793; incorporated c.1844.
Population: 1,783 (1990); 1,645 (2000); 1,645 (2010); Density: 45.6 persons per square mile (2010); Race: 97.9% White, 0.5% Black, 0.6% Asian, 0.2% American Indian/Alaska Native, 0.0% Native Hawaiian/Other Pacific Islander, 0.8% Other, 1.2% Hispanic of any race (2010); Average household size: 2.36 (2010); Median age: 46.2 (2010); Males per 100 females: 98.7 (2010); Marriage status: 23.3% never married, 57.6% now married, 9.6% widowed, 9.4% divorced (2006-2010 5-year est.); Foreign born: 2.2% (2006-2010 5-year est.); Ancestry (includes multiple ancestries): 23.4% German, 17.0% English, 13.3% Irish, 7.9% American, 5.5% French (2006-2010 5-year est.).
Economy: Single-family building permits issued: 2 (2011); Multi-family building permits issued: 0 (2011); Employment by occupation: 9.3% management, 4.6% professional, 11.3% services, 12.4% sales, 2.4% farming, 15.9% construction, 12.4% production (2006-2010 5-year est.).
Income: Per capita income: $20,676 (2006-2010 5-year est.); Median household income: $41,625 (2006-2010 5-year est.); Average household income: $48,030 (2006-2010 5-year est.); Percent of households with income of $100,000 or more: 8.8% (2006-2010 5-year est.); Poverty rate: 11.6% (2006-2010 5-year est.).
Education: Percent of population age 25 and over with: High school diploma (including GED) or higher: 92.2% (2006-2010 5-year est.); Bachelor's degree or higher: 23.4% (2006-2010 5-year est.); Master's degree or higher: 7.8% (2006-2010 5-year est.).
Housing: Homeownership rate: 78.7% (2010); Median home value: $110,400 (2006-2010 5-year est.); Median contract rent: $368 per month (2006-2010 5-year est.); Median year structure built: 1972 (2006-2010 5-year est.).
Hospitals: Troy Community Hospital (32 beds)
Newspapers: Gazette-Register (Local news; Circulation 1,000); The Troy Pennysaver (Community news; Circulation 12,851)
Transportation: Commute to work: 88.2% car, 0.0% public transportation, 4.2% walk, 6.5% work from home (2006-2010 5-year est.); Travel time to work: 41.5% less than 15 minutes, 28.2% 15 to 30 minutes, 19.5% 30 to 45 minutes, 8.2% 45 to 60 minutes, 2.6% 60 minutes or more (2006-2010 5-year est.)
Additional Information Contacts
Mansfield Chamber of Commerce, Inc. . . . . (570) 662-3442
http://www.mansfield.org

TUSCARORA (township). Covers a land area of 29.025 square miles and a water area of 0.520 square miles. Located at 41.70° N. Lat; 76.16° W. Long.
Population: 996 (1990); 1,072 (2000); 1,131 (2010); Density: 39.0 persons per square mile (2010); Race: 97.4% White, 0.4% Black, 0.3% Asian, 0.3% American Indian/Alaska Native, 0.0% Native Hawaiian/Other Pacific Islander, 1.6% Other, 1.3% Hispanic of any race (2010); Average household size: 2.62 (2010); Median age: 43.2 (2010); Males per 100 females: 95.7 (2010); Marriage status: 17.2% never married, 58.3% now married, 7.5% widowed, 17.1% divorced (2006-2010 5-year est.); Foreign born: 1.2% (2006-2010 5-year est.); Ancestry (includes multiple ancestries): 34.0% German, 20.3% English, 16.0% Irish, 9.3% French, 9.2% American (2006-2010 5-year est.).
Economy: Single-family building permits issued: 1 (2011); Multi-family building permits issued: 0 (2011); Employment by occupation: 13.0% management, 5.9% professional, 4.6% services, 11.4% sales, 5.7% farming, 13.2% construction, 18.0% production (2006-2010 5-year est.).
Income: Per capita income: $22,056 (2006-2010 5-year est.); Median household income: $50,688 (2006-2010 5-year est.); Average household income: $53,707 (2006-2010 5-year est.); Percent of households with income of $100,000 or more: 11.9% (2006-2010 5-year est.); Poverty rate: 8.5% (2006-2010 5-year est.).
Education: Percent of population age 25 and over with: High school diploma (including GED) or higher: 86.5% (2006-2010 5-year est.);

Bachelor's degree or higher: 16.0% (2006-2010 5-year est.); Master's degree or higher: 4.5% (2006-2010 5-year est.).
Housing: Homeownership rate: 80.7% (2010); Median home value: $154,300 (2006-2010 5-year est.); Median contract rent: $488 per month (2006-2010 5-year est.); Median year structure built: 1972 (2006-2010 5-year est.).
Transportation: Commute to work: 92.5% car, 0.0% public transportation, 2.4% walk, 5.1% work from home (2006-2010 5-year est.); Travel time to work: 21.5% less than 15 minutes, 47.9% 15 to 30 minutes, 16.2% 30 to 45 minutes, 4.9% 45 to 60 minutes, 9.5% 60 minutes or more (2006-2010 5-year est.)
Additional Information Contacts
Greater Wyalusing Chamber of Commerce . . . . (570) 746-4922
http://www.wyalusing.net

ULSTER (township). Covers a land area of 18.739 square miles and a water area of 0.789 square miles. Located at 41.86° N. Lat; 76.54° W. Long. Elevation is 745 feet.
Population: 1,295 (1990); 1,340 (2000); 1,337 (2010); Density: 71.4 persons per square mile (2010); Race: 98.1% White, 0.9% Black, 0.2% Asian, 0.1% American Indian/Alaska Native, 0.0% Native Hawaiian/Other Pacific Islander, 0.7% Other, 0.9% Hispanic of any race (2010); Average household size: 2.47 (2010); Median age: 42.2 (2010); Males per 100 females: 99.3 (2010); Marriage status: 21.4% never married, 58.9% now married, 6.6% widowed, 13.1% divorced (2006-2010 5-year est.); Foreign born: 1.5% (2006-2010 5-year est.); Ancestry (includes multiple ancestries): 33.3% German, 19.6% Irish, 14.2% English, 4.2% French, 4.1% American (2006-2010 5-year est.).
Economy: Single-family building permits issued: 3 (2011); Multi-family building permits issued: 0 (2011); Employment by occupation: 7.3% management, 2.2% professional, 13.5% services, 18.4% sales, 4.9% farming, 9.1% construction, 10.2% production (2006-2010 5-year est.).
Income: Per capita income: $22,269 (2006-2010 5-year est.); Median household income: $46,302 (2006-2010 5-year est.); Average household income: $56,786 (2006-2010 5-year est.); Percent of households with income of $100,000 or more: 11.6% (2006-2010 5-year est.); Poverty rate: 6.1% (2006-2010 5-year est.).
Education: Percent of population age 25 and over with: High school diploma (including GED) or higher: 92.5% (2006-2010 5-year est.); Bachelor's degree or higher: 15.5% (2006-2010 5-year est.); Master's degree or higher: 4.5% (2006-2010 5-year est.).

School District(s)
Athens Area SD (KG-12)
    2010-11 Enrollment: 2,271 . . . . (570) 888-7766
Housing: Homeownership rate: 71.2% (2010); Median home value: $104,500 (2006-2010 5-year est.); Median contract rent: $459 per month (2006-2010 5-year est.); Median year structure built: 1953 (2006-2010 5-year est.).
Transportation: Commute to work: 93.6% car, 0.7% public transportation, 2.3% walk, 2.4% work from home (2006-2010 5-year est.); Travel time to work: 23.8% less than 15 minutes, 55.1% 15 to 30 minutes, 13.0% 30 to 45 minutes, 3.2% 45 to 60 minutes, 4.8% 60 minutes or more (2006-2010 5-year est.)
Additional Information Contacts
Greater Wyalusing Chamber of Commerce . . . . (570) 746-4922
http://www.wyalusing.net

WARREN (township). Covers a land area of 42.509 square miles and a water area of 0.267 square miles. Located at 41.95° N. Lat; 76.19° W. Long.
Population: 927 (1990); 1,025 (2000); 959 (2010); Density: 22.6 persons per square mile (2010); Race: 98.3% White, 0.2% Black, 0.2% Asian, 0.0% American Indian/Alaska Native, 0.0% Native Hawaiian/Other Pacific Islander, 1.3% Other, 1.4% Hispanic of any race (2010); Average household size: 2.56 (2010); Median age: 44.7 (2010); Males per 100 females: 108.5 (2010); Marriage status: 16.8% never married, 69.4% now married, 4.7% widowed, 9.0% divorced (2006-2010 5-year est.); Foreign born: 1.0% (2006-2010 5-year est.); Ancestry (includes multiple ancestries): 22.8% German, 21.4% English, 20.5% Irish, 9.9% Welsh, 6.4% Italian (2006-2010 5-year est.).
Economy: Single-family building permits issued: 2 (2011); Multi-family building permits issued: 0 (2011); Employment by occupation: 6.5% management, 3.0% professional, 8.2% services, 21.2% sales, 7.2% farming, 11.2% construction, 11.4% production (2006-2010 5-year est.).

Income: Per capita income: $20,167 (2006-2010 5-year est.); Median household income: $34,907 (2006-2010 5-year est.); Average household income: $50,672 (2006-2010 5-year est.); Percent of households with income of $100,000 or more: 12.2% (2006-2010 5-year est.); Poverty rate: 22.2% (2006-2010 5-year est.).

Education: Percent of population age 25 and over with: High school diploma (including GED) or higher: 85.8% (2006-2010 5-year est.); Bachelor's degree or higher: 10.5% (2006-2010 5-year est.); Master's degree or higher: 2.5% (2006-2010 5-year est.).

Housing: Homeownership rate: 84.0% (2010); Median home value: $126,500 (2006-2010 5-year est.); Median contract rent: $318 per month (2006-2010 5-year est.); Median year structure built: 1971 (2006-2010 5-year est.).

Transportation: Commute to work: 92.2% car, 0.0% public transportation, 1.2% walk, 5.2% work from home (2006-2010 5-year est.); Travel time to work: 14.8% less than 15 minutes, 20.0% 15 to 30 minutes, 43.0% 30 to 45 minutes, 15.3% 45 to 60 minutes, 7.0% 60 minutes or more (2006-2010 5-year est.)

Additional Information Contacts

Greater Wyalusing Chamber of Commerce . . . . (570) 746-4922
 http://www.wyalusing.net

WARREN CENTER (unincorporated postal area)
Zip Code: 18851
 Covers a land area of 28.022 square miles and a water area of 0.242 square miles. Located at 41.93° N. Lat; 76.17° W. Long. Elevation is 1,316 feet. Population: 706 (2010); Density: 25.2 persons per square mile (2010); Race: 98.0% White, 0.3% Black, 0.3% Asian, 0.0% American Indian/Alaska Native, 0.0% Native Hawaiian/Other Pacific Islander, 1.4% Other, 1.8% Hispanic of any race (2010); Average household size: 2.42 (2010); Median age: 46.7 (2010); Males per 100 females: 112.0 (2010); Homeownership rate: 86.3% (2010)

WELLS (township). Covers a land area of 33.758 square miles and a water area of 0.100 square miles. Located at 41.95° N. Lat; 76.87° W. Long.
Population: 1,018 (1990); 1,278 (2000); 814 (2010); Density: 24.1 persons per square mile (2010); Race: 96.6% White, 0.4% Black, 0.0% Asian, 0.5% American Indian/Alaska Native, 0.0% Native Hawaiian/Other Pacific Islander, 2.5% Other, 1.5% Hispanic of any race (2010); Average household size: 2.68 (2010); Median age: 45.3 (2010); Males per 100 females: 110.3 (2010); Marriage status: 27.6% never married, 57.4% now married, 9.9% widowed, 5.1% divorced (2006-2010 5-year est.); Foreign born: 0.0% (2006-2010 5-year est.); Ancestry (includes multiple ancestries): 23.5% German, 22.2% English, 12.2% Irish, 11.0% American, 6.2% Dutch (2006-2010 5-year est.).

Economy: Single-family building permits issued: 0 (2011); Multi-family building permits issued: 0 (2011); Employment by occupation: 15.0% management, 3.0% professional, 12.0% services, 8.0% sales, 3.4% farming, 14.8% construction, 4.0% production (2006-2010 5-year est.).

Income: Per capita income: $21,491 (2006-2010 5-year est.); Median household income: $41,653 (2006-2010 5-year est.); Average household income: $52,152 (2006-2010 5-year est.); Percent of households with income of $100,000 or more: 9.6% (2006-2010 5-year est.); Poverty rate: 6.4% (2006-2010 5-year est.).

Education: Percent of population age 25 and over with: High school diploma (including GED) or higher: 87.6% (2006-2010 5-year est.); Bachelor's degree or higher: 9.0% (2006-2010 5-year est.); Master's degree or higher: 3.8% (2006-2010 5-year est.).

Housing: Homeownership rate: 88.1% (2010); Median home value: $88,200 (2006-2010 5-year est.); Median contract rent: $393 per month (2006-2010 5-year est.); Median year structure built: 1978 (2006-2010 5-year est.).

Transportation: Commute to work: 87.8% car, 0.0% public transportation, 3.4% walk, 5.3% work from home (2006-2010 5-year est.); Travel time to work: 14.7% less than 15 minutes, 37.8% 15 to 30 minutes, 33.9% 30 to 45 minutes, 7.0% 45 to 60 minutes, 6.6% 60 minutes or more (2006-2010 5-year est.)

Additional Information Contacts

Wellsboro Area Chamber of Commerce . . . . (570) 724-1926
 http://www.wellsboropa.com

WEST BURLINGTON (township). Covers a land area of 23.932 square miles and a water area of 0.191 square miles. Located at 41.78° N. Lat; 76.66° W. Long. Elevation is 974 feet.
Population: 417 (1990); 782 (2000); 696 (2010); Density: 29.1 persons per square mile (2010); Race: 97.7% White, 0.3% Black, 0.0% Asian, 0.7% American Indian/Alaska Native, 0.0% Native Hawaiian/Other Pacific Islander, 1.3% Other, 1.1% Hispanic of any race (2010); Average household size: 2.53 (2010); Median age: 48.6 (2010); Males per 100 females: 102.9 (2010); Marriage status: 17.6% never married, 60.7% now married, 16.9% widowed, 4.9% divorced (2006-2010 5-year est.); Foreign born: 1.2% (2006-2010 5-year est.); Ancestry (includes multiple ancestries): 20.0% German, 15.8% English, 7.9% Irish, 5.8% Scotch-Irish, 5.0% American (2006-2010 5-year est.).

Economy: Single-family building permits issued: 0 (2011); Multi-family building permits issued: 0 (2011); Employment by occupation: 13.0% management, 0.0% professional, 10.1% services, 14.0% sales, 3.9% farming, 5.8% construction, 6.8% production (2006-2010 5-year est.).

Income: Per capita income: $23,443 (2006-2010 5-year est.); Median household income: $44,038 (2006-2010 5-year est.); Average household income: $55,458 (2006-2010 5-year est.); Percent of households with income of $100,000 or more: 8.7% (2006-2010 5-year est.); Poverty rate: 10.7% (2006-2010 5-year est.).

Education: Percent of population age 25 and over with: High school diploma (including GED) or higher: 85.0% (2006-2010 5-year est.); Bachelor's degree or higher: 8.1% (2006-2010 5-year est.); Master's degree or higher: 1.3% (2006-2010 5-year est.).

Housing: Homeownership rate: 88.3% (2010); Median home value: $104,900 (2006-2010 5-year est.); Median contract rent: $758 per month (2006-2010 5-year est.); Median year structure built: 1975 (2006-2010 5-year est.).

Transportation: Commute to work: 92.2% car, 0.0% public transportation, 3.9% walk, 3.9% work from home (2006-2010 5-year est.); Travel time to work: 21.8% less than 15 minutes, 57.4% 15 to 30 minutes, 12.7% 30 to 45 minutes, 3.6% 45 to 60 minutes, 4.6% 60 minutes or more (2006-2010 5-year est.)

WILMOT (township). Covers a land area of 43.767 square miles and a water area of 0.972 square miles. Located at 41.59° N. Lat; 76.26° W. Long. Elevation is 1,181 feet.
Population: 1,050 (1990); 1,177 (2000); 1,204 (2010); Density: 27.5 persons per square mile (2010); Race: 97.0% White, 0.6% Black, 0.6% Asian, 0.3% American Indian/Alaska Native, 0.0% Native Hawaiian/Other Pacific Islander, 1.5% Other, 0.9% Hispanic of any race (2010); Average household size: 2.46 (2010); Median age: 46.4 (2010); Males per 100 females: 106.5 (2010); Marriage status: 18.3% never married, 65.0% now married, 5.7% widowed, 10.9% divorced (2006-2010 5-year est.); Foreign born: 1.6% (2006-2010 5-year est.); Ancestry (includes multiple ancestries): 23.9% Irish, 20.3% German, 14.2% American, 12.9% Dutch, 11.3% English (2006-2010 5-year est.).

Economy: Single-family building permits issued: 0 (2011); Multi-family building permits issued: 0 (2011); Employment by occupation: 6.0% management, 0.0% professional, 8.8% services, 13.6% sales, 1.3% farming, 12.9% construction, 17.9% production (2006-2010 5-year est.).

Income: Per capita income: $24,798 (2006-2010 5-year est.); Median household income: $51,691 (2006-2010 5-year est.); Average household income: $59,183 (2006-2010 5-year est.); Percent of households with income of $100,000 or more: 13.4% (2006-2010 5-year est.); Poverty rate: 5.4% (2006-2010 5-year est.).

Education: Percent of population age 25 and over with: High school diploma (including GED) or higher: 89.1% (2006-2010 5-year est.); Bachelor's degree or higher: 15.3% (2006-2010 5-year est.); Master's degree or higher: 5.1% (2006-2010 5-year est.).

Housing: Homeownership rate: 88.5% (2010); Median home value: $130,800 (2006-2010 5-year est.); Median contract rent: $214 per month (2006-2010 5-year est.); Median year structure built: 1974 (2006-2010 5-year est.).

Transportation: Commute to work: 90.4% car, 0.9% public transportation, 0.7% walk, 7.1% work from home (2006-2010 5-year est.); Travel time to work: 17.7% less than 15 minutes, 44.5% 15 to 30 minutes, 29.4% 30 to 45 minutes, 1.7% 45 to 60 minutes, 6.7% 60 minutes or more (2006-2010 5-year est.)

Additional Information Contacts

Greater Scranton Chamber of Commerce . . . . (570) 342-7711
 http://www.scrantonchamber.com

WINDHAM (township). Covers a land area of 32.056 square miles and a water area of 0.230 square miles. Located at 41.96° N. Lat; 76.32° W. Long. Elevation is 991 feet.

Population: 862 (1990); 967 (2000); 933 (2010); Density: 29.1 persons per square mile (2010); Race: 97.3% White, 0.3% Black, 0.6% Asian, 0.3% American Indian/Alaska Native, 0.0% Native Hawaiian/Other Pacific Islander, 1.5% Other, 1.1% Hispanic of any race (2010); Average household size: 2.54 (2010); Median age: 44.1 (2010); Males per 100 females: 104.2 (2010); Marriage status: 19.5% never married, 67.1% now married, 5.8% widowed, 7.6% divorced (2006-2010 5-year est.); Foreign born: 1.4% (2006-2010 5-year est.); Ancestry (includes multiple ancestries): 26.2% German, 25.7% English, 11.9% Irish, 8.2% American, 7.0% Scotch-Irish (2006-2010 5-year est.).

Economy: Single-family building permits issued: 2 (2011); Multi-family building permits issued: 0 (2011); Employment by occupation: 7.7% management, 3.9% professional, 13.9% services, 6.7% sales, 0.0% farming, 15.2% construction, 11.6% production (2006-2010 5-year est.).

Income: Per capita income: $20,894 (2006-2010 5-year est.); Median household income: $41,964 (2006-2010 5-year est.); Average household income: $48,788 (2006-2010 5-year est.); Percent of households with income of $100,000 or more: 11.0% (2006-2010 5-year est.); Poverty rate: 11.6% (2006-2010 5-year est.).

Education: Percent of population age 25 and over with: High school diploma (including GED) or higher: 86.0% (2006-2010 5-year est.); Bachelor's degree or higher: 10.1% (2006-2010 5-year est.); Master's degree or higher: 3.5% (2006-2010 5-year est.).

Housing: Homeownership rate: 85.0% (2010); Median home value: $112,500 (2006-2010 5-year est.); Median contract rent: $388 per month (2006-2010 5-year est.); Median year structure built: 1983 (2006-2010 5-year est.).

Transportation: Commute to work: 92.8% car, 0.0% public transportation, 0.0% walk, 6.4% work from home (2006-2010 5-year est.); Travel time to work: 11.0% less than 15 minutes, 38.7% 15 to 30 minutes, 31.9% 30 to 45 minutes, 14.8% 45 to 60 minutes, 3.6% 60 minutes or more (2006-2010 5-year est.)

WYALUSING (borough). Covers a land area of 0.726 square miles and a water area of 0.068 square miles. Located at 41.67° N. Lat; 76.26° W. Long. Elevation is 705 feet.

Population: 686 (1990); 564 (2000); 596 (2010); Density: 821.0 persons per square mile (2010); Race: 97.7% White, 0.2% Black, 0.0% Asian, 1.3% American Indian/Alaska Native, 0.0% Native Hawaiian/Other Pacific Islander, 0.8% Other, 2.0% Hispanic of any race (2010); Average household size: 2.18 (2010); Median age: 42.6 (2010); Males per 100 females: 72.8 (2010); Marriage status: 19.1% never married, 46.8% now married, 14.2% widowed, 19.9% divorced (2006-2010 5-year est.); Foreign born: 3.1% (2006-2010 5-year est.); Ancestry (includes multiple ancestries): 48.2% German, 39.2% English, 18.8% Irish, 7.6% Scottish, 7.2% Dutch (2006-2010 5-year est.).

Economy: Single-family building permits issued: 0 (2011); Multi-family building permits issued: 0 (2011); Employment by occupation: 8.5% management, 6.8% professional, 10.7% services, 20.3% sales, 8.5% farming, 6.2% construction, 2.8% production (2006-2010 5-year est.).

Income: Per capita income: $25,727 (2006-2010 5-year est.); Median household income: $29,432 (2006-2010 5-year est.); Average household income: $51,974 (2006-2010 5-year est.); Percent of households with income of $100,000 or more: 9.5% (2006-2010 5-year est.); Poverty rate: 14.6% (2006-2010 5-year est.).

Education: Percent of population age 25 and over with: High school diploma (including GED) or higher: 92.6% (2006-2010 5-year est.); Bachelor's degree or higher: 23.7% (2006-2010 5-year est.); Master's degree or higher: 7.4% (2006-2010 5-year est.).

School District(s)

Wyalusing Area SD (KG-12)
    2010-11 Enrollment: 1,435 . . . . (570) 746-1605

Housing: Homeownership rate: 57.3% (2010); Median home value: $120,700 (2006-2010 5-year est.); Median contract rent: $295 per month (2006-2010 5-year est.); Median year structure built: before 1940 (2006-2010 5-year est.).

Newspapers: Rocket-Shopper (Community news; Circulation 16,700); Wyalusing Rocket Courier (Local news; Circulation 5,000)

Transportation: Commute to work: 94.1% car, 0.0% public transportation, 3.6% walk, 2.4% work from home (2006-2010 5-year est.); Travel time to work: 61.8% less than 15 minutes, 13.9% 15 to 30 minutes, 18.2% 30 to

45 minutes, 0.0% 45 to 60 minutes, 6.1% 60 minutes or more (2006-2010 5-year est.)

WYALUSING (township). Covers a land area of 27.931 square miles and a water area of 0.888 square miles. Located at 41.69° N. Lat; 76.26° W. Long. Elevation is 705 feet.

History: French Azilum Historical Site to Northwest.

Population: 1,235 (1990); 1,341 (2000); 1,242 (2010); Density: 44.5 persons per square mile (2010); Race: 97.8% White, 0.5% Black, 0.5% Asian, 0.1% American Indian/Alaska Native, 0.0% Native Hawaiian/Other Pacific Islander, 1.1% Other, 1.1% Hispanic of any race (2010); Average household size: 2.44 (2010); Median age: 44.3 (2010); Males per 100 females: 93.5 (2010); Marriage status: 22.0% never married, 61.1% now married, 6.2% widowed, 10.7% divorced (2006-2010 5-year est.); Foreign born: 4.0% (2006-2010 5-year est.); Ancestry (includes multiple ancestries): 26.4% German, 23.0% English, 19.4% Irish, 8.6% Italian, 8.1% American (2006-2010 5-year est.).

Economy: Single-family building permits issued: 6 (2011); Multi-family building permits issued: 0 (2011); Employment by occupation: 8.7% management, 5.4% professional, 3.3% services, 14.2% sales, 0.5% farming, 11.4% construction, 13.6% production (2006-2010 5-year est.).

Income: Per capita income: $25,458 (2006-2010 5-year est.); Median household income: $48,636 (2006-2010 5-year est.); Average household income: $63,016 (2006-2010 5-year est.); Percent of households with income of $100,000 or more: 18.1% (2006-2010 5-year est.); Poverty rate: 8.9% (2006-2010 5-year est.).

Taxes: Total city taxes per capita: $165 (2009); City property taxes per capita: $45 (2009).

Education: Percent of population age 25 and over with: High school diploma (including GED) or higher: 90.0% (2006-2010 5-year est.); Bachelor's degree or higher: 18.6% (2006-2010 5-year est.); Master's degree or higher: 5.1% (2006-2010 5-year est.).

Housing: Homeownership rate: 82.8% (2010); Median home value: $134,100 (2006-2010 5-year est.); Median contract rent: $442 per month (2006-2010 5-year est.); Median year structure built: 1955 (2006-2010 5-year est.).

Newspapers: Rocket-Shopper (Community news; Circulation 16,700); Wyalusing Rocket Courier (Local news; Circulation 5,000)

Transportation: Commute to work: 95.8% car, 1.9% public transportation, 1.1% walk, 1.1% work from home (2006-2010 5-year est.); Travel time to work: 37.9% less than 15 minutes, 26.2% 15 to 30 minutes, 22.1% 30 to 45 minutes, 9.4% 45 to 60 minutes, 4.4% 60 minutes or more (2006-2010 5-year est.)

Additional Information Contacts

Greater Wyalusing Chamber of Commerce . . . . (570) 746-4922
    http://www.wyalusing.net

WYSOX (township). Covers a land area of 22.722 square miles and a water area of 0.601 square miles. Located at 41.81° N. Lat; 76.38° W. Long. Elevation is 715 feet.

Population: 1,685 (1990); 1,763 (2000); 1,721 (2010); Density: 75.7 persons per square mile (2010); Race: 96.7% White, 0.3% Black, 0.6% Asian, 0.5% American Indian/Alaska Native, 0.0% Native Hawaiian/Other Pacific Islander, 1.9% Other, 1.4% Hispanic of any race (2010); Average household size: 2.49 (2010); Median age: 44.6 (2010); Males per 100 females: 103.9 (2010); Marriage status: 20.1% never married, 59.6% now married, 8.1% widowed, 12.2% divorced (2006-2010 5-year est.); Foreign born: 1.7% (2006-2010 5-year est.); Ancestry (includes multiple ancestries): 25.0% German, 22.0% English, 12.5% Irish, 9.7% American, 5.7% French (2006-2010 5-year est.).

Economy: Single-family building permits issued: 1 (2011); Multi-family building permits issued: 0 (2011); Employment by occupation: 13.5% management, 2.4% professional, 9.2% services, 14.4% sales, 4.5% farming, 8.4% construction, 11.4% production (2006-2010 5-year est.).

Income: Per capita income: $24,151 (2006-2010 5-year est.); Median household income: $45,192 (2006-2010 5-year est.); Average household income: $58,635 (2006-2010 5-year est.); Percent of households with income of $100,000 or more: 10.6% (2006-2010 5-year est.); Poverty rate: 12.4% (2006-2010 5-year est.).

Education: Percent of population age 25 and over with: High school diploma (including GED) or higher: 85.0% (2006-2010 5-year est.); Bachelor's degree or higher: 19.9% (2006-2010 5-year est.); Master's degree or higher: 6.3% (2006-2010 5-year est.).

Housing: Homeownership rate: 77.0% (2010); Median home value: $125,000 (2006-2010 5-year est.); Median contract rent: $475 per month

(2006-2010 5-year est.); Median year structure built: 1969 (2006-2010 5-year est.).

Transportation: Commute to work: 91.8% car, 0.0% public transportation, 3.4% walk, 3.8% work from home (2006-2010 5-year est.); Travel time to work: 46.5% less than 15 minutes, 29.9% 15 to 30 minutes, 12.0% 30 to 45 minutes, 10.9% 45 to 60 minutes, 0.8% 60 minutes or more (2006-2010 5-year est.)

Additional Information Contacts

Central Bradford County Chamber of Commerce . . . . (570) 268-2732
  http://cbradchamber.org

Bucks County

Located in southeastern Pennsylvania; bounded on the east and southeast by the Delaware River and the New Jersey border. Covers a land area of 604.307 square miles, a water area of 17.567 square miles, and is located in the Eastern Time Zone at 40.34° N. Lat., 75.11° W. Long. The county was founded in 1682. County seat is Doylestown.

Bucks County is part of the Philadelphia-Camden-Wilmington, PA-NJ-DE-MD Metropolitan Statistical Area. The entire metro area includes: Camden, NJ Metropolitan Division (Burlington County, NJ; Camden County, NJ; Gloucester County, NJ); Philadelphia, PA Metropolitan Division (Bucks County, PA; Chester County, PA; Delaware County, PA; Montgomery County, PA; Philadelphia County, PA); Wilmington, DE-MD-NJ Metropolitan Division (New Castle County, DE; Cecil County, MD; Salem County, NJ)

Weather Station: Bucksville										Elevation: 459 feet		
	Jan	Feb	Mar	Apr	May	Jun	Jul	Aug	Sep	Oct	Nov	Dec
High	38	41	49	62	72	80	84	82	75	64	54	42
Low	19	21	28	38	48	57	62	61	53	41	32	24
Precip	3.5	2.9	4.0	4.4	4.2	4.3	5.3	4.0	4.6	4.4	3.8	4.3
Snow	7.7	7.1	4.8	1.5	0.0	tr	0.0	0.0	0.0	tr	0.6	3.3

High and Low temperatures in degrees Fahrenheit; Precipitation and Snow in inches

Weather Station: Neshaminy Falls										Elevation: 60 feet		
	Jan	Feb	Mar	Apr	May	Jun	Jul	Aug	Sep	Oct	Nov	Dec
High	42	45	53	64	74	83	87	86	79	67	57	45
Low	21	23	29	39	48	58	64	62	54	42	33	25
Precip	3.5	2.7	4.3	4.2	4.3	4.5	5.2	4.1	4.5	3.8	3.7	3.9
Snow	3.7	3.4	2.1	0.3	0.0	0.0	0.0	0.0	0.0	tr	tr	2.4

High and Low temperatures in degrees Fahrenheit; Precipitation and Snow in inches

Population: 541,176 (1990); 597,635 (2000); 625,249 (2010); Race: 89.2% White, 3.6% Black, 3.8% Asian, 0.2% American Indian/Alaska Native, 0.0% Native Hawaiian/Other Pacific Islander, 3.2% Other, 4.3% Hispanic of any race (2010); Density: 1,034.7 persons per square mile (2010); Average household size: 2.63 (2010); Median age: 42.0 (2010); Males per 100 females: 96.3 (2010).

Religion: Six largest groups: 51.5% Catholicism, 3.2% Lutheran, 3.2% Presbyterian-Reformed, 2.8% Methodist/Pietist, 2.2% Non-Denominational, 1.4% Judaism (2010)

Economy: Unemployment rate: 7.8% (August 2012); Total civilian labor force: 344,867 (August 2012); Leading industries: 16.6% health care and social assistance; 15.9% retail trade; 10.7% manufacturing (2010); Farms: 934 totaling 75,883 acres (2007); Companies that employ 500 or more persons: 20 (2010); Companies that employ 100 to 499 persons: 361 (2010); Companies that employ less than 100 persons: 18,440 (2010); Black-owned businesses: 976 (2007); Hispanic-owned businesses: 1,327 (2007); Asian-owned businesses: 2,290 (2007); Women-owned businesses: 16,205 (2007); Retail sales per capita: $18,168 (2010). Single-family building permits issued: 416 (2011); Multi-family building permits issued: 38 (2011).

Income: Per capita income: $35,687 (2006-2010 5-year est.); Median household income: $74,828 (2006-2010 5-year est.); Average household income: $94,979 (2006-2010 5-year est.); Percent of households with income of $100,000 or more: 35.0% (2006-2010 5-year est.); Poverty rate: 4.9% (2006-2010 5-year est.); Bankruptcy rate: 2.86% (2011).

Taxes: Total county taxes per capita: $279 (2009); County property taxes per capita: $279 (2009).

Education: Percent of population age 25 and over with: High school diploma (including GED) or higher: 91.9% (2006-2010 5-year est.); Bachelor's degree or higher: 34.5% (2006-2010 5-year est.); Master's degree or higher: 13.4% (2006-2010 5-year est.).

Housing: Homeownership rate: 77.1% (2010); Median home value: $321,500 (2006-2010 5-year est.); Median contract rent: $890 per month (2006-2010 5-year est.); Median year structure built: 1973 (2006-2010 5-year est.)

Health: Birth rate: 98.8 per 10,000 population (2011); Death rate: 84.2 per 10,000 population (2011); Age-adjusted cancer mortality rate: 176.6 deaths per 100,000 population (2009); Number of physicians: 29.5 per 10,000 population (2010); Hospital beds: 19.8 per 10,000 population (2008); Hospital admissions: 999.5 per 10,000 population (2008).

Environment: Air Quality Index: 68.2% good, 29.9% moderate, 1.9% unhealthy for sensitive individuals, 0.0% unhealthy (percent of days in 2011)

Elections: 2012 Presidential election results: 50.0% Obama, 48.8% Romney

National and State Parks: High Rocks State Park; Neshaminy State Park; Nockamixon State Park; Pennsbury Manor State Park; Ralph Stover State Park; Roosevelt State Park; Tyler State Park

Additional Information Contacts

Bucks County Government . . . . (215) 348-6000
  http://www.buckscounty.org
Lower Bucks County Chamber of Commerce . . . . (215) 943-7400
  http://www.lbccc.org

Bucks County Communities

BEDMINSTER (township). Covers a land area of 30.461 square miles and a water area of 0.779 square miles. Located at 40.43° N. Lat; 75.19° W. Long. Elevation is 423 feet.

Population: 4,597 (1990); 4,804 (2000); 6,574 (2010); Density: 215.8 persons per square mile (2010); Race: 94.9% White, 0.8% Black, 1.9% Asian, 0.2% American Indian/Alaska Native, 0.0% Native Hawaiian/Other Pacific Islander, 2.2% Other, 2.5% Hispanic of any race (2010); Average household size: 2.74 (2010); Median age: 40.1 (2010); Males per 100 females: 99.9 (2010); Marriage status: 24.3% never married, 62.8% now married, 7.1% widowed, 5.9% divorced (2006-2010 5-year est.); Foreign born: 2.6% (2006-2010 5-year est.); Ancestry (includes multiple ancestries): 42.3% German, 22.4% Irish, 12.7% English, 12.4% Italian, 10.6% Polish (2006-2010 5-year est.).

Economy: Single-family building permits issued: 33 (2011); Multi-family building permits issued: 0 (2011); Employment by occupation: 16.9% management, 7.4% professional, 7.7% services, 15.9% sales, 2.8% farming, 12.2% construction, 7.0% production (2006-2010 5-year est.).

Income: Per capita income: $34,856 (2006-2010 5-year est.); Median household income: $85,709 (2006-2010 5-year est.); Average household income: $95,815 (2006-2010 5-year est.); Percent of households with income of $100,000 or more: 41.5% (2006-2010 5-year est.); Poverty rate: 3.1% (2006-2010 5-year est.).

Education: Percent of population age 25 and over with: High school diploma (including GED) or higher: 93.1% (2006-2010 5-year est.); Bachelor's degree or higher: 35.2% (2006-2010 5-year est.); Master's degree or higher: 13.4% (2006-2010 5-year est.).

Housing: Homeownership rate: 85.1% (2010); Median home value: $404,900 (2006-2010 5-year est.); Median contract rent: $984 per month (2006-2010 5-year est.); Median year structure built: 1980 (2006-2010 5-year est.).

Safety: Violent crime rate: 4.5 per 10,000 population; Property crime rate: 74.3 per 10,000 population (2011).

Transportation: Commute to work: 94.7% car, 1.2% public transportation, 0.4% walk, 3.0% work from home (2006-2010 5-year est.); Travel time to work: 14.4% less than 15 minutes, 37.1% 15 to 30 minutes, 25.1% 30 to 45 minutes, 10.8% 45 to 60 minutes, 12.5% 60 minutes or more (2006-2010 5-year est.)

Additional Information Contacts

Bedminster Township . . . . (215) 795-2190
  http://www.bedminsterpa.org
Upper Bucks Chamber of Commerce . . . . (215) 536-3211
  http://www.ubcc.org

BENSALEM (township). Covers a land area of 19.838 square miles and a water area of 1.092 square miles. Located at 40.11° N. Lat; 74.94° W. Long. Elevation is 98 feet.

Population: 56,788 (1990); 58,434 (2000); 60,427 (2010); Density: 3,046.1 persons per square mile (2010); Race: 75.6% White, 7.3% Black, 10.2% Asian, 0.5% American Indian/Alaska Native, 0.0% Native Hawaiian/Other Pacific Islander, 6.4% Other, 8.4% Hispanic of any race

(2010); Average household size: 2.55 (2010); Median age: 39.6 (2010); Males per 100 females: 97.9 (2010); Marriage status: 30.9% never married, 53.0% now married, 6.9% widowed, 9.3% divorced (2006-2010 5-year est.); Foreign born: 15.7% (2006-2010 5-year est.); Ancestry (includes multiple ancestries): 26.5% Irish, 22.1% German, 14.5% Italian, 9.2% Polish, 7.8% English (2006-2010 5-year est.).

Economy: Unemployment rate: 8.5% (August 2012); Total civilian labor force: 34,836 (August 2012); Single-family building permits issued: 31 (2011); Multi-family building permits issued: 0 (2011); Employment by occupation: 9.5% management, 5.3% professional, 9.1% services, 19.2% sales, 5.3% farming, 9.3% construction, 6.6% production (2006-2010 5-year est.).

Income: Per capita income: $27,707 (2006-2010 5-year est.); Median household income: $59,668 (2006-2010 5-year est.); Average household income: $70,002 (2006-2010 5-year est.); Percent of households with income of $100,000 or more: 21.4% (2006-2010 5-year est.); Poverty rate: 6.4% (2006-2010 5-year est.).

Taxes: Total city taxes per capita: $296 (2009); City property taxes per capita: $188 (2009).

Education: Percent of population age 25 and over with: High school diploma (including GED) or higher: 87.7% (2006-2010 5-year est.); Bachelor's degree or higher: 22.7% (2006-2010 5-year est.); Master's degree or higher: 8.2% (2006-2010 5-year est.).

School District(s)

Bensalem Township SD (KG-12)
   2010-11 Enrollment: 6,120 . . . . (215) 750-2800
School Lane CS (KG-08)
   2010-11 Enrollment: 595. . . . . (215) 245-6055

Two-year College(s)

ITT Technical Institute-Bensalem (Private, For-profit)
   Fall 2010 Enrollment: 741 . . . . (215) 244-8871
   2011-12 Tuition: In-state $18,048; Out-of-state $18,048

Housing: Homeownership rate: 58.5% (2010); Median home value: $263,600 (2006-2010 5-year est.); Median contract rent: $913 per month (2006-2010 5-year est.); Median year structure built: 1973 (2006-2010 5-year est.).

Safety: Violent crime rate: 15.3 per 10,000 population; Property crime rate: 377.4 per 10,000 population (2011).

Transportation: Commute to work: 90.7% car, 5.2% public transportation, 1.7% walk, 1.8% work from home (2006-2010 5-year est.); Travel time to work: 23.9% less than 15 minutes, 39.1% 15 to 30 minutes, 20.3% 30 to 45 minutes, 8.9% 45 to 60 minutes, 7.7% 60 minutes or more (2006-2010 5-year est.)

Additional Information Contacts

Bensalem Township . . . . (215) 633-3654
   http://www.bensalem-township.net
Lower Bucks County Chamber of Commerce . . . . (215) 943-7400
   http://www.lbccc.org

BRIDGETON (township). Covers a land area of 6.583 square miles and a water area of 0.220 square miles. Located at 40.55° N. Lat; 75.12° W. Long.

Population: 1,408 (1990); 1,408 (2000); 1,277 (2010); Density: 194.0 persons per square mile (2010); Race: 98.0% White, 0.4% Black, 0.5% Asian, 0.1% American Indian/Alaska Native, 0.0% Native Hawaiian/Other Pacific Islander, 1.0% Other, 1.7% Hispanic of any race (2010); Average household size: 2.24 (2010); Median age: 48.4 (2010); Males per 100 females: 99.2 (2010); Marriage status: 21.2% never married, 59.2% now married, 6.3% widowed, 13.3% divorced (2006-2010 5-year est.); Foreign born: 4.0% (2006-2010 5-year est.); Ancestry (includes multiple ancestries): 37.7% German, 20.9% Irish, 13.8% English, 11.5% Italian, 6.0% Dutch (2006-2010 5-year est.).

Economy: Single-family building permits issued: 1 (2011); Multi-family building permits issued: 0 (2011); Employment by occupation: 12.9% management, 5.3% professional, 12.2% services, 10.3% sales, 3.4% farming, 15.5% construction, 10.3% production (2006-2010 5-year est.).

Income: Per capita income: $32,355 (2006-2010 5-year est.); Median household income: $59,632 (2006-2010 5-year est.); Average household income: $78,638 (2006-2010 5-year est.); Percent of households with income of $100,000 or more: 26.3% (2006-2010 5-year est.); Poverty rate: 8.8% (2006-2010 5-year est.).

Education: Percent of population age 25 and over with: High school diploma (including GED) or higher: 88.0% (2006-2010 5-year est.); Bachelor's degree or higher: 22.7% (2006-2010 5-year est.); Master's degree or higher: 8.3% (2006-2010 5-year est.).

Housing: Homeownership rate: 77.9% (2010); Median home value: $332,900 (2006-2010 5-year est.); Median contract rent: $732 per month (2006-2010 5-year est.); Median year structure built: 1957 (2006-2010 5-year est.).

Transportation: Commute to work: 89.8% car, 0.3% public transportation, 3.9% walk, 5.7% work from home (2006-2010 5-year est.); Travel time to work: 21.8% less than 15 minutes, 28.9% 15 to 30 minutes, 17.6% 30 to 45 minutes, 15.9% 45 to 60 minutes, 15.9% 60 minutes or more (2006-2010 5-year est.)

Additional Information Contacts

Lancaster Chamber of Commerce & Industry . . . . (717) 397-3531
   http://www.lancasterchamber.com

BRISTOL (borough). Covers a land area of 1.624 square miles and a water area of 0.231 square miles. Located at 40.10° N. Lat; 74.85° W. Long. Elevation is 20 feet.

History: Named for Bristol in Gloucestershire and Somerset, England, an important trade center. The state's third-oldest borough, it was once a busy river port with important shipbuilding activities. Among its historic structures is the Friends Meetinghouse, built c.1710. Historic Fallsington, a restoration of 17th- and 18th-century buildings is to the north, and Pennsburg Manor State Park, a replica of William Penn's country manor is to the northeast. Settled 1697. Incorporated 1720.

Population: 10,405 (1990); 9,923 (2000); 9,726 (2010); Density: 5,987.2 persons per square mile (2010); Race: 81.1% White, 9.5% Black, 0.6% Asian, 0.2% American Indian/Alaska Native, 0.0% Native Hawaiian/Other Pacific Islander, 8.6% Other, 14.2% Hispanic of any race (2010); Average household size: 2.45 (2010); Median age: 38.0 (2010); Males per 100 females: 93.7 (2010); Marriage status: 31.7% never married, 46.6% now married, 7.6% widowed, 14.1% divorced (2006-2010 5-year est.); Foreign born: 3.7% (2006-2010 5-year est.); Ancestry (includes multiple ancestries): 36.0% Irish, 27.7% Italian, 18.0% German, 9.4% English, 5.1% Polish (2006-2010 5-year est.).

Economy: Single-family building permits issued: 1 (2011); Multi-family building permits issued: 0 (2011); Employment by occupation: 8.6% management, 3.5% professional, 7.5% services, 21.4% sales, 3.8% farming, 8.3% construction, 7.0% production (2006-2010 5-year est.).

Income: Per capita income: $24,360 (2006-2010 5-year est.); Median household income: $47,693 (2006-2010 5-year est.); Average household income: $56,833 (2006-2010 5-year est.); Percent of households with income of $100,000 or more: 13.1% (2006-2010 5-year est.); Poverty rate: 9.4% (2006-2010 5-year est.).

Education: Percent of population age 25 and over with: High school diploma (including GED) or higher: 85.2% (2006-2010 5-year est.); Bachelor's degree or higher: 12.8% (2006-2010 5-year est.); Master's degree or higher: 5.6% (2006-2010 5-year est.).

School District(s)

Bristol Borough SD (PK-12)
   2010-11 Enrollment: 1,318 . . . . (215) 781-1011
Bristol Township SD (PK-12)
   2010-11 Enrollment: 6,228 . . . . (215) 943-3200

Two-year College(s)

Pennco Tech-Bristol (Private, For-profit)
   Fall 2010 Enrollment: 708 . . . . (215) 785-0111

Housing: Homeownership rate: 55.6% (2010); Median home value: $184,700 (2006-2010 5-year est.); Median contract rent: $708 per month (2006-2010 5-year est.); Median year structure built: 1951 (2006-2010 5-year est.).

Hospitals: Lower Bucks Hospital (150 beds)

Safety: Violent crime rate: 22.5 per 10,000 population; Property crime rate: 378.2 per 10,000 population (2011).

Newspapers: Bristol Express (Local news; Circulation 6,350); Bristol Pilot (Community news; Circulation 5,500); Burlington Mail (Local news; Circulation 6,235)

Transportation: Commute to work: 88.8% car, 3.8% public transportation, 3.9% walk, 2.7% work from home (2006-2010 5-year est.); Travel time to work: 33.3% less than 15 minutes, 40.0% 15 to 30 minutes, 18.2% 30 to 45 minutes, 5.2% 45 to 60 minutes, 3.3% 60 minutes or more (2006-2010 5-year est.)

Additional Information Contacts

Borough of Bristol . . . . (215) 785-0500
   http://www.bristoltownship.org
Lower Bucks County Chamber of Commerce . . . . (215) 943-7400
   http://www.lbccc.org

BRISTOL (township). Covers a land area of 15.942 square miles and a water area of 1.259 square miles. Located at 40.12° N. Lat; 74.87° W. Long. Elevation is 20 feet.

History: Bristol, settled in 1697, was an early port of call for river traffic, and completion in 1834 of the Easton to Bristol canal furthered local progress.

Population: 57,129 (1990); 55,521 (2000); 54,582 (2010); Density: 3,423.8 persons per square mile (2010); Race: 81.0% White, 10.2% Black, 2.8% Asian, 0.2% American Indian/Alaska Native, 0.0% Native Hawaiian/Other Pacific Islander, 5.8% Other, 7.4% Hispanic of any race (2010); Average household size: 2.73 (2010); Median age: 38.8 (2010); Males per 100 females: 98.8 (2010); Marriage status: 28.9% never married, 52.4% now married, 7.1% widowed, 11.6% divorced (2006-2010 5-year est.); Foreign born: 7.8% (2006-2010 5-year est.); Ancestry (includes multiple ancestries): 29.6% Irish, 25.4% German, 14.4% Italian, 10.0% English, 9.6% Polish (2006-2010 5-year est.).

Economy: Unemployment rate: 10.7% (August 2012); Total civilian labor force: 30,096 (August 2012); Single-family building permits issued: 3 (2011); Multi-family building permits issued: 0 (2011); Employment by occupation: 7.1% management, 2.9% professional, 9.2% services, 21.0% sales, 3.4% farming, 11.1% construction, 9.1% production (2006-2010 5-year est.).

Income: Per capita income: $24,364 (2006-2010 5-year est.); Median household income: $54,626 (2006-2010 5-year est.); Average household income: $63,657 (2006-2010 5-year est.); Percent of households with income of $100,000 or more: 16.6% (2006-2010 5-year est.); Poverty rate: 7.9% (2006-2010 5-year est.).

Taxes: Total city taxes per capita: $360 (2009); City property taxes per capita: $177 (2009).

Education: Percent of population age 25 and over with: High school diploma (including GED) or higher: 87.4% (2006-2010 5-year est.); Bachelor's degree or higher: 13.0% (2006-2010 5-year est.); Master's degree or higher: 3.7% (2006-2010 5-year est.).

Two-year College(s)

Pennco Tech-Bristol (Private, For-profit)

   Fall 2010 Enrollment: 708 . . . . (215) 785-0111

Housing: Homeownership rate: 74.3% (2010); Median home value: $223,100 (2006-2010 5-year est.); Median contract rent: $787 per month (2006-2010 5-year est.); Median year structure built: 1959 (2006-2010 5-year est.).

Hospitals: Lower Bucks Hospital (150 beds)

Safety: Violent crime rate: 23.0 per 10,000 population; Property crime rate: 329.6 per 10,000 population (2011).

Newspapers: Bristol Express (Local news; Circulation 6,350); Bristol Pilot (Community news; Circulation 5,500); Burlington Mail (Local news; Circulation 6,235).

Transportation: Commute to work: 94.4% car, 3.1% public transportation, 0.6% walk, 1.3% work from home (2006-2010 5-year est.); Travel time to work: 31.5% less than 15 minutes, 39.6% 15 to 30 minutes, 15.5% 30 to 45 minutes, 6.7% 45 to 60 minutes, 6.7% 60 minutes or more (2006-2010 5-year est.)

Additional Information Contacts

Bristol Township . . . . (215) 785-0500
   http://www.bristoltownship.org

Lower Bucks County Chamber of Commerce . . . . (215) 943-7400
   http://www.lbccc.org

BRITTANY FARMS-THE HIGHLANDS (CDP). Covers a land area of 1.192 square miles and a water area of 0.005 square miles. Located at 40.27° N. Lat; 75.21° W. Long.

Population: 2,747 (1990); 3,268 (2000); 3,695 (2010); Density: 3,100.6 persons per square mile (2010); Race: 92.6% White, 2.1% Black, 3.7% Asian, 0.0% American Indian/Alaska Native, 0.0% Native Hawaiian/Other Pacific Islander, 1.6% Other, 2.5% Hispanic of any race (2010); Average household size: 2.37 (2010); Median age: 42.1 (2010); Males per 100 females: 86.5 (2010); Marriage status: 18.4% never married, 59.1% now married, 13.2% widowed, 9.3% divorced (2006-2010 5-year est.); Foreign born: 8.4% (2006-2010 5-year est.); Ancestry (includes multiple ancestries): 35.3% Irish, 29.5% German, 15.4% Italian, 8.8% Polish, 7.2% English (2006-2010 5-year est.).

Economy: Employment by occupation: 14.1% management, 10.0% professional, 5.1% services, 22.6% sales, 2.5% farming, 5.0% construction, 3.0% production (2006-2010 5-year est.).

Income: Per capita income: $35,181 (2006-2010 5-year est.); Median household income: $85,104 (2006-2010 5-year est.); Average household income: $88,613 (2006-2010 5-year est.); Percent of households with income of $100,000 or more: 38.3% (2006-2010 5-year est.); Poverty rate: 5.7% (2006-2010 5-year est.).

Education: Percent of population age 25 and over with: High school diploma (including GED) or higher: 95.0% (2006-2010 5-year est.); Bachelor's degree or higher: 40.9% (2006-2010 5-year est.); Master's degree or higher: 17.7% (2006-2010 5-year est.).

Housing: Homeownership rate: 83.2% (2010); Median home value: $284,900 (2006-2010 5-year est.); Median contract rent: $1,252 per month (2006-2010 5-year est.); Median year structure built: 1982 (2006-2010 5-year est.).

Transportation: Commute to work: 86.6% car, 0.8% public transportation, 2.4% walk, 10.1% work from home (2006-2010 5-year est.); Travel time to work: 14.8% less than 15 minutes, 42.0% 15 to 30 minutes, 22.3% 30 to 45 minutes, 11.1% 45 to 60 minutes, 9.8% 60 minutes or more (2006-2010 5-year est.)

BUCKINGHAM (township). Covers a land area of 32.882 square miles and a water area of 0.138 square miles. Located at 40.32° N. Lat; 75.06° W. Long. Elevation is 236 feet.

History: Buckingham takes its name from Buckingham in Buckinghamshire known as Bucks County in England. Buckingham Township was once known as Greenville and was once the historic county seat of the English Bucks County.

Population: 9,364 (1990); 16,442 (2000); 20,075 (2010); Density: 610.5 persons per square mile (2010); Race: 93.8% White, 1.1% Black, 3.4% Asian, 0.1% American Indian/Alaska Native, 0.0% Native Hawaiian/Other Pacific Islander, 1.6% Other, 2.4% Hispanic of any race (2010); Average household size: 2.86 (2010); Median age: 43.2 (2010); Males per 100 females: 96.3 (2010); Marriage status: 21.3% never married, 67.0% now married, 6.2% widowed, 5.6% divorced (2006-2010 5-year est.); Foreign born: 7.0% (2006-2010 5-year est.); Ancestry (includes multiple ancestries): 28.5% Irish, 22.8% Italian, 20.7% German, 12.8% English, 8.0% Polish (2006-2010 5-year est.).

Economy: Single-family building permits issued: 43 (2011); Multi-family building permits issued: 0 (2011); Employment by occupation: 23.8% management, 4.9% professional, 4.0% services, 13.4% sales, 2.6% farming, 7.2% construction, 1.6% production (2006-2010 5-year est.).

Income: Per capita income: $47,957 (2006-2010 5-year est.); Median household income: $111,207 (2006-2010 5-year est.); Average household income: $137,621 (2006-2010 5-year est.); Percent of households with income of $100,000 or more: 55.5% (2006-2010 5-year est.); Poverty rate: 3.2% (2006-2010 5-year est.).

Taxes: Total city taxes per capita: $335 (2009); City property taxes per capita: $25 (2009).

Education: Percent of population age 25 and over with: High school diploma (including GED) or higher: 96.1% (2006-2010 5-year est.); Bachelor's degree or higher: 54.5% (2006-2010 5-year est.); Master's degree or higher: 24.9% (2006-2010 5-year est.).

School District(s)

Central Bucks SD (KG-12)

   2010-11 Enrollment: 20,432 . . . . (267) 893-2000

Housing: Homeownership rate: 92.4% (2010); Median home value: $546,200 (2006-2010 5-year est.); Median contract rent: $1,166 per month (2006-2010 5-year est.); Median year structure built: 1991 (2006-2010 5-year est.).

Safety: Violent crime rate: 4.5 per 10,000 population; Property crime rate: 61.6 per 10,000 population (2011).

Transportation: Commute to work: 87.7% car, 1.3% public transportation, 1.9% walk, 8.0% work from home (2006-2010 5-year est.); Travel time to work: 21.5% less than 15 minutes, 21.0% 15 to 30 minutes, 20.8% 30 to 45 minutes, 16.0% 45 to 60 minutes, 20.7% 60 minutes or more (2006-2010 5-year est.)

Additional Information Contacts

Buckingham Township . . . . (215) 794-8834
   http://www.buckinghampa.org

Central Bucks Chamber of Commerce . . . . (215) 348-3913
   http://www.centralbuckschamber.com

CARVERSVILLE (unincorporated postal area)

Zip Code: 18913

   Covers a land area of 1.470 square miles and a water area of 0.007 square miles. Located at 40.37° N. Lat; 75.06° W. Long. Elevation is 213 feet. Population: 185 (2010); Density: 125.8 persons per square mile (2010); Race: 95.7% White, 0.5% Black, 3.8% Asian, 0.0%

American Indian/Alaska Native, 0.0% Native Hawaiian/Other Pacific Islander, 0.0% Other, 0.0% Hispanic of any race (2010); Average household size: 2.03 (2010); Median age: 56.1 (2010); Males per 100 females: 98.9 (2010); Homeownership rate: 77.0% (2010)

CHALFONT (borough). Covers a land area of 1.618 square miles and a water area of 0.018 square miles. Located at 40.29° N. Lat; 75.21° W. Long. Elevation is 285 feet.

Population: 3,063 (1990); 3,900 (2000); 4,009 (2010); Density: 2,477.1 persons per square mile (2010); Race: 94.1% White, 1.4% Black, 3.0% Asian, 0.3% American Indian/Alaska Native, 0.0% Native Hawaiian/Other Pacific Islander, 1.2% Other, 1.7% Hispanic of any race (2010); Average household size: 2.70 (2010); Median age: 40.2 (2010); Males per 100 females: 94.9 (2010); Marriage status: 27.5% never married, 61.0% now married, 7.0% widowed, 4.5% divorced (2006-2010 5-year est.); Foreign born: 3.9% (2006-2010 5-year est.); Ancestry (includes multiple ancestries): 41.7% German, 26.4% Irish, 17.4% Italian, 11.6% English, 5.9% Polish (2006-2010 5-year est.).

Economy: Single-family building permits issued: 9 (2011); Multi-family building permits issued: 0 (2011); Employment by occupation: 13.6% management, 6.3% professional, 1.8% services, 23.8% sales, 3.2% farming, 4.4% construction, 1.0% production (2006-2010 5-year est.).

Income: Per capita income: $38,417 (2006-2010 5-year est.); Median household income: $91,019 (2006-2010 5-year est.); Average household income: $106,982 (2006-2010 5-year est.); Percent of households with income of $100,000 or more: 44.1% (2006-2010 5-year est.); Poverty rate: 4.4% (2006-2010 5-year est.).

Education: Percent of population age 25 and over with: High school diploma (including GED) or higher: 95.9% (2006-2010 5-year est.); Bachelor's degree or higher: 38.1% (2006-2010 5-year est.); Master's degree or higher: 18.3% (2006-2010 5-year est.).

School District(s)

Central Bucks SD (KG-12)

   2010-11 Enrollment: 20,432 . . . . (267) 893-2000

Housing: Homeownership rate: 85.3% (2010); Median home value: $351,200 (2006-2010 5-year est.); Median contract rent: $787 per month (2006-2010 5-year est.); Median year structure built: 1980 (2006-2010 5-year est.).

Safety: Violent crime rate: 9.9 per 10,000 population; Property crime rate: 156.6 per 10,000 population (2011).

Transportation: Commute to work: 94.0% car, 3.2% public transportation, 0.6% walk, 2.2% work from home (2006-2010 5-year est.); Travel time to work: 24.6% less than 15 minutes, 35.9% 15 to 30 minutes, 17.3% 30 to 45 minutes, 7.7% 45 to 60 minutes, 14.6% 60 minutes or more (2006-2010 5-year est.)

Additional Information Contacts

Borough of Chalfont . . . . (215) 822-7295
  http://www.chalfontborough.com

Central Bucks Chamber of Commerce . . . . (215) 348-3913
  http://www.centralbuckschamber.com

CHURCHVILLE (CDP). Covers a land area of 2.021 square miles and a water area of 0.023 square miles. Located at 40.20° N. Lat; 75.00° W. Long. Elevation is 203 feet.

History: Independent filmmaker Tom Quinn used the Churchville train station in his film "Lusting For Dust Words" The station, built in 1892, was a stop on the Reading Railroad's Newtown Line, and a replacement for another structure built in 1878.

Population: 4,255 (1990); 4,469 (2000); 4,128 (2010); Density: 2,043.1 persons per square mile (2010); Race: 96.4% White, 0.5% Black, 2.1% Asian, 0.0% American Indian/Alaska Native, 0.0% Native Hawaiian/Other Pacific Islander, 1.0% Other, 1.2% Hispanic of any race (2010); Average household size: 3.09 (2010); Median age: 44.7 (2010); Males per 100 females: 99.9 (2010); Marriage status: 24.8% never married, 70.5% now married, 2.9% widowed, 1.8% divorced (2006-2010 5-year est.); Foreign born: 6.4% (2006-2010 5-year est.); Ancestry (includes multiple ancestries): 37.5% Irish, 25.4% German, 12.3% Italian, 10.8% English, 9.9% Polish (2006-2010 5-year est.).

Economy: Employment by occupation: 22.0% management, 5.8% professional, 6.2% services, 11.6% sales, 3.6% farming, 8.0% construction, 2.3% production (2006-2010 5-year est.).

Income: Per capita income: $40,731 (2006-2010 5-year est.); Median household income: $107,763 (2006-2010 5-year est.); Average household income: $131,684 (2006-2010 5-year est.); Percent of households with

income of $100,000 or more: 56.2% (2006-2010 5-year est.); Poverty rate: 2.3% (2006-2010 5-year est.).

Education: Percent of population age 25 and over with: High school diploma (including GED) or higher: 96.3% (2006-2010 5-year est.); Bachelor's degree or higher: 47.2% (2006-2010 5-year est.); Master's degree or higher: 16.7% (2006-2010 5-year est.).

School District(s)

Council Rock SD (KG-12)

   2010-11 Enrollment: 11,882 . . . . (215) 944-1000

Housing: Homeownership rate: 97.9% (2010); Median home value: $435,900 (2006-2010 5-year est.); Median contract rent: n/a per month (2006-2010 5-year est.); Median year structure built: 1972 (2006-2010 5-year est.).

Transportation: Commute to work: 87.6% car, 4.0% public transportation, 0.0% walk, 8.4% work from home (2006-2010 5-year est.); Travel time to work: 21.3% less than 15 minutes, 29.8% 15 to 30 minutes, 19.7% 30 to 45 minutes, 9.2% 45 to 60 minutes, 20.0% 60 minutes or more (2006-2010 5-year est.)

Additional Information Contacts

Lower Bucks County Chamber of Commerce . . . . (215) 943-7400
  http://www.lbccc.org

CORNWELLS HEIGHTS (CDP). Covers a land area of 0.475 square miles and a water area of 0 square miles. Located at 40.08° N. Lat; 74.95° W. Long. Elevation is 79 feet.

Population: n/a (1990); n/a (2000); 1,391 (2010); Density: 2,926.1 persons per square mile (2010); Race: 92.8% White, 2.2% Black, 1.2% Asian, 0.1% American Indian/Alaska Native, 0.0% Native Hawaiian/Other Pacific Islander, 3.7% Other, 5.2% Hispanic of any race (2010); Average household size: 2.59 (2010); Median age: 44.3 (2010); Males per 100 females: 87.5 (2010); Marriage status: 33.4% never married, 50.9% now married, 8.9% widowed, 6.8% divorced (2006-2010 5-year est.); Foreign born: 5.3% (2006-2010 5-year est.); Ancestry (includes multiple ancestries): 30.6% German, 28.1% Irish, 15.6% American, 15.5% Italian, 9.4% English (2006-2010 5-year est.).

Economy: Employment by occupation: 5.8% management, 0.0% professional, 26.4% services, 16.6% sales, 7.5% farming, 21.6% construction, 13.8% production (2006-2010 5-year est.).

Income: Per capita income: $23,760 (2006-2010 5-year est.); Median household income: $60,000 (2006-2010 5-year est.); Average household income: $62,136 (2006-2010 5-year est.); Percent of households with income of $100,000 or more: 19.8% (2006-2010 5-year est.); Poverty rate: 5.1% (2006-2010 5-year est.).

Education: Percent of population age 25 and over with: High school diploma (including GED) or higher: 90.3% (2006-2010 5-year est.); Bachelor's degree or higher: 16.5% (2006-2010 5-year est.); Master's degree or higher: 1.2% (2006-2010 5-year est.).

Housing: Homeownership rate: 70.8% (2010); Median home value: $269,900 (2006-2010 5-year est.); Median contract rent: $702 per month (2006-2010 5-year est.); Median year structure built: 1954 (2006-2010 5-year est.).

Transportation: Commute to work: 92.1% car, 3.0% public transportation, 1.7% walk, 0.0% work from home (2006-2010 5-year est.); Travel time to work: 22.7% less than 15 minutes, 32.7% 15 to 30 minutes, 23.5% 30 to 45 minutes, 13.7% 45 to 60 minutes, 7.5% 60 minutes or more (2006-2010 5-year est.); Amtrak: train service available.

CROYDON (CDP). Covers a land area of 2.411 square miles and a water area of 0.042 square miles. Located at 40.09° N. Lat; 74.90° W. Long. Elevation is 20 feet.

Population: 10,024 (1990); 9,993 (2000); 9,950 (2010); Density: 4,127.0 persons per square mile (2010); Race: 86.6% White, 4.9% Black, 2.9% Asian, 0.3% American Indian/Alaska Native, 0.0% Native Hawaiian/Other Pacific Islander, 5.3% Other, 7.4% Hispanic of any race (2010); Average household size: 2.70 (2010); Median age: 39.1 (2010); Males per 100 females: 100.6 (2010); Marriage status: 33.8% never married, 49.3% now married, 8.6% widowed, 8.3% divorced (2006-2010 5-year est.); Foreign born: 6.7% (2006-2010 5-year est.); Ancestry (includes multiple ancestries): 32.7% Irish, 32.2% German, 12.0% English, 10.4% Italian, 7.7% Polish (2006-2010 5-year est.).

Economy: Employment by occupation: 4.7% management, 2.8% professional, 6.5% services, 24.7% sales, 3.1% farming, 15.4% construction, 10.9% production (2006-2010 5-year est.).

Income: Per capita income: $24,228 (2006-2010 5-year est.); Median household income: $53,809 (2006-2010 5-year est.); Average household

income: $60,172 (2006-2010 5-year est.); Percent of households with income of $100,000 or more: 14.4% (2006-2010 5-year est.); Poverty rate: 6.8% (2006-2010 5-year est.).

Education: Percent of population age 25 and over with: High school diploma (including GED) or higher: 80.8% (2006-2010 5-year est.); Bachelor's degree or higher: 10.5% (2006-2010 5-year est.); Master's degree or higher: 2.4% (2006-2010 5-year est.).

School District(s)

Bristol Township SD (PK-12)

    2010-11 Enrollment: 6,228 . . . . (215) 943-3200

Housing: Homeownership rate: 72.4% (2010); Median home value: $211,500 (2006-2010 5-year est.); Median contract rent: $726 per month (2006-2010 5-year est.); Median year structure built: 1958 (2006-2010 5-year est.).

Transportation: Commute to work: 94.3% car, 4.3% public transportation, 0.8% walk, 0.5% work from home (2006-2010 5-year est.); Travel time to work: 28.8% less than 15 minutes, 43.0% 15 to 30 minutes, 14.0% 30 to 45 minutes, 7.6% 45 to 60 minutes, 6.6% 60 minutes or more (2006-2010 5-year est.)

Additional Information Contacts

Lower Bucks County Chamber of Commerce . . . . (215) 943-7400

    http://www.lbccc.org

DOYLESTOWN (borough). County seat. Covers a land area of 2.157

square miles and a water area of 0.002 square miles. Located at 40.31° N. Lat; 75.13° W. Long. Elevation is 423 feet.

Population: 8,575 (1990); 8,227 (2000); 8,380 (2010); Density: 3,885.3 persons per square mile (2010); Race: 94.8% White, 1.3% Black, 1.9% Asian, 0.1% American Indian/Alaska Native, 0.1% Native Hawaiian/Other Pacific Islander, 1.8% Other, 2.0% Hispanic of any race (2010); Average household size: 2.00 (2010); Median age: 48.2 (2010); Males per 100 females: 81.1 (2010); Marriage status: 26.9% never married, 49.9% now married, 11.5% widowed, 11.8% divorced (2006-2010 5-year est.); Foreign born: 5.4% (2006-2010 5-year est.); Ancestry (includes multiple ancestries): 28.7% German, 26.3% Irish, 15.4% English, 13.0% Italian, 5.9% Polish (2006-2010 5-year est.).

Economy: Single-family building permits issued: 1 (2011); Multi-family building permits issued: 0 (2011); Employment by occupation: 18.2% management, 6.4% professional, 6.8% services, 15.4% sales, 3.3% farming, 3.3% construction, 2.1% production (2006-2010 5-year est.).

Income: Per capita income: $42,270 (2006-2010 5-year est.); Median household income: $61,733 (2006-2010 5-year est.); Average household income: $84,828 (2006-2010 5-year est.); Percent of households with income of $100,000 or more: 31.6% (2006-2010 5-year est.); Poverty rate: 5.0% (2006-2010 5-year est.).

Education: Percent of population age 25 and over with: High school diploma (including GED) or higher: 94.7% (2006-2010 5-year est.); Bachelor's degree or higher: 51.9% (2006-2010 5-year est.); Master's degree or higher: 25.9% (2006-2010 5-year est.).

School District(s)

Central Bucks SD (KG-12)

    2010-11 Enrollment: 20,432 . . . . (267) 893-2000

Four-year College(s)

Delaware Valley College (Private, Not-for-profit)

    Fall 2010 Enrollment: 2,129 . . . . (215) 345-1500

    2011-12 Tuition: In-state $30,704; Out-of-state $30,704

Housing: Homeownership rate: 50.2% (2010); Median home value: $379,100 (2006-2010 5-year est.); Median contract rent: $1,007 per month (2006-2010 5-year est.); Median year structure built: 1963 (2006-2010 5-year est.).

Hospitals: Doylestown Hospital (165 beds); Foundations Behavioral Health (54 beds)

Safety: Violent crime rate: 7.1 per 10,000 population; Property crime rate: 210.5 per 10,000 population (2011).

Newspapers: Doylestown Patriot (Community news; Circulation 6,000); The Intelligencer (Local news; Circulation 46,094); The Philadelphia Inquirer - Doylestown Bureau (Local news)

Transportation: Commute to work: 86.9% car, 3.2% public transportation, 3.8% walk, 5.4% work from home (2006-2010 5-year est.); Travel time to work: 40.8% less than 15 minutes, 22.7% 15 to 30 minutes, 13.9% 30 to 45 minutes, 9.2% 45 to 60 minutes, 13.4% 60 minutes or more (2006-2010 5-year est.)

Airports: Doylestown (general aviation)

Additional Information Contacts

Borough of Doylestown . . . . (215) 345-4140

    http://www.doylestownborough.net

Central Bucks Chamber of Commerce . . . . (215) 348-3913

    http://www.centralbuckschamber.com

DOYLESTOWN (township). Covers a land area of 15.320 square

miles and a water area of 0.310 square miles. Located at 40.30° N. Lat; 75.14° W. Long. Elevation is 423 feet.

History: Seat of Delaware Valley College of Science and Agriculture. Mercer Museum. Settled 1735, laid out 1778, incorporated 1838.

Population: 14,573 (1990); 17,619 (2000); 17,565 (2010); Density: 1,146.5 persons per square mile (2010); Race: 94.2% White, 2.3% Black, 1.4% Asian, 0.2% American Indian/Alaska Native, 0.1% Native Hawaiian/Other Pacific Islander, 1.8% Other, 2.8% Hispanic of any race (2010); Average household size: 2.53 (2010); Median age: 45.3 (2010); Males per 100 females: 100.0 (2010); Marriage status: 30.0% never married, 51.4% now married, 9.6% widowed, 9.0% divorced (2006-2010 5-year est.); Foreign born: 4.9% (2006-2010 5-year est.); Ancestry (includes multiple ancestries): 29.8% German, 24.7% Irish, 17.3% Italian, 15.9% English, 9.1% Polish (2006-2010 5-year est.).

Economy: Single-family building permits issued: 2 (2011); Multi-family building permits issued: 0 (2011); Employment by occupation: 19.1% management, 6.0% professional, 5.3% services, 15.9% sales, 2.6% farming, 4.8% construction, 3.2% production (2006-2010 5-year est.).

Income: Per capita income: $40,443 (2006-2010 5-year est.); Median household income: $99,926 (2006-2010 5-year est.); Average household income: $118,225 (2006-2010 5-year est.); Percent of households with income of $100,000 or more: 49.9% (2006-2010 5-year est.); Poverty rate: 3.4% (2006-2010 5-year est.).

Education: Percent of population age 25 and over with: High school diploma (including GED) or higher: 93.3% (2006-2010 5-year est.); Bachelor's degree or higher: 46.7% (2006-2010 5-year est.); Master's degree or higher: 19.3% (2006-2010 5-year est.).

Four-year College(s)

Delaware Valley College (Private, Not-for-profit)

    Fall 2010 Enrollment: 2,129 . . . . (215) 345-1500

    2011-12 Tuition: In-state $30,704; Out-of-state $30,704

Housing: Homeownership rate: 82.0% (2010); Median home value: $448,700 (2006-2010 5-year est.); Median contract rent: $1,325 per month (2006-2010 5-year est.); Median year structure built: 1979 (2006-2010 5-year est.).

Hospitals: Doylestown Hospital (165 beds); Foundations Behavioral Health (54 beds)

Safety: Violent crime rate: 8.5 per 10,000 population; Property crime rate: 164.0 per 10,000 population (2011).

Newspapers: Doylestown Patriot (Community news; Circulation 6,000); The Intelligencer (Local news; Circulation 46,094); The Philadelphia Inquirer - Doylestown Bureau (Local news)

Transportation: Commute to work: 91.1% car, 2.0% public transportation, 1.1% walk, 5.6% work from home (2006-2010 5-year est.); Travel time to work: 30.0% less than 15 minutes, 21.4% 15 to 30 minutes, 19.1% 30 to 45 minutes, 12.4% 45 to 60 minutes, 17.0% 60 minutes or more (2006-2010 5-year est.)

Airports: Doylestown (general aviation)

Additional Information Contacts

Central Bucks Chamber of Commerce . . . . (215) 348-3913

    http://www.centralbuckschamber.com

Doylestown Township . . . . (215) 348-9915

    http://www.doylestownpa.org

DUBLIN (borough). Covers a land area of 0.583 square miles and a

water area of <.001 square miles. Located at 40.38° N. Lat; 75.21° W. Long. Elevation is 581 feet.

Population: 1,985 (1990); 2,083 (2000); 2,158 (2010); Density: 3,702.4 persons per square mile (2010); Race: 90.5% White, 1.4% Black, 2.0% Asian, 0.1% American Indian/Alaska Native, 0.0% Native Hawaiian/Other Pacific Islander, 6.0% Other, 8.9% Hispanic of any race (2010); Average household size: 2.37 (2010); Median age: 36.6 (2010); Males per 100 females: 102.2 (2010); Marriage status: 32.7% never married, 46.0% now married, 4.2% widowed, 17.1% divorced (2006-2010 5-year est.); Foreign born: 6.3% (2006-2010 5-year est.); Ancestry (includes multiple ancestries): 31.9% German, 26.9% Irish, 11.2% American, 10.6% English, 9.8% Italian (2006-2010 5-year est.).

Economy: Single-family building permits issued: 0 (2011); Multi-family building permits issued: 0 (2011); Employment by occupation: 11.7% management, 8.4% professional, 10.5% services, 17.0% sales, 3.9% farming, 7.0% construction, 5.7% production (2006-2010 5-year est.).
Income: Per capita income: $25,851 (2006-2010 5-year est.); Median household income: $52,750 (2006-2010 5-year est.); Average household income: $62,676 (2006-2010 5-year est.); Percent of households with income of $100,000 or more: 19.8% (2006-2010 5-year est.); Poverty rate: 9.8% (2006-2010 5-year est.).
Education: Percent of population age 25 and over with: High school diploma (including GED) or higher: 85.2% (2006-2010 5-year est.); Bachelor's degree or higher: 22.7% (2006-2010 5-year est.); Master's degree or higher: 6.0% (2006-2010 5-year est.).
Housing: Homeownership rate: 46.9% (2010); Median home value: $305,800 (2006-2010 5-year est.); Median contract rent: $833 per month (2006-2010 5-year est.); Median year structure built: 1975 (2006-2010 5-year est.).
Safety: Violent crime rate: 32.3 per 10,000 population; Property crime rate: 69.3 per 10,000 population (2011).
Transportation: Commute to work: 94.6% car, 0.0% public transportation, 3.6% walk, 0.7% work from home (2006-2010 5-year est.); Travel time to work: 19.4% less than 15 minutes, 41.6% 15 to 30 minutes, 18.3% 30 to 45 minutes, 8.4% 45 to 60 minutes, 12.3% 60 minutes or more (2006-2010 5-year est.)

Additional Information Contacts
Central Bucks Chamber of Commerce . . . . (215) 348-3913
  http://www.centralbuckschamber.com

DURHAM (township). Covers a land area of 9.188 square miles and a water area of 0.181 square miles. Located at 40.57° N. Lat; 75.22° W. Long. Elevation is 230 feet.
Population: 1,211 (1990); 1,313 (2000); 1,144 (2010); Density: 124.5 persons per square mile (2010); Race: 97.8% White, 0.3% Black, 1.0% Asian, 0.1% American Indian/Alaska Native, 0.0% Native Hawaiian/Other Pacific Islander, 0.8% Other, 1.3% Hispanic of any race (2010); Average household size: 2.50 (2010); Median age: 48.8 (2010); Males per 100 females: 112.6 (2010); Marriage status: 19.7% never married, 70.2% now married, 5.0% widowed, 5.1% divorced (2006-2010 5-year est.); Foreign born: 9.5% (2006-2010 5-year est.); Ancestry (includes multiple ancestries): 28.7% German, 17.1% Irish, 13.9% English, 11.8% Italian, 9.3% Polish (2006-2010 5-year est.).
Economy: Single-family building permits issued: 0 (2011); Multi-family building permits issued: 0 (2011); Employment by occupation: 21.6% management, 5.4% professional, 4.8% services, 12.9% sales, 3.0% farming, 16.6% construction, 5.4% production (2006-2010 5-year est.).
Income: Per capita income: $44,729 (2006-2010 5-year est.); Median household income: $81,250 (2006-2010 5-year est.); Average household income: $116,121 (2006-2010 5-year est.); Percent of households with income of $100,000 or more: 40.0% (2006-2010 5-year est.); Poverty rate: 3.2% (2006-2010 5-year est.).
Education: Percent of population age 25 and over with: High school diploma (including GED) or higher: 92.7% (2006-2010 5-year est.); Bachelor's degree or higher: 44.1% (2006-2010 5-year est.); Master's degree or higher: 15.5% (2006-2010 5-year est.).
Housing: Homeownership rate: 89.1% (2010); Median home value: $472,000 (2006-2010 5-year est.); Median contract rent: $700 per month (2006-2010 5-year est.); Median year structure built: 1973 (2006-2010 5-year est.).
Transportation: Commute to work: 84.6% car, 0.3% public transportation, 1.3% walk, 13.3% work from home (2006-2010 5-year est.); Travel time to work: 15.6% less than 15 minutes, 22.3% 15 to 30 minutes, 30.4% 30 to 45 minutes, 10.1% 45 to 60 minutes, 21.6% 60 minutes or more (2006-2010 5-year est.)

Additional Information Contacts
Greater Lehigh Valley Chamber of Commerce . . . . (610) 841-5800
  http://www.lehighvalleychamber.org

EAST ROCKHILL (township). Covers a land area of 12.911 square miles and a water area of 0.178 square miles. Located at 40.41° N. Lat; 75.29° W. Long.
Population: 3,753 (1990); 5,199 (2000); 5,706 (2010); Density: 441.9 persons per square mile (2010); Race: 96.7% White, 0.7% Black, 0.6% Asian, 0.2% American Indian/Alaska Native, 0.0% Native Hawaiian/Other Pacific Islander, 1.8% Other, 1.6% Hispanic of any race (2010); Average household size: 2.79 (2010); Median age: 40.8 (2010); Males per 100

females: 101.9 (2010); Marriage status: 24.9% never married, 59.9% now married, 4.2% widowed, 11.1% divorced (2006-2010 5-year est.); Foreign born: 0.3% (2006-2010 5-year est.); Ancestry (includes multiple ancestries): 45.2% German, 25.6% Irish, 13.6% Italian, 11.4% English, 8.7% Polish (2006-2010 5-year est.).
Economy: Single-family building permits issued: 3 (2011); Multi-family building permits issued: 0 (2011); Employment by occupation: 10.7% management, 5.4% professional, 6.4% services, 18.4% sales, 2.2% farming, 12.0% construction, 5.9% production (2006-2010 5-year est.).
Income: Per capita income: $30,583 (2006-2010 5-year est.); Median household income: $79,142 (2006-2010 5-year est.); Average household income: $86,086 (2006-2010 5-year est.); Percent of households with income of $100,000 or more: 35.0% (2006-2010 5-year est.); Poverty rate: 2.5% (2006-2010 5-year est.).
Education: Percent of population age 25 and over with: High school diploma (including GED) or higher: 90.4% (2006-2010 5-year est.); Bachelor's degree or higher: 27.1% (2006-2010 5-year est.); Master's degree or higher: 9.7% (2006-2010 5-year est.).
Housing: Homeownership rate: 85.4% (2010); Median home value: $344,300 (2006-2010 5-year est.); Median contract rent: $647 per month (2006-2010 5-year est.); Median year structure built: 1985 (2006-2010 5-year est.).
Transportation: Commute to work: 96.0% car, 0.0% public transportation, 0.0% walk, 3.9% work from home (2006-2010 5-year est.); Travel time to work: 22.3% less than 15 minutes, 34.4% 15 to 30 minutes, 18.6% 30 to 45 minutes, 13.3% 45 to 60 minutes, 11.4% 60 minutes or more (2006-2010 5-year est.)

Additional Information Contacts
East Rockhill Township . . . . (215) 257-9156
  http://eastrockhilltownship.org
Pennridge Chamber of Commerce . . . . (215) 257-5390
  http://www.pennridge.com

EDDINGTON (CDP). Covers a land area of 0.553 square miles and a water area of 0 square miles. Located at 40.09° N. Lat; 74.94° W. Long. Elevation is 62 feet.
Population: n/a (1990); n/a (2000); 1,906 (2010); Density: 3,445.7 persons per square mile (2010); Race: 94.5% White, 0.4% Black, 2.2% Asian, 0.2% American Indian/Alaska Native, 0.1% Native Hawaiian/Other Pacific Islander, 2.6% Other, 3.8% Hispanic of any race (2010); Average household size: 2.78 (2010); Median age: 44.4 (2010); Males per 100 females: 103.2 (2010); Marriage status: 20.4% never married, 62.0% now married, 8.7% widowed, 8.9% divorced (2006-2010 5-year est.); Foreign born: 12.1% (2006-2010 5-year est.); Ancestry (includes multiple ancestries): 35.4% German, 31.1% Irish, 21.8% Italian, 13.9% Polish, 7.8% English (2006-2010 5-year est.).
Economy: Employment by occupation: 3.3% management, 2.1% professional, 18.5% services, 15.8% sales, 3.5% farming, 16.6% construction, 10.1% production (2006-2010 5-year est.).
Income: Per capita income: $23,686 (2006-2010 5-year est.); Median household income: $64,125 (2006-2010 5-year est.); Average household income: $66,859 (2006-2010 5-year est.); Percent of households with income of $100,000 or more: 11.7% (2006-2010 5-year est.); Poverty rate: 1.8% (2006-2010 5-year est.).
Education: Percent of population age 25 and over with: High school diploma (including GED) or higher: 75.6% (2006-2010 5-year est.); Bachelor's degree or higher: 6.0% (2006-2010 5-year est.); Master's degree or higher: 3.2% (2006-2010 5-year est.).
Housing: Homeownership rate: 91.1% (2010); Median home value: $272,900 (2006-2010 5-year est.); Median contract rent: $657 per month (2006-2010 5-year est.); Median year structure built: 1955 (2006-2010 5-year est.).
Transportation: Commute to work: 91.6% car, 2.2% public transportation, 2.3% walk, 3.1% work from home (2006-2010 5-year est.); Travel time to work: 34.6% less than 15 minutes, 17.8% 15 to 30 minutes, 33.5% 30 to 45 minutes, 8.2% 45 to 60 minutes, 5.9% 60 minutes or more (2006-2010 5-year est.)

ERWINNA (unincorporated postal area)
Zip Code: 18920
  Covers a land area of 2.729 square miles and a water area of 0.106 square miles. Located at 40.49° N. Lat; 75.08° W. Long. Elevation is 135 feet. Population: 361 (2010); Density: 132.3 persons per square mile (2010); Race: 95.8% White, 0.0% Black, 1.1% Asian, 0.0% American Indian/Alaska Native, 0.0% Native Hawaiian/Other Pacific

Islander, 3.1% Other, 3.3% Hispanic of any race (2010); Average household size: 2.38 (2010); Median age: 50.9 (2010); Males per 100 females: 118.8 (2010); Homeownership rate: 79.0% (2010)

FAIRLESS HILLS (CDP).
Covers a land area of 1.935 square miles and a water area of 0.013 square miles. Located at 40.18° N. Lat; 74.85° W. Long. Elevation is 108 feet.

History: Historic Fallsington with restored buildings to East.

Population: 9,026 (1990); 8,365 (2000); 8,466 (2010); Density: 4,375.0 persons per square mile (2010); Race: 87.3% White, 3.8% Black, 5.6% Asian, 0.1% American Indian/Alaska Native, 0.0% Native Hawaiian/Other Pacific Islander, 3.2% Other, 3.6% Hispanic of any race (2010); Average household size: 2.54 (2010); Median age: 40.0 (2010); Males per 100 females: 91.7 (2010); Marriage status: 32.3% never married, 49.8% now married, 7.4% widowed, 10.4% divorced (2006-2010 5-year est.); Foreign born: 9.5% (2006-2010 5-year est.); Ancestry (includes multiple ancestries): 30.3% Irish, 26.5% German, 14.7% English, 13.8% Italian, 6.0% Polish (2006-2010 5-year est.).

Economy: Employment by occupation: 9.4% management, 5.6% professional, 7.8% services, 21.6% sales, 4.0% farming, 11.2% construction, 9.7% production (2006-2010 5-year est.).

Income: Per capita income: $24,914 (2006-2010 5-year est.); Median household income: $59,360 (2006-2010 5-year est.); Average household income: $62,422 (2006-2010 5-year est.); Percent of households with income of $100,000 or more: 16.4% (2006-2010 5-year est.); Poverty rate: 5.6% (2006-2010 5-year est.).

Education: Percent of population age 25 and over with: High school diploma (including GED) or higher: 88.2% (2006-2010 5-year est.); Bachelor's degree or higher: 14.9% (2006-2010 5-year est.); Master's degree or higher: 4.3% (2006-2010 5-year est.).

School District(s)
Bristol Township SD (PK-12)
    2010-11 Enrollment: 6,228 . . . . (215) 943-3200
Bucks County Montessori CS (KG-06)
    2010-11 Enrollment: 183. . . . . (215) 428-6700
Bucks County Technical High School (09-12)
    2010-11 Enrollment: 1,355 . . . . (215) 949-1700
Pennsbury SD (KG-12)
    2010-11 Enrollment: 10,850 . . . . (215) 428-4100

Housing: Homeownership rate: 75.3% (2010); Median home value: $240,100 (2006-2010 5-year est.); Median contract rent: $817 per month (2006-2010 5-year est.); Median year structure built: 1959 (2006-2010 5-year est.).

Transportation: Commute to work: 92.9% car, 1.1% public transportation, 4.6% walk, 0.7% work from home (2006-2010 5-year est.); Travel time to work: 35.7% less than 15 minutes, 38.9% 15 to 30 minutes, 15.9% 30 to 45 minutes, 4.5% 45 to 60 minutes, 5.0% 60 minutes or more (2006-2010 5-year est.)

Additional Information Contacts
Lower Bucks County Chamber of Commerce . . . . (215) 943-7400
    http://www.lbccc.org

FALLS (township).
Covers a land area of 21.256 square miles and a water area of 5.312 square miles. Located at 40.18° N. Lat; 74.79° W. Long.

Population: 35,053 (1990); 34,865 (2000); 34,300 (2010); Density: 1,613.7 persons per square mile (2010); Race: 86.5% White, 5.8% Black, 4.2% Asian, 0.2% American Indian/Alaska Native, 0.0% Native Hawaiian/Other Pacific Islander, 3.3% Other, 4.4% Hispanic of any race (2010); Average household size: 2.61 (2010); Median age: 39.1 (2010); Males per 100 females: 95.2 (2010); Marriage status: 29.6% never married, 52.5% now married, 7.6% widowed, 10.3% divorced (2006-2010 5-year est.); Foreign born: 8.7% (2006-2010 5-year est.); Ancestry (includes multiple ancestries): 28.2% Irish, 27.8% German, 15.0% Italian, 12.7% English, 8.6% Polish (2006-2010 5-year est.).

Economy: Unemployment rate: 8.5% (August 2012); Total civilian labor force: 18,900 (August 2012); Single-family building permits issued: 7 (2011); Multi-family building permits issued: 0 (2011); Employment by occupation: 9.0% management, 6.1% professional, 8.6% services, 20.6% sales, 4.8% farming, 10.2% construction, 7.5% production (2006-2010 5-year est.).

Income: Per capita income: $27,054 (2006-2010 5-year est.); Median household income: $62,799 (2006-2010 5-year est.); Average household income: $69,635 (2006-2010 5-year est.); Percent of households with

income of $100,000 or more: 21.2% (2006-2010 5-year est.); Poverty rate: 6.4% (2006-2010 5-year est.).

Taxes: Total city taxes per capita: $120 (2009); City property taxes per capita: $68 (2009).

Education: Percent of population age 25 and over with: High school diploma (including GED) or higher: 89.4% (2006-2010 5-year est.); Bachelor's degree or higher: 19.7% (2006-2010 5-year est.); Master's degree or higher: 4.8% (2006-2010 5-year est.).

Housing: Homeownership rate: 71.7% (2010); Median home value: $240,100 (2006-2010 5-year est.); Median contract rent: $884 per month (2006-2010 5-year est.); Median year structure built: 1963 (2006-2010 5-year est.).

Safety: Violent crime rate: 14.0 per 10,000 population; Property crime rate: 281.6 per 10,000 population (2011).

Transportation: Commute to work: 94.6% car, 1.5% public transportation, 1.8% walk, 1.3% work from home (2006-2010 5-year est.); Travel time to work: 29.1% less than 15 minutes, 43.4% 15 to 30 minutes, 14.7% 30 to 45 minutes, 5.7% 45 to 60 minutes, 7.1% 60 minutes or more (2006-2010 5-year est.)

Additional Information Contacts
Falls Township . . . . (215) 949-9000
    http://www.fallstwp.com
Lower Bucks County Chamber of Commerce . . . . (215) 943-7400
    http://www.lbccc.org

FEASTERVILLE (CDP).
Covers a land area of 0.643 square miles and a water area of 0 square miles. Located at 40.15° N. Lat; 74.99° W. Long. Elevation is 220 feet.

Population: n/a (1990); n/a (2000); 3,074 (2010); Density: 4,777.2 persons per square mile (2010); Race: 89.3% White, 3.8% Black, 3.3% Asian, 0.1% American Indian/Alaska Native, 0.0% Native Hawaiian/Other Pacific Islander, 3.5% Other, 4.5% Hispanic of any race (2010); Average household size: 2.39 (2010); Median age: 38.3 (2010); Males per 100 females: 99.2 (2010); Marriage status: 34.5% never married, 50.8% now married, 5.7% widowed, 9.0% divorced (2006-2010 5-year est.); Foreign born: 14.7% (2006-2010 5-year est.); Ancestry (includes multiple ancestries): 33.6% Irish, 21.3% German, 12.1% Polish, 11.8% Italian, 8.0% English (2006-2010 5-year est.).

Economy: Employment by occupation: 8.6% management, 6.6% professional, 6.7% services, 25.1% sales, 0.8% farming, 11.8% construction, 4.2% production (2006-2010 5-year est.).

Income: Per capita income: $29,761 (2006-2010 5-year est.); Median household income: $61,786 (2006-2010 5-year est.); Average household income: $69,354 (2006-2010 5-year est.); Percent of households with income of $100,000 or more: 23.1% (2006-2010 5-year est.); Poverty rate: 3.0% (2006-2010 5-year est.).

Education: Percent of population age 25 and over with: High school diploma (including GED) or higher: 91.8% (2006-2010 5-year est.); Bachelor's degree or higher: 23.8% (2006-2010 5-year est.); Master's degree or higher: 6.7% (2006-2010 5-year est.).

School District(s)
Neshaminy SD (KG-12)
    2010-11 Enrollment: 8,587 . . . . (215) 809-6500

Housing: Homeownership rate: 45.9% (2010); Median home value: $283,900 (2006-2010 5-year est.); Median contract rent: $908 per month (2006-2010 5-year est.); Median year structure built: 1966 (2006-2010 5-year est.).

Transportation: Commute to work: 91.3% car, 2.2% public transportation, 3.3% walk, 2.6% work from home (2006-2010 5-year est.); Travel time to work: 16.4% less than 15 minutes, 49.2% 15 to 30 minutes, 15.1% 30 to 45 minutes, 11.6% 45 to 60 minutes, 7.6% 60 minutes or more (2006-2010 5-year est.)

FOUNTAINVILLE (unincorporated postal area)
Zip Code: 18923
    Covers a land area of 1.738 square miles and a water area of 0.001 square miles. Located at 40.35° N. Lat; 75.17° W. Long. Population: 998 (2010); Density: 574.1 persons per square mile (2010); Race: 91.6% White, 1.4% Black, 3.3% Asian, 0.1% American Indian/Alaska Native, 0.0% Native Hawaiian/Other Pacific Islander, 3.6% Other, 3.0% Hispanic of any race (2010); Average household size: 2.96 (2010); Median age: 35.0 (2010); Males per 100 females: 96.5 (2010); Homeownership rate: 85.2% (2010)

FURLONG (unincorporated postal area)

Zip Code: 18925

Covers a land area of 10.740 square miles and a water area of 0.088 square miles. Located at 40.28° N. Lat; 75.05° W. Long. Elevation is 322 feet. Population: 6,195 (2010); Density: 576.8 persons per square mile (2010); Race: 89.1% White, 1.8% Black, 6.6% Asian, 0.1% American Indian/Alaska Native, 0.0% Native Hawaiian/Other Pacific Islander, 2.4% Other, 2.7% Hispanic of any race (2010); Average household size: 2.99 (2010); Median age: 39.8 (2010); Males per 100 females: 95.8 (2010); Homeownership rate: 91.5% (2010)

HAYCOCK (township).

Covers a land area of 19.672 square miles and a water area of 1.362 square miles. Located at 40.47° N. Lat; 75.25° W. Long.

Population: 2,171 (1990); 2,191 (2000); 2,225 (2010); Density: 113.1 persons per square mile (2010); Race: 96.9% White, 1.0% Black, 0.5% Asian, 0.0% American Indian/Alaska Native, 0.0% Native Hawaiian/Other Pacific Islander, 1.6% Other, 1.0% Hispanic of any race (2010); Average household size: 2.49 (2010); Median age: 47.0 (2010); Males per 100 females: 108.7 (2010); Marriage status: 18.0% never married, 67.7% now married, 5.4% widowed, 9.0% divorced (2006-2010 5-year est.); Foreign born: 5.0% (2006-2010 5-year est.); Ancestry (includes multiple ancestries): 31.8% German, 16.9% Irish, 15.9% English, 11.9% Italian, 8.5% Polish (2006-2010 5-year est.).

Economy: Single-family building permits issued: 1 (2011); Multi-family building permits issued: 0 (2011); Employment by occupation: 15.2% management, 6.6% professional, 9.3% services, 17.7% sales, 3.4% farming, 14.0% construction, 7.2% production (2006-2010 5-year est.).

Income: Per capita income: $33,414 (2006-2010 5-year est.); Median household income: $80,509 (2006-2010 5-year est.); Average household income: $88,246 (2006-2010 5-year est.); Percent of households with income of $100,000 or more: 33.6% (2006-2010 5-year est.); Poverty rate: 4.1% (2006-2010 5-year est.).

Education: Percent of population age 25 and over with: High school diploma (including GED) or higher: 89.4% (2006-2010 5-year est.); Bachelor's degree or higher: 27.9% (2006-2010 5-year est.); Master's degree or higher: 6.8% (2006-2010 5-year est.).

Housing: Homeownership rate: 88.1% (2010); Median home value: $347,200 (2006-2010 5-year est.); Median contract rent: $875 per month (2006-2010 5-year est.); Median year structure built: 1976 (2006-2010 5-year est.).

Transportation: Commute to work: 91.4% car, 0.6% public transportation, 0.0% walk, 7.5% work from home (2006-2010 5-year est.); Travel time to work: 11.4% less than 15 minutes, 40.0% 15 to 30 minutes, 22.6% 30 to 45 minutes, 6.0% 45 to 60 minutes, 19.9% 60 minutes or more (2006-2010 5-year est.)

Additional Information Contacts

Upper Bucks Chamber of Commerce . . . . (215) 536-3211
  http://www.ubcc.org

HILLTOWN (township).

Covers a land area of 26.968 square miles and a water area of 0.065 square miles. Located at 40.34° N. Lat; 75.25° W. Long.

History: The first recorded history in Hilltown Township was made in 1683, when William Penn met the Indian Chiefs of the Delaware Nation on the land where Hilltown Village now sits.

Population: 10,582 (1990); 12,102 (2000); 15,029 (2010); Density: 557.3 persons per square mile (2010); Race: 92.7% White, 2.0% Black, 3.1% Asian, 0.1% American Indian/Alaska Native, 0.1% Native Hawaiian/Other Pacific Islander, 2.0% Other, 2.8% Hispanic of any race (2010); Average household size: 2.78 (2010); Median age: 40.6 (2010); Males per 100 females: 97.3 (2010); Marriage status: 21.0% never married, 66.6% now married, 4.7% widowed, 7.7% divorced (2006-2010 5-year est.); Foreign born: 5.1% (2006-2010 5-year est.); Ancestry (includes multiple ancestries): 40.1% German, 24.2% Irish, 14.1% Italian, 10.4% English, 5.2% Polish (2006-2010 5-year est.).

Economy: Single-family building permits issued: 26 (2011); Multi-family building permits issued: 0 (2011); Employment by occupation: 16.1% management, 5.4% professional, 7.1% services, 17.1% sales, 2.9% farming, 6.4% construction, 5.6% production (2006-2010 5-year est.).

Income: Per capita income: $34,840 (2006-2010 5-year est.); Median household income: $86,922 (2006-2010 5-year est.); Average household income: $97,064 (2006-2010 5-year est.); Percent of households with income of $100,000 or more: 39.4% (2006-2010 5-year est.); Poverty rate: 4.1% (2006-2010 5-year est.).

Education: Percent of population age 25 and over with: High school diploma (including GED) or higher: 92.4% (2006-2010 5-year est.); Bachelor's degree or higher: 36.8% (2006-2010 5-year est.); Master's degree or higher: 13.8% (2006-2010 5-year est.).

Housing: Homeownership rate: 80.4% (2010); Median home value: $347,200 (2006-2010 5-year est.); Median contract rent: $1,016 per month (2006-2010 5-year est.); Median year structure built: 1981 (2006-2010 5-year est.).

Safety: Violent crime rate: 6.6 per 10,000 population; Property crime rate: 187.0 per 10,000 population (2011).

Transportation: Commute to work: 91.1% car, 0.4% public transportation, 2.0% walk, 5.6% work from home (2006-2010 5-year est.); Travel time to work: 26.9% less than 15 minutes, 30.9% 15 to 30 minutes, 20.6% 30 to 45 minutes, 9.7% 45 to 60 minutes, 12.0% 60 minutes or more (2006-2010 5-year est.)

Additional Information Contacts

Hilltown Township . . . . (215) 453-6000
  http://www.hilltown.org
Indian Valley Chamber of Commerce . . . . (215) 723-9472
  http://indianvalleychamber.com

HULMEVILLE (borough).

Covers a land area of 0.356 square miles and a water area of 0.017 square miles. Located at 40.14° N. Lat; 74.91° W. Long. Elevation is 46 feet.

Population: 916 (1990); 893 (2000); 1,003 (2010); Density: 2,817.6 persons per square mile (2010); Race: 93.8% White, 0.7% Black, 3.0% Asian, 0.0% American Indian/Alaska Native, 0.0% Native Hawaiian/Other Pacific Islander, 2.5% Other, 1.0% Hispanic of any race (2010); Average household size: 2.67 (2010); Median age: 40.1 (2010); Males per 100 females: 92.5 (2010); Marriage status: 32.0% never married, 53.7% now married, 7.1% widowed, 7.1% divorced (2006-2010 5-year est.); Foreign born: 3.6% (2006-2010 5-year est.); Ancestry (includes multiple ancestries): 47.8% German, 25.6% Irish, 11.1% Italian, 6.6% English, 5.9% Polish (2006-2010 5-year est.).

Economy: Single-family building permits issued: 0 (2011); Multi-family building permits issued: 0 (2011); Employment by occupation: 10.4% management, 3.3% professional, 5.2% services, 14.8% sales, 1.1% farming, 16.1% construction, 8.7% production (2006-2010 5-year est.).

Income: Per capita income: $27,613 (2006-2010 5-year est.); Median household income: $64,018 (2006-2010 5-year est.); Average household income: $77,528 (2006-2010 5-year est.); Percent of households with income of $100,000 or more: 31.0% (2006-2010 5-year est.); Poverty rate: 8.9% (2006-2010 5-year est.).

Education: Percent of population age 25 and over with: High school diploma (including GED) or higher: 88.6% (2006-2010 5-year est.); Bachelor's degree or higher: 25.1% (2006-2010 5-year est.); Master's degree or higher: 12.3% (2006-2010 5-year est.).

Housing: Homeownership rate: 74.5% (2010); Median home value: $304,100 (2006-2010 5-year est.); Median contract rent: $792 per month (2006-2010 5-year est.); Median year structure built: 1960 (2006-2010 5-year est.).

Safety: Violent crime rate: 9.9 per 10,000 population; Property crime rate: 69.6 per 10,000 population (2011).

Transportation: Commute to work: 88.3% car, 3.4% public transportation, 3.8% walk, 3.8% work from home (2006-2010 5-year est.); Travel time to work: 31.5% less than 15 minutes, 44.6% 15 to 30 minutes, 9.2% 30 to 45 minutes, 8.0% 45 to 60 minutes, 6.8% 60 minutes or more (2006-2010 5-year est.)

IVYLAND (borough).

Covers a land area of 0.355 square miles and a water area of <.001 square miles. Located at 40.21° N. Lat; 75.07° W. Long. Elevation is 299 feet.

Population: 476 (1990); 492 (2000); 1,041 (2010); Density: 2,936.0 persons per square mile (2010); Race: 88.3% White, 0.4% Black, 7.8% Asian, 0.0% American Indian/Alaska Native, 0.0% Native Hawaiian/Other Pacific Islander, 3.5% Other, 2.4% Hispanic of any race (2010); Average household size: 2.87 (2010); Median age: 40.4 (2010); Males per 100 females: 84.9 (2010); Marriage status: 25.7% never married, 63.2% now married, 4.6% widowed, 6.5% divorced (2006-2010 5-year est.); Foreign born: 10.0% (2006-2010 5-year est.); Ancestry (includes multiple ancestries): 32.9% Irish, 28.2% German, 22.1% Italian, 13.8% English, 9.0% Polish (2006-2010 5-year est.).

Economy: Single-family building permits issued: 0 (2011); Multi-family building permits issued: 0 (2011); Employment by occupation: 16.2%

management, 5.3% professional, 11.9% services, 10.7% sales, 1.0% farming, 8.1% construction, 2.1% production (2006-2010 5-year est.).
Income: Per capita income: $36,101 (2006-2010 5-year est.); Median household income: $79,500 (2006-2010 5-year est.); Average household income: $96,305 (2006-2010 5-year est.); Percent of households with income of $100,000 or more: 36.4% (2006-2010 5-year est.); Poverty rate: 0.0% (2006-2010 5-year est.).
Education: Percent of population age 25 and over with: High school diploma (including GED) or higher: 92.3% (2006-2010 5-year est.); Bachelor's degree or higher: 40.0% (2006-2010 5-year est.); Master's degree or higher: 16.8% (2006-2010 5-year est.).
Housing: Homeownership rate: 86.3% (2010); Median home value: $394,900 (2006-2010 5-year est.); Median contract rent: $775 per month (2006-2010 5-year est.); Median year structure built: 1970 (2006-2010 5-year est.).
Safety: Violent crime rate: 0.0 per 10,000 population; Property crime rate: 86.2 per 10,000 population (2011).
Transportation: Commute to work: 94.4% car, 0.5% public transportation, 2.9% walk, 2.2% work from home (2006-2010 5-year est.); Travel time to work: 43.2% less than 15 minutes, 30.5% 15 to 30 minutes, 16.1% 30 to 45 minutes, 1.0% 45 to 60 minutes, 9.2% 60 minutes or more (2006-2010 5-year est.)
Additional Information Contacts
Borough of Ivyland . . . . (215) 675-0110
  http://www.ivylandborough.org

JAMISON (unincorporated postal area)
Zip Code: 18929
  Covers a land area of 8.124 square miles and a water area of 0.094 square miles. Located at 40.25° N. Lat; 75.08° W. Long. Elevation is 305 feet. Population: 9,306 (2010); Density: 1,145.4 persons per square mile (2010); Race: 93.2% White, 1.1% Black, 4.0% Asian, 0.2% American Indian/Alaska Native, 0.0% Native Hawaiian/Other Pacific Islander, 1.5% Other, 1.9% Hispanic of any race (2010); Average household size: 3.10 (2010); Median age: 39.7 (2010); Males per 100 females: 95.8 (2010); Homeownership rate: 94.5% (2010)

KINTNERSVILLE (unincorporated postal area)
Zip Code: 18930
  Covers a land area of 22.313 square miles and a water area of 0.786 square miles. Located at 40.52° N. Lat; 75.21° W. Long. Population: 2,721 (2010); Density: 121.9 persons per square mile (2010); Race: 98.1% White, 0.3% Black, 0.5% Asian, 0.1% American Indian/Alaska Native, 0.0% Native Hawaiian/Other Pacific Islander, 1.0% Other, 1.9% Hispanic of any race (2010); Average household size: 2.55 (2010); Median age: 47.0 (2010); Males per 100 females: 104.4 (2010); Homeownership rate: 84.6% (2010)

LANGHORNE (borough). Covers a land area of 0.492 square miles and a water area of 0.002 square miles. Located at 40.18° N. Lat; 74.92° W. Long. Elevation is 220 feet.
History: Sesame Place, theme park based upon . *SESAME STREETITAL TELEVISION SHOW, TO EAST, LAID OUT 1783, INCORPORATED 1874.*
Population: 1,361 (1990); 1,981 (2000); 1,622 (2010); Density: 3,296.9 persons per square mile (2010); Race: 87.7% White, 8.0% Black, 1.5% Asian, 0.1% American Indian/Alaska Native, 0.0% Native Hawaiian/Other Pacific Islander, 2.7% Other, 2.3% Hispanic of any race (2010); Average household size: 2.21 (2010); Median age: 41.3 (2010); Males per 100 females: 96.8 (2010); Marriage status: 48.5% never married, 37.6% now married, 6.4% widowed, 7.5% divorced (2006-2010 5-year est.); Foreign born: 1.3% (2006-2010 5-year est.); Ancestry (includes multiple ancestries): 18.3% German, 17.3% Irish, 11.9% English, 8.5% Italian, 3.7% Polish (2006-2010 5-year est.).
Economy: Single-family building permits issued: 0 (2011); Multi-family building permits issued: 0 (2011); Employment by occupation: 10.8% management, 5.6% professional, 6.3% services, 19.8% sales, 2.6% farming, 4.8% construction, 1.2% production (2006-2010 5-year est.).
Income: Per capita income: $22,894 (2006-2010 5-year est.); Median household income: $73,542 (2006-2010 5-year est.); Average household income: $90,636 (2006-2010 5-year est.); Percent of households with income of $100,000 or more: 38.3% (2006-2010 5-year est.); Poverty rate: 8.5% (2006-2010 5-year est.).
Education: Percent of population age 25 and over with: High school diploma (including GED) or higher: 96.7% (2006-2010 5-year est.);

Bachelor's degree or higher: 41.5% (2006-2010 5-year est.); Master's degree or higher: 17.7% (2006-2010 5-year est.).
School District(s)
Neshaminy SD (KG-12)
  2010-11 Enrollment: 8,587 . . . . (215) 809-6500
Four-year College(s)
Philadelphia Biblical University-Langhorne (Private, Not-for-profit)
  Fall 2010 Enrollment: 1,150 . . . . (215) 752-5800
  2011-12 Tuition: In-state $20,888; Out-of-state $20,888
Housing: Homeownership rate: 56.8% (2010); Median home value: $340,100 (2006-2010 5-year est.); Median contract rent: $800 per month (2006-2010 5-year est.); Median year structure built: 1941 (2006-2010 5-year est.).
Hospitals: St. Mary Medical Center (327 beds)
Safety: Violent crime rate: 12.3 per 10,000 population; Property crime rate: 159.8 per 10,000 population (2011).
Transportation: Commute to work: 85.4% car, 3.7% public transportation, 5.5% walk, 4.0% work from home (2006-2010 5-year est.); Travel time to work: 32.5% less than 15 minutes, 40.4% 15 to 30 minutes, 15.7% 30 to 45 minutes, 8.7% 45 to 60 minutes, 2.6% 60 minutes or more (2006-2010 5-year est.)
Additional Information Contacts
Lower Bucks County Chamber of Commerce . . . . (215) 943-7400
  http://www.lbccc.org

LANGHORNE MANOR (borough). Covers a land area of 0.598 square miles and a water area of 0.005 square miles. Located at 40.17° N. Lat; 74.92° W. Long. Elevation is 217 feet.
Population: 807 (1990); 927 (2000); 1,442 (2010); Density: 2,410.8 persons per square mile (2010); Race: 92.1% White, 4.1% Black, 1.5% Asian, 0.2% American Indian/Alaska Native, 0.0% Native Hawaiian/Other Pacific Islander, 2.1% Other, 3.3% Hispanic of any race (2010); Average household size: 2.70 (2010); Median age: 27.7 (2010); Males per 100 females: 85.3 (2010); Marriage status: 37.1% never married, 53.1% now married, 5.0% widowed, 4.8% divorced (2006-2010 5-year est.); Foreign born: 4.0% (2006-2010 5-year est.); Ancestry (includes multiple ancestries): 30.5% German, 26.6% Irish, 19.6% Italian, 16.4% English, 8.1% Polish (2006-2010 5-year est.).
Economy: Single-family building permits issued: 0 (2011); Multi-family building permits issued: 0 (2011); Employment by occupation: 15.5% management, 7.1% professional, 4.9% services, 19.2% sales, 2.4% farming, 5.6% construction, 2.8% production (2006-2010 5-year est.).
Income: Per capita income: $31,326 (2006-2010 5-year est.); Median household income: $93,393 (2006-2010 5-year est.); Average household income: $101,062 (2006-2010 5-year est.); Percent of households with income of $100,000 or more: 46.8% (2006-2010 5-year est.); Poverty rate: 3.8% (2006-2010 5-year est.).
Education: Percent of population age 25 and over with: High school diploma (including GED) or higher: 96.0% (2006-2010 5-year est.); Bachelor's degree or higher: 46.3% (2006-2010 5-year est.); Master's degree or higher: 24.9% (2006-2010 5-year est.).
Housing: Homeownership rate: 85.4% (2010); Median home value: $348,300 (2006-2010 5-year est.); Median contract rent: $911 per month (2006-2010 5-year est.); Median year structure built: 1954 (2006-2010 5-year est.).
Safety: Violent crime rate: 6.9 per 10,000 population; Property crime rate: 27.6 per 10,000 population (2011).
Transportation: Commute to work: 81.9% car, 5.1% public transportation, 7.5% walk, 4.9% work from home (2006-2010 5-year est.); Travel time to work: 32.9% less than 15 minutes, 35.8% 15 to 30 minutes, 11.2% 30 to 45 minutes, 10.6% 45 to 60 minutes, 9.5% 60 minutes or more (2006-2010 5-year est.)
Additional Information Contacts
Borough of Langhorne Manor . . . . (215) 752-5835
  http://langhornemanor.com

LEVITTOWN (CDP). Aka Fleetwing. Covers a land area of 10.159 square miles and a water area of 0.098 square miles. Located at 40.15° N. Lat; 74.85° W. Long. Elevation is 30 feet.
History: Named for William Levitt, developer of model suburban communities. It was the second housing development built (1951—1955) by Levitt and Sons, Incorporated, who repeated the low-cost residence plan of their Levittown, N.Y., development. The very name itself, Levittown, has come to symbolize the U.S. post-World War II suburban phenomenon,

which first gave middle-class families the option of inexpensive, single-unit housing outside the urban sector.

Population: 55,427 (1990); 53,966 (2000); 52,983 (2010); Density: 5,215.4 persons per square mile (2010); Race: 90.4% White, 3.8% Black, 1.7% Asian, 0.3% American Indian/Alaska Native, 0.0% Native Hawaiian/Other Pacific Islander, 3.8% Other, 5.1% Hispanic of any race (2010); Average household size: 2.85 (2010); Median age: 39.4 (2010); Males per 100 females: 98.0 (2010); Marriage status: 26.8% never married, 54.6% now married, 7.4% widowed, 11.1% divorced (2006-2010 5-year est.); Foreign born: 4.5% (2006-2010 5-year est.); Ancestry (includes multiple ancestries): 34.2% Irish, 30.5% German, 15.2% Italian, 11.0% Polish, 10.7% English (2006-2010 5-year est.).

Economy: Employment by occupation: 8.7% management, 3.5% professional, 9.3% services, 20.3% sales, 4.7% farming, 10.9% construction, 7.8% production (2006-2010 5-year est.).

Income: Per capita income: $25,345 (2006-2010 5-year est.); Median household income: $64,298 (2006-2010 5-year est.); Average household income: $70,393 (2006-2010 5-year est.); Percent of households with income of $100,000 or more: 21.1% (2006-2010 5-year est.); Poverty rate: 6.1% (2006-2010 5-year est.).

Education: Percent of population age 25 and over with: High school diploma (including GED) or higher: 90.8% (2006-2010 5-year est.); Bachelor's degree or higher: 15.6% (2006-2010 5-year est.); Master's degree or higher: 4.3% (2006-2010 5-year est.).

School District(s)

Bristol Township SD (PK-12)
2010-11 Enrollment: 6,228 . . . . (215) 943-3200
Center for Student Learning CS at Pennsbury (06-12)
2010-11 Enrollment: 147. . . . . (215) 269-7390
Neshaminy SD (KG-12)
2010-11 Enrollment: 8,587 . . . . (215) 809-6500
Pennsbury SD (KG-12)
2010-11 Enrollment: 10,850 . . . . (215) 428-4100

Vocational/Technical School(s)

Levittown Beauty Academy (Private, For-profit)
Fall 2010 Enrollment: 96. . . . . (215) 943-0298
2011-12 Tuition: $15,000

Housing: Homeownership rate: 83.8% (2010); Median home value: $235,800 (2006-2010 5-year est.); Median contract rent: $881 per month (2006-2010 5-year est.); Median year structure built: 1957 (2006-2010 5-year est.).

Newspapers: Bucks County Courier Times (Local news; Circulation 62,353); To Do - Bucks County Courier Times

Transportation: Commute to work: 95.2% car, 2.0% public transportation, 0.6% walk, 1.6% work from home (2006-2010 5-year est.); Travel time to work: 31.9% less than 15 minutes, 40.7% 15 to 30 minutes, 15.9% 30 to 45 minutes, 5.9% 45 to 60 minutes, 5.7% 60 minutes or more (2006-2010 5-year est.)

Additional Information Contacts

Lower Bucks County Chamber of Commerce . . . . (215) 943-7400
http://www.lbccc.org

LINE LEXINGTON (unincorporated postal area)

Zip Code: 18932
Covers a land area of 1.255 square miles and a water area of 0.001 square miles. Located at 40.29° N. Lat; 75.25° W. Long. Elevation is 387 feet. Population: 388 (2010); Density: 308.9 persons per square mile (2010); Race: 96.9% White, 0.5% Black, 1.0% Asian, 0.0% American Indian/Alaska Native, 0.0% Native Hawaiian/Other Pacific Islander, 1.6% Other, 2.3% Hispanic of any race (2010); Average household size: 2.66 (2010); Median age: 43.8 (2010); Males per 100 females: 99.0 (2010); Homeownership rate: 85.7% (2010)

LOWER MAKEFIELD (township). Covers a land area of 17.871 square miles and a water area of 0.413 square miles. Located at 40.23° N. Lat; 74.86° W. Long.

Population: 25,083 (1990); 32,681 (2000); 32,559 (2010); Density: 1,821.9 persons per square mile (2010); Race: 89.6% White, 2.3% Black, 6.3% Asian, 0.1% American Indian/Alaska Native, 0.0% Native Hawaiian/Other Pacific Islander, 1.7% Other, 2.4% Hispanic of any race (2010); Average household size: 2.74 (2010); Median age: 43.5 (2010); Males per 100 females: 93.5 (2010); Marriage status: 22.8% never married, 66.1% now married, 4.3% widowed, 6.8% divorced (2006-2010 5-year est.); Foreign born: 9.4% (2006-2010 5-year est.); Ancestry

(includes multiple ancestries): 24.8% Irish, 22.0% German, 16.3% Italian, 12.4% English, 8.1% Polish (2006-2010 5-year est.).

Economy: Unemployment rate: 5.8% (August 2012); Total civilian labor force: 17,657 (August 2012); Single-family building permits issued: 25 (2011); Multi-family building permits issued: 0 (2011); Employment by occupation: 27.1% management, 7.4% professional, 3.6% services, 13.6% sales, 2.5% farming, 2.5% construction, 1.6% production (2006-2010 5-year est.).

Income: Per capita income: $52,988 (2006-2010 5-year est.); Median household income: $121,260 (2006-2010 5-year est.); Average household income: $146,839 (2006-2010 5-year est.); Percent of households with income of $100,000 or more: 61.7% (2006-2010 5-year est.); Poverty rate: 1.6% (2006-2010 5-year est.).

Taxes: Total city taxes per capita: $303 (2009); City property taxes per capita: $241 (2009).

Education: Percent of population age 25 and over with: High school diploma (including GED) or higher: 97.7% (2006-2010 5-year est.); Bachelor's degree or higher: 61.9% (2006-2010 5-year est.); Master's degree or higher: 29.8% (2006-2010 5-year est.).

Housing: Homeownership rate: 88.0% (2010); Median home value: $449,000 (2006-2010 5-year est.); Median contract rent: $1,504 per month (2006-2010 5-year est.); Median year structure built: 1982 (2006-2010 5-year est.).

Safety: Violent crime rate: 8.0 per 10,000 population; Property crime rate: 147.9 per 10,000 population (2011).

Transportation: Commute to work: 82.4% car, 7.8% public transportation, 1.9% walk, 7.4% work from home (2006-2010 5-year est.); Travel time to work: 21.9% less than 15 minutes, 32.8% 15 to 30 minutes, 17.1% 30 to 45 minutes, 10.8% 45 to 60 minutes, 17.3% 60 minutes or more (2006-2010 5-year est.)

Additional Information Contacts

Lower Bucks County Chamber of Commerce . . . . (215) 943-7400
http://www.lbccc.org
Lower Makefield Township . . . . (215) 493-3646
http://www.lmt.org

LOWER SOUTHAMPTON (township). Covers a land area of 6.686 square miles and a water area of 0.041 square miles. Located at 40.15° N. Lat; 74.99° W. Long.

Population: 19,860 (1990); 19,276 (2000); 18,909 (2010); Density: 2,828.1 persons per square mile (2010); Race: 93.7% White, 1.8% Black, 2.5% Asian, 0.2% American Indian/Alaska Native, 0.0% Native Hawaiian/Other Pacific Islander, 1.8% Other, 2.8% Hispanic of any race (2010); Average household size: 2.64 (2010); Median age: 42.3 (2010); Males per 100 females: 97.3 (2010); Marriage status: 27.6% never married, 57.7% now married, 6.7% widowed, 8.1% divorced (2006-2010 5-year est.); Foreign born: 11.7% (2006-2010 5-year est.); Ancestry (includes multiple ancestries): 30.1% Irish, 26.1% German, 13.1% Italian, 9.7% Polish, 9.6% English (2006-2010 5-year est.).

Economy: Single-family building permits issued: 6 (2011); Multi-family building permits issued: 0 (2011); Employment by occupation: 12.4% management, 5.3% professional, 7.4% services, 17.3% sales, 4.7% farming, 11.1% construction, 6.5% production (2006-2010 5-year est.).

Income: Per capita income: $31,448 (2006-2010 5-year est.); Median household income: $74,193 (2006-2010 5-year est.); Average household income: $81,668 (2006-2010 5-year est.); Percent of households with income of $100,000 or more: 31.1% (2006-2010 5-year est.); Poverty rate: 2.2% (2006-2010 5-year est.).

Taxes: Total city taxes per capita: $487 (2009); City property taxes per capita: $251 (2009).

Education: Percent of population age 25 and over with: High school diploma (including GED) or higher: 92.4% (2006-2010 5-year est.); Bachelor's degree or higher: 25.4% (2006-2010 5-year est.); Master's degree or higher: 8.3% (2006-2010 5-year est.).

Housing: Homeownership rate: 80.9% (2010); Median home value: $300,700 (2006-2010 5-year est.); Median contract rent: $907 per month (2006-2010 5-year est.); Median year structure built: 1967 (2006-2010 5-year est.).

Transportation: Commute to work: 91.1% car, 3.2% public transportation, 1.4% walk, 2.6% work from home (2006-2010 5-year est.); Travel time to work: 20.9% less than 15 minutes, 40.3% 15 to 30 minutes, 19.1% 30 to 45 minutes, 10.9% 45 to 60 minutes, 8.8% 60 minutes or more (2006-2010 5-year est.)

Additional Information Contacts

Lower Bucks County Chamber of Commerce . . . . (215) 943-7400
http://www.lbccc.org

Lower Southampton Township . . . . (215) 357-7300
http://www.lowersouthamptontownship.org

MIDDLETOWN (township). Covers a land area of 18.899 square miles and a water area of 0.421 square miles. Located at 40.18° N. Lat; 74.91° W. Long.

Population: 43,063 (1990); 44,141 (2000); 45,436 (2010); Density: 2,404.2 persons per square mile (2010); Race: 90.1% White, 3.2% Black, 3.9% Asian, 0.2% American Indian/Alaska Native, 0.0% Native Hawaiian/Other Pacific Islander, 2.6% Other, 3.1% Hispanic of any race (2010); Average household size: 2.65 (2010); Median age: 42.6 (2010); Males per 100 females: 95.4 (2010); Marriage status: 32.4% never married, 51.8% now married, 7.9% widowed, 7.9% divorced (2006-2010 5-year est.); Foreign born: 5.8% (2006-2010 5-year est.); Ancestry (includes multiple ancestries): 29.2% Irish, 28.3% German, 16.4% Italian, 10.6% English, 9.4% Polish (2006-2010 5-year est.).

Economy: Unemployment rate: 7.8% (August 2012); Total civilian labor force: 24,970 (August 2012); Single-family building permits issued: 10 (2011); Multi-family building permits issued: 0 (2011); Employment by occupation: 14.3% management, 5.7% professional, 7.4% services, 18.4% sales, 4.8% farming, 7.0% construction, 3.7% production (2006-2010 5-year est.).

Income: Per capita income: $33,377 (2006-2010 5-year est.); Median household income: $78,861 (2006-2010 5-year est.); Average household income: $93,940 (2006-2010 5-year est.); Percent of households with income of $100,000 or more: 35.7% (2006-2010 5-year est.); Poverty rate: 5.7% (2006-2010 5-year est.).

Taxes: Total city taxes per capita: $285 (2009); City property taxes per capita: $170 (2009).

Education: Percent of population age 25 and over with: High school diploma (including GED) or higher: 91.6% (2006-2010 5-year est.); Bachelor's degree or higher: 31.1% (2006-2010 5-year est.); Master's degree or higher: 11.4% (2006-2010 5-year est.).

Housing: Homeownership rate: 75.6% (2010); Median home value: $316,700 (2006-2010 5-year est.); Median contract rent: $976 per month (2006-2010 5-year est.); Median year structure built: 1974 (2006-2010 5-year est.).

Safety: Violent crime rate: 8.3 per 10,000 population; Property crime rate: 312.9 per 10,000 population (2011).

Transportation: Commute to work: 92.2% car, 2.4% public transportation, 0.9% walk, 3.6% work from home (2006-2010 5-year est.); Travel time to work: 28.3% less than 15 minutes, 39.0% 15 to 30 minutes, 17.5% 30 to 45 minutes, 7.7% 45 to 60 minutes, 7.6% 60 minutes or more (2006-2010 5-year est.)

Additional Information Contacts

Lower Bucks County Chamber of Commerce . . . . (215) 943-7400
http://www.lbccc.org

Middletown Township . . . . (215) 750-3800
http://www.middletowntwpbucks.org

MILFORD (township). Covers a land area of 27.889 square miles and a water area of 0.081 square miles. Located at 40.43° N. Lat; 75.42° W. Long.

Population: 7,360 (1990); 8,810 (2000); 9,902 (2010); Density: 355.1 persons per square mile (2010); Race: 95.2% White, 1.5% Black, 1.4% Asian, 0.1% American Indian/Alaska Native, 0.0% Native Hawaiian/Other Pacific Islander, 1.8% Other, 1.8% Hispanic of any race (2010); Average household size: 2.75 (2010); Median age: 42.2 (2010); Males per 100 females: 99.3 (2010); Marriage status: 23.4% never married, 65.4% now married, 4.9% widowed, 6.2% divorced (2006-2010 5-year est.); Foreign born: 2.2% (2006-2010 5-year est.); Ancestry (includes multiple ancestries): 41.6% German, 17.3% Irish, 13.9% Italian, 8.5% English, 8.1% Polish (2006-2010 5-year est.).

Economy: Single-family building permits issued: 2 (2011); Multi-family building permits issued: 0 (2011); Employment by occupation: 12.6% management, 5.4% professional, 7.0% services, 16.5% sales, 2.1% farming, 12.1% construction, 7.8% production (2006-2010 5-year est.).

Income: Per capita income: $32,245 (2006-2010 5-year est.); Median household income: $81,740 (2006-2010 5-year est.); Average household income: $89,478 (2006-2010 5-year est.); Percent of households with income of $100,000 or more: 35.3% (2006-2010 5-year est.); Poverty rate: 3.2% (2006-2010 5-year est.).

Education: Percent of population age 25 and over with: High school diploma (including GED) or higher: 93.0% (2006-2010 5-year est.); Bachelor's degree or higher: 31.3% (2006-2010 5-year est.); Master's degree or higher: 9.3% (2006-2010 5-year est.).

Housing: Homeownership rate: 89.6% (2010); Median home value: $293,200 (2006-2010 5-year est.); Median contract rent: $656 per month (2006-2010 5-year est.); Median year structure built: 1976 (2006-2010 5-year est.).

Transportation: Commute to work: 90.7% car, 1.2% public transportation, 2.0% walk, 5.8% work from home (2006-2010 5-year est.); Travel time to work: 24.0% less than 15 minutes, 31.7% 15 to 30 minutes, 25.7% 30 to 45 minutes, 12.6% 45 to 60 minutes, 6.0% 60 minutes or more (2006-2010 5-year est.)

Additional Information Contacts

Milford Township . . . . (215) 536-2090
http://www.milfordtownship.org

Upper Bucks Chamber of Commerce . . . . (215) 536-3211
http://www.ubcc.org

MILFORD SQUARE (CDP). Covers a land area of 0.921 square miles and a water area of 0.001 square miles. Located at 40.43° N. Lat; 75.41° W. Long. Elevation is 509 feet.

Population: n/a (1990); n/a (2000); 897 (2010); Density: 974.2 persons per square mile (2010); Race: 96.1% White, 1.2% Black, 0.7% Asian, 0.1% American Indian/Alaska Native, 0.0% Native Hawaiian/Other Pacific Islander, 1.9% Other, 1.6% Hispanic of any race (2010); Average household size: 2.67 (2010); Median age: 36.9 (2010); Males per 100 females: 102.9 (2010); Marriage status: 25.0% never married, 53.9% now married, 5.5% widowed, 15.7% divorced (2006-2010 5-year est.); Foreign born: 6.4% (2006-2010 5-year est.); Ancestry (includes multiple ancestries): 47.7% German, 16.9% Italian, 9.6% English, 8.8% American, 4.1% Czech (2006-2010 5-year est.).

Economy: Employment by occupation: 3.1% management, 1.9% professional, 5.4% services, 16.9% sales, 2.5% farming, 14.0% construction, 16.9% production (2006-2010 5-year est.).

Income: Per capita income: $29,862 (2006-2010 5-year est.); Median household income: $76,108 (2006-2010 5-year est.); Average household income: $86,972 (2006-2010 5-year est.); Percent of households with income of $100,000 or more: 39.4% (2006-2010 5-year est.); Poverty rate: 5.9% (2006-2010 5-year est.).

Education: Percent of population age 25 and over with: High school diploma (including GED) or higher: 83.6% (2006-2010 5-year est.); Bachelor's degree or higher: 17.5% (2006-2010 5-year est.); Master's degree or higher: 0.0% (2006-2010 5-year est.).

Housing: Homeownership rate: 81.0% (2010); Median home value: $228,500 (2006-2010 5-year est.); Median contract rent: $664 per month (2006-2010 5-year est.); Median year structure built: 1967 (2006-2010 5-year est.).

Transportation: Commute to work: 90.8% car, 3.6% public transportation, 0.0% walk, 2.8% work from home (2006-2010 5-year est.); Travel time to work: 36.6% less than 15 minutes, 14.6% 15 to 30 minutes, 28.7% 30 to 45 minutes, 14.4% 45 to 60 minutes, 5.7% 60 minutes or more (2006-2010 5-year est.)

MORRISVILLE (borough). Covers a land area of 1.747 square miles and a water area of 0.225 square miles. Located at 40.21° N. Lat; 74.78° W. Long. Elevation is 98 feet.

History: George Washington had his headquarters here Dec. 8—14, 1776. Pennsbury Manor State Park, with reconstructed Pennsbury, which was William Penn's home, to south. Settled c.1624 by the Dutch West India Company, Incorporated 1804.

Population: 9,759 (1990); 10,023 (2000); 8,728 (2010); Density: 4,994.8 persons per square mile (2010); Race: 75.7% White, 15.4% Black, 2.0% Asian, 0.3% American Indian/Alaska Native, 0.0% Native Hawaiian/Other Pacific Islander, 6.6% Other, 10.2% Hispanic of any race (2010); Average household size: 2.38 (2010); Median age: 38.4 (2010); Males per 100 females: 94.6 (2010); Marriage status: 35.0% never married, 47.9% now married, 6.8% widowed, 10.3% divorced (2006-2010 5-year est.); Foreign born: 12.8% (2006-2010 5-year est.); Ancestry (includes multiple ancestries): 19.5% Irish, 19.4% German, 12.4% Italian, 10.6% English, 9.2% Polish (2006-2010 5-year est.).

Economy: Single-family building permits issued: 0 (2011); Multi-family building permits issued: 0 (2011); Employment by occupation: 11.8% management, 3.1% professional, 9.0% services, 17.8% sales, 3.5% farming, 7.2% construction, 5.4% production (2006-2010 5-year est.).

Income: Per capita income: $26,448 (2006-2010 5-year est.); Median household income: $50,980 (2006-2010 5-year est.); Average household income: $61,578 (2006-2010 5-year est.); Percent of households with income of $100,000 or more: 17.5% (2006-2010 5-year est.); Poverty rate: 8.8% (2006-2010 5-year est.).

Taxes: Total city taxes per capita: $269 (2009); City property taxes per capita: $232 (2009).

Education: Percent of population age 25 and over with: High school diploma (including GED) or higher: 84.1% (2006-2010 5-year est.); Bachelor's degree or higher: 25.4% (2006-2010 5-year est.); Master's degree or higher: 7.5% (2006-2010 5-year est.).

School District(s)

Morrisville Borough SD (PK-12)

   2010-11 Enrollment: 874 . . . . (215) 736-2681

Pennsbury SD (KG-12)

   2010-11 Enrollment: 10,850 . . . . (215) 428-4100

Housing: Homeownership rate: 62.3% (2010); Median home value: $223,400 (2006-2010 5-year est.); Median contract rent: $826 per month (2006-2010 5-year est.); Median year structure built: 1956 (2006-2010 5-year est.).

Transportation: Commute to work: 87.9% car, 1.8% public transportation, 1.6% walk, 5.7% work from home (2006-2010 5-year est.); Travel time to work: 22.0% less than 15 minutes, 43.1% 15 to 30 minutes, 18.8% 30 to 45 minutes, 5.9% 45 to 60 minutes, 10.2% 60 minutes or more (2006-2010 5-year est.)

Additional Information Contacts

Borough of Morrisville . . . . (215) 295-8112

   http://morrisville-boro-gov.com

Lower Bucks County Chamber of Commerce . . . . (215) 943-7400

   http://www.lbccc.org

NEW BRITAIN (borough). Covers a land area of 1.207 square miles and a water area of 0.003 square miles. Located at 40.30° N. Lat; 75.18° W. Long. Elevation is 289 feet.

Population: 2,111 (1990); 3,125 (2000); 3,152 (2010); Density: 2,611.5 persons per square mile (2010); Race: 94.3% White, 1.6% Black, 1.3% Asian, 0.2% American Indian/Alaska Native, 0.2% Native Hawaiian/Other Pacific Islander, 2.4% Other, 2.7% Hispanic of any race (2010); Average household size: 2.46 (2010); Median age: 28.6 (2010); Males per 100 females: 82.3 (2010); Marriage status: 42.3% never married, 47.0% now married, 3.9% widowed, 6.8% divorced (2006-2010 5-year est.); Foreign born: 2.5% (2006-2010 5-year est.); Ancestry (includes multiple ancestries): 28.9% German, 24.0% Irish, 15.9% Italian, 11.6% English, 11.1% American (2006-2010 5-year est.).

Economy: Single-family building permits issued: 0 (2011); Multi-family building permits issued: 0 (2011); Employment by occupation: 11.3% management, 6.2% professional, 7.9% services, 20.1% sales, 7.5% farming, 6.1% construction, 2.7% production (2006-2010 5-year est.).

Income: Per capita income: $27,702 (2006-2010 5-year est.); Median household income: $77,260 (2006-2010 5-year est.); Average household income: $84,725 (2006-2010 5-year est.); Percent of households with income of $100,000 or more: 30.3% (2006-2010 5-year est.); Poverty rate: 3.2% (2006-2010 5-year est.).

Education: Percent of population age 25 and over with: High school diploma (including GED) or higher: 97.2% (2006-2010 5-year est.); Bachelor's degree or higher: 45.9% (2006-2010 5-year est.); Master's degree or higher: 16.5% (2006-2010 5-year est.).

School District(s)

Central Bucks SD (KG-12)

   2010-11 Enrollment: 20,432 . . . . (267) 893-2000

Housing: Homeownership rate: 86.7% (2010); Median home value: $266,000 (2006-2010 5-year est.); Median contract rent: $981 per month (2006-2010 5-year est.); Median year structure built: 1969 (2006-2010 5-year est.).

Transportation: Commute to work: 82.7% car, 0.6% public transportation, 8.0% walk, 6.9% work from home (2006-2010 5-year est.); Travel time to work: 40.6% less than 15 minutes, 31.6% 15 to 30 minutes, 12.6% 30 to 45 minutes, 9.3% 45 to 60 minutes, 5.9% 60 minutes or more (2006-2010 5-year est.)

Additional Information Contacts

Central Bucks Chamber of Commerce . . . . (215) 348-3913

   http://www.centralbuckschamber.com

NEW BRITAIN (township). Covers a land area of 14.757 square miles and a water area of 0.531 square miles. Located at 40.31° N. Lat; 75.21° W. Long. Elevation is 289 feet.

History: New Britain Township was founded in 1723 and celebrated its 275th birthday in 1998. The Township was comprised more than 15,000 acres and included land which is now occupied by Chalfont and New Britain boroughs as well as Doylestown Township.

Population: 9,105 (1990); 10,698 (2000); 11,070 (2010); Density: 750.1 persons per square mile (2010); Race: 93.9% White, 1.6% Black, 3.3% Asian, 0.0% American Indian/Alaska Native, 0.0% Native Hawaiian/Other Pacific Islander, 1.2% Other, 2.4% Hispanic of any race (2010); Average household size: 2.67 (2010); Median age: 42.5 (2010); Males per 100 females: 93.5 (2010); Marriage status: 23.0% never married, 63.4% now married, 7.3% widowed, 6.3% divorced (2006-2010 5-year est.); Foreign born: 5.4% (2006-2010 5-year est.); Ancestry (includes multiple ancestries): 33.8% German, 30.6% Irish, 18.1% Italian, 10.2% English, 8.8% Polish (2006-2010 5-year est.).

Economy: Single-family building permits issued: 0 (2011); Multi-family building permits issued: 0 (2011); Employment by occupation: 18.3% management, 8.5% professional, 6.0% services, 18.6% sales, 1.8% farming, 6.7% construction, 3.5% production (2006-2010 5-year est.).

Income: Per capita income: $37,050 (2006-2010 5-year est.); Median household income: $91,163 (2006-2010 5-year est.); Average household income: $103,781 (2006-2010 5-year est.); Percent of households with income of $100,000 or more: 45.4% (2006-2010 5-year est.); Poverty rate: 4.5% (2006-2010 5-year est.).

Education: Percent of population age 25 and over with: High school diploma (including GED) or higher: 95.2% (2006-2010 5-year est.); Bachelor's degree or higher: 45.2% (2006-2010 5-year est.); Master's degree or higher: 17.9% (2006-2010 5-year est.).

Housing: Homeownership rate: 88.1% (2010); Median home value: $359,300 (2006-2010 5-year est.); Median contract rent: $1,307 per month (2006-2010 5-year est.); Median year structure built: 1978 (2006-2010 5-year est.).

Safety: Violent crime rate: 7.2 per 10,000 population; Property crime rate: 74.7 per 10,000 population (2011).

Transportation: Commute to work: 88.7% car, 1.2% public transportation, 1.0% walk, 9.1% work from home (2006-2010 5-year est.); Travel time to work: 20.8% less than 15 minutes, 39.2% 15 to 30 minutes, 18.7% 30 to 45 minutes, 10.5% 45 to 60 minutes, 10.7% 60 minutes or more (2006-2010 5-year est.)

Additional Information Contacts

Central Bucks Chamber of Commerce . . . . (215) 348-3913

   http://www.centralbuckschamber.com

New Britain Township . . . . (215) 822-1391

   http://www.newbritaintownship.org

NEW HOPE (borough). Aka Buckingham Valley. Covers a land area of 1.270 square miles and a water area of 0.149 square miles. Located at 40.36° N. Lat; 74.96° W. Long. Elevation is 69 feet.

History: Washington Crossing State Park to south, one of two places where George Washington crossed Delaware River in 1776. Settled c.1712, Incorporated 1837.

Population: 1,400 (1990); 2,252 (2000); 2,528 (2010); Density: 1,990.7 persons per square mile (2010); Race: 93.2% White, 1.1% Black, 1.9% Asian, 0.1% American Indian/Alaska Native, 0.0% Native Hawaiian/Other Pacific Islander, 3.7% Other, 7.3% Hispanic of any race (2010); Average household size: 2.01 (2010); Median age: 46.5 (2010); Males per 100 females: 108.4 (2010); Marriage status: 33.2% never married, 51.2% now married, 8.4% widowed, 7.1% divorced (2006-2010 5-year est.); Foreign born: 14.2% (2006-2010 5-year est.); Ancestry (includes multiple ancestries): 22.0% German, 17.3% English, 15.9% Irish, 15.0% Italian, 11.4% Polish (2006-2010 5-year est.).

Economy: Single-family building permits issued: 0 (2011); Multi-family building permits issued: 0 (2011); Employment by occupation: 19.4% management, 5.1% professional, 7.0% services, 13.7% sales, 2.7% farming, 3.6% construction, 2.3% production (2006-2010 5-year est.).

Income: Per capita income: $58,140 (2006-2010 5-year est.); Median household income: $84,167 (2006-2010 5-year est.); Average household income: $114,057 (2006-2010 5-year est.); Percent of households with income of $100,000 or more: 44.7% (2006-2010 5-year est.); Poverty rate: 3.8% (2006-2010 5-year est.).

Education: Percent of population age 25 and over with: High school diploma (including GED) or higher: 95.4% (2006-2010 5-year est.);

Bachelor's degree or higher: 56.2% (2006-2010 5-year est.); Master's degree or higher: 19.8% (2006-2010 5-year est.).

School District(s)

New Hope-Solebury SD (KG-12)

2010-11 Enrollment: 1,587 . . . . (215) 862-2552

Housing: Homeownership rate: 58.0% (2010); Median home value: $537,600 (2006-2010 5-year est.); Median contract rent: $1,073 per month (2006-2010 5-year est.); Median year structure built: 1977 (2006-2010 5-year est.).

Safety: Violent crime rate: 59.1 per 10,000 population; Property crime rate: 319.4 per 10,000 population (2011).

Newspapers: New Hope Gazette (Community news; Circulation 5,000)

Transportation: Commute to work: 77.4% car, 3.4% public transportation, 10.1% walk, 8.2% work from home (2006-2010 5-year est.); Travel time to work: 28.9% less than 15 minutes, 23.3% 15 to 30 minutes, 18.5% 30 to 45 minutes, 12.3% 45 to 60 minutes, 17.0% 60 minutes or more (2006-2010 5-year est.)

Additional Information Contacts

Central Bucks Chamber of Commerce . . . . (215) 348-3913
http://centralbuckschamber.com

NEWTOWN (borough).

Covers a land area of 0.552 square miles and a water area of <.001 square miles. Located at 40.23° N. Lat; 74.93° W. Long. Elevation is 157 feet.

Population: 2,343 (1990); 2,312 (2000); 2,248 (2010); Density: 4,071.1 persons per square mile (2010); Race: 96.2% White, 0.8% Black, 1.2% Asian, 0.2% American Indian/Alaska Native, 0.0% Native Hawaiian/Other Pacific Islander, 1.6% Other, 1.2% Hispanic of any race (2010); Average household size: 2.33 (2010); Median age: 45.4 (2010); Males per 100 females: 94.3 (2010); Marriage status: 23.4% never married, 54.7% now married, 12.5% widowed, 9.3% divorced (2006-2010 5-year est.); Foreign born: 7.1% (2006-2010 5-year est.); Ancestry (includes multiple ancestries): 24.5% German, 21.5% Irish, 14.1% English, 10.2% Italian, 6.0% Israeli (2006-2010 5-year est.).

Economy: Single-family building permits issued: 0 (2011); Multi-family building permits issued: 0 (2011); Employment by occupation: 20.8% management, 5.1% professional, 7.5% services, 15.7% sales, 1.9% farming, 4.0% construction, 0.8% production (2006-2010 5-year est.).

Income: Per capita income: $47,492 (2006-2010 5-year est.); Median household income: $74,000 (2006-2010 5-year est.); Average household income: $111,994 (2006-2010 5-year est.); Percent of households with income of $100,000 or more: 37.7% (2006-2010 5-year est.); Poverty rate: 4.8% (2006-2010 5-year est.).

Education: Percent of population age 25 and over with: High school diploma (including GED) or higher: 94.9% (2006-2010 5-year est.); Bachelor's degree or higher: 54.6% (2006-2010 5-year est.); Master's degree or higher: 25.9% (2006-2010 5-year est.).

School District(s)

Council Rock SD (KG-12)

2010-11 Enrollment: 11,882 . . . . (215) 944-1000

Two-year College(s)

Bucks County Community College (Public)

Fall 2010 Enrollment: 8,247 . . . . (215) 968-8000

2011-12 Tuition: In-state $7,410; Out-of-state $10,668

Housing: Homeownership rate: 67.1% (2010); Median home value: $489,600 (2006-2010 5-year est.); Median contract rent: $896 per month (2006-2010 5-year est.); Median year structure built: 1944 (2006-2010 5-year est.).

Safety: Violent crime rate: 8.9 per 10,000 population; Property crime rate: 133.0 per 10,000 population (2011).

Newspapers: Advance Of Bucks County (Community news; Circulation 6,000)

Transportation: Commute to work: 80.0% car, 8.6% public transportation, 4.3% walk, 7.1% work from home (2006-2010 5-year est.); Travel time to work: 33.5% less than 15 minutes, 29.1% 15 to 30 minutes, 12.5% 30 to 45 minutes, 9.7% 45 to 60 minutes, 15.3% 60 minutes or more (2006-2010 5-year est.)

Additional Information Contacts

Borough of Newtown . . . . (215) 968-3881
http://boro.newtown.pa.us

Lower Bucks County Chamber of Commerce . . . . (215) 943-7400
http://www.lbccc.org

NEWTOWN (township).

Covers a land area of 11.901 square miles and a water area of 0.079 square miles. Located at 40.24° N. Lat; 74.94° W. Long. Elevation is 157 feet.

History: Settled 1684, laid out 1733, incorporated 1838.

Population: 13,907 (1990); 18,206 (2000); 19,299 (2010); Density: 1,621.6 persons per square mile (2010); Race: 89.3% White, 1.2% Black, 7.9% Asian, 0.1% American Indian/Alaska Native, 0.0% Native Hawaiian/Other Pacific Islander, 1.5% Other, 1.9% Hispanic of any race (2010); Average household size: 2.59 (2010); Median age: 42.1 (2010); Males per 100 females: 91.5 (2010); Marriage status: 23.9% never married, 62.7% now married, 6.0% widowed, 7.5% divorced (2006-2010 5-year est.); Foreign born: 10.1% (2006-2010 5-year est.); Ancestry (includes multiple ancestries): 26.0% Irish, 20.8% German, 18.9% Italian, 12.4% English, 8.9% Polish (2006-2010 5-year est.).

Economy: Single-family building permits issued: 24 (2011); Multi-family building permits issued: 5 (2011); Employment by occupation: 23.3% management, 6.3% professional, 5.1% services, 12.6% sales, 2.5% farming, 4.0% construction, 3.2% production (2006-2010 5-year est.).

Income: Per capita income: $47,867 (2006-2010 5-year est.); Median household income: $107,430 (2006-2010 5-year est.); Average household income: $126,367 (2006-2010 5-year est.); Percent of households with income of $100,000 or more: 55.0% (2006-2010 5-year est.); Poverty rate: 3.1% (2006-2010 5-year est.).

Education: Percent of population age 25 and over with: High school diploma (including GED) or higher: 97.3% (2006-2010 5-year est.); Bachelor's degree or higher: 58.5% (2006-2010 5-year est.); Master's degree or higher: 24.8% (2006-2010 5-year est.).

Two-year College(s)

Bucks County Community College (Public)

Fall 2010 Enrollment: 8,247 . . . . (215) 968-8000

2011-12 Tuition: In-state $7,410; Out-of-state $10,668

Housing: Homeownership rate: 86.4% (2010); Median home value: $379,900 (2006-2010 5-year est.); Median contract rent: $1,341 per month (2006-2010 5-year est.); Median year structure built: 1987 (2006-2010 5-year est.).

Safety: Violent crime rate: 6.7 per 10,000 population; Property crime rate: 117.6 per 10,000 population (2011).

Newspapers: Advance Of Bucks County (Community news; Circulation 6,000)

Transportation: Commute to work: 90.7% car, 2.4% public transportation, 1.6% walk, 5.4% work from home (2006-2010 5-year est.); Travel time to work: 22.4% less than 15 minutes, 29.5% 15 to 30 minutes, 21.8% 30 to 45 minutes, 10.5% 45 to 60 minutes, 15.8% 60 minutes or more (2006-2010 5-year est.)

Additional Information Contacts

Lower Bucks County Chamber of Commerce . . . . (215) 943-7400
http://www.lbccc.org

Newtown Township . . . . (215) 968-2800
http://www.twp.newtown.pa.us

NEWTOWN GRANT (CDP).

Covers a land area of 0.771 square miles and a water area of <.001 square miles. Located at 40.26° N. Lat; 74.96° W. Long. Elevation is 289 feet.

History: Newtown Grant was built by Orleans, inc. builders. It is divided in to 12 subsections: Estates I-IV, Fawn Hollow, Phesant Walk, Raven's View, Greenbriar, Whispering Woods, Heather Wood, Quail Creek, and Society Place. Acquired from Jonapher Deisendorf.

Population: 2,141 (1990); 3,887 (2000); 3,620 (2010); Density: 4,694.6 persons per square mile (2010); Race: 87.7% White, 1.4% Black, 9.0% Asian, 0.1% American Indian/Alaska Native, 0.0% Native Hawaiian/Other Pacific Islander, 1.8% Other, 2.7% Hispanic of any race (2010); Average household size: 2.35 (2010); Median age: 40.7 (2010); Males per 100 females: 88.7 (2010); Marriage status: 26.8% never married, 60.2% now married, 4.2% widowed, 8.8% divorced (2006-2010 5-year est.); Foreign born: 14.4% (2006-2010 5-year est.); Ancestry (includes multiple ancestries): 27.1% Irish, 20.8% German, 18.8% Italian, 11.0% English, 7.8% Russian (2006-2010 5-year est.).

Economy: Employment by occupation: 25.7% management, 5.8% professional, 2.5% services, 12.9% sales, 1.7% farming, 3.0% construction, 3.4% production (2006-2010 5-year est.).

Income: Per capita income: $50,446 (2006-2010 5-year est.); Median household income: $104,151 (2006-2010 5-year est.); Average household income: $117,502 (2006-2010 5-year est.); Percent of households with income of $100,000 or more: 52.2% (2006-2010 5-year est.); Poverty rate: 1.8% (2006-2010 5-year est.).

Education: Percent of population age 25 and over with: High school diploma (including GED) or higher: 97.4% (2006-2010 5-year est.); Bachelor's degree or higher: 59.8% (2006-2010 5-year est.); Master's degree or higher: 19.4% (2006-2010 5-year est.).

Housing: Homeownership rate: 88.1% (2010); Median home value: $343,300 (2006-2010 5-year est.); Median contract rent: $1,231 per month (2006-2010 5-year est.); Median year structure built: 1991 (2006-2010 5-year est.).

Transportation: Commute to work: 94.9% car, 0.4% public transportation, 0.0% walk, 4.6% work from home (2006-2010 5-year est.); Travel time to work: 18.6% less than 15 minutes, 29.0% 15 to 30 minutes, 21.8% 30 to 45 minutes, 13.0% 45 to 60 minutes, 17.6% 60 minutes or more (2006-2010 5-year est.)

Additional Information Contacts

Lower Bucks County Chamber of Commerce . . . . (215) 943-7400
http://www.lbccc.org

NOCKAMIXON (township). Covers a land area of 22.046 square miles and a water area of 0.330 square miles. Located at 40.52° N. Lat; 75.17° W. Long.

Population: 3,299 (1990); 3,517 (2000); 3,441 (2010); Density: 156.1 persons per square mile (2010); Race: 97.4% White, 0.3% Black, 0.3% Asian, 0.1% American Indian/Alaska Native, 0.0% Native Hawaiian/Other Pacific Islander, 1.9% Other, 1.7% Hispanic of any race (2010); Average household size: 2.50 (2010); Median age: 46.3 (2010); Males per 100 females: 106.0 (2010); Marriage status: 20.6% never married, 62.3% now married, 6.9% widowed, 10.2% divorced (2006-2010 5-year est.); Foreign born: 4.7% (2006-2010 5-year est.); Ancestry (includes multiple ancestries): 41.4% German, 23.4% Irish, 12.3% English, 12.2% Italian, 6.2% Polish (2006-2010 5-year est.).

Economy: Single-family building permits issued: 0 (2011); Multi-family building permits issued: 0 (2011); Employment by occupation: 10.9% management, 6.4% professional, 7.9% services, 17.0% sales, 3.8% farming, 12.1% construction, 7.5% production (2006-2010 5-year est.).

Income: Per capita income: $36,614 (2006-2010 5-year est.); Median household income: $70,128 (2006-2010 5-year est.); Average household income: $92,932 (2006-2010 5-year est.); Percent of households with income of $100,000 or more: 33.0% (2006-2010 5-year est.); Poverty rate: 6.6% (2006-2010 5-year est.).

Education: Percent of population age 25 and over with: High school diploma (including GED) or higher: 93.8% (2006-2010 5-year est.); Bachelor's degree or higher: 29.8% (2006-2010 5-year est.); Master's degree or higher: 7.4% (2006-2010 5-year est.).

Housing: Homeownership rate: 81.0% (2010); Median home value: $363,500 (2006-2010 5-year est.); Median contract rent: $858 per month (2006-2010 5-year est.); Median year structure built: 1971 (2006-2010 5-year est.).

Transportation: Commute to work: 91.3% car, 0.0% public transportation, 1.7% walk, 6.9% work from home (2006-2010 5-year est.); Travel time to work: 25.5% less than 15 minutes, 26.3% 15 to 30 minutes, 29.8% 30 to 45 minutes, 8.1% 45 to 60 minutes, 10.4% 60 minutes or more (2006-2010 5-year est.)

Additional Information Contacts

Upper Bucks Chamber of Commerce . . . . (215) 536-3211
http://www.ubcc.org

NORTHAMPTON (township). Covers a land area of 25.680 square miles and a water area of 0.442 square miles. Located at 40.21° N. Lat; 75.00° W. Long.

Population: 35,406 (1990); 39,384 (2000); 39,726 (2010); Density: 1,546.9 persons per square mile (2010); Race: 94.9% White, 0.6% Black, 3.5% Asian, 0.1% American Indian/Alaska Native, 0.0% Native Hawaiian/Other Pacific Islander, 0.9% Other, 1.5% Hispanic of any race (2010); Average household size: 2.84 (2010); Median age: 44.4 (2010); Males per 100 females: 94.6 (2010); Marriage status: 25.1% never married, 65.9% now married, 4.5% widowed, 4.5% divorced (2006-2010 5-year est.); Foreign born: 10.5% (2006-2010 5-year est.); Ancestry (includes multiple ancestries): 29.0% Irish, 24.2% German, 17.6% Italian, 9.4% English, 8.6% Polish (2006-2010 5-year est.).

Economy: Unemployment rate: 7.3% (August 2012); Total civilian labor force: 21,924 (August 2012); Single-family building permits issued: 7 (2011); Multi-family building permits issued: 0 (2011); Employment by occupation: 19.0% management, 6.9% professional, 5.7% services, 14.9% sales, 3.5% farming, 6.0% construction, 3.3% production (2006-2010 5-year est.).

Income: Per capita income: $43,253 (2006-2010 5-year est.); Median household income: $105,148 (2006-2010 5-year est.); Average household income: $125,588 (2006-2010 5-year est.); Percent of households with income of $100,000 or more: 53.4% (2006-2010 5-year est.); Poverty rate: 2.3% (2006-2010 5-year est.).

Taxes: Total city taxes per capita: $326 (2009); City property taxes per capita: $133 (2009).

Education: Percent of population age 25 and over with: High school diploma (including GED) or higher: 95.9% (2006-2010 5-year est.); Bachelor's degree or higher: 47.1% (2006-2010 5-year est.); Master's degree or higher: 18.3% (2006-2010 5-year est.).

Housing: Homeownership rate: 91.8% (2010); Median home value: $415,500 (2006-2010 5-year est.); Median contract rent: $1,150 per month (2006-2010 5-year est.); Median year structure built: 1979 (2006-2010 5-year est.).

Safety: Violent crime rate: 0.5 per 10,000 population; Property crime rate: 70.3 per 10,000 population (2011).

Transportation: Commute to work: 89.8% car, 3.4% public transportation, 1.0% walk, 5.4% work from home (2006-2010 5-year est.); Travel time to work: 21.3% less than 15 minutes, 31.5% 15 to 30 minutes, 21.6% 30 to 45 minutes, 11.0% 45 to 60 minutes, 14.6% 60 minutes or more (2006-2010 5-year est.)

Additional Information Contacts

Lower Bucks County Chamber of Commerce . . . . (215) 943-7400
http://www.lbccc.org
Northampton Township . . . . (215) 357-6800
http://www.northamptontownship.com

OTTSVILLE (unincorporated postal area)

Zip Code: 18942

Covers a land area of 22.463 square miles and a water area of 0.269 square miles. Located at 40.47° N. Lat; 75.16° W. Long. Elevation is 397 feet. Population: 3,260 (2010); Density: 145.1 persons per square mile (2010); Race: 96.9% White, 0.6% Black, 0.6% Asian, 0.2% American Indian/Alaska Native, 0.0% Native Hawaiian/Other Pacific Islander, 1.7% Other, 2.0% Hispanic of any race (2010); Average household size: 2.50 (2010); Median age: 46.9 (2010); Males per 100 females: 104.9 (2010); Homeownership rate: 78.6% (2010)

PENNDEL (borough). Aka South Langhorne. Covers a land area of 0.418 square miles and a water area of 0 square miles. Located at 40.16° N. Lat; 74.91° W. Long. Elevation is 102 feet.

History: Formerly South Langhorne. Incorporated 1889.

Population: 2,703 (1990); 2,420 (2000); 2,328 (2010); Density: 5,572.8 persons per square mile (2010); Race: 84.2% White, 8.6% Black, 2.7% Asian, 0.0% American Indian/Alaska Native, 0.0% Native Hawaiian/Other Pacific Islander, 4.5% Other, 4.3% Hispanic of any race (2010); Average household size: 2.34 (2010); Median age: 35.6 (2010); Males per 100 females: 89.9 (2010); Marriage status: 40.5% never married, 43.9% now married, 6.4% widowed, 9.2% divorced (2006-2010 5-year est.); Foreign born: 6.3% (2006-2010 5-year est.); Ancestry (includes multiple ancestries): 40.4% Irish, 28.0% German, 14.1% English, 8.0% Italian, 7.2% Polish (2006-2010 5-year est.).

Economy: Single-family building permits issued: 4 (2011); Multi-family building permits issued: 0 (2011); Employment by occupation: 7.4% management, 3.2% professional, 17.1% services, 21.2% sales, 3.5% farming, 10.1% construction, 10.6% production (2006-2010 5-year est.).

Income: Per capita income: $24,076 (2006-2010 5-year est.); Median household income: $49,181 (2006-2010 5-year est.); Average household income: $63,240 (2006-2010 5-year est.); Percent of households with income of $100,000 or more: 18.1% (2006-2010 5-year est.); Poverty rate: 7.3% (2006-2010 5-year est.).

Education: Percent of population age 25 and over with: High school diploma (including GED) or higher: 95.9% (2006-2010 5-year est.); Bachelor's degree or higher: 24.2% (2006-2010 5-year est.); Master's degree or higher: 6.7% (2006-2010 5-year est.).

Housing: Homeownership rate: 53.3% (2010); Median home value: $275,500 (2006-2010 5-year est.); Median contract rent: $809 per month (2006-2010 5-year est.); Median year structure built: 1960 (2006-2010 5-year est.).

Safety: Violent crime rate: 51.4 per 10,000 population; Property crime rate: 141.3 per 10,000 population (2011).

Transportation: Commute to work: 83.1% car, 3.7% public transportation, 11.1% walk, 1.6% work from home (2006-2010 5-year est.); Travel time to work: 39.6% less than 15 minutes, 33.4% 15 to 30 minutes, 15.4% 30 to

45 minutes, 6.6% 45 to 60 minutes, 5.1% 60 minutes or more (2006-2010 5-year est.)

Additional Information Contacts

Lower Bucks County Chamber of Commerce . . . . (215) 943-7400
   http://www.lbccc.org

PERKASIE (borough).
Covers a land area of 2.535 square miles and a water area of 0.029 square miles. Located at 40.37° N. Lat; 75.29° W. Long. Elevation is 361 feet.

History: Incorporated 1876.

Population: 7,878 (1990); 8,828 (2000); 8,511 (2010); Density: 3,357.0 persons per square mile (2010); Race: 95.8% White, 1.0% Black, 1.0% Asian, 0.2% American Indian/Alaska Native, 0.0% Native Hawaiian/Other Pacific Islander, 2.0% Other, 2.5% Hispanic of any race (2010); Average household size: 2.57 (2010); Median age: 38.9 (2010); Males per 100 females: 96.8 (2010); Marriage status: 30.9% never married, 51.9% now married, 6.2% widowed, 11.1% divorced (2006-2010 5-year est.); Foreign born: 1.8% (2006-2010 5-year est.); Ancestry (includes multiple ancestries): 44.9% German, 24.5% Irish, 13.0% Italian, 12.1% English, 6.0% Pennsylvania German (2006-2010 5-year est.).

Economy: Single-family building permits issued: 3 (2011); Multi-family building permits issued: 0 (2011); Employment by occupation: 13.1% management, 5.0% professional, 8.5% services, 18.8% sales, 2.3% farming, 11.1% construction, 5.6% production (2006-2010 5-year est.).

Income: Per capita income: $29,898 (2006-2010 5-year est.); Median household income: $66,663 (2006-2010 5-year est.); Average household income: $77,086 (2006-2010 5-year est.); Percent of households with income of $100,000 or more: 28.5% (2006-2010 5-year est.); Poverty rate: 2.9% (2006-2010 5-year est.).

Taxes: Total city taxes per capita: $217 (2009); City property taxes per capita: $54 (2009).

Education: Percent of population age 25 and over with: High school diploma (including GED) or higher: 92.2% (2006-2010 5-year est.); Bachelor's degree or higher: 29.2% (2006-2010 5-year est.); Master's degree or higher: 9.3% (2006-2010 5-year est.).

School District(s)

Pennridge SD (KG-12)
   2010-11 Enrollment: 7,325 . . . . (215) 257-5011
Upper Bucks County Avts (09-12)
   2010-11 Enrollment: n/a . . . . (215) 795-2911

Housing: Homeownership rate: 70.0% (2010); Median home value: $268,300 (2006-2010 5-year est.); Median contract rent: $685 per month (2006-2010 5-year est.); Median year structure built: 1968 (2006-2010 5-year est.).

Safety: Violent crime rate: 16.4 per 10,000 population; Property crime rate: 246.0 per 10,000 population (2011).

Transportation: Commute to work: 95.1% car, 0.4% public transportation, 1.3% walk, 2.4% work from home (2006-2010 5-year est.); Travel time to work: 27.9% less than 15 minutes, 25.4% 15 to 30 minutes, 25.6% 30 to 45 minutes, 8.3% 45 to 60 minutes, 12.8% 60 minutes or more (2006-2010 5-year est.)

Additional Information Contacts

Borough of Perkasie . . . . (215) 257-5065
   http://www.perkasieborough.org
Pennridge Chamber of Commerce . . . . (215) 257-5390
   http://www.pennridge.com

PIPERSVILLE (unincorporated postal area)
Zip Code: 18947
   Covers a land area of 23.909 square miles and a water area of 0.134 square miles. Located at 40.42° N. Lat; 75.11° W. Long. Elevation is 436 feet. Population: 6,172 (2010); Density: 258.1 persons per square mile (2010); Race: 95.7% White, 0.4% Black, 0.7% Asian, 0.0% American Indian/Alaska Native, 0.0% Native Hawaiian/Other Pacific Islander, 3.2% Other, 4.0% Hispanic of any race (2010); Average household size: 2.86 (2010); Median age: 42.8 (2010); Males per 100 females: 103.2 (2010); Homeownership rate: 85.7% (2010)

PLUMSTEAD (township).
Covers a land area of 27.164 square miles and a water area of 0.117 square miles. Located at 40.38° N. Lat; 75.12° W. Long.

History: Plumstead Township was formed shortly after 1700 by English Quakers who came to Pennsylvania to help fulfill William Penn's dream of a land of religious freedom. Plumstead Friends Meeting, founded in 1727, was the township's first religious establishment, but diversity soon followed. In 1725, a petition was presented by a group of residents to the Bucks County Court, organizing Plumstead Township.

Population: 6,294 (1990); 11,409 (2000); 12,442 (2010); Density: 458.0 persons per square mile (2010); Race: 94.1% White, 0.7% Black, 1.7% Asian, 0.1% American Indian/Alaska Native, 0.0% Native Hawaiian/Other Pacific Islander, 3.4% Other, 4.7% Hispanic of any race (2010); Average household size: 2.90 (2010); Median age: 39.6 (2010); Males per 100 females: 99.9 (2010); Marriage status: 23.4% never married, 66.2% now married, 4.4% widowed, 6.1% divorced (2006-2010 5-year est.); Foreign born: 6.2% (2006-2010 5-year est.); Ancestry (includes multiple ancestries): 34.3% German, 24.5% Irish, 17.4% Italian, 9.6% English, 6.8% Polish (2006-2010 5-year est.).

Economy: Single-family building permits issued: 22 (2011); Multi-family building permits issued: 29 (2011); Employment by occupation: 21.6% management, 5.6% professional, 8.3% services, 13.9% sales, 2.5% farming, 6.9% construction, 3.0% production (2006-2010 5-year est.).

Income: Per capita income: $39,500 (2006-2010 5-year est.); Median household income: $97,925 (2006-2010 5-year est.); Average household income: $117,249 (2006-2010 5-year est.); Percent of households with income of $100,000 or more: 48.9% (2006-2010 5-year est.); Poverty rate: 5.7% (2006-2010 5-year est.).

Education: Percent of population age 25 and over with: High school diploma (including GED) or higher: 90.7% (2006-2010 5-year est.); Bachelor's degree or higher: 47.1% (2006-2010 5-year est.); Master's degree or higher: 18.8% (2006-2010 5-year est.).

Housing: Homeownership rate: 85.5% (2010); Median home value: $428,700 (2006-2010 5-year est.); Median contract rent: $1,094 per month (2006-2010 5-year est.); Median year structure built: 1991 (2006-2010 5-year est.).

Safety: Violent crime rate: 4.8 per 10,000 population; Property crime rate: 92.9 per 10,000 population (2011).

Transportation: Commute to work: 90.8% car, 1.5% public transportation, 1.4% walk, 6.0% work from home (2006-2010 5-year est.); Travel time to work: 24.2% less than 15 minutes, 27.4% 15 to 30 minutes, 19.1% 30 to 45 minutes, 13.8% 45 to 60 minutes, 15.5% 60 minutes or more (2006-2010 5-year est.)

Additional Information Contacts

Central Bucks Chamber of Commerce . . . . (215) 348-3913
   http://www.centralbuckschamber.com
Plumstead Township . . . . (215) 766-8914
   http://www.plumstead.org

PLUMSTEADVILLE (CDP).
Covers a land area of 2.387 square miles and a water area of 0.001 square miles. Located at 40.38° N. Lat; 75.14° W. Long. Elevation is 584 feet.

Population: n/a (1990); n/a (2000); 2,637 (2010); Density: 1,104.9 persons per square mile (2010); Race: 94.4% White, 0.3% Black, 1.1% Asian, 0.0% American Indian/Alaska Native, 0.0% Native Hawaiian/Other Pacific Islander, 4.2% Other, 5.0% Hispanic of any race (2010); Average household size: 3.20 (2010); Median age: 37.0 (2010); Males per 100 females: 96.5 (2010); Marriage status: 24.7% never married, 71.3% now married, 2.0% widowed, 1.9% divorced (2006-2010 5-year est.); Foreign born: 7.5% (2006-2010 5-year est.); Ancestry (includes multiple ancestries): 26.1% Italian, 24.1% Irish, 22.8% German, 9.8% English, 6.8% American (2006-2010 5-year est.).

Economy: Employment by occupation: 29.8% management, 5.4% professional, 6.7% services, 9.3% sales, 6.3% farming, 2.2% construction, 0.0% production (2006-2010 5-year est.).

Income: Per capita income: $43,578 (2006-2010 5-year est.); Median household income: $126,739 (2006-2010 5-year est.); Average household income: $157,499 (2006-2010 5-year est.); Percent of households with income of $100,000 or more: 72.4% (2006-2010 5-year est.); Poverty rate: 1.8% (2006-2010 5-year est.).

Education: Percent of population age 25 and over with: High school diploma (including GED) or higher: 87.1% (2006-2010 5-year est.); Bachelor's degree or higher: 53.4% (2006-2010 5-year est.); Master's degree or higher: 29.7% (2006-2010 5-year est.).

Housing: Homeownership rate: 85.9% (2010); Median home value: $414,300 (2006-2010 5-year est.); Median contract rent: $1,382 per month (2006-2010 5-year est.); Median year structure built: 1995 (2006-2010 5-year est.).

Transportation: Commute to work: 81.6% car, 4.8% public transportation, 1.0% walk, 12.6% work from home (2006-2010 5-year est.); Travel time to work: 19.0% less than 15 minutes, 31.1% 15 to 30 minutes, 16.8% 30 to

45 minutes, 10.8% 45 to 60 minutes, 22.3% 60 minutes or more (2006-2010 5-year est.)

POINT PLEASANT (unincorporated postal area)
Zip Code: 18950

Covers a land area of 1.161 square miles and a water area of 0.235 square miles. Located at 40.44° N. Lat; 75.07° W. Long. Elevation is 92 feet. Population: 252 (2010); Density: 216.9 persons per square mile (2010); Race: 81.7% White, 13.1% Black, 1.6% Asian, 0.4% American Indian/Alaska Native, 0.0% Native Hawaiian/Other Pacific Islander, 3.2% Other, 4.0% Hispanic of any race (2010); Average household size: 2.40 (2010); Median age: 46.6 (2010); Males per 100 females: 108.3 (2010); Homeownership rate: 85.4% (2010)

QUAKERTOWN (borough). Covers a land area of 2.032 square miles and a water area of 0.005 square miles. Located at 40.44° N. Lat; 75.35° W. Long. Elevation is 499 feet.
History: Settled c.1700, incorporated 1855.
Population: 8,982 (1990); 8,931 (2000); 8,979 (2010); Density: 4,419.1 persons per square mile (2010); Race: 90.6% White, 2.4% Black, 2.0% Asian, 0.3% American Indian/Alaska Native, 0.0% Native Hawaiian/Other Pacific Islander, 4.7% Other, 6.0% Hispanic of any race (2010); Average household size: 2.40 (2010); Median age: 38.0 (2010); Males per 100 females: 96.8 (2010); Marriage status: 33.3% never married, 47.1% now married, 10.9% widowed, 8.7% divorced (2006-2010 5-year est.); Foreign born: 5.2% (2006-2010 5-year est.); Ancestry (includes multiple ancestries): 39.6% German, 21.6% Irish, 9.5% English, 7.4% Italian, 6.5% American (2006-2010 5-year est.).
Economy: Single-family building permits issued: 0 (2011); Multi-family building permits issued: 0 (2011); Employment by occupation: 8.4% management, 2.8% professional, 9.7% services, 24.8% sales, 2.8% farming, 11.7% construction, 7.3% production (2006-2010 5-year est.).
Income: Per capita income: $23,634 (2006-2010 5-year est.); Median household income: $50,348 (2006-2010 5-year est.); Average household income: $58,961 (2006-2010 5-year est.); Percent of households with income of $100,000 or more: 13.7% (2006-2010 5-year est.); Poverty rate: 9.5% (2006-2010 5-year est.).
Taxes: Total city taxes per capita: $203 (2009); City property taxes per capita: $15 (2009).
Education: Percent of population age 25 and over with: High school diploma (including GED) or higher: 84.0% (2006-2010 5-year est.); Bachelor's degree or higher: 19.3% (2006-2010 5-year est.); Master's degree or higher: 3.7% (2006-2010 5-year est.).

School District(s)
Palisades SD (KG-12)
    2010-11 Enrollment: 1,901 . . . . (610) 847-5131
Quakertown Community SD (KG-12)
    2010-11 Enrollment: 5,333 . . . . (215) 529-2000
Housing: Homeownership rate: 58.7% (2010); Median home value: $190,300 (2006-2010 5-year est.); Median contract rent: $739 per month (2006-2010 5-year est.); Median year structure built: 1954 (2006-2010 5-year est.).
Hospitals: St. Luke's Quakertown Hospital (89 beds)
Safety: Violent crime rate: 44.4 per 10,000 population; Property crime rate: 341.9 per 10,000 population (2011).
Newspapers: The Free Press (Local news; Circulation 10,250); The Saucon News (Community news; Circulation 4,000)
Transportation: Commute to work: 93.3% car, 0.0% public transportation, 4.0% walk, 1.2% work from home (2006-2010 5-year est.); Travel time to work: 33.2% less than 15 minutes, 31.3% 15 to 30 minutes, 20.6% 30 to 45 minutes, 8.3% 45 to 60 minutes, 6.6% 60 minutes or more (2006-2010 5-year est.)

Additional Information Contacts
Borough of Quakertown . . . . (215) 536-5001
    http://www.quakertownboro.com
Upper Bucks Chamber of Commerce . . . . (215) 536-3211
    http://www.ubcc.org

RICHBORO (CDP). Covers a land area of 4.378 square miles and a water area of 0.029 square miles. Located at 40.23° N. Lat; 74.99° W. Long. Elevation is 262 feet.
History: The first Europeans to come to the area were English immigrants who arrived with William Penn in the late 1600's. Dutch farmers joined the English colonists to settle in places destined to become known as

Richboro, Holland, Churchville, Rocksville, Addisville, and Jacksonville - all located within Northampton Township.
Population: 5,536 (1990); 6,678 (2000); 6,563 (2010); Density: 1,499.0 persons per square mile (2010); Race: 95.4% White, 0.4% Black, 3.1% Asian, 0.1% American Indian/Alaska Native, 0.0% Native Hawaiian/Other Pacific Islander, 1.0% Other, 1.2% Hispanic of any race (2010); Average household size: 2.93 (2010); Median age: 45.6 (2010); Males per 100 females: 94.7 (2010); Marriage status: 27.0% never married, 65.0% now married, 5.4% widowed, 2.7% divorced (2006-2010 5-year est.); Foreign born: 9.5% (2006-2010 5-year est.); Ancestry (includes multiple ancestries): 26.7% Irish, 19.2% German, 15.6% Italian, 13.0% Polish, 11.5% English (2006-2010 5-year est.).
Economy: Employment by occupation: 18.6% management, 5.1% professional, 7.0% services, 15.1% sales, 3.6% farming, 6.9% construction, 2.1% production (2006-2010 5-year est.).
Income: Per capita income: $40,049 (2006-2010 5-year est.); Median household income: $116,422 (2006-2010 5-year est.); Average household income: $126,373 (2006-2010 5-year est.); Percent of households with income of $100,000 or more: 55.4% (2006-2010 5-year est.); Poverty rate: 1.9% (2006-2010 5-year est.).
Education: Percent of population age 25 and over with: High school diploma (including GED) or higher: 95.8% (2006-2010 5-year est.); Bachelor's degree or higher: 45.7% (2006-2010 5-year est.); Master's degree or higher: 16.0% (2006-2010 5-year est.).

School District(s)
Council Rock SD (KG-12)
    2010-11 Enrollment: 11,882 . . . . (215) 944-1000
Housing: Homeownership rate: 93.7% (2010); Median home value: $437,600 (2006-2010 5-year est.); Median contract rent: $1,328 per month (2006-2010 5-year est.); Median year structure built: 1978 (2006-2010 5-year est.).
Transportation: Commute to work: 92.4% car, 2.6% public transportation, 1.2% walk, 3.8% work from home (2006-2010 5-year est.); Travel time to work: 21.1% less than 15 minutes, 32.3% 15 to 30 minutes, 23.5% 30 to 45 minutes, 11.7% 45 to 60 minutes, 11.5% 60 minutes or more (2006-2010 5-year est.)

Additional Information Contacts
Lower Bucks County Chamber of Commerce . . . . (215) 943-7400
    http://www.lbccc.org

RICHLAND (township). Covers a land area of 20.651 square miles and a water area of 0.115 square miles. Located at 40.45° N. Lat; 75.34° W. Long.
Population: 8,554 (1990); 9,920 (2000); 13,052 (2010); Density: 632.0 persons per square mile (2010); Race: 92.2% White, 1.4% Black, 2.9% Asian, 0.3% American Indian/Alaska Native, 0.0% Native Hawaiian/Other Pacific Islander, 3.2% Other, 3.8% Hispanic of any race (2010); Average household size: 2.70 (2010); Median age: 37.8 (2010); Males per 100 females: 98.4 (2010); Marriage status: 21.3% never married, 64.8% now married, 5.4% widowed, 8.5% divorced (2006-2010 5-year est.); Foreign born: 6.3% (2006-2010 5-year est.); Ancestry (includes multiple ancestries): 37.7% German, 18.5% Irish, 13.5% Italian, 11.2% English, 7.5% Polish (2006-2010 5-year est.).
Economy: Single-family building permits issued: 28 (2011); Multi-family building permits issued: 0 (2011); Employment by occupation: 11.6% management, 3.6% professional, 7.5% services, 15.1% sales, 3.8% farming, 9.7% construction, 8.5% production (2006-2010 5-year est.).
Income: Per capita income: $29,625 (2006-2010 5-year est.); Median household income: $67,976 (2006-2010 5-year est.); Average household income: $79,205 (2006-2010 5-year est.); Percent of households with income of $100,000 or more: 32.6% (2006-2010 5-year est.); Poverty rate: 3.7% (2006-2010 5-year est.).
Education: Percent of population age 25 and over with: High school diploma (including GED) or higher: 88.4% (2006-2010 5-year est.); Bachelor's degree or higher: 26.8% (2006-2010 5-year est.); Master's degree or higher: 8.3% (2006-2010 5-year est.).
Housing: Homeownership rate: 87.5% (2010); Median home value: $243,200 (2006-2010 5-year est.); Median contract rent: $823 per month (2006-2010 5-year est.); Median year structure built: 1986 (2006-2010 5-year est.).
Safety: Violent crime rate: 4.6 per 10,000 population; Property crime rate: 217.7 per 10,000 population (2011).
Transportation: Commute to work: 92.0% car, 0.9% public transportation, 1.2% walk, 4.5% work from home (2006-2010 5-year est.); Travel time to work: 21.5% less than 15 minutes, 27.7% 15 to 30 minutes, 28.0% 30 to

45 minutes, 11.3% 45 to 60 minutes, 11.6% 60 minutes or more (2006-2010 5-year est.)

Additional Information Contacts
Richland Township . . . . (215) 536-4066
   http://www.richlandtownship.org
Upper Bucks Chamber of Commerce . . . . (215) 536-3211
   http://www.ubcc.org

RICHLANDTOWN (borough).
Covers a land area of 0.260 square miles and a water area of 0 square miles. Located at 40.47° N. Lat; 75.32° W. Long. Elevation is 525 feet.
Population: 1,195 (1990); 1,283 (2000); 1,327 (2010); Density: 5,097.1 persons per square mile (2010); Race: 95.7% White, 1.1% Black, 0.4% Asian, 0.0% American Indian/Alaska Native, 0.1% Native Hawaiian/Other Pacific Islander, 2.7% Other, 3.2% Hispanic of any race (2010); Average household size: 2.57 (2010); Median age: 39.5 (2010); Males per 100 females: 88.8 (2010); Marriage status: 25.9% never married, 58.3% now married, 9.1% widowed, 6.7% divorced (2006-2010 5-year est.); Foreign born: 1.0% (2006-2010 5-year est.); Ancestry (includes multiple ancestries): 46.3% German, 19.7% Irish, 12.3% Polish, 9.7% English, 9.4% Italian (2006-2010 5-year est.).
Economy: Single-family building permits issued: 0 (2011); Multi-family building permits issued: 0 (2011); Employment by occupation: 11.8% management, 1.7% professional, 13.5% services, 13.1% sales, 1.7% farming, 9.7% construction, 12.5% production (2006-2010 5-year est.).
Income: Per capita income: $25,870 (2006-2010 5-year est.); Median household income: $70,789 (2006-2010 5-year est.); Average household income: $72,825 (2006-2010 5-year est.); Percent of households with income of $100,000 or more: 23.9% (2006-2010 5-year est.); Poverty rate: 2.1% (2006-2010 5-year est.).
Education: Percent of population age 25 and over with: High school diploma (including GED) or higher: 91.2% (2006-2010 5-year est.); Bachelor's degree or higher: 11.4% (2006-2010 5-year est.); Master's degree or higher: 4.6% (2006-2010 5-year est.).
Housing: Homeownership rate: 68.4% (2010); Median home value: $238,700 (2006-2010 5-year est.); Median contract rent: $725 per month (2006-2010 5-year est.); Median year structure built: 1949 (2006-2010 5-year est.).
Transportation: Commute to work: 95.9% car, 0.0% public transportation, 0.3% walk, 3.1% work from home (2006-2010 5-year est.); Travel time to work: 21.2% less than 15 minutes, 27.6% 15 to 30 minutes, 24.4% 30 to 45 minutes, 12.3% 45 to 60 minutes, 14.5% 60 minutes or more (2006-2010 5-year est.)

Additional Information Contacts
Upper Bucks Chamber of Commerce . . . . (215) 536-3211
   http://www.ubcc.org

RIEGELSVILLE (borough).
Covers a land area of 1.007 square miles and a water area of 0.072 square miles. Located at 40.59° N. Lat; 75.20° W. Long. Elevation is 180 feet.
Population: 912 (1990); 863 (2000); 868 (2010); Density: 862.1 persons per square mile (2010); Race: 98.5% White, 0.2% Black, 0.2% Asian, 0.3% American Indian/Alaska Native, 0.0% Native Hawaiian/Other Pacific Islander, 0.8% Other, 2.0% Hispanic of any race (2010); Average household size: 2.32 (2010); Median age: 44.5 (2010); Males per 100 females: 103.8 (2010); Marriage status: 18.5% never married, 59.3% now married, 9.0% widowed, 13.2% divorced (2006-2010 5-year est.); Foreign born: 2.6% (2006-2010 5-year est.); Ancestry (includes multiple ancestries): 34.3% German, 26.6% Irish, 22.5% Italian, 13.4% English, 9.9% Polish (2006-2010 5-year est.).
Economy: Single-family building permits issued: 0 (2011); Multi-family building permits issued: 0 (2011); Employment by occupation: 6.1% management, 4.8% professional, 10.9% services, 15.1% sales, 8.0% farming, 11.6% construction, 7.4% production (2006-2010 5-year est.).
Income: Per capita income: $28,799 (2006-2010 5-year est.); Median household income: $52,578 (2006-2010 5-year est.); Average household income: $59,796 (2006-2010 5-year est.); Percent of households with income of $100,000 or more: 17.3% (2006-2010 5-year est.); Poverty rate: 6.1% (2006-2010 5-year est.).
Education: Percent of population age 25 and over with: High school diploma (including GED) or higher: 95.2% (2006-2010 5-year est.); Bachelor's degree or higher: 26.5% (2006-2010 5-year est.); Master's degree or higher: 7.7% (2006-2010 5-year est.).
Housing: Homeownership rate: 72.0% (2010); Median home value: $253,500 (2006-2010 5-year est.); Median contract rent: $874 per month

(2006-2010 5-year est.); Median year structure built: before 1940 (2006-2010 5-year est.).
Transportation: Commute to work: 82.6% car, 5.4% public transportation, 1.3% walk, 10.1% work from home (2006-2010 5-year est.); Travel time to work: 16.8% less than 15 minutes, 20.9% 15 to 30 minutes, 35.1% 30 to 45 minutes, 11.9% 45 to 60 minutes, 15.3% 60 minutes or more (2006-2010 5-year est.)

SELLERSVILLE (borough).
Covers a land area of 1.144 square miles and a water area of 0.025 square miles. Located at 40.36° N. Lat; 75.31° W. Long. Elevation is 341 feet.
History: Settled c.1730, incorporated 1874.
Population: 4,479 (1990); 4,564 (2000); 4,249 (2010); Density: 3,714.5 persons per square mile (2010); Race: 93.6% White, 1.8% Black, 1.0% Asian, 0.3% American Indian/Alaska Native, 0.0% Native Hawaiian/Other Pacific Islander, 3.3% Other, 3.4% Hispanic of any race (2010); Average household size: 2.45 (2010); Median age: 36.8 (2010); Males per 100 females: 103.0 (2010); Marriage status: 34.3% never married, 51.0% now married, 3.2% widowed, 11.5% divorced (2006-2010 5-year est.); Foreign born: 1.9% (2006-2010 5-year est.); Ancestry (includes multiple ancestries): 39.1% German, 28.3% Irish, 11.7% Italian, 11.0% English, 7.2% American (2006-2010 5-year est.).
Economy: Single-family building permits issued: 0 (2011); Multi-family building permits issued: 0 (2011); Employment by occupation: 12.3% management, 2.1% professional, 10.8% services, 20.7% sales, 4.9% farming, 10.0% construction, 6.2% production (2006-2010 5-year est.).
Income: Per capita income: $24,382 (2006-2010 5-year est.); Median household income: $56,023 (2006-2010 5-year est.); Average household income: $63,510 (2006-2010 5-year est.); Percent of households with income of $100,000 or more: 14.4% (2006-2010 5-year est.); Poverty rate: 7.2% (2006-2010 5-year est.).
Education: Percent of population age 25 and over with: High school diploma (including GED) or higher: 90.9% (2006-2010 5-year est.); Bachelor's degree or higher: 24.7% (2006-2010 5-year est.); Master's degree or higher: 5.9% (2006-2010 5-year est.).
School District(s)
Pennridge SD (KG-12)
   2010-11 Enrollment: 7,325 . . . . (215) 257-5011
Housing: Homeownership rate: 70.7% (2010); Median home value: $201,500 (2006-2010 5-year est.); Median contract rent: $797 per month (2006-2010 5-year est.); Median year structure built: 1958 (2006-2010 5-year est.).
Hospitals: Grand View Hospital (198 beds)
Transportation: Commute to work: 95.7% car, 1.2% public transportation, 1.3% walk, 1.1% work from home (2006-2010 5-year est.); Travel time to work: 30.0% less than 15 minutes, 29.7% 15 to 30 minutes, 19.0% 30 to 45 minutes, 11.6% 45 to 60 minutes, 9.7% 60 minutes or more (2006-2010 5-year est.)

Additional Information Contacts
Upper Bucks Chamber of Commerce . . . . (215) 536-3211
   http://www.ubcc.org

SILVERDALE (borough).
Covers a land area of 0.413 square miles and a water area of <.001 square miles. Located at 40.35° N. Lat; 75.27° W. Long. Elevation is 433 feet.
Population: 881 (1990); 1,001 (2000); 871 (2010); Density: 2,106.8 persons per square mile (2010); Race: 97.7% White, 0.8% Black, 0.0% Asian, 0.2% American Indian/Alaska Native, 0.0% Native Hawaiian/Other Pacific Islander, 1.3% Other, 1.4% Hispanic of any race (2010); Average household size: 2.70 (2010); Median age: 42.6 (2010); Males per 100 females: 94.9 (2010); Marriage status: 26.2% never married, 61.0% now married, 4.0% widowed, 8.8% divorced (2006-2010 5-year est.); Foreign born: 5.6% (2006-2010 5-year est.); Ancestry (includes multiple ancestries): 50.8% German, 29.3% Irish, 16.4% Italian, 15.0% English, 4.7% Polish (2006-2010 5-year est.).
Economy: Single-family building permits issued: 0 (2011); Multi-family building permits issued: 0 (2011); Employment by occupation: 12.6% management, 6.3% professional, 0.9% services, 21.6% sales, 4.0% farming, 10.5% construction, 5.8% production (2006-2010 5-year est.).
Income: Per capita income: $27,968 (2006-2010 5-year est.); Median household income: $64,231 (2006-2010 5-year est.); Average household income: $76,469 (2006-2010 5-year est.); Percent of households with income of $100,000 or more: 23.5% (2006-2010 5-year est.); Poverty rate: 5.5% (2006-2010 5-year est.).

Education: Percent of population age 25 and over with: High school diploma (including GED) or higher: 95.1% (2006-2010 5-year est.); Bachelor's degree or higher: 21.7% (2006-2010 5-year est.); Master's degree or higher: 7.3% (2006-2010 5-year est.).

Housing: Homeownership rate: 80.0% (2010); Median home value: $235,900 (2006-2010 5-year est.); Median contract rent: $681 per month (2006-2010 5-year est.); Median year structure built: 1982 (2006-2010 5-year est.).

Transportation: Commute to work: 95.1% car, 3.3% public transportation, 0.9% walk, 0.7% work from home (2006-2010 5-year est.); Travel time to work: 25.2% less than 15 minutes, 19.8% 15 to 30 minutes, 30.7% 30 to 45 minutes, 13.9% 45 to 60 minutes, 10.4% 60 minutes or more (2006-2010 5-year est.)

SOLEBURY (township).
Covers a land area of 26.567 square miles and a water area of 0.584 square miles. Located at 40.37° N. Lat; 75.01° W. Long. Elevation is 387 feet.

History: In July 1682, William Markham made the first treaty and purchase, before William Penn's arrival. It included the southeastern part of Bucks County, and was approved by 13 Native American tribal leaders. The area of Solebury Township was included in a 1686 treaty.

Population: 5,998 (1990); 7,743 (2000); 8,692 (2010); Density: 327.2 persons per square mile (2010); Race: 94.3% White, 0.9% Black, 2.9% Asian, 0.0% American Indian/Alaska Native, 0.1% Native Hawaiian/Other Pacific Islander, 1.8% Other, 2.7% Hispanic of any race (2010); Average household size: 2.51 (2010); Median age: 48.9 (2010); Males per 100 females: 103.1 (2010); Marriage status: 22.1% never married, 66.9% now married, 2.9% widowed, 8.0% divorced (2006-2010 5-year est.); Foreign born: 9.2% (2006-2010 5-year est.); Ancestry (includes multiple ancestries): 21.0% English, 19.5% Italian, 19.0% Irish, 18.9% German, 6.8% Polish (2006-2010 5-year est.).

Economy: Single-family building permits issued: 4 (2011); Multi-family building permits issued: 0 (2011); Employment by occupation: 28.4% management, 5.1% professional, 6.4% services, 11.9% sales, 4.6% farming, 7.2% construction, 2.3% production (2006-2010 5-year est.).

Income: Per capita income: $73,647 (2006-2010 5-year est.); Median household income: $116,364 (2006-2010 5-year est.); Average household income: $181,671 (2006-2010 5-year est.); Percent of households with income of $100,000 or more: 55.5% (2006-2010 5-year est.); Poverty rate: 3.4% (2006-2010 5-year est.).

Taxes: Total city taxes per capita: $777 (2009); City property taxes per capita: $397 (2009).

Education: Percent of population age 25 and over with: High school diploma (including GED) or higher: 98.1% (2006-2010 5-year est.); Bachelor's degree or higher: 62.9% (2006-2010 5-year est.); Master's degree or higher: 30.2% (2006-2010 5-year est.).

School District(s)
New Hope-Solebury SD (KG-12)

    2010-11 Enrollment: 1,587 . . . . (215) 862-2552

Housing: Homeownership rate: 89.7% (2010); Median home value: $565,900 (2006-2010 5-year est.); Median contract rent: $1,157 per month (2006-2010 5-year est.); Median year structure built: 1982 (2006-2010 5-year est.).

Safety: Violent crime rate: 4.6 per 10,000 population; Property crime rate: 73.4 per 10,000 population (2011).

Transportation: Commute to work: 85.5% car, 1.2% public transportation, 3.2% walk, 7.4% work from home (2006-2010 5-year est.); Travel time to work: 24.7% less than 15 minutes, 19.5% 15 to 30 minutes, 17.1% 30 to 45 minutes, 20.4% 45 to 60 minutes, 18.2% 60 minutes or more (2006-2010 5-year est.)

Additional Information Contacts

Central Bucks Chamber of Commerce . . . . (215) 348-3913
  http://www.centralbuckschamber.com
Solebury Township . . . . (215) 297-5656
  http://www.soleburytwp.org

SPINNERSTOWN (CDP).
Covers a land area of 1.886 square miles and a water area of 0.008 square miles. Located at 40.44° N. Lat; 75.45° W. Long. Elevation is 554 feet.

Population: n/a (1990); n/a (2000); 1,826 (2010); Density: 968.0 persons per square mile (2010); Race: 94.3% White, 1.4% Black, 1.9% Asian, 0.1% American Indian/Alaska Native, 0.1% Native Hawaiian/Other Pacific Islander, 2.2% Other, 2.0% Hispanic of any race (2010); Average household size: 3.15 (2010); Median age: 37.5 (2010); Males per 100 females: 99.6 (2010); Marriage status: 19.8% never married, 71.1% now

married, 4.0% widowed, 5.2% divorced (2006-2010 5-year est.); Foreign born: 1.6% (2006-2010 5-year est.); Ancestry (includes multiple ancestries): 34.2% German, 22.5% Irish, 16.3% Italian, 6.9% Polish, 5.4% English (2006-2010 5-year est.).

Economy: Employment by occupation: 10.0% management, 10.0% professional, 4.7% services, 21.4% sales, 2.5% farming, 7.7% construction, 4.9% production (2006-2010 5-year est.).

Income: Per capita income: $31,486 (2006-2010 5-year est.); Median household income: $93,661 (2006-2010 5-year est.); Average household income: $95,825 (2006-2010 5-year est.); Percent of households with income of $100,000 or more: 47.2% (2006-2010 5-year est.); Poverty rate: 1.6% (2006-2010 5-year est.).

Education: Percent of population age 25 and over with: High school diploma (including GED) or higher: 96.8% (2006-2010 5-year est.); Bachelor's degree or higher: 41.4% (2006-2010 5-year est.); Master's degree or higher: 10.5% (2006-2010 5-year est.).

Housing: Homeownership rate: 88.3% (2010); Median home value: $305,200 (2006-2010 5-year est.); Median contract rent: $908 per month (2006-2010 5-year est.); Median year structure built: 1996 (2006-2010 5-year est.).

Transportation: Commute to work: 93.2% car, 1.7% public transportation, 1.3% walk, 3.9% work from home (2006-2010 5-year est.); Travel time to work: 16.4% less than 15 minutes, 29.4% 15 to 30 minutes, 22.2% 30 to 45 minutes, 19.7% 45 to 60 minutes, 12.3% 60 minutes or more (2006-2010 5-year est.)

SPRINGFIELD (township).
Covers a land area of 30.602 square miles and a water area of 0.083 square miles. Located at 40.53° N. Lat; 75.30° W. Long.

Population: 5,177 (1990); 4,963 (2000); 5,035 (2010); Density: 164.5 persons per square mile (2010); Race: 97.6% White, 0.4% Black, 0.8% Asian, 0.1% American Indian/Alaska Native, 0.0% Native Hawaiian/Other Pacific Islander, 1.1% Other, 1.5% Hispanic of any race (2010); Average household size: 2.50 (2010); Median age: 47.3 (2010); Males per 100 females: 104.5 (2010); Marriage status: 20.9% never married, 64.7% now married, 6.3% widowed, 8.0% divorced (2006-2010 5-year est.); Foreign born: 0.7% (2006-2010 5-year est.); Ancestry (includes multiple ancestries): 44.0% German, 17.2% Irish, 14.2% Italian, 8.3% English, 7.6% American (2006-2010 5-year est.).

Economy: Single-family building permits issued: 3 (2011); Multi-family building permits issued: 0 (2011); Employment by occupation: 14.2% management, 4.1% professional, 6.8% services, 13.2% sales, 3.6% farming, 13.8% construction, 4.5% production (2006-2010 5-year est.).

Income: Per capita income: $33,586 (2006-2010 5-year est.); Median household income: $72,639 (2006-2010 5-year est.); Average household income: $87,194 (2006-2010 5-year est.); Percent of households with income of $100,000 or more: 32.5% (2006-2010 5-year est.); Poverty rate: 3.0% (2006-2010 5-year est.).

Education: Percent of population age 25 and over with: High school diploma (including GED) or higher: 94.1% (2006-2010 5-year est.); Bachelor's degree or higher: 33.4% (2006-2010 5-year est.); Master's degree or higher: 15.7% (2006-2010 5-year est.).

Housing: Homeownership rate: 86.0% (2010); Median home value: $348,900 (2006-2010 5-year est.); Median contract rent: $1,008 per month (2006-2010 5-year est.); Median year structure built: 1968 (2006-2010 5-year est.).

Transportation: Commute to work: 87.0% car, 0.0% public transportation, 1.5% walk, 11.2% work from home (2006-2010 5-year est.); Travel time to work: 13.8% less than 15 minutes, 24.6% 15 to 30 minutes, 32.7% 30 to 45 minutes, 7.9% 45 to 60 minutes, 21.0% 60 minutes or more (2006-2010 5-year est.)

Additional Information Contacts

Upper Bucks Chamber of Commerce . . . . (215) 536-3211
  http://www.ubcc.org

SPRINGTOWN (unincorporated postal area)
Zip Code: 18081

  Covers a land area of 0.526 square miles and a water area of 0.003 square miles. Located at 40.56° N. Lat; 75.28° W. Long. Elevation is 348 feet. Population: 357 (2010); Density: 677.6 persons per square mile (2010); Race: 97.8% White, 0.3% Black, 0.3% Asian, 0.0% American Indian/Alaska Native, 0.0% Native Hawaiian/Other Pacific Islander, 1.6% Other, 1.1% Hispanic of any race (2010); Average household size: 2.46 (2010); Median age: 43.7 (2010); Males per 100 females: 111.2 (2010); Homeownership rate: 82.1% (2010)

TINICUM (township). Covers a land area of 30.073 square miles and a water area of 0.954 square miles. Located at 40.49° N. Lat; 75.10° W. Long. Elevation is 384 feet.

Population: 4,167 (1990); 4,206 (2000); 3,995 (2010); Density: 132.8 persons per square mile (2010); Race: 96.0% White, 1.3% Black, 0.8% Asian, 0.2% American Indian/Alaska Native, 0.0% Native Hawaiian/Other Pacific Islander, 1.7% Other, 2.1% Hispanic of any race (2010); Average household size: 2.40 (2010); Median age: 48.6 (2010); Males per 100 females: 105.6 (2010); Marriage status: 19.0% never married, 65.3% now married, 4.1% widowed, 11.6% divorced (2006-2010 5-year est.); Foreign born: 1.9% (2006-2010 5-year est.); Ancestry (includes multiple ancestries): 29.0% German, 26.0% Irish, 15.2% English, 10.0% Italian, 8.5% Polish (2006-2010 5-year est.).

Economy: Single-family building permits issued: 0 (2011); Multi-family building permits issued: 0 (2011); Employment by occupation: 18.9% management, 5.8% professional, 10.0% services, 15.0% sales, 1.0% farming, 10.3% construction, 6.3% production (2006-2010 5-year est.).

Income: Per capita income: $45,384 (2006-2010 5-year est.); Median household income: $69,554 (2006-2010 5-year est.); Average household income: $107,472 (2006-2010 5-year est.); Percent of households with income of $100,000 or more: 35.4% (2006-2010 5-year est.); Poverty rate: 9.9% (2006-2010 5-year est.).

Education: Percent of population age 25 and over with: High school diploma (including GED) or higher: 91.7% (2006-2010 5-year est.); Bachelor's degree or higher: 30.9% (2006-2010 5-year est.); Master's degree or higher: 15.6% (2006-2010 5-year est.).

Housing: Homeownership rate: 79.9% (2010); Median home value: $449,800 (2006-2010 5-year est.); Median contract rent: $803 per month (2006-2010 5-year est.); Median year structure built: 1968 (2006-2010 5-year est.).

Safety: Violent crime rate: 7.5 per 10,000 population; Property crime rate: 72.4 per 10,000 population (2011).

Transportation: Commute to work: 83.2% car, 2.8% public transportation, 4.0% walk, 10.0% work from home (2006-2010 5-year est.); Travel time to work: 16.2% less than 15 minutes, 28.8% 15 to 30 minutes, 25.5% 30 to 45 minutes, 10.6% 45 to 60 minutes, 18.9% 60 minutes or more (2006-2010 5-year est.)

Additional Information Contacts

Central Bucks Chamber of Commerce . . . . (215) 348-3913
   http://www.centralbuckschamber.com

TREVOSE (CDP). Covers a land area of 0.706 square miles and a water area of 0 square miles. Located at 40.15° N. Lat; 74.98° W. Long. Elevation is 128 feet.

Population: n/a (1990); n/a (2000); 3,550 (2010); Density: 5,026.6 persons per square mile (2010); Race: 93.6% White, 1.9% Black, 2.4% Asian, 0.2% American Indian/Alaska Native, 0.1% Native Hawaiian/Other Pacific Islander, 1.8% Other, 2.8% Hispanic of any race (2010); Average household size: 2.67 (2010); Median age: 39.3 (2010); Males per 100 females: 101.4 (2010); Marriage status: 24.4% never married, 53.0% now married, 9.9% widowed, 12.7% divorced (2006-2010 5-year est.); Foreign born: 3.6% (2006-2010 5-year est.); Ancestry (includes multiple ancestries): 32.7% German, 26.3% Irish, 16.4% Italian, 13.1% English, 8.9% Polish (2006-2010 5-year est.).

Economy: Employment by occupation: 11.0% management, 1.3% professional, 7.1% services, 15.3% sales, 4.2% farming, 11.4% construction, 4.9% production (2006-2010 5-year est.).

Income: Per capita income: $25,900 (2006-2010 5-year est.); Median household income: $48,516 (2006-2010 5-year est.); Average household income: $60,443 (2006-2010 5-year est.); Percent of households with income of $100,000 or more: 19.0% (2006-2010 5-year est.); Poverty rate: 3.0% (2006-2010 5-year est.).

Education: Percent of population age 25 and over with: High school diploma (including GED) or higher: 91.9% (2006-2010 5-year est.); Bachelor's degree or higher: 15.6% (2006-2010 5-year est.); Master's degree or higher: 3.4% (2006-2010 5-year est.).

Four-year College(s)

Strayer University-Pennsylvania (Private, For-profit)
   Fall 2010 Enrollment: 2,244 . . . . (888) 378-7293
   2011-12 Tuition: In-state $14,805; Out-of-state $14,805

Housing: Homeownership rate: 75.7% (2010); Median home value: $267,000 (2006-2010 5-year est.); Median contract rent: $884 per month (2006-2010 5-year est.); Median year structure built: 1963 (2006-2010 5-year est.).

Transportation: Commute to work: 90.9% car, 3.6% public transportation, 1.4% walk, 3.0% work from home (2006-2010 5-year est.); Travel time to work: 20.8% less than 15 minutes, 34.1% 15 to 30 minutes, 27.3% 30 to 45 minutes, 11.5% 45 to 60 minutes, 6.3% 60 minutes or more (2006-2010 5-year est.)

TRUMBAUERSVILLE (borough). Aka Cressman. Covers a land area of 0.445 square miles and a water area of <.001 square miles. Located at 40.41° N. Lat; 75.38° W. Long. Elevation is 538 feet.

Population: 894 (1990); 1,059 (2000); 974 (2010); Density: 2,189.3 persons per square mile (2010); Race: 97.0% White, 0.6% Black, 0.8% Asian, 0.3% American Indian/Alaska Native, 0.1% Native Hawaiian/Other Pacific Islander, 1.2% Other, 3.1% Hispanic of any race (2010); Average household size: 2.70 (2010); Median age: 38.5 (2010); Males per 100 females: 106.4 (2010); Marriage status: 24.1% never married, 59.6% now married, 6.2% widowed, 10.2% divorced (2006-2010 5-year est.); Foreign born: 0.0% (2006-2010 5-year est.); Ancestry (includes multiple ancestries): 41.3% German, 20.6% Irish, 14.4% Italian, 12.6% Pennsylvania German, 8.9% English (2006-2010 5-year est.).

Economy: Single-family building permits issued: 0 (2011); Multi-family building permits issued: 0 (2011); Employment by occupation: 6.2% management, 1.6% professional, 11.4% services, 19.1% sales, 4.2% farming, 9.4% construction, 17.1% production (2006-2010 5-year est.).

Income: Per capita income: $25,686 (2006-2010 5-year est.); Median household income: $62,375 (2006-2010 5-year est.); Average household income: $69,347 (2006-2010 5-year est.); Percent of households with income of $100,000 or more: 20.6% (2006-2010 5-year est.); Poverty rate: 1.8% (2006-2010 5-year est.).

Education: Percent of population age 25 and over with: High school diploma (including GED) or higher: 81.6% (2006-2010 5-year est.); Bachelor's degree or higher: 14.5% (2006-2010 5-year est.); Master's degree or higher: 4.0% (2006-2010 5-year est.).

Housing: Homeownership rate: 72.8% (2010); Median home value: $234,800 (2006-2010 5-year est.); Median contract rent: $685 per month (2006-2010 5-year est.); Median year structure built: before 1940 (2006-2010 5-year est.).

Transportation: Commute to work: 85.7% car, 0.0% public transportation, 11.4% walk, 3.0% work from home (2006-2010 5-year est.); Travel time to work: 33.9% less than 15 minutes, 38.2% 15 to 30 minutes, 17.5% 30 to 45 minutes, 8.6% 45 to 60 minutes, 1.8% 60 minutes or more (2006-2010 5-year est.)

Additional Information Contacts

Borough of Trumbauersville . . . . (215) 536-1761
   http://www.trumbauersville.org
Upper Bucks Chamber of Commerce . . . . (215) 536-3211
   http://www.ubcc.org

TULLYTOWN (borough). Covers a land area of 1.516 square miles and a water area of 0.592 square miles. Located at 40.14° N. Lat; 74.81° W. Long. Elevation is 13 feet.

History: "Pennsbury Manor," restored home of William Penn, in Pennsbury Manor State Park, to East.

Population: 2,289 (1990); 2,031 (2000); 1,872 (2010); Density: 1,235.0 persons per square mile (2010); Race: 94.6% White, 3.2% Black, 0.4% Asian, 0.2% American Indian/Alaska Native, 0.0% Native Hawaiian/Other Pacific Islander, 1.6% Other, 3.0% Hispanic of any race (2010); Average household size: 2.46 (2010); Median age: 42.3 (2010); Males per 100 females: 94.0 (2010); Marriage status: 38.4% never married, 40.3% now married, 12.4% widowed, 8.9% divorced (2006-2010 5-year est.); Foreign born: 2.4% (2006-2010 5-year est.); Ancestry (includes multiple ancestries): 38.9% Irish, 32.0% German, 17.5% Italian, 12.4% Polish, 8.3% English (2006-2010 5-year est.).

Economy: Single-family building permits issued: 1 (2011); Multi-family building permits issued: 0 (2011); Employment by occupation: 10.1% management, 3.9% professional, 6.9% services, 20.7% sales, 5.7% farming, 12.8% construction, 5.6% production (2006-2010 5-year est.).

Income: Per capita income: $22,104 (2006-2010 5-year est.); Median household income: $50,677 (2006-2010 5-year est.); Average household income: $56,843 (2006-2010 5-year est.); Percent of households with income of $100,000 or more: 13.2% (2006-2010 5-year est.); Poverty rate: 8.5% (2006-2010 5-year est.).

Education: Percent of population age 25 and over with: High school diploma (including GED) or higher: 85.1% (2006-2010 5-year est.); Bachelor's degree or higher: 6.1% (2006-2010 5-year est.); Master's degree or higher: 3.0% (2006-2010 5-year est.).

Housing: Homeownership rate: 62.9% (2010); Median home value: $217,000 (2006-2010 5-year est.); Median contract rent: $645 per month (2006-2010 5-year est.); Median year structure built: 1957 (2006-2010 5-year est.).

Transportation: Commute to work: 96.5% car, 0.0% public transportation, 1.9% walk, 1.6% work from home (2006-2010 5-year est.); Travel time to work: 25.6% less than 15 minutes, 47.9% 15 to 30 minutes, 12.2% 30 to 45 minutes, 9.9% 45 to 60 minutes, 4.5% 60 minutes or more (2006-2010 5-year est.)

Additional Information Contacts

Lower Bucks County Chamber of Commerce . . . . (215) 943-7400
　http://www.lbccc.org

UPPER BLACK EDDY (unincorporated postal area)
Zip Code: 18972

Covers a land area of 23.538 square miles and a water area of 0.840 square miles. Located at 40.52° N. Lat; 75.12° W. Long. Population: 3,512 (2010); Density: 149.2 persons per square mile (2010); Race: 97.5% White, 0.4% Black, 0.4% Asian, 0.1% American Indian/Alaska Native, 0.0% Native Hawaiian/Other Pacific Islander, 1.6% Other, 1.3% Hispanic of any race (2010); Average household size: 2.32 (2010); Median age: 48.2 (2010); Males per 100 females: 103.9 (2010); Homeownership rate: 80.9% (2010)

UPPER MAKEFIELD (township). Covers a land area of 21.250 square miles and a water area of 0.550 square miles. Located at 40.30° N. Lat; 74.93° W. Long.

History: Founded in 1692, George Washington crossed the Delaware River here during the American Revolutionary War.

Population: 5,949 (1990); 7,180 (2000); 8,190 (2010); Density: 385.4 persons per square mile (2010); Race: 94.7% White, 1.1% Black, 2.5% Asian, 0.2% American Indian/Alaska Native, 0.0% Native Hawaiian/Other Pacific Islander, 1.5% Other, 2.3% Hispanic of any race (2010); Average household size: 2.76 (2010); Median age: 48.1 (2010); Males per 100 females: 97.2 (2010); Marriage status: 21.5% never married, 68.4% now married, 4.3% widowed, 5.8% divorced (2006-2010 5-year est.); Foreign born: 6.2% (2006-2010 5-year est.); Ancestry (includes multiple ancestries): 24.1% German, 21.0% Irish, 17.2% Italian, 15.7% English, 10.4% Polish (2006-2010 5-year est.).

Economy: Single-family building permits issued: 13 (2011); Multi-family building permits issued: 0 (2011); Employment by occupation: 26.6% management, 8.4% professional, 4.1% services, 13.9% sales, 2.0% farming, 3.8% construction, 1.4% production (2006-2010 5-year est.).

Income: Per capita income: $80,765 (2006-2010 5-year est.); Median household income: $155,221 (2006-2010 5-year est.); Average household income: $232,848 (2006-2010 5-year est.); Percent of households with income of $100,000 or more: 71.7% (2006-2010 5-year est.); Poverty rate: 4.3% (2006-2010 5-year est.).

Taxes: Total city taxes per capita: $800 (2009); City property taxes per capita: $331 (2009).

Education: Percent of population age 25 and over with: High school diploma (including GED) or higher: 98.3% (2006-2010 5-year est.); Bachelor's degree or higher: 64.2% (2006-2010 5-year est.); Master's degree or higher: 27.2% (2006-2010 5-year est.).

Housing: Homeownership rate: 94.8% (2010); Median home value: $693,000 (2006-2010 5-year est.); Median contract rent: n/a per month (2006-2010 5-year est.); Median year structure built: 1982 (2006-2010 5-year est.).

Safety: Violent crime rate: 4.9 per 10,000 population; Property crime rate: 70.6 per 10,000 population (2011).

Transportation: Commute to work: 85.7% car, 3.7% public transportation, 0.6% walk, 9.1% work from home (2006-2010 5-year est.); Travel time to work: 15.2% less than 15 minutes, 40.8% 15 to 30 minutes, 18.9% 30 to 45 minutes, 9.9% 45 to 60 minutes, 15.2% 60 minutes or more (2006-2010 5-year est.)

Additional Information Contacts

Central Bucks Chamber of Commerce . . . . (215) 348-3913
　http://www.centralbuckschamber.com
Upper Makefield Township . . . . (215) 968-3340
　http://www.upper-makefield.com

UPPER SOUTHAMPTON (township). Covers a land area of 6.620 square miles and a water area of 0.012 square miles. Located at 40.17° N. Lat; 75.03° W. Long.

Population: 16,076 (1990); 15,764 (2000); 15,152 (2010); Density: 2,289.0 persons per square mile (2010); Race: 95.8% White, 0.8% Black, 1.8% Asian, 0.1% American Indian/Alaska Native, 0.1% Native Hawaiian/Other Pacific Islander, 1.4% Other, 1.6% Hispanic of any race (2010); Average household size: 2.54 (2010); Median age: 47.4 (2010); Males per 100 females: 92.7 (2010); Marriage status: 22.0% never married, 61.7% now married, 9.9% widowed, 6.4% divorced (2006-2010 5-year est.); Foreign born: 9.5% (2006-2010 5-year est.); Ancestry (includes multiple ancestries): 31.9% Irish, 25.6% German, 13.7% Italian, 10.8% English, 7.9% Polish (2006-2010 5-year est.).

Economy: Single-family building permits issued: 7 (2011); Multi-family building permits issued: 0 (2011); Employment by occupation: 14.3% management, 6.0% professional, 5.5% services, 19.0% sales, 3.8% farming, 6.9% construction, 4.5% production (2006-2010 5-year est.).

Income: Per capita income: $33,777 (2006-2010 5-year est.); Median household income: $69,320 (2006-2010 5-year est.); Average household income: $85,322 (2006-2010 5-year est.); Percent of households with income of $100,000 or more: 35.4% (2006-2010 5-year est.); Poverty rate: 5.1% (2006-2010 5-year est.).

Education: Percent of population age 25 and over with: High school diploma (including GED) or higher: 94.9% (2006-2010 5-year est.); Bachelor's degree or higher: 36.2% (2006-2010 5-year est.); Master's degree or higher: 14.3% (2006-2010 5-year est.).

Housing: Homeownership rate: 84.7% (2010); Median home value: $334,500 (2006-2010 5-year est.); Median contract rent: $1,060 per month (2006-2010 5-year est.); Median year structure built: 1967 (2006-2010 5-year est.).

Safety: Violent crime rate: 5.3 per 10,000 population; Property crime rate: 105.9 per 10,000 population (2011).

Transportation: Commute to work: 90.7% car, 3.4% public transportation, 2.3% walk, 2.8% work from home (2006-2010 5-year est.); Travel time to work: 26.1% less than 15 minutes, 28.3% 15 to 30 minutes, 23.9% 30 to 45 minutes, 9.3% 45 to 60 minutes, 12.5% 60 minutes or more (2006-2010 5-year est.)

Additional Information Contacts

Central Bucks Chamber of Commerce . . . . (215) 348-3913
　http://www.centralbuckschamber.com
Upper Southampton Township . . . . (215) 322-9700
　http://www.southamptonpa.com

VILLAGE SHIRES (CDP). Covers a land area of 1.199 square miles and a water area of 0.001 square miles. Located at 40.20° N. Lat; 74.97° W. Long. Elevation is 161 feet.

Population: 4,364 (1990); 4,137 (2000); 3,949 (2010); Density: 3,294.0 persons per square mile (2010); Race: 95.7% White, 1.0% Black, 2.4% Asian, 0.1% American Indian/Alaska Native, 0.0% Native Hawaiian/Other Pacific Islander, 0.8% Other, 1.2% Hispanic of any race (2010); Average household size: 2.22 (2010); Median age: 45.6 (2010); Males per 100 females: 81.1 (2010); Marriage status: 25.5% never married, 55.7% now married, 11.4% widowed, 7.5% divorced (2006-2010 5-year est.); Foreign born: 10.3% (2006-2010 5-year est.); Ancestry (includes multiple ancestries): 31.2% Irish, 30.3% German, 19.3% Italian, 9.2% English, 7.7% Polish (2006-2010 5-year est.).

Economy: Employment by occupation: 14.5% management, 7.2% professional, 7.5% services, 22.4% sales, 2.8% farming, 5.2% construction, 4.8% production (2006-2010 5-year est.).

Income: Per capita income: $43,033 (2006-2010 5-year est.); Median household income: $67,932 (2006-2010 5-year est.); Average household income: $91,774 (2006-2010 5-year est.); Percent of households with income of $100,000 or more: 36.3% (2006-2010 5-year est.); Poverty rate: 2.0% (2006-2010 5-year est.).

Education: Percent of population age 25 and over with: High school diploma (including GED) or higher: 96.3% (2006-2010 5-year est.); Bachelor's degree or higher: 48.8% (2006-2010 5-year est.); Master's degree or higher: 20.5% (2006-2010 5-year est.).

Housing: Homeownership rate: 71.0% (2010); Median home value: $353,500 (2006-2010 5-year est.); Median contract rent: $1,609 per month (2006-2010 5-year est.); Median year structure built: 1982 (2006-2010 5-year est.).

Transportation: Commute to work: 88.8% car, 3.9% public pennsportation, 2.1% walk, 3.9% work from home (2006-2010 5-year est.); Travel time to work: 19.3% less than 15 minutes, 23.3% 15 to 30 minutes, 30.1% 30 to

45 minutes, 12.7% 45 to 60 minutes, 14.6% 60 minutes or more (2006-2010 5-year est.)

Additional Information Contacts

Lower Bucks County Chamber of Commerce . . . . (215) 943-7400
http://www.lbccc.org

WARMINSTER (township). Covers a land area of 10.162 square miles and a water area of 0.021 square miles. Located at 40.20° N. Lat; 75.09° W. Long. Elevation is 308 feet.

Population: 32,846 (1990); 31,383 (2000); 32,682 (2010); Density: 3,216.1 persons per square mile (2010); Race: 89.3% White, 3.1% Black, 1.9% Asian, 0.2% American Indian/Alaska Native, 0.1% Native Hawaiian/Other Pacific Islander, 5.4% Other, 7.7% Hispanic of any race (2010); Average household size: 2.51 (2010); Median age: 44.6 (2010); Males per 100 females: 94.0 (2010); Marriage status: 25.5% never married, 57.6% now married, 9.7% widowed, 7.2% divorced (2006-2010 5-year est.); Foreign born: 9.1% (2006-2010 5-year est.); Ancestry (includes multiple ancestries): 27.7% Irish, 27.2% German, 16.6% Italian, 10.6% English, 8.1% Polish (2006-2010 5-year est.).

Economy: Unemployment rate: 8.3% (August 2012); Total civilian labor force: 17,514 (August 2012); Single-family building permits issued: 43 (2011); Multi-family building permits issued: 0 (2011); Employment by occupation: 11.2% management, 4.2% professional, 10.3% services, 20.5% sales, 4.5% farming, 10.5% construction, 5.6% production (2006-2010 5-year est.).

Income: Per capita income: $28,280 (2006-2010 5-year est.); Median household income: $59,980 (2006-2010 5-year est.); Average household income: $72,268 (2006-2010 5-year est.); Percent of households with income of $100,000 or more: 23.8% (2006-2010 5-year est.); Poverty rate: 8.0% (2006-2010 5-year est.).

Education: Percent of population age 25 and over with: High school diploma (including GED) or higher: 89.7% (2006-2010 5-year est.); Bachelor's degree or higher: 24.5% (2006-2010 5-year est.); Master's degree or higher: 7.5% (2006-2010 5-year est.).

School District(s)

Centennial SD (KG-12)

   2010-11 Enrollment: 5,800 . . . . (215) 441-6000

Two-year College(s)

Automotive Training Center (Private, For-profit)

   Fall 2010 Enrollment: 581 . . . . (215) 259-1900

Vocational/Technical School(s)

Empire Beauty School-Warminster (Private, For-profit)

   Fall 2010 Enrollment: 168 . . . . (800) 223-3271
   2011-12 Tuition: $14,490

Housing: Homeownership rate: 71.0% (2010); Median home value: $306,100 (2006-2010 5-year est.); Median contract rent: $880 per month (2006-2010 5-year est.); Median year structure built: 1967 (2006-2010 5-year est.).

Hospitals: Warminster Hospital (145 beds)

Safety: Violent crime rate: 9.2 per 10,000 population; Property crime rate: 178.1 per 10,000 population (2011).

Transportation: Commute to work: 92.2% car, 3.3% public transportation, 1.2% walk, 2.8% work from home (2006-2010 5-year est.); Travel time to work: 29.3% less than 15 minutes, 31.7% 15 to 30 minutes, 23.2% 30 to 45 minutes, 7.8% 45 to 60 minutes, 8.0% 60 minutes or more (2006-2010 5-year est.)

Additional Information Contacts

Central Bucks Chamber of Commerce . . . . (215) 348-3913
http://www.centralbuckschamber.com

Warminster Township . . . . (215) 443-5414
http://www.warminstertownship.org

WARMINSTER HEIGHTS (CDP). Covers a land area of 0.630 square miles and a water area of 0 square miles. Located at 40.19° N. Lat; 75.08° W. Long. Elevation is 318 feet.

Population: 4,310 (1990); 4,191 (2000); 4,124 (2010); Density: 6,543.3 persons per square mile (2010); Race: 60.7% White, 10.6% Black, 3.3% Asian, 0.8% American Indian/Alaska Native, 0.2% Native Hawaiian/Other Pacific Islander, 24.4% Other, 35.1% Hispanic of any race (2010); Average household size: 2.67 (2010); Median age: 32.9 (2010); Males per 100 females: 99.3 (2010); Marriage status: 34.1% never married, 46.4% now married, 6.1% widowed, 13.5% divorced (2006-2010 5-year est.); Foreign born: 23.8% (2006-2010 5-year est.); Ancestry (includes multiple ancestries): 14.8% German, 12.6% Irish, 7.3% Italian, 5.0% English, 3.7% Polish (2006-2010 5-year est.).

Economy: Employment by occupation: 1.3% management, 0.7% professional, 14.5% services, 16.7% sales, 1.5% farming, 11.1% construction, 9.6% production (2006-2010 5-year est.).

Income: Per capita income: $15,162 (2006-2010 5-year est.); Median household income: $28,810 (2006-2010 5-year est.); Average household income: $40,646 (2006-2010 5-year est.); Percent of households with income of $100,000 or more: 4.6% (2006-2010 5-year est.); Poverty rate: 31.2% (2006-2010 5-year est.).

Education: Percent of population age 25 and over with: High school diploma (including GED) or higher: 71.9% (2006-2010 5-year est.); Bachelor's degree or higher: 9.6% (2006-2010 5-year est.); Master's degree or higher: 3.0% (2006-2010 5-year est.).

Housing: Homeownership rate: 21.3% (2010); Median home value: $277,300 (2006-2010 5-year est.); Median contract rent: $424 per month (2006-2010 5-year est.); Median year structure built: 1957 (2006-2010 5-year est.).

Transportation: Commute to work: 88.1% car, 4.8% public transportation, 4.2% walk, 1.2% work from home (2006-2010 5-year est.); Travel time to work: 31.7% less than 15 minutes, 40.8% 15 to 30 minutes, 17.6% 30 to 45 minutes, 5.5% 45 to 60 minutes, 4.3% 60 minutes or more (2006-2010 5-year est.)

Additional Information Contacts

Lower Bucks County Chamber of Commerce . . . . (215) 943-7400
http://www.lbccc.org

WARRINGTON (township). Covers a land area of 13.696 square miles and a water area of 0.094 square miles. Located at 40.25° N. Lat; 75.16° W. Long. Elevation is 394 feet.

History: Warrington Township was founded in October 1734, and is named after a town in Lancashire, England. The early township consisted of four villages: Warrington, Neshaminy, Tradesville, and Pleasantville.

Population: 12,169 (1990); 17,580 (2000); 23,418 (2010); Density: 1,709.8 persons per square mile (2010); Race: 88.5% White, 2.1% Black, 6.1% Asian, 0.2% American Indian/Alaska Native, 0.0% Native Hawaiian/Other Pacific Islander, 3.1% Other, 4.2% Hispanic of any race (2010); Average household size: 2.86 (2010); Median age: 39.8 (2010); Males per 100 females: 98.9 (2010); Marriage status: 23.3% never married, 65.7% now married, 5.0% widowed, 6.0% divorced (2006-2010 5-year est.); Foreign born: 10.7% (2006-2010 5-year est.); Ancestry (includes multiple ancestries): 30.0% Irish, 28.1% German, 17.9% Italian, 10.6% English, 8.2% Polish (2006-2010 5-year est.).

Economy: Single-family building permits issued: 5 (2011); Multi-family building permits issued: 0 (2011); Employment by occupation: 16.8% management, 8.6% professional, 4.2% services, 19.0% sales, 2.8% farming, 7.2% construction, 5.0% production (2006-2010 5-year est.).

Income: Per capita income: $36,805 (2006-2010 5-year est.); Median household income: $93,386 (2006-2010 5-year est.); Average household income: $105,949 (2006-2010 5-year est.); Percent of households with income of $100,000 or more: 45.5% (2006-2010 5-year est.); Poverty rate: 1.3% (2006-2010 5-year est.).

Taxes: Total city taxes per capita: $333 (2009); City property taxes per capita: $118 (2009).

Education: Percent of population age 25 and over with: High school diploma (including GED) or higher: 95.8% (2006-2010 5-year est.); Bachelor's degree or higher: 46.7% (2006-2010 5-year est.); Master's degree or higher: 17.8% (2006-2010 5-year est.).

School District(s)

Central Bucks SD (KG-12)

   2010-11 Enrollment: 20,432 . . . . (267) 893-2000

Housing: Homeownership rate: 83.7% (2010); Median home value: $392,000 (2006-2010 5-year est.); Median contract rent: $950 per month (2006-2010 5-year est.); Median year structure built: 1989 (2006-2010 5-year est.).

Safety: Violent crime rate: 10.6 per 10,000 population; Property crime rate: 94.9 per 10,000 population (2011).

Transportation: Commute to work: 91.4% car, 3.1% public transportation, 0.8% walk, 4.2% work from home (2006-2010 5-year est.); Travel time to work: 24.0% less than 15 minutes, 34.4% 15 to 30 minutes, 18.9% 30 to 45 minutes, 11.2% 45 to 60 minutes, 11.5% 60 minutes or more (2006-2010 5-year est.)

Additional Information Contacts

Central Bucks Chamber of Commerce . . . . (215) 348-3913
http://www.centralbuckschamber.com

Warrington Township . . . . (215) 343-9350
http://www.warringtontownship.org

WARWICK (township).
Covers a land area of 10.972 square miles and a water area of 0.140 square miles. Located at 40.25° N. Lat; 75.08° W. Long.

History: Warwick was formed by petition February 13, 1733 by eighteen residents. It was named after a town in central England and was the home to many Scots-Irish Presbyterians.

Population: 5,915 (1990); 11,977 (2000); 14,437 (2010); Density: 1,315.8 persons per square mile (2010); Race: 93.4% White, 1.3% Black, 3.7% Asian, 0.2% American Indian/Alaska Native, 0.0% Native Hawaiian/Other Pacific Islander, 1.4% Other, 2.1% Hispanic of any race (2010); Average household size: 2.82 (2010); Median age: 41.9 (2010); Males per 100 females: 94.8 (2010); Marriage status: 24.0% never married, 64.8% now married, 4.8% widowed, 6.4% divorced (2006-2010 5-year est.); Foreign born: 7.7% (2006-2010 5-year est.); Ancestry (includes multiple ancestries): 29.1% Irish, 28.4% German, 21.6% Italian, 10.9% Polish, 8.7% English (2006-2010 5-year est.).

Economy: Single-family building permits issued: 24 (2011); Multi-family building permits issued: 0 (2011); Employment by occupation: 21.9% management, 7.6% professional, 5.4% services, 16.0% sales, 2.4% farming, 5.4% construction, 5.6% production (2006-2010 5-year est.).

Income: Per capita income: $46,629 (2006-2010 5-year est.); Median household income: $110,561 (2006-2010 5-year est.); Average household income: $135,621 (2006-2010 5-year est.); Percent of households with income of $100,000 or more: 56.0% (2006-2010 5-year est.); Poverty rate: 1.1% (2006-2010 5-year est.).

Taxes: Total city taxes per capita: $385 (2009); City property taxes per capita: $170 (2009).

Education: Percent of population age 25 and over with: High school diploma (including GED) or higher: 96.7% (2006-2010 5-year est.); Bachelor's degree or higher: 50.9% (2006-2010 5-year est.); Master's degree or higher: 20.8% (2006-2010 5-year est.).

Housing: Homeownership rate: 94.5% (2010); Median home value: $409,300 (2006-2010 5-year est.); Median contract rent: $1,398 per month (2006-2010 5-year est.); Median year structure built: 1993 (2006-2010 5-year est.).

Safety: Violent crime rate: 8.3 per 10,000 population; Property crime rate: 71.1 per 10,000 population (2011).

Transportation: Commute to work: 88.6% car, 3.4% public transportation, 1.8% walk, 5.4% work from home (2006-2010 5-year est.); Travel time to work: 21.2% less than 15 minutes, 31.8% 15 to 30 minutes, 19.0% 30 to 45 minutes, 11.3% 45 to 60 minutes, 16.8% 60 minutes or more (2006-2010 5-year est.)

Additional Information Contacts
Greater Hatboro Chamber of Commerce . . . . (215) 956-9540
  http://hatborochamber.org
Warwick Township . . . . (215) 343-6100
  http://www.warwick-bucks.org

WASHINGTON CROSSING (unincorporated postal area)
Zip Code: 18977
  Covers a land area of 5.228 square miles and a water area of 0.448 square miles. Located at 40.28° N. Lat; 74.88° W. Long. Elevation is 43 feet. Population: 4,291 (2010); Density: 820.8 persons per square mile (2010); Race: 94.7% White, 1.1% Black, 2.5% Asian, 0.2% American Indian/Alaska Native, 0.0% Native Hawaiian/Other Pacific Islander, 1.5% Other, 2.4% Hispanic of any race (2010); Average household size: 2.56 (2010); Median age: 50.0 (2010); Males per 100 females: 95.0 (2010); Homeownership rate: 94.2% (2010)

WEST ROCKHILL (township).
Covers a land area of 16.304 square miles and a water area of 0.125 square miles. Located at 40.37° N. Lat; 75.35° W. Long.

Population: 4,518 (1990); 4,233 (2000); 5,256 (2010); Density: 322.4 persons per square mile (2010); Race: 96.1% White, 1.1% Black, 1.4% Asian, 0.2% American Indian/Alaska Native, 0.0% Native Hawaiian/Other Pacific Islander, 1.2% Other, 1.4% Hispanic of any race (2010); Average household size: 2.38 (2010); Median age: 47.4 (2010); Males per 100 females: 92.4 (2010); Marriage status: 18.8% never married, 60.2% now married, 12.6% widowed, 8.4% divorced (2006-2010 5-year est.); Foreign born: 3.8% (2006-2010 5-year est.); Ancestry (includes multiple ancestries): 39.0% German, 16.3% Irish, 12.9% English, 11.4% Italian, 6.6% Pennsylvania German (2006-2010 5-year est.).

Economy: Single-family building permits issued: 7 (2011); Multi-family building permits issued: 4 (2011); Employment by occupation: 10.4%

management, 2.0% professional, 9.9% services, 19.0% sales, 2.8% farming, 13.8% construction, 8.6% production (2006-2010 5-year est.).

Income: Per capita income: $32,014 (2006-2010 5-year est.); Median household income: $61,176 (2006-2010 5-year est.); Average household income: $76,059 (2006-2010 5-year est.); Percent of households with income of $100,000 or more: 24.0% (2006-2010 5-year est.); Poverty rate: 5.1% (2006-2010 5-year est.).

Education: Percent of population age 25 and over with: High school diploma (including GED) or higher: 85.2% (2006-2010 5-year est.); Bachelor's degree or higher: 21.9% (2006-2010 5-year est.); Master's degree or higher: 7.8% (2006-2010 5-year est.).

Housing: Homeownership rate: 73.5% (2010); Median home value: $303,800 (2006-2010 5-year est.); Median contract rent: $1,026 per month (2006-2010 5-year est.); Median year structure built: 1977 (2006-2010 5-year est.).

Transportation: Commute to work: 93.0% car, 2.7% public transportation, 0.0% walk, 3.2% work from home (2006-2010 5-year est.); Travel time to work: 37.4% less than 15 minutes, 18.9% 15 to 30 minutes, 17.5% 30 to 45 minutes, 14.3% 45 to 60 minutes, 11.8% 60 minutes or more (2006-2010 5-year est.)

Additional Information Contacts
Indian Valley Chamber of Commerce . . . . (215) 723-9472
  http://indianvalleychamber.com

WOODBOURNE (CDP).
Covers a land area of 1.233 square miles and a water area of 0.007 square miles. Located at 40.20° N. Lat; 74.89° W. Long. Elevation is 174 feet.

History: Woodbourne was sparsely populated before 1950; Then William Levitt began his second Levittown, which included land of four municipalities, including the area known today as Woodbourne. Over eight developments were constructed, each containing hundreds of homes.

Population: 2,953 (1990); 3,512 (2000); 3,851 (2010); Density: 3,123.6 persons per square mile (2010); Race: 90.0% White, 2.4% Black, 5.9% Asian, 0.1% American Indian/Alaska Native, 0.1% Native Hawaiian/Other Pacific Islander, 1.5% Other, 2.4% Hispanic of any race (2010); Average household size: 2.83 (2010); Median age: 40.5 (2010); Males per 100 females: 101.2 (2010); Marriage status: 24.9% never married, 66.8% now married, 1.5% widowed, 6.8% divorced (2006-2010 5-year est.); Foreign born: 1.8% (2006-2010 5-year est.); Ancestry (includes multiple ancestries): 29.0% German, 28.2% Irish, 21.1% Italian, 8.8% Polish, 8.2% English (2006-2010 5-year est.).

Economy: Employment by occupation: 21.2% management, 6.8% professional, 5.2% services, 13.8% sales, 3.0% farming, 4.6% construction, 1.0% production (2006-2010 5-year est.).

Income: Per capita income: $50,950 (2006-2010 5-year est.); Median household income: $127,955 (2006-2010 5-year est.); Average household income: $140,858 (2006-2010 5-year est.); Percent of households with income of $100,000 or more: 60.3% (2006-2010 5-year est.); Poverty rate: 2.6% (2006-2010 5-year est.).

Education: Percent of population age 25 and over with: High school diploma (including GED) or higher: 99.3% (2006-2010 5-year est.); Bachelor's degree or higher: 62.0% (2006-2010 5-year est.); Master's degree or higher: 25.4% (2006-2010 5-year est.).

Housing: Homeownership rate: 74.4% (2010); Median home value: $459,200 (2006-2010 5-year est.); Median contract rent: $1,386 per month (2006-2010 5-year est.); Median year structure built: 1988 (2006-2010 5-year est.).

Transportation: Commute to work: 90.0% car, 6.9% public transportation, 0.0% walk, 3.0% work from home (2006-2010 5-year est.); Travel time to work: 28.7% less than 15 minutes, 32.6% 15 to 30 minutes, 16.0% 30 to 45 minutes, 8.4% 45 to 60 minutes, 14.4% 60 minutes or more (2006-2010 5-year est.)

Additional Information Contacts
Lower Bucks County Chamber of Commerce . . . . (215) 943-7400
  http://www.lbccc.org

WOODSIDE (CDP).
Covers a land area of 1.023 square miles and a water area of <.001 square miles. Located at 40.23° N. Lat; 74.86° W. Long. Elevation is 157 feet.

Population: 2,947 (1990); 2,575 (2000); 2,425 (2010); Density: 2,369.8 persons per square mile (2010); Race: 89.5% White, 1.8% Black, 7.2% Asian, 0.1% American Indian/Alaska Native, 0.0% Native Hawaiian/Other Pacific Islander, 1.4% Other, 2.1% Hispanic of any race (2010); Average household size: 3.11 (2010); Median age: 44.3 (2010); Males per 100 females: 93.2 (2010); Marriage status: 14.9% never married, 80.3% now

married, 3.1% widowed, 1.7% divorced (2006-2010 5-year est.); Foreign born: 9.5% (2006-2010 5-year est.); Ancestry (includes multiple ancestries): 20.1% Irish, 18.6% German, 16.1% English, 15.8% Italian, 8.4% Russian (2006-2010 5-year est.).

Economy: Employment by occupation: 31.6% management, 8.7% professional, 1.7% services, 12.2% sales, 0.8% farming, 1.6% construction, 0.8% production (2006-2010 5-year est.).

Income: Per capita income: $66,365 (2006-2010 5-year est.); Median household income: $145,673 (2006-2010 5-year est.); Average household income: $192,632 (2006-2010 5-year est.); Percent of households with income of $100,000 or more: 78.1% (2006-2010 5-year est.); Poverty rate: 0.0% (2006-2010 5-year est.).

Education: Percent of population age 25 and over with: High school diploma (including GED) or higher: 99.4% (2006-2010 5-year est.); Bachelor's degree or higher: 74.7% (2006-2010 5-year est.); Master's degree or higher: 33.3% (2006-2010 5-year est.).

Housing: Homeownership rate: 99.4% (2010); Median home value: $532,400 (2006-2010 5-year est.); Median contract rent: n/a per month (2006-2010 5-year est.); Median year structure built: 1981 (2006-2010 5-year est.).

Transportation: Commute to work: 80.0% car, 8.4% public transportation, 0.0% walk, 11.6% work from home (2006-2010 5-year est.); Travel time to work: 20.7% less than 15 minutes, 36.9% 15 to 30 minutes, 13.0% 30 to 45 minutes, 9.4% 45 to 60 minutes, 20.1% 60 minutes or more (2006-2010 5-year est.)

Additional Information Contacts

Lower Bucks County Chamber of Commerce . . . . (215) 943-7400
   http://www.lbccc.org

WRIGHTSTOWN (township). Covers a land area of 9.702 square miles and a water area of 0.076 square miles. Located at 40.27° N. Lat; 75.00° W. Long. Elevation is 361 feet.

Population: 2,426 (1990); 2,839 (2000); 2,995 (2010); Density: 308.7 persons per square mile (2010); Race: 94.5% White, 1.4% Black, 2.8% Asian, 0.1% American Indian/Alaska Native, 0.0% Native Hawaiian/Other Pacific Islander, 1.2% Other, 1.4% Hispanic of any race (2010); Average household size: 2.89 (2010); Median age: 44.7 (2010); Males per 100 females: 99.1 (2010); Marriage status: 24.2% never married, 65.3% now married, 3.8% widowed, 6.7% divorced (2006-2010 5-year est.); Foreign born: 2.9% (2006-2010 5-year est.); Ancestry (includes multiple ancestries): 32.5% German, 29.7% Irish, 16.3% English, 16.3% Italian, 7.8% Polish (2006-2010 5-year est.).

Economy: Single-family building permits issued: 17 (2011); Multi-family building permits issued: 0 (2011); Employment by occupation: 16.6% management, 4.0% professional, 6.0% services, 16.0% sales, 3.7% farming, 6.4% construction, 3.7% production (2006-2010 5-year est.).

Income: Per capita income: $51,183 (2006-2010 5-year est.); Median household income: $101,071 (2006-2010 5-year est.); Average household income: $149,820 (2006-2010 5-year est.); Percent of households with income of $100,000 or more: 50.7% (2006-2010 5-year est.); Poverty rate: 3.5% (2006-2010 5-year est.).

Education: Percent of population age 25 and over with: High school diploma (including GED) or higher: 95.9% (2006-2010 5-year est.); Bachelor's degree or higher: 47.7% (2006-2010 5-year est.); Master's degree or higher: 18.7% (2006-2010 5-year est.).

School District(s)

Council Rock SD (KG-12)
   2010-11 Enrollment: 11,882 . . . . (215) 944-1000

Housing: Homeownership rate: 89.8% (2010); Median home value: $648,900 (2006-2010 5-year est.); Median contract rent: $1,060 per month (2006-2010 5-year est.); Median year structure built: 1972 (2006-2010 5-year est.).

Transportation: Commute to work: 92.2% car, 1.3% public transportation, 0.4% walk, 5.4% work from home (2006-2010 5-year est.); Travel time to work: 16.7% less than 15 minutes, 40.9% 15 to 30 minutes, 18.9% 30 to 45 minutes, 9.0% 45 to 60 minutes, 14.6% 60 minutes or more (2006-2010 5-year est.)

Additional Information Contacts

Lower Bucks County Chamber of Commerce . . . . (215) 943-7400
   http://www.lbccc.org

WYCOMBE (unincorporated postal area)

Zip Code: 18980

   Covers a land area of 2.376 square miles and a water area of 0.011 square miles. Located at 40.26° N. Lat; 75.01° W. Long. Elevation is

187 feet. Population: 510 (2010); Density: 214.6 persons per square mile (2010); Race: 97.8% White, 1.0% Black, 0.2% Asian, 0.0% American Indian/Alaska Native, 0.0% Native Hawaiian/Other Pacific Islander, 1.0% Other, 1.4% Hispanic of any race (2010); Average household size: 2.83 (2010); Median age: 46.1 (2010); Males per 100 females: 95.4 (2010); Homeownership rate: 86.7% (2010)

YARDLEY (borough). Covers a land area of 0.933 square miles and a water area of 0.087 square miles. Located at 40.24° N. Lat; 74.84° W. Long. Elevation is 72 feet.

History: Washington Crossing Historical Park, one of two places where George Washington crossed Delaware River, Dec. 25, 1776, to North. Settled 1682, incorporated c.1895.

Population: 2,288 (1990); 2,498 (2000); 2,434 (2010); Density: 2,607.7 persons per square mile (2010); Race: 91.4% White, 3.5% Black, 2.6% Asian, 0.0% American Indian/Alaska Native, 0.0% Native Hawaiian/Other Pacific Islander, 2.5% Other, 2.5% Hispanic of any race (2010); Average household size: 2.13 (2010); Median age: 42.7 (2010); Males per 100 females: 91.7 (2010); Marriage status: 27.0% never married, 46.2% now married, 9.8% widowed, 17.0% divorced (2006-2010 5-year est.); Foreign born: 5.2% (2006-2010 5-year est.); Ancestry (includes multiple ancestries): 22.4% Irish, 21.0% Italian, 20.1% German, 17.8% English, 11.0% Polish (2006-2010 5-year est.).

Economy: Single-family building permits issued: 0 (2011); Multi-family building permits issued: 0 (2011); Employment by occupation: 19.3% management, 5.0% professional, 6.4% services, 14.4% sales, 2.5% farming, 2.7% construction, 1.3% production (2006-2010 5-year est.).

Income: Per capita income: $44,258 (2006-2010 5-year est.); Median household income: $71,360 (2006-2010 5-year est.); Average household income: $85,881 (2006-2010 5-year est.); Percent of households with income of $100,000 or more: 33.5% (2006-2010 5-year est.); Poverty rate: 2.9% (2006-2010 5-year est.).

Education: Percent of population age 25 and over with: High school diploma (including GED) or higher: 98.2% (2006-2010 5-year est.); Bachelor's degree or higher: 48.7% (2006-2010 5-year est.); Master's degree or higher: 18.3% (2006-2010 5-year est.).

School District(s)

Pennsbury SD (KG-12)
   2010-11 Enrollment: 10,850 . . . . (215) 428-4100

Housing: Homeownership rate: 70.3% (2010); Median home value: $332,700 (2006-2010 5-year est.); Median contract rent: $931 per month (2006-2010 5-year est.); Median year structure built: 1954 (2006-2010 5-year est.).

Newspapers: Yardley News (Community news; Circulation 6,000)

Transportation: Commute to work: 87.7% car, 1.1% public transportation, 4.9% walk, 5.3% work from home (2006-2010 5-year est.); Travel time to work: 28.4% less than 15 minutes, 35.0% 15 to 30 minutes, 19.5% 30 to 45 minutes, 8.1% 45 to 60 minutes, 9.0% 60 minutes or more (2006-2010 5-year est.)

Additional Information Contacts

Lower Bucks County Chamber of Commerce . . . . (215) 943-7400
   http://www.lbccc.org

Butler County

Located in western Pennsylvania; drained by tributaries of the Beaver River. Covers a land area of 788.604 square miles, a water area of 6.147 square miles, and is located in the Eastern Time Zone at 40.91° N. Lat., 79.92° W. Long. The county was founded in 1800. County seat is Butler.

Butler County is part of the Pittsburgh, PA Metropolitan Statistical Area. The entire metro area includes: Allegheny County, PA; Armstrong County, PA; Beaver County, PA; Butler County, PA; Fayette County, PA; Washington County, PA; Westmoreland County, PA

Weather Station: Butler 2 SW   Elevation: 1,000 feet

	Jan	Feb	Mar	Apr	May	Jun	Jul	Aug	Sep	Oct	Nov	Dec
High	35	38	47	61	70	79	82	82	75	63	51	39
Low	18	19	26	36	45	54	58	58	50	39	32	23
Precip	2.8	2.4	3.3	3.4	4.1	4.0	4.4	3.8	3.7	2.8	3.5	3.1
Snow	11.7	8.1	5.4	0.8	tr	0.0	0.0	0.0	0.0	0.1	1.1	7.0

High and Low temperatures in degrees Fahrenheit; Precipitation and Snow in inches

Weather Station: Slippery Rock 1 SSW   Elevation: 1,250 feet

	Jan	Feb	Mar	Apr	May	Jun	Jul	Aug	Sep	Oct	Nov	Dec
High	35	39	48	60	71	79	83	82	75	63	51	39
Low	16	18	24	34	43	52	57	55	49	38	30	21
Precip	3.0	2.4	3.4	3.6	4.2	4.7	4.6	4.1	4.1	3.0	3.6	3.0
Snow	11.8	8.3	5.9	0.9	tr	0.0	0.0	0.0	0.0	0.1	1.8	8.3

High and Low temperatures in degrees Fahrenheit; Precipitation and Snow in inches

Population: 152,013 (1990); 174,083 (2000); 183,862 (2010); Race: 96.6% White, 1.1% Black, 1.0% Asian, 0.1% American Indian/Alaska Native, 0.0% Native Hawaiian/Other Pacific Islander, 1.2% Other, 1.1% Hispanic of any race (2010); Density: 233.1 persons per square mile (2010); Average household size: 2.45 (2010); Median age: 41.5 (2010); Males per 100 females: 96.9 (2010).

Religion: Six largest groups: 29.7% Catholicism, 6.2% Methodist/Pietist, 5.8% Presbyterian-Reformed, 5.6% Lutheran, 4.5% Non-Denominational, 3.5% Holiness (2010)

Economy: Unemployment rate: 6.7% (August 2012); Total civilian labor force: 102,404 (August 2012); Leading industries: 17.1% health care and social assistance; 15.9% manufacturing; 14.8% retail trade (2010); Farms: 1,116 totaling 129,850 acres (2007); Companies that employ 500 or more persons: 11 (2010); Companies that employ 100 to 499 persons: 104 (2010); Companies that employ less than 100 persons: 4,527 (2010); Black-owned businesses: n/a (2007); Hispanic-owned businesses: 96 (2007); Asian-owned businesses: n/a (2007); Women-owned businesses: 4,227 (2007); Retail sales per capita: $17,520 (2010). Single-family building permits issued: 429 (2011); Multi-family building permits issued: 80 (2011).

Income: Per capita income: $28,446 (2006-2010 5-year est.); Median household income: $56,878 (2006-2010 5-year est.); Average household income: $71,621 (2006-2010 5-year est.); Percent of households with income of $100,000 or more: 22.5% (2006-2010 5-year est.); Poverty rate: 8.3% (2006-2010 5-year est.); Bankruptcy rate: 2.57% (2011).

Taxes: Total county taxes per capita: $199 (2009); County property taxes per capita: $194 (2009).

Education: Percent of population age 25 and over with: High school diploma (including GED) or higher: 91.9% (2006-2010 5-year est.); Bachelor's degree or higher: 28.8% (2006-2010 5-year est.); Master's degree or higher: 9.4% (2006-2010 5-year est.).

Housing: Homeownership rate: 75.8% (2010); Median home value: $159,000 (2006-2010 5-year est.); Median contract rent: $545 per month (2006-2010 5-year est.); Median year structure built: 1974 (2006-2010 5-year est.)

Health: Birth rate: 96.7 per 10,000 population (2011); Death rate: 96.7 per 10,000 population (2011); Age-adjusted cancer mortality rate: 183.6 deaths per 100,000 population (2009); Number of physicians: 15.5 per 10,000 population (2010); Hospital beds: 20.9 per 10,000 population (2008); Hospital admissions: 702.1 per 10,000 population (2008).

Elections: 2012 Presidential election results: 31.9% Obama, 66.8% Romney

National and State Parks: Moraine State Park

Additional Information Contacts
Butler County Government . . . . (724) 285-4731
  http://www.co.butler.pa.us
Butler County Chamber of Commerce . . . . (724) 283-2222
  http://www.butlercountychamber.com

Butler County Communities

ADAMS (township). Covers a land area of 22.402 square miles and a water area of 0.019 square miles. Located at 40.72° N. Lat; 80.01° W. Long.

Population: 3,911 (1990); 6,774 (2000); 11,652 (2010); Density: 520.1 persons per square mile (2010); Race: 95.4% White, 1.0% Black, 2.3% Asian, 0.0% American Indian/Alaska Native, 0.0% Native Hawaiian/Other Pacific Islander, 1.3% Other, 1.4% Hispanic of any race (2010); Average household size: 2.64 (2010); Median age: 40.1 (2010); Males per 100 females: 95.1 (2010); Marriage status: 23.5% never married, 68.6% now married, 2.5% widowed, 5.3% divorced (2006-2010 5-year est.); Foreign born: 2.7% (2006-2010 5-year est.); Ancestry (includes multiple ancestries): 42.0% German, 22.6% Irish, 20.3% Italian, 10.5% English, 5.3% French (2006-2010 5-year est.).

Economy: Single-family building permits issued: 144 (2011); Multi-family building permits issued: 0 (2011); Employment by occupation: 21.7% management, 6.0% professional, 8.0% services, 14.0% sales, 3.0% farming, 5.1% construction, 2.4% production (2006-2010 5-year est.).

Income: Per capita income: $43,690 (2006-2010 5-year est.); Median household income: $96,667 (2006-2010 5-year est.); Average household income: $119,817 (2006-2010 5-year est.); Percent of households with income of $100,000 or more: 47.6% (2006-2010 5-year est.); Poverty rate: 2.6% (2006-2010 5-year est.).

Education: Percent of population age 25 and over with: High school diploma (including GED) or higher: 98.0% (2006-2010 5-year est.); Bachelor's degree or higher: 54.0% (2006-2010 5-year est.); Master's degree or higher: 21.6% (2006-2010 5-year est.).

Housing: Homeownership rate: 85.5% (2010); Median home value: $313,500 (2006-2010 5-year est.); Median contract rent: $994 per month (2006-2010 5-year est.); Median year structure built: 1998 (2006-2010 5-year est.).

Safety: Violent crime rate: 6.0 per 10,000 population; Property crime rate: 74.4 per 10,000 population (2011).

Transportation: Commute to work: 92.7% car, 0.4% public transportation, 0.6% walk, 5.8% work from home (2006-2010 5-year est.); Travel time to work: 20.7% less than 15 minutes, 30.4% 15 to 30 minutes, 29.2% 30 to 45 minutes, 14.0% 45 to 60 minutes, 5.7% 60 minutes or more (2006-2010 5-year est.)

Additional Information Contacts
Adams Township . . . . (724) 625-2221
  http://www.adamstwp.org
Butler County Chamber of Commerce . . . . (724) 283-2222
  http://www.butlercountychamber.com

ALLEGHENY (township). Covers a land area of 24.629 square miles and a water area of 0 square miles. Located at 41.14° N. Lat; 79.74° W. Long.

Population: 504 (1990); 555 (2000); 641 (2010); Density: 26.0 persons per square mile (2010); Race: 86.9% White, 11.5% Black, 0.6% Asian, 0.0% American Indian/Alaska Native, 0.0% Native Hawaiian/Other Pacific Islander, 1.0% Other, 1.7% Hispanic of any race (2010); Average household size: 2.39 (2010); Median age: 36.5 (2010); Males per 100 females: 129.7 (2010); Marriage status: 23.7% never married, 58.2% now married, 6.4% widowed, 11.7% divorced (2006-2010 5-year est.); Foreign born: 0.8% (2006-2010 5-year est.); Ancestry (includes multiple ancestries): 39.7% German, 12.4% Irish, 10.8% English, 7.2% Scotch-Irish, 6.6% American (2006-2010 5-year est.).

Economy: Single-family building permits issued: 1 (2011); Multi-family building permits issued: 0 (2011); Employment by occupation: 4.3% management, 4.3% professional, 8.6% services, 21.0% sales, 2.4% farming, 14.8% construction, 9.5% production (2006-2010 5-year est.).

Income: Per capita income: $19,701 (2006-2010 5-year est.); Median household income: $48,333 (2006-2010 5-year est.); Average household income: $47,939 (2006-2010 5-year est.); Percent of households with income of $100,000 or more: 3.9% (2006-2010 5-year est.); Poverty rate: 9.4% (2006-2010 5-year est.).

Education: Percent of population age 25 and over with: High school diploma (including GED) or higher: 88.0% (2006-2010 5-year est.); Bachelor's degree or higher: 5.9% (2006-2010 5-year est.); Master's degree or higher: 0.0% (2006-2010 5-year est.).

Housing: Homeownership rate: 82.1% (2010); Median home value: $88,900 (2006-2010 5-year est.); Median contract rent: $417 per month (2006-2010 5-year est.); Median year structure built: 1978 (2006-2010 5-year est.).

Transportation: Commute to work: 93.0% car, 0.0% public transportation, 1.5% walk, 5.5% work from home (2006-2010 5-year est.); Travel time to work: 23.4% less than 15 minutes, 18.6% 15 to 30 minutes, 29.8% 30 to 45 minutes, 18.6% 45 to 60 minutes, 9.6% 60 minutes or more (2006-2010 5-year est.)

BOYERS (unincorporated postal area)
Zip Code: 16020
  Covers a land area of 25.492 square miles and a water area of 0 square miles. Located at 41.11° N. Lat; 79.89° W. Long. Elevation is 1,211 feet. Population: 1,150 (2010); Density: 45.1 persons per square mile (2010); Race: 99.0% White, 0.2% Black, 0.2% Asian, 0.1% American Indian/Alaska Native, 0.0% Native Hawaiian/Other Pacific Islander, 0.5% Other, 0.3% Hispanic of any race (2010); Average household size: 2.69 (2010); Median age: 41.6 (2010); Males per 100 females: 107.6 (2010); Homeownership rate: 86.1% (2010)

BRADY (township). Covers a land area of 17.037 square miles and a water area of 0.347 square miles. Located at 40.99° N. Lat; 80.02° W. Long.

Population: 802 (1990); 1,452 (2000); 1,310 (2010); Density: 76.9 persons per square mile (2010); Race: 97.9% White, 0.4% Black, 0.5% Asian, 0.6% American Indian/Alaska Native, 0.0% Native Hawaiian/Other Pacific Islander, 0.6% Other, 0.8% Hispanic of any race (2010); Average household size: 2.55 (2010); Median age: 39.8 (2010); Males per 100 females: 100.0 (2010); Marriage status: 32.6% never married, 53.7% now married, 4.4% widowed, 9.3% divorced (2006-2010 5-year est.); Foreign born: 0.4% (2006-2010 5-year est.); Ancestry (includes multiple ancestries): 45.9% German, 16.7% Irish, 12.0% English, 10.0% Italian, 6.9% Polish (2006-2010 5-year est.).

Economy: Single-family building permits issued: 0 (2011); Multi-family building permits issued: 0 (2011); Employment by occupation: 9.9% management, 1.6% professional, 14.8% services, 17.8% sales, 2.2% farming, 7.0% construction, 7.0% production (2006-2010 5-year est.).

Income: Per capita income: $23,652 (2006-2010 5-year est.); Median household income: $37,813 (2006-2010 5-year est.); Average household income: $58,290 (2006-2010 5-year est.); Percent of households with income of $100,000 or more: 12.9% (2006-2010 5-year est.); Poverty rate: 21.3% (2006-2010 5-year est.).

Education: Percent of population age 25 and over with: High school diploma (including GED) or higher: 86.5% (2006-2010 5-year est.); Bachelor's degree or higher: 20.5% (2006-2010 5-year est.); Master's degree or higher: 8.6% (2006-2010 5-year est.).

Housing: Homeownership rate: 80.7% (2010); Median home value: $116,700 (2006-2010 5-year est.); Median contract rent: $503 per month (2006-2010 5-year est.); Median year structure built: 1980 (2006-2010 5-year est.).

Transportation: Commute to work: 94.5% car, 1.1% public transportation, 1.3% walk, 3.0% work from home (2006-2010 5-year est.); Travel time to work: 29.2% less than 15 minutes, 44.5% 15 to 30 minutes, 16.9% 30 to 45 minutes, 4.1% 45 to 60 minutes, 5.3% 60 minutes or more (2006-2010 5-year est.)

Additional Information Contacts

Butler County Chamber of Commerce . . . . (724) 283-2222
http://www.butlercountychamber.com

BRUIN (borough). Covers a land area of 1.826 square miles and a water area of 0 square miles. Located at 41.05° N. Lat; 79.73° W. Long. Elevation is 1,102 feet.

Population: 646 (1990); 534 (2000); 524 (2010); Density: 287.0 persons per square mile (2010); Race: 98.5% White, 0.0% Black, 0.4% Asian, 0.8% American Indian/Alaska Native, 0.0% Native Hawaiian/Other Pacific Islander, 0.3% Other, 1.9% Hispanic of any race (2010); Average household size: 2.73 (2010); Median age: 33.1 (2010); Males per 100 females: 89.2 (2010); Marriage status: 21.9% never married, 70.1% now married, 4.2% widowed, 3.8% divorced (2006-2010 5-year est.); Foreign born: 0.0% (2006-2010 5-year est.); Ancestry (includes multiple ancestries): 63.9% German, 23.9% Irish, 11.9% English, 9.4% Scotch-Irish, 6.1% Dutch (2006-2010 5-year est.).

Economy: Single-family building permits issued: 0 (2011); Multi-family building permits issued: 0 (2011); Employment by occupation: 4.0% management, 1.2% professional, 13.8% services, 19.0% sales, 1.2% farming, 22.9% construction, 12.6% production (2006-2010 5-year est.).

Income: Per capita income: $22,813 (2006-2010 5-year est.); Median household income: $49,773 (2006-2010 5-year est.); Average household income: $65,076 (2006-2010 5-year est.); Percent of households with income of $100,000 or more: 20.4% (2006-2010 5-year est.); Poverty rate: 10.9% (2006-2010 5-year est.).

Education: Percent of population age 25 and over with: High school diploma (including GED) or higher: 87.8% (2006-2010 5-year est.); Bachelor's degree or higher: 7.7% (2006-2010 5-year est.); Master's degree or higher: 2.8% (2006-2010 5-year est.).

School District(s)

Karns City Area SD (KG-12)
2010-11 Enrollment: 1,618 . . . . (724) 756-2030

Housing: Homeownership rate: 75.0% (2010); Median home value: $74,800 (2006-2010 5-year est.); Median contract rent: $463 per month (2006-2010 5-year est.); Median year structure built: before 1940 (2006-2010 5-year est.).

Transportation: Commute to work: 97.1% car, 1.6% public transportation, 1.2% walk, 0.0% work from home (2006-2010 5-year est.); Travel time to work: 34.0% less than 15 minutes, 25.8% 15 to 30 minutes, 22.1% 30 to

45 minutes, 2.9% 45 to 60 minutes, 15.2% 60 minutes or more (2006-2010 5-year est.)

BUFFALO (township). Covers a land area of 24.295 square miles and a water area of 0.058 square miles. Located at 40.71° N. Lat; 79.74° W. Long.

Population: 6,317 (1990); 6,827 (2000); 7,307 (2010); Density: 300.8 persons per square mile (2010); Race: 97.9% White, 0.4% Black, 0.7% Asian, 0.1% American Indian/Alaska Native, 0.0% Native Hawaiian/Other Pacific Islander, 0.9% Other, 0.8% Hispanic of any race (2010); Average household size: 2.58 (2010); Median age: 43.8 (2010); Males per 100 females: 99.5 (2010); Marriage status: 17.4% never married, 67.6% now married, 4.2% widowed, 10.7% divorced (2006-2010 5-year est.); Foreign born: 1.2% (2006-2010 5-year est.); Ancestry (includes multiple ancestries): 40.5% German, 14.0% Irish, 13.3% Italian, 12.2% English, 10.3% Polish (2006-2010 5-year est.).

Economy: Single-family building permits issued: 13 (2011); Multi-family building permits issued: 3 (2011); Employment by occupation: 11.4% management, 5.1% professional, 9.1% services, 16.0% sales, 4.7% farming, 8.8% construction, 5.7% production (2006-2010 5-year est.).

Income: Per capita income: $29,802 (2006-2010 5-year est.); Median household income: $69,500 (2006-2010 5-year est.); Average household income: $78,410 (2006-2010 5-year est.); Percent of households with income of $100,000 or more: 23.9% (2006-2010 5-year est.); Poverty rate: 5.5% (2006-2010 5-year est.).

Education: Percent of population age 25 and over with: High school diploma (including GED) or higher: 95.2% (2006-2010 5-year est.); Bachelor's degree or higher: 28.4% (2006-2010 5-year est.); Master's degree or higher: 10.0% (2006-2010 5-year est.).

Housing: Homeownership rate: 88.6% (2010); Median home value: $166,300 (2006-2010 5-year est.); Median contract rent: $571 per month (2006-2010 5-year est.); Median year structure built: 1974 (2006-2010 5-year est.).

Safety: Violent crime rate: 13.6 per 10,000 population; Property crime rate: 69.6 per 10,000 population (2011).

Transportation: Commute to work: 94.2% car, 0.0% public transportation, 0.4% walk, 5.4% work from home (2006-2010 5-year est.); Travel time to work: 23.7% less than 15 minutes, 35.0% 15 to 30 minutes, 24.7% 30 to 45 minutes, 10.1% 45 to 60 minutes, 6.5% 60 minutes or more (2006-2010 5-year est.)

Additional Information Contacts

Buffalo Township. . . . . (724) 295-2648
http://www.buffalotownship.com
Butler County Chamber of Commerce . . . . (724) 283-2222
http://www.butlercountychamber.com

BUTLER (city). County seat. Covers a land area of 2.719 square miles and a water area of 0 square miles. Located at 40.86° N. Lat; 79.90° W. Long. Elevation is 1,037 feet.

History: Named for Major General Richard Butler (1743-1791), who served in the American Revolution. Incorporated as a borough 1817, as a city 1917.

Population: 15,714 (1990); 15,121 (2000); 13,757 (2010); Density: 5,060.2 persons per square mile (2010); Race: 93.6% White, 2.7% Black, 0.5% Asian, 0.2% American Indian/Alaska Native, 0.0% Native Hawaiian/Other Pacific Islander, 3.0% Other, 2.4% Hispanic of any race (2010); Average household size: 2.18 (2010); Median age: 36.8 (2010); Males per 100 females: 95.4 (2010); Marriage status: 35.0% never married, 42.4% now married, 6.3% widowed, 16.3% divorced (2006-2010 5-year est.); Foreign born: 1.1% (2006-2010 5-year est.); Ancestry (includes multiple ancestries): 42.4% German, 22.6% Irish, 12.3% Italian, 10.5% English, 5.8% Polish (2006-2010 5-year est.).

Economy: Single-family building permits issued: 2 (2011); Multi-family building permits issued: 0 (2011); Employment by occupation: 7.9% management, 1.3% professional, 14.3% services, 19.1% sales, 4.7% farming, 7.3% construction, 6.1% production (2006-2010 5-year est.).

Income: Per capita income: $18,729 (2006-2010 5-year est.); Median household income: $30,317 (2006-2010 5-year est.); Average household income: $42,031 (2006-2010 5-year est.); Percent of households with income of $100,000 or more: 6.6% (2006-2010 5-year est.); Poverty rate: 22.4% (2006-2010 5-year est.).

Taxes: Total city taxes per capita: $368 (2009); City property taxes per capita: $176 (2009).

Education: Percent of population age 25 and over with: High school diploma (including GED) or higher: 83.3% (2006-2010 5-year est.);

Bachelor's degree or higher: 12.7% (2006-2010 5-year est.); Master's degree or higher: 3.3% (2006-2010 5-year est.).

School District(s)

Butler Area SD (KG-12)
2010-11 Enrollment: 7,630 . . . . (724) 287-8721
Butler County Avts (10-12)
2010-11 Enrollment: n/a . . . . (724) 282-0735

Two-year College(s)

Butler County Community College (Public)
Fall 2010 Enrollment: 3,042 . . . . (724) 287-8711
2011-12 Tuition: In-state $5,880; Out-of-state $8,520

Vocational/Technical School(s)

Butler Beauty School (Private, For-profit)
Fall 2010 Enrollment: 133 . . . . (724) 287-0708
2011-12 Tuition: $13,800

Housing: Homeownership rate: 41.7% (2010); Median home value: $84,900 (2006-2010 5-year est.); Median contract rent: $437 per month (2006-2010 5-year est.); Median year structure built: before 1940 (2006-2010 5-year est.).
Hospitals: Butler Memorial Hospital (268 beds); Department of Veterans Affairs Medical Center (180 beds)
Safety: Violent crime rate: 61.6 per 10,000 population; Property crime rate: 413.7 per 10,000 population (2011).
Newspapers: Butler Eagle (Regional news; Circulation 30,595)
Transportation: Commute to work: 86.0% car, 0.9% public transportation, 9.8% walk, 2.0% work from home (2006-2010 5-year est.); Travel time to work: 44.9% less than 15 minutes, 25.2% 15 to 30 minutes, 13.9% 30 to 45 minutes, 8.9% 45 to 60 minutes, 7.2% 60 minutes or more (2006-2010 5-year est.)

Additional Information Contacts

Butler County Chamber of Commerce . . . . (724) 283-2222
http://www.butlercountychamber.com
City of Butler . . . . (724) 283-3430
http://www.butlertwp.org

BUTLER (township). Covers a land area of 21.622 square miles and a water area of 0.126 square miles. Located at 40.85° N. Lat; 79.93° W. Long. Elevation is 1,037 feet.
History: Butler was laid out in 1803, and named for Richard Butler of York County, a military man. Coal, gas, limestone, and oil were the basis of its early livelihood.
Population: 17,313 (1990); 17,185 (2000); 17,248 (2010); Density: 797.7 persons per square mile (2010); Race: 97.4% White, 0.8% Black, 0.5% Asian, 0.1% American Indian/Alaska Native, 0.0% Native Hawaiian/Other Pacific Islander, 1.2% Other, 1.0% Hispanic of any race (2010); Average household size: 2.29 (2010); Median age: 46.3 (2010); Males per 100 females: 93.7 (2010); Marriage status: 22.9% never married, 57.5% now married, 8.4% widowed, 11.2% divorced (2006-2010 5-year est.); Foreign born: 1.2% (2006-2010 5-year est.); Ancestry (includes multiple ancestries): 42.4% German, 18.4% Irish, 13.7% Italian, 11.6% English, 9.0% Polish (2006-2010 5-year est.).
Economy: Single-family building permits issued: 6 (2011); Multi-family building permits issued: 0 (2011); Employment by occupation: 8.2% management, 4.2% professional, 10.7% services, 17.6% sales, 4.0% farming, 5.5% construction, 4.4% production (2006-2010 5-year est.).
Income: Per capita income: $28,950 (2006-2010 5-year est.); Median household income: $53,694 (2006-2010 5-year est.); Average household income: $68,253 (2006-2010 5-year est.); Percent of households with income of $100,000 or more: 19.3% (2006-2010 5-year est.); Poverty rate: 7.8% (2006-2010 5-year est.).
Education: Percent of population age 25 and over with: High school diploma (including GED) or higher: 91.4% (2006-2010 5-year est.); Bachelor's degree or higher: 25.0% (2006-2010 5-year est.); Master's degree or higher: 7.9% (2006-2010 5-year est.).

Two-year College(s)

Butler County Community College (Public)
Fall 2010 Enrollment: 3,042 . . . . (724) 287-8711
2011-12 Tuition: In-state $5,880; Out-of-state $8,520

Vocational/Technical School(s)

Butler Beauty School (Private, For-profit)
Fall 2010 Enrollment: 133 . . . . (724) 287-0708
2011-12 Tuition: $13,800

Housing: Homeownership rate: 76.5% (2010); Median home value: $137,400 (2006-2010 5-year est.); Median contract rent: $562 per month

(2006-2010 5-year est.); Median year structure built: 1962 (2006-2010 5-year est.).
Hospitals: Butler Memorial Hospital (268 beds); Department of Veterans Affairs Medical Center (180 beds)
Safety: Violent crime rate: 15.6 per 10,000 population; Property crime rate: 246.8 per 10,000 population (2011).
Newspapers: Butler Eagle (Regional news; Circulation 30,595)
Transportation: Commute to work: 95.2% car, 0.7% public transportation, 1.4% walk, 2.4% work from home (2006-2010 5-year est.); Travel time to work: 40.6% less than 15 minutes, 26.4% 15 to 30 minutes, 14.0% 30 to 45 minutes, 9.0% 45 to 60 minutes, 10.0% 60 minutes or more (2006-2010 5-year est.)
Airports: Butler County/K W Scholter Field (general aviation)

Additional Information Contacts

Butler County Chamber of Commerce . . . . (724) 283-2222
http://www.butlercountychamber.com
Butler Township . . . . (724) 283-3430
http://www.butlertwp.org

CABOT (unincorporated postal area)
Zip Code: 16023
Covers a land area of 26.301 square miles and a water area of 0 square miles. Located at 40.78° N. Lat; 79.75° W. Long. Elevation is 1,198 feet. Population: 4,169 (2010); Density: 158.5 persons per square mile (2010); Race: 98.9% White, 0.3% Black, 0.3% Asian, 0.1% American Indian/Alaska Native, 0.0% Native Hawaiian/Other Pacific Islander, 0.4% Other, 0.4% Hispanic of any race (2010); Average household size: 2.19 (2010); Median age: 50.2 (2010); Males per 100 females: 85.1 (2010); Homeownership rate: 66.8% (2010)

CALLERY (borough). Covers a land area of 0.537 square miles and a water area of 0 square miles. Located at 40.74° N. Lat; 80.04° W. Long. Elevation is 958 feet.
Population: 420 (1990); 444 (2000); 394 (2010); Density: 734.3 persons per square mile (2010); Race: 96.4% White, 0.0% Black, 0.5% Asian, 0.0% American Indian/Alaska Native, 0.0% Native Hawaiian/Other Pacific Islander, 3.1% Other, 0.5% Hispanic of any race (2010); Average household size: 2.58 (2010); Median age: 38.7 (2010); Males per 100 females: 111.8 (2010); Marriage status: 21.7% never married, 58.2% now married, 4.9% widowed, 15.1% divorced (2006-2010 5-year est.); Foreign born: 0.6% (2006-2010 5-year est.); Ancestry (includes multiple ancestries): 54.6% German, 36.6% Irish, 5.9% Italian, 4.5% Polish, 4.2% Scotch-Irish (2006-2010 5-year est.).
Economy: Single-family building permits issued: 0 (2011); Multi-family building permits issued: 0 (2011); Employment by occupation: 12.6% management, 1.0% professional, 15.0% services, 27.7% sales, 8.7% farming, 11.2% construction, 4.9% production (2006-2010 5-year est.).
Income: Per capita income: $27,068 (2006-2010 5-year est.); Median household income: $68,068 (2006-2010 5-year est.); Average household income: $66,242 (2006-2010 5-year est.); Percent of households with income of $100,000 or more: 19.1% (2006-2010 5-year est.); Poverty rate: 9.7% (2006-2010 5-year est.).
Education: Percent of population age 25 and over with: High school diploma (including GED) or higher: 91.0% (2006-2010 5-year est.); Bachelor's degree or higher: 12.5% (2006-2010 5-year est.); Master's degree or higher: 4.7% (2006-2010 5-year est.).
Housing: Homeownership rate: 75.1% (2010); Median home value: $161,300 (2006-2010 5-year est.); Median contract rent: $456 per month (2006-2010 5-year est.); Median year structure built: 1954 (2006-2010 5-year est.).
Transportation: Commute to work: 96.9% car, 0.0% public transportation, 0.0% walk, 3.1% work from home (2006-2010 5-year est.); Travel time to work: 32.6% less than 15 minutes, 45.3% 15 to 30 minutes, 8.9% 30 to 45 minutes, 8.9% 45 to 60 minutes, 4.2% 60 minutes or more (2006-2010 5-year est.)

CENTER (township). Covers a land area of 24.397 square miles and a water area of 0.042 square miles. Located at 40.92° N. Lat; 79.93° W. Long.
Population: 6,551 (1990); 8,182 (2000); 7,898 (2010); Density: 323.7 persons per square mile (2010); Race: 97.5% White, 0.5% Black, 1.0% Asian, 0.1% American Indian/Alaska Native, 0.0% Native Hawaiian/Other Pacific Islander, 0.9% Other, 0.8% Hispanic of any race (2010); Average household size: 2.29 (2010); Median age: 46.5 (2010); Males per 100 females: 91.0 (2010); Marriage status: 19.8% never married, 62.6% now

married, 8.3% widowed, 9.2% divorced (2006-2010 5-year est.); Foreign born: 1.1% (2006-2010 5-year est.); Ancestry (includes multiple ancestries): 43.0% German, 19.7% Irish, 16.3% Italian, 12.2% English, 6.2% American (2006-2010 5-year est.).

Economy: Single-family building permits issued: 4 (2011); Multi-family building permits issued: 0 (2011); Employment by occupation: 12.4% management, 4.5% professional, 11.2% services, 14.8% sales, 4.3% farming, 7.3% construction, 6.0% production (2006-2010 5-year est.).

Income: Per capita income: $28,878 (2006-2010 5-year est.); Median household income: $54,779 (2006-2010 5-year est.); Average household income: $66,705 (2006-2010 5-year est.); Percent of households with income of $100,000 or more: 20.0% (2006-2010 5-year est.); Poverty rate: 4.0% (2006-2010 5-year est.).

Education: Percent of population age 25 and over with: High school diploma (including GED) or higher: 93.7% (2006-2010 5-year est.); Bachelor's degree or higher: 31.4% (2006-2010 5-year est.); Master's degree or higher: 12.3% (2006-2010 5-year est.).

Housing: Homeownership rate: 77.4% (2010); Median home value: $165,000 (2006-2010 5-year est.); Median contract rent: $595 per month (2006-2010 5-year est.); Median year structure built: 1979 (2006-2010 5-year est.).

Transportation: Commute to work: 94.9% car, 0.0% public transportation, 0.7% walk, 3.5% work from home (2006-2010 5-year est.); Travel time to work: 34.8% less than 15 minutes, 37.1% 15 to 30 minutes, 14.3% 30 to 45 minutes, 7.0% 45 to 60 minutes, 6.8% 60 minutes or more (2006-2010 5-year est.)

Additional Information Contacts

Butler County Chamber of Commerce . . . . (724) 283-2222
  http://www.butlercountychamber.com
Center Township . . . . (724) 282-7805
  http://www.centertownship.net

CHERRY (township). Covers a land area of 25.618 square miles and a water area of 0.268 square miles. Located at 41.06° N. Lat; 79.92° W. Long.

Population: 814 (1990); 1,053 (2000); 1,106 (2010); Density: 43.2 persons per square mile (2010); Race: 97.4% White, 0.3% Black, 0.4% Asian, 0.2% American Indian/Alaska Native, 0.0% Native Hawaiian/Other Pacific Islander, 1.7% Other, 0.6% Hispanic of any race (2010); Average household size: 2.58 (2010); Median age: 42.6 (2010); Males per 100 females: 107.1 (2010); Marriage status: 27.4% never married, 58.5% now married, 5.1% widowed, 9.0% divorced (2006-2010 5-year est.); Foreign born: 0.3% (2006-2010 5-year est.); Ancestry (includes multiple ancestries): 42.9% German, 15.7% Irish, 9.9% Italian, 8.2% English, 5.3% American (2006-2010 5-year est.).

Economy: Single-family building permits issued: 2 (2011); Multi-family building permits issued: 0 (2011); Employment by occupation: 8.6% management, 4.4% professional, 13.6% services, 14.1% sales, 2.5% farming, 15.9% construction, 10.3% production (2006-2010 5-year est.).

Income: Per capita income: $21,138 (2006-2010 5-year est.); Median household income: $44,792 (2006-2010 5-year est.); Average household income: $54,319 (2006-2010 5-year est.); Percent of households with income of $100,000 or more: 14.0% (2006-2010 5-year est.); Poverty rate: 16.5% (2006-2010 5-year est.).

Education: Percent of population age 25 and over with: High school diploma (including GED) or higher: 79.6% (2006-2010 5-year est.); Bachelor's degree or higher: 14.7% (2006-2010 5-year est.); Master's degree or higher: 5.3% (2006-2010 5-year est.).

Housing: Homeownership rate: 87.2% (2010); Median home value: $123,500 (2006-2010 5-year est.); Median contract rent: $520 per month (2006-2010 5-year est.); Median year structure built: 1975 (2006-2010 5-year est.).

Transportation: Commute to work: 94.9% car, 0.0% public transportation, 2.9% walk, 2.1% work from home (2006-2010 5-year est.); Travel time to work: 37.5% less than 15 minutes, 22.0% 15 to 30 minutes, 16.2% 30 to 45 minutes, 10.0% 45 to 60 minutes, 14.4% 60 minutes or more (2006-2010 5-year est.)

Additional Information Contacts

Butler County Chamber of Commerce . . . . (724) 283-2222
  http://www.butlercountychamber.com

CHERRY VALLEY (borough). Covers a land area of 2.824 square miles and a water area of 0 square miles. Located at 41.16° N. Lat; 79.80° W. Long. Elevation is 1,329 feet.

Population: 96 (1990); 72 (2000); 66 (2010); Density: 23.4 persons per square mile (2010); Race: 98.5% White, 1.5% Black, 0.0% Asian, 0.0% American Indian/Alaska Native, 0.0% Native Hawaiian/Other Pacific Islander, 0.0% Other, 0.0% Hispanic of any race (2010); Average household size: 2.36 (2010); Median age: 46.5 (2010); Males per 100 females: 88.6 (2010); Marriage status: 32.1% never married, 47.2% now married, 17.0% widowed, 3.8% divorced (2006-2010 5-year est.); Foreign born: 0.0% (2006-2010 5-year est.); Ancestry (includes multiple ancestries): 36.4% German, 21.8% Irish, 9.1% American, 9.1% English, 9.1% Lithuanian (2006-2010 5-year est.).

Economy: Single-family building permits issued: 0 (2011); Multi-family building permits issued: 0 (2011); Employment by occupation: 0.0% management, 0.0% professional, 23.7% services, 10.5% sales, 0.0% farming, 13.2% construction, 10.5% production (2006-2010 5-year est.).

Income: Per capita income: $29,242 (2006-2010 5-year est.); Median household income: $56,250 (2006-2010 5-year est.); Average household income: $67,477 (2006-2010 5-year est.); Percent of households with income of $100,000 or more: 23.1% (2006-2010 5-year est.); Poverty rate: 0.0% (2006-2010 5-year est.).

Education: Percent of population age 25 and over with: High school diploma (including GED) or higher: 93.3% (2006-2010 5-year est.); Bachelor's degree or higher: 24.4% (2006-2010 5-year est.); Master's degree or higher: 6.7% (2006-2010 5-year est.).

Housing: Homeownership rate: 78.6% (2010); Median home value: $159,400 (2006-2010 5-year est.); Median contract rent: n/a per month (2006-2010 5-year est.); Median year structure built: before 1940 (2006-2010 5-year est.).

Transportation: Commute to work: 100.0% car, 0.0% public transportation, 0.0% walk, 0.0% work from home (2006-2010 5-year est.); Travel time to work: 18.4% less than 15 minutes, 36.8% 15 to 30 minutes, 15.8% 30 to 45 minutes, 18.4% 45 to 60 minutes, 10.5% 60 minutes or more (2006-2010 5-year est.)

CHICORA (borough). Covers a land area of 0.531 square miles and a water area of 0.002 square miles. Located at 40.95° N. Lat; 79.74° W. Long. Elevation is 1,211 feet.

History: Incorporated 1855.

Population: 1,052 (1990); 1,021 (2000); 1,043 (2010); Density: 1,964.3 persons per square mile (2010); Race: 98.9% White, 0.2% Black, 0.3% Asian, 0.0% American Indian/Alaska Native, 0.0% Native Hawaiian/Other Pacific Islander, 0.6% Other, 0.4% Hispanic of any race (2010); Average household size: 2.37 (2010); Median age: 41.3 (2010); Males per 100 females: 90.0 (2010); Marriage status: 18.8% never married, 63.1% now married, 8.4% widowed, 9.7% divorced (2006-2010 5-year est.); Foreign born: 0.2% (2006-2010 5-year est.); Ancestry (includes multiple ancestries): 52.6% German, 34.9% Irish, 9.9% Italian, 7.4% Dutch, 6.9% English (2006-2010 5-year est.).

Economy: Single-family building permits issued: 1 (2011); Multi-family building permits issued: 0 (2011); Employment by occupation: 6.7% management, 7.4% professional, 6.5% services, 14.7% sales, 5.8% farming, 7.6% construction, 4.9% production (2006-2010 5-year est.).

Income: Per capita income: $22,204 (2006-2010 5-year est.); Median household income: $39,167 (2006-2010 5-year est.); Average household income: $51,323 (2006-2010 5-year est.); Percent of households with income of $100,000 or more: 13.1% (2006-2010 5-year est.); Poverty rate: 12.4% (2006-2010 5-year est.).

Education: Percent of population age 25 and over with: High school diploma (including GED) or higher: 92.3% (2006-2010 5-year est.); Bachelor's degree or higher: 18.1% (2006-2010 5-year est.); Master's degree or higher: 6.2% (2006-2010 5-year est.).

School District(s)

Karns City Area SD (KG-12)
  2010-11 Enrollment: 1,618 . . . . (724) 756-2030

Housing: Homeownership rate: 67.1% (2010); Median home value: $101,500 (2006-2010 5-year est.); Median contract rent: $380 per month (2006-2010 5-year est.); Median year structure built: 1951 (2006-2010 5-year est.).

Transportation: Commute to work: 90.9% car, 0.0% public transportation, 3.4% walk, 5.3% work from home (2006-2010 5-year est.); Travel time to work: 39.7% less than 15 minutes, 22.8% 15 to 30 minutes, 18.5% 30 to 45 minutes, 8.4% 45 to 60 minutes, 10.6% 60 minutes or more (2006-2010 5-year est.)

CLAY (township). Covers a land area of 25.115 square miles and a water area of 0 square miles. Located at 40.99° N. Lat; 79.93° W. Long.
Population: 2,360 (1990); 2,628 (2000); 2,703 (2010); Density: 107.6 persons per square mile (2010); Race: 98.9% White, 0.0% Black, 0.2% Asian, 0.4% American Indian/Alaska Native, 0.0% Native Hawaiian/Other Pacific Islander, 0.5% Other, 0.7% Hispanic of any race (2010); Average household size: 2.55 (2010); Median age: 42.7 (2010); Males per 100 females: 106.5 (2010); Marriage status: 24.5% never married, 59.4% now married, 4.4% widowed, 11.7% divorced (2006-2010 5-year est.); Foreign born: 0.0% (2006-2010 5-year est.); Ancestry (includes multiple ancestries): 39.9% German, 25.2% Irish, 10.0% English, 8.9% American, 6.7% Scotch-Irish (2006-2010 5-year est.).
Economy: Single-family building permits issued: 4 (2011); Multi-family building permits issued: 0 (2011); Employment by occupation: 6.4% management, 0.4% professional, 15.7% services, 14.0% sales, 2.3% farming, 19.6% construction, 15.1% production (2006-2010 5-year est.).
Income: Per capita income: $20,567 (2006-2010 5-year est.); Median household income: $44,639 (2006-2010 5-year est.); Average household income: $51,851 (2006-2010 5-year est.); Percent of households with income of $100,000 or more: 7.0% (2006-2010 5-year est.); Poverty rate: 10.2% (2006-2010 5-year est.).
Education: Percent of population age 25 and over with: High school diploma (including GED) or higher: 84.2% (2006-2010 5-year est.); Bachelor's degree or higher: 8.6% (2006-2010 5-year est.); Master's degree or higher: 3.4% (2006-2010 5-year est.).
Housing: Homeownership rate: 86.9% (2010); Median home value: $117,200 (2006-2010 5-year est.); Median contract rent: $427 per month (2006-2010 5-year est.); Median year structure built: 1976 (2006-2010 5-year est.).
Transportation: Commute to work: 97.1% car, 0.0% public transportation, 1.4% walk, 1.5% work from home (2006-2010 5-year est.); Travel time to work: 17.8% less than 15 minutes, 43.7% 15 to 30 minutes, 22.2% 30 to 45 minutes, 2.6% 45 to 60 minutes, 13.8% 60 minutes or more (2006-2010 5-year est.)
Additional Information Contacts
Butler County Chamber of Commerce . . . . (724) 283-2222
　http://www.butlercountychamber.com

CLEARFIELD (township). Covers a land area of 23.639 square miles and a water area of 0.003 square miles. Located at 40.85° N. Lat; 79.74° W. Long.
Population: 2,635 (1990); 2,705 (2000); 2,645 (2010); Density: 111.9 persons per square mile (2010); Race: 99.1% White, 0.3% Black, 0.1% Asian, 0.2% American Indian/Alaska Native, 0.0% Native Hawaiian/Other Pacific Islander, 0.3% Other, 0.3% Hispanic of any race (2010); Average household size: 2.57 (2010); Median age: 43.5 (2010); Males per 100 females: 104.4 (2010); Marriage status: 21.8% never married, 65.8% now married, 3.6% widowed, 8.9% divorced (2006-2010 5-year est.); Foreign born: 0.3% (2006-2010 5-year est.); Ancestry (includes multiple ancestries): 49.4% German, 24.8% Irish, 6.5% Italian, 6.4% American, 5.9% Polish (2006-2010 5-year est.).
Economy: Single-family building permits issued: 4 (2011); Multi-family building permits issued: 0 (2011); Employment by occupation: 4.4% management, 4.0% professional, 11.1% services, 20.1% sales, 0.8% farming, 13.6% construction, 10.4% production (2006-2010 5-year est.).
Income: Per capita income: $20,992 (2006-2010 5-year est.); Median household income: $49,775 (2006-2010 5-year est.); Average household income: $56,635 (2006-2010 5-year est.); Percent of households with income of $100,000 or more: 12.5% (2006-2010 5-year est.); Poverty rate: 11.0% (2006-2010 5-year est.).
Education: Percent of population age 25 and over with: High school diploma (including GED) or higher: 88.9% (2006-2010 5-year est.); Bachelor's degree or higher: 9.5% (2006-2010 5-year est.); Master's degree or higher: 2.1% (2006-2010 5-year est.).
Housing: Homeownership rate: 81.8% (2010); Median home value: $128,100 (2006-2010 5-year est.); Median contract rent: $396 per month (2006-2010 5-year est.); Median year structure built: 1980 (2006-2010 5-year est.).
Transportation: Commute to work: 97.2% car, 0.0% public transportation, 1.1% walk, 1.6% work from home (2006-2010 5-year est.); Travel time to work: 19.0% less than 15 minutes, 46.0% 15 to 30 minutes, 16.4% 30 to 45 minutes, 9.3% 45 to 60 minutes, 9.2% 60 minutes or more (2006-2010 5-year est.)

Additional Information Contacts
Butler County Chamber of Commerce . . . . (724) 283-2222
　http://www.butlercountychamber.com

CLINTON (township). Covers a land area of 23.552 square miles and a water area of 0.008 square miles. Located at 40.71° N. Lat; 79.83° W. Long. Elevation is 1,257 feet.
Population: 2,556 (1990); 2,779 (2000); 2,864 (2010); Density: 121.6 persons per square mile (2010); Race: 98.6% White, 0.2% Black, 0.2% Asian, 0.2% American Indian/Alaska Native, 0.0% Native Hawaiian/Other Pacific Islander, 0.8% Other, 0.5% Hispanic of any race (2010); Average household size: 2.58 (2010); Median age: 44.7 (2010); Males per 100 females: 103.7 (2010); Marriage status: 22.5% never married, 62.9% now married, 5.7% widowed, 8.8% divorced (2006-2010 5-year est.); Foreign born: 0.8% (2006-2010 5-year est.); Ancestry (includes multiple ancestries): 44.7% German, 24.5% Irish, 11.7% English, 8.5% Polish, 6.6% Scottish (2006-2010 5-year est.).
Economy: Single-family building permits issued: 7 (2011); Multi-family building permits issued: 0 (2011); Employment by occupation: 9.4% management, 5.7% professional, 10.4% services, 17.9% sales, 3.7% farming, 12.3% construction, 6.7% production (2006-2010 5-year est.).
Income: Per capita income: $23,962 (2006-2010 5-year est.); Median household income: $53,265 (2006-2010 5-year est.); Average household income: $60,240 (2006-2010 5-year est.); Percent of households with income of $100,000 or more: 14.4% (2006-2010 5-year est.); Poverty rate: 8.3% (2006-2010 5-year est.).
Education: Percent of population age 25 and over with: High school diploma (including GED) or higher: 92.7% (2006-2010 5-year est.); Bachelor's degree or higher: 23.2% (2006-2010 5-year est.); Master's degree or higher: 8.8% (2006-2010 5-year est.).
Housing: Homeownership rate: 88.5% (2010); Median home value: $155,600 (2006-2010 5-year est.); Median contract rent: $603 per month (2006-2010 5-year est.); Median year structure built: 1972 (2006-2010 5-year est.).
Transportation: Commute to work: 91.7% car, 1.0% public transportation, 1.7% walk, 4.3% work from home (2006-2010 5-year est.); Travel time to work: 24.7% less than 15 minutes, 30.3% 15 to 30 minutes, 27.8% 30 to 45 minutes, 9.3% 45 to 60 minutes, 7.8% 60 minutes or more (2006-2010 5-year est.)
Additional Information Contacts
Butler County Chamber of Commerce . . . . (724) 283-2222
　http://www.butlercountychamber.com

CONCORD (township). Covers a land area of 24.185 square miles and a water area of 0.010 square miles. Located at 40.99° N. Lat; 79.83° W. Long.
Population: 1,336 (1990); 1,493 (2000); 1,505 (2010); Density: 62.2 persons per square mile (2010); Race: 97.5% White, 0.5% Black, 0.5% Asian, 0.0% American Indian/Alaska Native, 0.0% Native Hawaiian/Other Pacific Islander, 1.5% Other, 0.3% Hispanic of any race (2010); Average household size: 2.44 (2010); Median age: 44.0 (2010); Males per 100 females: 98.3 (2010); Marriage status: 22.4% never married, 64.3% now married, 4.1% widowed, 9.2% divorced (2006-2010 5-year est.); Foreign born: 0.7% (2006-2010 5-year est.); Ancestry (includes multiple ancestries): 44.1% German, 22.6% Irish, 8.0% Scotch-Irish, 7.3% Polish, 6.5% English (2006-2010 5-year est.).
Economy: Single-family building permits issued: 0 (2011); Multi-family building permits issued: 0 (2011); Employment by occupation: 6.1% management, 3.0% professional, 13.2% services, 21.2% sales, 2.2% farming, 16.5% construction, 14.3% production (2006-2010 5-year est.).
Income: Per capita income: $20,126 (2006-2010 5-year est.); Median household income: $44,770 (2006-2010 5-year est.); Average household income: $52,783 (2006-2010 5-year est.); Percent of households with income of $100,000 or more: 11.2% (2006-2010 5-year est.); Poverty rate: 5.3% (2006-2010 5-year est.).
Education: Percent of population age 25 and over with: High school diploma (including GED) or higher: 92.5% (2006-2010 5-year est.); Bachelor's degree or higher: 10.6% (2006-2010 5-year est.); Master's degree or higher: 3.9% (2006-2010 5-year est.).
Housing: Homeownership rate: 83.5% (2010); Median home value: $109,400 (2006-2010 5-year est.); Median contract rent: $407 per month (2006-2010 5-year est.); Median year structure built: 1975 (2006-2010 5-year est.).
Transportation: Commute to work: 92.7% car, 0.0% public transportation, 0.0% walk, 4.7% work from home (2006-2010 5-year est.); Travel time to

work: 10.6% less than 15 minutes, 45.4% 15 to 30 minutes, 22.9% 30 to 45 minutes, 9.0% 45 to 60 minutes, 12.2% 60 minutes or more (2006-2010 5-year est.)

Additional Information Contacts
Butler County Chamber of Commerce . . . . (724) 283-2222
http://www.butlercountychamber.com

CONNOQUENESSING (borough).
Covers a land area of 1.363 square miles and a water area of 0 square miles. Located at 40.82° N. Lat; 80.02° W. Long. Elevation is 1,299 feet.

Population: 507 (1990); 564 (2000); 528 (2010); Density: 387.5 persons per square mile (2010); Race: 98.7% White, 0.0% Black, 0.6% Asian, 0.2% American Indian/Alaska Native, 0.0% Native Hawaiian/Other Pacific Islander, 0.5% Other, 0.0% Hispanic of any race (2010); Average household size: 2.67 (2010); Median age: 39.4 (2010); Males per 100 females: 101.5 (2010); Marriage status: 10.8% never married, 72.2% now married, 6.4% widowed, 10.6% divorced (2006-2010 5-year est.); Foreign born: 0.5% (2006-2010 5-year est.); Ancestry (includes multiple ancestries): 68.7% German, 28.6% Irish, 10.4% English, 6.1% Italian, 5.4% Swedish (2006-2010 5-year est.).

Economy: Single-family building permits issued: 9 (2011); Multi-family building permits issued: 4 (2011); Employment by occupation: 6.3% management, 2.6% professional, 10.3% services, 23.8% sales, 3.3% farming, 12.3% construction, 6.0% production (2006-2010 5-year est.).

Income: Per capita income: $22,486 (2006-2010 5-year est.); Median household income: $49,688 (2006-2010 5-year est.); Average household income: $58,161 (2006-2010 5-year est.); Percent of households with income of $100,000 or more: 13.8% (2006-2010 5-year est.); Poverty rate: 12.1% (2006-2010 5-year est.).

Education: Percent of population age 25 and over with: High school diploma (including GED) or higher: 96.0% (2006-2010 5-year est.); Bachelor's degree or higher: 17.5% (2006-2010 5-year est.); Master's degree or higher: 0.8% (2006-2010 5-year est.).

Housing: Homeownership rate: 81.3% (2010); Median home value: $156,100 (2006-2010 5-year est.); Median contract rent: $572 per month (2006-2010 5-year est.); Median year structure built: 1941 (2006-2010 5-year est.).

Transportation: Commute to work: 93.3% car, 0.0% public transportation, 4.3% walk, 2.3% work from home (2006-2010 5-year est.); Travel time to work: 23.5% less than 15 minutes, 53.9% 15 to 30 minutes, 15.4% 30 to 45 minutes, 4.8% 45 to 60 minutes, 2.4% 60 minutes or more (2006-2010 5-year est.)

CONNOQUENESSING (township).
Covers a land area of 22.734 square miles and a water area of 0.008 square miles. Located at 40.86° N. Lat; 80.02° W. Long. Elevation is 1,299 feet.

History: Conoquenessing.

Population: 3,093 (1990); 3,653 (2000); 4,170 (2010); Density: 183.4 persons per square mile (2010); Race: 98.4% White, 0.0% Black, 0.8% Asian, 0.1% American Indian/Alaska Native, 0.0% Native Hawaiian/Other Pacific Islander, 0.7% Other, 0.4% Hispanic of any race (2010); Average household size: 2.41 (2010); Median age: 44.8 (2010); Males per 100 females: 103.1 (2010); Marriage status: 20.4% never married, 66.0% now married, 7.1% widowed, 6.4% divorced (2006-2010 5-year est.); Foreign born: 2.5% (2006-2010 5-year est.); Ancestry (includes multiple ancestries): 43.2% German, 15.8% Irish, 10.2% English, 9.3% Italian, 6.4% Scotch-Irish (2006-2010 5-year est.).

Economy: Single-family building permits issued: 0 (2011); Multi-family building permits issued: 0 (2011); Employment by occupation: 13.7% management, 4.2% professional, 7.0% services, 17.4% sales, 5.2% farming, 7.5% construction, 7.6% production (2006-2010 5-year est.).

Income: Per capita income: $26,395 (2006-2010 5-year est.); Median household income: $50,862 (2006-2010 5-year est.); Average household income: $63,025 (2006-2010 5-year est.); Percent of households with income of $100,000 or more: 20.5% (2006-2010 5-year est.); Poverty rate: 7.6% (2006-2010 5-year est.).

Education: Percent of population age 25 and over with: High school diploma (including GED) or higher: 90.1% (2006-2010 5-year est.); Bachelor's degree or higher: 24.8% (2006-2010 5-year est.); Master's degree or higher: 3.5% (2006-2010 5-year est.).

Housing: Homeownership rate: 87.9% (2010); Median home value: $172,100 (2006-2010 5-year est.); Median contract rent: $521 per month (2006-2010 5-year est.); Median year structure built: 1989 (2006-2010 5-year est.).

Transportation: Commute to work: 88.8% car, 0.3% public transportation, 0.8% walk, 9.2% work from home (2006-2010 5-year est.); Travel time to work: 24.4% less than 15 minutes, 37.4% 15 to 30 minutes, 20.7% 30 to 45 minutes, 12.9% 45 to 60 minutes, 4.6% 60 minutes or more (2006-2010 5-year est.)

Additional Information Contacts
Butler County Chamber of Commerce . . . . (724) 283-2222
http://www.butlercountychamber.com

CRANBERRY (township).
Covers a land area of 22.823 square miles and a water area of 0.005 square miles. Located at 40.71° N. Lat; 80.11° W. Long.

Population: 14,764 (1990); 23,625 (2000); 28,098 (2010); Density: 1,231.1 persons per square mile (2010); Race: 94.4% White, 1.2% Black, 2.8% Asian, 0.1% American Indian/Alaska Native, 0.0% Native Hawaiian/Other Pacific Islander, 1.5% Other, 1.6% Hispanic of any race (2010); Average household size: 2.72 (2010); Median age: 38.0 (2010); Males per 100 females: 97.1 (2010); Marriage status: 20.0% never married, 68.8% now married, 4.8% widowed, 6.4% divorced (2006-2010 5-year est.); Foreign born: 3.8% (2006-2010 5-year est.); Ancestry (includes multiple ancestries): 35.6% German, 22.4% Irish, 20.4% Italian, 9.0% English, 8.4% Polish (2006-2010 5-year est.).

Economy: Unemployment rate: 4.7% (August 2012); Total civilian labor force: 16,787 (August 2012); Single-family building permits issued: 127 (2011); Multi-family building permits issued: 64 (2011); Employment by occupation: 19.1% management, 10.2% professional, 7.0% services, 13.7% sales, 3.0% farming, 6.1% construction, 4.5% production (2006-2010 5-year est.).

Income: Per capita income: $37,726 (2006-2010 5-year est.); Median household income: $88,791 (2006-2010 5-year est.); Average household income: $101,589 (2006-2010 5-year est.); Percent of households with income of $100,000 or more: 43.3% (2006-2010 5-year est.); Poverty rate: 2.8% (2006-2010 5-year est.).

Taxes: Total city taxes per capita: $491 (2009); City property taxes per capita: $173 (2009).

Education: Percent of population age 25 and over with: High school diploma (including GED) or higher: 97.5% (2006-2010 5-year est.); Bachelor's degree or higher: 53.5% (2006-2010 5-year est.); Master's degree or higher: 17.6% (2006-2010 5-year est.).

School District(s)
Seneca Valley SD (KG-12)
    2010-11 Enrollment: 7,288 . . . . (724) 452-6040

Housing: Homeownership rate: 83.5% (2010); Median home value: $230,600 (2006-2010 5-year est.); Median contract rent: $828 per month (2006-2010 5-year est.); Median year structure built: 1990 (2006-2010 5-year est.).

Safety: Violent crime rate: 2.5 per 10,000 population; Property crime rate: 121.3 per 10,000 population (2011).

Newspapers: Cranberry Eagle (Local news; Circulation 20,000); Hampton-Richland Eagle (Local news; Circulation 12,000); News Weekly (Community news; Circulation 7,647); Pittsburgh Post-Gazette - North Bureau (Community news); Sunday Cranberry Eagle (Community news)

Transportation: Commute to work: 90.9% car, 1.5% public transportation, 1.2% walk, 5.4% work from home (2006-2010 5-year est.); Travel time to work: 27.2% less than 15 minutes, 20.8% 15 to 30 minutes, 33.1% 30 to 45 minutes, 13.4% 45 to 60 minutes, 5.5% 60 minutes or more (2006-2010 5-year est.)

Additional Information Contacts
Butler County Chamber of Commerce . . . . (724) 283-2222
http://www.butlercountychamber.com
Cranberry Township . . . . (724) 776-4806
http://www.twp.cranberry.pa.us

DONEGAL (township).
Covers a land area of 23.194 square miles and a water area of 0.015 square miles. Located at 40.92° N. Lat; 79.73° W. Long.

Population: 1,569 (1990); 1,722 (2000); 1,864 (2010); Density: 80.4 persons per square mile (2010); Race: 98.9% White, 0.5% Black, 0.1% Asian, 0.1% American Indian/Alaska Native, 0.1% Native Hawaiian/Other Pacific Islander, 0.3% Other, 0.4% Hispanic of any race (2010); Average household size: 2.58 (2010); Median age: 43.7 (2010); Males per 100 females: 96.4 (2010); Marriage status: 19.8% never married, 63.3% now married, 11.1% widowed, 5.8% divorced (2006-2010 5-year est.); Foreign born: 1.5% (2006-2010 5-year est.); Ancestry (includes multiple

ancestries): 55.6% German, 28.7% Irish, 7.5% English, 6.5% Italian, 5.1% Scotch-Irish (2006-2010 5-year est.).

Economy: Single-family building permits issued: 0 (2011); Multi-family building permits issued: 0 (2011); Employment by occupation: 8.8% management, 2.6% professional, 10.2% services, 17.2% sales, 2.7% farming, 15.9% construction, 8.1% production (2006-2010 5-year est.).

Income: Per capita income: $24,945 (2006-2010 5-year est.); Median household income: $52,500 (2006-2010 5-year est.); Average household income: $66,883 (2006-2010 5-year est.); Percent of households with income of $100,000 or more: 17.9% (2006-2010 5-year est.); Poverty rate: 6.8% (2006-2010 5-year est.).

Education: Percent of population age 25 and over with: High school diploma (including GED) or higher: 88.3% (2006-2010 5-year est.); Bachelor's degree or higher: 8.1% (2006-2010 5-year est.); Master's degree or higher: 2.6% (2006-2010 5-year est.).

Housing: Homeownership rate: 85.8% (2010); Median home value: $136,800 (2006-2010 5-year est.); Median contract rent: $469 per month (2006-2010 5-year est.); Median year structure built: 1977 (2006-2010 5-year est.).

Transportation: Commute to work: 96.8% car, 0.4% public transportation, 1.3% walk, 1.0% work from home (2006-2010 5-year est.); Travel time to work: 15.7% less than 15 minutes, 43.6% 15 to 30 minutes, 20.4% 30 to 45 minutes, 11.3% 45 to 60 minutes, 9.0% 60 minutes or more (2006-2010 5-year est.)

Additional Information Contacts

Butler County Chamber of Commerce . . . . (724) 283-2222
http://www.butlercountychamber.com

EAST BUTLER (borough). Covers a land area of 1.043 square miles and a water area of 0 square miles. Located at 40.88° N. Lat; 79.85° W. Long. Elevation is 1,063 feet.

Population: 725 (1990); 679 (2000); 732 (2010); Density: 702.0 persons per square mile (2010); Race: 97.0% White, 0.4% Black, 0.0% Asian, 0.0% American Indian/Alaska Native, 0.3% Native Hawaiian/Other Pacific Islander, 2.3% Other, 1.0% Hispanic of any race (2010); Average household size: 2.35 (2010); Median age: 41.2 (2010); Males per 100 females: 100.0 (2010); Marriage status: 20.4% never married, 60.6% now married, 9.5% widowed, 9.5% divorced (2006-2010 5-year est.); Foreign born: 0.4% (2006-2010 5-year est.); Ancestry (includes multiple ancestries): 56.6% German, 27.1% Irish, 9.5% Italian, 9.4% English, 7.0% Hungarian (2006-2010 5-year est.).

Economy: Single-family building permits issued: 0 (2011); Multi-family building permits issued: 0 (2011); Employment by occupation: 5.4% management, 3.4% professional, 17.5% services, 11.1% sales, 6.1% farming, 16.2% construction, 18.2% production (2006-2010 5-year est.).

Income: Per capita income: $22,643 (2006-2010 5-year est.); Median household income: $43,750 (2006-2010 5-year est.); Average household income: $51,539 (2006-2010 5-year est.); Percent of households with income of $100,000 or more: 10.7% (2006-2010 5-year est.); Poverty rate: 12.2% (2006-2010 5-year est.).

Education: Percent of population age 25 and over with: High school diploma (including GED) or higher: 90.2% (2006-2010 5-year est.); Bachelor's degree or higher: 13.3% (2006-2010 5-year est.); Master's degree or higher: 3.1% (2006-2010 5-year est.).

Housing: Homeownership rate: 79.2% (2010); Median home value: $98,300 (2006-2010 5-year est.); Median contract rent: $601 per month (2006-2010 5-year est.); Median year structure built: 1949 (2006-2010 5-year est.).

Transportation: Commute to work: 94.2% car, 0.0% public transportation, 1.0% walk, 4.8% work from home (2006-2010 5-year est.); Travel time to work: 45.7% less than 15 minutes, 32.5% 15 to 30 minutes, 15.7% 30 to 45 minutes, 0.7% 45 to 60 minutes, 5.4% 60 minutes or more (2006-2010 5-year est.)

EAU CLAIRE (borough). Covers a land area of 1.275 square miles and a water area of 0 square miles. Located at 41.14° N. Lat; 79.80° W. Long. Elevation is 1,519 feet.

Population: 371 (1990); 355 (2000); 316 (2010); Density: 247.9 persons per square mile (2010); Race: 99.4% White, 0.3% Black, 0.0% Asian, 0.0% American Indian/Alaska Native, 0.0% Native Hawaiian/Other Pacific Islander, 0.3% Other, 0.0% Hispanic of any race (2010); Average household size: 2.36 (2010); Median age: 38.2 (2010); Males per 100 females: 87.0 (2010); Marriage status: 26.0% never married, 57.2% now married, 5.3% widowed, 11.5% divorced (2006-2010 5-year est.); Foreign born: 0.0% (2006-2010 5-year est.); Ancestry (includes multiple

ancestries): 52.1% German, 28.8% Irish, 16.5% Scotch-Irish, 11.0% English, 6.4% Italian (2006-2010 5-year est.).

Economy: Single-family building permits issued: 0 (2011); Multi-family building permits issued: 0 (2011); Employment by occupation: 0.0% management, 12.4% professional, 12.4% services, 19.0% sales, 7.6% farming, 6.7% construction, 6.7% production (2006-2010 5-year est.).

Income: Per capita income: $24,581 (2006-2010 5-year est.); Median household income: $42,708 (2006-2010 5-year est.); Average household income: $50,950 (2006-2010 5-year est.); Percent of households with income of $100,000 or more: 4.4% (2006-2010 5-year est.); Poverty rate: 31.4% (2006-2010 5-year est.).

Education: Percent of population age 25 and over with: High school diploma (including GED) or higher: 91.8% (2006-2010 5-year est.); Bachelor's degree or higher: 17.5% (2006-2010 5-year est.); Master's degree or higher: 7.0% (2006-2010 5-year est.).

Housing: Homeownership rate: 65.6% (2010); Median home value: $103,800 (2006-2010 5-year est.); Median contract rent: $297 per month (2006-2010 5-year est.); Median year structure built: 1955 (2006-2010 5-year est.).

Transportation: Commute to work: 83.5% car, 0.0% public transportation, 5.8% walk, 10.7% work from home (2006-2010 5-year est.); Travel time to work: 22.8% less than 15 minutes, 15.2% 15 to 30 minutes, 16.3% 30 to 45 minutes, 21.7% 45 to 60 minutes, 23.9% 60 minutes or more (2006-2010 5-year est.)

EVANS CITY (borough). Aka Evansburg. Covers a land area of 0.818 square miles and a water area of 0 square miles. Located at 40.77° N. Lat; 80.06° W. Long. Elevation is 928 feet.

Population: 2,054 (1990); 2,009 (2000); 1,833 (2010); Density: 2,240.1 persons per square mile (2010); Race: 98.4% White, 0.4% Black, 0.5% Asian, 0.0% American Indian/Alaska Native, 0.1% Native Hawaiian/Other Pacific Islander, 0.6% Other, 0.8% Hispanic of any race (2010); Average household size: 2.37 (2010); Median age: 40.7 (2010); Males per 100 females: 92.1 (2010); Marriage status: 26.7% never married, 56.4% now married, 7.7% widowed, 9.1% divorced (2006-2010 5-year est.); Foreign born: 1.7% (2006-2010 5-year est.); Ancestry (includes multiple ancestries): 46.6% German, 20.0% Italian, 17.0% Irish, 12.6% English, 7.2% Scotch-Irish (2006-2010 5-year est.).

Economy: Single-family building permits issued: 1 (2011); Multi-family building permits issued: 0 (2011); Employment by occupation: 8.2% management, 4.0% professional, 10.0% services, 11.6% sales, 5.5% farming, 10.3% construction, 6.3% production (2006-2010 5-year est.).

Income: Per capita income: $23,269 (2006-2010 5-year est.); Median household income: $49,148 (2006-2010 5-year est.); Average household income: $55,647 (2006-2010 5-year est.); Percent of households with income of $100,000 or more: 8.8% (2006-2010 5-year est.); Poverty rate: 5.3% (2006-2010 5-year est.).

Education: Percent of population age 25 and over with: High school diploma (including GED) or higher: 90.6% (2006-2010 5-year est.); Bachelor's degree or higher: 23.7% (2006-2010 5-year est.); Master's degree or higher: 9.8% (2006-2010 5-year est.).

School District(s)

Seneca Valley SD (KG-12)
    2010-11 Enrollment: 7,288 . . . . (724) 452-6040

Housing: Homeownership rate: 64.3% (2010); Median home value: $131,200 (2006-2010 5-year est.); Median contract rent: $461 per month (2006-2010 5-year est.); Median year structure built: 1950 (2006-2010 5-year est.).

Safety: Violent crime rate: 0.0 per 10,000 population; Property crime rate: 81.6 per 10,000 population (2011).

Transportation: Commute to work: 93.9% car, 0.7% public transportation, 4.4% walk, 0.9% work from home (2006-2010 5-year est.); Travel time to work: 34.9% less than 15 minutes, 36.8% 15 to 30 minutes, 10.6% 30 to 45 minutes, 12.1% 45 to 60 minutes, 5.6% 60 minutes or more (2006-2010 5-year est.)

Additional Information Contacts

Butler County Chamber of Commerce . . . . (724) 283-2222
http://www.butlercountychamber.com

FAIRVIEW (borough). Aka Baldwin. Covers a land area of 0.113 square miles and a water area of 0 square miles. Located at 41.02° N. Lat; 79.74° W. Long. Elevation is 1,401 feet.

Population: 247 (1990); 220 (2000); 198 (2010); Density: 1,755.8 persons per square mile (2010); Race: 96.0% White, 2.5% Black, 0.0% Asian, 0.0% American Indian/Alaska Native, 0.0% Native Hawaiian/Other Pacific

Islander, 1.5% Other, 0.0% Hispanic of any race (2010); Average household size: 2.96 (2010); Median age: 37.5 (2010); Males per 100 females: 90.4 (2010); Marriage status: 32.2% never married, 55.9% now married, 8.5% widowed, 3.4% divorced (2006-2010 5-year est.); Foreign born: 0.0% (2006-2010 5-year est.); Ancestry (includes multiple ancestries): 46.8% German, 22.4% Irish, 13.5% Dutch, 8.9% English, 7.2% Scotch-Irish (2006-2010 5-year est.).

Economy: Single-family building permits issued: 1 (2011); Multi-family building permits issued: 0 (2011); Employment by occupation: 2.0% management, 0.0% professional, 21.8% services, 15.8% sales, 5.9% farming, 6.9% construction, 8.9% production (2006-2010 5-year est.).

Income: Per capita income: $19,785 (2006-2010 5-year est.); Median household income: $50,000 (2006-2010 5-year est.); Average household income: $55,740 (2006-2010 5-year est.); Percent of households with income of $100,000 or more: 6.0% (2006-2010 5-year est.); Poverty rate: 11.0% (2006-2010 5-year est.).

Education: Percent of population age 25 and over with: High school diploma (including GED) or higher: 94.9% (2006-2010 5-year est.); Bachelor's degree or higher: 11.4% (2006-2010 5-year est.); Master's degree or higher: 2.5% (2006-2010 5-year est.).

Housing: Homeownership rate: 83.5% (2010); Median home value: $73,800 (2006-2010 5-year est.); Median contract rent: $454 per month (2006-2010 5-year est.); Median year structure built: 1945 (2006-2010 5-year est.).

Transportation: Commute to work: 97.0% car, 0.0% public transportation, 3.0% walk, 0.0% work from home (2006-2010 5-year est.); Travel time to work: 23.0% less than 15 minutes, 28.0% 15 to 30 minutes, 24.0% 30 to 45 minutes, 5.0% 45 to 60 minutes, 20.0% 60 minutes or more (2006-2010 5-year est.)

FAIRVIEW (township). Aka Baldwin. Covers a land area of 24.206 square miles and a water area of 0.007 square miles. Located at 40.99° N. Lat; 79.74° W. Long. Elevation is 1,401 feet.

Population: 1,986 (1990); 2,061 (2000); 2,080 (2010); Density: 85.9 persons per square mile (2010); Race: 99.4% White, 0.1% Black, 0.0% Asian, 0.0% American Indian/Alaska Native, 0.0% Native Hawaiian/Other Pacific Islander, 0.5% Other, 0.3% Hispanic of any race (2010); Average household size: 2.65 (2010); Median age: 43.9 (2010); Males per 100 females: 103.7 (2010); Marriage status: 23.1% never married, 60.2% now married, 8.0% widowed, 8.7% divorced (2006-2010 5-year est.); Foreign born: 0.2% (2006-2010 5-year est.); Ancestry (includes multiple ancestries): 45.4% German, 20.5% Irish, 8.8% English, 7.4% American, 6.8% Italian (2006-2010 5-year est.).

Economy: Single-family building permits issued: 1 (2011); Multi-family building permits issued: 0 (2011); Employment by occupation: 6.6% management, 3.0% professional, 9.0% services, 13.6% sales, 3.5% farming, 16.1% construction, 12.1% production (2006-2010 5-year est.).

Income: Per capita income: $25,433 (2006-2010 5-year est.); Median household income: $54,179 (2006-2010 5-year est.); Average household income: $65,629 (2006-2010 5-year est.); Percent of households with income of $100,000 or more: 20.2% (2006-2010 5-year est.); Poverty rate: 7.5% (2006-2010 5-year est.).

Education: Percent of population age 25 and over with: High school diploma (including GED) or higher: 88.8% (2006-2010 5-year est.); Bachelor's degree or higher: 10.5% (2006-2010 5-year est.); Master's degree or higher: 2.8% (2006-2010 5-year est.).

Housing: Homeownership rate: 89.3% (2010); Median home value: $120,700 (2006-2010 5-year est.); Median contract rent: $456 per month (2006-2010 5-year est.); Median year structure built: 1970 (2006-2010 5-year est.).

Transportation: Commute to work: 95.1% car, 0.0% public transportation, 1.2% walk, 3.2% work from home (2006-2010 5-year est.); Travel time to work: 25.3% less than 15 minutes, 30.2% 15 to 30 minutes, 25.8% 30 to 45 minutes, 7.0% 45 to 60 minutes, 11.6% 60 minutes or more (2006-2010 5-year est.)

Additional Information Contacts
Butler County Chamber of Commerce . . . . (724) 283-2222
   http://www.butlercountychamber.com

FENELTON (unincorporated postal area)
Zip Code: 16034
   Covers a land area of 19.844 square miles and a water area of 0.009 square miles. Located at 40.86° N. Lat; 79.73° W. Long. Elevation is 1,096 feet. Population: 2,054 (2010); Density: 103.5 persons per square mile (2010); Race: 99.3% White, 0.3% Black, 0.1% Asian, 0.0%

American Indian/Alaska Native, 0.0% Native Hawaiian/Other Pacific Islander, 0.3% Other, 0.2% Hispanic of any race (2010); Average household size: 2.64 (2010); Median age: 42.5 (2010); Males per 100 females: 105.0 (2010); Homeownership rate: 81.4% (2010)

FERNWAY (CDP). Covers a land area of 5.384 square miles and a water area of 0 square miles. Located at 40.69° N. Lat; 80.13° W. Long. Elevation is 1,037 feet.

Population: 9,072 (1990); 12,188 (2000); 12,414 (2010); Density: 2,305.7 persons per square mile (2010); Race: 94.5% White, 1.2% Black, 2.5% Asian, 0.1% American Indian/Alaska Native, 0.0% Native Hawaiian/Other Pacific Islander, 1.7% Other, 1.9% Hispanic of any race (2010); Average household size: 2.62 (2010); Median age: 36.8 (2010); Males per 100 females: 97.4 (2010); Marriage status: 22.8% never married, 64.8% now married, 4.3% widowed, 8.1% divorced (2006-2010 5-year est.); Foreign born: 3.4% (2006-2010 5-year est.); Ancestry (includes multiple ancestries): 37.4% German, 22.1% Irish, 20.9% Italian, 9.6% English, 9.4% Polish (2006-2010 5-year est.).

Economy: Employment by occupation: 15.0% management, 10.8% professional, 6.8% services, 14.5% sales, 3.1% farming, 5.9% construction, 5.0% production (2006-2010 5-year est.).

Income: Per capita income: $36,178 (2006-2010 5-year est.); Median household income: $80,158 (2006-2010 5-year est.); Average household income: $93,850 (2006-2010 5-year est.); Percent of households with income of $100,000 or more: 40.3% (2006-2010 5-year est.); Poverty rate: 3.3% (2006-2010 5-year est.).

Education: Percent of population age 25 and over with: High school diploma (including GED) or higher: 97.1% (2006-2010 5-year est.); Bachelor's degree or higher: 51.7% (2006-2010 5-year est.); Master's degree or higher: 18.2% (2006-2010 5-year est.).

Housing: Homeownership rate: 85.3% (2010); Median home value: $187,800 (2006-2010 5-year est.); Median contract rent: $903 per month (2006-2010 5-year est.); Median year structure built: 1985 (2006-2010 5-year est.).

Transportation: Commute to work: 89.7% car, 2.6% public transportation, 1.3% walk, 5.8% work from home (2006-2010 5-year est.); Travel time to work: 28.9% less than 15 minutes, 22.5% 15 to 30 minutes, 28.6% 30 to 45 minutes, 15.1% 45 to 60 minutes, 4.9% 60 minutes or more (2006-2010 5-year est.)

Additional Information Contacts
The Chamber of Commerce, Inc. (724) 934-9700
   http://www.thechamberinc.com

FORWARD (township). Covers a land area of 23.030 square miles and a water area of 0.009 square miles. Located at 40.78° N. Lat; 80.03° W. Long.

Population: 2,339 (1990); 2,687 (2000); 2,531 (2010); Density: 109.9 persons per square mile (2010); Race: 98.5% White, 0.1% Black, 0.4% Asian, 0.2% American Indian/Alaska Native, 0.0% Native Hawaiian/Other Pacific Islander, 0.8% Other, 0.4% Hispanic of any race (2010); Average household size: 2.61 (2010); Median age: 43.9 (2010); Males per 100 females: 103.3 (2010); Marriage status: 25.0% never married, 64.4% now married, 3.7% widowed, 6.9% divorced (2006-2010 5-year est.); Foreign born: 0.0% (2006-2010 5-year est.); Ancestry (includes multiple ancestries): 51.2% German, 21.3% Irish, 14.2% Polish, 9.3% Italian, 9.3% English (2006-2010 5-year est.).

Economy: Single-family building permits issued: 1 (2011); Multi-family building permits issued: 0 (2011); Employment by occupation: 8.9% management, 3.3% professional, 11.9% services, 17.3% sales, 3.7% farming, 13.3% construction, 8.0% production (2006-2010 5-year est.).

Income: Per capita income: $27,866 (2006-2010 5-year est.); Median household income: $63,563 (2006-2010 5-year est.); Average household income: $75,371 (2006-2010 5-year est.); Percent of households with income of $100,000 or more: 24.9% (2006-2010 5-year est.); Poverty rate: 6.4% (2006-2010 5-year est.).

Education: Percent of population age 25 and over with: High school diploma (including GED) or higher: 87.8% (2006-2010 5-year est.); Bachelor's degree or higher: 17.3% (2006-2010 5-year est.); Master's degree or higher: 4.8% (2006-2010 5-year est.).

Housing: Homeownership rate: 87.9% (2010); Median home value: $165,200 (2006-2010 5-year est.); Median contract rent: $475 per month (2006-2010 5-year est.); Median year structure built: 1979 (2006-2010 5-year est.).

Transportation: Commute to work: 89.7% car, 0.8% public transportation, 1.5% walk, 4.0% work from home (2006-2010 5-year est.); Travel time to

work: 20.8% less than 15 minutes, 48.6% 15 to 30 minutes, 15.7% 30 to 45 minutes, 9.8% 45 to 60 minutes, 5.1% 60 minutes or more (2006-2010 5-year est.)

Additional Information Contacts
Butler County Chamber of Commerce . . . . (724) 283-2222
  http://www.butlercountychamber.com

FOX RUN (CDP). Covers a land area of 2.384 square miles and a water area of 0 square miles. Located at 40.70° N. Lat; 80.08° W. Long. Elevation is 1,083 feet.

Population: 2,603 (1990); 3,044 (2000); 3,282 (2010); Density: 1,376.6 persons per square mile (2010); Race: 95.7% White, 1.0% Black, 1.8% Asian, 0.2% American Indian/Alaska Native, 0.0% Native Hawaiian/Other Pacific Islander, 1.3% Other, 1.4% Hispanic of any race (2010); Average household size: 2.89 (2010); Median age: 39.2 (2010); Males per 100 females: 103.7 (2010); Marriage status: 13.3% never married, 80.6% now married, 1.2% widowed, 5.0% divorced (2006-2010 5-year est.); Foreign born: 2.0% (2006-2010 5-year est.); Ancestry (includes multiple ancestries): 33.2% German, 24.4% Irish, 20.6% Italian, 8.3% Polish, 3.5% English (2006-2010 5-year est.).
Economy: Employment by occupation: 19.8% management, 15.1% professional, 6.2% services, 13.9% sales, 4.2% farming, 4.8% construction, 4.8% production (2006-2010 5-year est.).
Income: Per capita income: $30,450 (2006-2010 5-year est.); Median household income: $91,033 (2006-2010 5-year est.); Average household income: $93,287 (2006-2010 5-year est.); Percent of households with income of $100,000 or more: 38.5% (2006-2010 5-year est.); Poverty rate: 4.3% (2006-2010 5-year est.).
Education: Percent of population age 25 and over with: High school diploma (including GED) or higher: 96.4% (2006-2010 5-year est.); Bachelor's degree or higher: 49.6% (2006-2010 5-year est.); Master's degree or higher: 11.7% (2006-2010 5-year est.).
Housing: Homeownership rate: 88.7% (2010); Median home value: $239,300 (2006-2010 5-year est.); Median contract rent: $721 per month (2006-2010 5-year est.); Median year structure built: 1987 (2006-2010 5-year est.).
Transportation: Commute to work: 89.1% car, 0.0% public transportation, 1.7% walk, 8.8% work from home (2006-2010 5-year est.); Travel time to work: 26.4% less than 15 minutes, 19.3% 15 to 30 minutes, 40.7% 30 to 45 minutes, 9.5% 45 to 60 minutes, 4.1% 60 minutes or more (2006-2010 5-year est.)

Additional Information Contacts
Greater Hatboro Chamber of Commerce . . . . (215) 956-9540
  http://hatborochamber.org

FRANKLIN (township). Covers a land area of 21.273 square miles and a water area of 1.609 square miles. Located at 40.93° N. Lat; 80.01° W. Long.

Population: 2,156 (1990); 2,292 (2000); 2,620 (2010); Density: 123.2 persons per square mile (2010); Race: 98.3% White, 0.3% Black, 0.3% Asian, 0.0% American Indian/Alaska Native, 0.2% Native Hawaiian/Other Pacific Islander, 0.9% Other, 0.7% Hispanic of any race (2010); Average household size: 2.45 (2010); Median age: 47.7 (2010); Males per 100 females: 98.8 (2010); Marriage status: 17.1% never married, 65.1% now married, 5.8% widowed, 12.0% divorced (2006-2010 5-year est.); Foreign born: 0.2% (2006-2010 5-year est.); Ancestry (includes multiple ancestries): 46.6% German, 25.2% Irish, 11.4% English, 8.0% Scotch-Irish, 5.5% Italian (2006-2010 5-year est.).
Economy: Single-family building permits issued: 14 (2011); Multi-family building permits issued: 4 (2011); Employment by occupation: 13.1% management, 4.0% professional, 8.5% services, 15.3% sales, 2.0% farming, 12.7% construction, 13.4% production (2006-2010 5-year est.).
Income: Per capita income: $27,287 (2006-2010 5-year est.); Median household income: $55,568 (2006-2010 5-year est.); Average household income: $65,142 (2006-2010 5-year est.); Percent of households with income of $100,000 or more: 21.1% (2006-2010 5-year est.); Poverty rate: 4.7% (2006-2010 5-year est.).
Education: Percent of population age 25 and over with: High school diploma (including GED) or higher: 93.6% (2006-2010 5-year est.); Bachelor's degree or higher: 19.0% (2006-2010 5-year est.); Master's degree or higher: 5.2% (2006-2010 5-year est.).
Housing: Homeownership rate: 86.7% (2010); Median home value: $166,700 (2006-2010 5-year est.); Median contract rent: $492 per month (2006-2010 5-year est.); Median year structure built: 1980 (2006-2010 5-year est.).

Transportation: Commute to work: 93.1% car, 0.5% public transportation, 2.8% walk, 1.6% work from home (2006-2010 5-year est.); Travel time to work: 28.2% less than 15 minutes, 33.5% 15 to 30 minutes, 25.9% 30 to 45 minutes, 6.8% 45 to 60 minutes, 5.6% 60 minutes or more (2006-2010 5-year est.)

Additional Information Contacts
Delaware County Chamber of Commerce. . . . . (610) 565-3677
  http://www.delcochamber.org

HARMONY (borough). Covers a land area of 0.396 square miles and a water area of 0.005 square miles. Located at 40.80° N. Lat; 80.12° W. Long. Elevation is 919 feet.

History: First settlement (1805) of Harmony Society.
Population: 1,059 (1990); 937 (2000); 890 (2010); Density: 2,249.8 persons per square mile (2010); Race: 97.9% White, 0.1% Black, 0.4% Asian, 0.0% American Indian/Alaska Native, 0.0% Native Hawaiian/Other Pacific Islander, 1.6% Other, 1.5% Hispanic of any race (2010); Average household size: 2.29 (2010); Median age: 45.1 (2010); Males per 100 females: 91.8 (2010); Marriage status: 24.4% never married, 58.6% now married, 4.9% widowed, 12.1% divorced (2006-2010 5-year est.); Foreign born: 0.4% (2006-2010 5-year est.); Ancestry (includes multiple ancestries): 49.2% German, 28.7% Irish, 17.5% English, 13.0% Italian, 7.8% Polish (2006-2010 5-year est.).
Economy: Single-family building permits issued: 0 (2011); Multi-family building permits issued: 0 (2011); Employment by occupation: 7.0% management, 6.2% professional, 9.9% services, 15.9% sales, 7.9% farming, 5.6% construction, 4.8% production (2006-2010 5-year est.).
Income: Per capita income: $26,451 (2006-2010 5-year est.); Median household income: $52,875 (2006-2010 5-year est.); Average household income: $60,860 (2006-2010 5-year est.); Percent of households with income of $100,000 or more: 9.6% (2006-2010 5-year est.); Poverty rate: 7.7% (2006-2010 5-year est.).
Education: Percent of population age 25 and over with: High school diploma (including GED) or higher: 92.7% (2006-2010 5-year est.); Bachelor's degree or higher: 28.2% (2006-2010 5-year est.); Master's degree or higher: 7.3% (2006-2010 5-year est.).

School District(s)
Seneca Valley SD (KG-12)
  2010-11 Enrollment: 7,288 . . . . (724) 452-6040
Housing: Homeownership rate: 73.3% (2010); Median home value: $158,400 (2006-2010 5-year est.); Median contract rent: $567 per month (2006-2010 5-year est.); Median year structure built: 1955 (2006-2010 5-year est.).
Transportation: Commute to work: 91.8% car, 0.8% public transportation, 1.9% walk, 5.5% work from home (2006-2010 5-year est.); Travel time to work: 24.6% less than 15 minutes, 36.9% 15 to 30 minutes, 21.3% 30 to 45 minutes, 7.4% 45 to 60 minutes, 9.8% 60 minutes or more (2006-2010 5-year est.)

HARRISVILLE (borough). Covers a land area of 0.804 square miles and a water area of 0.003 square miles. Located at 41.14° N. Lat; 80.01° W. Long. Elevation is 1,312 feet.

Population: 862 (1990); 883 (2000); 897 (2010); Density: 1,115.9 persons per square mile (2010); Race: 96.9% White, 1.2% Black, 0.0% Asian, 0.1% American Indian/Alaska Native, 0.0% Native Hawaiian/Other Pacific Islander, 1.8% Other, 1.0% Hispanic of any race (2010); Average household size: 2.46 (2010); Median age: 44.6 (2010); Males per 100 females: 96.7 (2010); Marriage status: 23.4% never married, 55.9% now married, 12.8% widowed, 7.9% divorced (2006-2010 5-year est.); Foreign born: 2.8% (2006-2010 5-year est.); Ancestry (includes multiple ancestries): 35.2% German, 20.7% Irish, 15.1% Italian, 14.8% Scotch-Irish, 7.3% English (2006-2010 5-year est.).
Economy: Single-family building permits issued: 0 (2011); Multi-family building permits issued: 0 (2011); Employment by occupation: 3.4% management, 1.0% professional, 15.7% services, 16.4% sales, 3.1% farming, 5.8% construction, 1.4% production (2006-2010 5-year est.).
Income: Per capita income: $18,240 (2006-2010 5-year est.); Median household income: $44,125 (2006-2010 5-year est.); Average household income: $49,720 (2006-2010 5-year est.); Percent of households with income of $100,000 or more: 4.3% (2006-2010 5-year est.); Poverty rate: 5.6% (2006-2010 5-year est.).
Education: Percent of population age 25 and over with: High school diploma (including GED) or higher: 77.3% (2006-2010 5-year est.); Bachelor's degree or higher: 15.1% (2006-2010 5-year est.); Master's degree or higher: 6.2% (2006-2010 5-year est.).

School District(s)

Franklin Area SD (KG-12)

    2010-11 Enrollment: 2,068 . . . . (814) 432-8917

Slippery Rock Area SD (KG-12)

    2010-11 Enrollment: 2,220 . . . . (724) 794-2960

Housing: Homeownership rate: 74.5% (2010); Median home value: $91,600 (2006-2010 5-year est.); Median contract rent: $419 per month (2006-2010 5-year est.); Median year structure built: 1945 (2006-2010 5-year est.).

Safety: Violent crime rate: 11.1 per 10,000 population; Property crime rate: 22.2 per 10,000 population (2011).

Transportation: Commute to work: 86.1% car, 0.0% public transportation, 8.9% walk, 5.1% work from home (2006-2010 5-year est.); Travel time to work: 40.3% less than 15 minutes, 32.0% 15 to 30 minutes, 15.7% 30 to 45 minutes, 8.0% 45 to 60 minutes, 4.0% 60 minutes or more (2006-2010 5-year est.)

HILLIARDS (unincorporated postal area)

Zip Code: 16040

    Covers a land area of 19.618 square miles and a water area of 0.003 square miles. Located at 41.09° N. Lat; 79.84° W. Long. Elevation is 1,276 feet. Population: 975 (2010); Density: 49.7 persons per square mile (2010); Race: 99.0% White, 0.0% Black, 0.0% Asian, 0.0% American Indian/Alaska Native, 0.5% Native Hawaiian/Other Pacific Islander, 0.5% Other, 0.0% Hispanic of any race (2010); Average household size: 2.54 (2010); Median age: 40.3 (2010); Males per 100 females: 95.4 (2010); Homeownership rate: 80.5% (2010)

HOMEACRE-LYNDORA (CDP). Covers a land area of 6.642 square miles and a water area of 0 square miles. Located at 40.87° N. Lat; 79.92° W. Long.

Population: 7,286 (1990); 6,685 (2000); 6,906 (2010); Density: 1,039.8 persons per square mile (2010); Race: 96.7% White, 1.1% Black, 0.7% Asian, 0.0% American Indian/Alaska Native, 0.0% Native Hawaiian/Other Pacific Islander, 1.5% Other, 1.3% Hispanic of any race (2010); Average household size: 2.19 (2010); Median age: 46.2 (2010); Males per 100 females: 93.2 (2010); Marriage status: 21.8% never married, 54.4% now married, 10.4% widowed, 13.4% divorced (2006-2010 5-year est.); Foreign born: 1.2% (2006-2010 5-year est.); Ancestry (includes multiple ancestries): 43.2% German, 18.9% Irish, 12.4% English, 12.3% Italian, 9.0% Polish (2006-2010 5-year est.).

Economy: Employment by occupation: 8.0% management, 3.8% professional, 13.0% services, 18.8% sales, 2.7% farming, 6.2% construction, 4.8% production (2006-2010 5-year est.).

Income: Per capita income: $28,031 (2006-2010 5-year est.); Median household income: $49,533 (2006-2010 5-year est.); Average household income: $63,669 (2006-2010 5-year est.); Percent of households with income of $100,000 or more: 14.7% (2006-2010 5-year est.); Poverty rate: 7.3% (2006-2010 5-year est.).

Education: Percent of population age 25 and over with: High school diploma (including GED) or higher: 92.4% (2006-2010 5-year est.); Bachelor's degree or higher: 22.5% (2006-2010 5-year est.); Master's degree or higher: 7.0% (2006-2010 5-year est.).

Housing: Homeownership rate: 70.8% (2010); Median home value: $124,800 (2006-2010 5-year est.); Median contract rent: $568 per month (2006-2010 5-year est.); Median year structure built: 1959 (2006-2010 5-year est.).

Transportation: Commute to work: 93.7% car, 1.3% public transportation, 2.6% walk, 2.3% work from home (2006-2010 5-year est.); Travel time to work: 41.9% less than 15 minutes, 21.6% 15 to 30 minutes, 16.2% 30 to 45 minutes, 9.6% 45 to 60 minutes, 10.7% 60 minutes or more (2006-2010 5-year est.).

Additional Information Contacts

Butler County Chamber of Commerce . . . . (724) 283-2222

    http://www.butlercountychamber.com

JACKSON (township). Covers a land area of 21.692 square miles and a water area of 0.037 square miles. Located at 40.78° N. Lat; 80.11° W. Long.

Population: 3,073 (1990); 3,645 (2000); 3,657 (2010); Density: 168.6 persons per square mile (2010); Race: 97.8% White, 0.5% Black, 0.4% Asian, 0.1% American Indian/Alaska Native, 0.1% Native Hawaiian/Other Pacific Islander, 1.1% Other, 1.0% Hispanic of any race (2010); Average household size: 2.50 (2010); Median age: 47.2 (2010); Males per 100 females: 98.6 (2010); Marriage status: 17.7% never married, 71.5% now

married, 5.9% widowed, 4.9% divorced (2006-2010 5-year est.); Foreign born: 2.4% (2006-2010 5-year est.); Ancestry (includes multiple ancestries): 48.3% German, 29.1% Irish, 11.0% English, 10.0% Polish, 9.2% Italian (2006-2010 5-year est.).

Economy: Single-family building permits issued: 9 (2011); Multi-family building permits issued: 0 (2011); Employment by occupation: 10.7% management, 1.7% professional, 5.9% services, 18.1% sales, 6.7% farming, 13.8% construction, 8.1% production (2006-2010 5-year est.).

Income: Per capita income: $27,395 (2006-2010 5-year est.); Median household income: $71,009 (2006-2010 5-year est.); Average household income: $71,438 (2006-2010 5-year est.); Percent of households with income of $100,000 or more: 19.6% (2006-2010 5-year est.); Poverty rate: 0.8% (2006-2010 5-year est.).

Education: Percent of population age 25 and over with: High school diploma (including GED) or higher: 92.5% (2006-2010 5-year est.); Bachelor's degree or higher: 29.8% (2006-2010 5-year est.); Master's degree or higher: 5.2% (2006-2010 5-year est.).

Housing: Homeownership rate: 85.7% (2010); Median home value: $157,100 (2006-2010 5-year est.); Median contract rent: $593 per month (2006-2010 5-year est.); Median year structure built: 1977 (2006-2010 5-year est.).

Safety: Violent crime rate: 21.8 per 10,000 population; Property crime rate: 81.8 per 10,000 population (2011).

Transportation: Commute to work: 89.8% car, 0.9% public transportation, 3.1% walk, 2.5% work from home (2006-2010 5-year est.); Travel time to work: 17.2% less than 15 minutes, 27.8% 15 to 30 minutes, 27.7% 30 to 45 minutes, 10.8% 45 to 60 minutes, 16.5% 60 minutes or more (2006-2010 5-year est.)

Additional Information Contacts

Butler County Chamber of Commerce . . . . (724) 283-2222

    http://www.butlercountychamber.com

JEFFERSON (township). Covers a land area of 22.939 square miles and a water area of 0.025 square miles. Located at 40.79° N. Lat; 79.83° W. Long.

Population: 4,812 (1990); 5,690 (2000); 5,504 (2010); Density: 239.9 persons per square mile (2010); Race: 98.7% White, 0.5% Black, 0.2% Asian, 0.1% American Indian/Alaska Native, 0.0% Native Hawaiian/Other Pacific Islander, 0.5% Other, 0.6% Hispanic of any race (2010); Average household size: 2.38 (2010); Median age: 47.9 (2010); Males per 100 females: 91.0 (2010); Marriage status: 18.0% never married, 64.0% now married, 10.2% widowed, 7.7% divorced (2006-2010 5-year est.); Foreign born: 1.0% (2006-2010 5-year est.); Ancestry (includes multiple ancestries): 55.4% German, 22.5% Irish, 8.7% French, 8.0% English, 7.0% Italian (2006-2010 5-year est.).

Economy: Single-family building permits issued: 5 (2011); Multi-family building permits issued: 0 (2011); Employment by occupation: 6.9% management, 4.1% professional, 15.1% services, 14.1% sales, 3.2% farming, 8.9% construction, 9.8% production (2006-2010 5-year est.).

Income: Per capita income: $25,221 (2006-2010 5-year est.); Median household income: $54,871 (2006-2010 5-year est.); Average household income: $63,428 (2006-2010 5-year est.); Percent of households with income of $100,000 or more: 17.1% (2006-2010 5-year est.); Poverty rate: 2.1% (2006-2010 5-year est.).

Education: Percent of population age 25 and over with: High school diploma (including GED) or higher: 93.1% (2006-2010 5-year est.); Bachelor's degree or higher: 17.8% (2006-2010 5-year est.); Master's degree or higher: 4.4% (2006-2010 5-year est.).

Housing: Homeownership rate: 75.5% (2010); Median home value: $157,400 (2006-2010 5-year est.); Median contract rent: $541 per month (2006-2010 5-year est.); Median year structure built: 1980 (2006-2010 5-year est.).

Transportation: Commute to work: 95.4% car, 0.0% public transportation, 2.3% walk, 2.3% work from home (2006-2010 5-year est.); Travel time to work: 32.1% less than 15 minutes, 30.0% 15 to 30 minutes, 16.3% 30 to 45 minutes, 7.7% 45 to 60 minutes, 13.9% 60 minutes or more (2006-2010 5-year est.)

Additional Information Contacts

Butler County Chamber of Commerce . . . . (724) 283-2222

    http://www.butlercountychamber.com

Jefferson Township . . . . (724) 352-2324

    http://jeffersonbutler.com

KARNS CITY (borough). Covers a land area of 0.363 square miles and a water area of 0 square miles. Located at 41.00° N. Lat; 79.73° W. Long. Elevation is 1,234 feet.

Population: 226 (1990); 244 (2000); 209 (2010); Density: 576.3 persons per square mile (2010); Race: 100.0% White, 0.0% Black, 0.0% Asian, 0.0% American Indian/Alaska Native, 0.0% Native Hawaiian/Other Pacific Islander, 0.0% Other, 0.0% Hispanic of any race (2010); Average household size: 2.38 (2010); Median age: 42.8 (2010); Males per 100 females: 102.9 (2010); Marriage status: 37.1% never married, 44.2% now married, 4.2% widowed, 14.6% divorced (2006-2010 5-year est.); Foreign born: 0.0% (2006-2010 5-year est.); Ancestry (includes multiple ancestries): 35.8% German, 25.9% Irish, 15.4% English, 6.4% Swedish, 6.1% French (2006-2010 5-year est.).

Economy: Single-family building permits issued: 0 (2011); Multi-family building permits issued: 0 (2011); Employment by occupation: 4.0% management, 2.6% professional, 33.1% services, 4.6% sales, 4.0% farming, 17.9% construction, 13.2% production (2006-2010 5-year est.).

Income: Per capita income: $17,172 (2006-2010 5-year est.); Median household income: $56,250 (2006-2010 5-year est.); Average household income: $55,698 (2006-2010 5-year est.); Percent of households with income of $100,000 or more: 12.7% (2006-2010 5-year est.); Poverty rate: 23.2% (2006-2010 5-year est.).

Education: Percent of population age 25 and over with: High school diploma (including GED) or higher: 85.2% (2006-2010 5-year est.); Bachelor's degree or higher: 8.0% (2006-2010 5-year est.); Master's degree or higher: 2.8% (2006-2010 5-year est.).

School District(s)

Karns City Area SD (KG-12)
    2010-11 Enrollment: 1,618 . . . . (724) 756-2030

Housing: Homeownership rate: 60.3% (2010); Median home value: $86,700 (2006-2010 5-year est.); Median contract rent: $486 per month (2006-2010 5-year est.); Median year structure built: 1943 (2006-2010 5-year est.).

Transportation: Commute to work: 92.1% car, 0.0% public transportation, 7.9% walk, 0.0% work from home (2006-2010 5-year est.); Travel time to work: 43.9% less than 15 minutes, 22.3% 15 to 30 minutes, 14.4% 30 to 45 minutes, 3.6% 45 to 60 minutes, 15.8% 60 minutes or more (2006-2010 5-year est.)

LAKE ARTHUR ESTATES (CDP). Covers a land area of 0.663 square miles and a water area of 0 square miles. Located at 40.96° N. Lat; 80.15° W. Long.

Population: n/a (1990); n/a (2000); 594 (2010); Density: 895.9 persons per square mile (2010); Race: 98.3% White, 0.0% Black, 0.0% Asian, 0.5% American Indian/Alaska Native, 0.0% Native Hawaiian/Other Pacific Islander, 1.2% Other, 1.0% Hispanic of any race (2010); Average household size: 2.12 (2010); Median age: 41.3 (2010); Males per 100 females: 94.8 (2010); Marriage status: 31.1% never married, 40.8% now married, 7.3% widowed, 20.8% divorced (2006-2010 5-year est.); Foreign born: 0.0% (2006-2010 5-year est.); Ancestry (includes multiple ancestries): 67.6% German, 18.4% Irish, 15.4% Italian, 10.5% English, 9.5% Polish (2006-2010 5-year est.).

Economy: Employment by occupation: 6.7% management, 0.0% professional, 23.4% services, 18.4% sales, 2.5% farming, 8.4% construction, 13.8% production (2006-2010 5-year est.).

Income: Per capita income: $15,553 (2006-2010 5-year est.); Median household income: $29,563 (2006-2010 5-year est.); Average household income: $34,191 (2006-2010 5-year est.); Percent of households with income of $100,000 or more: n/a (2006-2010 5-year est.); Poverty rate: 29.3% (2006-2010 5-year est.).

Education: Percent of population age 25 and over with: High school diploma (including GED) or higher: 88.4% (2006-2010 5-year est.); Bachelor's degree or higher: 1.3% (2006-2010 5-year est.); Master's degree or higher: 0.0% (2006-2010 5-year est.).

Housing: Homeownership rate: 91.8% (2010); Median home value: $19,300 (2006-2010 5-year est.); Median contract rent: n/a per month (2006-2010 5-year est.); Median year structure built: 1987 (2006-2010 5-year est.).

Transportation: Commute to work: 93.0% car, 0.0% public transportation, 3.2% walk, 3.8% work from home (2006-2010 5-year est.); Travel time to work: 16.9% less than 15 minutes, 41.6% 15 to 30 minutes, 29.8% 30 to 45 minutes, 11.8% 45 to 60 minutes, 0.0% 60 minutes or more (2006-2010 5-year est.)

LANCASTER (township). Covers a land area of 23.001 square miles and a water area of 0.007 square miles. Located at 40.84° N. Lat; 80.11° W. Long.

Population: 2,268 (1990); 2,511 (2000); 2,532 (2010); Density: 110.1 persons per square mile (2010); Race: 98.5% White, 0.3% Black, 0.4% Asian, 0.0% American Indian/Alaska Native, 0.0% Native Hawaiian/Other Pacific Islander, 0.8% Other, 0.7% Hispanic of any race (2010); Average household size: 2.66 (2010); Median age: 44.7 (2010); Males per 100 females: 104.5 (2010); Marriage status: 20.6% never married, 66.1% now married, 4.5% widowed, 8.8% divorced (2006-2010 5-year est.); Foreign born: 3.4% (2006-2010 5-year est.); Ancestry (includes multiple ancestries): 49.1% German, 23.3% Irish, 13.3% English, 12.1% Italian, 5.7% American (2006-2010 5-year est.).

Economy: Single-family building permits issued: 5 (2011); Multi-family building permits issued: 0 (2011); Employment by occupation: 16.2% management, 2.6% professional, 4.4% services, 17.9% sales, 3.9% farming, 14.7% construction, 9.2% production (2006-2010 5-year est.).

Income: Per capita income: $29,721 (2006-2010 5-year est.); Median household income: $69,805 (2006-2010 5-year est.); Average household income: $80,811 (2006-2010 5-year est.); Percent of households with income of $100,000 or more: 29.1% (2006-2010 5-year est.); Poverty rate: 3.9% (2006-2010 5-year est.).

Education: Percent of population age 25 and over with: High school diploma (including GED) or higher: 89.9% (2006-2010 5-year est.); Bachelor's degree or higher: 30.5% (2006-2010 5-year est.); Master's degree or higher: 13.6% (2006-2010 5-year est.).

Housing: Homeownership rate: 88.4% (2010); Median home value: $207,700 (2006-2010 5-year est.); Median contract rent: $633 per month (2006-2010 5-year est.); Median year structure built: 1974 (2006-2010 5-year est.).

Safety: Violent crime rate: 23.6 per 10,000 population; Property crime rate: 90.6 per 10,000 population (2011).

Transportation: Commute to work: 93.3% car, 0.0% public transportation, 1.8% walk, 4.4% work from home (2006-2010 5-year est.); Travel time to work: 23.4% less than 15 minutes, 34.1% 15 to 30 minutes, 22.1% 30 to 45 minutes, 14.2% 45 to 60 minutes, 6.2% 60 minutes or more (2006-2010 5-year est.)

Additional Information Contacts

Butler County Chamber of Commerce . . . . (724) 283-2222
http://www.butlercountychamber.com

LYNDORA (unincorporated postal area)

Zip Code: 16045

    Covers a land area of 0.577 square miles and a water area of 0 square miles. Located at 40.85° N. Lat; 79.91° W. Long. Elevation is 1,207 feet. Population: 1,195 (2010); Density: 2,068.4 persons per square mile (2010); Race: 94.1% White, 2.3% Black, 0.1% Asian, 0.2% American Indian/Alaska Native, 0.0% Native Hawaiian/Other Pacific Islander, 3.3% Other, 1.8% Hispanic of any race (2010); Average household size: 2.26 (2010); Median age: 38.9 (2010); Males per 100 females: 95.3 (2010); Homeownership rate: 51.3% (2010)

MARION (township). Covers a land area of 25.436 square miles and a water area of 0 square miles. Located at 41.14° N. Lat; 79.93° W. Long.

Population: 1,113 (1990); 1,330 (2000); 1,239 (2010); Density: 48.7 persons per square mile (2010); Race: 99.3% White, 0.2% Black, 0.0% Asian, 0.2% American Indian/Alaska Native, 0.0% Native Hawaiian/Other Pacific Islander, 0.3% Other, 0.1% Hispanic of any race (2010); Average household size: 2.66 (2010); Median age: 42.1 (2010); Males per 100 females: 101.8 (2010); Marriage status: 24.1% never married, 61.6% now married, 5.4% widowed, 8.9% divorced (2006-2010 5-year est.); Foreign born: 0.1% (2006-2010 5-year est.); Ancestry (includes multiple ancestries): 44.4% German, 26.0% Irish, 18.4% Italian, 10.7% English, 6.2% Scotch-Irish (2006-2010 5-year est.).

Economy: Single-family building permits issued: 0 (2011); Multi-family building permits issued: 0 (2011); Employment by occupation: 4.0% management, 0.0% professional, 18.4% services, 11.9% sales, 2.9% farming, 19.2% construction, 9.4% production (2006-2010 5-year est.).

Income: Per capita income: $23,575 (2006-2010 5-year est.); Median household income: $50,125 (2006-2010 5-year est.); Average household income: $68,288 (2006-2010 5-year est.); Percent of households with income of $100,000 or more: 13.4% (2006-2010 5-year est.); Poverty rate: 10.2% (2006-2010 5-year est.).

Education: Percent of population age 25 and over with: High school diploma (including GED) or higher: 88.4% (2006-2010 5-year est.);

Bachelor's degree or higher: 15.9% (2006-2010 5-year est.); Master's degree or higher: 5.5% (2006-2010 5-year est.).

Housing: Homeownership rate: 85.6% (2010); Median home value: $101,200 (2006-2010 5-year est.); Median contract rent: $497 per month (2006-2010 5-year est.); Median year structure built: 1970 (2006-2010 5-year est.).

Transportation: Commute to work: 95.2% car, 0.8% public transportation, 2.0% walk, 1.5% work from home (2006-2010 5-year est.); Travel time to work: 20.7% less than 15 minutes, 36.8% 15 to 30 minutes, 23.2% 30 to 45 minutes, 8.7% 45 to 60 minutes, 10.5% 60 minutes or more (2006-2010 5-year est.)

Additional Information Contacts

Butler County Chamber of Commerce . . . . (724) 283-2222
http://www.butlercountychamber.com

MARS (borough). Covers a land area of 0.471 square miles and a water area of 0 square miles. Located at 40.70° N. Lat; 80.01° W. Long. Elevation is 1,040 feet.

History: Incorporated 1882.

Population: 1,713 (1990); 1,746 (2000); 1,699 (2010); Density: 3,609.2 persons per square mile (2010); Race: 97.3% White, 0.7% Black, 0.8% Asian, 0.0% American Indian/Alaska Native, 0.0% Native Hawaiian/Other Pacific Islander, 1.2% Other, 1.4% Hispanic of any race (2010); Average household size: 2.08 (2010); Median age: 49.5 (2010); Males per 100 females: 78.1 (2010); Marriage status: 22.5% never married, 49.4% now married, 17.2% widowed, 10.9% divorced (2006-2010 5-year est.); Foreign born: 0.9% (2006-2010 5-year est.); Ancestry (includes multiple ancestries): 43.7% German, 21.5% Irish, 16.2% English, 8.9% Italian, 6.7% Scotch-Irish (2006-2010 5-year est.).

Economy: Single-family building permits issued: 0 (2011); Multi-family building permits issued: 0 (2011); Employment by occupation: 13.8% management, 2.3% professional, 14.5% services, 21.7% sales, 6.5% farming, 8.6% construction, 3.0% production (2006-2010 5-year est.).

Income: Per capita income: $25,151 (2006-2010 5-year est.); Median household income: $53,333 (2006-2010 5-year est.); Average household income: $59,597 (2006-2010 5-year est.); Percent of households with income of $100,000 or more: 16.2% (2006-2010 5-year est.); Poverty rate: 5.4% (2006-2010 5-year est.).

Education: Percent of population age 25 and over with: High school diploma (including GED) or higher: 87.1% (2006-2010 5-year est.); Bachelor's degree or higher: 23.8% (2006-2010 5-year est.); Master's degree or higher: 6.6% (2006-2010 5-year est.).

School District(s)

Mars Area SD (KG-12)

    2010-11 Enrollment: 3,162 . . . . (724) 625-1518

Housing: Homeownership rate: 54.2% (2010); Median home value: $160,000 (2006-2010 5-year est.); Median contract rent: $457 per month (2006-2010 5-year est.); Median year structure built: 1948 (2006-2010 5-year est.).

Safety: Violent crime rate: 5.9 per 10,000 population; Property crime rate: 76.3 per 10,000 population (2011).

Transportation: Commute to work: 91.7% car, 1.7% public transportation, 5.3% walk, 1.3% work from home (2006-2010 5-year est.); Travel time to work: 39.7% less than 15 minutes, 25.1% 15 to 30 minutes, 22.2% 30 to 45 minutes, 5.1% 45 to 60 minutes, 7.8% 60 minutes or more (2006-2010 5-year est.)

Additional Information Contacts

Butler County Chamber of Commerce . . . . (724) 283-2222
http://www.butlercountychamber.com

MEADOWOOD (CDP). Covers a land area of 1.566 square miles and a water area of 0.013 square miles. Located at 40.84° N. Lat; 79.90° W. Long. Elevation is 1,306 feet.

Population: 3,011 (1990); 2,912 (2000); 2,693 (2010); Density: 1,719.2 persons per square mile (2010); Race: 97.7% White, 0.8% Black, 0.5% Asian, 0.1% American Indian/Alaska Native, 0.0% Native Hawaiian/Other Pacific Islander, 0.9% Other, 0.3% Hispanic of any race (2010); Average household size: 2.38 (2010); Median age: 49.1 (2010); Males per 100 females: 92.1 (2010); Marriage status: 25.2% never married, 54.8% now married, 6.8% widowed, 13.1% divorced (2006-2010 5-year est.); Foreign born: 1.1% (2006-2010 5-year est.); Ancestry (includes multiple ancestries): 46.2% German, 19.1% Irish, 13.3% Italian, 8.1% English, 8.0% Polish (2006-2010 5-year est.).

Economy: Employment by occupation: 5.9% management, 2.6% professional, 14.9% services, 17.4% sales, 6.9% farming, 8.7% construction, 5.4% production (2006-2010 5-year est.).

Income: Per capita income: $23,080 (2006-2010 5-year est.); Median household income: $48,304 (2006-2010 5-year est.); Average household income: $57,859 (2006-2010 5-year est.); Percent of households with income of $100,000 or more: 13.7% (2006-2010 5-year est.); Poverty rate: 11.3% (2006-2010 5-year est.).

Education: Percent of population age 25 and over with: High school diploma (including GED) or higher: 89.5% (2006-2010 5-year est.); Bachelor's degree or higher: 24.2% (2006-2010 5-year est.); Master's degree or higher: 6.0% (2006-2010 5-year est.).

Housing: Homeownership rate: 88.6% (2010); Median home value: $118,900 (2006-2010 5-year est.); Median contract rent: $504 per month (2006-2010 5-year est.); Median year structure built: 1957 (2006-2010 5-year est.).

Transportation: Commute to work: 97.2% car, 0.0% public transportation, 0.0% walk, 2.8% work from home (2006-2010 5-year est.); Travel time to work: 46.2% less than 15 minutes, 22.8% 15 to 30 minutes, 9.6% 30 to 45 minutes, 7.5% 45 to 60 minutes, 13.8% 60 minutes or more (2006-2010 5-year est.)

Additional Information Contacts

Butler County Chamber of Commerce . . . . (724) 283-2222
http://www.butlercountychamber.com

MERCER (township). Covers a land area of 12.880 square miles and a water area of 0.008 square miles. Located at 41.12° N. Lat; 80.02° W. Long.

Population: 1,110 (1990); 1,183 (2000); 1,100 (2010); Density: 85.4 persons per square mile (2010); Race: 98.9% White, 0.4% Black, 0.3% Asian, 0.0% American Indian/Alaska Native, 0.0% Native Hawaiian/Other Pacific Islander, 0.4% Other, 0.1% Hispanic of any race (2010); Average household size: 2.49 (2010); Median age: 41.9 (2010); Males per 100 females: 105.6 (2010); Marriage status: 21.0% never married, 65.6% now married, 5.4% widowed, 8.0% divorced (2006-2010 5-year est.); Foreign born: 0.6% (2006-2010 5-year est.); Ancestry (includes multiple ancestries): 53.4% German, 28.4% Irish, 13.4% Italian, 9.4% Scotch-Irish, 8.2% English (2006-2010 5-year est.).

Economy: Single-family building permits issued: 0 (2011); Multi-family building permits issued: 0 (2011); Employment by occupation: 8.4% management, 1.2% professional, 12.0% services, 20.8% sales, 3.8% farming, 15.5% construction, 6.3% production (2006-2010 5-year est.).

Income: Per capita income: $24,807 (2006-2010 5-year est.); Median household income: $52,065 (2006-2010 5-year est.); Average household income: $61,017 (2006-2010 5-year est.); Percent of households with income of $100,000 or more: 16.4% (2006-2010 5-year est.); Poverty rate: 9.6% (2006-2010 5-year est.).

Education: Percent of population age 25 and over with: High school diploma (including GED) or higher: 88.4% (2006-2010 5-year est.); Bachelor's degree or higher: 13.1% (2006-2010 5-year est.); Master's degree or higher: 1.7% (2006-2010 5-year est.).

Housing: Homeownership rate: 84.2% (2010); Median home value: $124,600 (2006-2010 5-year est.); Median contract rent: $394 per month (2006-2010 5-year est.); Median year structure built: 1970 (2006-2010 5-year est.).

Transportation: Commute to work: 96.4% car, 0.0% public transportation, 2.0% walk, 1.7% work from home (2006-2010 5-year est.); Travel time to work: 36.0% less than 15 minutes, 29.5% 15 to 30 minutes, 17.5% 30 to 45 minutes, 9.4% 45 to 60 minutes, 7.5% 60 minutes or more (2006-2010 5-year est.)

Additional Information Contacts

Mercer Area Chamber of Commerce . . . . (724) 662-4185
http://www.mercerareachamber.com

MERIDIAN (CDP). Covers a land area of 2.817 square miles and a water area of 0.005 square miles. Located at 40.85° N. Lat; 79.95° W. Long. Elevation is 1,273 feet.

Population: 3,473 (1990); 3,794 (2000); 3,881 (2010); Density: 1,377.9 persons per square mile (2010); Race: 98.2% White, 0.4% Black, 0.2% Asian, 0.1% American Indian/Alaska Native, 0.1% Native Hawaiian/Other Pacific Islander, 1.0% Other, 1.1% Hispanic of any race (2010); Average household size: 2.48 (2010); Median age: 44.7 (2010); Males per 100 females: 95.8 (2010); Marriage status: 20.4% never married, 65.3% now married, 6.8% widowed, 7.4% divorced (2006-2010 5-year est.); Foreign born: 1.5% (2006-2010 5-year est.); Ancestry (includes multiple

ancestries): 44.3% German, 14.7% Irish, 14.2% Italian, 13.2% English, 7.9% Polish (2006-2010 5-year est.).

Economy: Employment by occupation: 11.1% management, 4.1% professional, 5.9% services, 21.1% sales, 2.5% farming, 2.9% construction, 2.4% production (2006-2010 5-year est.).

Income: Per capita income: $32,200 (2006-2010 5-year est.); Median household income: $63,304 (2006-2010 5-year est.); Average household income: $82,237 (2006-2010 5-year est.); Percent of households with income of $100,000 or more: 29.0% (2006-2010 5-year est.); Poverty rate: 5.8% (2006-2010 5-year est.).

Education: Percent of population age 25 and over with: High school diploma (including GED) or higher: 92.6% (2006-2010 5-year est.); Bachelor's degree or higher: 28.5% (2006-2010 5-year est.); Master's degree or higher: 9.4% (2006-2010 5-year est.).

Housing: Homeownership rate: 89.4% (2010); Median home value: $162,700 (2006-2010 5-year est.); Median contract rent: $449 per month (2006-2010 5-year est.); Median year structure built: 1967 (2006-2010 5-year est.).

Transportation: Commute to work: 96.3% car, 0.0% public transportation, 0.7% walk, 2.4% work from home (2006-2010 5-year est.); Travel time to work: 43.4% less than 15 minutes, 30.0% 15 to 30 minutes, 9.4% 30 to 45 minutes, 9.0% 45 to 60 minutes, 8.1% 60 minutes or more (2006-2010 5-year est.)

Additional Information Contacts
Butler County Chamber of Commerce . . . . (724) 283-2222
   http://www.butlercountychamber.com

MIDDLESEX (township). Covers a land area of 23.145 square miles and a water area of 0.073 square miles. Located at 40.71° N. Lat; 79.93° W. Long.

Population: 5,578 (1990); 5,586 (2000); 5,390 (2010); Density: 232.9 persons per square mile (2010); Race: 98.6% White, 0.3% Black, 0.5% Asian, 0.1% American Indian/Alaska Native, 0.0% Native Hawaiian/Other Pacific Islander, 0.5% Other, 0.8% Hispanic of any race (2010); Average household size: 2.55 (2010); Median age: 45.7 (2010); Males per 100 females: 100.1 (2010); Marriage status: 24.5% never married, 63.8% now married, 4.7% widowed, 7.0% divorced (2006-2010 5-year est.); Foreign born: 0.4% (2006-2010 5-year est.); Ancestry (includes multiple ancestries): 43.9% German, 26.0% Irish, 17.5% Italian, 7.7% Polish, 6.5% English (2006-2010 5-year est.).

Economy: Single-family building permits issued: 25 (2011); Multi-family building permits issued: 0 (2011); Employment by occupation: 7.8% management, 4.0% professional, 12.8% services, 19.3% sales, 3.9% farming, 14.7% construction, 10.7% production (2006-2010 5-year est.).

Income: Per capita income: $27,568 (2006-2010 5-year est.); Median household income: $68,734 (2006-2010 5-year est.); Average household income: $75,401 (2006-2010 5-year est.); Percent of households with income of $100,000 or more: 23.7% (2006-2010 5-year est.); Poverty rate: 8.9% (2006-2010 5-year est.).

Education: Percent of population age 25 and over with: High school diploma (including GED) or higher: 94.1% (2006-2010 5-year est.); Bachelor's degree or higher: 25.9% (2006-2010 5-year est.); Master's degree or higher: 7.0% (2006-2010 5-year est.).

Housing: Homeownership rate: 90.0% (2010); Median home value: $168,000 (2006-2010 5-year est.); Median contract rent: $511 per month (2006-2010 5-year est.); Median year structure built: 1969 (2006-2010 5-year est.).

Safety: Violent crime rate: 1.8 per 10,000 population; Property crime rate: 62.9 per 10,000 population (2011).

Transportation: Commute to work: 94.1% car, 0.5% public transportation, 0.4% walk, 3.3% work from home (2006-2010 5-year est.); Travel time to work: 26.2% less than 15 minutes, 38.5% 15 to 30 minutes, 16.7% 30 to 45 minutes, 11.3% 45 to 60 minutes, 7.3% 60 minutes or more (2006-2010 5-year est.)

Additional Information Contacts
Butler County Chamber of Commerce . . . . (724) 283-2222
   http://www.butlercountychamber.com
Middlesex Township . . . . (717) 249-4409
   http://www.middlesextownship.com

MUDDY CREEK (township). Covers a land area of 22.423 square miles and a water area of 1.970 square miles. Located at 40.93° N. Lat; 80.12° W. Long. Elevation is 1,220 feet.

Population: 2,139 (1990); 2,267 (2000); 2,254 (2010); Density: 100.5 persons per square mile (2010); Race: 97.9% White, 0.3% Black, 0.4%

Asian, 0.3% American Indian/Alaska Native, 0.0% Native Hawaiian/Other Pacific Islander, 1.1% Other, 0.8% Hispanic of any race (2010); Average household size: 2.38 (2010); Median age: 44.2 (2010); Males per 100 females: 98.6 (2010); Marriage status: 24.1% never married, 57.9% now married, 6.0% widowed, 12.1% divorced (2006-2010 5-year est.); Foreign born: 1.2% (2006-2010 5-year est.); Ancestry (includes multiple ancestries): 50.0% German, 20.6% Irish, 10.8% English, 8.4% Italian, 7.8% Scotch-Irish (2006-2010 5-year est.).

Economy: Single-family building permits issued: 3 (2011); Multi-family building permits issued: 0 (2011); Employment by occupation: 5.9% management, 2.3% professional, 11.6% services, 21.1% sales, 2.2% farming, 13.8% construction, 7.0% production (2006-2010 5-year est.).

Income: Per capita income: $23,930 (2006-2010 5-year est.); Median household income: $47,413 (2006-2010 5-year est.); Average household income: $55,307 (2006-2010 5-year est.); Percent of households with income of $100,000 or more: 14.5% (2006-2010 5-year est.); Poverty rate: 12.0% (2006-2010 5-year est.).

Education: Percent of population age 25 and over with: High school diploma (including GED) or higher: 91.1% (2006-2010 5-year est.); Bachelor's degree or higher: 20.2% (2006-2010 5-year est.); Master's degree or higher: 8.3% (2006-2010 5-year est.).

Housing: Homeownership rate: 88.4% (2010); Median home value: $116,300 (2006-2010 5-year est.); Median contract rent: $542 per month (2006-2010 5-year est.); Median year structure built: 1979 (2006-2010 5-year est.).

Transportation: Commute to work: 90.4% car, 1.3% public transportation, 3.8% walk, 3.9% work from home (2006-2010 5-year est.); Travel time to work: 17.9% less than 15 minutes, 37.9% 15 to 30 minutes, 24.4% 30 to 45 minutes, 10.0% 45 to 60 minutes, 9.7% 60 minutes or more (2006-2010 5-year est.)

Additional Information Contacts
Zelienople-Harmony Area Chamber of Commerce . . . . (724) 452-5232
   http://www.zhchamber.com

NIXON (CDP). Covers a land area of 2.691 square miles and a water area of 0.010 square miles. Located at 40.79° N. Lat; 79.94° W. Long. Elevation is 1,220 feet.

Population: 1,355 (1990); 1,404 (2000); 1,373 (2010); Density: 510.3 persons per square mile (2010); Race: 98.0% White, 0.1% Black, 1.2% Asian, 0.0% American Indian/Alaska Native, 0.0% Native Hawaiian/Other Pacific Islander, 0.7% Other, 0.5% Hispanic of any race (2010); Average household size: 2.63 (2010); Median age: 47.0 (2010); Males per 100 females: 109.0 (2010); Marriage status: 12.3% never married, 76.8% now married, 4.0% widowed, 6.9% divorced (2006-2010 5-year est.); Foreign born: 1.5% (2006-2010 5-year est.); Ancestry (includes multiple ancestries): 46.9% German, 29.6% Irish, 16.4% Italian, 9.2% English, 6.7% Russian (2006-2010 5-year est.).

Economy: Employment by occupation: 13.3% management, 2.2% professional, 7.2% services, 13.5% sales, 0.0% farming, 7.6% construction, 6.1% production (2006-2010 5-year est.).

Income: Per capita income: $34,153 (2006-2010 5-year est.); Median household income: $74,596 (2006-2010 5-year est.); Average household income: $89,959 (2006-2010 5-year est.); Percent of households with income of $100,000 or more: 39.1% (2006-2010 5-year est.); Poverty rate: 1.2% (2006-2010 5-year est.).

Education: Percent of population age 25 and over with: High school diploma (including GED) or higher: 95.4% (2006-2010 5-year est.); Bachelor's degree or higher: 47.4% (2006-2010 5-year est.); Master's degree or higher: 20.6% (2006-2010 5-year est.).

Housing: Homeownership rate: 94.7% (2010); Median home value: $224,500 (2006-2010 5-year est.); Median contract rent: n/a per month (2006-2010 5-year est.); Median year structure built: 1967 (2006-2010 5-year est.).

Transportation: Commute to work: 90.8% car, 3.8% public transportation, 0.0% walk, 4.1% work from home (2006-2010 5-year est.); Travel time to work: 21.5% less than 15 minutes, 47.2% 15 to 30 minutes, 16.4% 30 to 45 minutes, 5.1% 45 to 60 minutes, 9.8% 60 minutes or more (2006-2010 5-year est.)

Additional Information Contacts
Butler County Chamber of Commerce . . . . (724) 283-2222
   http://www.butlercountychamber.com

NORTH WASHINGTON (unincorporated postal area)
Zip Code: 16048

Covers a land area of 1.104 square miles and a water area of 0 square miles. Located at 41.05° N. Lat; 79.81° W. Long. Population: 139 (2010); Density: 125.8 persons per square mile (2010); Race: 97.8% White, 0.0% Black, 1.4% Asian, 0.0% American Indian/Alaska Native, 0.0% Native Hawaiian/Other Pacific Islander, 0.8% Other, 0.0% Hispanic of any race (2010); Average household size: 2.84 (2010); Median age: 46.1 (2010); Males per 100 females: 107.5 (2010); Homeownership rate: 83.7% (2010)

OAK HILLS (CDP). Covers a land area of 3.350 square miles and a water area of 0 square miles. Located at 40.83° N. Lat; 79.92° W. Long. Elevation is 1,224 feet.

Population: 2,245 (1990); 2,335 (2000); 2,333 (2010); Density: 696.5 persons per square mile (2010); Race: 97.0% White, 1.2% Black, 0.4% Asian, 0.1% American Indian/Alaska Native, 0.0% Native Hawaiian/Other Pacific Islander, 1.3% Other, 1.2% Hispanic of any race (2010); Average household size: 2.19 (2010); Median age: 43.9 (2010); Males per 100 females: 91.4 (2010); Marriage status: 27.4% never married, 58.8% now married, 6.2% widowed, 7.6% divorced (2006-2010 5-year est.); Foreign born: 0.4% (2006-2010 5-year est.); Ancestry (includes multiple ancestries): 31.9% German, 19.6% Irish, 19.5% Italian, 14.5% Polish, 7.9% Slovak (2006-2010 5-year est.).

Economy: Employment by occupation: 7.5% management, 9.1% professional, 9.4% services, 15.3% sales, 6.1% farming, 4.7% construction, 2.4% production (2006-2010 5-year est.).

Income: Per capita income: $31,025 (2006-2010 5-year est.); Median household income: $65,061 (2006-2010 5-year est.); Average household income: $76,945 (2006-2010 5-year est.); Percent of households with income of $100,000 or more: 27.5% (2006-2010 5-year est.); Poverty rate: 9.8% (2006-2010 5-year est.).

Education: Percent of population age 25 and over with: High school diploma (including GED) or higher: 90.7% (2006-2010 5-year est.); Bachelor's degree or higher: 31.3% (2006-2010 5-year est.); Master's degree or higher: 9.8% (2006-2010 5-year est.).

Housing: Homeownership rate: 59.3% (2010); Median home value: $165,400 (2006-2010 5-year est.); Median contract rent: $594 per month (2006-2010 5-year est.); Median year structure built: 1972 (2006-2010 5-year est.).

Transportation: Commute to work: 95.1% car, 0.0% public transportation, 1.4% walk, 3.6% work from home (2006-2010 5-year est.); Travel time to work: 30.3% less than 15 minutes, 38.2% 15 to 30 minutes, 17.0% 30 to 45 minutes, 7.6% 45 to 60 minutes, 6.9% 60 minutes or more (2006-2010 5-year est.).

Additional Information Contacts
Butler County Chamber of Commerce . . . . (724) 283-2222
http://www.butlercountychamber.com

OAKLAND (township). Covers a land area of 23.683 square miles and a water area of 0.328 square miles. Located at 40.92° N. Lat; 79.83° W. Long.

Population: 2,820 (1990); 3,074 (2000); 2,987 (2010); Density: 126.1 persons per square mile (2010); Race: 99.1% White, 0.1% Black, 0.2% Asian, 0.2% American Indian/Alaska Native, 0.0% Native Hawaiian/Other Pacific Islander, 0.4% Other, 0.2% Hispanic of any race (2010); Average household size: 2.62 (2010); Median age: 43.1 (2010); Males per 100 females: 105.4 (2010); Marriage status: 25.2% never married, 62.0% now married, 6.3% widowed, 6.5% divorced (2006-2010 5-year est.); Foreign born: 0.5% (2006-2010 5-year est.); Ancestry (includes multiple ancestries): 53.4% German, 28.4% Irish, 8.4% Scotch-Irish, 6.9% Italian, 5.9% French (2006-2010 5-year est.).

Economy: Single-family building permits issued: 2 (2011); Multi-family building permits issued: 0 (2011); Employment by occupation: 5.3% management, 5.9% professional, 7.6% services, 18.4% sales, 2.8% farming, 13.3% construction, 8.6% production (2006-2010 5-year est.).

Income: Per capita income: $26,021 (2006-2010 5-year est.); Median household income: $53,380 (2006-2010 5-year est.); Average household income: $63,904 (2006-2010 5-year est.); Percent of households with income of $100,000 or more: 15.9% (2006-2010 5-year est.); Poverty rate: 6.5% (2006-2010 5-year est.).

Education: Percent of population age 25 and over with: High school diploma (including GED) or higher: 91.0% (2006-2010 5-year est.); Bachelor's degree or higher: 16.2% (2006-2010 5-year est.); Master's degree or higher: 3.3% (2006-2010 5-year est.).

Housing: Homeownership rate: 86.6% (2010); Median home value: $134,600 (2006-2010 5-year est.); Median contract rent: $569 per month

(2006-2010 5-year est.); Median year structure built: 1977 (2006-2010 5-year est.).

Transportation: Commute to work: 97.5% car, 0.0% public transportation, 1.0% walk, 1.4% work from home (2006-2010 5-year est.); Travel time to work: 21.8% less than 15 minutes, 40.8% 15 to 30 minutes, 16.6% 30 to 45 minutes, 9.8% 45 to 60 minutes, 11.0% 60 minutes or more (2006-2010 5-year est.).

Additional Information Contacts
Butler County Chamber of Commerce . . . . (724) 283-2222
http://www.butlercountychamber.com

PARKER (township). Covers a land area of 22.942 square miles and a water area of 0 square miles. Located at 41.07° N. Lat; 79.74° W. Long.

Population: 601 (1990); 700 (2000); 632 (2010); Density: 27.5 persons per square mile (2010); Race: 98.9% White, 0.3% Black, 0.0% Asian, 0.3% American Indian/Alaska Native, 0.5% Native Hawaiian/Other Pacific Islander, 0.0% Other, 0.2% Hispanic of any race (2010); Average household size: 2.44 (2010); Median age: 44.3 (2010); Males per 100 females: 91.5 (2010); Marriage status: 18.7% never married, 61.6% now married, 12.3% widowed, 7.5% divorced (2006-2010 5-year est.); Foreign born: 0.0% (2006-2010 5-year est.); Ancestry (includes multiple ancestries): 34.8% German, 31.7% Irish, 14.4% English, 10.9% Italian, 9.0% American (2006-2010 5-year est.).

Economy: Single-family building permits issued: 3 (2011); Multi-family building permits issued: 0 (2011); Employment by occupation: 5.7% management, 1.7% professional, 16.0% services, 12.6% sales, 12.0% farming, 18.9% construction, 3.4% production (2006-2010 5-year est.).

Income: Per capita income: $24,657 (2006-2010 5-year est.); Median household income: $44,750 (2006-2010 5-year est.); Average household income: $55,215 (2006-2010 5-year est.); Percent of households with income of $100,000 or more: 12.3% (2006-2010 5-year est.); Poverty rate: 6.6% (2006-2010 5-year est.).

Education: Percent of population age 25 and over with: High school diploma (including GED) or higher: 91.8% (2006-2010 5-year est.); Bachelor's degree or higher: 7.3% (2006-2010 5-year est.); Master's degree or higher: 2.1% (2006-2010 5-year est.).

Housing: Homeownership rate: 83.8% (2010); Median home value: $94,300 (2006-2010 5-year est.); Median contract rent: $325 per month (2006-2010 5-year est.); Median year structure built: 1973 (2006-2010 5-year est.).

Transportation: Commute to work: 97.7% car, 0.0% public transportation, 0.0% walk, 2.3% work from home (2006-2010 5-year est.); Travel time to work: 8.2% less than 15 minutes, 31.0% 15 to 30 minutes, 30.4% 30 to 45 minutes, 8.8% 45 to 60 minutes, 21.6% 60 minutes or more (2006-2010 5-year est.).

PENN (township). Covers a land area of 24.271 square miles and a water area of 0.018 square miles. Located at 40.79° N. Lat; 79.93° W. Long.

Population: 5,080 (1990); 5,210 (2000); 5,071 (2010); Density: 208.9 persons per square mile (2010); Race: 98.5% White, 0.2% Black, 0.5% Asian, 0.1% American Indian/Alaska Native, 0.1% Native Hawaiian/Other Pacific Islander, 0.6% Other, 0.8% Hispanic of any race (2010); Average household size: 2.58 (2010); Median age: 46.2 (2010); Males per 100 females: 103.7 (2010); Marriage status: 21.7% never married, 69.7% now married, 3.3% widowed, 5.3% divorced (2006-2010 5-year est.); Foreign born: 0.8% (2006-2010 5-year est.); Ancestry (includes multiple ancestries): 45.2% German, 19.8% Irish, 16.3% Italian, 9.6% Polish, 8.1% English (2006-2010 5-year est.).

Economy: Single-family building permits issued: 3 (2011); Multi-family building permits issued: 0 (2011); Employment by occupation: 15.9% management, 3.7% professional, 7.2% services, 15.4% sales, 2.5% farming, 13.1% construction, 6.3% production (2006-2010 5-year est.).

Income: Per capita income: $31,439 (2006-2010 5-year est.); Median household income: $69,875 (2006-2010 5-year est.); Average household income: $86,282 (2006-2010 5-year est.); Percent of households with income of $100,000 or more: 31.4% (2006-2010 5-year est.); Poverty rate: 0.7% (2006-2010 5-year est.).

Education: Percent of population age 25 and over with: High school diploma (including GED) or higher: 92.9% (2006-2010 5-year est.); Bachelor's degree or higher: 31.2% (2006-2010 5-year est.); Master's degree or higher: 10.9% (2006-2010 5-year est.).

Housing: Homeownership rate: 89.1% (2010); Median home value: $189,600 (2006-2010 5-year est.); Median contract rent: $245 per month

(2006-2010 5-year est.); Median year structure built: 1965 (2006-2010 5-year est.).

Safety: Violent crime rate: 5.9 per 10,000 population; Property crime rate: 80.6 per 10,000 population (2011).

Transportation: Commute to work: 93.6% car, 1.0% public transportation, 0.0% walk, 4.6% work from home (2006-2010 5-year est.); Travel time to work: 26.6% less than 15 minutes, 35.3% 15 to 30 minutes, 17.9% 30 to 45 minutes, 9.1% 45 to 60 minutes, 11.1% 60 minutes or more (2006-2010 5-year est.)

Additional Information Contacts

Butler County Chamber of Commerce . . . . (724) 283-2222
   http://www.butlercountychamber.com
Penn Township . . . . (724) 586-1165
   http://www.penntownship.org

PETROLIA (borough). Covers a land area of 0.396 square miles and a water area of 0 square miles. Located at 41.02° N. Lat; 79.72° W. Long. Elevation is 1,175 feet.

History: Former oil producing center.

Population: 292 (1990); 218 (2000); 212 (2010); Density: 535.2 persons per square mile (2010); Race: 100.0% White, 0.0% Black, 0.0% Asian, 0.0% American Indian/Alaska Native, 0.0% Native Hawaiian/Other Pacific Islander, 0.0% Other, 0.5% Hispanic of any race (2010); Average household size: 2.49 (2010); Median age: 36.8 (2010); Males per 100 females: 98.1 (2010); Marriage status: 25.9% never married, 51.1% now married, 1.5% widowed, 21.5% divorced (2006-2010 5-year est.); Foreign born: 0.0% (2006-2010 5-year est.); Ancestry (includes multiple ancestries): 62.4% German, 27.1% Irish, 12.9% American, 8.2% Italian, 5.9% English (2006-2010 5-year est.).

Economy: Single-family building permits issued: 0 (2011); Multi-family building permits issued: 0 (2011); Employment by occupation: 10.7% management, 2.7% professional, 16.0% services, 18.7% sales, 0.0% farming, 20.0% construction, 10.7% production (2006-2010 5-year est.).

Income: Per capita income: $18,367 (2006-2010 5-year est.); Median household income: $37,946 (2006-2010 5-year est.); Average household income: $45,455 (2006-2010 5-year est.); Percent of households with income of $100,000 or more: 11.3% (2006-2010 5-year est.); Poverty rate: 28.5% (2006-2010 5-year est.).

Education: Percent of population age 25 and over with: High school diploma (including GED) or higher: 94.1% (2006-2010 5-year est.); Bachelor's degree or higher: 3.4% (2006-2010 5-year est.); Master's degree or higher: 0.0% (2006-2010 5-year est.).

Housing: Homeownership rate: 81.2% (2010); Median home value: $64,500 (2006-2010 5-year est.); Median contract rent: $505 per month (2006-2010 5-year est.); Median year structure built: 1947 (2006-2010 5-year est.).

Transportation: Commute to work: 94.7% car, 0.0% public transportation, 5.3% walk, 0.0% work from home (2006-2010 5-year est.); Travel time to work: 10.7% less than 15 minutes, 33.3% 15 to 30 minutes, 33.3% 30 to 45 minutes, 2.7% 45 to 60 minutes, 20.0% 60 minutes or more (2006-2010 5-year est.)

PORTERSVILLE (borough). Covers a land area of 0.795 square miles and a water area of 0 square miles. Located at 40.92° N. Lat; 80.15° W. Long. Elevation is 1,362 feet.

Population: 307 (1990); 268 (2000); 235 (2010); Density: 295.6 persons per square mile (2010); Race: 99.1% White, 0.0% Black, 0.0% Asian, 0.0% American Indian/Alaska Native, 0.0% Native Hawaiian/Other Pacific Islander, 0.9% Other, 0.9% Hispanic of any race (2010); Average household size: 2.26 (2010); Median age: 46.3 (2010); Males per 100 females: 100.9 (2010); Marriage status: 22.8% never married, 64.8% now married, 2.7% widowed, 9.6% divorced (2006-2010 5-year est.); Foreign born: 0.0% (2006-2010 5-year est.); Ancestry (includes multiple ancestries): 56.5% German, 19.6% Irish, 7.8% Dutch, 5.9% English, 4.7% American (2006-2010 5-year est.).

Economy: Single-family building permits issued: 0 (2011); Multi-family building permits issued: 0 (2011); Employment by occupation: 2.8% management, 3.5% professional, 7.6% services, 27.8% sales, 2.8% farming, 12.5% construction, 5.6% production (2006-2010 5-year est.).

Income: Per capita income: $24,354 (2006-2010 5-year est.); Median household income: $47,813 (2006-2010 5-year est.); Average household income: $55,688 (2006-2010 5-year est.); Percent of households with income of $100,000 or more: 9.0% (2006-2010 5-year est.); Poverty rate: 2.7% (2006-2010 5-year est.).

Education: Percent of population age 25 and over with: High school diploma (including GED) or higher: 96.8% (2006-2010 5-year est.); Bachelor's degree or higher: 24.9% (2006-2010 5-year est.); Master's degree or higher: 5.9% (2006-2010 5-year est.).

Housing: Homeownership rate: 76.0% (2010); Median home value: $104,400 (2006-2010 5-year est.); Median contract rent: $521 per month (2006-2010 5-year est.); Median year structure built: 1949 (2006-2010 5-year est.).

Transportation: Commute to work: 90.1% car, 0.0% public transportation, 3.5% walk, 6.3% work from home (2006-2010 5-year est.); Travel time to work: 30.8% less than 15 minutes, 42.9% 15 to 30 minutes, 23.3% 30 to 45 minutes, 1.5% 45 to 60 minutes, 1.5% 60 minutes or more (2006-2010 5-year est.)

PROSPECT (borough). Covers a land area of 4.082 square miles and a water area of 0 square miles. Located at 40.90° N. Lat; 80.05° W. Long. Elevation is 1,375 feet.

Population: 1,122 (1990); 1,234 (2000); 1,169 (2010); Density: 286.4 persons per square mile (2010); Race: 98.2% White, 0.3% Black, 0.4% Asian, 0.1% American Indian/Alaska Native, 0.0% Native Hawaiian/Other Pacific Islander, 1.0% Other, 0.7% Hispanic of any race (2010); Average household size: 2.44 (2010); Median age: 42.7 (2010); Males per 100 females: 102.6 (2010); Marriage status: 27.7% never married, 52.2% now married, 9.5% widowed, 10.6% divorced (2006-2010 5-year est.); Foreign born: 1.7% (2006-2010 5-year est.); Ancestry (includes multiple ancestries): 43.7% German, 20.4% Irish, 13.3% Italian, 10.3% English, 7.4% American (2006-2010 5-year est.).

Economy: Single-family building permits issued: 0 (2011); Multi-family building permits issued: 0 (2011); Employment by occupation: 8.5% management, 4.6% professional, 11.5% services, 11.8% sales, 2.5% farming, 10.4% construction, 9.5% production (2006-2010 5-year est.).

Income: Per capita income: $25,656 (2006-2010 5-year est.); Median household income: $46,719 (2006-2010 5-year est.); Average household income: $59,981 (2006-2010 5-year est.); Percent of households with income of $100,000 or more: 13.4% (2006-2010 5-year est.); Poverty rate: 10.6% (2006-2010 5-year est.).

Education: Percent of population age 25 and over with: High school diploma (including GED) or higher: 86.9% (2006-2010 5-year est.); Bachelor's degree or higher: 20.7% (2006-2010 5-year est.); Master's degree or higher: 5.1% (2006-2010 5-year est.).

School District(s)

Slippery Rock Area SD (KG-12)
   2010-11 Enrollment: 2,220 . . . . (724) 794-2960

Housing: Homeownership rate: 85.8% (2010); Median home value: $129,400 (2006-2010 5-year est.); Median contract rent: $516 per month (2006-2010 5-year est.); Median year structure built: 1972 (2006-2010 5-year est.).

Transportation: Commute to work: 93.3% car, 0.0% public transportation, 0.5% walk, 4.5% work from home (2006-2010 5-year est.); Travel time to work: 20.9% less than 15 minutes, 41.6% 15 to 30 minutes, 20.0% 30 to 45 minutes, 10.3% 45 to 60 minutes, 7.2% 60 minutes or more (2006-2010 5-year est.)

Additional Information Contacts

Butler County Chamber of Commerce . . . . (724) 283-2222
   http://www.butlercountychamber.com

RENFREW (unincorporated postal area)

Zip Code: 16053

   Covers a land area of 21.454 square miles and a water area of 0 square miles. Located at 40.81° N. Lat; 79.98° W. Long. Elevation is 978 feet. Population: 4,020 (2010); Density: 187.4 persons per square mile (2010); Race: 98.4% White, 0.1% Black, 0.6% Asian, 0.2% American Indian/Alaska Native, 0.0% Native Hawaiian/Other Pacific Islander, 0.7% Other, 0.5% Hispanic of any race (2010); Average household size: 2.47 (2010); Median age: 46.2 (2010); Males per 100 females: 98.9 (2010); Homeownership rate: 89.5% (2010)

SARVER (unincorporated postal area)

Zip Code: 16055

   Covers a land area of 38.944 square miles and a water area of 0.086 square miles. Located at 40.71° N. Lat; 79.74° W. Long. Elevation is 1,099 feet. Population: 8,486 (2010); Density: 217.9 persons per square mile (2010); Race: 98.5% White, 0.3% Black, 0.4% Asian, 0.1% American Indian/Alaska Native, 0.0% Native Hawaiian/Other Pacific Islander, 0.7% Other, 0.7% Hispanic of any race (2010); Average

household size: 2.57 (2010); Median age: 44.1 (2010); Males per 100 females: 98.9 (2010); Homeownership rate: 87.5% (2010)

SAXONBURG (borough). Covers a land area of 0.906 square miles and a water area of 0 square miles. Located at 40.75° N. Lat; 79.82° W. Long. Elevation is 1,296 feet.
Population: 1,345 (1990); 1,629 (2000); 1,525 (2010); Density: 1,683.3 persons per square mile (2010); Race: 99.2% White, 0.0% Black, 0.2% Asian, 0.0% American Indian/Alaska Native, 0.0% Native Hawaiian/Other Pacific Islander, 0.6% Other, 0.7% Hispanic of any race (2010); Average household size: 1.92 (2010); Median age: 53.1 (2010); Males per 100 females: 77.5 (2010); Marriage status: 19.4% never married, 47.7% now married, 28.2% widowed, 4.6% divorced (2006-2010 5-year est.); Foreign born: 0.5% (2006-2010 5-year est.); Ancestry (includes multiple ancestries): 33.1% German, 13.5% Irish, 12.3% Italian, 7.5% English, 6.8% Polish (2006-2010 5-year est.).
Economy: Single-family building permits issued: 5 (2011); Multi-family building permits issued: 0 (2011); Employment by occupation: 14.4% management, 3.4% professional, 13.4% services, 17.5% sales, 3.1% farming, 8.1% construction, 8.5% production (2006-2010 5-year est.).
Income: Per capita income: $25,133 (2006-2010 5-year est.); Median household income: $41,691 (2006-2010 5-year est.); Average household income: $55,180 (2006-2010 5-year est.); Percent of households with income of $100,000 or more: 12.0% (2006-2010 5-year est.); Poverty rate: 4.6% (2006-2010 5-year est.).
Education: Percent of population age 25 and over with: High school diploma (including GED) or higher: 87.7% (2006-2010 5-year est.); Bachelor's degree or higher: 17.5% (2006-2010 5-year est.); Master's degree or higher: 4.0% (2006-2010 5-year est.).
School District(s)
South Butler County SD (KG-12)
   2010-11 Enrollment: 2,658 . . . . (724) 352-1700
Housing: Homeownership rate: 58.4% (2010); Median home value: $142,900 (2006-2010 5-year est.); Median contract rent: $505 per month (2006-2010 5-year est.); Median year structure built: 1975 (2006-2010 5-year est.).
Transportation: Commute to work: 93.0% car, 0.4% public transportation, 2.2% walk, 3.9% work from home (2006-2010 5-year est.); Travel time to work: 30.4% less than 15 minutes, 36.3% 15 to 30 minutes, 20.5% 30 to 45 minutes, 8.2% 45 to 60 minutes, 4.6% 60 minutes or more (2006-2010 5-year est.)
Additional Information Contacts
Borough of Saxonburg . . . . (724) 352-1400
   http://www.saxonburgpa.org
Butler County Chamber of Commerce . . . . (724) 283-2222
   http://www.butlercountychamber.com

SEVEN FIELDS (borough). Covers a land area of 0.805 square miles and a water area of 0 square miles. Located at 40.69° N. Lat; 80.06° W. Long. Elevation is 1,106 feet.
Population: 608 (1990); 1,986 (2000); 2,887 (2010); Density: 3,585.1 persons per square mile (2010); Race: 93.0% White, 2.2% Black, 2.9% Asian, 0.0% American Indian/Alaska Native, 0.0% Native Hawaiian/Other Pacific Islander, 1.9% Other, 1.7% Hispanic of any race (2010); Average household size: 2.43 (2010); Median age: 36.3 (2010); Males per 100 females: 95.5 (2010); Marriage status: 18.4% never married, 69.8% now married, 3.1% widowed, 8.7% divorced (2006-2010 5-year est.); Foreign born: 4.6% (2006-2010 5-year est.); Ancestry (includes multiple ancestries): 34.5% German, 20.1% Irish, 18.4% Italian, 11.5% Polish, 9.4% English (2006-2010 5-year est.).
Economy: Single-family building permits issued: 0 (2011); Multi-family building permits issued: 5 (2011); Employment by occupation: 19.4% management, 11.2% professional, 6.0% services, 11.2% sales, 7.0% farming, 1.1% construction, 1.2% production (2006-2010 5-year est.).
Income: Per capita income: $43,305 (2006-2010 5-year est.); Median household income: $87,426 (2006-2010 5-year est.); Average household income: $107,843 (2006-2010 5-year est.); Percent of households with income of $100,000 or more: 45.3% (2006-2010 5-year est.); Poverty rate: 2.3% (2006-2010 5-year est.).
Education: Percent of population age 25 and over with: High school diploma (including GED) or higher: 99.3% (2006-2010 5-year est.); Bachelor's degree or higher: 65.8% (2006-2010 5-year est.); Master's degree or higher: 18.6% (2006-2010 5-year est.).
Housing: Homeownership rate: 73.0% (2010); Median home value: $267,400 (2006-2010 5-year est.); Median contract rent: $951 per month

(2006-2010 5-year est.); Median year structure built: 1997 (2006-2010 5-year est.).
Transportation: Commute to work: 88.2% car, 1.2% public transportation, 0.8% walk, 9.4% work from home (2006-2010 5-year est.); Travel time to work: 26.3% less than 15 minutes, 14.8% 15 to 30 minutes, 40.1% 30 to 45 minutes, 13.2% 45 to 60 minutes, 5.7% 60 minutes or more (2006-2010 5-year est.)
Additional Information Contacts
Borough of Seven Fields . . . . (724) 776-3090
   http://www.sevenfields.org
Butler County Chamber of Commerce . . . . (724) 283-2222
   http://www.butlercountychamber.com

SHANOR-NORTHVUE (CDP). Covers a land area of 6.753 square miles and a water area of 0.022 square miles. Located at 40.91° N. Lat; 79.92° W. Long.
Population: 3,517 (1990); 4,825 (2000); 5,051 (2010); Density: 747.9 persons per square mile (2010); Race: 97.1% White, 0.5% Black, 1.2% Asian, 0.1% American Indian/Alaska Native, 0.0% Native Hawaiian/Other Pacific Islander, 1.1% Other, 1.1% Hispanic of any race (2010); Average household size: 2.28 (2010); Median age: 46.7 (2010); Males per 100 females: 85.8 (2010); Marriage status: 20.4% never married, 60.4% now married, 9.4% widowed, 9.8% divorced (2006-2010 5-year est.); Foreign born: 1.0% (2006-2010 5-year est.); Ancestry (includes multiple ancestries): 43.9% German, 21.6% Irish, 18.1% Italian, 14.8% English, 6.3% American (2006-2010 5-year est.).
Economy: Employment by occupation: 14.0% management, 4.2% professional, 10.1% services, 17.5% sales, 4.5% farming, 6.3% construction, 4.3% production (2006-2010 5-year est.).
Income: Per capita income: $30,796 (2006-2010 5-year est.); Median household income: $62,384 (2006-2010 5-year est.); Average household income: $71,635 (2006-2010 5-year est.); Percent of households with income of $100,000 or more: 24.3% (2006-2010 5-year est.); Poverty rate: 4.9% (2006-2010 5-year est.).
Education: Percent of population age 25 and over with: High school diploma (including GED) or higher: 94.1% (2006-2010 5-year est.); Bachelor's degree or higher: 35.8% (2006-2010 5-year est.); Master's degree or higher: 14.6% (2006-2010 5-year est.).
Housing: Homeownership rate: 76.3% (2010); Median home value: $181,600 (2006-2010 5-year est.); Median contract rent: $604 per month (2006-2010 5-year est.); Median year structure built: 1987 (2006-2010 5-year est.).
Transportation: Commute to work: 95.1% car, 0.0% public transportation, 1.1% walk, 3.0% work from home (2006-2010 5-year est.); Travel time to work: 36.8% less than 15 minutes, 33.7% 15 to 30 minutes, 15.6% 30 to 45 minutes, 6.7% 45 to 60 minutes, 7.3% 60 minutes or more (2006-2010 5-year est.)
Additional Information Contacts
Butler County Chamber of Commerce . . . . (724) 283-2222
   http://www.butlercountychamber.com

SLIPPERY ROCK (borough). Covers a land area of 1.645 square miles and a water area of 0 square miles. Located at 41.07° N. Lat; 80.06° W. Long. Elevation is 1,302 feet.
Population: 3,008 (1990); 3,068 (2000); 3,625 (2010); Density: 2,203.1 persons per square mile (2010); Race: 90.0% White, 5.5% Black, 2.2% Asian, 0.1% American Indian/Alaska Native, 0.0% Native Hawaiian/Other Pacific Islander, 2.2% Other, 1.1% Hispanic of any race (2010); Average household size: 2.12 (2010); Median age: 21.7 (2010); Males per 100 females: 95.8 (2010); Marriage status: 64.3% never married, 27.8% now married, 4.0% widowed, 4.0% divorced (2006-2010 5-year est.); Foreign born: 6.3% (2006-2010 5-year est.); Ancestry (includes multiple ancestries): 41.9% German, 20.7% Irish, 14.5% Italian, 12.7% Polish, 6.9% English (2006-2010 5-year est.).
Economy: Single-family building permits issued: 4 (2011); Multi-family building permits issued: 0 (2011); Employment by occupation: 3.6% management, 2.5% professional, 29.9% services, 20.8% sales, 4.4% farming, 5.8% construction, 5.0% production (2006-2010 5-year est.).
Income: Per capita income: $18,247 (2006-2010 5-year est.); Median household income: $38,598 (2006-2010 5-year est.); Average household income: $52,796 (2006-2010 5-year est.); Percent of households with income of $100,000 or more: 17.1% (2006-2010 5-year est.); Poverty rate: 34.3% (2006-2010 5-year est.).
Education: Percent of population age 25 and over with: High school diploma (including GED) or higher: 93.4% (2006-2010 5-year est.);

Bachelor's degree or higher: 50.4% (2006-2010 5-year est.); Master's degree or higher: 25.7% (2006-2010 5-year est.).

School District(s)

Slippery Rock Area SD (KG-12)
  2010-11 Enrollment: 2,220 . . . . (724) 794-2960

Four-year College(s)

Slippery Rock University of Pennsylvania (Public)
  Fall 2010 Enrollment: 8,837 . . . . (724) 738-9000
  2011-12 Tuition: In-state $8,505; Out-of-state $11,804

Housing: Homeownership rate: 31.9% (2010); Median home value: $150,700 (2006-2010 5-year est.); Median contract rent: $548 per month (2006-2010 5-year est.); Median year structure built: 1970 (2006-2010 5-year est.).

Safety: Violent crime rate: 5.5 per 10,000 population; Property crime rate: 129.2 per 10,000 population (2011).

Newspapers: The Eagle (Community news; Circulation 12,325); Tri-County News (Community news; Circulation 21,047)

Transportation: Commute to work: 74.3% car, 1.7% public transportation, 19.5% walk, 2.3% work from home (2006-2010 5-year est.); Travel time to work: 52.8% less than 15 minutes, 32.5% 15 to 30 minutes, 6.7% 30 to 45 minutes, 4.1% 45 to 60 minutes, 3.9% 60 minutes or more (2006-2010 5-year est.)

Additional Information Contacts

Butler County Chamber of Commerce . . . . (724) 283-2222
  http://www.butlercountychamber.com

SLIPPERY ROCK (township). Covers a land area of 25.677 square miles and a water area of 0.016 square miles. Located at 41.06° N. Lat; 80.03° W. Long. Elevation is 1,302 feet.

History: Seat of Slippery Rock University of Pennsylvania. Incorporated 1851.

Population: 4,670 (1990); 5,251 (2000); 5,614 (2010); Density: 218.6 persons per square mile (2010); Race: 94.4% White, 3.2% Black, 0.9% Asian, 0.1% American Indian/Alaska Native, 0.1% Native Hawaiian/Other Pacific Islander, 1.3% Other, 1.2% Hispanic of any race (2010); Average household size: 2.45 (2010); Median age: 21.4 (2010); Males per 100 females: 88.0 (2010); Marriage status: 55.9% never married, 36.4% now married, 3.2% widowed, 4.5% divorced (2006-2010 5-year est.); Foreign born: 1.4% (2006-2010 5-year est.); Ancestry (includes multiple ancestries): 40.5% German, 27.0% Irish, 10.7% Italian, 6.3% English, 5.3% Polish (2006-2010 5-year est.).

Economy: Single-family building permits issued: 6 (2011); Multi-family building permits issued: 0 (2011); Employment by occupation: 9.7% management, 2.0% professional, 12.3% services, 18.3% sales, 1.8% farming, 14.9% construction, 6.5% production (2006-2010 5-year est.).

Income: Per capita income: $20,892 (2006-2010 5-year est.); Median household income: $39,242 (2006-2010 5-year est.); Average household income: $54,698 (2006-2010 5-year est.); Percent of households with income of $100,000 or more: 15.5% (2006-2010 5-year est.); Poverty rate: 30.8% (2006-2010 5-year est.).

Education: Percent of population age 25 and over with: High school diploma (including GED) or higher: 89.8% (2006-2010 5-year est.); Bachelor's degree or higher: 36.3% (2006-2010 5-year est.); Master's degree or higher: 10.6% (2006-2010 5-year est.).

Four-year College(s)

Slippery Rock University of Pennsylvania (Public)
  Fall 2010 Enrollment: 8,837 . . . . (724) 738-9000
  2011-12 Tuition: In-state $8,505; Out-of-state $11,804

Housing: Homeownership rate: 57.9% (2010); Median home value: $155,000 (2006-2010 5-year est.); Median contract rent: $583 per month (2006-2010 5-year est.); Median year structure built: 1982 (2006-2010 5-year est.).

Newspapers: The Eagle (Community news; Circulation 12,325); Tri-County News (Community news; Circulation 21,047)

Transportation: Commute to work: 91.3% car, 0.0% public transportation, 4.3% walk, 3.6% work from home (2006-2010 5-year est.); Travel time to work: 36.6% less than 15 minutes, 32.5% 15 to 30 minutes, 11.2% 30 to 45 minutes, 10.8% 45 to 60 minutes, 8.9% 60 minutes or more (2006-2010 5-year est.)

Additional Information Contacts

Butler County Chamber of Commerce . . . . (724) 283-2222
  http://www.butlercountychamber.com
Slippery Rock Township . . . . (724) 794-6391
  http://www.slippery-rock.com

SLIPPERY ROCK UNIVERSITY (CDP). Covers a land area of 0.551 square miles and a water area of 0 square miles. Located at 41.06° N. Lat; 80.04° W. Long.

Population: n/a (1990); n/a (2000); 1,898 (2010); Density: 3,447.5 persons per square mile (2010); Race: 90.0% White, 6.7% Black, 0.9% Asian, 0.2% American Indian/Alaska Native, 0.1% Native Hawaiian/Other Pacific Islander, 2.1% Other, 2.0% Hispanic of any race (2010); Average household size: 3.50 (2010); Median age: 19.7 (2010); Males per 100 females: 61.4 (2010); Marriage status: 99.1% never married, 0.9% now married, 0.0% widowed, 0.0% divorced (2006-2010 5-year est.); Foreign born: 4.3% (2006-2010 5-year est.); Ancestry (includes multiple ancestries): 27.7% German, 21.3% Polish, 18.0% Irish, 9.1% Italian, 4.6% French (2006-2010 5-year est.).

Economy: Employment by occupation: 9.9% management, 0.0% professional, 9.9% services, 53.0% sales, 0.0% farming, 9.9% construction, 0.0% production (2006-2010 5-year est.).

Income: Per capita income: $4,717 (2006-2010 5-year est.); Median household income: n/a (2006-2010 5-year est.); Average household income: n/a (2006-2010 5-year est.); Percent of households with income of $100,000 or more: n/a (2006-2010 5-year est.); Poverty rate: 0.0% (2006-2010 5-year est.).

Education: Percent of population age 25 and over with: High school diploma (including GED) or higher: 100.0% (2006-2010 5-year est.); Bachelor's degree or higher: 100.0% (2006-2010 5-year est.); Master's degree or higher: 0.0% (2006-2010 5-year est.).

Housing: Homeownership rate: 100.0% (2010); Median home value: n/a (2006-2010 5-year est.); Median contract rent: n/a per month (2006-2010 5-year est.); Median year structure built: before 1940 (2006-2010 5-year est.).

Transportation: Commute to work: 45.5% car, 0.0% public transportation, 6.5% walk, 44.2% work from home (2006-2010 5-year est.); Travel time to work: 25.6% less than 15 minutes, 34.9% 15 to 30 minutes, 4.7% 30 to 45 minutes, 0.0% 45 to 60 minutes, 34.9% 60 minutes or more (2006-2010 5-year est.)

SUMMIT (township). Covers a land area of 22.495 square miles and a water area of 0.041 square miles. Located at 40.85° N. Lat; 79.83° W. Long.

Population: 4,284 (1990); 4,728 (2000); 4,884 (2010); Density: 217.1 persons per square mile (2010); Race: 94.7% White, 4.1% Black, 0.2% Asian, 0.0% American Indian/Alaska Native, 0.0% Native Hawaiian/Other Pacific Islander, 1.0% Other, 1.3% Hispanic of any race (2010); Average household size: 2.50 (2010); Median age: 40.4 (2010); Males per 100 females: 116.9 (2010); Marriage status: 29.6% never married, 58.4% now married, 2.5% widowed, 9.5% divorced (2006-2010 5-year est.); Foreign born: 0.0% (2006-2010 5-year est.); Ancestry (includes multiple ancestries): 46.3% German, 15.5% Irish, 11.4% Italian, 10.4% English, 8.1% American (2006-2010 5-year est.).

Economy: Single-family building permits issued: 4 (2011); Multi-family building permits issued: 0 (2011); Employment by occupation: 9.0% management, 2.3% professional, 6.2% services, 23.9% sales, 2.9% farming, 18.8% construction, 11.5% production (2006-2010 5-year est.).

Income: Per capita income: $22,757 (2006-2010 5-year est.); Median household income: $49,816 (2006-2010 5-year est.); Average household income: $59,750 (2006-2010 5-year est.); Percent of households with income of $100,000 or more: 15.0% (2006-2010 5-year est.); Poverty rate: 14.6% (2006-2010 5-year est.).

Education: Percent of population age 25 and over with: High school diploma (including GED) or higher: 89.4% (2006-2010 5-year est.); Bachelor's degree or higher: 12.0% (2006-2010 5-year est.); Master's degree or higher: 2.8% (2006-2010 5-year est.).

Housing: Homeownership rate: 78.2% (2010); Median home value: $120,600 (2006-2010 5-year est.); Median contract rent: $514 per month (2006-2010 5-year est.); Median year structure built: 1969 (2006-2010 5-year est.).

Transportation: Commute to work: 93.6% car, 0.8% public transportation, 1.6% walk, 2.3% work from home (2006-2010 5-year est.); Travel time to work: 37.0% less than 15 minutes, 35.0% 15 to 30 minutes, 10.7% 30 to 45 minutes, 8.4% 45 to 60 minutes, 8.9% 60 minutes or more (2006-2010 5-year est.)

Additional Information Contacts

Butler County Chamber of Commerce . . . . (724) 283-2222
  http://www.butlercountychamber.com

UNIONVILLE (CDP). Covers a land area of 2.568 square miles and a water area of 0 square miles. Located at 40.94° N. Lat; 79.96° W. Long. Elevation is 1,263 feet.
Population: n/a (1990); n/a (2000); 962 (2010); Density: 374.5 persons per square mile (2010); Race: 98.4% White, 0.3% Black, 0.3% Asian, 0.0% American Indian/Alaska Native, 0.0% Native Hawaiian/Other Pacific Islander, 1.0% Other, 0.2% Hispanic of any race (2010); Average household size: 2.18 (2010); Median age: 44.7 (2010); Males per 100 females: 105.1 (2010); Marriage status: 21.3% never married, 57.3% now married, 9.7% widowed, 11.6% divorced (2006-2010 5-year est.); Foreign born: 0.0% (2006-2010 5-year est.); Ancestry (includes multiple ancestries): 41.3% German, 17.8% Irish, 10.7% American, 8.6% English, 8.6% Italian (2006-2010 5-year est.).
Economy: Employment by occupation: 12.1% management, 1.1% professional, 18.6% services, 10.0% sales, 6.6% farming, 8.1% construction, 7.8% production (2006-2010 5-year est.).
Income: Per capita income: $23,386 (2006-2010 5-year est.); Median household income: $41,019 (2006-2010 5-year est.); Average household income: $47,119 (2006-2010 5-year est.); Percent of households with income of $100,000 or more: 7.3% (2006-2010 5-year est.); Poverty rate: 2.2% (2006-2010 5-year est.).
Education: Percent of population age 25 and over with: High school diploma (including GED) or higher: 88.9% (2006-2010 5-year est.); Bachelor's degree or higher: 16.3% (2006-2010 5-year est.); Master's degree or higher: 2.7% (2006-2010 5-year est.).
Housing: Homeownership rate: 83.2% (2010); Median home value: $91,300 (2006-2010 5-year est.); Median contract rent: $335 per month (2006-2010 5-year est.); Median year structure built: 1982 (2006-2010 5-year est.).
Transportation: Commute to work: 97.5% car, 0.0% public transportation, 0.0% walk, 2.5% work from home (2006-2010 5-year est.); Travel time to work: 27.5% less than 15 minutes, 41.5% 15 to 30 minutes, 16.6% 30 to 45 minutes, 12.6% 45 to 60 minutes, 1.8% 60 minutes or more (2006-2010 5-year est.)

VALENCIA (borough). Covers a land area of 0.334 square miles and a water area of 0 square miles. Located at 40.68° N. Lat; 79.99° W. Long. Elevation is 1,063 feet.
Population: 364 (1990); 384 (2000); 551 (2010); Density: 1,649.8 persons per square mile (2010); Race: 99.5% White, 0.2% Black, 0.2% Asian, 0.0% American Indian/Alaska Native, 0.0% Native Hawaiian/Other Pacific Islander, 0.1% Other, 0.4% Hispanic of any race (2010); Average household size: 1.83 (2010); Median age: 76.2 (2010); Males per 100 females: 66.5 (2010); Marriage status: 21.9% never married, 52.5% now married, 16.1% widowed, 9.5% divorced (2006-2010 5-year est.); Foreign born: 2.4% (2006-2010 5-year est.); Ancestry (includes multiple ancestries): 54.4% German, 18.2% Irish, 17.1% Italian, 11.3% Polish, 9.1% English (2006-2010 5-year est.).
Economy: Single-family building permits issued: 2 (2011); Multi-family building permits issued: 0 (2011); Employment by occupation: 9.2% management, 2.3% professional, 20.0% services, 5.4% sales, 0.0% farming, 31.5% construction, 11.5% production (2006-2010 5-year est.).
Income: Per capita income: $28,544 (2006-2010 5-year est.); Median household income: $43,438 (2006-2010 5-year est.); Average household income: $61,881 (2006-2010 5-year est.); Percent of households with income of $100,000 or more: 17.9% (2006-2010 5-year est.); Poverty rate: 14.1% (2006-2010 5-year est.).
Education: Percent of population age 25 and over with: High school diploma (including GED) or higher: 93.1% (2006-2010 5-year est.); Bachelor's degree or higher: 35.2% (2006-2010 5-year est.); Master's degree or higher: 21.2% (2006-2010 5-year est.).
Housing: Homeownership rate: 23.1% (2010); Median home value: $122,700 (2006-2010 5-year est.); Median contract rent: n/a per month (2006-2010 5-year est.); Median year structure built: 1996 (2006-2010 5-year est.).
Transportation: Commute to work: 93.4% car, 1.6% public transportation, 4.1% walk, 0.8% work from home (2006-2010 5-year est.); Travel time to work: 37.2% less than 15 minutes, 32.2% 15 to 30 minutes, 12.4% 30 to 45 minutes, 14.9% 45 to 60 minutes, 3.3% 60 minutes or more (2006-2010 5-year est.)

VENANGO (township). Covers a land area of 20.989 square miles and a water area of 0 square miles. Located at 41.13° N. Lat; 79.84° W. Long.
Population: 707 (1990); 732 (2000); 868 (2010); Density: 41.4 persons per square mile (2010); Race: 98.7% White, 0.0% Black, 0.2% Asian,

0.2% American Indian/Alaska Native, 0.0% Native Hawaiian/Other Pacific Islander, 0.9% Other, 0.1% Hispanic of any race (2010); Average household size: 2.59 (2010); Median age: 40.1 (2010); Males per 100 females: 109.2 (2010); Marriage status: 22.3% never married, 65.2% now married, 5.0% widowed, 7.4% divorced (2006-2010 5-year est.); Foreign born: 0.0% (2006-2010 5-year est.); Ancestry (includes multiple ancestries): 38.6% German, 19.7% Irish, 9.2% Polish, 7.6% English, 5.5% French (2006-2010 5-year est.).
Economy: Single-family building permits issued: 1 (2011); Multi-family building permits issued: 0 (2011); Employment by occupation: 4.2% management, 1.7% professional, 17.5% services, 10.4% sales, 3.7% farming, 16.0% construction, 6.7% production (2006-2010 5-year est.).
Income: Per capita income: $18,286 (2006-2010 5-year est.); Median household income: $44,524 (2006-2010 5-year est.); Average household income: $49,265 (2006-2010 5-year est.); Percent of households with income of $100,000 or more: 5.5% (2006-2010 5-year est.); Poverty rate: 7.6% (2006-2010 5-year est.).
Education: Percent of population age 25 and over with: High school diploma (including GED) or higher: 82.2% (2006-2010 5-year est.); Bachelor's degree or higher: 8.5% (2006-2010 5-year est.); Master's degree or higher: 1.0% (2006-2010 5-year est.).
Housing: Homeownership rate: 84.7% (2010); Median home value: $115,300 (2006-2010 5-year est.); Median contract rent: $440 per month (2006-2010 5-year est.); Median year structure built: 1975 (2006-2010 5-year est.).
Transportation: Commute to work: 98.5% car, 0.0% public transportation, 0.0% walk, 0.7% work from home (2006-2010 5-year est.); Travel time to work: 16.4% less than 15 minutes, 25.6% 15 to 30 minutes, 28.4% 30 to 45 minutes, 15.9% 45 to 60 minutes, 13.7% 60 minutes or more (2006-2010 5-year est.)

WASHINGTON (township). Covers a land area of 24.936 square miles and a water area of 0.023 square miles. Located at 41.07° N. Lat; 79.83° W. Long.
Population: 1,280 (1990); 1,419 (2000); 1,300 (2010); Density: 52.1 persons per square mile (2010); Race: 99.2% White, 0.0% Black, 0.2% Asian, 0.0% American Indian/Alaska Native, 0.4% Native Hawaiian/Other Pacific Islander, 0.2% Other, 0.3% Hispanic of any race (2010); Average household size: 2.54 (2010); Median age: 42.7 (2010); Males per 100 females: 102.5 (2010); Marriage status: 25.6% never married, 61.4% now married, 4.8% widowed, 8.1% divorced (2006-2010 5-year est.); Foreign born: 0.6% (2006-2010 5-year est.); Ancestry (includes multiple ancestries): 50.4% German, 23.4% Irish, 8.4% English, 7.7% Scotch-Irish, 6.2% American (2006-2010 5-year est.).
Economy: Single-family building permits issued: 0 (2011); Multi-family building permits issued: 0 (2011); Employment by occupation: 3.5% management, 1.4% professional, 14.5% services, 15.4% sales, 9.4% farming, 13.2% construction, 7.4% production (2006-2010 5-year est.).
Income: Per capita income: $19,497 (2006-2010 5-year est.); Median household income: $42,286 (2006-2010 5-year est.); Average household income: $52,727 (2006-2010 5-year est.); Percent of households with income of $100,000 or more: 10.1% (2006-2010 5-year est.); Poverty rate: 5.3% (2006-2010 5-year est.).
Education: Percent of population age 25 and over with: High school diploma (including GED) or higher: 85.3% (2006-2010 5-year est.); Bachelor's degree or higher: 8.2% (2006-2010 5-year est.); Master's degree or higher: 1.7% (2006-2010 5-year est.).
Housing: Homeownership rate: 83.4% (2010); Median home value: $96,900 (2006-2010 5-year est.); Median contract rent: $509 per month (2006-2010 5-year est.); Median year structure built: 1957 (2006-2010 5-year est.).
Transportation: Commute to work: 94.4% car, 0.0% public transportation, 2.2% walk, 2.5% work from home (2006-2010 5-year est.); Travel time to work: 15.4% less than 15 minutes, 26.6% 15 to 30 minutes, 30.1% 30 to 45 minutes, 13.5% 45 to 60 minutes, 14.3% 60 minutes or more (2006-2010 5-year est.)
Additional Information Contacts
Butler County Chamber of Commerce . . . . (724) 283-2222
   http://www.butlercountychamber.com

WEST LIBERTY (borough). Covers a land area of 3.848 square miles and a water area of 0.030 square miles. Located at 41.01° N. Lat; 80.07° W. Long. Elevation is 1,211 feet.
Population: 282 (1990); 325 (2000); 343 (2010); Density: 89.1 persons per square mile (2010); Race: 95.6% White, 0.0% Black, 0.9% Asian,

0.0% American Indian/Alaska Native, 0.0% Native Hawaiian/Other Pacific Islander, 3.5% Other, 0.0% Hispanic of any race (2010); Average household size: 2.62 (2010); Median age: 43.3 (2010); Males per 100 females: 114.4 (2010); Marriage status: 25.1% never married, 61.1% now married, 5.6% widowed, 8.3% divorced (2006-2010 5-year est.); Foreign born: 0.0% (2006-2010 5-year est.); Ancestry (includes multiple ancestries): 39.0% German, 26.8% Irish, 8.9% English, 8.2% American, 7.4% Scotch-Irish (2006-2010 5-year est.).
Economy: Single-family building permits issued: 0 (2011); Multi-family building permits issued: 0 (2011); Employment by occupation: 5.9% management, 4.1% professional, 5.4% services, 24.0% sales, 4.5% farming, 20.4% construction, 5.0% production (2006-2010 5-year est.).
Income: Per capita income: $30,735 (2006-2010 5-year est.); Median household income: $58,125 (2006-2010 5-year est.); Average household income: $78,214 (2006-2010 5-year est.); Percent of households with income of $100,000 or more: 22.8% (2006-2010 5-year est.); Poverty rate: 5.9% (2006-2010 5-year est.).
Education: Percent of population age 25 and over with: High school diploma (including GED) or higher: 90.7% (2006-2010 5-year est.); Bachelor's degree or higher: 16.0% (2006-2010 5-year est.); Master's degree or higher: 5.2% (2006-2010 5-year est.).
Housing: Homeownership rate: 85.5% (2010); Median home value: $156,300 (2006-2010 5-year est.); Median contract rent: $475 per month (2006-2010 5-year est.); Median year structure built: 1971 (2006-2010 5-year est.).
Transportation: Commute to work: 95.3% car, 0.0% public transportation, 1.9% walk, 2.8% work from home (2006-2010 5-year est.); Travel time to work: 27.2% less than 15 minutes, 35.0% 15 to 30 minutes, 23.3% 30 to 45 minutes, 4.4% 45 to 60 minutes, 10.2% 60 minutes or more (2006-2010 5-year est.)

WEST SUNBURY (borough). Covers a land area of 0.110 square miles and a water area of 0 square miles. Located at 41.01° N. Lat; 79.90° W. Long. Elevation is 1,371 feet.

Population: 177 (1990); 104 (2000); 192 (2010); Density: 1,744.1 persons per square mile (2010); Race: 96.4% White, 2.1% Black, 0.5% Asian, 0.0% American Indian/Alaska Native, 0.0% Native Hawaiian/Other Pacific Islander, 1.0% Other, 0.5% Hispanic of any race (2010); Average household size: 2.49 (2010); Median age: 33.8 (2010); Males per 100 females: 100.0 (2010); Marriage status: 44.4% never married, 35.1% now married, 2.0% widowed, 18.5% divorced (2006-2010 5-year est.); Foreign born: 0.0% (2006-2010 5-year est.); Ancestry (includes multiple ancestries): 72.9% German, 45.7% Irish, 12.2% Croatian, 6.9% Swedish, 6.9% French (2006-2010 5-year est.).
Economy: Single-family building permits issued: 0 (2011); Multi-family building permits issued: 0 (2011); Employment by occupation: 2.1% management, 2.1% professional, 12.6% services, 33.7% sales, 0.0% farming, 14.7% construction, 10.5% production (2006-2010 5-year est.).
Income: Per capita income: $11,691 (2006-2010 5-year est.); Median household income: $35,673 (2006-2010 5-year est.); Average household income: $35,839 (2006-2010 5-year est.); Percent of households with income of $100,000 or more: n/a (2006-2010 5-year est.); Poverty rate: 13.8% (2006-2010 5-year est.).
Education: Percent of population age 25 and over with: High school diploma (including GED) or higher: 89.6% (2006-2010 5-year est.); Bachelor's degree or higher: 4.7% (2006-2010 5-year est.); Master's degree or higher: 0.0% (2006-2010 5-year est.).
School District(s)
Moniteau SD (KG-12)
    2010-11 Enrollment: 1,489 . . . . (724) 637-2117
Housing: Homeownership rate: 52.0% (2010); Median home value: $108,300 (2006-2010 5-year est.); Median contract rent: $410 per month (2006-2010 5-year est.); Median year structure built: before 1940 (2006-2010 5-year est.).
Transportation: Commute to work: 97.6% car, 0.0% public transportation, 2.4% walk, 0.0% work from home (2006-2010 5-year est.); Travel time to work: 28.9% less than 15 minutes, 51.8% 15 to 30 minutes, 8.4% 30 to 45 minutes, 8.4% 45 to 60 minutes, 2.4% 60 minutes or more (2006-2010 5-year est.)

WINFIELD (township). Covers a land area of 24.067 square miles and a water area of 0 square miles. Located at 40.78° N. Lat; 79.74° W. Long.

Population: 3,162 (1990); 3,585 (2000); 3,535 (2010); Density: 146.9 persons per square mile (2010); Race: 98.9% White, 0.3% Black, 0.2% Asian, 0.1% American Indian/Alaska Native, 0.0% Native Hawaiian/Other

Pacific Islander, 0.5% Other, 0.4% Hispanic of any race (2010); Average household size: 2.35 (2010); Median age: 47.0 (2010); Males per 100 females: 91.7 (2010); Marriage status: 20.3% never married, 63.3% now married, 11.1% widowed, 5.3% divorced (2006-2010 5-year est.); Foreign born: 0.6% (2006-2010 5-year est.); Ancestry (includes multiple ancestries): 48.6% German, 20.4% Irish, 9.7% Slovak, 8.5% English, 8.5% Polish (2006-2010 5-year est.).
Economy: Single-family building permits issued: 8 (2011); Multi-family building permits issued: 0 (2011); Employment by occupation: 11.9% management, 2.3% professional, 12.8% services, 13.5% sales, 4.2% farming, 15.2% construction, 7.0% production (2006-2010 5-year est.).
Income: Per capita income: $24,909 (2006-2010 5-year est.); Median household income: $48,580 (2006-2010 5-year est.); Average household income: $62,432 (2006-2010 5-year est.); Percent of households with income of $100,000 or more: 18.3% (2006-2010 5-year est.); Poverty rate: 3.0% (2006-2010 5-year est.).
Education: Percent of population age 25 and over with: High school diploma (including GED) or higher: 91.2% (2006-2010 5-year est.); Bachelor's degree or higher: 15.0% (2006-2010 5-year est.); Master's degree or higher: 6.9% (2006-2010 5-year est.).
Housing: Homeownership rate: 76.5% (2010); Median home value: $153,300 (2006-2010 5-year est.); Median contract rent: $819 per month (2006-2010 5-year est.); Median year structure built: 1985 (2006-2010 5-year est.).
Transportation: Commute to work: 95.1% car, 0.0% public transportation, 0.5% walk, 2.7% work from home (2006-2010 5-year est.); Travel time to work: 23.6% less than 15 minutes, 35.5% 15 to 30 minutes, 23.1% 30 to 45 minutes, 13.7% 45 to 60 minutes, 4.0% 60 minutes or more (2006-2010 5-year est.)
Additional Information Contacts
Central PA Chamber of Commerce. . . . . (570) 742-7341
    http://www.centralpachamber.com/index.php

WORTH (township). Covers a land area of 24.228 square miles and a water area of 0.981 square miles. Located at 41.00° N. Lat; 80.11° W. Long.

Population: 955 (1990); 1,331 (2000); 1,416 (2010); Density: 58.4 persons per square mile (2010); Race: 98.3% White, 0.4% Black, 0.4% Asian, 0.0% American Indian/Alaska Native, 0.0% Native Hawaiian/Other Pacific Islander, 0.9% Other, 0.9% Hispanic of any race (2010); Average household size: 2.27 (2010); Median age: 41.6 (2010); Males per 100 females: 107.0 (2010); Marriage status: 26.0% never married, 62.8% now married, 4.2% widowed, 7.1% divorced (2006-2010 5-year est.); Foreign born: 0.9% (2006-2010 5-year est.); Ancestry (includes multiple ancestries): 40.5% German, 26.9% Irish, 12.2% English, 11.6% Scotch-Irish, 10.9% Italian (2006-2010 5-year est.).
Economy: Single-family building permits issued: 1 (2011); Multi-family building permits issued: 0 (2011); Employment by occupation: 5.4% management, 3.8% professional, 11.0% services, 15.4% sales, 3.5% farming, 15.2% construction, 8.9% production (2006-2010 5-year est.).
Income: Per capita income: $23,268 (2006-2010 5-year est.); Median household income: $45,833 (2006-2010 5-year est.); Average household income: $52,209 (2006-2010 5-year est.); Percent of households with income of $100,000 or more: 9.8% (2006-2010 5-year est.); Poverty rate: 12.7% (2006-2010 5-year est.).
Education: Percent of population age 25 and over with: High school diploma (including GED) or higher: 91.1% (2006-2010 5-year est.); Bachelor's degree or higher: 22.7% (2006-2010 5-year est.); Master's degree or higher: 6.3% (2006-2010 5-year est.).
Housing: Homeownership rate: 68.7% (2010); Median home value: $143,100 (2006-2010 5-year est.); Median contract rent: $410 per month (2006-2010 5-year est.); Median year structure built: 1985 (2006-2010 5-year est.).
Transportation: Commute to work: 89.3% car, 0.3% public transportation, 3.6% walk, 5.0% work from home (2006-2010 5-year est.); Travel time to work: 21.0% less than 15 minutes, 28.4% 15 to 30 minutes, 28.3% 30 to 45 minutes, 13.7% 45 to 60 minutes, 8.5% 60 minutes or more (2006-2010 5-year est.)
Additional Information Contacts
Butler County Chamber of Commerce . . . . (724) 283-2222
    http://www.butlercountychamber.com

ZELIENOPLE (borough). Covers a land area of 2.049 square miles and a water area of 0.046 square miles. Located at 40.79° N. Lat; 80.14° W. Long. Elevation is 942 feet.

History: Settled by Germans; laid out c.1802, incorporated 1840.

Population: 4,158 (1990); 4,123 (2000); 3,812 (2010); Density: 1,860.7 persons per square mile (2010); Race: 97.5% White, 0.9% Black, 0.6% Asian, 0.1% American Indian/Alaska Native, 0.1% Native Hawaiian/Other Pacific Islander, 0.8% Other, 0.7% Hispanic of any race (2010); Average household size: 2.00 (2010); Median age: 47.2 (2010); Males per 100 females: 82.7 (2010); Marriage status: 20.2% never married, 56.8% now married, 15.4% widowed, 7.6% divorced (2006-2010 5-year est.); Foreign born: 3.1% (2006-2010 5-year est.); Ancestry (includes multiple ancestries): 40.7% German, 17.8% Irish, 15.2% English, 11.5% Italian, 5.6% Scotch-Irish (2006-2010 5-year est.).

Economy: Single-family building permits issued: 1 (2011); Multi-family building permits issued: 0 (2011); Employment by occupation: 8.4% management, 8.4% professional, 7.7% services, 19.7% sales, 3.9% farming, 5.9% construction, 6.3% production (2006-2010 5-year est.).

Income: Per capita income: $32,788 (2006-2010 5-year est.); Median household income: $48,100 (2006-2010 5-year est.); Average household income: $63,869 (2006-2010 5-year est.); Percent of households with income of $100,000 or more: 16.4% (2006-2010 5-year est.); Poverty rate: 2.6% (2006-2010 5-year est.).

Education: Percent of population age 25 and over with: High school diploma (including GED) or higher: 92.7% (2006-2010 5-year est.); Bachelor's degree or higher: 34.0% (2006-2010 5-year est.); Master's degree or higher: 11.1% (2006-2010 5-year est.).

School District(s)

Seneca Valley SD (KG-12)
    2010-11 Enrollment: 7,288 . . . . (724) 452-6040

Housing: Homeownership rate: 48.7% (2010); Median home value: $179,200 (2006-2010 5-year est.); Median contract rent: $609 per month (2006-2010 5-year est.); Median year structure built: 1965 (2006-2010 5-year est.).

Safety: Violent crime rate: 23.5 per 10,000 population; Property crime rate: 175.2 per 10,000 population (2011).

Transportation: Commute to work: 91.8% car, 1.4% public transportation, 2.6% walk, 3.5% work from home (2006-2010 5-year est.); Travel time to work: 29.3% less than 15 minutes, 40.8% 15 to 30 minutes, 16.6% 30 to 45 minutes, 7.9% 45 to 60 minutes, 5.4% 60 minutes or more (2006-2010 5-year est.)

Additional Information Contacts

Borough of Zelienople . . . . (724) 452-6610
    http://boro.zelienople.pa.us
Zelienople-Harmony Area Chamber of Commerce . . . . (724) 452-5232
    http://www.zhchamber.com

Cambria County

Located in central Pennsylvania; mountainous area, bounded on the southwest by Laurel Hill, and on the east by the Allegheny Mountains. Covers a land area of 688.351 square miles, a water area of 5.282 square miles, and is located in the Eastern Time Zone at 40.49° N. Lat., 78.72° W. Long. The county was founded in 1804. County seat is Ebensburg.

Cambria County is part of the Johnstown, PA Metropolitan Statistical Area. The entire metro area includes: Cambria County, PA

Weather Station: Ebensburg Sewage Plant										Elevation: 1,939 feet	
	Jan	Feb	Mar	Apr	May	Jun	Jul	Aug	Sep	Oct	Nov	Dec
High	35	39	48	61	70	78	81	80	73	62	51	39
Low	17	18	24	34	43	52	56	55	48	37	30	21
Precip	3.7	2.9	4.1	4.4	4.6	4.3	4.8	4.1	3.9	3.2	4.1	3.7
Snow	25.7	17.6	15.8	4.5	tr	0.0	0.0	0.0	tr	0.4	5.7	15.4

High and Low temperatures in degrees Fahrenheit; Precipitation and Snow in inches

Weather Station: Prince Gallitzin St Pk										Elevation: 1,520 feet	
	Jan	Feb	Mar	Apr	May	Jun	Jul	Aug	Sep	Oct	Nov	Dec
High	34	36	46	59	69	78	82	80	73	61	49	39
Low	16	17	24	34	43	53	57	55	48	37	30	21
Precip	2.7	2.3	3.4	3.5	3.7	3.7	3.7	3.9	3.5	2.8	3.4	2.7
Snow	na	na	7.6	0.8	tr	0.0	0.0	0.0	0.0	0.4	2.7	na

High and Low temperatures in degrees Fahrenheit; Precipitation and Snow in inches

Population: 163,029 (1990); 152,598 (2000); 143,679 (2010); Race: 94.1% White, 3.6% Black, 0.5% Asian, 0.1% American Indian/Alaska

Native, 0.0% Native Hawaiian/Other Pacific Islander, 1.7% Other, 1.4% Hispanic of any race (2010); Density: 208.7 persons per square mile (2010); Average household size: 2.30 (2010); Median age: 43.8 (2010); Males per 100 females: 97.7 (2010).

Religion: Six largest groups: 45.1% Catholicism, 11.0% Methodist/Pietist, 4.2% Lutheran, 2.0% Non-Denominational, 2.0% Baptist, 1.9% European Free-Church (2010)

Economy: Unemployment rate: 9.2% (August 2012); Total civilian labor force: 68,684 (August 2012); Leading industries: 24.1% health care and social assistance; 13.9% retail trade; 11.3% manufacturing (2010); Farms: 656 totaling 87,924 acres (2007); Companies that employ 500 or more persons: 4 (2010); Companies that employ 100 to 499 persons: 60 (2010); Companies that employ less than 100 persons: 3,373 (2010); Black-owned businesses: 100 (2007); Hispanic-owned businesses: n/a (2007); Asian-owned businesses: 143 (2007); Women-owned businesses: 2,316 (2007); Retail sales per capita: $13,321 (2010). Single-family building permits issued: 62 (2011); Multi-family building permits issued: 0 (2011).

Income: Per capita income: $21,278 (2006-2010 5-year est.); Median household income: $39,574 (2006-2010 5-year est.); Average household income: $50,473 (2006-2010 5-year est.); Percent of households with income of $100,000 or more: 9.4% (2006-2010 5-year est.); Poverty rate: 13.7% (2006-2010 5-year est.); Bankruptcy rate: 2.53% (2011).

Taxes: Total county taxes per capita: $192 (2009); County property taxes per capita: $189 (2009).

Education: Percent of population age 25 and over with: High school diploma (including GED) or higher: 87.6% (2006-2010 5-year est.); Bachelor's degree or higher: 17.5% (2006-2010 5-year est.); Master's degree or higher: 6.5% (2006-2010 5-year est.).

Housing: Homeownership rate: 73.6% (2010); Median home value: $86,000 (2006-2010 5-year est.); Median contract rent: $362 per month (2006-2010 5-year est.); Median year structure built: 1951 (2006-2010 5-year est.)

Health: Birth rate: 92.2 per 10,000 population (2011); Death rate: 125.4 per 10,000 population (2011); Age-adjusted cancer mortality rate: 172.1 deaths per 100,000 population (2009); Number of physicians: 27.1 per 10,000 population (2010); Hospital beds: 54.2 per 10,000 population (2008); Hospital admissions: 2,374.7 per 10,000 population (2008).

Environment: Air Quality Index: 66.5% good, 33.0% moderate, 0.6% unhealthy for sensitive individuals, 0.0% unhealthy (percent of days in 2011)

Elections: 2012 Presidential election results: 40.1% Obama, 58.1% Romney

National and State Parks: Allegheny Portage Railroad National Historic Site; Johnstown Flood National Memorial; Prince Gallitzin State Park

Additional Information Contacts

Cambria County Government . . . . (814) 472-5440
    http://www.co.cambria.pa.us
Greater Johnstown Cambria County Chamber of Commerce . . . . (814) 536-5107
    http://www.johnstownchamber.com

Cambria County Communities

ADAMS (township). Covers a land area of 46.083 square miles and a water area of 0.119 square miles. Located at 40.28° N. Lat; 78.74° W. Long.

Population: 6,771 (1990); 6,495 (2000); 5,972 (2010); Density: 129.6 persons per square mile (2010); Race: 98.9% White, 0.2% Black, 0.2% Asian, 0.0% American Indian/Alaska Native, 0.1% Native Hawaiian/Other Pacific Islander, 0.6% Other, 0.5% Hispanic of any race (2010); Average household size: 2.35 (2010); Median age: 45.8 (2010); Males per 100 females: 96.4 (2010); Marriage status: 21.5% never married, 60.1% now married, 8.7% widowed, 9.6% divorced (2006-2010 5-year est.); Foreign born: 0.0% (2006-2010 5-year est.); Ancestry (includes multiple ancestries): 33.5% German, 20.4% Irish, 12.5% Slovak, 10.6% English, 8.0% Italian (2006-2010 5-year est.).

Economy: Single-family building permits issued: 4 (2011); Multi-family building permits issued: 0 (2011); Employment by occupation: 10.6% management, 4.2% professional, 12.0% services, 17.3% sales, 1.5% farming, 9.8% construction, 8.1% production (2006-2010 5-year est.).

Income: Per capita income: $24,982 (2006-2010 5-year est.); Median household income: $44,890 (2006-2010 5-year est.); Average household income: $58,515 (2006-2010 5-year est.); Percent of households with income of $100,000 or more: 14.2% (2006-2010 5-year est.); Poverty rate: 10.2% (2006-2010 5-year est.).

Education: Percent of population age 25 and over with: High school diploma (including GED) or higher: 88.1% (2006-2010 5-year est.); Bachelor's degree or higher: 17.7% (2006-2010 5-year est.); Master's degree or higher: 6.5% (2006-2010 5-year est.).

Housing: Homeownership rate: 82.7% (2010); Median home value: $104,700 (2006-2010 5-year est.); Median contract rent: $383 per month (2006-2010 5-year est.); Median year structure built: 1966 (2006-2010 5-year est.).

Transportation: Commute to work: 91.8% car, 0.0% public transportation, 3.4% walk, 3.5% work from home (2006-2010 5-year est.); Travel time to work: 34.1% less than 15 minutes, 40.7% 15 to 30 minutes, 12.9% 30 to 45 minutes, 4.7% 45 to 60 minutes, 7.5% 60 minutes or more (2006-2010 5-year est.)

Additional Information Contacts

Adams Township. . . . . (814) 487-5054
  http://www.adamstwpcambria.com/news.html
Greater Johnstown Cambria County Chamber of Commerce . . . . (814) 536-5107
  http://www.johnstownchamber.com

ALLEGHENY (township). Covers a land area of 29.368 square miles and a water area of 0.053 square miles. Located at 40.54° N. Lat; 78.62° W. Long.

Population: 2,075 (1990); 2,498 (2000); 2,851 (2010); Density: 97.1 persons per square mile (2010); Race: 77.5% White, 15.9% Black, 0.6% Asian, 0.7% American Indian/Alaska Native, 0.0% Native Hawaiian/Other Pacific Islander, 5.3% Other, 8.6% Hispanic of any race (2010); Average household size: 2.74 (2010); Median age: 38.4 (2010); Males per 100 females: 200.4 (2010); Marriage status: 35.5% never married, 50.6% now married, 2.8% widowed, 11.1% divorced (2006-2010 5-year est.); Foreign born: 12.0% (2006-2010 5-year est.); Ancestry (includes multiple ancestries): 35.9% German, 20.8% Irish, 6.8% English, 6.5% Polish, 6.1% Italian (2006-2010 5-year est.).

Economy: Single-family building permits issued: 2 (2011); Multi-family building permits issued: 0 (2011); Employment by occupation: 10.7% management, 4.5% professional, 10.1% services, 12.7% sales, 1.8% farming, 18.6% construction, 9.7% production (2006-2010 5-year est.).

Income: Per capita income: $16,602 (2006-2010 5-year est.); Median household income: $60,667 (2006-2010 5-year est.); Average household income: $66,095 (2006-2010 5-year est.); Percent of households with income of $100,000 or more: 17.9% (2006-2010 5-year est.); Poverty rate: 8.5% (2006-2010 5-year est.).

Education: Percent of population age 25 and over with: High school diploma (including GED) or higher: 88.4% (2006-2010 5-year est.); Bachelor's degree or higher: 11.3% (2006-2010 5-year est.); Master's degree or higher: 3.7% (2006-2010 5-year est.).

Housing: Homeownership rate: 88.5% (2010); Median home value: $139,400 (2006-2010 5-year est.); Median contract rent: $388 per month (2006-2010 5-year est.); Median year structure built: 1978 (2006-2010 5-year est.).

Transportation: Commute to work: 97.8% car, 0.0% public transportation, 1.3% walk, 0.5% work from home (2006-2010 5-year est.); Travel time to work: 26.3% less than 15 minutes, 38.7% 15 to 30 minutes, 17.6% 30 to 45 minutes, 7.1% 45 to 60 minutes, 10.2% 60 minutes or more (2006-2010 5-year est.)

Additional Information Contacts

Blair County Chamber of Commerce . . . . (814) 943-8151
  http://www.blairchamber.com

ASHVILLE (borough). Covers a land area of 0.179 square miles and a water area of 0 square miles. Located at 40.56° N. Lat; 78.55° W. Long. Elevation is 1,647 feet.

Population: 306 (1990); 279 (2000); 227 (2010); Density: 1,270.2 persons per square mile (2010); Race: 97.4% White, 0.9% Black, 0.0% Asian, 0.0% American Indian/Alaska Native, 0.4% Native Hawaiian/Other Pacific Islander, 1.3% Other, 0.9% Hispanic of any race (2010); Average household size: 2.23 (2010); Median age: 40.3 (2010); Males per 100 females: 102.7 (2010); Marriage status: 23.8% never married, 52.4% now married, 13.7% widowed, 10.1% divorced (2006-2010 5-year est.); Foreign born: 0.0% (2006-2010 5-year est.); Ancestry (includes multiple ancestries): 40.6% German, 30.7% Irish, 17.0% Polish, 9.0% Italian, 7.5% Hungarian (2006-2010 5-year est.).

Economy: Single-family building permits issued: 0 (2011); Multi-family building permits issued: 0 (2011); Employment by occupation: 10.1%

management, 3.0% professional, 18.2% services, 16.2% sales, 0.0% farming, 20.2% construction, 5.1% production (2006-2010 5-year est.).

Income: Per capita income: $22,999 (2006-2010 5-year est.); Median household income: $38,409 (2006-2010 5-year est.); Average household income: $49,781 (2006-2010 5-year est.); Percent of households with income of $100,000 or more: 8.4% (2006-2010 5-year est.); Poverty rate: 15.6% (2006-2010 5-year est.).

Education: Percent of population age 25 and over with: High school diploma (including GED) or higher: 89.7% (2006-2010 5-year est.); Bachelor's degree or higher: 6.6% (2006-2010 5-year est.); Master's degree or higher: 0.0% (2006-2010 5-year est.).

Housing: Homeownership rate: 72.6% (2010); Median home value: $76,300 (2006-2010 5-year est.); Median contract rent: n/a per month (2006-2010 5-year est.); Median year structure built: before 1940 (2006-2010 5-year est.).

Transportation: Commute to work: 94.8% car, 0.0% public transportation, 4.1% walk, 1.0% work from home (2006-2010 5-year est.); Travel time to work: 12.5% less than 15 minutes, 45.8% 15 to 30 minutes, 21.9% 30 to 45 minutes, 3.1% 45 to 60 minutes, 16.7% 60 minutes or more (2006-2010 5-year est.)

BARR (township). Covers a land area of 31.354 square miles and a water area of 0.052 square miles. Located at 40.61° N. Lat; 78.82° W. Long.

Population: 2,260 (1990); 2,175 (2000); 2,056 (2010); Density: 65.6 persons per square mile (2010); Race: 99.1% White, 0.0% Black, 0.1% Asian, 0.2% American Indian/Alaska Native, 0.0% Native Hawaiian/Other Pacific Islander, 0.6% Other, 0.2% Hispanic of any race (2010); Average household size: 2.64 (2010); Median age: 43.9 (2010); Males per 100 females: 98.3 (2010); Marriage status: 24.7% never married, 61.0% now married, 5.0% widowed, 9.4% divorced (2006-2010 5-year est.); Foreign born: 2.5% (2006-2010 5-year est.); Ancestry (includes multiple ancestries): 44.4% German, 16.8% Italian, 13.4% Irish, 12.4% Polish, 8.3% English (2006-2010 5-year est.).

Economy: Single-family building permits issued: 6 (2011); Multi-family building permits issued: 0 (2011); Employment by occupation: 2.1% management, 3.1% professional, 11.7% services, 21.1% sales, 2.0% farming, 10.5% construction, 7.1% production (2006-2010 5-year est.).

Income: Per capita income: $20,195 (2006-2010 5-year est.); Median household income: $53,125 (2006-2010 5-year est.); Average household income: $55,031 (2006-2010 5-year est.); Percent of households with income of $100,000 or more: 7.6% (2006-2010 5-year est.); Poverty rate: 10.3% (2006-2010 5-year est.).

Education: Percent of population age 25 and over with: High school diploma (including GED) or higher: 87.5% (2006-2010 5-year est.); Bachelor's degree or higher: 13.9% (2006-2010 5-year est.); Master's degree or higher: 3.5% (2006-2010 5-year est.).

Housing: Homeownership rate: 87.4% (2010); Median home value: $96,300 (2006-2010 5-year est.); Median contract rent: $320 per month (2006-2010 5-year est.); Median year structure built: 1971 (2006-2010 5-year est.).

Transportation: Commute to work: 95.7% car, 0.0% public transportation, 2.1% walk, 2.1% work from home (2006-2010 5-year est.); Travel time to work: 26.6% less than 15 minutes, 28.7% 15 to 30 minutes, 24.8% 30 to 45 minutes, 17.3% 45 to 60 minutes, 2.6% 60 minutes or more (2006-2010 5-year est.)

Additional Information Contacts

Greater Scranton Chamber of Commerce . . . . (570) 342-7711
  http://www.scrantonchamber.com

BEAVERDALE (CDP). Covers a land area of 1.551 square miles and a water area of 0 square miles. Located at 40.32° N. Lat; 78.70° W. Long. Elevation is 1,919 feet.

Population: n/a (1990); n/a (2000); 1,035 (2010); Density: 667.4 persons per square mile (2010); Race: 99.4% White, 0.0% Black, 0.0% Asian, 0.0% American Indian/Alaska Native, 0.0% Native Hawaiian/Other Pacific Islander, 0.6% Other, 0.1% Hispanic of any race (2010); Average household size: 2.48 (2010); Median age: 39.6 (2010); Males per 100 females: 104.1 (2010); Marriage status: 31.2% never married, 44.0% now married, 12.9% widowed, 11.8% divorced (2006-2010 5-year est.); Foreign born: 0.0% (2006-2010 5-year est.); Ancestry (includes multiple ancestries): 26.9% German, 23.9% Slovak, 17.6% Irish, 9.8% English, 8.4% Polish (2006-2010 5-year est.).

Economy: Employment by occupation: 6.9% management, 5.4% professional, 9.5% services, 9.7% sales, 9.5% farming, 11.7% construction, 10.0% production (2006-2010 5-year est.).
Income: Per capita income: $19,235 (2006-2010 5-year est.); Median household income: $39,708 (2006-2010 5-year est.); Average household income: $50,238 (2006-2010 5-year est.); Percent of households with income of $100,000 or more: 1.4% (2006-2010 5-year est.); Poverty rate: 17.0% (2006-2010 5-year est.).
Education: Percent of population age 25 and over with: High school diploma (including GED) or higher: 87.0% (2006-2010 5-year est.); Bachelor's degree or higher: 17.0% (2006-2010 5-year est.); Master's degree or higher: 7.3% (2006-2010 5-year est.).
Housing: Homeownership rate: 87.0% (2010); Median home value: $67,100 (2006-2010 5-year est.); Median contract rent: $296 per month (2006-2010 5-year est.); Median year structure built: before 1940 (2006-2010 5-year est.).
Transportation: Commute to work: 95.0% car, 0.0% public transportation, 2.5% walk, 0.0% work from home (2006-2010 5-year est.); Travel time to work: 15.8% less than 15 minutes, 59.3% 15 to 30 minutes, 17.0% 30 to 45 minutes, 3.6% 45 to 60 minutes, 4.3% 60 minutes or more (2006-2010 5-year est.)

BELMONT (CDP).

Covers a land area of 1.757 square miles and a water area of 0.018 square miles. Located at 40.28° N. Lat; 78.88° W. Long. Elevation is 1,696 feet.
Population: 3,220 (1990); 2,846 (2000); 2,784 (2010); Density: 1,584.8 persons per square mile (2010); Race: 96.8% White, 1.1% Black, 1.1% Asian, 0.0% American Indian/Alaska Native, 0.0% Native Hawaiian/Other Pacific Islander, 1.0% Other, 0.8% Hispanic of any race (2010); Average household size: 2.06 (2010); Median age: 52.4 (2010); Males per 100 females: 80.1 (2010); Marriage status: 24.6% never married, 47.0% now married, 24.5% widowed, 3.8% divorced (2006-2010 5-year est.); Foreign born: 3.1% (2006-2010 5-year est.); Ancestry (includes multiple ancestries): 37.0% German, 17.1% Irish, 10.2% Polish, 9.3% Italian, 6.7% English (2006-2010 5-year est.).
Economy: Employment by occupation: 12.1% management, 7.9% professional, 14.6% services, 7.6% sales, 1.8% farming, 2.8% construction, 1.7% production (2006-2010 5-year est.).
Income: Per capita income: $24,633 (2006-2010 5-year est.); Median household income: $38,750 (2006-2010 5-year est.); Average household income: $48,280 (2006-2010 5-year est.); Percent of households with income of $100,000 or more: 11.9% (2006-2010 5-year est.); Poverty rate: 9.3% (2006-2010 5-year est.).
Education: Percent of population age 25 and over with: High school diploma (including GED) or higher: 85.9% (2006-2010 5-year est.); Bachelor's degree or higher: 22.0% (2006-2010 5-year est.); Master's degree or higher: 8.9% (2006-2010 5-year est.).
Housing: Homeownership rate: 71.6% (2010); Median home value: $96,400 (2006-2010 5-year est.); Median contract rent: $403 per month (2006-2010 5-year est.); Median year structure built: 1957 (2006-2010 5-year est.).
Transportation: Commute to work: 98.9% car, 1.1% public transportation, 0.0% walk, 0.0% work from home (2006-2010 5-year est.); Travel time to work: 58.5% less than 15 minutes, 25.5% 15 to 30 minutes, 8.8% 30 to 45 minutes, 2.4% 45 to 60 minutes, 4.8% 60 minutes or more (2006-2010 5-year est.)
Additional Information Contacts
Greater Johnstown Cambria County Chamber of Commerce . . . . (814) 536-5107
   http://www.johnstownchamber.com

BELSANO (unincorporated postal area)
Zip Code: 15922
   Covers a land area of 0.688 square miles and a water area of 0 square miles. Located at 40.51° N. Lat; 78.87° W. Long. Elevation is 1,831 feet. Population: 177 (2010); Density: 256.9 persons per square mile (2010); Race: 100.0% White, 0.0% Black, 0.0% Asian, 0.0% American Indian/Alaska Native, 0.0% Native Hawaiian/Other Pacific Islander, 0.0% Other, 0.0% Hispanic of any race (2010); Average household size: 2.37 (2010); Median age: 49.5 (2010); Males per 100 females: 105.8 (2010); Homeownership rate: 89.1% (2010)

BLACKLICK (township).

Covers a land area of 31.149 square miles and a water area of 0.047 square miles. Located at 40.52° N. Lat; 78.83° W. Long.
Population: 2,206 (1990); 2,200 (2000); 2,013 (2010); Density: 64.6 persons per square mile (2010); Race: 99.4% White, 0.1% Black, 0.1% Asian, 0.0% American Indian/Alaska Native, 0.0% Native Hawaiian/Other Pacific Islander, 0.4% Other, 0.4% Hispanic of any race (2010); Average household size: 2.46 (2010); Median age: 45.6 (2010); Males per 100 females: 99.9 (2010); Marriage status: 23.1% never married, 55.4% now married, 10.6% widowed, 11.0% divorced (2006-2010 5-year est.); Foreign born: 0.0% (2006-2010 5-year est.); Ancestry (includes multiple ancestries): 34.4% German, 22.3% Irish, 12.2% Polish, 9.3% English, 8.3% Slovak (2006-2010 5-year est.).
Economy: Single-family building permits issued: 2 (2011); Multi-family building permits issued: 0 (2011); Employment by occupation: 10.8% management, 4.2% professional, 11.4% services, 16.6% sales, 1.2% farming, 10.5% construction, 7.3% production (2006-2010 5-year est.).
Income: Per capita income: $19,840 (2006-2010 5-year est.); Median household income: $41,354 (2006-2010 5-year est.); Average household income: $48,089 (2006-2010 5-year est.); Percent of households with income of $100,000 or more: 6.3% (2006-2010 5-year est.); Poverty rate: 10.0% (2006-2010 5-year est.).
Education: Percent of population age 25 and over with: High school diploma (including GED) or higher: 83.2% (2006-2010 5-year est.); Bachelor's degree or higher: 14.0% (2006-2010 5-year est.); Master's degree or higher: 4.1% (2006-2010 5-year est.).
Housing: Homeownership rate: 86.3% (2010); Median home value: $87,800 (2006-2010 5-year est.); Median contract rent: $335 per month (2006-2010 5-year est.); Median year structure built: 1953 (2006-2010 5-year est.).
Safety: Violent crime rate: 0.0 per 10,000 population; Property crime rate: 0.0 per 10,000 population (2011).
Transportation: Commute to work: 96.6% car, 0.0% public transportation, 2.3% walk, 0.9% work from home (2006-2010 5-year est.); Travel time to work: 12.1% less than 15 minutes, 37.9% 15 to 30 minutes, 30.7% 30 to 45 minutes, 10.7% 45 to 60 minutes, 8.6% 60 minutes or more (2006-2010 5-year est.)
Additional Information Contacts
Greater Johnstown Cambria County Chamber of Commerce . . . . (814) 536-5107
   http://www.johnstownchamber.com

BLANDBURG (CDP).

Covers a land area of 0.484 square miles and a water area of 0 square miles. Located at 40.68° N. Lat; 78.42° W. Long. Elevation is 2,100 feet.
Population: n/a (1990); n/a (2000); 402 (2010); Density: 830.4 persons per square mile (2010); Race: 97.5% White, 1.2% Black, 0.2% Asian, 0.0% American Indian/Alaska Native, 0.0% Native Hawaiian/Other Pacific Islander, 1.1% Other, 0.0% Hispanic of any race (2010); Average household size: 2.34 (2010); Median age: 39.8 (2010); Males per 100 females: 116.1 (2010); Marriage status: 25.1% never married, 45.7% now married, 11.9% widowed, 17.4% divorced (2006-2010 5-year est.); Foreign born: 0.0% (2006-2010 5-year est.); Ancestry (includes multiple ancestries): 27.0% Irish, 27.0% German, 19.4% Polish, 18.7% Italian, 11.9% English (2006-2010 5-year est.).
Economy: Employment by occupation: 9.8% management, 0.0% professional, 13.0% services, 16.3% sales, 0.0% farming, 11.4% construction, 11.4% production (2006-2010 5-year est.).
Income: Per capita income: $17,344 (2006-2010 5-year est.); Median household income: $31,364 (2006-2010 5-year est.); Average household income: $33,270 (2006-2010 5-year est.); Percent of households with income of $100,000 or more: n/a (2006-2010 5-year est.); Poverty rate: 15.5% (2006-2010 5-year est.).
Education: Percent of population age 25 and over with: High school diploma (including GED) or higher: 91.8% (2006-2010 5-year est.); Bachelor's degree or higher: 3.8% (2006-2010 5-year est.); Master's degree or higher: 0.0% (2006-2010 5-year est.).
Housing: Homeownership rate: 84.7% (2010); Median home value: $60,500 (2006-2010 5-year est.); Median contract rent: $460 per month (2006-2010 5-year est.); Median year structure built: 1948 (2006-2010 5-year est.).
Transportation: Commute to work: 100.0% car, 0.0% public transportation, 0.0% walk, 0.0% work from home (2006-2010 5-year est.); Travel time to work: 2.6% less than 15 minutes, 43.0% 15 to 30 minutes,

27.2% 30 to 45 minutes, 11.4% 45 to 60 minutes, 15.8% 60 minutes or more (2006-2010 5-year est.).

BROWNSTOWN (borough). Covers a land area of 0.234 square miles and a water area of 0 square miles. Located at 40.33° N. Lat; 78.94° W. Long. Elevation is 1,516 feet.

Population: 937 (1990); 883 (2000); 744 (2010); Density: 3,175.6 persons per square mile (2010); Race: 99.3% White, 0.1% Black, 0.1% Asian, 0.0% American Indian/Alaska Native, 0.0% Native Hawaiian/Other Pacific Islander, 0.5% Other, 0.7% Hispanic of any race (2010); Average household size: 2.33 (2010); Median age: 44.8 (2010); Males per 100 females: 96.8 (2010); Marriage status: 29.1% never married, 60.8% now married, 7.1% widowed, 2.9% divorced (2006-2010 5-year est.); Foreign born: 0.8% (2006-2010 5-year est.); Ancestry (includes multiple ancestries): 32.8% German, 20.6% Slovak, 19.3% Irish, 9.9% Polish, 8.1% American (2006-2010 5-year est.).

Economy: Single-family building permits issued: 0 (2011); Multi-family building permits issued: 0 (2011); Employment by occupation: 4.8% management, 2.9% professional, 18.5% services, 18.0% sales, 5.3% farming, 3.7% construction, 2.9% production (2006-2010 5-year est.).

Income: Per capita income: $16,899 (2006-2010 5-year est.); Median household income: $37,891 (2006-2010 5-year est.); Average household income: $40,942 (2006-2010 5-year est.); Percent of households with income of $100,000 or more: n/a (2006-2010 5-year est.); Poverty rate: 6.9% (2006-2010 5-year est.).

Education: Percent of population age 25 and over with: High school diploma (including GED) or higher: 88.5% (2006-2010 5-year est.); Bachelor's degree or higher: 12.8% (2006-2010 5-year est.); Master's degree or higher: 3.8% (2006-2010 5-year est.).

Housing: Homeownership rate: 84.4% (2010); Median home value: $58,100 (2006-2010 5-year est.); Median contract rent: $313 per month (2006-2010 5-year est.); Median year structure built: 1941 (2006-2010 5-year est.).

Transportation: Commute to work: 97.0% car, 2.2% public transportation, 0.8% walk, 0.0% work from home (2006-2010 5-year est.); Travel time to work: 50.1% less than 15 minutes, 32.0% 15 to 30 minutes, 11.0% 30 to 45 minutes, 3.6% 45 to 60 minutes, 3.3% 60 minutes or more (2006-2010 5-year est.).

CAMBRIA (township). Covers a land area of 49.863 square miles and a water area of 0.338 square miles. Located at 40.49° N. Lat; 78.74° W. Long.

Population: 6,338 (1990); 6,323 (2000); 6,099 (2010); Density: 122.3 persons per square mile (2010); Race: 94.9% White, 3.7% Black, 0.5% Asian, 0.1% American Indian/Alaska Native, 0.0% Native Hawaiian/Other Pacific Islander, 0.8% Other, 1.1% Hispanic of any race (2010); Average household size: 2.50 (2010); Median age: 44.7 (2010); Males per 100 females: 110.7 (2010); Marriage status: 27.1% never married, 60.2% now married, 6.9% widowed, 5.8% divorced (2006-2010 5-year est.); Foreign born: 1.2% (2006-2010 5-year est.); Ancestry (includes multiple ancestries): 32.6% German, 29.0% Irish, 13.5% Italian, 12.9% Polish, 9.2% English (2006-2010 5-year est.).

Economy: Single-family building permits issued: 3 (2011); Multi-family building permits issued: 0 (2011); Employment by occupation: 5.0% management, 2.4% professional, 9.7% services, 14.4% sales, 3.5% farming, 10.4% construction, 4.8% production (2006-2010 5-year est.).

Income: Per capita income: $22,125 (2006-2010 5-year est.); Median household income: $41,392 (2006-2010 5-year est.); Average household income: $58,787 (2006-2010 5-year est.); Percent of households with income of $100,000 or more: 13.3% (2006-2010 5-year est.); Poverty rate: 20.5% (2006-2010 5-year est.).

Education: Percent of population age 25 and over with: High school diploma (including GED) or higher: 82.9% (2006-2010 5-year est.); Bachelor's degree or higher: 17.3% (2006-2010 5-year est.); Master's degree or higher: 5.7% (2006-2010 5-year est.).

Housing: Homeownership rate: 84.4% (2010); Median home value: $110,400 (2006-2010 5-year est.); Median contract rent: $318 per month (2006-2010 5-year est.); Median year structure built: 1950 (2006-2010 5-year est.).

Safety: Violent crime rate: 6.5 per 10,000 population; Property crime rate: 147.1 per 10,000 population (2011).

Transportation: Commute to work: 91.7% car, 2.0% public transportation, 0.0% walk, 2.5% work from home (2006-2010 5-year est.); Travel time to work: 40.4% less than 15 minutes, 30.2% 15 to 30 minutes, 20.0% 30 to

45 minutes, 9.2% 45 to 60 minutes, 0.2% 60 minutes or more (2006-2010 5-year est.).

Additional Information Contacts

Cambria Township . . . . (814) 472-8810
  http://www.cambriatownship.com
Greater Johnstown Cambria County Chamber of Commerce . . . . (814) 536-5107
  http://www.johnstownchamber.com

CARROLLTOWN (borough). Covers a land area of 0.692 square miles and a water area of 0 square miles. Located at 40.60° N. Lat; 78.71° W. Long. Elevation is 2,175 feet.

History: Laid out 1840, incorporated 1858.

Population: 1,286 (1990); 1,049 (2000); 853 (2010); Density: 1,232.8 persons per square mile (2010); Race: 98.8% White, 0.2% Black, 0.0% Asian, 0.0% American Indian/Alaska Native, 0.0% Native Hawaiian/Other Pacific Islander, 1.0% Other, 0.5% Hispanic of any race (2010); Average household size: 2.40 (2010); Median age: 45.3 (2010); Males per 100 females: 95.2 (2010); Marriage status: 24.3% never married, 60.4% now married, 9.8% widowed, 5.5% divorced (2006-2010 5-year est.); Foreign born: 0.6% (2006-2010 5-year est.); Ancestry (includes multiple ancestries): 47.3% German, 22.7% Irish, 19.1% Polish, 9.6% Italian, 6.7% English (2006-2010 5-year est.).

Economy: Single-family building permits issued: 0 (2011); Multi-family building permits issued: 0 (2011); Employment by occupation: 4.9% management, 1.3% professional, 13.5% services, 15.0% sales, 6.2% farming, 18.1% construction, 8.2% production (2006-2010 5-year est.).

Income: Per capita income: $21,420 (2006-2010 5-year est.); Median household income: $44,318 (2006-2010 5-year est.); Average household income: $48,876 (2006-2010 5-year est.); Percent of households with income of $100,000 or more: 6.2% (2006-2010 5-year est.); Poverty rate: 7.6% (2006-2010 5-year est.).

Education: Percent of population age 25 and over with: High school diploma (including GED) or higher: 92.7% (2006-2010 5-year est.); Bachelor's degree or higher: 9.3% (2006-2010 5-year est.); Master's degree or higher: 4.3% (2006-2010 5-year est.).

School District(s)

Cambria Heights SD (PK-12)
  2010-11 Enrollment: 1,465 . . . . (814) 674-3626

Housing: Homeownership rate: 82.5% (2010); Median home value: $80,900 (2006-2010 5-year est.); Median contract rent: $454 per month (2006-2010 5-year est.); Median year structure built: 1941 (2006-2010 5-year est.).

Safety: Violent crime rate: 0.0 per 10,000 population; Property crime rate: 140.2 per 10,000 population (2011).

Transportation: Commute to work: 94.2% car, 0.0% public transportation, 4.0% walk, 1.9% work from home (2006-2010 5-year est.); Travel time to work: 31.0% less than 15 minutes, 28.9% 15 to 30 minutes, 26.3% 30 to 45 minutes, 7.8% 45 to 60 minutes, 5.9% 60 minutes or more (2006-2010 5-year est.).

Additional Information Contacts

Borough of Carrolltown . . . . (814) 344-6650
  http://www.carrolltown.pa.us

CASSANDRA (borough). Covers a land area of 0.076 square miles and a water area of 0 square miles. Located at 40.41° N. Lat; 78.64° W. Long. Elevation is 1,808 feet.

Population: 192 (1990); 136 (2000); 147 (2010); Density: 1,924.1 persons per square mile (2010); Race: 97.3% White, 0.0% Black, 0.0% Asian, 0.0% American Indian/Alaska Native, 0.0% Native Hawaiian/Other Pacific Islander, 2.7% Other, 0.0% Hispanic of any race (2010); Average household size: 2.33 (2010); Median age: 43.1 (2010); Males per 100 females: 116.2 (2010); Marriage status: 20.2% never married, 58.0% now married, 9.2% widowed, 12.6% divorced (2006-2010 5-year est.); Foreign born: 0.0% (2006-2010 5-year est.); Ancestry (includes multiple ancestries): 43.4% German, 20.2% Polish, 19.4% Irish, 16.3% Slovak, 10.1% English (2006-2010 5-year est.).

Economy: Single-family building permits issued: 0 (2011); Multi-family building permits issued: 0 (2011); Employment by occupation: 16.3% management, 0.0% professional, 16.3% services, 8.8% sales, 0.0% farming, 18.8% construction, 16.3% production (2006-2010 5-year est.).

Income: Per capita income: $24,158 (2006-2010 5-year est.); Median household income: $33,750 (2006-2010 5-year est.); Average household income: $51,488 (2006-2010 5-year est.); Percent of households with

income of $100,000 or more: 11.6% (2006-2010 5-year est.); Poverty rate: 3.2% (2006-2010 5-year est.).

Education: Percent of population age 25 and over with: High school diploma (including GED) or higher: 81.4% (2006-2010 5-year est.); Bachelor's degree or higher: 5.2% (2006-2010 5-year est.); Master's degree or higher: 3.1% (2006-2010 5-year est.).

Housing: Homeownership rate: 74.6% (2010); Median home value: $56,700 (2006-2010 5-year est.); Median contract rent: $450 per month (2006-2010 5-year est.); Median year structure built: before 1940 (2006-2010 5-year est.).

Transportation: Commute to work: 91.0% car, 0.0% public transportation, 3.8% walk, 0.0% work from home (2006-2010 5-year est.); Travel time to work: 16.7% less than 15 minutes, 55.1% 15 to 30 minutes, 17.9% 30 to 45 minutes, 7.7% 45 to 60 minutes, 2.6% 60 minutes or more (2006-2010 5-year est.)

CHEST (township). Covers a land area of 29.122 square miles and a water area of 0.039 square miles. Located at 40.68° N. Lat; 78.62° W. Long.

Population: 312 (1990); 346 (2000); 349 (2010); Density: 12.0 persons per square mile (2010); Race: 98.0% White, 0.0% Black, 0.0% Asian, 0.6% American Indian/Alaska Native, 0.0% Native Hawaiian/Other Pacific Islander, 1.4% Other, 1.7% Hispanic of any race (2010); Average household size: 2.39 (2010); Median age: 52.3 (2010); Males per 100 females: 119.5 (2010); Marriage status: 18.6% never married, 68.2% now married, 5.1% widowed, 8.1% divorced (2006-2010 5-year est.); Foreign born: 0.6% (2006-2010 5-year est.); Ancestry (includes multiple ancestries): 39.7% German, 17.1% Polish, 15.4% Irish, 6.4% Scotch-Irish, 5.8% Dutch (2006-2010 5-year est.).

Economy: Single-family building permits issued: 3 (2011); Multi-family building permits issued: 0 (2011); Employment by occupation: 2.1% management, 4.6% professional, 3.1% services, 11.3% sales, 5.7% farming, 10.3% construction, 12.4% production (2006-2010 5-year est.).

Income: Per capita income: $21,517 (2006-2010 5-year est.); Median household income: $48,750 (2006-2010 5-year est.); Average household income: $57,988 (2006-2010 5-year est.); Percent of households with income of $100,000 or more: 10.3% (2006-2010 5-year est.); Poverty rate: 3.5% (2006-2010 5-year est.).

Education: Percent of population age 25 and over with: High school diploma (including GED) or higher: 91.7% (2006-2010 5-year est.); Bachelor's degree or higher: 11.9% (2006-2010 5-year est.); Master's degree or higher: 2.8% (2006-2010 5-year est.).

Housing: Homeownership rate: 93.8% (2010); Median home value: $116,300 (2006-2010 5-year est.); Median contract rent: <$101 per month (2006-2010 5-year est.); Median year structure built: 1975 (2006-2010 5-year est.).

Transportation: Commute to work: 95.3% car, 0.0% public transportation, 2.1% walk, 2.6% work from home (2006-2010 5-year est.); Travel time to work: 20.5% less than 15 minutes, 19.5% 15 to 30 minutes, 35.7% 30 to 45 minutes, 4.9% 45 to 60 minutes, 19.5% 60 minutes or more (2006-2010 5-year est.)

CHEST SPRINGS (borough). Covers a land area of 0.193 square miles and a water area of 0 square miles. Located at 40.58° N. Lat; 78.61° W. Long. Elevation is 1,991 feet.

Population: 166 (1990); 110 (2000); 149 (2010); Density: 773.0 persons per square mile (2010); Race: 100.0% White, 0.0% Black, 0.0% Asian, 0.0% American Indian/Alaska Native, 0.0% Native Hawaiian/Other Pacific Islander, 0.0% Other, 0.0% Hispanic of any race (2010); Average household size: 2.40 (2010); Median age: 36.3 (2010); Males per 100 females: 104.1 (2010); Marriage status: 22.9% never married, 53.2% now married, 7.3% widowed, 16.5% divorced (2006-2010 5-year est.); Foreign born: 0.0% (2006-2010 5-year est.); Ancestry (includes multiple ancestries): 63.0% German, 27.4% Irish, 6.7% American, 5.9% French, 4.4% Polish (2006-2010 5-year est.).

Economy: Single-family building permits issued: 0 (2011); Multi-family building permits issued: 0 (2011); Employment by occupation: 10.6% management, 0.0% professional, 21.2% services, 13.6% sales, 4.5% farming, 31.8% construction, 1.5% production (2006-2010 5-year est.).

Income: Per capita income: $20,927 (2006-2010 5-year est.); Median household income: $41,250 (2006-2010 5-year est.); Average household income: $50,196 (2006-2010 5-year est.); Percent of households with income of $100,000 or more: 7.2% (2006-2010 5-year est.); Poverty rate: 8.1% (2006-2010 5-year est.).

Education: Percent of population age 25 and over with: High school diploma (including GED) or higher: 88.7% (2006-2010 5-year est.); Bachelor's degree or higher: 14.4% (2006-2010 5-year est.); Master's degree or higher: 2.1% (2006-2010 5-year est.).

Housing: Homeownership rate: 85.5% (2010); Median home value: $89,000 (2006-2010 5-year est.); Median contract rent: $280 per month (2006-2010 5-year est.); Median year structure built: 1958 (2006-2010 5-year est.).

Transportation: Commute to work: 100.0% car, 0.0% public transportation, 0.0% walk, 0.0% work from home (2006-2010 5-year est.); Travel time to work: 24.2% less than 15 minutes, 40.9% 15 to 30 minutes, 15.2% 30 to 45 minutes, 6.1% 45 to 60 minutes, 13.6% 60 minutes or more (2006-2010 5-year est.)

CLEARFIELD (township). Covers a land area of 30.986 square miles and a water area of 0 square miles. Located at 40.61° N. Lat; 78.58° W. Long.

Population: 1,736 (1990); 1,680 (2000); 1,604 (2010); Density: 51.8 persons per square mile (2010); Race: 99.1% White, 0.4% Black, 0.1% Asian, 0.0% American Indian/Alaska Native, 0.0% Native Hawaiian/Other Pacific Islander, 0.4% Other, 0.9% Hispanic of any race (2010); Average household size: 2.70 (2010); Median age: 41.9 (2010); Males per 100 females: 106.7 (2010); Marriage status: 23.2% never married, 66.5% now married, 5.0% widowed, 5.3% divorced (2006-2010 5-year est.); Foreign born: 0.2% (2006-2010 5-year est.); Ancestry (includes multiple ancestries): 43.5% German, 28.3% Irish, 12.1% Italian, 11.1% English, 7.8% Polish (2006-2010 5-year est.).

Economy: Single-family building permits issued: 5 (2011); Multi-family building permits issued: 0 (2011); Employment by occupation: 6.9% management, 5.6% professional, 10.5% services, 19.8% sales, 1.9% farming, 19.3% construction, 8.3% production (2006-2010 5-year est.).

Income: Per capita income: $21,886 (2006-2010 5-year est.); Median household income: $52,321 (2006-2010 5-year est.); Average household income: $60,929 (2006-2010 5-year est.); Percent of households with income of $100,000 or more: 10.0% (2006-2010 5-year est.); Poverty rate: 7.5% (2006-2010 5-year est.).

Education: Percent of population age 25 and over with: High school diploma (including GED) or higher: 91.4% (2006-2010 5-year est.); Bachelor's degree or higher: 9.7% (2006-2010 5-year est.); Master's degree or higher: 2.7% (2006-2010 5-year est.).

Housing: Homeownership rate: 89.1% (2010); Median home value: $111,700 (2006-2010 5-year est.); Median contract rent: $292 per month (2006-2010 5-year est.); Median year structure built: 1973 (2006-2010 5-year est.).

Transportation: Commute to work: 92.6% car, 0.6% public transportation, 0.4% walk, 5.3% work from home (2006-2010 5-year est.); Travel time to work: 13.4% less than 15 minutes, 31.3% 15 to 30 minutes, 38.2% 30 to 45 minutes, 8.1% 45 to 60 minutes, 9.0% 60 minutes or more (2006-2010 5-year est.)

Additional Information Contacts

Blair County Chamber of Commerce . . . . (814) 943-8151
    http://www.blairchamber.com

COLVER (CDP). Covers a land area of 1.263 square miles and a water area of 0 square miles. Located at 40.54° N. Lat; 78.79° W. Long. Elevation is 2,169 feet.

Population: 1,054 (1990); 1,035 (2000); 959 (2010); Density: 759.0 persons per square mile (2010); Race: 98.6% White, 0.1% Black, 0.2% Asian, 0.3% American Indian/Alaska Native, 0.0% Native Hawaiian/Other Pacific Islander, 0.8% Other, 0.3% Hispanic of any race (2010); Average household size: 2.48 (2010); Median age: 38.5 (2010); Males per 100 females: 93.0 (2010); Marriage status: 34.2% never married, 52.8% now married, 11.4% widowed, 1.6% divorced (2006-2010 5-year est.); Foreign born: 0.0% (2006-2010 5-year est.); Ancestry (includes multiple ancestries): 46.9% German, 25.8% Irish, 17.2% Polish, 11.9% Italian, 8.8% French (2006-2010 5-year est.).

Economy: Employment by occupation: 9.1% management, 0.0% professional, 10.7% services, 15.0% sales, 0.0% farming, 13.4% construction, 10.7% production (2006-2010 5-year est.).

Income: Per capita income: $15,880 (2006-2010 5-year est.); Median household income: $29,127 (2006-2010 5-year est.); Average household income: $35,781 (2006-2010 5-year est.); Percent of households with income of $100,000 or more: 3.9% (2006-2010 5-year est.); Poverty rate: 31.6% (2006-2010 5-year est.).

Education: Percent of population age 25 and over with: High school diploma (including GED) or higher: 71.1% (2006-2010 5-year est.); Bachelor's degree or higher: 5.8% (2006-2010 5-year est.); Master's degree or higher: 0.0% (2006-2010 5-year est.).

Housing: Homeownership rate: 82.3% (2010); Median home value: $59,800 (2006-2010 5-year est.); Median contract rent: <$101 per month (2006-2010 5-year est.); Median year structure built: before 1940 (2006-2010 5-year est.).

Transportation: Commute to work: 100.0% car, 0.0% public transportation, 0.0% walk, 0.0% work from home (2006-2010 5-year est.); Travel time to work: 31.9% less than 15 minutes, 25.4% 15 to 30 minutes, 39.4% 30 to 45 minutes, 3.3% 45 to 60 minutes, 0.0% 60 minutes or more (2006-2010 5-year est.)

CONEMAUGH (township). Aka East Conemaugh. Covers a land area of 11.286 square miles and a water area of 0.090 square miles. Located at 40.35° N. Lat; 78.85° W. Long. Elevation is 1,217 feet.

History: Incorporated 1891.

Population: 2,399 (1990); 2,145 (2000); 2,012 (2010); Density: 178.3 persons per square mile (2010); Race: 97.5% White, 1.2% Black, 0.0% Asian, 0.3% American Indian/Alaska Native, 0.0% Native Hawaiian/Other Pacific Islander, 1.0% Other, 1.6% Hispanic of any race (2010); Average household size: 2.35 (2010); Median age: 48.1 (2010); Males per 100 females: 96.5 (2010); Marriage status: 25.5% never married, 59.2% now married, 9.2% widowed, 6.1% divorced (2006-2010 5-year est.); Foreign born: 0.0% (2006-2010 5-year est.); Ancestry (includes multiple ancestries): 37.2% German, 13.0% Polish, 11.9% Irish, 11.6% Italian, 6.8% American (2006-2010 5-year est.).

Economy: Single-family building permits issued: 0 (2011); Multi-family building permits issued: 0 (2011); Employment by occupation: 5.0% management, 3.2% professional, 11.9% services, 13.8% sales, 10.4% farming, 9.0% construction, 4.2% production (2006-2010 5-year est.).

Income: Per capita income: $23,146 (2006-2010 5-year est.); Median household income: $46,726 (2006-2010 5-year est.); Average household income: $53,269 (2006-2010 5-year est.); Percent of households with income of $100,000 or more: 8.9% (2006-2010 5-year est.); Poverty rate: 3.0% (2006-2010 5-year est.).

Education: Percent of population age 25 and over with: High school diploma (including GED) or higher: 85.8% (2006-2010 5-year est.); Bachelor's degree or higher: 16.3% (2006-2010 5-year est.); Master's degree or higher: 3.5% (2006-2010 5-year est.).

Housing: Homeownership rate: 89.5% (2010); Median home value: $88,500 (2006-2010 5-year est.); Median contract rent: $316 per month (2006-2010 5-year est.); Median year structure built: 1956 (2006-2010 5-year est.).

Transportation: Commute to work: 96.8% car, 1.1% public transportation, 0.7% walk, 0.7% work from home (2006-2010 5-year est.); Travel time to work: 39.5% less than 15 minutes, 45.1% 15 to 30 minutes, 8.9% 30 to 45 minutes, 3.6% 45 to 60 minutes, 3.0% 60 minutes or more (2006-2010 5-year est.)

Additional Information Contacts
Greater Johnstown Cambria County Chamber of Commerce . . . . (814) 536-5107
  http://www.johnstownchamber.com

CRESSON (borough). Covers a land area of 0.483 square miles and a water area of 0 square miles. Located at 40.46° N. Lat; 78.59° W. Long. Elevation is 2,018 feet.

Population: 1,784 (1990); 1,631 (2000); 1,711 (2010); Density: 3,542.9 persons per square mile (2010); Race: 98.8% White, 0.4% Black, 0.2% Asian, 0.1% American Indian/Alaska Native, 0.0% Native Hawaiian/Other Pacific Islander, 0.5% Other, 0.4% Hispanic of any race (2010); Average household size: 2.27 (2010); Median age: 37.3 (2010); Males per 100 females: 91.2 (2010); Marriage status: 38.1% never married, 41.1% now married, 10.7% widowed, 10.1% divorced (2006-2010 5-year est.); Foreign born: 2.2% (2006-2010 5-year est.); Ancestry (includes multiple ancestries): 37.1% German, 29.0% Irish, 14.6% Polish, 12.7% Italian, 5.4% English (2006-2010 5-year est.).

Economy: Single-family building permits issued: 0 (2011); Multi-family building permits issued: 0 (2011); Employment by occupation: 10.7% management, 0.8% professional, 17.0% services, 18.0% sales, 4.5% farming, 6.5% construction, 4.3% production (2006-2010 5-year est.).

Income: Per capita income: $18,661 (2006-2010 5-year est.); Median household income: $33,500 (2006-2010 5-year est.); Average household income: $45,173 (2006-2010 5-year est.); Percent of households with

income of $100,000 or more: 8.9% (2006-2010 5-year est.); Poverty rate: 21.1% (2006-2010 5-year est.).

Education: Percent of population age 25 and over with: High school diploma (including GED) or higher: 92.1% (2006-2010 5-year est.); Bachelor's degree or higher: 16.6% (2006-2010 5-year est.); Master's degree or higher: 6.4% (2006-2010 5-year est.).

School District(s)
Cresson Secure Treatment Unit (09-12)
  2010-11 Enrollment: 38 . . . . (814) 886-6258
Penn Cambria SD (PK-12)
  2010-11 Enrollment: 1,758 . . . . (814) 886-8121

Four-year College(s)
Mount Aloysius College (Private, Not-for-profit, Roman Catholic)
  Fall 2010 Enrollment: 1,491 . . . . (814) 886-4131
  2011-12 Tuition: In-state $18,750; Out-of-state $18,750

Housing: Homeownership rate: 60.2% (2010); Median home value: $93,300 (2006-2010 5-year est.); Median contract rent: $419 per month (2006-2010 5-year est.); Median year structure built: before 1940 (2006-2010 5-year est.).

Safety: Violent crime rate: 11.7 per 10,000 population; Property crime rate: 139.9 per 10,000 population (2011).

Newspapers: Cresson and Gallitzin Mainliner (Community news; Circulation 4,500); Cresson/Gallitzin Mainliner (Local news; Circulation 4,500); Tribune-Democrat - Cresson Bureau (Local news)

Transportation: Commute to work: 91.5% car, 0.0% public transportation, 7.6% walk, 0.9% work from home (2006-2010 5-year est.); Travel time to work: 39.8% less than 15 minutes, 34.4% 15 to 30 minutes, 18.6% 30 to 45 minutes, 3.1% 45 to 60 minutes, 4.1% 60 minutes or more (2006-2010 5-year est.)

Additional Information Contacts
Cresson Area Chamber of Commerce . . . . (814) 886-7710
  http://www.cressonarea.com

CRESSON (township). Covers a land area of 12.025 square miles and a water area of 0.022 square miles. Located at 40.45° N. Lat; 78.59° W. Long. Elevation is 2,018 feet.

History: Allegheny Portage Railroad National Historical Site to East. Birthplace of Robert E. Peary. Incorporated 1906.

Population: 3,284 (1990); 4,055 (2000); 4,336 (2010); Density: 360.6 persons per square mile (2010); Race: 80.7% White, 14.7% Black, 0.4% Asian, 0.0% American Indian/Alaska Native, 0.0% Native Hawaiian/Other Pacific Islander, 4.2% Other, 4.4% Hispanic of any race (2010); Average household size: 2.35 (2010); Median age: 38.3 (2010); Males per 100 females: 180.6 (2010); Marriage status: 30.2% never married, 47.8% now married, 8.0% widowed, 14.0% divorced (2006-2010 5-year est.); Foreign born: 1.0% (2006-2010 5-year est.); Ancestry (includes multiple ancestries): 26.2% German, 20.6% Irish, 11.8% Polish, 9.6% Italian, 4.7% English (2006-2010 5-year est.).

Economy: Single-family building permits issued: 2 (2011); Multi-family building permits issued: 0 (2011); Employment by occupation: 6.9% management, 1.6% professional, 9.4% services, 13.3% sales, 4.2% farming, 9.9% construction, 7.8% production (2006-2010 5-year est.).

Income: Per capita income: $19,892 (2006-2010 5-year est.); Median household income: $39,640 (2006-2010 5-year est.); Average household income: $52,106 (2006-2010 5-year est.); Percent of households with income of $100,000 or more: 9.7% (2006-2010 5-year est.); Poverty rate: 14.0% (2006-2010 5-year est.).

Education: Percent of population age 25 and over with: High school diploma (including GED) or higher: 82.7% (2006-2010 5-year est.); Bachelor's degree or higher: 18.2% (2006-2010 5-year est.); Master's degree or higher: 8.4% (2006-2010 5-year est.).

Four-year College(s)
Mount Aloysius College (Private, Not-for-profit, Roman Catholic)
  Fall 2010 Enrollment: 1,491 . . . . (814) 886-4131
  2011-12 Tuition: In-state $18,750; Out-of-state $18,750

Housing: Homeownership rate: 74.2% (2010); Median home value: $120,200 (2006-2010 5-year est.); Median contract rent: $345 per month (2006-2010 5-year est.); Median year structure built: 1981 (2006-2010 5-year est.).

Safety: Violent crime rate: 18.4 per 10,000 population; Property crime rate: 71.3 per 10,000 population (2011).

Newspapers: Cresson and Gallitzin Mainliner (Community news; Circulation 4,500); Cresson/Gallitzin Mainliner (Local news; Circulation 4,500); Tribune-Democrat - Cresson Bureau (Local news)

Transportation: Commute to work: 95.1% car, 0.0% public transportation, 2.4% walk, 2.5% work from home (2006-2010 5-year est.); Travel time to work: 34.9% less than 15 minutes, 41.7% 15 to 30 minutes, 18.7% 30 to 45 minutes, 2.7% 45 to 60 minutes, 1.9% 60 minutes or more (2006-2010 5-year est.)

Additional Information Contacts

Cresson Area Chamber of Commerce . . . . (814) 886-7710
http://www.cressonarea.com

CROYLE (township). Covers a land area of 18.328 square miles and a water area of 0.032 square miles. Located at 40.37° N. Lat; 78.76° W. Long.

Population: 2,475 (1990); 2,233 (2000); 2,339 (2010); Density: 127.6 persons per square mile (2010); Race: 99.2% White, 0.3% Black, 0.0% Asian, 0.1% American Indian/Alaska Native, 0.0% Native Hawaiian/Other Pacific Islander, 0.4% Other, 0.4% Hispanic of any race (2010); Average household size: 2.62 (2010); Median age: 41.7 (2010); Males per 100 females: 104.5 (2010); Marriage status: 30.3% never married, 57.0% now married, 8.0% widowed, 4.8% divorced (2006-2010 5-year est.); Foreign born: 0.2% (2006-2010 5-year est.); Ancestry (includes multiple ancestries): 51.6% German, 14.1% Irish, 9.9% Polish, 9.4% English, 8.6% Slovak (2006-2010 5-year est.).

Economy: Single-family building permits issued: 1 (2011); Multi-family building permits issued: 0 (2011); Employment by occupation: 4.5% management, 2.4% professional, 8.2% services, 15.3% sales, 1.5% farming, 18.9% construction, 8.1% production (2006-2010 5-year est.).

Income: Per capita income: $21,079 (2006-2010 5-year est.); Median household income: $50,262 (2006-2010 5-year est.); Average household income: $54,711 (2006-2010 5-year est.); Percent of households with income of $100,000 or more: 10.3% (2006-2010 5-year est.); Poverty rate: 10.2% (2006-2010 5-year est.).

Education: Percent of population age 25 and over with: High school diploma (including GED) or higher: 88.3% (2006-2010 5-year est.); Bachelor's degree or higher: 18.4% (2006-2010 5-year est.); Master's degree or higher: 5.6% (2006-2010 5-year est.).

Housing: Homeownership rate: 88.1% (2010); Median home value: $107,700 (2006-2010 5-year est.); Median contract rent: $347 per month (2006-2010 5-year est.); Median year structure built: 1958 (2006-2010 5-year est.).

Safety: Violent crime rate: 0.0 per 10,000 population; Property crime rate: 93.8 per 10,000 population (2011).

Transportation: Commute to work: 92.6% car, 0.0% public transportation, 0.0% walk, 6.9% work from home (2006-2010 5-year est.); Travel time to work: 25.8% less than 15 minutes, 47.3% 15 to 30 minutes, 14.7% 30 to 45 minutes, 8.9% 45 to 60 minutes, 3.3% 60 minutes or more (2006-2010 5-year est.)

Additional Information Contacts

Greater Johnstown Cambria County Chamber of Commerce . . . . (814) 536-5107
http://www.johnstownchamber.com

DAISYTOWN (borough). Covers a land area of 0.235 square miles and a water area of 0 square miles. Located at 40.32° N. Lat; 78.90° W. Long. Elevation is 1,801 feet.

Population: 367 (1990); 356 (2000); 326 (2010); Density: 1,384.9 persons per square mile (2010); Race: 100.0% White, 0.0% Black, 0.0% Asian, 0.0% American Indian/Alaska Native, 0.0% Native Hawaiian/Other Pacific Islander, 0.0% Other, 0.3% Hispanic of any race (2010); Average household size: 2.38 (2010); Median age: 49.5 (2010); Males per 100 females: 95.2 (2010); Marriage status: 31.2% never married, 54.5% now married, 9.5% widowed, 4.8% divorced (2006-2010 5-year est.); Foreign born: 0.7% (2006-2010 5-year est.); Ancestry (includes multiple ancestries): 44.1% German, 12.5% English, 12.5% American, 8.8% Polish, 8.8% Irish (2006-2010 5-year est.).

Economy: Single-family building permits issued: 0 (2011); Multi-family building permits issued: 0 (2011); Employment by occupation: 9.2% management, 0.0% professional, 11.8% services, 13.8% sales, 2.0% farming, 13.2% construction, 13.2% production (2006-2010 5-year est.).

Income: Per capita income: $22,988 (2006-2010 5-year est.); Median household income: $44,554 (2006-2010 5-year est.); Average household income: $59,155 (2006-2010 5-year est.); Percent of households with income of $100,000 or more: 13.5% (2006-2010 5-year est.); Poverty rate: 2.7% (2006-2010 5-year est.).

Education: Percent of population age 25 and over with: High school diploma (including GED) or higher: 90.3% (2006-2010 5-year est.);

Bachelor's degree or higher: 18.9% (2006-2010 5-year est.); Master's degree or higher: 8.7% (2006-2010 5-year est.).

Housing: Homeownership rate: 92.7% (2010); Median home value: $80,300 (2006-2010 5-year est.); Median contract rent: $233 per month (2006-2010 5-year est.); Median year structure built: 1954 (2006-2010 5-year est.).

Transportation: Commute to work: 89.2% car, 0.0% public transportation, 3.4% walk, 7.4% work from home (2006-2010 5-year est.); Travel time to work: 27.0% less than 15 minutes, 56.2% 15 to 30 minutes, 5.8% 30 to 45 minutes, 10.9% 45 to 60 minutes, 0.0% 60 minutes or more (2006-2010 5-year est.)

DALE (borough). Covers a land area of 0.176 square miles and a water area of 0 square miles. Located at 40.31° N. Lat; 78.90° W. Long. Elevation is 1,299 feet.

History: Incorporated 1891.

Population: 1,642 (1990); 1,503 (2000); 1,234 (2010); Density: 7,023.8 persons per square mile (2010); Race: 89.1% White, 6.1% Black, 0.2% Asian, 0.2% American Indian/Alaska Native, 0.1% Native Hawaiian/Other Pacific Islander, 4.3% Other, 2.6% Hispanic of any race (2010); Average household size: 2.21 (2010); Median age: 40.7 (2010); Males per 100 females: 82.0 (2010); Marriage status: 31.5% never married, 47.0% now married, 7.7% widowed, 13.7% divorced (2006-2010 5-year est.); Foreign born: 0.0% (2006-2010 5-year est.); Ancestry (includes multiple ancestries): 32.5% German, 26.8% Irish, 7.5% Dutch, 7.4% Italian, 7.4% Polish (2006-2010 5-year est.).

Economy: Single-family building permits issued: 0 (2011); Multi-family building permits issued: 0 (2011); Employment by occupation: 4.6% management, 1.1% professional, 17.7% services, 24.7% sales, 4.3% farming, 9.1% construction, 3.2% production (2006-2010 5-year est.).

Income: Per capita income: $14,736 (2006-2010 5-year est.); Median household income: $26,250 (2006-2010 5-year est.); Average household income: $35,000 (2006-2010 5-year est.); Percent of households with income of $100,000 or more: 2.7% (2006-2010 5-year est.); Poverty rate: 23.4% (2006-2010 5-year est.).

Education: Percent of population age 25 and over with: High school diploma (including GED) or higher: 83.4% (2006-2010 5-year est.); Bachelor's degree or higher: 7.9% (2006-2010 5-year est.); Master's degree or higher: 1.8% (2006-2010 5-year est.).

Housing: Homeownership rate: 44.4% (2010); Median home value: $40,000 (2006-2010 5-year est.); Median contract rent: $332 per month (2006-2010 5-year est.); Median year structure built: before 1940 (2006-2010 5-year est.).

Safety: Violent crime rate: 40.4 per 10,000 population; Property crime rate: 88.9 per 10,000 population (2011).

Transportation: Commute to work: 82.3% car, 5.6% public transportation, 8.7% walk, 2.1% work from home (2006-2010 5-year est.); Travel time to work: 41.8% less than 15 minutes, 41.5% 15 to 30 minutes, 4.7% 30 to 45 minutes, 4.5% 45 to 60 minutes, 7.5% 60 minutes or more (2006-2010 5-year est.)

Additional Information Contacts

Greater Johnstown Cambria County Chamber of Commerce . . . . (814) 536-5107
http://www.johnstownchamber.com

DEAN (township). Covers a land area of 20.865 square miles and a water area of 0 square miles. Located at 40.59° N. Lat; 78.49° W. Long. Elevation is 1,545 feet.

Population: 398 (1990); 408 (2000); 391 (2010); Density: 18.7 persons per square mile (2010); Race: 99.0% White, 0.8% Black, 0.0% Asian, 0.0% American Indian/Alaska Native, 0.0% Native Hawaiian/Other Pacific Islander, 0.2% Other, 0.0% Hispanic of any race (2010); Average household size: 2.40 (2010); Median age: 44.7 (2010); Males per 100 females: 104.7 (2010); Marriage status: 16.9% never married, 62.2% now married, 11.2% widowed, 9.7% divorced (2006-2010 5-year est.); Foreign born: 0.0% (2006-2010 5-year est.); Ancestry (includes multiple ancestries): 46.3% German, 26.1% Italian, 17.5% Polish, 16.7% Irish, 7.8% English (2006-2010 5-year est.).

Economy: Single-family building permits issued: 0 (2011); Multi-family building permits issued: 0 (2011); Employment by occupation: 9.0% management, 0.0% professional, 12.3% services, 20.0% sales, 2.6% farming, 27.1% construction, 2.6% production (2006-2010 5-year est.).

Income: Per capita income: $20,260 (2006-2010 5-year est.); Median household income: $30,000 (2006-2010 5-year est.); Average household income: $46,739 (2006-2010 5-year est.); Percent of households with

income of $100,000 or more: 4.1% (2006-2010 5-year est.); Poverty rate: 12.8% (2006-2010 5-year est.).

Education: Percent of population age 25 and over with: High school diploma (including GED) or higher: 84.5% (2006-2010 5-year est.); Bachelor's degree or higher: 6.9% (2006-2010 5-year est.); Master's degree or higher: 2.9% (2006-2010 5-year est.).

Housing: Homeownership rate: 90.2% (2010); Median home value: $87,000 (2006-2010 5-year est.); Median contract rent: $240 per month (2006-2010 5-year est.); Median year structure built: 1963 (2006-2010 5-year est.).

Transportation: Commute to work: 97.4% car, 0.0% public transportation, 0.0% walk, 2.6% work from home (2006-2010 5-year est.); Travel time to work: 18.1% less than 15 minutes, 47.0% 15 to 30 minutes, 23.5% 30 to 45 minutes, 1.3% 45 to 60 minutes, 10.1% 60 minutes or more (2006-2010 5-year est.)

DUNLO (CDP). Covers a land area of 0.523 square miles and a water area of 0 square miles. Located at 40.29° N. Lat; 78.72° W. Long. Elevation is 2,201 feet.

Population: n/a (1990); n/a (2000); 342 (2010); Density: 653.5 persons per square mile (2010); Race: 99.1% White, 0.3% Black, 0.3% Asian, 0.0% American Indian/Alaska Native, 0.0% Native Hawaiian/Other Pacific Islander, 0.3% Other, 0.3% Hispanic of any race (2010); Average household size: 2.30 (2010); Median age: 44.1 (2010); Males per 100 females: 112.4 (2010); Marriage status: 26.9% never married, 45.7% now married, 14.6% widowed, 12.8% divorced (2006-2010 5-year est.); Foreign born: 0.0% (2006-2010 5-year est.); Ancestry (includes multiple ancestries): 38.8% German, 35.6% English, 20.5% Scottish, 17.4% Welsh, 11.9% Italian (2006-2010 5-year est.).

Economy: Employment by occupation: 25.0% management, 0.0% professional, 28.1% services, 23.8% sales, 0.0% farming, 0.0% construction, 0.0% production (2006-2010 5-year est.).

Income: Per capita income: $17,122 (2006-2010 5-year est.); Median household income: $40,658 (2006-2010 5-year est.); Average household income: $33,741 (2006-2010 5-year est.); Percent of households with income of $100,000 or more: n/a (2006-2010 5-year est.); Poverty rate: 13.7% (2006-2010 5-year est.).

Education: Percent of population age 25 and over with: High school diploma (including GED) or higher: 67.1% (2006-2010 5-year est.); Bachelor's degree or higher: 51.4% (2006-2010 5-year est.); Master's degree or higher: 6.4% (2006-2010 5-year est.).

Housing: Homeownership rate: 83.9% (2010); Median home value: $83,600 (2006-2010 5-year est.); Median contract rent: n/a per month (2006-2010 5-year est.); Median year structure built: 1949 (2006-2010 5-year est.).

Transportation: Commute to work: 100.0% car, 0.0% public transportation, 0.0% walk, 0.0% work from home (2006-2010 5-year est.); Travel time to work: 6.9% less than 15 minutes, 93.1% 15 to 30 minutes, 0.0% 30 to 45 minutes, 0.0% 45 to 60 minutes, 0.0% 60 minutes or more (2006-2010 5-year est.)

DYSART (unincorporated postal area)

Zip Code: 16636

Covers a land area of 28.072 square miles and a water area of 0.006 square miles. Located at 40.60° N. Lat; 78.50° W. Long. Elevation is 1,575 feet. Population: 742 (2010); Density: 26.4 persons per square mile (2010); Race: 98.9% White, 0.5% Black, 0.0% Asian, 0.0% American Indian/Alaska Native, 0.0% Native Hawaiian/Other Pacific Islander, 0.6% Other, 0.0% Hispanic of any race (2010); Average household size: 2.41 (2010); Median age: 45.3 (2010); Males per 100 females: 103.3 (2010); Homeownership rate: 90.6% (2010)

EAST CARROLL (township). Covers a land area of 24.947 square miles and a water area of <.001 square miles. Located at 40.58° N. Lat; 78.69° W. Long.

Population: 1,823 (1990); 1,798 (2000); 1,654 (2010); Density: 66.3 persons per square mile (2010); Race: 99.8% White, 0.1% Black, 0.0% Asian, 0.1% American Indian/Alaska Native, 0.0% Native Hawaiian/Other Pacific Islander, 0.0% Other, 0.7% Hispanic of any race (2010); Average household size: 2.63 (2010); Median age: 44.8 (2010); Males per 100 females: 102.2 (2010); Marriage status: 28.1% never married, 54.6% now married, 7.7% widowed, 9.6% divorced (2006-2010 5-year est.); Foreign born: 0.0% (2006-2010 5-year est.); Ancestry (includes multiple ancestries): 48.6% German, 19.9% Irish, 13.0% Italian, 12.2% Polish, 10.4% English (2006-2010 5-year est.).

Economy: Single-family building permits issued: 2 (2011); Multi-family building permits issued: 0 (2011); Employment by occupation: 9.4% management, 5.0% professional, 10.7% services, 8.8% sales, 1.1% farming, 14.9% construction, 4.9% production (2006-2010 5-year est.).

Income: Per capita income: $22,502 (2006-2010 5-year est.); Median household income: $50,417 (2006-2010 5-year est.); Average household income: $59,614 (2006-2010 5-year est.); Percent of households with income of $100,000 or more: 11.1% (2006-2010 5-year est.); Poverty rate: 10.3% (2006-2010 5-year est.).

Education: Percent of population age 25 and over with: High school diploma (including GED) or higher: 92.0% (2006-2010 5-year est.); Bachelor's degree or higher: 12.8% (2006-2010 5-year est.); Master's degree or higher: 3.0% (2006-2010 5-year est.).

Housing: Homeownership rate: 88.4% (2010); Median home value: $104,900 (2006-2010 5-year est.); Median contract rent: $379 per month (2006-2010 5-year est.); Median year structure built: 1974 (2006-2010 5-year est.).

Transportation: Commute to work: 94.6% car, 0.0% public transportation, 0.0% walk, 3.0% work from home (2006-2010 5-year est.); Travel time to work: 28.2% less than 15 minutes, 32.7% 15 to 30 minutes, 24.5% 30 to 45 minutes, 6.1% 45 to 60 minutes, 8.5% 60 minutes or more (2006-2010 5-year est.)

Additional Information Contacts

Blair County Chamber of Commerce . . . . (814) 943-8151
   http://www.blairchamber.com

EAST CONEMAUGH (borough). Aka Conemaugh. Covers a land area of 0.270 square miles and a water area of 0.007 square miles. Located at 40.35° N. Lat; 78.89° W. Long. Elevation is 1,293 feet.

Population: 1,470 (1990); 1,291 (2000); 1,220 (2010); Density: 4,516.4 persons per square mile (2010); Race: 94.2% White, 4.3% Black, 0.0% Asian, 0.2% American Indian/Alaska Native, 0.0% Native Hawaiian/Other Pacific Islander, 1.3% Other, 1.8% Hispanic of any race (2010); Average household size: 2.30 (2010); Median age: 41.0 (2010); Males per 100 females: 91.5 (2010); Marriage status: 35.2% never married, 47.3% now married, 8.4% widowed, 9.1% divorced (2006-2010 5-year est.); Foreign born: 0.7% (2006-2010 5-year est.); Ancestry (includes multiple ancestries): 28.4% German, 15.7% Polish, 14.7% Irish, 10.3% Slovak, 9.7% Italian (2006-2010 5-year est.).

Economy: Single-family building permits issued: 0 (2011); Multi-family building permits issued: 0 (2011); Employment by occupation: 4.2% management, 0.6% professional, 16.5% services, 15.8% sales, 4.2% farming, 11.9% construction, 9.5% production (2006-2010 5-year est.).

Income: Per capita income: $15,481 (2006-2010 5-year est.); Median household income: $30,952 (2006-2010 5-year est.); Average household income: $36,676 (2006-2010 5-year est.); Percent of households with income of $100,000 or more: 0.9% (2006-2010 5-year est.); Poverty rate: 19.7% (2006-2010 5-year est.).

Education: Percent of population age 25 and over with: High school diploma (including GED) or higher: 80.3% (2006-2010 5-year est.); Bachelor's degree or higher: 5.5% (2006-2010 5-year est.); Master's degree or higher: 1.1% (2006-2010 5-year est.).

Housing: Homeownership rate: 65.0% (2010); Median home value: $35,200 (2006-2010 5-year est.); Median contract rent: $326 per month (2006-2010 5-year est.); Median year structure built: before 1940 (2006-2010 5-year est.).

Safety: Violent crime rate: 19.4 per 10,000 population; Property crime rate: 45.2 per 10,000 population (2011).

Transportation: Commute to work: 88.6% car, 4.5% public transportation, 6.9% walk, 0.0% work from home (2006-2010 5-year est.); Travel time to work: 29.9% less than 15 minutes, 46.9% 15 to 30 minutes, 10.1% 30 to 45 minutes, 8.2% 45 to 60 minutes, 4.9% 60 minutes or more (2006-2010 5-year est.)

Additional Information Contacts

Greater Johnstown Cambria County Chamber of Commerce . . . . (814) 536-5107
   http://www.johnstownchamber.com

EAST TAYLOR (township). Covers a land area of 8.810 square miles and a water area of 0.309 square miles. Located at 40.37° N. Lat; 78.86° W. Long.

Population: 3,073 (1990); 2,726 (2000); 2,726 (2010); Density: 309.4 persons per square mile (2010); Race: 97.5% White, 1.4% Black, 0.3% Asian, 0.1% American Indian/Alaska Native, 0.0% Native Hawaiian/Other Pacific Islander, 0.7% Other, 0.7% Hispanic of any race (2010); Average

household size: 2.49 (2010); Median age: 45.2 (2010); Males per 100 females: 92.9 (2010); Marriage status: 22.0% never married, 60.2% now married, 10.4% widowed, 7.4% divorced (2006-2010 5-year est.); Foreign born: 0.2% (2006-2010 5-year est.); Ancestry (includes multiple ancestries): 31.8% German, 14.2% Irish, 11.7% Polish, 9.7% Slovak, 9.4% English (2006-2010 5-year est.).

Economy: Single-family building permits issued: 0 (2011); Multi-family building permits issued: 0 (2011); Employment by occupation: 4.4% management, 3.3% professional, 10.9% services, 21.7% sales, 3.4% farming, 7.7% construction, 6.5% production (2006-2010 5-year est.).

Income: Per capita income: $19,738 (2006-2010 5-year est.); Median household income: $42,204 (2006-2010 5-year est.); Average household income: $51,570 (2006-2010 5-year est.); Percent of households with income of $100,000 or more: 8.4% (2006-2010 5-year est.); Poverty rate: 8.3% (2006-2010 5-year est.).

Education: Percent of population age 25 and over with: High school diploma (including GED) or higher: 85.5% (2006-2010 5-year est.); Bachelor's degree or higher: 8.5% (2006-2010 5-year est.); Master's degree or higher: 1.7% (2006-2010 5-year est.).

Housing: Homeownership rate: 89.1% (2010); Median home value: $85,600 (2006-2010 5-year est.); Median contract rent: $353 per month (2006-2010 5-year est.); Median year structure built: 1955 (2006-2010 5-year est.).

Safety: Violent crime rate: 14.6 per 10,000 population; Property crime rate: 58.5 per 10,000 population (2011).

Transportation: Commute to work: 93.5% car, 0.9% public transportation, 0.4% walk, 4.7% work from home (2006-2010 5-year est.); Travel time to work: 21.0% less than 15 minutes, 58.8% 15 to 30 minutes, 9.7% 30 to 45 minutes, 4.5% 45 to 60 minutes, 6.0% 60 minutes or more (2006-2010 5-year est.)

Additional Information Contacts
Greater Johnstown Cambria County Chamber of Commerce . . . . (814) 536-5107
   http://www.johnstownchamber.com

EBENSBURG (borough). County seat. Covers a land area of 1.653 square miles and a water area of 0.036 square miles. Located at 40.49° N. Lat; 78.73° W. Long. Elevation is 2,139 feet.

History: Cambria county Historic Site Museum. Settled 1796, laid out 1806, incorporated 1825.

Population: 3,891 (1990); 3,091 (2000); 3,351 (2010); Density: 2,027.4 persons per square mile (2010); Race: 98.3% White, 0.5% Black, 0.7% Asian, 0.1% American Indian/Alaska Native, 0.0% Native Hawaiian/Other Pacific Islander, 0.4% Other, 0.5% Hispanic of any race (2010); Average household size: 2.07 (2010); Median age: 43.9 (2010); Males per 100 females: 87.1 (2010); Marriage status: 24.3% never married, 59.4% now married, 5.9% widowed, 10.3% divorced (2006-2010 5-year est.); Foreign born: 0.0% (2006-2010 5-year est.); Ancestry (includes multiple ancestries): 35.0% German, 21.2% Irish, 12.4% Italian, 11.6% Polish, 11.6% English (2006-2010 5-year est.).

Economy: Single-family building permits issued: 2 (2011); Multi-family building permits issued: 0 (2011); Employment by occupation: 9.4% management, 2.8% professional, 11.5% services, 18.1% sales, 5.0% farming, 6.3% construction, 4.4% production (2006-2010 5-year est.).

Income: Per capita income: $25,609 (2006-2010 5-year est.); Median household income: $53,125 (2006-2010 5-year est.); Average household income: $53,097 (2006-2010 5-year est.); Percent of households with income of $100,000 or more: 9.4% (2006-2010 5-year est.); Poverty rate: 6.5% (2006-2010 5-year est.).

Education: Percent of population age 25 and over with: High school diploma (including GED) or higher: 95.2% (2006-2010 5-year est.); Bachelor's degree or higher: 35.7% (2006-2010 5-year est.); Master's degree or higher: 13.5% (2006-2010 5-year est.).

School District(s)
Admiral Peary Avts (10-12)
   2010-11 Enrollment: n/a . . . . (814) 472-6490
Central Cambria SD (KG-12)
   2010-11 Enrollment: 1,792 . . . . (814) 472-8870
Vocational/Technical School(s)
Pennsylvania Institute of Taxidermy Inc (Private, For-profit)
   Fall 2010 Enrollment: 19 . . . . (814) 472-4510
   2011-12 Tuition: $21,000

Housing: Homeownership rate: 53.7% (2010); Median home value: $113,900 (2006-2010 5-year est.); Median contract rent: $538 per month

(2006-2010 5-year est.); Median year structure built: 1948 (2006-2010 5-year est.).

Safety: Violent crime rate: 5.9 per 10,000 population; Property crime rate: 175.5 per 10,000 population (2011).

Newspapers: Ebensburg Mountaineer-Herald (Community news; Circulation 3,200); Ebensburg News Leader (Community news; Circulation 3,000); Nanty Glo Journal (Community news; Circulation 3,500); Tribune-Democrat - Ebensburg Bureau (Local news)

Transportation: Commute to work: 91.4% car, 0.0% public transportation, 3.8% walk, 4.8% work from home (2006-2010 5-year est.); Travel time to work: 45.1% less than 15 minutes, 26.0% 15 to 30 minutes, 16.9% 30 to 45 minutes, 5.5% 45 to 60 minutes, 6.4% 60 minutes or more (2006-2010 5-year est.)

Additional Information Contacts
Borough of Ebensburg . . . . (814) 472-8780
   http://www.ebensburgpa.com
Indiana County Chamber of Commerce . . . . (724) 465-2511
   http://www.indianapa.com/chamber

EHRENFELD (borough). Covers a land area of 0.432 square miles and a water area of 0.013 square miles. Located at 40.38° N. Lat; 78.78° W. Long. Elevation is 1,529 feet.

Population: 307 (1990); 234 (2000); 228 (2010); Density: 528.2 persons per square mile (2010); Race: 100.0% White, 0.0% Black, 0.0% Asian, 0.0% American Indian/Alaska Native, 0.0% Native Hawaiian/Other Pacific Islander, 0.0% Other, 1.8% Hispanic of any race (2010); Average household size: 2.68 (2010); Median age: 38.0 (2010); Males per 100 females: 91.6 (2010); Marriage status: 18.1% never married, 63.1% now married, 17.4% widowed, 1.3% divorced (2006-2010 5-year est.); Foreign born: 0.0% (2006-2010 5-year est.); Ancestry (includes multiple ancestries): 21.6% Italian, 17.1% German, 16.6% Irish, 16.6% Polish, 11.1% American (2006-2010 5-year est.).

Economy: Single-family building permits issued: 0 (2011); Multi-family building permits issued: 0 (2011); Employment by occupation: 6.0% management, 3.6% professional, 19.0% services, 10.7% sales, 3.6% farming, 8.3% construction, 8.3% production (2006-2010 5-year est.).

Income: Per capita income: $17,014 (2006-2010 5-year est.); Median household income: $34,375 (2006-2010 5-year est.); Average household income: $43,655 (2006-2010 5-year est.); Percent of households with income of $100,000 or more: 7.7% (2006-2010 5-year est.); Poverty rate: 20.1% (2006-2010 5-year est.).

Education: Percent of population age 25 and over with: High school diploma (including GED) or higher: 88.5% (2006-2010 5-year est.); Bachelor's degree or higher: 6.1% (2006-2010 5-year est.); Master's degree or higher: 6.1% (2006-2010 5-year est.).

Housing: Homeownership rate: 89.5% (2010); Median home value: $58,100 (2006-2010 5-year est.); Median contract rent: $358 per month (2006-2010 5-year est.); Median year structure built: before 1940 (2006-2010 5-year est.).

Transportation: Commute to work: 92.7% car, 0.0% public transportation, 0.0% walk, 7.3% work from home (2006-2010 5-year est.); Travel time to work: 21.1% less than 15 minutes, 50.0% 15 to 30 minutes, 18.4% 30 to 45 minutes, 3.9% 45 to 60 minutes, 6.6% 60 minutes or more (2006-2010 5-year est.)

ELDER (township). Covers a land area of 12.936 square miles and a water area of 0 square miles. Located at 40.68° N. Lat; 78.69° W. Long.

Population: 1,185 (1990); 990 (2000); 1,038 (2010); Density: 80.2 persons per square mile (2010); Race: 99.4% White, 0.1% Black, 0.1% Asian, 0.2% American Indian/Alaska Native, 0.1% Native Hawaiian/Other Pacific Islander, 0.1% Other, 0.4% Hispanic of any race (2010); Average household size: 2.51 (2010); Median age: 49.2 (2010); Males per 100 females: 95.5 (2010); Marriage status: 20.0% never married, 66.7% now married, 7.5% widowed, 5.9% divorced (2006-2010 5-year est.); Foreign born: 0.0% (2006-2010 5-year est.); Ancestry (includes multiple ancestries): 43.9% German, 21.4% Irish, 11.5% Italian, 9.1% Polish, 8.5% American (2006-2010 5-year est.).

Economy: Single-family building permits issued: 1 (2011); Multi-family building permits issued: 0 (2011); Employment by occupation: 11.4% management, 3.9% professional, 8.6% services, 16.0% sales, 4.6% farming, 22.5% construction, 12.5% production (2006-2010 5-year est.).

Income: Per capita income: $18,524 (2006-2010 5-year est.); Median household income: $40,000 (2006-2010 5-year est.); Average household income: $47,019 (2006-2010 5-year est.); Percent of households with

income of $100,000 or more: 8.8% (2006-2010 5-year est.); Poverty rate: 8.9% (2006-2010 5-year est.).

Education: Percent of population age 25 and over with: High school diploma (including GED) or higher: 89.1% (2006-2010 5-year est.); Bachelor's degree or higher: 8.2% (2006-2010 5-year est.); Master's degree or higher: 1.5% (2006-2010 5-year est.).

Housing: Homeownership rate: 92.3% (2010); Median home value: $82,800 (2006-2010 5-year est.); Median contract rent: $325 per month (2006-2010 5-year est.); Median year structure built: 1952 (2006-2010 5-year est.).

Transportation: Commute to work: 93.9% car, 0.7% public transportation, 3.0% walk, 2.3% work from home (2006-2010 5-year est.); Travel time to work: 23.4% less than 15 minutes, 24.4% 15 to 30 minutes, 23.4% 30 to 45 minutes, 11.5% 45 to 60 minutes, 17.2% 60 minutes or more (2006-2010 5-year est.)

ELIM (CDP). Covers a land area of 1.994 square miles and a water area of 0.031 square miles. Located at 40.30° N. Lat; 78.95° W. Long. Elevation is 1,654 feet.

Population: 4,208 (1990); 4,175 (2000); 3,727 (2010); Density: 1,869.5 persons per square mile (2010); Race: 95.7% White, 1.2% Black, 1.5% Asian, 0.2% American Indian/Alaska Native, 0.1% Native Hawaiian/Other Pacific Islander, 1.3% Other, 0.8% Hispanic of any race (2010); Average household size: 2.17 (2010); Median age: 48.1 (2010); Males per 100 females: 91.7 (2010); Marriage status: 32.2% never married, 49.6% now married, 10.4% widowed, 7.9% divorced (2006-2010 5-year est.); Foreign born: 1.7% (2006-2010 5-year est.); Ancestry (includes multiple ancestries): 40.8% German, 14.9% Slovak, 12.3% Polish, 11.9% Irish, 11.4% Italian (2006-2010 5-year est.).

Economy: Employment by occupation: 9.0% management, 5.7% professional, 7.0% services, 13.0% sales, 2.4% farming, 10.3% construction, 8.6% production (2006-2010 5-year est.).

Income: Per capita income: $23,818 (2006-2010 5-year est.); Median household income: $48,061 (2006-2010 5-year est.); Average household income: $54,609 (2006-2010 5-year est.); Percent of households with income of $100,000 or more: 10.5% (2006-2010 5-year est.); Poverty rate: 9.2% (2006-2010 5-year est.).

Education: Percent of population age 25 and over with: High school diploma (including GED) or higher: 90.4% (2006-2010 5-year est.); Bachelor's degree or higher: 25.5% (2006-2010 5-year est.); Master's degree or higher: 10.1% (2006-2010 5-year est.).

Housing: Homeownership rate: 77.3% (2010); Median home value: $107,600 (2006-2010 5-year est.); Median contract rent: $486 per month (2006-2010 5-year est.); Median year structure built: 1953 (2006-2010 5-year est.).

Transportation: Commute to work: 90.0% car, 0.0% public transportation, 2.7% walk, 3.1% work from home (2006-2010 5-year est.); Travel time to work: 50.0% less than 15 minutes, 37.4% 15 to 30 minutes, 4.3% 30 to 45 minutes, 5.2% 45 to 60 minutes, 3.0% 60 minutes or more (2006-2010 5-year est.)

Additional Information Contacts
Greater Johnstown Cambria County Chamber of Commerce . . . . (814) 536-5107
  http://www.johnstownchamber.com

ELMORA (unincorporated postal area)
Zip Code: 15737
  Covers a land area of 0.176 square miles and a water area of 0 square miles. Located at 40.60° N. Lat; 78.75° W. Long. Population: 83 (2010); Density: 469.8 persons per square mile (2010); Race: 100.0% White, 0.0% Black, 0.0% Asian, 0.0% American Indian/Alaska Native, 0.0% Native Hawaiian/Other Pacific Islander, 0.0% Other, 0.0% Hispanic of any race (2010); Average household size: 1.98 (2010); Median age: 51.5 (2010); Males per 100 females: 97.6 (2010); Homeownership rate: 95.2% (2010)

ELTON (unincorporated postal area)
Zip Code: 15934
  Covers a land area of 0.340 square miles and a water area of 0 square miles. Located at 40.27° N. Lat; 78.80° W. Long. Elevation is 2,044 feet. Population: 218 (2010); Density: 639.5 persons per square mile (2010); Race: 98.2% White, 0.0% Black, 0.9% Asian, 0.0% American Indian/Alaska Native, 0.0% Native Hawaiian/Other Pacific Islander, 0.9% Other, 0.5% Hispanic of any race (2010); Average household size:

2.20 (2010); Median age: 43.5 (2010); Males per 100 females: 109.6 (2010); Homeownership rate: 66.6% (2010)

EMEIGH (unincorporated postal area)
Zip Code: 15738
  Covers a land area of 2.621 square miles and a water area of 0 square miles. Located at 40.69° N. Lat; 78.78° W. Long. Elevation is 1,499 feet. Population: 265 (2010); Density: 101.1 persons per square mile (2010); Race: 100.0% White, 0.0% Black, 0.0% Asian, 0.0% American Indian/Alaska Native, 0.0% Native Hawaiian/Other Pacific Islander, 0.0% Other, 1.9% Hispanic of any race (2010); Average household size: 2.43 (2010); Median age: 43.1 (2010); Males per 100 females: 108.7 (2010); Homeownership rate: 84.4% (2010)

FALLENTIMBER (unincorporated postal area)
Zip Code: 16639
  Covers a land area of 36.124 square miles and a water area of 0.032 square miles. Located at 40.69° N. Lat; 78.44° W. Long. Population: 1,494 (2010); Density: 41.4 persons per square mile (2010); Race: 99.0% White, 0.3% Black, 0.0% Asian, 0.2% American Indian/Alaska Native, 0.0% Native Hawaiian/Other Pacific Islander, 0.5% Other, 0.1% Hispanic of any race (2010); Average household size: 2.47 (2010); Median age: 44.1 (2010); Males per 100 females: 102.2 (2010); Homeownership rate: 82.7% (2010)

FERNDALE (borough). Covers a land area of 0.389 square miles and a water area of 0.025 square miles. Located at 40.29° N. Lat; 78.92° W. Long. Elevation is 1,198 feet.

History: Incorporated 1896.

Population: 2,020 (1990); 1,834 (2000); 1,636 (2010); Density: 4,207.8 persons per square mile (2010); Race: 97.1% White, 1.2% Black, 0.1% Asian, 0.1% American Indian/Alaska Native, 0.0% Native Hawaiian/Other Pacific Islander, 1.5% Other, 1.4% Hispanic of any race (2010); Average household size: 2.25 (2010); Median age: 39.7 (2010); Males per 100 females: 90.5 (2010); Marriage status: 30.0% never married, 56.0% now married, 6.2% widowed, 7.7% divorced (2006-2010 5-year est.); Foreign born: 1.1% (2006-2010 5-year est.); Ancestry (includes multiple ancestries): 40.4% German, 21.5% Irish, 14.2% Italian, 11.4% English, 6.5% Slovak (2006-2010 5-year est.).

Economy: Single-family building permits issued: 0 (2011); Multi-family building permits issued: 0 (2011); Employment by occupation: 8.0% management, 1.8% professional, 12.2% services, 19.3% sales, 5.9% farming, 4.8% construction, 3.9% production (2006-2010 5-year est.).

Income: Per capita income: $19,533 (2006-2010 5-year est.); Median household income: $40,000 (2006-2010 5-year est.); Average household income: $44,317 (2006-2010 5-year est.); Percent of households with income of $100,000 or more: 2.3% (2006-2010 5-year est.); Poverty rate: 8.8% (2006-2010 5-year est.).

Education: Percent of population age 25 and over with: High school diploma (including GED) or higher: 93.3% (2006-2010 5-year est.); Bachelor's degree or higher: 16.1% (2006-2010 5-year est.); Master's degree or higher: 6.2% (2006-2010 5-year est.).

Housing: Homeownership rate: 67.9% (2010); Median home value: $73,600 (2006-2010 5-year est.); Median contract rent: $421 per month (2006-2010 5-year est.); Median year structure built: before 1940 (2006-2010 5-year est.).

Safety: Violent crime rate: 12.2 per 10,000 population; Property crime rate: 18.3 per 10,000 population (2011).

Transportation: Commute to work: 90.4% car, 3.0% public transportation, 1.3% walk, 4.8% work from home (2006-2010 5-year est.); Travel time to work: 38.9% less than 15 minutes, 45.0% 15 to 30 minutes, 4.5% 30 to 45 minutes, 6.5% 45 to 60 minutes, 5.2% 60 minutes or more (2006-2010 5-year est.)

Additional Information Contacts
Greater Johnstown Cambria County Chamber of Commerce . . . . (814) 536-5107
  http://www.johnstownchamber.com

FLINTON (unincorporated postal area)
Zip Code: 16640
  Covers a land area of 13.226 square miles and a water area of 0.104 square miles. Located at 40.70° N. Lat; 78.57° W. Long. Population: 817 (2010); Density: 61.8 persons per square mile (2010); Race: 97.8% White, 0.1% Black, 0.2% Asian, 0.2% American Indian/Alaska Native, 0.1% Native Hawaiian/Other Pacific Islander, 1.6% Other, 0.6%

Hispanic of any race (2010); Average household size: 2.33 (2010); Median age: 49.4 (2010); Males per 100 females: 103.7 (2010); Homeownership rate: 90.3% (2010)

FRANKLIN (borough). Covers a land area of 0.552 square miles and a water area of 0.015 square miles. Located at 40.34° N. Lat; 78.88° W. Long. Elevation is 1,253 feet.
Population: 565 (1990); 442 (2000); 323 (2010); Density: 585.1 persons per square mile (2010); Race: 93.2% White, 4.6% Black, 0.0% Asian, 0.0% American Indian/Alaska Native, 0.0% Native Hawaiian/Other Pacific Islander, 2.2% Other, 0.6% Hispanic of any race (2010); Average household size: 2.04 (2010); Median age: 47.1 (2010); Males per 100 females: 91.1 (2010); Marriage status: 46.8% never married, 34.3% now married, 12.8% widowed, 6.1% divorced (2006-2010 5-year est.); Foreign born: 0.0% (2006-2010 5-year est.); Ancestry (includes multiple ancestries): 20.2% Polish, 12.4% German, 10.4% Slovak, 9.8% Irish, 7.3% Italian (2006-2010 5-year est.).
Economy: Single-family building permits issued: 0 (2011); Multi-family building permits issued: 0 (2011); Employment by occupation: 1.1% management, 2.2% professional, 14.4% services, 30.9% sales, 6.1% farming, 2.2% construction, 3.9% production (2006-2010 5-year est.).
Income: Per capita income: $19,581 (2006-2010 5-year est.); Median household income: $27,386 (2006-2010 5-year est.); Average household income: $41,307 (2006-2010 5-year est.); Percent of households with income of $100,000 or more: 5.3% (2006-2010 5-year est.); Poverty rate: 11.5% (2006-2010 5-year est.).
Education: Percent of population age 25 and over with: High school diploma (including GED) or higher: 88.4% (2006-2010 5-year est.); Bachelor's degree or higher: 16.5% (2006-2010 5-year est.); Master's degree or higher: 4.1% (2006-2010 5-year est.).
Housing: Homeownership rate: 76.5% (2010); Median home value: $34,200 (2006-2010 5-year est.); Median contract rent: $304 per month (2006-2010 5-year est.); Median year structure built: before 1940 (2006-2010 5-year est.).
Transportation: Commute to work: 84.4% car, 0.0% public transportation, 2.2% walk, 0.0% work from home (2006-2010 5-year est.); Travel time to work: 36.3% less than 15 minutes, 57.5% 15 to 30 minutes, 0.0% 30 to 45 minutes, 2.8% 45 to 60 minutes, 3.4% 60 minutes or more (2006-2010 5-year est.)

GALLITZIN (borough). Covers a land area of 0.732 square miles and a water area of 0 square miles. Located at 40.48° N. Lat; 78.55° W. Long. Elevation is 2,182 feet.
Population: 2,003 (1990); 1,756 (2000); 1,668 (2010); Density: 2,278.8 persons per square mile (2010); Race: 98.5% White, 0.6% Black, 0.1% Asian, 0.0% American Indian/Alaska Native, 0.0% Native Hawaiian/Other Pacific Islander, 0.8% Other, 1.5% Hispanic of any race (2010); Average household size: 2.40 (2010); Median age: 39.7 (2010); Males per 100 females: 94.2 (2010); Marriage status: 29.6% never married, 49.0% now married, 10.1% widowed, 11.3% divorced (2006-2010 5-year est.); Foreign born: 1.8% (2006-2010 5-year est.); Ancestry (includes multiple ancestries): 35.4% German, 28.5% Irish, 19.8% Polish, 15.4% Italian, 4.6% English (2006-2010 5-year est.).
Economy: Single-family building permits issued: 1 (2011); Multi-family building permits issued: 0 (2011); Employment by occupation: 7.2% management, 1.8% professional, 14.5% services, 18.9% sales, 4.5% farming, 8.0% construction, 5.0% production (2006-2010 5-year est.).
Income: Per capita income: $18,432 (2006-2010 5-year est.); Median household income: $34,570 (2006-2010 5-year est.); Average household income: $43,074 (2006-2010 5-year est.); Percent of households with income of $100,000 or more: 4.8% (2006-2010 5-year est.); Poverty rate: 15.8% (2006-2010 5-year est.).
Education: Percent of population age 25 and over with: High school diploma (including GED) or higher: 83.8% (2006-2010 5-year est.); Bachelor's degree or higher: 9.7% (2006-2010 5-year est.); Master's degree or higher: 4.0% (2006-2010 5-year est.).
School District(s)
Penn Cambria SD (PK-12)
    2010-11 Enrollment: 1,758 . . . . (814) 886-8121
Housing: Homeownership rate: 75.0% (2010); Median home value: $58,700 (2006-2010 5-year est.); Median contract rent: $357 per month (2006-2010 5-year est.); Median year structure built: before 1940 (2006-2010 5-year est.).
Safety: Violent crime rate: 5.2 per 10,000 population; Property crime rate: 109.4 per 10,000 population (2011).

Transportation: Commute to work: 95.0% car, 0.0% public transportation, 3.6% walk, 1.0% work from home (2006-2010 5-year est.); Travel time to work: 29.0% less than 15 minutes, 33.8% 15 to 30 minutes, 23.7% 30 to 45 minutes, 6.3% 45 to 60 minutes, 7.2% 60 minutes or more (2006-2010 5-year est.).
Additional Information Contacts
Cresson Area Chamber of Commerce . . . . (814) 886-7710
    http://www.cressonarea.com

GALLITZIN (township). Covers a land area of 17.105 square miles and a water area of 0 square miles. Located at 40.52° N. Lat; 78.55° W. Long. Elevation is 2,182 feet.
History: Allegheny Portage Railroad National Historic Site to South. Settled c.1796.
Population: 1,289 (1990); 1,310 (2000); 1,324 (2010); Density: 77.4 persons per square mile (2010); Race: 99.4% White, 0.0% Black, 0.1% Asian, 0.1% American Indian/Alaska Native, 0.0% Native Hawaiian/Other Pacific Islander, 0.4% Other, 1.2% Hispanic of any race (2010); Average household size: 2.68 (2010); Median age: 43.5 (2010); Males per 100 females: 112.9 (2010); Marriage status: 23.0% never married, 66.7% now married, 3.6% widowed, 6.7% divorced (2006-2010 5-year est.); Foreign born: 0.0% (2006-2010 5-year est.); Ancestry (includes multiple ancestries): 39.1% German, 25.2% Irish, 19.5% Italian, 14.8% Polish, 9.0% English (2006-2010 5-year est.).
Economy: Single-family building permits issued: 3 (2011); Multi-family building permits issued: 0 (2011); Employment by occupation: 7.0% management, 1.2% professional, 11.8% services, 14.5% sales, 5.3% farming, 17.8% construction, 9.3% production (2006-2010 5-year est.).
Income: Per capita income: $18,959 (2006-2010 5-year est.); Median household income: $47,016 (2006-2010 5-year est.); Average household income: $52,499 (2006-2010 5-year est.); Percent of households with income of $100,000 or more: 7.5% (2006-2010 5-year est.); Poverty rate: 12.6% (2006-2010 5-year est.).
Education: Percent of population age 25 and over with: High school diploma (including GED) or higher: 89.4% (2006-2010 5-year est.); Bachelor's degree or higher: 11.2% (2006-2010 5-year est.); Master's degree or higher: 3.4% (2006-2010 5-year est.).
Housing: Homeownership rate: 92.2% (2010); Median home value: $95,400 (2006-2010 5-year est.); Median contract rent: $425 per month (2006-2010 5-year est.); Median year structure built: 1977 (2006-2010 5-year est.).
Safety: Violent crime rate: 7.5 per 10,000 population; Property crime rate: 22.6 per 10,000 population (2011).
Transportation: Commute to work: 91.0% car, 0.0% public transportation, 1.0% walk, 5.5% work from home (2006-2010 5-year est.); Travel time to work: 15.8% less than 15 minutes, 53.3% 15 to 30 minutes, 18.9% 30 to 45 minutes, 3.8% 45 to 60 minutes, 8.2% 60 minutes or more (2006-2010 5-year est.).
Additional Information Contacts
Cresson Area Chamber of Commerce . . . . (814) 886-7710
    http://www.cressonarea.com

GEISTOWN (borough). Covers a land area of 1.060 square miles and a water area of 0 square miles. Located at 40.29° N. Lat; 78.87° W. Long. Elevation is 1,893 feet.
History: University of Pittsburg-Johnstown Campus to Southeast.
Population: 2,749 (1990); 2,555 (2000); 2,467 (2010); Density: 2,328.0 persons per square mile (2010); Race: 97.3% White, 0.5% Black, 1.5% Asian, 0.0% American Indian/Alaska Native, 0.0% Native Hawaiian/Other Pacific Islander, 0.7% Other, 0.7% Hispanic of any race (2010); Average household size: 2.21 (2010); Median age: 47.6 (2010); Males per 100 females: 93.0 (2010); Marriage status: 26.2% never married, 56.1% now married, 10.7% widowed, 7.0% divorced (2006-2010 5-year est.); Foreign born: 0.9% (2006-2010 5-year est.); Ancestry (includes multiple ancestries): 38.2% German, 19.5% Irish, 14.9% Polish, 11.3% Italian, 7.7% English (2006-2010 5-year est.).
Economy: Single-family building permits issued: 0 (2011); Multi-family building permits issued: 0 (2011); Employment by occupation: 8.0% management, 1.1% professional, 16.2% services, 20.7% sales, 3.8% farming, 7.7% construction, 7.4% production (2006-2010 5-year est.).
Income: Per capita income: $22,530 (2006-2010 5-year est.); Median household income: $42,566 (2006-2010 5-year est.); Average household income: $50,432 (2006-2010 5-year est.); Percent of households with income of $100,000 or more: 7.6% (2006-2010 5-year est.); Poverty rate: 6.3% (2006-2010 5-year est.).

Education: Percent of population age 25 and over with: High school diploma (including GED) or higher: 91.5% (2006-2010 5-year est.); Bachelor's degree or higher: 17.8% (2006-2010 5-year est.); Master's degree or higher: 6.2% (2006-2010 5-year est.).
Housing: Homeownership rate: 74.6% (2010); Median home value: $101,700 (2006-2010 5-year est.); Median contract rent: $506 per month (2006-2010 5-year est.); Median year structure built: 1955 (2006-2010 5-year est.).
Safety: Violent crime rate: 4.0 per 10,000 population; Property crime rate: 173.7 per 10,000 population (2011).
Transportation: Commute to work: 98.0% car, 0.0% public transportation, 1.1% walk, 0.8% work from home (2006-2010 5-year est.); Travel time to work: 59.6% less than 15 minutes, 25.1% 15 to 30 minutes, 5.6% 30 to 45 minutes, 5.8% 45 to 60 minutes, 4.0% 60 minutes or more (2006-2010 5-year est.)
Additional Information Contacts
Greater Johnstown Cambria County Chamber of Commerce . . . . (814) 536-5107
  http://www.johnstownchamber.com

HASTINGS (borough). Covers a land area of 0.555 square miles and a water area of 0 square miles. Located at 40.66° N. Lat; 78.71° W. Long. Elevation is 1,765 feet.
History: Incorporated 1894.
Population: 1,431 (1990); 1,398 (2000); 1,278 (2010); Density: 2,303.7 persons per square mile (2010); Race: 98.8% White, 0.2% Black, 0.2% Asian, 0.1% American Indian/Alaska Native, 0.0% Native Hawaiian/Other Pacific Islander, 0.7% Other, 0.5% Hispanic of any race (2010); Average household size: 2.41 (2010); Median age: 42.6 (2010); Males per 100 females: 86.3 (2010); Marriage status: 25.3% never married, 58.5% now married, 10.7% widowed, 5.5% divorced (2006-2010 5-year est.); Foreign born: 1.0% (2006-2010 5-year est.); Ancestry (includes multiple ancestries): 44.8% German, 19.8% Irish, 15.1% Polish, 14.6% Italian, 9.7% Slovak (2006-2010 5-year est.).
Economy: Single-family building permits issued: 0 (2011); Multi-family building permits issued: 0 (2011); Employment by occupation: 4.9% management, 2.4% professional, 22.9% services, 9.6% sales, 1.5% farming, 16.7% construction, 6.4% production (2006-2010 5-year est.).
Income: Per capita income: $20,196 (2006-2010 5-year est.); Median household income: $35,938 (2006-2010 5-year est.); Average household income: $45,230 (2006-2010 5-year est.); Percent of households with income of $100,000 or more: 8.3% (2006-2010 5-year est.); Poverty rate: 6.6% (2006-2010 5-year est.).
Education: Percent of population age 25 and over with: High school diploma (including GED) or higher: 90.2% (2006-2010 5-year est.); Bachelor's degree or higher: 12.8% (2006-2010 5-year est.); Master's degree or higher: 4.2% (2006-2010 5-year est.).
Housing: Homeownership rate: 77.3% (2010); Median home value: $74,000 (2006-2010 5-year est.); Median contract rent: $323 per month (2006-2010 5-year est.); Median year structure built: before 1940 (2006-2010 5-year est.).
Hospitals: Miners Hospital Northern Cambria (30 beds)
Safety: Violent crime rate: 70.2 per 10,000 population; Property crime rate: 249.6 per 10,000 population (2011).
Transportation: Commute to work: 92.8% car, 0.0% public transportation, 5.0% walk, 1.5% work from home (2006-2010 5-year est.); Travel time to work: 42.5% less than 15 minutes, 18.9% 15 to 30 minutes, 16.3% 30 to 45 minutes, 14.5% 45 to 60 minutes, 7.8% 60 minutes or more (2006-2010 5-year est.)
Additional Information Contacts
Blair County Chamber of Commerce . . . . (814) 943-8151
  http://www.blairchamber.com

JACKSON (township). Covers a land area of 47.941 square miles and a water area of 0.055 square miles. Located at 40.43° N. Lat; 78.87° W. Long.
Population: 5,213 (1990); 4,925 (2000); 4,392 (2010); Density: 91.6 persons per square mile (2010); Race: 99.2% White, 0.1% Black, 0.2% Asian, 0.0% American Indian/Alaska Native, 0.0% Native Hawaiian/Other Pacific Islander, 0.5% Other, 0.3% Hispanic of any race (2010); Average household size: 2.38 (2010); Median age: 48.5 (2010); Males per 100 females: 99.6 (2010); Marriage status: 20.3% never married, 64.1% now married, 10.5% widowed, 5.1% divorced (2006-2010 5-year est.); Foreign born: 0.9% (2006-2010 5-year est.); Ancestry (includes multiple

ancestries): 40.8% German, 10.5% Irish, 9.7% English, 9.4% Polish, 7.6% Italian (2006-2010 5-year est.).
Economy: Single-family building permits issued: 1 (2011); Multi-family building permits issued: 0 (2011); Employment by occupation: 9.7% management, 6.2% professional, 5.3% services, 15.1% sales, 1.5% farming, 14.9% construction, 7.8% production (2006-2010 5-year est.).
Income: Per capita income: $24,994 (2006-2010 5-year est.); Median household income: $50,366 (2006-2010 5-year est.); Average household income: $57,372 (2006-2010 5-year est.); Percent of households with income of $100,000 or more: 15.0% (2006-2010 5-year est.); Poverty rate: 2.1% (2006-2010 5-year est.).
Education: Percent of population age 25 and over with: High school diploma (including GED) or higher: 91.5% (2006-2010 5-year est.); Bachelor's degree or higher: 16.4% (2006-2010 5-year est.); Master's degree or higher: 9.5% (2006-2010 5-year est.).
Housing: Homeownership rate: 88.1% (2010); Median home value: $126,100 (2006-2010 5-year est.); Median contract rent: $346 per month (2006-2010 5-year est.); Median year structure built: 1972 (2006-2010 5-year est.).
Safety: Violent crime rate: 2.3 per 10,000 population; Property crime rate: 54.5 per 10,000 population (2011).
Transportation: Commute to work: 95.8% car, 0.0% public transportation, 2.0% walk, 2.2% work from home (2006-2010 5-year est.); Travel time to work: 12.6% less than 15 minutes, 50.4% 15 to 30 minutes, 28.5% 30 to 45 minutes, 3.8% 45 to 60 minutes, 4.8% 60 minutes or more (2006-2010 5-year est.)
Additional Information Contacts
Greater Johnstown Cambria County Chamber of Commerce . . . . (814) 536-5107
  http://www.johnstownchamber.com
Jackson Township. . . . . (814) 749-0725
  http://www.jacksontwppa.com

JOHNSTOWN (city). Covers a land area of 5.893 square miles and a water area of 0.198 square miles. Located at 40.33° N. Lat; 78.92° W. Long. Elevation is 1,168 feet.
History: In 1800 a Swiss immigrant, Joseph Johns, laid out the town, then called Conemaugh, on a 249-acre tract. Early discovery of iron ore made the settlement an important supply point for Pittsburgh mills. With the subsequent discovery of bituminous coal, Johnstown became a steel center in its own right. Johnstown's location in a narrow river valley led to frequent flooding. The flood of 1889, when the South Fork Dam collapsed, was the most devastating.
Population: 28,134 (1990); 23,906 (2000); 20,978 (2010); Density: 3,559.8 persons per square mile (2010); Race: 80.0% White, 14.6% Black, 0.2% Asian, 0.2% American Indian/Alaska Native, 0.0% Native Hawaiian/Other Pacific Islander, 5.0% Other, 3.1% Hispanic of any race (2010); Average household size: 2.08 (2010); Median age: 41.8 (2010); Males per 100 females: 87.9 (2010); Marriage status: 34.3% never married, 41.1% now married, 10.8% widowed, 13.8% divorced (2006-2010 5-year est.); Foreign born: 1.6% (2006-2010 5-year est.); Ancestry (includes multiple ancestries): 24.2% German, 15.7% Irish, 12.7% Italian, 8.0% Slovak, 7.3% English (2006-2010 5-year est.).
Economy: Unemployment rate: 11.1% (August 2012); Total civilian labor force: 9,198 (August 2012); Single-family building permits issued: 0 (2011); Multi-family building permits issued: 0 (2011); Employment by occupation: 4.2% management, 1.7% professional, 16.9% services, 19.1% sales, 4.2% farming, 7.6% construction, 5.2% production (2006-2010 5-year est.).
Income: Per capita income: $16,383 (2006-2010 5-year est.); Median household income: $24,819 (2006-2010 5-year est.); Average household income: $32,931 (2006-2010 5-year est.); Percent of households with income of $100,000 or more: 3.2% (2006-2010 5-year est.); Poverty rate: 30.7% (2006-2010 5-year est.).
Taxes: Total city taxes per capita: $374 (2009); City property taxes per capita: $246 (2009).
Education: Percent of population age 25 and over with: High school diploma (including GED) or higher: 83.3% (2006-2010 5-year est.); Bachelor's degree or higher: 13.3% (2006-2010 5-year est.); Master's degree or higher: 4.2% (2006-2010 5-year est.).
School District(s)
Central Cambria SD (KG-12)
  2010-11 Enrollment: 1,792 . . . . (814) 472-8870
Conemaugh Township Area SD (KG-12)
  2010-11 Enrollment: 1,022 . . . . (814) 479-7575

Conemaugh Valley SD (PK-12)
   2010-11 Enrollment: 973 . . . . (814) 535-3957
Ferndale Area SD (KG-12)
   2010-11 Enrollment: 796 . . . . (814) 535-1507
Greater Johnstown CTC (10-12)
   2010-11 Enrollment: n/a . . . . (814) 266-6073
Greater Johnstown SD (PK-12)
   2010-11 Enrollment: 3,162 . . . . (814) 533-5651
Richland SD (KG-12)
   2010-11 Enrollment: 1,607 . . . . (814) 266-6063
Westmont Hilltop SD (KG-12)
   2010-11 Enrollment: 1,714 . . . . (814) 255-6751

Four-year College(s)
University of Pittsburgh-Johnstown (Public)
   Fall 2010 Enrollment: 2,866 . . . . (814) 269-7000
   2011-12 Tuition: In-state $12,528; Out-of-state $22,720

Two-year College(s)
Cambria-Rowe Business College-Johnstown (Private, For-profit)
   Fall 2010 Enrollment: 266 . . . . (814) 536-5168
   2011-12 Tuition: In-state $11,205; Out-of-state $11,205
Commonwealth Technical Institute (Private, Not-for-profit)
   Fall 2010 Enrollment: 288 . . . . (814) 255-8200
   2011-12 Tuition: In-state $16,836; Out-of-state $16,836
Conemaugh Valley Memorial Hospital (Private, Not-for-profit)
   Fall 2010 Enrollment: 187 . . . . (814) 534-9118
Pennsylvania Highlands Community College (Public)
   Fall 2010 Enrollment: 1,344 . . . . (814) 262-6400
   2011-12 Tuition: In-state $7,300; Out-of-state $10,200

Vocational/Technical School(s)
Greater Johnstown Career and Technology Center (Public)
   Fall 2010 Enrollment: 488 . . . . (814) 269-3874
   2011-12 Tuition: $12,780
Pennsylvania Academy of Cosmetology Arts and Sciences (Private, For-profit)
   Fall 2010 Enrollment: 59 . . . . (814) 269-3444
   2011-12 Tuition: $15,100

Housing: Homeownership rate: 48.2% (2010); Median home value: $44,800 (2006-2010 5-year est.); Median contract rent: $316 per month (2006-2010 5-year est.); Median year structure built: before 1940 (2006-2010 5-year est.).
Hospitals: Good Samaritan Medical Center (700 beds); Memorial Medical Center - Lee Campus (770 beds); Memorial Medical Center - Main Campus (474 beds)
Safety: Violent crime rate: 66.9 per 10,000 population; Property crime rate: 425.7 per 10,000 population (2011).
Newspapers: The Tribune-Democrat (Local news; Circulation 42,747)
Transportation: Commute to work: 81.0% car, 5.2% public transportation, 9.5% walk, 1.8% work from home (2006-2010 5-year est.); Travel time to work: 41.7% less than 15 minutes, 40.1% 15 to 30 minutes, 9.0% 30 to 45 minutes, 5.1% 45 to 60 minutes, 4.1% 60 minutes or more (2006-2010 5-year est.); Amtrak: train service available.
Airports: John Murtha Johnstown-Cambria County (commercial service)
Additional Information Contacts
City of Johnstown . . . . (814) 533-2001
   http://www.cityofjohnstownpa.net
Greater Johnstown Cambria County Chamber of Commerce . . . . (814) 536-5107
   http://www.johnstownchamber.com

LILLY (borough). Covers a land area of 0.503 square miles and a water area of 0 square miles. Located at 40.42° N. Lat; 78.62° W. Long. Elevation is 1,913 feet.
Population: 1,162 (1990); 948 (2000); 968 (2010); Density: 1,924.1 persons per square mile (2010); Race: 99.7% White, 0.0% Black, 0.0% Asian, 0.0% American Indian/Alaska Native, 0.0% Native Hawaiian/Other Pacific Islander, 0.3% Other, 0.2% Hispanic of any race (2010); Average household size: 2.36 (2010); Median age: 42.1 (2010); Males per 100 females: 91.7 (2010); Marriage status: 25.5% never married, 52.9% now married, 11.7% widowed, 9.9% divorced (2006-2010 5-year est.); Foreign born: 0.0% (2006-2010 5-year est.); Ancestry (includes multiple ancestries): 39.7% German, 28.3% Irish, 25.3% Polish, 14.4% Italian, 6.3% English (2006-2010 5-year est.).
Economy: Single-family building permits issued: 0 (2011); Multi-family building permits issued: 0 (2011); Employment by occupation: 3.3%

management, 0.7% professional, 21.9% services, 12.7% sales, 7.5% farming, 10.6% construction, 3.1% production (2006-2010 5-year est.).
Income: Per capita income: $20,175 (2006-2010 5-year est.); Median household income: $39,148 (2006-2010 5-year est.); Average household income: $43,794 (2006-2010 5-year est.); Percent of households with income of $100,000 or more: 6.1% (2006-2010 5-year est.); Poverty rate: 11.0% (2006-2010 5-year est.).
Education: Percent of population age 25 and over with: High school diploma (including GED) or higher: 92.5% (2006-2010 5-year est.); Bachelor's degree or higher: 10.7% (2006-2010 5-year est.); Master's degree or higher: 4.2% (2006-2010 5-year est.).
School District(s)
Penn Cambria SD (PK-12)
   2010-11 Enrollment: 1,758 . . . . (814) 886-8121
Housing: Homeownership rate: 78.6% (2010); Median home value: $73,000 (2006-2010 5-year est.); Median contract rent: $373 per month (2006-2010 5-year est.); Median year structure built: before 1940 (2006-2010 5-year est.).
Transportation: Commute to work: 95.6% car, 0.0% public transportation, 1.5% walk, 3.0% work from home (2006-2010 5-year est.); Travel time to work: 24.7% less than 15 minutes, 48.6% 15 to 30 minutes, 17.8% 30 to 45 minutes, 5.6% 45 to 60 minutes, 3.3% 60 minutes or more (2006-2010 5-year est.)

LORAIN (borough). Covers a land area of 0.339 square miles and a water area of 0 square miles. Located at 40.30° N. Lat; 78.90° W. Long. Elevation is 1,539 feet.
Population: 842 (1990); 747 (2000); 759 (2010); Density: 2,240.0 persons per square mile (2010); Race: 94.7% White, 2.4% Black, 0.3% Asian, 0.4% American Indian/Alaska Native, 0.0% Native Hawaiian/Other Pacific Islander, 2.2% Other, 0.5% Hispanic of any race (2010); Average household size: 2.25 (2010); Median age: 41.7 (2010); Males per 100 females: 94.6 (2010); Marriage status: 26.6% never married, 46.2% now married, 12.6% widowed, 14.6% divorced (2006-2010 5-year est.); Foreign born: 0.0% (2006-2010 5-year est.); Ancestry (includes multiple ancestries): 32.3% German, 14.4% Irish, 10.0% Scottish, 8.5% Polish, 6.9% Italian (2006-2010 5-year est.).
Economy: Single-family building permits issued: 0 (2011); Multi-family building permits issued: 0 (2011); Employment by occupation: 5.3% management, 0.0% professional, 14.8% services, 18.3% sales, 3.8% farming, 11.8% construction, 3.0% production (2006-2010 5-year est.).
Income: Per capita income: $15,142 (2006-2010 5-year est.); Median household income: $34,712 (2006-2010 5-year est.); Average household income: $37,723 (2006-2010 5-year est.); Percent of households with income of $100,000 or more: 3.9% (2006-2010 5-year est.); Poverty rate: 22.0% (2006-2010 5-year est.).
Education: Percent of population age 25 and over with: High school diploma (including GED) or higher: 84.0% (2006-2010 5-year est.); Bachelor's degree or higher: 11.7% (2006-2010 5-year est.); Master's degree or higher: 6.2% (2006-2010 5-year est.).
Housing: Homeownership rate: 76.9% (2010); Median home value: $47,000 (2006-2010 5-year est.); Median contract rent: $265 per month (2006-2010 5-year est.); Median year structure built: 1943 (2006-2010 5-year est.).
Transportation: Commute to work: 90.0% car, 0.0% public transportation, 3.5% walk, 0.8% work from home (2006-2010 5-year est.); Travel time to work: 44.2% less than 15 minutes, 32.9% 15 to 30 minutes, 5.8% 30 to 45 minutes, 8.1% 45 to 60 minutes, 8.9% 60 minutes or more (2006-2010 5-year est.)

LORETTO (borough). Covers a land area of 0.957 square miles and a water area of 0 square miles. Located at 40.51° N. Lat; 78.63° W. Long. Elevation is 1,952 feet.
History: St. Francis College here.
Population: 1,072 (1990); 1,190 (2000); 1,302 (2010); Density: 1,360.2 persons per square mile (2010); Race: 91.2% White, 5.8% Black, 0.9% Asian, 0.0% American Indian/Alaska Native, 0.2% Native Hawaiian/Other Pacific Islander, 1.9% Other, 2.2% Hispanic of any race (2010); Average household size: 2.40 (2010); Median age: 20.5 (2010); Males per 100 females: 78.4 (2010); Marriage status: 89.7% never married, 7.9% now married, 1.3% widowed, 1.2% divorced (2006-2010 5-year est.); Foreign born: 2.3% (2006-2010 5-year est.); Ancestry (includes multiple ancestries): 45.6% German, 30.2% Irish, 17.0% Italian, 16.2% Polish, 6.2% Slovak (2006-2010 5-year est.).

Economy: Single-family building permits issued: 0 (2011); Multi-family building permits issued: 0 (2011); Employment by occupation: 17.5% management, 0.0% professional, 19.7% services, 22.7% sales, 0.8% farming, 0.8% construction, 1.0% production (2006-2010 5-year est.).

Income: Per capita income: $6,373 (2006-2010 5-year est.); Median household income: $30,469 (2006-2010 5-year est.); Average household income: $34,138 (2006-2010 5-year est.); Percent of households with income of $100,000 or more: 3.6% (2006-2010 5-year est.); Poverty rate: 22.4% (2006-2010 5-year est.).

Education: Percent of population age 25 and over with: High school diploma (including GED) or higher: 94.9% (2006-2010 5-year est.); Bachelor's degree or higher: 43.0% (2006-2010 5-year est.); Master's degree or higher: 15.3% (2006-2010 5-year est.).

Four-year College(s)
Saint Francis University (Private, Not-for-profit, Roman Catholic)
    Fall 2010 Enrollment: 2,462 . . . . (814) 472-3000
    2011-12 Tuition: In-state $27,808; Out-of-state $27,808

Housing: Homeownership rate: 43.0% (2010); Median home value: $86,900 (2006-2010 5-year est.); Median contract rent: $519 per month (2006-2010 5-year est.); Median year structure built: 1950 (2006-2010 5-year est.).

Safety: Violent crime rate: 0.0 per 10,000 population; Property crime rate: 0.0 per 10,000 population (2011).

Transportation: Commute to work: 39.4% car, 1.2% public transportation, 41.9% walk, 17.5% work from home (2006-2010 5-year est.); Travel time to work: 75.4% less than 15 minutes, 17.3% 15 to 30 minutes, 3.4% 30 to 45 minutes, 2.7% 45 to 60 minutes, 1.2% 60 minutes or more (2006-2010 5-year est.)

Additional Information Contacts
Blair County Chamber of Commerce . . . . (814) 943-8151
    http://www.blairchamber.com

LOWER YODER (township). Covers a land area of 13.042 square miles and a water area of 0.085 square miles. Located at 40.34° N. Lat; 78.97° W. Long.

Population: 3,439 (1990); 3,029 (2000); 2,699 (2010); Density: 206.9 persons per square mile (2010); Race: 97.1% White, 1.5% Black, 0.4% Asian, 0.0% American Indian/Alaska Native, 0.0% Native Hawaiian/Other Pacific Islander, 1.0% Other, 0.9% Hispanic of any race (2010); Average household size: 2.01 (2010); Median age: 53.2 (2010); Males per 100 females: 91.7 (2010); Marriage status: 19.7% never married, 59.8% now married, 11.7% widowed, 8.8% divorced (2006-2010 5-year est.); Foreign born: 1.1% (2006-2010 5-year est.); Ancestry (includes multiple ancestries): 37.5% German, 17.4% Slovak, 14.3% Irish, 12.3% Italian, 9.3% Polish (2006-2010 5-year est.).

Economy: Single-family building permits issued: 0 (2011); Multi-family building permits issued: 0 (2011); Employment by occupation: 10.9% management, 1.6% professional, 9.3% services, 16.6% sales, 7.0% farming, 3.6% construction, 2.9% production (2006-2010 5-year est.).

Income: Per capita income: $23,120 (2006-2010 5-year est.); Median household income: $35,572 (2006-2010 5-year est.); Average household income: $46,552 (2006-2010 5-year est.); Percent of households with income of $100,000 or more: 6.9% (2006-2010 5-year est.); Poverty rate: 8.7% (2006-2010 5-year est.).

Education: Percent of population age 25 and over with: High school diploma (including GED) or higher: 90.1% (2006-2010 5-year est.); Bachelor's degree or higher: 16.5% (2006-2010 5-year est.); Master's degree or higher: 4.9% (2006-2010 5-year est.).

Housing: Homeownership rate: 80.0% (2010); Median home value: $70,300 (2006-2010 5-year est.); Median contract rent: $518 per month (2006-2010 5-year est.); Median year structure built: 1950 (2006-2010 5-year est.).

Transportation: Commute to work: 97.1% car, 0.0% public transportation, 1.3% walk, 1.6% work from home (2006-2010 5-year est.); Travel time to work: 42.4% less than 15 minutes, 44.2% 15 to 30 minutes, 9.2% 30 to 45 minutes, 2.4% 45 to 60 minutes, 1.8% 60 minutes or more (2006-2010 5-year est.)

Additional Information Contacts
Greater Johnstown Cambria County Chamber of Commerce . . . . (814) 536-5107
    http://www.johnstownchamber.com

MARSTELLER (unincorporated postal area)
Zip Code: 15760

Covers a land area of 1.575 square miles and a water area of 0 square miles. Located at 40.64° N. Lat; 78.80° W. Long. Population: 152 (2010); Density: 96.5 persons per square mile (2010); Race: 100.0% White, 0.0% Black, 0.0% Asian, 0.0% American Indian/Alaska Native, 0.0% Native Hawaiian/Other Pacific Islander, 0.0% Other, 0.0% Hispanic of any race (2010); Average household size: 2.92 (2010); Median age: 42.0 (2010); Males per 100 females: 100.0 (2010); Homeownership rate: 88.5% (2010)

MIDDLE TAYLOR (township). Covers a land area of 4.672 square miles and a water area of 0.103 square miles. Located at 40.37° N. Lat; 78.91° W. Long.

Population: 802 (1990); 792 (2000); 727 (2010); Density: 155.6 persons per square mile (2010); Race: 99.0% White, 0.7% Black, 0.0% Asian, 0.0% American Indian/Alaska Native, 0.0% Native Hawaiian/Other Pacific Islander, 0.3% Other, 1.2% Hispanic of any race (2010); Average household size: 2.40 (2010); Median age: 48.6 (2010); Males per 100 females: 93.4 (2010); Marriage status: 15.7% never married, 76.1% now married, 5.3% widowed, 3.0% divorced (2006-2010 5-year est.); Foreign born: 0.3% (2006-2010 5-year est.); Ancestry (includes multiple ancestries): 28.2% German, 14.3% Slovak, 11.8% English, 10.5% Italian, 8.3% Polish (2006-2010 5-year est.).

Economy: Single-family building permits issued: 0 (2011); Multi-family building permits issued: 0 (2011); Employment by occupation: 8.7% management, 5.1% professional, 11.6% services, 12.2% sales, 5.1% farming, 6.3% construction, 6.0% production (2006-2010 5-year est.).

Income: Per capita income: $26,673 (2006-2010 5-year est.); Median household income: $48,929 (2006-2010 5-year est.); Average household income: $58,964 (2006-2010 5-year est.); Percent of households with income of $100,000 or more: 9.5% (2006-2010 5-year est.); Poverty rate: 4.9% (2006-2010 5-year est.).

Education: Percent of population age 25 and over with: High school diploma (including GED) or higher: 86.1% (2006-2010 5-year est.); Bachelor's degree or higher: 17.8% (2006-2010 5-year est.); Master's degree or higher: 7.1% (2006-2010 5-year est.).

Housing: Homeownership rate: 88.8% (2010); Median home value: $87,900 (2006-2010 5-year est.); Median contract rent: $245 per month (2006-2010 5-year est.); Median year structure built: 1955 (2006-2010 5-year est.).

Transportation: Commute to work: 97.7% car, 0.0% public transportation, 0.0% walk, 2.3% work from home (2006-2010 5-year est.); Travel time to work: 26.6% less than 15 minutes, 56.0% 15 to 30 minutes, 14.4% 30 to 45 minutes, 1.2% 45 to 60 minutes, 1.8% 60 minutes or more (2006-2010 5-year est.)

MINERAL POINT (unincorporated postal area)
Zip Code: 15942

Covers a land area of 18.538 square miles and a water area of 0.219 square miles. Located at 40.39° N. Lat; 78.81° W. Long. Elevation is 1,378 feet. Population: 2,079 (2010); Density: 112.1 persons per square mile (2010); Race: 98.7% White, 0.3% Black, 0.4% Asian, 0.3% American Indian/Alaska Native, 0.0% Native Hawaiian/Other Pacific Islander, 0.3% Other, 0.5% Hispanic of any race (2010); Average household size: 2.45 (2010); Median age: 46.4 (2010); Males per 100 females: 99.1 (2010); Homeownership rate: 90.4% (2010)

MUNDYS CORNER (CDP). Covers a land area of 6.278 square miles and a water area of 0 square miles. Located at 40.44° N. Lat; 78.83° W. Long. Elevation is 1,890 feet.

Population: n/a (1990); n/a (2000); 1,651 (2010); Density: 263.0 persons per square mile (2010); Race: 99.6% White, 0.0% Black, 0.0% Asian, 0.0% American Indian/Alaska Native, 0.1% Native Hawaiian/Other Pacific Islander, 0.3% Other, 0.0% Hispanic of any race (2010); Average household size: 2.42 (2010); Median age: 45.8 (2010); Males per 100 females: 99.2 (2010); Marriage status: 27.5% never married, 62.5% now married, 7.6% widowed, 2.4% divorced (2006-2010 5-year est.); Foreign born: 1.9% (2006-2010 5-year est.); Ancestry (includes multiple ancestries): 43.1% German, 14.4% English, 10.8% Dutch, 9.9% American, 6.0% Welsh (2006-2010 5-year est.).

Economy: Employment by occupation: 5.8% management, 5.9% professional, 6.1% services, 13.6% sales, 3.2% farming, 21.3% construction, 11.7% production (2006-2010 5-year est.).

Income: Per capita income: $22,334 (2006-2010 5-year est.); Median household income: $48,319 (2006-2010 5-year est.); Average household income: $55,277 (2006-2010 5-year est.); Percent of households with

income of $100,000 or more: 9.4% (2006-2010 5-year est.); Poverty rate: 3.2% (2006-2010 5-year est.).

Education: Percent of population age 25 and over with: High school diploma (including GED) or higher: 94.0% (2006-2010 5-year est.); Bachelor's degree or higher: 11.7% (2006-2010 5-year est.); Master's degree or higher: 5.7% (2006-2010 5-year est.).

Housing: Homeownership rate: 83.2% (2010); Median home value: $98,400 (2006-2010 5-year est.); Median contract rent: $198 per month (2006-2010 5-year est.); Median year structure built: 1973 (2006-2010 5-year est.).

Transportation: Commute to work: 96.1% car, 0.0% public transportation, 2.0% walk, 2.0% work from home (2006-2010 5-year est.); Travel time to work: 19.8% less than 15 minutes, 49.7% 15 to 30 minutes, 27.9% 30 to 45 minutes, 2.6% 45 to 60 minutes, 0.0% 60 minutes or more (2006-2010 5-year est.)

MUNSTER (township). Covers a land area of 14.071 square miles and a water area of 0.059 square miles. Located at 40.45° N. Lat; 78.67° W. Long. Elevation is 1,982 feet.

Population: 688 (1990); 675 (2000); 690 (2010); Density: 49.0 persons per square mile (2010); Race: 99.1% White, 0.1% Black, 0.0% Asian, 0.1% American Indian/Alaska Native, 0.0% Native Hawaiian/Other Pacific Islander, 0.7% Other, 0.3% Hispanic of any race (2010); Average household size: 2.65 (2010); Median age: 41.4 (2010); Males per 100 females: 97.7 (2010); Marriage status: 23.3% never married, 58.3% now married, 7.6% widowed, 10.8% divorced (2006-2010 5-year est.); Foreign born: 0.0% (2006-2010 5-year est.); Ancestry (includes multiple ancestries): 60.5% German, 29.9% Irish, 16.8% Polish, 13.1% Italian, 4.8% American (2006-2010 5-year est.).

Economy: Single-family building permits issued: 6 (2011); Multi-family building permits issued: 0 (2011); Employment by occupation: 15.0% management, 1.9% professional, 8.6% services, 16.9% sales, 4.9% farming, 18.7% construction, 3.7% production (2006-2010 5-year est.).

Income: Per capita income: $20,530 (2006-2010 5-year est.); Median household income: $50,179 (2006-2010 5-year est.); Average household income: $52,840 (2006-2010 5-year est.); Percent of households with income of $100,000 or more: 7.8% (2006-2010 5-year est.); Poverty rate: 5.4% (2006-2010 5-year est.).

Education: Percent of population age 25 and over with: High school diploma (including GED) or higher: 93.1% (2006-2010 5-year est.); Bachelor's degree or higher: 24.5% (2006-2010 5-year est.); Master's degree or higher: 4.0% (2006-2010 5-year est.).

Housing: Homeownership rate: 84.6% (2010); Median home value: $152,000 (2006-2010 5-year est.); Median contract rent: $367 per month (2006-2010 5-year est.); Median year structure built: 1972 (2006-2010 5-year est.).

Transportation: Commute to work: 90.0% car, 0.0% public transportation, 4.6% walk, 5.4% work from home (2006-2010 5-year est.); Travel time to work: 34.4% less than 15 minutes, 30.0% 15 to 30 minutes, 24.7% 30 to 45 minutes, 7.3% 45 to 60 minutes, 3.6% 60 minutes or more (2006-2010 5-year est.)

NANTY-GLO (borough). Aka Nanty Glo. Covers a land area of 1.852 square miles and a water area of 0.001 square miles. Located at 40.47° N. Lat; 78.83° W. Long.

Population: 3,190 (1990); 3,054 (2000); 2,734 (2010); Density: 1,476.4 persons per square mile (2010); Race: 98.2% White, 0.4% Black, 0.1% Asian, 0.0% American Indian/Alaska Native, 0.0% Native Hawaiian/Other Pacific Islander, 1.3% Other, 0.9% Hispanic of any race (2010); Average household size: 2.33 (2010); Median age: 44.5 (2010); Males per 100 females: 92.9 (2010); Marriage status: 26.4% never married, 50.1% now married, 10.2% widowed, 13.4% divorced (2006-2010 5-year est.); Foreign born: 0.9% (2006-2010 5-year est.); Ancestry (includes multiple ancestries): 18.6% German, 15.9% Irish, 15.9% Italian, 8.8% Polish, 7.2% English (2006-2010 5-year est.).

Economy: Single-family building permits issued: 1 (2011); Multi-family building permits issued: 0 (2011); Employment by occupation: 6.1% management, 3.8% professional, 28.3% services, 12.6% sales, 0.8% farming, 15.6% construction, 5.6% production (2006-2010 5-year est.).

Income: Per capita income: $19,213 (2006-2010 5-year est.); Median household income: $37,356 (2006-2010 5-year est.); Average household income: $45,618 (2006-2010 5-year est.); Percent of households with income of $100,000 or more: 8.8% (2006-2010 5-year est.); Poverty rate: 11.3% (2006-2010 5-year est.).

Education: Percent of population age 25 and over with: High school diploma (including GED) or higher: 78.1% (2006-2010 5-year est.); Bachelor's degree or higher: 12.1% (2006-2010 5-year est.); Master's degree or higher: 7.0% (2006-2010 5-year est.).

School District(s)

Blacklick Valley SD (PK-12)

   2010-11 Enrollment: 689 . . . . (814) 749-9211

Housing: Homeownership rate: 74.4% (2010); Median home value: $68,300 (2006-2010 5-year est.); Median contract rent: $310 per month (2006-2010 5-year est.); Median year structure built: before 1940 (2006-2010 5-year est.).

Safety: Violent crime rate: 51.0 per 10,000 population; Property crime rate: 339.0 per 10,000 population (2011).

Transportation: Commute to work: 95.6% car, 0.6% public transportation, 2.0% walk, 1.7% work from home (2006-2010 5-year est.); Travel time to work: 28.5% less than 15 minutes, 35.8% 15 to 30 minutes, 27.5% 30 to 45 minutes, 1.9% 45 to 60 minutes, 6.3% 60 minutes or more (2006-2010 5-year est.)

Additional Information Contacts

Borough of Nanty-Glo . . . . (814) 472-5440

   http://www.co.cambria.pa.us

Greater Johnstown Cambria County Chamber of Commerce . . . . (814) 536-5107

   http://www.johnstownchamber.com

NICKTOWN (unincorporated postal area)

Zip Code: 15762

   Covers a land area of 13.365 square miles and a water area of 0.012 square miles. Located at 40.59° N. Lat; 78.82° W. Long. Elevation is 1,959 feet. Population: 823 (2010); Density: 61.6 persons per square mile (2010); Race: 99.4% White, 0.1% Black, 0.2% Asian, 0.0% American Indian/Alaska Native, 0.0% Native Hawaiian/Other Pacific Islander, 0.3% Other, 0.1% Hispanic of any race (2010); Average household size: 2.68 (2010); Median age: 43.9 (2010); Males per 100 females: 100.7 (2010); Homeownership rate: 88.2% (2010)

NORTHERN CAMBRIA (borough). Aka Barnesboro. Covers a land area of 2.984 square miles and a water area of <.001 square miles. Located at 40.66° N. Lat; 78.78° W. Long. Elevation is 1,519 feet.

Population: 4,598 (1990); 4,199 (2000); 3,835 (2010); Density: 1,285.3 persons per square mile (2010); Race: 98.5% White, 0.4% Black, 0.4% Asian, 0.1% American Indian/Alaska Native, 0.0% Native Hawaiian/Other Pacific Islander, 0.6% Other, 0.4% Hispanic of any race (2010); Average household size: 2.41 (2010); Median age: 41.4 (2010); Males per 100 females: 95.2 (2010); Marriage status: 26.2% never married, 56.6% now married, 8.7% widowed, 8.5% divorced (2006-2010 5-year est.); Foreign born: 0.3% (2006-2010 5-year est.); Ancestry (includes multiple ancestries): 24.6% German, 21.0% Polish, 17.4% Irish, 17.2% Italian, 8.5% Slovak (2006-2010 5-year est.).

Economy: Single-family building permits issued: 0 (2011); Multi-family building permits issued: 0 (2011); Employment by occupation: 4.5% management, 2.1% professional, 10.8% services, 12.9% sales, 2.8% farming, 20.7% construction, 10.2% production (2006-2010 5-year est.).

Income: Per capita income: $20,053 (2006-2010 5-year est.); Median household income: $38,843 (2006-2010 5-year est.); Average household income: $47,684 (2006-2010 5-year est.); Percent of households with income of $100,000 or more: 7.3% (2006-2010 5-year est.); Poverty rate: 13.1% (2006-2010 5-year est.).

Education: Percent of population age 25 and over with: High school diploma (including GED) or higher: 86.1% (2006-2010 5-year est.); Bachelor's degree or higher: 15.7% (2006-2010 5-year est.); Master's degree or higher: 5.5% (2006-2010 5-year est.).

School District(s)

Northern Cambria SD (KG-12)

   2010-11 Enrollment: 1,217 . . . . (814) 948-5481

Housing: Homeownership rate: 73.7% (2010); Median home value: $69,000 (2006-2010 5-year est.); Median contract rent: $392 per month (2006-2010 5-year est.); Median year structure built: before 1940 (2006-2010 5-year est.).

Safety: Violent crime rate: 10.4 per 10,000 population; Property crime rate: 223.6 per 10,000 population (2011).

Transportation: Commute to work: 96.6% car, 0.0% public transportation, 2.2% walk, 0.7% work from home (2006-2010 5-year est.); Travel time to work: 29.4% less than 15 minutes, 15.4% 15 to 30 minutes, 26.4% 30 to

45 minutes, 20.9% 45 to 60 minutes, 7.9% 60 minutes or more (2006-2010 5-year est.)

Additional Information Contacts
Indiana County Chamber of Commerce . . . . (724) 465-2511
　　http://www.indianapa.com/chamber

OAKLAND (CDP).
Covers a land area of 1.416 square miles and a water area of 0 square miles. Located at 40.31° N. Lat; 78.88° W. Long. Elevation is 1,591 feet.
Population: n/a (1990); n/a (2000); 1,578 (2010); Density: 1,114.0 persons per square mile (2010); Race: 96.9% White, 1.3% Black, 0.5% Asian, 0.1% American Indian/Alaska Native, 0.0% Native Hawaiian/Other Pacific Islander, 1.2% Other, 1.1% Hispanic of any race (2010); Average household size: 2.08 (2010); Median age: 53.3 (2010); Males per 100 females: 95.1 (2010); Marriage status: 23.6% never married, 61.0% now married, 9.1% widowed, 6.3% divorced (2006-2010 5-year est.); Foreign born: 6.7% (2006-2010 5-year est.); Ancestry (includes multiple ancestries): 39.8% German, 18.8% Irish, 10.9% English, 10.0% Italian, 7.6% Polish (2006-2010 5-year est.).
Economy: Employment by occupation: 8.3% management, 1.7% professional, 3.9% services, 26.0% sales, 7.7% farming, 5.0% construction, 3.0% production (2006-2010 5-year est.).
Income: Per capita income: $25,808 (2006-2010 5-year est.); Median household income: $45,904 (2006-2010 5-year est.); Average household income: $53,888 (2006-2010 5-year est.); Percent of households with income of $100,000 or more: 9.7% (2006-2010 5-year est.); Poverty rate: 2.7% (2006-2010 5-year est.).
Education: Percent of population age 25 and over with: High school diploma (including GED) or higher: 91.6% (2006-2010 5-year est.); Bachelor's degree or higher: 20.5% (2006-2010 5-year est.); Master's degree or higher: 5.5% (2006-2010 5-year est.).
Housing: Homeownership rate: 83.7% (2010); Median home value: $88,400 (2006-2010 5-year est.); Median contract rent: $397 per month (2006-2010 5-year est.); Median year structure built: 1955 (2006-2010 5-year est.).
Transportation: Commute to work: 93.7% car, 0.9% public transportation, 0.7% walk, 2.3% work from home (2006-2010 5-year est.); Travel time to work: 51.6% less than 15 minutes, 27.3% 15 to 30 minutes, 8.6% 30 to 45 minutes, 3.6% 45 to 60 minutes, 8.9% 60 minutes or more (2006-2010 5-year est.)

PARKHILL (unincorporated postal area)
Zip Code: 15945
　　Covers a land area of 0.588 square miles and a water area of 0.045 square miles. Located at 40.35° N. Lat; 78.86° W. Long. Elevation is 1,549 feet. Population: 198 (2010); Density: 336.3 persons per square mile (2010); Race: 97.5% White, 1.5% Black, 1.0% Asian, 0.0% American Indian/Alaska Native, 0.0% Native Hawaiian/Other Pacific Islander, 0.0% Other, 1.0% Hispanic of any race (2010); Average household size: 2.79 (2010); Median age: 43.5 (2010); Males per 100 females: 108.4 (2010); Homeownership rate: 92.9% (2010)

PATTON (borough).
Covers a land area of 0.880 square miles and a water area of 0 square miles. Located at 40.63° N. Lat; 78.65° W. Long. Elevation is 1,791 feet.
Population: 2,347 (1990); 2,023 (2000); 1,769 (2010); Density: 2,010.1 persons per square mile (2010); Race: 99.3% White, 0.1% Black, 0.2% Asian, 0.1% American Indian/Alaska Native, 0.0% Native Hawaiian/Other Pacific Islander, 0.3% Other, 0.4% Hispanic of any race (2010); Average household size: 2.19 (2010); Median age: 45.2 (2010); Males per 100 females: 92.3 (2010); Marriage status: 24.2% never married, 51.2% now married, 10.8% widowed, 13.7% divorced (2006-2010 5-year est.); Foreign born: 0.0% (2006-2010 5-year est.); Ancestry (includes multiple ancestries): 41.5% German, 17.7% Italian, 15.4% Irish, 6.5% Slovak, 6.5% English (2006-2010 5-year est.).
Economy: Single-family building permits issued: 0 (2011); Multi-family building permits issued: 0 (2011); Employment by occupation: 2.3% management, 4.8% professional, 11.0% services, 14.7% sales, 3.5% farming, 6.9% construction, 4.6% production (2006-2010 5-year est.).
Income: Per capita income: $15,938 (2006-2010 5-year est.); Median household income: $25,330 (2006-2010 5-year est.); Average household income: $33,878 (2006-2010 5-year est.); Percent of households with income of $100,000 or more: 2.7% (2006-2010 5-year est.); Poverty rate: 22.9% (2006-2010 5-year est.).

Education: Percent of population age 25 and over with: High school diploma (including GED) or higher: 84.0% (2006-2010 5-year est.); Bachelor's degree or higher: 9.3% (2006-2010 5-year est.); Master's degree or higher: 3.2% (2006-2010 5-year est.).
School District(s)
Cambria Heights SD (PK-12)
　　2010-11 Enrollment: 1,465 . . . . (814) 674-3626
Housing: Homeownership rate: 68.8% (2010); Median home value: $66,500 (2006-2010 5-year est.); Median contract rent: $254 per month (2006-2010 5-year est.); Median year structure built: before 1940 (2006-2010 5-year est.).
Safety: Violent crime rate: 5.6 per 10,000 population; Property crime rate: 22.5 per 10,000 population (2011).
Transportation: Commute to work: 83.2% car, 0.0% public transportation, 11.7% walk, 2.4% work from home (2006-2010 5-year est.); Travel time to work: 31.4% less than 15 minutes, 25.9% 15 to 30 minutes, 25.1% 30 to 45 minutes, 10.3% 45 to 60 minutes, 7.3% 60 minutes or more (2006-2010 5-year est.)
Additional Information Contacts
Blair County Chamber of Commerce . . . . (814) 943-8151
　　http://www.blairchamber.com
Borough of Patton . . . . (814) 674-3641
　　http://www.pattonboro.com

PORTAGE (borough).
Covers a land area of 0.658 square miles and a water area of 0 square miles. Located at 40.39° N. Lat; 78.67° W. Long. Elevation is 1,686 feet.
Population: 3,105 (1990); 2,837 (2000); 2,638 (2010); Density: 4,008.3 persons per square mile (2010); Race: 98.6% White, 0.3% Black, 0.0% Asian, 0.1% American Indian/Alaska Native, 0.0% Native Hawaiian/Other Pacific Islander, 1.0% Other, 0.5% Hispanic of any race (2010); Average household size: 2.25 (2010); Median age: 42.7 (2010); Males per 100 females: 92.0 (2010); Marriage status: 28.6% never married, 54.8% now married, 9.3% widowed, 7.3% divorced (2006-2010 5-year est.); Foreign born: 0.0% (2006-2010 5-year est.); Ancestry (includes multiple ancestries): 26.4% German, 14.3% Italian, 12.8% Polish, 12.7% English, 10.8% Russian (2006-2010 5-year est.).
Economy: Single-family building permits issued: 0 (2011); Multi-family building permits issued: 0 (2011); Employment by occupation: 6.4% management, 0.0% professional, 17.9% services, 16.0% sales, 2.9% farming, 6.4% construction, 8.1% production (2006-2010 5-year est.).
Income: Per capita income: $16,985 (2006-2010 5-year est.); Median household income: $32,656 (2006-2010 5-year est.); Average household income: $39,810 (2006-2010 5-year est.); Percent of households with income of $100,000 or more: 3.9% (2006-2010 5-year est.); Poverty rate: 14.6% (2006-2010 5-year est.).
Education: Percent of population age 25 and over with: High school diploma (including GED) or higher: 83.0% (2006-2010 5-year est.); Bachelor's degree or higher: 8.2% (2006-2010 5-year est.); Master's degree or higher: 4.5% (2006-2010 5-year est.).
School District(s)
Portage Area SD (KG-12)
　　2010-11 Enrollment: 934 . . . . (814) 736-9636
Housing: Homeownership rate: 65.6% (2010); Median home value: $66,500 (2006-2010 5-year est.); Median contract rent: $314 per month (2006-2010 5-year est.); Median year structure built: 1940 (2006-2010 5-year est.).
Safety: Violent crime rate: 26.5 per 10,000 population; Property crime rate: 313.7 per 10,000 population (2011).
Newspapers: Portage Dispatch (Community news; Circulation 5,285)
Transportation: Commute to work: 93.2% car, 0.0% public transportation, 5.1% walk, 0.0% work from home (2006-2010 5-year est.); Travel time to work: 24.5% less than 15 minutes, 43.9% 15 to 30 minutes, 19.0% 30 to 45 minutes, 4.4% 45 to 60 minutes, 8.1% 60 minutes or more (2006-2010 5-year est.)
Additional Information Contacts
Greater Johnstown Cambria County Chamber of Commerce . . . . (814) 536-5107
　　http://www.johnstownchamber.com

PORTAGE (township).
Covers a land area of 24.765 square miles and a water area of 0.097 square miles. Located at 40.38° N. Lat; 78.64° W. Long. Elevation is 1,686 feet.
Population: 4,089 (1990); 3,906 (2000); 3,640 (2010); Density: 147.0 persons per square mile (2010); Race: 98.8% White, 0.4% Black, 0.2%

Asian, 0.1% American Indian/Alaska Native, 0.0% Native Hawaiian/Other Pacific Islander, 0.5% Other, 0.4% Hispanic of any race (2010); Average household size: 2.47 (2010); Median age: 46.3 (2010); Males per 100 females: 102.1 (2010); Marriage status: 25.4% never married, 58.0% now married, 9.3% widowed, 7.3% divorced (2006-2010 5-year est.); Foreign born: 0.6% (2006-2010 5-year est.); Ancestry (includes multiple ancestries): 33.7% German, 26.8% Polish, 15.2% Irish, 8.4% Slovak, 8.0% English (2006-2010 5-year est.).

Economy: Single-family building permits issued: 3 (2011); Multi-family building permits issued: 0 (2011); Employment by occupation: 3.7% management, 1.2% professional, 21.0% services, 18.6% sales, 3.5% farming, 15.0% construction, 9.8% production (2006-2010 5-year est.).

Income: Per capita income: $20,809 (2006-2010 5-year est.); Median household income: $43,535 (2006-2010 5-year est.); Average household income: $50,143 (2006-2010 5-year est.); Percent of households with income of $100,000 or more: 8.4% (2006-2010 5-year est.); Poverty rate: 7.8% (2006-2010 5-year est.).

Education: Percent of population age 25 and over with: High school diploma (including GED) or higher: 85.2% (2006-2010 5-year est.); Bachelor's degree or higher: 10.1% (2006-2010 5-year est.); Master's degree or higher: 2.6% (2006-2010 5-year est.).

Housing: Homeownership rate: 87.7% (2010); Median home value: $74,400 (2006-2010 5-year est.); Median contract rent: $376 per month (2006-2010 5-year est.); Median year structure built: 1957 (2006-2010 5-year est.).

Newspapers: Portage Dispatch (Community news; Circulation 5,285)

Transportation: Commute to work: 93.3% car, 0.0% public transportation, 3.0% walk, 2.8% work from home (2006-2010 5-year est.); Travel time to work: 26.2% less than 15 minutes, 35.6% 15 to 30 minutes, 21.9% 30 to 45 minutes, 12.6% 45 to 60 minutes, 3.7% 60 minutes or more (2006-2010 5-year est.)

Additional Information Contacts
Greater Johnstown Cambria County Chamber of Commerce . . . . (814) 536-5107
   http://www.johnstownchamber.com

READE (township). Covers a land area of 38.665 square miles and a water area of 0.016 square miles. Located at 40.68° N. Lat; 78.46° W. Long.

Population: 1,716 (1990); 1,764 (2000); 1,619 (2010); Density: 41.9 persons per square mile (2010); Race: 98.6% White, 0.3% Black, 0.1% Asian, 0.2% American Indian/Alaska Native, 0.1% Native Hawaiian/Other Pacific Islander, 0.7% Other, 0.2% Hispanic of any race (2010); Average household size: 2.52 (2010); Median age: 42.0 (2010); Males per 100 females: 107.8 (2010); Marriage status: 21.7% never married, 55.0% now married, 9.2% widowed, 14.0% divorced (2006-2010 5-year est.); Foreign born: 0.0% (2006-2010 5-year est.); Ancestry (includes multiple ancestries): 33.2% German, 26.0% Irish, 12.1% Polish, 8.7% Italian, 6.8% English (2006-2010 5-year est.).

Economy: Single-family building permits issued: 2 (2011); Multi-family building permits issued: 0 (2011); Employment by occupation: 6.8% management, 2.3% professional, 16.3% services, 14.2% sales, 1.7% farming, 15.1% construction, 9.1% production (2006-2010 5-year est.).

Income: Per capita income: $17,833 (2006-2010 5-year est.); Median household income: $37,714 (2006-2010 5-year est.); Average household income: $42,766 (2006-2010 5-year est.); Percent of households with income of $100,000 or more: 4.9% (2006-2010 5-year est.); Poverty rate: 17.5% (2006-2010 5-year est.).

Education: Percent of population age 25 and over with: High school diploma (including GED) or higher: 81.8% (2006-2010 5-year est.); Bachelor's degree or higher: 5.2% (2006-2010 5-year est.); Master's degree or higher: 0.5% (2006-2010 5-year est.).

Housing: Homeownership rate: 83.4% (2010); Median home value: $62,700 (2006-2010 5-year est.); Median contract rent: $376 per month (2006-2010 5-year est.); Median year structure built: 1961 (2006-2010 5-year est.).

Transportation: Commute to work: 90.2% car, 0.0% public transportation, 1.9% walk, 3.5% work from home (2006-2010 5-year est.); Travel time to work: 20.6% less than 15 minutes, 23.4% 15 to 30 minutes, 35.8% 30 to 45 minutes, 12.9% 45 to 60 minutes, 7.4% 60 minutes or more (2006-2010 5-year est.)

Additional Information Contacts
Blair County Chamber of Commerce . . . . (814) 943-8151
   http://www.blairchamber.com

REVLOC (CDP). Covers a land area of 0.344 square miles and a water area of 0 square miles. Located at 40.49° N. Lat; 78.76° W. Long. Elevation is 2,067 feet.

Population: n/a (1990); n/a (2000); 570 (2010); Density: 1,658.5 persons per square mile (2010); Race: 96.8% White, 1.1% Black, 0.5% Asian, 0.0% American Indian/Alaska Native, 0.2% Native Hawaiian/Other Pacific Islander, 1.4% Other, 0.5% Hispanic of any race (2010); Average household size: 2.59 (2010); Median age: 37.8 (2010); Males per 100 females: 102.8 (2010); Marriage status: 12.7% never married, 77.5% now married, 9.8% widowed, 0.0% divorced (2006-2010 5-year est.); Foreign born: 0.0% (2006-2010 5-year est.); Ancestry (includes multiple ancestries): 51.6% Irish, 26.1% Italian, 11.4% Polish, 11.3% American, 10.8% English (2006-2010 5-year est.).

Economy: Employment by occupation: 0.0% management, 0.0% professional, 10.0% services, 16.7% sales, 0.0% farming, 9.0% construction, 3.3% production (2006-2010 5-year est.).

Income: Per capita income: $13,420 (2006-2010 5-year est.); Median household income: $25,959 (2006-2010 5-year est.); Average household income: $30,287 (2006-2010 5-year est.); Percent of households with income of $100,000 or more: 4.3% (2006-2010 5-year est.); Poverty rate: 23.6% (2006-2010 5-year est.).

Education: Percent of population age 25 and over with: High school diploma (including GED) or higher: 79.0% (2006-2010 5-year est.); Bachelor's degree or higher: 3.6% (2006-2010 5-year est.); Master's degree or higher: 0.0% (2006-2010 5-year est.).

Housing: Homeownership rate: 75.9% (2010); Median home value: $71,300 (2006-2010 5-year est.); Median contract rent: $325 per month (2006-2010 5-year est.); Median year structure built: before 1940 (2006-2010 5-year est.).

Transportation: Commute to work: 76.5% car, 0.0% public transportation, 0.0% walk, 0.0% work from home (2006-2010 5-year est.); Travel time to work: 34.0% less than 15 minutes, 52.3% 15 to 30 minutes, 10.2% 30 to 45 minutes, 3.5% 45 to 60 minutes, 0.0% 60 minutes or more (2006-2010 5-year est.)

RICHLAND (township). Covers a land area of 20.592 square miles and a water area of 0.032 square miles. Located at 40.29° N. Lat; 78.84° W. Long.

Population: 12,787 (1990); 12,598 (2000); 12,814 (2010); Density: 622.3 persons per square mile (2010); Race: 96.1% White, 1.0% Black, 1.9% Asian, 0.0% American Indian/Alaska Native, 0.0% Native Hawaiian/Other Pacific Islander, 1.0% Other, 1.0% Hispanic of any race (2010); Average household size: 2.20 (2010); Median age: 43.6 (2010); Males per 100 females: 92.1 (2010); Marriage status: 35.9% never married, 46.7% now married, 11.0% widowed, 6.5% divorced (2006-2010 5-year est.); Foreign born: 2.6% (2006-2010 5-year est.); Ancestry (includes multiple ancestries): 37.2% German, 18.3% Irish, 12.5% Italian, 10.0% Polish, 8.5% English (2006-2010 5-year est.).

Economy: Single-family building permits issued: 6 (2011); Multi-family building permits issued: 0 (2011); Employment by occupation: 11.9% management, 6.6% professional, 13.1% services, 17.6% sales, 3.9% farming, 5.3% construction, 2.8% production (2006-2010 5-year est.).

Income: Per capita income: $26,256 (2006-2010 5-year est.); Median household income: $46,992 (2006-2010 5-year est.); Average household income: $68,404 (2006-2010 5-year est.); Percent of households with income of $100,000 or more: 16.7% (2006-2010 5-year est.); Poverty rate: 7.5% (2006-2010 5-year est.).

Education: Percent of population age 25 and over with: High school diploma (including GED) or higher: 91.1% (2006-2010 5-year est.); Bachelor's degree or higher: 26.6% (2006-2010 5-year est.); Master's degree or higher: 10.7% (2006-2010 5-year est.).

Housing: Homeownership rate: 71.9% (2010); Median home value: $131,500 (2006-2010 5-year est.); Median contract rent: $483 per month (2006-2010 5-year est.); Median year structure built: 1969 (2006-2010 5-year est.).

Safety: Violent crime rate: 7.0 per 10,000 population; Property crime rate: 529.8 per 10,000 population (2011).

Transportation: Commute to work: 94.7% car, 0.3% public transportation, 1.0% walk, 3.4% work from home (2006-2010 5-year est.); Travel time to work: 55.1% less than 15 minutes, 27.9% 15 to 30 minutes, 8.3% 30 to 45 minutes, 2.4% 45 to 60 minutes, 6.2% 60 minutes or more (2006-2010 5-year est.)

Additional Information Contacts
Greater Johnstown Cambria County Chamber of Commerce . . . . (814) 536-5107
http://www.johnstownchamber.com
Richland Township . . . . (814) 266-2922
http://www.richlandtwp.com

RIVERSIDE (CDP). Covers a land area of 0.116 square miles and a water area of 0.016 square miles. Located at 40.28° N. Lat; 78.92° W. Long. Elevation is 1,234 feet.
Population: n/a (1990); n/a (2000); 381 (2010); Density: 3,279.3 persons per square mile (2010); Race: 96.9% White, 0.3% Black, 1.0% Asian, 0.0% American Indian/Alaska Native, 0.0% Native Hawaiian/Other Pacific Islander, 1.8% Other, 0.3% Hispanic of any race (2010); Average household size: 2.12 (2010); Median age: 44.3 (2010); Males per 100 females: 87.7 (2010); Marriage status: 27.9% never married, 38.4% now married, 8.8% widowed, 24.9% divorced (2006-2010 5-year est.); Foreign born: 0.0% (2006-2010 5-year est.); Ancestry (includes multiple ancestries): 53.2% German, 26.4% Irish, 18.5% English, 10.1% American, 5.0% Slovene (2006-2010 5-year est.).
Economy: Employment by occupation: 20.6% management, 7.8% professional, 0.0% services, 6.4% sales, 0.0% farming, 16.2% construction, 0.0% production (2006-2010 5-year est.).
Income: Per capita income: $37,234 (2006-2010 5-year est.); Median household income: $82,857 (2006-2010 5-year est.); Average household income: $82,200 (2006-2010 5-year est.); Percent of households with income of $100,000 or more: 25.3% (2006-2010 5-year est.); Poverty rate: 12.8% (2006-2010 5-year est.).
Education: Percent of population age 25 and over with: High school diploma (including GED) or higher: 81.1% (2006-2010 5-year est.); Bachelor's degree or higher: 29.3% (2006-2010 5-year est.); Master's degree or higher: 18.3% (2006-2010 5-year est.).
Housing: Homeownership rate: 80.6% (2010); Median home value: $66,200 (2006-2010 5-year est.); Median contract rent: $607 per month (2006-2010 5-year est.); Median year structure built: 1951 (2006-2010 5-year est.).
Transportation: Commute to work: 100.0% car, 0.0% public transportation, 0.0% walk, 0.0% work from home (2006-2010 5-year est.); Travel time to work: 19.0% less than 15 minutes, 46.7% 15 to 30 minutes, 9.2% 30 to 45 minutes, 25.1% 45 to 60 minutes, 0.0% 60 minutes or more (2006-2010 5-year est.)

SAINT BENEDICT (unincorporated postal area)
Zip Code: 15773
Covers a land area of 3.804 square miles and a water area of 0 square miles. Located at 40.62° N. Lat; 78.73° W. Long. Elevation is 1,854 feet. Population: 516 (2010); Density: 135.6 persons per square mile (2010); Race: 100.0% White, 0.0% Black, 0.0% Asian, 0.0% American Indian/Alaska Native, 0.0% Native Hawaiian/Other Pacific Islander, 0.0% Other, 0.4% Hispanic of any race (2010); Average household size: 2.61 (2010); Median age: 46.8 (2010); Males per 100 females: 95.5 (2010); Homeownership rate: 90.4% (2010)

SAINT MICHAEL (CDP). Covers a land area of 1.041 square miles and a water area of 0.011 square miles. Located at 40.32° N. Lat; 78.77° W. Long. Elevation is 1,598 feet.
Population: n/a (1990); n/a (2000); 408 (2010); Density: 392.0 persons per square mile (2010); Race: 99.5% White, 0.0% Black, 0.0% Asian, 0.0% American Indian/Alaska Native, 0.0% Native Hawaiian/Other Pacific Islander, 0.5% Other, 0.7% Hispanic of any race (2010); Average household size: 2.09 (2010); Median age: 48.2 (2010); Males per 100 females: 88.9 (2010); Marriage status: 16.7% never married, 31.0% now married, 18.3% widowed, 34.1% divorced (2006-2010 5-year est.); Foreign born: 0.0% (2006-2010 5-year est.); Ancestry (includes multiple ancestries): 67.5% German, 52.1% Irish, 10.4% Polish, 5.4% Slovak, 5.0% Dutch (2006-2010 5-year est.).
Economy: Employment by occupation: 0.0% management, 0.0% professional, 22.9% services, 0.0% sales, 0.0% farming, 0.0% construction, 0.0% production (2006-2010 5-year est.).
Income: Per capita income: $9,646 (2006-2010 5-year est.); Median household income: $19,375 (2006-2010 5-year est.); Average household income: $23,208 (2006-2010 5-year est.); Percent of households with income of $100,000 or more: n/a (2006-2010 5-year est.); Poverty rate: 21.1% (2006-2010 5-year est.).

Education: Percent of population age 25 and over with: High school diploma (including GED) or higher: 76.6% (2006-2010 5-year est.); Bachelor's degree or higher: 0.0% (2006-2010 5-year est.); Master's degree or higher: 0.0% (2006-2010 5-year est.).
Housing: Homeownership rate: 68.2% (2010); Median home value: $37,500 (2006-2010 5-year est.); Median contract rent: n/a per month (2006-2010 5-year est.); Median year structure built: before 1940 (2006-2010 5-year est.).
Transportation: Commute to work: 45.7% car, 0.0% public transportation, 54.3% walk, 0.0% work from home (2006-2010 5-year est.); Travel time to work: 67.6% less than 15 minutes, 19.0% 15 to 30 minutes, 13.3% 30 to 45 minutes, 0.0% 45 to 60 minutes, 0.0% 60 minutes or more (2006-2010 5-year est.)

SALIX (CDP). Covers a land area of 0.969 square miles and a water area of 0 square miles. Located at 40.29° N. Lat; 78.77° W. Long. Elevation is 2,051 feet.
Population: n/a (1990); n/a (2000); 1,149 (2010); Density: 1,185.5 persons per square mile (2010); Race: 99.1% White, 0.3% Black, 0.1% Asian, 0.0% American Indian/Alaska Native, 0.0% Native Hawaiian/Other Pacific Islander, 0.5% Other, 0.3% Hispanic of any race (2010); Average household size: 2.42 (2010); Median age: 42.8 (2010); Males per 100 females: 88.1 (2010); Marriage status: 28.7% never married, 53.4% now married, 6.2% widowed, 11.7% divorced (2006-2010 5-year est.); Foreign born: 0.0% (2006-2010 5-year est.); Ancestry (includes multiple ancestries): 30.0% German, 24.4% Irish, 12.9% Slovak, 9.4% Polish, 8.2% English (2006-2010 5-year est.).
Economy: Employment by occupation: 15.7% management, 3.1% professional, 16.5% services, 18.8% sales, 4.3% farming, 1.7% construction, 2.2% production (2006-2010 5-year est.).
Income: Per capita income: $21,127 (2006-2010 5-year est.); Median household income: $46,439 (2006-2010 5-year est.); Average household income: $49,355 (2006-2010 5-year est.); Percent of households with income of $100,000 or more: 5.4% (2006-2010 5-year est.); Poverty rate: 6.3% (2006-2010 5-year est.).
Education: Percent of population age 25 and over with: High school diploma (including GED) or higher: 88.2% (2006-2010 5-year est.); Bachelor's degree or higher: 20.6% (2006-2010 5-year est.); Master's degree or higher: 11.1% (2006-2010 5-year est.).
Housing: Homeownership rate: 72.0% (2010); Median home value: $104,800 (2006-2010 5-year est.); Median contract rent: $142 per month (2006-2010 5-year est.); Median year structure built: 1974 (2006-2010 5-year est.).
Transportation: Commute to work: 99.2% car, 0.0% public transportation, 0.0% walk, 0.8% work from home (2006-2010 5-year est.); Travel time to work: 33.1% less than 15 minutes, 39.1% 15 to 30 minutes, 15.1% 30 to 45 minutes, 2.9% 45 to 60 minutes, 9.7% 60 minutes or more (2006-2010 5-year est.)

SANKERTOWN (borough). Covers a land area of 0.295 square miles and a water area of 0 square miles. Located at 40.47° N. Lat; 78.59° W. Long. Elevation is 2,067 feet.
Population: 770 (1990); 680 (2000); 675 (2010); Density: 2,287.8 persons per square mile (2010); Race: 99.4% White, 0.1% Black, 0.1% Asian, 0.1% American Indian/Alaska Native, 0.0% Native Hawaiian/Other Pacific Islander, 0.3% Other, 0.1% Hispanic of any race (2010); Average household size: 2.26 (2010); Median age: 45.7 (2010); Males per 100 females: 89.1 (2010); Marriage status: 28.4% never married, 48.2% now married, 9.5% widowed, 14.0% divorced (2006-2010 5-year est.); Foreign born: 0.0% (2006-2010 5-year est.); Ancestry (includes multiple ancestries): 48.8% German, 30.0% Irish, 15.0% Polish, 9.4% Italian, 7.0% American (2006-2010 5-year est.).
Economy: Single-family building permits issued: 0 (2011); Multi-family building permits issued: 0 (2011); Employment by occupation: 2.7% management, 0.9% professional, 10.4% services, 21.7% sales, 2.1% farming, 10.7% construction, 7.4% production (2006-2010 5-year est.).
Income: Per capita income: $19,065 (2006-2010 5-year est.); Median household income: $43,375 (2006-2010 5-year est.); Average household income: $46,809 (2006-2010 5-year est.); Percent of households with income of $100,000 or more: 4.2% (2006-2010 5-year est.); Poverty rate: 8.6% (2006-2010 5-year est.).
Education: Percent of population age 25 and over with: High school diploma (including GED) or higher: 87.7% (2006-2010 5-year est.); Bachelor's degree or higher: 16.2% (2006-2010 5-year est.); Master's degree or higher: 5.2% (2006-2010 5-year est.).

Housing: Homeownership rate: 68.0% (2010); Median home value: $90,900 (2006-2010 5-year est.); Median contract rent: $363 per month (2006-2010 5-year est.); Median year structure built: 1945 (2006-2010 5-year est.).

Safety: Violent crime rate: 0.0 per 10,000 population; Property crime rate: 29.5 per 10,000 population (2011).

Transportation: Commute to work: 92.0% car, 0.0% public transportation, 3.7% walk, 4.3% work from home (2006-2010 5-year est.); Travel time to work: 30.4% less than 15 minutes, 31.4% 15 to 30 minutes, 28.5% 30 to 45 minutes, 6.5% 45 to 60 minutes, 3.2% 60 minutes or more (2006-2010 5-year est.)

SCALP LEVEL (borough). Covers a land area of 0.659 square miles and a water area of 0 square miles. Located at 40.25° N. Lat; 78.84° W. Long. Elevation is 1,762 feet.

History: University of Pittsburgh-Johnstown Campus to North. Incorporated 1898.

Population: 1,158 (1990); 851 (2000); 778 (2010); Density: 1,180.7 persons per square mile (2010); Race: 97.4% White, 0.9% Black, 1.0% Asian, 0.0% American Indian/Alaska Native, 0.0% Native Hawaiian/Other Pacific Islander, 0.7% Other, 0.3% Hispanic of any race (2010); Average household size: 2.34 (2010); Median age: 43.0 (2010); Males per 100 females: 86.6 (2010); Marriage status: 30.7% never married, 52.3% now married, 10.8% widowed, 6.2% divorced (2006-2010 5-year est.); Foreign born: 2.0% (2006-2010 5-year est.); Ancestry (includes multiple ancestries): 22.7% German, 14.6% Polish, 12.9% Italian, 11.9% Slovak, 8.0% Irish (2006-2010 5-year est.).

Economy: Single-family building permits issued: 0 (2011); Multi-family building permits issued: 0 (2011); Employment by occupation: 6.0% management, 4.3% professional, 12.1% services, 24.4% sales, 6.0% farming, 8.6% construction, 6.6% production (2006-2010 5-year est.).

Income: Per capita income: $21,074 (2006-2010 5-year est.); Median household income: $32,538 (2006-2010 5-year est.); Average household income: $46,575 (2006-2010 5-year est.); Percent of households with income of $100,000 or more: 9.3% (2006-2010 5-year est.); Poverty rate: 13.5% (2006-2010 5-year est.).

Education: Percent of population age 25 and over with: High school diploma (including GED) or higher: 80.3% (2006-2010 5-year est.); Bachelor's degree or higher: 11.9% (2006-2010 5-year est.); Master's degree or higher: 1.4% (2006-2010 5-year est.).

Housing: Homeownership rate: 79.5% (2010); Median home value: $51,500 (2006-2010 5-year est.); Median contract rent: $357 per month (2006-2010 5-year est.); Median year structure built: before 1940 (2006-2010 5-year est.).

Transportation: Commute to work: 94.0% car, 0.0% public transportation, 0.6% walk, 4.6% work from home (2006-2010 5-year est.); Travel time to work: 41.9% less than 15 minutes, 37.0% 15 to 30 minutes, 12.0% 30 to 45 minutes, 2.1% 45 to 60 minutes, 6.9% 60 minutes or more (2006-2010 5-year est.)

SIDMAN (CDP). Covers a land area of 0.992 square miles and a water area of 0 square miles. Located at 40.32° N. Lat; 78.75° W. Long. Elevation is 1,634 feet.

Population: n/a (1990); n/a (2000); 431 (2010); Density: 434.5 persons per square mile (2010); Race: 99.8% White, 0.0% Black, 0.0% Asian, 0.0% American Indian/Alaska Native, 0.2% Native Hawaiian/Other Pacific Islander, 0.0% Other, 0.0% Hispanic of any race (2010); Average household size: 2.29 (2010); Median age: 47.5 (2010); Males per 100 females: 86.6 (2010); Marriage status: 27.6% never married, 44.0% now married, 28.4% widowed, 0.0% divorced (2006-2010 5-year est.); Foreign born: 0.0% (2006-2010 5-year est.); Ancestry (includes multiple ancestries): 39.2% Pennsylvania German, 28.5% Italian, 18.8% Irish, 14.2% Slovak, 8.1% Croatian (2006-2010 5-year est.).

Economy: Employment by occupation: 0.0% management, 20.8% professional, 0.0% services, 23.8% sales, 0.0% farming, 20.8% construction, 0.0% production (2006-2010 5-year est.).

Income: Per capita income: $27,992 (2006-2010 5-year est.); Median household income: $22,589 (2006-2010 5-year est.); Average household income: $57,266 (2006-2010 5-year est.); Percent of households with income of $100,000 or more: 18.5% (2006-2010 5-year est.); Poverty rate: 16.5% (2006-2010 5-year est.).

Education: Percent of population age 25 and over with: High school diploma (including GED) or higher: 100.0% (2006-2010 5-year est.); Bachelor's degree or higher: 10.8% (2006-2010 5-year est.); Master's degree or higher: 0.0% (2006-2010 5-year est.).

School District(s)

Forest Hills SD (PK-12)

    2010-11 Enrollment: 2,006 . . . . (814) 487-7613

Housing: Homeownership rate: 83.0% (2010); Median home value: $93,400 (2006-2010 5-year est.); Median contract rent: n/a per month (2006-2010 5-year est.); Median year structure built: 1980 (2006-2010 5-year est.).

Transportation: Commute to work: 100.0% car, 0.0% public transportation, 0.0% walk, 0.0% work from home (2006-2010 5-year est.); Travel time to work: 9.2% less than 15 minutes, 58.5% 15 to 30 minutes, 11.5% 30 to 45 minutes, 20.8% 45 to 60 minutes, 0.0% 60 minutes or more (2006-2010 5-year est.)

SOUTH FORK (borough). Covers a land area of 0.472 square miles and a water area of 0.029 square miles. Located at 40.36° N. Lat; 78.79° W. Long. Elevation is 1,489 feet.

History: Break in South Fork Dam, 1 mile to South (Johnstown Flood National Memorial), 1889, caused Johnstown Flood, killing 2,200 people. Part of Allegheny Portage National Historic Site to West.

Population: 1,173 (1990); 1,138 (2000); 928 (2010); Density: 1,966.5 persons per square mile (2010); Race: 98.2% White, 0.5% Black, 0.0% Asian, 0.0% American Indian/Alaska Native, 0.0% Native Hawaiian/Other Pacific Islander, 1.3% Other, 0.2% Hispanic of any race (2010); Average household size: 2.23 (2010); Median age: 40.0 (2010); Males per 100 females: 95.8 (2010); Marriage status: 27.3% never married, 54.9% now married, 7.4% widowed, 10.3% divorced (2006-2010 5-year est.); Foreign born: 0.0% (2006-2010 5-year est.); Ancestry (includes multiple ancestries): 30.9% German, 15.4% English, 13.7% Irish, 12.6% Polish, 7.4% Italian (2006-2010 5-year est.).

Economy: Single-family building permits issued: 0 (2011); Multi-family building permits issued: 0 (2011); Employment by occupation: 2.3% management, 5.1% professional, 11.8% services, 22.9% sales, 2.5% farming, 12.5% construction, 8.1% production (2006-2010 5-year est.).

Income: Per capita income: $18,624 (2006-2010 5-year est.); Median household income: $40,000 (2006-2010 5-year est.); Average household income: $45,815 (2006-2010 5-year est.); Percent of households with income of $100,000 or more: 4.4% (2006-2010 5-year est.); Poverty rate: 8.8% (2006-2010 5-year est.).

Education: Percent of population age 25 and over with: High school diploma (including GED) or higher: 87.4% (2006-2010 5-year est.); Bachelor's degree or higher: 11.0% (2006-2010 5-year est.); Master's degree or higher: 3.3% (2006-2010 5-year est.).

Housing: Homeownership rate: 75.1% (2010); Median home value: $50,000 (2006-2010 5-year est.); Median contract rent: $359 per month (2006-2010 5-year est.); Median year structure built: before 1940 (2006-2010 5-year est.).

Safety: Violent crime rate: 10.7 per 10,000 population; Property crime rate: 32.2 per 10,000 population (2011).

Transportation: Commute to work: 87.4% car, 0.0% public transportation, 8.1% walk, 1.4% work from home (2006-2010 5-year est.); Travel time to work: 27.8% less than 15 minutes, 48.8% 15 to 30 minutes, 11.4% 30 to 45 minutes, 5.1% 45 to 60 minutes, 7.0% 60 minutes or more (2006-2010 5-year est.)

Additional Information Contacts

Greater Johnstown Cambria County Chamber of Commerce . . . . (814) 536-5107

    http://www.johnstownchamber.com

SOUTHMONT (borough). Covers a land area of 1.050 square miles and a water area of 0 square miles. Located at 40.31° N. Lat; 78.93° W. Long. Elevation is 1,591 feet.

Population: 2,415 (1990); 2,262 (2000); 2,284 (2010); Density: 2,175.9 persons per square mile (2010); Race: 95.8% White, 0.7% Black, 1.3% Asian, 0.2% American Indian/Alaska Native, 0.0% Native Hawaiian/Other Pacific Islander, 2.0% Other, 2.2% Hispanic of any race (2010); Average household size: 2.28 (2010); Median age: 46.1 (2010); Males per 100 females: 90.8 (2010); Marriage status: 20.3% never married, 63.8% now married, 7.4% widowed, 8.6% divorced (2006-2010 5-year est.); Foreign born: 3.2% (2006-2010 5-year est.); Ancestry (includes multiple ancestries): 40.3% German, 20.7% Irish, 15.2% Italian, 9.5% English, 7.1% Slovak (2006-2010 5-year est.).

Economy: Single-family building permits issued: 0 (2011); Multi-family building permits issued: 0 (2011); Employment by occupation: 15.7% management, 5.0% professional, 13.4% services, 14.7% sales, 2.1% farming, 5.2% construction, 3.8% production (2006-2010 5-year est.).

Income: Per capita income: $27,225 (2006-2010 5-year est.); Median household income: $49,841 (2006-2010 5-year est.); Average household income: $64,032 (2006-2010 5-year est.); Percent of households with income of $100,000 or more: 14.4% (2006-2010 5-year est.); Poverty rate: 9.1% (2006-2010 5-year est.).

Education: Percent of population age 25 and over with: High school diploma (including GED) or higher: 97.7% (2006-2010 5-year est.); Bachelor's degree or higher: 31.6% (2006-2010 5-year est.); Master's degree or higher: 9.9% (2006-2010 5-year est.).

Housing: Homeownership rate: 76.7% (2010); Median home value: $100,200 (2006-2010 5-year est.); Median contract rent: $473 per month (2006-2010 5-year est.); Median year structure built: 1947 (2006-2010 5-year est.).

Transportation: Commute to work: 95.6% car, 0.0% public transportation, 2.1% walk, 2.3% work from home (2006-2010 5-year est.); Travel time to work: 42.4% less than 15 minutes, 37.8% 15 to 30 minutes, 13.5% 30 to 45 minutes, 5.5% 45 to 60 minutes, 0.8% 60 minutes or more (2006-2010 5-year est.)

Additional Information Contacts

Greater Johnstown Cambria County Chamber of Commerce . . . . (814) 536-5107

   http://www.johnstownchamber.com

SPANGLER (unincorporated postal area)

Zip Code: 15775

   Covers a land area of 3.459 square miles and a water area of 0.005 square miles. Located at 40.63° N. Lat; 78.78° W. Long. Population: 751 (2010); Density: 217.1 persons per square mile (2010); Race: 98.8% White, 0.0% Black, 0.0% Asian, 0.0% American Indian/Alaska Native, 0.0% Native Hawaiian/Other Pacific Islander, 1.2% Other, 0.9% Hispanic of any race (2010); Average household size: 2.35 (2010); Median age: 47.7 (2010); Males per 100 females: 99.2 (2010); Homeownership rate: 87.7% (2010)

SPRING HILL (CDP). Covers a land area of 1.044 square miles and a water area of 0 square miles. Located at 40.37° N. Lat; 78.67° W. Long. Elevation is 1,893 feet.

Population: 1,014 (1990); 970 (2000); 839 (2010); Density: 803.9 persons per square mile (2010); Race: 99.0% White, 0.0% Black, 0.0% Asian, 0.1% American Indian/Alaska Native, 0.0% Native Hawaiian/Other Pacific Islander, 0.9% Other, 0.5% Hispanic of any race (2010); Average household size: 2.32 (2010); Median age: 47.1 (2010); Males per 100 females: 95.1 (2010); Marriage status: 19.0% never married, 66.0% now married, 9.1% widowed, 6.0% divorced (2006-2010 5-year est.); Foreign born: 0.0% (2006-2010 5-year est.); Ancestry (includes multiple ancestries): 38.8% German, 26.9% Polish, 23.5% Irish, 6.9% Slovak, 6.2% Czech (2006-2010 5-year est.).

Economy: Employment by occupation: 0.0% management, 2.8% professional, 19.7% services, 13.5% sales, 3.0% farming, 7.9% construction, 2.6% production (2006-2010 5-year est.).

Income: Per capita income: $21,392 (2006-2010 5-year est.); Median household income: $44,722 (2006-2010 5-year est.); Average household income: $50,226 (2006-2010 5-year est.); Percent of households with income of $100,000 or more: 10.3% (2006-2010 5-year est.); Poverty rate: 2.0% (2006-2010 5-year est.).

Education: Percent of population age 25 and over with: High school diploma (including GED) or higher: 89.2% (2006-2010 5-year est.); Bachelor's degree or higher: 10.3% (2006-2010 5-year est.); Master's degree or higher: 0.0% (2006-2010 5-year est.).

Housing: Homeownership rate: 88.6% (2010); Median home value: $69,400 (2006-2010 5-year est.); Median contract rent: $386 per month (2006-2010 5-year est.); Median year structure built: 1950 (2006-2010 5-year est.).

Transportation: Commute to work: 93.7% car, 0.0% public transportation, 2.1% walk, 4.2% work from home (2006-2010 5-year est.); Travel time to work: 32.4% less than 15 minutes, 33.2% 15 to 30 minutes, 14.8% 30 to 45 minutes, 19.6% 45 to 60 minutes, 0.0% 60 minutes or more (2006-2010 5-year est.)

STONYCREEK (township). Covers a land area of 3.494 square miles and a water area of 0.088 square miles. Located at 40.31° N. Lat; 78.87° W. Long. Elevation is 1,506 feet.

Population: 3,544 (1990); 3,204 (2000); 2,844 (2010); Density: 813.9 persons per square mile (2010); Race: 96.2% White, 1.6% Black, 0.7% Asian, 0.0% American Indian/Alaska Native, 0.0% Native Hawaiian/Other

Pacific Islander, 1.5% Other, 1.0% Hispanic of any race (2010); Average household size: 2.02 (2010); Median age: 51.8 (2010); Males per 100 females: 94.3 (2010); Marriage status: 25.2% never married, 55.2% now married, 10.2% widowed, 9.4% divorced (2006-2010 5-year est.); Foreign born: 4.9% (2006-2010 5-year est.); Ancestry (includes multiple ancestries): 38.5% German, 19.3% Irish, 11.8% English, 10.4% Italian, 8.2% Polish (2006-2010 5-year est.).

Economy: Single-family building permits issued: 0 (2011); Multi-family building permits issued: 0 (2011); Employment by occupation: 10.2% management, 2.8% professional, 4.1% services, 20.2% sales, 5.8% farming, 8.2% construction, 3.9% production (2006-2010 5-year est.).

Income: Per capita income: $25,168 (2006-2010 5-year est.); Median household income: $41,860 (2006-2010 5-year est.); Average household income: $51,176 (2006-2010 5-year est.); Percent of households with income of $100,000 or more: 11.3% (2006-2010 5-year est.); Poverty rate: 11.1% (2006-2010 5-year est.).

Education: Percent of population age 25 and over with: High school diploma (including GED) or higher: 87.4% (2006-2010 5-year est.); Bachelor's degree or higher: 20.8% (2006-2010 5-year est.); Master's degree or higher: 7.1% (2006-2010 5-year est.).

Housing: Homeownership rate: 76.4% (2010); Median home value: $86,500 (2006-2010 5-year est.); Median contract rent: $405 per month (2006-2010 5-year est.); Median year structure built: 1955 (2006-2010 5-year est.).

Transportation: Commute to work: 95.1% car, 1.4% public transportation, 0.5% walk, 1.5% work from home (2006-2010 5-year est.); Travel time to work: 46.5% less than 15 minutes, 31.6% 15 to 30 minutes, 7.5% 30 to 45 minutes, 7.9% 45 to 60 minutes, 6.5% 60 minutes or more (2006-2010 5-year est.)

Additional Information Contacts

Greater Johnstown Cambria County Chamber of Commerce . . . . (814) 536-5107

   http://www.johnstownchamber.com

SUMMERHILL (borough). Covers a land area of 0.328 square miles and a water area of 0.005 square miles. Located at 40.38° N. Lat; 78.76° W. Long. Elevation is 1,601 feet.

Population: 614 (1990); 521 (2000); 490 (2010); Density: 1,494.3 persons per square mile (2010); Race: 99.8% White, 0.0% Black, 0.0% Asian, 0.0% American Indian/Alaska Native, 0.0% Native Hawaiian/Other Pacific Islander, 0.2% Other, 0.8% Hispanic of any race (2010); Average household size: 2.23 (2010); Median age: 43.2 (2010); Males per 100 females: 84.2 (2010); Marriage status: 27.6% never married, 57.2% now married, 8.5% widowed, 6.8% divorced (2006-2010 5-year est.); Foreign born: 0.0% (2006-2010 5-year est.); Ancestry (includes multiple ancestries): 55.0% German, 16.3% English, 16.3% Irish, 9.8% Slovak, 4.4% Italian (2006-2010 5-year est.).

Economy: Single-family building permits issued: 0 (2011); Multi-family building permits issued: 0 (2011); Employment by occupation: 8.8% management, 2.5% professional, 12.6% services, 12.2% sales, 1.3% farming, 5.0% construction, 7.6% production (2006-2010 5-year est.).

Income: Per capita income: $24,229 (2006-2010 5-year est.); Median household income: $40,625 (2006-2010 5-year est.); Average household income: $47,423 (2006-2010 5-year est.); Percent of households with income of $100,000 or more: 8.7% (2006-2010 5-year est.); Poverty rate: 4.7% (2006-2010 5-year est.).

Education: Percent of population age 25 and over with: High school diploma (including GED) or higher: 93.4% (2006-2010 5-year est.); Bachelor's degree or higher: 15.2% (2006-2010 5-year est.); Master's degree or higher: 2.3% (2006-2010 5-year est.).

Housing: Homeownership rate: 79.6% (2010); Median home value: $86,500 (2006-2010 5-year est.); Median contract rent: $359 per month (2006-2010 5-year est.); Median year structure built: before 1940 (2006-2010 5-year est.).

Transportation: Commute to work: 94.9% car, 0.0% public transportation, 3.8% walk, 0.0% work from home (2006-2010 5-year est.); Travel time to work: 29.5% less than 15 minutes, 48.3% 15 to 30 minutes, 17.1% 30 to 45 minutes, 5.1% 45 to 60 minutes, 0.0% 60 minutes or more (2006-2010 5-year est.)

SUMMERHILL (township). Covers a land area of 28.904 square miles and a water area of 0.677 square miles. Located at 40.35° N. Lat; 78.69° W. Long. Elevation is 1,601 feet.

Population: 2,886 (1990); 2,724 (2000); 2,467 (2010); Density: 85.4 persons per square mile (2010); Race: 99.6% White, 0.0% Black, 0.0%

Asian, 0.0% American Indian/Alaska Native, 0.0% Native Hawaiian/Other Pacific Islander, 0.4% Other, 0.4% Hispanic of any race (2010); Average household size: 2.62 (2010); Median age: 40.4 (2010); Males per 100 females: 105.6 (2010); Marriage status: 28.3% never married, 52.9% now married, 8.8% widowed, 10.0% divorced (2006-2010 5-year est.); Foreign born: 0.7% (2006-2010 5-year est.); Ancestry (includes multiple ancestries): 32.9% German, 17.3% Irish, 11.7% Slovak, 8.9% Polish, 8.4% English (2006-2010 5-year est.).

Economy: Single-family building permits issued: 1 (2011); Multi-family building permits issued: 0 (2011); Employment by occupation: 8.3% management, 2.3% professional, 14.1% services, 9.6% sales, 6.3% farming, 12.1% construction, 12.0% production (2006-2010 5-year est.).

Income: Per capita income: $18,429 (2006-2010 5-year est.); Median household income: $45,139 (2006-2010 5-year est.); Average household income: $52,337 (2006-2010 5-year est.); Percent of households with income of $100,000 or more: 4.7% (2006-2010 5-year est.); Poverty rate: 14.8% (2006-2010 5-year est.).

Education: Percent of population age 25 and over with: High school diploma (including GED) or higher: 87.7% (2006-2010 5-year est.); Bachelor's degree or higher: 11.7% (2006-2010 5-year est.); Master's degree or higher: 4.1% (2006-2010 5-year est.).

Housing: Homeownership rate: 88.9% (2010); Median home value: $90,300 (2006-2010 5-year est.); Median contract rent: $313 per month (2006-2010 5-year est.); Median year structure built: 1957 (2006-2010 5-year est.).

Safety: Violent crime rate: 8.1 per 10,000 population; Property crime rate: 157.6 per 10,000 population (2011).

Transportation: Commute to work: 95.7% car, 0.0% public transportation, 1.0% walk, 2.3% work from home (2006-2010 5-year est.); Travel time to work: 24.3% less than 15 minutes, 44.6% 15 to 30 minutes, 17.5% 30 to 45 minutes, 8.3% 45 to 60 minutes, 5.4% 60 minutes or more (2006-2010 5-year est.)

Additional Information Contacts
Greater Johnstown Cambria County Chamber of Commerce . . . . (814) 536-5107
　http://www.johnstownchamber.com

SUSQUEHANNA (township). Covers a land area of 28.042 square miles and a water area of 0.004 square miles. Located at 40.69° N. Lat; 78.79° W. Long.

Population: 2,299 (1990); 2,198 (2000); 2,007 (2010); Density: 71.6 persons per square mile (2010); Race: 99.4% White, 0.2% Black, 0.0% Asian, 0.0% American Indian/Alaska Native, 0.0% Native Hawaiian/Other Pacific Islander, 0.4% Other, 0.3% Hispanic of any race (2010); Average household size: 2.54 (2010); Median age: 43.5 (2010); Males per 100 females: 100.9 (2010); Marriage status: 19.3% never married, 67.2% now married, 7.3% widowed, 6.2% divorced (2006-2010 5-year est.); Foreign born: 0.3% (2006-2010 5-year est.); Ancestry (includes multiple ancestries): 31.1% German, 16.7% Irish, 14.8% Polish, 9.5% Slovak, 8.0% Italian (2006-2010 5-year est.).

Economy: Single-family building permits issued: 0 (2011); Multi-family building permits issued: 0 (2011); Employment by occupation: 4.1% management, 2.0% professional, 11.9% services, 17.4% sales, 1.4% farming, 15.9% construction, 7.8% production (2006-2010 5-year est.).

Income: Per capita income: $20,920 (2006-2010 5-year est.); Median household income: $49,333 (2006-2010 5-year est.); Average household income: $55,170 (2006-2010 5-year est.); Percent of households with income of $100,000 or more: 5.8% (2006-2010 5-year est.); Poverty rate: 11.5% (2006-2010 5-year est.).

Education: Percent of population age 25 and over with: High school diploma (including GED) or higher: 83.1% (2006-2010 5-year est.); Bachelor's degree or higher: 13.0% (2006-2010 5-year est.); Master's degree or higher: 5.6% (2006-2010 5-year est.).

Housing: Homeownership rate: 88.3% (2010); Median home value: $75,600 (2006-2010 5-year est.); Median contract rent: $244 per month (2006-2010 5-year est.); Median year structure built: 1953 (2006-2010 5-year est.).

Transportation: Commute to work: 91.9% car, 0.7% public transportation, 2.5% walk, 3.5% work from home (2006-2010 5-year est.); Travel time to work: 35.8% less than 15 minutes, 22.6% 15 to 30 minutes, 15.6% 30 to 45 minutes, 16.3% 45 to 60 minutes, 9.8% 60 minutes or more (2006-2010 5-year est.)

Additional Information Contacts
Indiana County Chamber of Commerce . . . . (724) 465-2511
　http://www.indianapa.com/chamber

TUNNELHILL (borough). Covers a land area of 0.493 square miles and a water area of 0 square miles. Located at 40.48° N. Lat; 78.54° W. Long. Elevation is 2,320 feet.

History: Also spelled Tunnel Hill.

Population: 382 (1990); 409 (2000); 363 (2010); Density: 735.8 persons per square mile (2010); Race: 98.9% White, 0.0% Black, 1.1% Asian, 0.0% American Indian/Alaska Native, 0.0% Native Hawaiian/Other Pacific Islander, 0.0% Other, 0.0% Hispanic of any race (2010); Average household size: 2.43 (2010); Median age: 45.5 (2010); Males per 100 females: 105.1 (2010); Marriage status: 31.9% never married, 60.3% now married, 3.2% widowed, 4.7% divorced (2006-2010 5-year est.); Foreign born: 2.9% (2006-2010 5-year est.); Ancestry (includes multiple ancestries): 42.2% Irish, 34.6% German, 25.6% Polish, 6.3% English, 4.7% Italian (2006-2010 5-year est.).

Economy: Single-family building permits issued: 0 (2011); Multi-family building permits issued: 0 (2011); Employment by occupation: 3.6% management, 0.0% professional, 13.7% services, 18.5% sales, 4.8% farming, 11.3% construction, 6.0% production (2006-2010 5-year est.).

Income: Per capita income: $20,359 (2006-2010 5-year est.); Median household income: $42,500 (2006-2010 5-year est.); Average household income: $51,925 (2006-2010 5-year est.); Percent of households with income of $100,000 or more: 10.3% (2006-2010 5-year est.); Poverty rate: 12.9% (2006-2010 5-year est.).

Education: Percent of population age 25 and over with: High school diploma (including GED) or higher: 84.3% (2006-2010 5-year est.); Bachelor's degree or higher: 7.1% (2006-2010 5-year est.); Master's degree or higher: 2.6% (2006-2010 5-year est.).

Housing: Homeownership rate: 91.2% (2010); Median home value: $81,100 (2006-2010 5-year est.); Median contract rent: $338 per month (2006-2010 5-year est.); Median year structure built: 1945 (2006-2010 5-year est.).

Transportation: Commute to work: 95.7% car, 0.0% public transportation, 1.2% walk, 1.2% work from home (2006-2010 5-year est.); Travel time to work: 34.6% less than 15 minutes, 43.8% 15 to 30 minutes, 11.1% 30 to 45 minutes, 5.6% 45 to 60 minutes, 4.9% 60 minutes or more (2006-2010 5-year est.)

TWIN ROCKS (unincorporated postal area)
Zip Code: 15960
　Covers a land area of 4.727 square miles and a water area of 0.047 square miles. Located at 40.49° N. Lat; 78.88° W. Long. Elevation is 1,654 feet. Population: 425 (2010); Density: 89.9 persons per square mile (2010); Race: 99.3% White, 0.0% Black, 0.5% Asian, 0.0% American Indian/Alaska Native, 0.0% Native Hawaiian/Other Pacific Islander, 0.2% Other, 0.9% Hispanic of any race (2010); Average household size: 2.43 (2010); Median age: 42.1 (2010); Males per 100 females: 85.6 (2010); Homeownership rate: 80.0% (2010)

UNIVERSITY OF PITTSBURGH JOHNSTOWN (CDP). Covers a land area of 0.584 square miles and a water area of 0 square miles. Located at 40.26° N. Lat; 78.83° W. Long.

Population: n/a (1990); n/a (2000); 1,572 (2010); Density: 2,691.3 persons per square mile (2010); Race: 93.4% White, 3.0% Black, 1.7% Asian, 0.2% American Indian/Alaska Native, 0.1% Native Hawaiian/Other Pacific Islander, 1.6% Other, 1.7% Hispanic of any race (2010); Average household size: 2.00 (2010); Median age: 20.3 (2010); Males per 100 females: 127.2 (2010); Marriage status: 100.0% never married, 0.0% now married, 0.0% widowed, 0.0% divorced (2006-2010 5-year est.); Foreign born: 1.0% (2006-2010 5-year est.); Ancestry (includes multiple ancestries): 46.0% German, 26.3% Irish, 22.5% Italian, 11.8% Polish, 5.3% English (2006-2010 5-year est.).

Economy: Employment by occupation: 4.7% management, 0.0% professional, 12.9% services, 23.4% sales, 0.0% farming, 3.8% construction, 8.5% production (2006-2010 5-year est.).

Income: Per capita income: $3,010 (2006-2010 5-year est.); Median household income: n/a (2006-2010 5-year est.); Average household income: n/a (2006-2010 5-year est.); Percent of households with income of $100,000 or more: n/a (2006-2010 5-year est.); Poverty rate: n/a (2006-2010 5-year est.).

Education: Percent of population age 25 and over with: High school diploma (including GED) or higher: n/a (2006-2010 5-year est.); Bachelor's degree or higher: n/a (2006-2010 5-year est.); Master's degree or higher: n/a (2006-2010 5-year est.).

Housing: Homeownership rate: 100.0% (2010); Median home value: n/a (2006-2010 5-year est.); Median contract rent: n/a per month (2006-2010 5-year est.); Median year structure built: n/a (2006-2010 5-year est.).
Transportation: Commute to work: 71.1% car, 4.0% public transportation, 15.2% walk, 9.7% work from home (2006-2010 5-year est.); Travel time to work: 63.6% less than 15 minutes, 27.9% 15 to 30 minutes, 4.0% 30 to 45 minutes, 0.0% 45 to 60 minutes, 4.4% 60 minutes or more (2006-2010 5-year est.)

UPPER YODER (township). Covers a land area of 12.197 square miles and a water area of 0.033 square miles. Located at 40.30° N. Lat; 78.99° W. Long.
Population: 5,685 (1990); 5,862 (2000); 5,449 (2010); Density: 446.7 persons per square mile (2010); Race: 96.7% White, 0.9% Black, 1.3% Asian, 0.1% American Indian/Alaska Native, 0.1% Native Hawaiian/Other Pacific Islander, 0.9% Other, 0.8% Hispanic of any race (2010); Average household size: 2.22 (2010); Median age: 49.7 (2010); Males per 100 females: 90.1 (2010); Marriage status: 26.6% never married, 56.2% now married, 10.1% widowed, 7.0% divorced (2006-2010 5-year est.); Foreign born: 1.4% (2006-2010 5-year est.); Ancestry (includes multiple ancestries): 41.1% German, 14.7% Slovak, 11.9% Irish, 10.3% Italian, 10.1% Polish (2006-2010 5-year est.).
Economy: Single-family building permits issued: 3 (2011); Multi-family building permits issued: 0 (2011); Employment by occupation: 12.8% management, 6.0% professional, 8.5% services, 12.9% sales, 2.8% farming, 10.2% construction, 6.2% production (2006-2010 5-year est.).
Income: Per capita income: $25,952 (2006-2010 5-year est.); Median household income: $52,582 (2006-2010 5-year est.); Average household income: $61,625 (2006-2010 5-year est.); Percent of households with income of $100,000 or more: 14.3% (2006-2010 5-year est.); Poverty rate: 8.2% (2006-2010 5-year est.).
Education: Percent of population age 25 and over with: High school diploma (including GED) or higher: 93.1% (2006-2010 5-year est.); Bachelor's degree or higher: 27.5% (2006-2010 5-year est.); Master's degree or higher: 10.2% (2006-2010 5-year est.).
Housing: Homeownership rate: 77.7% (2010); Median home value: $119,500 (2006-2010 5-year est.); Median contract rent: $486 per month (2006-2010 5-year est.); Median year structure built: 1954 (2006-2010 5-year est.).
Safety: Violent crime rate: 23.8 per 10,000 population; Property crime rate: 23.8 per 10,000 population (2011).
Transportation: Commute to work: 91.2% car, 0.0% public transportation, 2.1% walk, 3.5% work from home (2006-2010 5-year est.); Travel time to work: 40.0% less than 15 minutes, 44.7% 15 to 30 minutes, 6.2% 30 to 45 minutes, 6.3% 45 to 60 minutes, 2.9% 60 minutes or more (2006-2010 5-year est.)
Additional Information Contacts
Greater Johnstown Cambria County Chamber of Commerce . . . . (814) 536-5107
  http://www.johnstownchamber.com
Upper Yoder Township . . . . (814) 255-5243
  http://www.co.cambria.pa.us/upperyoder/site/default.asp

VINCO (CDP). Covers a land area of 3.910 square miles and a water area of 0 square miles. Located at 40.41° N. Lat; 78.84° W. Long. Elevation is 1,732 feet.
Population: 1,749 (1990); 1,429 (2000); 1,305 (2010); Density: 333.8 persons per square mile (2010); Race: 98.6% White, 0.4% Black, 0.2% Asian, 0.1% American Indian/Alaska Native, 0.1% Native Hawaiian/Other Pacific Islander, 0.6% Other, 0.3% Hispanic of any race (2010); Average household size: 2.27 (2010); Median age: 48.7 (2010); Males per 100 females: 94.2 (2010); Marriage status: 15.7% never married, 68.6% now married, 11.4% widowed, 4.3% divorced (2006-2010 5-year est.); Foreign born: 0.0% (2006-2010 5-year est.); Ancestry (includes multiple ancestries): 41.0% German, 18.4% Irish, 15.8% Polish, 9.8% English, 7.4% Italian (2006-2010 5-year est.).
Economy: Employment by occupation: 14.2% management, 5.8% professional, 4.6% services, 5.7% sales, 1.6% farming, 8.4% construction, 1.5% production (2006-2010 5-year est.).
Income: Per capita income: $24,954 (2006-2010 5-year est.); Median household income: $46,510 (2006-2010 5-year est.); Average household income: $57,646 (2006-2010 5-year est.); Percent of households with income of $100,000 or more: 19.4% (2006-2010 5-year est.); Poverty rate: 2.9% (2006-2010 5-year est.).

Education: Percent of population age 25 and over with: High school diploma (including GED) or higher: 93.0% (2006-2010 5-year est.); Bachelor's degree or higher: 20.3% (2006-2010 5-year est.); Master's degree or higher: 13.1% (2006-2010 5-year est.).
Housing: Homeownership rate: 89.3% (2010); Median home value: $123,600 (2006-2010 5-year est.); Median contract rent: n/a per month (2006-2010 5-year est.); Median year structure built: 1964 (2006-2010 5-year est.).
Transportation: Commute to work: 95.8% car, 0.0% public transportation, 4.2% walk, 0.0% work from home (2006-2010 5-year est.); Travel time to work: 11.5% less than 15 minutes, 56.7% 15 to 30 minutes, 19.8% 30 to 45 minutes, 5.5% 45 to 60 minutes, 6.4% 60 minutes or more (2006-2010 5-year est.)
Additional Information Contacts
Greater Johnstown Cambria County Chamber of Commerce . . . . (814) 536-5107
  http://www.johnstownchamber.com

VINTONDALE (borough). Covers a land area of 0.470 square miles and a water area of 0.017 square miles. Located at 40.48° N. Lat; 78.91° W. Long. Elevation is 1,407 feet.
Population: 582 (1990); 528 (2000); 414 (2010); Density: 881.2 persons per square mile (2010); Race: 98.8% White, 0.0% Black, 0.5% Asian, 0.0% American Indian/Alaska Native, 0.0% Native Hawaiian/Other Pacific Islander, 0.7% Other, 0.0% Hispanic of any race (2010); Average household size: 2.30 (2010); Median age: 46.0 (2010); Males per 100 females: 99.0 (2010); Marriage status: 33.0% never married, 53.5% now married, 9.5% widowed, 3.9% divorced (2006-2010 5-year est.); Foreign born: 0.4% (2006-2010 5-year est.); Ancestry (includes multiple ancestries): 47.8% German, 24.0% Irish, 13.5% English, 9.9% Swiss, 9.9% Welsh (2006-2010 5-year est.).
Economy: Single-family building permits issued: 0 (2011); Multi-family building permits issued: 0 (2011); Employment by occupation: 0.0% management, 1.9% professional, 21.7% services, 10.8% sales, 8.3% farming, 22.3% construction, 2.5% production (2006-2010 5-year est.).
Income: Per capita income: $14,754 (2006-2010 5-year est.); Median household income: $31,458 (2006-2010 5-year est.); Average household income: $40,004 (2006-2010 5-year est.); Percent of households with income of $100,000 or more: 4.8% (2006-2010 5-year est.); Poverty rate: 24.0% (2006-2010 5-year est.).
Education: Percent of population age 25 and over with: High school diploma (including GED) or higher: 81.1% (2006-2010 5-year est.); Bachelor's degree or higher: 0.9% (2006-2010 5-year est.); Master's degree or higher: 0.0% (2006-2010 5-year est.).
Housing: Homeownership rate: 83.3% (2010); Median home value: $40,400 (2006-2010 5-year est.); Median contract rent: $269 per month (2006-2010 5-year est.); Median year structure built: before 1940 (2006-2010 5-year est.).
Safety: Violent crime rate: 0.0 per 10,000 population; Property crime rate: 0.0 per 10,000 population (2011).
Transportation: Commute to work: 86.0% car, 0.0% public transportation, 8.0% walk, 0.0% work from home (2006-2010 5-year est.); Travel time to work: 14.7% less than 15 minutes, 56.7% 15 to 30 minutes, 24.0% 30 to 45 minutes, 2.0% 45 to 60 minutes, 2.7% 60 minutes or more (2006-2010 5-year est.)

WASHINGTON (township). Covers a land area of 12.560 square miles and a water area of 0.019 square miles. Located at 40.41° N. Lat; 78.61° W. Long.
Population: 929 (1990); 921 (2000); 875 (2010); Density: 69.7 persons per square mile (2010); Race: 99.2% White, 0.3% Black, 0.1% Asian, 0.0% American Indian/Alaska Native, 0.0% Native Hawaiian/Other Pacific Islander, 0.4% Other, 0.7% Hispanic of any race (2010); Average household size: 2.54 (2010); Median age: 45.8 (2010); Males per 100 females: 106.4 (2010); Marriage status: 27.9% never married, 59.0% now married, 6.2% widowed, 6.9% divorced (2006-2010 5-year est.); Foreign born: 0.0% (2006-2010 5-year est.); Ancestry (includes multiple ancestries): 42.5% German, 31.9% Polish, 25.2% Irish, 8.5% Italian, 6.8% English (2006-2010 5-year est.).
Economy: Single-family building permits issued: 0 (2011); Multi-family building permits issued: 0 (2011); Employment by occupation: 2.6% management, 1.7% professional, 8.8% services, 24.3% sales, 3.9% farming, 11.2% construction, 6.5% production (2006-2010 5-year est.).
Income: Per capita income: $22,485 (2006-2010 5-year est.); Median household income: $56,000 (2006-2010 5-year est.); Average household

income: $60,223 (2006-2010 5-year est.); Percent of households with income of $100,000 or more: 10.6% (2006-2010 5-year est.); Poverty rate: 2.1% (2006-2010 5-year est.).

Education: Percent of population age 25 and over with: High school diploma (including GED) or higher: 92.7% (2006-2010 5-year est.); Bachelor's degree or higher: 15.1% (2006-2010 5-year est.); Master's degree or higher: 3.4% (2006-2010 5-year est.).

Housing: Homeownership rate: 93.0% (2010); Median home value: $90,200 (2006-2010 5-year est.); Median contract rent: $375 per month (2006-2010 5-year est.); Median year structure built: 1959 (2006-2010 5-year est.).

Transportation: Commute to work: 96.7% car, 0.0% public transportation, 0.7% walk, 0.4% work from home (2006-2010 5-year est.); Travel time to work: 27.1% less than 15 minutes, 47.1% 15 to 30 minutes, 13.6% 30 to 45 minutes, 6.2% 45 to 60 minutes, 6.0% 60 minutes or more (2006-2010 5-year est.)

WEST CARROLL (township). Covers a land area of 10.711 square miles and a water area of 0.006 square miles. Located at 40.61° N. Lat; 78.74° W. Long.

Population: 1,524 (1990); 1,445 (2000); 1,296 (2010); Density: 121.0 persons per square mile (2010); Race: 99.6% White, 0.3% Black, 0.0% Asian, 0.0% American Indian/Alaska Native, 0.0% Native Hawaiian/Other Pacific Islander, 0.1% Other, 0.2% Hispanic of any race (2010); Average household size: 2.48 (2010); Median age: 46.3 (2010); Males per 100 females: 100.6 (2010); Marriage status: 29.7% never married, 52.7% now married, 8.7% widowed, 8.9% divorced (2006-2010 5-year est.); Foreign born: 0.9% (2006-2010 5-year est.); Ancestry (includes multiple ancestries): 32.0% Polish, 31.0% German, 16.6% Italian, 16.6% Irish, 9.3% English (2006-2010 5-year est.).

Economy: Single-family building permits issued: 0 (2011); Multi-family building permits issued: 0 (2011); Employment by occupation: 9.5% management, 4.5% professional, 13.6% services, 14.7% sales, 7.2% farming, 13.6% construction, 7.2% production (2006-2010 5-year est.).

Income: Per capita income: $18,105 (2006-2010 5-year est.); Median household income: $35,917 (2006-2010 5-year est.); Average household income: $49,368 (2006-2010 5-year est.); Percent of households with income of $100,000 or more: 8.0% (2006-2010 5-year est.); Poverty rate: 18.0% (2006-2010 5-year est.).

Education: Percent of population age 25 and over with: High school diploma (including GED) or higher: 82.1% (2006-2010 5-year est.); Bachelor's degree or higher: 14.1% (2006-2010 5-year est.); Master's degree or higher: 2.9% (2006-2010 5-year est.).

Housing: Homeownership rate: 88.8% (2010); Median home value: $57,500 (2006-2010 5-year est.); Median contract rent: $348 per month (2006-2010 5-year est.); Median year structure built: before 1940 (2006-2010 5-year est.).

Safety: Violent crime rate: 7.7 per 10,000 population; Property crime rate: 38.5 per 10,000 population (2011).

Transportation: Commute to work: 90.5% car, 0.0% public transportation, 0.0% walk, 6.7% work from home (2006-2010 5-year est.); Travel time to work: 19.1% less than 15 minutes, 30.8% 15 to 30 minutes, 30.4% 30 to 45 minutes, 11.9% 45 to 60 minutes, 7.8% 60 minutes or more (2006-2010 5-year est.)

Additional Information Contacts
Blair County Chamber of Commerce . . . . (814) 943-8151
   http://www.blairchamber.com

WEST TAYLOR (township). Covers a land area of 6.021 square miles and a water area of 0.106 square miles. Located at 40.38° N. Lat; 78.93° W. Long.

Population: 995 (1990); 862 (2000); 795 (2010); Density: 132.0 persons per square mile (2010); Race: 97.7% White, 1.6% Black, 0.0% Asian, 0.1% American Indian/Alaska Native, 0.0% Native Hawaiian/Other Pacific Islander, 0.6% Other, 1.5% Hispanic of any race (2010); Average household size: 2.21 (2010); Median age: 46.9 (2010); Males per 100 females: 114.3 (2010); Marriage status: 24.5% never married, 63.2% now married, 7.0% widowed, 5.3% divorced (2006-2010 5-year est.); Foreign born: 0.0% (2006-2010 5-year est.); Ancestry (includes multiple ancestries): 30.7% German, 13.5% Irish, 9.3% Polish, 9.0% Slovak, 8.5% English (2006-2010 5-year est.).

Economy: Single-family building permits issued: 0 (2011); Multi-family building permits issued: 0 (2011); Employment by occupation: 8.6% management, 2.4% professional, 13.6% services, 18.2% sales, 2.4% farming, 13.4% construction, 3.7% production (2006-2010 5-year est.).

Income: Per capita income: $22,135 (2006-2010 5-year est.); Median household income: $38,611 (2006-2010 5-year est.); Average household income: $47,853 (2006-2010 5-year est.); Percent of households with income of $100,000 or more: 6.7% (2006-2010 5-year est.); Poverty rate: 5.3% (2006-2010 5-year est.).

Education: Percent of population age 25 and over with: High school diploma (including GED) or higher: 84.0% (2006-2010 5-year est.); Bachelor's degree or higher: 7.9% (2006-2010 5-year est.); Master's degree or higher: 3.3% (2006-2010 5-year est.).

Housing: Homeownership rate: 87.5% (2010); Median home value: $62,000 (2006-2010 5-year est.); Median contract rent: $258 per month (2006-2010 5-year est.); Median year structure built: 1946 (2006-2010 5-year est.).

Transportation: Commute to work: 97.7% car, 0.6% public transportation, 0.6% walk, 1.1% work from home (2006-2010 5-year est.); Travel time to work: 32.8% less than 15 minutes, 48.0% 15 to 30 minutes, 12.6% 30 to 45 minutes, 4.3% 45 to 60 minutes, 2.3% 60 minutes or more (2006-2010 5-year est.)

WESTMONT (borough). Covers a land area of 2.348 square miles and a water area of 0 square miles. Located at 40.32° N. Lat; 78.95° W. Long. Elevation is 1,755 feet.

Population: 5,442 (1990); 5,523 (2000); 5,181 (2010); Density: 2,206.9 persons per square mile (2010); Race: 95.9% White, 1.0% Black, 1.5% Asian, 0.1% American Indian/Alaska Native, 0.0% Native Hawaiian/Other Pacific Islander, 1.5% Other, 1.4% Hispanic of any race (2010); Average household size: 2.37 (2010); Median age: 46.4 (2010); Males per 100 females: 90.5 (2010); Marriage status: 22.9% never married, 62.6% now married, 8.6% widowed, 6.0% divorced (2006-2010 5-year est.); Foreign born: 4.5% (2006-2010 5-year est.); Ancestry (includes multiple ancestries): 30.7% German, 21.4% Irish, 18.6% Italian, 11.8% English, 8.4% Slovak (2006-2010 5-year est.).

Economy: Single-family building permits issued: 0 (2011); Multi-family building permits issued: 0 (2011); Employment by occupation: 17.4% management, 6.7% professional, 13.1% services, 12.0% sales, 0.9% farming, 5.4% construction, 4.0% production (2006-2010 5-year est.).

Income: Per capita income: $34,254 (2006-2010 5-year est.); Median household income: $74,044 (2006-2010 5-year est.); Average household income: $80,685 (2006-2010 5-year est.); Percent of households with income of $100,000 or more: 30.1% (2006-2010 5-year est.); Poverty rate: 4.5% (2006-2010 5-year est.).

Education: Percent of population age 25 and over with: High school diploma (including GED) or higher: 98.5% (2006-2010 5-year est.); Bachelor's degree or higher: 50.1% (2006-2010 5-year est.); Master's degree or higher: 24.4% (2006-2010 5-year est.).

Housing: Homeownership rate: 84.9% (2010); Median home value: $154,300 (2006-2010 5-year est.); Median contract rent: $473 per month (2006-2010 5-year est.); Median year structure built: 1950 (2006-2010 5-year est.).

Transportation: Commute to work: 90.3% car, 0.0% public transportation, 3.3% walk, 3.9% work from home (2006-2010 5-year est.); Travel time to work: 49.3% less than 15 minutes, 37.3% 15 to 30 minutes, 7.5% 30 to 45 minutes, 3.9% 45 to 60 minutes, 2.0% 60 minutes or more (2006-2010 5-year est.)

Additional Information Contacts
Borough of Westmont . . . . (814) 255-4145
   http://www.southmontborough.net
Greater Johnstown Cambria County Chamber of Commerce . . . . (814) 536-5107
   http://www.johnstownchamber.com

WHITE (township). Covers a land area of 20.288 square miles and a water area of 2.455 square miles. Located at 40.67° N. Lat; 78.54° W. Long.

Population: 553 (1990); 813 (2000); 836 (2010); Density: 41.2 persons per square mile (2010); Race: 98.2% White, 0.2% Black, 0.2% Asian, 0.2% American Indian/Alaska Native, 0.0% Native Hawaiian/Other Pacific Islander, 1.2% Other, 0.4% Hispanic of any race (2010); Average household size: 2.27 (2010); Median age: 48.4 (2010); Males per 100 females: 96.2 (2010); Marriage status: 20.4% never married, 60.9% now married, 3.6% widowed, 15.1% divorced (2006-2010 5-year est.); Foreign born: 0.0% (2006-2010 5-year est.); Ancestry (includes multiple ancestries): 51.1% German, 19.6% Irish, 19.3% English, 9.4% Italian, 7.2% Scottish (2006-2010 5-year est.).

Economy: Single-family building permits issued: 2 (2011); Multi-family building permits issued: 0 (2011); Employment by occupation: 9.2% management, 4.9% professional, 13.9% services, 16.3% sales, 0.8% farming, 16.0% construction, 2.2% production (2006-2010 5-year est.).

Income: Per capita income: $18,775 (2006-2010 5-year est.); Median household income: $38,269 (2006-2010 5-year est.); Average household income: $44,679 (2006-2010 5-year est.); Percent of households with income of $100,000 or more: 9.9% (2006-2010 5-year est.); Poverty rate: 18.7% (2006-2010 5-year est.).

Education: Percent of population age 25 and over with: High school diploma (including GED) or higher: 89.7% (2006-2010 5-year est.); Bachelor's degree or higher: 11.5% (2006-2010 5-year est.); Master's degree or higher: 3.1% (2006-2010 5-year est.).

Housing: Homeownership rate: 85.4% (2010); Median home value: $81,400 (2006-2010 5-year est.); Median contract rent: $454 per month (2006-2010 5-year est.); Median year structure built: 1977 (2006-2010 5-year est.).

Transportation: Commute to work: 96.0% car, 0.0% public transportation, 0.8% walk, 3.1% work from home (2006-2010 5-year est.); Travel time to work: 18.4% less than 15 minutes, 21.9% 15 to 30 minutes, 37.4% 30 to 45 minutes, 11.4% 45 to 60 minutes, 10.8% 60 minutes or more (2006-2010 5-year est.)

WILMORE (borough). Covers a land area of 0.332 square miles and a water area of 0 square miles. Located at 40.39° N. Lat; 78.72° W. Long. Elevation is 1,565 feet.

Population: 277 (1990); 252 (2000); 225 (2010); Density: 678.4 persons per square mile (2010); Race: 100.0% White, 0.0% Black, 0.0% Asian, 0.0% American Indian/Alaska Native, 0.0% Native Hawaiian/Other Pacific Islander, 0.0% Other, 0.0% Hispanic of any race (2010); Average household size: 2.68 (2010); Median age: 40.6 (2010); Males per 100 females: 95.7 (2010); Marriage status: 25.5% never married, 60.0% now married, 11.8% widowed, 2.7% divorced (2006-2010 5-year est.); Foreign born: 0.0% (2006-2010 5-year est.); Ancestry (includes multiple ancestries): 21.2% German, 14.4% Polish, 12.1% Italian, 7.6% Eastern European, 7.6% Russian (2006-2010 5-year est.).

Economy: Single-family building permits issued: 0 (2011); Multi-family building permits issued: 0 (2011); Employment by occupation: 16.9% management, 0.0% professional, 9.9% services, 9.9% sales, 0.0% farming, 2.8% construction, 8.5% production (2006-2010 5-year est.).

Income: Per capita income: $20,370 (2006-2010 5-year est.); Median household income: $33,906 (2006-2010 5-year est.); Average household income: $47,781 (2006-2010 5-year est.); Percent of households with income of $100,000 or more: 12.3% (2006-2010 5-year est.); Poverty rate: 6.1% (2006-2010 5-year est.).

Education: Percent of population age 25 and over with: High school diploma (including GED) or higher: 84.0% (2006-2010 5-year est.); Bachelor's degree or higher: 23.5% (2006-2010 5-year est.); Master's degree or higher: 2.5% (2006-2010 5-year est.).

Housing: Homeownership rate: 83.3% (2010); Median home value: $72,500 (2006-2010 5-year est.); Median contract rent: n/a per month (2006-2010 5-year est.); Median year structure built: 1978 (2006-2010 5-year est.).

Transportation: Commute to work: 97.1% car, 0.0% public transportation, 0.0% walk, 0.0% work from home (2006-2010 5-year est.); Travel time to work: 47.1% less than 15 minutes, 36.8% 15 to 30 minutes, 10.3% 30 to 45 minutes, 2.9% 45 to 60 minutes, 2.9% 60 minutes or more (2006-2010 5-year est.)

Cameron County

Located in north central Pennsylvania; mountainous area, drained by Sinnemahoning Creek. Covers a land area of 396.231 square miles, a water area of 2.187 square miles, and is located in the Eastern Time Zone at 41.44° N. Lat., 78.20° W. Long. The county was founded in 1860. County seat is Emporium.

Weather Station: Emporium   Elevation: 1,040 feet

	Jan	Feb	Mar	Apr	May	Jun	Jul	Aug	Sep	Oct	Nov	Dec
High	33	37	46	60	71	79	82	81	73	62	49	37
Low	16	16	24	34	43	53	58	57	49	38	30	21
Precip	2.6	2.1	3.2	3.6	4.0	4.7	4.3	4.2	4.0	3.3	3.7	2.7
Snow	11.9	8.5	9.0	0.8	tr	0.0	0.0	0.0	0.0	0.1	2.4	8.9

High and Low temperatures in degrees Fahrenheit; Precipitation and Snow in inches

Weather Station: Stevenson Dam   Elevation: 932 feet

	Jan	Feb	Mar	Apr	May	Jun	Jul	Aug	Sep	Oct	Nov	Dec
High	34	38	47	60	71	79	82	82	74	62	50	38
Low	16	17	24	34	43	54	58	58	51	39	31	22
Precip	2.4	2.3	3.3	3.5	3.7	4.2	4.2	3.9	4.0	3.2	3.7	2.9
Snow	10.3	7.3	6.6	0.9	tr	0.0	0.0	0.0	0.0	tr	1.6	5.6

High and Low temperatures in degrees Fahrenheit; Precipitation and Snow in inches

Population: 5,913 (1990); 5,974 (2000); 5,085 (2010); Race: 98.3% White, 0.3% Black, 0.3% Asian, 0.3% American Indian/Alaska Native, 0.0% Native Hawaiian/Other Pacific Islander, 0.8% Other, 0.4% Hispanic of any race (2010); Density: 12.8 persons per square mile (2010); Average household size: 2.20 (2010); Median age: 48.2 (2010); Males per 100 females: 96.6 (2010).

Religion: Six largest groups: 36.1% Catholicism, 10.0% Methodist/Pietist, 7.2% Baptist, 5.7% Holiness, 2.9% Non-Denominational, 2.3% Lutheran (2010)

Economy: Unemployment rate: 11.1% (August 2012); Total civilian labor force: 2,428 (August 2012); Leading industries: 55.0% manufacturing; 12.3% health care and social assistance; 12.1% retail trade (2010); Farms: 34 totaling 5,092 acres (2007); Companies that employ 500 or more persons: 0 (2010); Companies that employ 100 to 499 persons: 2 (2010); Companies that employ less than 100 persons: 119 (2010); Black-owned businesses: n/a (2007); Hispanic-owned businesses: n/a (2007); Asian-owned businesses: n/a (2007); Women-owned businesses: n/a (2007); Retail sales per capita: $7,723 (2010). Single-family building permits issued: 0 (2011); Multi-family building permits issued: 0 (2011).

Income: Per capita income: $21,375 (2006-2010 5-year est.); Median household income: $40,733 (2006-2010 5-year est.); Average household income: $48,765 (2006-2010 5-year est.); Percent of households with income of $100,000 or more: 7.7% (2006-2010 5-year est.); Poverty rate: 11.4% (2006-2010 5-year est.); Bankruptcy rate: 2.59% (2011).

Education: Percent of population age 25 and over with: High school diploma (including GED) or higher: 85.2% (2006-2010 5-year est.); Bachelor's degree or higher: 14.9% (2006-2010 5-year est.); Master's degree or higher: 3.9% (2006-2010 5-year est.).

Housing: Homeownership rate: 73.8% (2010); Median home value: $74,200 (2006-2010 5-year est.); Median contract rent: $362 per month (2006-2010 5-year est.); Median year structure built: 1958 (2006-2010 5-year est.)

Health: Birth rate: 77.8 per 10,000 population (2011); Death rate: 145.7 per 10,000 population (2011); Age-adjusted cancer mortality rate: Unreliable deaths per 100,000 population (2009); Number of physicians: 7.9 per 10,000 population (2010); Hospital beds: 0.0 per 10,000 population (2008); Hospital admissions: 0.0 per 10,000 population (2008).

Elections: 2012 Presidential election results: 34.3% Obama, 64.4% Romney

National and State Parks: Johnson Run State Forest Natural Area; Sinnemahoning State Park; Sizerville State Park; Wayside Memorial State Forest Picnic Area; Wykoff Run State Forest Natural Area

Additional Information Contacts

Cameron County Government . . . . (814) 486-2315
   http://www.cameroncountypa.com
Cameron County Chamber of Commerce . . . . (814) 486-4314
   http://www.cameroncountychamber.org

Cameron County Communities

DRIFTWOOD (borough). Covers a land area of 2.489 square miles and a water area of 0.068 square miles. Located at 41.34° N. Lat; 78.13° W. Long. Elevation is 850 feet.

Population: 116 (1990); 103 (2000); 67 (2010); Density: 26.9 persons per square mile (2010); Race: 94.0% White, 1.5% Black, 0.0% Asian, 0.0% American Indian/Alaska Native, 0.0% Native Hawaiian/Other Pacific Islander, 4.5% Other, 0.0% Hispanic of any race (2010); Average household size: 1.91 (2010); Median age: 51.3 (2010); Males per 100 females: 168.0 (2010); Marriage status: 24.7% never married, 53.4% now married, 15.1% widowed, 6.8% divorced (2006-2010 5-year est.); Foreign born: 0.0% (2006-2010 5-year est.); Ancestry (includes multiple ancestries): 47.6% German, 15.9% Italian, 13.4% Scotch-Irish, 9.8% Russian, 9.8% English (2006-2010 5-year est.).

Economy: Employment by occupation: 0.0% management, 8.3% professional, 5.6% services, 11.1% sales, 0.0% farming, 38.9% construction, 5.6% production (2006-2010 5-year est.).

Income: Per capita income: $22,060 (2006-2010 5-year est.); Median household income: $45,417 (2006-2010 5-year est.); Average household

income: $47,326 (2006-2010 5-year est.); Percent of households with income of $100,000 or more: 8.6% (2006-2010 5-year est.); Poverty rate: 9.8% (2006-2010 5-year est.).

Education: Percent of population age 25 and over with: High school diploma (including GED) or higher: 68.2% (2006-2010 5-year est.); Bachelor's degree or higher: 0.0% (2006-2010 5-year est.); Master's degree or higher: 0.0% (2006-2010 5-year est.).

Housing: Homeownership rate: 94.3% (2010); Median home value: $42,500 (2006-2010 5-year est.); Median contract rent: n/a per month (2006-2010 5-year est.); Median year structure built: 1975 (2006-2010 5-year est.).

Transportation: Commute to work: 91.2% car, 0.0% public transportation, 0.0% walk, 8.8% work from home (2006-2010 5-year est.); Travel time to work: 16.1% less than 15 minutes, 38.7% 15 to 30 minutes, 38.7% 30 to 45 minutes, 0.0% 45 to 60 minutes, 6.5% 60 minutes or more (2006-2010 5-year est.)

EMPORIUM (borough). County seat. Covers a land area of 0.710 square miles and a water area of 0.041 square miles. Located at 41.51° N. Lat; 78.23° W. Long. Elevation is 1,033 feet.

History: Emporium was settled in 1810. It grew with the lumber boom in the middle of the 19th century.

Population: 2,513 (1990); 2,526 (2000); 2,073 (2010); Density: 2,920.7 persons per square mile (2010); Race: 98.1% White, 0.5% Black, 0.4% Asian, 0.4% American Indian/Alaska Native, 0.0% Native Hawaiian/Other Pacific Islander, 0.6% Other, 0.6% Hispanic of any race (2010); Average household size: 2.09 (2010); Median age: 43.8 (2010); Males per 100 females: 88.6 (2010); Marriage status: 27.2% never married, 46.1% now married, 12.2% widowed, 14.5% divorced (2006-2010 5-year est.); Foreign born: 1.3% (2006-2010 5-year est.); Ancestry (includes multiple ancestries): 32.4% German, 15.8% Irish, 15.7% Italian, 12.4% English, 6.9% Swedish (2006-2010 5-year est.).

Economy: Single-family building permits issued: 0 (2011); Multi-family building permits issued: 0 (2011); Employment by occupation: 11.6% management, 3.3% professional, 10.2% services, 15.8% sales, 2.3% farming, 12.7% construction, 11.1% production (2006-2010 5-year est.).

Income: Per capita income: $18,713 (2006-2010 5-year est.); Median household income: $32,468 (2006-2010 5-year est.); Average household income: $41,975 (2006-2010 5-year est.); Percent of households with income of $100,000 or more: 5.0% (2006-2010 5-year est.); Poverty rate: 16.3% (2006-2010 5-year est.).

Education: Percent of population age 25 and over with: High school diploma (including GED) or higher: 85.1% (2006-2010 5-year est.); Bachelor's degree or higher: 13.2% (2006-2010 5-year est.); Master's degree or higher: 2.9% (2006-2010 5-year est.).

School District(s)

Cameron County SD (KG-12)

    2010-11 Enrollment: 731 . . . . (814) 486-4000

Housing: Homeownership rate: 54.3% (2010); Median home value: $63,700 (2006-2010 5-year est.); Median contract rent: $341 per month (2006-2010 5-year est.); Median year structure built: 1946 (2006-2010 5-year est.).

Safety: Violent crime rate: 0.0 per 10,000 population; Property crime rate: 72.1 per 10,000 population (2011).

Newspapers: Cameron County Echo (Community news; Circulation 4,000)

Transportation: Commute to work: 72.3% car, 0.0% public transportation, 22.0% walk, 3.9% work from home (2006-2010 5-year est.); Travel time to work: 72.5% less than 15 minutes, 7.2% 15 to 30 minutes, 10.7% 30 to 45 minutes, 7.3% 45 to 60 minutes, 2.2% 60 minutes or more (2006-2010 5-year est.)

Additional Information Contacts

Cameron County Chamber of Commerce . . . . (814) 486-4314
    http://www.cameroncountychamber.org

GIBSON (township). Covers a land area of 93.933 square miles and a water area of 0.634 square miles. Located at 41.31° N. Lat; 78.20° W. Long.

Population: 215 (1990); 222 (2000); 164 (2010); Density: 1.7 persons per square mile (2010); Race: 98.2% White, 0.0% Black, 0.0% Asian, 0.0% American Indian/Alaska Native, 0.0% Native Hawaiian/Other Pacific Islander, 1.8% Other, 0.0% Hispanic of any race (2010); Average household size: 1.89 (2010); Median age: 56.0 (2010); Males per 100 females: 100.0 (2010); Marriage status: 19.3% never married, 62.2% now married, 8.4% widowed, 10.1% divorced (2006-2010 5-year est.); Foreign

born: 0.0% (2006-2010 5-year est.); Ancestry (includes multiple ancestries): 25.4% German, 19.8% American, 15.1% Irish, 11.9% Dutch, 7.9% English (2006-2010 5-year est.).

Economy: Employment by occupation: 10.3% management, 3.4% professional, 6.9% services, 6.9% sales, 0.0% farming, 15.5% construction, 6.9% production (2006-2010 5-year est.).

Income: Per capita income: $29,579 (2006-2010 5-year est.); Median household income: $43,295 (2006-2010 5-year est.); Average household income: $64,154 (2006-2010 5-year est.); Percent of households with income of $100,000 or more: 11.5% (2006-2010 5-year est.); Poverty rate: 13.5% (2006-2010 5-year est.).

Education: Percent of population age 25 and over with: High school diploma (including GED) or higher: 86.6% (2006-2010 5-year est.); Bachelor's degree or higher: 18.8% (2006-2010 5-year est.); Master's degree or higher: 16.1% (2006-2010 5-year est.).

Housing: Homeownership rate: 86.2% (2010); Median home value: $67,500 (2006-2010 5-year est.); Median contract rent: n/a per month (2006-2010 5-year est.); Median year structure built: 1973 (2006-2010 5-year est.).

Transportation: Commute to work: 100.0% car, 0.0% public transportation, 0.0% walk, 0.0% work from home (2006-2010 5-year est.); Travel time to work: 21.8% less than 15 minutes, 29.1% 15 to 30 minutes, 21.8% 30 to 45 minutes, 7.3% 45 to 60 minutes, 20.0% 60 minutes or more (2006-2010 5-year est.)

GROVE (township). Covers a land area of 73.166 square miles and a water area of 0.761 square miles. Located at 41.40° N. Lat; 78.06° W. Long.

Population: 168 (1990); 129 (2000); 183 (2010); Density: 2.5 persons per square mile (2010); Race: 98.9% White, 0.0% Black, 0.0% Asian, 0.5% American Indian/Alaska Native, 0.0% Native Hawaiian/Other Pacific Islander, 0.6% Other, 0.0% Hispanic of any race (2010); Average household size: 1.93 (2010); Median age: 57.4 (2010); Males per 100 females: 108.0 (2010); Marriage status: 4.1% never married, 69.4% now married, 5.1% widowed, 21.4% divorced (2006-2010 5-year est.); Foreign born: 0.0% (2006-2010 5-year est.); Ancestry (includes multiple ancestries): 15.1% German, 9.4% English, 9.4% American, 7.5% Italian, 6.6% French (2006-2010 5-year est.).

Economy: Employment by occupation: 5.0% management, 0.0% professional, 50.0% services, 2.5% sales, 0.0% farming, 0.0% construction, 0.0% production (2006-2010 5-year est.).

Income: Per capita income: $24,619 (2006-2010 5-year est.); Median household income: $44,375 (2006-2010 5-year est.); Average household income: $44,996 (2006-2010 5-year est.); Percent of households with income of $100,000 or more: 4.1% (2006-2010 5-year est.); Poverty rate: 7.5% (2006-2010 5-year est.).

Education: Percent of population age 25 and over with: High school diploma (including GED) or higher: 85.7% (2006-2010 5-year est.); Bachelor's degree or higher: 2.0% (2006-2010 5-year est.); Master's degree or higher: 0.0% (2006-2010 5-year est.).

Housing: Homeownership rate: 89.5% (2010); Median home value: $90,000 (2006-2010 5-year est.); Median contract rent: n/a per month (2006-2010 5-year est.); Median year structure built: 1972 (2006-2010 5-year est.).

Transportation: Commute to work: 95.0% car, 0.0% public transportation, 5.0% walk, 0.0% work from home (2006-2010 5-year est.); Travel time to work: 65.0% less than 15 minutes, 17.5% 15 to 30 minutes, 12.5% 30 to 45 minutes, 0.0% 45 to 60 minutes, 5.0% 60 minutes or more (2006-2010 5-year est.)

LUMBER (township). Covers a land area of 54.941 square miles and a water area of 0.212 square miles. Located at 41.50° N. Lat; 78.15° W. Long.

Population: 195 (1990); 241 (2000); 195 (2010); Density: 3.5 persons per square mile (2010); Race: 97.9% White, 0.0% Black, 0.5% Asian, 0.0% American Indian/Alaska Native, 0.0% Native Hawaiian/Other Pacific Islander, 1.6% Other, 0.5% Hispanic of any race (2010); Average household size: 2.19 (2010); Median age: 54.9 (2010); Males per 100 females: 107.4 (2010); Marriage status: 10.8% never married, 67.0% now married, 11.4% widowed, 10.8% divorced (2006-2010 5-year est.); Foreign born: 0.0% (2006-2010 5-year est.); Ancestry (includes multiple ancestries): 27.2% German, 22.3% English, 15.5% Irish, 11.2% French, 10.7% Polish (2006-2010 5-year est.).

Economy: Employment by occupation: 8.3% management, 2.4% professional, 7.1% services, 8.3% sales, 0.0% farming, 16.7% construction, 14.3% production (2006-2010 5-year est.).

Income: Per capita income: $22,367 (2006-2010 5-year est.); Median household income: $44,375 (2006-2010 5-year est.); Average household income: $53,686 (2006-2010 5-year est.); Percent of households with income of $100,000 or more: 6.9% (2006-2010 5-year est.); Poverty rate: 3.9% (2006-2010 5-year est.).

Education: Percent of population age 25 and over with: High school diploma (including GED) or higher: 82.2% (2006-2010 5-year est.); Bachelor's degree or higher: 20.9% (2006-2010 5-year est.); Master's degree or higher: 0.0% (2006-2010 5-year est.).

Housing: Homeownership rate: 92.1% (2010); Median home value: $85,900 (2006-2010 5-year est.); Median contract rent: n/a per month (2006-2010 5-year est.); Median year structure built: 1980 (2006-2010 5-year est.).

Transportation: Commute to work: 97.5% car, 0.0% public transportation, 0.0% walk, 2.5% work from home (2006-2010 5-year est.); Travel time to work: 70.1% less than 15 minutes, 18.2% 15 to 30 minutes, 5.2% 30 to 45 minutes, 3.9% 45 to 60 minutes, 2.6% 60 minutes or more (2006-2010 5-year est.)

PORTAGE (township). Covers a land area of 14.368 square miles and a water area of 0.100 square miles. Located at 41.56° N. Lat; 78.19° W. Long.

Population: 211 (1990); 258 (2000); 171 (2010); Density: 11.9 persons per square mile (2010); Race: 99.4% White, 0.0% Black, 0.0% Asian, 0.6% American Indian/Alaska Native, 0.0% Native Hawaiian/Other Pacific Islander, 0.0% Other, 0.0% Hispanic of any race (2010); Average household size: 2.16 (2010); Median age: 45.4 (2010); Males per 100 females: 96.6 (2010); Marriage status: 26.8% never married, 56.3% now married, 11.6% widowed, 5.4% divorced (2006-2010 5-year est.); Foreign born: 0.0% (2006-2010 5-year est.); Ancestry (includes multiple ancestries): 40.0% German, 26.4% Irish, 17.1% Italian, 16.4% American, 10.7% Polish (2006-2010 5-year est.).

Economy: Employment by occupation: 13.6% management, 4.5% professional, 7.6% services, 13.6% sales, 0.0% farming, 9.1% construction, 7.6% production (2006-2010 5-year est.).

Income: Per capita income: $16,191 (2006-2010 5-year est.); Median household income: $43,125 (2006-2010 5-year est.); Average household income: $41,379 (2006-2010 5-year est.); Percent of households with income of $100,000 or more: 3.8% (2006-2010 5-year est.); Poverty rate: 27.9% (2006-2010 5-year est.).

Education: Percent of population age 25 and over with: High school diploma (including GED) or higher: 79.0% (2006-2010 5-year est.); Bachelor's degree or higher: 12.0% (2006-2010 5-year est.); Master's degree or higher: 4.0% (2006-2010 5-year est.).

Housing: Homeownership rate: 72.1% (2010); Median home value: $77,500 (2006-2010 5-year est.); Median contract rent: $363 per month (2006-2010 5-year est.); Median year structure built: 1960 (2006-2010 5-year est.).

Transportation: Commute to work: 89.4% car, 0.0% public transportation, 10.6% walk, 0.0% work from home (2006-2010 5-year est.); Travel time to work: 56.1% less than 15 minutes, 24.2% 15 to 30 minutes, 9.1% 30 to 45 minutes, 6.1% 45 to 60 minutes, 4.5% 60 minutes or more (2006-2010 5-year est.)

PROSPECT PARK (CDP). Covers a land area of 0.609 square miles and a water area of 0.006 square miles. Located at 41.52° N. Lat; 78.21° W. Long. Elevation is 1,030 feet.

Population: n/a (1990); n/a (2000); 327 (2010); Density: 537.0 persons per square mile (2010); Race: 99.7% White, 0.0% Black, 0.0% Asian, 0.3% American Indian/Alaska Native, 0.0% Native Hawaiian/Other Pacific Islander, 0.0% Other, 0.0% Hispanic of any race (2010); Average household size: 2.29 (2010); Median age: 47.1 (2010); Males per 100 females: 87.9 (2010); Marriage status: 15.4% never married, 51.4% now married, 14.5% widowed, 18.7% divorced (2006-2010 5-year est.); Foreign born: 0.0% (2006-2010 5-year est.); Ancestry (includes multiple ancestries): 28.6% German, 15.8% English, 12.8% Italian, 11.7% Irish, 7.7% American (2006-2010 5-year est.).

Economy: Employment by occupation: 7.0% management, 2.6% professional, 6.1% services, 0.0% sales, 2.6% farming, 24.3% construction, 14.8% production (2006-2010 5-year est.).

Income: Per capita income: $21,879 (2006-2010 5-year est.); Median household income: $41,563 (2006-2010 5-year est.); Average household

income: $47,666 (2006-2010 5-year est.); Percent of households with income of $100,000 or more: 2.4% (2006-2010 5-year est.); Poverty rate: 3.3% (2006-2010 5-year est.).

Education: Percent of population age 25 and over with: High school diploma (including GED) or higher: 79.1% (2006-2010 5-year est.); Bachelor's degree or higher: 13.3% (2006-2010 5-year est.); Master's degree or higher: 5.1% (2006-2010 5-year est.).

Housing: Homeownership rate: 83.3% (2010); Median home value: $73,400 (2006-2010 5-year est.); Median contract rent: $417 per month (2006-2010 5-year est.); Median year structure built: 1950 (2006-2010 5-year est.).

Transportation: Commute to work: 94.6% car, 0.0% public transportation, 0.0% walk, 0.0% work from home (2006-2010 5-year est.); Travel time to work: 48.6% less than 15 minutes, 8.1% 15 to 30 minutes, 21.6% 30 to 45 minutes, 18.9% 45 to 60 minutes, 2.7% 60 minutes or more (2006-2010 5-year est.)

SHIPPEN (township). Covers a land area of 156.624 square miles and a water area of 0.371 square miles. Located at 41.50° N. Lat; 78.32° W. Long.

Population: 2,495 (1990); 2,495 (2000); 2,232 (2010); Density: 14.3 persons per square mile (2010); Race: 98.6% White, 0.1% Black, 0.2% Asian, 0.1% American Indian/Alaska Native, 0.0% Native Hawaiian/Other Pacific Islander, 1.0% Other, 0.2% Hispanic of any race (2010); Average household size: 2.37 (2010); Median age: 49.3 (2010); Males per 100 females: 100.9 (2010); Marriage status: 20.8% never married, 62.4% now married, 8.7% widowed, 8.1% divorced (2006-2010 5-year est.); Foreign born: 0.7% (2006-2010 5-year est.); Ancestry (includes multiple ancestries): 38.2% German, 16.3% American, 12.9% Irish, 11.5% Italian, 11.3% English (2006-2010 5-year est.).

Economy: Employment by occupation: 9.1% management, 3.5% professional, 10.7% services, 14.5% sales, 2.1% farming, 11.0% construction, 11.3% production (2006-2010 5-year est.).

Income: Per capita income: $23,783 (2006-2010 5-year est.); Median household income: $44,891 (2006-2010 5-year est.); Average household income: $55,278 (2006-2010 5-year est.); Percent of households with income of $100,000 or more: 10.9% (2006-2010 5-year est.); Poverty rate: 6.1% (2006-2010 5-year est.).

Education: Percent of population age 25 and over with: High school diploma (including GED) or higher: 86.5% (2006-2010 5-year est.); Bachelor's degree or higher: 17.2% (2006-2010 5-year est.); Master's degree or higher: 4.7% (2006-2010 5-year est.).

Housing: Homeownership rate: 88.6% (2010); Median home value: $84,100 (2006-2010 5-year est.); Median contract rent: $421 per month (2006-2010 5-year est.); Median year structure built: 1955 (2006-2010 5-year est.).

Transportation: Commute to work: 93.2% car, 0.0% public transportation, 4.8% walk, 1.4% work from home (2006-2010 5-year est.); Travel time to work: 61.8% less than 15 minutes, 21.9% 15 to 30 minutes, 8.6% 30 to 45 minutes, 5.1% 45 to 60 minutes, 2.6% 60 minutes or more (2006-2010 5-year est.)

Additional Information Contacts
Cameron County Chamber of Commerce . . . . (814) 486-4314
http://www.cameroncountychamber.org

SINNAMAHONING (unincorporated postal area)
Zip Code: 15861
Covers a land area of 67.395 square miles and a water area of 0.615 square miles. Located at 41.30° N. Lat; 78.06° W. Long. Population: 174 (2010); Density: 2.6 persons per square mile (2010); Race: 98.3% White, 0.0% Black, 0.0% Asian, 0.6% American Indian/Alaska Native, 0.0% Native Hawaiian/Other Pacific Islander, 1.1% Other, 0.0% Hispanic of any race (2010); Average household size: 1.83 (2010); Median age: 57.3 (2010); Males per 100 females: 109.6 (2010); Homeownership rate: 89.4% (2010)

Carbon County

Located in eastern Pennsylvania; mountainous area, drained by the Lehigh River; bounded on the south by the Blue Mountains; the eastern part of the county is on the Pocono Plateau. Covers a land area of 381.460 square miles, a water area of 5.927 square miles, and is located in the Eastern Time Zone at 40.92° N. Lat., 75.71° W. Long. The county was founded in 1843. County seat is Jim Thorpe.

Carbon County is part of the Allentown-Bethlehem-Easton, PA-NJ Metropolitan Statistical Area. The entire metro area includes: Warren County, NJ; Carbon County, PA; Lehigh County, PA; Northampton County, PA

Population: 56,710 (1990); 58,802 (2000); 65,249 (2010); Race: 95.8% White, 1.5% Black, 0.5% Asian, 0.2% American Indian/Alaska Native, 0.0% Native Hawaiian/Other Pacific Islander, 2.0% Other, 3.3% Hispanic of any race (2010); Density: 171.1 persons per square mile (2010); Average household size: 2.42 (2010); Median age: 43.9 (2010); Males per 100 females: 97.3 (2010).
Religion: Six largest groups: 19.0% Catholicism, 13.6% Lutheran, 5.8% Presbyterian-Reformed, 3.2% Methodist/Pietist, 1.4% Non-Denominational, 0.9% Episcopalianism/Anglicanism (2010)
Economy: Unemployment rate: 9.5% (August 2012); Total civilian labor force: 32,518 (August 2012); Leading industries: 20.9% health care and social assistance; 15.9% retail trade; 15.0% manufacturing (2010); Farms: 207 totaling 20,035 acres (2007); Companies that employ 500 or more persons: 3 (2010); Companies that employ 100 to 499 persons: 15 (2010); Companies that employ less than 100 persons: 1,110 (2010); Black-owned businesses: 102 (2007); Hispanic-owned businesses: n/a (2007); Asian-owned businesses: n/a (2007); Women-owned businesses: 1,446 (2007); Retail sales per capita: $8,745 (2010). Single-family building permits issued: 97 (2011); Multi-family building permits issued: 0 (2011).
Income: Per capita income: $22,956 (2006-2010 5-year est.); Median household income: $47,744 (2006-2010 5-year est.); Average household income: $56,353 (2006-2010 5-year est.); Percent of households with income of $100,000 or more: 12.8% (2006-2010 5-year est.); Poverty rate: 10.5% (2006-2010 5-year est.); Bankruptcy rate: 3.44% (2011).
Education: Percent of population age 25 and over with: High school diploma (including GED) or higher: 86.7% (2006-2010 5-year est.); Bachelor's degree or higher: 14.6% (2006-2010 5-year est.); Master's degree or higher: 5.3% (2006-2010 5-year est.).
Housing: Homeownership rate: 77.3% (2010); Median home value: $139,800 (2006-2010 5-year est.); Median contract rent: $502 per month (2006-2010 5-year est.); Median year structure built: 1967 (2006-2010 5-year est.)
Health: Birth rate: 90.4 per 10,000 population (2011); Death rate: 120.9 per 10,000 population (2011); Age-adjusted cancer mortality rate: 210.7 deaths per 100,000 population (2009); Number of physicians: 9.5 per 10,000 population (2010); Hospital beds: 36.0 per 10,000 population (2008); Hospital admissions: 800.7 per 10,000 population (2008).
Elections: 2012 Presidential election results: 45.3% Obama, 52.8% Romney
National and State Parks: Beltzville State Park; Hickory Run State Park; Lehigh Gorge State Park; Weiser State Forest
Additional Information Contacts
Carbon County Government . . . . (570) 325-3611
  http://www.carboncounty.com
Carbon County Chamber of Commerce . . . . (610) 379-5000
  http://carboncountypa.org
Carbon County Chamber of Commerce . . . . (610) 379-5000
  http://carboncountypa.org/contact-us.html
Carbon County Chamber of Commerce . . . . (610) 379-5000
  http://www.carboncountychamber.org

Carbon County Communities

ALBRIGHTSVILLE (CDP). Covers a land area of 1.009 square miles and a water area of 0 square miles. Located at 41.01° N. Lat; 75.61° W. Long. Elevation is 1,509 feet.
Population: n/a (1990); n/a (2000); 202 (2010); Density: 200.3 persons per square mile (2010); Race: 94.6% White, 2.5% Black, 1.0% Asian, 0.0% American Indian/Alaska Native, 0.0% Native Hawaiian/Other Pacific Islander, 1.9% Other, 6.9% Hispanic of any race (2010); Average household size: 2.95 (2010); Median age: 39.6 (2010); Males per 100 females: 88.8 (2010); Marriage status: 17.5% never married, 57.7% now married, 24.8% widowed, 0.0% divorced (2006-2010 5-year est.); Foreign born: 8.2% (2006-2010 5-year est.); Ancestry (includes multiple ancestries): 27.7% Jamaican, 22.6% Italian, 19.0% American, 16.4% English, 13.3% German (2006-2010 5-year est.).
Economy: Employment by occupation: 13.2% management, 0.0% professional, 0.0% services, 39.5% sales, 36.8% farming, 0.0% construction, 0.0% production (2006-2010 5-year est.).

Income: Per capita income: $14,893 (2006-2010 5-year est.); Median household income: $27,500 (2006-2010 5-year est.); Average household income: $42,100 (2006-2010 5-year est.); Percent of households with income of $100,000 or more: 5.9% (2006-2010 5-year est.); Poverty rate: 0.0% (2006-2010 5-year est.).
Education: Percent of population age 25 and over with: High school diploma (including GED) or higher: 74.3% (2006-2010 5-year est.); Bachelor's degree or higher: 0.0% (2006-2010 5-year est.); Master's degree or higher: 0.0% (2006-2010 5-year est.).
School District(s)
Jim Thorpe Area SD (KG-12)
    2010-11 Enrollment: 2,229 . . . . (570) 325-3691
Housing: Homeownership rate: 87.6% (2010); Median home value: $158,100 (2006-2010 5-year est.); Median contract rent: n/a per month (2006-2010 5-year est.); Median year structure built: 1973 (2006-2010 5-year est.).
Transportation: Commute to work: 100.0% car, 0.0% public transportation, 0.0% walk, 0.0% work from home (2006-2010 5-year est.); Travel time to work: 0.0% less than 15 minutes, 23.7% 15 to 30 minutes, 65.8% 30 to 45 minutes, 0.0% 45 to 60 minutes, 10.5% 60 minutes or more (2006-2010 5-year est.)

ASHFIELD (unincorporated postal area)
Zip Code: 18212
    Covers a land area of 1.707 square miles and a water area of 0 square miles. Located at 40.77° N. Lat; 75.70° W. Long. Elevation is 548 feet. Population: 131 (2010); Density: 76.7 persons per square mile (2010); Race: 99.2% White, 0.0% Black, 0.8% Asian, 0.0% American Indian/Alaska Native, 0.0% Native Hawaiian/Other Pacific Islander, 0.0% Other, 3.1% Hispanic of any race (2010); Average household size: 2.34 (2010); Median age: 49.8 (2010); Males per 100 females: 101.5 (2010); Homeownership rate: 85.7% (2010)

BANKS (township). Covers a land area of 11.624 square miles and a water area of 0 square miles. Located at 40.93° N. Lat; 75.92° W. Long.
Population: 1,485 (1990); 1,359 (2000); 1,262 (2010); Density: 108.6 persons per square mile (2010); Race: 97.6% White, 0.5% Black, 0.8% Asian, 0.0% American Indian/Alaska Native, 0.0% Native Hawaiian/Other Pacific Islander, 1.1% Other, 2.0% Hispanic of any race (2010); Average household size: 2.31 (2010); Median age: 45.7 (2010); Males per 100 females: 94.2 (2010); Marriage status: 28.2% never married, 50.0% now married, 9.6% widowed, 12.1% divorced (2006-2010 5-year est.); Foreign born: 0.2% (2006-2010 5-year est.); Ancestry (includes multiple ancestries): 24.3% Slovak, 21.1% Italian, 16.3% Polish, 15.7% German, 11.2% Irish (2006-2010 5-year est.).
Economy: Single-family building permits issued: 0 (2011); Multi-family building permits issued: 0 (2011); Employment by occupation: 10.2% management, 2.1% professional, 10.0% services, 16.3% sales, 7.4% farming, 16.0% construction, 14.8% production (2006-2010 5-year est.).
Income: Per capita income: $24,225 (2006-2010 5-year est.); Median household income: $45,667 (2006-2010 5-year est.); Average household income: $54,710 (2006-2010 5-year est.); Percent of households with income of $100,000 or more: 8.0% (2006-2010 5-year est.); Poverty rate: 4.2% (2006-2010 5-year est.).
Education: Percent of population age 25 and over with: High school diploma (including GED) or higher: 88.7% (2006-2010 5-year est.); Bachelor's degree or higher: 11.1% (2006-2010 5-year est.); Master's degree or higher: 4.4% (2006-2010 5-year est.).
Housing: Homeownership rate: 77.0% (2010); Median home value: $89,000 (2006-2010 5-year est.); Median contract rent: $554 per month (2006-2010 5-year est.); Median year structure built: before 1940 (2006-2010 5-year est.).
Transportation: Commute to work: 89.1% car, 0.0% public transportation, 8.9% walk, 0.3% work from home (2006-2010 5-year est.); Travel time to work: 48.4% less than 15 minutes, 32.9% 15 to 30 minutes, 12.9% 30 to 45 minutes, 3.5% 45 to 60 minutes, 2.3% 60 minutes or more (2006-2010 5-year est.)
Additional Information Contacts
Carbon County Chamber of Commerce . . . . (610) 379-5000
  http://carboncountypa.org

BEAVER MEADOWS (borough). Aka Beaver Meadow Colliery. Covers a land area of 0.258 square miles and a water area of 0 square miles. Located at 40.93° N. Lat; 75.91° W. Long. Elevation is 1,585 feet.
History: Settled 1787.

Population: 985 (1990); 968 (2000); 869 (2010); Density: 3,366.2 persons per square mile (2010); Race: 97.0% White, 0.5% Black, 0.2% Asian, 0.1% American Indian/Alaska Native, 0.0% Native Hawaiian/Other Pacific Islander, 2.2% Other, 2.6% Hispanic of any race (2010); Average household size: 2.30 (2010); Median age: 43.2 (2010); Males per 100 females: 96.2 (2010); Marriage status: 31.1% never married, 44.2% now married, 13.5% widowed, 11.1% divorced (2006-2010 5-year est.); Foreign born: 0.0% (2006-2010 5-year est.); Ancestry (includes multiple ancestries): 24.1% Slovak, 20.3% Italian, 17.3% Irish, 12.7% German, 10.6% Polish (2006-2010 5-year est.).

Economy: Single-family building permits issued: 0 (2011); Multi-family building permits issued: 0 (2011); Employment by occupation: 4.2% management, 1.8% professional, 8.4% services, 25.1% sales, 2.9% farming, 20.6% construction, 9.9% production (2006-2010 5-year est.).

Income: Per capita income: $22,427 (2006-2010 5-year est.); Median household income: $45,268 (2006-2010 5-year est.); Average household income: $50,826 (2006-2010 5-year est.); Percent of households with income of $100,000 or more: 8.1% (2006-2010 5-year est.); Poverty rate: 11.4% (2006-2010 5-year est.).

Education: Percent of population age 25 and over with: High school diploma (including GED) or higher: 84.9% (2006-2010 5-year est.); Bachelor's degree or higher: 6.3% (2006-2010 5-year est.); Master's degree or higher: 1.8% (2006-2010 5-year est.).

Housing: Homeownership rate: 71.9% (2010); Median home value: $84,500 (2006-2010 5-year est.); Median contract rent: $517 per month (2006-2010 5-year est.); Median year structure built: before 1940 (2006-2010 5-year est.).

Transportation: Commute to work: 98.3% car, 0.0% public transportation, 0.8% walk, 0.0% work from home (2006-2010 5-year est.); Travel time to work: 34.7% less than 15 minutes, 37.5% 15 to 30 minutes, 14.0% 30 to 45 minutes, 3.9% 45 to 60 minutes, 9.9% 60 minutes or more (2006-2010 5-year est.)

BOWMANSTOWN (borough). Covers a land area of 0.769 square miles and a water area of 0.029 square miles. Located at 40.80° N. Lat; 75.66° W. Long. Elevation is 492 feet.

History: Appalachian Trail passes to South, on Blue Mt. Ridge.

Population: 888 (1990); 895 (2000); 937 (2010); Density: 1,218.0 persons per square mile (2010); Race: 96.3% White, 0.5% Black, 0.6% Asian, 0.4% American Indian/Alaska Native, 0.0% Native Hawaiian/Other Pacific Islander, 2.2% Other, 2.7% Hispanic of any race (2010); Average household size: 2.30 (2010); Median age: 43.5 (2010); Males per 100 females: 101.5 (2010); Marriage status: 18.6% never married, 66.1% now married, 8.1% widowed, 7.3% divorced (2006-2010 5-year est.); Foreign born: 1.3% (2006-2010 5-year est.); Ancestry (includes multiple ancestries): 50.3% German, 13.0% Pennsylvania German, 11.7% Italian, 7.2% American, 6.6% Irish (2006-2010 5-year est.).

Economy: Single-family building permits issued: 1 (2011); Multi-family building permits issued: 0 (2011); Employment by occupation: 2.1% management, 0.4% professional, 10.0% services, 17.7% sales, 2.1% farming, 15.0% construction, 7.1% production (2006-2010 5-year est.).

Income: Per capita income: $22,879 (2006-2010 5-year est.); Median household income: $48,333 (2006-2010 5-year est.); Average household income: $51,954 (2006-2010 5-year est.); Percent of households with income of $100,000 or more: 5.8% (2006-2010 5-year est.); Poverty rate: 5.5% (2006-2010 5-year est.).

Education: Percent of population age 25 and over with: High school diploma (including GED) or higher: 87.3% (2006-2010 5-year est.); Bachelor's degree or higher: 13.1% (2006-2010 5-year est.); Master's degree or higher: 3.5% (2006-2010 5-year est.).

Housing: Homeownership rate: 67.9% (2010); Median home value: $142,700 (2006-2010 5-year est.); Median contract rent: $443 per month (2006-2010 5-year est.); Median year structure built: before 1940 (2006-2010 5-year est.).

Transportation: Commute to work: 94.2% car, 0.4% public transportation, 0.6% walk, 4.7% work from home (2006-2010 5-year est.); Travel time to work: 23.9% less than 15 minutes, 21.2% 15 to 30 minutes, 32.7% 30 to 45 minutes, 15.3% 45 to 60 minutes, 6.8% 60 minutes or more (2006-2010 5-year est.)

EAST PENN (township). Covers a land area of 22.706 square miles and a water area of 0.135 square miles. Located at 40.78° N. Lat; 75.72° W. Long.

Population: 2,091 (1990); 2,461 (2000); 2,881 (2010); Density: 126.9 persons per square mile (2010); Race: 98.6% White, 0.2% Black, 0.1%

Asian, 0.1% American Indian/Alaska Native, 0.0% Native Hawaiian/Other Pacific Islander, 1.0% Other, 1.4% Hispanic of any race (2010); Average household size: 2.47 (2010); Median age: 47.5 (2010); Males per 100 females: 97.5 (2010); Marriage status: 20.8% never married, 63.5% now married, 6.1% widowed, 9.6% divorced (2006-2010 5-year est.); Foreign born: 1.0% (2006-2010 5-year est.); Ancestry (includes multiple ancestries): 42.5% German, 11.2% Pennsylvania German, 10.7% Irish, 7.8% American, 5.3% English (2006-2010 5-year est.).

Economy: Single-family building permits issued: 3 (2011); Multi-family building permits issued: 0 (2011); Employment by occupation: 8.3% management, 2.8% professional, 10.8% services, 19.1% sales, 3.9% farming, 13.0% construction, 9.2% production (2006-2010 5-year est.).

Income: Per capita income: $24,137 (2006-2010 5-year est.); Median household income: $53,844 (2006-2010 5-year est.); Average household income: $60,356 (2006-2010 5-year est.); Percent of households with income of $100,000 or more: 13.1% (2006-2010 5-year est.); Poverty rate: 9.2% (2006-2010 5-year est.).

Education: Percent of population age 25 and over with: High school diploma (including GED) or higher: 86.2% (2006-2010 5-year est.); Bachelor's degree or higher: 13.6% (2006-2010 5-year est.); Master's degree or higher: 5.0% (2006-2010 5-year est.).

Housing: Homeownership rate: 86.8% (2010); Median home value: $163,000 (2006-2010 5-year est.); Median contract rent: $606 per month (2006-2010 5-year est.); Median year structure built: 1979 (2006-2010 5-year est.).

Safety: Violent crime rate: 0.0 per 10,000 population; Property crime rate: 45.0 per 10,000 population (2011).

Transportation: Commute to work: 93.5% car, 0.0% public transportation, 0.5% walk, 5.1% work from home (2006-2010 5-year est.); Travel time to work: 24.2% less than 15 minutes, 25.2% 15 to 30 minutes, 21.7% 30 to 45 minutes, 21.9% 45 to 60 minutes, 7.0% 60 minutes or more (2006-2010 5-year est.)

Additional Information Contacts

Carbon County Chamber of Commerce . . . . (610) 379-5000
  http://carboncountypa.org/contact-us.html

EAST SIDE (borough). Covers a land area of 1.146 square miles and a water area of 0.006 square miles. Located at 41.06° N. Lat; 75.76° W. Long. Elevation is 1,125 feet.

Population: 330 (1990); 290 (2000); 317 (2010); Density: 276.5 persons per square mile (2010); Race: 95.6% White, 2.8% Black, 0.0% Asian, 0.9% American Indian/Alaska Native, 0.0% Native Hawaiian/Other Pacific Islander, 0.7% Other, 1.3% Hispanic of any race (2010); Average household size: 2.33 (2010); Median age: 44.4 (2010); Males per 100 females: 111.3 (2010); Marriage status: 29.7% never married, 43.3% now married, 9.6% widowed, 17.3% divorced (2006-2010 5-year est.); Foreign born: 0.8% (2006-2010 5-year est.); Ancestry (includes multiple ancestries): 43.4% German, 21.0% Irish, 16.5% Italian, 7.2% Pennsylvania German, 6.6% Polish (2006-2010 5-year est.).

Economy: Single-family building permits issued: 1 (2011); Multi-family building permits issued: 0 (2011); Employment by occupation: 4.8% management, 0.0% professional, 15.6% services, 16.2% sales, 2.4% farming, 7.8% construction, 1.8% production (2006-2010 5-year est.).

Income: Per capita income: $17,485 (2006-2010 5-year est.); Median household income: $36,875 (2006-2010 5-year est.); Average household income: $39,315 (2006-2010 5-year est.); Percent of households with income of $100,000 or more: 5.3% (2006-2010 5-year est.); Poverty rate: 25.8% (2006-2010 5-year est.).

Education: Percent of population age 25 and over with: High school diploma (including GED) or higher: 89.1% (2006-2010 5-year est.); Bachelor's degree or higher: 7.0% (2006-2010 5-year est.); Master's degree or higher: 3.9% (2006-2010 5-year est.).

Housing: Homeownership rate: 73.5% (2010); Median home value: $65,000 (2006-2010 5-year est.); Median contract rent: $383 per month (2006-2010 5-year est.); Median year structure built: 1969 (2006-2010 5-year est.).

Transportation: Commute to work: 90.1% car, 0.0% public transportation, 3.7% walk, 6.2% work from home (2006-2010 5-year est.); Travel time to work: 34.9% less than 15 minutes, 44.7% 15 to 30 minutes, 17.8% 30 to 45 minutes, 1.3% 45 to 60 minutes, 1.3% 60 minutes or more (2006-2010 5-year est.)

FRANKLIN (township).
Covers a land area of 15.158 square miles and a water area of 0.512 square miles. Located at 40.86° N. Lat; 75.66° W. Long.

Population: 3,706 (1990); 4,243 (2000); 4,262 (2010); Density: 281.2 persons per square mile (2010); Race: 98.1% White, 0.4% Black, 0.3% Asian, 0.1% American Indian/Alaska Native, 0.0% Native Hawaiian/Other Pacific Islander, 1.1% Other, 0.8% Hispanic of any race (2010); Average household size: 2.51 (2010); Median age: 44.3 (2010); Males per 100 females: 101.9 (2010); Marriage status: 21.7% never married, 64.7% now married, 4.4% widowed, 9.1% divorced (2006-2010 5-year est.); Foreign born: 4.7% (2006-2010 5-year est.); Ancestry (includes multiple ancestries): 42.1% German, 14.8% Irish, 11.7% Dutch, 9.7% Pennsylvania German, 8.1% Polish (2006-2010 5-year est.).
Economy: Single-family building permits issued: 0 (2011); Multi-family building permits issued: 0 (2011); Employment by occupation: 6.7% management, 1.0% professional, 12.3% services, 16.2% sales, 3.1% farming, 14.4% construction, 6.4% production (2006-2010 5-year est.).
Income: Per capita income: $27,590 (2006-2010 5-year est.); Median household income: $57,878 (2006-2010 5-year est.); Average household income: $71,030 (2006-2010 5-year est.); Percent of households with income of $100,000 or more: 19.7% (2006-2010 5-year est.); Poverty rate: 4.6% (2006-2010 5-year est.).
Education: Percent of population age 25 and over with: High school diploma (including GED) or higher: 86.8% (2006-2010 5-year est.); Bachelor's degree or higher: 14.4% (2006-2010 5-year est.); Master's degree or higher: 5.8% (2006-2010 5-year est.).
Housing: Homeownership rate: 84.9% (2010); Median home value: $173,200 (2006-2010 5-year est.); Median contract rent: $619 per month (2006-2010 5-year est.); Median year structure built: 1978 (2006-2010 5-year est.).
Safety: Violent crime rate: 32.7 per 10,000 population; Property crime rate: 91.2 per 10,000 population (2011).
Transportation: Commute to work: 93.7% car, 0.5% public transportation, 1.8% walk, 3.9% work from home (2006-2010 5-year est.); Travel time to work: 24.4% less than 15 minutes, 26.1% 15 to 30 minutes, 23.8% 30 to 45 minutes, 16.2% 45 to 60 minutes, 9.4% 60 minutes or more (2006-2010 5-year est.)
Additional Information Contacts
Carbon County Chamber of Commerce . . . . (610) 379-5000
  http://carboncountypa.org

HOLIDAY POCONO (CDP).
Covers a land area of 2.345 square miles and a water area of 0.042 square miles. Located at 41.03° N. Lat; 75.61° W. Long.

Population: n/a (1990); n/a (2000); 476 (2010); Density: 203.0 persons per square mile (2010); Race: 96.0% White, 1.1% Black, 0.2% Asian, 0.0% American Indian/Alaska Native, 0.0% Native Hawaiian/Other Pacific Islander, 2.7% Other, 8.4% Hispanic of any race (2010); Average household size: 2.18 (2010); Median age: 48.3 (2010); Males per 100 females: 120.4 (2010); Marriage status: 13.3% never married, 66.3% now married, 16.8% widowed, 3.5% divorced (2006-2010 5-year est.); Foreign born: 5.9% (2006-2010 5-year est.); Ancestry (includes multiple ancestries): 29.9% German, 29.5% Irish, 16.7% Italian, 15.4% Polish, 8.9% English (2006-2010 5-year est.).
Economy: Employment by occupation: 18.5% management, 0.0% professional, 0.0% services, 24.0% sales, 5.5% farming, 9.6% construction, 13.0% production (2006-2010 5-year est.).
Income: Per capita income: $20,175 (2006-2010 5-year est.); Median household income: $32,143 (2006-2010 5-year est.); Average household income: $41,285 (2006-2010 5-year est.); Percent of households with income of $100,000 or more: 8.4% (2006-2010 5-year est.); Poverty rate: 19.7% (2006-2010 5-year est.).
Education: Percent of population age 25 and over with: High school diploma (including GED) or higher: 77.7% (2006-2010 5-year est.); Bachelor's degree or higher: 10.9% (2006-2010 5-year est.); Master's degree or higher: 0.0% (2006-2010 5-year est.).
Housing: Homeownership rate: 85.8% (2010); Median home value: $159,200 (2006-2010 5-year est.); Median contract rent: $449 per month (2006-2010 5-year est.); Median year structure built: 1982 (2006-2010 5-year est.).
Transportation: Commute to work: 87.7% car, 0.0% public transportation, 0.0% walk, 12.3% work from home (2006-2010 5-year est.); Travel time to work: 7.4% less than 15 minutes, 30.6% 15 to 30 minutes, 23.1% 30 to 45 minutes, 3.3% 45 to 60 minutes, 35.5% 60 minutes or more (2006-2010 5-year est.)

JIM THORPE (borough).
Aka Mauch Chunk. County seat. Covers a land area of 14.598 square miles and a water area of 0.321 square miles. Located at 40.86° N. Lat; 75.77° W. Long. Elevation is 722 feet.
History: Borough created in the late 1950s by merging Mauch Chunk (the former county seat) and East Mauch Chunk boroughs. Borough named for Oklahoma football legend Jim Thorpe (1888-1953).
Population: 5,048 (1990); 4,804 (2000); 4,781 (2010); Density: 327.5 persons per square mile (2010); Race: 96.9% White, 0.4% Black, 0.6% Asian, 0.0% American Indian/Alaska Native, 0.1% Native Hawaiian/Other Pacific Islander, 2.0% Other, 2.5% Hispanic of any race (2010); Average household size: 2.40 (2010); Median age: 43.8 (2010); Males per 100 females: 93.6 (2010); Marriage status: 31.0% never married, 52.2% now married, 8.5% widowed, 8.2% divorced (2006-2010 5-year est.); Foreign born: 0.8% (2006-2010 5-year est.); Ancestry (includes multiple ancestries): 52.1% German, 22.5% Irish, 9.6% Italian, 7.7% English, 6.9% Slovak (2006-2010 5-year est.).
Economy: Single-family building permits issued: 2 (2011); Multi-family building permits issued: 0 (2011); Employment by occupation: 3.3% management, 5.6% professional, 7.8% services, 19.0% sales, 3.2% farming, 11.4% construction, 8.3% production (2006-2010 5-year est.).
Income: Per capita income: $25,384 (2006-2010 5-year est.); Median household income: $44,831 (2006-2010 5-year est.); Average household income: $62,930 (2006-2010 5-year est.); Percent of households with income of $100,000 or more: 16.5% (2006-2010 5-year est.); Poverty rate: 12.9% (2006-2010 5-year est.).
Education: Percent of population age 25 and over with: High school diploma (including GED) or higher: 88.1% (2006-2010 5-year est.); Bachelor's degree or higher: 17.6% (2006-2010 5-year est.); Master's degree or higher: 7.1% (2006-2010 5-year est.).

School District(s)
Carbon Career & Technical Institute (09-12)
  2010-11 Enrollment: 330 . . . . (570) 325-3682
Jim Thorpe Area SD (KG-12)
  2010-11 Enrollment: 2,229 . . . . (570) 325-3691
Housing: Homeownership rate: 75.8% (2010); Median home value: $129,500 (2006-2010 5-year est.); Median contract rent: $455 per month (2006-2010 5-year est.); Median year structure built: before 1940 (2006-2010 5-year est.).
Safety: Violent crime rate: 31.3 per 10,000 population; Property crime rate: 281.5 per 10,000 population (2011).
Transportation: Commute to work: 84.2% car, 1.6% public transportation, 8.8% walk, 3.6% work from home (2006-2010 5-year est.); Travel time to work: 34.3% less than 15 minutes, 28.1% 15 to 30 minutes, 9.6% 30 to 45 minutes, 17.7% 45 to 60 minutes, 10.3% 60 minutes or more (2006-2010 5-year est.)
Additional Information Contacts
Jim Thorpe Chamber of Commerce . . . . (570) 325-5810
  http://www.jimthorpe.org

JUNEDALE (unincorporated postal area)
Zip Code: 18230
  Covers a land area of 2.723 square miles and a water area of 0 square miles. Located at 40.92° N. Lat; 75.93° W. Long. Elevation is 1,670 feet. Population: 132 (2010); Density: 48.5 persons per square mile (2010); Race: 98.5% White, 0.0% Black, 0.0% Asian, 0.0% American Indian/Alaska Native, 0.0% Native Hawaiian/Other Pacific Islander, 1.5% Other, 1.5% Hispanic of any race (2010); Average household size: 2.28 (2010); Median age: 40.5 (2010); Males per 100 females: 97.0 (2010); Homeownership rate: 82.7% (2010)

KIDDER (township).
Covers a land area of 69.075 square miles and a water area of 0.723 square miles. Located at 41.06° N. Lat; 75.65° W. Long.
Population: 1,319 (1990); 1,185 (2000); 1,935 (2010); Density: 28.0 persons per square mile (2010); Race: 95.3% White, 2.0% Black, 0.7% Asian, 0.3% American Indian/Alaska Native, 0.0% Native Hawaiian/Other Pacific Islander, 1.7% Other, 5.0% Hispanic of any race (2010); Average household size: 2.11 (2010); Median age: 50.4 (2010); Males per 100 females: 109.6 (2010); Marriage status: 25.3% never married, 62.4% now married, 8.2% widowed, 4.0% divorced (2006-2010 5-year est.); Foreign born: 4.3% (2006-2010 5-year est.); Ancestry (includes multiple ancestries): 27.2% German, 24.6% Irish, 9.9% Italian, 8.8% American, 8.2% Polish (2006-2010 5-year est.).
Economy: Single-family building permits issued: 12 (2011); Multi-family building permits issued: 0 (2011); Employment by occupation: 11.8%

management, 10.1% professional, 6.9% services, 16.5% sales, 3.8% farming, 10.6% construction, 7.1% production (2006-2010 5-year est.).
Income: Per capita income: $24,195 (2006-2010 5-year est.); Median household income: $46,420 (2006-2010 5-year est.); Average household income: $66,857 (2006-2010 5-year est.); Percent of households with income of $100,000 or more: 18.8% (2006-2010 5-year est.); Poverty rate: 10.1% (2006-2010 5-year est.).
Education: Percent of population age 25 and over with: High school diploma (including GED) or higher: 88.2% (2006-2010 5-year est.); Bachelor's degree or higher: 21.9% (2006-2010 5-year est.); Master's degree or higher: 7.7% (2006-2010 5-year est.).
Housing: Homeownership rate: 85.6% (2010); Median home value: $168,600 (2006-2010 5-year est.); Median contract rent: $713 per month (2006-2010 5-year est.); Median year structure built: 1982 (2006-2010 5-year est.).
Safety: Violent crime rate: 61.8 per 10,000 population; Property crime rate: 577.0 per 10,000 population (2011).
Transportation: Commute to work: 84.4% car, 0.0% public transportation, 1.6% walk, 8.1% work from home (2006-2010 5-year est.); Travel time to work: 18.6% less than 15 minutes, 34.4% 15 to 30 minutes, 23.0% 30 to 45 minutes, 6.8% 45 to 60 minutes, 17.2% 60 minutes or more (2006-2010 5-year est.)
Additional Information Contacts
Carbon County Chamber of Commerce . . . . (610) 379-5000
  http://carboncountypa.org
Kidder Township . . . . (570) 722-0107
  http://www.kiddertownship.org

LAKE HARMONY (unincorporated postal area)
Zip Code: 18624
  Covers a land area of 16.057 square miles and a water area of 0.492 square miles. Located at 41.06° N. Lat; 75.64° W. Long. Elevation is 1,870 feet. Population: 718 (2010); Density: 44.7 persons per square mile (2010); Race: 95.8% White, 1.7% Black, 0.7% Asian, 0.1% American Indian/Alaska Native, 0.0% Native Hawaiian/Other Pacific Islander, 1.7% Other, 3.1% Hispanic of any race (2010); Average household size: 2.00 (2010); Median age: 52.1 (2010); Males per 100 females: 112.4 (2010); Homeownership rate: 85.0% (2010)

LANSFORD (borough). Covers a land area of 1.536 square miles and a water area of <.001 square miles. Located at 40.83° N. Lat; 75.88° W. Long. Elevation is 1,148 feet.
History: Founded 1846, incorporated 1877.
Population: 4,690 (1990); 4,230 (2000); 3,941 (2010); Density: 2,565.2 persons per square mile (2010); Race: 94.7% White, 1.0% Black, 0.3% Asian, 0.2% American Indian/Alaska Native, 0.0% Native Hawaiian/Other Pacific Islander, 3.8% Other, 4.3% Hispanic of any race (2010); Average household size: 2.28 (2010); Median age: 40.7 (2010); Males per 100 females: 91.6 (2010); Marriage status: 27.8% never married, 43.1% now married, 10.1% widowed, 19.0% divorced (2006-2010 5-year est.); Foreign born: 0.6% (2006-2010 5-year est.); Ancestry (includes multiple ancestries): 22.9% German, 16.0% Irish, 15.4% Slovak, 12.9% American, 12.3% Polish (2006-2010 5-year est.).
Economy: Single-family building permits issued: 0 (2011); Multi-family building permits issued: 0 (2011); Employment by occupation: 3.8% management, 1.7% professional, 11.1% services, 13.2% sales, 15.3% farming, 10.3% construction, 10.1% production (2006-2010 5-year est.).
Income: Per capita income: $18,395 (2006-2010 5-year est.); Median household income: $38,252 (2006-2010 5-year est.); Average household income: $40,294 (2006-2010 5-year est.); Percent of households with income of $100,000 or more: 2.6% (2006-2010 5-year est.); Poverty rate: 20.6% (2006-2010 5-year est.).
Education: Percent of population age 25 and over with: High school diploma (including GED) or higher: 87.5% (2006-2010 5-year est.); Bachelor's degree or higher: 7.6% (2006-2010 5-year est.); Master's degree or higher: 2.8% (2006-2010 5-year est.).
School District(s)
Panther Valley SD (KG-12)
  2010-11 Enrollment: 1,711 . . . . (570) 645-4248
Housing: Homeownership rate: 61.3% (2010); Median home value: $54,800 (2006-2010 5-year est.); Median contract rent: $447 per month (2006-2010 5-year est.); Median year structure built: before 1940 (2006-2010 5-year est.).
Safety: Violent crime rate: 17.7 per 10,000 population; Property crime rate: 78.4 per 10,000 population (2011).

Transportation: Commute to work: 91.7% car, 0.0% public transportation, 5.3% walk, 2.0% work from home (2006-2010 5-year est.); Travel time to work: 26.0% less than 15 minutes, 34.7% 15 to 30 minutes, 22.6% 30 to 45 minutes, 3.0% 45 to 60 minutes, 13.7% 60 minutes or more (2006-2010 5-year est.)
Additional Information Contacts
Carbon County Chamber of Commerce . . . . (610) 379-5000
  http://carboncountypa.org

LAUSANNE (township). Covers a land area of 5.955 square miles and a water area of 0 square miles. Located at 40.97° N. Lat; 75.82° W. Long.
Population: 237 (1990); 218 (2000); 237 (2010); Density: 39.8 persons per square mile (2010); Race: 97.0% White, 0.8% Black, 0.8% Asian, 0.0% American Indian/Alaska Native, 0.0% Native Hawaiian/Other Pacific Islander, 1.4% Other, 0.0% Hispanic of any race (2010); Average household size: 2.47 (2010); Median age: 45.9 (2010); Males per 100 females: 89.6 (2010); Marriage status: 30.8% never married, 52.8% now married, 8.8% widowed, 7.6% divorced (2006-2010 5-year est.); Foreign born: 2.4% (2006-2010 5-year est.); Ancestry (includes multiple ancestries): 34.4% German, 22.7% Polish, 16.5% Italian, 10.7% Irish, 9.3% English (2006-2010 5-year est.).
Economy: Single-family building permits issued: 0 (2011); Multi-family building permits issued: 0 (2011); Employment by occupation: 3.5% management, 1.4% professional, 9.9% services, 22.7% sales, 1.4% farming, 18.4% construction, 8.5% production (2006-2010 5-year est.).
Income: Per capita income: $21,502 (2006-2010 5-year est.); Median household income: $44,250 (2006-2010 5-year est.); Average household income: $56,258 (2006-2010 5-year est.); Percent of households with income of $100,000 or more: 9.0% (2006-2010 5-year est.); Poverty rate: 17.2% (2006-2010 5-year est.).
Education: Percent of population age 25 and over with: High school diploma (including GED) or higher: 81.7% (2006-2010 5-year est.); Bachelor's degree or higher: 9.9% (2006-2010 5-year est.); Master's degree or higher: 7.3% (2006-2010 5-year est.).
Housing: Homeownership rate: 93.8% (2010); Median home value: $166,800 (2006-2010 5-year est.); Median contract rent: n/a per month (2006-2010 5-year est.); Median year structure built: 1977 (2006-2010 5-year est.).
Transportation: Commute to work: 88.7% car, 2.8% public transportation, 0.0% walk, 8.5% work from home (2006-2010 5-year est.); Travel time to work: 18.6% less than 15 minutes, 24.8% 15 to 30 minutes, 42.6% 30 to 45 minutes, 0.0% 45 to 60 minutes, 14.0% 60 minutes or more (2006-2010 5-year est.)

LEHIGH (township). Covers a land area of 26.155 square miles and a water area of 0.297 square miles. Located at 40.96° N. Lat; 75.76° W. Long.
Population: 500 (1990); 527 (2000); 479 (2010); Density: 18.3 persons per square mile (2010); Race: 95.6% White, 0.2% Black, 1.5% Asian, 0.4% American Indian/Alaska Native, 0.0% Native Hawaiian/Other Pacific Islander, 2.3% Other, 2.3% Hispanic of any race (2010); Average household size: 2.35 (2010); Median age: 51.9 (2010); Males per 100 females: 97.1 (2010); Marriage status: 24.8% never married, 66.4% now married, 3.8% widowed, 5.0% divorced (2006-2010 5-year est.); Foreign born: 1.5% (2006-2010 5-year est.); Ancestry (includes multiple ancestries): 45.2% German, 16.0% Irish, 15.6% Polish, 9.3% Dutch, 6.6% Italian (2006-2010 5-year est.).
Economy: Single-family building permits issued: 0 (2011); Multi-family building permits issued: 0 (2011); Employment by occupation: 6.9% management, 1.9% professional, 16.6% services, 16.6% sales, 3.1% farming, 17.4% construction, 8.1% production (2006-2010 5-year est.).
Income: Per capita income: $24,555 (2006-2010 5-year est.); Median household income: $47,434 (2006-2010 5-year est.); Average household income: $56,751 (2006-2010 5-year est.); Percent of households with income of $100,000 or more: 9.6% (2006-2010 5-year est.); Poverty rate: 10.0% (2006-2010 5-year est.).
Education: Percent of population age 25 and over with: High school diploma (including GED) or higher: 88.3% (2006-2010 5-year est.); Bachelor's degree or higher: 14.9% (2006-2010 5-year est.); Master's degree or higher: 5.3% (2006-2010 5-year est.).
Housing: Homeownership rate: 88.1% (2010); Median home value: $145,200 (2006-2010 5-year est.); Median contract rent: $428 per month (2006-2010 5-year est.); Median year structure built: 1959 (2006-2010 5-year est.).

Transportation: Commute to work: 89.5% car, 1.2% public transportation, 3.6% walk, 2.4% work from home (2006-2010 5-year est.); Travel time to work: 26.6% less than 15 minutes, 27.0% 15 to 30 minutes, 30.7% 30 to 45 minutes, 10.8% 45 to 60 minutes, 5.0% 60 minutes or more (2006-2010 5-year est.)

LEHIGHTON (borough). Covers a land area of 1.623 square miles and a water area of 0.028 square miles. Located at 40.83° N. Lat; 75.72° W. Long. Elevation is 571 feet.

History: The site of Lehighton was settled by Moravians in 1746, but the village was destroyed in 1755. A new settlement was laid out in 1794 and incorporated as a borough in 1866.

Population: 5,914 (1990); 5,537 (2000); 5,500 (2010); Density: 3,388.6 persons per square mile (2010); Race: 96.5% White, 0.6% Black, 0.5% Asian, 0.2% American Indian/Alaska Native, 0.0% Native Hawaiian/Other Pacific Islander, 2.2% Other, 3.7% Hispanic of any race (2010); Average household size: 2.36 (2010); Median age: 40.6 (2010); Males per 100 females: 86.6 (2010); Marriage status: 28.4% never married, 48.9% now married, 11.2% widowed, 11.5% divorced (2006-2010 5-year est.); Foreign born: 0.8% (2006-2010 5-year est.); Ancestry (includes multiple ancestries): 41.1% German, 13.7% Irish, 7.5% Pennsylvania German, 7.1% Dutch, 6.6% American (2006-2010 5-year est.).

Economy: Single-family building permits issued: 0 (2011); Multi-family building permits issued: 0 (2011); Employment by occupation: 7.7% management, 0.4% professional, 15.6% services, 18.5% sales, 4.6% farming, 11.9% construction, 12.9% production (2006-2010 5-year est.).

Income: Per capita income: $21,800 (2006-2010 5-year est.); Median household income: $44,349 (2006-2010 5-year est.); Average household income: $49,794 (2006-2010 5-year est.); Percent of households with income of $100,000 or more: 9.7% (2006-2010 5-year est.); Poverty rate: 10.2% (2006-2010 5-year est.).

Education: Percent of population age 25 and over with: High school diploma (including GED) or higher: 86.2% (2006-2010 5-year est.); Bachelor's degree or higher: 13.5% (2006-2010 5-year est.); Master's degree or higher: 7.3% (2006-2010 5-year est.).

School District(s)

Lehighton Area SD (PK-12)
　　2010-11 Enrollment: 2,389 . . . . (610) 377-4490
Palmerton Area SD (KG-12)
　　2010-11 Enrollment: 1,896 . . . . (610) 826-2364

Housing: Homeownership rate: 55.1% (2010); Median home value: $117,800 (2006-2010 5-year est.); Median contract rent: $467 per month (2006-2010 5-year est.); Median year structure built: before 1940 (2006-2010 5-year est.).

Hospitals: Gnaden Huetten Memorial Hospital (202 beds)

Safety: Violent crime rate: 23.6 per 10,000 population; Property crime rate: 277.3 per 10,000 population (2011).

Newspapers: The Morning Call - Lehighton Bureau (Local news); Times News (Local news; Circulation 13,718)

Transportation: Commute to work: 88.5% car, 0.0% public transportation, 10.9% walk, 0.0% work from home (2006-2010 5-year est.); Travel time to work: 43.9% less than 15 minutes, 24.0% 15 to 30 minutes, 14.0% 30 to 45 minutes, 11.5% 45 to 60 minutes, 6.5% 60 minutes or more (2006-2010 5-year est.)

Airports: Jake Arner Memorial (general aviation)

Additional Information Contacts

Borough of Lehighton . . . . (610) 377-4002
　　http://www.lehightonborough.com
Lehighton Chamber of Commerce . . . . (610) 377-2191
　　http://lehigtonareacouncil.org

LOWER TOWAMENSING (township). Covers a land area of 21.255 square miles and a water area of 0.045 square miles. Located at 40.82° N. Lat; 75.57° W. Long.

Population: 2,969 (1990); 3,173 (2000); 3,228 (2010); Density: 151.9 persons per square mile (2010); Race: 99.0% White, 0.1% Black, 0.2% Asian, 0.1% American Indian/Alaska Native, 0.0% Native Hawaiian/Other Pacific Islander, 0.6% Other, 1.4% Hispanic of any race (2010); Average household size: 2.48 (2010); Median age: 45.1 (2010); Males per 100 females: 103.8 (2010); Marriage status: 13.1% never married, 71.6% now married, 6.3% widowed, 9.0% divorced (2006-2010 5-year est.); Foreign born: 1.7% (2006-2010 5-year est.); Ancestry (includes multiple ancestries): 43.9% German, 15.5% Pennsylvania German, 11.4% Irish, 6.1% Italian, 5.7% Dutch (2006-2010 5-year est.).

Economy: Single-family building permits issued: 3 (2011); Multi-family building permits issued: 0 (2011); Employment by occupation: 6.2% management, 2.7% professional, 16.9% services, 14.3% sales, 2.9% farming, 11.0% construction, 6.8% production (2006-2010 5-year est.).

Income: Per capita income: $25,020 (2006-2010 5-year est.); Median household income: $59,735 (2006-2010 5-year est.); Average household income: $60,828 (2006-2010 5-year est.); Percent of households with income of $100,000 or more: 16.8% (2006-2010 5-year est.); Poverty rate: 6.0% (2006-2010 5-year est.).

Education: Percent of population age 25 and over with: High school diploma (including GED) or higher: 83.3% (2006-2010 5-year est.); Bachelor's degree or higher: 17.2% (2006-2010 5-year est.); Master's degree or higher: 9.4% (2006-2010 5-year est.).

Housing: Homeownership rate: 84.1% (2010); Median home value: $153,600 (2006-2010 5-year est.); Median contract rent: $588 per month (2006-2010 5-year est.); Median year structure built: 1972 (2006-2010 5-year est.).

Transportation: Commute to work: 97.3% car, 0.0% public transportation, 0.0% walk, 2.7% work from home (2006-2010 5-year est.); Travel time to work: 26.6% less than 15 minutes, 21.8% 15 to 30 minutes, 27.7% 30 to 45 minutes, 16.3% 45 to 60 minutes, 7.7% 60 minutes or more (2006-2010 5-year est.)

Additional Information Contacts

Carbon County Chamber of Commerce . . . . (610) 379-5000
　　http://carboncountypa.org

MAHONING (township). Covers a land area of 23.663 square miles and a water area of 0.114 square miles. Located at 40.81° N. Lat; 75.77° W. Long.

Population: 4,198 (1990); 3,978 (2000); 4,305 (2010); Density: 181.9 persons per square mile (2010); Race: 98.0% White, 0.5% Black, 0.3% Asian, 0.3% American Indian/Alaska Native, 0.0% Native Hawaiian/Other Pacific Islander, 0.9% Other, 1.5% Hispanic of any race (2010); Average household size: 2.49 (2010); Median age: 46.3 (2010); Males per 100 females: 96.7 (2010); Marriage status: 26.0% never married, 54.0% now married, 10.1% widowed, 10.0% divorced (2006-2010 5-year est.); Foreign born: 4.1% (2006-2010 5-year est.); Ancestry (includes multiple ancestries): 37.0% German, 17.7% Irish, 11.4% Pennsylvania German, 8.8% American, 5.2% Polish (2006-2010 5-year est.).

Economy: Single-family building permits issued: 6 (2011); Multi-family building permits issued: 0 (2011); Employment by occupation: 2.9% management, 1.9% professional, 9.7% services, 14.5% sales, 6.6% farming, 16.3% construction, 10.8% production (2006-2010 5-year est.).

Income: Per capita income: $22,687 (2006-2010 5-year est.); Median household income: $52,647 (2006-2010 5-year est.); Average household income: $57,149 (2006-2010 5-year est.); Percent of households with income of $100,000 or more: 15.6% (2006-2010 5-year est.); Poverty rate: 10.8% (2006-2010 5-year est.).

Education: Percent of population age 25 and over with: High school diploma (including GED) or higher: 83.5% (2006-2010 5-year est.); Bachelor's degree or higher: 13.3% (2006-2010 5-year est.); Master's degree or higher: 5.3% (2006-2010 5-year est.).

Housing: Homeownership rate: 85.5% (2010); Median home value: $177,800 (2006-2010 5-year est.); Median contract rent: $541 per month (2006-2010 5-year est.); Median year structure built: 1970 (2006-2010 5-year est.).

Transportation: Commute to work: 90.3% car, 0.4% public transportation, 4.1% walk, 3.9% work from home (2006-2010 5-year est.); Travel time to work: 37.0% less than 15 minutes, 17.1% 15 to 30 minutes, 16.6% 30 to 45 minutes, 22.8% 45 to 60 minutes, 6.6% 60 minutes or more (2006-2010 5-year est.)

Additional Information Contacts

Carbon County Chamber of Commerce . . . . (610) 379-5000
　　http://carboncountypa.org

NESQUEHONING (borough). Covers a land area of 21.162 square miles and a water area of 0.388 square miles. Located at 40.88° N. Lat; 75.82° W. Long. Elevation is 820 feet.

Population: 3,364 (1990); 3,288 (2000); 3,349 (2010); Density: 158.3 persons per square mile (2010); Race: 96.7% White, 1.2% Black, 0.1% Asian, 0.2% American Indian/Alaska Native, 0.0% Native Hawaiian/Other Pacific Islander, 1.8% Other, 2.4% Hispanic of any race (2010); Average household size: 2.21 (2010); Median age: 45.1 (2010); Males per 100 females: 102.4 (2010); Marriage status: 30.8% never married, 57.4% now married, 7.3% widowed, 4.5% divorced (2006-2010 5-year est.); Foreign

born: 0.7% (2006-2010 5-year est.); Ancestry (includes multiple ancestries): 20.8% German, 20.2% Irish, 18.2% Italian, 18.0% Slovak, 5.5% Polish (2006-2010 5-year est.).

Economy: Single-family building permits issued: 1 (2011); Multi-family building permits issued: 0 (2011); Employment by occupation: 5.9% management, 1.3% professional, 13.4% services, 23.9% sales, 2.8% farming, 9.3% construction, 4.3% production (2006-2010 5-year est.).

Income: Per capita income: $18,692 (2006-2010 5-year est.); Median household income: $36,946 (2006-2010 5-year est.); Average household income: $44,560 (2006-2010 5-year est.); Percent of households with income of $100,000 or more: 6.4% (2006-2010 5-year est.); Poverty rate: 20.8% (2006-2010 5-year est.).

Education: Percent of population age 25 and over with: High school diploma (including GED) or higher: 90.5% (2006-2010 5-year est.); Bachelor's degree or higher: 13.2% (2006-2010 5-year est.); Master's degree or higher: 4.5% (2006-2010 5-year est.).

School District(s)
Panther Valley SD (KG-12)
   2010-11 Enrollment: 1,711 . . . . (570) 645-4248

Housing: Homeownership rate: 71.1% (2010); Median home value: $88,900 (2006-2010 5-year est.); Median contract rent: $511 per month (2006-2010 5-year est.); Median year structure built: before 1940 (2006-2010 5-year est.).

Safety: Violent crime rate: 17.9 per 10,000 population; Property crime rate: 288.7 per 10,000 population (2011).

Transportation: Commute to work: 85.6% car, 0.0% public transportation, 6.3% walk, 7.3% work from home (2006-2010 5-year est.); Travel time to work: 36.3% less than 15 minutes, 41.7% 15 to 30 minutes, 7.8% 30 to 45 minutes, 7.5% 45 to 60 minutes, 6.7% 60 minutes or more (2006-2010 5-year est.)

Additional Information Contacts
Carbon County Chamber of Commerce . . . . (610) 379-5000
   http://carboncountypa.org

PACKER (township). Covers a land area of 27.934 square miles and a water area of 0 square miles. Located at 40.90° N. Lat; 75.89° W. Long.

Population: 918 (1990); 986 (2000); 998 (2010); Density: 35.7 persons per square mile (2010); Race: 97.7% White, 0.1% Black, 0.1% Asian, 0.3% American Indian/Alaska Native, 0.0% Native Hawaiian/Other Pacific Islander, 1.8% Other, 1.5% Hispanic of any race (2010); Average household size: 2.52 (2010); Median age: 46.3 (2010); Males per 100 females: 102.4 (2010); Marriage status: 21.2% never married, 61.2% now married, 7.1% widowed, 10.5% divorced (2006-2010 5-year est.); Foreign born: 1.5% (2006-2010 5-year est.); Ancestry (includes multiple ancestries): 31.6% German, 16.4% Polish, 14.9% Italian, 10.7% Dutch, 8.4% Slovak (2006-2010 5-year est.).

Economy: Single-family building permits issued: 1 (2011); Multi-family building permits issued: 0 (2011); Employment by occupation: 12.7% management, 2.4% professional, 10.3% services, 17.2% sales, 2.4% farming, 15.1% construction, 14.1% production (2006-2010 5-year est.).

Income: Per capita income: $24,530 (2006-2010 5-year est.); Median household income: $58,281 (2006-2010 5-year est.); Average household income: $66,357 (2006-2010 5-year est.); Percent of households with income of $100,000 or more: 19.0% (2006-2010 5-year est.); Poverty rate: 7.5% (2006-2010 5-year est.).

Education: Percent of population age 25 and over with: High school diploma (including GED) or higher: 88.5% (2006-2010 5-year est.); Bachelor's degree or higher: 11.5% (2006-2010 5-year est.); Master's degree or higher: 2.7% (2006-2010 5-year est.).

Housing: Homeownership rate: 91.1% (2010); Median home value: $168,600 (2006-2010 5-year est.); Median contract rent: $442 per month (2006-2010 5-year est.); Median year structure built: 1975 (2006-2010 5-year est.).

Transportation: Commute to work: 96.6% car, 0.0% public transportation, 0.0% walk, 1.0% work from home (2006-2010 5-year est.); Travel time to work: 21.5% less than 15 minutes, 48.5% 15 to 30 minutes, 11.2% 30 to 45 minutes, 7.1% 45 to 60 minutes, 11.7% 60 minutes or more (2006-2010 5-year est.).

Additional Information Contacts
Greater Hazleton Chamber of Commerce. . . . . (570) 455-1509
   http://www.hazletonchamber.org

PALMERTON (borough). Covers a land area of 2.484 square miles and a water area of 0.051 square miles. Located at 40.80° N. Lat; 75.62° W. Long. Elevation is 400 feet.

History: Settled 1737, laid out 1898, incorporated 1912.

Population: 5,373 (1990); 5,248 (2000); 5,414 (2010); Density: 2,179.4 persons per square mile (2010); Race: 97.3% White, 0.5% Black, 0.5% Asian, 0.1% American Indian/Alaska Native, 0.0% Native Hawaiian/Other Pacific Islander, 1.6% Other, 3.9% Hispanic of any race (2010); Average household size: 2.38 (2010); Median age: 38.0 (2010); Males per 100 females: 93.2 (2010); Marriage status: 25.7% never married, 55.1% now married, 8.0% widowed, 11.2% divorced (2006-2010 5-year est.); Foreign born: 2.3% (2006-2010 5-year est.); Ancestry (includes multiple ancestries): 28.8% German, 17.0% Pennsylvania German, 12.3% Irish, 6.4% Italian, 4.9% American (2006-2010 5-year est.).

Economy: Single-family building permits issued: 2 (2011); Multi-family building permits issued: 0 (2011); Employment by occupation: 6.0% management, 4.7% professional, 15.4% services, 20.6% sales, 5.5% farming, 11.3% construction, 9.3% production (2006-2010 5-year est.).

Income: Per capita income: $20,378 (2006-2010 5-year est.); Median household income: $43,482 (2006-2010 5-year est.); Average household income: $47,401 (2006-2010 5-year est.); Percent of households with income of $100,000 or more: 7.3% (2006-2010 5-year est.); Poverty rate: 12.7% (2006-2010 5-year est.).

Education: Percent of population age 25 and over with: High school diploma (including GED) or higher: 84.2% (2006-2010 5-year est.); Bachelor's degree or higher: 13.7% (2006-2010 5-year est.); Master's degree or higher: 4.8% (2006-2010 5-year est.).

School District(s)
Palmerton Area SD (KG-12)
   2010-11 Enrollment: 1,896 . . . . (610) 826-2364

Housing: Homeownership rate: 64.8% (2010); Median home value: $116,200 (2006-2010 5-year est.); Median contract rent: $569 per month (2006-2010 5-year est.); Median year structure built: before 1940 (2006-2010 5-year est.).

Hospitals: Palmerton Hospital (70 beds)

Safety: Violent crime rate: 20.3 per 10,000 population; Property crime rate: 320.4 per 10,000 population (2011).

Newspapers: Panorama Latino News (Local news; Circulation 15,000)

Transportation: Commute to work: 94.8% car, 0.0% public transportation, 3.3% walk, 1.4% work from home (2006-2010 5-year est.); Travel time to work: 26.0% less than 15 minutes, 18.8% 15 to 30 minutes, 40.4% 30 to 45 minutes, 11.1% 45 to 60 minutes, 3.7% 60 minutes or more (2006-2010 5-year est.)

Additional Information Contacts
Borough of Palmerton . . . . (610) 826-2505
   http://palmertonpolice.ptd.net/palbor.html
Carbon County Chamber of Commerce . . . . (610) 379-5000
   http://carboncountypa.org

PARRYVILLE (borough). Covers a land area of 1.611 square miles and a water area of 0.017 square miles. Located at 40.82° N. Lat; 75.67° W. Long. Elevation is 446 feet.

Population: 488 (1990); 478 (2000); 525 (2010); Density: 325.9 persons per square mile (2010); Race: 98.3% White, 0.4% Black, 0.2% Asian, 0.4% American Indian/Alaska Native, 0.0% Native Hawaiian/Other Pacific Islander, 0.7% Other, 2.1% Hispanic of any race (2010); Average household size: 2.32 (2010); Median age: 44.8 (2010); Males per 100 females: 109.2 (2010); Marriage status: 19.1% never married, 71.1% now married, 2.3% widowed, 7.5% divorced (2006-2010 5-year est.); Foreign born: 1.0% (2006-2010 5-year est.); Ancestry (includes multiple ancestries): 52.1% German, 13.1% Pennsylvania German, 7.9% American, 6.7% Irish, 6.7% English (2006-2010 5-year est.).

Economy: Single-family building permits issued: 0 (2011); Multi-family building permits issued: 0 (2011); Employment by occupation: 0.5% management, 6.0% professional, 9.3% services, 14.0% sales, 8.8% farming, 20.0% construction, 15.3% production (2006-2010 5-year est.).

Income: Per capita income: $26,558 (2006-2010 5-year est.); Median household income: $55,000 (2006-2010 5-year est.); Average household income: $65,032 (2006-2010 5-year est.); Percent of households with income of $100,000 or more: 14.0% (2006-2010 5-year est.); Poverty rate: 1.9% (2006-2010 5-year est.).

Education: Percent of population age 25 and over with: High school diploma (including GED) or higher: 87.0% (2006-2010 5-year est.); Bachelor's degree or higher: 7.8% (2006-2010 5-year est.); Master's degree or higher: 1.4% (2006-2010 5-year est.).

Housing: Homeownership rate: 70.8% (2010); Median home value: $108,700 (2006-2010 5-year est.); Median contract rent: $498 per month (2006-2010 5-year est.); Median year structure built: 1951 (2006-2010 5-year est.).

Transportation: Commute to work: 96.2% car, 0.9% public transportation, 2.8% walk, 0.0% work from home (2006-2010 5-year est.); Travel time to work: 27.7% less than 15 minutes, 14.1% 15 to 30 minutes, 24.4% 30 to 45 minutes, 16.4% 45 to 60 minutes, 17.4% 60 minutes or more (2006-2010 5-year est.)

PENN FOREST (township). Covers a land area of 73.806 square miles and a water area of 1.048 square miles. Located at 40.96° N. Lat; 75.63° W. Long.

Population: 2,888 (1990); 5,439 (2000); 9,581 (2010); Density: 129.8 persons per square mile (2010); Race: 87.8% White, 6.7% Black, 1.0% Asian, 0.4% American Indian/Alaska Native, 0.0% Native Hawaiian/Other Pacific Islander, 4.1% Other, 7.7% Hispanic of any race (2010); Average household size: 2.55 (2010); Median age: 43.7 (2010); Males per 100 females: 101.5 (2010); Marriage status: 24.1% never married, 62.1% now married, 5.1% widowed, 8.7% divorced (2006-2010 5-year est.); Foreign born: 7.0% (2006-2010 5-year est.); Ancestry (includes multiple ancestries): 26.0% German, 23.4% Irish, 16.4% Italian, 8.4% American, 7.2% English (2006-2010 5-year est.).

Economy: Single-family building permits issued: 53 (2011); Multi-family building permits issued: 0 (2011); Employment by occupation: 7.5% management, 5.5% professional, 7.7% services, 20.0% sales, 3.1% farming, 15.0% construction, 8.4% production (2006-2010 5-year est.).

Income: Per capita income: $23,572 (2006-2010 5-year est.); Median household income: $54,901 (2006-2010 5-year est.); Average household income: $63,513 (2006-2010 5-year est.); Percent of households with income of $100,000 or more: 17.3% (2006-2010 5-year est.); Poverty rate: 3.6% (2006-2010 5-year est.).

Education: Percent of population age 25 and over with: High school diploma (including GED) or higher: 87.1% (2006-2010 5-year est.); Bachelor's degree or higher: 20.6% (2006-2010 5-year est.); Master's degree or higher: 5.8% (2006-2010 5-year est.).

Housing: Homeownership rate: 89.8% (2010); Median home value: $176,200 (2006-2010 5-year est.); Median contract rent: $815 per month (2006-2010 5-year est.); Median year structure built: 1986 (2006-2010 5-year est.).

Transportation: Commute to work: 93.0% car, 3.2% public transportation, 0.4% walk, 3.5% work from home (2006-2010 5-year est.); Travel time to work: 11.3% less than 15 minutes, 23.8% 15 to 30 minutes, 18.3% 30 to 45 minutes, 17.9% 45 to 60 minutes, 28.7% 60 minutes or more (2006-2010 5-year est.)

Additional Information Contacts

Carbon County Chamber of Commerce . . . . (610) 379-5000
  http://www.carboncountychamber.org
Penn Forest Township . . . . (570) 325-2768
  http://www.pennforesttownship.com

SUMMIT HILL (borough). Covers a land area of 8.691 square miles and a water area of 0.414 square miles. Located at 40.82° N. Lat; 75.85° W. Long. Elevation is 1,503 feet.

Population: 3,225 (1990); 2,974 (2000); 3,034 (2010); Density: 349.1 persons per square mile (2010); Race: 97.4% White, 0.7% Black, 0.3% Asian, 0.1% American Indian/Alaska Native, 0.1% Native Hawaiian/Other Pacific Islander, 1.4% Other, 1.8% Hispanic of any race (2010); Average household size: 2.35 (2010); Median age: 43.2 (2010); Males per 100 females: 97.9 (2010); Marriage status: 26.3% never married, 56.1% now married, 8.2% widowed, 9.4% divorced (2006-2010 5-year est.); Foreign born: 0.0% (2006-2010 5-year est.); Ancestry (includes multiple ancestries): 26.9% German, 24.3% Irish, 18.7% Italian, 14.4% Slovak, 11.1% Polish (2006-2010 5-year est.).

Economy: Single-family building permits issued: 2 (2011); Multi-family building permits issued: 0 (2011); Employment by occupation: 5.0% management, 3.4% professional, 11.5% services, 16.8% sales, 5.2% farming, 11.5% construction, 11.0% production (2006-2010 5-year est.).

Income: Per capita income: $21,987 (2006-2010 5-year est.); Median household income: $40,680 (2006-2010 5-year est.); Average household income: $52,064 (2006-2010 5-year est.); Percent of households with income of $100,000 or more: 9.9% (2006-2010 5-year est.); Poverty rate: 11.4% (2006-2010 5-year est.).

Taxes: Total city taxes per capita: $258 (2009); City property taxes per capita: $156 (2009).

Education: Percent of population age 25 and over with: High school diploma (including GED) or higher: 91.2% (2006-2010 5-year est.); Bachelor's degree or higher: 17.6% (2006-2010 5-year est.); Master's degree or higher: 3.7% (2006-2010 5-year est.).

Housing: Homeownership rate: 79.2% (2010); Median home value: $68,000 (2006-2010 5-year est.); Median contract rent: $502 per month (2006-2010 5-year est.); Median year structure built: before 1940 (2006-2010 5-year est.).

Safety: Violent crime rate: 6.6 per 10,000 population; Property crime rate: 16.4 per 10,000 population (2011).

Transportation: Commute to work: 95.6% car, 0.0% public transportation, 2.6% walk, 0.9% work from home (2006-2010 5-year est.); Travel time to work: 22.8% less than 15 minutes, 28.1% 15 to 30 minutes, 11.1% 30 to 45 minutes, 18.9% 45 to 60 minutes, 19.1% 60 minutes or more (2006-2010 5-year est.)

Additional Information Contacts

Carbon County Chamber of Commerce . . . . (610) 379-5000
  http://carboncountypa.org

TOWAMENSING (township). Covers a land area of 27.137 square miles and a water area of 1.778 square miles. Located at 40.87° N. Lat; 75.60° W. Long.

Population: 2,982 (1990); 3,475 (2000); 4,477 (2010); Density: 165.0 persons per square mile (2010); Race: 98.3% White, 0.2% Black, 0.3% Asian, 0.0% American Indian/Alaska Native, 0.3% Native Hawaiian/Other Pacific Islander, 0.9% Other, 2.1% Hispanic of any race (2010); Average household size: 2.66 (2010); Median age: 44.4 (2010); Males per 100 females: 104.4 (2010); Marriage status: 17.3% never married, 63.8% now married, 7.9% widowed, 10.9% divorced (2006-2010 5-year est.); Foreign born: 3.0% (2006-2010 5-year est.); Ancestry (includes multiple ancestries): 40.0% German, 12.4% Italian, 11.0% Pennsylvania German, 10.2% Irish, 9.8% Slovak (2006-2010 5-year est.).

Economy: Single-family building permits issued: 9 (2011); Multi-family building permits issued: 0 (2011); Employment by occupation: 12.5% management, 1.1% professional, 6.4% services, 18.1% sales, 6.9% farming, 17.6% construction, 9.0% production (2006-2010 5-year est.).

Income: Per capita income: $27,359 (2006-2010 5-year est.); Median household income: $60,000 (2006-2010 5-year est.); Average household income: $68,188 (2006-2010 5-year est.); Percent of households with income of $100,000 or more: 20.9% (2006-2010 5-year est.); Poverty rate: 12.5% (2006-2010 5-year est.).

Education: Percent of population age 25 and over with: High school diploma (including GED) or higher: 84.3% (2006-2010 5-year est.); Bachelor's degree or higher: 12.3% (2006-2010 5-year est.); Master's degree or higher: 3.7% (2006-2010 5-year est.).

Housing: Homeownership rate: 91.5% (2010); Median home value: $207,100 (2006-2010 5-year est.); Median contract rent: $548 per month (2006-2010 5-year est.); Median year structure built: 1986 (2006-2010 5-year est.).

Transportation: Commute to work: 96.7% car, 0.0% public transportation, 0.4% walk, 2.3% work from home (2006-2010 5-year est.); Travel time to work: 17.6% less than 15 minutes, 30.6% 15 to 30 minutes, 19.4% 30 to 45 minutes, 18.6% 45 to 60 minutes, 13.8% 60 minutes or more (2006-2010 5-year est.)

Additional Information Contacts

Lehighton Chamber of Commerce . . . . (610) 377-2191
  http://lehigtonareacouncil.org
Towamensing Township . . . . (610) 681-4202
  http://www.carboncounty.com

TOWAMENSING TRAILS (CDP). Covers a land area of 5.944 square miles and a water area of 0.288 square miles. Located at 40.99° N. Lat; 75.58° W. Long. Elevation is 1,631 feet.

Population: n/a (1990); n/a (2000); 2,292 (2010); Density: 385.6 persons per square mile (2010); Race: 88.2% White, 0.9% Black, 0.9% Asian, 0.3% American Indian/Alaska Native, 0.0% Native Hawaiian/Other Pacific Islander, 2.9% Other, 7.4% Hispanic of any race (2010); Average household size: 2.42 (2010); Median age: 47.1 (2010); Males per 100 females: 103.0 (2010); Marriage status: 7.3% never married, 63.6% now married, 7.1% widowed, 22.0% divorced (2006-2010 5-year est.); Foreign born: 1.6% (2006-2010 5-year est.); Ancestry (includes multiple ancestries): 22.7% Italian, 18.2% American, 17.5% Irish, 11.4% German, 10.0% English (2006-2010 5-year est.).

Economy: Employment by occupation: 6.8% management, 4.4% professional, 15.4% services, 11.3% sales, 3.8% farming, 0.0% construction, 10.9% production (2006-2010 5-year est.).

Income: Per capita income: $27,305 (2006-2010 5-year est.); Median household income: $41,852 (2006-2010 5-year est.); Average household income: $51,536 (2006-2010 5-year est.); Percent of households with income of $100,000 or more: 3.3% (2006-2010 5-year est.); Poverty rate: 0.0% (2006-2010 5-year est.).

Education: Percent of population age 25 and over with: High school diploma (including GED) or higher: 96.1% (2006-2010 5-year est.); Bachelor's degree or higher: 19.0% (2006-2010 5-year est.); Master's degree or higher: 5.1% (2006-2010 5-year est.).

Housing: Homeownership rate: 88.9% (2010); Median home value: $169,900 (2006-2010 5-year est.); Median contract rent: n/a per month (2006-2010 5-year est.); Median year structure built: 1986 (2006-2010 5-year est.).

Transportation: Commute to work: 100.0% car, 0.0% public transportation, 0.0% walk, 0.0% work from home (2006-2010 5-year est.); Travel time to work: 5.9% less than 15 minutes, 20.0% 15 to 30 minutes, 7.8% 30 to 45 minutes, 32.2% 45 to 60 minutes, 34.1% 60 minutes or more (2006-2010 5-year est.)

TRESCKOW (CDP). Covers a land area of 1.781 square miles and a water area of 0 square miles. Located at 40.92° N. Lat; 75.97° W. Long. Elevation is 1,778 feet.

History: In former anthracite coal-mining region.

Population: 1,041 (1990); 964 (2000); 880 (2010); Density: 494.0 persons per square mile (2010); Race: 98.8% White, 0.2% Black, 0.0% Asian, 0.0% American Indian/Alaska Native, 0.0% Native Hawaiian/Other Pacific Islander, 1.0% Other, 2.0% Hispanic of any race (2010); Average household size: 2.29 (2010); Median age: 47.2 (2010); Males per 100 females: 100.0 (2010); Marriage status: 31.7% never married, 49.7% now married, 6.6% widowed, 12.0% divorced (2006-2010 5-year est.); Foreign born: 0.2% (2006-2010 5-year est.); Ancestry (includes multiple ancestries): 30.3% Slovak, 25.6% Italian, 16.1% Polish, 15.4% German, 14.2% Irish (2006-2010 5-year est.).

Economy: Employment by occupation: 10.9% management, 3.1% professional, 8.6% services, 16.6% sales, 7.6% farming, 16.9% construction, 13.1% production (2006-2010 5-year est.).

Income: Per capita income: $25,967 (2006-2010 5-year est.); Median household income: $50,294 (2006-2010 5-year est.); Average household income: $61,106 (2006-2010 5-year est.); Percent of households with income of $100,000 or more: 11.5% (2006-2010 5-year est.); Poverty rate: 4.1% (2006-2010 5-year est.).

Education: Percent of population age 25 and over with: High school diploma (including GED) or higher: 87.8% (2006-2010 5-year est.); Bachelor's degree or higher: 12.9% (2006-2010 5-year est.); Master's degree or higher: 5.3% (2006-2010 5-year est.).

Housing: Homeownership rate: 77.9% (2010); Median home value: $94,400 (2006-2010 5-year est.); Median contract rent: $564 per month (2006-2010 5-year est.); Median year structure built: 1941 (2006-2010 5-year est.).

Transportation: Commute to work: 91.9% car, 0.0% public transportation, 5.1% walk, 0.5% work from home (2006-2010 5-year est.); Travel time to work: 47.5% less than 15 minutes, 34.5% 15 to 30 minutes, 13.3% 30 to 45 minutes, 2.5% 45 to 60 minutes, 2.2% 60 minutes or more (2006-2010 5-year est.)

WEATHERLY (borough). Covers a land area of 2.979 square miles and a water area of 0 square miles. Located at 40.94° N. Lat; 75.82° W. Long. Elevation is 1,086 feet.

History: Incorporated 1863.

Population: 2,640 (1990); 2,612 (2000); 2,525 (2010); Density: 847.6 persons per square mile (2010); Race: 96.6% White, 0.6% Black, 0.4% Asian, 0.1% American Indian/Alaska Native, 0.0% Native Hawaiian/Other Pacific Islander, 2.3% Other, 2.5% Hispanic of any race (2010); Average household size: 2.40 (2010); Median age: 46.1 (2010); Males per 100 females: 85.0 (2010); Marriage status: 22.2% never married, 58.1% now married, 11.7% widowed, 8.0% divorced (2006-2010 5-year est.); Foreign born: 2.5% (2006-2010 5-year est.); Ancestry (includes multiple ancestries): 30.6% German, 16.3% Italian, 13.3% Irish, 11.0% Polish, 7.5% Dutch (2006-2010 5-year est.).

Economy: Single-family building permits issued: 1 (2011); Multi-family building permits issued: 0 (2011); Employment by occupation: 3.9%

management, 7.0% professional, 12.7% services, 15.1% sales, 5.0% farming, 16.1% construction, 11.0% production (2006-2010 5-year est.).

Income: Per capita income: $18,544 (2006-2010 5-year est.); Median household income: $41,285 (2006-2010 5-year est.); Average household income: $48,578 (2006-2010 5-year est.); Percent of households with income of $100,000 or more: 10.1% (2006-2010 5-year est.); Poverty rate: 13.3% (2006-2010 5-year est.).

Education: Percent of population age 25 and over with: High school diploma (including GED) or higher: 91.3% (2006-2010 5-year est.); Bachelor's degree or higher: 11.2% (2006-2010 5-year est.); Master's degree or higher: 2.9% (2006-2010 5-year est.).

School District(s)

Weatherly Area SD (KG-12)

    2010-11 Enrollment: 688 . . . . (570) 427-8681

Housing: Homeownership rate: 73.9% (2010); Median home value: $105,400 (2006-2010 5-year est.); Median contract rent: $438 per month (2006-2010 5-year est.); Median year structure built: 1941 (2006-2010 5-year est.).

Safety: Violent crime rate: 75.0 per 10,000 population; Property crime rate: 367.2 per 10,000 population (2011).

Transportation: Commute to work: 87.0% car, 0.5% public transportation, 6.0% walk, 6.4% work from home (2006-2010 5-year est.); Travel time to work: 29.2% less than 15 minutes, 34.5% 15 to 30 minutes, 15.6% 30 to 45 minutes, 8.5% 45 to 60 minutes, 12.2% 60 minutes or more (2006-2010 5-year est.)

Additional Information Contacts

Carbon County Chamber of Commerce . . . . (610) 379-5000
    http://carboncountypa.org

WEISSPORT (borough). Covers a land area of 0.135 square miles and a water area of 0.022 square miles. Located at 40.83° N. Lat; 75.70° W. Long. Elevation is 509 feet.

Population: 472 (1990); 434 (2000); 412 (2010); Density: 3,049.6 persons per square mile (2010); Race: 93.4% White, 1.0% Black, 1.2% Asian, 0.5% American Indian/Alaska Native, 0.0% Native Hawaiian/Other Pacific Islander, 3.9% Other, 5.3% Hispanic of any race (2010); Average household size: 2.48 (2010); Median age: 38.5 (2010); Males per 100 females: 91.6 (2010); Marriage status: 32.1% never married, 52.7% now married, 4.4% widowed, 10.8% divorced (2006-2010 5-year est.); Foreign born: 6.3% (2006-2010 5-year est.); Ancestry (includes multiple ancestries): 38.0% German, 12.7% Pennsylvania German, 12.3% American, 3.4% Italian, 3.2% Irish (2006-2010 5-year est.).

Economy: Single-family building permits issued: 0 (2011); Multi-family building permits issued: 0 (2011); Employment by occupation: 2.9% management, 7.8% professional, 12.7% services, 13.5% sales, 5.3% farming, 16.4% construction, 6.1% production (2006-2010 5-year est.).

Income: Per capita income: $17,678 (2006-2010 5-year est.); Median household income: $40,417 (2006-2010 5-year est.); Average household income: $44,388 (2006-2010 5-year est.); Percent of households with income of $100,000 or more: 2.4% (2006-2010 5-year est.); Poverty rate: 15.5% (2006-2010 5-year est.).

Education: Percent of population age 25 and over with: High school diploma (including GED) or higher: 78.7% (2006-2010 5-year est.); Bachelor's degree or higher: 11.5% (2006-2010 5-year est.); Master's degree or higher: 4.4% (2006-2010 5-year est.).

Housing: Homeownership rate: 47.5% (2010); Median home value: $86,900 (2006-2010 5-year est.); Median contract rent: $514 per month (2006-2010 5-year est.); Median year structure built: before 1940 (2006-2010 5-year est.).

Transportation: Commute to work: 78.3% car, 0.0% public transportation, 12.2% walk, 6.1% work from home (2006-2010 5-year est.); Travel time to work: 40.3% less than 15 minutes, 14.4% 15 to 30 minutes, 23.1% 30 to 45 minutes, 15.7% 45 to 60 minutes, 6.5% 60 minutes or more (2006-2010 5-year est.)

WEISSPORT EAST (CDP). Covers a land area of 2.098 square miles and a water area of 0 square miles. Located at 40.84° N. Lat; 75.69° W. Long.

Population: 1,843 (1990); 1,936 (2000); 1,624 (2010); Density: 774.0 persons per square mile (2010); Race: 98.6% White, 0.3% Black, 0.4% Asian, 0.1% American Indian/Alaska Native, 0.1% Native Hawaiian/Other Pacific Islander, 0.5% Other, 1.0% Hispanic of any race (2010); Average household size: 2.34 (2010); Median age: 45.6 (2010); Males per 100 females: 100.0 (2010); Marriage status: 28.6% never married, 56.4% now married, 2.3% widowed, 12.7% divorced (2006-2010 5-year est.); Foreign

born: 0.0% (2006-2010 5-year est.); Ancestry (includes multiple ancestries): 52.8% German, 12.8% Dutch, 10.2% Irish, 9.2% Pennsylvania German, 5.1% Welsh (2006-2010 5-year est.).

Economy: Employment by occupation: 2.0% management, 0.0% professional, 12.1% services, 25.1% sales, 4.1% farming, 8.6% construction, 4.1% production (2006-2010 5-year est.).

Income: Per capita income: $24,136 (2006-2010 5-year est.); Median household income: $54,833 (2006-2010 5-year est.); Average household income: $54,972 (2006-2010 5-year est.); Percent of households with income of $100,000 or more: 8.2% (2006-2010 5-year est.); Poverty rate: 2.4% (2006-2010 5-year est.).

Education: Percent of population age 25 and over with: High school diploma (including GED) or higher: 87.1% (2006-2010 5-year est.); Bachelor's degree or higher: 8.9% (2006-2010 5-year est.); Master's degree or higher: 3.9% (2006-2010 5-year est.).

Housing: Homeownership rate: 76.8% (2010); Median home value: $124,200 (2006-2010 5-year est.); Median contract rent: $630 per month (2006-2010 5-year est.); Median year structure built: 1954 (2006-2010 5-year est.).

Transportation: Commute to work: 90.9% car, 1.6% public transportation, 5.5% walk, 2.0% work from home (2006-2010 5-year est.); Travel time to work: 35.6% less than 15 minutes, 22.2% 15 to 30 minutes, 19.6% 30 to 45 minutes, 12.0% 45 to 60 minutes, 10.6% 60 minutes or more (2006-2010 5-year est.)

Additional Information Contacts

Carbon County Chamber of Commerce . . . . (610) 379-5000
http://carboncountypa.org

Centre County

Located in central Pennsylvania; mountainous area, bounded on the northwest by the West Branch of the Susquehanna River; includes part of the Allegheny Mountains. Covers a land area of 1,109.921 square miles, a water area of 3.042 square miles, and is located in the Eastern Time Zone at 40.91° N. Lat., 77.85° W. Long. The county was founded in 1800. County seat is Bellefonte.

Centre County is part of the State College, PA Metropolitan Statistical Area. The entire metro area includes: Centre County, PA

Weather Station: State College   Elevation: 1,169 feet

	Jan	Feb	Mar	Apr	May	Jun	Jul	Aug	Sep	Oct	Nov	Dec
High	34	38	46	60	70	78	82	80	72	61	50	38
Low	19	21	27	38	48	57	61	60	52	41	33	24
Precip	2.7	2.5	3.4	3.3	3.4	4.1	3.5	3.8	3.6	3.0	3.4	2.8
Snow	12.5	10.4	10.3	1.4	tr	0.0	0.0	0.0	0.0	0.4	2.6	7.8

High and Low temperatures in degrees Fahrenheit; Precipitation and Snow in inches

Population: 123,786 (1990); 135,758 (2000); 153,990 (2010); Race: 89.4% White, 3.0% Black, 5.2% Asian, 0.1% American Indian/Alaska Native, 0.0% Native Hawaiian/Other Pacific Islander, 2.3% Other, 2.4% Hispanic of any race (2010); Density: 138.7 persons per square mile (2010); Average household size: 2.38 (2010); Median age: 28.7 (2010); Males per 100 females: 107.5 (2010).

Religion: Six largest groups: 12.5% Catholicism, 7.4% Methodist/Pietist, 4.4% Lutheran, 2.8% Presbyterian-Reformed, 2.3% Baptist, 1.8% European Free-Church (2010)

Economy: Unemployment rate: 6.3% (August 2012); Total civilian labor force: 75,921 (August 2012); Leading industries: 18.3% retail trade; 17.3% health care and social assistance; 14.7% accommodation & food services (2010); Farms: 1,146 totaling 148,464 acres (2007); Companies that employ 500 or more persons: 2 (2010); Companies that employ 100 to 499 persons: 56 (2010); Companies that employ less than 100 persons: 3,131 (2010); Black-owned businesses: 91 (2007); Hispanic-owned businesses: 104 (2007); Asian-owned businesses: 223 (2007); Women-owned businesses: 2,811 (2007); Retail sales per capita: $11,635 (2010). Single-family building permits issued: 207 (2011); Multi-family building permits issued: 52 (2011).

Income: Per capita income: $23,744 (2006-2010 5-year est.); Median household income: $47,016 (2006-2010 5-year est.); Average household income: $63,056 (2006-2010 5-year est.); Percent of households with income of $100,000 or more: 17.4% (2006-2010 5-year est.); Poverty rate: 18.5% (2006-2010 5-year est.); Bankruptcy rate: 1.17% (2011).

Taxes: Total county taxes per capita: $151 (2009); County property taxes per capita: $141 (2009).

Education: Percent of population age 25 and over with: High school diploma (including GED) or higher: 92.6% (2006-2010 5-year est.); Bachelor's degree or higher: 40.0% (2006-2010 5-year est.); Master's degree or higher: 19.2% (2006-2010 5-year est.).

Housing: Homeownership rate: 58.6% (2010); Median home value: $175,800 (2006-2010 5-year est.); Median contract rent: $711 per month (2006-2010 5-year est.); Median year structure built: 1975 (2006-2010 5-year est.)

Health: Birth rate: 81.2 per 10,000 population (2011); Death rate: 58.6 per 10,000 population (2011); Age-adjusted cancer mortality rate: 146.4 deaths per 100,000 population (2009); Number of physicians: 22.0 per 10,000 population (2010); Hospital beds: 28.4 per 10,000 population (2008); Hospital admissions: 1,344.8 per 10,000 population (2008).

Environment: Air Quality Index: 77.5% good, 21.4% moderate, 1.1% unhealthy for sensitive individuals, 0.0% unhealthy (percent of days in 2011)

Elections: 2012 Presidential election results: 49.1% Obama, 48.9% Romney

National and State Parks: Bald Eagle State Forest; Bald Eagle State Park; Black Moshannon State Park; McCall Dam State Park; Moshannon State Forest; Penn Roosevelt State Park; Poe Paddy State Park; Poe Valley State Park; Thickhead State Wildlife Area

Additional Information Contacts

Centre County Government . . . . (814) 355-6700
http://www.co.centre.pa.us
Chamber of Business & Industry of Centre County . . . . . . (814) 234-1829
http://www.cbicc.org

Centre County Communities

AARONSBURG (CDP). Covers a land area of 0.888 square miles and a water area of 0 square miles. Located at 40.90° N. Lat; 77.45° W. Long. Elevation is 1,175 feet.

Population: 427 (1990); 485 (2000); 613 (2010); Density: 690.5 persons per square mile (2010); Race: 99.2% White, 0.2% Black, 0.0% Asian, 0.0% American Indian/Alaska Native, 0.2% Native Hawaiian/Other Pacific Islander, 0.4% Other, 0.5% Hispanic of any race (2010); Average household size: 2.55 (2010); Median age: 40.9 (2010); Males per 100 females: 105.0 (2010); Marriage status: 32.5% never married, 44.3% now married, 5.7% widowed, 17.5% divorced (2006-2010 5-year est.); Foreign born: 0.0% (2006-2010 5-year est.); Ancestry (includes multiple ancestries): 53.9% German, 6.4% Polish, 6.0% Dutch, 5.6% Italian, 5.4% English (2006-2010 5-year est.).

Economy: Employment by occupation: 2.2% management, 9.9% professional, 20.5% services, 13.5% sales, 4.2% farming, 9.9% construction, 4.2% production (2006-2010 5-year est.).

Income: Per capita income: $19,611 (2006-2010 5-year est.); Median household income: $45,833 (2006-2010 5-year est.); Average household income: $49,621 (2006-2010 5-year est.); Percent of households with income of $100,000 or more: 8.5% (2006-2010 5-year est.); Poverty rate: 12.0% (2006-2010 5-year est.).

Education: Percent of population age 25 and over with: High school diploma (including GED) or higher: 91.8% (2006-2010 5-year est.); Bachelor's degree or higher: 21.1% (2006-2010 5-year est.); Master's degree or higher: 10.5% (2006-2010 5-year est.).

Housing: Homeownership rate: 88.4% (2010); Median home value: $135,900 (2006-2010 5-year est.); Median contract rent: $528 per month (2006-2010 5-year est.); Median year structure built: 1958 (2006-2010 5-year est.).

Transportation: Commute to work: 94.9% car, 0.0% public transportation, 0.0% walk, 4.2% work from home (2006-2010 5-year est.); Travel time to work: 30.1% less than 15 minutes, 16.4% 15 to 30 minutes, 44.1% 30 to 45 minutes, 4.7% 45 to 60 minutes, 4.7% 60 minutes or more (2006-2010 5-year est.)

BAILEYVILLE (CDP). Covers a land area of 1.242 square miles and a water area of 0.005 square miles. Located at 40.71° N. Lat; 78.00° W. Long. Elevation is 1,142 feet.

Population: n/a (1990); n/a (2000); 201 (2010); Density: 161.8 persons per square mile (2010); Race: 95.5% White, 0.0% Black, 0.5% Asian, 1.5% American Indian/Alaska Native, 0.0% Native Hawaiian/Other Pacific Islander, 2.5% Other, 1.5% Hispanic of any race (2010); Average household size: 2.61 (2010); Median age: 44.1 (2010); Males per 100 females: 125.8 (2010); Marriage status: 18.6% never married, 73.8% now married, 0.0% widowed, 7.7% divorced (2006-2010 5-year est.); Foreign

born: 0.0% (2006-2010 5-year est.); Ancestry (includes multiple ancestries): 43.9% Italian, 40.7% German, 33.5% Irish, 19.9% English, 16.3% Scottish (2006-2010 5-year est.).

Economy: Employment by occupation: 9.8% management, 9.2% professional, 11.5% services, 29.3% sales, 0.0% farming, 10.9% construction, 0.0% production (2006-2010 5-year est.).

Income: Per capita income: $26,103 (2006-2010 5-year est.); Median household income: $68,594 (2006-2010 5-year est.); Average household income: $66,902 (2006-2010 5-year est.); Percent of households with income of $100,000 or more: n/a (2006-2010 5-year est.); Poverty rate: 0.0% (2006-2010 5-year est.).

Education: Percent of population age 25 and over with: High school diploma (including GED) or higher: 94.5% (2006-2010 5-year est.); Bachelor's degree or higher: 8.6% (2006-2010 5-year est.); Master's degree or higher: 8.6% (2006-2010 5-year est.).

Housing: Homeownership rate: 90.9% (2010); Median home value: $215,800 (2006-2010 5-year est.); Median contract rent: n/a per month (2006-2010 5-year est.); Median year structure built: 1973 (2006-2010 5-year est.).

Transportation: Commute to work: 100.0% car, 0.0% public transportation, 0.0% walk, 0.0% work from home (2006-2010 5-year est.); Travel time to work: 0.0% less than 15 minutes, 81.8% 15 to 30 minutes, 18.2% 30 to 45 minutes, 0.0% 45 to 60 minutes, 0.0% 60 minutes or more (2006-2010 5-year est.)

BELLEFONTE (borough). County seat. Covers a land area of 1.850 square miles and a water area of 0 square miles. Located at 40.91° N. Lat; 77.77° W. Long. Elevation is 797 feet.

History: Centre County Library and Historical Museum. Laid out 1775, Incorporated 1806.

Population: 6,358 (1990); 6,395 (2000); 6,187 (2010); Density: 3,344.5 persons per square mile (2010); Race: 96.3% White, 1.5% Black, 0.5% Asian, 0.1% American Indian/Alaska Native, 0.0% Native Hawaiian/Other Pacific Islander, 1.6% Other, 1.4% Hispanic of any race (2010); Average household size: 2.10 (2010); Median age: 39.5 (2010); Males per 100 females: 89.0 (2010); Marriage status: 28.0% never married, 53.9% now married, 9.3% widowed, 8.7% divorced (2006-2010 5-year est.); Foreign born: 1.3% (2006-2010 5-year est.); Ancestry (includes multiple ancestries): 31.2% German, 13.2% Irish, 9.6% English, 8.8% Italian, 5.6% Polish (2006-2010 5-year est.).

Economy: Single-family building permits issued: 2 (2011); Multi-family building permits issued: 40 (2011); Employment by occupation: 12.5% management, 3.0% professional, 7.9% services, 12.1% sales, 5.7% farming, 7.2% construction, 3.6% production (2006-2010 5-year est.).

Income: Per capita income: $26,938 (2006-2010 5-year est.); Median household income: $48,211 (2006-2010 5-year est.); Average household income: $58,338 (2006-2010 5-year est.); Percent of households with income of $100,000 or more: 14.7% (2006-2010 5-year est.); Poverty rate: 10.2% (2006-2010 5-year est.).

Education: Percent of population age 25 and over with: High school diploma (including GED) or higher: 90.5% (2006-2010 5-year est.); Bachelor's degree or higher: 34.8% (2006-2010 5-year est.); Master's degree or higher: 14.4% (2006-2010 5-year est.).

School District(s)

Bellefonte Area SD (KG-12)
   2010-11 Enrollment: 2,909 . . . . (814) 355-4814

Housing: Homeownership rate: 49.1% (2010); Median home value: $166,400 (2006-2010 5-year est.); Median contract rent: $539 per month (2006-2010 5-year est.); Median year structure built: 1946 (2006-2010 5-year est.).

Safety: Violent crime rate: 17.7 per 10,000 population; Property crime rate: 167.6 per 10,000 population (2011).

Transportation: Commute to work: 91.7% car, 0.0% public transportation, 3.2% walk, 3.5% work from home (2006-2010 5-year est.); Travel time to work: 31.4% less than 15 minutes, 49.9% 15 to 30 minutes, 13.9% 30 to 45 minutes, 1.9% 45 to 60 minutes, 3.0% 60 minutes or more (2006-2010 5-year est.)

Additional Information Contacts

Bellefonte Intervalley Area Chamber of Commerce . . . . . . (814) 355-2917
   http://bellefontechamber.org/site/default.aspx?PageID=1
Borough of Bellefonte . . . . (814) 355-1501
   http://www.bellefonte.net

BENNER (township). Covers a land area of 28.353 square miles and a water area of 0 square miles. Located at 40.87° N. Lat; 77.82° W. Long.

Population: 5,078 (1990); 5,217 (2000); 6,188 (2010); Density: 218.2 persons per square mile (2010); Race: 78.8% White, 16.2% Black, 0.4% Asian, 0.1% American Indian/Alaska Native, 0.0% Native Hawaiian/Other Pacific Islander, 4.5% Other, 4.2% Hispanic of any race (2010); Average household size: 2.38 (2010); Median age: 39.8 (2010); Males per 100 females: 218.8 (2010); Marriage status: 24.5% never married, 56.6% now married, 5.8% widowed, 13.1% divorced (2006-2010 5-year est.); Foreign born: 1.5% (2006-2010 5-year est.); Ancestry (includes multiple ancestries): 21.9% German, 10.0% Irish, 9.9% American, 7.1% English, 5.7% Italian (2006-2010 5-year est.).

Economy: Single-family building permits issued: 2 (2011); Multi-family building permits issued: 0 (2011); Employment by occupation: 10.3% management, 6.9% professional, 9.1% services, 19.5% sales, 5.2% farming, 7.9% construction, 6.7% production (2006-2010 5-year est.).

Income: Per capita income: $24,092 (2006-2010 5-year est.); Median household income: $54,566 (2006-2010 5-year est.); Average household income: $74,282 (2006-2010 5-year est.); Percent of households with income of $100,000 or more: 21.4% (2006-2010 5-year est.); Poverty rate: 5.4% (2006-2010 5-year est.).

Education: Percent of population age 25 and over with: High school diploma (including GED) or higher: 87.7% (2006-2010 5-year est.); Bachelor's degree or higher: 18.6% (2006-2010 5-year est.); Master's degree or higher: 9.0% (2006-2010 5-year est.).

Housing: Homeownership rate: 89.2% (2010); Median home value: $154,300 (2006-2010 5-year est.); Median contract rent: $490 per month (2006-2010 5-year est.); Median year structure built: 1983 (2006-2010 5-year est.).

Transportation: Commute to work: 92.7% car, 0.4% public transportation, 1.9% walk, 5.0% work from home (2006-2010 5-year est.); Travel time to work: 33.6% less than 15 minutes, 57.7% 15 to 30 minutes, 6.3% 30 to 45 minutes, 0.9% 45 to 60 minutes, 1.6% 60 minutes or more (2006-2010 5-year est.)

Additional Information Contacts

Bellefonte Intervalley Area Chamber of Commerce . . . . . . (814) 355-2917
   http://bellefontechamber.org/site/default.aspx?PageID=1
Benner Township . . . . (814) 355-1419
   http://benner.centreconnect.org

BLANCHARD (CDP). Covers a land area of 1.219 square miles and a water area of 0 square miles. Located at 41.07° N. Lat; 77.61° W. Long. Elevation is 673 feet.

Population: 609 (1990); 621 (2000); 740 (2010); Density: 607.1 persons per square mile (2010); Race: 97.6% White, 0.0% Black, 0.3% Asian, 1.1% American Indian/Alaska Native, 0.0% Native Hawaiian/Other Pacific Islander, 1.0% Other, 0.4% Hispanic of any race (2010); Average household size: 2.53 (2010); Median age: 40.1 (2010); Males per 100 females: 99.5 (2010); Marriage status: 21.6% never married, 68.5% now married, 5.0% widowed, 5.0% divorced (2006-2010 5-year est.); Foreign born: 0.0% (2006-2010 5-year est.); Ancestry (includes multiple ancestries): 39.9% German, 19.3% Irish, 8.9% Dutch, 3.2% European, 3.0% Pennsylvania German (2006-2010 5-year est.).

Economy: Employment by occupation: 10.6% management, 5.5% professional, 12.2% services, 16.1% sales, 0.0% farming, 10.0% construction, 11.3% production (2006-2010 5-year est.).

Income: Per capita income: $19,064 (2006-2010 5-year est.); Median household income: $33,906 (2006-2010 5-year est.); Average household income: $49,497 (2006-2010 5-year est.); Percent of households with income of $100,000 or more: 10.9% (2006-2010 5-year est.); Poverty rate: 14.6% (2006-2010 5-year est.).

Education: Percent of population age 25 and over with: High school diploma (including GED) or higher: 86.2% (2006-2010 5-year est.); Bachelor's degree or higher: 14.7% (2006-2010 5-year est.); Master's degree or higher: 2.5% (2006-2010 5-year est.).

School District(s)

Keystone Central SD (KG-12)
   2010-11 Enrollment: 4,394 . . . . (570) 893-4900

Housing: Homeownership rate: 84.7% (2010); Median home value: $107,100 (2006-2010 5-year est.); Median contract rent: $272 per month (2006-2010 5-year est.); Median year structure built: 1973 (2006-2010 5-year est.).

Transportation: Commute to work: 96.7% car, 0.0% public pennsportation, 1.7% walk, 1.7% work from home (2006-2010 5-year est.); Travel time to work: 16.2% less than 15 minutes, 55.4% 15 to 30 minutes, 19.9% 30 to

45 minutes, 7.4% 45 to 60 minutes, 1.0% 60 minutes or more (2006-2010 5-year est.)

BOALSBURG (CDP).

Covers a land area of 5.794 square miles and a water area of 0 square miles. Located at 40.78° N. Lat; 77.77° W. Long. Elevation is 1,106 feet.

History: Columbus Chapel; Boal Mansion and Museum, Pennsylvania Military Museum. Was important stagecoach stop. Laid out 1810. Birthplace of Memorial Day.

Population: 3,384 (1990); 3,578 (2000); 3,722 (2010); Density: 642.4 persons per square mile (2010); Race: 93.5% White, 2.2% Black, 2.0% Asian, 0.1% American Indian/Alaska Native, 0.0% Native Hawaiian/Other Pacific Islander, 2.2% Other, 1.6% Hispanic of any race (2010); Average household size: 2.44 (2010); Median age: 42.8 (2010); Males per 100 females: 91.9 (2010); Marriage status: 21.3% never married, 65.3% now married, 5.3% widowed, 8.1% divorced (2006-2010 5-year est.); Foreign born: 9.5% (2006-2010 5-year est.); Ancestry (includes multiple ancestries): 23.8% German, 14.8% English, 11.0% Irish, 10.3% Italian, 9.9% American (2006-2010 5-year est.).

Economy: Employment by occupation: 14.0% management, 7.1% professional, 7.7% services, 13.8% sales, 3.0% farming, 7.6% construction, 4.6% production (2006-2010 5-year est.).

Income: Per capita income: $32,676 (2006-2010 5-year est.); Median household income: $62,289 (2006-2010 5-year est.); Average household income: $89,240 (2006-2010 5-year est.); Percent of households with income of $100,000 or more: 22.7% (2006-2010 5-year est.); Poverty rate: 6.0% (2006-2010 5-year est.).

Education: Percent of population age 25 and over with: High school diploma (including GED) or higher: 97.7% (2006-2010 5-year est.); Bachelor's degree or higher: 52.6% (2006-2010 5-year est.); Master's degree or higher: 27.1% (2006-2010 5-year est.).

Housing: Homeownership rate: 72.0% (2010); Median home value: $206,000 (2006-2010 5-year est.); Median contract rent: $710 per month (2006-2010 5-year est.); Median year structure built: 1971 (2006-2010 5-year est.).

Transportation: Commute to work: 93.8% car, 1.3% public transportation, 0.0% walk, 4.2% work from home (2006-2010 5-year est.); Travel time to work: 50.0% less than 15 minutes, 42.9% 15 to 30 minutes, 4.2% 30 to 45 minutes, 2.3% 45 to 60 minutes, 0.6% 60 minutes or more (2006-2010 5-year est.)

Additional Information Contacts
Chamber of Business & Industry of Centre County . . . . (814) 234-1829
    http://www.cbicc.org

BOGGS (township).

Covers a land area of 51.465 square miles and a water area of 0.153 square miles. Located at 40.99° N. Lat; 77.80° W. Long.

Population: 2,525 (1990); 2,834 (2000); 2,985 (2010); Density: 58.0 persons per square mile (2010); Race: 98.4% White, 0.2% Black, 0.1% Asian, 0.2% American Indian/Alaska Native, 0.0% Native Hawaiian/Other Pacific Islander, 1.1% Other, 0.8% Hispanic of any race (2010); Average household size: 2.49 (2010); Median age: 42.8 (2010); Males per 100 females: 101.3 (2010); Marriage status: 24.7% never married, 60.1% now married, 5.3% widowed, 9.9% divorced (2006-2010 5-year est.); Foreign born: 2.7% (2006-2010 5-year est.); Ancestry (includes multiple ancestries): 35.9% German, 15.3% American, 11.6% English, 10.7% Irish, 7.6% Dutch (2006-2010 5-year est.).

Economy: Single-family building permits issued: 3 (2011); Multi-family building permits issued: 0 (2011); Employment by occupation: 5.9% management, 2.4% professional, 13.5% services, 18.4% sales, 4.2% farming, 13.9% construction, 7.8% production (2006-2010 5-year est.).

Income: Per capita income: $21,024 (2006-2010 5-year est.); Median household income: $41,746 (2006-2010 5-year est.); Average household income: $52,214 (2006-2010 5-year est.); Percent of households with income of $100,000 or more: 8.8% (2006-2010 5-year est.); Poverty rate: 8.6% (2006-2010 5-year est.).

Education: Percent of population age 25 and over with: High school diploma (including GED) or higher: 91.2% (2006-2010 5-year est.); Bachelor's degree or higher: 11.5% (2006-2010 5-year est.); Master's degree or higher: 4.2% (2006-2010 5-year est.).

Housing: Homeownership rate: 79.4% (2010); Median home value: $123,100 (2006-2010 5-year est.); Median contract rent: $478 per month (2006-2010 5-year est.); Median year structure built: 1978 (2006-2010 5-year est.).

Transportation: Commute to work: 95.6% car, 0.0% public transportation, 0.8% walk, 3.5% work from home (2006-2010 5-year est.); Travel time to work: 25.3% less than 15 minutes, 40.7% 15 to 30 minutes, 28.5% 30 to 45 minutes, 3.5% 45 to 60 minutes, 2.0% 60 minutes or more (2006-2010 5-year est.)

Additional Information Contacts
Bellefonte Intervalley Area Chamber of Commerce . . . . . . (814) 355-2917
    http://bellefontechamber.org/site/default.aspx?PageID=1
Boggs Township . . . . (814) 355-3301
    http://www.boggstownship.org

BURNSIDE (township).

Covers a land area of 89.631 square miles and a water area of 0.783 square miles. Located at 41.15° N. Lat; 77.97° W. Long.

Population: 390 (1990); 410 (2000); 439 (2010); Density: 4.9 persons per square mile (2010); Race: 97.3% White, 0.2% Black, 0.2% Asian, 0.0% American Indian/Alaska Native, 0.0% Native Hawaiian/Other Pacific Islander, 2.3% Other, 3.6% Hispanic of any race (2010); Average household size: 2.54 (2010); Median age: 42.2 (2010); Males per 100 females: 119.5 (2010); Marriage status: 22.1% never married, 61.2% now married, 4.7% widowed, 11.9% divorced (2006-2010 5-year est.); Foreign born: 0.0% (2006-2010 5-year est.); Ancestry (includes multiple ancestries): 28.0% German, 11.2% Dutch, 9.3% Slovak, 8.5% Irish, 7.3% American (2006-2010 5-year est.).

Economy: Single-family building permits issued: 0 (2011); Multi-family building permits issued: 0 (2011); Employment by occupation: 9.2% management, 6.4% professional, 2.8% services, 17.0% sales, 4.1% farming, 15.1% construction, 11.9% production (2006-2010 5-year est.).

Income: Per capita income: $21,011 (2006-2010 5-year est.); Median household income: $52,625 (2006-2010 5-year est.); Average household income: $55,350 (2006-2010 5-year est.); Percent of households with income of $100,000 or more: 10.3% (2006-2010 5-year est.); Poverty rate: 12.4% (2006-2010 5-year est.).

Education: Percent of population age 25 and over with: High school diploma (including GED) or higher: 83.0% (2006-2010 5-year est.); Bachelor's degree or higher: 3.2% (2006-2010 5-year est.); Master's degree or higher: 2.0% (2006-2010 5-year est.).

Housing: Homeownership rate: 93.6% (2010); Median home value: $113,300 (2006-2010 5-year est.); Median contract rent: $580 per month (2006-2010 5-year est.); Median year structure built: 1967 (2006-2010 5-year est.).

Transportation: Commute to work: 94.1% car, 5.9% public transportation, 0.0% walk, 0.0% work from home (2006-2010 5-year est.); Travel time to work: 14.0% less than 15 minutes, 21.2% 15 to 30 minutes, 32.0% 30 to 45 minutes, 30.6% 45 to 60 minutes, 2.3% 60 minutes or more (2006-2010 5-year est.)

CENTRE HALL (borough).

Covers a land area of 0.622 square miles and a water area of 0 square miles. Located at 40.84° N. Lat; 77.69° W. Long. Elevation is 1,325 feet.

Population: 1,203 (1990); 1,079 (2000); 1,265 (2010); Density: 2,033.7 persons per square mile (2010); Race: 99.0% White, 0.1% Black, 0.3% Asian, 0.1% American Indian/Alaska Native, 0.0% Native Hawaiian/Other Pacific Islander, 0.5% Other, 0.6% Hispanic of any race (2010); Average household size: 2.31 (2010); Median age: 42.5 (2010); Males per 100 females: 88.2 (2010); Marriage status: 17.6% never married, 68.0% now married, 5.0% widowed, 9.4% divorced (2006-2010 5-year est.); Foreign born: 0.0% (2006-2010 5-year est.); Ancestry (includes multiple ancestries): 38.4% German, 16.1% Irish, 12.5% American, 6.7% Italian, 6.5% English (2006-2010 5-year est.).

Economy: Single-family building permits issued: 0 (2011); Multi-family building permits issued: 0 (2011); Employment by occupation: 14.1% management, 3.6% professional, 8.6% services, 18.7% sales, 2.5% farming, 9.8% construction, 6.1% production (2006-2010 5-year est.).

Income: Per capita income: $25,298 (2006-2010 5-year est.); Median household income: $50,556 (2006-2010 5-year est.); Average household income: $59,136 (2006-2010 5-year est.); Percent of households with income of $100,000 or more: 8.8% (2006-2010 5-year est.); Poverty rate: 6.0% (2006-2010 5-year est.).

Education: Percent of population age 25 and over with: High school diploma (including GED) or higher: 92.1% (2006-2010 5-year est.); Bachelor's degree or higher: 24.0% (2006-2010 5-year est.); Master's degree or higher: 3.4% (2006-2010 5-year est.).

School District(s)

Penns Valley Area SD (KG-12)

  2010-11 Enrollment: 1,459 . . . . (814) 422-2000

Housing: Homeownership rate: 70.8% (2010); Median home value: $164,000 (2006-2010 5-year est.); Median contract rent: $583 per month (2006-2010 5-year est.); Median year structure built: 1955 (2006-2010 5-year est.).

Hospitals: Meadows Psychiatric Center (101 beds)

Transportation: Commute to work: 91.2% car, 0.0% public transportation, 1.8% walk, 6.0% work from home (2006-2010 5-year est.); Travel time to work: 22.8% less than 15 minutes, 49.0% 15 to 30 minutes, 19.8% 30 to 45 minutes, 3.4% 45 to 60 minutes, 5.0% 60 minutes or more (2006-2010 5-year est.)

CLARENCE (CDP). Covers a land area of 1.648 square miles and a water area of 0 square miles. Located at 41.05° N. Lat; 77.95° W. Long. Elevation is 1,401 feet.

Population: 599 (1990); 577 (2000); 626 (2010); Density: 379.8 persons per square mile (2010); Race: 99.7% White, 0.0% Black, 0.0% Asian, 0.3% American Indian/Alaska Native, 0.0% Native Hawaiian/Other Pacific Islander, 0.0% Other, 0.3% Hispanic of any race (2010); Average household size: 2.50 (2010); Median age: 41.0 (2010); Males per 100 females: 103.9 (2010); Marriage status: 24.1% never married, 61.8% now married, 9.8% widowed, 4.2% divorced (2006-2010 5-year est.); Foreign born: 0.3% (2006-2010 5-year est.); Ancestry (includes multiple ancestries): 19.0% Slovak, 14.6% German, 14.2% Polish, 10.5% Dutch, 9.7% Irish (2006-2010 5-year est.).

Economy: Employment by occupation: 2.6% management, 4.6% professional, 14.9% services, 11.6% sales, 7.9% farming, 13.5% construction, 7.3% production (2006-2010 5-year est.).

Income: Per capita income: $21,122 (2006-2010 5-year est.); Median household income: $55,125 (2006-2010 5-year est.); Average household income: $53,370 (2006-2010 5-year est.); Percent of households with income of $100,000 or more: 3.8% (2006-2010 5-year est.); Poverty rate: 4.1% (2006-2010 5-year est.).

Education: Percent of population age 25 and over with: High school diploma (including GED) or higher: 78.5% (2006-2010 5-year est.); Bachelor's degree or higher: 4.6% (2006-2010 5-year est.); Master's degree or higher: 1.1% (2006-2010 5-year est.).

Housing: Homeownership rate: 91.6% (2010); Median home value: $95,200 (2006-2010 5-year est.); Median contract rent: $325 per month (2006-2010 5-year est.); Median year structure built: 1961 (2006-2010 5-year est.).

Transportation: Commute to work: 96.0% car, 0.0% public transportation, 1.0% walk, 1.7% work from home (2006-2010 5-year est.); Travel time to work: 24.3% less than 15 minutes, 17.5% 15 to 30 minutes, 37.3% 30 to 45 minutes, 5.8% 45 to 60 minutes, 15.1% 60 minutes or more (2006-2010 5-year est.)

COBURN (CDP). Covers a land area of 0.381 square miles and a water area of 0 square miles. Located at 40.87° N. Lat; 77.46° W. Long. Elevation is 1,037 feet.

Population: 130 (1990); 145 (2000); 236 (2010); Density: 619.8 persons per square mile (2010); Race: 97.9% White, 0.8% Black, 0.0% Asian, 0.0% American Indian/Alaska Native, 0.0% Native Hawaiian/Other Pacific Islander, 1.3% Other, 1.7% Hispanic of any race (2010); Average household size: 2.81 (2010); Median age: 35.0 (2010); Males per 100 females: 91.9 (2010); Marriage status: 47.9% never married, 47.9% now married, 4.3% widowed, 0.0% divorced (2006-2010 5-year est.); Foreign born: 0.0% (2006-2010 5-year est.); Ancestry (includes multiple ancestries): 41.4% German, 40.5% Irish, 15.5% English, 13.8% American, 12.9% French (2006-2010 5-year est.).

Economy: Employment by occupation: 19.6% management, 0.0% professional, 6.5% services, 6.5% sales, 23.9% farming, 15.2% construction, 13.0% production (2006-2010 5-year est.).

Income: Per capita income: $15,747 (2006-2010 5-year est.); Median household income: $51,667 (2006-2010 5-year est.); Average household income: $53,079 (2006-2010 5-year est.); Percent of households with income of $100,000 or more: 8.8% (2006-2010 5-year est.); Poverty rate: 32.8% (2006-2010 5-year est.).

Education: Percent of population age 25 and over with: High school diploma (including GED) or higher: 77.6% (2006-2010 5-year est.); Bachelor's degree or higher: 24.5% (2006-2010 5-year est.); Master's degree or higher: 6.1% (2006-2010 5-year est.).

Housing: Homeownership rate: 80.9% (2010); Median home value: $155,400 (2006-2010 5-year est.); Median contract rent: n/a per month (2006-2010 5-year est.); Median year structure built: before 1940 (2006-2010 5-year est.).

Transportation: Commute to work: 93.5% car, 0.0% public transportation, 6.5% walk, 0.0% work from home (2006-2010 5-year est.); Travel time to work: 13.0% less than 15 minutes, 0.0% 15 to 30 minutes, 28.3% 30 to 45 minutes, 58.7% 45 to 60 minutes, 0.0% 60 minutes or more (2006-2010 5-year est.)

COLLEGE (township). Covers a land area of 18.563 square miles and a water area of 0 square miles. Located at 40.81° N. Lat; 77.82° W. Long.

Population: 6,720 (1990); 8,489 (2000); 9,521 (2010); Density: 512.9 persons per square mile (2010); Race: 91.6% White, 2.4% Black, 3.4% Asian, 0.2% American Indian/Alaska Native, 0.1% Native Hawaiian/Other Pacific Islander, 2.3% Other, 2.4% Hispanic of any race (2010); Average household size: 2.30 (2010); Median age: 38.7 (2010); Males per 100 females: 96.8 (2010); Marriage status: 26.3% never married, 58.6% now married, 7.4% widowed, 7.7% divorced (2006-2010 5-year est.); Foreign born: 5.1% (2006-2010 5-year est.); Ancestry (includes multiple ancestries): 31.0% German, 14.4% English, 9.6% Irish, 8.7% American, 7.5% Italian (2006-2010 5-year est.).

Economy: Single-family building permits issued: 5 (2011); Multi-family building permits issued: 0 (2011); Employment by occupation: 16.9% management, 11.6% professional, 4.6% services, 11.7% sales, 3.3% farming, 4.0% construction, 4.4% production (2006-2010 5-year est.).

Income: Per capita income: $38,356 (2006-2010 5-year est.); Median household income: $73,977 (2006-2010 5-year est.); Average household income: $88,760 (2006-2010 5-year est.); Percent of households with income of $100,000 or more: 33.3% (2006-2010 5-year est.); Poverty rate: 6.6% (2006-2010 5-year est.).

Education: Percent of population age 25 and over with: High school diploma (including GED) or higher: 95.3% (2006-2010 5-year est.); Bachelor's degree or higher: 55.5% (2006-2010 5-year est.); Master's degree or higher: 26.8% (2006-2010 5-year est.).

Housing: Homeownership rate: 75.7% (2010); Median home value: $223,400 (2006-2010 5-year est.); Median contract rent: $623 per month (2006-2010 5-year est.); Median year structure built: 1984 (2006-2010 5-year est.).

Transportation: Commute to work: 86.4% car, 1.9% public transportation, 1.6% walk, 5.3% work from home (2006-2010 5-year est.); Travel time to work: 63.3% less than 15 minutes, 27.5% 15 to 30 minutes, 6.2% 30 to 45 minutes, 1.8% 45 to 60 minutes, 1.3% 60 minutes or more (2006-2010 5-year est.)

Additional Information Contacts

Chamber of Business & Industry of Centre County . . . . (814) 234-1829

  http://www.cbicc.org

College Township . . . . (814) 231-3021

  http://www.collegetownship.govoffice.com

CURTIN (township). Covers a land area of 43.280 square miles and a water area of 0 square miles. Located at 41.10° N. Lat; 77.77° W. Long. Elevation is 682 feet.

Population: 516 (1990); 551 (2000); 618 (2010); Density: 14.3 persons per square mile (2010); Race: 98.4% White, 0.6% Black, 0.2% Asian, 0.3% American Indian/Alaska Native, 0.0% Native Hawaiian/Other Pacific Islander, 0.5% Other, 0.3% Hispanic of any race (2010); Average household size: 2.45 (2010); Median age: 45.8 (2010); Males per 100 females: 113.1 (2010); Marriage status: 22.0% never married, 67.0% now married, 3.3% widowed, 7.7% divorced (2006-2010 5-year est.); Foreign born: 0.0% (2006-2010 5-year est.); Ancestry (includes multiple ancestries): 34.0% German, 17.4% American, 11.2% Scotch-Irish, 8.9% Dutch West Indian, 7.5% English (2006-2010 5-year est.).

Economy: Single-family building permits issued: 0 (2011); Multi-family building permits issued: 0 (2011); Employment by occupation: 4.7% management, 1.0% professional, 10.8% services, 19.9% sales, 3.7% farming, 13.9% construction, 5.4% production (2006-2010 5-year est.).

Income: Per capita income: $18,218 (2006-2010 5-year est.); Median household income: $41,188 (2006-2010 5-year est.); Average household income: $50,514 (2006-2010 5-year est.); Percent of households with income of $100,000 or more: 6.0% (2006-2010 5-year est.); Poverty rate: 7.9% (2006-2010 5-year est.).

Education: Percent of population age 25 and over with: High school diploma (including GED) or higher: 82.8% (2006-2010 5-year est.);

Bachelor's degree or higher: 12.5% (2006-2010 5-year est.); Master's degree or higher: 5.7% (2006-2010 5-year est.).
Housing: Homeownership rate: 86.1% (2010); Median home value: $105,400 (2006-2010 5-year est.); Median contract rent: $417 per month (2006-2010 5-year est.); Median year structure built: 1974 (2006-2010 5-year est.).
Transportation: Commute to work: 98.6% car, 0.0% public transportation, 0.0% walk, 1.4% work from home (2006-2010 5-year est.); Travel time to work: 10.6% less than 15 minutes, 28.8% 15 to 30 minutes, 38.0% 30 to 45 minutes, 15.4% 45 to 60 minutes, 7.2% 60 minutes or more (2006-2010 5-year est.)

EAGLEVILLE (CDP). Covers a land area of 0.945 square miles and a water area of 0 square miles. Located at 41.06° N. Lat; 77.59° W. Long. Elevation is 656 feet.
Population: n/a (1990); n/a (2000); 324 (2010); Density: 342.8 persons per square mile (2010); Race: 99.4% White, 0.0% Black, 0.0% Asian, 0.0% American Indian/Alaska Native, 0.0% Native Hawaiian/Other Pacific Islander, 0.6% Other, 1.5% Hispanic of any race (2010); Average household size: 2.55 (2010); Median age: 38.3 (2010); Males per 100 females: 109.0 (2010); Marriage status: 24.0% never married, 70.1% now married, 6.0% widowed, 0.0% divorced (2006-2010 5-year est.); Foreign born: 8.8% (2006-2010 5-year est.); Ancestry (includes multiple ancestries): 37.4% German, 13.0% Yugoslavian, 7.6% Slovak, 6.7% Canadian, 4.6% Irish (2006-2010 5-year est.).
Economy: Employment by occupation: 5.6% management, 0.0% professional, 5.6% services, 18.0% sales, 0.0% farming, 5.6% construction, 4.5% production (2006-2010 5-year est.).
Income: Per capita income: $20,219 (2006-2010 5-year est.); Median household income: $78,173 (2006-2010 5-year est.); Average household income: $68,790 (2006-2010 5-year est.); Percent of households with income of $100,000 or more: 7.5% (2006-2010 5-year est.); Poverty rate: 6.7% (2006-2010 5-year est.).
Education: Percent of population age 25 and over with: High school diploma (including GED) or higher: 70.1% (2006-2010 5-year est.); Bachelor's degree or higher: 19.7% (2006-2010 5-year est.); Master's degree or higher: 0.0% (2006-2010 5-year est.).
Housing: Homeownership rate: 90.6% (2010); Median home value: $134,800 (2006-2010 5-year est.); Median contract rent: n/a per month (2006-2010 5-year est.); Median year structure built: 1994 (2006-2010 5-year est.).
Transportation: Commute to work: 93.7% car, 0.0% public transportation, 6.3% walk, 0.0% work from home (2006-2010 5-year est.); Travel time to work: 13.9% less than 15 minutes, 65.8% 15 to 30 minutes, 7.6% 30 to 45 minutes, 0.0% 45 to 60 minutes, 12.7% 60 minutes or more (2006-2010 5-year est.)

FERGUSON (township). Covers a land area of 47.651 square miles and a water area of 0.005 square miles. Located at 40.74° N. Lat; 77.94° W. Long.
Population: 9,347 (1990); 14,063 (2000); 17,690 (2010); Density: 371.2 persons per square mile (2010); Race: 82.0% White, 3.2% Black, 11.4% Asian, 0.1% American Indian/Alaska Native, 0.0% Native Hawaiian/Other Pacific Islander, 3.3% Other, 3.0% Hispanic of any race (2010); Average household size: 2.45 (2010); Median age: 32.7 (2010); Males per 100 females: 102.8 (2010); Marriage status: 34.7% never married, 55.0% now married, 3.2% widowed, 7.2% divorced (2006-2010 5-year est.); Foreign born: 13.8% (2006-2010 5-year est.); Ancestry (includes multiple ancestries): 30.2% German, 14.0% Irish, 9.9% English, 9.5% Italian, 5.3% Polish (2006-2010 5-year est.).
Economy: Single-family building permits issued: 33 (2011); Multi-family building permits issued: 0 (2011); Employment by occupation: 10.2% management, 8.0% professional, 8.5% services, 14.7% sales, 2.0% farming, 4.6% construction, 3.4% production (2006-2010 5-year est.).
Income: Per capita income: $31,016 (2006-2010 5-year est.); Median household income: $57,459 (2006-2010 5-year est.); Average household income: $75,990 (2006-2010 5-year est.); Percent of households with income of $100,000 or more: 23.9% (2006-2010 5-year est.); Poverty rate: 15.6% (2006-2010 5-year est.).
Education: Percent of population age 25 and over with: High school diploma (including GED) or higher: 97.1% (2006-2010 5-year est.); Bachelor's degree or higher: 63.4% (2006-2010 5-year est.); Master's degree or higher: 33.1% (2006-2010 5-year est.).
Housing: Homeownership rate: 59.0% (2010); Median home value: $226,500 (2006-2010 5-year est.); Median contract rent: $743 per month

(2006-2010 5-year est.); Median year structure built: 1983 (2006-2010 5-year est.).
Safety: Violent crime rate: 7.3 per 10,000 population; Property crime rate: 102.6 per 10,000 population (2011).
Transportation: Commute to work: 75.7% car, 5.5% public transportation, 4.6% walk, 5.3% work from home (2006-2010 5-year est.); Travel time to work: 50.3% less than 15 minutes, 41.8% 15 to 30 minutes, 4.3% 30 to 45 minutes, 2.6% 45 to 60 minutes, 1.0% 60 minutes or more (2006-2010 5-year est.)
Additional Information Contacts
Chamber of Business & Industry of Centre County . . . . (814) 234-1829
    http://www.cbicc.org
Ferguson Township. . . . . (814) 238-4651
    http://www.twp.ferguson.pa.us

FLEMING (unincorporated postal area)
Zip Code: 16835
    Covers a land area of 0.166 square miles and a water area of 0 square miles. Located at 40.90° N. Lat; 77.87° W. Long. Population: 238 (2010); Density: 1,426.6 persons per square mile (2010); Race: 97.9% White, 0.4% Black, 0.4% Asian, 0.0% American Indian/Alaska Native, 0.0% Native Hawaiian/Other Pacific Islander, 1.3% Other, 0.8% Hispanic of any race (2010); Average household size: 2.33 (2010); Median age: 42.6 (2010); Males per 100 females: 87.4 (2010); Homeownership rate: 76.5% (2010)

GREGG (township). Covers a land area of 46.753 square miles and a water area of 0.009 square miles. Located at 40.87° N. Lat; 77.57° W. Long.
Population: 1,805 (1990); 2,119 (2000); 2,405 (2010); Density: 51.4 persons per square mile (2010); Race: 97.8% White, 0.2% Black, 0.5% Asian, 0.1% American Indian/Alaska Native, 0.0% Native Hawaiian/Other Pacific Islander, 1.4% Other, 1.2% Hispanic of any race (2010); Average household size: 2.53 (2010); Median age: 42.4 (2010); Males per 100 females: 100.2 (2010); Marriage status: 23.3% never married, 65.9% now married, 4.0% widowed, 6.8% divorced (2006-2010 5-year est.); Foreign born: 0.5% (2006-2010 5-year est.); Ancestry (includes multiple ancestries): 37.6% German, 9.6% American, 6.2% English, 5.3% Irish, 4.9% Dutch (2006-2010 5-year est.).
Economy: Single-family building permits issued: 5 (2011); Multi-family building permits issued: 0 (2011); Employment by occupation: 11.5% management, 1.7% professional, 12.8% services, 11.7% sales, 1.6% farming, 13.3% construction, 9.3% production (2006-2010 5-year est.).
Income: Per capita income: $21,167 (2006-2010 5-year est.); Median household income: $49,792 (2006-2010 5-year est.); Average household income: $58,393 (2006-2010 5-year est.); Percent of households with income of $100,000 or more: 12.6% (2006-2010 5-year est.); Poverty rate: 9.3% (2006-2010 5-year est.).
Education: Percent of population age 25 and over with: High school diploma (including GED) or higher: 93.2% (2006-2010 5-year est.); Bachelor's degree or higher: 23.9% (2006-2010 5-year est.); Master's degree or higher: 6.1% (2006-2010 5-year est.).
Housing: Homeownership rate: 78.3% (2010); Median home value: $168,700 (2006-2010 5-year est.); Median contract rent: $513 per month (2006-2010 5-year est.); Median year structure built: 1962 (2006-2010 5-year est.).
Transportation: Commute to work: 84.4% car, 0.0% public transportation, 3.0% walk, 8.9% work from home (2006-2010 5-year est.); Travel time to work: 23.6% less than 15 minutes, 32.1% 15 to 30 minutes, 39.4% 30 to 45 minutes, 0.6% 45 to 60 minutes, 4.2% 60 minutes or more (2006-2010 5-year est.)
Additional Information Contacts
Bellefonte Intervalley Area Chamber of Commerce . . . . . . (814) 355-2917
    http://bellefontechamber.org/site/default.aspx?PageID=1

HAINES (township). Covers a land area of 57.384 square miles and a water area of 0 square miles. Located at 40.90° N. Lat; 77.36° W. Long.
Population: 1,315 (1990); 1,479 (2000); 1,564 (2010); Density: 27.3 persons per square mile (2010); Race: 99.4% White, 0.2% Black, 0.1% Asian, 0.1% American Indian/Alaska Native, 0.1% Native Hawaiian/Other Pacific Islander, 0.1% Other, 0.3% Hispanic of any race (2010); Average household size: 2.75 (2010); Median age: 36.9 (2010); Males per 100 females: 104.2 (2010); Marriage status: 29.2% never married, 53.6% now married, 5.1% widowed, 12.1% divorced (2006-2010 5-year est.); Foreign born: 0.0% (2006-2010 5-year est.); Ancestry (includes multiple

ancestries): 37.1% German, 5.0% Irish, 4.5% Dutch, 3.3% Italian, 3.2% English (2006-2010 5-year est.).

Economy: Single-family building permits issued: 6 (2011); Multi-family building permits issued: 0 (2011); Employment by occupation: 6.1% management, 5.2% professional, 17.0% services, 16.2% sales, 4.6% farming, 13.8% construction, 5.2% production (2006-2010 5-year est.).

Income: Per capita income: $18,157 (2006-2010 5-year est.); Median household income: $44,643 (2006-2010 5-year est.); Average household income: $49,679 (2006-2010 5-year est.); Percent of households with income of $100,000 or more: 9.4% (2006-2010 5-year est.); Poverty rate: 17.5% (2006-2010 5-year est.).

Education: Percent of population age 25 and over with: High school diploma (including GED) or higher: 81.6% (2006-2010 5-year est.); Bachelor's degree or higher: 13.6% (2006-2010 5-year est.); Master's degree or higher: 5.1% (2006-2010 5-year est.).

Housing: Homeownership rate: 85.5% (2010); Median home value: $152,200 (2006-2010 5-year est.); Median contract rent: $540 per month (2006-2010 5-year est.); Median year structure built: 1970 (2006-2010 5-year est.).

Transportation: Commute to work: 82.0% car, 0.0% public transportation, 1.8% walk, 12.8% work from home (2006-2010 5-year est.); Travel time to work: 25.6% less than 15 minutes, 20.5% 15 to 30 minutes, 34.8% 30 to 45 minutes, 13.8% 45 to 60 minutes, 5.3% 60 minutes or more (2006-2010 5-year est.).

Additional Information Contacts
Clinton County Economic Partnership/Clinton County Chamber o . . . (570) 748-5782
   http://www.clintoncountyinfo.com

HALFMOON (township). Covers a land area of 23.596 square miles and a water area of 0 square miles. Located at 40.77° N. Lat; 78.02° W. Long.

Population: 1,469 (1990); 2,357 (2000); 2,667 (2010); Density: 113.0 persons per square mile (2010); Race: 97.3% White, 0.5% Black, 0.8% Asian, 0.0% American Indian/Alaska Native, 0.0% Native Hawaiian/Other Pacific Islander, 1.4% Other, 1.1% Hispanic of any race (2010); Average household size: 2.92 (2010); Median age: 41.0 (2010); Males per 100 females: 104.2 (2010); Marriage status: 17.7% never married, 75.5% now married, 2.3% widowed, 4.5% divorced (2006-2010 5-year est.); Foreign born: 1.5% (2006-2010 5-year est.); Ancestry (includes multiple ancestries): 37.1% German, 16.9% Irish, 10.9% English, 9.3% Polish, 7.1% American (2006-2010 5-year est.).

Economy: Single-family building permits issued: 1 (2011); Multi-family building permits issued: 0 (2011); Employment by occupation: 13.6% management, 12.0% professional, 6.9% services, 14.2% sales, 2.8% farming, 4.7% construction, 3.6% production (2006-2010 5-year est.).

Income: Per capita income: $36,018 (2006-2010 5-year est.); Median household income: $98,911 (2006-2010 5-year est.); Average household income: $107,294 (2006-2010 5-year est.); Percent of households with income of $100,000 or more: 48.5% (2006-2010 5-year est.); Poverty rate: 3.9% (2006-2010 5-year est.).

Education: Percent of population age 25 and over with: High school diploma (including GED) or higher: 99.2% (2006-2010 5-year est.); Bachelor's degree or higher: 50.8% (2006-2010 5-year est.); Master's degree or higher: 19.2% (2006-2010 5-year est.).

Housing: Homeownership rate: 91.9% (2010); Median home value: $236,500 (2006-2010 5-year est.); Median contract rent: $425 per month (2006-2010 5-year est.); Median year structure built: 1988 (2006-2010 5-year est.).

Transportation: Commute to work: 92.8% car, 0.0% public transportation, 0.4% walk, 6.3% work from home (2006-2010 5-year est.); Travel time to work: 8.3% less than 15 minutes, 70.5% 15 to 30 minutes, 13.4% 30 to 45 minutes, 2.3% 45 to 60 minutes, 5.5% 60 minutes or more (2006-2010 5-year est.).

Additional Information Contacts
Chamber of Business & Industry of Centre County . . . . (814) 234-1829
   http://www.cbicc.org

HARRIS (township). Covers a land area of 31.208 square miles and a water area of 0.002 square miles. Located at 40.77° N. Lat; 77.77° W. Long.

History: The Birthplace of Memorial Day.

Population: 4,167 (1990); 4,657 (2000); 4,873 (2010); Density: 156.1 persons per square mile (2010); Race: 94.2% White, 1.9% Black, 1.9% Asian, 0.1% American Indian/Alaska Native, 0.0% Native Hawaiian/Other

Pacific Islander, 1.9% Other, 1.7% Hispanic of any race (2010); Average household size: 2.45 (2010); Median age: 44.8 (2010); Males per 100 females: 95.0 (2010); Marriage status: 22.6% never married, 65.4% now married, 4.7% widowed, 7.4% divorced (2006-2010 5-year est.); Foreign born: 8.9% (2006-2010 5-year est.); Ancestry (includes multiple ancestries): 25.2% German, 15.3% English, 10.1% Irish, 10.1% Italian, 7.9% American (2006-2010 5-year est.).

Economy: Single-family building permits issued: 48 (2011); Multi-family building permits issued: 0 (2011); Employment by occupation: 14.9% management, 8.4% professional, 7.2% services, 13.7% sales, 4.0% farming, 7.0% construction, 4.7% production (2006-2010 5-year est.).

Income: Per capita income: $37,835 (2006-2010 5-year est.); Median household income: $68,920 (2006-2010 5-year est.); Average household income: $101,268 (2006-2010 5-year est.); Percent of households with income of $100,000 or more: 27.4% (2006-2010 5-year est.); Poverty rate: 5.1% (2006-2010 5-year est.).

Education: Percent of population age 25 and over with: High school diploma (including GED) or higher: 97.7% (2006-2010 5-year est.); Bachelor's degree or higher: 53.1% (2006-2010 5-year est.); Master's degree or higher: 25.9% (2006-2010 5-year est.).

Housing: Homeownership rate: 75.9% (2010); Median home value: $226,400 (2006-2010 5-year est.); Median contract rent: $691 per month (2006-2010 5-year est.); Median year structure built: 1972 (2006-2010 5-year est.).

Transportation: Commute to work: 91.4% car, 1.4% public transportation, 1.7% walk, 4.1% work from home (2006-2010 5-year est.); Travel time to work: 52.7% less than 15 minutes, 40.2% 15 to 30 minutes, 4.0% 30 to 45 minutes, 2.2% 45 to 60 minutes, 1.0% 60 minutes or more (2006-2010 5-year est.)

Additional Information Contacts
Chamber of Business & Industry of Centre County . . . . (814) 234-1829
   http://www.cbicc.org
Harris Township . . . . (814) 466-6228
   http://harris.centreconnect.org

HOUSERVILLE (CDP). Covers a land area of 1.095 square miles and a water area of 0 square miles. Located at 40.83° N. Lat; 77.82° W. Long. Elevation is 984 feet.

Population: 1,458 (1990); 1,809 (2000); 1,814 (2010); Density: 1,657.1 persons per square mile (2010); Race: 92.9% White, 1.9% Black, 1.8% Asian, 0.0% American Indian/Alaska Native, 0.1% Native Hawaiian/Other Pacific Islander, 3.3% Other, 1.5% Hispanic of any race (2010); Average household size: 2.47 (2010); Median age: 38.5 (2010); Males per 100 females: 101.3 (2010); Marriage status: 24.3% never married, 59.6% now married, 6.9% widowed, 9.2% divorced (2006-2010 5-year est.); Foreign born: 2.5% (2006-2010 5-year est.); Ancestry (includes multiple ancestries): 38.3% German, 12.5% English, 10.4% Italian, 7.9% American, 7.7% Irish (2006-2010 5-year est.).

Economy: Employment by occupation: 14.1% management, 8.5% professional, 11.0% services, 12.4% sales, 5.8% farming, 2.0% construction, 1.7% production (2006-2010 5-year est.).

Income: Per capita income: $29,246 (2006-2010 5-year est.); Median household income: $57,976 (2006-2010 5-year est.); Average household income: $70,286 (2006-2010 5-year est.); Percent of households with income of $100,000 or more: 19.3% (2006-2010 5-year est.); Poverty rate: 4.3% (2006-2010 5-year est.).

Education: Percent of population age 25 and over with: High school diploma (including GED) or higher: 95.9% (2006-2010 5-year est.); Bachelor's degree or higher: 44.1% (2006-2010 5-year est.); Master's degree or higher: 14.4% (2006-2010 5-year est.).

Housing: Homeownership rate: 84.4% (2010); Median home value: $164,300 (2006-2010 5-year est.); Median contract rent: $881 per month (2006-2010 5-year est.); Median year structure built: 1981 (2006-2010 5-year est.).

Transportation: Commute to work: 89.9% car, 2.4% public transportation, 0.7% walk, 0.8% work from home (2006-2010 5-year est.); Travel time to work: 59.0% less than 15 minutes, 33.9% 15 to 30 minutes, 7.2% 30 to 45 minutes, 0.0% 45 to 60 minutes, 0.0% 60 minutes or more (2006-2010 5-year est.)

Additional Information Contacts
Chamber of Business & Industry of Centre County . . . . (814) 234-1829
   http://www.cbicc.org

HOWARD (borough). Covers a land area of 0.364 square miles and a water area of 0 square miles. Located at 41.01° N. Lat; 77.66° W. Long. Elevation is 669 feet.

Population: 749 (1990); 699 (2000); 720 (2010); Density: 1,975.9 persons per square mile (2010); Race: 97.5% White, 0.4% Black, 0.3% Asian, 0.0% American Indian/Alaska Native, 0.0% Native Hawaiian/Other Pacific Islander, 1.8% Other, 1.4% Hispanic of any race (2010); Average household size: 2.48 (2010); Median age: 40.3 (2010); Males per 100 females: 105.1 (2010); Marriage status: 21.4% never married, 59.9% now married, 8.4% widowed, 10.3% divorced (2006-2010 5-year est.); Foreign born: 0.0% (2006-2010 5-year est.); Ancestry (includes multiple ancestries): 50.2% German, 15.2% Irish, 12.7% English, 6.3% Italian, 4.5% American (2006-2010 5-year est.).

Economy: Single-family building permits issued: 3 (2011); Multi-family building permits issued: 0 (2011); Employment by occupation: 8.2% management, 0.7% professional, 13.2% services, 13.2% sales, 1.0% farming, 14.1% construction, 11.8% production (2006-2010 5-year est.).

Income: Per capita income: $25,304 (2006-2010 5-year est.); Median household income: $51,548 (2006-2010 5-year est.); Average household income: $60,679 (2006-2010 5-year est.); Percent of households with income of $100,000 or more: 9.4% (2006-2010 5-year est.); Poverty rate: 8.0% (2006-2010 5-year est.).

Education: Percent of population age 25 and over with: High school diploma (including GED) or higher: 92.4% (2006-2010 5-year est.); Bachelor's degree or higher: 18.9% (2006-2010 5-year est.); Master's degree or higher: 7.2% (2006-2010 5-year est.).

School District(s)

Bald Eagle Area SD (KG-12)

　　2010-11 Enrollment: 1,864 . . . . (814) 355-4860

Housing: Homeownership rate: 71.7% (2010); Median home value: $134,100 (2006-2010 5-year est.); Median contract rent: $500 per month (2006-2010 5-year est.); Median year structure built: 1941 (2006-2010 5-year est.).

Transportation: Commute to work: 92.5% car, 0.0% public transportation, 0.0% walk, 7.5% work from home (2006-2010 5-year est.); Travel time to work: 14.9% less than 15 minutes, 42.7% 15 to 30 minutes, 28.8% 30 to 45 minutes, 10.6% 45 to 60 minutes, 3.0% 60 minutes or more (2006-2010 5-year est.)

HOWARD (township). Covers a land area of 18.002 square miles and a water area of 0.917 square miles. Located at 41.02° N. Lat; 77.69° W. Long. Elevation is 669 feet.

Population: 1,153 (1990); 924 (2000); 964 (2010); Density: 53.5 persons per square mile (2010); Race: 98.9% White, 0.3% Black, 0.0% Asian, 0.4% American Indian/Alaska Native, 0.2% Native Hawaiian/Other Pacific Islander, 0.2% Other, 0.3% Hispanic of any race (2010); Average household size: 2.61 (2010); Median age: 41.7 (2010); Males per 100 females: 97.5 (2010); Marriage status: 25.9% never married, 64.2% now married, 1.5% widowed, 8.4% divorced (2006-2010 5-year est.); Foreign born: 1.0% (2006-2010 5-year est.); Ancestry (includes multiple ancestries): 27.3% German, 14.2% Irish, 10.0% American, 4.6% English, 4.3% Italian (2006-2010 5-year est.).

Economy: Single-family building permits issued: 0 (2011); Multi-family building permits issued: 0 (2011); Employment by occupation: 8.6% management, 3.0% professional, 7.7% services, 13.9% sales, 5.6% farming, 12.6% construction, 10.5% production (2006-2010 5-year est.).

Income: Per capita income: $21,373 (2006-2010 5-year est.); Median household income: $47,188 (2006-2010 5-year est.); Average household income: $59,905 (2006-2010 5-year est.); Percent of households with income of $100,000 or more: 14.5% (2006-2010 5-year est.); Poverty rate: 10.9% (2006-2010 5-year est.).

Education: Percent of population age 25 and over with: High school diploma (including GED) or higher: 89.4% (2006-2010 5-year est.); Bachelor's degree or higher: 14.7% (2006-2010 5-year est.); Master's degree or higher: 5.4% (2006-2010 5-year est.).

Housing: Homeownership rate: 85.9% (2010); Median home value: $132,200 (2006-2010 5-year est.); Median contract rent: $625 per month (2006-2010 5-year est.); Median year structure built: 1975 (2006-2010 5-year est.).

Transportation: Commute to work: 90.3% car, 0.0% public transportation, 2.2% walk, 7.6% work from home (2006-2010 5-year est.); Travel time to work: 24.1% less than 15 minutes, 38.1% 15 to 30 minutes, 31.5% 30 to 45 minutes, 3.0% 45 to 60 minutes, 3.3% 60 minutes or more (2006-2010 5-year est.)

HUBLERSBURG (CDP). Covers a land area of 0.161 square miles and a water area of 0 square miles. Located at 40.96° N. Lat; 77.61° W. Long. Elevation is 938 feet.

Population: n/a (1990); n/a (2000); 104 (2010); Density: 644.0 persons per square mile (2010); Race: 99.0% White, 1.0% Black, 0.0% Asian, 0.0% American Indian/Alaska Native, 0.0% Native Hawaiian/Other Pacific Islander, 0.0% Other, 0.0% Hispanic of any race (2010); Average household size: 2.81 (2010); Median age: 36.0 (2010); Males per 100 females: 96.2 (2010); Marriage status: 52.0% never married, 48.0% now married, 0.0% widowed, 0.0% divorced (2006-2010 5-year est.); Foreign born: 0.0% (2006-2010 5-year est.); Ancestry (includes multiple ancestries): 100.0% Pennsylvania German, 54.0% Irish, 46.0% Italian (2006-2010 5-year est.).

Economy: Employment by occupation: 0.0% management, 0.0% professional, 0.0% services, 30.8% sales, 0.0% farming, 0.0% construction, 0.0% production (2006-2010 5-year est.).

Income: Per capita income: $15,154 (2006-2010 5-year est.); Median household income: n/a (2006-2010 5-year est.); Average household income: n/a (2006-2010 5-year est.); Percent of households with income of $100,000 or more: n/a (2006-2010 5-year est.); Poverty rate: 0.0% (2006-2010 5-year est.).

Education: Percent of population age 25 and over with: High school diploma (including GED) or higher: 100.0% (2006-2010 5-year est.); Bachelor's degree or higher: 0.0% (2006-2010 5-year est.); Master's degree or higher: 0.0% (2006-2010 5-year est.).

Housing: Homeownership rate: 67.5% (2010); Median home value: n/a (2006-2010 5-year est.); Median contract rent: n/a per month (2006-2010 5-year est.); Median year structure built: n/a (2006-2010 5-year est.).

Transportation: Commute to work: 100.0% car, 0.0% public transportation, 0.0% walk, 0.0% work from home (2006-2010 5-year est.); Travel time to work: 0.0% less than 15 minutes, 38.5% 15 to 30 minutes, 61.5% 30 to 45 minutes, 0.0% 45 to 60 minutes, 0.0% 60 minutes or more (2006-2010 5-year est.)

HUSTON (township). Covers a land area of 25.599 square miles and a water area of 0 square miles. Located at 40.87° N. Lat; 77.98° W. Long.

Population: 1,291 (1990); 1,311 (2000); 1,360 (2010); Density: 53.1 persons per square mile (2010); Race: 98.3% White, 0.1% Black, 0.2% Asian, 0.1% American Indian/Alaska Native, 0.0% Native Hawaiian/Other Pacific Islander, 1.3% Other, 0.7% Hispanic of any race (2010); Average household size: 2.58 (2010); Median age: 43.4 (2010); Males per 100 females: 106.7 (2010); Marriage status: 23.1% never married, 62.5% now married, 4.5% widowed, 9.9% divorced (2006-2010 5-year est.); Foreign born: 0.7% (2006-2010 5-year est.); Ancestry (includes multiple ancestries): 30.6% German, 14.9% American, 9.9% Irish, 7.6% English, 6.6% Polish (2006-2010 5-year est.).

Economy: Single-family building permits issued: 1 (2011); Multi-family building permits issued: 0 (2011); Employment by occupation: 8.1% management, 5.0% professional, 12.5% services, 14.3% sales, 6.6% farming, 10.7% construction, 8.7% production (2006-2010 5-year est.).

Income: Per capita income: $25,243 (2006-2010 5-year est.); Median household income: $59,426 (2006-2010 5-year est.); Average household income: $66,879 (2006-2010 5-year est.); Percent of households with income of $100,000 or more: 15.9% (2006-2010 5-year est.); Poverty rate: 9.4% (2006-2010 5-year est.).

Education: Percent of population age 25 and over with: High school diploma (including GED) or higher: 94.9% (2006-2010 5-year est.); Bachelor's degree or higher: 19.7% (2006-2010 5-year est.); Master's degree or higher: 8.7% (2006-2010 5-year est.).

Housing: Homeownership rate: 86.5% (2010); Median home value: $159,600 (2006-2010 5-year est.); Median contract rent: $436 per month (2006-2010 5-year est.); Median year structure built: 1978 (2006-2010 5-year est.).

Transportation: Commute to work: 94.8% car, 0.0% public transportation, 1.2% walk, 3.1% work from home (2006-2010 5-year est.); Travel time to work: 5.2% less than 15 minutes, 62.8% 15 to 30 minutes, 27.6% 30 to 45 minutes, 4.4% 45 to 60 minutes, 0.0% 60 minutes or more (2006-2010 5-year est.)

Additional Information Contacts

Chamber of Business & Industry of Centre County . . . . (814) 234-1829
　　http://www.cbicc.org

JACKSONVILLE (CDP). Covers a land area of 0.142 square miles and a water area of 0 square miles. Located at 40.99° N. Lat; 77.63° W. Long. Elevation is 912 feet.

Population: n/a (1990); n/a (2000); 95 (2010); Density: 668.5 persons per square mile (2010); Race: 98.9% White, 0.0% Black, 0.0% Asian, 0.0% American Indian/Alaska Native, 0.0% Native Hawaiian/Other Pacific Islander, 1.1% Other, 0.0% Hispanic of any race (2010); Average household size: 2.71 (2010); Median age: 38.8 (2010); Males per 100 females: 106.5 (2010); Marriage status: 49.4% never married, 30.6% now married, 10.6% widowed, 9.4% divorced (2006-2010 5-year est.); Foreign born: 0.0% (2006-2010 5-year est.); Ancestry (includes multiple ancestries): 28.7% German, 24.8% Welsh, 22.8% Dutch, 9.9% Italian, 7.9% American (2006-2010 5-year est.).

Economy: Employment by occupation: 10.4% management, 0.0% professional, 10.4% services, 0.0% sales, 0.0% farming, 29.2% construction, 43.8% production (2006-2010 5-year est.).

Income: Per capita income: $15,055 (2006-2010 5-year est.); Median household income: $29,821 (2006-2010 5-year est.); Average household income: $38,007 (2006-2010 5-year est.); Percent of households with income of $100,000 or more: 7.3% (2006-2010 5-year est.); Poverty rate: 49.5% (2006-2010 5-year est.).

Education: Percent of population age 25 and over with: High school diploma (including GED) or higher: 80.9% (2006-2010 5-year est.); Bachelor's degree or higher: 10.6% (2006-2010 5-year est.); Master's degree or higher: 6.4% (2006-2010 5-year est.).

Housing: Homeownership rate: 82.8% (2010); Median home value: $89,200 (2006-2010 5-year est.); Median contract rent: $623 per month (2006-2010 5-year est.); Median year structure built: before 1940 (2006-2010 5-year est.).

Transportation: Commute to work: 91.7% car, 0.0% public transportation, 0.0% walk, 0.0% work from home (2006-2010 5-year est.); Travel time to work: 16.7% less than 15 minutes, 62.5% 15 to 30 minutes, 20.8% 30 to 45 minutes, 0.0% 45 to 60 minutes, 0.0% 60 minutes or more (2006-2010 5-year est.)

JULIAN (CDP). Covers a land area of 0.148 square miles and a water area of 0 square miles. Located at 40.86° N. Lat; 77.94° W. Long. Elevation is 853 feet.

Population: 150 (1990); 152 (2000); 152 (2010); Density: 1,026.1 persons per square mile (2010); Race: 99.3% White, 0.0% Black, 0.0% Asian, 0.7% American Indian/Alaska Native, 0.0% Native Hawaiian/Other Pacific Islander, 0.0% Other, 0.0% Hispanic of any race (2010); Average household size: 2.58 (2010); Median age: 45.0 (2010); Males per 100 females: 111.1 (2010); Marriage status: 46.2% never married, 48.5% now married, 5.4% widowed, 0.0% divorced (2006-2010 5-year est.); Foreign born: 0.0% (2006-2010 5-year est.); Ancestry (includes multiple ancestries): 17.3% German, 15.8% Dutch, 13.5% Polish, 11.3% Irish, 10.5% American (2006-2010 5-year est.).

Economy: Employment by occupation: 0.0% management, 11.1% professional, 19.4% services, 20.8% sales, 0.0% farming, 13.9% construction, 4.2% production (2006-2010 5-year est.).

Income: Per capita income: $23,232 (2006-2010 5-year est.); Median household income: $58,750 (2006-2010 5-year est.); Average household income: $56,725 (2006-2010 5-year est.); Percent of households with income of $100,000 or more: 5.7% (2006-2010 5-year est.); Poverty rate: 14.3% (2006-2010 5-year est.).

Education: Percent of population age 25 and over with: High school diploma (including GED) or higher: 95.9% (2006-2010 5-year est.); Bachelor's degree or higher: 16.5% (2006-2010 5-year est.); Master's degree or higher: 4.1% (2006-2010 5-year est.).

Housing: Homeownership rate: 89.8% (2010); Median home value: $112,500 (2006-2010 5-year est.); Median contract rent: n/a per month (2006-2010 5-year est.); Median year structure built: 1943 (2006-2010 5-year est.).

Transportation: Commute to work: 100.0% car, 0.0% public transportation, 0.0% walk, 0.0% work from home (2006-2010 5-year est.); Travel time to work: 11.6% less than 15 minutes, 63.8% 15 to 30 minutes, 24.6% 30 to 45 minutes, 0.0% 45 to 60 minutes, 0.0% 60 minutes or more (2006-2010 5-year est.)

LEMONT (CDP). Covers a land area of 1.267 square miles and a water area of 0 square miles. Located at 40.81° N. Lat; 77.82° W. Long. Elevation is 1,014 feet.

Population: 1,889 (1990); 2,116 (2000); 2,270 (2010); Density: 1,792.1 persons per square mile (2010); Race: 94.2% White, 1.8% Black, 1.9%

Asian, 0.2% American Indian/Alaska Native, 0.0% Native Hawaiian/Other Pacific Islander, 1.9% Other, 1.3% Hispanic of any race (2010); Average household size: 2.45 (2010); Median age: 39.1 (2010); Males per 100 females: 100.2 (2010); Marriage status: 33.0% never married, 60.0% now married, 2.1% widowed, 4.9% divorced (2006-2010 5-year est.); Foreign born: 11.2% (2006-2010 5-year est.); Ancestry (includes multiple ancestries): 27.3% German, 14.5% English, 7.4% Italian, 7.3% Irish, 5.9% American (2006-2010 5-year est.).

Economy: Employment by occupation: 12.1% management, 18.4% professional, 1.9% services, 13.6% sales, 2.5% farming, 4.2% construction, 1.3% production (2006-2010 5-year est.).

Income: Per capita income: $33,795 (2006-2010 5-year est.); Median household income: $89,783 (2006-2010 5-year est.); Average household income: $86,395 (2006-2010 5-year est.); Percent of households with income of $100,000 or more: 38.7% (2006-2010 5-year est.); Poverty rate: 8.0% (2006-2010 5-year est.).

Education: Percent of population age 25 and over with: High school diploma (including GED) or higher: 94.5% (2006-2010 5-year est.); Bachelor's degree or higher: 63.3% (2006-2010 5-year est.); Master's degree or higher: 27.7% (2006-2010 5-year est.).

Housing: Homeownership rate: 75.5% (2010); Median home value: $229,800 (2006-2010 5-year est.); Median contract rent: $592 per month (2006-2010 5-year est.); Median year structure built: 1985 (2006-2010 5-year est.).

Transportation: Commute to work: 88.0% car, 0.0% public transportation, 1.0% walk, 2.9% work from home (2006-2010 5-year est.); Travel time to work: 57.9% less than 15 minutes, 31.5% 15 to 30 minutes, 9.5% 30 to 45 minutes, 0.0% 45 to 60 minutes, 1.1% 60 minutes or more (2006-2010 5-year est.)

Additional Information Contacts

Chamber of Business & Industry of Centre County . . . . (814) 234-1829
http://www.cbicc.org

LIBERTY (township). Covers a land area of 23.952 square miles and a water area of 0.740 square miles. Located at 41.06° N. Lat; 77.65° W. Long.

Population: 1,747 (1990); 1,830 (2000); 2,118 (2010); Density: 88.4 persons per square mile (2010); Race: 98.7% White, 0.0% Black, 0.3% Asian, 0.4% American Indian/Alaska Native, 0.0% Native Hawaiian/Other Pacific Islander, 0.6% Other, 0.7% Hispanic of any race (2010); Average household size: 2.53 (2010); Median age: 41.1 (2010); Males per 100 females: 103.1 (2010); Marriage status: 23.8% never married, 61.0% now married, 6.4% widowed, 8.9% divorced (2006-2010 5-year est.); Foreign born: 1.1% (2006-2010 5-year est.); Ancestry (includes multiple ancestries): 32.3% German, 10.4% Irish, 7.8% American, 5.8% English, 4.9% Dutch (2006-2010 5-year est.).

Economy: Single-family building permits issued: 7 (2011); Multi-family building permits issued: 0 (2011); Employment by occupation: 7.6% management, 1.8% professional, 12.6% services, 20.9% sales, 2.3% farming, 12.4% construction, 9.9% production (2006-2010 5-year est.).

Income: Per capita income: $19,727 (2006-2010 5-year est.); Median household income: $41,667 (2006-2010 5-year est.); Average household income: $52,135 (2006-2010 5-year est.); Percent of households with income of $100,000 or more: 10.6% (2006-2010 5-year est.); Poverty rate: 9.3% (2006-2010 5-year est.).

Education: Percent of population age 25 and over with: High school diploma (including GED) or higher: 83.6% (2006-2010 5-year est.); Bachelor's degree or higher: 11.1% (2006-2010 5-year est.); Master's degree or higher: 1.2% (2006-2010 5-year est.).

Housing: Homeownership rate: 87.6% (2010); Median home value: $97,900 (2006-2010 5-year est.); Median contract rent: $365 per month (2006-2010 5-year est.); Median year structure built: 1979 (2006-2010 5-year est.).

Transportation: Commute to work: 94.7% car, 0.0% public transportation, 1.1% walk, 4.2% work from home (2006-2010 5-year est.); Travel time to work: 10.4% less than 15 minutes, 50.6% 15 to 30 minutes, 26.2% 30 to 45 minutes, 9.6% 45 to 60 minutes, 3.1% 60 minutes or more (2006-2010 5-year est.)

Additional Information Contacts

Chamber of Business & Industry of Centre County . . . . (814) 234-1829
http://www.cbicc.org

MADISONBURG (CDP). Covers a land area of 0.079 square miles and a water area of 0 square miles. Located at 40.93° N. Lat; 77.52° W. Long. Elevation is 1,293 feet.

Population: 130 (1990); 135 (2000); 168 (2010); Density: 2,127.7 persons per square mile (2010); Race: 100.0% White, 0.0% Black, 0.0% Asian, 0.0% American Indian/Alaska Native, 0.0% Native Hawaiian/Other Pacific Islander, 0.0% Other, 0.0% Hispanic of any race (2010); Average household size: 2.67 (2010); Median age: 43.5 (2010); Males per 100 females: 104.9 (2010); Marriage status: 27.9% never married, 69.2% now married, 2.9% widowed, 0.0% divorced (2006-2010 5-year est.); Foreign born: 0.0% (2006-2010 5-year est.); Ancestry (includes multiple ancestries): 50.5% German, 39.3% Irish, 29.9% English, 20.6% Polish, 15.0% Dutch (2006-2010 5-year est.).

Economy: Employment by occupation: 5.6% management, 0.0% professional, 12.7% services, 5.6% sales, 0.0% farming, 12.7% construction, 22.5% production (2006-2010 5-year est.).

Income: Per capita income: $18,217 (2006-2010 5-year est.); Median household income: $52,083 (2006-2010 5-year est.); Average household income: $49,418 (2006-2010 5-year est.); Percent of households with income of $100,000 or more: n/a (2006-2010 5-year est.); Poverty rate: 15.0% (2006-2010 5-year est.).

Education: Percent of population age 25 and over with: High school diploma (including GED) or higher: 90.7% (2006-2010 5-year est.); Bachelor's degree or higher: 38.7% (2006-2010 5-year est.); Master's degree or higher: 0.0% (2006-2010 5-year est.).

Housing: Homeownership rate: 95.3% (2010); Median home value: $137,000 (2006-2010 5-year est.); Median contract rent: n/a per month (2006-2010 5-year est.); Median year structure built: before 1940 (2006-2010 5-year est.).

Transportation: Commute to work: 82.1% car, 0.0% public transportation, 0.0% walk, 0.0% work from home (2006-2010 5-year est.); Travel time to work: 22.4% less than 15 minutes, 32.8% 15 to 30 minutes, 35.8% 30 to 45 minutes, 9.0% 45 to 60 minutes, 0.0% 60 minutes or more (2006-2010 5-year est.)

MARION (township). Covers a land area of 22.048 square miles and a water area of 0 square miles. Located at 40.99° N. Lat; 77.64° W. Long.

Population: 730 (1990); 978 (2000); 1,224 (2010); Density: 55.5 persons per square mile (2010); Race: 98.3% White, 0.3% Black, 0.0% Asian, 0.3% American Indian/Alaska Native, 0.0% Native Hawaiian/Other Pacific Islander, 1.1% Other, 0.0% Hispanic of any race (2010); Average household size: 3.10 (2010); Median age: 37.3 (2010); Males per 100 females: 106.8 (2010); Marriage status: 21.8% never married, 68.3% now married, 3.4% widowed, 6.5% divorced (2006-2010 5-year est.); Foreign born: 0.0% (2006-2010 5-year est.); Ancestry (includes multiple ancestries): 29.2% German, 11.3% Irish, 10.1% Pennsylvania German, 9.6% English, 7.0% American (2006-2010 5-year est.).

Economy: Single-family building permits issued: 1 (2011); Multi-family building permits issued: 0 (2011); Employment by occupation: 16.6% management, 1.9% professional, 8.8% services, 18.6% sales, 3.4% farming, 13.6% construction, 8.5% production (2006-2010 5-year est.).

Income: Per capita income: $20,710 (2006-2010 5-year est.); Median household income: $53,098 (2006-2010 5-year est.); Average household income: $62,932 (2006-2010 5-year est.); Percent of households with income of $100,000 or more: 17.3% (2006-2010 5-year est.); Poverty rate: 10.1% (2006-2010 5-year est.).

Education: Percent of population age 25 and over with: High school diploma (including GED) or higher: 77.3% (2006-2010 5-year est.); Bachelor's degree or higher: 15.0% (2006-2010 5-year est.); Master's degree or higher: 6.2% (2006-2010 5-year est.).

Housing: Homeownership rate: 89.3% (2010); Median home value: $192,100 (2006-2010 5-year est.); Median contract rent: $550 per month (2006-2010 5-year est.); Median year structure built: 1984 (2006-2010 5-year est.).

Transportation: Commute to work: 85.4% car, 0.0% public transportation, 8.3% walk, 4.8% work from home (2006-2010 5-year est.); Travel time to work: 19.5% less than 15 minutes, 47.9% 15 to 30 minutes, 27.3% 30 to 45 minutes, 2.1% 45 to 60 minutes, 3.1% 60 minutes or more (2006-2010 5-year est.)

Additional Information Contacts

Indiana County Chamber of Commerce . . . . (724) 465-2511
http://www.indianapa.com/chamber

MILES (township). Covers a land area of 62.555 square miles and a water area of 0 square miles. Located at 40.96° N. Lat; 77.37° W. Long.

Population: 1,494 (1990); 1,573 (2000); 1,983 (2010); Density: 31.7 persons per square mile (2010); Race: 98.8% White, 0.2% Black, 0.2% Asian, 0.1% American Indian/Alaska Native, 0.1% Native Hawaiian/Other Pacific Islander, 0.6% Other, 0.1% Hispanic of any race (2010); Average household size: 3.33 (2010); Median age: 29.2 (2010); Males per 100 females: 93.7 (2010); Marriage status: 23.8% never married, 60.8% now married, 5.6% widowed, 9.7% divorced (2006-2010 5-year est.); Foreign born: 1.5% (2006-2010 5-year est.); Ancestry (includes multiple ancestries): 33.3% German, 7.9% Irish, 5.5% English, 4.4% American, 3.7% Palestinian (2006-2010 5-year est.).

Economy: Single-family building permits issued: 5 (2011); Multi-family building permits issued: 0 (2011); Employment by occupation: 12.0% management, 2.3% professional, 8.8% services, 16.0% sales, 3.0% farming, 16.7% construction, 13.4% production (2006-2010 5-year est.).

Income: Per capita income: $16,100 (2006-2010 5-year est.); Median household income: $39,844 (2006-2010 5-year est.); Average household income: $49,470 (2006-2010 5-year est.); Percent of households with income of $100,000 or more: 9.3% (2006-2010 5-year est.); Poverty rate: 13.5% (2006-2010 5-year est.).

Education: Percent of population age 25 and over with: High school diploma (including GED) or higher: 82.3% (2006-2010 5-year est.); Bachelor's degree or higher: 10.6% (2006-2010 5-year est.); Master's degree or higher: 3.4% (2006-2010 5-year est.).

Housing: Homeownership rate: 77.9% (2010); Median home value: $142,900 (2006-2010 5-year est.); Median contract rent: $548 per month (2006-2010 5-year est.); Median year structure built: 1963 (2006-2010 5-year est.).

Transportation: Commute to work: 68.8% car, 1.7% public transportation, 2.4% walk, 15.8% work from home (2006-2010 5-year est.); Travel time to work: 21.1% less than 15 minutes, 28.2% 15 to 30 minutes, 30.1% 30 to 45 minutes, 13.5% 45 to 60 minutes, 7.2% 60 minutes or more (2006-2010 5-year est.)

Additional Information Contacts

Chamber of Business & Industry of Centre County . . . . (814) 234-1829
http://www.cbicc.org

MILESBURG (borough). Covers a land area of 0.447 square miles and a water area of 0 square miles. Located at 40.94° N. Lat; 77.79° W. Long. Elevation is 696 feet.

Population: 1,156 (1990); 1,187 (2000); 1,123 (2010); Density: 2,514.9 persons per square mile (2010); Race: 98.7% White, 0.4% Black, 0.4% Asian, 0.1% American Indian/Alaska Native, 0.0% Native Hawaiian/Other Pacific Islander, 0.4% Other, 0.3% Hispanic of any race (2010); Average household size: 2.45 (2010); Median age: 42.3 (2010); Males per 100 females: 89.1 (2010); Marriage status: 20.7% never married, 60.7% now married, 3.5% widowed, 15.1% divorced (2006-2010 5-year est.); Foreign born: 0.0% (2006-2010 5-year est.); Ancestry (includes multiple ancestries): 38.3% German, 27.2% Irish, 7.8% Dutch, 7.3% English, 3.8% Polish (2006-2010 5-year est.).

Economy: Single-family building permits issued: 0 (2011); Multi-family building permits issued: 0 (2011); Employment by occupation: 3.8% management, 1.6% professional, 20.8% services, 19.0% sales, 5.6% farming, 10.2% construction, 7.7% production (2006-2010 5-year est.).

Income: Per capita income: $19,310 (2006-2010 5-year est.); Median household income: $45,588 (2006-2010 5-year est.); Average household income: $48,292 (2006-2010 5-year est.); Percent of households with income of $100,000 or more: 3.7% (2006-2010 5-year est.); Poverty rate: 7.2% (2006-2010 5-year est.).

Education: Percent of population age 25 and over with: High school diploma (including GED) or higher: 93.0% (2006-2010 5-year est.); Bachelor's degree or higher: 16.1% (2006-2010 5-year est.); Master's degree or higher: 5.1% (2006-2010 5-year est.).

Housing: Homeownership rate: 67.7% (2010); Median home value: $121,900 (2006-2010 5-year est.); Median contract rent: $505 per month (2006-2010 5-year est.); Median year structure built: 1954 (2006-2010 5-year est.).

Transportation: Commute to work: 95.1% car, 0.0% public transportation, 0.0% walk, 4.9% work from home (2006-2010 5-year est.); Travel time to work: 27.6% less than 15 minutes, 51.4% 15 to 30 minutes, 17.5% 30 to 45 minutes, 1.2% 45 to 60 minutes, 2.4% 60 minutes or more (2006-2010 5-year est.)

MILLHEIM (borough). Covers a land area of 1.323 square miles and a water area of 0 square miles. Located at 40.89° N. Lat; 77.48° W. Long. Elevation is 1,089 feet.
Population: 847 (1990); 749 (2000); 904 (2010); Density: 683.1 persons per square mile (2010); Race: 98.2% White, 0.1% Black, 0.0% Asian, 0.1% American Indian/Alaska Native, 0.0% Native Hawaiian/Other Pacific Islander, 1.6% Other, 0.2% Hispanic of any race (2010); Average household size: 2.40 (2010); Median age: 39.9 (2010); Males per 100 females: 92.8 (2010); Marriage status: 22.3% never married, 59.0% now married, 5.4% widowed, 13.4% divorced (2006-2010 5-year est.); Foreign born: 3.4% (2006-2010 5-year est.); Ancestry (includes multiple ancestries): 33.6% German, 18.7% Irish, 8.4% Italian, 3.0% English, 2.8% American (2006-2010 5-year est.).
Economy: Single-family building permits issued: 0 (2011); Multi-family building permits issued: 0 (2011); Employment by occupation: 13.4% management, 5.7% professional, 23.3% services, 14.9% sales, 3.5% farming, 5.9% construction, 7.9% production (2006-2010 5-year est.).
Income: Per capita income: $17,335 (2006-2010 5-year est.); Median household income: $43,077 (2006-2010 5-year est.); Average household income: $47,999 (2006-2010 5-year est.); Percent of households with income of $100,000 or more: 5.7% (2006-2010 5-year est.); Poverty rate: 10.7% (2006-2010 5-year est.).
Education: Percent of population age 25 and over with: High school diploma (including GED) or higher: 86.4% (2006-2010 5-year est.); Bachelor's degree or higher: 17.3% (2006-2010 5-year est.); Master's degree or higher: 4.7% (2006-2010 5-year est.).
Housing: Homeownership rate: 75.6% (2010); Median home value: $138,000 (2006-2010 5-year est.); Median contract rent: $427 per month (2006-2010 5-year est.); Median year structure built: 1941 (2006-2010 5-year est.).
Transportation: Commute to work: 82.8% car, 0.0% public transportation, 7.5% walk, 2.0% work from home (2006-2010 5-year est.); Travel time to work: 36.1% less than 15 minutes, 17.3% 15 to 30 minutes, 37.2% 30 to 45 minutes, 8.7% 45 to 60 minutes, 0.8% 60 minutes or more (2006-2010 5-year est.)

MINGOVILLE (CDP). Covers a land area of 1.832 square miles and a water area of 0 square miles. Located at 40.94° N. Lat; 77.66° W. Long. Elevation is 1,037 feet.
Population: n/a (1990); n/a (2000); 503 (2010); Density: 274.6 persons per square mile (2010); Race: 99.6% White, 0.0% Black, 0.2% Asian, 0.0% American Indian/Alaska Native, 0.0% Native Hawaiian/Other Pacific Islander, 0.2% Other, 0.6% Hispanic of any race (2010); Average household size: 2.57 (2010); Median age: 42.8 (2010); Males per 100 females: 99.6 (2010); Marriage status: 10.5% never married, 71.1% now married, 3.7% widowed, 14.8% divorced (2006-2010 5-year est.); Foreign born: 5.4% (2006-2010 5-year est.); Ancestry (includes multiple ancestries): 48.2% German, 11.4% European, 10.9% English, 8.4% Irish, 7.6% British (2006-2010 5-year est.).
Economy: Employment by occupation: 11.5% management, 13.9% professional, 9.4% services, 22.5% sales, 0.0% farming, 17.6% construction, 11.9% production (2006-2010 5-year est.).
Income: Per capita income: $34,964 (2006-2010 5-year est.); Median household income: $66,538 (2006-2010 5-year est.); Average household income: $75,799 (2006-2010 5-year est.); Percent of households with income of $100,000 or more: 28.5% (2006-2010 5-year est.); Poverty rate: 7.4% (2006-2010 5-year est.).
Education: Percent of population age 25 and over with: High school diploma (including GED) or higher: 97.7% (2006-2010 5-year est.); Bachelor's degree or higher: 32.5% (2006-2010 5-year est.); Master's degree or higher: 0.0% (2006-2010 5-year est.).
Housing: Homeownership rate: 87.2% (2010); Median home value: $197,000 (2006-2010 5-year est.); Median contract rent: n/a per month (2006-2010 5-year est.); Median year structure built: 1980 (2006-2010 5-year est.).
Transportation: Commute to work: 100.0% car, 0.0% public transportation, 0.0% walk, 0.0% work from home (2006-2010 5-year est.); Travel time to work: 3.5% less than 15 minutes, 74.4% 15 to 30 minutes, 17.2% 30 to 45 minutes, 4.8% 45 to 60 minutes, 0.0% 60 minutes or more (2006-2010 5-year est.)

MONUMENT (CDP). Covers a land area of 0.087 square miles and a water area of 0 square miles. Located at 41.11° N. Lat; 77.70° W. Long. Elevation is 755 feet.
Population: 133 (1990); 133 (2000); 150 (2010); Density: 1,722.9 persons per square mile (2010); Race: 100.0% White, 0.0% Black, 0.0% Asian, 0.0% American Indian/Alaska Native, 0.0% Native Hawaiian/Other Pacific Islander, 0.0% Other, 0.7% Hispanic of any race (2010); Average household size: 2.83 (2010); Median age: 39.3 (2010); Males per 100 females: 89.9 (2010); Marriage status: 33.1% never married, 58.5% now married, 1.5% widowed, 6.9% divorced (2006-2010 5-year est.); Foreign born: 0.0% (2006-2010 5-year est.); Ancestry (includes multiple ancestries): 22.3% German, 14.4% English, 10.8% American, 9.4% Northern European, 3.6% Dutch (2006-2010 5-year est.).
Economy: Employment by occupation: 0.0% management, 0.0% professional, 31.6% services, 13.2% sales, 6.6% farming, 19.7% construction, 7.9% production (2006-2010 5-year est.).
Income: Per capita income: $16,899 (2006-2010 5-year est.); Median household income: $40,625 (2006-2010 5-year est.); Average household income: $38,964 (2006-2010 5-year est.); Percent of households with income of $100,000 or more: n/a (2006-2010 5-year est.); Poverty rate: 6.5% (2006-2010 5-year est.).
Education: Percent of population age 25 and over with: High school diploma (including GED) or higher: 76.2% (2006-2010 5-year est.); Bachelor's degree or higher: 0.0% (2006-2010 5-year est.); Master's degree or higher: 0.0% (2006-2010 5-year est.).
Housing: Homeownership rate: 79.2% (2010); Median home value: $44,000 (2006-2010 5-year est.); Median contract rent: $355 per month (2006-2010 5-year est.); Median year structure built: before 1940 (2006-2010 5-year est.).
Transportation: Commute to work: 93.4% car, 0.0% public transportation, 0.0% walk, 6.6% work from home (2006-2010 5-year est.); Travel time to work: 0.0% less than 15 minutes, 8.5% 15 to 30 minutes, 87.3% 30 to 45 minutes, 0.0% 45 to 60 minutes, 4.2% 60 minutes or more (2006-2010 5-year est.)

MOSHANNON (CDP). Covers a land area of 0.343 square miles and a water area of 0 square miles. Located at 41.03° N. Lat; 78.01° W. Long. Elevation is 1,529 feet.
Population: n/a (1990); n/a (2000); 281 (2010); Density: 820.3 persons per square mile (2010); Race: 99.6% White, 0.0% Black, 0.4% Asian, 0.0% American Indian/Alaska Native, 0.0% Native Hawaiian/Other Pacific Islander, 0.0% Other, 0.0% Hispanic of any race (2010); Average household size: 2.36 (2010); Median age: 42.7 (2010); Males per 100 females: 84.9 (2010); Marriage status: 39.5% never married, 45.1% now married, 9.4% widowed, 6.0% divorced (2006-2010 5-year est.); Foreign born: 0.0% (2006-2010 5-year est.); Ancestry (includes multiple ancestries): 18.4% German, 10.5% French, 9.9% Dutch, 7.2% English, 5.6% Irish (2006-2010 5-year est.).
Economy: Employment by occupation: 0.0% management, 0.0% professional, 14.2% services, 14.2% sales, 0.0% farming, 9.0% construction, 7.5% production (2006-2010 5-year est.).
Income: Per capita income: $16,776 (2006-2010 5-year est.); Median household income: $45,417 (2006-2010 5-year est.); Average household income: $44,835 (2006-2010 5-year est.); Percent of households with income of $100,000 or more: n/a (2006-2010 5-year est.); Poverty rate: 13.8% (2006-2010 5-year est.).
Education: Percent of population age 25 and over with: High school diploma (including GED) or higher: 93.5% (2006-2010 5-year est.); Bachelor's degree or higher: 10.8% (2006-2010 5-year est.); Master's degree or higher: 0.0% (2006-2010 5-year est.).
Housing: Homeownership rate: 77.3% (2010); Median home value: $77,100 (2006-2010 5-year est.); Median contract rent: $330 per month (2006-2010 5-year est.); Median year structure built: 1969 (2006-2010 5-year est.).
Transportation: Commute to work: 97.0% car, 0.0% public transportation, 0.0% walk, 0.0% work from home (2006-2010 5-year est.); Travel time to work: 17.9% less than 15 minutes, 21.6% 15 to 30 minutes, 35.1% 30 to 45 minutes, 14.9% 45 to 60 minutes, 10.4% 60 minutes or more (2006-2010 5-year est.)

MOUNT EAGLE (CDP). Covers a land area of 0.256 square miles and a water area of 0 square miles. Located at 40.98° N. Lat; 77.71° W. Long. Elevation is 689 feet.
Population: n/a (1990); n/a (2000); 103 (2010); Density: 401.6 persons per square mile (2010); Race: 99.0% White, 0.0% Black, 0.0% Asian,

1.0% American Indian/Alaska Native, 0.0% Native Hawaiian/Other Pacific Islander, 0.0% Other, 0.0% Hispanic of any race (2010); Average household size: 2.19 (2010); Median age: 44.8 (2010); Males per 100 females: 83.9 (2010); Marriage status: 23.8% never married, 51.6% now married, 0.0% widowed, 24.6% divorced (2006-2010 5-year est.); Foreign born: 0.0% (2006-2010 5-year est.); Ancestry (includes multiple ancestries): 25.8% German, 19.7% Irish, 15.2% American, 6.8% French, 6.1% English (2006-2010 5-year est.).

Economy: Employment by occupation: 4.4% management, 0.0% professional, 11.8% services, 14.7% sales, 5.9% farming, 2.9% construction, 5.9% production (2006-2010 5-year est.).

Income: Per capita income: $19,398 (2006-2010 5-year est.); Median household income: $40,833 (2006-2010 5-year est.); Average household income: $43,084 (2006-2010 5-year est.); Percent of households with income of $100,000 or more: n/a (2006-2010 5-year est.); Poverty rate: 3.8% (2006-2010 5-year est.).

Education: Percent of population age 25 and over with: High school diploma (including GED) or higher: 82.9% (2006-2010 5-year est.); Bachelor's degree or higher: 0.0% (2006-2010 5-year est.); Master's degree or higher: 0.0% (2006-2010 5-year est.).

Housing: Homeownership rate: 80.8% (2010); Median home value: $104,700 (2006-2010 5-year est.); Median contract rent: $563 per month (2006-2010 5-year est.); Median year structure built: before 1940 (2006-2010 5-year est.).

Transportation: Commute to work: 92.6% car, 0.0% public transportation, 0.0% walk, 7.4% work from home (2006-2010 5-year est.); Travel time to work: 14.3% less than 15 minutes, 66.7% 15 to 30 minutes, 19.0% 30 to 45 minutes, 0.0% 45 to 60 minutes, 0.0% 60 minutes or more (2006-2010 5-year est.)

NITTANY (CDP).
Covers a land area of 1.416 square miles and a water area of 0 square miles. Located at 40.99° N. Lat; 77.55° W. Long. Elevation is 892 feet.

Population: n/a (1990); n/a (2000); 658 (2010); Density: 464.6 persons per square mile (2010); Race: 98.2% White, 0.6% Black, 0.2% Asian, 0.0% American Indian/Alaska Native, 0.0% Native Hawaiian/Other Pacific Islander, 1.0% Other, 0.6% Hispanic of any race (2010); Average household size: 2.41 (2010); Median age: 45.5 (2010); Males per 100 females: 101.8 (2010); Marriage status: 27.6% never married, 59.2% now married, 7.8% widowed, 5.3% divorced (2006-2010 5-year est.); Foreign born: 0.0% (2006-2010 5-year est.); Ancestry (includes multiple ancestries): 42.3% German, 32.0% American, 13.5% Dutch, 10.9% Irish, 4.7% Italian (2006-2010 5-year est.).

Economy: Employment by occupation: 2.3% management, 2.9% professional, 4.1% services, 26.8% sales, 3.1% farming, 24.1% construction, 8.3% production (2006-2010 5-year est.).

Income: Per capita income: $20,069 (2006-2010 5-year est.); Median household income: $45,417 (2006-2010 5-year est.); Average household income: $48,515 (2006-2010 5-year est.); Percent of households with income of $100,000 or more: n/a (2006-2010 5-year est.); Poverty rate: 2.9% (2006-2010 5-year est.).

Education: Percent of population age 25 and over with: High school diploma (including GED) or higher: 82.9% (2006-2010 5-year est.); Bachelor's degree or higher: 3.9% (2006-2010 5-year est.); Master's degree or higher: 2.0% (2006-2010 5-year est.).

Housing: Homeownership rate: 89.0% (2010); Median home value: $138,800 (2006-2010 5-year est.); Median contract rent: $435 per month (2006-2010 5-year est.); Median year structure built: 1973 (2006-2010 5-year est.).

Transportation: Commute to work: 98.1% car, 0.0% public transportation, 0.0% walk, 1.9% work from home (2006-2010 5-year est.); Travel time to work: 17.3% less than 15 minutes, 58.3% 15 to 30 minutes, 10.0% 30 to 45 minutes, 4.7% 45 to 60 minutes, 9.6% 60 minutes or more (2006-2010 5-year est.)

NORTH PHILIPSBURG (CDP).
Covers a land area of 0.756 square miles and a water area of 0 square miles. Located at 40.91° N. Lat; 78.21° W. Long. Elevation is 1,470 feet.

Population: 752 (1990); 697 (2000); 660 (2010); Density: 873.0 persons per square mile (2010); Race: 98.2% White, 0.0% Black, 0.2% Asian, 0.2% American Indian/Alaska Native, 0.0% Native Hawaiian/Other Pacific Islander, 1.4% Other, 0.5% Hispanic of any race (2010); Average household size: 2.10 (2010); Median age: 51.6 (2010); Males per 100 females: 76.9 (2010); Marriage status: 24.4% never married, 52.8% now married, 10.2% widowed, 12.6% divorced (2006-2010 5-year est.); Foreign born: 0.0% (2006-2010 5-year est.); Ancestry (includes multiple ancestries): 15.3% German, 14.3% Irish, 10.7% Slovak, 6.1% English, 5.5% Italian (2006-2010 5-year est.).

Economy: Employment by occupation: 13.3% management, 0.0% professional, 4.5% services, 26.6% sales, 4.2% farming, 18.5% construction, 14.7% production (2006-2010 5-year est.).

Income: Per capita income: $16,432 (2006-2010 5-year est.); Median household income: $36,598 (2006-2010 5-year est.); Average household income: $37,115 (2006-2010 5-year est.); Percent of households with income of $100,000 or more: n/a (2006-2010 5-year est.); Poverty rate: 10.5% (2006-2010 5-year est.).

Education: Percent of population age 25 and over with: High school diploma (including GED) or higher: 80.0% (2006-2010 5-year est.); Bachelor's degree or higher: 0.0% (2006-2010 5-year est.); Master's degree or higher: 0.0% (2006-2010 5-year est.).

Housing: Homeownership rate: 67.3% (2010); Median home value: $72,900 (2006-2010 5-year est.); Median contract rent: $398 per month (2006-2010 5-year est.); Median year structure built: 1964 (2006-2010 5-year est.).

Transportation: Commute to work: 90.6% car, 9.4% public transportation, 0.0% walk, 0.0% work from home (2006-2010 5-year est.); Travel time to work: 26.9% less than 15 minutes, 3.1% 15 to 30 minutes, 42.7% 30 to 45 minutes, 22.7% 45 to 60 minutes, 4.5% 60 minutes or more (2006-2010 5-year est.)

ORVISTON (CDP).
Covers a land area of 0.107 square miles and a water area of 0 square miles. Located at 41.11° N. Lat; 77.75° W. Long.

Population: n/a (1990); n/a (2000); 95 (2010); Density: 886.8 persons per square mile (2010); Race: 96.8% White, 0.0% Black, 2.1% American Indian/Alaska Native, 0.0% Native Hawaiian/Other Pacific Islander, 1.1% Other, 1.1% Hispanic of any race (2010); Average household size: 2.44 (2010); Median age: 46.8 (2010); Males per 100 females: 106.5 (2010); Marriage status: 31.0% never married, 55.2% now married, 0.0% widowed, 13.8% divorced (2006-2010 5-year est.); Foreign born: 0.0% (2006-2010 5-year est.); Ancestry (includes multiple ancestries): 35.5% American, 27.4% German, 17.7% English, 8.1% Dutch, 8.1% Irish (2006-2010 5-year est.).

Economy: Employment by occupation: 0.0% management, 0.0% professional, 0.0% services, 22.2% sales, 0.0% farming, 33.3% construction, 16.7% production (2006-2010 5-year est.).

Income: Per capita income: $16,677 (2006-2010 5-year est.); Median household income: $24,545 (2006-2010 5-year est.); Average household income: $34,429 (2006-2010 5-year est.); Percent of households with income of $100,000 or more: n/a (2006-2010 5-year est.); Poverty rate: 0.0% (2006-2010 5-year est.).

Education: Percent of population age 25 and over with: High school diploma (including GED) or higher: 44.8% (2006-2010 5-year est.); Bachelor's degree or higher: 0.0% (2006-2010 5-year est.); Master's degree or higher: 0.0% (2006-2010 5-year est.).

Housing: Homeownership rate: 87.2% (2010); Median home value: $25,000 (2006-2010 5-year est.); Median contract rent: n/a per month (2006-2010 5-year est.); Median year structure built: before 1940 (2006-2010 5-year est.).

Transportation: Commute to work: 100.0% car, 0.0% public transportation, 0.0% walk, 0.0% work from home (2006-2010 5-year est.); Travel time to work: 0.0% less than 15 minutes, 0.0% 15 to 30 minutes, 22.2% 30 to 45 minutes, 61.1% 45 to 60 minutes, 16.7% 60 minutes or more (2006-2010 5-year est.)

PARK FOREST VILLAGE (CDP).
Covers a land area of 2.453 square miles and a water area of 0 square miles. Located at 40.80° N. Lat; 77.91° W. Long. Elevation is 1,260 feet.

Population: 6,713 (1990); 8,830 (2000); 9,660 (2010); Density: 3,938.5 persons per square mile (2010); Race: 81.7% White, 3.8% Black, 10.8% Asian, 0.1% American Indian/Alaska Native, 0.0% Native Hawaiian/Other Pacific Islander, 3.6% Other, 3.2% Hispanic of any race (2010); Average household size: 2.45 (2010); Median age: 28.9 (2010); Males per 100 females: 105.5 (2010); Marriage status: 37.6% never married, 53.5% now married, 3.5% widowed, 5.4% divorced (2006-2010 5-year est.); Foreign born: 18.3% (2006-2010 5-year est.); Ancestry (includes multiple ancestries): 23.4% German, 14.4% Irish, 10.5% Italian, 7.9% English, 4.7% Polish (2006-2010 5-year est.).

Economy: Employment by occupation: 6.9% management, 8.9% professional, 7.8% services, 14.0% sales, 0.8% farming, 2.3% construction, 3.2% production (2006-2010 5-year est.).

Income: Per capita income: $29,387 (2006-2010 5-year est.); Median household income: $51,587 (2006-2010 5-year est.); Average household income: $71,609 (2006-2010 5-year est.); Percent of households with income of $100,000 or more: 22.8% (2006-2010 5-year est.); Poverty rate: 22.9% (2006-2010 5-year est.).

Education: Percent of population age 25 and over with: High school diploma (including GED) or higher: 97.0% (2006-2010 5-year est.); Bachelor's degree or higher: 71.7% (2006-2010 5-year est.); Master's degree or higher: 38.9% (2006-2010 5-year est.).

Housing: Homeownership rate: 53.8% (2010); Median home value: $216,200 (2006-2010 5-year est.); Median contract rent: $801 per month (2006-2010 5-year est.); Median year structure built: 1980 (2006-2010 5-year est.).

Transportation: Commute to work: 73.9% car, 9.7% public transportation, 4.3% walk, 5.5% work from home (2006-2010 5-year est.); Travel time to work: 47.6% less than 15 minutes, 40.7% 15 to 30 minutes, 6.9% 30 to 45 minutes, 3.7% 45 to 60 minutes, 1.0% 60 minutes or more (2006-2010 5-year est.)

Additional Information Contacts

Chamber of Business & Industry of Centre County . . . . (814) 234-1829
  http://www.cbicc.org

PATTON (township). Covers a land area of 24.531 square miles and a water area of 0.018 square miles. Located at 40.83° N. Lat; 77.92° W. Long.

Population: 9,969 (1990); 11,420 (2000); 15,311 (2010); Density: 624.1 persons per square mile (2010); Race: 83.3% White, 5.7% Black, 7.9% Asian, 0.1% American Indian/Alaska Native, 0.1% Native Hawaiian/Other Pacific Islander, 2.9% Other, 3.2% Hispanic of any race (2010); Average household size: 2.22 (2010); Median age: 27.0 (2010); Males per 100 females: 107.4 (2010); Marriage status: 49.2% never married, 41.8% now married, 3.3% widowed, 5.6% divorced (2006-2010 5-year est.); Foreign born: 11.8% (2006-2010 5-year est.); Ancestry (includes multiple ancestries): 27.3% German, 13.0% Irish, 9.2% English, 8.8% Italian, 6.8% Polish (2006-2010 5-year est.).

Economy: Single-family building permits issued: 40 (2011); Multi-family building permits issued: 0 (2011); Employment by occupation: 9.7% management, 9.4% professional, 5.1% services, 10.3% sales, 1.9% farming, 3.8% construction, 2.2% production (2006-2010 5-year est.).

Income: Per capita income: $31,201 (2006-2010 5-year est.); Median household income: $51,052 (2006-2010 5-year est.); Average household income: $71,705 (2006-2010 5-year est.); Percent of households with income of $100,000 or more: 22.6% (2006-2010 5-year est.); Poverty rate: 21.1% (2006-2010 5-year est.).

Taxes: Total city taxes per capita: $436 (2009); City property taxes per capita: $241 (2009).

Education: Percent of population age 25 and over with: High school diploma (including GED) or higher: 96.7% (2006-2010 5-year est.); Bachelor's degree or higher: 65.8% (2006-2010 5-year est.); Master's degree or higher: 34.7% (2006-2010 5-year est.).

Housing: Homeownership rate: 45.5% (2010); Median home value: $198,300 (2006-2010 5-year est.); Median contract rent: $850 per month (2006-2010 5-year est.); Median year structure built: 1986 (2006-2010 5-year est.).

Safety: Violent crime rate: 3.9 per 10,000 population; Property crime rate: 130.9 per 10,000 population (2011).

Transportation: Commute to work: 80.4% car, 9.1% public transportation, 3.7% walk, 4.7% work from home (2006-2010 5-year est.); Travel time to work: 54.4% less than 15 minutes, 34.8% 15 to 30 minutes, 6.1% 30 to 45 minutes, 3.1% 45 to 60 minutes, 1.5% 60 minutes or more (2006-2010 5-year est.)

Additional Information Contacts

Chamber of Business & Industry of Centre County . . . . (814) 234-1829
  http://www.cbicc.org
Patton Township . . . . (814) 234-0271
  http://twp.patton.pa.us

PENN (township). Covers a land area of 28.358 square miles and a water area of 0.019 square miles. Located at 40.86° N. Lat; 77.49° W. Long.

Population: 935 (1990); 1,044 (2000); 1,181 (2010); Density: 41.6 persons per square mile (2010); Race: 98.6% White, 0.2% Black, 0.5% Asian, 0.1% American Indian/Alaska Native, 0.0% Native Hawaiian/Other Pacific Islander, 0.6% Other, 0.8% Hispanic of any race (2010); Average household size: 2.74 (2010); Median age: 37.7 (2010); Males per 100

females: 109.0 (2010); Marriage status: 21.8% never married, 65.4% now married, 5.0% widowed, 7.9% divorced (2006-2010 5-year est.); Foreign born: 0.2% (2006-2010 5-year est.); Ancestry (includes multiple ancestries): 29.8% German, 15.3% Irish, 9.0% American, 6.3% English, 5.5% Italian (2006-2010 5-year est.).

Economy: Single-family building permits issued: 2 (2011); Multi-family building permits issued: 0 (2011); Employment by occupation: 5.8% management, 3.4% professional, 14.7% services, 13.5% sales, 5.6% farming, 21.0% construction, 14.7% production (2006-2010 5-year est.).

Income: Per capita income: $21,275 (2006-2010 5-year est.); Median household income: $53,636 (2006-2010 5-year est.); Average household income: $60,587 (2006-2010 5-year est.); Percent of households with income of $100,000 or more: 9.3% (2006-2010 5-year est.); Poverty rate: 17.5% (2006-2010 5-year est.).

Education: Percent of population age 25 and over with: High school diploma (including GED) or higher: 91.2% (2006-2010 5-year est.); Bachelor's degree or higher: 18.4% (2006-2010 5-year est.); Master's degree or higher: 6.0% (2006-2010 5-year est.).

Housing: Homeownership rate: 85.2% (2010); Median home value: $167,900 (2006-2010 5-year est.); Median contract rent: $592 per month (2006-2010 5-year est.); Median year structure built: 1964 (2006-2010 5-year est.).

Transportation: Commute to work: 90.3% car, 0.0% public transportation, 2.6% walk, 7.1% work from home (2006-2010 5-year est.); Travel time to work: 27.5% less than 15 minutes, 14.6% 15 to 30 minutes, 37.9% 30 to 45 minutes, 10.5% 45 to 60 minutes, 9.6% 60 minutes or more (2006-2010 5-year est.)

Additional Information Contacts

Chamber of Business & Industry of Centre County . . . . (814) 234-1829
  http://www.cbicc.org

PENNSYLVANIA FURNACE (unincorporated postal area)

Zip Code: 16865

  Covers a land area of 35.072 square miles and a water area of 0.010 square miles. Located at 40.71° N. Lat; 77.99° W. Long. Population: 1,839 (2010); Density: 52.4 persons per square mile (2010); Race: 96.6% White, 0.7% Black, 0.8% Asian, 0.2% American Indian/Alaska Native, 0.0% Native Hawaiian/Other Pacific Islander, 1.7% Other, 2.8% Hispanic of any race (2010); Average household size: 2.57 (2010); Median age: 43.9 (2010); Males per 100 females: 96.5 (2010); Homeownership rate: 89.8% (2010)

PHILIPSBURG (borough). Covers a land area of 0.868 square miles and a water area of 0.011 square miles. Located at 40.89° N. Lat; 78.22° W. Long. Elevation is 1,447 feet.

History: Laid out 1797, incorporated 1864.

Population: 3,002 (1990); 3,056 (2000); 2,770 (2010); Density: 3,190.8 persons per square mile (2010); Race: 97.5% White, 0.3% Black, 0.7% Asian, 0.2% American Indian/Alaska Native, 0.0% Native Hawaiian/Other Pacific Islander, 1.3% Other, 0.6% Hispanic of any race (2010); Average household size: 2.10 (2010); Median age: 41.7 (2010); Males per 100 females: 89.2 (2010); Marriage status: 26.5% never married, 51.1% now married, 8.9% widowed, 13.5% divorced (2006-2010 5-year est.); Foreign born: 2.0% (2006-2010 5-year est.); Ancestry (includes multiple ancestries): 28.8% German, 16.9% American, 16.0% Irish, 11.5% English, 5.2% Slovak (2006-2010 5-year est.).

Economy: Single-family building permits issued: 1 (2011); Multi-family building permits issued: 0 (2011); Employment by occupation: 5.1% management, 3.2% professional, 13.4% services, 15.3% sales, 6.2% farming, 5.6% construction, 4.5% production (2006-2010 5-year est.).

Income: Per capita income: $23,675 (2006-2010 5-year est.); Median household income: $31,903 (2006-2010 5-year est.); Average household income: $48,019 (2006-2010 5-year est.); Percent of households with income of $100,000 or more: 8.0% (2006-2010 5-year est.); Poverty rate: 16.8% (2006-2010 5-year est.).

Education: Percent of population age 25 and over with: High school diploma (including GED) or higher: 89.4% (2006-2010 5-year est.); Bachelor's degree or higher: 19.9% (2006-2010 5-year est.); Master's degree or higher: 10.2% (2006-2010 5-year est.).

School District(s)

Philipsburg-Osceola Area SD (PK-12)
  2010-11 Enrollment: 1,916 . . . . (814) 342-1050
Philipsburg-Osceola Area SD (PK-12)
  2010-11 Enrollment: 1,916 . . . . (814) 342-1050

Housing: Homeownership rate: 55.9% (2010); Median home value: $91,800 (2006-2010 5-year est.); Median contract rent: $356 per month (2006-2010 5-year est.); Median year structure built: 1948 (2006-2010 5-year est.).

Transportation: Commute to work: 91.0% car, 0.0% public transportation, 4.7% walk, 3.7% work from home (2006-2010 5-year est.); Travel time to work: 42.1% less than 15 minutes, 17.0% 15 to 30 minutes, 30.5% 30 to 45 minutes, 3.0% 45 to 60 minutes, 7.4% 60 minutes or more (2006-2010 5-year est.)

Additional Information Contacts

Chamber of Business & Industry of Centre County . . . . (814) 234-1829
http://www.cbicc.org

PINE GLEN (CDP). Covers a land area of 0.179 square miles and a water area of 0 square miles. Located at 41.09° N. Lat; 78.06° W. Long. Elevation is 1,526 feet.

Population: 200 (1990); 210 (2000); 190 (2010); Density: 1,062.7 persons per square mile (2010); Race: 100.0% White, 0.0% Black, 0.0% Asian, 0.0% American Indian/Alaska Native, 0.0% Native Hawaiian/Other Pacific Islander, 0.0% Other, 1.6% Hispanic of any race (2010); Average household size: 2.71 (2010); Median age: 37.2 (2010); Males per 100 females: 134.6 (2010); Marriage status: 19.0% never married, 55.0% now married, 12.0% widowed, 14.0% divorced (2006-2010 5-year est.); Foreign born: 0.0% (2006-2010 5-year est.); Ancestry (includes multiple ancestries): 26.3% German, 17.3% Irish, 10.5% Slovak, 6.8% Dutch, 6.0% Polish (2006-2010 5-year est.).

Economy: Employment by occupation: 8.9% management, 0.0% professional, 0.0% services, 13.3% sales, 0.0% farming, 13.3% construction, 20.0% production (2006-2010 5-year est.).

Income: Per capita income: $17,275 (2006-2010 5-year est.); Median household income: $46,667 (2006-2010 5-year est.); Average household income: $45,146 (2006-2010 5-year est.); Percent of households with income of $100,000 or more: n/a (2006-2010 5-year est.); Poverty rate: 22.1% (2006-2010 5-year est.).

Education: Percent of population age 25 and over with: High school diploma (including GED) or higher: 84.0% (2006-2010 5-year est.); Bachelor's degree or higher: 4.3% (2006-2010 5-year est.); Master's degree or higher: 0.0% (2006-2010 5-year est.).

Housing: Homeownership rate: 95.7% (2010); Median home value: $87,500 (2006-2010 5-year est.); Median contract rent: n/a per month (2006-2010 5-year est.); Median year structure built: 1956 (2006-2010 5-year est.).

Transportation: Commute to work: 100.0% car, 0.0% public transportation, 0.0% walk, 0.0% work from home (2006-2010 5-year est.); Travel time to work: 16.3% less than 15 minutes, 34.7% 15 to 30 minutes, 28.6% 30 to 45 minutes, 16.3% 45 to 60 minutes, 4.1% 60 minutes or more (2006-2010 5-year est.)

PINE GROVE MILLS (CDP). Covers a land area of 2.504 square miles and a water area of 0 square miles. Located at 40.73° N. Lat; 77.89° W. Long. Elevation is 1,296 feet.

Population: 1,147 (1990); 1,141 (2000); 1,502 (2010); Density: 599.8 persons per square mile (2010); Race: 93.9% White, 1.9% Black, 2.0% Asian, 0.1% American Indian/Alaska Native, 0.0% Native Hawaiian/Other Pacific Islander, 2.1% Other, 2.1% Hispanic of any race (2010); Average household size: 2.52 (2010); Median age: 38.9 (2010); Males per 100 females: 95.8 (2010); Marriage status: 20.6% never married, 66.3% now married, 1.4% widowed, 11.7% divorced (2006-2010 5-year est.); Foreign born: 5.2% (2006-2010 5-year est.); Ancestry (includes multiple ancestries): 49.5% German, 9.1% Irish, 6.1% American, 6.1% English, 5.5% Scottish (2006-2010 5-year est.).

Economy: Employment by occupation: 12.8% management, 1.1% professional, 7.8% services, 23.6% sales, 4.6% farming, 5.2% construction, 5.2% production (2006-2010 5-year est.).

Income: Per capita income: $27,494 (2006-2010 5-year est.); Median household income: $45,708 (2006-2010 5-year est.); Average household income: $60,973 (2006-2010 5-year est.); Percent of households with income of $100,000 or more: 16.3% (2006-2010 5-year est.); Poverty rate: 0.0% (2006-2010 5-year est.).

Education: Percent of population age 25 and over with: High school diploma (including GED) or higher: 100.0% (2006-2010 5-year est.); Bachelor's degree or higher: 35.7% (2006-2010 5-year est.); Master's degree or higher: 13.5% (2006-2010 5-year est.).

State College Area SD (KG-12)
2010-11 Enrollment: 6,944 . . . . (814) 231-1011
Housing: Homeownership rate: 81.2% (2010); Median home value: $172,900 (2006-2010 5-year est.); Median contract rent: $766 per month (2006-2010 5-year est.); Median year structure built: 1958 (2006-2010 5-year est.).

Transportation: Commute to work: 76.1% car, 0.0% public transportation, 0.0% walk, 20.2% work from home (2006-2010 5-year est.); Travel time to work: 78.3% less than 15 minutes, 19.5% 15 to 30 minutes, 2.3% 30 to 45 minutes, 0.0% 45 to 60 minutes, 0.0% 60 minutes or more (2006-2010 5-year est.)

Additional Information Contacts

Chamber of Business & Industry of Centre County . . . . (814) 234-1829
http://www.cbicc.org

PLEASANT GAP (CDP). Covers a land area of 1.626 square miles and a water area of 0 square miles. Located at 40.87° N. Lat; 77.74° W. Long. Elevation is 981 feet.

Population: 1,699 (1990); 1,611 (2000); 2,879 (2010); Density: 1,771.0 persons per square mile (2010); Race: 95.7% White, 1.9% Black, 1.0% Asian, 0.2% American Indian/Alaska Native, 0.0% Native Hawaiian/Other Pacific Islander, 1.2% Other, 0.8% Hispanic of any race (2010); Average household size: 2.40 (2010); Median age: 36.9 (2010); Males per 100 females: 96.1 (2010); Marriage status: 33.8% never married, 45.5% now married, 7.8% widowed, 12.9% divorced (2006-2010 5-year est.); Foreign born: 2.7% (2006-2010 5-year est.); Ancestry (includes multiple ancestries): 23.0% German, 13.6% Irish, 13.1% English, 11.9% Italian, 7.5% American (2006-2010 5-year est.).

Economy: Employment by occupation: 16.5% management, 6.2% professional, 7.0% services, 13.3% sales, 3.4% farming, 12.1% construction, 7.0% production (2006-2010 5-year est.).

Income: Per capita income: $25,350 (2006-2010 5-year est.); Median household income: $49,728 (2006-2010 5-year est.); Average household income: $56,686 (2006-2010 5-year est.); Percent of households with income of $100,000 or more: 11.9% (2006-2010 5-year est.); Poverty rate: 4.9% (2006-2010 5-year est.).

Education: Percent of population age 25 and over with: High school diploma (including GED) or higher: 85.9% (2006-2010 5-year est.); Bachelor's degree or higher: 24.9% (2006-2010 5-year est.); Master's degree or higher: 9.7% (2006-2010 5-year est.).

School District(s)
Bellefonte Area SD (KG-12)
2010-11 Enrollment: 2,909 . . . . (814) 355-4814
Central PA Institute of Science & Technology (09-12)
2010-11 Enrollment: n/a . . . . (814) 359-2793
Vocational/Technical School(s)
Central Pennsylvania Institute of Science and Technology (Public)
Fall 2010 Enrollment: 161 . . . . (814) 359-2793
2011-12 Tuition: $12,960
Housing: Homeownership rate: 73.1% (2010); Median home value: $154,800 (2006-2010 5-year est.); Median contract rent: $581 per month (2006-2010 5-year est.); Median year structure built: 1970 (2006-2010 5-year est.).

Hospitals: HealthSouth Nittany Valley Rehabilitation Hospital (87 beds)
Transportation: Commute to work: 86.1% car, 8.7% public transportation, 1.2% walk, 4.0% work from home (2006-2010 5-year est.); Travel time to work: 26.4% less than 15 minutes, 60.8% 15 to 30 minutes, 7.6% 30 to 45 minutes, 3.2% 45 to 60 minutes, 2.0% 60 minutes or more (2006-2010 5-year est.)

Additional Information Contacts

Chamber of Business & Industry of Centre County . . . . (814) 234-1829
http://www.cbicc.org

PORT MATILDA (borough). Covers a land area of 0.563 square miles and a water area of 0 square miles. Located at 40.80° N. Lat; 78.05° W. Long. Elevation is 1,027 feet.

Population: 669 (1990); 638 (2000); 606 (2010); Density: 1,077.0 persons per square mile (2010); Race: 98.0% White, 0.2% Black, 0.2% Asian, 0.2% American Indian/Alaska Native, 0.0% Native Hawaiian/Other Pacific Islander, 1.4% Other, 1.2% Hispanic of any race (2010); Average household size: 2.31 (2010); Median age: 39.9 (2010); Males per 100 females: 103.4 (2010); Marriage status: 24.6% never married, 58.4% now married, 8.8% widowed, 8.2% divorced (2006-2010 5-year est.); Foreign born: 0.0% (2006-2010 5-year est.); Ancestry (includes multiple

ancestries): 28.4% German, 13.9% Irish, 12.4% English, 12.1% Dutch, 8.1% American (2006-2010 5-year est.).
Economy: Single-family building permits issued: 0 (2011); Multi-family building permits issued: 2 (2011); Employment by occupation: 4.9% management, 1.6% professional, 18.8% services, 13.6% sales, 1.9% farming, 10.4% construction, 7.8% production (2006-2010 5-year est.).
Income: Per capita income: $19,418 (2006-2010 5-year est.); Median household income: $32,054 (2006-2010 5-year est.); Average household income: $42,418 (2006-2010 5-year est.); Percent of households with income of $100,000 or more: 4.1% (2006-2010 5-year est.); Poverty rate: 20.2% (2006-2010 5-year est.).
Education: Percent of population age 25 and over with: High school diploma (including GED) or higher: 91.2% (2006-2010 5-year est.); Bachelor's degree or higher: 9.0% (2006-2010 5-year est.); Master's degree or higher: 0.5% (2006-2010 5-year est.).

School District(s)
Bald Eagle Area SD (KG-12)
  2010-11 Enrollment: 1,864 . . . . (814) 355-4860
State College Area SD (KG-12)
  2010-11 Enrollment: 6,944 . . . . (814) 231-1011
Housing: Homeownership rate: 66.4% (2010); Median home value: $98,500 (2006-2010 5-year est.); Median contract rent: $379 per month (2006-2010 5-year est.); Median year structure built: 1945 (2006-2010 5-year est.).
Transportation: Commute to work: 92.7% car, 2.6% public transportation, 2.3% walk, 0.0% work from home (2006-2010 5-year est.); Travel time to work: 10.9% less than 15 minutes, 69.0% 15 to 30 minutes, 14.2% 30 to 45 minutes, 5.9% 45 to 60 minutes, 0.0% 60 minutes or more (2006-2010 5-year est.)

POTTER (township). Covers a land area of 58.856 square miles and a water area of 0.128 square miles. Located at 40.80° N. Lat; 77.65° W. Long.
Population: 3,020 (1990); 3,339 (2000); 3,517 (2010); Density: 59.8 persons per square mile (2010); Race: 98.4% White, 0.3% Black, 0.3% Asian, 0.1% American Indian/Alaska Native, 0.0% Native Hawaiian/Other Pacific Islander, 0.9% Other, 0.9% Hispanic of any race (2010); Average household size: 2.40 (2010); Median age: 46.1 (2010); Males per 100 females: 97.5 (2010); Marriage status: 27.1% never married, 64.6% now married, 5.8% widowed, 2.4% divorced (2006-2010 5-year est.); Foreign born: 2.5% (2006-2010 5-year est.); Ancestry (includes multiple ancestries): 35.1% German, 13.8% Irish, 8.9% English, 7.0% Dutch, 4.3% Pennsylvania German (2006-2010 5-year est.).
Economy: Single-family building permits issued: 8 (2011); Multi-family building permits issued: 0 (2011); Employment by occupation: 15.1% management, 7.4% professional, 7.5% services, 16.3% sales, 2.5% farming, 13.2% construction, 12.3% production (2006-2010 5-year est.).
Income: Per capita income: $26,683 (2006-2010 5-year est.); Median household income: $56,902 (2006-2010 5-year est.); Average household income: $67,866 (2006-2010 5-year est.); Percent of households with income of $100,000 or more: 16.5% (2006-2010 5-year est.); Poverty rate: 12.0% (2006-2010 5-year est.).
Education: Percent of population age 25 and over with: High school diploma (including GED) or higher: 91.1% (2006-2010 5-year est.); Bachelor's degree or higher: 27.0% (2006-2010 5-year est.); Master's degree or higher: 9.6% (2006-2010 5-year est.).
Housing: Homeownership rate: 84.8% (2010); Median home value: $182,600 (2006-2010 5-year est.); Median contract rent: $381 per month (2006-2010 5-year est.); Median year structure built: 1978 (2006-2010 5-year est.).
Transportation: Commute to work: 89.9% car, 0.0% public transportation, 2.2% walk, 5.8% work from home (2006-2010 5-year est.); Travel time to work: 15.2% less than 15 minutes, 58.9% 15 to 30 minutes, 22.2% 30 to 45 minutes, 0.7% 45 to 60 minutes, 3.0% 60 minutes or more (2006-2010 5-year est.)
Additional Information Contacts
Coudersport Area Chamber of Commerce . . . . (814) 274-8165
  http://www.coudersport.org

RAMBLEWOOD (CDP). Covers a land area of 3.099 square miles and a water area of 0 square miles. Located at 40.72° N. Lat; 77.94° W. Long. Elevation is 1,224 feet.
Population: 1,104 (1990); 1,054 (2000); 849 (2010); Density: 273.9 persons per square mile (2010); Race: 96.7% White, 0.0% Black, 1.1% Asian, 0.0% American Indian/Alaska Native, 0.0% Native Hawaiian/Other

Pacific Islander, 2.2% Other, 2.9% Hispanic of any race (2010); Average household size: 2.73 (2010); Median age: 42.6 (2010); Males per 100 females: 91.6 (2010); Marriage status: 21.0% never married, 58.5% now married, 13.9% widowed, 6.6% divorced (2006-2010 5-year est.); Foreign born: 2.2% (2006-2010 5-year est.); Ancestry (includes multiple ancestries): 48.4% German, 16.9% Polish, 16.5% French, 15.0% English, 10.7% Irish (2006-2010 5-year est.).
Economy: Employment by occupation: 8.3% management, 2.9% professional, 5.1% services, 10.9% sales, 8.3% farming, 7.0% construction, 0.0% production (2006-2010 5-year est.).
Income: Per capita income: $29,996 (2006-2010 5-year est.); Median household income: $54,464 (2006-2010 5-year est.); Average household income: $62,755 (2006-2010 5-year est.); Percent of households with income of $100,000 or more: 12.7% (2006-2010 5-year est.); Poverty rate: 0.0% (2006-2010 5-year est.).
Education: Percent of population age 25 and over with: High school diploma (including GED) or higher: 100.0% (2006-2010 5-year est.); Bachelor's degree or higher: 60.5% (2006-2010 5-year est.); Master's degree or higher: 24.0% (2006-2010 5-year est.).
Housing: Homeownership rate: 96.8% (2010); Median home value: $153,800 (2006-2010 5-year est.); Median contract rent: $545 per month (2006-2010 5-year est.); Median year structure built: 1976 (2006-2010 5-year est.).
Transportation: Commute to work: 97.3% car, 0.0% public transportation, 0.0% walk, 0.0% work from home (2006-2010 5-year est.); Travel time to work: 14.1% less than 15 minutes, 68.7% 15 to 30 minutes, 12.9% 30 to 45 minutes, 4.4% 45 to 60 minutes, 0.0% 60 minutes or more (2006-2010 5-year est.)
Additional Information Contacts
Chamber of Business & Industry of Centre County . . . . (814) 234-1829
  http://www.cbicc.org

REBERSBURG (CDP). Covers a land area of 1.360 square miles and a water area of 0 square miles. Located at 40.94° N. Lat; 77.44° W. Long. Elevation is 1,286 feet.
Population: 474 (1990); 492 (2000); 494 (2010); Density: 363.3 persons per square mile (2010); Race: 97.8% White, 0.4% Black, 0.6% Asian, 0.2% American Indian/Alaska Native, 0.0% Native Hawaiian/Other Pacific Islander, 1.0% Other, 0.0% Hispanic of any race (2010); Average household size: 2.76 (2010); Median age: 37.7 (2010); Males per 100 females: 87.1 (2010); Marriage status: 22.1% never married, 46.0% now married, 16.7% widowed, 15.2% divorced (2006-2010 5-year est.); Foreign born: 0.0% (2006-2010 5-year est.); Ancestry (includes multiple ancestries): 47.6% German, 6.8% Dutch, 5.6% Irish, 4.7% American, 4.1% Scotch-Irish (2006-2010 5-year est.).
Economy: Employment by occupation: 9.7% management, 5.2% professional, 11.2% services, 26.9% sales, 3.7% farming, 9.7% construction, 11.2% production (2006-2010 5-year est.).
Income: Per capita income: $21,702 (2006-2010 5-year est.); Median household income: $31,417 (2006-2010 5-year est.); Average household income: $43,183 (2006-2010 5-year est.); Percent of households with income of $100,000 or more: 8.9% (2006-2010 5-year est.); Poverty rate: 7.7% (2006-2010 5-year est.).
Education: Percent of population age 25 and over with: High school diploma (including GED) or higher: 88.6% (2006-2010 5-year est.); Bachelor's degree or higher: 13.9% (2006-2010 5-year est.); Master's degree or higher: 6.3% (2006-2010 5-year est.).

School District(s)
Penns Valley Area SD (KG-12)
  2010-11 Enrollment: 1,459 . . . . (814) 422-2000
Housing: Homeownership rate: 78.2% (2010); Median home value: $142,000 (2006-2010 5-year est.); Median contract rent: $592 per month (2006-2010 5-year est.); Median year structure built: 1945 (2006-2010 5-year est.).
Transportation: Commute to work: 80.9% car, 0.0% public transportation, 0.0% walk, 16.0% work from home (2006-2010 5-year est.); Travel time to work: 12.7% less than 15 minutes, 30.0% 15 to 30 minutes, 37.3% 30 to 45 minutes, 20.0% 45 to 60 minutes, 0.0% 60 minutes or more (2006-2010 5-year est.)

RUSH (township). Covers a land area of 148.072 square miles and a water area of 0.239 square miles. Located at 40.83° N. Lat; 78.18° W. Long.
Population: 3,457 (1990); 3,466 (2000); 4,008 (2010); Density: 27.1 persons per square mile (2010); Race: 99.2% White, 0.0% Black, 0.0%

Asian, 0.1% American Indian/Alaska Native, 0.0% Native Hawaiian/Other Pacific Islander, 0.7% Other, 0.4% Hispanic of any race (2010); Average household size: 2.33 (2010); Median age: 46.0 (2010); Males per 100 females: 97.6 (2010); Marriage status: 22.4% never married, 63.7% now married, 4.6% widowed, 9.3% divorced (2006-2010 5-year est.); Foreign born: 0.4% (2006-2010 5-year est.); Ancestry (includes multiple ancestries): 23.4% German, 18.9% Irish, 15.5% English, 11.3% American, 6.1% Slovak (2006-2010 5-year est.).

Economy: Single-family building permits issued: 3 (2011); Multi-family building permits issued: 0 (2011); Employment by occupation: 8.3% management, 3.1% professional, 10.4% services, 20.9% sales, 1.5% farming, 17.9% construction, 9.8% production (2006-2010 5-year est.).

Income: Per capita income: $24,068 (2006-2010 5-year est.); Median household income: $49,205 (2006-2010 5-year est.); Average household income: $57,815 (2006-2010 5-year est.); Percent of households with income of $100,000 or more: 15.7% (2006-2010 5-year est.); Poverty rate: 5.8% (2006-2010 5-year est.).

Education: Percent of population age 25 and over with: High school diploma (including GED) or higher: 90.2% (2006-2010 5-year est.); Bachelor's degree or higher: 9.8% (2006-2010 5-year est.); Master's degree or higher: 3.8% (2006-2010 5-year est.).

Housing: Homeownership rate: 85.5% (2010); Median home value: $94,000 (2006-2010 5-year est.); Median contract rent: $411 per month (2006-2010 5-year est.); Median year structure built: 1962 (2006-2010 5-year est.).

Transportation: Commute to work: 95.9% car, 1.5% public transportation, 0.5% walk, 1.9% work from home (2006-2010 5-year est.); Travel time to work: 24.0% less than 15 minutes, 19.2% 15 to 30 minutes, 33.2% 30 to 45 minutes, 14.0% 45 to 60 minutes, 9.6% 60 minutes or more (2006-2010 5-year est.).

Additional Information Contacts

Chamber of Business & Industry of Centre County . . . . . . (814) 234-1829
   http://www.cbicc.org

SANDY RIDGE (CDP).
Covers a land area of 0.637 square miles and a water area of 0 square miles. Located at 40.81° N. Lat; 78.23° W. Long. Elevation is 1,864 feet.

Population: 355 (1990); 340 (2000); 407 (2010); Density: 638.8 persons per square mile (2010); Race: 99.8% White, 0.0% Black, 0.0% Asian, 0.0% American Indian/Alaska Native, 0.0% Native Hawaiian/Other Pacific Islander, 0.2% Other, 0.5% Hispanic of any race (2010); Average household size: 2.39 (2010); Median age: 44.7 (2010); Males per 100 females: 95.7 (2010); Marriage status: 34.1% never married, 65.9% now married, 0.0% widowed, 0.0% divorced (2006-2010 5-year est.); Foreign born: 0.0% (2006-2010 5-year est.); Ancestry (includes multiple ancestries): 35.7% German, 27.6% American, 22.6% Russian, 21.3% Irish, 9.5% Polish (2006-2010 5-year est.).

Economy: Employment by occupation: 17.1% management, 11.6% professional, 19.2% services, 10.3% sales, 0.0% farming, 24.7% construction, 0.0% production (2006-2010 5-year est.).

Income: Per capita income: $24,197 (2006-2010 5-year est.); Median household income: $41,406 (2006-2010 5-year est.); Average household income: $56,547 (2006-2010 5-year est.); Percent of households with income of $100,000 or more: n/a (2006-2010 5-year est.); Poverty rate: 0.0% (2006-2010 5-year est.).

Education: Percent of population age 25 and over with: High school diploma (including GED) or higher: 80.2% (2006-2010 5-year est.); Bachelor's degree or higher: 0.0% (2006-2010 5-year est.); Master's degree or higher: 0.0% (2006-2010 5-year est.).

Housing: Homeownership rate: 91.7% (2010); Median home value: $65,900 (2006-2010 5-year est.); Median contract rent: n/a per month (2006-2010 5-year est.); Median year structure built: 1958 (2006-2010 5-year est.).

Transportation: Commute to work: 100.0% car, 0.0% public transportation, 0.0% walk, 0.0% work from home (2006-2010 5-year est.); Travel time to work: 10.3% less than 15 minutes, 21.2% 15 to 30 minutes, 21.9% 30 to 45 minutes, 26.0% 45 to 60 minutes, 20.5% 60 minutes or more (2006-2010 5-year est.)

SNOW SHOE (borough).
Covers a land area of 0.589 square miles and a water area of 0 square miles. Located at 41.03° N. Lat; 77.95° W. Long. Elevation is 1,542 feet.

Population: 800 (1990); 771 (2000); 765 (2010); Density: 1,298.9 persons per square mile (2010); Race: 99.6% White, 0.0% Black, 0.1% Asian, 0.0% American Indian/Alaska Native, 0.0% Native Hawaiian/Other Pacific

Islander, 0.3% Other, 0.1% Hispanic of any race (2010); Average household size: 2.64 (2010); Median age: 40.4 (2010); Males per 100 females: 98.2 (2010); Marriage status: 24.9% never married, 56.4% now married, 12.7% widowed, 6.0% divorced (2006-2010 5-year est.); Foreign born: 0.0% (2006-2010 5-year est.); Ancestry (includes multiple ancestries): 36.4% German, 21.4% Irish, 13.5% English, 8.6% Slovak, 8.0% American (2006-2010 5-year est.).

Economy: Single-family building permits issued: 3 (2011); Multi-family building permits issued: 0 (2011); Employment by occupation: 1.8% management, 4.2% professional, 11.1% services, 15.7% sales, 1.2% farming, 13.3% construction, 7.5% production (2006-2010 5-year est.).

Income: Per capita income: $21,225 (2006-2010 5-year est.); Median household income: $48,789 (2006-2010 5-year est.); Average household income: $53,717 (2006-2010 5-year est.); Percent of households with income of $100,000 or more: 8.6% (2006-2010 5-year est.); Poverty rate: 2.6% (2006-2010 5-year est.).

Education: Percent of population age 25 and over with: High school diploma (including GED) or higher: 92.4% (2006-2010 5-year est.); Bachelor's degree or higher: 16.5% (2006-2010 5-year est.); Master's degree or higher: 3.7% (2006-2010 5-year est.).

School District(s)

Bald Eagle Area SD (KG-12)
   2010-11 Enrollment: 1,864 . . . . (814) 355-4860

Housing: Homeownership rate: 83.8% (2010); Median home value: $114,900 (2006-2010 5-year est.); Median contract rent: $522 per month (2006-2010 5-year est.); Median year structure built: 1964 (2006-2010 5-year est.).

Transportation: Commute to work: 93.8% car, 0.0% public transportation, 4.0% walk, 2.2% work from home (2006-2010 5-year est.); Travel time to work: 10.8% less than 15 minutes, 27.5% 15 to 30 minutes, 44.3% 30 to 45 minutes, 10.1% 45 to 60 minutes, 7.3% 60 minutes or more (2006-2010 5-year est.)

SNOW SHOE (township).
Covers a land area of 84.000 square miles and a water area of 0.013 square miles. Located at 41.05° N. Lat; 77.93° W. Long. Elevation is 1,542 feet.

Population: 1,756 (1990); 1,760 (2000); 1,746 (2010); Density: 20.8 persons per square mile (2010); Race: 99.5% White, 0.0% Black, 0.1% Asian, 0.2% American Indian/Alaska Native, 0.0% Native Hawaiian/Other Pacific Islander, 0.2% Other, 0.8% Hispanic of any race (2010); Average household size: 2.42 (2010); Median age: 43.9 (2010); Males per 100 females: 102.1 (2010); Marriage status: 24.4% never married, 61.3% now married, 8.3% widowed, 6.0% divorced (2006-2010 5-year est.); Foreign born: 0.3% (2006-2010 5-year est.); Ancestry (includes multiple ancestries): 16.9% German, 16.3% Slovak, 12.0% Irish, 9.7% American, 8.3% Dutch (2006-2010 5-year est.).

Economy: Single-family building permits issued: 0 (2011); Multi-family building permits issued: 0 (2011); Employment by occupation: 3.5% management, 2.3% professional, 13.5% services, 14.7% sales, 4.7% farming, 13.0% construction, 8.9% production (2006-2010 5-year est.).

Income: Per capita income: $21,324 (2006-2010 5-year est.); Median household income: $49,250 (2006-2010 5-year est.); Average household income: $54,301 (2006-2010 5-year est.); Percent of households with income of $100,000 or more: 6.8% (2006-2010 5-year est.); Poverty rate: 7.2% (2006-2010 5-year est.).

Education: Percent of population age 25 and over with: High school diploma (including GED) or higher: 83.1% (2006-2010 5-year est.); Bachelor's degree or higher: 6.5% (2006-2010 5-year est.); Master's degree or higher: 1.1% (2006-2010 5-year est.).

Housing: Homeownership rate: 86.1% (2010); Median home value: $97,400 (2006-2010 5-year est.); Median contract rent: $352 per month (2006-2010 5-year est.); Median year structure built: 1969 (2006-2010 5-year est.).

Transportation: Commute to work: 96.2% car, 0.0% public transportation, 1.4% walk, 1.0% work from home (2006-2010 5-year est.); Travel time to work: 25.3% less than 15 minutes, 18.5% 15 to 30 minutes, 37.6% 30 to 45 minutes, 9.5% 45 to 60 minutes, 9.2% 60 minutes or more (2006-2010 5-year est.).

Additional Information Contacts

Chamber of Business & Industry of Centre County . . . . . . (814) 234-1829
   http://www.cbicc.org

SNYDERTOWN (CDP). Covers a land area of 3.055 square miles and a water area of 0 square miles. Located at 40.99° N. Lat; 77.60° W. Long. Elevation is 883 feet.

Population: n/a (1990); n/a (2000); 483 (2010); Density: 158.1 persons per square mile (2010); Race: 97.5% White, 0.4% Black, 0.0% Asian, 0.2% American Indian/Alaska Native, 0.0% Native Hawaiian/Other Pacific Islander, 1.9% Other, 0.2% Hispanic of any race (2010); Average household size: 2.95 (2010); Median age: 38.8 (2010); Males per 100 females: 102.9 (2010); Marriage status: 31.2% never married, 68.1% now married, 0.0% widowed, 0.7% divorced (2006-2010 5-year est.); Foreign born: 0.0% (2006-2010 5-year est.); Ancestry (includes multiple ancestries): 53.6% German, 7.5% American, 4.5% Italian, 4.5% Dutch, 3.0% Greek (2006-2010 5-year est.).

Economy: Employment by occupation: 17.6% management, 5.3% professional, 10.2% services, 1.6% sales, 13.9% farming, 8.2% construction, 1.6% production (2006-2010 5-year est.).

Income: Per capita income: $18,363 (2006-2010 5-year est.); Median household income: $58,462 (2006-2010 5-year est.); Average household income: $66,611 (2006-2010 5-year est.); Percent of households with income of $100,000 or more: 19.8% (2006-2010 5-year est.); Poverty rate: 23.5% (2006-2010 5-year est.).

Education: Percent of population age 25 and over with: High school diploma (including GED) or higher: 82.7% (2006-2010 5-year est.); Bachelor's degree or higher: 12.7% (2006-2010 5-year est.); Master's degree or higher: 3.4% (2006-2010 5-year est.).

Housing: Homeownership rate: 92.7% (2010); Median home value: $169,200 (2006-2010 5-year est.); Median contract rent: n/a per month (2006-2010 5-year est.); Median year structure built: 2001 (2006-2010 5-year est.).

Transportation: Commute to work: 85.3% car, 0.0% public transportation, 9.1% walk, 5.6% work from home (2006-2010 5-year est.); Travel time to work: 9.6% less than 15 minutes, 51.6% 15 to 30 minutes, 36.1% 30 to 45 minutes, 2.7% 45 to 60 minutes, 0.0% 60 minutes or more (2006-2010 5-year est.)

SOUTH PHILIPSBURG (CDP). Covers a land area of 0.260 square miles and a water area of 0 square miles. Located at 40.89° N. Lat; 78.22° W. Long. Elevation is 1,440 feet.

Population: 438 (1990); 438 (2000); 410 (2010); Density: 1,575.4 persons per square mile (2010); Race: 99.3% White, 0.0% Black, 0.0% Asian, 0.2% American Indian/Alaska Native, 0.0% Native Hawaiian/Other Pacific Islander, 0.5% Other, 1.2% Hispanic of any race (2010); Average household size: 2.28 (2010); Median age: 44.0 (2010); Males per 100 females: 100.0 (2010); Marriage status: 29.7% never married, 56.8% now married, 3.0% widowed, 10.4% divorced (2006-2010 5-year est.); Foreign born: 0.0% (2006-2010 5-year est.); Ancestry (includes multiple ancestries): 15.3% American, 14.6% German, 12.4% English, 6.5% Irish, 4.9% French (2006-2010 5-year est.).

Economy: Employment by occupation: 7.7% management, 1.1% professional, 13.2% services, 26.6% sales, 0.3% farming, 8.2% construction, 4.7% production (2006-2010 5-year est.).

Income: Per capita income: $21,359 (2006-2010 5-year est.); Median household income: $58,929 (2006-2010 5-year est.); Average household income: $65,600 (2006-2010 5-year est.); Percent of households with income of $100,000 or more: 17.8% (2006-2010 5-year est.); Poverty rate: 5.2% (2006-2010 5-year est.).

Education: Percent of population age 25 and over with: High school diploma (including GED) or higher: 89.3% (2006-2010 5-year est.); Bachelor's degree or higher: 16.6% (2006-2010 5-year est.); Master's degree or higher: 4.8% (2006-2010 5-year est.).

Housing: Homeownership rate: 86.1% (2010); Median home value: $76,000 (2006-2010 5-year est.); Median contract rent: $633 per month (2006-2010 5-year est.); Median year structure built: 1957 (2006-2010 5-year est.).

Transportation: Commute to work: 98.1% car, 0.8% public transportation, 0.0% walk, 0.0% work from home (2006-2010 5-year est.); Travel time to work: 20.3% less than 15 minutes, 16.3% 15 to 30 minutes, 42.3% 30 to 45 minutes, 8.4% 45 to 60 minutes, 12.7% 60 minutes or more (2006-2010 5-year est.)

SPRING (township). Covers a land area of 27.133 square miles and a water area of 0.005 square miles. Located at 40.89° N. Lat; 77.73° W. Long.

Population: 5,344 (1990); 6,117 (2000); 7,470 (2010); Density: 275.3 persons per square mile (2010); Race: 96.6% White, 1.0% Black, 0.7%

Asian, 0.1% American Indian/Alaska Native, 0.0% Native Hawaiian/Other Pacific Islander, 1.6% Other, 1.0% Hispanic of any race (2010); Average household size: 2.36 (2010); Median age: 40.1 (2010); Males per 100 females: 95.9 (2010); Marriage status: 26.6% never married, 58.3% now married, 5.7% widowed, 9.4% divorced (2006-2010 5-year est.); Foreign born: 2.9% (2006-2010 5-year est.); Ancestry (includes multiple ancestries): 29.9% German, 16.3% Irish, 8.5% English, 7.5% Italian, 6.9% American (2006-2010 5-year est.).

Economy: Single-family building permits issued: 17 (2011); Multi-family building permits issued: 10 (2011); Employment by occupation: 10.6% management, 6.3% professional, 8.9% services, 14.7% sales, 5.2% farming, 14.4% construction, 6.3% production (2006-2010 5-year est.).

Income: Per capita income: $23,485 (2006-2010 5-year est.); Median household income: $49,312 (2006-2010 5-year est.); Average household income: $56,926 (2006-2010 5-year est.); Percent of households with income of $100,000 or more: 14.1% (2006-2010 5-year est.); Poverty rate: 7.9% (2006-2010 5-year est.).

Education: Percent of population age 25 and over with: High school diploma (including GED) or higher: 88.5% (2006-2010 5-year est.); Bachelor's degree or higher: 23.5% (2006-2010 5-year est.); Master's degree or higher: 8.1% (2006-2010 5-year est.).

Housing: Homeownership rate: 71.4% (2010); Median home value: $159,200 (2006-2010 5-year est.); Median contract rent: $554 per month (2006-2010 5-year est.); Median year structure built: 1975 (2006-2010 5-year est.).

Safety: Violent crime rate: 5.3 per 10,000 population; Property crime rate: 38.7 per 10,000 population (2011).

Transportation: Commute to work: 93.1% car, 3.6% public transportation, 0.8% walk, 2.5% work from home (2006-2010 5-year est.); Travel time to work: 27.0% less than 15 minutes, 54.0% 15 to 30 minutes, 12.2% 30 to 45 minutes, 2.8% 45 to 60 minutes, 4.0% 60 minutes or more (2006-2010 5-year est.)

Additional Information Contacts

Chamber of Business & Industry of Centre County . . . . . . (814) 234-1829
  http://www.cbicc.org
Spring Township . . . . (814) 355-7543
  http://www.springtownship.org

SPRING MILLS (CDP). Aka Rising Springs. Covers a land area of 0.445 square miles and a water area of 0 square miles. Located at 40.85° N. Lat; 77.56° W. Long. Elevation is 1,106 feet.

Population: 278 (1990); 289 (2000); 268 (2010); Density: 602.6 persons per square mile (2010); Race: 99.6% White, 0.0% Black, 0.0% Asian, 0.0% American Indian/Alaska Native, 0.0% Native Hawaiian/Other Pacific Islander, 0.4% Other, 0.4% Hispanic of any race (2010); Average household size: 2.46 (2010); Median age: 41.6 (2010); Males per 100 females: 106.2 (2010); Marriage status: 13.5% never married, 60.9% now married, 3.8% widowed, 21.8% divorced (2006-2010 5-year est.); Foreign born: 0.0% (2006-2010 5-year est.); Ancestry (includes multiple ancestries): 40.8% German, 12.0% Irish, 11.5% Swiss, 11.5% Dutch, 8.4% French (2006-2010 5-year est.).

Economy: Employment by occupation: 19.6% management, 5.4% professional, 14.3% services, 0.0% sales, 0.0% farming, 14.3% construction, 0.0% production (2006-2010 5-year est.).

Income: Per capita income: $21,941 (2006-2010 5-year est.); Median household income: $38,542 (2006-2010 5-year est.); Average household income: $46,532 (2006-2010 5-year est.); Percent of households with income of $100,000 or more: n/a (2006-2010 5-year est.); Poverty rate: 7.3% (2006-2010 5-year est.).

Education: Percent of population age 25 and over with: High school diploma (including GED) or higher: 95.4% (2006-2010 5-year est.); Bachelor's degree or higher: 39.1% (2006-2010 5-year est.); Master's degree or higher: 0.0% (2006-2010 5-year est.).

School District(s)

Penns Valley Area SD (KG-12)
  2010-11 Enrollment: 1,459 . . . . (814) 422-2000

Housing: Homeownership rate: 70.7% (2010); Median home value: $133,300 (2006-2010 5-year est.); Median contract rent: $441 per month (2006-2010 5-year est.); Median year structure built: before 1940 (2006-2010 5-year est.).

Transportation: Commute to work: 88.4% car, 0.0% public transportation, 7.1% walk, 4.5% work from home (2006-2010 5-year est.); Travel time to work: 15.0% less than 15 minutes, 35.5% 15 to 30 minutes, 43.0% 30 to 45 minutes, 0.0% 45 to 60 minutes, 6.5% 60 minutes or more (2006-2010 5-year est.)

STATE COLLEGE (borough).

STATE COLLEGE (borough). Covers a land area of 4.557 square miles and a water area of 0 square miles. Located at 40.79° N. Lat; 77.86° W. Long. Elevation is 1,165 feet.

History: Pennsylvania State College began as a small State-aided farm school, chartered in 1855. It was originally called Farmers High School to teach better methods of soil cultivation. The borough of State College was incorporated from parts of two connecting townships.

Population: 38,933 (1990); 38,420 (2000); 42,034 (2010); Density: 9,223.2 persons per square mile (2010); Race: 83.2% White, 3.8% Black, 9.8% Asian, 0.2% American Indian/Alaska Native, 0.0% Native Hawaiian/Other Pacific Islander, 3.0% Other, 3.9% Hispanic of any race (2010); Average household size: 2.30 (2010); Median age: 21.5 (2010); Males per 100 females: 117.2 (2010); Marriage status: 82.6% never married, 13.8% now married, 1.3% widowed, 2.3% divorced (2006-2010 5-year est.); Foreign born: 9.8% (2006-2010 5-year est.); Ancestry (includes multiple ancestries): 21.3% German, 14.7% Irish, 10.0% Italian, 6.3% Polish, 5.5% English (2006-2010 5-year est.).

Economy: Unemployment rate: 7.2% (August 2012); Total civilian labor force: 18,853 (August 2012); Single-family building permits issued: 0 (2011); Multi-family building permits issued: 0 (2011); Employment by occupation: 6.4% management, 8.1% professional, 11.2% services, 16.3% sales, 4.2% farming, 3.4% construction, 1.9% production (2006-2010 5-year est.).

Income: Per capita income: $13,336 (2006-2010 5-year est.); Median household income: $23,513 (2006-2010 5-year est.); Average household income: $42,235 (2006-2010 5-year est.); Percent of households with income of $100,000 or more: 11.0% (2006-2010 5-year est.); Poverty rate: 48.4% (2006-2010 5-year est.).

Taxes: Total city taxes per capita: $262 (2009); City property taxes per capita: $112 (2009).

Education: Percent of population age 25 and over with: High school diploma (including GED) or higher: 95.3% (2006-2010 5-year est.); Bachelor's degree or higher: 66.0% (2006-2010 5-year est.); Master's degree or higher: 36.8% (2006-2010 5-year est.).

School District(s)

Centre Learning Community CS (05-08)
    2010-11 Enrollment: 94 . . . . (814) 861-7980
Nittany Valley CS (01-08)
    2010-11 Enrollment: 48 . . . . (814) 867-3842
State College Area SD (KG-12)
    2010-11 Enrollment: 6,944 . . . . (814) 231-1011
Wonderland CS (KG-KG)
    2010-11 Enrollment: 29 . . . . (814) 234-5886
Young Scholars of Central PA CS (KG-06)
    2010-11 Enrollment: 172 . . . . (814) 237-9727

Two-year College(s)

South Hills School of Business & Technology (Private, For-profit)
    Fall 2010 Enrollment: 975 . . . . (814) 234-7755
    2011-12 Tuition: In-state $14,961; Out-of-state $14,961

Vocational/Technical School(s)

Empire Beauty School-State College (Private, For-profit)
    Fall 2010 Enrollment: 79 . . . . (800) 223-3271
    2011-12 Tuition: $14,490

Housing: Homeownership rate: 20.3% (2010); Median home value: $237,900 (2006-2010 5-year est.); Median contract rent: $743 per month (2006-2010 5-year est.); Median year structure built: 1971 (2006-2010 5-year est.).

Hospitals: Mount Nittany Medical Center

Safety: Violent crime rate: 10.1 per 10,000 population; Property crime rate: 157.8 per 10,000 population (2011).

Newspapers: The Bargain Sheet (Community news; Circulation 38,000); Centre Daily Times (Local news; Circulation 31,259)

Transportation: Commute to work: 46.5% car, 6.1% public transportation, 39.4% walk, 4.0% work from home (2006-2010 5-year est.); Travel time to work: 55.0% less than 15 minutes, 35.2% 15 to 30 minutes, 6.4% 30 to 45 minutes, 1.5% 45 to 60 minutes, 2.0% 60 minutes or more (2006-2010 5-year est.).

Airports: University Park (primary service)

Additional Information Contacts

Borough of State College . . . . (814) 234-7100
    http://www.statecollegepa.us
Chamber of Business & Industry of Centre County . . . . . . (814) 234-1829
    http://www.cbicc.org

STORMSTOWN (CDP).

STORMSTOWN (CDP). Covers a land area of 7.950 square miles and a water area of 0 square miles. Located at 40.79° N. Lat; 78.02° W. Long. Elevation is 1,329 feet.

Population: 998 (1990); 1,602 (2000); 2,366 (2010); Density: 297.6 persons per square mile (2010); Race: 97.2% White, 0.5% Black, 0.9% Asian, 0.0% American Indian/Alaska Native, 0.0% Native Hawaiian/Other Pacific Islander, 1.4% Other, 1.2% Hispanic of any race (2010); Average household size: 3.00 (2010); Median age: 40.6 (2010); Males per 100 females: 103.6 (2010); Marriage status: 16.8% never married, 75.9% now married, 2.6% widowed, 4.8% divorced (2006-2010 5-year est.); Foreign born: 1.7% (2006-2010 5-year est.); Ancestry (includes multiple ancestries): 36.1% German, 17.5% Irish, 10.0% English, 8.4% Polish, 6.6% Italian (2006-2010 5-year est.).

Economy: Employment by occupation: 13.3% management, 12.0% professional, 7.0% services, 15.2% sales, 3.2% farming, 4.9% construction, 3.6% production (2006-2010 5-year est.).

Income: Per capita income: $34,855 (2006-2010 5-year est.); Median household income: $99,318 (2006-2010 5-year est.); Average household income: $103,990 (2006-2010 5-year est.); Percent of households with income of $100,000 or more: 49.6% (2006-2010 5-year est.); Poverty rate: 3.7% (2006-2010 5-year est.).

Education: Percent of population age 25 and over with: High school diploma (including GED) or higher: 99.1% (2006-2010 5-year est.); Bachelor's degree or higher: 51.4% (2006-2010 5-year est.); Master's degree or higher: 19.1% (2006-2010 5-year est.).

Housing: Homeownership rate: 92.4% (2010); Median home value: $236,200 (2006-2010 5-year est.); Median contract rent: $425 per month (2006-2010 5-year est.); Median year structure built: 1989 (2006-2010 5-year est.).

Transportation: Commute to work: 93.8% car, 0.0% public transportation, 0.0% walk, 5.7% work from home (2006-2010 5-year est.); Travel time to work: 7.3% less than 15 minutes, 73.2% 15 to 30 minutes, 11.2% 30 to 45 minutes, 2.6% 45 to 60 minutes, 5.7% 60 minutes or more (2006-2010 5-year est.).

Additional Information Contacts

Chamber of Business & Industry of Centre County . . . . . . (814) 234-1829
    http://www.cbicc.org

TAYLOR (township).

TAYLOR (township). Covers a land area of 30.754 square miles and a water area of 0 square miles. Located at 40.77° N. Lat; 78.16° W. Long.

Population: 714 (1990); 741 (2000); 853 (2010); Density: 27.7 persons per square mile (2010); Race: 99.3% White, 0.0% Black, 0.0% Asian, 0.0% American Indian/Alaska Native, 0.0% Native Hawaiian/Other Pacific Islander, 0.7% Other, 0.5% Hispanic of any race (2010); Average household size: 2.38 (2010); Median age: 45.2 (2010); Males per 100 females: 113.3 (2010); Marriage status: 18.5% never married, 67.4% now married, 6.0% widowed, 8.1% divorced (2006-2010 5-year est.); Foreign born: 0.0% (2006-2010 5-year est.); Ancestry (includes multiple ancestries): 21.9% German, 16.0% Irish, 15.5% American, 9.6% English, 5.9% Scotch-Irish (2006-2010 5-year est.).

Economy: Single-family building permits issued: 2 (2011); Multi-family building permits issued: 0 (2011); Employment by occupation: 5.4% management, 0.0% professional, 14.3% services, 24.3% sales, 3.1% farming, 16.1% construction, 2.7% production (2006-2010 5-year est.).

Income: Per capita income: $22,453 (2006-2010 5-year est.); Median household income: $46,420 (2006-2010 5-year est.); Average household income: $53,429 (2006-2010 5-year est.); Percent of households with income of $100,000 or more: 7.8% (2006-2010 5-year est.); Poverty rate: 8.7% (2006-2010 5-year est.).

Education: Percent of population age 25 and over with: High school diploma (including GED) or higher: 89.6% (2006-2010 5-year est.); Bachelor's degree or higher: 9.9% (2006-2010 5-year est.); Master's degree or higher: 4.2% (2006-2010 5-year est.).

Housing: Homeownership rate: 88.8% (2010); Median home value: $155,100 (2006-2010 5-year est.); Median contract rent: $342 per month (2006-2010 5-year est.); Median year structure built: 1975 (2006-2010 5-year est.).

Transportation: Commute to work: 97.4% car, 0.0% public transportation, 0.9% walk, 1.6% work from home (2006-2010 5-year est.); Travel time to work: 6.2% less than 15 minutes, 35.3% 15 to 30 minutes, 38.6% 30 to 45 minutes, 10.2% 45 to 60 minutes, 9.7% 60 minutes or more (2006-2010 5-year est.).

TOFTREES (CDP). Covers a land area of 0.878 square miles and a water area of 0 square miles. Located at 40.82° N. Lat; 77.89° W. Long.
Population: n/a (1990); n/a (2000); 2,053 (2010); Density: 2,337.8 persons per square mile (2010); Race: 86.6% White, 2.9% Black, 7.6% Asian, 0.0% American Indian/Alaska Native, 0.0% Native Hawaiian/Other Pacific Islander, 2.9% Other, 2.4% Hispanic of any race (2010); Average household size: 1.69 (2010); Median age: 31.2 (2010); Males per 100 females: 101.9 (2010); Marriage status: 44.1% never married, 47.6% now married, 5.0% widowed, 3.3% divorced (2006-2010 5-year est.); Foreign born: 11.9% (2006-2010 5-year est.); Ancestry (includes multiple ancestries): 40.9% German, 15.3% English, 13.4% Irish, 7.7% Italian, 4.6% French (2006-2010 5-year est.).
Economy: Employment by occupation: 9.0% management, 11.1% professional, 6.7% services, 5.2% sales, 2.8% farming, 2.5% construction, 2.0% production (2006-2010 5-year est.).
Income: Per capita income: $34,830 (2006-2010 5-year est.); Median household income: $51,027 (2006-2010 5-year est.); Average household income: $63,870 (2006-2010 5-year est.); Percent of households with income of $100,000 or more: 15.3% (2006-2010 5-year est.); Poverty rate: 12.8% (2006-2010 5-year est.).
Education: Percent of population age 25 and over with: High school diploma (including GED) or higher: 97.3% (2006-2010 5-year est.); Bachelor's degree or higher: 71.8% (2006-2010 5-year est.); Master's degree or higher: 38.2% (2006-2010 5-year est.).
Housing: Homeownership rate: 21.6% (2010); Median home value: $250,000 (2006-2010 5-year est.); Median contract rent: $820 per month (2006-2010 5-year est.); Median year structure built: 1983 (2006-2010 5-year est.).
Transportation: Commute to work: 85.0% car, 7.8% public transportation, 1.2% walk, 4.9% work from home (2006-2010 5-year est.); Travel time to work: 64.7% less than 15 minutes, 26.0% 15 to 30 minutes, 3.6% 30 to 45 minutes, 2.6% 45 to 60 minutes, 3.1% 60 minutes or more (2006-2010 5-year est.)

UNION (township). Covers a land area of 46.741 square miles and a water area of 0 square miles. Located at 40.94° N. Lat; 77.90° W. Long.
Population: 895 (1990); 1,200 (2000); 1,383 (2010); Density: 29.6 persons per square mile (2010); Race: 99.2% White, 0.1% Black, 0.0% Asian, 0.0% American Indian/Alaska Native, 0.3% Native Hawaiian/Other Pacific Islander, 0.4% Other, 0.5% Hispanic of any race (2010); Average household size: 2.52 (2010); Median age: 44.2 (2010); Males per 100 females: 101.6 (2010); Marriage status: 20.6% never married, 71.4% now married, 2.3% widowed, 5.6% divorced (2006-2010 5-year est.); Foreign born: 1.2% (2006-2010 5-year est.); Ancestry (includes multiple ancestries): 27.0% German, 14.5% English, 13.1% American, 11.3% Irish, 5.1% Dutch (2006-2010 5-year est.).
Economy: Single-family building permits issued: 3 (2011); Multi-family building permits issued: 0 (2011); Employment by occupation: 4.8% management, 6.2% professional, 10.6% services, 12.4% sales, 4.3% farming, 15.7% construction, 8.9% production (2006-2010 5-year est.).
Income: Per capita income: $23,686 (2006-2010 5-year est.); Median household income: $60,625 (2006-2010 5-year est.); Average household income: $65,167 (2006-2010 5-year est.); Percent of households with income of $100,000 or more: 14.2% (2006-2010 5-year est.); Poverty rate: 1.3% (2006-2010 5-year est.).
Education: Percent of population age 25 and over with: High school diploma (including GED) or higher: 91.2% (2006-2010 5-year est.); Bachelor's degree or higher: 22.0% (2006-2010 5-year est.); Master's degree or higher: 6.6% (2006-2010 5-year est.).
Housing: Homeownership rate: 90.0% (2010); Median home value: $135,600 (2006-2010 5-year est.); Median contract rent: $400 per month (2006-2010 5-year est.); Median year structure built: 1978 (2006-2010 5-year est.).
Transportation: Commute to work: 97.7% car, 0.4% public transportation, 0.4% walk, 1.5% work from home (2006-2010 5-year est.); Travel time to work: 10.1% less than 15 minutes, 49.4% 15 to 30 minutes, 32.6% 30 to 45 minutes, 2.5% 45 to 60 minutes, 5.4% 60 minutes or more (2006-2010 5-year est.)
Additional Information Contacts
Chamber of Business & Industry of Centre County . . . . (814) 234-1829
  http://www.cbicc.org

UNIONVILLE (borough). Aka Fleming. Covers a land area of 0.237 square miles and a water area of 0 square miles. Located at 40.91° N. Lat; 77.88° W. Long. Elevation is 787 feet.
Population: 284 (1990); 313 (2000); 291 (2010); Density: 1,229.3 persons per square mile (2010); Race: 97.6% White, 0.3% Black, 0.7% Asian, 0.0% American Indian/Alaska Native, 0.0% Native Hawaiian/Other Pacific Islander, 1.4% Other, 0.7% Hispanic of any race (2010); Average household size: 2.37 (2010); Median age: 42.4 (2010); Males per 100 females: 87.7 (2010); Marriage status: 32.0% never married, 49.5% now married, 7.6% widowed, 10.9% divorced (2006-2010 5-year est.); Foreign born: 0.0% (2006-2010 5-year est.); Ancestry (includes multiple ancestries): 37.0% German, 12.3% English, 11.3% Dutch, 8.9% Irish, 8.2% Scotch-Irish (2006-2010 5-year est.).
Economy: Single-family building permits issued: 0 (2011); Multi-family building permits issued: 0 (2011); Employment by occupation: 2.3% management, 0.0% professional, 13.6% services, 24.3% sales, 1.1% farming, 16.9% construction, 17.5% production (2006-2010 5-year est.).
Income: Per capita income: $21,735 (2006-2010 5-year est.); Median household income: $34,792 (2006-2010 5-year est.); Average household income: $44,313 (2006-2010 5-year est.); Percent of households with income of $100,000 or more: 7.8% (2006-2010 5-year est.); Poverty rate: 22.9% (2006-2010 5-year est.).
Education: Percent of population age 25 and over with: High school diploma (including GED) or higher: 94.7% (2006-2010 5-year est.); Bachelor's degree or higher: 10.7% (2006-2010 5-year est.); Master's degree or higher: 4.4% (2006-2010 5-year est.).
Housing: Homeownership rate: 74.8% (2010); Median home value: $94,700 (2006-2010 5-year est.); Median contract rent: $431 per month (2006-2010 5-year est.); Median year structure built: 1949 (2006-2010 5-year est.).
Transportation: Commute to work: 94.3% car, 0.0% public transportation, 2.3% walk, 3.4% work from home (2006-2010 5-year est.); Travel time to work: 16.6% less than 15 minutes, 66.9% 15 to 30 minutes, 16.6% 30 to 45 minutes, 0.0% 45 to 60 minutes, 0.0% 60 minutes or more (2006-2010 5-year est.)

UNIVERSITY PARK (unincorporated postal area)
Zip Code: 16802
  Covers a land area of 0.833 square miles and a water area of 0 square miles. Located at 40.80° N. Lat; 77.86° W. Long. Elevation is 1,142 feet.
  Population: 12,764 (2010); Density: 15,305.6 persons per square mile (2010); Race: 80.4% White, 6.3% Black, 9.1% Asian, 0.1% American Indian/Alaska Native, 0.0% Native Hawaiian/Other Pacific Islander, 4.1% Other, 5.6% Hispanic of any race (2010); Average household size: 2.20 (2010); Median age: 19.7 (2010); Males per 100 females: 102.3 (2010); Homeownership rate: 0.0% (2010)

WALKER (township). Covers a land area of 38.358 square miles and a water area of 0 square miles. Located at 40.95° N. Lat; 77.61° W. Long.
Population: 2,801 (1990); 3,299 (2000); 4,433 (2010); Density: 115.6 persons per square mile (2010); Race: 98.2% White, 0.4% Black, 0.2% Asian, 0.1% American Indian/Alaska Native, 0.0% Native Hawaiian/Other Pacific Islander, 1.1% Other, 0.5% Hispanic of any race (2010); Average household size: 2.63 (2010); Median age: 40.3 (2010); Males per 100 females: 98.2 (2010); Marriage status: 20.6% never married, 66.8% now married, 6.5% widowed, 6.1% divorced (2006-2010 5-year est.); Foreign born: 1.2% (2006-2010 5-year est.); Ancestry (includes multiple ancestries): 46.5% German, 14.7% American, 12.3% Irish, 7.3% English, 7.0% Italian (2006-2010 5-year est.).
Economy: Single-family building permits issued: 3 (2011); Multi-family building permits issued: 0 (2011); Employment by occupation: 9.4% management, 6.7% professional, 10.8% services, 17.6% sales, 2.8% farming, 13.7% construction, 5.3% production (2006-2010 5-year est.).
Income: Per capita income: $25,209 (2006-2010 5-year est.); Median household income: $56,528 (2006-2010 5-year est.); Average household income: $65,285 (2006-2010 5-year est.); Percent of households with income of $100,000 or more: 13.7% (2006-2010 5-year est.); Poverty rate: 7.0% (2006-2010 5-year est.).
Education: Percent of population age 25 and over with: High school diploma (including GED) or higher: 90.9% (2006-2010 5-year est.); Bachelor's degree or higher: 24.2% (2006-2010 5-year est.); Master's degree or higher: 5.3% (2006-2010 5-year est.).
Housing: Homeownership rate: 89.7% (2010); Median home value: $170,600 (2006-2010 5-year est.); Median contract rent: $526 per month

(2006-2010 5-year est.); Median year structure built: 1986 (2006-2010 5-year est.).

Transportation: Commute to work: 94.3% car, 0.0% public transportation, 1.6% walk, 3.5% work from home (2006-2010 5-year est.); Travel time to work: 16.6% less than 15 minutes, 59.8% 15 to 30 minutes, 16.1% 30 to 45 minutes, 2.6% 45 to 60 minutes, 4.9% 60 minutes or more (2006-2010 5-year est.)

Additional Information Contacts

Chamber of Business & Industry of Centre County . . . . (814) 234-1829
  http://www.cbicc.org

WOODWARD (CDP). Covers a land area of 0.590 square miles and a water area of 0 square miles. Located at 40.90° N. Lat; 77.35° W. Long. Elevation is 1,142 feet.

Population: 122 (1990); 126 (2000); 110 (2010); Density: 186.3 persons per square mile (2010); Race: 98.2% White, 0.9% Black, 0.0% Asian, 0.0% American Indian/Alaska Native, 0.0% Native Hawaiian/Other Pacific Islander, 0.9% Other, 0.0% Hispanic of any race (2010); Average household size: 2.00 (2010); Median age: 42.5 (2010); Males per 100 females: 107.5 (2010); Marriage status: 8.7% never married, 73.1% now married, 9.6% widowed, 8.7% divorced (2006-2010 5-year est.); Foreign born: 0.0% (2006-2010 5-year est.); Ancestry (includes multiple ancestries): 13.8% German, 3.4% Dutch (2006-2010 5-year est.).

Economy: Employment by occupation: 0.0% management, 0.0% professional, 27.0% services, 0.0% sales, 0.0% farming, 54.1% construction, 8.1% production (2006-2010 5-year est.).

Income: Per capita income: $7,711 (2006-2010 5-year est.); Median household income: $16,250 (2006-2010 5-year est.); Average household income: $20,838 (2006-2010 5-year est.); Percent of households with income of $100,000 or more: n/a (2006-2010 5-year est.); Poverty rate: 66.2% (2006-2010 5-year est.).

Education: Percent of population age 25 and over with: High school diploma (including GED) or higher: 88.4% (2006-2010 5-year est.); Bachelor's degree or higher: 0.0% (2006-2010 5-year est.); Master's degree or higher: 0.0% (2006-2010 5-year est.).

Housing: Homeownership rate: 76.4% (2010); Median home value: $95,500 (2006-2010 5-year est.); Median contract rent: n/a per month (2006-2010 5-year est.); Median year structure built: 1971 (2006-2010 5-year est.).

Transportation: Commute to work: 100.0% car, 0.0% public transportation, 0.0% walk, 0.0% work from home (2006-2010 5-year est.); Travel time to work: 37.8% less than 15 minutes, 32.4% 15 to 30 minutes, 29.7% 30 to 45 minutes, 0.0% 45 to 60 minutes, 0.0% 60 minutes or more (2006-2010 5-year est.)

WORTH (township). Covers a land area of 21.658 square miles and a water area of 0 square miles. Located at 40.82° N. Lat; 78.06° W. Long.

Population: 709 (1990); 835 (2000); 824 (2010); Density: 38.0 persons per square mile (2010); Race: 98.3% White, 0.4% Black, 0.2% Asian, 0.0% American Indian/Alaska Native, 0.0% Native Hawaiian/Other Pacific Islander, 1.1% Other, 1.0% Hispanic of any race (2010); Average household size: 2.46 (2010); Median age: 44.0 (2010); Males per 100 females: 107.0 (2010); Marriage status: 18.5% never married, 64.0% now married, 9.2% widowed, 8.3% divorced (2006-2010 5-year est.); Foreign born: 1.9% (2006-2010 5-year est.); Ancestry (includes multiple ancestries): 29.9% German, 12.3% Irish, 10.8% American, 8.4% European, 6.1% English (2006-2010 5-year est.).

Economy: Single-family building permits issued: 3 (2011); Multi-family building permits issued: 0 (2011); Employment by occupation: 13.2% management, 7.2% professional, 11.0% services, 10.0% sales, 4.5% farming, 16.5% construction, 9.7% production (2006-2010 5-year est.).

Income: Per capita income: $27,145 (2006-2010 5-year est.); Median household income: $47,143 (2006-2010 5-year est.); Average household income: $57,350 (2006-2010 5-year est.); Percent of households with income of $100,000 or more: 10.8% (2006-2010 5-year est.); Poverty rate: 7.7% (2006-2010 5-year est.).

Education: Percent of population age 25 and over with: High school diploma (including GED) or higher: 86.1% (2006-2010 5-year est.); Bachelor's degree or higher: 13.7% (2006-2010 5-year est.); Master's degree or higher: 4.9% (2006-2010 5-year est.).

Housing: Homeownership rate: 87.7% (2010); Median home value: $146,600 (2006-2010 5-year est.); Median contract rent: $213 per month (2006-2010 5-year est.); Median year structure built: 1976 (2006-2010 5-year est.).

Transportation: Commute to work: 88.5% car, 0.0% public transportation, 4.4% walk, 6.2% work from home (2006-2010 5-year est.); Travel time to work: 9.0% less than 15 minutes, 52.7% 15 to 30 minutes, 38.3% 30 to 45 minutes, 0.0% 45 to 60 minutes, 0.0% 60 minutes or more (2006-2010 5-year est.)

ZION (CDP). Covers a land area of 2.881 square miles and a water area of 0 square miles. Located at 40.92° N. Lat; 77.69° W. Long. Elevation is 1,014 feet.

Population: 1,573 (1990); 2,054 (2000); 2,030 (2010); Density: 704.7 persons per square mile (2010); Race: 98.2% White, 0.4% Black, 0.2% Asian, 0.0% American Indian/Alaska Native, 0.0% Native Hawaiian/Other Pacific Islander, 1.2% Other, 0.8% Hispanic of any race (2010); Average household size: 2.61 (2010); Median age: 38.6 (2010); Males per 100 females: 97.5 (2010); Marriage status: 19.0% never married, 68.8% now married, 6.0% widowed, 6.3% divorced (2006-2010 5-year est.); Foreign born: 1.8% (2006-2010 5-year est.); Ancestry (includes multiple ancestries): 44.8% German, 14.5% Irish, 14.1% Polish, 13.2% Italian, 11.9% English (2006-2010 5-year est.).

Economy: Employment by occupation: 13.7% management, 9.0% professional, 15.6% services, 14.8% sales, 1.4% farming, 8.1% construction, 1.5% production (2006-2010 5-year est.).

Income: Per capita income: $27,810 (2006-2010 5-year est.); Median household income: $57,477 (2006-2010 5-year est.); Average household income: $70,674 (2006-2010 5-year est.); Percent of households with income of $100,000 or more: 18.4% (2006-2010 5-year est.); Poverty rate: 4.9% (2006-2010 5-year est.).

Education: Percent of population age 25 and over with: High school diploma (including GED) or higher: 97.3% (2006-2010 5-year est.); Bachelor's degree or higher: 40.3% (2006-2010 5-year est.); Master's degree or higher: 10.2% (2006-2010 5-year est.).

Housing: Homeownership rate: 93.0% (2010); Median home value: $187,300 (2006-2010 5-year est.); Median contract rent: $543 per month (2006-2010 5-year est.); Median year structure built: 1992 (2006-2010 5-year est.).

Transportation: Commute to work: 93.8% car, 0.0% public transportation, 1.4% walk, 4.8% work from home (2006-2010 5-year est.); Travel time to work: 21.9% less than 15 minutes, 59.7% 15 to 30 minutes, 14.6% 30 to 45 minutes, 2.5% 45 to 60 minutes, 1.2% 60 minutes or more (2006-2010 5-year est.)

Additional Information Contacts

Chamber of Business & Industry of Centre County . . . . (814) 234-1829
  http://www.cbicc.org

Chester County

Located in southeastern Pennsylvania; drained by the Schuylkill River; includes the Chester Valley. Covers a land area of 750.508 square miles, a water area of 8.727 square miles, and is located in the Eastern Time Zone at 39.97° N. Lat., 75.75° W. Long. The county was founded in 1682. County seat is West Chester.

Chester County is part of the Philadelphia-Camden-Wilmington, PA-NJ-DE-MD Metropolitan Statistical Area. The entire metro area includes: Camden, NJ Metropolitan Division (Burlington County, NJ; Camden County, NJ; Gloucester County, NJ); Philadelphia, PA Metropolitan Division (Bucks County, PA; Chester County, PA; Delaware County, PA; Montgomery County, PA; Philadelphia County, PA); Wilmington, DE-MD-NJ Metropolitan Division (New Castle County, DE; Cecil County, MD; Salem County, NJ)

Weather Station: Coatesville 2 W									Elevation: 640 feet		
	Jan	Feb	Mar	Apr	May	Jun	Jul	Aug	Sep	Oct	Nov	Dec
High	38	41	50	62	72	81	85	83	75	65	54	42
Low	22	23	30	39	49	58	63	62	54	43	34	25
Precip	4.1	3.2	4.7	4.1	4.4	3.9	4.8	4.0	5.1	4.2	4.2	4.1
Snow	10.8	10.2	5.2	1.4	0.0	tr	0.0	0.0	0.0	tr	1.0	4.3

High and Low temperatures in degrees Fahrenheit; Precipitation and Snow in inches

Weather Station: Phoenixville 1 E									Elevation: 104 feet		
	Jan	Feb	Mar	Apr	May	Jun	Jul	Aug	Sep	Oct	Nov	Dec
High	41	44	52	64	74	82	86	85	78	67	55	44
Low	22	23	30	40	49	59	64	62	54	42	33	25
Precip	3.0	2.5	3.5	3.7	3.5	3.7	4.1	3.4	4.1	3.4	3.6	3.7
Snow	na	na	na	0.0	0.0	0.0	0.0	0.0	0.0	0.0	0.0	tr

High and Low temperatures in degrees Fahrenheit; Precipitation and Snow in inches

Population: 376,389 (1990); 433,501 (2000); 498,886 (2010); Race: 85.5% White, 6.1% Black, 3.9% Asian, 0.2% American Indian/Alaska Native, 0.0% Native Hawaiian/Other Pacific Islander, 4.3% Other, 6.5% Hispanic of any race (2010); Density: 664.7 persons per square mile (2010); Average household size: 2.65 (2010); Median age: 39.3 (2010); Males per 100 females: 96.6 (2010).

Religion: Six largest groups: 42.5% Catholicism, 4.4% Methodist/Pietist, 4.0% Presbyterian-Reformed, 3.4% Non-Denominational, 2.3% Lutheran, 1.4% Baptist (2010)

Economy: Unemployment rate: 6.8% (August 2012); Total civilian labor force: 269,490 (August 2012); Leading industries: 14.1% health care and social assistance; 11.7% retail trade; 10.2% finance & insurance (2010); Farms: 1,733 totaling 166,891 acres (2007); Companies that employ 500 or more persons: 39 (2010); Companies that employ 100 to 499 persons: 300 (2010); Companies that employ less than 100 persons: 13,448 (2010); Black-owned businesses: 1,158 (2007); Hispanic-owned businesses: 698 (2007); Asian-owned businesses: 1,395 (2007); Women-owned businesses: 13,183 (2007); Retail sales per capita: $21,035 (2010). Single-family building permits issued: 783 (2011); Multi-family building permits issued: 151 (2011).

Income: Per capita income: $41,251 (2006-2010 5-year est.); Median household income: $84,741 (2006-2010 5-year est.); Average household income: $110,798 (2006-2010 5-year est.); Percent of households with income of $100,000 or more: 41.4% (2006-2010 5-year est.); Poverty rate: 6.2% (2006-2010 5-year est.); Bankruptcy rate: 1.97% (2011).

Taxes: Total county taxes per capita: $288 (2009); County property taxes per capita: $283 (2009).

Education: Percent of population age 25 and over with: High school diploma (including GED) or higher: 92.5% (2006-2010 5-year est.); Bachelor's degree or higher: 47.8% (2006-2010 5-year est.); Master's degree or higher: 18.3% (2006-2010 5-year est.).

Housing: Homeownership rate: 76.2% (2010); Median home value: $334,300 (2006-2010 5-year est.); Median contract rent: $928 per month (2006-2010 5-year est.); Median year structure built: 1978 (2006-2010 5-year est.)

Health: Birth rate: 114.3 per 10,000 population (2011); Death rate: 69.9 per 10,000 population (2011); Age-adjusted cancer mortality rate: 166.2 deaths per 100,000 population (2009); Number of physicians: 28.6 per 10,000 population (2010); Hospital beds: 30.2 per 10,000 population (2008); Hospital admissions: 1,240.1 per 10,000 population (2008).

Environment: Air Quality Index: 67.4% good, 30.3% moderate, 2.3% unhealthy for sensitive individuals, 0.0% unhealthy (percent of days in 2011)

Elections: 2012 Presidential election results: 49.2% Obama, 49.6% Romney

National and State Parks: Marsh Creek State Park

Additional Information Contacts

Chester County Government . . . . (610) 344-6000
    http://dsf.chesco.org

Chester County Chamber of Business and Industry . . . . . . (610) 725-9100
    http://www.cccbi.org

Southern Chester County Chamber of Commerce . . . . (610) 444-0774
    http://www.scccc.com

Western Chester County Chamber of Commerce . . . . (610) 384-9550
    http://www.westernchestercounty.com

Chester County Communities

ATGLEN (borough). Covers a land area of 0.875 square miles and a water area of 0.008 square miles. Located at 39.95° N. Lat; 75.97° W. Long. Elevation is 489 feet.

Population: 825 (1990); 1,217 (2000); 1,406 (2010); Density: 1,607.6 persons per square mile (2010); Race: 89.0% White, 7.4% Black, 0.2% Asian, 0.1% American Indian/Alaska Native, 0.0% Native Hawaiian/Other Pacific Islander, 3.3% Other, 5.8% Hispanic of any race (2010); Average household size: 3.08 (2010); Median age: 32.4 (2010); Males per 100 females: 94.7 (2010); Marriage status: 28.7% never married, 60.8% now married, 2.9% widowed, 7.6% divorced (2006-2010 5-year est.); Foreign born: 2.3% (2006-2010 5-year est.); Ancestry (includes multiple ancestries): 26.9% German, 16.4% Irish, 15.7% Italian, 11.1% English, 5.8% American (2006-2010 5-year est.).

Economy: Single-family building permits issued: 0 (2011); Multi-family building permits issued: 0 (2011); Employment by occupation: 9.3% management, 2.8% professional, 15.1% services, 12.6% sales, 3.7% farming, 12.8% construction, 7.0% production (2006-2010 5-year est.).

Income: Per capita income: $27,265 (2006-2010 5-year est.); Median household income: $70,179 (2006-2010 5-year est.); Average household income: $78,467 (2006-2010 5-year est.); Percent of households with income of $100,000 or more: 24.0% (2006-2010 5-year est.); Poverty rate: 11.8% (2006-2010 5-year est.).

Education: Percent of population age 25 and over with: High school diploma (including GED) or higher: 87.5% (2006-2010 5-year est.); Bachelor's degree or higher: 24.6% (2006-2010 5-year est.); Master's degree or higher: 9.5% (2006-2010 5-year est.).

School District(s)

Octorara Area SD (KG-12)

    2010-11 Enrollment: 2,581 . . . . (610) 593-8238

Housing: Homeownership rate: 72.2% (2010); Median home value: $228,300 (2006-2010 5-year est.); Median contract rent: $669 per month (2006-2010 5-year est.); Median year structure built: 1955 (2006-2010 5-year est.).

Safety: Violent crime rate: 7.1 per 10,000 population; Property crime rate: 21.3 per 10,000 population (2011).

Transportation: Commute to work: 90.1% car, 1.2% public transportation, 2.7% walk, 2.7% work from home (2006-2010 5-year est.); Travel time to work: 21.7% less than 15 minutes, 26.9% 15 to 30 minutes, 21.8% 30 to 45 minutes, 16.6% 45 to 60 minutes, 13.0% 60 minutes or more (2006-2010 5-year est.)

Additional Information Contacts

Borough of Atglen . . . . (610) 593-6854
    http://www.atglen.org

Western Chester County Chamber of Commerce . . . . (610) 384-9550
    http://www.westernchestercounty.com

AVONDALE (borough). Covers a land area of 0.484 square miles and a water area of 0.012 square miles. Located at 39.83° N. Lat; 75.78° W. Long. Elevation is 269 feet.

Population: 954 (1990); 1,108 (2000); 1,265 (2010); Density: 2,616.2 persons per square mile (2010); Race: 57.7% White, 8.9% Black, 0.8% Asian, 1.4% American Indian/Alaska Native, 0.0% Native Hawaiian/Other Pacific Islander, 31.2% Other, 59.0% Hispanic of any race (2010); Average household size: 3.84 (2010); Median age: 27.8 (2010); Males per 100 females: 131.7 (2010); Marriage status: 31.1% never married, 61.5% now married, 3.7% widowed, 3.7% divorced (2006-2010 5-year est.); Foreign born: 44.3% (2006-2010 5-year est.); Ancestry (includes multiple ancestries): 7.6% German, 7.6% Irish, 6.4% Italian, 4.1% Polish, 3.4% French (2006-2010 5-year est.).

Economy: Single-family building permits issued: 20 (2011); Multi-family building permits issued: 0 (2011); Employment by occupation: 4.2% management, 1.9% professional, 7.7% services, 11.7% sales, 9.6% farming, 33.3% construction, 11.7% production (2006-2010 5-year est.).

Income: Per capita income: $17,253 (2006-2010 5-year est.); Median household income: $53,203 (2006-2010 5-year est.); Average household income: $60,814 (2006-2010 5-year est.); Percent of households with income of $100,000 or more: 13.3% (2006-2010 5-year est.); Poverty rate: 17.6% (2006-2010 5-year est.).

Education: Percent of population age 25 and over with: High school diploma (including GED) or higher: 56.9% (2006-2010 5-year est.); Bachelor's degree or higher: 8.3% (2006-2010 5-year est.); Master's degree or higher: 2.2% (2006-2010 5-year est.).

Housing: Homeownership rate: 53.2% (2010); Median home value: $215,800 (2006-2010 5-year est.); Median contract rent: $851 per month (2006-2010 5-year est.); Median year structure built: before 1940 (2006-2010 5-year est.).

Safety: Violent crime rate: 15.8 per 10,000 population; Property crime rate: 47.3 per 10,000 population (2011).

Transportation: Commute to work: 92.5% car, 2.2% public transportation, 4.7% walk, 0.4% work from home (2006-2010 5-year est.); Travel time to work: 42.2% less than 15 minutes, 33.6% 15 to 30 minutes, 18.2% 30 to 45 minutes, 1.3% 45 to 60 minutes, 4.7% 60 minutes or more (2006-2010 5-year est.)

Additional Information Contacts

Southern Chester County Chamber of Commerce . . . . (610) 444-0774
    http://www.scccc.com

BERWYN (CDP). Covers a land area of 1.863 square miles and a water area of 0.004 square miles. Located at 40.04° N. Lat; 75.44° W. Long. Elevation is 492 feet.

Population: n/a (1990); n/a (2000); 3,631 (2010); Density: 1,948.8 persons per square mile (2010); Race: 89.3% White, 4.6% Black, 4.1%

Asian, 0.2% American Indian/Alaska Native, 0.0% Native Hawaiian/Other Pacific Islander, 1.8% Other, 2.3% Hispanic of any race (2010); Average household size: 2.47 (2010); Median age: 44.0 (2010); Males per 100 females: 87.3 (2010); Marriage status: 31.1% never married, 55.5% now married, 7.0% widowed, 6.4% divorced (2006-2010 5-year est.); Foreign born: 6.6% (2006-2010 5-year est.); Ancestry (includes multiple ancestries): 25.7% Irish, 23.3% German, 18.6% Italian, 18.3% English, 4.9% American (2006-2010 5-year est.).

Economy: Employment by occupation: 18.3% management, 3.2% professional, 10.3% services, 19.8% sales, 2.2% farming, 3.4% construction, 8.4% production (2006-2010 5-year est.).

Income: Per capita income: $56,988 (2006-2010 5-year est.); Median household income: $78,417 (2006-2010 5-year est.); Average household income: $139,987 (2006-2010 5-year est.); Percent of households with income of $100,000 or more: 44.5% (2006-2010 5-year est.); Poverty rate: 4.6% (2006-2010 5-year est.).

Education: Percent of population age 25 and over with: High school diploma (including GED) or higher: 91.8% (2006-2010 5-year est.); Bachelor's degree or higher: 56.5% (2006-2010 5-year est.); Master's degree or higher: 19.8% (2006-2010 5-year est.).

School District(s)

Tredyffrin-Easttown SD (KG-12)
   2010-11 Enrollment: 6,334 . . . . (610) 240-1900

Housing: Homeownership rate: 69.4% (2010); Median home value: $448,200 (2006-2010 5-year est.); Median contract rent: $787 per month (2006-2010 5-year est.); Median year structure built: 1957 (2006-2010 5-year est.).

Transportation: Commute to work: 80.7% car, 6.9% public transportation, 1.8% walk, 9.9% work from home (2006-2010 5-year est.); Travel time to work: 26.4% less than 15 minutes, 46.2% 15 to 30 minutes, 14.4% 30 to 45 minutes, 9.5% 45 to 60 minutes, 3.6% 60 minutes or more (2006-2010 5-year est.)

BIRMINGHAM (township).

Covers a land area of 6.322 square miles and a water area of 0.108 square miles. Located at 39.90° N. Lat; 75.60° W. Long. Elevation is 377 feet.

History: Birmingham Township was the site of the American Revolutionary War, Battle of the Brandywine, September 11, 1777.

Population: 2,636 (1990); 4,221 (2000); 4,208 (2010); Density: 665.6 persons per square mile (2010); Race: 92.2% White, 1.4% Black, 5.2% Asian, 0.0% American Indian/Alaska Native, 0.0% Native Hawaiian/Other Pacific Islander, 1.2% Other, 2.1% Hispanic of any race (2010); Average household size: 2.96 (2010); Median age: 44.8 (2010); Males per 100 females: 98.3 (2010); Marriage status: 19.1% never married, 76.8% now married, 1.8% widowed, 2.3% divorced (2006-2010 5-year est.); Foreign born: 11.7% (2006-2010 5-year est.); Ancestry (includes multiple ancestries): 23.3% German, 22.7% Irish, 13.9% English, 12.8% Italian, 8.3% Polish (2006-2010 5-year est.).

Economy: Single-family building permits issued: 0 (2011); Multi-family building permits issued: 0 (2011); Employment by occupation: 23.4% management, 12.6% professional, 5.4% services, 14.3% sales, 3.0% farming, 1.7% construction, 2.6% production (2006-2010 5-year est.).

Income: Per capita income: $72,034 (2006-2010 5-year est.); Median household income: $165,833 (2006-2010 5-year est.); Average household income: $215,902 (2006-2010 5-year est.); Percent of households with income of $100,000 or more: 78.5% (2006-2010 5-year est.); Poverty rate: 0.2% (2006-2010 5-year est.).

Education: Percent of population age 25 and over with: High school diploma (including GED) or higher: 99.3% (2006-2010 5-year est.); Bachelor's degree or higher: 75.4% (2006-2010 5-year est.); Master's degree or higher: 32.1% (2006-2010 5-year est.).

Housing: Homeownership rate: 95.9% (2010); Median home value: $580,500 (2006-2010 5-year est.); Median contract rent: $1,216 per month (2006-2010 5-year est.); Median year structure built: 1989 (2006-2010 5-year est.).

Safety: Violent crime rate: 0.0 per 10,000 population; Property crime rate: 54.5 per 10,000 population (2011).

Transportation: Commute to work: 84.9% car, 0.5% public transportation, 1.4% walk, 11.3% work from home (2006-2010 5-year est.); Travel time to work: 15.3% less than 15 minutes, 49.6% 15 to 30 minutes, 14.9% 30 to 45 minutes, 8.9% 45 to 60 minutes, 11.3% 60 minutes or more (2006-2010 5-year est.)

Additional Information Contacts
Birmingham Township . . . . (610) 793-2600
   http://www.birminghamtownship.org

Tyron Area Chamber of Commerce . . . . (814) 684-0736
   http://www.tyronechamber.com

BRANDAMORE (unincorporated postal area)

Zip Code: 19316
   Covers a land area of 0.890 square miles and a water area of 0.004 square miles. Located at 40.05° N. Lat; 75.83° W. Long. Elevation is 620 feet. Population: 186 (2010); Density: 208.8 persons per square mile (2010); Race: 92.5% White, 1.1% Black, 1.1% Asian, 0.0% American Indian/Alaska Native, 0.0% Native Hawaiian/Other Pacific Islander, 5.3% Other, 3.2% Hispanic of any race (2010); Average household size: 2.66 (2010); Median age: 45.6 (2010); Males per 100 females: 93.8 (2010); Homeownership rate: 92.9% (2010)

CALN (CDP).

Covers a land area of 0.804 square miles and a water area of 0.003 square miles. Located at 40.00° N. Lat; 75.78° W. Long. Elevation is 328 feet.

Population: n/a (1990); n/a (2000); 1,519 (2010); Density: 1,890.2 persons per square mile (2010); Race: 65.2% White, 26.7% Black, 1.3% Asian, 0.4% American Indian/Alaska Native, 0.0% Native Hawaiian/Other Pacific Islander, 6.4% Other, 10.7% Hispanic of any race (2010); Average household size: 2.55 (2010); Median age: 35.1 (2010); Males per 100 females: 93.3 (2010); Marriage status: 24.2% never married, 53.7% now married, 12.7% widowed, 9.3% divorced (2006-2010 5-year est.); Foreign born: 0.0% (2006-2010 5-year est.); Ancestry (includes multiple ancestries): 25.9% Irish, 24.7% Italian, 17.6% German, 10.6% English, 6.6% Polish (2006-2010 5-year est.).

Economy: Employment by occupation: 0.0% management, 4.2% professional, 11.3% services, 16.2% sales, 2.3% farming, 16.3% construction, 7.5% production (2006-2010 5-year est.).

Income: Per capita income: $36,988 (2006-2010 5-year est.); Median household income: $73,990 (2006-2010 5-year est.); Average household income: $85,215 (2006-2010 5-year est.); Percent of households with income of $100,000 or more: 32.6% (2006-2010 5-year est.); Poverty rate: 3.3% (2006-2010 5-year est.).

Education: Percent of population age 25 and over with: High school diploma (including GED) or higher: 94.6% (2006-2010 5-year est.); Bachelor's degree or higher: 27.4% (2006-2010 5-year est.); Master's degree or higher: 4.6% (2006-2010 5-year est.).

Housing: Homeownership rate: 73.0% (2010); Median home value: $188,900 (2006-2010 5-year est.); Median contract rent: $856 per month (2006-2010 5-year est.); Median year structure built: 1973 (2006-2010 5-year est.).

Transportation: Commute to work: 88.8% car, 3.2% public transportation, 0.0% walk, 5.7% work from home (2006-2010 5-year est.); Travel time to work: 12.0% less than 15 minutes, 26.9% 15 to 30 minutes, 31.3% 30 to 45 minutes, 9.4% 45 to 60 minutes, 20.4% 60 minutes or more (2006-2010 5-year est.)

CALN (township).

Covers a land area of 8.856 square miles and a water area of 0.059 square miles. Located at 40.00° N. Lat; 75.76° W. Long. Elevation is 328 feet.

Population: 11,997 (1990); 11,916 (2000); 13,817 (2010); Density: 1,560.2 persons per square mile (2010); Race: 75.7% White, 16.2% Black, 3.9% Asian, 0.1% American Indian/Alaska Native, 0.1% Native Hawaiian/Other Pacific Islander, 4.0% Other, 5.5% Hispanic of any race (2010); Average household size: 2.51 (2010); Median age: 38.5 (2010); Males per 100 females: 101.4 (2010); Marriage status: 29.4% never married, 53.5% now married, 7.1% widowed, 9.9% divorced (2006-2010 5-year est.); Foreign born: 7.2% (2006-2010 5-year est.); Ancestry (includes multiple ancestries): 25.9% Irish, 19.3% German, 16.8% Italian, 9.3% English, 5.8% Polish (2006-2010 5-year est.).

Economy: Single-family building permits issued: 9 (2011); Multi-family building permits issued: 0 (2011); Employment by occupation: 11.4% management, 6.7% professional, 7.2% services, 16.3% sales, 4.3% farming, 10.2% construction, 7.2% production (2006-2010 5-year est.).

Income: Per capita income: $33,905 (2006-2010 5-year est.); Median household income: $74,227 (2006-2010 5-year est.); Average household income: $84,285 (2006-2010 5-year est.); Percent of households with income of $100,000 or more: 31.6% (2006-2010 5-year est.); Poverty rate: 7.5% (2006-2010 5-year est.).

Education: Percent of population age 25 and over with: High school diploma (including GED) or higher: 92.8% (2006-2010 5-year est.); Bachelor's degree or higher: 34.2% (2006-2010 5-year est.); Master's degree or higher: 8.9% (2006-2010 5-year est.).

Housing: Homeownership rate: 73.0% (2010); Median home value: $229,000 (2006-2010 5-year est.); Median contract rent: $1,078 per month (2006-2010 5-year est.); Median year structure built: 1978 (2006-2010 5-year est.).

Safety: Violent crime rate: 47.6 per 10,000 population; Property crime rate: 246.7 per 10,000 population (2011).

Transportation: Commute to work: 89.7% car, 3.2% public transportation, 2.6% walk, 3.0% work from home (2006-2010 5-year est.); Travel time to work: 17.5% less than 15 minutes, 36.6% 15 to 30 minutes, 24.1% 30 to 45 minutes, 9.5% 45 to 60 minutes, 12.3% 60 minutes or more (2006-2010 5-year est.)

Additional Information Contacts

Caln Township. . . . . (610) 384-0600
   http://www.calntownship.org

Western Chester County Chamber of Commerce. . . . . (610) 384-9550
   http://www.westernchestercounty.com

CHARLESTOWN (township). Covers a land area of 12.450 square miles and a water area of 0.074 square miles. Located at 40.09° N. Lat; 75.56° W. Long. Elevation is 223 feet.

History: The name, Charlestown, honors Charles Pickering, the friend to whom William Penn granted 5,383 acres along the creek where Pickering and his friend John Tinker, believed (mistakenly) that they had found silver.

Population: 2,754 (1990); 4,051 (2000); 5,671 (2010); Density: 455.5 persons per square mile (2010); Race: 85.9% White, 2.3% Black, 9.0% Asian, 0.2% American Indian/Alaska Native, 0.0% Native Hawaiian/Other Pacific Islander, 2.6% Other, 2.6% Hispanic of any race (2010); Average household size: 2.72 (2010); Median age: 39.3 (2010); Males per 100 females: 93.9 (2010); Marriage status: 30.0% never married, 58.4% now married, 3.1% widowed, 8.5% divorced (2006-2010 5-year est.); Foreign born: 11.4% (2006-2010 5-year est.); Ancestry (includes multiple ancestries): 21.3% Irish, 20.4% German, 17.6% Italian, 10.1% English, 8.9% Polish (2006-2010 5-year est.).

Economy: Single-family building permits issued: 4 (2011); Multi-family building permits issued: 0 (2011); Employment by occupation: 25.0% management, 9.9% professional, 5.5% services, 11.0% sales, 3.0% farming, 3.2% construction, 3.5% production (2006-2010 5-year est.).

Income: Per capita income: $57,618 (2006-2010 5-year est.); Median household income: $136,071 (2006-2010 5-year est.); Average household income: $181,670 (2006-2010 5-year est.); Percent of households with income of $100,000 or more: 69.5% (2006-2010 5-year est.); Poverty rate: 1.9% (2006-2010 5-year est.).

Education: Percent of population age 25 and over with: High school diploma (including GED) or higher: 97.1% (2006-2010 5-year est.); Bachelor's degree or higher: 66.0% (2006-2010 5-year est.); Master's degree or higher: 27.8% (2006-2010 5-year est.).

Housing: Homeownership rate: 91.3% (2010); Median home value: $455,400 (2006-2010 5-year est.); Median contract rent: n/a per month (2006-2010 5-year est.); Median year structure built: 1991 (2006-2010 5-year est.).

Transportation: Commute to work: 85.3% car, 1.5% public transportation, 6.3% walk, 6.3% work from home (2006-2010 5-year est.); Travel time to work: 28.6% less than 15 minutes, 35.7% 15 to 30 minutes, 18.7% 30 to 45 minutes, 5.6% 45 to 60 minutes, 11.3% 60 minutes or more (2006-2010 5-year est.)

Additional Information Contacts

Charlestown Township . . . . (610) 240-0326
   http://www.charlestown.pa.us

Chester County Chamber of Business and Industry . . . . . . (610) 725-9100
   http://www.cccbi.org

CHESTER SPRINGS (unincorporated postal area)

Zip Code: 19425

Covers a land area of 26.943 square miles and a water area of 0.226 square miles. Located at 40.10° N. Lat; 75.65° W. Long. Population: 13,922 (2010); Density: 516.7 persons per square mile (2010); Race: 85.1% White, 1.5% Black, 11.8% Asian, 0.0% American Indian/Alaska Native, 0.0% Native Hawaiian/Other Pacific Islander, 1.6% Other, 2.6% Hispanic of any race (2010); Average household size: 2.95 (2010); Median age: 37.9 (2010); Males per 100 females: 99.1 (2010); Homeownership rate: 91.7% (2010)

CHESTERBROOK (CDP). Covers a land area of 1.561 square miles and a water area of 0.007 square miles. Located at 40.07° N. Lat; 75.45° W. Long. Elevation is 161 feet.

History: As part of Chester County, (one of the three original counties of Pennsylvania created by William Penn in 1682), It is named for Cheshire, England.

Population: 4,451 (1990); 4,625 (2000); 4,589 (2010); Density: 2,939.4 persons per square mile (2010); Race: 79.1% White, 3.6% Black, 15.7% Asian, 0.0% American Indian/Alaska Native, 0.0% Native Hawaiian/Other Pacific Islander, 1.6% Other, 2.4% Hispanic of any race (2010); Average household size: 2.00 (2010); Median age: 43.4 (2010); Males per 100 females: 80.8 (2010); Marriage status: 34.6% never married, 43.5% now married, 9.1% widowed, 12.7% divorced (2006-2010 5-year est.); Foreign born: 10.3% (2006-2010 5-year est.); Ancestry (includes multiple ancestries): 19.6% Irish, 18.6% English, 17.9% German, 12.2% Italian, 4.6% Polish (2006-2010 5-year est.).

Economy: Employment by occupation: 19.2% management, 16.1% professional, 1.5% services, 9.1% sales, 1.4% farming, 2.9% construction, 2.3% production (2006-2010 5-year est.).

Income: Per capita income: $54,076 (2006-2010 5-year est.); Median household income: $86,667 (2006-2010 5-year est.); Average household income: $102,354 (2006-2010 5-year est.); Percent of households with income of $100,000 or more: 38.9% (2006-2010 5-year est.); Poverty rate: 4.3% (2006-2010 5-year est.).

Education: Percent of population age 25 and over with: High school diploma (including GED) or higher: 97.2% (2006-2010 5-year est.); Bachelor's degree or higher: 75.1% (2006-2010 5-year est.); Master's degree or higher: 32.6% (2006-2010 5-year est.).

Housing: Homeownership rate: 81.9% (2010); Median home value: $311,800 (2006-2010 5-year est.); Median contract rent: $1,645 per month (2006-2010 5-year est.); Median year structure built: 1984 (2006-2010 5-year est.).

Transportation: Commute to work: 88.9% car, 3.8% public transportation, 3.7% walk, 1.5% work from home (2006-2010 5-year est.); Travel time to work: 31.0% less than 15 minutes, 38.5% 15 to 30 minutes, 11.5% 30 to 45 minutes, 8.2% 45 to 60 minutes, 10.9% 60 minutes or more (2006-2010 5-year est.)

Additional Information Contacts

Main Line Chamber of Commerce . . . . (610) 687-6232
   http://www.mlcc.org

COATESVILLE (city). Covers a land area of 1.809 square miles and a water area of 0.019 square miles. Located at 39.99° N. Lat; 75.82° W. Long. Elevation is 318 feet.

History: Named for Moses Coates, the first postmaster, or for his grandfather. Settled c.1717. Incorporated 1916.

Population: 11,038 (1990); 10,838 (2000); 13,100 (2010); Density: 7,240.2 persons per square mile (2010); Race: 38.0% White, 46.4% Black, 0.8% Asian, 0.5% American Indian/Alaska Native, 0.1% Native Hawaiian/Other Pacific Islander, 14.2% Other, 23.0% Hispanic of any race (2010); Average household size: 2.86 (2010); Median age: 29.9 (2010); Males per 100 females: 97.5 (2010); Marriage status: 42.8% never married, 41.2% now married, 6.3% widowed, 9.7% divorced (2006-2010 5-year est.); Foreign born: 16.6% (2006-2010 5-year est.); Ancestry (includes multiple ancestries): 6.5% Irish, 5.9% German, 4.8% Italian, 3.4% English, 3.3% American (2006-2010 5-year est.).

Economy: Single-family building permits issued: 2 (2011); Multi-family building permits issued: 0 (2011); Employment by occupation: 7.0% management, 3.2% professional, 14.3% services, 14.6% sales, 1.9% farming, 11.1% construction, 10.9% production (2006-2010 5-year est.).

Income: Per capita income: $18,153 (2006-2010 5-year est.); Median household income: $35,553 (2006-2010 5-year est.); Average household income: $49,769 (2006-2010 5-year est.); Percent of households with income of $100,000 or more: 12.2% (2006-2010 5-year est.); Poverty rate: 25.2% (2006-2010 5-year est.).

Taxes: Total city taxes per capita: $473 (2009); City property taxes per capita: $218 (2009).

Education: Percent of population age 25 and over with: High school diploma (including GED) or higher: 79.6% (2006-2010 5-year est.); Bachelor's degree or higher: 14.7% (2006-2010 5-year est.); Master's degree or higher: 3.6% (2006-2010 5-year est.).

School District(s)

Center for Arts & Technology (09-12)
   2010-11 Enrollment: 517. . . . . (484) 237-5110

Coatesville Area SD (KG-12)
    2010-11 Enrollment: 6,891 . . . . (610) 466-2400
Graystone Academy CS (KG-08)
    2010-11 Enrollment: 444. . . . . (610) 383-4311
Vocational/Technical School(s)
Center for Arts and Technology-Brandywine Campus (Public)
    Fall 2010 Enrollment: 190 . . . . (610) 384-6214
    2011-12 Tuition: $16,185
Housing: Homeownership rate: 37.4% (2010); Median home value: $135,800 (2006-2010 5-year est.); Median contract rent: $679 per month (2006-2010 5-year est.); Median year structure built: 1946 (2006-2010 5-year est.).
Hospitals: Brandywine Hospital (168 beds); Veterans Affairs Medical Center
Safety: Violent crime rate: 113.4 per 10,000 population; Property crime rate: 351.5 per 10,000 population (2011).
Transportation: Commute to work: 86.1% car, 9.9% public transportation, 2.0% walk, 0.9% work from home (2006-2010 5-year est.); Travel time to work: 24.4% less than 15 minutes, 33.6% 15 to 30 minutes, 23.8% 30 to 45 minutes, 9.2% 45 to 60 minutes, 9.0% 60 minutes or more (2006-2010 5-year est.); Amtrak: train service available.
Airports: Chester County G O Carlson (general aviation)
Additional Information Contacts
City of Coatesville . . . . (610) 384-0300
    http://www.coatesville.org
Western Chester County Chamber of Commerce. . . . . (610) 384-9550
    http://www.westernchestercounty.com

COCHRANVILLE (CDP). Covers a land area of 1.117 square miles and a water area of 0.002 square miles. Located at 39.89° N. Lat; 75.92° W. Long. Elevation is 581 feet.
Population: n/a (1990); n/a (2000); 668 (2010); Density: 597.8 persons per square mile (2010); Race: 89.8% White, 1.3% Black, 2.4% Asian, 0.0% American Indian/Alaska Native, 0.0% Native Hawaiian/Other Pacific Islander, 6.5% Other, 9.3% Hispanic of any race (2010); Average household size: 2.60 (2010); Median age: 42.1 (2010); Males per 100 females: 98.8 (2010); Marriage status: 21.1% never married, 60.3% now married, 10.1% widowed, 8.6% divorced (2006-2010 5-year est.); Foreign born: 0.8% (2006-2010 5-year est.); Ancestry (includes multiple ancestries): 28.3% German, 18.8% Irish, 16.6% English, 9.9% Italian, 8.8% Scottish (2006-2010 5-year est.).
Economy: Employment by occupation: 6.3% management, 0.0% professional, 7.4% services, 15.3% sales, 9.8% farming, 11.4% construction, 6.8% production (2006-2010 5-year est.).
Income: Per capita income: $27,207 (2006-2010 5-year est.); Median household income: $70,000 (2006-2010 5-year est.); Average household income: $77,525 (2006-2010 5-year est.); Percent of households with income of $100,000 or more: 25.0% (2006-2010 5-year est.); Poverty rate: 2.7% (2006-2010 5-year est.).
Education: Percent of population age 25 and over with: High school diploma (including GED) or higher: 97.8% (2006-2010 5-year est.); Bachelor's degree or higher: 13.1% (2006-2010 5-year est.); Master's degree or higher: 5.1% (2006-2010 5-year est.).
Housing: Homeownership rate: 77.4% (2010); Median home value: $217,600 (2006-2010 5-year est.); Median contract rent: $913 per month (2006-2010 5-year est.); Median year structure built: 1959 (2006-2010 5-year est.).
Transportation: Commute to work: 94.6% car, 0.0% public transportation, 5.4% walk, 0.0% work from home (2006-2010 5-year est.); Travel time to work: 20.9% less than 15 minutes, 28.0% 15 to 30 minutes, 28.9% 30 to 45 minutes, 10.9% 45 to 60 minutes, 11.4% 60 minutes or more (2006-2010 5-year est.)

DEVON (CDP). Covers a land area of 0.611 square miles and a water area of <.001 square miles. Located at 40.05° N. Lat; 75.43° W. Long. Elevation is 499 feet.
Population: n/a (1990); n/a (2000); 1,515 (2010); Density: 2,481.5 persons per square mile (2010); Race: 92.5% White, 1.1% Black, 4.4% Asian, 0.0% American Indian/Alaska Native, 0.0% Native Hawaiian/Other Pacific Islander, 2.0% Other, 2.1% Hispanic of any race (2010); Average household size: 2.66 (2010); Median age: 42.4 (2010); Males per 100 females: 89.4 (2010); Marriage status: 21.3% never married, 71.3% now married, 0.9% widowed, 6.5% divorced (2006-2010 5-year est.); Foreign born: 8.8% (2006-2010 5-year est.); Ancestry (includes multiple

ancestries): 28.5% Irish, 21.1% Italian, 19.6% German, 5.1% Eastern European, 3.8% English (2006-2010 5-year est.).
Economy: Employment by occupation: 26.9% management, 8.0% professional, 2.2% services, 11.7% sales, 0.0% farming, 4.9% construction, 7.1% production (2006-2010 5-year est.).
Income: Per capita income: $57,480 (2006-2010 5-year est.); Median household income: $120,694 (2006-2010 5-year est.); Average household income: $165,798 (2006-2010 5-year est.); Percent of households with income of $100,000 or more: 60.6% (2006-2010 5-year est.); Poverty rate: 0.0% (2006-2010 5-year est.).
Education: Percent of population age 25 and over with: High school diploma (including GED) or higher: 100.0% (2006-2010 5-year est.); Bachelor's degree or higher: 78.0% (2006-2010 5-year est.); Master's degree or higher: 32.2% (2006-2010 5-year est.).
School District(s)
Tredyffrin-Easttown SD (KG-12)
    2010-11 Enrollment: 6,334 . . . . (610) 240-1900
Housing: Homeownership rate: 88.9% (2010); Median home value: $455,700 (2006-2010 5-year est.); Median contract rent: $1,325 per month (2006-2010 5-year est.); Median year structure built: 1955 (2006-2010 5-year est.).
Transportation: Commute to work: 84.2% car, 9.0% public transportation, 1.4% walk, 5.4% work from home (2006-2010 5-year est.); Travel time to work: 29.4% less than 15 minutes, 36.4% 15 to 30 minutes, 17.9% 30 to 45 minutes, 2.8% 45 to 60 minutes, 13.6% 60 minutes or more (2006-2010 5-year est.)

DOWNINGTOWN (borough). Covers a land area of 2.188 square miles and a water area of 0.036 square miles. Located at 40.01° N. Lat; 75.70° W. Long. Elevation is 233 feet.
History: Incorporated 1859.
Population: 7,749 (1990); 7,589 (2000); 7,891 (2010); Density: 3,606.7 persons per square mile (2010); Race: 79.3% White, 12.0% Black, 2.7% Asian, 0.1% American Indian/Alaska Native, 0.1% Native Hawaiian/Other Pacific Islander, 5.8% Other, 7.2% Hispanic of any race (2010); Average household size: 2.35 (2010); Median age: 35.8 (2010); Males per 100 females: 95.3 (2010); Marriage status: 32.6% never married, 47.3% now married, 8.0% widowed, 12.1% divorced (2006-2010 5-year est.); Foreign born: 6.3% (2006-2010 5-year est.); Ancestry (includes multiple ancestries): 25.6% Irish, 21.8% German, 20.1% Italian, 12.1% English, 5.4% Scotch-Irish (2006-2010 5-year est.).
Economy: Single-family building permits issued: 6 (2011); Multi-family building permits issued: 0 (2011); Employment by occupation: 11.2% management, 5.4% professional, 10.4% services, 19.3% sales, 4.2% farming, 7.8% construction, 4.3% production (2006-2010 5-year est.).
Income: Per capita income: $27,269 (2006-2010 5-year est.); Median household income: $50,062 (2006-2010 5-year est.); Average household income: $62,325 (2006-2010 5-year est.); Percent of households with income of $100,000 or more: 18.9% (2006-2010 5-year est.); Poverty rate: 6.3% (2006-2010 5-year est.).
Education: Percent of population age 25 and over with: High school diploma (including GED) or higher: 88.7% (2006-2010 5-year est.); Bachelor's degree or higher: 27.4% (2006-2010 5-year est.); Master's degree or higher: 7.9% (2006-2010 5-year est.).
School District(s)
21st Century Cyber CS (06-12)
    2010-11 Enrollment: 686. . . . . (484) 237-5206
Downingtown Area SD (PK-12)
    2010-11 Enrollment: 11,813 . . . . (610) 269-8460
Vocational/Technical School(s)
Pulse Beauty Academy-A Paul Mitchell Partner School (Private, For-profit)
    Fall 2010 Enrollment: 173. . . . . (610) 873-8600
    2011-12 Tuition: $15,750
Housing: Homeownership rate: 55.1% (2010); Median home value: $220,800 (2006-2010 5-year est.); Median contract rent: $824 per month (2006-2010 5-year est.); Median year structure built: 1964 (2006-2010 5-year est.).
Safety: Violent crime rate: 7.6 per 10,000 population; Property crime rate: 346.1 per 10,000 population (2011).
Newspapers: Coatesville Ledger (Community news; Circulation 3,500); Downington Ledger (Community news; Circulation 2,900)
Transportation: Commute to work: 93.1% car, 3.2% public transportation, 1.7% walk, 2.0% work from home (2006-2010 5-year est.); Travel time to work: 32.6% less than 15 minutes, 35.6% 15 to 30 minutes, 17.3% 30 to

45 minutes, 9.5% 45 to 60 minutes, 5.0% 60 minutes or more (2006-2010 5-year est.); Amtrak: train service available.

Additional Information Contacts

Borough of Downingtown . . . . (610) 269-0344
  http://www.downingtown.org
Western Chester County Chamber of Commerce. . . . . . . (610) 384-9550
  http://www.westernchestercounty.com

EAGLEVIEW (CDP). Covers a land area of 1.341 square miles and a water area of 0.014 square miles. Located at 40.06° N. Lat; 75.68° W. Long.

Population: n/a (1990); n/a (2000); 1,644 (2010); Density: 1,226.0 persons per square mile (2010); Race: 94.8% White, 1.6% Black, 2.6% Asian, 0.0% American Indian/Alaska Native, 0.0% Native Hawaiian/Other Pacific Islander, 1.0% Other, 1.8% Hispanic of any race (2010); Average household size: 2.24 (2010); Median age: 46.3 (2010); Males per 100 females: 84.7 (2010); Marriage status: 22.4% never married, 62.8% now married, 6.8% widowed, 8.0% divorced (2006-2010 5-year est.); Foreign born: 7.1% (2006-2010 5-year est.); Ancestry (includes multiple ancestries): 21.7% Irish, 16.1% German, 14.7% English, 9.7% Scotch-Irish, 9.4% Scottish (2006-2010 5-year est.).

Economy: Employment by occupation: 31.1% management, 13.1% professional, 2.6% services, 14.8% sales, 5.0% farming, 4.5% construction, 4.5% production (2006-2010 5-year est.).

Income: Per capita income: $59,837 (2006-2010 5-year est.); Median household income: $103,083 (2006-2010 5-year est.); Average household income: $126,886 (2006-2010 5-year est.); Percent of households with income of $100,000 or more: 50.9% (2006-2010 5-year est.); Poverty rate: 0.5% (2006-2010 5-year est.).

Education: Percent of population age 25 and over with: High school diploma (including GED) or higher: 98.5% (2006-2010 5-year est.); Bachelor's degree or higher: 64.7% (2006-2010 5-year est.); Master's degree or higher: 17.5% (2006-2010 5-year est.).

Housing: Homeownership rate: 62.4% (2010); Median home value: $409,400 (2006-2010 5-year est.); Median contract rent: $1,365 per month (2006-2010 5-year est.); Median year structure built: 2001 (2006-2010 5-year est.).

Transportation: Commute to work: 85.6% car, 5.3% public transportation, 1.3% walk, 6.9% work from home (2006-2010 5-year est.); Travel time to work: 34.3% less than 15 minutes, 22.1% 15 to 30 minutes, 28.1% 30 to 45 minutes, 8.8% 45 to 60 minutes, 6.7% 60 minutes or more (2006-2010 5-year est.)

EAST BRADFORD (township). Covers a land area of 14.934 square miles and a water area of 0.221 square miles. Located at 39.96° N. Lat; 75.65° W. Long.

History: The land consisting of East Bradford Township was part of the original land grant from King Charles II to William Penn in 1681. Bradford Township was established in 1705 and was named for Bradford, England.

Population: 6,440 (1990); 9,405 (2000); 9,942 (2010); Density: 665.7 persons per square mile (2010); Race: 92.8% White, 3.3% Black, 2.0% Asian, 0.1% American Indian/Alaska Native, 0.0% Native Hawaiian/Other Pacific Islander, 1.8% Other, 2.0% Hispanic of any race (2010); Average household size: 2.77 (2010); Median age: 40.2 (2010); Males per 100 females: 89.7 (2010); Marriage status: 26.6% never married, 63.9% now married, 5.8% widowed, 3.7% divorced (2006-2010 5-year est.); Foreign born: 4.7% (2006-2010 5-year est.); Ancestry (includes multiple ancestries): 25.6% Irish, 22.5% German, 22.1% English, 17.9% Italian, 6.1% Polish (2006-2010 5-year est.).

Economy: Single-family building permits issued: 0 (2011); Multi-family building permits issued: 0 (2011); Employment by occupation: 24.6% management, 8.4% professional, 4.4% services, 15.8% sales, 3.0% farming, 3.3% construction, 1.6% production (2006-2010 5-year est.).

Income: Per capita income: $53,249 (2006-2010 5-year est.); Median household income: $123,077 (2006-2010 5-year est.); Average household income: $157,031 (2006-2010 5-year est.); Percent of households with income of $100,000 or more: 63.4% (2006-2010 5-year est.); Poverty rate: 1.1% (2006-2010 5-year est.).

Education: Percent of population age 25 and over with: High school diploma (including GED) or higher: 96.5% (2006-2010 5-year est.); Bachelor's degree or higher: 66.3% (2006-2010 5-year est.); Master's degree or higher: 27.4% (2006-2010 5-year est.).

Housing: Homeownership rate: 89.0% (2010); Median home value: $468,400 (2006-2010 5-year est.); Median contract rent: $912 per month

(2006-2010 5-year est.); Median year structure built: 1986 (2006-2010 5-year est.).

Transportation: Commute to work: 89.1% car, 3.0% public transportation, 2.2% walk, 4.5% work from home (2006-2010 5-year est.); Travel time to work: 25.5% less than 15 minutes, 33.3% 15 to 30 minutes, 21.4% 30 to 45 minutes, 12.7% 45 to 60 minutes, 7.1% 60 minutes or more (2006-2010 5-year est.)

Additional Information Contacts

East Bradford Township . . . . (610) 436-5108
  http://www.eastbradford.org
Greater West Chester Chamber of Commerce . . . . (610) 696-4046
  http://www.gwcc.org

EAST BRANDYWINE (township). Covers a land area of 11.152 square miles and a water area of 0.103 square miles. Located at 40.03° N. Lat; 75.75° W. Long.

History: Brandywine Township was established in 1790. Another split occurred in 1844, and East and West Brandywine Townships were born.

Population: 5,179 (1990); 5,822 (2000); 6,742 (2010); Density: 604.6 persons per square mile (2010); Race: 94.8% White, 1.4% Black, 2.2% Asian, 0.1% American Indian/Alaska Native, 0.1% Native Hawaiian/Other Pacific Islander, 1.4% Other, 1.8% Hispanic of any race (2010); Average household size: 2.84 (2010); Median age: 41.6 (2010); Males per 100 females: 98.5 (2010); Marriage status: 24.0% never married, 69.3% now married, 3.4% widowed, 3.3% divorced (2006-2010 5-year est.); Foreign born: 4.0% (2006-2010 5-year est.); Ancestry (includes multiple ancestries): 31.4% German, 24.7% Irish, 18.1% English, 16.9% Italian, 8.4% Polish (2006-2010 5-year est.).

Economy: Single-family building permits issued: 90 (2011); Multi-family building permits issued: 0 (2011); Employment by occupation: 20.2% management, 9.0% professional, 6.1% services, 16.6% sales, 3.7% farming, 3.2% construction, 2.1% production (2006-2010 5-year est.).

Income: Per capita income: $39,960 (2006-2010 5-year est.); Median household income: $102,848 (2006-2010 5-year est.); Average household income: $115,280 (2006-2010 5-year est.); Percent of households with income of $100,000 or more: 52.9% (2006-2010 5-year est.); Poverty rate: 2.7% (2006-2010 5-year est.).

Education: Percent of population age 25 and over with: High school diploma (including GED) or higher: 94.9% (2006-2010 5-year est.); Bachelor's degree or higher: 55.9% (2006-2010 5-year est.); Master's degree or higher: 22.1% (2006-2010 5-year est.).

Housing: Homeownership rate: 92.4% (2010); Median home value: $349,400 (2006-2010 5-year est.); Median contract rent: $134 per month (2006-2010 5-year est.); Median year structure built: 1979 (2006-2010 5-year est.).

Safety: Violent crime rate: 5.9 per 10,000 population; Property crime rate: 68.0 per 10,000 population (2011).

Transportation: Commute to work: 87.1% car, 3.7% public transportation, 1.2% walk, 7.1% work from home (2006-2010 5-year est.); Travel time to work: 13.8% less than 15 minutes, 43.5% 15 to 30 minutes, 18.7% 30 to 45 minutes, 12.1% 45 to 60 minutes, 11.9% 60 minutes or more (2006-2010 5-year est.)

Additional Information Contacts

East Brandywine Township . . . . (610) 269-8230
  http://www.ebrandywine.org
Greater West Chester Chamber of Commerce . . . . (610) 696-4046
  http://www.gwcc.org

EAST CALN (township). Covers a land area of 3.584 square miles and a water area of 0.097 square miles. Located at 40.01° N. Lat; 75.68° W. Long.

History: East Caln Township was created in 1728 in the center of Chester County along the Lancaster Turnpike, which is now U.S. Rt. 30. East Caln is one of the oldest Townships in the County.

Population: 2,619 (1990); 2,857 (2000); 4,838 (2010); Density: 1,350.1 persons per square mile (2010); Race: 73.9% White, 6.1% Black, 17.0% Asian, 0.2% American Indian/Alaska Native, 0.0% Native Hawaiian/Other Pacific Islander, 2.8% Other, 2.8% Hispanic of any race (2010); Average household size: 2.38 (2010); Median age: 37.0 (2010); Males per 100 females: 89.6 (2010); Marriage status: 22.4% never married, 56.9% now married, 12.1% widowed, 8.6% divorced (2006-2010 5-year est.); Foreign born: 12.9% (2006-2010 5-year est.); Ancestry (includes multiple ancestries): 30.3% German, 17.2% Irish, 14.9% English, 11.4% Italian, 9.2% Polish (2006-2010 5-year est.).

Economy: Single-family building permits issued: 0 (2011); Multi-family building permits issued: 0 (2011); Employment by occupation: 20.8% management, 16.8% professional, 2.2% services, 13.9% sales, 2.8% farming, 3.0% construction, 2.5% production (2006-2010 5-year est.).
Income: Per capita income: $45,993 (2006-2010 5-year est.); Median household income: $91,939 (2006-2010 5-year est.); Average household income: $104,098 (2006-2010 5-year est.); Percent of households with income of $100,000 or more: 46.0% (2006-2010 5-year est.); Poverty rate: 1.7% (2006-2010 5-year est.).
Education: Percent of population age 25 and over with: High school diploma (including GED) or higher: 95.8% (2006-2010 5-year est.); Bachelor's degree or higher: 60.0% (2006-2010 5-year est.); Master's degree or higher: 26.5% (2006-2010 5-year est.).
Housing: Homeownership rate: 66.3% (2010); Median home value: $330,300 (2006-2010 5-year est.); Median contract rent: $1,418 per month (2006-2010 5-year est.); Median year structure built: 1992 (2006-2010 5-year est.).
Transportation: Commute to work: 88.4% car, 5.6% public transportation, 0.9% walk, 4.1% work from home (2006-2010 5-year est.); Travel time to work: 21.5% less than 15 minutes, 24.3% 15 to 30 minutes, 26.3% 30 to 45 minutes, 13.0% 45 to 60 minutes, 14.9% 60 minutes or more (2006-2010 5-year est.)
Additional Information Contacts
Greater West Chester Chamber of Commerce . . . . (610) 696-4046
    http://www.gwcc.org

EAST COVENTRY (township). Covers a land area of 10.658 square miles and a water area of 0.253 square miles. Located at 40.20° N. Lat; 75.61° W. Long.

Population: 4,450 (1990); 4,566 (2000); 6,636 (2010); Density: 622.6 persons per square mile (2010); Race: 93.6% White, 3.1% Black, 1.4% Asian, 0.1% American Indian/Alaska Native, 0.0% Native Hawaiian/Other Pacific Islander, 1.8% Other, 1.7% Hispanic of any race (2010); Average household size: 2.59 (2010); Median age: 40.1 (2010); Males per 100 females: 94.1 (2010); Marriage status: 23.7% never married, 58.2% now married, 7.5% widowed, 10.6% divorced (2006-2010 5-year est.); Foreign born: 4.9% (2006-2010 5-year est.); Ancestry (includes multiple ancestries): 31.5% German, 22.5% Irish, 15.1% Italian, 14.6% English, 5.8% Polish (2006-2010 5-year est.).
Economy: Single-family building permits issued: 4 (2011); Multi-family building permits issued: 0 (2011); Employment by occupation: 15.7% management, 2.9% professional, 9.1% services, 18.5% sales, 5.2% farming, 6.7% construction, 4.0% production (2006-2010 5-year est.).
Income: Per capita income: $36,728 (2006-2010 5-year est.); Median household income: $83,661 (2006-2010 5-year est.); Average household income: $98,085 (2006-2010 5-year est.); Percent of households with income of $100,000 or more: 40.3% (2006-2010 5-year est.); Poverty rate: 3.3% (2006-2010 5-year est.).
Education: Percent of population age 25 and over with: High school diploma (including GED) or higher: 93.0% (2006-2010 5-year est.); Bachelor's degree or higher: 34.1% (2006-2010 5-year est.); Master's degree or higher: 9.8% (2006-2010 5-year est.).
Housing: Homeownership rate: 79.8% (2010); Median home value: $272,700 (2006-2010 5-year est.); Median contract rent: $1,137 per month (2006-2010 5-year est.); Median year structure built: 1981 (2006-2010 5-year est.).
Safety: Violent crime rate: 4.5 per 10,000 population; Property crime rate: 76.6 per 10,000 population (2011).
Transportation: Commute to work: 93.3% car, 0.3% public transportation, 0.6% walk, 4.6% work from home (2006-2010 5-year est.); Travel time to work: 19.2% less than 15 minutes, 28.4% 15 to 30 minutes, 24.4% 30 to 45 minutes, 15.7% 45 to 60 minutes, 12.2% 60 minutes or more (2006-2010 5-year est.)
Additional Information Contacts
East Coventry Township . . . . (610) 495-5443
    http://www.eastcoventry-pa.gov
TriCounty Area Chamber of Commerce . . . . (610) 326-2900
    http://tricountyareachamber.com

EAST FALLOWFIELD (township). Covers a land area of 15.511 square miles and a water area of 0.104 square miles. Located at 39.95° N. Lat; 75.81° W. Long.

Population: 4,433 (1990); 5,157 (2000); 7,449 (2010); Density: 480.2 persons per square mile (2010); Race: 84.9% White, 9.3% Black, 1.8% Asian, 0.1% American Indian/Alaska Native, 0.0% Native Hawaiian/Other

Pacific Islander, 3.9% Other, 4.6% Hispanic of any race (2010); Average household size: 2.81 (2010); Median age: 37.9 (2010); Males per 100 females: 101.5 (2010); Marriage status: 26.0% never married, 64.0% now married, 3.7% widowed, 6.4% divorced (2006-2010 5-year est.); Foreign born: 7.0% (2006-2010 5-year est.); Ancestry (includes multiple ancestries): 22.8% Irish, 19.5% German, 13.7% English, 13.6% Italian, 5.5% Polish (2006-2010 5-year est.).
Economy: Single-family building permits issued: 6 (2011); Multi-family building permits issued: 0 (2011); Employment by occupation: 13.9% management, 5.6% professional, 4.6% services, 19.3% sales, 2.2% farming, 8.1% construction, 4.1% production (2006-2010 5-year est.).
Income: Per capita income: $31,851 (2006-2010 5-year est.); Median household income: $81,509 (2006-2010 5-year est.); Average household income: $89,294 (2006-2010 5-year est.); Percent of households with income of $100,000 or more: 35.5% (2006-2010 5-year est.); Poverty rate: 6.6% (2006-2010 5-year est.).
Education: Percent of population age 25 and over with: High school diploma (including GED) or higher: 92.3% (2006-2010 5-year est.); Bachelor's degree or higher: 43.5% (2006-2010 5-year est.); Master's degree or higher: 18.1% (2006-2010 5-year est.).
School District(s)
Coatesville Area SD (KG-12)
    2010-11 Enrollment: 6,891 . . . . (610) 466-2400
Housing: Homeownership rate: 91.6% (2010); Median home value: $270,800 (2006-2010 5-year est.); Median contract rent: $638 per month (2006-2010 5-year est.); Median year structure built: 1988 (2006-2010 5-year est.).
Transportation: Commute to work: 92.4% car, 2.7% public transportation, 0.2% walk, 4.4% work from home (2006-2010 5-year est.); Travel time to work: 9.1% less than 15 minutes, 36.4% 15 to 30 minutes, 27.0% 30 to 45 minutes, 12.2% 45 to 60 minutes, 15.3% 60 minutes or more (2006-2010 5-year est.)
Additional Information Contacts
East Fallowfield Township . . . . (610) 384-7144
    http://www.eastfallowfield.org
Southern Chester County Chamber of Commerce . . . . (610) 444-0774
    http://www.scccc.com

EAST GOSHEN (township). Covers a land area of 10.046 square miles and a water area of 0.117 square miles. Located at 39.99° N. Lat; 75.55° W. Long.

History: East Goshen Township was incorporated in 1817 when Goshen was divided, forming East and West Goshen Townships. The ten square miles of this land that is now the Township of East Goshen was part of a larger tract purchased from William Penn in Wales in September 1681.
Population: 15,209 (1990); 16,824 (2000); 18,026 (2010); Density: 1,794.3 persons per square mile (2010); Race: 92.6% White, 2.7% Black, 2.9% Asian, 0.1% American Indian/Alaska Native, 0.0% Native Hawaiian/Other Pacific Islander, 1.7% Other, 2.2% Hispanic of any race (2010); Average household size: 2.22 (2010); Median age: 47.3 (2010); Males per 100 females: 88.5 (2010); Marriage status: 26.1% never married, 55.7% now married, 8.9% widowed, 9.3% divorced (2006-2010 5-year est.); Foreign born: 4.9% (2006-2010 5-year est.); Ancestry (includes multiple ancestries): 32.1% Irish, 24.6% German, 20.8% Italian, 17.3% English, 6.3% Polish (2006-2010 5-year est.).
Economy: Single-family building permits issued: 2 (2011); Multi-family building permits issued: 0 (2011); Employment by occupation: 18.7% management, 6.6% professional, 4.5% services, 18.3% sales, 4.1% farming, 5.7% construction, 4.0% production (2006-2010 5-year est.).
Income: Per capita income: $47,359 (2006-2010 5-year est.); Median household income: $73,266 (2006-2010 5-year est.); Average household income: $105,201 (2006-2010 5-year est.); Percent of households with income of $100,000 or more: 35.8% (2006-2010 5-year est.); Poverty rate: 5.0% (2006-2010 5-year est.).
Education: Percent of population age 25 and over with: High school diploma (including GED) or higher: 96.1% (2006-2010 5-year est.); Bachelor's degree or higher: 54.5% (2006-2010 5-year est.); Master's degree or higher: 21.5% (2006-2010 5-year est.).
Housing: Homeownership rate: 71.3% (2010); Median home value: $410,700 (2006-2010 5-year est.); Median contract rent: $1,006 per month (2006-2010 5-year est.); Median year structure built: 1981 (2006-2010 5-year est.).
Transportation: Commute to work: 88.4% car, 2.6% public transportation, 0.3% walk, 7.5% work from home (2006-2010 5-year est.); Travel time to work: 23.8% less than 15 minutes, 38.9% 15 to 30 minutes, 22.3% 30 to

45 minutes, 7.0% 45 to 60 minutes, 8.1% 60 minutes or more (2006-2010 5-year est.)

Additional Information Contacts

East Goshen Township . . . . (610) 692-7171
    http://www.eastgoshentownship.org
Greater West Chester Chamber of Commerce . . . . (610) 696-4046
    http://www.gwcc.org

EAST MARLBOROUGH (township). Covers a land area of 15.453 square miles and a water area of 0.091 square miles. Located at 39.88° N. Lat; 75.72° W. Long.

History: East Marlborough and West Marlborough Townships were carved out of the larger Marlborough Township in 1729. The township is home to a large number of Penn Oak Trees, trees that were in existence when William Penn explored the area.

Population: 4,781 (1990); 6,317 (2000); 7,026 (2010); Density: 454.7 persons per square mile (2010); Race: 92.5% White, 1.4% Black, 3.6% Asian, 0.2% American Indian/Alaska Native, 0.1% Native Hawaiian/Other Pacific Islander, 2.2% Other, 4.6% Hispanic of any race (2010); Average household size: 2.69 (2010); Median age: 44.7 (2010); Males per 100 females: 99.0 (2010); Marriage status: 23.1% never married, 68.1% now married, 4.9% widowed, 4.0% divorced (2006-2010 5-year est.); Foreign born: 8.8% (2006-2010 5-year est.); Ancestry (includes multiple ancestries): 24.1% German, 20.9% Irish, 19.6% English, 12.5% Italian, 5.1% Scottish (2006-2010 5-year est.).

Economy: Single-family building permits issued: 19 (2011); Multi-family building permits issued: 0 (2011); Employment by occupation: 25.2% management, 6.4% professional, 8.1% services, 11.5% sales, 4.0% farming, 9.1% construction, 2.2% production (2006-2010 5-year est.).

Income: Per capita income: $54,340 (2006-2010 5-year est.); Median household income: $118,295 (2006-2010 5-year est.); Average household income: $151,175 (2006-2010 5-year est.); Percent of households with income of $100,000 or more: 56.8% (2006-2010 5-year est.); Poverty rate: 1.5% (2006-2010 5-year est.).

Education: Percent of population age 25 and over with: High school diploma (including GED) or higher: 95.4% (2006-2010 5-year est.); Bachelor's degree or higher: 64.8% (2006-2010 5-year est.); Master's degree or higher: 25.0% (2006-2010 5-year est.).

Housing: Homeownership rate: 89.1% (2010); Median home value: $443,600 (2006-2010 5-year est.); Median contract rent: $850 per month (2006-2010 5-year est.); Median year structure built: 1984 (2006-2010 5-year est.).

Safety: Violent crime rate: 0.0 per 10,000 population; Property crime rate: 21.3 per 10,000 population (2011).

Transportation: Commute to work: 87.2% car, 0.4% public transportation, 3.5% walk, 7.5% work from home (2006-2010 5-year est.); Travel time to work: 29.7% less than 15 minutes, 23.2% 15 to 30 minutes, 26.3% 30 to 45 minutes, 12.1% 45 to 60 minutes, 8.7% 60 minutes or more (2006-2010 5-year est.)

Additional Information Contacts

East Marlborough Township . . . . (610) 444-0725
    http://www.eastmarlborough.org
Southern Chester County Chamber of Commerce . . . . (610) 444-0774
    http://www.sccccc.com

EAST NANTMEAL (township). Covers a land area of 16.211 square miles and a water area of 0.172 square miles. Located at 40.13° N. Lat; 75.75° W. Long. Elevation is 722 feet.

Population: 1,448 (1990); 1,787 (2000); 1,803 (2010); Density: 111.2 persons per square mile (2010); Race: 97.4% White, 0.8% Black, 0.7% Asian, 0.1% American Indian/Alaska Native, 0.0% Native Hawaiian/Other Pacific Islander, 1.0% Other, 1.9% Hispanic of any race (2010); Average household size: 2.63 (2010); Median age: 45.4 (2010); Males per 100 females: 95.3 (2010); Marriage status: 26.0% never married, 60.9% now married, 4.8% widowed, 8.4% divorced (2006-2010 5-year est.); Foreign born: 7.6% (2006-2010 5-year est.); Ancestry (includes multiple ancestries): 31.0% German, 25.2% Irish, 16.9% English, 13.1% Italian, 4.4% Welsh (2006-2010 5-year est.).

Economy: Single-family building permits issued: 4 (2011); Multi-family building permits issued: 0 (2011); Employment by occupation: 24.2% management, 5.5% professional, 4.0% services, 15.1% sales, 1.1% farming, 9.7% construction, 4.9% production (2006-2010 5-year est.).

Income: Per capita income: $47,788 (2006-2010 5-year est.); Median household income: $100,000 (2006-2010 5-year est.); Average household income: $136,619 (2006-2010 5-year est.); Percent of households with

income of $100,000 or more: 50.0% (2006-2010 5-year est.); Poverty rate: 1.1% (2006-2010 5-year est.).

Education: Percent of population age 25 and over with: High school diploma (including GED) or higher: 97.0% (2006-2010 5-year est.); Bachelor's degree or higher: 53.9% (2006-2010 5-year est.); Master's degree or higher: 17.3% (2006-2010 5-year est.).

Housing: Homeownership rate: 87.2% (2010); Median home value: $452,100 (2006-2010 5-year est.); Median contract rent: $1,313 per month (2006-2010 5-year est.); Median year structure built: 1981 (2006-2010 5-year est.).

Transportation: Commute to work: 84.9% car, 2.9% public transportation, 2.8% walk, 8.7% work from home (2006-2010 5-year est.); Travel time to work: 19.3% less than 15 minutes, 28.3% 15 to 30 minutes, 23.3% 30 to 45 minutes, 14.7% 45 to 60 minutes, 14.4% 60 minutes or more (2006-2010 5-year est.)

Additional Information Contacts

Western Chester County Chamber of Commerce . . . . (610) 384-9550
    http://www.westernchestercounty.com

EAST NOTTINGHAM (township). Covers a land area of 20.026 square miles and a water area of 0.118 square miles. Located at 39.76° N. Lat; 75.97° W. Long.

Population: 3,818 (1990); 5,516 (2000); 8,650 (2010); Density: 431.9 persons per square mile (2010); Race: 90.0% White, 3.1% Black, 0.4% Asian, 0.0% American Indian/Alaska Native, 0.0% Native Hawaiian/Other Pacific Islander, 6.5% Other, 9.2% Hispanic of any race (2010); Average household size: 3.24 (2010); Median age: 35.0 (2010); Males per 100 females: 104.0 (2010); Marriage status: 27.4% never married, 66.2% now married, 1.2% widowed, 5.1% divorced (2006-2010 5-year est.); Foreign born: 2.9% (2006-2010 5-year est.); Ancestry (includes multiple ancestries): 26.0% German, 23.5% Irish, 17.4% Italian, 15.6% English, 5.9% American (2006-2010 5-year est.).

Economy: Single-family building permits issued: 11 (2011); Multi-family building permits issued: 0 (2011); Employment by occupation: 20.1% management, 6.5% professional, 5.4% services, 13.6% sales, 2.5% farming, 9.3% construction, 5.5% production (2006-2010 5-year est.).

Income: Per capita income: $30,189 (2006-2010 5-year est.); Median household income: $81,176 (2006-2010 5-year est.); Average household income: $93,053 (2006-2010 5-year est.); Percent of households with income of $100,000 or more: 38.6% (2006-2010 5-year est.); Poverty rate: 7.8% (2006-2010 5-year est.).

Education: Percent of population age 25 and over with: High school diploma (including GED) or higher: 89.7% (2006-2010 5-year est.); Bachelor's degree or higher: 33.6% (2006-2010 5-year est.); Master's degree or higher: 9.4% (2006-2010 5-year est.).

Housing: Homeownership rate: 88.2% (2010); Median home value: $296,800 (2006-2010 5-year est.); Median contract rent: $609 per month (2006-2010 5-year est.); Median year structure built: 1993 (2006-2010 5-year est.).

Transportation: Commute to work: 91.2% car, 0.3% public transportation, 1.1% walk, 7.2% work from home (2006-2010 5-year est.); Travel time to work: 19.5% less than 15 minutes, 23.4% 15 to 30 minutes, 16.3% 30 to 45 minutes, 22.0% 45 to 60 minutes, 18.8% 60 minutes or more (2006-2010 5-year est.)

Additional Information Contacts

East Nottingham Township . . . . (610) 932-8494
    http://www.eastnottingham.org
Oxford Area Chamber of Commerce . . . . (610) 932-0740
    http://www.oxfordpa.org

EAST PIKELAND (township). Covers a land area of 8.737 square miles and a water area of 0.157 square miles. Located at 40.13° N. Lat; 75.56° W. Long.

History: Pike's Land was the first name given to a grant of 10,000 acres by William Penn to Joseph Pike from County Cork, Ireland, in 1705. It was eventually sold by Pike's ancestors and in 1838 was split in two parts, East Pikeland and West Pikeland.

Population: 5,825 (1990); 6,551 (2000); 7,079 (2010); Density: 810.2 persons per square mile (2010); Race: 94.9% White, 1.9% Black, 1.9% Asian, 0.1% American Indian/Alaska Native, 0.0% Native Hawaiian/Other Pacific Islander, 1.2% Other, 1.6% Hispanic of any race (2010); Average household size: 2.45 (2010); Median age: 44.9 (2010); Males per 100 females: 92.2 (2010); Marriage status: 24.7% never married, 61.9% now married, 6.6% widowed, 6.8% divorced (2006-2010 5-year est.); Foreign born: 3.9% (2006-2010 5-year est.); Ancestry (includes multiple

ancestries): 32.4% German, 30.3% Irish, 15.7% Italian, 13.3% English, 6.2% Polish (2006-2010 5-year est.).

Economy: Single-family building permits issued: 26 (2011); Multi-family building permits issued: 0 (2011); Employment by occupation: 16.6% management, 8.8% professional, 7.3% services, 15.9% sales, 2.5% farming, 7.9% construction, 3.5% production (2006-2010 5-year est.).

Income: Per capita income: $44,039 (2006-2010 5-year est.); Median household income: $89,358 (2006-2010 5-year est.); Average household income: $109,640 (2006-2010 5-year est.); Percent of households with income of $100,000 or more: 45.1% (2006-2010 5-year est.); Poverty rate: 2.0% (2006-2010 5-year est.).

Education: Percent of population age 25 and over with: High school diploma (including GED) or higher: 94.4% (2006-2010 5-year est.); Bachelor's degree or higher: 47.4% (2006-2010 5-year est.); Master's degree or higher: 14.2% (2006-2010 5-year est.).

Housing: Homeownership rate: 87.7% (2010); Median home value: $288,700 (2006-2010 5-year est.); Median contract rent: $867 per month (2006-2010 5-year est.); Median year structure built: 1983 (2006-2010 5-year est.).

Safety: Violent crime rate: 14.1 per 10,000 population; Property crime rate: 88.7 per 10,000 population (2011).

Transportation: Commute to work: 94.4% car, 0.7% public transportation, 1.2% walk, 3.5% work from home (2006-2010 5-year est.); Travel time to work: 27.2% less than 15 minutes, 34.6% 15 to 30 minutes, 23.3% 30 to 45 minutes, 5.8% 45 to 60 minutes, 9.1% 60 minutes or more (2006-2010 5-year est.)

Additional Information Contacts

East Pikeland Township . . . . (610) 933-1770
  http://www.eastpikeland.org
TriCounty Area Chamber of Commerce . . . . (610) 326-2900
  http://tricountyareachamber.com

EAST VINCENT (township).

Covers a land area of 13.398 square miles and a water area of 0.252 square miles. Located at 40.17° N. Lat; 75.59° W. Long.

Population: 4,161 (1990); 5,493 (2000); 6,821 (2010); Density: 509.1 persons per square mile (2010); Race: 90.7% White, 4.9% Black, 2.2% Asian, 0.2% American Indian/Alaska Native, 0.1% Native Hawaiian/Other Pacific Islander, 1.9% Other, 2.1% Hispanic of any race (2010); Average household size: 2.88 (2010); Median age: 39.8 (2010); Males per 100 females: 106.1 (2010); Marriage status: 23.8% never married, 61.4% now married, 6.7% widowed, 8.1% divorced (2006-2010 5-year est.); Foreign born: 4.4% (2006-2010 5-year est.); Ancestry (includes multiple ancestries): 25.6% German, 23.5% Irish, 16.3% Italian, 11.3% Polish, 10.9% English (2006-2010 5-year est.).

Economy: Single-family building permits issued: 2 (2011); Multi-family building permits issued: 0 (2011); Employment by occupation: 18.9% management, 8.7% professional, 6.2% services, 13.8% sales, 3.3% farming, 5.1% construction, 3.1% production (2006-2010 5-year est.).

Income: Per capita income: $36,588 (2006-2010 5-year est.); Median household income: $83,405 (2006-2010 5-year est.); Average household income: $100,609 (2006-2010 5-year est.); Percent of households with income of $100,000 or more: 46.3% (2006-2010 5-year est.); Poverty rate: 6.9% (2006-2010 5-year est.).

Education: Percent of population age 25 and over with: High school diploma (including GED) or higher: 91.1% (2006-2010 5-year est.); Bachelor's degree or higher: 39.8% (2006-2010 5-year est.); Master's degree or higher: 16.6% (2006-2010 5-year est.).

Housing: Homeownership rate: 82.4% (2010); Median home value: $311,600 (2006-2010 5-year est.); Median contract rent: $261 per month (2006-2010 5-year est.); Median year structure built: 1983 (2006-2010 5-year est.).

Safety: Violent crime rate: 1.5 per 10,000 population; Property crime rate: 77.5 per 10,000 population (2011).

Transportation: Commute to work: 93.8% car, 0.5% public transportation, 1.2% walk, 4.1% work from home (2006-2010 5-year est.); Travel time to work: 16.5% less than 15 minutes, 44.6% 15 to 30 minutes, 19.4% 30 to 45 minutes, 5.5% 45 to 60 minutes, 14.0% 60 minutes or more (2006-2010 5-year est.)

Additional Information Contacts

East Vincent Township . . . . (610) 933-0115
  http://www.eastvincent.org
TriCounty Area Chamber of Commerce . . . . (610) 326-2900
  http://tricountyareachamber.com

EAST WHITELAND (township).

Covers a land area of 10.936 square miles and a water area of 0.067 square miles. Located at 40.05° N. Lat; 75.55° W. Long.

History: Founded in 1704, Whiteland Township was made up of what is today known as East and West Whiteland townships. The first European settlers were Welsh. The name Whiteland came from Whitford Garden in Flintshire, Wales. Whiteland Township was divided into two townships in 1765.

Population: 8,398 (1990); 9,333 (2000); 10,650 (2010); Density: 973.8 persons per square mile (2010); Race: 80.9% White, 3.3% Black, 11.6% Asian, 0.2% American Indian/Alaska Native, 0.0% Native Hawaiian/Other Pacific Islander, 4.0% Other, 6.9% Hispanic of any race (2010); Average household size: 2.73 (2010); Median age: 37.4 (2010); Males per 100 females: 91.1 (2010); Marriage status: 36.6% never married, 52.7% now married, 4.7% widowed, 6.0% divorced (2006-2010 5-year est.); Foreign born: 17.7% (2006-2010 5-year est.); Ancestry (includes multiple ancestries): 24.4% Irish, 21.8% German, 19.8% Italian, 11.9% English, 3.5% Polish (2006-2010 5-year est.).

Economy: Single-family building permits issued: 3 (2011); Multi-family building permits issued: 0 (2011); Employment by occupation: 15.3% management, 12.7% professional, 9.7% services, 12.9% sales, 5.3% farming, 5.7% construction, 2.9% production (2006-2010 5-year est.).

Income: Per capita income: $40,051 (2006-2010 5-year est.); Median household income: $88,277 (2006-2010 5-year est.); Average household income: $122,242 (2006-2010 5-year est.); Percent of households with income of $100,000 or more: 43.9% (2006-2010 5-year est.); Poverty rate: 7.1% (2006-2010 5-year est.).

Education: Percent of population age 25 and over with: High school diploma (including GED) or higher: 91.9% (2006-2010 5-year est.); Bachelor's degree or higher: 54.8% (2006-2010 5-year est.); Master's degree or higher: 22.1% (2006-2010 5-year est.).

Four-year College(s)

Immaculata University (Private, Not-for-profit, Roman Catholic)
  Fall 2010 Enrollment: 3,320 . . . . (610) 647-4400
    2011-12 Tuition: In-state $28,850; Out-of-state $28,850

Housing: Homeownership rate: 73.8% (2010); Median home value: $364,100 (2006-2010 5-year est.); Median contract rent: $1,159 per month (2006-2010 5-year est.); Median year structure built: 1977 (2006-2010 5-year est.).

Safety: Violent crime rate: 7.5 per 10,000 population; Property crime rate: 122.6 per 10,000 population (2011).

Transportation: Commute to work: 82.5% car, 4.4% public transportation, 6.0% walk, 4.3% work from home (2006-2010 5-year est.); Travel time to work: 36.9% less than 15 minutes, 29.7% 15 to 30 minutes, 17.7% 30 to 45 minutes, 6.9% 45 to 60 minutes, 8.8% 60 minutes or more (2006-2010 5-year est.)

Additional Information Contacts

Chester County Chamber of Business and Industry . . . . . . (610) 725-9100
  http://www.cccbi.org
East Whiteland Township . . . . (610) 648-0600
  http://www.eastwhiteland.org

EASTTOWN (township).

Covers a land area of 8.225 square miles and a water area of 0.042 square miles. Located at 40.03° N. Lat; 75.45° W. Long.

History: The land that eventually became Easttown Township was once part of the Welsh Tract, a large expanse of land promised by William Penn to a group of Welsh Quaker settlers in which they would be able to speak and conduct business in the Welsh language.

Population: 9,570 (1990); 10,270 (2000); 10,477 (2010); Density: 1,273.7 persons per square mile (2010); Race: 91.2% White, 2.0% Black, 5.3% Asian, 0.1% American Indian/Alaska Native, 0.0% Native Hawaiian/Other Pacific Islander, 1.4% Other, 2.0% Hispanic of any race (2010); Average household size: 2.72 (2010); Median age: 44.8 (2010); Males per 100 females: 90.9 (2010); Marriage status: 25.4% never married, 65.6% now married, 3.8% widowed, 5.2% divorced (2006-2010 5-year est.); Foreign born: 7.3% (2006-2010 5-year est.); Ancestry (includes multiple ancestries): 28.4% Irish, 21.1% German, 18.3% Italian, 15.5% English, 3.7% American (2006-2010 5-year est.).

Economy: Single-family building permits issued: 7 (2011); Multi-family building permits issued: 0 (2011); Employment by occupation: 25.3% management, 4.6% professional, 7.2% services, 14.7% sales, 1.7% farming, 3.1% construction, 4.4% production (2006-2010 5-year est.).

Income: Per capita income: $70,178 (2006-2010 5-year est.); Median household income: $128,984 (2006-2010 5-year est.); Average household

income: $200,971 (2006-2010 5-year est.); Percent of households with income of $100,000 or more: 57.0% (2006-2010 5-year est.); Poverty rate: 3.6% (2006-2010 5-year est.).

Education: Percent of population age 25 and over with: High school diploma (including GED) or higher: 96.4% (2006-2010 5-year est.); Bachelor's degree or higher: 70.5% (2006-2010 5-year est.); Master's degree or higher: 27.0% (2006-2010 5-year est.).

Housing: Homeownership rate: 85.0% (2010); Median home value: $611,200 (2006-2010 5-year est.); Median contract rent: $943 per month (2006-2010 5-year est.); Median year structure built: 1964 (2006-2010 5-year est.).

Safety: Violent crime rate: 1.9 per 10,000 population; Property crime rate: 87.5 per 10,000 population (2011).

Transportation: Commute to work: 80.8% car, 5.5% public transportation, 1.8% walk, 11.2% work from home (2006-2010 5-year est.); Travel time to work: 28.2% less than 15 minutes, 39.9% 15 to 30 minutes, 15.2% 30 to 45 minutes, 8.4% 45 to 60 minutes, 8.4% 60 minutes or more (2006-2010 5-year est.)

Additional Information Contacts
Chester County Chamber of Business and Industry . . . . . . (610) 725-9100
  http://www.cccbi.org
Easttown Township . . . . (610) 687-3000
  http://www.easttown.org

ELK (township). Covers a land area of 10.052 square miles and a water area of 0.073 square miles. Located at 39.74° N. Lat; 75.91° W. Long.

Population: 1,129 (1990); 1,485 (2000); 1,681 (2010); Density: 167.2 persons per square mile (2010); Race: 93.7% White, 1.6% Black, 1.2% Asian, 0.5% American Indian/Alaska Native, 0.0% Native Hawaiian/Other Pacific Islander, 3.0% Other, 5.7% Hispanic of any race (2010); Average household size: 2.83 (2010); Median age: 41.1 (2010); Males per 100 females: 98.2 (2010); Marriage status: 22.5% never married, 65.2% now married, 3.4% widowed, 8.9% divorced (2006-2010 5-year est.); Foreign born: 6.1% (2006-2010 5-year est.); Ancestry (includes multiple ancestries): 27.4% Irish, 24.2% German, 16.6% English, 10.6% Italian, 4.6% Polish (2006-2010 5-year est.).

Economy: Single-family building permits issued: 0 (2011); Multi-family building permits issued: 0 (2011); Employment by occupation: 20.2% management, 5.0% professional, 11.1% services, 10.8% sales, 3.0% farming, 11.4% construction, 8.5% production (2006-2010 5-year est.).

Income: Per capita income: $33,896 (2006-2010 5-year est.); Median household income: $83,287 (2006-2010 5-year est.); Average household income: $100,639 (2006-2010 5-year est.); Percent of households with income of $100,000 or more: 39.9% (2006-2010 5-year est.); Poverty rate: 8.3% (2006-2010 5-year est.).

Education: Percent of population age 25 and over with: High school diploma (including GED) or higher: 87.3% (2006-2010 5-year est.); Bachelor's degree or higher: 39.4% (2006-2010 5-year est.); Master's degree or higher: 11.7% (2006-2010 5-year est.).

Housing: Homeownership rate: 86.6% (2010); Median home value: $316,300 (2006-2010 5-year est.); Median contract rent: $661 per month (2006-2010 5-year est.); Median year structure built: 1984 (2006-2010 5-year est.).

Transportation: Commute to work: 89.2% car, 0.8% public transportation, 0.8% walk, 7.9% work from home (2006-2010 5-year est.); Travel time to work: 19.7% less than 15 minutes, 32.2% 15 to 30 minutes, 19.8% 30 to 45 minutes, 16.5% 45 to 60 minutes, 11.8% 60 minutes or more (2006-2010 5-year est.)

Additional Information Contacts
Oxford Area Chamber of Commerce . . . . (610) 932-0740
  http://www.oxfordpa.org

ELVERSON (borough). Covers a land area of 0.994 square miles and a water area of 0.011 square miles. Located at 40.15° N. Lat; 75.83° W. Long. Elevation is 673 feet.

Population: 470 (1990); 959 (2000); 1,225 (2010); Density: 1,232.2 persons per square mile (2010); Race: 98.1% White, 0.6% Black, 0.5% Asian, 0.1% American Indian/Alaska Native, 0.0% Native Hawaiian/Other Pacific Islander, 0.7% Other, 1.6% Hispanic of any race (2010); Average household size: 2.20 (2010); Median age: 56.7 (2010); Males per 100 females: 87.0 (2010); Marriage status: 16.4% never married, 65.5% now married, 9.6% widowed, 8.4% divorced (2006-2010 5-year est.); Foreign born: 2.1% (2006-2010 5-year est.); Ancestry (includes multiple ancestries): 39.7% German, 25.4% Irish, 16.7% English, 11.8% Italian, 6.1% American (2006-2010 5-year est.).

Economy: Single-family building permits issued: 5 (2011); Multi-family building permits issued: 0 (2011); Employment by occupation: 16.6% management, 4.8% professional, 6.7% services, 22.0% sales, 0.8% farming, 12.6% construction, 7.8% production (2006-2010 5-year est.).

Income: Per capita income: $32,621 (2006-2010 5-year est.); Median household income: $58,750 (2006-2010 5-year est.); Average household income: $68,577 (2006-2010 5-year est.); Percent of households with income of $100,000 or more: 21.8% (2006-2010 5-year est.); Poverty rate: 2.8% (2006-2010 5-year est.).

Education: Percent of population age 25 and over with: High school diploma (including GED) or higher: 96.8% (2006-2010 5-year est.); Bachelor's degree or higher: 31.5% (2006-2010 5-year est.); Master's degree or higher: 13.6% (2006-2010 5-year est.).

School District(s)
Twin Valley SD (KG-12)
  2010-11 Enrollment: 3,390 . . . . (610) 286-8600
Twin Valley SD (KG-12)
  2010-11 Enrollment: 3,390 . . . . (610) 286-8600

Housing: Homeownership rate: 82.8% (2010); Median home value: $287,200 (2006-2010 5-year est.); Median contract rent: $711 per month (2006-2010 5-year est.); Median year structure built: 1994 (2006-2010 5-year est.).

Transportation: Commute to work: 86.6% car, 1.2% public transportation, 6.3% walk, 6.0% work from home (2006-2010 5-year est.); Travel time to work: 29.8% less than 15 minutes, 24.1% 15 to 30 minutes, 18.6% 30 to 45 minutes, 17.3% 45 to 60 minutes, 10.2% 60 minutes or more (2006-2010 5-year est.)

Additional Information Contacts
Borough of Elverson . . . . (610) 286-6420
  http://www.elverson.org
TriCounty Area Chamber of Commerce . . . . (610) 326-2900
  http://tricountyareachamber.com

EXTON (CDP). Covers a land area of 3.127 square miles and a water area of 0.027 square miles. Located at 40.03° N. Lat; 75.63° W. Long. Elevation is 312 feet.

History: A theory exists that Exton was named as the "X" on the map, denoting this intersection, though more likely the village was named after one of the several Extons in the United Kingdom.

Population: 2,550 (1990); 4,267 (2000); 4,842 (2010); Density: 1,548.5 persons per square mile (2010); Race: 75.7% White, 4.1% Black, 17.5% Asian, 0.2% American Indian/Alaska Native, 0.0% Native Hawaiian/Other Pacific Islander, 2.5% Other, 1.9% Hispanic of any race (2010); Average household size: 2.20 (2010); Median age: 38.4 (2010); Males per 100 females: 95.1 (2010); Marriage status: 29.8% never married, 57.5% now married, 3.5% widowed, 9.3% divorced (2006-2010 5-year est.); Foreign born: 17.5% (2006-2010 5-year est.); Ancestry (includes multiple ancestries): 24.4% Irish, 22.1% German, 19.3% Italian, 9.5% English, 4.6% Polish (2006-2010 5-year est.).

Economy: Employment by occupation: 27.2% management, 14.1% professional, 3.2% services, 13.0% sales, 3.2% farming, 2.0% construction, 2.2% production (2006-2010 5-year est.).

Income: Per capita income: $51,084 (2006-2010 5-year est.); Median household income: $87,829 (2006-2010 5-year est.); Average household income: $100,991 (2006-2010 5-year est.); Percent of households with income of $100,000 or more: 39.5% (2006-2010 5-year est.); Poverty rate: 1.8% (2006-2010 5-year est.).

Education: Percent of population age 25 and over with: High school diploma (including GED) or higher: 95.7% (2006-2010 5-year est.); Bachelor's degree or higher: 59.0% (2006-2010 5-year est.); Master's degree or higher: 24.1% (2006-2010 5-year est.).

School District(s)
Achievement House CS (07-12)
  2010-11 Enrollment: 536 . . . . (484) 615-6200
Collegium CS (KG-12)
  2010-11 Enrollment: 1,562 . . . . (610) 903-1300
Downingtown Area SD (PK-12)
  2010-11 Enrollment: 11,813 . . . . (610) 269-8460
West Chester Area SD (KG-12)
  2010-11 Enrollment: 11,825 . . . . (484) 266-1000

Two-year College(s)
Automotive Training Center (Private, For-profit)
  Fall 2010 Enrollment: 559 . . . . (610) 363-6716
Universal Technical Institute of Pennsylvania Inc (Private, For-profit)
  Fall 2010 Enrollment: 2,339 . . . . (610) 458-5595

Vocational/Technical School(s)

Empire Beauty School-Exton (Private, For-profit)
Fall 2010 Enrollment: 224 . . . . (800) 223-3271
2011-12 Tuition: $14,490

Housing: Homeownership rate: 41.0% (2010); Median home value: $385,200 (2006-2010 5-year est.); Median contract rent: $1,156 per month (2006-2010 5-year est.); Median year structure built: 1990 (2006-2010 5-year est.).

Newspapers: Suburban Advertiser (Community news; Circulation 16,435)

Transportation: Commute to work: 90.5% car, 3.7% public transportation, 0.6% walk, 4.1% work from home (2006-2010 5-year est.); Travel time to work: 26.4% less than 15 minutes, 33.1% 15 to 30 minutes, 25.9% 30 to 45 minutes, 8.4% 45 to 60 minutes, 6.2% 60 minutes or more (2006-2010 5-year est.); Amtrak: train service available.

Additional Information Contacts

Exton Region Chamber of Commerce . . . . (610) 363-7746
http://www.ercc.net

FRANKLIN (township).

Covers a land area of 13.059 square miles and a water area of 0.083 square miles. Located at 39.76° N. Lat; 75.83° W. Long. Elevation is 305 feet.

History: The mailing addresses for the township include Landenberg, Lincoln University, and Kemblesville; Town administration is located in Kemblesville.

Population: 2,779 (1990); 3,850 (2000); 4,352 (2010); Density: 333.3 persons per square mile (2010); Race: 94.5% White, 1.9% Black, 1.1% Asian, 0.1% American Indian/Alaska Native, 0.0% Native Hawaiian/Other Pacific Islander, 2.4% Other, 3.3% Hispanic of any race (2010); Average household size: 3.04 (2010); Median age: 41.2 (2010); Males per 100 females: 102.3 (2010); Marriage status: 23.9% never married, 69.6% now married, 1.3% widowed, 5.3% divorced (2006-2010 5-year est.); Foreign born: 3.2% (2006-2010 5-year est.); Ancestry (includes multiple ancestries): 23.9% Irish, 22.3% German, 17.9% Italian, 13.6% English, 9.2% American (2006-2010 5-year est.).

Economy: Single-family building permits issued: 7 (2011); Multi-family building permits issued: 0 (2011); Employment by occupation: 21.3% management, 7.9% professional, 5.0% services, 15.0% sales, 3.9% farming, 9.7% construction, 4.0% production (2006-2010 5-year est.).

Income: Per capita income: $41,302 (2006-2010 5-year est.); Median household income: $115,692 (2006-2010 5-year est.); Average household income: $127,950 (2006-2010 5-year est.); Percent of households with income of $100,000 or more: 62.0% (2006-2010 5-year est.); Poverty rate: 1.5% (2006-2010 5-year est.).

Education: Percent of population age 25 and over with: High school diploma (including GED) or higher: 95.9% (2006-2010 5-year est.); Bachelor's degree or higher: 51.1% (2006-2010 5-year est.); Master's degree or higher: 22.4% (2006-2010 5-year est.).

Housing: Homeownership rate: 91.0% (2010); Median home value: $374,200 (2006-2010 5-year est.); Median contract rent: $994 per month (2006-2010 5-year est.); Median year structure built: 1985 (2006-2010 5-year est.).

Transportation: Commute to work: 88.4% car, 2.2% public transportation, 1.3% walk, 5.4% work from home (2006-2010 5-year est.); Travel time to work: 16.2% less than 15 minutes, 39.2% 15 to 30 minutes, 25.5% 30 to 45 minutes, 9.7% 45 to 60 minutes, 9.5% 60 minutes or more (2006-2010 5-year est.).

Additional Information Contacts

Chester County Chamber of Business and Industry . . . . . . (610) 725-9100
http://www.cccbi.org

GLENMOORE (unincorporated postal area)

Zip Code: 19343

Covers a land area of 27.099 square miles and a water area of 0.313 square miles. Located at 40.10° N. Lat; 75.75° W. Long. Elevation is 446 feet. Population: 8,142 (2010); Density: 300.5 persons per square mile (2010); Race: 95.2% White, 2.0% Black, 1.4% Asian, 0.2% American Indian/Alaska Native, 0.0% Native Hawaiian/Other Pacific Islander, 1.2% Other, 2.2% Hispanic of any race (2010); Average household size: 2.83 (2010); Median age: 41.4 (2010); Males per 100 females: 102.0 (2010); Homeownership rate: 85.6% (2010)

HIGHLAND (township).

Covers a land area of 17.114 square miles and a water area of 0.071 square miles. Located at 39.92° N. Lat; 75.90° W. Long.

Population: 1,199 (1990); 1,125 (2000); 1,272 (2010); Density: 74.3 persons per square mile (2010); Race: 90.3% White, 4.2% Black, 0.3% Asian, 0.2% American Indian/Alaska Native, 0.0% Native Hawaiian/Other Pacific Islander, 5.0% Other, 8.7% Hispanic of any race (2010); Average household size: 2.79 (2010); Median age: 41.1 (2010); Males per 100 females: 95.4 (2010); Marriage status: 23.2% never married, 64.5% now married, 6.8% widowed, 5.5% divorced (2006-2010 5-year est.); Foreign born: 4.2% (2006-2010 5-year est.); Ancestry (includes multiple ancestries): 26.6% German, 19.5% Irish, 15.5% English, 8.7% American, 5.7% Polish (2006-2010 5-year est.).

Economy: Single-family building permits issued: 3 (2011); Multi-family building permits issued: 0 (2011); Employment by occupation: 13.1% management, 1.9% professional, 15.5% services, 16.8% sales, 2.3% farming, 14.0% construction, 6.9% production (2006-2010 5-year est.).

Income: Per capita income: $26,591 (2006-2010 5-year est.); Median household income: $56,103 (2006-2010 5-year est.); Average household income: $69,905 (2006-2010 5-year est.); Percent of households with income of $100,000 or more: 23.3% (2006-2010 5-year est.); Poverty rate: 14.1% (2006-2010 5-year est.).

Education: Percent of population age 25 and over with: High school diploma (including GED) or higher: 82.6% (2006-2010 5-year est.); Bachelor's degree or higher: 23.0% (2006-2010 5-year est.); Master's degree or higher: 9.2% (2006-2010 5-year est.).

Housing: Homeownership rate: 79.1% (2010); Median home value: $230,900 (2006-2010 5-year est.); Median contract rent: $725 per month (2006-2010 5-year est.); Median year structure built: 1970 (2006-2010 5-year est.).

Safety: Violent crime rate: 0.0 per 10,000 population; Property crime rate: 7.8 per 10,000 population (2011).

Transportation: Commute to work: 84.0% car, 0.4% public transportation, 3.1% walk, 11.5% work from home (2006-2010 5-year est.); Travel time to work: 36.1% less than 15 minutes, 30.5% 15 to 30 minutes, 14.4% 30 to 45 minutes, 11.9% 45 to 60 minutes, 7.1% 60 minutes or more (2006-2010 5-year est.)

Additional Information Contacts

Kane Area Chamber of Commerce . . . . (814) 837-6565
http://www.kanepa.com

HONEY BROOK (borough).

Covers a land area of 0.479 square miles and a water area of <.001 square miles. Located at 40.09° N. Lat; 75.91° W. Long. Elevation is 741 feet.

Population: 1,184 (1990); 1,287 (2000); 1,713 (2010); Density: 3,576.3 persons per square mile (2010); Race: 94.5% White, 1.1% Black, 0.2% Asian, 0.0% American Indian/Alaska Native, 0.1% Native Hawaiian/Other Pacific Islander, 4.1% Other, 3.5% Hispanic of any race (2010); Average household size: 2.62 (2010); Median age: 34.1 (2010); Males per 100 females: 93.3 (2010); Marriage status: 32.0% never married, 52.7% now married, 5.9% widowed, 9.4% divorced (2006-2010 5-year est.); Foreign born: 2.4% (2006-2010 5-year est.); Ancestry (includes multiple ancestries): 34.3% German, 28.3% Irish, 16.4% English, 10.9% Italian, 5.9% American (2006-2010 5-year est.).

Economy: Single-family building permits issued: 8 (2011); Multi-family building permits issued: 0 (2011); Employment by occupation: 8.5% management, 4.1% professional, 7.0% services, 13.1% sales, 2.9% farming, 12.2% construction, 10.0% production (2006-2010 5-year est.).

Income: Per capita income: $28,259 (2006-2010 5-year est.); Median household income: $78,333 (2006-2010 5-year est.); Average household income: $76,157 (2006-2010 5-year est.); Percent of households with income of $100,000 or more: 23.1% (2006-2010 5-year est.); Poverty rate: 6.7% (2006-2010 5-year est.).

Education: Percent of population age 25 and over with: High school diploma (including GED) or higher: 91.0% (2006-2010 5-year est.); Bachelor's degree or higher: 21.4% (2006-2010 5-year est.); Master's degree or higher: 7.4% (2006-2010 5-year est.).

School District(s)

Twin Valley SD (KG-12)
2010-11 Enrollment: 3,390 . . . . (610) 286-8600

Housing: Homeownership rate: 70.1% (2010); Median home value: $218,900 (2006-2010 5-year est.); Median contract rent: $758 per month (2006-2010 5-year est.); Median year structure built: 1965 (2006-2010 5-year est.).

Safety: Violent crime rate: 0.0 per 10,000 population; Property crime rate: 17.5 per 10,000 population (2011).

Transportation: Commute to work: 97.1% car, 0.0% public transportation, 0.5% walk, 2.4% work from home (2006-2010 5-year est.); Travel time to work: 16.1% less than 15 minutes, 34.3% 15 to 30 minutes, 25.8% 30 to 45 minutes, 15.7% 45 to 60 minutes, 8.0% 60 minutes or more (2006-2010 5-year est.)

Additional Information Contacts

Western Chester County Chamber of Commerce . . . . (610) 384-9550
  http://www.westernchestercounty.com

HONEY BROOK (township).
Covers a land area of 24.751 square miles and a water area of 0.424 square miles. Located at 40.09° N. Lat; 75.89° W. Long. Elevation is 741 feet.

Population: 5,449 (1990); 6,278 (2000); 7,647 (2010); Density: 309.0 persons per square mile (2010); Race: 96.5% White, 1.0% Black, 0.5% Asian, 0.4% American Indian/Alaska Native, 0.0% Native Hawaiian/Other Pacific Islander, 1.6% Other, 1.7% Hispanic of any race (2010); Average household size: 2.82 (2010); Median age: 40.8 (2010); Males per 100 females: 87.2 (2010); Marriage status: 20.8% never married, 61.2% now married, 13.4% widowed, 4.6% divorced (2006-2010 5-year est.); Foreign born: 2.2% (2006-2010 5-year est.); Ancestry (includes multiple ancestries): 34.0% German, 15.2% Irish, 10.8% Italian, 10.6% English, 6.0% Polish (2006-2010 5-year est.).

Economy: Single-family building permits issued: 35 (2011); Multi-family building permits issued: 2 (2011); Employment by occupation: 12.7% management, 4.1% professional, 7.7% services, 18.9% sales, 4.8% farming, 10.2% construction, 6.7% production (2006-2010 5-year est.).

Income: Per capita income: $27,215 (2006-2010 5-year est.); Median household income: $73,355 (2006-2010 5-year est.); Average household income: $78,413 (2006-2010 5-year est.); Percent of households with income of $100,000 or more: 28.3% (2006-2010 5-year est.); Poverty rate: 11.1% (2006-2010 5-year est.).

Education: Percent of population age 25 and over with: High school diploma (including GED) or higher: 78.7% (2006-2010 5-year est.); Bachelor's degree or higher: 25.0% (2006-2010 5-year est.); Master's degree or higher: 9.9% (2006-2010 5-year est.).

Housing: Homeownership rate: 75.7% (2010); Median home value: $283,800 (2006-2010 5-year est.); Median contract rent: $939 per month (2006-2010 5-year est.); Median year structure built: 1992 (2006-2010 5-year est.).

Transportation: Commute to work: 89.9% car, 0.9% public transportation, 0.8% walk, 6.3% work from home (2006-2010 5-year est.); Travel time to work: 20.6% less than 15 minutes, 21.5% 15 to 30 minutes, 32.8% 30 to 45 minutes, 12.9% 45 to 60 minutes, 12.1% 60 minutes or more (2006-2010 5-year est.)

Additional Information Contacts

Honey Brook Township . . . . (610) 273-3129
  http://www.honeybrooktwp.com

Western Chester County Chamber of Commerce . . . . (610) 384-9550
  http://www.westernchestercounty.com

IMMACULATA (unincorporated postal area)
Zip Code: 19345

Covers a land area of 0.202 square miles and a water area of 0 square miles. Located at 40.02° N. Lat; 75.56° W. Long. Population: 689 (2010); Density: 3,408.4 persons per square mile (2010); Race: 92.0% White, 5.8% Black, 0.3% Asian, 0.0% American Indian/Alaska Native, 0.0% Native Hawaiian/Other Pacific Islander, 1.9% Other, 3.9% Hispanic of any race (2010); Average household size: 2.00 (2010); Median age: 21.3 (2010); Males per 100 females: 24.8 (2010); Homeownership rate: 100.0% (2010)

KENILWORTH (CDP).
Aka Madison. Covers a land area of 1.707 square miles and a water area of 0.040 square miles. Located at 40.22° N. Lat; 75.64° W. Long. Elevation is 177 feet.

Population: 1,847 (1990); 1,576 (2000); 1,907 (2010); Density: 1,117.4 persons per square mile (2010); Race: 93.6% White, 2.8% Black, 1.3% Asian, 0.3% American Indian/Alaska Native, 0.0% Native Hawaiian/Other Pacific Islander, 2.0% Other, 2.5% Hispanic of any race (2010); Average household size: 2.51 (2010); Median age: 38.7 (2010); Males per 100 females: 96.4 (2010); Marriage status: 24.7% never married, 57.5% now married, 7.1% widowed, 10.7% divorced (2006-2010 5-year est.); Foreign born: 1.2% (2006-2010 5-year est.); Ancestry (includes multiple

ancestries): 29.0% Italian, 28.2% Irish, 23.8% German, 5.2% English, 5.1% American (2006-2010 5-year est.).

Economy: Employment by occupation: 12.6% management, 5.7% professional, 2.9% services, 16.8% sales, 7.4% farming, 5.2% construction, 6.2% production (2006-2010 5-year est.).

Income: Per capita income: $31,777 (2006-2010 5-year est.); Median household income: $73,333 (2006-2010 5-year est.); Average household income: $75,742 (2006-2010 5-year est.); Percent of households with income of $100,000 or more: 32.6% (2006-2010 5-year est.); Poverty rate: 1.6% (2006-2010 5-year est.).

Education: Percent of population age 25 and over with: High school diploma (including GED) or higher: 90.8% (2006-2010 5-year est.); Bachelor's degree or higher: 30.8% (2006-2010 5-year est.); Master's degree or higher: 8.7% (2006-2010 5-year est.).

Housing: Homeownership rate: 70.6% (2010); Median home value: $249,000 (2006-2010 5-year est.); Median contract rent: $755 per month (2006-2010 5-year est.); Median year structure built: 1970 (2006-2010 5-year est.).

Transportation: Commute to work: 91.5% car, 4.5% public transportation, 1.3% walk, 2.6% work from home (2006-2010 5-year est.); Travel time to work: 33.5% less than 15 minutes, 18.1% 15 to 30 minutes, 27.3% 30 to 45 minutes, 14.6% 45 to 60 minutes, 6.4% 60 minutes or more (2006-2010 5-year est.)

Additional Information Contacts

TriCounty Area Chamber of Commerce . . . . (610) 326-2900
  http://www.tricountyareachamber.com

KENNETT (township).
Covers a land area of 15.339 square miles and a water area of 0.143 square miles. Located at 39.84° N. Lat; 75.68° W. Long.

History: Brandywine River Museum nearby. Settled c.1750, incorporated 1855.

Population: 4,624 (1990); 6,451 (2000); 7,565 (2010); Density: 493.2 persons per square mile (2010); Race: 88.9% White, 1.8% Black, 2.4% Asian, 0.4% American Indian/Alaska Native, 0.1% Native Hawaiian/Other Pacific Islander, 6.4% Other, 10.5% Hispanic of any race (2010); Average household size: 2.50 (2010); Median age: 46.0 (2010); Males per 100 females: 93.7 (2010); Marriage status: 19.8% never married, 66.7% now married, 6.5% widowed, 7.0% divorced (2006-2010 5-year est.); Foreign born: 15.8% (2006-2010 5-year est.); Ancestry (includes multiple ancestries): 19.5% Irish, 19.2% Italian, 18.2% English, 15.8% German, 6.6% American (2006-2010 5-year est.).

Economy: Single-family building permits issued: 14 (2011); Multi-family building permits issued: 48 (2011); Employment by occupation: 26.9% management, 4.3% professional, 3.5% services, 9.8% sales, 1.0% farming, 15.9% construction, 1.7% production (2006-2010 5-year est.).

Income: Per capita income: $60,971 (2006-2010 5-year est.); Median household income: $101,446 (2006-2010 5-year est.); Average household income: $152,389 (2006-2010 5-year est.); Percent of households with income of $100,000 or more: 51.0% (2006-2010 5-year est.); Poverty rate: 2.5% (2006-2010 5-year est.).

Education: Percent of population age 25 and over with: High school diploma (including GED) or higher: 93.8% (2006-2010 5-year est.); Bachelor's degree or higher: 63.9% (2006-2010 5-year est.); Master's degree or higher: 32.4% (2006-2010 5-year est.).

Housing: Homeownership rate: 78.7% (2010); Median home value: $464,000 (2006-2010 5-year est.); Median contract rent: $916 per month (2006-2010 5-year est.); Median year structure built: 1980 (2006-2010 5-year est.).

Transportation: Commute to work: 81.2% car, 0.2% public transportation, 6.7% walk, 11.2% work from home (2006-2010 5-year est.); Travel time to work: 27.8% less than 15 minutes, 35.7% 15 to 30 minutes, 22.3% 30 to 45 minutes, 6.0% 45 to 60 minutes, 8.2% 60 minutes or more (2006-2010 5-year est.)

Additional Information Contacts

Kennett Township . . . . (610) 388-1300
  http://www.kennett.pa.us

Southern Chester County Chamber of Commerce . . . . (610) 444-0774
  http://www.scccc.com

KENNETT SQUARE (borough).
Covers a land area of 1.065 square miles and a water area of 0.006 square miles. Located at 39.84° N. Lat; 75.71° W. Long. Elevation is 381 feet.

Population: 5,218 (1990); 5,273 (2000); 6,072 (2010); Density: 5,699.7 persons per square mile (2010); Race: 65.7% White, 7.2% Black, 0.8%

Asian, 0.4% American Indian/Alaska Native, 0.0% Native Hawaiian/Other Pacific Islander, 25.9% Other, 48.8% Hispanic of any race (2010); Average household size: 3.05 (2010); Median age: 32.3 (2010); Males per 100 females: 107.9 (2010); Marriage status: 26.1% never married, 63.5% now married, 3.2% widowed, 7.3% divorced (2006-2010 5-year est.); Foreign born: 34.5% (2006-2010 5-year est.); Ancestry (includes multiple ancestries): 10.9% German, 10.7% Irish, 8.6% English, 8.3% Italian, 4.0% Polish (2006-2010 5-year est.).
Economy: Single-family building permits issued: 3 (2011); Multi-family building permits issued: 0 (2011); Employment by occupation: 7.4% management, 2.0% professional, 9.8% services, 10.1% sales, 6.4% farming, 19.7% construction, 8.9% production (2006-2010 5-year est.).
Income: Per capita income: $24,057 (2006-2010 5-year est.); Median household income: $57,500 (2006-2010 5-year est.); Average household income: $68,242 (2006-2010 5-year est.); Percent of households with income of $100,000 or more: 19.0% (2006-2010 5-year est.); Poverty rate: 11.1% (2006-2010 5-year est.).
Taxes: Total city taxes per capita: $368 (2009); City property taxes per capita: $113 (2009).
Education: Percent of population age 25 and over with: High school diploma (including GED) or higher: 66.0% (2006-2010 5-year est.); Bachelor's degree or higher: 17.8% (2006-2010 5-year est.); Master's degree or higher: 5.9% (2006-2010 5-year est.).

School District(s)
Kennett Consolidated SD (KG-12)
    2010-11 Enrollment: 4,219 . . . . (610) 444-6600
Unionville-Chadds Ford SD (KG-12)
    2010-11 Enrollment: 4,089 . . . . (610) 347-0970
Housing: Homeownership rate: 54.0% (2010); Median home value: $221,900 (2006-2010 5-year est.); Median contract rent: $799 per month (2006-2010 5-year est.); Median year structure built: 1955 (2006-2010 5-year est.).
Safety: Violent crime rate: 27.9 per 10,000 population; Property crime rate: 177.3 per 10,000 population (2011).
Newspapers: Kennett Paper (Local news; Circulation 8,000)
Transportation: Commute to work: 92.3% car, 0.7% public transportation, 1.7% walk, 3.2% work from home (2006-2010 5-year est.); Travel time to work: 34.6% less than 15 minutes, 35.7% 15 to 30 minutes, 16.5% 30 to 45 minutes, 6.7% 45 to 60 minutes, 6.6% 60 minutes or more (2006-2010 5-year est.)
Additional Information Contacts
Borough of Kennett Square . . . . (610) 444-6020
    http://www.kennett-square.pa.us
Southern Chester County Chamber of Commerce . . . . (610) 444-0774
    http://www.scccc.com

KIMBERTON (unincorporated postal area)
Zip Code: 19442
    Covers a land area of 0.019 square miles and a water area of 0 square miles. Located at 40.12° N. Lat; 75.58° W. Long. Elevation is 207 feet. Population: 45 (2010); Density: 2,281.7 persons per square mile (2010); Race: 93.3% White, 0.0% Black, 2.2% Asian, 0.0% American Indian/Alaska Native, 0.0% Native Hawaiian/Other Pacific Islander, 4.5% Other, 0.0% Hispanic of any race (2010); Average household size: 2.81 (2010); Median age: 38.3 (2010); Males per 100 females: 150.0 (2010); Homeownership rate: 100.0% (2010)

LANDENBERG (unincorporated postal area)
Zip Code: 19350
    Covers a land area of 27.862 square miles and a water area of 0.278 square miles. Located at 39.76° N. Lat; 75.79° W. Long. Elevation is 187 feet. Population: 10,921 (2010); Density: 392.0 persons per square mile (2010); Race: 92.7% White, 1.8% Black, 2.0% Asian, 0.3% American Indian/Alaska Native, 0.0% Native Hawaiian/Other Pacific Islander, 3.2% Other, 6.1% Hispanic of any race (2010); Average household size: 2.92 (2010); Median age: 42.8 (2010); Males per 100 females: 104.6 (2010); Homeownership rate: 90.3% (2010)

LINCOLN UNIVERSITY (CDP). Covers a land area of 0.290 square miles and a water area of 0 square miles. Located at 39.81° N. Lat; 75.93° W. Long.
Population: n/a (1990); n/a (2000); 1,726 (2010); Density: 5,959.4 persons per square mile (2010); Race: 0.7% White, 94.9% Black, 0.1% Asian, 0.4% American Indian/Alaska Native, 0.1% Native Hawaiian/Other Pacific Islander, 3.8% Other, 4.3% Hispanic of any race (2010); Average

household size: 4.00 (2010); Median age: 20.3 (2010); Males per 100 females: 65.0 (2010); Marriage status: 98.0% never married, 2.0% now married, 0.0% widowed, 0.0% divorced (2006-2010 5-year est.); Foreign born: 7.2% (2006-2010 5-year est.); Ancestry (includes multiple ancestries): 4.9% Nigerian, 3.6% African, 3.5% Haitian, 2.3% American, 2.3% Guyanese (2006-2010 5-year est.).
Economy: Employment by occupation: 5.0% management, 0.0% professional, 12.4% services, 34.0% sales, 5.3% farming, 1.4% construction, 1.4% production (2006-2010 5-year est.).
Income: Per capita income: $2,902 (2006-2010 5-year est.); Median household income: n/a (2006-2010 5-year est.); Average household income: n/a (2006-2010 5-year est.); Percent of households with income of $100,000 or more: n/a (2006-2010 5-year est.); Poverty rate: 0.0% (2006-2010 5-year est.).
Education: Percent of population age 25 and over with: High school diploma (including GED) or higher: 100.0% (2006-2010 5-year est.); Bachelor's degree or higher: 0.0% (2006-2010 5-year est.); Master's degree or higher: 0.0% (2006-2010 5-year est.).
Housing: Homeownership rate: 100.0% (2010); Median home value: n/a (2006-2010 5-year est.); Median contract rent: n/a per month (2006-2010 5-year est.); Median year structure built: before 1940 (2006-2010 5-year est.).
Transportation: Commute to work: 8.2% car, 0.0% public transportation, 54.7% walk, 37.1% work from home (2006-2010 5-year est.); Travel time to work: 89.3% less than 15 minutes, 0.0% 15 to 30 minutes, 8.3% 30 to 45 minutes, 0.0% 45 to 60 minutes, 2.4% 60 minutes or more (2006-2010 5-year est.)

LIONVILLE (CDP). Covers a land area of 2.484 square miles and a water area of 0.012 square miles. Located at 40.05° N. Lat; 75.64° W. Long. Elevation is 541 feet.
Population: 6,488 (1990); 6,298 (2000); 6,189 (2010); Density: 2,491.9 persons per square mile (2010); Race: 86.8% White, 4.0% Black, 6.5% Asian, 0.1% American Indian/Alaska Native, 0.0% Native Hawaiian/Other Pacific Islander, 2.6% Other, 2.9% Hispanic of any race (2010); Average household size: 2.44 (2010); Median age: 37.8 (2010); Males per 100 females: 98.6 (2010); Marriage status: 27.7% never married, 58.0% now married, 5.5% widowed, 8.8% divorced (2006-2010 5-year est.); Foreign born: 7.1% (2006-2010 5-year est.); Ancestry (includes multiple ancestries): 28.4% German, 24.9% Irish, 13.1% Italian, 12.5% English, 6.0% Scotch-Irish (2006-2010 5-year est.).
Economy: Employment by occupation: 16.1% management, 15.7% professional, 4.0% services, 13.8% sales, 3.9% farming, 7.0% construction, 3.2% production (2006-2010 5-year est.).
Income: Per capita income: $37,001 (2006-2010 5-year est.); Median household income: $74,043 (2006-2010 5-year est.); Average household income: $85,742 (2006-2010 5-year est.); Percent of households with income of $100,000 or more: 34.2% (2006-2010 5-year est.); Poverty rate: 2.4% (2006-2010 5-year est.).
Education: Percent of population age 25 and over with: High school diploma (including GED) or higher: 95.3% (2006-2010 5-year est.); Bachelor's degree or higher: 51.5% (2006-2010 5-year est.); Master's degree or higher: 17.2% (2006-2010 5-year est.).
Housing: Homeownership rate: 65.7% (2010); Median home value: $305,600 (2006-2010 5-year est.); Median contract rent: $954 per month (2006-2010 5-year est.); Median year structure built: 1977 (2006-2010 5-year est.).
Transportation: Commute to work: 87.2% car, 6.8% public transportation, 1.9% walk, 3.5% work from home (2006-2010 5-year est.); Travel time to work: 28.1% less than 15 minutes, 38.4% 15 to 30 minutes, 11.1% 30 to 45 minutes, 12.1% 45 to 60 minutes, 10.4% 60 minutes or more (2006-2010 5-year est.)

LONDON BRITAIN (township). Covers a land area of 9.698 square miles and a water area of 0.088 square miles. Located at 39.75° N. Lat; 75.79° W. Long.
History: Established in 1725, The Township of London Britain was organized from a tract of land belonging to the London Company of Great Britain.
Population: 2,671 (1990); 2,797 (2000); 3,139 (2010); Density: 323.7 persons per square mile (2010); Race: 95.1% White, 1.3% Black, 1.4% Asian, 0.1% American Indian/Alaska Native, 0.0% Native Hawaiian/Other Pacific Islander, 2.1% Other, 2.3% Hispanic of any race (2010); Average household size: 2.87 (2010); Median age: 44.1 (2010); Males per 100 females: 104.2 (2010); Marriage status: 20.2% never married, 71.3% now

married, 2.7% widowed, 5.9% divorced (2006-2010 5-year est.); Foreign born: 6.4% (2006-2010 5-year est.); Ancestry (includes multiple ancestries): 24.7% Irish, 23.1% German, 21.0% English, 10.8% American, 9.6% Italian (2006-2010 5-year est.).

Economy: Single-family building permits issued: 7 (2011); Multi-family building permits issued: 0 (2011); Employment by occupation: 23.7% management, 9.2% professional, 5.7% services, 11.0% sales, 1.6% farming, 6.6% construction, 4.3% production (2006-2010 5-year est.).

Income: Per capita income: $51,811 (2006-2010 5-year est.); Median household income: $116,574 (2006-2010 5-year est.); Average household income: $151,069 (2006-2010 5-year est.); Percent of households with income of $100,000 or more: 59.8% (2006-2010 5-year est.); Poverty rate: 3.7% (2006-2010 5-year est.).

Education: Percent of population age 25 and over with: High school diploma (including GED) or higher: 96.7% (2006-2010 5-year est.); Bachelor's degree or higher: 57.5% (2006-2010 5-year est.); Master's degree or higher: 25.1% (2006-2010 5-year est.).

Housing: Homeownership rate: 94.1% (2010); Median home value: $375,100 (2006-2010 5-year est.); Median contract rent: $1,341 per month (2006-2010 5-year est.); Median year structure built: 1982 (2006-2010 5-year est.).

Transportation: Commute to work: 94.8% car, 0.8% public transportation, 0.0% walk, 4.0% work from home (2006-2010 5-year est.); Travel time to work: 13.6% less than 15 minutes, 41.8% 15 to 30 minutes, 25.3% 30 to 45 minutes, 10.5% 45 to 60 minutes, 8.8% 60 minutes or more (2006-2010 5-year est.)

Additional Information Contacts
Southern Chester County Chamber of Commerce . . . . (610) 444-0774
    http://www.scccc.com

LONDON GROVE (township). Covers a land area of 17.148 square miles and a water area of 0.108 square miles. Located at 39.83° N. Lat; 75.82° W. Long.

History: The Township traditionally has been an agricultural community. And while agriculture is still a major part of the Township, recently London Grove has become an attractive place to live as development pushes west from Philadelphia and north from Wilmington, Delaware.

Population: 3,922 (1990); 5,265 (2000); 7,475 (2010); Density: 435.9 persons per square mile (2010); Race: 84.6% White, 3.8% Black, 1.8% Asian, 0.1% American Indian/Alaska Native, 0.1% Native Hawaiian/Other Pacific Islander, 9.6% Other, 17.6% Hispanic of any race (2010); Average household size: 3.17 (2010); Median age: 36.4 (2010); Males per 100 females: 102.5 (2010); Marriage status: 25.6% never married, 65.7% now married, 4.0% widowed, 4.7% divorced (2006-2010 5-year est.); Foreign born: 16.0% (2006-2010 5-year est.); Ancestry (includes multiple ancestries): 19.3% Italian, 18.5% German, 18.3% Irish, 13.8% English, 5.5% American (2006-2010 5-year est.).

Economy: Single-family building permits issued: 80 (2011); Multi-family building permits issued: 0 (2011); Employment by occupation: 17.2% management, 5.1% professional, 7.7% services, 9.0% sales, 4.0% farming, 16.9% construction, 3.9% production (2006-2010 5-year est.).

Income: Per capita income: $34,088 (2006-2010 5-year est.); Median household income: $91,667 (2006-2010 5-year est.); Average household income: $115,729 (2006-2010 5-year est.); Percent of households with income of $100,000 or more: 42.4% (2006-2010 5-year est.); Poverty rate: 3.2% (2006-2010 5-year est.).

Education: Percent of population age 25 and over with: High school diploma (including GED) or higher: 89.4% (2006-2010 5-year est.); Bachelor's degree or higher: 41.7% (2006-2010 5-year est.); Master's degree or higher: 16.3% (2006-2010 5-year est.).

Housing: Homeownership rate: 86.9% (2010); Median home value: $340,900 (2006-2010 5-year est.); Median contract rent: $1,037 per month (2006-2010 5-year est.); Median year structure built: 1991 (2006-2010 5-year est.).

Transportation: Commute to work: 93.7% car, 0.3% public transportation, 2.8% walk, 2.5% work from home (2006-2010 5-year est.); Travel time to work: 23.1% less than 15 minutes, 29.6% 15 to 30 minutes, 25.0% 30 to 45 minutes, 12.7% 45 to 60 minutes, 9.7% 60 minutes or more (2006-2010 5-year est.)

Additional Information Contacts
London Grove Township . . . . (610) 345-0100
    http://www.london-grove.pa.us
Southern Chester County Chamber of Commerce . . . . (610) 444-0774
    http://www.scccc.com

LONDONDERRY (township). Covers a land area of 11.313 square miles and a water area of 0.046 square miles. Located at 39.88° N. Lat; 75.88° W. Long.

Population: 1,243 (1990); 1,632 (2000); 2,149 (2010); Density: 190.0 persons per square mile (2010); Race: 95.1% White, 1.0% Black, 0.8% Asian, 0.0% American Indian/Alaska Native, 0.0% Native Hawaiian/Other Pacific Islander, 3.1% Other, 6.2% Hispanic of any race (2010); Average household size: 2.83 (2010); Median age: 40.1 (2010); Males per 100 females: 99.9 (2010); Marriage status: 18.9% never married, 70.7% now married, 4.2% widowed, 6.3% divorced (2006-2010 5-year est.); Foreign born: 4.2% (2006-2010 5-year est.); Ancestry (includes multiple ancestries): 32.9% German, 21.0% Irish, 15.0% Italian, 13.6% English, 7.1% Polish (2006-2010 5-year est.).

Economy: Single-family building permits issued: 18 (2011); Multi-family building permits issued: 0 (2011); Employment by occupation: 14.3% management, 8.4% professional, 5.4% services, 12.6% sales, 4.5% farming, 11.4% construction, 6.4% production (2006-2010 5-year est.).

Income: Per capita income: $33,339 (2006-2010 5-year est.); Median household income: $95,132 (2006-2010 5-year est.); Average household income: $94,071 (2006-2010 5-year est.); Percent of households with income of $100,000 or more: 46.2% (2006-2010 5-year est.); Poverty rate: 5.0% (2006-2010 5-year est.).

Education: Percent of population age 25 and over with: High school diploma (including GED) or higher: 90.4% (2006-2010 5-year est.); Bachelor's degree or higher: 30.0% (2006-2010 5-year est.); Master's degree or higher: 11.2% (2006-2010 5-year est.).

Housing: Homeownership rate: 85.5% (2010); Median home value: $320,600 (2006-2010 5-year est.); Median contract rent: $810 per month (2006-2010 5-year est.); Median year structure built: 1983 (2006-2010 5-year est.).

Transportation: Commute to work: 93.0% car, 0.1% public transportation, 2.9% walk, 4.0% work from home (2006-2010 5-year est.); Travel time to work: 18.3% less than 15 minutes, 27.2% 15 to 30 minutes, 20.9% 30 to 45 minutes, 18.7% 45 to 60 minutes, 14.9% 60 minutes or more (2006-2010 5-year est.)

Additional Information Contacts
Southern Chester County Chamber of Commerce . . . . (610) 444-0774
    http://www.scccc.com

LOWER OXFORD (township). Covers a land area of 18.140 square miles and a water area of 0.383 square miles. Located at 39.81° N. Lat; 75.98° W. Long.

Population: 3,313 (1990); 4,319 (2000); 5,200 (2010); Density: 286.7 persons per square mile (2010); Race: 58.6% White, 35.1% Black, 0.3% Asian, 0.3% American Indian/Alaska Native, 0.1% Native Hawaiian/Other Pacific Islander, 5.6% Other, 10.6% Hispanic of any race (2010); Average household size: 3.14 (2010); Median age: 21.8 (2010); Males per 100 females: 88.1 (2010); Marriage status: 58.8% never married, 34.9% now married, 2.4% widowed, 3.9% divorced (2006-2010 5-year est.); Foreign born: 7.2% (2006-2010 5-year est.); Ancestry (includes multiple ancestries): 15.5% German, 8.8% Irish, 5.4% American, 4.9% Scotch-Irish, 4.8% Italian (2006-2010 5-year est.).

Economy: Single-family building permits issued: 6 (2011); Multi-family building permits issued: 0 (2011); Employment by occupation: 13.7% management, 3.1% professional, 7.7% services, 16.1% sales, 3.7% farming, 15.5% construction, 5.7% production (2006-2010 5-year est.).

Income: Per capita income: $17,816 (2006-2010 5-year est.); Median household income: $78,799 (2006-2010 5-year est.); Average household income: $83,789 (2006-2010 5-year est.); Percent of households with income of $100,000 or more: 30.9% (2006-2010 5-year est.); Poverty rate: 7.3% (2006-2010 5-year est.).

Education: Percent of population age 25 and over with: High school diploma (including GED) or higher: 82.0% (2006-2010 5-year est.); Bachelor's degree or higher: 17.0% (2006-2010 5-year est.); Master's degree or higher: 4.2% (2006-2010 5-year est.).

Housing: Homeownership rate: 81.8% (2010); Median home value: $264,500 (2006-2010 5-year est.); Median contract rent: $594 per month (2006-2010 5-year est.); Median year structure built: 1984 (2006-2010 5-year est.).

Transportation: Commute to work: 74.5% car, 0.7% public transportation, 9.7% walk, 12.9% work from home (2006-2010 5-year est.); Travel time to work: 32.9% less than 15 minutes, 21.9% 15 to 30 minutes, 20.3% 30 to 45 minutes, 12.8% 45 to 60 minutes, 12.0% 60 minutes or more (2006-2010 5-year est.)

Additional Information Contacts

Oxford Area Chamber of Commerce . . . . (610) 932-0740
  http://www.oxfordpa.org

MALVERN (borough). Covers a land area of 1.260 square miles and a water area of 0.006 square miles. Located at 40.03° N. Lat; 75.52° W. Long. Elevation is 564 feet.

History: Settled 1866, incorporated 1889.

Population: 2,944 (1990); 3,059 (2000); 2,998 (2010); Density: 2,378.6 persons per square mile (2010); Race: 90.0% White, 2.9% Black, 4.2% Asian, 0.3% American Indian/Alaska Native, 0.0% Native Hawaiian/Other Pacific Islander, 2.6% Other, 3.7% Hispanic of any race (2010); Average household size: 2.22 (2010); Median age: 41.6 (2010); Males per 100 females: 92.4 (2010); Marriage status: 24.7% never married, 54.3% now married, 8.5% widowed, 12.5% divorced (2006-2010 5-year est.); Foreign born: 6.5% (2006-2010 5-year est.); Ancestry (includes multiple ancestries): 36.3% Irish, 20.0% German, 19.2% English, 16.4% Italian, 5.7% Russian (2006-2010 5-year est.).

Economy: Single-family building permits issued: 6 (2011); Multi-family building permits issued: 0 (2011); Employment by occupation: 14.4% management, 6.1% professional, 7.0% services, 17.7% sales, 3.9% farming, 8.5% construction, 7.1% production (2006-2010 5-year est.).

Income: Per capita income: $38,970 (2006-2010 5-year est.); Median household income: $68,571 (2006-2010 5-year est.); Average household income: $86,623 (2006-2010 5-year est.); Percent of households with income of $100,000 or more: 33.0% (2006-2010 5-year est.); Poverty rate: 6.7% (2006-2010 5-year est.).

Education: Percent of population age 25 and over with: High school diploma (including GED) or higher: 97.6% (2006-2010 5-year est.); Bachelor's degree or higher: 54.5% (2006-2010 5-year est.); Master's degree or higher: 17.5% (2006-2010 5-year est.).

School District(s)

Great Valley SD (KG-12)
  2010-11 Enrollment: 4,079 . . . . (610) 889-2100

Four-year College(s)

Pennsylvania State University-Penn State Great Valley (Public)
  Fall 2010 Enrollment: 518 . . . . (610) 648-3200

Housing: Homeownership rate: 61.1% (2010); Median home value: $343,300 (2006-2010 5-year est.); Median contract rent: $1,137 per month (2006-2010 5-year est.); Median year structure built: 1966 (2006-2010 5-year est.).

Hospitals: Bryn Mawr Rehabilitation Hospital (141 beds); Devereux Foundation - Mapleton Psychiatric Institute (24 beds); Malvern Institute (53 beds)

Safety: Violent crime rate: 26.6 per 10,000 population; Property crime rate: 113.0 per 10,000 population (2011).

Transportation: Commute to work: 88.9% car, 3.2% public transportation, 0.4% walk, 5.6% work from home (2006-2010 5-year est.); Travel time to work: 39.0% less than 15 minutes, 31.8% 15 to 30 minutes, 15.1% 30 to 45 minutes, 9.8% 45 to 60 minutes, 4.3% 60 minutes or more (2006-2010 5-year est.)

Additional Information Contacts

Borough of Malvern . . . . (610) 644-2602
  http://www.malvern.org
Great Valley Regional Chamber of Commerce . . . . (610) 889-2069
  http://www.greatvalleyonline.com

MODENA (borough). Aka Paperville. Covers a land area of 0.344 square miles and a water area of 0.009 square miles. Located at 39.97° N. Lat; 75.81° W. Long. Elevation is 305 feet.

History: Formerly Paperville.

Population: 563 (1990); 610 (2000); 535 (2010); Density: 1,553.6 persons per square mile (2010); Race: 63.2% White, 22.6% Black, 0.6% Asian, 0.2% American Indian/Alaska Native, 0.0% Native Hawaiian/Other Pacific Islander, 13.4% Other, 17.4% Hispanic of any race (2010); Average household size: 2.82 (2010); Median age: 31.5 (2010); Males per 100 females: 106.6 (2010); Marriage status: 42.9% never married, 43.6% now married, 2.5% widowed, 11.0% divorced (2006-2010 5-year est.); Foreign born: 5.8% (2006-2010 5-year est.); Ancestry (includes multiple ancestries): 11.4% German, 10.5% Italian, 10.5% Irish, 7.9% English, 4.5% Polish (2006-2010 5-year est.).

Economy: Single-family building permits issued: 0 (2011); Multi-family building permits issued: 0 (2011); Employment by occupation: 9.1% management, 0.0% professional, 15.1% services, 17.4% sales, 0.0% farming, 17.0% construction, 2.6% production (2006-2010 5-year est.).

Income: Per capita income: $25,608 (2006-2010 5-year est.); Median household income: $51,875 (2006-2010 5-year est.); Average household income: $63,892 (2006-2010 5-year est.); Percent of households with income of $100,000 or more: 22.1% (2006-2010 5-year est.); Poverty rate: 9.9% (2006-2010 5-year est.).

Education: Percent of population age 25 and over with: High school diploma (including GED) or higher: 76.8% (2006-2010 5-year est.); Bachelor's degree or higher: 16.6% (2006-2010 5-year est.); Master's degree or higher: 3.0% (2006-2010 5-year est.).

Housing: Homeownership rate: 45.2% (2010); Median home value: $184,600 (2006-2010 5-year est.); Median contract rent: $712 per month (2006-2010 5-year est.); Median year structure built: 1942 (2006-2010 5-year est.).

Transportation: Commute to work: 93.3% car, 0.0% public transportation, 4.8% walk, 2.0% work from home (2006-2010 5-year est.); Travel time to work: 16.6% less than 15 minutes, 29.6% 15 to 30 minutes, 38.1% 30 to 45 minutes, 11.7% 45 to 60 minutes, 4.0% 60 minutes or more (2006-2010 5-year est.)

NEW GARDEN (township). Covers a land area of 16.109 square miles and a water area of 0.174 square miles. Located at 39.81° N. Lat; 75.76° W. Long. Elevation is 407 feet.

History: New Garden is the center of the mushroom agribusiness in southeastern Pennsylvania with a higher concentration of composting, mushroom growing, packaging, and shipping businesses than in any other municipality in the area. It was named for the 'New Garden Friends' Meeting House, an eighteenth century brick house of worship of the Religious Society of Friends, within its territorial limits.

Population: 5,430 (1990); 9,083 (2000); 11,984 (2010); Density: 743.9 persons per square mile (2010); Race: 78.2% White, 3.0% Black, 3.0% Asian, 0.5% American Indian/Alaska Native, 0.0% Native Hawaiian/Other Pacific Islander, 15.3% Other, 26.4% Hispanic of any race (2010); Average household size: 3.20 (2010); Median age: 37.0 (2010); Males per 100 females: 108.5 (2010); Marriage status: 23.5% never married, 69.2% now married, 3.2% widowed, 4.1% divorced (2006-2010 5-year est.); Foreign born: 23.6% (2006-2010 5-year est.); Ancestry (includes multiple ancestries): 16.9% Italian, 16.0% German, 13.3% Irish, 10.5% English, 5.3% Polish (2006-2010 5-year est.).

Economy: Single-family building permits issued: 3 (2011); Multi-family building permits issued: 0 (2011); Employment by occupation: 22.0% management, 4.5% professional, 7.2% services, 9.3% sales, 3.6% farming, 13.0% construction, 2.1% production (2006-2010 5-year est.).

Income: Per capita income: $46,281 (2006-2010 5-year est.); Median household income: $113,317 (2006-2010 5-year est.); Average household income: $145,288 (2006-2010 5-year est.); Percent of households with income of $100,000 or more: 54.2% (2006-2010 5-year est.); Poverty rate: 8.1% (2006-2010 5-year est.).

Education: Percent of population age 25 and over with: High school diploma (including GED) or higher: 84.6% (2006-2010 5-year est.); Bachelor's degree or higher: 49.9% (2006-2010 5-year est.); Master's degree or higher: 21.4% (2006-2010 5-year est.).

Housing: Homeownership rate: 76.1% (2010); Median home value: $435,000 (2006-2010 5-year est.); Median contract rent: $782 per month (2006-2010 5-year est.); Median year structure built: 1995 (2006-2010 5-year est.).

Safety: Violent crime rate: 8.3 per 10,000 population; Property crime rate: 145.6 per 10,000 population (2011).

Transportation: Commute to work: 85.9% car, 0.2% public transportation, 2.5% walk, 10.5% work from home (2006-2010 5-year est.); Travel time to work: 28.0% less than 15 minutes, 31.0% 15 to 30 minutes, 26.2% 30 to 45 minutes, 7.0% 45 to 60 minutes, 7.9% 60 minutes or more (2006-2010 5-year est.)

Additional Information Contacts

New Garden Township . . . . (610) 268-2915
  http://www.newgarden.org
Southern Chester County Chamber of Commerce . . . . (610) 444-0774
  http://www.scccc.com

NEW LONDON (township). Covers a land area of 11.651 square miles and a water area of 0.090 square miles. Located at 39.77° N. Lat; 75.88° W. Long. Elevation is 469 feet.

History: New London was originally the home of the Lenni Lenape Indian tribe. The London Company, a group of five entrepreneurs, purchased a large tract of land in order the break the tract into smaller lots and sell

them at a profit to immigrant farmers. This tract included present-day New London Township, which was chartered in 1723.

Population: 2,721 (1990); 4,583 (2000); 5,631 (2010); Density: 483.3 persons per square mile (2010); Race: 94.7% White, 1.4% Black, 0.9% Asian, 0.0% American Indian/Alaska Native, 0.0% Native Hawaiian/Other Pacific Islander, 3.0% Other, 4.9% Hispanic of any race (2010); Average household size: 3.24 (2010); Median age: 39.3 (2010); Males per 100 females: 102.8 (2010); Marriage status: 26.7% never married, 66.3% now married, 3.1% widowed, 4.0% divorced (2006-2010 5-year est.); Foreign born: 4.1% (2006-2010 5-year est.); Ancestry (includes multiple ancestries): 29.3% Irish, 20.9% German, 20.3% English, 16.8% Italian, 7.1% Polish (2006-2010 5-year est.).

Economy: Single-family building permits issued: 18 (2011); Multi-family building permits issued: 0 (2011); Employment by occupation: 21.3% management, 7.3% professional, 5.1% services, 14.8% sales, 4.0% farming, 4.6% construction, 4.1% production (2006-2010 5-year est.).

Income: Per capita income: $38,437 (2006-2010 5-year est.); Median household income: $119,471 (2006-2010 5-year est.); Average household income: $126,429 (2006-2010 5-year est.); Percent of households with income of $100,000 or more: 61.6% (2006-2010 5-year est.); Poverty rate: 5.1% (2006-2010 5-year est.).

Education: Percent of population age 25 and over with: High school diploma (including GED) or higher: 92.2% (2006-2010 5-year est.); Bachelor's degree or higher: 44.1% (2006-2010 5-year est.); Master's degree or higher: 17.9% (2006-2010 5-year est.).

Housing: Homeownership rate: 92.7% (2010); Median home value: $363,700 (2006-2010 5-year est.); Median contract rent: $680 per month (2006-2010 5-year est.); Median year structure built: 1993 (2006-2010 5-year est.).

Transportation: Commute to work: 92.7% car, 0.3% public transportation, 0.3% walk, 5.0% work from home (2006-2010 5-year est.); Travel time to work: 16.7% less than 15 minutes, 22.3% 15 to 30 minutes, 23.1% 30 to 45 minutes, 21.5% 45 to 60 minutes, 16.4% 60 minutes or more (2006-2010 5-year est.)

Additional Information Contacts
Oxford Area Chamber of Commerce. . . . . (610) 932-0740
　http://www.oxfordpa.org

NEWLIN (township). Covers a land area of 11.975 square miles and a water area of 0.146 square miles. Located at 39.92° N. Lat; 75.74° W. Long.

Population: 1,092 (1990); 1,150 (2000); 1,285 (2010); Density: 107.3 persons per square mile (2010); Race: 96.1% White, 0.6% Black, 0.9% Asian, 0.0% American Indian/Alaska Native, 0.0% Native Hawaiian/Other Pacific Islander, 2.4% Other, 2.9% Hispanic of any race (2010); Average household size: 2.67 (2010); Median age: 47.2 (2010); Males per 100 females: 104.6 (2010); Marriage status: 17.3% never married, 68.2% now married, 6.8% widowed, 7.7% divorced (2006-2010 5-year est.); Foreign born: 4.5% (2006-2010 5-year est.); Ancestry (includes multiple ancestries): 22.6% English, 21.8% German, 18.7% Irish, 10.1% Italian, 8.8% Scotch-Irish (2006-2010 5-year est.).

Economy: Single-family building permits issued: 2 (2011); Multi-family building permits issued: 0 (2011); Employment by occupation: 25.5% management, 2.1% professional, 3.8% services, 13.1% sales, 0.3% farming, 7.4% construction, 4.2% production (2006-2010 5-year est.).

Income: Per capita income: $60,900 (2006-2010 5-year est.); Median household income: $101,250 (2006-2010 5-year est.); Average household income: $170,025 (2006-2010 5-year est.); Percent of households with income of $100,000 or more: 50.4% (2006-2010 5-year est.); Poverty rate: 2.4% (2006-2010 5-year est.).

Education: Percent of population age 25 and over with: High school diploma (including GED) or higher: 95.0% (2006-2010 5-year est.); Bachelor's degree or higher: 55.0% (2006-2010 5-year est.); Master's degree or higher: 23.2% (2006-2010 5-year est.).

Housing: Homeownership rate: 86.8% (2010); Median home value: $439,100 (2006-2010 5-year est.); Median contract rent: $850 per month (2006-2010 5-year est.); Median year structure built: 1975 (2006-2010 5-year est.).

Transportation: Commute to work: 81.5% car, 1.2% public transportation, 2.0% walk, 14.2% work from home (2006-2010 5-year est.); Travel time to work: 17.3% less than 15 minutes, 31.7% 15 to 30 minutes, 27.0% 30 to 45 minutes, 10.5% 45 to 60 minutes, 13.5% 60 minutes or more (2006-2010 5-year est.)

Additional Information Contacts
Southern Chester County Chamber of Commerce . . . . (610) 444-0774
　http://www.scccc.com

NORTH COVENTRY (township). Covers a land area of 13.223 square miles and a water area of 0.287 square miles. Located at 40.22° N. Lat; 75.68° W. Long.

Population: 7,561 (1990); 7,381 (2000); 7,866 (2010); Density: 594.9 persons per square mile (2010); Race: 93.4% White, 2.7% Black, 1.2% Asian, 0.2% American Indian/Alaska Native, 0.0% Native Hawaiian/Other Pacific Islander, 2.5% Other, 2.3% Hispanic of any race (2010); Average household size: 2.50 (2010); Median age: 42.4 (2010); Males per 100 females: 98.6 (2010); Marriage status: 27.1% never married, 56.7% now married, 6.2% widowed, 10.0% divorced (2006-2010 5-year est.); Foreign born: 2.9% (2006-2010 5-year est.); Ancestry (includes multiple ancestries): 30.6% German, 25.3% Irish, 20.9% Italian, 11.1% English, 6.4% Polish (2006-2010 5-year est.).

Economy: Single-family building permits issued: 8 (2011); Multi-family building permits issued: 0 (2011); Employment by occupation: 11.5% management, 7.4% professional, 4.4% services, 19.5% sales, 6.3% farming, 11.8% construction, 9.7% production (2006-2010 5-year est.).

Income: Per capita income: $30,920 (2006-2010 5-year est.); Median household income: $68,355 (2006-2010 5-year est.); Average household income: $75,354 (2006-2010 5-year est.); Percent of households with income of $100,000 or more: 28.1% (2006-2010 5-year est.); Poverty rate: 6.1% (2006-2010 5-year est.).

Education: Percent of population age 25 and over with: High school diploma (including GED) or higher: 93.8% (2006-2010 5-year est.); Bachelor's degree or higher: 31.1% (2006-2010 5-year est.); Master's degree or higher: 10.3% (2006-2010 5-year est.).

Housing: Homeownership rate: 73.6% (2010); Median home value: $249,000 (2006-2010 5-year est.); Median contract rent: $773 per month (2006-2010 5-year est.); Median year structure built: 1970 (2006-2010 5-year est.).

Safety: Violent crime rate: 7.6 per 10,000 population; Property crime rate: 340.9 per 10,000 population (2011).

Transportation: Commute to work: 93.0% car, 2.6% public transportation, 1.6% walk, 2.5% work from home (2006-2010 5-year est.); Travel time to work: 25.5% less than 15 minutes, 29.4% 15 to 30 minutes, 25.7% 30 to 45 minutes, 12.4% 45 to 60 minutes, 7.0% 60 minutes or more (2006-2010 5-year est.)

Additional Information Contacts
North Coventry Township . . . . (610) 323-1694
　http://www.northcoventry.us
TriCounty Area Chamber of Commerce . . . . (610) 326-2900
　http://tricountyareachamber.com

OXFORD (borough). Covers a land area of 1.967 square miles and a water area of 0.002 square miles. Located at 39.79° N. Lat; 75.98° W. Long. Elevation is 561 feet.

History: Lincoln University to Northeast; 3 covered bridges to Southeast. Incorporated 1833.

Population: 3,769 (1990); 4,315 (2000); 5,077 (2010); Density: 2,581.0 persons per square mile (2010); Race: 70.8% White, 9.0% Black, 0.8% Asian, 0.4% American Indian/Alaska Native, 0.1% Native Hawaiian/Other Pacific Islander, 18.9% Other, 28.8% Hispanic of any race (2010); Average household size: 2.70 (2010); Median age: 33.7 (2010); Males per 100 females: 92.2 (2010); Marriage status: 31.0% never married, 49.4% now married, 10.1% widowed, 9.5% divorced (2006-2010 5-year est.); Foreign born: 14.2% (2006-2010 5-year est.); Ancestry (includes multiple ancestries): 15.5% German, 12.9% Irish, 12.3% American, 9.1% English, 7.2% Italian (2006-2010 5-year est.).

Economy: Single-family building permits issued: 4 (2011); Multi-family building permits issued: 0 (2011); Employment by occupation: 10.1% management, 0.4% professional, 21.2% services, 11.1% sales, 3.9% farming, 10.1% construction, 8.1% production (2006-2010 5-year est.).

Income: Per capita income: $19,663 (2006-2010 5-year est.); Median household income: $49,608 (2006-2010 5-year est.); Average household income: $58,279 (2006-2010 5-year est.); Percent of households with income of $100,000 or more: 12.4% (2006-2010 5-year est.); Poverty rate: 15.7% (2006-2010 5-year est.).

Education: Percent of population age 25 and over with: High school diploma (including GED) or higher: 79.1% (2006-2010 5-year est.); Bachelor's degree or higher: 20.5% (2006-2010 5-year est.); Master's degree or higher: 5.8% (2006-2010 5-year est.).

School District(s)

Oxford Area SD (KG-12)

   2010-11 Enrollment: 3,898 . . . . (610) 932-6600

Housing: Homeownership rate: 47.3% (2010); Median home value: $216,800 (2006-2010 5-year est.); Median contract rent: $668 per month (2006-2010 5-year est.); Median year structure built: 1964 (2006-2010 5-year est.).

Safety: Violent crime rate: 58.9 per 10,000 population; Property crime rate: 216.0 per 10,000 population (2011).

Newspapers: Chester County Press (Community news; Circulation 15,700); Oxford Tribune (Community news; Circulation 4,500); Unidad Latina (Regional news; Circulation 17,000)

Transportation: Commute to work: 93.2% car, 0.9% public transportation, 3.3% walk, 2.6% work from home (2006-2010 5-year est.); Travel time to work: 36.3% less than 15 minutes, 28.3% 15 to 30 minutes, 17.6% 30 to 45 minutes, 12.2% 45 to 60 minutes, 5.5% 60 minutes or more (2006-2010 5-year est.)

Additional Information Contacts

Southern Chester County Chamber of Commerce . . . . (610) 444-0774
   http://www.scccc.com

PAOLI (CDP). Covers a land area of 1.969 square miles and a water area of 0.002 square miles. Located at 40.04° N. Lat; 75.49° W. Long. Elevation is 509 feet.

History: Near here is birthplace of Gen. Wayne and scene of his defeat by British, 1777.

Population: 5,603 (1990); 5,425 (2000); 5,575 (2010); Density: 2,831.9 persons per square mile (2010); Race: 84.4% White, 6.9% Black, 6.6% Asian, 0.0% American Indian/Alaska Native, 0.0% Native Hawaiian/Other Pacific Islander, 2.1% Other, 2.3% Hispanic of any race (2010); Average household size: 2.24 (2010); Median age: 44.8 (2010); Males per 100 females: 85.4 (2010); Marriage status: 24.5% never married, 59.1% now married, 8.3% widowed, 8.1% divorced (2006-2010 5-year est.); Foreign born: 9.6% (2006-2010 5-year est.); Ancestry (includes multiple ancestries): 27.5% Irish, 21.8% German, 18.0% English, 14.7% Italian, 4.8% Scottish (2006-2010 5-year est.).

Economy: Employment by occupation: 18.0% management, 13.3% professional, 5.8% services, 11.8% sales, 3.5% farming, 4.2% construction, 1.6% production (2006-2010 5-year est.).

Income: Per capita income: $47,693 (2006-2010 5-year est.); Median household income: $86,207 (2006-2010 5-year est.); Average household income: $106,742 (2006-2010 5-year est.); Percent of households with income of $100,000 or more: 42.8% (2006-2010 5-year est.); Poverty rate: 3.4% (2006-2010 5-year est.).

Education: Percent of population age 25 and over with: High school diploma (including GED) or higher: 94.4% (2006-2010 5-year est.); Bachelor's degree or higher: 55.8% (2006-2010 5-year est.); Master's degree or higher: 26.0% (2006-2010 5-year est.).

Housing: Homeownership rate: 68.5% (2010); Median home value: $333,000 (2006-2010 5-year est.); Median contract rent: $992 per month (2006-2010 5-year est.); Median year structure built: 1959 (2006-2010 5-year est.).

Hospitals: Paoli Memorial Hospital (208 beds)

Transportation: Commute to work: 86.8% car, 7.4% public transportation, 2.5% walk, 2.8% work from home (2006-2010 5-year est.); Travel time to work: 30.3% less than 15 minutes, 41.5% 15 to 30 minutes, 14.7% 30 to 45 minutes, 4.9% 45 to 60 minutes, 8.6% 60 minutes or more (2006-2010 5-year est.); Amtrak: train service available.

Additional Information Contacts

Chester County Chamber of Business and Industry . . . . . . (610) 725-9100
   http://www.cccbi.org

PARKER FORD (unincorporated postal area)

Zip Code: 19457

   Covers a land area of 0.196 square miles and a water area of 0.002 square miles. Located at 40.20° N. Lat; 75.59° W. Long. Elevation is 125 feet. Population: 125 (2010); Density: 634.9 persons per square mile (2010); Race: 95.2% White, 0.0% Black, 1.6% Asian, 0.0% American Indian/Alaska Native, 0.0% Native Hawaiian/Other Pacific Islander, 3.2% Other, 4.0% Hispanic of any race (2010); Average household size: 2.84 (2010); Median age: 31.3 (2010); Males per 100 females: 92.3 (2010); Homeownership rate: 68.2% (2010)

PARKESBURG (borough). Covers a land area of 1.269 square miles and a water area of 0.005 square miles. Located at 39.96° N. Lat; 75.92° W. Long. Elevation is 525 feet.

History: Incorporated 1872.

Population: 2,981 (1990); 3,373 (2000); 3,593 (2010); Density: 2,830.7 persons per square mile (2010); Race: 86.1% White, 9.0% Black, 0.3% Asian, 0.9% American Indian/Alaska Native, 0.1% Native Hawaiian/Other Pacific Islander, 3.6% Other, 7.5% Hispanic of any race (2010); Average household size: 2.62 (2010); Median age: 36.1 (2010); Males per 100 females: 90.3 (2010); Marriage status: 26.7% never married, 59.0% now married, 7.9% widowed, 6.4% divorced (2006-2010 5-year est.); Foreign born: 7.5% (2006-2010 5-year est.); Ancestry (includes multiple ancestries): 24.4% German, 21.4% Italian, 21.1% Irish, 12.6% English, 3.5% Scottish (2006-2010 5-year est.).

Economy: Single-family building permits issued: 6 (2011); Multi-family building permits issued: 0 (2011); Employment by occupation: 13.3% management, 3.8% professional, 9.2% services, 17.3% sales, 2.9% farming, 17.0% construction, 5.7% production (2006-2010 5-year est.).

Income: Per capita income: $26,199 (2006-2010 5-year est.); Median household income: $65,016 (2006-2010 5-year est.); Average household income: $72,371 (2006-2010 5-year est.); Percent of households with income of $100,000 or more: 13.5% (2006-2010 5-year est.); Poverty rate: 8.0% (2006-2010 5-year est.).

Education: Percent of population age 25 and over with: High school diploma (including GED) or higher: 84.8% (2006-2010 5-year est.); Bachelor's degree or higher: 24.2% (2006-2010 5-year est.); Master's degree or higher: 7.9% (2006-2010 5-year est.).

Housing: Homeownership rate: 63.8% (2010); Median home value: $194,900 (2006-2010 5-year est.); Median contract rent: $718 per month (2006-2010 5-year est.); Median year structure built: 1958 (2006-2010 5-year est.).

Transportation: Commute to work: 94.2% car, 3.3% public transportation, 1.4% walk, 1.1% work from home (2006-2010 5-year est.); Travel time to work: 31.7% less than 15 minutes, 29.5% 15 to 30 minutes, 19.7% 30 to 45 minutes, 8.0% 45 to 60 minutes, 11.1% 60 minutes or more (2006-2010 5-year est.); Amtrak: train service available.

Additional Information Contacts

Borough of Parkesburg . . . . (610) 857-2616
   http://parkesburg.org
Southern Chester County Chamber of Commerce . . . . (610) 444-0774
   http://www.scccc.com

PENN (township). Covers a land area of 9.597 square miles and a water area of 0.053 square miles. Located at 39.82° N. Lat; 75.87° W. Long.

Population: 2,257 (1990); 2,812 (2000); 5,364 (2010); Density: 558.9 persons per square mile (2010); Race: 91.4% White, 2.9% Black, 1.6% Asian, 0.1% American Indian/Alaska Native, 0.1% Native Hawaiian/Other Pacific Islander, 3.9% Other, 8.1% Hispanic of any race (2010); Average household size: 2.43 (2010); Median age: 47.1 (2010); Males per 100 females: 87.2 (2010); Marriage status: 13.5% never married, 64.8% now married, 11.2% widowed, 10.6% divorced (2006-2010 5-year est.); Foreign born: 3.9% (2006-2010 5-year est.); Ancestry (includes multiple ancestries): 26.6% Irish, 22.1% German, 18.6% English, 14.4% Italian, 11.5% American (2006-2010 5-year est.).

Economy: Single-family building permits issued: 7 (2011); Multi-family building permits issued: 0 (2011); Employment by occupation: 18.6% management, 2.9% professional, 6.7% services, 12.7% sales, 5.1% farming, 9.0% construction, 3.0% production (2006-2010 5-year est.).

Income: Per capita income: $34,063 (2006-2010 5-year est.); Median household income: $71,563 (2006-2010 5-year est.); Average household income: $84,533 (2006-2010 5-year est.); Percent of households with income of $100,000 or more: 33.9% (2006-2010 5-year est.); Poverty rate: 3.7% (2006-2010 5-year est.).

Education: Percent of population age 25 and over with: High school diploma (including GED) or higher: 91.8% (2006-2010 5-year est.); Bachelor's degree or higher: 37.2% (2006-2010 5-year est.); Master's degree or higher: 11.7% (2006-2010 5-year est.).

Housing: Homeownership rate: 72.6% (2010); Median home value: $316,600 (2006-2010 5-year est.); Median contract rent: $525 per month (2006-2010 5-year est.); Median year structure built: 1999 (2006-2010 5-year est.).

Transportation: Commute to work: 93.9% car, 0.0% public transportation, 2.0% walk, 3.5% work from home (2006-2010 5-year est.); Travel time to work: 17.7% less than 15 minutes, 25.6% 15 to 30 minutes, 21.8% 30 to

45 minutes, 19.0% 45 to 60 minutes, 15.9% 60 minutes or more (2006-2010 5-year est.)
Additional Information Contacts
Southern Chester County Chamber of Commerce . . . . (610) 444-0774
  http://www.scccc.com

PENNSBURY (township). Covers a land area of 9.924 square miles and a water area of 0.131 square miles. Located at 39.87° N. Lat; 75.62° W. Long.

History: Peensbury township was established in 1770 and began as part of Kennett Township which was one of the original Townships from the grant to William Penn.
Population: 3,326 (1990); 3,500 (2000); 3,604 (2010); Density: 363.1 persons per square mile (2010); Race: 94.6% White, 0.7% Black, 3.1% Asian, 0.1% American Indian/Alaska Native, 0.0% Native Hawaiian/Other Pacific Islander, 1.5% Other, 1.4% Hispanic of any race (2010); Average household size: 2.42 (2010); Median age: 50.9 (2010); Males per 100 females: 89.6 (2010); Marriage status: 12.2% never married, 68.9% now married, 13.6% widowed, 5.4% divorced (2006-2010 5-year est.); Foreign born: 4.3% (2006-2010 5-year est.); Ancestry (includes multiple ancestries): 20.8% Irish, 19.0% German, 17.5% English, 15.7% Italian, 7.1% American (2006-2010 5-year est.).
Economy: Single-family building permits issued: 1 (2011); Multi-family building permits issued: 0 (2011); Employment by occupation: 28.0% management, 5.9% professional, 3.5% services, 8.0% sales, 2.0% farming, 4.2% construction, 0.0% production (2006-2010 5-year est.).
Income: Per capita income: $70,937 (2006-2010 5-year est.); Median household income: $122,381 (2006-2010 5-year est.); Average household income: $160,027 (2006-2010 5-year est.); Percent of households with income of $100,000 or more: 59.4% (2006-2010 5-year est.); Poverty rate: 1.1% (2006-2010 5-year est.).
Education: Percent of population age 25 and over with: High school diploma (including GED) or higher: 99.4% (2006-2010 5-year est.); Bachelor's degree or higher: 69.0% (2006-2010 5-year est.); Master's degree or higher: 34.3% (2006-2010 5-year est.).
Housing: Homeownership rate: 75.9% (2010); Median home value: $500,400 (2006-2010 5-year est.); Median contract rent: n/a per month (2006-2010 5-year est.); Median year structure built: 1978 (2006-2010 5-year est.).
Transportation: Commute to work: 88.0% car, 0.0% public transportation, 2.1% walk, 8.7% work from home (2006-2010 5-year est.); Travel time to work: 20.7% less than 15 minutes, 33.3% 15 to 30 minutes, 18.8% 30 to 45 minutes, 8.8% 45 to 60 minutes, 18.3% 60 minutes or more (2006-2010 5-year est.)
Additional Information Contacts
Pennsbury Township. . . . . (610) 388-7323
  http://www.pennsbury.pa.us
Southern Chester County Chamber of Commerce . . . . (610) 444-0774
  http://www.scccc.com

PHOENIXVILLE (borough). Covers a land area of 3.508 square miles and a water area of 0.211 square miles. Located at 40.14° N. Lat; 75.52° W. Long. Elevation is 138 feet.

History: Named for the Phoenix Iron Works, which was named for the bird of mythology. Iron deposits in the region led to the early development of an iron industry and later (1886) to the manufacturing of steel. Phoenixville was the westernmost point in the state reached (1777) by the British during the Revolutionary War. Several 18th-century stone houses are here. Valley Forge is a few miles to the southeast. Valley Forge National Historical Park to southeast. Settled 1720. Incorporated 1849.
Population: 15,066 (1990); 14,788 (2000); 16,440 (2010); Density: 4,686.5 persons per square mile (2010); Race: 81.9% White, 8.6% Black, 3.5% Asian, 0.2% American Indian/Alaska Native, 0.2% Native Hawaiian/Other Pacific Islander, 5.6% Other, 7.4% Hispanic of any race (2010); Average household size: 2.25 (2010); Median age: 35.1 (2010); Males per 100 females: 98.1 (2010); Marriage status: 28.9% never married, 50.9% now married, 6.2% widowed, 13.9% divorced (2006-2010 5-year est.); Foreign born: 9.1% (2006-2010 5-year est.); Ancestry (includes multiple ancestries): 26.8% Irish, 24.3% German, 16.8% Italian, 10.2% English, 7.1% Polish (2006-2010 5-year est.).
Economy: Single-family building permits issued: 6 (2011); Multi-family building permits issued: 0 (2011); Employment by occupation: 14.8% management, 10.0% professional, 9.8% services, 17.8% sales, 5.3% farming, 4.8% construction, 3.0% production (2006-2010 5-year est.).

Income: Per capita income: $33,492 (2006-2010 5-year est.); Median household income: $61,153 (2006-2010 5-year est.); Average household income: $74,856 (2006-2010 5-year est.); Percent of households with income of $100,000 or more: 23.8% (2006-2010 5-year est.); Poverty rate: 7.7% (2006-2010 5-year est.).
Taxes: Total city taxes per capita: $348 (2009); City property taxes per capita: $157 (2009).
Education: Percent of population age 25 and over with: High school diploma (including GED) or higher: 89.6% (2006-2010 5-year est.); Bachelor's degree or higher: 35.1% (2006-2010 5-year est.); Master's degree or higher: 10.0% (2006-2010 5-year est.).
School District(s)
Center for Arts & Technology (09-12)
  2010-11 Enrollment: 517. . . . . (484) 237-5110
Phoenixville Area SD (KG-12)
  2010-11 Enrollment: 3,296 . . . . (484) 927-5000
Renaissance Academy CS (KG-12)
  2010-11 Enrollment: 942. . . . . (610) 983-4080
Four-year College(s)
Valley Forge Christian College (Private, Not-for-profit, Assemblies of God Church)
  Fall 2010 Enrollment: 948. . . . . (610) 935-0450
  2011-12 Tuition: In-state $17,377; Out-of-state $17,377
Housing: Homeownership rate: 55.8% (2010); Median home value: $208,200 (2006-2010 5-year est.); Median contract rent: $839 per month (2006-2010 5-year est.); Median year structure built: 1962 (2006-2010 5-year est.).
Hospitals: Phoenixville Hospital (106 beds)
Safety: Violent crime rate: 22.4 per 10,000 population; Property crime rate: 239.5 per 10,000 population (2011).
Newspapers: The Phoenix (Local news; Circulation 3,872); Township Voice (Local news; Circulation 20,520)
Transportation: Commute to work: 91.2% car, 1.9% public transportation, 4.0% walk, 2.3% work from home (2006-2010 5-year est.); Travel time to work: 22.8% less than 15 minutes, 36.4% 15 to 30 minutes, 23.7% 30 to 45 minutes, 9.1% 45 to 60 minutes, 8.0% 60 minutes or more (2006-2010 5-year est.)
Additional Information Contacts
Borough of Phoenixville. . . . . (610) 933-8801
  http://www.phoenixville.org
Phoenixville Area Chamber of Commerce . . . . (610) 933-3070
  http://www.phoenixvillechamber.org

POCOPSON (township). Covers a land area of 8.187 square miles and a water area of 0.138 square miles. Located at 39.91° N. Lat; 75.66° W. Long. Elevation is 180 feet.

History: Pocopson township was started with a petition to the Court of Quarter Sessions in late 1848, signed by 28 male inhabitants of Pennsbury, West Bradford, New Marlborough, and Newlin townships pleading that 'they labor under great inconvenience for want of a new township to be composed of part of their existing townships'.
Population: 3,266 (1990); 3,350 (2000); 4,582 (2010); Density: 559.7 persons per square mile (2010); Race: 83.8% White, 8.4% Black, 4.3% Asian, 0.3% American Indian/Alaska Native, 0.1% Native Hawaiian/Other Pacific Islander, 3.1% Other, 4.4% Hispanic of any race (2010); Average household size: 2.95 (2010); Median age: 40.7 (2010); Males per 100 females: 126.2 (2010); Marriage status: 34.7% never married, 46.2% now married, 9.6% widowed, 9.6% divorced (2006-2010 5-year est.); Foreign born: 4.6% (2006-2010 5-year est.); Ancestry (includes multiple ancestries): 20.8% Irish, 20.7% German, 15.6% Italian, 14.4% English, 8.3% American (2006-2010 5-year est.).
Economy: Single-family building permits issued: 16 (2011); Multi-family building permits issued: 0 (2011); Employment by occupation: 28.7% management, 6.0% professional, 3.2% services, 13.4% sales, 1.5% farming, 6.0% construction, 2.3% production (2006-2010 5-year est.).
Income: Per capita income: $41,126 (2006-2010 5-year est.); Median household income: $145,089 (2006-2010 5-year est.); Average household income: $165,456 (2006-2010 5-year est.); Percent of households with income of $100,000 or more: 71.2% (2006-2010 5-year est.); Poverty rate: 2.7% (2006-2010 5-year est.).
Education: Percent of population age 25 and over with: High school diploma (including GED) or higher: 80.7% (2006-2010 5-year est.); Bachelor's degree or higher: 42.0% (2006-2010 5-year est.); Master's degree or higher: 18.5% (2006-2010 5-year est.).

Housing: Homeownership rate: 93.9% (2010); Median home value: $494,900 (2006-2010 5-year est.); Median contract rent: $1,113 per month (2006-2010 5-year est.); Median year structure built: 1981 (2006-2010 5-year est.).

Transportation: Commute to work: 87.8% car, 1.7% public transportation, 0.0% walk, 9.6% work from home (2006-2010 5-year est.); Travel time to work: 18.1% less than 15 minutes, 36.0% 15 to 30 minutes, 24.4% 30 to 45 minutes, 13.1% 45 to 60 minutes, 8.5% 60 minutes or more (2006-2010 5-year est.)

Additional Information Contacts

Greater West Chester Chamber of Commerce . . . . (610) 696-4046
    http://www.gwcc.org

POMEROY (CDP). Covers a land area of 0.327 square miles and a water area of 0.003 square miles. Located at 39.96° N. Lat; 75.88° W. Long. Elevation is 463 feet.

Population: n/a (1990); n/a (2000); 401 (2010); Density: 1,225.1 persons per square mile (2010); Race: 86.3% White, 5.5% Black, 2.0% Asian, 0.0% American Indian/Alaska Native, 0.7% Native Hawaiian/Other Pacific Islander, 5.5% Other, 7.2% Hispanic of any race (2010); Average household size: 2.29 (2010); Median age: 44.5 (2010); Males per 100 females: 91.9 (2010); Marriage status: 25.6% never married, 65.0% now married, 2.9% widowed, 6.5% divorced (2006-2010 5-year est.); Foreign born: 0.0% (2006-2010 5-year est.); Ancestry (includes multiple ancestries): 40.5% German, 40.2% Irish, 23.1% English, 11.8% Welsh, 5.8% Polish (2006-2010 5-year est.).

Economy: Employment by occupation: 20.0% management, 8.6% professional, 6.9% services, 33.7% sales, 0.0% farming, 0.0% construction, 0.0% production (2006-2010 5-year est.).

Income: Per capita income: $34,294 (2006-2010 5-year est.); Median household income: $67,083 (2006-2010 5-year est.); Average household income: $69,282 (2006-2010 5-year est.); Percent of households with income of $100,000 or more: 24.1% (2006-2010 5-year est.); Poverty rate: 14.2% (2006-2010 5-year est.).

Education: Percent of population age 25 and over with: High school diploma (including GED) or higher: 86.2% (2006-2010 5-year est.); Bachelor's degree or higher: 14.5% (2006-2010 5-year est.); Master's degree or higher: 9.4% (2006-2010 5-year est.).

Housing: Homeownership rate: 74.3% (2010); Median home value: $151,800 (2006-2010 5-year est.); Median contract rent: $510 per month (2006-2010 5-year est.); Median year structure built: before 1940 (2006-2010 5-year est.).

Transportation: Commute to work: 88.6% car, 0.0% public transportation, 0.0% walk, 11.4% work from home (2006-2010 5-year est.); Travel time to work: 56.8% less than 15 minutes, 18.1% 15 to 30 minutes, 17.4% 30 to 45 minutes, 7.7% 45 to 60 minutes, 0.0% 60 minutes or more (2006-2010 5-year est.)

SADSBURY (township). Covers a land area of 6.167 square miles and a water area of 0.029 square miles. Located at 39.98° N. Lat; 75.91° W. Long.

Population: 2,510 (1990); 2,582 (2000); 3,570 (2010); Density: 578.9 persons per square mile (2010); Race: 84.5% White, 8.5% Black, 2.6% Asian, 0.3% American Indian/Alaska Native, 0.1% Native Hawaiian/Other Pacific Islander, 4.0% Other, 4.1% Hispanic of any race (2010); Average household size: 2.72 (2010); Median age: 37.4 (2010); Males per 100 females: 102.8 (2010); Marriage status: 20.7% never married, 66.9% now married, 3.7% widowed, 8.7% divorced (2006-2010 5-year est.); Foreign born: 2.3% (2006-2010 5-year est.); Ancestry (includes multiple ancestries): 31.1% German, 20.3% Irish, 11.6% Italian, 10.6% English, 5.3% American (2006-2010 5-year est.).

Economy: Single-family building permits issued: 13 (2011); Multi-family building permits issued: 40 (2011); Employment by occupation: 13.8% management, 3.6% professional, 5.0% services, 17.6% sales, 3.0% farming, 10.9% construction, 8.5% production (2006-2010 5-year est.).

Income: Per capita income: $31,603 (2006-2010 5-year est.); Median household income: $77,551 (2006-2010 5-year est.); Average household income: $85,202 (2006-2010 5-year est.); Percent of households with income of $100,000 or more: 26.5% (2006-2010 5-year est.); Poverty rate: 2.8% (2006-2010 5-year est.).

Taxes: Total city taxes per capita: $186 (2009); City property taxes per capita: $17 (2009).

Education: Percent of population age 25 and over with: High school diploma (including GED) or higher: 90.2% (2006-2010 5-year est.);

Bachelor's degree or higher: 26.3% (2006-2010 5-year est.); Master's degree or higher: 9.4% (2006-2010 5-year est.).

Housing: Homeownership rate: 86.3% (2010); Median home value: $225,400 (2006-2010 5-year est.); Median contract rent: $498 per month (2006-2010 5-year est.); Median year structure built: 1973 (2006-2010 5-year est.).

Safety: Violent crime rate: 11.2 per 10,000 population; Property crime rate: 22.3 per 10,000 population (2011).

Transportation: Commute to work: 90.2% car, 2.2% public transportation, 0.4% walk, 6.1% work from home (2006-2010 5-year est.); Travel time to work: 19.9% less than 15 minutes, 24.1% 15 to 30 minutes, 33.7% 30 to 45 minutes, 14.0% 45 to 60 minutes, 8.3% 60 minutes or more (2006-2010 5-year est.)

Additional Information Contacts

Western Chester County Chamber of Commerce . . . . (610) 384-9550
    http://www.westernchestercounty.com

SCHUYLKILL (township). Covers a land area of 8.508 square miles and a water area of 0.404 square miles. Located at 40.11° N. Lat; 75.49° W. Long.

History: On November 4, 1826, the Chester County Court declared, "...it is agreed that the Township of Charlestown be divided according to the report of the Court and that the Eastern section thereof be called the Township of Schuylkill." In 1849, the establishment of the Borough of Phoenixville further defined the limits of the township.

Population: 5,538 (1990); 6,960 (2000); 8,516 (2010); Density: 1,001.0 persons per square mile (2010); Race: 91.7% White, 2.1% Black, 4.0% Asian, 0.1% American Indian/Alaska Native, 0.0% Native Hawaiian/Other Pacific Islander, 2.1% Other, 2.6% Hispanic of any race (2010); Average household size: 2.78 (2010); Median age: 41.3 (2010); Males per 100 females: 101.5 (2010); Marriage status: 23.2% never married, 63.7% now married, 4.4% widowed, 8.7% divorced (2006-2010 5-year est.); Foreign born: 7.0% (2006-2010 5-year est.); Ancestry (includes multiple ancestries): 31.3% Irish, 25.9% German, 15.8% Italian, 13.1% English, 5.7% Polish (2006-2010 5-year est.).

Economy: Single-family building permits issued: 3 (2011); Multi-family building permits issued: 0 (2011); Employment by occupation: 18.6% management, 6.2% professional, 3.4% services, 16.2% sales, 2.0% farming, 5.4% construction, 3.5% production (2006-2010 5-year est.).

Income: Per capita income: $52,051 (2006-2010 5-year est.); Median household income: $118,882 (2006-2010 5-year est.); Average household income: $148,080 (2006-2010 5-year est.); Percent of households with income of $100,000 or more: 58.0% (2006-2010 5-year est.); Poverty rate: 4.5% (2006-2010 5-year est.).

Education: Percent of population age 25 and over with: High school diploma (including GED) or higher: 96.1% (2006-2010 5-year est.); Bachelor's degree or higher: 56.2% (2006-2010 5-year est.); Master's degree or higher: 22.6% (2006-2010 5-year est.).

Housing: Homeownership rate: 90.8% (2010); Median home value: $409,200 (2006-2010 5-year est.); Median contract rent: $961 per month (2006-2010 5-year est.); Median year structure built: 1974 (2006-2010 5-year est.).

Safety: Violent crime rate: 16.4 per 10,000 population; Property crime rate: 144.0 per 10,000 population (2011).

Transportation: Commute to work: 92.6% car, 1.6% public transportation, 1.2% walk, 3.5% work from home (2006-2010 5-year est.); Travel time to work: 25.0% less than 15 minutes, 39.3% 15 to 30 minutes, 18.9% 30 to 45 minutes, 5.5% 45 to 60 minutes, 11.3% 60 minutes or more (2006-2010 5-year est.)

Additional Information Contacts

Great Valley Regional Chamber of Commerce . . . . (610) 889-2069
    http://www.greatvalleyonline.com
Schuylkill Township . . . . (610) 933-5843
    http://www.schuylkilltwp.com

SOUTH COATESVILLE (borough). Covers a land area of 1.736 square miles and a water area of 0.028 square miles. Located at 39.97° N. Lat; 75.81° W. Long. Elevation is 374 feet.

History: Incorporated 1921.

Population: 1,026 (1990); 997 (2000); 1,303 (2010); Density: 750.6 persons per square mile (2010); Race: 41.6% White, 47.9% Black, 0.3% Asian, 0.2% American Indian/Alaska Native, 0.0% Native Hawaiian/Other Pacific Islander, 10.0% Other, 13.0% Hispanic of any race (2010); Average household size: 2.60 (2010); Median age: 32.9 (2010); Males per 100 females: 88.0 (2010); Marriage status: 38.3% never married, 43.1% now

married, 8.7% widowed, 9.9% divorced (2006-2010 5-year est.); Foreign born: 6.3% (2006-2010 5-year est.); Ancestry (includes multiple ancestries): 16.9% Italian, 14.3% Irish, 9.4% German, 9.2% English, 6.0% Scotch-Irish (2006-2010 5-year est.).

Economy: Single-family building permits issued: 16 (2011); Multi-family building permits issued: 0 (2011); Employment by occupation: 7.8% management, 4.2% professional, 15.5% services, 18.2% sales, 3.5% farming, 7.4% construction, 5.1% production (2006-2010 5-year est.).

Income: Per capita income: $26,448 (2006-2010 5-year est.); Median household income: $41,944 (2006-2010 5-year est.); Average household income: $61,428 (2006-2010 5-year est.); Percent of households with income of $100,000 or more: 15.0% (2006-2010 5-year est.); Poverty rate: 21.3% (2006-2010 5-year est.).

Education: Percent of population age 25 and over with: High school diploma (including GED) or higher: 87.8% (2006-2010 5-year est.); Bachelor's degree or higher: 25.9% (2006-2010 5-year est.); Master's degree or higher: 8.5% (2006-2010 5-year est.).

Housing: Homeownership rate: 58.3% (2010); Median home value: $167,100 (2006-2010 5-year est.); Median contract rent: $746 per month (2006-2010 5-year est.); Median year structure built: 1959 (2006-2010 5-year est.).

Safety: Violent crime rate: 68.9 per 10,000 population; Property crime rate: 84.2 per 10,000 population (2011).

Transportation: Commute to work: 91.8% car, 4.1% public transportation, 0.3% walk, 2.1% work from home (2006-2010 5-year est.); Travel time to work: 22.5% less than 15 minutes, 26.5% 15 to 30 minutes, 26.2% 30 to 45 minutes, 10.0% 45 to 60 minutes, 14.7% 60 minutes or more (2006-2010 5-year est.)

Additional Information Contacts

Western Chester County Chamber of Commerce . . . . (610) 384-9550
    http://www.westernchestercounty.com

SOUTH COVENTRY (township). Covers a land area of 7.538 square miles and a water area of 0.059 square miles. Located at 40.18° N. Lat; 75.68° W. Long.

Population: 1,627 (1990); 1,895 (2000); 2,604 (2010); Density: 345.5 persons per square mile (2010); Race: 96.9% White, 0.5% Black, 1.0% Asian, 0.2% American Indian/Alaska Native, 0.0% Native Hawaiian/Other Pacific Islander, 1.4% Other, 1.7% Hispanic of any race (2010); Average household size: 2.73 (2010); Median age: 40.8 (2010); Males per 100 females: 101.7 (2010); Marriage status: 18.7% never married, 72.0% now married, 2.9% widowed, 6.4% divorced (2006-2010 5-year est.); Foreign born: 5.5% (2006-2010 5-year est.); Ancestry (includes multiple ancestries): 36.2% German, 30.3% Irish, 18.6% English, 12.3% Italian, 8.0% Polish (2006-2010 5-year est.).

Economy: Single-family building permits issued: 1 (2011); Multi-family building permits issued: 0 (2011); Employment by occupation: 20.6% management, 8.9% professional, 7.0% services, 13.4% sales, 3.2% farming, 8.9% construction, 5.4% production (2006-2010 5-year est.).

Income: Per capita income: $37,734 (2006-2010 5-year est.); Median household income: $91,042 (2006-2010 5-year est.); Average household income: $102,842 (2006-2010 5-year est.); Percent of households with income of $100,000 or more: 42.6% (2006-2010 5-year est.); Poverty rate: 3.0% (2006-2010 5-year est.).

Taxes: Total city taxes per capita: $251 (2009); City property taxes per capita: $35 (2009).

Education: Percent of population age 25 and over with: High school diploma (including GED) or higher: 95.3% (2006-2010 5-year est.); Bachelor's degree or higher: 45.7% (2006-2010 5-year est.); Master's degree or higher: 18.1% (2006-2010 5-year est.).

Housing: Homeownership rate: 87.6% (2010); Median home value: $310,400 (2006-2010 5-year est.); Median contract rent: $776 per month (2006-2010 5-year est.); Median year structure built: 1975 (2006-2010 5-year est.).

Transportation: Commute to work: 92.4% car, 1.2% public transportation, 0.3% walk, 5.9% work from home (2006-2010 5-year est.); Travel time to work: 17.6% less than 15 minutes, 28.2% 15 to 30 minutes, 28.3% 30 to 45 minutes, 11.8% 45 to 60 minutes, 14.1% 60 minutes or more (2006-2010 5-year est.)

Additional Information Contacts

South Coventry Township . . . . (610) 469-0444
    http://www.southcoventry.org
TriCounty Area Chamber of Commerce . . . . (610) 326-2900
    http://tricountyareachamber.com

SOUTH POTTSTOWN (CDP). Covers a land area of 1.523 square miles and a water area of 0.103 square miles. Located at 40.24° N. Lat; 75.66° W. Long. Elevation is 141 feet.

History: Hopewell Furnace National Historic Site to Southwest.

Population: 2,009 (1990); 2,135 (2000); 2,081 (2010); Density: 1,366.2 persons per square mile (2010); Race: 89.0% White, 5.7% Black, 1.2% Asian, 0.2% American Indian/Alaska Native, 0.0% Native Hawaiian/Other Pacific Islander, 3.9% Other, 3.5% Hispanic of any race (2010); Average household size: 2.19 (2010); Median age: 35.8 (2010); Males per 100 females: 98.8 (2010); Marriage status: 37.4% never married, 43.0% now married, 4.8% widowed, 14.8% divorced (2006-2010 5-year est.); Foreign born: 5.9% (2006-2010 5-year est.); Ancestry (includes multiple ancestries): 31.3% German, 14.5% Italian, 11.7% English, 11.4% Irish, 7.8% Polish (2006-2010 5-year est.).

Economy: Employment by occupation: 11.6% management, 1.8% professional, 5.1% services, 17.2% sales, 10.6% farming, 11.2% construction, 12.6% production (2006-2010 5-year est.).

Income: Per capita income: $26,163 (2006-2010 5-year est.); Median household income: $48,710 (2006-2010 5-year est.); Average household income: $54,216 (2006-2010 5-year est.); Percent of households with income of $100,000 or more: 8.4% (2006-2010 5-year est.); Poverty rate: 9.9% (2006-2010 5-year est.).

Education: Percent of population age 25 and over with: High school diploma (including GED) or higher: 94.2% (2006-2010 5-year est.); Bachelor's degree or higher: 21.4% (2006-2010 5-year est.); Master's degree or higher: 3.9% (2006-2010 5-year est.).

Housing: Homeownership rate: 44.6% (2010); Median home value: $181,400 (2006-2010 5-year est.); Median contract rent: $775 per month (2006-2010 5-year est.); Median year structure built: 1964 (2006-2010 5-year est.).

Transportation: Commute to work: 94.8% car, 4.1% public transportation, 1.1% walk, 0.0% work from home (2006-2010 5-year est.); Travel time to work: 22.3% less than 15 minutes, 34.0% 15 to 30 minutes, 21.8% 30 to 45 minutes, 12.7% 45 to 60 minutes, 9.1% 60 minutes or more (2006-2010 5-year est.)

Additional Information Contacts

TriCounty Area Chamber of Commerce . . . . (610) 326-2900
    http://www.tricountyareachamber.com

SPRING CITY (borough). Aka Hiestand. Covers a land area of 0.767 square miles and a water area of 0.054 square miles. Located at 40.18° N. Lat; 75.55° W. Long. Elevation is 161 feet.

History: Incorporated 1867 as Springville; renamed 1872.

Population: 3,433 (1990); 3,305 (2000); 3,323 (2010); Density: 4,331.0 persons per square mile (2010); Race: 91.4% White, 3.6% Black, 1.4% Asian, 0.1% American Indian/Alaska Native, 0.0% Native Hawaiian/Other Pacific Islander, 3.5% Other, 3.4% Hispanic of any race (2010); Average household size: 2.21 (2010); Median age: 39.2 (2010); Males per 100 females: 105.9 (2010); Marriage status: 40.3% never married, 42.4% now married, 4.0% widowed, 13.4% divorced (2006-2010 5-year est.); Foreign born: 3.8% (2006-2010 5-year est.); Ancestry (includes multiple ancestries): 41.4% German, 26.9% Irish, 12.2% Italian, 11.6% English, 9.0% Dutch (2006-2010 5-year est.).

Economy: Single-family building permits issued: 0 (2011); Multi-family building permits issued: 0 (2011); Employment by occupation: 12.1% management, 6.2% professional, 9.4% services, 21.1% sales, 2.2% farming, 6.7% construction, 7.1% production (2006-2010 5-year est.).

Income: Per capita income: $27,555 (2006-2010 5-year est.); Median household income: $52,694 (2006-2010 5-year est.); Average household income: $60,108 (2006-2010 5-year est.); Percent of households with income of $100,000 or more: 12.4% (2006-2010 5-year est.); Poverty rate: 5.2% (2006-2010 5-year est.).

Education: Percent of population age 25 and over with: High school diploma (including GED) or higher: 93.9% (2006-2010 5-year est.); Bachelor's degree or higher: 15.1% (2006-2010 5-year est.); Master's degree or higher: 6.6% (2006-2010 5-year est.).

School District(s)

Owen J Roberts SD (KG-12)
    2010-11 Enrollment: 5,026 . . . . (610) 469-5100
Spring-Ford Area SD (KG-12)
    2010-11 Enrollment: 7,730 . . . . (610) 705-6000

Housing: Homeownership rate: 50.0% (2010); Median home value: $163,600 (2006-2010 5-year est.); Median contract rent: $694 per month (2006-2010 5-year est.); Median year structure built: before 1940 (2006-2010 5-year est.).

Transportation: Commute to work: 94.3% car, 1.9% public transportation, 2.1% walk, 1.0% work from home (2006-2010 5-year est.); Travel time to work: 30.8% less than 15 minutes, 34.5% 15 to 30 minutes, 18.3% 30 to 45 minutes, 7.8% 45 to 60 minutes, 8.5% 60 minutes or more (2006-2010 5-year est.)

Additional Information Contacts

Spring-Ford Chamber of Commerce . . . . (610) 489-7200
http://www.springfordchamber.com

THORNBURY (township). Covers a land area of 3.832 square miles and a water area of 0.032 square miles. Located at 39.92° N. Lat; 75.56° W. Long.

Population: 1,131 (1990); 2,678 (2000); 3,017 (2010); Density: 787.2 persons per square mile (2010); Race: 87.2% White, 3.4% Black, 7.6% Asian, 0.1% American Indian/Alaska Native, 0.0% Native Hawaiian/Other Pacific Islander, 1.7% Other, 1.9% Hispanic of any race (2010); Average household size: 2.68 (2010); Median age: 41.6 (2010); Males per 100 females: 99.4 (2010); Marriage status: 28.1% never married, 59.8% now married, 3.5% widowed, 8.6% divorced (2006-2010 5-year est.); Foreign born: 8.4% (2006-2010 5-year est.); Ancestry (includes multiple ancestries): 33.4% Irish, 23.3% German, 23.0% Italian, 8.6% English, 5.7% Polish (2006-2010 5-year est.).

Economy: Single-family building permits issued: 11 (2011); Multi-family building permits issued: 0 (2011); Employment by occupation: 24.3% management, 11.6% professional, 4.1% services, 16.1% sales, 1.4% farming, 2.0% construction, 0.7% production (2006-2010 5-year est.).

Income: Per capita income: $57,965 (2006-2010 5-year est.); Median household income: $121,186 (2006-2010 5-year est.); Average household income: $153,162 (2006-2010 5-year est.); Percent of households with income of $100,000 or more: 63.4% (2006-2010 5-year est.); Poverty rate: 3.1% (2006-2010 5-year est.).

Education: Percent of population age 25 and over with: High school diploma (including GED) or higher: 96.3% (2006-2010 5-year est.); Bachelor's degree or higher: 66.2% (2006-2010 5-year est.); Master's degree or higher: 26.2% (2006-2010 5-year est.).

Housing: Homeownership rate: 78.2% (2010); Median home value: $443,000 (2006-2010 5-year est.); Median contract rent: $1,327 per month (2006-2010 5-year est.); Median year structure built: 1993 (2006-2010 5-year est.).

Transportation: Commute to work: 88.8% car, 1.6% public transportation, 2.0% walk, 7.3% work from home (2006-2010 5-year est.); Travel time to work: 22.1% less than 15 minutes, 37.0% 15 to 30 minutes, 23.9% 30 to 45 minutes, 8.9% 45 to 60 minutes, 8.0% 60 minutes or more (2006-2010 5-year est.)

Additional Information Contacts

Chester County Chamber of Business and Industry . . . . . . (610) 725-9100
http://www.cccbi.org
Thornbury Township . . . . (610) 399-1425
http://www.thornburytwp.com

THORNDALE (CDP). Covers a land area of 1.845 square miles and a water area of 0.017 square miles. Located at 40.00° N. Lat; 75.75° W. Long. Elevation is 344 feet.

Population: 3,503 (1990); 3,561 (2000); 3,407 (2010); Density: 1,847.0 persons per square mile (2010); Race: 84.9% White, 8.9% Black, 3.1% Asian, 0.1% American Indian/Alaska Native, 0.0% Native Hawaiian/Other Pacific Islander, 3.0% Other, 4.3% Hispanic of any race (2010); Average household size: 2.46 (2010); Median age: 36.7 (2010); Males per 100 females: 98.4 (2010); Marriage status: 30.1% never married, 59.2% now married, 6.0% widowed, 4.7% divorced (2006-2010 5-year est.); Foreign born: 8.9% (2006-2010 5-year est.); Ancestry (includes multiple ancestries): 24.2% German, 19.2% Irish, 17.6% Italian, 9.2% English, 6.5% Polish (2006-2010 5-year est.).

Economy: Employment by occupation: 10.5% management, 3.1% professional, 11.1% services, 9.2% sales, 4.3% farming, 9.0% construction, 6.1% production (2006-2010 5-year est.).

Income: Per capita income: $34,687 (2006-2010 5-year est.); Median household income: $61,389 (2006-2010 5-year est.); Average household income: $79,768 (2006-2010 5-year est.); Percent of households with income of $100,000 or more: 26.2% (2006-2010 5-year est.); Poverty rate: 9.9% (2006-2010 5-year est.).

Education: Percent of population age 25 and over with: High school diploma (including GED) or higher: 92.8% (2006-2010 5-year est.); Bachelor's degree or higher: 34.2% (2006-2010 5-year est.); Master's degree or higher: 7.6% (2006-2010 5-year est.).

School District(s)

Coatesville Area SD (KG-12)
2010-11 Enrollment: 6,891 . . . . (610) 466-2400

Housing: Homeownership rate: 67.7% (2010); Median home value: $232,100 (2006-2010 5-year est.); Median contract rent: $973 per month (2006-2010 5-year est.); Median year structure built: 1973 (2006-2010 5-year est.).

Transportation: Commute to work: 91.3% car, 2.4% public transportation, 1.7% walk, 2.4% work from home (2006-2010 5-year est.); Travel time to work: 18.0% less than 15 minutes, 46.9% 15 to 30 minutes, 20.0% 30 to 45 minutes, 6.1% 45 to 60 minutes, 9.0% 60 minutes or more (2006-2010 5-year est.)

Additional Information Contacts

Western Chester County Chamber of Commerce . . . . (610) 384-9550
http://www.westernchestercounty.com

TOUGHKENAMON (CDP). Covers a land area of 2.063 square miles and a water area of 0.021 square miles. Located at 39.83° N. Lat; 75.76° W. Long. Elevation is 338 feet.

Population: 1,273 (1990); 1,375 (2000); 1,492 (2010); Density: 723.3 persons per square mile (2010); Race: 60.8% White, 2.9% Black, 0.1% Asian, 0.7% American Indian/Alaska Native, 0.0% Native Hawaiian/Other Pacific Islander, 35.5% Other, 58.0% Hispanic of any race (2010); Average household size: 3.63 (2010); Median age: 29.8 (2010); Males per 100 females: 143.4 (2010); Marriage status: 17.8% never married, 79.1% now married, 0.0% widowed, 3.2% divorced (2006-2010 5-year est.); Foreign born: 56.8% (2006-2010 5-year est.); Ancestry (includes multiple ancestries): 9.9% Irish, 6.8% German, 5.1% English, 4.6% American, 4.1% Portuguese (2006-2010 5-year est.).

Economy: Employment by occupation: 17.3% management, 4.1% professional, 0.0% services, 7.5% sales, 11.8% farming, 11.8% construction, 0.0% production (2006-2010 5-year est.).

Income: Per capita income: $14,355 (2006-2010 5-year est.); Median household income: $50,893 (2006-2010 5-year est.); Average household income: $68,632 (2006-2010 5-year est.); Percent of households with income of $100,000 or more: 27.6% (2006-2010 5-year est.); Poverty rate: 28.4% (2006-2010 5-year est.).

Education: Percent of population age 25 and over with: High school diploma (including GED) or higher: 59.6% (2006-2010 5-year est.); Bachelor's degree or higher: 10.2% (2006-2010 5-year est.); Master's degree or higher: 2.3% (2006-2010 5-year est.).

School District(s)

Kennett Consolidated SD (KG-12)
2010-11 Enrollment: 4,219 . . . . (610) 444-6600

Housing: Homeownership rate: 49.3% (2010); Median home value: $248,400 (2006-2010 5-year est.); Median contract rent: $675 per month (2006-2010 5-year est.); Median year structure built: 1991 (2006-2010 5-year est.).

Transportation: Commute to work: 90.0% car, 0.0% public transportation, 0.0% walk, 10.0% work from home (2006-2010 5-year est.); Travel time to work: 47.2% less than 15 minutes, 19.9% 15 to 30 minutes, 10.0% 30 to 45 minutes, 17.3% 45 to 60 minutes, 5.7% 60 minutes or more (2006-2010 5-year est.)

Airports: New Garden (general aviation)

Additional Information Contacts

Southern Chester County Chamber of Commerce . . . . (610) 444-0774
http://www.scccc.com

TREDYFFRIN (township). Covers a land area of 19.765 square miles and a water area of 0.085 square miles. Located at 40.07° N. Lat; 75.45° W. Long.

Population: 28,021 (1990); 29,062 (2000); 29,332 (2010); Density: 1,484.1 persons per square mile (2010); Race: 85.1% White, 3.3% Black, 9.8% Asian, 0.1% American Indian/Alaska Native, 0.0% Native Hawaiian/Other Pacific Islander, 1.7% Other, 2.2% Hispanic of any race (2010); Average household size: 2.42 (2010); Median age: 42.9 (2010); Males per 100 females: 89.5 (2010); Marriage status: 26.6% never married, 59.3% now married, 6.1% widowed, 8.0% divorced (2006-2010 5-year est.); Foreign born: 10.1% (2006-2010 5-year est.); Ancestry (includes multiple ancestries): 24.9% Irish, 23.9% German, 16.4% English, 14.8% Italian, 4.6% Polish (2006-2010 5-year est.).

Economy: Unemployment rate: 5.9% (August 2012); Total civilian labor force: 15,887 (August 2012); Single-family building permits issued: 4 (2011); Multi-family building permits issued: 0 (2011); Employment by occupation: 20.6% management, 12.4% professional, 3.3% services,

11.8% sales, 2.0% farming, 2.6% construction, 1.3% production (2006-2010 5-year est.).

Income: Per capita income: $59,231 (2006-2010 5-year est.); Median household income: $99,728 (2006-2010 5-year est.); Average household income: $138,788 (2006-2010 5-year est.); Percent of households with income of $100,000 or more: 49.9% (2006-2010 5-year est.); Poverty rate: 4.3% (2006-2010 5-year est.).

Taxes: Total city taxes per capita: $434 (2009); City property taxes per capita: $265 (2009).

Education: Percent of population age 25 and over with: High school diploma (including GED) or higher: 97.4% (2006-2010 5-year est.); Bachelor's degree or higher: 72.3% (2006-2010 5-year est.); Master's degree or higher: 34.4% (2006-2010 5-year est.).

Housing: Homeownership rate: 78.5% (2010); Median home value: $447,700 (2006-2010 5-year est.); Median contract rent: $1,099 per month (2006-2010 5-year est.); Median year structure built: 1971 (2006-2010 5-year est.).

Safety: Violent crime rate: 4.1 per 10,000 population; Property crime rate: 89.7 per 10,000 population (2011).

Transportation: Commute to work: 82.5% car, 7.7% public transportation, 1.8% walk, 6.8% work from home (2006-2010 5-year est.); Travel time to work: 32.1% less than 15 minutes, 34.4% 15 to 30 minutes, 14.8% 30 to 45 minutes, 7.9% 45 to 60 minutes, 10.9% 60 minutes or more (2006-2010 5-year est.).

Additional Information Contacts

Main Line Chamber of Commerce . . . . (610) 687-6232
http://www.mlcc.org

Tredyffrin Township . . . . (610) 644-1400
http://www.tredyffrin.org

UPPER OXFORD (township). Covers a land area of 16.636 square miles and a water area of 0.098 square miles. Located at 39.84° N. Lat; 75.96° W. Long.

Population: 1,615 (1990); 2,095 (2000); 2,484 (2010); Density: 149.3 persons per square mile (2010); Race: 90.5% White, 3.7% Black, 0.3% Asian, 0.4% American Indian/Alaska Native, 0.0% Native Hawaiian/Other Pacific Islander, 5.1% Other, 7.8% Hispanic of any race (2010); Average household size: 3.03 (2010); Median age: 38.5 (2010); Males per 100 females: 99.2 (2010); Marriage status: 22.0% never married, 69.1% now married, 3.8% widowed, 5.2% divorced (2006-2010 5-year est.); Foreign born: 2.1% (2006-2010 5-year est.); Ancestry (includes multiple ancestries): 25.1% Irish, 20.6% German, 12.1% Italian, 11.5% English, 8.7% American (2006-2010 5-year est.).

Economy: Single-family building permits issued: 0 (2011); Multi-family building permits issued: 0 (2011); Employment by occupation: 12.9% management, 7.7% professional, 8.5% services, 15.2% sales, 1.7% farming, 10.9% construction, 11.4% production (2006-2010 5-year est.).

Income: Per capita income: $27,873 (2006-2010 5-year est.); Median household income: $80,000 (2006-2010 5-year est.); Average household income: $89,057 (2006-2010 5-year est.); Percent of households with income of $100,000 or more: 36.8% (2006-2010 5-year est.); Poverty rate: 10.1% (2006-2010 5-year est.).

Education: Percent of population age 25 and over with: High school diploma (including GED) or higher: 89.1% (2006-2010 5-year est.); Bachelor's degree or higher: 24.6% (2006-2010 5-year est.); Master's degree or higher: 4.5% (2006-2010 5-year est.).

Housing: Homeownership rate: 84.5% (2010); Median home value: $293,600 (2006-2010 5-year est.); Median contract rent: $696 per month (2006-2010 5-year est.); Median year structure built: 1983 (2006-2010 5-year est.).

Transportation: Commute to work: 86.9% car, 0.7% public transportation, 2.4% walk, 5.8% work from home (2006-2010 5-year est.); Travel time to work: 27.9% less than 15 minutes, 21.4% 15 to 30 minutes, 23.9% 30 to 45 minutes, 15.9% 45 to 60 minutes, 10.8% 60 minutes or more (2006-2010 5-year est.)

Additional Information Contacts

Oxford Area Chamber of Commerce . . . . (610) 932-0740
http://www.oxfordpa.org

UPPER UWCHLAN (township). Covers a land area of 10.893 square miles and a water area of 0.829 square miles. Located at 40.08° N. Lat; 75.71° W. Long.

History: Upper Uwchlan Township was incorporated as a Municipality in 1858. For over one hundred and twenty-five years, it had been the upper part of greater Uwchlan Township.

Population: 4,396 (1990); 6,850 (2000); 11,227 (2010); Density: 1,030.7 persons per square mile (2010); Race: 82.7% White, 1.4% Black, 14.1% Asian, 0.0% American Indian/Alaska Native, 0.0% Native Hawaiian/Other Pacific Islander, 1.8% Other, 2.4% Hispanic of any race (2010); Average household size: 3.14 (2010); Median age: 36.3 (2010); Males per 100 females: 100.3 (2010); Marriage status: 19.2% never married, 74.1% now married, 2.7% widowed, 4.0% divorced (2006-2010 5-year est.); Foreign born: 14.2% (2006-2010 5-year est.); Ancestry (includes multiple ancestries): 24.6% Irish, 24.1% German, 15.8% Italian, 12.9% English, 6.8% Polish (2006-2010 5-year est.).

Economy: Single-family building permits issued: 13 (2011); Multi-family building permits issued: 0 (2011); Employment by occupation: 23.6% management, 15.3% professional, 4.4% services, 11.6% sales, 2.4% farming, 2.9% construction, 1.5% production (2006-2010 5-year est.).

Income: Per capita income: $52,868 (2006-2010 5-year est.); Median household income: $159,694 (2006-2010 5-year est.); Average household income: $165,293 (2006-2010 5-year est.); Percent of households with income of $100,000 or more: 76.0% (2006-2010 5-year est.); Poverty rate: 1.3% (2006-2010 5-year est.).

Education: Percent of population age 25 and over with: High school diploma (including GED) or higher: 98.6% (2006-2010 5-year est.); Bachelor's degree or higher: 70.3% (2006-2010 5-year est.); Master's degree or higher: 28.1% (2006-2010 5-year est.).

Housing: Homeownership rate: 93.8% (2010); Median home value: $427,500 (2006-2010 5-year est.); Median contract rent: $1,636 per month (2006-2010 5-year est.); Median year structure built: 1995 (2006-2010 5-year est.).

Safety: Violent crime rate: 1.8 per 10,000 population; Property crime rate: 32.9 per 10,000 population (2011).

Transportation: Commute to work: 88.3% car, 1.9% public transportation, 0.5% walk, 7.3% work from home (2006-2010 5-year est.); Travel time to work: 11.1% less than 15 minutes, 32.4% 15 to 30 minutes, 32.8% 30 to 45 minutes, 12.8% 45 to 60 minutes, 10.8% 60 minutes or more (2006-2010 5-year est.)

Additional Information Contacts

Greater West Chester Chamber of Commerce . . . . (610) 696-4046
http://www.gwcc.org

Upper Uwchlan Township . . . . (610) 458-9400
http://www.upperuwchlan-pa.gov

UWCHLAN (township). Covers a land area of 10.398 square miles and a water area of 0.058 square miles. Located at 40.05° N. Lat; 75.67° W. Long.

History: Uwchlan Township (pronounced /yu kl?n/), in the original Welsh has the meaning "land above the valley".

Population: 12,999 (1990); 16,576 (2000); 18,088 (2010); Density: 1,739.5 persons per square mile (2010); Race: 90.4% White, 2.5% Black, 5.2% Asian, 0.1% American Indian/Alaska Native, 0.0% Native Hawaiian/Other Pacific Islander, 1.8% Other, 2.3% Hispanic of any race (2010); Average household size: 2.74 (2010); Median age: 39.5 (2010); Males per 100 females: 96.8 (2010); Marriage status: 22.7% never married, 68.2% now married, 3.2% widowed, 5.9% divorced (2006-2010 5-year est.); Foreign born: 7.3% (2006-2010 5-year est.); Ancestry (includes multiple ancestries): 27.3% Irish, 26.4% German, 14.2% Italian, 12.4% English, 5.1% Polish (2006-2010 5-year est.).

Economy: Single-family building permits issued: 8 (2011); Multi-family building permits issued: 50 (2011); Employment by occupation: 22.8% management, 12.2% professional, 4.7% services, 14.5% sales, 3.3% farming, 4.7% construction, 2.9% production (2006-2010 5-year est.).

Income: Per capita income: $44,314 (2006-2010 5-year est.); Median household income: $103,617 (2006-2010 5-year est.); Average household income: $118,226 (2006-2010 5-year est.); Percent of households with income of $100,000 or more: 52.5% (2006-2010 5-year est.); Poverty rate: 1.2% (2006-2010 5-year est.).

Taxes: Total city taxes per capita: $339 (2009); City property taxes per capita: $9 (2009).

Education: Percent of population age 25 and over with: High school diploma (including GED) or higher: 96.8% (2006-2010 5-year est.); Bachelor's degree or higher: 63.6% (2006-2010 5-year est.); Master's degree or higher: 21.3% (2006-2010 5-year est.).

Housing: Homeownership rate: 80.7% (2010); Median home value: $364,400 (2006-2010 5-year est.); Median contract rent: $978 per month (2006-2010 5-year est.); Median year structure built: 1985 (2006-2010 5-year est.).

Safety: Violent crime rate: 9.9 per 10,000 population; Property crime rate: 93.1 per 10,000 population (2011).

Transportation: Commute to work: 86.5% car, 4.3% public transportation, 1.0% walk, 7.5% work from home (2006-2010 5-year est.); Travel time to work: 28.6% less than 15 minutes, 31.2% 15 to 30 minutes, 19.7% 30 to 45 minutes, 9.5% 45 to 60 minutes, 11.0% 60 minutes or more (2006-2010 5-year est.)

Additional Information Contacts

Chester County Chamber of Business and Industry . . . . . . (610) 725-9100
   http://www.cccbi.org
Uwchlan Township . . . . (610) 363-9450
   http://www.uwchlan.com

VALLEY (township). Covers a land area of 5.934 square miles and a water area of 0.032 square miles. Located at 39.99° N. Lat; 75.85° W. Long.

Population: 4,007 (1990); 5,116 (2000); 6,794 (2010); Density: 1,145.0 persons per square mile (2010); Race: 67.9% White, 23.8% Black, 1.5% Asian, 0.2% American Indian/Alaska Native, 0.0% Native Hawaiian/Other Pacific Islander, 6.6% Other, 7.5% Hispanic of any race (2010); Average household size: 2.54 (2010); Median age: 37.2 (2010); Males per 100 females: 92.8 (2010); Marriage status: 19.9% never married, 63.4% now married, 7.5% widowed, 9.2% divorced (2006-2010 5-year est.); Foreign born: 4.5% (2006-2010 5-year est.); Ancestry (includes multiple ancestries): 19.8% Irish, 17.0% German, 14.1% Italian, 7.7% English, 4.8% Polish (2006-2010 5-year est.).

Economy: Single-family building permits issued: 64 (2011); Multi-family building permits issued: 0 (2011); Employment by occupation: 12.1% management, 7.1% professional, 8.8% services, 16.8% sales, 3.1% farming, 10.8% construction, 7.1% production (2006-2010 5-year est.).

Income: Per capita income: $28,707 (2006-2010 5-year est.); Median household income: $61,366 (2006-2010 5-year est.); Average household income: $72,729 (2006-2010 5-year est.); Percent of households with income of $100,000 or more: 23.2% (2006-2010 5-year est.); Poverty rate: 9.7% (2006-2010 5-year est.).

Education: Percent of population age 25 and over with: High school diploma (including GED) or higher: 88.8% (2006-2010 5-year est.); Bachelor's degree or higher: 30.4% (2006-2010 5-year est.); Master's degree or higher: 7.9% (2006-2010 5-year est.).

Housing: Homeownership rate: 82.6% (2010); Median home value: $217,600 (2006-2010 5-year est.); Median contract rent: $892 per month (2006-2010 5-year est.); Median year structure built: 1989 (2006-2010 5-year est.).

Safety: Violent crime rate: 64.6 per 10,000 population; Property crime rate: 201.0 per 10,000 population (2011).

Transportation: Commute to work: 92.6% car, 2.5% public transportation, 1.1% walk, 2.6% work from home (2006-2010 5-year est.); Travel time to work: 21.5% less than 15 minutes, 29.3% 15 to 30 minutes, 27.9% 30 to 45 minutes, 10.2% 45 to 60 minutes, 11.2% 60 minutes or more (2006-2010 5-year est.)

Additional Information Contacts

Chester County Chamber of Business and Industry . . . . . . (610) 725-9100
   http://www.cccbi.org
Valley Township . . . . (570) 275-2449
   http://www.valleytownshippa.net

WALLACE (township). Covers a land area of 11.961 square miles and a water area of 0.166 square miles. Located at 40.08° N. Lat; 75.78° W. Long. Elevation is 564 feet.

History: Wallace Township was formed through a division of West Nantmeal Township in 1852. The Township-as defined by its current boundaries-includes nearly the same territory as the early eighteenth century Springton Manor, minus a small portion of land that was granted to Uwchlan Township in 1853.

Population: 2,541 (1990); 3,240 (2000); 3,458 (2010); Density: 289.1 persons per square mile (2010); Race: 94.1% White, 3.2% Black, 1.4% Asian, 0.1% American Indian/Alaska Native, 0.0% Native Hawaiian/Other Pacific Islander, 1.2% Other, 1.6% Hispanic of any race (2010); Average household size: 2.95 (2010); Median age: 41.4 (2010); Males per 100 females: 108.3 (2010); Marriage status: 19.8% never married, 66.1% now married, 5.3% widowed, 8.8% divorced (2006-2010 5-year est.); Foreign born: 4.0% (2006-2010 5-year est.); Ancestry (includes multiple ancestries): 34.1% German, 28.3% Irish, 15.6% English, 12.1% Italian, 5.1% American (2006-2010 5-year est.).

Economy: Single-family building permits issued: 12 (2011); Multi-family building permits issued: 0 (2011); Employment by occupation: 18.6% management, 7.8% professional, 7.2% services, 15.9% sales, 3.0% farming, 9.0% construction, 3.9% production (2006-2010 5-year est.).

Income: Per capita income: $38,413 (2006-2010 5-year est.); Median household income: $108,229 (2006-2010 5-year est.); Average household income: $120,732 (2006-2010 5-year est.); Percent of households with income of $100,000 or more: 55.3% (2006-2010 5-year est.); Poverty rate: 4.2% (2006-2010 5-year est.).

Education: Percent of population age 25 and over with: High school diploma (including GED) or higher: 95.4% (2006-2010 5-year est.); Bachelor's degree or higher: 45.9% (2006-2010 5-year est.); Master's degree or higher: 17.1% (2006-2010 5-year est.).

Housing: Homeownership rate: 89.5% (2010); Median home value: $405,100 (2006-2010 5-year est.); Median contract rent: $958 per month (2006-2010 5-year est.); Median year structure built: 1980 (2006-2010 5-year est.).

Transportation: Commute to work: 89.9% car, 0.6% public transportation, 0.0% walk, 6.2% work from home (2006-2010 5-year est.); Travel time to work: 17.0% less than 15 minutes, 30.1% 15 to 30 minutes, 29.8% 30 to 45 minutes, 11.1% 45 to 60 minutes, 11.9% 60 minutes or more (2006-2010 5-year est.)

Additional Information Contacts

Greater West Chester Chamber of Commerce . . . . (610) 696-4046
   http://www.gwcc.org
Wallace Township . . . . (610) 942-2880
   http://www.wallacetwp.org

WARWICK (township). Aka Saint Marys. Covers a land area of 18.747 square miles and a water area of 0.149 square miles. Located at 40.18° N. Lat; 75.76° W. Long. Elevation is 643 feet.

Population: 2,575 (1990); 2,556 (2000); 2,507 (2010); Density: 133.7 persons per square mile (2010); Race: 97.4% White, 0.3% Black, 0.8% Asian, 0.1% American Indian/Alaska Native, 0.0% Native Hawaiian/Other Pacific Islander, 1.4% Other, 1.6% Hispanic of any race (2010); Average household size: 2.57 (2010); Median age: 46.3 (2010); Males per 100 females: 99.3 (2010); Marriage status: 21.8% never married, 67.5% now married, 3.7% widowed, 7.0% divorced (2006-2010 5-year est.); Foreign born: 2.8% (2006-2010 5-year est.); Ancestry (includes multiple ancestries): 32.0% German, 28.5% Irish, 15.1% English, 11.5% Italian, 5.2% Dutch (2006-2010 5-year est.).

Economy: Single-family building permits issued: 2 (2011); Multi-family building permits issued: 0 (2011); Employment by occupation: 10.6% management, 11.7% professional, 9.0% services, 17.9% sales, 2.7% farming, 12.1% construction, 10.3% production (2006-2010 5-year est.).

Income: Per capita income: $42,593 (2006-2010 5-year est.); Median household income: $72,048 (2006-2010 5-year est.); Average household income: $107,917 (2006-2010 5-year est.); Percent of households with income of $100,000 or more: 35.7% (2006-2010 5-year est.); Poverty rate: 5.2% (2006-2010 5-year est.).

Education: Percent of population age 25 and over with: High school diploma (including GED) or higher: 96.2% (2006-2010 5-year est.); Bachelor's degree or higher: 36.1% (2006-2010 5-year est.); Master's degree or higher: 11.2% (2006-2010 5-year est.).

Housing: Homeownership rate: 87.0% (2010); Median home value: $317,500 (2006-2010 5-year est.); Median contract rent: $828 per month (2006-2010 5-year est.); Median year structure built: 1972 (2006-2010 5-year est.).

Transportation: Commute to work: 90.4% car, 0.0% public transportation, 3.6% walk, 6.0% work from home (2006-2010 5-year est.); Travel time to work: 15.0% less than 15 minutes, 28.4% 15 to 30 minutes, 35.8% 30 to 45 minutes, 10.6% 45 to 60 minutes, 10.2% 60 minutes or more (2006-2010 5-year est.)

Additional Information Contacts

TriCounty Area Chamber of Commerce . . . . (610) 326-2900
   http://tricountyareachamber.com

WEST BRADFORD (township). Covers a land area of 18.498 square miles and a water area of 0.097 square miles. Located at 39.96° N. Lat; 75.72° W. Long.

History: West Bradford Township was originally part of Bradford Township; organized in 1705. It was divided into East and West Bradford in 1731. Its boundaries changed in 1849, when a portion in the southeast was included in the formation of Pocopson Township. Bradford's earliest settlers were English Quakers.

Population: 10,406 (1990); 10,775 (2000); 12,223 (2010); Density: 660.8 persons per square mile (2010); Race: 92.4% White, 2.9% Black, 2.6% Asian, 0.2% American Indian/Alaska Native, 0.0% Native Hawaiian/Other Pacific Islander, 1.9% Other, 2.0% Hispanic of any race (2010); Average household size: 2.96 (2010); Median age: 39.6 (2010); Males per 100 females: 100.1 (2010); Marriage status: 22.2% never married, 70.4% now married, 3.0% widowed, 4.4% divorced (2006-2010 5-year est.); Foreign born: 4.2% (2006-2010 5-year est.); Ancestry (includes multiple ancestries): 30.1% Irish, 28.6% German, 16.5% Italian, 14.4% English, 9.6% Polish (2006-2010 5-year est.).

Economy: Single-family building permits issued: 28 (2011); Multi-family building permits issued: 0 (2011); Employment by occupation: 21.4% management, 7.3% professional, 7.0% services, 15.2% sales, 3.2% farming, 6.7% construction, 4.2% production (2006-2010 5-year est.).

Income: Per capita income: $39,759 (2006-2010 5-year est.); Median household income: $102,535 (2006-2010 5-year est.); Average household income: $122,641 (2006-2010 5-year est.); Percent of households with income of $100,000 or more: 51.6% (2006-2010 5-year est.); Poverty rate: 2.3% (2006-2010 5-year est.).

Education: Percent of population age 25 and over with: High school diploma (including GED) or higher: 97.8% (2006-2010 5-year est.); Bachelor's degree or higher: 54.1% (2006-2010 5-year est.); Master's degree or higher: 15.7% (2006-2010 5-year est.).

Housing: Homeownership rate: 94.7% (2010); Median home value: $320,700 (2006-2010 5-year est.); Median contract rent: $594 per month (2006-2010 5-year est.); Median year structure built: 1980 (2006-2010 5-year est.).

Transportation: Commute to work: 93.4% car, 1.6% public transportation, 0.8% walk, 4.0% work from home (2006-2010 5-year est.); Travel time to work: 18.9% less than 15 minutes, 37.2% 15 to 30 minutes, 22.0% 30 to 45 minutes, 8.9% 45 to 60 minutes, 13.0% 60 minutes or more (2006-2010 5-year est.).

Additional Information Contacts

Greater West Chester Chamber of Commerce . . . . (610) 696-4046
  http://www.gwcc.org
West Bradford Township . . . . (610) 269-4174
  http://www.westbradford.org

WEST BRANDYWINE (township). Covers a land area of 13.119 square miles and a water area of 0.137 square miles. Located at 40.04° N. Lat; 75.81° W. Long.

Population: 5,984 (1990); 7,153 (2000); 7,394 (2010); Density: 563.6 persons per square mile (2010); Race: 93.8% White, 3.5% Black, 0.9% Asian, 0.1% American Indian/Alaska Native, 0.0% Native Hawaiian/Other Pacific Islander, 1.7% Other, 2.6% Hispanic of any race (2010); Average household size: 2.56 (2010); Median age: 45.5 (2010); Males per 100 females: 94.4 (2010); Marriage status: 19.8% never married, 67.6% now married, 6.6% widowed, 5.9% divorced (2006-2010 5-year est.); Foreign born: 2.2% (2006-2010 5-year est.); Ancestry (includes multiple ancestries): 37.2% Irish, 25.6% German, 16.0% English, 15.8% Italian, 5.8% Polish (2006-2010 5-year est.).

Economy: Single-family building permits issued: 2 (2011); Multi-family building permits issued: 0 (2011); Employment by occupation: 16.9% management, 5.8% professional, 10.7% services, 20.3% sales, 2.5% farming, 5.6% construction, 3.3% production (2006-2010 5-year est.).

Income: Per capita income: $37,377 (2006-2010 5-year est.); Median household income: $84,167 (2006-2010 5-year est.); Average household income: $100,082 (2006-2010 5-year est.); Percent of households with income of $100,000 or more: 43.0% (2006-2010 5-year est.); Poverty rate: 3.0% (2006-2010 5-year est.).

Education: Percent of population age 25 and over with: High school diploma (including GED) or higher: 92.4% (2006-2010 5-year est.); Bachelor's degree or higher: 37.7% (2006-2010 5-year est.); Master's degree or higher: 12.4% (2006-2010 5-year est.).

Housing: Homeownership rate: 88.5% (2010); Median home value: $287,400 (2006-2010 5-year est.); Median contract rent: $668 per month (2006-2010 5-year est.); Median year structure built: 1989 (2006-2010 5-year est.).

Safety: Violent crime rate: 17.5 per 10,000 population; Property crime rate: 132.1 per 10,000 population (2011).

Transportation: Commute to work: 92.1% car, 2.0% public transportation, 1.1% walk, 4.3% work from home (2006-2010 5-year est.); Travel time to work: 12.0% less than 15 minutes, 32.8% 15 to 30 minutes, 27.6% 30 to 45 minutes, 13.4% 45 to 60 minutes, 14.2% 60 minutes or more (2006-2010 5-year est.)

Additional Information Contacts

Southern Chester County Chamber of Commerce . . . . (610) 444-0774
  http://www.scccc.com
West Brandywine Township . . . . (610) 380-8200
  http://www.wbrandywine.org

WEST CALN (township). Covers a land area of 21.598 square miles and a water area of 0.322 square miles. Located at 40.02° N. Lat; 75.89° W. Long.

Population: 6,143 (1990); 7,054 (2000); 9,014 (2010); Density: 417.3 persons per square mile (2010); Race: 92.9% White, 3.9% Black, 0.7% Asian, 0.2% American Indian/Alaska Native, 0.0% Native Hawaiian/Other Pacific Islander, 2.3% Other, 2.3% Hispanic of any race (2010); Average household size: 2.76 (2010); Median age: 41.9 (2010); Males per 100 females: 101.4 (2010); Marriage status: 24.7% never married, 61.6% now married, 4.8% widowed, 8.9% divorced (2006-2010 5-year est.); Foreign born: 2.0% (2006-2010 5-year est.); Ancestry (includes multiple ancestries): 25.7% German, 22.1% Irish, 16.8% English, 13.9% Italian, 9.3% American (2006-2010 5-year est.).

Economy: Single-family building permits issued: 2 (2011); Multi-family building permits issued: 0 (2011); Employment by occupation: 14.4% management, 5.5% professional, 7.9% services, 16.2% sales, 7.2% farming, 13.3% construction, 10.2% production (2006-2010 5-year est.).

Income: Per capita income: $31,075 (2006-2010 5-year est.); Median household income: $75,717 (2006-2010 5-year est.); Average household income: $83,842 (2006-2010 5-year est.); Percent of households with income of $100,000 or more: 29.9% (2006-2010 5-year est.); Poverty rate: 4.9% (2006-2010 5-year est.).

Education: Percent of population age 25 and over with: High school diploma (including GED) or higher: 91.3% (2006-2010 5-year est.); Bachelor's degree or higher: 25.1% (2006-2010 5-year est.); Master's degree or higher: 7.4% (2006-2010 5-year est.).

Housing: Homeownership rate: 91.0% (2010); Median home value: $231,900 (2006-2010 5-year est.); Median contract rent: $800 per month (2006-2010 5-year est.); Median year structure built: 1985 (2006-2010 5-year est.).

Transportation: Commute to work: 93.9% car, 1.2% public transportation, 0.0% walk, 3.8% work from home (2006-2010 5-year est.); Travel time to work: 17.8% less than 15 minutes, 27.5% 15 to 30 minutes, 33.8% 30 to 45 minutes, 11.4% 45 to 60 minutes, 9.6% 60 minutes or more (2006-2010 5-year est.)

Additional Information Contacts

West Caln Township . . . . (610) 384-5643
  http://www.wcaln.org
Western Chester County Chamber of Commerce . . . . (610) 384-9550
  http://www.westernchestercounty.com

WEST CHESTER (borough). County seat. Covers a land area of 1.846 square miles and a water area of <.001 square miles. Located at 39.96° N. Lat; 75.61° W. Long. Elevation is 459 feet.

History: Named for the town and county of Chester in England. West Chester's early growth involved a prolonged and sometimes violent dispute with the town of Chester over the location of the Chester County seat, which West Chester finally won.

Population: 18,041 (1990); 17,861 (2000); 18,461 (2010); Density: 9,999.4 persons per square mile (2010); Race: 78.7% White, 12.1% Black, 1.4% Asian, 0.2% American Indian/Alaska Native, 0.0% Native Hawaiian/Other Pacific Islander, 7.6% Other, 13.4% Hispanic of any race (2010); Average household size: 2.32 (2010); Median age: 23.9 (2010); Males per 100 females: 93.5 (2010); Marriage status: 65.8% never married, 24.7% now married, 4.0% widowed, 5.4% divorced (2006-2010 5-year est.); Foreign born: 7.2% (2006-2010 5-year est.); Ancestry (includes multiple ancestries): 22.9% Irish, 20.8% German, 16.2% Italian, 9.7% English, 5.4% Polish (2006-2010 5-year est.).

Economy: Single-family building permits issued: 31 (2011); Multi-family building permits issued: 0 (2011); Employment by occupation: 10.8% management, 5.0% professional, 16.2% services, 17.5% sales, 4.5% farming, 4.4% construction, 2.4% production (2006-2010 5-year est.).

Income: Per capita income: $23,742 (2006-2010 5-year est.); Median household income: $45,052 (2006-2010 5-year est.); Average household income: $62,700 (2006-2010 5-year est.); Percent of households with income of $100,000 or more: 17.7% (2006-2010 5-year est.); Poverty rate: 24.9% (2006-2010 5-year est.).

Taxes: Total city taxes per capita: $494 (2009); City property taxes per capita: $195 (2009).

Education: Percent of population age 25 and over with: High school diploma (including GED) or higher: 90.0% (2006-2010 5-year est.); Bachelor's degree or higher: 43.9% (2006-2010 5-year est.); Master's degree or higher: 14.1% (2006-2010 5-year est.).

School District(s)

Chester Co Family Academy CS (KG-02)
    2010-11 Enrollment: 58. . . . . (610) 696-5910
Pennsylvania Leadership Charter School (PK-12)
    2010-11 Enrollment: 2,155 . . . . (610) 701-3333
Sankofa Academy CS (05-12)
    2010-11 Enrollment: 67. . . . . (610) 696-0333
Unionville-Chadds Ford SD (KG-12)
    2010-11 Enrollment: 4,089 . . . . (610) 347-0970
West Chester Area SD (KG-12)
    2010-11 Enrollment: 11,825 . . . . (484) 266-1000

Four-year College(s)

West Chester University of Pennsylvania (Public)
    Fall 2010 Enrollment: 13,548 . . . . (610) 436-1000
    2011-12 Tuition: In-state $8,274; Out-of-state $17,634

Housing: Homeownership rate: 34.7% (2010); Median home value: $296,800 (2006-2010 5-year est.); Median contract rent: $927 per month (2006-2010 5-year est.); Median year structure built: before 1940 (2006-2010 5-year est.).

Hospitals: Chester County Hospital (261 beds)

Safety: Violent crime rate: 52.9 per 10,000 population; Property crime rate: 267.3 per 10,000 population (2011).

Newspapers: Daily Local News (Local news; Circulation 25,767); The Philadelphia Inquirer - Chester County Bureau (Local news)

Transportation: Commute to work: 77.9% car, 3.7% public transportation, 11.6% walk, 3.2% work from home (2006-2010 5-year est.); Travel time to work: 38.6% less than 15 minutes, 33.7% 15 to 30 minutes, 17.3% 30 to 45 minutes, 5.2% 45 to 60 minutes, 5.2% 60 minutes or more (2006-2010 5-year est.)

Airports: Brandywine (general aviation)

Additional Information Contacts
Borough of West Chester . . . . (610) 692-7574
    http://www.west-chester.com
Greater West Chester Chamber of Commerce . . . . (610) 696-4046
    http://www.gwcc.org

WEST FALLOWFIELD (township).

Covers a land area of 18.149 square miles and a water area of 0.104 square miles. Located at 39.90° N. Lat; 75.96° W. Long.

Population: 2,342 (1990); 2,485 (2000); 2,566 (2010); Density: 141.4 persons per square mile (2010); Race: 93.0% White, 1.5% Black, 0.9% Asian, 0.0% American Indian/Alaska Native, 0.0% Native Hawaiian/Other Pacific Islander, 4.6% Other, 6.8% Hispanic of any race (2010); Average household size: 2.99 (2010); Median age: 38.8 (2010); Males per 100 females: 102.8 (2010); Marriage status: 22.8% never married, 65.4% now married, 5.5% widowed, 6.3% divorced (2006-2010 5-year est.); Foreign born: 1.4% (2006-2010 5-year est.); Ancestry (includes multiple ancestries): 34.0% German, 18.7% Irish, 11.4% English, 7.7% Italian, 5.3% Pennsylvania German (2006-2010 5-year est.).

Economy: Single-family building permits issued: 2 (2011); Multi-family building permits issued: 0 (2011); Employment by occupation: 12.8% management, 1.0% professional, 6.1% services, 16.5% sales, 6.7% farming, 14.1% construction, 5.6% production (2006-2010 5-year est.).

Income: Per capita income: $21,158 (2006-2010 5-year est.); Median household income: $55,128 (2006-2010 5-year est.); Average household income: $67,182 (2006-2010 5-year est.); Percent of households with income of $100,000 or more: 21.0% (2006-2010 5-year est.); Poverty rate: 25.8% (2006-2010 5-year est.).

Education: Percent of population age 25 and over with: High school diploma (including GED) or higher: 82.5% (2006-2010 5-year est.); Bachelor's degree or higher: 14.5% (2006-2010 5-year est.); Master's degree or higher: 4.0% (2006-2010 5-year est.).

Housing: Homeownership rate: 79.1% (2010); Median home value: $243,400 (2006-2010 5-year est.); Median contract rent: $829 per month (2006-2010 5-year est.); Median year structure built: 1972 (2006-2010 5-year est.).

Safety: Violent crime rate: 3.9 per 10,000 population; Property crime rate: 143.7 per 10,000 population (2011).

Transportation: Commute to work: 86.7% car, 0.5% public transportation, 9.0% walk, 3.7% work from home (2006-2010 5-year est.); Travel time to work: 31.3% less than 15 minutes, 29.5% 15 to 30 minutes, 22.2% 30 to

45 minutes, 9.3% 45 to 60 minutes, 7.7% 60 minutes or more (2006-2010 5-year est.)

Additional Information Contacts
Oxford Area Chamber of Commerce. . . . . (610) 932-0740
    http://www.oxfordpa.org

WEST GOSHEN (township).

Covers a land area of 11.852 square miles and a water area of 0.149 square miles. Located at 39.98° N. Lat; 75.59° W. Long. Elevation is 436 feet.

History: The lands of Goshen were purchased in 1681 from William Penn as part of the Welsh tract of Westtown. In 1788, the formation of the Borough of West Chester reduced the size of Goshen. Finally, in 1817, the Township divided into East and West Goshen Townships.

Population: 18,110 (1990); 20,495 (2000); 21,866 (2010); Density: 1,844.9 persons per square mile (2010); Race: 88.8% White, 3.7% Black, 4.7% Asian, 0.2% American Indian/Alaska Native, 0.0% Native Hawaiian/Other Pacific Islander, 2.6% Other, 3.7% Hispanic of any race (2010); Average household size: 2.70 (2010); Median age: 38.7 (2010); Males per 100 females: 95.8 (2010); Marriage status: 27.9% never married, 61.0% now married, 4.5% widowed, 6.6% divorced (2006-2010 5-year est.); Foreign born: 7.2% (2006-2010 5-year est.); Ancestry (includes multiple ancestries): 29.4% Irish, 24.1% German, 19.1% Italian, 16.3% English, 4.5% Polish (2006-2010 5-year est.).

Economy: Single-family building permits issued: 34 (2011); Multi-family building permits issued: 7 (2011); Employment by occupation: 19.1% management, 7.5% professional, 6.3% services, 16.4% sales, 3.7% farming, 7.8% construction, 3.7% production (2006-2010 5-year est.).

Income: Per capita income: $38,891 (2006-2010 5-year est.); Median household income: $89,233 (2006-2010 5-year est.); Average household income: $103,888 (2006-2010 5-year est.); Percent of households with income of $100,000 or more: 40.6% (2006-2010 5-year est.); Poverty rate: 6.1% (2006-2010 5-year est.).

Education: Percent of population age 25 and over with: High school diploma (including GED) or higher: 95.6% (2006-2010 5-year est.); Bachelor's degree or higher: 50.6% (2006-2010 5-year est.); Master's degree or higher: 18.2% (2006-2010 5-year est.).

Housing: Homeownership rate: 74.3% (2010); Median home value: $362,300 (2006-2010 5-year est.); Median contract rent: $1,025 per month (2006-2010 5-year est.); Median year structure built: 1974 (2006-2010 5-year est.).

Safety: Violent crime rate: 10.9 per 10,000 population; Property crime rate: 177.8 per 10,000 population (2011).

Transportation: Commute to work: 92.0% car, 1.2% public transportation, 1.0% walk, 5.2% work from home (2006-2010 5-year est.); Travel time to work: 34.4% less than 15 minutes, 27.8% 15 to 30 minutes, 20.5% 30 to 45 minutes, 10.5% 45 to 60 minutes, 6.8% 60 minutes or more (2006-2010 5-year est.)

Additional Information Contacts
Greater West Chester Chamber of Commerce . . . . (610) 696-4046
    http://www.gwcc.org
West Goshen Township . . . . (610) 696-5266
    http://www.wgoshen.org

WEST GROVE (borough).

Covers a land area of 0.651 square miles and a water area of <.001 square miles. Located at 39.82° N. Lat; 75.83° W. Long. Elevation is 394 feet.

Population: 2,128 (1990); 2,652 (2000); 2,854 (2010); Density: 4,384.6 persons per square mile (2010); Race: 75.5% White, 6.0% Black, 0.8% Asian, 0.8% American Indian/Alaska Native, 0.0% Native Hawaiian/Other Pacific Islander, 16.9% Other, 35.2% Hispanic of any race (2010); Average household size: 3.18 (2010); Median age: 31.5 (2010); Males per 100 females: 101.6 (2010); Marriage status: 30.1% never married, 52.1% now married, 5.8% widowed, 12.0% divorced (2006-2010 5-year est.); Foreign born: 20.0% (2006-2010 5-year est.); Ancestry (includes multiple ancestries): 17.8% German, 16.7% Irish, 9.8% Italian, 9.6% American, 4.8% Scotch-Irish (2006-2010 5-year est.).

Economy: Single-family building permits issued: 1 (2011); Multi-family building permits issued: 0 (2011); Employment by occupation: 8.7% management, 1.9% professional, 7.2% services, 14.1% sales, 6.3% farming, 12.9% construction, 5.8% production (2006-2010 5-year est.).

Income: Per capita income: $25,463 (2006-2010 5-year est.); Median household income: $63,988 (2006-2010 5-year est.); Average household income: $73,794 (2006-2010 5-year est.); Percent of households with income of $100,000 or more: 28.9% (2006-2010 5-year est.); Poverty rate: 10.2% (2006-2010 5-year est.).

Education: Percent of population age 25 and over with: High school diploma (including GED) or higher: 77.3% (2006-2010 5-year est.); Bachelor's degree or higher: 26.0% (2006-2010 5-year est.); Master's degree or higher: 6.4% (2006-2010 5-year est.).

School District(s)

Avon Grove CS (KG-12)
  2010-11 Enrollment: 1,463 . . . . (484) 667-5000
Avon Grove SD (KG-12)
  2010-11 Enrollment: 5,391 . . . . (610) 869-2441
Center for Arts & Technology (09-12)
  2010-11 Enrollment: 517 . . . . (484) 237-5110

Housing: Homeownership rate: 75.2% (2010); Median home value: $198,200 (2006-2010 5-year est.); Median contract rent: $919 per month (2006-2010 5-year est.); Median year structure built: 1965 (2006-2010 5-year est.).

Hospitals: Jennersville Regional Hospital (64 beds)

Transportation: Commute to work: 96.4% car, 0.9% public transportation, 0.9% walk, 1.1% work from home (2006-2010 5-year est.); Travel time to work: 35.7% less than 15 minutes, 27.4% 15 to 30 minutes, 17.2% 30 to 45 minutes, 9.5% 45 to 60 minutes, 10.2% 60 minutes or more (2006-2010 5-year est.)

Additional Information Contacts

Southern Chester County Chamber of Commerce . . . . (610) 444-0774
  http://www.scccc.com

WEST MARLBOROUGH (township). Covers a land area of 16.985 square miles and a water area of 0.093 square miles. Located at 39.89° N. Lat; 75.81° W. Long.

Population: 874 (1990); 859 (2000); 814 (2010); Density: 47.9 persons per square mile (2010); Race: 97.1% White, 0.7% Black, 0.6% Asian, 0.1% American Indian/Alaska Native, 0.0% Native Hawaiian/Other Pacific Islander, 1.5% Other, 8.7% Hispanic of any race (2010); Average household size: 2.37 (2010); Median age: 43.3 (2010); Males per 100 females: 96.1 (2010); Marriage status: 26.9% never married, 53.6% now married, 7.3% widowed, 12.1% divorced (2006-2010 5-year est.); Foreign born: 6.0% (2006-2010 5-year est.); Ancestry (includes multiple ancestries): 22.5% Irish, 20.5% English, 20.2% German, 12.0% American, 6.3% Scottish (2006-2010 5-year est.).

Economy: Single-family building permits issued: 1 (2011); Multi-family building permits issued: 0 (2011); Employment by occupation: 20.2% management, 1.3% professional, 16.1% services, 12.8% sales, 1.5% farming, 8.5% construction, 3.5% production (2006-2010 5-year est.).

Income: Per capita income: $58,094 (2006-2010 5-year est.); Median household income: $87,222 (2006-2010 5-year est.); Average household income: $144,448 (2006-2010 5-year est.); Percent of households with income of $100,000 or more: 40.3% (2006-2010 5-year est.); Poverty rate: 2.0% (2006-2010 5-year est.).

Education: Percent of population age 25 and over with: High school diploma (including GED) or higher: 89.8% (2006-2010 5-year est.); Bachelor's degree or higher: 40.7% (2006-2010 5-year est.); Master's degree or higher: 14.3% (2006-2010 5-year est.).

Housing: Homeownership rate: 52.8% (2010); Median home value: $338,500 (2006-2010 5-year est.); Median contract rent: $888 per month (2006-2010 5-year est.); Median year structure built: 1963 (2006-2010 5-year est.).

Transportation: Commute to work: 85.8% car, 1.7% public transportation, 4.1% walk, 7.6% work from home (2006-2010 5-year est.); Travel time to work: 26.2% less than 15 minutes, 37.6% 15 to 30 minutes, 21.0% 30 to 45 minutes, 9.5% 45 to 60 minutes, 5.7% 60 minutes or more (2006-2010 5-year est.)

WEST NANTMEAL (township). Covers a land area of 13.330 square miles and a water area of 0.212 square miles. Located at 40.12° N. Lat; 75.82° W. Long.

Population: 1,958 (1990); 2,031 (2000); 2,170 (2010); Density: 162.8 persons per square mile (2010); Race: 96.1% White, 1.1% Black, 0.6% Asian, 0.3% American Indian/Alaska Native, 0.1% Native Hawaiian/Other Pacific Islander, 1.8% Other, 2.3% Hispanic of any race (2010); Average household size: 2.64 (2010); Median age: 46.0 (2010); Males per 100 females: 103.6 (2010); Marriage status: 20.2% never married, 65.7% now married, 7.3% widowed, 6.8% divorced (2006-2010 5-year est.); Foreign born: 3.9% (2006-2010 5-year est.); Ancestry (includes multiple ancestries): 32.6% German, 18.4% Irish, 16.9% English, 10.5% Italian, 7.0% Polish (2006-2010 5-year est.).

Economy: Single-family building permits issued: 1 (2011); Multi-family building permits issued: 0 (2011); Employment by occupation: 17.5% management, 4.8% professional, 7.2% services, 18.6% sales, 4.0% farming, 13.7% construction, 9.9% production (2006-2010 5-year est.).

Income: Per capita income: $34,376 (2006-2010 5-year est.); Median household income: $67,375 (2006-2010 5-year est.); Average household income: $89,180 (2006-2010 5-year est.); Percent of households with income of $100,000 or more: 33.9% (2006-2010 5-year est.); Poverty rate: 3.4% (2006-2010 5-year est.).

Education: Percent of population age 25 and over with: High school diploma (including GED) or higher: 88.7% (2006-2010 5-year est.); Bachelor's degree or higher: 26.5% (2006-2010 5-year est.); Master's degree or higher: 8.3% (2006-2010 5-year est.).

Housing: Homeownership rate: 82.3% (2010); Median home value: $319,700 (2006-2010 5-year est.); Median contract rent: $606 per month (2006-2010 5-year est.); Median year structure built: 1978 (2006-2010 5-year est.).

Transportation: Commute to work: 90.0% car, 1.0% public transportation, 1.1% walk, 7.6% work from home (2006-2010 5-year est.); Travel time to work: 13.5% less than 15 minutes, 29.0% 15 to 30 minutes, 22.8% 30 to 45 minutes, 18.5% 45 to 60 minutes, 16.2% 60 minutes or more (2006-2010 5-year est.)

Additional Information Contacts

TriCounty Area Chamber of Commerce . . . . (610) 326-2900
  http://tricountyareachamber.com

WEST NOTTINGHAM (township). Covers a land area of 13.810 square miles and a water area of 0.171 square miles. Located at 39.73° N. Lat; 76.04° W. Long.

Population: 2,157 (1990); 2,634 (2000); 2,722 (2010); Density: 197.1 persons per square mile (2010); Race: 91.3% White, 2.0% Black, 0.3% Asian, 0.6% American Indian/Alaska Native, 0.0% Native Hawaiian/Other Pacific Islander, 5.8% Other, 8.3% Hispanic of any race (2010); Average household size: 2.72 (2010); Median age: 40.2 (2010); Males per 100 females: 105.4 (2010); Marriage status: 23.3% never married, 60.7% now married, 4.6% widowed, 11.4% divorced (2006-2010 5-year est.); Foreign born: 2.8% (2006-2010 5-year est.); Ancestry (includes multiple ancestries): 21.6% German, 19.2% Irish, 11.2% American, 8.5% Italian, 8.0% English (2006-2010 5-year est.).

Economy: Single-family building permits issued: 1 (2011); Multi-family building permits issued: 0 (2011); Employment by occupation: 7.6% management, 6.2% professional, 7.5% services, 16.4% sales, 0.6% farming, 18.4% construction, 10.6% production (2006-2010 5-year est.).

Income: Per capita income: $22,686 (2006-2010 5-year est.); Median household income: $58,466 (2006-2010 5-year est.); Average household income: $62,972 (2006-2010 5-year est.); Percent of households with income of $100,000 or more: 17.8% (2006-2010 5-year est.); Poverty rate: 8.0% (2006-2010 5-year est.).

Education: Percent of population age 25 and over with: High school diploma (including GED) or higher: 81.3% (2006-2010 5-year est.); Bachelor's degree or higher: 11.9% (2006-2010 5-year est.); Master's degree or higher: 3.6% (2006-2010 5-year est.).

Housing: Homeownership rate: 84.4% (2010); Median home value: $169,600 (2006-2010 5-year est.); Median contract rent: $827 per month (2006-2010 5-year est.); Median year structure built: 1990 (2006-2010 5-year est.).

Safety: Violent crime rate: 3.7 per 10,000 population; Property crime rate: 33.0 per 10,000 population (2011).

Transportation: Commute to work: 93.3% car, 0.0% public transportation, 1.7% walk, 4.7% work from home (2006-2010 5-year est.); Travel time to work: 23.8% less than 15 minutes, 21.0% 15 to 30 minutes, 23.7% 30 to 45 minutes, 15.3% 45 to 60 minutes, 16.3% 60 minutes or more (2006-2010 5-year est.)

Additional Information Contacts

Oxford Area Chamber of Commerce. . . . . (610) 932-0740
  http://www.oxfordpa.org

WEST PIKELAND (township). Covers a land area of 9.867 square miles and a water area of 0.093 square miles. Located at 40.09° N. Lat; 75.62° W. Long. Elevation is 377 feet.

History: West Pikeland Township was organized in 1849. The Historic Village of Yellow Springs is a significant part of the rich cultural and historic heritage of West Pikeland. General Washington and his staff stayed at Yellow Springs after the Battle at Brandywine.

Population: 2,323 (1990); 3,551 (2000); 4,024 (2010); Density: 407.8 persons per square mile (2010); Race: 95.2% White, 0.8% Black, 2.7% Asian, 0.1% American Indian/Alaska Native, 0.0% Native Hawaiian/Other Pacific Islander, 1.2% Other, 2.3% Hispanic of any race (2010); Average household size: 2.92 (2010); Median age: 43.8 (2010); Males per 100 females: 101.4 (2010); Marriage status: 20.2% never married, 70.0% now married, 2.0% widowed, 7.8% divorced (2006-2010 5-year est.); Foreign born: 4.8% (2006-2010 5-year est.); Ancestry (includes multiple ancestries): 27.0% Irish, 21.6% English, 18.8% Italian, 17.2% German, 10.3% Polish (2006-2010 5-year est.).

Economy: Single-family building permits issued: 4 (2011); Multi-family building permits issued: 0 (2011); Employment by occupation: 34.4% management, 2.5% professional, 3.0% services, 13.1% sales, 2.6% farming, 5.5% construction, 1.4% production (2006-2010 5-year est.).

Income: Per capita income: $63,117 (2006-2010 5-year est.); Median household income: $135,667 (2006-2010 5-year est.); Average household income: $184,726 (2006-2010 5-year est.); Percent of households with income of $100,000 or more: 64.3% (2006-2010 5-year est.); Poverty rate: 1.4% (2006-2010 5-year est.).

Education: Percent of population age 25 and over with: High school diploma (including GED) or higher: 98.2% (2006-2010 5-year est.); Bachelor's degree or higher: 68.5% (2006-2010 5-year est.); Master's degree or higher: 26.9% (2006-2010 5-year est.).

Housing: Homeownership rate: 93.6% (2010); Median home value: $547,500 (2006-2010 5-year est.); Median contract rent: n/a per month (2006-2010 5-year est.); Median year structure built: 1986 (2006-2010 5-year est.).

Transportation: Commute to work: 89.2% car, 1.2% public transportation, 1.2% walk, 6.9% work from home (2006-2010 5-year est.); Travel time to work: 21.5% less than 15 minutes, 44.1% 15 to 30 minutes, 18.7% 30 to 45 minutes, 10.2% 45 to 60 minutes, 5.6% 60 minutes or more (2006-2010 5-year est.)

Additional Information Contacts
Southern Chester County Chamber of Commerce . . . . (610) 444-0774
    http://www.scccc.com
West Pikeland Township . . . . (610) 827-7660
    http://www.westpikeland.com

WEST SADSBURY (township). Covers a land area of 10.612 square miles and a water area of 0.040 square miles. Located at 39.97° N. Lat; 75.96° W. Long.

Population: 2,160 (1990); 2,444 (2000); 2,444 (2010); Density: 230.3 persons per square mile (2010); Race: 91.9% White, 5.0% Black, 0.4% Asian, 0.1% American Indian/Alaska Native, 0.0% Native Hawaiian/Other Pacific Islander, 2.6% Other, 2.4% Hispanic of any race (2010); Average household size: 3.13 (2010); Median age: 36.8 (2010); Males per 100 females: 96.9 (2010); Marriage status: 28.0% never married, 61.2% now married, 4.5% widowed, 6.4% divorced (2006-2010 5-year est.); Foreign born: 1.4% (2006-2010 5-year est.); Ancestry (includes multiple ancestries): 36.6% German, 31.8% Irish, 7.8% English, 7.4% American, 7.2% Italian (2006-2010 5-year est.).

Economy: Single-family building permits issued: 2 (2011); Multi-family building permits issued: 0 (2011); Employment by occupation: 12.5% management, 1.2% professional, 5.3% services, 19.6% sales, 2.4% farming, 17.3% construction, 8.6% production (2006-2010 5-year est.).

Income: Per capita income: $25,582 (2006-2010 5-year est.); Median household income: $72,563 (2006-2010 5-year est.); Average household income: $80,619 (2006-2010 5-year est.); Percent of households with income of $100,000 or more: 23.2% (2006-2010 5-year est.); Poverty rate: 2.1% (2006-2010 5-year est.).

Education: Percent of population age 25 and over with: High school diploma (including GED) or higher: 85.3% (2006-2010 5-year est.); Bachelor's degree or higher: 23.0% (2006-2010 5-year est.); Master's degree or higher: 6.3% (2006-2010 5-year est.).

Housing: Homeownership rate: 79.8% (2010); Median home value: $241,900 (2006-2010 5-year est.); Median contract rent: $619 per month (2006-2010 5-year est.); Median year structure built: 1976 (2006-2010 5-year est.).

Safety: Violent crime rate: 4.1 per 10,000 population; Property crime rate: 330.3 per 10,000 population (2011).

Transportation: Commute to work: 94.8% car, 0.0% public transportation, 0.8% walk, 4.0% work from home (2006-2010 5-year est.); Travel time to work: 28.8% less than 15 minutes, 27.9% 15 to 30 minutes, 25.5% 30 to 45 minutes, 7.3% 45 to 60 minutes, 10.5% 60 minutes or more (2006-2010 5-year est.)

Additional Information Contacts
Western Chester County Chamber of Commerce . . . . (610) 384-9550
    http://www.westernchestercounty.com

WEST VINCENT (township). Covers a land area of 17.677 square miles and a water area of 0.164 square miles. Located at 40.13° N. Lat; 75.65° W. Long.

History: An interesting feature of West Vincent Township is its "missing quarter". In 1715, founder Sir Mathias Vincent and others failed to pay taxes to William Penn, who took them to court. In the end, 467 acres (1.89 sq. km.) in southern West Vincent Township were seized and given to Upper Uwlchlan Township.

Population: 2,262 (1990); 3,170 (2000); 4,567 (2010); Density: 258.4 persons per square mile (2010); Race: 95.3% White, 1.1% Black, 2.1% Asian, 0.1% American Indian/Alaska Native, 0.0% Native Hawaiian/Other Pacific Islander, 1.4% Other, 1.9% Hispanic of any race (2010); Average household size: 2.71 (2010); Median age: 43.2 (2010); Males per 100 females: 100.3 (2010); Marriage status: 26.1% never married, 64.5% now married, 2.0% widowed, 7.4% divorced (2006-2010 5-year est.); Foreign born: 2.9% (2006-2010 5-year est.); Ancestry (includes multiple ancestries): 33.0% German, 20.7% Irish, 16.6% English, 11.0% Italian, 6.3% Scottish (2006-2010 5-year est.).

Economy: Single-family building permits issued: 39 (2011); Multi-family building permits issued: 0 (2011); Employment by occupation: 21.7% management, 3.9% professional, 4.5% services, 14.2% sales, 1.9% farming, 7.7% construction, 4.1% production (2006-2010 5-year est.).

Income: Per capita income: $57,422 (2006-2010 5-year est.); Median household income: $118,375 (2006-2010 5-year est.); Average household income: $170,329 (2006-2010 5-year est.); Percent of households with income of $100,000 or more: 61.8% (2006-2010 5-year est.); Poverty rate: 9.7% (2006-2010 5-year est.).

Taxes: Total city taxes per capita: $674 (2009); City property taxes per capita: $365 (2009).

Education: Percent of population age 25 and over with: High school diploma (including GED) or higher: 94.6% (2006-2010 5-year est.); Bachelor's degree or higher: 61.6% (2006-2010 5-year est.); Master's degree or higher: 21.6% (2006-2010 5-year est.).

Housing: Homeownership rate: 81.4% (2010); Median home value: $529,500 (2006-2010 5-year est.); Median contract rent: $1,234 per month (2006-2010 5-year est.); Median year structure built: 1984 (2006-2010 5-year est.).

Safety: Violent crime rate: 2.2 per 10,000 population; Property crime rate: 65.5 per 10,000 population (2011).

Transportation: Commute to work: 78.8% car, 3.2% public transportation, 0.6% walk, 15.0% work from home (2006-2010 5-year est.); Travel time to work: 13.4% less than 15 minutes, 35.8% 15 to 30 minutes, 26.8% 30 to 45 minutes, 8.9% 45 to 60 minutes, 15.1% 60 minutes or more (2006-2010 5-year est.)

Additional Information Contacts
TriCounty Area Chamber of Commerce . . . . (610) 326-2900
    http://tricountyareachamber.com
West Vincent Township . . . . (610) 458-1601
    http://www.westvincenttwp.org

WEST WHITELAND (township). Covers a land area of 12.835 square miles and a water area of 0.089 square miles. Located at 40.02° N. Lat; 75.62° W. Long.

History: West Whiteland Township was incorporated in 1765 and exists as a Township of the Second Class under Pennsylvania law.

Population: 12,403 (1990); 16,499 (2000); 18,274 (2010); Density: 1,423.8 persons per square mile (2010); Race: 80.5% White, 5.1% Black, 11.4% Asian, 0.2% American Indian/Alaska Native, 0.0% Native Hawaiian/Other Pacific Islander, 2.8% Other, 3.0% Hispanic of any race (2010); Average household size: 2.47 (2010); Median age: 38.1 (2010); Males per 100 females: 96.9 (2010); Marriage status: 25.5% never married, 61.6% now married, 3.8% widowed, 9.1% divorced (2006-2010 5-year est.); Foreign born: 13.3% (2006-2010 5-year est.); Ancestry (includes multiple ancestries): 25.5% German, 24.3% Irish, 18.5% Italian, 13.1% English, 5.2% Polish (2006-2010 5-year est.).

Economy: Single-family building permits issued: 3 (2011); Multi-family building permits issued: 0 (2011); Employment by occupation: 20.0% management, 12.2% professional, 5.3% services, 14.4% sales, 3.7% farming, 4.1% construction, 3.1% production (2006-2010 5-year est.).

Income: Per capita income: $45,360 (2006-2010 5-year est.); Median household income: $93,542 (2006-2010 5-year est.); Average household

income: $110,375 (2006-2010 5-year est.); Percent of households with income of $100,000 or more: 46.1% (2006-2010 5-year est.); Poverty rate: 2.7% (2006-2010 5-year est.).

Education: Percent of population age 25 and over with: High school diploma (including GED) or higher: 96.9% (2006-2010 5-year est.); Bachelor's degree or higher: 58.6% (2006-2010 5-year est.); Master's degree or higher: 21.3% (2006-2010 5-year est.).

Housing: Homeownership rate: 71.9% (2010); Median home value: $333,100 (2006-2010 5-year est.); Median contract rent: $1,136 per month (2006-2010 5-year est.); Median year structure built: 1986 (2006-2010 5-year est.).

Safety: Violent crime rate: 5.5 per 10,000 population; Property crime rate: 265.7 per 10,000 population (2011).

Transportation: Commute to work: 90.0% car, 4.2% public transportation, 0.2% walk, 4.3% work from home (2006-2010 5-year est.); Travel time to work: 28.0% less than 15 minutes, 35.4% 15 to 30 minutes, 18.8% 30 to 45 minutes, 9.2% 45 to 60 minutes, 8.6% 60 minutes or more (2006-2010 5-year est.)

Additional Information Contacts

Greater West Chester Chamber of Commerce . . . . (610) 696-4046
    http://www.gwcc.org
West Whiteland Township. . . . . (610) 363-9525
    http://www.westwhiteland.org

WESTTOWN (township).
Covers a land area of 8.664 square miles and a water area of 0.074 square miles. Located at 39.94° N. Lat; 75.56° W. Long. Elevation is 259 feet.

History: Westtown was established in 1685 and is the second township in Chester County. Westtown was established three years after the formation of Chester County by William Penn. The first settlers were English Quakers, who came to Westtown to establish dairy farms and orchards.

Population: 9,840 (1990); 10,352 (2000); 10,827 (2010); Density: 1,249.6 persons per square mile (2010); Race: 91.0% White, 3.8% Black, 3.2% Asian, 0.1% American Indian/Alaska Native, 0.1% Native Hawaiian/Other Pacific Islander, 1.8% Other, 2.4% Hispanic of any race (2010); Average household size: 2.75 (2010); Median age: 40.5 (2010); Males per 100 females: 93.8 (2010); Marriage status: 22.4% never married, 67.2% now married, 3.6% widowed, 6.8% divorced (2006-2010 5-year est.); Foreign born: 6.2% (2006-2010 5-year est.); Ancestry (includes multiple ancestries): 35.3% Irish, 22.0% German, 21.7% Italian, 15.2% English, 5.6% American (2006-2010 5-year est.).

Economy: Single-family building permits issued: 0 (2011); Multi-family building permits issued: 0 (2011); Employment by occupation: 21.2% management, 7.4% professional, 3.8% services, 17.1% sales, 1.8% farming, 6.2% construction, 3.5% production (2006-2010 5-year est.).

Income: Per capita income: $47,434 (2006-2010 5-year est.); Median household income: $107,524 (2006-2010 5-year est.); Average household income: $128,545 (2006-2010 5-year est.); Percent of households with income of $100,000 or more: 54.9% (2006-2010 5-year est.); Poverty rate: 2.3% (2006-2010 5-year est.).

Taxes: Total city taxes per capita: $393 (2009); City property taxes per capita: $138 (2009).

Education: Percent of population age 25 and over with: High school diploma (including GED) or higher: 97.8% (2006-2010 5-year est.); Bachelor's degree or higher: 55.8% (2006-2010 5-year est.); Master's degree or higher: 24.6% (2006-2010 5-year est.).

Housing: Homeownership rate: 81.0% (2010); Median home value: $401,400 (2006-2010 5-year est.); Median contract rent: $1,237 per month (2006-2010 5-year est.); Median year structure built: 1979 (2006-2010 5-year est.).

Transportation: Commute to work: 92.2% car, 1.9% public transportation, 0.5% walk, 5.0% work from home (2006-2010 5-year est.); Travel time to work: 20.7% less than 15 minutes, 36.3% 15 to 30 minutes, 23.7% 30 to 45 minutes, 7.8% 45 to 60 minutes, 11.4% 60 minutes or more (2006-2010 5-year est.)

Additional Information Contacts

Greater West Chester Chamber of Commerce . . . . (610) 696-4046
    http://www.gwcc.org
Westtown Township . . . . (610) 692-1930
    http://www.westtownpa.org

WESTWOOD (CDP).
Covers a land area of 0.456 square miles and a water area of 0.003 square miles. Located at 39.97° N. Lat; 75.86° W. Long. Elevation is 361 feet.

Population: n/a (1990); n/a (2000); 950 (2010); Density: 2,082.4 persons per square mile (2010); Race: 76.6% White, 16.5% Black, 0.6% Asian, 0.2% American Indian/Alaska Native, 0.3% Native Hawaiian/Other Pacific Islander, 5.8% Other, 9.2% Hispanic of any race (2010); Average household size: 2.58 (2010); Median age: 36.3 (2010); Males per 100 females: 95.1 (2010); Marriage status: 17.0% never married, 48.5% now married, 12.0% widowed, 22.5% divorced (2006-2010 5-year est.); Foreign born: 0.0% (2006-2010 5-year est.); Ancestry (includes multiple ancestries): 44.3% German, 16.3% English, 12.8% Dutch, 12.5% Italian, 10.3% Irish (2006-2010 5-year est.).

Economy: Employment by occupation: 0.0% management, 6.2% professional, 20.0% services, 7.1% sales, 0.0% farming, 15.2% construction, 23.8% production (2006-2010 5-year est.).

Income: Per capita income: $22,282 (2006-2010 5-year est.); Median household income: $39,755 (2006-2010 5-year est.); Average household income: $46,155 (2006-2010 5-year est.); Percent of households with income of $100,000 or more: 6.8% (2006-2010 5-year est.); Poverty rate: 7.2% (2006-2010 5-year est.).

Education: Percent of population age 25 and over with: High school diploma (including GED) or higher: 71.0% (2006-2010 5-year est.); Bachelor's degree or higher: 15.2% (2006-2010 5-year est.); Master's degree or higher: 4.5% (2006-2010 5-year est.).

Housing: Homeownership rate: 80.7% (2010); Median home value: $118,500 (2006-2010 5-year est.); Median contract rent: $613 per month (2006-2010 5-year est.); Median year structure built: 1950 (2006-2010 5-year est.).

Transportation: Commute to work: 87.1% car, 0.0% public transportation, 7.1% walk, 0.0% work from home (2006-2010 5-year est.); Travel time to work: 29.0% less than 15 minutes, 25.7% 15 to 30 minutes, 22.4% 30 to 45 minutes, 6.2% 45 to 60 minutes, 16.7% 60 minutes or more (2006-2010 5-year est.)

WILLISTOWN (township).
Covers a land area of 18.109 square miles and a water area of 0.161 square miles. Located at 40.00° N. Lat; 75.50° W. Long. Elevation is 351 feet.

History: Originally settled by Lenni Lenape Indians, Willistown Township was part of the 50,000 acre Welsh Tract surveyed for William Penn in 1684. The Holmes Map of 1681 is the first reference to Willistown, calling it "Willeston". In 1704, Willistown was organized as a township.

Population: 9,378 (1990); 10,011 (2000); 10,497 (2010); Density: 579.7 persons per square mile (2010); Race: 93.3% White, 2.1% Black, 3.6% Asian, 0.0% American Indian/Alaska Native, 0.0% Native Hawaiian/Other Pacific Islander, 1.0% Other, 1.5% Hispanic of any race (2010); Average household size: 2.43 (2010); Median age: 48.2 (2010); Males per 100 females: 90.5 (2010); Marriage status: 23.8% never married, 63.4% now married, 5.4% widowed, 7.4% divorced (2006-2010 5-year est.); Foreign born: 6.4% (2006-2010 5-year est.); Ancestry (includes multiple ancestries): 30.1% Irish, 25.2% German, 19.2% English, 18.3% Italian, 4.3% American (2006-2010 5-year est.).

Economy: Single-family building permits issued: 7 (2011); Multi-family building permits issued: 4 (2011); Employment by occupation: 23.2% management, 8.0% professional, 4.8% services, 14.1% sales, 2.7% farming, 4.1% construction, 1.8% production (2006-2010 5-year est.).

Income: Per capita income: $59,899 (2006-2010 5-year est.); Median household income: $100,905 (2006-2010 5-year est.); Average household income: $150,494 (2006-2010 5-year est.); Percent of households with income of $100,000 or more: 50.5% (2006-2010 5-year est.); Poverty rate: 4.3% (2006-2010 5-year est.).

Taxes: Total city taxes per capita: $657 (2009); City property taxes per capita: $36 (2009).

Education: Percent of population age 25 and over with: High school diploma (including GED) or higher: 96.0% (2006-2010 5-year est.); Bachelor's degree or higher: 60.5% (2006-2010 5-year est.); Master's degree or higher: 30.0% (2006-2010 5-year est.).

Housing: Homeownership rate: 87.9% (2010); Median home value: $391,300 (2006-2010 5-year est.); Median contract rent: $1,309 per month (2006-2010 5-year est.); Median year structure built: 1969 (2006-2010 5-year est.).

Safety: Violent crime rate: 8.5 per 10,000 population; Property crime rate: 84.5 per 10,000 population (2011).

Transportation: Commute to work: 87.3% car, 6.2% public transportation, 0.8% walk, 5.1% work from home (2006-2010 5-year est.); Travel time to

work: 24.1% less than 15 minutes, 37.6% 15 to 30 minutes, 20.5% 30 to 45 minutes, 10.1% 45 to 60 minutes, 7.7% 60 minutes or more (2006-2010 5-year est.)

Additional Information Contacts
Chester County Chamber of Business and Industry . . . . . . (610) 725-9100
  http://www.cccbi.org
Willistown Township . . . . (610) 647-5300
  http://www.willistown.pa.us

Clarion County

Located in west central Pennsylvania; plateau area, bounded on the southwest by the Allegheny River, and on the south by Redbank Creek. Covers a land area of 600.834 square miles, a water area of 9.010 square miles, and is located in the Eastern Time Zone at 41.20° N. Lat., 79.42° W. Long. The county was founded in 1839. County seat is Clarion.

Weather Station: Clarion 3 SW — Elevation: 1,040 feet

	Jan	Feb	Mar	Apr	May	Jun	Jul	Aug	Sep	Oct	Nov	Dec
High	34	37	47	61	72	79	83	82	74	62	49	37
Low	17	17	24	34	44	53	57	56	50	38	31	22
Precip	3.0	2.5	3.2	3.7	4.2	5.0	5.0	4.5	4.5	3.3	4.0	3.4
Snow	10.2	7.5	5.1	0.8	0.0	0.0	0.0	0.0	0.0	tr	1.5	7.3

High and Low temperatures in degrees Fahrenheit; Precipitation and Snow in inches

Population: 41,699 (1990); 41,765 (2000); 39,988 (2010); Race: 97.2% White, 1.2% Black, 0.5% Asian, 0.1% American Indian/Alaska Native, 0.0% Native Hawaiian/Other Pacific Islander, 1.0% Other, 0.6% Hispanic of any race (2010); Density: 66.6 persons per square mile (2010); Average household size: 2.37 (2010); Median age: 39.4 (2010); Males per 100 females: 93.9 (2010).
Religion: Six largest groups: 22.7% Catholicism, 12.7% Methodist/Pietist, 4.7% Presbyterian-Reformed, 3.9% Non-Denominational, 3.7% Lutheran, 3.6% Baptist (2010)
Economy: Unemployment rate: 9.0% (August 2012); Total civilian labor force: 19,515 (August 2012); Leading industries: 22.7% health care and social assistance; 17.2% retail trade; 15.3% manufacturing (2010); Farms: 872 totaling 132,140 acres (2007); Companies that employ 500 or more persons: 0 (2010); Companies that employ 100 to 499 persons: 14 (2010); Companies that employ less than 100 persons: 946 (2010); Black-owned businesses: n/a (2007); Hispanic-owned businesses: n/a (2007); Asian-owned businesses: n/a (2007); Women-owned businesses: n/a (2007); Retail sales per capita: $12,011 (2010). Single-family building permits issued: 29 (2011); Multi-family building permits issued: 15 (2011).
Income: Per capita income: $20,259 (2006-2010 5-year est.); Median household income: $40,028 (2006-2010 5-year est.); Average household income: $50,290 (2006-2010 5-year est.); Percent of households with income of $100,000 or more: 8.9% (2006-2010 5-year est.); Poverty rate: 15.8% (2006-2010 5-year est.); Bankruptcy rate: 1.89% (2011).
Education: Percent of population age 25 and over with: High school diploma (including GED) or higher: 87.2% (2006-2010 5-year est.); Bachelor's degree or higher: 17.2% (2006-2010 5-year est.); Master's degree or higher: 6.3% (2006-2010 5-year est.).
Housing: Homeownership rate: 68.3% (2010); Median home value: $97,800 (2006-2010 5-year est.); Median contract rent: $396 per month (2006-2010 5-year est.); Median year structure built: 1963 (2006-2010 5-year est.)
Health: Birth rate: 100.2 per 10,000 population (2011); Death rate: 105.2 per 10,000 population (2011); Age-adjusted cancer mortality rate: 186.5 deaths per 100,000 population (2009); Number of physicians: 14.0 per 10,000 population (2010); Hospital beds: 38.7 per 10,000 population (2008); Hospital admissions: 1,370.2 per 10,000 population (2008).
Elections: 2012 Presidential election results: 31.2% Obama, 66.9% Romney

Additional Information Contacts
Clarion County Government . . . . (814) 226-4000
  http://www.co.clarion.pa.us

Clarion County Communities

ASHLAND (township). Covers a land area of 22.433 square miles and a water area of 0.090 square miles. Located at 41.28° N. Lat; 79.56° W. Long.
Population: 1,019 (1990); 1,081 (2000); 1,114 (2010); Density: 49.7 persons per square mile (2010); Race: 98.8% White, 0.2% Black, 0.1%

Asian, 0.3% American Indian/Alaska Native, 0.0% Native Hawaiian/Other Pacific Islander, 0.6% Other, 0.1% Hispanic of any race (2010); Average household size: 2.66 (2010); Median age: 40.1 (2010); Males per 100 females: 105.5 (2010); Marriage status: 22.4% never married, 69.5% now married, 1.5% widowed, 6.6% divorced (2006-2010 5-year est.); Foreign born: 0.3% (2006-2010 5-year est.); Ancestry (includes multiple ancestries): 46.0% German, 13.9% Irish, 11.2% American, 5.6% English, 5.1% Scotch-Irish (2006-2010 5-year est.).
Economy: Single-family building permits issued: 2 (2011); Multi-family building permits issued: 0 (2011); Employment by occupation: 6.3% management, 0.7% professional, 12.3% services, 15.7% sales, 6.1% farming, 13.3% construction, 5.4% production (2006-2010 5-year est.).
Income: Per capita income: $17,461 (2006-2010 5-year est.); Median household income: $43,073 (2006-2010 5-year est.); Average household income: $48,837 (2006-2010 5-year est.); Percent of households with income of $100,000 or more: 6.1% (2006-2010 5-year est.); Poverty rate: 9.9% (2006-2010 5-year est.).
Education: Percent of population age 25 and over with: High school diploma (including GED) or higher: 83.4% (2006-2010 5-year est.); Bachelor's degree or higher: 17.1% (2006-2010 5-year est.); Master's degree or higher: 5.8% (2006-2010 5-year est.).
Housing: Homeownership rate: 83.9% (2010); Median home value: $109,500 (2006-2010 5-year est.); Median contract rent: $340 per month (2006-2010 5-year est.); Median year structure built: 1970 (2006-2010 5-year est.).
Transportation: Commute to work: 85.7% car, 0.0% public transportation, 3.5% walk, 5.8% work from home (2006-2010 5-year est.); Travel time to work: 29.5% less than 15 minutes, 53.2% 15 to 30 minutes, 12.8% 30 to 45 minutes, 2.2% 45 to 60 minutes, 2.2% 60 minutes or more (2006-2010 5-year est.)

Additional Information Contacts
Clarion Chamber of Business & Industry . . . . (814) 226-9161
  http://www.clarionpa.com

BEAVER (township). Covers a land area of 33.421 square miles and a water area of 0.316 square miles. Located at 41.20° N. Lat; 79.52° W. Long.
Population: 1,840 (1990); 1,753 (2000); 1,761 (2010); Density: 52.7 persons per square mile (2010); Race: 98.4% White, 0.7% Black, 0.1% Asian, 0.1% American Indian/Alaska Native, 0.0% Native Hawaiian/Other Pacific Islander, 0.7% Other, 0.1% Hispanic of any race (2010); Average household size: 2.48 (2010); Median age: 42.8 (2010); Males per 100 females: 102.9 (2010); Marriage status: 22.0% never married, 64.8% now married, 5.3% widowed, 7.9% divorced (2006-2010 5-year est.); Foreign born: 0.2% (2006-2010 5-year est.); Ancestry (includes multiple ancestries): 50.1% German, 16.2% Irish, 5.6% English, 4.5% Dutch, 4.3% Scotch-Irish (2006-2010 5-year est.).
Economy: Single-family building permits issued: 1 (2011); Multi-family building permits issued: 0 (2011); Employment by occupation: 5.2% management, 1.2% professional, 16.1% services, 21.2% sales, 1.2% farming, 14.1% construction, 8.2% production (2006-2010 5-year est.).
Income: Per capita income: $18,722 (2006-2010 5-year est.); Median household income: $38,618 (2006-2010 5-year est.); Average household income: $46,862 (2006-2010 5-year est.); Percent of households with income of $100,000 or more: 9.4% (2006-2010 5-year est.); Poverty rate: 13.3% (2006-2010 5-year est.).
Education: Percent of population age 25 and over with: High school diploma (including GED) or higher: 86.8% (2006-2010 5-year est.); Bachelor's degree or higher: 10.7% (2006-2010 5-year est.); Master's degree or higher: 3.4% (2006-2010 5-year est.).
Housing: Homeownership rate: 79.9% (2010); Median home value: $98,700 (2006-2010 5-year est.); Median contract rent: $331 per month (2006-2010 5-year est.); Median year structure built: 1967 (2006-2010 5-year est.).
Transportation: Commute to work: 90.5% car, 0.0% public transportation, 2.2% walk, 6.3% work from home (2006-2010 5-year est.); Travel time to work: 34.5% less than 15 minutes, 41.9% 15 to 30 minutes, 14.4% 30 to 45 minutes, 7.6% 45 to 60 minutes, 1.6% 60 minutes or more (2006-2010 5-year est.)

Additional Information Contacts
Clarion Chamber of Business & Industry . . . . (814) 226-9161
  http://www.clarionpa.com

BRADY (township). Covers a land area of 1.653 square miles and a water area of 0.596 square miles. Located at 40.98° N. Lat; 79.60° W. Long.

History: Laid out 1866.

Population: 78 (1990); 62 (2000); 55 (2010); Density: 33.3 persons per square mile (2010); Race: 98.2% White, 1.8% Black, 0.0% Asian, 0.0% American Indian/Alaska Native, 0.0% Native Hawaiian/Other Pacific Islander, 0.0% Other, 0.0% Hispanic of any race (2010); Average household size: 2.39 (2010); Median age: 39.9 (2010); Males per 100 females: 120.0 (2010); Marriage status: 14.7% never married, 75.0% now married, 10.3% widowed, 0.0% divorced (2006-2010 5-year est.); Foreign born: 0.0% (2006-2010 5-year est.); Ancestry (includes multiple ancestries): 39.5% Italian, 16.3% German, 14.0% Irish, 10.5% English, 5.8% American (2006-2010 5-year est.).

Economy: Single-family building permits issued: 0 (2011); Multi-family building permits issued: 0 (2011); Employment by occupation: 5.4% management, 0.0% professional, 5.4% services, 24.3% sales, 0.0% farming, 29.7% construction, 0.0% production (2006-2010 5-year est.).

Income: Per capita income: $17,529 (2006-2010 5-year est.); Median household income: $38,750 (2006-2010 5-year est.); Average household income: $45,347 (2006-2010 5-year est.); Percent of households with income of $100,000 or more: n/a (2006-2010 5-year est.); Poverty rate: 9.3% (2006-2010 5-year est.).

Education: Percent of population age 25 and over with: High school diploma (including GED) or higher: 96.8% (2006-2010 5-year est.); Bachelor's degree or higher: 17.7% (2006-2010 5-year est.); Master's degree or higher: 0.0% (2006-2010 5-year est.).

Housing: Homeownership rate: 91.3% (2010); Median home value: $55,800 (2006-2010 5-year est.); Median contract rent: n/a per month (2006-2010 5-year est.); Median year structure built: 1959 (2006-2010 5-year est.).

Transportation: Commute to work: 100.0% car, 0.0% public transportation, 0.0% walk, 0.0% work from home (2006-2010 5-year est.); Travel time to work: 21.6% less than 15 minutes, 35.1% 15 to 30 minutes, 32.4% 30 to 45 minutes, 0.0% 45 to 60 minutes, 10.8% 60 minutes or more (2006-2010 5-year est.)

CALLENSBURG (borough). Covers a land area of 0.145 square miles and a water area of <.001 square miles. Located at 41.13° N. Lat; 79.56° W. Long. Elevation is 1,115 feet.

Population: 205 (1990); 224 (2000); 207 (2010); Density: 1,429.9 persons per square mile (2010); Race: 99.5% White, 0.0% Black, 0.0% Asian, 0.5% American Indian/Alaska Native, 0.0% Native Hawaiian/Other Pacific Islander, 0.0% Other, 1.0% Hispanic of any race (2010); Average household size: 2.27 (2010); Median age: 43.8 (2010); Males per 100 females: 81.6 (2010); Marriage status: 47.7% never married, 30.7% now married, 17.0% widowed, 4.5% divorced (2006-2010 5-year est.); Foreign born: 0.0% (2006-2010 5-year est.); Ancestry (includes multiple ancestries): 21.9% Polish, 18.8% Irish, 7.0% German, 5.5% English, 5.5% Italian (2006-2010 5-year est.).

Economy: Single-family building permits issued: 0 (2011); Multi-family building permits issued: 0 (2011); Employment by occupation: 3.8% management, 0.0% professional, 13.5% services, 23.1% sales, 0.0% farming, 0.0% construction, 0.0% production (2006-2010 5-year est.).

Income: Per capita income: $9,698 (2006-2010 5-year est.); Median household income: $21,944 (2006-2010 5-year est.); Average household income: $25,171 (2006-2010 5-year est.); Percent of households with income of $100,000 or more: n/a (2006-2010 5-year est.); Poverty rate: 17.2% (2006-2010 5-year est.).

Education: Percent of population age 25 and over with: High school diploma (including GED) or higher: 79.4% (2006-2010 5-year est.); Bachelor's degree or higher: 0.0% (2006-2010 5-year est.); Master's degree or higher: 0.0% (2006-2010 5-year est.).

Housing: Homeownership rate: 70.4% (2010); Median home value: $94,200 (2006-2010 5-year est.); Median contract rent: $404 per month (2006-2010 5-year est.); Median year structure built: before 1940 (2006-2010 5-year est.).

Transportation: Commute to work: 100.0% car, 0.0% public transportation, 0.0% walk, 0.0% work from home (2006-2010 5-year est.); Travel time to work: 40.4% less than 15 minutes, 25.0% 15 to 30 minutes, 23.1% 30 to 45 minutes, 11.5% 45 to 60 minutes, 0.0% 60 minutes or more (2006-2010 5-year est.)

CLARION (borough). County seat. Covers a land area of 1.574 square miles and a water area of 0.044 square miles. Located at 41.21° N. Lat; 79.38° W. Long. Elevation is 1,516 feet.

History: Clarion was laid out on a plateau along the Clarion River in 1840, after the site had been chosen as the Clarion County seat because of its central location on the Bellefonte-Meanville Turnpike.

Population: 6,457 (1990); 6,185 (2000); 5,276 (2010); Density: 3,351.1 persons per square mile (2010); Race: 91.0% White, 5.0% Black, 1.9% Asian, 0.1% American Indian/Alaska Native, 0.0% Native Hawaiian/Other Pacific Islander, 2.0% Other, 1.0% Hispanic of any race (2010); Average household size: 2.11 (2010); Median age: 22.0 (2010); Males per 100 females: 77.8 (2010); Marriage status: 69.3% never married, 19.3% now married, 5.1% widowed, 6.2% divorced (2006-2010 5-year est.); Foreign born: 3.1% (2006-2010 5-year est.); Ancestry (includes multiple ancestries): 45.5% German, 24.6% Irish, 13.8% Italian, 9.0% Polish, 8.2% English (2006-2010 5-year est.).

Economy: Single-family building permits issued: 0 (2011); Multi-family building permits issued: 15 (2011); Employment by occupation: 2.7% management, 3.5% professional, 19.8% services, 23.2% sales, 2.2% farming, 5.5% construction, 2.5% production (2006-2010 5-year est.).

Income: Per capita income: $13,465 (2006-2010 5-year est.); Median household income: $23,750 (2006-2010 5-year est.); Average household income: $37,921 (2006-2010 5-year est.); Percent of households with income of $100,000 or more: 9.6% (2006-2010 5-year est.); Poverty rate: 35.1% (2006-2010 5-year est.).

Education: Percent of population age 25 and over with: High school diploma (including GED) or higher: 92.3% (2006-2010 5-year est.); Bachelor's degree or higher: 32.1% (2006-2010 5-year est.); Master's degree or higher: 15.2% (2006-2010 5-year est.).

School District(s)

Clarion Area SD (PK-12)

    2010-11 Enrollment: 814 . . . . (814) 226-6110

Four-year College(s)

Clarion University of Pennsylvania (Public)

    Fall 2010 Enrollment: 6,155 . . . . (814) 393-2000

    2011-12 Tuition: In-state $8,340; Out-of-state $14,680

Housing: Homeownership rate: 34.6% (2010); Median home value: $127,800 (2006-2010 5-year est.); Median contract rent: $425 per month (2006-2010 5-year est.); Median year structure built: 1962 (2006-2010 5-year est.).

Hospitals: Clarion Hospital (96 beds); Clarion Psychiatric Center (52 beds)

Safety: Violent crime rate: 5.7 per 10,000 population; Property crime rate: 196.5 per 10,000 population (2011).

Newspapers: The Clarion News (Local news; Circulation 7,000); The Midweek (Local news; Circulation 16,456)

Transportation: Commute to work: 72.9% car, 1.4% public transportation, 21.0% walk, 4.8% work from home (2006-2010 5-year est.); Travel time to work: 71.6% less than 15 minutes, 14.7% 15 to 30 minutes, 8.6% 30 to 45 minutes, 4.1% 45 to 60 minutes, 1.0% 60 minutes or more (2006-2010 5-year est.)

Airports: Clarion County (general aviation)

Additional Information Contacts

Borough of Clarion . . . . (814) 226-7707

    http://www.clarionboro.org

Clarion Chamber of Business & Industry . . . . (814) 226-9161

    http://www.clarionpa.com

CLARION (township). Covers a land area of 31.261 square miles and a water area of 0.273 square miles. Located at 41.19° N. Lat; 79.30° W. Long. Elevation is 1,516 feet.

History: Seat of Clarion University of Pa. Laid out 1840, incorporated 1841.

Population: 3,306 (1990); 3,273 (2000); 4,116 (2010); Density: 131.7 persons per square mile (2010); Race: 95.1% White, 2.8% Black, 0.5% Asian, 0.3% American Indian/Alaska Native, 0.1% Native Hawaiian/Other Pacific Islander, 1.2% Other, 0.9% Hispanic of any race (2010); Average household size: 2.24 (2010); Median age: 27.1 (2010); Males per 100 females: 86.6 (2010); Marriage status: 35.4% never married, 49.9% now married, 4.8% widowed, 10.0% divorced (2006-2010 5-year est.); Foreign born: 0.4% (2006-2010 5-year est.); Ancestry (includes multiple ancestries): 35.5% German, 13.9% Irish, 7.7% English, 7.0% Italian, 4.3% American (2006-2010 5-year est.).

Economy: Single-family building permits issued: 6 (2011); Multi-family building permits issued: 0 (2011); Employment by occupation: 8.9%

management, 13.5% professional, 13.7% services, 10.9% sales, 4.2% farming, 7.1% construction, 4.6% production (2006-2010 5-year est.). **Income:** Per capita income: $22,487 (2006-2010 5-year est.); Median household income: $40,625 (2006-2010 5-year est.); Average household income: $49,630 (2006-2010 5-year est.); Percent of households with income of $100,000 or more: 9.5% (2006-2010 5-year est.); Poverty rate: 21.7% (2006-2010 5-year est.). **Education:** Percent of population age 25 and over with: High school diploma (including GED) or higher: 87.5% (2006-2010 5-year est.); Bachelor's degree or higher: 16.1% (2006-2010 5-year est.); Master's degree or higher: 6.1% (2006-2010 5-year est.).

Four-year College(s)
Clarion University of Pennsylvania (Public)
Fall 2010 Enrollment: 6,155 . . . . (814) 393-2000
2011-12 Tuition: In-state $8,340; Out-of-state $14,680

Housing: Homeownership rate: 47.0% (2010); Median home value: $122,800 (2006-2010 5-year est.); Median contract rent: $412 per month (2006-2010 5-year est.); Median year structure built: 1973 (2006-2010 5-year est.). **Hospitals:** Clarion Hospital (96 beds); Clarion Psychiatric Center (52 beds) **Newspapers:** The Clarion News (Local news; Circulation 7,000); The Midweek (Local news; Circulation 16,456) **Transportation:** Commute to work: 84.4% car, 0.0% public transportation, 15.6% walk, 0.0% work from home (2006-2010 5-year est.); Travel time to work: 47.7% less than 15 minutes, 35.7% 15 to 30 minutes, 4.2% 30 to 45 minutes, 8.1% 45 to 60 minutes, 4.3% 60 minutes or more (2006-2010 5-year est.) **Airports:** Clarion County (general aviation)

Additional Information Contacts
Clarion Chamber of Business & Industry . . . . (814) 226-9161
http://www.clarionpa.com

CROWN (CDP). Covers a land area of 2.535 square miles and a water area of 0.016 square miles. Located at 41.39° N. Lat; 79.26° W. Long. Elevation is 1,647 feet.
Population: n/a (1990); n/a (2000); 183 (2010); Density: 72.2 persons per square mile (2010); Race: 98.9% White, 0.0% Black, 0.5% Asian, 0.0% American Indian/Alaska Native, 0.0% Native Hawaiian/Other Pacific Islander, 0.6% Other, 0.5% Hispanic of any race (2010); Average household size: 2.32 (2010); Median age: 43.5 (2010); Males per 100 females: 110.3 (2010); Marriage status: 22.0% never married, 60.2% now married, 12.7% widowed, 5.1% divorced (2006-2010 5-year est.); Foreign born: 0.0% (2006-2010 5-year est.); Ancestry (includes multiple ancestries): 39.0% German, 27.1% Irish, 22.0% Croatian, 11.9% English, 5.9% American (2006-2010 5-year est.). **Economy:** Employment by occupation: 23.1% management, 0.0% professional, 0.0% services, 0.0% sales, 0.0% farming, 0.0% construction, 0.0% production (2006-2010 5-year est.). **Income:** Per capita income: $21,031 (2006-2010 5-year est.); Median household income: $37,500 (2006-2010 5-year est.); Average household income: $42,252 (2006-2010 5-year est.); Percent of households with income of $100,000 or more: 12.1% (2006-2010 5-year est.); Poverty rate: 12.7% (2006-2010 5-year est.). **Education:** Percent of population age 25 and over with: High school diploma (including GED) or higher: 74.3% (2006-2010 5-year est.); Bachelor's degree or higher: 16.8% (2006-2010 5-year est.); Master's degree or higher: 0.0% (2006-2010 5-year est.). **Housing:** Homeownership rate: 78.4% (2010); Median home value: $120,500 (2006-2010 5-year est.); Median contract rent: n/a per month (2006-2010 5-year est.); Median year structure built: 1951 (2006-2010 5-year est.). **Transportation:** Commute to work: 100.0% car, 0.0% public transportation, 0.0% walk, 0.0% work from home (2006-2010 5-year est.); Travel time to work: 23.1% less than 15 minutes, 43.6% 15 to 30 minutes, 15.4% 30 to 45 minutes, 0.0% 45 to 60 minutes, 17.9% 60 minutes or more (2006-2010 5-year est.)

EAST BRADY (borough). Covers a land area of 0.809 square miles and a water area of 0.299 square miles. Located at 40.98° N. Lat; 79.61° W. Long. Elevation is 965 feet.
Population: 1,047 (1990); 1,038 (2000); 942 (2010); Density: 1,164.3 persons per square mile (2010); Race: 98.7% White, 0.1% Black, 0.0% Asian, 0.1% American Indian/Alaska Native, 0.0% Native Hawaiian/Other Pacific Islander, 1.1% Other, 0.6% Hispanic of any race (2010); Average

household size: 2.12 (2010); Median age: 49.1 (2010); Males per 100 females: 99.6 (2010); Marriage status: 26.6% never married, 55.5% now married, 8.2% widowed, 9.8% divorced (2006-2010 5-year est.); Foreign born: 0.2% (2006-2010 5-year est.); Ancestry (includes multiple ancestries): 36.8% German, 27.5% Irish, 12.7% English, 8.4% Italian, 7.0% Dutch (2006-2010 5-year est.). **Economy:** Single-family building permits issued: 0 (2011); Multi-family building permits issued: 0 (2011); Employment by occupation: 7.6% management, 1.8% professional, 9.7% services, 8.4% sales, 1.0% farming, 15.3% construction, 6.9% production (2006-2010 5-year est.). **Income:** Per capita income: $16,706 (2006-2010 5-year est.); Median household income: $26,927 (2006-2010 5-year est.); Average household income: $37,642 (2006-2010 5-year est.); Percent of households with income of $100,000 or more: 6.3% (2006-2010 5-year est.); Poverty rate: 24.3% (2006-2010 5-year est.). **Education:** Percent of population age 25 and over with: High school diploma (including GED) or higher: 85.5% (2006-2010 5-year est.); Bachelor's degree or higher: 11.6% (2006-2010 5-year est.); Master's degree or higher: 3.3% (2006-2010 5-year est.). **Housing:** Homeownership rate: 56.8% (2010); Median home value: $86,400 (2006-2010 5-year est.); Median contract rent: $343 per month (2006-2010 5-year est.); Median year structure built: 1951 (2006-2010 5-year est.). **Transportation:** Commute to work: 89.8% car, 0.0% public transportation, 4.6% walk, 5.6% work from home (2006-2010 5-year est.); Travel time to work: 41.0% less than 15 minutes, 17.8% 15 to 30 minutes, 26.7% 30 to 45 minutes, 12.9% 45 to 60 minutes, 1.6% 60 minutes or more (2006-2010 5-year est.)

ELK (township). Covers a land area of 31.539 square miles and a water area of 0.111 square miles. Located at 41.28° N. Lat; 79.49° W. Long.
Population: 1,526 (1990); 1,519 (2000); 1,490 (2010); Density: 47.2 persons per square mile (2010); Race: 98.9% White, 0.1% Black, 0.5% Asian, 0.1% American Indian/Alaska Native, 0.0% Native Hawaiian/Other Pacific Islander, 0.4% Other, 0.1% Hispanic of any race (2010); Average household size: 2.43 (2010); Median age: 45.7 (2010); Males per 100 females: 100.0 (2010); Marriage status: 22.2% never married, 62.0% now married, 5.7% widowed, 10.1% divorced (2006-2010 5-year est.); Foreign born: 0.5% (2006-2010 5-year est.); Ancestry (includes multiple ancestries): 56.4% German, 13.4% Irish, 7.8% English, 4.1% French, 3.7% Scottish (2006-2010 5-year est.). **Economy:** Single-family building permits issued: 0 (2011); Multi-family building permits issued: 0 (2011); Employment by occupation: 8.2% management, 1.4% professional, 10.3% services, 14.9% sales, 3.9% farming, 15.3% construction, 6.9% production (2006-2010 5-year est.). **Income:** Per capita income: $21,240 (2006-2010 5-year est.); Median household income: $42,000 (2006-2010 5-year est.); Average household income: $50,677 (2006-2010 5-year est.); Percent of households with income of $100,000 or more: 9.2% (2006-2010 5-year est.); Poverty rate: 14.2% (2006-2010 5-year est.). **Education:** Percent of population age 25 and over with: High school diploma (including GED) or higher: 89.5% (2006-2010 5-year est.); Bachelor's degree or higher: 15.2% (2006-2010 5-year est.); Master's degree or higher: 4.9% (2006-2010 5-year est.). **Housing:** Homeownership rate: 82.2% (2010); Median home value: $114,500 (2006-2010 5-year est.); Median contract rent: $465 per month (2006-2010 5-year est.); Median year structure built: 1967 (2006-2010 5-year est.). **Transportation:** Commute to work: 94.4% car, 0.0% public transportation, 0.0% walk, 4.5% work from home (2006-2010 5-year est.); Travel time to work: 32.9% less than 15 minutes, 41.3% 15 to 30 minutes, 13.4% 30 to 45 minutes, 7.8% 45 to 60 minutes, 4.7% 60 minutes or more (2006-2010 5-year est.)

Additional Information Contacts
Clarion Chamber of Business & Industry . . . . (814) 226-9161
http://www.clarionpa.com

FAIRMOUNT CITY (unincorporated postal area)
Zip Code: 16224
Covers a land area of 20.053 square miles and a water area of 0.095 square miles. Located at 41.06° N. Lat; 79.29° W. Long. Population: 1,181 (2010); Density: 58.9 persons per square mile (2010); Race: 98.5% White, 0.3% Black, 0.0% Asian, 0.0% American Indian/Alaska Native, 0.3% Native Hawaiian/Other Pacific Islander, 0.9% Other, 1.7% Hispanic of any race (2010); Average household size: 2.44 (2010);

Median age: 43.0 (2010); Males per 100 females: 96.5 (2010); Homeownership rate: 76.3% (2010)

FARMINGTON (township). Covers a land area of 62.288 square miles and a water area of 0.226 square miles. Located at 41.37° N. Lat; 79.28° W. Long.

Population: 2,008 (1990); 1,986 (2000); 1,934 (2010); Density: 31.0 persons per square mile (2010); Race: 99.2% White, 0.1% Black, 0.1% Asian, 0.1% American Indian/Alaska Native, 0.0% Native Hawaiian/Other Pacific Islander, 0.5% Other, 0.6% Hispanic of any race (2010); Average household size: 2.42 (2010); Median age: 44.0 (2010); Males per 100 females: 102.7 (2010); Marriage status: 19.7% never married, 60.0% now married, 7.5% widowed, 12.8% divorced (2006-2010 5-year est.); Foreign born: 0.3% (2006-2010 5-year est.); Ancestry (includes multiple ancestries): 60.0% German, 14.3% Irish, 9.7% English, 5.9% Italian, 4.1% Scottish (2006-2010 5-year est.).
Economy: Single-family building permits issued: 6 (2011); Multi-family building permits issued: 0 (2011); Employment by occupation: 10.4% management, 2.2% professional, 15.1% services, 14.2% sales, 3.8% farming, 7.1% construction, 5.3% production (2006-2010 5-year est.).
Income: Per capita income: $21,726 (2006-2010 5-year est.); Median household income: $47,667 (2006-2010 5-year est.); Average household income: $50,865 (2006-2010 5-year est.); Percent of households with income of $100,000 or more: 8.1% (2006-2010 5-year est.); Poverty rate: 10.8% (2006-2010 5-year est.).
Education: Percent of population age 25 and over with: High school diploma (including GED) or higher: 83.7% (2006-2010 5-year est.); Bachelor's degree or higher: 14.3% (2006-2010 5-year est.); Master's degree or higher: 4.1% (2006-2010 5-year est.).
Housing: Homeownership rate: 84.9% (2010); Median home value: $97,100 (2006-2010 5-year est.); Median contract rent: $397 per month (2006-2010 5-year est.); Median year structure built: 1962 (2006-2010 5-year est.).
Transportation: Commute to work: 87.6% car, 0.0% public transportation, 2.9% walk, 4.8% work from home (2006-2010 5-year est.); Travel time to work: 18.8% less than 15 minutes, 44.1% 15 to 30 minutes, 16.9% 30 to 45 minutes, 9.5% 45 to 60 minutes, 10.6% 60 minutes or more (2006-2010 5-year est.)
Additional Information Contacts
Clarion Chamber of Business & Industry . . . . (814) 226-9161
  http://www.clarionpa.com

FOXBURG (borough). Covers a land area of 0.368 square miles and a water area of 0.132 square miles. Located at 41.14° N. Lat; 79.68° W. Long. Elevation is 997 feet.

History: First golf course in the United States.
Population: 262 (1990); 275 (2000); 183 (2010); Density: 497.6 persons per square mile (2010); Race: 97.8% White, 0.0% Black, 0.5% Asian, 0.0% American Indian/Alaska Native, 0.0% Native Hawaiian/Other Pacific Islander, 1.7% Other, 1.6% Hispanic of any race (2010); Average household size: 2.32 (2010); Median age: 47.3 (2010); Males per 100 females: 88.7 (2010); Marriage status: 25.0% never married, 53.3% now married, 10.0% widowed, 11.7% divorced (2006-2010 5-year est.); Foreign born: 3.1% (2006-2010 5-year est.); Ancestry (includes multiple ancestries): 39.9% German, 26.4% Irish, 9.8% Scottish, 7.8% English, 7.3% Dutch (2006-2010 5-year est.).
Economy: Single-family building permits issued: 0 (2011); Multi-family building permits issued: 0 (2011); Employment by occupation: 14.3% management, 0.0% professional, 14.3% services, 14.3% sales, 0.0% farming, 3.2% construction, 3.2% production (2006-2010 5-year est.).
Income: Per capita income: $21,567 (2006-2010 5-year est.); Median household income: $41,250 (2006-2010 5-year est.); Average household income: $49,771 (2006-2010 5-year est.); Percent of households with income of $100,000 or more: 9.7% (2006-2010 5-year est.); Poverty rate: 5.2% (2006-2010 5-year est.).
Education: Percent of population age 25 and over with: High school diploma (including GED) or higher: 92.4% (2006-2010 5-year est.); Bachelor's degree or higher: 24.1% (2006-2010 5-year est.); Master's degree or higher: 6.9% (2006-2010 5-year est.).
School District(s)
Allegheny-Clarion Valley SD (PK-12)
  2010-11 Enrollment: 792. . . . . (724) 659-5820
Housing: Homeownership rate: 81.0% (2010); Median home value: $85,000 (2006-2010 5-year est.); Median contract rent: n/a per month

(2006-2010 5-year est.); Median year structure built: before 1940 (2006-2010 5-year est.).
Transportation: Commute to work: 93.7% car, 0.0% public transportation, 0.0% walk, 1.6% work from home (2006-2010 5-year est.); Travel time to work: 35.5% less than 15 minutes, 25.8% 15 to 30 minutes, 30.6% 30 to 45 minutes, 3.2% 45 to 60 minutes, 4.8% 60 minutes or more (2006-2010 5-year est.)

FRYBURG (unincorporated postal area)
Zip Code: 16326
  Covers a land area of 6.832 square miles and a water area of 0.007 square miles. Located at 41.37° N. Lat; 79.43° W. Long. Elevation is 1,706 feet. Population: 391 (2010); Density: 57.2 persons per square mile (2010); Race: 100.0% White, 0.0% Black, 0.0% Asian, 0.0% American Indian/Alaska Native, 0.0% Native Hawaiian/Other Pacific Islander, 0.0% Other, 0.3% Hispanic of any race (2010); Average household size: 2.66 (2010); Median age: 41.8 (2010); Males per 100 females: 117.2 (2010); Homeownership rate: 83.0% (2010)

HAWTHORN (borough). Covers a land area of 1.025 square miles and a water area of 0.060 square miles. Located at 41.02° N. Lat; 79.28° W. Long. Elevation is 1,106 feet.

Population: 528 (1990); 587 (2000); 494 (2010); Density: 482.1 persons per square mile (2010); Race: 99.8% White, 0.0% Black, 0.0% Asian, 0.0% American Indian/Alaska Native, 0.0% Native Hawaiian/Other Pacific Islander, 0.2% Other, 0.0% Hispanic of any race (2010); Average household size: 2.67 (2010); Median age: 36.9 (2010); Males per 100 females: 90.7 (2010); Marriage status: 16.2% never married, 58.4% now married, 12.8% widowed, 12.6% divorced (2006-2010 5-year est.); Foreign born: 0.7% (2006-2010 5-year est.); Ancestry (includes multiple ancestries): 43.0% German, 12.4% Dutch, 10.7% Irish, 10.1% English, 7.8% American (2006-2010 5-year est.).
Economy: Single-family building permits issued: 0 (2011); Multi-family building permits issued: 0 (2011); Employment by occupation: 6.8% management, 1.8% professional, 11.3% services, 6.8% sales, 1.4% farming, 23.0% construction, 6.8% production (2006-2010 5-year est.).
Income: Per capita income: $16,578 (2006-2010 5-year est.); Median household income: $35,417 (2006-2010 5-year est.); Average household income: $43,544 (2006-2010 5-year est.); Percent of households with income of $100,000 or more: 1.4% (2006-2010 5-year est.); Poverty rate: 12.6% (2006-2010 5-year est.).
Education: Percent of population age 25 and over with: High school diploma (including GED) or higher: 87.5% (2006-2010 5-year est.); Bachelor's degree or higher: 1.7% (2006-2010 5-year est.); Master's degree or higher: 0.8% (2006-2010 5-year est.).
School District(s)
Redbank Valley SD (KG-12)
  2010-11 Enrollment: 1,168 . . . . (814) 275-2426
Housing: Homeownership rate: 77.8% (2010); Median home value: $74,500 (2006-2010 5-year est.); Median contract rent: $371 per month (2006-2010 5-year est.); Median year structure built: before 1940 (2006-2010 5-year est.).
Transportation: Commute to work: 98.6% car, 0.0% public transportation, 0.0% walk, 1.4% work from home (2006-2010 5-year est.); Travel time to work: 29.2% less than 15 minutes, 40.6% 15 to 30 minutes, 15.5% 30 to 45 minutes, 10.5% 45 to 60 minutes, 4.1% 60 minutes or more (2006-2010 5-year est.)

HIGHLAND (township). Covers a land area of 19.913 square miles and a water area of 0.328 square miles. Located at 41.27° N. Lat; 79.33° W. Long.

Population: 565 (1990); 633 (2000); 525 (2010); Density: 26.4 persons per square mile (2010); Race: 98.9% White, 0.8% Black, 0.2% Asian, 0.0% American Indian/Alaska Native, 0.0% Native Hawaiian/Other Pacific Islander, 0.1% Other, 0.0% Hispanic of any race (2010); Average household size: 2.24 (2010); Median age: 49.9 (2010); Males per 100 females: 98.1 (2010); Marriage status: 24.0% never married, 63.4% now married, 4.4% widowed, 8.2% divorced (2006-2010 5-year est.); Foreign born: 4.3% (2006-2010 5-year est.); Ancestry (includes multiple ancestries): 44.5% German, 11.1% Italian, 10.6% American, 9.0% Irish, 7.4% English (2006-2010 5-year est.).
Economy: Single-family building permits issued: 0 (2011); Multi-family building permits issued: 0 (2011); Employment by occupation: 12.3% management, 0.9% professional, 9.5% services, 20.3% sales, 3.7% farming, 14.8% construction, 2.8% production (2006-2010 5-year est.).

Income: Per capita income: $38,390 (2006-2010 5-year est.); Median household income: $52,500 (2006-2010 5-year est.); Average household income: $91,427 (2006-2010 5-year est.); Percent of households with income of $100,000 or more: 9.1% (2006-2010 5-year est.); Poverty rate: 3.5% (2006-2010 5-year est.).

Education: Percent of population age 25 and over with: High school diploma (including GED) or higher: 93.4% (2006-2010 5-year est.); Bachelor's degree or higher: 20.9% (2006-2010 5-year est.); Master's degree or higher: 6.6% (2006-2010 5-year est.).

Housing: Homeownership rate: 87.6% (2010); Median home value: $136,800 (2006-2010 5-year est.); Median contract rent: $325 per month (2006-2010 5-year est.); Median year structure built: 1973 (2006-2010 5-year est.).

Transportation: Commute to work: 96.3% car, 0.0% public transportation, 0.0% walk, 3.1% work from home (2006-2010 5-year est.); Travel time to work: 37.7% less than 15 minutes, 41.6% 15 to 30 minutes, 11.3% 30 to 45 minutes, 4.8% 45 to 60 minutes, 4.5% 60 minutes or more (2006-2010 5-year est.)

KNOX (borough). Aka Edenburg. Covers a land area of 0.562 square miles and a water area of 0.004 square miles. Located at 41.23° N. Lat; 79.54° W. Long. Elevation is 1,391 feet.

Population: 1,182 (1990); 1,176 (2000); 1,146 (2010); Density: 2,038.3 persons per square mile (2010); Race: 98.2% White, 0.4% Black, 0.7% Asian, 0.1% American Indian/Alaska Native, 0.0% Native Hawaiian/Other Pacific Islander, 0.6% Other, 0.5% Hispanic of any race (2010); Average household size: 2.14 (2010); Median age: 45.2 (2010); Males per 100 females: 90.0 (2010); Marriage status: 24.7% never married, 57.7% now married, 8.5% widowed, 9.1% divorced (2006-2010 5-year est.); Foreign born: 1.4% (2006-2010 5-year est.); Ancestry (includes multiple ancestries): 53.1% German, 10.5% Irish, 9.2% Scotch-Irish, 9.1% English, 6.9% Dutch (2006-2010 5-year est.).

Economy: Single-family building permits issued: 0 (2011); Multi-family building permits issued: 0 (2011); Employment by occupation: 8.3% management, 1.8% professional, 3.7% services, 16.1% sales, 6.7% farming, 5.1% construction, 7.1% production (2006-2010 5-year est.).

Income: Per capita income: $22,533 (2006-2010 5-year est.); Median household income: $40,357 (2006-2010 5-year est.); Average household income: $47,899 (2006-2010 5-year est.); Percent of households with income of $100,000 or more: 8.7% (2006-2010 5-year est.); Poverty rate: 11.2% (2006-2010 5-year est.).

Education: Percent of population age 25 and over with: High school diploma (including GED) or higher: 88.7% (2006-2010 5-year est.); Bachelor's degree or higher: 19.9% (2006-2010 5-year est.); Master's degree or higher: 5.2% (2006-2010 5-year est.).

School District(s)

Keystone SD (KG-12)

   2010-11 Enrollment: 1,124 . . . . (814) 797-5921

Housing: Homeownership rate: 62.8% (2010); Median home value: $90,500 (2006-2010 5-year est.); Median contract rent: $325 per month (2006-2010 5-year est.); Median year structure built: 1949 (2006-2010 5-year est.).

Safety: Violent crime rate: 8.7 per 10,000 population; Property crime rate: 217.4 per 10,000 population (2011).

Transportation: Commute to work: 93.3% car, 0.0% public transportation, 4.6% walk, 2.0% work from home (2006-2010 5-year est.); Travel time to work: 33.8% less than 15 minutes, 47.1% 15 to 30 minutes, 10.2% 30 to 45 minutes, 4.7% 45 to 60 minutes, 4.2% 60 minutes or more (2006-2010 5-year est.)

Additional Information Contacts

Clarion Chamber of Business & Industry . . . . (814) 226-9161

   http://www.clarionpa.com

KNOX (township). Aka Edenburg. Covers a land area of 16.024 square miles and a water area of 0.052 square miles. Located at 41.31° N. Lat; 79.38° W. Long.

History: Name changed from Edenburg to its post office name in 1933.

Population: 1,208 (1990); 1,045 (2000); 1,036 (2010); Density: 64.7 persons per square mile (2010); Race: 99.8% White, 0.0% Black, 0.0% Asian, 0.0% American Indian/Alaska Native, 0.0% Native Hawaiian/Other Pacific Islander, 0.2% Other, 0.1% Hispanic of any race (2010); Average household size: 2.52 (2010); Median age: 42.6 (2010); Males per 100 females: 92.2 (2010); Marriage status: 28.1% never married, 56.1% now married, 8.4% widowed, 7.4% divorced (2006-2010 5-year est.); Foreign born: 0.0% (2006-2010 5-year est.); Ancestry (includes multiple

ancestries): 76.8% German, 12.9% Irish, 6.2% Italian, 3.7% English, 3.7% Swedish (2006-2010 5-year est.).

Economy: Single-family building permits issued: 0 (2011); Multi-family building permits issued: 0 (2011); Employment by occupation: 11.0% management, 1.2% professional, 8.6% services, 15.5% sales, 0.6% farming, 16.5% construction, 8.4% production (2006-2010 5-year est.).

Income: Per capita income: $21,296 (2006-2010 5-year est.); Median household income: $41,000 (2006-2010 5-year est.); Average household income: $45,722 (2006-2010 5-year est.); Percent of households with income of $100,000 or more: 3.8% (2006-2010 5-year est.); Poverty rate: 8.6% (2006-2010 5-year est.).

Education: Percent of population age 25 and over with: High school diploma (including GED) or higher: 92.5% (2006-2010 5-year est.); Bachelor's degree or higher: 13.6% (2006-2010 5-year est.); Master's degree or higher: 5.2% (2006-2010 5-year est.).

Housing: Homeownership rate: 89.7% (2010); Median home value: $109,800 (2006-2010 5-year est.); Median contract rent: $389 per month (2006-2010 5-year est.); Median year structure built: 1960 (2006-2010 5-year est.).

Transportation: Commute to work: 94.9% car, 0.0% public transportation, 1.0% walk, 4.1% work from home (2006-2010 5-year est.); Travel time to work: 27.4% less than 15 minutes, 55.8% 15 to 30 minutes, 8.5% 30 to 45 minutes, 4.3% 45 to 60 minutes, 4.1% 60 minutes or more (2006-2010 5-year est.)

KOSSUTH (unincorporated postal area)

Zip Code: 16331

   Covers a land area of 1.316 square miles and a water area of 0.005 square miles. Located at 41.29° N. Lat; 79.55° W. Long. Elevation is 1,555 feet. Population: 88 (2010); Density: 66.8 persons per square mile (2010); Race: 98.9% White, 0.0% Black, 0.0% Asian, 0.0% American Indian/Alaska Native, 0.0% Native Hawaiian/Other Pacific Islander, 1.1% Other, 1.1% Hispanic of any race (2010); Average household size: 2.93 (2010); Median age: 43.0 (2010); Males per 100 females: 109.5 (2010); Homeownership rate: 86.7% (2010)

LEEPER (CDP). Covers a land area of 0.524 square miles and a water area of 0 square miles. Located at 41.37° N. Lat; 79.31° W. Long. Elevation is 1,644 feet.

Population: n/a (1990); n/a (2000); 158 (2010); Density: 301.6 persons per square mile (2010); Race: 99.4% White, 0.0% Black, 0.0% Asian, 0.0% American Indian/Alaska Native, 0.0% Native Hawaiian/Other Pacific Islander, 0.6% Other, 0.0% Hispanic of any race (2010); Average household size: 2.47 (2010); Median age: 39.7 (2010); Males per 100 females: 79.5 (2010); Marriage status: 22.1% never married, 57.4% now married, 0.0% widowed, 20.6% divorced (2006-2010 5-year est.); Foreign born: 0.0% (2006-2010 5-year est.); Ancestry (includes multiple ancestries): 79.9% German, 27.7% English, 22.0% Irish, 9.4% Scottish, 5.7% French (2006-2010 5-year est.).

Economy: Employment by occupation: 10.2% management, 0.0% professional, 11.2% services, 15.3% sales, 0.0% farming, 16.3% construction, 29.6% production (2006-2010 5-year est.).

Income: Per capita income: $27,998 (2006-2010 5-year est.); Median household income: $68,472 (2006-2010 5-year est.); Average household income: $60,582 (2006-2010 5-year est.); Percent of households with income of $100,000 or more: n/a (2006-2010 5-year est.); Poverty rate: 0.0% (2006-2010 5-year est.).

Education: Percent of population age 25 and over with: High school diploma (including GED) or higher: 92.4% (2006-2010 5-year est.); Bachelor's degree or higher: 14.3% (2006-2010 5-year est.); Master's degree or higher: 14.3% (2006-2010 5-year est.).

Housing: Homeownership rate: 76.5% (2010); Median home value: $78,400 (2006-2010 5-year est.); Median contract rent: n/a per month (2006-2010 5-year est.); Median year structure built: 1961 (2006-2010 5-year est.).

Transportation: Commute to work: 100.0% car, 0.0% public transportation, 0.0% walk, 0.0% work from home (2006-2010 5-year est.); Travel time to work: 28.6% less than 15 minutes, 61.2% 15 to 30 minutes, 0.0% 30 to 45 minutes, 10.2% 45 to 60 minutes, 0.0% 60 minutes or more (2006-2010 5-year est.)

LICKING (township). Covers a land area of 17.520 square miles and a water area of 0.402 square miles. Located at 41.14° N. Lat; 79.55° W. Long.

Population: 483 (1990); 479 (2000); 536 (2010); Density: 30.6 persons per square mile (2010); Race: 98.7% White, 0.0% Black, 0.6% Asian, 0.0% American Indian/Alaska Native, 0.0% Native Hawaiian/Other Pacific Islander, 0.7% Other, 0.0% Hispanic of any race (2010); Average household size: 2.76 (2010); Median age: 37.5 (2010); Males per 100 females: 109.4 (2010); Marriage status: 13.9% never married, 65.7% now married, 6.5% widowed, 13.9% divorced (2006-2010 5-year est.); Foreign born: 0.0% (2006-2010 5-year est.); Ancestry (includes multiple ancestries): 30.9% German, 11.6% Irish, 5.1% Polish, 4.9% English, 3.7% Scottish (2006-2010 5-year est.).

Economy: Single-family building permits issued: 3 (2011); Multi-family building permits issued: 0 (2011); Employment by occupation: 7.3% management, 0.8% professional, 15.8% services, 18.5% sales, 0.8% farming, 15.8% construction, 4.6% production (2006-2010 5-year est.).

Income: Per capita income: $19,861 (2006-2010 5-year est.); Median household income: $38,304 (2006-2010 5-year est.); Average household income: $45,930 (2006-2010 5-year est.); Percent of households with income of $100,000 or more: 7.2% (2006-2010 5-year est.); Poverty rate: 10.3% (2006-2010 5-year est.).

Education: Percent of population age 25 and over with: High school diploma (including GED) or higher: 88.1% (2006-2010 5-year est.); Bachelor's degree or higher: 8.2% (2006-2010 5-year est.); Master's degree or higher: 1.1% (2006-2010 5-year est.).

Housing: Homeownership rate: 81.9% (2010); Median home value: $92,100 (2006-2010 5-year est.); Median contract rent: $430 per month (2006-2010 5-year est.); Median year structure built: 1954 (2006-2010 5-year est.).

Transportation: Commute to work: 90.1% car, 0.0% public transportation, 4.4% walk, 5.6% work from home (2006-2010 5-year est.); Travel time to work: 24.4% less than 15 minutes, 41.2% 15 to 30 minutes, 24.4% 30 to 45 minutes, 5.9% 45 to 60 minutes, 4.2% 60 minutes or more (2006-2010 5-year est.)

LICKINGVILLE (unincorporated postal area)

Zip Code: 16332

Covers a land area of 2.997 square miles and a water area of 0.009 square miles. Located at 41.35° N. Lat; 79.36° W. Long. Elevation is 1,591 feet. Population: 53 (2010); Density: 17.7 persons per square mile (2010); Race: 96.2% White, 0.0% Black, 0.0% Asian, 3.8% American Indian/Alaska Native, 0.0% Native Hawaiian/Other Pacific Islander, 0.0% Other, 0.0% Hispanic of any race (2010); Average household size: 2.04 (2010); Median age: 41.5 (2010); Males per 100 females: 120.8 (2010); Homeownership rate: 57.7% (2010)

LIMESTONE (township). Covers a land area of 37.833 square miles and a water area of 0.116 square miles. Located at 41.14° N. Lat; 79.29° W. Long. Elevation is 1,296 feet.

Population: 1,686 (1990); 1,773 (2000); 1,858 (2010); Density: 49.1 persons per square mile (2010); Race: 99.1% White, 0.2% Black, 0.1% Asian, 0.1% American Indian/Alaska Native, 0.1% Native Hawaiian/Other Pacific Islander, 0.4% Other, 0.2% Hispanic of any race (2010); Average household size: 2.53 (2010); Median age: 42.7 (2010); Males per 100 females: 99.1 (2010); Marriage status: 23.7% never married, 63.5% now married, 6.5% widowed, 6.2% divorced (2006-2010 5-year est.); Foreign born: 0.6% (2006-2010 5-year est.); Ancestry (includes multiple ancestries): 46.6% German, 13.3% Irish, 8.6% American, 5.8% Dutch, 5.7% English (2006-2010 5-year est.).

Economy: Single-family building permits issued: 1 (2011); Multi-family building permits issued: 0 (2011); Employment by occupation: 11.5% management, 2.0% professional, 8.1% services, 19.4% sales, 3.3% farming, 13.7% construction, 6.0% production (2006-2010 5-year est.).

Income: Per capita income: $24,676 (2006-2010 5-year est.); Median household income: $51,518 (2006-2010 5-year est.); Average household income: $61,976 (2006-2010 5-year est.); Percent of households with income of $100,000 or more: 14.0% (2006-2010 5-year est.); Poverty rate: 4.2% (2006-2010 5-year est.).

Education: Percent of population age 25 and over with: High school diploma (including GED) or higher: 89.5% (2006-2010 5-year est.); Bachelor's degree or higher: 17.9% (2006-2010 5-year est.); Master's degree or higher: 6.1% (2006-2010 5-year est.).

Housing: Homeownership rate: 83.4% (2010); Median home value: $123,900 (2006-2010 5-year est.); Median contract rent: $446 per month

(2006-2010 5-year est.); Median year structure built: 1977 (2006-2010 5-year est.).

Transportation: Commute to work: 93.9% car, 1.7% public transportation, 1.6% walk, 2.9% work from home (2006-2010 5-year est.); Travel time to work: 34.1% less than 15 minutes, 48.6% 15 to 30 minutes, 8.6% 30 to 45 minutes, 3.4% 45 to 60 minutes, 5.3% 60 minutes or more (2006-2010 5-year est.)

Additional Information Contacts

Clarion Chamber of Business & Industry . . . . (814) 226-9161
http://www.clarionpa.com

LUCINDA (unincorporated postal area)

Zip Code: 16235

Covers a land area of 28.169 square miles and a water area of 0.096 square miles. Located at 41.32° N. Lat; 79.35° W. Long. Elevation is 1,542 feet. Population: 1,256 (2010); Density: 44.6 persons per square mile (2010); Race: 99.2% White, 0.1% Black, 0.1% Asian, 0.0% American Indian/Alaska Native, 0.0% Native Hawaiian/Other Pacific Islander, 0.6% Other, 0.1% Hispanic of any race (2010); Average household size: 2.51 (2010); Median age: 43.2 (2010); Males per 100 females: 97.5 (2010); Homeownership rate: 87.6% (2010)

MADISON (township). Covers a land area of 26.678 square miles and a water area of 1.075 square miles. Located at 41.01° N. Lat; 79.52° W. Long.

Population: 1,423 (1990); 1,442 (2000); 1,207 (2010); Density: 45.2 persons per square mile (2010); Race: 99.0% White, 0.4% Black, 0.2% Asian, 0.0% American Indian/Alaska Native, 0.0% Native Hawaiian/Other Pacific Islander, 0.4% Other, 0.4% Hispanic of any race (2010); Average household size: 2.38 (2010); Median age: 45.5 (2010); Males per 100 females: 102.2 (2010); Marriage status: 29.6% never married, 55.5% now married, 8.2% widowed, 6.6% divorced (2006-2010 5-year est.); Foreign born: 0.4% (2006-2010 5-year est.); Ancestry (includes multiple ancestries): 27.6% German, 13.0% American, 7.9% English, 7.4% Italian, 6.8% Irish (2006-2010 5-year est.).

Economy: Single-family building permits issued: 0 (2011); Multi-family building permits issued: 0 (2011); Employment by occupation: 5.7% management, 1.3% professional, 13.9% services, 20.4% sales, 2.4% farming, 14.6% construction, 10.4% production (2006-2010 5-year est.).

Income: Per capita income: $16,662 (2006-2010 5-year est.); Median household income: $38,571 (2006-2010 5-year est.); Average household income: $43,306 (2006-2010 5-year est.); Percent of households with income of $100,000 or more: 3.3% (2006-2010 5-year est.); Poverty rate: 12.6% (2006-2010 5-year est.).

Education: Percent of population age 25 and over with: High school diploma (including GED) or higher: 78.1% (2006-2010 5-year est.); Bachelor's degree or higher: 5.5% (2006-2010 5-year est.); Master's degree or higher: 2.3% (2006-2010 5-year est.).

Housing: Homeownership rate: 79.1% (2010); Median home value: $71,700 (2006-2010 5-year est.); Median contract rent: $253 per month (2006-2010 5-year est.); Median year structure built: 1958 (2006-2010 5-year est.).

Transportation: Commute to work: 95.6% car, 0.0% public transportation, 0.4% walk, 3.7% work from home (2006-2010 5-year est.); Travel time to work: 20.8% less than 15 minutes, 34.1% 15 to 30 minutes, 31.5% 30 to 45 minutes, 8.6% 45 to 60 minutes, 5.0% 60 minutes or more (2006-2010 5-year est.)

Additional Information Contacts

Clarion Chamber of Business & Industry . . . . (814) 226-9161
http://www.clarionpa.com

MARBLE (unincorporated postal area)

Zip Code: 16334

Covers a land area of 5.440 square miles and a water area of 0.001 square miles. Located at 41.29° N. Lat; 79.44° W. Long. Elevation is 1,568 feet. Population: 338 (2010); Density: 62.1 persons per square mile (2010); Race: 99.7% White, 0.0% Black, 0.3% Asian, 0.0% American Indian/Alaska Native, 0.0% Native Hawaiian/Other Pacific Islander, 0.0% Other, 0.0% Hispanic of any race (2010); Average household size: 2.52 (2010); Median age: 43.3 (2010); Males per 100 females: 101.2 (2010); Homeownership rate: 85.1% (2010)

MARIANNE (CDP). Covers a land area of 1.449 square miles and a water area of 0.008 square miles. Located at 41.24° N. Lat; 79.43° W. Long. Elevation is 1,450 feet.
Population: n/a (1990); n/a (2000); 1,167 (2010); Density: 805.1 persons per square mile (2010); Race: 96.6% White, 0.9% Black, 0.9% Asian, 0.3% American Indian/Alaska Native, 0.0% Native Hawaiian/Other Pacific Islander, 1.3% Other, 2.1% Hispanic of any race (2010); Average household size: 2.21 (2010); Median age: 49.4 (2010); Males per 100 females: 92.3 (2010); Marriage status: 18.3% never married, 57.1% now married, 15.7% widowed, 8.9% divorced (2006-2010 5-year est.); Foreign born: 3.2% (2006-2010 5-year est.); Ancestry (includes multiple ancestries): 35.4% German, 16.7% Irish, 11.1% English, 6.5% Scotch-Irish, 5.4% Scottish (2006-2010 5-year est.).
Economy: Employment by occupation: 17.0% management, 1.7% professional, 17.9% services, 6.3% sales, 2.3% farming, 4.6% construction, 0.9% production (2006-2010 5-year est.).
Income: Per capita income: $33,905 (2006-2010 5-year est.); Median household income: $46,750 (2006-2010 5-year est.); Average household income: $79,436 (2006-2010 5-year est.); Percent of households with income of $100,000 or more: 17.9% (2006-2010 5-year est.); Poverty rate: 13.6% (2006-2010 5-year est.).
Education: Percent of population age 25 and over with: High school diploma (including GED) or higher: 88.1% (2006-2010 5-year est.); Bachelor's degree or higher: 31.8% (2006-2010 5-year est.); Master's degree or higher: 18.8% (2006-2010 5-year est.).
Housing: Homeownership rate: 88.2% (2010); Median home value: $126,500 (2006-2010 5-year est.); Median contract rent: $473 per month (2006-2010 5-year est.); Median year structure built: 1977 (2006-2010 5-year est.).
Transportation: Commute to work: 98.8% car, 0.0% public transportation, 0.0% walk, 1.2% work from home (2006-2010 5-year est.); Travel time to work: 56.3% less than 15 minutes, 25.1% 15 to 30 minutes, 11.7% 30 to 45 minutes, 4.5% 45 to 60 minutes, 2.4% 60 minutes or more (2006-2010 5-year est.)

MAYPORT (unincorporated postal area)
Zip Code: 16240
Covers a land area of 53.661 square miles and a water area of 0.393 square miles. Located at 41.03° N. Lat; 79.22° W. Long. Population: 1,533 (2010); Density: 28.6 persons per square mile (2010); Race: 99.1% White, 0.4% Black, 0.0% Asian, 0.0% American Indian/Alaska Native, 0.0% Native Hawaiian/Other Pacific Islander, 0.5% Other, 0.3% Hispanic of any race (2010); Average household size: 2.39 (2010); Median age: 44.0 (2010); Males per 100 females: 108.6 (2010); Homeownership rate: 77.0% (2010)

MILLCREEK (township). Covers a land area of 28.942 square miles and a water area of 0.309 square miles. Located at 41.26° N. Lat; 79.25° W. Long.
Population: 407 (1990); 415 (2000); 396 (2010); Density: 13.7 persons per square mile (2010); Race: 99.5% White, 0.0% Black, 0.0% Asian, 0.3% American Indian/Alaska Native, 0.0% Native Hawaiian/Other Pacific Islander, 0.2% Other, 0.3% Hispanic of any race (2010); Average household size: 2.29 (2010); Median age: 49.5 (2010); Males per 100 females: 110.6 (2010); Marriage status: 18.1% never married, 58.6% now married, 11.4% widowed, 11.9% divorced (2006-2010 5-year est.); Foreign born: 0.0% (2006-2010 5-year est.); Ancestry (includes multiple ancestries): 40.1% German, 16.8% American, 15.0% Irish, 10.8% Dutch, 8.1% Scottish (2006-2010 5-year est.).
Economy: Single-family building permits issued: 0 (2011); Multi-family building permits issued: 0 (2011); Employment by occupation: 3.8% management, 0.0% professional, 19.8% services, 13.7% sales, 1.9% farming, 11.3% construction, 7.1% production (2006-2010 5-year est.).
Income: Per capita income: $26,911 (2006-2010 5-year est.); Median household income: $41,932 (2006-2010 5-year est.); Average household income: $59,584 (2006-2010 5-year est.); Percent of households with income of $100,000 or more: 10.0% (2006-2010 5-year est.); Poverty rate: 9.0% (2006-2010 5-year est.).
Education: Percent of population age 25 and over with: High school diploma (including GED) or higher: 79.7% (2006-2010 5-year est.); Bachelor's degree or higher: 12.1% (2006-2010 5-year est.); Master's degree or higher: 3.9% (2006-2010 5-year est.).
Housing: Homeownership rate: 87.3% (2010); Median home value: $106,300 (2006-2010 5-year est.); Median contract rent: $386 per month

(2006-2010 5-year est.); Median year structure built: 1971 (2006-2010 5-year est.).
Transportation: Commute to work: 96.2% car, 1.4% public transportation, 1.4% walk, 0.9% work from home (2006-2010 5-year est.); Travel time to work: 10.5% less than 15 minutes, 56.7% 15 to 30 minutes, 23.3% 30 to 45 minutes, 3.8% 45 to 60 minutes, 5.7% 60 minutes or more (2006-2010 5-year est.)

MONROE (township). Covers a land area of 29.451 square miles and a water area of 0.402 square miles. Located at 41.13° N. Lat; 79.41° W. Long.
Population: 1,314 (1990); 1,587 (2000); 1,544 (2010); Density: 52.4 persons per square mile (2010); Race: 97.0% White, 0.7% Black, 0.8% Asian, 0.1% American Indian/Alaska Native, 0.0% Native Hawaiian/Other Pacific Islander, 1.4% Other, 0.4% Hispanic of any race (2010); Average household size: 2.39 (2010); Median age: 43.8 (2010); Males per 100 females: 98.7 (2010); Marriage status: 28.0% never married, 61.3% now married, 5.1% widowed, 5.6% divorced (2006-2010 5-year est.); Foreign born: 0.8% (2006-2010 5-year est.); Ancestry (includes multiple ancestries): 42.4% German, 17.3% Irish, 6.6% English, 6.1% American, 4.6% Italian (2006-2010 5-year est.).
Economy: Single-family building permits issued: 1 (2011); Multi-family building permits issued: 0 (2011); Employment by occupation: 5.2% management, 2.7% professional, 9.2% services, 19.3% sales, 2.6% farming, 9.1% construction, 5.0% production (2006-2010 5-year est.).
Income: Per capita income: $26,984 (2006-2010 5-year est.); Median household income: $62,143 (2006-2010 5-year est.); Average household income: $74,688 (2006-2010 5-year est.); Percent of households with income of $100,000 or more: 21.3% (2006-2010 5-year est.); Poverty rate: 8.2% (2006-2010 5-year est.).
Education: Percent of population age 25 and over with: High school diploma (including GED) or higher: 90.3% (2006-2010 5-year est.); Bachelor's degree or higher: 28.4% (2006-2010 5-year est.); Master's degree or higher: 12.3% (2006-2010 5-year est.).
Housing: Homeownership rate: 73.4% (2010); Median home value: $124,800 (2006-2010 5-year est.); Median contract rent: $427 per month (2006-2010 5-year est.); Median year structure built: 1972 (2006-2010 5-year est.).
Transportation: Commute to work: 91.5% car, 0.0% public transportation, 1.7% walk, 5.1% work from home (2006-2010 5-year est.); Travel time to work: 40.1% less than 15 minutes, 38.1% 15 to 30 minutes, 14.2% 30 to 45 minutes, 0.6% 45 to 60 minutes, 7.0% 60 minutes or more (2006-2010 5-year est.)
Additional Information Contacts
Clarion Chamber of Business & Industry . . . . (814) 226-9161
http://www.clarionpa.com

NEW BETHLEHEM (borough). Covers a land area of 0.466 square miles and a water area of 0.051 square miles. Located at 41.00° N. Lat; 79.33° W. Long. Elevation is 1,073 feet.
History: Settled 1785, laid out 1840, incorporated 1853.
Population: 1,151 (1990); 1,057 (2000); 989 (2010); Density: 2,121.3 persons per square mile (2010); Race: 99.4% White, 0.1% Black, 0.1% Asian, 0.1% American Indian/Alaska Native, 0.0% Native Hawaiian/Other Pacific Islander, 0.3% Other, 0.1% Hispanic of any race (2010); Average household size: 2.12 (2010); Median age: 42.1 (2010); Males per 100 females: 88.0 (2010); Marriage status: 21.5% never married, 55.3% now married, 14.7% widowed, 8.5% divorced (2006-2010 5-year est.); Foreign born: 0.0% (2006-2010 5-year est.); Ancestry (includes multiple ancestries): 43.0% German, 15.7% Irish, 9.8% Dutch, 8.8% English, 8.4% Scottish (2006-2010 5-year est.).
Economy: Single-family building permits issued: 0 (2011); Multi-family building permits issued: 0 (2011); Employment by occupation: 14.2% management, 0.0% professional, 8.4% services, 6.9% sales, 3.5% farming, 15.9% construction, 8.7% production (2006-2010 5-year est.).
Income: Per capita income: $27,552 (2006-2010 5-year est.); Median household income: $30,000 (2006-2010 5-year est.); Average household income: $55,280 (2006-2010 5-year est.); Percent of households with income of $100,000 or more: 9.8% (2006-2010 5-year est.); Poverty rate: 15.2% (2006-2010 5-year est.).
Education: Percent of population age 25 and over with: High school diploma (including GED) or higher: 80.7% (2006-2010 5-year est.); Bachelor's degree or higher: 18.3% (2006-2010 5-year est.); Master's degree or higher: 6.9% (2006-2010 5-year est.).

School District(s)

Redbank Valley SD (KG-12)
   2010-11 Enrollment: 1,168 . . . . (814) 275-2426
Redbank Valley SD (KG-12)
   2010-11 Enrollment: 1,168 . . . . (814) 275-2426

Housing: Homeownership rate: 51.8% (2010); Median home value: $87,900 (2006-2010 5-year est.); Median contract rent: $332 per month (2006-2010 5-year est.); Median year structure built: 1941 (2006-2010 5-year est.).

Safety: Violent crime rate: 10.1 per 10,000 population; Property crime rate: 131.0 per 10,000 population (2011).

Newspapers: Leader Vindicator (Local news; Circulation 5,500)

Transportation: Commute to work: 86.3% car, 0.0% public transportation, 10.2% walk, 0.9% work from home (2006-2010 5-year est.); Travel time to work: 38.9% less than 15 minutes, 34.2% 15 to 30 minutes, 20.1% 30 to 45 minutes, 3.8% 45 to 60 minutes, 2.9% 60 minutes or more (2006-2010 5-year est.)

Additional Information Contacts

Redbank Valley Chamber of Commerce . . . . (814) 275-3929
   http://www.newbethlehemarea.com

PAINT (township). Covers a land area of 20.329 square miles and a water area of 0.354 square miles. Located at 41.24° N. Lat; 79.41° W. Long.

Population: 1,730 (1990); 1,778 (2000); 1,699 (2010); Density: 83.6 persons per square mile (2010); Race: 96.5% White, 1.1% Black, 0.8% Asian, 0.5% American Indian/Alaska Native, 0.0% Native Hawaiian/Other Pacific Islander, 1.1% Other, 2.1% Hispanic of any race (2010); Average household size: 2.23 (2010); Median age: 47.7 (2010); Males per 100 females: 98.7 (2010); Marriage status: 21.0% never married, 56.2% now married, 13.4% widowed, 9.4% divorced (2006-2010 5-year est.); Foreign born: 2.3% (2006-2010 5-year est.); Ancestry (includes multiple ancestries): 46.7% German, 16.1% Irish, 9.2% English, 5.8% Italian, 5.7% Scotch-Irish (2006-2010 5-year est.).

Economy: Single-family building permits issued: 0 (2011); Multi-family building permits issued: 0 (2011); Employment by occupation: 14.7% management, 2.0% professional, 14.0% services, 17.0% sales, 2.3% farming, 5.0% construction, 1.6% production (2006-2010 5-year est.).

Income: Per capita income: $30,617 (2006-2010 5-year est.); Median household income: $46,167 (2006-2010 5-year est.); Average household income: $71,265 (2006-2010 5-year est.); Percent of households with income of $100,000 or more: 15.0% (2006-2010 5-year est.); Poverty rate: 12.7% (2006-2010 5-year est.).

Education: Percent of population age 25 and over with: High school diploma (including GED) or higher: 88.9% (2006-2010 5-year est.); Bachelor's degree or higher: 26.3% (2006-2010 5-year est.); Master's degree or higher: 14.9% (2006-2010 5-year est.).

Housing: Homeownership rate: 82.7% (2010); Median home value: $116,700 (2006-2010 5-year est.); Median contract rent: $485 per month (2006-2010 5-year est.); Median year structure built: 1976 (2006-2010 5-year est.).

Transportation: Commute to work: 92.9% car, 0.0% public transportation, 5.1% walk, 2.0% work from home (2006-2010 5-year est.); Travel time to work: 56.4% less than 15 minutes, 25.5% 15 to 30 minutes, 10.8% 30 to 45 minutes, 4.5% 45 to 60 minutes, 2.8% 60 minutes or more (2006-2010 5-year est.)

Additional Information Contacts

Clarion Chamber of Business & Industry . . . . (814) 226-9161
   http://www.clarionpa.com

PERRY (township). Covers a land area of 28.805 square miles and a water area of 1.336 square miles. Located at 41.09° N. Lat; 79.64° W. Long.

Population: 1,076 (1990); 1,064 (2000); 947 (2010); Density: 32.9 persons per square mile (2010); Race: 99.3% White, 0.1% Black, 0.0% Asian, 0.4% American Indian/Alaska Native, 0.0% Native Hawaiian/Other Pacific Islander, 0.2% Other, 0.6% Hispanic of any race (2010); Average household size: 2.49 (2010); Median age: 45.1 (2010); Males per 100 females: 102.4 (2010); Marriage status: 26.5% never married, 63.4% now married, 5.1% widowed, 5.0% divorced (2006-2010 5-year est.); Foreign born: 0.3% (2006-2010 5-year est.); Ancestry (includes multiple ancestries): 44.4% German, 21.0% Irish, 10.3% American, 9.1% Dutch, 5.4% English (2006-2010 5-year est.).

Economy: Single-family building permits issued: 2 (2011); Multi-family building permits issued: 0 (2011); Employment by occupation: 12.2%

management, 0.0% professional, 10.9% services, 15.4% sales, 2.5% farming, 15.1% construction, 13.0% production (2006-2010 5-year est.).

Income: Per capita income: $19,360 (2006-2010 5-year est.); Median household income: $46,818 (2006-2010 5-year est.); Average household income: $48,526 (2006-2010 5-year est.); Percent of households with income of $100,000 or more: 5.1% (2006-2010 5-year est.); Poverty rate: 10.8% (2006-2010 5-year est.).

Education: Percent of population age 25 and over with: High school diploma (including GED) or higher: 87.5% (2006-2010 5-year est.); Bachelor's degree or higher: 11.2% (2006-2010 5-year est.); Master's degree or higher: 4.6% (2006-2010 5-year est.).

Housing: Homeownership rate: 85.8% (2010); Median home value: $68,800 (2006-2010 5-year est.); Median contract rent: $348 per month (2006-2010 5-year est.); Median year structure built: 1946 (2006-2010 5-year est.).

Transportation: Commute to work: 95.7% car, 0.0% public transportation, 1.9% walk, 2.4% work from home (2006-2010 5-year est.); Travel time to work: 19.3% less than 15 minutes, 32.9% 15 to 30 minutes, 24.4% 30 to 45 minutes, 13.6% 45 to 60 minutes, 9.8% 60 minutes or more (2006-2010 5-year est.)

Additional Information Contacts

Clarion Chamber of Business & Industry . . . . (814) 226-9161
   http://www.clarionpa.com

PINEY (township). Covers a land area of 17.769 square miles and a water area of 0.208 square miles. Located at 41.14° N. Lat; 79.47° W. Long.

Population: 515 (1990); 516 (2000); 453 (2010); Density: 25.5 persons per square mile (2010); Race: 99.1% White, 0.0% Black, 0.0% Asian, 0.2% American Indian/Alaska Native, 0.0% Native Hawaiian/Other Pacific Islander, 0.7% Other, 1.1% Hispanic of any race (2010); Average household size: 2.25 (2010); Median age: 53.5 (2010); Males per 100 females: 79.1 (2010); Marriage status: 18.2% never married, 67.9% now married, 8.6% widowed, 5.3% divorced (2006-2010 5-year est.); Foreign born: 0.0% (2006-2010 5-year est.); Ancestry (includes multiple ancestries): 43.0% German, 27.9% Irish, 16.9% American, 2.9% English, 2.2% Dutch (2006-2010 5-year est.).

Economy: Single-family building permits issued: 0 (2011); Multi-family building permits issued: 0 (2011); Employment by occupation: 6.0% management, 2.6% professional, 14.7% services, 12.9% sales, 3.4% farming, 17.2% construction, 12.1% production (2006-2010 5-year est.).

Income: Per capita income: $19,463 (2006-2010 5-year est.); Median household income: $37,375 (2006-2010 5-year est.); Average household income: $47,486 (2006-2010 5-year est.); Percent of households with income of $100,000 or more: 6.4% (2006-2010 5-year est.); Poverty rate: 8.5% (2006-2010 5-year est.).

Education: Percent of population age 25 and over with: High school diploma (including GED) or higher: 89.3% (2006-2010 5-year est.); Bachelor's degree or higher: 10.7% (2006-2010 5-year est.); Master's degree or higher: 1.7% (2006-2010 5-year est.).

Housing: Homeownership rate: 67.1% (2010); Median home value: $105,000 (2006-2010 5-year est.); Median contract rent: $263 per month (2006-2010 5-year est.); Median year structure built: 1951 (2006-2010 5-year est.).

Transportation: Commute to work: 95.2% car, 0.0% public transportation, 4.8% walk, 0.0% work from home (2006-2010 5-year est.); Travel time to work: 26.9% less than 15 minutes, 47.1% 15 to 30 minutes, 5.8% 30 to 45 minutes, 8.7% 45 to 60 minutes, 11.5% 60 minutes or more (2006-2010 5-year est.)

PORTER (township). Covers a land area of 43.881 square miles and a water area of 0.598 square miles. Located at 41.05° N. Lat; 79.41° W. Long.

Population: 1,564 (1990); 1,466 (2000); 1,348 (2010); Density: 30.7 persons per square mile (2010); Race: 98.8% White, 0.1% Black, 0.0% Asian, 0.0% American Indian/Alaska Native, 0.0% Native Hawaiian/Other Pacific Islander, 1.1% Other, 0.4% Hispanic of any race (2010); Average household size: 2.58 (2010); Median age: 43.4 (2010); Males per 100 females: 88.3 (2010); Marriage status: 27.5% never married, 60.4% now married, 5.8% widowed, 6.3% divorced (2006-2010 5-year est.); Foreign born: 0.0% (2006-2010 5-year est.); Ancestry (includes multiple ancestries): 47.0% German, 15.6% Irish, 11.1% Dutch, 9.1% English, 6.6% Italian (2006-2010 5-year est.).

Economy: Single-family building permits issued: 0 (2011); Multi-family building permits issued: 0 (2011); Employment by occupation: 6.0%

management, 1.7% professional, 12.1% services, 14.1% sales, 2.1% farming, 17.2% construction, 9.2% production (2006-2010 5-year est.).
Income: Per capita income: $20,143 (2006-2010 5-year est.); Median household income: $43,750 (2006-2010 5-year est.); Average household income: $53,451 (2006-2010 5-year est.); Percent of households with income of $100,000 or more: 10.1% (2006-2010 5-year est.); Poverty rate: 8.8% (2006-2010 5-year est.).
Education: Percent of population age 25 and over with: High school diploma (including GED) or higher: 88.3% (2006-2010 5-year est.); Bachelor's degree or higher: 16.4% (2006-2010 5-year est.); Master's degree or higher: 5.0% (2006-2010 5-year est.).
Housing: Homeownership rate: 81.6% (2010); Median home value: $102,600 (2006-2010 5-year est.); Median contract rent: $382 per month (2006-2010 5-year est.); Median year structure built: 1963 (2006-2010 5-year est.).
Transportation: Commute to work: 91.3% car, 0.7% public transportation, 3.5% walk, 3.1% work from home (2006-2010 5-year est.); Travel time to work: 34.6% less than 15 minutes, 33.2% 15 to 30 minutes, 20.5% 30 to 45 minutes, 4.7% 45 to 60 minutes, 7.0% 60 minutes or more (2006-2010 5-year est.)

Additional Information Contacts
Clarion Chamber of Business & Industry . . . . (814) 226-9161
  http://www.clarionpa.com

REDBANK (township).
Covers a land area of 30.053 square miles and a water area of 0.222 square miles. Located at 41.07° N. Lat; 79.27° W. Long.
Population: 1,576 (1990); 1,502 (2000); 1,370 (2010); Density: 45.6 persons per square mile (2010); Race: 98.2% White, 0.4% Black, 0.0% Asian, 0.0% American Indian/Alaska Native, 0.2% Native Hawaiian/Other Pacific Islander, 1.2% Other, 1.6% Hispanic of any race (2010); Average household size: 2.41 (2010); Median age: 45.5 (2010); Males per 100 females: 102.7 (2010); Marriage status: 28.2% never married, 57.8% now married, 6.9% widowed, 7.1% divorced (2006-2010 5-year est.); Foreign born: 0.2% (2006-2010 5-year est.); Ancestry (includes multiple ancestries): 38.7% German, 9.8% Dutch, 8.4% Irish, 8.2% American, 4.9% Scottish (2006-2010 5-year est.).
Economy: Single-family building permits issued: 2 (2011); Multi-family building permits issued: 0 (2011); Employment by occupation: 8.8% management, 2.1% professional, 12.9% services, 7.9% sales, 2.7% farming, 16.4% construction, 13.0% production (2006-2010 5-year est.).
Income: Per capita income: $21,805 (2006-2010 5-year est.); Median household income: $44,375 (2006-2010 5-year est.); Average household income: $53,558 (2006-2010 5-year est.); Percent of households with income of $100,000 or more: 10.0% (2006-2010 5-year est.); Poverty rate: 13.5% (2006-2010 5-year est.).
Education: Percent of population age 25 and over with: High school diploma (including GED) or higher: 86.4% (2006-2010 5-year est.); Bachelor's degree or higher: 15.2% (2006-2010 5-year est.); Master's degree or higher: 10.0% (2006-2010 5-year est.).
Housing: Homeownership rate: 75.5% (2010); Median home value: $84,900 (2006-2010 5-year est.); Median contract rent: $369 per month (2006-2010 5-year est.); Median year structure built: 1956 (2006-2010 5-year est.).
Transportation: Commute to work: 93.6% car, 0.0% public transportation, 2.2% walk, 2.2% work from home (2006-2010 5-year est.); Travel time to work: 29.4% less than 15 minutes, 35.6% 15 to 30 minutes, 23.6% 30 to 45 minutes, 3.5% 45 to 60 minutes, 7.8% 60 minutes or more (2006-2010 5-year est.)

Additional Information Contacts
Clarion Chamber of Business & Industry . . . . (814) 226-9161
  http://www.clarionpa.com

RICHLAND (township).
Covers a land area of 15.074 square miles and a water area of 0.712 square miles. Located at 41.17° N. Lat; 79.64° W. Long.
Population: 442 (1990); 553 (2000); 494 (2010); Density: 32.8 persons per square mile (2010); Race: 99.2% White, 0.0% Black, 0.4% Asian, 0.0% American Indian/Alaska Native, 0.0% Native Hawaiian/Other Pacific Islander, 0.4% Other, 0.2% Hispanic of any race (2010); Average household size: 2.52 (2010); Median age: 43.8 (2010); Males per 100 females: 96.8 (2010); Marriage status: 20.8% never married, 66.8% now married, 3.2% widowed, 9.2% divorced (2006-2010 5-year est.); Foreign born: 0.0% (2006-2010 5-year est.); Ancestry (includes multiple

ancestries): 40.8% German, 33.1% Irish, 13.2% English, 11.0% Swedish, 4.4% Scotch-Irish (2006-2010 5-year est.).
Economy: Single-family building permits issued: 0 (2011); Multi-family building permits issued: 0 (2011); Employment by occupation: 1.1% management, 0.0% professional, 6.9% services, 19.1% sales, 4.3% farming, 9.0% construction, 5.3% production (2006-2010 5-year est.).
Income: Per capita income: $21,502 (2006-2010 5-year est.); Median household income: $41,875 (2006-2010 5-year est.); Average household income: $52,333 (2006-2010 5-year est.); Percent of households with income of $100,000 or more: 12.9% (2006-2010 5-year est.); Poverty rate: 5.9% (2006-2010 5-year est.).
Education: Percent of population age 25 and over with: High school diploma (including GED) or higher: 80.3% (2006-2010 5-year est.); Bachelor's degree or higher: 15.6% (2006-2010 5-year est.); Master's degree or higher: 4.7% (2006-2010 5-year est.).
Housing: Homeownership rate: 85.2% (2010); Median home value: $106,500 (2006-2010 5-year est.); Median contract rent: $246 per month (2006-2010 5-year est.); Median year structure built: 1956 (2006-2010 5-year est.).
Transportation: Commute to work: 100.0% car, 0.0% public transportation, 0.0% walk, 0.0% work from home (2006-2010 5-year est.); Travel time to work: 19.1% less than 15 minutes, 44.1% 15 to 30 minutes, 30.9% 30 to 45 minutes, 4.3% 45 to 60 minutes, 1.6% 60 minutes or more (2006-2010 5-year est.)

RIMERSBURG (borough).
Covers a land area of 0.364 square miles and a water area of 0 square miles. Located at 41.04° N. Lat; 79.50° W. Long. Elevation is 1,486 feet.
History: Settled 1829; laid out 1839; incorporated 1853.
Population: 1,053 (1990); 1,051 (2000); 951 (2010); Density: 2,614.7 persons per square mile (2010); Race: 98.2% White, 0.6% Black, 0.1% Asian, 0.0% American Indian/Alaska Native, 0.0% Native Hawaiian/Other Pacific Islander, 1.1% Other, 0.4% Hispanic of any race (2010); Average household size: 2.40 (2010); Median age: 38.1 (2010); Males per 100 females: 87.2 (2010); Marriage status: 30.5% never married, 46.4% now married, 10.9% widowed, 12.3% divorced (2006-2010 5-year est.); Foreign born: 0.0% (2006-2010 5-year est.); Ancestry (includes multiple ancestries): 35.4% German, 12.9% Irish, 7.3% American, 7.3% Dutch, 6.0% English (2006-2010 5-year est.).
Economy: Single-family building permits issued: 1 (2011); Multi-family building permits issued: 0 (2011); Employment by occupation: 5.4% management, 3.6% professional, 13.5% services, 14.1% sales, 4.3% farming, 10.1% construction, 16.6% production (2006-2010 5-year est.).
Income: Per capita income: $17,952 (2006-2010 5-year est.); Median household income: $38,942 (2006-2010 5-year est.); Average household income: $42,300 (2006-2010 5-year est.); Percent of households with income of $100,000 or more: 4.8% (2006-2010 5-year est.); Poverty rate: 29.4% (2006-2010 5-year est.).
Education: Percent of population age 25 and over with: High school diploma (including GED) or higher: 81.9% (2006-2010 5-year est.); Bachelor's degree or higher: 11.9% (2006-2010 5-year est.); Master's degree or higher: 4.2% (2006-2010 5-year est.).

School District(s)
Union SD (KG-12)
  2010-11 Enrollment: 593 . . . . (814) 473-6311
Housing: Homeownership rate: 53.7% (2010); Median home value: $77,600 (2006-2010 5-year est.); Median contract rent: $226 per month (2006-2010 5-year est.); Median year structure built: 1951 (2006-2010 5-year est.).
Transportation: Commute to work: 94.2% car, 0.0% public transportation, 1.2% walk, 3.5% work from home (2006-2010 5-year est.); Travel time to work: 34.0% less than 15 minutes, 22.0% 15 to 30 minutes, 25.6% 30 to 45 minutes, 9.6% 45 to 60 minutes, 8.9% 60 minutes or more (2006-2010 5-year est.)

Additional Information Contacts
Clarion Chamber of Business & Industry . . . . (814) 226-9161
  http://www.clarionpa.com

SAINT PETERSBURG (borough).
Covers a land area of 0.319 square miles and a water area of 0 square miles. Located at 41.16° N. Lat; 79.65° W. Long. Elevation is 1,401 feet.
Population: 397 (1990); 405 (2000); 400 (2010); Density: 1,253.9 persons per square mile (2010); Race: 99.5% White, 0.0% Black, 0.5% Asian, 0.0% American Indian/Alaska Native, 0.0% Native Hawaiian/Other Pacific Islander, 0.0% Other, 0.0% Hispanic of any race (2010); Average

household size: 2.40 (2010); Median age: 39.9 (2010); Males per 100 females: 97.0 (2010); Marriage status: 16.7% never married, 62.6% now married, 3.3% widowed, 17.4% divorced (2006-2010 5-year est.); Foreign born: 6.3% (2006-2010 5-year est.); Ancestry (includes multiple ancestries): 30.5% Irish, 29.8% German, 20.0% Italian, 6.3% Russian, 5.4% Dutch (2006-2010 5-year est.).

Economy: Single-family building permits issued: 0 (2011); Multi-family building permits issued: 0 (2011); Employment by occupation: 2.0% management, 4.0% professional, 12.7% services, 11.3% sales, 0.0% farming, 8.0% construction, 9.3% production (2006-2010 5-year est.).

Income: Per capita income: $19,879 (2006-2010 5-year est.); Median household income: $43,250 (2006-2010 5-year est.); Average household income: $48,914 (2006-2010 5-year est.); Percent of households with income of $100,000 or more: 10.8% (2006-2010 5-year est.); Poverty rate: 10.5% (2006-2010 5-year est.).

Education: Percent of population age 25 and over with: High school diploma (including GED) or higher: 86.1% (2006-2010 5-year est.); Bachelor's degree or higher: 8.9% (2006-2010 5-year est.); Master's degree or higher: 3.8% (2006-2010 5-year est.).

Housing: Homeownership rate: 73.6% (2010); Median home value: $104,000 (2006-2010 5-year est.); Median contract rent: $442 per month (2006-2010 5-year est.); Median year structure built: before 1940 (2006-2010 5-year est.).

Transportation: Commute to work: 97.3% car, 0.0% public transportation, 0.0% walk, 2.7% work from home (2006-2010 5-year est.); Travel time to work: 35.7% less than 15 minutes, 32.2% 15 to 30 minutes, 22.4% 30 to 45 minutes, 1.4% 45 to 60 minutes, 8.4% 60 minutes or more (2006-2010 5-year est.)

SALEM (township). Covers a land area of 16.037 square miles and a water area of 0.282 square miles. Located at 41.22° N. Lat; 79.62° W. Long.

Population: 893 (1990); 852 (2000); 881 (2010); Density: 54.9 persons per square mile (2010); Race: 99.4% White, 0.1% Black, 0.1% Asian, 0.0% American Indian/Alaska Native, 0.0% Native Hawaiian/Other Pacific Islander, 0.4% Other, 0.0% Hispanic of any race (2010); Average household size: 2.65 (2010); Median age: 40.1 (2010); Males per 100 females: 98.0 (2010); Marriage status: 24.6% never married, 56.5% now married, 9.1% widowed, 9.8% divorced (2006-2010 5-year est.); Foreign born: 0.3% (2006-2010 5-year est.); Ancestry (includes multiple ancestries): 57.6% German, 15.5% Irish, 8.9% English, 7.2% Scotch-Irish, 4.5% Dutch (2006-2010 5-year est.).

Economy: Single-family building permits issued: 1 (2011); Multi-family building permits issued: 0 (2011); Employment by occupation: 6.3% management, 6.3% professional, 9.6% services, 12.6% sales, 2.2% farming, 16.9% construction, 9.3% production (2006-2010 5-year est.).

Income: Per capita income: $19,917 (2006-2010 5-year est.); Median household income: $49,545 (2006-2010 5-year est.); Average household income: $54,057 (2006-2010 5-year est.); Percent of households with income of $100,000 or more: 9.9% (2006-2010 5-year est.); Poverty rate: 14.8% (2006-2010 5-year est.).

Education: Percent of population age 25 and over with: High school diploma (including GED) or higher: 93.2% (2006-2010 5-year est.); Bachelor's degree or higher: 25.2% (2006-2010 5-year est.); Master's degree or higher: 6.0% (2006-2010 5-year est.).

Housing: Homeownership rate: 83.1% (2010); Median home value: $105,600 (2006-2010 5-year est.); Median contract rent: $428 per month (2006-2010 5-year est.); Median year structure built: 1955 (2006-2010 5-year est.).

Transportation: Commute to work: 89.1% car, 0.0% public transportation, 3.7% walk, 5.1% work from home (2006-2010 5-year est.); Travel time to work: 25.2% less than 15 minutes, 45.3% 15 to 30 minutes, 17.4% 30 to 45 minutes, 2.4% 45 to 60 minutes, 9.8% 60 minutes or more (2006-2010 5-year est.)

SHIPPENVILLE (borough). Covers a land area of 0.307 square miles and a water area of 0 square miles. Located at 41.25° N. Lat; 79.46° W. Long. Elevation is 1,378 feet.

Population: 474 (1990); 505 (2000); 480 (2010); Density: 1,565.4 persons per square mile (2010); Race: 98.8% White, 0.0% Black, 0.4% Asian, 0.0% American Indian/Alaska Native, 0.0% Native Hawaiian/Other Pacific Islander, 0.8% Other, 0.2% Hispanic of any race (2010); Average household size: 2.30 (2010); Median age: 36.7 (2010); Males per 100 females: 99.2 (2010); Marriage status: 32.7% never married, 43.8% now married, 9.9% widowed, 13.6% divorced (2006-2010 5-year est.); Foreign

born: 0.6% (2006-2010 5-year est.); Ancestry (includes multiple ancestries): 40.5% German, 19.8% Irish, 14.2% American, 9.1% English, 5.7% Dutch (2006-2010 5-year est.).

Economy: Single-family building permits issued: 0 (2011); Multi-family building permits issued: 0 (2011); Employment by occupation: 6.1% management, 0.0% professional, 10.5% services, 19.5% sales, 6.1% farming, 11.2% construction, 6.5% production (2006-2010 5-year est.).

Income: Per capita income: $22,969 (2006-2010 5-year est.); Median household income: $44,375 (2006-2010 5-year est.); Average household income: $49,207 (2006-2010 5-year est.); Percent of households with income of $100,000 or more: 6.3% (2006-2010 5-year est.); Poverty rate: 7.0% (2006-2010 5-year est.).

Education: Percent of population age 25 and over with: High school diploma (including GED) or higher: 89.0% (2006-2010 5-year est.); Bachelor's degree or higher: 19.5% (2006-2010 5-year est.); Master's degree or higher: 4.8% (2006-2010 5-year est.).

School District(s)

Clarion County Career Center (09-12)

    2010-11 Enrollment: n/a . . . . (814) 226-4391

Vocational/Technical School(s)

Clarion County Career Center Practical Nursing Program (Public)

    Fall 2010 Enrollment: 74 . . . . (814) 226-5857

    2011-12 Tuition: $12,275

Housing: Homeownership rate: 63.8% (2010); Median home value: $79,300 (2006-2010 5-year est.); Median contract rent: $452 per month (2006-2010 5-year est.); Median year structure built: 1943 (2006-2010 5-year est.).

Transportation: Commute to work: 87.7% car, 0.0% public transportation, 5.2% walk, 3.7% work from home (2006-2010 5-year est.); Travel time to work: 49.4% less than 15 minutes, 31.3% 15 to 30 minutes, 7.7% 30 to 45 minutes, 8.1% 45 to 60 minutes, 3.5% 60 minutes or more (2006-2010 5-year est.)

SLIGO (borough). Covers a land area of 1.407 square miles and a water area of 0.003 square miles. Located at 41.11° N. Lat; 79.50° W. Long. Elevation is 1,152 feet.

Population: 706 (1990); 728 (2000); 720 (2010); Density: 511.7 persons per square mile (2010); Race: 98.2% White, 0.7% Black, 1.0% Asian, 0.0% American Indian/Alaska Native, 0.0% Native Hawaiian/Other Pacific Islander, 0.1% Other, 0.1% Hispanic of any race (2010); Average household size: 2.58 (2010); Median age: 37.1 (2010); Males per 100 females: 95.1 (2010); Marriage status: 26.6% never married, 59.4% now married, 9.0% widowed, 5.0% divorced (2006-2010 5-year est.); Foreign born: 0.0% (2006-2010 5-year est.); Ancestry (includes multiple ancestries): 31.9% German, 16.4% Irish, 5.2% American, 5.2% Italian, 5.2% Dutch (2006-2010 5-year est.).

Economy: Single-family building permits issued: 0 (2011); Multi-family building permits issued: 0 (2011); Employment by occupation: 4.3% management, 0.0% professional, 14.6% services, 11.3% sales, 4.3% farming, 12.1% construction, 12.1% production (2006-2010 5-year est.).

Income: Per capita income: $17,511 (2006-2010 5-year est.); Median household income: $41,429 (2006-2010 5-year est.); Average household income: $47,897 (2006-2010 5-year est.); Percent of households with income of $100,000 or more: 5.1% (2006-2010 5-year est.); Poverty rate: 9.7% (2006-2010 5-year est.).

Education: Percent of population age 25 and over with: High school diploma (including GED) or higher: 89.0% (2006-2010 5-year est.); Bachelor's degree or higher: 21.1% (2006-2010 5-year est.); Master's degree or higher: 5.4% (2006-2010 5-year est.).

School District(s)

Union SD (KG-12)

    2010-11 Enrollment: 593 . . . . (814) 473-6311

Housing: Homeownership rate: 65.3% (2010); Median home value: $66,400 (2006-2010 5-year est.); Median contract rent: $460 per month (2006-2010 5-year est.); Median year structure built: 1943 (2006-2010 5-year est.).

Transportation: Commute to work: 89.1% car, 0.0% public transportation, 4.4% walk, 0.9% work from home (2006-2010 5-year est.); Travel time to work: 33.0% less than 15 minutes, 50.0% 15 to 30 minutes, 10.1% 30 to 45 minutes, 4.8% 45 to 60 minutes, 2.1% 60 minutes or more (2006-2010 5-year est.)

STRATTANVILLE (borough). Aka Strattonville. Covers a land area of 0.505 square miles and a water area of 0 square miles. Located at 41.20° N. Lat; 79.33° W. Long. Elevation is 1,532 feet.

Population: 490 (1990); 542 (2000); 550 (2010); Density: 1,089.1 persons per square mile (2010); Race: 95.5% White, 1.1% Black, 0.4% Asian, 0.7% American Indian/Alaska Native, 0.0% Native Hawaiian/Other Pacific Islander, 2.3% Other, 2.2% Hispanic of any race (2010); Average household size: 2.15 (2010); Median age: 38.9 (2010); Males per 100 females: 86.4 (2010); Marriage status: 32.6% never married, 46.0% now married, 9.5% widowed, 12.0% divorced (2006-2010 5-year est.); Foreign born: 1.4% (2006-2010 5-year est.); Ancestry (includes multiple ancestries): 45.4% German, 14.2% Irish, 8.9% Italian, 7.3% English, 5.5% Portuguese (2006-2010 5-year est.).

Economy: Single-family building permits issued: 0 (2011); Multi-family building permits issued: 0 (2011); Employment by occupation: 2.8% management, 1.0% professional, 19.2% services, 22.4% sales, 0.0% farming, 16.8% construction, 15.0% production (2006-2010 5-year est.).

Income: Per capita income: $15,415 (2006-2010 5-year est.); Median household income: $27,283 (2006-2010 5-year est.); Average household income: $36,073 (2006-2010 5-year est.); Percent of households with income of $100,000 or more: 4.5% (2006-2010 5-year est.); Poverty rate: 25.8% (2006-2010 5-year est.).

Education: Percent of population age 25 and over with: High school diploma (including GED) or higher: 82.9% (2006-2010 5-year est.); Bachelor's degree or higher: 18.5% (2006-2010 5-year est.); Master's degree or higher: 5.2% (2006-2010 5-year est.).

School District(s)

Clarion-Limestone Area SD (KG-12)

2010-11 Enrollment: 964 . . . . (814) 764-5111

Housing: Homeownership rate: 52.3% (2010); Median home value: $67,400 (2006-2010 5-year est.); Median contract rent: $421 per month (2006-2010 5-year est.); Median year structure built: 1957 (2006-2010 5-year est.).

Transportation: Commute to work: 93.0% car, 0.0% public transportation, 4.2% walk, 0.0% work from home (2006-2010 5-year est.); Travel time to work: 45.8% less than 15 minutes, 36.4% 15 to 30 minutes, 14.7% 30 to 45 minutes, 0.0% 45 to 60 minutes, 3.1% 60 minutes or more (2006-2010 5-year est.)

TOBY (township). Covers a land area of 29.041 square miles and a water area of 0.334 square miles. Located at 41.07° N. Lat; 79.53° W. Long. Elevation is 1,171 feet.

Population: 1,153 (1990); 1,166 (2000); 991 (2010); Density: 34.1 persons per square mile (2010); Race: 98.1% White, 0.7% Black, 0.1% Asian, 0.0% American Indian/Alaska Native, 0.0% Native Hawaiian/Other Pacific Islander, 1.1% Other, 0.7% Hispanic of any race (2010); Average household size: 2.50 (2010); Median age: 42.9 (2010); Males per 100 females: 106.0 (2010); Marriage status: 21.5% never married, 59.1% now married, 6.2% widowed, 13.3% divorced (2006-2010 5-year est.); Foreign born: 0.0% (2006-2010 5-year est.); Ancestry (includes multiple ancestries): 32.1% German, 14.9% Irish, 12.3% American, 9.8% Italian, 7.1% Dutch (2006-2010 5-year est.).

Economy: Single-family building permits issued: 1 (2011); Multi-family building permits issued: 0 (2011); Employment by occupation: 3.5% management, 0.0% professional, 10.7% services, 19.0% sales, 0.0% farming, 12.9% construction, 11.0% production (2006-2010 5-year est.).

Income: Per capita income: $20,257 (2006-2010 5-year est.); Median household income: $41,719 (2006-2010 5-year est.); Average household income: $50,162 (2006-2010 5-year est.); Percent of households with income of $100,000 or more: 10.3% (2006-2010 5-year est.); Poverty rate: 13.0% (2006-2010 5-year est.).

Education: Percent of population age 25 and over with: High school diploma (including GED) or higher: 80.3% (2006-2010 5-year est.); Bachelor's degree or higher: 12.1% (2006-2010 5-year est.); Master's degree or higher: 3.1% (2006-2010 5-year est.).

Housing: Homeownership rate: 76.4% (2010); Median home value: $65,700 (2006-2010 5-year est.); Median contract rent: $316 per month (2006-2010 5-year est.); Median year structure built: 1952 (2006-2010 5-year est.).

Transportation: Commute to work: 93.7% car, 0.0% public transportation, 2.7% walk, 3.5% work from home (2006-2010 5-year est.); Travel time to work: 30.8% less than 15 minutes, 23.4% 15 to 30 minutes, 26.6% 30 to 45 minutes, 6.8% 45 to 60 minutes, 12.4% 60 minutes or more (2006-2010 5-year est.)

Additional Information Contacts

Clarion Chamber of Business & Industry . . . . (814) 226-9161
http://www.clarionpa.com

TYLERSBURG (CDP). Covers a land area of 0.591 square miles and a water area of 0.003 square miles. Located at 41.38° N. Lat; 79.32° W. Long. Elevation is 1,562 feet.

Population: n/a (1990); n/a (2000); 196 (2010); Density: 331.8 persons per square mile (2010); Race: 99.0% White, 0.0% Black, 0.0% Asian, 0.0% American Indian/Alaska Native, 0.0% Native Hawaiian/Other Pacific Islander, 1.0% Other, 2.0% Hispanic of any race (2010); Average household size: 2.65 (2010); Median age: 43.5 (2010); Males per 100 females: 102.1 (2010); Marriage status: 17.4% never married, 56.5% now married, 0.0% widowed, 26.1% divorced (2006-2010 5-year est.); Foreign born: 0.0% (2006-2010 5-year est.); Ancestry (includes multiple ancestries): 61.5% German, 22.6% English, 19.2% Italian, 10.2% Scottish, 7.2% Irish (2006-2010 5-year est.).

Economy: Employment by occupation: 0.0% management, 16.8% professional, 9.7% services, 6.2% sales, 0.0% farming, 0.0% construction, 0.0% production (2006-2010 5-year est.).

Income: Per capita income: $17,800 (2006-2010 5-year est.); Median household income: $60,263 (2006-2010 5-year est.); Average household income: $59,344 (2006-2010 5-year est.); Percent of households with income of $100,000 or more: 7.5% (2006-2010 5-year est.); Poverty rate: 13.6% (2006-2010 5-year est.).

Education: Percent of population age 25 and over with: High school diploma (including GED) or higher: 100.0% (2006-2010 5-year est.); Bachelor's degree or higher: 23.3% (2006-2010 5-year est.); Master's degree or higher: 0.0% (2006-2010 5-year est.).

Housing: Homeownership rate: 83.8% (2010); Median home value: $121,600 (2006-2010 5-year est.); Median contract rent: $664 per month (2006-2010 5-year est.); Median year structure built: 1952 (2006-2010 5-year est.).

Transportation: Commute to work: 78.3% car, 0.0% public transportation, 0.0% walk, 0.0% work from home (2006-2010 5-year est.); Travel time to work: 0.0% less than 15 minutes, 49.1% 15 to 30 minutes, 10.4% 30 to 45 minutes, 22.6% 45 to 60 minutes, 17.9% 60 minutes or more (2006-2010 5-year est.)

VOWINCKEL (CDP). Covers a land area of 2.465 square miles and a water area of 0.003 square miles. Located at 41.40° N. Lat; 79.23° W. Long. Elevation is 1,634 feet.

Population: n/a (1990); n/a (2000); 139 (2010); Density: 56.4 persons per square mile (2010); Race: 99.3% White, 0.0% Black, 0.0% Asian, 0.0% American Indian/Alaska Native, 0.0% Native Hawaiian/Other Pacific Islander, 0.7% Other, 0.7% Hispanic of any race (2010); Average household size: 2.40 (2010); Median age: 42.3 (2010); Males per 100 females: 98.6 (2010); Marriage status: 18.9% never married, 66.2% now married, 14.9% widowed, 0.0% divorced (2006-2010 5-year est.); Foreign born: 0.0% (2006-2010 5-year est.); Ancestry (includes multiple ancestries): 15.0% German, 10.3% Dutch, 5.6% Irish, 4.7% Scotch-Irish (2006-2010 5-year est.).

Economy: Employment by occupation: 0.0% management, 0.0% professional, 60.7% services, 39.3% sales, 0.0% farming, 0.0% construction, 0.0% production (2006-2010 5-year est.).

Income: Per capita income: $11,495 (2006-2010 5-year est.); Median household income: $22,708 (2006-2010 5-year est.); Average household income: $26,660 (2006-2010 5-year est.); Percent of households with income of $100,000 or more: n/a (2006-2010 5-year est.); Poverty rate: 14.0% (2006-2010 5-year est.).

Education: Percent of population age 25 and over with: High school diploma (including GED) or higher: 71.6% (2006-2010 5-year est.); Bachelor's degree or higher: 0.0% (2006-2010 5-year est.); Master's degree or higher: 0.0% (2006-2010 5-year est.).

Housing: Homeownership rate: 91.4% (2010); Median home value: $69,700 (2006-2010 5-year est.); Median contract rent: n/a per month (2006-2010 5-year est.); Median year structure built: 1948 (2006-2010 5-year est.).

Transportation: Commute to work: 100.0% car, 0.0% public transportation, 0.0% walk, 0.0% work from home (2006-2010 5-year est.); Travel time to work: 39.3% less than 15 minutes, 0.0% 15 to 30 minutes, 17.9% 30 to 45 minutes, 42.9% 45 to 60 minutes, 0.0% 60 minutes or more (2006-2010 5-year est.)

WASHINGTON (township). Covers a land area of 32.943 square miles and a water area of 0.070 square miles. Located at 41.37° N. Lat; 79.42° W. Long.
Population: 1,925 (1990); 2,037 (2000); 1,887 (2010); Density: 57.3 persons per square mile (2010); Race: 98.8% White, 0.2% Black, 0.0% Asian, 0.4% American Indian/Alaska Native, 0.0% Native Hawaiian/Other Pacific Islander, 0.6% Other, 0.4% Hispanic of any race (2010); Average household size: 2.61 (2010); Median age: 39.3 (2010); Males per 100 females: 104.7 (2010); Marriage status: 22.7% never married, 63.1% now married, 6.1% widowed, 8.1% divorced (2006-2010 5-year est.); Foreign born: 0.0% (2006-2010 5-year est.); Ancestry (includes multiple ancestries): 44.5% German, 12.0% Irish, 9.7% Pennsylvania German, 3.4% Italian, 3.0% English (2006-2010 5-year est.).
Economy: Single-family building permits issued: 2 (2011); Multi-family building permits issued: 0 (2011); Employment by occupation: 11.0% management, 2.3% professional, 7.2% services, 13.2% sales, 2.2% farming, 13.6% construction, 7.5% production (2006-2010 5-year est.).
Income: Per capita income: $14,550 (2006-2010 5-year est.); Median household income: $36,713 (2006-2010 5-year est.); Average household income: $42,709 (2006-2010 5-year est.); Percent of households with income of $100,000 or more: 4.8% (2006-2010 5-year est.); Poverty rate: 22.3% (2006-2010 5-year est.).
Education: Percent of population age 25 and over with: High school diploma (including GED) or higher: 87.9% (2006-2010 5-year est.); Bachelor's degree or higher: 16.1% (2006-2010 5-year est.); Master's degree or higher: 2.5% (2006-2010 5-year est.).
Housing: Homeownership rate: 81.7% (2010); Median home value: $98,700 (2006-2010 5-year est.); Median contract rent: $418 per month (2006-2010 5-year est.); Median year structure built: 1970 (2006-2010 5-year est.).
Transportation: Commute to work: 92.9% car, 0.0% public transportation, 2.8% walk, 4.0% work from home (2006-2010 5-year est.); Travel time to work: 35.3% less than 15 minutes, 40.1% 15 to 30 minutes, 19.2% 30 to 45 minutes, 3.3% 45 to 60 minutes, 2.1% 60 minutes or more (2006-2010 5-year est.)
Additional Information Contacts
Clarion Chamber of Business & Industry . . . . (814) 226-9161
  http://www.clarionpa.com

Clearfield County

Located in central Pennsylvania; upland area, drained by the West Branch of the Susquehanna River. Covers a land area of 1,144.722 square miles, a water area of 9.241 square miles, and is located in the Eastern Time Zone at 41.00° N. Lat., 78.47° W. Long. The county was founded in 1804. County seat is Clearfield.

Clearfield County is part of the DuBois, PA Micropolitan Statistical Area. The entire metro area includes: Clearfield County, PA

Population: 78,097 (1990); 83,382 (2000); 81,642 (2010); Race: 95.4% White, 2.3% Black, 0.5% Asian, 0.1% American Indian/Alaska Native, 0.0% Native Hawaiian/Other Pacific Islander, 1.7% Other, 2.3% Hispanic of any race (2010); Density: 71.3 persons per square mile (2010); Average household size: 2.37 (2010); Median age: 42.9 (2010); Males per 100 females: 106.6 (2010).
Religion: Six largest groups: 23.7% Catholicism, 12.1% Methodist/Pietist, 4.9% Holiness, 3.9% Lutheran, 2.6% Presbyterian-Reformed, 1.3% Non-Denominational (2010)
Economy: Unemployment rate: 8.7% (August 2012); Total civilian labor force: 41,667 (August 2012); Leading industries: 23.2% health care and social assistance; 17.7% retail trade; 11.5% transportation & warehousing (2010); Farms: 473 totaling 62,721 acres (2007); Companies that employ 500 or more persons: 3 (2010); Companies that employ 100 to 499 persons: 29 (2010); Companies that employ less than 100 persons: 1,945 (2010); Black-owned businesses: n/a (2007); Hispanic-owned businesses: n/a (2007); Asian-owned businesses: n/a (2007); Women-owned businesses: 1,400 (2007); Retail sales per capita: $11,718 (2010). Single-family building permits issued: 62 (2011); Multi-family building permits issued: 0 (2011).
Income: Per capita income: $20,142 (2006-2010 5-year est.); Median household income: $37,130 (2006-2010 5-year est.); Average household income: $47,022 (2006-2010 5-year est.); Percent of households with income of $100,000 or more: 7.6% (2006-2010 5-year est.); Poverty rate: 14.7% (2006-2010 5-year est.); Bankruptcy rate: 2.72% (2011).

Education: Percent of population age 25 and over with: High school diploma (including GED) or higher: 86.0% (2006-2010 5-year est.); Bachelor's degree or higher: 12.3% (2006-2010 5-year est.); Master's degree or higher: 3.8% (2006-2010 5-year est.).
Housing: Homeownership rate: 76.9% (2010); Median home value: $82,900 (2006-2010 5-year est.); Median contract rent: $384 per month (2006-2010 5-year est.); Median year structure built: 1960 (2006-2010 5-year est.)
Health: Birth rate: 86.9 per 10,000 population (2011); Death rate: 110.3 per 10,000 population (2011); Age-adjusted cancer mortality rate: 183.5 deaths per 100,000 population (2009); Number of physicians: 19.1 per 10,000 population (2010); Hospital beds: 36.2 per 10,000 population (2008); Hospital admissions: 1,577.1 per 10,000 population (2008).
Environment: Air Quality Index: 92.9% good, 6.8% moderate, 0.3% unhealthy for sensitive individuals, 0.0% unhealthy (percent of days in 2011)
Elections: 2012 Presidential election results: 34.8% Obama, 63.6% Romney
National and State Parks: Curwensville State Park; Parker Dam State Park; S B Elliott State Park
Additional Information Contacts
Clearfield County Government . . . . (814) 765-2641
  http://www.clearfieldco.org

Clearfield County Communities

ALLPORT (CDP). Covers a land area of 0.597 square miles and a water area of 0.002 square miles. Located at 40.97° N. Lat; 78.20° W. Long. Elevation is 1,611 feet.
Population: n/a (1990); n/a (2000); 264 (2010); Density: 442.3 persons per square mile (2010); Race: 98.9% White, 0.4% Black, 0.0% Asian, 0.0% American Indian/Alaska Native, 0.0% Native Hawaiian/Other Pacific Islander, 0.7% Other, 1.1% Hispanic of any race (2010); Average household size: 2.64 (2010); Median age: 42.1 (2010); Males per 100 females: 87.2 (2010); Marriage status: 14.2% never married, 65.5% now married, 16.8% widowed, 3.6% divorced (2006-2010 5-year est.); Foreign born: 9.4% (2006-2010 5-year est.); Ancestry (includes multiple ancestries): 27.5% Dutch, 25.4% Polish, 18.0% English, 17.2% German, 9.4% Russian (2006-2010 5-year est.).
Economy: Employment by occupation: 16.9% management, 0.0% professional, 14.6% services, 0.0% sales, 0.0% farming, 23.6% construction, 14.6% production (2006-2010 5-year est.).
Income: Per capita income: $16,767 (2006-2010 5-year est.); Median household income: $52,792 (2006-2010 5-year est.); Average household income: $49,470 (2006-2010 5-year est.); Percent of households with income of $100,000 or more: n/a (2006-2010 5-year est.); Poverty rate: 2.9% (2006-2010 5-year est.).
Education: Percent of population age 25 and over with: High school diploma (including GED) or higher: 93.5% (2006-2010 5-year est.); Bachelor's degree or higher: 11.8% (2006-2010 5-year est.); Master's degree or higher: 0.0% (2006-2010 5-year est.).
Housing: Homeownership rate: 88.0% (2010); Median home value: $118,500 (2006-2010 5-year est.); Median contract rent: n/a per month (2006-2010 5-year est.); Median year structure built: 1984 (2006-2010 5-year est.).
Transportation: Commute to work: 100.0% car, 0.0% public transportation, 0.0% walk, 0.0% work from home (2006-2010 5-year est.); Travel time to work: 58.4% less than 15 minutes, 0.0% 15 to 30 minutes, 16.9% 30 to 45 minutes, 16.9% 45 to 60 minutes, 7.9% 60 minutes or more (2006-2010 5-year est.)

BECCARIA (township). Covers a land area of 35.769 square miles and a water area of 0.229 square miles. Located at 40.76° N. Lat; 78.52° W. Long.
Population: 1,869 (1990); 1,835 (2000); 1,782 (2010); Density: 49.8 persons per square mile (2010); Race: 99.3% White, 0.1% Black, 0.0% Asian, 0.0% American Indian/Alaska Native, 0.0% Native Hawaiian/Other Pacific Islander, 0.6% Other, 0.4% Hispanic of any race (2010); Average household size: 2.43 (2010); Median age: 45.0 (2010); Males per 100 females: 96.9 (2010); Marriage status: 21.6% never married, 54.6% now married, 8.5% widowed, 15.4% divorced (2006-2010 5-year est.); Foreign born: 0.2% (2006-2010 5-year est.); Ancestry (includes multiple ancestries): 36.3% German, 17.4% Irish, 14.2% English, 9.6% Polish, 6.2% American (2006-2010 5-year est.).

Economy: Single-family building permits issued: 3 (2011); Multi-family building permits issued: 0 (2011); Employment by occupation: 4.1% management, 2.1% professional, 13.2% services, 9.1% sales, 3.0% farming, 21.5% construction, 11.4% production (2006-2010 5-year est.).
Income: Per capita income: $18,347 (2006-2010 5-year est.); Median household income: $33,214 (2006-2010 5-year est.); Average household income: $40,340 (2006-2010 5-year est.); Percent of households with income of $100,000 or more: 5.7% (2006-2010 5-year est.); Poverty rate: 16.1% (2006-2010 5-year est.).
Education: Percent of population age 25 and over with: High school diploma (including GED) or higher: 83.3% (2006-2010 5-year est.); Bachelor's degree or higher: 5.9% (2006-2010 5-year est.); Master's degree or higher: 1.3% (2006-2010 5-year est.).
Housing: Homeownership rate: 88.1% (2010); Median home value: $70,800 (2006-2010 5-year est.); Median contract rent: $263 per month (2006-2010 5-year est.); Median year structure built: 1959 (2006-2010 5-year est.).
Transportation: Commute to work: 95.3% car, 0.0% public transportation, 2.0% walk, 2.1% work from home (2006-2010 5-year est.); Travel time to work: 20.1% less than 15 minutes, 22.3% 15 to 30 minutes, 29.3% 30 to 45 minutes, 14.4% 45 to 60 minutes, 13.9% 60 minutes or more (2006-2010 5-year est.)
Additional Information Contacts
Tyron Area Chamber of Commerce . . . . (814) 684-0736
 http://www.tyronechamber.com

BELL (township). Covers a land area of 56.681 square miles and a water area of 0.244 square miles. Located at 40.92° N. Lat; 78.75° W. Long.
Population: 925 (1990); 825 (2000); 760 (2010); Density: 13.4 persons per square mile (2010); Race: 99.3% White, 0.0% Black, 0.0% Asian, 0.3% American Indian/Alaska Native, 0.0% Native Hawaiian/Other Pacific Islander, 0.4% Other, 0.4% Hispanic of any race (2010); Average household size: 2.48 (2010); Median age: 45.4 (2010); Males per 100 females: 101.1 (2010); Marriage status: 20.7% never married, 56.0% now married, 7.4% widowed, 16.0% divorced (2006-2010 5-year est.); Foreign born: 0.3% (2006-2010 5-year est.); Ancestry (includes multiple ancestries): 31.5% German, 14.0% American, 13.1% English, 9.7% Italian, 7.1% Irish (2006-2010 5-year est.).
Economy: Single-family building permits issued: 2 (2011); Multi-family building permits issued: 0 (2011); Employment by occupation: 5.6% management, 3.8% professional, 14.6% services, 17.1% sales, 0.7% farming, 18.5% construction, 9.4% production (2006-2010 5-year est.).
Income: Per capita income: $15,651 (2006-2010 5-year est.); Median household income: $31,250 (2006-2010 5-year est.); Average household income: $40,861 (2006-2010 5-year est.); Percent of households with income of $100,000 or more: 3.4% (2006-2010 5-year est.); Poverty rate: 12.9% (2006-2010 5-year est.).
Education: Percent of population age 25 and over with: High school diploma (including GED) or higher: 87.0% (2006-2010 5-year est.); Bachelor's degree or higher: 6.7% (2006-2010 5-year est.); Master's degree or higher: 2.3% (2006-2010 5-year est.).
Housing: Homeownership rate: 87.0% (2010); Median home value: $92,500 (2006-2010 5-year est.); Median contract rent: $555 per month (2006-2010 5-year est.); Median year structure built: 1972 (2006-2010 5-year est.).
Transportation: Commute to work: 86.8% car, 1.4% public transportation, 2.1% walk, 7.0% work from home (2006-2010 5-year est.); Travel time to work: 22.5% less than 15 minutes, 19.9% 15 to 30 minutes, 30.7% 30 to 45 minutes, 13.1% 45 to 60 minutes, 13.9% 60 minutes or more (2006-2010 5-year est.)

BIGLER (CDP). Covers a land area of 1.210 square miles and a water area of 0.008 square miles. Located at 40.99° N. Lat; 78.31° W. Long. Elevation is 1,690 feet.
Population: n/a (1990); n/a (2000); 398 (2010); Density: 329.0 persons per square mile (2010); Race: 98.5% White, 0.0% Black, 0.0% Asian, 0.0% American Indian/Alaska Native, 0.8% Native Hawaiian/Other Pacific Islander, 0.7% Other, 0.8% Hispanic of any race (2010); Average household size: 2.47 (2010); Median age: 44.4 (2010); Males per 100 females: 104.1 (2010); Marriage status: 17.1% never married, 34.3% now married, 33.1% widowed, 15.4% divorced (2006-2010 5-year est.); Foreign born: 0.0% (2006-2010 5-year est.); Ancestry (includes multiple ancestries): 34.9% German, 27.4% American, 21.1% English, 19.4% French, 18.9% Irish (2006-2010 5-year est.).

Economy: Employment by occupation: 0.0% management, 0.0% professional, 14.5% services, 0.0% sales, 0.0% farming, 0.0% construction, 25.5% production (2006-2010 5-year est.).
Income: Per capita income: $24,769 (2006-2010 5-year est.); Median household income: $16,659 (2006-2010 5-year est.); Average household income: $33,828 (2006-2010 5-year est.); Percent of households with income of $100,000 or more: 9.3% (2006-2010 5-year est.); Poverty rate: 14.9% (2006-2010 5-year est.).
Education: Percent of population age 25 and over with: High school diploma (including GED) or higher: 84.2% (2006-2010 5-year est.); Bachelor's degree or higher: 15.2% (2006-2010 5-year est.); Master's degree or higher: 15.2% (2006-2010 5-year est.).
School District(s)
Clearfield Area SD (KG-12)
 2010-11 Enrollment: 2,401 . . . . (814) 765-5511
Housing: Homeownership rate: 86.3% (2010); Median home value: $111,100 (2006-2010 5-year est.); Median contract rent: n/a per month (2006-2010 5-year est.); Median year structure built: before 1940 (2006-2010 5-year est.).
Transportation: Commute to work: 78.2% car, 0.0% public transportation, 21.8% walk, 0.0% work from home (2006-2010 5-year est.); Travel time to work: 21.8% less than 15 minutes, 78.2% 15 to 30 minutes, 0.0% 30 to 45 minutes, 0.0% 45 to 60 minutes, 0.0% 60 minutes or more (2006-2010 5-year est.)

BIGLER (township). Covers a land area of 24.278 square miles and a water area of 0.299 square miles. Located at 40.83° N. Lat; 78.46° W. Long. Elevation is 1,690 feet.
Population: 1,391 (1990); 1,368 (2000); 1,289 (2010); Density: 53.1 persons per square mile (2010); Race: 99.5% White, 0.1% Black, 0.2% Asian, 0.0% American Indian/Alaska Native, 0.0% Native Hawaiian/Other Pacific Islander, 0.2% Other, 0.7% Hispanic of any race (2010); Average household size: 2.48 (2010); Median age: 41.8 (2010); Males per 100 females: 100.5 (2010); Marriage status: 23.6% never married, 53.6% now married, 7.0% widowed, 15.8% divorced (2006-2010 5-year est.); Foreign born: 0.0% (2006-2010 5-year est.); Ancestry (includes multiple ancestries): 36.5% German, 18.9% English, 16.1% Irish, 14.9% Polish, 6.2% Slovak (2006-2010 5-year est.).
Economy: Single-family building permits issued: 1 (2011); Multi-family building permits issued: 0 (2011); Employment by occupation: 3.7% management, 0.0% professional, 16.2% services, 14.5% sales, 2.9% farming, 16.6% construction, 9.7% production (2006-2010 5-year est.).
Income: Per capita income: $17,441 (2006-2010 5-year est.); Median household income: $34,063 (2006-2010 5-year est.); Average household income: $43,873 (2006-2010 5-year est.); Percent of households with income of $100,000 or more: 7.7% (2006-2010 5-year est.); Poverty rate: 20.6% (2006-2010 5-year est.).
Education: Percent of population age 25 and over with: High school diploma (including GED) or higher: 78.1% (2006-2010 5-year est.); Bachelor's degree or higher: 7.6% (2006-2010 5-year est.); Master's degree or higher: 2.0% (2006-2010 5-year est.).
Housing: Homeownership rate: 84.3% (2010); Median home value: $61,200 (2006-2010 5-year est.); Median contract rent: $345 per month (2006-2010 5-year est.); Median year structure built: before 1940 (2006-2010 5-year est.).
Transportation: Commute to work: 90.2% car, 1.6% public transportation, 3.1% walk, 3.9% work from home (2006-2010 5-year est.); Travel time to work: 19.0% less than 15 minutes, 26.8% 15 to 30 minutes, 19.2% 30 to 45 minutes, 15.7% 45 to 60 minutes, 19.2% 60 minutes or more (2006-2010 5-year est.)
Additional Information Contacts
Clearfield Chamber of Commerce. . . . . (814) 765-7567
 http://www.clearfieldchamber.com

BLOOM (township). Covers a land area of 18.832 square miles and a water area of 0.058 square miles. Located at 41.02° N. Lat; 78.62° W. Long.
Population: 393 (1990); 412 (2000); 414 (2010); Density: 22.0 persons per square mile (2010); Race: 99.0% White, 0.0% Black, 0.0% Asian, 0.0% American Indian/Alaska Native, 0.0% Native Hawaiian/Other Pacific Islander, 1.0% Other, 0.5% Hispanic of any race (2010); Average household size: 2.38 (2010); Median age: 47.4 (2010); Males per 100 females: 99.0 (2010); Marriage status: 24.8% never married, 63.7% now married, 3.6% widowed, 7.8% divorced (2006-2010 5-year est.); Foreign born: 0.0% (2006-2010 5-year est.); Ancestry (includes multiple

ancestries): 31.8% German, 20.4% American, 16.0% Irish, 9.6% English, 5.3% Dutch (2006-2010 5-year est.).

Economy: Single-family building permits issued: 0 (2011); Multi-family building permits issued: 0 (2011); Employment by occupation: 4.7% management, 0.0% professional, 9.1% services, 13.0% sales, 4.7% farming, 9.4% construction, 5.9% production (2006-2010 5-year est.).

Income: Per capita income: $22,267 (2006-2010 5-year est.); Median household income: $44,583 (2006-2010 5-year est.); Average household income: $56,971 (2006-2010 5-year est.); Percent of households with income of $100,000 or more: 15.3% (2006-2010 5-year est.); Poverty rate: 8.9% (2006-2010 5-year est.).

Education: Percent of population age 25 and over with: High school diploma (including GED) or higher: 83.4% (2006-2010 5-year est.); Bachelor's degree or higher: 11.2% (2006-2010 5-year est.); Master's degree or higher: 2.6% (2006-2010 5-year est.).

Housing: Homeownership rate: 86.8% (2010); Median home value: $77,400 (2006-2010 5-year est.); Median contract rent: $467 per month (2006-2010 5-year est.); Median year structure built: 1944 (2006-2010 5-year est.).

Transportation: Commute to work: 88.5% car, 0.0% public transportation, 2.0% walk, 8.3% work from home (2006-2010 5-year est.); Travel time to work: 19.5% less than 15 minutes, 52.4% 15 to 30 minutes, 19.5% 30 to 45 minutes, 1.3% 45 to 60 minutes, 7.4% 60 minutes or more (2006-2010 5-year est.)

BOGGS (township). Covers a land area of 36.194 square miles and a water area of 0.322 square miles. Located at 40.94° N. Lat; 78.35° W. Long.

Population: 1,907 (1990); 1,837 (2000); 1,751 (2010); Density: 48.4 persons per square mile (2010); Race: 99.2% White, 0.1% Black, 0.1% Asian, 0.3% American Indian/Alaska Native, 0.0% Native Hawaiian/Other Pacific Islander, 0.3% Other, 0.5% Hispanic of any race (2010); Average household size: 2.44 (2010); Median age: 44.1 (2010); Males per 100 females: 98.8 (2010); Marriage status: 23.5% never married, 62.7% now married, 7.4% widowed, 6.4% divorced (2006-2010 5-year est.); Foreign born: 0.6% (2006-2010 5-year est.); Ancestry (includes multiple ancestries): 30.2% American, 16.8% German, 7.5% Irish, 6.8% English, 6.2% French (2006-2010 5-year est.).

Economy: Single-family building permits issued: 7 (2011); Multi-family building permits issued: 0 (2011); Employment by occupation: 5.5% management, 0.9% professional, 12.2% services, 16.1% sales, 3.0% farming, 18.1% construction, 8.5% production (2006-2010 5-year est.).

Income: Per capita income: $19,525 (2006-2010 5-year est.); Median household income: $41,010 (2006-2010 5-year est.); Average household income: $48,041 (2006-2010 5-year est.); Percent of households with income of $100,000 or more: 10.1% (2006-2010 5-year est.); Poverty rate: 12.2% (2006-2010 5-year est.).

Education: Percent of population age 25 and over with: High school diploma (including GED) or higher: 77.4% (2006-2010 5-year est.); Bachelor's degree or higher: 6.0% (2006-2010 5-year est.); Master's degree or higher: 0.7% (2006-2010 5-year est.).

Housing: Homeownership rate: 87.7% (2010); Median home value: $84,900 (2006-2010 5-year est.); Median contract rent: $368 per month (2006-2010 5-year est.); Median year structure built: 1972 (2006-2010 5-year est.).

Transportation: Commute to work: 95.4% car, 0.0% public transportation, 0.9% walk, 2.4% work from home (2006-2010 5-year est.); Travel time to work: 23.2% less than 15 minutes, 43.3% 15 to 30 minutes, 15.4% 30 to 45 minutes, 5.8% 45 to 60 minutes, 12.4% 60 minutes or more (2006-2010 5-year est.)

Additional Information Contacts

Chamber of Commerce of Clearfield . . . . (814) 765-7567
　http://www.clearfieldchamber.com

BRADFORD (township). Covers a land area of 38.328 square miles and a water area of 0.527 square miles. Located at 41.03° N. Lat; 78.32° W. Long.

Population: 2,504 (1990); 3,314 (2000); 3,034 (2010); Density: 79.2 persons per square mile (2010); Race: 98.7% White, 0.1% Black, 0.2% Asian, 0.3% American Indian/Alaska Native, 0.1% Native Hawaiian/Other Pacific Islander, 0.6% Other, 0.6% Hispanic of any race (2010); Average household size: 2.57 (2010); Median age: 42.8 (2010); Males per 100 females: 102.3 (2010); Marriage status: 21.1% never married, 62.1% now married, 10.1% widowed, 6.7% divorced (2006-2010 5-year est.); Foreign born: 0.0% (2006-2010 5-year est.); Ancestry (includes multiple

---

ancestries): 34.1% American, 16.7% German, 9.0% English, 7.4% Irish, 6.2% French (2006-2010 5-year est.).

Economy: Employment by occupation: 5.9% management, 0.2% professional, 14.3% services, 14.7% sales, 2.4% farming, 15.1% construction, 12.7% production (2006-2010 5-year est.).

Income: Per capita income: $16,676 (2006-2010 5-year est.); Median household income: $34,247 (2006-2010 5-year est.); Average household income: $44,193 (2006-2010 5-year est.); Percent of households with income of $100,000 or more: 12.4% (2006-2010 5-year est.); Poverty rate: 17.4% (2006-2010 5-year est.).

Education: Percent of population age 25 and over with: High school diploma (including GED) or higher: 76.0% (2006-2010 5-year est.); Bachelor's degree or higher: 3.6% (2006-2010 5-year est.); Master's degree or higher: 1.6% (2006-2010 5-year est.).

Housing: Homeownership rate: 87.4% (2010); Median home value: $98,500 (2006-2010 5-year est.); Median contract rent: $323 per month (2006-2010 5-year est.); Median year structure built: 1959 (2006-2010 5-year est.).

Transportation: Commute to work: 93.1% car, 0.0% public transportation, 0.9% walk, 5.6% work from home (2006-2010 5-year est.); Travel time to work: 25.7% less than 15 minutes, 41.8% 15 to 30 minutes, 14.1% 30 to 45 minutes, 8.8% 45 to 60 minutes, 9.5% 60 minutes or more (2006-2010 5-year est.)

Additional Information Contacts

Chamber of Commerce of Clearfield . . . . (814) 765-7567
　http://www.clearfieldchamber.com

BRADY (township). Covers a land area of 37.233 square miles and a water area of 0.134 square miles. Located at 41.04° N. Lat; 78.73° W. Long.

Population: 2,041 (1990); 2,010 (2000); 2,000 (2010); Density: 53.7 persons per square mile (2010); Race: 98.4% White, 0.5% Black, 0.3% Asian, 0.0% American Indian/Alaska Native, 0.0% Native Hawaiian/Other Pacific Islander, 0.8% Other, 0.9% Hispanic of any race (2010); Average household size: 2.60 (2010); Median age: 43.0 (2010); Males per 100 females: 103.7 (2010); Marriage status: 20.3% never married, 67.0% now married, 6.0% widowed, 6.7% divorced (2006-2010 5-year est.); Foreign born: 0.5% (2006-2010 5-year est.); Ancestry (includes multiple ancestries): 24.4% American, 24.2% German, 10.6% English, 9.5% Irish, 7.7% Italian (2006-2010 5-year est.).

Economy: Single-family building permits issued: 3 (2011); Multi-family building permits issued: 0 (2011); Employment by occupation: 7.9% management, 1.2% professional, 13.9% services, 16.5% sales, 4.3% farming, 16.8% construction, 8.1% production (2006-2010 5-year est.).

Income: Per capita income: $18,313 (2006-2010 5-year est.); Median household income: $42,432 (2006-2010 5-year est.); Average household income: $46,619 (2006-2010 5-year est.); Percent of households with income of $100,000 or more: 6.3% (2006-2010 5-year est.); Poverty rate: 12.0% (2006-2010 5-year est.).

Education: Percent of population age 25 and over with: High school diploma (including GED) or higher: 87.1% (2006-2010 5-year est.); Bachelor's degree or higher: 15.3% (2006-2010 5-year est.); Master's degree or higher: 6.6% (2006-2010 5-year est.).

Housing: Homeownership rate: 85.0% (2010); Median home value: $87,300 (2006-2010 5-year est.); Median contract rent: $463 per month (2006-2010 5-year est.); Median year structure built: 1972 (2006-2010 5-year est.).

Transportation: Commute to work: 88.4% car, 0.5% public transportation, 2.8% walk, 4.9% work from home (2006-2010 5-year est.); Travel time to work: 37.5% less than 15 minutes, 41.4% 15 to 30 minutes, 13.7% 30 to 45 minutes, 2.5% 45 to 60 minutes, 5.1% 60 minutes or more (2006-2010 5-year est.)

Additional Information Contacts

Chamber of Commerce of Clearfield . . . . (814) 765-7567
　http://www.clearfieldchamber.com

BRISBIN (borough). Covers a land area of 0.714 square miles and a water area of 0.014 square miles. Located at 40.84° N. Lat; 78.35° W. Long. Elevation is 1,588 feet.

Population: 369 (1990); 413 (2000); 411 (2010); Density: 575.5 persons per square mile (2010); Race: 98.3% White, 0.2% Black, 0.0% Asian, 0.2% American Indian/Alaska Native, 0.0% Native Hawaiian/Other Pacific Islander, 1.3% Other, 2.2% Hispanic of any race (2010); Average household size: 2.38 (2010); Median age: 43.1 (2010); Males per 100 females: 86.8 (2010); Marriage status: 23.6% never married, 58.1% now

married, 3.9% widowed, 14.3% divorced (2006-2010 5-year est.); Foreign born: 0.0% (2006-2010 5-year est.); Ancestry (includes multiple ancestries): 32.0% German, 22.8% English, 13.1% Polish, 9.7% Irish, 5.7% Slovak (2006-2010 5-year est.).
Economy: Single-family building permits issued: 0 (2011); Multi-family building permits issued: 0 (2011); Employment by occupation: 6.0% management, 0.0% professional, 11.0% services, 15.0% sales, 0.0% farming, 17.0% construction, 7.5% production (2006-2010 5-year est.).
Income: Per capita income: $18,677 (2006-2010 5-year est.); Median household income: $36,042 (2006-2010 5-year est.); Average household income: $44,585 (2006-2010 5-year est.); Percent of households with income of $100,000 or more: 5.1% (2006-2010 5-year est.); Poverty rate: 15.5% (2006-2010 5-year est.).
Education: Percent of population age 25 and over with: High school diploma (including GED) or higher: 68.9% (2006-2010 5-year est.); Bachelor's degree or higher: 7.0% (2006-2010 5-year est.); Master's degree or higher: 1.0% (2006-2010 5-year est.).
Housing: Homeownership rate: 78.6% (2010); Median home value: $62,600 (2006-2010 5-year est.); Median contract rent: $375 per month (2006-2010 5-year est.); Median year structure built: 1956 (2006-2010 5-year est.).
Transportation: Commute to work: 90.0% car, 1.0% public transportation, 0.0% walk, 6.5% work from home (2006-2010 5-year est.); Travel time to work: 18.7% less than 15 minutes, 31.6% 15 to 30 minutes, 17.1% 30 to 45 minutes, 17.1% 45 to 60 minutes, 15.5% 60 minutes or more (2006-2010 5-year est.)

BURNSIDE (borough). Covers a land area of 1.680 square miles and a water area of 0.055 square miles. Located at 40.81° N. Lat; 78.80° W. Long. Elevation is 1,339 feet.
Population: 350 (1990); 283 (2000); 234 (2010); Density: 139.3 persons per square mile (2010); Race: 100.0% White, 0.0% Black, 0.0% Asian, 0.0% American Indian/Alaska Native, 0.0% Native Hawaiian/Other Pacific Islander, 0.0% Other, 0.4% Hispanic of any race (2010); Average household size: 2.60 (2010); Median age: 42.0 (2010); Males per 100 females: 122.9 (2010); Marriage status: 17.1% never married, 65.2% now married, 7.0% widowed, 10.8% divorced (2006-2010 5-year est.); Foreign born: 0.0% (2006-2010 5-year est.); Ancestry (includes multiple ancestries): 52.9% German, 26.5% American, 15.2% Irish, 8.8% French, 7.4% Hungarian (2006-2010 5-year est.).
Economy: Single-family building permits issued: 0 (2011); Multi-family building permits issued: 0 (2011); Employment by occupation: 10.8% management, 0.0% professional, 5.4% services, 16.2% sales, 0.0% farming, 27.0% construction, 4.1% production (2006-2010 5-year est.).
Income: Per capita income: $16,263 (2006-2010 5-year est.); Median household income: $33,750 (2006-2010 5-year est.); Average household income: $38,974 (2006-2010 5-year est.); Percent of households with income of $100,000 or more: n/a (2006-2010 5-year est.); Poverty rate: 17.6% (2006-2010 5-year est.).
Education: Percent of population age 25 and over with: High school diploma (including GED) or higher: 86.3% (2006-2010 5-year est.); Bachelor's degree or higher: 3.4% (2006-2010 5-year est.); Master's degree or higher: 1.4% (2006-2010 5-year est.).
Housing: Homeownership rate: 88.9% (2010); Median home value: $61,500 (2006-2010 5-year est.); Median contract rent: $475 per month (2006-2010 5-year est.); Median year structure built: before 1940 (2006-2010 5-year est.).
Transportation: Commute to work: 95.8% car, 0.0% public transportation, 4.2% walk, 0.0% work from home (2006-2010 5-year est.); Travel time to work: 6.9% less than 15 minutes, 25.0% 15 to 30 minutes, 19.4% 30 to 45 minutes, 29.2% 45 to 60 minutes, 19.4% 60 minutes or more (2006-2010 5-year est.)

BURNSIDE (township). Covers a land area of 44.002 square miles and a water area of 0.222 square miles. Located at 40.78° N. Lat; 78.76° W. Long. Elevation is 1,339 feet.
Population: 1,137 (1990); 1,128 (2000); 1,076 (2010); Density: 24.5 persons per square mile (2010); Race: 98.8% White, 0.1% Black, 0.3% Asian, 0.0% American Indian/Alaska Native, 0.0% Native Hawaiian/Other Pacific Islander, 0.8% Other, 0.2% Hispanic of any race (2010); Average household size: 2.63 (2010); Median age: 43.5 (2010); Males per 100 females: 106.5 (2010); Marriage status: 20.2% never married, 65.8% now married, 8.0% widowed, 6.1% divorced (2006-2010 5-year est.); Foreign born: 0.4% (2006-2010 5-year est.); Ancestry (includes multiple

ancestries): 28.8% German, 15.2% Irish, 13.8% English, 13.1% American, 7.3% Italian (2006-2010 5-year est.).
Economy: Single-family building permits issued: 0 (2011); Multi-family building permits issued: 0 (2011); Employment by occupation: 11.8% management, 1.5% professional, 11.3% services, 11.8% sales, 1.3% farming, 21.0% construction, 11.5% production (2006-2010 5-year est.).
Income: Per capita income: $18,405 (2006-2010 5-year est.); Median household income: $31,250 (2006-2010 5-year est.); Average household income: $44,106 (2006-2010 5-year est.); Percent of households with income of $100,000 or more: 10.6% (2006-2010 5-year est.); Poverty rate: 21.6% (2006-2010 5-year est.).
Education: Percent of population age 25 and over with: High school diploma (including GED) or higher: 86.3% (2006-2010 5-year est.); Bachelor's degree or higher: 6.5% (2006-2010 5-year est.); Master's degree or higher: 2.2% (2006-2010 5-year est.).
Housing: Homeownership rate: 86.0% (2010); Median home value: $72,600 (2006-2010 5-year est.); Median contract rent: $330 per month (2006-2010 5-year est.); Median year structure built: 1970 (2006-2010 5-year est.).
Transportation: Commute to work: 93.3% car, 0.0% public transportation, 0.8% walk, 3.7% work from home (2006-2010 5-year est.); Travel time to work: 23.1% less than 15 minutes, 16.1% 15 to 30 minutes, 13.3% 30 to 45 minutes, 26.4% 45 to 60 minutes, 21.1% 60 minutes or more (2006-2010 5-year est.)
Additional Information Contacts
Punxsutawney Area Chamber of Commerce . . . . (814) 938-7700
   http://www.punxsutawney.com/chamber

CHEST (township). Covers a land area of 35.801 square miles and a water area of 0.180 square miles. Located at 40.77° N. Lat; 78.65° W. Long.
Population: 565 (1990); 547 (2000); 515 (2010); Density: 14.4 persons per square mile (2010); Race: 99.4% White, 0.2% Black, 0.0% Asian, 0.0% American Indian/Alaska Native, 0.0% Native Hawaiian/Other Pacific Islander, 0.4% Other, 0.6% Hispanic of any race (2010); Average household size: 2.49 (2010); Median age: 45.0 (2010); Males per 100 females: 99.6 (2010); Marriage status: 26.5% never married, 60.9% now married, 5.7% widowed, 6.9% divorced (2006-2010 5-year est.); Foreign born: 0.0% (2006-2010 5-year est.); Ancestry (includes multiple ancestries): 33.6% German, 23.9% American, 18.7% Irish, 13.1% English, 5.2% Polish (2006-2010 5-year est.).
Economy: Single-family building permits issued: 0 (2011); Multi-family building permits issued: 0 (2011); Employment by occupation: 0.0% management, 0.0% professional, 12.9% services, 13.4% sales, 3.5% farming, 16.9% construction, 13.4% production (2006-2010 5-year est.).
Income: Per capita income: $13,678 (2006-2010 5-year est.); Median household income: $33,438 (2006-2010 5-year est.); Average household income: $35,002 (2006-2010 5-year est.); Percent of households with income of $100,000 or more: 1.1% (2006-2010 5-year est.); Poverty rate: 18.5% (2006-2010 5-year est.).
Education: Percent of population age 25 and over with: High school diploma (including GED) or higher: 82.2% (2006-2010 5-year est.); Bachelor's degree or higher: 3.2% (2006-2010 5-year est.); Master's degree or higher: 0.0% (2006-2010 5-year est.).
Housing: Homeownership rate: 88.4% (2010); Median home value: $65,000 (2006-2010 5-year est.); Median contract rent: $363 per month (2006-2010 5-year est.); Median year structure built: 1969 (2006-2010 5-year est.).
Transportation: Commute to work: 95.5% car, 0.0% public transportation, 1.5% walk, 2.0% work from home (2006-2010 5-year est.); Travel time to work: 23.9% less than 15 minutes, 16.8% 15 to 30 minutes, 28.9% 30 to 45 minutes, 23.9% 45 to 60 minutes, 6.6% 60 minutes or more (2006-2010 5-year est.)

CHESTER HILL (borough). Aka Wigton. Covers a land area of 0.439 square miles and a water area of 0.035 square miles. Located at 40.89° N. Lat; 78.23° W. Long. Elevation is 1,467 feet.
Population: 945 (1990); 918 (2000); 883 (2010); Density: 2,011.8 persons per square mile (2010); Race: 96.9% White, 0.6% Black, 0.9% Asian, 0.0% American Indian/Alaska Native, 0.0% Native Hawaiian/Other Pacific Islander, 1.6% Other, 0.6% Hispanic of any race (2010); Average household size: 2.31 (2010); Median age: 36.1 (2010); Males per 100 females: 93.2 (2010); Marriage status: 25.6% never married, 49.0% now married, 8.5% widowed, 17.0% divorced (2006-2010 5-year est.); Foreign born: 1.5% (2006-2010 5-year est.); Ancestry (includes multiple

ancestries): 16.4% German, 14.9% English, 12.8% Irish, 9.8% Italian, 4.5% Dutch (2006-2010 5-year est.).

Economy: Single-family building permits issued: 0 (2011); Multi-family building permits issued: 0 (2011); Employment by occupation: 7.5% management, 0.0% professional, 13.9% services, 15.0% sales, 2.9% farming, 15.0% construction, 13.0% production (2006-2010 5-year est.).

Income: Per capita income: $17,320 (2006-2010 5-year est.); Median household income: $26,500 (2006-2010 5-year est.); Average household income: $40,142 (2006-2010 5-year est.); Percent of households with income of $100,000 or more: 5.9% (2006-2010 5-year est.); Poverty rate: 33.0% (2006-2010 5-year est.).

Education: Percent of population age 25 and over with: High school diploma (including GED) or higher: 86.4% (2006-2010 5-year est.); Bachelor's degree or higher: 17.6% (2006-2010 5-year est.); Master's degree or higher: 5.3% (2006-2010 5-year est.).

Housing: Homeownership rate: 62.9% (2010); Median home value: $82,000 (2006-2010 5-year est.); Median contract rent: $266 per month (2006-2010 5-year est.); Median year structure built: 1959 (2006-2010 5-year est.).

Transportation: Commute to work: 92.8% car, 0.0% public transportation, 2.4% walk, 1.8% work from home (2006-2010 5-year est.); Travel time to work: 56.8% less than 15 minutes, 10.6% 15 to 30 minutes, 22.8% 30 to 45 minutes, 7.3% 45 to 60 minutes, 2.4% 60 minutes or more (2006-2010 5-year est.)

CLEARFIELD (borough). Aka Janesville. County seat. Covers a land area of 1.803 square miles and a water area of 0.078 square miles. Located at 41.02° N. Lat; 78.44° W. Long. Elevation is 1,089 feet.

History: Laid out 1805, incorporated 1840.

Population: 6,633 (1990); 6,631 (2000); 6,215 (2010); Density: 3,447.4 persons per square mile (2010); Race: 97.3% White, 0.8% Black, 0.4% Asian, 0.1% American Indian/Alaska Native, 0.0% Native Hawaiian/Other Pacific Islander, 1.4% Other, 0.9% Hispanic of any race (2010); Average household size: 2.11 (2010); Median age: 42.8 (2010); Males per 100 females: 92.1 (2010); Marriage status: 26.6% never married, 47.5% now married, 9.1% widowed, 16.8% divorced (2006-2010 5-year est.); Foreign born: 0.5% (2006-2010 5-year est.); Ancestry (includes multiple ancestries): 29.6% German, 14.7% Irish, 13.9% English, 11.2% Italian, 10.6% American (2006-2010 5-year est.).

Economy: Single-family building permits issued: 0 (2011); Multi-family building permits issued: 0 (2011); Employment by occupation: 6.9% management, 3.6% professional, 14.8% services, 20.4% sales, 3.4% farming, 5.3% construction, 4.5% production (2006-2010 5-year est.).

Income: Per capita income: $22,029 (2006-2010 5-year est.); Median household income: $30,646 (2006-2010 5-year est.); Average household income: $45,576 (2006-2010 5-year est.); Percent of households with income of $100,000 or more: 7.0% (2006-2010 5-year est.); Poverty rate: 14.5% (2006-2010 5-year est.).

Taxes: Total city taxes per capita: $234 (2009); City property taxes per capita: $134 (2009).

Education: Percent of population age 25 and over with: High school diploma (including GED) or higher: 89.7% (2006-2010 5-year est.); Bachelor's degree or higher: 20.0% (2006-2010 5-year est.); Master's degree or higher: 6.2% (2006-2010 5-year est.).

School District(s)

Clearfield Area SD (KG-12)
    2010-11 Enrollment: 2,401 . . . . (814) 765-5511
Clearfield County CTC (09-12)
    2010-11 Enrollment: n/a . . . . (814) 765-5308

Vocational/Technical School(s)

Clearfield County Career and Technology Center (Public)
    Fall 2010 Enrollment: 94 . . . . (814) 765-4047
    2011-12 Tuition: $12,000

Housing: Homeownership rate: 55.2% (2010); Median home value: $76,600 (2006-2010 5-year est.); Median contract rent: $378 per month (2006-2010 5-year est.); Median year structure built: before 1940 (2006-2010 5-year est.).

Hospitals: Clearfield Hospital (83 beds)

Safety: Violent crime rate: 20.9 per 10,000 population; Property crime rate: 391.3 per 10,000 population (2011).

Newspapers: Penn Hills Progress (Community news; Circulation 7,665); The Progress (Local news; Circulation 15,000)

Transportation: Commute to work: 91.4% car, 0.0% public transportation, 5.8% walk, 1.3% work from home (2006-2010 5-year est.); Travel time to work: 59.6% less than 15 minutes, 22.0% 15 to 30 minutes, 6.2% 30 to 45

minutes, 3.5% 45 to 60 minutes, 8.7% 60 minutes or more (2006-2010 5-year est.)

Additional Information Contacts

Borough of Clearfield . . . . (814) 765-7817
    http://clearfield.blogware.com
Chamber of Commerce of Clearfield . . . . (814) 765-7567
    http://www.clearfieldchamber.com

COALPORT (borough). Covers a land area of 0.374 square miles and a water area of 0.005 square miles. Located at 40.75° N. Lat; 78.53° W. Long. Elevation is 1,407 feet.

History: Incorporated 1883.

Population: 573 (1990); 490 (2000); 523 (2010); Density: 1,398.1 persons per square mile (2010); Race: 97.9% White, 0.0% Black, 0.2% Asian, 0.0% American Indian/Alaska Native, 0.0% Native Hawaiian/Other Pacific Islander, 1.9% Other, 0.6% Hispanic of any race (2010); Average household size: 2.26 (2010); Median age: 42.6 (2010); Males per 100 females: 98.9 (2010); Marriage status: 26.3% never married, 43.7% now married, 17.6% widowed, 12.4% divorced (2006-2010 5-year est.); Foreign born: 0.0% (2006-2010 5-year est.); Ancestry (includes multiple ancestries): 35.3% German, 19.2% Irish, 14.1% English, 11.0% Polish, 10.2% Scottish (2006-2010 5-year est.).

Economy: Single-family building permits issued: 0 (2011); Multi-family building permits issued: 0 (2011); Employment by occupation: 0.9% management, 1.9% professional, 18.0% services, 15.6% sales, 5.2% farming, 17.1% construction, 11.8% production (2006-2010 5-year est.).

Income: Per capita income: $14,203 (2006-2010 5-year est.); Median household income: $23,438 (2006-2010 5-year est.); Average household income: $33,268 (2006-2010 5-year est.); Percent of households with income of $100,000 or more: 1.6% (2006-2010 5-year est.); Poverty rate: 27.1% (2006-2010 5-year est.).

Education: Percent of population age 25 and over with: High school diploma (including GED) or higher: 86.3% (2006-2010 5-year est.); Bachelor's degree or higher: 5.0% (2006-2010 5-year est.); Master's degree or higher: 0.0% (2006-2010 5-year est.).

Housing: Homeownership rate: 62.7% (2010); Median home value: $65,200 (2006-2010 5-year est.); Median contract rent: $297 per month (2006-2010 5-year est.); Median year structure built: before 1940 (2006-2010 5-year est.).

Transportation: Commute to work: 90.5% car, 0.0% public transportation, 3.8% walk, 5.7% work from home (2006-2010 5-year est.); Travel time to work: 27.1% less than 15 minutes, 18.6% 15 to 30 minutes, 28.6% 30 to 45 minutes, 14.1% 45 to 60 minutes, 11.6% 60 minutes or more (2006-2010 5-year est.)

COOPER (township). Covers a land area of 40.929 square miles and a water area of 0.317 square miles. Located at 41.01° N. Lat; 78.11° W. Long.

Population: 2,590 (1990); 2,731 (2000); 2,704 (2010); Density: 66.1 persons per square mile (2010); Race: 99.5% White, 0.1% Black, 0.0% Asian, 0.1% American Indian/Alaska Native, 0.0% Native Hawaiian/Other Pacific Islander, 0.3% Other, 0.2% Hispanic of any race (2010); Average household size: 2.53 (2010); Median age: 42.0 (2010); Males per 100 females: 101.8 (2010); Marriage status: 21.6% never married, 61.3% now married, 4.9% widowed, 12.2% divorced (2006-2010 5-year est.); Foreign born: 0.0% (2006-2010 5-year est.); Ancestry (includes multiple ancestries): 27.5% German, 15.8% Slovak, 11.6% Italian, 11.5% Irish, 10.2% English (2006-2010 5-year est.).

Economy: Single-family building permits issued: 3 (2011); Multi-family building permits issued: 0 (2011); Employment by occupation: 4.9% management, 3.0% professional, 11.6% services, 14.8% sales, 0.9% farming, 16.6% construction, 8.0% production (2006-2010 5-year est.).

Income: Per capita income: $17,597 (2006-2010 5-year est.); Median household income: $34,769 (2006-2010 5-year est.); Average household income: $42,229 (2006-2010 5-year est.); Percent of households with income of $100,000 or more: 4.2% (2006-2010 5-year est.); Poverty rate: 18.0% (2006-2010 5-year est.).

Education: Percent of population age 25 and over with: High school diploma (including GED) or higher: 87.8% (2006-2010 5-year est.); Bachelor's degree or higher: 6.8% (2006-2010 5-year est.); Master's degree or higher: 1.6% (2006-2010 5-year est.).

Housing: Homeownership rate: 85.0% (2010); Median home value: $80,100 (2006-2010 5-year est.); Median contract rent: $386 per month (2006-2010 5-year est.); Median year structure built: 1946 (2006-2010 5-year est.).

Transportation: Commute to work: 94.7% car, 0.0% public transportation, 3.0% walk, 2.3% work from home (2006-2010 5-year est.); Travel time to work: 24.6% less than 15 minutes, 38.2% 15 to 30 minutes, 15.9% 30 to 45 minutes, 11.2% 45 to 60 minutes, 10.1% 60 minutes or more (2006-2010 5-year est.)

Additional Information Contacts
Chamber of Commerce of Clearfield. . . . . (814) 765-7567
http://www.clearfieldchamber.com

COVINGTON (township). Covers a land area of 52.876 square miles and a water area of 0.223 square miles. Located at 41.13° N. Lat; 78.19° W. Long.
Population: 648 (1990); 621 (2000); 526 (2010); Density: 9.9 persons per square mile (2010); Race: 98.9% White, 0.2% Black, 0.2% Asian, 0.0% American Indian/Alaska Native, 0.2% Native Hawaiian/Other Pacific Islander, 0.5% Other, 0.6% Hispanic of any race (2010); Average household size: 2.28 (2010); Median age: 48.4 (2010); Males per 100 females: 107.9 (2010); Marriage status: 24.7% never married, 61.1% now married, 5.1% widowed, 9.1% divorced (2006-2010 5-year est.); Foreign born: 0.6% (2006-2010 5-year est.); Ancestry (includes multiple ancestries): 30.6% German, 24.4% Irish, 17.3% French, 16.2% Slovak, 9.0% Dutch (2006-2010 5-year est.).
Economy: Single-family building permits issued: 0 (2011); Multi-family building permits issued: 0 (2011); Employment by occupation: 10.6% management, 0.0% professional, 6.4% services, 25.1% sales, 3.2% farming, 18.4% construction, 8.8% production (2006-2010 5-year est.).
Income: Per capita income: $20,233 (2006-2010 5-year est.); Median household income: $50,667 (2006-2010 5-year est.); Average household income: $51,245 (2006-2010 5-year est.); Percent of households with income of $100,000 or more: 6.3% (2006-2010 5-year est.); Poverty rate: 4.1% (2006-2010 5-year est.).
Education: Percent of population age 25 and over with: High school diploma (including GED) or higher: 89.7% (2006-2010 5-year est.); Bachelor's degree or higher: 4.7% (2006-2010 5-year est.); Master's degree or higher: 0.8% (2006-2010 5-year est.).
Housing: Homeownership rate: 90.0% (2010); Median home value: $93,100 (2006-2010 5-year est.); Median contract rent: n/a per month (2006-2010 5-year est.); Median year structure built: 1979 (2006-2010 5-year est.).
Transportation: Commute to work: 93.9% car, 3.6% public transportation, 2.5% walk, 0.0% work from home (2006-2010 5-year est.); Travel time to work: 18.3% less than 15 minutes, 20.8% 15 to 30 minutes, 19.4% 30 to 45 minutes, 23.7% 45 to 60 minutes, 17.9% 60 minutes or more (2006-2010 5-year est.)

CURWENSVILLE (borough). Aka Lumber. Covers a land area of 2.228 square miles and a water area of 0.105 square miles. Located at 40.97° N. Lat; 78.52° W. Long. Elevation is 1,191 feet.
History: Settled c.1800, incorporated c.1832.
Population: 2,924 (1990); 2,650 (2000); 2,542 (2010); Density: 1,140.9 persons per square mile (2010); Race: 98.7% White, 0.5% Black, 0.1% Asian, 0.1% American Indian/Alaska Native, 0.0% Native Hawaiian/Other Pacific Islander, 0.6% Other, 0.2% Hispanic of any race (2010); Average household size: 2.27 (2010); Median age: 44.4 (2010); Males per 100 females: 87.0 (2010); Marriage status: 20.0% never married, 44.7% now married, 13.5% widowed, 21.8% divorced (2006-2010 5-year est.); Foreign born: 0.0% (2006-2010 5-year est.); Ancestry (includes multiple ancestries): 27.8% German, 16.7% English, 15.5% Irish, 12.3% Italian, 9.6% Dutch (2006-2010 5-year est.).
Economy: Single-family building permits issued: 0 (2011); Multi-family building permits issued: 0 (2011); Employment by occupation: 6.1% management, 0.0% professional, 18.1% services, 19.7% sales, 1.1% farming, 9.2% construction, 4.3% production (2006-2010 5-year est.).
Income: Per capita income: $16,433 (2006-2010 5-year est.); Median household income: $28,586 (2006-2010 5-year est.); Average household income: $33,464 (2006-2010 5-year est.); Percent of households with income of $100,000 or more: 2.2% (2006-2010 5-year est.); Poverty rate: 18.1% (2006-2010 5-year est.).
Education: Percent of population age 25 and over with: High school diploma (including GED) or higher: 88.4% (2006-2010 5-year est.); Bachelor's degree or higher: 7.8% (2006-2010 5-year est.); Master's degree or higher: 1.0% (2006-2010 5-year est.).
School District(s)
Curwensville Area SD (KG-12)
    2010-11 Enrollment: 1,154 . . . . (814) 236-1101

Housing: Homeownership rate: 68.7% (2010); Median home value: $63,300 (2006-2010 5-year est.); Median contract rent: $324 per month (2006-2010 5-year est.); Median year structure built: 1956 (2006-2010 5-year est.).
Safety: Violent crime rate: 39.2 per 10,000 population; Property crime rate: 156.9 per 10,000 population (2011).
Transportation: Commute to work: 97.9% car, 0.0% public transportation, 2.1% walk, 0.0% work from home (2006-2010 5-year est.); Travel time to work: 44.6% less than 15 minutes, 33.9% 15 to 30 minutes, 6.3% 30 to 45 minutes, 6.8% 45 to 60 minutes, 8.5% 60 minutes or more (2006-2010 5-year est.)
Additional Information Contacts
Chamber of Commerce of Clearfield. . . . . (814) 765-7567
http://www.clearfieldchamber.com

DECATUR (township). Covers a land area of 37.376 square miles and a water area of 0.249 square miles. Located at 40.88° N. Lat; 78.31° W. Long.
Population: 3,000 (1990); 2,974 (2000); 4,548 (2010); Density: 121.7 persons per square mile (2010); Race: 79.7% White, 7.1% Black, 1.9% Asian, 0.5% American Indian/Alaska Native, 0.0% Native Hawaiian/Other Pacific Islander, 10.8% Other, 24.8% Hispanic of any race (2010); Average household size: 2.39 (2010); Median age: 41.9 (2010); Males per 100 females: 190.4 (2010); Marriage status: 20.4% never married, 58.0% now married, 11.8% widowed, 9.9% divorced (2006-2010 5-year est.); Foreign born: 0.4% (2006-2010 5-year est.); Ancestry (includes multiple ancestries): 23.0% German, 18.0% English, 13.4% Irish, 11.0% American, 5.9% Scottish (2006-2010 5-year est.).
Economy: Single-family building permits issued: 3 (2011); Multi-family building permits issued: 0 (2011); Employment by occupation: 9.6% management, 0.0% professional, 7.2% services, 15.7% sales, 3.2% farming, 14.6% construction, 13.3% production (2006-2010 5-year est.).
Income: Per capita income: $18,299 (2006-2010 5-year est.); Median household income: $33,234 (2006-2010 5-year est.); Average household income: $37,528 (2006-2010 5-year est.); Percent of households with income of $100,000 or more: 2.7% (2006-2010 5-year est.); Poverty rate: 12.6% (2006-2010 5-year est.).
Taxes: Total city taxes per capita: $106 (2009); City property taxes per capita: $40 (2009).
Education: Percent of population age 25 and over with: High school diploma (including GED) or higher: 82.0% (2006-2010 5-year est.); Bachelor's degree or higher: 4.6% (2006-2010 5-year est.); Master's degree or higher: 0.6% (2006-2010 5-year est.).
Housing: Homeownership rate: 83.9% (2010); Median home value: $71,600 (2006-2010 5-year est.); Median contract rent: $189 per month (2006-2010 5-year est.); Median year structure built: 1972 (2006-2010 5-year est.).
Safety: Violent crime rate: 48.2 per 10,000 population; Property crime rate: 153.4 per 10,000 population (2011).
Transportation: Commute to work: 95.6% car, 0.0% public transportation, 1.8% walk, 0.0% work from home (2006-2010 5-year est.); Travel time to work: 38.8% less than 15 minutes, 19.5% 15 to 30 minutes, 14.0% 30 to 45 minutes, 7.1% 45 to 60 minutes, 20.7% 60 minutes or more (2006-2010 5-year est.)
Additional Information Contacts
Chamber of Commerce of Clearfield. . . . . (814) 765-7567
http://www.clearfieldchamber.com

DRIFTING (unincorporated postal area)
Zip Code: 16834
    Covers a land area of 18.225 square miles and a water area of 0.247 square miles. Located at 41.05° N. Lat; 78.08° W. Long. Population: 299 (2010); Density: 16.4 persons per square mile (2010); Race: 99.3% White, 0.0% Black, 0.0% Asian, 0.0% American Indian/Alaska Native, 0.0% Native Hawaiian/Other Pacific Islander, 0.7% Other, 0.0% Hispanic of any race (2010); Average household size: 2.56 (2010); Median age: 45.4 (2010); Males per 100 females: 110.6 (2010); Homeownership rate: 90.6% (2010)

DUBOIS (city). Covers a land area of 3.177 square miles and a water area of 0.040 square miles. Located at 41.12° N. Lat; 78.76° W. Long. Elevation is 1,411 feet.
History: DuBois was settled in 1865 and later named for John E. DuBois, a major landholder. Lumbering, mining, and industry were among early activities.

Population: 8,038 (1990); 8,123 (2000); 7,794 (2010); Density: 2,453.4 persons per square mile (2010); Race: 97.0% White, 0.6% Black, 0.9% Asian, 0.1% American Indian/Alaska Native, 0.0% Native Hawaiian/Other Pacific Islander, 1.4% Other, 1.2% Hispanic of any race (2010); Average household size: 2.22 (2010); Median age: 38.5 (2010); Males per 100 females: 90.6 (2010); Marriage status: 30.0% never married, 48.0% now married, 9.4% widowed, 12.6% divorced (2006-2010 5-year est.); Foreign born: 0.9% (2006-2010 5-year est.); Ancestry (includes multiple ancestries): 23.0% German, 19.3% American, 16.4% Irish, 11.6% Italian, 10.3% English (2006-2010 5-year est.).
Economy: Single-family building permits issued: 1 (2011); Multi-family building permits issued: 0 (2011); Employment by occupation: 5.0% management, 2.4% professional, 13.1% services, 14.0% sales, 2.9% farming, 8.4% construction, 7.8% production (2006-2010 5-year est.).
Income: Per capita income: $17,928 (2006-2010 5-year est.); Median household income: $31,494 (2006-2010 5-year est.); Average household income: $39,646 (2006-2010 5-year est.); Percent of households with income of $100,000 or more: 4.2% (2006-2010 5-year est.); Poverty rate: 22.7% (2006-2010 5-year est.).
Taxes: Total city taxes per capita: $300 (2009); City property taxes per capita: $168 (2009).
Education: Percent of population age 25 and over with: High school diploma (including GED) or higher: 93.7% (2006-2010 5-year est.); Bachelor's degree or higher: 17.8% (2006-2010 5-year est.); Master's degree or higher: 7.7% (2006-2010 5-year est.).

School District(s)

Dubois Area SD (KG-12)
   2010-11 Enrollment: 4,077 . . . . (814) 371-2700

Four-year College(s)

Pennsylvania State University-Penn State Dubois (Public)
   Fall 2010 Enrollment: 836 . . . . (814) 375-4700
   2011-12 Tuition: In-state $12,994; Out-of-state $19,434

Two-year College(s)

Du Bois Business College-Du Bois (Private, For-profit)
   Fall 2010 Enrollment: 275 . . . . (814) 371-6920
   2011-12 Tuition: In-state $10,305; Out-of-state $10,305

Vocational/Technical School(s)

Pennsylvania Academy of Cosmetology Arts and Sciences (Private, For-profit)
   Fall 2010 Enrollment: 50 . . . . (814) 371-4151
   2011-12 Tuition: $15,100

Housing: Homeownership rate: 57.5% (2010); Median home value: $84,500 (2006-2010 5-year est.); Median contract rent: $408 per month (2006-2010 5-year est.); Median year structure built: before 1940 (2006-2010 5-year est.).
Hospitals: DuBois Regional Medical Center (214 beds)
Safety: Violent crime rate: 30.7 per 10,000 population; Property crime rate: 365.8 per 10,000 population (2011).
Newspapers: Courier-Express (Local news; Circulation 10,198); Tri-County Sunday (Community news; Circulation 14,937)
Transportation: Commute to work: 80.2% car, 0.9% public transportation, 14.4% walk, 2.9% work from home (2006-2010 5-year est.); Travel time to work: 62.2% less than 15 minutes, 22.6% 15 to 30 minutes, 8.0% 30 to 45 minutes, 5.2% 45 to 60 minutes, 2.0% 60 minutes or more (2006-2010 5-year est.)

Additional Information Contacts

City of Du Bois. . . . . (814) 371-2000
   http://www.duboispa.gov
Greater DuBois Chamber of Commerce & Economic Development . . (814) 371-5010
   http://www.duboispachamber.com

FERGUSON (township). Covers a land area of 23.365 square miles and a water area of 0.055 square miles. Located at 40.87° N. Lat; 78.61° W. Long.
Population: 437 (1990); 410 (2000); 444 (2010); Density: 19.0 persons per square mile (2010); Race: 99.5% White, 0.0% Black, 0.2% Asian, 0.0% American Indian/Alaska Native, 0.0% Native Hawaiian/Other Pacific Islander, 0.3% Other, 0.0% Hispanic of any race (2010); Average household size: 2.69 (2010); Median age: 41.2 (2010); Males per 100 females: 109.4 (2010); Marriage status: 20.8% never married, 71.0% now married, 4.8% widowed, 3.3% divorced (2006-2010 5-year est.); Foreign born: 0.5% (2006-2010 5-year est.); Ancestry (includes multiple ancestries): 37.6% German, 17.7% English, 13.1% American, 9.8% Irish, 6.3% Dutch (2006-2010 5-year est.).

Economy: Single-family building permits issued: 1 (2011); Multi-family building permits issued: 0 (2011); Employment by occupation: 6.6% management, 2.5% professional, 12.7% services, 10.7% sales, 2.5% farming, 15.2% construction, 4.6% production (2006-2010 5-year est.).
Income: Per capita income: $19,039 (2006-2010 5-year est.); Median household income: $40,000 (2006-2010 5-year est.); Average household income: $48,047 (2006-2010 5-year est.); Percent of households with income of $100,000 or more: 7.6% (2006-2010 5-year est.); Poverty rate: 12.4% (2006-2010 5-year est.).
Education: Percent of population age 25 and over with: High school diploma (including GED) or higher: 80.1% (2006-2010 5-year est.); Bachelor's degree or higher: 11.0% (2006-2010 5-year est.); Master's degree or higher: 3.9% (2006-2010 5-year est.).
Housing: Homeownership rate: 89.1% (2010); Median home value: $76,000 (2006-2010 5-year est.); Median contract rent: $193 per month (2006-2010 5-year est.); Median year structure built: 1970 (2006-2010 5-year est.).
Transportation: Commute to work: 91.8% car, 0.0% public transportation, 2.7% walk, 5.5% work from home (2006-2010 5-year est.); Travel time to work: 10.4% less than 15 minutes, 40.5% 15 to 30 minutes, 42.8% 30 to 45 minutes, 1.2% 45 to 60 minutes, 5.2% 60 minutes or more (2006-2010 5-year est.)

FRENCHVILLE (unincorporated postal area)
Zip Code: 16836
   Covers a land area of 122.026 square miles and a water area of 0.670 square miles. Located at 41.15° N. Lat; 78.27° W. Long. Population: 1,152 (2010); Density: 9.4 persons per square mile (2010); Race: 98.6% White, 0.2% Black, 0.1% Asian, 0.0% American Indian/Alaska Native, 0.2% Native Hawaiian/Other Pacific Islander, 0.9% Other, 0.4% Hispanic of any race (2010); Average household size: 2.30 (2010); Median age: 46.3 (2010); Males per 100 females: 108.3 (2010); Homeownership rate: 90.0% (2010)

GIRARD (township). Covers a land area of 63.221 square miles and a water area of 0.340 square miles. Located at 41.14° N. Lat; 78.29° W. Long.
Population: 630 (1990); 674 (2000); 534 (2010); Density: 8.4 persons per square mile (2010); Race: 98.3% White, 0.2% Black, 0.0% Asian, 0.0% American Indian/Alaska Native, 0.2% Native Hawaiian/Other Pacific Islander, 1.3% Other, 0.4% Hispanic of any race (2010); Average household size: 2.35 (2010); Median age: 44.9 (2010); Males per 100 females: 100.0 (2010); Marriage status: 34.5% never married, 49.1% now married, 7.7% widowed, 8.7% divorced (2006-2010 5-year est.); Foreign born: 0.0% (2006-2010 5-year est.); Ancestry (includes multiple ancestries): 26.1% German, 14.6% French, 14.0% Irish, 8.1% American, 5.5% English (2006-2010 5-year est.).
Economy: Single-family building permits issued: 2 (2011); Multi-family building permits issued: 0 (2011); Employment by occupation: 4.3% management, 0.0% professional, 7.9% services, 19.1% sales, 5.6% farming, 17.4% construction, 4.9% production (2006-2010 5-year est.).
Income: Per capita income: $21,262 (2006-2010 5-year est.); Median household income: $41,625 (2006-2010 5-year est.); Average household income: $50,502 (2006-2010 5-year est.); Percent of households with income of $100,000 or more: 13.1% (2006-2010 5-year est.); Poverty rate: 11.8% (2006-2010 5-year est.).
Education: Percent of population age 25 and over with: High school diploma (including GED) or higher: 85.9% (2006-2010 5-year est.); Bachelor's degree or higher: 3.5% (2006-2010 5-year est.); Master's degree or higher: 1.0% (2006-2010 5-year est.).
Housing: Homeownership rate: 91.2% (2010); Median home value: $88,500 (2006-2010 5-year est.); Median contract rent: $477 per month (2006-2010 5-year est.); Median year structure built: 1959 (2006-2010 5-year est.).
Transportation: Commute to work: 98.0% car, 0.0% public transportation, 0.0% walk, 1.3% work from home (2006-2010 5-year est.); Travel time to work: 15.0% less than 15 minutes, 48.3% 15 to 30 minutes, 16.0% 30 to 45 minutes, 5.3% 45 to 60 minutes, 15.3% 60 minutes or more (2006-2010 5-year est.)

GLEN HOPE (borough). Aka Glenhope. Covers a land area of 2.129 square miles and a water area of 0.045 square miles. Located at 40.80° N. Lat; 78.50° W. Long. Elevation is 1,358 feet.
History: Also spelled Glenhope.

Population: 187 (1990); 149 (2000); 142 (2010); Density: 66.7 persons per square mile (2010); Race: 100.0% White, 0.0% Black, 0.0% Asian, 0.0% American Indian/Alaska Native, 0.0% Native Hawaiian/Other Pacific Islander, 0.0% Other, 0.0% Hispanic of any race (2010); Average household size: 2.33 (2010); Median age: 50.8 (2010); Males per 100 females: 102.9 (2010); Marriage status: 24.2% never married, 53.1% now married, 19.5% widowed, 3.1% divorced (2006-2010 5-year est.); Foreign born: 0.0% (2006-2010 5-year est.); Ancestry (includes multiple ancestries): 48.3% German, 29.4% Irish, 14.7% Polish, 11.2% English, 8.4% Scotch-Irish (2006-2010 5-year est.).
Economy: Employment by occupation: 4.0% management, 6.0% professional, 10.0% services, 18.0% sales, 0.0% farming, 16.0% construction, 12.0% production (2006-2010 5-year est.).
Income: Per capita income: $17,985 (2006-2010 5-year est.); Median household income: $26,667 (2006-2010 5-year est.); Average household income: $42,419 (2006-2010 5-year est.); Percent of households with income of $100,000 or more: 13.8% (2006-2010 5-year est.); Poverty rate: 12.6% (2006-2010 5-year est.).
Education: Percent of population age 25 and over with: High school diploma (including GED) or higher: 84.1% (2006-2010 5-year est.); Bachelor's degree or higher: 6.2% (2006-2010 5-year est.); Master's degree or higher: 0.0% (2006-2010 5-year est.).
Housing: Homeownership rate: 86.9% (2010); Median home value: $45,600 (2006-2010 5-year est.); Median contract rent: n/a per month (2006-2010 5-year est.); Median year structure built: before 1940 (2006-2010 5-year est.).
Transportation: Commute to work: 96.0% car, 0.0% public transportation, 4.0% walk, 0.0% work from home (2006-2010 5-year est.); Travel time to work: 20.0% less than 15 minutes, 44.0% 15 to 30 minutes, 12.0% 30 to 45 minutes, 6.0% 45 to 60 minutes, 18.0% 60 minutes or more (2006-2010 5-year est.)

GLEN RICHEY (unincorporated postal area)
Zip Code: 16837

Covers a land area of 0.846 square miles and a water area of 0.002 square miles. Located at 40.94° N. Lat; 78.47° W. Long. Elevation is 1,391 feet. Population: 186 (2010); Density: 219.8 persons per square mile (2010); Race: 98.4% White, 0.0% Black, 0.0% Asian, 0.0% American Indian/Alaska Native, 0.0% Native Hawaiian/Other Pacific Islander, 1.6% Other, 0.0% Hispanic of any race (2010); Average household size: 2.62 (2010); Median age: 39.5 (2010); Males per 100 females: 95.8 (2010); Homeownership rate: 86.0% (2010)

GOSHEN (township). Covers a land area of 48.571 square miles and a water area of 0.255 square miles. Located at 41.14° N. Lat; 78.38° W. Long. Elevation is 1,453 feet.
Population: 369 (1990); 496 (2000); 435 (2010); Density: 9.0 persons per square mile (2010); Race: 98.6% White, 0.0% Black, 0.0% Asian, 0.0% American Indian/Alaska Native, 0.0% Native Hawaiian/Other Pacific Islander, 1.4% Other, 0.5% Hispanic of any race (2010); Average household size: 2.34 (2010); Median age: 43.6 (2010); Males per 100 females: 106.2 (2010); Marriage status: 27.9% never married, 58.3% now married, 10.4% widowed, 3.4% divorced (2006-2010 5-year est.); Foreign born: 0.8% (2006-2010 5-year est.); Ancestry (includes multiple ancestries): 27.0% Irish, 26.5% German, 10.1% Italian, 7.5% English, 7.5% American (2006-2010 5-year est.).
Economy: Single-family building permits issued: 0 (2011); Multi-family building permits issued: 0 (2011); Employment by occupation: 9.2% management, 1.4% professional, 15.5% services, 8.5% sales, 12.0% farming, 10.6% construction, 16.9% production (2006-2010 5-year est.).
Income: Per capita income: $16,151 (2006-2010 5-year est.); Median household income: $35,208 (2006-2010 5-year est.); Average household income: $42,806 (2006-2010 5-year est.); Percent of households with income of $100,000 or more: 2.8% (2006-2010 5-year est.); Poverty rate: 22.6% (2006-2010 5-year est.).
Education: Percent of population age 25 and over with: High school diploma (including GED) or higher: 71.9% (2006-2010 5-year est.); Bachelor's degree or higher: 8.3% (2006-2010 5-year est.); Master's degree or higher: 4.0% (2006-2010 5-year est.).
Housing: Homeownership rate: 81.1% (2010); Median home value: $89,700 (2006-2010 5-year est.); Median contract rent: $400 per month (2006-2010 5-year est.); Median year structure built: 1971 (2006-2010 5-year est.).
Transportation: Commute to work: 91.4% car, 0.0% public transportation, 2.2% walk, 5.0% work from home (2006-2010 5-year est.); Travel time to

work: 13.6% less than 15 minutes, 59.1% 15 to 30 minutes, 17.4% 30 to 45 minutes, 4.5% 45 to 60 minutes, 5.3% 60 minutes or more (2006-2010 5-year est.)

GRAHAM (township). Covers a land area of 29.706 square miles and a water area of 0.227 square miles. Located at 41.01° N. Lat; 78.22° W. Long. Elevation is 1,437 feet.
Population: 1,220 (1990); 1,236 (2000); 1,383 (2010); Density: 46.6 persons per square mile (2010); Race: 99.1% White, 0.1% Black, 0.3% Asian, 0.0% American Indian/Alaska Native, 0.0% Native Hawaiian/Other Pacific Islander, 0.5% Other, 0.7% Hispanic of any race (2010); Average household size: 2.59 (2010); Median age: 43.3 (2010); Males per 100 females: 101.9 (2010); Marriage status: 21.2% never married, 67.3% now married, 5.1% widowed, 6.4% divorced (2006-2010 5-year est.); Foreign born: 0.0% (2006-2010 5-year est.); Ancestry (includes multiple ancestries): 22.1% German, 16.5% English, 13.7% American, 9.9% Irish, 5.1% Polish (2006-2010 5-year est.).
Economy: Single-family building permits issued: 1 (2011); Multi-family building permits issued: 0 (2011); Employment by occupation: 2.6% management, 4.5% professional, 9.7% services, 13.6% sales, 3.0% farming, 21.3% construction, 8.0% production (2006-2010 5-year est.).
Income: Per capita income: $18,795 (2006-2010 5-year est.); Median household income: $47,072 (2006-2010 5-year est.); Average household income: $55,326 (2006-2010 5-year est.); Percent of households with income of $100,000 or more: 10.0% (2006-2010 5-year est.); Poverty rate: 4.5% (2006-2010 5-year est.).
Education: Percent of population age 25 and over with: High school diploma (including GED) or higher: 83.0% (2006-2010 5-year est.); Bachelor's degree or higher: 5.9% (2006-2010 5-year est.); Master's degree or higher: 2.4% (2006-2010 5-year est.).
Housing: Homeownership rate: 89.7% (2010); Median home value: $111,400 (2006-2010 5-year est.); Median contract rent: $227 per month (2006-2010 5-year est.); Median year structure built: 1979 (2006-2010 5-year est.).
Transportation: Commute to work: 97.1% car, 0.0% public transportation, 0.7% walk, 1.7% work from home (2006-2010 5-year est.); Travel time to work: 26.5% less than 15 minutes, 35.3% 15 to 30 minutes, 13.4% 30 to 45 minutes, 15.7% 45 to 60 minutes, 9.0% 60 minutes or more (2006-2010 5-year est.)
Additional Information Contacts
Moshannon Valley EDP & Chamber Services . . . . (814) 342-2260
  http://www.mvedp.org

GRAMPIAN (borough). Covers a land area of 0.282 square miles and a water area of <.001 square miles. Located at 40.96° N. Lat; 78.61° W. Long. Elevation is 1,591 feet.
Population: 395 (1990); 441 (2000); 356 (2010); Density: 1,263.8 persons per square mile (2010); Race: 99.7% White, 0.3% Black, 0.0% Asian, 0.0% American Indian/Alaska Native, 0.0% Native Hawaiian/Other Pacific Islander, 0.0% Other, 0.0% Hispanic of any race (2010); Average household size: 2.47 (2010); Median age: 33.8 (2010); Males per 100 females: 103.4 (2010); Marriage status: 21.1% never married, 64.8% now married, 6.0% widowed, 8.2% divorced (2006-2010 5-year est.); Foreign born: 0.8% (2006-2010 5-year est.); Ancestry (includes multiple ancestries): 33.4% German, 19.7% Irish, 15.3% American, 7.6% English, 5.0% Dutch (2006-2010 5-year est.).
Economy: Single-family building permits issued: 0 (2011); Multi-family building permits issued: 0 (2011); Employment by occupation: 3.5% management, 0.0% professional, 11.6% services, 12.1% sales, 5.1% farming, 11.1% construction, 5.6% production (2006-2010 5-year est.).
Income: Per capita income: $22,211 (2006-2010 5-year est.); Median household income: $38,750 (2006-2010 5-year est.); Average household income: $54,442 (2006-2010 5-year est.); Percent of households with income of $100,000 or more: 9.2% (2006-2010 5-year est.); Poverty rate: 7.1% (2006-2010 5-year est.).
Education: Percent of population age 25 and over with: High school diploma (including GED) or higher: 86.1% (2006-2010 5-year est.); Bachelor's degree or higher: 18.8% (2006-2010 5-year est.); Master's degree or higher: 6.8% (2006-2010 5-year est.).
School District(s)
Curwensville Area SD (KG-12)
  2010-11 Enrollment: 1,154 . . . . (814) 236-1101
Housing: Homeownership rate: 74.4% (2010); Median home value: $59,600 (2006-2010 5-year est.); Median contract rent: $369 per month

(2006-2010 5-year est.); Median year structure built: before 1940 (2006-2010 5-year est.).
Transportation: Commute to work: 95.9% car, 0.0% public transportation, 3.1% walk, 0.0% work from home (2006-2010 5-year est.); Travel time to work: 26.7% less than 15 minutes, 31.3% 15 to 30 minutes, 32.8% 30 to 45 minutes, 3.6% 45 to 60 minutes, 5.6% 60 minutes or more (2006-2010 5-year est.)

GRASSFLAT (CDP).
Covers a land area of 1.131 square miles and a water area of 0.001 square miles. Located at 41.00° N. Lat; 78.11° W. Long. Elevation is 1,470 feet.
Population: n/a (1990); n/a (2000); 511 (2010); Density: 451.8 persons per square mile (2010); Race: 99.4% White, 0.2% Black, 0.0% Asian, 0.2% American Indian/Alaska Native, 0.0% Native Hawaiian/Other Pacific Islander, 0.2% Other, 0.8% Hispanic of any race (2010); Average household size: 2.46 (2010); Median age: 43.3 (2010); Males per 100 females: 102.0 (2010); Marriage status: 31.0% never married, 55.6% now married, 2.9% widowed, 10.6% divorced (2006-2010 5-year est.); Foreign born: 0.0% (2006-2010 5-year est.); Ancestry (includes multiple ancestries): 21.6% German, 17.3% Slovak, 11.9% English, 9.7% French, 7.9% Swedish (2006-2010 5-year est.).
Economy: Employment by occupation: 0.0% management, 0.0% professional, 21.1% services, 16.6% sales, 0.0% farming, 20.6% construction, 5.5% production (2006-2010 5-year est.).
Income: Per capita income: $14,572 (2006-2010 5-year est.); Median household income: $34,318 (2006-2010 5-year est.); Average household income: $44,280 (2006-2010 5-year est.); Percent of households with income of $100,000 or more: n/a (2006-2010 5-year est.); Poverty rate: 23.0% (2006-2010 5-year est.).
Education: Percent of population age 25 and over with: High school diploma (including GED) or higher: 83.2% (2006-2010 5-year est.); Bachelor's degree or higher: 0.0% (2006-2010 5-year est.); Master's degree or higher: 0.0% (2006-2010 5-year est.).
Housing: Homeownership rate: 89.9% (2010); Median home value: $67,500 (2006-2010 5-year est.); Median contract rent: n/a per month (2006-2010 5-year est.); Median year structure built: before 1940 (2006-2010 5-year est.).
Transportation: Commute to work: 100.0% car, 0.0% public transportation, 0.0% walk, 0.0% work from home (2006-2010 5-year est.); Travel time to work: 12.3% less than 15 minutes, 45.5% 15 to 30 minutes, 6.4% 30 to 45 minutes, 20.3% 45 to 60 minutes, 15.5% 60 minutes or more (2006-2010 5-year est.)

GREENWOOD (township).
Covers a land area of 20.414 square miles and a water area of 0.283 square miles. Located at 40.92° N. Lat; 78.66° W. Long.
Population: 415 (1990); 424 (2000); 372 (2010); Density: 18.2 persons per square mile (2010); Race: 98.1% White, 0.8% Black, 0.0% Asian, 0.0% American Indian/Alaska Native, 0.0% Native Hawaiian/Other Pacific Islander, 1.1% Other, 0.0% Hispanic of any race (2010); Average household size: 2.34 (2010); Median age: 48.3 (2010); Males per 100 females: 105.5 (2010); Marriage status: 27.4% never married, 58.4% now married, 3.7% widowed, 10.5% divorced (2006-2010 5-year est.); Foreign born: 0.0% (2006-2010 5-year est.); Ancestry (includes multiple ancestries): 24.3% German, 20.5% English, 20.2% Irish, 18.8% American, 3.8% Dutch (2006-2010 5-year est.).
Economy: Employment by occupation: 8.9% management, 0.0% professional, 9.6% services, 17.8% sales, 8.9% farming, 21.9% construction, 18.5% production (2006-2010 5-year est.).
Income: Per capita income: $14,944 (2006-2010 5-year est.); Median household income: $33,750 (2006-2010 5-year est.); Average household income: $38,459 (2006-2010 5-year est.); Percent of households with income of $100,000 or more: 3.0% (2006-2010 5-year est.); Poverty rate: 12.9% (2006-2010 5-year est.).
Education: Percent of population age 25 and over with: High school diploma (including GED) or higher: 90.8% (2006-2010 5-year est.); Bachelor's degree or higher: 7.2% (2006-2010 5-year est.); Master's degree or higher: 2.0% (2006-2010 5-year est.).
Housing: Homeownership rate: 87.4% (2010); Median home value: $81,200 (2006-2010 5-year est.); Median contract rent: $308 per month (2006-2010 5-year est.); Median year structure built: 1969 (2006-2010 5-year est.).
Transportation: Commute to work: 92.3% car, 0.0% public transportation, 3.5% walk, 4.2% work from home (2006-2010 5-year est.); Travel time to work: 22.1% less than 15 minutes, 28.7% 15 to 30 minutes, 30.9% 30 to

45 minutes, 8.8% 45 to 60 minutes, 9.6% 60 minutes or more (2006-2010 5-year est.)

GULICH (township).
Covers a land area of 19.875 square miles and a water area of 0.098 square miles. Located at 40.77° N. Lat; 78.41° W. Long.
Population: 1,192 (1990); 1,275 (2000); 1,235 (2010); Density: 62.1 persons per square mile (2010); Race: 99.4% White, 0.1% Black, 0.2% Asian, 0.0% American Indian/Alaska Native, 0.0% Native Hawaiian/Other Pacific Islander, 0.3% Other, 0.2% Hispanic of any race (2010); Average household size: 2.42 (2010); Median age: 42.3 (2010); Males per 100 females: 99.8 (2010); Marriage status: 23.9% never married, 58.7% now married, 8.9% widowed, 8.5% divorced (2006-2010 5-year est.); Foreign born: 0.0% (2006-2010 5-year est.); Ancestry (includes multiple ancestries): 32.7% German, 12.8% English, 12.6% Irish, 11.8% Polish, 10.9% Italian (2006-2010 5-year est.).
Economy: Single-family building permits issued: 5 (2011); Multi-family building permits issued: 0 (2011); Employment by occupation: 10.8% management, 5.0% professional, 5.5% services, 14.0% sales, 3.3% farming, 13.5% construction, 7.0% production (2006-2010 5-year est.).
Income: Per capita income: $20,090 (2006-2010 5-year est.); Median household income: $43,942 (2006-2010 5-year est.); Average household income: $48,533 (2006-2010 5-year est.); Percent of households with income of $100,000 or more: 8.2% (2006-2010 5-year est.); Poverty rate: 12.6% (2006-2010 5-year est.).
Education: Percent of population age 25 and over with: High school diploma (including GED) or higher: 87.9% (2006-2010 5-year est.); Bachelor's degree or higher: 14.7% (2006-2010 5-year est.); Master's degree or higher: 3.5% (2006-2010 5-year est.).
Housing: Homeownership rate: 87.4% (2010); Median home value: $88,800 (2006-2010 5-year est.); Median contract rent: $230 per month (2006-2010 5-year est.); Median year structure built: 1966 (2006-2010 5-year est.).
Transportation: Commute to work: 92.9% car, 0.0% public transportation, 0.0% walk, 7.1% work from home (2006-2010 5-year est.); Travel time to work: 16.9% less than 15 minutes, 22.2% 15 to 30 minutes, 24.5% 30 to 45 minutes, 18.0% 45 to 60 minutes, 18.4% 60 minutes or more (2006-2010 5-year est.)
Additional Information Contacts
Tyrone Area Chamber of Commerce . . . . (814) 684-0736
  http://www.tyronechamber.com

HAWK RUN (CDP).
Covers a land area of 0.804 square miles and a water area of 0.007 square miles. Located at 40.92° N. Lat; 78.20° W. Long. Elevation is 1,467 feet.
Population: n/a (1990); n/a (2000); 534 (2010); Density: 664.4 persons per square mile (2010); Race: 98.5% White, 0.2% Black, 0.0% Asian, 0.2% American Indian/Alaska Native, 0.0% Native Hawaiian/Other Pacific Islander, 1.1% Other, 0.0% Hispanic of any race (2010); Average household size: 2.17 (2010); Median age: 46.3 (2010); Males per 100 females: 94.2 (2010); Marriage status: 21.7% never married, 31.7% now married, 22.1% widowed, 24.6% divorced (2006-2010 5-year est.); Foreign born: 1.9% (2006-2010 5-year est.); Ancestry (includes multiple ancestries): 27.0% Slovak, 22.5% Italian, 20.3% Irish, 10.0% German, 6.4% Czech (2006-2010 5-year est.).
Economy: Employment by occupation: 9.2% management, 0.0% professional, 21.8% services, 21.8% sales, 8.4% farming, 20.2% construction, 15.1% production (2006-2010 5-year est.).
Income: Per capita income: $15,070 (2006-2010 5-year est.); Median household income: $16,528 (2006-2010 5-year est.); Average household income: $22,348 (2006-2010 5-year est.); Percent of households with income of $100,000 or more: n/a (2006-2010 5-year est.); Poverty rate: 23.2% (2006-2010 5-year est.).
Education: Percent of population age 25 and over with: High school diploma (including GED) or higher: 63.6% (2006-2010 5-year est.); Bachelor's degree or higher: 8.4% (2006-2010 5-year est.); Master's degree or higher: 0.0% (2006-2010 5-year est.).
Housing: Homeownership rate: 73.1% (2010); Median home value: $77,100 (2006-2010 5-year est.); Median contract rent: $402 per month (2006-2010 5-year est.); Median year structure built: 1961 (2006-2010 5-year est.).
Transportation: Commute to work: 91.6% car, 0.0% public transportation, 0.0% walk, 0.0% work from home (2006-2010 5-year est.); Travel time to work: 66.4% less than 15 minutes, 5.0% 15 to 30 minutes, 16.8% 30 to 45

minutes, 11.8% 45 to 60 minutes, 0.0% 60 minutes or more (2006-2010 5-year est.)

HOUTZDALE (borough). Covers a land area of 0.383 square miles and a water area of 0 square miles. Located at 40.83° N. Lat; 78.35° W. Long. Elevation is 1,526 feet.

History: Laid out 1870, incorporated 1872.

Population: 914 (1990); 941 (2000); 797 (2010); Density: 2,081.6 persons per square mile (2010); Race: 99.2% White, 0.0% Black, 0.0% Asian, 0.0% American Indian/Alaska Native, 0.0% Native Hawaiian/Other Pacific Islander, 0.8% Other, 0.1% Hispanic of any race (2010); Average household size: 2.39 (2010); Median age: 41.5 (2010); Males per 100 females: 97.8 (2010); Marriage status: 29.9% never married, 50.1% now married, 7.6% widowed, 12.4% divorced (2006-2010 5-year est.); Foreign born: 0.0% (2006-2010 5-year est.); Ancestry (includes multiple ancestries): 19.8% German, 14.8% English, 14.7% Irish, 13.2% Polish, 12.6% American (2006-2010 5-year est.).

Economy: Single-family building permits issued: 0 (2011); Multi-family building permits issued: 0 (2011); Employment by occupation: 6.0% management, 3.3% professional, 12.1% services, 12.3% sales, 6.3% farming, 13.1% construction, 8.0% production (2006-2010 5-year est.).

Income: Per capita income: $18,322 (2006-2010 5-year est.); Median household income: $39,659 (2006-2010 5-year est.); Average household income: $49,609 (2006-2010 5-year est.); Percent of households with income of $100,000 or more: 7.0% (2006-2010 5-year est.); Poverty rate: 18.4% (2006-2010 5-year est.).

Education: Percent of population age 25 and over with: High school diploma (including GED) or higher: 86.0% (2006-2010 5-year est.); Bachelor's degree or higher: 11.9% (2006-2010 5-year est.); Master's degree or higher: 4.1% (2006-2010 5-year est.).

School District(s)

Moshannon Valley SD (KG-12)

   2010-11 Enrollment: 948 . . . . (814) 378-7609

Housing: Homeownership rate: 75.9% (2010); Median home value: $75,500 (2006-2010 5-year est.); Median contract rent: $359 per month (2006-2010 5-year est.); Median year structure built: 1941 (2006-2010 5-year est.).

Transportation: Commute to work: 97.5% car, 0.0% public transportation, 2.5% walk, 0.0% work from home (2006-2010 5-year est.); Travel time to work: 32.5% less than 15 minutes, 23.8% 15 to 30 minutes, 16.3% 30 to 45 minutes, 20.5% 45 to 60 minutes, 7.0% 60 minutes or more (2006-2010 5-year est.)

HUSTON (township). Covers a land area of 63.996 square miles and a water area of 0.212 square miles. Located at 41.20° N. Lat; 78.57° W. Long.

Population: 1,352 (1990); 1,468 (2000); 1,433 (2010); Density: 22.4 persons per square mile (2010); Race: 99.1% White, 0.1% Black, 0.3% Asian, 0.1% American Indian/Alaska Native, 0.0% Native Hawaiian/Other Pacific Islander, 0.4% Other, 0.9% Hispanic of any race (2010); Average household size: 2.40 (2010); Median age: 43.1 (2010); Males per 100 females: 100.1 (2010); Marriage status: 21.1% never married, 54.4% now married, 7.9% widowed, 16.5% divorced (2006-2010 5-year est.); Foreign born: 0.9% (2006-2010 5-year est.); Ancestry (includes multiple ancestries): 33.9% American, 20.8% German, 15.0% Italian, 10.0% Irish, 9.0% Polish (2006-2010 5-year est.).

Economy: Single-family building permits issued: 1 (2011); Multi-family building permits issued: 0 (2011); Employment by occupation: 6.3% management, 1.4% professional, 13.2% services, 18.3% sales, 1.3% farming, 17.4% construction, 13.6% production (2006-2010 5-year est.).

Income: Per capita income: $17,935 (2006-2010 5-year est.); Median household income: $35,761 (2006-2010 5-year est.); Average household income: $42,459 (2006-2010 5-year est.); Percent of households with income of $100,000 or more: 4.9% (2006-2010 5-year est.); Poverty rate: 17.6% (2006-2010 5-year est.).

Education: Percent of population age 25 and over with: High school diploma (including GED) or higher: 85.3% (2006-2010 5-year est.); Bachelor's degree or higher: 7.6% (2006-2010 5-year est.); Master's degree or higher: 1.2% (2006-2010 5-year est.).

Housing: Homeownership rate: 79.9% (2010); Median home value: $64,500 (2006-2010 5-year est.); Median contract rent: $448 per month (2006-2010 5-year est.); Median year structure built: 1969 (2006-2010 5-year est.).

Transportation: Commute to work: 95.2% car, 0.0% public transportation, 2.2% walk, 2.6% work from home (2006-2010 5-year est.); Travel time to

work: 17.9% less than 15 minutes, 49.0% 15 to 30 minutes, 25.6% 30 to 45 minutes, 4.0% 45 to 60 minutes, 3.6% 60 minutes or more (2006-2010 5-year est.)

Additional Information Contacts

Greater DuBois Area Chamber of Commerce . . . . (814) 371-5010
   http://www.duboispachamber.com

HYDE (CDP). Covers a land area of 1.667 square miles and a water area of 0.008 square miles. Located at 41.01° N. Lat; 78.48° W. Long. Elevation is 1,086 feet.

Population: 1,644 (1990); 1,491 (2000); 1,399 (2010); Density: 839.5 persons per square mile (2010); Race: 98.1% White, 0.6% Black, 0.1% Asian, 0.1% American Indian/Alaska Native, 0.0% Native Hawaiian/Other Pacific Islander, 1.1% Other, 0.6% Hispanic of any race (2010); Average household size: 2.30 (2010); Median age: 41.1 (2010); Males per 100 females: 85.1 (2010); Marriage status: 27.2% never married, 43.6% now married, 8.8% widowed, 20.4% divorced (2006-2010 5-year est.); Foreign born: 0.0% (2006-2010 5-year est.); Ancestry (includes multiple ancestries): 36.1% German, 20.4% Irish, 15.5% English, 9.3% Italian, 6.6% Dutch (2006-2010 5-year est.).

Economy: Employment by occupation: 0.0% management, 0.0% professional, 2.6% services, 21.6% sales, 0.0% farming, 11.6% construction, 3.7% production (2006-2010 5-year est.).

Income: Per capita income: $13,611 (2006-2010 5-year est.); Median household income: $22,782 (2006-2010 5-year est.); Average household income: $29,359 (2006-2010 5-year est.); Percent of households with income of $100,000 or more: n/a (2006-2010 5-year est.); Poverty rate: 29.7% (2006-2010 5-year est.).

Education: Percent of population age 25 and over with: High school diploma (including GED) or higher: 75.9% (2006-2010 5-year est.); Bachelor's degree or higher: 4.4% (2006-2010 5-year est.); Master's degree or higher: 0.0% (2006-2010 5-year est.).

Housing: Homeownership rate: 67.1% (2010); Median home value: $78,900 (2006-2010 5-year est.); Median contract rent: $238 per month (2006-2010 5-year est.); Median year structure built: 1969 (2006-2010 5-year est.).

Transportation: Commute to work: 95.8% car, 0.0% public transportation, 0.0% walk, 4.2% work from home (2006-2010 5-year est.); Travel time to work: 60.4% less than 15 minutes, 20.1% 15 to 30 minutes, 16.2% 30 to 45 minutes, 0.0% 45 to 60 minutes, 3.3% 60 minutes or more (2006-2010 5-year est.)

Additional Information Contacts

Chamber of Commerce of Clearfield . . . . (814) 765-7567
   http://www.clearfieldchamber.com

IRVONA (borough). Covers a land area of 0.929 square miles and a water area of 0.020 square miles. Located at 40.77° N. Lat; 78.55° W. Long. Elevation is 1,391 feet.

Population: 719 (1990); 680 (2000); 647 (2010); Density: 696.2 persons per square mile (2010); Race: 98.6% White, 0.0% Black, 0.2% Asian, 0.0% American Indian/Alaska Native, 0.0% Native Hawaiian/Other Pacific Islander, 1.2% Other, 0.2% Hispanic of any race (2010); Average household size: 2.72 (2010); Median age: 40.8 (2010); Males per 100 females: 86.5 (2010); Marriage status: 29.1% never married, 57.2% now married, 6.0% widowed, 7.7% divorced (2006-2010 5-year est.); Foreign born: 0.0% (2006-2010 5-year est.); Ancestry (includes multiple ancestries): 27.4% German, 11.7% Italian, 11.4% English, 10.9% Irish, 10.3% Dutch (2006-2010 5-year est.).

Economy: Single-family building permits issued: 0 (2011); Multi-family building permits issued: 0 (2011); Employment by occupation: 5.2% management, 0.0% professional, 15.5% services, 19.3% sales, 0.0% farming, 16.6% construction, 14.1% production (2006-2010 5-year est.).

Income: Per capita income: $12,850 (2006-2010 5-year est.); Median household income: $24,821 (2006-2010 5-year est.); Average household income: $34,862 (2006-2010 5-year est.); Percent of households with income of $100,000 or more: 2.0% (2006-2010 5-year est.); Poverty rate: 29.4% (2006-2010 5-year est.).

Education: Percent of population age 25 and over with: High school diploma (including GED) or higher: 85.5% (2006-2010 5-year est.); Bachelor's degree or higher: 4.8% (2006-2010 5-year est.); Master's degree or higher: 0.0% (2006-2010 5-year est.).

Housing: Homeownership rate: 87.8% (2010); Median home value: $64,500 (2006-2010 5-year est.); Median contract rent: $382 per month (2006-2010 5-year est.); Median year structure built: before 1940 (2006-2010 5-year est.).

Transportation: Commute to work: 93.7% car, 0.0% public transportation, 3.5% walk, 1.7% work from home (2006-2010 5-year est.); Travel time to work: 29.2% less than 15 minutes, 9.3% 15 to 30 minutes, 40.6% 30 to 45 minutes, 7.5% 45 to 60 minutes, 13.5% 60 minutes or more (2006-2010 5-year est.)

JORDAN (township). Covers a land area of 23.262 square miles and a water area of 0.088 square miles. Located at 40.84° N. Lat; 78.56° W. Long.
Population: 533 (1990); 543 (2000); 461 (2010); Density: 19.8 persons per square mile (2010); Race: 97.6% White, 0.7% Black, 0.7% Asian, 0.0% American Indian/Alaska Native, 0.0% Native Hawaiian/Other Pacific Islander, 1.0% Other, 0.0% Hispanic of any race (2010); Average household size: 2.51 (2010); Median age: 42.7 (2010); Males per 100 females: 106.7 (2010); Marriage status: 31.5% never married, 53.5% now married, 4.9% widowed, 10.1% divorced (2006-2010 5-year est.); Foreign born: 0.0% (2006-2010 5-year est.); Ancestry (includes multiple ancestries): 30.2% Irish, 28.5% German, 10.1% Italian, 6.8% English, 5.3% Scottish (2006-2010 5-year est.).
Economy: Single-family building permits issued: 0 (2011); Multi-family building permits issued: 0 (2011); Employment by occupation: 3.8% management, 0.0% professional, 14.6% services, 14.2% sales, 7.3% farming, 22.9% construction, 21.2% production (2006-2010 5-year est.).
Income: Per capita income: $16,488 (2006-2010 5-year est.); Median household income: $35,536 (2006-2010 5-year est.); Average household income: $42,858 (2006-2010 5-year est.); Percent of households with income of $100,000 or more: 5.0% (2006-2010 5-year est.); Poverty rate: 18.3% (2006-2010 5-year est.).
Education: Percent of population age 25 and over with: High school diploma (including GED) or higher: 83.6% (2006-2010 5-year est.); Bachelor's degree or higher: 10.1% (2006-2010 5-year est.); Master's degree or higher: 1.4% (2006-2010 5-year est.).
Housing: Homeownership rate: 90.3% (2010); Median home value: $66,400 (2006-2010 5-year est.); Median contract rent: $335 per month (2006-2010 5-year est.); Median year structure built: 1959 (2006-2010 5-year est.).
Transportation: Commute to work: 92.5% car, 0.0% public transportation, 3.9% walk, 2.5% work from home (2006-2010 5-year est.); Travel time to work: 20.9% less than 15 minutes, 20.1% 15 to 30 minutes, 33.0% 30 to 45 minutes, 16.1% 45 to 60 minutes, 9.9% 60 minutes or more (2006-2010 5-year est.)

KARTHAUS (township). Covers a land area of 35.382 square miles and a water area of 0.439 square miles. Located at 41.16° N. Lat; 78.11° W. Long. Elevation is 906 feet.
Population: 547 (1990); 811 (2000); 811 (2010); Density: 22.9 persons per square mile (2010); Race: 74.1% White, 18.2% Black, 0.1% Asian, 0.0% American Indian/Alaska Native, 0.0% Native Hawaiian/Other Pacific Islander, 7.6% Other, 7.3% Hispanic of any race (2010); Average household size: 2.17 (2010); Median age: 32.9 (2010); Males per 100 females: 186.6 (2010); Marriage status: 35.1% never married, 50.8% now married, 2.9% widowed, 11.1% divorced (2006-2010 5-year est.); Foreign born: 0.0% (2006-2010 5-year est.); Ancestry (includes multiple ancestries): 25.2% German, 9.7% Irish, 5.3% French, 3.0% Polish, 2.6% American (2006-2010 5-year est.).
Economy: Single-family building permits issued: 0 (2011); Multi-family building permits issued: 0 (2011); Employment by occupation: 7.9% management, 0.0% professional, 8.5% services, 13.3% sales, 3.0% farming, 24.5% construction, 8.2% production (2006-2010 5-year est.).
Income: Per capita income: $22,512 (2006-2010 5-year est.); Median household income: $36,111 (2006-2010 5-year est.); Average household income: $45,718 (2006-2010 5-year est.); Percent of households with income of $100,000 or more: 11.6% (2006-2010 5-year est.); Poverty rate: 7.8% (2006-2010 5-year est.).
Education: Percent of population age 25 and over with: High school diploma (including GED) or higher: 87.8% (2006-2010 5-year est.); Bachelor's degree or higher: 7.0% (2006-2010 5-year est.); Master's degree or higher: 0.0% (2006-2010 5-year est.).
Housing: Homeownership rate: 85.6% (2010); Median home value: $77,200 (2006-2010 5-year est.); Median contract rent: $454 per month (2006-2010 5-year est.); Median year structure built: 1964 (2006-2010 5-year est.).
Transportation: Commute to work: 97.5% car, 0.0% public transportation, 2.5% walk, 0.0% work from home (2006-2010 5-year est.); Travel time to work: 31.1% less than 15 minutes, 31.1% 15 to 30 minutes, 17.5% 30 to

45 minutes, 15.1% 45 to 60 minutes, 5.2% 60 minutes or more (2006-2010 5-year est.)

KNOX (township). Covers a land area of 25.809 square miles and a water area of 0.169 square miles. Located at 40.89° N. Lat; 78.48° W. Long.
Population: 704 (1990); 705 (2000); 647 (2010); Density: 25.1 persons per square mile (2010); Race: 98.6% White, 0.2% Black, 0.0% Asian, 0.3% American Indian/Alaska Native, 0.0% Native Hawaiian/Other Pacific Islander, 0.9% Other, 0.2% Hispanic of any race (2010); Average household size: 2.41 (2010); Median age: 44.5 (2010); Males per 100 females: 107.4 (2010); Marriage status: 15.8% never married, 60.6% now married, 4.5% widowed, 19.1% divorced (2006-2010 5-year est.); Foreign born: 0.0% (2006-2010 5-year est.); Ancestry (includes multiple ancestries): 29.5% German, 14.1% Irish, 9.8% English, 7.9% French, 5.5% Dutch (2006-2010 5-year est.).
Economy: Single-family building permits issued: 0 (2011); Multi-family building permits issued: 0 (2011); Employment by occupation: 0.8% management, 4.8% professional, 8.3% services, 17.1% sales, 0.8% farming, 21.4% construction, 15.5% production (2006-2010 5-year est.).
Income: Per capita income: $19,766 (2006-2010 5-year est.); Median household income: $35,000 (2006-2010 5-year est.); Average household income: $40,686 (2006-2010 5-year est.); Percent of households with income of $100,000 or more: 1.9% (2006-2010 5-year est.); Poverty rate: 15.4% (2006-2010 5-year est.).
Education: Percent of population age 25 and over with: High school diploma (including GED) or higher: 81.5% (2006-2010 5-year est.); Bachelor's degree or higher: 8.7% (2006-2010 5-year est.); Master's degree or higher: 2.0% (2006-2010 5-year est.).
Housing: Homeownership rate: 87.0% (2010); Median home value: $85,300 (2006-2010 5-year est.); Median contract rent: $456 per month (2006-2010 5-year est.); Median year structure built: 1962 (2006-2010 5-year est.).
Transportation: Commute to work: 94.8% car, 0.0% public transportation, 0.0% walk, 4.4% work from home (2006-2010 5-year est.); Travel time to work: 26.1% less than 15 minutes, 49.8% 15 to 30 minutes, 17.4% 30 to 45 minutes, 2.5% 45 to 60 minutes, 4.1% 60 minutes or more (2006-2010 5-year est.)

KYLERTOWN (CDP). Covers a land area of 1.715 square miles and a water area of 0.001 square miles. Located at 41.00° N. Lat; 78.17° W. Long. Elevation is 1,650 feet.
Population: n/a (1990); n/a (2000); 340 (2010); Density: 198.2 persons per square mile (2010); Race: 99.7% White, 0.3% Black, 0.0% Asian, 0.0% American Indian/Alaska Native, 0.0% Native Hawaiian/Other Pacific Islander, 0.0% Other, 0.0% Hispanic of any race (2010); Average household size: 2.58 (2010); Median age: 37.2 (2010); Males per 100 females: 88.9 (2010); Marriage status: 9.2% never married, 81.0% now married, 0.0% widowed, 9.8% divorced (2006-2010 5-year est.); Foreign born: 0.0% (2006-2010 5-year est.); Ancestry (includes multiple ancestries): 37.0% German, 17.5% Slovak, 15.0% Irish, 9.4% Italian, 8.3% English (2006-2010 5-year est.).
Economy: Employment by occupation: 0.0% management, 0.0% professional, 0.0% services, 20.2% sales, 5.2% farming, 13.6% construction, 5.2% production (2006-2010 5-year est.).
Income: Per capita income: $18,827 (2006-2010 5-year est.); Median household income: $50,625 (2006-2010 5-year est.); Average household income: $52,895 (2006-2010 5-year est.); Percent of households with income of $100,000 or more: n/a (2006-2010 5-year est.); Poverty rate: 2.4% (2006-2010 5-year est.).
Education: Percent of population age 25 and over with: High school diploma (including GED) or higher: 74.4% (2006-2010 5-year est.); Bachelor's degree or higher: 3.9% (2006-2010 5-year est.); Master's degree or higher: 0.0% (2006-2010 5-year est.).
Housing: Homeownership rate: 81.8% (2010); Median home value: $84,100 (2006-2010 5-year est.); Median contract rent: $515 per month (2006-2010 5-year est.); Median year structure built: before 1940 (2006-2010 5-year est.).
Transportation: Commute to work: 94.8% car, 0.0% public transportation, 0.0% walk, 5.2% work from home (2006-2010 5-year est.); Travel time to work: 16.8% less than 15 minutes, 46.2% 15 to 30 minutes, 19.0% 30 to 45 minutes, 0.0% 45 to 60 minutes, 17.9% 60 minutes or more (2006-2010 5-year est.)

LA JOSE (unincorporated postal area)

Zip Code: 15753

Covers a land area of 39.131 square miles and a water area of 0.170 square miles. Located at 40.79° N. Lat; 78.65° W. Long. Population: 513 (2010); Density: 13.1 persons per square mile (2010); Race: 99.6% White, 0.2% Black, 0.0% Asian, 0.0% American Indian/Alaska Native, 0.0% Native Hawaiian/Other Pacific Islander, 0.2% Other, 0.6% Hispanic of any race (2010); Average household size: 2.39 (2010); Median age: 44.2 (2010); Males per 100 females: 102.8 (2010); Homeownership rate: 87.5% (2010).

LANSE (unincorporated postal area)

Zip Code: 16849

Covers a land area of 4.115 square miles and a water area of 0.004 square miles. Located at 40.96° N. Lat; 78.11° W. Long. Elevation is 1,591 feet. Population: 331 (2010); Density: 80.4 persons per square mile (2010); Race: 100.0% White, 0.0% Black, 0.0% Asian, 0.0% American Indian/Alaska Native, 0.0% Native Hawaiian/Other Pacific Islander, 0.0% Other, 0.0% Hispanic of any race (2010); Average household size: 2.38 (2010); Median age: 47.1 (2010); Males per 100 females: 99.4 (2010); Homeownership rate: 89.9% (2010).

LAWRENCE (township). Covers a land area of 82.544 square miles and a water area of 0.707 square miles. Located at 41.08° N. Lat; 78.47° W. Long.

Population: 7,977 (1990); 7,712 (2000); 7,681 (2010); Density: 93.1 persons per square mile (2010); Race: 98.1% White, 0.6% Black, 0.5% Asian, 0.1% American Indian/Alaska Native, 0.1% Native Hawaiian/Other Pacific Islander, 0.6% Other, 0.5% Hispanic of any race (2010); Average household size: 2.30 (2010); Median age: 46.0 (2010); Males per 100 females: 93.9 (2010); Marriage status: 21.2% never married, 55.1% now married, 11.5% widowed, 12.3% divorced (2006-2010 5-year est.); Foreign born: 0.6% (2006-2010 5-year est.); Ancestry (includes multiple ancestries): 32.5% German, 13.7% Irish, 12.9% American, 11.8% English, 8.4% Italian (2006-2010 5-year est.).

Economy: Single-family building permits issued: 3 (2011); Multi-family building permits issued: 0 (2011); Employment by occupation: 8.5% management, 3.9% professional, 9.8% services, 16.9% sales, 3.3% farming, 10.3% construction, 7.8% production (2006-2010 5-year est.).

Income: Per capita income: $20,358 (2006-2010 5-year est.); Median household income: $35,930 (2006-2010 5-year est.); Average household income: $46,871 (2006-2010 5-year est.); Percent of households with income of $100,000 or more: 8.3% (2006-2010 5-year est.); Poverty rate: 16.9% (2006-2010 5-year est.).

Education: Percent of population age 25 and over with: High school diploma (including GED) or higher: 83.1% (2006-2010 5-year est.); Bachelor's degree or higher: 13.9% (2006-2010 5-year est.); Master's degree or higher: 4.1% (2006-2010 5-year est.).

Housing: Homeownership rate: 75.0% (2010); Median home value: $82,700 (2006-2010 5-year est.); Median contract rent: $362 per month (2006-2010 5-year est.); Median year structure built: 1965 (2006-2010 5-year est.).

Safety: Violent crime rate: 105.1 per 10,000 population; Property crime rate: 410.1 per 10,000 population (2011).

Transportation: Commute to work: 92.4% car, 0.3% public transportation, 1.3% walk, 1.9% work from home (2006-2010 5-year est.); Travel time to work: 53.7% less than 15 minutes, 26.4% 15 to 30 minutes, 10.3% 30 to 45 minutes, 2.7% 45 to 60 minutes, 6.9% 60 minutes or more (2006-2010 5-year est.).

Additional Information Contacts

Chamber of Commerce of Clearfield . . . . (814) 765-7567
    http://www.clearfieldchamber.com
Lawrence Township . . . . (814) 765-4551
    http://www.lawrencetwp.net

LUMBER CITY (borough). Aka Lumber. Covers a land area of 2.741 square miles and a water area of 0.145 square miles. Located at 40.93° N. Lat; 78.58° W. Long. Elevation is 1,266 feet.

Population: 83 (1990); 86 (2000); 76 (2010); Density: 27.7 persons per square mile (2010); Race: 100.0% White, 0.0% Black, 0.0% Asian, 0.0% American Indian/Alaska Native, 0.0% Native Hawaiian/Other Pacific Islander, 0.0% Other, 0.0% Hispanic of any race (2010); Average household size: 2.00 (2010); Median age: 50.3 (2010); Males per 100 females: 117.1 (2010); Marriage status: 6.3% never married, 82.5% now married, 0.0% widowed, 11.1% divorced (2006-2010 5-year est.); Foreign born: 0.0% (2006-2010 5-year est.); Ancestry (includes multiple ancestries): 35.3% German, 16.2% Scotch-Irish, 13.2% Irish, 10.3% English, 8.8% American (2006-2010 5-year est.).

Economy: Employment by occupation: 4.3% management, 0.0% professional, 15.2% services, 6.5% sales, 4.3% farming, 10.9% construction, 4.3% production (2006-2010 5-year est.).

Income: Per capita income: $14,796 (2006-2010 5-year est.); Median household income: $23,068 (2006-2010 5-year est.); Average household income: $26,528 (2006-2010 5-year est.); Percent of households with income of $100,000 or more: n/a (2006-2010 5-year est.); Poverty rate: 11.8% (2006-2010 5-year est.).

Education: Percent of population age 25 and over with: High school diploma (including GED) or higher: 77.8% (2006-2010 5-year est.); Bachelor's degree or higher: 0.0% (2006-2010 5-year est.); Master's degree or higher: 0.0% (2006-2010 5-year est.).

Housing: Homeownership rate: 81.6% (2010); Median home value: $71,700 (2006-2010 5-year est.); Median contract rent: n/a per month (2006-2010 5-year est.); Median year structure built: 1968 (2006-2010 5-year est.).

Transportation: Commute to work: 89.1% car, 0.0% public transportation, 0.0% walk, 10.9% work from home (2006-2010 5-year est.); Travel time to work: 0.0% less than 15 minutes, 92.7% 15 to 30 minutes, 7.3% 30 to 45 minutes, 0.0% 45 to 60 minutes, 0.0% 60 minutes or more (2006-2010 5-year est.).

LUTHERSBURG (unincorporated postal area)

Zip Code: 15848

Covers a land area of 20.196 square miles and a water area of 0.096 square miles. Located at 41.02° N. Lat; 78.73° W. Long. Population: 1,027 (2010); Density: 50.9 persons per square mile (2010); Race: 97.8% White, 0.9% Black, 0.4% Asian, 0.0% American Indian/Alaska Native, 0.0% Native Hawaiian/Other Pacific Islander, 0.9% Other, 0.7% Hispanic of any race (2010); Average household size: 2.83 (2010); Median age: 40.6 (2010); Males per 100 females: 102.2 (2010); Homeownership rate: 87.8% (2010).

MADERA (unincorporated postal area)

Zip Code: 16661

Covers a land area of 20.233 square miles and a water area of 0.284 square miles. Located at 40.83° N. Lat; 78.46° W. Long. Population: 951 (2010); Density: 47.0 persons per square mile (2010); Race: 99.3% White, 0.3% Black, 0.2% Asian, 0.0% American Indian/Alaska Native, 0.0% Native Hawaiian/Other Pacific Islander, 0.2% Other, 0.7% Hispanic of any race (2010); Average household size: 2.48 (2010); Median age: 41.3 (2010); Males per 100 females: 104.1 (2010); Homeownership rate: 83.8% (2010).

MAHAFFEY (borough). Covers a land area of 0.428 square miles and a water area of 0.008 square miles. Located at 40.88° N. Lat; 78.73° W. Long. Elevation is 1,335 feet.

Population: 341 (1990); 402 (2000); 368 (2010); Density: 859.6 persons per square mile (2010); Race: 99.2% White, 0.0% Black, 0.0% Asian, 0.3% American Indian/Alaska Native, 0.0% Native Hawaiian/Other Pacific Islander, 0.5% Other, 0.0% Hispanic of any race (2010); Average household size: 2.61 (2010); Median age: 39.4 (2010); Males per 100 females: 107.9 (2010); Marriage status: 29.4% never married, 55.9% now married, 7.5% widowed, 7.2% divorced (2006-2010 5-year est.); Foreign born: 0.0% (2006-2010 5-year est.); Ancestry (includes multiple ancestries): 28.4% Irish, 23.7% American, 17.1% German, 10.6% Italian, 10.2% English (2006-2010 5-year est.).

Economy: Single-family building permits issued: 0 (2011); Multi-family building permits issued: 0 (2011); Employment by occupation: 0.0% management, 0.0% professional, 20.7% services, 16.8% sales, 1.7% farming, 20.1% construction, 2.2% production (2006-2010 5-year est.).

Income: Per capita income: $12,686 (2006-2010 5-year est.); Median household income: $21,250 (2006-2010 5-year est.); Average household income: $30,702 (2006-2010 5-year est.); Percent of households with income of $100,000 or more: n/a (2006-2010 5-year est.); Poverty rate: 19.3% (2006-2010 5-year est.).

Education: Percent of population age 25 and over with: High school diploma (including GED) or higher: 80.0% (2006-2010 5-year est.); Bachelor's degree or higher: 5.0% (2006-2010 5-year est.); Master's degree or higher: 0.0% (2006-2010 5-year est.).

Purchase Line SD (KG-12)
2010-11 Enrollment: 1,035 . . . . (724) 254-4312
Housing: Homeownership rate: 75.8% (2010); Median home value: $54,000 (2006-2010 5-year est.); Median contract rent: $502 per month (2006-2010 5-year est.); Median year structure built: before 1940 (2006-2010 5-year est.).
Transportation: Commute to work: 92.8% car, 0.0% public transportation, 3.0% walk, 1.2% work from home (2006-2010 5-year est.); Travel time to work: 19.4% less than 15 minutes, 34.5% 15 to 30 minutes, 20.6% 30 to 45 minutes, 15.8% 45 to 60 minutes, 9.7% 60 minutes or more (2006-2010 5-year est.)

MINERAL SPRINGS (unincorporated postal area)
Zip Code: 16855
Covers a land area of 2.675 square miles and a water area of 0.029 square miles. Located at 40.99° N. Lat; 78.37° W. Long. Elevation is 1,398 feet. Population: 282 (2010); Density: 105.4 persons per square mile (2010); Race: 97.5% White, 0.4% Black, 0.0% Asian, 1.4% American Indian/Alaska Native, 0.0% Native Hawaiian/Other Pacific Islander, 0.7% Other, 0.0% Hispanic of any race (2010); Average household size: 2.45 (2010); Median age: 42.5 (2010); Males per 100 females: 90.5 (2010); Homeownership rate: 89.5% (2010)

MORRIS (township).
Covers a land area of 19.751 square miles and a water area of 0.124 square miles. Located at 40.95° N. Lat; 78.21° W. Long.
Population: 2,695 (1990); 3,063 (2000); 2,938 (2010); Density: 148.8 persons per square mile (2010); Race: 98.8% White, 0.2% Black, 0.0% Asian, 0.3% American Indian/Alaska Native, 0.0% Native Hawaiian/Other Pacific Islander, 0.7% Other, 0.7% Hispanic of any race (2010); Average household size: 2.39 (2010); Median age: 42.9 (2010); Males per 100 females: 96.1 (2010); Marriage status: 23.5% never married, 58.1% now married, 7.0% widowed, 11.5% divorced (2006-2010 5-year est.); Foreign born: 1.0% (2006-2010 5-year est.); Ancestry (includes multiple ancestries): 18.0% German, 16.8% English, 15.6% Slovak, 11.0% Italian, 9.8% Polish (2006-2010 5-year est.).
Economy: Single-family building permits issued: 1 (2011); Multi-family building permits issued: 0 (2011); Employment by occupation: 4.4% management, 2.4% professional, 10.5% services, 16.7% sales, 6.2% farming, 17.4% construction, 8.9% production (2006-2010 5-year est.).
Income: Per capita income: $21,753 (2006-2010 5-year est.); Median household income: $40,875 (2006-2010 5-year est.); Average household income: $51,464 (2006-2010 5-year est.); Percent of households with income of $100,000 or more: 10.3% (2006-2010 5-year est.); Poverty rate: 7.2% (2006-2010 5-year est.).
Education: Percent of population age 25 and over with: High school diploma (including GED) or higher: 86.5% (2006-2010 5-year est.); Bachelor's degree or higher: 12.1% (2006-2010 5-year est.); Master's degree or higher: 0.0% (2006-2010 5-year est.).
Housing: Homeownership rate: 81.1% (2010); Median home value: $79,500 (2006-2010 5-year est.); Median contract rent: $377 per month (2006-2010 5-year est.); Median year structure built: 1968 (2006-2010 5-year est.).
Transportation: Commute to work: 94.6% car, 0.0% public transportation, 0.5% walk, 2.3% work from home (2006-2010 5-year est.); Travel time to work: 47.8% less than 15 minutes, 13.2% 15 to 30 minutes, 18.6% 30 to 45 minutes, 15.2% 45 to 60 minutes, 5.3% 60 minutes or more (2006-2010 5-year est.)
Additional Information Contacts
Chamber of Commerce of Clearfield . . . . (814) 765-7567
http://www.clearfieldchamber.com

MORRISDALE (CDP).
Covers a land area of 1.684 square miles and a water area of 0.004 square miles. Located at 40.95° N. Lat; 78.23° W. Long. Elevation is 1,640 feet.
Population: n/a (1990); n/a (2000); 754 (2010); Density: 447.7 persons per square mile (2010); Race: 97.3% White, 0.7% Black, 0.0% Asian, 1.1% American Indian/Alaska Native, 0.0% Native Hawaiian/Other Pacific Islander, 0.9% Other, 0.4% Hispanic of any race (2010); Average household size: 2.42 (2010); Median age: 39.0 (2010); Males per 100 females: 92.3 (2010); Marriage status: 12.4% never married, 66.8% now married, 5.1% widowed, 15.7% divorced (2006-2010 5-year est.); Foreign born: 0.0% (2006-2010 5-year est.); Ancestry (includes multiple

ancestries): 17.4% English, 12.8% German, 9.2% Irish, 8.3% Slovak, 7.9% American (2006-2010 5-year est.).
Economy: Employment by occupation: 0.0% management, 0.0% professional, 14.4% services, 4.6% sales, 16.3% farming, 16.3% construction, 16.3% production (2006-2010 5-year est.).
Income: Per capita income: $16,687 (2006-2010 5-year est.); Median household income: $29,514 (2006-2010 5-year est.); Average household income: $34,470 (2006-2010 5-year est.); Percent of households with income of $100,000 or more: 3.4% (2006-2010 5-year est.); Poverty rate: 12.4% (2006-2010 5-year est.).
Education: Percent of population age 25 and over with: High school diploma (including GED) or higher: 88.7% (2006-2010 5-year est.); Bachelor's degree or higher: 3.4% (2006-2010 5-year est.); Master's degree or higher: 0.0% (2006-2010 5-year est.).

West Branch Area SD (KG-12)
2010-11 Enrollment: 1,160 . . . . (814) 345-6832
Housing: Homeownership rate: 72.1% (2010); Median home value: $65,500 (2006-2010 5-year est.); Median contract rent: $375 per month (2006-2010 5-year est.); Median year structure built: 1947 (2006-2010 5-year est.).
Transportation: Commute to work: 90.1% car, 0.0% public transportation, 0.0% walk, 0.0% work from home (2006-2010 5-year est.); Travel time to work: 63.1% less than 15 minutes, 17.1% 15 to 30 minutes, 15.2% 30 to 45 minutes, 0.0% 45 to 60 minutes, 4.6% 60 minutes or more (2006-2010 5-year est.)

MUNSON (unincorporated postal area)
Zip Code: 16860
Covers a land area of 5.441 square miles and a water area of 0.014 square miles. Located at 40.93° N. Lat; 78.17° W. Long. Population: 451 (2010); Density: 82.9 persons per square mile (2010); Race: 99.6% White, 0.0% Black, 0.0% Asian, 0.0% American Indian/Alaska Native, 0.0% Native Hawaiian/Other Pacific Islander, 0.4% Other, 2.9% Hispanic of any race (2010); Average household size: 2.29 (2010); Median age: 46.9 (2010); Males per 100 females: 115.8 (2010); Homeownership rate: 89.8% (2010)

NEW MILLPORT (unincorporated postal area)
Zip Code: 16861
Covers a land area of 12.123 square miles and a water area of 0.028 square miles. Located at 40.85° N. Lat; 78.52° W. Long. Elevation is 1,365 feet. Population: 311 (2010); Density: 25.7 persons per square mile (2010); Race: 97.4% White, 0.3% Black, 0.3% Asian, 0.3% American Indian/Alaska Native, 0.0% Native Hawaiian/Other Pacific Islander, 1.7% Other, 0.0% Hispanic of any race (2010); Average household size: 2.36 (2010); Median age: 42.8 (2010); Males per 100 females: 98.1 (2010); Homeownership rate: 84.9% (2010)

NEW WASHINGTON (borough).
Covers a land area of 2.292 square miles and a water area of 0.004 square miles. Located at 40.82° N. Lat; 78.70° W. Long. Elevation is 1,693 feet.
Population: 78 (1990); 89 (2000); 59 (2010); Density: 25.7 persons per square mile (2010); Race: 100.0% White, 0.0% Black, 0.0% Asian, 0.0% American Indian/Alaska Native, 0.0% Native Hawaiian/Other Pacific Islander, 0.0% Other, 0.0% Hispanic of any race (2010); Average household size: 2.36 (2010); Median age: 50.5 (2010); Males per 100 females: 118.5 (2010); Marriage status: 28.7% never married, 51.2% now married, 8.8% widowed, 11.3% divorced (2006-2010 5-year est.); Foreign born: 0.0% (2006-2010 5-year est.); Ancestry (includes multiple ancestries): 50.0% German, 24.5% Irish, 12.2% Scotch-Irish, 11.2% American, 9.2% Polish (2006-2010 5-year est.).
Economy: Single-family building permits issued: 0 (2011); Multi-family building permits issued: 0 (2011); Employment by occupation: 22.2% management, 0.0% professional, 4.4% services, 17.8% sales, 6.7% farming, 17.8% construction, 0.0% production (2006-2010 5-year est.).
Income: Per capita income: $19,092 (2006-2010 5-year est.); Median household income: $48,125 (2006-2010 5-year est.); Average household income: $46,397 (2006-2010 5-year est.); Percent of households with income of $100,000 or more: n/a (2006-2010 5-year est.); Poverty rate: 15.3% (2006-2010 5-year est.).
Education: Percent of population age 25 and over with: High school diploma (including GED) or higher: 85.1% (2006-2010 5-year est.); Bachelor's degree or higher: 25.4% (2006-2010 5-year est.); Master's degree or higher: 7.5% (2006-2010 5-year est.).

Housing: Homeownership rate: 92.0% (2010); Median home value: $61,000 (2006-2010 5-year est.); Median contract rent: n/a per month (2006-2010 5-year est.); Median year structure built: before 1940 (2006-2010 5-year est.).
Transportation: Commute to work: 95.6% car, 0.0% public transportation, 0.0% walk, 4.4% work from home (2006-2010 5-year est.); Travel time to work: 55.8% less than 15 minutes, 14.0% 15 to 30 minutes, 7.0% 30 to 45 minutes, 23.3% 45 to 60 minutes, 0.0% 60 minutes or more (2006-2010 5-year est.)

NEWBURG (borough). Aka La Jose. Covers a land area of 1.844 square miles and a water area of 0.009 square miles. Located at 40.84° N. Lat; 78.69° W. Long. Elevation is 1,302 feet.
Population: 117 (1990); 81 (2000); 92 (2010); Density: 49.9 persons per square mile (2010); Race: 100.0% White, 0.0% Black, 0.0% Asian, 0.0% American Indian/Alaska Native, 0.0% Native Hawaiian/Other Pacific Islander, 0.0% Other, 0.0% Hispanic of any race (2010); Average household size: 2.42 (2010); Median age: 38.5 (2010); Males per 100 females: 104.4 (2010); Marriage status: 34.9% never married, 48.4% now married, 5.6% widowed, 11.1% divorced (2006-2010 5-year est.); Foreign born: 0.0% (2006-2010 5-year est.); Ancestry (includes multiple ancestries): 23.8% German, 22.3% Polish, 17.7% Dutch, 13.8% Scottish, 10.0% English (2006-2010 5-year est.).
Economy: Employment by occupation: 12.3% management, 0.0% professional, 13.7% services, 16.4% sales, 6.8% farming, 0.0% construction, 0.0% production (2006-2010 5-year est.).
Income: Per capita income: $18,754 (2006-2010 5-year est.); Median household income: $50,481 (2006-2010 5-year est.); Average household income: $49,194 (2006-2010 5-year est.); Percent of households with income of $100,000 or more: 4.1% (2006-2010 5-year est.); Poverty rate: 5.4% (2006-2010 5-year est.).
Education: Percent of population age 25 and over with: High school diploma (including GED) or higher: 92.7% (2006-2010 5-year est.); Bachelor's degree or higher: 2.1% (2006-2010 5-year est.); Master's degree or higher: 2.1% (2006-2010 5-year est.).
Housing: Homeownership rate: 78.9% (2010); Median home value: $72,500 (2006-2010 5-year est.); Median contract rent: n/a per month (2006-2010 5-year est.); Median year structure built: 1949 (2006-2010 5-year est.).
Transportation: Commute to work: 91.8% car, 0.0% public transportation, 0.0% walk, 5.5% work from home (2006-2010 5-year est.); Travel time to work: 49.3% less than 15 minutes, 7.2% 15 to 30 minutes, 29.0% 30 to 45 minutes, 7.2% 45 to 60 minutes, 7.2% 60 minutes or more (2006-2010 5-year est.)

OKLAHOMA (CDP). Covers a land area of 0.765 square miles and a water area of <.001 square miles. Located at 41.11° N. Lat; 78.73° W. Long. Elevation is 1,444 feet.
Population: n/a (1990); n/a (2000); 782 (2010); Density: 1,021.7 persons per square mile (2010); Race: 95.7% White, 1.0% Black, 1.2% Asian, 0.0% American Indian/Alaska Native, 0.0% Native Hawaiian/Other Pacific Islander, 2.1% Other, 0.6% Hispanic of any race (2010); Average household size: 2.35 (2010); Median age: 40.6 (2010); Males per 100 females: 87.1 (2010); Marriage status: 31.0% never married, 54.0% now married, 1.7% widowed, 13.3% divorced (2006-2010 5-year est.); Foreign born: 4.9% (2006-2010 5-year est.); Ancestry (includes multiple ancestries): 39.1% American, 9.9% Polish, 8.5% English, 8.0% German, 7.8% Swedish (2006-2010 5-year est.).
Economy: Employment by occupation: 10.2% management, 0.0% professional, 11.3% services, 17.3% sales, 0.0% farming, 2.8% construction, 3.2% production (2006-2010 5-year est.).
Income: Per capita income: $31,394 (2006-2010 5-year est.); Median household income: $27,386 (2006-2010 5-year est.); Average household income: $100,759 (2006-2010 5-year est.); Percent of households with income of $100,000 or more: 24.0% (2006-2010 5-year est.); Poverty rate: 40.1% (2006-2010 5-year est.).
Education: Percent of population age 25 and over with: High school diploma (including GED) or higher: 91.0% (2006-2010 5-year est.); Bachelor's degree or higher: 23.0% (2006-2010 5-year est.); Master's degree or higher: 16.8% (2006-2010 5-year est.).
Housing: Homeownership rate: 56.7% (2010); Median home value: $173,400 (2006-2010 5-year est.); Median contract rent: $392 per month (2006-2010 5-year est.); Median year structure built: 1975 (2006-2010 5-year est.).

Transportation: Commute to work: 96.7% car, 0.0% public transportation, 3.3% walk, 0.0% work from home (2006-2010 5-year est.); Travel time to work: 58.0% less than 15 minutes, 22.3% 15 to 30 minutes, 16.4% 30 to 45 minutes, 0.0% 45 to 60 minutes, 3.3% 60 minutes or more (2006-2010 5-year est.)

OLANTA (unincorporated postal area)
Zip Code: 16863
Covers a land area of 25.419 square miles and a water area of 0.359 square miles. Located at 40.90° N. Lat; 78.47° W. Long. Elevation is 1,322 feet. Population: 718 (2010); Density: 28.2 persons per square mile (2010); Race: 99.6% White, 0.0% Black, 0.0% Asian, 0.1% American Indian/Alaska Native, 0.0% Native Hawaiian/Other Pacific Islander, 0.3% Other, 0.3% Hispanic of any race (2010); Average household size: 2.42 (2010); Median age: 46.9 (2010); Males per 100 females: 105.1 (2010); Homeownership rate: 91.3% (2010)

OSCEOLA MILLS (borough). Aka Osceola. Covers a land area of 0.330 square miles and a water area of 0 square miles. Located at 40.85° N. Lat; 78.27° W. Long. Elevation is 1,499 feet.
History: Laid out c.1857, incorporated 1864.
Population: 1,310 (1990); 1,249 (2000); 1,141 (2010); Density: 3,460.1 persons per square mile (2010); Race: 98.2% White, 0.2% Black, 0.4% Asian, 0.1% American Indian/Alaska Native, 0.0% Native Hawaiian/Other Pacific Islander, 1.1% Other, 1.2% Hispanic of any race (2010); Average household size: 2.45 (2010); Median age: 40.0 (2010); Males per 100 females: 94.0 (2010); Marriage status: 30.4% never married, 53.8% now married, 6.3% widowed, 9.5% divorced (2006-2010 5-year est.); Foreign born: 0.1% (2006-2010 5-year est.); Ancestry (includes multiple ancestries): 21.7% German, 12.7% English, 12.5% Irish, 11.4% Polish, 5.9% American (2006-2010 5-year est.).
Economy: Single-family building permits issued: 0 (2011); Multi-family building permits issued: 0 (2011); Employment by occupation: 4.1% management, 2.7% professional, 11.4% services, 10.9% sales, 3.6% farming, 12.9% construction, 8.1% production (2006-2010 5-year est.).
Income: Per capita income: $16,700 (2006-2010 5-year est.); Median household income: $39,342 (2006-2010 5-year est.); Average household income: $43,855 (2006-2010 5-year est.); Percent of households with income of $100,000 or more: 4.4% (2006-2010 5-year est.); Poverty rate: 13.6% (2006-2010 5-year est.).
Education: Percent of population age 25 and over with: High school diploma (including GED) or higher: 86.7% (2006-2010 5-year est.); Bachelor's degree or higher: 13.5% (2006-2010 5-year est.); Master's degree or higher: 4.7% (2006-2010 5-year est.).
School District(s)
Philipsburg-Osceola Area SD (PK-12)
    2010-11 Enrollment: 1,916 . . . . (814) 342-1050
Housing: Homeownership rate: 73.6% (2010); Median home value: $69,100 (2006-2010 5-year est.); Median contract rent: $405 per month (2006-2010 5-year est.); Median year structure built: before 1940 (2006-2010 5-year est.).
Transportation: Commute to work: 93.5% car, 0.0% public transportation, 4.8% walk, 1.4% work from home (2006-2010 5-year est.); Travel time to work: 31.5% less than 15 minutes, 19.9% 15 to 30 minutes, 18.3% 30 to 45 minutes, 19.1% 45 to 60 minutes, 11.1% 60 minutes or more (2006-2010 5-year est.)
Additional Information Contacts
Tyrone Area Chamber of Commerce . . . . (814) 684-0736
   http://www.tyronechamber.com

PENFIELD (unincorporated postal area)
Zip Code: 15849
Covers a land area of 78.339 square miles and a water area of 0.201 square miles. Located at 41.16° N. Lat; 78.58° W. Long. Elevation is 1,253 feet. Population: 1,399 (2010); Density: 17.9 persons per square mile (2010); Race: 98.9% White, 0.1% Black, 0.3% Asian, 0.1% American Indian/Alaska Native, 0.0% Native Hawaiian/Other Pacific Islander, 0.6% Other, 1.1% Hispanic of any race (2010); Average household size: 2.39 (2010); Median age: 43.5 (2010); Males per 100 females: 101.9 (2010); Homeownership rate: 80.1% (2010)

PENN (township). Covers a land area of 24.118 square miles and a water area of 0.110 square miles. Located at 40.96° N. Lat; 78.64° W. Long.

Population: 1,372 (1990); 1,326 (2000); 1,264 (2010); Density: 52.4 persons per square mile (2010); Race: 99.2% White, 0.1% Black, 0.1% Asian, 0.2% American Indian/Alaska Native, 0.0% Native Hawaiian/Other Pacific Islander, 0.4% Other, 0.8% Hispanic of any race (2010); Average household size: 2.43 (2010); Median age: 45.9 (2010); Males per 100 females: 99.4 (2010); Marriage status: 23.8% never married, 68.4% now married, 3.9% widowed, 3.9% divorced (2006-2010 5-year est.); Foreign born: 0.3% (2006-2010 5-year est.); Ancestry (includes multiple ancestries): 27.7% German, 22.4% American, 20.4% Irish, 13.1% English, 5.7% Dutch (2006-2010 5-year est.).

Economy: Single-family building permits issued: 0 (2011); Multi-family building permits issued: 0 (2011); Employment by occupation: 3.4% management, 1.8% professional, 12.2% services, 12.6% sales, 1.8% farming, 23.0% construction, 14.6% production (2006-2010 5-year est.).

Income: Per capita income: $19,902 (2006-2010 5-year est.); Median household income: $37,788 (2006-2010 5-year est.); Average household income: $51,128 (2006-2010 5-year est.); Percent of households with income of $100,000 or more: 9.8% (2006-2010 5-year est.); Poverty rate: 14.3% (2006-2010 5-year est.).

Education: Percent of population age 25 and over with: High school diploma (including GED) or higher: 87.0% (2006-2010 5-year est.); Bachelor's degree or higher: 9.4% (2006-2010 5-year est.); Master's degree or higher: 3.5% (2006-2010 5-year est.).

Housing: Homeownership rate: 87.1% (2010); Median home value: $73,900 (2006-2010 5-year est.); Median contract rent: $344 per month (2006-2010 5-year est.); Median year structure built: 1971 (2006-2010 5-year est.).

Transportation: Commute to work: 95.1% car, 0.0% public transportation, 1.3% walk, 3.6% work from home (2006-2010 5-year est.); Travel time to work: 14.5% less than 15 minutes, 46.2% 15 to 30 minutes, 26.6% 30 to 45 minutes, 5.1% 45 to 60 minutes, 7.5% 60 minutes or more (2006-2010 5-year est.)

Additional Information Contacts
Chamber of Commerce of Clearfield . . . . (814) 765-7567
    http://www.clearfieldchamber.com

PIKE (township). Covers a land area of 41.837 square miles and a water area of 0.926 square miles. Located at 40.99° N. Lat; 78.53° W. Long.

Population: 2,083 (1990); 2,309 (2000); 2,311 (2010); Density: 55.2 persons per square mile (2010); Race: 99.2% White, 0.3% Black, 0.1% Asian, 0.0% American Indian/Alaska Native, 0.0% Native Hawaiian/Other Pacific Islander, 0.4% Other, 0.8% Hispanic of any race (2010); Average household size: 2.43 (2010); Median age: 46.4 (2010); Males per 100 females: 102.7 (2010); Marriage status: 17.7% never married, 71.0% now married, 5.8% widowed, 5.5% divorced (2006-2010 5-year est.); Foreign born: 0.2% (2006-2010 5-year est.); Ancestry (includes multiple ancestries): 32.2% German, 17.3% Irish, 10.7% English, 9.4% Dutch, 9.4% Polish (2006-2010 5-year est.).

Economy: Single-family building permits issued: 7 (2011); Multi-family building permits issued: 0 (2011); Employment by occupation: 5.6% management, 1.3% professional, 12.2% services, 21.0% sales, 1.1% farming, 17.9% construction, 12.1% production (2006-2010 5-year est.).

Income: Per capita income: $20,160 (2006-2010 5-year est.); Median household income: $45,170 (2006-2010 5-year est.); Average household income: $50,359 (2006-2010 5-year est.); Percent of households with income of $100,000 or more: 8.5% (2006-2010 5-year est.); Poverty rate: 6.9% (2006-2010 5-year est.).

Education: Percent of population age 25 and over with: High school diploma (including GED) or higher: 86.9% (2006-2010 5-year est.); Bachelor's degree or higher: 11.8% (2006-2010 5-year est.); Master's degree or higher: 5.0% (2006-2010 5-year est.).

Housing: Homeownership rate: 85.0% (2010); Median home value: $94,300 (2006-2010 5-year est.); Median contract rent: $406 per month (2006-2010 5-year est.); Median year structure built: 1973 (2006-2010 5-year est.).

Transportation: Commute to work: 97.8% car, 0.0% public transportation, 0.0% walk, 1.6% work from home (2006-2010 5-year est.); Travel time to work: 27.1% less than 15 minutes, 37.1% 15 to 30 minutes, 20.5% 30 to 45 minutes, 3.0% 45 to 60 minutes, 12.3% 60 minutes or more (2006-2010 5-year est.)

Additional Information Contacts
Chamber of Commerce of Clearfield . . . . (814) 765-7567
    http://www.clearfieldchamber.com

PINE (township). Covers a land area of 31.874 square miles and a water area of 0.008 square miles. Located at 41.09° N. Lat; 78.53° W. Long.

Population: 43 (1990); 77 (2000); 60 (2010); Density: 1.9 persons per square mile (2010); Race: 100.0% White, 0.0% Black, 0.0% Asian, 0.0% American Indian/Alaska Native, 0.0% Native Hawaiian/Other Pacific Islander, 0.0% Other, 0.0% Hispanic of any race (2010); Average household size: 2.07 (2010); Median age: 52.0 (2010); Males per 100 females: 106.9 (2010); Marriage status: 24.3% never married, 68.9% now married, 0.0% widowed, 6.8% divorced (2006-2010 5-year est.); Foreign born: 0.0% (2006-2010 5-year est.); Ancestry (includes multiple ancestries): 24.4% German, 20.9% American, 15.1% Irish, 14.0% English, 8.1% Polish (2006-2010 5-year est.).

Economy: Single-family building permits issued: 0 (2011); Multi-family building permits issued: 0 (2011); Employment by occupation: 16.7% management, 19.0% professional, 7.1% services, 4.8% sales, 0.0% farming, 0.0% construction, 0.0% production (2006-2010 5-year est.).

Income: Per capita income: $23,350 (2006-2010 5-year est.); Median household income: $63,750 (2006-2010 5-year est.); Average household income: $66,990 (2006-2010 5-year est.); Percent of households with income of $100,000 or more: 13.4% (2006-2010 5-year est.); Poverty rate: 2.3% (2006-2010 5-year est.).

Education: Percent of population age 25 and over with: High school diploma (including GED) or higher: 100.0% (2006-2010 5-year est.); Bachelor's degree or higher: 20.4% (2006-2010 5-year est.); Master's degree or higher: 7.4% (2006-2010 5-year est.).

Housing: Homeownership rate: 96.6% (2010); Median home value: $141,700 (2006-2010 5-year est.); Median contract rent: $525 per month (2006-2010 5-year est.); Median year structure built: 1959 (2006-2010 5-year est.).

Transportation: Commute to work: 90.9% car, 0.0% public transportation, 0.0% walk, 4.5% work from home (2006-2010 5-year est.); Travel time to work: 23.8% less than 15 minutes, 54.8% 15 to 30 minutes, 14.3% 30 to 45 minutes, 0.0% 45 to 60 minutes, 7.1% 60 minutes or more (2006-2010 5-year est.)

PLYMPTONVILLE (CDP). Covers a land area of 1.298 square miles and a water area of 0.006 square miles. Located at 41.04° N. Lat; 78.45° W. Long. Elevation is 1,378 feet.

Population: 1,074 (1990); 1,040 (2000); 981 (2010); Density: 755.9 persons per square mile (2010); Race: 98.3% White, 0.5% Black, 0.3% Asian, 0.1% American Indian/Alaska Native, 0.0% Native Hawaiian/Other Pacific Islander, 0.8% Other, 0.3% Hispanic of any race (2010); Average household size: 2.24 (2010); Median age: 43.7 (2010); Males per 100 females: 97.8 (2010); Marriage status: 23.5% never married, 47.1% now married, 18.9% widowed, 10.6% divorced (2006-2010 5-year est.); Foreign born: 1.1% (2006-2010 5-year est.); Ancestry (includes multiple ancestries): 22.5% German, 22.5% American, 15.9% French, 13.1% English, 10.7% Irish (2006-2010 5-year est.).

Economy: Employment by occupation: 20.5% management, 0.0% professional, 10.6% services, 17.6% sales, 10.1% farming, 10.6% construction, 9.6% production (2006-2010 5-year est.).

Income: Per capita income: $20,487 (2006-2010 5-year est.); Median household income: $27,222 (2006-2010 5-year est.); Average household income: $38,592 (2006-2010 5-year est.); Percent of households with income of $100,000 or more: 5.6% (2006-2010 5-year est.); Poverty rate: 13.1% (2006-2010 5-year est.).

Education: Percent of population age 25 and over with: High school diploma (including GED) or higher: 81.3% (2006-2010 5-year est.); Bachelor's degree or higher: 10.0% (2006-2010 5-year est.); Master's degree or higher: 2.1% (2006-2010 5-year est.).

Housing: Homeownership rate: 73.9% (2010); Median home value: $66,500 (2006-2010 5-year est.); Median contract rent: $289 per month (2006-2010 5-year est.); Median year structure built: 1948 (2006-2010 5-year est.).

Transportation: Commute to work: 95.9% car, 0.0% public transportation, 2.6% walk, 1.5% work from home (2006-2010 5-year est.); Travel time to work: 66.4% less than 15 minutes, 21.6% 15 to 30 minutes, 2.3% 30 to 45 minutes, 2.1% 45 to 60 minutes, 7.6% 60 minutes or more (2006-2010 5-year est.)

Additional Information Contacts

Chamber of Commerce of Clearfield . . . . (814) 765-7567
http://www.clearfieldchamber.com

POTTERSDALE (unincorporated postal area)

Zip Code: 16871

Covers a land area of 24.915 square miles and a water area of 0.347 square miles. Located at 41.18° N. Lat; 78.02° W. Long. Population: 46 (2010); Density: 1.8 persons per square mile (2010); Race: 100.0% White, 0.0% Black, 0.0% Asian, 0.0% American Indian/Alaska Native, 0.0% Native Hawaiian/Other Pacific Islander, 0.0% Other, 0.0% Hispanic of any race (2010); Average household size: 1.84 (2010); Median age: 64.0 (2010); Males per 100 females: 142.1 (2010); Homeownership rate: 84.0% (2010)

RAMEY (borough).

Covers a land area of 0.928 square miles and a water area of 0.004 square miles. Located at 40.80° N. Lat; 78.40° W. Long. Elevation is 1,604 feet.

Population: 536 (1990); 525 (2000); 451 (2010); Density: 486.2 persons per square mile (2010); Race: 100.0% White, 0.0% Black, 0.0% Asian, 0.0% American Indian/Alaska Native, 0.0% Native Hawaiian/Other Pacific Islander, 0.0% Other, 0.4% Hispanic of any race (2010); Average household size: 2.36 (2010); Median age: 45.1 (2010); Males per 100 females: 96.1 (2010); Marriage status: 28.6% never married, 52.7% now married, 10.6% widowed, 8.1% divorced (2006-2010 5-year est.); Foreign born: 0.0% (2006-2010 5-year est.); Ancestry (includes multiple ancestries): 25.7% German, 20.7% Polish, 14.1% Irish, 11.6% Italian, 10.0% English (2006-2010 5-year est.).

Economy: Single-family building permits issued: 0 (2011); Multi-family building permits issued: 0 (2011); Employment by occupation: 5.0% management, 6.7% professional, 3.9% services, 17.8% sales, 5.6% farming, 7.8% construction, 5.0% production (2006-2010 5-year est.).

Income: Per capita income: $19,662 (2006-2010 5-year est.); Median household income: $38,068 (2006-2010 5-year est.); Average household income: $44,364 (2006-2010 5-year est.); Percent of households with income of $100,000 or more: 7.9% (2006-2010 5-year est.); Poverty rate: 18.0% (2006-2010 5-year est.).

Education: Percent of population age 25 and over with: High school diploma (including GED) or higher: 87.5% (2006-2010 5-year est.); Bachelor's degree or higher: 15.3% (2006-2010 5-year est.); Master's degree or higher: 5.4% (2006-2010 5-year est.).

Housing: Homeownership rate: 83.8% (2010); Median home value: $86,300 (2006-2010 5-year est.); Median contract rent: $438 per month (2006-2010 5-year est.); Median year structure built: before 1940 (2006-2010 5-year est.).

Transportation: Commute to work: 91.7% car, 0.0% public transportation, 5.6% walk, 2.8% work from home (2006-2010 5-year est.); Travel time to work: 28.6% less than 15 minutes, 27.4% 15 to 30 minutes, 21.1% 30 to 45 minutes, 13.1% 45 to 60 minutes, 9.7% 60 minutes or more (2006-2010 5-year est.)

ROCKTON (unincorporated postal area)

Zip Code: 15856

Covers a land area of 36.341 square miles and a water area of 0.383 square miles. Located at 41.08° N. Lat; 78.61° W. Long. Population: 889 (2010); Density: 24.5 persons per square mile (2010); Race: 99.3% White, 0.2% Black, 0.0% Asian, 0.1% American Indian/Alaska Native, 0.0% Native Hawaiian/Other Pacific Islander, 0.4% Other, 0.1% Hispanic of any race (2010); Average household size: 2.37 (2010); Median age: 48.7 (2010); Males per 100 females: 111.2 (2010); Homeownership rate: 87.5% (2010)

SANDY (CDP).

Covers a land area of 1.386 square miles and a water area of 0.003 square miles. Located at 41.10° N. Lat; 78.78° W. Long. Elevation is 1,430 feet.

Population: 1,774 (1990); 1,687 (2000); 1,429 (2010); Density: 1,031.3 persons per square mile (2010); Race: 98.1% White, 0.7% Black, 0.4% Asian, 0.0% American Indian/Alaska Native, 0.1% Native Hawaiian/Other Pacific Islander, 0.7% Other, 0.7% Hispanic of any race (2010); Average household size: 2.28 (2010); Median age: 45.1 (2010); Males per 100 females: 94.4 (2010); Marriage status: 26.5% never married, 46.7% now married, 12.1% widowed, 14.7% divorced (2006-2010 5-year est.); Foreign born: 0.0% (2006-2010 5-year est.); Ancestry (includes multiple ancestries): 20.7% German, 19.2% American, 9.1% Irish, 8.2% English, 7.9% Swedish (2006-2010 5-year est.).

Economy: Employment by occupation: 12.0% management, 2.2% professional, 16.1% services, 11.6% sales, 6.3% farming, 13.4% construction, 7.3% production (2006-2010 5-year est.).

Income: Per capita income: $19,904 (2006-2010 5-year est.); Median household income: $35,679 (2006-2010 5-year est.); Average household income: $44,698 (2006-2010 5-year est.); Percent of households with income of $100,000 or more: 6.3% (2006-2010 5-year est.); Poverty rate: 21.0% (2006-2010 5-year est.).

Education: Percent of population age 25 and over with: High school diploma (including GED) or higher: 87.6% (2006-2010 5-year est.); Bachelor's degree or higher: 4.2% (2006-2010 5-year est.); Master's degree or higher: 0.0% (2006-2010 5-year est.).

Housing: Homeownership rate: 75.9% (2010); Median home value: $73,400 (2006-2010 5-year est.); Median contract rent: $423 per month (2006-2010 5-year est.); Median year structure built: 1942 (2006-2010 5-year est.).

Transportation: Commute to work: 100.0% car, 0.0% public transportation, 0.0% walk, 0.0% work from home (2006-2010 5-year est.); Travel time to work: 72.4% less than 15 minutes, 14.8% 15 to 30 minutes, 1.0% 30 to 45 minutes, 4.5% 45 to 60 minutes, 7.3% 60 minutes or more (2006-2010 5-year est.)

Additional Information Contacts

Chamber of Commerce of Clearfield . . . . (814) 765-7567
http://www.clearfieldchamber.com

SANDY (township).

Covers a land area of 51.960 square miles and a water area of 1.033 square miles. Located at 41.15° N. Lat; 78.73° W. Long. Elevation is 1,430 feet.

Population: 9,253 (1990); 11,556 (2000); 10,625 (2010); Density: 204.5 persons per square mile (2010); Race: 97.6% White, 0.3% Black, 1.0% Asian, 0.0% American Indian/Alaska Native, 0.0% Native Hawaiian/Other Pacific Islander, 1.1% Other, 0.8% Hispanic of any race (2010); Average household size: 2.42 (2010); Median age: 46.4 (2010); Males per 100 females: 94.9 (2010); Marriage status: 19.1% never married, 61.8% now married, 10.3% widowed, 8.8% divorced (2006-2010 5-year est.); Foreign born: 3.5% (2006-2010 5-year est.); Ancestry (includes multiple ancestries): 30.3% American, 19.0% German, 10.1% Italian, 8.6% Irish, 7.9% English (2006-2010 5-year est.).

Economy: Single-family building permits issued: 19 (2011); Multi-family building permits issued: 0 (2011); Employment by occupation: 10.7% management, 3.0% professional, 12.8% services, 14.4% sales, 2.5% farming, 9.3% construction, 6.8% production (2006-2010 5-year est.).

Income: Per capita income: $26,154 (2006-2010 5-year est.); Median household income: $53,401 (2006-2010 5-year est.); Average household income: $66,425 (2006-2010 5-year est.); Percent of households with income of $100,000 or more: 15.4% (2006-2010 5-year est.); Poverty rate: 8.6% (2006-2010 5-year est.).

Education: Percent of population age 25 and over with: High school diploma (including GED) or higher: 90.8% (2006-2010 5-year est.); Bachelor's degree or higher: 21.3% (2006-2010 5-year est.); Master's degree or higher: 8.1% (2006-2010 5-year est.).

Housing: Homeownership rate: 83.1% (2010); Median home value: $132,100 (2006-2010 5-year est.); Median contract rent: $465 per month (2006-2010 5-year est.); Median year structure built: 1981 (2006-2010 5-year est.).

Safety: Violent crime rate: 18.8 per 10,000 population; Property crime rate: 273.9 per 10,000 population (2011).

Transportation: Commute to work: 95.8% car, 0.2% public transportation, 1.4% walk, 1.6% work from home (2006-2010 5-year est.); Travel time to work: 43.8% less than 15 minutes, 34.7% 15 to 30 minutes, 12.1% 30 to 45 minutes, 3.2% 45 to 60 minutes, 6.3% 60 minutes or more (2006-2010 5-year est.)

Additional Information Contacts

Greater DuBois Chamber of Commerce & Economic Development . . (814) 371-5010
http://www.duboispachamber.com
Sandy Township . . . . (814) 371-4220
http://www.sandytownship.org

SMITHMILL (unincorporated postal area)

Zip Code: 16680

Covers a land area of 6.754 square miles and a water area of 0.022 square miles. Located at 40.74° N. Lat; 78.37° W. Long. Population: 427 (2010); Density: 63.2 persons per square mile (2010); Race: 99.3% White, 0.0% Black, 0.5% Asian, 0.0% American Indian/Alaska Native,

0.0% Native Hawaiian/Other Pacific Islander, 0.2% Other, 0.0% Hispanic of any race (2010); Average household size: 2.40 (2010); Median age: 42.1 (2010); Males per 100 females: 102.4 (2010); Homeownership rate: 84.8% (2010)

TREASURE LAKE (CDP). Covers a land area of 10.659 square miles and a water area of 0.780 square miles. Located at 41.17° N. Lat; 78.72° W. Long. Elevation is 1,755 feet.
Population: 2,249 (1990); 4,507 (2000); 3,861 (2010); Density: 362.2 persons per square mile (2010); Race: 96.5% White, 0.3% Black, 2.0% Asian, 0.0% American Indian/Alaska Native, 0.0% Native Hawaiian/Other Pacific Islander, 1.2% Other, 0.8% Hispanic of any race (2010); Average household size: 2.58 (2010); Median age: 45.5 (2010); Males per 100 females: 100.1 (2010); Marriage status: 15.8% never married, 71.1% now married, 5.8% widowed, 7.4% divorced (2006-2010 5-year est.); Foreign born: 3.5% (2006-2010 5-year est.); Ancestry (includes multiple ancestries): 35.9% American, 20.2% German, 13.3% Italian, 10.9% Irish, 8.4% English (2006-2010 5-year est.).
Economy: Employment by occupation: 14.3% management, 4.4% professional, 8.8% services, 12.9% sales, 2.4% farming, 8.2% construction, 8.0% production (2006-2010 5-year est.).
Income: Per capita income: $31,543 (2006-2010 5-year est.); Median household income: $66,950 (2006-2010 5-year est.); Average household income: $76,790 (2006-2010 5-year est.); Percent of households with income of $100,000 or more: 21.0% (2006-2010 5-year est.); Poverty rate: 2.4% (2006-2010 5-year est.).
Education: Percent of population age 25 and over with: High school diploma (including GED) or higher: 96.2% (2006-2010 5-year est.); Bachelor's degree or higher: 41.5% (2006-2010 5-year est.); Master's degree or higher: 16.0% (2006-2010 5-year est.).
Housing: Homeownership rate: 92.6% (2010); Median home value: $160,800 (2006-2010 5-year est.); Median contract rent: $601 per month (2006-2010 5-year est.); Median year structure built: 1987 (2006-2010 5-year est.).
Transportation: Commute to work: 95.8% car, 0.0% public transportation, 0.8% walk, 2.8% work from home (2006-2010 5-year est.); Travel time to work: 21.9% less than 15 minutes, 46.4% 15 to 30 minutes, 20.4% 30 to 45 minutes, 4.0% 45 to 60 minutes, 7.3% 60 minutes or more (2006-2010 5-year est.).
Additional Information Contacts
Greater DuBois Chamber of Commerce & Economic Development . . (814) 371-5010
  http://www.duboispachamber.com

TROUTVILLE (borough). Covers a land area of 0.771 square miles and a water area of <.001 square miles. Located at 41.03° N. Lat; 78.79° W. Long. Elevation is 1,585 feet.
Population: 226 (1990); 224 (2000); 243 (2010); Density: 315.2 persons per square mile (2010); Race: 100.0% White, 0.0% Black, 0.0% Asian, 0.0% American Indian/Alaska Native, 0.0% Native Hawaiian/Other Pacific Islander, 0.0% Other, 1.6% Hispanic of any race (2010); Average household size: 2.86 (2010); Median age: 37.8 (2010); Males per 100 females: 102.5 (2010); Marriage status: 22.0% never married, 61.9% now married, 4.5% widowed, 11.7% divorced (2006-2010 5-year est.); Foreign born: 0.0% (2006-2010 5-year est.); Ancestry (includes multiple ancestries): 37.5% American, 29.6% German, 11.1% Irish, 10.4% Italian, 7.1% Pennsylvania German (2006-2010 5-year est.).
Economy: Single-family building permits issued: 0 (2011); Multi-family building permits issued: 0 (2011); Employment by occupation: 19.1% management, 0.0% professional, 10.4% services, 11.3% sales, 6.1% farming, 21.7% construction, 10.4% production (2006-2010 5-year est.).
Income: Per capita income: $54,996 (2006-2010 5-year est.); Median household income: $48,500 (2006-2010 5-year est.); Average household income: $151,622 (2006-2010 5-year est.); Percent of households with income of $100,000 or more: 22.6% (2006-2010 5-year est.); Poverty rate: 32.1% (2006-2010 5-year est.).
Education: Percent of population age 25 and over with: High school diploma (including GED) or higher: 90.4% (2006-2010 5-year est.); Bachelor's degree or higher: 19.2% (2006-2010 5-year est.); Master's degree or higher: 0.0% (2006-2010 5-year est.).
Housing: Homeownership rate: 90.6% (2010); Median home value: $85,000 (2006-2010 5-year est.); Median contract rent: $525 per month (2006-2010 5-year est.); Median year structure built: before 1940 (2006-2010 5-year est.).

Transportation: Commute to work: 100.0% car, 0.0% public transportation, 0.0% walk, 0.0% work from home (2006-2010 5-year est.); Travel time to work: 20.0% less than 15 minutes, 62.6% 15 to 30 minutes, 13.9% 30 to 45 minutes, 0.0% 45 to 60 minutes, 3.5% 60 minutes or more (2006-2010 5-year est.)

UNION (township). Covers a land area of 31.196 square miles and a water area of 0.387 square miles. Located at 41.09° N. Lat; 78.63° W. Long.
Population: 837 (1990); 918 (2000); 892 (2010); Density: 28.6 persons per square mile (2010); Race: 99.3% White, 0.2% Black, 0.0% Asian, 0.1% American Indian/Alaska Native, 0.0% Native Hawaiian/Other Pacific Islander, 0.4% Other, 0.1% Hispanic of any race (2010); Average household size: 2.41 (2010); Median age: 48.1 (2010); Males per 100 females: 110.4 (2010); Marriage status: 29.1% never married, 51.4% now married, 8.1% widowed, 11.3% divorced (2006-2010 5-year est.); Foreign born: 0.0% (2006-2010 5-year est.); Ancestry (includes multiple ancestries): 36.4% German, 23.1% American, 18.1% Irish, 14.0% English, 5.9% Polish (2006-2010 5-year est.).
Economy: Single-family building permits issued: 2 (2011); Multi-family building permits issued: 0 (2011); Employment by occupation: 2.5% management, 1.4% professional, 15.7% services, 16.1% sales, 4.1% farming, 8.0% construction, 4.5% production (2006-2010 5-year est.).
Income: Per capita income: $22,043 (2006-2010 5-year est.); Median household income: $44,760 (2006-2010 5-year est.); Average household income: $56,583 (2006-2010 5-year est.); Percent of households with income of $100,000 or more: 10.2% (2006-2010 5-year est.); Poverty rate: 2.5% (2006-2010 5-year est.).
Education: Percent of population age 25 and over with: High school diploma (including GED) or higher: 94.7% (2006-2010 5-year est.); Bachelor's degree or higher: 10.8% (2006-2010 5-year est.); Master's degree or higher: 2.0% (2006-2010 5-year est.).
Housing: Homeownership rate: 87.0% (2010); Median home value: $106,300 (2006-2010 5-year est.); Median contract rent: $335 per month (2006-2010 5-year est.); Median year structure built: 1974 (2006-2010 5-year est.).
Transportation: Commute to work: 95.3% car, 0.0% public transportation, 0.0% walk, 3.8% work from home (2006-2010 5-year est.); Travel time to work: 31.1% less than 15 minutes, 55.8% 15 to 30 minutes, 6.0% 30 to 45 minutes, 6.4% 45 to 60 minutes, 0.7% 60 minutes or more (2006-2010 5-year est.)

WALLACETON (borough). Covers a land area of 0.764 square miles and a water area of 0.002 square miles. Located at 40.97° N. Lat; 78.29° W. Long. Elevation is 1,745 feet.
Population: 319 (1990); 350 (2000); 313 (2010); Density: 409.7 persons per square mile (2010); Race: 99.7% White, 0.3% Black, 0.0% Asian, 0.0% American Indian/Alaska Native, 0.0% Native Hawaiian/Other Pacific Islander, 0.0% Other, 0.0% Hispanic of any race (2010); Average household size: 2.65 (2010); Median age: 41.1 (2010); Males per 100 females: 90.9 (2010); Marriage status: 27.7% never married, 64.0% now married, 3.2% widowed, 5.1% divorced (2006-2010 5-year est.); Foreign born: 0.0% (2006-2010 5-year est.); Ancestry (includes multiple ancestries): 47.9% American, 22.1% German, 12.1% English, 6.6% Irish, 5.2% Scottish (2006-2010 5-year est.).
Economy: Employment by occupation: 2.5% management, 0.0% professional, 23.3% services, 19.2% sales, 0.0% farming, 17.5% construction, 0.0% production (2006-2010 5-year est.).
Income: Per capita income: $17,300 (2006-2010 5-year est.); Median household income: $39,750 (2006-2010 5-year est.); Average household income: $43,126 (2006-2010 5-year est.); Percent of households with income of $100,000 or more: 4.4% (2006-2010 5-year est.); Poverty rate: 6.6% (2006-2010 5-year est.).
Education: Percent of population age 25 and over with: High school diploma (including GED) or higher: 75.6% (2006-2010 5-year est.); Bachelor's degree or higher: 4.1% (2006-2010 5-year est.); Master's degree or higher: 0.0% (2006-2010 5-year est.).
Housing: Homeownership rate: 89.0% (2010); Median home value: $78,300 (2006-2010 5-year est.); Median contract rent: $425 per month (2006-2010 5-year est.); Median year structure built: 1955 (2006-2010 5-year est.).
Transportation: Commute to work: 94.0% car, 0.0% public transportation, 0.0% walk, 3.4% work from home (2006-2010 5-year est.); Travel time to work: 17.7% less than 15 minutes, 29.2% 15 to 30 minutes, 36.3% 30 to

45 minutes, 9.7% 45 to 60 minutes, 7.1% 60 minutes or more (2006-2010 5-year est.)

WEST DECATUR (CDP). Covers a land area of 1.400 square miles and a water area of <.001 square miles. Located at 40.93° N. Lat; 78.28° W. Long. Elevation is 1,526 feet.

Population: n/a (1990); n/a (2000); 533 (2010); Density: 380.7 persons per square mile (2010); Race: 99.4% White, 0.2% Black, 0.0% Asian, 0.2% American Indian/Alaska Native, 0.0% Native Hawaiian/Other Pacific Islander, 0.2% Other, 0.4% Hispanic of any race (2010); Average household size: 2.43 (2010); Median age: 40.6 (2010); Males per 100 females: 96.7 (2010); Marriage status: 20.1% never married, 60.7% now married, 9.5% widowed, 9.8% divorced (2006-2010 5-year est.); Foreign born: 1.4% (2006-2010 5-year est.); Ancestry (includes multiple ancestries): 29.0% American, 19.6% German, 6.8% Irish, 4.7% Polish, 4.0% French (2006-2010 5-year est.).
Economy: Employment by occupation: 1.4% management, 2.0% professional, 8.2% services, 19.7% sales, 5.4% farming, 22.4% construction, 10.9% production (2006-2010 5-year est.).
Income: Per capita income: $15,976 (2006-2010 5-year est.); Median household income: $35,438 (2006-2010 5-year est.); Average household income: $40,171 (2006-2010 5-year est.); Percent of households with income of $100,000 or more: 4.8% (2006-2010 5-year est.); Poverty rate: 23.8% (2006-2010 5-year est.).
Education: Percent of population age 25 and over with: High school diploma (including GED) or higher: 73.9% (2006-2010 5-year est.); Bachelor's degree or higher: 4.1% (2006-2010 5-year est.); Master's degree or higher: 1.7% (2006-2010 5-year est.).
Housing: Homeownership rate: 81.7% (2010); Median home value: $74,200 (2006-2010 5-year est.); Median contract rent: $384 per month (2006-2010 5-year est.); Median year structure built: before 1940 (2006-2010 5-year est.).
Transportation: Commute to work: 100.0% car, 0.0% public transportation, 0.0% walk, 0.0% work from home (2006-2010 5-year est.); Travel time to work: 29.9% less than 15 minutes, 32.7% 15 to 30 minutes, 15.6% 30 to 45 minutes, 8.8% 45 to 60 minutes, 12.9% 60 minutes or more (2006-2010 5-year est.)

WESTOVER (borough). Covers a land area of 2.696 square miles and a water area of 0.054 square miles. Located at 40.74° N. Lat; 78.69° W. Long. Elevation is 1,385 feet.

Population: 446 (1990); 458 (2000); 390 (2010); Density: 144.6 persons per square mile (2010); Race: 99.7% White, 0.0% Black, 0.3% Asian, 0.0% American Indian/Alaska Native, 0.0% Native Hawaiian/Other Pacific Islander, 0.0% Other, 0.0% Hispanic of any race (2010); Average household size: 2.52 (2010); Median age: 39.1 (2010); Males per 100 females: 113.1 (2010); Marriage status: 34.6% never married, 51.6% now married, 6.1% widowed, 7.8% divorced (2006-2010 5-year est.); Foreign born: 0.0% (2006-2010 5-year est.); Ancestry (includes multiple ancestries): 53.4% German, 10.8% English, 10.3% Irish, 8.0% French, 7.6% American (2006-2010 5-year est.).
Economy: Single-family building permits issued: 2 (2011); Multi-family building permits issued: 0 (2011); Employment by occupation: 4.8% management, 0.0% professional, 11.6% services, 15.6% sales, 2.0% farming, 4.8% construction, 4.8% production (2006-2010 5-year est.).
Income: Per capita income: $13,918 (2006-2010 5-year est.); Median household income: $33,365 (2006-2010 5-year est.); Average household income: $40,306 (2006-2010 5-year est.); Percent of households with income of $100,000 or more: 6.0% (2006-2010 5-year est.); Poverty rate: 17.5% (2006-2010 5-year est.).
Education: Percent of population age 25 and over with: High school diploma (including GED) or higher: 82.9% (2006-2010 5-year est.); Bachelor's degree or higher: 7.6% (2006-2010 5-year est.); Master's degree or higher: 1.9% (2006-2010 5-year est.).

School District(s)
Harmony Area SD (PK-12)
   2010-11 Enrollment: 382 . . . . (814) 845-7918
Housing: Homeownership rate: 77.4% (2010); Median home value: $53,400 (2006-2010 5-year est.); Median contract rent: $302 per month (2006-2010 5-year est.); Median year structure built: before 1940 (2006-2010 5-year est.).
Transportation: Commute to work: 93.8% car, 0.0% public transportation, 0.0% walk, 6.2% work from home (2006-2010 5-year est.); Travel time to work: 15.7% less than 15 minutes, 11.6% 15 to 30 minutes, 29.8% 30 to

45 minutes, 15.7% 45 to 60 minutes, 27.3% 60 minutes or more (2006-2010 5-year est.)

WINBURNE (unincorporated postal area)
Zip Code: 16879
   Covers a land area of 2.171 square miles and a water area of 0.006 square miles. Located at 40.96° N. Lat; 78.15° W. Long. Population: 532 (2010); Density: 244.9 persons per square mile (2010); Race: 99.1% White, 0.2% Black, 0.0% Asian, 0.2% American Indian/Alaska Native, 0.0% Native Hawaiian/Other Pacific Islander, 0.5% Other, 0.0% Hispanic of any race (2010); Average household size: 2.71 (2010); Median age: 38.9 (2010); Males per 100 females: 104.6 (2010); Homeownership rate: 76.6% (2010)

WOODLAND (unincorporated postal area)
Zip Code: 16881
   Covers a land area of 31.382 square miles and a water area of 0.418 square miles. Located at 41.02° N. Lat; 78.32° W. Long. Elevation is 1,496 feet. Population: 2,232 (2010); Density: 71.1 persons per square mile (2010); Race: 99.0% White, 0.1% Black, 0.3% Asian, 0.0% American Indian/Alaska Native, 0.1% Native Hawaiian/Other Pacific Islander, 0.5% Other, 0.7% Hispanic of any race (2010); Average household size: 2.61 (2010); Median age: 42.4 (2010); Males per 100 females: 102.7 (2010); Homeownership rate: 87.6% (2010)

WOODWARD (township). Covers a land area of 22.567 square miles and a water area of 0.157 square miles. Located at 40.85° N. Lat; 78.38° W. Long.

Population: 1,911 (1990); 3,550 (2000); 3,992 (2010); Density: 176.9 persons per square mile (2010); Race: 65.6% White, 28.5% Black, 0.2% Asian, 0.0% American Indian/Alaska Native, 0.0% Native Hawaiian/Other Pacific Islander, 5.7% Other, 6.0% Hispanic of any race (2010); Average household size: 2.28 (2010); Median age: 36.6 (2010); Males per 100 females: 334.4 (2010); Marriage status: 44.4% never married, 39.3% now married, 4.9% widowed, 11.4% divorced (2006-2010 5-year est.); Foreign born: 2.5% (2006-2010 5-year est.); Ancestry (includes multiple ancestries): 9.7% German, 6.9% Polish, 5.7% English, 4.4% American, 4.2% Irish (2006-2010 5-year est.).
Economy: Single-family building permits issued: 0 (2011); Multi-family building permits issued: 0 (2011); Employment by occupation: 13.0% management, 0.0% professional, 15.6% services, 16.4% sales, 5.5% farming, 11.6% construction, 5.6% production (2006-2010 5-year est.).
Income: Per capita income: $22,771 (2006-2010 5-year est.); Median household income: $38,534 (2006-2010 5-year est.); Average household income: $42,859 (2006-2010 5-year est.); Percent of households with income of $100,000 or more: 6.7% (2006-2010 5-year est.); Poverty rate: 10.6% (2006-2010 5-year est.).
Education: Percent of population age 25 and over with: High school diploma (including GED) or higher: 75.7% (2006-2010 5-year est.); Bachelor's degree or higher: 6.0% (2006-2010 5-year est.); Master's degree or higher: 1.1% (2006-2010 5-year est.).
Housing: Homeownership rate: 77.5% (2010); Median home value: $77,700 (2006-2010 5-year est.); Median contract rent: $371 per month (2006-2010 5-year est.); Median year structure built: 1954 (2006-2010 5-year est.).
Transportation: Commute to work: 97.3% car, 0.0% public transportation, 2.1% walk, 0.7% work from home (2006-2010 5-year est.); Travel time to work: 30.4% less than 15 minutes, 35.3% 15 to 30 minutes, 16.3% 30 to 45 minutes, 6.1% 45 to 60 minutes, 11.9% 60 minutes or more (2006-2010 5-year est.)
Additional Information Contacts
Chamber of Commerce of Clearfield . . . . (814) 765-7567
   http://www.clearfieldchamber.com

Clinton County

Located in north central Pennsylvania; mountainous area, drained by the West Branch of the Susquehanna River. Covers a land area of 887.984 square miles, a water area of 8.949 square miles, and is located in the Eastern Time Zone at 41.25° N. Lat., 77.65° W. Long. The county was founded in 1839. County seat is Lock Haven.

Clinton County is part of the Lock Haven, PA Micropolitan Statistical Area. The entire metro area includes: Clinton County, PA

Weather Station: Lock Haven Sewage Plant   Elevation: 565 feet

	Jan	Feb	Mar	Apr	May	Jun	Jul	Aug	Sep	Oct	Nov	Dec
High	35	39	48	62	73	80	84	83	75	63	51	39
Low	18	19	26	36	46	55	60	58	51	39	31	23
Precip	2.4	2.2	3.2	3.4	3.7	4.5	4.0	4.0	4.0	3.2	3.4	2.6
Snow	9.2	6.1	6.7	0.7	0.0	0.0	0.0	0.0	0.0	tr	1.1	4.9

High and Low temperatures in degrees Fahrenheit; Precipitation and Snow in inches

Weather Station: Renovo   Elevation: 660 feet

	Jan	Feb	Mar	Apr	May	Jun	Jul	Aug	Sep	Oct	Nov	Dec
High	35	38	47	61	72	80	84	82	74	63	50	39
Low	18	19	26	36	45	54	59	58	51	40	32	23
Precip	2.4	2.3	3.1	3.3	3.4	4.3	3.7	3.8	3.8	3.1	3.5	2.7
Snow	9.7	7.3	5.7	0.5	0.0	0.0	0.0	0.0	0.0	0.1	1.2	6.1

High and Low temperatures in degrees Fahrenheit; Precipitation and Snow in inches

Population: 37,182 (1990); 37,914 (2000); 39,238 (2010); Race: 96.5% White, 1.6% Black, 0.5% Asian, 0.1% American Indian/Alaska Native, 0.0% Native Hawaiian/Other Pacific Islander, 1.3% Other, 1.1% Hispanic of any race (2010); Density: 44.2 persons per square mile (2010); Average household size: 2.42 (2010); Median age: 38.5 (2010); Males per 100 females: 96.1 (2010).
Religion: Six largest groups: 9.3% Methodist/Pietist, 6.7% Catholicism, 3.6% European Free-Church, 3.3% Baptist, 2.6% Lutheran, 2.3% Holiness (2010)
Economy: Unemployment rate: 8.7% (August 2012); Total civilian labor force: 20,603 (August 2012); Leading industries: 29.5% manufacturing; 18.4% retail trade; 11.4% health care and social assistance (2010); Farms: 537 totaling 56,626 acres (2007); Companies that employ 500 or more persons: 1 (2010); Companies that employ 100 to 499 persons: 18 (2010); Companies that employ less than 100 persons: 717 (2010); Black-owned businesses: n/a (2007); Hispanic-owned businesses: n/a (2007); Asian-owned businesses: n/a (2007); Women-owned businesses: 609 (2007); Retail sales per capita: $12,591 (2010). Single-family building permits issued: 27 (2011); Multi-family building permits issued: 8 (2011).
Income: Per capita income: $19,261 (2006-2010 5-year est.); Median household income: $39,354 (2006-2010 5-year est.); Average household income: $47,851 (2006-2010 5-year est.); Percent of households with income of $100,000 or more: 7.9% (2006-2010 5-year est.); Poverty rate: 15.5% (2006-2010 5-year est.); Bankruptcy rate: 1.73% (2011).
Education: Percent of population age 25 and over with: High school diploma (including GED) or higher: 85.6% (2006-2010 5-year est.); Bachelor's degree or higher: 16.7% (2006-2010 5-year est.); Master's degree or higher: 5.6% (2006-2010 5-year est.).
Housing: Homeownership rate: 70.9% (2010); Median home value: $98,400 (2006-2010 5-year est.); Median contract rent: $487 per month (2006-2010 5-year est.); Median year structure built: 1963 (2006-2010 5-year est.)
Health: Birth rate: 100.7 per 10,000 population (2011); Death rate: 97.4 per 10,000 population (2011); Age-adjusted cancer mortality rate: 194.6 deaths per 100,000 population (2009); Number of physicians: 9.7 per 10,000 population (2010); Hospital beds: 63.0 per 10,000 population (2008); Hospital admissions: 825.9 per 10,000 population (2008).
Elections: 2012 Presidential election results: 43.2% Obama, 55.1% Romney
National and State Parks: Hyner Run State Park; Kettle Creek State Park; Ravensburg State Park; Sproul State Forest
Additional Information Contacts
Clinton County Government . . . . (570) 893-4000
http://www.clintoncountypa.com
Clinton County Economic Partnership . . . . (570) 748-5782
http://www.clintoncountyinfo.com

Clinton County Communities

ALLISON (township). Covers a land area of 1.523 square miles and a water area of 0.104 square miles. Located at 41.15° N. Lat; 77.48° W. Long.
Population: 191 (1990); 198 (2000); 193 (2010); Density: 126.7 persons per square mile (2010); Race: 100.0% White, 0.0% Black, 0.0% Asian, 0.0% American Indian/Alaska Native, 0.0% Native Hawaiian/Other Pacific Islander, 0.0% Other, 0.0% Hispanic of any race (2010); Average household size: 2.51 (2010); Median age: 45.2 (2010); Males per 100 females: 116.9 (2010); Marriage status: 14.3% never married, 53.8% now married, 23.1% widowed, 8.8% divorced (2006-2010 5-year est.); Foreign born: 0.0% (2006-2010 5-year est.); Ancestry (includes multiple

ancestries): 34.2% German, 18.8% Irish, 12.8% American, 6.0% English, 5.1% Swiss (2006-2010 5-year est.).
Economy: Single-family building permits issued: 0 (2011); Multi-family building permits issued: 0 (2011); Employment by occupation: 12.2% management, 0.0% professional, 9.8% services, 17.1% sales, 9.8% farming, 4.9% construction, 14.6% production (2006-2010 5-year est.).
Income: Per capita income: $19,568 (2006-2010 5-year est.); Median household income: $24,750 (2006-2010 5-year est.); Average household income: $40,324 (2006-2010 5-year est.); Percent of households with income of $100,000 or more: 7.3% (2006-2010 5-year est.); Poverty rate: 15.4% (2006-2010 5-year est.).
Education: Percent of population age 25 and over with: High school diploma (including GED) or higher: 77.9% (2006-2010 5-year est.); Bachelor's degree or higher: 9.3% (2006-2010 5-year est.); Master's degree or higher: 4.7% (2006-2010 5-year est.).
Housing: Homeownership rate: 89.6% (2010); Median home value: $103,100 (2006-2010 5-year est.); Median contract rent: n/a per month (2006-2010 5-year est.); Median year structure built: 1958 (2006-2010 5-year est.).
Transportation: Commute to work: 100.0% car, 0.0% public transportation, 0.0% walk, 0.0% work from home (2006-2010 5-year est.); Travel time to work: 43.9% less than 15 minutes, 43.9% 15 to 30 minutes, 9.8% 30 to 45 minutes, 2.4% 45 to 60 minutes, 0.0% 60 minutes or more (2006-2010 5-year est.)

AVIS (borough). Covers a land area of 0.495 square miles and a water area of 0 square miles. Located at 41.19° N. Lat; 77.32° W. Long. Elevation is 597 feet.
Population: 1,506 (1990); 1,492 (2000); 1,484 (2010); Density: 2,999.2 persons per square mile (2010); Race: 98.7% White, 0.5% Black, 0.3% Asian, 0.0% American Indian/Alaska Native, 0.0% Native Hawaiian/Other Pacific Islander, 0.5% Other, 0.5% Hispanic of any race (2010); Average household size: 2.35 (2010); Median age: 41.5 (2010); Males per 100 females: 92.7 (2010); Marriage status: 21.0% never married, 57.1% now married, 6.1% widowed, 15.8% divorced (2006-2010 5-year est.); Foreign born: 0.1% (2006-2010 5-year est.); Ancestry (includes multiple ancestries): 45.4% German, 16.7% English, 13.4% Irish, 7.0% Italian, 3.1% Dutch (2006-2010 5-year est.).
Economy: Single-family building permits issued: 1 (2011); Multi-family building permits issued: 8 (2011); Employment by occupation: 3.6% management, 0.4% professional, 12.0% services, 10.8% sales, 4.1% farming, 13.9% construction, 14.0% production (2006-2010 5-year est.).
Income: Per capita income: $20,396 (2006-2010 5-year est.); Median household income: $39,531 (2006-2010 5-year est.); Average household income: $47,901 (2006-2010 5-year est.); Percent of households with income of $100,000 or more: 3.3% (2006-2010 5-year est.); Poverty rate: 14.0% (2006-2010 5-year est.).
Education: Percent of population age 25 and over with: High school diploma (including GED) or higher: 88.5% (2006-2010 5-year est.); Bachelor's degree or higher: 8.0% (2006-2010 5-year est.); Master's degree or higher: 3.4% (2006-2010 5-year est.).
Housing: Homeownership rate: 73.6% (2010); Median home value: $99,500 (2006-2010 5-year est.); Median contract rent: $407 per month (2006-2010 5-year est.); Median year structure built: 1965 (2006-2010 5-year est.).
Safety: Violent crime rate: 20.1 per 10,000 population; Property crime rate: 53.7 per 10,000 population (2011).
Transportation: Commute to work: 93.7% car, 0.0% public transportation, 3.1% walk, 3.2% work from home (2006-2010 5-year est.); Travel time to work: 37.2% less than 15 minutes, 40.4% 15 to 30 minutes, 14.5% 30 to 45 minutes, 1.1% 45 to 60 minutes, 6.8% 60 minutes or more (2006-2010 5-year est.)
Additional Information Contacts
Williamsport/Lycoming Chamber of Commerce . . . . (570) 326-1971
http://www.williamsport.org

BALD EAGLE (township). Covers a land area of 41.634 square miles and a water area of 0.421 square miles. Located at 41.14° N. Lat; 77.57° W. Long.
Population: 1,803 (1990); 1,898 (2000); 2,065 (2010); Density: 49.6 persons per square mile (2010); Race: 96.7% White, 1.1% Black, 0.6% Asian, 0.1% American Indian/Alaska Native, 0.0% Native Hawaiian/Other Pacific Islander, 1.5% Other, 0.6% Hispanic of any race (2010); Average household size: 2.57 (2010); Median age: 41.5 (2010); Males per 100 females: 99.9 (2010); Marriage status: 26.1% never married, 61.1% now

married, 5.0% widowed, 7.8% divorced (2006-2010 5-year est.); Foreign born: 0.1% (2006-2010 5-year est.); Ancestry (includes multiple ancestries): 34.4% German, 10.5% Irish, 8.6% Italian, 8.4% English, 7.7% American (2006-2010 5-year est.).

Economy: Single-family building permits issued: 2 (2011); Multi-family building permits issued: 0 (2011); Employment by occupation: 12.2% management, 0.9% professional, 12.4% services, 14.9% sales, 3.9% farming, 14.1% construction, 12.5% production (2006-2010 5-year est.).

Income: Per capita income: $22,695 (2006-2010 5-year est.); Median household income: $44,688 (2006-2010 5-year est.); Average household income: $57,860 (2006-2010 5-year est.); Percent of households with income of $100,000 or more: 13.9% (2006-2010 5-year est.); Poverty rate: 9.0% (2006-2010 5-year est.).

Education: Percent of population age 25 and over with: High school diploma (including GED) or higher: 86.2% (2006-2010 5-year est.); Bachelor's degree or higher: 22.0% (2006-2010 5-year est.); Master's degree or higher: 8.7% (2006-2010 5-year est.).

Housing: Homeownership rate: 85.0% (2010); Median home value: $110,100 (2006-2010 5-year est.); Median contract rent: $510 per month (2006-2010 5-year est.); Median year structure built: 1975 (2006-2010 5-year est.).

Transportation: Commute to work: 95.7% car, 0.0% public transportation, 0.8% walk, 2.2% work from home (2006-2010 5-year est.); Travel time to work: 38.1% less than 15 minutes, 37.2% 15 to 30 minutes, 14.1% 30 to 45 minutes, 4.0% 45 to 60 minutes, 6.5% 60 minutes or more (2006-2010 5-year est.)

Additional Information Contacts

Tyron Area Chamber of Commerce . . . . (814) 684-0736
http://www.tyronechamber.com

BEECH CREEK (borough). Covers a land area of 0.542 square miles and a water area of 0.014 square miles. Located at 41.07° N. Lat; 77.59° W. Long. Elevation is 640 feet.

Population: 716 (1990); 717 (2000); 701 (2010); Density: 1,293.5 persons per square mile (2010); Race: 99.3% White, 0.0% Black, 0.1% Asian, 0.1% American Indian/Alaska Native, 0.0% Native Hawaiian/Other Pacific Islander, 0.5% Other, 0.6% Hispanic of any race (2010); Average household size: 2.42 (2010); Median age: 42.4 (2010); Males per 100 females: 99.1 (2010); Marriage status: 12.3% never married, 72.2% now married, 8.8% widowed, 6.7% divorced (2006-2010 5-year est.); Foreign born: 0.0% (2006-2010 5-year est.); Ancestry (includes multiple ancestries): 46.1% German, 14.1% Irish, 3.5% Dutch, 3.4% English, 2.9% Pennsylvania German (2006-2010 5-year est.).

Economy: Single-family building permits issued: 0 (2011); Multi-family building permits issued: 0 (2011); Employment by occupation: 4.3% management, 5.0% professional, 15.9% services, 6.6% sales, 5.0% farming, 3.5% construction, 8.9% production (2006-2010 5-year est.).

Income: Per capita income: $21,142 (2006-2010 5-year est.); Median household income: $40,625 (2006-2010 5-year est.); Average household income: $45,278 (2006-2010 5-year est.); Percent of households with income of $100,000 or more: 6.3% (2006-2010 5-year est.); Poverty rate: 7.7% (2006-2010 5-year est.).

Education: Percent of population age 25 and over with: High school diploma (including GED) or higher: 84.6% (2006-2010 5-year est.); Bachelor's degree or higher: 9.9% (2006-2010 5-year est.); Master's degree or higher: 4.3% (2006-2010 5-year est.).

Housing: Homeownership rate: 73.1% (2010); Median home value: $92,200 (2006-2010 5-year est.); Median contract rent: $220 per month (2006-2010 5-year est.); Median year structure built: 1957 (2006-2010 5-year est.).

Transportation: Commute to work: 98.0% car, 0.0% public transportation, 0.0% walk, 0.0% work from home (2006-2010 5-year est.); Travel time to work: 19.0% less than 15 minutes, 35.1% 15 to 30 minutes, 32.3% 30 to 45 minutes, 8.5% 45 to 60 minutes, 5.2% 60 minutes or more (2006-2010 5-year est.)

BEECH CREEK (township). Covers a land area of 94.251 square miles and a water area of 0.250 square miles. Located at 41.16° N. Lat; 77.72° W. Long. Elevation is 640 feet.

Population: 1,007 (1990); 1,010 (2000); 1,015 (2010); Density: 10.8 persons per square mile (2010); Race: 98.8% White, 0.1% Black, 0.5% Asian, 0.0% American Indian/Alaska Native, 0.0% Native Hawaiian/Other Pacific Islander, 0.6% Other, 0.2% Hispanic of any race (2010); Average household size: 2.46 (2010); Median age: 44.0 (2010); Males per 100 females: 103.0 (2010); Marriage status: 18.0% never married, 68.5% now

married, 5.1% widowed, 8.5% divorced (2006-2010 5-year est.); Foreign born: 0.5% (2006-2010 5-year est.); Ancestry (includes multiple ancestries): 33.8% German, 22.1% Irish, 11.2% English, 5.7% American, 4.9% Polish (2006-2010 5-year est.).

Economy: Single-family building permits issued: 0 (2011); Multi-family building permits issued: 0 (2011); Employment by occupation: 4.5% management, 0.6% professional, 11.5% services, 19.8% sales, 1.5% farming, 18.1% construction, 13.6% production (2006-2010 5-year est.).

Income: Per capita income: $20,119 (2006-2010 5-year est.); Median household income: $45,652 (2006-2010 5-year est.); Average household income: $51,255 (2006-2010 5-year est.); Percent of households with income of $100,000 or more: 11.4% (2006-2010 5-year est.); Poverty rate: 3.9% (2006-2010 5-year est.).

Education: Percent of population age 25 and over with: High school diploma (including GED) or higher: 92.1% (2006-2010 5-year est.); Bachelor's degree or higher: 14.6% (2006-2010 5-year est.); Master's degree or higher: 1.8% (2006-2010 5-year est.).

Housing: Homeownership rate: 86.2% (2010); Median home value: $99,400 (2006-2010 5-year est.); Median contract rent: $444 per month (2006-2010 5-year est.); Median year structure built: 1979 (2006-2010 5-year est.).

Transportation: Commute to work: 96.2% car, 0.0% public transportation, 1.9% walk, 1.9% work from home (2006-2010 5-year est.); Travel time to work: 21.1% less than 15 minutes, 38.1% 15 to 30 minutes, 27.0% 30 to 45 minutes, 10.7% 45 to 60 minutes, 3.1% 60 minutes or more (2006-2010 5-year est.)

CASTANEA (CDP). Covers a land area of 1.364 square miles and a water area of 0.027 square miles. Located at 41.12° N. Lat; 77.43° W. Long. Elevation is 597 feet.

Population: 1,123 (1990); 1,189 (2000); 1,125 (2010); Density: 824.8 persons per square mile (2010); Race: 98.0% White, 0.2% Black, 0.3% Asian, 0.1% American Indian/Alaska Native, 0.0% Native Hawaiian/Other Pacific Islander, 1.4% Other, 0.4% Hispanic of any race (2010); Average household size: 2.25 (2010); Median age: 43.9 (2010); Males per 100 females: 102.0 (2010); Marriage status: 17.4% never married, 58.7% now married, 9.8% widowed, 14.0% divorced (2006-2010 5-year est.); Foreign born: 0.1% (2006-2010 5-year est.); Ancestry (includes multiple ancestries): 44.3% German, 11.7% Italian, 9.9% Irish, 9.8% American, 8.8% English (2006-2010 5-year est.).

Economy: Employment by occupation: 2.0% management, 0.4% professional, 9.4% services, 13.6% sales, 3.1% farming, 10.3% construction, 6.6% production (2006-2010 5-year est.).

Income: Per capita income: $19,823 (2006-2010 5-year est.); Median household income: $38,188 (2006-2010 5-year est.); Average household income: $41,939 (2006-2010 5-year est.); Percent of households with income of $100,000 or more: 4.5% (2006-2010 5-year est.); Poverty rate: 12.0% (2006-2010 5-year est.).

Education: Percent of population age 25 and over with: High school diploma (including GED) or higher: 86.3% (2006-2010 5-year est.); Bachelor's degree or higher: 12.9% (2006-2010 5-year est.); Master's degree or higher: 6.4% (2006-2010 5-year est.).

Housing: Homeownership rate: 74.2% (2010); Median home value: $91,600 (2006-2010 5-year est.); Median contract rent: $571 per month (2006-2010 5-year est.); Median year structure built: 1969 (2006-2010 5-year est.).

Transportation: Commute to work: 99.3% car, 0.7% public transportation, 0.0% walk, 0.0% work from home (2006-2010 5-year est.); Travel time to work: 40.4% less than 15 minutes, 30.4% 15 to 30 minutes, 18.4% 30 to 45 minutes, 6.0% 45 to 60 minutes, 4.9% 60 minutes or more (2006-2010 5-year est.)

Additional Information Contacts

Clinton County Economic Partnership. . . . . (570) 748-5782
http://www.clintoncountyinfo.com

CASTANEA (township). Covers a land area of 5.512 square miles and a water area of 0.348 square miles. Located at 41.12° N. Lat; 77.42° W. Long. Elevation is 597 feet.

Population: 1,183 (1990); 1,233 (2000); 1,185 (2010); Density: 215.0 persons per square mile (2010); Race: 98.0% White, 0.2% Black, 0.3% Asian, 0.1% American Indian/Alaska Native, 0.0% Native Hawaiian/Other Pacific Islander, 1.4% Other, 0.3% Hispanic of any race (2010); Average household size: 2.25 (2010); Median age: 44.2 (2010); Males per 100 females: 101.9 (2010); Marriage status: 18.4% never married, 58.6% now married, 9.5% widowed, 13.5% divorced (2006-2010 5-year est.); Foreign

born: 0.1% (2006-2010 5-year est.); Ancestry (includes multiple ancestries): 44.5% German, 11.3% Italian, 9.6% American, 9.6% Irish, 9.4% English (2006-2010 5-year est.).

Economy: Single-family building permits issued: 0 (2011); Multi-family building permits issued: 0 (2011); Employment by occupation: 1.9% management, 1.1% professional, 9.9% services, 14.7% sales, 2.9% farming, 9.9% construction, 6.3% production (2006-2010 5-year est.).

Income: Per capita income: $19,851 (2006-2010 5-year est.); Median household income: $38,313 (2006-2010 5-year est.); Average household income: $42,110 (2006-2010 5-year est.); Percent of households with income of $100,000 or more: 4.4% (2006-2010 5-year est.); Poverty rate: 11.9% (2006-2010 5-year est.).

Education: Percent of population age 25 and over with: High school diploma (including GED) or higher: 86.7% (2006-2010 5-year est.); Bachelor's degree or higher: 12.8% (2006-2010 5-year est.); Master's degree or higher: 6.2% (2006-2010 5-year est.).

Housing: Homeownership rate: 73.6% (2010); Median home value: $92,000 (2006-2010 5-year est.); Median contract rent: $561 per month (2006-2010 5-year est.); Median year structure built: 1969 (2006-2010 5-year est.).

Transportation: Commute to work: 99.4% car, 0.6% public transportation, 0.0% walk, 0.0% work from home (2006-2010 5-year est.); Travel time to work: 40.0% less than 15 minutes, 30.9% 15 to 30 minutes, 18.3% 30 to 45 minutes, 5.7% 45 to 60 minutes, 5.1% 60 minutes or more (2006-2010 5-year est.).

Additional Information Contacts

Clinton County Economic Partnership . . . . (570) 748-5782
  http://www.clintoncountyinfo.com

CHAPMAN (township). Covers a land area of 100.077 square miles and a water area of 0.897 square miles. Located at 41.41° N. Lat; 77.66° W. Long.

Population: 978 (1990); 993 (2000); 848 (2010); Density: 8.5 persons per square mile (2010); Race: 100.0% White, 0.0% Black, 0.0% Asian, 0.0% American Indian/Alaska Native, 0.0% Native Hawaiian/Other Pacific Islander, 0.0% Other, 0.1% Hispanic of any race (2010); Average household size: 2.28 (2010); Median age: 49.4 (2010); Males per 100 females: 100.5 (2010); Marriage status: 15.7% never married, 60.3% now married, 13.7% widowed, 10.4% divorced (2006-2010 5-year est.); Foreign born: 0.4% (2006-2010 5-year est.); Ancestry (includes multiple ancestries): 37.8% German, 25.5% Irish, 16.7% Italian, 10.0% English, 7.2% Swedish (2006-2010 5-year est.).

Economy: Single-family building permits issued: 2 (2011); Multi-family building permits issued: 0 (2011); Employment by occupation: 3.2% management, 4.3% professional, 9.0% services, 15.8% sales, 4.7% farming, 7.9% construction, 8.2% production (2006-2010 5-year est.).

Income: Per capita income: $20,841 (2006-2010 5-year est.); Median household income: $31,607 (2006-2010 5-year est.); Average household income: $43,348 (2006-2010 5-year est.); Percent of households with income of $100,000 or more: 9.8% (2006-2010 5-year est.); Poverty rate: 9.3% (2006-2010 5-year est.).

Education: Percent of population age 25 and over with: High school diploma (including GED) or higher: 87.2% (2006-2010 5-year est.); Bachelor's degree or higher: 15.8% (2006-2010 5-year est.); Master's degree or higher: 9.2% (2006-2010 5-year est.).

Housing: Homeownership rate: 87.3% (2010); Median home value: $68,300 (2006-2010 5-year est.); Median contract rent: $375 per month (2006-2010 5-year est.); Median year structure built: 1953 (2006-2010 5-year est.).

Transportation: Commute to work: 89.3% car, 1.9% public transportation, 6.9% walk, 1.9% work from home (2006-2010 5-year est.); Travel time to work: 32.8% less than 15 minutes, 23.8% 15 to 30 minutes, 13.3% 30 to 45 minutes, 13.7% 45 to 60 minutes, 16.4% 60 minutes or more (2006-2010 5-year est.)

COLEBROOK (township). Covers a land area of 18.131 square miles and a water area of 0.498 square miles. Located at 41.21° N. Lat; 77.52° W. Long.

Population: 180 (1990); 179 (2000); 199 (2010); Density: 11.0 persons per square mile (2010); Race: 93.5% White, 3.0% Black, 0.0% Asian, 1.5% American Indian/Alaska Native, 0.0% Native Hawaiian/Other Pacific Islander, 2.0% Other, 1.0% Hispanic of any race (2010); Average household size: 2.29 (2010); Median age: 43.8 (2010); Males per 100 females: 84.3 (2010); Marriage status: 13.3% never married, 67.7% now married, 4.3% widowed, 14.7% divorced (2006-2010 5-year est.); Foreign

born: 0.0% (2006-2010 5-year est.); Ancestry (includes multiple ancestries): 65.9% German, 17.5% Irish, 5.0% Finnish, 3.3% Slovak, 3.3% Italian (2006-2010 5-year est.).

Economy: Employment by occupation: 1.2% management, 0.0% professional, 5.8% services, 16.8% sales, 2.3% farming, 6.9% construction, 8.1% production (2006-2010 5-year est.).

Income: Per capita income: $20,974 (2006-2010 5-year est.); Median household income: $39,583 (2006-2010 5-year est.); Average household income: $44,900 (2006-2010 5-year est.); Percent of households with income of $100,000 or more: n/a (2006-2010 5-year est.); Poverty rate: 13.9% (2006-2010 5-year est.).

Education: Percent of population age 25 and over with: High school diploma (including GED) or higher: 87.8% (2006-2010 5-year est.); Bachelor's degree or higher: 4.1% (2006-2010 5-year est.); Master's degree or higher: 0.0% (2006-2010 5-year est.).

Housing: Homeownership rate: 64.4% (2010); Median home value: $84,200 (2006-2010 5-year est.); Median contract rent: $360 per month (2006-2010 5-year est.); Median year structure built: before 1940 (2006-2010 5-year est.).

Transportation: Commute to work: 100.0% car, 0.0% public transportation, 0.0% walk, 0.0% work from home (2006-2010 5-year est.); Travel time to work: 9.2% less than 15 minutes, 30.1% 15 to 30 minutes, 22.5% 30 to 45 minutes, 6.9% 45 to 60 minutes, 31.2% 60 minutes or more (2006-2010 5-year est.)

CRAWFORD (township). Covers a land area of 22.119 square miles and a water area of 0.015 square miles. Located at 41.11° N. Lat; 77.26° W. Long.

Population: 665 (1990); 848 (2000); 939 (2010); Density: 42.5 persons per square mile (2010); Race: 99.1% White, 0.5% Black, 0.1% Asian, 0.0% American Indian/Alaska Native, 0.0% Native Hawaiian/Other Pacific Islander, 0.3% Other, 0.4% Hispanic of any race (2010); Average household size: 2.75 (2010); Median age: 40.6 (2010); Males per 100 females: 105.9 (2010); Marriage status: 20.4% never married, 67.0% now married, 4.1% widowed, 8.4% divorced (2006-2010 5-year est.); Foreign born: 1.4% (2006-2010 5-year est.); Ancestry (includes multiple ancestries): 52.9% German, 10.5% Irish, 7.9% Italian, 7.4% American, 5.3% Dutch (2006-2010 5-year est.).

Economy: Employment by occupation: 4.7% management, 0.8% professional, 8.5% services, 13.8% sales, 4.1% farming, 19.9% construction, 14.8% production (2006-2010 5-year est.).

Income: Per capita income: $19,984 (2006-2010 5-year est.); Median household income: $50,703 (2006-2010 5-year est.); Average household income: $54,499 (2006-2010 5-year est.); Percent of households with income of $100,000 or more: 8.3% (2006-2010 5-year est.); Poverty rate: 5.3% (2006-2010 5-year est.).

Education: Percent of population age 25 and over with: High school diploma (including GED) or higher: 86.2% (2006-2010 5-year est.); Bachelor's degree or higher: 10.3% (2006-2010 5-year est.); Master's degree or higher: 0.9% (2006-2010 5-year est.).

Housing: Homeownership rate: 87.4% (2010); Median home value: $133,900 (2006-2010 5-year est.); Median contract rent: $438 per month (2006-2010 5-year est.); Median year structure built: 1977 (2006-2010 5-year est.).

Transportation: Commute to work: 96.2% car, 0.0% public transportation, 1.8% walk, 2.0% work from home (2006-2010 5-year est.); Travel time to work: 14.3% less than 15 minutes, 38.8% 15 to 30 minutes, 37.1% 30 to 45 minutes, 4.3% 45 to 60 minutes, 5.5% 60 minutes or more (2006-2010 5-year est.)

DUNNSTABLE (township). Covers a land area of 9.375 square miles and a water area of 0.235 square miles. Located at 41.17° N. Lat; 77.39° W. Long.

Population: 846 (1990); 945 (2000); 1,008 (2010); Density: 107.5 persons per square mile (2010); Race: 98.1% White, 0.1% Black, 0.5% Asian, 0.0% American Indian/Alaska Native, 0.0% Native Hawaiian/Other Pacific Islander, 1.3% Other, 0.3% Hispanic of any race (2010); Average household size: 2.53 (2010); Median age: 45.6 (2010); Males per 100 females: 97.6 (2010); Marriage status: 10.1% never married, 62.0% now married, 7.9% widowed, 20.0% divorced (2006-2010 5-year est.); Foreign born: 1.2% (2006-2010 5-year est.); Ancestry (includes multiple ancestries): 49.4% German, 13.8% Irish, 11.7% English, 8.4% Dutch, 7.8% Italian (2006-2010 5-year est.).

Economy: Single-family building permits issued: 0 (2011); Multi-family building permits issued: 0 (2011); Employment by occupation: 6.7%

management, 6.7% professional, 5.6% services, 15.8% sales, 2.7% farming, 10.0% construction, 11.8% production (2006-2010 5-year est.).
Income: Per capita income: $24,770 (2006-2010 5-year est.); Median household income: $47,500 (2006-2010 5-year est.); Average household income: $56,946 (2006-2010 5-year est.); Percent of households with income of $100,000 or more: 11.7% (2006-2010 5-year est.); Poverty rate: 7.7% (2006-2010 5-year est.).
Education: Percent of population age 25 and over with: High school diploma (including GED) or higher: 90.3% (2006-2010 5-year est.); Bachelor's degree or higher: 22.1% (2006-2010 5-year est.); Master's degree or higher: 13.2% (2006-2010 5-year est.).
Housing: Homeownership rate: 90.5% (2010); Median home value: $144,200 (2006-2010 5-year est.); Median contract rent: $563 per month (2006-2010 5-year est.); Median year structure built: 1969 (2006-2010 5-year est.).
Safety: Violent crime rate: 9.9 per 10,000 population; Property crime rate: 49.5 per 10,000 population (2011).
Transportation: Commute to work: 93.7% car, 0.7% public transportation, 3.1% walk, 2.5% work from home (2006-2010 5-year est.); Travel time to work: 30.7% less than 15 minutes, 38.3% 15 to 30 minutes, 18.3% 30 to 45 minutes, 4.8% 45 to 60 minutes, 7.8% 60 minutes or more (2006-2010 5-year est.)

DUNNSTOWN (CDP). Covers a land area of 0.822 square miles and a water area of 0.016 square miles. Located at 41.15° N. Lat; 77.42° W. Long. Elevation is 646 feet.
Population: 1,486 (1990); 1,365 (2000); 1,360 (2010); Density: 1,654.6 persons per square mile (2010); Race: 98.5% White, 1.0% Black, 0.1% Asian, 0.0% American Indian/Alaska Native, 0.0% Native Hawaiian/Other Pacific Islander, 0.4% Other, 0.9% Hispanic of any race (2010); Average household size: 2.37 (2010); Median age: 44.9 (2010); Males per 100 females: 94.6 (2010); Marriage status: 17.6% never married, 62.2% now married, 6.0% widowed, 14.2% divorced (2006-2010 5-year est.); Foreign born: 0.6% (2006-2010 5-year est.); Ancestry (includes multiple ancestries): 38.4% German, 16.7% Irish, 12.1% American, 9.5% Italian, 7.9% English (2006-2010 5-year est.).
Economy: Employment by occupation: 15.6% management, 4.0% professional, 14.8% services, 15.8% sales, 1.5% farming, 10.3% construction, 3.5% production (2006-2010 5-year est.).
Income: Per capita income: $25,980 (2006-2010 5-year est.); Median household income: $44,318 (2006-2010 5-year est.); Average household income: $55,262 (2006-2010 5-year est.); Percent of households with income of $100,000 or more: 13.7% (2006-2010 5-year est.); Poverty rate: 5.3% (2006-2010 5-year est.).
Education: Percent of population age 25 and over with: High school diploma (including GED) or higher: 94.3% (2006-2010 5-year est.); Bachelor's degree or higher: 19.5% (2006-2010 5-year est.); Master's degree or higher: 10.0% (2006-2010 5-year est.).
Housing: Homeownership rate: 85.0% (2010); Median home value: $128,700 (2006-2010 5-year est.); Median contract rent: $398 per month (2006-2010 5-year est.); Median year structure built: 1971 (2006-2010 5-year est.).
Transportation: Commute to work: 91.5% car, 0.9% public transportation, 1.9% walk, 1.1% work from home (2006-2010 5-year est.); Travel time to work: 58.9% less than 15 minutes, 16.3% 15 to 30 minutes, 13.7% 30 to 45 minutes, 4.9% 45 to 60 minutes, 6.2% 60 minutes or more (2006-2010 5-year est.)
Additional Information Contacts
Clinton County Economic Partnership. . . . . (570) 748-5782
http://www.clintoncountyinfo.com

EAST KEATING (township). Covers a land area of 50.665 square miles and a water area of 0.719 square miles. Located at 41.32° N. Lat; 77.97° W. Long.
Population: 22 (1990); 24 (2000); 11 (2010); Density: 0.2 persons per square mile (2010); Race: 100.0% White, 0.0% Black, 0.0% Asian, 0.0% American Indian/Alaska Native, 0.0% Native Hawaiian/Other Pacific Islander, 0.0% Other, 0.0% Hispanic of any race (2010); Average household size: 1.57 (2010); Median age: 69.2 (2010); Males per 100 females: 175.0 (2010); Marriage status: 17.6% never married, 58.8% now married, 23.5% widowed, 0.0% divorced (2006-2010 5-year est.); Foreign born: 0.0% (2006-2010 5-year est.); Ancestry (includes multiple ancestries): 29.4% Irish, 23.5% German, 17.6% Swedish, 17.6% Czechoslovakian (2006-2010 5-year est.).

Economy: Income: Per capita income: $15,559 (2006-2010 5-year est.); Median household income: $22,500 (2006-2010 5-year est.); Average household income: $29,250 (2006-2010 5-year est.); Percent of households with income of $100,000 or more: n/a (2006-2010 5-year est.); Poverty rate: 35.3% (2006-2010 5-year est.).
Education: Percent of population age 25 and over with: High school diploma (including GED) or higher: 76.5% (2006-2010 5-year est.); Bachelor's degree or higher: 0.0% (2006-2010 5-year est.); Master's degree or higher: 0.0% (2006-2010 5-year est.).
Housing: Homeownership rate: 85.7% (2010); Median home value: $158,300 (2006-2010 5-year est.); Median contract rent: n/a per month (2006-2010 5-year est.); Median year structure built: 1957 (2006-2010 5-year est.).
Transportation: Commute to work: 100.0% car, 0.0% public transportation, 0.0% walk, 0.0% work from home (2006-2010 5-year est.); Travel time to work: 0.0% less than 15 minutes, 0.0% 15 to 30 minutes, 0.0% 30 to 45 minutes, 0.0% 45 to 60 minutes, 100.0% 60 minutes or more (2006-2010 5-year est.)

FLEMINGTON (borough). Covers a land area of 0.450 square miles and a water area of 0.006 square miles. Located at 41.13° N. Lat; 77.47° W. Long. Elevation is 650 feet.
History: Incorporated 1864.
Population: 1,326 (1990); 1,319 (2000); 1,330 (2010); Density: 2,953.0 persons per square mile (2010); Race: 96.6% White, 0.8% Black, 1.4% Asian, 0.0% American Indian/Alaska Native, 0.0% Native Hawaiian/Other Pacific Islander, 1.2% Other, 0.8% Hispanic of any race (2010); Average household size: 2.30 (2010); Median age: 43.2 (2010); Males per 100 females: 92.8 (2010); Marriage status: 22.0% never married, 57.2% now married, 11.6% widowed, 9.2% divorced (2006-2010 5-year est.); Foreign born: 0.0% (2006-2010 5-year est.); Ancestry (includes multiple ancestries): 35.6% German, 14.0% Irish, 9.4% Italian, 9.0% American, 7.0% English (2006-2010 5-year est.).
Economy: Single-family building permits issued: 0 (2011); Multi-family building permits issued: 0 (2011); Employment by occupation: 8.1% management, 2.1% professional, 9.6% services, 15.1% sales, 2.9% farming, 12.5% construction, 11.4% production (2006-2010 5-year est.).
Income: Per capita income: $21,761 (2006-2010 5-year est.); Median household income: $37,632 (2006-2010 5-year est.); Average household income: $45,910 (2006-2010 5-year est.); Percent of households with income of $100,000 or more: 4.6% (2006-2010 5-year est.); Poverty rate: 9.0% (2006-2010 5-year est.).
Education: Percent of population age 25 and over with: High school diploma (including GED) or higher: 89.7% (2006-2010 5-year est.); Bachelor's degree or higher: 17.3% (2006-2010 5-year est.); Master's degree or higher: 5.5% (2006-2010 5-year est.).
Housing: Homeownership rate: 76.2% (2010); Median home value: $92,700 (2006-2010 5-year est.); Median contract rent: $495 per month (2006-2010 5-year est.); Median year structure built: 1953 (2006-2010 5-year est.).
Transportation: Commute to work: 94.6% car, 0.0% public transportation, 2.8% walk, 1.3% work from home (2006-2010 5-year est.); Travel time to work: 54.5% less than 15 minutes, 19.0% 15 to 30 minutes, 10.1% 30 to 45 minutes, 8.9% 45 to 60 minutes, 7.5% 60 minutes or more (2006-2010 5-year est.)
Additional Information Contacts
Clinton County Economic Partnership/Clinton County Chamber o . . . (570) 748-5782
http://www.clintoncountyinfo.com

GALLAGHER (township). Covers a land area of 53.716 square miles and a water area of 0.020 square miles. Located at 41.28° N. Lat; 77.48° W. Long. Elevation is 1,608 feet.
Population: 213 (1990); 340 (2000); 381 (2010); Density: 7.1 persons per square mile (2010); Race: 99.5% White, 0.0% Black, 0.3% Asian, 0.0% American Indian/Alaska Native, 0.0% Native Hawaiian/Other Pacific Islander, 0.2% Other, 0.3% Hispanic of any race (2010); Average household size: 2.37 (2010); Median age: 46.9 (2010); Males per 100 females: 107.1 (2010); Marriage status: 17.2% never married, 62.5% now married, 7.1% widowed, 13.1% divorced (2006-2010 5-year est.); Foreign born: 0.0% (2006-2010 5-year est.); Ancestry (includes multiple ancestries): 49.3% German, 22.2% Irish, 12.0% Italian, 7.7% Swiss, 5.6% American (2006-2010 5-year est.).

Economy: Employment by occupation: 6.3% management, 1.3% professional, 6.3% services, 20.3% sales, 8.2% farming, 20.9% construction, 19.0% production (2006-2010 5-year est.).

Income: Per capita income: $21,079 (2006-2010 5-year est.); Median household income: $41,750 (2006-2010 5-year est.); Average household income: $48,860 (2006-2010 5-year est.); Percent of households with income of $100,000 or more: 8.4% (2006-2010 5-year est.); Poverty rate: 6.3% (2006-2010 5-year est.).

Education: Percent of population age 25 and over with: High school diploma (including GED) or higher: 89.2% (2006-2010 5-year est.); Bachelor's degree or higher: 10.0% (2006-2010 5-year est.); Master's degree or higher: 1.7% (2006-2010 5-year est.).

Housing: Homeownership rate: 91.9% (2010); Median home value: $185,000 (2006-2010 5-year est.); Median contract rent: n/a per month (2006-2010 5-year est.); Median year structure built: 1992 (2006-2010 5-year est.).

Transportation: Commute to work: 99.3% car, 0.0% public transportation, 0.0% walk, 0.0% work from home (2006-2010 5-year est.); Travel time to work: 3.9% less than 15 minutes, 36.2% 15 to 30 minutes, 39.5% 30 to 45 minutes, 6.6% 45 to 60 minutes, 13.8% 60 minutes or more (2006-2010 5-year est.)

GREENE (township). Covers a land area of 46.772 square miles and a water area of 0.222 square miles. Located at 41.05° N. Lat; 77.26° W. Long.

Population: 1,153 (1990); 1,464 (2000); 1,695 (2010); Density: 36.2 persons per square mile (2010); Race: 98.1% White, 0.1% Black, 0.2% Asian, 0.0% American Indian/Alaska Native, 0.0% Native Hawaiian/Other Pacific Islander, 1.6% Other, 1.7% Hispanic of any race (2010); Average household size: 3.19 (2010); Median age: 32.8 (2010); Males per 100 females: 111.6 (2010); Marriage status: 19.6% never married, 69.8% now married, 3.8% widowed, 6.8% divorced (2006-2010 5-year est.); Foreign born: 0.5% (2006-2010 5-year est.); Ancestry (includes multiple ancestries): 40.3% German, 17.5% Pennsylvania German, 8.9% English, 8.2% American, 4.9% Dutch (2006-2010 5-year est.).

Economy: Employment by occupation: 12.0% management, 1.8% professional, 13.8% services, 11.6% sales, 2.7% farming, 16.5% construction, 9.1% production (2006-2010 5-year est.).

Income: Per capita income: $19,243 (2006-2010 5-year est.); Median household income: $49,583 (2006-2010 5-year est.); Average household income: $62,598 (2006-2010 5-year est.); Percent of households with income of $100,000 or more: 12.9% (2006-2010 5-year est.); Poverty rate: 6.8% (2006-2010 5-year est.).

Education: Percent of population age 25 and over with: High school diploma (including GED) or higher: 75.3% (2006-2010 5-year est.); Bachelor's degree or higher: 11.5% (2006-2010 5-year est.); Master's degree or higher: 2.4% (2006-2010 5-year est.).

Housing: Homeownership rate: 82.7% (2010); Median home value: $131,300 (2006-2010 5-year est.); Median contract rent: $467 per month (2006-2010 5-year est.); Median year structure built: 1973 (2006-2010 5-year est.).

Transportation: Commute to work: 83.3% car, 0.4% public transportation, 5.5% walk, 10.4% work from home (2006-2010 5-year est.); Travel time to work: 16.0% less than 15 minutes, 37.7% 15 to 30 minutes, 24.0% 30 to 45 minutes, 10.5% 45 to 60 minutes, 11.8% 60 minutes or more (2006-2010 5-year est.)

Additional Information Contacts
Clinton County Economic Partnership/Clinton County Chamber o . . . (570) 748-5782
  http://www.clintoncountyinfo.com

GRUGAN (township). Covers a land area of 68.270 square miles and a water area of 1.111 square miles. Located at 41.28° N. Lat; 77.62° W. Long.

Population: 52 (1990); 52 (2000); 51 (2010); Density: 0.7 persons per square mile (2010); Race: 90.2% White, 2.0% Black, 0.0% Asian, 3.9% American Indian/Alaska Native, 0.0% Native Hawaiian/Other Pacific Islander, 3.9% Other, 2.0% Hispanic of any race (2010); Average household size: 1.89 (2010); Median age: 56.8 (2010); Males per 100 females: 112.5 (2010); Marriage status: 22.2% never married, 77.8% now married, 0.0% widowed, 0.0% divorced (2006-2010 5-year est.); Foreign born: 0.0% (2006-2010 5-year est.); Ancestry (includes multiple ancestries): 73.1% German, 71.6% Irish, 14.9% Polish, 9.0% Swedish, 6.0% English (2006-2010 5-year est.).

Economy: Employment by occupation: 0.0% management, 0.0% professional, 8.0% services, 44.0% sales, 0.0% farming, 12.0% construction, 0.0% production (2006-2010 5-year est.).

Income: Per capita income: $11,164 (2006-2010 5-year est.); Median household income: $16,875 (2006-2010 5-year est.); Average household income: $36,352 (2006-2010 5-year est.); Percent of households with income of $100,000 or more: n/a (2006-2010 5-year est.); Poverty rate: 52.2% (2006-2010 5-year est.).

Education: Percent of population age 25 and over with: High school diploma (including GED) or higher: 86.7% (2006-2010 5-year est.); Bachelor's degree or higher: 10.0% (2006-2010 5-year est.); Master's degree or higher: 0.0% (2006-2010 5-year est.).

Housing: Homeownership rate: 77.7% (2010); Median home value: $154,500 (2006-2010 5-year est.); Median contract rent: n/a per month (2006-2010 5-year est.); Median year structure built: 1976 (2006-2010 5-year est.).

Transportation: Commute to work: 100.0% car, 0.0% public transportation, 0.0% walk, 0.0% work from home (2006-2010 5-year est.); Travel time to work: 8.0% less than 15 minutes, 24.0% 15 to 30 minutes, 32.0% 30 to 45 minutes, 36.0% 45 to 60 minutes, 0.0% 60 minutes or more (2006-2010 5-year est.)

LAMAR (CDP). Covers a land area of 1.115 square miles and a water area of 0.013 square miles. Located at 41.01° N. Lat; 77.52° W. Long. Elevation is 823 feet.

Population: n/a (1990); n/a (2000); 562 (2010); Density: 504.2 persons per square mile (2010); Race: 98.4% White, 0.0% Black, 0.2% Asian, 0.2% American Indian/Alaska Native, 0.0% Native Hawaiian/Other Pacific Islander, 1.2% Other, 0.5% Hispanic of any race (2010); Average household size: 2.38 (2010); Median age: 42.3 (2010); Males per 100 females: 100.7 (2010); Marriage status: 18.8% never married, 61.3% now married, 9.5% widowed, 10.5% divorced (2006-2010 5-year est.); Foreign born: 0.1% (2006-2010 5-year est.); Ancestry (includes multiple ancestries): 53.5% German, 15.3% Irish, 10.4% Pennsylvania German, 6.6% English, 6.6% Italian (2006-2010 5-year est.).

Economy: Employment by occupation: 2.4% management, 0.0% professional, 15.6% services, 20.0% sales, 1.2% farming, 20.4% construction, 11.2% production (2006-2010 5-year est.).

Income: Per capita income: $17,018 (2006-2010 5-year est.); Median household income: $32,863 (2006-2010 5-year est.); Average household income: $39,227 (2006-2010 5-year est.); Percent of households with income of $100,000 or more: 6.3% (2006-2010 5-year est.); Poverty rate: 16.5% (2006-2010 5-year est.).

Education: Percent of population age 25 and over with: High school diploma (including GED) or higher: 75.7% (2006-2010 5-year est.); Bachelor's degree or higher: 10.1% (2006-2010 5-year est.); Master's degree or higher: 6.8% (2006-2010 5-year est.).

Housing: Homeownership rate: 88.1% (2010); Median home value: $98,800 (2006-2010 5-year est.); Median contract rent: $568 per month (2006-2010 5-year est.); Median year structure built: 1961 (2006-2010 5-year est.).

Transportation: Commute to work: 85.5% car, 0.0% public transportation, 4.4% walk, 10.0% work from home (2006-2010 5-year est.); Travel time to work: 29.5% less than 15 minutes, 43.8% 15 to 30 minutes, 16.5% 30 to 45 minutes, 1.3% 45 to 60 minutes, 8.9% 60 minutes or more (2006-2010 5-year est.)

LAMAR (township). Covers a land area of 40.892 square miles and a water area of 0.111 square miles. Located at 41.07° N. Lat; 77.40° W. Long.

Population: 2,345 (1990); 2,450 (2000); 2,517 (2010); Density: 61.6 persons per square mile (2010); Race: 98.8% White, 0.3% Black, 0.3% Asian, 0.0% American Indian/Alaska Native, 0.0% Native Hawaiian/Other Pacific Islander, 0.6% Other, 0.9% Hispanic of any race (2010); Average household size: 2.64 (2010); Median age: 41.4 (2010); Males per 100 females: 95.4 (2010); Marriage status: 19.0% never married, 62.7% now married, 5.7% widowed, 12.6% divorced (2006-2010 5-year est.); Foreign born: 1.2% (2006-2010 5-year est.); Ancestry (includes multiple ancestries): 28.8% German, 14.4% Irish, 7.3% American, 5.6% English, 5.0% Dutch (2006-2010 5-year est.).

Economy: Single-family building permits issued: 3 (2011); Multi-family building permits issued: 0 (2011); Employment by occupation: 3.8% management, 0.9% professional, 10.7% services, 9.8% sales, 4.2% farming, 13.4% construction, 13.1% production (2006-2010 5-year est.).

Income: Per capita income: $24,271 (2006-2010 5-year est.); Median household income: $53,281 (2006-2010 5-year est.); Average household income: $55,793 (2006-2010 5-year est.); Percent of households with income of $100,000 or more: 9.9% (2006-2010 5-year est.); Poverty rate: 9.8% (2006-2010 5-year est.).

Education: Percent of population age 25 and over with: High school diploma (including GED) or higher: 87.6% (2006-2010 5-year est.); Bachelor's degree or higher: 23.4% (2006-2010 5-year est.); Master's degree or higher: 8.1% (2006-2010 5-year est.).

Housing: Homeownership rate: 85.8% (2010); Median home value: $104,500 (2006-2010 5-year est.); Median contract rent: $558 per month (2006-2010 5-year est.); Median year structure built: 1969 (2006-2010 5-year est.).

Safety: Violent crime rate: 4.0 per 10,000 population; Property crime rate: 59.4 per 10,000 population (2011).

Transportation: Commute to work: 95.1% car, 0.0% public transportation, 0.5% walk, 3.6% work from home (2006-2010 5-year est.); Travel time to work: 32.7% less than 15 minutes, 37.5% 15 to 30 minutes, 14.7% 30 to 45 minutes, 7.5% 45 to 60 minutes, 7.6% 60 minutes or more (2006-2010 5-year est.)

Additional Information Contacts

Clinton County Economic Partnership/Clinton County Chamber o . . . (570) 748-5782
    http://www.clintoncountyinfo.com

LEIDY (township). Covers a land area of 96.541 square miles and a water area of 0.606 square miles. Located at 41.40° N. Lat; 77.86° W. Long. Elevation is 883 feet.

Population: 214 (1990); 229 (2000); 180 (2010); Density: 1.9 persons per square mile (2010); Race: 98.9% White, 0.0% Black, 0.0% Asian, 1.1% American Indian/Alaska Native, 0.0% Native Hawaiian/Other Pacific Islander, 0.0% Other, 0.0% Hispanic of any race (2010); Average household size: 1.91 (2010); Median age: 60.0 (2010); Males per 100 females: 119.5 (2010); Marriage status: 8.1% never married, 72.7% now married, 10.1% widowed, 9.1% divorced (2006-2010 5-year est.); Foreign born: 0.0% (2006-2010 5-year est.); Ancestry (includes multiple ancestries): 32.5% German, 10.8% Irish, 8.3% American, 8.3% Dutch, 6.7% English (2006-2010 5-year est.).

Economy: Single-family building permits issued: 0 (2011); Multi-family building permits issued: 0 (2011); Employment by occupation: 0.0% management, 4.8% professional, 4.8% services, 9.5% sales, 0.0% farming, 26.2% construction, 28.6% production (2006-2010 5-year est.).

Income: Per capita income: $21,208 (2006-2010 5-year est.); Median household income: $37,083 (2006-2010 5-year est.); Average household income: $43,154 (2006-2010 5-year est.); Percent of households with income of $100,000 or more: 6.8% (2006-2010 5-year est.); Poverty rate: 15.0% (2006-2010 5-year est.).

Education: Percent of population age 25 and over with: High school diploma (including GED) or higher: 72.6% (2006-2010 5-year est.); Bachelor's degree or higher: 4.2% (2006-2010 5-year est.); Master's degree or higher: 0.0% (2006-2010 5-year est.).

Housing: Homeownership rate: 85.1% (2010); Median home value: $111,500 (2006-2010 5-year est.); Median contract rent: <$101 per month (2006-2010 5-year est.); Median year structure built: 1965 (2006-2010 5-year est.).

Transportation: Commute to work: 78.4% car, 0.0% public transportation, 16.2% walk, 5.4% work from home (2006-2010 5-year est.); Travel time to work: 45.7% less than 15 minutes, 0.0% 15 to 30 minutes, 25.7% 30 to 45 minutes, 0.0% 45 to 60 minutes, 28.6% 60 minutes or more (2006-2010 5-year est.)

LOCK HAVEN (city). County seat. Covers a land area of 2.496 square miles and a water area of 0.172 square miles. Located at 41.14° N. Lat; 77.45° W. Long. Elevation is 561 feet.

History: Lock Haven was a rude frontier settlement in 1834. In the late 1800's it became a lumber center frequented by woodsmen and rivermen.

Population: 9,230 (1990); 9,149 (2000); 9,772 (2010); Density: 3,914.4 persons per square mile (2010); Race: 92.8% White, 4.2% Black, 1.0% Asian, 0.1% American Indian/Alaska Native, 0.1% Native Hawaiian/Other Pacific Islander, 1.8% Other, 1.9% Hispanic of any race (2010); Average household size: 2.26 (2010); Median age: 22.7 (2010); Males per 100 females: 85.6 (2010); Marriage status: 62.8% never married, 23.5% now married, 5.2% widowed, 8.4% divorced (2006-2010 5-year est.); Foreign born: 1.3% (2006-2010 5-year est.); Ancestry (includes multiple

ancestries): 30.5% German, 17.8% Irish, 12.7% Italian, 5.8% Polish, 4.3% English (2006-2010 5-year est.).

Economy: Single-family building permits issued: 1 (2011); Multi-family building permits issued: 0 (2011); Employment by occupation: 2.7% management, 1.7% professional, 17.8% services, 22.7% sales, 7.5% farming, 5.8% construction, 5.0% production (2006-2010 5-year est.).

Income: Per capita income: $13,170 (2006-2010 5-year est.); Median household income: $25,579 (2006-2010 5-year est.); Average household income: $36,709 (2006-2010 5-year est.); Percent of households with income of $100,000 or more: 4.2% (2006-2010 5-year est.); Poverty rate: 36.3% (2006-2010 5-year est.).

Education: Percent of population age 25 and over with: High school diploma (including GED) or higher: 83.0% (2006-2010 5-year est.); Bachelor's degree or higher: 22.6% (2006-2010 5-year est.); Master's degree or higher: 5.6% (2006-2010 5-year est.).

School District(s)

Keystone Central SD (KG-12)
    2010-11 Enrollment: 4,394 . . . . (570) 893-4900

Four-year College(s)

Lock Haven University (Public)
    Fall 2010 Enrollment: 5,360 . . . . (570) 484-2011
    2011-12 Tuition: In-state $8,239; Out-of-state $15,777

Housing: Homeownership rate: 34.0% (2010); Median home value: $89,700 (2006-2010 5-year est.); Median contract rent: $533 per month (2006-2010 5-year est.); Median year structure built: 1953 (2006-2010 5-year est.).

Hospitals: Lock Haven Hospital & Extended Care Unit (137 beds)

Safety: Violent crime rate: 24.5 per 10,000 population; Property crime rate: 271.3 per 10,000 population (2011).

Newspapers: The Express (Local news; Circulation 9,384)

Transportation: Commute to work: 77.8% car, 0.0% public transportation, 16.9% walk, 3.8% work from home (2006-2010 5-year est.); Travel time to work: 59.9% less than 15 minutes, 22.0% 15 to 30 minutes, 7.5% 30 to 45 minutes, 4.6% 45 to 60 minutes, 6.0% 60 minutes or more (2006-2010 5-year est.)

Airports: William T. Piper Memorial (general aviation)

Additional Information Contacts

City of Lock Haven . . . . (570) 893-5900
    http://www.lockhavencity.org
Clinton County Economic Partnership/Clinton County Chamber o . . . (570) 748-5782
    http://www.clintoncountyinfo.com

LOGAN (township). Covers a land area of 24.176 square miles and a water area of 0.078 square miles. Located at 41.01° N. Lat; 77.42° W. Long.

Population: 730 (1990); 773 (2000); 817 (2010); Density: 33.8 persons per square mile (2010); Race: 98.2% White, 0.0% Black, 0.1% Asian, 0.1% American Indian/Alaska Native, 0.1% Native Hawaiian/Other Pacific Islander, 1.5% Other, 0.4% Hispanic of any race (2010); Average household size: 2.96 (2010); Median age: 35.7 (2010); Males per 100 females: 99.3 (2010); Marriage status: 20.8% never married, 65.7% now married, 8.3% widowed, 5.3% divorced (2006-2010 5-year est.); Foreign born: 1.9% (2006-2010 5-year est.); Ancestry (includes multiple ancestries): 41.9% German, 16.3% American, 9.2% Irish, 6.8% English, 4.4% Other Arab (2006-2010 5-year est.).

Economy: Employment by occupation: 11.0% management, 1.2% professional, 12.2% services, 19.6% sales, 0.4% farming, 16.1% construction, 10.2% production (2006-2010 5-year est.).

Income: Per capita income: $18,859 (2006-2010 5-year est.); Median household income: $44,167 (2006-2010 5-year est.); Average household income: $52,896 (2006-2010 5-year est.); Percent of households with income of $100,000 or more: 8.8% (2006-2010 5-year est.); Poverty rate: 12.6% (2006-2010 5-year est.).

Education: Percent of population age 25 and over with: High school diploma (including GED) or higher: 80.4% (2006-2010 5-year est.); Bachelor's degree or higher: 8.6% (2006-2010 5-year est.); Master's degree or higher: 2.6% (2006-2010 5-year est.).

Housing: Homeownership rate: 84.8% (2010); Median home value: $104,300 (2006-2010 5-year est.); Median contract rent: $634 per month (2006-2010 5-year est.); Median year structure built: 1950 (2006-2010 5-year est.).

Transportation: Commute to work: 91.5% car, 0.0% public transportation, 0.0% walk, 6.5% work from home (2006-2010 5-year est.); Travel time to work: 5.6% less than 15 minutes, 19.9% 15 to 30 minutes, 40.3% 30 to 45

minutes, 19.5% 45 to 60 minutes, 14.7% 60 minutes or more (2006-2010 5-year est.)

LOGANTON (borough). Covers a land area of 1.053 square miles and a water area of 0.003 square miles. Located at 41.03° N. Lat; 77.30° W. Long. Elevation is 1,302 feet.

Population: 443 (1990); 435 (2000); 468 (2010); Density: 444.6 persons per square mile (2010); Race: 97.0% White, 0.2% Black, 0.0% Asian, 0.0% American Indian/Alaska Native, 0.0% Native Hawaiian/Other Pacific Islander, 2.8% Other, 2.1% Hispanic of any race (2010); Average household size: 2.57 (2010); Median age: 39.8 (2010); Males per 100 females: 95.0 (2010); Marriage status: 23.7% never married, 58.8% now married, 8.6% widowed, 8.9% divorced (2006-2010 5-year est.); Foreign born: 0.9% (2006-2010 5-year est.); Ancestry (includes multiple ancestries): 47.1% German, 14.6% American, 13.9% Irish, 11.1% English, 3.9% Dutch (2006-2010 5-year est.).
Economy: Single-family building permits issued: 1 (2011); Multi-family building permits issued: 0 (2011); Employment by occupation: 4.1% management, 2.3% professional, 8.1% services, 21.7% sales, 2.3% farming, 14.0% construction, 6.3% production (2006-2010 5-year est.).
Income: Per capita income: $19,695 (2006-2010 5-year est.); Median household income: $44,625 (2006-2010 5-year est.); Average household income: $48,536 (2006-2010 5-year est.); Percent of households with income of $100,000 or more: 4.6% (2006-2010 5-year est.); Poverty rate: 5.6% (2006-2010 5-year est.).
Education: Percent of population age 25 and over with: High school diploma (including GED) or higher: 89.0% (2006-2010 5-year est.); Bachelor's degree or higher: 10.0% (2006-2010 5-year est.); Master's degree or higher: 3.3% (2006-2010 5-year est.).

School District(s)
Keystone Central SD (KG-12)
   2010-11 Enrollment: 4,394 . . . . (570) 893-4900
Sugar Valley Rural CS (KG-12)
   2010-11 Enrollment: 261 . . . . (570) 725-7822
Housing: Homeownership rate: 84.6% (2010); Median home value: $96,500 (2006-2010 5-year est.); Median contract rent: $421 per month (2006-2010 5-year est.); Median year structure built: 1950 (2006-2010 5-year est.).
Transportation: Commute to work: 93.3% car, 0.0% public transportation, 1.8% walk, 4.0% work from home (2006-2010 5-year est.); Travel time to work: 23.8% less than 15 minutes, 26.2% 15 to 30 minutes, 32.2% 30 to 45 minutes, 8.9% 45 to 60 minutes, 8.9% 60 minutes or more (2006-2010 5-year est.)

MACKEYVILLE (unincorporated postal area)
Zip Code: 17750
   Covers a land area of 1.519 square miles and a water area of 0.006 square miles. Located at 41.05° N. Lat; 77.48° W. Long. Elevation is 656 feet. Population: 167 (2010); Density: 109.9 persons per square mile (2010); Race: 100.0% White, 0.0% Black, 0.0% Asian, 0.0% American Indian/Alaska Native, 0.0% Native Hawaiian/Other Pacific Islander, 0.0% Other, 0.0% Hispanic of any race (2010); Average household size: 2.83 (2010); Median age: 36.5 (2010); Males per 100 females: 92.0 (2010); Homeownership rate: 86.4% (2010)

MCELHATTAN (CDP). Covers a land area of 1.344 square miles and a water area of 0.090 square miles. Located at 41.16° N. Lat; 77.36° W. Long. Elevation is 574 feet.

Population: n/a (1990); n/a (2000); 598 (2010); Density: 445.1 persons per square mile (2010); Race: 97.7% White, 0.5% Black, 0.0% Asian, 0.8% American Indian/Alaska Native, 0.0% Native Hawaiian/Other Pacific Islander, 1.0% Other, 1.0% Hispanic of any race (2010); Average household size: 2.34 (2010); Median age: 47.6 (2010); Males per 100 females: 94.8 (2010); Marriage status: 19.5% never married, 60.2% now married, 12.4% widowed, 7.9% divorced (2006-2010 5-year est.); Foreign born: 0.6% (2006-2010 5-year est.); Ancestry (includes multiple ancestries): 42.2% German, 14.4% Irish, 9.1% Dutch, 7.8% English, 5.0% Italian (2006-2010 5-year est.).
Economy: Employment by occupation: 13.8% management, 1.9% professional, 7.3% services, 20.8% sales, 0.0% farming, 7.7% construction, 15.8% production (2006-2010 5-year est.).
Income: Per capita income: $20,469 (2006-2010 5-year est.); Median household income: $40,792 (2006-2010 5-year est.); Average household income: $44,039 (2006-2010 5-year est.); Percent of households with

income of $100,000 or more: 4.5% (2006-2010 5-year est.); Poverty rate: 13.3% (2006-2010 5-year est.).
Education: Percent of population age 25 and over with: High school diploma (including GED) or higher: 85.9% (2006-2010 5-year est.); Bachelor's degree or higher: 11.8% (2006-2010 5-year est.); Master's degree or higher: 1.4% (2006-2010 5-year est.).
Housing: Homeownership rate: 86.7% (2010); Median home value: $72,500 (2006-2010 5-year est.); Median contract rent: $429 per month (2006-2010 5-year est.); Median year structure built: 1984 (2006-2010 5-year est.).
Transportation: Commute to work: 95.0% car, 0.0% public transportation, 1.5% walk, 3.5% work from home (2006-2010 5-year est.); Travel time to work: 31.5% less than 15 minutes, 45.4% 15 to 30 minutes, 13.5% 30 to 45 minutes, 7.6% 45 to 60 minutes, 2.0% 60 minutes or more (2006-2010 5-year est.)

MILL HALL (borough). Covers a land area of 0.921 square miles and a water area of 0.027 square miles. Located at 41.11° N. Lat; 77.49° W. Long. Elevation is 571 feet.

History: Laid out 1806, incorporated 1850.
Population: 1,708 (1990); 1,568 (2000); 1,613 (2010); Density: 1,750.9 persons per square mile (2010); Race: 98.2% White, 0.3% Black, 0.7% Asian, 0.1% American Indian/Alaska Native, 0.0% Native Hawaiian/Other Pacific Islander, 0.7% Other, 0.5% Hispanic of any race (2010); Average household size: 2.31 (2010); Median age: 40.6 (2010); Males per 100 females: 91.1 (2010); Marriage status: 23.2% never married, 58.3% now married, 7.7% widowed, 10.9% divorced (2006-2010 5-year est.); Foreign born: 1.8% (2006-2010 5-year est.); Ancestry (includes multiple ancestries): 38.3% German, 10.3% American, 8.9% Irish, 7.8% English, 7.0% Italian (2006-2010 5-year est.).
Economy: Single-family building permits issued: 0 (2011); Multi-family building permits issued: 0 (2011); Employment by occupation: 3.0% management, 2.3% professional, 11.1% services, 18.6% sales, 3.7% farming, 9.0% construction, 9.1% production (2006-2010 5-year est.).
Income: Per capita income: $19,000 (2006-2010 5-year est.); Median household income: $41,161 (2006-2010 5-year est.); Average household income: $46,159 (2006-2010 5-year est.); Percent of households with income of $100,000 or more: 3.2% (2006-2010 5-year est.); Poverty rate: 8.0% (2006-2010 5-year est.).
Education: Percent of population age 25 and over with: High school diploma (including GED) or higher: 89.7% (2006-2010 5-year est.); Bachelor's degree or higher: 12.5% (2006-2010 5-year est.); Master's degree or higher: 3.3% (2006-2010 5-year est.).

School District(s)
Keystone Central CTC (09-12)
   2010-11 Enrollment: n/a . . . . (570) 748-6584
Keystone Central SD (KG-12)
   2010-11 Enrollment: 4,394 . . . . (570) 893-4900
Housing: Homeownership rate: 66.4% (2010); Median home value: $96,200 (2006-2010 5-year est.); Median contract rent: $485 per month (2006-2010 5-year est.); Median year structure built: 1953 (2006-2010 5-year est.).
Transportation: Commute to work: 93.9% car, 0.0% public transportation, 2.8% walk, 1.8% work from home (2006-2010 5-year est.); Travel time to work: 52.4% less than 15 minutes, 18.7% 15 to 30 minutes, 16.3% 30 to 45 minutes, 9.5% 45 to 60 minutes, 3.1% 60 minutes or more (2006-2010 5-year est.)
Additional Information Contacts
Clinton County Economic Partnership/Clinton County Chamber o . . . (570) 748-5782
   http://www.clintoncountyinfo.com

NORTH BEND (unincorporated postal area)
Zip Code: 17760
   Covers a land area of 82.935 square miles and a water area of 0.660 square miles. Located at 41.41° N. Lat; 77.65° W. Long. Elevation is 669 feet. Population: 557 (2010); Density: 6.7 persons per square mile (2010); Race: 100.0% White, 0.0% Black, 0.0% Asian, 0.0% American Indian/Alaska Native, 0.0% Native Hawaiian/Other Pacific Islander, 0.0% Other, 0.2% Hispanic of any race (2010); Average household size: 2.29 (2010); Median age: 48.9 (2010); Males per 100 females: 102.5 (2010); Homeownership rate: 89.3% (2010)

NOYES (township). Covers a land area of 88.813 square miles and a water area of 1.159 square miles. Located at 41.28° N. Lat; 77.79° W. Long.

Population: 463 (1990); 419 (2000); 357 (2010); Density: 4.0 persons per square mile (2010); Race: 99.7% White, 0.0% Black, 0.0% Asian, 0.0% American Indian/Alaska Native, 0.0% Native Hawaiian/Other Pacific Islander, 0.3% Other, 0.0% Hispanic of any race (2010); Average household size: 2.14 (2010); Median age: 53.5 (2010); Males per 100 females: 117.7 (2010); Marriage status: 16.1% never married, 59.5% now married, 10.8% widowed, 13.6% divorced (2006-2010 5-year est.); Foreign born: 0.9% (2006-2010 5-year est.); Ancestry (includes multiple ancestries): 26.0% German, 13.0% English, 12.4% Italian, 11.5% Welsh, 8.7% Irish (2006-2010 5-year est.).

Economy: Employment by occupation: 7.8% management, 7.8% professional, 7.8% services, 13.3% sales, 0.0% farming, 10.2% construction, 5.5% production (2006-2010 5-year est.).

Income: Per capita income: $22,135 (2006-2010 5-year est.); Median household income: $38,281 (2006-2010 5-year est.); Average household income: $47,274 (2006-2010 5-year est.); Percent of households with income of $100,000 or more: 6.7% (2006-2010 5-year est.); Poverty rate: 10.2% (2006-2010 5-year est.).

Education: Percent of population age 25 and over with: High school diploma (including GED) or higher: 83.6% (2006-2010 5-year est.); Bachelor's degree or higher: 12.6% (2006-2010 5-year est.); Master's degree or higher: 3.3% (2006-2010 5-year est.).

Housing: Homeownership rate: 91.0% (2010); Median home value: $70,500 (2006-2010 5-year est.); Median contract rent: n/a per month (2006-2010 5-year est.); Median year structure built: 1954 (2006-2010 5-year est.).

Transportation: Commute to work: 79.7% car, 0.0% public transportation, 10.2% walk, 1.6% work from home (2006-2010 5-year est.); Travel time to work: 26.2% less than 15 minutes, 25.4% 15 to 30 minutes, 18.3% 30 to 45 minutes, 11.9% 45 to 60 minutes, 18.3% 60 minutes or more (2006-2010 5-year est.)

PINE CREEK (township). Covers a land area of 14.406 square miles and a water area of 0.504 square miles. Located at 41.19° N. Lat; 77.33° W. Long.

Population: 3,188 (1990); 3,184 (2000); 3,215 (2010); Density: 223.2 persons per square mile (2010); Race: 98.5% White, 0.2% Black, 0.6% Asian, 0.1% American Indian/Alaska Native, 0.2% Native Hawaiian/Other Pacific Islander, 0.4% Other, 0.1% Hispanic of any race (2010); Average household size: 2.35 (2010); Median age: 47.1 (2010); Males per 100 females: 99.2 (2010); Marriage status: 17.8% never married, 57.9% now married, 10.3% widowed, 13.9% divorced (2006-2010 5-year est.); Foreign born: 0.3% (2006-2010 5-year est.); Ancestry (includes multiple ancestries): 47.2% German, 18.1% Irish, 10.7% English, 8.5% Italian, 4.8% Dutch (2006-2010 5-year est.).

Economy: Single-family building permits issued: 6 (2011); Multi-family building permits issued: 0 (2011); Employment by occupation: 13.6% management, 1.5% professional, 13.6% services, 14.3% sales, 2.5% farming, 12.1% construction, 6.5% production (2006-2010 5-year est.).

Income: Per capita income: $24,219 (2006-2010 5-year est.); Median household income: $45,262 (2006-2010 5-year est.); Average household income: $53,807 (2006-2010 5-year est.); Percent of households with income of $100,000 or more: 10.3% (2006-2010 5-year est.); Poverty rate: 5.4% (2006-2010 5-year est.).

Education: Percent of population age 25 and over with: High school diploma (including GED) or higher: 87.5% (2006-2010 5-year est.); Bachelor's degree or higher: 17.3% (2006-2010 5-year est.); Master's degree or higher: 6.4% (2006-2010 5-year est.).

Housing: Homeownership rate: 84.3% (2010); Median home value: $96,000 (2006-2010 5-year est.); Median contract rent: $452 per month (2006-2010 5-year est.); Median year structure built: 1974 (2006-2010 5-year est.).

Safety: Violent crime rate: 12.4 per 10,000 population; Property crime rate: 43.4 per 10,000 population (2011).

Transportation: Commute to work: 90.9% car, 0.0% public transportation, 5.4% walk, 3.7% work from home (2006-2010 5-year est.); Travel time to work: 33.4% less than 15 minutes, 32.9% 15 to 30 minutes, 19.3% 30 to 45 minutes, 6.9% 45 to 60 minutes, 7.5% 60 minutes or more (2006-2010 5-year est.)

Additional Information Contacts
Clinton County Economic Partnership/Clinton County Chamber o . . . (570) 748-5782
http://www.clintoncountyinfo.com

PORTER (township). Covers a land area of 25.554 square miles and a water area of 0.116 square miles. Located at 41.03° N. Lat; 77.51° W. Long.

Population: 1,437 (1990); 1,419 (2000); 1,460 (2010); Density: 57.1 persons per square mile (2010); Race: 98.2% White, 0.3% Black, 0.1% Asian, 0.2% American Indian/Alaska Native, 0.0% Native Hawaiian/Other Pacific Islander, 1.2% Other, 1.8% Hispanic of any race (2010); Average household size: 2.58 (2010); Median age: 41.7 (2010); Males per 100 females: 98.1 (2010); Marriage status: 17.5% never married, 65.7% now married, 6.1% widowed, 10.7% divorced (2006-2010 5-year est.); Foreign born: 1.1% (2006-2010 5-year est.); Ancestry (includes multiple ancestries): 45.3% German, 12.8% Irish, 6.6% Pennsylvania German, 6.4% English, 6.4% Italian (2006-2010 5-year est.).

Economy: Single-family building permits issued: 6 (2011); Multi-family building permits issued: 0 (2011); Employment by occupation: 8.8% management, 1.3% professional, 10.9% services, 15.8% sales, 5.3% farming, 23.7% construction, 10.6% production (2006-2010 5-year est.).

Income: Per capita income: $20,138 (2006-2010 5-year est.); Median household income: $36,228 (2006-2010 5-year est.); Average household income: $48,716 (2006-2010 5-year est.); Percent of households with income of $100,000 or more: 8.8% (2006-2010 5-year est.); Poverty rate: 11.5% (2006-2010 5-year est.).

Education: Percent of population age 25 and over with: High school diploma (including GED) or higher: 79.1% (2006-2010 5-year est.); Bachelor's degree or higher: 14.8% (2006-2010 5-year est.); Master's degree or higher: 5.6% (2006-2010 5-year est.).

Housing: Homeownership rate: 87.1% (2010); Median home value: $117,900 (2006-2010 5-year est.); Median contract rent: $501 per month (2006-2010 5-year est.); Median year structure built: 1965 (2006-2010 5-year est.).

Transportation: Commute to work: 83.9% car, 1.9% public transportation, 4.6% walk, 9.6% work from home (2006-2010 5-year est.); Travel time to work: 34.1% less than 15 minutes, 33.9% 15 to 30 minutes, 18.8% 30 to 45 minutes, 5.1% 45 to 60 minutes, 8.1% 60 minutes or more (2006-2010 5-year est.)

Additional Information Contacts
Clinton County Economic Partnership/Clinton County Chamber o . . . (570) 748-5782
http://www.clintoncountyinfo.com

RAUCHTOWN (CDP). Covers a land area of 1.782 square miles and a water area of 0.003 square miles. Located at 41.13° N. Lat; 77.24° W. Long. Elevation is 886 feet.

Population: n/a (1990); n/a (2000); 726 (2010); Density: 407.3 persons per square mile (2010); Race: 99.0% White, 0.6% Black, 0.1% Asian, 0.0% American Indian/Alaska Native, 0.0% Native Hawaiian/Other Pacific Islander, 0.3% Other, 0.3% Hispanic of any race (2010); Average household size: 2.61 (2010); Median age: 42.9 (2010); Males per 100 females: 107.4 (2010); Marriage status: 17.0% never married, 68.5% now married, 4.9% widowed, 9.6% divorced (2006-2010 5-year est.); Foreign born: 1.7% (2006-2010 5-year est.); Ancestry (includes multiple ancestries): 53.6% German, 12.1% Irish, 9.9% Italian, 6.4% English, 5.0% Dutch (2006-2010 5-year est.).

Economy: Employment by occupation: 5.8% management, 1.0% professional, 9.4% services, 15.6% sales, 5.0% farming, 12.9% construction, 9.4% production (2006-2010 5-year est.).

Income: Per capita income: $20,480 (2006-2010 5-year est.); Median household income: $48,417 (2006-2010 5-year est.); Average household income: $53,209 (2006-2010 5-year est.); Percent of households with income of $100,000 or more: 7.6% (2006-2010 5-year est.); Poverty rate: 5.5% (2006-2010 5-year est.).

Education: Percent of population age 25 and over with: High school diploma (including GED) or higher: 85.5% (2006-2010 5-year est.); Bachelor's degree or higher: 12.0% (2006-2010 5-year est.); Master's degree or higher: 1.0% (2006-2010 5-year est.).

Housing: Homeownership rate: 87.1% (2010); Median home value: $120,500 (2006-2010 5-year est.); Median contract rent: $400 per month (2006-2010 5-year est.); Median year structure built: 1976 (2006-2010 5-year est.).

Transportation: Commute to work: 94.6% car, 0.0% public transportation, 2.2% walk, 3.2% work from home (2006-2010 5-year est.); Travel time to work: 14.6% less than 15 minutes, 37.3% 15 to 30 minutes, 38.5% 30 to 45 minutes, 2.0% 45 to 60 minutes, 7.6% 60 minutes or more (2006-2010 5-year est.)

RENOVO (borough). Covers a land area of 1.126 square miles and a water area of 0.005 square miles. Located at 41.33° N. Lat; 77.74° W. Long. Elevation is 659 feet.
History: Laid out 1862, incorporated 1866.
Population: 1,526 (1990); 1,318 (2000); 1,228 (2010); Density: 1,091.0 persons per square mile (2010); Race: 97.9% White, 0.1% Black, 0.0% Asian, 0.1% American Indian/Alaska Native, 0.0% Native Hawaiian/Other Pacific Islander, 1.9% Other, 1.1% Hispanic of any race (2010); Average household size: 2.31 (2010); Median age: 39.2 (2010); Males per 100 females: 91.0 (2010); Marriage status: 29.7% never married, 41.9% now married, 12.6% widowed, 15.9% divorced (2006-2010 5-year est.); Foreign born: 0.0% (2006-2010 5-year est.); Ancestry (includes multiple ancestries): 39.6% German, 16.7% Irish, 15.4% Italian, 12.6% English, 3.9% Dutch (2006-2010 5-year est.).
Economy: Single-family building permits issued: 0 (2011); Multi-family building permits issued: 0 (2011); Employment by occupation: 2.5% management, 2.5% professional, 18.6% services, 18.6% sales, 2.2% farming, 15.2% construction, 10.0% production (2006-2010 5-year est.).
Income: Per capita income: $12,757 (2006-2010 5-year est.); Median household income: $18,397 (2006-2010 5-year est.); Average household income: $26,459 (2006-2010 5-year est.); Percent of households with income of $100,000 or more: 1.0% (2006-2010 5-year est.); Poverty rate: 36.7% (2006-2010 5-year est.).
Education: Percent of population age 25 and over with: High school diploma (including GED) or higher: 81.4% (2006-2010 5-year est.); Bachelor's degree or higher: 5.4% (2006-2010 5-year est.); Master's degree or higher: 2.1% (2006-2010 5-year est.).

School District(s)
Keystone Central SD (KG-12)
   2010-11 Enrollment: 4,394 . . . . (570) 893-4900
Housing: Homeownership rate: 58.7% (2010); Median home value: $34,800 (2006-2010 5-year est.); Median contract rent: $271 per month (2006-2010 5-year est.); Median year structure built: before 1940 (2006-2010 5-year est.).
Newspapers: The Record (Community news; Circulation 2,700)
Transportation: Commute to work: 85.9% car, 0.0% public transportation, 8.5% walk, 4.5% work from home (2006-2010 5-year est.); Travel time to work: 44.1% less than 15 minutes, 5.3% 15 to 30 minutes, 17.8% 30 to 45 minutes, 16.0% 45 to 60 minutes, 16.9% 60 minutes or more (2006-2010 5-year est.)
Additional Information Contacts
Clinton County Economic Partnership/Clinton County Chamber o . . . (570) 748-5782
   http://www.clintoncountyinfo.com

ROTE (CDP). Covers a land area of 1.088 square miles and a water area of 0 square miles. Located at 41.08° N. Lat; 77.41° W. Long. Elevation is 751 feet.
Population: n/a (1990); n/a (2000); 507 (2010); Density: 466.0 persons per square mile (2010); Race: 98.4% White, 0.0% Black, 0.6% Asian, 0.0% American Indian/Alaska Native, 0.0% Native Hawaiian/Other Pacific Islander, 1.0% Other, 1.4% Hispanic of any race (2010); Average household size: 2.44 (2010); Median age: 47.3 (2010); Males per 100 females: 101.2 (2010); Marriage status: 22.6% never married, 62.4% now married, 5.9% widowed, 9.1% divorced (2006-2010 5-year est.); Foreign born: 0.0% (2006-2010 5-year est.); Ancestry (includes multiple ancestries): 33.4% German, 13.7% American, 6.1% English, 6.1% Irish, 5.1% Russian (2006-2010 5-year est.).
Economy: Employment by occupation: 0.0% management, 4.3% professional, 9.4% services, 8.7% sales, 0.0% farming, 21.3% construction, 13.4% production (2006-2010 5-year est.).
Income: Per capita income: $20,865 (2006-2010 5-year est.); Median household income: $50,227 (2006-2010 5-year est.); Average household income: $51,638 (2006-2010 5-year est.); Percent of households with income of $100,000 or more: 7.3% (2006-2010 5-year est.); Poverty rate: 7.5% (2006-2010 5-year est.).
Education: Percent of population age 25 and over with: High school diploma (including GED) or higher: 80.3% (2006-2010 5-year est.);

Bachelor's degree or higher: 17.4% (2006-2010 5-year est.); Master's degree or higher: 8.9% (2006-2010 5-year est.).
Housing: Homeownership rate: 92.8% (2010); Median home value: $116,000 (2006-2010 5-year est.); Median contract rent: n/a per month (2006-2010 5-year est.); Median year structure built: 1976 (2006-2010 5-year est.).
Transportation: Commute to work: 96.0% car, 0.0% public transportation, 0.0% walk, 4.0% work from home (2006-2010 5-year est.); Travel time to work: 16.5% less than 15 minutes, 40.5% 15 to 30 minutes, 19.8% 30 to 45 minutes, 10.1% 45 to 60 minutes, 13.1% 60 minutes or more (2006-2010 5-year est.)

SALONA (unincorporated postal area)
Zip Code: 17767
   Covers a land area of 0.025 square miles and a water area of 0 square miles. Located at 41.08° N. Lat; 77.46° W. Long. Elevation is 614 feet. Population: 91 (2010); Density: 3,531.2 persons per square mile (2010); Race: 100.0% White, 0.0% Black, 0.0% Asian, 0.0% American Indian/Alaska Native, 0.0% Native Hawaiian/Other Pacific Islander, 0.0% Other, 0.0% Hispanic of any race (2010); Average household size: 2.39 (2010); Median age: 34.5 (2010); Males per 100 females: 85.7 (2010); Homeownership rate: 65.8% (2010)

SOUTH RENOVO (borough). Covers a land area of 0.204 square miles and a water area of 0.029 square miles. Located at 41.32° N. Lat; 77.74° W. Long. Elevation is 699 feet.
Population: 579 (1990); 557 (2000); 439 (2010); Density: 2,153.9 persons per square mile (2010); Race: 99.1% White, 0.0% Black, 0.2% Asian, 0.0% American Indian/Alaska Native, 0.2% Native Hawaiian/Other Pacific Islander, 0.5% Other, 0.5% Hispanic of any race (2010); Average household size: 2.23 (2010); Median age: 53.1 (2010); Males per 100 females: 86.8 (2010); Marriage status: 21.5% never married, 50.0% now married, 17.9% widowed, 10.5% divorced (2006-2010 5-year est.); Foreign born: 1.4% (2006-2010 5-year est.); Ancestry (includes multiple ancestries): 38.0% German, 18.6% Irish, 11.7% Italian, 8.3% Dutch, 7.2% English (2006-2010 5-year est.).
Economy: Single-family building permits issued: 0 (2011); Multi-family building permits issued: 0 (2011); Employment by occupation: 5.5% management, 0.5% professional, 14.6% services, 11.1% sales, 2.0% farming, 17.1% construction, 19.6% production (2006-2010 5-year est.).
Income: Per capita income: $16,895 (2006-2010 5-year est.); Median household income: $36,458 (2006-2010 5-year est.); Average household income: $41,966 (2006-2010 5-year est.); Percent of households with income of $100,000 or more: 3.8% (2006-2010 5-year est.); Poverty rate: 19.8% (2006-2010 5-year est.).
Education: Percent of population age 25 and over with: High school diploma (including GED) or higher: 77.0% (2006-2010 5-year est.); Bachelor's degree or higher: 11.1% (2006-2010 5-year est.); Master's degree or higher: 1.8% (2006-2010 5-year est.).
Housing: Homeownership rate: 88.0% (2010); Median home value: $38,900 (2006-2010 5-year est.); Median contract rent: $313 per month (2006-2010 5-year est.); Median year structure built: before 1940 (2006-2010 5-year est.).
Transportation: Commute to work: 93.9% car, 1.0% public transportation, 1.0% walk, 0.0% work from home (2006-2010 5-year est.); Travel time to work: 40.3% less than 15 minutes, 10.7% 15 to 30 minutes, 16.3% 30 to 45 minutes, 14.8% 45 to 60 minutes, 17.9% 60 minutes or more (2006-2010 5-year est.)

WAYNE (township). Covers a land area of 22.313 square miles and a water area of 0.548 square miles. Located at 41.14° N. Lat; 77.33° W. Long.
Population: 782 (1990); 1,363 (2000); 1,666 (2010); Density: 74.7 persons per square mile (2010); Race: 88.3% White, 7.1% Black, 0.4% Asian, 0.3% American Indian/Alaska Native, 0.2% Native Hawaiian/Other Pacific Islander, 3.7% Other, 3.8% Hispanic of any race (2010); Average household size: 2.44 (2010); Median age: 41.6 (2010); Males per 100 females: 136.3 (2010); Marriage status: 32.1% never married, 52.3% now married, 5.5% widowed, 10.1% divorced (2006-2010 5-year est.); Foreign born: 14.0% (2006-2010 5-year est.); Ancestry (includes multiple ancestries): 26.2% German, 14.0% Irish, 7.0% English, 4.7% Italian, 4.3% Dutch (2006-2010 5-year est.).
Economy: Single-family building permits issued: 2 (2011); Multi-family building permits issued: 0 (2011); Employment by occupation: 12.5%

management, 0.9% professional, 7.9% services, 18.5% sales, 0.9% farming, 9.9% construction, 10.6% production (2006-2010 5-year est.).
Income: Per capita income: $19,422 (2006-2010 5-year est.); Median household income: $46,023 (2006-2010 5-year est.); Average household income: $55,515 (2006-2010 5-year est.); Percent of households with income of $100,000 or more: 11.1% (2006-2010 5-year est.); Poverty rate: 8.0% (2006-2010 5-year est.).
Education: Percent of population age 25 and over with: High school diploma (including GED) or higher: 84.1% (2006-2010 5-year est.); Bachelor's degree or higher: 13.2% (2006-2010 5-year est.); Master's degree or higher: 4.5% (2006-2010 5-year est.).
Housing: Homeownership rate: 88.0% (2010); Median home value: $107,000 (2006-2010 5-year est.); Median contract rent: $428 per month (2006-2010 5-year est.); Median year structure built: 1985 (2006-2010 5-year est.).
Transportation: Commute to work: 95.7% car, 0.0% public transportation, 1.6% walk, 2.8% work from home (2006-2010 5-year est.); Travel time to work: 31.3% less than 15 minutes, 45.1% 15 to 30 minutes, 15.1% 30 to 45 minutes, 6.6% 45 to 60 minutes, 2.0% 60 minutes or more (2006-2010 5-year est.)
Additional Information Contacts
Williamsport/Lycoming Chamber of Commerce . . . . (570) 326-1971
   http://www.williamsport.org

WEST KEATING (township). Covers a land area of 38.128 square miles and a water area of 0.349 square miles. Located at 41.21° N. Lat; 78.02° W. Long.

Population: 34 (1990); 42 (2000); 29 (2010); Density: 0.8 persons per square mile (2010); Race: 100.0% White, 0.0% Black, 0.0% Asian, 0.0% American Indian/Alaska Native, 0.0% Native Hawaiian/Other Pacific Islander, 0.0% Other, 0.0% Hispanic of any race (2010); Average household size: 1.93 (2010); Median age: 62.3 (2010); Males per 100 females: 141.7 (2010); Marriage status: 15.0% never married, 85.0% now married, 0.0% widowed, 0.0% divorced (2006-2010 5-year est.); Foreign born: 0.0% (2006-2010 5-year est.); Ancestry (includes multiple ancestries): 30.0% German, 15.0% Dutch, 15.0% English (2006-2010 5-year est.).
Economy: Employment by occupation: 0.0% management, 0.0% professional, 0.0% services, 0.0% sales, 0.0% farming, 60.0% construction, 0.0% production (2006-2010 5-year est.).
Income: Per capita income: $16,430 (2006-2010 5-year est.); Median household income: $34,375 (2006-2010 5-year est.); Average household income: $34,444 (2006-2010 5-year est.); Percent of households with income of $100,000 or more: n/a (2006-2010 5-year est.); Poverty rate: 0.0% (2006-2010 5-year est.).
Education: Percent of population age 25 and over with: High school diploma (including GED) or higher: 65.0% (2006-2010 5-year est.); Bachelor's degree or higher: 0.0% (2006-2010 5-year est.); Master's degree or higher: 0.0% (2006-2010 5-year est.).
Housing: Homeownership rate: 86.7% (2010); Median home value: $162,500 (2006-2010 5-year est.); Median contract rent: n/a per month (2006-2010 5-year est.); Median year structure built: 1963 (2006-2010 5-year est.).
Transportation: Commute to work: 100.0% car, 0.0% public transportation, 0.0% walk, 0.0% work from home (2006-2010 5-year est.); Travel time to work: 60.0% less than 15 minutes, 0.0% 15 to 30 minutes, 0.0% 30 to 45 minutes, 0.0% 45 to 60 minutes, 40.0% 60 minutes or more (2006-2010 5-year est.)

WESTPORT (unincorporated postal area)
Zip Code: 17778
   Covers a land area of 87.303 square miles and a water area of 0.833 square miles. Located at 41.28° N. Lat; 77.98° W. Long. Population: 102 (2010); Density: 1.2 persons per square mile (2010); Race: 99.0% White, 0.0% Black, 0.0% Asian, 0.0% American Indian/Alaska Native, 0.0% Native Hawaiian/Other Pacific Islander, 1.0% Other, 0.0% Hispanic of any race (2010); Average household size: 1.85 (2010); Median age: 57.3 (2010); Males per 100 females: 137.2 (2010); Homeownership rate: 83.6% (2010)

WOODWARD (township). Covers a land area of 17.828 square miles and a water area of 0.384 square miles. Located at 41.19° N. Lat; 77.45° W. Long.
Population: 2,662 (1990); 2,296 (2000); 2,372 (2010); Density: 133.0 persons per square mile (2010); Race: 98.6% White, 0.6% Black, 0.2%

Asian, 0.0% American Indian/Alaska Native, 0.0% Native Hawaiian/Other Pacific Islander, 0.6% Other, 0.8% Hispanic of any race (2010); Average household size: 2.40 (2010); Median age: 45.8 (2010); Males per 100 females: 91.9 (2010); Marriage status: 18.5% never married, 64.5% now married, 7.1% widowed, 9.8% divorced (2006-2010 5-year est.); Foreign born: 1.5% (2006-2010 5-year est.); Ancestry (includes multiple ancestries): 36.2% German, 15.8% Irish, 14.8% American, 11.5% English, 10.4% Italian (2006-2010 5-year est.).
Economy: Single-family building permits issued: 3 (2011); Multi-family building permits issued: 0 (2011); Employment by occupation: 16.5% management, 3.6% professional, 10.8% services, 16.9% sales, 1.5% farming, 10.3% construction, 6.9% production (2006-2010 5-year est.).
Income: Per capita income: $25,983 (2006-2010 5-year est.); Median household income: $47,197 (2006-2010 5-year est.); Average household income: $59,931 (2006-2010 5-year est.); Percent of households with income of $100,000 or more: 19.3% (2006-2010 5-year est.); Poverty rate: 6.7% (2006-2010 5-year est.).
Education: Percent of population age 25 and over with: High school diploma (including GED) or higher: 91.8% (2006-2010 5-year est.); Bachelor's degree or higher: 26.0% (2006-2010 5-year est.); Master's degree or higher: 10.0% (2006-2010 5-year est.).
Housing: Homeownership rate: 84.6% (2010); Median home value: $124,800 (2006-2010 5-year est.); Median contract rent: $381 per month (2006-2010 5-year est.); Median year structure built: 1969 (2006-2010 5-year est.).
Safety: Violent crime rate: 0.0 per 10,000 population; Property crime rate: 357.1 per 10,000 population (2011).
Transportation: Commute to work: 92.6% car, 1.7% public transportation, 1.0% walk, 1.5% work from home (2006-2010 5-year est.); Travel time to work: 54.9% less than 15 minutes, 20.5% 15 to 30 minutes, 17.3% 30 to 45 minutes, 3.2% 45 to 60 minutes, 4.0% 60 minutes or more (2006-2010 5-year est.)
Additional Information Contacts
Clinton County Economic Partnership/Clinton County Chamber o . . . (570) 748-5782
   http://www.clintoncountyinfo.com

WOOLRICH (unincorporated postal area)
Zip Code: 17779
   Covers a land area of 1.454 square miles and a water area of 0.003 square miles. Located at 41.20° N. Lat; 77.37° W. Long. Elevation is 719 feet. Population: 235 (2010); Density: 161.6 persons per square mile (2010); Race: 98.7% White, 0.9% Black, 0.4% Asian, 0.0% American Indian/Alaska Native, 0.0% Native Hawaiian/Other Pacific Islander, 0.0% Other, 0.0% Hispanic of any race (2010); Average household size: 1.96 (2010); Median age: 50.9 (2010); Males per 100 females: 95.8 (2010); Homeownership rate: 55.8% (2010)

Columbia County

Located in east central Pennsylvania; hilly area on the Pocono Plateau; drained by the Susquehanna River. Covers a land area of 483.108 square miles, a water area of 7.051 square miles, and is located in the Eastern Time Zone at 41.05° N. Lat., 76.40° W. Long. The county was founded in 1813. County seat is Bloomsburg.

Columbia County is part of the Bloomsburg-Berwick, PA Micropolitan Statistical Area. The entire metro area includes: Columbia County, PA; Montour County, PA

Population: 63,202 (1990); 64,151 (2000); 67,295 (2010); Race: 95.4% White, 1.9% Black, 0.8% Asian, 0.1% American Indian/Alaska Native, 0.0% Native Hawaiian/Other Pacific Islander, 1.8% Other, 2.0% Hispanic of any race (2010); Density: 139.3 persons per square mile (2010); Average household size: 2.38 (2010); Median age: 39.5 (2010); Males per 100 females: 92.2 (2010).
Religion: Six largest groups: 12.7% Methodist/Pietist, 11.9% Catholicism, 7.3% Lutheran, 4.2% Non-Denominational, 4.1% Baptist, 2.8% Presbyterian-Reformed (2010)
Economy: Unemployment rate: 8.1% (August 2012); Total civilian labor force: 36,709 (August 2012); Leading industries: 24.4% manufacturing; 18.2% health care and social assistance; 17.2% retail trade (2010); Farms: 962 totaling 122,621 acres (2007); Companies that employ 500 or more persons: 2 (2010); Companies that employ 100 to 499 persons: 35 (2010); Companies that employ less than 100 persons: 1,398 (2010); Black-owned

businesses: n/a (2007); Hispanic-owned businesses: n/a (2007); Asian-owned businesses: n/a (2007); Women-owned businesses: 1,239 (2007); Retail sales per capita: $14,789 (2010). Single-family building permits issued: 71 (2011); Multi-family building permits issued: 18 (2011).

Income: Per capita income: $22,403 (2006-2010 5-year est.); Median household income: $42,788 (2006-2010 5-year est.); Average household income: $55,485 (2006-2010 5-year est.); Percent of households with income of $100,000 or more: 11.3% (2006-2010 5-year est.); Poverty rate: 13.7% (2006-2010 5-year est.); Bankruptcy rate: 1.70% (2011).

Education: Percent of population age 25 and over with: High school diploma (including GED) or higher: 86.7% (2006-2010 5-year est.); Bachelor's degree or higher: 18.3% (2006-2010 5-year est.); Master's degree or higher: 6.6% (2006-2010 5-year est.).

Housing: Homeownership rate: 69.4% (2010); Median home value: $118,800 (2006-2010 5-year est.); Median contract rent: $494 per month (2006-2010 5-year est.); Median year structure built: 1958 (2006-2010 5-year est.).

Health: Birth rate: 91.3 per 10,000 population (2011); Death rate: 104.2 per 10,000 population (2011); Age-adjusted cancer mortality rate: 182.3 deaths per 100,000 population (2009); Number of physicians: 19.9 per 10,000 population (2010); Hospital beds: 63.5 per 10,000 population (2008); Hospital admissions: 1,058.3 per 10,000 population (2008).

Elections: 2012 Presidential election results: 42.7% Obama, 55.6% Romney

Additional Information Contacts

Columbia County Government . . . . (570) 389-5600
http://www.columbiapa.org

Columbia County Communities

ALMEDIA (CDP). Covers a land area of 0.571 square miles and a water area of 0.207 square miles. Located at 41.01° N. Lat; 76.38° W. Long. Elevation is 499 feet.

Population: 1,134 (1990); 1,056 (2000); 1,078 (2010); Density: 1,888.7 persons per square mile (2010); Race: 97.6% White, 0.8% Black, 0.6% Asian, 0.0% American Indian/Alaska Native, 0.0% Native Hawaiian/Other Pacific Islander, 1.0% Other, 0.4% Hispanic of any race (2010); Average household size: 2.24 (2010); Median age: 49.4 (2010); Males per 100 females: 92.5 (2010); Marriage status: 17.7% never married, 58.6% now married, 6.9% widowed, 16.8% divorced (2006-2010 5-year est.); Foreign born: 0.0% (2006-2010 5-year est.); Ancestry (includes multiple ancestries): 37.9% German, 14.5% Irish, 13.9% English, 8.1% Italian, 6.6% American (2006-2010 5-year est.).

Economy: Employment by occupation: 1.9% management, 0.0% professional, 8.1% services, 18.3% sales, 9.6% farming, 8.9% construction, 8.5% production (2006-2010 5-year est.).

Income: Per capita income: $25,726 (2006-2010 5-year est.); Median household income: $44,773 (2006-2010 5-year est.); Average household income: $57,251 (2006-2010 5-year est.); Percent of households with income of $100,000 or more: 18.6% (2006-2010 5-year est.); Poverty rate: 6.3% (2006-2010 5-year est.).

Education: Percent of population age 25 and over with: High school diploma (including GED) or higher: 87.9% (2006-2010 5-year est.); Bachelor's degree or higher: 14.6% (2006-2010 5-year est.); Master's degree or higher: 7.1% (2006-2010 5-year est.).

Housing: Homeownership rate: 80.9% (2010); Median home value: $115,600 (2006-2010 5-year est.); Median contract rent: $526 per month (2006-2010 5-year est.); Median year structure built: 1958 (2006-2010 5-year est.).

Transportation: Commute to work: 96.6% car, 0.0% public transportation, 2.2% walk, 1.2% work from home (2006-2010 5-year est.); Travel time to work: 51.5% less than 15 minutes, 27.4% 15 to 30 minutes, 12.4% 30 to 45 minutes, 8.7% 45 to 60 minutes, 0.0% 60 minutes or more (2006-2010 5-year est.)

ARISTES (CDP). Covers a land area of 0.372 square miles and a water area of 0.002 square miles. Located at 40.81° N. Lat; 76.34° W. Long. Elevation is 1,716 feet.

Population: 303 (1990); 230 (2000); 311 (2010); Density: 835.6 persons per square mile (2010); Race: 100.0% White, 0.0% Black, 0.0% Asian, 0.0% American Indian/Alaska Native, 0.0% Native Hawaiian/Other Pacific Islander, 0.0% Other, 0.0% Hispanic of any race (2010); Average household size: 2.27 (2010); Median age: 47.3 (2010); Males per 100 females: 92.0 (2010); Marriage status: 16.2% never married, 78.9% now married, 3.6% widowed, 1.2% divorced (2006-2010 5-year est.); Foreign

born: 2.4% (2006-2010 5-year est.); Ancestry (includes multiple ancestries): 46.6% German, 27.2% Irish, 13.1% Polish, 9.0% Russian, 8.6% Dutch (2006-2010 5-year est.).

Economy: Employment by occupation: 0.0% management, 2.1% professional, 4.3% services, 4.3% sales, 2.1% farming, 16.4% construction, 23.6% production (2006-2010 5-year est.).

Income: Per capita income: $20,333 (2006-2010 5-year est.); Median household income: $49,375 (2006-2010 5-year est.); Average household income: $52,953 (2006-2010 5-year est.); Percent of households with income of $100,000 or more: 13.3% (2006-2010 5-year est.); Poverty rate: 4.1% (2006-2010 5-year est.).

Education: Percent of population age 25 and over with: High school diploma (including GED) or higher: 88.8% (2006-2010 5-year est.); Bachelor's degree or higher: 6.5% (2006-2010 5-year est.); Master's degree or higher: 5.1% (2006-2010 5-year est.).

Housing: Homeownership rate: 89.8% (2010); Median home value: $70,000 (2006-2010 5-year est.); Median contract rent: $344 per month (2006-2010 5-year est.); Median year structure built: before 1940 (2006-2010 5-year est.).

Transportation: Commute to work: 97.1% car, 0.0% public transportation, 2.9% walk, 0.0% work from home (2006-2010 5-year est.); Travel time to work: 17.9% less than 15 minutes, 28.6% 15 to 30 minutes, 38.6% 30 to 45 minutes, 12.9% 45 to 60 minutes, 2.1% 60 minutes or more (2006-2010 5-year est.)

BEAVER (township). Covers a land area of 35.394 square miles and a water area of 0.396 square miles. Located at 40.96° N. Lat; 76.27° W. Long.

Population: 928 (1990); 885 (2000); 917 (2010); Density: 25.9 persons per square mile (2010); Race: 97.7% White, 0.0% Black, 0.7% Asian, 0.9% American Indian/Alaska Native, 0.0% Native Hawaiian/Other Pacific Islander, 0.7% Other, 1.5% Hispanic of any race (2010); Average household size: 2.57 (2010); Median age: 44.8 (2010); Males per 100 females: 103.3 (2010); Marriage status: 21.9% never married, 60.9% now married, 6.0% widowed, 11.1% divorced (2006-2010 5-year est.); Foreign born: 0.3% (2006-2010 5-year est.); Ancestry (includes multiple ancestries): 42.1% German, 13.3% Dutch, 11.5% Polish, 9.6% Irish, 8.1% English (2006-2010 5-year est.).

Economy: Single-family building permits issued: 1 (2011); Multi-family building permits issued: 0 (2011); Employment by occupation: 8.1% management, 2.5% professional, 4.3% services, 21.3% sales, 2.9% farming, 20.5% construction, 15.5% production (2006-2010 5-year est.).

Income: Per capita income: $21,056 (2006-2010 5-year est.); Median household income: $46,359 (2006-2010 5-year est.); Average household income: $56,576 (2006-2010 5-year est.); Percent of households with income of $100,000 or more: 17.2% (2006-2010 5-year est.); Poverty rate: 8.6% (2006-2010 5-year est.).

Education: Percent of population age 25 and over with: High school diploma (including GED) or higher: 90.0% (2006-2010 5-year est.); Bachelor's degree or higher: 8.7% (2006-2010 5-year est.); Master's degree or higher: 2.7% (2006-2010 5-year est.).

Housing: Homeownership rate: 90.2% (2010); Median home value: $123,100 (2006-2010 5-year est.); Median contract rent: $413 per month (2006-2010 5-year est.); Median year structure built: 1976 (2006-2010 5-year est.).

Transportation: Commute to work: 92.9% car, 0.0% public transportation, 1.7% walk, 4.2% work from home (2006-2010 5-year est.); Travel time to work: 14.4% less than 15 minutes, 37.3% 15 to 30 minutes, 36.5% 30 to 45 minutes, 5.9% 45 to 60 minutes, 5.9% 60 minutes or more (2006-2010 5-year est.)

BENTON (borough). Aka Derk. Covers a land area of 0.597 square miles and a water area of 0.018 square miles. Located at 41.20° N. Lat; 76.38° W. Long. Elevation is 764 feet.

Population: 958 (1990); 955 (2000); 824 (2010); Density: 1,380.4 persons per square mile (2010); Race: 98.7% White, 0.2% Black, 0.5% Asian, 0.0% American Indian/Alaska Native, 0.0% Native Hawaiian/Other Pacific Islander, 0.6% Other, 1.5% Hispanic of any race (2010); Average household size: 2.27 (2010); Median age: 42.6 (2010); Males per 100 females: 86.4 (2010); Marriage status: 29.3% never married, 46.9% now married, 9.6% widowed, 14.1% divorced (2006-2010 5-year est.); Foreign born: 2.2% (2006-2010 5-year est.); Ancestry (includes multiple ancestries): 36.6% German, 15.1% Irish, 9.6% Polish, 8.8% Italian, 6.8% Scottish (2006-2010 5-year est.).

Economy: Single-family building permits issued: 0 (2011); Multi-family building permits issued: 0 (2011); Employment by occupation: 7.8% management, 2.2% professional, 19.4% services, 21.1% sales, 4.4% farming, 13.6% construction, 8.6% production (2006-2010 5-year est.).
Income: Per capita income: $18,451 (2006-2010 5-year est.); Median household income: $33,977 (2006-2010 5-year est.); Average household income: $44,103 (2006-2010 5-year est.); Percent of households with income of $100,000 or more: 13.4% (2006-2010 5-year est.); Poverty rate: 13.2% (2006-2010 5-year est.).
Education: Percent of population age 25 and over with: High school diploma (including GED) or higher: 85.1% (2006-2010 5-year est.); Bachelor's degree or higher: 10.4% (2006-2010 5-year est.); Master's degree or higher: 3.7% (2006-2010 5-year est.).
School District(s)
Benton Area SD (KG-12)
   2010-11 Enrollment: 709. . . . . (570) 925-6651
Housing: Homeownership rate: 59.3% (2010); Median home value: $108,700 (2006-2010 5-year est.); Median contract rent: $426 per month (2006-2010 5-year est.); Median year structure built: before 1940 (2006-2010 5-year est.).
Transportation: Commute to work: 79.5% car, 0.0% public transportation, 13.8% walk, 5.9% work from home (2006-2010 5-year est.); Travel time to work: 37.6% less than 15 minutes, 19.7% 15 to 30 minutes, 32.2% 30 to 45 minutes, 6.3% 45 to 60 minutes, 4.2% 60 minutes or more (2006-2010 5-year est.)

BENTON (township). Aka Derk. Covers a land area of 19.672 square miles and a water area of 0.263 square miles. Located at 41.20° N. Lat; 76.37° W. Long. Elevation is 764 feet.
Population: 1,094 (1990); 1,216 (2000); 1,245 (2010); Density: 63.3 persons per square mile (2010); Race: 99.4% White, 0.0% Black, 0.1% Asian, 0.1% American Indian/Alaska Native, 0.0% Native Hawaiian/Other Pacific Islander, 0.4% Other, 0.2% Hispanic of any race (2010); Average household size: 2.39 (2010); Median age: 46.1 (2010); Males per 100 females: 103.4 (2010); Marriage status: 20.3% never married, 61.9% now married, 8.4% widowed, 9.4% divorced (2006-2010 5-year est.); Foreign born: 0.5% (2006-2010 5-year est.); Ancestry (includes multiple ancestries): 34.2% German, 15.1% Irish, 13.3% English, 10.1% Dutch, 8.6% Italian (2006-2010 5-year est.).
Economy: Single-family building permits issued: 2 (2011); Multi-family building permits issued: 0 (2011); Employment by occupation: 5.7% management, 1.7% professional, 16.2% services, 8.0% sales, 7.4% farming, 13.4% construction, 8.7% production (2006-2010 5-year est.).
Income: Per capita income: $22,760 (2006-2010 5-year est.); Median household income: $43,529 (2006-2010 5-year est.); Average household income: $50,703 (2006-2010 5-year est.); Percent of households with income of $100,000 or more: 8.1% (2006-2010 5-year est.); Poverty rate: 7.2% (2006-2010 5-year est.).
Education: Percent of population age 25 and over with: High school diploma (including GED) or higher: 87.0% (2006-2010 5-year est.); Bachelor's degree or higher: 14.0% (2006-2010 5-year est.); Master's degree or higher: 5.0% (2006-2010 5-year est.).
Housing: Homeownership rate: 87.0% (2010); Median home value: $123,000 (2006-2010 5-year est.); Median contract rent: $440 per month (2006-2010 5-year est.); Median year structure built: 1971 (2006-2010 5-year est.).
Transportation: Commute to work: 89.6% car, 0.6% public transportation, 1.5% walk, 8.3% work from home (2006-2010 5-year est.); Travel time to work: 14.6% less than 15 minutes, 24.3% 15 to 30 minutes, 35.8% 30 to 45 minutes, 10.1% 45 to 60 minutes, 15.2% 60 minutes or more (2006-2010 5-year est.)
Additional Information Contacts
Columbia Montour Chamber of Commerce. . . . . (570) 784-2522
   http://www.bloomsburg.org

BERWICK (borough). Covers a land area of 3.076 square miles and a water area of 0.177 square miles. Located at 41.06° N. Lat; 76.25° W. Long. Elevation is 558 feet.
History: Settled 1783, incorporated 1818.
Population: 10,976 (1990); 10,774 (2000); 10,477 (2010); Density: 3,405.6 persons per square mile (2010); Race: 94.4% White, 1.5% Black, 0.8% Asian, 0.2% American Indian/Alaska Native, 0.0% Native Hawaiian/Other Pacific Islander, 3.1% Other, 3.7% Hispanic of any race (2010); Average household size: 2.29 (2010); Median age: 40.3 (2010); Males per 100 females: 91.3 (2010); Marriage status: 29.7% never

married, 45.3% now married, 11.3% widowed, 13.7% divorced (2006-2010 5-year est.); Foreign born: 1.7% (2006-2010 5-year est.); Ancestry (includes multiple ancestries): 29.9% German, 12.5% Irish, 12.5% Italian, 8.2% English, 7.8% Dutch (2006-2010 5-year est.).
Economy: Single-family building permits issued: 2 (2011); Multi-family building permits issued: 0 (2011); Employment by occupation: 2.2% management, 1.7% professional, 7.3% services, 16.0% sales, 5.6% farming, 8.7% construction, 11.3% production (2006-2010 5-year est.).
Income: Per capita income: $17,206 (2006-2010 5-year est.); Median household income: $32,103 (2006-2010 5-year est.); Average household income: $39,232 (2006-2010 5-year est.); Percent of households with income of $100,000 or more: 4.0% (2006-2010 5-year est.); Poverty rate: 13.7% (2006-2010 5-year est.).
Education: Percent of population age 25 and over with: High school diploma (including GED) or higher: 81.5% (2006-2010 5-year est.); Bachelor's degree or higher: 9.9% (2006-2010 5-year est.); Master's degree or higher: 2.9% (2006-2010 5-year est.).
School District(s)
Berwick Area SD (KG-12)
   2010-11 Enrollment: 3,014 . . . . (570) 759-6400
Berwick Area SD (KG-12)
   2010-11 Enrollment: 3,014 . . . . (570) 759-6400
Housing: Homeownership rate: 58.1% (2010); Median home value: $86,500 (2006-2010 5-year est.); Median contract rent: $442 per month (2006-2010 5-year est.); Median year structure built: 1941 (2006-2010 5-year est.).
Hospitals: Berwick Hospital Center (130 beds)
Safety: Violent crime rate: 34.3 per 10,000 population; Property crime rate: 412.9 per 10,000 population (2011).
Transportation: Commute to work: 90.1% car, 0.0% public transportation, 3.3% walk, 4.7% work from home (2006-2010 5-year est.); Travel time to work: 49.8% less than 15 minutes, 28.5% 15 to 30 minutes, 13.5% 30 to 45 minutes, 4.2% 45 to 60 minutes, 3.9% 60 minutes or more (2006-2010 5-year est.)
Additional Information Contacts
Borough of Berwick. . . . . (570) 752-2723
   http://www.berwickpa.com
Columbia Montour Chamber of Commerce. . . . . (570) 784-2522
   http://www.bloomsburg.org

BLOOMSBURG (town). County seat. Covers a land area of 4.350 square miles and a water area of 0.338 square miles. Located at 41.00° N. Lat; 76.46° W. Long. Elevation is 531 feet.
History: Bloomsburg was laid out in 1802. It was incorporated as a town.
Population: 12,439 (1990); 12,375 (2000); 14,855 (2010); Density: 3,414.8 persons per square mile (2010); Race: 89.6% White, 6.2% Black, 1.6% Asian, 0.1% American Indian/Alaska Native, 0.0% Native Hawaiian/Other Pacific Islander, 2.5% Other, 3.4% Hispanic of any race (2010); Average household size: 2.30 (2010); Median age: 22.0 (2010); Males per 100 females: 82.5 (2010); Marriage status: 66.1% never married, 22.8% now married, 3.6% widowed, 7.5% divorced (2006-2010 5-year est.); Foreign born: 2.4% (2006-2010 5-year est.); Ancestry (includes multiple ancestries): 33.6% German, 16.5% Irish, 10.4% English, 9.6% Italian, 7.9% Polish (2006-2010 5-year est.).
Economy: Single-family building permits issued: 7 (2011); Multi-family building permits issued: 18 (2011); Employment by occupation: 5.9% management, 2.1% professional, 21.4% services, 20.5% sales, 4.3% farming, 3.8% construction, 3.6% production (2006-2010 5-year est.).
Income: Per capita income: $14,550 (2006-2010 5-year est.); Median household income: $29,978 (2006-2010 5-year est.); Average household income: $41,482 (2006-2010 5-year est.); Percent of households with income of $100,000 or more: 7.1% (2006-2010 5-year est.); Poverty rate: 33.8% (2006-2010 5-year est.).
Education: Percent of population age 25 and over with: High school diploma (including GED) or higher: 93.1% (2006-2010 5-year est.); Bachelor's degree or higher: 26.9% (2006-2010 5-year est.); Master's degree or higher: 9.0% (2006-2010 5-year est.).
School District(s)
Bloomsburg Area SD (KG-12)
   2010-11 Enrollment: 1,645 . . . . (570) 784-5000
Central Columbia SD (KG-12)
   2010-11 Enrollment: 1,953 . . . . (570) 784-2850
Columbia-Montour Avts (09-12)
   2010-11 Enrollment: 633. . . . . (570) 784-8040

Susq-Cyber CS (09-12)
    2010-11 Enrollment: 192. . . . . (570) 245-0252
Four-year College(s)
Bloomsburg University of Pennsylvania (Public)
    Fall 2010 Enrollment: 9,772 . . . . (570) 389-4000
    2011-12 Tuition: In-state $8,082; Out-of-state $17,620
Housing: Homeownership rate: 32.7% (2010); Median home value:
$110,000 (2006-2010 5-year est.); Median contract rent: $527 per month
(2006-2010 5-year est.); Median year structure built: before 1940
(2006-2010 5-year est.).
Hospitals: Bloomsburg Hospital (117 beds)
Safety: Violent crime rate: 17.4 per 10,000 population; Property crime rate:
188.6 per 10,000 population (2011).
Newspapers: Press-Enterprise (Local news; Circulation 23,000)
Transportation: Commute to work: 75.7% car, 1.5% public transportation,
17.8% walk, 4.5% work from home (2006-2010 5-year est.); Travel time to
work: 60.3% less than 15 minutes, 25.8% 15 to 30 minutes, 8.3% 30 to 45
minutes, 2.6% 45 to 60 minutes, 3.0% 60 minutes or more (2006-2010
5-year est.)
Additional Information Contacts
Columbia Montour Chamber of Commerce. . . . . (570) 784-2522
    http://www.bloomsburg.org
Town of Bloomsburg . . . . (570) 784-7703
    http://www.bloomsburgpa.org

BRIAR CREEK (borough). Covers a land area of 1.650 square miles
and a water area of 0.191 square miles. Located at 41.05° N. Lat; 76.28°
W. Long. Elevation is 495 feet.
Population: 616 (1990); 651 (2000); 660 (2010); Density: 399.9 persons
per square mile (2010); Race: 97.4% White, 0.3% Black, 0.5% Asian,
0.2% American Indian/Alaska Native, 0.0% Native Hawaiian/Other Pacific
Islander, 1.6% Other, 0.6% Hispanic of any race (2010); Average
household size: 2.14 (2010); Median age: 49.3 (2010); Males per 100
females: 78.4 (2010); Marriage status: 15.1% never married, 54.9% now
married, 8.9% widowed, 21.1% divorced (2006-2010 5-year est.); Foreign
born: 0.0% (2006-2010 5-year est.); Ancestry (includes multiple
ancestries): 33.2% German, 20.3% Italian, 14.9% Irish, 10.6% English,
10.1% Polish (2006-2010 5-year est.).
Economy: Single-family building permits issued: 0 (2011); Multi-family
building permits issued: 0 (2011); Employment by occupation: 6.7%
management, 0.0% professional, 29.1% services, 4.2% sales, 0.0%
farming, 21.2% construction, 16.4% production (2006-2010 5-year est.).
Income: Per capita income: $15,747 (2006-2010 5-year est.); Median
household income: $27,206 (2006-2010 5-year est.); Average household
income: $29,776 (2006-2010 5-year est.); Percent of households with
income of $100,000 or more: 2.4% (2006-2010 5-year est.); Poverty rate:
32.5% (2006-2010 5-year est.).
Education: Percent of population age 25 and over with: High school
diploma (including GED) or higher: 67.6% (2006-2010 5-year est.);
Bachelor's degree or higher: 12.5% (2006-2010 5-year est.); Master's
degree or higher: 3.0% (2006-2010 5-year est.).
Housing: Homeownership rate: 61.9% (2010); Median home value:
$71,700 (2006-2010 5-year est.); Median contract rent: $463 per month
(2006-2010 5-year est.); Median year structure built: 1981 (2006-2010
5-year est.).
Transportation: Commute to work: 89.2% car, 0.0% public transportation,
0.0% walk, 10.8% work from home (2006-2010 5-year est.); Travel time to
work: 47.5% less than 15 minutes, 36.2% 15 to 30 minutes, 13.5% 30 to
45 minutes, 0.0% 45 to 60 minutes, 2.8% 60 minutes or more (2006-2010
5-year est.)

BRIAR CREEK (township). Covers a land area of 20.955 square
miles and a water area of 0.221 square miles. Located at 41.09° N. Lat;
76.27° W. Long. Elevation is 495 feet.
Population: 3,010 (1990); 3,061 (2000); 3,016 (2010); Density: 143.9
persons per square mile (2010); Race: 97.7% White, 0.3% Black, 0.5%
Asian, 0.1% American Indian/Alaska Native, 0.0% Native Hawaiian/Other
Pacific Islander, 1.4% Other, 1.0% Hispanic of any race (2010); Average
household size: 2.43 (2010); Median age: 46.5 (2010); Males per 100
females: 96.1 (2010); Marriage status: 20.7% never married, 65.4% now
married, 7.9% widowed, 6.1% divorced (2006-2010 5-year est.); Foreign
born: 1.5% (2006-2010 5-year est.); Ancestry (includes multiple
ancestries): 45.4% German, 9.7% Irish, 8.7% American, 7.6% Dutch, 6.7%
English (2006-2010 5-year est.).

Economy: Single-family building permits issued: 4 (2011); Multi-family
building permits issued: 0 (2011); Employment by occupation: 8.4%
management, 4.1% professional, 9.3% services, 18.7% sales, 1.7%
farming, 6.8% construction, 9.0% production (2006-2010 5-year est.).
Income: Per capita income: $25,108 (2006-2010 5-year est.); Median
household income: $56,419 (2006-2010 5-year est.); Average household
income: $59,550 (2006-2010 5-year est.); Percent of households with
income of $100,000 or more: 19.2% (2006-2010 5-year est.); Poverty rate:
9.9% (2006-2010 5-year est.).
Education: Percent of population age 25 and over with: High school
diploma (including GED) or higher: 88.0% (2006-2010 5-year est.);
Bachelor's degree or higher: 10.8% (2006-2010 5-year est.); Master's
degree or higher: 3.7% (2006-2010 5-year est.).
Housing: Homeownership rate: 86.5% (2010); Median home value:
$123,800 (2006-2010 5-year est.); Median contract rent: $425 per month
(2006-2010 5-year est.); Median year structure built: 1971 (2006-2010
5-year est.).
Transportation: Commute to work: 95.4% car, 1.5% public transportation,
0.7% walk, 2.4% work from home (2006-2010 5-year est.); Travel time to
work: 50.9% less than 15 minutes, 22.4% 15 to 30 minutes, 18.8% 30 to
45 minutes, 5.6% 45 to 60 minutes, 2.2% 60 minutes or more (2006-2010
5-year est.)
Additional Information Contacts
Columbia Montour Chamber of Commerce. . . . . (570) 784-2522
    http://www.bloomsburg.org

BUCKHORN (CDP). Covers a land area of 0.672 square miles and a
water area of 0.005 square miles. Located at 41.02° N. Lat; 76.49° W.
Long. Elevation is 600 feet.
Population: 144 (1990); 176 (2000); 318 (2010); Density: 472.9 persons
per square mile (2010); Race: 94.0% White, 0.9% Black, 3.5% Asian,
0.0% American Indian/Alaska Native, 0.0% Native Hawaiian/Other Pacific
Islander, 1.6% Other, 2.8% Hispanic of any race (2010); Average
household size: 2.55 (2010); Median age: 45.0 (2010); Males per 100
females: 92.7 (2010); Marriage status: 32.8% never married, 61.5% now
married, 2.0% widowed, 3.7% divorced (2006-2010 5-year est.); Foreign
born: 0.0% (2006-2010 5-year est.); Ancestry (includes multiple
ancestries): 50.8% German, 12.1% Dutch, 7.0% Scottish, 6.7% Polish,
5.1% Welsh (2006-2010 5-year est.).
Economy: Employment by occupation: 13.9% management, 0.0%
professional, 9.5% services, 10.8% sales, 1.9% farming, 2.5%
construction, 15.2% production (2006-2010 5-year est.).
Income: Per capita income: $25,373 (2006-2010 5-year est.); Median
household income: $73,875 (2006-2010 5-year est.); Average household
income: $84,777 (2006-2010 5-year est.); Percent of households with
income of $100,000 or more: 25.1% (2006-2010 5-year est.); Poverty rate:
0.0% (2006-2010 5-year est.).
Education: Percent of population age 25 and over with: High school
diploma (including GED) or higher: 98.2% (2006-2010 5-year est.);
Bachelor's degree or higher: 33.7% (2006-2010 5-year est.); Master's
degree or higher: 19.6% (2006-2010 5-year est.).
Housing: Homeownership rate: 92.0% (2010); Median home value:
$122,500 (2006-2010 5-year est.); Median contract rent: n/a per month
(2006-2010 5-year est.); Median year structure built: 1953 (2006-2010
5-year est.).
Transportation: Commute to work: 96.2% car, 0.0% public transportation,
0.0% walk, 3.8% work from home (2006-2010 5-year est.); Travel time to
work: 29.6% less than 15 minutes, 40.1% 15 to 30 minutes, 30.3% 30 to
45 minutes, 0.0% 45 to 60 minutes, 0.0% 60 minutes or more (2006-2010
5-year est.)

CATAWISSA (borough). Covers a land area of 0.513 square miles
and a water area of 0.024 square miles. Located at 40.95° N. Lat; 76.46°
W. Long. Elevation is 518 feet.
Population: 1,683 (1990); 1,589 (2000); 1,552 (2010); Density: 3,023.3
persons per square mile (2010); Race: 97.1% White, 0.5% Black, 0.2%
Asian, 0.1% American Indian/Alaska Native, 0.3% Native Hawaiian/Other
Pacific Islander, 1.8% Other, 1.6% Hispanic of any race (2010); Average
household size: 2.21 (2010); Median age: 37.0 (2010); Males per 100
females: 85.2 (2010); Marriage status: 35.3% never married, 44.8% now
married, 7.2% widowed, 12.7% divorced (2006-2010 5-year est.); Foreign
born: 0.2% (2006-2010 5-year est.); Ancestry (includes multiple
ancestries): 38.4% German, 20.0% Irish, 9.7% Italian, 8.9% Dutch, 7.7%
English (2006-2010 5-year est.).

Economy: Single-family building permits issued: 0 (2011); Multi-family building permits issued: 0 (2011); Employment by occupation: 5.1% management, 2.0% professional, 13.5% services, 14.5% sales, 4.2% farming, 11.4% construction, 7.7% production (2006-2010 5-year est.).
Income: Per capita income: $18,478 (2006-2010 5-year est.); Median household income: $37,344 (2006-2010 5-year est.); Average household income: $41,540 (2006-2010 5-year est.); Percent of households with income of $100,000 or more: 3.8% (2006-2010 5-year est.); Poverty rate: 16.7% (2006-2010 5-year est.).
Education: Percent of population age 25 and over with: High school diploma (including GED) or higher: 84.0% (2006-2010 5-year est.); Bachelor's degree or higher: 14.6% (2006-2010 5-year est.); Master's degree or higher: 4.6% (2006-2010 5-year est.).

School District(s)
Southern Columbia Area SD (KG-12)
   2010-11 Enrollment: 1,428 . . . . (570) 356-2331
Housing: Homeownership rate: 53.8% (2010); Median home value: $84,800 (2006-2010 5-year est.); Median contract rent: $442 per month (2006-2010 5-year est.); Median year structure built: before 1940 (2006-2010 5-year est.).
Safety: Violent crime rate: 25.7 per 10,000 population; Property crime rate: 366.1 per 10,000 population (2011).
Transportation: Commute to work: 95.2% car, 0.0% public transportation, 2.2% walk, 1.3% work from home (2006-2010 5-year est.); Travel time to work: 24.3% less than 15 minutes, 49.2% 15 to 30 minutes, 17.5% 30 to 45 minutes, 5.2% 45 to 60 minutes, 3.8% 60 minutes or more (2006-2010 5-year est.)
Additional Information Contacts
Columbia Montour Chamber of Commerce. . . . . (570) 784-2522
   http://www.bloomsburg.org

CATAWISSA (township). Covers a land area of 12.363 square miles and a water area of 0.517 square miles. Located at 40.95° N. Lat; 76.44° W. Long. Elevation is 518 feet.
History: Several covered bridges to South on Roaring Creek and its South Branch. Laid out 1787, incorporated 1892.
Population: 1,037 (1990); 944 (2000); 932 (2010); Density: 75.4 persons per square mile (2010); Race: 98.4% White, 0.1% Black, 0.9% Asian, 0.0% American Indian/Alaska Native, 0.0% Native Hawaiian/Other Pacific Islander, 0.6% Other, 0.2% Hispanic of any race (2010); Average household size: 2.44 (2010); Median age: 48.4 (2010); Males per 100 females: 92.2 (2010); Marriage status: 18.7% never married, 66.5% now married, 8.4% widowed, 6.4% divorced (2006-2010 5-year est.); Foreign born: 0.8% (2006-2010 5-year est.); Ancestry (includes multiple ancestries): 48.8% German, 14.8% Irish, 9.6% Polish, 8.7% English, 6.7% Dutch (2006-2010 5-year est.).
Economy: Employment by occupation: 7.6% management, 5.9% professional, 8.7% services, 14.0% sales, 4.9% farming, 7.6% construction, 5.7% production (2006-2010 5-year est.).
Income: Per capita income: $32,103 (2006-2010 5-year est.); Median household income: $57,000 (2006-2010 5-year est.); Average household income: $76,723 (2006-2010 5-year est.); Percent of households with income of $100,000 or more: 18.9% (2006-2010 5-year est.); Poverty rate: 5.4% (2006-2010 5-year est.).
Education: Percent of population age 25 and over with: High school diploma (including GED) or higher: 88.2% (2006-2010 5-year est.); Bachelor's degree or higher: 20.2% (2006-2010 5-year est.); Master's degree or higher: 6.2% (2006-2010 5-year est.).
Housing: Homeownership rate: 93.4% (2010); Median home value: $144,400 (2006-2010 5-year est.); Median contract rent: n/a per month (2006-2010 5-year est.); Median year structure built: 1972 (2006-2010 5-year est.).
Transportation: Commute to work: 95.1% car, 0.0% public transportation, 0.0% walk, 4.5% work from home (2006-2010 5-year est.); Travel time to work: 26.5% less than 15 minutes, 50.0% 15 to 30 minutes, 19.5% 30 to 45 minutes, 2.2% 45 to 60 minutes, 1.8% 60 minutes or more (2006-2010 5-year est.)

CENTRALIA (borough). Covers a land area of 0.239 square miles and a water area of <.001 square miles. Located at 40.80° N. Lat; 76.34° W. Long. Elevation is 1,460 feet.
History: Former anthracite-coal center. Incorporated 1866.
Population: 63 (1990); 21 (2000); 10 (2010); Density: 41.9 persons per square mile (2010); Race: 100.0% White, 0.0% Black, 0.0% Asian, 0.0% American Indian/Alaska Native, 0.0% Native Hawaiian/Other Pacific

Islander, 0.0% Other, 0.0% Hispanic of any race (2010); Average household size: 2.00 (2010); Median age: 62.5 (2010); Males per 100 females: 100.0 (2010); Marriage status: n/a never married, n/a now married, n/a widowed, n/a divorced (2006-2010 5-year est.); Foreign born: n/a (2006-2010 5-year est.); Ancestry (includes multiple ancestries): n/a (2006-2010 5-year est.).
Economy: Employment by occupation: n/a management, n/a professional, n/a services, n/a sales, n/a farming, n/a construction, n/a production (2006-2010 5-year est.).
Income: Per capita income: n/a (2006-2010 5-year est.); Median household income: n/a (2006-2010 5-year est.); Average household income: n/a (2006-2010 5-year est.); Percent of households with income of $100,000 or more: n/a (2006-2010 5-year est.); Poverty rate: n/a (2006-2010 5-year est.).
Education: Percent of population age 25 and over with: High school diploma (including GED) or higher: n/a (2006-2010 5-year est.); Bachelor's degree or higher: n/a (2006-2010 5-year est.); Master's degree or higher: n/a (2006-2010 5-year est.).
Housing: Homeownership rate: 40.0% (2010); Median home value: n/a (2006-2010 5-year est.); Median contract rent: n/a per month (2006-2010 5-year est.); Median year structure built: n/a (2006-2010 5-year est.).
Transportation: Commute to work: n/a car, n/a public transportation, n/a walk, n/a work from home (2006-2010 5-year est.); Travel time to work: n/a less than 15 minutes, n/a 15 to 30 minutes, n/a 30 to 45 minutes, n/a 45 to 60 minutes, n/a 60 minutes or more (2006-2010 5-year est.)

CLEVELAND (township). Covers a land area of 23.191 square miles and a water area of 0.165 square miles. Located at 40.87° N. Lat; 76.45° W. Long.
Population: 997 (1990); 1,004 (2000); 1,110 (2010); Density: 47.9 persons per square mile (2010); Race: 98.4% White, 0.5% Black, 0.0% Asian, 0.1% American Indian/Alaska Native, 0.1% Native Hawaiian/Other Pacific Islander, 0.9% Other, 0.9% Hispanic of any race (2010); Average household size: 2.44 (2010); Median age: 46.6 (2010); Males per 100 females: 106.3 (2010); Marriage status: 26.8% never married, 60.9% now married, 6.2% widowed, 6.1% divorced (2006-2010 5-year est.); Foreign born: 0.4% (2006-2010 5-year est.); Ancestry (includes multiple ancestries): 33.2% German, 23.4% Polish, 9.9% Irish, 9.0% English, 8.1% Dutch (2006-2010 5-year est.).
Economy: Single-family building permits issued: 0 (2011); Multi-family building permits issued: 0 (2011); Employment by occupation: 11.8% management, 1.6% professional, 5.3% services, 18.7% sales, 3.7% farming, 13.2% construction, 12.3% production (2006-2010 5-year est.).
Income: Per capita income: $24,974 (2006-2010 5-year est.); Median household income: $61,583 (2006-2010 5-year est.); Average household income: $64,127 (2006-2010 5-year est.); Percent of households with income of $100,000 or more: 16.0% (2006-2010 5-year est.); Poverty rate: 3.8% (2006-2010 5-year est.).
Education: Percent of population age 25 and over with: High school diploma (including GED) or higher: 90.4% (2006-2010 5-year est.); Bachelor's degree or higher: 21.0% (2006-2010 5-year est.); Master's degree or higher: 4.6% (2006-2010 5-year est.).
Housing: Homeownership rate: 90.1% (2010); Median home value: $158,300 (2006-2010 5-year est.); Median contract rent: $610 per month (2006-2010 5-year est.); Median year structure built: 1958 (2006-2010 5-year est.).
Transportation: Commute to work: 91.7% car, 0.0% public transportation, 1.6% walk, 4.1% work from home (2006-2010 5-year est.); Travel time to work: 16.9% less than 15 minutes, 43.1% 15 to 30 minutes, 23.6% 30 to 45 minutes, 6.0% 45 to 60 minutes, 10.5% 60 minutes or more (2006-2010 5-year est.)

CONYNGHAM (township). Covers a land area of 20.240 square miles and a water area of 0.243 square miles. Located at 40.82° N. Lat; 76.35° W. Long.
Population: 1,038 (1990); 792 (2000); 758 (2010); Density: 37.5 persons per square mile (2010); Race: 99.9% White, 0.0% Black, 0.1% Asian, 0.0% American Indian/Alaska Native, 0.0% Native Hawaiian/Other Pacific Islander, 0.0% Other, 0.0% Hispanic of any race (2010); Average household size: 2.29 (2010); Median age: 46.7 (2010); Males per 100 females: 101.6 (2010); Marriage status: 12.6% never married, 75.7% now married, 7.5% widowed, 4.1% divorced (2006-2010 5-year est.); Foreign born: 1.0% (2006-2010 5-year est.); Ancestry (includes multiple ancestries): 34.0% German, 25.7% Irish, 15.6% Polish, 10.8% Dutch, 7.6% English (2006-2010 5-year est.).

Economy: Employment by occupation: 2.9% management, 0.9% professional, 7.5% services, 4.9% sales, 4.9% farming, 13.5% construction, 15.0% production (2006-2010 5-year est.).
Income: Per capita income: $22,442 (2006-2010 5-year est.); Median household income: $48,125 (2006-2010 5-year est.); Average household income: $54,840 (2006-2010 5-year est.); Percent of households with income of $100,000 or more: 13.4% (2006-2010 5-year est.); Poverty rate: 4.4% (2006-2010 5-year est.).
Education: Percent of population age 25 and over with: High school diploma (including GED) or higher: 85.3% (2006-2010 5-year est.); Bachelor's degree or higher: 12.3% (2006-2010 5-year est.); Master's degree or higher: 4.7% (2006-2010 5-year est.).
Housing: Homeownership rate: 88.9% (2010); Median home value: $72,900 (2006-2010 5-year est.); Median contract rent: $200 per month (2006-2010 5-year est.); Median year structure built: before 1940 (2006-2010 5-year est.).
Transportation: Commute to work: 95.1% car, 0.9% public transportation, 2.9% walk, 1.2% work from home (2006-2010 5-year est.); Travel time to work: 28.9% less than 15 minutes, 27.7% 15 to 30 minutes, 27.1% 30 to 45 minutes, 11.7% 45 to 60 minutes, 4.7% 60 minutes or more (2006-2010 5-year est.)

ESPY (CDP). Covers a land area of 0.916 square miles and a water area of 0.202 square miles. Located at 41.01° N. Lat; 76.42° W. Long. Elevation is 486 feet.
Population: 1,430 (1990); 1,428 (2000); 1,642 (2010); Density: 1,792.3 persons per square mile (2010); Race: 96.5% White, 1.2% Black, 1.0% Asian, 0.0% American Indian/Alaska Native, 0.0% Native Hawaiian/Other Pacific Islander, 1.3% Other, 1.8% Hispanic of any race (2010); Average household size: 2.15 (2010); Median age: 43.5 (2010); Males per 100 females: 90.5 (2010); Marriage status: 27.3% never married, 55.1% now married, 7.3% widowed, 10.3% divorced (2006-2010 5-year est.); Foreign born: 5.7% (2006-2010 5-year est.); Ancestry (includes multiple ancestries): 43.0% German, 17.6% Irish, 10.5% Dutch, 7.9% English, 7.1% Italian (2006-2010 5-year est.).
Economy: Employment by occupation: 10.2% management, 5.3% professional, 5.1% services, 15.9% sales, 16.8% farming, 6.9% construction, 6.7% production (2006-2010 5-year est.).
Income: Per capita income: $26,151 (2006-2010 5-year est.); Median household income: $53,152 (2006-2010 5-year est.); Average household income: $52,539 (2006-2010 5-year est.); Percent of households with income of $100,000 or more: 9.9% (2006-2010 5-year est.); Poverty rate: 12.5% (2006-2010 5-year est.).
Education: Percent of population age 25 and over with: High school diploma (including GED) or higher: 91.6% (2006-2010 5-year est.); Bachelor's degree or higher: 22.0% (2006-2010 5-year est.); Master's degree or higher: 8.9% (2006-2010 5-year est.).
Housing: Homeownership rate: 63.9% (2010); Median home value: $107,900 (2006-2010 5-year est.); Median contract rent: $535 per month (2006-2010 5-year est.); Median year structure built: 1961 (2006-2010 5-year est.).
Transportation: Commute to work: 93.9% car, 0.0% public transportation, 1.3% walk, 2.0% work from home (2006-2010 5-year est.); Travel time to work: 45.8% less than 15 minutes, 31.7% 15 to 30 minutes, 11.9% 30 to 45 minutes, 9.4% 45 to 60 minutes, 1.1% 60 minutes or more (2006-2010 5-year est.)

Additional Information Contacts
Columbia Montour Chamber of Commerce. . . . . (570) 784-2522
  http://www.bloomsburg.org

EYERS GROVE (CDP). Covers a land area of 0.217 square miles and a water area of 0.005 square miles. Located at 41.10° N. Lat; 76.52° W. Long. Elevation is 584 feet.
Population: 90 (1990); 86 (2000); 105 (2010); Density: 484.3 persons per square mile (2010); Race: 99.0% White, 1.0% Black, 0.0% Asian, 0.0% American Indian/Alaska Native, 0.0% Native Hawaiian/Other Pacific Islander, 0.0% Other, 1.0% Hispanic of any race (2010); Average household size: 2.33 (2010); Median age: 38.5 (2010); Males per 100 females: 101.9 (2010); Marriage status: 26.7% never married, 58.9% now married, 14.4% widowed, 0.0% divorced (2006-2010 5-year est.); Foreign born: 0.0% (2006-2010 5-year est.); Ancestry (includes multiple ancestries): 47.0% German, 20.0% English, 11.0% French, 11.0% American, 9.0% Northern European (2006-2010 5-year est.).

Economy: Employment by occupation: 0.0% management, 0.0% professional, 0.0% services, 8.9% sales, 16.1% farming, 3.6% construction, 3.6% production (2006-2010 5-year est.).
Income: Per capita income: $22,313 (2006-2010 5-year est.); Median household income: $35,694 (2006-2010 5-year est.); Average household income: $52,073 (2006-2010 5-year est.); Percent of households with income of $100,000 or more: 22.0% (2006-2010 5-year est.); Poverty rate: 0.0% (2006-2010 5-year est.).
Education: Percent of population age 25 and over with: High school diploma (including GED) or higher: 97.4% (2006-2010 5-year est.); Bachelor's degree or higher: 44.9% (2006-2010 5-year est.); Master's degree or higher: 25.6% (2006-2010 5-year est.).
Housing: Homeownership rate: 73.4% (2010); Median home value: $205,600 (2006-2010 5-year est.); Median contract rent: n/a per month (2006-2010 5-year est.); Median year structure built: before 1940 (2006-2010 5-year est.).
Transportation: Commute to work: 100.0% car, 0.0% public transportation, 0.0% walk, 0.0% work from home (2006-2010 5-year est.); Travel time to work: 16.1% less than 15 minutes, 50.0% 15 to 30 minutes, 19.6% 30 to 45 minutes, 0.0% 45 to 60 minutes, 14.3% 60 minutes or more (2006-2010 5-year est.)

FERNVILLE (CDP). Covers a land area of 0.808 square miles and a water area of 0.019 square miles. Located at 41.00° N. Lat; 76.48° W. Long. Elevation is 486 feet.
Population: 399 (1990); 488 (2000); 556 (2010); Density: 688.5 persons per square mile (2010); Race: 97.5% White, 0.2% Black, 1.1% Asian, 0.0% American Indian/Alaska Native, 0.0% Native Hawaiian/Other Pacific Islander, 1.2% Other, 1.4% Hispanic of any race (2010); Average household size: 2.42 (2010); Median age: 41.8 (2010); Males per 100 females: 92.4 (2010); Marriage status: 18.9% never married, 72.4% now married, 4.3% widowed, 4.3% divorced (2006-2010 5-year est.); Foreign born: 19.1% (2006-2010 5-year est.); Ancestry (includes multiple ancestries): 21.9% German, 20.8% Polish, 10.1% Italian, 9.4% English, 9.0% Irish (2006-2010 5-year est.).
Economy: Employment by occupation: 7.1% management, 2.1% professional, 4.2% services, 12.9% sales, 3.3% farming, 5.4% construction, 5.4% production (2006-2010 5-year est.).
Income: Per capita income: $40,230 (2006-2010 5-year est.); Median household income: $72,083 (2006-2010 5-year est.); Average household income: $101,566 (2006-2010 5-year est.); Percent of households with income of $100,000 or more: 22.4% (2006-2010 5-year est.); Poverty rate: 3.3% (2006-2010 5-year est.).
Education: Percent of population age 25 and over with: High school diploma (including GED) or higher: 91.5% (2006-2010 5-year est.); Bachelor's degree or higher: 45.6% (2006-2010 5-year est.); Master's degree or higher: 26.9% (2006-2010 5-year est.).
Housing: Homeownership rate: 85.2% (2010); Median home value: $187,500 (2006-2010 5-year est.); Median contract rent: $530 per month (2006-2010 5-year est.); Median year structure built: 1961 (2006-2010 5-year est.).
Transportation: Commute to work: 94.6% car, 0.0% public transportation, 0.0% walk, 5.4% work from home (2006-2010 5-year est.); Travel time to work: 42.7% less than 15 minutes, 35.2% 15 to 30 minutes, 9.3% 30 to 45 minutes, 7.9% 45 to 60 minutes, 4.8% 60 minutes or more (2006-2010 5-year est.)

FISHING CREEK (township). Covers a land area of 28.427 square miles and a water area of 0.304 square miles. Located at 41.14° N. Lat; 76.35° W. Long.
Population: 1,484 (1990); 1,393 (2000); 1,416 (2010); Density: 49.8 persons per square mile (2010); Race: 98.9% White, 0.1% Black, 0.2% Asian, 0.1% American Indian/Alaska Native, 0.0% Native Hawaiian/Other Pacific Islander, 0.7% Other, 0.3% Hispanic of any race (2010); Average household size: 2.40 (2010); Median age: 48.2 (2010); Males per 100 females: 102.3 (2010); Marriage status: 17.9% never married, 65.8% now married, 8.6% widowed, 7.8% divorced (2006-2010 5-year est.); Foreign born: 0.5% (2006-2010 5-year est.); Ancestry (includes multiple ancestries): 42.4% German, 10.4% Irish, 10.3% English, 9.2% American, 8.1% Polish (2006-2010 5-year est.).
Economy: Single-family building permits issued: 3 (2011); Multi-family building permits issued: 0 (2011); Employment by occupation: 6.5% management, 1.3% professional, 10.5% services, 13.9% sales, 3.5% farming, 13.3% construction, 9.5% production (2006-2010 5-year est.).

Income: Per capita income: $23,010 (2006-2010 5-year est.); Median household income: $50,147 (2006-2010 5-year est.); Average household income: $58,569 (2006-2010 5-year est.); Percent of households with income of $100,000 or more: 14.9% (2006-2010 5-year est.); Poverty rate: 8.2% (2006-2010 5-year est.).

Education: Percent of population age 25 and over with: High school diploma (including GED) or higher: 86.1% (2006-2010 5-year est.); Bachelor's degree or higher: 15.7% (2006-2010 5-year est.); Master's degree or higher: 8.6% (2006-2010 5-year est.).

Housing: Homeownership rate: 89.0% (2010); Median home value: $158,800 (2006-2010 5-year est.); Median contract rent: $471 per month (2006-2010 5-year est.); Median year structure built: 1968 (2006-2010 5-year est.).

Transportation: Commute to work: 93.8% car, 0.0% public transportation, 0.3% walk, 5.0% work from home (2006-2010 5-year est.); Travel time to work: 19.4% less than 15 minutes, 53.6% 15 to 30 minutes, 15.6% 30 to 45 minutes, 6.4% 45 to 60 minutes, 5.0% 60 minutes or more (2006-2010 5-year est.)

Additional Information Contacts

Columbia Montour Chamber of Commerce . . . . (570) 784-2522
   http://columbiamontourchamber.com

FOUNDRYVILLE (CDP). Covers a land area of 0.543 square miles and a water area of 0.008 square miles. Located at 41.08° N. Lat; 76.23° W. Long. Elevation is 636 feet.

Population: 225 (1990); 265 (2000); 256 (2010); Density: 471.5 persons per square mile (2010); Race: 96.5% White, 0.0% Black, 0.4% Asian, 0.0% American Indian/Alaska Native, 0.0% Native Hawaiian/Other Pacific Islander, 3.1% Other, 2.0% Hispanic of any race (2010); Average household size: 2.56 (2010); Median age: 41.0 (2010); Males per 100 females: 104.8 (2010); Marriage status: 25.5% never married, 39.8% now married, 15.3% widowed, 19.4% divorced (2006-2010 5-year est.); Foreign born: 0.0% (2006-2010 5-year est.); Ancestry (includes multiple ancestries): 45.4% Dutch, 34.7% German, 15.8% Irish, 12.2% Norwegian, 6.1% Ukrainian (2006-2010 5-year est.).

Economy: Employment by occupation: 0.0% management, 0.0% professional, 35.1% services, 0.0% sales, 0.0% farming, 0.0% construction, 30.5% production (2006-2010 5-year est.).

Income: Per capita income: $21,552 (2006-2010 5-year est.); Median household income: $32,237 (2006-2010 5-year est.); Average household income: $39,496 (2006-2010 5-year est.); Percent of households with income of $100,000 or more: n/a (2006-2010 5-year est.); Poverty rate: 0.0% (2006-2010 5-year est.).

Education: Percent of population age 25 and over with: High school diploma (including GED) or higher: 100.0% (2006-2010 5-year est.); Bachelor's degree or higher: 0.0% (2006-2010 5-year est.); Master's degree or higher: 0.0% (2006-2010 5-year est.).

Housing: Homeownership rate: 81.0% (2010); Median home value: $85,000 (2006-2010 5-year est.); Median contract rent: n/a per month (2006-2010 5-year est.); Median year structure built: before 1940 (2006-2010 5-year est.).

Transportation: Commute to work: 100.0% car, 0.0% public transportation, 0.0% walk, 0.0% work from home (2006-2010 5-year est.); Travel time to work: 62.3% less than 15 minutes, 29.9% 15 to 30 minutes, 7.8% 30 to 45 minutes, 0.0% 45 to 60 minutes, 0.0% 60 minutes or more (2006-2010 5-year est.)

FRANKLIN (township). Covers a land area of 13.091 square miles and a water area of 0.439 square miles. Located at 40.92° N. Lat; 76.50° W. Long.

Population: 624 (1990); 597 (2000); 595 (2010); Density: 45.5 persons per square mile (2010); Race: 99.5% White, 0.0% Black, 0.0% Asian, 0.0% American Indian/Alaska Native, 0.0% Native Hawaiian/Other Pacific Islander, 0.5% Other, 1.0% Hispanic of any race (2010); Average household size: 2.44 (2010); Median age: 47.6 (2010); Males per 100 females: 109.5 (2010); Marriage status: 19.8% never married, 66.7% now married, 3.2% widowed, 10.2% divorced (2006-2010 5-year est.); Foreign born: 0.5% (2006-2010 5-year est.); Ancestry (includes multiple ancestries): 50.6% German, 9.7% English, 8.3% Polish, 7.8% Dutch, 5.5% American (2006-2010 5-year est.).

Economy: Single-family building permits issued: 0 (2011); Multi-family building permits issued: 0 (2011); Employment by occupation: 6.1% management, 4.0% professional, 11.4% services, 13.5% sales, 6.4% farming, 12.5% construction, 8.4% production (2006-2010 5-year est.).

Income: Per capita income: $25,048 (2006-2010 5-year est.); Median household income: $52,105 (2006-2010 5-year est.); Average household income: $59,645 (2006-2010 5-year est.); Percent of households with income of $100,000 or more: 14.1% (2006-2010 5-year est.); Poverty rate: 4.6% (2006-2010 5-year est.).

Education: Percent of population age 25 and over with: High school diploma (including GED) or higher: 82.3% (2006-2010 5-year est.); Bachelor's degree or higher: 12.4% (2006-2010 5-year est.); Master's degree or higher: 4.1% (2006-2010 5-year est.).

Housing: Homeownership rate: 86.9% (2010); Median home value: $115,700 (2006-2010 5-year est.); Median contract rent: $658 per month (2006-2010 5-year est.); Median year structure built: 1971 (2006-2010 5-year est.).

Transportation: Commute to work: 97.5% car, 0.0% public transportation, 1.5% walk, 1.1% work from home (2006-2010 5-year est.); Travel time to work: 18.8% less than 15 minutes, 64.0% 15 to 30 minutes, 11.8% 30 to 45 minutes, 3.3% 45 to 60 minutes, 2.2% 60 minutes or more (2006-2010 5-year est.)

GREENWOOD (township). Covers a land area of 28.337 square miles and a water area of 0.105 square miles. Located at 41.15° N. Lat; 76.47° W. Long. Elevation is 787 feet.

Population: 1,972 (1990); 1,932 (2000); 1,952 (2010); Density: 68.9 persons per square mile (2010); Race: 98.4% White, 0.6% Black, 0.1% Asian, 0.1% American Indian/Alaska Native, 0.0% Native Hawaiian/Other Pacific Islander, 0.8% Other, 1.1% Hispanic of any race (2010); Average household size: 2.56 (2010); Median age: 43.8 (2010); Males per 100 females: 101.2 (2010); Marriage status: 17.8% never married, 65.4% now married, 7.5% widowed, 9.3% divorced (2006-2010 5-year est.); Foreign born: 1.7% (2006-2010 5-year est.); Ancestry (includes multiple ancestries): 42.7% German, 12.8% English, 12.0% Dutch, 12.0% Irish, 6.7% American (2006-2010 5-year est.).

Economy: Single-family building permits issued: 0 (2011); Multi-family building permits issued: 0 (2011); Employment by occupation: 7.5% management, 2.1% professional, 13.0% services, 11.0% sales, 3.9% farming, 13.1% construction, 11.8% production (2006-2010 5-year est.).

Income: Per capita income: $29,937 (2006-2010 5-year est.); Median household income: $42,379 (2006-2010 5-year est.); Average household income: $67,921 (2006-2010 5-year est.); Percent of households with income of $100,000 or more: 9.8% (2006-2010 5-year est.); Poverty rate: 8.6% (2006-2010 5-year est.).

Education: Percent of population age 25 and over with: High school diploma (including GED) or higher: 80.2% (2006-2010 5-year est.); Bachelor's degree or higher: 15.2% (2006-2010 5-year est.); Master's degree or higher: 6.4% (2006-2010 5-year est.).

Housing: Homeownership rate: 85.4% (2010); Median home value: $129,900 (2006-2010 5-year est.); Median contract rent: $467 per month (2006-2010 5-year est.); Median year structure built: 1968 (2006-2010 5-year est.).

Safety: Violent crime rate: 0.0 per 10,000 population; Property crime rate: 0.0 per 10,000 population (2011).

Transportation: Commute to work: 84.5% car, 0.0% public transportation, 2.4% walk, 8.3% work from home (2006-2010 5-year est.); Travel time to work: 18.3% less than 15 minutes, 48.2% 15 to 30 minutes, 27.4% 30 to 45 minutes, 3.1% 45 to 60 minutes, 3.1% 60 minutes or more (2006-2010 5-year est.)

Additional Information Contacts

Columbia Montour Chamber of Commerce . . . . (570) 784-2522
   http://www.bloomsburg.org

HEMLOCK (township). Covers a land area of 17.555 square miles and a water area of 0.090 square miles. Located at 41.02° N. Lat; 76.52° W. Long.

Population: 1,534 (1990); 1,874 (2000); 2,249 (2010); Density: 128.1 persons per square mile (2010); Race: 97.2% White, 0.4% Black, 1.2% Asian, 0.0% American Indian/Alaska Native, 0.0% Native Hawaiian/Other Pacific Islander, 1.2% Other, 1.4% Hispanic of any race (2010); Average household size: 2.55 (2010); Median age: 43.6 (2010); Males per 100 females: 98.7 (2010); Marriage status: 22.8% never married, 63.8% now married, 6.0% widowed, 7.5% divorced (2006-2010 5-year est.); Foreign born: 4.3% (2006-2010 5-year est.); Ancestry (includes multiple ancestries): 37.8% German, 11.0% English, 10.3% Polish, 7.2% Irish, 5.4% French (2006-2010 5-year est.).

Economy: Single-family building permits issued: 2 (2011); Multi-family building permits issued: 0 (2011); Employment by occupation: 10.1%

management, 1.7% professional, 7.6% services, 15.3% sales, 2.9% farming, 9.2% construction, 11.5% production (2006-2010 5-year est.).
Income: Per capita income: $32,081 (2006-2010 5-year est.); Median household income: $64,891 (2006-2010 5-year est.); Average household income: $79,747 (2006-2010 5-year est.); Percent of households with income of $100,000 or more: 18.3% (2006-2010 5-year est.); Poverty rate: 2.5% (2006-2010 5-year est.).
Education: Percent of population age 25 and over with: High school diploma (including GED) or higher: 89.6% (2006-2010 5-year est.); Bachelor's degree or higher: 34.0% (2006-2010 5-year est.); Master's degree or higher: 18.6% (2006-2010 5-year est.).
Housing: Homeownership rate: 87.7% (2010); Median home value: $159,300 (2006-2010 5-year est.); Median contract rent: $500 per month (2006-2010 5-year est.); Median year structure built: 1979 (2006-2010 5-year est.).
Safety: Violent crime rate: 4.4 per 10,000 population; Property crime rate: 518.6 per 10,000 population (2011).
Transportation: Commute to work: 95.9% car, 0.0% public transportation, 0.0% walk, 3.0% work from home (2006-2010 5-year est.); Travel time to work: 35.4% less than 15 minutes, 42.4% 15 to 30 minutes, 13.1% 30 to 45 minutes, 4.9% 45 to 60 minutes, 4.2% 60 minutes or more (2006-2010 5-year est.)

Additional Information Contacts
Columbia Montour Chamber of Commerce............ (570) 784-2522
  http://columbiamontourchamber.com

IOLA (CDP). Covers a land area of 0.272 square miles and a water area of 0.004 square miles. Located at 41.13° N. Lat; 76.53° W. Long. Elevation is 663 feet.
Population: 136 (1990); 129 (2000); 144 (2010); Density: 530.3 persons per square mile (2010); Race: 97.2% White, 0.0% Black, 0.7% Asian, 0.0% American Indian/Alaska Native, 0.0% Native Hawaiian/Other Pacific Islander, 2.1% Other, 4.9% Hispanic of any race (2010); Average household size: 2.36 (2010); Median age: 36.8 (2010); Males per 100 females: 77.8 (2010); Marriage status: 29.9% never married, 48.8% now married, 2.4% widowed, 18.9% divorced (2006-2010 5-year est.); Foreign born: 0.0% (2006-2010 5-year est.); Ancestry (includes multiple ancestries): 60.2% German, 13.8% Irish, 10.5% Italian, 9.9% English, 2.2% American (2006-2010 5-year est.).
Economy: Employment by occupation: 6.2% management, 0.0% professional, 23.1% services, 13.8% sales, 4.6% farming, 4.6% construction, 13.8% production (2006-2010 5-year est.).
Income: Per capita income: $9,284 (2006-2010 5-year est.); Median household income: $27,813 (2006-2010 5-year est.); Average household income: $29,890 (2006-2010 5-year est.); Percent of households with income of $100,000 or more: 4.1% (2006-2010 5-year est.); Poverty rate: 33.7% (2006-2010 5-year est.).
Education: Percent of population age 25 and over with: High school diploma (including GED) or higher: 72.7% (2006-2010 5-year est.); Bachelor's degree or higher: 3.0% (2006-2010 5-year est.); Master's degree or higher: 3.0% (2006-2010 5-year est.).
Housing: Homeownership rate: 62.3% (2010); Median home value: $107,100 (2006-2010 5-year est.); Median contract rent: $450 per month (2006-2010 5-year est.); Median year structure built: before 1940 (2006-2010 5-year est.).
Transportation: Commute to work: 95.4% car, 0.0% public transportation, 4.6% walk, 0.0% work from home (2006-2010 5-year est.); Travel time to work: 16.9% less than 15 minutes, 56.9% 15 to 30 minutes, 21.5% 30 to 45 minutes, 4.6% 45 to 60 minutes, 0.0% 60 minutes or more (2006-2010 5-year est.)

JACKSON (township). Covers a land area of 18.391 square miles and a water area of 0.036 square miles. Located at 41.23° N. Lat; 76.43° W. Long. Elevation is 1,191 feet.
Population: 508 (1990); 598 (2000); 626 (2010); Density: 34.0 persons per square mile (2010); Race: 99.4% White, 0.2% Black, 0.2% Asian, 0.0% American Indian/Alaska Native, 0.0% Native Hawaiian/Other Pacific Islander, 0.2% Other, 0.2% Hispanic of any race (2010); Average household size: 2.51 (2010); Median age: 44.7 (2010); Males per 100 females: 103.9 (2010); Marriage status: 17.8% never married, 67.5% now married, 4.6% widowed, 10.1% divorced (2006-2010 5-year est.); Foreign born: 0.0% (2006-2010 5-year est.); Ancestry (includes multiple ancestries): 34.0% German, 14.2% Irish, 10.8% American, 8.7% English, 7.2% Dutch (2006-2010 5-year est.).

Economy: Single-family building permits issued: 0 (2011); Multi-family building permits issued: 0 (2011); Employment by occupation: 10.6% management, 1.4% professional, 6.4% services, 17.4% sales, 1.4% farming, 6.9% construction, 10.6% production (2006-2010 5-year est.).
Income: Per capita income: $29,135 (2006-2010 5-year est.); Median household income: $42,333 (2006-2010 5-year est.); Average household income: $69,263 (2006-2010 5-year est.); Percent of households with income of $100,000 or more: 15.1% (2006-2010 5-year est.); Poverty rate: 4.7% (2006-2010 5-year est.).
Education: Percent of population age 25 and over with: High school diploma (including GED) or higher: 82.0% (2006-2010 5-year est.); Bachelor's degree or higher: 18.0% (2006-2010 5-year est.); Master's degree or higher: 9.1% (2006-2010 5-year est.).
Housing: Homeownership rate: 88.0% (2010); Median home value: $181,900 (2006-2010 5-year est.); Median contract rent: $470 per month (2006-2010 5-year est.); Median year structure built: 1980 (2006-2010 5-year est.).
Transportation: Commute to work: 93.5% car, 0.0% public transportation, 2.3% walk, 2.8% work from home (2006-2010 5-year est.); Travel time to work: 12.0% less than 15 minutes, 29.8% 15 to 30 minutes, 31.7% 30 to 45 minutes, 15.9% 45 to 60 minutes, 10.6% 60 minutes or more (2006-2010 5-year est.)

JAMISON CITY (CDP). Covers a land area of 0.388 square miles and a water area of <.001 square miles. Located at 41.30° N. Lat; 76.37° W. Long. Elevation is 1,063 feet.
Population: 90 (1990); 102 (2000); 134 (2010); Density: 345.1 persons per square mile (2010); Race: 99.3% White, 0.0% Black, 0.0% Asian, 0.7% American Indian/Alaska Native, 0.0% Native Hawaiian/Other Pacific Islander, 0.0% Other, 0.0% Hispanic of any race (2010); Average household size: 2.09 (2010); Median age: 53.3 (2010); Males per 100 females: 109.4 (2010); Marriage status: 20.2% never married, 71.3% now married, 5.3% widowed, 3.2% divorced (2006-2010 5-year est.); Foreign born: 0.0% (2006-2010 5-year est.); Ancestry (includes multiple ancestries): 31.4% German, 19.0% Welsh, 15.2% Italian, 13.3% Austrian, 10.5% Scotch-Irish (2006-2010 5-year est.).
Economy: Employment by occupation: 8.0% management, 0.0% professional, 8.0% services, 10.0% sales, 6.0% farming, 30.0% construction, 8.0% production (2006-2010 5-year est.).
Income: Per capita income: $19,370 (2006-2010 5-year est.); Median household income: $28,333 (2006-2010 5-year est.); Average household income: $37,631 (2006-2010 5-year est.); Percent of households with income of $100,000 or more: n/a (2006-2010 5-year est.); Poverty rate: 14.3% (2006-2010 5-year est.).
Education: Percent of population age 25 and over with: High school diploma (including GED) or higher: 86.1% (2006-2010 5-year est.); Bachelor's degree or higher: 0.0% (2006-2010 5-year est.); Master's degree or higher: 0.0% (2006-2010 5-year est.).
Housing: Homeownership rate: 87.5% (2010); Median home value: $128,100 (2006-2010 5-year est.); Median contract rent: n/a per month (2006-2010 5-year est.); Median year structure built: before 1940 (2006-2010 5-year est.).
Transportation: Commute to work: 88.0% car, 0.0% public transportation, 8.0% walk, 4.0% work from home (2006-2010 5-year est.); Travel time to work: 41.7% less than 15 minutes, 16.7% 15 to 30 minutes, 20.8% 30 to 45 minutes, 20.8% 45 to 60 minutes, 0.0% 60 minutes or more (2006-2010 5-year est.)

JERSEYTOWN (CDP). Covers a land area of 0.725 square miles and a water area of 0.002 square miles. Located at 41.09° N. Lat; 76.58° W. Long. Elevation is 636 feet.
Population: 150 (1990); 150 (2000); 184 (2010); Density: 253.8 persons per square mile (2010); Race: 97.8% White, 0.0% Black, 0.5% Asian, 1.1% American Indian/Alaska Native, 0.0% Native Hawaiian/Other Pacific Islander, 0.6% Other, 0.5% Hispanic of any race (2010); Average household size: 2.67 (2010); Median age: 36.0 (2010); Males per 100 females: 78.6 (2010); Marriage status: 17.9% never married, 71.5% now married, 8.6% widowed, 2.0% divorced (2006-2010 5-year est.); Foreign born: 0.0% (2006-2010 5-year est.); Ancestry (includes multiple ancestries): 55.7% German, 7.5% Irish, 5.5% English, 5.0% Scottish, 3.5% Polish (2006-2010 5-year est.).
Economy: Employment by occupation: 3.4% management, 0.0% professional, 5.2% services, 39.7% sales, 0.0% farming, 19.8% construction, 15.5% production (2006-2010 5-year est.).

Income: Per capita income: $21,942 (2006-2010 5-year est.); Median household income: $58,500 (2006-2010 5-year est.); Average household income: $60,849 (2006-2010 5-year est.); Percent of households with income of $100,000 or more: 8.4% (2006-2010 5-year est.); Poverty rate: 6.0% (2006-2010 5-year est.).

Education: Percent of population age 25 and over with: High school diploma (including GED) or higher: 97.9% (2006-2010 5-year est.); Bachelor's degree or higher: 18.2% (2006-2010 5-year est.); Master's degree or higher: 4.9% (2006-2010 5-year est.).

Housing: Homeownership rate: 79.7% (2010); Median home value: $133,000 (2006-2010 5-year est.); Median contract rent: n/a per month (2006-2010 5-year est.); Median year structure built: 1941 (2006-2010 5-year est.).

Transportation: Commute to work: 67.6% car, 0.0% public transportation, 27.0% walk, 2.7% work from home (2006-2010 5-year est.); Travel time to work: 33.3% less than 15 minutes, 38.0% 15 to 30 minutes, 25.9% 30 to 45 minutes, 0.0% 45 to 60 minutes, 2.8% 60 minutes or more (2006-2010 5-year est.)

JONESTOWN (CDP). Covers a land area of 0.367 square miles and a water area of 0.021 square miles. Located at 41.13° N. Lat; 76.31° W. Long. Elevation is 696 feet.

Population: 37 (1990); 34 (2000); 64 (2010); Density: 174.5 persons per square mile (2010); Race: 100.0% White, 0.0% Black, 0.0% Asian, 0.0% American Indian/Alaska Native, 0.0% Native Hawaiian/Other Pacific Islander, 0.0% Other, 0.0% Hispanic of any race (2010); Average household size: 2.29 (2010); Median age: 44.7 (2010); Males per 100 females: 77.8 (2010); Marriage status: 25.2% never married, 27.8% now married, 47.0% widowed, 0.0% divorced (2006-2010 5-year est.); Foreign born: 0.0% (2006-2010 5-year est.); Ancestry (includes multiple ancestries): 6.8% Scottish, 6.8% Italian, 6.8% Dutch, 4.2% English, 4.2% Irish (2006-2010 5-year est.).

Economy: Employment by occupation: 0.0% management, 0.0% professional, 35.1% services, 0.0% sales, 0.0% farming, 5.4% construction, 0.0% production (2006-2010 5-year est.).

Income: Per capita income: $7,878 (2006-2010 5-year est.); Median household income: $32,500 (2006-2010 5-year est.); Average household income: $29,796 (2006-2010 5-year est.); Percent of households with income of $100,000 or more: n/a (2006-2010 5-year est.); Poverty rate: 4.2% (2006-2010 5-year est.).

Education: Percent of population age 25 and over with: High school diploma (including GED) or higher: 53.3% (2006-2010 5-year est.); Bachelor's degree or higher: 10.5% (2006-2010 5-year est.); Master's degree or higher: 0.0% (2006-2010 5-year est.).

Housing: Homeownership rate: 96.4% (2010); Median home value: $81,800 (2006-2010 5-year est.); Median contract rent: n/a per month (2006-2010 5-year est.); Median year structure built: before 1940 (2006-2010 5-year est.).

Transportation: Commute to work: 100.0% car, 0.0% public transportation, 0.0% walk, 0.0% work from home (2006-2010 5-year est.); Travel time to work: 0.0% less than 15 minutes, 94.6% 15 to 30 minutes, 0.0% 30 to 45 minutes, 5.4% 45 to 60 minutes, 0.0% 60 minutes or more (2006-2010 5-year est.)

LIGHTSTREET (CDP). Covers a land area of 0.973 square miles and a water area of 0.013 square miles. Located at 41.04° N. Lat; 76.42° W. Long. Elevation is 548 feet.

Population: 726 (1990); 881 (2000); 1,093 (2010); Density: 1,123.3 persons per square mile (2010); Race: 96.5% White, 0.5% Black, 1.6% Asian, 0.2% American Indian/Alaska Native, 0.0% Native Hawaiian/Other Pacific Islander, 1.2% Other, 0.3% Hispanic of any race (2010); Average household size: 2.12 (2010); Median age: 49.6 (2010); Males per 100 females: 85.6 (2010); Marriage status: 14.0% never married, 56.1% now married, 19.1% widowed, 10.8% divorced (2006-2010 5-year est.); Foreign born: 8.2% (2006-2010 5-year est.); Ancestry (includes multiple ancestries): 23.2% German, 17.5% Dutch, 15.7% English, 9.3% American, 6.2% Pennsylvania German (2006-2010 5-year est.).

Economy: Employment by occupation: 7.2% management, 6.0% professional, 9.4% services, 20.3% sales, 11.3% farming, 11.8% construction, 10.4% production (2006-2010 5-year est.).

Income: Per capita income: $60,927 (2006-2010 5-year est.); Median household income: $42,639 (2006-2010 5-year est.); Average household income: $121,408 (2006-2010 5-year est.); Percent of households with income of $100,000 or more: 17.2% (2006-2010 5-year est.); Poverty rate: 4.0% (2006-2010 5-year est.).

Education: Percent of population age 25 and over with: High school diploma (including GED) or higher: 75.8% (2006-2010 5-year est.); Bachelor's degree or higher: 15.6% (2006-2010 5-year est.); Master's degree or higher: 7.5% (2006-2010 5-year est.).

Housing: Homeownership rate: 79.4% (2010); Median home value: $82,000 (2006-2010 5-year est.); Median contract rent: $292 per month (2006-2010 5-year est.); Median year structure built: 1987 (2006-2010 5-year est.).

Transportation: Commute to work: 97.6% car, 0.0% public transportation, 0.0% walk, 2.4% work from home (2006-2010 5-year est.); Travel time to work: 41.3% less than 15 minutes, 33.1% 15 to 30 minutes, 14.0% 30 to 45 minutes, 1.9% 45 to 60 minutes, 9.7% 60 minutes or more (2006-2010 5-year est.)

LIME RIDGE (CDP). Covers a land area of 1.296 square miles and a water area of 0.287 square miles. Located at 41.02° N. Lat; 76.35° W. Long. Elevation is 502 feet.

Population: 1,033 (1990); 951 (2000); 890 (2010); Density: 687.0 persons per square mile (2010); Race: 96.5% White, 0.4% Black, 0.6% Asian, 0.0% American Indian/Alaska Native, 0.0% Native Hawaiian/Other Pacific Islander, 2.5% Other, 2.5% Hispanic of any race (2010); Average household size: 2.37 (2010); Median age: 44.2 (2010); Males per 100 females: 89.8 (2010); Marriage status: 29.0% never married, 48.0% now married, 5.9% widowed, 17.1% divorced (2006-2010 5-year est.); Foreign born: 0.8% (2006-2010 5-year est.); Ancestry (includes multiple ancestries): 35.8% German, 12.9% Pennsylvania German, 10.2% English, 10.2% Italian, 8.9% Irish (2006-2010 5-year est.).

Economy: Employment by occupation: 2.5% management, 1.1% professional, 22.6% services, 14.3% sales, 2.1% farming, 5.5% construction, 8.2% production (2006-2010 5-year est.).

Income: Per capita income: $20,026 (2006-2010 5-year est.); Median household income: $39,185 (2006-2010 5-year est.); Average household income: $48,011 (2006-2010 5-year est.); Percent of households with income of $100,000 or more: 6.0% (2006-2010 5-year est.); Poverty rate: 12.3% (2006-2010 5-year est.).

Education: Percent of population age 25 and over with: High school diploma (including GED) or higher: 85.9% (2006-2010 5-year est.); Bachelor's degree or higher: 9.3% (2006-2010 5-year est.); Master's degree or higher: 5.5% (2006-2010 5-year est.).

Housing: Homeownership rate: 84.1% (2010); Median home value: $89,800 (2006-2010 5-year est.); Median contract rent: $561 per month (2006-2010 5-year est.); Median year structure built: 1960 (2006-2010 5-year est.).

Transportation: Commute to work: 93.7% car, 0.0% public transportation, 1.2% walk, 2.0% work from home (2006-2010 5-year est.); Travel time to work: 39.6% less than 15 minutes, 32.3% 15 to 30 minutes, 19.2% 30 to 45 minutes, 1.3% 45 to 60 minutes, 7.7% 60 minutes or more (2006-2010 5-year est.)

LOCUST (township). Covers a land area of 17.790 square miles and a water area of 0.108 square miles. Located at 40.87° N. Lat; 76.39° W. Long.

Population: 1,308 (1990); 1,410 (2000); 1,404 (2010); Density: 78.9 persons per square mile (2010); Race: 99.0% White, 0.1% Black, 0.3% Asian, 0.1% American Indian/Alaska Native, 0.0% Native Hawaiian/Other Pacific Islander, 0.5% Other, 0.5% Hispanic of any race (2010); Average household size: 2.42 (2010); Median age: 44.9 (2010); Males per 100 females: 97.7 (2010); Marriage status: 18.1% never married, 66.9% now married, 5.9% widowed, 9.2% divorced (2006-2010 5-year est.); Foreign born: 0.4% (2006-2010 5-year est.); Ancestry (includes multiple ancestries): 38.2% German, 11.3% Polish, 9.7% Irish, 8.2% Italian, 8.0% Dutch (2006-2010 5-year est.).

Economy: Single-family building permits issued: 2 (2011); Multi-family building permits issued: 0 (2011); Employment by occupation: 10.8% management, 2.8% professional, 5.6% services, 17.4% sales, 3.2% farming, 11.1% construction, 11.5% production (2006-2010 5-year est.).

Income: Per capita income: $23,807 (2006-2010 5-year est.); Median household income: $47,414 (2006-2010 5-year est.); Average household income: $56,963 (2006-2010 5-year est.); Percent of households with income of $100,000 or more: 9.9% (2006-2010 5-year est.); Poverty rate: 8.6% (2006-2010 5-year est.).

Education: Percent of population age 25 and over with: High school diploma (including GED) or higher: 90.3% (2006-2010 5-year est.); Bachelor's degree or higher: 16.2% (2006-2010 5-year est.); Master's degree or higher: 3.9% (2006-2010 5-year est.).

Housing: Homeownership rate: 88.1% (2010); Median home value: $169,100 (2006-2010 5-year est.); Median contract rent: $250 per month (2006-2010 5-year est.); Median year structure built: 1970 (2006-2010 5-year est.).

Transportation: Commute to work: 90.3% car, 0.4% public transportation, 1.8% walk, 7.0% work from home (2006-2010 5-year est.); Travel time to work: 13.2% less than 15 minutes, 50.1% 15 to 30 minutes, 16.1% 30 to 45 minutes, 15.4% 45 to 60 minutes, 5.3% 60 minutes or more (2006-2010 5-year est.)

Additional Information Contacts

Punxsutawney Area Chamber of Commerce . . . . (814) 938-7700
    http://www.punxsutawney.com

LOCUSTDALE (CDP). Aka Locust Dale. Covers a land area of 0.085 square miles and a water area of 0 square miles. Located at 40.78° N. Lat; 76.37° W. Long. Elevation is 1,024 feet.

Population: 92 (1990); 70 (2000); 177 (2010); Density: 2,079.6 persons per square mile (2010); Race: 99.4% White, 0.0% Black, 0.0% Asian, 0.0% American Indian/Alaska Native, 0.0% Native Hawaiian/Other Pacific Islander, 0.6% Other, 0.6% Hispanic of any race (2010); Average household size: 2.24 (2010); Median age: 46.6 (2010); Males per 100 females: 94.5 (2010); Marriage status: 0.0% never married, 74.7% now married, 16.5% widowed, 8.9% divorced (2006-2010 5-year est.); Foreign born: 0.0% (2006-2010 5-year est.); Ancestry (includes multiple ancestries): 70.9% German, 17.7% Irish, 8.9% Italian, 8.9% English, 7.6% Dutch (2006-2010 5-year est.).

Economy: Employment by occupation: 0.0% management, 0.0% professional, 15.2% services, 30.4% sales, 0.0% farming, 0.0% construction, 0.0% production (2006-2010 5-year est.).

Income: Per capita income: $18,889 (2006-2010 5-year est.); Median household income: $40,833 (2006-2010 5-year est.); Average household income: $31,340 (2006-2010 5-year est.); Percent of households with income of $100,000 or more: n/a (2006-2010 5-year est.); Poverty rate: 10.1% (2006-2010 5-year est.).

Education: Percent of population age 25 and over with: High school diploma (including GED) or higher: 68.4% (2006-2010 5-year est.); Bachelor's degree or higher: 0.0% (2006-2010 5-year est.); Master's degree or higher: 0.0% (2006-2010 5-year est.).

Housing: Homeownership rate: 82.3% (2010); Median home value: $35,000 (2006-2010 5-year est.); Median contract rent: n/a per month (2006-2010 5-year est.); Median year structure built: before 1940 (2006-2010 5-year est.).

Transportation: Commute to work: 100.0% car, 0.0% public transportation, 0.0% walk, 0.0% work from home (2006-2010 5-year est.); Travel time to work: 30.4% less than 15 minutes, 54.3% 15 to 30 minutes, 6.5% 30 to 45 minutes, 0.0% 45 to 60 minutes, 8.7% 60 minutes or more (2006-2010 5-year est.)

MADISON (township). Covers a land area of 35.155 square miles and a water area of 0.106 square miles. Located at 41.10° N. Lat; 76.57° W. Long.

Population: 1,577 (1990); 1,590 (2000); 1,605 (2010); Density: 45.7 persons per square mile (2010); Race: 98.6% White, 0.3% Black, 0.1% Asian, 0.1% American Indian/Alaska Native, 0.0% Native Hawaiian/Other Pacific Islander, 0.9% Other, 0.8% Hispanic of any race (2010); Average household size: 2.58 (2010); Median age: 44.7 (2010); Males per 100 females: 92.9 (2010); Marriage status: 18.0% never married, 68.6% now married, 5.1% widowed, 8.3% divorced (2006-2010 5-year est.); Foreign born: 0.3% (2006-2010 5-year est.); Ancestry (includes multiple ancestries): 43.8% German, 11.2% Irish, 10.8% English, 6.6% Italian, 6.5% American (2006-2010 5-year est.).

Economy: Single-family building permits issued: 2 (2011); Multi-family building permits issued: 0 (2011); Employment by occupation: 11.8% management, 3.1% professional, 11.8% services, 13.9% sales, 3.5% farming, 10.8% construction, 8.3% production (2006-2010 5-year est.).

Income: Per capita income: $25,226 (2006-2010 5-year est.); Median household income: $51,875 (2006-2010 5-year est.); Average household income: $60,695 (2006-2010 5-year est.); Percent of households with income of $100,000 or more: 11.6% (2006-2010 5-year est.); Poverty rate: 8.8% (2006-2010 5-year est.).

Education: Percent of population age 25 and over with: High school diploma (including GED) or higher: 89.9% (2006-2010 5-year est.); Bachelor's degree or higher: 18.7% (2006-2010 5-year est.); Master's degree or higher: 6.3% (2006-2010 5-year est.).

Housing: Homeownership rate: 85.6% (2010); Median home value: $148,400 (2006-2010 5-year est.); Median contract rent: $444 per month (2006-2010 5-year est.); Median year structure built: 1974 (2006-2010 5-year est.).

Safety: Violent crime rate: 0.0 per 10,000 population; Property crime rate: 0.0 per 10,000 population (2011).

Transportation: Commute to work: 83.5% car, 0.0% public transportation, 4.9% walk, 10.1% work from home (2006-2010 5-year est.); Travel time to work: 15.7% less than 15 minutes, 56.1% 15 to 30 minutes, 17.8% 30 to 45 minutes, 5.0% 45 to 60 minutes, 5.3% 60 minutes or more (2006-2010 5-year est.)

Additional Information Contacts

Columbia Montour Chamber of Commerce . . . . (570) 784-2522
    http://www.bloomsburg.org

MAIN (township). Covers a land area of 16.146 square miles and a water area of 0.514 square miles. Located at 40.98° N. Lat; 76.38° W. Long.

Population: 1,241 (1990); 1,289 (2000); 1,236 (2010); Density: 76.6 persons per square mile (2010); Race: 98.5% White, 0.3% Black, 0.4% Asian, 0.1% American Indian/Alaska Native, 0.0% Native Hawaiian/Other Pacific Islander, 0.7% Other, 1.3% Hispanic of any race (2010); Average household size: 2.58 (2010); Median age: 43.0 (2010); Males per 100 females: 100.0 (2010); Marriage status: 24.6% never married, 59.6% now married, 6.1% widowed, 9.8% divorced (2006-2010 5-year est.); Foreign born: 1.1% (2006-2010 5-year est.); Ancestry (includes multiple ancestries): 42.6% German, 14.4% Irish, 9.0% American, 7.7% Polish, 7.2% Dutch (2006-2010 5-year est.).

Economy: Single-family building permits issued: 22 (2011); Multi-family building permits issued: 0 (2011); Employment by occupation: 10.8% management, 2.6% professional, 7.9% services, 17.9% sales, 3.9% farming, 13.5% construction, 6.4% production (2006-2010 5-year est.).

Income: Per capita income: $23,918 (2006-2010 5-year est.); Median household income: $51,858 (2006-2010 5-year est.); Average household income: $64,645 (2006-2010 5-year est.); Percent of households with income of $100,000 or more: 17.1% (2006-2010 5-year est.); Poverty rate: 4.8% (2006-2010 5-year est.).

Education: Percent of population age 25 and over with: High school diploma (including GED) or higher: 89.4% (2006-2010 5-year est.); Bachelor's degree or higher: 25.1% (2006-2010 5-year est.); Master's degree or higher: 10.5% (2006-2010 5-year est.).

Housing: Homeownership rate: 87.7% (2010); Median home value: $135,800 (2006-2010 5-year est.); Median contract rent: $625 per month (2006-2010 5-year est.); Median year structure built: 1975 (2006-2010 5-year est.).

Transportation: Commute to work: 94.5% car, 0.0% public transportation, 0.0% walk, 5.0% work from home (2006-2010 5-year est.); Travel time to work: 34.6% less than 15 minutes, 41.2% 15 to 30 minutes, 14.0% 30 to 45 minutes, 4.7% 45 to 60 minutes, 5.5% 60 minutes or more (2006-2010 5-year est.)

Additional Information Contacts

Main Line Chamber of Commerce . . . . (610) 687-6232
    http://www.mlcc.org

MAINVILLE (CDP). Covers a land area of 0.738 square miles and a water area of 0.008 square miles. Located at 40.98° N. Lat; 76.37° W. Long. Elevation is 541 feet.

Population: 82 (1990); 83 (2000); 132 (2010); Density: 178.7 persons per square mile (2010); Race: 99.2% White, 0.0% Black, 0.0% Asian, 0.0% American Indian/Alaska Native, 0.0% Native Hawaiian/Other Pacific Islander, 0.8% Other, 0.0% Hispanic of any race (2010); Average household size: 2.44 (2010); Median age: 39.5 (2010); Males per 100 females: 112.9 (2010); Marriage status: 34.2% never married, 43.8% now married, 9.6% widowed, 12.3% divorced (2006-2010 5-year est.); Foreign born: 0.0% (2006-2010 5-year est.); Ancestry (includes multiple ancestries): 32.9% Irish, 27.1% German, 9.7% English, 6.5% American, 6.5% Pennsylvania German (2006-2010 5-year est.).

Economy: Employment by occupation: 10.6% management, 5.3% professional, 8.5% services, 30.9% sales, 3.2% farming, 20.2% construction, 7.4% production (2006-2010 5-year est.).

Income: Per capita income: $25,085 (2006-2010 5-year est.); Median household income: $51,500 (2006-2010 5-year est.); Average household income: $65,653 (2006-2010 5-year est.); Percent of households with income of $100,000 or more: 22.4% (2006-2010 5-year est.); Poverty rate: 5.8% (2006-2010 5-year est.).

Education: Percent of population age 25 and over with: High school diploma (including GED) or higher: 79.8% (2006-2010 5-year est.); Bachelor's degree or higher: 13.2% (2006-2010 5-year est.); Master's degree or higher: 0.0% (2006-2010 5-year est.).

Housing: Homeownership rate: 75.9% (2010); Median home value: $97,000 (2006-2010 5-year est.); Median contract rent: $392 per month (2006-2010 5-year est.); Median year structure built: before 1940 (2006-2010 5-year est.).

Transportation: Commute to work: 89.4% car, 0.0% public transportation, 0.0% walk, 10.6% work from home (2006-2010 5-year est.); Travel time to work: 17.9% less than 15 minutes, 64.3% 15 to 30 minutes, 11.9% 30 to 45 minutes, 6.0% 45 to 60 minutes, 0.0% 60 minutes or more (2006-2010 5-year est.)

MIFFLIN (township). Covers a land area of 19.220 square miles and a water area of 0.642 square miles. Located at 41.02° N. Lat; 76.28° W. Long.

Population: 2,305 (1990); 2,251 (2000); 2,322 (2010); Density: 120.8 persons per square mile (2010); Race: 98.6% White, 0.1% Black, 0.3% Asian, 0.0% American Indian/Alaska Native, 0.0% Native Hawaiian/Other Pacific Islander, 1.0% Other, 1.9% Hispanic of any race (2010); Average household size: 2.44 (2010); Median age: 45.2 (2010); Males per 100 females: 96.9 (2010); Marriage status: 21.8% never married, 68.3% now married, 3.7% widowed, 6.2% divorced (2006-2010 5-year est.); Foreign born: 2.0% (2006-2010 5-year est.); Ancestry (includes multiple ancestries): 35.0% German, 14.8% Dutch, 12.0% Irish, 9.3% Italian, 5.9% Pennsylvania German (2006-2010 5-year est.).

Economy: Single-family building permits issued: 0 (2011); Multi-family building permits issued: 0 (2011); Employment by occupation: 8.1% management, 2.8% professional, 12.1% services, 11.7% sales, 10.1% farming, 7.9% construction, 8.7% production (2006-2010 5-year est.).

Income: Per capita income: $30,542 (2006-2010 5-year est.); Median household income: $55,625 (2006-2010 5-year est.); Average household income: $78,236 (2006-2010 5-year est.); Percent of households with income of $100,000 or more: 14.9% (2006-2010 5-year est.); Poverty rate: 9.1% (2006-2010 5-year est.).

Education: Percent of population age 25 and over with: High school diploma (including GED) or higher: 84.8% (2006-2010 5-year est.); Bachelor's degree or higher: 17.2% (2006-2010 5-year est.); Master's degree or higher: 4.5% (2006-2010 5-year est.).

Housing: Homeownership rate: 81.9% (2010); Median home value: $134,600 (2006-2010 5-year est.); Median contract rent: $535 per month (2006-2010 5-year est.); Median year structure built: 1971 (2006-2010 5-year est.).

Transportation: Commute to work: 89.4% car, 0.0% public transportation, 2.8% walk, 6.9% work from home (2006-2010 5-year est.); Travel time to work: 29.7% less than 15 minutes, 50.5% 15 to 30 minutes, 15.0% 30 to 45 minutes, 2.8% 45 to 60 minutes, 2.0% 60 minutes or more (2006-2010 5-year est.)

Additional Information Contacts

Columbia Montour Chamber of Commerce. . . . . (570) 784-2522
http://www.bloomsburg.org

MIFFLINVILLE (CDP). Aka Creasy. Covers a land area of 1.370 square miles and a water area of 0.007 square miles. Located at 41.03° N. Lat; 76.30° W. Long. Elevation is 515 feet.

Population: 1,329 (1990); 1,213 (2000); 1,253 (2010); Density: 914.6 persons per square mile (2010); Race: 98.5% White, 0.2% Black, 0.0% Asian, 0.0% American Indian/Alaska Native, 0.0% Native Hawaiian/Other Pacific Islander, 1.3% Other, 2.1% Hispanic of any race (2010); Average household size: 2.38 (2010); Median age: 46.9 (2010); Males per 100 females: 93.1 (2010); Marriage status: 21.6% never married, 65.2% now married, 5.1% widowed, 8.2% divorced (2006-2010 5-year est.); Foreign born: 0.7% (2006-2010 5-year est.); Ancestry (includes multiple ancestries): 34.9% German, 14.0% Dutch, 11.3% Irish, 8.1% Italian, 8.1% Pennsylvania German (2006-2010 5-year est.).

Economy: Employment by occupation: 9.7% management, 3.8% professional, 6.8% services, 15.8% sales, 7.8% farming, 5.6% construction, 2.2% production (2006-2010 5-year est.).

Income: Per capita income: $27,499 (2006-2010 5-year est.); Median household income: $54,276 (2006-2010 5-year est.); Average household income: $69,597 (2006-2010 5-year est.); Percent of households with income of $100,000 or more: 19.2% (2006-2010 5-year est.); Poverty rate: 8.0% (2006-2010 5-year est.).

Education: Percent of population age 25 and over with: High school diploma (including GED) or higher: 88.6% (2006-2010 5-year est.); Bachelor's degree or higher: 17.2% (2006-2010 5-year est.); Master's degree or higher: 4.7% (2006-2010 5-year est.).

Housing: Homeownership rate: 81.6% (2010); Median home value: $134,000 (2006-2010 5-year est.); Median contract rent: $566 per month (2006-2010 5-year est.); Median year structure built: 1960 (2006-2010 5-year est.).

Transportation: Commute to work: 90.6% car, 0.0% public transportation, 5.4% walk, 2.3% work from home (2006-2010 5-year est.); Travel time to work: 26.6% less than 15 minutes, 55.5% 15 to 30 minutes, 17.9% 30 to 45 minutes, 0.0% 45 to 60 minutes, 0.0% 60 minutes or more (2006-2010 5-year est.)

Additional Information Contacts

Columbia Montour Chamber of Commerce. . . . . (570) 784-2522
http://www.bloomsburg.org

MILLVILLE (borough). Covers a land area of 0.981 square miles and a water area of 0.008 square miles. Located at 41.12° N. Lat; 76.53° W. Long. Elevation is 653 feet.

History: Covered bridges in area.

Population: 969 (1990); 991 (2000); 948 (2010); Density: 966.0 persons per square mile (2010); Race: 97.9% White, 0.7% Black, 0.3% Asian, 0.0% American Indian/Alaska Native, 0.0% Native Hawaiian/Other Pacific Islander, 1.1% Other, 1.3% Hispanic of any race (2010); Average household size: 2.26 (2010); Median age: 43.1 (2010); Males per 100 females: 83.0 (2010); Marriage status: 20.3% never married, 46.0% now married, 18.2% widowed, 15.4% divorced (2006-2010 5-year est.); Foreign born: 1.6% (2006-2010 5-year est.); Ancestry (includes multiple ancestries): 46.1% German, 12.6% Irish, 5.0% Dutch, 4.8% English, 4.1% Polish (2006-2010 5-year est.).

Economy: Single-family building permits issued: 0 (2011); Multi-family building permits issued: 0 (2011); Employment by occupation: 5.2% management, 2.6% professional, 6.9% services, 23.1% sales, 2.6% farming, 12.4% construction, 7.2% production (2006-2010 5-year est.).

Income: Per capita income: $18,714 (2006-2010 5-year est.); Median household income: $34,044 (2006-2010 5-year est.); Average household income: $44,222 (2006-2010 5-year est.); Percent of households with income of $100,000 or more: 7.4% (2006-2010 5-year est.); Poverty rate: 22.7% (2006-2010 5-year est.).

Education: Percent of population age 25 and over with: High school diploma (including GED) or higher: 85.7% (2006-2010 5-year est.); Bachelor's degree or higher: 17.9% (2006-2010 5-year est.); Master's degree or higher: 4.1% (2006-2010 5-year est.).

School District(s)

Millville Area SD (KG-12)
    2010-11 Enrollment: 708. . . . . (570) 458-5538

Housing: Homeownership rate: 52.7% (2010); Median home value: $103,300 (2006-2010 5-year est.); Median contract rent: $351 per month (2006-2010 5-year est.); Median year structure built: before 1940 (2006-2010 5-year est.).

Safety: Violent crime rate: 0.0 per 10,000 population; Property crime rate: 0.0 per 10,000 population (2011).

Transportation: Commute to work: 88.7% car, 0.0% public transportation, 2.5% walk, 5.2% work from home (2006-2010 5-year est.); Travel time to work: 34.6% less than 15 minutes, 44.0% 15 to 30 minutes, 13.9% 30 to 45 minutes, 4.9% 45 to 60 minutes, 2.6% 60 minutes or more (2006-2010 5-year est.)

MONTOUR (township). Covers a land area of 9.155 square miles and a water area of 0.449 square miles. Located at 40.97° N. Lat; 76.51° W. Long.

Population: 1,419 (1990); 1,437 (2000); 1,344 (2010); Density: 146.8 persons per square mile (2010); Race: 95.8% White, 0.5% Black, 0.7% Asian, 0.7% American Indian/Alaska Native, 0.0% Native Hawaiian/Other Pacific Islander, 2.3% Other, 1.4% Hispanic of any race (2010); Average household size: 2.35 (2010); Median age: 45.3 (2010); Males per 100 females: 102.1 (2010); Marriage status: 25.2% never married, 55.9% now married, 7.8% widowed, 11.1% divorced (2006-2010 5-year est.); Foreign born: 2.0% (2006-2010 5-year est.); Ancestry (includes multiple ancestries): 43.0% German, 11.6% Irish, 9.5% English, 8.6% Dutch, 7.6% Italian (2006-2010 5-year est.).

Economy: Single-family building permits issued: 1 (2011); Multi-family building permits issued: 0 (2011); Employment by occupation: 7.9%

management, 1.5% professional, 13.5% services, 13.3% sales, 6.6% farming, 13.0% construction, 11.3% production (2006-2010 5-year est.).
Income: Per capita income: $23,434 (2006-2010 5-year est.); Median household income: $48,542 (2006-2010 5-year est.); Average household income: $56,335 (2006-2010 5-year est.); Percent of households with income of $100,000 or more: 11.5% (2006-2010 5-year est.); Poverty rate: 12.4% (2006-2010 5-year est.).
Education: Percent of population age 25 and over with: High school diploma (including GED) or higher: 88.0% (2006-2010 5-year est.); Bachelor's degree or higher: 21.4% (2006-2010 5-year est.); Master's degree or higher: 8.4% (2006-2010 5-year est.).
Housing: Homeownership rate: 81.0% (2010); Median home value: $139,600 (2006-2010 5-year est.); Median contract rent: $525 per month (2006-2010 5-year est.); Median year structure built: 1966 (2006-2010 5-year est.).
Transportation: Commute to work: 95.3% car, 0.0% public transportation, 1.9% walk, 2.2% work from home (2006-2010 5-year est.); Travel time to work: 41.1% less than 15 minutes, 38.5% 15 to 30 minutes, 16.3% 30 to 45 minutes, 1.6% 45 to 60 minutes, 2.6% 60 minutes or more (2006-2010 5-year est.)

Additional Information Contacts
Columbia Montour Chamber of Commerce. . . . . (570) 784-2522
  http://www.bloomsburg.org

MOUNT PLEASANT (township). Covers a land area of 16.754 square miles and a water area of 0.157 square miles. Located at 41.07° N. Lat; 76.48° W. Long.
Population: 1,383 (1990); 1,459 (2000); 1,609 (2010); Density: 96.0 persons per square mile (2010); Race: 96.7% White, 1.4% Black, 0.6% Asian, 0.1% American Indian/Alaska Native, 0.4% Native Hawaiian/Other Pacific Islander, 0.8% Other, 0.9% Hispanic of any race (2010); Average household size: 2.67 (2010); Median age: 42.9 (2010); Males per 100 females: 101.9 (2010); Marriage status: 21.7% never married, 68.0% now married, 3.5% widowed, 6.9% divorced (2006-2010 5-year est.); Foreign born: 1.6% (2006-2010 5-year est.); Ancestry (includes multiple ancestries): 40.5% German, 18.6% Irish, 9.3% Italian, 7.5% English, 6.1% American (2006-2010 5-year est.).
Economy: Single-family building permits issued: 3 (2011); Multi-family building permits issued: 0 (2011); Employment by occupation: 7.9% management, 1.0% professional, 7.2% services, 18.0% sales, 1.9% farming, 12.9% construction, 6.2% production (2006-2010 5-year est.).
Income: Per capita income: $26,448 (2006-2010 5-year est.); Median household income: $62,542 (2006-2010 5-year est.); Average household income: $70,104 (2006-2010 5-year est.); Percent of households with income of $100,000 or more: 19.9% (2006-2010 5-year est.); Poverty rate: 10.2% (2006-2010 5-year est.).
Education: Percent of population age 25 and over with: High school diploma (including GED) or higher: 88.4% (2006-2010 5-year est.); Bachelor's degree or higher: 21.3% (2006-2010 5-year est.); Master's degree or higher: 8.2% (2006-2010 5-year est.).
Housing: Homeownership rate: 86.9% (2010); Median home value: $158,700 (2006-2010 5-year est.); Median contract rent: $398 per month (2006-2010 5-year est.); Median year structure built: 1977 (2006-2010 5-year est.).
Transportation: Commute to work: 97.3% car, 0.0% public transportation, 0.0% walk, 1.5% work from home (2006-2010 5-year est.); Travel time to work: 23.6% less than 15 minutes, 45.3% 15 to 30 minutes, 18.4% 30 to 45 minutes, 7.8% 45 to 60 minutes, 4.8% 60 minutes or more (2006-2010 5-year est.)

Additional Information Contacts
Columbia Montour Chamber of Commerce. . . . . (570) 784-2522
  http://www.bloomsburg.org

NORTH CENTRE (township). Covers a land area of 14.960 square miles and a water area of 0.045 square miles. Located at 41.06° N. Lat; 76.36° W. Long. Elevation is 919 feet.
Population: 1,821 (1990); 2,009 (2000); 2,105 (2010); Density: 140.7 persons per square mile (2010); Race: 97.7% White, 1.0% Black, 0.2% Asian, 0.1% American Indian/Alaska Native, 0.0% Native Hawaiian/Other Pacific Islander, 1.0% Other, 0.9% Hispanic of any race (2010); Average household size: 2.57 (2010); Median age: 45.5 (2010); Males per 100 females: 92.6 (2010); Marriage status: 25.0% never married, 63.5% now married, 3.1% widowed, 8.4% divorced (2006-2010 5-year est.); Foreign born: 0.0% (2006-2010 5-year est.); Ancestry (includes multiple

ancestries): 38.4% German, 15.5% English, 13.4% Irish, 7.3% Italian, 6.5% Polish (2006-2010 5-year est.).
Economy: Single-family building permits issued: 3 (2011); Multi-family building permits issued: 0 (2011); Employment by occupation: 6.2% management, 3.6% professional, 6.4% services, 20.7% sales, 2.6% farming, 8.9% construction, 9.4% production (2006-2010 5-year est.).
Income: Per capita income: $24,008 (2006-2010 5-year est.); Median household income: $55,673 (2006-2010 5-year est.); Average household income: $66,364 (2006-2010 5-year est.); Percent of households with income of $100,000 or more: 16.5% (2006-2010 5-year est.); Poverty rate: 7.2% (2006-2010 5-year est.).
Education: Percent of population age 25 and over with: High school diploma (including GED) or higher: 87.0% (2006-2010 5-year est.); Bachelor's degree or higher: 23.0% (2006-2010 5-year est.); Master's degree or higher: 6.2% (2006-2010 5-year est.).
Housing: Homeownership rate: 92.2% (2010); Median home value: $151,800 (2006-2010 5-year est.); Median contract rent: $504 per month (2006-2010 5-year est.); Median year structure built: 1980 (2006-2010 5-year est.).
Transportation: Commute to work: 97.4% car, 0.0% public transportation, 0.0% walk, 2.1% work from home (2006-2010 5-year est.); Travel time to work: 28.2% less than 15 minutes, 50.3% 15 to 30 minutes, 11.8% 30 to 45 minutes, 6.4% 45 to 60 minutes, 3.2% 60 minutes or more (2006-2010 5-year est.)

Additional Information Contacts
Columbia Montour Chamber of Commerce. . . . . (570) 784-2522
  http://columbiamontourchamber.com

NUMIDIA (CDP). Covers a land area of 1.055 square miles and a water area of 0.006 square miles. Located at 40.88° N. Lat; 76.40° W. Long. Elevation is 988 feet.
Population: 242 (1990); 254 (2000); 244 (2010); Density: 231.3 persons per square mile (2010); Race: 98.0% White, 0.4% Black, 0.0% Asian, 0.4% American Indian/Alaska Native, 0.0% Native Hawaiian/Other Pacific Islander, 1.2% Other, 0.8% Hispanic of any race (2010); Average household size: 2.46 (2010); Median age: 44.5 (2010); Males per 100 females: 90.6 (2010); Marriage status: 14.2% never married, 57.9% now married, 7.1% widowed, 20.8% divorced (2006-2010 5-year est.); Foreign born: 0.0% (2006-2010 5-year est.); Ancestry (includes multiple ancestries): 41.4% German, 18.9% Irish, 18.2% Italian, 9.8% Polish, 7.2% Pennsylvania German (2006-2010 5-year est.).
Economy: Employment by occupation: 5.1% management, 0.0% professional, 10.9% services, 7.2% sales, 2.2% farming, 1.4% construction, 12.3% production (2006-2010 5-year est.).
Income: Per capita income: $22,668 (2006-2010 5-year est.); Median household income: $51,667 (2006-2010 5-year est.); Average household income: $59,299 (2006-2010 5-year est.); Percent of households with income of $100,000 or more: 5.2% (2006-2010 5-year est.); Poverty rate: 0.0% (2006-2010 5-year est.).
Education: Percent of population age 25 and over with: High school diploma (including GED) or higher: 84.9% (2006-2010 5-year est.); Bachelor's degree or higher: 16.0% (2006-2010 5-year est.); Master's degree or higher: 4.6% (2006-2010 5-year est.).
Housing: Homeownership rate: 89.9% (2010); Median home value: $150,000 (2006-2010 5-year est.); Median contract rent: n/a per month (2006-2010 5-year est.); Median year structure built: 1945 (2006-2010 5-year est.).
Transportation: Commute to work: 100.0% car, 0.0% public transportation, 0.0% walk, 0.0% work from home (2006-2010 5-year est.); Travel time to work: 6.5% less than 15 minutes, 54.3% 15 to 30 minutes, 23.2% 30 to 45 minutes, 15.9% 45 to 60 minutes, 0.0% 60 minutes or more (2006-2010 5-year est.)

ORANGE (township). Covers a land area of 12.874 square miles and a water area of 0.154 square miles. Located at 41.09° N. Lat; 76.42° W. Long.
History: Covered bridges in area.
Population: 1,021 (1990); 1,148 (2000); 1,257 (2010); Density: 97.6 persons per square mile (2010); Race: 97.9% White, 0.3% Black, 0.3% Asian, 0.4% American Indian/Alaska Native, 0.0% Native Hawaiian/Other Pacific Islander, 1.1% Other, 0.8% Hispanic of any race (2010); Average household size: 2.64 (2010); Median age: 43.9 (2010); Males per 100 females: 100.8 (2010); Marriage status: 19.3% never married, 67.4% now married, 5.8% widowed, 7.6% divorced (2006-2010 5-year est.); Foreign born: 2.3% (2006-2010 5-year est.); Ancestry (includes multiple

ancestries): 46.8% German, 15.5% Irish, 13.2% English, 10.2% Italian, 9.7% Dutch (2006-2010 5-year est.).

Economy: Single-family building permits issued: 0 (2011); Multi-family building permits issued: 0 (2011); Employment by occupation: 9.6% management, 5.5% professional, 9.1% services, 16.5% sales, 3.1% farming, 10.6% construction, 9.6% production (2006-2010 5-year est.).
Income: Per capita income: $25,776 (2006-2010 5-year est.); Median household income: $53,125 (2006-2010 5-year est.); Average household income: $63,716 (2006-2010 5-year est.); Percent of households with income of $100,000 or more: 18.2% (2006-2010 5-year est.); Poverty rate: 4.3% (2006-2010 5-year est.).
Education: Percent of population age 25 and over with: High school diploma (including GED) or higher: 92.0% (2006-2010 5-year est.); Bachelor's degree or higher: 22.2% (2006-2010 5-year est.); Master's degree or higher: 9.1% (2006-2010 5-year est.).
Housing: Homeownership rate: 88.4% (2010); Median home value: $168,900 (2006-2010 5-year est.); Median contract rent: $444 per month (2006-2010 5-year est.); Median year structure built: 1982 (2006-2010 5-year est.).
Transportation: Commute to work: 94.7% car, 0.0% public transportation, 0.8% walk, 4.1% work from home (2006-2010 5-year est.); Travel time to work: 28.6% less than 15 minutes, 51.5% 15 to 30 minutes, 12.3% 30 to 45 minutes, 5.0% 45 to 60 minutes, 2.6% 60 minutes or more (2006-2010 5-year est.)
Additional Information Contacts
Columbia Montour Chamber of Commerce............ (570) 784-2522
   http://columbiamontourchamber.com

ORANGEVILLE (borough). Covers a land area of 0.445 square miles and a water area of 0.008 square miles. Located at 41.08° N. Lat; 76.41° W. Long. Elevation is 587 feet.

Population: 504 (1990); 500 (2000); 508 (2010); Density: 1,141.2 persons per square mile (2010); Race: 97.8% White, 0.4% Black, 0.2% Asian, 0.4% American Indian/Alaska Native, 0.0% Native Hawaiian/Other Pacific Islander, 1.2% Other, 1.4% Hispanic of any race (2010); Average household size: 2.36 (2010); Median age: 51.8 (2010); Males per 100 females: 97.7 (2010); Marriage status: 21.3% never married, 40.2% now married, 26.5% widowed, 12.0% divorced (2006-2010 5-year est.); Foreign born: 5.2% (2006-2010 5-year est.); Ancestry (includes multiple ancestries): 48.8% German, 7.4% English, 6.9% Irish, 6.9% Dutch, 6.5% Polish (2006-2010 5-year est.).
Economy: Single-family building permits issued: 0 (2011); Multi-family building permits issued: 0 (2011); Employment by occupation: 6.3% management, 8.1% professional, 10.8% services, 18.5% sales, 6.3% farming, 15.3% construction, 5.0% production (2006-2010 5-year est.).
Income: Per capita income: $26,922 (2006-2010 5-year est.); Median household income: $53,672 (2006-2010 5-year est.); Average household income: $79,199 (2006-2010 5-year est.); Percent of households with income of $100,000 or more: 12.1% (2006-2010 5-year est.); Poverty rate: 10.5% (2006-2010 5-year est.).
Education: Percent of population age 25 and over with: High school diploma (including GED) or higher: 75.9% (2006-2010 5-year est.); Bachelor's degree or higher: 13.5% (2006-2010 5-year est.); Master's degree or higher: 8.8% (2006-2010 5-year est.).
Housing: Homeownership rate: 65.6% (2010); Median home value: $116,300 (2006-2010 5-year est.); Median contract rent: $702 per month (2006-2010 5-year est.); Median year structure built: before 1940 (2006-2010 5-year est.).
Safety: Violent crime rate: 0.0 per 10,000 population; Property crime rate: 5.6 per 10,000 population (2011).
Transportation: Commute to work: 94.1% car, 0.0% public transportation, 0.9% walk, 5.0% work from home (2006-2010 5-year est.); Travel time to work: 41.7% less than 15 minutes, 40.8% 15 to 30 minutes, 8.1% 30 to 45 minutes, 9.5% 45 to 60 minutes, 0.0% 60 minutes or more (2006-2010 5-year est.)

PINE (township). Covers a land area of 26.434 square miles and a water area of 0.052 square miles. Located at 41.19° N. Lat; 76.52° W. Long.
Population: 990 (1990); 1,092 (2000); 1,046 (2010); Density: 39.6 persons per square mile (2010); Race: 98.9% White, 0.0% Black, 0.2% Asian, 0.0% American Indian/Alaska Native, 0.0% Native Hawaiian/Other Pacific Islander, 0.9% Other, 1.0% Hispanic of any race (2010); Average household size: 2.42 (2010); Median age: 46.2 (2010); Males per 100 females: 101.9 (2010); Marriage status: 20.5% never married, 64.4% now married, 2.4% widowed, 12.6% divorced (2006-2010 5-year est.); Foreign

born: 3.2% (2006-2010 5-year est.); Ancestry (includes multiple ancestries): 44.9% German, 15.1% English, 13.5% Irish, 11.9% Dutch, 4.9% American (2006-2010 5-year est.).
Economy: Single-family building permits issued: 0 (2011); Multi-family building permits issued: 0 (2011); Employment by occupation: 9.3% management, 1.1% professional, 7.6% services, 18.1% sales, 2.7% farming, 14.3% construction, 9.3% production (2006-2010 5-year est.).
Income: Per capita income: $22,471 (2006-2010 5-year est.); Median household income: $39,115 (2006-2010 5-year est.); Average household income: $51,913 (2006-2010 5-year est.); Percent of households with income of $100,000 or more: 7.4% (2006-2010 5-year est.); Poverty rate: 7.5% (2006-2010 5-year est.).
Education: Percent of population age 25 and over with: High school diploma (including GED) or higher: 84.0% (2006-2010 5-year est.); Bachelor's degree or higher: 13.7% (2006-2010 5-year est.); Master's degree or higher: 4.4% (2006-2010 5-year est.).
Housing: Homeownership rate: 88.2% (2010); Median home value: $120,600 (2006-2010 5-year est.); Median contract rent: $438 per month (2006-2010 5-year est.); Median year structure built: 1971 (2006-2010 5-year est.).
Transportation: Commute to work: 93.2% car, 0.0% public transportation, 0.6% walk, 6.2% work from home (2006-2010 5-year est.); Travel time to work: 23.1% less than 15 minutes, 35.1% 15 to 30 minutes, 29.5% 30 to 45 minutes, 7.5% 45 to 60 minutes, 4.8% 60 minutes or more (2006-2010 5-year est.)
Additional Information Contacts
Columbia Montour Chamber of Commerce............ (570) 784-2522
   http://www.bloomsburg.org

ROARING CREEK (township). Aka Slabtown. Covers a land area of 23.461 square miles and a water area of 0.080 square miles. Located at 40.90° N. Lat; 76.33° W. Long.
Population: 478 (1990); 495 (2000); 545 (2010); Density: 23.2 persons per square mile (2010); Race: 98.9% White, 0.0% Black, 0.0% Asian, 0.0% American Indian/Alaska Native, 0.0% Native Hawaiian/Other Pacific Islander, 1.1% Other, 2.8% Hispanic of any race (2010); Average household size: 2.45 (2010); Median age: 48.0 (2010); Males per 100 females: 99.6 (2010); Marriage status: 14.7% never married, 70.9% now married, 7.9% widowed, 6.5% divorced (2006-2010 5-year est.); Foreign born: 0.0% (2006-2010 5-year est.); Ancestry (includes multiple ancestries): 41.9% German, 10.3% Polish, 9.5% Italian, 8.3% Dutch, 6.0% American (2006-2010 5-year est.).
Economy: Single-family building permits issued: 2 (2011); Multi-family building permits issued: 0 (2011); Employment by occupation: 5.3% management, 3.7% professional, 8.2% services, 14.0% sales, 1.6% farming, 15.2% construction, 10.3% production (2006-2010 5-year est.).
Income: Per capita income: $20,599 (2006-2010 5-year est.); Median household income: $48,125 (2006-2010 5-year est.); Average household income: $52,350 (2006-2010 5-year est.); Percent of households with income of $100,000 or more: 6.7% (2006-2010 5-year est.); Poverty rate: 6.0% (2006-2010 5-year est.).
Education: Percent of population age 25 and over with: High school diploma (including GED) or higher: 88.8% (2006-2010 5-year est.); Bachelor's degree or higher: 18.0% (2006-2010 5-year est.); Master's degree or higher: 5.5% (2006-2010 5-year est.).
Housing: Homeownership rate: 91.0% (2010); Median home value: $148,900 (2006-2010 5-year est.); Median contract rent: n/a per month (2006-2010 5-year est.); Median year structure built: 1973 (2006-2010 5-year est.).
Transportation: Commute to work: 99.2% car, 0.0% public transportation, 0.0% walk, 0.0% work from home (2006-2010 5-year est.); Travel time to work: 13.9% less than 15 minutes, 60.3% 15 to 30 minutes, 18.1% 30 to 45 minutes, 7.6% 45 to 60 minutes, 0.0% 60 minutes or more (2006-2010 5-year est.)

ROHRSBURG (CDP). Covers a land area of 0.708 square miles and a water area of 0.006 square miles. Located at 41.13° N. Lat; 76.43° W. Long. Elevation is 656 feet.
Population: 172 (1990); 164 (2000); 145 (2010); Density: 204.8 persons per square mile (2010); Race: 97.9% White, 1.4% Black, 0.7% Asian, 0.0% American Indian/Alaska Native, 0.0% Native Hawaiian/Other Pacific Islander, 0.0% Other, 0.7% Hispanic of any race (2010); Average household size: 2.69 (2010); Median age: 37.5 (2010); Males per 100 females: 107.1 (2010); Marriage status: 23.5% never married, 63.0% now married, 13.6% widowed, 0.0% divorced (2006-2010 5-year est.); Foreign

born: 0.0% (2006-2010 5-year est.); Ancestry (includes multiple ancestries): 27.0% German, 21.6% Irish, 14.4% Dutch, 13.5% Scottish, 12.6% English (2006-2010 5-year est.).

Economy: Employment by occupation: 7.1% management, 7.1% professional, 9.5% services, 7.1% sales, 0.0% farming, 28.6% construction, 7.1% production (2006-2010 5-year est.).

Income: Per capita income: $143,735 (2006-2010 5-year est.); Median household income: $67,250 (2006-2010 5-year est.); Average household income: $274,021 (2006-2010 5-year est.); Percent of households with income of $100,000 or more: 16.3% (2006-2010 5-year est.); Poverty rate: 1.8% (2006-2010 5-year est.).

Education: Percent of population age 25 and over with: High school diploma (including GED) or higher: 82.4% (2006-2010 5-year est.); Bachelor's degree or higher: 4.4% (2006-2010 5-year est.); Master's degree or higher: 0.0% (2006-2010 5-year est.).

Housing: Homeownership rate: 79.6% (2010); Median home value: $86,700 (2006-2010 5-year est.); Median contract rent: n/a per month (2006-2010 5-year est.); Median year structure built: before 1940 (2006-2010 5-year est.).

Transportation: Commute to work: 100.0% car, 0.0% public transportation, 0.0% walk, 0.0% work from home (2006-2010 5-year est.); Travel time to work: 0.0% less than 15 minutes, 45.2% 15 to 30 minutes, 54.8% 30 to 45 minutes, 0.0% 45 to 60 minutes, 0.0% 60 minutes or more (2006-2010 5-year est.).

RUPERT (CDP). Covers a land area of 0.905 square miles and a water area of 0.036 square miles. Located at 40.98° N. Lat; 76.48° W. Long. Elevation is 502 feet.

Population: 172 (1990); 174 (2000); 183 (2010); Density: 202.2 persons per square mile (2010); Race: 100.0% White, 0.0% Black, 0.0% Asian, 0.0% American Indian/Alaska Native, 0.0% Native Hawaiian/Other Pacific Islander, 0.0% Other, 1.1% Hispanic of any race (2010); Average household size: 2.58 (2010); Median age: 46.8 (2010); Males per 100 females: 96.8 (2010); Marriage status: 27.7% never married, 65.9% now married, 2.9% widowed, 3.5% divorced (2006-2010 5-year est.); Foreign born: 2.7% (2006-2010 5-year est.); Ancestry (includes multiple ancestries): 39.0% German, 25.1% Irish, 16.6% English, 9.1% Polish, 4.8% Ukrainian (2006-2010 5-year est.).

Economy: Employment by occupation: 3.1% management, 6.1% professional, 7.1% services, 14.3% sales, 4.1% farming, 10.2% construction, 11.2% production (2006-2010 5-year est.).

Income: Per capita income: $22,456 (2006-2010 5-year est.); Median household income: $52,917 (2006-2010 5-year est.); Average household income: $57,286 (2006-2010 5-year est.); Percent of households with income of $100,000 or more: 10.0% (2006-2010 5-year est.); Poverty rate: 9.1% (2006-2010 5-year est.).

Education: Percent of population age 25 and over with: High school diploma (including GED) or higher: 89.7% (2006-2010 5-year est.); Bachelor's degree or higher: 14.4% (2006-2010 5-year est.); Master's degree or higher: 5.5% (2006-2010 5-year est.).

Housing: Homeownership rate: 88.7% (2010); Median home value: $105,800 (2006-2010 5-year est.); Median contract rent: n/a per month (2006-2010 5-year est.); Median year structure built: before 1940 (2006-2010 5-year est.).

Transportation: Commute to work: 100.0% car, 0.0% public transportation, 0.0% walk, 0.0% work from home (2006-2010 5-year est.); Travel time to work: 30.9% less than 15 minutes, 50.5% 15 to 30 minutes, 18.6% 30 to 45 minutes, 0.0% 45 to 60 minutes, 0.0% 60 minutes or more (2006-2010 5-year est.).

SCOTT (township). Covers a land area of 6.995 square miles and a water area of 0.469 square miles. Located at 41.02° N. Lat; 76.41° W. Long.

Population: 4,378 (1990); 4,768 (2000); 5,113 (2010); Density: 731.0 persons per square mile (2010); Race: 96.1% White, 0.6% Black, 2.0% Asian, 0.1% American Indian/Alaska Native, 0.0% Native Hawaiian/Other Pacific Islander, 1.2% Other, 1.0% Hispanic of any race (2010); Average household size: 2.26 (2010); Median age: 47.2 (2010); Males per 100 females: 89.1 (2010); Marriage status: 18.8% never married, 59.9% now married, 10.8% widowed, 10.6% divorced (2006-2010 5-year est.); Foreign born: 4.5% (2006-2010 5-year est.); Ancestry (includes multiple ancestries): 36.3% German, 15.2% Irish, 11.0% English, 9.4% Dutch, 6.6% Italian (2006-2010 5-year est.).

Economy: Single-family building permits issued: 10 (2011); Multi-family building permits issued: 0 (2011); Employment by occupation: 8.8%

management, 3.1% professional, 6.9% services, 16.7% sales, 10.3% farming, 7.8% construction, 6.5% production (2006-2010 5-year est.).

Income: Per capita income: $37,859 (2006-2010 5-year est.); Median household income: $56,303 (2006-2010 5-year est.); Average household income: $81,525 (2006-2010 5-year est.); Percent of households with income of $100,000 or more: 20.2% (2006-2010 5-year est.); Poverty rate: 7.6% (2006-2010 5-year est.).

Education: Percent of population age 25 and over with: High school diploma (including GED) or higher: 88.4% (2006-2010 5-year est.); Bachelor's degree or higher: 26.4% (2006-2010 5-year est.); Master's degree or higher: 11.3% (2006-2010 5-year est.).

Housing: Homeownership rate: 78.8% (2010); Median home value: $129,900 (2006-2010 5-year est.); Median contract rent: $540 per month (2006-2010 5-year est.); Median year structure built: 1972 (2006-2010 5-year est.).

Safety: Violent crime rate: 2.0 per 10,000 population; Property crime rate: 122.8 per 10,000 population (2011).

Transportation: Commute to work: 96.4% car, 0.0% public transportation, 1.5% walk, 1.2% work from home (2006-2010 5-year est.); Travel time to work: 50.1% less than 15 minutes, 30.3% 15 to 30 minutes, 12.3% 30 to 45 minutes, 5.0% 45 to 60 minutes, 2.4% 60 minutes or more (2006-2010 5-year est.).

Additional Information Contacts
Columbia Montour Chamber of Commerce . . . . (570) 784-2522
    http://columbiamontourchamber.com
Scott Township . . . . (570) 784-9114
    http://www.scott-township.com

SLABTOWN (CDP). Aka Roaring Creek. Covers a land area of 0.477 square miles and a water area of 0.014 square miles. Located at 40.90° N. Lat; 76.40° W. Long. Elevation is 794 feet.

Population: 94 (1990); 105 (2000); 156 (2010); Density: 327.2 persons per square mile (2010); Race: 100.0% White, 0.0% Black, 0.0% Asian, 0.0% American Indian/Alaska Native, 0.0% Native Hawaiian/Other Pacific Islander, 0.0% Other, 0.0% Hispanic of any race (2010); Average household size: 2.36 (2010); Median age: 41.0 (2010); Males per 100 females: 97.5 (2010); Marriage status: 11.8% never married, 74.3% now married, 6.6% widowed, 7.4% divorced (2006-2010 5-year est.); Foreign born: 1.8% (2006-2010 5-year est.); Ancestry (includes multiple ancestries): 21.2% German, 12.1% Dutch, 9.1% Irish, 7.3% Polish, 6.1% French (2006-2010 5-year est.).

Economy: Employment by occupation: 0.0% management, 8.0% professional, 4.0% services, 24.0% sales, 0.0% farming, 14.7% construction, 14.7% production (2006-2010 5-year est.).

Income: Per capita income: $20,488 (2006-2010 5-year est.); Median household income: $50,417 (2006-2010 5-year est.); Average household income: $49,074 (2006-2010 5-year est.); Percent of households with income of $100,000 or more: n/a (2006-2010 5-year est.); Poverty rate: 0.0% (2006-2010 5-year est.).

Education: Percent of population age 25 and over with: High school diploma (including GED) or higher: 83.1% (2006-2010 5-year est.); Bachelor's degree or higher: 2.4% (2006-2010 5-year est.); Master's degree or higher: 0.0% (2006-2010 5-year est.).

Housing: Homeownership rate: 74.2% (2010); Median home value: $75,000 (2006-2010 5-year est.); Median contract rent: $425 per month (2006-2010 5-year est.); Median year structure built: 1953 (2006-2010 5-year est.).

Transportation: Commute to work: 100.0% car, 0.0% public transportation, 0.0% walk, 0.0% work from home (2006-2010 5-year est.); Travel time to work: 4.0% less than 15 minutes, 29.3% 15 to 30 minutes, 28.0% 30 to 45 minutes, 38.7% 45 to 60 minutes, 0.0% 60 minutes or more (2006-2010 5-year est.)

SOUTH CENTRE (township). Covers a land area of 5.432 square miles and a water area of 0.526 square miles. Located at 41.03° N. Lat; 76.36° W. Long.

Population: 1,891 (1990); 1,972 (2000); 1,937 (2010); Density: 356.6 persons per square mile (2010); Race: 96.1% White, 0.5% Black, 0.9% Asian, 0.2% American Indian/Alaska Native, 0.1% Native Hawaiian/Other Pacific Islander, 2.2% Other, 2.2% Hispanic of any race (2010); Average household size: 2.39 (2010); Median age: 44.4 (2010); Males per 100 females: 95.9 (2010); Marriage status: 25.8% never married, 55.6% now married, 5.6% widowed, 13.0% divorced (2006-2010 5-year est.); Foreign born: 1.6% (2006-2010 5-year est.); Ancestry (includes multiple

ancestries): 36.1% German, 8.6% English, 8.0% Dutch, 7.7% Italian, 7.6% Welsh (2006-2010 5-year est.).

Economy: Single-family building permits issued: 1 (2011); Multi-family building permits issued: 0 (2011); Employment by occupation: 4.0% management, 2.0% professional, 17.0% services, 14.6% sales, 4.8% farming, 6.0% construction, 8.4% production (2006-2010 5-year est.).

Income: Per capita income: $24,728 (2006-2010 5-year est.); Median household income: $45,139 (2006-2010 5-year est.); Average household income: $62,699 (2006-2010 5-year est.); Percent of households with income of $100,000 or more: 13.5% (2006-2010 5-year est.); Poverty rate: 7.0% (2006-2010 5-year est.).

Education: Percent of population age 25 and over with: High school diploma (including GED) or higher: 85.8% (2006-2010 5-year est.); Bachelor's degree or higher: 15.7% (2006-2010 5-year est.); Master's degree or higher: 5.6% (2006-2010 5-year est.).

Housing: Homeownership rate: 82.8% (2010); Median home value: $108,400 (2006-2010 5-year est.); Median contract rent: $502 per month (2006-2010 5-year est.); Median year structure built: 1974 (2006-2010 5-year est.).

Safety: Violent crime rate: 10.3 per 10,000 population; Property crime rate: 159.5 per 10,000 population (2011).

Transportation: Commute to work: 93.8% car, 0.0% public transportation, 1.3% walk, 3.3% work from home (2006-2010 5-year est.); Travel time to work: 41.1% less than 15 minutes, 32.7% 15 to 30 minutes, 15.4% 30 to 45 minutes, 3.3% 45 to 60 minutes, 7.5% 60 minutes or more (2006-2010 5-year est.)

Additional Information Contacts

Columbia Montour Chamber of Commerce . . . . (570) 784-2522
    http://columbiamontourchamber.com

STILLWATER (borough).
Covers a land area of 3.114 square miles and a water area of 0.042 square miles. Located at 41.15° N. Lat; 76.38° W. Long. Elevation is 696 feet.

History: Covered bridges in area.

Population: 223 (1990); 194 (2000); 209 (2010); Density: 67.1 persons per square mile (2010); Race: 97.6% White, 1.4% Black, 0.0% Asian, 0.0% American Indian/Alaska Native, 0.0% Native Hawaiian/Other Pacific Islander, 1.0% Other, 1.0% Hispanic of any race (2010); Average household size: 2.40 (2010); Median age: 42.6 (2010); Males per 100 females: 90.0 (2010); Marriage status: 21.3% never married, 53.8% now married, 4.1% widowed, 20.7% divorced (2006-2010 5-year est.); Foreign born: 0.0% (2006-2010 5-year est.); Ancestry (includes multiple ancestries): 35.1% Irish, 25.2% German, 22.1% Dutch, 18.9% English, 9.0% Scottish (2006-2010 5-year est.).

Economy: Single-family building permits issued: 1 (2011); Multi-family building permits issued: 0 (2011); Employment by occupation: 12.5% management, 11.5% professional, 5.2% services, 18.8% sales, 2.1% farming, 7.3% construction, 7.3% production (2006-2010 5-year est.).

Income: Per capita income: $20,229 (2006-2010 5-year est.); Median household income: $45,250 (2006-2010 5-year est.); Average household income: $53,243 (2006-2010 5-year est.); Percent of households with income of $100,000 or more: 14.5% (2006-2010 5-year est.); Poverty rate: 4.5% (2006-2010 5-year est.).

Education: Percent of population age 25 and over with: High school diploma (including GED) or higher: 96.5% (2006-2010 5-year est.); Bachelor's degree or higher: 28.2% (2006-2010 5-year est.); Master's degree or higher: 2.8% (2006-2010 5-year est.).

Housing: Homeownership rate: 72.4% (2010); Median home value: $132,800 (2006-2010 5-year est.); Median contract rent: $511 per month (2006-2010 5-year est.); Median year structure built: before 1940 (2006-2010 5-year est.).

Transportation: Commute to work: 91.4% car, 0.0% public transportation, 2.2% walk, 3.2% work from home (2006-2010 5-year est.); Travel time to work: 33.3% less than 15 minutes, 41.1% 15 to 30 minutes, 18.9% 30 to 45 minutes, 4.4% 45 to 60 minutes, 2.2% 60 minutes or more (2006-2010 5-year est.)

SUGARLOAF (township).
Covers a land area of 26.139 square miles and a water area of 0.161 square miles. Located at 41.27° N. Lat; 76.36° W. Long.

Population: 730 (1990); 885 (2000); 913 (2010); Density: 34.9 persons per square mile (2010); Race: 98.9% White, 0.0% Black, 0.4% Asian, 0.1% American Indian/Alaska Native, 0.0% Native Hawaiian/Other Pacific Islander, 0.6% Other, 1.0% Hispanic of any race (2010); Average household size: 2.26 (2010); Median age: 50.4 (2010); Males per 100

females: 96.8 (2010); Marriage status: 23.0% never married, 61.0% now married, 9.5% widowed, 6.4% divorced (2006-2010 5-year est.); Foreign born: 2.5% (2006-2010 5-year est.); Ancestry (includes multiple ancestries): 26.6% German, 12.9% English, 9.5% Irish, 6.9% Italian, 6.6% Polish (2006-2010 5-year est.).

Economy: Single-family building permits issued: 3 (2011); Multi-family building permits issued: 0 (2011); Employment by occupation: 4.5% management, 0.0% professional, 18.7% services, 6.6% sales, 2.1% farming, 18.1% construction, 20.2% production (2006-2010 5-year est.).

Income: Per capita income: $19,716 (2006-2010 5-year est.); Median household income: $36,571 (2006-2010 5-year est.); Average household income: $42,088 (2006-2010 5-year est.); Percent of households with income of $100,000 or more: 2.0% (2006-2010 5-year est.); Poverty rate: 8.1% (2006-2010 5-year est.).

Education: Percent of population age 25 and over with: High school diploma (including GED) or higher: 82.1% (2006-2010 5-year est.); Bachelor's degree or higher: 8.0% (2006-2010 5-year est.); Master's degree or higher: 3.6% (2006-2010 5-year est.).

Housing: Homeownership rate: 88.1% (2010); Median home value: $124,700 (2006-2010 5-year est.); Median contract rent: $423 per month (2006-2010 5-year est.); Median year structure built: 1966 (2006-2010 5-year est.).

Transportation: Commute to work: 93.5% car, 0.0% public transportation, 2.2% walk, 4.3% work from home (2006-2010 5-year est.); Travel time to work: 26.9% less than 15 minutes, 15.9% 15 to 30 minutes, 41.7% 30 to 45 minutes, 10.7% 45 to 60 minutes, 4.9% 60 minutes or more (2006-2010 5-year est.)

WALLER (CDP).
Covers a land area of 1.280 square miles and a water area of <.001 square miles. Located at 41.24° N. Lat; 76.42° W. Long. Elevation is 1,260 feet.

Population: 47 (1990); 55 (2000); 48 (2010); Density: 37.5 persons per square mile (2010); Race: 100.0% White, 0.0% Black, 0.0% Asian, 0.0% American Indian/Alaska Native, 0.0% Native Hawaiian/Other Pacific Islander, 0.0% Other, 0.0% Hispanic of any race (2010); Average household size: 2.40 (2010); Median age: 53.0 (2010); Males per 100 females: 108.7 (2010); Marriage status: 8.9% never married, 68.9% now married, 15.6% widowed, 6.7% divorced (2006-2010 5-year est.); Foreign born: 0.0% (2006-2010 5-year est.); Ancestry (includes multiple ancestries): 64.3% German, 41.1% Irish, 7.1% Pennsylvania German, 7.1% French, 7.1% English (2006-2010 5-year est.).

Economy: Employment by occupation: 0.0% management, 12.0% professional, 0.0% services, 0.0% sales, 0.0% farming, 28.0% construction, 24.0% production (2006-2010 5-year est.).

Income: Per capita income: $35,086 (2006-2010 5-year est.); Median household income: $70,313 (2006-2010 5-year est.); Average household income: $73,704 (2006-2010 5-year est.); Percent of households with income of $100,000 or more: 37.0% (2006-2010 5-year est.); Poverty rate: 0.0% (2006-2010 5-year est.).

Education: Percent of population age 25 and over with: High school diploma (including GED) or higher: 100.0% (2006-2010 5-year est.); Bachelor's degree or higher: 17.8% (2006-2010 5-year est.); Master's degree or higher: 8.9% (2006-2010 5-year est.).

Housing: Homeownership rate: 95.0% (2010); Median home value: $237,500 (2006-2010 5-year est.); Median contract rent: n/a per month (2006-2010 5-year est.); Median year structure built: 1976 (2006-2010 5-year est.).

Transportation: Commute to work: 85.7% car, 0.0% public transportation, 0.0% walk, 0.0% work from home (2006-2010 5-year est.); Travel time to work: 14.3% less than 15 minutes, 14.3% 15 to 30 minutes, 57.1% 30 to 45 minutes, 14.3% 45 to 60 minutes, 0.0% 60 minutes or more (2006-2010 5-year est.)

WILBURTON (unincorporated postal area)
Zip Code: 17888

Covers a land area of 2.847 square miles and a water area of 0.013 square miles. Located at 40.80° N. Lat; 76.37° W. Long. Elevation is 1,778 feet. Population: 326 (2010); Density: 114.5 persons per square mile (2010); Race: 99.7% White, 0.0% Black, 0.3% Asian, 0.0% American Indian/Alaska Native, 0.0% Native Hawaiian/Other Pacific Islander, 0.0% Other, 0.0% Hispanic of any race (2010); Average household size: 2.38 (2010); Median age: 44.2 (2010); Males per 100 females: 115.9 (2010); Homeownership rate: 87.6% (2010)

WILBURTON NUMBER ONE (CDP).
Covers a land area of 0.106 square miles and a water area of 0 square miles. Located at 40.81° N. Lat; 76.39° W. Long. Elevation is 1,522 feet.

Population: 326 (1990); 248 (2000); 196 (2010); Density: 1,845.4 persons per square mile (2010); Race: 99.5% White, 0.0% Black, 0.5% Asian, 0.0% American Indian/Alaska Native, 0.0% Native Hawaiian/Other Pacific Islander, 0.0% Other, 0.0% Hispanic of any race (2010); Average household size: 2.33 (2010); Median age: 46.0 (2010); Males per 100 females: 108.5 (2010); Marriage status: 8.0% never married, 74.8% now married, 8.6% widowed, 8.6% divorced (2006-2010 5-year est.); Foreign born: 0.0% (2006-2010 5-year est.); Ancestry (includes multiple ancestries): 29.3% Irish, 26.3% Polish, 14.6% Dutch, 14.6% German, 11.7% English (2006-2010 5-year est.).

Economy: Employment by occupation: 5.8% management, 0.0% professional, 4.9% services, 7.8% sales, 10.7% farming, 10.7% construction, 12.6% production (2006-2010 5-year est.).

Income: Per capita income: $23,000 (2006-2010 5-year est.); Median household income: $50,625 (2006-2010 5-year est.); Average household income: $58,552 (2006-2010 5-year est.); Percent of households with income of $100,000 or more: 11.1% (2006-2010 5-year est.); Poverty rate: 2.4% (2006-2010 5-year est.).

Education: Percent of population age 25 and over with: High school diploma (including GED) or higher: 86.8% (2006-2010 5-year est.); Bachelor's degree or higher: 15.7% (2006-2010 5-year est.); Master's degree or higher: 0.0% (2006-2010 5-year est.).

Housing: Homeownership rate: 86.9% (2010); Median home value: $90,400 (2006-2010 5-year est.); Median contract rent: n/a per month (2006-2010 5-year est.); Median year structure built: before 1940 (2006-2010 5-year est.).

Transportation: Commute to work: 97.1% car, 2.9% public transportation, 0.0% walk, 0.0% work from home (2006-2010 5-year est.); Travel time to work: 58.3% less than 15 minutes, 16.5% 15 to 30 minutes, 5.8% 30 to 45 minutes, 14.6% 45 to 60 minutes, 4.9% 60 minutes or more (2006-2010 5-year est.)

WILBURTON NUMBER TWO (CDP).
Covers a land area of 0.749 square miles and a water area of 0.001 square miles. Located at 40.82° N. Lat; 76.38° W. Long. Elevation is 1,781 feet.

Population: 101 (1990); 77 (2000); 96 (2010); Density: 128.2 persons per square mile (2010); Race: 100.0% White, 0.0% Black, 0.0% Asian, 0.0% American Indian/Alaska Native, 0.0% Native Hawaiian/Other Pacific Islander, 0.0% Other, 0.0% Hispanic of any race (2010); Average household size: 2.67 (2010); Median age: 35.5 (2010); Males per 100 females: 123.3 (2010); Marriage status: 6.2% never married, 89.2% now married, 4.6% widowed, 0.0% divorced (2006-2010 5-year est.); Foreign born: 0.0% (2006-2010 5-year est.); Ancestry (includes multiple ancestries): 25.3% German, 24.1% Pennsylvania German, 18.1% Polish, 10.8% Irish, 9.6% Dutch (2006-2010 5-year est.).

Economy: Employment by occupation: 8.9% management, 0.0% professional, 6.7% services, 6.7% sales, 6.7% farming, 20.0% construction, 13.3% production (2006-2010 5-year est.).

Income: Per capita income: $18,065 (2006-2010 5-year est.); Median household income: $39,583 (2006-2010 5-year est.); Average household income: $47,258 (2006-2010 5-year est.); Percent of households with income of $100,000 or more: n/a (2006-2010 5-year est.); Poverty rate: 0.0% (2006-2010 5-year est.).

Education: Percent of population age 25 and over with: High school diploma (including GED) or higher: 93.4% (2006-2010 5-year est.); Bachelor's degree or higher: 14.8% (2006-2010 5-year est.); Master's degree or higher: 0.0% (2006-2010 5-year est.).

Housing: Homeownership rate: 86.1% (2010); Median home value: $61,300 (2006-2010 5-year est.); Median contract rent: n/a per month (2006-2010 5-year est.); Median year structure built: before 1940 (2006-2010 5-year est.).

Transportation: Commute to work: 86.7% car, 0.0% public transportation, 4.4% walk, 8.9% work from home (2006-2010 5-year est.); Travel time to work: 19.5% less than 15 minutes, 34.1% 15 to 30 minutes, 29.3% 30 to 45 minutes, 7.3% 45 to 60 minutes, 9.8% 60 minutes or more (2006-2010 5-year est.)

Crawford County

Located in northwestern Pennsylvania; bounded on the west by Ohio; drained by French Creek. Covers a land area of 1,012.298 square miles, a water area of 25.217 square miles, and is located in the Eastern Time Zone at 41.69° N. Lat., 80.11° W. Long. The county was founded in 1800. County seat is Meadville.

Crawford County is part of the Meadville, PA Micropolitan Statistical Area. The entire metro area includes: Crawford County, PA

Weather Station: Jamestown 2 NW										Elevation: 1,040 feet	
	Jan	Feb	Mar	Apr	May	Jun	Jul	Aug	Sep	Oct	Nov	Dec
High	33	36	45	58	69	77	81	80	73	61	49	37
Low	16	17	25	35	45	54	58	57	50	39	32	22
Precip	2.7	2.3	2.9	3.6	3.9	4.1	4.6	4.0	4.2	3.3	3.6	3.2
Snow	17.6	12.6	9.9	2.9	0.0	0.0	0.0	0.0	0.0	0.4	6.1	15.8

High and Low temperatures in degrees Fahrenheit; Precipitation and Snow in inches

Weather Station: Linesville 1 S										Elevation: 1,029 feet	
	Jan	Feb	Mar	Apr	May	Jun	Jul	Aug	Sep	Oct	Nov	Dec
High	33	35	44	57	67	77	80	79	72	60	48	36
Low	17	17	25	36	46	56	60	58	51	41	33	22
Precip	2.5	2.0	2.4	3.5	3.7	4.6	4.3	3.7	4.3	3.5	3.4	2.8
Snow	18.4	11.5	8.9	2.6	tr	0.0	0.0	0.0	0.0	tr	5.5	15.9

High and Low temperatures in degrees Fahrenheit; Precipitation and Snow in inches

Weather Station: Titusville Water Works										Elevation: 1,220 feet	
	Jan	Feb	Mar	Apr	May	Jun	Jul	Aug	Sep	Oct	Nov	Dec
High	32	35	44	58	69	77	81	79	72	61	48	36
Low	15	15	22	33	42	52	56	55	48	37	30	20
Precip	2.9	2.6	3.2	3.9	4.2	4.7	4.8	3.9	4.4	3.9	3.9	3.5
Snow	21.0	15.4	11.8	2.9	tr	0.0	0.0	0.0	0.0	0.8	7.4	20.4

High and Low temperatures in degrees Fahrenheit; Precipitation and Snow in inches

Population: 86,155 (1990); 90,366 (2000); 88,765 (2010); Race: 96.3% White, 1.7% Black, 0.5% Asian, 0.2% American Indian/Alaska Native, 0.0% Native Hawaiian/Other Pacific Islander, 1.3% Other, 0.9% Hispanic of any race (2010); Density: 87.7 persons per square mile (2010); Average household size: 2.42 (2010); Median age: 41.7 (2010); Males per 100 females: 95.4 (2010).

Religion: Six largest groups: 15.0% Catholicism, 9.2% Methodist/Pietist, 4.3% European Free-Church, 3.6% Presbyterian-Reformed, 3.1% Non-Denominational, 3.1% Holiness (2010)

Economy: Unemployment rate: 8.1% (August 2012); Total civilian labor force: 43,273 (August 2012); Leading industries: 24.9% manufacturing; 19.2% health care and social assistance; 13.3% retail trade (2010); Farms: 1,468 totaling 232,093 acres (2007); Companies that employ 500 or more persons: 2 (2010); Companies that employ 100 to 499 persons: 35 (2010); Companies that employ less than 100 persons: 2,011 (2010); Black-owned businesses: n/a (2007); Hispanic-owned businesses: n/a (2007); Asian-owned businesses: n/a (2007); Women-owned businesses: 1,474 (2007); Retail sales per capita: $10,873 (2010). Single-family building permits issued: 60 (2011); Multi-family building permits issued: 0 (2011).

Income: Per capita income: $20,383 (2006-2010 5-year est.); Median household income: $38,924 (2006-2010 5-year est.); Average household income: $50,213 (2006-2010 5-year est.); Percent of households with income of $100,000 or more: 9.9% (2006-2010 5-year est.); Poverty rate: 15.8% (2006-2010 5-year est.); Bankruptcy rate: 3.10% (2011).

Education: Percent of population age 25 and over with: High school diploma (including GED) or higher: 85.8% (2006-2010 5-year est.); Bachelor's degree or higher: 18.3% (2006-2010 5-year est.); Master's degree or higher: 6.7% (2006-2010 5-year est.).

Housing: Homeownership rate: 73.7% (2010); Median home value: $97,900 (2006-2010 5-year est.); Median contract rent: $400 per month (2006-2010 5-year est.); Median year structure built: 1962 (2006-2010 5-year est.).

Health: Birth rate: 103.9 per 10,000 population (2011); Death rate: 106.7 per 10,000 population (2011); Age-adjusted cancer mortality rate: 204.5 deaths per 100,000 population (2009); Number of physicians: 17.2 per 10,000 population (2010); Hospital beds: 32.3 per 10,000 population (2008); Hospital admissions: 1,206.1 per 10,000 population (2008).

Elections: 2012 Presidential election results: 39.4% Obama, 58.9% Romney

National and State Parks: Erie National Wildlife Refuge; Pymatuning State Park

Additional Information Contacts
Crawford County Government. . . . . (814) 333-7400
 http://www.crawfordcountypa.net

Meadville-Western Crawford County Chamber of Commerce....... (814) 337-8030

　http://www.meadvillechamber.com

Crawford County Communities

ADAMSVILLE (CDP). Covers a land area of 0.179 square miles and a water area of 0 square miles. Located at 41.51° N. Lat; 80.37° W. Long. Elevation is 1,047 feet.

Population: 121 (1990); 117 (2000); 67 (2010); Density: 374.1 persons per square mile (2010); Race: 91.0% White, 9.0% Black, 0.0% Asian, 0.0% American Indian/Alaska Native, 0.0% Native Hawaiian/Other Pacific Islander, 0.0% Other, 0.0% Hispanic of any race (2010); Average household size: 2.31 (2010); Median age: 48.5 (2010); Males per 100 females: 81.1 (2010); Marriage status: 0.0% never married, 94.1% now married, 5.9% widowed, 0.0% divorced (2006-2010 5-year est.); Foreign born: 0.0% (2006-2010 5-year est.); Ancestry (includes multiple ancestries): 48.9% English, 47.9% German, 11.7% American, 10.6% Scotch-Irish, 7.4% Irish (2006-2010 5-year est.).

Economy: Employment by occupation: 13.8% management, 0.0% professional, 10.3% services, 0.0% sales, 0.0% farming, 17.2% construction, 17.2% production (2006-2010 5-year est.).

Income: Per capita income: $13,503 (2006-2010 5-year est.); Median household income: $31,125 (2006-2010 5-year est.); Average household income: $30,968 (2006-2010 5-year est.); Percent of households with income of $100,000 or more: n/a (2006-2010 5-year est.); Poverty rate: 0.0% (2006-2010 5-year est.).

Education: Percent of population age 25 and over with: High school diploma (including GED) or higher: 69.2% (2006-2010 5-year est.); Bachelor's degree or higher: 6.2% (2006-2010 5-year est.); Master's degree or higher: 0.0% (2006-2010 5-year est.).

Housing: Homeownership rate: 86.2% (2010); Median home value: $48,600 (2006-2010 5-year est.); Median contract rent: n/a per month (2006-2010 5-year est.); Median year structure built: 1952 (2006-2010 5-year est.).

Transportation: Commute to work: 100.0% car, 0.0% public transportation, 0.0% walk, 0.0% work from home (2006-2010 5-year est.); Travel time to work: 0.0% less than 15 minutes, 79.3% 15 to 30 minutes, 10.3% 30 to 45 minutes, 10.3% 45 to 60 minutes, 0.0% 60 minutes or more (2006-2010 5-year est.)

ATHENS (township). Covers a land area of 28.266 square miles and a water area of 0.035 square miles. Located at 41.75° N. Lat; 79.85° W. Long.

Population: 699 (1990); 775 (2000); 734 (2010); Density: 26.0 persons per square mile (2010); Race: 98.6% White, 0.5% Black, 0.0% Asian, 0.5% American Indian/Alaska Native, 0.0% Native Hawaiian/Other Pacific Islander, 0.4% Other, 0.7% Hispanic of any race (2010); Average household size: 2.58 (2010); Median age: 44.7 (2010); Males per 100 females: 103.9 (2010); Marriage status: 30.3% never married, 59.6% now married, 4.9% widowed, 5.2% divorced (2006-2010 5-year est.); Foreign born: 2.0% (2006-2010 5-year est.); Ancestry (includes multiple ancestries): 33.4% German, 16.8% English, 13.9% Irish, 9.7% American, 6.7% Polish (2006-2010 5-year est.).

Economy: Single-family building permits issued: 3 (2011); Multi-family building permits issued: 0 (2011); Employment by occupation: 14.7% management, 1.4% professional, 17.0% services, 7.5% sales, 3.7% farming, 12.8% construction, 9.6% production (2006-2010 5-year est.).

Income: Per capita income: $18,381 (2006-2010 5-year est.); Median household income: $42,750 (2006-2010 5-year est.); Average household income: $49,407 (2006-2010 5-year est.); Percent of households with income of $100,000 or more: 10.4% (2006-2010 5-year est.); Poverty rate: 7.1% (2006-2010 5-year est.).

Education: Percent of population age 25 and over with: High school diploma (including GED) or higher: 86.4% (2006-2010 5-year est.); Bachelor's degree or higher: 15.5% (2006-2010 5-year est.); Master's degree or higher: 2.5% (2006-2010 5-year est.).

Housing: Homeownership rate: 82.5% (2010); Median home value: $93,300 (2006-2010 5-year est.); Median contract rent: $275 per month (2006-2010 5-year est.); Median year structure built: 1964 (2006-2010 5-year est.).

Transportation: Commute to work: 83.7% car, 0.0% public transportation, 3.4% walk, 10.5% work from home (2006-2010 5-year est.); Travel time to work: 9.0% less than 15 minutes, 41.1% 15 to 30 minutes, 25.1% 30 to 45

minutes, 15.8% 45 to 60 minutes, 9.0% 60 minutes or more (2006-2010 5-year est.)

ATLANTIC (CDP). Covers a land area of 0.148 square miles and a water area of 0 square miles. Located at 41.51° N. Lat; 80.34° W. Long. Elevation is 1,161 feet.

Population: 35 (1990); 43 (2000); 77 (2010); Density: 520.7 persons per square mile (2010); Race: 100.0% White, 0.0% Black, 0.0% Asian, 0.0% American Indian/Alaska Native, 0.0% Native Hawaiian/Other Pacific Islander, 0.0% Other, 0.0% Hispanic of any race (2010); Average household size: 3.67 (2010); Median age: 25.5 (2010); Males per 100 females: 87.8 (2010); Marriage status: 16.7% never married, 75.0% now married, 0.0% widowed, 8.3% divorced (2006-2010 5-year est.); Foreign born: 0.0% (2006-2010 5-year est.); Ancestry (includes multiple ancestries): 34.0% Irish, 34.0% German, 26.0% Pennsylvania German (2006-2010 5-year est.).

Economy: Employment by occupation: 0.0% management, 0.0% professional, 25.0% services, 0.0% sales, 0.0% farming, 50.0% construction, 25.0% production (2006-2010 5-year est.).

Income: Per capita income: $6,892 (2006-2010 5-year est.); Median household income: $35,417 (2006-2010 5-year est.); Average household income: $31,327 (2006-2010 5-year est.); Percent of households with income of $100,000 or more: n/a (2006-2010 5-year est.); Poverty rate: 4.0% (2006-2010 5-year est.).

Education: Percent of population age 25 and over with: High school diploma (including GED) or higher: 45.0% (2006-2010 5-year est.); Bachelor's degree or higher: 0.0% (2006-2010 5-year est.); Master's degree or higher: 0.0% (2006-2010 5-year est.).

Housing: Homeownership rate: 85.7% (2010); Median home value: $85,000 (2006-2010 5-year est.); Median contract rent: n/a per month (2006-2010 5-year est.); Median year structure built: 1975 (2006-2010 5-year est.).

Transportation: Commute to work: 100.0% car, 0.0% public transportation, 0.0% walk, 0.0% work from home (2006-2010 5-year est.); Travel time to work: 25.0% less than 15 minutes, 0.0% 15 to 30 minutes, 75.0% 30 to 45 minutes, 0.0% 45 to 60 minutes, 0.0% 60 minutes or more (2006-2010 5-year est.)

BEAVER (township). Covers a land area of 36.648 square miles and a water area of <.001 square miles. Located at 41.81° N. Lat; 80.46° W. Long.

Population: 804 (1990); 903 (2000); 902 (2010); Density: 24.6 persons per square mile (2010); Race: 97.9% White, 0.8% Black, 0.0% Asian, 0.0% American Indian/Alaska Native, 0.0% Native Hawaiian/Other Pacific Islander, 1.3% Other, 0.3% Hispanic of any race (2010); Average household size: 2.85 (2010); Median age: 38.9 (2010); Males per 100 females: 103.6 (2010); Marriage status: 26.0% never married, 63.3% now married, 3.5% widowed, 7.2% divorced (2006-2010 5-year est.); Foreign born: 1.2% (2006-2010 5-year est.); Ancestry (includes multiple ancestries): 48.6% German, 15.3% Swiss, 13.9% Irish, 8.8% English, 7.3% Polish (2006-2010 5-year est.).

Economy: Single-family building permits issued: 0 (2011); Multi-family building permits issued: 0 (2011); Employment by occupation: 11.9% management, 5.1% professional, 4.8% services, 19.6% sales, 3.4% farming, 23.9% construction, 8.5% production (2006-2010 5-year est.).

Income: Per capita income: $17,173 (2006-2010 5-year est.); Median household income: $43,500 (2006-2010 5-year est.); Average household income: $44,993 (2006-2010 5-year est.); Percent of households with income of $100,000 or more: 5.3% (2006-2010 5-year est.); Poverty rate: 23.3% (2006-2010 5-year est.).

Education: Percent of population age 25 and over with: High school diploma (including GED) or higher: 75.5% (2006-2010 5-year est.); Bachelor's degree or higher: 4.8% (2006-2010 5-year est.); Master's degree or higher: 1.7% (2006-2010 5-year est.).

Housing: Homeownership rate: 83.8% (2010); Median home value: $108,200 (2006-2010 5-year est.); Median contract rent: $258 per month (2006-2010 5-year est.); Median year structure built: 1968 (2006-2010 5-year est.).

Transportation: Commute to work: 74.6% car, 0.0% public transportation, 2.6% walk, 15.9% work from home (2006-2010 5-year est.); Travel time to work: 28.5% less than 15 minutes, 24.1% 15 to 30 minutes, 28.9% 30 to 45 minutes, 13.4% 45 to 60 minutes, 5.2% 60 minutes or more (2006-2010 5-year est.)

BLOOMFIELD (township). Covers a land area of 37.913 square miles and a water area of 0.327 square miles. Located at 41.81° N. Lat; 79.84° W. Long.

Population: 1,839 (1990); 2,051 (2000); 1,919 (2010); Density: 50.6 persons per square mile (2010); Race: 98.3% White, 0.4% Black, 0.1% Asian, 0.1% American Indian/Alaska Native, 0.1% Native Hawaiian/Other Pacific Islander, 1.0% Other, 0.8% Hispanic of any race (2010); Average household size: 2.54 (2010); Median age: 42.5 (2010); Males per 100 females: 102.4 (2010); Marriage status: 28.0% never married, 56.4% now married, 5.4% widowed, 10.2% divorced (2006-2010 5-year est.); Foreign born: 1.4% (2006-2010 5-year est.); Ancestry (includes multiple ancestries): 30.1% German, 16.3% Irish, 11.8% English, 7.4% Italian, 7.4% American (2006-2010 5-year est.).

Economy: Single-family building permits issued: 1 (2011); Multi-family building permits issued: 0 (2011); Employment by occupation: 4.4% management, 2.0% professional, 12.8% services, 15.9% sales, 4.2% farming, 13.6% construction, 6.0% production (2006-2010 5-year est.).

Income: Per capita income: $19,222 (2006-2010 5-year est.); Median household income: $38,281 (2006-2010 5-year est.); Average household income: $48,498 (2006-2010 5-year est.); Percent of households with income of $100,000 or more: 10.0% (2006-2010 5-year est.); Poverty rate: 15.0% (2006-2010 5-year est.).

Education: Percent of population age 25 and over with: High school diploma (including GED) or higher: 86.4% (2006-2010 5-year est.); Bachelor's degree or higher: 17.0% (2006-2010 5-year est.); Master's degree or higher: 4.4% (2006-2010 5-year est.).

Housing: Homeownership rate: 82.6% (2010); Median home value: $94,400 (2006-2010 5-year est.); Median contract rent: $366 per month (2006-2010 5-year est.); Median year structure built: 1964 (2006-2010 5-year est.).

Transportation: Commute to work: 88.1% car, 1.3% public transportation, 4.3% walk, 4.6% work from home (2006-2010 5-year est.); Travel time to work: 17.6% less than 15 minutes, 28.4% 15 to 30 minutes, 22.0% 30 to 45 minutes, 22.0% 45 to 60 minutes, 10.0% 60 minutes or more (2006-2010 5-year est.)

Additional Information Contacts

Meadville-Western Crawford County Chamber of Commerce . . . . (814) 337-8030

  http://www.meadvillechamber.com

BLOOMING VALLEY (borough). Covers a land area of 1.944 square miles and a water area of 0.022 square miles. Located at 41.67° N. Lat; 80.04° W. Long. Elevation is 1,283 feet.

Population: 391 (1990); 378 (2000); 337 (2010); Density: 173.4 persons per square mile (2010); Race: 99.4% White, 0.3% Black, 0.0% Asian, 0.0% American Indian/Alaska Native, 0.0% Native Hawaiian/Other Pacific Islander, 0.3% Other, 0.3% Hispanic of any race (2010); Average household size: 2.44 (2010); Median age: 42.0 (2010); Males per 100 females: 99.4 (2010); Marriage status: 26.1% never married, 55.8% now married, 8.2% widowed, 9.9% divorced (2006-2010 5-year est.); Foreign born: 3.2% (2006-2010 5-year est.); Ancestry (includes multiple ancestries): 41.2% German, 17.2% Irish, 8.8% English, 6.3% American, 4.8% Pennsylvania German (2006-2010 5-year est.).

Economy: Single-family building permits issued: 0 (2011); Multi-family building permits issued: 0 (2011); Employment by occupation: 10.6% management, 3.7% professional, 10.1% services, 11.5% sales, 1.8% farming, 9.2% construction, 14.7% production (2006-2010 5-year est.).

Income: Per capita income: $20,393 (2006-2010 5-year est.); Median household income: $55,000 (2006-2010 5-year est.); Average household income: $57,025 (2006-2010 5-year est.); Percent of households with income of $100,000 or more: 10.2% (2006-2010 5-year est.); Poverty rate: 7.6% (2006-2010 5-year est.).

Education: Percent of population age 25 and over with: High school diploma (including GED) or higher: 91.5% (2006-2010 5-year est.); Bachelor's degree or higher: 19.2% (2006-2010 5-year est.); Master's degree or higher: 3.2% (2006-2010 5-year est.).

Housing: Homeownership rate: 84.1% (2010); Median home value: $96,700 (2006-2010 5-year est.); Median contract rent: $420 per month (2006-2010 5-year est.); Median year structure built: 1968 (2006-2010 5-year est.).

Transportation: Commute to work: 96.1% car, 0.0% public transportation, 1.0% walk, 2.9% work from home (2006-2010 5-year est.); Travel time to work: 28.8% less than 15 minutes, 49.5% 15 to 30 minutes, 12.1% 30 to 45 minutes, 1.0% 45 to 60 minutes, 8.6% 60 minutes or more (2006-2010 5-year est.)

CAMBRIDGE (township). Covers a land area of 21.450 square miles and a water area of 0.138 square miles. Located at 41.83° N. Lat; 80.02° W. Long.

Population: 1,341 (1990); 1,486 (2000); 1,563 (2010); Density: 72.9 persons per square mile (2010); Race: 98.9% White, 0.1% Black, 0.1% Asian, 0.2% American Indian/Alaska Native, 0.0% Native Hawaiian/Other Pacific Islander, 0.7% Other, 0.7% Hispanic of any race (2010); Average household size: 2.53 (2010); Median age: 43.1 (2010); Males per 100 females: 102.7 (2010); Marriage status: 20.8% never married, 62.3% now married, 6.2% widowed, 10.7% divorced (2006-2010 5-year est.); Foreign born: 0.6% (2006-2010 5-year est.); Ancestry (includes multiple ancestries): 37.7% German, 18.4% Irish, 15.3% English, 13.1% Polish, 11.0% Italian (2006-2010 5-year est.).

Economy: Single-family building permits issued: 0 (2011); Multi-family building permits issued: 0 (2011); Employment by occupation: 7.1% management, 2.7% professional, 13.0% services, 16.3% sales, 1.9% farming, 12.7% construction, 7.4% production (2006-2010 5-year est.).

Income: Per capita income: $22,699 (2006-2010 5-year est.); Median household income: $50,645 (2006-2010 5-year est.); Average household income: $58,019 (2006-2010 5-year est.); Percent of households with income of $100,000 or more: 9.7% (2006-2010 5-year est.); Poverty rate: 10.6% (2006-2010 5-year est.).

Education: Percent of population age 25 and over with: High school diploma (including GED) or higher: 88.7% (2006-2010 5-year est.); Bachelor's degree or higher: 19.7% (2006-2010 5-year est.); Master's degree or higher: 5.1% (2006-2010 5-year est.).

Housing: Homeownership rate: 89.5% (2010); Median home value: $127,200 (2006-2010 5-year est.); Median contract rent: $413 per month (2006-2010 5-year est.); Median year structure built: 1971 (2006-2010 5-year est.).

Transportation: Commute to work: 91.6% car, 0.0% public transportation, 5.3% walk, 2.7% work from home (2006-2010 5-year est.); Travel time to work: 41.1% less than 15 minutes, 25.7% 15 to 30 minutes, 17.5% 30 to 45 minutes, 10.6% 45 to 60 minutes, 5.0% 60 minutes or more (2006-2010 5-year est.)

Additional Information Contacts

Meadville-Western Crawford County Chamber of Commerce . . . . (814) 337-8030

  http://www.meadvillechamber.com

CAMBRIDGE SPRINGS (borough). Aka Brown Hill. Covers a land area of 0.872 square miles and a water area of 0 square miles. Located at 41.80° N. Lat; 80.06° W. Long. Elevation is 1,158 feet.

Population: 1,992 (1990); 2,363 (2000); 2,595 (2010); Density: 2,976.2 persons per square mile (2010); Race: 84.9% White, 12.8% Black, 0.3% Asian, 0.3% American Indian/Alaska Native, 0.1% Native Hawaiian/Other Pacific Islander, 1.6% Other, 3.5% Hispanic of any race (2010); Average household size: 2.28 (2010); Median age: 38.0 (2010); Males per 100 females: 43.1 (2010); Marriage status: 30.3% never married, 48.6% now married, 5.5% widowed, 15.6% divorced (2006-2010 5-year est.); Foreign born: 1.1% (2006-2010 5-year est.); Ancestry (includes multiple ancestries): 31.5% German, 13.6% Irish, 10.2% English, 8.5% Polish, 6.5% Italian (2006-2010 5-year est.).

Economy: Single-family building permits issued: 0 (2011); Multi-family building permits issued: 0 (2011); Employment by occupation: 4.1% management, 3.0% professional, 16.9% services, 10.6% sales, 1.8% farming, 6.3% construction, 7.6% production (2006-2010 5-year est.).

Income: Per capita income: $15,004 (2006-2010 5-year est.); Median household income: $40,238 (2006-2010 5-year est.); Average household income: $45,341 (2006-2010 5-year est.); Percent of households with income of $100,000 or more: 6.8% (2006-2010 5-year est.); Poverty rate: 12.1% (2006-2010 5-year est.).

Education: Percent of population age 25 and over with: High school diploma (including GED) or higher: 83.5% (2006-2010 5-year est.); Bachelor's degree or higher: 19.7% (2006-2010 5-year est.); Master's degree or higher: 5.6% (2006-2010 5-year est.).

School District(s)

Penncrest SD (PK-12)

  2010-11 Enrollment: 3,459 . . . . (814) 763-2323

Housing: Homeownership rate: 54.1% (2010); Median home value: $88,900 (2006-2010 5-year est.); Median contract rent: $416 per month (2006-2010 5-year est.); Median year structure built: before 1940 (2006-2010 5-year est.).

Safety: Violent crime rate: 3.8 per 10,000 population; Property crime rate: 7.7 per 10,000 population (2011).

Transportation: Commute to work: 89.7% car, 0.0% public transportation, 8.4% walk, 1.3% work from home (2006-2010 5-year est.); Travel time to work: 37.3% less than 15 minutes, 32.9% 15 to 30 minutes, 19.6% 30 to 45 minutes, 5.6% 45 to 60 minutes, 4.5% 60 minutes or more (2006-2010 5-year est.)

Additional Information Contacts

Meadville-Western Crawford County Chamber of Commerce . . . . (814) 337-8030

http://www.meadvillechamber.com

CANADOHTA LAKE (CDP). Covers a land area of 1.195 square miles and a water area of 0.266 square miles. Located at 41.81° N. Lat; 79.84° W. Long. Elevation is 1,391 feet.

Population: 499 (1990); 572 (2000); 516 (2010); Density: 431.7 persons per square mile (2010); Race: 98.8% White, 0.0% Black, 0.0% Asian, 0.0% American Indian/Alaska Native, 0.0% Native Hawaiian/Other Pacific Islander, 1.2% Other, 1.2% Hispanic of any race (2010); Average household size: 2.18 (2010); Median age: 46.6 (2010); Males per 100 females: 104.0 (2010); Marriage status: 22.4% never married, 55.4% now married, 9.3% widowed, 12.9% divorced (2006-2010 5-year est.); Foreign born: 1.1% (2006-2010 5-year est.); Ancestry (includes multiple ancestries): 39.5% German, 24.4% Irish, 14.4% Italian, 12.1% English, 8.8% Polish (2006-2010 5-year est.).

Economy: Employment by occupation: 5.0% management, 1.3% professional, 17.1% services, 20.4% sales, 4.6% farming, 7.9% construction, 1.3% production (2006-2010 5-year est.).

Income: Per capita income: $18,998 (2006-2010 5-year est.); Median household income: $29,904 (2006-2010 5-year est.); Average household income: $40,647 (2006-2010 5-year est.); Percent of households with income of $100,000 or more: 8.9% (2006-2010 5-year est.); Poverty rate: 21.1% (2006-2010 5-year est.).

Education: Percent of population age 25 and over with: High school diploma (including GED) or higher: 86.1% (2006-2010 5-year est.); Bachelor's degree or higher: 17.4% (2006-2010 5-year est.); Master's degree or higher: 5.8% (2006-2010 5-year est.).

Housing: Homeownership rate: 78.0% (2010); Median home value: $85,500 (2006-2010 5-year est.); Median contract rent: $391 per month (2006-2010 5-year est.); Median year structure built: 1958 (2006-2010 5-year est.).

Transportation: Commute to work: 83.3% car, 5.3% public transportation, 9.2% walk, 2.2% work from home (2006-2010 5-year est.); Travel time to work: 17.9% less than 15 minutes, 22.9% 15 to 30 minutes, 23.8% 30 to 45 minutes, 35.4% 45 to 60 minutes, 0.0% 60 minutes or more (2006-2010 5-year est.)

CENTERVILLE (borough). Covers a land area of 1.770 square miles and a water area of 0 square miles. Located at 41.74° N. Lat; 79.76° W. Long. Elevation is 1,306 feet.

Population: 249 (1990); 247 (2000); 218 (2010); Density: 123.1 persons per square mile (2010); Race: 100.0% White, 0.0% Black, 0.0% Asian, 0.0% American Indian/Alaska Native, 0.0% Native Hawaiian/Other Pacific Islander, 0.0% Other, 0.5% Hispanic of any race (2010); Average household size: 2.51 (2010); Median age: 42.5 (2010); Males per 100 females: 94.6 (2010); Marriage status: 33.5% never married, 43.5% now married, 9.6% widowed, 13.4% divorced (2006-2010 5-year est.); Foreign born: 0.0% (2006-2010 5-year est.); Ancestry (includes multiple ancestries): 39.1% German, 10.5% English, 8.2% Irish, 8.2% American, 7.0% Polish (2006-2010 5-year est.).

Economy: Single-family building permits issued: 0 (2011); Multi-family building permits issued: 0 (2011); Employment by occupation: 2.7% management, 4.5% professional, 22.7% services, 1.8% sales, 0.0% farming, 17.3% construction, 6.4% production (2006-2010 5-year est.).

Income: Per capita income: $17,191 (2006-2010 5-year est.); Median household income: $40,694 (2006-2010 5-year est.); Average household income: $46,531 (2006-2010 5-year est.); Percent of households with income of $100,000 or more: 4.4% (2006-2010 5-year est.); Poverty rate: 11.7% (2006-2010 5-year est.).

Education: Percent of population age 25 and over with: High school diploma (including GED) or higher: 78.1% (2006-2010 5-year est.); Bachelor's degree or higher: 12.6% (2006-2010 5-year est.); Master's degree or higher: 6.0% (2006-2010 5-year est.).

Housing: Homeownership rate: 82.8% (2010); Median home value: $79,000 (2006-2010 5-year est.); Median contract rent: $340 per month (2006-2010 5-year est.); Median year structure built: 1972 (2006-2010 5-year est.).

Transportation: Commute to work: 93.6% car, 0.0% public transportation, 1.8% walk, 4.5% work from home (2006-2010 5-year est.); Travel time to work: 11.4% less than 15 minutes, 46.7% 15 to 30 minutes, 21.9% 30 to 45 minutes, 13.3% 45 to 60 minutes, 6.7% 60 minutes or more (2006-2010 5-year est.)

COCHRANTON (borough). Covers a land area of 1.197 square miles and a water area of 0 square miles. Located at 41.52° N. Lat; 80.05° W. Long. Elevation is 1,070 feet.

Population: 1,174 (1990); 1,148 (2000); 1,136 (2010); Density: 949.0 persons per square mile (2010); Race: 98.2% White, 0.3% Black, 0.4% Asian, 0.0% American Indian/Alaska Native, 0.0% Native Hawaiian/Other Pacific Islander, 1.1% Other, 0.9% Hispanic of any race (2010); Average household size: 2.47 (2010); Median age: 43.8 (2010); Males per 100 females: 95.5 (2010); Marriage status: 20.1% never married, 64.9% now married, 8.8% widowed, 6.1% divorced (2006-2010 5-year est.); Foreign born: 1.9% (2006-2010 5-year est.); Ancestry (includes multiple ancestries): 35.7% German, 19.3% Irish, 13.3% English, 10.2% Swedish, 7.5% Scotch-Irish (2006-2010 5-year est.).

Economy: Single-family building permits issued: 1 (2011); Multi-family building permits issued: 0 (2011); Employment by occupation: 11.8% management, 6.3% professional, 8.1% services, 14.4% sales, 3.3% farming, 9.4% construction, 11.4% production (2006-2010 5-year est.).

Income: Per capita income: $23,174 (2006-2010 5-year est.); Median household income: $48,807 (2006-2010 5-year est.); Average household income: $55,019 (2006-2010 5-year est.); Percent of households with income of $100,000 or more: 10.4% (2006-2010 5-year est.); Poverty rate: 15.9% (2006-2010 5-year est.).

Education: Percent of population age 25 and over with: High school diploma (including GED) or higher: 94.6% (2006-2010 5-year est.); Bachelor's degree or higher: 20.1% (2006-2010 5-year est.); Master's degree or higher: 9.1% (2006-2010 5-year est.).

School District(s)

Crawford Central SD (KG-12)

    2010-11 Enrollment: 3,972 . . . . (814) 724-3960

Housing: Homeownership rate: 73.3% (2010); Median home value: $88,200 (2006-2010 5-year est.); Median contract rent: $364 per month (2006-2010 5-year est.); Median year structure built: 1940 (2006-2010 5-year est.).

Safety: Violent crime rate: 0.0 per 10,000 population; Property crime rate: 96.5 per 10,000 population (2011).

Newspapers: Area Shopper (Community news; Circulation 2,500)

Transportation: Commute to work: 84.6% car, 0.7% public transportation, 9.4% walk, 4.8% work from home (2006-2010 5-year est.); Travel time to work: 26.3% less than 15 minutes, 49.3% 15 to 30 minutes, 13.8% 30 to 45 minutes, 6.9% 45 to 60 minutes, 3.7% 60 minutes or more (2006-2010 5-year est.)

CONNEAUT (township). Covers a land area of 40.875 square miles and a water area of 0.784 square miles. Located at 41.70° N. Lat; 80.46° W. Long.

Population: 1,399 (1990); 1,550 (2000); 1,476 (2010); Density: 36.1 persons per square mile (2010); Race: 98.9% White, 0.2% Black, 0.3% Asian, 0.1% American Indian/Alaska Native, 0.0% Native Hawaiian/Other Pacific Islander, 0.5% Other, 0.7% Hispanic of any race (2010); Average household size: 2.55 (2010); Median age: 45.3 (2010); Males per 100 females: 114.2 (2010); Marriage status: 26.3% never married, 56.8% now married, 7.4% widowed, 9.5% divorced (2006-2010 5-year est.); Foreign born: 0.2% (2006-2010 5-year est.); Ancestry (includes multiple ancestries): 28.9% German, 15.8% English, 11.8% Irish, 7.9% American, 5.2% Czech (2006-2010 5-year est.).

Economy: Single-family building permits issued: 0 (2011); Multi-family building permits issued: 0 (2011); Employment by occupation: 8.4% management, 4.4% professional, 15.6% services, 12.5% sales, 1.1% farming, 18.9% construction, 11.2% production (2006-2010 5-year est.).

Income: Per capita income: $17,139 (2006-2010 5-year est.); Median household income: $34,737 (2006-2010 5-year est.); Average household income: $45,526 (2006-2010 5-year est.); Percent of households with income of $100,000 or more: 8.1% (2006-2010 5-year est.); Poverty rate: 18.8% (2006-2010 5-year est.).

Education: Percent of population age 25 and over with: High school diploma (including GED) or higher: 85.0% (2006-2010 5-year est.); Bachelor's degree or higher: 10.3% (2006-2010 5-year est.); Master's degree or higher: 2.6% (2006-2010 5-year est.).

Housing: Homeownership rate: 87.2% (2010); Median home value: $90,000 (2006-2010 5-year est.); Median contract rent: $546 per month (2006-2010 5-year est.); Median year structure built: 1966 (2006-2010 5-year est.).

Transportation: Commute to work: 89.6% car, 0.6% public transportation, 6.1% walk, 3.0% work from home (2006-2010 5-year est.); Travel time to work: 30.7% less than 15 minutes, 32.1% 15 to 30 minutes, 22.1% 30 to 45 minutes, 8.2% 45 to 60 minutes, 6.8% 60 minutes or more (2006-2010 5-year est.).

Additional Information Contacts
Meadville-Western Crawford County Chamber of Commerce . . . . (814) 337-8030
  http://www.meadvillechamber.com

CONNEAUT LAKE (borough). Covers a land area of 0.362 square miles and a water area of 0 square miles. Located at 41.60° N. Lat; 80.31° W. Long. Elevation is 1,083 feet.

Population: 605 (1990); 708 (2000); 653 (2010); Density: 1,801.5 persons per square mile (2010); Race: 98.0% White, 0.0% Black, 0.3% Asian, 0.0% American Indian/Alaska Native, 0.0% Native Hawaiian/Other Pacific Islander, 1.7% Other, 0.6% Hispanic of any race (2010); Average household size: 2.03 (2010); Median age: 46.7 (2010); Males per 100 females: 97.3 (2010); Marriage status: 15.8% never married, 55.8% now married, 12.1% widowed, 16.3% divorced (2006-2010 5-year est.); Foreign born: 3.2% (2006-2010 5-year est.); Ancestry (includes multiple ancestries): 35.7% German, 18.6% English, 12.4% Irish, 10.1% Scotch-Irish, 8.8% Italian (2006-2010 5-year est.).

Economy: Single-family building permits issued: 0 (2011); Multi-family building permits issued: 0 (2011); Employment by occupation: 13.3% management, 7.0% professional, 15.0% services, 12.0% sales, 0.7% farming, 7.3% construction, 2.3% production (2006-2010 5-year est.).

Income: Per capita income: $26,058 (2006-2010 5-year est.); Median household income: $46,094 (2006-2010 5-year est.); Average household income: $56,457 (2006-2010 5-year est.); Percent of households with income of $100,000 or more: 9.9% (2006-2010 5-year est.); Poverty rate: 2.1% (2006-2010 5-year est.).

Education: Percent of population age 25 and over with: High school diploma (including GED) or higher: 90.3% (2006-2010 5-year est.); Bachelor's degree or higher: 29.0% (2006-2010 5-year est.); Master's degree or higher: 7.5% (2006-2010 5-year est.).

School District(s)
Conneaut SD (KG-12)
  2010-11 Enrollment: 2,456 . . . . (814) 683-5900

Housing: Homeownership rate: 67.1% (2010); Median home value: $92,200 (2006-2010 5-year est.); Median contract rent: $434 per month (2006-2010 5-year est.); Median year structure built: 1958 (2006-2010 5-year est.).

Transportation: Commute to work: 83.3% car, 0.0% public transportation, 11.8% walk, 4.9% work from home (2006-2010 5-year est.); Travel time to work: 33.0% less than 15 minutes, 48.7% 15 to 30 minutes, 0.0% 30 to 45 minutes, 9.5% 45 to 60 minutes, 8.8% 60 minutes or more (2006-2010 5-year est.).

CONNEAUT LAKESHORE (CDP). Covers a land area of 5.186 square miles and a water area of 1.487 square miles. Located at 41.62° N. Lat; 80.31° W. Long.

Population: 1,930 (1990); 2,502 (2000); 2,395 (2010); Density: 461.8 persons per square mile (2010); Race: 98.0% White, 0.5% Black, 0.3% Asian, 0.1% American Indian/Alaska Native, 0.1% Native Hawaiian/Other Pacific Islander, 1.0% Other, 0.9% Hispanic of any race (2010); Average household size: 2.08 (2010); Median age: 50.8 (2010); Males per 100 females: 94.7 (2010); Marriage status: 17.4% never married, 60.7% now married, 11.3% widowed, 10.6% divorced (2006-2010 5-year est.); Foreign born: 1.1% (2006-2010 5-year est.); Ancestry (includes multiple ancestries): 36.0% German, 20.3% Irish, 13.6% English, 10.1% Scotch-Irish, 8.5% American (2006-2010 5-year est.).

Economy: Employment by occupation: 15.0% management, 2.6% professional, 4.3% services, 22.9% sales, 1.5% farming, 6.4% construction, 3.7% production (2006-2010 5-year est.).

Income: Per capita income: $26,767 (2006-2010 5-year est.); Median household income: $37,192 (2006-2010 5-year est.); Average household income: $56,453 (2006-2010 5-year est.); Percent of households with income of $100,000 or more: 14.1% (2006-2010 5-year est.); Poverty rate: 16.6% (2006-2010 5-year est.).

Education: Percent of population age 25 and over with: High school diploma (including GED) or higher: 93.2% (2006-2010 5-year est.); Bachelor's degree or higher: 25.2% (2006-2010 5-year est.); Master's degree or higher: 9.2% (2006-2010 5-year est.).

Housing: Homeownership rate: 77.5% (2010); Median home value: $141,900 (2006-2010 5-year est.); Median contract rent: $388 per month (2006-2010 5-year est.); Median year structure built: 1970 (2006-2010 5-year est.).

Transportation: Commute to work: 91.5% car, 0.0% public transportation, 3.5% walk, 3.7% work from home (2006-2010 5-year est.); Travel time to work: 43.4% less than 15 minutes, 41.6% 15 to 30 minutes, 6.3% 30 to 45 minutes, 5.9% 45 to 60 minutes, 2.9% 60 minutes or more (2006-2010 5-year est.).

Additional Information Contacts
Meadville-Western Crawford County Chamber of Commerce . . . . (814) 337-8030
  http://www.meadvillechamber.com

CONNEAUTVILLE (borough). Covers a land area of 1.031 square miles and a water area of 0.006 square miles. Located at 41.76° N. Lat; 80.37° W. Long. Elevation is 948 feet.

Population: 822 (1990); 848 (2000); 774 (2010); Density: 751.0 persons per square mile (2010); Race: 96.9% White, 1.2% Black, 0.1% Asian, 0.4% American Indian/Alaska Native, 0.0% Native Hawaiian/Other Pacific Islander, 1.4% Other, 0.8% Hispanic of any race (2010); Average household size: 2.44 (2010); Median age: 42.9 (2010); Males per 100 females: 88.8 (2010); Marriage status: 27.3% never married, 51.7% now married, 9.0% widowed, 12.0% divorced (2006-2010 5-year est.); Foreign born: 1.3% (2006-2010 5-year est.); Ancestry (includes multiple ancestries): 30.6% German, 17.7% English, 14.3% Irish, 6.6% Polish, 6.6% Scotch-Irish (2006-2010 5-year est.).

Economy: Single-family building permits issued: 0 (2011); Multi-family building permits issued: 0 (2011); Employment by occupation: 7.4% management, 1.1% professional, 16.8% services, 14.4% sales, 0.8% farming, 16.2% construction, 11.7% production (2006-2010 5-year est.).

Income: Per capita income: $16,980 (2006-2010 5-year est.); Median household income: $32,050 (2006-2010 5-year est.); Average household income: $40,235 (2006-2010 5-year est.); Percent of households with income of $100,000 or more: 3.5% (2006-2010 5-year est.); Poverty rate: 13.5% (2006-2010 5-year est.).

Education: Percent of population age 25 and over with: High school diploma (including GED) or higher: 84.8% (2006-2010 5-year est.); Bachelor's degree or higher: 12.0% (2006-2010 5-year est.); Master's degree or higher: 5.0% (2006-2010 5-year est.).

School District(s)
Conneaut SD (KG-12)
  2010-11 Enrollment: 2,456 . . . . (814) 683-5900

Housing: Homeownership rate: 68.8% (2010); Median home value: $71,800 (2006-2010 5-year est.); Median contract rent: $344 per month (2006-2010 5-year est.); Median year structure built: 1945 (2006-2010 5-year est.).

Transportation: Commute to work: 89.7% car, 0.0% public transportation, 9.5% walk, 0.0% work from home (2006-2010 5-year est.); Travel time to work: 23.7% less than 15 minutes, 49.4% 15 to 30 minutes, 23.7% 30 to 45 minutes, 3.1% 45 to 60 minutes, 0.0% 60 minutes or more (2006-2010 5-year est.).

CUSSEWAGO (township). Covers a land area of 40.826 square miles and a water area of 0.099 square miles. Located at 41.80° N. Lat; 80.21° W. Long.

Population: 1,436 (1990); 1,597 (2000); 1,559 (2010); Density: 38.2 persons per square mile (2010); Race: 97.9% White, 0.6% Black, 0.4% Asian, 0.2% American Indian/Alaska Native, 0.0% Native Hawaiian/Other Pacific Islander, 0.9% Other, 0.7% Hispanic of any race (2010); Average household size: 2.62 (2010); Median age: 41.8 (2010); Males per 100 females: 101.9 (2010); Marriage status: 24.1% never married, 61.9% now married, 5.1% widowed, 8.9% divorced (2006-2010 5-year est.); Foreign born: 0.6% (2006-2010 5-year est.); Ancestry (includes multiple ancestries): 36.4% German, 17.9% Irish, 12.1% Polish, 9.8% Italian, 9.6% English (2006-2010 5-year est.).

Economy: Single-family building permits issued: 4 (2011); Multi-family building permits issued: 0 (2011); Employment by occupation: 11.4% management, 1.8% professional, 11.7% services, 12.6% sales, 1.3% farming, 10.9% construction, 7.4% production (2006-2010 5-year est.).

Income: Per capita income: $25,043 (2006-2010 5-year est.); Median household income: $55,259 (2006-2010 5-year est.); Average household income: $65,072 (2006-2010 5-year est.); Percent of households with income of $100,000 or more: 15.3% (2006-2010 5-year est.); Poverty rate: 7.4% (2006-2010 5-year est.).

Education: Percent of population age 25 and over with: High school diploma (including GED) or higher: 87.3% (2006-2010 5-year est.); Bachelor's degree or higher: 21.4% (2006-2010 5-year est.); Master's degree or higher: 6.3% (2006-2010 5-year est.).

Housing: Homeownership rate: 85.6% (2010); Median home value: $133,600 (2006-2010 5-year est.); Median contract rent: $458 per month (2006-2010 5-year est.); Median year structure built: 1974 (2006-2010 5-year est.).

Transportation: Commute to work: 92.2% car, 0.2% public transportation, 2.0% walk, 4.3% work from home (2006-2010 5-year est.); Travel time to work: 21.8% less than 15 minutes, 44.4% 15 to 30 minutes, 24.4% 30 to 45 minutes, 6.1% 45 to 60 minutes, 3.2% 60 minutes or more (2006-2010 5-year est.)

Additional Information Contacts
Meadville-Western Crawford County Chamber of Commerce . . . . (814) 337-8030
  http://www.meadvillechamber.com

EAST FAIRFIELD (township). Covers a land area of 12.836 square miles and a water area of <.001 square miles. Located at 41.55° N. Lat; 80.08° W. Long.

Population: 890 (1990); 848 (2000); 922 (2010); Density: 71.8 persons per square mile (2010); Race: 98.8% White, 0.2% Black, 0.0% Asian, 0.0% American Indian/Alaska Native, 0.0% Native Hawaiian/Other Pacific Islander, 1.0% Other, 0.7% Hispanic of any race (2010); Average household size: 2.58 (2010); Median age: 41.3 (2010); Males per 100 females: 100.0 (2010); Marriage status: 20.0% never married, 67.6% now married, 5.9% widowed, 6.6% divorced (2006-2010 5-year est.); Foreign born: 0.2% (2006-2010 5-year est.); Ancestry (includes multiple ancestries): 40.7% German, 15.0% Irish, 12.2% English, 6.6% American, 5.9% Italian (2006-2010 5-year est.).

Economy: Single-family building permits issued: 1 (2011); Multi-family building permits issued: 0 (2011); Employment by occupation: 16.9% management, 5.0% professional, 8.8% services, 18.1% sales, 1.7% farming, 6.5% construction, 4.4% production (2006-2010 5-year est.).

Income: Per capita income: $22,199 (2006-2010 5-year est.); Median household income: $58,641 (2006-2010 5-year est.); Average household income: $60,126 (2006-2010 5-year est.); Percent of households with income of $100,000 or more: 10.1% (2006-2010 5-year est.); Poverty rate: 12.9% (2006-2010 5-year est.).

Education: Percent of population age 25 and over with: High school diploma (including GED) or higher: 87.3% (2006-2010 5-year est.); Bachelor's degree or higher: 16.1% (2006-2010 5-year est.); Master's degree or higher: 4.9% (2006-2010 5-year est.).

Housing: Homeownership rate: 89.4% (2010); Median home value: $108,800 (2006-2010 5-year est.); Median contract rent: <$101 per month (2006-2010 5-year est.); Median year structure built: 1970 (2006-2010 5-year est.).

Transportation: Commute to work: 91.9% car, 0.0% public transportation, 2.3% walk, 5.2% work from home (2006-2010 5-year est.); Travel time to work: 31.6% less than 15 minutes, 49.0% 15 to 30 minutes, 11.0% 30 to 45 minutes, 1.5% 45 to 60 minutes, 6.8% 60 minutes or more (2006-2010 5-year est.)

Additional Information Contacts
Meadville-Western Crawford County Chamber of Commerce . . . . (814) 337-8030
  http://www.meadvillechamber.com

EAST FALLOWFIELD (township). Covers a land area of 28.055 square miles and a water area of 0.039 square miles. Located at 41.53° N. Lat; 80.32° W. Long.

Population: 1,280 (1990); 1,434 (2000); 1,620 (2010); Density: 57.7 persons per square mile (2010); Race: 99.4% White, 0.2% Black, 0.1% Asian, 0.0% American Indian/Alaska Native, 0.1% Native Hawaiian/Other Pacific Islander, 0.2% Other, 0.4% Hispanic of any race (2010); Average household size: 3.21 (2010); Median age: 30.8 (2010); Males per 100 females: 103.8 (2010); Marriage status: 17.7% never married, 70.0% now married, 5.3% widowed, 7.0% divorced (2006-2010 5-year est.); Foreign born: 0.0% (2006-2010 5-year est.); Ancestry (includes multiple

ancestries): 28.1% German, 13.8% Pennsylvania German, 13.0% Irish, 10.8% English, 5.9% American (2006-2010 5-year est.).

Economy: Single-family building permits issued: 1 (2011); Multi-family building permits issued: 0 (2011); Employment by occupation: 4.5% management, 0.0% professional, 13.2% services, 8.3% sales, 1.9% farming, 22.7% construction, 8.5% production (2006-2010 5-year est.).

Income: Per capita income: $18,062 (2006-2010 5-year est.); Median household income: $40,658 (2006-2010 5-year est.); Average household income: $53,439 (2006-2010 5-year est.); Percent of households with income of $100,000 or more: 11.0% (2006-2010 5-year est.); Poverty rate: 24.0% (2006-2010 5-year est.).

Education: Percent of population age 25 and over with: High school diploma (including GED) or higher: 64.9% (2006-2010 5-year est.); Bachelor's degree or higher: 11.2% (2006-2010 5-year est.); Master's degree or higher: 2.4% (2006-2010 5-year est.).

Housing: Homeownership rate: 83.9% (2010); Median home value: $111,000 (2006-2010 5-year est.); Median contract rent: $345 per month (2006-2010 5-year est.); Median year structure built: 1975 (2006-2010 5-year est.).

Transportation: Commute to work: 79.8% car, 0.4% public transportation, 3.4% walk, 12.6% work from home (2006-2010 5-year est.); Travel time to work: 14.8% less than 15 minutes, 44.5% 15 to 30 minutes, 23.8% 30 to 45 minutes, 4.1% 45 to 60 minutes, 12.7% 60 minutes or more (2006-2010 5-year est.)

Additional Information Contacts
Meadville-Western Crawford County Chamber of Commerce . . . . (814) 337-8030
  http://www.meadvillechamber.com

EAST MEAD (township). Covers a land area of 22.858 square miles and a water area of 0.431 square miles. Located at 41.62° N. Lat; 80.06° W. Long.

Population: 1,441 (1990); 1,485 (2000); 1,493 (2010); Density: 65.3 persons per square mile (2010); Race: 98.1% White, 0.3% Black, 0.3% Asian, 0.1% American Indian/Alaska Native, 0.0% Native Hawaiian/Other Pacific Islander, 1.2% Other, 0.7% Hispanic of any race (2010); Average household size: 2.53 (2010); Median age: 41.1 (2010); Males per 100 females: 101.5 (2010); Marriage status: 18.9% never married, 67.8% now married, 4.5% widowed, 8.8% divorced (2006-2010 5-year est.); Foreign born: 1.5% (2006-2010 5-year est.); Ancestry (includes multiple ancestries): 39.4% German, 20.6% Irish, 13.5% English, 13.3% French, 9.9% Italian (2006-2010 5-year est.).

Economy: Single-family building permits issued: 1 (2011); Multi-family building permits issued: 0 (2011); Employment by occupation: 9.0% management, 1.7% professional, 9.0% services, 16.3% sales, 6.9% farming, 13.9% construction, 10.7% production (2006-2010 5-year est.).

Income: Per capita income: $23,603 (2006-2010 5-year est.); Median household income: $50,714 (2006-2010 5-year est.); Average household income: $58,474 (2006-2010 5-year est.); Percent of households with income of $100,000 or more: 12.0% (2006-2010 5-year est.); Poverty rate: 9.9% (2006-2010 5-year est.).

Education: Percent of population age 25 and over with: High school diploma (including GED) or higher: 86.8% (2006-2010 5-year est.); Bachelor's degree or higher: 14.1% (2006-2010 5-year est.); Master's degree or higher: 4.4% (2006-2010 5-year est.).

Housing: Homeownership rate: 84.1% (2010); Median home value: $106,700 (2006-2010 5-year est.); Median contract rent: $388 per month (2006-2010 5-year est.); Median year structure built: 1972 (2006-2010 5-year est.).

Transportation: Commute to work: 86.4% car, 0.0% public transportation, 6.8% walk, 5.1% work from home (2006-2010 5-year est.); Travel time to work: 35.4% less than 15 minutes, 47.6% 15 to 30 minutes, 7.0% 30 to 45 minutes, 6.3% 45 to 60 minutes, 3.7% 60 minutes or more (2006-2010 5-year est.)

Additional Information Contacts
Meadville-Western Crawford County Chamber of Commerce . . . . (814) 337-8030
  http://www.meadvillechamber.com

FAIRFIELD (township). Covers a land area of 19.318 square miles and a water area of 0.020 square miles. Located at 41.51° N. Lat; 80.11° W. Long.

Population: 997 (1990); 1,104 (2000); 1,023 (2010); Density: 53.0 persons per square mile (2010); Race: 99.0% White, 0.2% Black, 0.0% Asian, 0.1% American Indian/Alaska Native, 0.0% Native Hawaiian/Other

Pacific Islander, 0.7% Other, 0.6% Hispanic of any race (2010); Average household size: 2.50 (2010); Median age: 45.0 (2010); Males per 100 females: 103.4 (2010); Marriage status: 19.2% never married, 63.8% now married, 6.5% widowed, 10.6% divorced (2006-2010 5-year est.); Foreign born: 0.8% (2006-2010 5-year est.); Ancestry (includes multiple ancestries): 37.4% German, 18.1% Irish, 10.3% English, 8.9% Italian, 7.7% French (2006-2010 5-year est.).

Economy: Single-family building permits issued: 0 (2011); Multi-family building permits issued: 0 (2011); Employment by occupation: 5.4% management, 1.6% professional, 10.9% services, 14.9% sales, 2.6% farming, 12.3% construction, 11.7% production (2006-2010 5-year est.).

Income: Per capita income: $18,920 (2006-2010 5-year est.); Median household income: $42,396 (2006-2010 5-year est.); Average household income: $48,452 (2006-2010 5-year est.); Percent of households with income of $100,000 or more: 8.2% (2006-2010 5-year est.); Poverty rate: 7.9% (2006-2010 5-year est.).

Education: Percent of population age 25 and over with: High school diploma (including GED) or higher: 83.1% (2006-2010 5-year est.); Bachelor's degree or higher: 9.0% (2006-2010 5-year est.); Master's degree or higher: 3.5% (2006-2010 5-year est.).

Housing: Homeownership rate: 86.8% (2010); Median home value: $119,300 (2006-2010 5-year est.); Median contract rent: $431 per month (2006-2010 5-year est.); Median year structure built: 1962 (2006-2010 5-year est.).

Transportation: Commute to work: 91.5% car, 0.0% public transportation, 2.8% walk, 5.6% work from home (2006-2010 5-year est.); Travel time to work: 25.7% less than 15 minutes, 45.0% 15 to 30 minutes, 16.0% 30 to 45 minutes, 9.0% 45 to 60 minutes, 4.3% 60 minutes or more (2006-2010 5-year est.)

Additional Information Contacts
Meadville-Western Crawford County Chamber of Commerce . . . . (814) 337-8030
  http://www.meadvillechamber.com

FREDERICKSBURG (CDP). Covers a land area of 1.751 square miles and a water area of 0 square miles. Located at 41.64° N. Lat; 80.18° W. Long. Elevation is 1,125 feet.

Population: 1,253 (1990); 1,140 (2000); 733 (2010); Density: 418.6 persons per square mile (2010); Race: 96.6% White, 1.5% Black, 0.3% Asian, 0.4% American Indian/Alaska Native, 0.1% Native Hawaiian/Other Pacific Islander, 1.1% Other, 1.4% Hispanic of any race (2010); Average household size: 2.16 (2010); Median age: 44.9 (2010); Males per 100 females: 91.4 (2010); Marriage status: 20.5% never married, 32.4% now married, 10.8% widowed, 36.3% divorced (2006-2010 5-year est.); Foreign born: 0.0% (2006-2010 5-year est.); Ancestry (includes multiple ancestries): 26.5% German, 20.1% Polish, 15.2% English, 11.7% Irish, 8.7% Welsh (2006-2010 5-year est.).

Economy: Employment by occupation: 3.8% management, 4.2% professional, 5.3% services, 14.3% sales, 0.0% farming, 13.6% construction, 11.7% production (2006-2010 5-year est.).

Income: Per capita income: $24,863 (2006-2010 5-year est.); Median household income: $43,977 (2006-2010 5-year est.); Average household income: $40,805 (2006-2010 5-year est.); Percent of households with income of $100,000 or more: n/a (2006-2010 5-year est.); Poverty rate: 8.9% (2006-2010 5-year est.).

Education: Percent of population age 25 and over with: High school diploma (including GED) or higher: 97.2% (2006-2010 5-year est.); Bachelor's degree or higher: 19.8% (2006-2010 5-year est.); Master's degree or higher: 5.8% (2006-2010 5-year est.).

Housing: Homeownership rate: 74.4% (2010); Median home value: $71,900 (2006-2010 5-year est.); Median contract rent: $330 per month (2006-2010 5-year est.); Median year structure built: 1953 (2006-2010 5-year est.).

Transportation: Commute to work: 88.7% car, 0.0% public transportation, 0.0% walk, 0.0% work from home (2006-2010 5-year est.); Travel time to work: 46.8% less than 15 minutes, 26.8% 15 to 30 minutes, 13.2% 30 to 45 minutes, 9.4% 45 to 60 minutes, 3.8% 60 minutes or more (2006-2010 5-year est.)

GENEVA (CDP). Covers a land area of 0.218 square miles and a water area of 0 square miles. Located at 41.56° N. Lat; 80.23° W. Long. Elevation is 1,129 feet.

Population: 103 (1990); 115 (2000); 109 (2010); Density: 499.7 persons per square mile (2010); Race: 97.2% White, 0.9% Black, 0.0% Asian, 0.0% American Indian/Alaska Native, 0.0% Native Hawaiian/Other Pacific

Islander, 1.9% Other, 0.0% Hispanic of any race (2010); Average household size: 2.10 (2010); Median age: 50.2 (2010); Males per 100 females: 84.7 (2010); Marriage status: 6.4% never married, 84.0% now married, 3.2% widowed, 6.4% divorced (2006-2010 5-year est.); Foreign born: 0.0% (2006-2010 5-year est.); Ancestry (includes multiple ancestries): 18.7% American, 17.1% Polish, 17.1% French, 16.3% German, 12.2% Irish (2006-2010 5-year est.).

Economy: Employment by occupation: 0.0% management, 5.2% professional, 0.0% services, 25.9% sales, 5.2% farming, 3.4% construction, 0.0% production (2006-2010 5-year est.).

Income: Per capita income: $16,702 (2006-2010 5-year est.); Median household income: $43,750 (2006-2010 5-year est.); Average household income: $45,209 (2006-2010 5-year est.); Percent of households with income of $100,000 or more: n/a (2006-2010 5-year est.); Poverty rate: 22.8% (2006-2010 5-year est.).

Education: Percent of population age 25 and over with: High school diploma (including GED) or higher: 79.5% (2006-2010 5-year est.); Bachelor's degree or higher: 10.2% (2006-2010 5-year est.); Master's degree or higher: 6.8% (2006-2010 5-year est.).

Housing: Homeownership rate: 69.3% (2010); Median home value: $76,000 (2006-2010 5-year est.); Median contract rent: n/a per month (2006-2010 5-year est.); Median year structure built: 1945 (2006-2010 5-year est.).

Transportation: Commute to work: 94.4% car, 5.6% public transportation, 0.0% walk, 0.0% work from home (2006-2010 5-year est.); Travel time to work: 29.6% less than 15 minutes, 51.9% 15 to 30 minutes, 7.4% 30 to 45 minutes, 0.0% 45 to 60 minutes, 11.1% 60 minutes or more (2006-2010 5-year est.)

GREENWOOD (township). Covers a land area of 36.427 square miles and a water area of 0.180 square miles. Located at 41.53° N. Lat; 80.23° W. Long.

Population: 1,361 (1990); 1,487 (2000); 1,454 (2010); Density: 39.9 persons per square mile (2010); Race: 98.6% White, 0.1% Black, 0.1% Asian, 0.0% American Indian/Alaska Native, 0.0% Native Hawaiian/Other Pacific Islander, 1.2% Other, 0.2% Hispanic of any race (2010); Average household size: 2.59 (2010); Median age: 41.6 (2010); Males per 100 females: 101.1 (2010); Marriage status: 18.8% never married, 65.6% now married, 6.5% widowed, 9.1% divorced (2006-2010 5-year est.); Foreign born: 0.9% (2006-2010 5-year est.); Ancestry (includes multiple ancestries): 36.1% German, 21.4% Irish, 12.1% English, 8.2% Polish, 8.1% American (2006-2010 5-year est.).

Economy: Single-family building permits issued: 2 (2011); Multi-family building permits issued: 0 (2011); Employment by occupation: 7.3% management, 1.2% professional, 10.0% services, 12.3% sales, 3.4% farming, 9.8% construction, 5.8% production (2006-2010 5-year est.).

Income: Per capita income: $21,742 (2006-2010 5-year est.); Median household income: $47,188 (2006-2010 5-year est.); Average household income: $56,281 (2006-2010 5-year est.); Percent of households with income of $100,000 or more: 11.2% (2006-2010 5-year est.); Poverty rate: 10.9% (2006-2010 5-year est.).

Education: Percent of population age 25 and over with: High school diploma (including GED) or higher: 82.1% (2006-2010 5-year est.); Bachelor's degree or higher: 11.7% (2006-2010 5-year est.); Master's degree or higher: 5.8% (2006-2010 5-year est.).

Housing: Homeownership rate: 87.1% (2010); Median home value: $95,700 (2006-2010 5-year est.); Median contract rent: $343 per month (2006-2010 5-year est.); Median year structure built: 1973 (2006-2010 5-year est.).

Transportation: Commute to work: 91.2% car, 0.4% public transportation, 0.5% walk, 7.3% work from home (2006-2010 5-year est.); Travel time to work: 19.9% less than 15 minutes, 56.2% 15 to 30 minutes, 11.2% 30 to 45 minutes, 4.4% 45 to 60 minutes, 8.3% 60 minutes or more (2006-2010 5-year est.)

Additional Information Contacts
Meadville-Western Crawford County Chamber of Commerce . . . . (814) 337-8030
  http://www.meadvillechamber.com

GUYS MILLS (CDP). Covers a land area of 0.155 square miles and a water area of 0 square miles. Located at 41.63° N. Lat; 79.98° W. Long. Elevation is 1,388 feet.

Population: 136 (1990); 133 (2000); 124 (2010); Density: 801.5 persons per square mile (2010); Race: 96.8% White, 0.8% Black, 0.0% Asian, 0.0% American Indian/Alaska Native, 0.0% Native Hawaiian/Other Pacific

Islander, 2.4% Other, 0.8% Hispanic of any race (2010); Average household size: 2.72 (2010); Median age: 27.3 (2010); Males per 100 females: 79.7 (2010); Marriage status: 66.2% never married, 29.7% now married, 2.1% widowed, 2.1% divorced (2006-2010 5-year est.); Foreign born: 1.9% (2006-2010 5-year est.); Ancestry (includes multiple ancestries): 40.5% German, 16.5% Swiss, 7.6% Swedish, 7.6% Irish, 7.0% Polish (2006-2010 5-year est.).
Economy: Employment by occupation: 0.0% management, 11.8% professional, 25.5% services, 13.7% sales, 0.0% farming, 0.0% construction, 0.0% production (2006-2010 5-year est.).
Income: Per capita income: $19,512 (2006-2010 5-year est.); Median household income: $50,833 (2006-2010 5-year est.); Average household income: $88,717 (2006-2010 5-year est.); Percent of households with income of $100,000 or more: 20.0% (2006-2010 5-year est.); Poverty rate: 0.0% (2006-2010 5-year est.).
Education: Percent of population age 25 and over with: High school diploma (including GED) or higher: 73.2% (2006-2010 5-year est.); Bachelor's degree or higher: 18.3% (2006-2010 5-year est.); Master's degree or higher: 14.6% (2006-2010 5-year est.).

School District(s)

Penncrest SD (PK-12)
   2010-11 Enrollment: 3,459 . . . . (814) 763-2323
Housing: Homeownership rate: 79.3% (2010); Median home value: $95,000 (2006-2010 5-year est.); Median contract rent: n/a per month (2006-2010 5-year est.); Median year structure built: before 1940 (2006-2010 5-year est.).
Transportation: Commute to work: 56.9% car, 0.0% public transportation, 13.7% walk, 23.5% work from home (2006-2010 5-year est.); Travel time to work: 30.8% less than 15 minutes, 46.2% 15 to 30 minutes, 7.7% 30 to 45 minutes, 0.0% 45 to 60 minutes, 15.4% 60 minutes or more (2006-2010 5-year est.)

HARMONSBURG (CDP). Covers a land area of 1.377 square miles and a water area of 0 square miles. Located at 41.67° N. Lat; 80.31° W. Long. Elevation is 1,119 feet.
Population: 351 (1990); 356 (2000); 401 (2010); Density: 291.3 persons per square mile (2010); Race: 97.0% White, 0.2% Black, 0.0% Asian, 0.2% American Indian/Alaska Native, 0.0% Native Hawaiian/Other Pacific Islander, 2.6% Other, 1.7% Hispanic of any race (2010); Average household size: 2.49 (2010); Median age: 43.9 (2010); Males per 100 females: 103.6 (2010); Marriage status: 5.3% never married, 87.8% now married, 6.9% widowed, 0.0% divorced (2006-2010 5-year est.); Foreign born: 3.1% (2006-2010 5-year est.); Ancestry (includes multiple ancestries): 49.3% German, 21.1% English, 14.5% Irish, 13.7% Italian, 9.3% Pennsylvania German (2006-2010 5-year est.).
Economy: Employment by occupation: 8.2% management, 0.0% professional, 5.5% services, 15.1% sales, 27.4% farming, 0.0% construction, 6.8% production (2006-2010 5-year est.).
Income: Per capita income: $14,401 (2006-2010 5-year est.); Median household income: $30,357 (2006-2010 5-year est.); Average household income: $33,302 (2006-2010 5-year est.); Percent of households with income of $100,000 or more: n/a (2006-2010 5-year est.); Poverty rate: 6.0% (2006-2010 5-year est.).
Education: Percent of population age 25 and over with: High school diploma (including GED) or higher: 89.9% (2006-2010 5-year est.); Bachelor's degree or higher: 3.9% (2006-2010 5-year est.); Master's degree or higher: 3.9% (2006-2010 5-year est.).
Housing: Homeownership rate: 87.6% (2010); Median home value: $66,800 (2006-2010 5-year est.); Median contract rent: n/a per month (2006-2010 5-year est.); Median year structure built: 1975 (2006-2010 5-year est.).
Transportation: Commute to work: 90.6% car, 0.0% public transportation, 0.0% walk, 0.0% work from home (2006-2010 5-year est.); Travel time to work: 47.2% less than 15 minutes, 45.3% 15 to 30 minutes, 7.5% 30 to 45 minutes, 0.0% 45 to 60 minutes, 0.0% 60 minutes or more (2006-2010 5-year est.)

HARTSTOWN (CDP). Covers a land area of 0.809 square miles and a water area of 0.012 square miles. Located at 41.55° N. Lat; 80.38° W. Long. Elevation is 1,040 feet.
Population: 265 (1990); 246 (2000); 201 (2010); Density: 248.4 persons per square mile (2010); Race: 99.0% White, 0.5% Black, 0.0% Asian, 0.0% American Indian/Alaska Native, 0.0% Native Hawaiian/Other Pacific Islander, 0.5% Other, 0.0% Hispanic of any race (2010); Average household size: 2.42 (2010); Median age: 39.6 (2010); Males per 100

females: 109.4 (2010); Marriage status: 23.3% never married, 64.3% now married, 6.2% widowed, 6.2% divorced (2006-2010 5-year est.); Foreign born: 0.0% (2006-2010 5-year est.); Ancestry (includes multiple ancestries): 25.0% German, 8.9% Irish, 6.1% Swedish, 5.6% Scottish, 5.0% American (2006-2010 5-year est.).
Economy: Employment by occupation: 0.0% management, 0.0% professional, 14.6% services, 6.3% sales, 0.0% farming, 12.5% construction, 6.3% production (2006-2010 5-year est.).
Income: Per capita income: $12,993 (2006-2010 5-year est.); Median household income: $35,192 (2006-2010 5-year est.); Average household income: $36,152 (2006-2010 5-year est.); Percent of households with income of $100,000 or more: n/a (2006-2010 5-year est.); Poverty rate: 15.6% (2006-2010 5-year est.).
Education: Percent of population age 25 and over with: High school diploma (including GED) or higher: 70.8% (2006-2010 5-year est.); Bachelor's degree or higher: 13.3% (2006-2010 5-year est.); Master's degree or higher: 2.7% (2006-2010 5-year est.).
Housing: Homeownership rate: 74.7% (2010); Median home value: $70,900 (2006-2010 5-year est.); Median contract rent: n/a per month (2006-2010 5-year est.); Median year structure built: 1969 (2006-2010 5-year est.).
Transportation: Commute to work: 93.2% car, 0.0% public transportation, 0.0% walk, 0.0% work from home (2006-2010 5-year est.); Travel time to work: 13.6% less than 15 minutes, 68.2% 15 to 30 minutes, 6.8% 30 to 45 minutes, 6.8% 45 to 60 minutes, 4.5% 60 minutes or more (2006-2010 5-year est.)

HAYFIELD (township). Covers a land area of 38.840 square miles and a water area of 0.062 square miles. Located at 41.71° N. Lat; 80.20° W. Long.
Population: 2,910 (1990); 3,092 (2000); 2,940 (2010); Density: 75.7 persons per square mile (2010); Race: 98.8% White, 0.3% Black, 0.1% Asian, 0.0% American Indian/Alaska Native, 0.0% Native Hawaiian/Other Pacific Islander, 0.8% Other, 0.4% Hispanic of any race (2010); Average household size: 2.51 (2010); Median age: 44.3 (2010); Males per 100 females: 104.0 (2010); Marriage status: 22.7% never married, 64.5% now married, 5.1% widowed, 7.7% divorced (2006-2010 5-year est.); Foreign born: 0.9% (2006-2010 5-year est.); Ancestry (includes multiple ancestries): 40.6% German, 14.1% Irish, 13.7% English, 8.1% Polish, 7.5% Italian (2006-2010 5-year est.).
Economy: Single-family building permits issued: 0 (2011); Multi-family building permits issued: 0 (2011); Employment by occupation: 6.0% management, 2.1% professional, 8.3% services, 15.1% sales, 3.5% farming, 11.3% construction, 12.3% production (2006-2010 5-year est.).
Income: Per capita income: $21,001 (2006-2010 5-year est.); Median household income: $45,259 (2006-2010 5-year est.); Average household income: $51,393 (2006-2010 5-year est.); Percent of households with income of $100,000 or more: 6.5% (2006-2010 5-year est.); Poverty rate: 9.6% (2006-2010 5-year est.).
Education: Percent of population age 25 and over with: High school diploma (including GED) or higher: 88.3% (2006-2010 5-year est.); Bachelor's degree or higher: 17.8% (2006-2010 5-year est.); Master's degree or higher: 6.5% (2006-2010 5-year est.).
Housing: Homeownership rate: 88.2% (2010); Median home value: $97,800 (2006-2010 5-year est.); Median contract rent: $334 per month (2006-2010 5-year est.); Median year structure built: 1973 (2006-2010 5-year est.).
Transportation: Commute to work: 95.3% car, 0.0% public transportation, 2.3% walk, 1.7% work from home (2006-2010 5-year est.); Travel time to work: 36.2% less than 15 minutes, 47.8% 15 to 30 minutes, 10.7% 30 to 45 minutes, 1.5% 45 to 60 minutes, 3.8% 60 minutes or more (2006-2010 5-year est.)
Additional Information Contacts
Meadville-Western Crawford County Chamber of Commerce . . . . (814) 337-8030
   http://www.meadvillechamber.com

HYDETOWN (borough). Covers a land area of 2.255 square miles and a water area of 0 square miles. Located at 41.65° N. Lat; 79.72° W. Long. Elevation is 1,247 feet.
Population: 681 (1990); 605 (2000); 526 (2010); Density: 233.3 persons per square mile (2010); Race: 98.7% White, 0.0% Black, 0.8% Asian, 0.2% American Indian/Alaska Native, 0.0% Native Hawaiian/Other Pacific Islander, 0.3% Other, 1.0% Hispanic of any race (2010); Average household size: 2.26 (2010); Median age: 48.3 (2010); Males per 100

females: 92.7 (2010); Marriage status: 13.6% never married, 63.3% now married, 11.2% widowed, 11.9% divorced (2006-2010 5-year est.); Foreign born: 0.7% (2006-2010 5-year est.); Ancestry (includes multiple ancestries): 36.2% German, 19.2% Irish, 14.6% English, 11.2% American, 6.9% Swedish (2006-2010 5-year est.).

Economy: Single-family building permits issued: 0 (2011); Multi-family building permits issued: 0 (2011); Employment by occupation: 8.5% management, 0.0% professional, 8.0% services, 26.9% sales, 0.0% farming, 10.4% construction, 15.6% production (2006-2010 5-year est.).

Income: Per capita income: $22,125 (2006-2010 5-year est.); Median household income: $35,417 (2006-2010 5-year est.); Average household income: $51,723 (2006-2010 5-year est.); Percent of households with income of $100,000 or more: 11.4% (2006-2010 5-year est.); Poverty rate: 14.5% (2006-2010 5-year est.).

Education: Percent of population age 25 and over with: High school diploma (including GED) or higher: 88.2% (2006-2010 5-year est.); Bachelor's degree or higher: 21.3% (2006-2010 5-year est.); Master's degree or higher: 7.3% (2006-2010 5-year est.).

Housing: Homeownership rate: 81.1% (2010); Median home value: $77,300 (2006-2010 5-year est.); Median contract rent: $349 per month (2006-2010 5-year est.); Median year structure built: before 1940 (2006-2010 5-year est.).

Transportation: Commute to work: 95.1% car, 0.0% public transportation, 2.0% walk, 2.9% work from home (2006-2010 5-year est.); Travel time to work: 43.9% less than 15 minutes, 21.2% 15 to 30 minutes, 16.7% 30 to 45 minutes, 6.6% 45 to 60 minutes, 11.6% 60 minutes or more (2006-2010 5-year est.)

KERRTOWN (CDP). Covers a land area of 0.846 square miles and a water area of 0 square miles. Located at 41.63° N. Lat; 80.17° W. Long. Elevation is 1,076 feet.

Population: n/a (1990); n/a (2000); 305 (2010); Density: 360.4 persons per square mile (2010); Race: 93.1% White, 1.6% Black, 2.0% Asian, 0.0% American Indian/Alaska Native, 0.0% Native Hawaiian/Other Pacific Islander, 3.3% Other, 2.0% Hispanic of any race (2010); Average household size: 2.40 (2010); Median age: 43.1 (2010); Males per 100 females: 99.3 (2010); Marriage status: 26.3% never married, 60.0% now married, 0.0% widowed, 13.7% divorced (2006-2010 5-year est.); Foreign born: 0.0% (2006-2010 5-year est.); Ancestry (includes multiple ancestries): 24.9% Italian, 17.3% German, 13.4% Scotch-Irish, 11.6% Slavic, 8.2% Irish (2006-2010 5-year est.).

Economy: Employment by occupation: 0.0% management, 0.0% professional, 19.6% services, 7.0% sales, 0.0% farming, 14.6% construction, 13.6% production (2006-2010 5-year est.).

Income: Per capita income: $14,753 (2006-2010 5-year est.); Median household income: $22,685 (2006-2010 5-year est.); Average household income: $37,423 (2006-2010 5-year est.); Percent of households with income of $100,000 or more: 10.9% (2006-2010 5-year est.); Poverty rate: 55.6% (2006-2010 5-year est.).

Education: Percent of population age 25 and over with: High school diploma (including GED) or higher: 72.0% (2006-2010 5-year est.); Bachelor's degree or higher: 0.0% (2006-2010 5-year est.); Master's degree or higher: 0.0% (2006-2010 5-year est.).

Housing: Homeownership rate: 61.4% (2010); Median home value: $37,500 (2006-2010 5-year est.); Median contract rent: $374 per month (2006-2010 5-year est.); Median year structure built: before 1940 (2006-2010 5-year est.).

Transportation: Commute to work: 74.9% car, 0.0% public transportation, 25.1% walk, 0.0% work from home (2006-2010 5-year est.); Travel time to work: 73.4% less than 15 minutes, 26.6% 15 to 30 minutes, 0.0% 30 to 45 minutes, 0.0% 45 to 60 minutes, 0.0% 60 minutes or more (2006-2010 5-year est.)

LINCOLNVILLE (CDP). Covers a land area of 0.268 square miles and a water area of 0 square miles. Located at 41.79° N. Lat; 79.84° W. Long. Elevation is 1,371 feet.

Population: 98 (1990); 112 (2000); 96 (2010); Density: 357.6 persons per square mile (2010); Race: 97.9% White, 1.0% Black, 0.0% Asian, 0.0% American Indian/Alaska Native, 0.0% Native Hawaiian/Other Pacific Islander, 1.1% Other, 0.0% Hispanic of any race (2010); Average household size: 2.67 (2010); Median age: 38.0 (2010); Males per 100 females: 108.7 (2010); Marriage status: 33.3% never married, 44.1% now married, 0.0% widowed, 22.6% divorced (2006-2010 5-year est.); Foreign born: 9.7% (2006-2010 5-year est.); Ancestry (includes multiple

ancestries): 25.8% American, 21.5% German, 12.9% English, 8.6% Polish, 5.4% Swedish (2006-2010 5-year est.).

Economy: Employment by occupation: 9.3% management, 0.0% professional, 48.1% services, 0.0% sales, 0.0% farming, 0.0% construction, 0.0% production (2006-2010 5-year est.).

Income: Per capita income: $26,334 (2006-2010 5-year est.); Median household income: $33,750 (2006-2010 5-year est.); Average household income: $48,840 (2006-2010 5-year est.); Percent of households with income of $100,000 or more: 10.0% (2006-2010 5-year est.); Poverty rate: 0.0% (2006-2010 5-year est.).

Education: Percent of population age 25 and over with: High school diploma (including GED) or higher: 86.3% (2006-2010 5-year est.); Bachelor's degree or higher: 28.8% (2006-2010 5-year est.); Master's degree or higher: 13.7% (2006-2010 5-year est.).

Housing: Homeownership rate: 83.3% (2010); Median home value: $63,600 (2006-2010 5-year est.); Median contract rent: n/a per month (2006-2010 5-year est.); Median year structure built: 1948 (2006-2010 5-year est.).

Transportation: Commute to work: 83.3% car, 0.0% public transportation, 0.0% walk, 16.7% work from home (2006-2010 5-year est.); Travel time to work: 26.7% less than 15 minutes, 62.2% 15 to 30 minutes, 0.0% 30 to 45 minutes, 11.1% 45 to 60 minutes, 0.0% 60 minutes or more (2006-2010 5-year est.)

LINESVILLE (borough). Covers a land area of 0.771 square miles and a water area of 0 square miles. Located at 41.66° N. Lat; 80.42° W. Long. Elevation is 1,050 feet.

History: Incorporated 1862.

Population: 1,166 (1990); 1,155 (2000); 1,040 (2010); Density: 1,348.9 persons per square mile (2010); Race: 97.2% White, 0.1% Black, 0.1% Asian, 0.7% American Indian/Alaska Native, 0.0% Native Hawaiian/Other Pacific Islander, 1.9% Other, 1.0% Hispanic of any race (2010); Average household size: 2.32 (2010); Median age: 42.5 (2010); Males per 100 females: 92.9 (2010); Marriage status: 28.8% never married, 49.4% now married, 9.1% widowed, 12.7% divorced (2006-2010 5-year est.); Foreign born: 0.3% (2006-2010 5-year est.); Ancestry (includes multiple ancestries): 45.2% German, 17.0% Irish, 12.5% English, 4.1% Polish, 3.6% Dutch (2006-2010 5-year est.).

Economy: Single-family building permits issued: 0 (2011); Multi-family building permits issued: 0 (2011); Employment by occupation: 2.9% management, 1.7% professional, 23.9% services, 13.5% sales, 2.4% farming, 11.6% construction, 11.8% production (2006-2010 5-year est.).

Income: Per capita income: $18,886 (2006-2010 5-year est.); Median household income: $31,250 (2006-2010 5-year est.); Average household income: $42,614 (2006-2010 5-year est.); Percent of households with income of $100,000 or more: 7.5% (2006-2010 5-year est.); Poverty rate: 22.3% (2006-2010 5-year est.).

Education: Percent of population age 25 and over with: High school diploma (including GED) or higher: 93.2% (2006-2010 5-year est.); Bachelor's degree or higher: 7.6% (2006-2010 5-year est.); Master's degree or higher: 2.9% (2006-2010 5-year est.).

School District(s)

Conneaut SD (KG-12)

   2010-11 Enrollment: 2,456 . . . . (814) 683-5900

Housing: Homeownership rate: 57.4% (2010); Median home value: $90,400 (2006-2010 5-year est.); Median contract rent: $368 per month (2006-2010 5-year est.); Median year structure built: 1945 (2006-2010 5-year est.).

Safety: Violent crime rate: 19.2 per 10,000 population; Property crime rate: 76.7 per 10,000 population (2011).

Transportation: Commute to work: 91.6% car, 0.0% public transportation, 7.4% walk, 1.0% work from home (2006-2010 5-year est.); Travel time to work: 28.0% less than 15 minutes, 42.0% 15 to 30 minutes, 18.8% 30 to 45 minutes, 7.5% 45 to 60 minutes, 3.8% 60 minutes or more (2006-2010 5-year est.)

MEADVILLE (city). Aka Nebbons Hill. County seat. Covers a land area of 4.375 square miles and a water area of 0.004 square miles. Located at 41.65° N. Lat; 80.15° W. Long. Elevation is 1,099 feet.

History: Meadville was settled in 1788 by David Mead, his brothers, and other pioneers from Sunbury. It has been known as the home of the first successful slide fastener factory and as the seat of Allegheny College, founded in 1815.

Population: 14,272 (1990); 13,685 (2000); 13,388 (2010); Density: 3,060.0 persons per square mile (2010); Race: 90.6% White, 5.0% Black,

1.1% Asian, 0.2% American Indian/Alaska Native, 0.0% Native Hawaiian/Other Pacific Islander, 3.1% Other, 1.7% Hispanic of any race (2010); Average household size: 2.15 (2010); Median age: 33.0 (2010); Males per 100 females: 89.0 (2010); Marriage status: 41.8% never married, 39.2% now married, 7.4% widowed, 11.5% divorced (2006-2010 5-year est.); Foreign born: 1.7% (2006-2010 5-year est.); Ancestry (includes multiple ancestries): 32.4% German, 19.8% Irish, 13.9% Italian, 11.3% English, 8.3% Polish (2006-2010 5-year est.).

Economy: Single-family building permits issued: 0 (2011); Multi-family building permits issued: 0 (2011); Employment by occupation: 8.0% management, 2.1% professional, 14.8% services, 12.4% sales, 5.3% farming, 5.1% construction, 5.8% production (2006-2010 5-year est.).

Income: Per capita income: $18,698 (2006-2010 5-year est.); Median household income: $28,052 (2006-2010 5-year est.); Average household income: $42,440 (2006-2010 5-year est.); Percent of households with income of $100,000 or more: 9.1% (2006-2010 5-year est.); Poverty rate: 27.8% (2006-2010 5-year est.).

Education: Percent of population age 25 and over with: High school diploma (including GED) or higher: 89.0% (2006-2010 5-year est.); Bachelor's degree or higher: 26.2% (2006-2010 5-year est.); Master's degree or higher: 12.9% (2006-2010 5-year est.).

School District(s)

Crawford Central SD (KG-12)
  2010-11 Enrollment: 3,972 . . . . (814) 724-3960
Crawford County CTC (10-12)
  2010-11 Enrollment: n/a . . . . (814) 724-6024

Four-year College(s)

Allegheny College (Private, Not-for-profit, United Methodist)
  Fall 2010 Enrollment: 2,081 . . . . (814) 332-3100
  2011-12 Tuition: In-state $36,190; Out-of-state $36,190

Vocational/Technical School(s)

Crawford County Career and Technical Center Practical Nursing Program (Public)
  Fall 2010 Enrollment: 43 . . . . (814) 724-6028
  2011-12 Tuition: $12,250
Precision Manufacturing Institute (Private, Not-for-profit)
  Fall 2010 Enrollment: 196 . . . . (814) 333-2415
  2011-12 Tuition: $21,350

Housing: Homeownership rate: 42.8% (2010); Median home value: $95,100 (2006-2010 5-year est.); Median contract rent: $394 per month (2006-2010 5-year est.); Median year structure built: 1947 (2006-2010 5-year est.).

Hospitals: Meadville Medical Center (277 beds)

Safety: Violent crime rate: 17.9 per 10,000 population; Property crime rate: 230.8 per 10,000 population (2011).

Newspapers: The Meadville Tribune (Local news; Circulation 13,779)

Transportation: Commute to work: 69.3% car, 3.1% public transportation, 22.8% walk, 3.7% work from home (2006-2010 5-year est.); Travel time to work: 65.4% less than 15 minutes, 22.1% 15 to 30 minutes, 7.4% 30 to 45 minutes, 2.3% 45 to 60 minutes, 2.7% 60 minutes or more (2006-2010 5-year est.)

Airports: Port Meadville (general aviation)

Additional Information Contacts

City of Meadville . . . . (814) 724-6000
  http://www.cityofmeadville.org
Meadville-Western Crawford County Chamber of Commerce . . . . (814) 337-8030
  http://www.meadvillechamber.com

NORTH SHENANGO (township). Covers a land area of 18.750 square miles and a water area of 7.405 square miles. Located at 41.61° N. Lat; 80.47° W. Long.

Population: 902 (1990); 1,387 (2000); 1,410 (2010); Density: 75.2 persons per square mile (2010); Race: 98.4% White, 0.4% Black, 0.1% Asian, 0.2% American Indian/Alaska Native, 0.0% Native Hawaiian/Other Pacific Islander, 0.9% Other, 0.2% Hispanic of any race (2010); Average household size: 2.09 (2010); Median age: 53.7 (2010); Males per 100 females: 100.9 (2010); Marriage status: 17.5% never married, 60.5% now married, 6.4% widowed, 15.6% divorced (2006-2010 5-year est.); Foreign born: 1.4% (2006-2010 5-year est.); Ancestry (includes multiple ancestries): 33.5% German, 18.8% Irish, 11.0% Italian, 10.2% English, 7.5% Polish (2006-2010 5-year est.).

Economy: Single-family building permits issued: 1 (2011); Multi-family building permits issued: 0 (2011); Employment by occupation: 4.5%

management, 4.7% professional, 11.5% services, 20.1% sales, 6.2% farming, 13.5% construction, 11.1% production (2006-2010 5-year est.).

Income: Per capita income: $18,076 (2006-2010 5-year est.); Median household income: $31,996 (2006-2010 5-year est.); Average household income: $39,321 (2006-2010 5-year est.); Percent of households with income of $100,000 or more: 2.4% (2006-2010 5-year est.); Poverty rate: 16.4% (2006-2010 5-year est.).

Education: Percent of population age 25 and over with: High school diploma (including GED) or higher: 82.1% (2006-2010 5-year est.); Bachelor's degree or higher: 9.6% (2006-2010 5-year est.); Master's degree or higher: 2.5% (2006-2010 5-year est.).

Housing: Homeownership rate: 88.0% (2010); Median home value: $83,800 (2006-2010 5-year est.); Median contract rent: $507 per month (2006-2010 5-year est.); Median year structure built: 1970 (2006-2010 5-year est.).

Transportation: Commute to work: 93.2% car, 0.0% public transportation, 2.0% walk, 4.1% work from home (2006-2010 5-year est.); Travel time to work: 15.3% less than 15 minutes, 35.3% 15 to 30 minutes, 29.8% 30 to 45 minutes, 10.0% 45 to 60 minutes, 9.6% 60 minutes or more (2006-2010 5-year est.)

Additional Information Contacts

Meadville-Western Crawford County Chamber of Commerce . . . . (814) 337-8030
  http://www.meadvillechamber.com

OIL CREEK (township). Covers a land area of 32.196 square miles and a water area of 0 square miles. Located at 41.66° N. Lat; 79.68° W. Long.

Population: 2,133 (1990); 1,880 (2000); 1,877 (2010); Density: 58.3 persons per square mile (2010); Race: 98.4% White, 0.5% Black, 0.5% Asian, 0.1% American Indian/Alaska Native, 0.0% Native Hawaiian/Other Pacific Islander, 0.5% Other, 0.7% Hispanic of any race (2010); Average household size: 2.43 (2010); Median age: 45.4 (2010); Males per 100 females: 105.8 (2010); Marriage status: 25.7% never married, 62.2% now married, 5.5% widowed, 6.6% divorced (2006-2010 5-year est.); Foreign born: 0.7% (2006-2010 5-year est.); Ancestry (includes multiple ancestries): 39.0% German, 23.2% Irish, 11.8% English, 7.0% American, 6.8% Scotch-Irish (2006-2010 5-year est.).

Economy: Single-family building permits issued: 0 (2011); Multi-family building permits issued: 0 (2011); Employment by occupation: 10.1% management, 2.5% professional, 10.1% services, 16.3% sales, 0.0% farming, 5.5% construction, 5.9% production (2006-2010 5-year est.).

Income: Per capita income: $20,351 (2006-2010 5-year est.); Median household income: $40,625 (2006-2010 5-year est.); Average household income: $49,445 (2006-2010 5-year est.); Percent of households with income of $100,000 or more: 8.8% (2006-2010 5-year est.); Poverty rate: 9.7% (2006-2010 5-year est.).

Education: Percent of population age 25 and over with: High school diploma (including GED) or higher: 86.7% (2006-2010 5-year est.); Bachelor's degree or higher: 14.3% (2006-2010 5-year est.); Master's degree or higher: 5.8% (2006-2010 5-year est.).

Housing: Homeownership rate: 83.7% (2010); Median home value: $71,400 (2006-2010 5-year est.); Median contract rent: $385 per month (2006-2010 5-year est.); Median year structure built: 1969 (2006-2010 5-year est.).

Transportation: Commute to work: 91.7% car, 0.0% public transportation, 4.4% walk, 2.5% work from home (2006-2010 5-year est.); Travel time to work: 55.4% less than 15 minutes, 20.7% 15 to 30 minutes, 10.2% 30 to 45 minutes, 3.3% 45 to 60 minutes, 10.3% 60 minutes or more (2006-2010 5-year est.)

Additional Information Contacts

Titusville Area Chamber of Commerce . . . . (814) 827-2941
  http://titusvillechamber.com

PINE (township). Covers a land area of 6.516 square miles and a water area of 6.081 square miles. Located at 41.65° N. Lat; 80.43° W. Long.

Population: 455 (1990); 531 (2000); 462 (2010); Density: 70.9 persons per square mile (2010); Race: 98.1% White, 0.0% Black, 0.4% Asian, 1.3% American Indian/Alaska Native, 0.0% Native Hawaiian/Other Pacific Islander, 0.2% Other, 0.2% Hispanic of any race (2010); Average household size: 2.31 (2010); Median age: 47.8 (2010); Males per 100 females: 96.6 (2010); Marriage status: 21.9% never married, 57.2% now married, 12.6% widowed, 8.2% divorced (2006-2010 5-year est.); Foreign born: 1.7% (2006-2010 5-year est.); Ancestry (includes multiple

ancestries): 28.7% German, 17.1% Irish, 10.4% Scotch-Irish, 8.9% Italian, 7.8% American (2006-2010 5-year est.).

Economy: Single-family building permits issued: 0 (2011); Multi-family building permits issued: 0 (2011); Employment by occupation: 3.0% management, 0.0% professional, 3.0% services, 14.8% sales, 2.4% farming, 12.4% construction, 14.2% production (2006-2010 5-year est.).

Income: Per capita income: $19,291 (2006-2010 5-year est.); Median household income: $40,000 (2006-2010 5-year est.); Average household income: $47,963 (2006-2010 5-year est.); Percent of households with income of $100,000 or more: 2.2% (2006-2010 5-year est.); Poverty rate: 5.2% (2006-2010 5-year est.).

Education: Percent of population age 25 and over with: High school diploma (including GED) or higher: 89.2% (2006-2010 5-year est.); Bachelor's degree or higher: 9.3% (2006-2010 5-year est.); Master's degree or higher: 4.1% (2006-2010 5-year est.).

Housing: Homeownership rate: 84.0% (2010); Median home value: $98,300 (2006-2010 5-year est.); Median contract rent: $367 per month (2006-2010 5-year est.); Median year structure built: 1979 (2006-2010 5-year est.).

Transportation: Commute to work: 84.0% car, 0.0% public transportation, 8.3% walk, 1.8% work from home (2006-2010 5-year est.); Travel time to work: 25.9% less than 15 minutes, 29.5% 15 to 30 minutes, 28.9% 30 to 45 minutes, 12.7% 45 to 60 minutes, 3.0% 60 minutes or more (2006-2010 5-year est.)

PYMATUNING CENTRAL (CDP). Covers a land area of 16.369 square miles and a water area of 0.063 square miles. Located at 41.59° N. Lat; 80.48° W. Long.

Population: 1,430 (1990); 2,216 (2000); 2,269 (2010); Density: 138.6 persons per square mile (2010); Race: 98.8% White, 0.2% Black, 0.1% Asian, 0.2% American Indian/Alaska Native, 0.0% Native Hawaiian/Other Pacific Islander, 0.7% Other, 0.3% Hispanic of any race (2010); Average household size: 2.13 (2010); Median age: 52.6 (2010); Males per 100 females: 101.9 (2010); Marriage status: 20.5% never married, 63.6% now married, 5.4% widowed, 10.4% divorced (2006-2010 5-year est.); Foreign born: 2.6% (2006-2010 5-year est.); Ancestry (includes multiple ancestries): 34.1% German, 16.3% Irish, 11.1% English, 9.1% Italian, 5.6% Polish (2006-2010 5-year est.).

Economy: Employment by occupation: 2.1% management, 3.3% professional, 14.0% services, 16.0% sales, 4.0% farming, 13.5% construction, 7.9% production (2006-2010 5-year est.).

Income: Per capita income: $19,103 (2006-2010 5-year est.); Median household income: $32,191 (2006-2010 5-year est.); Average household income: $44,066 (2006-2010 5-year est.); Percent of households with income of $100,000 or more: 6.2% (2006-2010 5-year est.); Poverty rate: 22.0% (2006-2010 5-year est.).

Education: Percent of population age 25 and over with: High school diploma (including GED) or higher: 85.9% (2006-2010 5-year est.); Bachelor's degree or higher: 11.8% (2006-2010 5-year est.); Master's degree or higher: 3.1% (2006-2010 5-year est.).

Housing: Homeownership rate: 88.0% (2010); Median home value: $88,400 (2006-2010 5-year est.); Median contract rent: $508 per month (2006-2010 5-year est.); Median year structure built: 1970 (2006-2010 5-year est.).

Transportation: Commute to work: 89.5% car, 2.0% public transportation, 2.1% walk, 5.6% work from home (2006-2010 5-year est.); Travel time to work: 16.4% less than 15 minutes, 34.1% 15 to 30 minutes, 33.5% 30 to 45 minutes, 7.0% 45 to 60 minutes, 9.0% 60 minutes or more (2006-2010 5-year est.).

Additional Information Contacts

Meadville-Western Crawford County Chamber of Commerce . . . . (814) 337-8030
  http://www.meadvillechamber.com

PYMATUNING NORTH (CDP). Covers a land area of 1.903 square miles and a water area of 0.003 square miles. Located at 41.67° N. Lat; 80.47° W. Long.

Population: 287 (1990); 325 (2000); 311 (2010); Density: 163.4 persons per square mile (2010); Race: 98.1% White, 0.0% Black, 0.6% Asian, 1.3% American Indian/Alaska Native, 0.0% Native Hawaiian/Other Pacific Islander, 0.0% Other, 0.0% Hispanic of any race (2010); Average household size: 2.10 (2010); Median age: 51.9 (2010); Males per 100 females: 107.3 (2010); Marriage status: 17.6% never married, 60.2% now married, 6.5% widowed, 15.8% divorced (2006-2010 5-year est.); Foreign born: 0.6% (2006-2010 5-year est.); Ancestry (includes multiple

ancestries): 35.0% German, 12.7% English, 12.1% Irish, 9.2% Italian, 7.0% Polish (2006-2010 5-year est.).

Economy: Employment by occupation: 5.8% management, 2.9% professional, 9.6% services, 5.8% sales, 0.0% farming, 28.8% construction, 23.1% production (2006-2010 5-year est.).

Income: Per capita income: $19,610 (2006-2010 5-year est.); Median household income: $31,583 (2006-2010 5-year est.); Average household income: $41,029 (2006-2010 5-year est.); Percent of households with income of $100,000 or more: 6.1% (2006-2010 5-year est.); Poverty rate: 6.4% (2006-2010 5-year est.).

Education: Percent of population age 25 and over with: High school diploma (including GED) or higher: 80.4% (2006-2010 5-year est.); Bachelor's degree or higher: 15.6% (2006-2010 5-year est.); Master's degree or higher: 3.2% (2006-2010 5-year est.).

Housing: Homeownership rate: 82.4% (2010); Median home value: $79,400 (2006-2010 5-year est.); Median contract rent: $511 per month (2006-2010 5-year est.); Median year structure built: 1979 (2006-2010 5-year est.).

Transportation: Commute to work: 83.3% car, 0.0% public transportation, 0.0% walk, 8.3% work from home (2006-2010 5-year est.); Travel time to work: 15.9% less than 15 minutes, 19.3% 15 to 30 minutes, 46.6% 30 to 45 minutes, 11.4% 45 to 60 minutes, 6.8% 60 minutes or more (2006-2010 5-year est.)

PYMATUNING SOUTH (CDP). Covers a land area of 2.589 square miles and a water area of 0.011 square miles. Located at 41.51° N. Lat; 80.48° W. Long.

Population: 375 (1990); 467 (2000); 479 (2010); Density: 185.0 persons per square mile (2010); Race: 98.5% White, 0.0% Black, 0.8% Asian, 0.2% American Indian/Alaska Native, 0.0% Native Hawaiian/Other Pacific Islander, 0.5% Other, 0.4% Hispanic of any race (2010); Average household size: 2.22 (2010); Median age: 48.9 (2010); Males per 100 females: 97.9 (2010); Marriage status: 33.1% never married, 53.8% now married, 3.5% widowed, 9.6% divorced (2006-2010 5-year est.); Foreign born: 2.8% (2006-2010 5-year est.); Ancestry (includes multiple ancestries): 30.4% German, 15.3% Irish, 10.1% French, 9.5% Italian, 8.2% Polish (2006-2010 5-year est.).

Economy: Employment by occupation: 7.9% management, 0.4% professional, 11.7% services, 14.2% sales, 6.7% farming, 3.3% construction, 10.0% production (2006-2010 5-year est.).

Income: Per capita income: $20,515 (2006-2010 5-year est.); Median household income: $38,750 (2006-2010 5-year est.); Average household income: $48,512 (2006-2010 5-year est.); Percent of households with income of $100,000 or more: 9.0% (2006-2010 5-year est.); Poverty rate: 22.2% (2006-2010 5-year est.).

Education: Percent of population age 25 and over with: High school diploma (including GED) or higher: 91.4% (2006-2010 5-year est.); Bachelor's degree or higher: 14.6% (2006-2010 5-year est.); Master's degree or higher: 7.1% (2006-2010 5-year est.).

Housing: Homeownership rate: 78.7% (2010); Median home value: $88,700 (2006-2010 5-year est.); Median contract rent: $588 per month (2006-2010 5-year est.); Median year structure built: 1957 (2006-2010 5-year est.).

Transportation: Commute to work: 96.2% car, 0.0% public transportation, 0.0% walk, 3.8% work from home (2006-2010 5-year est.); Travel time to work: 29.6% less than 15 minutes, 35.8% 15 to 30 minutes, 14.2% 30 to 45 minutes, 6.2% 45 to 60 minutes, 14.2% 60 minutes or more (2006-2010 5-year est.)

RANDOLPH (township). Covers a land area of 42.749 square miles and a water area of 0.333 square miles. Located at 41.62° N. Lat; 79.96° W. Long.

Population: 1,661 (1990); 1,838 (2000); 1,782 (2010); Density: 41.7 persons per square mile (2010); Race: 98.5% White, 0.4% Black, 0.3% Asian, 0.0% American Indian/Alaska Native, 0.0% Native Hawaiian/Other Pacific Islander, 0.8% Other, 0.4% Hispanic of any race (2010); Average household size: 2.67 (2010); Median age: 40.4 (2010); Males per 100 females: 103.4 (2010); Marriage status: 31.7% never married, 57.2% now married, 6.1% widowed, 5.0% divorced (2006-2010 5-year est.); Foreign born: 2.8% (2006-2010 5-year est.); Ancestry (includes multiple ancestries): 38.0% German, 18.0% Irish, 9.2% French, 8.8% English, 7.3% Italian (2006-2010 5-year est.).

Economy: Single-family building permits issued: 0 (2011); Multi-family building permits issued: 0 (2011); Employment by occupation: 5.9%

management, 3.5% professional, 18.4% services, 14.3% sales, 3.2% farming, 8.8% construction, 5.9% production (2006-2010 5-year est.).
Income: Per capita income: $21,267 (2006-2010 5-year est.); Median household income: $45,119 (2006-2010 5-year est.); Average household income: $59,505 (2006-2010 5-year est.); Percent of households with income of $100,000 or more: 9.0% (2006-2010 5-year est.); Poverty rate: 6.6% (2006-2010 5-year est.).
Education: Percent of population age 25 and over with: High school diploma (including GED) or higher: 82.5% (2006-2010 5-year est.); Bachelor's degree or higher: 12.9% (2006-2010 5-year est.); Master's degree or higher: 2.3% (2006-2010 5-year est.).
Housing: Homeownership rate: 88.5% (2010); Median home value: $103,900 (2006-2010 5-year est.); Median contract rent: $475 per month (2006-2010 5-year est.); Median year structure built: 1960 (2006-2010 5-year est.).
Transportation: Commute to work: 86.2% car, 0.4% public transportation, 5.4% walk, 6.1% work from home (2006-2010 5-year est.); Travel time to work: 22.8% less than 15 minutes, 49.9% 15 to 30 minutes, 13.8% 30 to 45 minutes, 6.4% 45 to 60 minutes, 7.0% 60 minutes or more (2006-2010 5-year est.)
Additional Information Contacts
Titusville Area Chamber of Commerce . . . . (814) 827-2941
http://titusvillechamber.com

RICEVILLE (CDP). Covers a land area of 0.426 square miles and a water area of 0 square miles. Located at 41.78° N. Lat; 79.80° W. Long. Elevation is 1,358 feet.
Population: 79 (1990); 82 (2000); 68 (2010); Density: 159.6 persons per square mile (2010); Race: 100.0% White, 0.0% Black, 0.0% Asian, 0.0% American Indian/Alaska Native, 0.0% Native Hawaiian/Other Pacific Islander, 0.0% Other, 0.0% Hispanic of any race (2010); Average household size: 2.52 (2010); Median age: 47.2 (2010); Males per 100 females: 100.0 (2010); Marriage status: 37.3% never married, 28.8% now married, 15.3% widowed, 18.6% divorced (2006-2010 5-year est.); Foreign born: 0.0% (2006-2010 5-year est.); Ancestry (includes multiple ancestries): 13.6% Swiss, 8.5% German, 8.5% Welsh, 5.1% American, 5.1% Pennsylvania German (2006-2010 5-year est.).
Economy: Employment by occupation: 0.0% management, 0.0% professional, 13.6% services, 27.3% sales, 0.0% farming, 0.0% construction, 0.0% production (2006-2010 5-year est.).
Income: Per capita income: $20,200 (2006-2010 5-year est.); Median household income: $14,773 (2006-2010 5-year est.); Average household income: $37,231 (2006-2010 5-year est.); Percent of households with income of $100,000 or more: n/a (2006-2010 5-year est.); Poverty rate: 20.3% (2006-2010 5-year est.).
Education: Percent of population age 25 and over with: High school diploma (including GED) or higher: 92.3% (2006-2010 5-year est.); Bachelor's degree or higher: 7.7% (2006-2010 5-year est.); Master's degree or higher: 0.0% (2006-2010 5-year est.).
Housing: Homeownership rate: 85.1% (2010); Median home value: $51,700 (2006-2010 5-year est.); Median contract rent: n/a per month (2006-2010 5-year est.); Median year structure built: before 1940 (2006-2010 5-year est.).
Transportation: Commute to work: 100.0% car, 0.0% public transportation, 0.0% walk, 0.0% work from home (2006-2010 5-year est.); Travel time to work: 0.0% less than 15 minutes, 68.2% 15 to 30 minutes, 22.7% 30 to 45 minutes, 9.1% 45 to 60 minutes, 0.0% 60 minutes or more (2006-2010 5-year est.)

RICHMOND (township). Covers a land area of 36.691 square miles and a water area of 0.069 square miles. Located at 41.72° N. Lat; 79.96° W. Long.
Population: 1,341 (1990); 1,379 (2000); 1,475 (2010); Density: 40.2 persons per square mile (2010); Race: 97.6% White, 0.2% Black, 0.3% Asian, 0.5% American Indian/Alaska Native, 0.1% Native Hawaiian/Other Pacific Islander, 1.3% Other, 0.9% Hispanic of any race (2010); Average household size: 2.74 (2010); Median age: 41.1 (2010); Males per 100 females: 105.7 (2010); Marriage status: 21.3% never married, 68.8% now married, 2.7% widowed, 7.2% divorced (2006-2010 5-year est.); Foreign born: 1.0% (2006-2010 5-year est.); Ancestry (includes multiple ancestries): 31.3% German, 15.8% Irish, 15.0% English, 6.8% American, 5.8% Polish (2006-2010 5-year est.).
Economy: Single-family building permits issued: 0 (2011); Multi-family building permits issued: 0 (2011); Employment by occupation: 11.1%

management, 0.6% professional, 9.8% services, 16.5% sales, 1.8% farming, 10.1% construction, 7.7% production (2006-2010 5-year est.).
Income: Per capita income: $20,100 (2006-2010 5-year est.); Median household income: $53,553 (2006-2010 5-year est.); Average household income: $59,330 (2006-2010 5-year est.); Percent of households with income of $100,000 or more: 11.0% (2006-2010 5-year est.); Poverty rate: 8.6% (2006-2010 5-year est.).
Education: Percent of population age 25 and over with: High school diploma (including GED) or higher: 89.6% (2006-2010 5-year est.); Bachelor's degree or higher: 18.5% (2006-2010 5-year est.); Master's degree or higher: 6.0% (2006-2010 5-year est.).
Housing: Homeownership rate: 88.9% (2010); Median home value: $108,200 (2006-2010 5-year est.); Median contract rent: $465 per month (2006-2010 5-year est.); Median year structure built: 1971 (2006-2010 5-year est.).
Transportation: Commute to work: 89.9% car, 0.5% public transportation, 2.2% walk, 6.3% work from home (2006-2010 5-year est.); Travel time to work: 18.7% less than 15 minutes, 51.0% 15 to 30 minutes, 14.9% 30 to 45 minutes, 7.2% 45 to 60 minutes, 8.2% 60 minutes or more (2006-2010 5-year est.)
Additional Information Contacts
Meadville-Western Crawford County Chamber of Commerce . . . . (814) 337-8030
http://www.meadvillechamber.com

ROCKDALE (township). Covers a land area of 36.033 square miles and a water area of 0.181 square miles. Located at 41.81° N. Lat; 79.97° W. Long.
Population: 1,074 (1990); 1,343 (2000); 1,506 (2010); Density: 41.8 persons per square mile (2010); Race: 97.7% White, 0.5% Black, 0.2% Asian, 0.1% American Indian/Alaska Native, 0.0% Native Hawaiian/Other Pacific Islander, 1.5% Other, 0.9% Hispanic of any race (2010); Average household size: 2.82 (2010); Median age: 38.1 (2010); Males per 100 females: 109.7 (2010); Marriage status: 28.6% never married, 57.4% now married, 3.9% widowed, 10.1% divorced (2006-2010 5-year est.); Foreign born: 0.2% (2006-2010 5-year est.); Ancestry (includes multiple ancestries): 26.9% German, 12.7% American, 10.4% Irish, 10.0% English, 7.5% Polish (2006-2010 5-year est.).
Economy: Single-family building permits issued: 1 (2011); Multi-family building permits issued: 0 (2011); Employment by occupation: 9.5% management, 4.2% professional, 13.5% services, 5.5% sales, 1.7% farming, 19.6% construction, 8.6% production (2006-2010 5-year est.).
Income: Per capita income: $18,318 (2006-2010 5-year est.); Median household income: $41,250 (2006-2010 5-year est.); Average household income: $48,103 (2006-2010 5-year est.); Percent of households with income of $100,000 or more: 6.3% (2006-2010 5-year est.); Poverty rate: 14.7% (2006-2010 5-year est.).
Education: Percent of population age 25 and over with: High school diploma (including GED) or higher: 82.7% (2006-2010 5-year est.); Bachelor's degree or higher: 15.1% (2006-2010 5-year est.); Master's degree or higher: 5.1% (2006-2010 5-year est.).
Housing: Homeownership rate: 83.7% (2010); Median home value: $89,900 (2006-2010 5-year est.); Median contract rent: $444 per month (2006-2010 5-year est.); Median year structure built: 1969 (2006-2010 5-year est.).
Transportation: Commute to work: 82.7% car, 0.6% public transportation, 4.4% walk, 6.1% work from home (2006-2010 5-year est.); Travel time to work: 15.3% less than 15 minutes, 38.7% 15 to 30 minutes, 27.3% 30 to 45 minutes, 13.5% 45 to 60 minutes, 5.2% 60 minutes or more (2006-2010 5-year est.)
Additional Information Contacts
Meadville-Western Crawford County Chamber of Commerce . . . . (814) 337-8030
http://www.meadvillechamber.com

ROME (township). Covers a land area of 41.339 square miles and a water area of 0 square miles. Located at 41.74° N. Lat; 79.69° W. Long.
Population: 1,491 (1990); 1,745 (2000); 1,840 (2010); Density: 44.5 persons per square mile (2010); Race: 99.1% White, 0.1% Black, 0.0% Asian, 0.0% American Indian/Alaska Native, 0.0% Native Hawaiian/Other Pacific Islander, 0.8% Other, 0.3% Hispanic of any race (2010); Average household size: 3.43 (2010); Median age: 27.2 (2010); Males per 100 females: 99.3 (2010); Marriage status: 32.9% never married, 53.7% now married, 7.2% widowed, 6.1% divorced (2006-2010 5-year est.); Foreign born: 0.1% (2006-2010 5-year est.); Ancestry (includes multiple

ancestries): 36.3% German, 12.4% Irish, 6.9% English, 6.7% American, 5.4% Swiss (2006-2010 5-year est.).

Economy: Single-family building permits issued: 3 (2011); Multi-family building permits issued: 0 (2011); Employment by occupation: 9.8% management, 1.8% professional, 13.7% services, 14.3% sales, 0.4% farming, 13.1% construction, 5.1% production (2006-2010 5-year est.).

Income: Per capita income: $14,077 (2006-2010 5-year est.); Median household income: $38,824 (2006-2010 5-year est.); Average household income: $48,975 (2006-2010 5-year est.); Percent of households with income of $100,000 or more: 10.3% (2006-2010 5-year est.); Poverty rate: 21.9% (2006-2010 5-year est.).

Education: Percent of population age 25 and over with: High school diploma (including GED) or higher: 68.7% (2006-2010 5-year est.); Bachelor's degree or higher: 7.7% (2006-2010 5-year est.); Master's degree or higher: 2.4% (2006-2010 5-year est.).

Housing: Homeownership rate: 81.5% (2010); Median home value: $104,500 (2006-2010 5-year est.); Median contract rent: $367 per month (2006-2010 5-year est.); Median year structure built: 1976 (2006-2010 5-year est.).

Transportation: Commute to work: 74.3% car, 0.0% public transportation, 16.1% walk, 3.7% work from home (2006-2010 5-year est.); Travel time to work: 35.1% less than 15 minutes, 35.1% 15 to 30 minutes, 11.5% 30 to 45 minutes, 7.0% 45 to 60 minutes, 11.3% 60 minutes or more (2006-2010 5-year est.)

Additional Information Contacts

Meadville-Western Crawford County Chamber of Commerce . . . . (814) 337-8030
   http://www.meadvillechamber.com

SADSBURY (township).

Covers a land area of 23.673 square miles and a water area of 1.403 square miles. Located at 41.61° N. Lat; 80.33° W. Long.

Population: 2,657 (1990); 2,941 (2000); 2,933 (2010); Density: 123.9 persons per square mile (2010); Race: 98.7% White, 0.3% Black, 0.3% Asian, 0.1% American Indian/Alaska Native, 0.0% Native Hawaiian/Other Pacific Islander, 0.6% Other, 0.9% Hispanic of any race (2010); Average household size: 2.14 (2010); Median age: 50.5 (2010); Males per 100 females: 96.7 (2010); Marriage status: 17.5% never married, 61.3% now married, 10.8% widowed, 10.5% divorced (2006-2010 5-year est.); Foreign born: 0.6% (2006-2010 5-year est.); Ancestry (includes multiple ancestries): 35.4% German, 24.0% Irish, 10.8% English, 10.1% American, 9.6% Scotch-Irish (2006-2010 5-year est.).

Economy: Single-family building permits issued: 5 (2011); Multi-family building permits issued: 0 (2011); Employment by occupation: 14.1% management, 1.0% professional, 6.4% services, 17.0% sales, 5.5% farming, 7.1% construction, 0.8% production (2006-2010 5-year est.).

Income: Per capita income: $28,492 (2006-2010 5-year est.); Median household income: $43,788 (2006-2010 5-year est.); Average household income: $61,118 (2006-2010 5-year est.); Percent of households with income of $100,000 or more: 16.0% (2006-2010 5-year est.); Poverty rate: 12.1% (2006-2010 5-year est.).

Education: Percent of population age 25 and over with: High school diploma (including GED) or higher: 91.3% (2006-2010 5-year est.); Bachelor's degree or higher: 25.0% (2006-2010 5-year est.); Master's degree or higher: 9.8% (2006-2010 5-year est.).

Housing: Homeownership rate: 79.4% (2010); Median home value: $137,600 (2006-2010 5-year est.); Median contract rent: $408 per month (2006-2010 5-year est.); Median year structure built: 1969 (2006-2010 5-year est.)

Transportation: Commute to work: 92.9% car, 0.0% public transportation, 3.3% walk, 2.8% work from home (2006-2010 5-year est.); Travel time to work: 42.4% less than 15 minutes, 41.3% 15 to 30 minutes, 6.3% 30 to 45 minutes, 5.5% 45 to 60 minutes, 4.5% 60 minutes or more (2006-2010 5-year est.)

Additional Information Contacts

Meadville-Western Crawford County Chamber of Commerce . . . . (814) 337-8030
   http://www.meadvillechamber.com
Sadsbury Township . . . . (814) 382-8579
   http://www.sadsburytownship.com

SAEGERTOWN (borough).

Covers a land area of 1.540 square miles and a water area of <.001 square miles. Located at 41.71° N. Lat; 80.13° W. Long. Elevation is 1,109 feet.

Population: 1,066 (1990); 1,071 (2000); 997 (2010); Density: 647.4 persons per square mile (2010); Race: 94.5% White, 3.5% Black, 0.1% Asian, 0.1% American Indian/Alaska Native, 0.0% Native Hawaiian/Other Pacific Islander, 1.8% Other, 1.2% Hispanic of any race (2010); Average household size: 2.26 (2010); Median age: 39.4 (2010); Males per 100 females: 136.3 (2010); Marriage status: 40.1% never married, 47.0% now married, 3.5% widowed, 9.4% divorced (2006-2010 5-year est.); Foreign born: 0.8% (2006-2010 5-year est.); Ancestry (includes multiple ancestries): 44.3% German, 14.8% Irish, 12.1% Italian, 8.6% English, 7.8% Polish (2006-2010 5-year est.).

Economy: Single-family building permits issued: 0 (2011); Multi-family building permits issued: 0 (2011); Employment by occupation: 13.7% management, 9.8% professional, 7.5% services, 17.0% sales, 6.1% farming, 4.5% construction, 6.1% production (2006-2010 5-year est.).

Income: Per capita income: $18,265 (2006-2010 5-year est.); Median household income: $44,659 (2006-2010 5-year est.); Average household income: $46,781 (2006-2010 5-year est.); Percent of households with income of $100,000 or more: 5.1% (2006-2010 5-year est.); Poverty rate: 4.2% (2006-2010 5-year est.).

Education: Percent of population age 25 and over with: High school diploma (including GED) or higher: 87.8% (2006-2010 5-year est.); Bachelor's degree or higher: 10.5% (2006-2010 5-year est.); Master's degree or higher: 1.4% (2006-2010 5-year est.).

School District(s)

Penncrest SD (PK-12)
   2010-11 Enrollment: 3,459 . . . . (814) 763-2323

Housing: Homeownership rate: 66.7% (2010); Median home value: $98,200 (2006-2010 5-year est.); Median contract rent: $443 per month (2006-2010 5-year est.); Median year structure built: 1952 (2006-2010 5-year est.).

Transportation: Commute to work: 89.9% car, 0.0% public transportation, 7.7% walk, 1.8% work from home (2006-2010 5-year est.); Travel time to work: 58.1% less than 15 minutes, 23.5% 15 to 30 minutes, 8.7% 30 to 45 minutes, 8.4% 45 to 60 minutes, 1.2% 60 minutes or more (2006-2010 5-year est.)

SOUTH SHENANGO (township).

Covers a land area of 26.566 square miles and a water area of 3.356 square miles. Located at 41.54° N. Lat; 80.45° W. Long.

Population: 1,560 (1990); 2,047 (2000); 2,037 (2010); Density: 76.7 persons per square mile (2010); Race: 98.7% White, 0.1% Black, 0.3% Asian, 0.2% American Indian/Alaska Native, 0.0% Native Hawaiian/Other Pacific Islander, 0.7% Other, 0.5% Hispanic of any race (2010); Average household size: 2.30 (2010); Median age: 50.1 (2010); Males per 100 females: 99.7 (2010); Marriage status: 27.5% never married, 61.4% now married, 4.5% widowed, 6.6% divorced (2006-2010 5-year est.); Foreign born: 2.3% (2006-2010 5-year est.); Ancestry (includes multiple ancestries): 32.3% German, 19.2% Irish, 12.0% English, 6.9% Italian, 6.2% Scotch-Irish (2006-2010 5-year est.).

Economy: Single-family building permits issued: 10 (2011); Multi-family building permits issued: 0 (2011); Employment by occupation: 3.3% management, 2.0% professional, 13.3% services, 14.0% sales, 1.5% farming, 10.9% construction, 7.4% production (2006-2010 5-year est.).

Income: Per capita income: $21,669 (2006-2010 5-year est.); Median household income: $37,171 (2006-2010 5-year est.); Average household income: $52,616 (2006-2010 5-year est.); Percent of households with income of $100,000 or more: 13.2% (2006-2010 5-year est.); Poverty rate: 23.0% (2006-2010 5-year est.).

Education: Percent of population age 25 and over with: High school diploma (including GED) or higher: 89.3% (2006-2010 5-year est.); Bachelor's degree or higher: 17.0% (2006-2010 5-year est.); Master's degree or higher: 5.7% (2006-2010 5-year est.).

Housing: Homeownership rate: 86.5% (2010); Median home value: $90,300 (2006-2010 5-year est.); Median contract rent: $528 per month (2006-2010 5-year est.); Median year structure built: 1969 (2006-2010 5-year est.).

Transportation: Commute to work: 91.1% car, 2.0% public transportation, 0.9% walk, 5.2% work from home (2006-2010 5-year est.); Travel time to work: 19.3% less than 15 minutes, 37.7% 15 to 30 minutes, 26.2% 30 to 45 minutes, 4.4% 45 to 60 minutes, 12.5% 60 minutes or more (2006-2010 5-year est.)

Corry Area SD (PK-12)

2010-11 Enrollment: 2,319 . . . . (814) 664-4677

Housing: Homeownership rate: 78.6% (2010); Median home value: $75,200 (2006-2010 5-year est.); Median contract rent: $488 per month (2006-2010 5-year est.); Median year structure built: before 1940 (2006-2010 5-year est.).

Transportation: Commute to work: 86.1% car, 0.0% public transportation, 10.9% walk, 2.9% work from home (2006-2010 5-year est.); Travel time to work: 35.3% less than 15 minutes, 37.6% 15 to 30 minutes, 6.8% 30 to 45 minutes, 9.8% 45 to 60 minutes, 10.5% 60 minutes or more (2006-2010 5-year est.)

SPRING (township). Covers a land area of 45.677 square miles and a water area of 0.014 square miles. Located at 41.81° N. Lat; 80.34° W. Long. Elevation is 1,227 feet.

Population: 1,561 (1990); 1,571 (2000); 1,548 (2010); Density: 33.9 persons per square mile (2010); Race: 97.9% White, 0.3% Black, 0.3% Asian, 0.1% American Indian/Alaska Native, 0.1% Native Hawaiian/Other Pacific Islander, 1.3% Other, 0.4% Hispanic of any race (2010); Average household size: 2.55 (2010); Median age: 41.4 (2010); Males per 100 females: 100.5 (2010); Marriage status: 26.2% never married, 55.9% now married, 5.9% widowed, 11.9% divorced (2006-2010 5-year est.); Foreign born: 0.2% (2006-2010 5-year est.); Ancestry (includes multiple ancestries): 37.7% German, 15.2% Irish, 12.9% English, 8.7% Italian, 7.8% Polish (2006-2010 5-year est.).

Economy: Single-family building permits issued: 3 (2011); Multi-family building permits issued: 0 (2011); Employment by occupation: 9.6% management, 2.4% professional, 16.5% services, 15.9% sales, 2.3% farming, 13.4% construction, 9.0% production (2006-2010 5-year est.).

Income: Per capita income: $23,010 (2006-2010 5-year est.); Median household income: $46,719 (2006-2010 5-year est.); Average household income: $64,122 (2006-2010 5-year est.); Percent of households with income of $100,000 or more: 9.2% (2006-2010 5-year est.); Poverty rate: 11.7% (2006-2010 5-year est.).

Education: Percent of population age 25 and over with: High school diploma (including GED) or higher: 80.8% (2006-2010 5-year est.); Bachelor's degree or higher: 16.4% (2006-2010 5-year est.); Master's degree or higher: 4.9% (2006-2010 5-year est.).

Housing: Homeownership rate: 80.9% (2010); Median home value: $107,500 (2006-2010 5-year est.); Median contract rent: $517 per month (2006-2010 5-year est.); Median year structure built: 1971 (2006-2010 5-year est.).

Transportation: Commute to work: 82.9% car, 0.4% public transportation, 3.1% walk, 9.9% work from home (2006-2010 5-year est.); Travel time to work: 13.5% less than 15 minutes, 37.2% 15 to 30 minutes, 32.1% 30 to 45 minutes, 10.1% 45 to 60 minutes, 7.1% 60 minutes or more (2006-2010 5-year est.)

Additional Information Contacts

Meadville-Western Crawford County Chamber of Commerce . . . . (814) 337-8030

http://www.meadvillechamber.com

SPRINGBORO (borough). Covers a land area of 0.829 square miles and a water area of 0 square miles. Located at 41.80° N. Lat; 80.37° W. Long. Elevation is 942 feet.

Population: 471 (1990); 491 (2000); 477 (2010); Density: 575.5 persons per square mile (2010); Race: 97.5% White, 1.0% Black, 0.0% Asian, 0.0% American Indian/Alaska Native, 0.4% Native Hawaiian/Other Pacific Islander, 1.1% Other, 1.9% Hispanic of any race (2010); Average household size: 2.66 (2010); Median age: 38.5 (2010); Males per 100 females: 102.1 (2010); Marriage status: 22.9% never married, 66.0% now married, 3.2% widowed, 7.9% divorced (2006-2010 5-year est.); Foreign born: 1.4% (2006-2010 5-year est.); Ancestry (includes multiple ancestries): 26.7% German, 15.7% Italian, 9.8% Irish, 9.3% Polish, 5.5% Scotch-Irish (2006-2010 5-year est.).

Economy: Single-family building permits issued: 0 (2011); Multi-family building permits issued: 0 (2011); Employment by occupation: 3.5% management, 1.5% professional, 10.5% services, 16.5% sales, 1.5% farming, 15.0% construction, 18.5% production (2006-2010 5-year est.).

Income: Per capita income: $16,384 (2006-2010 5-year est.); Median household income: $44,375 (2006-2010 5-year est.); Average household income: $46,173 (2006-2010 5-year est.); Percent of households with income of $100,000 or more: 5.4% (2006-2010 5-year est.); Poverty rate: 11.1% (2006-2010 5-year est.).

Additional Information Contacts

Meadville-Western Crawford County Chamber of Commerce . . . . (814) 337-8030

http://www.meadvillechamber.com

SPARTA (township). Covers a land area of 41.814 square miles and a water area of 0.188 square miles. Located at 41.82° N. Lat; 79.70° W. Long.

Population: 1,554 (1990); 1,740 (2000); 1,832 (2010); Density: 43.8 persons per square mile (2010); Race: 98.1% White, 0.3% Black, 0.0% Asian, 0.5% American Indian/Alaska Native, 0.0% Native Hawaiian/Other Pacific Islander, 1.1% Other, 0.8% Hispanic of any race (2010); Average household size: 3.29 (2010); Median age: 28.5 (2010); Males per 100 females: 102.7 (2010); Marriage status: 22.3% never married, 66.5% now married, 5.0% widowed, 6.2% divorced (2006-2010 5-year est.); Foreign born: 0.2% (2006-2010 5-year est.); Ancestry (includes multiple ancestries): 34.4% German, 10.8% English, 10.0% Irish, 5.8% Pennsylvania German, 5.6% American (2006-2010 5-year est.).

Economy: Single-family building permits issued: 1 (2011); Multi-family building permits issued: 0 (2011); Employment by occupation: 7.6% management, 1.1% professional, 10.8% services, 8.3% sales, 2.1% farming, 23.2% construction, 10.1% production (2006-2010 5-year est.).

Income: Per capita income: $13,440 (2006-2010 5-year est.); Median household income: $33,583 (2006-2010 5-year est.); Average household income: $44,675 (2006-2010 5-year est.); Percent of households with income of $100,000 or more: 6.3% (2006-2010 5-year est.); Poverty rate: 28.6% (2006-2010 5-year est.).

Education: Percent of population age 25 and over with: High school diploma (including GED) or higher: 66.7% (2006-2010 5-year est.); Bachelor's degree or higher: 6.1% (2006-2010 5-year est.); Master's degree or higher: 1.3% (2006-2010 5-year est.).

Housing: Homeownership rate: 82.3% (2010); Median home value: $98,700 (2006-2010 5-year est.); Median contract rent: $319 per month (2006-2010 5-year est.); Median year structure built: 1976 (2006-2010 5-year est.).

Transportation: Commute to work: 77.3% car, 0.0% public transportation, 8.7% walk, 5.8% work from home (2006-2010 5-year est.); Travel time to work: 36.1% less than 15 minutes, 28.2% 15 to 30 minutes, 13.5% 30 to 45 minutes, 12.4% 45 to 60 minutes, 9.8% 60 minutes or more (2006-2010 5-year est.)

Additional Information Contacts

Meadville-Western Crawford County Chamber of Commerce . . . . (814) 337-8030

http://www.meadvillechamber.com

SPARTANSBURG (borough). Covers a land area of 0.679 square miles and a water area of 0.030 square miles. Located at 41.82° N. Lat; 79.68° W. Long. Elevation is 1,450 feet.

Population: 403 (1990); 333 (2000); 305 (2010); Density: 449.5 persons per square mile (2010); Race: 100.0% White, 0.0% Black, 0.0% Asian, 0.0% American Indian/Alaska Native, 0.0% Native Hawaiian/Other Pacific Islander, 0.0% Other, 0.0% Hispanic of any race (2010); Average household size: 2.42 (2010); Median age: 43.1 (2010); Males per 100 females: 113.3 (2010); Marriage status: 19.4% never married, 56.7% now married, 11.5% widowed, 12.3% divorced (2006-2010 5-year est.); Foreign born: 0.0% (2006-2010 5-year est.); Ancestry (includes multiple ancestries): 25.6% German, 15.3% English, 11.2% Irish, 10.5% Dutch, 8.0% American (2006-2010 5-year est.).

Economy: Single-family building permits issued: 0 (2011); Multi-family building permits issued: 0 (2011); Employment by occupation: 5.2% management, 3.7% professional, 5.2% services, 22.4% sales, 3.7% farming, 11.9% construction, 11.9% production (2006-2010 5-year est.).

Income: Per capita income: $18,615 (2006-2010 5-year est.); Median household income: $36,250 (2006-2010 5-year est.); Average household income: $47,436 (2006-2010 5-year est.); Percent of households with income of $100,000 or more: 5.8% (2006-2010 5-year est.); Poverty rate: 23.6% (2006-2010 5-year est.).

Taxes: Total city taxes per capita: $123 (2009); City property taxes per capita: $28 (2009).

Education: Percent of population age 25 and over with: High school diploma (including GED) or higher: 86.3% (2006-2010 5-year est.); Bachelor's degree or higher: 11.5% (2006-2010 5-year est.); Master's degree or higher: 4.9% (2006-2010 5-year est.).

Education: Percent of population age 25 and over with: High school diploma (including GED) or higher: 78.1% (2006-2010 5-year est.); Bachelor's degree or higher: 7.8% (2006-2010 5-year est.); Master's degree or higher: 3.1% (2006-2010 5-year est.).

Housing: Homeownership rate: 76.0% (2010); Median home value: $72,700 (2006-2010 5-year est.); Median contract rent: $411 per month (2006-2010 5-year est.); Median year structure built: before 1940 (2006-2010 5-year est.).

Transportation: Commute to work: 95.8% car, 0.0% public transportation, 0.0% walk, 4.2% work from home (2006-2010 5-year est.); Travel time to work: 27.3% less than 15 minutes, 18.6% 15 to 30 minutes, 39.9% 30 to 45 minutes, 8.7% 45 to 60 minutes, 5.5% 60 minutes or more (2006-2010 5-year est.)

STEUBEN (township). Covers a land area of 24.537 square miles and a water area of 0.018 square miles. Located at 41.70° N. Lat; 79.83° W. Long.

Population: 820 (1990); 908 (2000); 804 (2010); Density: 32.8 persons per square mile (2010); Race: 99.3% White, 0.1% Black, 0.0% Asian, 0.1% American Indian/Alaska Native, 0.0% Native Hawaiian/Other Pacific Islander, 0.5% Other, 0.2% Hispanic of any race (2010); Average household size: 2.50 (2010); Median age: 43.4 (2010); Males per 100 females: 116.7 (2010); Marriage status: 27.3% never married, 57.9% now married, 6.3% widowed, 8.5% divorced (2006-2010 5-year est.); Foreign born: 4.8% (2006-2010 5-year est.); Ancestry (includes multiple ancestries): 31.0% German, 19.8% Irish, 13.3% English, 6.9% American, 4.7% Dutch (2006-2010 5-year est.).

Economy: Single-family building permits issued: 3 (2011); Multi-family building permits issued: 0 (2011); Employment by occupation: 10.7% management, 2.3% professional, 10.7% services, 13.6% sales, 4.1% farming, 17.3% construction, 8.4% production (2006-2010 5-year est.).

Income: Per capita income: $19,375 (2006-2010 5-year est.); Median household income: $42,500 (2006-2010 5-year est.); Average household income: $50,944 (2006-2010 5-year est.); Percent of households with income of $100,000 or more: 14.7% (2006-2010 5-year est.); Poverty rate: 17.8% (2006-2010 5-year est.).

Education: Percent of population age 25 and over with: High school diploma (including GED) or higher: 80.8% (2006-2010 5-year est.); Bachelor's degree or higher: 7.1% (2006-2010 5-year est.); Master's degree or higher: 1.0% (2006-2010 5-year est.).

Housing: Homeownership rate: 82.6% (2010); Median home value: $88,600 (2006-2010 5-year est.); Median contract rent: $336 per month (2006-2010 5-year est.); Median year structure built: 1971 (2006-2010 5-year est.).

Transportation: Commute to work: 79.5% car, 0.7% public transportation, 10.0% walk, 8.1% work from home (2006-2010 5-year est.); Travel time to work: 28.4% less than 15 minutes, 33.4% 15 to 30 minutes, 26.8% 30 to 45 minutes, 0.8% 45 to 60 minutes, 10.6% 60 minutes or more (2006-2010 5-year est.)

SUMMERHILL (township). Covers a land area of 25.381 square miles and a water area of 0.020 square miles. Located at 41.72° N. Lat; 80.33° W. Long.

Population: 1,284 (1990); 1,350 (2000); 1,236 (2010); Density: 48.7 persons per square mile (2010); Race: 98.3% White, 0.6% Black, 0.0% Asian, 0.2% American Indian/Alaska Native, 0.0% Native Hawaiian/Other Pacific Islander, 0.9% Other, 0.6% Hispanic of any race (2010); Average household size: 2.67 (2010); Median age: 44.5 (2010); Males per 100 females: 92.8 (2010); Marriage status: 23.8% never married, 51.8% now married, 18.2% widowed, 6.2% divorced (2006-2010 5-year est.); Foreign born: 1.1% (2006-2010 5-year est.); Ancestry (includes multiple ancestries): 30.3% German, 13.0% Irish, 8.0% Italian, 7.5% English, 5.1% American (2006-2010 5-year est.).

Economy: Single-family building permits issued: 5 (2011); Multi-family building permits issued: 0 (2011); Employment by occupation: 9.7% management, 4.8% professional, 12.6% services, 13.3% sales, 2.1% farming, 8.6% construction, 4.2% production (2006-2010 5-year est.).

Income: Per capita income: $19,667 (2006-2010 5-year est.); Median household income: $44,306 (2006-2010 5-year est.); Average household income: $52,127 (2006-2010 5-year est.); Percent of households with income of $100,000 or more: 10.0% (2006-2010 5-year est.); Poverty rate: 14.3% (2006-2010 5-year est.).

Education: Percent of population age 25 and over with: High school diploma (including GED) or higher: 75.6% (2006-2010 5-year est.);

Bachelor's degree or higher: 14.1% (2006-2010 5-year est.); Master's degree or higher: 4.9% (2006-2010 5-year est.).

Housing: Homeownership rate: 87.2% (2010); Median home value: $114,100 (2006-2010 5-year est.); Median contract rent: $388 per month (2006-2010 5-year est.); Median year structure built: 1958 (2006-2010 5-year est.).

Transportation: Commute to work: 87.3% car, 0.8% public transportation, 2.0% walk, 6.1% work from home (2006-2010 5-year est.); Travel time to work: 23.4% less than 15 minutes, 47.0% 15 to 30 minutes, 22.2% 30 to 45 minutes, 5.7% 45 to 60 minutes, 1.7% 60 minutes or more (2006-2010 5-year est.)

Additional Information Contacts

Meadville-Western Crawford County Chamber of Commerce . . . . . . (814) 337-8030

  http://www.meadvillechamber.com

SUMMIT (township). Covers a land area of 25.823 square miles and a water area of 0.212 square miles. Located at 41.67° N. Lat; 80.33° W. Long.

Population: 1,882 (1990); 2,172 (2000); 2,027 (2010); Density: 78.5 persons per square mile (2010); Race: 97.8% White, 0.6% Black, 0.3% Asian, 0.1% American Indian/Alaska Native, 0.1% Native Hawaiian/Other Pacific Islander, 1.1% Other, 0.7% Hispanic of any race (2010); Average household size: 2.30 (2010); Median age: 46.6 (2010); Males per 100 females: 108.1 (2010); Marriage status: 27.6% never married, 55.8% now married, 5.2% widowed, 11.4% divorced (2006-2010 5-year est.); Foreign born: 1.4% (2006-2010 5-year est.); Ancestry (includes multiple ancestries): 39.2% German, 18.7% Irish, 17.6% English, 8.1% Italian, 5.1% Hungarian (2006-2010 5-year est.).

Economy: Single-family building permits issued: 3 (2011); Multi-family building permits issued: 0 (2011); Employment by occupation: 8.0% management, 5.5% professional, 10.7% services, 16.4% sales, 6.2% farming, 11.6% construction, 9.8% production (2006-2010 5-year est.).

Income: Per capita income: $19,354 (2006-2010 5-year est.); Median household income: $35,333 (2006-2010 5-year est.); Average household income: $45,574 (2006-2010 5-year est.); Percent of households with income of $100,000 or more: 6.3% (2006-2010 5-year est.); Poverty rate: 18.4% (2006-2010 5-year est.).

Education: Percent of population age 25 and over with: High school diploma (including GED) or higher: 89.8% (2006-2010 5-year est.); Bachelor's degree or higher: 15.5% (2006-2010 5-year est.); Master's degree or higher: 4.5% (2006-2010 5-year est.).

Housing: Homeownership rate: 83.7% (2010); Median home value: $121,900 (2006-2010 5-year est.); Median contract rent: $347 per month (2006-2010 5-year est.); Median year structure built: 1972 (2006-2010 5-year est.).

Transportation: Commute to work: 93.9% car, 0.0% public transportation, 0.9% walk, 4.5% work from home (2006-2010 5-year est.); Travel time to work: 28.6% less than 15 minutes, 49.9% 15 to 30 minutes, 10.4% 30 to 45 minutes, 4.9% 45 to 60 minutes, 6.2% 60 minutes or more (2006-2010 5-year est.)

Additional Information Contacts

Meadville-Western Crawford County Chamber of Commerce . . . . . . (814) 337-8030

  http://www.meadvillechamber.com

TITUSVILLE (city). Covers a land area of 2.901 square miles and a water area of 0 square miles. Located at 41.63° N. Lat; 79.67° W. Long. Elevation is 1,198 feet.

History: Drake Well Memorial Park and Museum marks site of first successful oil well (1859) in U.S. The city grew in oil boom of 1860s; its last oil refinery closed in 1950. Settled 1796, laid out 1809, Incorporated as borough 1847, as city 1866.

Population: 6,383 (1990); 6,146 (2000); 5,601 (2010); Density: 1,930.8 persons per square mile (2010); Race: 95.9% White, 1.8% Black, 0.7% Asian, 0.3% American Indian/Alaska Native, 0.0% Native Hawaiian/Other Pacific Islander, 1.3% Other, 1.2% Hispanic of any race (2010); Average household size: 2.23 (2010); Median age: 40.1 (2010); Males per 100 females: 84.8 (2010); Marriage status: 25.1% never married, 51.0% now married, 8.8% widowed, 15.1% divorced (2006-2010 5-year est.); Foreign born: 0.9% (2006-2010 5-year est.); Ancestry (includes multiple ancestries): 30.5% German, 17.5% Irish, 11.8% English, 8.2% Italian, 8.1% American (2006-2010 5-year est.).

Economy: Single-family building permits issued: 1 (2011); Multi-family building permits issued: 0 (2011); Employment by occupation: 7.8%

management, 2.3% professional, 13.8% services, 14.2% sales, 4.8% farming, 4.4% construction, 6.7% production (2006-2010 5-year est.).
Income: Per capita income: $17,311 (2006-2010 5-year est.); Median household income: $30,682 (2006-2010 5-year est.); Average household income: $39,245 (2006-2010 5-year est.); Percent of households with income of $100,000 or more: 8.2% (2006-2010 5-year est.); Poverty rate: 24.5% (2006-2010 5-year est.).
Education: Percent of population age 25 and over with: High school diploma (including GED) or higher: 80.4% (2006-2010 5-year est.); Bachelor's degree or higher: 18.4% (2006-2010 5-year est.); Master's degree or higher: 4.7% (2006-2010 5-year est.).

School District(s)
Titusville Area SD (KG-12)
 2010-11 Enrollment: 2,077 . . . . (814) 827-2715
Two-year College(s)
University of Pittsburgh-Titusville (Public)
 Fall 2010 Enrollment: 448 . . . . (888) 878-0462
 2011-12 Tuition: In-state $11,118; Out-of-state $20,308
Housing: Homeownership rate: 54.3% (2010); Median home value: $71,600 (2006-2010 5-year est.); Median contract rent: $382 per month (2006-2010 5-year est.); Median year structure built: 1941 (2006-2010 5-year est.).
Hospitals: Titusville Area Hospital (95 beds)
Safety: Violent crime rate: 10.7 per 10,000 population; Property crime rate: 325.7 per 10,000 population (2011).
Newspapers: The Titusville Herald (Local news; Circulation 5,000)
Transportation: Commute to work: 85.7% car, 0.0% public transportation, 9.6% walk, 1.9% work from home (2006-2010 5-year est.); Travel time to work: 59.0% less than 15 minutes, 12.8% 15 to 30 minutes, 15.6% 30 to 45 minutes, 10.3% 45 to 60 minutes, 2.3% 60 minutes or more (2006-2010 5-year est.)
Additional Information Contacts
City of Titusville . . . . (814) 827-5300
 http://www.titusvillecityhall.com
Titusville Area Chamber of Commerce . . . . (814) 827-2941
 http://titusvillechamber.com

TOWNVILLE (borough). Covers a land area of 0.514 square miles and a water area of 0 square miles. Located at 41.68° N. Lat; 79.88° W. Long. Elevation is 1,411 feet.
Population: 358 (1990); 306 (2000); 323 (2010); Density: 628.3 persons per square mile (2010); Race: 100.0% White, 0.0% Black, 0.0% Asian, 0.0% American Indian/Alaska Native, 0.0% Native Hawaiian/Other Pacific Islander, 0.0% Other, 0.6% Hispanic of any race (2010); Average household size: 2.48 (2010); Median age: 38.3 (2010); Males per 100 females: 93.4 (2010); Marriage status: 19.7% never married, 63.1% now married, 7.3% widowed, 9.9% divorced (2006-2010 5-year est.); Foreign born: 0.6% (2006-2010 5-year est.); Ancestry (includes multiple ancestries): 19.5% Irish, 19.5% German, 18.9% English, 8.7% American, 6.0% French (2006-2010 5-year est.).
Economy: Single-family building permits issued: 0 (2011); Multi-family building permits issued: 0 (2011); Employment by occupation: 5.6% management, 3.5% professional, 13.9% services, 13.2% sales, 4.2% farming, 9.0% construction, 8.3% production (2006-2010 5-year est.).
Income: Per capita income: $22,438 (2006-2010 5-year est.); Median household income: $38,750 (2006-2010 5-year est.); Average household income: $48,326 (2006-2010 5-year est.); Percent of households with income of $100,000 or more: 8.3% (2006-2010 5-year est.); Poverty rate: 3.1% (2006-2010 5-year est.).
Education: Percent of population age 25 and over with: High school diploma (including GED) or higher: 88.8% (2006-2010 5-year est.); Bachelor's degree or higher: 11.6% (2006-2010 5-year est.); Master's degree or higher: 2.1% (2006-2010 5-year est.).
School District(s)
Penncrest SD (PK-12)
 2010-11 Enrollment: 3,459 . . . . (814) 763-2323
Housing: Homeownership rate: 70.7% (2010); Median home value: $76,900 (2006-2010 5-year est.); Median contract rent: $355 per month (2006-2010 5-year est.); Median year structure built: before 1940 (2006-2010 5-year est.).
Transportation: Commute to work: 98.6% car, 0.0% public transportation, 1.4% walk, 0.0% work from home (2006-2010 5-year est.); Travel time to work: 32.1% less than 15 minutes, 34.3% 15 to 30 minutes, 27.9% 30 to 45 minutes, 4.3% 45 to 60 minutes, 1.4% 60 minutes or more (2006-2010 5-year est.)

TROY (township). Covers a land area of 31.689 square miles and a water area of 0.044 square miles. Located at 41.63° N. Lat; 79.83° W. Long.
Population: 1,235 (1990); 1,339 (2000); 1,235 (2010); Density: 39.0 persons per square mile (2010); Race: 97.8% White, 0.2% Black, 0.1% Asian, 0.4% American Indian/Alaska Native, 0.0% Native Hawaiian/Other Pacific Islander, 1.5% Other, 0.5% Hispanic of any race (2010); Average household size: 2.75 (2010); Median age: 40.7 (2010); Males per 100 females: 102.1 (2010); Marriage status: 25.3% never married, 54.5% now married, 9.4% widowed, 10.8% divorced (2006-2010 5-year est.); Foreign born: 0.6% (2006-2010 5-year est.); Ancestry (includes multiple ancestries): 38.6% German, 23.1% Irish, 16.2% English, 6.0% Italian, 4.5% American (2006-2010 5-year est.).
Economy: Single-family building permits issued: 0 (2011); Multi-family building permits issued: 0 (2011); Employment by occupation: 5.8% management, 0.9% professional, 10.7% services, 17.5% sales, 2.1% farming, 9.8% construction, 6.8% production (2006-2010 5-year est.).
Income: Per capita income: $18,096 (2006-2010 5-year est.); Median household income: $40,000 (2006-2010 5-year est.); Average household income: $47,705 (2006-2010 5-year est.); Percent of households with income of $100,000 or more: 6.4% (2006-2010 5-year est.); Poverty rate: 12.0% (2006-2010 5-year est.).
Education: Percent of population age 25 and over with: High school diploma (including GED) or higher: 83.7% (2006-2010 5-year est.); Bachelor's degree or higher: 13.4% (2006-2010 5-year est.); Master's degree or higher: 3.2% (2006-2010 5-year est.).
Housing: Homeownership rate: 88.2% (2010); Median home value: $87,200 (2006-2010 5-year est.); Median contract rent: $365 per month (2006-2010 5-year est.); Median year structure built: 1966 (2006-2010 5-year est.).
Transportation: Commute to work: 87.6% car, 0.0% public transportation, 5.7% walk, 6.7% work from home (2006-2010 5-year est.); Travel time to work: 26.2% less than 15 minutes, 31.1% 15 to 30 minutes, 27.8% 30 to 45 minutes, 5.5% 45 to 60 minutes, 9.4% 60 minutes or more (2006-2010 5-year est.)
Additional Information Contacts
Meadville-Western Crawford County Chamber of Commerce . . . . (814) 337-8030
 http://www.meadvillechamber.com

UNION (township). Covers a land area of 15.798 square miles and a water area of 0.088 square miles. Located at 41.57° N. Lat; 80.16° W. Long.
Population: 895 (1990); 1,049 (2000); 1,010 (2010); Density: 63.9 persons per square mile (2010); Race: 97.2% White, 0.9% Black, 0.1% Asian, 0.8% American Indian/Alaska Native, 0.0% Native Hawaiian/Other Pacific Islander, 1.0% Other, 0.3% Hispanic of any race (2010); Average household size: 2.32 (2010); Median age: 45.1 (2010); Males per 100 females: 95.4 (2010); Marriage status: 26.8% never married, 54.9% now married, 5.3% widowed, 13.0% divorced (2006-2010 5-year est.); Foreign born: 1.2% (2006-2010 5-year est.); Ancestry (includes multiple ancestries): 29.9% German, 17.5% Irish, 11.7% English, 9.5% Italian, 5.2% Dutch (2006-2010 5-year est.).
Economy: Single-family building permits issued: 0 (2011); Multi-family building permits issued: 0 (2011); Employment by occupation: 6.3% management, 0.9% professional, 14.3% services, 16.8% sales, 4.9% farming, 13.8% construction, 12.1% production (2006-2010 5-year est.).
Income: Per capita income: $17,653 (2006-2010 5-year est.); Median household income: $36,458 (2006-2010 5-year est.); Average household income: $47,110 (2006-2010 5-year est.); Percent of households with income of $100,000 or more: 7.0% (2006-2010 5-year est.); Poverty rate: 17.2% (2006-2010 5-year est.).
Education: Percent of population age 25 and over with: High school diploma (including GED) or higher: 80.6% (2006-2010 5-year est.); Bachelor's degree or higher: 15.3% (2006-2010 5-year est.); Master's degree or higher: 3.9% (2006-2010 5-year est.).
Housing: Homeownership rate: 82.3% (2010); Median home value: $80,200 (2006-2010 5-year est.); Median contract rent: $325 per month (2006-2010 5-year est.); Median year structure built: 1978 (2006-2010 5-year est.).
Transportation: Commute to work: 96.0% car, 0.0% public transportation, 0.0% walk, 2.1% work from home (2006-2010 5-year est.); Travel time to work: 48.4% less than 15 minutes, 37.2% 15 to 30 minutes, 7.7% 30 to 45 minutes, 1.2% 45 to 60 minutes, 5.5% 60 minutes or more (2006-2010 5-year est.)

Additional Information Contacts
Meadville-Western Crawford County Chamber of Commerce . . . . (814) 337-8030
  http://www.meadvillechamber.com

VENANGO (borough). Covers a land area of 0.275 square miles and a water area of 0 square miles. Located at 41.77° N. Lat; 80.11° W. Long. Elevation is 1,145 feet.

Population: 289 (1990); 288 (2000); 239 (2010); Density: 870.3 persons per square mile (2010); Race: 98.3% White, 0.4% Black, 0.0% Asian, 0.0% American Indian/Alaska Native, 0.0% Native Hawaiian/Other Pacific Islander, 1.3% Other, 0.0% Hispanic of any race (2010); Average household size: 2.46 (2010); Median age: 45.8 (2010); Males per 100 females: 97.5 (2010); Marriage status: 28.0% never married, 53.8% now married, 7.0% widowed, 11.3% divorced (2006-2010 5-year est.); Foreign born: 0.0% (2006-2010 5-year est.); Ancestry (includes multiple ancestries): 33.5% German, 16.3% Irish, 13.3% English, 11.3% Italian, 11.3% Polish (2006-2010 5-year est.).

Economy: Single-family building permits issued: 0 (2011); Multi-family building permits issued: 0 (2011); Employment by occupation: 5.9% management, 0.0% professional, 20.8% services, 12.9% sales, 4.0% farming, 1.0% construction, 5.9% production (2006-2010 5-year est.).

Income: Per capita income: $23,223 (2006-2010 5-year est.); Median household income: $32,045 (2006-2010 5-year est.); Average household income: $47,467 (2006-2010 5-year est.); Percent of households with income of $100,000 or more: 13.6% (2006-2010 5-year est.); Poverty rate: 10.8% (2006-2010 5-year est.).

Education: Percent of population age 25 and over with: High school diploma (including GED) or higher: 93.9% (2006-2010 5-year est.); Bachelor's degree or higher: 21.5% (2006-2010 5-year est.); Master's degree or higher: 11.0% (2006-2010 5-year est.).

Housing: Homeownership rate: 82.5% (2010); Median home value: $73,400 (2006-2010 5-year est.); Median contract rent: $385 per month (2006-2010 5-year est.); Median year structure built: before 1940 (2006-2010 5-year est.).

Transportation: Commute to work: 86.9% car, 0.0% public transportation, 6.1% walk, 7.1% work from home (2006-2010 5-year est.); Travel time to work: 35.9% less than 15 minutes, 31.5% 15 to 30 minutes, 23.9% 30 to 45 minutes, 3.3% 45 to 60 minutes, 5.4% 60 minutes or more (2006-2010 5-year est.).

VENANGO (township). Covers a land area of 16.878 square miles and a water area of 0.034 square miles. Located at 41.82° N. Lat; 80.12° W. Long. Elevation is 1,145 feet.

Population: 729 (1990); 956 (2000); 997 (2010); Density: 59.1 persons per square mile (2010); Race: 97.2% White, 1.4% Black, 0.2% Asian, 0.2% American Indian/Alaska Native, 0.0% Native Hawaiian/Other Pacific Islander, 1.0% Other, 0.9% Hispanic of any race (2010); Average household size: 2.62 (2010); Median age: 39.7 (2010); Males per 100 females: 108.6 (2010); Marriage status: 22.9% never married, 64.0% now married, 4.7% widowed, 8.4% divorced (2006-2010 5-year est.); Foreign born: 0.0% (2006-2010 5-year est.); Ancestry (includes multiple ancestries): 36.1% German, 33.9% Irish, 12.0% English, 10.2% Polish, 5.5% European (2006-2010 5-year est.).

Economy: Single-family building permits issued: 1 (2011); Multi-family building permits issued: 0 (2011); Employment by occupation: 10.0% management, 4.0% professional, 13.8% services, 18.8% sales, 0.6% farming, 9.2% construction, 5.4% production (2006-2010 5-year est.).

Income: Per capita income: $20,049 (2006-2010 5-year est.); Median household income: $45,833 (2006-2010 5-year est.); Average household income: $56,159 (2006-2010 5-year est.); Percent of households with income of $100,000 or more: 15.2% (2006-2010 5-year est.); Poverty rate: 9.4% (2006-2010 5-year est.).

Education: Percent of population age 25 and over with: High school diploma (including GED) or higher: 92.5% (2006-2010 5-year est.); Bachelor's degree or higher: 27.7% (2006-2010 5-year est.); Master's degree or higher: 13.8% (2006-2010 5-year est.).

Housing: Homeownership rate: 86.5% (2010); Median home value: $150,200 (2006-2010 5-year est.); Median contract rent: $347 per month (2006-2010 5-year est.); Median year structure built: 1976 (2006-2010 5-year est.).

Transportation: Commute to work: 94.3% car, 0.0% public transportation, 2.1% walk, 3.6% work from home (2006-2010 5-year est.); Travel time to work: 31.7% less than 15 minutes, 48.2% 15 to 30 minutes, 13.0% 30 to

45 minutes, 5.1% 45 to 60 minutes, 2.0% 60 minutes or more (2006-2010 5-year est.)

VERNON (township). Covers a land area of 29.558 square miles and a water area of 0.009 square miles. Located at 41.63° N. Lat; 80.21° W. Long.

Population: 5,605 (1990); 5,499 (2000); 5,630 (2010); Density: 190.5 persons per square mile (2010); Race: 96.4% White, 1.1% Black, 1.1% Asian, 0.2% American Indian/Alaska Native, 0.0% Native Hawaiian/Other Pacific Islander, 1.2% Other, 0.7% Hispanic of any race (2010); Average household size: 2.26 (2010); Median age: 47.1 (2010); Males per 100 females: 93.7 (2010); Marriage status: 18.4% never married, 59.3% now married, 8.0% widowed, 14.4% divorced (2006-2010 5-year est.); Foreign born: 1.8% (2006-2010 5-year est.); Ancestry (includes multiple ancestries): 38.5% German, 19.5% Irish, 12.5% English, 9.5% Italian, 8.0% Polish (2006-2010 5-year est.).

Economy: Single-family building permits issued: 1 (2011); Multi-family building permits issued: 0 (2011); Employment by occupation: 9.8% management, 3.2% professional, 9.6% services, 17.2% sales, 1.4% farming, 10.4% construction, 7.4% production (2006-2010 5-year est.).

Income: Per capita income: $25,765 (2006-2010 5-year est.); Median household income: $42,254 (2006-2010 5-year est.); Average household income: $54,183 (2006-2010 5-year est.); Percent of households with income of $100,000 or more: 13.2% (2006-2010 5-year est.); Poverty rate: 11.6% (2006-2010 5-year est.).

Education: Percent of population age 25 and over with: High school diploma (including GED) or higher: 91.7% (2006-2010 5-year est.); Bachelor's degree or higher: 22.7% (2006-2010 5-year est.); Master's degree or higher: 9.5% (2006-2010 5-year est.).

Housing: Homeownership rate: 77.5% (2010); Median home value: $105,700 (2006-2010 5-year est.); Median contract rent: $524 per month (2006-2010 5-year est.); Median year structure built: 1969 (2006-2010 5-year est.).

Safety: Violent crime rate: 1.8 per 10,000 population; Property crime rate: 175.3 per 10,000 population (2011).

Transportation: Commute to work: 93.9% car, 0.0% public transportation, 3.3% walk, 0.8% work from home (2006-2010 5-year est.); Travel time to work: 48.2% less than 15 minutes, 28.9% 15 to 30 minutes, 8.6% 30 to 45 minutes, 8.6% 45 to 60 minutes, 5.8% 60 minutes or more (2006-2010 5-year est.).

Additional Information Contacts
Meadville-Western Crawford County Chamber of Commerce . . . . (814) 337-8030
  http://www.meadvillechamber.com
Vernon Township . . . . (814) 337-8126
  http://www.vernontwp-pa.gov

WAYNE (township). Covers a land area of 35.237 square miles and a water area of 0.269 square miles. Located at 41.56° N. Lat; 79.98° W. Long.

Population: 1,401 (1990); 1,558 (2000); 1,539 (2010); Density: 43.7 persons per square mile (2010); Race: 98.7% White, 0.2% Black, 0.4% Asian, 0.0% American Indian/Alaska Native, 0.1% Native Hawaiian/Other Pacific Islander, 0.6% Other, 0.3% Hispanic of any race (2010); Average household size: 2.75 (2010); Median age: 41.3 (2010); Males per 100 females: 96.8 (2010); Marriage status: 21.2% never married, 65.5% now married, 5.3% widowed, 8.0% divorced (2006-2010 5-year est.); Foreign born: 0.8% (2006-2010 5-year est.); Ancestry (includes multiple ancestries): 32.3% German, 18.8% Irish, 13.5% English, 11.2% American, 5.7% Italian (2006-2010 5-year est.).

Economy: Single-family building permits issued: 1 (2011); Multi-family building permits issued: 0 (2011); Employment by occupation: 8.0% management, 2.7% professional, 9.1% services, 15.4% sales, 2.4% farming, 14.6% construction, 12.0% production (2006-2010 5-year est.).

Income: Per capita income: $18,844 (2006-2010 5-year est.); Median household income: $46,500 (2006-2010 5-year est.); Average household income: $51,948 (2006-2010 5-year est.); Percent of households with income of $100,000 or more: 6.8% (2006-2010 5-year est.); Poverty rate: 11.3% (2006-2010 5-year est.).

Education: Percent of population age 25 and over with: High school diploma (including GED) or higher: 85.5% (2006-2010 5-year est.); Bachelor's degree or higher: 8.9% (2006-2010 5-year est.); Master's degree or higher: 2.6% (2006-2010 5-year est.).

Housing: Homeownership rate: 88.8% (2010); Median home value: $118,300 (2006-2010 5-year est.); Median contract rent: $513 per month

(2006-2010 5-year est.); Median year structure built: 1976 (2006-2010 5-year est.).

Transportation: Commute to work: 87.8% car, 0.0% public transportation, 4.9% walk, 6.3% work from home (2006-2010 5-year est.); Travel time to work: 30.6% less than 15 minutes, 42.7% 15 to 30 minutes, 15.7% 30 to 45 minutes, 5.9% 45 to 60 minutes, 5.0% 60 minutes or more (2006-2010 5-year est.)

Additional Information Contacts
Meadville-Western Crawford County Chamber of Commerce. . . . . . . (814) 337-8030
   http://www.meadvillechamber.com

WEST FALLOWFIELD (township). Covers a land area of 11.602 square miles and a water area of 0.106 square miles. Located at 41.53° N. Lat; 80.39° W. Long.

Population: 693 (1990); 659 (2000); 605 (2010); Density: 52.1 persons per square mile (2010); Race: 98.2% White, 1.7% Black, 0.0% Asian, 0.0% American Indian/Alaska Native, 0.0% Native Hawaiian/Other Pacific Islander, 0.1% Other, 0.2% Hispanic of any race (2010); Average household size: 2.47 (2010); Median age: 43.1 (2010); Males per 100 females: 103.7 (2010); Marriage status: 19.4% never married, 67.5% now married, 8.0% widowed, 5.1% divorced (2006-2010 5-year est.); Foreign born: 0.0% (2006-2010 5-year est.); Ancestry (includes multiple ancestries): 44.1% German, 14.4% English, 14.3% Irish, 8.8% American, 4.4% Italian (2006-2010 5-year est.).

Economy: Single-family building permits issued: 0 (2011); Multi-family building permits issued: 0 (2011); Employment by occupation: 2.0% management, 2.0% professional, 12.5% services, 13.5% sales, 1.5% farming, 8.5% construction, 7.0% production (2006-2010 5-year est.).

Income: Per capita income: $16,723 (2006-2010 5-year est.); Median household income: $35,000 (2006-2010 5-year est.); Average household income: $43,275 (2006-2010 5-year est.); Percent of households with income of $100,000 or more: 3.2% (2006-2010 5-year est.); Poverty rate: 9.3% (2006-2010 5-year est.).

Education: Percent of population age 25 and over with: High school diploma (including GED) or higher: 76.2% (2006-2010 5-year est.); Bachelor's degree or higher: 12.6% (2006-2010 5-year est.); Master's degree or higher: 3.9% (2006-2010 5-year est.).

Housing: Homeownership rate: 81.6% (2010); Median home value: $80,800 (2006-2010 5-year est.); Median contract rent: $288 per month (2006-2010 5-year est.); Median year structure built: 1970 (2006-2010 5-year est.).

Transportation: Commute to work: 92.3% car, 0.0% public transportation, 1.5% walk, 1.5% work from home (2006-2010 5-year est.); Travel time to work: 18.1% less than 15 minutes, 52.8% 15 to 30 minutes, 15.5% 30 to 45 minutes, 8.3% 45 to 60 minutes, 5.2% 60 minutes or more (2006-2010 5-year est.)

WEST MEAD (township). Covers a land area of 18.286 square miles and a water area of 0.497 square miles. Located at 41.63° N. Lat; 80.13° W. Long.

Population: 5,447 (1990); 5,227 (2000); 5,249 (2010); Density: 287.1 persons per square mile (2010); Race: 95.8% White, 2.0% Black, 0.5% Asian, 0.1% American Indian/Alaska Native, 0.0% Native Hawaiian/Other Pacific Islander, 1.6% Other, 1.0% Hispanic of any race (2010); Average household size: 2.38 (2010); Median age: 44.1 (2010); Males per 100 females: 94.9 (2010); Marriage status: 22.0% never married, 59.1% now married, 6.9% widowed, 11.9% divorced (2006-2010 5-year est.); Foreign born: 1.9% (2006-2010 5-year est.); Ancestry (includes multiple ancestries): 31.5% German, 19.1% Irish, 13.2% English, 11.9% Italian, 6.6% Polish (2006-2010 5-year est.).

Economy: Single-family building permits issued: 4 (2011); Multi-family building permits issued: 0 (2011); Employment by occupation: 12.3% management, 1.8% professional, 11.4% services, 14.4% sales, 5.3% farming, 7.9% construction, 6.3% production (2006-2010 5-year est.).

Income: Per capita income: $25,946 (2006-2010 5-year est.); Median household income: $43,985 (2006-2010 5-year est.); Average household income: $59,320 (2006-2010 5-year est.); Percent of households with income of $100,000 or more: 14.9% (2006-2010 5-year est.); Poverty rate: 7.8% (2006-2010 5-year est.).

Education: Percent of population age 25 and over with: High school diploma (including GED) or higher: 88.3% (2006-2010 5-year est.); Bachelor's degree or higher: 27.5% (2006-2010 5-year est.); Master's degree or higher: 9.9% (2006-2010 5-year est.).

Housing: Homeownership rate: 77.1% (2010); Median home value: $106,900 (2006-2010 5-year est.); Median contract rent: $515 per month (2006-2010 5-year est.); Median year structure built: 1960 (2006-2010 5-year est.).

Safety: Violent crime rate: 0.0 per 10,000 population; Property crime rate: 28.5 per 10,000 population (2011).

Transportation: Commute to work: 95.0% car, 0.0% public transportation, 1.4% walk, 2.3% work from home (2006-2010 5-year est.); Travel time to work: 62.0% less than 15 minutes, 25.4% 15 to 30 minutes, 6.1% 30 to 45 minutes, 5.7% 45 to 60 minutes, 0.8% 60 minutes or more (2006-2010 5-year est.)

Additional Information Contacts
Meadville-Western Crawford County Chamber of Commerce. . . . . . . (814) 337-8030
   http://www.meadvillechamber.com
West Mead Township . . . . (814) 337-7510

WEST SHENANGO (township). Covers a land area of 6.827 square miles and a water area of 2.176 square miles. Located at 41.51° N. Lat; 80.49° W. Long.

Population: 496 (1990); 541 (2000); 504 (2010); Density: 73.8 persons per square mile (2010); Race: 99.4% White, 0.0% Black, 0.0% Asian, 0.0% American Indian/Alaska Native, 0.0% Native Hawaiian/Other Pacific Islander, 0.6% Other, 0.6% Hispanic of any race (2010); Average household size: 2.25 (2010); Median age: 48.1 (2010); Males per 100 females: 96.1 (2010); Marriage status: 26.4% never married, 53.8% now married, 12.5% widowed, 7.4% divorced (2006-2010 5-year est.); Foreign born: 2.1% (2006-2010 5-year est.); Ancestry (includes multiple ancestries): 33.8% German, 23.2% Irish, 11.3% Italian, 9.8% Polish, 9.3% English (2006-2010 5-year est.).

Economy: Single-family building permits issued: 1 (2011); Multi-family building permits issued: 0 (2011); Employment by occupation: 9.0% management, 0.4% professional, 7.1% services, 13.9% sales, 5.3% farming, 10.2% construction, 9.0% production (2006-2010 5-year est.).

Income: Per capita income: $18,210 (2006-2010 5-year est.); Median household income: $41,250 (2006-2010 5-year est.); Average household income: $46,444 (2006-2010 5-year est.); Percent of households with income of $100,000 or more: 6.3% (2006-2010 5-year est.); Poverty rate: 19.4% (2006-2010 5-year est.).

Education: Percent of population age 25 and over with: High school diploma (including GED) or higher: 84.7% (2006-2010 5-year est.); Bachelor's degree or higher: 14.8% (2006-2010 5-year est.); Master's degree or higher: 4.0% (2006-2010 5-year est.).

Housing: Homeownership rate: 77.1% (2010); Median home value: $85,800 (2006-2010 5-year est.); Median contract rent: $391 per month (2006-2010 5-year est.); Median year structure built: 1963 (2006-2010 5-year est.).

Transportation: Commute to work: 93.1% car, 0.0% public transportation, 1.1% walk, 5.0% work from home (2006-2010 5-year est.); Travel time to work: 32.1% less than 15 minutes, 35.7% 15 to 30 minutes, 18.9% 30 to 45 minutes, 6.8% 45 to 60 minutes, 6.4% 60 minutes or more (2006-2010 5-year est.)

WOODCOCK (borough). Covers a land area of 0.664 square miles and a water area of 0 square miles. Located at 41.75° N. Lat; 80.08° W. Long. Elevation is 1,201 feet.

Population: 148 (1990); 146 (2000); 157 (2010); Density: 236.5 persons per square mile (2010); Race: 100.0% White, 0.0% Black, 0.0% Asian, 0.0% American Indian/Alaska Native, 0.0% Native Hawaiian/Other Pacific Islander, 0.0% Other, 0.0% Hispanic of any race (2010); Average household size: 2.71 (2010); Median age: 42.9 (2010); Males per 100 females: 96.3 (2010); Marriage status: 20.6% never married, 70.6% now married, 2.4% widowed, 6.5% divorced (2006-2010 5-year est.); Foreign born: 0.0% (2006-2010 5-year est.); Ancestry (includes multiple ancestries): 38.5% German, 32.0% Irish, 13.9% English, 12.1% Italian, 6.5% American (2006-2010 5-year est.).

Economy: Single-family building permits issued: 0 (2011); Multi-family building permits issued: 0 (2011); Employment by occupation: 3.2% management, 0.0% professional, 3.2% services, 6.5% sales, 15.3% farming, 3.2% construction, 12.9% production (2006-2010 5-year est.).

Income: Per capita income: $18,961 (2006-2010 5-year est.); Median household income: $55,250 (2006-2010 5-year est.); Average household income: $55,356 (2006-2010 5-year est.); Percent of households with income of $100,000 or more: 5.1% (2006-2010 5-year est.); Poverty rate: 13.0% (2006-2010 5-year est.).

Education: Percent of population age 25 and over with: High school diploma (including GED) or higher: 80.4% (2006-2010 5-year est.); Bachelor's degree or higher: 13.1% (2006-2010 5-year est.); Master's degree or higher: 0.0% (2006-2010 5-year est.).
Housing: Homeownership rate: 91.4% (2010); Median home value: $156,300 (2006-2010 5-year est.); Median contract rent: $428 per month (2006-2010 5-year est.); Median year structure built: 1971 (2006-2010 5-year est.).
Transportation: Commute to work: 70.7% car, 0.0% public transportation, 17.2% walk, 0.0% work from home (2006-2010 5-year est.); Travel time to work: 34.3% less than 15 minutes, 39.4% 15 to 30 minutes, 12.1% 30 to 45 minutes, 4.0% 45 to 60 minutes, 10.1% 60 minutes or more (2006-2010 5-year est.)

WOODCOCK (township). Covers a land area of 32.385 square miles and a water area of 0.532 square miles. Located at 41.72° N. Lat; 80.08° W. Long. Elevation is 1,201 feet.
Population: 2,412 (1990); 2,976 (2000); 2,856 (2010); Density: 88.2 persons per square mile (2010); Race: 96.4% White, 1.7% Black, 0.6% Asian, 0.1% American Indian/Alaska Native, 0.0% Native Hawaiian/Other Pacific Islander, 1.2% Other, 0.7% Hispanic of any race (2010); Average household size: 2.60 (2010); Median age: 44.0 (2010); Males per 100 females: 93.8 (2010); Marriage status: 18.7% never married, 65.7% now married, 5.0% widowed, 10.6% divorced (2006-2010 5-year est.); Foreign born: 0.9% (2006-2010 5-year est.); Ancestry (includes multiple ancestries): 34.0% German, 21.8% Irish, 12.3% English, 6.4% American, 5.8% Italian (2006-2010 5-year est.).
Economy: Single-family building permits issued: 2 (2011); Multi-family building permits issued: 0 (2011); Employment by occupation: 12.7% management, 1.7% professional, 14.3% services, 15.6% sales, 2.5% farming, 9.1% construction, 8.8% production (2006-2010 5-year est.).
Income: Per capita income: $22,431 (2006-2010 5-year est.); Median household income: $50,353 (2006-2010 5-year est.); Average household income: $57,786 (2006-2010 5-year est.); Percent of households with income of $100,000 or more: 12.1% (2006-2010 5-year est.); Poverty rate: 10.1% (2006-2010 5-year est.).
Education: Percent of population age 25 and over with: High school diploma (including GED) or higher: 87.6% (2006-2010 5-year est.); Bachelor's degree or higher: 15.2% (2006-2010 5-year est.); Master's degree or higher: 5.3% (2006-2010 5-year est.).
Housing: Homeownership rate: 88.7% (2010); Median home value: $102,600 (2006-2010 5-year est.); Median contract rent: $490 per month (2006-2010 5-year est.); Median year structure built: 1973 (2006-2010 5-year est.).
Transportation: Commute to work: 88.6% car, 0.7% public transportation, 2.2% walk, 6.3% work from home (2006-2010 5-year est.); Travel time to work: 43.0% less than 15 minutes, 44.7% 15 to 30 minutes, 3.0% 30 to 45 minutes, 4.8% 45 to 60 minutes, 4.4% 60 minutes or more (2006-2010 5-year est.)

Additional Information Contacts
Meadville-Western Crawford County Chamber of Commerce . . . . (814) 337-8030
  http://www.meadvillechamber.com

Cumberland County

Located in southern Pennsylvania; includes the Blue Mountains in the north and the South Mountains in the south, with the Cumberland Valley between; bounded on the east by the Susquehanna River. Covers a land area of 545.459 square miles, a water area of 4.843 square miles, and is located in the Eastern Time Zone at 40.16° N. Lat, 77.26° W. Long. The county was founded in 1750. County seat is Carlisle.

Cumberland County is part of the Harrisburg-Carlisle, PA Metropolitan Statistical Area. The entire metro area includes: Cumberland County, PA; Dauphin County, PA; Perry County, PA

Weather Station: Bloserville 1 N										Elevation: 700 feet	
	Jan	Feb	Mar	Apr	May	Jun	Jul	Aug	Sep	Oct	Nov	Dec
High	37	40	48	60	71	79	84	82	75	63	52	41
Low	21	23	30	40	49	58	63	61	54	42	35	25
Precip	2.7	2.5	3.4	3.6	3.9	3.9	4.1	3.7	4.0	3.3	3.3	2.8
Snow	7.0	6.5	3.6	0.4	0.0	0.0	0.0	0.0	0.0	tr	0.6	3.5

High and Low temperatures in degrees Fahrenheit; Precipitation and Snow in inches

Weather Station: Shippensburg										Elevation: 680 feet	
	Jan	Feb	Mar	Apr	May	Jun	Jul	Aug	Sep	Oct	Nov	Dec
High	37	41	51	63	73	82	86	84	76	65	53	41
Low	22	24	31	41	50	60	64	62	55	44	35	26
Precip	2.9	2.6	3.7	3.5	4.0	3.7	3.8	3.1	3.6	3.0	3.2	3.1
Snow	10.6	9.4	6.4	0.9	0.0	0.0	0.0	0.0	0.0	tr	1.6	6.1

High and Low temperatures in degrees Fahrenheit; Precipitation and Snow in inches

Population: 195,257 (1990); 213,674 (2000); 235,406 (2010); Race: 90.9% White, 3.2% Black, 3.0% Asian, 0.2% American Indian/Alaska Native, 0.0% Native Hawaiian/Other Pacific Islander, 2.7% Other, 2.7% Hispanic of any race (2010); Density: 431.6 persons per square mile (2010); Average household size: 2.37 (2010); Median age: 40.3 (2010); Males per 100 females: 96.5 (2010).
Religion: Six largest groups: 15.4% Catholicism, 9.9% Methodist/Pietist, 6.0% Lutheran, 5.9% Presbyterian-Reformed, 3.0% Non-Denominational, 2.8% Hindu (2010)
Economy: Unemployment rate: 7.1% (August 2012); Total civilian labor force: 126,235 (August 2012); Leading industries: 14.1% retail trade; 13.7% health care and social assistance; 11.3% transportation & warehousing (2010); Farms: 1,550 totaling 157,388 acres (2007); Companies that employ 500 or more persons: 24 (2010); Companies that employ 100 to 499 persons: 154 (2010); Companies that employ less than 100 persons: 5,547 (2010); Black-owned businesses: 284 (2007); Hispanic-owned businesses: n/a (2007); Asian-owned businesses: 469 (2007); Women-owned businesses: 4,339 (2007); Retail sales per capita: $15,819 (2010); Single-family building permits issued: 503 (2011); Multi-family building permits issued: 149 (2011).
Income: Per capita income: $30,119 (2006-2010 5-year est.); Median household income: $60,219 (2006-2010 5-year est.); Average household income: $73,430 (2006-2010 5-year est.); Percent of households with income of $100,000 or more: 22.5% (2006-2010 5-year est.); Poverty rate: 6.5% (2006-2010 5-year est.); Bankruptcy rate: 2.42% (2011).
Taxes: Total county taxes per capita: $175 (2009); County property taxes per capita: $168 (2009).
Education: Percent of population age 25 and over with: High school diploma (including GED) or higher: 90.4% (2006-2010 5-year est.); Bachelor's degree or higher: 32.3% (2006-2010 5-year est.); Master's degree or higher: 12.0% (2006-2010 5-year est.).
Housing: Homeownership rate: 72.0% (2010); Median home value: $174,600 (2006-2010 5-year est.); Median contract rent: $628 per month (2006-2010 5-year est.); Median year structure built: 1973 (2006-2010 5-year est.)
Health: Birth rate: 98.7 per 10,000 population (2011); Death rate: 85.8 per 10,000 population (2011); Age-adjusted cancer mortality rate: 152.1 deaths per 100,000 population (2009); Number of physicians: 28.3 per 10,000 population (2010); Hospital beds: 30.1 per 10,000 population (2008); Hospital admissions: 1,168.8 per 10,000 population (2008).
Environment: Air Quality Index: 61.0% good, 38.4% moderate, 0.6% unhealthy for sensitive individuals, 0.0% unhealthy (percent of days in 2011)
Elections: 2012 Presidential election results: 40.0% Obama, 58.5% Romney
National and State Parks: Colonel Denning State Park; Kings Gap State Park; Pine Grove Furnace State Park
Additional Information Contacts
Cumberland County Government . . . . (717) 240-6100
  http://www.ccpa.net/index.asp

Cumberland County Communities

BOILING SPRINGS (CDP). Covers a land area of 2.469 square miles and a water area of 0.012 square miles. Located at 40.16° N. Lat; 77.14° W. Long. Elevation is 472 feet.
History: Appalachian Trail passes to South and East.
Population: 2,166 (1990); 2,769 (2000); 3,225 (2010); Density: 1,306.4 persons per square mile (2010); Race: 96.2% White, 0.6% Black, 1.4% Asian, 0.1% American Indian/Alaska Native, 0.1% Native Hawaiian/Other Pacific Islander, 1.6% Other, 2.1% Hispanic of any race (2010); Average household size: 2.65 (2010); Median age: 43.8 (2010); Males per 100 females: 94.7 (2010); Marriage status: 25.6% never married, 65.2% now married, 4.1% widowed, 5.1% divorced (2006-2010 5-year est.); Foreign born: 1.4% (2006-2010 5-year est.); Ancestry (includes multiple ancestries): 53.5% German, 15.1% Irish, 9.3% English, 5.9% Italian, 5.4% American (2006-2010 5-year est.).

Economy: Employment by occupation: 19.5% management, 6.5% professional, 5.3% services, 9.9% sales, 1.7% farming, 5.7% construction, 5.1% production (2006-2010 5-year est.).

Income: Per capita income: $38,262 (2006-2010 5-year est.); Median household income: $74,247 (2006-2010 5-year est.); Average household income: $97,935 (2006-2010 5-year est.); Percent of households with income of $100,000 or more: 35.3% (2006-2010 5-year est.); Poverty rate: 2.4% (2006-2010 5-year est.).

Education: Percent of population age 25 and over with: High school diploma (including GED) or higher: 95.8% (2006-2010 5-year est.); Bachelor's degree or higher: 52.2% (2006-2010 5-year est.); Master's degree or higher: 13.8% (2006-2010 5-year est.).

School District(s)

Cumberland Valley SD (KG-12)
    2010-11 Enrollment: 7,743 . . . . (717) 697-8261
South Middleton SD (KG-12)
    2010-11 Enrollment: 2,203 . . . . (717) 258-6484

Housing: Homeownership rate: 83.1% (2010); Median home value: $196,800 (2006-2010 5-year est.); Median contract rent: $807 per month (2006-2010 5-year est.); Median year structure built: 1984 (2006-2010 5-year est.).

Transportation: Commute to work: 93.3% car, 0.0% public transportation, 2.0% walk, 2.8% work from home (2006-2010 5-year est.); Travel time to work: 35.4% less than 15 minutes, 41.6% 15 to 30 minutes, 17.1% 30 to 45 minutes, 2.5% 45 to 60 minutes, 3.4% 60 minutes or more (2006-2010 5-year est.)

Additional Information Contacts

Greater Carlisle Area Chamber of Commerce . . . . (717) 243-4515
    http://carlislechamber.org

CAMP HILL (borough). Aka Lemoyne-Camp Hill. Covers a land area of 2.122 square miles and a water area of 0 square miles. Located at 40.24° N. Lat; 76.93° W. Long. Elevation is 443 feet.

History: Founded 1756.

Population: 7,831 (1990); 7,636 (2000); 7,888 (2010); Density: 3,717.4 persons per square mile (2010); Race: 88.8% White, 1.8% Black, 6.7% Asian, 0.1% American Indian/Alaska Native, 0.0% Native Hawaiian/Other Pacific Islander, 2.6% Other, 2.7% Hispanic of any race (2010); Average household size: 2.30 (2010); Median age: 42.3 (2010); Males per 100 females: 92.2 (2010); Marriage status: 23.6% never married, 55.7% now married, 9.1% widowed, 11.6% divorced (2006-2010 5-year est.); Foreign born: 8.4% (2006-2010 5-year est.); Ancestry (includes multiple ancestries): 37.3% German, 21.0% Irish, 12.9% English, 6.5% Italian, 4.7% American (2006-2010 5-year est.).

Economy: Single-family building permits issued: 2 (2011); Multi-family building permits issued: 0 (2011); Employment by occupation: 14.5% management, 8.6% professional, 7.8% services, 17.1% sales, 4.9% farming, 3.0% construction, 3.5% production (2006-2010 5-year est.).

Income: Per capita income: $35,470 (2006-2010 5-year est.); Median household income: $60,083 (2006-2010 5-year est.); Average household income: $79,928 (2006-2010 5-year est.); Percent of households with income of $100,000 or more: 27.7% (2006-2010 5-year est.); Poverty rate: 3.9% (2006-2010 5-year est.).

Taxes: Total city taxes per capita: $521 (2009); City property taxes per capita: $319 (2009).

Education: Percent of population age 25 and over with: High school diploma (including GED) or higher: 95.8% (2006-2010 5-year est.); Bachelor's degree or higher: 46.2% (2006-2010 5-year est.); Master's degree or higher: 17.8% (2006-2010 5-year est.).

School District(s)

Camp Hill SD (KG-12)
    2010-11 Enrollment: 1,198 . . . . (717) 901-2400
East Pennsboro Area SD (KG-12)
    2010-11 Enrollment: 2,785 . . . . (717) 732-3601
West Shore SD (KG-12)
    2010-11 Enrollment: 7,943 . . . . (717) 938-9577

Housing: Homeownership rate: 72.9% (2010); Median home value: $194,800 (2006-2010 5-year est.); Median contract rent: $787 per month (2006-2010 5-year est.); Median year structure built: 1952 (2006-2010 5-year est.).

Hospitals: Holy Spirit Hospital (332 beds); State Correctional Institution at Camp Hill (34 beds)

Safety: Violent crime rate: 2.5 per 10,000 population; Property crime rate: 158.0 per 10,000 population (2011).

Newspapers: The Patriot-News - Camp Hill Bureau (Local news)

Transportation: Commute to work: 90.6% car, 2.3% public transportation, 3.1% walk, 3.3% work from home (2006-2010 5-year est.); Travel time to work: 49.5% less than 15 minutes, 39.3% 15 to 30 minutes, 9.1% 30 to 45 minutes, 1.4% 45 to 60 minutes, 0.7% 60 minutes or more (2006-2010 5-year est.)

Additional Information Contacts

Borough of Camp Hill . . . . (717) 737-3456
    http://www.camphillborough.com
West Shore Chamber of Commerce . . . . (717) 761-0702
    http://www.wschamber.org

CARLISLE (borough). County seat. Covers a land area of 5.532 square miles and a water area of 0.008 square miles. Located at 40.20° N. Lat; 77.20° W. Long. Elevation is 479 feet.

History: The town of Carlisle was laid out in 1751 by Nicholas Scull, Surveyor General of the Province, and was named Carlisle for the county seat of Cumberland County, England. The early settlers were Scots-Irish, and later Germans. Agriculture and iron were the major occupations.

Population: 18,439 (1990); 17,970 (2000); 18,682 (2010); Density: 3,376.8 persons per square mile (2010); Race: 84.3% White, 8.3% Black, 2.3% Asian, 0.2% American Indian/Alaska Native, 0.0% Native Hawaiian/Other Pacific Islander, 4.9% Other, 4.5% Hispanic of any race (2010); Average household size: 2.14 (2010); Median age: 34.1 (2010); Males per 100 females: 87.1 (2010); Marriage status: 41.1% never married, 42.0% now married, 7.5% widowed, 9.4% divorced (2006-2010 5-year est.); Foreign born: 6.9% (2006-2010 5-year est.); Ancestry (includes multiple ancestries): 30.7% German, 15.9% Irish, 8.8% English, 6.9% Italian, 4.5% Scotch-Irish (2006-2010 5-year est.).

Economy: Single-family building permits issued: 5 (2011); Multi-family building permits issued: 0 (2011); Employment by occupation: 9.8% management, 4.4% professional, 11.1% services, 17.8% sales, 4.6% farming, 4.6% construction, 4.1% production (2006-2010 5-year est.).

Income: Per capita income: $25,288 (2006-2010 5-year est.); Median household income: $43,922 (2006-2010 5-year est.); Average household income: $59,559 (2006-2010 5-year est.); Percent of households with income of $100,000 or more: 15.9% (2006-2010 5-year est.); Poverty rate: 12.9% (2006-2010 5-year est.).

Taxes: Total city taxes per capita: $324 (2009); City property taxes per capita: $175 (2009).

Education: Percent of population age 25 and over with: High school diploma (including GED) or higher: 90.1% (2006-2010 5-year est.); Bachelor's degree or higher: 36.1% (2006-2010 5-year est.); Master's degree or higher: 17.4% (2006-2010 5-year est.).

School District(s)

Big Spring SD (KG-12)
    2010-11 Enrollment: 2,846 . . . . (717) 776-2000
Carlisle Area SD (KG-12)
    2010-11 Enrollment: 4,803 . . . . (717) 240-6800
Cumberland Valley SD (KG-12)
    2010-11 Enrollment: 7,743 . . . . (717) 697-8261

Four-year College(s)

Dickinson College (Private, Not-for-profit)
    Fall 2010 Enrollment: 2,547 . . . . (717) 243-5121
    2011-12 Tuition: In-state $43,060; Out-of-state $43,060
The Dickinson School of Law of the Pennsylvania State University (Public)
    Fall 2010 Enrollment: 291 . . . . (717) 240-5000

Housing: Homeownership rate: 49.9% (2010); Median home value: $165,200 (2006-2010 5-year est.); Median contract rent: $562 per month (2006-2010 5-year est.); Median year structure built: 1950 (2006-2010 5-year est.).

Hospitals: Carlisle Regional Medical Center (200 beds)

Safety: Violent crime rate: 30.9 per 10,000 population; Property crime rate: 247.6 per 10,000 population (2011).

Newspapers: The Sentinel (Community news; Circulation 14,572)

Transportation: Commute to work: 77.2% car, 0.1% public transportation, 18.4% walk, 3.1% work from home (2006-2010 5-year est.); Travel time to work: 52.5% less than 15 minutes, 23.2% 15 to 30 minutes, 17.7% 30 to 45 minutes, 2.9% 45 to 60 minutes, 3.7% 60 minutes or more (2006-2010 5-year est.)

Additional Information Contacts

Borough of Carlisle . . . . (717) 249-4422
    http://www.carlislepa.org
Greater Carlisle Area Chamber of Commerce . . . . (717) 243-4515
    http://carlislechamber.org

COOKE (township). Covers a land area of 19.787 square miles and a water area of 0.076 square miles. Located at 40.03° N. Lat; 77.32° W. Long.

Population: 90 (1990); 117 (2000); 179 (2010); Density: 9.0 persons per square mile (2010); Race: 98.9% White, 1.1% Black, 0.0% Asian, 0.0% American Indian/Alaska Native, 0.0% Native Hawaiian/Other Pacific Islander, 0.0% Other, 0.0% Hispanic of any race (2010); Average household size: 2.24 (2010); Median age: 45.6 (2010); Males per 100 females: 92.5 (2010); Marriage status: 9.1% never married, 75.8% now married, 9.1% widowed, 6.1% divorced (2006-2010 5-year est.); Foreign born: 5.9% (2006-2010 5-year est.); Ancestry (includes multiple ancestries): 31.4% German, 14.2% Irish, 10.3% American, 9.8% Scotch-Irish, 9.3% English (2006-2010 5-year est.).
Economy: Single-family building permits issued: 0 (2011); Multi-family building permits issued: 0 (2011); Employment by occupation: 16.8% management, 2.0% professional, 12.9% services, 12.9% sales, 4.0% farming, 8.9% construction, 4.0% production (2006-2010 5-year est.).
Income: Per capita income: $31,798 (2006-2010 5-year est.); Median household income: $66,042 (2006-2010 5-year est.); Average household income: $67,062 (2006-2010 5-year est.); Percent of households with income of $100,000 or more: 14.7% (2006-2010 5-year est.); Poverty rate: 5.4% (2006-2010 5-year est.).
Education: Percent of population age 25 and over with: High school diploma (including GED) or higher: 93.8% (2006-2010 5-year est.); Bachelor's degree or higher: 27.2% (2006-2010 5-year est.); Master's degree or higher: 20.4% (2006-2010 5-year est.).
Housing: Homeownership rate: 93.8% (2010); Median home value: $207,500 (2006-2010 5-year est.); Median contract rent: $1,054 per month (2006-2010 5-year est.); Median year structure built: 1993 (2006-2010 5-year est.).
Transportation: Commute to work: 95.8% car, 0.0% public transportation, 0.0% walk, 4.2% work from home (2006-2010 5-year est.); Travel time to work: 6.5% less than 15 minutes, 31.5% 15 to 30 minutes, 23.9% 30 to 45 minutes, 19.6% 45 to 60 minutes, 18.5% 60 minutes or more (2006-2010 5-year est.)

DICKINSON (township). Covers a land area of 45.808 square miles and a water area of 0.221 square miles. Located at 40.09° N. Lat; 77.26° W. Long. Elevation is 692 feet.
Population: 3,870 (1990); 4,702 (2000); 5,223 (2010); Density: 114.0 persons per square mile (2010); Race: 96.8% White, 0.9% Black, 0.6% Asian, 0.2% American Indian/Alaska Native, 0.0% Native Hawaiian/Other Pacific Islander, 1.5% Other, 1.3% Hispanic of any race (2010); Average household size: 2.64 (2010); Median age: 45.3 (2010); Males per 100 females: 100.7 (2010); Marriage status: 17.0% never married, 71.6% now married, 4.5% widowed, 6.9% divorced (2006-2010 5-year est.); Foreign born: 0.8% (2006-2010 5-year est.); Ancestry (includes multiple ancestries): 39.5% German, 15.8% Irish, 13.3% American, 7.6% Polish, 5.3% English (2006-2010 5-year est.).
Economy: Single-family building permits issued: 9 (2011); Multi-family building permits issued: 0 (2011); Employment by occupation: 14.5% management, 4.2% professional, 10.7% services, 13.5% sales, 3.0% farming, 9.1% construction, 8.1% production (2006-2010 5-year est.).
Income: Per capita income: $34,470 (2006-2010 5-year est.); Median household income: $77,734 (2006-2010 5-year est.); Average household income: $90,869 (2006-2010 5-year est.); Percent of households with income of $100,000 or more: 36.7% (2006-2010 5-year est.); Poverty rate: 2.4% (2006-2010 5-year est.).
Education: Percent of population age 25 and over with: High school diploma (including GED) or higher: 86.7% (2006-2010 5-year est.); Bachelor's degree or higher: 34.6% (2006-2010 5-year est.); Master's degree or higher: 14.5% (2006-2010 5-year est.).
Housing: Homeownership rate: 90.2% (2010); Median home value: $208,600 (2006-2010 5-year est.); Median contract rent: $648 per month (2006-2010 5-year est.); Median year structure built: 1981 (2006-2010 5-year est.).
Transportation: Commute to work: 91.1% car, 0.6% public transportation, 0.0% walk, 8.0% work from home (2006-2010 5-year est.); Travel time to work: 21.0% less than 15 minutes, 45.5% 15 to 30 minutes, 19.8% 30 to 45 minutes, 9.0% 45 to 60 minutes, 4.6% 60 minutes or more (2006-2010 5-year est.)
Additional Information Contacts
Greater Carlisle Area Chamber of Commerce . . . . (717) 243-4515
  http://carlislechamber.org

EAST PENNSBORO (township). Covers a land area of 10.391 square miles and a water area of 0.310 square miles. Located at 40.29° N. Lat; 76.94° W. Long.
Population: 16,588 (1990); 18,254 (2000); 20,228 (2010); Density: 1,946.6 persons per square mile (2010); Race: 89.0% White, 2.7% Black, 5.1% Asian, 0.1% American Indian/Alaska Native, 0.0% Native Hawaiian/Other Pacific Islander, 3.1% Other, 2.8% Hispanic of any race (2010); Average household size: 2.35 (2010); Median age: 40.5 (2010); Males per 100 females: 92.3 (2010); Marriage status: 28.6% never married, 55.9% now married, 6.1% widowed, 9.4% divorced (2006-2010 5-year est.); Foreign born: 7.4% (2006-2010 5-year est.); Ancestry (includes multiple ancestries): 39.8% German, 17.9% Irish, 9.7% Italian, 7.7% English, 5.5% American (2006-2010 5-year est.).
Economy: Single-family building permits issued: 20 (2011); Multi-family building permits issued: 96 (2011); Employment by occupation: 12.5% management, 8.1% professional, 10.2% services, 23.8% sales, 5.2% farming, 6.4% construction, 4.2% production (2006-2010 5-year est.).
Income: Per capita income: $28,334 (2006-2010 5-year est.); Median household income: $59,155 (2006-2010 5-year est.); Average household income: $70,264 (2006-2010 5-year est.); Percent of households with income of $100,000 or more: 21.1% (2006-2010 5-year est.); Poverty rate: 6.0% (2006-2010 5-year est.).
Taxes: Total city taxes per capita: $259 (2009); City property taxes per capita: $77 (2009).
Education: Percent of population age 25 and over with: High school diploma (including GED) or higher: 89.1% (2006-2010 5-year est.); Bachelor's degree or higher: 28.8% (2006-2010 5-year est.); Master's degree or higher: 10.0% (2006-2010 5-year est.).
Housing: Homeownership rate: 70.0% (2010); Median home value: $162,100 (2006-2010 5-year est.); Median contract rent: $634 per month (2006-2010 5-year est.); Median year structure built: 1972 (2006-2010 5-year est.).
Safety: Violent crime rate: 6.4 per 10,000 population; Property crime rate: 171.0 per 10,000 population (2011).
Transportation: Commute to work: 91.2% car, 1.5% public transportation, 4.0% walk, 2.7% work from home (2006-2010 5-year est.); Travel time to work: 35.0% less than 15 minutes, 48.5% 15 to 30 minutes, 11.7% 30 to 45 minutes, 2.1% 45 to 60 minutes, 2.7% 60 minutes or more (2006-2010 5-year est.)
Additional Information Contacts
East Pennsboro Township . . . . (717) 732-0711
  http://eastpennsboro.net
West Shore Chamber of Commerce . . . . (717) 761-0702
  http://www.wschamber.org

ENOLA (CDP). Covers a land area of 1.886 square miles and a water area of 0.020 square miles. Located at 40.29° N. Lat; 76.94° W. Long. Elevation is 446 feet.
Population: 5,980 (1990); 5,627 (2000); 6,111 (2010); Density: 3,239.6 persons per square mile (2010); Race: 89.9% White, 3.4% Black, 1.8% Asian, 0.3% American Indian/Alaska Native, 0.0% Native Hawaiian/Other Pacific Islander, 4.6% Other, 4.0% Hispanic of any race (2010); Average household size: 2.23 (2010); Median age: 35.3 (2010); Males per 100 females: 94.1 (2010); Marriage status: 43.7% never married, 40.2% now married, 5.6% widowed, 10.4% divorced (2006-2010 5-year est.); Foreign born: 5.7% (2006-2010 5-year est.); Ancestry (includes multiple ancestries): 40.7% German, 18.4% Irish, 8.5% Italian, 5.9% English, 5.1% American (2006-2010 5-year est.).
Economy: Employment by occupation: 8.6% management, 6.9% professional, 9.6% services, 30.7% sales, 4.0% farming, 8.8% construction, 4.9% production (2006-2010 5-year est.).
Income: Per capita income: $20,293 (2006-2010 5-year est.); Median household income: $44,710 (2006-2010 5-year est.); Average household income: $50,867 (2006-2010 5-year est.); Percent of households with income of $100,000 or more: 8.5% (2006-2010 5-year est.); Poverty rate: 8.9% (2006-2010 5-year est.).
Education: Percent of population age 25 and over with: High school diploma (including GED) or higher: 83.4% (2006-2010 5-year est.); Bachelor's degree or higher: 16.5% (2006-2010 5-year est.); Master's degree or higher: 4.5% (2006-2010 5-year est.).
School District(s)
Cumberland Valley SD (KG-12)
  2010-11 Enrollment: 7,743 . . . . (717) 697-8261
East Pennsboro Area SD (KG-12)
  2010-11 Enrollment: 2,785 . . . . (717) 732-3601

Four-year College(s)

Central Penn College (Private, For-profit)
    Fall 2010 Enrollment: 1,549 .... (800) 759-2727
    2011-12 Tuition: In-state $14,991; Out-of-state $14,991

Housing: Homeownership rate: 53.6% (2010); Median home value: $123,200 (2006-2010 5-year est.); Median contract rent: $612 per month (2006-2010 5-year est.); Median year structure built: 1957 (2006-2010 5-year est.).

Transportation: Commute to work: 85.3% car, 3.0% public transportation, 9.9% walk, 1.6% work from home (2006-2010 5-year est.); Travel time to work: 41.1% less than 15 minutes, 42.1% 15 to 30 minutes, 13.1% 30 to 45 minutes, 1.3% 45 to 60 minutes, 2.3% 60 minutes or more (2006-2010 5-year est.).

Additional Information Contacts

Harrisburg Regional Chamber & CREDC .... (717) 232-4099
    http://www.harrisburgregionalchamber.org

GRANTHAM (unincorporated postal area)

Zip Code: 17027
    Covers a land area of 0.374 square miles and a water area of 0.012 square miles. Located at 40.15° N. Lat; 76.99° W. Long. Elevation is 446 feet. Population: 2,141 (2010); Density: 5,714.7 persons per square mile (2010); Race: 93.9% White, 1.9% Black, 2.2% Asian, 0.1% American Indian/Alaska Native, 0.0% Native Hawaiian/Other Pacific Islander, 1.9% Other, 2.4% Hispanic of any race (2010); Average household size: 2.65 (2010); Median age: 20.7 (2010); Males per 100 females: 64.4 (2010); Homeownership rate: 71.8% (2010)

HAMPDEN (township). Covers a land area of 17.342 square miles and a water area of 0.523 square miles. Located at 40.26° N. Lat; 76.98° W. Long.

Population: 20,384 (1990); 24,135 (2000); 28,044 (2010); Density: 1,617.1 persons per square mile (2010); Race: 88.9% White, 1.7% Black, 7.1% Asian, 0.1% American Indian/Alaska Native, 0.0% Native Hawaiian/Other Pacific Islander, 2.2% Other, 2.0% Hispanic of any race (2010); Average household size: 2.44 (2010); Median age: 42.6 (2010); Males per 100 females: 93.5 (2010); Marriage status: 21.8% never married, 64.8% now married, 6.3% widowed, 7.2% divorced (2006-2010 5-year est.); Foreign born: 7.6% (2006-2010 5-year est.); Ancestry (includes multiple ancestries): 34.0% German, 19.5% Irish, 10.6% English, 10.4% Italian, 5.9% Polish (2006-2010 5-year est.).

Economy: Unemployment rate: 5.3% (August 2012); Total civilian labor force: 15,498 (August 2012); Single-family building permits issued: 103 (2011); Multi-family building permits issued: 0 (2011); Employment by occupation: 17.0% management, 9.3% professional, 5.5% services, 16.8% sales, 4.5% farming, 3.3% construction, 3.8% production (2006-2010 5-year est.).

Income: Per capita income: $42,904 (2006-2010 5-year est.); Median household income: $82,674 (2006-2010 5-year est.); Average household income: $102,762 (2006-2010 5-year est.); Percent of households with income of $100,000 or more: 39.0% (2006-2010 5-year est.); Poverty rate: 3.7% (2006-2010 5-year est.).

Taxes: Total city taxes per capita: $281 (2009); City property taxes per capita: $21 (2009).

Education: Percent of population age 25 and over with: High school diploma (including GED) or higher: 96.1% (2006-2010 5-year est.); Bachelor's degree or higher: 48.4% (2006-2010 5-year est.); Master's degree or higher: 18.8% (2006-2010 5-year est.).

Housing: Homeownership rate: 79.8% (2010); Median home value: $228,500 (2006-2010 5-year est.); Median contract rent: $719 per month (2006-2010 5-year est.); Median year structure built: 1983 (2006-2010 5-year est.).

Safety: Violent crime rate: 3.9 per 10,000 population; Property crime rate: 127.3 per 10,000 population (2011).

Transportation: Commute to work: 94.1% car, 0.4% public transportation, 1.0% walk, 3.9% work from home (2006-2010 5-year est.); Travel time to work: 28.8% less than 15 minutes, 53.6% 15 to 30 minutes, 11.5% 30 to 45 minutes, 3.4% 45 to 60 minutes, 2.7% 60 minutes or more (2006-2010 5-year est.)

Additional Information Contacts

Hampden Township .... (717) 761-0119
    http://www.hampdentownship.us/hampden.htm
West Shore Chamber of Commerce .... (717) 761-0702
    http://www.wschamber.org

HOPEWELL (township). Covers a land area of 27.672 square miles and a water area of 0.155 square miles. Located at 40.15° N. Lat; 77.55° W. Long.

Population: 1,992 (1990); 2,096 (2000); 2,329 (2010); Density: 84.2 persons per square mile (2010); Race: 97.9% White, 0.5% Black, 0.1% Asian, 0.0% American Indian/Alaska Native, 0.0% Native Hawaiian/Other Pacific Islander, 1.5% Other, 0.6% Hispanic of any race (2010); Average household size: 2.96 (2010); Median age: 37.9 (2010); Males per 100 females: 103.1 (2010); Marriage status: 22.2% never married, 70.0% now married, 4.3% widowed, 3.6% divorced (2006-2010 5-year est.); Foreign born: 1.3% (2006-2010 5-year est.); Ancestry (includes multiple ancestries): 41.6% German, 12.1% Pennsylvania German, 12.0% American, 9.4% Irish, 7.1% English (2006-2010 5-year est.).

Economy: Single-family building permits issued: 7 (2011); Multi-family building permits issued: 0 (2011); Employment by occupation: 12.1% management, 1.7% professional, 7.2% services, 19.5% sales, 1.6% farming, 17.0% construction, 6.0% production (2006-2010 5-year est.).

Income: Per capita income: $19,830 (2006-2010 5-year est.); Median household income: $60,078 (2006-2010 5-year est.); Average household income: $65,139 (2006-2010 5-year est.); Percent of households with income of $100,000 or more: 16.8% (2006-2010 5-year est.); Poverty rate: 7.0% (2006-2010 5-year est.).

Education: Percent of population age 25 and over with: High school diploma (including GED) or higher: 74.4% (2006-2010 5-year est.); Bachelor's degree or higher: 13.0% (2006-2010 5-year est.); Master's degree or higher: 6.8% (2006-2010 5-year est.).

Housing: Homeownership rate: 87.8% (2010); Median home value: $178,900 (2006-2010 5-year est.); Median contract rent: $528 per month (2006-2010 5-year est.); Median year structure built: 1979 (2006-2010 5-year est.).

Transportation: Commute to work: 83.8% car, 0.3% public transportation, 3.6% walk, 11.2% work from home (2006-2010 5-year est.); Travel time to work: 23.3% less than 15 minutes, 34.1% 15 to 30 minutes, 25.5% 30 to 45 minutes, 11.0% 45 to 60 minutes, 6.1% 60 minutes or more (2006-2010 5-year est.)

Additional Information Contacts

Shippensburg Area Chamber of Commerce .... (717) 532-5509
    http://www.shippensburg.org

LEMOYNE (borough). Covers a land area of 1.612 square miles and a water area of <.001 square miles. Located at 40.24° N. Lat; 76.90° W. Long. Elevation is 390 feet.

History: Northernmost point of Confederate advance, 1863.

Population: 3,959 (1990); 3,995 (2000); 4,553 (2010); Density: 2,824.6 persons per square mile (2010); Race: 90.4% White, 2.6% Black, 1.6% Asian, 0.3% American Indian/Alaska Native, 0.0% Native Hawaiian/Other Pacific Islander, 5.1% Other, 5.1% Hispanic of any race (2010); Average household size: 2.11 (2010); Median age: 38.3 (2010); Males per 100 females: 96.0 (2010); Marriage status: 34.4% never married, 41.3% now married, 6.1% widowed, 18.2% divorced (2006-2010 5-year est.); Foreign born: 4.3% (2006-2010 5-year est.); Ancestry (includes multiple ancestries): 42.5% German, 19.5% Irish, 10.9% Italian, 9.3% English, 4.8% Polish (2006-2010 5-year est.).

Economy: Single-family building permits issued: 0 (2011); Multi-family building permits issued: 29 (2011); Employment by occupation: 7.4% management, 1.8% professional, 7.1% services, 20.0% sales, 10.9% farming, 7.0% construction, 3.7% production (2006-2010 5-year est.).

Income: Per capita income: $27,304 (2006-2010 5-year est.); Median household income: $47,863 (2006-2010 5-year est.); Average household income: $53,708 (2006-2010 5-year est.); Percent of households with income of $100,000 or more: 7.3% (2006-2010 5-year est.); Poverty rate: 9.9% (2006-2010 5-year est.).

Education: Percent of population age 25 and over with: High school diploma (including GED) or higher: 93.4% (2006-2010 5-year est.); Bachelor's degree or higher: 26.0% (2006-2010 5-year est.); Master's degree or higher: 7.6% (2006-2010 5-year est.).

School District(s)

West Shore SD (KG-12)
    2010-11 Enrollment: 7,943 .... (717) 938-9577

Housing: Homeownership rate: 53.8% (2010); Median home value: $127,700 (2006-2010 5-year est.); Median contract rent: $582 per month (2006-2010 5-year est.); Median year structure built: 1949 (2006-2010 5-year est.).

Transportation: Commute to work: 91.3% car, 3.4% public transportation, 3.4% walk, 2.0% work from home (2006-2010 5-year est.); Travel time to

work: 42.0% less than 15 minutes, 37.6% 15 to 30 minutes, 16.1% 30 to 45 minutes, 2.9% 45 to 60 minutes, 1.5% 60 minutes or more (2006-2010 5-year est.)

Additional Information Contacts
West Shore Chamber of Commerce . . . . (717) 761-0702
  http://www.cbicc.org

LOWER ALLEN (CDP). Covers a land area of 2.197 square miles and a water area of 0.034 square miles. Located at 40.23° N. Lat; 76.90° W. Long. Elevation is 384 feet.
Population: 6,329 (1990); 6,619 (2000); 6,694 (2010); Density: 3,046.3 persons per square mile (2010); Race: 92.6% White, 3.1% Black, 1.7% Asian, 0.1% American Indian/Alaska Native, 0.0% Native Hawaiian/Other Pacific Islander, 2.5% Other, 3.7% Hispanic of any race (2010); Average household size: 2.15 (2010); Median age: 43.8 (2010); Males per 100 females: 86.7 (2010); Marriage status: 23.6% never married, 59.1% now married, 9.9% widowed, 7.4% divorced (2006-2010 5-year est.); Foreign born: 3.6% (2006-2010 5-year est.); Ancestry (includes multiple ancestries): 42.6% German, 12.3% Irish, 11.1% English, 8.4% Italian, 4.7% Polish (2006-2010 5-year est.).
Economy: Employment by occupation: 16.8% management, 7.6% professional, 8.7% services, 18.4% sales, 5.8% farming, 4.8% construction, 3.9% production (2006-2010 5-year est.).
Income: Per capita income: $31,793 (2006-2010 5-year est.); Median household income: $61,916 (2006-2010 5-year est.); Average household income: $70,147 (2006-2010 5-year est.); Percent of households with income of $100,000 or more: 19.4% (2006-2010 5-year est.); Poverty rate: 6.5% (2006-2010 5-year est.).
Education: Percent of population age 25 and over with: High school diploma (including GED) or higher: 94.8% (2006-2010 5-year est.); Bachelor's degree or higher: 36.2% (2006-2010 5-year est.); Master's degree or higher: 13.2% (2006-2010 5-year est.).
Housing: Homeownership rate: 72.2% (2010); Median home value: $164,200 (2006-2010 5-year est.); Median contract rent: $638 per month (2006-2010 5-year est.); Median year structure built: 1964 (2006-2010 5-year est.).
Transportation: Commute to work: 93.5% car, 1.1% public transportation, 0.7% walk, 4.4% work from home (2006-2010 5-year est.); Travel time to work: 36.5% less than 15 minutes, 48.8% 15 to 30 minutes, 9.3% 30 to 45 minutes, 3.2% 45 to 60 minutes, 2.1% 60 minutes or more (2006-2010 5-year est.)

Additional Information Contacts
Harrisburg Regional Chamber & CREDC . . . . (717) 232-4099
  http://www.harrisburgregionalchamber.org

LOWER ALLEN (township). Covers a land area of 10.127 square miles and a water area of 0.202 square miles. Located at 40.21° N. Lat; 76.93° W. Long. Elevation is 384 feet.
Population: 15,254 (1990); 17,437 (2000); 17,980 (2010); Density: 1,775.4 persons per square mile (2010); Race: 82.5% White, 10.3% Black, 2.3% Asian, 0.1% American Indian/Alaska Native, 0.1% Native Hawaiian/Other Pacific Islander, 4.7% Other, 5.3% Hispanic of any race (2010); Average household size: 2.09 (2010); Median age: 41.4 (2010); Males per 100 females: 129.6 (2010); Marriage status: 25.8% never married, 53.8% now married, 10.2% widowed, 10.1% divorced (2006-2010 5-year est.); Foreign born: 5.8% (2006-2010 5-year est.); Ancestry (includes multiple ancestries): 31.9% German, 9.7% Irish, 8.0% Italian, 8.0% English, 5.4% American (2006-2010 5-year est.).
Economy: Single-family building permits issued: 23 (2011); Multi-family building permits issued: 0 (2011); Employment by occupation: 14.4% management, 7.9% professional, 9.0% services, 17.4% sales, 6.8% farming, 4.8% construction, 4.6% production (2006-2010 5-year est.).
Income: Per capita income: $30,563 (2006-2010 5-year est.); Median household income: $60,456 (2006-2010 5-year est.); Average household income: $72,181 (2006-2010 5-year est.); Percent of households with income of $100,000 or more: 20.1% (2006-2010 5-year est.); Poverty rate: 5.1% (2006-2010 5-year est.).
Education: Percent of population age 25 and over with: High school diploma (including GED) or higher: 89.8% (2006-2010 5-year est.); Bachelor's degree or higher: 27.7% (2006-2010 5-year est.); Master's degree or higher: 9.7% (2006-2010 5-year est.).
Housing: Homeownership rate: 66.1% (2010); Median home value: $161,500 (2006-2010 5-year est.); Median contract rent: $772 per month (2006-2010 5-year est.); Median year structure built: 1969 (2006-2010 5-year est.).

Safety: Violent crime rate: 4.4 per 10,000 population; Property crime rate: 162.4 per 10,000 population (2011).
Transportation: Commute to work: 93.3% car, 1.2% public transportation, 1.0% walk, 4.2% work from home (2006-2010 5-year est.); Travel time to work: 37.1% less than 15 minutes, 42.2% 15 to 30 minutes, 13.9% 30 to 45 minutes, 3.7% 45 to 60 minutes, 3.1% 60 minutes or more (2006-2010 5-year est.)

Additional Information Contacts
Harrisburg Regional Chamber & CREDC . . . . (717) 232-4099
  http://www.harrisburgregionalchamber.org
Lower Allen Township . . . . (717) 975-7575
  http://www.lower-allen.pa.us

LOWER FRANKFORD (township). Covers a land area of 14.680 square miles and a water area of 0.317 square miles. Located at 40.24° N. Lat; 77.29° W. Long.
Population: 1,491 (1990); 1,823 (2000); 1,732 (2010); Density: 118.0 persons per square mile (2010); Race: 98.2% White, 0.6% Black, 0.0% Asian, 0.2% American Indian/Alaska Native, 0.0% Native Hawaiian/Other Pacific Islander, 1.0% Other, 1.0% Hispanic of any race (2010); Average household size: 2.55 (2010); Median age: 45.5 (2010); Males per 100 females: 100.7 (2010); Marriage status: 20.3% never married, 63.6% now married, 5.8% widowed, 10.2% divorced (2006-2010 5-year est.); Foreign born: 2.2% (2006-2010 5-year est.); Ancestry (includes multiple ancestries): 38.8% German, 14.1% American, 11.7% Irish, 4.6% English, 3.2% Polish (2006-2010 5-year est.).
Economy: Single-family building permits issued: 0 (2011); Multi-family building permits issued: 0 (2011); Employment by occupation: 7.6% management, 5.1% professional, 12.3% services, 14.1% sales, 3.5% farming, 16.1% construction, 12.6% production (2006-2010 5-year est.).
Income: Per capita income: $23,706 (2006-2010 5-year est.); Median household income: $53,036 (2006-2010 5-year est.); Average household income: $60,965 (2006-2010 5-year est.); Percent of households with income of $100,000 or more: 16.3% (2006-2010 5-year est.); Poverty rate: 9.1% (2006-2010 5-year est.).
Education: Percent of population age 25 and over with: High school diploma (including GED) or higher: 79.3% (2006-2010 5-year est.); Bachelor's degree or higher: 14.0% (2006-2010 5-year est.); Master's degree or higher: 6.2% (2006-2010 5-year est.).
Housing: Homeownership rate: 82.8% (2010); Median home value: $168,300 (2006-2010 5-year est.); Median contract rent: $556 per month (2006-2010 5-year est.); Median year structure built: 1975 (2006-2010 5-year est.).
Transportation: Commute to work: 92.3% car, 0.9% public transportation, 1.7% walk, 3.1% work from home (2006-2010 5-year est.); Travel time to work: 15.6% less than 15 minutes, 49.0% 15 to 30 minutes, 23.3% 30 to 45 minutes, 7.9% 45 to 60 minutes, 4.2% 60 minutes or more (2006-2010 5-year est.)

Additional Information Contacts
Greater Carlisle Area Chamber of Commerce . . . . (717) 243-4515
  http://carlislechamber.org

LOWER MIFFLIN (township). Covers a land area of 23.768 square miles and a water area of 0.138 square miles. Located at 40.25° N. Lat; 77.43° W. Long.
Population: 1,700 (1990); 1,620 (2000); 1,783 (2010); Density: 75.0 persons per square mile (2010); Race: 97.9% White, 0.4% Black, 0.2% Asian, 0.0% American Indian/Alaska Native, 0.1% Native Hawaiian/Other Pacific Islander, 1.4% Other, 0.4% Hispanic of any race (2010); Average household size: 2.63 (2010); Median age: 41.0 (2010); Males per 100 females: 101.0 (2010); Marriage status: 20.2% never married, 67.9% now married, 3.6% widowed, 8.3% divorced (2006-2010 5-year est.); Foreign born: 0.4% (2006-2010 5-year est.); Ancestry (includes multiple ancestries): 43.5% German, 12.5% American, 9.5% Irish, 5.3% English, 3.8% Scotch-Irish (2006-2010 5-year est.).
Economy: Single-family building permits issued: 0 (2011); Multi-family building permits issued: 0 (2011); Employment by occupation: 5.9% management, 1.4% professional, 12.4% services, 17.4% sales, 4.9% farming, 11.8% construction, 10.8% production (2006-2010 5-year est.).
Income: Per capita income: $24,015 (2006-2010 5-year est.); Median household income: $56,563 (2006-2010 5-year est.); Average household income: $59,530 (2006-2010 5-year est.); Percent of households with income of $100,000 or more: 8.8% (2006-2010 5-year est.); Poverty rate: 8.7% (2006-2010 5-year est.).

Education: Percent of population age 25 and over with: High school diploma (including GED) or higher: 81.2% (2006-2010 5-year est.); Bachelor's degree or higher: 10.4% (2006-2010 5-year est.); Master's degree or higher: 4.2% (2006-2010 5-year est.).

Housing: Homeownership rate: 85.8% (2010); Median home value: $147,300 (2006-2010 5-year est.); Median contract rent: $489 per month (2006-2010 5-year est.); Median year structure built: 1982 (2006-2010 5-year est.).

Transportation: Commute to work: 94.5% car, 0.2% public transportation, 2.1% walk, 2.4% work from home (2006-2010 5-year est.); Travel time to work: 11.9% less than 15 minutes, 29.7% 15 to 30 minutes, 35.1% 30 to 45 minutes, 15.1% 45 to 60 minutes, 8.3% 60 minutes or more (2006-2010 5-year est.)

Additional Information Contacts

Juniata River Valley Chamber of Commerce . . . . (717) 248-6713
http://www.juniatarivervalley.org

MECHANICSBURG (borough). Covers a land area of 2.410 square miles and a water area of 0.002 square miles. Located at 40.21° N. Lat; 77.01° W. Long. Elevation is 433 feet.

History: Appalachian Trail passes to west. Settled c.1790, Incorporated 1828.

Population: 9,452 (1990); 9,042 (2000); 8,981 (2010); Density: 3,725.8 persons per square mile (2010); Race: 92.3% White, 2.2% Black, 1.8% Asian, 0.3% American Indian/Alaska Native, 0.0% Native Hawaiian/Other Pacific Islander, 3.4% Other, 3.5% Hispanic of any race (2010); Average household size: 2.22 (2010); Median age: 39.9 (2010); Males per 100 females: 96.4 (2010); Marriage status: 30.7% never married, 50.9% now married, 6.1% widowed, 12.3% divorced (2006-2010 5-year est.); Foreign born: 1.8% (2006-2010 5-year est.); Ancestry (includes multiple ancestries): 45.2% German, 16.8% Irish, 13.3% Italian, 9.9% English, 5.5% American (2006-2010 5-year est.).

Economy: Single-family building permits issued: 0 (2011); Multi-family building permits issued: 0 (2011); Employment by occupation: 12.3% management, 6.0% professional, 12.5% services, 16.2% sales, 4.6% farming, 4.8% construction, 6.8% production (2006-2010 5-year est.).

Income: Per capita income: $27,336 (2006-2010 5-year est.); Median household income: $49,789 (2006-2010 5-year est.); Average household income: $57,013 (2006-2010 5-year est.); Percent of households with income of $100,000 or more: 12.3% (2006-2010 5-year est.); Poverty rate: 7.6% (2006-2010 5-year est.).

Education: Percent of population age 25 and over with: High school diploma (including GED) or higher: 91.1% (2006-2010 5-year est.); Bachelor's degree or higher: 29.1% (2006-2010 5-year est.); Master's degree or higher: 11.0% (2006-2010 5-year est.).

School District(s)

Cumberland Valley SD (KG-12)
    2010-11 Enrollment: 7,743 . . . . (717) 697-8261
Cumberland-Perry Avts (10-12)
    2010-11 Enrollment: n/a . . . . (717) 697-0354
Mechanicsburg Area SD (KG-12)
    2010-11 Enrollment: 3,724 . . . . (717) 691-4500
West Shore SD (KG-12)
    2010-11 Enrollment: 7,943 . . . . (717) 938-9577

Two-year College(s)

ITT Technical Institute-Harrisburg (Private, For-profit)
    Fall 2010 Enrollment: 439 . . . . (717) 565-1700
    2011-12 Tuition: In-state $18,048; Out-of-state $18,048
YTI Career Institute-Capital Region (Private, For-profit)
    Fall 2010 Enrollment: 239 . . . . (717) 761-1481

Housing: Homeownership rate: 62.3% (2010); Median home value: $160,400 (2006-2010 5-year est.); Median contract rent: $606 per month (2006-2010 5-year est.); Median year structure built: 1952 (2006-2010 5-year est.).

Hospitals: HealthSouth Rehabilitation of Mechanicsburg (103 beds); Seidle Memorial Hospital (15 beds)

Safety: Violent crime rate: 63.3 per 10,000 population; Property crime rate: 258.6 per 10,000 population (2011).

Newspapers: Guide News (National news; Circulation 176,543)

Transportation: Commute to work: 90.4% car, 0.8% public transportation, 3.0% walk, 4.0% work from home (2006-2010 5-year est.); Travel time to work: 35.7% less than 15 minutes, 47.5% 15 to 30 minutes, 10.5% 30 to 45 minutes, 3.3% 45 to 60 minutes, 2.9% 60 minutes or more (2006-2010 5-year est.)

Additional Information Contacts

Borough of Mechanicsburg . . . . (717) 691-3310
    http://www.mechanicsburgborough.org
Mechanicsburg Chamber of Commerce . . . . (717) 796-0811
    http://mechanicsburgchamber.org

MESSIAH COLLEGE (CDP). Covers a land area of 0.321 square miles and a water area of 0.015 square miles. Located at 40.16° N. Lat; 76.98° W. Long.

Population: n/a (1990); n/a (2000); 2,215 (2010); Density: 6,909.3 persons per square mile (2010); Race: 92.7% White, 2.5% Black, 2.5% Asian, 0.1% American Indian/Alaska Native, 0.0% Native Hawaiian/Other Pacific Islander, 2.2% Other, 2.9% Hispanic of any race (2010); Average household size: 4.20 (2010); Median age: 20.4 (2010); Males per 100 females: 60.5 (2010); Marriage status: 99.1% never married, 0.9% now married, 0.0% widowed, 0.0% divorced (2006-2010 5-year est.); Foreign born: 2.4% (2006-2010 5-year est.); Ancestry (includes multiple ancestries): 42.5% German, 15.3% Irish, 12.9% Italian, 11.1% English, 5.3% Polish (2006-2010 5-year est.).

Economy: Employment by occupation: 10.4% management, 1.0% professional, 43.0% services, 13.7% sales, 1.2% farming, 2.0% construction, 2.2% production (2006-2010 5-year est.).

Income: Per capita income: $10,399 (2006-2010 5-year est.); Median household income: $250 (2006-2010 5-year est.); Average household income: n/a (2006-2010 5-year est.); Percent of households with income of $100,000 or more: 100.0% (2006-2010 5-year est.); Poverty rate: 0.0% (2006-2010 5-year est.).

Education: Percent of population age 25 and over with: High school diploma (including GED) or higher: 100.0% (2006-2010 5-year est.); Bachelor's degree or higher: 32.4% (2006-2010 5-year est.); Master's degree or higher: 5.9% (2006-2010 5-year est.).

Housing: Homeownership rate: 80.0% (2010); Median home value: $1 (2006-2010 5-year est.); Median contract rent: n/a per month (2006-2010 5-year est.); Median year structure built: n/a (2006-2010 5-year est.).

Transportation: Commute to work: 26.5% car, 1.1% public transportation, 64.6% walk, 7.9% work from home (2006-2010 5-year est.); Travel time to work: 80.3% less than 15 minutes, 15.0% 15 to 30 minutes, 3.6% 30 to 45 minutes, 0.0% 45 to 60 minutes, 1.2% 60 minutes or more (2006-2010 5-year est.)

MIDDLESEX (township). Covers a land area of 25.692 square miles and a water area of 0.272 square miles. Located at 40.25° N. Lat; 77.13° W. Long. Elevation is 436 feet.

Population: 5,597 (1990); 6,669 (2000); 7,040 (2010); Density: 274.0 persons per square mile (2010); Race: 94.2% White, 2.0% Black, 1.6% Asian, 0.2% American Indian/Alaska Native, 0.0% Native Hawaiian/Other Pacific Islander, 2.0% Other, 1.9% Hispanic of any race (2010); Average household size: 2.47 (2010); Median age: 43.8 (2010); Males per 100 females: 103.6 (2010); Marriage status: 22.8% never married, 59.0% now married, 6.3% widowed, 12.0% divorced (2006-2010 5-year est.); Foreign born: 2.2% (2006-2010 5-year est.); Ancestry (includes multiple ancestries): 42.5% German, 17.4% Irish, 10.3% English, 7.5% American, 7.1% Italian (2006-2010 5-year est.).

Economy: Single-family building permits issued: 11 (2011); Multi-family building permits issued: 20 (2011); Employment by occupation: 7.3% management, 7.5% professional, 6.5% services, 20.8% sales, 3.7% farming, 11.9% construction, 8.8% production (2006-2010 5-year est.).

Income: Per capita income: $28,042 (2006-2010 5-year est.); Median household income: $56,429 (2006-2010 5-year est.); Average household income: $64,244 (2006-2010 5-year est.); Percent of households with income of $100,000 or more: 22.4% (2006-2010 5-year est.); Poverty rate: 5.1% (2006-2010 5-year est.).

Education: Percent of population age 25 and over with: High school diploma (including GED) or higher: 88.6% (2006-2010 5-year est.); Bachelor's degree or higher: 24.5% (2006-2010 5-year est.); Master's degree or higher: 8.1% (2006-2010 5-year est.).

Housing: Homeownership rate: 84.7% (2010); Median home value: $154,100 (2006-2010 5-year est.); Median contract rent: $504 per month (2006-2010 5-year est.); Median year structure built: 1979 (2006-2010 5-year est.).

Transportation: Commute to work: 94.7% car, 0.6% public transportation, 0.3% walk, 3.9% work from home (2006-2010 5-year est.); Travel time to work: 23.8% less than 15 minutes, 46.9% 15 to 30 minutes, 22.5% 30 to 45 minutes, 2.1% 45 to 60 minutes, 4.6% 60 minutes or more (2006-2010 5-year est.)

Additional Information Contacts
Greater Carlisle Area Chamber of Commerce . . . . (717) 243-4515
  http://carlislechamber.org
Middlesex Township . . . . (717) 249-4409
  http://www.ccpa.net/index.asp?NID=2343

MONROE (township). Covers a land area of 26.088 square miles and a water area of 0.214 square miles. Located at 40.16° N. Lat; 77.07° W. Long.
Population: 5,542 (1990); 5,530 (2000); 5,823 (2010); Density: 223.2 persons per square mile (2010); Race: 96.9% White, 0.3% Black, 1.3% Asian, 0.2% American Indian/Alaska Native, 0.0% Native Hawaiian/Other Pacific Islander, 1.3% Other, 1.4% Hispanic of any race (2010); Average household size: 2.57 (2010); Median age: 45.8 (2010); Males per 100 females: 103.9 (2010); Marriage status: 20.9% never married, 65.7% now married, 4.0% widowed, 9.4% divorced (2006-2010 5-year est.); Foreign born: 3.1% (2006-2010 5-year est.); Ancestry (includes multiple ancestries): 46.9% German, 12.1% Irish, 7.2% American, 6.9% English, 5.2% Dutch (2006-2010 5-year est.).
Economy: Single-family building permits issued: 7 (2011); Multi-family building permits issued: 0 (2011); Employment by occupation: 13.9% management, 6.6% professional, 11.9% services, 17.9% sales, 4.7% farming, 11.1% construction, 2.6% production (2006-2010 5-year est.).
Income: Per capita income: $37,444 (2006-2010 5-year est.); Median household income: $83,327 (2006-2010 5-year est.); Average household income: $95,476 (2006-2010 5-year est.); Percent of households with income of $100,000 or more: 35.2% (2006-2010 5-year est.); Poverty rate: 3.5% (2006-2010 5-year est.).
Education: Percent of population age 25 and over with: High school diploma (including GED) or higher: 91.8% (2006-2010 5-year est.); Bachelor's degree or higher: 35.1% (2006-2010 5-year est.); Master's degree or higher: 13.6% (2006-2010 5-year est.).
Housing: Homeownership rate: 88.8% (2010); Median home value: $207,300 (2006-2010 5-year est.); Median contract rent: $540 per month (2006-2010 5-year est.); Median year structure built: 1975 (2006-2010 5-year est.).
Transportation: Commute to work: 92.6% car, 1.1% public transportation, 1.6% walk, 4.8% work from home (2006-2010 5-year est.); Travel time to work: 27.3% less than 15 minutes, 40.3% 15 to 30 minutes, 21.0% 30 to 45 minutes, 6.8% 45 to 60 minutes, 4.7% 60 minutes or more (2006-2010 5-year est.)
Additional Information Contacts
Greater Carlisle Area Chamber of Commerce . . . . (717) 243-4515
  http://carlislechamber.org
Monroe Township . . . . (717) 258-6642
  http://www.monroetwp.net

MOUNT HOLLY SPRINGS (borough). Covers a land area of 1.358 square miles and a water area of 0.094 square miles. Located at 40.11° N. Lat; 77.18° W. Long. Elevation is 551 feet.
History: Appalachian Trail passes to South. Laid out 1815.
Population: 1,925 (1990); 1,925 (2000); 2,030 (2010); Density: 1,494.8 persons per square mile (2010); Race: 92.4% White, 2.8% Black, 0.3% Asian, 0.2% American Indian/Alaska Native, 0.3% Native Hawaiian/Other Pacific Islander, 4.0% Other, 4.5% Hispanic of any race (2010); Average household size: 2.36 (2010); Median age: 39.1 (2010); Males per 100 females: 94.6 (2010); Marriage status: 26.7% never married, 52.3% now married, 5.9% widowed, 15.1% divorced (2006-2010 5-year est.); Foreign born: 2.0% (2006-2010 5-year est.); Ancestry (includes multiple ancestries): 41.0% German, 14.4% American, 12.2% Irish, 7.2% Italian, 6.4% English (2006-2010 5-year est.).
Economy: Single-family building permits issued: 0 (2011); Multi-family building permits issued: 0 (2011); Employment by occupation: 3.7% management, 2.1% professional, 6.5% services, 23.2% sales, 5.3% farming, 10.9% construction, 9.7% production (2006-2010 5-year est.).
Income: Per capita income: $20,914 (2006-2010 5-year est.); Median household income: $40,887 (2006-2010 5-year est.); Average household income: $45,275 (2006-2010 5-year est.); Percent of households with income of $100,000 or more: 5.8% (2006-2010 5-year est.); Poverty rate: 9.8% (2006-2010 5-year est.).
Education: Percent of population age 25 and over with: High school diploma (including GED) or higher: 85.6% (2006-2010 5-year est.); Bachelor's degree or higher: 9.6% (2006-2010 5-year est.); Master's degree or higher: 4.1% (2006-2010 5-year est.).

School District(s)
Carlisle Area SD (KG-12)
  2010-11 Enrollment: 4,803 . . . . (717) 240-6800
South Middleton SD (KG-12)
  2010-11 Enrollment: 2,203 . . . . (717) 258-6484
Housing: Homeownership rate: 65.1% (2010); Median home value: $119,000 (2006-2010 5-year est.); Median contract rent: $548 per month (2006-2010 5-year est.); Median year structure built: 1962 (2006-2010 5-year est.).
Safety: Violent crime rate: 19.6 per 10,000 population; Property crime rate: 152.3 per 10,000 population (2011).
Transportation: Commute to work: 95.4% car, 0.0% public transportation, 1.1% walk, 3.2% work from home (2006-2010 5-year est.); Travel time to work: 20.7% less than 15 minutes, 45.8% 15 to 30 minutes, 22.4% 30 to 45 minutes, 6.2% 45 to 60 minutes, 5.0% 60 minutes or more (2006-2010 5-year est.)
Additional Information Contacts
Greater Carlisle Area Chamber of Commerce . . . . (717) 243-4515
  http://carlislechamber.org

NEW CUMBERLAND (borough). Covers a land area of 1.674 square miles and a water area of 0.011 square miles. Located at 40.23° N. Lat; 76.88° W. Long. Elevation is 390 feet.
History: Laid out c.1810, incorporated 1831.
Population: 7,665 (1990); 7,349 (2000); 7,277 (2010); Density: 4,346.6 persons per square mile (2010); Race: 94.6% White, 1.5% Black, 1.0% Asian, 0.1% American Indian/Alaska Native, 0.0% Native Hawaiian/Other Pacific Islander, 2.8% Other, 3.5% Hispanic of any race (2010); Average household size: 2.21 (2010); Median age: 40.7 (2010); Males per 100 females: 94.2 (2010); Marriage status: 26.5% never married, 54.5% now married, 6.3% widowed, 12.6% divorced (2006-2010 5-year est.); Foreign born: 3.5% (2006-2010 5-year est.); Ancestry (includes multiple ancestries): 45.4% German, 19.7% Irish, 9.7% English, 7.9% Italian, 5.4% American (2006-2010 5-year est.).
Economy: Single-family building permits issued: 1 (2011); Multi-family building permits issued: 0 (2011); Employment by occupation: 14.6% management, 7.6% professional, 6.9% services, 18.7% sales, 4.5% farming, 3.7% construction, 3.5% production (2006-2010 5-year est.).
Income: Per capita income: $29,995 (2006-2010 5-year est.); Median household income: $59,706 (2006-2010 5-year est.); Average household income: $66,875 (2006-2010 5-year est.); Percent of households with income of $100,000 or more: 19.3% (2006-2010 5-year est.); Poverty rate: 3.4% (2006-2010 5-year est.).
Education: Percent of population age 25 and over with: High school diploma (including GED) or higher: 93.0% (2006-2010 5-year est.); Bachelor's degree or higher: 33.5% (2006-2010 5-year est.); Master's degree or higher: 9.4% (2006-2010 5-year est.).
School District(s)
West Shore SD (KG-12)
  2010-11 Enrollment: 7,943 . . . . (717) 938-9577
West Shore SD (KG-12)
  2010-11 Enrollment: 7,943 . . . . (717) 938-9577
Housing: Homeownership rate: 70.1% (2010); Median home value: $150,200 (2006-2010 5-year est.); Median contract rent: $544 per month (2006-2010 5-year est.); Median year structure built: 1951 (2006-2010 5-year est.).
Safety: Violent crime rate: 15.1 per 10,000 population; Property crime rate: 171.2 per 10,000 population (2011).
Transportation: Commute to work: 95.0% car, 0.3% public transportation, 2.6% walk, 1.7% work from home (2006-2010 5-year est.); Travel time to work: 33.2% less than 15 minutes, 51.7% 15 to 30 minutes, 7.2% 30 to 45 minutes, 2.4% 45 to 60 minutes, 5.5% 60 minutes or more (2006-2010 5-year est.)
Airports: Capital City (general aviation)
Additional Information Contacts
Borough of New Cumberland . . . . (717) 774-0404
  http://www.newcumberlandborough.com
West Shore Chamber of Commerce . . . . (717) 761-0702
  http://www.wschamber.org

NEW KINGSTOWN (CDP). Aka New Kingston. Covers a land area of 1.593 square miles and a water area of 0.001 square miles. Located at 40.23° N. Lat; 77.07° W. Long. Elevation is 443 feet.
Population: 368 (1990); 539 (2000); 495 (2010); Density: 310.8 persons per square mile (2010); Race: 90.9% White, 2.8% Black, 2.4% Asian,

0.2% American Indian/Alaska Native, 0.0% Native Hawaiian/Other Pacific Islander, 3.7% Other, 2.4% Hispanic of any race (2010); Average household size: 2.37 (2010); Median age: 40.3 (2010); Males per 100 females: 98.0 (2010); Marriage status: 16.3% never married, 74.3% now married, 6.1% widowed, 3.3% divorced (2006-2010 5-year est.); Foreign born: 0.0% (2006-2010 5-year est.); Ancestry (includes multiple ancestries): 50.9% German, 32.8% French, 14.2% English, 9.1% Scottish, 7.2% Irish (2006-2010 5-year est.).

Economy: Employment by occupation: 25.8% management, 15.3% professional, 4.8% services, 14.3% sales, 0.0% farming, 6.4% construction, 4.3% production (2006-2010 5-year est.).

Income: Per capita income: $27,119 (2006-2010 5-year est.); Median household income: $72,353 (2006-2010 5-year est.); Average household income: $72,195 (2006-2010 5-year est.); Percent of households with income of $100,000 or more: 7.8% (2006-2010 5-year est.); Poverty rate: 1.2% (2006-2010 5-year est.).

Education: Percent of population age 25 and over with: High school diploma (including GED) or higher: 91.5% (2006-2010 5-year est.); Bachelor's degree or higher: 30.0% (2006-2010 5-year est.); Master's degree or higher: 5.6% (2006-2010 5-year est.).

Housing: Homeownership rate: 69.9% (2010); Median home value: $146,500 (2006-2010 5-year est.); Median contract rent: $938 per month (2006-2010 5-year est.); Median year structure built: before 1940 (2006-2010 5-year est.).

Transportation: Commute to work: 95.9% car, 0.0% public transportation, 4.1% walk, 0.0% work from home (2006-2010 5-year est.); Travel time to work: 24.5% less than 15 minutes, 37.2% 15 to 30 minutes, 20.6% 30 to 45 minutes, 17.7% 45 to 60 minutes, 0.0% 60 minutes or more (2006-2010 5-year est.)

NEWBURG (borough). Covers a land area of 0.185 square miles and a water area of 0 square miles. Located at 40.14° N. Lat; 77.55° W. Long. Elevation is 587 feet.

Population: 233 (1990); 372 (2000); 336 (2010); Density: 1,820.1 persons per square mile (2010); Race: 98.8% White, 0.0% Black, 0.0% Asian, 0.3% American Indian/Alaska Native, 0.0% Native Hawaiian/Other Pacific Islander, 0.9% Other, 0.9% Hispanic of any race (2010); Average household size: 2.51 (2010); Median age: 38.3 (2010); Males per 100 females: 110.0 (2010); Marriage status: 22.0% never married, 57.5% now married, 4.0% widowed, 16.5% divorced (2006-2010 5-year est.); Foreign born: 7.7% (2006-2010 5-year est.); Ancestry (includes multiple ancestries): 44.3% German, 12.2% American, 9.8% Italian, 8.3% Scottish, 7.1% Irish (2006-2010 5-year est.).

Economy: Single-family building permits issued: 0 (2011); Multi-family building permits issued: 0 (2011); Employment by occupation: 8.0% management, 2.9% professional, 3.4% services, 14.4% sales, 4.6% farming, 6.9% construction, 9.2% production (2006-2010 5-year est.).

Income: Per capita income: $22,028 (2006-2010 5-year est.); Median household income: $48,021 (2006-2010 5-year est.); Average household income: $53,600 (2006-2010 5-year est.); Percent of households with income of $100,000 or more: 10.8% (2006-2010 5-year est.); Poverty rate: 19.3% (2006-2010 5-year est.).

Education: Percent of population age 25 and over with: High school diploma (including GED) or higher: 82.1% (2006-2010 5-year est.); Bachelor's degree or higher: 24.2% (2006-2010 5-year est.); Master's degree or higher: 4.9% (2006-2010 5-year est.).

Housing: Homeownership rate: 82.1% (2010); Median home value: $152,100 (2006-2010 5-year est.); Median contract rent: $433 per month (2006-2010 5-year est.); Median year structure built: before 1940 (2006-2010 5-year est.).

Transportation: Commute to work: 93.0% car, 0.0% public transportation, 4.1% walk, 1.8% work from home (2006-2010 5-year est.); Travel time to work: 25.0% less than 15 minutes, 35.7% 15 to 30 minutes, 25.6% 30 to 45 minutes, 6.0% 45 to 60 minutes, 7.7% 60 minutes or more (2006-2010 5-year est.)

NEWVILLE (borough). Covers a land area of 0.419 square miles and a water area of 0.009 square miles. Located at 40.17° N. Lat; 77.40° W. Long. Elevation is 518 feet.

History: Laid out 1794, incorporated 1817.

Population: 1,360 (1990); 1,367 (2000); 1,326 (2010); Density: 3,161.4 persons per square mile (2010); Race: 97.5% White, 0.7% Black, 0.2% Asian, 0.3% American Indian/Alaska Native, 0.0% Native Hawaiian/Other Pacific Islander, 1.3% Other, 0.8% Hispanic of any race (2010); Average household size: 2.45 (2010); Median age: 36.2 (2010); Males per 100

females: 95.0 (2010); Marriage status: 25.6% never married, 54.4% now married, 6.9% widowed, 13.0% divorced (2006-2010 5-year est.); Foreign born: 0.2% (2006-2010 5-year est.); Ancestry (includes multiple ancestries): 38.5% German, 10.8% American, 9.0% Irish, 6.6% English, 5.2% Scotch-Irish (2006-2010 5-year est.).

Economy: Single-family building permits issued: 1 (2011); Multi-family building permits issued: 0 (2011); Employment by occupation: 5.0% management, 6.3% professional, 12.3% services, 22.6% sales, 1.4% farming, 9.9% construction, 9.9% production (2006-2010 5-year est.).

Income: Per capita income: $20,363 (2006-2010 5-year est.); Median household income: $40,670 (2006-2010 5-year est.); Average household income: $45,215 (2006-2010 5-year est.); Percent of households with income of $100,000 or more: 3.1% (2006-2010 5-year est.); Poverty rate: 10.1% (2006-2010 5-year est.).

Education: Percent of population age 25 and over with: High school diploma (including GED) or higher: 84.2% (2006-2010 5-year est.); Bachelor's degree or higher: 20.4% (2006-2010 5-year est.); Master's degree or higher: 5.2% (2006-2010 5-year est.).

School District(s)

Big Spring SD (KG-12)
    2010-11 Enrollment: 2,846 . . . . (717) 776-2000

Housing: Homeownership rate: 51.7% (2010); Median home value: $123,500 (2006-2010 5-year est.); Median contract rent: $476 per month (2006-2010 5-year est.); Median year structure built: before 1940 (2006-2010 5-year est.).

Safety: Violent crime rate: 7.5 per 10,000 population; Property crime rate: 315.8 per 10,000 population (2011).

Transportation: Commute to work: 93.9% car, 0.0% public transportation, 4.4% walk, 1.6% work from home (2006-2010 5-year est.); Travel time to work: 23.5% less than 15 minutes, 46.0% 15 to 30 minutes, 21.7% 30 to 45 minutes, 6.3% 45 to 60 minutes, 2.5% 60 minutes or more (2006-2010 5-year est.)

Additional Information Contacts

Greater Carlisle Area Chamber of Commerce . . . . (717) 243-4515
    http://carlislechamber.org

NORTH MIDDLETON (township). Covers a land area of 23.193 square miles and a water area of 0.336 square miles. Located at 40.25° N. Lat; 77.21° W. Long.

Population: 9,996 (1990); 10,197 (2000); 11,143 (2010); Density: 480.4 persons per square mile (2010); Race: 91.6% White, 3.9% Black, 1.4% Asian, 0.2% American Indian/Alaska Native, 0.0% Native Hawaiian/Other Pacific Islander, 2.9% Other, 2.7% Hispanic of any race (2010); Average household size: 2.51 (2010); Median age: 41.4 (2010); Males per 100 females: 96.2 (2010); Marriage status: 17.2% never married, 66.8% now married, 6.0% widowed, 10.1% divorced (2006-2010 5-year est.); Foreign born: 6.9% (2006-2010 5-year est.); Ancestry (includes multiple ancestries): 30.2% German, 16.5% Irish, 9.9% English, 9.4% American, 8.3% Italian (2006-2010 5-year est.).

Economy: Single-family building permits issued: 15 (2011); Multi-family building permits issued: 4 (2011); Employment by occupation: 10.9% management, 6.0% professional, 8.7% services, 14.2% sales, 6.1% farming, 9.6% construction, 11.9% production (2006-2010 5-year est.).

Income: Per capita income: $27,634 (2006-2010 5-year est.); Median household income: $61,656 (2006-2010 5-year est.); Average household income: $70,318 (2006-2010 5-year est.); Percent of households with income of $100,000 or more: 21.1% (2006-2010 5-year est.); Poverty rate: 6.5% (2006-2010 5-year est.).

Education: Percent of population age 25 and over with: High school diploma (including GED) or higher: 86.4% (2006-2010 5-year est.); Bachelor's degree or higher: 25.9% (2006-2010 5-year est.); Master's degree or higher: 9.9% (2006-2010 5-year est.).

Housing: Homeownership rate: 74.5% (2010); Median home value: $160,000 (2006-2010 5-year est.); Median contract rent: $649 per month (2006-2010 5-year est.); Median year structure built: 1975 (2006-2010 5-year est.).

Safety: Violent crime rate: 4.5 per 10,000 population; Property crime rate: 59.0 per 10,000 population (2011).

Transportation: Commute to work: 91.7% car, 0.2% public transportation, 3.8% walk, 3.6% work from home (2006-2010 5-year est.); Travel time to work: 33.1% less than 15 minutes, 35.2% 15 to 30 minutes, 23.1% 30 to 45 minutes, 5.4% 45 to 60 minutes, 3.2% 60 minutes or more (2006-2010 5-year est.)

Additional Information Contacts

Greater Carlisle Area Chamber of Commerce .... (717) 243-4515
  http://carlislechamber.org
North Middleton Township. .... (717) 243-8550
  http://www.northmiddleton-township.org

NORTH NEWTON (township). Covers a land area of 22.765 square miles and a water area of 0.084 square miles. Located at 40.14° N. Lat; 77.45° W. Long.

Population: 1,779 (1990); 2,169 (2000); 2,430 (2010); Density: 106.7 persons per square mile (2010); Race: 97.8% White, 0.0% Black, 0.4% Asian, 0.1% American Indian/Alaska Native, 0.0% Native Hawaiian/Other Pacific Islander, 1.7% Other, 1.0% Hispanic of any race (2010); Average household size: 2.81 (2010); Median age: 38.1 (2010); Males per 100 females: 100.2 (2010); Marriage status: 19.7% never married, 61.7% now married, 7.6% widowed, 11.0% divorced (2006-2010 5-year est.); Foreign born: 0.5% (2006-2010 5-year est.); Ancestry (includes multiple ancestries): 38.6% German, 13.3% Irish, 11.8% American, 5.8% English, 3.0% Swiss (2006-2010 5-year est.).

Economy: Single-family building permits issued: 2 (2011); Multi-family building permits issued: 0 (2011); Employment by occupation: 4.8% management, 2.2% professional, 10.8% services, 17.5% sales, 2.3% farming, 21.4% construction, 12.2% production (2006-2010 5-year est.).

Income: Per capita income: $24,203 (2006-2010 5-year est.); Median household income: $50,846 (2006-2010 5-year est.); Average household income: $61,269 (2006-2010 5-year est.); Percent of households with income of $100,000 or more: 12.7% (2006-2010 5-year est.); Poverty rate: 5.6% (2006-2010 5-year est.).

Education: Percent of population age 25 and over with: High school diploma (including GED) or higher: 82.4% (2006-2010 5-year est.); Bachelor's degree or higher: 10.9% (2006-2010 5-year est.); Master's degree or higher: 4.0% (2006-2010 5-year est.).

Housing: Homeownership rate: 85.6% (2010); Median home value: $182,200 (2006-2010 5-year est.); Median contract rent: $436 per month (2006-2010 5-year est.); Median year structure built: 1979 (2006-2010 5-year est.).

Transportation: Commute to work: 89.7% car, 2.1% public transportation, 0.0% walk, 7.7% work from home (2006-2010 5-year est.); Travel time to work: 31.1% less than 15 minutes, 24.6% 15 to 30 minutes, 25.7% 30 to 45 minutes, 10.1% 45 to 60 minutes, 8.5% 60 minutes or more (2006-2010 5-year est.)

Additional Information Contacts

Shippensburg Area Chamber of Commerce .... (717) 532-5509
  http://www.shippensburg.org

PENN (township). Covers a land area of 29.565 square miles and a water area of 0.069 square miles. Located at 40.10° N. Lat; 77.34° W. Long.

Population: 2,412 (1990); 2,807 (2000); 2,924 (2010); Density: 98.9 persons per square mile (2010); Race: 97.9% White, 0.8% Black, 0.2% Asian, 0.3% American Indian/Alaska Native, 0.1% Native Hawaiian/Other Pacific Islander, 0.7% Other, 1.1% Hispanic of any race (2010); Average household size: 2.70 (2010); Median age: 41.3 (2010); Males per 100 females: 101.2 (2010); Marriage status: 22.5% never married, 68.4% now married, 4.1% widowed, 5.0% divorced (2006-2010 5-year est.); Foreign born: 1.0% (2006-2010 5-year est.); Ancestry (includes multiple ancestries): 44.4% German, 12.1% Irish, 9.0% English, 7.8% American, 4.8% French (2006-2010 5-year est.).

Economy: Single-family building permits issued: 5 (2011); Multi-family building permits issued: 0 (2011); Employment by occupation: 8.4% management, 3.0% professional, 14.0% services, 20.6% sales, 4.5% farming, 13.9% construction, 7.7% production (2006-2010 5-year est.).

Income: Per capita income: $24,571 (2006-2010 5-year est.); Median household income: $56,286 (2006-2010 5-year est.); Average household income: $64,052 (2006-2010 5-year est.); Percent of households with income of $100,000 or more: 14.4% (2006-2010 5-year est.); Poverty rate: 10.3% (2006-2010 5-year est.).

Education: Percent of population age 25 and over with: High school diploma (including GED) or higher: 85.5% (2006-2010 5-year est.); Bachelor's degree or higher: 15.6% (2006-2010 5-year est.); Master's degree or higher: 4.8% (2006-2010 5-year est.).

Housing: Homeownership rate: 88.2% (2010); Median home value: $161,200 (2006-2010 5-year est.); Median contract rent: $585 per month (2006-2010 5-year est.); Median year structure built: 1976 (2006-2010 5-year est.).

Transportation: Commute to work: 91.3% car, 0.5% public transportation, 1.8% walk, 5.2% work from home (2006-2010 5-year est.); Travel time to work: 13.7% less than 15 minutes, 44.0% 15 to 30 minutes, 23.2% 30 to 45 minutes, 14.2% 45 to 60 minutes, 4.9% 60 minutes or more (2006-2010 5-year est.)

Additional Information Contacts

Greater Carlisle Area Chamber of Commerce .... (717) 243-4515
  http://carlislechamber.org

PLAINFIELD (CDP). Covers a land area of 0.646 square miles and a water area of 0 square miles. Located at 40.20° N. Lat; 77.28° W. Long. Elevation is 495 feet.

Population: 397 (1990); 376 (2000); 399 (2010); Density: 617.7 persons per square mile (2010); Race: 97.2% White, 1.5% Black, 0.3% Asian, 0.0% American Indian/Alaska Native, 0.0% Native Hawaiian/Other Pacific Islander, 1.0% Other, 1.8% Hispanic of any race (2010); Average household size: 2.43 (2010); Median age: 38.1 (2010); Males per 100 females: 100.5 (2010); Marriage status: 21.3% never married, 44.3% now married, 26.2% widowed, 8.2% divorced (2006-2010 5-year est.); Foreign born: 0.0% (2006-2010 5-year est.); Ancestry (includes multiple ancestries): 73.8% German, 34.4% English, 21.3% Irish (2006-2010 5-year est.).

Economy: Employment by occupation: 0.0% management, 0.0% professional, 0.0% services, 0.0% sales, 0.0% farming, 0.0% construction, 43.8% production (2006-2010 5-year est.).

Income: Per capita income: $34,118 (2006-2010 5-year est.); Median household income: $39,095 (2006-2010 5-year est.); Average household income: $43,715 (2006-2010 5-year est.); Percent of households with income of $100,000 or more: n/a (2006-2010 5-year est.); Poverty rate: 0.0% (2006-2010 5-year est.).

Education: Percent of population age 25 and over with: High school diploma (including GED) or higher: 100.0% (2006-2010 5-year est.); Bachelor's degree or higher: 47.5% (2006-2010 5-year est.); Master's degree or higher: 21.3% (2006-2010 5-year est.).

Housing: Homeownership rate: 70.2% (2010); Median home value: $96,200 (2006-2010 5-year est.); Median contract rent: n/a per month (2006-2010 5-year est.); Median year structure built: 1944 (2006-2010 5-year est.).

Transportation: Commute to work: 100.0% car, 0.0% public transportation, 0.0% walk, 0.0% work from home (2006-2010 5-year est.); Travel time to work: 56.3% less than 15 minutes, 43.8% 15 to 30 minutes, 0.0% 30 to 45 minutes, 0.0% 45 to 60 minutes, 0.0% 60 minutes or more (2006-2010 5-year est.)

SCHLUSSER (CDP). Covers a land area of 2.918 square miles and a water area of 0.075 square miles. Located at 40.24° N. Lat; 77.18° W. Long. Elevation is 423 feet.

Population: 4,804 (1990); 4,750 (2000); 5,265 (2010); Density: 1,804.6 persons per square mile (2010); Race: 91.0% White, 3.8% Black, 1.9% Asian, 0.2% American Indian/Alaska Native, 0.0% Native Hawaiian/Other Pacific Islander, 3.1% Other, 2.5% Hispanic of any race (2010); Average household size: 2.41 (2010); Median age: 40.3 (2010); Males per 100 females: 95.9 (2010); Marriage status: 14.2% never married, 69.3% now married, 3.3% widowed, 13.3% divorced (2006-2010 5-year est.); Foreign born: 9.7% (2006-2010 5-year est.); Ancestry (includes multiple ancestries): 30.7% German, 19.2% Irish, 12.6% Italian, 9.4% English, 8.5% American (2006-2010 5-year est.).

Economy: Employment by occupation: 8.2% management, 5.3% professional, 9.8% services, 17.9% sales, 4.4% farming, 11.6% construction, 14.2% production (2006-2010 5-year est.).

Income: Per capita income: $27,503 (2006-2010 5-year est.); Median household income: $61,948 (2006-2010 5-year est.); Average household income: $68,796 (2006-2010 5-year est.); Percent of households with income of $100,000 or more: 19.4% (2006-2010 5-year est.); Poverty rate: 1.7% (2006-2010 5-year est.).

Education: Percent of population age 25 and over with: High school diploma (including GED) or higher: 91.1% (2006-2010 5-year est.); Bachelor's degree or higher: 22.8% (2006-2010 5-year est.); Master's degree or higher: 7.9% (2006-2010 5-year est.).

Housing: Homeownership rate: 76.2% (2010); Median home value: $149,400 (2006-2010 5-year est.); Median contract rent: $546 per month (2006-2010 5-year est.); Median year structure built: 1975 (2006-2010 5-year est.).

Transportation: Commute to work: 97.9% car, 0.0% public transportation, 0.0% walk, 2.0% work from home (2006-2010 5-year est.); Travel time to

work: 26.5% less than 15 minutes, 36.6% 15 to 30 minutes, 26.0% 30 to 45 minutes, 7.1% 45 to 60 minutes, 3.8% 60 minutes or more (2006-2010 5-year est.)

Additional Information Contacts
Mechanicsburg Chamber of Commerce . . . . (717) 796-0811
  http://mechanicsburgchamber.org

SHIPPENSBURG (borough). Covers a land area of 1.990 square miles and a water area of 0.004 square miles. Located at 40.05° N. Lat; 77.52° W. Long. Elevation is 656 feet.

Population: 5,331 (1990); 5,586 (2000); 5,492 (2010); Density: 2,759.3 persons per square mile (2010); Race: 90.6% White, 4.4% Black, 1.2% Asian, 0.3% American Indian/Alaska Native, 0.0% Native Hawaiian/Other Pacific Islander, 3.5% Other, 3.3% Hispanic of any race (2010); Average household size: 2.23 (2010); Median age: 29.0 (2010); Males per 100 females: 91.9 (2010); Marriage status: 46.2% never married, 35.7% now married, 8.9% widowed, 9.2% divorced (2006-2010 5-year est.); Foreign born: 3.1% (2006-2010 5-year est.); Ancestry (includes multiple ancestries): 38.6% German, 14.7% Irish, 10.6% English, 5.1% Italian, 4.1% American (2006-2010 5-year est.).
Economy: Single-family building permits issued: 0 (2011); Multi-family building permits issued: 0 (2011); Employment by occupation: 7.4% management, 3.4% professional, 12.2% services, 13.2% sales, 6.8% farming, 7.0% construction, 7.1% production (2006-2010 5-year est.).
Income: Per capita income: $20,511 (2006-2010 5-year est.); Median household income: $38,011 (2006-2010 5-year est.); Average household income: $44,446 (2006-2010 5-year est.); Percent of households with income of $100,000 or more: 6.7% (2006-2010 5-year est.); Poverty rate: 18.6% (2006-2010 5-year est.).
Education: Percent of population age 25 and over with: High school diploma (including GED) or higher: 85.7% (2006-2010 5-year est.); Bachelor's degree or higher: 29.6% (2006-2010 5-year est.); Master's degree or higher: 11.3% (2006-2010 5-year est.).

School District(s)
Shippensburg Area SD (KG-12)
  2010-11 Enrollment: 3,420 . . . . (717) 530-2700
Shippensburg Area SD (KG-12)
  2010-11 Enrollment: 3,420 . . . . (717) 530-2700

Four-year College(s)
Shippensburg University of Pennsylvania (Public)
  Fall 2010 Enrollment: 7,594 . . . . (717) 477-7447
  2011-12 Tuition: In-state $8,856; Out-of-state $18,394
Housing: Homeownership rate: 39.6% (2010); Median home value: $137,600 (2006-2010 5-year est.); Median contract rent: $510 per month (2006-2010 5-year est.); Median year structure built: 1952 (2006-2010 5-year est.).
Safety: Violent crime rate: 0.0 per 10,000 population; Property crime rate: 163.3 per 10,000 population (2011).
Newspapers: News Chronicle (Community news; Circulation 6,400); The Sentinel - Shippensburg Bureau (Community news); Valley Times-Star (Community news; Circulation 3,200)
Transportation: Commute to work: 88.1% car, 2.3% public transportation, 6.9% walk, 2.8% work from home (2006-2010 5-year est.); Travel time to work: 53.1% less than 15 minutes, 25.9% 15 to 30 minutes, 10.7% 30 to 45 minutes, 7.0% 45 to 60 minutes, 3.3% 60 minutes or more (2006-2010 5-year est.)

Additional Information Contacts
Borough of Shippensburg . . . . (717) 532-2147
  http://www.borough.shippensburg.pa.us
Shippensburg Area Chamber of Commerce . . . . (717) 532-5509
  http://www.shippensburg.org

SHIPPENSBURG (township). Covers a land area of 2.517 square miles and a water area of 0.013 square miles. Located at 40.06° N. Lat; 77.51° W. Long. Elevation is 656 feet.

Population: 4,606 (1990); 4,504 (2000); 5,429 (2010); Density: 2,157.2 persons per square mile (2010); Race: 89.6% White, 6.6% Black, 1.2% Asian, 0.0% American Indian/Alaska Native, 0.0% Native Hawaiian/Other Pacific Islander, 2.6% Other, 2.4% Hispanic of any race (2010); Average household size: 2.36 (2010); Median age: 20.7 (2010); Males per 100 females: 97.5 (2010); Marriage status: 84.3% never married, 8.8% now married, 2.2% widowed, 4.7% divorced (2006-2010 5-year est.); Foreign born: 0.9% (2006-2010 5-year est.); Ancestry (includes multiple ancestries): 36.6% German, 18.1% Irish, 14.8% Italian, 7.7% Polish, 4.6% English (2006-2010 5-year est.).

Economy: Single-family building permits issued: 4 (2011); Multi-family building permits issued: 0 (2011); Employment by occupation: 3.9% management, 1.9% professional, 19.7% services, 26.0% sales, 6.4% farming, 6.0% construction, 3.2% production (2006-2010 5-year est.).
Income: Per capita income: $8,886 (2006-2010 5-year est.); Median household income: $26,011 (2006-2010 5-year est.); Average household income: $34,423 (2006-2010 5-year est.); Percent of households with income of $100,000 or more: 4.6% (2006-2010 5-year est.); Poverty rate: 41.0% (2006-2010 5-year est.).
Taxes: Total city taxes per capita: $107 (2009); City property taxes per capita: $23 (2009).
Education: Percent of population age 25 and over with: High school diploma (including GED) or higher: 73.5% (2006-2010 5-year est.); Bachelor's degree or higher: 15.7% (2006-2010 5-year est.); Master's degree or higher: 6.7% (2006-2010 5-year est.).

Four-year College(s)
Shippensburg University of Pennsylvania (Public)
  Fall 2010 Enrollment: 7,594 . . . . (717) 477-7447
  2011-12 Tuition: In-state $8,856; Out-of-state $18,394
Housing: Homeownership rate: 35.7% (2010); Median home value: $47,500 (2006-2010 5-year est.); Median contract rent: $743 per month (2006-2010 5-year est.); Median year structure built: 1983 (2006-2010 5-year est.).
Newspapers: News Chronicle (Community news; Circulation 6,400); The Sentinel - Shippensburg Bureau (Community news); Valley Times-Star (Community news; Circulation 3,200)
Transportation: Commute to work: 70.2% car, 0.0% public transportation, 24.2% walk, 5.2% work from home (2006-2010 5-year est.); Travel time to work: 48.7% less than 15 minutes, 32.9% 15 to 30 minutes, 11.1% 30 to 45 minutes, 4.4% 45 to 60 minutes, 2.8% 60 minutes or more (2006-2010 5-year est.)

Additional Information Contacts
Shippensburg Area Chamber of Commerce . . . . (717) 532-5509
  http://www.shippensburg.org

SHIPPENSBURG UNIVERSITY (CDP). Covers a land area of 0.279 square miles and a water area of <.001 square miles. Located at 40.06° N. Lat; 77.52° W. Long.

Population: n/a (1990); n/a (2000); 2,625 (2010); Density: 9,403.4 persons per square mile (2010); Race: 85.7% White, 10.0% Black, 1.2% Asian, 0.1% American Indian/Alaska Native, 0.0% Native Hawaiian/Other Pacific Islander, 3.0% Other, 3.4% Hispanic of any race (2010); Average household size: 2.61 (2010); Median age: 19.7 (2010); Males per 100 females: 96.9 (2010); Marriage status: 98.8% never married, 0.0% now married, 0.0% widowed, 1.2% divorced (2006-2010 5-year est.); Foreign born: 0.9% (2006-2010 5-year est.); Ancestry (includes multiple ancestries): 37.9% German, 19.8% Irish, 18.4% Italian, 8.1% Polish, 3.5% Scottish (2006-2010 5-year est.).
Economy: Employment by occupation: 1.8% management, 1.6% professional, 22.2% services, 33.8% sales, 6.6% farming, 3.2% construction, 1.6% production (2006-2010 5-year est.).
Income: Per capita income: $5,365 (2006-2010 5-year est.); Median household income: $13,306 (2006-2010 5-year est.); Average household income: $13,916 (2006-2010 5-year est.); Percent of households with income of $100,000 or more: n/a (2006-2010 5-year est.); Poverty rate: 100.0% (2006-2010 5-year est.).
Education: Percent of population age 25 and over with: High school diploma (including GED) or higher: 54.8% (2006-2010 5-year est.); Bachelor's degree or higher: 7.1% (2006-2010 5-year est.); Master's degree or higher: 7.1% (2006-2010 5-year est.).
Housing: Homeownership rate: 0.0% (2010); Median home value: n/a (2006-2010 5-year est.); Median contract rent: $628 per month (2006-2010 5-year est.); Median year structure built: 1976 (2006-2010 5-year est.).
Transportation: Commute to work: 57.3% car, 0.0% public transportation, 33.6% walk, 8.4% work from home (2006-2010 5-year est.); Travel time to work: 62.2% less than 15 minutes, 30.1% 15 to 30 minutes, 0.8% 30 to 45 minutes, 5.3% 45 to 60 minutes, 1.8% 60 minutes or more (2006-2010 5-year est.)

SHIREMANSTOWN (borough). Covers a land area of 0.297 square miles and a water area of 0 square miles. Located at 40.22° N. Lat; 76.96° W. Long. Elevation is 420 feet.

Population: 1,567 (1990); 1,521 (2000); 1,569 (2010); Density: 5,283.8 persons per square mile (2010); Race: 93.1% White, 2.3% Black, 1.5% Asian, 0.0% American Indian/Alaska Native, 0.3% Native Hawaiian/Other

Pacific Islander, 2.8% Other, 4.9% Hispanic of any race (2010); Average household size: 2.19 (2010); Median age: 38.8 (2010); Males per 100 females: 91.8 (2010); Marriage status: 25.6% never married, 48.6% now married, 11.6% widowed, 14.3% divorced (2006-2010 5-year est.); Foreign born: 4.9% (2006-2010 5-year est.); Ancestry (includes multiple ancestries): 41.6% German, 17.9% Irish, 13.7% English, 9.0% Italian, 3.9% Scotch-Irish (2006-2010 5-year est.).

Economy: Single-family building permits issued: 0 (2011); Multi-family building permits issued: 0 (2011); Employment by occupation: 14.7% management, 4.9% professional, 10.3% services, 21.2% sales, 2.7% farming, 7.8% construction, 6.5% production (2006-2010 5-year est.).

Income: Per capita income: $29,111 (2006-2010 5-year est.); Median household income: $45,938 (2006-2010 5-year est.); Average household income: $56,551 (2006-2010 5-year est.); Percent of households with income of $100,000 or more: 11.9% (2006-2010 5-year est.); Poverty rate: 7.1% (2006-2010 5-year est.).

Education: Percent of population age 25 and over with: High school diploma (including GED) or higher: 92.3% (2006-2010 5-year est.); Bachelor's degree or higher: 28.6% (2006-2010 5-year est.); Master's degree or higher: 4.4% (2006-2010 5-year est.).

Housing: Homeownership rate: 61.4% (2010); Median home value: $161,200 (2006-2010 5-year est.); Median contract rent: $591 per month (2006-2010 5-year est.); Median year structure built: 1961 (2006-2010 5-year est.).

Transportation: Commute to work: 92.3% car, 1.3% public transportation, 2.0% walk, 0.6% work from home (2006-2010 5-year est.); Travel time to work: 41.7% less than 15 minutes, 38.4% 15 to 30 minutes, 13.3% 30 to 45 minutes, 3.2% 45 to 60 minutes, 3.4% 60 minutes or more (2006-2010 5-year est.).

Additional Information Contacts

West Shore Chamber of Commerce . . . . (717) 761-0702
  http://www.wschamber.org

SILVER SPRING (township). Covers a land area of 32.314 square miles and a water area of 0.507 square miles. Located at 40.25° N. Lat; 77.06° W. Long.

Population: 8,369 (1990); 10,592 (2000); 13,657 (2010); Density: 422.6 persons per square mile (2010); Race: 90.8% White, 1.4% Black, 5.4% Asian, 0.1% American Indian/Alaska Native, 0.0% Native Hawaiian/Other Pacific Islander, 2.3% Other, 2.0% Hispanic of any race (2010); Average household size: 2.45 (2010); Median age: 43.8 (2010); Males per 100 females: 96.1 (2010); Marriage status: 21.4% never married, 64.2% now married, 6.2% widowed, 8.2% divorced (2006-2010 5-year est.); Foreign born: 5.2% (2006-2010 5-year est.); Ancestry (includes multiple ancestries): 38.8% German, 14.8% Irish, 12.8% English, 7.9% Italian, 6.5% American (2006-2010 5-year est.).

Economy: Single-family building permits issued: 175 (2011); Multi-family building permits issued: 0 (2011); Employment by occupation: 14.1% management, 7.6% professional, 7.8% services, 15.2% sales, 5.3% farming, 4.7% construction, 4.2% production (2006-2010 5-year est.).

Income: Per capita income: $36,246 (2006-2010 5-year est.); Median household income: $75,498 (2006-2010 5-year est.); Average household income: $90,654 (2006-2010 5-year est.); Percent of households with income of $100,000 or more: 32.0% (2006-2010 5-year est.); Poverty rate: 3.3% (2006-2010 5-year est.).

Taxes: Total city taxes per capita: $354 (2009); City property taxes per capita: $114 (2009).

Education: Percent of population age 25 and over with: High school diploma (including GED) or higher: 94.7% (2006-2010 5-year est.); Bachelor's degree or higher: 35.9% (2006-2010 5-year est.); Master's degree or higher: 14.1% (2006-2010 5-year est.).

Housing: Homeownership rate: 81.3% (2010); Median home value: $203,500 (2006-2010 5-year est.); Median contract rent: $900 per month (2006-2010 5-year est.); Median year structure built: 1988 (2006-2010 5-year est.).

Safety: Violent crime rate: 4.4 per 10,000 population; Property crime rate: 137.2 per 10,000 population (2011).

Transportation: Commute to work: 94.3% car, 0.3% public transportation, 1.1% walk, 2.9% work from home (2006-2010 5-year est.); Travel time to work: 23.8% less than 15 minutes, 49.1% 15 to 30 minutes, 17.8% 30 to 45 minutes, 5.6% 45 to 60 minutes, 3.8% 60 minutes or more (2006-2010 5-year est.)

Additional Information Contacts

Lancaster Chamber of Commerce & Industry . . . . (717) 397-3531
  http://www.lancasterchamber.com

Silver Spring Township . . . . (717) 766-0178
  http://www.silverspringtwp-pa.gov

SOUTH MIDDLETON (township). Covers a land area of 48.714 square miles and a water area of 0.308 square miles. Located at 40.14° N. Lat; 77.17° W. Long.

Population: 10,248 (1990); 12,939 (2000); 14,663 (2010); Density: 301.0 persons per square mile (2010); Race: 96.2% White, 0.9% Black, 1.2% Asian, 0.2% American Indian/Alaska Native, 0.0% Native Hawaiian/Other Pacific Islander, 1.5% Other, 1.7% Hispanic of any race (2010); Average household size: 2.44 (2010); Median age: 45.9 (2010); Males per 100 females: 92.7 (2010); Marriage status: 18.2% never married, 65.9% now married, 7.0% widowed, 9.0% divorced (2006-2010 5-year est.); Foreign born: 2.5% (2006-2010 5-year est.); Ancestry (includes multiple ancestries): 43.2% German, 16.3% Irish, 10.0% English, 7.3% American, 5.6% Italian (2006-2010 5-year est.).

Economy: Single-family building permits issued: 33 (2011); Multi-family building permits issued: 0 (2011); Employment by occupation: 10.3% management, 6.0% professional, 7.2% services, 16.4% sales, 5.6% farming, 8.5% construction, 6.6% production (2006-2010 5-year est.).

Income: Per capita income: $30,889 (2006-2010 5-year est.); Median household income: $66,579 (2006-2010 5-year est.); Average household income: $76,445 (2006-2010 5-year est.); Percent of households with income of $100,000 or more: 24.7% (2006-2010 5-year est.); Poverty rate: 2.7% (2006-2010 5-year est.).

Education: Percent of population age 25 and over with: High school diploma (including GED) or higher: 91.0% (2006-2010 5-year est.); Bachelor's degree or higher: 32.8% (2006-2010 5-year est.); Master's degree or higher: 10.7% (2006-2010 5-year est.).

Housing: Homeownership rate: 83.4% (2010); Median home value: $181,000 (2006-2010 5-year est.); Median contract rent: $625 per month (2006-2010 5-year est.); Median year structure built: 1982 (2006-2010 5-year est.).

Transportation: Commute to work: 91.6% car, 0.3% public transportation, 2.9% walk, 4.0% work from home (2006-2010 5-year est.); Travel time to work: 34.5% less than 15 minutes, 36.1% 15 to 30 minutes, 21.3% 30 to 45 minutes, 5.7% 45 to 60 minutes, 2.4% 60 minutes or more (2006-2010 5-year est.).

Additional Information Contacts

Greater Carlisle Area Chamber of Commerce . . . . (717) 243-4515
  http://carlislechamber.org
South Middleton Township . . . . (717) 258-5324
  http://www.smiddleton.com

SOUTH NEWTON (township). Covers a land area of 11.319 square miles and a water area of 0.071 square miles. Located at 40.07° N. Lat; 77.39° W. Long.

Population: 1,166 (1990); 1,290 (2000); 1,383 (2010); Density: 122.2 persons per square mile (2010); Race: 97.5% White, 0.8% Black, 0.1% Asian, 0.2% American Indian/Alaska Native, 0.0% Native Hawaiian/Other Pacific Islander, 1.4% Other, 0.9% Hispanic of any race (2010); Average household size: 2.85 (2010); Median age: 38.8 (2010); Males per 100 females: 101.9 (2010); Marriage status: 25.4% never married, 58.8% now married, 8.3% widowed, 7.5% divorced (2006-2010 5-year est.); Foreign born: 0.5% (2006-2010 5-year est.); Ancestry (includes multiple ancestries): 40.5% German, 11.8% Irish, 8.0% American, 5.6% Swiss, 5.5% English (2006-2010 5-year est.).

Economy: Single-family building permits issued: 3 (2011); Multi-family building permits issued: 0 (2011); Employment by occupation: 17.3% management, 1.2% professional, 9.3% services, 11.3% sales, 1.8% farming, 20.8% construction, 15.2% production (2006-2010 5-year est.).

Income: Per capita income: $24,214 (2006-2010 5-year est.); Median household income: $58,241 (2006-2010 5-year est.); Average household income: $69,181 (2006-2010 5-year est.); Percent of households with income of $100,000 or more: 18.9% (2006-2010 5-year est.); Poverty rate: 6.8% (2006-2010 5-year est.).

Education: Percent of population age 25 and over with: High school diploma (including GED) or higher: 75.2% (2006-2010 5-year est.); Bachelor's degree or higher: 15.5% (2006-2010 5-year est.); Master's degree or higher: 4.8% (2006-2010 5-year est.).

Housing: Homeownership rate: 84.6% (2010); Median home value: $155,600 (2006-2010 5-year est.); Median contract rent: $535 per month (2006-2010 5-year est.); Median year structure built: 1973 (2006-2010 5-year est.).

Transportation: Commute to work: 88.0% car, 2.0% public transportation, 1.5% walk, 7.0% work from home (2006-2010 5-year est.); Travel time to work: 13.9% less than 15 minutes, 45.8% 15 to 30 minutes, 30.0% 30 to 45 minutes, 5.6% 45 to 60 minutes, 4.7% 60 minutes or more (2006-2010 5-year est.)

Additional Information Contacts

Lower Bucks County Chamber of Commerce . . . . (215) 943-7400
  http://www.lbccc.org

SOUTHAMPTON (township). Covers a land area of 51.433 square miles and a water area of 0.166 square miles. Located at 40.04° N. Lat; 77.46° W. Long.

Population: 3,552 (1990); 4,787 (2000); 6,359 (2010); Density: 123.6 persons per square mile (2010); Race: 96.6% White, 0.8% Black, 1.1% Asian, 0.1% American Indian/Alaska Native, 0.0% Native Hawaiian/Other Pacific Islander, 1.4% Other, 1.5% Hispanic of any race (2010); Average household size: 2.72 (2010); Median age: 36.5 (2010); Males per 100 females: 97.9 (2010); Marriage status: 19.4% never married, 71.2% now married, 4.7% widowed, 4.8% divorced (2006-2010 5-year est.); Foreign born: 1.9% (2006-2010 5-year est.); Ancestry (includes multiple ancestries): 32.2% German, 14.8% American, 9.6% Irish, 6.9% English, 4.9% French (2006-2010 5-year est.).

Economy: Single-family building permits issued: 8 (2011); Multi-family building permits issued: 0 (2011); Employment by occupation: 6.3% management, 4.0% professional, 9.3% services, 19.8% sales, 3.5% farming, 11.7% construction, 7.4% production (2006-2010 5-year est.).

Income: Per capita income: $23,301 (2006-2010 5-year est.); Median household income: $55,522 (2006-2010 5-year est.); Average household income: $59,832 (2006-2010 5-year est.); Percent of households with income of $100,000 or more: 14.1% (2006-2010 5-year est.); Poverty rate: 7.7% (2006-2010 5-year est.).

Education: Percent of population age 25 and over with: High school diploma (including GED) or higher: 82.1% (2006-2010 5-year est.); Bachelor's degree or higher: 19.8% (2006-2010 5-year est.); Master's degree or higher: 6.1% (2006-2010 5-year est.).

Housing: Homeownership rate: 85.1% (2010); Median home value: $165,700 (2006-2010 5-year est.); Median contract rent: $541 per month (2006-2010 5-year est.); Median year structure built: 1990 (2006-2010 5-year est.).

Transportation: Commute to work: 90.4% car, 0.9% public transportation, 0.0% walk, 6.3% work from home (2006-2010 5-year est.); Travel time to work: 32.8% less than 15 minutes, 36.3% 15 to 30 minutes, 17.4% 30 to 45 minutes, 11.2% 45 to 60 minutes, 2.3% 60 minutes or more (2006-2010 5-year est.)

Additional Information Contacts

Shippensburg Area Chamber of Commerce . . . . (717) 532-5509
  http://www.shippensburg.org

SUMMERDALE (unincorporated postal area)

Zip Code: 17093

Covers a land area of 0.374 square miles and a water area of <.001 square miles. Located at 40.30° N. Lat; 76.93° W. Long. Elevation is 381 feet. Population: 801 (2010); Density: 2,136.3 persons per square mile (2010); Race: 94.0% White, 2.4% Black, 1.9% Asian, 0.2% American Indian/Alaska Native, 0.0% Native Hawaiian/Other Pacific Islander, 1.5% Other, 1.1% Hispanic of any race (2010); Average household size: 2.30 (2010); Median age: 38.9 (2010); Males per 100 females: 96.3 (2010); Homeownership rate: 82.1% (2010)

UPPER ALLEN (township). Covers a land area of 13.198 square miles and a water area of 0.104 square miles. Located at 40.18° N. Lat; 76.98° W. Long.

Population: 13,365 (1990); 15,338 (2000); 18,059 (2010); Density: 1,368.4 persons per square mile (2010); Race: 91.6% White, 3.3% Black, 2.3% Asian, 0.1% American Indian/Alaska Native, 0.0% Native Hawaiian/Other Pacific Islander, 2.7% Other, 2.6% Hispanic of any race (2010); Average household size: 2.33 (2010); Median age: 38.2 (2010); Males per 100 females: 84.7 (2010); Marriage status: 35.4% never married, 51.0% now married, 6.0% widowed, 7.7% divorced (2006-2010 5-year est.); Foreign born: 4.0% (2006-2010 5-year est.); Ancestry (includes multiple ancestries): 36.9% German, 15.9% Irish, 10.9% Italian, 10.4% English, 6.0% Polish (2006-2010 5-year est.).

Economy: Single-family building permits issued: 64 (2011); Multi-family building permits issued: 0 (2011); Employment by occupation: 15.0%

management, 6.7% professional, 11.0% services, 17.3% sales, 4.9% farming, 4.3% construction, 4.1% production (2006-2010 5-year est.).

Income: Per capita income: $30,585 (2006-2010 5-year est.); Median household income: $66,565 (2006-2010 5-year est.); Average household income: $81,173 (2006-2010 5-year est.); Percent of households with income of $100,000 or more: 27.3% (2006-2010 5-year est.); Poverty rate: 6.1% (2006-2010 5-year est.).

Education: Percent of population age 25 and over with: High school diploma (including GED) or higher: 96.0% (2006-2010 5-year est.); Bachelor's degree or higher: 42.7% (2006-2010 5-year est.); Master's degree or higher: 15.3% (2006-2010 5-year est.).

Four-year College(s)

Messiah College (Private, Not-for-profit, Interdenominational)
  Fall 2010 Enrollment: 2,988 . . . . (717) 766-2511
  2011-12 Tuition: In-state $28,356; Out-of-state $28,356

Housing: Homeownership rate: 76.2% (2010); Median home value: $187,100 (2006-2010 5-year est.); Median contract rent: $754 per month (2006-2010 5-year est.); Median year structure built: 1981 (2006-2010 5-year est.).

Safety: Violent crime rate: 1.7 per 10,000 population; Property crime rate: 115.9 per 10,000 population (2011).

Transportation: Commute to work: 82.9% car, 0.6% public transportation, 12.5% walk, 3.2% work from home (2006-2010 5-year est.); Travel time to work: 40.4% less than 15 minutes, 40.7% 15 to 30 minutes, 12.6% 30 to 45 minutes, 3.4% 45 to 60 minutes, 3.0% 60 minutes or more (2006-2010 5-year est.)

Additional Information Contacts

Mechanicsburg Chamber of Commerce . . . . (717) 796-0811
  http://mechanicsburgchamber.org
Upper Allen Township . . . . (717) 766-0756
  http://www.upperallentwp.org

UPPER FRANKFORD (township). Covers a land area of 19.427 square miles and a water area of 0.187 square miles. Located at 40.24° N. Lat; 77.37° W. Long.

Population: 1,703 (1990); 1,807 (2000); 2,005 (2010); Density: 103.2 persons per square mile (2010); Race: 99.4% White, 0.1% Black, 0.2% Asian, 0.0% American Indian/Alaska Native, 0.0% Native Hawaiian/Other Pacific Islander, 0.3% Other, 1.0% Hispanic of any race (2010); Average household size: 2.55 (2010); Median age: 42.5 (2010); Males per 100 females: 102.7 (2010); Marriage status: 21.7% never married, 67.6% now married, 3.1% widowed, 7.6% divorced (2006-2010 5-year est.); Foreign born: 0.4% (2006-2010 5-year est.); Ancestry (includes multiple ancestries): 37.0% German, 11.9% Irish, 9.3% American, 6.0% English, 4.2% Scottish (2006-2010 5-year est.).

Economy: Single-family building permits issued: 1 (2011); Multi-family building permits issued: 0 (2011); Employment by occupation: 8.1% management, 1.9% professional, 8.6% services, 21.9% sales, 2.1% farming, 12.4% construction, 16.0% production (2006-2010 5-year est.).

Income: Per capita income: $23,282 (2006-2010 5-year est.); Median household income: $53,581 (2006-2010 5-year est.); Average household income: $62,624 (2006-2010 5-year est.); Percent of households with income of $100,000 or more: 15.3% (2006-2010 5-year est.); Poverty rate: 3.9% (2006-2010 5-year est.).

Education: Percent of population age 25 and over with: High school diploma (including GED) or higher: 83.8% (2006-2010 5-year est.); Bachelor's degree or higher: 12.7% (2006-2010 5-year est.); Master's degree or higher: 3.0% (2006-2010 5-year est.).

Housing: Homeownership rate: 87.9% (2010); Median home value: $118,700 (2006-2010 5-year est.); Median contract rent: $478 per month (2006-2010 5-year est.); Median year structure built: 1979 (2006-2010 5-year est.).

Transportation: Commute to work: 94.7% car, 0.9% public transportation, 2.0% walk, 2.1% work from home (2006-2010 5-year est.); Travel time to work: 13.3% less than 15 minutes, 48.3% 15 to 30 minutes, 19.6% 30 to 45 minutes, 12.3% 45 to 60 minutes, 6.5% 60 minutes or more (2006-2010 5-year est.)

Additional Information Contacts

Greater Carlisle Area Chamber of Commerce . . . . (717) 243-4515
  http://carlislechamber.org

UPPER MIFFLIN (township). Covers a land area of 21.717 square miles and a water area of 0.389 square miles. Located at 40.19° N. Lat; 77.50° W. Long.

Population: 1,013 (1990); 1,347 (2000); 1,304 (2010); Density: 60.0 persons per square mile (2010); Race: 98.3% White, 0.3% Black, 0.2% Asian, 0.0% American Indian/Alaska Native, 0.0% Native Hawaiian/Other Pacific Islander, 1.2% Other, 0.9% Hispanic of any race (2010); Average household size: 2.73 (2010); Median age: 41.3 (2010); Males per 100 females: 105.7 (2010); Marriage status: 20.9% never married, 69.7% now married, 3.8% widowed, 5.6% divorced (2006-2010 5-year est.); Foreign born: 0.7% (2006-2010 5-year est.); Ancestry (includes multiple ancestries): 40.6% German, 10.5% Irish, 8.6% English, 8.3% American, 4.1% French (2006-2010 5-year est.).

Economy: Single-family building permits issued: 1 (2011); Multi-family building permits issued: 0 (2011); Employment by occupation: 8.1% management, 1.4% professional, 14.8% services, 14.3% sales, 1.4% farming, 12.1% construction, 12.4% production (2006-2010 5-year est.).

Income: Per capita income: $21,949 (2006-2010 5-year est.); Median household income: $55,078 (2006-2010 5-year est.); Average household income: $60,673 (2006-2010 5-year est.); Percent of households with income of $100,000 or more: 11.2% (2006-2010 5-year est.); Poverty rate: 3.2% (2006-2010 5-year est.).

Education: Percent of population age 25 and over with: High school diploma (including GED) or higher: 82.3% (2006-2010 5-year est.); Bachelor's degree or higher: 9.3% (2006-2010 5-year est.); Master's degree or higher: 2.0% (2006-2010 5-year est.).

Housing: Homeownership rate: 88.1% (2010); Median home value: $155,400 (2006-2010 5-year est.); Median contract rent: $524 per month (2006-2010 5-year est.); Median year structure built: 1978 (2006-2010 5-year est.).

Transportation: Commute to work: 93.0% car, 1.7% public transportation, 0.9% walk, 4.4% work from home (2006-2010 5-year est.); Travel time to work: 13.1% less than 15 minutes, 22.2% 15 to 30 minutes, 37.2% 30 to 45 minutes, 13.2% 45 to 60 minutes, 14.4% 60 minutes or more (2006-2010 5-year est.)

Additional Information Contacts
Juniata River Valley Chamber of Commerce . . . . (717) 248-6713
  http://www.juniatarivervalley.org

WALNUT BOTTOM (unincorporated postal area)
Zip Code: 17266
  Covers a land area of 1.345 square miles and a water area of 0.001 square miles. Located at 40.08° N. Lat; 77.41° W. Long. Elevation is 728 feet. Population: 581 (2010); Density: 431.8 persons per square mile (2010); Race: 96.0% White, 1.0% Black, 0.0% Asian, 0.5% American Indian/Alaska Native, 0.0% Native Hawaiian/Other Pacific Islander, 2.5% Other, 1.2% Hispanic of any race (2010); Average household size: 2.61 (2010); Median age: 39.7 (2010); Males per 100 females: 95.6 (2010); Homeownership rate: 76.7% (2010)

WEST FAIRVIEW (CDP). Covers a land area of 0.322 square miles and a water area of 0.013 square miles. Located at 40.28° N. Lat; 76.92° W. Long. Elevation is 331 feet.

Population: n/a (1990); n/a (2000); 1,282 (2010); Density: 3,979.5 persons per square mile (2010); Race: 92.5% White, 3.4% Black, 1.2% Asian, 0.2% American Indian/Alaska Native, 0.0% Native Hawaiian/Other Pacific Islander, 2.7% Other, 3.8% Hispanic of any race (2010); Average household size: 2.36 (2010); Median age: 37.1 (2010); Males per 100 females: 95.1 (2010); Marriage status: 26.8% never married, 53.4% now married, 6.8% widowed, 13.0% divorced (2006-2010 5-year est.); Foreign born: 2.0% (2006-2010 5-year est.); Ancestry (includes multiple ancestries): 41.7% German, 22.6% Irish, 12.5% American, 11.2% Italian, 5.9% French (2006-2010 5-year est.).

Economy: Employment by occupation: 2.6% management, 2.4% professional, 12.5% services, 42.7% sales, 5.3% farming, 13.8% construction, 1.5% production (2006-2010 5-year est.).

Income: Per capita income: $21,164 (2006-2010 5-year est.); Median household income: $39,146 (2006-2010 5-year est.); Average household income: $45,500 (2006-2010 5-year est.); Percent of households with income of $100,000 or more: 9.0% (2006-2010 5-year est.); Poverty rate: 12.4% (2006-2010 5-year est.).

Education: Percent of population age 25 and over with: High school diploma (including GED) or higher: 82.1% (2006-2010 5-year est.); Bachelor's degree or higher: 8.9% (2006-2010 5-year est.); Master's degree or higher: 0.0% (2006-2010 5-year est.).

Housing: Homeownership rate: 55.2% (2010); Median home value: $97,400 (2006-2010 5-year est.); Median contract rent: $527 per month (2006-2010 5-year est.); Median year structure built: before 1940 (2006-2010 5-year est.).

Transportation: Commute to work: 91.0% car, 4.2% public transportation, 2.8% walk, 2.1% work from home (2006-2010 5-year est.); Travel time to work: 22.5% less than 15 minutes, 52.7% 15 to 30 minutes, 22.8% 30 to 45 minutes, 0.0% 45 to 60 minutes, 1.9% 60 minutes or more (2006-2010 5-year est.)

WEST PENNSBORO (township). Covers a land area of 30.229 square miles and a water area of 0.047 square miles. Located at 40.18° N. Lat; 77.34° W. Long.

Population: 4,934 (1990); 5,263 (2000); 5,561 (2010); Density: 184.0 persons per square mile (2010); Race: 97.2% White, 0.7% Black, 0.5% Asian, 0.2% American Indian/Alaska Native, 0.0% Native Hawaiian/Other Pacific Islander, 1.4% Other, 1.5% Hispanic of any race (2010); Average household size: 2.54 (2010); Median age: 44.1 (2010); Males per 100 females: 96.6 (2010); Marriage status: 16.3% never married, 67.3% now married, 7.5% widowed, 8.9% divorced (2006-2010 5-year est.); Foreign born: 1.2% (2006-2010 5-year est.); Ancestry (includes multiple ancestries): 41.6% German, 15.2% Irish, 8.9% American, 7.5% English, 5.2% Italian (2006-2010 5-year est.).

Economy: Single-family building permits issued: 3 (2011); Multi-family building permits issued: 0 (2011); Employment by occupation: 6.6% management, 4.3% professional, 11.2% services, 22.2% sales, 0.6% farming, 10.4% construction, 8.2% production (2006-2010 5-year est.).

Income: Per capita income: $25,522 (2006-2010 5-year est.); Median household income: $58,371 (2006-2010 5-year est.); Average household income: $62,180 (2006-2010 5-year est.); Percent of households with income of $100,000 or more: 14.5% (2006-2010 5-year est.); Poverty rate: 6.2% (2006-2010 5-year est.).

Education: Percent of population age 25 and over with: High school diploma (including GED) or higher: 86.6% (2006-2010 5-year est.); Bachelor's degree or higher: 17.3% (2006-2010 5-year est.); Master's degree or higher: 5.8% (2006-2010 5-year est.).

Housing: Homeownership rate: 82.8% (2010); Median home value: $159,600 (2006-2010 5-year est.); Median contract rent: $765 per month (2006-2010 5-year est.); Median year structure built: 1979 (2006-2010 5-year est.).

Transportation: Commute to work: 92.2% car, 0.9% public transportation, 0.0% walk, 5.3% work from home (2006-2010 5-year est.); Travel time to work: 24.0% less than 15 minutes, 44.0% 15 to 30 minutes, 23.1% 30 to 45 minutes, 3.7% 45 to 60 minutes, 5.1% 60 minutes or more (2006-2010 5-year est.)

Additional Information Contacts
Greater Carlisle Area Chamber of Commerce . . . . (717) 243-4515
  http://carlislechamber.org
West Pennsboro Township . . . . (717) 243-0028

WORMLEYSBURG (borough). Covers a land area of 0.795 square miles and a water area of 0.011 square miles. Located at 40.26° N. Lat; 76.91° W. Long. Elevation is 443 feet.

History: Laid out 1815.

Population: 2,847 (1990); 2,607 (2000); 3,070 (2010); Density: 3,861.9 persons per square mile (2010); Race: 79.1% White, 4.6% Black, 12.6% Asian, 0.3% American Indian/Alaska Native, 0.1% Native Hawaiian/Other Pacific Islander, 3.3% Other, 3.7% Hispanic of any race (2010); Average household size: 2.15 (2010); Median age: 34.1 (2010); Males per 100 females: 98.1 (2010); Marriage status: 42.6% never married, 42.7% now married, 6.4% widowed, 8.2% divorced (2006-2010 5-year est.); Foreign born: 12.3% (2006-2010 5-year est.); Ancestry (includes multiple ancestries): 35.8% German, 12.1% Irish, 8.3% Italian, 7.3% English, 6.2% Polish (2006-2010 5-year est.).

Economy: Single-family building permits issued: 0 (2011); Multi-family building permits issued: 0 (2011); Employment by occupation: 19.9% management, 3.2% professional, 8.4% services, 19.1% sales, 7.3% farming, 4.7% construction, 5.1% production (2006-2010 5-year est.).

Income: Per capita income: $32,837 (2006-2010 5-year est.); Median household income: $53,594 (2006-2010 5-year est.); Average household income: $67,433 (2006-2010 5-year est.); Percent of households with income of $100,000 or more: 15.8% (2006-2010 5-year est.); Poverty rate: 8.4% (2006-2010 5-year est.).

Education: Percent of population age 25 and over with: High school diploma (including GED) or higher: 89.5% (2006-2010 5-year est.);

Bachelor's degree or higher: 39.8% (2006-2010 5-year est.); Master's degree or higher: 15.3% (2006-2010 5-year est.).
Housing: Homeownership rate: 43.3% (2010); Median home value: $151,800 (2006-2010 5-year est.); Median contract rent: $702 per month (2006-2010 5-year est.); Median year structure built: 1967 (2006-2010 5-year est.).
Transportation: Commute to work: 87.4% car, 0.0% public transportation, 6.2% walk, 3.5% work from home (2006-2010 5-year est.); Travel time to work: 41.8% less than 15 minutes, 42.7% 15 to 30 minutes, 7.0% 30 to 45 minutes, 3.7% 45 to 60 minutes, 4.7% 60 minutes or more (2006-2010 5-year est.)
Additional Information Contacts
Borough of Wormleysburg . . . . (717) 763-4483
  http://borough.wormleysburg.pa.us
West Shore Chamber of Commerce . . . . (717) 761-0702
  http://www.wschamber.org

Dauphin County

Located in south central Pennsylvania; bounded on the west by the Susquehanna River; crossed by the Blue Mountains. Covers a land area of 525.047 square miles, a water area of 33.131 square miles, and is located in the Eastern Time Zone at 40.41° N. Lat., 76.79° W. Long. The county was founded in 1785. County seat is Harrisburg.

Dauphin County is part of the Harrisburg-Carlisle, PA Metropolitan Statistical Area. The entire metro area includes: Cumberland County, PA; Dauphin County, PA; Perry County, PA

Population: 237,813 (1990); 251,798 (2000); 268,100 (2010); Race: 72.7% White, 18.0% Black, 3.2% Asian, 0.2% American Indian/Alaska Native, 0.0% Native Hawaiian/Other Pacific Islander, 5.9% Other, 7.0% Hispanic of any race (2010); Density: 510.6 persons per square mile (2010); Average household size: 2.37 (2010); Median age: 39.4 (2010); Males per 100 females: 93.6 (2010).
Religion: Six largest groups: 14.8% Catholicism, 9.4% Methodist/Pietist, 5.1% Lutheran, 4.4% Presbyterian-Reformed, 3.5% Non-Denominational, 2.3% Baptist (2010)
Economy: Unemployment rate: 7.9% (August 2012); Total civilian labor force: 141,697 (August 2012); Leading industries: 21.2% health care and social assistance; 10.9% retail trade; 8.8% accommodation & food services (2010); Farms: 836 totaling 89,533 acres (2007); Companies that employ 500 or more persons: 28 (2010); Companies that employ 100 to 499 persons: 193 (2010); Companies that employ less than 100 persons: 6,668 (2010); Black-owned businesses: 1,536 (2007); Hispanic-owned businesses: n/a (2007); Asian-owned businesses: 759 (2007); Women-owned businesses: 4,736 (2007); Retail sales per capita: $15,500 (2010). Single-family building permits issued: 373 (2011); Multi-family building permits issued: 12 (2011).
Income: Per capita income: $27,727 (2006-2010 5-year est.); Median household income: $52,371 (2006-2010 5-year est.); Average household income: $66,069 (2006-2010 5-year est.); Percent of households with income of $100,000 or more: 18.9% (2006-2010 5-year est.); Poverty rate: 11.9% (2006-2010 5-year est.); Bankruptcy rate: 2.75% (2011).
Taxes: Total county taxes per capita: $406 (2009); County property taxes per capita: $374 (2009).
Education: Percent of population age 25 and over with: High school diploma (including GED) or higher: 88.5% (2006-2010 5-year est.); Bachelor's degree or higher: 27.1% (2006-2010 5-year est.); Master's degree or higher: 10.1% (2006-2010 5-year est.).
Housing: Homeownership rate: 64.8% (2010); Median home value: $153,100 (2006-2010 5-year est.); Median contract rent: $626 per month (2006-2010 5-year est.); Median year structure built: 1963 (2006-2010 5-year est.).
Health: Birth rate: 126.7 per 10,000 population (2011); Death rate: 85.5 per 10,000 population (2011); Age-adjusted cancer mortality rate: 169.1 deaths per 100,000 population (2009); Number of physicians: 63.0 per 10,000 population (2010); Hospital beds: 59.2 per 10,000 population (2008); Hospital admissions: 3,192.4 per 10,000 population (2008).
Environment: Air Quality Index: 68.2% good, 30.1% moderate, 1.6% unhealthy for sensitive individuals, 0.0% unhealthy (percent of days in 2011)
Elections: 2012 Presidential election results: 52.3% Obama, 46.4% Romney
National and State Parks: Haldeman State Forest

Additional Information Contacts
Dauphin County Government . . . . (717) 780-6300
  http://www.dauphincounty.org

Dauphin County Communities

BERRYSBURG (borough). Covers a land area of 0.606 square miles and a water area of 0 square miles. Located at 40.60° N. Lat; 76.81° W. Long. Elevation is 722 feet.
Population: 376 (1990); 354 (2000); 368 (2010); Density: 607.1 persons per square mile (2010); Race: 100.0% White, 0.0% Black, 0.0% Asian, 0.0% American Indian/Alaska Native, 0.0% Native Hawaiian/Other Pacific Islander, 0.0% Other, 0.0% Hispanic of any race (2010); Average household size: 2.42 (2010); Median age: 43.2 (2010); Males per 100 females: 92.7 (2010); Marriage status: 24.1% never married, 60.0% now married, 4.4% widowed, 11.4% divorced (2006-2010 5-year est.); Foreign born: 0.0% (2006-2010 5-year est.); Ancestry (includes multiple ancestries): 71.5% German, 7.2% English, 6.4% Dutch, 5.6% Italian, 5.3% Pennsylvania German (2006-2010 5-year est.).
Economy: Single-family building permits issued: 0 (2011); Multi-family building permits issued: 0 (2011); Employment by occupation: 8.4% management, 0.0% professional, 14.5% services, 19.6% sales, 9.5% farming, 7.3% construction, 2.8% production (2006-2010 5-year est.).
Income: Per capita income: $19,456 (2006-2010 5-year est.); Median household income: $44,432 (2006-2010 5-year est.); Average household income: $52,765 (2006-2010 5-year est.); Percent of households with income of $100,000 or more: 5.8% (2006-2010 5-year est.); Poverty rate: 9.6% (2006-2010 5-year est.).
Education: Percent of population age 25 and over with: High school diploma (including GED) or higher: 88.9% (2006-2010 5-year est.); Bachelor's degree or higher: 6.1% (2006-2010 5-year est.); Master's degree or higher: 2.5% (2006-2010 5-year est.).
Housing: Homeownership rate: 79.6% (2010); Median home value: $85,800 (2006-2010 5-year est.); Median contract rent: $348 per month (2006-2010 5-year est.); Median year structure built: before 1940 (2006-2010 5-year est.).
Transportation: Commute to work: 83.8% car, 0.0% public transportation, 3.9% walk, 4.5% work from home (2006-2010 5-year est.); Travel time to work: 56.1% less than 15 minutes, 14.6% 15 to 30 minutes, 3.5% 30 to 45 minutes, 13.5% 45 to 60 minutes, 12.3% 60 minutes or more (2006-2010 5-year est.)

BRESSLER (CDP). Covers a land area of 0.312 square miles and a water area of 0 square miles. Located at 40.23° N. Lat; 76.82° W. Long. Elevation is 489 feet.
Population: n/a (1990); n/a (2000); 1,437 (2010); Density: 4,607.6 persons per square mile (2010); Race: 73.7% White, 17.9% Black, 0.5% Asian, 0.1% American Indian/Alaska Native, 0.0% Native Hawaiian/Other Pacific Islander, 7.8% Other, 10.3% Hispanic of any race (2010); Average household size: 2.43 (2010); Median age: 40.6 (2010); Males per 100 females: 97.9 (2010); Marriage status: 39.1% never married, 43.7% now married, 5.1% widowed, 12.0% divorced (2006-2010 5-year est.); Foreign born: 4.2% (2006-2010 5-year est.); Ancestry (includes multiple ancestries): 35.8% German, 15.8% Irish, 13.0% Croatian, 8.0% Italian, 6.5% American (2006-2010 5-year est.).
Economy: Employment by occupation: 4.5% management, 3.8% professional, 6.1% services, 22.2% sales, 11.0% farming, 7.5% construction, 4.8% production (2006-2010 5-year est.).
Income: Per capita income: $21,100 (2006-2010 5-year est.); Median household income: $44,694 (2006-2010 5-year est.); Average household income: $50,817 (2006-2010 5-year est.); Percent of households with income of $100,000 or more: 5.7% (2006-2010 5-year est.); Poverty rate: 8.3% (2006-2010 5-year est.).
Education: Percent of population age 25 and over with: High school diploma (including GED) or higher: 86.6% (2006-2010 5-year est.); Bachelor's degree or higher: 7.0% (2006-2010 5-year est.); Master's degree or higher: 1.0% (2006-2010 5-year est.).
Housing: Homeownership rate: 79.2% (2010); Median home value: $115,200 (2006-2010 5-year est.); Median contract rent: $525 per month (2006-2010 5-year est.); Median year structure built: 1956 (2006-2010 5-year est.).
Transportation: Commute to work: 90.2% car, 0.0% public transportation, 0.0% walk, 4.3% work from home (2006-2010 5-year est.); Travel time to work: 43.5% less than 15 minutes, 46.1% 15 to 30 minutes, 3.9% 30 to 45

minutes, 0.0% 45 to 60 minutes, 6.5% 60 minutes or more (2006-2010 5-year est.)

COLONIAL PARK (CDP). Covers a land area of 4.757 square miles and a water area of 0 square miles. Located at 40.30° N. Lat; 76.81° W. Long. Elevation is 499 feet.

Population: 13,647 (1990); 13,259 (2000); 13,229 (2010); Density: 2,780.8 persons per square mile (2010); Race: 72.9% White, 15.9% Black, 4.6% Asian, 0.2% American Indian/Alaska Native, 0.1% Native Hawaiian/Other Pacific Islander, 6.3% Other, 7.8% Hispanic of any race (2010); Average household size: 2.19 (2010); Median age: 38.2 (2010); Males per 100 females: 93.2 (2010); Marriage status: 32.9% never married, 46.1% now married, 6.6% widowed, 14.4% divorced (2006-2010 5-year est.); Foreign born: 9.4% (2006-2010 5-year est.); Ancestry (includes multiple ancestries): 32.4% German, 13.0% Irish, 8.6% Italian, 7.2% English, 3.9% Polish (2006-2010 5-year est.).

Economy: Employment by occupation: 10.2% management, 6.7% professional, 10.0% services, 21.6% sales, 6.4% farming, 5.7% construction, 5.9% production (2006-2010 5-year est.).

Income: Per capita income: $28,215 (2006-2010 5-year est.); Median household income: $48,433 (2006-2010 5-year est.); Average household income: $59,281 (2006-2010 5-year est.); Percent of households with income of $100,000 or more: 14.3% (2006-2010 5-year est.); Poverty rate: 9.3% (2006-2010 5-year est.).

Education: Percent of population age 25 and over with: High school diploma (including GED) or higher: 91.2% (2006-2010 5-year est.); Bachelor's degree or higher: 27.6% (2006-2010 5-year est.); Master's degree or higher: 8.6% (2006-2010 5-year est.).

Housing: Homeownership rate: 49.5% (2010); Median home value: $144,100 (2006-2010 5-year est.); Median contract rent: $708 per month (2006-2010 5-year est.); Median year structure built: 1964 (2006-2010 5-year est.).

Transportation: Commute to work: 92.8% car, 1.7% public transportation, 3.0% walk, 1.4% work from home (2006-2010 5-year est.); Travel time to work: 30.2% less than 15 minutes, 53.5% 15 to 30 minutes, 12.5% 30 to 45 minutes, 1.7% 45 to 60 minutes, 2.1% 60 minutes or more (2006-2010 5-year est.)

Additional Information Contacts

West Shore Chamber of Commerce . . . . (717) 761-0702
http://www.wschamber.org

CONEWAGO (township). Covers a land area of 16.733 square miles and a water area of 0 square miles. Located at 40.22° N. Lat; 76.62° W. Long.

Population: 2,832 (1990); 2,847 (2000); 2,997 (2010); Density: 179.1 persons per square mile (2010); Race: 96.0% White, 1.1% Black, 0.6% Asian, 0.3% American Indian/Alaska Native, 0.0% Native Hawaiian/Other Pacific Islander, 2.0% Other, 1.8% Hispanic of any race (2010); Average household size: 2.68 (2010); Median age: 42.1 (2010); Males per 100 females: 100.1 (2010); Marriage status: 21.6% never married, 64.5% now married, 4.6% widowed, 9.3% divorced (2006-2010 5-year est.); Foreign born: 2.3% (2006-2010 5-year est.); Ancestry (includes multiple ancestries): 39.1% German, 13.5% Irish, 12.8% Italian, 10.1% English, 5.5% Polish (2006-2010 5-year est.).

Economy: Single-family building permits issued: 2 (2011); Multi-family building permits issued: 0 (2011); Employment by occupation: 7.9% management, 6.3% professional, 9.0% services, 14.6% sales, 2.6% farming, 9.3% construction, 9.1% production (2006-2010 5-year est.).

Income: Per capita income: $38,809 (2006-2010 5-year est.); Median household income: $75,938 (2006-2010 5-year est.); Average household income: $103,306 (2006-2010 5-year est.); Percent of households with income of $100,000 or more: 39.9% (2006-2010 5-year est.); Poverty rate: 5.9% (2006-2010 5-year est.).

Education: Percent of population age 25 and over with: High school diploma (including GED) or higher: 93.7% (2006-2010 5-year est.); Bachelor's degree or higher: 41.8% (2006-2010 5-year est.); Master's degree or higher: 19.5% (2006-2010 5-year est.).

Housing: Homeownership rate: 84.3% (2010); Median home value: $221,500 (2006-2010 5-year est.); Median contract rent: $666 per month (2006-2010 5-year est.); Median year structure built: 1977 (2006-2010 5-year est.).

Transportation: Commute to work: 92.9% car, 0.4% public transportation, 2.2% walk, 4.5% work from home (2006-2010 5-year est.); Travel time to work: 34.7% less than 15 minutes, 46.1% 15 to 30 minutes, 14.6% 30 to

---

45 minutes, 1.8% 45 to 60 minutes, 2.8% 60 minutes or more (2006-2010 5-year est.)

Additional Information Contacts

Elizabethtown Area Chamber of Commerce . . . . (717) 361-7188
http://www.elizabethtowncoc.com

DAUPHIN (borough). Covers a land area of 0.428 square miles and a water area of 0.005 square miles. Located at 40.37° N. Lat; 76.93° W. Long. Elevation is 364 feet.

History: Appalachian Trail passes to North on Peters Mt. ridge. Fort Hunter Mansion (1814) to South..

Population: 845 (1990); 773 (2000); 791 (2010); Density: 1,848.2 persons per square mile (2010); Race: 97.3% White, 0.8% Black, 0.5% Asian, 0.0% American Indian/Alaska Native, 0.0% Native Hawaiian/Other Pacific Islander, 1.4% Other, 1.4% Hispanic of any race (2010); Average household size: 2.38 (2010); Median age: 40.7 (2010); Males per 100 females: 99.7 (2010); Marriage status: 23.8% never married, 62.1% now married, 3.2% widowed, 10.9% divorced (2006-2010 5-year est.); Foreign born: 0.8% (2006-2010 5-year est.); Ancestry (includes multiple ancestries): 49.4% German, 27.4% Irish, 8.5% Italian, 6.1% English, 4.5% French (2006-2010 5-year est.).

Economy: Single-family building permits issued: 1 (2011); Multi-family building permits issued: 0 (2011); Employment by occupation: 10.9% management, 4.0% professional, 13.6% services, 17.8% sales, 6.4% farming, 10.1% construction, 7.2% production (2006-2010 5-year est.).

Income: Per capita income: $30,130 (2006-2010 5-year est.); Median household income: $56,500 (2006-2010 5-year est.); Average household income: $73,310 (2006-2010 5-year est.); Percent of households with income of $100,000 or more: 26.5% (2006-2010 5-year est.); Poverty rate: 8.8% (2006-2010 5-year est.).

Education: Percent of population age 25 and over with: High school diploma (including GED) or higher: 97.1% (2006-2010 5-year est.); Bachelor's degree or higher: 22.4% (2006-2010 5-year est.); Master's degree or higher: 11.4% (2006-2010 5-year est.).

School District(s)

Central Dauphin SD (KG-12)
    2010-11 Enrollment: 10,937 . . . . (717) 545-4703

Housing: Homeownership rate: 76.0% (2010); Median home value: $153,100 (2006-2010 5-year est.); Median contract rent: $480 per month (2006-2010 5-year est.); Median year structure built: 1955 (2006-2010 5-year est.).

Transportation: Commute to work: 96.9% car, 0.0% public transportation, 0.8% walk, 1.6% work from home (2006-2010 5-year est.); Travel time to work: 15.9% less than 15 minutes, 49.5% 15 to 30 minutes, 29.1% 30 to 45 minutes, 4.5% 45 to 60 minutes, 1.1% 60 minutes or more (2006-2010 5-year est.)

DERRY (township). Covers a land area of 27.203 square miles and a water area of 0.195 square miles. Located at 40.27° N. Lat; 76.65° W. Long.

History: The Township of Derry was incorporated on August 1, 1729, when Lancaster County divided the territory for tax purposes. It was named after the city of Derry in Ireland.

Population: 18,408 (1990); 21,273 (2000); 24,679 (2010); Density: 907.2 persons per square mile (2010); Race: 84.7% White, 4.5% Black, 7.5% Asian, 0.2% American Indian/Alaska Native, 0.0% Native Hawaiian/Other Pacific Islander, 3.1% Other, 3.0% Hispanic of any race (2010); Average household size: 2.33 (2010); Median age: 38.3 (2010); Males per 100 females: 90.5 (2010); Marriage status: 27.2% never married, 57.7% now married, 6.9% widowed, 8.2% divorced (2006-2010 5-year est.); Foreign born: 9.2% (2006-2010 5-year est.); Ancestry (includes multiple ancestries): 35.6% German, 17.7% Irish, 14.5% Italian, 12.0% English, 3.7% Polish (2006-2010 5-year est.).

Economy: Single-family building permits issued: 22 (2011); Multi-family building permits issued: 12 (2011); Employment by occupation: 14.3% management, 6.6% professional, 8.7% services, 13.5% sales, 2.3% farming, 4.0% construction, 4.7% production (2006-2010 5-year est.).

Income: Per capita income: $37,797 (2006-2010 5-year est.); Median household income: $65,427 (2006-2010 5-year est.); Average household income: $89,499 (2006-2010 5-year est.); Percent of households with income of $100,000 or more: 29.4% (2006-2010 5-year est.); Poverty rate: 6.7% (2006-2010 5-year est.).

Taxes: Total city taxes per capita: $460 (2009); City property taxes per capita: $92 (2009).

Education: Percent of population age 25 and over with: High school diploma (including GED) or higher: 95.2% (2006-2010 5-year est.); Bachelor's degree or higher: 51.4% (2006-2010 5-year est.); Master's degree or higher: 25.0% (2006-2010 5-year est.).

Housing: Homeownership rate: 63.1% (2010); Median home value: $234,500 (2006-2010 5-year est.); Median contract rent: $751 per month (2006-2010 5-year est.); Median year structure built: 1975 (2006-2010 5-year est.).

Safety: Violent crime rate: 15.8 per 10,000 population; Property crime rate: 214.9 per 10,000 population (2011).

Transportation: Commute to work: 87.5% car, 0.5% public transportation, 7.4% walk, 3.6% work from home (2006-2010 5-year est.); Travel time to work: 46.2% less than 15 minutes, 30.9% 15 to 30 minutes, 14.1% 30 to 45 minutes, 4.0% 45 to 60 minutes, 4.8% 60 minutes or more (2006-2010 5-year est.)

Additional Information Contacts

Derry Township . . . . (717) 533-2057
  http://www.derrytownship.org
Harrisburg Regional Chamber & CREDC . . . . (717) 232-4099
  http://www.harrisburgregionalchamber.org

EAST HANOVER (township).

Covers a land area of 40.200 square miles and a water area of 0.020 square miles. Located at 40.39° N. Lat; 76.68° W. Long.

Population: 4,558 (1990); 5,322 (2000); 5,718 (2010); Density: 142.2 persons per square mile (2010); Race: 95.3% White, 0.8% Black, 1.1% Asian, 0.1% American Indian/Alaska Native, 0.0% Native Hawaiian/Other Pacific Islander, 2.7% Other, 4.4% Hispanic of any race (2010); Average household size: 2.57 (2010); Median age: 43.3 (2010); Males per 100 females: 103.4 (2010); Marriage status: 21.5% never married, 58.4% now married, 5.6% widowed, 14.6% divorced (2006-2010 5-year est.); Foreign born: 2.8% (2006-2010 5-year est.); Ancestry (includes multiple ancestries): 44.8% German, 16.6% Irish, 9.1% Italian, 5.7% American, 5.4% English (2006-2010 5-year est.).

Economy: Single-family building permits issued: 29 (2011); Multi-family building permits issued: 0 (2011); Employment by occupation: 9.2% management, 4.1% professional, 13.1% services, 20.2% sales, 3.4% farming, 5.9% construction, 9.6% production (2006-2010 5-year est.).

Income: Per capita income: $25,669 (2006-2010 5-year est.); Median household income: $57,003 (2006-2010 5-year est.); Average household income: $69,788 (2006-2010 5-year est.); Percent of households with income of $100,000 or more: 22.1% (2006-2010 5-year est.); Poverty rate: 8.3% (2006-2010 5-year est.).

Education: Percent of population age 25 and over with: High school diploma (including GED) or higher: 84.8% (2006-2010 5-year est.); Bachelor's degree or higher: 19.6% (2006-2010 5-year est.); Master's degree or higher: 7.7% (2006-2010 5-year est.).

Housing: Homeownership rate: 86.3% (2010); Median home value: $171,000 (2006-2010 5-year est.); Median contract rent: $550 per month (2006-2010 5-year est.); Median year structure built: 1982 (2006-2010 5-year est.).

Transportation: Commute to work: 90.5% car, 0.0% public transportation, 1.4% walk, 3.6% work from home (2006-2010 5-year est.); Travel time to work: 25.4% less than 15 minutes, 34.4% 15 to 30 minutes, 27.6% 30 to 45 minutes, 9.5% 45 to 60 minutes, 3.1% 60 minutes or more (2006-2010 5-year est.)

Additional Information Contacts

East Hanover Township . . . . (717) 469-0833
  http://www.easthanoverpa.com
Harrisburg Regional Chamber & CREDC . . . . (717) 232-4099
  http://www.harrisburgregionalchamber.org

ELIZABETHVILLE (borough).

Covers a land area of 0.546 square miles and a water area of 0 square miles. Located at 40.55° N. Lat; 76.82° W. Long. Elevation is 676 feet.

History: Settled 1817.

Population: 1,411 (1990); 1,344 (2000); 1,510 (2010); Density: 2,765.5 persons per square mile (2010); Race: 97.7% White, 0.4% Black, 0.7% Asian, 0.0% American Indian/Alaska Native, 0.0% Native Hawaiian/Other Pacific Islander, 1.2% Other, 0.7% Hispanic of any race (2010); Average household size: 2.31 (2010); Median age: 38.8 (2010); Males per 100 females: 103.2 (2010); Marriage status: 30.9% never married, 49.7% now married, 9.1% widowed, 10.3% divorced (2006-2010 5-year est.); Foreign born: 0.3% (2006-2010 5-year est.); Ancestry (includes multiple

ancestries): 59.1% German, 8.3% Irish, 6.7% English, 4.9% Italian, 3.6% American (2006-2010 5-year est.).

Economy: Single-family building permits issued: 0 (2011); Multi-family building permits issued: 0 (2011); Employment by occupation: 4.4% management, 2.1% professional, 11.4% services, 26.8% sales, 2.0% farming, 9.0% construction, 9.0% production (2006-2010 5-year est.).

Income: Per capita income: $19,827 (2006-2010 5-year est.); Median household income: $39,808 (2006-2010 5-year est.); Average household income: $48,525 (2006-2010 5-year est.); Percent of households with income of $100,000 or more: 8.0% (2006-2010 5-year est.); Poverty rate: 16.1% (2006-2010 5-year est.).

Education: Percent of population age 25 and over with: High school diploma (including GED) or higher: 81.7% (2006-2010 5-year est.); Bachelor's degree or higher: 7.7% (2006-2010 5-year est.); Master's degree or higher: 2.3% (2006-2010 5-year est.).

School District(s)

Upper Dauphin Area SD (KG-12)
  2010-11 Enrollment: 1,278 . . . . (717) 362-8134

Housing: Homeownership rate: 54.5% (2010); Median home value: $93,600 (2006-2010 5-year est.); Median contract rent: $406 per month (2006-2010 5-year est.); Median year structure built: 1943 (2006-2010 5-year est.).

Transportation: Commute to work: 91.0% car, 0.4% public transportation, 5.7% walk, 1.3% work from home (2006-2010 5-year est.); Travel time to work: 35.8% less than 15 minutes, 18.5% 15 to 30 minutes, 10.5% 30 to 45 minutes, 22.7% 45 to 60 minutes, 12.6% 60 minutes or more (2006-2010 5-year est.)

Additional Information Contacts

Harrisburg Regional Chamber & CREDC . . . . (717) 232-4099
  http://www.harrisburgregionalchamber.org

ENHAUT (CDP).

Covers a land area of 0.231 square miles and a water area of 0 square miles. Located at 40.23° N. Lat; 76.83° W. Long. Elevation is 492 feet.

Population: n/a (1990); n/a (2000); 1,007 (2010); Density: 4,366.6 persons per square mile (2010); Race: 78.3% White, 11.4% Black, 0.4% Asian, 0.4% American Indian/Alaska Native, 0.0% Native Hawaiian/Other Pacific Islander, 9.5% Other, 8.6% Hispanic of any race (2010); Average household size: 2.49 (2010); Median age: 37.6 (2010); Males per 100 females: 85.8 (2010); Marriage status: 28.3% never married, 40.6% now married, 13.9% widowed, 17.3% divorced (2006-2010 5-year est.); Foreign born: 10.5% (2006-2010 5-year est.); Ancestry (includes multiple ancestries): 16.4% Croatian, 14.0% German, 13.5% Irish, 9.2% English, 5.3% Dutch (2006-2010 5-year est.).

Economy: Employment by occupation: 6.1% management, 0.0% professional, 3.1% services, 16.9% sales, 0.0% farming, 13.3% construction, 3.3% production (2006-2010 5-year est.).

Income: Per capita income: $19,762 (2006-2010 5-year est.); Median household income: $42,667 (2006-2010 5-year est.); Average household income: $51,102 (2006-2010 5-year est.); Percent of households with income of $100,000 or more: 11.4% (2006-2010 5-year est.); Poverty rate: 23.0% (2006-2010 5-year est.).

Education: Percent of population age 25 and over with: High school diploma (including GED) or higher: 91.3% (2006-2010 5-year est.); Bachelor's degree or higher: 9.2% (2006-2010 5-year est.); Master's degree or higher: 2.0% (2006-2010 5-year est.).

Housing: Homeownership rate: 76.1% (2010); Median home value: $104,200 (2006-2010 5-year est.); Median contract rent: $655 per month (2006-2010 5-year est.); Median year structure built: before 1940 (2006-2010 5-year est.).

Transportation: Commute to work: 96.6% car, 3.4% public transportation, 0.0% walk, 0.0% work from home (2006-2010 5-year est.); Travel time to work: 35.1% less than 15 minutes, 54.3% 15 to 30 minutes, 7.8% 30 to 45 minutes, 0.0% 45 to 60 minutes, 2.9% 60 minutes or more (2006-2010 5-year est.)

GRANTVILLE (unincorporated postal area)

Zip Code: 17028

Covers a land area of 24.365 square miles and a water area of 0.011 square miles. Located at 40.39° N. Lat; 76.65° W. Long. Population: 3,720 (2010); Density: 152.7 persons per square mile (2010); Race: 93.3% White, 1.6% Black, 1.1% Asian, 0.2% American Indian/Alaska Native, 0.0% Native Hawaiian/Other Pacific Islander, 3.8% Other, 6.5% Hispanic of any race (2010); Average household size: 2.40 (2010);

Median age: 43.0 (2010); Males per 100 females: 108.2 (2010); Homeownership rate: 81.4% (2010)

GRATZ (borough). Covers a land area of 2.949 square miles and a water area of 0 square miles. Located at 40.61° N. Lat; 76.72° W. Long. Elevation is 817 feet.
Population: 703 (1990); 676 (2000); 765 (2010); Density: 259.4 persons per square mile (2010); Race: 97.0% White, 0.5% Black, 0.9% Asian, 0.0% American Indian/Alaska Native, 0.0% Native Hawaiian/Other Pacific Islander, 1.6% Other, 1.4% Hispanic of any race (2010); Average household size: 2.39 (2010); Median age: 43.7 (2010); Males per 100 females: 94.2 (2010); Marriage status: 23.6% never married, 52.5% now married, 14.2% widowed, 9.7% divorced (2006-2010 5-year est.); Foreign born: 0.0% (2006-2010 5-year est.); Ancestry (includes multiple ancestries): 67.6% German, 8.2% Polish, 6.8% Scottish, 6.8% English, 5.1% Pennsylvania German (2006-2010 5-year est.).
Economy: Single-family building permits issued: 0 (2011); Multi-family building permits issued: 0 (2011); Employment by occupation: 6.0% management, 6.3% professional, 5.6% services, 19.2% sales, 5.3% farming, 6.0% construction, 6.0% production (2006-2010 5-year est.).
Income: Per capita income: $20,558 (2006-2010 5-year est.); Median household income: $31,000 (2006-2010 5-year est.); Average household income: $42,946 (2006-2010 5-year est.); Percent of households with income of $100,000 or more: 13.7% (2006-2010 5-year est.); Poverty rate: 11.0% (2006-2010 5-year est.).
Education: Percent of population age 25 and over with: High school diploma (including GED) or higher: 73.3% (2006-2010 5-year est.); Bachelor's degree or higher: 8.7% (2006-2010 5-year est.); Master's degree or higher: 3.8% (2006-2010 5-year est.).
Housing: Homeownership rate: 73.8% (2010); Median home value: $97,800 (2006-2010 5-year est.); Median contract rent: $381 per month (2006-2010 5-year est.); Median year structure built: 1954 (2006-2010 5-year est.).
Transportation: Commute to work: 85.4% car, 3.0% public transportation, 3.6% walk, 7.9% work from home (2006-2010 5-year est.); Travel time to work: 34.2% less than 15 minutes, 28.4% 15 to 30 minutes, 9.4% 30 to 45 minutes, 20.1% 45 to 60 minutes, 7.9% 60 minutes or more (2006-2010 5-year est.).

HALIFAX (borough). Covers a land area of 0.336 square miles and a water area of 0 square miles. Located at 40.46° N. Lat; 76.93° W. Long. Elevation is 413 feet.
Population: 911 (1990); 875 (2000); 841 (2010); Density: 2,506.2 persons per square mile (2010); Race: 94.9% White, 1.3% Black, 0.2% Asian, 0.0% American Indian/Alaska Native, 0.0% Native Hawaiian/Other Pacific Islander, 3.6% Other, 2.0% Hispanic of any race (2010); Average household size: 2.40 (2010); Median age: 36.8 (2010); Males per 100 females: 94.2 (2010); Marriage status: 33.0% never married, 38.1% now married, 5.6% widowed, 23.3% divorced (2006-2010 5-year est.); Foreign born: 0.9% (2006-2010 5-year est.); Ancestry (includes multiple ancestries): 59.5% German, 12.7% Irish, 10.2% Italian, 9.4% Dutch, 6.2% English (2006-2010 5-year est.).
Economy: Single-family building permits issued: 0 (2011); Multi-family building permits issued: 0 (2011); Employment by occupation: 4.9% management, 6.2% professional, 17.9% services, 16.3% sales, 10.1% farming, 5.9% construction, 8.1% production (2006-2010 5-year est.).
Income: Per capita income: $17,410 (2006-2010 5-year est.); Median household income: $32,500 (2006-2010 5-year est.); Average household income: $37,672 (2006-2010 5-year est.); Percent of households with income of $100,000 or more: 5.0% (2006-2010 5-year est.); Poverty rate: 22.2% (2006-2010 5-year est.).
Education: Percent of population age 25 and over with: High school diploma (including GED) or higher: 79.3% (2006-2010 5-year est.); Bachelor's degree or higher: 6.8% (2006-2010 5-year est.); Master's degree or higher: 0.0% (2006-2010 5-year est.).
School District(s)
Halifax Area SD (PK-12)
    2010-11 Enrollment: 1,143 . . . . (717) 896-3416
Housing: Homeownership rate: 49.5% (2010); Median home value: $82,800 (2006-2010 5-year est.); Median contract rent: $454 per month (2006-2010 5-year est.); Median year structure built: before 1940 (2006-2010 5-year est.).
Transportation: Commute to work: 89.5% car, 1.3% public transportation, 4.3% walk, 1.0% work from home (2006-2010 5-year est.); Travel time to work: 19.6% less than 15 minutes, 25.6% 15 to 30 minutes, 43.5% 30 to

45 minutes, 9.3% 45 to 60 minutes, 2.0% 60 minutes or more (2006-2010 5-year est.)

HALIFAX (township). Covers a land area of 27.654 square miles and a water area of 4.130 square miles. Located at 40.47° N. Lat; 76.93° W. Long. Elevation is 413 feet.
History: Appalachian Trail passes to South on Peters Mt. ridge.
Population: 3,449 (1990); 3,329 (2000); 3,483 (2010); Density: 125.9 persons per square mile (2010); Race: 98.6% White, 0.5% Black, 0.3% Asian, 0.1% American Indian/Alaska Native, 0.0% Native Hawaiian/Other Pacific Islander, 0.5% Other, 1.2% Hispanic of any race (2010); Average household size: 2.50 (2010); Median age: 42.9 (2010); Males per 100 females: 101.6 (2010); Marriage status: 26.8% never married, 58.5% now married, 5.0% widowed, 9.8% divorced (2006-2010 5-year est.); Foreign born: 0.0% (2006-2010 5-year est.); Ancestry (includes multiple ancestries): 60.6% German, 12.6% Irish, 8.6% English, 8.2% American, 6.8% Italian (2006-2010 5-year est.).
Economy: Single-family building permits issued: 2 (2011); Multi-family building permits issued: 0 (2011); Employment by occupation: 11.2% management, 3.9% professional, 12.1% services, 17.7% sales, 4.4% farming, 10.8% construction, 8.7% production (2006-2010 5-year est.).
Income: Per capita income: $25,203 (2006-2010 5-year est.); Median household income: $59,292 (2006-2010 5-year est.); Average household income: $65,056 (2006-2010 5-year est.); Percent of households with income of $100,000 or more: 16.4% (2006-2010 5-year est.); Poverty rate: 15.4% (2006-2010 5-year est.).
Education: Percent of population age 25 and over with: High school diploma (including GED) or higher: 86.5% (2006-2010 5-year est.); Bachelor's degree or higher: 14.0% (2006-2010 5-year est.); Master's degree or higher: 2.8% (2006-2010 5-year est.).
Housing: Homeownership rate: 82.8% (2010); Median home value: $150,900 (2006-2010 5-year est.); Median contract rent: $547 per month (2006-2010 5-year est.); Median year structure built: 1979 (2006-2010 5-year est.).
Transportation: Commute to work: 88.2% car, 1.0% public transportation, 1.6% walk, 8.3% work from home (2006-2010 5-year est.); Travel time to work: 20.7% less than 15 minutes, 21.4% 15 to 30 minutes, 39.3% 30 to 45 minutes, 15.0% 45 to 60 minutes, 3.7% 60 minutes or more (2006-2010 5-year est.).
Additional Information Contacts
Harrisburg Regional Chamber & CREDC . . . . (717) 232-4099
    http://www.harrisburgregionalchamber.org

HARRISBURG (city). County seat. Covers a land area of 8.130 square miles and a water area of 3.734 square miles. Located at 40.28° N. Lat; 76.89° W. Long. Elevation is 335 feet.
History: In the beginning, Harrisburg's population was mainly Scots-Irish and German. The area around Harrisburg was originally called Peshtank or Peixtan ("swampy") by the Native Americans, who once had a large village on the site. The name was corrupted to Paxtang and settled by John Harris, a trader, about 1712. He and a son operated a ferry known as Harris' Ferry. The town was known as Louisbourg for a time, until the younger Harris declared: "You may Louisbourg all you please, but I'll not sell an inch more of land except in Harrisburg." The borough developed first as a canal and then as a railroad center. It became the state capital in 1812 and was incorporated as a city in 1860.
Population: 52,376 (1990); 48,950 (2000); 49,528 (2010); Density: 6,092.1 persons per square mile (2010); Race: 30.7% White, 52.4% Black, 3.5% Asian, 0.5% American Indian/Alaska Native, 0.1% Native Hawaiian/Other Pacific Islander, 12.8% Other, 18.0% Hispanic of any race (2010); Average household size: 2.36 (2010); Median age: 32.2 (2010); Males per 100 females: 92.7 (2010); Marriage status: 49.5% never married, 30.8% now married, 7.2% widowed, 12.5% divorced (2006-2010 5-year est.); Foreign born: 7.1% (2006-2010 5-year est.); Ancestry (includes multiple ancestries): 11.4% German, 5.9% Irish, 3.8% Italian, 2.5% English, 1.6% Polish (2006-2010 5-year est.).
Economy: Unemployment rate: 11.0% (August 2012); Total civilian labor force: 23,784 (August 2012); Single-family building permits issued: 12 (2011); Multi-family building permits issued: 0 (2011); Employment by occupation: 7.6% management, 2.7% professional, 11.2% services, 22.6% sales, 4.7% farming, 4.7% construction, 6.8% production (2006-2010 5-year est.).
Income: Per capita income: $18,009 (2006-2010 5-year est.); Median household income: $31,525 (2006-2010 5-year est.); Average household income: $40,740 (2006-2010 5-year est.); Percent of households with

income of $100,000 or more: 6.6% (2006-2010 5-year est.); Poverty rate: 30.2% (2006-2010 5-year est.).

Taxes: Total city taxes per capita: $603 (2009); City property taxes per capita: $338 (2009).

Education: Percent of population age 25 and over with: High school diploma (including GED) or higher: 78.5% (2006-2010 5-year est.); Bachelor's degree or higher: 16.6% (2006-2010 5-year est.); Master's degree or higher: 6.1% (2006-2010 5-year est.).

School District(s)

Central Dauphin SD (KG-12)
    2010-11 Enrollment: 10,937 . . . . (717) 545-4703
Commonwealth Connections Academy CS (KG-12)
    2010-11 Enrollment: 4,424 . . . . (717) 605-8900
Dauphin County Technical School (09-12)
    2010-11 Enrollment: 792 . . . . (717) 652-3170
Harrisburg City SD (PK-12)
    2010-11 Enrollment: 7,944 . . . . (717) 703-4000
Susquehanna Township SD (KG-12)
    2010-11 Enrollment: 2,966 . . . . (717) 657-5100
Sylvan Heights Science CS (KG-04)
    2010-11 Enrollment: 219 . . . . (717) 232-9220

Four-year College(s)

Harrisburg University of Science and Technology (Private, Not-for-profit)
    Fall 2010 Enrollment: 281 . . . . (717) 901-5152
    2011-12 Tuition: In-state $22,500; Out-of-state $22,500
University of Phoenix-Harrisburg Campus (Private, For-profit)
    Fall 2010 Enrollment: 68 . . . . (717) 540-3300
    2011-12 Tuition: In-state $9,859; Out-of-state $9,859
Widener University-Harrisburg Campus (Private, Not-for-profit)
    Fall 2010 Enrollment: 605 . . . . (717) 541-3900

Two-year College(s)

Harrisburg Area Community College-Harrisburg (Public)
    Fall 2010 Enrollment: 14,621 . . . . (717) 780-2300
    2011-12 Tuition: In-state $6,675; Out-of-state $9,660
Kaplan Career Institute-Harrisburg (Private, For-profit)
    Fall 2010 Enrollment: 987 . . . . (717) 558-1300
Keystone Technical Institute (Private, For-profit)
    Fall 2010 Enrollment: 679 . . . . (717) 545-4747

Vocational/Technical School(s)

Empire Beauty School-Harrisburg (Private, For-profit)
    Fall 2010 Enrollment: 342 . . . . (800) 223-3271
    2011-12 Tuition: $14,490

Housing: Homeownership rate: 38.8% (2010); Median home value: $79,200 (2006-2010 5-year est.); Median contract rent: $560 per month (2006-2010 5-year est.); Median year structure built: before 1940 (2006-2010 5-year est.).

Hospitals: Community General/Pinnacle Health (126 beds); Pinnacle Health System (599 beds)

Safety: Violent crime rate: 140.3 per 10,000 population; Property crime rate: 506.2 per 10,000 population (2011).

Newspapers: Catholic Witness (Local news; Circulation 77,000); The Morning Call - Harrisburg Bureau (Local news); The Patriot-News (Local news; Circulation 144,210); The Paxton Herald (Community news; Circulation 30,000); The Philadelphia Inquirer - Harrisburg Bureau (Regional news); Pittsburgh Post-Gazette - Harrisburg Bureau (Local news; Circulation 220,000); Pittsburgh Tribune-Review - Harrisburg Bureau (Regional news); York Daily Record - Harrisburg Bureau (Local news)

Transportation: Commute to work: 76.8% car, 8.4% public transportation, 9.2% walk, 1.3% work from home (2006-2010 5-year est.); Travel time to work: 38.6% less than 15 minutes, 44.1% 15 to 30 minutes, 11.1% 30 to 45 minutes, 3.0% 45 to 60 minutes, 3.2% 60 minutes or more (2006-2010 5-year est.); Amtrak: train service available.

Airports: Harrisburg International (primary service/small hub)

Additional Information Contacts

City of Harrisburg . . . . (717) 255-3060
    http://www.harrisburgpa.gov
Harrisburg Regional Chamber & CREDC . . . . (717) 232-4099
    http://www.harrisburgregionalchamber.org

HERSHEY (CDP). Covers a land area of 14.359 square miles and a water area of 0.060 square miles. Located at 40.28° N. Lat; 76.64° W. Long. Elevation is 423 feet.

History: Company town owned by Hershey Corp. Hershey Park, theme park; Hershey's Chocolate World; Hershey Museum; ZooAmerica (North American wildlife); Indian Echo Caverns to Southwest. Founded 1903.

Population: 11,815 (1990); 12,771 (2000); 14,257 (2010); Density: 992.9 persons per square mile (2010); Race: 83.5% White, 6.2% Black, 6.6% Asian, 0.2% American Indian/Alaska Native, 0.1% Native Hawaiian/Other Pacific Islander, 3.4% Other, 3.4% Hispanic of any race (2010); Average household size: 2.21 (2010); Median age: 35.3 (2010); Males per 100 females: 89.8 (2010); Marriage status: 28.2% never married, 54.0% now married, 8.6% widowed, 9.3% divorced (2006-2010 5-year est.); Foreign born: 10.4% (2006-2010 5-year est.); Ancestry (includes multiple ancestries): 35.0% German, 19.8% Irish, 15.9% Italian, 9.3% English, 4.5% Polish (2006-2010 5-year est.).

Economy: Employment by occupation: 13.3% management, 7.6% professional, 9.9% services, 15.0% sales, 1.9% farming, 4.3% construction, 3.9% production (2006-2010 5-year est.).

Income: Per capita income: $35,387 (2006-2010 5-year est.); Median household income: $58,162 (2006-2010 5-year est.); Average household income: $78,736 (2006-2010 5-year est.); Percent of households with income of $100,000 or more: 25.3% (2006-2010 5-year est.); Poverty rate: 9.3% (2006-2010 5-year est.).

Education: Percent of population age 25 and over with: High school diploma (including GED) or higher: 95.3% (2006-2010 5-year est.); Bachelor's degree or higher: 52.1% (2006-2010 5-year est.); Master's degree or higher: 24.6% (2006-2010 5-year est.).

School District(s)

Derry Township SD (KG-12)
    2010-11 Enrollment: 3,596 . . . . (717) 534-2501
Lower Dauphin SD (KG-12)
    2010-11 Enrollment: 3,832 . . . . (717) 566-5300

Four-year College(s)

Pennsylvania State University-College of Medicine (Public)
    Fall 2010 Enrollment: 1,313 . . . . (717) 531-8521

Housing: Homeownership rate: 52.2% (2010); Median home value: $233,700 (2006-2010 5-year est.); Median contract rent: $742 per month (2006-2010 5-year est.); Median year structure built: 1969 (2006-2010 5-year est.).

Hospitals: Milton S Hershey Medical Center (504 beds)

Newspapers: Hershey Chronicle (Community news; Circulation 4,500)

Transportation: Commute to work: 83.3% car, 0.5% public transportation, 10.6% walk, 4.2% work from home (2006-2010 5-year est.); Travel time to work: 48.5% less than 15 minutes, 29.2% 15 to 30 minutes, 15.5% 30 to 45 minutes, 4.2% 45 to 60 minutes, 2.6% 60 minutes or more (2006-2010 5-year est.)

Additional Information Contacts

Hershey Partnership Chamber of Commerce . . . . (717) 298-1359
    http://www.hersheypartnership.com

HIGHSPIRE (borough). Aka High Spire. Covers a land area of 0.719 square miles and a water area of 0.022 square miles. Located at 40.21° N. Lat; 76.79° W. Long. Elevation is 318 feet.

History: Settled 1775, laid out 1814, incorporated 1867.

Population: 2,668 (1990); 2,720 (2000); 2,399 (2010); Density: 3,338.5 persons per square mile (2010); Race: 80.5% White, 10.8% Black, 1.2% Asian, 0.4% American Indian/Alaska Native, 0.0% Native Hawaiian/Other Pacific Islander, 7.1% Other, 8.8% Hispanic of any race (2010); Average household size: 2.05 (2010); Median age: 40.4 (2010); Males per 100 females: 96.3 (2010); Marriage status: 36.3% never married, 41.4% now married, 9.1% widowed, 13.2% divorced (2006-2010 5-year est.); Foreign born: 1.3% (2006-2010 5-year est.); Ancestry (includes multiple ancestries): 31.7% German, 14.5% Irish, 11.9% Italian, 7.6% Polish, 7.4% English (2006-2010 5-year est.).

Economy: Single-family building permits issued: 0 (2011); Multi-family building permits issued: 0 (2011); Employment by occupation: 7.1% management, 0.8% professional, 9.6% services, 22.4% sales, 7.2% farming, 7.2% construction, 6.8% production (2006-2010 5-year est.).

Income: Per capita income: $23,902 (2006-2010 5-year est.); Median household income: $40,100 (2006-2010 5-year est.); Average household income: $49,067 (2006-2010 5-year est.); Percent of households with income of $100,000 or more: 9.5% (2006-2010 5-year est.); Poverty rate: 15.3% (2006-2010 5-year est.).

Education: Percent of population age 25 and over with: High school diploma (including GED) or higher: 90.8% (2006-2010 5-year est.); Bachelor's degree or higher: 12.3% (2006-2010 5-year est.); Master's degree or higher: 3.7% (2006-2010 5-year est.).

Housing: Homeownership rate: 56.4% (2010); Median home value: $84,400 (2006-2010 5-year est.); Median contract rent: $544 per month (2006-2010 5-year est.); Median year structure built: 1959 (2006-2010 5-year est.).

Safety: Violent crime rate: 58.2 per 10,000 population; Property crime rate: 153.7 per 10,000 population (2011).

Transportation: Commute to work: 91.0% car, 0.0% public transportation, 5.3% walk, 2.1% work from home (2006-2010 5-year est.); Travel time to work: 33.2% less than 15 minutes, 46.1% 15 to 30 minutes, 14.3% 30 to 45 minutes, 3.7% 45 to 60 minutes, 2.7% 60 minutes or more (2006-2010 5-year est.)

Additional Information Contacts

Harrisburg Regional Chamber & CREDC . . . . (717) 232-4099
http://www.harrisburgregionalchamber.org

HUMMELSTOWN (borough). Covers a land area of 1.227 square miles and a water area of 0.083 square miles. Located at 40.27° N. Lat; 76.71° W. Long. Elevation is 384 feet.

History: Founded c.1740, laid out 1762, incorporated 1874.

Population: 3,981 (1990); 4,360 (2000); 4,538 (2010); Density: 3,697.6 persons per square mile (2010); Race: 94.6% White, 1.1% Black, 1.4% Asian, 0.2% American Indian/Alaska Native, 0.1% Native Hawaiian/Other Pacific Islander, 2.6% Other, 3.0% Hispanic of any race (2010); Average household size: 2.34 (2010); Median age: 39.0 (2010); Males per 100 females: 93.6 (2010); Marriage status: 34.9% never married, 47.3% now married, 4.0% widowed, 13.8% divorced (2006-2010 5-year est.); Foreign born: 1.5% (2006-2010 5-year est.); Ancestry (includes multiple ancestries): 53.4% German, 13.5% Irish, 9.7% Italian, 9.4% English, 6.4% Polish (2006-2010 5-year est.).

Economy: Single-family building permits issued: 1 (2011); Multi-family building permits issued: 0 (2011); Employment by occupation: 16.5% management, 2.6% professional, 6.5% services, 18.0% sales, 1.6% farming, 6.2% construction, 3.6% production (2006-2010 5-year est.).

Income: Per capita income: $29,191 (2006-2010 5-year est.); Median household income: $58,325 (2006-2010 5-year est.); Average household income: $62,715 (2006-2010 5-year est.); Percent of households with income of $100,000 or more: 14.9% (2006-2010 5-year est.); Poverty rate: 4.5% (2006-2010 5-year est.).

Education: Percent of population age 25 and over with: High school diploma (including GED) or higher: 92.6% (2006-2010 5-year est.); Bachelor's degree or higher: 29.3% (2006-2010 5-year est.); Master's degree or higher: 13.1% (2006-2010 5-year est.).

School District(s)

Lower Dauphin SD (KG-12)

    2010-11 Enrollment: 3,832 . . . . (717) 566-5300

Housing: Homeownership rate: 60.3% (2010); Median home value: $153,300 (2006-2010 5-year est.); Median contract rent: $593 per month (2006-2010 5-year est.); Median year structure built: 1956 (2006-2010 5-year est.).

Newspapers: Sun (Local news; Circulation 6,400)

Transportation: Commute to work: 90.8% car, 1.3% public transportation, 3.2% walk, 3.6% work from home (2006-2010 5-year est.); Travel time to work: 42.1% less than 15 minutes, 36.7% 15 to 30 minutes, 17.2% 30 to 45 minutes, 2.0% 45 to 60 minutes, 2.0% 60 minutes or more (2006-2010 5-year est.)

Additional Information Contacts

Hershey Partnership Chamber of Commerce . . . . (717) 298-1359
http://www.hersheypartnership.com

JACKSON (township). Covers a land area of 40.066 square miles and a water area of 0 square miles. Located at 40.53° N. Lat; 76.78° W. Long.

Population: 1,797 (1990); 1,728 (2000); 1,941 (2010); Density: 48.4 persons per square mile (2010); Race: 98.7% White, 0.3% Black, 0.3% Asian, 0.1% American Indian/Alaska Native, 0.0% Native Hawaiian/Other Pacific Islander, 0.6% Other, 0.7% Hispanic of any race (2010); Average household size: 2.62 (2010); Median age: 43.7 (2010); Males per 100 females: 103.7 (2010); Marriage status: 22.2% never married, 66.9% now married, 5.0% widowed, 5.9% divorced (2006-2010 5-year est.); Foreign born: 0.3% (2006-2010 5-year est.); Ancestry (includes multiple ancestries): 54.1% German, 10.7% English, 9.5% American, 6.3% Irish, 4.7% Pennsylvania German (2006-2010 5-year est.).

Economy: Single-family building permits issued: 4 (2011); Multi-family building permits issued: 0 (2011); Employment by occupation: 6.9% management, 4.6% professional, 8.3% services, 21.5% sales, 3.5% farming, 16.2% construction, 8.6% production (2006-2010 5-year est.).

Income: Per capita income: $26,455 (2006-2010 5-year est.); Median household income: $61,250 (2006-2010 5-year est.); Average household income: $71,002 (2006-2010 5-year est.); Percent of households with income of $100,000 or more: 22.8% (2006-2010 5-year est.); Poverty rate: 4.6% (2006-2010 5-year est.).

Education: Percent of population age 25 and over with: High school diploma (including GED) or higher: 88.3% (2006-2010 5-year est.); Bachelor's degree or higher: 11.8% (2006-2010 5-year est.); Master's degree or higher: 3.1% (2006-2010 5-year est.).

Housing: Homeownership rate: 90.2% (2010); Median home value: $140,200 (2006-2010 5-year est.); Median contract rent: $463 per month (2006-2010 5-year est.); Median year structure built: 1976 (2006-2010 5-year est.).

Transportation: Commute to work: 92.7% car, 2.3% public transportation, 1.1% walk, 3.9% work from home (2006-2010 5-year est.); Travel time to work: 16.0% less than 15 minutes, 14.9% 15 to 30 minutes, 21.6% 30 to 45 minutes, 31.1% 45 to 60 minutes, 16.4% 60 minutes or more (2006-2010 5-year est.)

Additional Information Contacts

Harrisburg Regional Chamber & CREDC . . . . (717) 232-4099
http://www.harrisburgregionalchamber.org

JEFFERSON (township). Covers a land area of 24.356 square miles and a water area of 0 square miles. Located at 40.51° N. Lat; 76.70° W. Long.

Population: 385 (1990); 327 (2000); 362 (2010); Density: 14.9 persons per square mile (2010); Race: 98.9% White, 0.0% Black, 0.3% Asian, 0.6% American Indian/Alaska Native, 0.0% Native Hawaiian/Other Pacific Islander, 0.2% Other, 0.3% Hispanic of any race (2010); Average household size: 2.41 (2010); Median age: 48.0 (2010); Males per 100 females: 100.0 (2010); Marriage status: 24.7% never married, 56.3% now married, 10.8% widowed, 8.1% divorced (2006-2010 5-year est.); Foreign born: 0.5% (2006-2010 5-year est.); Ancestry (includes multiple ancestries): 42.3% German, 17.5% Irish, 11.2% English, 9.9% American, 8.9% Pennsylvania German (2006-2010 5-year est.).

Economy: Single-family building permits issued: 0 (2011); Multi-family building permits issued: 0 (2011); Employment by occupation: 8.9% management, 3.4% professional, 10.6% services, 16.8% sales, 7.8% farming, 16.2% construction, 12.3% production (2006-2010 5-year est.).

Income: Per capita income: $27,674 (2006-2010 5-year est.); Median household income: $60,714 (2006-2010 5-year est.); Average household income: $71,926 (2006-2010 5-year est.); Percent of households with income of $100,000 or more: 19.7% (2006-2010 5-year est.); Poverty rate: 16.2% (2006-2010 5-year est.).

Education: Percent of population age 25 and over with: High school diploma (including GED) or higher: 78.3% (2006-2010 5-year est.); Bachelor's degree or higher: 10.8% (2006-2010 5-year est.); Master's degree or higher: 4.5% (2006-2010 5-year est.).

Housing: Homeownership rate: 79.4% (2010); Median home value: $173,700 (2006-2010 5-year est.); Median contract rent: $338 per month (2006-2010 5-year est.); Median year structure built: 1968 (2006-2010 5-year est.).

Transportation: Commute to work: 95.5% car, 0.0% public transportation, 1.1% walk, 2.2% work from home (2006-2010 5-year est.); Travel time to work: 11.4% less than 15 minutes, 33.7% 15 to 30 minutes, 22.9% 30 to 45 minutes, 21.7% 45 to 60 minutes, 10.3% 60 minutes or more (2006-2010 5-year est.)

LAWNTON (CDP). Covers a land area of 1.158 square miles and a water area of 0 square miles. Located at 40.26° N. Lat; 76.80° W. Long. Elevation is 390 feet.

Population: 3,189 (1990); 3,787 (2000); 3,813 (2010); Density: 3,292.3 persons per square mile (2010); Race: 69.9% White, 18.8% Black, 4.3% Asian, 0.3% American Indian/Alaska Native, 0.0% Native Hawaiian/Other Pacific Islander, 6.7% Other, 7.0% Hispanic of any race (2010); Average household size: 2.29 (2010); Median age: 40.7 (2010); Males per 100 females: 87.8 (2010); Marriage status: 32.6% never married, 54.5% now married, 3.9% widowed, 9.0% divorced (2006-2010 5-year est.); Foreign born: 7.0% (2006-2010 5-year est.); Ancestry (includes multiple ancestries): 28.9% German, 18.1% Irish, 11.3% Italian, 10.6% English, 6.6% Polish (2006-2010 5-year est.).

Economy: Employment by occupation: 13.0% management, 6.2% professional, 9.5% services, 18.2% sales, 4.8% farming, 5.3% construction, 6.8% production (2006-2010 5-year est.).
Income: Per capita income: $29,307 (2006-2010 5-year est.); Median household income: $61,939 (2006-2010 5-year est.); Average household income: $67,439 (2006-2010 5-year est.); Percent of households with income of $100,000 or more: 16.1% (2006-2010 5-year est.); Poverty rate: 2.3% (2006-2010 5-year est.).
Education: Percent of population age 25 and over with: High school diploma (including GED) or higher: 92.0% (2006-2010 5-year est.); Bachelor's degree or higher: 27.4% (2006-2010 5-year est.); Master's degree or higher: 11.5% (2006-2010 5-year est.).
Housing: Homeownership rate: 66.0% (2010); Median home value: $147,800 (2006-2010 5-year est.); Median contract rent: $570 per month (2006-2010 5-year est.); Median year structure built: 1971 (2006-2010 5-year est.).
Transportation: Commute to work: 96.0% car, 0.9% public transportation, 0.0% walk, 0.6% work from home (2006-2010 5-year est.); Travel time to work: 39.2% less than 15 minutes, 46.0% 15 to 30 minutes, 9.6% 30 to 45 minutes, 4.1% 45 to 60 minutes, 1.1% 60 minutes or more (2006-2010 5-year est.)

Additional Information Contacts
Harrisburg Regional Chamber & CREDC . . . . (717) 232-4099
   http://www.harrisburgregionalchamber.org

LENKERVILLE (CDP).
Covers a land area of 0.335 square miles and a water area of 0 square miles. Located at 40.53° N. Lat; 76.96° W. Long. Elevation is 413 feet.
Population: n/a (1990); n/a (2000); 550 (2010); Density: 1,639.8 persons per square mile (2010); Race: 96.0% White, 2.4% Black, 0.4% Asian, 0.2% American Indian/Alaska Native, 0.0% Native Hawaiian/Other Pacific Islander, 1.0% Other, 1.5% Hispanic of any race (2010); Average household size: 2.40 (2010); Median age: 37.4 (2010); Males per 100 females: 91.0 (2010); Marriage status: 24.2% never married, 51.2% now married, 4.3% widowed, 20.3% divorced (2006-2010 5-year est.); Foreign born: 0.0% (2006-2010 5-year est.); Ancestry (includes multiple ancestries): 56.0% German, 18.9% American, 7.9% Scotch-Irish, 4.9% Pennsylvania German, 4.4% Italian (2006-2010 5-year est.).
Economy: Employment by occupation: 7.9% management, 0.0% professional, 0.0% services, 41.3% sales, 6.3% farming, 19.0% construction, 6.7% production (2006-2010 5-year est.).
Income: Per capita income: $24,483 (2006-2010 5-year est.); Median household income: $47,772 (2006-2010 5-year est.); Average household income: $45,299 (2006-2010 5-year est.); Percent of households with income of $100,000 or more: 2.3% (2006-2010 5-year est.); Poverty rate: 17.5% (2006-2010 5-year est.).
Education: Percent of population age 25 and over with: High school diploma (including GED) or higher: 86.8% (2006-2010 5-year est.); Bachelor's degree or higher: 15.2% (2006-2010 5-year est.); Master's degree or higher: 10.6% (2006-2010 5-year est.).
Housing: Homeownership rate: 59.0% (2010); Median home value: $92,600 (2006-2010 5-year est.); Median contract rent: $395 per month (2006-2010 5-year est.); Median year structure built: 1972 (2006-2010 5-year est.).
Transportation: Commute to work: 74.9% car, 0.0% public transportation, 25.1% walk, 0.0% work from home (2006-2010 5-year est.); Travel time to work: 35.0% less than 15 minutes, 4.6% 15 to 30 minutes, 37.6% 30 to 45 minutes, 10.9% 45 to 60 minutes, 11.9% 60 minutes or more (2006-2010 5-year est.)

LINGLESTOWN (CDP).
Covers a land area of 3.827 square miles and a water area of 0 square miles. Located at 40.34° N. Lat; 76.79° W. Long. Elevation is 541 feet.
Population: 5,862 (1990); 6,414 (2000); 6,334 (2010); Density: 1,655.2 persons per square mile (2010); Race: 91.1% White, 4.2% Black, 2.0% Asian, 0.2% American Indian/Alaska Native, 0.0% Native Hawaiian/Other Pacific Islander, 2.5% Other, 2.5% Hispanic of any race (2010); Average household size: 2.45 (2010); Median age: 44.3 (2010); Males per 100 females: 92.9 (2010); Marriage status: 28.1% never married, 58.4% now married, 5.2% widowed, 8.3% divorced (2006-2010 5-year est.); Foreign born: 3.4% (2006-2010 5-year est.); Ancestry (includes multiple ancestries): 42.3% German, 18.5% Irish, 10.4% Italian, 9.7% English, 4.9% American (2006-2010 5-year est.).

Economy: Employment by occupation: 18.6% management, 7.1% professional, 6.7% services, 18.1% sales, 5.7% farming, 6.5% construction, 4.9% production (2006-2010 5-year est.).
Income: Per capita income: $31,673 (2006-2010 5-year est.); Median household income: $71,439 (2006-2010 5-year est.); Average household income: $81,631 (2006-2010 5-year est.); Percent of households with income of $100,000 or more: 30.1% (2006-2010 5-year est.); Poverty rate: 3.3% (2006-2010 5-year est.).
Education: Percent of population age 25 and over with: High school diploma (including GED) or higher: 93.8% (2006-2010 5-year est.); Bachelor's degree or higher: 35.3% (2006-2010 5-year est.); Master's degree or higher: 10.6% (2006-2010 5-year est.).
Housing: Homeownership rate: 86.7% (2010); Median home value: $170,800 (2006-2010 5-year est.); Median contract rent: $825 per month (2006-2010 5-year est.); Median year structure built: 1974 (2006-2010 5-year est.).
Transportation: Commute to work: 92.5% car, 0.9% public transportation, 1.3% walk, 3.5% work from home (2006-2010 5-year est.); Travel time to work: 30.1% less than 15 minutes, 53.8% 15 to 30 minutes, 10.2% 30 to 45 minutes, 3.9% 45 to 60 minutes, 2.1% 60 minutes or more (2006-2010 5-year est.)

Additional Information Contacts
Harrisburg Regional Chamber & CREDC . . . . (717) 232-4099
   http://www.harrisburgregionalchamber.org

LONDONDERRY (township).
Covers a land area of 22.755 square miles and a water area of 4.171 square miles. Located at 40.18° N. Lat; 76.70° W. Long.
Population: 4,926 (1990); 5,224 (2000); 5,235 (2010); Density: 230.1 persons per square mile (2010); Race: 96.9% White, 0.6% Black, 0.4% Asian, 0.1% American Indian/Alaska Native, 0.0% Native Hawaiian/Other Pacific Islander, 2.0% Other, 3.2% Hispanic of any race (2010); Average household size: 2.56 (2010); Median age: 43.4 (2010); Males per 100 females: 99.5 (2010); Marriage status: 25.1% never married, 58.3% now married, 7.7% widowed, 9.0% divorced (2006-2010 5-year est.); Foreign born: 0.5% (2006-2010 5-year est.); Ancestry (includes multiple ancestries): 44.5% German, 18.5% Irish, 8.4% Italian, 6.8% American, 6.0% English (2006-2010 5-year est.).
Economy: Single-family building permits issued: 3 (2011); Multi-family building permits issued: 0 (2011); Employment by occupation: 6.6% management, 4.5% professional, 7.7% services, 19.8% sales, 5.0% farming, 11.4% construction, 11.4% production (2006-2010 5-year est.).
Income: Per capita income: $24,319 (2006-2010 5-year est.); Median household income: $61,528 (2006-2010 5-year est.); Average household income: $69,960 (2006-2010 5-year est.); Percent of households with income of $100,000 or more: 21.9% (2006-2010 5-year est.); Poverty rate: 9.6% (2006-2010 5-year est.).
Education: Percent of population age 25 and over with: High school diploma (including GED) or higher: 83.0% (2006-2010 5-year est.); Bachelor's degree or higher: 10.7% (2006-2010 5-year est.); Master's degree or higher: 4.1% (2006-2010 5-year est.).
Housing: Homeownership rate: 86.7% (2010); Median home value: $133,500 (2006-2010 5-year est.); Median contract rent: $468 per month (2006-2010 5-year est.); Median year structure built: 1971 (2006-2010 5-year est.).
Transportation: Commute to work: 95.8% car, 0.0% public transportation, 1.8% walk, 1.4% work from home (2006-2010 5-year est.); Travel time to work: 31.4% less than 15 minutes, 45.1% 15 to 30 minutes, 15.9% 30 to 45 minutes, 2.3% 45 to 60 minutes, 5.3% 60 minutes or more (2006-2010 5-year est.)

Additional Information Contacts
Elizabethtown Area Chamber of Commerce . . . . (717) 361-7188
   http://www.elizabethtowncoc.com
Londonderry Township . . . . (717) 944-1803
   http://www.londonderrypa.org

LOWER PAXTON (township).
Covers a land area of 28.171 square miles and a water area of 0 square miles. Located at 40.32° N. Lat; 76.80° W. Long.
Population: 39,128 (1990); 44,424 (2000); 47,360 (2010); Density: 1,681.2 persons per square mile (2010); Race: 78.8% White, 12.2% Black, 4.6% Asian, 0.1% American Indian/Alaska Native, 0.0% Native Hawaiian/Other Pacific Islander, 4.3% Other, 4.6% Hispanic of any race (2010); Average household size: 2.34 (2010); Median age: 41.2 (2010); Males per 100 females: 92.0 (2010); Marriage status: 29.3% never

married, 53.7% now married, 5.9% widowed, 11.1% divorced (2006-2010 5-year est.); Foreign born: 7.4% (2006-2010 5-year est.); Ancestry (includes multiple ancestries): 34.1% German, 14.0% Irish, 9.7% Italian, 8.1% English, 5.4% American (2006-2010 5-year est.).

Economy: Unemployment rate: 6.7% (August 2012); Total civilian labor force: 26,995 (August 2012); Single-family building permits issued: 55 (2011); Multi-family building permits issued: 0 (2011); Employment by occupation: 15.6% management, 7.0% professional, 7.3% services, 19.5% sales, 4.9% farming, 5.2% construction, 4.1% production (2006-2010 5-year est.).

Income: Per capita income: $33,767 (2006-2010 5-year est.); Median household income: $64,758 (2006-2010 5-year est.); Average household income: $78,513 (2006-2010 5-year est.); Percent of households with income of $100,000 or more: 26.2% (2006-2010 5-year est.); Poverty rate: 5.4% (2006-2010 5-year est.).

Taxes: Total city taxes per capita: $265 (2009); City property taxes per capita: $56 (2009).

Education: Percent of population age 25 and over with: High school diploma (including GED) or higher: 94.4% (2006-2010 5-year est.); Bachelor's degree or higher: 34.9% (2006-2010 5-year est.); Master's degree or higher: 12.2% (2006-2010 5-year est.).

Housing: Homeownership rate: 67.1% (2010); Median home value: $177,900 (2006-2010 5-year est.); Median contract rent: $741 per month (2006-2010 5-year est.); Median year structure built: 1975 (2006-2010 5-year est.).

Safety: Violent crime rate: 25.0 per 10,000 population; Property crime rate: 256.4 per 10,000 population (2011).

Transportation: Commute to work: 94.2% car, 1.1% public transportation, 1.8% walk, 2.1% work from home (2006-2010 5-year est.); Travel time to work: 30.2% less than 15 minutes, 53.2% 15 to 30 minutes, 11.5% 30 to 45 minutes, 2.4% 45 to 60 minutes, 2.7% 60 minutes or more (2006-2010 5-year est.)

Additional Information Contacts
Harrisburg Regional Chamber & CREDC . . . . (717) 232-4099
    http://www.harrisburgregionalchamber.org
Lower Paxton Township . . . . (717) 657-5600
    http://www.lowerpaxton-pa.gov

LOWER SWATARA (township). Covers a land area of 12.319 square miles and a water area of 2.486 square miles. Located at 40.22° N. Lat; 76.76° W. Long.

Population: 7,072 (1990); 8,149 (2000); 8,268 (2010); Density: 671.2 persons per square mile (2010); Race: 89.5% White, 4.8% Black, 1.4% Asian, 0.2% American Indian/Alaska Native, 0.0% Native Hawaiian/Other Pacific Islander, 4.1% Other, 4.0% Hispanic of any race (2010); Average household size: 2.41 (2010); Median age: 42.7 (2010); Males per 100 females: 93.3 (2010); Marriage status: 29.5% never married, 58.1% now married, 6.3% widowed, 6.2% divorced (2006-2010 5-year est.); Foreign born: 5.7% (2006-2010 5-year est.); Ancestry (includes multiple ancestries): 37.5% German, 13.8% Irish, 7.6% American, 6.7% Italian, 6.6% Polish (2006-2010 5-year est.).

Economy: Single-family building permits issued: 12 (2011); Multi-family building permits issued: 0 (2011); Employment by occupation: 10.1% management, 4.3% professional, 6.4% services, 20.3% sales, 4.6% farming, 8.0% construction, 8.0% production (2006-2010 5-year est.).

Income: Per capita income: $28,870 (2006-2010 5-year est.); Median household income: $67,321 (2006-2010 5-year est.); Average household income: $74,661 (2006-2010 5-year est.); Percent of households with income of $100,000 or more: 23.2% (2006-2010 5-year est.); Poverty rate: 4.2% (2006-2010 5-year est.).

Taxes: Total city taxes per capita: $459 (2009); City property taxes per capita: $248 (2009).

Education: Percent of population age 25 and over with: High school diploma (including GED) or higher: 90.8% (2006-2010 5-year est.); Bachelor's degree or higher: 28.0% (2006-2010 5-year est.); Master's degree or higher: 9.2% (2006-2010 5-year est.).

Housing: Homeownership rate: 87.4% (2010); Median home value: $144,400 (2006-2010 5-year est.); Median contract rent: $621 per month (2006-2010 5-year est.); Median year structure built: 1978 (2006-2010 5-year est.).

Safety: Violent crime rate: 20.5 per 10,000 population; Property crime rate: 156.7 per 10,000 population (2011).

Transportation: Commute to work: 92.5% car, 0.4% public transportation, 2.0% walk, 3.1% work from home (2006-2010 5-year est.); Travel time to work: 33.6% less than 15 minutes, 50.1% 15 to 30 minutes, 13.6% 30 to

45 minutes, 1.9% 45 to 60 minutes, 0.8% 60 minutes or more (2006-2010 5-year est.)

Additional Information Contacts
Harrisburg Regional Chamber & CREDC . . . . (717) 232-4099
    http://www.harrisburgregionalchamber.org
Lower Swatara Township . . . . (717) 939-9377
    http://lowerswatara.org

LYKENS (borough). Covers a land area of 1.220 square miles and a water area of 0 square miles. Located at 40.56° N. Lat; 76.70° W. Long. Elevation is 689 feet.

Population: 1,986 (1990); 1,937 (2000); 1,779 (2010); Density: 1,458.7 persons per square mile (2010); Race: 96.6% White, 0.1% Black, 1.1% Asian, 0.0% American Indian/Alaska Native, 0.0% Native Hawaiian/Other Pacific Islander, 2.2% Other, 2.2% Hispanic of any race (2010); Average household size: 2.30 (2010); Median age: 43.0 (2010); Males per 100 females: 97.9 (2010); Marriage status: 20.8% never married, 60.3% now married, 8.2% widowed, 10.8% divorced (2006-2010 5-year est.); Foreign born: 0.7% (2006-2010 5-year est.); Ancestry (includes multiple ancestries): 47.5% German, 13.9% English, 10.3% Irish, 9.2% American, 7.4% Dutch (2006-2010 5-year est.).

Economy: Single-family building permits issued: 0 (2011); Multi-family building permits issued: 0 (2011); Employment by occupation: 2.0% management, 1.4% professional, 10.4% services, 21.7% sales, 2.8% farming, 12.8% construction, 11.6% production (2006-2010 5-year est.).

Income: Per capita income: $21,956 (2006-2010 5-year est.); Median household income: $45,662 (2006-2010 5-year est.); Average household income: $53,043 (2006-2010 5-year est.); Percent of households with income of $100,000 or more: 9.0% (2006-2010 5-year est.); Poverty rate: 5.5% (2006-2010 5-year est.).

Education: Percent of population age 25 and over with: High school diploma (including GED) or higher: 88.5% (2006-2010 5-year est.); Bachelor's degree or higher: 8.7% (2006-2010 5-year est.); Master's degree or higher: 1.8% (2006-2010 5-year est.).

School District(s)
Upper Dauphin Area SD (KG-12)
    2010-11 Enrollment: 1,278 . . . . (717) 362-8134

Housing: Homeownership rate: 73.3% (2010); Median home value: $68,800 (2006-2010 5-year est.); Median contract rent: $465 per month (2006-2010 5-year est.); Median year structure built: before 1940 (2006-2010 5-year est.).

Safety: Violent crime rate: 5.6 per 10,000 population; Property crime rate: 106.4 per 10,000 population (2011).

Transportation: Commute to work: 84.6% car, 1.5% public transportation, 5.5% walk, 2.4% work from home (2006-2010 5-year est.); Travel time to work: 34.1% less than 15 minutes, 19.7% 15 to 30 minutes, 10.8% 30 to 45 minutes, 17.6% 45 to 60 minutes, 17.7% 60 minutes or more (2006-2010 5-year est.)

Additional Information Contacts
Harrisburg Regional Chamber & CREDC . . . . (717) 232-4099
    http://www.harrisburgregionalchamber.org

LYKENS (township). Covers a land area of 26.476 square miles and a water area of 0.007 square miles. Located at 40.62° N. Lat; 76.73° W. Long. Elevation is 689 feet.

History: Settled c.1740; laid out 1848; incorporated 1872.

Population: 1,231 (1990); 1,095 (2000); 1,618 (2010); Density: 61.1 persons per square mile (2010); Race: 98.3% White, 0.2% Black, 0.1% Asian, 0.1% American Indian/Alaska Native, 0.1% Native Hawaiian/Other Pacific Islander, 1.2% Other, 0.9% Hispanic of any race (2010); Average household size: 3.21 (2010); Median age: 31.6 (2010); Males per 100 females: 111.0 (2010); Marriage status: 23.2% never married, 65.1% now married, 6.9% widowed, 4.8% divorced (2006-2010 5-year est.); Foreign born: 0.0% (2006-2010 5-year est.); Ancestry (includes multiple ancestries): 62.0% German, 11.7% Pennsylvania German, 7.4% Swiss, 7.2% Dutch, 4.2% Irish (2006-2010 5-year est.).

Economy: Single-family building permits issued: 3 (2011); Multi-family building permits issued: 0 (2011); Employment by occupation: 10.0% management, 2.6% professional, 10.6% services, 14.9% sales, 4.2% farming, 14.9% construction, 10.6% production (2006-2010 5-year est.).

Income: Per capita income: $19,545 (2006-2010 5-year est.); Median household income: $53,333 (2006-2010 5-year est.); Average household income: $61,442 (2006-2010 5-year est.); Percent of households with income of $100,000 or more: 12.7% (2006-2010 5-year est.); Poverty rate: 5.2% (2006-2010 5-year est.).

Education: Percent of population age 25 and over with: High school diploma (including GED) or higher: 71.0% (2006-2010 5-year est.); Bachelor's degree or higher: 6.6% (2006-2010 5-year est.); Master's degree or higher: 1.7% (2006-2010 5-year est.).
Housing: Homeownership rate: 80.0% (2010); Median home value: $119,000 (2006-2010 5-year est.); Median contract rent: $508 per month (2006-2010 5-year est.); Median year structure built: 1967 (2006-2010 5-year est.).
Transportation: Commute to work: 84.3% car, 0.4% public transportation, 2.0% walk, 12.2% work from home (2006-2010 5-year est.); Travel time to work: 37.1% less than 15 minutes, 25.1% 15 to 30 minutes, 11.4% 30 to 45 minutes, 11.4% 45 to 60 minutes, 15.1% 60 minutes or more (2006-2010 5-year est.)
Additional Information Contacts
Harrisburg Regional Chamber & CREDC . . . . (717) 232-4099
    http://www.harrisburgregionalchamber.org

MIDDLE PAXTON (township). Covers a land area of 54.408 square miles and a water area of 4.735 square miles. Located at 40.39° N. Lat; 76.89° W. Long.
Population: 5,056 (1990); 4,823 (2000); 4,976 (2010); Density: 91.5 persons per square mile (2010); Race: 97.0% White, 0.9% Black, 0.5% Asian, 0.1% American Indian/Alaska Native, 0.0% Native Hawaiian/Other Pacific Islander, 1.5% Other, 1.8% Hispanic of any race (2010); Average household size: 2.41 (2010); Median age: 47.7 (2010); Males per 100 females: 99.9 (2010); Marriage status: 17.8% never married, 66.3% now married, 3.8% widowed, 12.1% divorced (2006-2010 5-year est.); Foreign born: 0.7% (2006-2010 5-year est.); Ancestry (includes multiple ancestries): 47.8% German, 14.5% Irish, 8.8% Italian, 7.5% English, 4.4% Dutch (2006-2010 5-year est.).
Economy: Single-family building permits issued: 15 (2011); Multi-family building permits issued: 0 (2011); Employment by occupation: 6.3% management, 4.4% professional, 6.1% services, 19.5% sales, 5.0% farming, 13.9% construction, 3.4% production (2006-2010 5-year est.).
Income: Per capita income: $31,592 (2006-2010 5-year est.); Median household income: $63,982 (2006-2010 5-year est.); Average household income: $70,670 (2006-2010 5-year est.); Percent of households with income of $100,000 or more: 26.1% (2006-2010 5-year est.); Poverty rate: 3.5% (2006-2010 5-year est.).
Education: Percent of population age 25 and over with: High school diploma (including GED) or higher: 87.9% (2006-2010 5-year est.); Bachelor's degree or higher: 32.9% (2006-2010 5-year est.); Master's degree or higher: 13.1% (2006-2010 5-year est.).
Housing: Homeownership rate: 87.2% (2010); Median home value: $180,700 (2006-2010 5-year est.); Median contract rent: $580 per month (2006-2010 5-year est.); Median year structure built: 1972 (2006-2010 5-year est.).
Transportation: Commute to work: 94.2% car, 0.0% public transportation, 0.7% walk, 4.5% work from home (2006-2010 5-year est.); Travel time to work: 13.1% less than 15 minutes, 60.7% 15 to 30 minutes, 20.7% 30 to 45 minutes, 4.2% 45 to 60 minutes, 1.3% 60 minutes or more (2006-2010 5-year est.)
Additional Information Contacts
Harrisburg Regional Chamber & CREDC . . . . (717) 232-4099
    http://www.harrisburgregionalchamber.org

MIDDLETOWN (borough). Covers a land area of 2.039 square miles and a water area of 0.049 square miles. Located at 40.20° N. Lat; 76.73° W. Long. Elevation is 361 feet.
History: Penn State Harrisburg, Capital College is here. Laid out 1755; incorporated 1828.
Population: 9,254 (1990); 9,242 (2000); 8,901 (2010); Density: 4,366.0 persons per square mile (2010); Race: 83.6% White, 8.3% Black, 1.8% Asian, 0.1% American Indian/Alaska Native, 0.0% Native Hawaiian/Other Pacific Islander, 6.2% Other, 5.7% Hispanic of any race (2010); Average household size: 2.22 (2010); Median age: 37.2 (2010); Males per 100 females: 92.5 (2010); Marriage status: 38.9% never married, 42.3% now married, 8.1% widowed, 10.7% divorced (2006-2010 5-year est.); Foreign born: 3.1% (2006-2010 5-year est.); Ancestry (includes multiple ancestries): 35.3% German, 15.1% Irish, 11.3% Italian, 7.2% English, 6.4% American (2006-2010 5-year est.).
Economy: Single-family building permits issued: 2 (2011); Multi-family building permits issued: 0 (2011); Employment by occupation: 6.7% management, 1.9% professional, 11.3% services, 21.3% sales, 4.4% farming, 6.5% construction, 5.8% production (2006-2010 5-year est.).

Income: Per capita income: $24,054 (2006-2010 5-year est.); Median household income: $50,212 (2006-2010 5-year est.); Average household income: $56,434 (2006-2010 5-year est.); Percent of households with income of $100,000 or more: 12.6% (2006-2010 5-year est.); Poverty rate: 12.8% (2006-2010 5-year est.).
Taxes: Total city taxes per capita: $295 (2009); City property taxes per capita: $168 (2009).
Education: Percent of population age 25 and over with: High school diploma (including GED) or higher: 86.6% (2006-2010 5-year est.); Bachelor's degree or higher: 15.1% (2006-2010 5-year est.); Master's degree or higher: 3.7% (2006-2010 5-year est.).

School District(s)
Lower Dauphin SD (KG-12)
    2010-11 Enrollment: 3,832 . . . . (717) 566-5300
Middletown Area SD (KG-12)
    2010-11 Enrollment: 2,309 . . . . (717) 948-3300
Four-year College(s)
Pennsylvania State University-Penn State Harrisburg (Public)
    Fall 2010 Enrollment: 3,556 . . . . (717) 948-6452
    2011-12 Tuition: In-state $13,628; Out-of-state $20,400
Housing: Homeownership rate: 50.3% (2010); Median home value: $114,500 (2006-2010 5-year est.); Median contract rent: $611 per month (2006-2010 5-year est.); Median year structure built: 1956 (2006-2010 5-year est.).
Safety: Violent crime rate: 21.3 per 10,000 population; Property crime rate: 160.2 per 10,000 population (2011).
Newspapers: Jednota (Regional news; Circulation 17,000); Press & Journal (Local news; Circulation 10,000)
Transportation: Commute to work: 89.7% car, 2.9% public transportation, 4.2% walk, 1.8% work from home (2006-2010 5-year est.); Travel time to work: 33.2% less than 15 minutes, 43.1% 15 to 30 minutes, 15.7% 30 to 45 minutes, 1.4% 45 to 60 minutes, 6.7% 60 minutes or more (2006-2010 5-year est.); Amtrak: train service available.
Additional Information Contacts
Borough of Middletown . . . . (717) 948-3050
    http://www.middletownborough.com
Elizabethtown Area Chamber of Commerce . . . . (717) 361-7188
    http://www.elizabethtowncoc.com

MIFFLIN (township). Covers a land area of 15.498 square miles and a water area of 0 square miles. Located at 40.60° N. Lat; 76.84° W. Long.
Population: 651 (1990); 662 (2000); 784 (2010); Density: 50.6 persons per square mile (2010); Race: 98.9% White, 0.8% Black, 0.1% Asian, 0.1% American Indian/Alaska Native, 0.0% Native Hawaiian/Other Pacific Islander, 0.1% Other, 0.5% Hispanic of any race (2010); Average household size: 3.20 (2010); Median age: 31.9 (2010); Males per 100 females: 114.2 (2010); Marriage status: 21.1% never married, 73.4% now married, 3.8% widowed, 1.6% divorced (2006-2010 5-year est.); Foreign born: 1.0% (2006-2010 5-year est.); Ancestry (includes multiple ancestries): 67.7% German, 10.1% American, 9.0% English, 5.9% Pennsylvania German, 2.5% Dutch (2006-2010 5-year est.).
Economy: Single-family building permits issued: 2 (2011); Multi-family building permits issued: 0 (2011); Employment by occupation: 12.0% management, 2.1% professional, 9.4% services, 12.3% sales, 4.0% farming, 13.7% construction, 12.3% production (2006-2010 5-year est.).
Income: Per capita income: $22,285 (2006-2010 5-year est.); Median household income: $57,813 (2006-2010 5-year est.); Average household income: $71,806 (2006-2010 5-year est.); Percent of households with income of $100,000 or more: 22.0% (2006-2010 5-year est.); Poverty rate: 13.8% (2006-2010 5-year est.).
Education: Percent of population age 25 and over with: High school diploma (including GED) or higher: 61.8% (2006-2010 5-year est.); Bachelor's degree or higher: 7.4% (2006-2010 5-year est.); Master's degree or higher: 4.7% (2006-2010 5-year est.).
Housing: Homeownership rate: 80.8% (2010); Median home value: $150,900 (2006-2010 5-year est.); Median contract rent: $442 per month (2006-2010 5-year est.); Median year structure built: 1966 (2006-2010 5-year est.).
Transportation: Commute to work: 82.1% car, 0.0% public transportation, 1.5% walk, 13.3% work from home (2006-2010 5-year est.); Travel time to work: 32.1% less than 15 minutes, 27.9% 15 to 30 minutes, 13.2% 30 to 45 minutes, 9.7% 45 to 60 minutes, 17.1% 60 minutes or more (2006-2010 5-year est.)

MILLERSBURG (borough). Covers a land area of 0.759 square miles and a water area of <.001 square miles. Located at 40.54° N. Lat; 76.95° W. Long. Elevation is 430 feet.

History: Settled c.1790, laid out 1807, incorporated 1850.

Population: 2,748 (1990); 2,562 (2000); 2,557 (2010); Density: 3,368.2 persons per square mile (2010); Race: 97.6% White, 1.2% Black, 0.2% Asian, 0.1% American Indian/Alaska Native, 0.0% Native Hawaiian/Other Pacific Islander, 0.9% Other, 1.2% Hispanic of any race (2010); Average household size: 2.14 (2010); Median age: 40.4 (2010); Males per 100 females: 90.7 (2010); Marriage status: 24.3% never married, 48.4% now married, 13.4% widowed, 13.8% divorced (2006-2010 5-year est.); Foreign born: 0.3% (2006-2010 5-year est.); Ancestry (includes multiple ancestries): 54.1% German, 11.5% Irish, 10.9% Italian, 5.6% American, 5.5% Pennsylvania German (2006-2010 5-year est.).

Economy: Single-family building permits issued: 0 (2011); Multi-family building permits issued: 0 (2011); Employment by occupation: 10.7% management, 0.0% professional, 17.4% services, 15.1% sales, 5.3% farming, 7.5% construction, 7.2% production (2006-2010 5-year est.).

Income: Per capita income: $22,142 (2006-2010 5-year est.); Median household income: $41,888 (2006-2010 5-year est.); Average household income: $48,679 (2006-2010 5-year est.); Percent of households with income of $100,000 or more: 5.2% (2006-2010 5-year est.); Poverty rate: 6.5% (2006-2010 5-year est.).

Education: Percent of population age 25 and over with: High school diploma (including GED) or higher: 85.6% (2006-2010 5-year est.); Bachelor's degree or higher: 10.8% (2006-2010 5-year est.); Master's degree or higher: 4.5% (2006-2010 5-year est.).

School District(s)

Millersburg Area SD (KG-12)

    2010-11 Enrollment: 842 . . . . (717) 692-2108

Housing: Homeownership rate: 52.8% (2010); Median home value: $92,300 (2006-2010 5-year est.); Median contract rent: $454 per month (2006-2010 5-year est.); Median year structure built: 1953 (2006-2010 5-year est.).

Safety: Violent crime rate: 42.9 per 10,000 population; Property crime rate: 109.2 per 10,000 population (2011).

Newspapers: Upper Dauphin Sentinel (Community news; Circulation 9,000)

Transportation: Commute to work: 91.8% car, 0.0% public transportation, 5.2% walk, 3.0% work from home (2006-2010 5-year est.); Travel time to work: 38.8% less than 15 minutes, 12.1% 15 to 30 minutes, 24.2% 30 to 45 minutes, 19.9% 45 to 60 minutes, 5.0% 60 minutes or more (2006-2010 5-year est.)

Additional Information Contacts

Perry County Chamber of Commerce . . . . (717) 582-4523
    http://www.perrycountychamber.org

OBERLIN (CDP). Covers a land area of 0.130 square miles and a water area of 0 square miles. Located at 40.24° N. Lat; 76.82° W. Long. Elevation is 571 feet.

Population: n/a (1990); n/a (2000); 588 (2010); Density: 4,521.7 persons per square mile (2010); Race: 75.0% White, 11.7% Black, 2.4% Asian, 0.5% American Indian/Alaska Native, 0.0% Native Hawaiian/Other Pacific Islander, 10.4% Other, 11.6% Hispanic of any race (2010); Average household size: 2.65 (2010); Median age: 38.3 (2010); Males per 100 females: 90.3 (2010); Marriage status: 13.1% never married, 78.1% now married, 2.9% widowed, 5.9% divorced (2006-2010 5-year est.); Foreign born: 14.1% (2006-2010 5-year est.); Ancestry (includes multiple ancestries): 23.4% German, 9.7% American, 8.2% French, 5.9% Irish, 2.9% Scottish (2006-2010 5-year est.).

Economy: Employment by occupation: 4.3% management, 0.0% professional, 7.0% services, 9.0% sales, 14.8% farming, 5.2% construction, 25.5% production (2006-2010 5-year est.).

Income: Per capita income: $18,195 (2006-2010 5-year est.); Median household income: $51,605 (2006-2010 5-year est.); Average household income: $50,076 (2006-2010 5-year est.); Percent of households with income of $100,000 or more: n/a (2006-2010 5-year est.); Poverty rate: 6.9% (2006-2010 5-year est.).

Education: Percent of population age 25 and over with: High school diploma (including GED) or higher: 82.4% (2006-2010 5-year est.); Bachelor's degree or higher: 4.0% (2006-2010 5-year est.); Master's degree or higher: 0.0% (2006-2010 5-year est.).

Housing: Homeownership rate: 76.2% (2010); Median home value: $112,500 (2006-2010 5-year est.); Median contract rent: $655 per month (2006-2010 5-year est.); Median year structure built: 1956 (2006-2010 5-year est.).

Transportation: Commute to work: 87.2% car, 0.0% public transportation, 12.8% walk, 0.0% work from home (2006-2010 5-year est.); Travel time to work: 37.4% less than 15 minutes, 58.3% 15 to 30 minutes, 4.4% 30 to 45 minutes, 0.0% 45 to 60 minutes, 0.0% 60 minutes or more (2006-2010 5-year est.)

PALMDALE (CDP). Covers a land area of 1.488 square miles and a water area of 0 square miles. Located at 40.30° N. Lat; 76.62° W. Long. Elevation is 433 feet.

Population: n/a (1990); n/a (2000); 1,308 (2010); Density: 879.2 persons per square mile (2010); Race: 86.2% White, 4.4% Black, 4.5% Asian, 0.6% American Indian/Alaska Native, 0.1% Native Hawaiian/Other Pacific Islander, 4.2% Other, 4.5% Hispanic of any race (2010); Average household size: 2.26 (2010); Median age: 36.5 (2010); Males per 100 females: 91.8 (2010); Marriage status: 39.7% never married, 48.3% now married, 4.2% widowed, 7.8% divorced (2006-2010 5-year est.); Foreign born: 5.3% (2006-2010 5-year est.); Ancestry (includes multiple ancestries): 31.3% German, 15.8% English, 15.1% Italian, 9.6% Irish, 5.3% Norwegian (2006-2010 5-year est.).

Economy: Employment by occupation: 4.0% management, 4.2% professional, 20.8% services, 8.8% sales, 0.8% farming, 3.4% construction, 2.6% production (2006-2010 5-year est.).

Income: Per capita income: $21,902 (2006-2010 5-year est.); Median household income: $48,621 (2006-2010 5-year est.); Average household income: $60,442 (2006-2010 5-year est.); Percent of households with income of $100,000 or more: 15.7% (2006-2010 5-year est.); Poverty rate: 5.2% (2006-2010 5-year est.).

Education: Percent of population age 25 and over with: High school diploma (including GED) or higher: 91.6% (2006-2010 5-year est.); Bachelor's degree or higher: 30.5% (2006-2010 5-year est.); Master's degree or higher: 12.6% (2006-2010 5-year est.).

Housing: Homeownership rate: 59.1% (2010); Median home value: $143,900 (2006-2010 5-year est.); Median contract rent: $587 per month (2006-2010 5-year est.); Median year structure built: 1961 (2006-2010 5-year est.).

Transportation: Commute to work: 87.7% car, 0.0% public transportation, 10.1% walk, 1.4% work from home (2006-2010 5-year est.); Travel time to work: 35.1% less than 15 minutes, 25.4% 15 to 30 minutes, 17.9% 30 to 45 minutes, 9.6% 45 to 60 minutes, 11.9% 60 minutes or more (2006-2010 5-year est.)

PAXTANG (borough). Covers a land area of 0.406 square miles and a water area of 0 square miles. Located at 40.26° N. Lat; 76.83° W. Long. Elevation is 364 feet.

History: Here occurred (1763) uprising of Paxtang (Paxton) Boys against Native Americans.

Population: 1,613 (1990); 1,570 (2000); 1,561 (2010); Density: 3,846.3 persons per square mile (2010); Race: 79.0% White, 10.6% Black, 1.9% Asian, 0.1% American Indian/Alaska Native, 0.0% Native Hawaiian/Other Pacific Islander, 8.4% Other, 9.1% Hispanic of any race (2010); Average household size: 2.37 (2010); Median age: 37.6 (2010); Males per 100 females: 93.0 (2010); Marriage status: 27.8% never married, 55.3% now married, 6.4% widowed, 10.4% divorced (2006-2010 5-year est.); Foreign born: 11.1% (2006-2010 5-year est.); Ancestry (includes multiple ancestries): 28.8% German, 13.1% Irish, 7.8% Italian, 6.9% English, 5.4% Egyptian (2006-2010 5-year est.).

Economy: Single-family building permits issued: 0 (2011); Multi-family building permits issued: 0 (2011); Employment by occupation: 16.3% management, 4.3% professional, 8.7% services, 15.2% sales, 4.1% farming, 4.6% construction, 7.0% production (2006-2010 5-year est.).

Income: Per capita income: $26,821 (2006-2010 5-year est.); Median household income: $56,364 (2006-2010 5-year est.); Average household income: $62,731 (2006-2010 5-year est.); Percent of households with income of $100,000 or more: 17.9% (2006-2010 5-year est.); Poverty rate: 7.2% (2006-2010 5-year est.).

Education: Percent of population age 25 and over with: High school diploma (including GED) or higher: 95.4% (2006-2010 5-year est.); Bachelor's degree or higher: 37.6% (2006-2010 5-year est.); Master's degree or higher: 13.4% (2006-2010 5-year est.).

Housing: Homeownership rate: 74.2% (2010); Median home value: $139,300 (2006-2010 5-year est.); Median contract rent: $638 per month (2006-2010 5-year est.); Median year structure built: before 1940 (2006-2010 5-year est.).

Safety: Violent crime rate: 25.5 per 10,000 population; Property crime rate: 478.9 per 10,000 population (2011).

Transportation: Commute to work: 87.1% car, 4.9% public transportation, 2.6% walk, 3.3% work from home (2006-2010 5-year est.); Travel time to work: 41.2% less than 15 minutes, 43.4% 15 to 30 minutes, 11.9% 30 to 45 minutes, 0.9% 45 to 60 minutes, 2.6% 60 minutes or more (2006-2010 5-year est.)

Additional Information Contacts

Harrisburg Regional Chamber & CREDC . . . . (717) 232-4099
   http://www.harrisburgregionalchamber.org

PAXTONIA (CDP). Covers a land area of 2.313 square miles and a water area of 0 square miles. Located at 40.32° N. Lat; 76.79° W. Long. Elevation is 522 feet.

Population: 4,809 (1990); 5,254 (2000); 5,412 (2010); Density: 2,339.9 persons per square mile (2010); Race: 86.4% White, 6.2% Black, 3.9% Asian, 0.1% American Indian/Alaska Native, 0.0% Native Hawaiian/Other Pacific Islander, 3.4% Other, 2.9% Hispanic of any race (2010); Average household size: 2.46 (2010); Median age: 40.2 (2010); Males per 100 females: 92.1 (2010); Marriage status: 30.0% never married, 52.2% now married, 6.0% widowed, 11.8% divorced (2006-2010 5-year est.); Foreign born: 2.2% (2006-2010 5-year est.); Ancestry (includes multiple ancestries): 34.5% German, 18.1% Irish, 11.9% American, 10.5% English, 8.4% Italian (2006-2010 5-year est.).

Economy: Employment by occupation: 11.1% management, 5.9% professional, 8.5% services, 23.4% sales, 4.0% farming, 8.8% construction, 4.6% production (2006-2010 5-year est.).

Income: Per capita income: $30,888 (2006-2010 5-year est.); Median household income: $64,960 (2006-2010 5-year est.); Average household income: $73,593 (2006-2010 5-year est.); Percent of households with income of $100,000 or more: 24.0% (2006-2010 5-year est.); Poverty rate: 2.4% (2006-2010 5-year est.).

Education: Percent of population age 25 and over with: High school diploma (including GED) or higher: 93.5% (2006-2010 5-year est.); Bachelor's degree or higher: 31.8% (2006-2010 5-year est.); Master's degree or higher: 8.3% (2006-2010 5-year est.).

Housing: Homeownership rate: 74.5% (2010); Median home value: $163,200 (2006-2010 5-year est.); Median contract rent: $749 per month (2006-2010 5-year est.); Median year structure built: 1971 (2006-2010 5-year est.).

Transportation: Commute to work: 94.9% car, 0.0% public transportation, 2.1% walk, 2.6% work from home (2006-2010 5-year est.); Travel time to work: 37.2% less than 15 minutes, 50.2% 15 to 30 minutes, 9.1% 30 to 45 minutes, 1.9% 45 to 60 minutes, 1.6% 60 minutes or more (2006-2010 5-year est.)

Additional Information Contacts

Harrisburg Regional Chamber & CREDC . . . . (717) 232-4099
   http://www.harrisburgregionalchamber.org

PENBROOK (borough). Covers a land area of 0.447 square miles and a water area of 0 square miles. Located at 40.28° N. Lat; 76.85° W. Long. Elevation is 486 feet.

Population: 2,784 (1990); 3,044 (2000); 3,008 (2010); Density: 6,735.2 persons per square mile (2010); Race: 57.1% White, 29.0% Black, 2.9% Asian, 0.4% American Indian/Alaska Native, 0.0% Native Hawaiian/Other Pacific Islander, 10.6% Other, 9.5% Hispanic of any race (2010); Average household size: 2.35 (2010); Median age: 35.1 (2010); Males per 100 females: 91.7 (2010); Marriage status: 38.6% never married, 45.0% now married, 4.3% widowed, 12.0% divorced (2006-2010 5-year est.); Foreign born: 2.3% (2006-2010 5-year est.); Ancestry (includes multiple ancestries): 33.3% German, 14.5% Irish, 9.4% Italian, 7.5% American, 5.2% English (2006-2010 5-year est.).

Economy: Single-family building permits issued: 0 (2011); Multi-family building permits issued: 0 (2011); Employment by occupation: 8.2% management, 3.9% professional, 6.6% services, 22.6% sales, 6.7% farming, 10.6% construction, 3.9% production (2006-2010 5-year est.).

Income: Per capita income: $21,648 (2006-2010 5-year est.); Median household income: $35,938 (2006-2010 5-year est.); Average household income: $50,754 (2006-2010 5-year est.); Percent of households with income of $100,000 or more: 9.5% (2006-2010 5-year est.); Poverty rate: 13.1% (2006-2010 5-year est.).

Education: Percent of population age 25 and over with: High school diploma (including GED) or higher: 89.0% (2006-2010 5-year est.); Bachelor's degree or higher: 14.5% (2006-2010 5-year est.); Master's degree or higher: 6.0% (2006-2010 5-year est.).

School District(s)

Infinity CS (KG-08)
   2010-11 Enrollment: 122 . . . . (717) 238-1880

Housing: Homeownership rate: 55.5% (2010); Median home value: $105,100 (2006-2010 5-year est.); Median contract rent: $553 per month (2006-2010 5-year est.); Median year structure built: 1944 (2006-2010 5-year est.).

Safety: Violent crime rate: 29.8 per 10,000 population; Property crime rate: 222.0 per 10,000 population (2011).

Transportation: Commute to work: 88.5% car, 3.6% public transportation, 3.0% walk, 0.0% work from home (2006-2010 5-year est.); Travel time to work: 48.7% less than 15 minutes, 42.3% 15 to 30 minutes, 4.3% 30 to 45 minutes, 3.0% 45 to 60 minutes, 1.8% 60 minutes or more (2006-2010 5-year est.)

Additional Information Contacts

Harrisburg Regional Chamber & CREDC . . . . (717) 232-4099
   http://www.harrisburgregionalchamber.org

PILLOW (borough). Aka Uniontown. Covers a land area of 0.493 square miles and a water area of 0 square miles. Located at 40.64° N. Lat; 76.80° W. Long. Elevation is 545 feet.

Population: 366 (1990); 304 (2000); 298 (2010); Density: 604.0 persons per square mile (2010); Race: 97.7% White, 0.0% Black, 0.0% Asian, 0.3% American Indian/Alaska Native, 0.0% Native Hawaiian/Other Pacific Islander, 2.0% Other, 5.0% Hispanic of any race (2010); Average household size: 2.40 (2010); Median age: 40.3 (2010); Males per 100 females: 93.5 (2010); Marriage status: 29.1% never married, 59.8% now married, 8.0% widowed, 3.0% divorced (2006-2010 5-year est.); Foreign born: 0.0% (2006-2010 5-year est.); Ancestry (includes multiple ancestries): 63.7% German, 12.8% Pennsylvania German, 12.0% English, 5.6% French, 5.1% Polish (2006-2010 5-year est.).

Economy: Single-family building permits issued: 0 (2011); Multi-family building permits issued: 0 (2011); Employment by occupation: 7.4% management, 9.1% professional, 7.4% services, 8.3% sales, 12.4% farming, 19.8% construction, 19.8% production (2006-2010 5-year est.).

Income: Per capita income: $20,939 (2006-2010 5-year est.); Median household income: $36,042 (2006-2010 5-year est.); Average household income: $44,998 (2006-2010 5-year est.); Percent of households with income of $100,000 or more: 4.6% (2006-2010 5-year est.); Poverty rate: 3.4% (2006-2010 5-year est.).

Education: Percent of population age 25 and over with: High school diploma (including GED) or higher: 90.1% (2006-2010 5-year est.); Bachelor's degree or higher: 8.2% (2006-2010 5-year est.); Master's degree or higher: 0.0% (2006-2010 5-year est.).

Housing: Homeownership rate: 76.6% (2010); Median home value: $85,300 (2006-2010 5-year est.); Median contract rent: $342 per month (2006-2010 5-year est.); Median year structure built: before 1940 (2006-2010 5-year est.).

Transportation: Commute to work: 100.0% car, 0.0% public transportation, 0.0% walk, 0.0% work from home (2006-2010 5-year est.); Travel time to work: 28.1% less than 15 minutes, 34.7% 15 to 30 minutes, 2.5% 30 to 45 minutes, 8.3% 45 to 60 minutes, 26.4% 60 minutes or more (2006-2010 5-year est.)

PROGRESS (CDP). Covers a land area of 2.802 square miles and a water area of 0 square miles. Located at 40.29° N. Lat; 76.84° W. Long. Elevation is 495 feet.

Population: 10,021 (1990); 9,647 (2000); 9,765 (2010); Density: 3,485.3 persons per square mile (2010); Race: 62.6% White, 26.4% Black, 3.7% Asian, 0.2% American Indian/Alaska Native, 0.0% Native Hawaiian/Other Pacific Islander, 7.1% Other, 7.4% Hispanic of any race (2010); Average household size: 2.25 (2010); Median age: 39.8 (2010); Males per 100 females: 87.6 (2010); Marriage status: 38.2% never married, 40.1% now married, 6.4% widowed, 15.4% divorced (2006-2010 5-year est.); Foreign born: 7.5% (2006-2010 5-year est.); Ancestry (includes multiple ancestries): 30.0% German, 12.6% Irish, 7.2% English, 4.4% Italian, 3.4% Polish (2006-2010 5-year est.).

Economy: Employment by occupation: 10.9% management, 4.9% professional, 7.4% services, 23.1% sales, 6.0% farming, 4.4% construction, 5.7% production (2006-2010 5-year est.).

Income: Per capita income: $26,759 (2006-2010 5-year est.); Median household income: $49,101 (2006-2010 5-year est.); Average household income: $58,626 (2006-2010 5-year est.); Percent of households with income of $100,000 or more: 16.1% (2006-2010 5-year est.); Poverty rate: 8.5% (2006-2010 5-year est.).

Education: Percent of population age 25 and over with: High school diploma (including GED) or higher: 92.0% (2006-2010 5-year est.); Bachelor's degree or higher: 25.0% (2006-2010 5-year est.); Master's degree or higher: 9.3% (2006-2010 5-year est.).
Housing: Homeownership rate: 62.9% (2010); Median home value: $147,200 (2006-2010 5-year est.); Median contract rent: $737 per month (2006-2010 5-year est.); Median year structure built: 1957 (2006-2010 5-year est.).
Transportation: Commute to work: 92.2% car, 5.3% public transportation, 0.5% walk, 1.2% work from home (2006-2010 5-year est.); Travel time to work: 38.5% less than 15 minutes, 47.7% 15 to 30 minutes, 8.4% 30 to 45 minutes, 2.5% 45 to 60 minutes, 2.9% 60 minutes or more (2006-2010 5-year est.)
Additional Information Contacts
Columbia Montour Chamber of Commerce . . . . (570) 784-2522
  http://www.bloomsburg.org

REED (township). Covers a land area of 5.924 square miles and a water area of 2.649 square miles. Located at 40.41° N. Lat; 76.99° W. Long.
Population: 259 (1990); 182 (2000); 239 (2010); Density: 40.3 persons per square mile (2010); Race: 97.5% White, 1.7% Black, 0.0% Asian, 0.0% American Indian/Alaska Native, 0.0% Native Hawaiian/Other Pacific Islander, 0.8% Other, 1.7% Hispanic of any race (2010); Average household size: 2.46 (2010); Median age: 48.1 (2010); Males per 100 females: 115.3 (2010); Marriage status: 15.2% never married, 58.6% now married, 14.8% widowed, 11.4% divorced (2006-2010 5-year est.); Foreign born: 0.0% (2006-2010 5-year est.); Ancestry (includes multiple ancestries): 46.7% German, 22.9% Irish, 9.6% English, 8.3% American, 6.3% Dutch (2006-2010 5-year est.).
Economy: Single-family building permits issued: 0 (2011); Multi-family building permits issued: 0 (2011); Employment by occupation: 18.3% management, 8.3% professional, 3.3% services, 15.0% sales, 1.7% farming, 10.8% construction, 4.2% production (2006-2010 5-year est.).
Income: Per capita income: $25,749 (2006-2010 5-year est.); Median household income: $42,411 (2006-2010 5-year est.); Average household income: $54,431 (2006-2010 5-year est.); Percent of households with income of $100,000 or more: 12.4% (2006-2010 5-year est.); Poverty rate: 6.3% (2006-2010 5-year est.).
Education: Percent of population age 25 and over with: High school diploma (including GED) or higher: 85.5% (2006-2010 5-year est.); Bachelor's degree or higher: 21.2% (2006-2010 5-year est.); Master's degree or higher: 5.0% (2006-2010 5-year est.).
Housing: Homeownership rate: 83.5% (2010); Median home value: $96,700 (2006-2010 5-year est.); Median contract rent: $425 per month (2006-2010 5-year est.); Median year structure built: 1967 (2006-2010 5-year est.).
Transportation: Commute to work: 94.8% car, 0.0% public transportation, 0.0% walk, 0.0% work from home (2006-2010 5-year est.); Travel time to work: 12.1% less than 15 minutes, 42.2% 15 to 30 minutes, 44.0% 30 to 45 minutes, 1.7% 45 to 60 minutes, 0.0% 60 minutes or more (2006-2010 5-year est.)

ROYALTON (borough). Covers a land area of 0.303 square miles and a water area of 0.032 square miles. Located at 40.19° N. Lat; 76.72° W. Long. Elevation is 295 feet.
Population: 1,120 (1990); 963 (2000); 907 (2010); Density: 2,994.8 persons per square mile (2010); Race: 90.6% White, 3.0% Black, 0.2% Asian, 0.8% American Indian/Alaska Native, 0.0% Native Hawaiian/Other Pacific Islander, 5.4% Other, 4.3% Hispanic of any race (2010); Average household size: 2.33 (2010); Median age: 42.8 (2010); Males per 100 females: 94.2 (2010); Marriage status: 30.8% never married, 51.3% now married, 5.4% widowed, 12.6% divorced (2006-2010 5-year est.); Foreign born: 2.8% (2006-2010 5-year est.); Ancestry (includes multiple ancestries): 42.1% German, 14.5% Italian, 10.0% Irish, 6.2% Dutch, 5.3% Pennsylvania German (2006-2010 5-year est.).
Economy: Single-family building permits issued: 0 (2011); Multi-family building permits issued: 0 (2011); Employment by occupation: 9.7% management, 4.5% professional, 9.5% services, 14.5% sales, 7.5% farming, 10.7% construction, 10.5% production (2006-2010 5-year est.).
Income: Per capita income: $23,224 (2006-2010 5-year est.); Median household income: $45,938 (2006-2010 5-year est.); Average household income: $53,900 (2006-2010 5-year est.); Percent of households with income of $100,000 or more: 12.3% (2006-2010 5-year est.); Poverty rate: 13.8% (2006-2010 5-year est.).

Education: Percent of population age 25 and over with: High school diploma (including GED) or higher: 84.4% (2006-2010 5-year est.); Bachelor's degree or higher: 14.1% (2006-2010 5-year est.); Master's degree or higher: 2.5% (2006-2010 5-year est.).
Housing: Homeownership rate: 70.8% (2010); Median home value: $110,800 (2006-2010 5-year est.); Median contract rent: $558 per month (2006-2010 5-year est.); Median year structure built: 1960 (2006-2010 5-year est.).
Safety: Violent crime rate: 0.0 per 10,000 population; Property crime rate: 22.0 per 10,000 population (2011).
Transportation: Commute to work: 93.6% car, 0.3% public transportation, 3.9% walk, 1.0% work from home (2006-2010 5-year est.); Travel time to work: 26.4% less than 15 minutes, 42.1% 15 to 30 minutes, 22.7% 30 to 45 minutes, 0.0% 45 to 60 minutes, 8.9% 60 minutes or more (2006-2010 5-year est.)

RUSH (township). Covers a land area of 23.533 square miles and a water area of 0.932 square miles. Located at 40.52° N. Lat; 76.64° W. Long.
Population: 201 (1990); 180 (2000); 231 (2010); Density: 9.8 persons per square mile (2010); Race: 99.1% White, 0.0% Black, 0.0% Asian, 0.0% American Indian/Alaska Native, 0.0% Native Hawaiian/Other Pacific Islander, 0.9% Other, 1.7% Hispanic of any race (2010); Average household size: 2.41 (2010); Median age: 42.2 (2010); Males per 100 females: 126.5 (2010); Marriage status: 21.0% never married, 67.9% now married, 4.9% widowed, 6.2% divorced (2006-2010 5-year est.); Foreign born: 2.1% (2006-2010 5-year est.); Ancestry (includes multiple ancestries): 26.8% German, 17.0% Hungarian, 15.7% Italian, 15.7% Irish, 14.0% Swiss (2006-2010 5-year est.).
Economy: Single-family building permits issued: 0 (2011); Multi-family building permits issued: 0 (2011); Employment by occupation: 14.3% management, 0.0% professional, 9.9% services, 23.1% sales, 3.3% farming, 15.4% construction, 15.4% production (2006-2010 5-year est.).
Income: Per capita income: $19,944 (2006-2010 5-year est.); Median household income: $60,469 (2006-2010 5-year est.); Average household income: $62,105 (2006-2010 5-year est.); Percent of households with income of $100,000 or more: 10.7% (2006-2010 5-year est.); Poverty rate: 5.5% (2006-2010 5-year est.).
Education: Percent of population age 25 and over with: High school diploma (including GED) or higher: 95.6% (2006-2010 5-year est.); Bachelor's degree or higher: 2.9% (2006-2010 5-year est.); Master's degree or higher: 1.5% (2006-2010 5-year est.).
Housing: Homeownership rate: 88.6% (2010); Median home value: $159,800 (2006-2010 5-year est.); Median contract rent: n/a per month (2006-2010 5-year est.); Median year structure built: 1974 (2006-2010 5-year est.).
Transportation: Commute to work: 100.0% car, 0.0% public transportation, 0.0% walk, 0.0% work from home (2006-2010 5-year est.); Travel time to work: 12.1% less than 15 minutes, 37.4% 15 to 30 minutes, 27.5% 30 to 45 minutes, 17.6% 45 to 60 minutes, 5.5% 60 minutes or more (2006-2010 5-year est.)

RUTHERFORD (CDP). Covers a land area of 1.275 square miles and a water area of 0 square miles. Located at 40.27° N. Lat; 76.77° W. Long. Elevation is 518 feet.
Population: 3,547 (1990); 3,859 (2000); 4,303 (2010); Density: 3,374.4 persons per square mile (2010); Race: 77.6% White, 12.0% Black, 4.5% Asian, 0.0% American Indian/Alaska Native, 0.0% Native Hawaiian/Other Pacific Islander, 5.9% Other, 6.9% Hispanic of any race (2010); Average household size: 2.37 (2010); Median age: 40.0 (2010); Males per 100 females: 89.1 (2010); Marriage status: 27.1% never married, 53.1% now married, 10.5% widowed, 9.3% divorced (2006-2010 5-year est.); Foreign born: 10.1% (2006-2010 5-year est.); Ancestry (includes multiple ancestries): 31.4% German, 11.9% Irish, 11.6% American, 7.2% Italian, 6.0% English (2006-2010 5-year est.).
Economy: Employment by occupation: 10.7% management, 7.4% professional, 7.1% services, 18.6% sales, 9.8% farming, 7.2% construction, 11.1% production (2006-2010 5-year est.).
Income: Per capita income: $27,231 (2006-2010 5-year est.); Median household income: $58,226 (2006-2010 5-year est.); Average household income: $65,553 (2006-2010 5-year est.); Percent of households with income of $100,000 or more: 12.9% (2006-2010 5-year est.); Poverty rate: 6.1% (2006-2010 5-year est.).
Education: Percent of population age 25 and over with: High school diploma (including GED) or higher: 88.5% (2006-2010 5-year est.);

Bachelor's degree or higher: 23.3% (2006-2010 5-year est.); Master's degree or higher: 4.6% (2006-2010 5-year est.).
Housing: Homeownership rate: 79.6% (2010); Median home value: $144,000 (2006-2010 5-year est.); Median contract rent: $702 per month (2006-2010 5-year est.); Median year structure built: 1969 (2006-2010 5-year est.).
Transportation: Commute to work: 95.8% car, 2.1% public transportation, 0.0% walk, 1.4% work from home (2006-2010 5-year est.); Travel time to work: 26.2% less than 15 minutes, 55.5% 15 to 30 minutes, 13.0% 30 to 45 minutes, 1.4% 45 to 60 minutes, 3.9% 60 minutes or more (2006-2010 5-year est.)
Additional Information Contacts
Harrisburg Regional Chamber & CREDC . . . . (717) 232-4099
  http://www.harrisburgregionalchamber.org

SKYLINE VIEW (CDP). Covers a land area of 2.674 square miles and a water area of 0 square miles. Located at 40.34° N. Lat; 76.73° W. Long. Elevation is 502 feet.
Population: 2,370 (1990); 2,307 (2000); 4,003 (2010); Density: 1,496.7 persons per square mile (2010); Race: 92.2% White, 2.4% Black, 2.8% Asian, 0.2% American Indian/Alaska Native, 0.0% Native Hawaiian/Other Pacific Islander, 2.4% Other, 2.1% Hispanic of any race (2010); Average household size: 2.43 (2010); Median age: 43.8 (2010); Males per 100 females: 94.7 (2010); Marriage status: 15.8% never married, 70.1% now married, 5.7% widowed, 8.4% divorced (2006-2010 5-year est.); Foreign born: 0.7% (2006-2010 5-year est.); Ancestry (includes multiple ancestries): 42.1% German, 16.2% Irish, 12.1% Italian, 6.2% English, 5.8% Polish (2006-2010 5-year est.).
Economy: Employment by occupation: 12.6% management, 11.2% professional, 11.1% services, 11.8% sales, 3.4% farming, 1.6% construction, 2.0% production (2006-2010 5-year est.).
Income: Per capita income: $35,791 (2006-2010 5-year est.); Median household income: $83,259 (2006-2010 5-year est.); Average household income: $83,723 (2006-2010 5-year est.); Percent of households with income of $100,000 or more: 32.2% (2006-2010 5-year est.); Poverty rate: 1.9% (2006-2010 5-year est.).
Education: Percent of population age 25 and over with: High school diploma (including GED) or higher: 95.1% (2006-2010 5-year est.); Bachelor's degree or higher: 32.1% (2006-2010 5-year est.); Master's degree or higher: 12.9% (2006-2010 5-year est.).
Housing: Homeownership rate: 94.2% (2010); Median home value: $209,700 (2006-2010 5-year est.); Median contract rent: $960 per month (2006-2010 5-year est.); Median year structure built: 1998 (2006-2010 5-year est.).
Transportation: Commute to work: 97.8% car, 0.0% public transportation, 0.0% walk, 1.3% work from home (2006-2010 5-year est.); Travel time to work: 25.2% less than 15 minutes, 51.4% 15 to 30 minutes, 19.9% 30 to 45 minutes, 1.0% 45 to 60 minutes, 2.5% 60 minutes or more (2006-2010 5-year est.)
Additional Information Contacts
Harrisburg Regional Chamber & CREDC . . . . (717) 232-4099
  http://www.harrisburgregionalchamber.org

SOUTH HANOVER (township). Covers a land area of 11.276 square miles and a water area of 0.125 square miles. Located at 40.29° N. Lat; 76.71° W. Long.
Population: 4,668 (1990); 4,793 (2000); 6,248 (2010); Density: 554.1 persons per square mile (2010); Race: 91.6% White, 2.6% Black, 3.4% Asian, 0.1% American Indian/Alaska Native, 0.0% Native Hawaiian/Other Pacific Islander, 2.3% Other, 2.3% Hispanic of any race (2010); Average household size: 2.56 (2010); Median age: 40.8 (2010); Males per 100 females: 96.7 (2010); Marriage status: 23.9% never married, 67.3% now married, 2.3% widowed, 6.5% divorced (2006-2010 5-year est.); Foreign born: 4.7% (2006-2010 5-year est.); Ancestry (includes multiple ancestries): 42.2% German, 13.9% Irish, 9.9% English, 9.6% Italian, 5.2% American (2006-2010 5-year est.).
Economy: Single-family building permits issued: 58 (2011); Multi-family building permits issued: 0 (2011); Employment by occupation: 15.8% management, 6.7% professional, 6.3% services, 16.0% sales, 3.8% farming, 4.8% construction, 2.3% production (2006-2010 5-year est.).
Income: Per capita income: $36,644 (2006-2010 5-year est.); Median household income: $87,500 (2006-2010 5-year est.); Average household income: $98,718 (2006-2010 5-year est.); Percent of households with income of $100,000 or more: 40.9% (2006-2010 5-year est.); Poverty rate: 1.8% (2006-2010 5-year est.).

Education: Percent of population age 25 and over with: High school diploma (including GED) or higher: 97.1% (2006-2010 5-year est.); Bachelor's degree or higher: 40.1% (2006-2010 5-year est.); Master's degree or higher: 14.2% (2006-2010 5-year est.).
Housing: Homeownership rate: 79.1% (2010); Median home value: $238,500 (2006-2010 5-year est.); Median contract rent: $949 per month (2006-2010 5-year est.); Median year structure built: 1982 (2006-2010 5-year est.).
Transportation: Commute to work: 93.4% car, 0.3% public transportation, 2.3% walk, 3.3% work from home (2006-2010 5-year est.); Travel time to work: 31.0% less than 15 minutes, 38.7% 15 to 30 minutes, 22.1% 30 to 45 minutes, 4.2% 45 to 60 minutes, 4.0% 60 minutes or more (2006-2010 5-year est.)
Additional Information Contacts
Harrisburg Regional Chamber & CREDC . . . . (717) 232-4099
  http://www.harrisburgregionalchamber.org

STEELTON (borough). Covers a land area of 1.896 square miles and a water area of 0 square miles. Located at 40.23° N. Lat; 76.83° W. Long. Elevation is 318 feet.
History: Site of Oberllin Gardens. First practical production of Bessemer steel in US here, 1867. Once a steel-producing center. Settled 1865.
Population: 5,152 (1990); 5,858 (2000); 5,990 (2010); Density: 3,160.0 persons per square mile (2010); Race: 48.7% White, 38.1% Black, 0.7% Asian, 0.2% American Indian/Alaska Native, 0.0% Native Hawaiian/Other Pacific Islander, 12.3% Other, 14.6% Hispanic of any race (2010); Average household size: 2.60 (2010); Median age: 33.5 (2010); Males per 100 females: 86.9 (2010); Marriage status: 43.2% never married, 29.4% now married, 8.8% widowed, 18.5% divorced (2006-2010 5-year est.); Foreign born: 3.1% (2006-2010 5-year est.); Ancestry (includes multiple ancestries): 18.8% German, 9.0% Italian, 6.4% Irish, 4.4% Croatian, 2.4% English (2006-2010 5-year est.).
Economy: Single-family building permits issued: 0 (2011); Multi-family building permits issued: 0 (2011); Employment by occupation: 4.1% management, 3.5% professional, 8.6% services, 18.4% sales, 12.2% farming, 5.5% construction, 3.1% production (2006-2010 5-year est.).
Income: Per capita income: $16,953 (2006-2010 5-year est.); Median household income: $36,075 (2006-2010 5-year est.); Average household income: $43,489 (2006-2010 5-year est.); Percent of households with income of $100,000 or more: 5.9% (2006-2010 5-year est.); Poverty rate: 23.9% (2006-2010 5-year est.).
Education: Percent of population age 25 and over with: High school diploma (including GED) or higher: 89.0% (2006-2010 5-year est.); Bachelor's degree or higher: 11.5% (2006-2010 5-year est.); Master's degree or higher: 2.8% (2006-2010 5-year est.).
School District(s)
Central Dauphin SD (KG-12)
    2010-11 Enrollment: 10,937 . . . . (717) 545-4703
Steelton-Highspire SD (KG-12)
    2010-11 Enrollment: 1,213 . . . . (717) 704-3800
Housing: Homeownership rate: 55.6% (2010); Median home value: $81,600 (2006-2010 5-year est.); Median contract rent: $518 per month (2006-2010 5-year est.); Median year structure built: before 1940 (2006-2010 5-year est.).
Safety: Violent crime rate: 44.9 per 10,000 population; Property crime rate: 426.0 per 10,000 population (2011).
Transportation: Commute to work: 87.9% car, 5.4% public transportation, 3.4% walk, 1.3% work from home (2006-2010 5-year est.); Travel time to work: 36.3% less than 15 minutes, 48.4% 15 to 30 minutes, 8.2% 30 to 45 minutes, 1.3% 45 to 60 minutes, 5.8% 60 minutes or more (2006-2010 5-year est.)
Additional Information Contacts
Borough of Steelton . . . . (717) 939-9842
  http://www.steeltonpa.com
Harrisburg Regional Chamber & CREDC . . . . (717) 232-4099
  http://www.harrisburgregionalchamber.org

SUSQUEHANNA (township). Covers a land area of 13.339 square miles and a water area of 1.933 square miles. Located at 40.31° N. Lat; 76.87° W. Long.
Population: 18,643 (1990); 21,895 (2000); 24,036 (2010); Density: 1,802.0 persons per square mile (2010); Race: 67.3% White, 23.6% Black, 3.6% Asian, 0.1% American Indian/Alaska Native, 0.0% Native Hawaiian/Other Pacific Islander, 5.4% Other, 4.9% Hispanic of any race (2010); Average household size: 2.20 (2010); Median age: 42.3 (2010);

Males per 100 females: 86.0 (2010); Marriage status: 28.6% never married, 50.2% now married, 8.3% widowed, 12.9% divorced (2006-2010 5-year est.); Foreign born: 6.3% (2006-2010 5-year est.); Ancestry (includes multiple ancestries): 31.3% German, 14.2% Irish, 7.0% English, 6.9% Italian, 3.8% Polish (2006-2010 5-year est.).

Economy: Single-family building permits issued: 40 (2011); Multi-family building permits issued: 0 (2011); Employment by occupation: 13.6% management, 6.3% professional, 5.5% services, 21.0% sales, 5.6% farming, 5.7% construction, 4.2% production (2006-2010 5-year est.).

Income: Per capita income: $33,889 (2006-2010 5-year est.); Median household income: $60,758 (2006-2010 5-year est.); Average household income: $74,265 (2006-2010 5-year est.); Percent of households with income of $100,000 or more: 23.0% (2006-2010 5-year est.); Poverty rate: 5.4% (2006-2010 5-year est.).

Taxes: Total city taxes per capita: $369 (2009); City property taxes per capita: $124 (2009).

Education: Percent of population age 25 and over with: High school diploma (including GED) or higher: 92.0% (2006-2010 5-year est.); Bachelor's degree or higher: 36.8% (2006-2010 5-year est.); Master's degree or higher: 12.8% (2006-2010 5-year est.).

Housing: Homeownership rate: 70.0% (2010); Median home value: $159,600 (2006-2010 5-year est.); Median contract rent: $761 per month (2006-2010 5-year est.); Median year structure built: 1972 (2006-2010 5-year est.).

Safety: Violent crime rate: 18.7 per 10,000 population; Property crime rate: 177.5 per 10,000 population (2011).

Transportation: Commute to work: 94.4% car, 2.3% public transportation, 0.5% walk, 1.7% work from home (2006-2010 5-year est.); Travel time to work: 36.5% less than 15 minutes, 49.8% 15 to 30 minutes, 8.3% 30 to 45 minutes, 2.9% 45 to 60 minutes, 2.6% 60 minutes or more (2006-2010 5-year est.)

Additional Information Contacts
Harrisburg Regional Chamber & CREDC . . . . (717) 232-4099
    http://www.harrisburgregionalchamber.org
Susquehanna Township . . . . (717) 545-4751
    http://www.susquehannatwp.com

SWATARA (township).
Covers a land area of 13.051 square miles and a water area of 2.480 square miles. Located at 40.25° N. Lat; 76.80° W. Long. Elevation is 417 feet.

Population: 19,681 (1990); 22,611 (2000); 23,362 (2010); Density: 1,790.1 persons per square mile (2010); Race: 71.0% White, 18.4% Black, 3.4% Asian, 0.1% American Indian/Alaska Native, 0.1% Native Hawaiian/Other Pacific Islander, 7.0% Other, 8.3% Hispanic of any race (2010); Average household size: 2.35 (2010); Median age: 40.0 (2010); Males per 100 females: 97.4 (2010); Marriage status: 35.8% never married, 47.2% now married, 6.8% widowed, 10.2% divorced (2006-2010 5-year est.); Foreign born: 8.9% (2006-2010 5-year est.); Ancestry (includes multiple ancestries): 26.4% German, 12.2% Irish, 7.1% Italian, 5.6% English, 5.2% American (2006-2010 5-year est.).

Economy: Single-family building permits issued: 64 (2011); Multi-family building permits issued: 0 (2011); Employment by occupation: 10.6% management, 4.8% professional, 8.1% services, 17.3% sales, 6.8% farming, 6.6% construction, 8.9% production (2006-2010 5-year est.).

Income: Per capita income: $24,981 (2006-2010 5-year est.); Median household income: $53,673 (2006-2010 5-year est.); Average household income: $62,289 (2006-2010 5-year est.); Percent of households with income of $100,000 or more: 15.1% (2006-2010 5-year est.); Poverty rate: 9.8% (2006-2010 5-year est.).

Education: Percent of population age 25 and over with: High school diploma (including GED) or higher: 87.6% (2006-2010 5-year est.); Bachelor's degree or higher: 22.6% (2006-2010 5-year est.); Master's degree or higher: 6.7% (2006-2010 5-year est.).

Housing: Homeownership rate: 70.1% (2010); Median home value: $149,700 (2006-2010 5-year est.); Median contract rent: $630 per month (2006-2010 5-year est.); Median year structure built: 1969 (2006-2010 5-year est.).

Safety: Violent crime rate: 68.3 per 10,000 population; Property crime rate: 339.6 per 10,000 population (2011).

Transportation: Commute to work: 94.5% car, 1.1% public transportation, 1.0% walk, 1.9% work from home (2006-2010 5-year est.); Travel time to work: 35.5% less than 15 minutes, 50.3% 15 to 30 minutes, 9.7% 30 to 45 minutes, 2.3% 45 to 60 minutes, 2.2% 60 minutes or more (2006-2010 5-year est.)

Additional Information Contacts
Harrisburg Regional Chamber & CREDC . . . . (717) 232-4099
    http://www.harrisburgregionalchamber.org
Swatara Township . . . . (717) 564-2551
    http://www.swataratwp.com

UNION DEPOSIT (CDP).
Covers a land area of 0.299 square miles and a water area of 0.013 square miles. Located at 40.29° N. Lat; 76.68° W. Long. Elevation is 387 feet.

Population: n/a (1990); n/a (2000); 407 (2010); Density: 1,359.1 persons per square mile (2010); Race: 91.9% White, 1.2% Black, 4.9% Asian, 0.5% American Indian/Alaska Native, 0.0% Native Hawaiian/Other Pacific Islander, 1.5% Other, 1.2% Hispanic of any race (2010); Average household size: 2.33 (2010); Median age: 36.1 (2010); Males per 100 females: 113.1 (2010); Marriage status: 28.5% never married, 64.8% now married, 0.0% widowed, 6.7% divorced (2006-2010 5-year est.); Foreign born: 0.0% (2006-2010 5-year est.); Ancestry (includes multiple ancestries): 30.8% German, 24.3% Dutch, 8.4% Swiss, 8.2% Italian, 8.1% American (2006-2010 5-year est.).

Economy: Employment by occupation: 21.0% management, 3.0% professional, 2.7% services, 26.6% sales, 3.3% farming, 12.6% construction, 3.6% production (2006-2010 5-year est.).

Income: Per capita income: $24,178 (2006-2010 5-year est.); Median household income: $66,563 (2006-2010 5-year est.); Average household income: $62,906 (2006-2010 5-year est.); Percent of households with income of $100,000 or more: 14.7% (2006-2010 5-year est.); Poverty rate: 0.0% (2006-2010 5-year est.).

Education: Percent of population age 25 and over with: High school diploma (including GED) or higher: 100.0% (2006-2010 5-year est.); Bachelor's degree or higher: 42.5% (2006-2010 5-year est.); Master's degree or higher: 2.3% (2006-2010 5-year est.).

Housing: Homeownership rate: 59.4% (2010); Median home value: $159,400 (2006-2010 5-year est.); Median contract rent: $478 per month (2006-2010 5-year est.); Median year structure built: before 1940 (2006-2010 5-year est.).

Transportation: Commute to work: 94.6% car, 0.0% public transportation, 2.7% walk, 2.7% work from home (2006-2010 5-year est.); Travel time to work: 36.6% less than 15 minutes, 18.8% 15 to 30 minutes, 28.3% 30 to 45 minutes, 4.0% 45 to 60 minutes, 12.3% 60 minutes or more (2006-2010 5-year est.)

UPPER PAXTON (township).
Covers a land area of 25.896 square miles and a water area of 5.343 square miles. Located at 40.57° N. Lat; 76.93° W. Long.

Population: 3,661 (1990); 3,930 (2000); 4,161 (2010); Density: 160.7 persons per square mile (2010); Race: 98.3% White, 0.6% Black, 0.3% Asian, 0.0% American Indian/Alaska Native, 0.0% Native Hawaiian/Other Pacific Islander, 0.8% Other, 0.7% Hispanic of any race (2010); Average household size: 2.48 (2010); Median age: 45.7 (2010); Males per 100 females: 94.9 (2010); Marriage status: 18.7% never married, 61.8% now married, 8.7% widowed, 10.7% divorced (2006-2010 5-year est.); Foreign born: 0.0% (2006-2010 5-year est.); Ancestry (includes multiple ancestries): 53.3% German, 8.4% American, 7.6% English, 7.3% Irish, 4.7% Dutch (2006-2010 5-year est.).

Economy: Single-family building permits issued: 2 (2011); Multi-family building permits issued: 0 (2011); Employment by occupation: 9.3% management, 4.0% professional, 8.9% services, 17.9% sales, 6.6% farming, 9.9% construction, 7.5% production (2006-2010 5-year est.).

Income: Per capita income: $27,922 (2006-2010 5-year est.); Median household income: $52,050 (2006-2010 5-year est.); Average household income: $66,436 (2006-2010 5-year est.); Percent of households with income of $100,000 or more: 15.1% (2006-2010 5-year est.); Poverty rate: 7.1% (2006-2010 5-year est.).

Education: Percent of population age 25 and over with: High school diploma (including GED) or higher: 82.6% (2006-2010 5-year est.); Bachelor's degree or higher: 15.4% (2006-2010 5-year est.); Master's degree or higher: 7.0% (2006-2010 5-year est.).

Housing: Homeownership rate: 80.3% (2010); Median home value: $124,300 (2006-2010 5-year est.); Median contract rent: $438 per month (2006-2010 5-year est.); Median year structure built: 1974 (2006-2010 5-year est.).

Transportation: Commute to work: 89.3% car, 0.0% public transportation, 5.3% walk, 4.2% work from home (2006-2010 5-year est.); Travel time to work: 37.2% less than 15 minutes, 13.3% 15 to 30 minutes, 21.3% 30 to

45 minutes, 18.8% 45 to 60 minutes, 9.4% 60 minutes or more (2006-2010 5-year est.)
Additional Information Contacts
Harrisburg Regional Chamber & CREDC . . . . (717) 232-4099
  http://www.harrisburgregionalchamber.org

WASHINGTON (township). Covers a land area of 17.714 square miles and a water area of 0 square miles. Located at 40.56° N. Lat; 76.81° W. Long.
Population: 1,872 (1990); 2,047 (2000); 2,268 (2010); Density: 128.0 persons per square mile (2010); Race: 97.4% White, 0.6% Black, 0.5% Asian, 0.1% American Indian/Alaska Native, 0.0% Native Hawaiian/Other Pacific Islander, 1.4% Other, 1.5% Hispanic of any race (2010); Average household size: 2.55 (2010); Median age: 42.8 (2010); Males per 100 females: 97.4 (2010); Marriage status: 22.2% never married, 60.5% now married, 9.2% widowed, 8.0% divorced (2006-2010 5-year est.); Foreign born: 0.8% (2006-2010 5-year est.); Ancestry (includes multiple ancestries): 58.9% German, 7.5% American, 7.2% Irish, 4.7% Pennsylvania German, 3.2% Italian (2006-2010 5-year est.).
Economy: Single-family building permits issued: 3 (2011); Multi-family building permits issued: 0 (2011); Employment by occupation: 11.6% management, 4.2% professional, 5.4% services, 19.0% sales, 3.2% farming, 16.2% construction, 9.7% production (2006-2010 5-year est.).
Income: Per capita income: $26,821 (2006-2010 5-year est.); Median household income: $57,639 (2006-2010 5-year est.); Average household income: $67,465 (2006-2010 5-year est.); Percent of households with income of $100,000 or more: 15.8% (2006-2010 5-year est.); Poverty rate: 8.7% (2006-2010 5-year est.).
Education: Percent of population age 25 and over with: High school diploma (including GED) or higher: 86.3% (2006-2010 5-year est.); Bachelor's degree or higher: 14.7% (2006-2010 5-year est.); Master's degree or higher: 5.2% (2006-2010 5-year est.).
Housing: Homeownership rate: 84.9% (2010); Median home value: $153,900 (2006-2010 5-year est.); Median contract rent: $350 per month (2006-2010 5-year est.); Median year structure built: 1977 (2006-2010 5-year est.).
Transportation: Commute to work: 90.7% car, 1.0% public transportation, 1.2% walk, 6.6% work from home (2006-2010 5-year est.); Travel time to work: 30.0% less than 15 minutes, 13.6% 15 to 30 minutes, 11.0% 30 to 45 minutes, 33.5% 45 to 60 minutes, 11.9% 60 minutes or more (2006-2010 5-year est.)
Additional Information Contacts
Washington County Chamber of Commerce . . . . (724) 225-3010
  http://www.washcochamber.com

WAYNE (township). Covers a land area of 13.908 square miles and a water area of 0 square miles. Located at 40.46° N. Lat; 76.84° W. Long.
Population: 847 (1990); 1,184 (2000); 1,341 (2010); Density: 96.4 persons per square mile (2010); Race: 96.9% White, 0.0% Black, 1.2% Asian, 0.4% American Indian/Alaska Native, 0.0% Native Hawaiian/Other Pacific Islander, 1.5% Other, 1.9% Hispanic of any race (2010); Average household size: 2.81 (2010); Median age: 41.9 (2010); Males per 100 females: 100.1 (2010); Marriage status: 17.8% never married, 72.4% now married, 5.8% widowed, 4.1% divorced (2006-2010 5-year est.); Foreign born: 0.4% (2006-2010 5-year est.); Ancestry (includes multiple ancestries): 57.5% German, 10.8% American, 8.5% English, 7.6% Italian, 7.3% Irish (2006-2010 5-year est.).
Economy: Single-family building permits issued: 0 (2011); Multi-family building permits issued: 0 (2011); Employment by occupation: 16.3% management, 3.5% professional, 9.0% services, 14.8% sales, 5.7% farming, 11.5% construction, 7.4% production (2006-2010 5-year est.).
Income: Per capita income: $28,986 (2006-2010 5-year est.); Median household income: $73,750 (2006-2010 5-year est.); Average household income: $79,321 (2006-2010 5-year est.); Percent of households with income of $100,000 or more: 29.8% (2006-2010 5-year est.); Poverty rate: 2.6% (2006-2010 5-year est.).
Education: Percent of population age 25 and over with: High school diploma (including GED) or higher: 91.9% (2006-2010 5-year est.); Bachelor's degree or higher: 22.3% (2006-2010 5-year est.); Master's degree or higher: 5.0% (2006-2010 5-year est.).
Housing: Homeownership rate: 92.1% (2010); Median home value: $172,900 (2006-2010 5-year est.); Median contract rent: $525 per month (2006-2010 5-year est.); Median year structure built: 1985 (2006-2010 5-year est.).

Transportation: Commute to work: 95.5% car, 0.0% public transportation, 0.0% walk, 3.9% work from home (2006-2010 5-year est.); Travel time to work: 10.9% less than 15 minutes, 26.3% 15 to 30 minutes, 36.1% 30 to 45 minutes, 20.4% 45 to 60 minutes, 6.3% 60 minutes or more (2006-2010 5-year est.)
Additional Information Contacts
Harrisburg Regional Chamber & CREDC . . . . (717) 232-4099
  http://www.harrisburgregionalchamber.org

WEST HANOVER (township). Covers a land area of 23.214 square miles and a water area of 0.002 square miles. Located at 40.36° N. Lat; 76.74° W. Long.
Population: 6,167 (1990); 6,505 (2000); 9,343 (2010); Density: 402.5 persons per square mile (2010); Race: 92.5% White, 3.3% Black, 2.0% Asian, 0.2% American Indian/Alaska Native, 0.0% Native Hawaiian/Other Pacific Islander, 2.0% Other, 2.3% Hispanic of any race (2010); Average household size: 2.47 (2010); Median age: 43.1 (2010); Males per 100 females: 99.5 (2010); Marriage status: 26.5% never married, 59.3% now married, 6.5% widowed, 7.7% divorced (2006-2010 5-year est.); Foreign born: 2.1% (2006-2010 5-year est.); Ancestry (includes multiple ancestries): 37.5% German, 12.5% Irish, 12.1% Italian, 9.3% English, 7.1% American (2006-2010 5-year est.).
Economy: Single-family building permits issued: 40 (2011); Multi-family building permits issued: 0 (2011); Employment by occupation: 11.0% management, 7.8% professional, 9.7% services, 13.9% sales, 3.9% farming, 7.4% construction, 4.1% production (2006-2010 5-year est.).
Income: Per capita income: $30,201 (2006-2010 5-year est.); Median household income: $70,047 (2006-2010 5-year est.); Average household income: $78,565 (2006-2010 5-year est.); Percent of households with income of $100,000 or more: 25.7% (2006-2010 5-year est.); Poverty rate: 5.8% (2006-2010 5-year est.).
Education: Percent of population age 25 and over with: High school diploma (including GED) or higher: 90.0% (2006-2010 5-year est.); Bachelor's degree or higher: 27.7% (2006-2010 5-year est.); Master's degree or higher: 10.2% (2006-2010 5-year est.).
Housing: Homeownership rate: 90.6% (2010); Median home value: $183,200 (2006-2010 5-year est.); Median contract rent: $826 per month (2006-2010 5-year est.); Median year structure built: 1978 (2006-2010 5-year est.).
Transportation: Commute to work: 94.3% car, 0.2% public transportation, 1.6% walk, 2.8% work from home (2006-2010 5-year est.); Travel time to work: 24.1% less than 15 minutes, 51.1% 15 to 30 minutes, 19.1% 30 to 45 minutes, 3.2% 45 to 60 minutes, 2.6% 60 minutes or more (2006-2010 5-year est.)
Additional Information Contacts
Harrisburg Regional Chamber & CREDC . . . . (717) 232-4099
  http://www.harrisburgregionalchamber.org
West Hanover Township . . . . (717) 652-4841
  http://www.westhanover.com

WICONISCO (township). Covers a land area of 9.761 square miles and a water area of 0 square miles. Located at 40.58° N. Lat; 76.70° W. Long. Elevation is 738 feet.
Population: 1,372 (1990); 1,168 (2000); 1,210 (2010); Density: 124.0 persons per square mile (2010); Race: 97.1% White, 0.3% Black, 0.4% Asian, 0.5% American Indian/Alaska Native, 0.0% Native Hawaiian/Other Pacific Islander, 1.7% Other, 2.9% Hispanic of any race (2010); Average household size: 2.42 (2010); Median age: 42.4 (2010); Males per 100 females: 99.0 (2010); Marriage status: 22.8% never married, 58.1% now married, 10.1% widowed, 9.0% divorced (2006-2010 5-year est.); Foreign born: 0.4% (2006-2010 5-year est.); Ancestry (includes multiple ancestries): 48.2% German, 11.7% Irish, 11.5% English, 8.1% Polish, 6.8% Dutch (2006-2010 5-year est.).
Economy: Single-family building permits issued: 0 (2011); Multi-family building permits issued: 0 (2011); Employment by occupation: 6.7% management, 8.3% professional, 9.1% services, 17.8% sales, 3.1% farming, 9.2% construction, 6.5% production (2006-2010 5-year est.).
Income: Per capita income: $20,346 (2006-2010 5-year est.); Median household income: $45,208 (2006-2010 5-year est.); Average household income: $55,359 (2006-2010 5-year est.); Percent of households with income of $100,000 or more: 9.8% (2006-2010 5-year est.); Poverty rate: 12.4% (2006-2010 5-year est.).
Education: Percent of population age 25 and over with: High school diploma (including GED) or higher: 81.4% (2006-2010 5-year est.);

Bachelor's degree or higher: 8.1% (2006-2010 5-year est.); Master's degree or higher: 0.7% (2006-2010 5-year est.).
Housing: Homeownership rate: 82.2% (2010); Median home value: $76,800 (2006-2010 5-year est.); Median contract rent: $434 per month (2006-2010 5-year est.); Median year structure built: before 1940 (2006-2010 5-year est.).
Safety: Violent crime rate: 0.0 per 10,000 population; Property crime rate: 24.7 per 10,000 population (2011).
Transportation: Commute to work: 89.7% car, 0.5% public transportation, 4.2% walk, 2.9% work from home (2006-2010 5-year est.); Travel time to work: 23.6% less than 15 minutes, 22.7% 15 to 30 minutes, 15.2% 30 to 45 minutes, 15.1% 45 to 60 minutes, 23.4% 60 minutes or more (2006-2010 5-year est.)

WICONSICO (CDP). Covers a land area of 1.090 square miles and a water area of 0 square miles. Located at 40.57° N. Lat; 76.68° W. Long. Elevation is 738 feet.
Population: n/a (1990); n/a (2000); 921 (2010); Density: 844.7 persons per square mile (2010); Race: 97.3% White, 0.4% Black, 0.5% Asian, 0.1% American Indian/Alaska Native, 0.0% Native Hawaiian/Other Pacific Islander, 1.7% Other, 2.5% Hispanic of any race (2010); Average household size: 2.43 (2010); Median age: 43.5 (2010); Males per 100 females: 97.2 (2010); Marriage status: 24.7% never married, 57.7% now married, 9.5% widowed, 8.1% divorced (2006-2010 5-year est.); Foreign born: 0.5% (2006-2010 5-year est.); Ancestry (includes multiple ancestries): 43.9% German, 10.9% Irish, 10.7% Polish, 7.9% Dutch, 7.8% American (2006-2010 5-year est.).
Economy: Employment by occupation: 2.3% management, 5.7% professional, 8.9% services, 19.3% sales, 3.6% farming, 10.9% construction, 8.6% production (2006-2010 5-year est.).
Income: Per capita income: $19,767 (2006-2010 5-year est.); Median household income: $46,023 (2006-2010 5-year est.); Average household income: $53,157 (2006-2010 5-year est.); Percent of households with income of $100,000 or more: 8.9% (2006-2010 5-year est.); Poverty rate: 11.0% (2006-2010 5-year est.).
Education: Percent of population age 25 and over with: High school diploma (including GED) or higher: 78.9% (2006-2010 5-year est.); Bachelor's degree or higher: 4.5% (2006-2010 5-year est.); Master's degree or higher: 0.4% (2006-2010 5-year est.).
Housing: Homeownership rate: 85.0% (2010); Median home value: $68,200 (2006-2010 5-year est.); Median contract rent: $444 per month (2006-2010 5-year est.); Median year structure built: before 1940 (2006-2010 5-year est.).
Transportation: Commute to work: 93.2% car, 0.8% public transportation, 2.1% walk, 0.0% work from home (2006-2010 5-year est.); Travel time to work: 17.8% less than 15 minutes, 27.3% 15 to 30 minutes, 17.1% 30 to 45 minutes, 13.4% 45 to 60 minutes, 24.4% 60 minutes or more (2006-2010 5-year est.)

WILLIAMS (township). Covers a land area of 8.832 square miles and a water area of 0 square miles. Located at 40.59° N. Lat; 76.63° W. Long.
History: Laid out 1869.
Population: 1,146 (1990); 1,135 (2000); 1,112 (2010); Density: 125.9 persons per square mile (2010); Race: 97.1% White, 0.4% Black, 0.1% Asian, 0.1% American Indian/Alaska Native, 0.0% Native Hawaiian/Other Pacific Islander, 2.3% Other, 2.1% Hispanic of any race (2010); Average household size: 2.41 (2010); Median age: 45.3 (2010); Males per 100 females: 102.6 (2010); Marriage status: 28.9% never married, 55.1% now married, 7.1% widowed, 9.0% divorced (2006-2010 5-year est.); Foreign born: 1.0% (2006-2010 5-year est.); Ancestry (includes multiple ancestries): 40.7% German, 16.9% Irish, 8.8% Pennsylvania German, 8.6% English, 8.4% Dutch (2006-2010 5-year est.).
Economy: Single-family building permits issued: 1 (2011); Multi-family building permits issued: 0 (2011); Employment by occupation: 6.5% management, 4.1% professional, 8.9% services, 18.3% sales, 4.8% farming, 10.6% construction, 7.2% production (2006-2010 5-year est.).
Income: Per capita income: $22,268 (2006-2010 5-year est.); Median household income: $41,641 (2006-2010 5-year est.); Average household income: $57,145 (2006-2010 5-year est.); Percent of households with income of $100,000 or more: 11.7% (2006-2010 5-year est.); Poverty rate: 21.8% (2006-2010 5-year est.).
Education: Percent of population age 25 and over with: High school diploma (including GED) or higher: 82.4% (2006-2010 5-year est.); Bachelor's degree or higher: 8.0% (2006-2010 5-year est.); Master's degree or higher: 1.9% (2006-2010 5-year est.).

Housing: Homeownership rate: 82.2% (2010); Median home value: $94,800 (2006-2010 5-year est.); Median contract rent: $199 per month (2006-2010 5-year est.); Median year structure built: 1956 (2006-2010 5-year est.).
Transportation: Commute to work: 96.7% car, 1.1% public transportation, 0.4% walk, 1.3% work from home (2006-2010 5-year est.); Travel time to work: 13.9% less than 15 minutes, 25.6% 15 to 30 minutes, 15.6% 30 to 45 minutes, 20.4% 45 to 60 minutes, 24.6% 60 minutes or more (2006-2010 5-year est.)
Additional Information Contacts
Harrisburg Regional Chamber & CREDC . . . . (717) 232-4099
  http://www.harrisburgregionalchamber.org

WILLIAMSTOWN (borough). Covers a land area of 0.259 square miles and a water area of 0 square miles. Located at 40.58° N. Lat; 76.62° W. Long. Elevation is 732 feet.
Population: 1,509 (1990); 1,433 (2000); 1,387 (2010); Density: 5,350.4 persons per square mile (2010); Race: 96.9% White, 1.5% Black, 0.8% Asian, 0.1% American Indian/Alaska Native, 0.0% Native Hawaiian/Other Pacific Islander, 0.7% Other, 0.5% Hispanic of any race (2010); Average household size: 2.45 (2010); Median age: 38.7 (2010); Males per 100 females: 90.3 (2010); Marriage status: 26.3% never married, 52.1% now married, 10.2% widowed, 11.4% divorced (2006-2010 5-year est.); Foreign born: 1.5% (2006-2010 5-year est.); Ancestry (includes multiple ancestries): 35.9% German, 20.6% Irish, 9.8% American, 8.5% Polish, 7.1% English (2006-2010 5-year est.).
Economy: Single-family building permits issued: 0 (2011); Multi-family building permits issued: 0 (2011); Employment by occupation: 3.9% management, 2.1% professional, 12.8% services, 17.4% sales, 7.8% farming, 13.0% construction, 14.3% production (2006-2010 5-year est.).
Income: Per capita income: $18,267 (2006-2010 5-year est.); Median household income: $47,628 (2006-2010 5-year est.); Average household income: $45,271 (2006-2010 5-year est.); Percent of households with income of $100,000 or more: 5.7% (2006-2010 5-year est.); Poverty rate: 12.4% (2006-2010 5-year est.).
Education: Percent of population age 25 and over with: High school diploma (including GED) or higher: 84.8% (2006-2010 5-year est.); Bachelor's degree or higher: 9.2% (2006-2010 5-year est.); Master's degree or higher: 2.1% (2006-2010 5-year est.).
Housing: Homeownership rate: 73.6% (2010); Median home value: $72,700 (2006-2010 5-year est.); Median contract rent: $367 per month (2006-2010 5-year est.); Median year structure built: before 1940 (2006-2010 5-year est.).
Transportation: Commute to work: 95.7% car, 0.0% public transportation, 1.2% walk, 2.0% work from home (2006-2010 5-year est.); Travel time to work: 13.5% less than 15 minutes, 28.0% 15 to 30 minutes, 20.1% 30 to 45 minutes, 17.9% 45 to 60 minutes, 20.5% 60 minutes or more (2006-2010 5-year est.)
Additional Information Contacts
Brush Valley Regional Chamber of Commerce . . . . (570) 648-4675
  http://www.brushvalleychamber.com

Delaware County

Located in southeastern Pennsylvania; bounded on the southeast by the Delaware River, and on the south by the Delware border. Covers a land area of 183.843 square miles, a water area of 6.760 square miles, and is located in the Eastern Time Zone at 39.92° N. Lat., 75.40° W. Long. The county was founded in 1789. County seat is Media.

Delaware County is part of the Philadelphia-Camden-Wilmington, PA-NJ-DE-MD Metropolitan Statistical Area. The entire metro area includes: Camden, NJ Metropolitan Division (Burlington County, NJ; Camden County, NJ; Gloucester County, NJ); Philadelphia, PA Metropolitan Division (Bucks County, PA; Chester County, PA; Delaware County, PA; Montgomery County, PA; Philadelphia County, PA); Wilmington, DE-MD-NJ Metropolitan Division (New Castle County, DE; Cecil County, MD; Salem County, NJ)

Weather Station: Marcus Hook											Elevation: 9 feet
	Jan	Feb	Mar	Apr	May	Jun	Jul	Aug	Sep	Oct	Nov	Dec
High	40	44	51	64	74	83	87	85	77	65	55	44
Low	28	30	36	46	56	65	70	69	62	50	41	33
Precip	2.4	2.3	3.2	3.2	3.7	2.9	4.1	2.8	4.3	3.0	3.1	2.9
Snow	na	2.7	na	tr	0.0	0.0	0.0	0.0	0.0	0.0	tr	na

High and Low temperatures in degrees Fahrenheit; Precipitation and Snow in inches

Population: 547,658 (1990); 550,864 (2000); 558,979 (2010); Race: 72.5% White, 19.7% Black, 4.7% Asian, 0.2% American Indian/Alaska Native, 0.0% Native Hawaiian/Other Pacific Islander, 2.9% Other, 3.0% Hispanic of any race (2010); Density: 3,040.5 persons per square mile (2010); Average household size: 2.57 (2010); Median age: 38.7 (2010); Males per 100 females: 92.0 (2010).

Religion: Six largest groups: 47.0% Catholicism, 3.1% Methodist/Pietist, 2.7% Non-Denominational, 2.4% Presbyterian-Reformed, 1.9% Baptist, 1.9% Episcopalianism/Anglicanism (2010)

Economy: Unemployment rate: 8.5% (August 2012); Total civilian labor force: 283,137 (August 2012); Leading industries: 18.6% health care and social assistance; 12.4% retail trade; 8.0% accommodation & food services (2010); Farms: 79 totaling 4,361 acres (2007); Companies that employ 500 or more persons: 40 (2010); Companies that employ 100 to 499 persons: 257 (2010); Companies that employ less than 100 persons: 12,475 (2010); Black-owned businesses: 4,032 (2007); Hispanic-owned businesses: n/a (2007); Asian-owned businesses: 2,647 (2007); Women-owned businesses: 13,590 (2007); Retail sales per capita: $11,148 (2010). Single-family building permits issued: 190 (2011); Multi-family building permits issued: 0 (2011).

Income: Per capita income: $32,067 (2006-2010 5-year est.); Median household income: $61,876 (2006-2010 5-year est.); Average household income: $84,070 (2006-2010 5-year est.); Percent of households with income of $100,000 or more: 28.2% (2006-2010 5-year est.); Poverty rate: 9.4% (2006-2010 5-year est.); Bankruptcy rate: 2.22% (2011).

Taxes: Total county taxes per capita: $277 (2009); County property taxes per capita: $259 (2009).

Education: Percent of population age 25 and over with: High school diploma (including GED) or higher: 90.5% (2006-2010 5-year est.); Bachelor's degree or higher: 34.7% (2006-2010 5-year est.); Master's degree or higher: 14.5% (2006-2010 5-year est.).

Housing: Homeownership rate: 70.6% (2010); Median home value: $232,300 (2006-2010 5-year est.); Median contract rent: $771 per month (2006-2010 5-year est.); Median year structure built: 1955 (2006-2010 5-year est.)

Health: Birth rate: 122.0 per 10,000 population (2011); Death rate: 94.1 per 10,000 population (2011); Age-adjusted cancer mortality rate: 192.7 deaths per 100,000 population (2009); Number of physicians: 50.6 per 10,000 population (2010); Hospital beds: 27.7 per 10,000 population (2008); Hospital admissions: 1,495.3 per 10,000 population (2008).

Environment: Air Quality Index: 69.3% good, 29.0% moderate, 1.6% unhealthy for sensitive individuals, 0.0% unhealthy (percent of days in 2011)

Elections: 2012 Presidential election results: 60.4% Obama, 38.6% Romney

National and State Parks: Brandywine Battlefield State Park; Ridley Creek State Park

Additional Information Contacts
Delaware County Government . . . . (610) 891-4000
   http://www.co.delaware.pa.us
Delaware County Chamber of Commerce. . . . . (610) 565-3677
   http://www.delcochamber.org

Delaware County Communities

ALDAN (borough). Covers a land area of 0.597 square miles and a water area of 0 square miles. Located at 39.92° N. Lat; 75.29° W. Long. Elevation is 131 feet.

Population: 4,549 (1990); 4,313 (2000); 4,152 (2010); Density: 6,958.0 persons per square mile (2010); Race: 76.3% White, 18.5% Black, 2.6% Asian, 0.1% American Indian/Alaska Native, 0.0% Native Hawaiian/Other Pacific Islander, 2.5% Other, 2.1% Hispanic of any race (2010); Average household size: 2.39 (2010); Median age: 42.1 (2010); Males per 100 females: 89.1 (2010); Marriage status: 33.8% never married, 44.7% now married, 7.2% widowed, 14.2% divorced (2006-2010 5-year est.); Foreign born: 6.4% (2006-2010 5-year est.); Ancestry (includes multiple ancestries): 30.4% Irish, 27.2% Italian, 16.9% German, 11.3% English, 7.1% Polish (2006-2010 5-year est.).

Economy: Single-family building permits issued: 0 (2011); Multi-family building permits issued: 0 (2011); Employment by occupation: 10.3% management, 1.3% professional, 6.9% services, 25.5% sales, 4.4% farming, 7.4% construction, 5.0% production (2006-2010 5-year est.).

Income: Per capita income: $31,358 (2006-2010 5-year est.); Median household income: $62,319 (2006-2010 5-year est.); Average household income: $74,114 (2006-2010 5-year est.); Percent of households with income of $100,000 or more: 26.0% (2006-2010 5-year est.); Poverty rate: 5.7% (2006-2010 5-year est.).

Education: Percent of population age 25 and over with: High school diploma (including GED) or higher: 92.6% (2006-2010 5-year est.); Bachelor's degree or higher: 23.1% (2006-2010 5-year est.); Master's degree or higher: 9.5% (2006-2010 5-year est.).

School District(s)
William Penn SD (KG-12)
   2010-11 Enrollment: 5,305 . . . . (610) 284-8000

Housing: Homeownership rate: 76.4% (2010); Median home value: $188,000 (2006-2010 5-year est.); Median contract rent: $733 per month (2006-2010 5-year est.); Median year structure built: 1952 (2006-2010 5-year est.).

Safety: Violent crime rate: 24.0 per 10,000 population; Property crime rate: 372.1 per 10,000 population (2011).

Transportation: Commute to work: 80.2% car, 12.8% public transportation, 4.6% walk, 1.4% work from home (2006-2010 5-year est.); Travel time to work: 17.7% less than 15 minutes, 38.5% 15 to 30 minutes, 16.5% 30 to 45 minutes, 12.9% 45 to 60 minutes, 14.4% 60 minutes or more (2006-2010 5-year est.)

Additional Information Contacts
Aldan Borough . . . . (610) 626-3554
   http://www.aldan-boro.org
Greater Philadelphia Chamber of Commerce . . . . (215) 545-1234
   http://www.greaterphilachamber.com

ASTON (township). Aka Aston Mills. Covers a land area of 5.844 square miles and a water area of 0.002 square miles. Located at 39.87° N. Lat; 75.44° W. Long.

Population: 15,079 (1990); 16,203 (2000); 16,592 (2010); Density: 2,839.1 persons per square mile (2010); Race: 94.3% White, 2.8% Black, 1.6% Asian, 0.1% American Indian/Alaska Native, 0.0% Native Hawaiian/Other Pacific Islander, 1.2% Other, 1.6% Hispanic of any race (2010); Average household size: 2.63 (2010); Median age: 40.0 (2010); Males per 100 females: 91.0 (2010); Marriage status: 28.6% never married, 57.3% now married, 7.0% widowed, 7.2% divorced (2006-2010 5-year est.); Foreign born: 3.1% (2006-2010 5-year est.); Ancestry (includes multiple ancestries): 34.0% Irish, 27.5% Italian, 22.4% German, 11.7% English, 10.3% Polish (2006-2010 5-year est.).

Economy: Single-family building permits issued: 8 (2011); Multi-family building permits issued: 0 (2011); Employment by occupation: 12.5% management, 6.2% professional, 6.2% services, 16.1% sales, 4.0% farming, 11.6% construction, 6.8% production (2006-2010 5-year est.).

Income: Per capita income: $32,209 (2006-2010 5-year est.); Median household income: $78,317 (2006-2010 5-year est.); Average household income: $87,555 (2006-2010 5-year est.); Percent of households with income of $100,000 or more: 33.1% (2006-2010 5-year est.); Poverty rate: 4.1% (2006-2010 5-year est.).

Taxes: Total city taxes per capita: $427 (2009); City property taxes per capita: $197 (2009).

Education: Percent of population age 25 and over with: High school diploma (including GED) or higher: 91.2% (2006-2010 5-year est.); Bachelor's degree or higher: 30.2% (2006-2010 5-year est.); Master's degree or higher: 10.1% (2006-2010 5-year est.).

School District(s)
Chichester SD (KG-12)
   2010-11 Enrollment: 3,411 . . . . (610) 485-6881
Delaware County Technical High School (10-12)
   2010-11 Enrollment: n/a . . . . (610) 583-7620
Penn-Delco SD (KG-12)
   2010-11 Enrollment: 3,356 . . . . (610) 497-6300

Four-year College(s)
Neumann University (Private, Not-for-profit, Roman Catholic)
   Fall 2010 Enrollment: 2,683 . . . . (610) 459-0905
   2011-12 Tuition: In-state $23,350; Out-of-state $23,350

Housing: Homeownership rate: 90.1% (2010); Median home value: $248,300 (2006-2010 5-year est.); Median contract rent: $752 per month (2006-2010 5-year est.); Median year structure built: 1967 (2006-2010 5-year est.).

Safety: Violent crime rate: 11.4 per 10,000 population; Property crime rate: 189.2 per 10,000 population (2011).

Transportation: Commute to work: 93.5% car, 2.7% public transportation, 1.9% walk, 1.4% work from home (2006-2010 5-year est.); Travel time to work: 27.4% less than 15 minutes, 36.3% 15 to 30 minutes, 21.3% 30 to 45 minutes, 9.1% 45 to 60 minutes, 5.9% 60 minutes or more (2006-2010 5-year est.)

Additional Information Contacts
Aston Township . . . . (610) 494-1636
   http://www.astontownship.net
Greater Philadelphia Chamber of Commerce . . . . (215) 545-1234
   http://www.greaterphilachamber.com

BETHEL (township). Covers a land area of 5.411 square miles and a water area of 0 square miles. Located at 39.85° N. Lat; 75.49° W. Long.
History: The township is mentioned as early as 1683.
Population: 3,330 (1990); 6,421 (2000); 8,791 (2010); Density: 1,624.5 persons per square mile (2010); Race: 90.3% White, 1.8% Black, 6.1% Asian, 0.2% American Indian/Alaska Native, 0.0% Native Hawaiian/Other Pacific Islander, 1.6% Other, 2.2% Hispanic of any race (2010); Average household size: 2.91 (2010); Median age: 41.9 (2010); Males per 100 females: 98.9 (2010); Marriage status: 22.4% never married, 68.3% now married, 4.1% widowed, 5.1% divorced (2006-2010 5-year est.); Foreign born: 5.3% (2006-2010 5-year est.); Ancestry (includes multiple ancestries): 34.2% Italian, 32.2% Irish, 19.4% German, 16.6% English, 6.6% Polish (2006-2010 5-year est.).
Economy: Single-family building permits issued: 27 (2011); Multi-family building permits issued: 0 (2011); Employment by occupation: 17.5% management, 7.3% professional, 6.4% services, 14.0% sales, 1.6% farming, 8.2% construction, 3.5% production (2006-2010 5-year est.).
Income: Per capita income: $40,524 (2006-2010 5-year est.); Median household income: $109,453 (2006-2010 5-year est.); Average household income: $127,416 (2006-2010 5-year est.); Percent of households with income of $100,000 or more: 56.9% (2006-2010 5-year est.); Poverty rate: 1.8% (2006-2010 5-year est.).
Education: Percent of population age 25 and over with: High school diploma (including GED) or higher: 95.5% (2006-2010 5-year est.); Bachelor's degree or higher: 46.0% (2006-2010 5-year est.); Master's degree or higher: 20.6% (2006-2010 5-year est.).
Housing: Homeownership rate: 96.8% (2010); Median home value: $395,600 (2006-2010 5-year est.); Median contract rent: $1,911 per month (2006-2010 5-year est.); Median year structure built: 1995 (2006-2010 5-year est.).
Safety: Violent crime rate: 12.5 per 10,000 population; Property crime rate: 137.2 per 10,000 population (2011).
Transportation: Commute to work: 90.6% car, 1.4% public transportation, 1.2% walk, 6.0% work from home (2006-2010 5-year est.); Travel time to work: 24.7% less than 15 minutes, 37.5% 15 to 30 minutes, 22.8% 30 to 45 minutes, 8.5% 45 to 60 minutes, 6.5% 60 minutes or more (2006-2010 5-year est.)
Additional Information Contacts
Bethel Township . . . . (610) 459-1529
   http://www.twp.bethel.pa.us
Delaware County Chamber of Commerce . . . . (610) 565-3677
   http://www.delcochamber.org

BOOTHWYN (CDP). Covers a land area of 1.247 square miles and a water area of 0 square miles. Located at 39.84° N. Lat; 75.45° W. Long. Elevation is 98 feet.
Population: 5,022 (1990); 5,206 (2000); 4,933 (2010); Density: 3,954.3 persons per square mile (2010); Race: 87.3% White, 8.1% Black, 1.7% Asian, 0.3% American Indian/Alaska Native, 0.0% Native Hawaiian/Other Pacific Islander, 2.6% Other, 2.6% Hispanic of any race (2010); Average household size: 2.50 (2010); Median age: 39.8 (2010); Males per 100 females: 92.8 (2010); Marriage status: 30.7% never married, 52.0% now married, 7.1% widowed, 10.2% divorced (2006-2010 5-year est.); Foreign born: 2.3% (2006-2010 5-year est.); Ancestry (includes multiple ancestries): 27.6% Irish, 26.5% Italian, 23.1% German, 10.0% Polish, 8.4% Scotch-Irish (2006-2010 5-year est.).
Economy: Employment by occupation: 11.3% management, 3.2% professional, 10.8% services, 21.5% sales, 4.3% farming, 14.7% construction, 7.9% production (2006-2010 5-year est.).
Income: Per capita income: $28,490 (2006-2010 5-year est.); Median household income: $66,332 (2006-2010 5-year est.); Average household income: $70,895 (2006-2010 5-year est.); Percent of households with income of $100,000 or more: 20.7% (2006-2010 5-year est.); Poverty rate: 6.0% (2006-2010 5-year est.).

Education: Percent of population age 25 and over with: High school diploma (including GED) or higher: 88.3% (2006-2010 5-year est.); Bachelor's degree or higher: 16.1% (2006-2010 5-year est.); Master's degree or higher: 5.5% (2006-2010 5-year est.).
School District(s)
Chichester SD (KG-12)
   2010-11 Enrollment: 3,411 . . . . (610) 485-6881
Garnet Valley SD (KG-12)
   2010-11 Enrollment: 4,832 . . . . (610) 579-7300
Housing: Homeownership rate: 64.6% (2010); Median home value: $211,900 (2006-2010 5-year est.); Median contract rent: $775 per month (2006-2010 5-year est.); Median year structure built: 1968 (2006-2010 5-year est.).
Transportation: Commute to work: 93.4% car, 2.7% public transportation, 0.5% walk, 2.1% work from home (2006-2010 5-year est.); Travel time to work: 22.9% less than 15 minutes, 38.8% 15 to 30 minutes, 24.3% 30 to 45 minutes, 6.6% 45 to 60 minutes, 7.3% 60 minutes or more (2006-2010 5-year est.)
Additional Information Contacts
Delaware County Chamber of Commerce . . . . (610) 565-3677
   http://www.delcochamber.org

BROOKHAVEN (borough). Covers a land area of 1.707 square miles and a water area of 0.003 square miles. Located at 39.87° N. Lat; 75.39° W. Long. Elevation is 98 feet.
Population: 8,567 (1990); 7,985 (2000); 8,006 (2010); Density: 4,691.3 persons per square mile (2010); Race: 92.4% White, 3.7% Black, 1.9% Asian, 0.1% American Indian/Alaska Native, 0.0% Native Hawaiian/Other Pacific Islander, 1.9% Other, 2.0% Hispanic of any race (2010); Average household size: 2.26 (2010); Median age: 42.5 (2010); Males per 100 females: 88.9 (2010); Marriage status: 25.7% never married, 57.7% now married, 8.4% widowed, 8.2% divorced (2006-2010 5-year est.); Foreign born: 7.2% (2006-2010 5-year est.); Ancestry (includes multiple ancestries): 29.0% Irish, 28.9% Italian, 16.2% German, 10.8% English, 7.7% Polish (2006-2010 5-year est.).
Economy: Single-family building permits issued: 0 (2011); Multi-family building permits issued: 0 (2011); Employment by occupation: 7.4% management, 6.1% professional, 8.0% services, 21.5% sales, 3.1% farming, 10.5% construction, 5.9% production (2006-2010 5-year est.).
Income: Per capita income: $30,811 (2006-2010 5-year est.); Median household income: $64,345 (2006-2010 5-year est.); Average household income: $70,452 (2006-2010 5-year est.); Percent of households with income of $100,000 or more: 23.8% (2006-2010 5-year est.); Poverty rate: 8.6% (2006-2010 5-year est.).
Taxes: Total city taxes per capita: $395 (2009); City property taxes per capita: $191 (2009).
Education: Percent of population age 25 and over with: High school diploma (including GED) or higher: 91.6% (2006-2010 5-year est.); Bachelor's degree or higher: 21.8% (2006-2010 5-year est.); Master's degree or higher: 5.4% (2006-2010 5-year est.).
School District(s)
Chester-Upland SD (PK-12)
   2010-11 Enrollment: 4,244 . . . . (610) 447-3600
Penn-Delco SD (KG-12)
   2010-11 Enrollment: 3,356 . . . . (610) 497-6300
Housing: Homeownership rate: 84.8% (2010); Median home value: $206,300 (2006-2010 5-year est.); Median contract rent: $819 per month (2006-2010 5-year est.); Median year structure built: 1969 (2006-2010 5-year est.).
Safety: Violent crime rate: 13.7 per 10,000 population; Property crime rate: 241.5 per 10,000 population (2011).
Transportation: Commute to work: 95.2% car, 0.8% public transportation, 1.2% walk, 2.9% work from home (2006-2010 5-year est.); Travel time to work: 24.0% less than 15 minutes, 45.0% 15 to 30 minutes, 21.5% 30 to 45 minutes, 5.6% 45 to 60 minutes, 3.8% 60 minutes or more (2006-2010 5-year est.)
Additional Information Contacts
Borough of Brookhaven . . . . (610) 874-2557
   http://www.brookhavenboro.com
Delaware County Chamber of Commerce . . . . (610) 565-3677
   http://www.delcochamber.org

BROOMALL (CDP). Aka Marple Township. Covers a land area of 2.890 square miles and a water area of 0 square miles. Located at 39.97° N. Lat; 75.35° W. Long. Elevation is 351 feet.

Population: 10,930 (1990); 11,046 (2000); 10,789 (2010); Density: 3,732.9 persons per square mile (2010); Race: 89.1% White, 1.8% Black, 7.7% Asian, 0.0% American Indian/Alaska Native, 0.0% Native Hawaiian/Other Pacific Islander, 1.4% Other, 1.4% Hispanic of any race (2010); Average household size: 2.55 (2010); Median age: 45.8 (2010); Males per 100 females: 92.8 (2010); Marriage status: 26.7% never married, 59.3% now married, 7.0% widowed, 7.0% divorced (2006-2010 5-year est.); Foreign born: 16.0% (2006-2010 5-year est.); Ancestry (includes multiple ancestries): 29.9% Italian, 25.4% Irish, 13.4% German, 8.3% English, 4.0% Polish (2006-2010 5-year est.).

Economy: Employment by occupation: 11.5% management, 5.9% professional, 7.7% services, 16.6% sales, 4.1% farming, 11.4% construction, 4.0% production (2006-2010 5-year est.).

Income: Per capita income: $31,357 (2006-2010 5-year est.); Median household income: $71,691 (2006-2010 5-year est.); Average household income: $82,624 (2006-2010 5-year est.); Percent of households with income of $100,000 or more: 33.9% (2006-2010 5-year est.); Poverty rate: 4.3% (2006-2010 5-year est.).

Education: Percent of population age 25 and over with: High school diploma (including GED) or higher: 89.3% (2006-2010 5-year est.); Bachelor's degree or higher: 29.1% (2006-2010 5-year est.); Master's degree or higher: 10.0% (2006-2010 5-year est.).

School District(s)
Marple Newtown SD (KG-12)
   2010-11 Enrollment: 3,496 . . . . (610) 359-4256

Two-year College(s)
Kaplan Career Institute (Private, For-profit)
   Fall 2010 Enrollment: 1,253 . . . . (610) 353-7630

Housing: Homeownership rate: 80.3% (2010); Median home value: $325,900 (2006-2010 5-year est.); Median contract rent: $870 per month (2006-2010 5-year est.); Median year structure built: 1957 (2006-2010 5-year est.).

Transportation: Commute to work: 90.4% car, 3.6% public transportation, 2.4% walk, 2.3% work from home (2006-2010 5-year est.); Travel time to work: 24.3% less than 15 minutes, 37.4% 15 to 30 minutes, 24.8% 30 to 45 minutes, 7.8% 45 to 60 minutes, 5.8% 60 minutes or more (2006-2010 5-year est.)

Additional Information Contacts
Main Line Chamber of Commerce . . . . (610) 687-6232
   http://www.mlcc.org

CHADDS FORD (township). Covers a land area of 8.660 square miles and a water area of 0.061 square miles. Located at 39.86° N. Lat; 75.57° W. Long. Elevation is 164 feet.

History: A ford is a shallow place in a body of water that can be crossed without a boat. Chadds Ford became known as such because "Ye Great Road to Nottingham" crossed the Brandywine at the property of John Chads.

Population: 3,118 (1990); 3,170 (2000); 3,640 (2010); Density: 420.3 persons per square mile (2010); Race: 89.4% White, 1.4% Black, 7.6% Asian, 0.0% American Indian/Alaska Native, 0.0% Native Hawaiian/Other Pacific Islander, 1.6% Other, 2.9% Hispanic of any race (2010); Average household size: 2.53 (2010); Median age: 44.5 (2010); Males per 100 females: 93.5 (2010); Marriage status: 22.7% never married, 59.7% now married, 6.5% widowed, 11.1% divorced (2006-2010 5-year est.); Foreign born: 6.4% (2006-2010 5-year est.); Ancestry (includes multiple ancestries): 28.2% Irish, 25.5% German, 23.8% Italian, 19.1% English, 9.0% Polish (2006-2010 5-year est.).

Economy: Single-family building permits issued: 3 (2011); Multi-family building permits issued: 0 (2011); Employment by occupation: 23.5% management, 6.5% professional, 7.0% services, 19.1% sales, 1.1% farming, 4.0% construction, 1.6% production (2006-2010 5-year est.).

Income: Per capita income: $68,840 (2006-2010 5-year est.); Median household income: $96,318 (2006-2010 5-year est.); Average household income: $165,895 (2006-2010 5-year est.); Percent of households with income of $100,000 or more: 47.3% (2006-2010 5-year est.); Poverty rate: 1.4% (2006-2010 5-year est.).

Education: Percent of population age 25 and over with: High school diploma (including GED) or higher: 96.9% (2006-2010 5-year est.); Bachelor's degree or higher: 62.9% (2006-2010 5-year est.); Master's degree or higher: 24.5% (2006-2010 5-year est.).

School District(s)
Unionville-Chadds Ford SD (KG-12)
   2010-11 Enrollment: 4,089 . . . . (610) 347-0970

Housing: Homeownership rate: 88.4% (2010); Median home value: $368,000 (2006-2010 5-year est.); Median contract rent: $1,881 per month (2006-2010 5-year est.); Median year structure built: 1982 (2006-2010 5-year est.).

Transportation: Commute to work: 91.6% car, 1.4% public transportation, 1.2% walk, 5.0% work from home (2006-2010 5-year est.); Travel time to work: 24.4% less than 15 minutes, 31.6% 15 to 30 minutes, 26.6% 30 to 45 minutes, 10.6% 45 to 60 minutes, 6.8% 60 minutes or more (2006-2010 5-year est.)

Additional Information Contacts
Southern Chester County Chamber of Commerce . . . . (610) 444-0774
   http://www.scccc.com

CHESTER (city). Aka Aston Mills. Covers a land area of 4.839 square miles and a water area of 1.167 square miles. Located at 39.85° N. Lat; 75.37° W. Long. Elevation is 13 feet.

History: Named for Chester, England, by William Penn. Chester was settled by Swedes in 1644, when the Swedish crown granted part of the area to Joran Kyn, one of the bodyguards of Governor Printz. Swedish control ended in 1655, when the Dutch took over. They were followed by the English, then Dutch again, and finally the English. Chester was the most important town in Pennsylvania until 1683.

Population: 42,042 (1990); 36,854 (2000); 33,972 (2010); Density: 7,020.3 persons per square mile (2010); Race: 17.2% White, 74.7% Black, 0.6% Asian, 0.4% American Indian/Alaska Native, 0.1% Native Hawaiian/Other Pacific Islander, 7.0% Other, 9.0% Hispanic of any race (2010); Average household size: 2.64 (2010); Median age: 29.9 (2010); Males per 100 females: 89.5 (2010); Marriage status: 56.0% never married, 27.5% now married, 7.4% widowed, 9.2% divorced (2006-2010 5-year est.); Foreign born: 2.8% (2006-2010 5-year est.); Ancestry (includes multiple ancestries): 2.9% Irish, 2.3% German, 1.9% Italian, 1.4% English, 1.1% Polish (2006-2010 5-year est.).

Economy: Unemployment rate: 15.1% (August 2012); Total civilian labor force: 14,152 (August 2012); Single-family building permits issued: 2 (2011); Multi-family building permits issued: 0 (2011); Employment by occupation: 4.5% management, 2.2% professional, 17.9% services, 18.7% sales, 2.0% farming, 5.9% construction, 7.4% production (2006-2010 5-year est.).

Income: Per capita income: $14,251 (2006-2010 5-year est.); Median household income: $26,787 (2006-2010 5-year est.); Average household income: $36,576 (2006-2010 5-year est.); Percent of households with income of $100,000 or more: 4.5% (2006-2010 5-year est.); Poverty rate: 35.1% (2006-2010 5-year est.).

Taxes: Total city taxes per capita: $513 (2009); City property taxes per capita: $189 (2009).

Education: Percent of population age 25 and over with: High school diploma (including GED) or higher: 76.9% (2006-2010 5-year est.); Bachelor's degree or higher: 8.7% (2006-2010 5-year est.); Master's degree or higher: 3.1% (2006-2010 5-year est.).

School District(s)
Chester Community CS (KG-08)
   2010-11 Enrollment: 2,734 . . . . (610) 447-0400
Chester-Upland SD (PK-12)
   2010-11 Enrollment: 4,244 . . . . (610) 447-3600
Chester-Upland SD (PK-12)
   2010-11 Enrollment: 4,244 . . . . (610) 447-3600
Widener Partnership CS (KG-05)
   2010-11 Enrollment: 294 . . . . (610) 872-1358

Four-year College(s)
Widener University-Main Campus (Private, Not-for-profit)
   Fall 2010 Enrollment: 4,251 . . . . (610) 499-4000
   2011-12 Tuition: In-state $34,762; Out-of-state $34,762

Housing: Homeownership rate: 38.5% (2010); Median home value: $66,900 (2006-2010 5-year est.); Median contract rent: $610 per month (2006-2010 5-year est.); Median year structure built: 1951 (2006-2010 5-year est.).

Hospitals: Keystone Center (84 beds)

Safety: Violent crime rate: n/a per 10,000 population; Property crime rate: 387.9 per 10,000 population (2011).

Transportation: Commute to work: 74.1% car, 15.0% public transportation, 6.6% walk, 3.1% work from home (2006-2010 5-year est.); Travel time to work: 31.2% less than 15 minutes, 40.6% 15 to 30 minutes,

16.6% 30 to 45 minutes, 7.3% 45 to 60 minutes, 4.4% 60 minutes or more (2006-2010 5-year est.)

Additional Information Contacts

City of Chester. . . . . (610) 447-7700
http://www.chestercity.com

Delaware County Chamber of Commerce. . . . . (610) 565-3677
http://www.delcochamber.org

CHESTER (township). Covers a land area of 1.428 square miles and a water area of 0 square miles. Located at 39.85° N. Lat; 75.40° W. Long. Elevation is 13 feet.

Population: 5,400 (1990); 4,604 (2000); 3,940 (2010); Density: 2,758.8 persons per square mile (2010); Race: 16.9% White, 78.3% Black, 0.5% Asian, 0.2% American Indian/Alaska Native, 0.0% Native Hawaiian/Other Pacific Islander, 4.1% Other, 3.9% Hispanic of any race (2010); Average household size: 2.79 (2010); Median age: 32.7 (2010); Males per 100 females: 79.2 (2010); Marriage status: 47.2% never married, 38.5% now married, 6.3% widowed, 8.1% divorced (2006-2010 5-year est.); Foreign born: 5.3% (2006-2010 5-year est.); Ancestry (includes multiple ancestries): 7.7% German, 5.8% Irish, 3.8% Italian, 3.0% English, 2.7% Ghanian (2006-2010 5-year est.).

Economy: Single-family building permits issued: 0 (2011); Multi-family building permits issued: 0 (2011); Employment by occupation: 5.4% management, 2.1% professional, 16.0% services, 19.3% sales, 3.7% farming, 7.3% construction, 6.0% production (2006-2010 5-year est.).

Income: Per capita income: $19,913 (2006-2010 5-year est.); Median household income: $50,441 (2006-2010 5-year est.); Average household income: $60,000 (2006-2010 5-year est.); Percent of households with income of $100,000 or more: 14.3% (2006-2010 5-year est.); Poverty rate: 13.6% (2006-2010 5-year est.).

Education: Percent of population age 25 and over with: High school diploma (including GED) or higher: 89.2% (2006-2010 5-year est.); Bachelor's degree or higher: 16.7% (2006-2010 5-year est.); Master's degree or higher: 5.0% (2006-2010 5-year est.).

Four-year College(s)

Widener University-Main Campus (Private, Not-for-profit)
Fall 2010 Enrollment: 4,251 . . . . (610) 499-4000
2011-12 Tuition: In-state $34,762; Out-of-state $34,762

Housing: Homeownership rate: 59.8% (2010); Median home value: $93,200 (2006-2010 5-year est.); Median contract rent: $704 per month (2006-2010 5-year est.); Median year structure built: 1972 (2006-2010 5-year est.).

Hospitals: Keystone Center (84 beds)

Safety: Violent crime rate: 151.8 per 10,000 population; Property crime rate: 392.1 per 10,000 population (2011).

Transportation: Commute to work: 79.8% car, 16.8% public transportation, 3.4% walk, 0.0% work from home (2006-2010 5-year est.); Travel time to work: 23.3% less than 15 minutes, 37.5% 15 to 30 minutes, 21.8% 30 to 45 minutes, 7.8% 45 to 60 minutes, 9.6% 60 minutes or more (2006-2010 5-year est.)

Additional Information Contacts

Delaware County Chamber of Commerce. . . . . (610) 565-3677
http://www.delcochamber.org

CHESTER HEIGHTS (borough). Covers a land area of 2.214 square miles and a water area of 0.002 square miles. Located at 39.89° N. Lat; 75.47° W. Long. Elevation is 331 feet.

Population: 2,273 (1990); 2,481 (2000); 2,531 (2010); Density: 1,143.4 persons per square mile (2010); Race: 92.1% White, 3.3% Black, 3.2% Asian, 0.0% American Indian/Alaska Native, 0.0% Native Hawaiian/Other Pacific Islander, 1.4% Other, 1.5% Hispanic of any race (2010); Average household size: 2.12 (2010); Median age: 43.5 (2010); Males per 100 females: 82.5 (2010); Marriage status: 31.5% never married, 52.5% now married, 6.4% widowed, 9.5% divorced (2006-2010 5-year est.); Foreign born: 1.9% (2006-2010 5-year est.); Ancestry (includes multiple ancestries): 29.3% Italian, 27.4% Irish, 19.5% German, 14.4% English, 5.5% Polish (2006-2010 5-year est.).

Economy: Single-family building permits issued: 0 (2011); Multi-family building permits issued: 0 (2011); Employment by occupation: 22.3% management, 6.7% professional, 3.4% services, 14.7% sales, 7.5% farming, 3.1% construction, 1.2% production (2006-2010 5-year est.).

Income: Per capita income: $40,897 (2006-2010 5-year est.); Median household income: $72,829 (2006-2010 5-year est.); Average household income: $92,373 (2006-2010 5-year est.); Percent of households with

income of $100,000 or more: 35.3% (2006-2010 5-year est.); Poverty rate: 3.0% (2006-2010 5-year est.).

Education: Percent of population age 25 and over with: High school diploma (including GED) or higher: 92.3% (2006-2010 5-year est.); Bachelor's degree or higher: 48.4% (2006-2010 5-year est.); Master's degree or higher: 19.1% (2006-2010 5-year est.).

Housing: Homeownership rate: 69.9% (2010); Median home value: $249,200 (2006-2010 5-year est.); Median contract rent: $1,196 per month (2006-2010 5-year est.); Median year structure built: 1984 (2006-2010 5-year est.).

Transportation: Commute to work: 91.1% car, 5.0% public transportation, 0.0% walk, 2.7% work from home (2006-2010 5-year est.); Travel time to work: 19.1% less than 15 minutes, 30.5% 15 to 30 minutes, 25.1% 30 to 45 minutes, 16.9% 45 to 60 minutes, 8.4% 60 minutes or more (2006-2010 5-year est.)

Additional Information Contacts

Greater West Chester Chamber of Commerce . . . . (610) 696-4046
http://www.gwcc.org

CHEYNEY (unincorporated postal area)

Zip Code: 19319

Covers a land area of 0.632 square miles and a water area of <.001 square miles. Located at 39.92° N. Lat; 75.52° W. Long. Elevation is 259 feet. Population: 1,130 (2010); Density: 1,785.8 persons per square mile (2010); Race: 13.8% White, 81.9% Black, 0.3% Asian, 0.6% American Indian/Alaska Native, 0.0% Native Hawaiian/Other Pacific Islander, 3.4% Other, 4.0% Hispanic of any race (2010); Average household size: 2.78 (2010); Median age: 20.5 (2010); Males per 100 females: 100.0 (2010); Homeownership rate: 85.2% (2010)

CHEYNEY UNIVERSITY (CDP). Covers a land area of 0.233 square miles and a water area of 0 square miles. Located at 39.93° N. Lat; 75.53° W. Long.

Population: n/a (1990); n/a (2000); 988 (2010); Density: 4,236.1 persons per square mile (2010); Race: 2.7% White, 92.6% Black, 0.2% Asian, 0.7% American Indian/Alaska Native, 0.0% Native Hawaiian/Other Pacific Islander, 3.8% Other, 3.9% Hispanic of any race (2010); Average household size: 2.00 (2010); Median age: 20.3 (2010); Males per 100 females: 96.8 (2010); Marriage status: 96.3% never married, 1.7% now married, 0.0% widowed, 2.0% divorced (2006-2010 5-year est.); Foreign born: 0.0% (2006-2010 5-year est.); Ancestry (includes multiple ancestries): 1.7% French (2006-2010 5-year est.).

Economy: Employment by occupation: 0.0% management, 0.0% professional, 7.0% services, 36.6% sales, 7.0% farming, 14.1% construction, 7.0% production (2006-2010 5-year est.).

Income: Per capita income: $3,328 (2006-2010 5-year est.); Median household income: n/a (2006-2010 5-year est.); Average household income: n/a (2006-2010 5-year est.); Percent of households with income of $100,000 or more: n/a (2006-2010 5-year est.); Poverty rate: 0.0% (2006-2010 5-year est.).

Education: Percent of population age 25 and over with: High school diploma (including GED) or higher: 100.0% (2006-2010 5-year est.); Bachelor's degree or higher: 0.0% (2006-2010 5-year est.); Master's degree or higher: 0.0% (2006-2010 5-year est.).

Housing: Homeownership rate: 25.0% (2010); Median home value: n/a (2006-2010 5-year est.); Median contract rent: n/a per month (2006-2010 5-year est.); Median year structure built: before 1940 (2006-2010 5-year est.).

Transportation: Commute to work: 26.3% car, 13.6% public transportation, 46.5% walk, 13.6% work from home (2006-2010 5-year est.); Travel time to work: 74.8% less than 15 minutes, 9.0% 15 to 30 minutes, 0.0% 30 to 45 minutes, 7.6% 45 to 60 minutes, 8.6% 60 minutes or more (2006-2010 5-year est.)

CLIFTON HEIGHTS (borough). Aka Clifton. Covers a land area of 0.630 square miles and a water area of 0 square miles. Located at 39.93° N. Lat; 75.30° W. Long. Elevation is 161 feet.

Population: 7,111 (1990); 6,779 (2000); 6,652 (2010); Density: 10,553.1 persons per square mile (2010); Race: 82.3% White, 11.4% Black, 3.3% Asian, 0.2% American Indian/Alaska Native, 0.0% Native Hawaiian/Other Pacific Islander, 2.8% Other, 2.2% Hispanic of any race (2010); Average household size: 2.48 (2010); Median age: 35.1 (2010); Males per 100 females: 96.3 (2010); Marriage status: 44.3% never married, 31.3% now married, 8.5% widowed, 15.9% divorced (2006-2010 5-year est.); Foreign born: 8.8% (2006-2010 5-year est.); Ancestry (includes multiple

ancestries): 40.0% Irish, 24.8% German, 22.7% Italian, 12.0% English, 5.6% Polish (2006-2010 5-year est.).

Economy: Single-family building permits issued: 1 (2011); Multi-family building permits issued: 0 (2011); Employment by occupation: 7.4% management, 4.4% professional, 13.6% services, 22.3% sales, 4.2% farming, 8.2% construction, 8.7% production (2006-2010 5-year est.).

Income: Per capita income: $21,415 (2006-2010 5-year est.); Median household income: $43,417 (2006-2010 5-year est.); Average household income: $49,424 (2006-2010 5-year est.); Percent of households with income of $100,000 or more: 7.7% (2006-2010 5-year est.); Poverty rate: 14.9% (2006-2010 5-year est.).

Education: Percent of population age 25 and over with: High school diploma (including GED) or higher: 89.3% (2006-2010 5-year est.); Bachelor's degree or higher: 17.4% (2006-2010 5-year est.); Master's degree or higher: 2.5% (2006-2010 5-year est.).

School District(s)

Upper Darby SD (KG-12)

   2010-11 Enrollment: 12,269 . . . . (610) 789-7200

Housing: Homeownership rate: 61.3% (2010); Median home value: $138,800 (2006-2010 5-year est.); Median contract rent: $711 per month (2006-2010 5-year est.); Median year structure built: 1949 (2006-2010 5-year est.).

Transportation: Commute to work: 80.5% car, 13.4% public transportation, 4.8% walk, 1.0% work from home (2006-2010 5-year est.); Travel time to work: 27.3% less than 15 minutes, 27.7% 15 to 30 minutes, 18.1% 30 to 45 minutes, 15.0% 45 to 60 minutes, 11.9% 60 minutes or more (2006-2010 5-year est.)

Additional Information Contacts

Borough of Clifton Heights . . . . (610) 623-1000
Greater Philadelphia Chamber of Commerce . . . . (215) 545-1234
   http://www.greaterphilachamber.com

COLLINGDALE (borough). Covers a land area of 0.869 square miles and a water area of 0 square miles. Located at 39.92° N. Lat; 75.28° W. Long. Elevation is 98 feet.

Population: 9,175 (1990); 8,664 (2000); 8,786 (2010); Density: 10,104.9 persons per square mile (2010); Race: 55.9% White, 36.3% Black, 2.9% Asian, 0.3% American Indian/Alaska Native, 0.0% Native Hawaiian/Other Pacific Islander, 4.6% Other, 3.1% Hispanic of any race (2010); Average household size: 2.75 (2010); Median age: 32.5 (2010); Males per 100 females: 91.2 (2010); Marriage status: 41.4% never married, 43.7% now married, 6.9% widowed, 8.0% divorced (2006-2010 5-year est.); Foreign born: 5.9% (2006-2010 5-year est.); Ancestry (includes multiple ancestries): 26.1% Irish, 14.6% German, 13.8% Italian, 8.6% English, 3.0% Polish (2006-2010 5-year est.).

Economy: Single-family building permits issued: 0 (2011); Multi-family building permits issued: 0 (2011); Employment by occupation: 8.6% management, 3.3% professional, 14.8% services, 18.8% sales, 3.3% farming, 8.5% construction, 7.8% production (2006-2010 5-year est.).

Income: Per capita income: $19,293 (2006-2010 5-year est.); Median household income: $43,340 (2006-2010 5-year est.); Average household income: $51,217 (2006-2010 5-year est.); Percent of households with income of $100,000 or more: 11.3% (2006-2010 5-year est.); Poverty rate: 15.3% (2006-2010 5-year est.).

Education: Percent of population age 25 and over with: High school diploma (including GED) or higher: 87.8% (2006-2010 5-year est.); Bachelor's degree or higher: 13.4% (2006-2010 5-year est.); Master's degree or higher: 4.4% (2006-2010 5-year est.).

School District(s)

Southeast Delco SD (KG-12)

   2010-11 Enrollment: 4,051 . . . . (610) 522-4300

Housing: Homeownership rate: 64.6% (2010); Median home value: $116,900 (2006-2010 5-year est.); Median contract rent: $670 per month (2006-2010 5-year est.); Median year structure built: 1946 (2006-2010 5-year est.).

Safety: Violent crime rate: 120.3 per 10,000 population; Property crime rate: 313.1 per 10,000 population (2011).

Transportation: Commute to work: 83.0% car, 11.1% public transportation, 4.3% walk, 0.7% work from home (2006-2010 5-year est.); Travel time to work: 19.5% less than 15 minutes, 28.2% 15 to 30 minutes, 29.9% 30 to 45 minutes, 13.1% 45 to 60 minutes, 9.3% 60 minutes or more (2006-2010 5-year est.)

Additional Information Contacts

Borough of Collingdale . . . . (610) 586-0500

Greater Philadelphia Chamber of Commerce . . . . (215) 545-1234
   http://www.greaterphilachamber.com

COLWYN (borough). Covers a land area of 0.258 square miles and a water area of 0 square miles. Located at 39.91° N. Lat; 75.25° W. Long. Elevation is 56 feet.

Population: 2,613 (1990); 2,453 (2000); 2,546 (2010); Density: 9,850.6 persons per square mile (2010); Race: 15.9% White, 80.1% Black, 0.7% Asian, 0.0% American Indian/Alaska Native, 0.0% Native Hawaiian/Other Pacific Islander, 3.3% Other, 1.6% Hispanic of any race (2010); Average household size: 3.09 (2010); Median age: 29.3 (2010); Males per 100 females: 83.2 (2010); Marriage status: 49.5% never married, 33.4% now married, 5.6% widowed, 11.5% divorced (2006-2010 5-year est.); Foreign born: 23.1% (2006-2010 5-year est.); Ancestry (includes multiple ancestries): 9.7% African, 9.2% Sierra Leonean, 6.3% Irish, 5.8% Italian, 4.5% German (2006-2010 5-year est.).

Economy: Single-family building permits issued: 0 (2011); Multi-family building permits issued: 0 (2011); Employment by occupation: 5.4% management, 0.0% professional, 10.4% services, 22.8% sales, 5.0% farming, 1.9% construction, 0.6% production (2006-2010 5-year est.).

Income: Per capita income: $24,877 (2006-2010 5-year est.); Median household income: $49,453 (2006-2010 5-year est.); Average household income: $77,304 (2006-2010 5-year est.); Percent of households with income of $100,000 or more: 11.5% (2006-2010 5-year est.); Poverty rate: 17.3% (2006-2010 5-year est.).

Education: Percent of population age 25 and over with: High school diploma (including GED) or higher: 85.2% (2006-2010 5-year est.); Bachelor's degree or higher: 20.5% (2006-2010 5-year est.); Master's degree or higher: 5.1% (2006-2010 5-year est.).

School District(s)

William Penn SD (KG-12)

   2010-11 Enrollment: 5,305 . . . . (610) 284-8000

Housing: Homeownership rate: 63.0% (2010); Median home value: $89,800 (2006-2010 5-year est.); Median contract rent: $613 per month (2006-2010 5-year est.); Median year structure built: before 1940 (2006-2010 5-year est.).

Safety: Violent crime rate: 66.6 per 10,000 population; Property crime rate: 340.6 per 10,000 population (2011).

Transportation: Commute to work: 65.9% car, 29.9% public transportation, 1.7% walk, 0.0% work from home (2006-2010 5-year est.); Travel time to work: 8.7% less than 15 minutes, 23.1% 15 to 30 minutes, 26.3% 30 to 45 minutes, 18.8% 45 to 60 minutes, 23.2% 60 minutes or more (2006-2010 5-year est.)

Additional Information Contacts

Delaware County Chamber of Commerce. . . . . (610) 565-3677
   http://www.delcochamber.org

CONCORD (township). Covers a land area of 13.623 square miles and a water area of 0.022 square miles. Located at 39.87° N. Lat; 75.51° W. Long.

History: The name "Concord" was believed to have been given by the earliest European settlers of the township and reflects the harmonious feelings among them at the time. Title to all real estate in the township can be traced back to a grant from William Penn.

Population: 6,607 (1990); 9,933 (2000); 17,231 (2010); Density: 1,264.8 persons per square mile (2010); Race: 86.1% White, 6.9% Black, 5.1% Asian, 0.1% American Indian/Alaska Native, 0.0% Native Hawaiian/Other Pacific Islander, 1.8% Other, 2.0% Hispanic of any race (2010); Average household size: 2.50 (2010); Median age: 43.4 (2010); Males per 100 females: 104.3 (2010); Marriage status: 26.4% never married, 59.2% now married, 7.5% widowed, 6.9% divorced (2006-2010 5-year est.); Foreign born: 5.6% (2006-2010 5-year est.); Ancestry (includes multiple ancestries): 24.4% Irish, 17.8% Italian, 16.8% German, 13.5% English, 5.3% Polish (2006-2010 5-year est.).

Economy: Single-family building permits issued: 16 (2011); Multi-family building permits issued: 0 (2011); Employment by occupation: 22.9% management, 7.2% professional, 6.5% services, 12.9% sales, 2.0% farming, 5.8% construction, 4.1% production (2006-2010 5-year est.).

Income: Per capita income: $42,358 (2006-2010 5-year est.); Median household income: $86,680 (2006-2010 5-year est.); Average household income: $122,624 (2006-2010 5-year est.); Percent of households with income of $100,000 or more: 45.9% (2006-2010 5-year est.); Poverty rate: 4.8% (2006-2010 5-year est.).

Education: Percent of population age 25 and over with: High school diploma (including GED) or higher: 92.2% (2006-2010 5-year est.);

Bachelor's degree or higher: 47.6% (2006-2010 5-year est.); Master's degree or higher: 21.1% (2006-2010 5-year est.).
Housing: Homeownership rate: 69.6% (2010); Median home value: $428,200 (2006-2010 5-year est.); Median contract rent: $1,540 per month (2006-2010 5-year est.); Median year structure built: 1994 (2006-2010 5-year est.).
Transportation: Commute to work: 91.1% car, 0.9% public transportation, 1.3% walk, 6.3% work from home (2006-2010 5-year est.); Travel time to work: 19.9% less than 15 minutes, 32.9% 15 to 30 minutes, 30.5% 30 to 45 minutes, 8.0% 45 to 60 minutes, 8.6% 60 minutes or more (2006-2010 5-year est.).
Additional Information Contacts
Concord Township . . . . (610) 459-8911
    http://www.twp.concord.pa.us
Delaware County Chamber of Commerce. . . . . (610) 565-3677
    http://www.delcochamber.org

CRUM LYNNE (unincorporated postal area)
Zip Code: 19022
    Covers a land area of 1.315 square miles and a water area of 0 square miles. Located at 39.86° N. Lat; 75.33° W. Long. Elevation is 62 feet. Population: 3,669 (2010); Density: 2,788.2 persons per square mile (2010); Race: 79.4% White, 14.6% Black, 1.3% Asian, 0.1% American Indian/Alaska Native, 0.0% Native Hawaiian/Other Pacific Islander, 4.6% Other, 3.5% Hispanic of any race (2010); Average household size: 2.55 (2010); Median age: 36.1 (2010); Males per 100 females: 96.8 (2010); Homeownership rate: 53.7% (2010)

DARBY (borough). Covers a land area of 0.842 square miles and a water area of 0 square miles. Located at 39.92° N. Lat; 75.26° W. Long. Elevation is 49 feet.
Population: 11,140 (1990); 10,299 (2000); 10,687 (2010); Density: 12,688.9 persons per square mile (2010); Race: 16.2% White, 78.9% Black, 0.7% Asian, 0.2% American Indian/Alaska Native, 0.0% Native Hawaiian/Other Pacific Islander, 4.0% Other, 2.1% Hispanic of any race (2010); Average household size: 3.03 (2010); Median age: 29.4 (2010); Males per 100 females: 83.4 (2010); Marriage status: 49.8% never married, 29.9% now married, 10.8% widowed, 9.4% divorced (2006-2010 5-year est.); Foreign born: 14.6% (2006-2010 5-year est.); Ancestry (includes multiple ancestries): 7.3% African, 7.2% Italian, 6.1% Irish, 5.3% Liberian, 4.1% German (2006-2010 5-year est.).
Economy: Single-family building permits issued: 0 (2011); Multi-family building permits issued: 0 (2011); Employment by occupation: 5.1% management, 0.4% professional, 26.4% services, 19.9% sales, 2.7% farming, 6.5% construction, 5.1% production (2006-2010 5-year est.).
Income: Per capita income: $13,833 (2006-2010 5-year est.); Median household income: $34,458 (2006-2010 5-year est.); Average household income: $39,690 (2006-2010 5-year est.); Percent of households with income of $100,000 or more: 6.0% (2006-2010 5-year est.); Poverty rate: 33.1% (2006-2010 5-year est.).
Education: Percent of population age 25 and over with: High school diploma (including GED) or higher: 83.7% (2006-2010 5-year est.); Bachelor's degree or higher: 12.7% (2006-2010 5-year est.); Master's degree or higher: 4.4% (2006-2010 5-year est.).
School District(s)
William Penn SD (KG-12)
    2010-11 Enrollment: 5,305 . . . . (610) 284-8000
Housing: Homeownership rate: 52.4% (2010); Median home value: $83,000 (2006-2010 5-year est.); Median contract rent: $724 per month (2006-2010 5-year est.); Median year structure built: before 1940 (2006-2010 5-year est.).
Hospitals: Mercy Fitzgerald Hospital (218 beds)
Safety: Violent crime rate: 378.7 per 10,000 population; Property crime rate: 548.5 per 10,000 population (2011).
Transportation: Commute to work: 69.1% car, 24.9% public transportation, 3.7% walk, 1.6% work from home (2006-2010 5-year est.); Travel time to work: 16.2% less than 15 minutes, 30.0% 15 to 30 minutes, 24.0% 30 to 45 minutes, 13.0% 45 to 60 minutes, 16.7% 60 minutes or more (2006-2010 5-year est.).
Additional Information Contacts
Borough of Darby . . . . (610) 586-1102
    http://www.darbyborough.com
Delaware County Chamber of Commerce. . . . . (610) 565-3677
    http://www.delcochamber.org

DARBY (township). Aka Darby Township CDP. Covers a land area of 1.416 square miles and a water area of 0.007 square miles. Located at 39.90° N. Lat; 75.27° W. Long. Elevation is 49 feet.
Population: 10,955 (1990); 9,622 (2000); 9,264 (2010); Density: 6,544.5 persons per square mile (2010); Race: 57.7% White, 38.9% Black, 0.6% Asian, 0.1% American Indian/Alaska Native, 0.0% Native Hawaiian/Other Pacific Islander, 2.7% Other, 2.0% Hispanic of any race (2010); Average household size: 2.48 (2010); Median age: 37.4 (2010); Males per 100 females: 85.9 (2010); Marriage status: 37.7% never married, 41.1% now married, 10.0% widowed, 11.3% divorced (2006-2010 5-year est.); Foreign born: 0.5% (2006-2010 5-year est.); Ancestry (includes multiple ancestries): 31.3% Irish, 22.7% Italian, 10.9% German, 5.4% Polish, 4.9% English (2006-2010 5-year est.).
Economy: Single-family building permits issued: 0 (2011); Multi-family building permits issued: 0 (2011); Employment by occupation: 8.6% management, 2.7% professional, 14.3% services, 21.2% sales, 5.1% farming, 4.5% construction, 5.6% production (2006-2010 5-year est.).
Income: Per capita income: $23,693 (2006-2010 5-year est.); Median household income: $49,258 (2006-2010 5-year est.); Average household income: $60,318 (2006-2010 5-year est.); Percent of households with income of $100,000 or more: 14.6% (2006-2010 5-year est.); Poverty rate: 13.2% (2006-2010 5-year est.).
Education: Percent of population age 25 and over with: High school diploma (including GED) or higher: 87.4% (2006-2010 5-year est.); Bachelor's degree or higher: 17.0% (2006-2010 5-year est.); Master's degree or higher: 7.2% (2006-2010 5-year est.).
Housing: Homeownership rate: 74.1% (2010); Median home value: $142,300 (2006-2010 5-year est.); Median contract rent: $617 per month (2006-2010 5-year est.); Median year structure built: 1955 (2006-2010 5-year est.).
Hospitals: Mercy Fitzgerald Hospital (218 beds)
Safety: Violent crime rate: 63.5 per 10,000 population; Property crime rate: 248.5 per 10,000 population (2011).
Transportation: Commute to work: 86.7% car, 8.7% public transportation, 3.5% walk, 0.6% work from home (2006-2010 5-year est.); Travel time to work: 21.1% less than 15 minutes, 42.0% 15 to 30 minutes, 23.2% 30 to 45 minutes, 7.1% 45 to 60 minutes, 6.7% 60 minutes or more (2006-2010 5-year est.)
Additional Information Contacts
Darby Township . . . . (610) 586-1514
Delaware County Chamber of Commerce. . . . . (610) 565-3677
    http://www.delcochamber.org

DREXEL HILL (CDP). Covers a land area of 3.194 square miles and a water area of 0 square miles. Located at 39.95° N. Lat; 75.30° W. Long. Elevation is 246 feet.
Population: 29,744 (1990); 29,364 (2000); 28,043 (2010); Density: 8,779.4 persons per square mile (2010); Race: 85.5% White, 7.7% Black, 4.3% Asian, 0.1% American Indian/Alaska Native, 0.0% Native Hawaiian/Other Pacific Islander, 2.4% Other, 2.6% Hispanic of any race (2010); Average household size: 2.48 (2010); Median age: 37.5 (2010); Males per 100 females: 93.1 (2010); Marriage status: 32.7% never married, 52.0% now married, 6.7% widowed, 8.5% divorced (2006-2010 5-year est.); Foreign born: 9.0% (2006-2010 5-year est.); Ancestry (includes multiple ancestries): 39.7% Irish, 25.0% Italian, 17.9% German, 6.5% English, 4.5% Polish (2006-2010 5-year est.).
Economy: Employment by occupation: 13.3% management, 5.4% professional, 6.4% services, 19.5% sales, 3.6% farming, 8.0% construction, 3.8% production (2006-2010 5-year est.).
Income: Per capita income: $31,575 (2006-2010 5-year est.); Median household income: $66,287 (2006-2010 5-year est.); Average household income: $78,116 (2006-2010 5-year est.); Percent of households with income of $100,000 or more: 29.3% (2006-2010 5-year est.); Poverty rate: 4.7% (2006-2010 5-year est.).
Education: Percent of population age 25 and over with: High school diploma (including GED) or higher: 93.2% (2006-2010 5-year est.); Bachelor's degree or higher: 39.2% (2006-2010 5-year est.); Master's degree or higher: 15.4% (2006-2010 5-year est.).
School District(s)
Upper Darby SD (KG-12)
    2010-11 Enrollment: 12,269 . . . . (610) 789-7200
Housing: Homeownership rate: 67.6% (2010); Median home value: $204,400 (2006-2010 5-year est.); Median contract rent: $798 per month (2006-2010 5-year est.); Median year structure built: 1949 (2006-2010 5-year est.).

Hospitals: Delaware County Memorial Hospital (225 beds)
Newspapers: Marcus Hook Press (Community news; Circulation 2,500); Ridley Press (Community news; Circulation 2,500); Upper Darby Press (Community news; Circulation 2,500); Yeadon Times (Community news; Circulation 2,500)
Transportation: Commute to work: 82.9% car, 10.3% public transportation, 2.5% walk, 3.5% work from home (2006-2010 5-year est.); Travel time to work: 20.8% less than 15 minutes, 25.5% 15 to 30 minutes, 28.1% 30 to 45 minutes, 15.7% 45 to 60 minutes, 9.9% 60 minutes or more (2006-2010 5-year est.)
Additional Information Contacts
Delaware County Chamber of Commerce. . . . . (610) 565-3677
    http://www.delcochamber.org

EAST LANSDOWNE (borough).

Covers a land area of 0.206 square miles and a water area of 0 square miles. Located at 39.94° N. Lat; 75.26° W. Long. Elevation is 131 feet.
Population: 2,691 (1990); 2,586 (2000); 2,668 (2010); Density: 12,931.0 persons per square mile (2010); Race: 30.5% White, 55.8% Black, 8.8% Asian, 0.1% American Indian/Alaska Native, 0.2% Native Hawaiian/Other Pacific Islander, 4.6% Other, 4.3% Hispanic of any race (2010); Average household size: 2.88 (2010); Median age: 34.7 (2010); Males per 100 females: 98.7 (2010); Marriage status: 44.1% never married, 44.4% now married, 6.3% widowed, 5.2% divorced (2006-2010 5-year est.); Foreign born: 22.1% (2006-2010 5-year est.); Ancestry (includes multiple ancestries): 18.3% Irish, 8.5% German, 6.4% Haitian, 5.5% Jamaican, 4.9% Italian (2006-2010 5-year est.).
Economy: Single-family building permits issued: 0 (2011); Multi-family building permits issued: 0 (2011); Employment by occupation: 8.8% management, 1.3% professional, 12.1% services, 14.1% sales, 5.0% farming, 9.9% construction, 6.8% production (2006-2010 5-year est.).
Income: Per capita income: $24,014 (2006-2010 5-year est.); Median household income: $55,574 (2006-2010 5-year est.); Average household income: $64,612 (2006-2010 5-year est.); Percent of households with income of $100,000 or more: 14.5% (2006-2010 5-year est.); Poverty rate: 10.5% (2006-2010 5-year est.).
Education: Percent of population age 25 and over with: High school diploma (including GED) or higher: 90.0% (2006-2010 5-year est.); Bachelor's degree or higher: 22.5% (2006-2010 5-year est.); Master's degree or higher: 6.7% (2006-2010 5-year est.).
School District(s)
William Penn SD (KG-12)
    2010-11 Enrollment: 5,305 . . . . (610) 284-8000
Housing: Homeownership rate: 67.0% (2010); Median home value: $146,500 (2006-2010 5-year est.); Median contract rent: $692 per month (2006-2010 5-year est.); Median year structure built: before 1940 (2006-2010 5-year est.).
Safety: Violent crime rate: 100.9 per 10,000 population; Property crime rate: 250.3 per 10,000 population (2011).
Transportation: Commute to work: 83.0% car, 8.7% public transportation, 5.4% walk, 0.5% work from home (2006-2010 5-year est.); Travel time to work: 24.8% less than 15 minutes, 29.0% 15 to 30 minutes, 25.3% 30 to 45 minutes, 13.3% 45 to 60 minutes, 7.5% 60 minutes or more (2006-2010 5-year est.)
Additional Information Contacts
Delaware County Chamber of Commerce. . . . . (610) 565-3677
    http://www.delcochamber.org

EDDYSTONE (borough).

Covers a land area of 0.995 square miles and a water area of 0.529 square miles. Located at 39.85° N. Lat; 75.34° W. Long. Elevation is 16 feet.
Population: 2,446 (1990); 2,442 (2000); 2,410 (2010); Density: 2,423.2 persons per square mile (2010); Race: 82.7% White, 11.7% Black, 1.3% Asian, 0.1% American Indian/Alaska Native, 0.0% Native Hawaiian/Other Pacific Islander, 4.2% Other, 4.4% Hispanic of any race (2010); Average household size: 2.60 (2010); Median age: 34.8 (2010); Males per 100 females: 97.1 (2010); Marriage status: 39.8% never married, 39.9% now married, 8.7% widowed, 11.6% divorced (2006-2010 5-year est.); Foreign born: 0.8% (2006-2010 5-year est.); Ancestry (includes multiple ancestries): 52.7% Irish, 21.9% German, 18.3% English, 17.9% Italian, 6.2% Polish (2006-2010 5-year est.).
Economy: Single-family building permits issued: 0 (2011); Multi-family building permits issued: 0 (2011); Employment by occupation: 6.9% management, 4.2% professional, 11.7% services, 23.4% sales, 3.8% farming, 12.7% construction, 10.9% production (2006-2010 5-year est.).

Income: Per capita income: $18,625 (2006-2010 5-year est.); Median household income: $40,365 (2006-2010 5-year est.); Average household income: $47,370 (2006-2010 5-year est.); Percent of households with income of $100,000 or more: 7.8% (2006-2010 5-year est.); Poverty rate: 11.6% (2006-2010 5-year est.).
Education: Percent of population age 25 and over with: High school diploma (including GED) or higher: 85.9% (2006-2010 5-year est.); Bachelor's degree or higher: 8.3% (2006-2010 5-year est.); Master's degree or higher: 1.7% (2006-2010 5-year est.).
School District(s)
Ridley SD (KG-12)
    2010-11 Enrollment: 5,847 . . . . (610) 534-1900
Housing: Homeownership rate: 57.6% (2010); Median home value: $112,900 (2006-2010 5-year est.); Median contract rent: $553 per month (2006-2010 5-year est.); Median year structure built: 1945 (2006-2010 5-year est.).
Safety: Violent crime rate: 45.5 per 10,000 population; Property crime rate: 1,335.8 per 10,000 population (2011).
Transportation: Commute to work: 78.7% car, 8.9% public transportation, 12.4% walk, 0.0% work from home (2006-2010 5-year est.); Travel time to work: 33.1% less than 15 minutes, 38.5% 15 to 30 minutes, 12.7% 30 to 45 minutes, 11.4% 45 to 60 minutes, 4.3% 60 minutes or more (2006-2010 5-year est.)
Additional Information Contacts
Borough of Eddystone. . . . . (610) 974-1100
    http://www.eddystoneboro.com
Delaware County Chamber of Commerce. . . . . (610) 565-3677
    http://www.delcochamber.org

EDGMONT (township).

Aka Edgemont. Covers a land area of 9.707 square miles and a water area of 0.023 square miles. Located at 39.95° N. Lat; 75.46° W. Long.
History: Edgmont Township, otherwise known by the post office name of Edgemont (19028) is a semi-rural suburban area in Western Delaware County. It was one of the first townships in Pennsylvania, founded in the late 1680s.
Population: 2,735 (1990); 3,918 (2000); 3,987 (2010); Density: 410.7 persons per square mile (2010); Race: 93.7% White, 1.1% Black, 3.8% Asian, 0.1% American Indian/Alaska Native, 0.0% Native Hawaiian/Other Pacific Islander, 1.3% Other, 0.9% Hispanic of any race (2010); Average household size: 2.36 (2010); Median age: 50.6 (2010); Males per 100 females: 86.5 (2010); Marriage status: 24.3% never married, 58.8% now married, 11.7% widowed, 5.2% divorced (2006-2010 5-year est.); Foreign born: 4.5% (2006-2010 5-year est.); Ancestry (includes multiple ancestries): 25.1% Irish, 21.6% Italian, 17.9% German, 15.3% English, 7.3% Polish (2006-2010 5-year est.).
Economy: Single-family building permits issued: 4 (2011); Multi-family building permits issued: 0 (2011); Employment by occupation: 21.4% management, 2.3% professional, 3.0% services, 12.7% sales, 2.8% farming, 10.0% construction, 5.0% production (2006-2010 5-year est.).
Income: Per capita income: $66,289 (2006-2010 5-year est.); Median household income: $112,321 (2006-2010 5-year est.); Average household income: $161,074 (2006-2010 5-year est.); Percent of households with income of $100,000 or more: 57.3% (2006-2010 5-year est.); Poverty rate: 2.7% (2006-2010 5-year est.).
Education: Percent of population age 25 and over with: High school diploma (including GED) or higher: 98.5% (2006-2010 5-year est.); Bachelor's degree or higher: 61.1% (2006-2010 5-year est.); Master's degree or higher: 24.2% (2006-2010 5-year est.).
Housing: Homeownership rate: 73.8% (2010); Median home value: $580,500 (2006-2010 5-year est.); Median contract rent: n/a per month (2006-2010 5-year est.); Median year structure built: 1986 (2006-2010 5-year est.).
Transportation: Commute to work: 90.4% car, 1.2% public transportation, 1.2% walk, 5.8% work from home (2006-2010 5-year est.); Travel time to work: 14.3% less than 15 minutes, 42.3% 15 to 30 minutes, 25.2% 30 to 45 minutes, 9.5% 45 to 60 minutes, 8.7% 60 minutes or more (2006-2010 5-year est.)
Additional Information Contacts
Delaware County Chamber of Commerce. . . . . (610) 565-3677
    http://www.delcochamber.org

ESSINGTON (unincorporated postal area)
Zip Code: 19029

Covers a land area of 2.311 square miles and a water area of 0.125 square miles. Located at 39.86° N. Lat; 75.29° W. Long. Elevation is 10 feet. Population: 3,971 (2010); Density: 1,717.8 persons per square mile (2010); Race: 93.8% White, 1.7% Black, 2.1% Asian, 0.2% American Indian/Alaska Native, 0.0% Native Hawaiian/Other Pacific Islander, 2.2% Other, 2.3% Hispanic of any race (2010); Average household size: 2.42 (2010); Median age: 41.9 (2010); Males per 100 females: 102.5 (2010); Homeownership rate: 67.9% (2010)

FOLCROFT (borough). Covers a land area of 1.245 square miles and a water area of 0.176 square miles. Located at 39.89° N. Lat; 75.28° W. Long. Elevation is 72 feet.
Population: 7,506 (1990); 6,978 (2000); 6,606 (2010); Density: 5,304.8 persons per square mile (2010); Race: 67.1% White, 26.0% Black, 2.9% Asian, 0.3% American Indian/Alaska Native, 0.0% Native Hawaiian/Other Pacific Islander, 3.7% Other, 4.6% Hispanic of any race (2010); Average household size: 2.68 (2010); Median age: 35.1 (2010); Males per 100 females: 94.8 (2010); Marriage status: 41.3% never married, 44.3% now married, 6.1% widowed, 8.3% divorced (2006-2010 5-year est.); Foreign born: 4.1% (2006-2010 5-year est.); Ancestry (includes multiple ancestries): 38.3% Irish, 17.2% Italian, 16.3% German, 6.6% English, 5.7% Polish (2006-2010 5-year est.).
Economy: Single-family building permits issued: 0 (2011); Multi-family building permits issued: 0 (2011); Employment by occupation: 10.6% management, 4.4% professional, 9.1% services, 23.0% sales, 5.7% farming, 8.3% construction, 5.3% production (2006-2010 5-year est.).
Income: Per capita income: $23,649 (2006-2010 5-year est.); Median household income: $53,476 (2006-2010 5-year est.); Average household income: $60,450 (2006-2010 5-year est.); Percent of households with income of $100,000 or more: 16.2% (2006-2010 5-year est.); Poverty rate: 9.5% (2006-2010 5-year est.).
Education: Percent of population age 25 and over with: High school diploma (including GED) or higher: 88.3% (2006-2010 5-year est.); Bachelor's degree or higher: 15.4% (2006-2010 5-year est.); Master's degree or higher: 4.1% (2006-2010 5-year est.).
School District(s)
Delaware County Technical High School (10-12)
    2010-11 Enrollment: n/a . . . . (610) 583-7620
Southeast Delco SD (KG-12)
    2010-11 Enrollment: 4,051 . . . . (610) 522-4300
Vocational/Technical School(s)
Delaware County Technical School-Practical Nursing Program (Public)
    Fall 2010 Enrollment: 169 . . . . (484) 423-7000
    2011-12 Tuition: $14,915
Housing: Homeownership rate: 74.6% (2010); Median home value: $127,700 (2006-2010 5-year est.); Median contract rent: $828 per month (2006-2010 5-year est.); Median year structure built: 1955 (2006-2010 5-year est.).
Safety: Violent crime rate: 52.8 per 10,000 population; Property crime rate: 229.4 per 10,000 population (2011).
Transportation: Commute to work: 87.4% car, 7.1% public transportation, 4.3% walk, 0.6% work from home (2006-2010 5-year est.); Travel time to work: 24.6% less than 15 minutes, 32.6% 15 to 30 minutes, 25.0% 30 to 45 minutes, 12.7% 45 to 60 minutes, 5.0% 60 minutes or more (2006-2010 5-year est.)
Additional Information Contacts
Borough of Folcroft . . . . (610) 522-1305
   http://www.folcroftpa.net
Greater Philadelphia Chamber of Commerce . . . . (215) 545-1234
   http://www.greaterphilachamber.com

FOLSOM (CDP). Covers a land area of 1.250 square miles and a water area of 0 square miles. Located at 39.89° N. Lat; 75.33° W. Long. Elevation is 102 feet.
Population: 8,173 (1990); 8,072 (2000); 8,323 (2010); Density: 6,659.0 persons per square mile (2010); Race: 93.1% White, 3.4% Black, 1.8% Asian, 0.1% American Indian/Alaska Native, 0.0% Native Hawaiian/Other Pacific Islander, 1.6% Other, 1.8% Hispanic of any race (2010); Average household size: 2.65 (2010); Median age: 40.8 (2010); Males per 100 females: 94.9 (2010); Marriage status: 29.7% never married, 55.0% now married, 8.6% widowed, 6.8% divorced (2006-2010 5-year est.); Foreign born: 2.4% (2006-2010 5-year est.); Ancestry (includes multiple ancestries): 46.7% Irish, 31.6% Italian, 20.4% German, 11.7% English, 6.2% Polish (2006-2010 5-year est.).

Economy: Employment by occupation: 11.2% management, 6.0% professional, 8.0% services, 19.8% sales, 4.7% farming, 15.2% construction, 7.9% production (2006-2010 5-year est.).
Income: Per capita income: $27,585 (2006-2010 5-year est.); Median household income: $58,478 (2006-2010 5-year est.); Average household income: $70,076 (2006-2010 5-year est.); Percent of households with income of $100,000 or more: 22.9% (2006-2010 5-year est.); Poverty rate: 2.9% (2006-2010 5-year est.).
Education: Percent of population age 25 and over with: High school diploma (including GED) or higher: 89.2% (2006-2010 5-year est.); Bachelor's degree or higher: 23.4% (2006-2010 5-year est.); Master's degree or higher: 7.1% (2006-2010 5-year est.).
School District(s)
Ridley SD (KG-12)
    2010-11 Enrollment: 5,847 . . . . (610) 534-1900
Housing: Homeownership rate: 81.9% (2010); Median home value: $206,400 (2006-2010 5-year est.); Median contract rent: $822 per month (2006-2010 5-year est.); Median year structure built: 1956 (2006-2010 5-year est.).
Transportation: Commute to work: 91.9% car, 3.6% public transportation, 1.4% walk, 1.8% work from home (2006-2010 5-year est.); Travel time to work: 30.3% less than 15 minutes, 32.6% 15 to 30 minutes, 23.0% 30 to 45 minutes, 10.2% 45 to 60 minutes, 3.9% 60 minutes or more (2006-2010 5-year est.)
Additional Information Contacts
Delaware County Chamber of Commerce . . . . (610) 565-3677
   http://www.delcochamber.org

GLEN MILLS (unincorporated postal area)
Zip Code: 19342
   Covers a land area of 19.502 square miles and a water area of 0.039 square miles. Located at 39.90° N. Lat; 75.49° W. Long. Elevation is 213 feet. Population: 18,099 (2010); Density: 928.1 persons per square mile (2010); Race: 88.8% White, 5.2% Black, 4.1% Asian, 0.1% American Indian/Alaska Native, 0.0% Native Hawaiian/Other Pacific Islander, 1.8% Other, 2.1% Hispanic of any race (2010); Average household size: 2.41 (2010); Median age: 45.3 (2010); Males per 100 females: 97.5 (2010); Homeownership rate: 71.6% (2010)

GLENOLDEN (borough). Covers a land area of 0.975 square miles and a water area of 0 square miles. Located at 39.90° N. Lat; 75.29° W. Long. Elevation is 92 feet.
Population: 7,260 (1990); 7,476 (2000); 7,153 (2010); Density: 7,337.9 persons per square mile (2010); Race: 86.9% White, 8.5% Black, 1.7% Asian, 0.1% American Indian/Alaska Native, 0.1% Native Hawaiian/Other Pacific Islander, 2.7% Other, 2.2% Hispanic of any race (2010); Average household size: 2.42 (2010); Median age: 37.9 (2010); Males per 100 females: 91.4 (2010); Marriage status: 34.9% never married, 43.1% now married, 9.7% widowed, 12.3% divorced (2006-2010 5-year est.); Foreign born: 7.6% (2006-2010 5-year est.); Ancestry (includes multiple ancestries): 38.5% Irish, 25.7% German, 22.1% Italian, 11.8% English, 5.4% Polish (2006-2010 5-year est.).
Economy: Single-family building permits issued: 0 (2011); Multi-family building permits issued: 0 (2011); Employment by occupation: 8.6% management, 3.4% professional, 8.2% services, 18.1% sales, 6.1% farming, 12.5% construction, 7.8% production (2006-2010 5-year est.).
Income: Per capita income: $23,509 (2006-2010 5-year est.); Median household income: $48,760 (2006-2010 5-year est.); Average household income: $56,059 (2006-2010 5-year est.); Percent of households with income of $100,000 or more: 10.6% (2006-2010 5-year est.); Poverty rate: 10.5% (2006-2010 5-year est.).
Education: Percent of population age 25 and over with: High school diploma (including GED) or higher: 90.4% (2006-2010 5-year est.); Bachelor's degree or higher: 16.4% (2006-2010 5-year est.); Master's degree or higher: 6.2% (2006-2010 5-year est.).
School District(s)
Interboro SD (KG-12)
    2010-11 Enrollment: 3,631 . . . . (610) 461-6700
Southeast Delco SD (KG-12)
    2010-11 Enrollment: 4,051 . . . . (610) 522-4300
Upper Darby SD (KG-12)
    2010-11 Enrollment: 12,269 . . . . (610) 789-7200
Housing: Homeownership rate: 65.6% (2010); Median home value: $163,100 (2006-2010 5-year est.); Median contract rent: $797 per month

(2006-2010 5-year est.); Median year structure built: 1952 (2006-2010 5-year est.).

Safety: Violent crime rate: 25.1 per 10,000 population; Property crime rate: 274.5 per 10,000 population (2011).

Transportation: Commute to work: 89.4% car, 5.1% public transportation, 2.7% walk, 1.6% work from home (2006-2010 5-year est.); Travel time to work: 23.1% less than 15 minutes, 36.4% 15 to 30 minutes, 23.9% 30 to 45 minutes, 11.2% 45 to 60 minutes, 5.4% 60 minutes or more (2006-2010 5-year est.)

Additional Information Contacts

Borough of Glenolden . . . . (610) 583-3221
  http://www.glenoldenborough.com
Delaware County Chamber of Commerce. . . . . (610) 565-3677
  http://www.delcochamber.org

HAVERFORD (township). Aka Haverford Township. Covers a land area of 9.945 square miles and a water area of 0 square miles. Located at 39.99° N. Lat; 75.32° W. Long.

Population: 49,848 (1990); 48,498 (2000); 48,491 (2010); Density: 4,875.8 persons per square mile (2010); Race: 91.2% White, 2.7% Black, 4.2% Asian, 0.1% American Indian/Alaska Native, 0.0% Native Hawaiian/Other Pacific Islander, 1.8% Other, 1.9% Hispanic of any race (2010); Average household size: 2.63 (2010); Median age: 40.5 (2010); Males per 100 females: 90.8 (2010); Marriage status: 29.5% never married, 56.6% now married, 7.7% widowed, 6.1% divorced (2006-2010 5-year est.); Foreign born: 7.1% (2006-2010 5-year est.); Ancestry (includes multiple ancestries): 38.1% Irish, 20.1% German, 20.0% Italian, 10.2% English, 4.6% Polish (2006-2010 5-year est.).

Economy: Unemployment rate: 6.2% (August 2012); Total civilian labor force: 25,518 (August 2012); Single-family building permits issued: 24 (2011); Multi-family building permits issued: 0 (2011); Employment by occupation: 18.2% management, 5.8% professional, 5.4% services, 13.7% sales, 3.3% farming, 5.9% construction, 2.6% production (2006-2010 5-year est.).

Income: Per capita income: $40,825 (2006-2010 5-year est.); Median household income: $86,451 (2006-2010 5-year est.); Average household income: $106,521 (2006-2010 5-year est.); Percent of households with income of $100,000 or more: 42.7% (2006-2010 5-year est.); Poverty rate: 3.3% (2006-2010 5-year est.).

Taxes: Total city taxes per capita: $437 (2009); City property taxes per capita: $352 (2009).

Education: Percent of population age 25 and over with: High school diploma (including GED) or higher: 95.6% (2006-2010 5-year est.); Bachelor's degree or higher: 53.4% (2006-2010 5-year est.); Master's degree or higher: 24.8% (2006-2010 5-year est.).

Four-year College(s)

Haverford College (Private, Not-for-profit)
  Fall 2010 Enrollment: 1,222 . . . . (610) 896-1000
  2011-12 Tuition: In-state $42,208; Out-of-state $42,208

Housing: Homeownership rate: 85.2% (2010); Median home value: $309,400 (2006-2010 5-year est.); Median contract rent: $898 per month (2006-2010 5-year est.); Median year structure built: 1951 (2006-2010 5-year est.).

Safety: Violent crime rate: 6.8 per 10,000 population; Property crime rate: 134.4 per 10,000 population (2011).

Transportation: Commute to work: 85.1% car, 6.8% public transportation, 3.0% walk, 4.1% work from home (2006-2010 5-year est.); Travel time to work: 22.5% less than 15 minutes, 34.1% 15 to 30 minutes, 27.1% 30 to 45 minutes, 10.7% 45 to 60 minutes, 5.6% 60 minutes or more (2006-2010 5-year est.)

Additional Information Contacts

Delaware County Chamber of Commerce. . . . . (610) 565-3677
  http://www.delcochamber.org
Haverford Township . . . . (610) 446-1000
  http://www.haverfordtownship.com

HAVERFORD COLLEGE (CDP). Covers a land area of 0.299 square miles and a water area of 0.004 square miles. Located at 40.01° N. Lat; 75.31° W. Long.

Population: n/a (1990); n/a (2000); 1,331 (2010); Density: 4,455.2 persons per square mile (2010); Race: 77.4% White, 5.6% Black, 7.4% Asian, 0.2% American Indian/Alaska Native, 0.0% Native Hawaiian/Other Pacific Islander, 9.4% Other, 7.7% Hispanic of any race (2010); Average household size: 2.48 (2010); Median age: 20.4 (2010); Males per 100 females: 82.3 (2010); Marriage status: 85.1% never married, 11.8% now

married, 0.0% widowed, 3.1% divorced (2006-2010 5-year est.); Foreign born: 14.4% (2006-2010 5-year est.); Ancestry (includes multiple ancestries): 25.4% Irish, 14.3% German, 14.0% English, 8.2% Austrian, 8.2% Scottish (2006-2010 5-year est.).

Economy: Employment by occupation: 4.3% management, 0.0% professional, 18.8% services, 15.6% sales, 8.5% farming, 0.0% construction, 0.0% production (2006-2010 5-year est.).

Income: Per capita income: $12,873 (2006-2010 5-year est.); Median household income: $50,104 (2006-2010 5-year est.); Average household income: $105,973 (2006-2010 5-year est.); Percent of households with income of $100,000 or more: 21.6% (2006-2010 5-year est.); Poverty rate: 30.5% (2006-2010 5-year est.).

Education: Percent of population age 25 and over with: High school diploma (including GED) or higher: 100.0% (2006-2010 5-year est.); Bachelor's degree or higher: 64.9% (2006-2010 5-year est.); Master's degree or higher: 58.9% (2006-2010 5-year est.).

Housing: Homeownership rate: 4.9% (2010); Median home value: n/a (2006-2010 5-year est.); Median contract rent: $809 per month (2006-2010 5-year est.); Median year structure built: before 1940 (2006-2010 5-year est.).

Transportation: Commute to work: 19.6% car, 0.0% public transportation, 63.5% walk, 16.9% work from home (2006-2010 5-year est.); Travel time to work: 87.1% less than 15 minutes, 3.4% 15 to 30 minutes, 9.5% 30 to 45 minutes, 0.0% 45 to 60 minutes, 0.0% 60 minutes or more (2006-2010 5-year est.)

HAVERTOWN (unincorporated postal area)

Zip Code: 19083

Covers a land area of 5.556 square miles and a water area of 0 square miles. Located at 39.97° N. Lat; 75.31° W. Long. Elevation is 276 feet. Population: 35,878 (2010); Density: 6,456.8 persons per square mile (2010); Race: 91.9% White, 2.1% Black, 4.4% Asian, 0.1% American Indian/Alaska Native, 0.0% Native Hawaiian/Other Pacific Islander, 1.5% Other, 1.7% Hispanic of any race (2010); Average household size: 2.70 (2010); Median age: 40.1 (2010); Males per 100 females: 92.9 (2010); Homeownership rate: 86.6% (2010)

HOLMES (unincorporated postal area)

Zip Code: 19043

Covers a land area of 0.395 square miles and a water area of 0 square miles. Located at 39.90° N. Lat; 75.30° W. Long. Elevation is 108 feet. Population: 2,664 (2010); Density: 6,729.8 persons per square mile (2010); Race: 95.4% White, 2.1% Black, 1.0% Asian, 0.1% American Indian/Alaska Native, 0.0% Native Hawaiian/Other Pacific Islander, 1.4% Other, 2.7% Hispanic of any race (2010); Average household size: 2.60 (2010); Median age: 38.8 (2010); Males per 100 females: 94.6 (2010); Homeownership rate: 72.8% (2010)

LANSDOWNE (borough). Covers a land area of 1.181 square miles and a water area of 0 square miles. Located at 39.94° N. Lat; 75.28° W. Long. Elevation is 131 feet.

Population: 11,712 (1990); 11,044 (2000); 10,620 (2010); Density: 8,990.2 persons per square mile (2010); Race: 47.1% White, 44.6% Black, 3.6% Asian, 0.2% American Indian/Alaska Native, 0.0% Native Hawaiian/Other Pacific Islander, 4.5% Other, 3.3% Hispanic of any race (2010); Average household size: 2.31 (2010); Median age: 39.7 (2010); Males per 100 females: 86.1 (2010); Marriage status: 39.1% never married, 45.3% now married, 5.8% widowed, 9.8% divorced (2006-2010 5-year est.); Foreign born: 10.4% (2006-2010 5-year est.); Ancestry (includes multiple ancestries): 22.9% Irish, 13.2% German, 9.4% Italian, 6.2% English, 6.1% Polish (2006-2010 5-year est.).

Economy: Single-family building permits issued: 2 (2011); Multi-family building permits issued: 0 (2011); Employment by occupation: 11.7% management, 4.8% professional, 7.5% services, 13.0% sales, 4.5% farming, 7.1% construction, 2.7% production (2006-2010 5-year est.).

Income: Per capita income: $30,352 (2006-2010 5-year est.); Median household income: $63,009 (2006-2010 5-year est.); Average household income: $71,331 (2006-2010 5-year est.); Percent of households with income of $100,000 or more: 20.8% (2006-2010 5-year est.); Poverty rate: 8.1% (2006-2010 5-year est.).

Education: Percent of population age 25 and over with: High school diploma (including GED) or higher: 95.3% (2006-2010 5-year est.); Bachelor's degree or higher: 36.9% (2006-2010 5-year est.); Master's degree or higher: 14.5% (2006-2010 5-year est.).

School District(s)

William Penn SD (KG-12)

  2010-11 Enrollment: 5,305 . . . . (610) 284-8000

Housing: Homeownership rate: 64.0% (2010); Median home value: $180,700 (2006-2010 5-year est.); Median contract rent: $745 per month (2006-2010 5-year est.); Median year structure built: 1941 (2006-2010 5-year est.).

Safety: Violent crime rate: 27.2 per 10,000 population; Property crime rate: 245.0 per 10,000 population (2011).

Transportation: Commute to work: 77.8% car, 18.1% public transportation, 1.6% walk, 1.9% work from home (2006-2010 5-year est.); Travel time to work: 11.4% less than 15 minutes, 29.4% 15 to 30 minutes, 26.8% 30 to 45 minutes, 16.3% 45 to 60 minutes, 16.2% 60 minutes or more (2006-2010 5-year est.)

Additional Information Contacts

Borough of Lansdowne . . . . (610) 623-7300

  http://www.lansdowneborough.com

Delaware County Chamber of Commerce . . . . (610) 565-3677

  http://www.delcochamber.org

LIMA (CDP). Covers a land area of 1.470 square miles and a water area of 0 square miles. Located at 39.92° N. Lat; 75.44° W. Long. Elevation is 348 feet.

Population: 2,670 (1990); 3,225 (2000); 2,735 (2010); Density: 1,861.1 persons per square mile (2010); Race: 91.0% White, 6.4% Black, 1.5% Asian, 0.1% American Indian/Alaska Native, 0.0% Native Hawaiian/Other Pacific Islander, 1.0% Other, 0.9% Hispanic of any race (2010); Average household size: 1.67 (2010); Median age: 79.0 (2010); Males per 100 females: 54.1 (2010); Marriage status: 21.3% never married, 32.2% now married, 37.6% widowed, 8.9% divorced (2006-2010 5-year est.); Foreign born: 4.4% (2006-2010 5-year est.); Ancestry (includes multiple ancestries): 24.9% Irish, 14.1% German, 13.2% English, 10.7% Italian, 3.1% Scottish (2006-2010 5-year est.).

Economy: Employment by occupation: 15.5% management, 5.8% professional, 5.3% services, 23.5% sales, 3.0% farming, 0.0% construction, 3.6% production (2006-2010 5-year est.).

Income: Per capita income: $31,258 (2006-2010 5-year est.); Median household income: $48,281 (2006-2010 5-year est.); Average household income: $69,071 (2006-2010 5-year est.); Percent of households with income of $100,000 or more: 22.6% (2006-2010 5-year est.); Poverty rate: 2.4% (2006-2010 5-year est.).

Education: Percent of population age 25 and over with: High school diploma (including GED) or higher: 82.5% (2006-2010 5-year est.); Bachelor's degree or higher: 28.4% (2006-2010 5-year est.); Master's degree or higher: 7.2% (2006-2010 5-year est.).

Housing: Homeownership rate: 43.9% (2010); Median home value: $260,600 (2006-2010 5-year est.); Median contract rent: $1,915 per month (2006-2010 5-year est.); Median year structure built: 1982 (2006-2010 5-year est.).

Transportation: Commute to work: 88.2% car, 0.0% public transportation, 1.3% walk, 10.5% work from home (2006-2010 5-year est.); Travel time to work: 8.9% less than 15 minutes, 53.6% 15 to 30 minutes, 18.0% 30 to 45 minutes, 9.1% 45 to 60 minutes, 10.3% 60 minutes or more (2006-2010 5-year est.)

Additional Information Contacts

Delaware County Chamber of Commerce . . . . (610) 565-3677

  http://www.delcochamber.org

LINWOOD (CDP). Aka Lower Chichester Township. Covers a land area of 0.512 square miles and a water area of 0 square miles. Located at 39.82° N. Lat; 75.42° W. Long. Elevation is 102 feet.

Population: 3,425 (1990); 3,374 (2000); 3,281 (2010); Density: 6,410.5 persons per square mile (2010); Race: 87.6% White, 8.0% Black, 0.6% Asian, 0.1% American Indian/Alaska Native, 0.0% Native Hawaiian/Other Pacific Islander, 3.7% Other, 3.7% Hispanic of any race (2010); Average household size: 2.78 (2010); Median age: 32.7 (2010); Males per 100 females: 94.3 (2010); Marriage status: 36.3% never married, 49.1% now married, 5.6% widowed, 9.0% divorced (2006-2010 5-year est.); Foreign born: 0.7% (2006-2010 5-year est.); Ancestry (includes multiple ancestries): 44.8% Irish, 20.9% Italian, 18.4% German, 11.8% English, 8.6% Polish (2006-2010 5-year est.).

Economy: Employment by occupation: 1.9% management, 2.0% professional, 14.2% services, 18.1% sales, 5.8% farming, 14.2% construction, 6.0% production (2006-2010 5-year est.).

Income: Per capita income: $23,784 (2006-2010 5-year est.); Median household income: $51,214 (2006-2010 5-year est.); Average household income: $56,636 (2006-2010 5-year est.); Percent of households with income of $100,000 or more: 13.6% (2006-2010 5-year est.); Poverty rate: 10.9% (2006-2010 5-year est.).

Education: Percent of population age 25 and over with: High school diploma (including GED) or higher: 85.5% (2006-2010 5-year est.); Bachelor's degree or higher: 6.6% (2006-2010 5-year est.); Master's degree or higher: 1.8% (2006-2010 5-year est.).

Housing: Homeownership rate: 68.3% (2010); Median home value: $107,600 (2006-2010 5-year est.); Median contract rent: $631 per month (2006-2010 5-year est.); Median year structure built: 1953 (2006-2010 5-year est.).

Transportation: Commute to work: 90.4% car, 0.0% public transportation, 6.3% walk, 3.3% work from home (2006-2010 5-year est.); Travel time to work: 43.8% less than 15 minutes, 35.6% 15 to 30 minutes, 11.9% 30 to 45 minutes, 4.9% 45 to 60 minutes, 3.8% 60 minutes or more (2006-2010 5-year est.)

Additional Information Contacts

Delaware County Chamber of Commerce . . . . (610) 565-3677

  http://www.delcochamber.org

LOWER CHICHESTER (township). Covers a land area of 1.073 square miles and a water area of 0 square miles. Located at 39.82° N. Lat; 75.43° W. Long.

Population: 3,660 (1990); 3,591 (2000); 3,469 (2010); Density: 3,234.3 persons per square mile (2010); Race: 87.6% White, 7.9% Black, 0.6% Asian, 0.1% American Indian/Alaska Native, 0.0% Native Hawaiian/Other Pacific Islander, 3.8% Other, 3.9% Hispanic of any race (2010); Average household size: 2.78 (2010); Median age: 32.4 (2010); Males per 100 females: 94.1 (2010); Marriage status: 35.7% never married, 50.5% now married, 5.3% widowed, 8.5% divorced (2006-2010 5-year est.); Foreign born: 0.6% (2006-2010 5-year est.); Ancestry (includes multiple ancestries): 42.8% Irish, 20.9% Italian, 19.2% German, 11.1% English, 8.1% Polish (2006-2010 5-year est.).

Economy: Single-family building permits issued: 0 (2011); Multi-family building permits issued: 0 (2011); Employment by occupation: 1.8% management, 1.9% professional, 13.8% services, 17.9% sales, 5.5% farming, 14.3% construction, 5.7% production (2006-2010 5-year est.).

Income: Per capita income: $23,942 (2006-2010 5-year est.); Median household income: $51,571 (2006-2010 5-year est.); Average household income: $58,022 (2006-2010 5-year est.); Percent of households with income of $100,000 or more: 14.2% (2006-2010 5-year est.); Poverty rate: 10.3% (2006-2010 5-year est.).

Education: Percent of population age 25 and over with: High school diploma (including GED) or higher: 84.4% (2006-2010 5-year est.); Bachelor's degree or higher: 6.2% (2006-2010 5-year est.); Master's degree or higher: 1.7% (2006-2010 5-year est.).

Housing: Homeownership rate: 67.8% (2010); Median home value: $107,100 (2006-2010 5-year est.); Median contract rent: $636 per month (2006-2010 5-year est.); Median year structure built: 1953 (2006-2010 5-year est.).

Transportation: Commute to work: 90.9% car, 0.0% public transportation, 5.9% walk, 3.1% work from home (2006-2010 5-year est.); Travel time to work: 43.3% less than 15 minutes, 34.9% 15 to 30 minutes, 13.5% 30 to 45 minutes, 4.6% 45 to 60 minutes, 3.6% 60 minutes or more (2006-2010 5-year est.)

Additional Information Contacts

Delaware County Chamber of Commerce . . . . (610) 565-3677

  http://www.delcochamber.org

MARCUS HOOK (borough). Covers a land area of 1.111 square miles and a water area of 0.514 square miles. Located at 39.81° N. Lat; 75.42° W. Long. Elevation is 30 feet.

Population: 2,546 (1990); 2,314 (2000); 2,397 (2010); Density: 2,157.8 persons per square mile (2010); Race: 82.3% White, 13.6% Black, 0.1% Asian, 0.1% American Indian/Alaska Native, 0.0% Native Hawaiian/Other Pacific Islander, 3.9% Other, 3.0% Hispanic of any race (2010); Average household size: 2.64 (2010); Median age: 33.1 (2010); Males per 100 females: 93.3 (2010); Marriage status: 39.1% never married, 39.6% now married, 7.6% widowed, 13.6% divorced (2006-2010 5-year est.); Foreign born: 3.6% (2006-2010 5-year est.); Ancestry (includes multiple ancestries): 34.7% Irish, 12.4% German, 12.1% Polish, 11.5% Italian, 4.7% English (2006-2010 5-year est.).

Economy: Single-family building permits issued: 0 (2011); Multi-family building permits issued: 0 (2011); Employment by occupation: 4.5% management, 0.5% professional, 15.5% services, 26.2% sales, 12.1% farming, 9.7% construction, 8.7% production (2006-2010 5-year est.).
Income: Per capita income: $17,209 (2006-2010 5-year est.); Median household income: $33,571 (2006-2010 5-year est.); Average household income: $44,658 (2006-2010 5-year est.); Percent of households with income of $100,000 or more: 8.8% (2006-2010 5-year est.); Poverty rate: 17.0% (2006-2010 5-year est.).
Education: Percent of population age 25 and over with: High school diploma (including GED) or higher: 75.8% (2006-2010 5-year est.); Bachelor's degree or higher: 6.2% (2006-2010 5-year est.); Master's degree or higher: 0.9% (2006-2010 5-year est.).
Housing: Homeownership rate: 48.9% (2010); Median home value: $82,300 (2006-2010 5-year est.); Median contract rent: $581 per month (2006-2010 5-year est.); Median year structure built: before 1940 (2006-2010 5-year est.).
Safety: Violent crime rate: 149.7 per 10,000 population; Property crime rate: 428.3 per 10,000 population (2011).
Transportation: Commute to work: 82.6% car, 8.1% public transportation, 8.3% walk, 0.0% work from home (2006-2010 5-year est.); Travel time to work: 30.3% less than 15 minutes, 33.1% 15 to 30 minutes, 19.2% 30 to 45 minutes, 6.9% 45 to 60 minutes, 10.4% 60 minutes or more (2006-2010 5-year est.)
Additional Information Contacts
Delaware County Chamber of Commerce . . . . (610) 565-3677
   http://www.delcochamber.org

MARPLE (township). Covers a land area of 10.202 square miles and a water area of 0.314 square miles. Located at 39.97° N. Lat; 75.36° W. Long. Elevation is 410 feet.
Population: 23,111 (1990); 23,737 (2000); 23,428 (2010); Density: 2,296.4 persons per square mile (2010); Race: 89.6% White, 2.1% Black, 7.0% Asian, 0.1% American Indian/Alaska Native, 0.0% Native Hawaiian/Other Pacific Islander, 1.2% Other, 1.3% Hispanic of any race (2010); Average household size: 2.61 (2010); Median age: 46.7 (2010); Males per 100 females: 91.5 (2010); Marriage status: 27.1% never married, 57.4% now married, 9.1% widowed, 6.4% divorced (2006-2010 5-year est.); Foreign born: 12.5% (2006-2010 5-year est.); Ancestry (includes multiple ancestries): 27.2% Irish, 26.0% Italian, 16.2% German, 9.4% English, 4.2% Polish (2006-2010 5-year est.).
Economy: Single-family building permits issued: 17 (2011); Multi-family building permits issued: 0 (2011); Employment by occupation: 13.1% management, 4.7% professional, 7.0% services, 16.3% sales, 3.5% farming, 9.7% construction, 3.7% production (2006-2010 5-year est.).
Income: Per capita income: $34,639 (2006-2010 5-year est.); Median household income: $76,723 (2006-2010 5-year est.); Average household income: $93,928 (2006-2010 5-year est.); Percent of households with income of $100,000 or more: 36.9% (2006-2010 5-year est.); Poverty rate: 4.4% (2006-2010 5-year est.).
Taxes: Total city taxes per capita: $405 (2009); City property taxes per capita: $251 (2009).
Education: Percent of population age 25 and over with: High school diploma (including GED) or higher: 89.6% (2006-2010 5-year est.); Bachelor's degree or higher: 34.9% (2006-2010 5-year est.); Master's degree or higher: 13.7% (2006-2010 5-year est.).
Housing: Homeownership rate: 84.7% (2010); Median home value: $345,700 (2006-2010 5-year est.); Median contract rent: $846 per month (2006-2010 5-year est.); Median year structure built: 1959 (2006-2010 5-year est.).
Safety: Violent crime rate: 4.3 per 10,000 population; Property crime rate: 171.9 per 10,000 population (2011).
Transportation: Commute to work: 88.2% car, 4.2% public transportation, 1.9% walk, 4.7% work from home (2006-2010 5-year est.); Travel time to work: 22.6% less than 15 minutes, 36.2% 15 to 30 minutes, 27.0% 30 to 45 minutes, 8.3% 45 to 60 minutes, 5.8% 60 minutes or more (2006-2010 5-year est.)
Additional Information Contacts
Delaware County Chamber of Commerce . . . . (610) 565-3677
   http://www.delcochamber.org
Marple Township . . . . (610) 356-4040
   http://www.marpletwp.com

MEDIA (borough). Aka Darling. County seat. Covers a land area of 0.759 square miles and a water area of 0.003 square miles. Located at 39.92° N. Lat; 75.39° W. Long. Elevation is 285 feet.
Population: 5,957 (1990); 5,533 (2000); 5,327 (2010); Density: 7,016.3 persons per square mile (2010); Race: 83.4% White, 10.6% Black, 3.5% Asian, 0.0% American Indian/Alaska Native, 0.0% Native Hawaiian/Other Pacific Islander, 2.5% Other, 2.5% Hispanic of any race (2010); Average household size: 1.86 (2010); Median age: 40.0 (2010); Males per 100 females: 91.5 (2010); Marriage status: 41.7% never married, 33.8% now married, 10.3% widowed, 14.2% divorced (2006-2010 5-year est.); Foreign born: 8.2% (2006-2010 5-year est.); Ancestry (includes multiple ancestries): 25.8% Irish, 16.9% German, 15.7% English, 15.4% Italian, 5.6% Welsh (2006-2010 5-year est.).
Economy: Single-family building permits issued: 0 (2011); Multi-family building permits issued: 0 (2011); Employment by occupation: 12.0% management, 9.0% professional, 7.8% services, 19.6% sales, 2.3% farming, 7.5% construction, 3.4% production (2006-2010 5-year est.).
Income: Per capita income: $34,670 (2006-2010 5-year est.); Median household income: $56,472 (2006-2010 5-year est.); Average household income: $66,335 (2006-2010 5-year est.); Percent of households with income of $100,000 or more: 18.6% (2006-2010 5-year est.); Poverty rate: 7.4% (2006-2010 5-year est.).
Taxes: Total city taxes per capita: $1,054 (2009); City property taxes per capita: $224 (2009).
Education: Percent of population age 25 and over with: High school diploma (including GED) or higher: 93.3% (2006-2010 5-year est.); Bachelor's degree or higher: 42.3% (2006-2010 5-year est.); Master's degree or higher: 20.5% (2006-2010 5-year est.).
School District(s)
Rose Tree Media SD (KG-12)
   2010-11 Enrollment: 3,706 . . . . (610) 627-6000
Four-year College(s)
Pennsylvania State University-Penn State Brandywine (Public)
   Fall 2010 Enrollment: 1,556 . . . . (610) 892-1200
   2011-12 Tuition: In-state $13,102; Out-of-state $19,542
Two-year College(s)
Delaware County Community College (Public)
   Fall 2010 Enrollment: 8,889 . . . . (610) 359-5000
   2011-12 Tuition: In-state $7,450; Out-of-state $10,570
Pennsylvania Institute of Technology (Private, Not-for-profit)
   Fall 2010 Enrollment: 1,136 . . . . (610) 565-7900
   2011-12 Tuition: In-state $11,400; Out-of-state $11,400
Housing: Homeownership rate: 41.4% (2010); Median home value: $263,100 (2006-2010 5-year est.); Median contract rent: $852 per month (2006-2010 5-year est.); Median year structure built: 1954 (2006-2010 5-year est.).
Hospitals: Riddle Memorial Hospital (248 beds)
Safety: Violent crime rate: 56.1 per 10,000 population; Property crime rate: 160.9 per 10,000 population (2011).
Transportation: Commute to work: 76.7% car, 9.9% public transportation, 7.0% walk, 5.0% work from home (2006-2010 5-year est.); Travel time to work: 27.6% less than 15 minutes, 23.2% 15 to 30 minutes, 27.2% 30 to 45 minutes, 15.9% 45 to 60 minutes, 6.1% 60 minutes or more (2006-2010 5-year est.)
Additional Information Contacts
Borough of Media . . . . (610) 566-5210
   http://www.mediaborough.com
Delaware County Chamber of Commerce . . . . (610) 565-3677
   http://www.delcochamber.org

MIDDLETOWN (township). Covers a land area of 13.466 square miles and a water area of <.001 square miles. Located at 39.91° N. Lat; 75.43° W. Long.
Population: 14,130 (1990); 16,064 (2000); 15,807 (2010); Density: 1,173.9 persons per square mile (2010); Race: 92.3% White, 3.4% Black, 2.8% Asian, 0.1% American Indian/Alaska Native, 0.0% Native Hawaiian/Other Pacific Islander, 1.4% Other, 1.6% Hispanic of any race (2010); Average household size: 2.41 (2010); Median age: 49.4 (2010); Males per 100 females: 87.3 (2010); Marriage status: 24.8% never married, 53.7% now married, 15.1% widowed, 6.3% divorced (2006-2010 5-year est.); Foreign born: 4.5% (2006-2010 5-year est.); Ancestry (includes multiple ancestries): 32.2% Irish, 23.6% German, 17.3% Italian, 14.5% English, 3.7% Polish (2006-2010 5-year est.).
Economy: Single-family building permits issued: 2 (2011); Multi-family building permits issued: 0 (2011); Employment by occupation: 23.1%

management, 6.4% professional, 6.2% services, 15.8% sales, 2.8% farming, 7.4% construction, 3.7% production (2006-2010 5-year est.).
Income: Per capita income: $39,648 (2006-2010 5-year est.); Median household income: $81,448 (2006-2010 5-year est.); Average household income: $102,523 (2006-2010 5-year est.); Percent of households with income of $100,000 or more: 41.6% (2006-2010 5-year est.); Poverty rate: 2.3% (2006-2010 5-year est.).
Taxes: Total city taxes per capita: $215 (2009); City property taxes per capita: $96 (2009).
Education: Percent of population age 25 and over with: High school diploma (including GED) or higher: 90.7% (2006-2010 5-year est.); Bachelor's degree or higher: 41.8% (2006-2010 5-year est.); Master's degree or higher: 16.5% (2006-2010 5-year est.).
Housing: Homeownership rate: 74.8% (2010); Median home value: $343,500 (2006-2010 5-year est.); Median contract rent: $1,740 per month (2006-2010 5-year est.); Median year structure built: 1972 (2006-2010 5-year est.).
Transportation: Commute to work: 88.0% car, 5.2% public transportation, 1.8% walk, 4.5% work from home (2006-2010 5-year est.); Travel time to work: 24.3% less than 15 minutes, 34.9% 15 to 30 minutes, 24.1% 30 to 45 minutes, 10.1% 45 to 60 minutes, 6.6% 60 minutes or more (2006-2010 5-year est.)
Additional Information Contacts
Delaware County Chamber of Commerce . . . . (610) 565-3677
    http://www.delcochamber.org
Middletown Township . . . . (610) 565-2700
    http://www.middletowntownship.org

MILLBOURNE (borough). Covers a land area of 0.074 square miles and a water area of 0 square miles. Located at 39.96° N. Lat; 75.25° W. Long. Elevation is 102 feet.
Population: 831 (1990); 943 (2000); 1,159 (2010); Density: 15,636.6 persons per square mile (2010); Race: 13.7% White, 20.1% Black, 56.3% Asian, 0.6% American Indian/Alaska Native, 0.9% Native Hawaiian/Other Pacific Islander, 8.4% Other, 8.5% Hispanic of any race (2010); Average household size: 3.03 (2010); Median age: 32.8 (2010); Males per 100 females: 129.5 (2010); Marriage status: 31.5% never married, 61.2% now married, 3.5% widowed, 3.8% divorced (2006-2010 5-year est.); Foreign born: 56.8% (2006-2010 5-year est.); Ancestry (includes multiple ancestries): 6.3% Irish, 4.2% Sudanese, 4.1% Italian, 3.5% Haitian, 1.9% Other Subsaharan African (2006-2010 5-year est.).
Economy: Single-family building permits issued: 0 (2011); Multi-family building permits issued: 0 (2011); Employment by occupation: 3.3% management, 2.8% professional, 13.5% services, 12.6% sales, 4.8% farming, 8.0% construction, 9.3% production (2006-2010 5-year est.).
Income: Per capita income: $16,722 (2006-2010 5-year est.); Median household income: $34,479 (2006-2010 5-year est.); Average household income: $45,032 (2006-2010 5-year est.); Percent of households with income of $100,000 or more: 8.0% (2006-2010 5-year est.); Poverty rate: 13.3% (2006-2010 5-year est.).
Education: Percent of population age 25 and over with: High school diploma (including GED) or higher: 83.3% (2006-2010 5-year est.); Bachelor's degree or higher: 29.6% (2006-2010 5-year est.); Master's degree or higher: 9.5% (2006-2010 5-year est.).
Housing: Homeownership rate: 25.1% (2010); Median home value: $117,700 (2006-2010 5-year est.); Median contract rent: $609 per month (2006-2010 5-year est.); Median year structure built: 1950 (2006-2010 5-year est.).
Safety: Violent crime rate: 129.0 per 10,000 population; Property crime rate: 215.0 per 10,000 population (2011).
Transportation: Commute to work: 67.4% car, 29.1% public transportation, 3.1% walk, 0.0% work from home (2006-2010 5-year est.); Travel time to work: 10.3% less than 15 minutes, 29.7% 15 to 30 minutes, 32.0% 30 to 45 minutes, 14.0% 45 to 60 minutes, 14.0% 60 minutes or more (2006-2010 5-year est.)

MORTON (borough). Covers a land area of 0.358 square miles and a water area of 0 square miles. Located at 39.91° N. Lat; 75.33° W. Long. Elevation is 135 feet.
Population: 2,851 (1990); 2,715 (2000); 2,669 (2010); Density: 7,450.7 persons per square mile (2010); Race: 65.1% White, 25.4% Black, 6.0% Asian, 0.3% American Indian/Alaska Native, 0.0% Native Hawaiian/Other Pacific Islander, 3.2% Other, 2.2% Hispanic of any race (2010); Average household size: 2.35 (2010); Median age: 39.5 (2010); Males per 100 females: 90.6 (2010); Marriage status: 32.8% never married, 47.3% now

married, 7.7% widowed, 12.1% divorced (2006-2010 5-year est.); Foreign born: 5.4% (2006-2010 5-year est.); Ancestry (includes multiple ancestries): 28.0% Irish, 17.1% Italian, 17.0% German, 7.5% English, 5.7% Polish (2006-2010 5-year est.).
Economy: Single-family building permits issued: 0 (2011); Multi-family building permits issued: 0 (2011); Employment by occupation: 7.1% management, 3.7% professional, 8.8% services, 17.2% sales, 5.2% farming, 13.4% construction, 6.7% production (2006-2010 5-year est.).
Income: Per capita income: $28,265 (2006-2010 5-year est.); Median household income: $54,076 (2006-2010 5-year est.); Average household income: $65,263 (2006-2010 5-year est.); Percent of households with income of $100,000 or more: 22.1% (2006-2010 5-year est.); Poverty rate: 5.0% (2006-2010 5-year est.).
Education: Percent of population age 25 and over with: High school diploma (including GED) or higher: 90.3% (2006-2010 5-year est.); Bachelor's degree or higher: 32.3% (2006-2010 5-year est.); Master's degree or higher: 8.0% (2006-2010 5-year est.).
School District(s)
Ridley SD (KG-12)
    2010-11 Enrollment: 5,847 . . . . (610) 534-1900
Housing: Homeownership rate: 54.2% (2010); Median home value: $215,900 (2006-2010 5-year est.); Median contract rent: $732 per month (2006-2010 5-year est.); Median year structure built: 1963 (2006-2010 5-year est.).
Safety: Violent crime rate: 14.9 per 10,000 population; Property crime rate: 556.4 per 10,000 population (2011).
Transportation: Commute to work: 82.6% car, 10.8% public transportation, 1.8% walk, 2.9% work from home (2006-2010 5-year est.); Travel time to work: 23.7% less than 15 minutes, 25.9% 15 to 30 minutes, 31.3% 30 to 45 minutes, 13.0% 45 to 60 minutes, 6.0% 60 minutes or more (2006-2010 5-year est.)
Additional Information Contacts
Delaware County Chamber of Commerce . . . . (610) 565-3677
    http://www.delcochamber.org

NETHER PROVIDENCE (township). Covers a land area of 4.714 square miles and a water area of 0.008 square miles. Located at 39.90° N. Lat; 75.37° W. Long.
History: The first recorded inhabitants of Nether Providence Township were Native Americans of the Lenape tribe, who lived in the area for about five hundred years. By 1740 few Lenape remained in the area.
Population: 13,229 (1990); 13,456 (2000); 13,706 (2010); Density: 2,907.7 persons per square mile (2010); Race: 85.6% White, 7.0% Black, 5.2% Asian, 0.1% American Indian/Alaska Native, 0.0% Native Hawaiian/Other Pacific Islander, 2.1% Other, 2.0% Hispanic of any race (2010); Average household size: 2.63 (2010); Median age: 44.0 (2010); Males per 100 females: 91.5 (2010); Marriage status: 24.7% never married, 63.4% now married, 6.7% widowed, 5.2% divorced (2006-2010 5-year est.); Foreign born: 7.1% (2006-2010 5-year est.); Ancestry (includes multiple ancestries): 28.2% Irish, 18.7% German, 14.5% English, 13.7% Italian, 7.9% Polish (2006-2010 5-year est.).
Economy: Single-family building permits issued: 3 (2011); Multi-family building permits issued: 0 (2011); Employment by occupation: 16.7% management, 7.0% professional, 4.2% services, 12.6% sales, 3.2% farming, 3.2% construction, 1.5% production (2006-2010 5-year est.).
Income: Per capita income: $42,760 (2006-2010 5-year est.); Median household income: $96,435 (2006-2010 5-year est.); Average household income: $114,988 (2006-2010 5-year est.); Percent of households with income of $100,000 or more: 48.3% (2006-2010 5-year est.); Poverty rate: 5.5% (2006-2010 5-year est.).
Education: Percent of population age 25 and over with: High school diploma (including GED) or higher: 94.9% (2006-2010 5-year est.); Bachelor's degree or higher: 58.2% (2006-2010 5-year est.); Master's degree or higher: 32.0% (2006-2010 5-year est.).
Housing: Homeownership rate: 87.4% (2010); Median home value: $318,500 (2006-2010 5-year est.); Median contract rent: $960 per month (2006-2010 5-year est.); Median year structure built: 1958 (2006-2010 5-year est.).
Safety: Violent crime rate: 18.2 per 10,000 population; Property crime rate: 137.5 per 10,000 population (2011).
Transportation: Commute to work: 82.2% car, 8.2% public transportation, 3.1% walk, 5.6% work from home (2006-2010 5-year est.); Travel time to work: 27.0% less than 15 minutes, 28.3% 15 to 30 minutes, 28.0% 30 to 45 minutes, 10.1% 45 to 60 minutes, 6.6% 60 minutes or more (2006-2010 5-year est.)

Additional Information Contacts
Delaware County Chamber of Commerce . . . . (610) 565-3677
   http://www.delcochamber.org
Nether Providence Township . . . . (610) 566-4516
   http://www.netherprovidence.org

NEWTOWN (township). Covers a land area of 10.018 square miles
and a water area of 0.073 square miles. Located at 39.99° N. Lat; 75.41°
W. Long.
History: Newtown Township was settled in 1681 and incorporated as a
Township in 1684. In 1681, William Penn planned the "first inland town
west of Philadelphia" at the intersection of Goshen Road (laid out in 1687)
and Newtown Street Road (laid out in 1683).
Population: 11,366 (1990); 11,700 (2000); 12,216 (2010); Density:
1,219.4 persons per square mile (2010); Race: 94.6% White, 0.9% Black,
3.3% Asian, 0.1% American Indian/Alaska Native, 0.0% Native
Hawaiian/Other Pacific Islander, 1.1% Other, 1.2% Hispanic of any race
(2010); Average household size: 2.46 (2010); Median age: 47.3 (2010);
Males per 100 females: 91.2 (2010); Marriage status: 26.4% never
married, 59.1% now married, 9.1% widowed, 5.4% divorced (2006-2010
5-year est.); Foreign born: 6.3% (2006-2010 5-year est.); Ancestry
(includes multiple ancestries): 32.0% Irish, 23.8% Italian, 21.8% German,
14.7% English, 3.9% American (2006-2010 5-year est.).
Economy: Single-family building permits issued: 10 (2011); Multi-family
building permits issued: 0 (2011); Employment by occupation: 17.8%
management, 5.2% professional, 3.4% services, 21.0% sales, 1.7%
farming, 7.0% construction, 3.9% production (2006-2010 5-year est.).
Income: Per capita income: $50,694 (2006-2010 5-year est.); Median
household income: $92,833 (2006-2010 5-year est.); Average household
income: $131,172 (2006-2010 5-year est.); Percent of households with
income of $100,000 or more: 46.8% (2006-2010 5-year est.); Poverty rate:
3.4% (2006-2010 5-year est.).
Education: Percent of population age 25 and over with: High school
diploma (including GED) or higher: 96.3% (2006-2010 5-year est.);
Bachelor's degree or higher: 51.8% (2006-2010 5-year est.); Master's
degree or higher: 24.6% (2006-2010 5-year est.).
Housing: Homeownership rate: 79.0% (2010); Median home value:
$392,000 (2006-2010 5-year est.); Median contract rent: $1,026 per month
(2006-2010 5-year est.); Median year structure built: 1961 (2006-2010
5-year est.).
Transportation: Commute to work: 91.0% car, 2.5% public transportation,
1.6% walk, 4.1% work from home (2006-2010 5-year est.); Travel time to
work: 23.8% less than 15 minutes, 42.2% 15 to 30 minutes, 21.1% 30 to
45 minutes, 8.8% 45 to 60 minutes, 4.1% 60 minutes or more (2006-2010
5-year est.)
Additional Information Contacts
Delaware County Chamber of Commerce . . . . (610) 565-3677
   http://www.delcochamber.org
Newtown Township . . . . (215) 968-2800
   http://www.twp.newtown.pa.us

NEWTOWN SQUARE (unincorporated postal area)
Zip Code: 19073
   Covers a land area of 20.699 square miles and a water area of 0.391
square miles. Located at 39.97° N. Lat; 75.43° W. Long. Elevation is
417 feet. Population: 18,332 (2010); Density: 885.6 persons per square
mile (2010); Race: 93.5% White, 1.1% Black, 4.1% Asian, 0.1%
American Indian/Alaska Native, 0.0% Native Hawaiian/Other Pacific
Islander, 1.2% Other, 1.3% Hispanic of any race (2010); Average
household size: 2.40 (2010); Median age: 48.5 (2010); Males per 100
females: 89.8 (2010); Homeownership rate: 79.9% (2010)

NORWOOD (borough). Covers a land area of 0.777 square miles and
a water area of 0.037 square miles. Located at 39.89° N. Lat; 75.30° W.
Long. Elevation is 89 feet.
Population: 6,162 (1990); 5,985 (2000); 5,890 (2010); Density: 7,579.0
persons per square mile (2010); Race: 95.0% White, 1.5% Black, 2.0%
Asian, 0.1% American Indian/Alaska Native, 0.0% Native Hawaiian/Other
Pacific Islander, 1.4% Other, 1.4% Hispanic of any race (2010); Average
household size: 2.63 (2010); Median age: 39.5 (2010); Males per 100
females: 97.0 (2010); Marriage status: 30.5% never married, 54.4% now
married, 6.2% widowed, 8.9% divorced (2006-2010 5-year est.); Foreign
born: 1.1% (2006-2010 5-year est.); Ancestry (includes multiple
ancestries): 47.3% Irish, 24.0% Italian, 22.6% German, 12.7% English,
6.0% Polish (2006-2010 5-year est.).

Economy: Single-family building permits issued: 0 (2011); Multi-family
building permits issued: 0 (2011); Employment by occupation: 7.4%
management, 5.9% professional, 8.7% services, 22.3% sales, 2.4%
farming, 15.3% construction, 8.6% production (2006-2010 5-year est.).
Income: Per capita income: $26,414 (2006-2010 5-year est.); Median
household income: $61,139 (2006-2010 5-year est.); Average household
income: $68,855 (2006-2010 5-year est.); Percent of households with
income of $100,000 or more: 20.5% (2006-2010 5-year est.); Poverty rate:
2.5% (2006-2010 5-year est.).
Education: Percent of population age 25 and over with: High school
diploma (including GED) or higher: 90.7% (2006-2010 5-year est.);
Bachelor's degree or higher: 17.0% (2006-2010 5-year est.); Master's
degree or higher: 5.1% (2006-2010 5-year est.).
School District(s)
Interboro SD (KG-12)
   2010-11 Enrollment: 3,631 . . . . (610) 461-6700
Housing: Homeownership rate: 74.0% (2010); Median home value:
$180,300 (2006-2010 5-year est.); Median contract rent: $711 per month
(2006-2010 5-year est.); Median year structure built: 1949 (2006-2010
5-year est.).
Safety: Violent crime rate: 20.3 per 10,000 population; Property crime rate:
192.9 per 10,000 population (2011).
Transportation: Commute to work: 88.9% car, 2.1% public transportation,
5.9% walk, 1.2% work from home (2006-2010 5-year est.); Travel time to
work: 26.9% less than 15 minutes, 31.8% 15 to 30 minutes, 22.1% 30 to
45 minutes, 9.6% 45 to 60 minutes, 9.5% 60 minutes or more (2006-2010
5-year est.)
Additional Information Contacts
Borough of Norwood . . . . (610) 586-5800
Greater Philadelphia Chamber of Commerce . . . . (215) 545-1234
   http://www.greaterphilachamber.com

PARKSIDE (borough). Covers a land area of 0.206 square miles and a
water area of 0 square miles. Located at 39.87° N. Lat; 75.38° W. Long.
Elevation is 95 feet.
Population: 2,369 (1990); 2,267 (2000); 2,328 (2010); Density: 11,311.9
persons per square mile (2010); Race: 80.5% White, 12.9% Black, 2.4%
Asian, 0.8% American Indian/Alaska Native, 0.0% Native Hawaiian/Other
Pacific Islander, 3.4% Other, 3.5% Hispanic of any race (2010); Average
household size: 2.66 (2010); Median age: 35.1 (2010); Males per 100
females: 90.0 (2010); Marriage status: 27.5% never married, 56.1% now
married, 6.3% widowed, 10.2% divorced (2006-2010 5-year est.); Foreign
born: 2.3% (2006-2010 5-year est.); Ancestry (includes multiple
ancestries): 28.7% Irish, 23.5% German, 22.2% Italian, 13.7% English,
6.1% Polish (2006-2010 5-year est.).
Economy: Single-family building permits issued: 0 (2011); Multi-family
building permits issued: 0 (2011); Employment by occupation: 11.5%
management, 1.5% professional, 11.9% services, 16.8% sales, 6.5%
farming, 11.0% construction, 3.9% production (2006-2010 5-year est.).
Income: Per capita income: $22,752 (2006-2010 5-year est.); Median
household income: $54,464 (2006-2010 5-year est.); Average household
income: $58,315 (2006-2010 5-year est.); Percent of households with
income of $100,000 or more: 10.7% (2006-2010 5-year est.); Poverty rate:
12.2% (2006-2010 5-year est.).
Education: Percent of population age 25 and over with: High school
diploma (including GED) or higher: 91.5% (2006-2010 5-year est.);
Bachelor's degree or higher: 18.6% (2006-2010 5-year est.); Master's
degree or higher: 4.6% (2006-2010 5-year est.).
School District(s)
Penn-Delco SD (KG-12)
   2010-11 Enrollment: 3,356 . . . . (610) 497-6300
Housing: Homeownership rate: 78.4% (2010); Median home value:
$145,900 (2006-2010 5-year est.); Median contract rent: $761 per month
(2006-2010 5-year est.); Median year structure built: 1951 (2006-2010
5-year est.).
Transportation: Commute to work: 91.7% car, 1.2% public transportation,
1.0% walk, 4.6% work from home (2006-2010 5-year est.); Travel time to
work: 27.9% less than 15 minutes, 43.0% 15 to 30 minutes, 15.7% 30 to
45 minutes, 7.1% 45 to 60 minutes, 6.3% 60 minutes or more (2006-2010
5-year est.)
Additional Information Contacts
Delaware County Chamber of Commerce . . . . (610) 565-3677
   http://www.delcochamber.org

PROSPECT PARK (borough). Aka Moore. Covers a land area of 0.729 square miles and a water area of 0.012 square miles. Located at 39.89° N. Lat; 75.31° W. Long. Elevation is 89 feet.

Population: 6,764 (1990); 6,594 (2000); 6,454 (2010); Density: 8,852.8 persons per square mile (2010); Race: 92.6% White, 3.0% Black, 1.8% Asian, 0.2% American Indian/Alaska Native, 0.0% Native Hawaiian/Other Pacific Islander, 2.4% Other, 1.9% Hispanic of any race (2010); Average household size: 2.49 (2010); Median age: 38.5 (2010); Males per 100 females: 99.6 (2010); Marriage status: 35.1% never married, 46.1% now married, 6.9% widowed, 11.8% divorced (2006-2010 5-year est.); Foreign born: 3.5% (2006-2010 5-year est.); Ancestry (includes multiple ancestries): 41.0% Irish, 23.9% German, 18.3% Italian, 11.7% English, 8.2% Polish (2006-2010 5-year est.).

Economy: Single-family building permits issued: 5 (2011); Multi-family building permits issued: 0 (2011); Employment by occupation: 9.2% management, 4.2% professional, 13.6% services, 21.2% sales, 4.1% farming, 12.0% construction, 10.1% production (2006-2010 5-year est.).

Income: Per capita income: $27,256 (2006-2010 5-year est.); Median household income: $70,090 (2006-2010 5-year est.); Average household income: $69,447 (2006-2010 5-year est.); Percent of households with income of $100,000 or more: 19.3% (2006-2010 5-year est.); Poverty rate: 5.2% (2006-2010 5-year est.).

Education: Percent of population age 25 and over with: High school diploma (including GED) or higher: 86.9% (2006-2010 5-year est.); Bachelor's degree or higher: 16.9% (2006-2010 5-year est.); Master's degree or higher: 5.2% (2006-2010 5-year est.).

School District(s)
Interboro SD (KG-12)
   2010-11 Enrollment: 3,631 . . . . (610) 461-6700

Housing: Homeownership rate: 63.0% (2010); Median home value: $189,800 (2006-2010 5-year est.); Median contract rent: $651 per month (2006-2010 5-year est.); Median year structure built: 1946 (2006-2010 5-year est.).

Safety: Violent crime rate: 51.0 per 10,000 population; Property crime rate: 274.9 per 10,000 population (2011).

Transportation: Commute to work: 83.3% car, 7.8% public transportation, 6.5% walk, 1.2% work from home (2006-2010 5-year est.); Travel time to work: 31.9% less than 15 minutes, 32.2% 15 to 30 minutes, 23.8% 30 to 45 minutes, 9.7% 45 to 60 minutes, 2.4% 60 minutes or more (2006-2010 5-year est.)

Additional Information Contacts
Borough of Prospect Park . . . . (610) 534-7275
   http://www.prospectpark.boroughs.org
Delaware County Chamber of Commerce. . . . . (610) 565-3677
   http://www.delcochamber.org

RADNOR (township). Covers a land area of 13.776 square miles and a water area of 0.014 square miles. Located at 40.02° N. Lat; 75.37° W. Long. Elevation is 433 feet.

Population: 28,710 (1990); 30,878 (2000); 31,531 (2010); Density: 2,288.8 persons per square mile (2010); Race: 85.8% White, 3.9% Black, 7.9% Asian, 0.1% American Indian/Alaska Native, 0.0% Native Hawaiian/Other Pacific Islander, 2.3% Other, 3.0% Hispanic of any race (2010); Average household size: 2.46 (2010); Median age: 27.5 (2010); Males per 100 females: 91.5 (2010); Marriage status: 46.2% never married, 43.8% now married, 4.7% widowed, 5.4% divorced (2006-2010 5-year est.); Foreign born: 11.6% (2006-2010 5-year est.); Ancestry (includes multiple ancestries): 25.6% Irish, 15.4% German, 14.1% Italian, 13.5% English, 5.0% Polish (2006-2010 5-year est.).

Economy: Unemployment rate: 6.9% (August 2012); Total civilian labor force: 14,579 (August 2012); Single-family building permits issued: 7 (2011); Multi-family building permits issued: 0 (2011); Employment by occupation: 19.2% management, 5.6% professional, 7.5% services, 16.3% sales, 3.9% farming, 2.6% construction, 1.7% production (2006-2010 5-year est.).

Income: Per capita income: $49,482 (2006-2010 5-year est.); Median household income: $85,942 (2006-2010 5-year est.); Average household income: $146,789 (2006-2010 5-year est.); Percent of households with income of $100,000 or more: 43.9% (2006-2010 5-year est.); Poverty rate: 6.8% (2006-2010 5-year est.).

Taxes: Total city taxes per capita: $755 (2009); City property taxes per capita: $299 (2009).

Education: Percent of population age 25 and over with: High school diploma (including GED) or higher: 96.4% (2006-2010 5-year est.);

Bachelor's degree or higher: 71.3% (2006-2010 5-year est.); Master's degree or higher: 36.0% (2006-2010 5-year est.).

School District(s)
Radnor Township SD (KG-12)
   2010-11 Enrollment: 3,584 . . . . (610) 688-8100
Radnor Township SD (KG-12)
   2010-11 Enrollment: 3,584 . . . . (610) 688-8100

Four-year College(s)
Cabrini College (Private, Not-for-profit, Roman Catholic)
   Fall 2010 Enrollment: 2,740 . . . . (610) 902-8100
   2011-12 Tuition: In-state $33,176; Out-of-state $33,176
Eastern University (Private, Not-for-profit, American Baptist)
   Fall 2010 Enrollment: 3,649 . . . . (610) 341-5800
   2011-12 Tuition: In-state $25,850; Out-of-state $25,850
University of Phoenix-Philadelphia Campus (Private, For-profit)
   Fall 2010 Enrollment: 663 . . . . (610) 989-0880
   2011-12 Tuition: In-state $9,859; Out-of-state $9,859

Two-year College(s)
Valley Forge Military College (Private, Not-for-profit)
   Fall 2010 Enrollment: 331 . . . . (610) 989-1203
   2011-12 Tuition: In-state $25,360; Out-of-state $25,360

Housing: Homeownership rate: 65.1% (2010); Median home value: $609,600 (2006-2010 5-year est.); Median contract rent: $1,185 per month (2006-2010 5-year est.); Median year structure built: 1960 (2006-2010 5-year est.).

Safety: Violent crime rate: 4.7 per 10,000 population; Property crime rate: 119.8 per 10,000 population (2011).

Newspapers: King of Prussia Courier (Community news; Circulation 8,900); Suburban and Wayne Times (Community news); Technology Times (Regional news; Circulation 170,000)

Transportation: Commute to work: 71.5% car, 7.4% public transportation, 12.3% walk, 7.1% work from home (2006-2010 5-year est.); Travel time to work: 35.9% less than 15 minutes, 29.6% 15 to 30 minutes, 19.9% 30 to 45 minutes, 9.0% 45 to 60 minutes, 5.5% 60 minutes or more (2006-2010 5-year est.)

Additional Information Contacts
Main Line Chamber of Commerce . . . . (610) 687-6232
   http://www.mlcc.org
Radnor Township . . . . (610) 688-5600
   http://www.radnor.com

RIDLEY (township). Covers a land area of 5.119 square miles and a water area of 0.192 square miles. Located at 39.89° N. Lat; 75.33° W. Long.

Population: 31,175 (1990); 30,791 (2000); 30,768 (2010); Density: 6,010.9 persons per square mile (2010); Race: 90.0% White, 5.7% Black, 2.2% Asian, 0.1% American Indian/Alaska Native, 0.0% Native Hawaiian/Other Pacific Islander, 2.0% Other, 1.9% Hispanic of any race (2010); Average household size: 2.55 (2010); Median age: 40.1 (2010); Males per 100 females: 93.5 (2010); Marriage status: 32.6% never married, 50.4% now married, 8.2% widowed, 8.8% divorced (2006-2010 5-year est.); Foreign born: 4.4% (2006-2010 5-year est.); Ancestry (includes multiple ancestries): 42.9% Irish, 26.9% Italian, 19.9% German, 11.4% English, 5.0% Polish (2006-2010 5-year est.).

Economy: Unemployment rate: 8.5% (August 2012); Total civilian labor force: 15,870 (August 2012); Single-family building permits issued: 5 (2011); Multi-family building permits issued: 0 (2011); Employment by occupation: 11.3% management, 4.5% professional, 9.2% services, 19.5% sales, 5.3% farming, 11.7% construction, 6.8% production (2006-2010 5-year est.).

Income: Per capita income: $26,847 (2006-2010 5-year est.); Median household income: $57,558 (2006-2010 5-year est.); Average household income: $66,920 (2006-2010 5-year est.); Percent of households with income of $100,000 or more: 21.2% (2006-2010 5-year est.); Poverty rate: 7.3% (2006-2010 5-year est.).

Taxes: Total city taxes per capita: $408 (2009); City property taxes per capita: $315 (2009).

Education: Percent of population age 25 and over with: High school diploma (including GED) or higher: 88.6% (2006-2010 5-year est.); Bachelor's degree or higher: 21.5% (2006-2010 5-year est.); Master's degree or higher: 7.6% (2006-2010 5-year est.).

Housing: Homeownership rate: 75.2% (2010); Median home value: $199,500 (2006-2010 5-year est.); Median contract rent: $773 per month (2006-2010 5-year est.); Median year structure built: 1955 (2006-2010 5-year est.).

Safety: Violent crime rate: 17.2 per 10,000 population; Property crime rate: 180.3 per 10,000 population (2011).

Transportation: Commute to work: 89.2% car, 4.4% public transportation, 3.8% walk, 1.6% work from home (2006-2010 5-year est.); Travel time to work: 31.1% less than 15 minutes, 32.0% 15 to 30 minutes, 22.2% 30 to 45 minutes, 10.4% 45 to 60 minutes, 4.3% 60 minutes or more (2006-2010 5-year est.)

Additional Information Contacts

Delaware County Chamber of Commerce. . . . . (610) 565-3677
    http://www.delcochamber.org
Ridley Township . . . . (610) 534-4806
    http://www.twp.ridley.pa.us

RIDLEY PARK (borough). Covers a land area of 1.079 square miles and a water area of 0.005 square miles. Located at 39.88° N. Lat; 75.33° W. Long. Elevation is 92 feet.

Population: 7,586 (1990); 7,196 (2000); 7,002 (2010); Density: 6,491.7 persons per square mile (2010); Race: 95.3% White, 2.0% Black, 1.2% Asian, 0.1% American Indian/Alaska Native, 0.0% Native Hawaiian/Other Pacific Islander, 1.4% Other, 1.4% Hispanic of any race (2010); Average household size: 2.34 (2010); Median age: 43.4 (2010); Males per 100 females: 93.5 (2010); Marriage status: 29.8% never married, 49.8% now married, 8.3% widowed, 12.1% divorced (2006-2010 5-year est.); Foreign born: 3.2% (2006-2010 5-year est.); Ancestry (includes multiple ancestries): 46.8% Irish, 26.7% Italian, 23.7% German, 12.3% English, 7.8% Polish (2006-2010 5-year est.).

Economy: Single-family building permits issued: 0 (2011); Multi-family building permits issued: 0 (2011); Employment by occupation: 10.3% management, 6.5% professional, 7.0% services, 23.5% sales, 4.9% farming, 9.3% construction, 6.3% production (2006-2010 5-year est.).

Income: Per capita income: $30,121 (2006-2010 5-year est.); Median household income: $60,561 (2006-2010 5-year est.); Average household income: $71,001 (2006-2010 5-year est.); Percent of households with income of $100,000 or more: 21.9% (2006-2010 5-year est.); Poverty rate: 6.4% (2006-2010 5-year est.).

Education: Percent of population age 25 and over with: High school diploma (including GED) or higher: 92.0% (2006-2010 5-year est.); Bachelor's degree or higher: 25.6% (2006-2010 5-year est.); Master's degree or higher: 7.4% (2006-2010 5-year est.).

School District(s)

Ridley SD (KG-12)
    2010-11 Enrollment: 5,847 . . . . (610) 534-1900

Housing: Homeownership rate: 67.0% (2010); Median home value: $215,500 (2006-2010 5-year est.); Median contract rent: $761 per month (2006-2010 5-year est.); Median year structure built: 1953 (2006-2010 5-year est.).

Hospitals: Taylor Hospital (151 beds)

Safety: Violent crime rate: 14.2 per 10,000 population; Property crime rate: 112.5 per 10,000 population (2011).

Transportation: Commute to work: 87.2% car, 6.5% public transportation, 1.9% walk, 2.7% work from home (2006-2010 5-year est.); Travel time to work: 27.5% less than 15 minutes, 31.5% 15 to 30 minutes, 22.0% 30 to 45 minutes, 11.2% 45 to 60 minutes, 7.8% 60 minutes or more (2006-2010 5-year est.)

Additional Information Contacts

Borough of Ridley Park . . . . (610) 532-2100
    http://www.ridleyparkborough.org
Delaware County Chamber of Commerce. . . . . (610) 565-3677
    http://www.delcochamber.org

ROSE VALLEY (borough). Covers a land area of 0.732 square miles and a water area of 0 square miles. Located at 39.89° N. Lat; 75.39° W. Long. Elevation is 115 feet.

Population: 982 (1990); 944 (2000); 913 (2010); Density: 1,247.2 persons per square mile (2010); Race: 93.1% White, 1.6% Black, 2.8% Asian, 0.1% American Indian/Alaska Native, 0.0% Native Hawaiian/Other Pacific Islander, 2.4% Other, 2.1% Hispanic of any race (2010); Average household size: 2.57 (2010); Median age: 50.6 (2010); Males per 100 females: 98.5 (2010); Marriage status: 22.8% never married, 72.0% now married, 1.9% widowed, 3.3% divorced (2006-2010 5-year est.); Foreign born: 7.0% (2006-2010 5-year est.); Ancestry (includes multiple ancestries): 23.6% Irish, 20.9% German, 17.6% English, 11.6% Italian, 5.4% Ukrainian (2006-2010 5-year est.).

Economy: Single-family building permits issued: 0 (2011); Multi-family building permits issued: 0 (2011); Employment by occupation: 23.2%

management, 3.6% professional, 3.4% services, 8.0% sales, 5.3% farming, 5.1% construction, 2.3% production (2006-2010 5-year est.).

Income: Per capita income: $69,535 (2006-2010 5-year est.); Median household income: $151,477 (2006-2010 5-year est.); Average household income: $186,421 (2006-2010 5-year est.); Percent of households with income of $100,000 or more: 69.0% (2006-2010 5-year est.); Poverty rate: 3.9% (2006-2010 5-year est.).

Education: Percent of population age 25 and over with: High school diploma (including GED) or higher: 98.0% (2006-2010 5-year est.); Bachelor's degree or higher: 73.1% (2006-2010 5-year est.); Master's degree or higher: 43.8% (2006-2010 5-year est.).

Housing: Homeownership rate: 96.9% (2010); Median home value: $482,300 (2006-2010 5-year est.); Median contract rent: $783 per month (2006-2010 5-year est.); Median year structure built: 1958 (2006-2010 5-year est.).

Transportation: Commute to work: 80.0% car, 7.5% public transportation, 1.7% walk, 9.8% work from home (2006-2010 5-year est.); Travel time to work: 23.2% less than 15 minutes, 25.3% 15 to 30 minutes, 40.6% 30 to 45 minutes, 4.5% 45 to 60 minutes, 6.4% 60 minutes or more (2006-2010 5-year est.)

RUTLEDGE (borough). Covers a land area of 0.143 square miles and a water area of 0 square miles. Located at 39.90° N. Lat; 75.33° W. Long. Elevation is 131 feet.

Population: 843 (1990); 860 (2000); 784 (2010); Density: 5,483.0 persons per square mile (2010); Race: 91.7% White, 2.9% Black, 3.1% Asian, 0.0% American Indian/Alaska Native, 0.0% Native Hawaiian/Other Pacific Islander, 2.3% Other, 1.8% Hispanic of any race (2010); Average household size: 2.77 (2010); Median age: 43.1 (2010); Males per 100 females: 92.6 (2010); Marriage status: 37.0% never married, 53.8% now married, 4.9% widowed, 4.3% divorced (2006-2010 5-year est.); Foreign born: 6.2% (2006-2010 5-year est.); Ancestry (includes multiple ancestries): 32.6% Irish, 22.9% English, 21.4% German, 17.7% Italian, 6.4% Scotch-Irish (2006-2010 5-year est.).

Economy: Single-family building permits issued: 0 (2011); Multi-family building permits issued: 0 (2011); Employment by occupation: 12.1% management, 5.2% professional, 12.3% services, 17.1% sales, 1.6% farming, 10.2% construction, 6.2% production (2006-2010 5-year est.).

Income: Per capita income: $33,774 (2006-2010 5-year est.); Median household income: $96,146 (2006-2010 5-year est.); Average household income: $104,631 (2006-2010 5-year est.); Percent of households with income of $100,000 or more: 47.8% (2006-2010 5-year est.); Poverty rate: 1.3% (2006-2010 5-year est.).

Education: Percent of population age 25 and over with: High school diploma (including GED) or higher: 94.3% (2006-2010 5-year est.); Bachelor's degree or higher: 44.8% (2006-2010 5-year est.); Master's degree or higher: 18.2% (2006-2010 5-year est.).

Housing: Homeownership rate: 86.5% (2010); Median home value: $293,100 (2006-2010 5-year est.); Median contract rent: $695 per month (2006-2010 5-year est.); Median year structure built: before 1940 (2006-2010 5-year est.).

Transportation: Commute to work: 82.2% car, 10.5% public transportation, 2.3% walk, 0.7% work from home (2006-2010 5-year est.); Travel time to work: 24.1% less than 15 minutes, 31.6% 15 to 30 minutes, 24.6% 30 to 45 minutes, 14.5% 45 to 60 minutes, 5.2% 60 minutes or more (2006-2010 5-year est.)

SHARON HILL (borough). Covers a land area of 0.772 square miles and a water area of 0 square miles. Located at 39.91° N. Lat; 75.27° W. Long. Elevation is 75 feet.

Population: 5,771 (1990); 5,468 (2000); 5,697 (2010); Density: 7,382.8 persons per square mile (2010); Race: 32.6% White, 60.6% Black, 2.1% Asian, 0.3% American Indian/Alaska Native, 0.0% Native Hawaiian/Other Pacific Islander, 4.4% Other, 3.2% Hispanic of any race (2010); Average household size: 2.70 (2010); Median age: 34.2 (2010); Males per 100 females: 86.4 (2010); Marriage status: 40.3% never married, 40.9% now married, 8.1% widowed, 10.7% divorced (2006-2010 5-year est.); Foreign born: 11.3% (2006-2010 5-year est.); Ancestry (includes multiple ancestries): 18.2% Irish, 12.2% Italian, 9.3% German, 4.6% English, 3.5% Other Subsaharan African (2006-2010 5-year est.).

Economy: Single-family building permits issued: 0 (2011); Multi-family building permits issued: 0 (2011); Employment by occupation: 11.6% management, 0.8% professional, 12.3% services, 15.3% sales, 2.2% farming, 8.0% construction, 2.6% production (2006-2010 5-year est.).

Income: Per capita income: $20,955 (2006-2010 5-year est.); Median household income: $46,389 (2006-2010 5-year est.); Average household income: $52,711 (2006-2010 5-year est.); Percent of households with income of $100,000 or more: 9.4% (2006-2010 5-year est.); Poverty rate: 12.9% (2006-2010 5-year est.).

Education: Percent of population age 25 and over with: High school diploma (including GED) or higher: 91.0% (2006-2010 5-year est.); Bachelor's degree or higher: 20.7% (2006-2010 5-year est.); Master's degree or higher: 6.5% (2006-2010 5-year est.).

School District(s)

Southeast Delco SD (KG-12)
   2010-11 Enrollment: 4,051 . . . . (610) 522-4300

Vocational/Technical School(s)

Venus Beauty Academy (Private, For-profit)
   Fall 2010 Enrollment: 122 . . . . (610) 586-2500
   2011-12 Tuition: $15,725

Housing: Homeownership rate: 70.0% (2010); Median home value: $117,800 (2006-2010 5-year est.); Median contract rent: $670 per month (2006-2010 5-year est.); Median year structure built: 1948 (2006-2010 5-year est.).

Safety: Violent crime rate: 113.7 per 10,000 population; Property crime rate: 414.7 per 10,000 population (2011).

Transportation: Commute to work: 78.8% car, 10.6% public transportation, 7.6% walk, 0.7% work from home (2006-2010 5-year est.); Travel time to work: 16.5% less than 15 minutes, 48.3% 15 to 30 minutes, 17.4% 30 to 45 minutes, 6.6% 45 to 60 minutes, 11.2% 60 minutes or more (2006-2010 5-year est.)

Additional Information Contacts

Borough of Sharon Hill . . . . (610) 586-8200
   http://www.sharonhillboro.com
Greater Philadelphia Chamber of Commerce . . . . (215) 545-1234
   http://www.greaterphilachamber.com

SPRINGFIELD (township). Covers a land area of 6.321 square miles and a water area of 0.018 square miles. Located at 39.93° N. Lat; 75.34° W. Long. Elevation is 249 feet.

Population: 24,172 (1990); 23,677 (2000); 24,211 (2010); Density: 3,830.5 persons per square mile (2010); Race: 93.4% White, 1.7% Black, 3.8% Asian, 0.1% American Indian/Alaska Native, 0.0% Native Hawaiian/Other Pacific Islander, 1.0% Other, 1.1% Hispanic of any race (2010); Average household size: 2.76 (2010); Median age: 43.2 (2010); Males per 100 females: 93.1 (2010); Marriage status: 25.5% never married, 58.9% now married, 9.1% widowed, 6.5% divorced (2006-2010 5-year est.); Foreign born: 4.4% (2006-2010 5-year est.); Ancestry (includes multiple ancestries): 43.4% Irish, 31.1% Italian, 19.1% German, 10.7% English, 4.0% Polish (2006-2010 5-year est.).

Economy: Single-family building permits issued: 4 (2011); Multi-family building permits issued: 0 (2011); Employment by occupation: 15.5% management, 5.8% professional, 5.6% services, 18.3% sales, 3.6% farming, 8.0% construction, 4.4% production (2006-2010 5-year est.).

Income: Per capita income: $36,391 (2006-2010 5-year est.); Median household income: $88,613 (2006-2010 5-year est.); Average household income: $102,141 (2006-2010 5-year est.); Percent of households with income of $100,000 or more: 45.3% (2006-2010 5-year est.); Poverty rate: 3.8% (2006-2010 5-year est.).

Education: Percent of population age 25 and over with: High school diploma (including GED) or higher: 94.1% (2006-2010 5-year est.); Bachelor's degree or higher: 40.4% (2006-2010 5-year est.); Master's degree or higher: 13.1% (2006-2010 5-year est.).

School District(s)

Springfield SD (KG-12)
   2010-11 Enrollment: 3,675 . . . . (610) 938-6004

Vocational/Technical School(s)

Anthem Institute-Springfield (Private, For-profit)
   Fall 2010 Enrollment: 590 . . . . (610) 338-2300
   2011-12 Tuition: $15,112
Empire Beauty School-Springfield (Private, For-profit)
   Fall 2010 Enrollment: 209 . . . . (800) 233-3271
   2011-12 Tuition: $15,120

Housing: Homeownership rate: 91.1% (2010); Median home value: $298,600 (2006-2010 5-year est.); Median contract rent: $903 per month (2006-2010 5-year est.); Median year structure built: 1955 (2006-2010 5-year est.).

Hospitals: Crozer-Chester Medical Center (424 beds); Springfield Hospital

Safety: Violent crime rate: 6.2 per 10,000 population; Property crime rate: 320.7 per 10,000 population (2011).

Transportation: Commute to work: 89.1% car, 6.3% public transportation, 1.0% walk, 3.0% work from home (2006-2010 5-year est.); Travel time to work: 18.5% less than 15 minutes, 31.4% 15 to 30 minutes, 28.4% 30 to 45 minutes, 14.0% 45 to 60 minutes, 7.6% 60 minutes or more (2006-2010 5-year est.)

Additional Information Contacts

Delaware County Chamber of Commerce. . . . . (610) 565-3677
   http://www.delcochamber.org
Springfield Township. . . . . (610) 544-1300
   http://www.springfielddelco.org

SWARTHMORE (borough). Covers a land area of 1.400 square miles and a water area of 0 square miles. Located at 39.90° N. Lat; 75.35° W. Long. Elevation is 128 feet.

History: Swarthmore was originally named Westdale in honor of noted painter Benjamin West, who was one of the early residents of the town. The name was changed to Swarthmore after the establishment of Swarthmore College.

Population: 6,157 (1990); 6,170 (2000); 6,194 (2010); Density: 4,424.6 persons per square mile (2010); Race: 82.5% White, 5.0% Black, 7.7% Asian, 0.3% American Indian/Alaska Native, 0.1% Native Hawaiian/Other Pacific Islander, 4.4% Other, 4.9% Hispanic of any race (2010); Average household size: 2.48 (2010); Median age: 30.8 (2010); Males per 100 females: 89.5 (2010); Marriage status: 43.6% never married, 49.5% now married, 4.4% widowed, 2.5% divorced (2006-2010 5-year est.); Foreign born: 14.6% (2006-2010 5-year est.); Ancestry (includes multiple ancestries): 17.5% German, 17.5% Irish, 17.3% English, 5.5% Scotch-Irish, 5.2% Italian (2006-2010 5-year est.).

Economy: Single-family building permits issued: 0 (2011); Multi-family building permits issued: 0 (2011); Employment by occupation: 14.3% management, 5.0% professional, 9.2% services, 11.3% sales, 4.8% farming, 0.6% construction, 1.1% production (2006-2010 5-year est.).

Income: Per capita income: $48,350 (2006-2010 5-year est.); Median household income: $119,342 (2006-2010 5-year est.); Average household income: $154,120 (2006-2010 5-year est.); Percent of households with income of $100,000 or more: 57.2% (2006-2010 5-year est.); Poverty rate: 4.2% (2006-2010 5-year est.).

Education: Percent of population age 25 and over with: High school diploma (including GED) or higher: 96.7% (2006-2010 5-year est.); Bachelor's degree or higher: 80.9% (2006-2010 5-year est.); Master's degree or higher: 57.7% (2006-2010 5-year est.).

School District(s)

Ridley SD (KG-12)
   2010-11 Enrollment: 5,847 . . . . (610) 534-1900
Wallingford-Swarthmore SD (KG-12)
   2010-11 Enrollment: 3,432 . . . . (610) 892-3470

Four-year College(s)

Swarthmore College (Private, Not-for-profit)
   Fall 2010 Enrollment: 1,556 . . . . (610) 328-8000
   2011-12 Tuition: In-state $41,150; Out-of-state $41,150

Housing: Homeownership rate: 71.8% (2010); Median home value: $432,500 (2006-2010 5-year est.); Median contract rent: $910 per month (2006-2010 5-year est.); Median year structure built: 1947 (2006-2010 5-year est.).

Newspapers: Swarthmorean (Community news; Circulation 2,400)

Transportation: Commute to work: 52.2% car, 13.6% public transportation, 22.8% walk, 10.2% work from home (2006-2010 5-year est.); Travel time to work: 40.5% less than 15 minutes, 19.8% 15 to 30 minutes, 21.0% 30 to 45 minutes, 14.8% 45 to 60 minutes, 3.9% 60 minutes or more (2006-2010 5-year est.)

Additional Information Contacts

Borough of Swarthmore . . . . (610) 891-4000
   http://www.co.delaware.pa.us
Delaware County Chamber of Commerce. . . . . (610) 565-3677
   http://www.delcochamber.org

THORNBURY (township). Covers a land area of 9.237 square miles and a water area of 0.032 square miles. Located at 39.92° N. Lat; 75.52° W. Long.

History: The Court of Equity in Chester recognized a separate Thornbury Township in 1687, and appointed township officers. At the time, the area was only in Chester County, one of the original counties chartered by William Penn; Delaware County had not yet been formed. Thornbury was

named after the English birthplace of the wife of George Pearce, who in 1685 had been granted title to 490 acres (198 hectares) in the Township. **Population:** 5,382 (1990); 7,093 (2000); 8,028 (2010); Density: 869.1 persons per square mile (2010); Race: 72.4% White, 20.6% Black, 4.1% Asian, 0.2% American Indian/Alaska Native, 0.0% Native Hawaiian/Other Pacific Islander, 2.7% Other, 2.4% Hispanic of any race (2010); Average household size: 2.98 (2010); Median age: 30.1 (2010); Males per 100 females: 117.2 (2010); Marriage status: 40.6% never married, 51.2% now married, 3.0% widowed, 5.2% divorced (2006-2010 5-year est.); Foreign born: 3.1% (2006-2010 5-year est.); Ancestry (includes multiple ancestries): 28.2% Irish, 22.0% Italian, 18.5% German, 10.4% English, 5.5% Polish (2006-2010 5-year est.).
Economy: Single-family building permits issued: 4 (2011); Multi-family building permits issued: 0 (2011); Employment by occupation: 25.4% management, 5.3% professional, 6.2% services, 18.3% sales, 3.0% farming, 5.3% construction, 2.0% production (2006-2010 5-year est.).
Income: Per capita income: $39,986 (2006-2010 5-year est.); Median household income: $112,146 (2006-2010 5-year est.); Average household income: $138,569 (2006-2010 5-year est.); Percent of households with income of $100,000 or more: 58.6% (2006-2010 5-year est.); Poverty rate: 2.6% (2006-2010 5-year est.).
Education: Percent of population age 25 and over with: High school diploma (including GED) or higher: 97.9% (2006-2010 5-year est.); Bachelor's degree or higher: 59.7% (2006-2010 5-year est.); Master's degree or higher: 28.3% (2006-2010 5-year est.).
Housing: Homeownership rate: 91.1% (2010); Median home value: $489,300 (2006-2010 5-year est.); Median contract rent: $975 per month (2006-2010 5-year est.); Median year structure built: 1987 (2006-2010 5-year est.).
Transportation: Commute to work: 84.5% car, 2.4% public transportation, 3.6% walk, 8.4% work from home (2006-2010 5-year est.); Travel time to work: 28.9% less than 15 minutes, 36.6% 15 to 30 minutes, 21.0% 30 to 45 minutes, 6.1% 45 to 60 minutes, 7.4% 60 minutes or more (2006-2010 5-year est.)
Additional Information Contacts
Delaware County Chamber of Commerce. . . . . (610) 565-3677
    http://www.delcochamber.org
Thornbury Township . . . . (610) 399-8383
    http://thornbury.websecurestores.net

THORNTON (unincorporated postal area)
Zip Code: 19373
    Covers a land area of 4.142 square miles and a water area of 0.014 square miles. Located at 39.90° N. Lat; 75.53° W. Long. Elevation is 459 feet. Population: 4,273 (2010); Density: 1,031.4 persons per square mile (2010); Race: 73.9% White, 21.7% Black, 2.3% Asian, 0.2% American Indian/Alaska Native, 0.0% Native Hawaiian/Other Pacific Islander, 1.9% Other, 1.9% Hispanic of any race (2010); Average household size: 3.18 (2010); Median age: 34.8 (2010); Males per 100 females: 181.9 (2010); Homeownership rate: 94.9% (2010)

TINICUM (township). Covers a land area of 5.769 square miles and a water area of 3.015 square miles. Located at 39.86° N. Lat; 75.26° W. Long.
Population: 4,440 (1990); 4,353 (2000); 4,091 (2010); Density: 709.2 persons per square mile (2010); Race: 93.7% White, 1.7% Black, 2.0% Asian, 0.2% American Indian/Alaska Native, 0.0% Native Hawaiian/Other Pacific Islander, 2.4% Other, 2.2% Hispanic of any race (2010); Average household size: 2.42 (2010); Median age: 41.9 (2010); Males per 100 females: 103.4 (2010); Marriage status: 34.6% never married, 42.1% now married, 8.5% widowed, 14.8% divorced (2006-2010 5-year est.); Foreign born: 3.1% (2006-2010 5-year est.); Ancestry (includes multiple ancestries): 36.4% Irish, 28.7% German, 20.1% Italian, 13.0% Polish, 8.8% English (2006-2010 5-year est.).
Economy: Single-family building permits issued: 0 (2011); Multi-family building permits issued: 0 (2011); Employment by occupation: 6.6% management, 6.4% professional, 4.2% services, 16.1% sales, 4.2% farming, 15.3% construction, 10.5% production (2006-2010 5-year est.).
Income: Per capita income: $26,793 (2006-2010 5-year est.); Median household income: $46,848 (2006-2010 5-year est.); Average household income: $64,241 (2006-2010 5-year est.); Percent of households with income of $100,000 or more: 19.4% (2006-2010 5-year est.); Poverty rate: 10.0% (2006-2010 5-year est.).
Taxes: Total city taxes per capita: $1,727 (2009); City property taxes per capita: $440 (2009).

Education: Percent of population age 25 and over with: High school diploma (including GED) or higher: 88.5% (2006-2010 5-year est.); Bachelor's degree or higher: 10.6% (2006-2010 5-year est.); Master's degree or higher: 2.4% (2006-2010 5-year est.).
Housing: Homeownership rate: 67.7% (2010); Median home value: $165,400 (2006-2010 5-year est.); Median contract rent: $677 per month (2006-2010 5-year est.); Median year structure built: 1953 (2006-2010 5-year est.).
Safety: Violent crime rate: 63.4 per 10,000 population; Property crime rate: 521.4 per 10,000 population (2011).
Transportation: Commute to work: 92.0% car, 2.2% public transportation, 4.0% walk, 1.8% work from home (2006-2010 5-year est.); Travel time to work: 38.2% less than 15 minutes, 31.0% 15 to 30 minutes, 18.5% 30 to 45 minutes, 7.9% 45 to 60 minutes, 4.4% 60 minutes or more (2006-2010 5-year est.)
Additional Information Contacts
Delaware County Chamber of Commerce. . . . . (610) 565-3677
    http://www.delcochamber.org

TRAINER (borough). Covers a land area of 1.059 square miles and a water area of 0.315 square miles. Located at 39.82° N. Lat; 75.40° W. Long. Elevation is 72 feet.
Population: 2,085 (1990); 1,901 (2000); 1,828 (2010); Density: 1,725.7 persons per square mile (2010); Race: 76.4% White, 18.9% Black, 0.5% Asian, 0.3% American Indian/Alaska Native, 0.0% Native Hawaiian/Other Pacific Islander, 3.9% Other, 5.5% Hispanic of any race (2010); Average household size: 2.92 (2010); Median age: 33.2 (2010); Males per 100 females: 92.2 (2010); Marriage status: 36.5% never married, 45.8% now married, 6.2% widowed, 11.5% divorced (2006-2010 5-year est.); Foreign born: 2.6% (2006-2010 5-year est.); Ancestry (includes multiple ancestries): 25.4% Irish, 19.3% Italian, 14.9% German, 11.0% English, 8.0% Polish (2006-2010 5-year est.).
Economy: Single-family building permits issued: 0 (2011); Multi-family building permits issued: 0 (2011); Employment by occupation: 6.2% management, 2.3% professional, 11.3% services, 18.7% sales, 4.8% farming, 17.0% construction, 6.6% production (2006-2010 5-year est.).
Income: Per capita income: $20,728 (2006-2010 5-year est.); Median household income: $44,667 (2006-2010 5-year est.); Average household income: $52,455 (2006-2010 5-year est.); Percent of households with income of $100,000 or more: 11.5% (2006-2010 5-year est.); Poverty rate: 14.3% (2006-2010 5-year est.).
Education: Percent of population age 25 and over with: High school diploma (including GED) or higher: 77.9% (2006-2010 5-year est.); Bachelor's degree or higher: 8.6% (2006-2010 5-year est.); Master's degree or higher: 2.8% (2006-2010 5-year est.).
Housing: Homeownership rate: 72.6% (2010); Median home value: $106,300 (2006-2010 5-year est.); Median contract rent: $813 per month (2006-2010 5-year est.); Median year structure built: 1953 (2006-2010 5-year est.).
Transportation: Commute to work: 90.9% car, 1.5% public transportation, 5.1% walk, 2.4% work from home (2006-2010 5-year est.); Travel time to work: 42.9% less than 15 minutes, 32.0% 15 to 30 minutes, 14.8% 30 to 45 minutes, 5.3% 45 to 60 minutes, 5.0% 60 minutes or more (2006-2010 5-year est.)
Additional Information Contacts
Delaware County Chamber of Commerce. . . . . (610) 565-3677
    http://www.delcochamber.org

UPLAND (borough). Covers a land area of 0.649 square miles and a water area of 0 square miles. Located at 39.86° N. Lat; 75.38° W. Long. Elevation is 33 feet.
Population: 3,334 (1990); 2,977 (2000); 3,239 (2010); Density: 4,991.9 persons per square mile (2010); Race: 51.3% White, 41.3% Black, 0.8% Asian, 0.3% American Indian/Alaska Native, 0.1% Native Hawaiian/Other Pacific Islander, 6.2% Other, 5.8% Hispanic of any race (2010); Average household size: 2.62 (2010); Median age: 33.8 (2010); Males per 100 females: 85.4 (2010); Marriage status: 36.2% never married, 38.8% now married, 9.4% widowed, 15.6% divorced (2006-2010 5-year est.); Foreign born: 2.4% (2006-2010 5-year est.); Ancestry (includes multiple ancestries): 22.3% Irish, 13.1% Italian, 11.1% German, 10.0% English, 5.1% Polish (2006-2010 5-year est.).
Economy: Single-family building permits issued: 0 (2011); Multi-family building permits issued: 0 (2011); Employment by occupation: 10.0% management, 6.2% professional, 8.0% services, 15.4% sales, 10.0% farming, 12.0% construction, 9.1% production (2006-2010 5-year est.).

Income: Per capita income: $20,317 (2006-2010 5-year est.); Median household income: $42,206 (2006-2010 5-year est.); Average household income: $49,599 (2006-2010 5-year est.); Percent of households with income of $100,000 or more: 8.9% (2006-2010 5-year est.); Poverty rate: 22.9% (2006-2010 5-year est.).

Education: Percent of population age 25 and over with: High school diploma (including GED) or higher: 87.7% (2006-2010 5-year est.); Bachelor's degree or higher: 17.3% (2006-2010 5-year est.); Master's degree or higher: 4.4% (2006-2010 5-year est.).

School District(s)

Chester-Upland SD (PK-12)

   2010-11 Enrollment: 4,244 . . . . (610) 447-3600

Housing: Homeownership rate: 45.5% (2010); Median home value: $103,700 (2006-2010 5-year est.); Median contract rent: $352 per month (2006-2010 5-year est.); Median year structure built: 1956 (2006-2010 5-year est.).

Hospitals: Crozer-Chester Medical Center (422 beds)

Safety: Violent crime rate: 310.9 per 10,000 population; Property crime rate: 440.1 per 10,000 population (2011).

Transportation: Commute to work: 93.4% car, 3.3% public transportation, 0.0% walk, 3.3% work from home (2006-2010 5-year est.); Travel time to work: 28.2% less than 15 minutes, 33.2% 15 to 30 minutes, 24.1% 30 to 45 minutes, 12.4% 45 to 60 minutes, 2.2% 60 minutes or more (2006-2010 5-year est.)

Additional Information Contacts

Delaware County Chamber of Commerce. . . . . (610) 565-3677
  http://www.delcochamber.org

UPPER CHICHESTER (township).

UPPER CHICHESTER (township). Covers a land area of 6.687 square miles and a water area of 0.010 square miles. Located at 39.84° N. Lat; 75.44° W. Long.

Population: 15,004 (1990); 16,842 (2000); 16,738 (2010); Density: 2,503.1 persons per square mile (2010); Race: 84.0% White, 10.7% Black, 2.7% Asian, 0.3% American Indian/Alaska Native, 0.0% Native Hawaiian/Other Pacific Islander, 2.3% Other, 2.4% Hispanic of any race (2010); Average household size: 2.50 (2010); Median age: 41.5 (2010); Males per 100 females: 91.9 (2010); Marriage status: 30.5% never married, 54.4% now married, 7.3% widowed, 7.8% divorced (2006-2010 5-year est.); Foreign born: 5.2% (2006-2010 5-year est.); Ancestry (includes multiple ancestries): 28.9% Irish, 20.2% Italian, 19.0% German, 9.6% English, 8.6% Polish (2006-2010 5-year est.).

Economy: Single-family building permits issued: 17 (2011); Multi-family building permits issued: 0 (2011); Employment by occupation: 12.5% management, 4.3% professional, 7.8% services, 18.2% sales, 3.8% farming, 10.2% construction, 6.4% production (2006-2010 5-year est.).

Income: Per capita income: $29,425 (2006-2010 5-year est.); Median household income: $66,988 (2006-2010 5-year est.); Average household income: $75,512 (2006-2010 5-year est.); Percent of households with income of $100,000 or more: 26.3% (2006-2010 5-year est.); Poverty rate: 7.5% (2006-2010 5-year est.).

Education: Percent of population age 25 and over with: High school diploma (including GED) or higher: 89.0% (2006-2010 5-year est.); Bachelor's degree or higher: 26.0% (2006-2010 5-year est.); Master's degree or higher: 8.9% (2006-2010 5-year est.).

Housing: Homeownership rate: 71.7% (2010); Median home value: $230,900 (2006-2010 5-year est.); Median contract rent: $788 per month (2006-2010 5-year est.); Median year structure built: 1974 (2006-2010 5-year est.).

Safety: Violent crime rate: 28.0 per 10,000 population; Property crime rate: 309.1 per 10,000 population (2011).

Transportation: Commute to work: 91.9% car, 3.1% public transportation, 1.8% walk, 2.2% work from home (2006-2010 5-year est.); Travel time to work: 26.1% less than 15 minutes, 36.3% 15 to 30 minutes, 23.4% 30 to 45 minutes, 7.1% 45 to 60 minutes, 7.0% 60 minutes or more (2006-2010 5-year est.)

Additional Information Contacts

Delaware County Chamber of Commerce. . . . . (610) 565-3677
  http://www.delcochamber.org
Upper Chichester Township . . . . (610) 485-5881
  http://www.upperchichester.org

UPPER DARBY (township).

UPPER DARBY (township). Covers a land area of 7.825 square miles and a water area of 0 square miles. Located at 39.95° N. Lat; 75.29° W. Long. Elevation is 66 feet.

Population: 81,177 (1990); 81,821 (2000); 82,795 (2010); Density: 10,580.3 persons per square mile (2010); Race: 56.6% White, 27.5% Black, 11.1% Asian, 0.2% American Indian/Alaska Native, 0.0% Native Hawaiian/Other Pacific Islander, 4.6% Other, 4.5% Hispanic of any race (2010); Average household size: 2.60 (2010); Median age: 34.7 (2010); Males per 100 females: 92.8 (2010); Marriage status: 37.6% never married, 48.6% now married, 5.7% widowed, 8.1% divorced (2006-2010 5-year est.); Foreign born: 18.4% (2006-2010 5-year est.); Ancestry (includes multiple ancestries): 27.3% Irish, 15.7% Italian, 11.9% German, 5.4% English, 3.3% Polish (2006-2010 5-year est.).

Economy: Unemployment rate: 8.7% (August 2012); Total civilian labor force: 43,588 (August 2012); Single-family building permits issued: 0 (2011); Multi-family building permits issued: 0 (2011); Employment by occupation: 10.6% management, 4.2% professional, 10.8% services, 19.6% sales, 4.4% farming, 6.7% construction, 4.4% production (2006-2010 5-year est.).

Income: Per capita income: $25,278 (2006-2010 5-year est.); Median household income: $52,572 (2006-2010 5-year est.); Average household income: $65,355 (2006-2010 5-year est.); Percent of households with income of $100,000 or more: 20.0% (2006-2010 5-year est.); Poverty rate: 11.5% (2006-2010 5-year est.).

Taxes: Total city taxes per capita: $527 (2009); City property taxes per capita: $467 (2009).

Education: Percent of population age 25 and over with: High school diploma (including GED) or higher: 87.8% (2006-2010 5-year est.); Bachelor's degree or higher: 29.7% (2006-2010 5-year est.); Master's degree or higher: 11.1% (2006-2010 5-year est.).

School District(s)

Upper Darby SD (KG-12)

   2010-11 Enrollment: 12,269 . . . . (610) 789-7200

Two-year College(s)

PJA School (Private, For-profit)

   Fall 2010 Enrollment: 893 . . . . (610) 789-6700
   2011-12 Tuition: In-state $22,915; Out-of-state $22,915

Vocational/Technical School(s)

Harris School of Business-Upper Darby Campus (Private, For-profit)

   Fall 2010 Enrollment: 824 . . . . (484) 463-3800
   2011-12 Tuition: $12,875

Housing: Homeownership rate: 60.5% (2010); Median home value: $163,600 (2006-2010 5-year est.); Median contract rent: $753 per month (2006-2010 5-year est.); Median year structure built: 1948 (2006-2010 5-year est.).

Safety: Violent crime rate: 50.9 per 10,000 population; Property crime rate: 268.8 per 10,000 population (2011).

Newspapers: El Hispano (Regional news; Circulation 48,000)

Transportation: Commute to work: 78.1% car, 14.9% public transportation, 3.3% walk, 2.4% work from home (2006-2010 5-year est.); Travel time to work: 17.3% less than 15 minutes, 27.6% 15 to 30 minutes, 29.7% 30 to 45 minutes, 14.9% 45 to 60 minutes, 10.5% 60 minutes or more (2006-2010 5-year est.)

Additional Information Contacts

Delaware County Chamber of Commerce. . . . . (610) 565-3677
  http://www.delcochamber.org
Upper Darby Township . . . . (610) 734-7600
  http://www.upperdarby.org

UPPER PROVIDENCE (township).

UPPER PROVIDENCE (township). Covers a land area of 5.602 square miles and a water area of 0.207 square miles. Located at 39.94° N. Lat; 75.40° W. Long. Elevation is 328 feet.

History: The area was settled about 1683 and formed into Providence Township. On October 17, 1683, the residents of Providence Township petitioned the Court of Chester County, of which they were then a part, to establish a road from Providence to Chester.

Population: 9,727 (1990); 10,509 (2000); 10,142 (2010); Density: 1,810.3 persons per square mile (2010); Race: 89.8% White, 3.9% Black, 4.3% Asian, 0.0% American Indian/Alaska Native, 0.0% Native Hawaiian/Other Pacific Islander, 2.0% Other, 1.5% Hispanic of any race (2010); Average household size: 2.45 (2010); Median age: 43.9 (2010); Males per 100 females: 96.0 (2010); Marriage status: 29.6% never married, 59.7% now married, 5.5% widowed, 5.3% divorced (2006-2010 5-year est.); Foreign born: 7.7% (2006-2010 5-year est.); Ancestry (includes multiple

ancestries): 33.4% Irish, 20.8% Italian, 19.9% German, 9.8% English, 5.8% Polish (2006-2010 5-year est.).

Economy: Single-family building permits issued: 29 (2011); Multi-family building permits issued: 0 (2011); Employment by occupation: 18.8% management, 7.2% professional, 6.4% services, 15.2% sales, 3.6% farming, 4.8% construction, 2.9% production (2006-2010 5-year est.).

Income: Per capita income: $46,756 (2006-2010 5-year est.); Median household income: $88,073 (2006-2010 5-year est.); Average household income: $118,562 (2006-2010 5-year est.); Percent of households with income of $100,000 or more: 44.2% (2006-2010 5-year est.); Poverty rate: 2.5% (2006-2010 5-year est.).

Education: Percent of population age 25 and over with: High school diploma (including GED) or higher: 97.2% (2006-2010 5-year est.); Bachelor's degree or higher: 55.1% (2006-2010 5-year est.); Master's degree or higher: 25.5% (2006-2010 5-year est.).

Housing: Homeownership rate: 74.1% (2010); Median home value: $429,900 (2006-2010 5-year est.); Median contract rent: $849 per month (2006-2010 5-year est.); Median year structure built: 1967 (2006-2010 5-year est.).

Transportation: Commute to work: 87.0% car, 5.7% public transportation, 0.7% walk, 6.4% work from home (2006-2010 5-year est.); Travel time to work: 22.1% less than 15 minutes, 32.4% 15 to 30 minutes, 27.2% 30 to 45 minutes, 11.3% 45 to 60 minutes, 7.0% 60 minutes or more (2006-2010 5-year est.)

Additional Information Contacts

Delaware County Chamber of Commerce. . . . . (610) 565-3677
   http://www.delcochamber.org
Upper Providence Township . . . . (610) 565-4944
   http://www.upperprovidence.org

VILLAGE GREEN-GREEN RIDGE (CDP). Covers a land area of 1.871 square miles and a water area of 0 square miles. Located at 39.86° N. Lat; 75.43° W. Long.

Population: 9,026 (1990); 8,279 (2000); 7,822 (2010); Density: 4,181.5 persons per square mile (2010); Race: 96.6% White, 1.4% Black, 0.7% Asian, 0.1% American Indian/Alaska Native, 0.0% Native Hawaiian/Other Pacific Islander, 1.2% Other, 1.8% Hispanic of any race (2010); Average household size: 2.58 (2010); Median age: 43.1 (2010); Males per 100 females: 94.9 (2010); Marriage status: 26.4% never married, 56.2% now married, 7.4% widowed, 10.0% divorced (2006-2010 5-year est.); Foreign born: 2.4% (2006-2010 5-year est.); Ancestry (includes multiple ancestries): 35.1% Irish, 29.7% Italian, 21.5% German, 15.5% English, 9.9% Polish (2006-2010 5-year est.).

Economy: Employment by occupation: 13.2% management, 5.5% professional, 6.3% services, 15.1% sales, 4.1% farming, 11.4% construction, 7.6% production (2006-2010 5-year est.).

Income: Per capita income: $32,386 (2006-2010 5-year est.); Median household income: $69,787 (2006-2010 5-year est.); Average household income: $83,129 (2006-2010 5-year est.); Percent of households with income of $100,000 or more: 30.3% (2006-2010 5-year est.); Poverty rate: 5.6% (2006-2010 5-year est.).

Education: Percent of population age 25 and over with: High school diploma (including GED) or higher: 88.2% (2006-2010 5-year est.); Bachelor's degree or higher: 19.6% (2006-2010 5-year est.); Master's degree or higher: 6.0% (2006-2010 5-year est.).

Housing: Homeownership rate: 88.0% (2010); Median home value: $239,800 (2006-2010 5-year est.); Median contract rent: $751 per month (2006-2010 5-year est.); Median year structure built: 1960 (2006-2010 5-year est.).

Transportation: Commute to work: 95.1% car, 2.2% public transportation, 1.1% walk, 1.1% work from home (2006-2010 5-year est.); Travel time to work: 27.3% less than 15 minutes, 41.5% 15 to 30 minutes, 18.9% 30 to 45 minutes, 8.2% 45 to 60 minutes, 4.1% 60 minutes or more (2006-2010 5-year est.)

Additional Information Contacts

Delaware County Chamber of Commerce. . . . . (610) 565-3677
   http://www.delcochamber.org

VILLANOVA (unincorporated postal area)

Zip Code: 19085

Covers a land area of 6.043 square miles and a water area of 0.004 square miles. Located at 40.03° N. Lat; 75.34° W. Long. Elevation is 394 feet. Population: 8,932 (2010); Density: 1,477.9 persons per square mile (2010); Race: 89.1% White, 2.8% Black, 5.6% Asian, 0.0% American Indian/Alaska Native, 0.0% Native Hawaiian/Other Pacific

Islander, 2.5% Other, 3.2% Hispanic of any race (2010); Average household size: 2.89 (2010); Median age: 21.3 (2010); Males per 100 females: 92.1 (2010); Homeownership rate: 93.9% (2010)

WALLINGFORD (unincorporated postal area)

Zip Code: 19086

Covers a land area of 3.853 square miles and a water area of 0 square miles. Located at 39.89° N. Lat; 75.37° W. Long. Elevation is 131 feet. Population: 11,420 (2010); Density: 2,963.9 persons per square mile (2010); Race: 88.7% White, 3.9% Black, 5.2% Asian, 0.1% American Indian/Alaska Native, 0.1% Native Hawaiian/Other Pacific Islander, 2.0% Other, 2.0% Hispanic of any race (2010); Average household size: 2.59 (2010); Median age: 44.5 (2010); Males per 100 females: 90.9 (2010); Homeownership rate: 87.4% (2010)

WOODLYN (CDP). Covers a land area of 1.674 square miles and a water area of 0 square miles. Located at 39.88° N. Lat; 75.34° W. Long. Elevation is 66 feet.

Population: 10,157 (1990); 10,036 (2000); 9,485 (2010); Density: 5,665.1 persons per square mile (2010); Race: 85.5% White, 10.6% Black, 1.3% Asian, 0.2% American Indian/Alaska Native, 0.0% Native Hawaiian/Other Pacific Islander, 2.4% Other, 2.3% Hispanic of any race (2010); Average household size: 2.51 (2010); Median age: 39.8 (2010); Males per 100 females: 92.1 (2010); Marriage status: 33.7% never married, 48.1% now married, 7.8% widowed, 10.4% divorced (2006-2010 5-year est.); Foreign born: 3.5% (2006-2010 5-year est.); Ancestry (includes multiple ancestries): 37.9% Irish, 25.0% Italian, 17.9% German, 10.8% English, 5.9% Polish (2006-2010 5-year est.).

Economy: Employment by occupation: 10.6% management, 3.8% professional, 6.5% services, 22.0% sales, 6.5% farming, 9.5% construction, 5.0% production (2006-2010 5-year est.).

Income: Per capita income: $25,256 (2006-2010 5-year est.); Median household income: $53,238 (2006-2010 5-year est.); Average household income: $60,873 (2006-2010 5-year est.); Percent of households with income of $100,000 or more: 16.6% (2006-2010 5-year est.); Poverty rate: 10.6% (2006-2010 5-year est.).

Education: Percent of population age 25 and over with: High school diploma (including GED) or higher: 88.4% (2006-2010 5-year est.); Bachelor's degree or higher: 20.0% (2006-2010 5-year est.); Master's degree or higher: 7.5% (2006-2010 5-year est.).

School District(s)

Ridley SD (KG-12)
   2010-11 Enrollment: 5,847 . . . . (610) 534-1900

Housing: Homeownership rate: 71.7% (2010); Median home value: $196,000 (2006-2010 5-year est.); Median contract rent: $600 per month (2006-2010 5-year est.); Median year structure built: 1955 (2006-2010 5-year est.).

Transportation: Commute to work: 91.8% car, 1.9% public transportation, 5.2% walk, 1.0% work from home (2006-2010 5-year est.); Travel time to work: 33.6% less than 15 minutes, 36.4% 15 to 30 minutes, 21.3% 30 to 45 minutes, 6.8% 45 to 60 minutes, 1.9% 60 minutes or more (2006-2010 5-year est.)

Additional Information Contacts

Delaware County Chamber of Commerce. . . . . (610) 565-3677
   http://www.delcochamber.org

YEADON (borough). Covers a land area of 1.595 square miles and a water area of 0 square miles. Located at 39.93° N. Lat; 75.25° W. Long. Elevation is 112 feet.

Population: 11,980 (1990); 11,762 (2000); 11,443 (2010); Density: 7,175.0 persons per square mile (2010); Race: 7.5% White, 88.6% Black, 0.8% Asian, 0.2% American Indian/Alaska Native, 0.1% Native Hawaiian/Other Pacific Islander, 2.8% Other, 1.9% Hispanic of any race (2010); Average household size: 2.46 (2010); Median age: 38.9 (2010); Males per 100 females: 82.3 (2010); Marriage status: 41.0% never married, 40.2% now married, 9.6% widowed, 9.2% divorced (2006-2010 5-year est.); Foreign born: 13.3% (2006-2010 5-year est.); Ancestry (includes multiple ancestries): 5.3% Liberian, 5.0% Jamaican, 3.4% African, 1.9% Irish, 1.7% Sierra Leonean (2006-2010 5-year est.).

Economy: Single-family building permits issued: 0 (2011); Multi-family building permits issued: 0 (2011); Employment by occupation: 10.3% management, 2.5% professional, 10.2% services, 24.1% sales, 4.5% farming, 4.5% construction, 3.3% production (2006-2010 5-year est.).

Income: Per capita income: $24,676 (2006-2010 5-year est.); Median household income: $46,629 (2006-2010 5-year est.); Average household

income: $56,919 (2006-2010 5-year est.); Percent of households with income of $100,000 or more: 11.9% (2006-2010 5-year est.); Poverty rate: 10.4% (2006-2010 5-year est.).

Education: Percent of population age 25 and over with: High school diploma (including GED) or higher: 88.7% (2006-2010 5-year est.); Bachelor's degree or higher: 26.8% (2006-2010 5-year est.); Master's degree or higher: 11.1% (2006-2010 5-year est.).

School District(s)

William Penn SD (KG-12)
    2010-11 Enrollment: 5,305 . . . . (610) 284-8000

Housing: Homeownership rate: 62.8% (2010); Median home value: $149,500 (2006-2010 5-year est.); Median contract rent: $655 per month (2006-2010 5-year est.); Median year structure built: 1949 (2006-2010 5-year est.).

Safety: Violent crime rate: 61.0 per 10,000 population; Property crime rate: 339.8 per 10,000 population (2011).

Transportation: Commute to work: 73.9% car, 21.7% public transportation, 1.6% walk, 1.1% work from home (2006-2010 5-year est.); Travel time to work: 13.8% less than 15 minutes, 27.7% 15 to 30 minutes, 24.1% 30 to 45 minutes, 20.0% 45 to 60 minutes, 14.3% 60 minutes or more (2006-2010 5-year est.)

Additional Information Contacts

Borough of Yeadon . . . . (610) 284-1606
    http://www.yeadon.boroughs.org/index.htm
Greater Philadelphia Chamber of Commerce . . . . (215) 545-1234
    http://www.greaterphilachamber.com

Elk County

Located in north central Pennsylvania; drained by the Clarion River. Covers a land area of 827.358 square miles, a water area of 4.949 square miles, and is located in the Eastern Time Zone at 41.43° N. Lat., 78.65° W. Long. The county was founded in 1843. County seat is Ridgway.

Elk County is part of the St. Marys, PA Micropolitan Statistical Area. The entire metro area includes: Elk County, PA

Weather Station: Ridgway									Elevation: 1,359 feet		
	Jan	Feb	Mar	Apr	May	Jun	Jul	Aug	Sep	Oct	Nov	Dec
High	32	36	44	58	68	76	80	79	72	60	48	36
Low	14	15	21	31	40	50	54	53	46	36	28	19
Precip	2.9	2.3	3.3	3.6	4.4	4.7	4.9	4.0	3.8	3.4	3.8	3.0
Snow	13.9	10.4	7.6	1.4	tr	0.0	0.0	0.0	0.0	0.3	3.2	10.8

High and Low temperatures in degrees Fahrenheit; Precipitation and Snow in inches

Population: 34,878 (1990); 35,112 (2000); 31,946 (2010); Race: 98.5% White, 0.3% Black, 0.3% Asian, 0.1% American Indian/Alaska Native, 0.0% Native Hawaiian/Other Pacific Islander, 0.8% Other, 0.6% Hispanic of any race (2010); Density: 38.6 persons per square mile (2010); Average household size: 2.31 (2010); Median age: 45.1 (2010); Males per 100 females: 98.7 (2010).

Religion: Six largest groups: 70.4% Catholicism, 7.3% Methodist/Pietist, 4.3% Lutheran, 2.7% Presbyterian-Reformed, 1.4% Holiness, 0.8% Baptist (2010)

Economy: Unemployment rate: 7.2% (August 2012); Total civilian labor force: 17,871 (August 2012); Leading industries: 47.4% manufacturing; 15.1% health care and social assistance; 10.7% retail trade (2010); Farms: 376 totaling 33,258 acres (2007); Companies that employ 500 or more persons: 2 (2010); Companies that employ 100 to 499 persons: 21 (2010); Companies that employ less than 100 persons: 883 (2010); Black-owned businesses: n/a (2007); Hispanic-owned businesses: n/a (2007); Asian-owned businesses: n/a (2007); Women-owned businesses: n/a (2007); Retail sales per capita: $10,104 (2010). Single-family building permits issued: 20 (2011); Multi-family building permits issued: 0 (2011).

Income: Per capita income: $22,729 (2006-2010 5-year est.); Median household income: $43,745 (2006-2010 5-year est.); Average household income: $52,172 (2006-2010 5-year est.); Percent of households with income of $100,000 or more: 10.0% (2006-2010 5-year est.); Poverty rate: 11.0% (2006-2010 5-year est.); Bankruptcy rate: 2.42% (2011).

Education: Percent of population age 25 and over with: High school diploma (including GED) or higher: 89.8% (2006-2010 5-year est.); Bachelor's degree or higher: 16.2% (2006-2010 5-year est.); Master's degree or higher: 4.9% (2006-2010 5-year est.).

Housing: Homeownership rate: 78.5% (2010); Median home value: $91,300 (2006-2010 5-year est.); Median contract rent: $379 per month

(2006-2010 5-year est.); Median year structure built: 1957 (2006-2010 5-year est.)

Health: Birth rate: 82.5 per 10,000 population (2011); Death rate: 119.1 per 10,000 population (2011); Age-adjusted cancer mortality rate: 198.3 deaths per 100,000 population (2009); Number of physicians: 13.5 per 10,000 population (2010); Hospital beds: 67.5 per 10,000 population (2008); Hospital admissions: 1,077.0 per 10,000 population (2008).

Environment: Air Quality Index: 94.3% good, 5.7% moderate, 0.0% unhealthy for sensitive individuals, 0.0% unhealthy (percent of days in 2011)

Elections: 2012 Presidential election results: 41.3% Obama, 57.3% Romney

National and State Parks: Bendigo State Park; Elk State Forest; Elk State Forest; Elk State Park

Additional Information Contacts

Elk County Government . . . . (814) 776-1161
    http://www.co.elk.pa.us
Ridgway-Elk County Chamber of Commerce . . . . (814) 776-1424
    http://www.ridgwaychamber.com

Elk County Communities

BENEZETT (unincorporated postal area)

Zip Code: 15821

    Covers a land area of 35.521 square miles and a water area of 0.257 square miles. Located at 41.35° N. Lat; 78.36° W. Long. Population: 164 (2010); Density: 4.6 persons per square mile (2010); Race: 97.6% White, 0.0% Black, 0.0% Asian, 0.0% American Indian/Alaska Native, 0.0% Native Hawaiian/Other Pacific Islander, 2.4% Other, 0.0% Hispanic of any race (2010); Average household size: 2.05 (2010); Median age: 53.0 (2010); Males per 100 females: 110.3 (2010); Homeownership rate: 91.3% (2010)

BENEZETTE (township). Covers a land area of 106.665 square miles and a water area of 0.489 square miles. Located at 41.30° N. Lat; 78.33° W. Long. Elevation is 991 feet.

Population: 243 (1990); 227 (2000); 207 (2010); Density: 1.9 persons per square mile (2010); Race: 97.1% White, 0.0% Black, 0.0% Asian, 0.0% American Indian/Alaska Native, 0.0% Native Hawaiian/Other Pacific Islander, 2.9% Other, 0.0% Hispanic of any race (2010); Average household size: 1.97 (2010); Median age: 53.1 (2010); Males per 100 females: 115.6 (2010); Marriage status: 24.6% never married, 30.6% now married, 27.9% widowed, 16.9% divorced (2006-2010 5-year est.); Foreign born: 0.0% (2006-2010 5-year est.); Ancestry (includes multiple ancestries): 29.1% English, 27.6% German, 25.6% Irish, 13.8% Italian, 13.3% American (2006-2010 5-year est.).

Economy: Single-family building permits issued: 0 (2011); Multi-family building permits issued: 0 (2011); Employment by occupation: 0.0% management, 0.0% professional, 0.0% services, 45.9% sales, 0.0% farming, 9.8% construction, 6.6% production (2006-2010 5-year est.).

Income: Per capita income: $19,325 (2006-2010 5-year est.); Median household income: $22,292 (2006-2010 5-year est.); Average household income: $31,473 (2006-2010 5-year est.); Percent of households with income of $100,000 or more: 4.1% (2006-2010 5-year est.); Poverty rate: 6.4% (2006-2010 5-year est.).

Education: Percent of population age 25 and over with: High school diploma (including GED) or higher: 81.9% (2006-2010 5-year est.); Bachelor's degree or higher: 7.6% (2006-2010 5-year est.); Master's degree or higher: 1.8% (2006-2010 5-year est.).

Housing: Homeownership rate: 91.4% (2010); Median home value: $77,500 (2006-2010 5-year est.); Median contract rent: n/a per month (2006-2010 5-year est.); Median year structure built: 1970 (2006-2010 5-year est.).

Transportation: Commute to work: 100.0% car, 0.0% public transportation, 0.0% walk, 0.0% work from home (2006-2010 5-year est.); Travel time to work: 15.3% less than 15 minutes, 28.8% 15 to 30 minutes, 30.5% 30 to 45 minutes, 23.7% 45 to 60 minutes, 1.7% 60 minutes or more (2006-2010 5-year est.)

BROCKPORT (unincorporated postal area)

Zip Code: 15823

    Covers a land area of 36.841 square miles and a water area of 0.092 square miles. Located at 41.25° N. Lat; 78.71° W. Long. Elevation is 1,473 feet. Population: 1,431 (2010); Density: 38.8 persons per square mile (2010); Race: 99.0% White, 0.0% Black, 0.1% Asian, 0.1%

American Indian/Alaska Native, 0.0% Native Hawaiian/Other Pacific Islander, 0.8% Other, 0.8% Hispanic of any race (2010); Average household size: 2.35 (2010); Median age: 45.5 (2010); Males per 100 females: 109.8 (2010); Homeownership rate: 84.7% (2010)

BYRNEDALE (CDP). Covers a land area of 1.250 square miles and a water area of <.001 square miles. Located at 41.29° N. Lat; 78.50° W. Long. Elevation is 1,224 feet.

Population: n/a (1990); n/a (2000); 427 (2010); Density: 341.5 persons per square mile (2010); Race: 96.0% White, 0.2% Black, 0.5% Asian, 0.0% American Indian/Alaska Native, 0.0% Native Hawaiian/Other Pacific Islander, 3.3% Other, 0.0% Hispanic of any race (2010); Average household size: 2.44 (2010); Median age: 43.8 (2010); Males per 100 females: 97.7 (2010); Marriage status: 22.4% never married, 55.9% now married, 5.4% widowed, 16.2% divorced (2006-2010 5-year est.); Foreign born: 1.0% (2006-2010 5-year est.); Ancestry (includes multiple ancestries): 40.0% German, 31.8% Italian, 8.4% Swedish, 8.2% Polish, 7.7% Irish (2006-2010 5-year est.).

Economy: Employment by occupation: 5.3% management, 4.8% professional, 7.9% services, 10.1% sales, 3.1% farming, 14.1% construction, 12.3% production (2006-2010 5-year est.).

Income: Per capita income: $19,050 (2006-2010 5-year est.); Median household income: $40,469 (2006-2010 5-year est.); Average household income: $48,003 (2006-2010 5-year est.); Percent of households with income of $100,000 or more: 11.8% (2006-2010 5-year est.); Poverty rate: 4.8% (2006-2010 5-year est.).

Education: Percent of population age 25 and over with: High school diploma (including GED) or higher: 97.4% (2006-2010 5-year est.); Bachelor's degree or higher: 15.5% (2006-2010 5-year est.); Master's degree or higher: 3.2% (2006-2010 5-year est.).

Housing: Homeownership rate: 82.2% (2010); Median home value: $101,100 (2006-2010 5-year est.); Median contract rent: $327 per month (2006-2010 5-year est.); Median year structure built: 1971 (2006-2010 5-year est.).

Transportation: Commute to work: 100.0% car, 0.0% public transportation, 0.0% walk, 0.0% work from home (2006-2010 5-year est.); Travel time to work: 28.2% less than 15 minutes, 42.3% 15 to 30 minutes, 18.5% 30 to 45 minutes, 9.7% 45 to 60 minutes, 1.3% 60 minutes or more (2006-2010 5-year est.)

DE YOUNG (unincorporated postal area)
Zip Code: 16728

Covers a land area of 5.575 square miles and a water area of 0 square miles. Located at 41.56° N. Lat; 78.92° W. Long. Population: 25 (2010); Density: 4.5 persons per square mile (2010); Race: 100.0% White, 0.0% Black, 0.0% Asian, 0.0% American Indian/Alaska Native, 0.0% Native Hawaiian/Other Pacific Islander, 0.0% Other, 0.0% Hispanic of any race (2010); Average household size: 1.92 (2010); Median age: 48.8 (2010); Males per 100 females: 127.3 (2010); Homeownership rate: 92.3% (2010)

FORCE (CDP). Covers a land area of 0.213 square miles and a water area of 0.003 square miles. Located at 41.26° N. Lat; 78.50° W. Long. Elevation is 1,227 feet.

Population: n/a (1990); n/a (2000); 253 (2010); Density: 1,189.0 persons per square mile (2010); Race: 99.6% White, 0.0% Black, 0.0% Asian, 0.0% American Indian/Alaska Native, 0.0% Native Hawaiian/Other Pacific Islander, 0.4% Other, 1.2% Hispanic of any race (2010); Average household size: 2.50 (2010); Median age: 40.9 (2010); Males per 100 females: 97.7 (2010); Marriage status: 38.9% never married, 56.2% now married, 2.7% widowed, 2.2% divorced (2006-2010 5-year est.); Foreign born: 0.0% (2006-2010 5-year est.); Ancestry (includes multiple ancestries): 37.8% Polish, 33.2% Lithuanian, 25.5% Italian, 16.3% German, 10.2% Swedish (2006-2010 5-year est.).

Economy: Employment by occupation: 0.0% management, 10.1% professional, 4.5% services, 0.0% sales, 5.6% farming, 11.2% construction, 16.9% production (2006-2010 5-year est.).

Income: Per capita income: $31,341 (2006-2010 5-year est.); Median household income: $57,750 (2006-2010 5-year est.); Average household income: $72,587 (2006-2010 5-year est.); Percent of households with income of $100,000 or more: 13.3% (2006-2010 5-year est.); Poverty rate: 0.0% (2006-2010 5-year est.).

Education: Percent of population age 25 and over with: High school diploma (including GED) or higher: 88.1% (2006-2010 5-year est.);

Bachelor's degree or higher: 22.5% (2006-2010 5-year est.); Master's degree or higher: 9.3% (2006-2010 5-year est.).

Housing: Homeownership rate: 80.2% (2010); Median home value: $57,300 (2006-2010 5-year est.); Median contract rent: n/a per month (2006-2010 5-year est.); Median year structure built: before 1940 (2006-2010 5-year est.).

Transportation: Commute to work: 87.6% car, 0.0% public transportation, 12.4% walk, 0.0% work from home (2006-2010 5-year est.); Travel time to work: 22.5% less than 15 minutes, 49.4% 15 to 30 minutes, 21.3% 30 to 45 minutes, 6.7% 45 to 60 minutes, 0.0% 60 minutes or more (2006-2010 5-year est.)

FOX (township). Covers a land area of 67.168 square miles and a water area of 0.059 square miles. Located at 41.32° N. Lat; 78.62° W. Long.

Population: 3,392 (1990); 3,734 (2000); 3,630 (2010); Density: 54.0 persons per square mile (2010); Race: 99.2% White, 0.1% Black, 0.1% Asian, 0.1% American Indian/Alaska Native, 0.0% Native Hawaiian/Other Pacific Islander, 0.5% Other, 0.3% Hispanic of any race (2010); Average household size: 2.42 (2010); Median age: 43.2 (2010); Males per 100 females: 102.1 (2010); Marriage status: 22.6% never married, 56.1% now married, 7.0% widowed, 14.3% divorced (2006-2010 5-year est.); Foreign born: 0.8% (2006-2010 5-year est.); Ancestry (includes multiple ancestries): 58.5% German, 21.9% Italian, 14.9% Irish, 8.6% Swedish, 5.5% American (2006-2010 5-year est.).

Economy: Single-family building permits issued: 7 (2011); Multi-family building permits issued: 0 (2011); Employment by occupation: 5.1% management, 3.2% professional, 11.3% services, 13.2% sales, 2.7% farming, 15.7% construction, 15.0% production (2006-2010 5-year est.).

Income: Per capita income: $22,235 (2006-2010 5-year est.); Median household income: $47,000 (2006-2010 5-year est.); Average household income: $52,431 (2006-2010 5-year est.); Percent of households with income of $100,000 or more: 9.2% (2006-2010 5-year est.); Poverty rate: 6.1% (2006-2010 5-year est.).

Education: Percent of population age 25 and over with: High school diploma (including GED) or higher: 87.9% (2006-2010 5-year est.); Bachelor's degree or higher: 11.9% (2006-2010 5-year est.); Master's degree or higher: 3.0% (2006-2010 5-year est.).

Housing: Homeownership rate: 86.7% (2010); Median home value: $94,600 (2006-2010 5-year est.); Median contract rent: $412 per month (2006-2010 5-year est.); Median year structure built: 1971 (2006-2010 5-year est.).

Transportation: Commute to work: 95.9% car, 1.1% public transportation, 0.0% walk, 2.5% work from home (2006-2010 5-year est.); Travel time to work: 42.0% less than 15 minutes, 41.7% 15 to 30 minutes, 7.5% 30 to 45 minutes, 1.7% 45 to 60 minutes, 7.2% 60 minutes or more (2006-2010 5-year est.)

Additional Information Contacts
Ridgway-Elk County Chamber of Commerce . . . . (814) 776-1424
http://www.ridgwaychamber.com

HIGHLAND (township). Covers a land area of 86.859 square miles and a water area of 0.090 square miles. Located at 41.54° N. Lat; 78.88° W. Long.

Population: 551 (1990); 509 (2000); 492 (2010); Density: 5.7 persons per square mile (2010); Race: 98.6% White, 0.0% Black, 0.0% Asian, 0.0% American Indian/Alaska Native, 0.0% Native Hawaiian/Other Pacific Islander, 1.4% Other, 0.0% Hispanic of any race (2010); Average household size: 2.28 (2010); Median age: 45.8 (2010); Males per 100 females: 118.7 (2010); Marriage status: 28.8% never married, 38.5% now married, 11.9% widowed, 20.8% divorced (2006-2010 5-year est.); Foreign born: 0.0% (2006-2010 5-year est.); Ancestry (includes multiple ancestries): 35.5% German, 20.4% Irish, 13.5% Swedish, 10.4% Italian, 9.0% American (2006-2010 5-year est.).

Economy: Single-family building permits issued: 0 (2011); Multi-family building permits issued: 0 (2011); Employment by occupation: 1.7% management, 2.2% professional, 32.0% services, 11.8% sales, 4.5% farming, 16.9% construction, 4.5% production (2006-2010 5-year est.).

Income: Per capita income: $19,610 (2006-2010 5-year est.); Median household income: $43,654 (2006-2010 5-year est.); Average household income: $47,526 (2006-2010 5-year est.); Percent of households with income of $100,000 or more: 4.8% (2006-2010 5-year est.); Poverty rate: 14.5% (2006-2010 5-year est.).

Education: Percent of population age 25 and over with: High school diploma (including GED) or higher: 84.7% (2006-2010 5-year est.);

Bachelor's degree or higher: 2.3% (2006-2010 5-year est.); Master's degree or higher: 0.0% (2006-2010 5-year est.).
Housing: Homeownership rate: 84.3% (2010); Median home value: $75,400 (2006-2010 5-year est.); Median contract rent: n/a per month (2006-2010 5-year est.); Median year structure built: 1944 (2006-2010 5-year est.).
Transportation: Commute to work: 94.9% car, 0.0% public transportation, 5.1% walk, 0.0% work from home (2006-2010 5-year est.); Travel time to work: 24.2% less than 15 minutes, 52.8% 15 to 30 minutes, 10.7% 30 to 45 minutes, 5.1% 45 to 60 minutes, 7.3% 60 minutes or more (2006-2010 5-year est.)

HORTON (township). Covers a land area of 56.992 square miles and a water area of 0.090 square miles. Located at 41.28° N. Lat; 78.72° W. Long.
Population: 1,655 (1990); 1,574 (2000); 1,452 (2010); Density: 25.5 persons per square mile (2010); Race: 99.0% White, 0.1% Black, 0.1% Asian, 0.1% American Indian/Alaska Native, 0.0% Native Hawaiian/Other Pacific Islander, 0.7% Other, 0.7% Hispanic of any race (2010); Average household size: 2.30 (2010); Median age: 46.1 (2010); Males per 100 females: 110.7 (2010); Marriage status: 23.0% never married, 58.4% now married, 6.0% widowed, 12.6% divorced (2006-2010 5-year est.); Foreign born: 0.5% (2006-2010 5-year est.); Ancestry (includes multiple ancestries): 31.5% German, 21.6% Irish, 17.8% Italian, 12.4% Swedish, 12.2% English (2006-2010 5-year est.).
Economy: Employment by occupation: 5.2% management, 2.0% professional, 9.0% services, 11.7% sales, 4.0% farming, 21.8% construction, 22.3% production (2006-2010 5-year est.).
Income: Per capita income: $21,094 (2006-2010 5-year est.); Median household income: $41,758 (2006-2010 5-year est.); Average household income: $48,622 (2006-2010 5-year est.); Percent of households with income of $100,000 or more: 7.7% (2006-2010 5-year est.); Poverty rate: 6.7% (2006-2010 5-year est.).
Education: Percent of population age 25 and over with: High school diploma (including GED) or higher: 84.5% (2006-2010 5-year est.); Bachelor's degree or higher: 9.1% (2006-2010 5-year est.); Master's degree or higher: 3.6% (2006-2010 5-year est.).
Housing: Homeownership rate: 84.6% (2010); Median home value: $82,200 (2006-2010 5-year est.); Median contract rent: $231 per month (2006-2010 5-year est.); Median year structure built: 1965 (2006-2010 5-year est.).
Transportation: Commute to work: 93.0% car, 2.4% public transportation, 1.9% walk, 2.7% work from home (2006-2010 5-year est.); Travel time to work: 27.2% less than 15 minutes, 41.0% 15 to 30 minutes, 25.9% 30 to 45 minutes, 3.0% 45 to 60 minutes, 3.0% 60 minutes or more (2006-2010 5-year est.)
Additional Information Contacts
Ridgway-Elk County Chamber of Commerce . . . . (814) 776-1424
http://www.ridgwaychamber.com

JAMES CITY (CDP). Covers a land area of 0.691 square miles and a water area of 0.001 square miles. Located at 41.62° N. Lat; 78.85° W. Long. Elevation is 1,955 feet.
Population: n/a (1990); n/a (2000); 287 (2010); Density: 415.1 persons per square mile (2010); Race: 99.7% White, 0.0% Black, 0.0% Asian, 0.0% American Indian/Alaska Native, 0.0% Native Hawaiian/Other Pacific Islander, 0.3% Other, 0.0% Hispanic of any race (2010); Average household size: 2.45 (2010); Median age: 43.1 (2010); Males per 100 females: 112.6 (2010); Marriage status: 39.7% never married, 44.4% now married, 9.1% widowed, 6.9% divorced (2006-2010 5-year est.); Foreign born: 0.0% (2006-2010 5-year est.); Ancestry (includes multiple ancestries): 35.3% German, 28.1% Irish, 17.3% Swedish, 8.6% Italian, 2.5% English (2006-2010 5-year est.).
Economy: Employment by occupation: 0.0% management, 0.0% professional, 24.0% services, 16.8% sales, 4.8% farming, 18.4% construction, 6.4% production (2006-2010 5-year est.).
Income: Per capita income: $17,480 (2006-2010 5-year est.); Median household income: $43,077 (2006-2010 5-year est.); Average household income: $51,278 (2006-2010 5-year est.); Percent of households with income of $100,000 or more: 4.3% (2006-2010 5-year est.); Poverty rate: 14.4% (2006-2010 5-year est.).
Education: Percent of population age 25 and over with: High school diploma (including GED) or higher: 95.5% (2006-2010 5-year est.); Bachelor's degree or higher: 0.0% (2006-2010 5-year est.); Master's degree or higher: 0.0% (2006-2010 5-year est.).

Housing: Homeownership rate: 86.3% (2010); Median home value: $71,700 (2006-2010 5-year est.); Median contract rent: n/a per month (2006-2010 5-year est.); Median year structure built: before 1940 (2006-2010 5-year est.).
Transportation: Commute to work: 95.2% car, 0.0% public transportation, 4.8% walk, 0.0% work from home (2006-2010 5-year est.); Travel time to work: 27.2% less than 15 minutes, 51.2% 15 to 30 minutes, 11.2% 30 to 45 minutes, 3.2% 45 to 60 minutes, 7.2% 60 minutes or more (2006-2010 5-year est.)

JAY (township). Covers a land area of 67.700 square miles and a water area of 0.229 square miles. Located at 41.32° N. Lat; 78.49° W. Long.
Population: 2,087 (1990); 2,094 (2000); 2,072 (2010); Density: 30.6 persons per square mile (2010); Race: 98.5% White, 0.1% Black, 0.1% Asian, 0.1% American Indian/Alaska Native, 0.0% Native Hawaiian/Other Pacific Islander, 1.2% Other, 1.3% Hispanic of any race (2010); Average household size: 2.35 (2010); Median age: 45.8 (2010); Males per 100 females: 96.8 (2010); Marriage status: 23.7% never married, 63.4% now married, 5.5% widowed, 7.4% divorced (2006-2010 5-year est.); Foreign born: 0.5% (2006-2010 5-year est.); Ancestry (includes multiple ancestries): 33.6% German, 26.3% Italian, 10.7% Polish, 9.7% Irish, 7.6% American (2006-2010 5-year est.).
Economy: Single-family building permits issued: 0 (2011); Multi-family building permits issued: 0 (2011); Employment by occupation: 5.4% management, 3.6% professional, 5.6% services, 10.0% sales, 1.2% farming, 13.1% construction, 18.0% production (2006-2010 5-year est.).
Income: Per capita income: $20,981 (2006-2010 5-year est.); Median household income: $45,813 (2006-2010 5-year est.); Average household income: $50,711 (2006-2010 5-year est.); Percent of households with income of $100,000 or more: 6.6% (2006-2010 5-year est.); Poverty rate: 7.9% (2006-2010 5-year est.).
Education: Percent of population age 25 and over with: High school diploma (including GED) or higher: 88.3% (2006-2010 5-year est.); Bachelor's degree or higher: 14.3% (2006-2010 5-year est.); Master's degree or higher: 5.3% (2006-2010 5-year est.).
Housing: Homeownership rate: 82.9% (2010); Median home value: $82,600 (2006-2010 5-year est.); Median contract rent: $347 per month (2006-2010 5-year est.); Median year structure built: 1963 (2006-2010 5-year est.).
Transportation: Commute to work: 96.1% car, 0.8% public transportation, 1.7% walk, 0.6% work from home (2006-2010 5-year est.); Travel time to work: 18.3% less than 15 minutes, 49.7% 15 to 30 minutes, 26.7% 30 to 45 minutes, 3.1% 45 to 60 minutes, 2.3% 60 minutes or more (2006-2010 5-year est.)
Additional Information Contacts
Ridgway-Elk County Chamber of Commerce . . . . (814) 776-1424
http://www.ridgwaychamber.com

JOHNSONBURG (borough). Covers a land area of 2.884 square miles and a water area of 0.042 square miles. Located at 41.49° N. Lat; 78.68° W. Long. Elevation is 1,457 feet.
History: Settled 1810, laid out 1888.
Population: 3,350 (1990); 3,003 (2000); 2,483 (2010); Density: 860.8 persons per square mile (2010); Race: 98.1% White, 0.1% Black, 0.3% Asian, 0.2% American Indian/Alaska Native, 0.0% Native Hawaiian/Other Pacific Islander, 1.3% Other, 1.5% Hispanic of any race (2010); Average household size: 2.21 (2010); Median age: 42.1 (2010); Males per 100 females: 96.6 (2010); Marriage status: 23.7% never married, 55.4% now married, 10.9% widowed, 10.0% divorced (2006-2010 5-year est.); Foreign born: 3.3% (2006-2010 5-year est.); Ancestry (includes multiple ancestries): 30.6% German, 28.4% Italian, 25.2% Irish, 13.0% Swedish, 12.3% Polish (2006-2010 5-year est.).
Economy: Single-family building permits issued: 0 (2011); Multi-family building permits issued: 0 (2011); Employment by occupation: 6.4% management, 0.0% professional, 19.4% services, 11.3% sales, 3.7% farming, 7.3% construction, 16.3% production (2006-2010 5-year est.).
Income: Per capita income: $16,438 (2006-2010 5-year est.); Median household income: $30,856 (2006-2010 5-year est.); Average household income: $36,805 (2006-2010 5-year est.); Percent of households with income of $100,000 or more: 4.1% (2006-2010 5-year est.); Poverty rate: 16.9% (2006-2010 5-year est.).
Education: Percent of population age 25 and over with: High school diploma (including GED) or higher: 85.2% (2006-2010 5-year est.); Bachelor's degree or higher: 9.0% (2006-2010 5-year est.); Master's degree or higher: 5.2% (2006-2010 5-year est.).

School District(s)

Johnsonburg Area SD (KG-12)

   2010-11 Enrollment: 639. . . . . (814) 965-2536

Housing: Homeownership rate: 68.8% (2010); Median home value: $47,100 (2006-2010 5-year est.); Median contract rent: $340 per month (2006-2010 5-year est.); Median year structure built: 1942 (2006-2010 5-year est.).

Safety: Violent crime rate: 20.1 per 10,000 population; Property crime rate: 216.8 per 10,000 population (2011).

Newspapers: Johnsonburg Press (Community news; Circulation 2,200)

Transportation: Commute to work: 92.0% car, 0.0% public transportation, 6.1% walk, 0.0% work from home (2006-2010 5-year est.); Travel time to work: 45.2% less than 15 minutes, 39.7% 15 to 30 minutes, 6.0% 30 to 45 minutes, 3.4% 45 to 60 minutes, 5.7% 60 minutes or more (2006-2010 5-year est.)

Additional Information Contacts

Ridgway-Elk County Chamber of Commerce . . . . (814) 776-1424
   http://www.ridgwaychamber.com

JONES (township). Covers a land area of 145.146 square miles and a water area of 1.946 square miles. Located at 41.57° N. Lat; 78.62° W. Long.

Population: 1,870 (1990); 1,721 (2000); 1,624 (2010); Density: 11.2 persons per square mile (2010); Race: 98.3% White, 0.6% Black, 0.1% Asian, 0.2% American Indian/Alaska Native, 0.0% Native Hawaiian/Other Pacific Islander, 0.8% Other, 0.4% Hispanic of any race (2010); Average household size: 2.36 (2010); Median age: 46.6 (2010); Males per 100 females: 108.2 (2010); Marriage status: 25.5% never married, 61.6% now married, 6.0% widowed, 6.9% divorced (2006-2010 5-year est.); Foreign born: 1.1% (2006-2010 5-year est.); Ancestry (includes multiple ancestries): 38.0% German, 12.2% American, 11.9% Irish, 11.3% Swedish, 11.0% Polish (2006-2010 5-year est.).

Economy: Single-family building permits issued: 5 (2011); Multi-family building permits issued: 0 (2011); Employment by occupation: 4.3% management, 3.1% professional, 10.8% services, 12.9% sales, 2.1% farming, 11.2% construction, 12.5% production (2006-2010 5-year est.).

Income: Per capita income: $26,451 (2006-2010 5-year est.); Median household income: $50,776 (2006-2010 5-year est.); Average household income: $60,531 (2006-2010 5-year est.); Percent of households with income of $100,000 or more: 13.0% (2006-2010 5-year est.); Poverty rate: 4.2% (2006-2010 5-year est.).

Education: Percent of population age 25 and over with: High school diploma (including GED) or higher: 90.5% (2006-2010 5-year est.); Bachelor's degree or higher: 13.4% (2006-2010 5-year est.); Master's degree or higher: 4.7% (2006-2010 5-year est.).

Housing: Homeownership rate: 85.8% (2010); Median home value: $99,600 (2006-2010 5-year est.); Median contract rent: $407 per month (2006-2010 5-year est.); Median year structure built: 1961 (2006-2010 5-year est.).

Transportation: Commute to work: 96.5% car, 0.0% public transportation, 1.1% walk, 1.0% work from home (2006-2010 5-year est.); Travel time to work: 25.8% less than 15 minutes, 47.3% 15 to 30 minutes, 19.4% 30 to 45 minutes, 4.3% 45 to 60 minutes, 3.3% 60 minutes or more (2006-2010 5-year est.)

Additional Information Contacts

St. Mary's Area Chamber of Commerce . . . . (814) 781-3804
   http://www.stmaryschamber.org

KERSEY (CDP). Covers a land area of 1.558 square miles and a water area of 0.002 square miles. Located at 41.36° N. Lat; 78.61° W. Long. Elevation is 1,975 feet.

Population: n/a (1990); n/a (2000); 937 (2010); Density: 601.3 persons per square mile (2010); Race: 99.5% White, 0.0% Black, 0.0% Asian, 0.2% American Indian/Alaska Native, 0.0% Native Hawaiian/Other Pacific Islander, 0.3% Other, 0.5% Hispanic of any race (2010); Average household size: 2.39 (2010); Median age: 42.8 (2010); Males per 100 females: 100.2 (2010); Marriage status: 31.9% never married, 50.3% now married, 6.7% widowed, 11.0% divorced (2006-2010 5-year est.); Foreign born: 0.0% (2006-2010 5-year est.); Ancestry (includes multiple ancestries): 42.3% German, 27.4% Italian, 26.0% Swedish, 16.2% Irish, 4.2% American (2006-2010 5-year est.).

Economy: Employment by occupation: 4.6% management, 1.8% professional, 5.7% services, 12.4% sales, 5.3% farming, 19.3% construction, 24.1% production (2006-2010 5-year est.).

Income: Per capita income: $24,194 (2006-2010 5-year est.); Median household income: $52,604 (2006-2010 5-year est.); Average household income: $52,967 (2006-2010 5-year est.); Percent of households with income of $100,000 or more: 4.7% (2006-2010 5-year est.); Poverty rate: 3.3% (2006-2010 5-year est.).

Education: Percent of population age 25 and over with: High school diploma (including GED) or higher: 94.0% (2006-2010 5-year est.); Bachelor's degree or higher: 7.2% (2006-2010 5-year est.); Master's degree or higher: 0.0% (2006-2010 5-year est.).

School District(s)

Saint Marys Area SD (KG-12)

   2010-11 Enrollment: 2,263 . . . . (814) 834-7831

Housing: Homeownership rate: 82.9% (2010); Median home value: $81,100 (2006-2010 5-year est.); Median contract rent: n/a per month (2006-2010 5-year est.); Median year structure built: 1959 (2006-2010 5-year est.).

Transportation: Commute to work: 100.0% car, 0.0% public transportation, 0.0% walk, 0.0% work from home (2006-2010 5-year est.); Travel time to work: 46.1% less than 15 minutes, 41.1% 15 to 30 minutes, 0.0% 30 to 45 minutes, 2.7% 45 to 60 minutes, 10.1% 60 minutes or more (2006-2010 5-year est.)

MILLSTONE (township). Covers a land area of 41.475 square miles and a water area of 0.126 square miles. Located at 41.42° N. Lat; 79.01° W. Long. Elevation is 1,204 feet.

Population: 85 (1990); 95 (2000); 82 (2010); Density: 2.0 persons per square mile (2010); Race: 100.0% White, 0.0% Black, 0.0% Asian, 0.0% American Indian/Alaska Native, 0.0% Native Hawaiian/Other Pacific Islander, 0.0% Other, 0.0% Hispanic of any race (2010); Average household size: 1.95 (2010); Median age: 55.5 (2010); Males per 100 females: 115.8 (2010); Marriage status: 34.6% never married, 65.4% now married, 0.0% widowed, 0.0% divorced (2006-2010 5-year est.); Foreign born: 0.0% (2006-2010 5-year est.); Ancestry (includes multiple ancestries): 22.9% German, 14.3% Irish, 8.6% Italian, 8.6% Polish, 5.7% Slovak (2006-2010 5-year est.).

Economy: Single-family building permits issued: 0 (2011); Multi-family building permits issued: 0 (2011); Employment by occupation: 30.8% management, 0.0% professional, 0.0% services, 23.1% sales, 0.0% farming, 0.0% construction, 0.0% production (2006-2010 5-year est.).

Income: Per capita income: $18,691 (2006-2010 5-year est.); Median household income: $43,333 (2006-2010 5-year est.); Average household income: $48,700 (2006-2010 5-year est.); Percent of households with income of $100,000 or more: n/a (2006-2010 5-year est.); Poverty rate: 0.0% (2006-2010 5-year est.).

Education: Percent of population age 25 and over with: High school diploma (including GED) or higher: 88.5% (2006-2010 5-year est.); Bachelor's degree or higher: 0.0% (2006-2010 5-year est.); Master's degree or higher: 0.0% (2006-2010 5-year est.).

Housing: Homeownership rate: 88.1% (2010); Median home value: $129,200 (2006-2010 5-year est.); Median contract rent: n/a per month (2006-2010 5-year est.); Median year structure built: 1958 (2006-2010 5-year est.).

Transportation: Commute to work: 100.0% car, 0.0% public transportation, 0.0% walk, 0.0% work from home (2006-2010 5-year est.); Travel time to work: 0.0% less than 15 minutes, 11.1% 15 to 30 minutes, 88.9% 30 to 45 minutes, 0.0% 45 to 60 minutes, 0.0% 60 minutes or more (2006-2010 5-year est.)

RIDGWAY (borough). County seat. Covers a land area of 2.613 square miles and a water area of 0.055 square miles. Located at 41.43° N. Lat; 78.73° W. Long. Elevation is 1,427 feet.

Population: 4,793 (1990); 4,591 (2000); 4,078 (2010); Density: 1,560.8 persons per square mile (2010); Race: 97.7% White, 0.6% Black, 0.6% Asian, 0.0% American Indian/Alaska Native, 0.0% Native Hawaiian/Other Pacific Islander, 1.1% Other, 0.6% Hispanic of any race (2010); Average household size: 2.25 (2010); Median age: 43.1 (2010); Males per 100 females: 95.5 (2010); Marriage status: 30.3% never married, 46.5% now married, 8.5% widowed, 14.7% divorced (2006-2010 5-year est.); Foreign born: 1.7% (2006-2010 5-year est.); Ancestry (includes multiple ancestries): 34.1% German, 24.0% Italian, 15.8% Irish, 10.7% English, 9.3% Swedish (2006-2010 5-year est.).

Economy: Single-family building permits issued: 0 (2011); Multi-family building permits issued: 0 (2011); Employment by occupation: 3.9% management, 3.2% professional, 9.4% services, 16.0% sales, 1.9% farming, 7.9% construction, 13.6% production (2006-2010 5-year est.).

Income: Per capita income: $22,415 (2006-2010 5-year est.); Median household income: $37,917 (2006-2010 5-year est.); Average household income: $49,302 (2006-2010 5-year est.); Percent of households with income of $100,000 or more: 7.1% (2006-2010 5-year est.); Poverty rate: 18.1% (2006-2010 5-year est.).

Taxes: Total city taxes per capita: $334 (2009); City property taxes per capita: $188 (2009).

Education: Percent of population age 25 and over with: High school diploma (including GED) or higher: 89.3% (2006-2010 5-year est.); Bachelor's degree or higher: 22.9% (2006-2010 5-year est.); Master's degree or higher: 4.2% (2006-2010 5-year est.).

School District(s)

Ridgway Area SD (KG-12)

  2010-11 Enrollment: 996 . . . . (814) 773-3146

Housing: Homeownership rate: 70.2% (2010); Median home value: $68,000 (2006-2010 5-year est.); Median contract rent: $345 per month (2006-2010 5-year est.); Median year structure built: 1940 (2006-2010 5-year est.).

Safety: Violent crime rate: 9.8 per 10,000 population; Property crime rate: 310.4 per 10,000 population (2011).

Newspapers: The Ridgway Record (Local news; Circulation 3,238)

Transportation: Commute to work: 91.2% car, 1.3% public transportation, 5.0% walk, 2.1% work from home (2006-2010 5-year est.); Travel time to work: 54.9% less than 15 minutes, 27.5% 15 to 30 minutes, 10.8% 30 to 45 minutes, 5.2% 45 to 60 minutes, 1.6% 60 minutes or more (2006-2010 5-year est.).

Additional Information Contacts

Ridgway-Elk County Chamber of Commerce . . . . (814) 776-1424
  http://www.ridgwaychamber.com

RIDGWAY (township). Covers a land area of 86.904 square miles and a water area of 0.908 square miles. Located at 41.44° N. Lat; 78.73° W. Long. Elevation is 1,427 feet.

History: Settled 1822, laid out 1833, incorporated 1881.

Population: 2,617 (1990); 2,802 (2000); 2,523 (2010); Density: 29.0 persons per square mile (2010); Race: 99.4% White, 0.1% Black, 0.0% Asian, 0.0% American Indian/Alaska Native, 0.0% Native Hawaiian/Other Pacific Islander, 0.5% Other, 0.6% Hispanic of any race (2010); Average household size: 2.44 (2010); Median age: 46.0 (2010); Males per 100 females: 101.7 (2010); Marriage status: 28.9% never married, 55.8% now married, 5.9% widowed, 9.3% divorced (2006-2010 5-year est.); Foreign born: 0.3% (2006-2010 5-year est.); Ancestry (includes multiple ancestries): 42.3% German, 30.9% Italian, 21.7% Irish, 13.4% Swedish, 10.4% Polish (2006-2010 5-year est.).

Economy: Single-family building permits issued: 2 (2011); Multi-family building permits issued: 0 (2011); Employment by occupation: 10.7% management, 3.3% professional, 11.9% services, 18.1% sales, 1.8% farming, 10.8% construction, 8.5% production (2006-2010 5-year est.).

Income: Per capita income: $23,574 (2006-2010 5-year est.); Median household income: $48,134 (2006-2010 5-year est.); Average household income: $57,004 (2006-2010 5-year est.); Percent of households with income of $100,000 or more: 14.1% (2006-2010 5-year est.); Poverty rate: 6.6% (2006-2010 5-year est.).

Education: Percent of population age 25 and over with: High school diploma (including GED) or higher: 93.4% (2006-2010 5-year est.); Bachelor's degree or higher: 11.8% (2006-2010 5-year est.); Master's degree or higher: 4.6% (2006-2010 5-year est.).

Housing: Homeownership rate: 83.7% (2010); Median home value: $110,400 (2006-2010 5-year est.); Median contract rent: $331 per month (2006-2010 5-year est.); Median year structure built: 1967 (2006-2010 5-year est.).

Newspapers: The Ridgway Record (Local news; Circulation 3,238)

Transportation: Commute to work: 94.3% car, 0.0% public transportation, 4.7% walk, 1.1% work from home (2006-2010 5-year est.); Travel time to work: 54.8% less than 15 minutes, 29.6% 15 to 30 minutes, 8.9% 30 to 45 minutes, 3.1% 45 to 60 minutes, 3.6% 60 minutes or more (2006-2010 5-year est.).

Additional Information Contacts

Ridgway-Elk County Chamber of Commerce . . . . (814) 776-1424
  http://www.ridgwaychamber.com

SAINT MARYS (city). Covers a land area of 99.322 square miles and a water area of 0.201 square miles. Located at 41.46° N. Lat; 78.52° W. Long. Elevation is 1,667 feet.

History: St. Marys had its beginning in 1842 when Philadelphia and Baltimore German Catholics, who had fled the "Know Nothing" persecution, settled on land owned by the German Catholic Brotherhood. During the 1860's, German Catholic predominance was diluted by an influx of Irish Catholic railroad laborers.

Population: 14,020 (1990); 14,502 (2000); 13,070 (2010); Density: 131.6 persons per square mile (2010); Race: 98.5% White, 0.3% Black, 0.4% Asian, 0.1% American Indian/Alaska Native, 0.0% Native Hawaiian/Other Pacific Islander, 0.7% Other, 0.4% Hispanic of any race (2010); Average household size: 2.29 (2010); Median age: 45.6 (2010); Males per 100 females: 95.1 (2010); Marriage status: 27.0% never married, 54.2% now married, 9.5% widowed, 9.2% divorced (2006-2010 5-year est.); Foreign born: 0.9% (2006-2010 5-year est.); Ancestry (includes multiple ancestries): 58.4% German, 17.7% Italian, 12.9% Irish, 8.1% Polish, 6.3% English (2006-2010 5-year est.).

Economy: Single-family building permits issued: 5 (2011); Multi-family building permits issued: 0 (2011); Employment by occupation: 9.5% management, 3.8% professional, 10.5% services, 14.7% sales, 2.6% farming, 8.3% construction, 13.7% production (2006-2010 5-year est.).

Income: Per capita income: $24,208 (2006-2010 5-year est.); Median household income: $45,802 (2006-2010 5-year est.); Average household income: $55,793 (2006-2010 5-year est.); Percent of households with income of $100,000 or more: 12.3% (2006-2010 5-year est.); Poverty rate: 11.4% (2006-2010 5-year est.).

Taxes: Total city taxes per capita: $379 (2009); City property taxes per capita: $258 (2009).

Education: Percent of population age 25 and over with: High school diploma (including GED) or higher: 91.6% (2006-2010 5-year est.); Bachelor's degree or higher: 19.3% (2006-2010 5-year est.); Master's degree or higher: 5.8% (2006-2010 5-year est.).

School District(s)

Saint Marys Area SD (KG-12)

  2010-11 Enrollment: 2,263 . . . . (814) 834-7831

Housing: Homeownership rate: 76.9% (2010); Median home value: $111,900 (2006-2010 5-year est.); Median contract rent: $430 per month (2006-2010 5-year est.); Median year structure built: 1959 (2006-2010 5-year est.).

Hospitals: Elk Regional Health Center (89 beds); Elk Regional Health Center (89 beds)

Safety: Violent crime rate: 11.4 per 10,000 population; Property crime rate: 173.1 per 10,000 population (2011).

Newspapers: The Daily Press (Local news; Circulation 5,300)

Transportation: Commute to work: 94.2% car, 0.9% public transportation, 2.6% walk, 1.1% work from home (2006-2010 5-year est.); Travel time to work: 68.2% less than 15 minutes, 19.8% 15 to 30 minutes, 6.2% 30 to 45 minutes, 3.1% 45 to 60 minutes, 2.6% 60 minutes or more (2006-2010 5-year est.)

Airports: St Marys Municipal (general aviation)

Additional Information Contacts

City of Saint Marys . . . . (814) 781-1718
  http://www.cityofstmarys.com

St. Marys Area Chamber of Commerce . . . . (814) 781-3804
  http://www.stmaryschamber.org

SPRING CREEK (township). Covers a land area of 63.632 square miles and a water area of 0.714 square miles. Located at 41.40° N. Lat; 78.87° W. Long.

Population: 215 (1990); 260 (2000); 233 (2010); Density: 3.7 persons per square mile (2010); Race: 96.1% White, 0.0% Black, 0.0% Asian, 2.6% American Indian/Alaska Native, 0.0% Native Hawaiian/Other Pacific Islander, 1.3% Other, 0.0% Hispanic of any race (2010); Average household size: 2.06 (2010); Median age: 51.6 (2010); Males per 100 females: 140.2 (2010); Marriage status: 25.7% never married, 39.8% now married, 18.6% widowed, 15.9% divorced (2006-2010 5-year est.); Foreign born: 0.0% (2006-2010 5-year est.); Ancestry (includes multiple ancestries): 32.5% German, 25.6% American, 17.1% Irish, 13.7% English, 6.8% Italian (2006-2010 5-year est.).

Economy: Single-family building permits issued: 1 (2011); Multi-family building permits issued: 0 (2011); Employment by occupation: 10.9% management, 0.0% professional, 5.5% services, 12.7% sales, 3.6% farming, 3.6% construction, 5.5% production (2006-2010 5-year est.).

Income: Per capita income: $27,308 (2006-2010 5-year est.); Median household income: $35,625 (2006-2010 5-year est.); Average household income: $47,802 (2006-2010 5-year est.); Percent of households with income of $100,000 or more: 6.3% (2006-2010 5-year est.); Poverty rate: 13.7% (2006-2010 5-year est.).
Education: Percent of population age 25 and over with: High school diploma (including GED) or higher: 96.3% (2006-2010 5-year est.); Bachelor's degree or higher: 15.0% (2006-2010 5-year est.); Master's degree or higher: 10.3% (2006-2010 5-year est.).
Housing: Homeownership rate: 92.0% (2010); Median home value: $81,900 (2006-2010 5-year est.); Median contract rent: $263 per month (2006-2010 5-year est.); Median year structure built: 1955 (2006-2010 5-year est.).
Transportation: Commute to work: 88.0% car, 0.0% public transportation, 0.0% walk, 12.0% work from home (2006-2010 5-year est.); Travel time to work: 15.9% less than 15 minutes, 43.2% 15 to 30 minutes, 34.1% 30 to 45 minutes, 6.8% 45 to 60 minutes, 0.0% 60 minutes or more (2006-2010 5-year est.)

WEEDVILLE (CDP). Covers a land area of 1.952 square miles and a water area of 0.049 square miles. Located at 41.28° N. Lat; 78.49° W. Long. Elevation is 1,171 feet.
Population: n/a (1990); n/a (2000); 542 (2010); Density: 277.7 persons per square mile (2010); Race: 98.7% White, 0.0% Black, 0.2% Asian, 0.4% American Indian/Alaska Native, 0.0% Native Hawaiian/Other Pacific Islander, 0.7% Other, 2.4% Hispanic of any race (2010); Average household size: 2.11 (2010); Median age: 50.9 (2010); Males per 100 females: 84.4 (2010); Marriage status: 23.8% never married, 62.9% now married, 8.4% widowed, 4.9% divorced (2006-2010 5-year est.); Foreign born: 0.0% (2006-2010 5-year est.); Ancestry (includes multiple ancestries): 40.0% Italian, 22.6% German, 17.1% Polish, 10.0% Lithuanian, 9.2% Swedish (2006-2010 5-year est.).
Economy: Employment by occupation: 5.9% management, 3.4% professional, 5.9% services, 13.5% sales, 0.0% farming, 10.5% construction, 12.2% production (2006-2010 5-year est.).
Income: Per capita income: $24,571 (2006-2010 5-year est.); Median household income: $45,921 (2006-2010 5-year est.); Average household income: $49,849 (2006-2010 5-year est.); Percent of households with income of $100,000 or more: 1.8% (2006-2010 5-year est.); Poverty rate: 6.0% (2006-2010 5-year est.).
Education: Percent of population age 25 and over with: High school diploma (including GED) or higher: 87.7% (2006-2010 5-year est.); Bachelor's degree or higher: 17.2% (2006-2010 5-year est.); Master's degree or higher: 9.3% (2006-2010 5-year est.).
School District(s)
Saint Marys Area SD (KG-12)
    2010-11 Enrollment: 2,263 . . . . (814) 834-7831
Housing: Homeownership rate: 71.6% (2010); Median home value: $88,200 (2006-2010 5-year est.); Median contract rent: $304 per month (2006-2010 5-year est.); Median year structure built: 1957 (2006-2010 5-year est.).
Transportation: Commute to work: 92.1% car, 3.5% public transportation, 2.6% walk, 1.7% work from home (2006-2010 5-year est.); Travel time to work: 19.1% less than 15 minutes, 46.2% 15 to 30 minutes, 32.0% 30 to 45 minutes, 0.0% 45 to 60 minutes, 2.7% 60 minutes or more (2006-2010 5-year est.)

WILCOX (CDP). Covers a land area of 0.513 square miles and a water area of 0.004 square miles. Located at 41.57° N. Lat; 78.69° W. Long. Elevation is 1,526 feet.
Population: n/a (1990); n/a (2000); 383 (2010); Density: 746.5 persons per square mile (2010); Race: 98.2% White, 0.3% Black, 0.3% Asian, 0.3% American Indian/Alaska Native, 0.0% Native Hawaiian/Other Pacific Islander, 0.9% Other, 1.0% Hispanic of any race (2010); Average household size: 2.36 (2010); Median age: 42.5 (2010); Males per 100 females: 94.4 (2010); Marriage status: 31.7% never married, 51.0% now married, 8.5% widowed, 8.8% divorced (2006-2010 5-year est.); Foreign born: 0.0% (2006-2010 5-year est.); Ancestry (includes multiple ancestries): 34.7% German, 13.4% Irish, 11.5% American, 10.4% Swedish, 9.3% Polish (2006-2010 5-year est.).
Economy: Employment by occupation: 3.0% management, 3.0% professional, 9.5% services, 11.9% sales, 0.0% farming, 12.5% construction, 8.3% production (2006-2010 5-year est.).
Income: Per capita income: $20,765 (2006-2010 5-year est.); Median household income: $33,750 (2006-2010 5-year est.); Average household

income: $44,103 (2006-2010 5-year est.); Percent of households with income of $100,000 or more: 6.4% (2006-2010 5-year est.); Poverty rate: 14.8% (2006-2010 5-year est.).
Education: Percent of population age 25 and over with: High school diploma (including GED) or higher: 85.1% (2006-2010 5-year est.); Bachelor's degree or higher: 12.5% (2006-2010 5-year est.); Master's degree or higher: 3.5% (2006-2010 5-year est.).
Housing: Homeownership rate: 77.1% (2010); Median home value: $86,700 (2006-2010 5-year est.); Median contract rent: $343 per month (2006-2010 5-year est.); Median year structure built: before 1940 (2006-2010 5-year est.).
Transportation: Commute to work: 100.0% car, 0.0% public transportation, 0.0% walk, 0.0% work from home (2006-2010 5-year est.); Travel time to work: 18.5% less than 15 minutes, 60.7% 15 to 30 minutes, 17.3% 30 to 45 minutes, 1.8% 45 to 60 minutes, 1.8% 60 minutes or more (2006-2010 5-year est.)

Erie County

Located in northwestern Pennsylvania; bounded on the north by Lake Erie, on the northeast by New York, and on the west by Ohio; drained by tributaries of the Allegheny River. Covers a land area of 799.154 square miles, a water area of 759.077 square miles, and is located in the Eastern Time Zone at 42.12° N. Lat., 80.10° W. Long. The county was founded in 1800. County seat is Erie.

Erie County is part of the Erie, PA Metropolitan Statistical Area. The entire metro area includes: Erie County, PA

Weather Station: Erie Intl Arpt										Elevation: 729 feet		
	Jan	Feb	Mar	Apr	May	Jun	Jul	Aug	Sep	Oct	Nov	Dec
High	34	35	44	56	66	76	80	79	72	61	50	38
Low	21	21	28	38	48	58	64	63	56	45	37	27
Precip	2.9	2.4	3.0	3.4	3.4	3.8	3.5	3.6	4.7	4.1	3.9	3.8
Snow	29.0	17.3	14.0	3.3	tr	tr	tr	tr	tr	0.2	7.9	27.9

High and Low temperatures in degrees Fahrenheit; Precipitation and Snow in inches

Population: 275,603 (1990); 280,843 (2000); 280,566 (2010); Race: 88.2% White, 7.2% Black, 1.1% Asian, 0.2% American Indian/Alaska Native, 0.0% Native Hawaiian/Other Pacific Islander, 3.3% Other, 3.4% Hispanic of any race (2010); Density: 351.1 persons per square mile (2010); Average household size: 2.42 (2010); Median age: 38.6 (2010); Males per 100 females: 96.7 (2010).
Religion: Six largest groups: 33.5% Catholicism, 5.7% Methodist/Pietist, 3.3% Holiness, 3.0% Lutheran, 2.2% Pentecostal, 2.2% Baptist (2010)
Economy: Unemployment rate: 7.6% (August 2012); Total civilian labor force: 146,385 (August 2012); Leading industries: 20.6% health care and social assistance; 19.6% manufacturing; 13.7% retail trade (2010); Farms: 1,609 totaling 173,125 acres (2007); Companies that employ 500 or more persons: 11 (2010); Companies that employ 100 to 499 persons: 154 (2010); Companies that employ less than 100 persons: 6,122 (2010); Black-owned businesses: 635 (2007); Hispanic-owned businesses: 227 (2007); Asian-owned businesses: n/a (2007); Women-owned businesses: 4,610 (2007); Retail sales per capita: $14,333 (2010). Single-family building permits issued: 140 (2011); Multi-family building permits issued: 171 (2011).
Income: Per capita income: $22,644 (2006-2010 5-year est.); Median household income: $43,595 (2006-2010 5-year est.); Average household income: $56,435 (2006-2010 5-year est.); Percent of households with income of $100,000 or more: 13.3% (2006-2010 5-year est.); Poverty rate: 15.6% (2006-2010 5-year est.); Bankruptcy rate: 3.22% (2011).
Taxes: Total county taxes per capita: $206 (2009); County property taxes per capita: $206 (2009).
Education: Percent of population age 25 and over with: High school diploma (including GED) or higher: 89.0% (2006-2010 5-year est.); Bachelor's degree or higher: 23.3% (2006-2010 5-year est.); Master's degree or higher: 8.7% (2006-2010 5-year est.).
Housing: Homeownership rate: 66.9% (2010); Median home value: $111,300 (2006-2010 5-year est.); Median contract rent: $474 per month (2006-2010 5-year est.); Median year structure built: 1959 (2006-2010 5-year est.)
Health: Birth rate: 113.4 per 10,000 population (2011); Death rate: 95.6 per 10,000 population (2011); Age-adjusted cancer mortality rate: 182.3 deaths per 100,000 population (2009); Number of physicians: 26.4 per 10,000 population (2010); Hospital beds: 44.2 per 10,000 population (2008); Hospital admissions: 1,679.4 per 10,000 population (2008).

Environment: Air Quality Index: 76.7% good, 22.7% moderate, 0.5% unhealthy for sensitive individuals, 0.0% unhealthy (percent of days in 2011)
Elections: 2012 Presidential election results: 57.4% Obama, 41.3% Romney
National and State Parks: Presque Isle State Park
Additional Information Contacts
Erie County Government. . . . . (814) 451-6000
  http://www.eriecountygov.org

Erie County Communities

ALBION (borough). Covers a land area of 1.078 square miles and a water area of 0.014 square miles. Located at 41.89° N. Lat; 80.36° W. Long. Elevation is 889 feet.
History: Covered bridges to the West. Settled 1815, incorporated 1861.
Population: 1,575 (1990); 1,607 (2000); 1,516 (2010); Density: 1,405.8 persons per square mile (2010); Race: 96.6% White, 0.9% Black, 0.1% Asian, 0.3% American Indian/Alaska Native, 0.0% Native Hawaiian/Other Pacific Islander, 2.1% Other, 1.8% Hispanic of any race (2010); Average household size: 2.35 (2010); Median age: 40.2 (2010); Males per 100 females: 85.6 (2010); Marriage status: 22.9% never married, 57.2% now married, 7.2% widowed, 12.6% divorced (2006-2010 5-year est.); Foreign born: 0.9% (2006-2010 5-year est.); Ancestry (includes multiple ancestries): 37.0% German, 22.6% Irish, 10.1% Italian, 9.6% English, 8.0% American (2006-2010 5-year est.).
Economy: Single-family building permits issued: 0 (2011); Multi-family building permits issued: 0 (2011); Employment by occupation: 6.1% management, 0.3% professional, 12.4% services, 17.3% sales, 3.3% farming, 9.6% construction, 7.2% production (2006-2010 5-year est.).
Income: Per capita income: $19,604 (2006-2010 5-year est.); Median household income: $42,153 (2006-2010 5-year est.); Average household income: $48,504 (2006-2010 5-year est.); Percent of households with income of $100,000 or more: 6.5% (2006-2010 5-year est.); Poverty rate: 13.4% (2006-2010 5-year est.).
Education: Percent of population age 25 and over with: High school diploma (including GED) or higher: 89.1% (2006-2010 5-year est.); Bachelor's degree or higher: 14.5% (2006-2010 5-year est.); Master's degree or higher: 4.8% (2006-2010 5-year est.).
School District(s)
Northwestern SD (KG-12)
  2010-11 Enrollment: 1,648 . . . . (814) 756-9400
Housing: Homeownership rate: 66.1% (2010); Median home value: $92,400 (2006-2010 5-year est.); Median contract rent: $340 per month (2006-2010 5-year est.); Median year structure built: 1955 (2006-2010 5-year est.).
Newspapers: The Albion News (Community news; Circulation 3,600)
Transportation: Commute to work: 93.5% car, 0.0% public transportation, 3.6% walk, 2.3% work from home (2006-2010 5-year est.); Travel time to work: 28.4% less than 15 minutes, 26.2% 15 to 30 minutes, 32.8% 30 to 45 minutes, 7.8% 45 to 60 minutes, 4.8% 60 minutes or more (2006-2010 5-year est.)
Additional Information Contacts
Albion Area Chamber of Commerce . . . . (814) 756-3660
  http://www.albionareachamber.com

AMITY (township). Covers a land area of 28.019 square miles and a water area of 0.155 square miles. Located at 41.97° N. Lat; 79.83° W. Long.
Population: 1,034 (1990); 1,140 (2000); 1,073 (2010); Density: 38.3 persons per square mile (2010); Race: 98.9% White, 0.3% Black, 0.0% Asian, 0.3% American Indian/Alaska Native, 0.0% Native Hawaiian/Other Pacific Islander, 0.5% Other, 0.2% Hispanic of any race (2010); Average household size: 2.84 (2010); Median age: 43.9 (2010); Males per 100 females: 106.7 (2010); Marriage status: 22.1% never married, 67.3% now married, 3.4% widowed, 7.2% divorced (2006-2010 5-year est.); Foreign born: 0.0% (2006-2010 5-year est.); Ancestry (includes multiple ancestries): 36.6% German, 13.6% Polish, 12.7% Irish, 10.7% American, 10.1% English (2006-2010 5-year est.).
Economy: Single-family building permits issued: 3 (2011); Multi-family building permits issued: 0 (2011); Employment by occupation: 5.9% management, 4.3% professional, 10.0% services, 20.4% sales, 3.7% farming, 17.4% construction, 11.3% production (2006-2010 5-year est.).
Income: Per capita income: $20,688 (2006-2010 5-year est.); Median household income: $52,083 (2006-2010 5-year est.); Average household

income: $57,627 (2006-2010 5-year est.); Percent of households with income of $100,000 or more: 12.5% (2006-2010 5-year est.); Poverty rate: 11.5% (2006-2010 5-year est.).
Education: Percent of population age 25 and over with: High school diploma (including GED) or higher: 88.0% (2006-2010 5-year est.); Bachelor's degree or higher: 16.9% (2006-2010 5-year est.); Master's degree or higher: 5.2% (2006-2010 5-year est.).
Housing: Homeownership rate: 92.9% (2010); Median home value: $128,400 (2006-2010 5-year est.); Median contract rent: $542 per month (2006-2010 5-year est.); Median year structure built: 1974 (2006-2010 5-year est.).
Transportation: Commute to work: 89.5% car, 0.0% public transportation, 2.0% walk, 5.4% work from home (2006-2010 5-year est.); Travel time to work: 13.9% less than 15 minutes, 35.8% 15 to 30 minutes, 40.3% 30 to 45 minutes, 9.9% 45 to 60 minutes, 0.0% 60 minutes or more (2006-2010 5-year est.)
Additional Information Contacts
Corry Area Chamber of Commerce. . . . . (814) 665-9925
  http://www.corrychamber.com

AVONIA (CDP). Covers a land area of 2.657 square miles and a water area of 0.003 square miles. Located at 42.05° N. Lat; 80.28° W. Long. Elevation is 673 feet.
Population: 1,371 (1990); 1,331 (2000); 1,205 (2010); Density: 453.5 persons per square mile (2010); Race: 98.5% White, 0.1% Black, 0.6% Asian, 0.0% American Indian/Alaska Native, 0.0% Native Hawaiian/Other Pacific Islander, 0.8% Other, 0.8% Hispanic of any race (2010); Average household size: 2.54 (2010); Median age: 46.2 (2010); Males per 100 females: 105.3 (2010); Marriage status: 20.1% never married, 71.8% now married, 2.4% widowed, 5.7% divorced (2006-2010 5-year est.); Foreign born: 2.5% (2006-2010 5-year est.); Ancestry (includes multiple ancestries): 40.7% German, 22.1% Irish, 13.7% Polish, 10.9% English, 7.4% Italian (2006-2010 5-year est.).
Economy: Employment by occupation: 17.8% management, 2.0% professional, 5.4% services, 23.1% sales, 3.9% farming, 8.0% construction, 3.7% production (2006-2010 5-year est.).
Income: Per capita income: $35,210 (2006-2010 5-year est.); Median household income: $66,818 (2006-2010 5-year est.); Average household income: $90,511 (2006-2010 5-year est.); Percent of households with income of $100,000 or more: 29.9% (2006-2010 5-year est.); Poverty rate: 6.4% (2006-2010 5-year est.).
Education: Percent of population age 25 and over with: High school diploma (including GED) or higher: 97.5% (2006-2010 5-year est.); Bachelor's degree or higher: 44.8% (2006-2010 5-year est.); Master's degree or higher: 15.9% (2006-2010 5-year est.).
Housing: Homeownership rate: 90.3% (2010); Median home value: $196,100 (2006-2010 5-year est.); Median contract rent: $508 per month (2006-2010 5-year est.); Median year structure built: 1970 (2006-2010 5-year est.).
Transportation: Commute to work: 95.5% car, 0.0% public transportation, 1.7% walk, 2.8% work from home (2006-2010 5-year est.); Travel time to work: 26.2% less than 15 minutes, 40.2% 15 to 30 minutes, 29.4% 30 to 45 minutes, 4.2% 45 to 60 minutes, 0.0% 60 minutes or more (2006-2010 5-year est.)
Additional Information Contacts
Greater Philadelphia Chamber of Commerce . . . . (215) 545-1234
  http://www.greaterphilachamber.com

CONCORD (township). Covers a land area of 33.108 square miles and a water area of 0.070 square miles. Located at 41.88° N. Lat; 79.69° W. Long. Elevation is 1,358 feet.
Population: 1,384 (1990); 1,361 (2000); 1,344 (2010); Density: 40.6 persons per square mile (2010); Race: 98.1% White, 0.1% Black, 0.1% Asian, 0.1% American Indian/Alaska Native, 0.0% Native Hawaiian/Other Pacific Islander, 1.6% Other, 0.7% Hispanic of any race (2010); Average household size: 2.72 (2010); Median age: 41.4 (2010); Males per 100 females: 97.4 (2010); Marriage status: 26.6% never married, 56.0% now married, 4.7% widowed, 12.8% divorced (2006-2010 5-year est.); Foreign born: 0.7% (2006-2010 5-year est.); Ancestry (includes multiple ancestries): 24.8% German, 15.3% Irish, 15.2% English, 13.5% American, 10.7% Polish (2006-2010 5-year est.).
Economy: Single-family building permits issued: 1 (2011); Multi-family building permits issued: 0 (2011); Employment by occupation: 9.2% management, 1.7% professional, 14.6% services, 11.7% sales, 4.4% farming, 11.3% construction, 9.2% production (2006-2010 5-year est.).

Income: Per capita income: $20,045 (2006-2010 5-year est.); Median household income: $48,438 (2006-2010 5-year est.); Average household income: $55,121 (2006-2010 5-year est.); Percent of households with income of $100,000 or more: 8.1% (2006-2010 5-year est.); Poverty rate: 7.8% (2006-2010 5-year est.).

Education: Percent of population age 25 and over with: High school diploma (including GED) or higher: 85.8% (2006-2010 5-year est.); Bachelor's degree or higher: 12.2% (2006-2010 5-year est.); Master's degree or higher: 3.1% (2006-2010 5-year est.).

Housing: Homeownership rate: 85.0% (2010); Median home value: $104,200 (2006-2010 5-year est.); Median contract rent: $408 per month (2006-2010 5-year est.); Median year structure built: 1969 (2006-2010 5-year est.).

Transportation: Commute to work: 96.0% car, 0.5% public transportation, 0.0% walk, 3.0% work from home (2006-2010 5-year est.); Travel time to work: 44.7% less than 15 minutes, 28.4% 15 to 30 minutes, 7.1% 30 to 45 minutes, 13.6% 45 to 60 minutes, 6.2% 60 minutes or more (2006-2010 5-year est.)

Additional Information Contacts

Corry Area Chamber of Commerce. . . . . (814) 665-9925
http://www.corrychamber.com

CONNEAUT (township).
Covers a land area of 43.072 square miles and a water area of 0.356 square miles. Located at 41.88° N. Lat; 80.44° W. Long.

Population: 1,956 (1990); 3,908 (2000); 4,290 (2010); Density: 99.6 persons per square mile (2010); Race: 70.2% White, 24.4% Black, 0.5% Asian, 0.4% American Indian/Alaska Native, 0.0% Native Hawaiian/Other Pacific Islander, 4.5% Other, 5.0% Hispanic of any race (2010); Average household size: 2.66 (2010); Median age: 37.6 (2010); Males per 100 females: 314.1 (2010); Marriage status: 37.1% never married, 44.5% now married, 5.8% widowed, 12.7% divorced (2006-2010 5-year est.); Foreign born: 2.0% (2006-2010 5-year est.); Ancestry (includes multiple ancestries): 19.1% German, 7.4% English, 6.3% Italian, 6.0% Irish, 3.9% American (2006-2010 5-year est.).

Economy: Employment by occupation: 1.9% management, 1.1% professional, 15.1% services, 14.6% sales, 1.6% farming, 13.2% construction, 14.2% production (2006-2010 5-year est.).

Income: Per capita income: $11,805 (2006-2010 5-year est.); Median household income: $39,393 (2006-2010 5-year est.); Average household income: $46,771 (2006-2010 5-year est.); Percent of households with income of $100,000 or more: 5.3% (2006-2010 5-year est.); Poverty rate: 18.1% (2006-2010 5-year est.).

Education: Percent of population age 25 and over with: High school diploma (including GED) or higher: 78.1% (2006-2010 5-year est.); Bachelor's degree or higher: 8.7% (2006-2010 5-year est.); Master's degree or higher: 4.1% (2006-2010 5-year est.).

Housing: Homeownership rate: 81.4% (2010); Median home value: $110,300 (2006-2010 5-year est.); Median contract rent: $434 per month (2006-2010 5-year est.); Median year structure built: 1970 (2006-2010 5-year est.).

Transportation: Commute to work: 91.6% car, 1.0% public transportation, 4.7% walk, 1.6% work from home (2006-2010 5-year est.); Travel time to work: 19.7% less than 15 minutes, 33.0% 15 to 30 minutes, 29.3% 30 to 45 minutes, 8.4% 45 to 60 minutes, 9.5% 60 minutes or more (2006-2010 5-year est.)

Additional Information Contacts

Girard-Lake City Chamber of Commerce . . . . (814) 774-3535
http://www.girardlakecity.org

CORRY (city).
Covers a land area of 5.994 square miles and a water area of 0.014 square miles. Located at 41.93° N. Lat; 79.63° W. Long. Elevation is 1,434 feet.

History: Settled 1795, incorporated as borough 1863, as city 1866.

Population: 7,216 (1990); 6,834 (2000); 6,605 (2010); Density: 1,102.0 persons per square mile (2010); Race: 97.5% White, 0.5% Black, 0.3% Asian, 0.2% American Indian/Alaska Native, 0.0% Native Hawaiian/Other Pacific Islander, 1.5% Other, 0.8% Hispanic of any race (2010); Average household size: 2.45 (2010); Median age: 37.7 (2010); Males per 100 females: 90.3 (2010); Marriage status: 28.3% never married, 49.1% now married, 10.0% widowed, 12.6% divorced (2006-2010 5-year est.); Foreign born: 0.7% (2006-2010 5-year est.); Ancestry (includes multiple ancestries): 28.7% German, 16.0% English, 14.1% Irish, 10.7% Italian, 7.6% Polish (2006-2010 5-year est.).

Economy: Single-family building permits issued: 0 (2011); Multi-family building permits issued: 0 (2011); Employment by occupation: 8.2% management, 2.9% professional, 8.6% services, 15.3% sales, 4.0% farming, 7.6% construction, 12.8% production (2006-2010 5-year est.).

Income: Per capita income: $16,913 (2006-2010 5-year est.); Median household income: $28,985 (2006-2010 5-year est.); Average household income: $41,594 (2006-2010 5-year est.); Percent of households with income of $100,000 or more: 5.5% (2006-2010 5-year est.); Poverty rate: 26.9% (2006-2010 5-year est.).

Education: Percent of population age 25 and over with: High school diploma (including GED) or higher: 85.0% (2006-2010 5-year est.); Bachelor's degree or higher: 11.2% (2006-2010 5-year est.); Master's degree or higher: 2.3% (2006-2010 5-year est.).

School District(s)

Corry Area SD (PK-12)
    2010-11 Enrollment: 2,319 . . . . (814) 664-4677

Housing: Homeownership rate: 56.6% (2010); Median home value: $72,000 (2006-2010 5-year est.); Median contract rent: $329 per month (2006-2010 5-year est.); Median year structure built: 1947 (2006-2010 5-year est.).

Hospitals: Corry Memorial Hospital (55 beds)

Safety: Violent crime rate: 45.3 per 10,000 population; Property crime rate: 369.8 per 10,000 population (2011).

Newspapers: The Corry Journal (Community news; Circulation 4,000)

Transportation: Commute to work: 88.7% car, 1.2% public transportation, 6.6% walk, 1.9% work from home (2006-2010 5-year est.); Travel time to work: 63.3% less than 15 minutes, 18.2% 15 to 30 minutes, 8.4% 30 to 45 minutes, 7.8% 45 to 60 minutes, 2.3% 60 minutes or more (2006-2010 5-year est.)

Additional Information Contacts

City of Corry . . . . (814) 664-9211
http://www.corrypa.com
Corry Area Chamber of Commerce. . . . . (814) 665-9925
http://www.corrychamber.com

CRANESVILLE (borough).
Covers a land area of 0.935 square miles and a water area of 0.005 square miles. Located at 41.90° N. Lat; 80.34° W. Long. Elevation is 945 feet.

Population: 598 (1990); 600 (2000); 638 (2010); Density: 682.2 persons per square mile (2010); Race: 98.0% White, 0.0% Black, 0.0% Asian, 0.0% American Indian/Alaska Native, 0.2% Native Hawaiian/Other Pacific Islander, 1.8% Other, 0.6% Hispanic of any race (2010); Average household size: 2.65 (2010); Median age: 37.8 (2010); Males per 100 females: 96.3 (2010); Marriage status: 25.9% never married, 64.7% now married, 4.8% widowed, 4.6% divorced (2006-2010 5-year est.); Foreign born: 0.5% (2006-2010 5-year est.); Ancestry (includes multiple ancestries): 35.3% German, 19.6% Irish, 16.1% English, 8.9% Italian, 5.4% Polish (2006-2010 5-year est.).

Economy: Single-family building permits issued: 0 (2011); Multi-family building permits issued: 0 (2011); Employment by occupation: 3.3% management, 0.0% professional, 13.7% services, 12.6% sales, 5.6% farming, 15.2% construction, 3.7% production (2006-2010 5-year est.).

Income: Per capita income: $16,946 (2006-2010 5-year est.); Median household income: $41,667 (2006-2010 5-year est.); Average household income: $43,278 (2006-2010 5-year est.); Percent of households with income of $100,000 or more: 5.4% (2006-2010 5-year est.); Poverty rate: 9.7% (2006-2010 5-year est.).

Education: Percent of population age 25 and over with: High school diploma (including GED) or higher: 82.7% (2006-2010 5-year est.); Bachelor's degree or higher: 9.3% (2006-2010 5-year est.); Master's degree or higher: 2.3% (2006-2010 5-year est.).

Housing: Homeownership rate: 77.6% (2010); Median home value: $84,700 (2006-2010 5-year est.); Median contract rent: $583 per month (2006-2010 5-year est.); Median year structure built: before 1940 (2006-2010 5-year est.).

Transportation: Commute to work: 97.8% car, 0.0% public transportation, 1.5% walk, 0.7% work from home (2006-2010 5-year est.); Travel time to work: 24.7% less than 15 minutes, 40.6% 15 to 30 minutes, 26.2% 30 to 45 minutes, 5.5% 45 to 60 minutes, 3.0% 60 minutes or more (2006-2010 5-year est.)

EAST SPRINGFIELD (unincorporated postal area)
Zip Code: 16411
    Covers a land area of 17.768 square miles and a water area of 2.000 square miles. Located at 41.97° N. Lat; 80.44° W. Long. Elevation is

748 feet. Population: 1,477 (2010); Density: 83.1 persons per square mile (2010); Race: 98.2% White, 0.4% Black, 0.2% Asian, 0.1% American Indian/Alaska Native, 0.0% Native Hawaiian/Other Pacific Islander, 1.1% Other, 0.9% Hispanic of any race (2010); Average household size: 2.60 (2010); Median age: 42.0 (2010); Males per 100 females: 104.9 (2010); Homeownership rate: 86.1% (2010)

EDINBORO (borough).
Covers a land area of 2.286 square miles and a water area of 0.119 square miles. Located at 41.87° N. Lat; 80.12° W. Long. Elevation is 1,214 feet.

History: Seat of Edinboro University of Pennsylvania.

Population: 7,664 (1990); 6,950 (2000); 6,438 (2010); Density: 2,815.7 persons per square mile (2010); Race: 92.0% White, 4.8% Black, 1.0% Asian, 0.2% American Indian/Alaska Native, 0.0% Native Hawaiian/Other Pacific Islander, 2.0% Other, 1.4% Hispanic of any race (2010); Average household size: 2.17 (2010); Median age: 22.0 (2010); Males per 100 females: 86.7 (2010); Marriage status: 59.6% never married, 30.1% now married, 4.6% widowed, 5.7% divorced (2006-2010 5-year est.); Foreign born: 8.0% (2006-2010 5-year est.); Ancestry (includes multiple ancestries): 28.8% German, 25.8% Irish, 11.8% Italian, 11.2% Polish, 9.0% English (2006-2010 5-year est.).

Economy: Single-family building permits issued: 2 (2011); Multi-family building permits issued: 0 (2011); Employment by occupation: 6.3% management, 8.1% professional, 23.8% services, 18.1% sales, 5.4% farming, 2.4% construction, 4.7% production (2006-2010 5-year est.).

Income: Per capita income: $19,369 (2006-2010 5-year est.); Median household income: $29,746 (2006-2010 5-year est.); Average household income: $47,210 (2006-2010 5-year est.); Percent of households with income of $100,000 or more: 13.8% (2006-2010 5-year est.); Poverty rate: 28.6% (2006-2010 5-year est.).

Education: Percent of population age 25 and over with: High school diploma (including GED) or higher: 93.9% (2006-2010 5-year est.); Bachelor's degree or higher: 42.1% (2006-2010 5-year est.); Master's degree or higher: 21.6% (2006-2010 5-year est.).

School District(s)
General Mclane SD (KG-12)
   2010-11 Enrollment: 2,148 . . . . (814) 273-1033

Four-year College(s)
Edinboro University of Pennsylvania (Public)
   Fall 2010 Enrollment: 7,438 . . . . (814) 732-2000
   2011-12 Tuition: In-state $8,360; Out-of-state $11,988

Housing: Homeownership rate: 36.3% (2010); Median home value: $145,200 (2006-2010 5-year est.); Median contract rent: $526 per month (2006-2010 5-year est.); Median year structure built: 1972 (2006-2010 5-year est.).

Safety: Violent crime rate: 4.6 per 10,000 population; Property crime rate: 171.9 per 10,000 population (2011).

Transportation: Commute to work: 75.2% car, 0.0% public transportation, 22.7% walk, 1.0% work from home (2006-2010 5-year est.); Travel time to work: 49.4% less than 15 minutes, 29.3% 15 to 30 minutes, 19.3% 30 to 45 minutes, 1.0% 45 to 60 minutes, 1.0% 60 minutes or more (2006-2010 5-year est.)

Additional Information Contacts
Borough of Edinboro . . . . (814) 734-1812
   http://www.edinboro.net
Girard-Lake City Chamber of Commerce . . . . (814) 774-3535
   http://www.girardlakecity.org

ELGIN (borough).
Covers a land area of 1.474 square miles and a water area of 0 square miles. Located at 41.91° N. Lat; 79.75° W. Long. Elevation is 1,388 feet.

Population: 229 (1990); 236 (2000); 218 (2010); Density: 147.9 persons per square mile (2010); Race: 99.5% White, 0.5% Black, 0.0% Asian, 0.0% American Indian/Alaska Native, 0.0% Native Hawaiian/Other Pacific Islander, 0.0% Other, 0.0% Hispanic of any race (2010); Average household size: 2.79 (2010); Median age: 39.4 (2010); Males per 100 females: 113.7 (2010); Marriage status: 26.7% never married, 63.9% now married, 2.6% widowed, 6.8% divorced (2006-2010 5-year est.); Foreign born: 0.8% (2006-2010 5-year est.); Ancestry (includes multiple ancestries): 20.4% English, 19.6% Polish, 17.2% German, 12.8% Irish, 7.2% American (2006-2010 5-year est.).

Economy: Single-family building permits issued: 0 (2011); Multi-family building permits issued: 0 (2011); Employment by occupation: 9.6% management, 0.0% professional, 15.2% services, 14.4% sales, 0.0% farming, 20.8% construction, 11.2% production (2006-2010 5-year est.).

Income: Per capita income: $19,658 (2006-2010 5-year est.); Median household income: $41,250 (2006-2010 5-year est.); Average household income: $51,707 (2006-2010 5-year est.); Percent of households with income of $100,000 or more: 5.2% (2006-2010 5-year est.); Poverty rate: 6.3% (2006-2010 5-year est.).

Education: Percent of population age 25 and over with: High school diploma (including GED) or higher: 92.3% (2006-2010 5-year est.); Bachelor's degree or higher: 11.0% (2006-2010 5-year est.); Master's degree or higher: 3.2% (2006-2010 5-year est.).

Housing: Homeownership rate: 88.5% (2010); Median home value: $91,400 (2006-2010 5-year est.); Median contract rent: $300 per month (2006-2010 5-year est.); Median year structure built: 1951 (2006-2010 5-year est.).

Transportation: Commute to work: 96.0% car, 0.0% public transportation, 2.4% walk, 1.6% work from home (2006-2010 5-year est.); Travel time to work: 31.7% less than 15 minutes, 25.2% 15 to 30 minutes, 12.2% 30 to 45 minutes, 23.6% 45 to 60 minutes, 7.3% 60 minutes or more (2006-2010 5-year est.)

ELK CREEK (township).
Covers a land area of 34.737 square miles and a water area of 0.104 square miles. Located at 41.89° N. Lat; 80.29° W. Long.

Population: 1,747 (1990); 1,800 (2000); 1,798 (2010); Density: 51.8 persons per square mile (2010); Race: 98.4% White, 0.5% Black, 0.1% Asian, 0.2% American Indian/Alaska Native, 0.0% Native Hawaiian/Other Pacific Islander, 0.8% Other, 1.4% Hispanic of any race (2010); Average household size: 2.62 (2010); Median age: 43.6 (2010); Males per 100 females: 103.9 (2010); Marriage status: 25.8% never married, 60.8% now married, 3.7% widowed, 9.8% divorced (2006-2010 5-year est.); Foreign born: 0.7% (2006-2010 5-year est.); Ancestry (includes multiple ancestries): 39.9% German, 12.9% English, 11.2% Irish, 10.6% Polish, 9.5% Italian (2006-2010 5-year est.).

Economy: Single-family building permits issued: 2 (2011); Multi-family building permits issued: 0 (2011); Employment by occupation: 6.2% management, 4.7% professional, 11.5% services, 16.9% sales, 2.6% farming, 11.7% construction, 6.7% production (2006-2010 5-year est.).

Income: Per capita income: $22,337 (2006-2010 5-year est.); Median household income: $57,216 (2006-2010 5-year est.); Average household income: $63,726 (2006-2010 5-year est.); Percent of households with income of $100,000 or more: 18.4% (2006-2010 5-year est.); Poverty rate: 4.1% (2006-2010 5-year est.).

Education: Percent of population age 25 and over with: High school diploma (including GED) or higher: 93.2% (2006-2010 5-year est.); Bachelor's degree or higher: 17.0% (2006-2010 5-year est.); Master's degree or higher: 4.5% (2006-2010 5-year est.).

Housing: Homeownership rate: 89.8% (2010); Median home value: $139,200 (2006-2010 5-year est.); Median contract rent: $496 per month (2006-2010 5-year est.); Median year structure built: 1974 (2006-2010 5-year est.).

Transportation: Commute to work: 92.6% car, 0.0% public transportation, 2.6% walk, 3.9% work from home (2006-2010 5-year est.); Travel time to work: 20.8% less than 15 minutes, 36.9% 15 to 30 minutes, 31.3% 30 to 45 minutes, 9.3% 45 to 60 minutes, 1.7% 60 minutes or more (2006-2010 5-year est.)

Additional Information Contacts
Girard-Lake City Chamber of Commerce . . . . (814) 774-3535
   http://www.girardlakecity.org

ERIE (city).
County seat. Covers a land area of 19.081 square miles and a water area of 0.198 square miles. Located at 42.12° N. Lat; 80.07° W. Long. Elevation is 653 feet.

History: Erie's first known inhabitants were members of the Eriez nation, from which the lake and later the city received their names. They were exterminated by the Seneca about 1654. In 1753, a French force, recognizing strategic possibilities, established a fort. By 1760, the fort had been abandoned to the conquering English. A permanent settlement was laid out in 1795 by Major Andrew Ellicott and General William Irvine. Its major development came after the opening of the Erie & Pittsburgh Canal in 1844 and the advent of the railroads in the 1850's. It was incorporated as a city in 1851.

Population: 108,718 (1990); 103,717 (2000); 101,786 (2010); Density: 5,334.5 persons per square mile (2010); Race: 75.0% White, 16.8% Black, 1.5% Asian, 0.3% American Indian/Alaska Native, 0.1% Native Hawaiian/Other Pacific Islander, 6.3% Other, 6.9% Hispanic of any race (2010); Average household size: 2.36 (2010); Median age: 33.2 (2010);

Males per 100 females: 93.3 (2010); Marriage status: 41.2% never married, 39.9% now married, 7.7% widowed, 11.2% divorced (2006-2010 5-year est.); Foreign born: 5.7% (2006-2010 5-year est.); Ancestry (includes multiple ancestries): 27.3% German, 17.4% Irish, 15.5% Italian, 12.7% Polish, 5.8% English (2006-2010 5-year est.).

Economy: Unemployment rate: 8.9% (August 2012); Total civilian labor force: 50,362 (August 2012); Single-family building permits issued: 6 (2011); Multi-family building permits issued: 9 (2011); Employment by occupation: 7.2% management, 3.1% professional, 13.6% services, 18.4% sales, 4.5% farming, 6.3% construction, 6.9% production (2006-2010 5-year est.).

Income: Per capita income: $18,242 (2006-2010 5-year est.); Median household income: $32,218 (2006-2010 5-year est.); Average household income: $43,955 (2006-2010 5-year est.); Percent of households with income of $100,000 or more: 6.8% (2006-2010 5-year est.); Poverty rate: 25.0% (2006-2010 5-year est.).

Taxes: Total city taxes per capita: $441 (2009); City property taxes per capita: $262 (2009).

Education: Percent of population age 25 and over with: High school diploma (including GED) or higher: 85.4% (2006-2010 5-year est.); Bachelor's degree or higher: 19.5% (2006-2010 5-year est.); Master's degree or higher: 6.8% (2006-2010 5-year est.).

School District(s)

Erie City SD (KG-12)
    2010-11 Enrollment: 12,452 . . . . (814) 874-6000
Erie County Technical School (10-12)
    2010-11 Enrollment: n/a . . . . (814) 464-8600
Fort Leboeuf SD (KG-12)
    2010-11 Enrollment: 2,175 . . . . (814) 796-2638
Harbor Creek SD (KG-12)
    2010-11 Enrollment: 1,996 . . . . (814) 897-2100
Iroquois SD (PK-12)
    2010-11 Enrollment: 1,292 . . . . (814) 899-7643
Millcreek Township SD (KG-12)
    2010-11 Enrollment: 7,295 . . . . (814) 835-5300
Montessori Regional CS (KG-06)
    2010-11 Enrollment: 262 . . . . (814) 833-7771
Perseus House CS of Excellence (07-12)
    2010-11 Enrollment: 435 . . . . (814) 480-5962
Robert Benjamin Wiley Community CS (PK-12)
    2010-11 Enrollment: 377 . . . . (814) 461-9600
Wattsburg Area SD (KG-12)
    2010-11 Enrollment: 1,584 . . . . (814) 824-4145

Four-year College(s)

Gannon University (Private, Not-for-profit, Roman Catholic)
    Fall 2010 Enrollment: 3,782 . . . . (814) 871-7000
    2011-12 Tuition: In-state $25,522; Out-of-state $25,522
Lake Erie College of Osteopathic Medicine (Private, Not-for-profit)
    Fall 2010 Enrollment: 9,450 . . . . (814) 866-6641
Mercyhurst College (Private, Not-for-profit, Roman Catholic)
    Fall 2010 Enrollment: 3,864 . . . . (814) 824-2000
    2011-12 Tuition: In-state $27,657; Out-of-state $27,657
Pennsylvania State University-Penn State Erie-Behrend College (Public)
    Fall 2010 Enrollment: 4,333 . . . . (814) 898-6000
    2011-12 Tuition: In-state $13,636; Out-of-state $20,408

Two-year College(s)

Erie Business Center-Erie (Private, For-profit)
    Fall 2010 Enrollment: 282 . . . . (814) 456-7504
    2011-12 Tuition: In-state $9,364; Out-of-state $9,364
Erie Institute of Technology Inc (Private, For-profit)
    Fall 2010 Enrollment: 490 . . . . (814) 868-9900
    2011-12 Tuition: In-state $12,769; Out-of-state $12,769
Fortis Institute-Erie (Private, For-profit)
    Fall 2010 Enrollment: 1,475 . . . . (814) 838-7673
    2011-12 Tuition: In-state $13,000; Out-of-state $13,000
Great Lakes Institute of Technology (Private, For-profit)
    Fall 2010 Enrollment: 559 . . . . (814) 864-6666
Northwest Regional Technology Institute (Private, For-profit)
    Fall 2010 Enrollment: 89 . . . . (814) 455-4446
Triangle Tech Inc-Erie (Private, For-profit)
    Fall 2010 Enrollment: 271 . . . . (814) 453-6016
    2011-12 Tuition: In-state $15,604; Out-of-state $15,604

Housing: Homeownership rate: 52.3% (2010); Median home value: $82,400 (2006-2010 5-year est.); Median contract rent: $454 per month

(2006-2010 5-year est.); Median year structure built: 1946 (2006-2010 5-year est.).

Hospitals: Hamot Medical Center (360 beds); HealthSouth Rehabilitation Hospital of Erie (100 beds); Millcreek Community Hospital; Saint Vincent Health Center (490 beds); Shriners Hospital for Children (30 beds); Veterans Affairs Medical Center (81 beds)

Safety: Violent crime rate: 42.2 per 10,000 population; Property crime rate: 366.1 per 10,000 population (2011).

Newspapers: The Catholic Peace Voice (Regional news; Circulation 14,500); Erie Gay News (Community news); Erie Times-News (Local news; Circulation 78,909); Lake Shore Visitor (Local news); Sportsweek - Erie Times-News

Transportation: Commute to work: 87.8% car, 3.8% public transportation, 5.3% walk, 1.6% work from home (2006-2010 5-year est.); Travel time to work: 45.1% less than 15 minutes, 40.4% 15 to 30 minutes, 10.3% 30 to 45 minutes, 1.9% 45 to 60 minutes, 2.2% 60 minutes or more (2006-2010 5-year est.); Amtrak: train service available.

Airports: Erie International/Tom Ridge Field (primary service)

Additional Information Contacts
City of Erie. . . . . (814) 870-1234
    http://www.erie.pa.us
Erie Regional Chamber and Growth Partnership . . . . (814) 454-7191
    http://www.eriepa.com

FAIRVIEW (CDP). Covers a land area of 3.518 square miles and a water area of 0.027 square miles. Located at 42.02° N. Lat; 80.25° W. Long. Elevation is 797 feet.

Population: n/a (1990); n/a (2000); 2,348 (2010); Density: 667.5 persons per square mile (2010); Race: 97.9% White, 0.6% Black, 0.4% Asian, 0.1% American Indian/Alaska Native, 0.0% Native Hawaiian/Other Pacific Islander, 1.0% Other, 1.7% Hispanic of any race (2010); Average household size: 2.44 (2010); Median age: 47.5 (2010); Males per 100 females: 80.2 (2010); Marriage status: 24.4% never married, 59.6% now married, 10.4% widowed, 5.5% divorced (2006-2010 5-year est.); Foreign born: 0.0% (2006-2010 5-year est.); Ancestry (includes multiple ancestries): 30.9% German, 20.3% Italian, 16.0% Irish, 9.9% English, 9.6% Polish (2006-2010 5-year est.).

Economy: Employment by occupation: 15.8% management, 5.1% professional, 11.2% services, 13.9% sales, 3.8% farming, 6.9% construction, 5.7% production (2006-2010 5-year est.).

Income: Per capita income: $19,725 (2006-2010 5-year est.); Median household income: $55,352 (2006-2010 5-year est.); Average household income: $57,808 (2006-2010 5-year est.); Percent of households with income of $100,000 or more: 9.8% (2006-2010 5-year est.); Poverty rate: 10.0% (2006-2010 5-year est.).

Education: Percent of population age 25 and over with: High school diploma (including GED) or higher: 83.9% (2006-2010 5-year est.); Bachelor's degree or higher: 22.2% (2006-2010 5-year est.); Master's degree or higher: 7.1% (2006-2010 5-year est.).

School District(s)

Fairview SD (KG-12)
    2010-11 Enrollment: 1,583 . . . . (814) 474-2600
Millcreek Township SD (KG-12)
    2010-11 Enrollment: 7,295 . . . . (814) 835-5300

Housing: Homeownership rate: 77.3% (2010); Median home value: $130,200 (2006-2010 5-year est.); Median contract rent: $654 per month (2006-2010 5-year est.); Median year structure built: 1962 (2006-2010 5-year est.).

Transportation: Commute to work: 91.9% car, 0.0% public transportation, 2.9% walk, 5.2% work from home (2006-2010 5-year est.); Travel time to work: 21.8% less than 15 minutes, 48.5% 15 to 30 minutes, 27.9% 30 to 45 minutes, 0.0% 45 to 60 minutes, 1.9% 60 minutes or more (2006-2010 5-year est.)

FAIRVIEW (township). Covers a land area of 28.969 square miles and a water area of 0.192 square miles. Located at 42.03° N. Lat; 80.24° W. Long. Elevation is 797 feet.

Population: 9,827 (1990); 10,140 (2000); 10,102 (2010); Density: 348.7 persons per square mile (2010); Race: 97.6% White, 0.6% Black, 0.7% Asian, 0.2% American Indian/Alaska Native, 0.0% Native Hawaiian/Other Pacific Islander, 0.9% Other, 1.4% Hispanic of any race (2010); Average household size: 2.53 (2010); Median age: 47.4 (2010); Males per 100 females: 91.9 (2010); Marriage status: 22.4% never married, 61.9% now married, 9.6% widowed, 6.1% divorced (2006-2010 5-year est.); Foreign born: 2.4% (2006-2010 5-year est.); Ancestry (includes multiple

ancestries): 35.4% German, 19.2% Irish, 15.8% Italian, 14.1% English, 10.6% Polish (2006-2010 5-year est.).

Economy: Single-family building permits issued: 17 (2011); Multi-family building permits issued: 0 (2011); Employment by occupation: 20.1% management, 3.6% professional, 9.2% services, 15.9% sales, 3.5% farming, 5.0% construction, 3.1% production (2006-2010 5-year est.).

Income: Per capita income: $31,971 (2006-2010 5-year est.); Median household income: $67,482 (2006-2010 5-year est.); Average household income: $85,760 (2006-2010 5-year est.); Percent of households with income of $100,000 or more: 26.9% (2006-2010 5-year est.); Poverty rate: 4.8% (2006-2010 5-year est.).

Education: Percent of population age 25 and over with: High school diploma (including GED) or higher: 92.6% (2006-2010 5-year est.); Bachelor's degree or higher: 35.8% (2006-2010 5-year est.); Master's degree or higher: 13.9% (2006-2010 5-year est.).

Housing: Homeownership rate: 87.6% (2010); Median home value: $178,000 (2006-2010 5-year est.); Median contract rent: $562 per month (2006-2010 5-year est.); Median year structure built: 1969 (2006-2010 5-year est.).

Transportation: Commute to work: 93.1% car, 0.0% public transportation, 1.2% walk, 5.0% work from home (2006-2010 5-year est.); Travel time to work: 23.0% less than 15 minutes, 53.3% 15 to 30 minutes, 19.5% 30 to 45 minutes, 2.0% 45 to 60 minutes, 2.2% 60 minutes or more (2006-2010 5-year est.).

Additional Information Contacts

Erie Regional Chamber and Growth Partnership . . . . (814) 454-7191
    http://www.eriepa.com
Fairview Township. . . . . (814) 474-5942
    http://www.fairviewtownship.com

FRANKLIN (township). Covers a land area of 28.663 square miles and a water area of 0.039 square miles. Located at 41.93° N. Lat; 80.22° W. Long.

Population: 1,429 (1990); 1,609 (2000); 1,633 (2010); Density: 57.0 persons per square mile (2010); Race: 97.9% White, 0.7% Black, 0.4% Asian, 0.0% American Indian/Alaska Native, 0.0% Native Hawaiian/Other Pacific Islander, 1.0% Other, 0.6% Hispanic of any race (2010); Average household size: 2.76 (2010); Median age: 42.8 (2010); Males per 100 females: 111.5 (2010); Marriage status: 22.6% never married, 71.4% now married, 1.9% widowed, 4.2% divorced (2006-2010 5-year est.); Foreign born: 0.8% (2006-2010 5-year est.); Ancestry (includes multiple ancestries): 40.1% German, 15.4% English, 13.6% Polish, 13.5% Irish, 9.8% Italian (2006-2010 5-year est.).

Economy: Single-family building permits issued: 1 (2011); Multi-family building permits issued: 0 (2011); Employment by occupation: 12.7% management, 5.5% professional, 10.8% services, 14.8% sales, 4.0% farming, 11.5% construction, 6.9% production (2006-2010 5-year est.).

Income: Per capita income: $27,118 (2006-2010 5-year est.); Median household income: $65,000 (2006-2010 5-year est.); Average household income: $73,788 (2006-2010 5-year est.); Percent of households with income of $100,000 or more: 21.4% (2006-2010 5-year est.); Poverty rate: 5.4% (2006-2010 5-year est.).

Education: Percent of population age 25 and over with: High school diploma (including GED) or higher: 89.1% (2006-2010 5-year est.); Bachelor's degree or higher: 25.3% (2006-2010 5-year est.); Master's degree or higher: 10.0% (2006-2010 5-year est.).

Housing: Homeownership rate: 90.9% (2010); Median home value: $169,400 (2006-2010 5-year est.); Median contract rent: $544 per month (2006-2010 5-year est.); Median year structure built: 1976 (2006-2010 5-year est.).

Transportation: Commute to work: 95.2% car, 0.0% public transportation, 0.0% walk, 3.1% work from home (2006-2010 5-year est.); Travel time to work: 21.0% less than 15 minutes, 40.3% 15 to 30 minutes, 28.8% 30 to 45 minutes, 4.5% 45 to 60 minutes, 5.4% 60 minutes or more (2006-2010 5-year est.)

Additional Information Contacts

Fulton County Chamber of Commerce and Tourism . . . . . . (717) 485-4064
    http://www.fultoncountypa.com

GIRARD (borough). Covers a land area of 2.344 square miles and a water area of 0.019 square miles. Located at 42.00° N. Lat; 80.32° W. Long. Elevation is 771 feet.

Population: 2,879 (1990); 3,164 (2000); 3,104 (2010); Density: 1,324.5 persons per square mile (2010); Race: 97.2% White, 0.7% Black, 0.6% Asian, 0.3% American Indian/Alaska Native, 0.0% Native Hawaiian/Other

Pacific Islander, 1.2% Other, 0.7% Hispanic of any race (2010); Average household size: 2.40 (2010); Median age: 39.7 (2010); Males per 100 females: 90.9 (2010); Marriage status: 21.1% never married, 63.7% now married, 3.2% widowed, 12.0% divorced (2006-2010 5-year est.); Foreign born: 1.6% (2006-2010 5-year est.); Ancestry (includes multiple ancestries): 44.4% German, 26.7% Irish, 16.3% Polish, 16.2% Italian, 4.7% English (2006-2010 5-year est.).

Economy: Single-family building permits issued: 0 (2011); Multi-family building permits issued: 0 (2011); Employment by occupation: 6.3% management, 1.9% professional, 7.1% services, 24.0% sales, 3.4% farming, 7.8% construction, 9.3% production (2006-2010 5-year est.).

Income: Per capita income: $20,557 (2006-2010 5-year est.); Median household income: $40,372 (2006-2010 5-year est.); Average household income: $48,282 (2006-2010 5-year est.); Percent of households with income of $100,000 or more: 6.5% (2006-2010 5-year est.); Poverty rate: 16.2% (2006-2010 5-year est.).

Education: Percent of population age 25 and over with: High school diploma (including GED) or higher: 96.2% (2006-2010 5-year est.); Bachelor's degree or higher: 9.9% (2006-2010 5-year est.); Master's degree or higher: 3.6% (2006-2010 5-year est.).

School District(s)

Girard SD (PK-12)
    2010-11 Enrollment: 1,979 . . . . (814) 774-5666

Housing: Homeownership rate: 71.8% (2010); Median home value: $99,400 (2006-2010 5-year est.); Median contract rent: $411 per month (2006-2010 5-year est.); Median year structure built: 1961 (2006-2010 5-year est.).

Safety: Violent crime rate: 28.9 per 10,000 population; Property crime rate: 96.3 per 10,000 population (2011).

Transportation: Commute to work: 95.9% car, 0.0% public transportation, 2.9% walk, 0.0% work from home (2006-2010 5-year est.); Travel time to work: 39.2% less than 15 minutes, 36.7% 15 to 30 minutes, 20.7% 30 to 45 minutes, 3.4% 45 to 60 minutes, 0.0% 60 minutes or more (2006-2010 5-year est.)

Additional Information Contacts

Girard-Lake City Chamber of Commerce . . . . (814) 774-3535
    http://www.girardlakecity.org

GIRARD (township). Covers a land area of 31.499 square miles and a water area of 0.251 square miles. Located at 41.98° N. Lat; 80.32° W. Long. Elevation is 771 feet.

History: Settled c.1800, incorporated 1846.

Population: 4,729 (1990); 5,133 (2000); 5,102 (2010); Density: 162.0 persons per square mile (2010); Race: 97.8% White, 0.3% Black, 0.2% Asian, 0.3% American Indian/Alaska Native, 0.2% Native Hawaiian/Other Pacific Islander, 1.2% Other, 1.0% Hispanic of any race (2010); Average household size: 2.45 (2010); Median age: 44.4 (2010); Males per 100 females: 100.7 (2010); Marriage status: 22.5% never married, 61.8% now married, 6.5% widowed, 9.2% divorced (2006-2010 5-year est.); Foreign born: 0.0% (2006-2010 5-year est.); Ancestry (includes multiple ancestries): 38.6% German, 17.4% Irish, 16.7% Polish, 12.7% Italian, 12.0% English (2006-2010 5-year est.).

Economy: Single-family building permits issued: 5 (2011); Multi-family building permits issued: 0 (2011); Employment by occupation: 10.9% management, 1.2% professional, 7.9% services, 17.6% sales, 2.0% farming, 13.9% construction, 11.9% production (2006-2010 5-year est.).

Income: Per capita income: $26,772 (2006-2010 5-year est.); Median household income: $50,119 (2006-2010 5-year est.); Average household income: $62,825 (2006-2010 5-year est.); Percent of households with income of $100,000 or more: 16.7% (2006-2010 5-year est.); Poverty rate: 6.1% (2006-2010 5-year est.).

Education: Percent of population age 25 and over with: High school diploma (including GED) or higher: 90.8% (2006-2010 5-year est.); Bachelor's degree or higher: 17.4% (2006-2010 5-year est.); Master's degree or higher: 6.0% (2006-2010 5-year est.).

Housing: Homeownership rate: 84.0% (2010); Median home value: $117,500 (2006-2010 5-year est.); Median contract rent: $383 per month (2006-2010 5-year est.); Median year structure built: 1978 (2006-2010 5-year est.).

Transportation: Commute to work: 97.0% car, 0.0% public transportation, 0.0% walk, 1.9% work from home (2006-2010 5-year est.); Travel time to work: 26.1% less than 15 minutes, 36.9% 15 to 30 minutes, 27.5% 30 to 45 minutes, 8.0% 45 to 60 minutes, 1.4% 60 minutes or more (2006-2010 5-year est.)

Additional Information Contacts
Girard Township . . . . (814) 774-4738
http://www.girardtownship.com
Girard-Lake City Chamber of Commerce . . . . (814) 774-3535
http://www.girardlakecity.org

GREENE (township).

Covers a land area of 37.385 square miles and a water area of 0.119 square miles. Located at 42.05° N. Lat; 79.95° W. Long.

Population: 4,959 (1990); 4,768 (2000); 4,706 (2010); Density: 125.9 persons per square mile (2010); Race: 98.5% White, 0.3% Black, 0.4% Asian, 0.1% American Indian/Alaska Native, 0.0% Native Hawaiian/Other Pacific Islander, 0.7% Other, 0.6% Hispanic of any race (2010); Average household size: 2.64 (2010); Median age: 43.9 (2010); Males per 100 females: 102.7 (2010); Marriage status: 23.9% never married, 56.9% now married, 8.2% widowed, 11.0% divorced (2006-2010 5-year est.); Foreign born: 1.2% (2006-2010 5-year est.); Ancestry (includes multiple ancestries): 43.0% German, 21.2% Polish, 13.5% Irish, 13.3% Italian, 8.8% English (2006-2010 5-year est.).

Economy: Single-family building permits issued: 1 (2011); Multi-family building permits issued: 0 (2011); Employment by occupation: 6.8% management, 4.2% professional, 10.8% services, 17.4% sales, 1.8% farming, 11.0% construction, 8.0% production (2006-2010 5-year est.).

Income: Per capita income: $27,972 (2006-2010 5-year est.); Median household income: $57,397 (2006-2010 5-year est.); Average household income: $70,483 (2006-2010 5-year est.); Percent of households with income of $100,000 or more: 22.2% (2006-2010 5-year est.); Poverty rate: 8.1% (2006-2010 5-year est.).

Education: Percent of population age 25 and over with: High school diploma (including GED) or higher: 89.6% (2006-2010 5-year est.); Bachelor's degree or higher: 20.2% (2006-2010 5-year est.); Master's degree or higher: 7.6% (2006-2010 5-year est.).

Housing: Homeownership rate: 91.0% (2010); Median home value: $150,100 (2006-2010 5-year est.); Median contract rent: $514 per month (2006-2010 5-year est.); Median year structure built: 1969 (2006-2010 5-year est.).

Transportation: Commute to work: 95.2% car, 0.0% public transportation, 0.9% walk, 3.1% work from home (2006-2010 5-year est.); Travel time to work: 26.9% less than 15 minutes, 57.8% 15 to 30 minutes, 12.8% 30 to 45 minutes, 0.0% 45 to 60 minutes, 2.5% 60 minutes or more (2006-2010 5-year est.)

Additional Information Contacts
Erie Regional Chamber and Growth Partnership . . . . (814) 454-7191
http://www.eriepa.com

GREENFIELD (township).

Covers a land area of 33.772 square miles and a water area of 0.380 square miles. Located at 42.12° N. Lat; 79.84° W. Long.

Population: 1,770 (1990); 1,909 (2000); 1,933 (2010); Density: 57.2 persons per square mile (2010); Race: 98.4% White, 0.2% Black, 0.3% Asian, 0.1% American Indian/Alaska Native, 0.0% Native Hawaiian/Other Pacific Islander, 1.0% Other, 0.6% Hispanic of any race (2010); Average household size: 2.73 (2010); Median age: 41.7 (2010); Males per 100 females: 107.4 (2010); Marriage status: 20.7% never married, 65.7% now married, 4.5% widowed, 9.1% divorced (2006-2010 5-year est.); Foreign born: 1.7% (2006-2010 5-year est.); Ancestry (includes multiple ancestries): 35.8% German, 18.2% Irish, 17.9% Polish, 12.8% English, 10.5% Italian (2006-2010 5-year est.).

Economy: Single-family building permits issued: 3 (2011); Multi-family building permits issued: 0 (2011); Employment by occupation: 10.7% management, 3.3% professional, 6.7% services, 17.2% sales, 3.4% farming, 14.8% construction, 9.5% production (2006-2010 5-year est.).

Income: Per capita income: $26,228 (2006-2010 5-year est.); Median household income: $56,250 (2006-2010 5-year est.); Average household income: $65,124 (2006-2010 5-year est.); Percent of households with income of $100,000 or more: 22.2% (2006-2010 5-year est.); Poverty rate: 7.2% (2006-2010 5-year est.).

Education: Percent of population age 25 and over with: High school diploma (including GED) or higher: 87.4% (2006-2010 5-year est.); Bachelor's degree or higher: 14.8% (2006-2010 5-year est.); Master's degree or higher: 4.2% (2006-2010 5-year est.).

Housing: Homeownership rate: 91.8% (2010); Median home value: $140,000 (2006-2010 5-year est.); Median contract rent: $327 per month (2006-2010 5-year est.); Median year structure built: 1978 (2006-2010 5-year est.).

Transportation: Commute to work: 94.5% car, 0.0% public transportation, 1.3% walk, 2.8% work from home (2006-2010 5-year est.); Travel time to work: 21.3% less than 15 minutes, 56.5% 15 to 30 minutes, 18.3% 30 to 45 minutes, 1.0% 45 to 60 minutes, 2.8% 60 minutes or more (2006-2010 5-year est.)

Additional Information Contacts
North East Area Chamber of Commerce . . . . (814) 725-4262
http://www.nechamber.org/about

HARBORCREEK (township).

Aka Harbor Creek. Covers a land area of 34.086 square miles and a water area of 0.025 square miles. Located at 42.15° N. Lat; 79.96° W. Long. Elevation is 732 feet.

Population: 15,108 (1990); 15,178 (2000); 17,234 (2010); Density: 505.6 persons per square mile (2010); Race: 96.7% White, 1.4% Black, 0.8% Asian, 0.1% American Indian/Alaska Native, 0.0% Native Hawaiian/Other Pacific Islander, 1.0% Other, 1.0% Hispanic of any race (2010); Average household size: 2.49 (2010); Median age: 41.5 (2010); Males per 100 females: 102.8 (2010); Marriage status: 31.8% never married, 54.2% now married, 6.2% widowed, 7.8% divorced (2006-2010 5-year est.); Foreign born: 1.8% (2006-2010 5-year est.); Ancestry (includes multiple ancestries): 36.5% German, 19.7% Polish, 15.8% Irish, 14.3% Italian, 10.3% English (2006-2010 5-year est.).

Economy: Single-family building permits issued: 10 (2011); Multi-family building permits issued: 0 (2011); Employment by occupation: 8.7% management, 4.3% professional, 10.0% services, 16.9% sales, 4.6% farming, 8.6% construction, 6.2% production (2006-2010 5-year est.).

Income: Per capita income: $23,733 (2006-2010 5-year est.); Median household income: $59,346 (2006-2010 5-year est.); Average household income: $65,772 (2006-2010 5-year est.); Percent of households with income of $100,000 or more: 20.1% (2006-2010 5-year est.); Poverty rate: 8.7% (2006-2010 5-year est.).

Education: Percent of population age 25 and over with: High school diploma (including GED) or higher: 91.6% (2006-2010 5-year est.); Bachelor's degree or higher: 26.4% (2006-2010 5-year est.); Master's degree or higher: 9.8% (2006-2010 5-year est.).

School District(s)

Harbor Creek SD (KG-12)
    2010-11 Enrollment: 1,996 . . . . (814) 897-2100

Housing: Homeownership rate: 79.5% (2010); Median home value: $146,500 (2006-2010 5-year est.); Median contract rent: $494 per month (2006-2010 5-year est.); Median year structure built: 1971 (2006-2010 5-year est.).

Transportation: Commute to work: 91.0% car, 0.4% public transportation, 4.9% walk, 3.2% work from home (2006-2010 5-year est.); Travel time to work: 37.8% less than 15 minutes, 47.3% 15 to 30 minutes, 11.3% 30 to 45 minutes, 1.6% 45 to 60 minutes, 2.0% 60 minutes or more (2006-2010 5-year est.)

Additional Information Contacts
Harborcreek Township . . . . (814) 899-3171
http://www.harborcreektownship.org
North East Area Chamber of Commerce . . . . (814) 725-4262
http://www.nechamber.org

LAKE CITY (borough).

Aka North Girard. Covers a land area of 1.798 square miles and a water area of 0.008 square miles. Located at 42.02° N. Lat; 80.35° W. Long. Elevation is 719 feet.

History: Borough formally called North Girard.

Population: 2,519 (1990); 2,811 (2000); 3,031 (2010); Density: 1,685.6 persons per square mile (2010); Race: 97.0% White, 0.9% Black, 0.2% Asian, 0.2% American Indian/Alaska Native, 0.1% Native Hawaiian/Other Pacific Islander, 1.6% Other, 1.3% Hispanic of any race (2010); Average household size: 2.70 (2010); Median age: 35.3 (2010); Males per 100 females: 93.3 (2010); Marriage status: 29.7% never married, 55.6% now married, 7.2% widowed, 7.5% divorced (2006-2010 5-year est.); Foreign born: 4.4% (2006-2010 5-year est.); Ancestry (includes multiple ancestries): 30.0% German, 15.1% Irish, 11.9% Polish, 11.5% English, 11.2% Italian (2006-2010 5-year est.).

Economy: Single-family building permits issued: 0 (2011); Multi-family building permits issued: 0 (2011); Employment by occupation: 4.9% management, 1.3% professional, 13.2% services, 15.8% sales, 2.6% farming, 10.7% construction, 10.6% production (2006-2010 5-year est.).

Income: Per capita income: $17,753 (2006-2010 5-year est.); Median household income: $43,837 (2006-2010 5-year est.); Average household income: $47,921 (2006-2010 5-year est.); Percent of households with

income of $100,000 or more: 6.4% (2006-2010 5-year est.); Poverty rate: 11.2% (2006-2010 5-year est.).

Education: Percent of population age 25 and over with: High school diploma (including GED) or higher: 88.8% (2006-2010 5-year est.); Bachelor's degree or higher: 11.9% (2006-2010 5-year est.); Master's degree or higher: 4.5% (2006-2010 5-year est.).

School District(s)

Girard SD (PK-12)

   2010-11 Enrollment: 1,979 . . . . (814) 774-5666

Housing: Homeownership rate: 77.7% (2010); Median home value: $102,000 (2006-2010 5-year est.); Median contract rent: $471 per month (2006-2010 5-year est.); Median year structure built: 1960 (2006-2010 5-year est.).

Safety: Violent crime rate: 16.4 per 10,000 population; Property crime rate: 226.9 per 10,000 population (2011).

Transportation: Commute to work: 93.9% car, 0.0% public transportation, 2.6% walk, 1.0% work from home (2006-2010 5-year est.); Travel time to work: 32.2% less than 15 minutes, 38.1% 15 to 30 minutes, 24.6% 30 to 45 minutes, 4.7% 45 to 60 minutes, 0.4% 60 minutes or more (2006-2010 5-year est.)

Additional Information Contacts

Girard-Lake City Chamber of Commerce . . . . (814) 774-3535
  http://www.girardlakecity.org

LAWRENCE PARK (cdp/township).
Covers a land area of 1.836 square miles and a water area of 0 square miles. Located at 42.15° N. Lat; 80.02° W. Long. Elevation is 650 feet.

Population: 4,310 (1990); 4,048 (2000); 3,982 (2010); Density: 2,168.3 persons per square mile (2010); Race: 96.1% White, 1.9% Black, 0.2% Asian, 0.2% American Indian/Alaska Native, 0.0% Native Hawaiian/Other Pacific Islander, 1.6% Other, 1.9% Hispanic of any race (2010); Average household size: 2.54 (2010); Median age: 39.4 (2010); Males per 100 females: 88.9 (2010); Marriage status: 23.1% never married, 56.9% now married, 10.0% widowed, 10.0% divorced (2006-2010 5-year est.); Foreign born: 1.0% (2006-2010 5-year est.); Ancestry (includes multiple ancestries): 36.1% German, 19.9% Irish, 12.7% Italian, 11.9% Polish, 8.5% English (2006-2010 5-year est.).

Economy: Single-family building permits issued: 0 (2011); Multi-family building permits issued: 0 (2011); Employment by occupation: 6.8% management, 4.0% professional, 13.4% services, 14.5% sales, 3.1% farming, 7.2% construction, 9.4% production (2006-2010 5-year est.).

Income: Per capita income: $23,128 (2006-2010 5-year est.); Median household income: $56,237 (2006-2010 5-year est.); Average household income: $60,094 (2006-2010 5-year est.); Percent of households with income of $100,000 or more: 10.2% (2006-2010 5-year est.); Poverty rate: 7.4% (2006-2010 5-year est.).

Education: Percent of population age 25 and over with: High school diploma (including GED) or higher: 90.5% (2006-2010 5-year est.); Bachelor's degree or higher: 15.0% (2006-2010 5-year est.); Master's degree or higher: 4.2% (2006-2010 5-year est.).

Housing: Homeownership rate: 80.3% (2010); Median home value: $98,000 (2006-2010 5-year est.); Median contract rent: $454 per month (2006-2010 5-year est.); Median year structure built: 1945 (2006-2010 5-year est.).

Transportation: Commute to work: 93.9% car, 0.9% public transportation, 4.8% walk, 0.4% work from home (2006-2010 5-year est.); Travel time to work: 42.4% less than 15 minutes, 40.1% 15 to 30 minutes, 11.8% 30 to 45 minutes, 1.6% 45 to 60 minutes, 4.1% 60 minutes or more (2006-2010 5-year est.)

LEBOEUF (township).
Covers a land area of 33.468 square miles and a water area of 0.412 square miles. Located at 41.88° N. Lat; 79.96° W. Long.

Population: 1,521 (1990); 1,680 (2000); 1,698 (2010); Density: 50.7 persons per square mile (2010); Race: 98.7% White, 0.1% Black, 0.4% Asian, 0.2% American Indian/Alaska Native, 0.0% Native Hawaiian/Other Pacific Islander, 0.6% Other, 0.3% Hispanic of any race (2010); Average household size: 2.76 (2010); Median age: 40.4 (2010); Males per 100 females: 100.9 (2010); Marriage status: 22.9% never married, 65.3% now married, 3.8% widowed, 8.0% divorced (2006-2010 5-year est.); Foreign born: 1.3% (2006-2010 5-year est.); Ancestry (includes multiple ancestries): 37.4% German, 22.7% Irish, 15.4% Polish, 9.0% English, 7.5% Italian (2006-2010 5-year est.).

Economy: Single-family building permits issued: 2 (2011); Multi-family building permits issued: 0 (2011); Employment by occupation: 9.8%

management, 5.4% professional, 8.1% services, 13.8% sales, 2.8% farming, 12.0% construction, 8.4% production (2006-2010 5-year est.).

Income: Per capita income: $21,345 (2006-2010 5-year est.); Median household income: $60,260 (2006-2010 5-year est.); Average household income: $62,053 (2006-2010 5-year est.); Percent of households with income of $100,000 or more: 14.7% (2006-2010 5-year est.); Poverty rate: 11.4% (2006-2010 5-year est.).

Education: Percent of population age 25 and over with: High school diploma (including GED) or higher: 91.9% (2006-2010 5-year est.); Bachelor's degree or higher: 21.9% (2006-2010 5-year est.); Master's degree or higher: 7.1% (2006-2010 5-year est.).

Housing: Homeownership rate: 87.7% (2010); Median home value: $149,500 (2006-2010 5-year est.); Median contract rent: $476 per month (2006-2010 5-year est.); Median year structure built: 1974 (2006-2010 5-year est.).

Transportation: Commute to work: 90.0% car, 0.4% public transportation, 1.3% walk, 6.7% work from home (2006-2010 5-year est.); Travel time to work: 21.1% less than 15 minutes, 32.9% 15 to 30 minutes, 30.8% 30 to 45 minutes, 10.7% 45 to 60 minutes, 4.5% 60 minutes or more (2006-2010 5-year est.)

Additional Information Contacts

Corry Area Chamber of Commerce. . . . . (814) 665-9925
  http://www.corrychamber.com

MCKEAN (borough).
Aka Middleboro. Covers a land area of 0.572 square miles and a water area of 0.011 square miles. Located at 42.00° N. Lat; 80.14° W. Long. Elevation is 1,047 feet.

Population: 418 (1990); 389 (2000); 388 (2010); Density: 678.5 persons per square mile (2010); Race: 96.9% White, 1.3% Black, 0.0% Asian, 0.3% American Indian/Alaska Native, 0.0% Native Hawaiian/Other Pacific Islander, 1.5% Other, 0.3% Hispanic of any race (2010); Average household size: 2.43 (2010); Median age: 41.3 (2010); Males per 100 females: 99.0 (2010); Marriage status: 33.0% never married, 48.6% now married, 9.4% widowed, 9.0% divorced (2006-2010 5-year est.); Foreign born: 0.6% (2006-2010 5-year est.); Ancestry (includes multiple ancestries): 36.2% German, 20.2% English, 18.7% Irish, 15.3% Polish, 9.2% Italian (2006-2010 5-year est.).

Economy: Single-family building permits issued: 1 (2011); Multi-family building permits issued: 0 (2011); Employment by occupation: 6.0% management, 3.5% professional, 8.5% services, 19.4% sales, 4.5% farming, 6.5% construction, 6.5% production (2006-2010 5-year est.).

Income: Per capita income: $24,906 (2006-2010 5-year est.); Median household income: $48,500 (2006-2010 5-year est.); Average household income: $52,305 (2006-2010 5-year est.); Percent of households with income of $100,000 or more: 7.5% (2006-2010 5-year est.); Poverty rate: 5.2% (2006-2010 5-year est.).

Education: Percent of population age 25 and over with: High school diploma (including GED) or higher: 96.7% (2006-2010 5-year est.); Bachelor's degree or higher: 24.9% (2006-2010 5-year est.); Master's degree or higher: 6.5% (2006-2010 5-year est.).

School District(s)

General Mclane SD (KG-12)

   2010-11 Enrollment: 2,148 . . . . (814) 273-1033

Housing: Homeownership rate: 61.9% (2010); Median home value: $125,700 (2006-2010 5-year est.); Median contract rent: $475 per month (2006-2010 5-year est.); Median year structure built: before 1940 (2006-2010 5-year est.).

Transportation: Commute to work: 94.0% car, 0.0% public transportation, 3.5% walk, 2.5% work from home (2006-2010 5-year est.); Travel time to work: 35.2% less than 15 minutes, 37.2% 15 to 30 minutes, 18.4% 30 to 45 minutes, 3.6% 45 to 60 minutes, 5.6% 60 minutes or more (2006-2010 5-year est.)

MCKEAN (township).
Aka Middleboro. Covers a land area of 36.801 square miles and a water area of 0.151 square miles. Located at 42.00° N. Lat; 80.13° W. Long.

History: Formerly called Middleboro.

Population: 4,500 (1990); 4,619 (2000); 4,409 (2010); Density: 119.8 persons per square mile (2010); Race: 98.2% White, 0.3% Black, 0.2% Asian, 0.3% American Indian/Alaska Native, 0.0% Native Hawaiian/Other Pacific Islander, 1.0% Other, 0.8% Hispanic of any race (2010); Average household size: 2.63 (2010); Median age: 43.6 (2010); Males per 100 females: 105.0 (2010); Marriage status: 21.9% never married, 65.5% now married, 4.7% widowed, 7.9% divorced (2006-2010 5-year est.); Foreign born: 0.9% (2006-2010 5-year est.); Ancestry (includes multiple

ancestries): 35.6% German, 23.2% Polish, 17.0% Italian, 13.2% Irish, 9.1% English (2006-2010 5-year est.).

Economy: Single-family building permits issued: 4 (2011); Multi-family building permits issued: 0 (2011); Employment by occupation: 15.8% management, 4.6% professional, 9.9% services, 18.8% sales, 2.8% farming, 7.9% construction, 7.3% production (2006-2010 5-year est.).

Income: Per capita income: $26,818 (2006-2010 5-year est.); Median household income: $55,508 (2006-2010 5-year est.); Average household income: $68,134 (2006-2010 5-year est.); Percent of households with income of $100,000 or more: 17.7% (2006-2010 5-year est.); Poverty rate: 4.2% (2006-2010 5-year est.).

Education: Percent of population age 25 and over with: High school diploma (including GED) or higher: 91.2% (2006-2010 5-year est.); Bachelor's degree or higher: 24.8% (2006-2010 5-year est.); Master's degree or higher: 10.3% (2006-2010 5-year est.).

Housing: Homeownership rate: 91.8% (2010); Median home value: $139,500 (2006-2010 5-year est.); Median contract rent: $501 per month (2006-2010 5-year est.); Median year structure built: 1976 (2006-2010 5-year est.).

Transportation: Commute to work: 96.8% car, 0.0% public transportation, 0.8% walk, 1.4% work from home (2006-2010 5-year est.); Travel time to work: 17.1% less than 15 minutes, 55.5% 15 to 30 minutes, 22.9% 30 to 45 minutes, 4.0% 45 to 60 minutes, 0.5% 60 minutes or more (2006-2010 5-year est.)

Additional Information Contacts

Erie Regional Chamber and Growth Partnership . . . . (814) 454-7191
    http://www.eriepa.com

MILL VILLAGE (borough). Covers a land area of 0.919 square miles and a water area of 0 square miles. Located at 41.88° N. Lat; 79.97° W. Long. Elevation is 1,204 feet.

Population: 429 (1990); 412 (2000); 412 (2010); Density: 448.5 persons per square mile (2010); Race: 97.3% White, 0.2% Black, 0.5% Asian, 0.0% American Indian/Alaska Native, 0.0% Native Hawaiian/Other Pacific Islander, 2.0% Other, 0.0% Hispanic of any race (2010); Average household size: 2.71 (2010); Median age: 40.6 (2010); Males per 100 females: 107.0 (2010); Marriage status: 28.4% never married, 56.5% now married, 8.4% widowed, 6.7% divorced (2006-2010 5-year est.); Foreign born: 7.3% (2006-2010 5-year est.); Ancestry (includes multiple ancestries): 23.6% German, 13.9% English, 8.0% Swedish, 7.3% Ukrainian, 6.9% Irish (2006-2010 5-year est.).

Economy: Single-family building permits issued: 0 (2011); Multi-family building permits issued: 0 (2011); Employment by occupation: 1.0% management, 0.0% professional, 2.6% services, 16.9% sales, 7.2% farming, 8.7% construction, 9.2% production (2006-2010 5-year est.).

Income: Per capita income: $19,552 (2006-2010 5-year est.); Median household income: $47,813 (2006-2010 5-year est.); Average household income: $47,847 (2006-2010 5-year est.); Percent of households with income of $100,000 or more: 8.9% (2006-2010 5-year est.); Poverty rate: 8.7% (2006-2010 5-year est.).

Education: Percent of population age 25 and over with: High school diploma (including GED) or higher: 91.0% (2006-2010 5-year est.); Bachelor's degree or higher: 9.4% (2006-2010 5-year est.); Master's degree or higher: 3.6% (2006-2010 5-year est.).

School District(s)

Fort Leboeuf SD (KG-12)
    2010-11 Enrollment: 2,175 . . . . (814) 796-2638

Housing: Homeownership rate: 81.6% (2010); Median home value: $110,500 (2006-2010 5-year est.); Median contract rent: $400 per month (2006-2010 5-year est.); Median year structure built: 1961 (2006-2010 5-year est.).

Transportation: Commute to work: 97.4% car, 0.0% public transportation, 1.0% walk, 0.0% work from home (2006-2010 5-year est.); Travel time to work: 22.3% less than 15 minutes, 32.6% 15 to 30 minutes, 30.6% 30 to 45 minutes, 13.5% 45 to 60 minutes, 1.0% 60 minutes or more (2006-2010 5-year est.)

MILLCREEK (township). Covers a land area of 32.073 square miles and a water area of 0.721 square miles. Located at 42.09° N. Lat; 80.12° W. Long.

Population: 46,820 (1990); 52,129 (2000); 53,515 (2010); Density: 1,668.5 persons per square mile (2010); Race: 94.7% White, 1.5% Black, 1.8% Asian, 0.1% American Indian/Alaska Native, 0.0% Native Hawaiian/Other Pacific Islander, 1.9% Other, 1.8% Hispanic of any race (2010); Average household size: 2.32 (2010); Median age: 42.8 (2010);

Males per 100 females: 92.8 (2010); Marriage status: 26.8% never married, 55.6% now married, 7.6% widowed, 10.0% divorced (2006-2010 5-year est.); Foreign born: 4.9% (2006-2010 5-year est.); Ancestry (includes multiple ancestries): 35.7% German, 20.1% Irish, 17.1% Italian, 12.6% Polish, 10.0% English (2006-2010 5-year est.).

Economy: Unemployment rate: 6.4% (August 2012); Total civilian labor force: 29,648 (August 2012); Single-family building permits issued: 44 (2011); Multi-family building permits issued: 154 (2011); Employment by occupation: 11.7% management, 4.8% professional, 7.1% services, 17.6% sales, 3.5% farming, 6.0% construction, 4.6% production (2006-2010 5-year est.).

Income: Per capita income: $30,051 (2006-2010 5-year est.); Median household income: $53,745 (2006-2010 5-year est.); Average household income: $70,505 (2006-2010 5-year est.); Percent of households with income of $100,000 or more: 21.4% (2006-2010 5-year est.); Poverty rate: 7.2% (2006-2010 5-year est.).

Taxes: Total city taxes per capita: $306 (2009); City property taxes per capita: $145 (2009).

Education: Percent of population age 25 and over with: High school diploma (including GED) or higher: 93.9% (2006-2010 5-year est.); Bachelor's degree or higher: 33.6% (2006-2010 5-year est.); Master's degree or higher: 13.4% (2006-2010 5-year est.).

Housing: Homeownership rate: 69.9% (2010); Median home value: $142,500 (2006-2010 5-year est.); Median contract rent: $612 per month (2006-2010 5-year est.); Median year structure built: 1973 (2006-2010 5-year est.).

Safety: Violent crime rate: 8.6 per 10,000 population; Property crime rate: 204.7 per 10,000 population (2011).

Transportation: Commute to work: 94.8% car, 0.2% public transportation, 1.8% walk, 2.2% work from home (2006-2010 5-year est.); Travel time to work: 40.8% less than 15 minutes, 49.8% 15 to 30 minutes, 7.0% 30 to 45 minutes, 0.7% 45 to 60 minutes, 1.7% 60 minutes or more (2006-2010 5-year est.)

Additional Information Contacts

Erie Regional Chamber and Growth Partnership . . . . (814) 454-7191
    http://www.eriepa.com
Millcreek Township . . . . (814) 833-1111
    http://www.millcreektownship.com

NORTH EAST (borough). Covers a land area of 1.303 square miles and a water area of 0 square miles. Located at 42.21° N. Lat; 79.83° W. Long. Elevation is 797 feet.

Population: 4,617 (1990); 4,601 (2000); 4,294 (2010); Density: 3,295.7 persons per square mile (2010); Race: 97.2% White, 1.0% Black, 0.3% Asian, 0.1% American Indian/Alaska Native, 0.0% Native Hawaiian/Other Pacific Islander, 1.4% Other, 2.1% Hispanic of any race (2010); Average household size: 2.45 (2010); Median age: 36.7 (2010); Males per 100 females: 96.3 (2010); Marriage status: 29.6% never married, 48.4% now married, 11.4% widowed, 10.6% divorced (2006-2010 5-year est.); Foreign born: 2.8% (2006-2010 5-year est.); Ancestry (includes multiple ancestries): 32.9% German, 15.2% Italian, 14.3% Irish, 11.8% English, 8.1% Polish (2006-2010 5-year est.).

Economy: Single-family building permits issued: 1 (2011); Multi-family building permits issued: 0 (2011); Employment by occupation: 7.3% management, 2.2% professional, 12.3% services, 12.9% sales, 3.5% farming, 9.2% construction, 10.2% production (2006-2010 5-year est.).

Income: Per capita income: $17,499 (2006-2010 5-year est.); Median household income: $36,875 (2006-2010 5-year est.); Average household income: $43,249 (2006-2010 5-year est.); Percent of households with income of $100,000 or more: 5.5% (2006-2010 5-year est.); Poverty rate: 22.1% (2006-2010 5-year est.).

Education: Percent of population age 25 and over with: High school diploma (including GED) or higher: 89.5% (2006-2010 5-year est.); Bachelor's degree or higher: 16.0% (2006-2010 5-year est.); Master's degree or higher: 3.9% (2006-2010 5-year est.).

School District(s)

North East SD (KG-12)
    2010-11 Enrollment: 1,711 . . . . (814) 725-8671

Housing: Homeownership rate: 56.9% (2010); Median home value: $109,300 (2006-2010 5-year est.); Median contract rent: $439 per month (2006-2010 5-year est.); Median year structure built: 1940 (2006-2010 5-year est.).

Newspapers: Erie Times-News - North East Bureau (Local news); North East News Journal (Community news; Circulation 9,000)

Transportation: Commute to work: 87.9% car, 0.0% public transportation, 7.9% walk, 3.5% work from home (2006-2010 5-year est.); Travel time to work: 43.4% less than 15 minutes, 34.2% 15 to 30 minutes, 14.6% 30 to 45 minutes, 3.2% 45 to 60 minutes, 4.7% 60 minutes or more (2006-2010 5-year est.)

Additional Information Contacts
North East Chamber of Commerce . . . . (814) 725-4262
  http://www.nechamber.org

NORTH EAST (township). Covers a land area of 42.148 square miles and a water area of 0.235 square miles. Located at 42.20° N. Lat; 79.83° W. Long. Elevation is 797 feet.

History: Lake Shore Railroad Museum here. Settled c.1800, incorporated 1834.

Population: 6,283 (1990); 7,702 (2000); 6,315 (2010); Density: 149.8 persons per square mile (2010); Race: 97.4% White, 1.1% Black, 0.3% Asian, 0.1% American Indian/Alaska Native, 0.0% Native Hawaiian/Other Pacific Islander, 1.1% Other, 1.5% Hispanic of any race (2010); Average household size: 2.53 (2010); Median age: 43.3 (2010); Males per 100 females: 99.5 (2010); Marriage status: 24.2% never married, 58.0% now married, 7.2% widowed, 10.6% divorced (2006-2010 5-year est.); Foreign born: 2.4% (2006-2010 5-year est.); Ancestry (includes multiple ancestries): 33.5% German, 17.3% Irish, 9.7% English, 8.7% Polish, 6.6% Italian (2006-2010 5-year est.).

Economy: Single-family building permits issued: 8 (2011); Multi-family building permits issued: 0 (2011); Employment by occupation: 8.8% management, 1.3% professional, 14.4% services, 16.9% sales, 4.8% farming, 9.4% construction, 4.7% production (2006-2010 5-year est.).

Income: Per capita income: $24,254 (2006-2010 5-year est.); Median household income: $53,320 (2006-2010 5-year est.); Average household income: $62,601 (2006-2010 5-year est.); Percent of households with income of $100,000 or more: 14.7% (2006-2010 5-year est.); Poverty rate: 6.1% (2006-2010 5-year est.).

Education: Percent of population age 25 and over with: High school diploma (including GED) or higher: 91.1% (2006-2010 5-year est.); Bachelor's degree or higher: 25.2% (2006-2010 5-year est.); Master's degree or higher: 12.6% (2006-2010 5-year est.).

Housing: Homeownership rate: 85.7% (2010); Median home value: $134,200 (2006-2010 5-year est.); Median contract rent: $386 per month (2006-2010 5-year est.); Median year structure built: 1969 (2006-2010 5-year est.).

Safety: Violent crime rate: 16.2 per 10,000 population; Property crime rate: 348.2 per 10,000 population (2011).

Newspapers: Erie Times-News - North East Bureau (Local news); North East News Journal (Community news; Circulation 9,000)

Transportation: Commute to work: 92.1% car, 0.0% public transportation, 3.7% walk, 3.8% work from home (2006-2010 5-year est.); Travel time to work: 37.3% less than 15 minutes, 33.2% 15 to 30 minutes, 21.3% 30 to 45 minutes, 5.3% 45 to 60 minutes, 2.9% 60 minutes or more (2006-2010 5-year est.)

Additional Information Contacts
North East Chamber of Commerce . . . . (814) 725-4262
  http://www.nechamber.org
North East Township . . . . (814) 725-8606
  http://www.northeastborough.com

NORTHWEST HARBORCREEK (CDP). Covers a land area of 5.004 square miles and a water area of <.001 square miles. Located at 42.15° N. Lat; 79.99° W. Long.

Population: 7,983 (1990); 8,658 (2000); 8,949 (2010); Density: 1,788.4 persons per square mile (2010); Race: 96.6% White, 1.7% Black, 0.7% Asian, 0.1% American Indian/Alaska Native, 0.0% Native Hawaiian/Other Pacific Islander, 0.9% Other, 1.3% Hispanic of any race (2010); Average household size: 2.45 (2010); Median age: 45.8 (2010); Males per 100 females: 95.2 (2010); Marriage status: 22.8% never married, 62.2% now married, 7.2% widowed, 7.8% divorced (2006-2010 5-year est.); Foreign born: 1.6% (2006-2010 5-year est.); Ancestry (includes multiple ancestries): 34.7% German, 24.1% Polish, 15.4% Irish, 13.0% Italian, 10.6% English (2006-2010 5-year est.).

Economy: Employment by occupation: 10.2% management, 6.1% professional, 8.0% services, 16.1% sales, 4.3% farming, 9.5% construction, 6.4% production (2006-2010 5-year est.).

Income: Per capita income: $25,166 (2006-2010 5-year est.); Median household income: $60,234 (2006-2010 5-year est.); Average household income: $64,927 (2006-2010 5-year est.); Percent of households with

income of $100,000 or more: 22.5% (2006-2010 5-year est.); Poverty rate: 8.7% (2006-2010 5-year est.).

Education: Percent of population age 25 and over with: High school diploma (including GED) or higher: 90.9% (2006-2010 5-year est.); Bachelor's degree or higher: 23.9% (2006-2010 5-year est.); Master's degree or higher: 7.0% (2006-2010 5-year est.).

Housing: Homeownership rate: 80.2% (2010); Median home value: $142,000 (2006-2010 5-year est.); Median contract rent: $511 per month (2006-2010 5-year est.); Median year structure built: 1973 (2006-2010 5-year est.).

Transportation: Commute to work: 94.8% car, 0.3% public transportation, 0.9% walk, 2.9% work from home (2006-2010 5-year est.); Travel time to work: 38.0% less than 15 minutes, 47.2% 15 to 30 minutes, 10.9% 30 to 45 minutes, 1.6% 45 to 60 minutes, 2.3% 60 minutes or more (2006-2010 5-year est.)

Additional Information Contacts
Erie Regional Chamber and Growth Partnership . . . . (814) 454-7191
  http://www.eriepa.com

PENN STATE ERIE (BEHREND) (CDP). Covers a land area of 0.784 square miles and a water area of 0.001 square miles. Located at 42.12° N. Lat; 79.98° W. Long.

Population: n/a (1990); n/a (2000); 1,629 (2010); Density: 2,078.1 persons per square mile (2010); Race: 90.4% White, 3.3% Black, 3.3% Asian, 0.1% American Indian/Alaska Native, 0.0% Native Hawaiian/Other Pacific Islander, 2.9% Other, 2.0% Hispanic of any race (2010); Average household size: 2.00 (2010); Median age: 19.8 (2010); Males per 100 females: 167.5 (2010); Marriage status: 100.0% never married, 0.0% now married, 0.0% widowed, 0.0% divorced (2006-2010 5-year est.); Foreign born: 3.9% (2006-2010 5-year est.); Ancestry (includes multiple ancestries): 33.5% German, 25.4% Irish, 21.8% Italian, 13.0% Polish, 2.9% English (2006-2010 5-year est.).

Economy: Employment by occupation: 2.7% management, 2.9% professional, 19.8% services, 13.9% sales, 5.3% farming, 5.7% construction, 5.7% production (2006-2010 5-year est.).

Income: Per capita income: $4,074 (2006-2010 5-year est.); Median household income: n/a (2006-2010 5-year est.); Average household income: n/a (2006-2010 5-year est.); Percent of households with income of $100,000 or more: n/a (2006-2010 5-year est.); Poverty rate: n/a (2006-2010 5-year est.).

Education: Percent of population age 25 and over with: High school diploma (including GED) or higher: 100.0% (2006-2010 5-year est.); Bachelor's degree or higher: 12.5% (2006-2010 5-year est.); Master's degree or higher: 12.5% (2006-2010 5-year est.).

Housing: Homeownership rate: 100.0% (2010); Median home value: n/a (2006-2010 5-year est.); Median contract rent: n/a per month (2006-2010 5-year est.); Median year structure built: n/a (2006-2010 5-year est.).

Transportation: Commute to work: 38.7% car, 0.0% public transportation, 58.6% walk, 2.7% work from home (2006-2010 5-year est.); Travel time to work: 69.0% less than 15 minutes, 28.2% 15 to 30 minutes, 0.0% 30 to 45 minutes, 0.0% 45 to 60 minutes, 2.7% 60 minutes or more (2006-2010 5-year est.)

PLATEA (borough). Covers a land area of 3.343 square miles and a water area of 0 square miles. Located at 41.95° N. Lat; 80.33° W. Long. Elevation is 869 feet.

Population: 467 (1990); 474 (2000); 430 (2010); Density: 128.6 persons per square mile (2010); Race: 98.6% White, 0.2% Black, 0.2% Asian, 0.0% American Indian/Alaska Native, 0.0% Native Hawaiian/Other Pacific Islander, 1.0% Other, 0.5% Hispanic of any race (2010); Average household size: 2.74 (2010); Median age: 43.8 (2010); Males per 100 females: 104.8 (2010); Marriage status: 18.1% never married, 63.0% now married, 6.8% widowed, 12.1% divorced (2006-2010 5-year est.); Foreign born: 0.8% (2006-2010 5-year est.); Ancestry (includes multiple ancestries): 33.4% German, 21.1% Irish, 14.9% English, 14.6% American, 8.1% Italian (2006-2010 5-year est.).

Economy: Single-family building permits issued: 0 (2011); Multi-family building permits issued: 0 (2011); Employment by occupation: 5.9% management, 0.5% professional, 10.7% services, 16.0% sales, 8.0% farming, 8.6% construction, 5.3% production (2006-2010 5-year est.).

Income: Per capita income: $21,301 (2006-2010 5-year est.); Median household income: $53,393 (2006-2010 5-year est.); Average household income: $52,450 (2006-2010 5-year est.); Percent of households with income of $100,000 or more: 4.2% (2006-2010 5-year est.); Poverty rate: 10.2% (2006-2010 5-year est.).

Education: Percent of population age 25 and over with: High school diploma (including GED) or higher: 93.0% (2006-2010 5-year est.); Bachelor's degree or higher: 11.9% (2006-2010 5-year est.); Master's degree or higher: 5.3% (2006-2010 5-year est.).

Housing: Homeownership rate: 86.7% (2010); Median home value: $99,600 (2006-2010 5-year est.); Median contract rent: $590 per month (2006-2010 5-year est.); Median year structure built: 1972 (2006-2010 5-year est.).

Transportation: Commute to work: 93.3% car, 0.0% public transportation, 3.4% walk, 2.2% work from home (2006-2010 5-year est.); Travel time to work: 24.1% less than 15 minutes, 39.1% 15 to 30 minutes, 28.2% 30 to 45 minutes, 6.3% 45 to 60 minutes, 2.3% 60 minutes or more (2006-2010 5-year est.)

SPRINGFIELD (township). Covers a land area of 37.383 square miles and a water area of 0.280 square miles. Located at 41.96° N. Lat; 80.45° W. Long.

Population: 3,211 (1990); 3,378 (2000); 3,425 (2010); Density: 91.6 persons per square mile (2010); Race: 97.6% White, 0.4% Black, 0.1% Asian, 0.1% American Indian/Alaska Native, 0.0% Native Hawaiian/Other Pacific Islander, 1.8% Other, 0.9% Hispanic of any race (2010); Average household size: 2.60 (2010); Median age: 40.8 (2010); Males per 100 females: 104.5 (2010); Marriage status: 25.3% never married, 59.6% now married, 4.5% widowed, 10.6% divorced (2006-2010 5-year est.); Foreign born: 1.2% (2006-2010 5-year est.); Ancestry (includes multiple ancestries): 37.5% German, 21.0% Irish, 12.4% English, 9.2% Italian, 6.9% American (2006-2010 5-year est.).

Economy: Single-family building permits issued: 2 (2011); Multi-family building permits issued: 0 (2011); Employment by occupation: 7.5% management, 3.2% professional, 8.4% services, 13.3% sales, 6.7% farming, 6.8% construction, 8.4% production (2006-2010 5-year est.).

Income: Per capita income: $19,966 (2006-2010 5-year est.); Median household income: $41,453 (2006-2010 5-year est.); Average household income: $51,277 (2006-2010 5-year est.); Percent of households with income of $100,000 or more: 9.8% (2006-2010 5-year est.); Poverty rate: 19.0% (2006-2010 5-year est.).

Education: Percent of population age 25 and over with: High school diploma (including GED) or higher: 90.9% (2006-2010 5-year est.); Bachelor's degree or higher: 18.6% (2006-2010 5-year est.); Master's degree or higher: 7.0% (2006-2010 5-year est.).

Housing: Homeownership rate: 83.0% (2010); Median home value: $109,800 (2006-2010 5-year est.); Median contract rent: $544 per month (2006-2010 5-year est.); Median year structure built: 1972 (2006-2010 5-year est.).

Transportation: Commute to work: 96.5% car, 0.0% public transportation, 1.5% walk, 1.9% work from home (2006-2010 5-year est.); Travel time to work: 15.7% less than 15 minutes, 46.8% 15 to 30 minutes, 29.9% 30 to 45 minutes, 3.9% 45 to 60 minutes, 3.8% 60 minutes or more (2006-2010 5-year est.)

Additional Information Contacts

Erie Regional Chamber and Growth Partnership . . . . (814) 454-7191
   http://www.eriepa.com

SUMMIT (township). Covers a land area of 24.050 square miles and a water area of 0.014 square miles. Located at 42.04° N. Lat; 80.05° W. Long.

Population: 5,287 (1990); 5,529 (2000); 6,603 (2010); Density: 274.6 persons per square mile (2010); Race: 96.8% White, 0.9% Black, 1.1% Asian, 0.2% American Indian/Alaska Native, 0.0% Native Hawaiian/Other Pacific Islander, 1.0% Other, 0.7% Hispanic of any race (2010); Average household size: 2.42 (2010); Median age: 46.3 (2010); Males per 100 females: 97.0 (2010); Marriage status: 22.5% never married, 60.1% now married, 5.4% widowed, 12.0% divorced (2006-2010 5-year est.); Foreign born: 1.5% (2006-2010 5-year est.); Ancestry (includes multiple ancestries): 33.3% German, 21.3% Irish, 15.1% Polish, 15.1% English, 14.3% Italian (2006-2010 5-year est.).

Economy: Single-family building permits issued: 16 (2011); Multi-family building permits issued: 0 (2011); Employment by occupation: 11.3% management, 4.3% professional, 8.3% services, 18.2% sales, 2.9% farming, 10.1% construction, 7.6% production (2006-2010 5-year est.).

Income: Per capita income: $26,205 (2006-2010 5-year est.); Median household income: $55,825 (2006-2010 5-year est.); Average household income: $65,899 (2006-2010 5-year est.); Percent of households with income of $100,000 or more: 17.3% (2006-2010 5-year est.); Poverty rate: 6.1% (2006-2010 5-year est.).

Education: Percent of population age 25 and over with: High school diploma (including GED) or higher: 87.5% (2006-2010 5-year est.); Bachelor's degree or higher: 20.0% (2006-2010 5-year est.); Master's degree or higher: 6.5% (2006-2010 5-year est.).

Housing: Homeownership rate: 89.1% (2010); Median home value: $154,700 (2006-2010 5-year est.); Median contract rent: $315 per month (2006-2010 5-year est.); Median year structure built: 1973 (2006-2010 5-year est.).

Transportation: Commute to work: 93.0% car, 0.0% public transportation, 2.9% walk, 2.7% work from home (2006-2010 5-year est.); Travel time to work: 28.8% less than 15 minutes, 58.0% 15 to 30 minutes, 9.9% 30 to 45 minutes, 1.3% 45 to 60 minutes, 2.0% 60 minutes or more (2006-2010 5-year est.)

Additional Information Contacts

Erie Regional Chamber and Growth Partnership . . . . (814) 454-7191
   http://www.eriepa.com
Summit Township . . . . (814) 868-9686
   http://www.summittownship.com

UNION (township). Covers a land area of 36.466 square miles and a water area of 0.180 square miles. Located at 41.90° N. Lat; 79.82° W. Long.

Population: 1,735 (1990); 1,663 (2000); 1,655 (2010); Density: 45.4 persons per square mile (2010); Race: 99.4% White, 0.3% Black, 0.1% Asian, 0.1% American Indian/Alaska Native, 0.0% Native Hawaiian/Other Pacific Islander, 0.1% Other, 0.4% Hispanic of any race (2010); Average household size: 2.67 (2010); Median age: 43.4 (2010); Males per 100 females: 103.3 (2010); Marriage status: 23.4% never married, 59.6% now married, 7.3% widowed, 9.7% divorced (2006-2010 5-year est.); Foreign born: 1.0% (2006-2010 5-year est.); Ancestry (includes multiple ancestries): 24.5% Irish, 22.2% German, 14.7% Polish, 10.9% English, 8.8% American (2006-2010 5-year est.).

Economy: Single-family building permits issued: 2 (2011); Multi-family building permits issued: 0 (2011); Employment by occupation: 8.1% management, 3.4% professional, 7.3% services, 21.5% sales, 2.8% farming, 16.6% construction, 14.3% production (2006-2010 5-year est.).

Income: Per capita income: $22,684 (2006-2010 5-year est.); Median household income: $56,835 (2006-2010 5-year est.); Average household income: $62,739 (2006-2010 5-year est.); Percent of households with income of $100,000 or more: 12.8% (2006-2010 5-year est.); Poverty rate: 7.4% (2006-2010 5-year est.).

Education: Percent of population age 25 and over with: High school diploma (including GED) or higher: 85.1% (2006-2010 5-year est.); Bachelor's degree or higher: 16.6% (2006-2010 5-year est.); Master's degree or higher: 5.8% (2006-2010 5-year est.).

Housing: Homeownership rate: 87.6% (2010); Median home value: $112,700 (2006-2010 5-year est.); Median contract rent: $407 per month (2006-2010 5-year est.); Median year structure built: 1961 (2006-2010 5-year est.).

Transportation: Commute to work: 93.1% car, 0.0% public transportation, 1.8% walk, 4.5% work from home (2006-2010 5-year est.); Travel time to work: 23.6% less than 15 minutes, 35.2% 15 to 30 minutes, 24.2% 30 to 45 minutes, 7.8% 45 to 60 minutes, 9.1% 60 minutes or more (2006-2010 5-year est.)

Additional Information Contacts

Erie Regional Chamber and Growth Partnership . . . . (814) 454-7191
   http://www.eriepa.com

UNION CITY (borough). Covers a land area of 1.830 square miles and a water area of 0.025 square miles. Located at 41.90° N. Lat; 79.84° W. Long. Elevation is 1,263 feet.

History: Growth stimulated by oil boom of 1860s. Union City American Historical Museum to south. Settled c.1785, Incorporated 1863.

Population: 3,537 (1990); 3,463 (2000); 3,320 (2010); Density: 1,814.1 persons per square mile (2010); Race: 97.7% White, 0.4% Black, 0.5% Asian, 0.2% American Indian/Alaska Native, 0.0% Native Hawaiian/Other Pacific Islander, 1.2% Other, 1.6% Hispanic of any race (2010); Average household size: 2.55 (2010); Median age: 34.7 (2010); Males per 100 females: 91.4 (2010); Marriage status: 24.9% never married, 59.2% now married, 5.4% widowed, 10.5% divorced (2006-2010 5-year est.); Foreign born: 2.8% (2006-2010 5-year est.); Ancestry (includes multiple ancestries): 30.2% German, 12.3% English, 10.8% Irish, 8.9% American, 8.0% Polish (2006-2010 5-year est.).

Economy: Single-family building permits issued: 0 (2011); Multi-family building permits issued: 0 (2011); Employment by occupation: 5.0%

management, 2.6% professional, 13.6% services, 9.9% sales, 3.3% farming, 11.6% construction, 18.0% production (2006-2010 5-year est.).
Income: Per capita income: $17,302 (2006-2010 5-year est.); Median household income: $40,042 (2006-2010 5-year est.); Average household income: $44,519 (2006-2010 5-year est.); Percent of households with income of $100,000 or more: 5.3% (2006-2010 5-year est.); Poverty rate: 12.3% (2006-2010 5-year est.).
Education: Percent of population age 25 and over with: High school diploma (including GED) or higher: 86.6% (2006-2010 5-year est.); Bachelor's degree or higher: 15.0% (2006-2010 5-year est.); Master's degree or higher: 3.5% (2006-2010 5-year est.).

School District(s)

Union City Area SD (KG-12)
   2010-11 Enrollment: 1,254 . . . . (814) 438-3804
Housing: Homeownership rate: 57.5% (2010); Median home value: $72,000 (2006-2010 5-year est.); Median contract rent: $363 per month (2006-2010 5-year est.); Median year structure built: before 1940 (2006-2010 5-year est.).
Safety: Violent crime rate: 12.0 per 10,000 population; Property crime rate: 276.2 per 10,000 population (2011).
Newspapers: Times-Leader (Community news; Circulation 9,710)
Transportation: Commute to work: 92.4% car, 0.0% public transportation, 4.9% walk, 2.6% work from home (2006-2010 5-year est.); Travel time to work: 29.1% less than 15 minutes, 28.8% 15 to 30 minutes, 31.8% 30 to 45 minutes, 7.0% 45 to 60 minutes, 3.3% 60 minutes or more (2006-2010 5-year est.)

Additional Information Contacts
Erie Regional Chamber and Growth Partnership . . . . (814) 454-7191
   http://www.eriepa.com

VENANGO (township). Covers a land area of 43.422 square miles and a water area of 0.376 square miles. Located at 42.05° N. Lat; 79.83° W. Long.

Population: 2,230 (1990); 2,277 (2000); 2,297 (2010); Density: 52.9 persons per square mile (2010); Race: 98.6% White, 0.2% Black, 0.2% Asian, 0.2% American Indian/Alaska Native, 0.0% Native Hawaiian/Other Pacific Islander, 0.8% Other, 0.4% Hispanic of any race (2010); Average household size: 2.79 (2010); Median age: 42.3 (2010); Males per 100 females: 104.0 (2010); Marriage status: 22.3% never married, 67.1% now married, 4.0% widowed, 6.6% divorced (2006-2010 5-year est.); Foreign born: 1.3% (2006-2010 5-year est.); Ancestry (includes multiple ancestries): 31.3% German, 21.9% Irish, 16.6% English, 16.2% Polish, 9.8% American (2006-2010 5-year est.).
Economy: Single-family building permits issued: 4 (2011); Multi-family building permits issued: 0 (2011); Employment by occupation: 13.2% management, 1.9% professional, 9.3% services, 15.0% sales, 1.7% farming, 12.4% construction, 9.7% production (2006-2010 5-year est.).
Income: Per capita income: $21,779 (2006-2010 5-year est.); Median household income: $57,361 (2006-2010 5-year est.); Average household income: $59,964 (2006-2010 5-year est.); Percent of households with income of $100,000 or more: 12.6% (2006-2010 5-year est.); Poverty rate: 11.4% (2006-2010 5-year est.).
Education: Percent of population age 25 and over with: High school diploma (including GED) or higher: 89.5% (2006-2010 5-year est.); Bachelor's degree or higher: 19.0% (2006-2010 5-year est.); Master's degree or higher: 3.4% (2006-2010 5-year est.).
Housing: Homeownership rate: 90.6% (2010); Median home value: $133,400 (2006-2010 5-year est.); Median contract rent: $478 per month (2006-2010 5-year est.); Median year structure built: 1974 (2006-2010 5-year est.).
Transportation: Commute to work: 89.8% car, 0.0% public transportation, 1.2% walk, 6.6% work from home (2006-2010 5-year est.); Travel time to work: 16.8% less than 15 minutes, 45.7% 15 to 30 minutes, 27.3% 30 to 45 minutes, 6.6% 45 to 60 minutes, 3.6% 60 minutes or more (2006-2010 5-year est.)

Additional Information Contacts
Venango Area Chamber of Commerce . . . . (814) 676-8521
   http://www.venangochamber.org

WASHINGTON (township). Covers a land area of 45.165 square miles and a water area of 0.452 square miles. Located at 41.89° N. Lat; 80.11° W. Long.

Population: 4,174 (1990); 4,526 (2000); 4,432 (2010); Density: 98.1 persons per square mile (2010); Race: 98.3% White, 0.3% Black, 0.3% Asian, 0.1% American Indian/Alaska Native, 0.0% Native Hawaiian/Other

Pacific Islander, 1.0% Other, 0.5% Hispanic of any race (2010); Average household size: 2.59 (2010); Median age: 43.3 (2010); Males per 100 females: 100.9 (2010); Marriage status: 30.3% never married, 58.3% now married, 3.6% widowed, 7.7% divorced (2006-2010 5-year est.); Foreign born: 0.8% (2006-2010 5-year est.); Ancestry (includes multiple ancestries): 34.5% German, 23.3% Irish, 12.0% Polish, 8.9% English, 8.0% Italian (2006-2010 5-year est.).
Economy: Single-family building permits issued: 2 (2011); Multi-family building permits issued: 0 (2011); Employment by occupation: 11.1% management, 5.0% professional, 7.8% services, 13.0% sales, 3.9% farming, 7.2% construction, 4.7% production (2006-2010 5-year est.).
Income: Per capita income: $29,205 (2006-2010 5-year est.); Median household income: $73,750 (2006-2010 5-year est.); Average household income: $82,458 (2006-2010 5-year est.); Percent of households with income of $100,000 or more: 28.3% (2006-2010 5-year est.); Poverty rate: 11.4% (2006-2010 5-year est.).
Education: Percent of population age 25 and over with: High school diploma (including GED) or higher: 92.9% (2006-2010 5-year est.); Bachelor's degree or higher: 47.1% (2006-2010 5-year est.); Master's degree or higher: 19.1% (2006-2010 5-year est.).
Housing: Homeownership rate: 87.3% (2010); Median home value: $166,500 (2006-2010 5-year est.); Median contract rent: $615 per month (2006-2010 5-year est.); Median year structure built: 1977 (2006-2010 5-year est.).
Transportation: Commute to work: 93.2% car, 0.0% public transportation, 2.4% walk, 3.9% work from home (2006-2010 5-year est.); Travel time to work: 30.0% less than 15 minutes, 32.0% 15 to 30 minutes, 27.8% 30 to 45 minutes, 7.5% 45 to 60 minutes, 2.7% 60 minutes or more (2006-2010 5-year est.)

Additional Information Contacts
Erie Regional Chamber and Growth Partnership . . . . (814) 454-7191
   http://www.eriepa.com

WATERFORD (borough). Covers a land area of 1.226 square miles and a water area of 0.015 square miles. Located at 41.95° N. Lat; 79.99° W. Long. Elevation is 1,204 feet.

Population: 1,492 (1990); 1,449 (2000); 1,517 (2010); Density: 1,237.8 persons per square mile (2010); Race: 98.5% White, 0.4% Black, 0.3% Asian, 0.3% American Indian/Alaska Native, 0.0% Native Hawaiian/Other Pacific Islander, 0.5% Other, 0.9% Hispanic of any race (2010); Average household size: 2.43 (2010); Median age: 39.6 (2010); Males per 100 females: 91.1 (2010); Marriage status: 24.8% never married, 58.2% now married, 10.4% widowed, 6.6% divorced (2006-2010 5-year est.); Foreign born: 1.9% (2006-2010 5-year est.); Ancestry (includes multiple ancestries): 32.1% German, 23.4% Irish, 16.1% English, 9.2% Polish, 8.2% Italian (2006-2010 5-year est.).
Economy: Single-family building permits issued: 0 (2011); Multi-family building permits issued: 8 (2011); Employment by occupation: 5.0% management, 3.7% professional, 11.2% services, 21.1% sales, 1.6% farming, 10.1% construction, 10.9% production (2006-2010 5-year est.).
Income: Per capita income: $21,173 (2006-2010 5-year est.); Median household income: $43,550 (2006-2010 5-year est.); Average household income: $51,975 (2006-2010 5-year est.); Percent of households with income of $100,000 or more: 8.9% (2006-2010 5-year est.); Poverty rate: 9.7% (2006-2010 5-year est.).
Education: Percent of population age 25 and over with: High school diploma (including GED) or higher: 88.7% (2006-2010 5-year est.); Bachelor's degree or higher: 15.6% (2006-2010 5-year est.); Master's degree or higher: 5.0% (2006-2010 5-year est.).

School District(s)

Fort Leboeuf SD (KG-12)
   2010-11 Enrollment: 2,175 . . . . (814) 796-2638
Housing: Homeownership rate: 63.6% (2010); Median home value: $99,200 (2006-2010 5-year est.); Median contract rent: $434 per month (2006-2010 5-year est.); Median year structure built: 1960 (2006-2010 5-year est.).
Transportation: Commute to work: 92.2% car, 0.0% public transportation, 4.9% walk, 2.5% work from home (2006-2010 5-year est.); Travel time to work: 28.3% less than 15 minutes, 36.5% 15 to 30 minutes, 25.9% 30 to 45 minutes, 7.7% 45 to 60 minutes, 1.6% 60 minutes or more (2006-2010 5-year est.)

Additional Information Contacts
Borough of Waterford . . . . (814) 796-4411
Erie Regional Chamber and Growth Partnership . . . . (814) 454-7191
   http://www.eriepa.com

WATERFORD (township). Covers a land area of 49.952 square miles and a water area of 0.329 square miles. Located at 41.96° N. Lat; 79.98° W. Long. Elevation is 1,204 feet.

History: Ruins of Fort Le Boeuf, built 1753 by French, here.

Population: 3,402 (1990); 3,878 (2000); 3,920 (2010); Density: 78.5 persons per square mile (2010); Race: 98.1% White, 0.6% Black, 0.2% Asian, 0.1% American Indian/Alaska Native, 0.0% Native Hawaiian/Other Pacific Islander, 1.0% Other, 0.6% Hispanic of any race (2010); Average household size: 2.70 (2010); Median age: 41.3 (2010); Males per 100 females: 100.1 (2010); Marriage status: 25.6% never married, 60.5% now married, 4.6% widowed, 9.2% divorced (2006-2010 5-year est.); Foreign born: 0.0% (2006-2010 5-year est.); Ancestry (includes multiple ancestries): 38.8% German, 17.0% Irish, 13.9% Italian, 11.9% English, 9.2% Polish (2006-2010 5-year est.).

Economy: Single-family building permits issued: 2 (2011); Multi-family building permits issued: 0 (2011); Employment by occupation: 5.7% management, 3.4% professional, 5.7% services, 12.0% sales, 1.8% farming, 15.7% construction, 12.3% production (2006-2010 5-year est.).

Income: Per capita income: $25,413 (2006-2010 5-year est.); Median household income: $49,375 (2006-2010 5-year est.); Average household income: $66,853 (2006-2010 5-year est.); Percent of households with income of $100,000 or more: 18.3% (2006-2010 5-year est.); Poverty rate: 15.1% (2006-2010 5-year est.).

Education: Percent of population age 25 and over with: High school diploma (including GED) or higher: 88.1% (2006-2010 5-year est.); Bachelor's degree or higher: 20.2% (2006-2010 5-year est.); Master's degree or higher: 9.5% (2006-2010 5-year est.).

Housing: Homeownership rate: 84.6% (2010); Median home value: $137,400 (2006-2010 5-year est.); Median contract rent: $337 per month (2006-2010 5-year est.); Median year structure built: 1976 (2006-2010 5-year est.).

Transportation: Commute to work: 92.2% car, 0.0% public transportation, 0.0% walk, 4.5% work from home (2006-2010 5-year est.); Travel time to work: 22.6% less than 15 minutes, 33.6% 15 to 30 minutes, 35.0% 30 to 45 minutes, 7.1% 45 to 60 minutes, 1.6% 60 minutes or more (2006-2010 5-year est.)

Additional Information Contacts

Erie Regional Chamber and Growth Partnership . . . . (814) 454-7191
    http://www.eriepa.com

WATTSBURG (borough). Covers a land area of 0.298 square miles and a water area of 0.011 square miles. Located at 42.00° N. Lat; 79.80° W. Long. Elevation is 1,283 feet.

History: Ida M. Tarbell born near here.

Population: 491 (1990); 378 (2000); 403 (2010); Density: 1,353.9 persons per square mile (2010); Race: 99.3% White, 0.2% Black, 0.0% Asian, 0.0% American Indian/Alaska Native, 0.0% Native Hawaiian/Other Pacific Islander, 0.5% Other, 1.5% Hispanic of any race (2010); Average household size: 2.62 (2010); Median age: 34.1 (2010); Males per 100 females: 108.8 (2010); Marriage status: 22.3% never married, 56.1% now married, 3.8% widowed, 17.8% divorced (2006-2010 5-year est.); Foreign born: 2.1% (2006-2010 5-year est.); Ancestry (includes multiple ancestries): 25.9% German, 15.7% American, 12.3% Irish, 12.0% English, 11.2% Italian (2006-2010 5-year est.).

Economy: Single-family building permits issued: 0 (2011); Multi-family building permits issued: 0 (2011); Employment by occupation: 5.1% management, 0.0% professional, 12.8% services, 10.2% sales, 7.1% farming, 6.6% construction, 14.8% production (2006-2010 5-year est.).

Income: Per capita income: $19,973 (2006-2010 5-year est.); Median household income: $46,875 (2006-2010 5-year est.); Average household income: $54,044 (2006-2010 5-year est.); Percent of households with income of $100,000 or more: 8.4% (2006-2010 5-year est.); Poverty rate: 8.6% (2006-2010 5-year est.).

Education: Percent of population age 25 and over with: High school diploma (including GED) or higher: 82.1% (2006-2010 5-year est.); Bachelor's degree or higher: 3.3% (2006-2010 5-year est.); Master's degree or higher: 1.3% (2006-2010 5-year est.).

Housing: Homeownership rate: 57.8% (2010); Median home value: $75,000 (2006-2010 5-year est.); Median contract rent: $367 per month (2006-2010 5-year est.); Median year structure built: before 1940 (2006-2010 5-year est.).

Transportation: Commute to work: 91.1% car, 0.0% public transportation, 2.1% walk, 4.2% work from home (2006-2010 5-year est.); Travel time to work: 12.0% less than 15 minutes, 34.2% 15 to 30 minutes, 44.6% 30 to 45 minutes, 7.1% 45 to 60 minutes, 2.2% 60 minutes or more (2006-2010 5-year est.)

WAYNE (township). Covers a land area of 38.071 square miles and a water area of 0.076 square miles. Located at 41.95° N. Lat; 79.69° W. Long.

Population: 1,683 (1990); 1,766 (2000); 1,659 (2010); Density: 43.6 persons per square mile (2010); Race: 98.6% White, 0.2% Black, 0.4% Asian, 0.1% American Indian/Alaska Native, 0.0% Native Hawaiian/Other Pacific Islander, 0.7% Other, 0.1% Hispanic of any race (2010); Average household size: 2.58 (2010); Median age: 44.1 (2010); Males per 100 females: 102.6 (2010); Marriage status: 24.3% never married, 63.0% now married, 6.5% widowed, 6.3% divorced (2006-2010 5-year est.); Foreign born: 0.3% (2006-2010 5-year est.); Ancestry (includes multiple ancestries): 30.6% German, 16.0% Irish, 13.6% English, 8.6% Polish, 5.8% American (2006-2010 5-year est.).

Economy: Single-family building permits issued: 1 (2011); Multi-family building permits issued: 0 (2011); Employment by occupation: 10.4% management, 3.3% professional, 10.3% services, 17.5% sales, 2.0% farming, 15.1% construction, 12.3% production (2006-2010 5-year est.).

Income: Per capita income: $20,308 (2006-2010 5-year est.); Median household income: $45,223 (2006-2010 5-year est.); Average household income: $51,059 (2006-2010 5-year est.); Percent of households with income of $100,000 or more: 10.4% (2006-2010 5-year est.); Poverty rate: 12.1% (2006-2010 5-year est.).

Education: Percent of population age 25 and over with: High school diploma (including GED) or higher: 88.3% (2006-2010 5-year est.); Bachelor's degree or higher: 13.8% (2006-2010 5-year est.); Master's degree or higher: 4.0% (2006-2010 5-year est.).

Housing: Homeownership rate: 90.4% (2010); Median home value: $107,300 (2006-2010 5-year est.); Median contract rent: $384 per month (2006-2010 5-year est.); Median year structure built: 1972 (2006-2010 5-year est.).

Transportation: Commute to work: 91.0% car, 0.6% public transportation, 1.6% walk, 6.8% work from home (2006-2010 5-year est.); Travel time to work: 43.7% less than 15 minutes, 22.9% 15 to 30 minutes, 14.6% 30 to 45 minutes, 13.0% 45 to 60 minutes, 5.7% 60 minutes or more (2006-2010 5-year est.)

Additional Information Contacts

Erie Regional Chamber and Growth Partnership . . . . (814) 454-7191
    http://www.eriepa.com

WESLEYVILLE (borough). Covers a land area of 0.529 square miles and a water area of 0.001 square miles. Located at 42.14° N. Lat; 80.01° W. Long. Elevation is 722 feet.

History: Pennsylvania State University, Behrend Campus, to Southeast. Settled 1797, laid out 1828, incorporated 1912.

Population: 3,655 (1990); 3,617 (2000); 3,341 (2010); Density: 6,318.3 persons per square mile (2010); Race: 94.5% White, 1.5% Black, 0.6% Asian, 0.1% American Indian/Alaska Native, 0.1% Native Hawaiian/Other Pacific Islander, 3.2% Other, 3.0% Hispanic of any race (2010); Average household size: 2.45 (2010); Median age: 36.0 (2010); Males per 100 females: 102.0 (2010); Marriage status: 30.4% never married, 49.1% now married, 5.5% widowed, 15.0% divorced (2006-2010 5-year est.); Foreign born: 0.7% (2006-2010 5-year est.); Ancestry (includes multiple ancestries): 33.9% German, 21.9% Irish, 12.3% Polish, 10.1% English, 6.7% Italian (2006-2010 5-year est.).

Economy: Single-family building permits issued: 0 (2011); Multi-family building permits issued: 0 (2011); Employment by occupation: 7.3% management, 0.9% professional, 15.3% services, 13.0% sales, 5.0% farming, 8.8% construction, 4.2% production (2006-2010 5-year est.).

Income: Per capita income: $20,566 (2006-2010 5-year est.); Median household income: $41,379 (2006-2010 5-year est.); Average household income: $49,478 (2006-2010 5-year est.); Percent of households with income of $100,000 or more: 7.6% (2006-2010 5-year est.); Poverty rate: 16.5% (2006-2010 5-year est.).

Education: Percent of population age 25 and over with: High school diploma (including GED) or higher: 86.7% (2006-2010 5-year est.); Bachelor's degree or higher: 14.8% (2006-2010 5-year est.); Master's degree or higher: 3.1% (2006-2010 5-year est.).

Housing: Homeownership rate: 69.5% (2010); Median home value: $75,500 (2006-2010 5-year est.); Median contract rent: $522 per month (2006-2010 5-year est.); Median year structure built: 1952 (2006-2010 5-year est.).

Transportation: Commute to work: 89.8% car, 0.0% public transportation, 8.1% walk, 1.7% work from home (2006-2010 5-year est.); Travel time to work: 47.1% less than 15 minutes, 47.0% 15 to 30 minutes, 4.6% 30 to 45 minutes, 0.0% 45 to 60 minutes, 1.3% 60 minutes or more (2006-2010 5-year est.)

Additional Information Contacts
Erie Regional Chamber and Growth Partnership . . . . (814) 454-7191
  http://www.eriepa.com

WEST SPRINGFIELD (unincorporated postal area)

Zip Code: 16443

Covers a land area of 11.276 square miles and a water area of 0.123 square miles. Located at 41.93° N. Lat; 80.48° W. Long. Elevation is 712 feet. Population: 1,425 (2010); Density: 126.4 persons per square mile (2010); Race: 97.4% White, 0.6% Black, 0.1% Asian, 0.1% American Indian/Alaska Native, 0.1% Native Hawaiian/Other Pacific Islander, 1.7% Other, 1.0% Hispanic of any race (2010); Average household size: 2.61 (2010); Median age: 39.4 (2010); Males per 100 females: 106.8 (2010); Homeownership rate: 79.1% (2010)

Fayette County

Located in southwestern Pennsylvania; bounded on the west by the Monongahela River, and on the south by West Virginia; drained by the Youghiogheny River; crossed by Chestnut Ridge. Covers a land area of 790.339 square miles, a water area of 7.971 square miles, and is located in the Eastern Time Zone at 39.91° N. Lat., 79.64° W. Long. The county was founded in 1783. County seat is Uniontown.

Fayette County is part of the Pittsburgh, PA Metropolitan Statistical Area. The entire metro area includes: Allegheny County, PA; Armstrong County, PA; Beaver County, PA; Butler County, PA; Fayette County, PA; Washington County, PA; Westmoreland County, PA

Weather Station: Chalk Hill 2 ENE									Elevation: 1,979 feet		
	Jan	Feb	Mar	Apr	May	Jun	Jul	Aug	Sep	Oct	Nov	Dec
High	35	39	48	61	69	75	78	77	70	60	50	39
Low	19	21	28	37	46	55	59	58	51	40	32	23
Precip	4.2	3.7	4.8	5.0	5.4	5.1	5.4	4.3	4.4	3.6	4.4	4.2
Snow	26.0	18.1	14.8	5.0	0.1	0.0	0.0	0.0	0.0	0.7	6.4	16.6

High and Low temperatures in degrees Fahrenheit; Precipitation and Snow in inches

Weather Station: Uniontown 1 NE									Elevation: 956 feet		
	Jan	Feb	Mar	Apr	May	Jun	Jul	Aug	Sep	Oct	Nov	Dec
High	39	42	51	63	72	80	84	83	77	65	54	43
Low	21	22	27	37	46	55	60	59	51	40	32	24
Precip	3.0	2.7	3.7	3.7	4.5	4.3	4.7	3.7	3.4	3.0	3.7	3.1
Snow	8.9	5.3	4.7	0.4	tr	0.0	0.0	0.0	0.0	tr	0.9	4.4

High and Low temperatures in degrees Fahrenheit; Precipitation and Snow in inches

Population: 145,351 (1990); 148,644 (2000); 136,606 (2010); Race: 93.3% White, 4.6% Black, 0.3% Asian, 0.1% American Indian/Alaska Native, 0.0% Native Hawaiian/Other Pacific Islander, 1.7% Other, 0.8% Hispanic of any race (2010); Density: 172.8 persons per square mile (2010); Average household size: 2.36 (2010); Median age: 43.6 (2010); Males per 100 females: 96.3 (2010).
Religion: Six largest groups: 18.0% Catholicism, 7.1% Methodist/Pietist, 5.2% Baptist, 3.0% Non-Denominational, 3.0% Presbyterian-Reformed, 2.3% Lutheran (2010)
Economy: Unemployment rate: 9.2% (August 2012); Total civilian labor force: 65,464 (August 2012); Leading industries: 21.5% health care and social assistance; 17.6% retail trade; 14.9% accommodation & food services (2010); Farms: 1,220 totaling 140,688 acres (2007); Companies that employ 500 or more persons: 5 (2010); Companies that employ 100 to 499 persons: 49 (2010); Companies that employ less than 100 persons: 2,688 (2010); Black-owned businesses: 132 (2007); Hispanic-owned businesses: n/a (2007); Asian-owned businesses: n/a (2007); Women-owned businesses: 2,069 (2007); Retail sales per capita: $13,528 (2010). Single-family building permits issued: 159 (2011); Multi-family building permits issued: 0 (2011).
Income: Per capita income: $19,209 (2006-2010 5-year est.); Median household income: $34,796 (2006-2010 5-year est.); Average household income: $46,026 (2006-2010 5-year est.); Percent of households with income of $100,000 or more: 8.4% (2006-2010 5-year est.); Poverty rate: 19.2% (2006-2010 5-year est.); Bankruptcy rate: 3.96% (2011).

Taxes: Total county taxes per capita: $111 (2009); County property taxes per capita: $107 (2009).
Education: Percent of population age 25 and over with: High school diploma (including GED) or higher: 82.9% (2006-2010 5-year est.); Bachelor's degree or higher: 13.9% (2006-2010 5-year est.); Master's degree or higher: 4.6% (2006-2010 5-year est.).
Housing: Homeownership rate: 71.9% (2010); Median home value: $82,500 (2006-2010 5-year est.); Median contract rent: $386 per month (2006-2010 5-year est.); Median year structure built: 1954 (2006-2010 5-year est.)
Health: Birth rate: 97.9 per 10,000 population (2011); Death rate: 133.9 per 10,000 population (2011); Age-adjusted cancer mortality rate: 202.1 deaths per 100,000 population (2009); Number of physicians: 11.9 per 10,000 population (2010); Hospital beds: 19.5 per 10,000 population (2008); Hospital admissions: 949.8 per 10,000 population (2008).
Elections: 2012 Presidential election results: 45.3% Obama, 53.6% Romney
National and State Parks: Braddock Grave State Park; Forbes State Forest; Fort Necessity National Battlefield; Fort Necessity State Park; Friendship Hill National Historic Site; Laural Ridge State Park; Ohiopyle State Park
Additional Information Contacts
Fayette County Government . . . . (724) 430-1200
  http://www.co.fayette.pa.us

Fayette County Communities

ADAH (unincorporated postal area)

Zip Code: 15410

Covers a land area of 10.581 square miles and a water area of 0.228 square miles. Located at 39.91° N. Lat; 79.90° W. Long. Elevation is 860 feet. Population: 905 (2010); Density: 85.5 persons per square mile (2010); Race: 96.6% White, 2.1% Black, 0.1% Asian, 0.3% American Indian/Alaska Native, 0.0% Native Hawaiian/Other Pacific Islander, 0.9% Other, 0.1% Hispanic of any race (2010); Average household size: 2.33 (2010); Median age: 44.4 (2010); Males per 100 females: 95.0 (2010); Homeownership rate: 78.7% (2010)

ALLISON (CDP). Covers a land area of 0.669 square miles and a water area of 0.002 square miles. Located at 39.99° N. Lat; 79.87° W. Long. Elevation is 1,066 feet.

Population: n/a (1990); n/a (2000); 625 (2010); Density: 934.9 persons per square mile (2010); Race: 89.0% White, 8.3% Black, 0.5% Asian, 0.2% American Indian/Alaska Native, 0.0% Native Hawaiian/Other Pacific Islander, 2.0% Other, 0.2% Hispanic of any race (2010); Average household size: 2.39 (2010); Median age: 40.6 (2010); Males per 100 females: 101.0 (2010); Marriage status: 19.4% never married, 66.0% now married, 9.8% widowed, 4.7% divorced (2006-2010 5-year est.); Foreign born: 0.0% (2006-2010 5-year est.); Ancestry (includes multiple ancestries): 23.2% German, 19.7% Irish, 13.3% African, 13.3% Hungarian, 9.4% Polish (2006-2010 5-year est.).
Economy: Employment by occupation: 11.7% management, 8.6% professional, 5.7% services, 27.3% sales, 4.4% farming, 5.7% construction, 0.0% production (2006-2010 5-year est.).
Income: Per capita income: $22,804 (2006-2010 5-year est.); Median household income: $49,038 (2006-2010 5-year est.); Average household income: $56,618 (2006-2010 5-year est.); Percent of households with income of $100,000 or more: 17.0% (2006-2010 5-year est.); Poverty rate: 2.3% (2006-2010 5-year est.).
Education: Percent of population age 25 and over with: High school diploma (including GED) or higher: 92.3% (2006-2010 5-year est.); Bachelor's degree or higher: 24.9% (2006-2010 5-year est.); Master's degree or higher: 0.0% (2006-2010 5-year est.).
Housing: Homeownership rate: 79.3% (2010); Median home value: $51,000 (2006-2010 5-year est.); Median contract rent: $381 per month (2006-2010 5-year est.); Median year structure built: before 1940 (2006-2010 5-year est.).
Transportation: Commute to work: 100.0% car, 0.0% public transportation, 0.0% walk, 0.0% work from home (2006-2010 5-year est.); Travel time to work: 16.2% less than 15 minutes, 39.7% 15 to 30 minutes, 15.9% 30 to 45 minutes, 16.8% 45 to 60 minutes, 11.4% 60 minutes or more (2006-2010 5-year est.)

ARNOLD CITY (CDP). Covers a land area of 0.449 square miles and a water area of 0 square miles. Located at 40.12° N. Lat; 79.82° W. Long. Elevation is 945 feet.
Population: n/a (1990); n/a (2000); 498 (2010); Density: 1,110.0 persons per square mile (2010); Race: 82.3% White, 9.2% Black, 0.2% Asian, 0.0% American Indian/Alaska Native, 0.0% Native Hawaiian/Other Pacific Islander, 8.3% Other, 1.6% Hispanic of any race (2010); Average household size: 2.49 (2010); Median age: 33.8 (2010); Males per 100 females: 82.4 (2010); Marriage status: 21.9% never married, 50.5% now married, 13.6% widowed, 14.1% divorced (2006-2010 5-year est.); Foreign born: 0.0% (2006-2010 5-year est.); Ancestry (includes multiple ancestries): 27.8% German, 16.6% Italian, 13.3% Polish, 5.2% Ukrainian, 4.2% English (2006-2010 5-year est.).
Economy: Employment by occupation: 0.0% management, 0.0% professional, 9.1% services, 18.6% sales, 15.7% farming, 10.2% construction, 0.0% production (2006-2010 5-year est.).
Income: Per capita income: $12,418 (2006-2010 5-year est.); Median household income: $21,250 (2006-2010 5-year est.); Average household income: $30,347 (2006-2010 5-year est.); Percent of households with income of $100,000 or more: 6.5% (2006-2010 5-year est.); Poverty rate: 52.2% (2006-2010 5-year est.).
Education: Percent of population age 25 and over with: High school diploma (including GED) or higher: 69.4% (2006-2010 5-year est.); Bachelor's degree or higher: 13.6% (2006-2010 5-year est.); Master's degree or higher: 2.0% (2006-2010 5-year est.).
Housing: Homeownership rate: 45.0% (2010); Median home value: $68,800 (2006-2010 5-year est.); Median contract rent: $306 per month (2006-2010 5-year est.); Median year structure built: 1961 (2006-2010 5-year est.).
Transportation: Commute to work: 100.0% car, 0.0% public transportation, 0.0% walk, 0.0% work from home (2006-2010 5-year est.); Travel time to work: 27.4% less than 15 minutes, 46.7% 15 to 30 minutes, 25.9% 30 to 45 minutes, 0.0% 45 to 60 minutes, 0.0% 60 minutes or more (2006-2010 5-year est.)

BEAR ROCKS (CDP). Covers a land area of 2.648 square miles and a water area of <.001 square miles. Located at 40.13° N. Lat; 79.46° W. Long. Elevation is 1,995 feet.
Population: n/a (1990); n/a (2000); 1,048 (2010); Density: 395.8 persons per square mile (2010); Race: 98.8% White, 0.1% Black, 0.3% Asian, 0.3% American Indian/Alaska Native, 0.0% Native Hawaiian/Other Pacific Islander, 0.5% Other, 0.5% Hispanic of any race (2010); Average household size: 2.29 (2010); Median age: 46.7 (2010); Males per 100 females: 103.9 (2010); Marriage status: 10.9% never married, 76.8% now married, 5.0% widowed, 7.3% divorced (2006-2010 5-year est.); Foreign born: 4.4% (2006-2010 5-year est.); Ancestry (includes multiple ancestries): 24.9% German, 17.3% Italian, 7.0% Irish, 5.3% American, 5.1% Slovak (2006-2010 5-year est.).
Economy: Employment by occupation: 1.9% management, 12.5% professional, 19.6% services, 19.9% sales, 0.0% farming, 3.8% construction, 7.4% production (2006-2010 5-year est.).
Income: Per capita income: $24,990 (2006-2010 5-year est.); Median household income: $51,017 (2006-2010 5-year est.); Average household income: $60,484 (2006-2010 5-year est.); Percent of households with income of $100,000 or more: 11.0% (2006-2010 5-year est.); Poverty rate: 2.2% (2006-2010 5-year est.).
Education: Percent of population age 25 and over with: High school diploma (including GED) or higher: 98.9% (2006-2010 5-year est.); Bachelor's degree or higher: 32.4% (2006-2010 5-year est.); Master's degree or higher: 11.7% (2006-2010 5-year est.).
Housing: Homeownership rate: 91.4% (2010); Median home value: $118,800 (2006-2010 5-year est.); Median contract rent: n/a per month (2006-2010 5-year est.); Median year structure built: 1973 (2006-2010 5-year est.).
Transportation: Commute to work: 100.0% car, 0.0% public transportation, 0.0% walk, 0.0% work from home (2006-2010 5-year est.); Travel time to work: 9.0% less than 15 minutes, 38.5% 15 to 30 minutes, 25.1% 30 to 45 minutes, 13.6% 45 to 60 minutes, 13.7% 60 minutes or more (2006-2010 5-year est.)

BELLE VERNON (borough). Covers a land area of 0.250 square miles and a water area of 0.064 square miles. Located at 40.13° N. Lat; 79.87° W. Long. Elevation is 807 feet.
Population: 1,213 (1990); 1,211 (2000); 1,093 (2010); Density: 4,366.0 persons per square mile (2010); Race: 94.4% White, 3.5% Black, 0.5%

Asian, 0.2% American Indian/Alaska Native, 0.0% Native Hawaiian/Other Pacific Islander, 1.4% Other, 1.6% Hispanic of any race (2010); Average household size: 1.90 (2010); Median age: 49.5 (2010); Males per 100 females: 82.8 (2010); Marriage status: 31.6% never married, 37.9% now married, 17.1% widowed, 13.3% divorced (2006-2010 5-year est.); Foreign born: 0.1% (2006-2010 5-year est.); Ancestry (includes multiple ancestries): 24.8% Italian, 22.4% German, 12.9% English, 12.0% Polish, 11.7% Irish (2006-2010 5-year est.).
Economy: Employment by occupation: 9.5% management, 2.9% professional, 19.1% services, 18.9% sales, 2.2% farming, 10.3% construction, 6.2% production (2006-2010 5-year est.).
Income: Per capita income: $20,329 (2006-2010 5-year est.); Median household income: $25,795 (2006-2010 5-year est.); Average household income: $39,802 (2006-2010 5-year est.); Percent of households with income of $100,000 or more: 4.4% (2006-2010 5-year est.); Poverty rate: 12.7% (2006-2010 5-year est.).
Education: Percent of population age 25 and over with: High school diploma (including GED) or higher: 80.8% (2006-2010 5-year est.); Bachelor's degree or higher: 12.2% (2006-2010 5-year est.); Master's degree or higher: 4.1% (2006-2010 5-year est.).

School District(s)

Belle Vernon Area SD (KG-12)
    2010-11 Enrollment: 2,677 . . . . (724) 808-2500
Belle Vernon Area SD (KG-12)
    2010-11 Enrollment: 2,677 . . . . (724) 808-2500
Housing: Homeownership rate: 39.7% (2010); Median home value: $67,300 (2006-2010 5-year est.); Median contract rent: $365 per month (2006-2010 5-year est.); Median year structure built: 1949 (2006-2010 5-year est.).
Transportation: Commute to work: 94.7% car, 0.7% public transportation, 3.7% walk, 0.0% work from home (2006-2010 5-year est.); Travel time to work: 45.4% less than 15 minutes, 32.0% 15 to 30 minutes, 17.1% 30 to 45 minutes, 2.3% 45 to 60 minutes, 3.2% 60 minutes or more (2006-2010 5-year est.)
Additional Information Contacts
Greater Rostraver Chamber of Commerce . . . . (724) 929-3329
    http://www.greaterrostraverchamber.org

BROWNSVILLE (borough). Covers a land area of 0.977 square miles and a water area of 0.114 square miles. Located at 40.02° N. Lat; 79.89° W. Long. Elevation is 846 feet.
Population: 3,164 (1990); 2,804 (2000); 2,331 (2010); Density: 2,386.2 persons per square mile (2010); Race: 81.4% White, 13.5% Black, 0.1% Asian, 0.1% American Indian/Alaska Native, 0.0% Native Hawaiian/Other Pacific Islander, 4.9% Other, 0.6% Hispanic of any race (2010); Average household size: 2.16 (2010); Median age: 41.9 (2010); Males per 100 females: 91.2 (2010); Marriage status: 31.7% never married, 42.6% now married, 11.0% widowed, 14.7% divorced (2006-2010 5-year est.); Foreign born: 0.0% (2006-2010 5-year est.); Ancestry (includes multiple ancestries): 22.0% Italian, 19.3% Irish, 11.1% German, 10.3% English, 8.0% Polish (2006-2010 5-year est.).
Economy: Employment by occupation: 10.7% management, 3.0% professional, 13.6% services, 23.1% sales, 1.8% farming, 16.7% construction, 6.2% production (2006-2010 5-year est.).
Income: Per capita income: $14,694 (2006-2010 5-year est.); Median household income: $21,794 (2006-2010 5-year est.); Average household income: $30,912 (2006-2010 5-year est.); Percent of households with income of $100,000 or more: 3.8% (2006-2010 5-year est.); Poverty rate: 35.0% (2006-2010 5-year est.).
Education: Percent of population age 25 and over with: High school diploma (including GED) or higher: 83.3% (2006-2010 5-year est.); Bachelor's degree or higher: 7.1% (2006-2010 5-year est.); Master's degree or higher: 2.9% (2006-2010 5-year est.).

School District(s)

Brownsville Area SD (KG-12)
    2010-11 Enrollment: 1,885 . . . . (724) 785-2021
Housing: Homeownership rate: 54.3% (2010); Median home value: $55,200 (2006-2010 5-year est.); Median contract rent: $260 per month (2006-2010 5-year est.); Median year structure built: before 1940 (2006-2010 5-year est.).
Hospitals: Brownsville General Hospital (109 beds)
Safety: Violent crime rate: 29.9 per 10,000 population; Property crime rate: 243.8 per 10,000 population (2011).
Newspapers: Herald-Standard - Brownsville Bureau (Local news)

Transportation: Commute to work: 84.8% car, 3.0% public transportation, 8.9% walk, 3.2% work from home (2006-2010 5-year est.); Travel time to work: 31.9% less than 15 minutes, 16.8% 15 to 30 minutes, 28.3% 30 to 45 minutes, 12.3% 45 to 60 minutes, 10.8% 60 minutes or more (2006-2010 5-year est.)

Additional Information Contacts

Mon Valley Regional Chamber of Commerce . . . . (724) 483-3507
http://www.mvrchamber.org

BROWNSVILLE (township). Covers a land area of 1.502 square miles and a water area of 0.045 square miles. Located at 40.02° N. Lat; 79.87° W. Long. Elevation is 846 feet.

History: Pioneers on Cumberland Road transferred here to water travel on Mississippi River system. Laid out 1785, incorporated 1815; consolidated 1933 with South Brownsville.

Population: 847 (1990); 769 (2000); 683 (2010); Density: 454.7 persons per square mile (2010); Race: 91.9% White, 5.9% Black, 0.0% Asian, 0.4% American Indian/Alaska Native, 0.0% Native Hawaiian/Other Pacific Islander, 1.8% Other, 0.9% Hispanic of any race (2010); Average household size: 2.31 (2010); Median age: 45.8 (2010); Males per 100 females: 88.2 (2010); Marriage status: 20.6% never married, 55.5% now married, 7.5% widowed, 16.4% divorced (2006-2010 5-year est.); Foreign born: 1.2% (2006-2010 5-year est.); Ancestry (includes multiple ancestries): 17.8% Irish, 10.2% German, 9.0% Italian, 7.4% Slovak, 6.8% English (2006-2010 5-year est.).

Economy: Employment by occupation: 0.0% management, 2.5% professional, 5.4% services, 18.2% sales, 2.9% farming, 8.9% construction, 5.4% production (2006-2010 5-year est.).

Income: Per capita income: $15,513 (2006-2010 5-year est.); Median household income: $29,306 (2006-2010 5-year est.); Average household income: $39,315 (2006-2010 5-year est.); Percent of households with income of $100,000 or more: 6.3% (2006-2010 5-year est.); Poverty rate: 30.5% (2006-2010 5-year est.).

Education: Percent of population age 25 and over with: High school diploma (including GED) or higher: 80.4% (2006-2010 5-year est.); Bachelor's degree or higher: 5.9% (2006-2010 5-year est.); Master's degree or higher: 2.9% (2006-2010 5-year est.).

Housing: Homeownership rate: 81.1% (2010); Median home value: $45,800 (2006-2010 5-year est.); Median contract rent: $421 per month (2006-2010 5-year est.); Median year structure built: 1943 (2006-2010 5-year est.).

Hospitals: Brownsville General Hospital (109 beds)

Newspapers: Herald-Standard - Brownsville Bureau (Local news)

Transportation: Commute to work: 100.0% car, 0.0% public transportation, 0.0% walk, 0.0% work from home (2006-2010 5-year est.); Travel time to work: 28.2% less than 15 minutes, 40.4% 15 to 30 minutes, 19.5% 30 to 45 minutes, 8.3% 45 to 60 minutes, 3.6% 60 minutes or more (2006-2010 5-year est.)

Additional Information Contacts

Mon Valley Regional Chamber of Commerce . . . . (724) 483-3507
http://www.mvrchamber.org

BUFFINGTON (CDP). Covers a land area of 0.162 square miles and a water area of 0 square miles. Located at 39.93° N. Lat; 79.84° W. Long. Elevation is 1,027 feet.

Population: n/a (1990); n/a (2000); 292 (2010); Density: 1,799.9 persons per square mile (2010); Race: 84.2% White, 14.0% Black, 0.3% Asian, 0.0% American Indian/Alaska Native, 0.0% Native Hawaiian/Other Pacific Islander, 1.5% Other, 0.3% Hispanic of any race (2010); Average household size: 2.30 (2010); Median age: 47.0 (2010); Males per 100 females: 73.8 (2010); Marriage status: 25.2% never married, 15.1% now married, 19.5% widowed, 40.3% divorced (2006-2010 5-year est.); Foreign born: 0.0% (2006-2010 5-year est.); Ancestry (includes multiple ancestries): 19.5% Polish, 19.5% Russian, 16.4% Irish, 15.1% German, 7.5% Dutch (2006-2010 5-year est.).

Economy: Employment by occupation: 0.0% management, 0.0% professional, 34.2% services, 15.8% sales, 0.0% farming, 0.0% construction, 0.0% production (2006-2010 5-year est.).

Income: Per capita income: $16,002 (2006-2010 5-year est.); Median household income: $22,702 (2006-2010 5-year est.); Average household income: $19,777 (2006-2010 5-year est.); Percent of households with income of $100,000 or more: n/a (2006-2010 5-year est.); Poverty rate: 40.3% (2006-2010 5-year est.).

Education: Percent of population age 25 and over with: High school diploma (including GED) or higher: 56.6% (2006-2010 5-year est.);

Bachelor's degree or higher: 0.0% (2006-2010 5-year est.); Master's degree or higher: 0.0% (2006-2010 5-year est.).

Housing: Homeownership rate: 71.0% (2010); Median home value: $18,600 (2006-2010 5-year est.); Median contract rent: n/a per month (2006-2010 5-year est.); Median year structure built: before 1940 (2006-2010 5-year est.).

Transportation: Commute to work: 100.0% car, 0.0% public transportation, 0.0% walk, 0.0% work from home (2006-2010 5-year est.); Travel time to work: 50.0% less than 15 minutes, 50.0% 15 to 30 minutes, 0.0% 30 to 45 minutes, 0.0% 45 to 60 minutes, 0.0% 60 minutes or more (2006-2010 5-year est.)

BULLSKIN (township). Covers a land area of 43.532 square miles and a water area of 0.105 square miles. Located at 40.08° N. Lat; 79.51° W. Long.

Population: 7,323 (1990); 7,782 (2000); 6,966 (2010); Density: 160.0 persons per square mile (2010); Race: 99.0% White, 0.2% Black, 0.2% Asian, 0.1% American Indian/Alaska Native, 0.0% Native Hawaiian/Other Pacific Islander, 0.5% Other, 0.2% Hispanic of any race (2010); Average household size: 2.42 (2010); Median age: 44.7 (2010); Males per 100 females: 101.0 (2010); Marriage status: 24.5% never married, 59.1% now married, 6.9% widowed, 9.5% divorced (2006-2010 5-year est.); Foreign born: 2.1% (2006-2010 5-year est.); Ancestry (includes multiple ancestries): 38.0% German, 14.6% Irish, 13.5% English, 10.3% American, 8.9% Italian (2006-2010 5-year est.).

Economy: Employment by occupation: 5.5% management, 3.8% professional, 11.1% services, 18.2% sales, 4.5% farming, 13.8% construction, 11.4% production (2006-2010 5-year est.).

Income: Per capita income: $22,642 (2006-2010 5-year est.); Median household income: $46,092 (2006-2010 5-year est.); Average household income: $53,155 (2006-2010 5-year est.); Percent of households with income of $100,000 or more: 11.3% (2006-2010 5-year est.); Poverty rate: 8.6% (2006-2010 5-year est.).

Education: Percent of population age 25 and over with: High school diploma (including GED) or higher: 86.8% (2006-2010 5-year est.); Bachelor's degree or higher: 17.3% (2006-2010 5-year est.); Master's degree or higher: 6.7% (2006-2010 5-year est.).

Housing: Homeownership rate: 84.1% (2010); Median home value: $109,100 (2006-2010 5-year est.); Median contract rent: $379 per month (2006-2010 5-year est.); Median year structure built: 1972 (2006-2010 5-year est.).

Transportation: Commute to work: 96.4% car, 0.0% public transportation, 0.5% walk, 2.5% work from home (2006-2010 5-year est.); Travel time to work: 24.8% less than 15 minutes, 37.2% 15 to 30 minutes, 21.0% 30 to 45 minutes, 9.0% 45 to 60 minutes, 8.0% 60 minutes or more (2006-2010 5-year est.)

Additional Information Contacts

Bullskin Township . . . . (724) 628-7630
http://bullskintownship.com

Laurel Highlands Chamber of Commerce . . . . (724) 547-7521
http://www.laurelhighlandschamber.com

CARDALE (unincorporated postal area)

Zip Code: 15420

Covers a land area of 0.458 square miles and a water area of 0 square miles. Located at 39.96° N. Lat; 79.86° W. Long. Elevation is 965 feet. Population: 251 (2010); Density: 547.0 persons per square mile (2010); Race: 64.1% White, 26.3% Black, 0.0% Asian, 0.4% American Indian/Alaska Native, 0.0% Native Hawaiian/Other Pacific Islander, 9.2% Other, 0.0% Hispanic of any race (2010); Average household size: 2.64 (2010); Median age: 38.9 (2010); Males per 100 females: 88.7 (2010); Homeownership rate: 70.5% (2010)

CHALK HILL (unincorporated postal area)

Zip Code: 15421

Covers a land area of 0.216 square miles and a water area of 0 square miles. Located at 39.84° N. Lat; 79.59° W. Long. Population: 112 (2010); Density: 516.2 persons per square mile (2010); Race: 95.5% White, 0.0% Black, 0.0% Asian, 0.0% American Indian/Alaska Native, 0.0% Native Hawaiian/Other Pacific Islander, 4.5% Other, 0.0% Hispanic of any race (2010); Average household size: 1.96 (2010); Median age: 51.0 (2010); Males per 100 females: 96.5 (2010); Homeownership rate: 94.7% (2010)

CHALKHILL (CDP). Covers a land area of 0.819 square miles and a water area of 0.010 square miles. Located at 39.85° N. Lat; 79.62° W. Long. Elevation is 2,070 feet.

Population: n/a (1990); n/a (2000); 141 (2010); Density: 172.2 persons per square mile (2010); Race: 100.0% White, 0.0% Black, 0.0% Asian, 0.0% American Indian/Alaska Native, 0.0% Native Hawaiian/Other Pacific Islander, 0.0% Other, 0.0% Hispanic of any race (2010); Average household size: 2.20 (2010); Median age: 52.3 (2010); Males per 100 females: 93.2 (2010); Marriage status: 47.6% never married, 29.8% now married, 0.0% widowed, 22.6% divorced (2006-2010 5-year est.); Foreign born: 14.3% (2006-2010 5-year est.); Ancestry (includes multiple ancestries): 72.6% German, 15.5% Swedish, 15.5% French, 11.9% Hungarian, 10.7% Irish (2006-2010 5-year est.).

Economy: Employment by occupation: 44.0% management, 0.0% professional, 0.0% services, 25.3% sales, 0.0% farming, 17.3% construction, 0.0% production (2006-2010 5-year est.).

Income: Per capita income: $28,125 (2006-2010 5-year est.); Median household income: $58,512 (2006-2010 5-year est.); Average household income: $54,077 (2006-2010 5-year est.); Percent of households with income of $100,000 or more: n/a (2006-2010 5-year est.); Poverty rate: 0.0% (2006-2010 5-year est.).

Education: Percent of population age 25 and over with: High school diploma (including GED) or higher: 100.0% (2006-2010 5-year est.); Bachelor's degree or higher: 0.0% (2006-2010 5-year est.); Master's degree or higher: 0.0% (2006-2010 5-year est.).

Housing: Homeownership rate: 68.7% (2010); Median home value: n/a (2006-2010 5-year est.); Median contract rent: n/a per month (2006-2010 5-year est.); Median year structure built: 1980 (2006-2010 5-year est.).

Transportation: Commute to work: 100.0% car, 0.0% public transportation, 0.0% walk, 0.0% work from home (2006-2010 5-year est.); Travel time to work: 0.0% less than 15 minutes, 42.7% 15 to 30 minutes, 0.0% 30 to 45 minutes, 44.0% 45 to 60 minutes, 13.3% 60 minutes or more (2006-2010 5-year est.)

CHESTNUT RIDGE (unincorporated postal area)

Zip Code: 15422

Covers a land area of 0.090 square miles and a water area of 0 square miles. Located at 39.98° N. Lat; 79.81° W. Long. Elevation is 1,024 feet. Population: 220 (2010); Density: 2,432.5 persons per square mile (2010); Race: 97.3% White, 1.8% Black, 0.0% Asian, 0.0% American Indian/Alaska Native, 0.0% Native Hawaiian/Other Pacific Islander, 0.9% Other, 0.0% Hispanic of any race (2010); Average household size: 2.56 (2010); Median age: 40.8 (2010); Males per 100 females: 98.2 (2010); Homeownership rate: 77.9% (2010)

CONNELLSVILLE (city). Covers a land area of 2.180 square miles and a water area of 0.106 square miles. Located at 40.02° N. Lat; 79.59° W. Long. Elevation is 948 feet.

History: The attack on Henry C. Frick by the anarchist Alexander Berkman occurred (1892) in Connellsville during the Homestead Strike. Settled c.1770, Incorporated as a borough 1806, as a city 1911.

Population: 9,229 (1990); 9,146 (2000); 7,637 (2010); Density: 3,502.5 persons per square mile (2010); Race: 93.2% White, 4.5% Black, 0.4% Asian, 0.1% American Indian/Alaska Native, 0.1% Native Hawaiian/Other Pacific Islander, 1.7% Other, 0.7% Hispanic of any race (2010); Average household size: 2.26 (2010); Median age: 39.5 (2010); Males per 100 females: 89.6 (2010); Marriage status: 33.9% never married, 45.9% now married, 8.9% widowed, 11.3% divorced (2006-2010 5-year est.); Foreign born: 1.0% (2006-2010 5-year est.); Ancestry (includes multiple ancestries): 32.5% German, 17.6% Irish, 12.7% Italian, 11.7% Polish, 11.4% English (2006-2010 5-year est.).

Economy: Employment by occupation: 7.6% management, 1.8% professional, 16.2% services, 18.9% sales, 4.9% farming, 7.4% construction, 5.1% production (2006-2010 5-year est.).

Income: Per capita income: $15,964 (2006-2010 5-year est.); Median household income: $30,073 (2006-2010 5-year est.); Average household income: $37,316 (2006-2010 5-year est.); Percent of households with income of $100,000 or more: 2.8% (2006-2010 5-year est.); Poverty rate: 28.2% (2006-2010 5-year est.).

Education: Percent of population age 25 and over with: High school diploma (including GED) or higher: 81.4% (2006-2010 5-year est.); Bachelor's degree or higher: 11.6% (2006-2010 5-year est.); Master's degree or higher: 2.1% (2006-2010 5-year est.).

School District(s)

Connellsville Area Career & Technical Center (09-12)
    2010-11 Enrollment: 428 . . . . (724) 626-0236
Connellsville Area SD (KG-12)
    2010-11 Enrollment: 4,886 . . . . (724) 628-3300

Housing: Homeownership rate: 51.4% (2010); Median home value: $76,300 (2006-2010 5-year est.); Median contract rent: $383 per month (2006-2010 5-year est.); Median year structure built: 1941 (2006-2010 5-year est.).

Hospitals: Highlands Hospital (87 beds)

Safety: Violent crime rate: 32.6 per 10,000 population; Property crime rate: 449.0 per 10,000 population (2011).

Newspapers: The Daily Courier (Local news; Circulation 8,507); Herald-Standard - Connellsville Bureau (Local news)

Transportation: Commute to work: 91.3% car, 0.0% public transportation, 6.8% walk, 1.9% work from home (2006-2010 5-year est.); Travel time to work: 44.7% less than 15 minutes, 31.9% 15 to 30 minutes, 13.4% 30 to 45 minutes, 7.4% 45 to 60 minutes, 2.5% 60 minutes or more (2006-2010 5-year est.); Amtrak: train service available.

Additional Information Contacts

City of Connellsville . . . . (724) 628-2020
    http://www.connellsville.org
Greater Connellsville Chamber of Commerce . . . . (724) 628-5500
    http://www.greaterconnellsville.org

CONNELLSVILLE (township). Covers a land area of 11.347 square miles and a water area of 0.152 square miles. Located at 40.00° N. Lat; 79.55° W. Long. Elevation is 948 feet.

Population: 2,553 (1990); 2,483 (2000); 2,391 (2010); Density: 210.7 persons per square mile (2010); Race: 98.5% White, 0.8% Black, 0.0% Asian, 0.1% American Indian/Alaska Native, 0.0% Native Hawaiian/Other Pacific Islander, 0.6% Other, 0.6% Hispanic of any race (2010); Average household size: 2.31 (2010); Median age: 46.9 (2010); Males per 100 females: 98.4 (2010); Marriage status: 29.1% never married, 55.9% now married, 7.0% widowed, 8.0% divorced (2006-2010 5-year est.); Foreign born: 0.3% (2006-2010 5-year est.); Ancestry (includes multiple ancestries): 40.4% German, 18.4% Irish, 14.4% Italian, 14.1% English, 5.2% Slovak (2006-2010 5-year est.).

Economy: Single-family building permits issued: 1 (2011); Multi-family building permits issued: 0 (2011); Employment by occupation: 7.9% management, 2.0% professional, 9.8% services, 19.6% sales, 6.6% farming, 15.2% construction, 6.2% production (2006-2010 5-year est.).

Income: Per capita income: $21,070 (2006-2010 5-year est.); Median household income: $36,571 (2006-2010 5-year est.); Average household income: $48,743 (2006-2010 5-year est.); Percent of households with income of $100,000 or more: 13.8% (2006-2010 5-year est.); Poverty rate: 20.2% (2006-2010 5-year est.).

Education: Percent of population age 25 and over with: High school diploma (including GED) or higher: 82.7% (2006-2010 5-year est.); Bachelor's degree or higher: 16.9% (2006-2010 5-year est.); Master's degree or higher: 5.6% (2006-2010 5-year est.).

Housing: Homeownership rate: 81.6% (2010); Median home value: $80,200 (2006-2010 5-year est.); Median contract rent: $397 per month (2006-2010 5-year est.); Median year structure built: 1959 (2006-2010 5-year est.).

Hospitals: Highlands Hospital (87 beds)

Newspapers: The Daily Courier (Local news; Circulation 8,507); Herald-Standard - Connellsville Bureau (Local news)

Transportation: Commute to work: 98.1% car, 0.0% public transportation, 1.3% walk, 0.6% work from home (2006-2010 5-year est.); Travel time to work: 39.6% less than 15 minutes, 29.4% 15 to 30 minutes, 18.3% 30 to 45 minutes, 7.9% 45 to 60 minutes, 4.8% 60 minutes or more (2006-2010 5-year est.); Amtrak: train service available.

Additional Information Contacts

Greater Connellsville Chamber of Commerce . . . . (724) 628-5500
    http://www.greaterconnellsville.org

DAWSON (borough). Aka Stickel. Covers a land area of 0.161 square miles and a water area of 0.050 square miles. Located at 40.05° N. Lat; 79.66° W. Long. Elevation is 856 feet.

Population: 535 (1990); 451 (2000); 367 (2010); Density: 2,274.2 persons per square mile (2010); Race: 96.2% White, 1.1% Black, 0.0% Asian, 0.3% American Indian/Alaska Native, 0.0% Native Hawaiian/Other Pacific Islander, 2.4% Other, 0.0% Hispanic of any race (2010); Average household size: 2.46 (2010); Median age: 41.9 (2010); Males per 100

females: 98.4 (2010); Marriage status: 15.4% never married, 61.5% now married, 7.3% widowed, 15.8% divorced (2006-2010 5-year est.); Foreign born: 0.0% (2006-2010 5-year est.); Ancestry (includes multiple ancestries): 36.0% German, 23.7% Irish, 14.1% Italian, 9.5% English, 7.8% Scotch-Irish (2006-2010 5-year est.).

Economy: Employment by occupation: 6.0% management, 0.0% professional, 4.3% services, 19.8% sales, 10.3% farming, 20.7% construction, 10.3% production (2006-2010 5-year est.).

Income: Per capita income: $19,282 (2006-2010 5-year est.); Median household income: $35,139 (2006-2010 5-year est.); Average household income: $40,385 (2006-2010 5-year est.); Percent of households with income of $100,000 or more: 6.1% (2006-2010 5-year est.); Poverty rate: 20.1% (2006-2010 5-year est.).

Education: Percent of population age 25 and over with: High school diploma (including GED) or higher: 90.1% (2006-2010 5-year est.); Bachelor's degree or higher: 9.9% (2006-2010 5-year est.); Master's degree or higher: 1.9% (2006-2010 5-year est.).

Housing: Homeownership rate: 71.1% (2010); Median home value: $55,800 (2006-2010 5-year est.); Median contract rent: $404 per month (2006-2010 5-year est.); Median year structure built: before 1940 (2006-2010 5-year est.).

Transportation: Commute to work: 91.2% car, 0.0% public transportation, 0.0% walk, 8.8% work from home (2006-2010 5-year est.); Travel time to work: 21.2% less than 15 minutes, 42.3% 15 to 30 minutes, 25.0% 30 to 45 minutes, 5.8% 45 to 60 minutes, 5.8% 60 minutes or more (2006-2010 5-year est.)

DEER LAKE (CDP). Covers a land area of 1.515 square miles and a water area of 0.091 square miles. Located at 39.85° N. Lat; 79.59° W. Long. Elevation is 1,975 feet.

Population: n/a (1990); n/a (2000); 495 (2010); Density: 326.8 persons per square mile (2010); Race: 98.8% White, 0.2% Black, 0.0% Asian, 0.0% American Indian/Alaska Native, 0.0% Native Hawaiian/Other Pacific Islander, 1.0% Other, 0.2% Hispanic of any race (2010); Average household size: 2.27 (2010); Median age: 48.6 (2010); Males per 100 females: 97.2 (2010); Marriage status: 13.4% never married, 68.8% now married, 4.9% widowed, 12.9% divorced (2006-2010 5-year est.); Foreign born: 0.0% (2006-2010 5-year est.); Ancestry (includes multiple ancestries): 16.5% German, 14.2% Irish, 11.8% Greek, 11.3% Italian, 8.0% Dutch (2006-2010 5-year est.).

Economy: Employment by occupation: 29.4% management, 0.0% professional, 6.9% services, 18.3% sales, 0.0% farming, 3.6% construction, 0.0% production (2006-2010 5-year est.).

Income: Per capita income: $25,871 (2006-2010 5-year est.); Median household income: $61,097 (2006-2010 5-year est.); Average household income: $57,670 (2006-2010 5-year est.); Percent of households with income of $100,000 or more: 5.5% (2006-2010 5-year est.); Poverty rate: 6.2% (2006-2010 5-year est.).

Education: Percent of population age 25 and over with: High school diploma (including GED) or higher: 95.3% (2006-2010 5-year est.); Bachelor's degree or higher: 41.2% (2006-2010 5-year est.); Master's degree or higher: 13.6% (2006-2010 5-year est.).

Housing: Homeownership rate: 91.7% (2010); Median home value: $192,400 (2006-2010 5-year est.); Median contract rent: n/a per month (2006-2010 5-year est.); Median year structure built: 1976 (2006-2010 5-year est.).

Transportation: Commute to work: 96.1% car, 0.0% public transportation, 0.0% walk, 3.9% work from home (2006-2010 5-year est.); Travel time to work: 7.5% less than 15 minutes, 58.4% 15 to 30 minutes, 25.6% 30 to 45 minutes, 4.7% 45 to 60 minutes, 3.8% 60 minutes or more (2006-2010 5-year est.)

DICKERSON RUN (unincorporated postal area)
Zip Code: 15430
Covers a land area of 0.354 square miles and a water area of 0.036 square miles. Located at 40.03° N. Lat; 79.65° W. Long. Elevation is 968 feet. Population: 314 (2010); Density: 884.7 persons per square mile (2010); Race: 96.2% White, 1.3% Black, 0.0% Asian, 0.0% American Indian/Alaska Native, 0.0% Native Hawaiian/Other Pacific Islander, 2.5% Other, 1.9% Hispanic of any race (2010); Average household size: 2.71 (2010); Median age: 38.7 (2010); Males per 100 females: 105.2 (2010); Homeownership rate: 78.4% (2010)

DUNBAR (borough). Covers a land area of 0.607 square miles and a water area of 0 square miles. Located at 39.98° N. Lat; 79.61° W. Long. Elevation is 1,047 feet.

Population: 1,213 (1990); 1,219 (2000); 1,042 (2010); Density: 1,717.7 persons per square mile (2010); Race: 98.2% White, 0.6% Black, 0.3% Asian, 0.1% American Indian/Alaska Native, 0.0% Native Hawaiian/Other Pacific Islander, 0.8% Other, 0.9% Hispanic of any race (2010); Average household size: 2.34 (2010); Median age: 42.3 (2010); Males per 100 females: 92.3 (2010); Marriage status: 29.0% never married, 54.3% now married, 6.3% widowed, 10.3% divorced (2006-2010 5-year est.); Foreign born: 0.0% (2006-2010 5-year est.); Ancestry (includes multiple ancestries): 38.1% German, 30.0% Irish, 23.6% Italian, 9.0% English, 8.9% Dutch (2006-2010 5-year est.).

Economy: Employment by occupation: 2.9% management, 0.6% professional, 14.0% services, 25.0% sales, 4.5% farming, 9.0% construction, 9.7% production (2006-2010 5-year est.).

Income: Per capita income: $16,333 (2006-2010 5-year est.); Median household income: $34,402 (2006-2010 5-year est.); Average household income: $40,075 (2006-2010 5-year est.); Percent of households with income of $100,000 or more: 3.0% (2006-2010 5-year est.); Poverty rate: 21.6% (2006-2010 5-year est.).

Education: Percent of population age 25 and over with: High school diploma (including GED) or higher: 82.3% (2006-2010 5-year est.); Bachelor's degree or higher: 7.9% (2006-2010 5-year est.); Master's degree or higher: 4.0% (2006-2010 5-year est.).

School District(s)
Connellsville Area SD (KG-12)
   2010-11 Enrollment: 4,886 . . . . (724) 628-3300

Housing: Homeownership rate: 74.0% (2010); Median home value: $63,300 (2006-2010 5-year est.); Median contract rent: $331 per month (2006-2010 5-year est.); Median year structure built: before 1940 (2006-2010 5-year est.).

Transportation: Commute to work: 93.7% car, 1.2% public transportation, 4.2% walk, 0.6% work from home (2006-2010 5-year est.); Travel time to work: 33.1% less than 15 minutes, 40.3% 15 to 30 minutes, 15.4% 30 to 45 minutes, 6.4% 45 to 60 minutes, 4.8% 60 minutes or more (2006-2010 5-year est.)

Additional Information Contacts
Greater Connellsville Chamber of Commerce . . . . (724) 628-5500
  http://www.greaterconnellsville.org

DUNBAR (township). Covers a land area of 59.098 square miles and a water area of 0.443 square miles. Located at 39.96° N. Lat; 79.61° W. Long. Elevation is 1,047 feet.

Population: 7,460 (1990); 7,562 (2000); 7,126 (2010); Density: 120.6 persons per square mile (2010); Race: 97.5% White, 1.4% Black, 0.2% Asian, 0.2% American Indian/Alaska Native, 0.0% Native Hawaiian/Other Pacific Islander, 0.7% Other, 0.7% Hispanic of any race (2010); Average household size: 2.46 (2010); Median age: 44.1 (2010); Males per 100 females: 97.1 (2010); Marriage status: 25.9% never married, 57.4% now married, 7.5% widowed, 9.3% divorced (2006-2010 5-year est.); Foreign born: 0.0% (2006-2010 5-year est.); Ancestry (includes multiple ancestries): 32.4% German, 19.5% Irish, 15.0% Italian, 8.7% Polish, 8.3% Slovak (2006-2010 5-year est.).

Economy: Employment by occupation: 7.1% management, 0.4% professional, 12.3% services, 18.3% sales, 1.8% farming, 14.2% construction, 13.3% production (2006-2010 5-year est.).

Income: Per capita income: $19,864 (2006-2010 5-year est.); Median household income: $35,333 (2006-2010 5-year est.); Average household income: $47,909 (2006-2010 5-year est.); Percent of households with income of $100,000 or more: 10.1% (2006-2010 5-year est.); Poverty rate: 18.3% (2006-2010 5-year est.).

Education: Percent of population age 25 and over with: High school diploma (including GED) or higher: 82.1% (2006-2010 5-year est.); Bachelor's degree or higher: 10.4% (2006-2010 5-year est.); Master's degree or higher: 3.8% (2006-2010 5-year est.).

Housing: Homeownership rate: 80.9% (2010); Median home value: $85,700 (2006-2010 5-year est.); Median contract rent: $368 per month (2006-2010 5-year est.); Median year structure built: 1958 (2006-2010 5-year est.).

Transportation: Commute to work: 97.7% car, 0.5% public transportation, 0.0% walk, 0.5% work from home (2006-2010 5-year est.); Travel time to work: 33.4% less than 15 minutes, 36.5% 15 to 30 minutes, 14.3% 30 to 45 minutes, 9.0% 45 to 60 minutes, 6.7% 60 minutes or more (2006-2010 5-year est.)

Additional Information Contacts
Dunbar Township . . . . (724) 626-1941
Greater Connellsville Chamber of Commerce . . . . (724) 628-5500
http://www.greaterconnellsville.org

EAST MILLSBORO (unincorporated postal area)
Zip Code: 15433
Covers a land area of 14.359 square miles and a water area of 0.805 square miles. Located at 39.98° N. Lat; 79.94° W. Long. Population: 741 (2010); Density: 51.6 persons per square mile (2010); Race: 98.2% White, 0.9% Black, 0.0% Asian, 0.0% American Indian/Alaska Native, 0.0% Native Hawaiian/Other Pacific Islander, 0.9% Other, 0.8% Hispanic of any race (2010); Average household size: 2.43 (2010); Median age: 47.7 (2010); Males per 100 females: 97.1 (2010); Homeownership rate: 87.2% (2010)

EAST UNIONTOWN (CDP). Covers a land area of 1.999 square
miles and a water area of 0 square miles. Located at 39.90° N. Lat; 79.70° W. Long. Elevation is 1,227 feet.
Population: 2,686 (1990); 2,760 (2000); 2,419 (2010); Density: 1,210.1 persons per square mile (2010); Race: 90.2% White, 6.8% Black, 0.5% Asian, 0.2% American Indian/Alaska Native, 0.0% Native Hawaiian/Other Pacific Islander, 2.3% Other, 0.8% Hispanic of any race (2010); Average household size: 2.26 (2010); Median age: 42.7 (2010); Males per 100 females: 87.4 (2010); Marriage status: 28.3% never married, 50.9% now married, 13.2% widowed, 7.6% divorced (2006-2010 5-year est.); Foreign born: 0.0% (2006-2010 5-year est.); Ancestry (includes multiple ancestries): 28.0% German, 15.3% Irish, 14.7% Italian, 10.2% English, 8.1% Polish (2006-2010 5-year est.).
Economy: Employment by occupation: 4.9% management, 2.6% professional, 11.2% services, 23.7% sales, 0.0% farming, 11.2% construction, 2.6% production (2006-2010 5-year est.).
Income: Per capita income: $17,299 (2006-2010 5-year est.); Median household income: $34,515 (2006-2010 5-year est.); Average household income: $39,515 (2006-2010 5-year est.); Percent of households with income of $100,000 or more: 1.4% (2006-2010 5-year est.); Poverty rate: 26.4% (2006-2010 5-year est.).
Education: Percent of population age 25 and over with: High school diploma (including GED) or higher: 83.4% (2006-2010 5-year est.); Bachelor's degree or higher: 16.1% (2006-2010 5-year est.); Master's degree or higher: 4.1% (2006-2010 5-year est.).
Housing: Homeownership rate: 62.2% (2010); Median home value: $75,400 (2006-2010 5-year est.); Median contract rent: $358 per month (2006-2010 5-year est.); Median year structure built: 1953 (2006-2010 5-year est.).
Transportation: Commute to work: 92.6% car, 0.0% public transportation, 0.0% walk, 3.6% work from home (2006-2010 5-year est.); Travel time to work: 33.4% less than 15 minutes, 42.9% 15 to 30 minutes, 8.8% 30 to 45 minutes, 5.1% 45 to 60 minutes, 9.9% 60 minutes or more (2006-2010 5-year est.)

Additional Information Contacts
Greater Connellsville Chamber of Commerce . . . . (724) 628-5500
http://www.greaterconnellsville.org

EDENBORN (CDP). Covers a land area of 0.379 square miles and a
water area of 0 square miles. Located at 39.88° N. Lat; 79.89° W. Long. Elevation is 1,168 feet.
Population: n/a (1990); n/a (2000); 294 (2010); Density: 775.0 persons per square mile (2010); Race: 51.4% White, 43.2% Black, 0.0% Asian, 0.0% American Indian/Alaska Native, 0.0% Native Hawaiian/Other Pacific Islander, 5.4% Other, 1.0% Hispanic of any race (2010); Average household size: 2.39 (2010); Median age: 41.3 (2010); Males per 100 females: 90.9 (2010); Marriage status: 0.0% never married, 100.0% now married, 0.0% widowed, 0.0% divorced (2006-2010 5-year est.); Foreign born: 0.0% (2006-2010 5-year est.); Ancestry (includes multiple ancestries): 79.4% Irish, 60.8% Swedish, 20.6% Slovak (2006-2010 5-year est.).
Economy: Income: Per capita income: $50,723 (2006-2010 5-year est.); Median household income: $65,827 (2006-2010 5-year est.); Average household income: n/a (2006-2010 5-year est.); Percent of households with income of $100,000 or more: n/a (2006-2010 5-year est.); Poverty rate: 0.0% (2006-2010 5-year est.).
Education: Percent of population age 25 and over with: High school diploma (including GED) or higher: 100.0% (2006-2010 5-year est.);

Bachelor's degree or higher: 0.0% (2006-2010 5-year est.); Master's degree or higher: 0.0% (2006-2010 5-year est.).
Housing: Homeownership rate: 73.2% (2010); Median home value: $93,300 (2006-2010 5-year est.); Median contract rent: n/a per month (2006-2010 5-year est.); Median year structure built: before 1940 (2006-2010 5-year est.).
Transportation: Commute to work: 100.0% car, 0.0% public transportation, 0.0% walk, 0.0% work from home (2006-2010 5-year est.); Travel time to work: 0.0% less than 15 minutes, 0.0% 15 to 30 minutes, 0.0% 30 to 45 minutes, 0.0% 45 to 60 minutes, 100.0% 60 minutes or more (2006-2010 5-year est.)

EVERSON (borough). Covers a land area of 0.193 square miles and a
water area of 0 square miles. Located at 40.09° N. Lat; 79.59° W. Long. Elevation is 1,063 feet.
History: Laid out 1874.
Population: 939 (1990); 842 (2000); 793 (2010); Density: 4,105.0 persons per square mile (2010); Race: 95.5% White, 2.1% Black, 0.5% Asian, 0.0% American Indian/Alaska Native, 0.0% Native Hawaiian/Other Pacific Islander, 1.9% Other, 1.5% Hispanic of any race (2010); Average household size: 2.37 (2010); Median age: 39.8 (2010); Males per 100 females: 89.3 (2010); Marriage status: 33.7% never married, 44.1% now married, 5.7% widowed, 16.6% divorced (2006-2010 5-year est.); Foreign born: 1.4% (2006-2010 5-year est.); Ancestry (includes multiple ancestries): 28.7% German, 19.6% Polish, 14.0% Italian, 12.2% Irish, 5.1% English (2006-2010 5-year est.).
Economy: Employment by occupation: 5.9% management, 2.0% professional, 17.5% services, 15.3% sales, 1.5% farming, 19.5% construction, 12.8% production (2006-2010 5-year est.).
Income: Per capita income: $15,161 (2006-2010 5-year est.); Median household income: $34,620 (2006-2010 5-year est.); Average household income: $38,516 (2006-2010 5-year est.); Percent of households with income of $100,000 or more: 1.0% (2006-2010 5-year est.); Poverty rate: 12.4% (2006-2010 5-year est.).
Education: Percent of population age 25 and over with: High school diploma (including GED) or higher: 86.9% (2006-2010 5-year est.); Bachelor's degree or higher: 8.9% (2006-2010 5-year est.); Master's degree or higher: 2.4% (2006-2010 5-year est.).
Housing: Homeownership rate: 64.5% (2010); Median home value: $61,600 (2006-2010 5-year est.); Median contract rent: $432 per month (2006-2010 5-year est.); Median year structure built: before 1940 (2006-2010 5-year est.).
Safety: Violent crime rate: 0.0 per 10,000 population; Property crime rate: 0.0 per 10,000 population (2011).
Transportation: Commute to work: 94.1% car, 1.0% public transportation, 4.9% walk, 0.0% work from home (2006-2010 5-year est.); Travel time to work: 29.6% less than 15 minutes, 43.0% 15 to 30 minutes, 19.3% 30 to 45 minutes, 6.2% 45 to 60 minutes, 1.8% 60 minutes or more (2006-2010 5-year est.)

FAIRBANK (unincorporated postal area)
Zip Code: 15435
Covers a land area of 1.097 square miles and a water area of 0.011 square miles. Located at 39.94° N. Lat; 79.85° W. Long. Population: 437 (2010); Density: 398.1 persons per square mile (2010); Race: 89.2% White, 8.7% Black, 0.0% Asian, 0.0% American Indian/Alaska Native, 0.0% Native Hawaiian/Other Pacific Islander, 2.1% Other, 0.0% Hispanic of any race (2010); Average household size: 2.35 (2010); Median age: 44.1 (2010); Males per 100 females: 89.2 (2010); Homeownership rate: 76.3% (2010)

FAIRCHANCE (borough). Covers a land area of 1.202 square miles
and a water area of 0 square miles. Located at 39.83° N. Lat; 79.75° W. Long. Elevation is 1,102 feet.
Population: 1,910 (1990); 2,174 (2000); 1,975 (2010); Density: 1,642.6 persons per square mile (2010); Race: 95.9% White, 2.7% Black, 0.0% Asian, 0.2% American Indian/Alaska Native, 0.0% Native Hawaiian/Other Pacific Islander, 1.2% Other, 0.6% Hispanic of any race (2010); Average household size: 2.51 (2010); Median age: 40.5 (2010); Males per 100 females: 84.4 (2010); Marriage status: 27.2% never married, 46.7% now married, 12.4% widowed, 13.8% divorced (2006-2010 5-year est.); Foreign born: 0.3% (2006-2010 5-year est.); Ancestry (includes multiple ancestries): 24.4% German, 22.1% Irish, 14.3% Italian, 10.2% American, 10.0% English (2006-2010 5-year est.).

Economy: Employment by occupation: 3.2% management, 1.8% professional, 16.5% services, 18.9% sales, 4.0% farming, 8.4% construction, 7.5% production (2006-2010 5-year est.).
Income: Per capita income: $16,639 (2006-2010 5-year est.); Median household income: $27,159 (2006-2010 5-year est.); Average household income: $39,707 (2006-2010 5-year est.); Percent of households with income of $100,000 or more: 7.1% (2006-2010 5-year est.); Poverty rate: 21.8% (2006-2010 5-year est.).
Education: Percent of population age 25 and over with: High school diploma (including GED) or higher: 85.6% (2006-2010 5-year est.); Bachelor's degree or higher: 13.0% (2006-2010 5-year est.); Master's degree or higher: 3.2% (2006-2010 5-year est.).

School District(s)
Albert Gallatin Area SD (KG-12)
   2010-11 Enrollment: 3,596 . . . . (724) 564-7190
Housing: Homeownership rate: 64.8% (2010); Median home value: $74,900 (2006-2010 5-year est.); Median contract rent: $356 per month (2006-2010 5-year est.); Median year structure built: 1951 (2006-2010 5-year est.).
Transportation: Commute to work: 94.3% car, 0.0% public transportation, 1.8% walk, 0.9% work from home (2006-2010 5-year est.); Travel time to work: 33.4% less than 15 minutes, 38.3% 15 to 30 minutes, 14.6% 30 to 45 minutes, 4.3% 45 to 60 minutes, 9.4% 60 minutes or more (2006-2010 5-year est.)
Additional Information Contacts
Greater Connellsville Chamber of Commerce. . . . . (724) 628-5500
  http://www.greaterconnellsville.org

FAIRHOPE (CDP). Covers a land area of 0.835 square miles and a water area of 0 square miles. Located at 40.12° N. Lat; 79.84° W. Long. Elevation is 942 feet.
Population: n/a (1990); n/a (2000); 1,151 (2010); Density: 1,377.9 persons per square mile (2010); Race: 99.0% White, 0.5% Black, 0.2% Asian, 0.1% American Indian/Alaska Native, 0.0% Native Hawaiian/Other Pacific Islander, 0.2% Other, 0.2% Hispanic of any race (2010); Average household size: 2.24 (2010); Median age: 47.6 (2010); Males per 100 females: 92.2 (2010); Marriage status: 19.5% never married, 48.1% now married, 17.5% widowed, 14.9% divorced (2006-2010 5-year est.); Foreign born: 0.0% (2006-2010 5-year est.); Ancestry (includes multiple ancestries): 28.5% German, 20.4% Italian, 14.7% English, 14.3% Hungarian, 11.3% Irish (2006-2010 5-year est.).
Economy: Employment by occupation: 10.9% management, 0.0% professional, 19.0% services, 14.9% sales, 0.0% farming, 6.3% construction, 12.2% production (2006-2010 5-year est.).
Income: Per capita income: $24,054 (2006-2010 5-year est.); Median household income: $40,492 (2006-2010 5-year est.); Average household income: $45,652 (2006-2010 5-year est.); Percent of households with income of $100,000 or more: 6.6% (2006-2010 5-year est.); Poverty rate: 17.4% (2006-2010 5-year est.).
Education: Percent of population age 25 and over with: High school diploma (including GED) or higher: 83.5% (2006-2010 5-year est.); Bachelor's degree or higher: 7.7% (2006-2010 5-year est.); Master's degree or higher: 5.3% (2006-2010 5-year est.).
Housing: Homeownership rate: 77.2% (2010); Median home value: $83,300 (2006-2010 5-year est.); Median contract rent: $423 per month (2006-2010 5-year est.); Median year structure built: 1952 (2006-2010 5-year est.).
Transportation: Commute to work: 93.7% car, 0.0% public transportation, 2.5% walk, 3.8% work from home (2006-2010 5-year est.); Travel time to work: 31.1% less than 15 minutes, 25.5% 15 to 30 minutes, 18.4% 30 to 45 minutes, 6.8% 45 to 60 minutes, 18.2% 60 minutes or more (2006-2010 5-year est.)

FARMINGTON (CDP). Covers a land area of 2.545 square miles and a water area of 0.041 square miles. Located at 39.81° N. Lat; 79.56° W. Long. Elevation is 1,837 feet.
Population: n/a (1990); n/a (2000); 767 (2010); Density: 301.4 persons per square mile (2010); Race: 98.8% White, 0.1% Black, 0.4% Asian, 0.0% American Indian/Alaska Native, 0.0% Native Hawaiian/Other Pacific Islander, 0.7% Other, 0.5% Hispanic of any race (2010); Average household size: 2.40 (2010); Median age: 42.2 (2010); Males per 100 females: 92.7 (2010); Marriage status: 43.7% never married, 42.4% now married, 6.6% widowed, 7.2% divorced (2006-2010 5-year est.); Foreign born: 15.4% (2006-2010 5-year est.); Ancestry (includes multiple

ancestries): 38.1% German, 16.2% English, 15.6% Swiss, 11.4% American, 11.4% British (2006-2010 5-year est.).
Economy: Employment by occupation: 0.0% management, 0.0% professional, 21.9% services, 0.0% sales, 0.0% farming, 32.8% construction, 32.8% production (2006-2010 5-year est.).
Income: Per capita income: $5,111 (2006-2010 5-year est.); Median household income: $69,524 (2006-2010 5-year est.); Average household income: n/a (2006-2010 5-year est.); Percent of households with income of $100,000 or more: n/a (2006-2010 5-year est.); Poverty rate: 83.6% (2006-2010 5-year est.).
Education: Percent of population age 25 and over with: High school diploma (including GED) or higher: 80.4% (2006-2010 5-year est.); Bachelor's degree or higher: 20.0% (2006-2010 5-year est.); Master's degree or higher: 1.8% (2006-2010 5-year est.).

School District(s)
Uniontown Area SD (KG-12)
   2010-11 Enrollment: 3,022 . . . . (724) 438-4501
Housing: Homeownership rate: 70.8% (2010); Median home value: $24,000 (2006-2010 5-year est.); Median contract rent: n/a per month (2006-2010 5-year est.); Median year structure built: 1985 (2006-2010 5-year est.).
Transportation: Commute to work: 78.1% car, 0.0% public transportation, 0.0% walk, 21.9% work from home (2006-2010 5-year est.); Travel time to work: 42.0% less than 15 minutes, 0.0% 15 to 30 minutes, 0.0% 30 to 45 minutes, 58.0% 45 to 60 minutes, 0.0% 60 minutes or more (2006-2010 5-year est.)

FAYETTE CITY (borough). Covers a land area of 0.192 square miles and a water area of 0.062 square miles. Located at 40.10° N. Lat; 79.84° W. Long. Elevation is 768 feet.
History: Settled 1794.
Population: 713 (1990); 714 (2000); 596 (2010); Density: 3,104.8 persons per square mile (2010); Race: 97.7% White, 0.2% Black, 1.0% Asian, 0.0% American Indian/Alaska Native, 0.0% Native Hawaiian/Other Pacific Islander, 1.1% Other, 1.5% Hispanic of any race (2010); Average household size: 2.54 (2010); Median age: 37.9 (2010); Males per 100 females: 83.4 (2010); Marriage status: 30.2% never married, 41.0% now married, 12.4% widowed, 16.5% divorced (2006-2010 5-year est.); Foreign born: 0.7% (2006-2010 5-year est.); Ancestry (includes multiple ancestries): 30.4% English, 20.0% Irish, 20.0% German, 13.0% Italian, 9.0% Polish (2006-2010 5-year est.).
Economy: Employment by occupation: 0.0% management, 4.0% professional, 21.3% services, 28.7% sales, 4.7% farming, 2.0% construction, 2.0% production (2006-2010 5-year est.).
Income: Per capita income: $14,777 (2006-2010 5-year est.); Median household income: $21,563 (2006-2010 5-year est.); Average household income: $32,258 (2006-2010 5-year est.); Percent of households with income of $100,000 or more: 2.8% (2006-2010 5-year est.); Poverty rate: 39.9% (2006-2010 5-year est.).
Education: Percent of population age 25 and over with: High school diploma (including GED) or higher: 88.8% (2006-2010 5-year est.); Bachelor's degree or higher: 11.9% (2006-2010 5-year est.); Master's degree or higher: 1.2% (2006-2010 5-year est.).
Housing: Homeownership rate: 64.3% (2010); Median home value: $71,500 (2006-2010 5-year est.); Median contract rent: $374 per month (2006-2010 5-year est.); Median year structure built: before 1940 (2006-2010 5-year est.).
Safety: Violent crime rate: 0.0 per 10,000 population; Property crime rate: 100.3 per 10,000 population (2011).
Transportation: Commute to work: 90.7% car, 0.0% public transportation, 6.0% walk, 3.3% work from home (2006-2010 5-year est.); Travel time to work: 37.9% less than 15 minutes, 31.7% 15 to 30 minutes, 13.8% 30 to 45 minutes, 8.3% 45 to 60 minutes, 8.3% 60 minutes or more (2006-2010 5-year est.)

FRANKLIN (township). Covers a land area of 29.600 square miles and a water area of 0.150 square miles. Located at 40.00° N. Lat; 79.75° W. Long.
Population: 2,640 (1990); 2,628 (2000); 2,528 (2010); Density: 85.4 persons per square mile (2010); Race: 98.0% White, 0.9% Black, 0.1% Asian, 0.1% American Indian/Alaska Native, 0.0% Native Hawaiian/Other Pacific Islander, 0.9% Other, 0.2% Hispanic of any race (2010); Average household size: 2.55 (2010); Median age: 44.4 (2010); Males per 100 females: 101.1 (2010); Marriage status: 28.1% never married, 54.3% now married, 12.4% widowed, 5.2% divorced (2006-2010 5-year est.); Foreign

born: 0.7% (2006-2010 5-year est.); Ancestry (includes multiple ancestries): 24.7% German, 14.8% Irish, 14.1% Italian, 11.1% Polish, 10.4% English (2006-2010 5-year est.).

Economy: Employment by occupation: 11.6% management, 3.4% professional, 6.4% services, 13.7% sales, 1.6% farming, 15.5% construction, 10.0% production (2006-2010 5-year est.).

Income: Per capita income: $17,296 (2006-2010 5-year est.); Median household income: $38,935 (2006-2010 5-year est.); Average household income: $44,686 (2006-2010 5-year est.); Percent of households with income of $100,000 or more: 6.9% (2006-2010 5-year est.); Poverty rate: 13.8% (2006-2010 5-year est.).

Education: Percent of population age 25 and over with: High school diploma (including GED) or higher: 84.1% (2006-2010 5-year est.); Bachelor's degree or higher: 12.6% (2006-2010 5-year est.); Master's degree or higher: 2.5% (2006-2010 5-year est.).

Housing: Homeownership rate: 84.6% (2010); Median home value: $79,600 (2006-2010 5-year est.); Median contract rent: $396 per month (2006-2010 5-year est.); Median year structure built: 1964 (2006-2010 5-year est.).

Transportation: Commute to work: 91.0% car, 0.0% public transportation, 7.0% walk, 2.0% work from home (2006-2010 5-year est.); Travel time to work: 20.9% less than 15 minutes, 42.6% 15 to 30 minutes, 18.7% 30 to 45 minutes, 13.7% 45 to 60 minutes, 4.2% 60 minutes or more (2006-2010 5-year est.)

Additional Information Contacts
Greater Connellsville Chamber of Commerce . . . . (724) 628-5500
   http://www.greaterconnellsville.org

GEORGES (township). Covers a land area of 47.614 square miles and a water area of 0.013 square miles. Located at 39.85° N. Lat; 79.79° W. Long.

Population: 6,533 (1990); 6,752 (2000); 6,612 (2010); Density: 138.9 persons per square mile (2010); Race: 98.2% White, 0.8% Black, 0.1% Asian, 0.1% American Indian/Alaska Native, 0.0% Native Hawaiian/Other Pacific Islander, 0.8% Other, 0.6% Hispanic of any race (2010); Average household size: 2.50 (2010); Median age: 42.7 (2010); Males per 100 females: 96.4 (2010); Marriage status: 32.1% never married, 52.0% now married, 6.2% widowed, 9.7% divorced (2006-2010 5-year est.); Foreign born: 0.0% (2006-2010 5-year est.); Ancestry (includes multiple ancestries): 19.5% Irish, 17.1% German, 12.9% Italian, 10.4% American, 9.1% Slovak (2006-2010 5-year est.).

Economy: Employment by occupation: 7.6% management, 1.4% professional, 13.9% services, 19.9% sales, 4.7% farming, 8.9% construction, 4.3% production (2006-2010 5-year est.).

Income: Per capita income: $16,594 (2006-2010 5-year est.); Median household income: $31,358 (2006-2010 5-year est.); Average household income: $42,329 (2006-2010 5-year est.); Percent of households with income of $100,000 or more: 7.6% (2006-2010 5-year est.); Poverty rate: 19.1% (2006-2010 5-year est.).

Education: Percent of population age 25 and over with: High school diploma (including GED) or higher: 78.7% (2006-2010 5-year est.); Bachelor's degree or higher: 8.2% (2006-2010 5-year est.); Master's degree or higher: 2.3% (2006-2010 5-year est.).

Housing: Homeownership rate: 78.4% (2010); Median home value: $76,200 (2006-2010 5-year est.); Median contract rent: $411 per month (2006-2010 5-year est.); Median year structure built: 1966 (2006-2010 5-year est.).

Transportation: Commute to work: 95.0% car, 0.3% public transportation, 0.0% walk, 2.5% work from home (2006-2010 5-year est.); Travel time to work: 31.0% less than 15 minutes, 36.6% 15 to 30 minutes, 15.5% 30 to 45 minutes, 7.6% 45 to 60 minutes, 9.3% 60 minutes or more (2006-2010 5-year est.).

Additional Information Contacts
Georges Township . . . . (724) 430-4884
York County Chamber of Commerce . . . . (717) 848-4000
   http://www.yorkchamber.com

GERMAN (township). Covers a land area of 33.477 square miles and a water area of 0.373 square miles. Located at 39.88° N. Lat; 79.87° W. Long.

Population: 5,596 (1990); 5,595 (2000); 5,097 (2010); Density: 152.3 persons per square mile (2010); Race: 92.8% White, 5.9% Black, 0.1% Asian, 0.1% American Indian/Alaska Native, 0.0% Native Hawaiian/Other Pacific Islander, 1.1% Other, 0.3% Hispanic of any race (2010); Average household size: 2.52 (2010); Median age: 42.8 (2010); Males per 100

females: 94.1 (2010); Marriage status: 25.1% never married, 53.1% now married, 11.7% widowed, 10.1% divorced (2006-2010 5-year est.); Foreign born: 0.3% (2006-2010 5-year est.); Ancestry (includes multiple ancestries): 18.1% Italian, 17.8% German, 16.9% Irish, 10.9% Polish, 10.9% English (2006-2010 5-year est.).

Economy: Employment by occupation: 14.3% management, 0.0% professional, 10.9% services, 14.1% sales, 3.4% farming, 8.2% construction, 1.9% production (2006-2010 5-year est.).

Income: Per capita income: $18,899 (2006-2010 5-year est.); Median household income: $29,107 (2006-2010 5-year est.); Average household income: $43,009 (2006-2010 5-year est.); Percent of households with income of $100,000 or more: 7.2% (2006-2010 5-year est.); Poverty rate: 24.4% (2006-2010 5-year est.).

Education: Percent of population age 25 and over with: High school diploma (including GED) or higher: 78.8% (2006-2010 5-year est.); Bachelor's degree or higher: 10.9% (2006-2010 5-year est.); Master's degree or higher: 3.2% (2006-2010 5-year est.).

Housing: Homeownership rate: 78.8% (2010); Median home value: $76,600 (2006-2010 5-year est.); Median contract rent: $416 per month (2006-2010 5-year est.); Median year structure built: before 1940 (2006-2010 5-year est.).

Transportation: Commute to work: 97.5% car, 0.0% public transportation, 0.5% walk, 2.0% work from home (2006-2010 5-year est.); Travel time to work: 28.6% less than 15 minutes, 43.4% 15 to 30 minutes, 12.4% 30 to 45 minutes, 4.1% 45 to 60 minutes, 11.4% 60 minutes or more (2006-2010 5-year est.)

Additional Information Contacts
German Township . . . . (724) 737-5130
Waynesburg Area Chamber of Commerce . . . . (724) 627-5925
   http://www.waynesburgchamber.com

GIBBON GLADE (unincorporated postal area)
Zip Code: 15440

Covers a land area of 15.168 square miles and a water area of 0 square miles. Located at 39.73° N. Lat; 79.61° W. Long. Elevation is 1,686 feet. Population: 349 (2010); Density: 23.0 persons per square mile (2010); Race: 99.7% White, 0.0% Black, 0.0% Asian, 0.0% American Indian/Alaska Native, 0.0% Native Hawaiian/Other Pacific Islander, 0.3% Other, 0.3% Hispanic of any race (2010); Average household size: 2.46 (2010); Median age: 43.7 (2010); Males per 100 females: 91.8 (2010); Homeownership rate: 84.5% (2010)

GRINDSTONE (CDP). Covers a land area of 1.276 square miles and a water area of 0 square miles. Located at 40.02° N. Lat; 79.82° W. Long. Elevation is 817 feet.

Population: n/a (1990); n/a (2000); 498 (2010); Density: 390.3 persons per square mile (2010); Race: 96.8% White, 2.2% Black, 0.2% Asian, 0.2% American Indian/Alaska Native, 0.0% Native Hawaiian/Other Pacific Islander, 0.6% Other, 0.0% Hispanic of any race (2010); Average household size: 2.28 (2010); Median age: 39.7 (2010); Males per 100 females: 83.1 (2010); Marriage status: 19.1% never married, 52.7% now married, 11.1% widowed, 17.0% divorced (2006-2010 5-year est.); Foreign born: 1.7% (2006-2010 5-year est.); Ancestry (includes multiple ancestries): 26.6% Polish, 18.0% German, 16.2% Russian, 11.4% Slovak, 7.5% Norwegian (2006-2010 5-year est.).

Economy: Employment by occupation: 0.0% management, 0.0% professional, 14.6% services, 16.6% sales, 13.0% farming, 13.0% construction, 21.3% production (2006-2010 5-year est.).

Income: Per capita income: $15,776 (2006-2010 5-year est.); Median household income: $44,444 (2006-2010 5-year est.); Average household income: $39,871 (2006-2010 5-year est.); Percent of households with income of $100,000 or more: 6.3% (2006-2010 5-year est.); Poverty rate: 11.5% (2006-2010 5-year est.).

Education: Percent of population age 25 and over with: High school diploma (including GED) or higher: 73.5% (2006-2010 5-year est.); Bachelor's degree or higher: 3.8% (2006-2010 5-year est.); Master's degree or higher: 0.0% (2006-2010 5-year est.).

Housing: Homeownership rate: 65.6% (2010); Median home value: $66,200 (2006-2010 5-year est.); Median contract rent: $288 per month (2006-2010 5-year est.); Median year structure built: before 1940 (2006-2010 5-year est.).

Transportation: Commute to work: 92.0% car, 0.0% public transportation, 8.0% walk, 0.0% work from home (2006-2010 5-year est.); Travel time to work: 11.6% less than 15 minutes, 39.2% 15 to 30 minutes, 43.9% 30 to

45 minutes, 0.0% 45 to 60 minutes, 5.3% 60 minutes or more (2006-2010 5-year est.)

HENRY CLAY (township). Covers a land area of 51.242 square miles and a water area of 1.811 square miles. Located at 39.77° N. Lat; 79.45° W. Long.

Population: 1,860 (1990); 1,984 (2000); 2,066 (2010); Density: 40.3 persons per square mile (2010); Race: 97.6% White, 0.2% Black, 0.5% Asian, 0.4% American Indian/Alaska Native, 0.0% Native Hawaiian/Other Pacific Islander, 1.3% Other, 1.3% Hispanic of any race (2010); Average household size: 2.46 (2010); Median age: 43.4 (2010); Males per 100 females: 106.4 (2010); Marriage status: 29.8% never married, 52.9% now married, 8.0% widowed, 9.3% divorced (2006-2010 5-year est.); Foreign born: 6.5% (2006-2010 5-year est.); Ancestry (includes multiple ancestries): 40.8% German, 14.9% Irish, 12.0% English, 5.6% American, 5.0% Dutch (2006-2010 5-year est.).

Economy: Employment by occupation: 8.8% management, 0.9% professional, 14.2% services, 13.3% sales, 2.1% farming, 13.9% construction, 5.6% production (2006-2010 5-year est.).

Income: Per capita income: $20,612 (2006-2010 5-year est.); Median household income: $35,217 (2006-2010 5-year est.); Average household income: $49,987 (2006-2010 5-year est.); Percent of households with income of $100,000 or more: 12.7% (2006-2010 5-year est.); Poverty rate: 22.7% (2006-2010 5-year est.).

Education: Percent of population age 25 and over with: High school diploma (including GED) or higher: 88.8% (2006-2010 5-year est.); Bachelor's degree or higher: 10.6% (2006-2010 5-year est.); Master's degree or higher: 6.0% (2006-2010 5-year est.).

Housing: Homeownership rate: 73.7% (2010); Median home value: $89,000 (2006-2010 5-year est.); Median contract rent: $370 per month (2006-2010 5-year est.); Median year structure built: 1971 (2006-2010 5-year est.).

Transportation: Commute to work: 92.2% car, 0.0% public transportation, 6.2% walk, 1.2% work from home (2006-2010 5-year est.); Travel time to work: 40.9% less than 15 minutes, 20.0% 15 to 30 minutes, 14.2% 30 to 45 minutes, 16.1% 45 to 60 minutes, 8.9% 60 minutes or more (2006-2010 5-year est.).

Additional Information Contacts
Greater Connellsville Chamber of Commerce. . . . . (724) 628-5500
http://www.greaterconnellsville.org

HIBBS (unincorporated postal area)
Zip Code: 15443
Covers a land area of 1.697 square miles and a water area of 0 square miles. Located at 39.91° N. Lat; 79.88° W. Long. Elevation is 997 feet. Population: 377 (2010); Density: 222.1 persons per square mile (2010); Race: 93.9% White, 5.0% Black, 0.0% Asian, 0.0% American Indian/Alaska Native, 0.0% Native Hawaiian/Other Pacific Islander, 1.1% Other, 0.5% Hispanic of any race (2010); Average household size: 2.77 (2010); Median age: 33.6 (2010); Males per 100 females: 93.3 (2010); Homeownership rate: 77.2% (2010)

HILLER (CDP). Covers a land area of 1.522 square miles and a water area of 0.048 square miles. Located at 40.01° N. Lat; 79.90° W. Long. Elevation is 1,024 feet.

Population: 1,420 (1990); 1,234 (2000); 1,155 (2010); Density: 758.7 persons per square mile (2010); Race: 92.6% White, 4.7% Black, 0.3% Asian, 0.1% American Indian/Alaska Native, 0.0% Native Hawaiian/Other Pacific Islander, 2.3% Other, 0.3% Hispanic of any race (2010); Average household size: 2.20 (2010); Median age: 49.1 (2010); Males per 100 females: 86.0 (2010); Marriage status: 28.8% never married, 59.2% now married, 6.9% widowed, 5.1% divorced (2006-2010 5-year est.); Foreign born: 1.1% (2006-2010 5-year est.); Ancestry (includes multiple ancestries): 18.5% Irish, 18.1% Hungarian, 15.2% German, 12.3% Welsh, 11.5% Italian (2006-2010 5-year est.).

Economy: Employment by occupation: 0.0% management, 0.0% professional, 9.9% services, 26.2% sales, 5.8% farming, 0.0% construction, 4.7% production (2006-2010 5-year est.).

Income: Per capita income: $22,003 (2006-2010 5-year est.); Median household income: $45,530 (2006-2010 5-year est.); Average household income: $55,669 (2006-2010 5-year est.); Percent of households with income of $100,000 or more: 20.5% (2006-2010 5-year est.); Poverty rate: 1.0% (2006-2010 5-year est.).

Education: Percent of population age 25 and over with: High school diploma (including GED) or higher: 94.3% (2006-2010 5-year est.);

Bachelor's degree or higher: 21.3% (2006-2010 5-year est.); Master's degree or higher: 3.7% (2006-2010 5-year est.).

Housing: Homeownership rate: 81.5% (2010); Median home value: $88,300 (2006-2010 5-year est.); Median contract rent: $511 per month (2006-2010 5-year est.); Median year structure built: 1944 (2006-2010 5-year est.).

Transportation: Commute to work: 97.5% car, 0.0% public transportation, 0.0% walk, 2.5% work from home (2006-2010 5-year est.); Travel time to work: 42.9% less than 15 minutes, 13.1% 15 to 30 minutes, 22.4% 30 to 45 minutes, 12.1% 45 to 60 minutes, 9.5% 60 minutes or more (2006-2010 5-year est.)

Additional Information Contacts
Greater Connellsville Chamber of Commerce. . . . . (724) 628-5500
http://www.greaterconnellsville.org

HOPWOOD (CDP). Covers a land area of 1.886 square miles and a water area of 0 square miles. Located at 39.88° N. Lat; 79.70° W. Long. Elevation is 1,112 feet.

History: Founded 1791.

Population: 2,033 (1990); 2,006 (2000); 2,090 (2010); Density: 1,108.4 persons per square mile (2010); Race: 97.7% White, 0.8% Black, 0.8% Asian, 0.0% American Indian/Alaska Native, 0.0% Native Hawaiian/Other Pacific Islander, 0.7% Other, 0.5% Hispanic of any race (2010); Average household size: 2.27 (2010); Median age: 47.4 (2010); Males per 100 females: 92.8 (2010); Marriage status: 22.7% never married, 50.4% now married, 7.5% widowed, 19.5% divorced (2006-2010 5-year est.); Foreign born: 5.2% (2006-2010 5-year est.); Ancestry (includes multiple ancestries): 23.8% Italian, 22.7% German, 21.1% Irish, 21.0% English, 8.6% Polish (2006-2010 5-year est.).

Economy: Employment by occupation: 4.3% management, 11.8% professional, 9.1% services, 16.4% sales, 0.0% farming, 9.7% construction, 4.4% production (2006-2010 5-year est.).

Income: Per capita income: $26,518 (2006-2010 5-year est.); Median household income: $45,826 (2006-2010 5-year est.); Average household income: $56,228 (2006-2010 5-year est.); Percent of households with income of $100,000 or more: 16.6% (2006-2010 5-year est.); Poverty rate: 8.3% (2006-2010 5-year est.).

Education: Percent of population age 25 and over with: High school diploma (including GED) or higher: 91.9% (2006-2010 5-year est.); Bachelor's degree or higher: 25.6% (2006-2010 5-year est.); Master's degree or higher: 10.9% (2006-2010 5-year est.).

Housing: Homeownership rate: 71.5% (2010); Median home value: $133,100 (2006-2010 5-year est.); Median contract rent: $460 per month (2006-2010 5-year est.); Median year structure built: 1954 (2006-2010 5-year est.).

Transportation: Commute to work: 95.9% car, 0.0% public transportation, 1.2% walk, 0.0% work from home (2006-2010 5-year est.); Travel time to work: 50.5% less than 15 minutes, 26.7% 15 to 30 minutes, 4.6% 30 to 45 minutes, 9.5% 45 to 60 minutes, 8.7% 60 minutes or more (2006-2010 5-year est.)

Additional Information Contacts
Greater Connellsville Chamber of Commerce. . . . . (724) 628-5500
http://www.greaterconnellsville.org

INDIAN HEAD (unincorporated postal area)
Zip Code: 15446
Covers a land area of 1.499 square miles and a water area of 0 square miles. Located at 40.03° N. Lat; 79.40° W. Long. Elevation is 1,407 feet. Population: 324 (2010); Density: 216.1 persons per square mile (2010); Race: 98.1% White, 0.0% Black, 0.0% Asian, 0.0% American Indian/Alaska Native, 0.0% Native Hawaiian/Other Pacific Islander, 1.9% Other, 0.0% Hispanic of any race (2010); Average household size: 2.33 (2010); Median age: 50.0 (2010); Males per 100 females: 97.6 (2010); Homeownership rate: 77.0% (2010)

ISABELLA (unincorporated postal area)
Zip Code: 15447
Covers a land area of 0.391 square miles and a water area of 0 square miles. Located at 39.94° N. Lat; 79.93° W. Long. Elevation is 919 feet. Population: 181 (2010); Density: 462.7 persons per square mile (2010); Race: 97.8% White, 0.6% Black, 0.6% Asian, 0.0% American Indian/Alaska Native, 0.0% Native Hawaiian/Other Pacific Islander, 1.0% Other, 1.1% Hispanic of any race (2010); Average household size: 2.42 (2010); Median age: 41.6 (2010); Males per 100 females: 82.8 (2010); Homeownership rate: 80.3% (2010)

JEFFERSON (township). Covers a land area of 20.061 square miles and a water area of 0.288 square miles. Located at 40.05° N. Lat; 79.82° W. Long.

Population: 2,047 (1990); 2,259 (2000); 2,015 (2010); Density: 100.4 persons per square mile (2010); Race: 98.0% White, 1.0% Black, 0.3% Asian, 0.1% American Indian/Alaska Native, 0.0% Native Hawaiian/Other Pacific Islander, 0.6% Other, 0.5% Hispanic of any race (2010); Average household size: 2.45 (2010); Median age: 45.2 (2010); Males per 100 females: 97.9 (2010); Marriage status: 20.4% never married, 61.8% now married, 9.5% widowed, 8.3% divorced (2006-2010 5-year est.); Foreign born: 0.6% (2006-2010 5-year est.); Ancestry (includes multiple ancestries): 20.3% Polish, 16.5% Slovak, 13.4% German, 12.5% Italian, 7.9% English (2006-2010 5-year est.).

Economy: Employment by occupation: 4.4% management, 2.8% professional, 6.7% services, 18.3% sales, 5.5% farming, 14.9% construction, 11.7% production (2006-2010 5-year est.).

Income: Per capita income: $19,629 (2006-2010 5-year est.); Median household income: $46,089 (2006-2010 5-year est.); Average household income: $50,650 (2006-2010 5-year est.); Percent of households with income of $100,000 or more: 10.2% (2006-2010 5-year est.); Poverty rate: 10.4% (2006-2010 5-year est.).

Education: Percent of population age 25 and over with: High school diploma (including GED) or higher: 85.9% (2006-2010 5-year est.); Bachelor's degree or higher: 16.5% (2006-2010 5-year est.); Master's degree or higher: 3.4% (2006-2010 5-year est.).

Housing: Homeownership rate: 83.3% (2010); Median home value: $86,500 (2006-2010 5-year est.); Median contract rent: $316 per month (2006-2010 5-year est.); Median year structure built: 1957 (2006-2010 5-year est.).

Transportation: Commute to work: 94.0% car, 0.8% public transportation, 2.8% walk, 2.4% work from home (2006-2010 5-year est.); Travel time to work: 17.1% less than 15 minutes, 32.7% 15 to 30 minutes, 26.7% 30 to 45 minutes, 9.7% 45 to 60 minutes, 13.8% 60 minutes or more (2006-2010 5-year est.)

Additional Information Contacts
Mon Valley Regional Chamber of Commerce . . . . (724) 483-3507
  http://www.mvrchamber.org

KEISTERVILLE (unincorporated postal area)
Zip Code: 15449
  Covers a land area of 0.156 square miles and a water area of 0 square miles. Located at 39.96° N. Lat; 79.78° W. Long. Elevation is 1,171 feet. Population: 184 (2010); Density: 1,179.0 persons per square mile (2010); Race: 100.0% White, 0.0% Black, 0.0% Asian, 0.0% American Indian/Alaska Native, 0.0% Native Hawaiian/Other Pacific Islander, 0.0% Other, 0.0% Hispanic of any race (2010); Average household size: 2.33 (2010); Median age: 42.6 (2010); Males per 100 females: 93.7 (2010); Homeownership rate: 89.9% (2010)

LA BELLE (unincorporated postal area)
Zip Code: 15450
  Covers a land area of 1.593 square miles and a water area of 0.207 square miles. Located at 40.00° N. Lat; 79.97° W. Long. Elevation is 1,007 feet. Population: 2,323 (2010); Density: 1,458.1 persons per square mile (2010); Race: 42.1% White, 48.7% Black, 0.3% Asian, 0.0% American Indian/Alaska Native, 0.0% Native Hawaiian/Other Pacific Islander, 8.9% Other, 8.7% Hispanic of any race (2010); Average household size: 2.54 (2010); Median age: 35.7 (2010); Males per 100 females: ***.* (2010); Homeownership rate: 89.0% (2010)

LAKE LYNN (unincorporated postal area)
Zip Code: 15451
  Covers a land area of 10.162 square miles and a water area of 0.136 square miles. Located at 39.73° N. Lat; 79.83° W. Long. Population: 955 (2010); Density: 94.0 persons per square mile (2010); Race: 97.8% White, 1.0% Black, 0.2% Asian, 0.3% American Indian/Alaska Native, 0.0% Native Hawaiian/Other Pacific Islander, 0.7% Other, 0.6% Hispanic of any race (2010); Average household size: 2.54 (2010); Median age: 41.0 (2010); Males per 100 females: 91.8 (2010); Homeownership rate: 78.0% (2010)

LECKRONE (unincorporated postal area)
Zip Code: 15454
  Covers a land area of 1.290 square miles and a water area of 0 square miles. Located at 39.86° N. Lat; 79.87° W. Long. Elevation is 965 feet.

Population: 237 (2010); Density: 183.6 persons per square mile (2010); Race: 95.8% White, 3.8% Black, 0.0% Asian, 0.0% American Indian/Alaska Native, 0.0% Native Hawaiian/Other Pacific Islander, 0.4% Other, 1.3% Hispanic of any race (2010); Average household size: 2.86 (2010); Median age: 37.2 (2010); Males per 100 females: 94.3 (2010); Homeownership rate: 81.9% (2010)

LEISENRING (unincorporated postal area)
Zip Code: 15455
  Covers a land area of 0.402 square miles and a water area of 0 square miles. Located at 40.00° N. Lat; 79.64° W. Long. Elevation is 1,043 feet. Population: 298 (2010); Density: 740.6 persons per square mile (2010); Race: 94.6% White, 3.0% Black, 0.0% Asian, 1.7% American Indian/Alaska Native, 0.0% Native Hawaiian/Other Pacific Islander, 0.7% Other, 0.3% Hispanic of any race (2010); Average household size: 2.31 (2010); Median age: 43.4 (2010); Males per 100 females: 87.4 (2010); Homeownership rate: 83.0% (2010)

LEITH-HATFIELD (CDP). Covers a land area of 1.850 square miles and a water area of 0 square miles. Located at 39.88° N. Lat; 79.73° W. Long.

Population: 2,438 (1990); 2,820 (2000); 2,546 (2010); Density: 1,375.9 persons per square mile (2010); Race: 95.6% White, 1.2% Black, 2.3% Asian, 0.0% American Indian/Alaska Native, 0.0% Native Hawaiian/Other Pacific Islander, 0.9% Other, 0.5% Hispanic of any race (2010); Average household size: 2.30 (2010); Median age: 50.9 (2010); Males per 100 females: 86.4 (2010); Marriage status: 21.7% never married, 61.3% now married, 9.6% widowed, 7.4% divorced (2006-2010 5-year est.); Foreign born: 3.0% (2006-2010 5-year est.); Ancestry (includes multiple ancestries): 24.4% Italian, 21.4% German, 18.8% Slovak, 18.3% Irish, 9.4% English (2006-2010 5-year est.).

Economy: Employment by occupation: 11.5% management, 3.4% professional, 8.2% services, 13.0% sales, 3.9% farming, 8.2% construction, 2.4% production (2006-2010 5-year est.).

Income: Per capita income: $32,765 (2006-2010 5-year est.); Median household income: $81,087 (2006-2010 5-year est.); Average household income: $85,231 (2006-2010 5-year est.); Percent of households with income of $100,000 or more: 30.3% (2006-2010 5-year est.); Poverty rate: 7.4% (2006-2010 5-year est.).

Education: Percent of population age 25 and over with: High school diploma (including GED) or higher: 88.1% (2006-2010 5-year est.); Bachelor's degree or higher: 32.5% (2006-2010 5-year est.); Master's degree or higher: 14.9% (2006-2010 5-year est.).

Housing: Homeownership rate: 86.6% (2010); Median home value: $154,200 (2006-2010 5-year est.); Median contract rent: $520 per month (2006-2010 5-year est.); Median year structure built: 1968 (2006-2010 5-year est.).

Transportation: Commute to work: 96.9% car, 0.0% public transportation, 0.0% walk, 2.3% work from home (2006-2010 5-year est.); Travel time to work: 64.9% less than 15 minutes, 18.8% 15 to 30 minutes, 7.8% 30 to 45 minutes, 4.1% 45 to 60 minutes, 4.4% 60 minutes or more (2006-2010 5-year est.)

Additional Information Contacts
Hatfield Chamber of Commerce . . . . (215) 855-3335
  http://www.hatfieldchamber.com

LEMONT FURNACE (CDP). Covers a land area of 1.023 square miles and a water area of 0.006 square miles. Located at 39.91° N. Lat; 79.66° W. Long. Elevation is 1,043 feet.

Population: n/a (1990); n/a (2000); 827 (2010); Density: 808.5 persons per square mile (2010); Race: 94.1% White, 3.0% Black, 0.0% Asian, 0.1% American Indian/Alaska Native, 0.0% Native Hawaiian/Other Pacific Islander, 2.8% Other, 2.1% Hispanic of any race (2010); Average household size: 2.59 (2010); Median age: 38.3 (2010); Males per 100 females: 105.7 (2010); Marriage status: 16.7% never married, 63.5% now married, 8.4% widowed, 11.4% divorced (2006-2010 5-year est.); Foreign born: 0.0% (2006-2010 5-year est.); Ancestry (includes multiple ancestries): 19.8% Irish, 9.3% Slovak, 9.0% Polish, 8.9% Scottish, 7.0% German (2006-2010 5-year est.).

Economy: Employment by occupation: 4.4% management, 0.0% professional, 16.5% services, 20.6% sales, 0.0% farming, 13.3% construction, 5.4% production (2006-2010 5-year est.).

Income: Per capita income: $14,975 (2006-2010 5-year est.); Median household income: $33,917 (2006-2010 5-year est.); Average household income: $36,058 (2006-2010 5-year est.); Percent of households with

income of $100,000 or more: n/a (2006-2010 5-year est.); Poverty rate: 27.1% (2006-2010 5-year est.).
Education: Percent of population age 25 and over with: High school diploma (including GED) or higher: 81.2% (2006-2010 5-year est.); Bachelor's degree or higher: 9.4% (2006-2010 5-year est.); Master's degree or higher: 6.1% (2006-2010 5-year est.).
Housing: Homeownership rate: 65.2% (2010); Median home value: $59,500 (2006-2010 5-year est.); Median contract rent: $388 per month (2006-2010 5-year est.); Median year structure built: before 1940 (2006-2010 5-year est.).
Transportation: Commute to work: 100.0% car, 0.0% public transportation, 0.0% walk, 0.0% work from home (2006-2010 5-year est.); Travel time to work: 36.5% less than 15 minutes, 36.5% 15 to 30 minutes, 9.8% 30 to 45 minutes, 0.0% 45 to 60 minutes, 17.1% 60 minutes or more (2006-2010 5-year est.)

LOWER TYRONE (township). Covers a land area of 15.876 square miles and a water area of 0.253 square miles. Located at 40.07° N. Lat; 79.66° W. Long.
Population: 1,138 (1990); 1,171 (2000); 1,123 (2010); Density: 70.7 persons per square mile (2010); Race: 98.8% White, 0.8% Black, 0.0% Asian, 0.0% American Indian/Alaska Native, 0.0% Native Hawaiian/Other Pacific Islander, 0.4% Other, 0.4% Hispanic of any race (2010); Average household size: 2.51 (2010); Median age: 44.4 (2010); Males per 100 females: 107.2 (2010); Marriage status: 27.5% never married, 54.1% now married, 9.0% widowed, 9.5% divorced (2006-2010 5-year est.); Foreign born: 0.0% (2006-2010 5-year est.); Ancestry (includes multiple ancestries): 34.7% German, 21.4% Irish, 12.9% English, 8.6% Italian, 6.9% Scottish (2006-2010 5-year est.).
Economy: Employment by occupation: 5.2% management, 1.5% professional, 8.7% services, 20.2% sales, 1.2% farming, 15.0% construction, 15.2% production (2006-2010 5-year est.).
Income: Per capita income: $19,866 (2006-2010 5-year est.); Median household income: $37,778 (2006-2010 5-year est.); Average household income: $46,131 (2006-2010 5-year est.); Percent of households with income of $100,000 or more: 5.4% (2006-2010 5-year est.); Poverty rate: 13.0% (2006-2010 5-year est.).
Education: Percent of population age 25 and over with: High school diploma (including GED) or higher: 88.5% (2006-2010 5-year est.); Bachelor's degree or higher: 7.7% (2006-2010 5-year est.); Master's degree or higher: 1.9% (2006-2010 5-year est.).
Housing: Homeownership rate: 85.5% (2010); Median home value: $86,600 (2006-2010 5-year est.); Median contract rent: $388 per month (2006-2010 5-year est.); Median year structure built: 1973 (2006-2010 5-year est.).
Transportation: Commute to work: 93.4% car, 0.0% public transportation, 0.0% walk, 4.8% work from home (2006-2010 5-year est.); Travel time to work: 12.4% less than 15 minutes, 35.2% 15 to 30 minutes, 32.3% 30 to 45 minutes, 11.0% 45 to 60 minutes, 9.1% 60 minutes or more (2006-2010 5-year est.)
Additional Information Contacts
Tyrone Chamber of Commerce. . . . . (814) 684-0736
  http://www.tyronechamber.com

LUZERNE (township). Covers a land area of 29.533 square miles and a water area of 1.206 square miles. Located at 39.97° N. Lat; 79.93° W. Long. Elevation is 758 feet.
Population: 4,904 (1990); 4,683 (2000); 5,965 (2010); Density: 202.0 persons per square mile (2010); Race: 74.7% White, 20.7% Black, 0.2% Asian, 0.1% American Indian/Alaska Native, 0.0% Native Hawaiian/Other Pacific Islander, 4.3% Other, 3.9% Hispanic of any race (2010); Average household size: 2.33 (2010); Median age: 41.3 (2010); Males per 100 females: 185.1 (2010); Marriage status: 28.8% never married, 52.7% now married, 8.0% widowed, 10.6% divorced (2006-2010 5-year est.); Foreign born: 0.5% (2006-2010 5-year est.); Ancestry (includes multiple ancestries): 14.4% German, 13.0% Irish, 9.8% Polish, 6.6% Hungarian, 5.7% Italian (2006-2010 5-year est.).
Economy: Employment by occupation: 6.1% management, 2.0% professional, 10.2% services, 21.2% sales, 2.1% farming, 9.7% construction, 2.9% production (2006-2010 5-year est.).
Income: Per capita income: $15,505 (2006-2010 5-year est.); Median household income: $36,653 (2006-2010 5-year est.); Average household income: $43,317 (2006-2010 5-year est.); Percent of households with income of $100,000 or more: 7.3% (2006-2010 5-year est.); Poverty rate: 10.5% (2006-2010 5-year est.).

Education: Percent of population age 25 and over with: High school diploma (including GED) or higher: 78.6% (2006-2010 5-year est.); Bachelor's degree or higher: 13.3% (2006-2010 5-year est.); Master's degree or higher: 3.9% (2006-2010 5-year est.).
Housing: Homeownership rate: 82.6% (2010); Median home value: $79,100 (2006-2010 5-year est.); Median contract rent: $290 per month (2006-2010 5-year est.); Median year structure built: 1945 (2006-2010 5-year est.).
Safety: Violent crime rate: 5.0 per 10,000 population; Property crime rate: 53.5 per 10,000 population (2011).
Transportation: Commute to work: 99.1% car, 0.0% public transportation, 0.0% walk, 0.9% work from home (2006-2010 5-year est.); Travel time to work: 22.7% less than 15 minutes, 31.7% 15 to 30 minutes, 20.4% 30 to 45 minutes, 15.7% 45 to 60 minutes, 9.4% 60 minutes or more (2006-2010 5-year est.)
Additional Information Contacts
Greater Hazelton Chamber of Commerce. . . . . (570) 455-1509
  http://www.hazletonchamber.org

MARKLEYSBURG (borough). Covers a land area of 0.300 square miles and a water area of 0 square miles. Located at 39.74° N. Lat; 79.45° W. Long. Elevation is 2,021 feet.
Population: 320 (1990); 282 (2000); 284 (2010); Density: 945.7 persons per square mile (2010); Race: 96.8% White, 2.5% Black, 0.0% Asian, 0.0% American Indian/Alaska Native, 0.0% Native Hawaiian/Other Pacific Islander, 0.7% Other, 0.4% Hispanic of any race (2010); Average household size: 2.57 (2010); Median age: 46.3 (2010); Males per 100 females: 115.2 (2010); Marriage status: 21.6% never married, 57.9% now married, 8.2% widowed, 12.3% divorced (2006-2010 5-year est.); Foreign born: 1.4% (2006-2010 5-year est.); Ancestry (includes multiple ancestries): 41.1% German, 15.8% Dutch, 15.3% Irish, 11.0% Italian, 4.8% Scottish (2006-2010 5-year est.).
Economy: Employment by occupation: 8.0% management, 9.1% professional, 12.5% services, 18.2% sales, 0.0% farming, 26.1% construction, 6.8% production (2006-2010 5-year est.).
Income: Per capita income: $16,582 (2006-2010 5-year est.); Median household income: $43,125 (2006-2010 5-year est.); Average household income: $44,251 (2006-2010 5-year est.); Percent of households with income of $100,000 or more: n/a (2006-2010 5-year est.); Poverty rate: 1.9% (2006-2010 5-year est.).
Education: Percent of population age 25 and over with: High school diploma (including GED) or higher: 78.4% (2006-2010 5-year est.); Bachelor's degree or higher: 1.4% (2006-2010 5-year est.); Master's degree or higher: 1.4% (2006-2010 5-year est.).
School District(s)
Uniontown Area SD (KG-12)
  2010-11 Enrollment: 3,022 . . . . (724) 438-4501
Housing: Homeownership rate: 67.1% (2010); Median home value: $76,900 (2006-2010 5-year est.); Median contract rent: $464 per month (2006-2010 5-year est.); Median year structure built: 1954 (2006-2010 5-year est.).
Transportation: Commute to work: 98.8% car, 0.0% public transportation, 0.0% walk, 1.2% work from home (2006-2010 5-year est.); Travel time to work: 56.5% less than 15 minutes, 9.4% 15 to 30 minutes, 3.5% 30 to 45 minutes, 15.3% 45 to 60 minutes, 15.3% 60 minutes or more (2006-2010 5-year est.)

MARTIN (unincorporated postal area)
Zip Code: 15460
  Covers a land area of 0.418 square miles and a water area of 0.070 square miles. Located at 39.80° N. Lat; 79.90° W. Long. Elevation is 988 feet. Population: 120 (2010); Density: 286.7 persons per square mile (2010); Race: 87.5% White, 0.0% Black, 0.0% Asian, 1.7% American Indian/Alaska Native, 1.7% Native Hawaiian/Other Pacific Islander, 9.1% Other, 2.5% Hispanic of any race (2010); Average household size: 2.79 (2010); Median age: 46.5 (2010); Males per 100 females: 103.4 (2010); Homeownership rate: 88.4% (2010)

MASONTOWN (borough). Covers a land area of 1.511 square miles and a water area of 0.032 square miles. Located at 39.85° N. Lat; 79.91° W. Long. Elevation is 1,047 feet.
History: Friendship Hill National Historic Site to South. Incorporated 1876.
Population: 3,759 (1990); 3,611 (2000); 3,450 (2010); Density: 2,283.9 persons per square mile (2010); Race: 91.5% White, 5.4% Black, 0.4% Asian, 0.2% American Indian/Alaska Native, 0.0% Native Hawaiian/Other

Pacific Islander, 2.5% Other, 0.9% Hispanic of any race (2010); Average household size: 2.35 (2010); Median age: 41.6 (2010); Males per 100 females: 89.5 (2010); Marriage status: 29.2% never married, 46.7% now married, 8.2% widowed, 15.9% divorced (2006-2010 5-year est.); Foreign born: 0.3% (2006-2010 5-year est.); Ancestry (includes multiple ancestries): 23.3% Italian, 18.3% German, 12.5% Irish, 11.6% Polish, 10.4% Russian (2006-2010 5-year est.).

Economy: Employment by occupation: 4.7% management, 1.3% professional, 13.2% services, 16.6% sales, 3.8% farming, 18.4% construction, 5.7% production (2006-2010 5-year est.).

Income: Per capita income: $18,741 (2006-2010 5-year est.); Median household income: $29,049 (2006-2010 5-year est.); Average household income: $41,113 (2006-2010 5-year est.); Percent of households with income of $100,000 or more: 6.3% (2006-2010 5-year est.); Poverty rate: 24.7% (2006-2010 5-year est.).

Education: Percent of population age 25 and over with: High school diploma (including GED) or higher: 88.1% (2006-2010 5-year est.); Bachelor's degree or higher: 12.6% (2006-2010 5-year est.); Master's degree or higher: 7.1% (2006-2010 5-year est.).

School District(s)
Albert Gallatin Area SD (KG-12)
   2010-11 Enrollment: 3,596 . . . . (724) 564-7190

Housing: Homeownership rate: 67.8% (2010); Median home value: $72,100 (2006-2010 5-year est.); Median contract rent: $397 per month (2006-2010 5-year est.); Median year structure built: 1952 (2006-2010 5-year est.).

Safety: Violent crime rate: 20.2 per 10,000 population; Property crime rate: 245.6 per 10,000 population (2011).

Newspapers: Masontown Sentinel (Local news; Circulation 3,500)

Transportation: Commute to work: 92.5% car, 0.0% public transportation, 6.5% walk, 0.9% work from home (2006-2010 5-year est.); Travel time to work: 32.3% less than 15 minutes, 24.4% 15 to 30 minutes, 18.0% 30 to 45 minutes, 13.3% 45 to 60 minutes, 12.0% 60 minutes or more (2006-2010 5-year est.)

Additional Information Contacts
Greater Connellsville Chamber of Commerce . . . . (724) 628-5500
   http://www.greaterconnellsville.org

MCCLELLANDTOWN (unincorporated postal area)
Zip Code: 15458
   Covers a land area of 15.652 square miles and a water area of 0 square miles. Located at 39.89° N. Lat; 79.85° W. Long. Elevation is 1,102 feet. Population: 2,379 (2010); Density: 152.0 persons per square mile (2010); Race: 90.0% White, 8.5% Black, 0.1% Asian, 0.1% American Indian/Alaska Native, 0.0% Native Hawaiian/Other Pacific Islander, 1.3% Other, 0.2% Hispanic of any race (2010); Average household size: 2.49 (2010); Median age: 45.0 (2010); Males per 100 females: 98.6 (2010); Homeownership rate: 80.7% (2010)

MELCROFT (unincorporated postal area)
Zip Code: 15462
   Covers a land area of 1.414 square miles and a water area of 0 square miles. Located at 40.06° N. Lat; 79.37° W. Long. Elevation is 1,417 feet. Population: 398 (2010); Density: 281.4 persons per square mile (2010); Race: 98.2% White, 0.0% Black, 0.3% Asian, 0.0% American Indian/Alaska Native, 0.0% Native Hawaiian/Other Pacific Islander, 1.5% Other, 0.8% Hispanic of any race (2010); Average household size: 2.64 (2010); Median age: 34.8 (2010); Males per 100 females: 108.4 (2010); Homeownership rate: 77.5% (2010)

MENALLEN (township). Covers a land area of 21.290 square miles and a water area of 0.048 square miles. Located at 39.94° N. Lat; 79.78° W. Long.
Population: 4,739 (1990); 4,644 (2000); 4,205 (2010); Density: 197.5 persons per square mile (2010); Race: 95.1% White, 3.2% Black, 0.1% Asian, 0.0% American Indian/Alaska Native, 0.0% Native Hawaiian/Other Pacific Islander, 1.6% Other, 0.2% Hispanic of any race (2010); Average household size: 2.38 (2010); Median age: 43.7 (2010); Males per 100 females: 89.8 (2010); Marriage status: 25.9% never married, 53.9% now married, 10.3% widowed, 9.9% divorced (2006-2010 5-year est.); Foreign born: 0.3% (2006-2010 5-year est.); Ancestry (includes multiple ancestries): 20.4% German, 19.2% Irish, 16.7% Polish, 14.0% Slovak, 11.6% Italian (2006-2010 5-year est.).

Economy: Employment by occupation: 10.2% management, 0.7% professional, 14.1% services, 11.4% sales, 7.7% farming, 10.1% construction, 6.7% production (2006-2010 5-year est.).

Income: Per capita income: $21,277 (2006-2010 5-year est.); Median household income: $39,087 (2006-2010 5-year est.); Average household income: $47,098 (2006-2010 5-year est.); Percent of households with income of $100,000 or more: 8.5% (2006-2010 5-year est.); Poverty rate: 17.2% (2006-2010 5-year est.).

Education: Percent of population age 25 and over with: High school diploma (including GED) or higher: 82.9% (2006-2010 5-year est.); Bachelor's degree or higher: 17.2% (2006-2010 5-year est.); Master's degree or higher: 5.5% (2006-2010 5-year est.).

Housing: Homeownership rate: 76.8% (2010); Median home value: $79,600 (2006-2010 5-year est.); Median contract rent: $385 per month (2006-2010 5-year est.); Median year structure built: before 1940 (2006-2010 5-year est.).

Transportation: Commute to work: 91.1% car, 3.6% public transportation, 2.4% walk, 2.9% work from home (2006-2010 5-year est.); Travel time to work: 34.8% less than 15 minutes, 42.4% 15 to 30 minutes, 5.5% 30 to 45 minutes, 6.8% 45 to 60 minutes, 10.5% 60 minutes or more (2006-2010 5-year est.)

Additional Information Contacts
Greater Connellsville Chamber of Commerce . . . . (724) 628-5500
   http://www.greaterconnellsville.org

MERRITTSTOWN (unincorporated postal area)
Zip Code: 15463
   Covers a land area of 0.315 square miles and a water area of 0 square miles. Located at 39.96° N. Lat; 79.89° W. Long. Elevation is 1,033 feet. Population: 64 (2010); Density: 203.0 persons per square mile (2010); Race: 87.5% White, 12.5% Black, 0.0% Asian, 0.0% American Indian/Alaska Native, 0.0% Native Hawaiian/Other Pacific Islander, 0.0% Other, 0.0% Hispanic of any race (2010); Average household size: 2.29 (2010); Median age: 49.2 (2010); Males per 100 females: 120.7 (2010); Homeownership rate: 85.7% (2010)

MILL RUN (unincorporated postal area)
Zip Code: 15464
   Covers a land area of 45.974 square miles and a water area of 0.542 square miles. Located at 39.93° N. Lat; 79.43° W. Long. Population: 1,536 (2010); Density: 33.4 persons per square mile (2010); Race: 98.4% White, 0.5% Black, 0.1% Asian, 0.0% American Indian/Alaska Native, 0.0% Native Hawaiian/Other Pacific Islander, 1.0% Other, 0.3% Hispanic of any race (2010); Average household size: 2.61 (2010); Median age: 41.7 (2010); Males per 100 females: 102.6 (2010); Homeownership rate: 79.4% (2010)

NAOMI (CDP). Covers a land area of 0.222 square miles and a water area of 0.067 square miles. Located at 40.11° N. Lat; 79.85° W. Long. Elevation is 807 feet.
Population: n/a (1990); n/a (2000); 69 (2010); Density: 311.2 persons per square mile (2010); Race: 92.8% White, 0.0% Black, 0.0% Asian, 0.0% American Indian/Alaska Native, 7.2% Native Hawaiian/Other Pacific Islander, 0.0% Other, 0.0% Hispanic of any race (2010); Average household size: 2.23 (2010); Median age: 40.5 (2010); Males per 100 females: 97.1 (2010); Marriage status: 30.7% never married, 69.3% now married, 0.0% widowed, 0.0% divorced (2006-2010 5-year est.); Foreign born: 14.9% (2006-2010 5-year est.); Ancestry (includes multiple ancestries): 22.8% German, 20.2% English, 14.9% Dutch, 9.6% French, 9.6% Croatian (2006-2010 5-year est.).

Economy: Employment by occupation: 0.0% management, 0.0% professional, 0.0% services, 0.0% sales, 0.0% farming, 38.3% construction, 74.5% production (2006-2010 5-year est.).

Income: Per capita income: $18,229 (2006-2010 5-year est.); Median household income: $23,750 (2006-2010 5-year est.); Average household income: $36,998 (2006-2010 5-year est.); Percent of households with income of $100,000 or more: n/a (2006-2010 5-year est.); Poverty rate: 16.7% (2006-2010 5-year est.).

Education: Percent of population age 25 and over with: High school diploma (including GED) or higher: 83.3% (2006-2010 5-year est.); Bachelor's degree or higher: 0.0% (2006-2010 5-year est.); Master's degree or higher: 0.0% (2006-2010 5-year est.).

Housing: Homeownership rate: 71.0% (2010); Median home value: $69,000 (2006-2010 5-year est.); Median contract rent: n/a per month

(2006-2010 5-year est.); Median year structure built: 1974 (2006-2010 5-year est.).

Transportation: Commute to work: 100.0% car, 0.0% public transportation, 0.0% walk, 0.0% work from home (2006-2010 5-year est.); Travel time to work: 0.0% less than 15 minutes, 100.0% 15 to 30 minutes, 0.0% 30 to 45 minutes, 0.0% 45 to 60 minutes, 0.0% 60 minutes or more (2006-2010 5-year est.)

NEW GENEVA (unincorporated postal area)
Zip Code: 15467

Covers a land area of 1.000 square miles and a water area of 0.148 square miles. Located at 39.78° N. Lat; 79.92° W. Long. Elevation is 971 feet. Population: 141 (2010); Density: 141.0 persons per square mile (2010); Race: 100.0% White, 0.0% Black, 0.0% Asian, 0.0% American Indian/Alaska Native, 0.0% Native Hawaiian/Other Pacific Islander, 0.0% Other, 0.0% Hispanic of any race (2010); Average household size: 2.39 (2010); Median age: 43.5 (2010); Males per 100 females: 110.4 (2010); Homeownership rate: 83.1% (2010)

NEW SALEM (CDP). Covers a land area of 1.159 square miles and a water area of 0 square miles. Located at 39.93° N. Lat; 79.83° W. Long. Elevation is 1,040 feet.
Population: n/a (1990); n/a (2000); 579 (2010); Density: 499.4 persons per square mile (2010); Race: 96.9% White, 1.6% Black, 0.0% Asian, 0.2% American Indian/Alaska Native, 0.2% Native Hawaiian/Other Pacific Islander, 1.1% Other, 0.5% Hispanic of any race (2010); Average household size: 2.42 (2010); Median age: 42.7 (2010); Males per 100 females: 96.3 (2010); Marriage status: 19.6% never married, 65.3% now married, 10.6% widowed, 4.6% divorced (2006-2010 5-year est.); Foreign born: 2.1% (2006-2010 5-year est.); Ancestry (includes multiple ancestries): 27.0% Irish, 26.0% German, 20.8% Polish, 13.7% Dutch, 8.7% English (2006-2010 5-year est.).
Economy: Employment by occupation: 26.3% management, 0.0% professional, 31.6% services, 0.0% sales, 0.0% farming, 4.3% construction, 0.0% production (2006-2010 5-year est.).
Income: Per capita income: $21,265 (2006-2010 5-year est.); Median household income: $38,281 (2006-2010 5-year est.); Average household income: $41,255 (2006-2010 5-year est.); Percent of households with income of $100,000 or more: 3.3% (2006-2010 5-year est.); Poverty rate: 5.8% (2006-2010 5-year est.).
Education: Percent of population age 25 and over with: High school diploma (including GED) or higher: 76.9% (2006-2010 5-year est.); Bachelor's degree or higher: 17.9% (2006-2010 5-year est.); Master's degree or higher: 3.8% (2006-2010 5-year est.).
Housing: Homeownership rate: 77.0% (2010); Median home value: $64,200 (2006-2010 5-year est.); Median contract rent: $136 per month (2006-2010 5-year est.); Median year structure built: before 1940 (2006-2010 5-year est.).
Transportation: Commute to work: 96.3% car, 3.7% public transportation, 0.0% walk, 0.0% work from home (2006-2010 5-year est.); Travel time to work: 39.6% less than 15 minutes, 53.9% 15 to 30 minutes, 0.0% 30 to 45 minutes, 0.0% 45 to 60 minutes, 6.5% 60 minutes or more (2006-2010 5-year est.)

NEWELL (borough). Covers a land area of 0.623 square miles and a water area of 0.140 square miles. Located at 40.08° N. Lat; 79.89° W. Long. Elevation is 774 feet.
Population: 518 (1990); 551 (2000); 541 (2010); Density: 868.0 persons per square mile (2010); Race: 97.8% White, 0.4% Black, 0.0% Asian, 0.0% American Indian/Alaska Native, 0.0% Native Hawaiian/Other Pacific Islander, 1.8% Other, 1.3% Hispanic of any race (2010); Average household size: 2.52 (2010); Median age: 40.5 (2010); Males per 100 females: 103.4 (2010); Marriage status: 23.5% never married, 55.3% now married, 12.3% widowed, 8.9% divorced (2006-2010 5-year est.); Foreign born: 1.4% (2006-2010 5-year est.); Ancestry (includes multiple ancestries): 31.7% Irish, 29.5% Italian, 28.1% German, 7.3% Polish, 5.5% Austrian (2006-2010 5-year est.).
Economy: Employment by occupation: 4.5% management, 3.4% professional, 15.0% services, 27.3% sales, 0.0% farming, 7.9% construction, 4.5% production (2006-2010 5-year est.).
Income: Per capita income: $21,096 (2006-2010 5-year est.); Median household income: $46,786 (2006-2010 5-year est.); Average household income: $47,974 (2006-2010 5-year est.); Percent of households with income of $100,000 or more: 5.3% (2006-2010 5-year est.); Poverty rate: 6.0% (2006-2010 5-year est.).

Education: Percent of population age 25 and over with: High school diploma (including GED) or higher: 95.7% (2006-2010 5-year est.); Bachelor's degree or higher: 14.1% (2006-2010 5-year est.); Master's degree or higher: 3.0% (2006-2010 5-year est.).
Housing: Homeownership rate: 85.1% (2010); Median home value: $68,800 (2006-2010 5-year est.); Median contract rent: $495 per month (2006-2010 5-year est.); Median year structure built: 1940 (2006-2010 5-year est.).
Transportation: Commute to work: 94.0% car, 0.0% public transportation, 0.0% walk, 3.8% work from home (2006-2010 5-year est.); Travel time to work: 14.5% less than 15 minutes, 51.4% 15 to 30 minutes, 12.9% 30 to 45 minutes, 8.2% 45 to 60 minutes, 12.9% 60 minutes or more (2006-2010 5-year est.)

NICHOLSON (township). Covers a land area of 21.811 square miles and a water area of 0.160 square miles. Located at 39.81° N. Lat; 79.87° W. Long.
Population: 1,995 (1990); 1,989 (2000); 1,805 (2010); Density: 82.8 persons per square mile (2010); Race: 97.8% White, 0.4% Black, 0.1% Asian, 0.2% American Indian/Alaska Native, 0.1% Native Hawaiian/Other Pacific Islander, 1.4% Other, 0.4% Hispanic of any race (2010); Average household size: 2.58 (2010); Median age: 44.2 (2010); Males per 100 females: 100.3 (2010); Marriage status: 29.6% never married, 52.0% now married, 10.6% widowed, 7.8% divorced (2006-2010 5-year est.); Foreign born: 0.2% (2006-2010 5-year est.); Ancestry (includes multiple ancestries): 23.8% German, 15.6% Irish, 12.1% Italian, 8.4% Polish, 8.3% English (2006-2010 5-year est.).
Economy: Employment by occupation: 9.3% management, 1.1% professional, 14.1% services, 15.8% sales, 4.8% farming, 16.1% construction, 9.0% production (2006-2010 5-year est.).
Income: Per capita income: $21,748 (2006-2010 5-year est.); Median household income: $38,633 (2006-2010 5-year est.); Average household income: $55,340 (2006-2010 5-year est.); Percent of households with income of $100,000 or more: 13.7% (2006-2010 5-year est.); Poverty rate: 16.8% (2006-2010 5-year est.).
Education: Percent of population age 25 and over with: High school diploma (including GED) or higher: 76.8% (2006-2010 5-year est.); Bachelor's degree or higher: 10.3% (2006-2010 5-year est.); Master's degree or higher: 3.8% (2006-2010 5-year est.).
Housing: Homeownership rate: 80.7% (2010); Median home value: $82,300 (2006-2010 5-year est.); Median contract rent: $300 per month (2006-2010 5-year est.); Median year structure built: 1964 (2006-2010 5-year est.).
Transportation: Commute to work: 95.0% car, 0.5% public transportation, 0.8% walk, 2.3% work from home (2006-2010 5-year est.); Travel time to work: 18.7% less than 15 minutes, 42.4% 15 to 30 minutes, 27.5% 30 to 45 minutes, 5.6% 45 to 60 minutes, 5.9% 60 minutes or more (2006-2010 5-year est.)
Additional Information Contacts
Greater Connellsville Chamber of Commerce . . . . (724) 628-5500
  http://www.greaterconnellsville.org

NORMALVILLE (unincorporated postal area)
Zip Code: 15469

Covers a land area of 33.954 square miles and a water area of 0.106 square miles. Located at 40.00° N. Lat; 79.41° W. Long. Elevation is 1,673 feet. Population: 2,331 (2010); Density: 68.7 persons per square mile (2010); Race: 99.0% White, 0.3% Black, 0.1% Asian, 0.0% American Indian/Alaska Native, 0.0% Native Hawaiian/Other Pacific Islander, 0.6% Other, 0.2% Hispanic of any race (2010); Average household size: 2.63 (2010); Median age: 39.3 (2010); Males per 100 females: 99.2 (2010); Homeownership rate: 79.5% (2010)

NORTH UNION (township). Covers a land area of 39.020 square miles and a water area of 0.011 square miles. Located at 39.91° N. Lat; 79.67° W. Long.
Population: 13,910 (1990); 14,140 (2000); 12,728 (2010); Density: 326.2 persons per square mile (2010); Race: 95.1% White, 2.8% Black, 0.3% Asian, 0.1% American Indian/Alaska Native, 0.0% Native Hawaiian/Other Pacific Islander, 1.7% Other, 0.8% Hispanic of any race (2010); Average household size: 2.29 (2010); Median age: 45.6 (2010); Males per 100 females: 90.2 (2010); Marriage status: 24.7% never married, 51.8% now married, 11.4% widowed, 12.1% divorced (2006-2010 5-year est.); Foreign born: 0.8% (2006-2010 5-year est.); Ancestry (includes multiple

ancestries): 23.2% German, 16.4% Irish, 15.2% Italian, 12.2% Polish, 10.2% English (2006-2010 5-year est.).

Economy: Employment by occupation: 6.7% management, 2.3% professional, 10.3% services, 20.9% sales, 3.2% farming, 12.1% construction, 6.9% production (2006-2010 5-year est.).

Income: Per capita income: $18,960 (2006-2010 5-year est.); Median household income: $36,937 (2006-2010 5-year est.); Average household income: $44,583 (2006-2010 5-year est.); Percent of households with income of $100,000 or more: 6.2% (2006-2010 5-year est.); Poverty rate: 15.0% (2006-2010 5-year est.).

Education: Percent of population age 25 and over with: High school diploma (including GED) or higher: 84.6% (2006-2010 5-year est.); Bachelor's degree or higher: 13.0% (2006-2010 5-year est.); Master's degree or higher: 3.3% (2006-2010 5-year est.).

Housing: Homeownership rate: 71.3% (2010); Median home value: $77,800 (2006-2010 5-year est.); Median contract rent: $386 per month (2006-2010 5-year est.); Median year structure built: 1957 (2006-2010 5-year est.).

Transportation: Commute to work: 94.9% car, 0.2% public transportation, 2.8% walk, 1.2% work from home (2006-2010 5-year est.); Travel time to work: 45.7% less than 15 minutes, 30.3% 15 to 30 minutes, 11.1% 30 to 45 minutes, 6.4% 45 to 60 minutes, 6.5% 60 minutes or more (2006-2010 5-year est.).

Additional Information Contacts
Greater Connellsville Chamber of Commerce . . . . (724) 628-5500
   http://www.greaterconnellsville.org
North Union Township . . . . (724) 438-6316
   http://northuniontownship-pa.gov

OHIOPYLE (borough). Aka Ohio Pyle. Covers a land area of 0.418 square miles and a water area of 0.080 square miles. Located at 39.87° N. Lat; 79.49° W. Long. Elevation is 1,217 feet.

History: Fallingwater, a home designed by Frank Lloyd Wright in 1936, is to North.

Population: 81 (1990); 77 (2000); 59 (2010); Density: 141.2 persons per square mile (2010); Race: 100.0% White, 0.0% Black, 0.0% Asian, 0.0% American Indian/Alaska Native, 0.0% Native Hawaiian/Other Pacific Islander, 0.0% Other, 0.0% Hispanic of any race (2010); Average household size: 2.19 (2010); Median age: 47.5 (2010); Males per 100 females: 103.4 (2010); Marriage status: 31.3% never married, 34.4% now married, 18.8% widowed, 15.6% divorced (2006-2010 5-year est.); Foreign born: 0.0% (2006-2010 5-year est.); Ancestry (includes multiple ancestries): 21.9% Irish, 21.9% Italian, 18.8% German, 12.5% American, 9.4% Pennsylvania German (2006-2010 5-year est.).

Economy: Employment by occupation: 28.6% management, 0.0% professional, 0.0% services, 0.0% sales, 42.9% farming, 0.0% construction, 28.6% production (2006-2010 5-year est.).

Income: Per capita income: $16,284 (2006-2010 5-year est.); Median household income: $16,500 (2006-2010 5-year est.); Average household income: $20,813 (2006-2010 5-year est.); Percent of households with income of $100,000 or more: n/a (2006-2010 5-year est.); Poverty rate: 6.3% (2006-2010 5-year est.).

Education: Percent of population age 25 and over with: High school diploma (including GED) or higher: 87.5% (2006-2010 5-year est.); Bachelor's degree or higher: 21.9% (2006-2010 5-year est.); Master's degree or higher: 0.0% (2006-2010 5-year est.).

Housing: Homeownership rate: 66.6% (2010); Median home value: $97,500 (2006-2010 5-year est.); Median contract rent: n/a per month (2006-2010 5-year est.); Median year structure built: before 1940 (2006-2010 5-year est.).

Transportation: Commute to work: 100.0% car, 0.0% public transportation, 0.0% walk, 0.0% work from home (2006-2010 5-year est.); Travel time to work: 28.6% less than 15 minutes, 0.0% 15 to 30 minutes, 28.6% 30 to 45 minutes, 0.0% 45 to 60 minutes, 42.9% 60 minutes or more (2006-2010 5-year est.).

OLIVER (CDP). Covers a land area of 2.216 square miles and a water area of 0 square miles. Located at 39.92° N. Lat; 79.72° W. Long. Elevation is 1,004 feet.

Population: 3,315 (1990); 2,925 (2000); 2,535 (2010); Density: 1,143.7 persons per square mile (2010); Race: 92.1% White, 5.5% Black, 0.1% Asian, 0.1% American Indian/Alaska Native, 0.0% Native Hawaiian/Other Pacific Islander, 2.2% Other, 0.8% Hispanic of any race (2010); Average household size: 2.23 (2010); Median age: 46.0 (2010); Males per 100 females: 83.8 (2010); Marriage status: 29.4% never married, 44.5% now

married, 9.4% widowed, 16.6% divorced (2006-2010 5-year est.); Foreign born: 0.0% (2006-2010 5-year est.); Ancestry (includes multiple ancestries): 20.4% German, 15.0% Italian, 13.1% Polish, 11.0% Irish, 10.0% English (2006-2010 5-year est.).

Economy: Employment by occupation: 11.7% management, 1.5% professional, 7.3% services, 20.6% sales, 1.6% farming, 6.4% construction, 5.7% production (2006-2010 5-year est.).

Income: Per capita income: $20,397 (2006-2010 5-year est.); Median household income: $28,719 (2006-2010 5-year est.); Average household income: $41,949 (2006-2010 5-year est.); Percent of households with income of $100,000 or more: 7.4% (2006-2010 5-year est.); Poverty rate: 23.6% (2006-2010 5-year est.).

Education: Percent of population age 25 and over with: High school diploma (including GED) or higher: 84.5% (2006-2010 5-year est.); Bachelor's degree or higher: 11.8% (2006-2010 5-year est.); Master's degree or higher: 2.6% (2006-2010 5-year est.).

Housing: Homeownership rate: 63.1% (2010); Median home value: $69,300 (2006-2010 5-year est.); Median contract rent: $392 per month (2006-2010 5-year est.); Median year structure built: 1956 (2006-2010 5-year est.).

Transportation: Commute to work: 88.3% car, 0.0% public transportation, 7.9% walk, 3.9% work from home (2006-2010 5-year est.); Travel time to work: 60.3% less than 15 minutes, 24.4% 15 to 30 minutes, 4.7% 30 to 45 minutes, 4.9% 45 to 60 minutes, 5.7% 60 minutes or more (2006-2010 5-year est.)

Additional Information Contacts
Greater Connellsville Chamber of Commerce . . . . (724) 628-5500
   http://www.greaterconnellsville.org

PERRY (township). Covers a land area of 20.236 square miles and a water area of 0.447 square miles. Located at 40.10° N. Lat; 79.77° W. Long.

History: George Washington Grist Mill here.

Population: 2,817 (1990); 2,786 (2000); 2,552 (2010); Density: 126.1 persons per square mile (2010); Race: 97.2% White, 1.5% Black, 0.2% Asian, 0.1% American Indian/Alaska Native, 0.0% Native Hawaiian/Other Pacific Islander, 1.0% Other, 0.2% Hispanic of any race (2010); Average household size: 2.33 (2010); Median age: 47.2 (2010); Males per 100 females: 99.4 (2010); Marriage status: 25.5% never married, 54.9% now married, 10.1% widowed, 9.4% divorced (2006-2010 5-year est.); Foreign born: 0.3% (2006-2010 5-year est.); Ancestry (includes multiple ancestries): 19.9% German, 18.4% Italian, 15.9% Slovak, 14.1% English, 9.3% Irish (2006-2010 5-year est.).

Economy: Employment by occupation: 4.8% management, 2.3% professional, 12.8% services, 22.3% sales, 5.5% farming, 18.4% construction, 6.6% production (2006-2010 5-year est.).

Income: Per capita income: $18,552 (2006-2010 5-year est.); Median household income: $28,438 (2006-2010 5-year est.); Average household income: $42,993 (2006-2010 5-year est.); Percent of households with income of $100,000 or more: 8.0% (2006-2010 5-year est.); Poverty rate: 20.3% (2006-2010 5-year est.).

Education: Percent of population age 25 and over with: High school diploma (including GED) or higher: 80.6% (2006-2010 5-year est.); Bachelor's degree or higher: 10.7% (2006-2010 5-year est.); Master's degree or higher: 3.8% (2006-2010 5-year est.).

Housing: Homeownership rate: 79.6% (2010); Median home value: $100,000 (2006-2010 5-year est.); Median contract rent: $380 per month (2006-2010 5-year est.); Median year structure built: 1965 (2006-2010 5-year est.).

Transportation: Commute to work: 93.7% car, 0.0% public transportation, 0.0% walk, 3.2% work from home (2006-2010 5-year est.); Travel time to work: 33.5% less than 15 minutes, 28.4% 15 to 30 minutes, 28.4% 30 to 45 minutes, 3.7% 45 to 60 minutes, 6.1% 60 minutes or more (2006-2010 5-year est.)

Additional Information Contacts
Greater Connellsville Chamber of Commerce . . . . (724) 628-5500
   http://www.greaterconnellsville.org

PERRYOPOLIS (borough). Covers a land area of 1.532 square miles and a water area of 0 square miles. Located at 40.09° N. Lat; 79.75° W. Long. Elevation is 1,010 feet.

Population: 1,833 (1990); 1,764 (2000); 1,784 (2010); Density: 1,164.6 persons per square mile (2010); Race: 97.9% White, 0.3% Black, 0.4% Asian, 0.1% American Indian/Alaska Native, 0.1% Native Hawaiian/Other Pacific Islander, 1.2% Other, 0.2% Hispanic of any race (2010); Average

household size: 2.29 (2010); Median age: 46.9 (2010); Males per 100 females: 90.8 (2010); Marriage status: 16.8% never married, 61.0% now married, 8.8% widowed, 13.4% divorced (2006-2010 5-year est.); Foreign born: 0.0% (2006-2010 5-year est.); Ancestry (includes multiple ancestries): 24.0% German, 18.9% Italian, 16.2% Slovak, 15.2% Irish, 10.2% English (2006-2010 5-year est.).

Economy: Employment by occupation: 5.0% management, 4.7% professional, 17.6% services, 19.6% sales, 6.6% farming, 7.5% construction, 7.9% production (2006-2010 5-year est.).

Income: Per capita income: $22,258 (2006-2010 5-year est.); Median household income: $40,899 (2006-2010 5-year est.); Average household income: $50,032 (2006-2010 5-year est.); Percent of households with income of $100,000 or more: 9.7% (2006-2010 5-year est.); Poverty rate: 13.9% (2006-2010 5-year est.).

Education: Percent of population age 25 and over with: High school diploma (including GED) or higher: 85.4% (2006-2010 5-year est.); Bachelor's degree or higher: 18.9% (2006-2010 5-year est.); Master's degree or higher: 4.4% (2006-2010 5-year est.).

School District(s)

Frazier SD (PK-12)

    2010-11 Enrollment: 1,200 . . . . (724) 736-4432

Housing: Homeownership rate: 78.0% (2010); Median home value: $108,700 (2006-2010 5-year est.); Median contract rent: $327 per month (2006-2010 5-year est.); Median year structure built: 1962 (2006-2010 5-year est.).

Safety: Violent crime rate: 0.0 per 10,000 population; Property crime rate: 201.1 per 10,000 population (2011).

Transportation: Commute to work: 97.8% car, 0.7% public transportation, 0.0% walk, 1.5% work from home (2006-2010 5-year est.); Travel time to work: 32.5% less than 15 minutes, 24.8% 15 to 30 minutes, 28.4% 30 to 45 minutes, 3.9% 45 to 60 minutes, 10.4% 60 minutes or more (2006-2010 5-year est.).

Additional Information Contacts

Mon Valley Regional Chamber of Commerce . . . . (724) 483-3507
   http://www.mvrchamber.org

POINT MARION (borough). Covers a land area of 0.394 square miles and a water area of 0.074 square miles. Located at 39.74° N. Lat; 79.90° W. Long. Elevation is 833 feet.

History: Friendship Hill National Historic Site to North. Laid out 1842.

Population: 1,344 (1990); 1,333 (2000); 1,159 (2010); Density: 2,945.0 persons per square mile (2010); Race: 98.1% White, 0.6% Black, 0.1% Asian, 0.1% American Indian/Alaska Native, 0.0% Native Hawaiian/Other Pacific Islander, 1.1% Other, 1.0% Hispanic of any race (2010); Average household size: 2.33 (2010); Median age: 42.3 (2010); Males per 100 females: 93.5 (2010); Marriage status: 28.5% never married, 53.1% now married, 7.7% widowed, 10.7% divorced (2006-2010 5-year est.); Foreign born: 0.4% (2006-2010 5-year est.); Ancestry (includes multiple ancestries): 24.8% German, 18.7% Irish, 13.4% Italian, 11.1% American, 10.6% English (2006-2010 5-year est.).

Economy: Employment by occupation: 8.3% management, 3.8% professional, 9.7% services, 11.9% sales, 2.0% farming, 23.4% construction, 11.9% production (2006-2010 5-year est.).

Income: Per capita income: $21,155 (2006-2010 5-year est.); Median household income: $33,269 (2006-2010 5-year est.); Average household income: $48,048 (2006-2010 5-year est.); Percent of households with income of $100,000 or more: 13.2% (2006-2010 5-year est.); Poverty rate: 20.2% (2006-2010 5-year est.).

Education: Percent of population age 25 and over with: High school diploma (including GED) or higher: 79.9% (2006-2010 5-year est.); Bachelor's degree or higher: 19.9% (2006-2010 5-year est.); Master's degree or higher: 4.6% (2006-2010 5-year est.).

School District(s)

Albert Gallatin Area SD (KG-12)

    2010-11 Enrollment: 3,596 . . . . (724) 564-7190

Housing: Homeownership rate: 60.1% (2010); Median home value: $64,400 (2006-2010 5-year est.); Median contract rent: $398 per month (2006-2010 5-year est.); Median year structure built: before 1940 (2006-2010 5-year est.).

Safety: Violent crime rate: 43.0 per 10,000 population; Property crime rate: 189.2 per 10,000 population (2011).

Transportation: Commute to work: 90.2% car, 0.0% public transportation, 7.7% walk, 1.2% work from home (2006-2010 5-year est.); Travel time to work: 22.6% less than 15 minutes, 46.7% 15 to 30 minutes, 18.4% 30 to

45 minutes, 5.9% 45 to 60 minutes, 6.4% 60 minutes or more (2006-2010 5-year est.)

Additional Information Contacts

Waynesburg Area Chamber of Commerce . . . . (724) 627-5926
   http://www.waynesburgchamber.com

REDSTONE (township). Covers a land area of 22.761 square miles and a water area of 0.061 square miles. Located at 39.98° N. Lat; 79.85° W. Long. Elevation is 902 feet.

Population: 6,459 (1990); 6,397 (2000); 5,566 (2010); Density: 244.5 persons per square mile (2010); Race: 87.0% White, 9.9% Black, 0.2% Asian, 0.3% American Indian/Alaska Native, 0.0% Native Hawaiian/Other Pacific Islander, 2.6% Other, 0.4% Hispanic of any race (2010); Average household size: 2.34 (2010); Median age: 42.8 (2010); Males per 100 females: 88.4 (2010); Marriage status: 21.9% never married, 54.7% now married, 12.0% widowed, 11.3% divorced (2006-2010 5-year est.); Foreign born: 1.0% (2006-2010 5-year est.); Ancestry (includes multiple ancestries): 21.1% Italian, 18.5% Irish, 14.4% Polish, 12.7% German, 6.0% Slovak (2006-2010 5-year est.).

Economy: Employment by occupation: 8.2% management, 0.9% professional, 8.4% services, 16.8% sales, 1.7% farming, 8.9% construction, 5.2% production (2006-2010 5-year est.).

Income: Per capita income: $15,125 (2006-2010 5-year est.); Median household income: $26,321 (2006-2010 5-year est.); Average household income: $36,824 (2006-2010 5-year est.); Percent of households with income of $100,000 or more: 5.1% (2006-2010 5-year est.); Poverty rate: 16.4% (2006-2010 5-year est.).

Education: Percent of population age 25 and over with: High school diploma (including GED) or higher: 82.0% (2006-2010 5-year est.); Bachelor's degree or higher: 12.2% (2006-2010 5-year est.); Master's degree or higher: 2.9% (2006-2010 5-year est.).

Housing: Homeownership rate: 69.0% (2010); Median home value: $58,600 (2006-2010 5-year est.); Median contract rent: $294 per month (2006-2010 5-year est.); Median year structure built: before 1940 (2006-2010 5-year est.).

Transportation: Commute to work: 93.8% car, 0.0% public transportation, 3.0% walk, 3.1% work from home (2006-2010 5-year est.); Travel time to work: 35.7% less than 15 minutes, 45.0% 15 to 30 minutes, 9.6% 30 to 45 minutes, 5.7% 45 to 60 minutes, 4.0% 60 minutes or more (2006-2010 5-year est.)

Additional Information Contacts

Mon Valley Regional Chamber of Commerce . . . . (724) 483-3507
   http://www.mvrchamber.org
Redstone Township. . . . . (724) 246-1910
   http://www.redstonetownship.com

REPUBLIC (CDP). Covers a land area of 0.723 square miles and a water area of 0 square miles. Located at 39.97° N. Lat; 79.88° W. Long. Elevation is 997 feet.

Population: 1,577 (1990); 1,396 (2000); 1,096 (2010); Density: 1,515.1 persons per square mile (2010); Race: 92.0% White, 6.1% Black, 0.2% Asian, 0.4% American Indian/Alaska Native, 0.0% Native Hawaiian/Other Pacific Islander, 1.3% Other, 0.5% Hispanic of any race (2010); Average household size: 2.26 (2010); Median age: 42.5 (2010); Males per 100 females: 86.4 (2010); Marriage status: 23.7% never married, 55.6% now married, 11.3% widowed, 9.3% divorced (2006-2010 5-year est.); Foreign born: 0.0% (2006-2010 5-year est.); Ancestry (includes multiple ancestries): 32.9% Italian, 30.0% Irish, 14.3% Dutch, 11.0% Russian, 8.0% German (2006-2010 5-year est.).

Economy: Employment by occupation: 3.9% management, 0.0% professional, 20.5% services, 23.0% sales, 0.0% farming, 0.0% construction, 0.0% production (2006-2010 5-year est.).

Income: Per capita income: $12,560 (2006-2010 5-year est.); Median household income: $24,429 (2006-2010 5-year est.); Average household income: $31,254 (2006-2010 5-year est.); Percent of households with income of $100,000 or more: 4.6% (2006-2010 5-year est.); Poverty rate: 22.6% (2006-2010 5-year est.).

Education: Percent of population age 25 and over with: High school diploma (including GED) or higher: 73.7% (2006-2010 5-year est.); Bachelor's degree or higher: 7.8% (2006-2010 5-year est.); Master's degree or higher: 3.8% (2006-2010 5-year est.).

Housing: Homeownership rate: 64.8% (2010); Median home value: $56,200 (2006-2010 5-year est.); Median contract rent: $340 per month (2006-2010 5-year est.); Median year structure built: before 1940 (2006-2010 5-year est.).

Transportation: Commute to work: 94.9% car, 0.0% public transportation, 5.1% walk, 0.0% work from home (2006-2010 5-year est.); Travel time to work: 30.8% less than 15 minutes, 48.7% 15 to 30 minutes, 16.4% 30 to 45 minutes, 0.0% 45 to 60 minutes, 4.1% 60 minutes or more (2006-2010 5-year est.)

Additional Information Contacts
Greater Connellsville Chamber of Commerce . . . . (724) 628-5500
  http://www.greaterconnellsville.org

RONCO (CDP). Covers a land area of 0.510 square miles and a water area of 0.055 square miles. Located at 39.87° N. Lat; 79.92° W. Long. Elevation is 1,030 feet.
Population: n/a (1990); n/a (2000); 256 (2010); Density: 501.8 persons per square mile (2010); Race: 89.5% White, 10.2% Black, 0.0% Asian, 0.0% American Indian/Alaska Native, 0.0% Native Hawaiian/Other Pacific Islander, 0.3% Other, 0.0% Hispanic of any race (2010); Average household size: 2.59 (2010); Median age: 40.1 (2010); Males per 100 females: 86.9 (2010); Marriage status: 30.5% never married, 41.6% now married, 17.8% widowed, 10.2% divorced (2006-2010 5-year est.); Foreign born: 0.0% (2006-2010 5-year est.); Ancestry (includes multiple ancestries): 45.4% German, 20.6% Italian, 16.0% Slovak, 15.3% Polish (2006-2010 5-year est.).
Economy: Employment by occupation: 0.0% management, 0.0% professional, 0.0% services, 0.0% sales, 100.0% farming, 0.0% construction, 0.0% production (2006-2010 5-year est.).
Income: Per capita income: $9,602 (2006-2010 5-year est.); Median household income: $12,255 (2006-2010 5-year est.); Average household income: $20,569 (2006-2010 5-year est.); Percent of households with income of $100,000 or more: n/a (2006-2010 5-year est.); Poverty rate: 55.2% (2006-2010 5-year est.).
Education: Percent of population age 25 and over with: High school diploma (including GED) or higher: 89.1% (2006-2010 5-year est.); Bachelor's degree or higher: 0.0% (2006-2010 5-year est.); Master's degree or higher: 0.0% (2006-2010 5-year est.).
Housing: Homeownership rate: 71.7% (2010); Median home value: $82,600 (2006-2010 5-year est.); Median contract rent: n/a per month (2006-2010 5-year est.); Median year structure built: before 1940 (2006-2010 5-year est.).
Transportation: Commute to work: 100.0% car, 0.0% public transportation, 0.0% walk, 0.0% work from home (2006-2010 5-year est.); Travel time to work: 0.0% less than 15 minutes, 0.0% 15 to 30 minutes, 0.0% 30 to 45 minutes, 0.0% 45 to 60 minutes, 100.0% 60 minutes or more (2006-2010 5-year est.)

ROWES RUN (CDP). Covers a land area of 1.232 square miles and a water area of 0 square miles. Located at 40.01° N. Lat; 79.82° W. Long. Elevation is 925 feet.
Population: n/a (1990); n/a (2000); 564 (2010); Density: 457.9 persons per square mile (2010); Race: 97.7% White, 0.4% Black, 0.0% Asian, 0.5% American Indian/Alaska Native, 0.0% Native Hawaiian/Other Pacific Islander, 1.4% Other, 0.5% Hispanic of any race (2010); Average household size: 2.31 (2010); Median age: 45.7 (2010); Males per 100 females: 92.5 (2010); Marriage status: 24.5% never married, 44.6% now married, 14.0% widowed, 16.9% divorced (2006-2010 5-year est.); Foreign born: 0.0% (2006-2010 5-year est.); Ancestry (includes multiple ancestries): 27.6% Irish, 20.2% Polish, 12.8% German, 11.7% Italian, 11.1% Slovak (2006-2010 5-year est.).
Economy: Employment by occupation: 2.6% management, 0.0% professional, 5.2% services, 16.9% sales, 5.2% farming, 13.1% construction, 5.0% production (2006-2010 5-year est.).
Income: Per capita income: $18,134 (2006-2010 5-year est.); Median household income: $30,739 (2006-2010 5-year est.); Average household income: $44,313 (2006-2010 5-year est.); Percent of households with income of $100,000 or more: 6.9% (2006-2010 5-year est.); Poverty rate: 6.0% (2006-2010 5-year est.).
Education: Percent of population age 25 and over with: High school diploma (including GED) or higher: 84.8% (2006-2010 5-year est.); Bachelor's degree or higher: 3.8% (2006-2010 5-year est.); Master's degree or higher: 0.0% (2006-2010 5-year est.).
Housing: Homeownership rate: 80.8% (2010); Median home value: $30,200 (2006-2010 5-year est.); Median contract rent: n/a per month (2006-2010 5-year est.); Median year structure built: before 1940 (2006-2010 5-year est.).
Transportation: Commute to work: 90.4% car, 0.0% public transportation, 5.5% walk, 4.1% work from home (2006-2010 5-year est.); Travel time to

work: 29.5% less than 15 minutes, 42.6% 15 to 30 minutes, 0.0% 30 to 45 minutes, 12.2% 45 to 60 minutes, 15.8% 60 minutes or more (2006-2010 5-year est.)

SALTLICK (township). Covers a land area of 37.630 square miles and a water area of 0.005 square miles. Located at 40.05° N. Lat; 79.39° W. Long.
Population: 3,253 (1990); 3,715 (2000); 3,461 (2010); Density: 92.0 persons per square mile (2010); Race: 99.2% White, 0.0% Black, 0.1% Asian, 0.0% American Indian/Alaska Native, 0.0% Native Hawaiian/Other Pacific Islander, 0.7% Other, 0.3% Hispanic of any race (2010); Average household size: 2.50 (2010); Median age: 41.9 (2010); Males per 100 females: 104.3 (2010); Marriage status: 27.5% never married, 58.2% now married, 6.5% widowed, 7.9% divorced (2006-2010 5-year est.); Foreign born: 0.5% (2006-2010 5-year est.); Ancestry (includes multiple ancestries): 47.9% German, 10.4% American, 9.8% Irish, 8.6% English, 7.2% Dutch (2006-2010 5-year est.).
Economy: Employment by occupation: 6.6% management, 0.0% professional, 25.6% services, 12.7% sales, 4.1% farming, 17.7% construction, 5.2% production (2006-2010 5-year est.).
Income: Per capita income: $17,888 (2006-2010 5-year est.); Median household income: $33,945 (2006-2010 5-year est.); Average household income: $41,210 (2006-2010 5-year est.); Percent of households with income of $100,000 or more: 2.9% (2006-2010 5-year est.); Poverty rate: 15.6% (2006-2010 5-year est.).
Education: Percent of population age 25 and over with: High school diploma (including GED) or higher: 80.2% (2006-2010 5-year est.); Bachelor's degree or higher: 9.1% (2006-2010 5-year est.); Master's degree or higher: 2.7% (2006-2010 5-year est.).
Housing: Homeownership rate: 80.9% (2010); Median home value: $91,300 (2006-2010 5-year est.); Median contract rent: $390 per month (2006-2010 5-year est.); Median year structure built: 1973 (2006-2010 5-year est.).
Transportation: Commute to work: 93.4% car, 0.0% public transportation, 3.3% walk, 3.3% work from home (2006-2010 5-year est.); Travel time to work: 38.6% less than 15 minutes, 29.1% 15 to 30 minutes, 11.8% 30 to 45 minutes, 10.9% 45 to 60 minutes, 9.6% 60 minutes or more (2006-2010 5-year est.)

Additional Information Contacts
Greater Connellsville Chamber of Commerce . . . . (724) 628-5500
  http://www.greaterconnellsville.org

SEVEN SPRINGS (borough). Covers a land area of 0.111 square miles and a water area of 0 square miles. Located at 40.03° N. Lat; 79.30° W. Long.
Population: n/a (1990); 1 (2000); 15 (2010); Density: 135.4 persons per square mile (2010); Race: 100.0% White, 0.0% Black, 0.0% Asian, 0.0% American Indian/Alaska Native, 0.0% Native Hawaiian/Other Pacific Islander, 0.0% Other, 0.0% Hispanic of any race (2010); Average household size: 1.00 (2010); Median age: 49.5 (2010); Males per 100 females: 114.3 (2010); Marriage status: 100.0% never married, 0.0% now married, 0.0% widowed, 0.0% divorced (2006-2010 5-year est.); Foreign born: 0.0% (2006-2010 5-year est.); Ancestry (includes multiple ancestries): 100.0% German, 100.0% Lithuanian (2006-2010 5-year est.).
Economy: Income: Per capita income: $-1 (2006-2010 5-year est.); Median household income: n/a (2006-2010 5-year est.); Average household income: n/a (2006-2010 5-year est.); Percent of households with income of $100,000 or more: n/a (2006-2010 5-year est.); Poverty rate: 100.0% (2006-2010 5-year est.).
Education: Percent of population age 25 and over with: High school diploma (including GED) or higher: n/a (2006-2010 5-year est.); Bachelor's degree or higher: n/a (2006-2010 5-year est.); Master's degree or higher: n/a (2006-2010 5-year est.).
Housing: Homeownership rate: 90.9% (2010); Median home value: n/a (2006-2010 5-year est.); Median contract rent: <$101 per month (2006-2010 5-year est.); Median year structure built: n/a (2006-2010 5-year est.).
Transportation: Commute to work: 100.0% car, 0.0% public transportation, 0.0% walk, 0.0% work from home (2006-2010 5-year est.); Travel time to work: 100.0% less than 15 minutes, 0.0% 15 to 30 minutes, 0.0% 30 to 45 minutes, 0.0% 45 to 60 minutes, 0.0% 60 minutes or more (2006-2010 5-year est.)

SEVEN SPRINGS (borough). Covers a land area of 1.083 square miles and a water area of 0 square miles. Located at 40.03° N. Lat; 79.29° W. Long.
Population: 22 (1990); 127 (2000); 26 (2010); Density: 24.0 persons per square mile (2010); Race: 100.0% White, 0.0% Black, 0.0% Asian, 0.0% American Indian/Alaska Native, 0.0% Native Hawaiian/Other Pacific Islander, 0.0% Other, 0.0% Hispanic of any race (2010); Average household size: 1.10 (2010); Median age: 68.0 (2010); Males per 100 females: 100.0 (2010); Marriage status: 15.9% never married, 75.0% now married, 0.0% widowed, 9.1% divorced (2006-2010 5-year est.); Foreign born: 0.0% (2006-2010 5-year est.); Ancestry (includes multiple ancestries): 40.9% German, 34.1% English, 18.2% Polish, 13.6% Irish, 13.6% Italian (2006-2010 5-year est.).
Economy: Employment by occupation: 0.0% management, 0.0% professional, 26.1% services, 8.7% sales, 0.0% farming, 0.0% construction, 0.0% production (2006-2010 5-year est.).
Income: Per capita income: $85,130 (2006-2010 5-year est.); Median household income: $89,063 (2006-2010 5-year est.); Average household income: $140,778 (2006-2010 5-year est.); Percent of households with income of $100,000 or more: 37.0% (2006-2010 5-year est.); Poverty rate: 9.1% (2006-2010 5-year est.).
Education: Percent of population age 25 and over with: High school diploma (including GED) or higher: 100.0% (2006-2010 5-year est.); Bachelor's degree or higher: 56.4% (2006-2010 5-year est.); Master's degree or higher: 43.6% (2006-2010 5-year est.).
Housing: Homeownership rate: 80.0% (2010); Median home value: $312,500 (2006-2010 5-year est.); Median contract rent: <$101 per month (2006-2010 5-year est.); Median year structure built: 1986 (2006-2010 5-year est.).
Transportation: Commute to work: 100.0% car, 0.0% public transportation, 0.0% walk, 0.0% work from home (2006-2010 5-year est.); Travel time to work: 39.1% less than 15 minutes, 52.2% 15 to 30 minutes, 0.0% 30 to 45 minutes, 0.0% 45 to 60 minutes, 8.7% 60 minutes or more (2006-2010 5-year est.)

SMITHFIELD (borough). Aka Shoaf Ovens. Covers a land area of 0.710 square miles and a water area of 0 square miles. Located at 39.80° N. Lat; 79.81° W. Long. Elevation is 1,086 feet.
Population: 1,000 (1990); 854 (2000); 875 (2010); Density: 1,233.1 persons per square mile (2010); Race: 98.5% White, 0.6% Black, 0.2% Asian, 0.1% American Indian/Alaska Native, 0.0% Native Hawaiian/Other Pacific Islander, 0.6% Other, 0.5% Hispanic of any race (2010); Average household size: 2.41 (2010); Median age: 40.7 (2010); Males per 100 females: 102.1 (2010); Marriage status: 26.5% never married, 54.3% now married, 11.2% widowed, 8.0% divorced (2006-2010 5-year est.); Foreign born: 0.0% (2006-2010 5-year est.); Ancestry (includes multiple ancestries): 21.7% German, 20.2% Irish, 9.6% Italian, 7.6% Polish, 6.6% English (2006-2010 5-year est.).
Economy: Employment by occupation: 5.4% management, 1.6% professional, 15.6% services, 8.6% sales, 4.0% farming, 11.9% construction, 7.5% production (2006-2010 5-year est.).
Income: Per capita income: $18,308 (2006-2010 5-year est.); Median household income: $33,359 (2006-2010 5-year est.); Average household income: $46,563 (2006-2010 5-year est.); Percent of households with income of $100,000 or more: 9.5% (2006-2010 5-year est.); Poverty rate: 22.6% (2006-2010 5-year est.).
Education: Percent of population age 25 and over with: High school diploma (including GED) or higher: 86.1% (2006-2010 5-year est.); Bachelor's degree or higher: 14.3% (2006-2010 5-year est.); Master's degree or higher: 5.9% (2006-2010 5-year est.).
School District(s)
Albert Gallatin Area SD (KG-12)
    2010-11 Enrollment: 3,596 . . . . (724) 564-7190
Housing: Homeownership rate: 67.8% (2010); Median home value: $84,600 (2006-2010 5-year est.); Median contract rent: $480 per month (2006-2010 5-year est.); Median year structure built: 1949 (2006-2010 5-year est.).
Safety: Violent crime rate: 0.0 per 10,000 population; Property crime rate: 0.0 per 10,000 population (2011).
Transportation: Commute to work: 94.0% car, 0.0% public transportation, 3.8% walk, 2.2% work from home (2006-2010 5-year est.); Travel time to work: 12.0% less than 15 minutes, 48.2% 15 to 30 minutes, 27.5% 30 to 45 minutes, 5.3% 45 to 60 minutes, 7.0% 60 minutes or more (2006-2010 5-year est.)

SMOCK (CDP). Covers a land area of 1.562 square miles and a water area of 0 square miles. Located at 40.00° N. Lat; 79.78° W. Long. Elevation is 883 feet.
Population: n/a (1990); n/a (2000); 583 (2010); Density: 373.2 persons per square mile (2010); Race: 93.7% White, 2.7% Black, 0.0% Asian, 0.0% American Indian/Alaska Native, 0.0% Native Hawaiian/Other Pacific Islander, 3.6% Other, 0.2% Hispanic of any race (2010); Average household size: 2.52 (2010); Median age: 43.5 (2010); Males per 100 females: 99.0 (2010); Marriage status: 23.8% never married, 48.5% now married, 14.0% widowed, 13.6% divorced (2006-2010 5-year est.); Foreign born: 0.0% (2006-2010 5-year est.); Ancestry (includes multiple ancestries): 32.3% English, 24.3% Irish, 20.4% German, 14.9% Slovak, 9.3% Swiss (2006-2010 5-year est.).
Economy: Employment by occupation: 13.9% management, 0.0% professional, 2.3% services, 33.5% sales, 0.0% farming, 3.5% construction, 3.5% production (2006-2010 5-year est.).
Income: Per capita income: $14,356 (2006-2010 5-year est.); Median household income: $36,250 (2006-2010 5-year est.); Average household income: $37,104 (2006-2010 5-year est.); Percent of households with income of $100,000 or more: 2.9% (2006-2010 5-year est.); Poverty rate: 19.0% (2006-2010 5-year est.).
Education: Percent of population age 25 and over with: High school diploma (including GED) or higher: 74.3% (2006-2010 5-year est.); Bachelor's degree or higher: 7.0% (2006-2010 5-year est.); Master's degree or higher: 0.9% (2006-2010 5-year est.).
Housing: Homeownership rate: 75.7% (2010); Median home value: $65,900 (2006-2010 5-year est.); Median contract rent: $435 per month (2006-2010 5-year est.); Median year structure built: before 1940 (2006-2010 5-year est.).
Transportation: Commute to work: 63.6% car, 0.0% public transportation, 23.1% walk, 13.3% work from home (2006-2010 5-year est.); Travel time to work: 29.3% less than 15 minutes, 17.3% 15 to 30 minutes, 16.0% 30 to 45 minutes, 37.3% 45 to 60 minutes, 0.0% 60 minutes or more (2006-2010 5-year est.)

SOUTH CONNELLSVILLE (borough). Covers a land area of 1.661 square miles and a water area of 0.067 square miles. Located at 39.99° N. Lat; 79.58° W. Long. Elevation is 1,050 feet.
Population: 2,204 (1990); 2,281 (2000); 1,970 (2010); Density: 1,186.0 persons per square mile (2010); Race: 97.4% White, 1.2% Black, 0.2% Asian, 0.1% American Indian/Alaska Native, 0.0% Native Hawaiian/Other Pacific Islander, 1.1% Other, 0.8% Hispanic of any race (2010); Average household size: 2.41 (2010); Median age: 43.4 (2010); Males per 100 females: 97.8 (2010); Marriage status: 26.7% never married, 53.8% now married, 11.3% widowed, 8.2% divorced (2006-2010 5-year est.); Foreign born: 0.0% (2006-2010 5-year est.); Ancestry (includes multiple ancestries): 34.2% German, 25.2% Irish, 11.7% English, 9.7% Dutch, 9.4% Italian (2006-2010 5-year est.).
Economy: Employment by occupation: 3.2% management, 0.8% professional, 12.4% services, 19.4% sales, 9.3% farming, 8.4% construction, 12.5% production (2006-2010 5-year est.).
Income: Per capita income: $15,628 (2006-2010 5-year est.); Median household income: $32,093 (2006-2010 5-year est.); Average household income: $40,298 (2006-2010 5-year est.); Percent of households with income of $100,000 or more: 2.2% (2006-2010 5-year est.); Poverty rate: 27.0% (2006-2010 5-year est.).
Education: Percent of population age 25 and over with: High school diploma (including GED) or higher: 84.2% (2006-2010 5-year est.); Bachelor's degree or higher: 8.9% (2006-2010 5-year est.); Master's degree or higher: 3.7% (2006-2010 5-year est.).
Housing: Homeownership rate: 75.5% (2010); Median home value: $72,800 (2006-2010 5-year est.); Median contract rent: $415 per month (2006-2010 5-year est.); Median year structure built: 1960 (2006-2010 5-year est.).
Safety: Violent crime rate: 5.1 per 10,000 population; Property crime rate: 50.6 per 10,000 population (2011).
Transportation: Commute to work: 96.1% car, 0.0% public transportation, 0.8% walk, 0.5% work from home (2006-2010 5-year est.); Travel time to work: 26.3% less than 15 minutes, 36.9% 15 to 30 minutes, 21.2% 30 to 45 minutes, 7.6% 45 to 60 minutes, 8.0% 60 minutes or more (2006-2010 5-year est.)
Additional Information Contacts
Greater Connellsville Chamber of Commerce . . . . (724) 628-5500
    http://www.greaterconnellsville.org

SOUTH UNION (township). Covers a land area of 16.762 square miles and a water area of 0.034 square miles. Located at 39.87° N. Lat; 79.72° W. Long.
Population: 10,223 (1990); 11,337 (2000); 10,681 (2010); Density: 637.2 persons per square mile (2010); Race: 93.4% White, 3.8% Black, 1.2% Asian, 0.1% American Indian/Alaska Native, 0.0% Native Hawaiian/Other Pacific Islander, 1.5% Other, 0.6% Hispanic of any race (2010); Average household size: 2.31 (2010); Median age: 47.9 (2010); Males per 100 females: 87.3 (2010); Marriage status: 24.5% never married, 54.3% now married, 10.8% widowed, 10.4% divorced (2006-2010 5-year est.); Foreign born: 1.5% (2006-2010 5-year est.); Ancestry (includes multiple ancestries): 21.7% German, 20.3% Irish, 19.1% Italian, 12.4% Polish, 12.0% English (2006-2010 5-year est.).
Economy: Single-family building permits issued: 18 (2011); Multi-family building permits issued: 0 (2011); Employment by occupation: 10.9% management, 5.1% professional, 9.0% services, 14.3% sales, 2.6% farming, 9.1% construction, 4.1% production (2006-2010 5-year est.).
Income: Per capita income: $26,093 (2006-2010 5-year est.); Median household income: $45,683 (2006-2010 5-year est.); Average household income: $61,273 (2006-2010 5-year est.); Percent of households with income of $100,000 or more: 18.2% (2006-2010 5-year est.); Poverty rate: 13.9% (2006-2010 5-year est.).
Education: Percent of population age 25 and over with: High school diploma (including GED) or higher: 88.1% (2006-2010 5-year est.); Bachelor's degree or higher: 26.8% (2006-2010 5-year est.); Master's degree or higher: 10.8% (2006-2010 5-year est.).
Housing: Homeownership rate: 73.9% (2010); Median home value: $126,700 (2006-2010 5-year est.); Median contract rent: $458 per month (2006-2010 5-year est.); Median year structure built: 1962 (2006-2010 5-year est.).
Transportation: Commute to work: 94.2% car, 0.2% public transportation, 1.7% walk, 2.6% work from home (2006-2010 5-year est.); Travel time to work: 54.4% less than 15 minutes, 26.4% 15 to 30 minutes, 7.2% 30 to 45 minutes, 6.6% 45 to 60 minutes, 5.4% 60 minutes or more (2006-2010 5-year est.)
Additional Information Contacts
Mansfield Chamber of Commerce, Inc. . . . . (570) 662-3442
　http://www.mansfield.org
South Union Township . . . . (724) 438-5647

SOUTH UNIONTOWN (CDP). Covers a land area of 0.455 square miles and a water area of 0 square miles. Located at 39.89° N. Lat; 79.75° W. Long. Elevation is 1,079 feet.
Population: n/a (1990); n/a (2000); 1,360 (2010); Density: 2,990.8 persons per square mile (2010); Race: 92.5% White, 4.9% Black, 0.1% Asian, 0.3% American Indian/Alaska Native, 0.0% Native Hawaiian/Other Pacific Islander, 2.2% Other, 0.9% Hispanic of any race (2010); Average household size: 2.41 (2010); Median age: 42.2 (2010); Males per 100 females: 92.4 (2010); Marriage status: 32.0% never married, 45.0% now married, 12.6% widowed, 10.4% divorced (2006-2010 5-year est.); Foreign born: 0.0% (2006-2010 5-year est.); Ancestry (includes multiple ancestries): 26.9% Irish, 25.4% German, 12.8% Slovak, 12.3% Italian, 12.3% Polish (2006-2010 5-year est.).
Economy: Employment by occupation: 11.9% management, 2.9% professional, 15.1% services, 20.1% sales, 0.0% farming, 15.0% construction, 5.4% production (2006-2010 5-year est.).
Income: Per capita income: $21,380 (2006-2010 5-year est.); Median household income: $38,445 (2006-2010 5-year est.); Average household income: $47,468 (2006-2010 5-year est.); Percent of households with income of $100,000 or more: 4.6% (2006-2010 5-year est.); Poverty rate: 2.3% (2006-2010 5-year est.).
Education: Percent of population age 25 and over with: High school diploma (including GED) or higher: 88.3% (2006-2010 5-year est.); Bachelor's degree or higher: 19.8% (2006-2010 5-year est.); Master's degree or higher: 7.4% (2006-2010 5-year est.).
Housing: Homeownership rate: 79.5% (2010); Median home value: $85,900 (2006-2010 5-year est.); Median contract rent: $494 per month (2006-2010 5-year est.); Median year structure built: 1951 (2006-2010 5-year est.).
Transportation: Commute to work: 94.5% car, 1.4% public transportation, 0.0% walk, 4.1% work from home (2006-2010 5-year est.); Travel time to work: 43.0% less than 15 minutes, 34.1% 15 to 30 minutes, 6.3% 30 to 45 minutes, 7.3% 45 to 60 minutes, 9.3% 60 minutes or more (2006-2010 5-year est.)

SPRINGFIELD (township). Covers a land area of 59.404 square miles and a water area of 0.227 square miles. Located at 39.98° N. Lat; 79.44° W. Long.
Population: 2,968 (1990); 3,111 (2000); 3,043 (2010); Density: 51.2 persons per square mile (2010); Race: 98.3% White, 0.5% Black, 0.1% Asian, 0.0% American Indian/Alaska Native, 0.0% Native Hawaiian/Other Pacific Islander, 1.1% Other, 0.4% Hispanic of any race (2010); Average household size: 2.63 (2010); Median age: 39.8 (2010); Males per 100 females: 97.9 (2010); Marriage status: 21.3% never married, 65.1% now married, 7.7% widowed, 5.9% divorced (2006-2010 5-year est.); Foreign born: 0.6% (2006-2010 5-year est.); Ancestry (includes multiple ancestries): 40.9% German, 14.6% Irish, 10.0% English, 7.5% American, 6.5% Dutch (2006-2010 5-year est.).
Economy: Employment by occupation: 6.3% management, 2.0% professional, 20.8% services, 10.0% sales, 1.3% farming, 22.6% construction, 12.7% production (2006-2010 5-year est.).
Income: Per capita income: $18,399 (2006-2010 5-year est.); Median household income: $39,263 (2006-2010 5-year est.); Average household income: $47,924 (2006-2010 5-year est.); Percent of households with income of $100,000 or more: 5.1% (2006-2010 5-year est.); Poverty rate: 20.0% (2006-2010 5-year est.).
Education: Percent of population age 25 and over with: High school diploma (including GED) or higher: 76.4% (2006-2010 5-year est.); Bachelor's degree or higher: 6.7% (2006-2010 5-year est.); Master's degree or higher: 2.9% (2006-2010 5-year est.).
Housing: Homeownership rate: 79.1% (2010); Median home value: $89,100 (2006-2010 5-year est.); Median contract rent: $242 per month (2006-2010 5-year est.); Median year structure built: 1974 (2006-2010 5-year est.).
Transportation: Commute to work: 91.0% car, 0.9% public transportation, 2.0% walk, 3.7% work from home (2006-2010 5-year est.); Travel time to work: 20.1% less than 15 minutes, 31.8% 15 to 30 minutes, 16.8% 30 to 45 minutes, 13.8% 45 to 60 minutes, 17.5% 60 minutes or more (2006-2010 5-year est.)
Additional Information Contacts
Greater Connellsville Chamber of Commerce . . . . (724) 628-5500
　http://www.greaterconnellsville.org

SPRINGHILL (township). Covers a land area of 33.780 square miles and a water area of 0.510 square miles. Located at 39.75° N. Lat; 79.84° W. Long. Elevation is 1,053 feet.
Population: 2,800 (1990); 2,974 (2000); 2,907 (2010); Density: 86.1 persons per square mile (2010); Race: 98.1% White, 0.6% Black, 0.1% Asian, 0.3% American Indian/Alaska Native, 0.0% Native Hawaiian/Other Pacific Islander, 0.9% Other, 0.6% Hispanic of any race (2010); Average household size: 2.52 (2010); Median age: 41.2 (2010); Males per 100 females: 94.6 (2010); Marriage status: 23.2% never married, 55.2% now married, 10.0% widowed, 11.6% divorced (2006-2010 5-year est.); Foreign born: 0.0% (2006-2010 5-year est.); Ancestry (includes multiple ancestries): 29.2% Irish, 26.5% German, 14.1% Italian, 6.2% English, 6.1% Polish (2006-2010 5-year est.).
Economy: Employment by occupation: 6.3% management, 1.8% professional, 16.0% services, 9.7% sales, 1.1% farming, 13.7% construction, 7.7% production (2006-2010 5-year est.).
Income: Per capita income: $16,978 (2006-2010 5-year est.); Median household income: $38,005 (2006-2010 5-year est.); Average household income: $44,837 (2006-2010 5-year est.); Percent of households with income of $100,000 or more: 9.9% (2006-2010 5-year est.); Poverty rate: 33.2% (2006-2010 5-year est.).
Education: Percent of population age 25 and over with: High school diploma (including GED) or higher: 80.4% (2006-2010 5-year est.); Bachelor's degree or higher: 9.5% (2006-2010 5-year est.); Master's degree or higher: 3.4% (2006-2010 5-year est.).
Housing: Homeownership rate: 75.0% (2010); Median home value: $66,500 (2006-2010 5-year est.); Median contract rent: $351 per month (2006-2010 5-year est.); Median year structure built: 1965 (2006-2010 5-year est.).
Transportation: Commute to work: 85.8% car, 0.0% public transportation, 2.7% walk, 9.9% work from home (2006-2010 5-year est.); Travel time to work: 17.3% less than 15 minutes, 44.3% 15 to 30 minutes, 26.1% 30 to 45 minutes, 5.3% 45 to 60 minutes, 7.0% 60 minutes or more (2006-2010 5-year est.)
Additional Information Contacts
Greater Connellsville Chamber of Commerce . . . . (724) 628-5500
　http://www.greaterconnellsville.org

STAR JUNCTION (CDP). Covers a land area of 1.188 square miles and a water area of 0.017 square miles. Located at 40.06° N. Lat; 79.77° W. Long. Elevation is 997 feet.

Population: n/a (1990); n/a (2000); 616 (2010); Density: 518.5 persons per square mile (2010); Race: 98.2% White, 0.2% Black, 0.0% Asian, 0.2% American Indian/Alaska Native, 0.0% Native Hawaiian/Other Pacific Islander, 1.4% Other, 0.0% Hispanic of any race (2010); Average household size: 2.37 (2010); Median age: 41.5 (2010); Males per 100 females: 92.5 (2010); Marriage status: 29.2% never married, 48.8% now married, 13.9% widowed, 8.1% divorced (2006-2010 5-year est.); Foreign born: 0.0% (2006-2010 5-year est.); Ancestry (includes multiple ancestries): 15.6% Slovak, 13.2% German, 8.6% Polish, 6.5% Italian, 6.3% English (2006-2010 5-year est.).

Economy: Employment by occupation: 0.0% management, 0.0% professional, 17.6% services, 11.5% sales, 12.1% farming, 18.3% construction, 7.1% production (2006-2010 5-year est.).

Income: Per capita income: $13,994 (2006-2010 5-year est.); Median household income: $24,375 (2006-2010 5-year est.); Average household income: $31,276 (2006-2010 5-year est.); Percent of households with income of $100,000 or more: 1.1% (2006-2010 5-year est.); Poverty rate: 23.9% (2006-2010 5-year est.).

Education: Percent of population age 25 and over with: High school diploma (including GED) or higher: 69.7% (2006-2010 5-year est.); Bachelor's degree or higher: 0.0% (2006-2010 5-year est.); Master's degree or higher: 0.0% (2006-2010 5-year est.).

Housing: Homeownership rate: 58.1% (2010); Median home value: $51,800 (2006-2010 5-year est.); Median contract rent: $401 per month (2006-2010 5-year est.); Median year structure built: before 1940 (2006-2010 5-year est.).

Transportation: Commute to work: 89.4% car, 0.0% public transportation, 0.0% walk, 10.6% work from home (2006-2010 5-year est.); Travel time to work: 53.3% less than 15 minutes, 29.9% 15 to 30 minutes, 14.9% 30 to 45 minutes, 0.0% 45 to 60 minutes, 1.9% 60 minutes or more (2006-2010 5-year est.)

STEWART (township). Covers a land area of 50.402 square miles and a water area of 0.473 square miles. Located at 39.88° N. Lat; 79.48° W. Long.

Population: 734 (1990); 743 (2000); 731 (2010); Density: 14.5 persons per square mile (2010); Race: 98.1% White, 0.0% Black, 0.0% Asian, 0.1% American Indian/Alaska Native, 0.0% Native Hawaiian/Other Pacific Islander, 1.8% Other, 1.0% Hispanic of any race (2010); Average household size: 2.49 (2010); Median age: 44.9 (2010); Males per 100 females: 111.3 (2010); Marriage status: 22.5% never married, 59.1% now married, 11.7% widowed, 6.8% divorced (2006-2010 5-year est.); Foreign born: 1.1% (2006-2010 5-year est.); Ancestry (includes multiple ancestries): 38.8% German, 15.8% Irish, 14.9% English, 12.8% Dutch, 12.5% American (2006-2010 5-year est.).

Economy: Employment by occupation: 2.7% management, 0.0% professional, 16.1% services, 16.5% sales, 4.2% farming, 11.9% construction, 9.6% production (2006-2010 5-year est.).

Income: Per capita income: $17,829 (2006-2010 5-year est.); Median household income: $45,347 (2006-2010 5-year est.); Average household income: $45,852 (2006-2010 5-year est.); Percent of households with income of $100,000 or more: 4.4% (2006-2010 5-year est.); Poverty rate: 12.8% (2006-2010 5-year est.).

Education: Percent of population age 25 and over with: High school diploma (including GED) or higher: 77.6% (2006-2010 5-year est.); Bachelor's degree or higher: 10.9% (2006-2010 5-year est.); Master's degree or higher: 2.0% (2006-2010 5-year est.).

Housing: Homeownership rate: 81.9% (2010); Median home value: $94,200 (2006-2010 5-year est.); Median contract rent: $602 per month (2006-2010 5-year est.); Median year structure built: 1970 (2006-2010 5-year est.).

Transportation: Commute to work: 95.8% car, 0.0% public transportation, 0.0% walk, 4.2% work from home (2006-2010 5-year est.); Travel time to work: 26.0% less than 15 minutes, 23.6% 15 to 30 minutes, 29.2% 30 to 45 minutes, 8.4% 45 to 60 minutes, 12.8% 60 minutes or more (2006-2010 5-year est.)

ULEDI (unincorporated postal area). Zip Code: 15484

Covers a land area of 0.636 square miles and a water area of 0 square miles. Located at 39.89° N. Lat; 79.78° W. Long. Elevation is 1,188 feet. Population: 328 (2010); Density: 515.5 persons per square mile (2010);

Race: 86.9% White, 7.0% Black, 2.1% Asian, 0.0% American Indian/Alaska Native, 0.0% Native Hawaiian/Other Pacific Islander, 4.0% Other, 0.0% Hispanic of any race (2010); Average household size: 2.48 (2010); Median age: 43.7 (2010); Males per 100 females: 95.2 (2010); Homeownership rate: 68.9% (2010)

UNIONTOWN (city). Aka Evans Manor. County seat. Covers a land area of 2.041 square miles and a water area of 0 square miles. Located at 39.90° N. Lat; 79.72° W. Long. Elevation is 1,076 feet.

History: Named for its location on two farms whose owners could not agree on a name. Uniontown was founded by Henry Beeson, a Quaker, in 1769. It was incorporated as a borough in 1796 and as a city in 1916.

Population: 12,034 (1990); 12,422 (2000); 10,372 (2010); Density: 5,082.0 persons per square mile (2010); Race: 77.4% White, 18.1% Black, 0.5% Asian, 0.3% American Indian/Alaska Native, 0.0% Native Hawaiian/Other Pacific Islander, 3.7% Other, 1.4% Hispanic of any race (2010); Average household size: 2.18 (2010); Median age: 40.1 (2010); Males per 100 females: 88.1 (2010); Marriage status: 38.8% never married, 36.7% now married, 9.6% widowed, 14.9% divorced (2006-2010 5-year est.); Foreign born: 1.9% (2006-2010 5-year est.); Ancestry (includes multiple ancestries): 18.6% German, 16.6% Irish, 13.6% Italian, 8.8% Polish, 6.5% Dutch (2006-2010 5-year est.).

Economy: Single-family building permits issued: 2 (2011); Multi-family building permits issued: 0 (2011); Employment by occupation: 6.1% management, 1.3% professional, 15.6% services, 23.9% sales, 2.7% farming, 4.9% construction, 5.0% production (2006-2010 5-year est.).

Income: Per capita income: $20,140 (2006-2010 5-year est.); Median household income: $30,005 (2006-2010 5-year est.); Average household income: $47,292 (2006-2010 5-year est.); Percent of households with income of $100,000 or more: 8.8% (2006-2010 5-year est.); Poverty rate: 28.0% (2006-2010 5-year est.).

Taxes: Total city taxes per capita: $306 (2009); City property taxes per capita: $191 (2009).

Education: Percent of population age 25 and over with: High school diploma (including GED) or higher: 82.3% (2006-2010 5-year est.); Bachelor's degree or higher: 15.4% (2006-2010 5-year est.); Master's degree or higher: 5.7% (2006-2010 5-year est.).

School District(s)

Albert Gallatin Area SD (KG-12)
  2010-11 Enrollment: 3,596 . . . . (724) 564-7190
Fayette County Avts (10-12)
  2010-11 Enrollment: n/a . . . . (724) 437-2721
Laurel Highlands SD (KG-12)
  2010-11 Enrollment: 3,331 . . . . (724) 437-2821
Uniontown Area SD (KG-12)
  2010-11 Enrollment: 3,022 . . . . (724) 438-4501

Four-year College(s)

Pennsylvania State University-Penn State Fayette- Eberly Campus (Public)
  Fall 2010 Enrollment: 942 . . . . (724) 430-4100
  2011-12 Tuition: In-state $13,040; Out-of-state $19,480

Two-year College(s)

Laurel Business Institute (Private, For-profit)
  Fall 2010 Enrollment: 405 . . . . (724) 439-4900
  2011-12 Tuition: In-state $9,379; Out-of-state $9,379

Vocational/Technical School(s)

Fayette County Career & Technical Institute Practical Nursing Program (Public)
  Fall 2010 Enrollment: 113 . . . . (724) 437-2721
  2011-12 Tuition: $6,863

Housing: Homeownership rate: 47.7% (2010); Median home value: $73,000 (2006-2010 5-year est.); Median contract rent: $403 per month (2006-2010 5-year est.); Median year structure built: before 1940 (2006-2010 5-year est.).

Hospitals: Uniontown Hospital (209 beds)

Safety: Violent crime rate: 51.9 per 10,000 population; Property crime rate: 497.8 per 10,000 population (2011).

Newspapers: Herald-Standard (Local news; Circulation 25,635)

Transportation: Commute to work: 89.8% car, 0.0% public transportation, 6.1% walk, 1.8% work from home (2006-2010 5-year est.); Travel time to work: 61.3% less than 15 minutes, 21.3% 15 to 30 minutes, 7.4% 30 to 45 minutes, 3.4% 45 to 60 minutes, 6.6% 60 minutes or more (2006-2010 5-year est.)

Additional Information Contacts

City of Uniontown . . . . (724) 430-4884
  http://www.uniontown.org

Greater Connellsville Chamber of Commerce. . . . . (724) 628-5500
http://www.greaterconnellsville.org

UPPER TYRONE (township).
Covers a land area of 7.799 square miles and a water area of 0.021 square miles. Located at 40.08° N. Lat; 79.59° W. Long.
Population: 1,995 (1990); 2,244 (2000); 2,059 (2010); Density: 264.0 persons per square mile (2010); Race: 98.2% White, 0.8% Black, 0.0% Asian, 0.1% American Indian/Alaska Native, 0.0% Native Hawaiian/Other Pacific Islander, 0.9% Other, 0.2% Hispanic of any race (2010); Average household size: 2.54 (2010); Median age: 42.5 (2010); Males per 100 females: 103.3 (2010); Marriage status: 27.8% never married, 52.2% now married, 4.3% widowed, 15.7% divorced (2006-2010 5-year est.); Foreign born: 0.5% (2006-2010 5-year est.); Ancestry (includes multiple ancestries): 34.4% German, 19.1% English, 17.0% Irish, 13.0% Italian, 10.5% Scotch-Irish (2006-2010 5-year est.).
Economy: Employment by occupation: 4.2% management, 1.2% professional, 14.6% services, 18.9% sales, 2.3% farming, 15.1% construction, 15.6% production (2006-2010 5-year est.).
Income: Per capita income: $20,580 (2006-2010 5-year est.); Median household income: $44,764 (2006-2010 5-year est.); Average household income: $52,127 (2006-2010 5-year est.); Percent of households with income of $100,000 or more: 12.5% (2006-2010 5-year est.); Poverty rate: 12.8% (2006-2010 5-year est.).
Education: Percent of population age 25 and over with: High school diploma (including GED) or higher: 82.7% (2006-2010 5-year est.); Bachelor's degree or higher: 9.7% (2006-2010 5-year est.); Master's degree or higher: 5.2% (2006-2010 5-year est.).
Housing: Homeownership rate: 81.3% (2010); Median home value: $78,500 (2006-2010 5-year est.); Median contract rent: $466 per month (2006-2010 5-year est.); Median year structure built: 1971 (2006-2010 5-year est.).
Transportation: Commute to work: 97.1% car, 0.0% public transportation, 1.9% walk, 0.0% work from home (2006-2010 5-year est.); Travel time to work: 37.2% less than 15 minutes, 25.0% 15 to 30 minutes, 25.1% 30 to 45 minutes, 3.3% 45 to 60 minutes, 9.4% 60 minutes or more (2006-2010 5-year est.)
Additional Information Contacts
Greater Connellsville Chamber of Commerce. . . . . (724) 628-5500
http://www.greaterconnellsville.org

VANDERBILT (borough).
Covers a land area of 0.175 square miles and a water area of 0 square miles. Located at 40.03° N. Lat; 79.66° W. Long. Elevation is 958 feet.
Population: 545 (1990); 553 (2000); 476 (2010); Density: 2,715.6 persons per square mile (2010); Race: 95.8% White, 1.9% Black, 0.0% Asian, 0.0% American Indian/Alaska Native, 0.0% Native Hawaiian/Other Pacific Islander, 2.3% Other, 0.2% Hispanic of any race (2010); Average household size: 2.42 (2010); Median age: 42.0 (2010); Males per 100 females: 86.7 (2010); Marriage status: 25.1% never married, 52.3% now married, 7.8% widowed, 14.7% divorced (2006-2010 5-year est.); Foreign born: 0.0% (2006-2010 5-year est.); Ancestry (includes multiple ancestries): 32.7% German, 29.9% Irish, 18.6% English, 11.6% Italian, 9.8% Dutch (2006-2010 5-year est.).
Economy: Employment by occupation: 3.4% management, 0.0% professional, 28.8% services, 0.0% sales, 0.0% farming, 14.4% construction, 6.8% production (2006-2010 5-year est.).
Income: Per capita income: $15,274 (2006-2010 5-year est.); Median household income: $31,923 (2006-2010 5-year est.); Average household income: $35,315 (2006-2010 5-year est.); Percent of households with income of $100,000 or more: 1.8% (2006-2010 5-year est.); Poverty rate: 11.6% (2006-2010 5-year est.).
Education: Percent of population age 25 and over with: High school diploma (including GED) or higher: 72.2% (2006-2010 5-year est.); Bachelor's degree or higher: 4.0% (2006-2010 5-year est.); Master's degree or higher: 3.0% (2006-2010 5-year est.).
School District(s)
Uniontown Area SD (KG-12)
    2010-11 Enrollment: 3,022 . . . . (724) 438-4501
Housing: Homeownership rate: 71.5% (2010); Median home value: $52,200 (2006-2010 5-year est.); Median contract rent: $272 per month (2006-2010 5-year est.); Median year structure built: before 1940 (2006-2010 5-year est.).
Transportation: Commute to work: 100.0% car, 0.0% public transportation, 0.0% walk, 0.0% work from home (2006-2010 5-year est.);

Travel time to work: 2.8% less than 15 minutes, 76.1% 15 to 30 minutes, 4.2% 30 to 45 minutes, 12.7% 45 to 60 minutes, 4.2% 60 minutes or more (2006-2010 5-year est.)

WASHINGTON (township).
Covers a land area of 9.705 square miles and a water area of 0.176 square miles. Located at 40.11° N. Lat; 79.82° W. Long.
Population: 4,613 (1990); 4,461 (2000); 3,902 (2010); Density: 402.1 persons per square mile (2010); Race: 96.7% White, 1.4% Black, 0.2% Asian, 0.2% American Indian/Alaska Native, 0.1% Native Hawaiian/Other Pacific Islander, 1.4% Other, 0.3% Hispanic of any race (2010); Average household size: 2.28 (2010); Median age: 48.5 (2010); Males per 100 females: 93.1 (2010); Marriage status: 20.7% never married, 56.7% now married, 13.7% widowed, 8.8% divorced (2006-2010 5-year est.); Foreign born: 4.1% (2006-2010 5-year est.); Ancestry (includes multiple ancestries): 21.9% German, 19.0% Italian, 12.2% Polish, 11.6% English, 7.3% Irish (2006-2010 5-year est.).
Economy: Single-family building permits issued: 3 (2011); Multi-family building permits issued: 0 (2011); Employment by occupation: 6.8% management, 1.4% professional, 17.2% services, 14.2% sales, 4.7% farming, 13.1% construction, 7.9% production (2006-2010 5-year est.).
Income: Per capita income: $20,289 (2006-2010 5-year est.); Median household income: $38,750 (2006-2010 5-year est.); Average household income: $45,620 (2006-2010 5-year est.); Percent of households with income of $100,000 or more: 6.4% (2006-2010 5-year est.); Poverty rate: 19.4% (2006-2010 5-year est.).
Education: Percent of population age 25 and over with: High school diploma (including GED) or higher: 83.1% (2006-2010 5-year est.); Bachelor's degree or higher: 15.5% (2006-2010 5-year est.); Master's degree or higher: 4.3% (2006-2010 5-year est.).
Housing: Homeownership rate: 77.3% (2010); Median home value: $87,800 (2006-2010 5-year est.); Median contract rent: $407 per month (2006-2010 5-year est.); Median year structure built: 1957 (2006-2010 5-year est.).
Safety: Violent crime rate: 25.5 per 10,000 population; Property crime rate: 158.4 per 10,000 population (2011).
Transportation: Commute to work: 98.4% car, 0.0% public transportation, 0.6% walk, 0.9% work from home (2006-2010 5-year est.); Travel time to work: 38.0% less than 15 minutes, 29.4% 15 to 30 minutes, 20.2% 30 to 45 minutes, 5.5% 45 to 60 minutes, 6.9% 60 minutes or more (2006-2010 5-year est.)
Additional Information Contacts
Greater Connellsville Chamber of Commerce. . . . . (724) 628-5500
http://www.greaterconnellsville.org

WEST LEISENRING (unincorporated postal area)
Zip Code: 15489
    Covers a land area of 0.933 square miles and a water area of 0 square miles. Located at 39.96° N. Lat; 79.69° W. Long. Elevation is 1,043 feet.
    Population: 389 (2010); Density: 416.8 persons per square mile (2010); Race: 99.2% White, 0.3% Black, 0.0% Asian, 0.0% American Indian/Alaska Native, 0.0% Native Hawaiian/Other Pacific Islander, 0.5% Other, 0.5% Hispanic of any race (2010); Average household size: 2.52 (2010); Median age: 40.1 (2010); Males per 100 females: 96.5 (2010); Homeownership rate: 77.7% (2010)

WHARTON (township).
Covers a land area of 91.620 square miles and a water area of 0.171 square miles. Located at 39.78° N. Lat; 79.61° W. Long.
Population: 3,390 (1990); 4,145 (2000); 3,575 (2010); Density: 39.0 persons per square mile (2010); Race: 98.9% White, 0.1% Black, 0.1% Asian, 0.1% American Indian/Alaska Native, 0.0% Native Hawaiian/Other Pacific Islander, 0.8% Other, 0.3% Hispanic of any race (2010); Average household size: 2.33 (2010); Median age: 45.5 (2010); Males per 100 females: 96.3 (2010); Marriage status: 34.3% never married, 52.1% now married, 4.5% widowed, 9.1% divorced (2006-2010 5-year est.); Foreign born: 3.8% (2006-2010 5-year est.); Ancestry (includes multiple ancestries): 31.1% German, 22.3% Irish, 10.0% English, 8.5% Italian, 6.6% Dutch (2006-2010 5-year est.).
Economy: Employment by occupation: 17.5% management, 0.6% professional, 10.6% services, 10.4% sales, 6.5% farming, 8.2% construction, 4.1% production (2006-2010 5-year est.).
Income: Per capita income: $20,075 (2006-2010 5-year est.); Median household income: $58,074 (2006-2010 5-year est.); Average household income: $57,234 (2006-2010 5-year est.); Percent of households with

income of $100,000 or more: 13.7% (2006-2010 5-year est.); Poverty rate: 23.2% (2006-2010 5-year est.).

Education: Percent of population age 25 and over with: High school diploma (including GED) or higher: 80.1% (2006-2010 5-year est.); Bachelor's degree or higher: 21.5% (2006-2010 5-year est.); Master's degree or higher: 6.0% (2006-2010 5-year est.).

Housing: Homeownership rate: 78.6% (2010); Median home value: $142,700 (2006-2010 5-year est.); Median contract rent: $414 per month (2006-2010 5-year est.); Median year structure built: 1972 (2006-2010 5-year est.).

Transportation: Commute to work: 95.7% car, 0.0% public transportation, 2.5% walk, 1.8% work from home (2006-2010 5-year est.); Travel time to work: 34.8% less than 15 minutes, 29.2% 15 to 30 minutes, 11.1% 30 to 45 minutes, 18.7% 45 to 60 minutes, 6.3% 60 minutes or more (2006-2010 5-year est.)

Additional Information Contacts

Cameron County Chamber of Commerce . . . . (814) 486-4314
    http://www.cameroncountychamber.org/#

WICKHAVEN (unincorporated postal area)

Zip Code: 15492

Covers a land area of 0.602 square miles and a water area of 0.064 square miles. Located at 40.11° N. Lat; 79.76° W. Long. Elevation is 981 feet. Population: 108 (2010); Density: 179.2 persons per square mile (2010); Race: 100.0% White, 0.0% Black, 0.0% Asian, 0.0% American Indian/Alaska Native, 0.0% Native Hawaiian/Other Pacific Islander, 0.0% Other, 0.0% Hispanic of any race (2010); Average household size: 2.25 (2010); Median age: 43.5 (2010); Males per 100 females: 107.7 (2010); Homeownership rate: 89.6% (2010)

Forest County

Located in northwestern Pennsylvania; drained by the Allegheny and Clarion Rivers. Covers a land area of 427.185 square miles, a water area of 3.311 square miles, and is located in the Eastern Time Zone at 41.51° N. Lat., 79.25° W. Long. The county was founded in 1848. County seat is Tionesta.

Weather Station: Tionesta 2 SE Lake   Elevation: 1,200 feet

	Jan	Feb	Mar	Apr	May	Jun	Jul	Aug	Sep	Oct	Nov	Dec
High	33	36	45	59	70	78	81	80	73	61	49	37
Low	15	15	22	32	43	52	57	56	49	37	30	20
Precip	3.0	2.3	3.2	3.6	4.2	4.8	5.1	4.2	4.2	3.3	3.6	3.1
Snow	13.4	9.3	8.8	1.4	0.0	0.0	0.0	0.0	0.0	0.2	3.2	11.5

High and Low temperatures in degrees Fahrenheit; Precipitation and Snow in inches

Population: 4,802 (1990); 4,946 (2000); 7,716 (2010); Race: 76.9% White, 18.0% Black, 0.2% Asian, 0.2% American Indian/Alaska Native, 0.0% Native Hawaiian/Other Pacific Islander, 4.7% Other, 5.4% Hispanic of any race (2010); Density: 18.1 persons per square mile (2010); Average household size: 2.08 (2010); Median age: 43.0 (2010); Males per 100 females: 202.4 (2010).

Religion: Six largest groups: 16.7% Methodist/Pietist, 6.3% Catholicism, 3.1% Holiness, 2.0% European Free-Church, 1.8% Lutheran, 1.5% Non-Denominational (2010)

Economy: Unemployment rate: 10.2% (August 2012); Total civilian labor force: 2,617 (August 2012); Leading industries: 18.1% manufacturing; 2.5% construction; 2.2% other services (except public administration) (2010); Farms: 84 totaling 10,728 acres (2007); Companies that employ 500 or more persons: 0 (2010); Companies that employ 100 to 499 persons: 3 (2010); Companies that employ less than 100 persons: 110 (2010); Black-owned businesses: n/a (2007); Hispanic-owned businesses: n/a (2007); Asian-owned businesses: n/a (2007); Women-owned businesses: n/a (2007); Retail sales per capita: $5,293 (2011). Single-family building permits issued: 7 (2011); Multi-family building permits issued: 0 (2011).

Income: Per capita income: $14,325 (2006-2010 5-year est.); Median household income: $35,150 (2006-2010 5-year est.); Average household income: $42,062 (2006-2010 5-year est.); Percent of households with income of $100,000 or more: 5.4% (2006-2010 5-year est.); Poverty rate: 11.7% (2006-2010 5-year est.); Bankruptcy rate: 2.36% (2011).

Education: Percent of population age 25 and over with: High school diploma (including GED) or higher: 80.7% (2006-2010 5-year est.); Bachelor's degree or higher: 9.6% (2006-2010 5-year est.); Master's degree or higher: 5.2% (2006-2010 5-year est.).

Housing: Homeownership rate: 82.0% (2010); Median home value: $79,700 (2006-2010 5-year est.); Median contract rent: $342 per month (2006-2010 5-year est.); Median year structure built: 1971 (2006-2010 5-year est.)

Health: Birth rate: 42.2 per 10,000 population (2011); Death rate: 123.9 per 10,000 population (2011); Age-adjusted cancer mortality rate: 254.3 deaths per 100,000 population (2009); Number of physicians: 1.3 per 10,000 population (2010); Hospital beds: 0.0 per 10,000 population (2008); Hospital admissions: 0.0 per 10,000 population (2008).

Elections: 2012 Presidential election results: 38.8% Obama, 59.8% Romney

Additional Information Contacts

Forest County Government . . . . (814) 755-3537
    http://www.co.forest.pa.us

Forest County Communities

BARNETT (township). Covers a land area of 34.342 square miles and a water area of 0.009 square miles. Located at 41.37° N. Lat; 79.14° W. Long.

Population: 400 (1990); 349 (2000); 361 (2010); Density: 10.5 persons per square mile (2010); Race: 97.5% White, 1.4% Black, 0.0% Asian, 0.0% American Indian/Alaska Native, 0.0% Native Hawaiian/Other Pacific Islander, 1.1% Other, 5.5% Hispanic of any race (2010); Average household size: 1.88 (2010); Median age: 57.2 (2010); Males per 100 females: 96.2 (2010); Marriage status: 24.2% never married, 56.1% now married, 16.0% widowed, 3.8% divorced (2006-2010 5-year est.); Foreign born: 0.0% (2006-2010 5-year est.); Ancestry (includes multiple ancestries): 47.4% German, 13.8% French, 12.1% Irish, 8.6% Dutch, 8.4% Italian (2006-2010 5-year est.).

Economy: Single-family building permits issued: 0 (2011); Multi-family building permits issued: 0 (2011); Employment by occupation: 4.9% management, 3.1% professional, 15.4% services, 11.1% sales, 3.1% farming, 4.3% construction, 27.8% production (2006-2010 5-year est.).

Income: Per capita income: $22,437 (2006-2010 5-year est.); Median household income: $32,500 (2006-2010 5-year est.); Average household income: $46,322 (2006-2010 5-year est.); Percent of households with income of $100,000 or more: 11.9% (2006-2010 5-year est.); Poverty rate: 4.7% (2006-2010 5-year est.).

Education: Percent of population age 25 and over with: High school diploma (including GED) or higher: 83.8% (2006-2010 5-year est.); Bachelor's degree or higher: 12.0% (2006-2010 5-year est.); Master's degree or higher: 5.3% (2006-2010 5-year est.).

Housing: Homeownership rate: 87.0% (2010); Median home value: $105,700 (2006-2010 5-year est.); Median contract rent: n/a per month (2006-2010 5-year est.); Median year structure built: 1974 (2006-2010 5-year est.).

Transportation: Commute to work: 86.4% car, 0.0% public transportation, 7.4% walk, 4.9% work from home (2006-2010 5-year est.); Travel time to work: 20.1% less than 15 minutes, 37.0% 15 to 30 minutes, 3.9% 30 to 45 minutes, 35.7% 45 to 60 minutes, 3.2% 60 minutes or more (2006-2010 5-year est.)

CLARINGTON (unincorporated postal area)

Zip Code: 15828

Covers a land area of 23.483 square miles and a water area of 0.394 square miles. Located at 41.38° N. Lat; 79.11° W. Long. Population: 286 (2010); Density: 12.2 persons per square mile (2010); Race: 97.2% White, 1.4% Black, 0.0% Asian, 0.0% American Indian/Alaska Native, 0.3% Native Hawaiian/Other Pacific Islander, 1.1% Other, 1.7% Hispanic of any race (2010); Average household size: 2.06 (2010); Median age: 54.3 (2010); Males per 100 females: 98.6 (2010); Homeownership rate: 91.4% (2010)

COOKSBURG (unincorporated postal area)

Zip Code: 16217

Covers a land area of 5.639 square miles and a water area of 0.044 square miles. Located at 41.33° N. Lat; 79.17° W. Long. Population: 101 (2010); Density: 17.9 persons per square mile (2010); Race: 100.0% White, 0.0% Black, 0.0% Asian, 0.0% American Indian/Alaska Native, 0.0% Native Hawaiian/Other Pacific Islander, 0.0% Other, 3.0% Hispanic of any race (2010); Average household size: 2.06 (2010); Median age: 55.5 (2010); Males per 100 females: 87.0 (2010); Homeownership rate: 77.5% (2010)

EAST HICKORY (unincorporated postal area)

Zip Code: 16321

Covers a land area of 1.273 square miles and a water area of 0 square miles. Located at 41.57° N. Lat; 79.39° W. Long. Elevation is 1,079 feet. Population: 76 (2010); Density: 59.7 persons per square mile (2010); Race: 98.7% White, 0.0% Black, 0.0% Asian, 1.3% American Indian/Alaska Native, 0.0% Native Hawaiian/Other Pacific Islander, 0.0% Other, 0.0% Hispanic of any race (2010); Average household size: 2.11 (2010); Median age: 48.5 (2010); Males per 100 females: 145.2 (2010); Homeownership rate: 91.6% (2010)

ENDEAVOR (unincorporated postal area)

Zip Code: 16322

Covers a land area of 6.105 square miles and a water area of 0 square miles. Located at 41.59° N. Lat; 79.37° W. Long. Elevation is 1,112 feet. Population: 158 (2010); Density: 25.9 persons per square mile (2010); Race: 96.8% White, 0.0% Black, 0.0% Asian, 0.0% American Indian/Alaska Native, 0.0% Native Hawaiian/Other Pacific Islander, 3.2% Other, 0.0% Hispanic of any race (2010); Average household size: 2.19 (2010); Median age: 48.0 (2010); Males per 100 females: 119.4 (2010); Homeownership rate: 90.3% (2010)

GREEN (township).

Covers a land area of 42.042 square miles and a water area of 0.361 square miles. Located at 41.48° N. Lat; 79.34° W. Long.

Population: 335 (1990); 397 (2000); 522 (2010); Density: 12.4 persons per square mile (2010); Race: 98.1% White, 0.0% Black, 0.0% Asian, 0.6% American Indian/Alaska Native, 0.0% Native Hawaiian/Other Pacific Islander, 1.3% Other, 0.8% Hispanic of any race (2010); Average household size: 2.17 (2010); Median age: 50.7 (2010); Males per 100 females: 116.6 (2010); Marriage status: 37.0% never married, 37.5% now married, 9.6% widowed, 15.9% divorced (2006-2010 5-year est.); Foreign born: 0.0% (2006-2010 5-year est.); Ancestry (includes multiple ancestries): 42.9% German, 31.5% Irish, 20.2% American, 12.4% English, 5.9% Italian (2006-2010 5-year est.).
Economy: Single-family building permits issued: 1 (2011); Multi-family building permits issued: 0 (2011); Employment by occupation: 0.0% management, 0.0% professional, 9.3% services, 26.2% sales, 3.5% farming, 18.6% construction, 8.1% production (2006-2010 5-year est.).
Income: Per capita income: $15,310 (2006-2010 5-year est.); Median household income: $30,000 (2006-2010 5-year est.); Average household income: $32,164 (2006-2010 5-year est.); Percent of households with income of $100,000 or more: 0.7% (2006-2010 5-year est.); Poverty rate: 19.3% (2006-2010 5-year est.).
Education: Percent of population age 25 and over with: High school diploma (including GED) or higher: 69.8% (2006-2010 5-year est.); Bachelor's degree or higher: 2.7% (2006-2010 5-year est.); Master's degree or higher: 0.0% (2006-2010 5-year est.).
Housing: Homeownership rate: 93.8% (2010); Median home value: $50,900 (2006-2010 5-year est.); Median contract rent: $240 per month (2006-2010 5-year est.); Median year structure built: 1972 (2006-2010 5-year est.).
Transportation: Commute to work: 100.0% car, 0.0% public transportation, 0.0% walk, 0.0% work from home (2006-2010 5-year est.); Travel time to work: 17.4% less than 15 minutes, 40.1% 15 to 30 minutes, 23.8% 30 to 45 minutes, 18.6% 45 to 60 minutes, 0.0% 60 minutes or more (2006-2010 5-year est.)

HARMONY (township).

Covers a land area of 34.070 square miles and a water area of 0.439 square miles. Located at 41.57° N. Lat; 79.46° W. Long.

Population: 499 (1990); 511 (2000); 666 (2010); Density: 19.5 persons per square mile (2010); Race: 99.2% White, 0.0% Black, 0.3% Asian, 0.2% American Indian/Alaska Native, 0.0% Native Hawaiian/Other Pacific Islander, 0.3% Other, 0.2% Hispanic of any race (2010); Average household size: 2.23 (2010); Median age: 50.9 (2010); Males per 100 females: 122.7 (2010); Marriage status: 38.4% never married, 50.9% now married, 3.2% widowed, 7.5% divorced (2006-2010 5-year est.); Foreign born: 0.0% (2006-2010 5-year est.); Ancestry (includes multiple ancestries): 50.8% German, 19.0% Irish, 10.2% Dutch, 8.2% Scotch-Irish, 5.5% Polish (2006-2010 5-year est.).
Economy: Single-family building permits issued: 0 (2011); Multi-family building permits issued: 0 (2011); Employment by occupation: 8.4% management, 0.0% professional, 28.6% services, 11.0% sales, 8.1% farming, 5.5% construction, 5.2% production (2006-2010 5-year est.).

Income: Per capita income: $14,959 (2006-2010 5-year est.); Median household income: $36,806 (2006-2010 5-year est.); Average household income: $44,583 (2006-2010 5-year est.); Percent of households with income of $100,000 or more: 8.8% (2006-2010 5-year est.); Poverty rate: 13.8% (2006-2010 5-year est.).
Education: Percent of population age 25 and over with: High school diploma (including GED) or higher: 90.6% (2006-2010 5-year est.); Bachelor's degree or higher: 6.5% (2006-2010 5-year est.); Master's degree or higher: 2.7% (2006-2010 5-year est.).
Housing: Homeownership rate: 89.0% (2010); Median home value: $69,400 (2006-2010 5-year est.); Median contract rent: $606 per month (2006-2010 5-year est.); Median year structure built: 1972 (2006-2010 5-year est.).
Transportation: Commute to work: 93.4% car, 0.0% public transportation, 4.0% walk, 1.7% work from home (2006-2010 5-year est.); Travel time to work: 47.1% less than 15 minutes, 21.5% 15 to 30 minutes, 18.5% 30 to 45 minutes, 5.0% 45 to 60 minutes, 7.9% 60 minutes or more (2006-2010 5-year est.)

HICKORY (township).

Covers a land area of 37.600 square miles and a water area of 0.421 square miles. Located at 41.58° N. Lat; 79.36° W. Long.

Population: 513 (1990); 525 (2000); 558 (2010); Density: 14.8 persons per square mile (2010); Race: 98.2% White, 0.0% Black, 0.2% Asian, 0.2% American Indian/Alaska Native, 0.0% Native Hawaiian/Other Pacific Islander, 1.4% Other, 1.3% Hispanic of any race (2010); Average household size: 2.11 (2010); Median age: 51.0 (2010); Males per 100 females: 124.1 (2010); Marriage status: 23.8% never married, 59.5% now married, 1.8% widowed, 14.8% divorced (2006-2010 5-year est.); Foreign born: 1.1% (2006-2010 5-year est.); Ancestry (includes multiple ancestries): 40.9% German, 20.5% Irish, 12.1% Italian, 10.1% English, 5.4% Swedish (2006-2010 5-year est.).
Economy: Single-family building permits issued: 0 (2011); Multi-family building permits issued: 0 (2011); Employment by occupation: 8.5% management, 0.0% professional, 15.3% services, 18.7% sales, 4.3% farming, 11.9% construction, 13.2% production (2006-2010 5-year est.).
Income: Per capita income: $14,281 (2006-2010 5-year est.); Median household income: $30,521 (2006-2010 5-year est.); Average household income: $34,828 (2006-2010 5-year est.); Percent of households with income of $100,000 or more: n/a (2006-2010 5-year est.); Poverty rate: 22.4% (2006-2010 5-year est.).
Education: Percent of population age 25 and over with: High school diploma (including GED) or higher: 79.4% (2006-2010 5-year est.); Bachelor's degree or higher: 5.5% (2006-2010 5-year est.); Master's degree or higher: 2.5% (2006-2010 5-year est.).
Housing: Homeownership rate: 88.7% (2010); Median home value: $73,800 (2006-2010 5-year est.); Median contract rent: n/a per month (2006-2010 5-year est.); Median year structure built: 1972 (2006-2010 5-year est.).
Transportation: Commute to work: 92.5% car, 0.0% public transportation, 2.2% walk, 3.5% work from home (2006-2010 5-year est.); Travel time to work: 27.1% less than 15 minutes, 33.5% 15 to 30 minutes, 10.1% 30 to 45 minutes, 11.0% 45 to 60 minutes, 18.3% 60 minutes or more (2006-2010 5-year est.)

HOWE (township).

Covers a land area of 87.509 square miles and a water area of 0.001 square miles. Located at 41.58° N. Lat; 79.08° W. Long.

Population: 300 (1990); 417 (2000); 405 (2010); Density: 4.6 persons per square mile (2010); Race: 64.7% White, 34.6% Black, 0.2% Asian, 0.0% American Indian/Alaska Native, 0.0% Native Hawaiian/Other Pacific Islander, 0.5% Other, 8.6% Hispanic of any race (2010); Average household size: 1.78 (2010); Median age: 18.6 (2010); Males per 100 females: 412.7 (2010); Marriage status: 12.8% never married, 45.0% now married, 16.1% widowed, 26.1% divorced (2006-2010 5-year est.); Foreign born: 0.0% (2006-2010 5-year est.); Ancestry (includes multiple ancestries): 32.4% German, 22.7% English, 18.9% Irish, 8.1% Italian, 4.9% Scotch-Irish (2006-2010 5-year est.).
Economy: Single-family building permits issued: 0 (2011); Multi-family building permits issued: 0 (2011); Employment by occupation: 12.9% management, 0.0% professional, 4.3% services, 35.7% sales, 0.0% farming, 4.3% construction, 0.0% production (2006-2010 5-year est.).
Income: Per capita income: $29,333 (2006-2010 5-year est.); Median household income: $50,000 (2006-2010 5-year est.); Average household income: $46,726 (2006-2010 5-year est.); Percent of households with

income of $100,000 or more: n/a (2006-2010 5-year est.); Poverty rate: 6.5% (2006-2010 5-year est.).

Education: Percent of population age 25 and over with: High school diploma (including GED) or higher: 88.5% (2006-2010 5-year est.); Bachelor's degree or higher: 5.2% (2006-2010 5-year est.); Master's degree or higher: 4.6% (2006-2010 5-year est.).

Housing: Homeownership rate: 90.0% (2010); Median home value: $88,100 (2006-2010 5-year est.); Median contract rent: $583 per month (2006-2010 5-year est.); Median year structure built: 1967 (2006-2010 5-year est.).

Transportation: Commute to work: 100.0% car, 0.0% public transportation, 0.0% walk, 0.0% work from home (2006-2010 5-year est.); Travel time to work: 14.3% less than 15 minutes, 30.0% 15 to 30 minutes, 52.9% 30 to 45 minutes, 2.9% 45 to 60 minutes, 0.0% 60 minutes or more (2006-2010 5-year est.)

Additional Information Contacts

Kane Area Chamber of Commerce . . . . (814) 837-6565
  http://www.kanepa.com

JENKS (township). Covers a land area of 84.445 square miles and a water area of 0.170 square miles. Located at 41.48° N. Lat; 79.10° W. Long.

Population: 1,321 (1990); 1,261 (2000); 3,629 (2010); Density: 43.0 persons per square mile (2010); Race: 56.6% White, 34.3% Black, 0.2% Asian, 0.2% American Indian/Alaska Native, 0.0% Native Hawaiian/Other Pacific Islander, 8.7% Other, 9.2% Hispanic of any race (2010); Average household size: 2.12 (2010); Median age: 35.3 (2010); Males per 100 females: 402.6 (2010); Marriage status: 36.9% never married, 43.6% now married, 5.0% widowed, 14.5% divorced (2006-2010 5-year est.); Foreign born: 1.2% (2006-2010 5-year est.); Ancestry (includes multiple ancestries): 17.6% German, 6.7% English, 6.2% Irish, 3.3% Polish, 3.0% Italian (2006-2010 5-year est.).

Economy: Single-family building permits issued: 1 (2011); Multi-family building permits issued: 0 (2011); Employment by occupation: 3.8% management, 9.6% professional, 13.9% services, 16.9% sales, 0.0% farming, 6.6% construction, 4.9% production (2006-2010 5-year est.).

Income: Per capita income: $9,612 (2006-2010 5-year est.); Median household income: $36,656 (2006-2010 5-year est.); Average household income: $41,370 (2006-2010 5-year est.); Percent of households with income of $100,000 or more: 3.8% (2006-2010 5-year est.); Poverty rate: 9.7% (2006-2010 5-year est.).

Taxes: Total city taxes per capita: $86 (2009); City property taxes per capita: $46 (2009).

Education: Percent of population age 25 and over with: High school diploma (including GED) or higher: 76.8% (2006-2010 5-year est.); Bachelor's degree or higher: 10.1% (2006-2010 5-year est.); Master's degree or higher: 6.4% (2006-2010 5-year est.).

Housing: Homeownership rate: 71.7% (2010); Median home value: $81,600 (2006-2010 5-year est.); Median contract rent: $315 per month (2006-2010 5-year est.); Median year structure built: 1963 (2006-2010 5-year est.).

Transportation: Commute to work: 87.6% car, 0.0% public transportation, 5.0% walk, 4.0% work from home (2006-2010 5-year est.); Travel time to work: 53.6% less than 15 minutes, 19.1% 15 to 30 minutes, 8.5% 30 to 45 minutes, 11.1% 45 to 60 minutes, 7.7% 60 minutes or more (2006-2010 5-year est.)

Additional Information Contacts

Punxsutawney Area Chamber of Commerce . . . . (814) 938-7700
  http://www.punxsutawney.com

KINGSLEY (township). Covers a land area of 60.826 square miles and a water area of 0.430 square miles. Located at 41.54° N. Lat; 79.27° W. Long.

Population: 218 (1990); 261 (2000); 363 (2010); Density: 6.0 persons per square mile (2010); Race: 99.4% White, 0.0% Black, 0.0% Asian, 0.3% American Indian/Alaska Native, 0.0% Native Hawaiian/Other Pacific Islander, 0.3% Other, 0.0% Hispanic of any race (2010); Average household size: 1.88 (2010); Median age: 55.8 (2010); Males per 100 females: 121.3 (2010); Marriage status: 23.9% never married, 46.4% now married, 7.8% widowed, 21.8% divorced (2006-2010 5-year est.); Foreign born: 0.7% (2006-2010 5-year est.); Ancestry (includes multiple ancestries): 43.1% German, 11.8% American, 9.2% Irish, 9.2% Polish, 6.9% English (2006-2010 5-year est.).

Economy: Single-family building permits issued: 0 (2011); Multi-family building permits issued: 0 (2011); Employment by occupation: 6.3%

management, 0.0% professional, 11.6% services, 13.7% sales, 12.6% farming, 18.9% construction, 11.6% production (2006-2010 5-year est.).

Income: Per capita income: $18,328 (2006-2010 5-year est.); Median household income: $26,136 (2006-2010 5-year est.); Average household income: $36,477 (2006-2010 5-year est.); Percent of households with income of $100,000 or more: 3.2% (2006-2010 5-year est.); Poverty rate: 12.7% (2006-2010 5-year est.).

Education: Percent of population age 25 and over with: High school diploma (including GED) or higher: 78.2% (2006-2010 5-year est.); Bachelor's degree or higher: 1.5% (2006-2010 5-year est.); Master's degree or higher: 0.0% (2006-2010 5-year est.).

Housing: Homeownership rate: 92.3% (2010); Median home value: $67,200 (2006-2010 5-year est.); Median contract rent: $369 per month (2006-2010 5-year est.); Median year structure built: 1973 (2006-2010 5-year est.).

Transportation: Commute to work: 93.7% car, 0.0% public transportation, 3.2% walk, 0.0% work from home (2006-2010 5-year est.); Travel time to work: 28.4% less than 15 minutes, 16.8% 15 to 30 minutes, 10.5% 30 to 45 minutes, 16.8% 45 to 60 minutes, 27.4% 60 minutes or more (2006-2010 5-year est.)

MARIENVILLE (CDP). Covers a land area of 6.045 square miles and a water area of 0 square miles. Located at 41.47° N. Lat; 79.12° W. Long. Elevation is 1,732 feet.

Population: n/a (1990); n/a (2000); 3,137 (2010); Density: 518.9 persons per square mile (2010); Race: 50.1% White, 39.6% Black, 0.2% Asian, 0.1% American Indian/Alaska Native, 0.0% Native Hawaiian/Other Pacific Islander, 10.0% Other, 10.3% Hispanic of any race (2010); Average household size: 2.12 (2010); Median age: 33.4 (2010); Males per 100 females: 549.5 (2010); Marriage status: 17.4% never married, 50.1% now married, 15.6% widowed, 16.9% divorced (2006-2010 5-year est.); Foreign born: 0.0% (2006-2010 5-year est.); Ancestry (includes multiple ancestries): 52.1% German, 24.7% English, 16.3% Irish, 9.4% Polish, 5.0% Italian (2006-2010 5-year est.).

Economy: Employment by occupation: 2.6% management, 7.5% professional, 10.1% services, 23.8% sales, 0.0% farming, 2.2% construction, 4.4% production (2006-2010 5-year est.).

Income: Per capita income: $16,844 (2006-2010 5-year est.); Median household income: $35,580 (2006-2010 5-year est.); Average household income: $41,280 (2006-2010 5-year est.); Percent of households with income of $100,000 or more: 4.5% (2006-2010 5-year est.); Poverty rate: 5.5% (2006-2010 5-year est.).

Education: Percent of population age 25 and over with: High school diploma (including GED) or higher: 87.9% (2006-2010 5-year est.); Bachelor's degree or higher: 18.5% (2006-2010 5-year est.); Master's degree or higher: 7.2% (2006-2010 5-year est.).

School District(s)

Forest Area SD (PK-12)
  2010-11 Enrollment: 558 . . . . (814) 755-4491

Housing: Homeownership rate: 64.5% (2010); Median home value: $76,500 (2006-2010 5-year est.); Median contract rent: $308 per month (2006-2010 5-year est.); Median year structure built: 1961 (2006-2010 5-year est.).

Transportation: Commute to work: 82.6% car, 0.0% public transportation, 6.9% walk, 4.1% work from home (2006-2010 5-year est.); Travel time to work: 59.3% less than 15 minutes, 8.1% 15 to 30 minutes, 11.5% 30 to 45 minutes, 18.2% 45 to 60 minutes, 2.9% 60 minutes or more (2006-2010 5-year est.)

TIONESTA (borough). County seat. Covers a land area of 1.375 square miles and a water area of <.001 square miles. Located at 41.50° N. Lat; 79.45° W. Long. Elevation is 1,086 feet.

Population: 634 (1990); 615 (2000); 483 (2010); Density: 351.4 persons per square mile (2010); Race: 98.8% White, 0.2% Black, 0.0% Asian, 0.0% American Indian/Alaska Native, 0.2% Native Hawaiian/Other Pacific Islander, 0.8% Other, 0.8% Hispanic of any race (2010); Average household size: 2.00 (2010); Median age: 54.5 (2010); Males per 100 females: 93.2 (2010); Marriage status: 23.5% never married, 55.4% now married, 10.8% widowed, 10.3% divorced (2006-2010 5-year est.); Foreign born: 2.9% (2006-2010 5-year est.); Ancestry (includes multiple ancestries): 36.7% German, 17.6% Irish, 15.1% English, 5.7% Dutch, 4.4% American (2006-2010 5-year est.).

Economy: Single-family building permits issued: 0 (2011); Multi-family building permits issued: 0 (2011); Employment by occupation: 3.6%

management, 1.4% professional, 20.5% services, 20.5% sales, 0.0% farming, 18.6% construction, 4.1% production (2006-2010 5-year est.).
Income: Per capita income: $23,697 (2006-2010 5-year est.); Median household income: $29,911 (2006-2010 5-year est.); Average household income: $44,415 (2006-2010 5-year est.); Percent of households with income of $100,000 or more: 9.4% (2006-2010 5-year est.); Poverty rate: 10.3% (2006-2010 5-year est.).
Education: Percent of population age 25 and over with: High school diploma (including GED) or higher: 90.7% (2006-2010 5-year est.); Bachelor's degree or higher: 16.9% (2006-2010 5-year est.); Master's degree or higher: 8.1% (2006-2010 5-year est.).

School District(s)
Forest Area SD (PK-12)
   2010-11 Enrollment: 558. . . . . (814) 755-4491
North Clarion County SD (PK-12)
   2010-11 Enrollment: 614. . . . . (814) 744-8536
Housing: Homeownership rate: 63.7% (2010); Median home value: $90,000 (2006-2010 5-year est.); Median contract rent: $252 per month (2006-2010 5-year est.); Median year structure built: 1959 (2006-2010 5-year est.).
Newspapers: Forest Press (Community news; Circulation 4,500)
Transportation: Commute to work: 77.9% car, 0.0% public transportation, 20.2% walk, 1.9% work from home (2006-2010 5-year est.); Travel time to work: 54.1% less than 15 minutes, 13.4% 15 to 30 minutes, 28.2% 30 to 45 minutes, 4.3% 45 to 60 minutes, 0.0% 60 minutes or more (2006-2010 5-year est.)

TIONESTA (township).
Covers a land area of 44.975 square miles and a water area of 1.481 square miles. Located at 41.47° N. Lat; 79.46° W. Long. Elevation is 1,086 feet.
Population: 582 (1990); 610 (2000); 729 (2010); Density: 16.2 persons per square mile (2010); Race: 97.3% White, 0.0% Black, 0.1% Asian, 0.0% American Indian/Alaska Native, 0.0% Native Hawaiian/Other Pacific Islander, 2.6% Other, 1.8% Hispanic of any race (2010); Average household size: 2.15 (2010); Median age: 49.2 (2010); Males per 100 females: 100.3 (2010); Marriage status: 18.9% never married, 67.7% now married, 6.5% widowed, 6.9% divorced (2006-2010 5-year est.); Foreign born: 0.6% (2006-2010 5-year est.); Ancestry (includes multiple ancestries): 52.7% German, 20.4% Irish, 15.1% English, 9.8% Dutch, 6.6% French (2006-2010 5-year est.).
Economy: Single-family building permits issued: 5 (2011); Multi-family building permits issued: 0 (2011); Employment by occupation: 9.5% management, 0.0% professional, 12.6% services, 21.2% sales, 0.0% farming, 15.2% construction, 12.6% production (2006-2010 5-year est.).
Income: Per capita income: $18,254 (2006-2010 5-year est.); Median household income: $44,231 (2006-2010 5-year est.); Average household income: $48,946 (2006-2010 5-year est.); Percent of households with income of $100,000 or more: 6.7% (2006-2010 5-year est.); Poverty rate: 4.9% (2006-2010 5-year est.).
Education: Percent of population age 25 and over with: High school diploma (including GED) or higher: 86.4% (2006-2010 5-year est.); Bachelor's degree or higher: 17.8% (2006-2010 5-year est.); Master's degree or higher: 8.8% (2006-2010 5-year est.).
Housing: Homeownership rate: 84.4% (2010); Median home value: $90,400 (2006-2010 5-year est.); Median contract rent: $388 per month (2006-2010 5-year est.); Median year structure built: 1973 (2006-2010 5-year est.).
Newspapers: Forest Press (Community news; Circulation 4,500)
Transportation: Commute to work: 94.3% car, 0.0% public transportation, 2.2% walk, 2.2% work from home (2006-2010 5-year est.); Travel time to work: 30.5% less than 15 minutes, 17.9% 15 to 30 minutes, 20.6% 30 to 45 minutes, 15.7% 45 to 60 minutes, 15.2% 60 minutes or more (2006-2010 5-year est.)

WEST HICKORY (unincorporated postal area)
Zip Code: 16370
   Covers a land area of 12.581 square miles and a water area of 0.438 square miles. Located at 41.57° N. Lat; 79.46° W. Long. Population: 358 (2010); Density: 28.5 persons per square mile (2010); Race: 98.6% White, 0.0% Black, 0.6% Asian, 0.3% American Indian/Alaska Native, 0.0% Native Hawaiian/Other Pacific Islander, 0.5% Other, 0.3% Hispanic of any race (2010); Average household size: 2.14 (2010); Median age: 53.3 (2010); Males per 100 females: 119.6 (2010); Homeownership rate: 89.2% (2010)

Franklin County

Located in southern Pennsylvania; bounded on the south by Maryland; includes the Tuscarora Mountains along the western border, parts of the Cove Mountains in the southwest, the South Mountains in the southeast, and the Blue Mountains in the north. Covers a land area of 772.224 square miles, a water area of 0.597 square miles, and is located in the Eastern Time Zone at 39.93° N. Lat., 77.72° W. Long. The county was founded in 1784. County seat is Chambersburg.

Franklin County is part of the Chambersburg, PA Micropolitan Statistical Area. The entire metro area includes: Franklin County, PA

Weather Station: Chambersburg 1 ESE   Elevation: 640 feet

	Jan	Feb	Mar	Apr	May	Jun	Jul	Aug	Sep	Oct	Nov	Dec
High	37	41	51	63	73	81	85	84	76	64	53	41
Low	22	24	31	41	50	59	63	62	54	43	35	26
Precip	3.0	2.6	3.6	3.8	4.1	3.8	3.6	3.6	3.4	3.3	3.4	3.2
Snow	10.3	8.8	5.1	0.6	0.0	0.0	0.0	0.0	0.0	tr	1.2	5.7

High and Low temperatures in degrees Fahrenheit; Precipitation and Snow in inches

Population: 121,082 (1990); 129,313 (2000); 149,618 (2010); Race: 92.0% White, 3.1% Black, 0.9% Asian, 0.2% American Indian/Alaska Native, 0.0% Native Hawaiian/Other Pacific Islander, 3.8% Other, 4.3% Hispanic of any race (2010); Density: 193.7 persons per square mile (2010); Average household size: 2.52 (2010); Median age: 40.1 (2010); Males per 100 females: 95.7 (2010).
Religion: Six largest groups: 7.9% Methodist/Pietist, 6.9% Catholicism, 4.5% Presbyterian-Reformed, 3.6% Lutheran, 3.4% Non-Denominational, 3.2% European Free-Church (2010)
Economy: Unemployment rate: 6.8% (August 2012); Total civilian labor force: 82,241 (August 2012); Leading industries: 16.6% health care and social assistance; 15.7% manufacturing; 15.4% retail trade (2010); Farms: 1,540 totaling 242,634 acres (2007); Companies that employ 500 or more persons: 9 (2010); Companies that employ 100 to 499 persons: 58 (2010); Companies that employ less than 100 persons: 2,963 (2010); Black-owned businesses: n/a (2007); Hispanic-owned businesses: 116 (2007); Asian-owned businesses: n/a (2007); Women-owned businesses: 2,900 (2007); Retail sales per capita: $10,957 (2010). Single-family building permits issued: 211 (2011); Multi-family building permits issued: 16 (2011).
Income: Per capita income: $25,307 (2006-2010 5-year est.); Median household income: $51,035 (2006-2010 5-year est.); Average household income: $63,104 (2006-2010 5-year est.); Percent of households with income of $100,000 or more: 15.5% (2006-2010 5-year est.); Poverty rate: 8.2% (2006-2010 5-year est.); Bankruptcy rate: 2.82% (2011).
Taxes: Total county taxes per capita: $198 (2009); County property taxes per capita: $195 (2009).
Education: Percent of population age 25 and over with: High school diploma (including GED) or higher: 83.8% (2006-2010 5-year est.); Bachelor's degree or higher: 18.3% (2006-2010 5-year est.); Master's degree or higher: 7.0% (2006-2010 5-year est.).
Housing: Homeownership rate: 73.5% (2010); Median home value: $175,000 (2006-2010 5-year est.); Median contract rent: $544 per month (2006-2010 5-year est.); Median year structure built: 1973 (2006-2010 5-year est.)
Health: Birth rate: 116.4 per 10,000 population (2011); Death rate: 93.7 per 10,000 population (2011); Age-adjusted cancer mortality rate: 197.5 deaths per 100,000 population (2009); Number of physicians: 14.6 per 10,000 population (2010); Hospital beds: 21.1 per 10,000 population (2008); Hospital admissions: 1,159.4 per 10,000 population (2008).
Environment: Air Quality Index: 91.9% good, 8.1% moderate, 0.0% unhealthy for sensitive individuals, 0.0% unhealthy (percent of days in 2011)
Elections: 2012 Presidential election results: 30.1% Obama, 68.6% Romney
National and State Parks: Caledonia State Park; Mont Alto State Forest; Mont Alto State Park; State Game Refuge
Additional Information Contacts
Franklin County Government . . . . (717) 264-4125
   http://www.co.franklin.pa.us

Franklin County Communities

AMBERSON (unincorporated postal area)
Zip Code: 17210

Covers a land area of 11.980 square miles and a water area of 0.005 square miles. Located at 40.20° N. Lat; 77.65° W. Long. Elevation is 938 feet. Population: 193 (2010); Density: 16.1 persons per square mile (2010); Race: 98.4% White, 0.0% Black, 0.5% Asian, 0.0% American Indian/Alaska Native, 0.0% Native Hawaiian/Other Pacific Islander, 1.1% Other, 0.0% Hispanic of any race (2010); Average household size: 2.27 (2010); Median age: 45.8 (2010); Males per 100 females: 109.8 (2010); Homeownership rate: 91.7% (2010)

ANTRIM (township).

Covers a land area of 70.243 square miles and a water area of 0.069 square miles. Located at 39.83° N. Lat; 77.68° W. Long.

Population: 10,107 (1990); 12,504 (2000); 14,893 (2010); Density: 212.0 persons per square mile (2010); Race: 95.6% White, 1.5% Black, 0.8% Asian, 0.2% American Indian/Alaska Native, 0.0% Native Hawaiian/Other Pacific Islander, 1.9% Other, 1.7% Hispanic of any race (2010); Average household size: 2.77 (2010); Median age: 39.2 (2010); Males per 100 females: 98.7 (2010); Marriage status: 23.0% never married, 63.0% now married, 4.4% widowed, 9.6% divorced (2006-2010 5-year est.); Foreign born: 1.5% (2006-2010 5-year est.); Ancestry (includes multiple ancestries): 42.3% German, 12.9% American, 9.9% Irish, 7.4% English, 4.6% Italian (2006-2010 5-year est.).
Economy: Single-family building permits issued: 23 (2011); Multi-family building permits issued: 0 (2011); Employment by occupation: 11.1% management, 2.8% professional, 8.1% services, 18.2% sales, 4.5% farming, 10.4% construction, 8.1% production (2006-2010 5-year est.).
Income: Per capita income: $27,605 (2006-2010 5-year est.); Median household income: $61,662 (2006-2010 5-year est.); Average household income: $73,030 (2006-2010 5-year est.); Percent of households with income of $100,000 or more: 22.3% (2006-2010 5-year est.); Poverty rate: 5.4% (2006-2010 5-year est.).
Taxes: Total city taxes per capita: $176 (2009); City property taxes per capita: $23 (2009).
Education: Percent of population age 25 and over with: High school diploma (including GED) or higher: 85.8% (2006-2010 5-year est.); Bachelor's degree or higher: 18.2% (2006-2010 5-year est.); Master's degree or higher: 7.1% (2006-2010 5-year est.).
Housing: Homeownership rate: 83.5% (2010); Median home value: $199,800 (2006-2010 5-year est.); Median contract rent: $662 per month (2006-2010 5-year est.); Median year structure built: 1983 (2006-2010 5-year est.).
Transportation: Commute to work: 91.5% car, 0.2% public transportation, 2.9% walk, 4.5% work from home (2006-2010 5-year est.); Travel time to work: 31.4% less than 15 minutes, 47.2% 15 to 30 minutes, 9.8% 30 to 45 minutes, 4.8% 45 to 60 minutes, 6.7% 60 minutes or more (2006-2010 5-year est.)
Additional Information Contacts
Antrim Township . . . . (717) 597-3818
    http://www.twp.antrim.pa.us
Greencastle-Antrim Chamber of Commerce . . . . (717) 597-4610
    http://www.greencastlepachamber.org

BLUE RIDGE SUMMIT (CDP).

Covers a land area of 0.718 square miles and a water area of 0 square miles. Located at 39.73° N. Lat; 77.47° W. Long. Elevation is 1,345 feet.
Population: n/a (1990); n/a (2000); 891 (2010); Density: 1,241.1 persons per square mile (2010); Race: 92.9% White, 1.8% Black, 2.2% Asian, 0.3% American Indian/Alaska Native, 0.0% Native Hawaiian/Other Pacific Islander, 2.8% Other, 1.8% Hispanic of any race (2010); Average household size: 2.33 (2010); Median age: 40.8 (2010); Males per 100 females: 111.1 (2010); Marriage status: 26.7% never married, 36.9% now married, 10.0% widowed, 26.4% divorced (2006-2010 5-year est.); Foreign born: 2.2% (2006-2010 5-year est.); Ancestry (includes multiple ancestries): 47.4% German, 29.3% Irish, 7.6% American, 5.4% French, 2.4% Italian (2006-2010 5-year est.).
Economy: Employment by occupation: 17.1% management, 2.5% professional, 19.4% services, 8.8% sales, 0.0% farming, 10.1% construction, 1.6% production (2006-2010 5-year est.).
Income: Per capita income: $30,122 (2006-2010 5-year est.); Median household income: $56,711 (2006-2010 5-year est.); Average household income: $62,018 (2006-2010 5-year est.); Percent of households with income of $100,000 or more: 15.3% (2006-2010 5-year est.); Poverty rate: 4.8% (2006-2010 5-year est.).
Education: Percent of population age 25 and over with: High school diploma (including GED) or higher: 86.3% (2006-2010 5-year est.);

Bachelor's degree or higher: 17.2% (2006-2010 5-year est.); Master's degree or higher: 10.4% (2006-2010 5-year est.).
Housing: Homeownership rate: 56.8% (2010); Median home value: $219,800 (2006-2010 5-year est.); Median contract rent: $586 per month (2006-2010 5-year est.); Median year structure built: 1960 (2006-2010 5-year est.).
Transportation: Commute to work: 84.8% car, 0.0% public transportation, 15.2% walk, 0.0% work from home (2006-2010 5-year est.); Travel time to work: 37.0% less than 15 minutes, 31.5% 15 to 30 minutes, 6.5% 30 to 45 minutes, 7.4% 45 to 60 minutes, 17.5% 60 minutes or more (2006-2010 5-year est.)

CHAMBERSBURG (borough).

Aka Beautiful. County seat. Covers a land area of 6.925 square miles and a water area of 0 square miles. Located at 39.93° N. Lat; 77.66° W. Long. Elevation is 617 feet.
History: Chambersburg was settled by Benjamin Chambers. John Brown lived in Chambersburg in 1859, prior to his attack on Harpers Ferry.
Population: 16,251 (1990); 17,862 (2000); 20,268 (2010); Density: 2,926.9 persons per square mile (2010); Race: 77.0% White, 9.2% Black, 1.4% Asian, 0.3% American Indian/Alaska Native, 0.1% Native Hawaiian/Other Pacific Islander, 12.0% Other, 15.7% Hispanic of any race (2010); Average household size: 2.33 (2010); Median age: 37.1 (2010); Males per 100 females: 87.3 (2010); Marriage status: 31.1% never married, 45.4% now married, 10.6% widowed, 12.8% divorced (2006-2010 5-year est.); Foreign born: 10.8% (2006-2010 5-year est.); Ancestry (includes multiple ancestries): 30.9% German, 13.0% Irish, 6.8% English, 6.1% American, 3.2% Italian (2006-2010 5-year est.).
Economy: Single-family building permits issued: 34 (2011); Multi-family building permits issued: 0 (2011); Employment by occupation: 8.8% management, 4.0% professional, 8.8% services, 17.7% sales, 3.5% farming, 9.0% construction, 7.5% production (2006-2010 5-year est.).
Income: Per capita income: $21,351 (2006-2010 5-year est.); Median household income: $38,547 (2006-2010 5-year est.); Average household income: $49,632 (2006-2010 5-year est.); Percent of households with income of $100,000 or more: 10.2% (2006-2010 5-year est.); Poverty rate: 20.5% (2006-2010 5-year est.).
Taxes: Total city taxes per capita: $389 (2009); City property taxes per capita: $199 (2009).
Education: Percent of population age 25 and over with: High school diploma (including GED) or higher: 78.8% (2006-2010 5-year est.); Bachelor's degree or higher: 20.9% (2006-2010 5-year est.); Master's degree or higher: 8.3% (2006-2010 5-year est.).

School District(s)
Chambersburg Area SD (KG-12)
    2010-11 Enrollment: 8,523 . . . . (717) 263-9281
Franklin County CTC (10-12)
    2010-11 Enrollment: n/a . . . . (717) 263-9033
Four-year College(s)
Wilson College (Private, Not-for-profit, Presbyterian Church (USA))
    Fall 2010 Enrollment: 629 . . . . (717) 264-4141
    2011-12 Tuition: In-state $29,340; Out-of-state $29,340
Vocational/Technical School(s)
Chambersburg Beauty School (Private, For-profit)
    Fall 2010 Enrollment: 88 . . . . (717) 267-0075
    2011-12 Tuition: $15,900
Franklin County Career and Technology Center (Public)
    Fall 2010 Enrollment: 66 . . . . (717) 263-5667
    2011-12 Tuition: $10,700
Housing: Homeownership rate: 48.5% (2010); Median home value: $152,700 (2006-2010 5-year est.); Median contract rent: $533 per month (2006-2010 5-year est.); Median year structure built: 1956 (2006-2010 5-year est.).
Hospitals: Chambersburg Hospital (248 beds)
Safety: Violent crime rate: 34.9 per 10,000 population; Property crime rate: 336.9 per 10,000 population (2011).
Newspapers: Public Opinion (Local news; Circulation 20,711)
Transportation: Commute to work: 92.1% car, 0.2% public transportation, 4.5% walk, 2.2% work from home (2006-2010 5-year est.); Travel time to work: 46.7% less than 15 minutes, 29.2% 15 to 30 minutes, 16.5% 30 to 45 minutes, 3.6% 45 to 60 minutes, 4.0% 60 minutes or more (2006-2010 5-year est.)
Additional Information Contacts
Borough of Chambersburg . . . . (717) 264-5151
    http://www.borough.chambersburg.pa.us

Greater Chambersburg Chamber of Commerce . . . . (717) 264-7101
http://chambersburg.org

DOYLESBURG (unincorporated postal area)
Zip Code: 17219

Covers a land area of 13.089 square miles and a water area of 0.001 square miles. Located at 40.24° N. Lat; 77.68° W. Long. Elevation is 1,040 feet. Population: 405 (2010); Density: 30.9 persons per square mile (2010); Race: 97.3% White, 0.7% Black, 0.0% Asian, 0.0% American Indian/Alaska Native, 0.0% Native Hawaiian/Other Pacific Islander, 2.0% Other, 2.0% Hispanic of any race (2010); Average household size: 2.85 (2010); Median age: 39.8 (2010); Males per 100 females: 100.5 (2010); Homeownership rate: 83.1% (2010)

DRY RUN (unincorporated postal area)
Zip Code: 17220

Covers a land area of 13.049 square miles and a water area of 0.005 square miles. Located at 40.19° N. Lat; 77.73° W. Long. Population: 534 (2010); Density: 40.9 persons per square mile (2010); Race: 99.4% White, 0.0% Black, 0.0% Asian, 0.0% American Indian/Alaska Native, 0.0% Native Hawaiian/Other Pacific Islander, 0.6% Other, 0.4% Hispanic of any race (2010); Average household size: 3.14 (2010); Median age: 30.0 (2010); Males per 100 females: 90.7 (2010); Homeownership rate: 78.3% (2010)

FANNETT (township). Covers a land area of 68.199 square miles and a water area of 0.015 square miles. Located at 40.17° N. Lat; 77.73° W. Long.
Population: 2,309 (1990); 2,370 (2000); 2,548 (2010); Density: 37.4 persons per square mile (2010); Race: 98.7% White, 0.2% Black, 0.2% Asian, 0.0% American Indian/Alaska Native, 0.0% Native Hawaiian/Other Pacific Islander, 0.9% Other, 0.6% Hispanic of any race (2010); Average household size: 2.86 (2010); Median age: 35.8 (2010); Males per 100 females: 97.1 (2010); Marriage status: 18.4% never married, 68.8% now married, 6.3% widowed, 6.5% divorced (2006-2010 5-year est.); Foreign born: 0.0% (2006-2010 5-year est.); Ancestry (includes multiple ancestries): 26.2% German, 12.9% Irish, 11.2% Pennsylvania German, 9.2% European, 7.5% American (2006-2010 5-year est.).
Economy: Single-family building permits issued: 3 (2011); Multi-family building permits issued: 0 (2011); Employment by occupation: 12.7% management, 1.4% professional, 6.3% services, 13.4% sales, 6.6% farming, 19.4% construction, 8.2% production (2006-2010 5-year est.).
Income: Per capita income: $20,671 (2006-2010 5-year est.); Median household income: $42,885 (2006-2010 5-year est.); Average household income: $58,020 (2006-2010 5-year est.); Percent of households with income of $100,000 or more: 13.9% (2006-2010 5-year est.); Poverty rate: 10.2% (2006-2010 5-year est.).
Education: Percent of population age 25 and over with: High school diploma (including GED) or higher: 67.1% (2006-2010 5-year est.); Bachelor's degree or higher: 8.3% (2006-2010 5-year est.); Master's degree or higher: 3.8% (2006-2010 5-year est.).
Housing: Homeownership rate: 80.5% (2010); Median home value: $176,200 (2006-2010 5-year est.); Median contract rent: $348 per month (2006-2010 5-year est.); Median year structure built: 1967 (2006-2010 5-year est.).
Transportation: Commute to work: 81.6% car, 0.0% public transportation, 7.6% walk, 7.3% work from home (2006-2010 5-year est.); Travel time to work: 20.4% less than 15 minutes, 15.6% 15 to 30 minutes, 34.5% 30 to 45 minutes, 14.7% 45 to 60 minutes, 14.8% 60 minutes or more (2006-2010 5-year est.)
Additional Information Contacts
Shippensburg Area Chamber of Commerce . . . . (717) 532-5509
http://www.shippensburg.org

FANNETTSBURG (unincorporated postal area)
Zip Code: 17221

Covers a land area of 10.312 square miles and a water area of 0.068 square miles. Located at 40.06° N. Lat; 77.81° W. Long. Elevation is 866 feet. Population: 637 (2010); Density: 61.8 persons per square mile (2010); Race: 98.3% White, 0.3% Black, 0.3% Asian, 0.0% American Indian/Alaska Native, 0.0% Native Hawaiian/Other Pacific Islander, 1.1% Other, 0.3% Hispanic of any race (2010); Average household size: 2.53 (2010); Median age: 40.8 (2010); Males per 100 females: 97.2 (2010); Homeownership rate: 80.9% (2010)

FAYETTEVILLE (CDP). Covers a land area of 3.173 square miles and a water area of 0 square miles. Located at 39.91° N. Lat; 77.57° W. Long. Elevation is 817 feet.
History: Appalachian Trail passes to East.
Population: 2,990 (1990); 2,774 (2000); 3,128 (2010); Density: 985.9 persons per square mile (2010); Race: 91.0% White, 4.1% Black, 0.6% Asian, 0.4% American Indian/Alaska Native, 0.0% Native Hawaiian/Other Pacific Islander, 3.9% Other, 3.7% Hispanic of any race (2010); Average household size: 2.48 (2010); Median age: 41.6 (2010); Males per 100 females: 95.6 (2010); Marriage status: 27.2% never married, 52.2% now married, 10.6% widowed, 10.0% divorced (2006-2010 5-year est.); Foreign born: 3.7% (2006-2010 5-year est.); Ancestry (includes multiple ancestries): 34.0% German, 10.6% Irish, 8.7% American, 8.4% English, 6.9% Moroccan (2006-2010 5-year est.).
Economy: Employment by occupation: 9.0% management, 4.3% professional, 10.8% services, 26.4% sales, 0.7% farming, 9.7% construction, 5.1% production (2006-2010 5-year est.).
Income: Per capita income: $26,652 (2006-2010 5-year est.); Median household income: $45,236 (2006-2010 5-year est.); Average household income: $58,183 (2006-2010 5-year est.); Percent of households with income of $100,000 or more: 10.0% (2006-2010 5-year est.); Poverty rate: 4.7% (2006-2010 5-year est.).
Education: Percent of population age 25 and over with: High school diploma (including GED) or higher: 88.4% (2006-2010 5-year est.); Bachelor's degree or higher: 20.5% (2006-2010 5-year est.); Master's degree or higher: 4.9% (2006-2010 5-year est.).

School District(s)
Chambersburg Area SD (KG-12)
2010-11 Enrollment: 8,523 . . . . (717) 263-9281
Housing: Homeownership rate: 80.4% (2010); Median home value: $136,800 (2006-2010 5-year est.); Median contract rent: $527 per month (2006-2010 5-year est.); Median year structure built: 1962 (2006-2010 5-year est.).
Transportation: Commute to work: 95.4% car, 0.0% public transportation, 0.0% walk, 4.6% work from home (2006-2010 5-year est.); Travel time to work: 26.5% less than 15 minutes, 38.3% 15 to 30 minutes, 16.1% 30 to 45 minutes, 8.7% 45 to 60 minutes, 10.5% 60 minutes or more (2006-2010 5-year est.)
Additional Information Contacts
Greater Chambersburg Chamber of Commerce . . . . (717) 264-7101
http://chambersburg.org

FORT LOUDON (CDP). Covers a land area of 4.259 square miles and a water area of 0 square miles. Located at 39.92° N. Lat; 77.91° W. Long. Elevation is 633 feet.
Population: n/a (1990); n/a (2000); 886 (2010); Density: 208.0 persons per square mile (2010); Race: 96.8% White, 0.5% Black, 0.3% Asian, 0.1% American Indian/Alaska Native, 0.0% Native Hawaiian/Other Pacific Islander, 2.3% Other, 2.0% Hispanic of any race (2010); Average household size: 2.58 (2010); Median age: 44.1 (2010); Males per 100 females: 99.1 (2010); Marriage status: 9.9% never married, 79.2% now married, 1.6% widowed, 9.2% divorced (2006-2010 5-year est.); Foreign born: 0.0% (2006-2010 5-year est.); Ancestry (includes multiple ancestries): 44.7% German, 15.7% Scottish, 14.5% English, 7.1% American, 6.8% Italian (2006-2010 5-year est.).
Economy: Employment by occupation: 7.7% management, 5.7% professional, 20.8% services, 10.9% sales, 3.6% farming, 8.1% construction, 0.0% production (2006-2010 5-year est.).
Income: Per capita income: $18,119 (2006-2010 5-year est.); Median household income: $46,231 (2006-2010 5-year est.); Average household income: $44,826 (2006-2010 5-year est.); Percent of households with income of $100,000 or more: 4.1% (2006-2010 5-year est.); Poverty rate: 15.1% (2006-2010 5-year est.).
Education: Percent of population age 25 and over with: High school diploma (including GED) or higher: 62.7% (2006-2010 5-year est.); Bachelor's degree or higher: 6.8% (2006-2010 5-year est.); Master's degree or higher: 3.9% (2006-2010 5-year est.).
Housing: Homeownership rate: 71.5% (2010); Median home value: $145,700 (2006-2010 5-year est.); Median contract rent: $563 per month (2006-2010 5-year est.); Median year structure built: 1971 (2006-2010 5-year est.).
Transportation: Commute to work: 96.2% car, 0.0% public transportation, 0.0% walk, 3.8% work from home (2006-2010 5-year est.); Travel time to work: 13.0% less than 15 minutes, 39.5% 15 to 30 minutes, 27.2% 30 to

45 minutes, 9.5% 45 to 60 minutes, 10.9% 60 minutes or more (2006-2010 5-year est.)

GREENCASTLE (borough).
Covers a land area of 1.588 square miles and a water area of 0 square miles. Located at 39.79° N. Lat; 77.73° W. Long. Elevation is 584 feet.

History: Laid out 1784, incorporated 1805.

Population: 3,600 (1990); 3,722 (2000); 3,996 (2010); Density: 2,517.1 persons per square mile (2010); Race: 94.4% White, 2.5% Black, 1.2% Asian, 0.2% American Indian/Alaska Native, 0.0% Native Hawaiian/Other Pacific Islander, 1.7% Other, 1.6% Hispanic of any race (2010); Average household size: 2.30 (2010); Median age: 39.7 (2010); Males per 100 females: 91.7 (2010); Marriage status: 23.2% never married, 56.9% now married, 8.3% widowed, 11.6% divorced (2006-2010 5-year est.); Foreign born: 2.8% (2006-2010 5-year est.); Ancestry (includes multiple ancestries): 42.3% German, 10.0% American, 9.4% Irish, 8.8% English, 5.9% Italian (2006-2010 5-year est.).

Economy: Single-family building permits issued: 1 (2011); Multi-family building permits issued: 6 (2011); Employment by occupation: 8.8% management, 1.7% professional, 10.5% services, 16.6% sales, 6.6% farming, 8.1% construction, 5.5% production (2006-2010 5-year est.).

Income: Per capita income: $37,241 (2006-2010 5-year est.); Median household income: $48,190 (2006-2010 5-year est.); Average household income: $80,577 (2006-2010 5-year est.); Percent of households with income of $100,000 or more: 22.2% (2006-2010 5-year est.); Poverty rate: 6.0% (2006-2010 5-year est.).

Education: Percent of population age 25 and over with: High school diploma (including GED) or higher: 85.2% (2006-2010 5-year est.); Bachelor's degree or higher: 21.6% (2006-2010 5-year est.); Master's degree or higher: 9.6% (2006-2010 5-year est.).

School District(s)
Greencastle-Antrim SD (KG-12)
    2010-11 Enrollment: 3,044 . . . . (717) 597-3226

Housing: Homeownership rate: 58.5% (2010); Median home value: $217,800 (2006-2010 5-year est.); Median contract rent: $536 per month (2006-2010 5-year est.); Median year structure built: 1971 (2006-2010 5-year est.).

Safety: Violent crime rate: 10.0 per 10,000 population; Property crime rate: 212.0 per 10,000 population (2011).

Newspapers: Echo Pilot (Community news; Circulation 2,500)

Transportation: Commute to work: 93.1% car, 0.0% public transportation, 3.3% walk, 1.2% work from home (2006-2010 5-year est.); Travel time to work: 28.9% less than 15 minutes, 49.6% 15 to 30 minutes, 12.6% 30 to 45 minutes, 5.4% 45 to 60 minutes, 3.5% 60 minutes or more (2006-2010 5-year est.)

Additional Information Contacts
Greencastle-Antrim Chamber of Commerce . . . . (717) 597-4610
    http://www.greencastlepachamber.org

GREENE (township).
Covers a land area of 57.303 square miles and a water area of 0.012 square miles. Located at 39.96° N. Lat; 77.57° W. Long.

Population: 12,326 (1990); 12,284 (2000); 16,700 (2010); Density: 291.4 persons per square mile (2010); Race: 92.8% White, 2.7% Black, 1.2% Asian, 0.1% American Indian/Alaska Native, 0.0% Native Hawaiian/Other Pacific Islander, 3.2% Other, 3.1% Hispanic of any race (2010); Average household size: 2.44 (2010); Median age: 43.4 (2010); Males per 100 females: 95.3 (2010); Marriage status: 21.1% never married, 62.9% now married, 8.2% widowed, 7.7% divorced (2006-2010 5-year est.); Foreign born: 2.6% (2006-2010 5-year est.); Ancestry (includes multiple ancestries): 42.8% German, 13.1% Irish, 8.2% American, 8.0% English, 4.2% Italian (2006-2010 5-year est.).

Economy: Single-family building permits issued: 40 (2011); Multi-family building permits issued: 6 (2011); Employment by occupation: 13.0% management, 2.3% professional, 8.5% services, 14.8% sales, 4.8% farming, 7.6% construction, 6.3% production (2006-2010 5-year est.).

Income: Per capita income: $26,893 (2006-2010 5-year est.); Median household income: $55,264 (2006-2010 5-year est.); Average household income: $66,370 (2006-2010 5-year est.); Percent of households with income of $100,000 or more: 15.9% (2006-2010 5-year est.); Poverty rate: 6.5% (2006-2010 5-year est.).

Education: Percent of population age 25 and over with: High school diploma (including GED) or higher: 84.6% (2006-2010 5-year est.); Bachelor's degree or higher: 21.3% (2006-2010 5-year est.); Master's degree or higher: 6.8% (2006-2010 5-year est.).

Housing: Homeownership rate: 81.8% (2010); Median home value: $174,100 (2006-2010 5-year est.); Median contract rent: $584 per month (2006-2010 5-year est.); Median year structure built: 1981 (2006-2010 5-year est.).

Transportation: Commute to work: 95.0% car, 0.0% public transportation, 1.2% walk, 2.8% work from home (2006-2010 5-year est.); Travel time to work: 37.1% less than 15 minutes, 43.3% 15 to 30 minutes, 7.9% 30 to 45 minutes, 6.1% 45 to 60 minutes, 5.6% 60 minutes or more (2006-2010 5-year est.)

Additional Information Contacts
Greater Chambersburg Chamber of Commerce . . . . (717) 264-7101
    http://chambersburg.org
Greene Township . . . . (717) 263-9160
    http://www.twp.greene.franklin.pa.us

GUILFORD (CDP).
Covers a land area of 1.319 square miles and a water area of 0 square miles. Located at 39.92° N. Lat; 77.60° W. Long. Elevation is 830 feet.

Population: 1,577 (1990); 1,835 (2000); 2,138 (2010); Density: 1,620.6 persons per square mile (2010); Race: 90.4% White, 2.9% Black, 2.9% Asian, 0.0% American Indian/Alaska Native, 0.0% Native Hawaiian/Other Pacific Islander, 3.8% Other, 5.2% Hispanic of any race (2010); Average household size: 2.56 (2010); Median age: 46.3 (2010); Males per 100 females: 94.7 (2010); Marriage status: 18.1% never married, 66.3% now married, 7.5% widowed, 8.1% divorced (2006-2010 5-year est.); Foreign born: 2.1% (2006-2010 5-year est.); Ancestry (includes multiple ancestries): 31.4% German, 14.8% Irish, 12.5% Italian, 12.5% American, 11.8% English (2006-2010 5-year est.).

Economy: Employment by occupation: 12.1% management, 3.1% professional, 5.0% services, 10.2% sales, 6.0% farming, 9.7% construction, 11.6% production (2006-2010 5-year est.).

Income: Per capita income: $29,830 (2006-2010 5-year est.); Median household income: $57,713 (2006-2010 5-year est.); Average household income: $69,990 (2006-2010 5-year est.); Percent of households with income of $100,000 or more: 16.2% (2006-2010 5-year est.); Poverty rate: 1.8% (2006-2010 5-year est.).

Education: Percent of population age 25 and over with: High school diploma (including GED) or higher: 94.6% (2006-2010 5-year est.); Bachelor's degree or higher: 27.5% (2006-2010 5-year est.); Master's degree or higher: 15.9% (2006-2010 5-year est.).

Housing: Homeownership rate: 91.3% (2010); Median home value: $195,100 (2006-2010 5-year est.); Median contract rent: $1,083 per month (2006-2010 5-year est.); Median year structure built: 1969 (2006-2010 5-year est.).

Transportation: Commute to work: 93.6% car, 1.2% public transportation, 0.0% walk, 5.3% work from home (2006-2010 5-year est.); Travel time to work: 29.8% less than 15 minutes, 35.0% 15 to 30 minutes, 9.4% 30 to 45 minutes, 10.0% 45 to 60 minutes, 16.0% 60 minutes or more (2006-2010 5-year est.)

Additional Information Contacts
Greater Chambersburg Chamber of Commerce . . . . (717) 264-7101
    http://chambersburg.org

GUILFORD (township).
Covers a land area of 51.017 square miles and a water area of 0.018 square miles. Located at 39.88° N. Lat; 77.60° W. Long. Elevation is 830 feet.

Population: 11,893 (1990); 13,100 (2000); 14,531 (2010); Density: 284.8 persons per square mile (2010); Race: 93.2% White, 2.7% Black, 0.9% Asian, 0.2% American Indian/Alaska Native, 0.0% Native Hawaiian/Other Pacific Islander, 3.0% Other, 3.7% Hispanic of any race (2010); Average household size: 2.46 (2010); Median age: 45.5 (2010); Males per 100 females: 97.4 (2010); Marriage status: 20.0% never married, 64.9% now married, 6.8% widowed, 8.3% divorced (2006-2010 5-year est.); Foreign born: 2.0% (2006-2010 5-year est.); Ancestry (includes multiple ancestries): 39.0% German, 12.6% American, 11.5% English, 11.4% Irish, 7.1% Italian (2006-2010 5-year est.).

Economy: Single-family building permits issued: 8 (2011); Multi-family building permits issued: 0 (2011); Employment by occupation: 11.8% management, 3.2% professional, 8.8% services, 18.2% sales, 3.2% farming, 13.0% construction, 9.8% production (2006-2010 5-year est.).

Income: Per capita income: $30,643 (2006-2010 5-year est.); Median household income: $56,659 (2006-2010 5-year est.); Average household income: $72,863 (2006-2010 5-year est.); Percent of households with income of $100,000 or more: 16.9% (2006-2010 5-year est.); Poverty rate: 4.1% (2006-2010 5-year est.).

Education: Percent of population age 25 and over with: High school diploma (including GED) or higher: 90.7% (2006-2010 5-year est.); Bachelor's degree or higher: 22.7% (2006-2010 5-year est.); Master's degree or higher: 8.5% (2006-2010 5-year est.).

Housing: Homeownership rate: 80.0% (2010); Median home value: $192,100 (2006-2010 5-year est.); Median contract rent: $610 per month (2006-2010 5-year est.); Median year structure built: 1977 (2006-2010 5-year est.).

Transportation: Commute to work: 92.0% car, 0.4% public transportation, 1.2% walk, 6.0% work from home (2006-2010 5-year est.); Travel time to work: 34.3% less than 15 minutes, 41.8% 15 to 30 minutes, 13.6% 30 to 45 minutes, 4.6% 45 to 60 minutes, 5.8% 60 minutes or more (2006-2010 5-year est.)

Additional Information Contacts

Greater Chambersburg Chamber of Commerce . . . . (717) 264-7101
  http://chambersburg.org
Guilford Township . . . . (717) 264-6626

HAMILTON (township). Covers a land area of 35.540 square miles and a water area of 0 square miles. Located at 39.94° N. Lat; 77.73° W. Long.

Population: 7,745 (1990); 8,949 (2000); 10,788 (2010); Density: 303.5 persons per square mile (2010); Race: 91.9% White, 3.3% Black, 0.7% Asian, 0.1% American Indian/Alaska Native, 0.0% Native Hawaiian/Other Pacific Islander, 4.0% Other, 4.2% Hispanic of any race (2010); Average household size: 2.60 (2010); Median age: 39.3 (2010); Males per 100 females: 97.6 (2010); Marriage status: 25.2% never married, 60.3% now married, 5.5% widowed, 9.0% divorced (2006-2010 5-year est.); Foreign born: 3.8% (2006-2010 5-year est.); Ancestry (includes multiple ancestries): 38.3% German, 15.8% Irish, 10.3% American, 7.5% English, 2.7% Italian (2006-2010 5-year est.).

Economy: Single-family building permits issued: 10 (2011); Multi-family building permits issued: 0 (2011); Employment by occupation: 10.3% management, 3.1% professional, 12.6% services, 14.7% sales, 3.4% farming, 12.8% construction, 9.8% production (2006-2010 5-year est.).

Income: Per capita income: $25,096 (2006-2010 5-year est.); Median household income: $51,617 (2006-2010 5-year est.); Average household income: $62,463 (2006-2010 5-year est.); Percent of households with income of $100,000 or more: 20.8% (2006-2010 5-year est.); Poverty rate: 6.3% (2006-2010 5-year est.).

Education: Percent of population age 25 and over with: High school diploma (including GED) or higher: 88.9% (2006-2010 5-year est.); Bachelor's degree or higher: 21.8% (2006-2010 5-year est.); Master's degree or higher: 8.8% (2006-2010 5-year est.).

Housing: Homeownership rate: 81.1% (2010); Median home value: $174,300 (2006-2010 5-year est.); Median contract rent: $547 per month (2006-2010 5-year est.); Median year structure built: 1979 (2006-2010 5-year est.).

Transportation: Commute to work: 95.6% car, 0.0% public transportation, 0.8% walk, 2.5% work from home (2006-2010 5-year est.); Travel time to work: 27.7% less than 15 minutes, 44.2% 15 to 30 minutes, 15.4% 30 to 45 minutes, 5.1% 45 to 60 minutes, 7.7% 60 minutes or more (2006-2010 5-year est.).

Additional Information Contacts

Greater Chambersburg Chamber of Commerce . . . . (717) 264-7101
  http://chambersburg.org
Hamilton Township . . . . (717) 491-3963
  http://www.hamiltontownship.org

LETTERKENNY (township). Covers a land area of 70.377 square miles and a water area of 0.134 square miles. Located at 40.04° N. Lat; 77.73° W. Long.

Population: 2,251 (1990); 2,074 (2000); 2,318 (2010); Density: 32.9 persons per square mile (2010); Race: 97.8% White, 1.1% Black, 0.2% Asian, 0.0% American Indian/Alaska Native, 0.0% Native Hawaiian/Other Pacific Islander, 0.9% Other, 0.6% Hispanic of any race (2010); Average household size: 2.56 (2010); Median age: 42.2 (2010); Males per 100 females: 102.8 (2010); Marriage status: 18.7% never married, 65.6% now married, 3.5% widowed, 12.3% divorced (2006-2010 5-year est.); Foreign born: 1.0% (2006-2010 5-year est.); Ancestry (includes multiple ancestries): 33.0% German, 18.4% American, 15.5% Irish, 7.1% English, 3.7% European (2006-2010 5-year est.).

Economy: Single-family building permits issued: 2 (2011); Multi-family building permits issued: 0 (2011); Employment by occupation: 7.0%

management, 2.8% professional, 9.1% services, 16.3% sales, 2.9% farming, 18.2% construction, 15.7% production (2006-2010 5-year est.).

Income: Per capita income: $23,029 (2006-2010 5-year est.); Median household income: $51,700 (2006-2010 5-year est.); Average household income: $61,713 (2006-2010 5-year est.); Percent of households with income of $100,000 or more: 13.5% (2006-2010 5-year est.); Poverty rate: 9.4% (2006-2010 5-year est.).

Education: Percent of population age 25 and over with: High school diploma (including GED) or higher: 81.8% (2006-2010 5-year est.); Bachelor's degree or higher: 13.0% (2006-2010 5-year est.); Master's degree or higher: 4.3% (2006-2010 5-year est.).

Housing: Homeownership rate: 84.2% (2010); Median home value: $165,000 (2006-2010 5-year est.); Median contract rent: $539 per month (2006-2010 5-year est.); Median year structure built: 1977 (2006-2010 5-year est.).

Transportation: Commute to work: 94.6% car, 0.6% public transportation, 1.0% walk, 3.2% work from home (2006-2010 5-year est.); Travel time to work: 22.5% less than 15 minutes, 44.7% 15 to 30 minutes, 23.4% 30 to 45 minutes, 3.3% 45 to 60 minutes, 6.3% 60 minutes or more (2006-2010 5-year est.)

Additional Information Contacts

Greater Chambersburg Chamber of Commerce . . . . (717) 264-7101
  http://chambersburg.org

LURGAN (township). Covers a land area of 32.718 square miles and a water area of 0.111 square miles. Located at 40.12° N. Lat; 77.63° W. Long. Elevation is 735 feet.

Population: 2,026 (1990); 2,014 (2000); 2,151 (2010); Density: 65.7 persons per square mile (2010); Race: 98.6% White, 0.4% Black, 0.1% Asian, 0.4% American Indian/Alaska Native, 0.0% Native Hawaiian/Other Pacific Islander, 0.5% Other, 0.5% Hispanic of any race (2010); Average household size: 2.87 (2010); Median age: 36.4 (2010); Males per 100 females: 101.4 (2010); Marriage status: 19.1% never married, 66.0% now married, 6.7% widowed, 8.1% divorced (2006-2010 5-year est.); Foreign born: 0.9% (2006-2010 5-year est.); Ancestry (includes multiple ancestries): 38.7% German, 17.8% American, 10.2% Irish, 7.7% Pennsylvania German, 5.9% English (2006-2010 5-year est.).

Economy: Single-family building permits issued: 3 (2011); Multi-family building permits issued: 0 (2011); Employment by occupation: 9.7% management, 2.6% professional, 9.1% services, 16.8% sales, 4.4% farming, 18.7% construction, 14.7% production (2006-2010 5-year est.).

Income: Per capita income: $22,260 (2006-2010 5-year est.); Median household income: $50,994 (2006-2010 5-year est.); Average household income: $63,914 (2006-2010 5-year est.); Percent of households with income of $100,000 or more: 16.5% (2006-2010 5-year est.); Poverty rate: 9.7% (2006-2010 5-year est.).

Education: Percent of population age 25 and over with: High school diploma (including GED) or higher: 72.0% (2006-2010 5-year est.); Bachelor's degree or higher: 9.0% (2006-2010 5-year est.); Master's degree or higher: 2.5% (2006-2010 5-year est.).

School District(s)

Chambersburg Area SD (KG-12)
  2010-11 Enrollment: 8,523 . . . . (717) 263-9281

Housing: Homeownership rate: 81.3% (2010); Median home value: $171,200 (2006-2010 5-year est.); Median contract rent: $459 per month (2006-2010 5-year est.); Median year structure built: 1973 (2006-2010 5-year est.).

Transportation: Commute to work: 81.7% car, 1.3% public transportation, 4.4% walk, 8.2% work from home (2006-2010 5-year est.); Travel time to work: 22.4% less than 15 minutes, 39.7% 15 to 30 minutes, 21.5% 30 to 45 minutes, 7.0% 45 to 60 minutes, 9.4% 60 minutes or more (2006-2010 5-year est.)

Additional Information Contacts

Shippensburg Area Chamber of Commerce . . . . (717) 532-5509
  http://www.shippensburg.org

MARION (CDP). Covers a land area of 1.977 square miles and a water area of 0 square miles. Located at 39.86° N. Lat; 77.70° W. Long. Elevation is 633 feet.

Population: n/a (1990); n/a (2000); 953 (2010); Density: 482.0 persons per square mile (2010); Race: 92.4% White, 1.5% Black, 0.1% Asian, 0.1% American Indian/Alaska Native, 0.1% Native Hawaiian/Other Pacific Islander, 5.8% Other, 7.3% Hispanic of any race (2010); Average household size: 2.62 (2010); Median age: 38.2 (2010); Males per 100 females: 104.1 (2010); Marriage status: 20.5% never married, 60.3% now

married, 9.5% widowed, 9.7% divorced (2006-2010 5-year est.); Foreign born: 2.5% (2006-2010 5-year est.); Ancestry (includes multiple ancestries): 54.5% German, 41.1% English, 10.1% American, 7.1% Irish, 6.7% Swiss (2006-2010 5-year est.).

Economy: Employment by occupation: 4.8% management, 0.0% professional, 12.7% services, 17.5% sales, 0.0% farming, 20.9% construction, 25.7% production (2006-2010 5-year est.).

Income: Per capita income: $23,169 (2006-2010 5-year est.); Median household income: $49,185 (2006-2010 5-year est.); Average household income: $52,443 (2006-2010 5-year est.); Percent of households with income of $100,000 or more: 7.7% (2006-2010 5-year est.); Poverty rate: 10.3% (2006-2010 5-year est.).

Education: Percent of population age 25 and over with: High school diploma (including GED) or higher: 96.6% (2006-2010 5-year est.); Bachelor's degree or higher: 33.5% (2006-2010 5-year est.); Master's degree or higher: 3.9% (2006-2010 5-year est.).

School District(s)

Chambersburg Area SD (KG-12)

    2010-11 Enrollment: 8,523 . . . . (717) 263-9281

Housing: Homeownership rate: 73.4% (2010); Median home value: $220,600 (2006-2010 5-year est.); Median contract rent: $503 per month (2006-2010 5-year est.); Median year structure built: 1946 (2006-2010 5-year est.).

Transportation: Commute to work: 100.0% car, 0.0% public transportation, 0.0% walk, 0.0% work from home (2006-2010 5-year est.); Travel time to work: 44.5% less than 15 minutes, 47.9% 15 to 30 minutes, 7.5% 30 to 45 minutes, 0.0% 45 to 60 minutes, 0.0% 60 minutes or more (2006-2010 5-year est.)

MERCERSBURG (borough). Covers a land area of 0.902 square miles and a water area of 0 square miles. Located at 39.83° N. Lat; 77.90° W. Long. Elevation is 568 feet.

History: Buchanan's Birthplace Historic State Park to Northwest. Settled c.1729, laid out 1780, incorporated 1831.

Population: 1,640 (1990); 1,540 (2000); 1,561 (2010); Density: 1,730.7 persons per square mile (2010); Race: 91.9% White, 4.9% Black, 0.4% Asian, 0.1% American Indian/Alaska Native, 0.0% Native Hawaiian/Other Pacific Islander, 2.7% Other, 2.9% Hispanic of any race (2010); Average household size: 2.34 (2010); Median age: 37.9 (2010); Males per 100 females: 89.2 (2010); Marriage status: 27.1% never married, 54.2% now married, 7.6% widowed, 11.1% divorced (2006-2010 5-year est.); Foreign born: 1.7% (2006-2010 5-year est.); Ancestry (includes multiple ancestries): 40.5% German, 11.0% English, 11.0% American, 9.8% Irish, 8.3% Italian (2006-2010 5-year est.).

Economy: Single-family building permits issued: 0 (2011); Multi-family building permits issued: 0 (2011); Employment by occupation: 10.2% management, 2.9% professional, 10.8% services, 18.9% sales, 2.9% farming, 9.8% construction, 8.8% production (2006-2010 5-year est.).

Income: Per capita income: $23,076 (2006-2010 5-year est.); Median household income: $47,266 (2006-2010 5-year est.); Average household income: $56,374 (2006-2010 5-year est.); Percent of households with income of $100,000 or more: 12.5% (2006-2010 5-year est.); Poverty rate: 7.8% (2006-2010 5-year est.).

Education: Percent of population age 25 and over with: High school diploma (including GED) or higher: 78.2% (2006-2010 5-year est.); Bachelor's degree or higher: 27.7% (2006-2010 5-year est.); Master's degree or higher: 11.8% (2006-2010 5-year est.).

School District(s)

Tuscarora SD (KG-12)

    2010-11 Enrollment: 2,593 . . . . (717) 328-3127

Housing: Homeownership rate: 51.9% (2010); Median home value: $156,800 (2006-2010 5-year est.); Median contract rent: $447 per month (2006-2010 5-year est.); Median year structure built: before 1940 (2006-2010 5-year est.).

Safety: Violent crime rate: 0.0 per 10,000 population; Property crime rate: 338.4 per 10,000 population (2011).

Newspapers: Mercersburg Journal (Community news; Circulation 8,200)

Transportation: Commute to work: 87.1% car, 0.4% public transportation, 8.7% walk, 3.1% work from home (2006-2010 5-year est.); Travel time to work: 34.7% less than 15 minutes, 20.4% 15 to 30 minutes, 33.5% 30 to 45 minutes, 5.3% 45 to 60 minutes, 6.2% 60 minutes or more (2006-2010 5-year est.)

Additional Information Contacts

Tuscarora Area Chamber of Commerce . . . . (717) 328-5827
    http://www.tachamber.org/contactus.php

METAL (township). Covers a land area of 44.534 square miles and a water area of 0.068 square miles. Located at 40.04° N. Lat; 77.85° W. Long. Elevation is 699 feet.

Population: 1,612 (1990); 1,721 (2000); 1,866 (2010); Density: 41.9 persons per square mile (2010); Race: 98.3% White, 0.5% Black, 0.2% Asian, 0.1% American Indian/Alaska Native, 0.0% Native Hawaiian/Other Pacific Islander, 0.9% Other, 0.5% Hispanic of any race (2010); Average household size: 2.60 (2010); Median age: 42.5 (2010); Males per 100 females: 100.6 (2010); Marriage status: 21.9% never married, 63.1% now married, 6.6% widowed, 8.5% divorced (2006-2010 5-year est.); Foreign born: 1.0% (2006-2010 5-year est.); Ancestry (includes multiple ancestries): 36.6% German, 14.7% Irish, 10.1% American, 7.8% English, 3.7% Dutch (2006-2010 5-year est.).

Economy: Single-family building permits issued: 4 (2011); Multi-family building permits issued: 0 (2011); Employment by occupation: 6.7% management, 3.1% professional, 10.7% services, 16.1% sales, 3.2% farming, 16.0% construction, 9.8% production (2006-2010 5-year est.).

Income: Per capita income: $24,751 (2006-2010 5-year est.); Median household income: $46,953 (2006-2010 5-year est.); Average household income: $63,057 (2006-2010 5-year est.); Percent of households with income of $100,000 or more: 12.2% (2006-2010 5-year est.); Poverty rate: 9.4% (2006-2010 5-year est.).

Education: Percent of population age 25 and over with: High school diploma (including GED) or higher: 77.3% (2006-2010 5-year est.); Bachelor's degree or higher: 8.7% (2006-2010 5-year est.); Master's degree or higher: 2.9% (2006-2010 5-year est.).

Housing: Homeownership rate: 84.5% (2010); Median home value: $125,500 (2006-2010 5-year est.); Median contract rent: $539 per month (2006-2010 5-year est.); Median year structure built: 1973 (2006-2010 5-year est.).

Transportation: Commute to work: 87.4% car, 0.0% public transportation, 4.2% walk, 6.0% work from home (2006-2010 5-year est.); Travel time to work: 23.9% less than 15 minutes, 20.4% 15 to 30 minutes, 28.9% 30 to 45 minutes, 16.5% 45 to 60 minutes, 10.2% 60 minutes or more (2006-2010 5-year est.)

Additional Information Contacts

Greater Chambersburg Chamber of Commerce . . . . (717) 264-7101
    http://chambersburg.org

MONT ALTO (borough). Covers a land area of 0.568 square miles and a water area of 0 square miles. Located at 39.84° N. Lat; 77.56° W. Long. Elevation is 846 feet.

History: Appalachian Trail passes to East.

Population: 1,395 (1990); 1,357 (2000); 1,705 (2010); Density: 3,000.3 persons per square mile (2010); Race: 92.9% White, 4.0% Black, 0.7% Asian, 0.2% American Indian/Alaska Native, 0.0% Native Hawaiian/Other Pacific Islander, 2.2% Other, 2.1% Hispanic of any race (2010); Average household size: 2.53 (2010); Median age: 33.0 (2010); Males per 100 females: 96.4 (2010); Marriage status: 16.0% never married, 68.4% now married, 6.7% widowed, 8.8% divorced (2006-2010 5-year est.); Foreign born: 1.8% (2006-2010 5-year est.); Ancestry (includes multiple ancestries): 36.2% German, 9.5% Irish, 8.7% American, 7.2% English, 5.7% Italian (2006-2010 5-year est.).

Economy: Single-family building permits issued: 0 (2011); Multi-family building permits issued: 0 (2011); Employment by occupation: 7.4% management, 3.3% professional, 10.9% services, 21.6% sales, 2.4% farming, 10.3% construction, 9.4% production (2006-2010 5-year est.).

Income: Per capita income: $20,652 (2006-2010 5-year est.); Median household income: $42,469 (2006-2010 5-year est.); Average household income: $50,150 (2006-2010 5-year est.); Percent of households with income of $100,000 or more: 4.7% (2006-2010 5-year est.); Poverty rate: 2.9% (2006-2010 5-year est.).

Education: Percent of population age 25 and over with: High school diploma (including GED) or higher: 80.9% (2006-2010 5-year est.); Bachelor's degree or higher: 6.4% (2006-2010 5-year est.); Master's degree or higher: 1.6% (2006-2010 5-year est.).

Four-year College(s)

Pennsylvania State University-Penn State Mont Alto (Public)

    Fall 2010 Enrollment: 1,138 . . . . (717) 749-6000
    2011-12 Tuition: In-state $13,102; Out-of-state $19,542

Housing: Homeownership rate: 76.4% (2010); Median home value: $152,900 (2006-2010 5-year est.); Median contract rent: $504 per month (2006-2010 5-year est.); Median year structure built: 1965 (2006-2010 5-year est.).

Transportation: Commute to work: 94.3% car, 0.0% public transportation, 1.5% walk, 2.9% work from home (2006-2010 5-year est.); Travel time to work: 17.4% less than 15 minutes, 37.4% 15 to 30 minutes, 34.0% 30 to 45 minutes, 7.4% 45 to 60 minutes, 3.8% 60 minutes or more (2006-2010 5-year est.)

Additional Information Contacts
Greater Chambersburg Chamber of Commerce . . . . (717) 264-7101
    http://chambersburg.org

MONTGOMERY (township).
Covers a land area of 67.364 square miles and a water area of 0.074 square miles. Located at 39.77° N. Lat; 77.90° W. Long.

Population: 4,558 (1990); 4,949 (2000); 6,116 (2010); Density: 90.8 persons per square mile (2010); Race: 95.7% White, 1.2% Black, 1.0% Asian, 0.2% American Indian/Alaska Native, 0.0% Native Hawaiian/Other Pacific Islander, 1.9% Other, 1.6% Hispanic of any race (2010); Average household size: 2.69 (2010); Median age: 39.3 (2010); Males per 100 females: 105.4 (2010); Marriage status: 24.0% never married, 64.8% now married, 2.1% widowed, 9.1% divorced (2006-2010 5-year est.); Foreign born: 0.6% (2006-2010 5-year est.); Ancestry (includes multiple ancestries): 36.9% German, 14.1% American, 10.3% Irish, 6.1% English, 3.5% Italian (2006-2010 5-year est.).
Economy: Single-family building permits issued: 6 (2011); Multi-family building permits issued: 0 (2011); Employment by occupation: 16.5% management, 3.4% professional, 5.4% services, 17.5% sales, 2.9% farming, 13.9% construction, 12.7% production (2006-2010 5-year est.).
Income: Per capita income: $27,793 (2006-2010 5-year est.); Median household income: $59,731 (2006-2010 5-year est.); Average household income: $75,955 (2006-2010 5-year est.); Percent of households with income of $100,000 or more: 24.8% (2006-2010 5-year est.); Poverty rate: 2.1% (2006-2010 5-year est.).
Education: Percent of population age 25 and over with: High school diploma (including GED) or higher: 81.6% (2006-2010 5-year est.); Bachelor's degree or higher: 16.0% (2006-2010 5-year est.); Master's degree or higher: 7.1% (2006-2010 5-year est.).
Housing: Homeownership rate: 85.2% (2010); Median home value: $200,000 (2006-2010 5-year est.); Median contract rent: $610 per month (2006-2010 5-year est.); Median year structure built: 1970 (2006-2010 5-year est.).
Transportation: Commute to work: 87.6% car, 0.0% public transportation, 2.8% walk, 8.5% work from home (2006-2010 5-year est.); Travel time to work: 23.6% less than 15 minutes, 32.7% 15 to 30 minutes, 22.8% 30 to 45 minutes, 12.2% 45 to 60 minutes, 8.7% 60 minutes or more (2006-2010 5-year est.)

Additional Information Contacts
Tuscarora Area Chamber of Commerce . . . . (717) 328-5827
    http://www.tachamber.org/contactus.php

ORRSTOWN (borough).
Covers a land area of 0.064 square miles and a water area of 0 square miles. Located at 40.06° N. Lat; 77.61° W. Long. Elevation is 686 feet.

Population: 220 (1990); 231 (2000); 262 (2010); Density: 4,123.6 persons per square mile (2010); Race: 96.9% White, 2.3% Black, 0.0% Asian, 0.0% American Indian/Alaska Native, 0.0% Native Hawaiian/Other Pacific Islander, 0.8% Other, 0.0% Hispanic of any race (2010); Average household size: 2.35 (2010); Median age: 47.6 (2010); Males per 100 females: 70.1 (2010); Marriage status: 18.2% never married, 52.4% now married, 21.4% widowed, 8.0% divorced (2006-2010 5-year est.); Foreign born: 0.0% (2006-2010 5-year est.); Ancestry (includes multiple ancestries): 30.8% German, 23.3% Irish, 18.9% American, 5.7% English, 4.4% French (2006-2010 5-year est.).
Economy: Single-family building permits issued: 0 (2011); Multi-family building permits issued: 0 (2011); Employment by occupation: 5.7% management, 5.7% professional, 14.2% services, 17.0% sales, 4.7% farming, 9.4% construction, 17.0% production (2006-2010 5-year est.).
Income: Per capita income: $20,904 (2006-2010 5-year est.); Median household income: $51,250 (2006-2010 5-year est.); Average household income: $48,669 (2006-2010 5-year est.); Percent of households with income of $100,000 or more: 2.0% (2006-2010 5-year est.); Poverty rate: 1.8% (2006-2010 5-year est.).
Education: Percent of population age 25 and over with: High school diploma (including GED) or higher: 78.3% (2006-2010 5-year est.); Bachelor's degree or higher: 5.6% (2006-2010 5-year est.); Master's degree or higher: 0.0% (2006-2010 5-year est.).

Housing: Homeownership rate: 65.0% (2010); Median home value: $118,200 (2006-2010 5-year est.); Median contract rent: $538 per month (2006-2010 5-year est.); Median year structure built: before 1940 (2006-2010 5-year est.).
Transportation: Commute to work: 98.1% car, 0.0% public transportation, 1.9% walk, 0.0% work from home (2006-2010 5-year est.); Travel time to work: 34.9% less than 15 minutes, 50.0% 15 to 30 minutes, 7.5% 30 to 45 minutes, 3.8% 45 to 60 minutes, 3.8% 60 minutes or more (2006-2010 5-year est.)

PEN MAR (CDP).
Covers a land area of 0.739 square miles and a water area of 0.007 square miles. Located at 39.73° N. Lat; 77.52° W. Long. Elevation is 1,237 feet.

Population: n/a (1990); n/a (2000); 929 (2010); Density: 1,257.8 persons per square mile (2010); Race: 94.4% White, 2.8% Black, 0.9% Asian, 0.2% American Indian/Alaska Native, 0.0% Native Hawaiian/Other Pacific Islander, 1.7% Other, 1.0% Hispanic of any race (2010); Average household size: 2.62 (2010); Median age: 40.9 (2010); Males per 100 females: 96.0 (2010); Marriage status: 15.5% never married, 71.0% now married, 8.5% widowed, 4.9% divorced (2006-2010 5-year est.); Foreign born: 5.5% (2006-2010 5-year est.); Ancestry (includes multiple ancestries): 27.6% German, 18.2% American, 10.3% English, 8.4% Irish, 2.7% Dutch (2006-2010 5-year est.).
Economy: Employment by occupation: 2.2% management, 5.4% professional, 25.4% services, 14.8% sales, 9.9% farming, 6.7% construction, 2.0% production (2006-2010 5-year est.).
Income: Per capita income: $26,020 (2006-2010 5-year est.); Median household income: $55,481 (2006-2010 5-year est.); Average household income: $56,039 (2006-2010 5-year est.); Percent of households with income of $100,000 or more: 9.9% (2006-2010 5-year est.); Poverty rate: 0.0% (2006-2010 5-year est.).
Education: Percent of population age 25 and over with: High school diploma (including GED) or higher: 87.3% (2006-2010 5-year est.); Bachelor's degree or higher: 10.6% (2006-2010 5-year est.); Master's degree or higher: 5.9% (2006-2010 5-year est.).
Housing: Homeownership rate: 86.4% (2010); Median home value: $175,000 (2006-2010 5-year est.); Median contract rent: n/a per month (2006-2010 5-year est.); Median year structure built: 1978 (2006-2010 5-year est.).
Transportation: Commute to work: 79.8% car, 3.9% public transportation, 0.0% walk, 14.1% work from home (2006-2010 5-year est.); Travel time to work: 41.8% less than 15 minutes, 18.2% 15 to 30 minutes, 26.1% 30 to 45 minutes, 0.0% 45 to 60 minutes, 13.9% 60 minutes or more (2006-2010 5-year est.)

PETERS (township).
Covers a land area of 55.808 square miles and a water area of 0.043 square miles. Located at 39.88° N. Lat; 77.88° W. Long.

Population: 4,090 (1990); 4,251 (2000); 4,430 (2010); Density: 79.4 persons per square mile (2010); Race: 96.9% White, 1.2% Black, 0.4% Asian, 0.1% American Indian/Alaska Native, 0.0% Native Hawaiian/Other Pacific Islander, 1.4% Other, 1.0% Hispanic of any race (2010); Average household size: 2.57 (2010); Median age: 41.6 (2010); Males per 100 females: 97.0 (2010); Marriage status: 19.7% never married, 67.9% now married, 5.1% widowed, 7.4% divorced (2006-2010 5-year est.); Foreign born: 0.0% (2006-2010 5-year est.); Ancestry (includes multiple ancestries): 45.5% German, 17.0% American, 6.3% Irish, 4.4% English, 3.9% Scottish (2006-2010 5-year est.).
Economy: Single-family building permits issued: 3 (2011); Multi-family building permits issued: 0 (2011); Employment by occupation: 8.9% management, 3.4% professional, 11.6% services, 16.3% sales, 4.4% farming, 12.4% construction, 9.5% production (2006-2010 5-year est.).
Income: Per capita income: $24,434 (2006-2010 5-year est.); Median household income: $52,703 (2006-2010 5-year est.); Average household income: $60,927 (2006-2010 5-year est.); Percent of households with income of $100,000 or more: 15.4% (2006-2010 5-year est.); Poverty rate: 6.0% (2006-2010 5-year est.).
Education: Percent of population age 25 and over with: High school diploma (including GED) or higher: 80.8% (2006-2010 5-year est.); Bachelor's degree or higher: 8.1% (2006-2010 5-year est.); Master's degree or higher: 3.9% (2006-2010 5-year est.).
Housing: Homeownership rate: 77.9% (2010); Median home value: $160,200 (2006-2010 5-year est.); Median contract rent: $440 per month (2006-2010 5-year est.); Median year structure built: 1965 (2006-2010 5-year est.).

Transportation: Commute to work: 93.5% car, 0.0% public transportation, 1.8% walk, 4.2% work from home (2006-2010 5-year est.); Travel time to work: 21.8% less than 15 minutes, 40.7% 15 to 30 minutes, 25.1% 30 to 45 minutes, 6.7% 45 to 60 minutes, 5.7% 60 minutes or more (2006-2010 5-year est.)

Additional Information Contacts

Tuscarora Area Chamber of Commerce . . . . (717) 328-5827
http://www.tachamber.org/contactus.php

PLEASANT HALL (unincorporated postal area)

Zip Code: 17246

Covers a land area of 1.627 square miles and a water area of 0 square miles. Located at 40.05° N. Lat; 77.66° W. Long. Elevation is 702 feet. Population: 195 (2010); Density: 119.9 persons per square mile (2010); Race: 99.5% White, 0.0% Black, 0.0% Asian, 0.0% American Indian/Alaska Native, 0.0% Native Hawaiian/Other Pacific Islander, 0.5% Other, 0.0% Hispanic of any race (2010); Average household size: 2.50 (2010); Median age: 41.8 (2010); Males per 100 females: 101.0 (2010); Homeownership rate: 84.6% (2010)

QUINCY (township).

Covers a land area of 45.201 square miles and a water area of 0.007 square miles. Located at 39.81° N. Lat; 77.55° W. Long. Elevation is 712 feet.

Population: 5,704 (1990); 5,846 (2000); 5,541 (2010); Density: 122.6 persons per square mile (2010); Race: 93.5% White, 3.4% Black, 0.5% Asian, 0.2% American Indian/Alaska Native, 0.0% Native Hawaiian/Other Pacific Islander, 2.4% Other, 2.0% Hispanic of any race (2010); Average household size: 2.55 (2010); Median age: 41.3 (2010); Males per 100 females: 101.9 (2010); Marriage status: 37.6% never married, 48.8% now married, 7.5% widowed, 6.1% divorced (2006-2010 5-year est.); Foreign born: 2.4% (2006-2010 5-year est.); Ancestry (includes multiple ancestries): 33.8% German, 11.6% American, 9.2% Irish, 7.3% English, 5.7% Italian (2006-2010 5-year est.).

Economy: Single-family building permits issued: 4 (2011); Multi-family building permits issued: 0 (2011); Employment by occupation: 14.5% management, 1.7% professional, 12.1% services, 17.5% sales, 2.0% farming, 14.6% construction, 8.7% production (2006-2010 5-year est.).

Income: Per capita income: $18,673 (2006-2010 5-year est.); Median household income: $49,665 (2006-2010 5-year est.); Average household income: $58,501 (2006-2010 5-year est.); Percent of households with income of $100,000 or more: 7.9% (2006-2010 5-year est.); Poverty rate: 8.7% (2006-2010 5-year est.).

Education: Percent of population age 25 and over with: High school diploma (including GED) or higher: 76.2% (2006-2010 5-year est.); Bachelor's degree or higher: 10.3% (2006-2010 5-year est.); Master's degree or higher: 2.6% (2006-2010 5-year est.).

Housing: Homeownership rate: 75.2% (2010); Median home value: $175,500 (2006-2010 5-year est.); Median contract rent: $588 per month (2006-2010 5-year est.); Median year structure built: 1974 (2006-2010 5-year est.).

Transportation: Commute to work: 83.9% car, 0.8% public transportation, 5.7% walk, 9.6% work from home (2006-2010 5-year est.); Travel time to work: 35.3% less than 15 minutes, 39.1% 15 to 30 minutes, 12.3% 30 to 45 minutes, 8.2% 45 to 60 minutes, 5.0% 60 minutes or more (2006-2010 5-year est.)

Additional Information Contacts

Greater Waynesboro Chamber of Commerce . . . . (717) 762-7123
http://www.waynesboro.org
Quincy Township . . . . (717) 762-5679

ROUZERVILLE (CDP).

Covers a land area of 0.654 square miles and a water area of 0 square miles. Located at 39.73° N. Lat; 77.53° W. Long. Elevation is 686 feet.

History: Appalachian Trail passes to East.

Population: 1,073 (1990); 862 (2000); 917 (2010); Density: 1,403.0 persons per square mile (2010); Race: 98.4% White, 0.7% Black, 0.0% Asian, 0.1% American Indian/Alaska Native, 0.0% Native Hawaiian/Other Pacific Islander, 0.8% Other, 2.3% Hispanic of any race (2010); Average household size: 2.41 (2010); Median age: 43.0 (2010); Males per 100 females: 101.1 (2010); Marriage status: 21.1% never married, 62.2% now married, 8.4% widowed, 8.2% divorced (2006-2010 5-year est.); Foreign born: 0.0% (2006-2010 5-year est.); Ancestry (includes multiple ancestries): 23.9% German, 13.3% English, 13.0% American, 7.1% Irish, 4.3% Scotch-Irish (2006-2010 5-year est.).

Economy: Employment by occupation: 0.0% management, 2.2% professional, 6.8% services, 21.8% sales, 2.9% farming, 14.5% construction, 10.4% production (2006-2010 5-year est.).

Income: Per capita income: $25,603 (2006-2010 5-year est.); Median household income: $50,777 (2006-2010 5-year est.); Average household income: $53,483 (2006-2010 5-year est.); Percent of households with income of $100,000 or more: 13.0% (2006-2010 5-year est.); Poverty rate: 5.7% (2006-2010 5-year est.).

Education: Percent of population age 25 and over with: High school diploma (including GED) or higher: 81.0% (2006-2010 5-year est.); Bachelor's degree or higher: 7.7% (2006-2010 5-year est.); Master's degree or higher: 2.7% (2006-2010 5-year est.).

Housing: Homeownership rate: 78.4% (2010); Median home value: $136,300 (2006-2010 5-year est.); Median contract rent: $517 per month (2006-2010 5-year est.); Median year structure built: 1945 (2006-2010 5-year est.).

Transportation: Commute to work: 97.1% car, 0.0% public transportation, 2.9% walk, 0.0% work from home (2006-2010 5-year est.); Travel time to work: 39.5% less than 15 minutes, 36.8% 15 to 30 minutes, 13.8% 30 to 45 minutes, 0.0% 45 to 60 minutes, 9.9% 60 minutes or more (2006-2010 5-year est.)

ROXBURY (unincorporated postal area)

Zip Code: 17251

Covers a land area of 2.228 square miles and a water area of 0.040 square miles. Located at 40.13° N. Lat; 77.68° W. Long. Elevation is 741 feet. Population: 158 (2010); Density: 70.9 persons per square mile (2010); Race: 98.7% White, 0.0% Black, 0.0% Asian, 0.6% American Indian/Alaska Native, 0.0% Native Hawaiian/Other Pacific Islander, 0.7% Other, 0.0% Hispanic of any race (2010); Average household size: 2.19 (2010); Median age: 41.9 (2010); Males per 100 females: 102.6 (2010); Homeownership rate: 72.2% (2010)

SAINT THOMAS (township).

Covers a land area of 51.867 square miles and a water area of 0.029 square miles. Located at 39.93° N. Lat; 77.81° W. Long.

Population: 5,861 (1990); 5,775 (2000); 5,935 (2010); Density: 114.4 persons per square mile (2010); Race: 96.1% White, 1.1% Black, 0.3% Asian, 0.4% American Indian/Alaska Native, 0.0% Native Hawaiian/Other Pacific Islander, 2.1% Other, 2.3% Hispanic of any race (2010); Average household size: 2.69 (2010); Median age: 40.0 (2010); Males per 100 females: 100.5 (2010); Marriage status: 24.0% never married, 62.6% now married, 5.8% widowed, 7.6% divorced (2006-2010 5-year est.); Foreign born: 2.6% (2006-2010 5-year est.); Ancestry (includes multiple ancestries): 49.8% German, 16.7% Irish, 6.8% English, 6.7% American, 4.5% Scottish (2006-2010 5-year est.).

Economy: Single-family building permits issued: 2 (2011); Multi-family building permits issued: 0 (2011); Employment by occupation: 11.5% management, 3.4% professional, 11.3% services, 15.6% sales, 3.3% farming, 16.2% construction, 15.0% production (2006-2010 5-year est.).

Income: Per capita income: $22,617 (2006-2010 5-year est.); Median household income: $50,516 (2006-2010 5-year est.); Average household income: $58,803 (2006-2010 5-year est.); Percent of households with income of $100,000 or more: 9.6% (2006-2010 5-year est.); Poverty rate: 3.0% (2006-2010 5-year est.).

Education: Percent of population age 25 and over with: High school diploma (including GED) or higher: 82.3% (2006-2010 5-year est.); Bachelor's degree or higher: 12.0% (2006-2010 5-year est.); Master's degree or higher: 2.9% (2006-2010 5-year est.).

School District(s)

Tuscarora SD (KG-12)
2010-11 Enrollment: 2,593 . . . . (717) 328-3127

Housing: Homeownership rate: 84.1% (2010); Median home value: $159,800 (2006-2010 5-year est.); Median contract rent: $509 per month (2006-2010 5-year est.); Median year structure built: 1969 (2006-2010 5-year est.).

Transportation: Commute to work: 90.8% car, 0.0% public transportation, 4.1% walk, 4.4% work from home (2006-2010 5-year est.); Travel time to work: 20.8% less than 15 minutes, 54.9% 15 to 30 minutes, 13.7% 30 to 45 minutes, 2.9% 45 to 60 minutes, 7.7% 60 minutes or more (2006-2010 5-year est.)

Additional Information Contacts

Greater Chambersburg Chamber of Commerce . . . . (717) 264-7101
http://chambersburg.org
Saint Thomas Township . . . . (717) 369-2144

SCOTLAND (CDP).
Covers a land area of 0.824 square miles and a water area of 0 square miles. Located at 39.97° N. Lat; 77.58° W. Long. Elevation is 699 feet.

Population: n/a (1990); n/a (2000); 1,395 (2010); Density: 1,692.8 persons per square mile (2010); Race: 94.2% White, 2.5% Black, 0.6% Asian, 0.0% American Indian/Alaska Native, 0.1% Native Hawaiian/Other Pacific Islander, 2.6% Other, 1.9% Hispanic of any race (2010); Average household size: 2.61 (2010); Median age: 38.6 (2010); Males per 100 females: 99.3 (2010); Marriage status: 17.2% never married, 63.8% now married, 13.2% widowed, 5.7% divorced (2006-2010 5-year est.); Foreign born: 2.9% (2006-2010 5-year est.); Ancestry (includes multiple ancestries): 35.6% German, 13.4% Italian, 7.7% American, 6.2% Polish, 5.9% Dutch (2006-2010 5-year est.).

Economy: Employment by occupation: 14.2% management, 4.6% professional, 17.3% services, 12.1% sales, 4.4% farming, 4.5% construction, 1.5% production (2006-2010 5-year est.).

Income: Per capita income: $22,923 (2006-2010 5-year est.); Median household income: $55,541 (2006-2010 5-year est.); Average household income: $62,039 (2006-2010 5-year est.); Percent of households with income of $100,000 or more: 12.5% (2006-2010 5-year est.); Poverty rate: 7.5% (2006-2010 5-year est.).

Education: Percent of population age 25 and over with: High school diploma (including GED) or higher: 82.2% (2006-2010 5-year est.); Bachelor's degree or higher: 23.3% (2006-2010 5-year est.); Master's degree or higher: 7.8% (2006-2010 5-year est.).

School District(s)
Chambersburg Area SD (KG-12)

   2010-11 Enrollment: 8,523 . . . . (717) 263-9281

Scotland Sch Veterans Children (-)

   2010-11 Enrollment: n/a . . . . (717) 264-7187

Housing: Homeownership rate: 85.4% (2010); Median home value: $178,400 (2006-2010 5-year est.); Median contract rent: $841 per month (2006-2010 5-year est.); Median year structure built: 1984 (2006-2010 5-year est.).

Transportation: Commute to work: 96.0% car, 0.0% public transportation, 2.0% walk, 1.9% work from home (2006-2010 5-year est.); Travel time to work: 42.4% less than 15 minutes, 33.8% 15 to 30 minutes, 3.3% 30 to 45 minutes, 15.7% 45 to 60 minutes, 4.9% 60 minutes or more (2006-2010 5-year est.)

SHADY GROVE (unincorporated postal area)
Zip Code: 17256

Covers a land area of 0.106 square miles and a water area of 0 square miles. Located at 39.78° N. Lat; 77.67° W. Long. Elevation is 797 feet. Population: 91 (2010); Density: 856.8 persons per square mile (2010); Race: 96.7% White, 0.0% Black, 1.1% Asian, 0.0% American Indian/Alaska Native, 0.0% Native Hawaiian/Other Pacific Islander, 2.2% Other, 1.1% Hispanic of any race (2010); Average household size: 3.03 (2010); Median age: 37.9 (2010); Males per 100 females: 97.8 (2010); Homeownership rate: 73.3% (2010)

SOUTH MOUNTAIN (unincorporated postal area)
Zip Code: 17261

Covers a land area of 2.401 square miles and a water area of 0 square miles. Located at 39.86° N. Lat; 77.50° W. Long. Population: 193 (2010); Density: 80.4 persons per square mile (2010); Race: 59.6% White, 32.1% Black, 0.5% Asian, 0.0% American Indian/Alaska Native, 0.5% Native Hawaiian/Other Pacific Islander, 7.3% Other, 8.8% Hispanic of any race (2010); Average household size: 0.00 (2010); Median age: 59.5 (2010); Males per 100 females: 206.3 (2010); Homeownership rate: 0.0% (2010)

SOUTHAMPTON (township).
Covers a land area of 38.230 square miles and a water area of 0.008 square miles. Located at 40.02° N. Lat; 77.55° W. Long.

Population: 5,484 (1990); 6,138 (2000); 7,987 (2010); Density: 208.9 persons per square mile (2010); Race: 94.8% White, 2.1% Black, 0.9% Asian, 0.2% American Indian/Alaska Native, 0.0% Native Hawaiian/Other Pacific Islander, 2.0% Other, 2.3% Hispanic of any race (2010); Average household size: 2.71 (2010); Median age: 37.0 (2010); Males per 100 females: 96.6 (2010); Marriage status: 23.9% never married, 62.6% now married, 5.4% widowed, 8.2% divorced (2006-2010 5-year est.); Foreign born: 4.5% (2006-2010 5-year est.); Ancestry (includes multiple ancestries): 46.4% German, 14.7% Irish, 10.6% American, 7.7% English, 7.1% Italian (2006-2010 5-year est.).

Economy: Single-family building permits issued: 40 (2011); Multi-family building permits issued: 0 (2011); Employment by occupation: 10.1% management, 3.0% professional, 5.9% services, 17.1% sales, 2.7% farming, 13.7% construction, 8.0% production (2006-2010 5-year est.).

Income: Per capita income: $23,463 (2006-2010 5-year est.); Median household income: $52,489 (2006-2010 5-year est.); Average household income: $62,066 (2006-2010 5-year est.); Percent of households with income of $100,000 or more: 15.3% (2006-2010 5-year est.); Poverty rate: 7.0% (2006-2010 5-year est.).

Education: Percent of population age 25 and over with: High school diploma (including GED) or higher: 82.1% (2006-2010 5-year est.); Bachelor's degree or higher: 17.3% (2006-2010 5-year est.); Master's degree or higher: 10.3% (2006-2010 5-year est.).

Housing: Homeownership rate: 82.6% (2010); Median home value: $160,800 (2006-2010 5-year est.); Median contract rent: $508 per month (2006-2010 5-year est.); Median year structure built: 1980 (2006-2010 5-year est.).

Transportation: Commute to work: 93.6% car, 0.3% public transportation, 0.4% walk, 4.8% work from home (2006-2010 5-year est.); Travel time to work: 32.9% less than 15 minutes, 38.5% 15 to 30 minutes, 16.2% 30 to 45 minutes, 6.2% 45 to 60 minutes, 6.2% 60 minutes or more (2006-2010 5-year est.)

Additional Information Contacts

Franklin Area Chamber of Commerce. . . . . (814) 432-5823
   http://www.franklinareachamber.org

Southampton Township. . . . . (717) 369-5890
   http://www.southamptontownship.org

SPRING RUN (unincorporated postal area)
Zip Code: 17262

Covers a land area of 26.908 square miles and a water area of 0.002 square miles. Located at 40.14° N. Lat; 77.74° W. Long. Population: 1,462 (2010); Density: 54.3 persons per square mile (2010); Race: 98.8% White, 0.1% Black, 0.3% Asian, 0.0% American Indian/Alaska Native, 0.0% Native Hawaiian/Other Pacific Islander, 0.8% Other, 0.4% Hispanic of any race (2010); Average household size: 2.95 (2010); Median age: 35.3 (2010); Males per 100 females: 97.6 (2010); Homeownership rate: 78.1% (2010)

STATE LINE (CDP).
Covers a land area of 2.738 square miles and a water area of 0 square miles. Located at 39.73° N. Lat; 77.72° W. Long. Elevation is 702 feet.

Population: n/a (1990); n/a (2000); 2,709 (2010); Density: 989.3 persons per square mile (2010); Race: 93.5% White, 2.3% Black, 1.8% Asian, 0.0% American Indian/Alaska Native, 0.0% Native Hawaiian/Other Pacific Islander, 2.4% Other, 2.7% Hispanic of any race (2010); Average household size: 2.63 (2010); Median age: 36.3 (2010); Males per 100 females: 95.5 (2010); Marriage status: 30.4% never married, 57.5% now married, 1.3% widowed, 10.8% divorced (2006-2010 5-year est.); Foreign born: 2.5% (2006-2010 5-year est.); Ancestry (includes multiple ancestries): 52.6% German, 11.1% Irish, 8.0% English, 6.5% French, 6.5% Italian (2006-2010 5-year est.).

Economy: Employment by occupation: 11.4% management, 0.7% professional, 8.3% services, 22.5% sales, 5.3% farming, 9.5% construction, 8.0% production (2006-2010 5-year est.).

Income: Per capita income: $27,547 (2006-2010 5-year est.); Median household income: $60,781 (2006-2010 5-year est.); Average household income: $67,072 (2006-2010 5-year est.); Percent of households with income of $100,000 or more: 22.8% (2006-2010 5-year est.); Poverty rate: 7.9% (2006-2010 5-year est.).

Education: Percent of population age 25 and over with: High school diploma (including GED) or higher: 89.4% (2006-2010 5-year est.); Bachelor's degree or higher: 19.5% (2006-2010 5-year est.); Master's degree or higher: 6.6% (2006-2010 5-year est.).

Housing: Homeownership rate: 75.7% (2010); Median home value: $154,000 (2006-2010 5-year est.); Median contract rent: $664 per month (2006-2010 5-year est.); Median year structure built: 1990 (2006-2010 5-year est.).

Transportation: Commute to work: 84.9% car, 0.0% public transportation, 6.5% walk, 7.6% work from home (2006-2010 5-year est.); Travel time to work: 34.4% less than 15 minutes, 40.6% 15 to 30 minutes, 8.0% 30 to 45 minutes, 7.9% 45 to 60 minutes, 9.0% 60 minutes or more (2006-2010 5-year est.)

UPPERSTRASBURG (unincorporated postal area)

Zip Code: 17265

Covers a land area of 37.928 square miles and a water area of 0.047 square miles. Located at 40.02° N. Lat; 77.78° W. Long. Population: 496 (2010); Density: 13.1 persons per square mile (2010); Race: 99.0% White, 0.4% Black, 0.0% Asian, 0.0% American Indian/Alaska Native, 0.0% Native Hawaiian/Other Pacific Islander, 0.6% Other, 0.2% Hispanic of any race (2010); Average household size: 2.35 (2010); Median age: 45.7 (2010); Males per 100 females: 105.8 (2010); Homeownership rate: 80.5% (2010)

WARREN (township).

Covers a land area of 30.634 square miles and a water area of 0 square miles. Located at 39.78° N. Lat; 78.01° W. Long.
Population: 310 (1990); 334 (2000); 369 (2010); Density: 12.0 persons per square mile (2010); Race: 98.1% White, 1.1% Black, 0.5% Asian, 0.3% American Indian/Alaska Native, 0.0% Native Hawaiian/Other Pacific Islander, 0.0% Other, 0.3% Hispanic of any race (2010); Average household size: 2.58 (2010); Median age: 44.1 (2010); Males per 100 females: 102.7 (2010); Marriage status: 16.7% never married, 60.2% now married, 4.0% widowed, 19.1% divorced (2006-2010 5-year est.); Foreign born: 0.6% (2006-2010 5-year est.); Ancestry (includes multiple ancestries): 45.1% German, 16.2% American, 6.4% English, 6.2% Irish, 2.0% Scottish (2006-2010 5-year est.).
Economy: Single-family building permits issued: 0 (2011); Multi-family building permits issued: 0 (2011); Employment by occupation: 16.2% management, 3.2% professional, 7.6% services, 13.5% sales, 9.7% farming, 12.4% construction, 9.7% production (2006-2010 5-year est.).
Income: Per capita income: $28,531 (2006-2010 5-year est.); Median household income: $52,292 (2006-2010 5-year est.); Average household income: $66,421 (2006-2010 5-year est.); Percent of households with income of $100,000 or more: 15.5% (2006-2010 5-year est.); Poverty rate: 5.3% (2006-2010 5-year est.).
Education: Percent of population age 25 and over with: High school diploma (including GED) or higher: 84.2% (2006-2010 5-year est.); Bachelor's degree or higher: 12.0% (2006-2010 5-year est.); Master's degree or higher: 6.4% (2006-2010 5-year est.).
Housing: Homeownership rate: 82.6% (2010); Median home value: $269,400 (2006-2010 5-year est.); Median contract rent: $455 per month (2006-2010 5-year est.); Median year structure built: 1982 (2006-2010 5-year est.).
Transportation: Commute to work: 93.4% car, 0.5% public transportation, 3.3% walk, 2.7% work from home (2006-2010 5-year est.); Travel time to work: 26.4% less than 15 minutes, 10.7% 15 to 30 minutes, 39.9% 30 to 45 minutes, 15.2% 45 to 60 minutes, 7.9% 60 minutes or more (2006-2010 5-year est.)

WASHINGTON (township).

Covers a land area of 39.050 square miles and a water area of 0.008 square miles. Located at 39.75° N. Lat; 77.56° W. Long.
Population: 11,128 (1990); 11,559 (2000); 14,009 (2010); Density: 358.7 persons per square mile (2010); Race: 95.1% White, 1.7% Black, 1.1% Asian, 0.2% American Indian/Alaska Native, 0.0% Native Hawaiian/Other Pacific Islander, 1.9% Other, 2.3% Hispanic of any race (2010); Average household size: 2.52 (2010); Median age: 42.0 (2010); Males per 100 females: 96.9 (2010); Marriage status: 18.9% never married, 65.7% now married, 7.2% widowed, 8.3% divorced (2006-2010 5-year est.); Foreign born: 3.5% (2006-2010 5-year est.); Ancestry (includes multiple ancestries): 42.6% German, 14.5% Irish, 8.5% English, 8.2% American, 3.2% Polish (2006-2010 5-year est.).
Economy: Single-family building permits issued: 9 (2011); Multi-family building permits issued: 4 (2011); Employment by occupation: 13.5% management, 5.1% professional, 13.7% services, 14.3% sales, 3.0% farming, 9.1% construction, 5.6% production (2006-2010 5-year est.).
Income: Per capita income: $28,406 (2006-2010 5-year est.); Median household income: $56,840 (2006-2010 5-year est.); Average household income: $69,228 (2006-2010 5-year est.); Percent of households with income of $100,000 or more: 21.4% (2006-2010 5-year est.); Poverty rate: 6.5% (2006-2010 5-year est.).
Education: Percent of population age 25 and over with: High school diploma (including GED) or higher: 88.4% (2006-2010 5-year est.); Bachelor's degree or higher: 20.1% (2006-2010 5-year est.); Master's degree or higher: 7.5% (2006-2010 5-year est.).
Housing: Homeownership rate: 81.0% (2010); Median home value: $206,200 (2006-2010 5-year est.); Median contract rent: $598 per month

(2006-2010 5-year est.); Median year structure built: 1974 (2006-2010 5-year est.).
Safety: Violent crime rate: 8.5 per 10,000 population; Property crime rate: 182.9 per 10,000 population (2011).
Transportation: Commute to work: 91.4% car, 1.1% public transportation, 2.9% walk, 3.0% work from home (2006-2010 5-year est.); Travel time to work: 35.6% less than 15 minutes, 30.1% 15 to 30 minutes, 19.0% 30 to 45 minutes, 5.8% 45 to 60 minutes, 9.4% 60 minutes or more (2006-2010 5-year est.)
Additional Information Contacts
Franklin Area Chamber of Commerce . . . . (814) 432-5823
   http://www.franklinareachamber.org
Washington Township . . . . (717) 762-1145
   http://www.wtwp.com

WAYNE HEIGHTS (CDP).

Covers a land area of 2.133 square miles and a water area of 0 square miles. Located at 39.75° N. Lat; 77.54° W. Long. Elevation is 636 feet.
History: Appalachian Trail passes to East on South Mt.
Population: 1,683 (1990); 1,805 (2000); 2,545 (2010); Density: 1,193.2 persons per square mile (2010); Race: 91.7% White, 3.3% Black, 2.0% Asian, 0.5% American Indian/Alaska Native, 0.0% Native Hawaiian/Other Pacific Islander, 2.5% Other, 2.8% Hispanic of any race (2010); Average household size: 2.46 (2010); Median age: 40.6 (2010); Males per 100 females: 90.6 (2010); Marriage status: 20.9% never married, 64.7% now married, 6.9% widowed, 7.5% divorced (2006-2010 5-year est.); Foreign born: 6.3% (2006-2010 5-year est.); Ancestry (includes multiple ancestries): 45.3% German, 15.0% English, 15.0% Irish, 8.5% Polish, 5.8% Italian (2006-2010 5-year est.).
Economy: Employment by occupation: 21.4% management, 6.2% professional, 13.1% services, 16.4% sales, 3.8% farming, 7.5% construction, 6.6% production (2006-2010 5-year est.).
Income: Per capita income: $31,520 (2006-2010 5-year est.); Median household income: $60,500 (2006-2010 5-year est.); Average household income: $73,233 (2006-2010 5-year est.); Percent of households with income of $100,000 or more: 26.8% (2006-2010 5-year est.); Poverty rate: 4.3% (2006-2010 5-year est.).
Education: Percent of population age 25 and over with: High school diploma (including GED) or higher: 87.4% (2006-2010 5-year est.); Bachelor's degree or higher: 22.0% (2006-2010 5-year est.); Master's degree or higher: 5.4% (2006-2010 5-year est.).
Housing: Homeownership rate: 72.0% (2010); Median home value: $209,000 (2006-2010 5-year est.); Median contract rent: $739 per month (2006-2010 5-year est.); Median year structure built: 1975 (2006-2010 5-year est.).
Transportation: Commute to work: 96.0% car, 0.0% public transportation, 2.7% walk, 1.4% work from home (2006-2010 5-year est.); Travel time to work: 36.2% less than 15 minutes, 30.7% 15 to 30 minutes, 18.2% 30 to 45 minutes, 8.7% 45 to 60 minutes, 6.1% 60 minutes or more (2006-2010 5-year est.)
Additional Information Contacts
Greater Waynesboro Chamber of Commerce . . . . (717) 762-7123
   http://www.waynesboro.org

WAYNESBORO (borough).

Covers a land area of 3.412 square miles and a water area of 0 square miles. Located at 39.75° N. Lat; 77.58° W. Long. Elevation is 709 feet.
History: Appalachian Trail passes to east. Settled 1798, Incorporated 1818.
Population: 9,569 (1990); 9,614 (2000); 10,568 (2010); Density: 3,097.1 persons per square mile (2010); Race: 92.4% White, 3.0% Black, 0.6% Asian, 0.4% American Indian/Alaska Native, 0.0% Native Hawaiian/Other Pacific Islander, 3.6% Other, 3.7% Hispanic of any race (2010); Average household size: 2.33 (2010); Median age: 36.6 (2010); Males per 100 females: 91.9 (2010); Marriage status: 29.0% never married, 51.3% now married, 7.2% widowed, 12.5% divorced (2006-2010 5-year est.); Foreign born: 0.9% (2006-2010 5-year est.); Ancestry (includes multiple ancestries): 40.5% German, 17.1% Irish, 9.7% English, 8.5% American, 4.9% Italian (2006-2010 5-year est.).
Economy: Single-family building permits issued: 19 (2011); Multi-family building permits issued: 0 (2011); Employment by occupation: 7.0% management, 3.5% professional, 14.4% services, 17.7% sales, 8.5% farming, 8.9% construction, 6.5% production (2006-2010 5-year est.).
Income: Per capita income: $20,638 (2006-2010 5-year est.); Median household income: $41,155 (2006-2010 5-year est.); Average household

income: $48,379 (2006-2010 5-year est.); Percent of households with income of $100,000 or more: 6.4% (2006-2010 5-year est.); Poverty rate: 11.7% (2006-2010 5-year est.).

Education: Percent of population age 25 and over with: High school diploma (including GED) or higher: 83.0% (2006-2010 5-year est.); Bachelor's degree or higher: 14.6% (2006-2010 5-year est.); Master's degree or higher: 5.4% (2006-2010 5-year est.).

School District(s)

Waynesboro Area SD (KG-12)

2010-11 Enrollment: 4,219 . . . . (717) 762-1191

Housing: Homeownership rate: 52.6% (2010); Median home value: $157,100 (2006-2010 5-year est.); Median contract rent: $521 per month (2006-2010 5-year est.); Median year structure built: 1948 (2006-2010 5-year est.).

Hospitals: Waynesboro Hospital (64 beds)

Safety: Violent crime rate: 20.8 per 10,000 population; Property crime rate: 167.0 per 10,000 population (2011).

Newspapers: The Record Herald (Local news; Circulation 10,375)

Transportation: Commute to work: 92.2% car, 0.5% public transportation, 4.7% walk, 1.5% work from home (2006-2010 5-year est.); Travel time to work: 34.8% less than 15 minutes, 30.0% 15 to 30 minutes, 20.1% 30 to 45 minutes, 8.0% 45 to 60 minutes, 7.1% 60 minutes or more (2006-2010 5-year est.)

Additional Information Contacts

Borough of Waynesboro . . . . (717) 762-2101
http://www.waynesboropa.org

Greater Waynesboro Chamber of Commerce . . . . (717) 762-7123
http://www.waynesboro.org

WILLIAMSON (unincorporated postal area)

Zip Code: 17270

Covers a land area of 0.097 square miles and a water area of 0 square miles. Located at 39.85° N. Lat; 77.79° W. Long. Elevation is 486 feet. Population: 115 (2010); Density: 1,174.1 persons per square mile (2010); Race: 100.0% White, 0.0% Black, 0.0% Asian, 0.0% American Indian/Alaska Native, 0.0% Native Hawaiian/Other Pacific Islander, 0.0% Other, 0.0% Hispanic of any race (2010); Average household size: 2.67 (2010); Median age: 36.8 (2010); Males per 100 females: 117.0 (2010); Homeownership rate: 95.4% (2010)

WILLOW HILL (unincorporated postal area)

Zip Code: 17271

Covers a land area of 10.650 square miles and a water area of 0 square miles. Located at 40.09° N. Lat; 77.80° W. Long. Elevation is 797 feet. Population: 339 (2010); Density: 31.8 persons per square mile (2010); Race: 98.2% White, 0.3% Black, 0.0% Asian, 0.3% American Indian/Alaska Native, 0.0% Native Hawaiian/Other Pacific Islander, 1.2% Other, 1.2% Hispanic of any race (2010); Average household size: 2.73 (2010); Median age: 42.2 (2010); Males per 100 females: 97.1 (2010); Homeownership rate: 87.9% (2010)

ZULLINGER (unincorporated postal area)

Zip Code: 17272

Covers a land area of 0.183 square miles and a water area of 0 square miles. Located at 39.76° N. Lat; 77.62° W. Long. Elevation is 745 feet. Population: 294 (2010); Density: 1,604.8 persons per square mile (2010); Race: 96.3% White, 0.7% Black, 0.0% Asian, 0.0% American Indian/Alaska Native, 0.0% Native Hawaiian/Other Pacific Islander, 3.0% Other, 1.4% Hispanic of any race (2010); Average household size: 2.19 (2010); Median age: 37.9 (2010); Males per 100 females: 88.5 (2010); Homeownership rate: 82.1% (2010)

Fulton County

Located in southern Pennsylvania; mountainous area with the Tuscarora Mountains in the east and Sideling Hill in the west; bounded on the south by Maryland. Covers a land area of 437.551 square miles, a water area of 0.504 square miles, and is located in the Eastern Time Zone at 39.91° N. Lat., 78.12° W. Long. The county was founded in 1850. County seat is McConnellsburg.

Population: 13,837 (1990); 14,261 (2000); 14,845 (2010); Race: 97.3% White, 1.0% Black, 0.1% Asian, 0.2% American Indian/Alaska Native, 0.0% Native Hawaiian/Other Pacific Islander, 1.4% Other, 0.8% Hispanic of any race (2010); Density: 33.9 persons per square mile (2010); Average

household size: 2.45 (2010); Median age: 41.8 (2010); Males per 100 females: 101.3 (2010).

Religion: Six largest groups: 10.0% Methodist/Pietist, 6.4% Non-Denominational, 6.1% Presbyterian-Reformed, 2.6% European Free-Church, 1.5% Pentecostal, 1.3% Catholicism (2010)

Economy: Unemployment rate: 8.6% (August 2012); Total civilian labor force: 7,968 (August 2012); Leading industries: 8.3% retail trade; 4.9% construction; 4.8% accommodation & food services (2010); Farms: 608 totaling 103,516 acres (2007); Companies that employ 500 or more persons: 1 (2010); Companies that employ 100 to 499 persons: 4 (2010); Companies that employ less than 100 persons: 271 (2010); Black-owned businesses: n/a (2007); Hispanic-owned businesses: n/a (2007); Asian-owned businesses: n/a (2007); Women-owned businesses: 313 (2007); Retail sales per capita: $9,294 (2010). Single-family building permits issued: 17 (2011); Multi-family building permits issued: 0 (2011).

Income: Per capita income: $21,739 (2006-2010 5-year est.); Median household income: $45,240 (2006-2010 5-year est.); Average household income: $54,226 (2006-2010 5-year est.); Percent of households with income of $100,000 or more: 11.5% (2006-2010 5-year est.); Poverty rate: 13.3% (2006-2010 5-year est.); Bankruptcy rate: 2.29% (2011).

Education: Percent of population age 25 and over with: High school diploma (including GED) or higher: 83.4% (2006-2010 5-year est.); Bachelor's degree or higher: 9.9% (2006-2010 5-year est.); Master's degree or higher: 3.9% (2006-2010 5-year est.).

Housing: Homeownership rate: 76.8% (2010); Median home value: $157,500 (2006-2010 5-year est.); Median contract rent: $422 per month (2006-2010 5-year est.); Median year structure built: 1972 (2006-2010 5-year est.)

Health: Birth rate: 104.0 per 10,000 population (2011); Death rate: 92.6 per 10,000 population (2011); Age-adjusted cancer mortality rate: 188.8 deaths per 100,000 population (2009); Number of physicians: 4.7 per 10,000 population (2010); Hospital beds: 58.9 per 10,000 population (2008); Hospital admissions: 694.2 per 10,000 population (2008).

Elections: 2012 Presidential election results: 21.2% Obama, 77.7% Romney

National and State Parks: Cowans Gap State Park

Additional Information Contacts

Fulton County Government . . . . (717) 485-3691
http://www.co.fulton.pa.us

Fulton County Chamber of Commerce and Tourism . . . . . . (717) 485-4064
http://www.fultoncountypa.com

Fulton County Communities

AYR (township). Covers a land area of 46.257 square miles and a water area of 0.308 square miles. Located at 39.87° N. Lat; 78.03° W. Long.

Population: 2,167 (1990); 1,982 (2000); 1,942 (2010); Density: 42.0 persons per square mile (2010); Race: 98.7% White, 0.7% Black, 0.1% Asian, 0.1% American Indian/Alaska Native, 0.0% Native Hawaiian/Other Pacific Islander, 0.4% Other, 0.3% Hispanic of any race (2010); Average household size: 2.46 (2010); Median age: 43.5 (2010); Males per 100 females: 105.9 (2010); Marriage status: 14.2% never married, 65.4% now married, 3.0% widowed, 17.3% divorced (2006-2010 5-year est.); Foreign born: 0.0% (2006-2010 5-year est.); Ancestry (includes multiple ancestries): 29.1% German, 16.0% American, 14.3% Irish, 4.2% Italian, 3.9% English (2006-2010 5-year est.).

Economy: Single-family building permits issued: 1 (2011); Multi-family building permits issued: 0 (2011); Employment by occupation: 6.0% management, 0.7% professional, 9.6% services, 14.8% sales, 8.9% farming, 15.3% construction, 6.6% production (2006-2010 5-year est.).

Income: Per capita income: $24,856 (2006-2010 5-year est.); Median household income: $51,875 (2006-2010 5-year est.); Average household income: $61,212 (2006-2010 5-year est.); Percent of households with income of $100,000 or more: 15.8% (2006-2010 5-year est.); Poverty rate: 9.3% (2006-2010 5-year est.).

Education: Percent of population age 25 and over with: High school diploma (including GED) or higher: 82.6% (2006-2010 5-year est.); Bachelor's degree or higher: 8.9% (2006-2010 5-year est.); Master's degree or higher: 4.1% (2006-2010 5-year est.).

Housing: Homeownership rate: 80.0% (2010); Median home value: $186,000 (2006-2010 5-year est.); Median contract rent: $459 per month (2006-2010 5-year est.); Median year structure built: 1974 (2006-2010 5-year est.).

Transportation: Commute to work: 88.4% car, 0.0% public transportation, 5.0% walk, 4.8% work from home (2006-2010 5-year est.); Travel time to

work: 50.8% less than 15 minutes, 11.4% 15 to 30 minutes, 9.6% 30 to 45 minutes, 19.5% 45 to 60 minutes, 8.7% 60 minutes or more (2006-2010 5-year est.)

Additional Information Contacts
Fulton County Chamber of Commerce and Tourism . . . . . . (717) 485-4064
http://www.fultoncountypa.com

BELFAST (township).
Covers a land area of 50.147 square miles and a water area of 0 square miles. Located at 39.88° N. Lat; 78.14° W. Long.
Population: 1,208 (1990); 1,341 (2000); 1,448 (2010); Density: 28.9 persons per square mile (2010); Race: 98.8% White, 0.1% Black, 0.3% Asian, 0.0% American Indian/Alaska Native, 0.0% Native Hawaiian/Other Pacific Islander, 0.8% Other, 0.3% Hispanic of any race (2010); Average household size: 2.63 (2010); Median age: 41.1 (2010); Males per 100 females: 101.7 (2010); Marriage status: 21.3% never married, 69.4% now married, 5.3% widowed, 3.9% divorced (2006-2010 5-year est.); Foreign born: 0.6% (2006-2010 5-year est.); Ancestry (includes multiple ancestries): 38.3% German, 14.5% American, 11.9% Irish, 8.2% French, 4.4% English (2006-2010 5-year est.).
Economy: Single-family building permits issued: 3 (2011); Multi-family building permits issued: 0 (2011); Employment by occupation: 12.9% management, 2.1% professional, 9.9% services, 15.3% sales, 4.8% farming, 16.6% construction, 11.8% production (2006-2010 5-year est.).
Income: Per capita income: $22,234 (2006-2010 5-year est.); Median household income: $48,846 (2006-2010 5-year est.); Average household income: $57,844 (2006-2010 5-year est.); Percent of households with income of $100,000 or more: 11.6% (2006-2010 5-year est.); Poverty rate: 7.3% (2006-2010 5-year est.).
Education: Percent of population age 25 and over with: High school diploma (including GED) or higher: 85.5% (2006-2010 5-year est.); Bachelor's degree or higher: 10.3% (2006-2010 5-year est.); Master's degree or higher: 2.3% (2006-2010 5-year est.).
Housing: Homeownership rate: 83.3% (2010); Median home value: $186,400 (2006-2010 5-year est.); Median contract rent: $446 per month (2006-2010 5-year est.); Median year structure built: 1966 (2006-2010 5-year est.).
Transportation: Commute to work: 89.8% car, 0.5% public transportation, 2.0% walk, 5.0% work from home (2006-2010 5-year est.); Travel time to work: 22.6% less than 15 minutes, 32.2% 15 to 30 minutes, 12.9% 30 to 45 minutes, 16.2% 45 to 60 minutes, 16.2% 60 minutes or more (2006-2010 5-year est.)

Additional Information Contacts
Fulton County Chamber of Commerce and Tourism . . . . . . (717) 485-4064
http://www.fultoncountypa.com

BETHEL (township).
Covers a land area of 37.064 square miles and a water area of 0.007 square miles. Located at 39.78° N. Lat; 78.22° W. Long.
Population: 1,326 (1990); 1,420 (2000); 1,508 (2010); Density: 40.7 persons per square mile (2010); Race: 98.3% White, 0.3% Black, 0.1% Asian, 0.3% American Indian/Alaska Native, 0.0% Native Hawaiian/Other Pacific Islander, 1.0% Other, 1.1% Hispanic of any race (2010); Average household size: 2.50 (2010); Median age: 40.8 (2010); Males per 100 females: 100.8 (2010); Marriage status: 23.6% never married, 58.3% now married, 6.6% widowed, 11.4% divorced (2006-2010 5-year est.); Foreign born: 0.3% (2006-2010 5-year est.); Ancestry (includes multiple ancestries): 45.6% German, 15.0% Irish, 12.4% English, 8.5% American, 3.3% French (2006-2010 5-year est.).
Economy: Single-family building permits issued: 2 (2011); Multi-family building permits issued: 0 (2011); Employment by occupation: 7.2% management, 1.3% professional, 5.9% services, 22.6% sales, 1.5% farming, 22.2% construction, 20.6% production (2006-2010 5-year est.).
Income: Per capita income: $22,623 (2006-2010 5-year est.); Median household income: $53,984 (2006-2010 5-year est.); Average household income: $57,353 (2006-2010 5-year est.); Percent of households with income of $100,000 or more: 13.1% (2006-2010 5-year est.); Poverty rate: 13.4% (2006-2010 5-year est.).
Education: Percent of population age 25 and over with: High school diploma (including GED) or higher: 82.8% (2006-2010 5-year est.); Bachelor's degree or higher: 11.6% (2006-2010 5-year est.); Master's degree or higher: 4.2% (2006-2010 5-year est.).
Housing: Homeownership rate: 76.8% (2010); Median home value: $185,000 (2006-2010 5-year est.); Median contract rent: $416 per month (2006-2010 5-year est.); Median year structure built: 1971 (2006-2010 5-year est.).

Transportation: Commute to work: 94.1% car, 0.0% public transportation, 2.1% walk, 2.5% work from home (2006-2010 5-year est.); Travel time to work: 20.0% less than 15 minutes, 18.3% 15 to 30 minutes, 23.0% 30 to 45 minutes, 23.9% 45 to 60 minutes, 14.8% 60 minutes or more (2006-2010 5-year est.)

Additional Information Contacts
Fulton County Chamber of Commerce and Tourism . . . . . . (717) 485-4064
http://www.fultoncountypa.com

BIG COVE TANNERY (unincorporated postal area)
Zip Code: 17212
Covers a land area of 35.241 square miles and a water area of 0.002 square miles. Located at 39.81° N. Lat; 78.06° W. Long. Population: 702 (2010); Density: 19.9 persons per square mile (2010); Race: 98.0% White, 0.9% Black, 0.3% Asian, 0.0% American Indian/Alaska Native, 0.0% Native Hawaiian/Other Pacific Islander, 0.8% Other, 0.7% Hispanic of any race (2010); Average household size: 2.53 (2010); Median age: 42.7 (2010); Males per 100 females: 109.6 (2010); Homeownership rate: 79.1% (2010)

BRUSH CREEK (township).
Covers a land area of 54.289 square miles and a water area of <.001 square miles. Located at 39.94° N. Lat; 78.21° W. Long.
Population: 634 (1990); 730 (2000); 819 (2010); Density: 15.1 persons per square mile (2010); Race: 94.9% White, 3.2% Black, 0.0% Asian, 0.2% American Indian/Alaska Native, 0.0% Native Hawaiian/Other Pacific Islander, 1.7% Other, 1.8% Hispanic of any race (2010); Average household size: 2.33 (2010); Median age: 44.9 (2010); Males per 100 females: 93.6 (2010); Marriage status: 23.2% never married, 59.7% now married, 7.5% widowed, 9.6% divorced (2006-2010 5-year est.); Foreign born: 1.5% (2006-2010 5-year est.); Ancestry (includes multiple ancestries): 32.5% German, 12.9% Irish, 10.6% American, 9.0% Italian, 8.9% English (2006-2010 5-year est.).
Economy: Single-family building permits issued: 1 (2011); Multi-family building permits issued: 0 (2011); Employment by occupation: 12.6% management, 1.0% professional, 15.7% services, 9.0% sales, 2.3% farming, 15.2% construction, 9.5% production (2006-2010 5-year est.).
Income: Per capita income: $18,626 (2006-2010 5-year est.); Median household income: $44,659 (2006-2010 5-year est.); Average household income: $50,103 (2006-2010 5-year est.); Percent of households with income of $100,000 or more: 9.3% (2006-2010 5-year est.); Poverty rate: 17.4% (2006-2010 5-year est.).
Education: Percent of population age 25 and over with: High school diploma (including GED) or higher: 89.5% (2006-2010 5-year est.); Bachelor's degree or higher: 3.7% (2006-2010 5-year est.); Master's degree or higher: 1.9% (2006-2010 5-year est.).
Housing: Homeownership rate: 78.2% (2010); Median home value: $153,600 (2006-2010 5-year est.); Median contract rent: $343 per month (2006-2010 5-year est.); Median year structure built: 1970 (2006-2010 5-year est.).
Transportation: Commute to work: 87.0% car, 0.0% public transportation, 4.2% walk, 7.8% work from home (2006-2010 5-year est.); Travel time to work: 37.6% less than 15 minutes, 41.0% 15 to 30 minutes, 6.2% 30 to 45 minutes, 2.3% 45 to 60 minutes, 13.0% 60 minutes or more (2006-2010 5-year est.)

BURNT CABINS (unincorporated postal area)
Zip Code: 17215
Covers a land area of 11.919 square miles and a water area of 0.006 square miles. Located at 40.07° N. Lat; 77.89° W. Long. Elevation is 889 feet. Population: 347 (2010); Density: 29.1 persons per square mile (2010); Race: 98.6% White, 0.0% Black, 0.0% Asian, 0.9% American Indian/Alaska Native, 0.0% Native Hawaiian/Other Pacific Islander, 0.5% Other, 0.0% Hispanic of any race (2010); Average household size: 2.82 (2010); Median age: 36.3 (2010); Males per 100 females: 94.9 (2010); Homeownership rate: 74.8% (2010)

CRYSTAL SPRING (unincorporated postal area)
Zip Code: 15536
Covers a land area of 34.004 square miles and a water area of <.001 square miles. Located at 39.95° N. Lat; 78.20° W. Long. Population: 459 (2010); Density: 13.5 persons per square mile (2010); Race: 98.5% White, 0.2% Black, 0.0% Asian, 0.2% American Indian/Alaska Native, 0.0% Native Hawaiian/Other Pacific Islander, 1.1% Other, 1.1% Hispanic of any race (2010); Average household size: 2.40 (2010);

Median age: 43.1 (2010); Males per 100 females: 93.7 (2010); Homeownership rate: 76.9% (2010)

DUBLIN (township). Covers a land area of 36.917 square miles and a water area of 0.025 square miles. Located at 40.06° N. Lat; 77.96° W. Long.
Population: 1,146 (1990); 1,277 (2000); 1,264 (2010); Density: 34.2 persons per square mile (2010); Race: 99.1% White, 0.0% Black, 0.0% Asian, 0.3% American Indian/Alaska Native, 0.0% Native Hawaiian/Other Pacific Islander, 0.6% Other, 0.0% Hispanic of any race (2010); Average household size: 2.44 (2010); Median age: 43.5 (2010); Males per 100 females: 90.6 (2010); Marriage status: 18.1% never married, 63.2% now married, 7.4% widowed, 11.3% divorced (2006-2010 5-year est.); Foreign born: 0.0% (2006-2010 5-year est.); Ancestry (includes multiple ancestries): 42.0% German, 15.1% Irish, 13.1% American, 7.2% English, 4.8% Dutch (2006-2010 5-year est.).
Economy: Single-family building permits issued: 0 (2011); Multi-family building permits issued: 0 (2011); Employment by occupation: 8.2% management, 1.3% professional, 11.9% services, 23.0% sales, 1.3% farming, 23.7% construction, 15.0% production (2006-2010 5-year est.).
Income: Per capita income: $18,752 (2006-2010 5-year est.); Median household income: $40,170 (2006-2010 5-year est.); Average household income: $45,876 (2006-2010 5-year est.); Percent of households with income of $100,000 or more: 7.1% (2006-2010 5-year est.); Poverty rate: 20.4% (2006-2010 5-year est.).
Education: Percent of population age 25 and over with: High school diploma (including GED) or higher: 78.0% (2006-2010 5-year est.); Bachelor's degree or higher: 5.6% (2006-2010 5-year est.); Master's degree or higher: 3.6% (2006-2010 5-year est.).
Housing: Homeownership rate: 78.4% (2010); Median home value: $130,400 (2006-2010 5-year est.); Median contract rent: $388 per month (2006-2010 5-year est.); Median year structure built: 1972 (2006-2010 5-year est.).
Transportation: Commute to work: 91.0% car, 0.0% public transportation, 0.0% walk, 8.5% work from home (2006-2010 5-year est.); Travel time to work: 27.3% less than 15 minutes, 39.8% 15 to 30 minutes, 8.6% 30 to 45 minutes, 12.3% 45 to 60 minutes, 11.9% 60 minutes or more (2006-2010 5-year est.)
Additional Information Contacts
Fulton County Chamber of Commerce and Tourism . . . . . . (717) 485-4064
    http://www.fultoncountypa.com

FORT LITTLETON (unincorporated postal area)
Zip Code: 17223
    Covers a land area of 10.889 square miles and a water area of 0.018 square miles. Located at 40.08° N. Lat; 77.94° W. Long. Population: 289 (2010); Density: 26.5 persons per square mile (2010); Race: 99.7% White, 0.0% Black, 0.0% Asian, 0.3% American Indian/Alaska Native, 0.0% Native Hawaiian/Other Pacific Islander, 0.0% Other, 0.0% Hispanic of any race (2010); Average household size: 2.37 (2010); Median age: 44.9 (2010); Males per 100 females: 97.9 (2010); Homeownership rate: 74.5% (2010)

HARRISONVILLE (unincorporated postal area)
Zip Code: 17228
    Covers a land area of 28.676 square miles and a water area of 0 square miles. Located at 39.98° N. Lat; 78.09° W. Long. Elevation is 781 feet. Population: 1,183 (2010); Density: 41.3 persons per square mile (2010); Race: 99.0% White, 0.2% Black, 0.1% Asian, 0.0% American Indian/Alaska Native, 0.1% Native Hawaiian/Other Pacific Islander, 0.6% Other, 0.8% Hispanic of any race (2010); Average household size: 2.57 (2010); Median age: 38.8 (2010); Males per 100 females: 107.5 (2010); Homeownership rate: 80.9% (2010)

HUSTONTOWN (unincorporated postal area)
Zip Code: 17229
    Covers a land area of 27.169 square miles and a water area of 0.005 square miles. Located at 40.08° N. Lat; 78.01° W. Long. Population: 1,276 (2010); Density: 47.0 persons per square mile (2010); Race: 98.9% White, 0.0% Black, 0.0% Asian, 0.4% American Indian/Alaska Native, 0.0% Native Hawaiian/Other Pacific Islander, 0.7% Other, 0.4% Hispanic of any race (2010); Average household size: 2.46 (2010); Median age: 41.6 (2010); Males per 100 females: 97.5 (2010); Homeownership rate: 80.5% (2010)

LICKING CREEK (township). Covers a land area of 44.664 square miles and a water area of 0 square miles. Located at 39.98° N. Lat; 78.08° W. Long.
Population: 1,410 (1990); 1,532 (2000); 1,703 (2010); Density: 38.1 persons per square mile (2010); Race: 98.4% White, 0.1% Black, 0.2% Asian, 0.0% American Indian/Alaska Native, 0.1% Native Hawaiian/Other Pacific Islander, 1.2% Other, 1.1% Hispanic of any race (2010); Average household size: 2.60 (2010); Median age: 38.5 (2010); Males per 100 females: 111.0 (2010); Marriage status: 19.5% never married, 61.3% now married, 8.6% widowed, 10.6% divorced (2006-2010 5-year est.); Foreign born: 0.9% (2006-2010 5-year est.); Ancestry (includes multiple ancestries): 35.9% German, 15.6% American, 7.6% French, 5.8% English, 5.8% Irish (2006-2010 5-year est.).
Economy: Single-family building permits issued: 2 (2011); Multi-family building permits issued: 0 (2011); Employment by occupation: 8.5% management, 3.4% professional, 8.3% services, 16.1% sales, 2.4% farming, 21.7% construction, 10.4% production (2006-2010 5-year est.).
Income: Per capita income: $22,274 (2006-2010 5-year est.); Median household income: $41,711 (2006-2010 5-year est.); Average household income: $54,862 (2006-2010 5-year est.); Percent of households with income of $100,000 or more: 13.6% (2006-2010 5-year est.); Poverty rate: 13.1% (2006-2010 5-year est.).
Education: Percent of population age 25 and over with: High school diploma (including GED) or higher: 82.8% (2006-2010 5-year est.); Bachelor's degree or higher: 8.6% (2006-2010 5-year est.); Master's degree or higher: 4.2% (2006-2010 5-year est.).
Housing: Homeownership rate: 82.2% (2010); Median home value: $146,300 (2006-2010 5-year est.); Median contract rent: $383 per month (2006-2010 5-year est.); Median year structure built: 1975 (2006-2010 5-year est.).
Transportation: Commute to work: 86.5% car, 0.0% public transportation, 5.4% walk, 4.6% work from home (2006-2010 5-year est.); Travel time to work: 22.2% less than 15 minutes, 32.1% 15 to 30 minutes, 10.0% 30 to 45 minutes, 19.8% 45 to 60 minutes, 15.9% 60 minutes or more (2006-2010 5-year est.)
Additional Information Contacts
Fulton County Chamber of Commerce and Tourism . . . . . . (717) 485-4064
    http://www.fultoncountypa.com

MCCONNELLSBURG (borough). County seat. Covers a land area of 0.359 square miles and a water area of 0 square miles. Located at 39.93° N. Lat; 78.00° W. Long. Elevation is 892 feet.
History: James Buchanan's Birthplace State Historical Park to Southeast. Settled c.1730, laid out 1786, incorporated 1814.
Population: 1,106 (1990); 1,073 (2000); 1,220 (2010); Density: 3,393.9 persons per square mile (2010); Race: 92.5% White, 4.2% Black, 0.1% Asian, 0.2% American Indian/Alaska Native, 0.0% Native Hawaiian/Other Pacific Islander, 3.0% Other, 0.5% Hispanic of any race (2010); Average household size: 2.08 (2010); Median age: 36.3 (2010); Males per 100 females: 83.2 (2010); Marriage status: 26.0% never married, 52.2% now married, 10.6% widowed, 11.2% divorced (2006-2010 5-year est.); Foreign born: 2.0% (2006-2010 5-year est.); Ancestry (includes multiple ancestries): 41.4% German, 12.5% Irish, 12.1% American, 5.2% English, 4.2% French (2006-2010 5-year est.).
Economy: Single-family building permits issued: 0 (2011); Multi-family building permits issued: 0 (2011); Employment by occupation: 7.7% management, 0.5% professional, 9.9% services, 19.6% sales, 7.7% farming, 8.3% construction, 9.2% production (2006-2010 5-year est.).
Income: Per capita income: $21,538 (2006-2010 5-year est.); Median household income: $29,948 (2006-2010 5-year est.); Average household income: $45,847 (2006-2010 5-year est.); Percent of households with income of $100,000 or more: 7.3% (2006-2010 5-year est.); Poverty rate: 18.1% (2006-2010 5-year est.).
Education: Percent of population age 25 and over with: High school diploma (including GED) or higher: 79.8% (2006-2010 5-year est.); Bachelor's degree or higher: 13.1% (2006-2010 5-year est.); Master's degree or higher: 4.7% (2006-2010 5-year est.).
School District(s)
Central Fulton SD (PK-12)
    2010-11 Enrollment: 977 . . . . (717) 485-3195
Fulton County Avts (09-12)
    2010-11 Enrollment: n/a . . . . (717) 485-5813
Housing: Homeownership rate: 41.5% (2010); Median home value: $133,600 (2006-2010 5-year est.); Median contract rent: $437 per month

(2006-2010 5-year est.); Median year structure built: 1961 (2006-2010 5-year est.).

Hospitals: Fulton County Medical Center (82 beds)

Newspapers: The Fulton County News (Community news; Circulation 6,800)

Transportation: Commute to work: 93.4% car, 0.0% public transportation, 4.8% walk, 1.8% work from home (2006-2010 5-year est.); Travel time to work: 46.4% less than 15 minutes, 9.8% 15 to 30 minutes, 24.1% 30 to 45 minutes, 7.5% 45 to 60 minutes, 12.2% 60 minutes or more (2006-2010 5-year est.)

Additional Information Contacts

Fulton County Chamber of Commerce and Tourism . . . . . . (717) 485-4064
http://www.fultoncountypa.com

NEEDMORE (CDP). Covers a land area of 0.454 square miles and a water area of 0 square miles. Located at 39.85° N. Lat; 78.14° W. Long. Elevation is 623 feet.

Population: n/a (1990); n/a (2000); 170 (2010); Density: 374.1 persons per square mile (2010); Race: 98.2% White, 0.0% Black, 0.0% Asian, 0.0% American Indian/Alaska Native, 0.0% Native Hawaiian/Other Pacific Islander, 1.8% Other, 0.6% Hispanic of any race (2010); Average household size: 2.58 (2010); Median age: 37.5 (2010); Males per 100 females: 97.7 (2010); Marriage status: 23.8% never married, 65.2% now married, 9.1% widowed, 1.8% divorced (2006-2010 5-year est.); Foreign born: 0.0% (2006-2010 5-year est.); Ancestry (includes multiple ancestries): 48.6% German, 6.5% English, 6.1% Irish, 5.1% American, 3.3% Swedish (2006-2010 5-year est.).

Economy: Employment by occupation: 3.6% management, 3.6% professional, 0.9% services, 22.3% sales, 2.7% farming, 24.1% construction, 24.1% production (2006-2010 5-year est.).

Income: Per capita income: $17,622 (2006-2010 5-year est.); Median household income: $45,417 (2006-2010 5-year est.); Average household income: $49,418 (2006-2010 5-year est.); Percent of households with income of $100,000 or more: n/a (2006-2010 5-year est.); Poverty rate: 3.8% (2006-2010 5-year est.).

Education: Percent of population age 25 and over with: High school diploma (including GED) or higher: 83.5% (2006-2010 5-year est.); Bachelor's degree or higher: 0.0% (2006-2010 5-year est.); Master's degree or higher: 0.0% (2006-2010 5-year est.).

Housing: Homeownership rate: 80.3% (2010); Median home value: $146,900 (2006-2010 5-year est.); Median contract rent: $433 per month (2006-2010 5-year est.); Median year structure built: 1951 (2006-2010 5-year est.).

Transportation: Commute to work: 91.4% car, 0.0% public transportation, 4.8% walk, 0.0% work from home (2006-2010 5-year est.); Travel time to work: 26.7% less than 15 minutes, 28.6% 15 to 30 minutes, 8.6% 30 to 45 minutes, 15.2% 45 to 60 minutes, 21.0% 60 minutes or more (2006-2010 5-year est.)

TAYLOR (township). Covers a land area of 32.641 square miles and a water area of 0.005 square miles. Located at 40.08° N. Lat; 78.05° W. Long.

Population: 1,172 (1990); 1,237 (2000); 1,118 (2010); Density: 34.3 persons per square mile (2010); Race: 98.1% White, 0.1% Black, 0.0% Asian, 0.5% American Indian/Alaska Native, 0.0% Native Hawaiian/Other Pacific Islander, 1.3% Other, 1.5% Hispanic of any race (2010); Average household size: 2.58 (2010); Median age: 40.0 (2010); Males per 100 females: 105.5 (2010); Marriage status: 20.8% never married, 67.2% now married, 6.1% widowed, 5.8% divorced (2006-2010 5-year est.); Foreign born: 0.3% (2006-2010 5-year est.); Ancestry (includes multiple ancestries): 36.7% German, 17.3% Irish, 15.6% American, 9.5% English, 6.6% French (2006-2010 5-year est.).

Economy: Single-family building permits issued: 1 (2011); Multi-family building permits issued: 0 (2011); Employment by occupation: 7.6% management, 1.9% professional, 7.6% services, 11.1% sales, 3.3% farming, 17.9% construction, 15.5% production (2006-2010 5-year est.).

Income: Per capita income: $22,137 (2006-2010 5-year est.); Median household income: $47,614 (2006-2010 5-year est.); Average household income: $54,924 (2006-2010 5-year est.); Percent of households with income of $100,000 or more: 10.0% (2006-2010 5-year est.); Poverty rate: 6.6% (2006-2010 5-year est.).

Education: Percent of population age 25 and over with: High school diploma (including GED) or higher: 86.4% (2006-2010 5-year est.); Bachelor's degree or higher: 16.3% (2006-2010 5-year est.); Master's degree or higher: 5.9% (2006-2010 5-year est.).

Housing: Homeownership rate: 82.0% (2010); Median home value: $151,800 (2006-2010 5-year est.); Median contract rent: $425 per month (2006-2010 5-year est.); Median year structure built: 1967 (2006-2010 5-year est.).

Transportation: Commute to work: 90.3% car, 0.0% public transportation, 1.9% walk, 6.9% work from home (2006-2010 5-year est.); Travel time to work: 19.8% less than 15 minutes, 34.8% 15 to 30 minutes, 9.0% 30 to 45 minutes, 9.4% 45 to 60 minutes, 27.0% 60 minutes or more (2006-2010 5-year est.)

Additional Information Contacts

Fulton County Chamber of Commerce and Tourism . . . . . . (717) 485-4064
http://www.fultoncountypa.com

THOMPSON (township). Covers a land area of 37.917 square miles and a water area of 0.028 square miles. Located at 39.79° N. Lat; 78.11° W. Long.

Population: 1,048 (1990); 998 (2000); 1,098 (2010); Density: 29.0 persons per square mile (2010); Race: 99.0% White, 0.0% Black, 0.0% Asian, 0.3% American Indian/Alaska Native, 0.0% Native Hawaiian/Other Pacific Islander, 0.7% Other, 0.5% Hispanic of any race (2010); Average household size: 2.54 (2010); Median age: 43.8 (2010); Males per 100 females: 108.0 (2010); Marriage status: 23.4% never married, 65.4% now married, 6.0% widowed, 5.2% divorced (2006-2010 5-year est.); Foreign born: 2.9% (2006-2010 5-year est.); Ancestry (includes multiple ancestries): 41.4% German, 19.6% Irish, 10.3% American, 8.8% English, 6.2% French (2006-2010 5-year est.).

Economy: Single-family building permits issued: 1 (2011); Multi-family building permits issued: 0 (2011); Employment by occupation: 11.3% management, 0.8% professional, 9.1% services, 24.1% sales, 2.4% farming, 13.1% construction, 6.4% production (2006-2010 5-year est.).

Income: Per capita income: $21,669 (2006-2010 5-year est.); Median household income: $49,464 (2006-2010 5-year est.); Average household income: $59,541 (2006-2010 5-year est.); Percent of households with income of $100,000 or more: 10.6% (2006-2010 5-year est.); Poverty rate: 7.4% (2006-2010 5-year est.).

Education: Percent of population age 25 and over with: High school diploma (including GED) or higher: 83.3% (2006-2010 5-year est.); Bachelor's degree or higher: 8.8% (2006-2010 5-year est.); Master's degree or higher: 2.9% (2006-2010 5-year est.).

Housing: Homeownership rate: 82.7% (2010); Median home value: $172,100 (2006-2010 5-year est.); Median contract rent: $435 per month (2006-2010 5-year est.); Median year structure built: 1969 (2006-2010 5-year est.).

Transportation: Commute to work: 89.2% car, 0.0% public transportation, 3.5% walk, 5.2% work from home (2006-2010 5-year est.); Travel time to work: 23.2% less than 15 minutes, 16.2% 15 to 30 minutes, 19.7% 30 to 45 minutes, 13.6% 45 to 60 minutes, 27.2% 60 minutes or more (2006-2010 5-year est.)

Additional Information Contacts

Fulton County Chamber of Commerce and Tourism . . . . . . (717) 485-4064
http://www.fultoncountypa.com

TODD (township). Covers a land area of 28.923 square miles and a water area of 0.065 square miles. Located at 39.97° N. Lat; 77.96° W. Long.

Population: 1,434 (1990); 1,488 (2000); 1,527 (2010); Density: 52.8 persons per square mile (2010); Race: 94.0% White, 3.3% Black, 0.3% Asian, 0.1% American Indian/Alaska Native, 0.0% Native Hawaiian/Other Pacific Islander, 2.3% Other, 1.2% Hispanic of any race (2010); Average household size: 2.34 (2010); Median age: 43.0 (2010); Males per 100 females: 103.1 (2010); Marriage status: 26.0% never married, 55.0% now married, 6.7% widowed, 12.3% divorced (2006-2010 5-year est.); Foreign born: 0.3% (2006-2010 5-year est.); Ancestry (includes multiple ancestries): 36.7% German, 12.4% Irish, 12.4% American, 7.5% English, 3.9% Italian (2006-2010 5-year est.).

Economy: Single-family building permits issued: 5 (2011); Multi-family building permits issued: 0 (2011); Employment by occupation: 7.3% management, 1.1% professional, 12.0% services, 13.6% sales, 1.7% farming, 16.8% construction, 10.0% production (2006-2010 5-year est.).

Income: Per capita income: $20,980 (2006-2010 5-year est.); Median household income: $40,313 (2006-2010 5-year est.); Average household income: $49,056 (2006-2010 5-year est.); Percent of households with income of $100,000 or more: 11.5% (2006-2010 5-year est.); Poverty rate: 19.2% (2006-2010 5-year est.).

Education: Percent of population age 25 and over with: High school diploma (including GED) or higher: 82.4% (2006-2010 5-year est.); Bachelor's degree or higher: 11.5% (2006-2010 5-year est.); Master's degree or higher: 4.4% (2006-2010 5-year est.).
Housing: Homeownership rate: 78.9% (2010); Median home value: $139,100 (2006-2010 5-year est.); Median contract rent: $402 per month (2006-2010 5-year est.); Median year structure built: 1981 (2006-2010 5-year est.).
Transportation: Commute to work: 93.5% car, 0.0% public transportation, 1.8% walk, 2.4% work from home (2006-2010 5-year est.); Travel time to work: 55.6% less than 15 minutes, 9.8% 15 to 30 minutes, 18.2% 30 to 45 minutes, 6.6% 45 to 60 minutes, 9.8% 60 minutes or more (2006-2010 5-year est.)

UNION (township). Covers a land area of 30.497 square miles and a water area of 0 square miles. Located at 39.77° N. Lat; 78.30° W. Long.
Population: 623 (1990); 634 (2000); 706 (2010); Density: 23.1 persons per square mile (2010); Race: 97.9% White, 0.1% Black, 0.3% Asian, 0.6% American Indian/Alaska Native, 0.0% Native Hawaiian/Other Pacific Islander, 1.1% Other, 0.6% Hispanic of any race (2010); Average household size: 2.56 (2010); Median age: 42.6 (2010); Males per 100 females: 110.1 (2010); Marriage status: 26.8% never married, 58.2% now married, 7.9% widowed, 7.1% divorced (2006-2010 5-year est.); Foreign born: 1.0% (2006-2010 5-year est.); Ancestry (includes multiple ancestries): 40.1% German, 22.7% Irish, 7.9% English, 6.1% American, 4.5% Dutch (2006-2010 5-year est.).
Economy: Single-family building permits issued: 1 (2011); Multi-family building permits issued: 0 (2011); Employment by occupation: 11.5% management, 1.2% professional, 9.0% services, 11.2% sales, 6.8% farming, 18.0% construction, 9.9% production (2006-2010 5-year est.).
Income: Per capita income: $22,981 (2006-2010 5-year est.); Median household income: $52,813 (2006-2010 5-year est.); Average household income: $62,849 (2006-2010 5-year est.); Percent of households with income of $100,000 or more: 15.0% (2006-2010 5-year est.); Poverty rate: 14.1% (2006-2010 5-year est.).
Education: Percent of population age 25 and over with: High school diploma (including GED) or higher: 89.1% (2006-2010 5-year est.); Bachelor's degree or higher: 14.0% (2006-2010 5-year est.); Master's degree or higher: 4.6% (2006-2010 5-year est.).
Housing: Homeownership rate: 80.4% (2010); Median home value: $157,700 (2006-2010 5-year est.); Median contract rent: $568 per month (2006-2010 5-year est.); Median year structure built: 1972 (2006-2010 5-year est.).
Transportation: Commute to work: 90.5% car, 0.0% public transportation, 1.0% walk, 3.5% work from home (2006-2010 5-year est.); Travel time to work: 11.8% less than 15 minutes, 30.3% 15 to 30 minutes, 8.6% 30 to 45 minutes, 19.1% 45 to 60 minutes, 30.3% 60 minutes or more (2006-2010 5-year est.)

VALLEY-HI (borough). Covers a land area of 0.504 square miles and a water area of 0.065 square miles. Located at 40.03° N. Lat; 78.19° W. Long. Elevation is 1,342 feet.
Population: 19 (1990); 20 (2000); 15 (2010); Density: 29.8 persons per square mile (2010); Race: 100.0% White, 0.0% Black, 0.0% Asian, 0.0% American Indian/Alaska Native, 0.0% Native Hawaiian/Other Pacific Islander, 0.0% Other, 0.0% Hispanic of any race (2010); Average household size: 2.50 (2010); Median age: 38.5 (2010); Males per 100 females: 114.3 (2010); Marriage status: 100.0% never married, 0.0% now married, 0.0% widowed, 0.0% divorced (2006-2010 5-year est.); Foreign born: 0.0% (2006-2010 5-year est.); Ancestry (includes multiple ancestries): 100.0% Welsh, 100.0% German (2006-2010 5-year est.).
Economy: Employment by occupation: 0.0% management, 0.0% professional, 100.0% services, 0.0% sales, 0.0% farming, 0.0% construction, 0.0% production (2006-2010 5-year est.).
Income: Per capita income: $-1 (2006-2010 5-year est.); Median household income: n/a (2006-2010 5-year est.); Average household income: n/a (2006-2010 5-year est.); Percent of households with income of $100,000 or more: n/a (2006-2010 5-year est.); Poverty rate: 0.0% (2006-2010 5-year est.).
Education: Percent of population age 25 and over with: High school diploma (including GED) or higher: 100.0% (2006-2010 5-year est.); Bachelor's degree or higher: 100.0% (2006-2010 5-year est.); Master's degree or higher: 0.0% (2006-2010 5-year est.).
Housing: Homeownership rate: 83.3% (2010); Median home value: $85,000 (2006-2010 5-year est.); Median contract rent: n/a per month

(2006-2010 5-year est.); Median year structure built: 1977 (2006-2010 5-year est.).
Transportation: Commute to work: 100.0% car, 0.0% public transportation, 0.0% walk, 0.0% work from home (2006-2010 5-year est.); Travel time to work: 0.0% less than 15 minutes, 100.0% 15 to 30 minutes, 0.0% 30 to 45 minutes, 0.0% 45 to 60 minutes, 0.0% 60 minutes or more (2006-2010 5-year est.)

WARFORDSBURG (unincorporated postal area)
Zip Code: 17267
Covers a land area of 95.808 square miles and a water area of 0.007 square miles. Located at 39.80° N. Lat; 78.23° W. Long. Elevation is 554 feet. Population: 2,810 (2010); Density: 29.3 persons per square mile (2010); Race: 97.3% White, 1.1% Black, 0.1% Asian, 0.3% American Indian/Alaska Native, 0.0% Native Hawaiian/Other Pacific Islander, 1.2% Other, 1.1% Hispanic of any race (2010); Average household size: 2.51 (2010); Median age: 41.6 (2010); Males per 100 females: 101.1 (2010); Homeownership rate: 77.8% (2010)

WATERFALL (unincorporated postal area)
Zip Code: 16689
Covers a land area of 20.490 square miles and a water area of 0 square miles. Located at 40.12° N. Lat; 78.12° W. Long. Elevation is 853 feet. Population: 462 (2010); Density: 22.5 persons per square mile (2010); Race: 99.1% White, 0.2% Black, 0.0% Asian, 0.0% American Indian/Alaska Native, 0.0% Native Hawaiian/Other Pacific Islander, 0.7% Other, 0.9% Hispanic of any race (2010); Average household size: 2.48 (2010); Median age: 45.3 (2010); Males per 100 females: 99.1 (2010); Homeownership rate: 87.1% (2010)

WELLS (township). Covers a land area of 37.373 square miles and a water area of 0 square miles. Located at 40.09° N. Lat; 78.14° W. Long.
Population: 544 (1990); 529 (2000); 477 (2010); Density: 12.8 persons per square mile (2010); Race: 96.9% White, 0.0% Black, 0.0% Asian, 0.0% American Indian/Alaska Native, 0.0% Native Hawaiian/Other Pacific Islander, 3.1% Other, 2.1% Hispanic of any race (2010); Average household size: 2.27 (2010); Median age: 48.3 (2010); Males per 100 females: 102.1 (2010); Marriage status: 19.4% never married, 59.3% now married, 9.4% widowed, 11.9% divorced (2006-2010 5-year est.); Foreign born: 0.4% (2006-2010 5-year est.); Ancestry (includes multiple ancestries): 39.8% German, 11.8% Irish, 10.6% American, 6.6% English, 5.4% Dutch (2006-2010 5-year est.).
Economy: Single-family building permits issued: 0 (2011); Multi-family building permits issued: 0 (2011); Employment by occupation: 8.1% management, 1.4% professional, 7.4% services, 13.7% sales, 1.4% farming, 26.3% construction, 21.8% production (2006-2010 5-year est.).
Income: Per capita income: $18,904 (2006-2010 5-year est.); Median household income: $43,625 (2006-2010 5-year est.); Average household income: $53,194 (2006-2010 5-year est.); Percent of households with income of $100,000 or more: 10.0% (2006-2010 5-year est.); Poverty rate: 15.2% (2006-2010 5-year est.).
Education: Percent of population age 25 and over with: High school diploma (including GED) or higher: 85.2% (2006-2010 5-year est.); Bachelor's degree or higher: 5.8% (2006-2010 5-year est.); Master's degree or higher: 3.2% (2006-2010 5-year est.).
Housing: Homeownership rate: 89.1% (2010); Median home value: $108,600 (2006-2010 5-year est.); Median contract rent: $606 per month (2006-2010 5-year est.); Median year structure built: 1971 (2006-2010 5-year est.).
Transportation: Commute to work: 93.3% car, 2.1% public transportation, 0.0% walk, 4.6% work from home (2006-2010 5-year est.); Travel time to work: 5.9% less than 15 minutes, 35.3% 15 to 30 minutes, 27.9% 30 to 45 minutes, 5.1% 45 to 60 minutes, 25.7% 60 minutes or more (2006-2010 5-year est.)

WELLS TANNERY (unincorporated postal area)
Zip Code: 16691
Covers a land area of 28.881 square miles and a water area of 0 square miles. Located at 40.07° N. Lat; 78.14° W. Long. Population: 314 (2010); Density: 10.9 persons per square mile (2010); Race: 95.9% White, 0.0% Black, 0.0% Asian, 0.0% American Indian/Alaska Native, 0.0% Native Hawaiian/Other Pacific Islander, 4.1% Other, 3.2% Hispanic of any race (2010); Average household size: 2.21 (2010); Median age: 48.6 (2010); Males per 100 females: 109.3 (2010); Homeownership rate: 88.7% (2010)

Greene County

Located in southwestern Pennsylvania; bounded on the south and west by West Virginia, and on the east by the Monongahela River. Covers a land area of 575.949 square miles, a water area of 2.029 square miles, and is located in the Eastern Time Zone at 39.85° N. Lat., 80.23° W. Long. The county was founded in 1796. County seat is Waynesburg.

Weather Station: Waynesburg 1 E										Elevation: 939 feet	
	Jan	Feb	Mar	Apr	May	Jun	Jul	Aug	Sep	Oct	Nov	Dec
High	39	42	51	63	72	80	84	83	76	65	54	42
Low	19	21	27	36	46	55	59	58	50	38	31	23
Precip	2.9	2.5	3.7	3.2	4.4	3.8	4.2	3.9	3.1	2.8	3.4	2.8
Snow	9.2	6.2	5.2	1.0	tr	0.0	0.0	0.0	0.0	0.2	1.3	4.9

High and Low temperatures in degrees Fahrenheit; Precipitation and Snow in inches

Population: 39,550 (1990); 40,672 (2000); 38,686 (2010); Race: 94.6% White, 3.3% Black, 0.3% Asian, 0.2% American Indian/Alaska Native, 0.0% Native Hawaiian/Other Pacific Islander, 1.6% Other, 1.2% Hispanic of any race (2010); Density: 67.2 persons per square mile (2010); Average household size: 2.42 (2010); Median age: 41.1 (2010); Males per 100 females: 106.2 (2010).
Religion: Six largest groups: 12.1% Catholicism, 10.8% Methodist/Pietist, 7.6% Baptist, 4.6% Pentecostal, 3.0% Presbyterian-Reformed, 2.0% Holiness (2010)
Economy: Unemployment rate: 7.6% (August 2012); Total civilian labor force: 21,296 (August 2012); Leading industries: 31.1% mining; 19.0% retail trade; 11.6% health care and social assistance (2010); Farms: 1,245 totaling 150,203 acres (2007); Companies that employ 500 or more persons: 5 (2010); Companies that employ 100 to 499 persons: 11 (2010); Companies that employ less than 100 persons: 713 (2010); Black-owned businesses: n/a (2007); Hispanic-owned businesses: n/a (2007); Asian-owned businesses: n/a (2007); Women-owned businesses: 544 (2007); Retail sales per capita: $11,044 (2010). Single-family building permits issued: 37 (2011); Multi-family building permits issued: 0 (2011).
Income: Per capita income: $20,258 (2006-2010 5-year est.); Median household income: $40,498 (2006-2010 5-year est.); Average household income: $51,860 (2006-2010 5-year est.); Percent of households with income of $100,000 or more: 11.9% (2006-2010 5-year est.); Poverty rate: 16.7% (2006-2010 5-year est.); Bankruptcy rate: 2.22% (2011).
Education: Percent of population age 25 and over with: High school diploma (including GED) or higher: 83.9% (2006-2010 5-year est.); Bachelor's degree or higher: 14.6% (2006-2010 5-year est.); Master's degree or higher: 4.7% (2006-2010 5-year est.).
Housing: Homeownership rate: 72.6% (2010); Median home value: $81,800 (2006-2010 5-year est.); Median contract rent: $351 per month (2006-2010 5-year est.); Median year structure built: 1955 (2006-2010 5-year est.)
Health: Birth rate: 98.6 per 10,000 population (2011); Death rate: 114.7 per 10,000 population (2011); Age-adjusted cancer mortality rate: 177.4 deaths per 100,000 population (2009); Number of physicians: 6.2 per 10,000 population (2010); Hospital beds: 17.5 per 10,000 population (2008); Hospital admissions: 821.7 per 10,000 population (2008).
Environment: Air Quality Index: 92.1% good, 7.9% moderate, 0.0% unhealthy for sensitive individuals, 0.0% unhealthy (percent of days in 2011)
Elections: 2012 Presidential election results: 40.5% Obama, 58.3% Romney
National and State Parks: Ryerson Station State Park
Additional Information Contacts
Greene County Government . . . . (724) 852-5210
  http://www.co.greene.pa.us

Greene County Communities

ALEPPO (township). Covers a land area of 27.955 square miles and a water area of 0 square miles. Located at 39.82° N. Lat; 80.46° W. Long. Elevation is 1,063 feet.
Population: 656 (1990); 597 (2000); 502 (2010); Density: 18.0 persons per square mile (2010); Race: 98.0% White, 0.0% Black, 0.2% Asian, 0.0% American Indian/Alaska Native, 0.0% Native Hawaiian/Other Pacific Islander, 1.8% Other, 0.2% Hispanic of any race (2010); Average household size: 2.44 (2010); Median age: 45.4 (2010); Males per 100 females: 107.4 (2010); Marriage status: 27.9% never married, 54.8% now married, 6.0% widowed, 11.3% divorced (2006-2010 5-year est.); Foreign born: 1.8% (2006-2010 5-year est.); Ancestry (includes multiple

ancestries): 44.9% German, 31.9% Irish, 9.2% Dutch, 7.8% American, 6.0% Italian (2006-2010 5-year est.).
Economy: Single-family building permits issued: 4 (2011); Multi-family building permits issued: 0 (2011); Employment by occupation: 1.9% management, 0.0% professional, 7.8% services, 10.9% sales, 5.4% farming, 28.4% construction, 1.6% production (2006-2010 5-year est.).
Income: Per capita income: $26,524 (2006-2010 5-year est.); Median household income: $50,313 (2006-2010 5-year est.); Average household income: $69,846 (2006-2010 5-year est.); Percent of households with income of $100,000 or more: 22.9% (2006-2010 5-year est.); Poverty rate: 27.1% (2006-2010 5-year est.).
Education: Percent of population age 25 and over with: High school diploma (including GED) or higher: 78.0% (2006-2010 5-year est.); Bachelor's degree or higher: 9.6% (2006-2010 5-year est.); Master's degree or higher: 1.1% (2006-2010 5-year est.).
Housing: Homeownership rate: 79.7% (2010); Median home value: $83,300 (2006-2010 5-year est.); Median contract rent: $242 per month (2006-2010 5-year est.); Median year structure built: 1945 (2006-2010 5-year est.).
Transportation: Commute to work: 94.5% car, 0.0% public transportation, 2.8% walk, 2.8% work from home (2006-2010 5-year est.); Travel time to work: 5.7% less than 15 minutes, 15.9% 15 to 30 minutes, 47.2% 30 to 45 minutes, 17.5% 45 to 60 minutes, 13.8% 60 minutes or more (2006-2010 5-year est.)

BOBTOWN (CDP). Covers a land area of 0.633 square miles and a water area of 0 square miles. Located at 39.76° N. Lat; 79.98° W. Long. Elevation is 1,188 feet.
Population: n/a (1990); n/a (2000); 757 (2010); Density: 1,195.1 persons per square mile (2010); Race: 96.7% White, 0.4% Black, 0.4% Asian, 0.3% American Indian/Alaska Native, 0.0% Native Hawaiian/Other Pacific Islander, 2.2% Other, 1.5% Hispanic of any race (2010); Average household size: 2.41 (2010); Median age: 41.8 (2010); Males per 100 females: 94.6 (2010); Marriage status: 20.9% never married, 62.8% now married, 11.3% widowed, 5.0% divorced (2006-2010 5-year est.); Foreign born: 0.4% (2006-2010 5-year est.); Ancestry (includes multiple ancestries): 16.9% Slovak, 16.4% German, 16.0% American, 15.4% Polish, 11.0% Irish (2006-2010 5-year est.).
Economy: Employment by occupation: 14.8% management, 0.0% professional, 15.8% services, 12.9% sales, 4.3% farming, 19.6% construction, 4.3% production (2006-2010 5-year est.).
Income: Per capita income: $16,937 (2006-2010 5-year est.); Median household income: $41,071 (2006-2010 5-year est.); Average household income: $45,527 (2006-2010 5-year est.); Percent of households with income of $100,000 or more: 5.9% (2006-2010 5-year est.); Poverty rate: 18.1% (2006-2010 5-year est.).
Education: Percent of population age 25 and over with: High school diploma (including GED) or higher: 86.8% (2006-2010 5-year est.); Bachelor's degree or higher: 7.2% (2006-2010 5-year est.); Master's degree or higher: 1.1% (2006-2010 5-year est.).
School District(s)
Southeastern Greene SD (KG-12)
  2010-11 Enrollment: 625. . . . . (724) 943-3630
Housing: Homeownership rate: 79.7% (2010); Median home value: $40,000 (2006-2010 5-year est.); Median contract rent: $339 per month (2006-2010 5-year est.); Median year structure built: before 1940 (2006-2010 5-year est.).
Transportation: Commute to work: 89.8% car, 0.0% public transportation, 2.1% walk, 8.0% work from home (2006-2010 5-year est.); Travel time to work: 8.7% less than 15 minutes, 43.7% 15 to 30 minutes, 33.8% 30 to 45 minutes, 3.8% 45 to 60 minutes, 9.9% 60 minutes or more (2006-2010 5-year est.)

BRAVE (CDP). Covers a land area of 0.889 square miles and a water area of <.001 square miles. Located at 39.73° N. Lat; 80.26° W. Long. Elevation is 965 feet.
Population: n/a (1990); n/a (2000); 201 (2010); Density: 226.0 persons per square mile (2010); Race: 98.5% White, 0.0% Black, 0.0% Asian, 1.0% American Indian/Alaska Native, 0.0% Native Hawaiian/Other Pacific Islander, 0.5% Other, 0.0% Hispanic of any race (2010); Average household size: 2.72 (2010); Median age: 35.9 (2010); Males per 100 females: 91.4 (2010); Marriage status: 19.8% never married, 68.3% now married, 3.0% widowed, 9.0% divorced (2006-2010 5-year est.); Foreign born: 0.0% (2006-2010 5-year est.); Ancestry (includes multiple

ancestries): 43.5% Irish, 13.0% Hungarian, 11.1% American, 10.1% Dutch, 10.1% Scottish (2006-2010 5-year est.).
Economy: Employment by occupation: 0.0% management, 0.0% professional, 28.0% services, 14.0% sales, 0.0% farming, 40.0% construction, 8.0% production (2006-2010 5-year est.).
Income: Per capita income: $10,601 (2006-2010 5-year est.); Median household income: $19,833 (2006-2010 5-year est.); Average household income: $26,540 (2006-2010 5-year est.); Percent of households with income of $100,000 or more: 8.5% (2006-2010 5-year est.); Poverty rate: 46.4% (2006-2010 5-year est.).
Education: Percent of population age 25 and over with: High school diploma (including GED) or higher: 62.3% (2006-2010 5-year est.); Bachelor's degree or higher: 0.0% (2006-2010 5-year est.); Master's degree or higher: 0.0% (2006-2010 5-year est.).
Housing: Homeownership rate: 83.8% (2010); Median home value: $33,900 (2006-2010 5-year est.); Median contract rent: $356 per month (2006-2010 5-year est.); Median year structure built: 1943 (2006-2010 5-year est.).
Transportation: Commute to work: 100.0% car, 0.0% public transportation, 0.0% walk, 0.0% work from home (2006-2010 5-year est.); Travel time to work: 32.0% less than 15 minutes, 32.0% 15 to 30 minutes, 18.0% 30 to 45 minutes, 18.0% 45 to 60 minutes, 0.0% 60 minutes or more (2006-2010 5-year est.)

CARMICHAELS (borough).
Covers a land area of 0.165 square miles and a water area of 0.005 square miles. Located at 39.90° N. Lat; 79.97° W. Long. Elevation is 1,010 feet.
Population: 532 (1990); 556 (2000); 483 (2010); Density: 2,929.0 persons per square mile (2010); Race: 96.7% White, 0.8% Black, 0.0% Asian, 0.0% American Indian/Alaska Native, 0.0% Native Hawaiian/Other Pacific Islander, 2.5% Other, 0.4% Hispanic of any race (2010); Average household size: 2.37 (2010); Median age: 44.5 (2010); Males per 100 females: 104.7 (2010); Marriage status: 20.8% never married, 51.3% now married, 6.7% widowed, 21.3% divorced (2006-2010 5-year est.); Foreign born: 0.4% (2006-2010 5-year est.); Ancestry (includes multiple ancestries): 18.0% Irish, 17.6% German, 17.1% English, 9.1% Slovak, 6.1% Polish (2006-2010 5-year est.).
Economy: Single-family building permits issued: 1 (2011); Multi-family building permits issued: 0 (2011); Employment by occupation: 11.2% management, 0.0% professional, 0.9% services, 11.7% sales, 5.1% farming, 24.3% construction, 15.0% production (2006-2010 5-year est.).
Income: Per capita income: $30,881 (2006-2010 5-year est.); Median household income: $55,417 (2006-2010 5-year est.); Average household income: $63,114 (2006-2010 5-year est.); Percent of households with income of $100,000 or more: 31.8% (2006-2010 5-year est.); Poverty rate: 22.6% (2006-2010 5-year est.).
Education: Percent of population age 25 and over with: High school diploma (including GED) or higher: 89.1% (2006-2010 5-year est.); Bachelor's degree or higher: 12.0% (2006-2010 5-year est.); Master's degree or higher: 3.6% (2006-2010 5-year est.).

School District(s)
Carmichaels Area SD (KG-12)
   2010-11 Enrollment: 1,126 . . . . (724) 966-5045
Housing: Homeownership rate: 67.1% (2010); Median home value: $83,000 (2006-2010 5-year est.); Median contract rent: $551 per month (2006-2010 5-year est.); Median year structure built: 1949 (2006-2010 5-year est.).
Safety: Violent crime rate: 0.0 per 10,000 population; Property crime rate: 20.6 per 10,000 population (2011).
Transportation: Commute to work: 94.4% car, 0.0% public transportation, 1.9% walk, 3.7% work from home (2006-2010 5-year est.); Travel time to work: 27.7% less than 15 minutes, 30.6% 15 to 30 minutes, 33.5% 30 to 45 minutes, 3.4% 45 to 60 minutes, 4.9% 60 minutes or more (2006-2010 5-year est.)

CENTER (township).
Covers a land area of 48.945 square miles and a water area of 0.004 square miles. Located at 39.88° N. Lat; 80.30° W. Long.
Population: 1,460 (1990); 1,393 (2000); 1,267 (2010); Density: 25.9 persons per square mile (2010); Race: 98.7% White, 0.2% Black, 0.0% Asian, 0.0% American Indian/Alaska Native, 0.1% Native Hawaiian/Other Pacific Islander, 1.0% Other, 0.6% Hispanic of any race (2010); Average household size: 2.61 (2010); Median age: 43.8 (2010); Males per 100 females: 102.7 (2010); Marriage status: 24.8% never married, 57.4% now married, 5.8% widowed, 12.1% divorced (2006-2010 5-year est.); Foreign

born: 0.5% (2006-2010 5-year est.); Ancestry (includes multiple ancestries): 31.7% German, 17.6% Irish, 17.2% English, 5.6% Scotch-Irish, 4.7% American (2006-2010 5-year est.).
Economy: Single-family building permits issued: 2 (2011); Multi-family building permits issued: 0 (2011); Employment by occupation: 9.2% management, 4.4% professional, 12.0% services, 15.7% sales, 1.1% farming, 21.7% construction, 8.0% production (2006-2010 5-year est.).
Income: Per capita income: $21,828 (2006-2010 5-year est.); Median household income: $46,667 (2006-2010 5-year est.); Average household income: $53,674 (2006-2010 5-year est.); Percent of households with income of $100,000 or more: 11.9% (2006-2010 5-year est.); Poverty rate: 15.6% (2006-2010 5-year est.).
Education: Percent of population age 25 and over with: High school diploma (including GED) or higher: 87.4% (2006-2010 5-year est.); Bachelor's degree or higher: 13.4% (2006-2010 5-year est.); Master's degree or higher: 4.2% (2006-2010 5-year est.).
Housing: Homeownership rate: 79.1% (2010); Median home value: $81,700 (2006-2010 5-year est.); Median contract rent: $308 per month (2006-2010 5-year est.); Median year structure built: 1944 (2006-2010 5-year est.).
Transportation: Commute to work: 94.3% car, 1.3% public transportation, 2.2% walk, 2.2% work from home (2006-2010 5-year est.); Travel time to work: 15.3% less than 15 minutes, 36.6% 15 to 30 minutes, 19.8% 30 to 45 minutes, 14.9% 45 to 60 minutes, 13.4% 60 minutes or more (2006-2010 5-year est.)
Additional Information Contacts
Waynesburg Area Chamber of Commerce . . . . (724) 627-5926
   http://www.waynesburgchamber.com

CLARKSVILLE (borough).
Covers a land area of 0.097 square miles and a water area of 0 square miles. Located at 39.97° N. Lat; 80.04° W. Long. Elevation is 804 feet.
Population: 211 (1990); 234 (2000); 230 (2010); Density: 2,363.8 persons per square mile (2010); Race: 97.4% White, 2.2% Black, 0.0% Asian, 0.0% American Indian/Alaska Native, 0.0% Native Hawaiian/Other Pacific Islander, 0.4% Other, 0.4% Hispanic of any race (2010); Average household size: 2.79 (2010); Median age: 41.7 (2010); Males per 100 females: 101.8 (2010); Marriage status: 31.7% never married, 49.5% now married, 9.1% widowed, 9.6% divorced (2006-2010 5-year est.); Foreign born: 0.0% (2006-2010 5-year est.); Ancestry (includes multiple ancestries): 29.5% Irish, 26.2% German, 20.3% Polish, 10.3% Scotch-Irish, 8.5% Italian (2006-2010 5-year est.).
Economy: Single-family building permits issued: 0 (2011); Multi-family building permits issued: 0 (2011); Employment by occupation: 0.0% management, 0.0% professional, 16.4% services, 32.8% sales, 0.0% farming, 18.0% construction, 4.9% production (2006-2010 5-year est.).
Income: Per capita income: $10,914 (2006-2010 5-year est.); Median household income: $28,000 (2006-2010 5-year est.); Average household income: $31,880 (2006-2010 5-year est.); Percent of households with income of $100,000 or more: n/a (2006-2010 5-year est.); Poverty rate: 35.4% (2006-2010 5-year est.).
Education: Percent of population age 25 and over with: High school diploma (including GED) or higher: 87.7% (2006-2010 5-year est.); Bachelor's degree or higher: 8.4% (2006-2010 5-year est.); Master's degree or higher: 1.3% (2006-2010 5-year est.).
Housing: Homeownership rate: 84.7% (2010); Median home value: $70,800 (2006-2010 5-year est.); Median contract rent: $421 per month (2006-2010 5-year est.); Median year structure built: before 1940 (2006-2010 5-year est.).
Transportation: Commute to work: 82.8% car, 0.0% public transportation, 5.2% walk, 3.4% work from home (2006-2010 5-year est.); Travel time to work: 26.8% less than 15 minutes, 41.1% 15 to 30 minutes, 10.7% 30 to 45 minutes, 8.9% 45 to 60 minutes, 12.5% 60 minutes or more (2006-2010 5-year est.)

CRUCIBLE (CDP).
Covers a land area of 1.152 square miles and a water area of 0.113 square miles. Located at 39.95° N. Lat; 79.97° W. Long. Elevation is 1,076 feet.
Population: n/a (1990); n/a (2000); 725 (2010); Density: 629.3 persons per square mile (2010); Race: 97.7% White, 0.0% Black, 0.0% Asian, 0.3% American Indian/Alaska Native, 0.1% Native Hawaiian/Other Pacific Islander, 1.9% Other, 1.0% Hispanic of any race (2010); Average household size: 2.60 (2010); Median age: 39.2 (2010); Males per 100 females: 89.8 (2010); Marriage status: 27.9% never married, 60.3% now married, 7.8% widowed, 4.0% divorced (2006-2010 5-year est.); Foreign

born: 2.4% (2006-2010 5-year est.); Ancestry (includes multiple ancestries): 52.5% German, 29.3% Italian, 17.2% Irish, 9.6% Dutch, 8.4% Croatian (2006-2010 5-year est.).

Economy: Employment by occupation: 19.9% management, 0.0% professional, 10.2% services, 20.4% sales, 0.0% farming, 7.7% construction, 6.6% production (2006-2010 5-year est.).

Income: Per capita income: $11,130 (2006-2010 5-year est.); Median household income: $22,083 (2006-2010 5-year est.); Average household income: $28,118 (2006-2010 5-year est.); Percent of households with income of $100,000 or more: n/a (2006-2010 5-year est.); Poverty rate: 56.8% (2006-2010 5-year est.).

Education: Percent of population age 25 and over with: High school diploma (including GED) or higher: 78.0% (2006-2010 5-year est.); Bachelor's degree or higher: 3.9% (2006-2010 5-year est.); Master's degree or higher: 0.0% (2006-2010 5-year est.).

Housing: Homeownership rate: 72.7% (2010); Median home value: $68,100 (2006-2010 5-year est.); Median contract rent: $378 per month (2006-2010 5-year est.); Median year structure built: 1943 (2006-2010 5-year est.).

Transportation: Commute to work: 69.1% car, 0.0% public transportation, 0.0% walk, 21.5% work from home (2006-2010 5-year est.); Travel time to work: 0.0% less than 15 minutes, 52.8% 15 to 30 minutes, 12.0% 30 to 45 minutes, 0.0% 45 to 60 minutes, 35.2% 60 minutes or more (2006-2010 5-year est.)

CUMBERLAND (township). Covers a land area of 38.256 square miles and a water area of 0.647 square miles. Located at 39.89° N. Lat; 79.99° W. Long.

Population: 6,742 (1990); 6,564 (2000); 6,623 (2010); Density: 173.1 persons per square mile (2010); Race: 98.2% White, 0.3% Black, 0.2% Asian, 0.2% American Indian/Alaska Native, 0.0% Native Hawaiian/Other Pacific Islander, 1.1% Other, 0.7% Hispanic of any race (2010); Average household size: 2.40 (2010); Median age: 41.7 (2010); Males per 100 females: 91.6 (2010); Marriage status: 21.8% never married, 58.9% now married, 7.8% widowed, 11.5% divorced (2006-2010 5-year est.); Foreign born: 1.7% (2006-2010 5-year est.); Ancestry (includes multiple ancestries): 28.0% German, 20.2% Irish, 16.3% Italian, 8.3% English, 7.5% American (2006-2010 5-year est.).

Economy: Single-family building permits issued: 4 (2011); Multi-family building permits issued: 0 (2011); Employment by occupation: 4.8% management, 4.2% professional, 9.6% services, 14.9% sales, 3.0% farming, 15.2% construction, 14.3% production (2006-2010 5-year est.).

Income: Per capita income: $19,533 (2006-2010 5-year est.); Median household income: $34,710 (2006-2010 5-year est.); Average household income: $46,733 (2006-2010 5-year est.); Percent of households with income of $100,000 or more: 11.2% (2006-2010 5-year est.); Poverty rate: 18.9% (2006-2010 5-year est.).

Education: Percent of population age 25 and over with: High school diploma (including GED) or higher: 84.5% (2006-2010 5-year est.); Bachelor's degree or higher: 17.6% (2006-2010 5-year est.); Master's degree or higher: 5.6% (2006-2010 5-year est.).

Housing: Homeownership rate: 72.3% (2010); Median home value: $90,300 (2006-2010 5-year est.); Median contract rent: $352 per month (2006-2010 5-year est.); Median year structure built: 1954 (2006-2010 5-year est.).

Safety: Violent crime rate: 15.1 per 10,000 population; Property crime rate: 252.9 per 10,000 population (2011).

Transportation: Commute to work: 91.3% car, 0.9% public transportation, 2.4% walk, 4.8% work from home (2006-2010 5-year est.); Travel time to work: 34.9% less than 15 minutes, 25.5% 15 to 30 minutes, 24.2% 30 to 45 minutes, 8.7% 45 to 60 minutes, 6.7% 60 minutes or more (2006-2010 5-year est.)

Additional Information Contacts

Cumberland Township . . . . (724) 966-5805
    http://www.co.greene.pa.us/secured/gc/depts/eo/twp/cumberland.htm
Waynesburg Area Chamber of Commerce . . . . (724) 627-5926
    http://www.waynesburgchamber.com

DILLINER (unincorporated postal area)
Zip Code: 15327
    Covers a land area of 19.878 square miles and a water area of 0.296 square miles. Located at 39.74° N. Lat; 79.96° W. Long. Population: 1,527 (2010); Density: 76.8 persons per square mile (2010); Race: 97.8% White, 0.2% Black, 0.0% Asian, 0.5% American Indian/Alaska Native, 0.0% Native Hawaiian/Other Pacific Islander, 1.5% Other, 0.7%

Hispanic of any race (2010); Average household size: 2.58 (2010); Median age: 41.7 (2010); Males per 100 females: 102.0 (2010); Homeownership rate: 78.8% (2010)

DRY TAVERN (CDP). Covers a land area of 1.352 square miles and a water area of 0 square miles. Located at 39.94° N. Lat; 80.01° W. Long. Elevation is 1,001 feet.

Population: n/a (1990); n/a (2000); 697 (2010); Density: 515.6 persons per square mile (2010); Race: 97.8% White, 0.3% Black, 0.7% Asian, 0.0% American Indian/Alaska Native, 0.0% Native Hawaiian/Other Pacific Islander, 1.2% Other, 1.0% Hispanic of any race (2010); Average household size: 2.34 (2010); Median age: 48.2 (2010); Males per 100 females: 98.6 (2010); Marriage status: 38.9% never married, 52.5% now married, 2.3% widowed, 6.3% divorced (2006-2010 5-year est.); Foreign born: 1.3% (2006-2010 5-year est.); Ancestry (includes multiple ancestries): 25.2% Irish, 23.4% German, 10.9% Scotch-Irish, 10.2% Italian, 6.8% English (2006-2010 5-year est.).

Economy: Employment by occupation: 5.8% management, 5.3% professional, 5.8% services, 13.7% sales, 5.3% farming, 24.8% construction, 6.2% production (2006-2010 5-year est.).

Income: Per capita income: $19,828 (2006-2010 5-year est.); Median household income: $46,447 (2006-2010 5-year est.); Average household income: $56,621 (2006-2010 5-year est.); Percent of households with income of $100,000 or more: 11.6% (2006-2010 5-year est.); Poverty rate: 22.1% (2006-2010 5-year est.).

Education: Percent of population age 25 and over with: High school diploma (including GED) or higher: 85.5% (2006-2010 5-year est.); Bachelor's degree or higher: 12.9% (2006-2010 5-year est.); Master's degree or higher: 1.2% (2006-2010 5-year est.).

Housing: Homeownership rate: 87.2% (2010); Median home value: $97,400 (2006-2010 5-year est.); Median contract rent: $458 per month (2006-2010 5-year est.); Median year structure built: 1963 (2006-2010 5-year est.).

Transportation: Commute to work: 100.0% car, 0.0% public transportation, 0.0% walk, 0.0% work from home (2006-2010 5-year est.); Travel time to work: 18.2% less than 15 minutes, 20.6% 15 to 30 minutes, 26.6% 30 to 45 minutes, 25.2% 45 to 60 minutes, 9.3% 60 minutes or more (2006-2010 5-year est.)

DUNKARD (township). Aka Taylortown. Covers a land area of 31.569 square miles and a water area of 0.297 square miles. Located at 39.75° N. Lat; 79.99° W. Long. Elevation is 928 feet.

Population: 2,386 (1990); 2,358 (2000); 2,372 (2010); Density: 75.1 persons per square mile (2010); Race: 97.4% White, 0.2% Black, 0.1% Asian, 0.3% American Indian/Alaska Native, 0.0% Native Hawaiian/Other Pacific Islander, 2.0% Other, 1.1% Hispanic of any race (2010); Average household size: 2.52 (2010); Median age: 41.6 (2010); Males per 100 females: 101.0 (2010); Marriage status: 22.3% never married, 61.1% now married, 10.0% widowed, 6.7% divorced (2006-2010 5-year est.); Foreign born: 0.2% (2006-2010 5-year est.); Ancestry (includes multiple ancestries): 27.5% German, 13.2% Italian, 12.5% Irish, 11.8% American, 10.2% English (2006-2010 5-year est.).

Economy: Employment by occupation: 12.6% management, 4.2% professional, 14.6% services, 16.3% sales, 3.1% farming, 21.3% construction, 6.2% production (2006-2010 5-year est.).

Income: Per capita income: $18,232 (2006-2010 5-year est.); Median household income: $40,262 (2006-2010 5-year est.); Average household income: $47,248 (2006-2010 5-year est.); Percent of households with income of $100,000 or more: 10.0% (2006-2010 5-year est.); Poverty rate: 13.6% (2006-2010 5-year est.).

Education: Percent of population age 25 and over with: High school diploma (including GED) or higher: 85.0% (2006-2010 5-year est.); Bachelor's degree or higher: 8.0% (2006-2010 5-year est.); Master's degree or higher: 0.9% (2006-2010 5-year est.).

Housing: Homeownership rate: 79.6% (2010); Median home value: $52,600 (2006-2010 5-year est.); Median contract rent: $342 per month (2006-2010 5-year est.); Median year structure built: before 1940 (2006-2010 5-year est.).

Transportation: Commute to work: 92.7% car, 0.0% public transportation, 2.6% walk, 4.7% work from home (2006-2010 5-year est.); Travel time to work: 15.1% less than 15 minutes, 29.3% 15 to 30 minutes, 35.3% 30 to 45 minutes, 11.9% 45 to 60 minutes, 8.5% 60 minutes or more (2006-2010 5-year est.)

Additional Information Contacts
Waynesburg Area Chamber of Commerce . . . . (724) 627-5926
http://www.waynesburgchamber.com

FAIRDALE (CDP). Covers a land area of 1.435 square miles and a water area of 0 square miles. Located at 39.89° N. Lat; 79.97° W. Long. Elevation is 1,017 feet.

Population: 2,049 (1990); 1,955 (2000); 2,059 (2010); Density: 1,435.0 persons per square mile (2010); Race: 98.9% White, 0.0% Black, 0.3% Asian, 0.0% American Indian/Alaska Native, 0.0% Native Hawaiian/Other Pacific Islander, 0.8% Other, 0.4% Hispanic of any race (2010); Average household size: 2.21 (2010); Median age: 44.7 (2010); Males per 100 females: 84.2 (2010); Marriage status: 16.5% never married, 68.9% now married, 5.4% widowed, 9.1% divorced (2006-2010 5-year est.); Foreign born: 2.6% (2006-2010 5-year est.); Ancestry (includes multiple ancestries): 22.6% Irish, 21.3% German, 11.1% Italian, 9.3% English, 7.1% Polish (2006-2010 5-year est.).

Economy: Employment by occupation: 0.0% management, 7.2% professional, 4.5% services, 13.9% sales, 3.1% farming, 16.6% construction, 12.9% production (2006-2010 5-year est.).

Income: Per capita income: $21,641 (2006-2010 5-year est.); Median household income: $33,750 (2006-2010 5-year est.); Average household income: $47,431 (2006-2010 5-year est.); Percent of households with income of $100,000 or more: 12.5% (2006-2010 5-year est.); Poverty rate: 15.1% (2006-2010 5-year est.).

Education: Percent of population age 25 and over with: High school diploma (including GED) or higher: 86.4% (2006-2010 5-year est.); Bachelor's degree or higher: 20.3% (2006-2010 5-year est.); Master's degree or higher: 8.2% (2006-2010 5-year est.).

Housing: Homeownership rate: 63.1% (2010); Median home value: $95,000 (2006-2010 5-year est.); Median contract rent: $284 per month (2006-2010 5-year est.); Median year structure built: 1959 (2006-2010 5-year est.).

Transportation: Commute to work: 88.7% car, 2.8% public transportation, 8.0% walk, 0.4% work from home (2006-2010 5-year est.); Travel time to work: 35.4% less than 15 minutes, 26.9% 15 to 30 minutes, 20.5% 30 to 45 minutes, 9.1% 45 to 60 minutes, 8.1% 60 minutes or more (2006-2010 5-year est.).

Additional Information Contacts
Waynesburg Area Chamber of Commerce . . . . (724) 627-5926
http://www.waynesburgchamber.com

FRANKLIN (township). Covers a land area of 40.588 square miles and a water area of 0.035 square miles. Located at 39.87° N. Lat; 80.19° W. Long.

Population: 5,556 (1990); 7,694 (2000); 7,280 (2010); Density: 179.4 persons per square mile (2010); Race: 80.7% White, 14.8% Black, 0.8% Asian, 0.2% American Indian/Alaska Native, 0.0% Native Hawaiian/Other Pacific Islander, 3.5% Other, 3.4% Hispanic of any race (2010); Average household size: 2.34 (2010); Median age: 40.2 (2010); Males per 100 females: 148.7 (2010); Marriage status: 28.5% never married, 47.0% now married, 12.3% widowed, 12.2% divorced (2006-2010 5-year est.); Foreign born: 0.4% (2006-2010 5-year est.); Ancestry (includes multiple ancestries): 21.1% German, 18.7% Irish, 7.5% American, 7.5% English, 6.0% Italian (2006-2010 5-year est.).

Economy: Single-family building permits issued: 8 (2011); Multi-family building permits issued: 0 (2011); Employment by occupation: 7.5% management, 1.6% professional, 10.7% services, 18.9% sales, 4.2% farming, 16.1% construction, 6.7% production (2006-2010 5-year est.).

Income: Per capita income: $18,929 (2006-2010 5-year est.); Median household income: $39,227 (2006-2010 5-year est.); Average household income: $52,330 (2006-2010 5-year est.); Percent of households with income of $100,000 or more: 13.9% (2006-2010 5-year est.); Poverty rate: 16.5% (2006-2010 5-year est.).

Education: Percent of population age 25 and over with: High school diploma (including GED) or higher: 80.0% (2006-2010 5-year est.); Bachelor's degree or higher: 13.0% (2006-2010 5-year est.); Master's degree or higher: 5.1% (2006-2010 5-year est.).

Housing: Homeownership rate: 63.4% (2010); Median home value: $95,000 (2006-2010 5-year est.); Median contract rent: $378 per month (2006-2010 5-year est.); Median year structure built: 1970 (2006-2010 5-year est.).

Transportation: Commute to work: 92.8% car, 0.0% public transportation, 2.8% walk, 4.1% work from home (2006-2010 5-year est.); Travel time to work: 43.8% less than 15 minutes, 25.7% 15 to 30 minutes, 20.8% 30 to

45 minutes, 4.4% 45 to 60 minutes, 5.2% 60 minutes or more (2006-2010 5-year est.).

Additional Information Contacts
Franklin Township . . . . (724) 627-5473
http://www.co.greene.pa.us/secured/gc/depts/eo/twp/franklin.htm
Waynesburg Area Chamber of Commerce . . . . (724) 627-5926
http://www.waynesburgchamber.com

FREEPORT (township). Covers a land area of 8.094 square miles and a water area of 0 square miles. Located at 39.75° N. Lat; 80.42° W. Long.

Population: 327 (1990); 302 (2000); 310 (2010); Density: 38.3 persons per square mile (2010); Race: 96.8% White, 0.0% Black, 0.0% Asian, 0.0% American Indian/Alaska Native, 0.0% Native Hawaiian/Other Pacific Islander, 3.2% Other, 0.3% Hispanic of any race (2010); Average household size: 2.61 (2010); Median age: 40.8 (2010); Males per 100 females: 95.0 (2010); Marriage status: 33.8% never married, 34.3% now married, 4.6% widowed, 27.3% divorced (2006-2010 5-year est.); Foreign born: 0.0% (2006-2010 5-year est.); Ancestry (includes multiple ancestries): 35.7% Irish, 23.3% German, 18.9% English, 10.4% American, 7.6% Polish (2006-2010 5-year est.).

Economy: Employment by occupation: 11.7% management, 0.0% professional, 18.3% services, 11.7% sales, 6.7% farming, 28.3% construction, 5.0% production (2006-2010 5-year est.).

Income: Per capita income: $15,207 (2006-2010 5-year est.); Median household income: $30,859 (2006-2010 5-year est.); Average household income: $40,448 (2006-2010 5-year est.); Percent of households with income of $100,000 or more: 7.8% (2006-2010 5-year est.); Poverty rate: 47.4% (2006-2010 5-year est.).

Education: Percent of population age 25 and over with: High school diploma (including GED) or higher: 75.9% (2006-2010 5-year est.); Bachelor's degree or higher: 9.6% (2006-2010 5-year est.); Master's degree or higher: 1.8% (2006-2010 5-year est.).

Housing: Homeownership rate: 77.3% (2010); Median home value: $112,500 (2006-2010 5-year est.); Median contract rent: $325 per month (2006-2010 5-year est.); Median year structure built: 1965 (2006-2010 5-year est.).

Transportation: Commute to work: 72.7% car, 0.0% public transportation, 12.7% walk, 14.5% work from home (2006-2010 5-year est.); Travel time to work: 42.6% less than 15 minutes, 12.8% 15 to 30 minutes, 29.8% 30 to 45 minutes, 14.9% 45 to 60 minutes, 0.0% 60 minutes or more (2006-2010 5-year est.).

GARARDS FORT (unincorporated postal area)
Zip Code: 15334

Covers a land area of 1.896 square miles and a water area of 0 square miles. Located at 39.80° N. Lat; 79.96° W. Long. Elevation is 971 feet. Population: 113 (2010); Density: 59.6 persons per square mile (2010); Race: 99.1% White, 0.0% Black, 0.0% Asian, 0.0% American Indian/Alaska Native, 0.0% Native Hawaiian/Other Pacific Islander, 0.9% Other, 0.0% Hispanic of any race (2010); Average household size: 2.51 (2010); Median age: 41.8 (2010); Males per 100 females: 85.2 (2010); Homeownership rate: 80.0% (2010)

GILMORE (township). Covers a land area of 23.035 square miles and a water area of 0 square miles. Located at 39.75° N. Lat; 80.35° W. Long.

Population: 365 (1990); 295 (2000); 260 (2010); Density: 11.3 persons per square mile (2010); Race: 97.3% White, 1.9% Black, 0.0% Asian, 0.0% American Indian/Alaska Native, 0.0% Native Hawaiian/Other Pacific Islander, 0.8% Other, 0.4% Hispanic of any race (2010); Average household size: 2.50 (2010); Median age: 42.7 (2010); Males per 100 females: 114.9 (2010); Marriage status: 19.2% never married, 61.1% now married, 8.8% widowed, 10.9% divorced (2006-2010 5-year est.); Foreign born: 0.0% (2006-2010 5-year est.); Ancestry (includes multiple ancestries): 35.3% German, 18.1% Irish, 11.8% American, 10.4% Polish, 7.7% Italian (2006-2010 5-year est.).

Economy: Single-family building permits issued: 0 (2011); Multi-family building permits issued: 0 (2011); Employment by occupation: 11.8% management, 0.0% professional, 8.2% services, 4.7% sales, 7.1% farming, 37.6% construction, 11.8% production (2006-2010 5-year est.).

Income: Per capita income: $26,488 (2006-2010 5-year est.); Median household income: $34,464 (2006-2010 5-year est.); Average household income: $58,223 (2006-2010 5-year est.); Percent of households with income of $100,000 or more: 20.2% (2006-2010 5-year est.); Poverty rate: 29.4% (2006-2010 5-year est.).

Education: Percent of population age 25 and over with: High school diploma (including GED) or higher: 79.1% (2006-2010 5-year est.); Bachelor's degree or higher: 13.3% (2006-2010 5-year est.); Master's degree or higher: 2.5% (2006-2010 5-year est.).
Housing: Homeownership rate: 78.8% (2010); Median home value: $91,700 (2006-2010 5-year est.); Median contract rent: $217 per month (2006-2010 5-year est.); Median year structure built: 1967 (2006-2010 5-year est.).
Transportation: Commute to work: 100.0% car, 0.0% public transportation, 0.0% walk, 0.0% work from home (2006-2010 5-year est.); Travel time to work: 10.6% less than 15 minutes, 38.8% 15 to 30 minutes, 24.7% 30 to 45 minutes, 11.8% 45 to 60 minutes, 14.1% 60 minutes or more (2006-2010 5-year est.)

GRAY (township). Covers a land area of 4.237 square miles and a water area of 0 square miles. Located at 39.93° N. Lat; 80.38° W. Long.
Population: 220 (1990); 236 (2000); 219 (2010); Density: 51.7 persons per square mile (2010); Race: 97.7% White, 0.0% Black, 0.0% Asian, 0.0% American Indian/Alaska Native, 0.0% Native Hawaiian/Other Pacific Islander, 2.3% Other, 2.3% Hispanic of any race (2010); Average household size: 2.61 (2010); Median age: 39.3 (2010); Males per 100 females: 104.7 (2010); Marriage status: 20.5% never married, 69.5% now married, 2.6% widowed, 7.4% divorced (2006-2010 5-year est.); Foreign born: 0.0% (2006-2010 5-year est.); Ancestry (includes multiple ancestries): 25.3% German, 18.0% Irish, 11.4% English, 10.2% American, 5.7% Italian (2006-2010 5-year est.).
Economy: Single-family building permits issued: 1 (2011); Multi-family building permits issued: 0 (2011); Employment by occupation: 7.8% management, 3.3% professional, 7.8% services, 12.2% sales, 2.2% farming, 35.6% construction, 6.7% production (2006-2010 5-year est.).
Income: Per capita income: $18,083 (2006-2010 5-year est.); Median household income: $39,107 (2006-2010 5-year est.); Average household income: $50,600 (2006-2010 5-year est.); Percent of households with income of $100,000 or more: 15.7% (2006-2010 5-year est.); Poverty rate: 24.9% (2006-2010 5-year est.).
Education: Percent of population age 25 and over with: High school diploma (including GED) or higher: 77.8% (2006-2010 5-year est.); Bachelor's degree or higher: 14.8% (2006-2010 5-year est.); Master's degree or higher: 4.3% (2006-2010 5-year est.).
Housing: Homeownership rate: 63.1% (2010); Median home value: $95,000 (2006-2010 5-year est.); Median contract rent: $420 per month (2006-2010 5-year est.); Median year structure built: 1962 (2006-2010 5-year est.).
Transportation: Commute to work: 97.8% car, 0.0% public transportation, 2.2% walk, 0.0% work from home (2006-2010 5-year est.); Travel time to work: 37.8% less than 15 minutes, 10.0% 15 to 30 minutes, 32.2% 30 to 45 minutes, 5.6% 45 to 60 minutes, 14.4% 60 minutes or more (2006-2010 5-year est.)

GRAYSVILLE (unincorporated postal area)
Zip Code: 15337
Covers a land area of 31.915 square miles and a water area of 0.006 square miles. Located at 39.95° N. Lat; 80.37° W. Long. Population: 744 (2010); Density: 23.3 persons per square mile (2010); Race: 98.3% White, 0.8% Black, 0.0% Asian, 0.0% American Indian/Alaska Native, 0.0% Native Hawaiian/Other Pacific Islander, 0.9% Other, 1.3% Hispanic of any race (2010); Average household size: 2.61 (2010); Median age: 43.1 (2010); Males per 100 females: 109.0 (2010); Homeownership rate: 75.2% (2010)

GREENE (township). Covers a land area of 18.508 square miles and a water area of 0.004 square miles. Located at 39.82° N. Lat; 80.03° W. Long.
Population: 494 (1990); 445 (2000); 445 (2010); Density: 24.0 persons per square mile (2010); Race: 98.7% White, 0.2% Black, 0.0% Asian, 0.2% American Indian/Alaska Native, 0.0% Native Hawaiian/Other Pacific Islander, 0.9% Other, 0.9% Hispanic of any race (2010); Average household size: 2.42 (2010); Median age: 43.0 (2010); Males per 100 females: 100.5 (2010); Marriage status: 16.0% never married, 68.0% now married, 8.0% widowed, 8.0% divorced (2006-2010 5-year est.); Foreign born: 0.0% (2006-2010 5-year est.); Ancestry (includes multiple ancestries): 34.6% Irish, 31.7% German, 20.1% English, 10.4% Hungarian, 7.5% Italian (2006-2010 5-year est.).
Economy: Single-family building permits issued: 0 (2011); Multi-family building permits issued: 0 (2011); Employment by occupation: 9.6%

management, 4.2% professional, 10.0% services, 17.2% sales, 12.1% farming, 10.9% construction, 2.9% production (2006-2010 5-year est.).
Income: Per capita income: $35,082 (2006-2010 5-year est.); Median household income: $53,646 (2006-2010 5-year est.); Average household income: $79,428 (2006-2010 5-year est.); Percent of households with income of $100,000 or more: 18.3% (2006-2010 5-year est.); Poverty rate: 10.6% (2006-2010 5-year est.).
Education: Percent of population age 25 and over with: High school diploma (including GED) or higher: 91.8% (2006-2010 5-year est.); Bachelor's degree or higher: 21.9% (2006-2010 5-year est.); Master's degree or higher: 7.1% (2006-2010 5-year est.).
Housing: Homeownership rate: 79.9% (2010); Median home value: $85,300 (2006-2010 5-year est.); Median contract rent: $286 per month (2006-2010 5-year est.); Median year structure built: 1960 (2006-2010 5-year est.).
Transportation: Commute to work: 96.2% car, 0.9% public transportation, 0.0% walk, 3.0% work from home (2006-2010 5-year est.); Travel time to work: 33.5% less than 15 minutes, 37.4% 15 to 30 minutes, 19.8% 30 to 45 minutes, 2.6% 45 to 60 minutes, 6.6% 60 minutes or more (2006-2010 5-year est.)

GREENSBORO (borough). Covers a land area of 0.108 square miles and a water area of 0.038 square miles. Located at 39.79° N. Lat; 79.91° W. Long. Elevation is 797 feet.
Population: 307 (1990); 295 (2000); 260 (2010); Density: 2,401.6 persons per square mile (2010); Race: 95.0% White, 1.5% Black, 0.0% Asian, 0.4% American Indian/Alaska Native, 0.0% Native Hawaiian/Other Pacific Islander, 3.1% Other, 1.2% Hispanic of any race (2010); Average household size: 2.36 (2010); Median age: 41.0 (2010); Males per 100 females: 78.1 (2010); Marriage status: 32.2% never married, 58.8% now married, 5.7% widowed, 3.3% divorced (2006-2010 5-year est.); Foreign born: 0.0% (2006-2010 5-year est.); Ancestry (includes multiple ancestries): 42.7% Irish, 25.2% German, 13.7% Polish, 11.8% Slovak, 9.5% Dutch (2006-2010 5-year est.).
Economy: Single-family building permits issued: 1 (2011); Multi-family building permits issued: 0 (2011); Employment by occupation: 15.3% management, 3.5% professional, 7.1% services, 17.6% sales, 0.0% farming, 4.7% construction, 7.1% production (2006-2010 5-year est.).
Income: Per capita income: $14,611 (2006-2010 5-year est.); Median household income: $32,361 (2006-2010 5-year est.); Average household income: $41,645 (2006-2010 5-year est.); Percent of households with income of $100,000 or more: 5.6% (2006-2010 5-year est.); Poverty rate: 23.7% (2006-2010 5-year est.).
Education: Percent of population age 25 and over with: High school diploma (including GED) or higher: 84.8% (2006-2010 5-year est.); Bachelor's degree or higher: 18.9% (2006-2010 5-year est.); Master's degree or higher: 1.8% (2006-2010 5-year est.).

School District(s)
Southeastern Greene SD (KG-12)
  2010-11 Enrollment: 625. . . . . (724) 943-3630
Housing: Homeownership rate: 76.4% (2010); Median home value: $51,800 (2006-2010 5-year est.); Median contract rent: $206 per month (2006-2010 5-year est.); Median year structure built: before 1940 (2006-2010 5-year est.).
Transportation: Commute to work: 84.7% car, 0.0% public transportation, 0.0% walk, 15.3% work from home (2006-2010 5-year est.); Travel time to work: 22.2% less than 15 minutes, 31.9% 15 to 30 minutes, 34.7% 30 to 45 minutes, 6.9% 45 to 60 minutes, 4.2% 60 minutes or more (2006-2010 5-year est.)

HOLBROOK (unincorporated postal area)
Zip Code: 15341
Covers a land area of 49.205 square miles and a water area of 0.007 square miles. Located at 39.82° N. Lat; 80.34° W. Long. Population: 869 (2010); Density: 17.7 persons per square mile (2010); Race: 99.1% White, 0.2% Black, 0.0% Asian, 0.0% American Indian/Alaska Native, 0.0% Native Hawaiian/Other Pacific Islander, 0.7% Other, 0.0% Hispanic of any race (2010); Average household size: 2.53 (2010); Median age: 43.4 (2010); Males per 100 females: 114.0 (2010); Homeownership rate: 77.3% (2010)

JACKSON (township). Covers a land area of 28.727 square miles and a water area of 0.013 square miles. Located at 39.82° N. Lat; 80.37° W. Long.

Population: 546 (1990); 516 (2000); 487 (2010); Density: 17.0 persons per square mile (2010); Race: 99.0% White, 0.0% Black, 0.4% Asian, 0.0% American Indian/Alaska Native, 0.0% Native Hawaiian/Other Pacific Islander, 0.6% Other, 0.0% Hispanic of any race (2010); Average household size: 2.52 (2010); Median age: 43.5 (2010); Males per 100 females: 114.5 (2010); Marriage status: 19.9% never married, 69.9% now married, 5.9% widowed, 4.3% divorced (2006-2010 5-year est.); Foreign born: 0.9% (2006-2010 5-year est.); Ancestry (includes multiple ancestries): 25.5% German, 23.1% Irish, 20.8% English, 8.6% American, 7.5% Dutch (2006-2010 5-year est.).

Economy: Single-family building permits issued: 2 (2011); Multi-family building permits issued: 0 (2011); Employment by occupation: 10.6% management, 4.1% professional, 12.8% services, 11.9% sales, 6.0% farming, 18.8% construction, 6.0% production (2006-2010 5-year est.).

Income: Per capita income: $22,188 (2006-2010 5-year est.); Median household income: $47,500 (2006-2010 5-year est.); Average household income: $55,034 (2006-2010 5-year est.); Percent of households with income of $100,000 or more: 11.3% (2006-2010 5-year est.); Poverty rate: 9.1% (2006-2010 5-year est.).

Education: Percent of population age 25 and over with: High school diploma (including GED) or higher: 83.6% (2006-2010 5-year est.); Bachelor's degree or higher: 23.0% (2006-2010 5-year est.); Master's degree or higher: 4.8% (2006-2010 5-year est.).

Housing: Homeownership rate: 77.7% (2010); Median home value: $98,300 (2006-2010 5-year est.); Median contract rent: $367 per month (2006-2010 5-year est.); Median year structure built: 1949 (2006-2010 5-year est.).

Transportation: Commute to work: 95.5% car, 0.0% public transportation, 0.0% walk, 4.5% work from home (2006-2010 5-year est.); Travel time to work: 7.8% less than 15 minutes, 23.3% 15 to 30 minutes, 20.2% 30 to 45 minutes, 9.3% 45 to 60 minutes, 39.4% 60 minutes or more (2006-2010 5-year est.)

JEFFERSON (borough). Covers a land area of 0.188 square miles and a water area of 0 square miles. Located at 39.93° N. Lat; 80.06° W. Long. Elevation is 961 feet.

Population: 355 (1990); 337 (2000); 270 (2010); Density: 1,437.0 persons per square mile (2010); Race: 99.3% White, 0.0% Black, 0.0% Asian, 0.0% American Indian/Alaska Native, 0.0% Native Hawaiian/Other Pacific Islander, 0.7% Other, 0.4% Hispanic of any race (2010); Average household size: 2.20 (2010); Median age: 46.4 (2010); Males per 100 females: 100.0 (2010); Marriage status: 27.5% never married, 40.8% now married, 16.9% widowed, 14.9% divorced (2006-2010 5-year est.); Foreign born: 0.7% (2006-2010 5-year est.); Ancestry (includes multiple ancestries): 36.1% German, 19.1% Irish, 7.6% Polish, 7.3% Scotch-Irish, 5.6% English (2006-2010 5-year est.).

Economy: Employment by occupation: 4.6% management, 3.7% professional, 13.8% services, 28.4% sales, 5.5% farming, 16.5% construction, 3.7% production (2006-2010 5-year est.).

Income: Per capita income: $15,903 (2006-2010 5-year est.); Median household income: $29,167 (2006-2010 5-year est.); Average household income: $35,505 (2006-2010 5-year est.); Percent of households with income of $100,000 or more: 4.2% (2006-2010 5-year est.); Poverty rate: 32.3% (2006-2010 5-year est.).

Education: Percent of population age 25 and over with: High school diploma (including GED) or higher: 73.3% (2006-2010 5-year est.); Bachelor's degree or higher: 12.9% (2006-2010 5-year est.); Master's degree or higher: 2.5% (2006-2010 5-year est.).

School District(s)

Jefferson-Morgan SD (KG-12)

   2010-11 Enrollment: 845 . . . . (724) 883-2310

Housing: Homeownership rate: 76.4% (2010); Median home value: $69,200 (2006-2010 5-year est.); Median contract rent: $355 per month (2006-2010 5-year est.); Median year structure built: 1941 (2006-2010 5-year est.).

Transportation: Commute to work: 79.0% car, 0.0% public transportation, 9.5% walk, 8.6% work from home (2006-2010 5-year est.); Travel time to work: 32.3% less than 15 minutes, 24.0% 15 to 30 minutes, 6.3% 30 to 45 minutes, 12.5% 45 to 60 minutes, 25.0% 60 minutes or more (2006-2010 5-year est.)

JEFFERSON (township). Covers a land area of 21.542 square miles and a water area of 0.122 square miles. Located at 39.92° N. Lat; 80.05° W. Long. Elevation is 961 feet.

Population: 2,536 (1990); 2,528 (2000); 2,352 (2010); Density: 109.2 persons per square mile (2010); Race: 96.8% White, 1.7% Black, 0.5% Asian, 0.2% American Indian/Alaska Native, 0.0% Native Hawaiian/Other Pacific Islander, 0.8% Other, 0.6% Hispanic of any race (2010); Average household size: 2.32 (2010); Median age: 47.7 (2010); Males per 100 females: 98.3 (2010); Marriage status: 27.9% never married, 54.7% now married, 6.9% widowed, 10.5% divorced (2006-2010 5-year est.); Foreign born: 1.6% (2006-2010 5-year est.); Ancestry (includes multiple ancestries): 24.2% German, 20.5% Irish, 15.2% English, 7.9% Italian, 6.2% Polish (2006-2010 5-year est.).

Economy: Single-family building permits issued: 4 (2011); Multi-family building permits issued: 0 (2011); Employment by occupation: 9.3% management, 3.2% professional, 10.8% services, 20.2% sales, 2.8% farming, 16.2% construction, 4.0% production (2006-2010 5-year est.).

Income: Per capita income: $21,345 (2006-2010 5-year est.); Median household income: $44,225 (2006-2010 5-year est.); Average household income: $54,743 (2006-2010 5-year est.); Percent of households with income of $100,000 or more: 12.9% (2006-2010 5-year est.); Poverty rate: 11.0% (2006-2010 5-year est.).

Education: Percent of population age 25 and over with: High school diploma (including GED) or higher: 86.2% (2006-2010 5-year est.); Bachelor's degree or higher: 11.5% (2006-2010 5-year est.); Master's degree or higher: 2.5% (2006-2010 5-year est.).

Housing: Homeownership rate: 84.4% (2010); Median home value: $84,600 (2006-2010 5-year est.); Median contract rent: $402 per month (2006-2010 5-year est.); Median year structure built: 1957 (2006-2010 5-year est.).

Transportation: Commute to work: 98.1% car, 0.0% public transportation, 1.1% walk, 0.2% work from home (2006-2010 5-year est.); Travel time to work: 28.2% less than 15 minutes, 30.9% 15 to 30 minutes, 21.8% 30 to 45 minutes, 10.4% 45 to 60 minutes, 8.6% 60 minutes or more (2006-2010 5-year est.)

Additional Information Contacts

Waynesburg Area Chamber of Commerce . . . . (724) 627-5926

  http://www.waynesburgchamber.com

MAPLETOWN (CDP). Covers a land area of 0.398 square miles and a water area of 0 square miles. Located at 39.81° N. Lat; 79.94° W. Long. Elevation is 965 feet.

Population: n/a (1990); n/a (2000); 130 (2010); Density: 327.0 persons per square mile (2010); Race: 100.0% White, 0.0% Black, 0.0% Asian, 0.0% American Indian/Alaska Native, 0.0% Native Hawaiian/Other Pacific Islander, 0.0% Other, 0.0% Hispanic of any race (2010); Average household size: 2.45 (2010); Median age: 46.5 (2010); Males per 100 females: 97.0 (2010); Marriage status: 38.8% never married, 37.1% now married, 22.4% widowed, 1.7% divorced (2006-2010 5-year est.); Foreign born: 0.0% (2006-2010 5-year est.); Ancestry (includes multiple ancestries): 50.0% Irish, 28.4% German, 15.5% Dutch, 9.5% American, 8.6% Yugoslavian (2006-2010 5-year est.).

Economy: Employment by occupation: 0.0% management, 37.3% professional, 0.0% services, 6.7% sales, 0.0% farming, 20.0% construction, 20.0% production (2006-2010 5-year est.).

Income: Per capita income: $20,473 (2006-2010 5-year est.); Median household income: $29,167 (2006-2010 5-year est.); Average household income: $43,640 (2006-2010 5-year est.); Percent of households with income of $100,000 or more: n/a (2006-2010 5-year est.); Poverty rate: 3.4% (2006-2010 5-year est.).

Education: Percent of population age 25 and over with: High school diploma (including GED) or higher: 78.3% (2006-2010 5-year est.); Bachelor's degree or higher: 26.5% (2006-2010 5-year est.); Master's degree or higher: 26.5% (2006-2010 5-year est.).

Housing: Homeownership rate: 81.2% (2010); Median home value: $75,000 (2006-2010 5-year est.); Median contract rent: n/a per month (2006-2010 5-year est.); Median year structure built: 1957 (2006-2010 5-year est.).

Transportation: Commute to work: 84.0% car, 0.0% public transportation, 16.0% walk, 0.0% work from home (2006-2010 5-year est.); Travel time to work: 20.0% less than 15 minutes, 53.3% 15 to 30 minutes, 26.7% 30 to 45 minutes, 0.0% 45 to 60 minutes, 0.0% 60 minutes or more (2006-2010 5-year est.)

MATHER (CDP). Covers a land area of 0.879 square miles and a water area of 0.003 square miles. Located at 39.94° N. Lat; 80.07° W. Long. Elevation is 955 feet.

Population: n/a (1990); n/a (2000); 737 (2010); Density: 838.7 persons per square mile (2010); Race: 97.4% White, 1.1% Black, 0.0% Asian, 0.4% American Indian/Alaska Native, 0.0% Native Hawaiian/Other Pacific Islander, 1.1% Other, 1.5% Hispanic of any race (2010); Average household size: 2.56 (2010); Median age: 41.0 (2010); Males per 100 females: 104.7 (2010); Marriage status: 30.1% never married, 56.1% now married, 2.5% widowed, 11.3% divorced (2006-2010 5-year est.); Foreign born: 0.9% (2006-2010 5-year est.); Ancestry (includes multiple ancestries): 38.9% German, 29.4% Irish, 13.3% Italian, 12.2% Polish, 9.5% English (2006-2010 5-year est.).

Economy: Employment by occupation: 0.0% management, 0.0% professional, 9.8% services, 10.4% sales, 5.7% farming, 20.3% construction, 8.9% production (2006-2010 5-year est.).

Income: Per capita income: $21,407 (2006-2010 5-year est.); Median household income: $62,120 (2006-2010 5-year est.); Average household income: $59,991 (2006-2010 5-year est.); Percent of households with income of $100,000 or more: 10.6% (2006-2010 5-year est.); Poverty rate: 7.9% (2006-2010 5-year est.).

Education: Percent of population age 25 and over with: High school diploma (including GED) or higher: 86.2% (2006-2010 5-year est.); Bachelor's degree or higher: 8.8% (2006-2010 5-year est.); Master's degree or higher: 4.6% (2006-2010 5-year est.).

Housing: Homeownership rate: 80.5% (2010); Median home value: $54,800 (2006-2010 5-year est.); Median contract rent: n/a per month (2006-2010 5-year est.); Median year structure built: before 1940 (2006-2010 5-year est.).

Transportation: Commute to work: 98.1% car, 1.9% public transportation, 0.0% walk, 0.0% work from home (2006-2010 5-year est.); Travel time to work: 22.5% less than 15 minutes, 26.3% 15 to 30 minutes, 28.8% 30 to 45 minutes, 12.7% 45 to 60 minutes, 9.8% 60 minutes or more (2006-2010 5-year est.)

MONONGAHELA (township). Covers a land area of 17.434 square miles and a water area of 0.549 square miles. Located at 39.81° N. Lat; 79.95° W. Long.

Population: 1,858 (1990); 1,714 (2000); 1,572 (2010); Density: 90.2 persons per square mile (2010); Race: 98.5% White, 0.3% Black, 0.2% Asian, 0.2% American Indian/Alaska Native, 0.0% Native Hawaiian/Other Pacific Islander, 0.8% Other, 1.0% Hispanic of any race (2010); Average household size: 2.54 (2010); Median age: 42.7 (2010); Males per 100 females: 99.7 (2010); Marriage status: 25.8% never married, 54.0% now married, 7.3% widowed, 12.8% divorced (2006-2010 5-year est.); Foreign born: 0.6% (2006-2010 5-year est.); Ancestry (includes multiple ancestries): 26.3% German, 17.5% Irish, 9.7% Italian, 9.5% English, 7.9% Polish (2006-2010 5-year est.).

Economy: Single-family building permits issued: 1 (2011); Multi-family building permits issued: 0 (2011); Employment by occupation: 9.3% management, 7.8% professional, 6.3% services, 8.4% sales, 3.1% farming, 13.9% construction, 11.5% production (2006-2010 5-year est.).

Income: Per capita income: $20,789 (2006-2010 5-year est.); Median household income: $40,766 (2006-2010 5-year est.); Average household income: $52,402 (2006-2010 5-year est.); Percent of households with income of $100,000 or more: 13.8% (2006-2010 5-year est.); Poverty rate: 21.1% (2006-2010 5-year est.).

Education: Percent of population age 25 and over with: High school diploma (including GED) or higher: 83.8% (2006-2010 5-year est.); Bachelor's degree or higher: 16.0% (2006-2010 5-year est.); Master's degree or higher: 7.3% (2006-2010 5-year est.).

Housing: Homeownership rate: 80.3% (2010); Median home value: $82,800 (2006-2010 5-year est.); Median contract rent: $375 per month (2006-2010 5-year est.); Median year structure built: 1960 (2006-2010 5-year est.).

Transportation: Commute to work: 92.3% car, 0.9% public transportation, 3.3% walk, 3.5% work from home (2006-2010 5-year est.); Travel time to work: 20.2% less than 15 minutes, 33.1% 15 to 30 minutes, 30.6% 30 to 45 minutes, 6.3% 45 to 60 minutes, 9.9% 60 minutes or more (2006-2010 5-year est.)

Additional Information Contacts
Waynesburg Area Chamber of Commerce . . . . (724) 627-5926
  http://www.waynesburgchamber.com

MORGAN (township). Covers a land area of 24.705 square miles and a water area of 0.016 square miles. Located at 39.95° N. Lat; 80.11° W. Long.

Population: 2,887 (1990); 2,600 (2000); 2,587 (2010); Density: 104.7 persons per square mile (2010); Race: 98.4% White, 0.5% Black, 0.0% Asian, 0.2% American Indian/Alaska Native, 0.0% Native Hawaiian/Other Pacific Islander, 0.9% Other, 0.9% Hispanic of any race (2010); Average household size: 2.51 (2010); Median age: 42.3 (2010); Males per 100 females: 102.6 (2010); Marriage status: 24.1% never married, 57.1% now married, 7.1% widowed, 11.7% divorced (2006-2010 5-year est.); Foreign born: 1.0% (2006-2010 5-year est.); Ancestry (includes multiple ancestries): 24.9% German, 18.7% Irish, 16.3% English, 8.8% Italian, 8.4% Polish (2006-2010 5-year est.).

Economy: Single-family building permits issued: 3 (2011); Multi-family building permits issued: 0 (2011); Employment by occupation: 5.6% management, 0.0% professional, 20.2% services, 12.7% sales, 5.1% farming, 13.0% construction, 6.8% production (2006-2010 5-year est.).

Income: Per capita income: $21,608 (2006-2010 5-year est.); Median household income: $40,735 (2006-2010 5-year est.); Average household income: $53,589 (2006-2010 5-year est.); Percent of households with income of $100,000 or more: 12.1% (2006-2010 5-year est.); Poverty rate: 11.1% (2006-2010 5-year est.).

Education: Percent of population age 25 and over with: High school diploma (including GED) or higher: 86.8% (2006-2010 5-year est.); Bachelor's degree or higher: 12.7% (2006-2010 5-year est.); Master's degree or higher: 3.8% (2006-2010 5-year est.).

Housing: Homeownership rate: 82.2% (2010); Median home value: $59,800 (2006-2010 5-year est.); Median contract rent: $373 per month (2006-2010 5-year est.); Median year structure built: 1947 (2006-2010 5-year est.).

Transportation: Commute to work: 91.4% car, 0.6% public transportation, 3.5% walk, 2.8% work from home (2006-2010 5-year est.); Travel time to work: 21.7% less than 15 minutes, 37.8% 15 to 30 minutes, 22.5% 30 to 45 minutes, 8.8% 45 to 60 minutes, 9.2% 60 minutes or more (2006-2010 5-year est.)

Additional Information Contacts
South West Communities Chamber of Commerce . . . . (412) 221-4100
  http://www.swccoc.org

MORRIS (township). Covers a land area of 35.688 square miles and a water area of 0.018 square miles. Located at 39.97° N. Lat; 80.31° W. Long.

Population: 898 (1990); 1,040 (2000); 818 (2010); Density: 22.9 persons per square mile (2010); Race: 97.3% White, 0.7% Black, 0.0% Asian, 0.1% American Indian/Alaska Native, 0.0% Native Hawaiian/Other Pacific Islander, 1.9% Other, 2.1% Hispanic of any race (2010); Average household size: 2.60 (2010); Median age: 45.5 (2010); Males per 100 females: 113.0 (2010); Marriage status: 24.2% never married, 63.9% now married, 4.0% widowed, 8.0% divorced (2006-2010 5-year est.); Foreign born: 0.0% (2006-2010 5-year est.); Ancestry (includes multiple ancestries): 40.3% German, 17.7% Irish, 15.5% English, 10.9% American, 6.7% Scotch-Irish (2006-2010 5-year est.).

Economy: Single-family building permits issued: 3 (2011); Multi-family building permits issued: 0 (2011); Employment by occupation: 11.8% management, 0.0% professional, 11.4% services, 15.3% sales, 6.4% farming, 18.0% construction, 7.3% production (2006-2010 5-year est.).

Income: Per capita income: $20,683 (2006-2010 5-year est.); Median household income: $47,986 (2006-2010 5-year est.); Average household income: $53,506 (2006-2010 5-year est.); Percent of households with income of $100,000 or more: 10.2% (2006-2010 5-year est.); Poverty rate: 6.2% (2006-2010 5-year est.).

Education: Percent of population age 25 and over with: High school diploma (including GED) or higher: 87.8% (2006-2010 5-year est.); Bachelor's degree or higher: 15.5% (2006-2010 5-year est.); Master's degree or higher: 3.6% (2006-2010 5-year est.).

Housing: Homeownership rate: 81.5% (2010); Median home value: $95,500 (2006-2010 5-year est.); Median contract rent: $343 per month (2006-2010 5-year est.); Median year structure built: 1942 (2006-2010 5-year est.).

Transportation: Commute to work: 92.3% car, 0.0% public transportation, 1.1% walk, 5.0% work from home (2006-2010 5-year est.); Travel time to work: 6.5% less than 15 minutes, 42.9% 15 to 30 minutes, 27.1% 30 to 45 minutes, 12.2% 45 to 60 minutes, 11.3% 60 minutes or more (2006-2010 5-year est.)

MORRISVILLE (CDP). Covers a land area of 1.550 square miles and a water area of 0 square miles. Located at 39.90° N. Lat; 80.17° W. Long. Elevation is 978 feet.

Population: 1,388 (1990); 1,443 (2000); 1,265 (2010); Density: 816.1 persons per square mile (2010); Race: 96.0% White, 1.7% Black, 0.8% Asian, 0.6% American Indian/Alaska Native, 0.0% Native Hawaiian/Other Pacific Islander, 0.9% Other, 1.5% Hispanic of any race (2010); Average household size: 2.09 (2010); Median age: 44.7 (2010); Males per 100 females: 92.0 (2010); Marriage status: 25.8% never married, 33.2% now married, 24.2% widowed, 16.9% divorced (2006-2010 5-year est.); Foreign born: 0.0% (2006-2010 5-year est.); Ancestry (includes multiple ancestries): 25.4% Irish, 21.5% German, 11.4% American, 9.2% Scotch-Irish, 8.1% English (2006-2010 5-year est.).

Economy: Employment by occupation: 9.3% management, 2.2% professional, 11.2% services, 29.0% sales, 7.1% farming, 11.0% construction, 0.0% production (2006-2010 5-year est.).

Income: Per capita income: $18,660 (2006-2010 5-year est.); Median household income: $31,250 (2006-2010 5-year est.); Average household income: $38,407 (2006-2010 5-year est.); Percent of households with income of $100,000 or more: 1.6% (2006-2010 5-year est.); Poverty rate: 11.5% (2006-2010 5-year est.).

Education: Percent of population age 25 and over with: High school diploma (including GED) or higher: 89.7% (2006-2010 5-year est.); Bachelor's degree or higher: 14.5% (2006-2010 5-year est.); Master's degree or higher: 5.4% (2006-2010 5-year est.).

Housing: Homeownership rate: 61.0% (2010); Median home value: $65,700 (2006-2010 5-year est.); Median contract rent: $416 per month (2006-2010 5-year est.); Median year structure built: 1967 (2006-2010 5-year est.).

Transportation: Commute to work: 96.7% car, 0.0% public transportation, 1.7% walk, 1.6% work from home (2006-2010 5-year est.); Travel time to work: 74.5% less than 15 minutes, 0.0% 15 to 30 minutes, 21.9% 30 to 45 minutes, 3.5% 45 to 60 minutes, 0.0% 60 minutes or more (2006-2010 5-year est.)

Additional Information Contacts

Waynesburg Area Chamber of Commerce . . . . (724) 627-5926
  http://www.waynesburgchamber.com

MOUNT MORRIS (CDP). Covers a land area of 2.677 square miles and a water area of 0.007 square miles. Located at 39.73° N. Lat; 80.08° W. Long. Elevation is 938 feet.

Population: n/a (1990); n/a (2000); 737 (2010); Density: 275.3 persons per square mile (2010); Race: 98.9% White, 0.3% Black, 0.0% Asian, 0.3% American Indian/Alaska Native, 0.0% Native Hawaiian/Other Pacific Islander, 0.5% Other, 0.0% Hispanic of any race (2010); Average household size: 2.28 (2010); Median age: 45.6 (2010); Males per 100 females: 95.5 (2010); Marriage status: 22.5% never married, 60.7% now married, 6.6% widowed, 10.2% divorced (2006-2010 5-year est.); Foreign born: 0.8% (2006-2010 5-year est.); Ancestry (includes multiple ancestries): 24.2% Irish, 24.0% German, 12.9% Italian, 12.3% English, 7.0% American (2006-2010 5-year est.).

Economy: Employment by occupation: 3.4% management, 2.1% professional, 13.4% services, 21.7% sales, 2.1% farming, 12.4% construction, 1.7% production (2006-2010 5-year est.).

Income: Per capita income: $21,171 (2006-2010 5-year est.); Median household income: $45,179 (2006-2010 5-year est.); Average household income: $49,060 (2006-2010 5-year est.); Percent of households with income of $100,000 or more: 7.4% (2006-2010 5-year est.); Poverty rate: 10.6% (2006-2010 5-year est.).

Education: Percent of population age 25 and over with: High school diploma (including GED) or higher: 82.0% (2006-2010 5-year est.); Bachelor's degree or higher: 16.2% (2006-2010 5-year est.); Master's degree or higher: 8.6% (2006-2010 5-year est.).

School District(s)

Central Greene SD (KG-12)
  2010-11 Enrollment: 1,991 . . . . (724) 627-8151

Housing: Homeownership rate: 76.8% (2010); Median home value: $91,600 (2006-2010 5-year est.); Median contract rent: $437 per month (2006-2010 5-year est.); Median year structure built: 1954 (2006-2010 5-year est.).

Transportation: Commute to work: 94.9% car, 0.0% public transportation, 0.0% walk, 5.1% work from home (2006-2010 5-year est.); Travel time to work: 12.6% less than 15 minutes, 55.0% 15 to 30 minutes, 26.0% 30 to 45 minutes, 3.4% 45 to 60 minutes, 3.1% 60 minutes or more (2006-2010 5-year est.)

NEMACOLIN (CDP). Covers a land area of 1.432 square miles and a water area of 0.134 square miles. Located at 39.88° N. Lat; 79.93° W. Long. Elevation is 1,040 feet.

Population: 1,140 (1990); 1,034 (2000); 937 (2010); Density: 654.5 persons per square mile (2010); Race: 98.1% White, 0.5% Black, 0.1% Asian, 0.2% American Indian/Alaska Native, 0.0% Native Hawaiian/Other Pacific Islander, 1.1% Other, 0.4% Hispanic of any race (2010); Average household size: 2.63 (2010); Median age: 34.9 (2010); Males per 100 females: 100.6 (2010); Marriage status: 23.0% never married, 33.6% now married, 20.1% widowed, 23.4% divorced (2006-2010 5-year est.); Foreign born: 0.0% (2006-2010 5-year est.); Ancestry (includes multiple ancestries): 33.2% Italian, 30.3% German, 17.5% Polish, 9.0% Irish, 6.3% American (2006-2010 5-year est.).

Economy: Employment by occupation: 0.0% management, 0.0% professional, 4.2% services, 22.6% sales, 11.1% farming, 7.2% construction, 7.2% production (2006-2010 5-year est.).

Income: Per capita income: $13,298 (2006-2010 5-year est.); Median household income: $30,174 (2006-2010 5-year est.); Average household income: $30,974 (2006-2010 5-year est.); Percent of households with income of $100,000 or more: n/a (2006-2010 5-year est.); Poverty rate: 7.1% (2006-2010 5-year est.).

Education: Percent of population age 25 and over with: High school diploma (including GED) or higher: 92.5% (2006-2010 5-year est.); Bachelor's degree or higher: 5.1% (2006-2010 5-year est.); Master's degree or higher: 0.0% (2006-2010 5-year est.).

Housing: Homeownership rate: 64.9% (2010); Median home value: $19,400 (2006-2010 5-year est.); Median contract rent: $367 per month (2006-2010 5-year est.); Median year structure built: 1943 (2006-2010 5-year est.).

Transportation: Commute to work: 100.0% car, 0.0% public transportation, 0.0% walk, 0.0% work from home (2006-2010 5-year est.); Travel time to work: 49.4% less than 15 minutes, 12.3% 15 to 30 minutes, 30.4% 30 to 45 minutes, 7.8% 45 to 60 minutes, 0.0% 60 minutes or more (2006-2010 5-year est.)

NEW FREEPORT (CDP). Covers a land area of 0.663 square miles and a water area of 0 square miles. Located at 39.76° N. Lat; 80.43° W. Long. Elevation is 1,063 feet.

Population: n/a (1990); n/a (2000); 112 (2010); Density: 168.8 persons per square mile (2010); Race: 98.2% White, 0.0% Black, 0.0% Asian, 0.0% American Indian/Alaska Native, 0.0% Native Hawaiian/Other Pacific Islander, 1.8% Other, 0.9% Hispanic of any race (2010); Average household size: 2.60 (2010); Median age: 44.0 (2010); Males per 100 females: 77.8 (2010); Marriage status: 18.6% never married, 67.8% now married, 1.7% widowed, 11.9% divorced (2006-2010 5-year est.); Foreign born: 0.0% (2006-2010 5-year est.); Ancestry (includes multiple ancestries): 24.4% Polish, 21.8% English, 19.2% American, 16.7% Irish, 16.7% Slovak (2006-2010 5-year est.).

Economy: Employment by occupation: 0.0% management, 0.0% professional, 16.7% services, 16.7% sales, 0.0% farming, 25.0% construction, 25.0% production (2006-2010 5-year est.).

Income: Per capita income: $9,687 (2006-2010 5-year est.); Median household income: $18,750 (2006-2010 5-year est.); Average household income: $26,057 (2006-2010 5-year est.); Percent of households with income of $100,000 or more: n/a (2006-2010 5-year est.); Poverty rate: 41.0% (2006-2010 5-year est.).

Education: Percent of population age 25 and over with: High school diploma (including GED) or higher: 96.2% (2006-2010 5-year est.); Bachelor's degree or higher: 25.0% (2006-2010 5-year est.); Master's degree or higher: 0.0% (2006-2010 5-year est.).

School District(s)

West Greene SD (KG-12)
  2010-11 Enrollment: 800 . . . . (724) 499-5183

Housing: Homeownership rate: 65.2% (2010); Median home value: $94,200 (2006-2010 5-year est.); Median contract rent: $267 per month (2006-2010 5-year est.); Median year structure built: 1969 (2006-2010 5-year est.).

Transportation: Commute to work: 100.0% car, 0.0% public transportation, 0.0% walk, 0.0% work from home (2006-2010 5-year est.); Travel time to work: 28.6% less than 15 minutes, 0.0% 15 to 30 minutes, 71.4% 30 to 45 minutes, 0.0% 45 to 60 minutes, 0.0% 60 minutes or more (2006-2010 5-year est.)

NINEVEH (unincorporated postal area)
Zip Code: 15353

Covers a land area of 0.059 square miles and a water area of 0 square miles. Located at 39.96° N. Lat; 80.31° W. Long. Elevation is 1,030 feet. Population: 64 (2010); Density: 1,081.1 persons per square mile (2010); Race: 79.7% White, 0.0% Black, 0.0% Asian, 0.0% American Indian/Alaska Native, 0.0% Native Hawaiian/Other Pacific Islander, 20.3% Other, 18.8% Hispanic of any race (2010); Average household size: 2.91 (2010); Median age: 34.0 (2010); Males per 100 females: 128.6 (2010); Homeownership rate: 72.8% (2010)

PERRY (township). Covers a land area of 30.229 square miles and a water area of 0.013 square miles. Located at 39.77° N. Lat; 80.12° W. Long.

Population: 1,719 (1990); 1,720 (2000); 1,521 (2010); Density: 50.3 persons per square mile (2010); Race: 98.9% White, 0.3% Black, 0.1% Asian, 0.2% American Indian/Alaska Native, 0.0% Native Hawaiian/Other Pacific Islander, 0.5% Other, 0.3% Hispanic of any race (2010); Average household size: 2.37 (2010); Median age: 43.8 (2010); Males per 100 females: 101.7 (2010); Marriage status: 20.8% never married, 64.2% now married, 6.0% widowed, 8.9% divorced (2006-2010 5-year est.); Foreign born: 0.9% (2006-2010 5-year est.); Ancestry (includes multiple ancestries): 29.2% German, 21.1% Irish, 14.6% English, 13.5% Italian, 7.1% American (2006-2010 5-year est.).
Economy: Single-family building permits issued: 0 (2011); Multi-family building permits issued: 0 (2011); Employment by occupation: 4.4% management, 2.8% professional, 12.7% services, 19.7% sales, 3.4% farming, 16.6% construction, 4.2% production (2006-2010 5-year est.).
Income: Per capita income: $23,096 (2006-2010 5-year est.); Median household income: $50,500 (2006-2010 5-year est.); Average household income: $57,732 (2006-2010 5-year est.); Percent of households with income of $100,000 or more: 10.7% (2006-2010 5-year est.); Poverty rate: 7.0% (2006-2010 5-year est.).
Education: Percent of population age 25 and over with: High school diploma (including GED) or higher: 82.7% (2006-2010 5-year est.); Bachelor's degree or higher: 17.0% (2006-2010 5-year est.); Master's degree or higher: 10.1% (2006-2010 5-year est.).
Housing: Homeownership rate: 80.4% (2010); Median home value: $89,000 (2006-2010 5-year est.); Median contract rent: $440 per month (2006-2010 5-year est.); Median year structure built: 1958 (2006-2010 5-year est.).
Transportation: Commute to work: 95.1% car, 0.0% public transportation, 0.9% walk, 4.1% work from home (2006-2010 5-year est.); Travel time to work: 11.0% less than 15 minutes, 44.8% 15 to 30 minutes, 30.6% 30 to 45 minutes, 9.0% 45 to 60 minutes, 4.6% 60 minutes or more (2006-2010 5-year est.)
Additional Information Contacts
Waynesburg Area Chamber of Commerce . . . . (724) 627-5926
http://www.waynesburgchamber.com

RICES LANDING (borough). Covers a land area of 0.794 square miles and a water area of 0.117 square miles. Located at 39.94° N. Lat; 80.00° W. Long. Elevation is 961 feet.
Population: 457 (1990); 443 (2000); 463 (2010); Density: 582.9 persons per square mile (2010); Race: 97.6% White, 1.3% Black, 0.0% Asian, 0.2% American Indian/Alaska Native, 0.0% Native Hawaiian/Other Pacific Islander, 0.9% Other, 0.9% Hispanic of any race (2010); Average household size: 2.54 (2010); Median age: 45.7 (2010); Males per 100 females: 95.4 (2010); Marriage status: 21.0% never married, 57.7% now married, 13.1% widowed, 8.2% divorced (2006-2010 5-year est.); Foreign born: 0.4% (2006-2010 5-year est.); Ancestry (includes multiple ancestries): 20.3% German, 19.1% Irish, 17.0% Polish, 13.4% English, 8.0% Italian (2006-2010 5-year est.).
Economy: Single-family building permits issued: 1 (2011); Multi-family building permits issued: 0 (2011); Employment by occupation: 5.1% management, 3.0% professional, 8.1% services, 11.7% sales, 4.6% farming, 18.8% construction, 5.6% production (2006-2010 5-year est.).
Income: Per capita income: $21,168 (2006-2010 5-year est.); Median household income: $40,893 (2006-2010 5-year est.); Average household income: $49,783 (2006-2010 5-year est.); Percent of households with income of $100,000 or more: 7.0% (2006-2010 5-year est.); Poverty rate: 7.0% (2006-2010 5-year est.).
Education: Percent of population age 25 and over with: High school diploma (including GED) or higher: 92.1% (2006-2010 5-year est.); Bachelor's degree or higher: 19.0% (2006-2010 5-year est.); Master's degree or higher: 9.6% (2006-2010 5-year est.).

Housing: Homeownership rate: 87.7% (2010); Median home value: $79,200 (2006-2010 5-year est.); Median contract rent: $263 per month (2006-2010 5-year est.); Median year structure built: before 1940 (2006-2010 5-year est.).
Transportation: Commute to work: 99.0% car, 0.0% public transportation, 0.0% walk, 1.0% work from home (2006-2010 5-year est.); Travel time to work: 11.6% less than 15 minutes, 36.8% 15 to 30 minutes, 25.8% 30 to 45 minutes, 17.4% 45 to 60 minutes, 8.4% 60 minutes or more (2006-2010 5-year est.)

RICHHILL (township). Covers a land area of 54.279 square miles and a water area of 0.081 square miles. Located at 39.91° N. Lat; 80.45° W. Long.
Population: 1,102 (1990); 1,062 (2000); 896 (2010); Density: 16.5 persons per square mile (2010); Race: 98.1% White, 0.0% Black, 0.0% Asian, 0.6% American Indian/Alaska Native, 0.0% Native Hawaiian/Other Pacific Islander, 1.3% Other, 0.0% Hispanic of any race (2010); Average household size: 2.52 (2010); Median age: 41.5 (2010); Males per 100 females: 111.3 (2010); Marriage status: 21.2% never married, 59.1% now married, 7.9% widowed, 11.8% divorced (2006-2010 5-year est.); Foreign born: 0.6% (2006-2010 5-year est.); Ancestry (includes multiple ancestries): 31.2% German, 18.1% Irish, 14.7% American, 12.6% English, 5.1% Scottish (2006-2010 5-year est.).
Economy: Single-family building permits issued: 0 (2011); Multi-family building permits issued: 0 (2011); Employment by occupation: 5.7% management, 6.2% professional, 9.5% services, 16.0% sales, 5.7% farming, 19.1% construction, 5.7% production (2006-2010 5-year est.).
Income: Per capita income: $23,832 (2006-2010 5-year est.); Median household income: $52,656 (2006-2010 5-year est.); Average household income: $61,543 (2006-2010 5-year est.); Percent of households with income of $100,000 or more: 12.1% (2006-2010 5-year est.); Poverty rate: 11.3% (2006-2010 5-year est.).
Education: Percent of population age 25 and over with: High school diploma (including GED) or higher: 83.7% (2006-2010 5-year est.); Bachelor's degree or higher: 16.2% (2006-2010 5-year est.); Master's degree or higher: 3.5% (2006-2010 5-year est.).
Housing: Homeownership rate: 72.0% (2010); Median home value: $107,800 (2006-2010 5-year est.); Median contract rent: $348 per month (2006-2010 5-year est.); Median year structure built: 1959 (2006-2010 5-year est.).
Transportation: Commute to work: 95.1% car, 0.0% public transportation, 3.6% walk, 1.3% work from home (2006-2010 5-year est.); Travel time to work: 24.8% less than 15 minutes, 23.0% 15 to 30 minutes, 17.0% 30 to 45 minutes, 18.3% 45 to 60 minutes, 17.0% 60 minutes or more (2006-2010 5-year est.)

ROGERSVILLE (CDP). Covers a land area of 0.408 square miles and a water area of 0 square miles. Located at 39.88° N. Lat; 80.27° W. Long. Elevation is 991 feet.
Population: n/a (1990); n/a (2000); 249 (2010); Density: 609.7 persons per square mile (2010); Race: 98.0% White, 0.0% Black, 0.0% Asian, 0.0% American Indian/Alaska Native, 0.0% Native Hawaiian/Other Pacific Islander, 2.0% Other, 1.6% Hispanic of any race (2010); Average household size: 2.37 (2010); Median age: 47.5 (2010); Males per 100 females: 88.6 (2010); Marriage status: 29.1% never married, 52.8% now married, 13.1% widowed, 5.0% divorced (2006-2010 5-year est.); Foreign born: 2.5% (2006-2010 5-year est.); Ancestry (includes multiple ancestries): 42.9% German, 18.3% Irish, 17.1% English, 12.1% Scotch-Irish, 7.9% Italian (2006-2010 5-year est.).
Economy: Employment by occupation: 19.2% management, 5.8% professional, 7.7% services, 26.0% sales, 0.0% farming, 7.7% construction, 1.9% production (2006-2010 5-year est.).
Income: Per capita income: $18,105 (2006-2010 5-year est.); Median household income: $48,750 (2006-2010 5-year est.); Average household income: $47,623 (2006-2010 5-year est.); Percent of households with income of $100,000 or more: n/a (2006-2010 5-year est.); Poverty rate: 11.7% (2006-2010 5-year est.).
Education: Percent of population age 25 and over with: High school diploma (including GED) or higher: 91.9% (2006-2010 5-year est.); Bachelor's degree or higher: 15.0% (2006-2010 5-year est.); Master's degree or higher: 3.8% (2006-2010 5-year est.).
Housing: Homeownership rate: 84.4% (2010); Median home value: $77,500 (2006-2010 5-year est.); Median contract rent: $125 per month (2006-2010 5-year est.); Median year structure built: before 1940 (2006-2010 5-year est.).

Transportation: Commute to work: 81.7% car, 6.7% public transportation, 11.5% walk, 0.0% work from home (2006-2010 5-year est.); Travel time to work: 34.6% less than 15 minutes, 30.8% 15 to 30 minutes, 4.8% 30 to 45 minutes, 15.4% 45 to 60 minutes, 14.4% 60 minutes or more (2006-2010 5-year est.)

SPRAGGS (unincorporated postal area)
Zip Code: 15362

Covers a land area of 25.885 square miles and a water area of 0.042 square miles. Located at 39.77° N. Lat; 80.21° W. Long. Elevation is 1,066 feet. Population: 767 (2010); Density: 29.6 persons per square mile (2010); Race: 98.3% White, 1.0% Black, 0.1% Asian, 0.1% American Indian/Alaska Native, 0.0% Native Hawaiian/Other Pacific Islander, 0.5% Other, 0.5% Hispanic of any race (2010); Average household size: 2.42 (2010); Median age: 42.1 (2010); Males per 100 females: 108.4 (2010); Homeownership rate: 78.5% (2010)

SPRINGHILL (township). Covers a land area of 21.954 square miles and a water area of 0.008 square miles. Located at 39.76° N. Lat; 80.47° W. Long.
Population: 506 (1990); 476 (2000); 349 (2010); Density: 15.9 persons per square mile (2010); Race: 99.7% White, 0.0% Black, 0.0% Asian, 0.0% American Indian/Alaska Native, 0.0% Native Hawaiian/Other Pacific Islander, 0.3% Other, 0.0% Hispanic of any race (2010); Average household size: 2.19 (2010); Median age: 46.5 (2010); Males per 100 females: 90.7 (2010); Marriage status: 30.7% never married, 46.5% now married, 12.9% widowed, 9.9% divorced (2006-2010 5-year est.); Foreign born: 0.0% (2006-2010 5-year est.); Ancestry (includes multiple ancestries): 27.9% German, 24.3% English, 14.7% American, 10.6% Irish, 4.1% Scottish (2006-2010 5-year est.).
Economy: Employment by occupation: 11.0% management, 2.0% professional, 4.0% services, 13.0% sales, 9.0% farming, 32.0% construction, 12.0% production (2006-2010 5-year est.).
Income: Per capita income: $14,900 (2006-2010 5-year est.); Median household income: $23,000 (2006-2010 5-year est.); Average household income: $35,557 (2006-2010 5-year est.); Percent of households with income of $100,000 or more: 7.3% (2006-2010 5-year est.); Poverty rate: 33.6% (2006-2010 5-year est.).
Education: Percent of population age 25 and over with: High school diploma (including GED) or higher: 64.8% (2006-2010 5-year est.); Bachelor's degree or higher: 6.9% (2006-2010 5-year est.); Master's degree or higher: 3.8% (2006-2010 5-year est.).
Housing: Homeownership rate: 83.6% (2010); Median home value: $61,500 (2006-2010 5-year est.); Median contract rent: $204 per month (2006-2010 5-year est.); Median year structure built: 1973 (2006-2010 5-year est.).
Transportation: Commute to work: 88.8% car, 0.0% public transportation, 1.0% walk, 8.2% work from home (2006-2010 5-year est.); Travel time to work: 18.9% less than 15 minutes, 15.6% 15 to 30 minutes, 30.0% 30 to 45 minutes, 20.0% 45 to 60 minutes, 15.6% 60 minutes or more (2006-2010 5-year est.)

SYCAMORE (unincorporated postal area)
Zip Code: 15364

Covers a land area of 37.209 square miles and a water area of 0.011 square miles. Located at 39.94° N. Lat; 80.30° W. Long. Population: 869 (2010); Density: 23.4 persons per square mile (2010); Race: 99.2% White, 0.1% Black, 0.0% Asian, 0.1% American Indian/Alaska Native, 0.0% Native Hawaiian/Other Pacific Islander, 0.6% Other, 0.1% Hispanic of any race (2010); Average household size: 2.59 (2010); Median age: 42.8 (2010); Males per 100 females: 101.6 (2010); Homeownership rate: 82.4% (2010)

WASHINGTON (township). Covers a land area of 27.146 square miles and a water area of 0.018 square miles. Located at 39.97° N. Lat; 80.21° W. Long.
Population: 1,071 (1990); 1,106 (2000); 1,098 (2010); Density: 40.4 persons per square mile (2010); Race: 98.4% White, 0.4% Black, 0.2% Asian, 0.0% American Indian/Alaska Native, 0.0% Native Hawaiian/Other Pacific Islander, 1.0% Other, 0.4% Hispanic of any race (2010); Average household size: 2.61 (2010); Median age: 43.9 (2010); Males per 100 females: 92.6 (2010); Marriage status: 19.2% never married, 69.3% now married, 3.9% widowed, 7.6% divorced (2006-2010 5-year est.); Foreign born: 0.7% (2006-2010 5-year est.); Ancestry (includes multiple ancestries): 30.9% German, 29.2% Irish, 18.9% English, 9.4% American, 6.0% Scotch-Irish (2006-2010 5-year est.).
Economy: Single-family building permits issued: 0 (2011); Multi-family building permits issued: 0 (2011); Employment by occupation: 10.0% management, 1.1% professional, 11.7% services, 14.4% sales, 5.3% farming, 12.5% construction, 4.7% production (2006-2010 5-year est.).
Income: Per capita income: $19,838 (2006-2010 5-year est.); Median household income: $55,641 (2006-2010 5-year est.); Average household income: $57,489 (2006-2010 5-year est.); Percent of households with income of $100,000 or more: 12.5% (2006-2010 5-year est.); Poverty rate: 10.6% (2006-2010 5-year est.).
Education: Percent of population age 25 and over with: High school diploma (including GED) or higher: 91.3% (2006-2010 5-year est.); Bachelor's degree or higher: 20.5% (2006-2010 5-year est.); Master's degree or higher: 7.7% (2006-2010 5-year est.).
Housing: Homeownership rate: 82.6% (2010); Median home value: $152,000 (2006-2010 5-year est.); Median contract rent: $275 per month (2006-2010 5-year est.); Median year structure built: 1975 (2006-2010 5-year est.).
Transportation: Commute to work: 91.4% car, 0.0% public transportation, 0.6% walk, 7.4% work from home (2006-2010 5-year est.); Travel time to work: 18.9% less than 15 minutes, 44.3% 15 to 30 minutes, 26.3% 30 to 45 minutes, 5.7% 45 to 60 minutes, 4.8% 60 minutes or more (2006-2010 5-year est.)

WAYNE (township). Covers a land area of 39.245 square miles and a water area of 0.041 square miles. Located at 39.77° N. Lat; 80.24° W. Long.
Population: 1,311 (1990); 1,223 (2000); 1,197 (2010); Density: 30.5 persons per square mile (2010); Race: 98.5% White, 0.7% Black, 0.0% Asian, 0.3% American Indian/Alaska Native, 0.0% Native Hawaiian/Other Pacific Islander, 0.5% Other, 0.2% Hispanic of any race (2010); Average household size: 2.55 (2010); Median age: 40.6 (2010); Males per 100 females: 104.3 (2010); Marriage status: 25.7% never married, 54.6% now married, 8.5% widowed, 11.2% divorced (2006-2010 5-year est.); Foreign born: 0.4% (2006-2010 5-year est.); Ancestry (includes multiple ancestries): 25.3% German, 24.6% Irish, 9.6% English, 8.4% Dutch, 7.1% American (2006-2010 5-year est.).
Economy: Single-family building permits issued: 0 (2011); Multi-family building permits issued: 0 (2011); Employment by occupation: 8.9% management, 1.3% professional, 7.3% services, 22.9% sales, 5.6% farming, 19.4% construction, 3.7% production (2006-2010 5-year est.).
Income: Per capita income: $20,785 (2006-2010 5-year est.); Median household income: $37,500 (2006-2010 5-year est.); Average household income: $49,762 (2006-2010 5-year est.); Percent of households with income of $100,000 or more: 15.1% (2006-2010 5-year est.); Poverty rate: 13.1% (2006-2010 5-year est.).
Education: Percent of population age 25 and over with: High school diploma (including GED) or higher: 78.0% (2006-2010 5-year est.); Bachelor's degree or higher: 12.6% (2006-2010 5-year est.); Master's degree or higher: 5.3% (2006-2010 5-year est.).
Housing: Homeownership rate: 81.0% (2010); Median home value: $78,000 (2006-2010 5-year est.); Median contract rent: $331 per month (2006-2010 5-year est.); Median year structure built: 1970 (2006-2010 5-year est.).
Transportation: Commute to work: 94.7% car, 1.0% public transportation, 0.8% walk, 3.6% work from home (2006-2010 5-year est.); Travel time to work: 12.8% less than 15 minutes, 31.8% 15 to 30 minutes, 24.1% 30 to 45 minutes, 14.0% 45 to 60 minutes, 17.4% 60 minutes or more (2006-2010 5-year est.)
Additional Information Contacts
Waynesburg Area Chamber of Commerce . . . . (724) 627-5926
    http://www.waynesburgchamber.com

WAYNESBURG (borough). County seat. Covers a land area of 0.800 square miles and a water area of 0 square miles. Located at 39.90° N. Lat; 80.19° W. Long. Elevation is 971 feet.
History: Waynesburg was laid out in 1796 and named for General Anthony Wayne.
Population: 4,270 (1990); 4,184 (2000); 4,176 (2010); Density: 5,219.7 persons per square mile (2010); Race: 95.9% White, 1.8% Black, 0.5% Asian, 0.2% American Indian/Alaska Native, 0.1% Native Hawaiian/Other Pacific Islander, 1.5% Other, 0.7% Hispanic of any race (2010); Average household size: 2.21 (2010); Median age: 27.7 (2010); Males per 100 females: 94.1 (2010); Marriage status: 42.5% never married, 37.4% now

married, 6.0% widowed, 14.1% divorced (2006-2010 5-year est.); Foreign born: 0.7% (2006-2010 5-year est.); Ancestry (includes multiple ancestries): 26.7% German, 11.4% English, 11.3% Italian, 10.4% Irish, 5.9% American (2006-2010 5-year est.).

Economy: Single-family building permits issued: 0 (2011); Multi-family building permits issued: 0 (2011); Employment by occupation: 2.9% management, 4.4% professional, 14.6% services, 16.9% sales, 4.5% farming, 18.7% construction, 6.6% production (2006-2010 5-year est.).

Income: Per capita income: $17,189 (2006-2010 5-year est.); Median household income: $38,287 (2006-2010 5-year est.); Average household income: $46,246 (2006-2010 5-year est.); Percent of households with income of $100,000 or more: 6.3% (2006-2010 5-year est.); Poverty rate: 26.1% (2006-2010 5-year est.).

Education: Percent of population age 25 and over with: High school diploma (including GED) or higher: 87.6% (2006-2010 5-year est.); Bachelor's degree or higher: 19.1% (2006-2010 5-year est.); Master's degree or higher: 4.2% (2006-2010 5-year est.).

School District(s)

Central Greene SD (KG-12)
  2010-11 Enrollment: 1,991 . . . . (724) 627-8151
Greene County CTC (10-12)
  2010-11 Enrollment: n/a . . . . (724) 627-3106
West Greene SD (KG-12)
  2010-11 Enrollment: 800 . . . . (724) 499-5183

Four-year College(s)

Waynesburg University (Private, Not-for-profit, Presbyterian Church (USA))
  Fall 2010 Enrollment: 2,344 . . . . (724) 627-8191
  2011-12 Tuition: In-state $19,090; Out-of-state $19,090

Vocational/Technical School(s)

Greene County Career and Technology Center (Public)
  Fall 2010 Enrollment: 64 . . . . (724) 627-3106
  2011-12 Tuition: $11,033

Housing: Homeownership rate: 43.9% (2010); Median home value: $80,300 (2006-2010 5-year est.); Median contract rent: $335 per month (2006-2010 5-year est.); Median year structure built: 1943 (2006-2010 5-year est.).

Hospitals: Greene County Memorial Hospital (54 beds)

Safety: Violent crime rate: 28.6 per 10,000 population; Property crime rate: 188.6 per 10,000 population (2011).

Newspapers: Greene County Messenger (Community news; Circulation 7,000)

Transportation: Commute to work: 86.3% car, 0.7% public transportation, 10.6% walk, 2.4% work from home (2006-2010 5-year est.); Travel time to work: 47.3% less than 15 minutes, 18.0% 15 to 30 minutes, 15.9% 30 to 45 minutes, 10.3% 45 to 60 minutes, 8.5% 60 minutes or more (2006-2010 5-year est.)

Additional Information Contacts

Waynesburg Area Chamber of Commerce . . . . (724) 627-5926
  http://www.waynesburgchamber.com

WEST WAYNESBURG (CDP).

Covers a land area of 0.216 square miles and a water area of 0 square miles. Located at 39.90° N. Lat; 80.20° W. Long. Elevation is 994 feet.

Population: n/a (1990); n/a (2000); 446 (2010); Density: 2,066.5 persons per square mile (2010); Race: 98.2% White, 0.2% Black, 0.0% Asian, 0.2% American Indian/Alaska Native, 0.0% Native Hawaiian/Other Pacific Islander, 1.4% Other, 0.2% Hispanic of any race (2010); Average household size: 2.13 (2010); Median age: 40.9 (2010); Males per 100 females: 69.6 (2010); Marriage status: 37.2% never married, 50.0% now married, 12.8% widowed, 0.0% divorced (2006-2010 5-year est.); Foreign born: 0.0% (2006-2010 5-year est.); Ancestry (includes multiple ancestries): 19.9% German, 19.2% American, 18.4% Irish, 12.3% English, 6.1% Dutch (2006-2010 5-year est.).

Economy: Employment by occupation: 13.0% management, 0.0% professional, 8.3% services, 18.9% sales, 0.0% farming, 21.3% construction, 6.5% production (2006-2010 5-year est.).

Income: Per capita income: $17,412 (2006-2010 5-year est.); Median household income: $28,203 (2006-2010 5-year est.); Average household income: $40,689 (2006-2010 5-year est.); Percent of households with income of $100,000 or more: n/a (2006-2010 5-year est.); Poverty rate: 22.3% (2006-2010 5-year est.).

Education: Percent of population age 25 and over with: High school diploma (including GED) or higher: 72.0% (2006-2010 5-year est.); Bachelor's degree or higher: 4.5% (2006-2010 5-year est.); Master's degree or higher: 0.0% (2006-2010 5-year est.).

Housing: Homeownership rate: 35.9% (2010); Median home value: $52,200 (2006-2010 5-year est.); Median contract rent: $394 per month (2006-2010 5-year est.); Median year structure built: 1951 (2006-2010 5-year est.).

Transportation: Commute to work: 94.7% car, 0.0% public transportation, 0.0% walk, 5.3% work from home (2006-2010 5-year est.); Travel time to work: 59.4% less than 15 minutes, 31.9% 15 to 30 minutes, 0.0% 30 to 45 minutes, 8.8% 45 to 60 minutes, 0.0% 60 minutes or more (2006-2010 5-year est.)

WHITELEY (township).

Covers a land area of 31.660 square miles and a water area of 0.004 square miles. Located at 39.82° N. Lat; 80.14° W. Long.

Population: 778 (1990); 754 (2000); 649 (2010); Density: 20.5 persons per square mile (2010); Race: 99.1% White, 0.2% Black, 0.0% Asian, 0.0% American Indian/Alaska Native, 0.0% Native Hawaiian/Other Pacific Islander, 0.7% Other, 0.8% Hispanic of any race (2010); Average household size: 2.57 (2010); Median age: 44.2 (2010); Males per 100 females: 102.8 (2010); Marriage status: 28.8% never married, 52.1% now married, 8.2% widowed, 10.9% divorced (2006-2010 5-year est.); Foreign born: 1.6% (2006-2010 5-year est.); Ancestry (includes multiple ancestries): 28.9% German, 23.1% Irish, 11.1% American, 8.1% English, 7.0% Dutch (2006-2010 5-year est.).

Economy: Single-family building permits issued: 2 (2011); Multi-family building permits issued: 0 (2011); Employment by occupation: 4.1% management, 3.5% professional, 15.5% services, 19.6% sales, 7.3% farming, 30.5% construction, 5.0% production (2006-2010 5-year est.).

Income: Per capita income: $28,111 (2006-2010 5-year est.); Median household income: $45,750 (2006-2010 5-year est.); Average household income: $76,489 (2006-2010 5-year est.); Percent of households with income of $100,000 or more: 14.2% (2006-2010 5-year est.); Poverty rate: 10.8% (2006-2010 5-year est.).

Education: Percent of population age 25 and over with: High school diploma (including GED) or higher: 78.7% (2006-2010 5-year est.); Bachelor's degree or higher: 11.0% (2006-2010 5-year est.); Master's degree or higher: 1.1% (2006-2010 5-year est.).

Housing: Homeownership rate: 80.7% (2010); Median home value: $129,000 (2006-2010 5-year est.); Median contract rent: $314 per month (2006-2010 5-year est.); Median year structure built: 1978 (2006-2010 5-year est.).

Transportation: Commute to work: 94.9% car, 0.0% public transportation, 0.0% walk, 5.1% work from home (2006-2010 5-year est.); Travel time to work: 23.2% less than 15 minutes, 42.5% 15 to 30 minutes, 20.3% 30 to 45 minutes, 6.0% 45 to 60 minutes, 7.9% 60 minutes or more (2006-2010 5-year est.)

WIND RIDGE (CDP).

Covers a land area of 3.146 square miles and a water area of 0 square miles. Located at 39.91° N. Lat; 80.43° W. Long. Elevation is 1,434 feet.

Population: n/a (1990); n/a (2000); 215 (2010); Density: 68.3 persons per square mile (2010); Race: 99.5% White, 0.0% Black, 0.0% Asian, 0.0% American Indian/Alaska Native, 0.0% Native Hawaiian/Other Pacific Islander, 0.5% Other, 0.0% Hispanic of any race (2010); Average household size: 2.19 (2010); Median age: 41.6 (2010); Males per 100 females: 92.0 (2010); Marriage status: 22.6% never married, 57.5% now married, 2.8% widowed, 17.1% divorced (2006-2010 5-year est.); Foreign born: 1.7% (2006-2010 5-year est.); Ancestry (includes multiple ancestries): 47.9% German, 19.5% Irish, 9.2% English, 8.6% Scottish, 6.3% Scotch-Irish (2006-2010 5-year est.).

Economy: Employment by occupation: 7.6% management, 10.6% professional, 4.5% services, 23.5% sales, 6.1% farming, 14.4% construction, 6.8% production (2006-2010 5-year est.).

Income: Per capita income: $27,521 (2006-2010 5-year est.); Median household income: $48,750 (2006-2010 5-year est.); Average household income: $73,978 (2006-2010 5-year est.); Percent of households with income of $100,000 or more: 15.3% (2006-2010 5-year est.); Poverty rate: 13.5% (2006-2010 5-year est.).

Education: Percent of population age 25 and over with: High school diploma (including GED) or higher: 90.9% (2006-2010 5-year est.); Bachelor's degree or higher: 17.4% (2006-2010 5-year est.); Master's degree or higher: 2.6% (2006-2010 5-year est.).

Housing: Homeownership rate: 71.5% (2010); Median home value: $68,300 (2006-2010 5-year est.); Median contract rent: $350 per month (2006-2010 5-year est.); Median year structure built: 1948 (2006-2010 5-year est.).

Transportation: Commute to work: 92.4% car, 0.0% public transportation, 7.6% walk, 0.0% work from home (2006-2010 5-year est.); Travel time to work: 27.3% less than 15 minutes, 19.7% 15 to 30 minutes, 20.5% 30 to 45 minutes, 25.8% 45 to 60 minutes, 6.8% 60 minutes or more (2006-2010 5-year est.)

Huntingdon County

Located in south central Pennsylvania; hilly area, drained by the Juniata River; includes the Tussey Mountains on the west and north, and the Tuscarora Mountains on the southeast. Covers a land area of 874.639 square miles, a water area of 14.627 square miles, and is located in the Eastern Time Zone at 40.42° N. Lat., 77.97° W. Long. The county was founded in 1787. County seat is Huntingdon.

Huntingdon County is part of the Huntingdon, PA Micropolitan Statistical Area. The entire metro area includes: Huntingdon County, PA

Weather Station: Raystown Lake 2   Elevation: 839 feet

	Jan	Feb	Mar	Apr	May	Jun	Jul	Aug	Sep	Oct	Nov	Dec
High	36	39	48	61	71	79	84	83	75	63	52	41
Low	20	21	27	38	47	56	61	60	53	41	33	25
Precip	2.5	2.1	3.1	3.5	4.0	3.7	3.4	3.3	3.3	3.1	3.4	2.7
Snow	6.4	6.7	3.5	0.6	0.0	0.0	0.0	0.0	0.0	tr	0.9	3.7

High and Low temperatures in degrees Fahrenheit; Precipitation and Snow in inches

Population: 44,165 (1990); 45,586 (2000); 45,913 (2010); Race: 92.5% White, 5.2% Black, 0.4% Asian, 0.1% American Indian/Alaska Native, 0.0% Native Hawaiian/Other Pacific Islander, 1.8% Other, 1.6% Hispanic of any race (2010); Density: 52.5 persons per square mile (2010); Average household size: 2.39 (2010); Median age: 41.2 (2010); Males per 100 females: 112.2 (2010).

Religion: Six largest groups: 9.7% Methodist/Pietist, 5.6% Catholicism, 4.8% Non-Denominational, 4.2% Presbyterian-Reformed, 3.4% European Free-Church, 3.3% Holiness (2010)

Economy: Unemployment rate: 9.0% (August 2012); Total civilian labor force: 22,775 (August 2012); Leading industries: 21.0% manufacturing; 18.9% health care and social assistance; 15.5% retail trade (2010); Farms: 930 totaling 148,289 acres (2007); Companies that employ 500 or more persons: 0 (2010); Companies that employ 100 to 499 persons: 14 (2010); Companies that employ less than 100 persons: 828 (2010); Black-owned businesses: n/a (2007); Hispanic-owned businesses: n/a (2007); Asian-owned businesses: n/a (2007); Women-owned businesses: 884 (2007); Retail sales per capita: $7,786 (2010). Single-family building permits issued: 65 (2011); Multi-family building permits issued: 10 (2011).

Income: Per capita income: $20,616 (2006-2010 5-year est.); Median household income: $41,700 (2006-2010 5-year est.); Average household income: $51,846 (2006-2010 5-year est.); Percent of households with income of $100,000 or more: 9.4% (2006-2010 5-year est.); Poverty rate: 11.4% (2006-2010 5-year est.); Bankruptcy rate: 2.04% (2011).

Taxes: Total county taxes per capita: $149 (2009); County property taxes per capita: $145 (2009).

Education: Percent of population age 25 and over with: High school diploma (including GED) or higher: 85.5% (2006-2010 5-year est.); Bachelor's degree or higher: 13.8% (2006-2010 5-year est.); Master's degree or higher: 4.9% (2006-2010 5-year est.).

Housing: Homeownership rate: 76.0% (2010); Median home value: $105,800 (2006-2010 5-year est.); Median contract rent: $384 per month (2006-2010 5-year est.); Median year structure built: 1965 (2006-2010 5-year est.)

Health: Birth rate: 96.6 per 10,000 population (2011); Death rate: 100.5 per 10,000 population (2011); Age-adjusted cancer mortality rate: 170.4 deaths per 100,000 population (2009); Number of physicians: 9.1 per 10,000 population (2010); Hospital beds: 16.0 per 10,000 population (2008); Hospital admissions: 658.9 per 10,000 population (2008).

Elections: 2012 Presidential election results: 30.6% Obama, 68.0% Romney

National and State Parks: Greenwood Furnace State Park; Rothrock State Forest; Trough Creek State Park; Whipple Dam State Park

Additional Information Contacts

Huntingdon County Government. . . . . (814) 643-3091
    http://huntingdoncounty.net

Huntingdon County Communities

ALEXANDRIA (borough). Covers a land area of 0.106 square miles and a water area of 0 square miles. Located at 40.56° N. Lat; 78.10° W. Long. Elevation is 696 feet.

Population: 411 (1990); 401 (2000); 346 (2010); Density: 3,276.2 persons per square mile (2010); Race: 98.6% White, 0.3% Black, 0.3% Asian, 0.0% American Indian/Alaska Native, 0.0% Native Hawaiian/Other Pacific Islander, 0.8% Other, 1.4% Hispanic of any race (2010); Average household size: 2.49 (2010); Median age: 38.5 (2010); Males per 100 females: 97.7 (2010); Marriage status: 26.1% never married, 56.6% now married, 7.6% widowed, 9.7% divorced (2006-2010 5-year est.); Foreign born: 0.0% (2006-2010 5-year est.); Ancestry (includes multiple ancestries): 50.6% German, 11.6% Irish, 7.6% Scotch-Irish, 6.5% Swedish, 4.5% Italian (2006-2010 5-year est.).

Economy: Single-family building permits issued: 0 (2011); Multi-family building permits issued: 0 (2011); Employment by occupation: 11.5% management, 3.3% professional, 10.4% services, 19.2% sales, 4.9% farming, 3.8% construction, 8.2% production (2006-2010 5-year est.).

Income: Per capita income: $21,111 (2006-2010 5-year est.); Median household income: $40,556 (2006-2010 5-year est.); Average household income: $51,069 (2006-2010 5-year est.); Percent of households with income of $100,000 or more: 6.9% (2006-2010 5-year est.); Poverty rate: 3.0% (2006-2010 5-year est.).

Education: Percent of population age 25 and over with: High school diploma (including GED) or higher: 94.8% (2006-2010 5-year est.); Bachelor's degree or higher: 18.1% (2006-2010 5-year est.); Master's degree or higher: 6.5% (2006-2010 5-year est.).

School District(s)

Juniata Valley SD (KG-12)
    2010-11 Enrollment: 806. . . . . (814) 669-9150

Housing: Homeownership rate: 71.9% (2010); Median home value: $86,900 (2006-2010 5-year est.); Median contract rent: $450 per month (2006-2010 5-year est.); Median year structure built: before 1940 (2006-2010 5-year est.).

Transportation: Commute to work: 86.3% car, 0.0% public transportation, 2.2% walk, 8.8% work from home (2006-2010 5-year est.); Travel time to work: 33.1% less than 15 minutes, 24.7% 15 to 30 minutes, 24.7% 30 to 45 minutes, 9.6% 45 to 60 minutes, 7.8% 60 minutes or more (2006-2010 5-year est.)

ALLENPORT (CDP). Covers a land area of 0.970 square miles and a water area of 0.070 square miles. Located at 40.37° N. Lat; 77.87° W. Long. Elevation is 581 feet.

Population: n/a (1990); n/a (2000); 648 (2010); Density: 668.1 persons per square mile (2010); Race: 98.3% White, 0.9% Black, 0.0% Asian, 0.0% American Indian/Alaska Native, 0.0% Native Hawaiian/Other Pacific Islander, 0.8% Other, 1.4% Hispanic of any race (2010); Average household size: 2.49 (2010); Median age: 39.2 (2010); Males per 100 females: 94.0 (2010); Marriage status: 30.6% never married, 42.2% now married, 12.1% widowed, 15.2% divorced (2006-2010 5-year est.); Foreign born: 0.0% (2006-2010 5-year est.); Ancestry (includes multiple ancestries): 38.5% German, 19.0% American, 17.2% Scotch-Irish, 16.8% Irish, 13.7% Dutch (2006-2010 5-year est.).

Economy: Employment by occupation: 0.0% management, 0.0% professional, 4.6% services, 50.3% sales, 0.0% farming, 0.0% construction, 0.0% production (2006-2010 5-year est.).

Income: Per capita income: $13,458 (2006-2010 5-year est.); Median household income: $22,383 (2006-2010 5-year est.); Average household income: $29,526 (2006-2010 5-year est.); Percent of households with income of $100,000 or more: n/a (2006-2010 5-year est.); Poverty rate: 11.6% (2006-2010 5-year est.).

Education: Percent of population age 25 and over with: High school diploma (including GED) or higher: 82.4% (2006-2010 5-year est.); Bachelor's degree or higher: 9.3% (2006-2010 5-year est.); Master's degree or higher: 0.0% (2006-2010 5-year est.).

Housing: Homeownership rate: 80.4% (2010); Median home value: $72,600 (2006-2010 5-year est.); Median contract rent: $171 per month (2006-2010 5-year est.); Median year structure built: 1965 (2006-2010 5-year est.).

Transportation: Commute to work: 96.0% car, 0.0% public transportation, 0.0% walk, 4.0% work from home (2006-2010 5-year est.); Travel time to work: 45.2% less than 15 minutes, 32.5% 15 to 30 minutes, 17.5% 30 to

45 minutes, 4.8% 45 to 60 minutes, 0.0% 60 minutes or more (2006-2010 5-year est.).

BARREE (township). Covers a land area of 23.994 square miles and a water area of 0.115 square miles. Located at 40.64° N. Lat; 77.92° W. Long. Elevation is 705 feet.

Population: 450 (1990); 460 (2000); 469 (2010); Density: 19.5 persons per square mile (2010); Race: 100.0% White, 0.0% Black, 0.0% Asian, 0.0% American Indian/Alaska Native, 0.0% Native Hawaiian/Other Pacific Islander, 0.0% Other, 0.2% Hispanic of any race (2010); Average household size: 2.44 (2010); Median age: 43.9 (2010); Males per 100 females: 104.8 (2010); Marriage status: 19.6% never married, 65.6% now married, 4.1% widowed, 10.7% divorced (2006-2010 5-year est.); Foreign born: 0.0% (2006-2010 5-year est.); Ancestry (includes multiple ancestries): 37.5% German, 16.8% Irish, 16.8% Pennsylvania German, 5.0% English, 4.3% American (2006-2010 5-year est.).
Economy: Single-family building permits issued: 1 (2011); Multi-family building permits issued: 0 (2011); Employment by occupation: 11.6% management, 0.7% professional, 11.2% services, 11.2% sales, 4.5% farming, 21.3% construction, 7.5% production (2006-2010 5-year est.).
Income: Per capita income: $24,111 (2006-2010 5-year est.); Median household income: $54,844 (2006-2010 5-year est.); Average household income: $71,558 (2006-2010 5-year est.); Percent of households with income of $100,000 or more: 20.8% (2006-2010 5-year est.); Poverty rate: 3.7% (2006-2010 5-year est.).
Education: Percent of population age 25 and over with: High school diploma (including GED) or higher: 92.1% (2006-2010 5-year est.); Bachelor's degree or higher: 19.3% (2006-2010 5-year est.); Master's degree or higher: 7.6% (2006-2010 5-year est.).
Housing: Homeownership rate: 80.7% (2010); Median home value: $150,000 (2006-2010 5-year est.); Median contract rent: $433 per month (2006-2010 5-year est.); Median year structure built: 1975 (2006-2010 5-year est.).
Transportation: Commute to work: 92.5% car, 0.0% public transportation, 0.0% walk, 6.4% work from home (2006-2010 5-year est.); Travel time to work: 6.5% less than 15 minutes, 30.2% 15 to 30 minutes, 47.6% 30 to 45 minutes, 4.4% 45 to 60 minutes, 11.3% 60 minutes or more (2006-2010 5-year est.).

BIRMINGHAM (borough). Covers a land area of 0.063 square miles and a water area of 0 square miles. Located at 40.65° N. Lat; 78.20° W. Long. Elevation is 974 feet.

Population: 122 (1990); 91 (2000); 90 (2010); Density: 1,432.9 persons per square mile (2010); Race: 97.8% White, 0.0% Black, 1.1% Asian, 0.0% American Indian/Alaska Native, 0.0% Native Hawaiian/Other Pacific Islander, 1.1% Other, 6.7% Hispanic of any race (2010); Average household size: 2.14 (2010); Median age: 45.3 (2010); Males per 100 females: 95.7 (2010); Marriage status: 17.7% never married, 67.1% now married, 5.1% widowed, 10.1% divorced (2006-2010 5-year est.); Foreign born: 0.0% (2006-2010 5-year est.); Ancestry (includes multiple ancestries): 43.1% Irish, 21.6% Scotch-Irish, 15.7% English, 10.8% German, 9.8% Italian (2006-2010 5-year est.).
Economy: Employment by occupation: 7.3% management, 0.0% professional, 19.5% services, 22.0% sales, 4.9% farming, 0.0% construction, 0.0% production (2006-2010 5-year est.).
Income: Per capita income: $22,532 (2006-2010 5-year est.); Median household income: $58,750 (2006-2010 5-year est.); Average household income: $63,309 (2006-2010 5-year est.); Percent of households with income of $100,000 or more: 17.6% (2006-2010 5-year est.); Poverty rate: 20.6% (2006-2010 5-year est.).
Education: Percent of population age 25 and over with: High school diploma (including GED) or higher: 91.3% (2006-2010 5-year est.); Bachelor's degree or higher: 26.1% (2006-2010 5-year est.); Master's degree or higher: 5.8% (2006-2010 5-year est.).
Housing: Homeownership rate: 57.1% (2010); Median home value: $87,500 (2006-2010 5-year est.); Median contract rent: n/a per month (2006-2010 5-year est.); Median year structure built: before 1940 (2006-2010 5-year est.).
Transportation: Commute to work: 87.8% car, 0.0% public transportation, 12.2% walk, 0.0% work from home (2006-2010 5-year est.); Travel time to work: 34.1% less than 15 minutes, 26.8% 15 to 30 minutes, 22.0% 30 to 45 minutes, 4.9% 45 to 60 minutes, 12.2% 60 minutes or more (2006-2010 5-year est.).

BLAIRS MILLS (unincorporated postal area)
Zip Code: 17213
Covers a land area of 39.819 square miles and a water area of 0.003 square miles. Located at 40.24° N. Lat; 77.77° W. Long. Population: 639 (2010); Density: 16.0 persons per square mile (2010); Race: 98.6% White, 0.6% Black, 0.2% Asian, 0.2% American Indian/Alaska Native, 0.0% Native Hawaiian/Other Pacific Islander, 0.4% Other, 0.6% Hispanic of any race (2010); Average household size: 2.59 (2010); Median age: 42.5 (2010); Males per 100 females: 108.8 (2010); Homeownership rate: 85.2% (2010)

BRADY (township). Covers a land area of 31.204 square miles and a water area of 0.164 square miles. Located at 40.47° N. Lat; 77.89° W. Long.

Population: 1,054 (1990); 1,035 (2000); 1,172 (2010); Density: 37.6 persons per square mile (2010); Race: 98.7% White, 0.0% Black, 0.3% Asian, 0.0% American Indian/Alaska Native, 0.0% Native Hawaiian/Other Pacific Islander, 1.0% Other, 0.3% Hispanic of any race (2010); Average household size: 2.89 (2010); Median age: 36.8 (2010); Males per 100 females: 111.2 (2010); Marriage status: 18.9% never married, 68.3% now married, 4.8% widowed, 8.0% divorced (2006-2010 5-year est.); Foreign born: 0.2% (2006-2010 5-year est.); Ancestry (includes multiple ancestries): 34.8% German, 16.3% Irish, 10.1% American, 8.7% Pennsylvania German, 8.3% Scotch-Irish (2006-2010 5-year est.).
Economy: Single-family building permits issued: 0 (2011); Multi-family building permits issued: 0 (2011); Employment by occupation: 6.0% management, 1.8% professional, 14.2% services, 15.0% sales, 2.3% farming, 17.3% construction, 6.8% production (2006-2010 5-year est.).
Income: Per capita income: $18,537 (2006-2010 5-year est.); Median household income: $39,083 (2006-2010 5-year est.); Average household income: $49,968 (2006-2010 5-year est.); Percent of households with income of $100,000 or more: 8.0% (2006-2010 5-year est.); Poverty rate: 12.5% (2006-2010 5-year est.).
Education: Percent of population age 25 and over with: High school diploma (including GED) or higher: 82.5% (2006-2010 5-year est.); Bachelor's degree or higher: 9.4% (2006-2010 5-year est.); Master's degree or higher: 1.4% (2006-2010 5-year est.).
Housing: Homeownership rate: 86.2% (2010); Median home value: $96,800 (2006-2010 5-year est.); Median contract rent: $343 per month (2006-2010 5-year est.); Median year structure built: 1967 (2006-2010 5-year est.).
Transportation: Commute to work: 88.5% car, 0.0% public transportation, 5.5% walk, 2.9% work from home (2006-2010 5-year est.); Travel time to work: 30.6% less than 15 minutes, 49.6% 15 to 30 minutes, 7.1% 30 to 45 minutes, 6.3% 45 to 60 minutes, 6.5% 60 minutes or more (2006-2010 5-year est.).

BROAD TOP CITY (borough). Aka Broad Top. Covers a land area of 0.677 square miles and a water area of 0 square miles. Located at 40.20° N. Lat; 78.14° W. Long. Elevation is 1,972 feet.

Population: 331 (1990); 384 (2000); 452 (2010); Density: 667.9 persons per square mile (2010); Race: 98.5% White, 0.0% Black, 0.0% Asian, 0.0% American Indian/Alaska Native, 0.0% Native Hawaiian/Other Pacific Islander, 1.5% Other, 0.4% Hispanic of any race (2010); Average household size: 2.61 (2010); Median age: 41.6 (2010); Males per 100 females: 105.5 (2010); Marriage status: 25.8% never married, 54.1% now married, 7.5% widowed, 12.5% divorced (2006-2010 5-year est.); Foreign born: 0.0% (2006-2010 5-year est.); Ancestry (includes multiple ancestries): 31.7% German, 25.5% Irish, 7.7% Italian, 7.1% Welsh, 7.1% English (2006-2010 5-year est.).
Economy: Single-family building permits issued: 1 (2011); Multi-family building permits issued: 0 (2011); Employment by occupation: 0.0% management, 0.0% professional, 25.6% services, 14.4% sales, 0.0% farming, 11.2% construction, 19.2% production (2006-2010 5-year est.).
Income: Per capita income: $19,232 (2006-2010 5-year est.); Median household income: $40,250 (2006-2010 5-year est.); Average household income: $45,748 (2006-2010 5-year est.); Percent of households with income of $100,000 or more: 5.4% (2006-2010 5-year est.); Poverty rate: 19.7% (2006-2010 5-year est.).
Education: Percent of population age 25 and over with: High school diploma (including GED) or higher: 78.3% (2006-2010 5-year est.); Bachelor's degree or higher: 4.7% (2006-2010 5-year est.); Master's degree or higher: 3.4% (2006-2010 5-year est.).
Housing: Homeownership rate: 82.1% (2010); Median home value: $87,500 (2006-2010 5-year est.); Median contract rent: $385 per month

(2006-2010 5-year est.); Median year structure built: 1971 (2006-2010 5-year est.).

Transportation: Commute to work: 81.3% car, 0.0% public transportation, 2.4% walk, 5.7% work from home (2006-2010 5-year est.); Travel time to work: 13.8% less than 15 minutes, 23.3% 15 to 30 minutes, 22.4% 30 to 45 minutes, 16.4% 45 to 60 minutes, 24.1% 60 minutes or more (2006-2010 5-year est.)

CALVIN (unincorporated postal area)

Zip Code: 16622

Covers a land area of 7.447 square miles and a water area of 0 square miles. Located at 40.32° N. Lat; 78.06° W. Long. Population: 175 (2010); Density: 23.5 persons per square mile (2010); Race: 99.4% White, 0.6% Black, 0.0% Asian, 0.0% American Indian/Alaska Native, 0.0% Native Hawaiian/Other Pacific Islander, 0.0% Other, 0.0% Hispanic of any race (2010); Average household size: 2.36 (2010); Median age: 46.4 (2010); Males per 100 females: 92.3 (2010); Homeownership rate: 83.8% (2010)

CARBON (township). Covers a land area of 18.584 square miles and a water area of 0 square miles. Located at 40.22° N. Lat; 78.17° W. Long.

Population: 438 (1990); 428 (2000); 375 (2010); Density: 20.2 persons per square mile (2010); Race: 99.5% White, 0.0% Black, 0.0% Asian, 0.0% American Indian/Alaska Native, 0.0% Native Hawaiian/Other Pacific Islander, 0.5% Other, 0.0% Hispanic of any race (2010); Average household size: 2.26 (2010); Median age: 47.2 (2010); Males per 100 females: 111.9 (2010); Marriage status: 20.7% never married, 68.3% now married, 3.9% widowed, 7.2% divorced (2006-2010 5-year est.); Foreign born: 0.0% (2006-2010 5-year est.); Ancestry (includes multiple ancestries): 36.7% German, 20.1% Irish, 7.3% Dutch, 5.1% Italian, 4.4% Polish (2006-2010 5-year est.).

Economy: Single-family building permits issued: 1 (2011); Multi-family building permits issued: 0 (2011); Employment by occupation: 11.5% management, 1.9% professional, 13.9% services, 16.7% sales, 3.3% farming, 15.3% construction, 10.0% production (2006-2010 5-year est.).

Income: Per capita income: $25,064 (2006-2010 5-year est.); Median household income: $46,250 (2006-2010 5-year est.); Average household income: $56,797 (2006-2010 5-year est.); Percent of households with income of $100,000 or more: 9.0% (2006-2010 5-year est.); Poverty rate: 3.9% (2006-2010 5-year est.).

Education: Percent of population age 25 and over with: High school diploma (including GED) or higher: 85.9% (2006-2010 5-year est.); Bachelor's degree or higher: 9.2% (2006-2010 5-year est.); Master's degree or higher: 1.8% (2006-2010 5-year est.).

Housing: Homeownership rate: 84.3% (2010); Median home value: $70,000 (2006-2010 5-year est.); Median contract rent: n/a per month (2006-2010 5-year est.); Median year structure built: 1954 (2006-2010 5-year est.).

Transportation: Commute to work: 80.3% car, 0.0% public transportation, 5.1% walk, 9.6% work from home (2006-2010 5-year est.); Travel time to work: 36.3% less than 15 minutes, 16.2% 15 to 30 minutes, 15.6% 30 to 45 minutes, 9.5% 45 to 60 minutes, 22.3% 60 minutes or more (2006-2010 5-year est.)

CASS (township). Covers a land area of 32.975 square miles and a water area of 0 square miles. Located at 40.29° N. Lat; 78.04° W. Long.

Population: 1,041 (1990); 1,062 (2000); 1,119 (2010); Density: 33.9 persons per square mile (2010); Race: 99.2% White, 0.1% Black, 0.0% Asian, 0.1% American Indian/Alaska Native, 0.0% Native Hawaiian/Other Pacific Islander, 0.6% Other, 0.1% Hispanic of any race (2010); Average household size: 2.59 (2010); Median age: 41.9 (2010); Males per 100 females: 98.4 (2010); Marriage status: 19.2% never married, 67.1% now married, 8.1% widowed, 5.7% divorced (2006-2010 5-year est.); Foreign born: 0.0% (2006-2010 5-year est.); Ancestry (includes multiple ancestries): 30.1% German, 12.4% English, 12.1% Irish, 8.2% American, 7.1% Italian (2006-2010 5-year est.).

Economy: Single-family building permits issued: 0 (2011); Multi-family building permits issued: 0 (2011); Employment by occupation: 6.5% management, 0.0% professional, 10.5% services, 14.5% sales, 2.8% farming, 17.7% construction, 6.9% production (2006-2010 5-year est.).

Income: Per capita income: $19,319 (2006-2010 5-year est.); Median household income: $47,298 (2006-2010 5-year est.); Average household income: $54,865 (2006-2010 5-year est.); Percent of households with income of $100,000 or more: 11.5% (2006-2010 5-year est.); Poverty rate: 13.7% (2006-2010 5-year est.).

Education: Percent of population age 25 and over with: High school diploma (including GED) or higher: 90.0% (2006-2010 5-year est.); Bachelor's degree or higher: 13.4% (2006-2010 5-year est.); Master's degree or higher: 5.8% (2006-2010 5-year est.).

Housing: Homeownership rate: 86.8% (2010); Median home value: $113,000 (2006-2010 5-year est.); Median contract rent: $415 per month (2006-2010 5-year est.); Median year structure built: 1976 (2006-2010 5-year est.).

Transportation: Commute to work: 95.8% car, 0.0% public transportation, 2.3% walk, 1.2% work from home (2006-2010 5-year est.); Travel time to work: 24.7% less than 15 minutes, 26.0% 15 to 30 minutes, 26.5% 30 to 45 minutes, 7.7% 45 to 60 minutes, 15.1% 60 minutes or more (2006-2010 5-year est.)

Additional Information Contacts

Huntingdon County Chamber of Commerce . . . . (814) 643-1110
    http://www.huntingdonchamber.com

CASSVILLE (borough). Covers a land area of 0.593 square miles and a water area of 0 square miles. Located at 40.29° N. Lat; 78.03° W. Long. Elevation is 1,234 feet.

Population: 140 (1990); 152 (2000); 143 (2010); Density: 241.2 persons per square mile (2010); Race: 99.3% White, 0.0% Black, 0.0% Asian, 0.0% American Indian/Alaska Native, 0.0% Native Hawaiian/Other Pacific Islander, 0.7% Other, 0.0% Hispanic of any race (2010); Average household size: 2.38 (2010); Median age: 46.8 (2010); Males per 100 females: 95.9 (2010); Marriage status: 16.7% never married, 69.8% now married, 9.3% widowed, 4.3% divorced (2006-2010 5-year est.); Foreign born: 0.0% (2006-2010 5-year est.); Ancestry (includes multiple ancestries): 41.8% German, 18.0% Irish, 13.8% American, 6.9% Italian, 4.8% Dutch (2006-2010 5-year est.).

Economy: Single-family building permits issued: 0 (2011); Multi-family building permits issued: 0 (2011); Employment by occupation: 4.9% management, 3.9% professional, 6.9% services, 15.7% sales, 0.0% farming, 5.9% construction, 17.6% production (2006-2010 5-year est.).

Income: Per capita income: $20,762 (2006-2010 5-year est.); Median household income: $45,278 (2006-2010 5-year est.); Average household income: $45,343 (2006-2010 5-year est.); Percent of households with income of $100,000 or more: n/a (2006-2010 5-year est.); Poverty rate: 3.7% (2006-2010 5-year est.).

Education: Percent of population age 25 and over with: High school diploma (including GED) or higher: 93.0% (2006-2010 5-year est.); Bachelor's degree or higher: 10.8% (2006-2010 5-year est.); Master's degree or higher: 3.2% (2006-2010 5-year est.).

School District(s)

Southern Huntingdon County SD (KG-12)
    2010-11 Enrollment: 1,313 . . . . (814) 447-5529

Housing: Homeownership rate: 81.6% (2010); Median home value: $105,500 (2006-2010 5-year est.); Median contract rent: $275 per month (2006-2010 5-year est.); Median year structure built: 1951 (2006-2010 5-year est.).

Transportation: Commute to work: 100.0% car, 0.0% public transportation, 0.0% walk, 0.0% work from home (2006-2010 5-year est.); Travel time to work: 2.2% less than 15 minutes, 21.5% 15 to 30 minutes, 31.2% 30 to 45 minutes, 1.1% 45 to 60 minutes, 44.1% 60 minutes or more (2006-2010 5-year est.)

CLAY (township). Covers a land area of 28.464 square miles and a water area of 0 square miles. Located at 40.18° N. Lat; 78.02° W. Long.

Population: 895 (1990); 920 (2000); 926 (2010); Density: 32.5 persons per square mile (2010); Race: 99.6% White, 0.2% Black, 0.0% Asian, 0.1% American Indian/Alaska Native, 0.0% Native Hawaiian/Other Pacific Islander, 0.1% Other, 0.3% Hispanic of any race (2010); Average household size: 2.44 (2010); Median age: 41.2 (2010); Males per 100 females: 100.9 (2010); Marriage status: 15.9% never married, 71.6% now married, 5.8% widowed, 6.7% divorced (2006-2010 5-year est.); Foreign born: 0.8% (2006-2010 5-year est.); Ancestry (includes multiple ancestries): 34.4% German, 11.1% American, 10.0% Irish, 8.3% English, 4.0% Pennsylvania German (2006-2010 5-year est.).

Economy: Single-family building permits issued: 1 (2011); Multi-family building permits issued: 0 (2011); Employment by occupation: 10.2% management, 0.8% professional, 13.5% services, 10.2% sales, 4.3% farming, 19.3% construction, 10.7% production (2006-2010 5-year est.).

Income: Per capita income: $19,380 (2006-2010 5-year est.); Median household income: $46,875 (2006-2010 5-year est.); Average household income: $51,409 (2006-2010 5-year est.); Percent of households with

income of $100,000 or more: 10.1% (2006-2010 5-year est.); Poverty rate: 15.2% (2006-2010 5-year est.).
Education: Percent of population age 25 and over with: High school diploma (including GED) or higher: 76.6% (2006-2010 5-year est.); Bachelor's degree or higher: 10.3% (2006-2010 5-year est.); Master's degree or higher: 2.5% (2006-2010 5-year est.).
Housing: Homeownership rate: 82.3% (2010); Median home value: $119,900 (2006-2010 5-year est.); Median contract rent: $293 per month (2006-2010 5-year est.); Median year structure built: 1969 (2006-2010 5-year est.).
Transportation: Commute to work: 86.4% car, 0.0% public transportation, 3.1% walk, 3.3% work from home (2006-2010 5-year est.); Travel time to work: 11.4% less than 15 minutes, 20.9% 15 to 30 minutes, 37.8% 30 to 45 minutes, 11.6% 45 to 60 minutes, 18.3% 60 minutes or more (2006-2010 5-year est.)

COALMONT (borough). Covers a land area of 0.120 square miles and a water area of 0 square miles. Located at 40.21° N. Lat; 78.20° W. Long. Elevation is 1,106 feet.
Population: 109 (1990); 128 (2000); 106 (2010); Density: 883.7 persons per square mile (2010); Race: 99.1% White, 0.0% Black, 0.0% Asian, 0.0% American Indian/Alaska Native, 0.0% Native Hawaiian/Other Pacific Islander, 0.9% Other, 0.0% Hispanic of any race (2010); Average household size: 2.59 (2010); Median age: 44.7 (2010); Males per 100 females: 89.3 (2010); Marriage status: 32.1% never married, 45.3% now married, 22.6% widowed, 0.0% divorced (2006-2010 5-year est.); Foreign born: 0.0% (2006-2010 5-year est.); Ancestry (includes multiple ancestries): 47.5% Irish, 39.0% German, 10.2% English, 6.8% American, 5.1% Welsh (2006-2010 5-year est.).
Economy: Single-family building permits issued: 0 (2011); Multi-family building permits issued: 0 (2011); Employment by occupation: 0.0% management, 0.0% professional, 0.0% services, 11.1% sales, 0.0% farming, 55.6% construction, 0.0% production (2006-2010 5-year est.).
Income: Per capita income: $21,342 (2006-2010 5-year est.); Median household income: $24,583 (2006-2010 5-year est.); Average household income: $37,334 (2006-2010 5-year est.); Percent of households with income of $100,000 or more: 10.3% (2006-2010 5-year est.); Poverty rate: 28.8% (2006-2010 5-year est.).
Education: Percent of population age 25 and over with: High school diploma (including GED) or higher: 72.5% (2006-2010 5-year est.); Bachelor's degree or higher: 5.9% (2006-2010 5-year est.); Master's degree or higher: 5.9% (2006-2010 5-year est.).
Housing: Homeownership rate: 82.9% (2010); Median home value: $77,000 (2006-2010 5-year est.); Median contract rent: $450 per month (2006-2010 5-year est.); Median year structure built: 1957 (2006-2010 5-year est.).
Transportation: Commute to work: 88.9% car, 0.0% public transportation, 0.0% walk, 11.1% work from home (2006-2010 5-year est.); Travel time to work: 18.8% less than 15 minutes, 18.8% 15 to 30 minutes, 31.3% 30 to 45 minutes, 0.0% 45 to 60 minutes, 31.3% 60 minutes or more (2006-2010 5-year est.)

CROMWELL (township). Covers a land area of 50.844 square miles and a water area of 0 square miles. Located at 40.24° N. Lat; 77.91° W. Long.
Population: 1,645 (1990); 1,632 (2000); 1,510 (2010); Density: 29.7 persons per square mile (2010); Race: 99.1% White, 0.3% Black, 0.1% Asian, 0.0% American Indian/Alaska Native, 0.0% Native Hawaiian/Other Pacific Islander, 0.5% Other, 0.4% Hispanic of any race (2010); Average household size: 2.54 (2010); Median age: 40.8 (2010); Males per 100 females: 109.1 (2010); Marriage status: 26.3% never married, 59.9% now married, 8.1% widowed, 5.7% divorced (2006-2010 5-year est.); Foreign born: 0.3% (2006-2010 5-year est.); Ancestry (includes multiple ancestries): 41.8% German, 11.2% English, 8.8% Irish, 7.5% American, 2.8% Scotch-Irish (2006-2010 5-year est.).
Economy: Single-family building permits issued: 2 (2011); Multi-family building permits issued: 0 (2011); Employment by occupation: 9.3% management, 2.3% professional, 10.4% services, 8.1% sales, 1.1% farming, 24.3% construction, 13.1% production (2006-2010 5-year est.).
Income: Per capita income: $22,829 (2006-2010 5-year est.); Median household income: $41,406 (2006-2010 5-year est.); Average household income: $52,821 (2006-2010 5-year est.); Percent of households with income of $100,000 or more: 10.2% (2006-2010 5-year est.); Poverty rate: 8.1% (2006-2010 5-year est.).

Education: Percent of population age 25 and over with: High school diploma (including GED) or higher: 83.6% (2006-2010 5-year est.); Bachelor's degree or higher: 11.0% (2006-2010 5-year est.); Master's degree or higher: 5.0% (2006-2010 5-year est.).
Housing: Homeownership rate: 85.5% (2010); Median home value: $111,300 (2006-2010 5-year est.); Median contract rent: $393 per month (2006-2010 5-year est.); Median year structure built: 1974 (2006-2010 5-year est.).
Transportation: Commute to work: 89.6% car, 0.0% public transportation, 0.5% walk, 5.9% work from home (2006-2010 5-year est.); Travel time to work: 27.6% less than 15 minutes, 30.3% 15 to 30 minutes, 12.2% 30 to 45 minutes, 16.1% 45 to 60 minutes, 13.8% 60 minutes or more (2006-2010 5-year est.)
Additional Information Contacts
Huntingdon County Chamber of Commerce . . . . (814) 643-1110
http://www.huntingdonchamber.com

DUBLIN (township). Covers a land area of 36.813 square miles and a water area of 0.004 square miles. Located at 40.15° N. Lat; 77.85° W. Long.
Population: 1,119 (1990); 1,280 (2000); 1,290 (2010); Density: 35.0 persons per square mile (2010); Race: 99.3% White, 0.1% Black, 0.2% Asian, 0.0% American Indian/Alaska Native, 0.0% Native Hawaiian/Other Pacific Islander, 0.4% Other, 0.5% Hispanic of any race (2010); Average household size: 2.50 (2010); Median age: 42.6 (2010); Males per 100 females: 104.8 (2010); Marriage status: 26.5% never married, 63.4% now married, 6.3% widowed, 3.8% divorced (2006-2010 5-year est.); Foreign born: 0.0% (2006-2010 5-year est.); Ancestry (includes multiple ancestries): 47.8% German, 19.6% Irish, 9.1% English, 4.6% Dutch, 4.1% American (2006-2010 5-year est.).
Economy: Single-family building permits issued: 3 (2011); Multi-family building permits issued: 0 (2011); Employment by occupation: 8.2% management, 0.0% professional, 16.3% services, 12.0% sales, 0.8% farming, 25.3% construction, 19.2% production (2006-2010 5-year est.).
Income: Per capita income: $26,130 (2006-2010 5-year est.); Median household income: $53,409 (2006-2010 5-year est.); Average household income: $73,521 (2006-2010 5-year est.); Percent of households with income of $100,000 or more: 10.1% (2006-2010 5-year est.); Poverty rate: 4.4% (2006-2010 5-year est.).
Education: Percent of population age 25 and over with: High school diploma (including GED) or higher: 80.9% (2006-2010 5-year est.); Bachelor's degree or higher: 6.6% (2006-2010 5-year est.); Master's degree or higher: 2.2% (2006-2010 5-year est.).
Housing: Homeownership rate: 86.2% (2010); Median home value: $151,000 (2006-2010 5-year est.); Median contract rent: $214 per month (2006-2010 5-year est.); Median year structure built: 1971 (2006-2010 5-year est.).
Transportation: Commute to work: 88.4% car, 0.0% public transportation, 3.3% walk, 4.8% work from home (2006-2010 5-year est.); Travel time to work: 10.9% less than 15 minutes, 23.8% 15 to 30 minutes, 24.9% 30 to 45 minutes, 21.0% 45 to 60 minutes, 19.4% 60 minutes or more (2006-2010 5-year est.)
Additional Information Contacts
Greater Chambersburg Chamber of Commerce . . . . (717) 264-7101
http://www.chambersburg.org

DUDLEY (borough). Aka Barnett. Covers a land area of 0.328 square miles and a water area of 0 square miles. Located at 40.21° N. Lat; 78.18° W. Long. Elevation is 1,542 feet.
Population: 232 (1990); 192 (2000); 184 (2010); Density: 560.5 persons per square mile (2010); Race: 99.5% White, 0.5% Black, 0.0% Asian, 0.0% American Indian/Alaska Native, 0.0% Native Hawaiian/Other Pacific Islander, 0.0% Other, 0.0% Hispanic of any race (2010); Average household size: 2.45 (2010); Median age: 44.4 (2010); Males per 100 females: 116.5 (2010); Marriage status: 17.6% never married, 71.2% now married, 7.2% widowed, 4.0% divorced (2006-2010 5-year est.); Foreign born: 0.0% (2006-2010 5-year est.); Ancestry (includes multiple ancestries): 22.9% Irish, 21.6% German, 11.8% English, 11.1% Pennsylvania German, 6.5% Italian (2006-2010 5-year est.).
Economy: Single-family building permits issued: 0 (2011); Multi-family building permits issued: 0 (2011); Employment by occupation: 5.6% management, 0.0% professional, 5.6% services, 13.0% sales, 0.0% farming, 13.0% construction, 0.0% production (2006-2010 5-year est.).
Income: Per capita income: $23,923 (2006-2010 5-year est.); Median household income: $54,375 (2006-2010 5-year est.); Average household

income: $60,088 (2006-2010 5-year est.); Percent of households with income of $100,000 or more: 10.6% (2006-2010 5-year est.); Poverty rate: 15.0% (2006-2010 5-year est.).

Education: Percent of population age 25 and over with: High school diploma (including GED) or higher: 90.8% (2006-2010 5-year est.); Bachelor's degree or higher: 8.3% (2006-2010 5-year est.); Master's degree or higher: 0.0% (2006-2010 5-year est.).

Housing: Homeownership rate: 78.7% (2010); Median home value: $84,400 (2006-2010 5-year est.); Median contract rent: n/a per month (2006-2010 5-year est.); Median year structure built: before 1940 (2006-2010 5-year est.).

Transportation: Commute to work: 92.2% car, 0.0% public transportation, 0.0% walk, 0.0% work from home (2006-2010 5-year est.); Travel time to work: 27.5% less than 15 minutes, 19.6% 15 to 30 minutes, 13.7% 30 to 45 minutes, 19.6% 45 to 60 minutes, 19.6% 60 minutes or more (2006-2010 5-year est.)

ENTRIKEN (unincorporated postal area)
Zip Code: 16638

Covers a land area of 0.687 square miles and a water area of 0 square miles. Located at 40.33° N. Lat; 78.20° W. Long. Elevation is 906 feet. Population: 67 (2010); Density: 97.4 persons per square mile (2010); Race: 98.5% White, 0.0% Black, 1.5% Asian, 0.0% American Indian/Alaska Native, 0.0% Native Hawaiian/Other Pacific Islander, 0.0% Other, 0.0% Hispanic of any race (2010); Average household size: 2.48 (2010); Median age: 41.9 (2010); Males per 100 females: 116.1 (2010); Homeownership rate: 77.7% (2010)

FRANKLIN (township). Covers a land area of 31.468 square miles and a water area of 0.005 square miles. Located at 40.69° N. Lat; 78.06° W. Long.

Population: 466 (1990); 447 (2000); 466 (2010); Density: 14.8 persons per square mile (2010); Race: 98.3% White, 0.6% Black, 0.2% Asian, 0.2% American Indian/Alaska Native, 0.0% Native Hawaiian/Other Pacific Islander, 0.7% Other, 6.4% Hispanic of any race (2010); Average household size: 2.32 (2010); Median age: 41.9 (2010); Males per 100 females: 115.7 (2010); Marriage status: 29.9% never married, 56.6% now married, 8.6% widowed, 4.9% divorced (2006-2010 5-year est.); Foreign born: 5.6% (2006-2010 5-year est.); Ancestry (includes multiple ancestries): 43.6% German, 19.6% Irish, 6.4% Dutch, 3.5% English, 3.5% American (2006-2010 5-year est.).

Economy: Single-family building permits issued: 0 (2011); Multi-family building permits issued: 0 (2011); Employment by occupation: 12.4% management, 5.3% professional, 6.4% services, 8.9% sales, 6.0% farming, 30.9% construction, 9.2% production (2006-2010 5-year est.).

Income: Per capita income: $23,119 (2006-2010 5-year est.); Median household income: $52,639 (2006-2010 5-year est.); Average household income: $60,361 (2006-2010 5-year est.); Percent of households with income of $100,000 or more: 17.2% (2006-2010 5-year est.); Poverty rate: 9.3% (2006-2010 5-year est.).

Education: Percent of population age 25 and over with: High school diploma (including GED) or higher: 88.6% (2006-2010 5-year est.); Bachelor's degree or higher: 31.2% (2006-2010 5-year est.); Master's degree or higher: 12.5% (2006-2010 5-year est.).

Housing: Homeownership rate: 70.6% (2010); Median home value: $142,200 (2006-2010 5-year est.); Median contract rent: $475 per month (2006-2010 5-year est.); Median year structure built: 1948 (2006-2010 5-year est.).

Transportation: Commute to work: 76.4% car, 0.0% public transportation, 19.2% walk, 4.3% work from home (2006-2010 5-year est.); Travel time to work: 40.2% less than 15 minutes, 33.7% 15 to 30 minutes, 20.1% 30 to 45 minutes, 3.4% 45 to 60 minutes, 2.7% 60 minutes or more (2006-2010 5-year est.)

HENDERSON (township). Covers a land area of 26.163 square miles and a water area of 0.128 square miles. Located at 40.50° N. Lat; 77.94° W. Long.

Population: 933 (1990); 972 (2000); 933 (2010); Density: 35.7 persons per square mile (2010); Race: 99.1% White, 0.3% Black, 0.0% Asian, 0.0% American Indian/Alaska Native, 0.0% Native Hawaiian/Other Pacific Islander, 0.6% Other, 0.4% Hispanic of any race (2010); Average household size: 2.37 (2010); Median age: 48.2 (2010); Males per 100 females: 102.8 (2010); Marriage status: 20.5% never married, 57.0% now married, 6.4% widowed, 16.1% divorced (2006-2010 5-year est.); Foreign born: 1.4% (2006-2010 5-year est.); Ancestry (includes multiple

ancestries): 42.0% German, 14.7% American, 11.6% Irish, 8.9% English, 4.5% Dutch (2006-2010 5-year est.).

Economy: Single-family building permits issued: 0 (2011); Multi-family building permits issued: 0 (2011); Employment by occupation: 8.8% management, 0.9% professional, 6.7% services, 19.4% sales, 5.9% farming, 15.8% construction, 4.7% production (2006-2010 5-year est.).

Income: Per capita income: $23,332 (2006-2010 5-year est.); Median household income: $45,486 (2006-2010 5-year est.); Average household income: $53,965 (2006-2010 5-year est.); Percent of households with income of $100,000 or more: 9.5% (2006-2010 5-year est.); Poverty rate: 11.9% (2006-2010 5-year est.).

Education: Percent of population age 25 and over with: High school diploma (including GED) or higher: 91.2% (2006-2010 5-year est.); Bachelor's degree or higher: 11.2% (2006-2010 5-year est.); Master's degree or higher: 4.3% (2006-2010 5-year est.).

Housing: Homeownership rate: 84.8% (2010); Median home value: $107,600 (2006-2010 5-year est.); Median contract rent: $246 per month (2006-2010 5-year est.); Median year structure built: 1975 (2006-2010 5-year est.).

Transportation: Commute to work: 94.3% car, 0.0% public transportation, 4.8% walk, 0.0% work from home (2006-2010 5-year est.); Travel time to work: 27.9% less than 15 minutes, 31.5% 15 to 30 minutes, 15.9% 30 to 45 minutes, 13.2% 45 to 60 minutes, 11.4% 60 minutes or more (2006-2010 5-year est.)

HESSTON (unincorporated postal area)
Zip Code: 16647

Covers a land area of 22.010 square miles and a water area of 5.942 square miles. Located at 40.40° N. Lat; 78.10° W. Long. Elevation is 781 feet. Population: 764 (2010); Density: 34.7 persons per square mile (2010); Race: 99.7% White, 0.3% Black, 0.0% Asian, 0.0% American Indian/Alaska Native, 0.0% Native Hawaiian/Other Pacific Islander, 0.0% Other, 0.4% Hispanic of any race (2010); Average household size: 2.32 (2010); Median age: 49.2 (2010); Males per 100 females: 93.9 (2010); Homeownership rate: 86.6% (2010)

HOPEWELL (township). Covers a land area of 15.306 square miles and a water area of 1.434 square miles. Located at 40.27° N. Lat; 78.23° W. Long.

Population: 540 (1990); 587 (2000); 586 (2010); Density: 38.3 persons per square mile (2010); Race: 98.8% White, 0.2% Black, 0.2% Asian, 0.3% American Indian/Alaska Native, 0.0% Native Hawaiian/Other Pacific Islander, 0.5% Other, 0.9% Hispanic of any race (2010); Average household size: 2.39 (2010); Median age: 46.2 (2010); Males per 100 females: 98.6 (2010); Marriage status: 20.3% never married, 63.0% now married, 6.5% widowed, 10.1% divorced (2006-2010 5-year est.); Foreign born: 0.0% (2006-2010 5-year est.); Ancestry (includes multiple ancestries): 34.0% German, 23.9% Irish, 16.4% Dutch, 12.2% English, 9.5% American (2006-2010 5-year est.).

Economy: Single-family building permits issued: 1 (2011); Multi-family building permits issued: 0 (2011); Employment by occupation: 3.9% management, 1.9% professional, 10.1% services, 19.8% sales, 1.9% farming, 9.7% construction, 13.5% production (2006-2010 5-year est.).

Income: Per capita income: $16,327 (2006-2010 5-year est.); Median household income: $34,792 (2006-2010 5-year est.); Average household income: $40,771 (2006-2010 5-year est.); Percent of households with income of $100,000 or more: 6.9% (2006-2010 5-year est.); Poverty rate: 17.4% (2006-2010 5-year est.).

Education: Percent of population age 25 and over with: High school diploma (including GED) or higher: 85.0% (2006-2010 5-year est.); Bachelor's degree or higher: 8.6% (2006-2010 5-year est.); Master's degree or higher: 5.6% (2006-2010 5-year est.).

Housing: Homeownership rate: 80.8% (2010); Median home value: $94,300 (2006-2010 5-year est.); Median contract rent: $319 per month (2006-2010 5-year est.); Median year structure built: 1973 (2006-2010 5-year est.).

Transportation: Commute to work: 90.1% car, 0.0% public transportation, 0.0% walk, 5.4% work from home (2006-2010 5-year est.); Travel time to work: 25.0% less than 15 minutes, 27.1% 15 to 30 minutes, 14.1% 30 to 45 minutes, 19.3% 45 to 60 minutes, 14.6% 60 minutes or more (2006-2010 5-year est.)

HUNTINGDON (borough). Aka South Huntingdon. County seat.
Covers a land area of 3.617 square miles and a water area of 0.093

square miles. Located at 40.50° N. Lat; 78.00° W. Long. Elevation is 633 feet.

History: The settlement at Huntingdon was laid out in 1767 by Dr. William Smith, first Provost of the University of Pennsylvania, and named for Selina Hastings, Countess of Huntingdon, who assisted with funding for the university.

Population: 6,843 (1990); 6,918 (2000); 7,093 (2010); Density: 1,960.9 persons per square mile (2010); Race: 94.6% White, 1.9% Black, 1.5% Asian, 0.1% American Indian/Alaska Native, 0.0% Native Hawaiian/Other Pacific Islander, 1.9% Other, 1.5% Hispanic of any race (2010); Average household size: 2.16 (2010); Median age: 32.8 (2010); Males per 100 females: 87.5 (2010); Marriage status: 46.0% never married, 34.1% now married, 6.6% widowed, 13.3% divorced (2006-2010 5-year est.); Foreign born: 2.3% (2006-2010 5-year est.); Ancestry (includes multiple ancestries): 38.2% German, 16.6% Irish, 11.0% English, 7.4% Italian, 4.4% Polish (2006-2010 5-year est.).

Economy: Single-family building permits issued: 1 (2011); Multi-family building permits issued: 10 (2011); Employment by occupation: 9.4% management, 1.8% professional, 11.7% services, 16.1% sales, 3.4% farming, 8.6% construction, 5.1% production (2006-2010 5-year est.).

Income: Per capita income: $19,070 (2006-2010 5-year est.); Median household income: $35,057 (2006-2010 5-year est.); Average household income: $45,256 (2006-2010 5-year est.); Percent of households with income of $100,000 or more: 7.7% (2006-2010 5-year est.); Poverty rate: 15.3% (2006-2010 5-year est.).

Taxes: Total city taxes per capita: $225 (2009); City property taxes per capita: $126 (2009).

Education: Percent of population age 25 and over with: High school diploma (including GED) or higher: 93.1% (2006-2010 5-year est.); Bachelor's degree or higher: 24.8% (2006-2010 5-year est.); Master's degree or higher: 9.0% (2006-2010 5-year est.).

School District(s)

Huntingdon Area SD (KG-12)
    2010-11 Enrollment: 2,082 . . . . (814) 643-4140
New Day Charter School (07-12)
    2010-11 Enrollment: 119. . . . . (814) 643-7112

Four-year College(s)

Juniata College (Private, Not-for-profit)
    Fall 2010 Enrollment: 1,543 . . . . (814) 641-3000
    2011-12 Tuition: In-state $34,090; Out-of-state $34,090

Two-year College(s)

Du Bois Business College-Huntingdon (Private, For-profit)
    Fall 2010 Enrollment: 58 . . . . (814) 371-6920
    2011-12 Tuition: In-state $10,305; Out-of-state $10,305

Housing: Homeownership rate: 55.6% (2010); Median home value: $104,200 (2006-2010 5-year est.); Median contract rent: $366 per month (2006-2010 5-year est.); Median year structure built: before 1940 (2006-2010 5-year est.).

Hospitals: JC Blair Memorial Hospital (104 beds)

Safety: Violent crime rate: 2.8 per 10,000 population; Property crime rate: 136.3 per 10,000 population (2011).

Newspapers: Huntingdon Daily News (Local news; Circulation 12,000)

Transportation: Commute to work: 77.5% car, 0.0% public transportation, 18.0% walk, 2.2% work from home (2006-2010 5-year est.); Travel time to work: 68.8% less than 15 minutes, 14.0% 15 to 30 minutes, 4.2% 30 to 45 minutes, 5.1% 45 to 60 minutes, 7.9% 60 minutes or more (2006-2010 5-year est.); Amtrak: train service available.

Additional Information Contacts

Borough of Huntingdon . . . . (814) 643-3966
    http://www.huntingdonboro.com
Huntingdon County Chamber of Commerce . . . . (814) 643-1110
    http://www.huntingdonchamber.com

JACKSON (township). Covers a land area of 72.475 square miles and a water area of 0.045 square miles. Located at 40.67° N. Lat; 77.81° W. Long.

Population: 816 (1990); 882 (2000); 872 (2010); Density: 12.0 persons per square mile (2010); Race: 99.0% White, 0.3% Black, 0.0% Asian, 0.1% American Indian/Alaska Native, 0.0% Native Hawaiian/Other Pacific Islander, 0.6% Other, 0.1% Hispanic of any race (2010); Average household size: 2.46 (2010); Median age: 45.0 (2010); Males per 100 females: 104.7 (2010); Marriage status: 22.6% never married, 63.1% now married, 7.0% widowed, 7.3% divorced (2006-2010 5-year est.); Foreign born: 0.4% (2006-2010 5-year est.); Ancestry (includes multiple

ancestries): 29.8% German, 16.2% Irish, 11.6% English, 7.8% Pennsylvania German, 6.7% American (2006-2010 5-year est.).

Economy: Single-family building permits issued: 4 (2011); Multi-family building permits issued: 0 (2011); Employment by occupation: 5.4% management, 3.6% professional, 10.2% services, 14.3% sales, 0.8% farming, 20.5% construction, 4.1% production (2006-2010 5-year est.).

Income: Per capita income: $24,104 (2006-2010 5-year est.); Median household income: $41,806 (2006-2010 5-year est.); Average household income: $56,762 (2006-2010 5-year est.); Percent of households with income of $100,000 or more: 9.2% (2006-2010 5-year est.); Poverty rate: 8.7% (2006-2010 5-year est.).

Education: Percent of population age 25 and over with: High school diploma (including GED) or higher: 85.0% (2006-2010 5-year est.); Bachelor's degree or higher: 16.6% (2006-2010 5-year est.); Master's degree or higher: 3.0% (2006-2010 5-year est.).

Housing: Homeownership rate: 86.2% (2010); Median home value: $114,600 (2006-2010 5-year est.); Median contract rent: $309 per month (2006-2010 5-year est.); Median year structure built: 1971 (2006-2010 5-year est.).

Transportation: Commute to work: 93.1% car, 0.0% public transportation, 2.6% walk, 2.6% work from home (2006-2010 5-year est.); Travel time to work: 12.1% less than 15 minutes, 47.0% 15 to 30 minutes, 32.0% 30 to 45 minutes, 3.9% 45 to 60 minutes, 5.0% 60 minutes or more (2006-2010 5-year est.)

JAMES CREEK (unincorporated postal area)

Zip Code: 16657

    Covers a land area of 52.012 square miles and a water area of 2.720 square miles. Located at 40.32° N. Lat; 78.18° W. Long. Population: 1,343 (2010); Density: 25.8 persons per square mile (2010); Race: 97.5% White, 1.0% Black, 0.3% Asian, 0.1% American Indian/Alaska Native, 0.0% Native Hawaiian/Other Pacific Islander, 1.1% Other, 1.3% Hispanic of any race (2010); Average household size: 2.40 (2010); Median age: 45.5 (2010); Males per 100 females: 106.3 (2010); Homeownership rate: 86.7% (2010)

JUNIATA (township). Covers a land area of 16.720 square miles and a water area of 3.450 square miles. Located at 40.42° N. Lat; 78.02° W. Long.

Population: 429 (1990); 553 (2000); 554 (2010); Density: 33.1 persons per square mile (2010); Race: 99.5% White, 0.2% Black, 0.2% Asian, 0.0% American Indian/Alaska Native, 0.0% Native Hawaiian/Other Pacific Islander, 0.1% Other, 0.2% Hispanic of any race (2010); Average household size: 2.36 (2010); Median age: 49.1 (2010); Males per 100 females: 96.5 (2010); Marriage status: 19.1% never married, 64.3% now married, 7.1% widowed, 9.4% divorced (2006-2010 5-year est.); Foreign born: 0.6% (2006-2010 5-year est.); Ancestry (includes multiple ancestries): 37.4% German, 21.0% American, 14.7% Irish, 5.2% Italian, 5.0% Dutch (2006-2010 5-year est.).

Economy: Single-family building permits issued: 3 (2011); Multi-family building permits issued: 0 (2011); Employment by occupation: 8.4% management, 0.0% professional, 10.0% services, 9.6% sales, 8.4% farming, 20.7% construction, 11.6% production (2006-2010 5-year est.).

Income: Per capita income: $22,481 (2006-2010 5-year est.); Median household income: $44,500 (2006-2010 5-year est.); Average household income: $54,815 (2006-2010 5-year est.); Percent of households with income of $100,000 or more: 10.2% (2006-2010 5-year est.); Poverty rate: 1.7% (2006-2010 5-year est.).

Education: Percent of population age 25 and over with: High school diploma (including GED) or higher: 90.7% (2006-2010 5-year est.); Bachelor's degree or higher: 14.3% (2006-2010 5-year est.); Master's degree or higher: 8.5% (2006-2010 5-year est.).

Housing: Homeownership rate: 82.1% (2010); Median home value: $158,200 (2006-2010 5-year est.); Median contract rent: $381 per month (2006-2010 5-year est.); Median year structure built: 1982 (2006-2010 5-year est.).

Transportation: Commute to work: 92.9% car, 0.0% public transportation, 2.1% walk, 5.0% work from home (2006-2010 5-year est.); Travel time to work: 39.4% less than 15 minutes, 37.2% 15 to 30 minutes, 10.2% 30 to 45 minutes, 2.2% 45 to 60 minutes, 11.1% 60 minutes or more (2006-2010 5-year est.)

LINCOLN (township). Covers a land area of 18.862 square miles and a water area of 2.090 square miles. Located at 40.34° N. Lat; 78.19° W. Long.

Population: 320 (1990); 319 (2000); 338 (2010); Density: 17.9 persons per square mile (2010); Race: 98.8% White, 0.3% Black, 0.9% Asian, 0.0% American Indian/Alaska Native, 0.0% Native Hawaiian/Other Pacific Islander, 0.0% Other, 0.0% Hispanic of any race (2010); Average household size: 2.38 (2010); Median age: 44.4 (2010); Males per 100 females: 116.7 (2010); Marriage status: 21.4% never married, 64.5% now married, 10.1% widowed, 4.0% divorced (2006-2010 5-year est.); Foreign born: 3.1% (2006-2010 5-year est.); Ancestry (includes multiple ancestries): 46.9% German, 23.1% Irish, 16.4% English, 7.0% American, 4.9% French (2006-2010 5-year est.).

Economy: Single-family building permits issued: 0 (2011); Multi-family building permits issued: 0 (2011); Employment by occupation: 9.7% management, 1.4% professional, 2.8% services, 21.5% sales, 2.1% farming, 16.7% construction, 9.0% production (2006-2010 5-year est.).

Income: Per capita income: $22,437 (2006-2010 5-year est.); Median household income: $41,500 (2006-2010 5-year est.); Average household income: $47,418 (2006-2010 5-year est.); Percent of households with income of $100,000 or more: 8.2% (2006-2010 5-year est.); Poverty rate: 7.3% (2006-2010 5-year est.).

Education: Percent of population age 25 and over with: High school diploma (including GED) or higher: 91.3% (2006-2010 5-year est.); Bachelor's degree or higher: 31.5% (2006-2010 5-year est.); Master's degree or higher: 5.9% (2006-2010 5-year est.).

Housing: Homeownership rate: 86.0% (2010); Median home value: $133,300 (2006-2010 5-year est.); Median contract rent: $238 per month (2006-2010 5-year est.); Median year structure built: 1973 (2006-2010 5-year est.).

Transportation: Commute to work: 88.7% car, 0.0% public transportation, 1.4% walk, 9.9% work from home (2006-2010 5-year est.); Travel time to work: 13.4% less than 15 minutes, 36.2% 15 to 30 minutes, 17.3% 30 to 45 minutes, 16.5% 45 to 60 minutes, 16.5% 60 minutes or more (2006-2010 5-year est.)

LOGAN (township). Covers a land area of 22.870 square miles and a water area of 0.154 square miles. Located at 40.59° N. Lat; 78.04° W. Long.

Population: 684 (1990); 703 (2000); 678 (2010); Density: 29.6 persons per square mile (2010); Race: 98.2% White, 0.4% Black, 0.4% Asian, 0.0% American Indian/Alaska Native, 0.0% Native Hawaiian/Other Pacific Islander, 1.0% Other, 0.4% Hispanic of any race (2010); Average household size: 2.47 (2010); Median age: 43.6 (2010); Males per 100 females: 97.7 (2010); Marriage status: 19.2% never married, 58.3% now married, 3.8% widowed, 18.7% divorced (2006-2010 5-year est.); Foreign born: 1.3% (2006-2010 5-year est.); Ancestry (includes multiple ancestries): 54.0% German, 22.5% Irish, 10.7% English, 6.7% Dutch, 6.1% American (2006-2010 5-year est.).

Economy: Single-family building permits issued: 2 (2011); Multi-family building permits issued: 0 (2011); Employment by occupation: 3.8% management, 4.5% professional, 13.5% services, 24.2% sales, 0.0% farming, 19.4% construction, 12.5% production (2006-2010 5-year est.).

Income: Per capita income: $19,467 (2006-2010 5-year est.); Median household income: $44,167 (2006-2010 5-year est.); Average household income: $50,128 (2006-2010 5-year est.); Percent of households with income of $100,000 or more: 6.6% (2006-2010 5-year est.); Poverty rate: 8.7% (2006-2010 5-year est.).

Education: Percent of population age 25 and over with: High school diploma (including GED) or higher: 87.6% (2006-2010 5-year est.); Bachelor's degree or higher: 8.8% (2006-2010 5-year est.); Master's degree or higher: 1.4% (2006-2010 5-year est.).

Housing: Homeownership rate: 79.9% (2010); Median home value: $110,600 (2006-2010 5-year est.); Median contract rent: $335 per month (2006-2010 5-year est.); Median year structure built: 1964 (2006-2010 5-year est.).

Transportation: Commute to work: 96.5% car, 0.0% public transportation, 0.0% walk, 2.4% work from home (2006-2010 5-year est.); Travel time to work: 12.1% less than 15 minutes, 36.9% 15 to 30 minutes, 24.1% 30 to 45 minutes, 6.7% 45 to 60 minutes, 20.2% 60 minutes or more (2006-2010 5-year est.)

MAPLETON (borough). Aka Mapleton Depot. Covers a land area of 0.183 square miles and a water area of 0.008 square miles. Located at 40.39° N. Lat; 77.94° W. Long. Elevation is 591 feet.

Population: 529 (1990); 473 (2000); 441 (2010); Density: 2,408.7 persons per square mile (2010); Race: 97.5% White, 0.5% Black, 0.0% Asian, 0.2% American Indian/Alaska Native, 0.0% Native Hawaiian/Other Pacific Islander, 1.8% Other, 1.4% Hispanic of any race (2010); Average household size: 2.52 (2010); Median age: 36.8 (2010); Males per 100 females: 87.7 (2010); Marriage status: 16.3% never married, 59.6% now married, 8.6% widowed, 15.5% divorced (2006-2010 5-year est.); Foreign born: 0.0% (2006-2010 5-year est.); Ancestry (includes multiple ancestries): 47.6% German, 24.0% Irish, 11.7% French, 8.9% Italian, 5.8% English (2006-2010 5-year est.).

Economy: Single-family building permits issued: 0 (2011); Multi-family building permits issued: 0 (2011); Employment by occupation: 2.2% management, 1.7% professional, 10.1% services, 11.2% sales, 1.7% farming, 18.4% construction, 13.4% production (2006-2010 5-year est.).

Income: Per capita income: $13,806 (2006-2010 5-year est.); Median household income: $34,205 (2006-2010 5-year est.); Average household income: $37,272 (2006-2010 5-year est.); Percent of households with income of $100,000 or more: n/a (2006-2010 5-year est.); Poverty rate: 26.4% (2006-2010 5-year est.).

Education: Percent of population age 25 and over with: High school diploma (including GED) or higher: 78.9% (2006-2010 5-year est.); Bachelor's degree or higher: 2.5% (2006-2010 5-year est.); Master's degree or higher: 0.8% (2006-2010 5-year est.).

Housing: Homeownership rate: 70.3% (2010); Median home value: $60,200 (2006-2010 5-year est.); Median contract rent: $419 per month (2006-2010 5-year est.); Median year structure built: before 1940 (2006-2010 5-year est.).

Transportation: Commute to work: 94.0% car, 0.0% public transportation, 0.0% walk, 0.0% work from home (2006-2010 5-year est.); Travel time to work: 35.5% less than 15 minutes, 31.9% 15 to 30 minutes, 9.6% 30 to 45 minutes, 1.8% 45 to 60 minutes, 21.1% 60 minutes or more (2006-2010 5-year est.)

MAPLETON DEPOT (unincorporated postal area)

Zip Code: 17052

Covers a land area of 40.130 square miles and a water area of 0.253 square miles. Located at 40.27° N. Lat; 77.98° W. Long. Population: 1,635 (2010); Density: 40.7 persons per square mile (2010); Race: 98.8% White, 0.2% Black, 0.0% Asian, 0.1% American Indian/Alaska Native, 0.0% Native Hawaiian/Other Pacific Islander, 0.9% Other, 0.6% Hispanic of any race (2010); Average household size: 2.52 (2010); Median age: 41.2 (2010); Males per 100 females: 96.0 (2010); Homeownership rate: 83.6% (2010)

MARKLESBURG (borough). Aka James Creek. Covers a land area of 1.036 square miles and a water area of 0.014 square miles. Located at 40.38° N. Lat; 78.17° W. Long. Elevation is 889 feet.

Population: 165 (1990); 216 (2000); 204 (2010); Density: 196.9 persons per square mile (2010); Race: 97.5% White, 0.5% Black, 0.0% Asian, 0.0% American Indian/Alaska Native, 0.0% Native Hawaiian/Other Pacific Islander, 2.0% Other, 0.0% Hispanic of any race (2010); Average household size: 2.34 (2010); Median age: 43.0 (2010); Males per 100 females: 82.1 (2010); Marriage status: 26.1% never married, 63.0% now married, 6.7% widowed, 4.2% divorced (2006-2010 5-year est.); Foreign born: 0.0% (2006-2010 5-year est.); Ancestry (includes multiple ancestries): 46.0% German, 29.2% Irish, 10.9% English, 5.4% Pennsylvania German, 5.4% European (2006-2010 5-year est.).

Economy: Single-family building permits issued: 1 (2011); Multi-family building permits issued: 0 (2011); Employment by occupation: 3.1% management, 0.0% professional, 9.4% services, 29.2% sales, 3.1% farming, 16.7% construction, 10.4% production (2006-2010 5-year est.).

Income: Per capita income: $21,635 (2006-2010 5-year est.); Median household income: $40,000 (2006-2010 5-year est.); Average household income: $46,843 (2006-2010 5-year est.); Percent of households with income of $100,000 or more: 7.6% (2006-2010 5-year est.); Poverty rate: 7.9% (2006-2010 5-year est.).

Education: Percent of population age 25 and over with: High school diploma (including GED) or higher: 90.1% (2006-2010 5-year est.); Bachelor's degree or higher: 10.6% (2006-2010 5-year est.); Master's degree or higher: 4.0% (2006-2010 5-year est.).

Housing: Homeownership rate: 81.9% (2010); Median home value: $107,000 (2006-2010 5-year est.); Median contract rent: $425 per month

(2006-2010 5-year est.); Median year structure built: 1953 (2006-2010 5-year est.).

Transportation: Commute to work: 87.5% car, 0.0% public transportation, 3.1% walk, 9.4% work from home (2006-2010 5-year est.); Travel time to work: 17.2% less than 15 minutes, 34.5% 15 to 30 minutes, 4.6% 30 to 45 minutes, 17.2% 45 to 60 minutes, 26.4% 60 minutes or more (2006-2010 5-year est.).

MCCONNELLSTOWN (CDP). Covers a land area of 3.212 square miles and a water area of 0 square miles. Located at 40.46° N. Lat; 78.07° W. Long. Elevation is 709 feet.

Population: n/a (1990); n/a (2000); 1,194 (2010); Density: 371.8 persons per square mile (2010); Race: 98.0% White, 0.2% Black, 0.6% Asian, 0.3% American Indian/Alaska Native, 0.0% Native Hawaiian/Other Pacific Islander, 0.9% Other, 0.5% Hispanic of any race (2010); Average household size: 2.54 (2010); Median age: 42.9 (2010); Males per 100 females: 96.1 (2010); Marriage status: 17.7% never married, 71.7% now married, 6.9% widowed, 3.7% divorced (2006-2010 5-year est.); Foreign born: 0.3% (2006-2010 5-year est.); Ancestry (includes multiple ancestries): 46.8% German, 18.3% Irish, 11.8% English, 7.0% Italian, 6.5% Scotch-Irish (2006-2010 5-year est.).

Economy: Employment by occupation: 9.8% management, 3.4% professional, 5.2% services, 21.5% sales, 5.1% farming, 8.1% construction, 2.0% production (2006-2010 5-year est.).

Income: Per capita income: $25,023 (2006-2010 5-year est.); Median household income: $57,625 (2006-2010 5-year est.); Average household income: $67,350 (2006-2010 5-year est.); Percent of households with income of $100,000 or more: 15.6% (2006-2010 5-year est.); Poverty rate: 5.4% (2006-2010 5-year est.).

Education: Percent of population age 25 and over with: High school diploma (including GED) or higher: 93.7% (2006-2010 5-year est.); Bachelor's degree or higher: 20.7% (2006-2010 5-year est.); Master's degree or higher: 7.2% (2006-2010 5-year est.).

Housing: Homeownership rate: 87.1% (2010); Median home value: $134,400 (2006-2010 5-year est.); Median contract rent: $456 per month (2006-2010 5-year est.); Median year structure built: 1967 (2006-2010 5-year est.).

Transportation: Commute to work: 95.3% car, 0.0% public transportation, 1.1% walk, 0.0% work from home (2006-2010 5-year est.); Travel time to work: 53.5% less than 15 minutes, 20.4% 15 to 30 minutes, 15.0% 30 to 45 minutes, 7.2% 45 to 60 minutes, 3.8% 60 minutes or more (2006-2010 5-year est.).

MILL CREEK (borough). Covers a land area of 0.301 square miles and a water area of 0.025 square miles. Located at 40.44° N. Lat; 77.93° W. Long. Elevation is 650 feet.

History: Swigart Museum, vintage autos.

Population: 392 (1990); 351 (2000); 328 (2010); Density: 1,088.8 persons per square mile (2010); Race: 97.9% White, 0.3% Black, 0.9% Asian, 0.3% American Indian/Alaska Native, 0.0% Native Hawaiian/Other Pacific Islander, 0.6% Other, 0.0% Hispanic of any race (2010); Average household size: 2.56 (2010); Median age: 37.8 (2010); Males per 100 females: 97.6 (2010); Marriage status: 22.7% never married, 65.0% now married, 6.8% widowed, 5.5% divorced (2006-2010 5-year est.); Foreign born: 0.0% (2006-2010 5-year est.); Ancestry (includes multiple ancestries): 51.5% German, 18.5% Irish, 10.8% Dutch, 9.2% English, 5.4% Czech (2006-2010 5-year est.).

Economy: Single-family building permits issued: 0 (2011); Multi-family building permits issued: 0 (2011); Employment by occupation: 10.6% management, 2.3% professional, 24.2% services, 9.8% sales, 2.3% farming, 8.3% construction, 9.8% production (2006-2010 5-year est.).

Income: Per capita income: $20,837 (2006-2010 5-year est.); Median household income: $44,583 (2006-2010 5-year est.); Average household income: $50,204 (2006-2010 5-year est.); Percent of households with income of $100,000 or more: 6.7% (2006-2010 5-year est.); Poverty rate: 4.2% (2006-2010 5-year est.).

Education: Percent of population age 25 and over with: High school diploma (including GED) or higher: 78.0% (2006-2010 5-year est.); Bachelor's degree or higher: 5.2% (2006-2010 5-year est.); Master's degree or higher: 1.7% (2006-2010 5-year est.).

School District(s)
Huntingdon Area SD (KG-12)
    2010-11 Enrollment: 2,082 . . . . (814) 643-4140
Huntingdon County CTC (10-12)
    2010-11 Enrollment: n/a . . . . (814) 643-0951

Vocational/Technical School(s)
Huntingdon County Career and Technology Center (Public)
    Fall 2010 Enrollment: 31 . . . . (814) 643-0951
    2011-12 Tuition: $11,515

Housing: Homeownership rate: 73.4% (2010); Median home value: $81,700 (2006-2010 5-year est.); Median contract rent: $400 per month (2006-2010 5-year est.); Median year structure built: before 1940 (2006-2010 5-year est.).

Transportation: Commute to work: 98.6% car, 0.0% public transportation, 0.0% walk, 0.0% work from home (2006-2010 5-year est.); Travel time to work: 29.7% less than 15 minutes, 34.8% 15 to 30 minutes, 15.9% 30 to 45 minutes, 10.1% 45 to 60 minutes, 9.4% 60 minutes or more (2006-2010 5-year est.).

MILLER (township). Covers a land area of 22.214 square miles and a water area of 0 square miles. Located at 40.58° N. Lat; 77.87° W. Long.

Population: 474 (1990); 514 (2000); 462 (2010); Density: 20.8 persons per square mile (2010); Race: 98.1% White, 1.5% Black, 0.4% Asian, 0.0% American Indian/Alaska Native, 0.0% Native Hawaiian/Other Pacific Islander, 0.0% Other, 0.4% Hispanic of any race (2010); Average household size: 2.37 (2010); Median age: 47.9 (2010); Males per 100 females: 99.1 (2010); Marriage status: 13.6% never married, 73.4% now married, 8.4% widowed, 4.7% divorced (2006-2010 5-year est.); Foreign born: 0.0% (2006-2010 5-year est.); Ancestry (includes multiple ancestries): 42.4% German, 13.7% Irish, 10.5% English, 6.8% American, 6.6% Dutch (2006-2010 5-year est.).

Economy: Single-family building permits issued: 0 (2011); Multi-family building permits issued: 0 (2011); Employment by occupation: 10.5% management, 7.8% professional, 11.4% services, 24.7% sales, 1.4% farming, 14.6% construction, 6.4% production (2006-2010 5-year est.).

Income: Per capita income: $27,799 (2006-2010 5-year est.); Median household income: $49,821 (2006-2010 5-year est.); Average household income: $55,864 (2006-2010 5-year est.); Percent of households with income of $100,000 or more: 8.6% (2006-2010 5-year est.); Poverty rate: 9.3% (2006-2010 5-year est.).

Education: Percent of population age 25 and over with: High school diploma (including GED) or higher: 91.1% (2006-2010 5-year est.); Bachelor's degree or higher: 14.5% (2006-2010 5-year est.); Master's degree or higher: 4.2% (2006-2010 5-year est.).

Housing: Homeownership rate: 87.6% (2010); Median home value: $155,000 (2006-2010 5-year est.); Median contract rent: $392 per month (2006-2010 5-year est.); Median year structure built: 1977 (2006-2010 5-year est.).

Transportation: Commute to work: 90.5% car, 0.0% public transportation, 1.0% walk, 7.5% work from home (2006-2010 5-year est.); Travel time to work: 7.0% less than 15 minutes, 45.7% 15 to 30 minutes, 28.0% 30 to 45 minutes, 10.2% 45 to 60 minutes, 9.1% 60 minutes or more (2006-2010 5-year est.).

MORRIS (township). Covers a land area of 12.155 square miles and a water area of 0 square miles. Located at 40.57° N. Lat; 78.16° W. Long.

Population: 415 (1990); 416 (2000); 410 (2010); Density: 33.7 persons per square mile (2010); Race: 100.0% White, 0.0% Black, 0.0% Asian, 0.0% American Indian/Alaska Native, 0.0% Native Hawaiian/Other Pacific Islander, 0.0% Other, 1.2% Hispanic of any race (2010); Average household size: 2.73 (2010); Median age: 38.3 (2010); Males per 100 females: 109.2 (2010); Marriage status: 21.9% never married, 75.6% now married, 1.0% widowed, 1.5% divorced (2006-2010 5-year est.); Foreign born: 0.0% (2006-2010 5-year est.); Ancestry (includes multiple ancestries): 42.2% German, 25.8% Irish, 9.4% English, 8.2% Pennsylvania German, 6.9% French (2006-2010 5-year est.).

Economy: Single-family building permits issued: 1 (2011); Multi-family building permits issued: 0 (2011); Employment by occupation: 8.7% management, 7.7% professional, 16.0% services, 18.1% sales, 0.0% farming, 12.5% construction, 0.3% production (2006-2010 5-year est.).

Income: Per capita income: $20,812 (2006-2010 5-year est.); Median household income: $53,393 (2006-2010 5-year est.); Average household income: $62,866 (2006-2010 5-year est.); Percent of households with income of $100,000 or more: 21.3% (2006-2010 5-year est.); Poverty rate: 7.1% (2006-2010 5-year est.).

Education: Percent of population age 25 and over with: High school diploma (including GED) or higher: 84.9% (2006-2010 5-year est.); Bachelor's degree or higher: 14.1% (2006-2010 5-year est.); Master's degree or higher: 4.2% (2006-2010 5-year est.).

Housing: Homeownership rate: 85.3% (2010); Median home value: $125,000 (2006-2010 5-year est.); Median contract rent: $506 per month (2006-2010 5-year est.); Median year structure built: 1974 (2006-2010 5-year est.).

Transportation: Commute to work: 96.7% car, 0.0% public transportation, 0.0% walk, 3.3% work from home (2006-2010 5-year est.); Travel time to work: 38.4% less than 15 minutes, 17.1% 15 to 30 minutes, 17.1% 30 to 45 minutes, 11.4% 45 to 60 minutes, 16.0% 60 minutes or more (2006-2010 5-year est.)

MOUNT UNION (borough). Aka Allenton. Covers a land area of 1.160 square miles and a water area of 0.077 square miles. Located at 40.38° N. Lat; 77.88° W. Long. Elevation is 610 feet.

Population: 2,878 (1990); 2,504 (2000); 2,447 (2010); Density: 2,110.1 persons per square mile (2010); Race: 84.4% White, 10.4% Black, 0.2% Asian, 0.1% American Indian/Alaska Native, 0.0% Native Hawaiian/Other Pacific Islander, 4.9% Other, 1.7% Hispanic of any race (2010); Average household size: 2.18 (2010); Median age: 38.5 (2010); Males per 100 females: 86.7 (2010); Marriage status: 39.5% never married, 39.8% now married, 10.1% widowed, 10.5% divorced (2006-2010 5-year est.); Foreign born: 0.9% (2006-2010 5-year est.); Ancestry (includes multiple ancestries): 37.6% German, 17.5% Irish, 10.5% English, 8.9% Dutch, 6.1% Italian (2006-2010 5-year est.).

Economy: Single-family building permits issued: 0 (2011); Multi-family building permits issued: 0 (2011); Employment by occupation: 3.8% management, 0.0% professional, 20.7% services, 13.0% sales, 0.0% farming, 7.9% construction, 13.1% production (2006-2010 5-year est.).

Income: Per capita income: $17,286 (2006-2010 5-year est.); Median household income: $29,042 (2006-2010 5-year est.); Average household income: $37,188 (2006-2010 5-year est.); Percent of households with income of $100,000 or more: 4.0% (2006-2010 5-year est.); Poverty rate: 21.0% (2006-2010 5-year est.).

Education: Percent of population age 25 and over with: High school diploma (including GED) or higher: 83.2% (2006-2010 5-year est.); Bachelor's degree or higher: 10.5% (2006-2010 5-year est.); Master's degree or higher: 1.9% (2006-2010 5-year est.).

School District(s)
Mount Union Area SD (KG-12)
    2010-11 Enrollment: 1,496 . . . . (814) 542-8631
Mount Union Area SD (KG-12)
    2010-11 Enrollment: 1,496 . . . . (814) 542-8631

Housing: Homeownership rate: 49.5% (2010); Median home value: $72,200 (2006-2010 5-year est.); Median contract rent: $414 per month (2006-2010 5-year est.); Median year structure built: 1952 (2006-2010 5-year est.).

Safety: Violent crime rate: 0.0 per 10,000 population; Property crime rate: 118.1 per 10,000 population (2011).

Transportation: Commute to work: 81.9% car, 0.0% public transportation, 6.1% walk, 4.8% work from home (2006-2010 5-year est.); Travel time to work: 38.6% less than 15 minutes, 30.8% 15 to 30 minutes, 14.4% 30 to 45 minutes, 4.4% 45 to 60 minutes, 11.8% 60 minutes or more (2006-2010 5-year est.)

Additional Information Contacts
Mount Union Area Chamber of Commerce . . . . (814) 542-9413
    http://www.mountunionchamber.org

NEELYTON (unincorporated postal area)
Zip Code: 17239
    Covers a land area of 8.959 square miles and a water area of 0 square miles. Located at 40.13° N. Lat; 77.83° W. Long. Population: 203 (2010); Density: 22.7 persons per square mile (2010); Race: 100.0% White, 0.0% Black, 0.0% Asian, 0.0% American Indian/Alaska Native, 0.0% Native Hawaiian/Other Pacific Islander, 0.0% Other, 0.0% Hispanic of any race (2010); Average household size: 2.51 (2010); Median age: 40.5 (2010); Males per 100 females: 109.3 (2010); Homeownership rate: 84.0% (2010)

ONEIDA (township). Covers a land area of 17.546 square miles and a water area of 0.025 square miles. Located at 40.54° N. Lat; 77.97° W. Long.

Population: 1,085 (1990); 1,129 (2000); 1,077 (2010); Density: 61.4 persons per square mile (2010); Race: 98.7% White, 0.4% Black, 0.1% Asian, 0.3% American Indian/Alaska Native, 0.0% Native Hawaiian/Other Pacific Islander, 0.5% Other, 0.7% Hispanic of any race (2010); Average household size: 2.34 (2010); Median age: 48.4 (2010); Males per 100

females: 99.8 (2010); Marriage status: 15.6% never married, 69.1% now married, 7.1% widowed, 8.2% divorced (2006-2010 5-year est.); Foreign born: 0.3% (2006-2010 5-year est.); Ancestry (includes multiple ancestries): 49.5% German, 13.8% Irish, 8.3% English, 6.7% Dutch, 6.5% Italian (2006-2010 5-year est.).

Economy: Single-family building permits issued: 3 (2011); Multi-family building permits issued: 0 (2011); Employment by occupation: 8.4% management, 3.6% professional, 10.3% services, 14.2% sales, 3.6% farming, 8.8% construction, 7.1% production (2006-2010 5-year est.).

Income: Per capita income: $22,779 (2006-2010 5-year est.); Median household income: $45,848 (2006-2010 5-year est.); Average household income: $53,808 (2006-2010 5-year est.); Percent of households with income of $100,000 or more: 11.4% (2006-2010 5-year est.); Poverty rate: 9.7% (2006-2010 5-year est.).

Education: Percent of population age 25 and over with: High school diploma (including GED) or higher: 89.2% (2006-2010 5-year est.); Bachelor's degree or higher: 21.9% (2006-2010 5-year est.); Master's degree or higher: 9.0% (2006-2010 5-year est.).

Housing: Homeownership rate: 84.2% (2010); Median home value: $116,200 (2006-2010 5-year est.); Median contract rent: $342 per month (2006-2010 5-year est.); Median year structure built: 1966 (2006-2010 5-year est.).

Transportation: Commute to work: 91.8% car, 0.0% public transportation, 0.0% walk, 6.3% work from home (2006-2010 5-year est.); Travel time to work: 39.5% less than 15 minutes, 28.7% 15 to 30 minutes, 15.6% 30 to 45 minutes, 8.5% 45 to 60 minutes, 7.6% 60 minutes or more (2006-2010 5-year est.)

Additional Information Contacts
Greater Hazelton Chamber of Commerce . . . . (570) 455-1509
    http://www.hazletonchamber.org

ORBISONIA (borough). Covers a land area of 0.098 square miles and a water area of 0 square miles. Located at 40.24° N. Lat; 77.89° W. Long. Elevation is 636 feet.

Population: 319 (1990); 425 (2000); 428 (2010); Density: 4,385.1 persons per square mile (2010); Race: 99.1% White, 0.2% Black, 0.5% Asian, 0.0% American Indian/Alaska Native, 0.0% Native Hawaiian/Other Pacific Islander, 0.2% Other, 0.7% Hispanic of any race (2010); Average household size: 2.09 (2010); Median age: 44.6 (2010); Males per 100 females: 90.2 (2010); Marriage status: 17.5% never married, 37.0% now married, 34.6% widowed, 10.8% divorced (2006-2010 5-year est.); Foreign born: 0.4% (2006-2010 5-year est.); Ancestry (includes multiple ancestries): 36.1% German, 27.9% Irish, 6.4% American, 3.1% Pennsylvania German, 2.9% Italian (2006-2010 5-year est.).

Economy: Single-family building permits issued: 1 (2011); Multi-family building permits issued: 0 (2011); Employment by occupation: 4.3% management, 0.9% professional, 20.9% services, 20.9% sales, 3.3% farming, 12.8% construction, 12.8% production (2006-2010 5-year est.).

Income: Per capita income: $20,842 (2006-2010 5-year est.); Median household income: $37,500 (2006-2010 5-year est.); Average household income: $60,082 (2006-2010 5-year est.); Percent of households with income of $100,000 or more: 10.2% (2006-2010 5-year est.); Poverty rate: 10.5% (2006-2010 5-year est.).

Education: Percent of population age 25 and over with: High school diploma (including GED) or higher: 65.9% (2006-2010 5-year est.); Bachelor's degree or higher: 5.3% (2006-2010 5-year est.); Master's degree or higher: 2.7% (2006-2010 5-year est.).

Housing: Homeownership rate: 59.1% (2010); Median home value: $104,200 (2006-2010 5-year est.); Median contract rent: $363 per month (2006-2010 5-year est.); Median year structure built: before 1940 (2006-2010 5-year est.).

Newspapers: The Valley Log (Community news; Circulation 3,500)

Transportation: Commute to work: 85.1% car, 0.0% public transportation, 4.1% walk, 5.1% work from home (2006-2010 5-year est.); Travel time to work: 40.5% less than 15 minutes, 5.9% 15 to 30 minutes, 26.5% 30 to 45 minutes, 16.8% 45 to 60 minutes, 10.3% 60 minutes or more (2006-2010 5-year est.)

PENN (township). Covers a land area of 28.647 square miles and a water area of 5.948 square miles. Located at 40.38° N. Lat; 78.12° W. Long.

Population: 956 (1990); 1,054 (2000); 1,077 (2010); Density: 37.6 persons per square mile (2010); Race: 99.2% White, 0.5% Black, 0.0% Asian, 0.0% American Indian/Alaska Native, 0.0% Native Hawaiian/Other Pacific Islander, 0.3% Other, 0.5% Hispanic of any race (2010); Average

household size: 2.33 (2010); Median age: 48.4 (2010); Males per 100 females: 101.3 (2010); Marriage status: 23.9% never married, 55.2% now married, 8.5% widowed, 12.4% divorced (2006-2010 5-year est.); Foreign born: 0.9% (2006-2010 5-year est.); Ancestry (includes multiple ancestries): 45.8% German, 17.5% Irish, 12.5% English, 8.5% American, 3.9% Scotch-Irish (2006-2010 5-year est.).

Economy: Single-family building permits issued: 3 (2011); Multi-family building permits issued: 0 (2011); Employment by occupation: 8.1% management, 1.3% professional, 8.3% services, 23.2% sales, 2.4% farming, 15.1% construction, 9.0% production (2006-2010 5-year est.).

Income: Per capita income: $24,081 (2006-2010 5-year est.); Median household income: $45,625 (2006-2010 5-year est.); Average household income: $55,476 (2006-2010 5-year est.); Percent of households with income of $100,000 or more: 10.3% (2006-2010 5-year est.); Poverty rate: 9.9% (2006-2010 5-year est.).

Education: Percent of population age 25 and over with: High school diploma (including GED) or higher: 92.2% (2006-2010 5-year est.); Bachelor's degree or higher: 18.3% (2006-2010 5-year est.); Master's degree or higher: 5.8% (2006-2010 5-year est.).

Housing: Homeownership rate: 88.1% (2010); Median home value: $137,500 (2006-2010 5-year est.); Median contract rent: $375 per month (2006-2010 5-year est.); Median year structure built: 1982 (2006-2010 5-year est.).

Transportation: Commute to work: 89.5% car, 1.1% public transportation, 2.6% walk, 3.9% work from home (2006-2010 5-year est.); Travel time to work: 18.0% less than 15 minutes, 49.9% 15 to 30 minutes, 14.6% 30 to 45 minutes, 4.3% 45 to 60 minutes, 13.2% 60 minutes or more (2006-2010 5-year est.)

Additional Information Contacts
Huntingdon County Chamber of Commerce . . . . (814) 643-1110
  http://www.huntingdonchamber.com

PETERSBURG (borough). Covers a land area of 0.333 square miles and a water area of 0 square miles. Located at 40.57° N. Lat; 78.05° W. Long. Elevation is 738 feet.

History: Indian Caverns to Northwest at Spence Creek.

Population: 469 (1990); 455 (2000); 480 (2010); Density: 1,442.9 persons per square mile (2010); Race: 98.8% White, 0.0% Black, 0.2% Asian, 0.0% American Indian/Alaska Native, 0.0% Native Hawaiian/Other Pacific Islander, 1.0% Other, 1.3% Hispanic of any race (2010); Average household size: 2.74 (2010); Median age: 34.7 (2010); Males per 100 females: 81.1 (2010); Marriage status: 27.6% never married, 59.0% now married, 2.8% widowed, 10.6% divorced (2006-2010 5-year est.); Foreign born: 0.0% (2006-2010 5-year est.); Ancestry (includes multiple ancestries): 54.4% German, 21.6% Irish, 4.5% English, 4.1% Dutch, 3.2% Italian (2006-2010 5-year est.).

Economy: Single-family building permits issued: 0 (2011); Multi-family building permits issued: 0 (2011); Employment by occupation: 3.2% management, 0.0% professional, 21.8% services, 21.8% sales, 5.6% farming, 10.2% construction, 3.7% production (2006-2010 5-year est.).

Income: Per capita income: $13,880 (2006-2010 5-year est.); Median household income: $35,625 (2006-2010 5-year est.); Average household income: $39,378 (2006-2010 5-year est.); Percent of households with income of $100,000 or more: 1.1% (2006-2010 5-year est.); Poverty rate: 23.6% (2006-2010 5-year est.).

Education: Percent of population age 25 and over with: High school diploma (including GED) or higher: 87.9% (2006-2010 5-year est.); Bachelor's degree or higher: 6.4% (2006-2010 5-year est.); Master's degree or higher: 1.2% (2006-2010 5-year est.).

Housing: Homeownership rate: 62.8% (2010); Median home value: $80,000 (2006-2010 5-year est.); Median contract rent: $427 per month (2006-2010 5-year est.); Median year structure built: before 1940 (2006-2010 5-year est.).

Transportation: Commute to work: 92.1% car, 0.0% public transportation, 2.3% walk, 5.6% work from home (2006-2010 5-year est.); Travel time to work: 30.2% less than 15 minutes, 35.6% 15 to 30 minutes, 14.4% 30 to 45 minutes, 16.8% 45 to 60 minutes, 3.0% 60 minutes or more (2006-2010 5-year est.)

PORTER (township). Covers a land area of 35.249 square miles and a water area of 0.223 square miles. Located at 40.54° N. Lat; 78.10° W. Long.

Population: 1,942 (1990); 1,917 (2000); 1,968 (2010); Density: 55.8 persons per square mile (2010); Race: 98.5% White, 0.1% Black, 0.1% Asian, 0.3% American Indian/Alaska Native, 0.0% Native Hawaiian/Other

Pacific Islander, 1.0% Other, 1.3% Hispanic of any race (2010); Average household size: 2.40 (2010); Median age: 46.2 (2010); Males per 100 females: 100.2 (2010); Marriage status: 25.9% never married, 64.5% now married, 3.2% widowed, 6.5% divorced (2006-2010 5-year est.); Foreign born: 2.4% (2006-2010 5-year est.); Ancestry (includes multiple ancestries): 42.8% German, 16.5% Irish, 6.9% American, 6.1% English, 4.0% Pennsylvania German (2006-2010 5-year est.).

Economy: Single-family building permits issued: 6 (2011); Multi-family building permits issued: 0 (2011); Employment by occupation: 6.1% management, 3.2% professional, 5.3% services, 13.2% sales, 5.0% farming, 14.7% construction, 9.9% production (2006-2010 5-year est.).

Income: Per capita income: $22,858 (2006-2010 5-year est.); Median household income: $52,215 (2006-2010 5-year est.); Average household income: $58,503 (2006-2010 5-year est.); Percent of households with income of $100,000 or more: 10.1% (2006-2010 5-year est.); Poverty rate: 6.6% (2006-2010 5-year est.).

Education: Percent of population age 25 and over with: High school diploma (including GED) or higher: 90.6% (2006-2010 5-year est.); Bachelor's degree or higher: 15.8% (2006-2010 5-year est.); Master's degree or higher: 5.0% (2006-2010 5-year est.).

Housing: Homeownership rate: 84.7% (2010); Median home value: $127,400 (2006-2010 5-year est.); Median contract rent: $425 per month (2006-2010 5-year est.); Median year structure built: 1974 (2006-2010 5-year est.).

Transportation: Commute to work: 91.0% car, 0.0% public transportation, 2.8% walk, 4.6% work from home (2006-2010 5-year est.); Travel time to work: 30.3% less than 15 minutes, 33.8% 15 to 30 minutes, 16.5% 30 to 45 minutes, 12.2% 45 to 60 minutes, 7.1% 60 minutes or more (2006-2010 5-year est.)

Additional Information Contacts
Huntingdon County Chamber of Commerce . . . . (814) 643-1110
  http://www.huntingdonchamber.com

ROBERTSDALE (unincorporated postal area)
Zip Code: 16674

Covers a land area of 22.591 square miles and a water area of 0 square miles. Located at 40.18° N. Lat; 78.08° W. Long. Elevation is 1,785 feet. Population: 736 (2010); Density: 32.6 persons per square mile (2010); Race: 98.4% White, 0.1% Black, 0.4% Asian, 0.1% American Indian/Alaska Native, 0.0% Native Hawaiian/Other Pacific Islander, 1.0% Other, 0.4% Hispanic of any race (2010); Average household size: 2.51 (2010); Median age: 41.5 (2010); Males per 100 females: 91.2 (2010); Homeownership rate: 80.6% (2010)

ROCKHILL (borough). Covers a land area of 0.291 square miles and a water area of 0 square miles. Located at 40.24° N. Lat; 77.90° W. Long. Elevation is 620 feet.

Population: n/a (1990); n/a (2000); 371 (2010); Density: 1,274.6 persons per square mile (2010); Race: 98.7% White, 0.5% Black, 0.0% Asian, 0.0% American Indian/Alaska Native, 0.0% Native Hawaiian/Other Pacific Islander, 0.8% Other, 1.1% Hispanic of any race (2010); Average household size: 2.32 (2010); Median age: 44.3 (2010); Males per 100 females: 88.3 (2010); Marriage status: 26.1% never married, 49.2% now married, 16.3% widowed, 8.3% divorced (2006-2010 5-year est.); Foreign born: 0.0% (2006-2010 5-year est.); Ancestry (includes multiple ancestries): 59.2% German, 16.0% Irish, 7.3% English, 6.5% French, 6.3% Dutch (2006-2010 5-year est.).

Economy: Single-family building permits issued: 0 (2011); Multi-family building permits issued: 0 (2011); Employment by occupation: 2.8% management, 1.9% professional, 12.0% services, 15.7% sales, 5.6% farming, 17.6% construction, 17.6% production (2006-2010 5-year est.).

Income: Per capita income: $15,795 (2006-2010 5-year est.); Median household income: $35,833 (2006-2010 5-year est.); Average household income: $41,168 (2006-2010 5-year est.); Percent of households with income of $100,000 or more: 6.6% (2006-2010 5-year est.); Poverty rate: 5.0% (2006-2010 5-year est.).

Education: Percent of population age 25 and over with: High school diploma (including GED) or higher: 77.7% (2006-2010 5-year est.); Bachelor's degree or higher: 4.7% (2006-2010 5-year est.); Master's degree or higher: 0.0% (2006-2010 5-year est.).

Housing: Homeownership rate: 88.2% (2010); Median home value: $76,300 (2006-2010 5-year est.); Median contract rent: $417 per month (2006-2010 5-year est.); Median year structure built: 1942 (2006-2010 5-year est.).

Transportation: Commute to work: 93.5% car, 0.0% public transportation, 0.0% walk, 6.5% work from home (2006-2010 5-year est.); Travel time to work: 37.6% less than 15 minutes, 15.8% 15 to 30 minutes, 15.8% 30 to 45 minutes, 7.9% 45 to 60 minutes, 22.8% 60 minutes or more (2006-2010 5-year est.)

ROCKHILL FURNACE (unincorporated postal area)
Zip Code: 17249

Covers a land area of 0.312 square miles and a water area of 0 square miles. Located at 40.24° N. Lat; 77.89° W. Long. Population: 371 (2010); Density: 1,187.2 persons per square mile (2010); Race: 98.7% White, 0.5% Black, 0.0% Asian, 0.0% American Indian/Alaska Native, 0.0% Native Hawaiian/Other Pacific Islander, 0.8% Other, 1.1% Hispanic of any race (2010); Average household size: 2.32 (2010); Median age: 44.3 (2010); Males per 100 females: 88.3 (2010); Homeownership rate: 88.2% (2010)

SALTILLO (borough).
Covers a land area of 0.252 square miles and a water area of 0 square miles. Located at 40.21° N. Lat; 78.01° W. Long. Elevation is 794 feet.

Population: 347 (1990); 343 (2000); 346 (2010); Density: 1,373.4 persons per square mile (2010); Race: 98.6% White, 0.3% Black, 0.0% Asian, 0.6% American Indian/Alaska Native, 0.0% Native Hawaiian/Other Pacific Islander, 0.5% Other, 0.3% Hispanic of any race (2010); Average household size: 2.68 (2010); Median age: 37.9 (2010); Males per 100 females: 93.3 (2010); Marriage status: 18.1% never married, 58.9% now married, 8.3% widowed, 14.7% divorced (2006-2010 5-year est.); Foreign born: 0.9% (2006-2010 5-year est.); Ancestry (includes multiple ancestries): 32.0% German, 22.3% Irish, 7.8% English, 6.0% Italian, 5.6% American (2006-2010 5-year est.).
Economy: Single-family building permits issued: 0 (2011); Multi-family building permits issued: 0 (2011); Employment by occupation: 8.6% management, 0.0% professional, 9.4% services, 14.4% sales, 2.2% farming, 18.0% construction, 14.4% production (2006-2010 5-year est.).
Income: Per capita income: $19,814 (2006-2010 5-year est.); Median household income: $40,556 (2006-2010 5-year est.); Average household income: $45,031 (2006-2010 5-year est.); Percent of households with income of $100,000 or more: 4.3% (2006-2010 5-year est.); Poverty rate: 16.0% (2006-2010 5-year est.).
Education: Percent of population age 25 and over with: High school diploma (including GED) or higher: 83.3% (2006-2010 5-year est.); Bachelor's degree or higher: 6.8% (2006-2010 5-year est.); Master's degree or higher: 2.7% (2006-2010 5-year est.).
Housing: Homeownership rate: 84.5% (2010); Median home value: $94,000 (2006-2010 5-year est.); Median contract rent: $380 per month (2006-2010 5-year est.); Median year structure built: 1944 (2006-2010 5-year est.).
Transportation: Commute to work: 91.5% car, 0.0% public transportation, 2.3% walk, 0.0% work from home (2006-2010 5-year est.); Travel time to work: 26.9% less than 15 minutes, 1.5% 15 to 30 minutes, 51.5% 30 to 45 minutes, 4.6% 45 to 60 minutes, 15.4% 60 minutes or more (2006-2010 5-year est.)

SHADE GAP (borough).
Covers a land area of 0.032 square miles and a water area of 0 square miles. Located at 40.18° N. Lat; 77.87° W. Long. Elevation is 991 feet.
History: Covered bridge to South Tuscarora Tunnel, through Tuscarora Mountains on Pennsylvania Turnpike 6 miles South Southeast.
Population: 113 (1990); 97 (2000); 105 (2010); Density: 3,322.7 persons per square mile (2010); Race: 99.0% White, 0.0% Black, 0.0% Asian, 0.0% American Indian/Alaska Native, 0.0% Native Hawaiian/Other Pacific Islander, 1.0% Other, 0.0% Hispanic of any race (2010); Average household size: 2.39 (2010); Median age: 37.5 (2010); Males per 100 females: 90.9 (2010); Marriage status: 34.6% never married, 34.6% now married, 0.0% widowed, 30.8% divorced (2006-2010 5-year est.); Foreign born: 10.3% (2006-2010 5-year est.); Ancestry (includes multiple ancestries): 60.3% German, 29.5% Irish, 10.3% Polish, 7.7% Dutch, 6.4% Swedish (2006-2010 5-year est.).
Economy: Employment by occupation: 5.6% management, 0.0% professional, 8.3% services, 13.9% sales, 0.0% farming, 27.8% construction, 38.9% production (2006-2010 5-year est.).
Income: Per capita income: $17,959 (2006-2010 5-year est.); Median household income: $16,250 (2006-2010 5-year est.); Average household income: $43,354 (2006-2010 5-year est.); Percent of households with income of $100,000 or more: 17.9% (2006-2010 5-year est.); Poverty rate: 51.3% (2006-2010 5-year est.).
Education: Percent of population age 25 and over with: High school diploma (including GED) or higher: 94.1% (2006-2010 5-year est.); Bachelor's degree or higher: 0.0% (2006-2010 5-year est.); Master's degree or higher: 0.0% (2006-2010 5-year est.).

School District(s)
Southern Huntingdon County SD (KG-12)
2010-11 Enrollment: 1,313 . . . . (814) 447-5529
Housing: Homeownership rate: 79.5% (2010); Median home value: $105,000 (2006-2010 5-year est.); Median contract rent: n/a per month (2006-2010 5-year est.); Median year structure built: before 1940 (2006-2010 5-year est.).
Transportation: Commute to work: 94.4% car, 0.0% public transportation, 0.0% walk, 0.0% work from home (2006-2010 5-year est.); Travel time to work: 36.1% less than 15 minutes, 25.0% 15 to 30 minutes, 5.6% 30 to 45 minutes, 16.7% 45 to 60 minutes, 16.7% 60 minutes or more (2006-2010 5-year est.)

SHIRLEY (township).
Covers a land area of 58.418 square miles and a water area of 0.253 square miles. Located at 40.35° N. Lat; 77.84° W. Long.
Population: 2,494 (1990); 2,526 (2000); 2,524 (2010); Density: 43.2 persons per square mile (2010); Race: 97.8% White, 0.5% Black, 0.2% Asian, 0.2% American Indian/Alaska Native, 0.0% Native Hawaiian/Other Pacific Islander, 1.3% Other, 0.7% Hispanic of any race (2010); Average household size: 2.46 (2010); Median age: 43.6 (2010); Males per 100 females: 99.4 (2010); Marriage status: 18.9% never married, 58.4% now married, 9.3% widowed, 13.4% divorced (2006-2010 5-year est.); Foreign born: 0.0% (2006-2010 5-year est.); Ancestry (includes multiple ancestries): 39.4% German, 28.4% Irish, 8.5% Dutch, 8.0% American, 5.5% English (2006-2010 5-year est.).
Economy: Single-family building permits issued: 5 (2011); Multi-family building permits issued: 0 (2011); Employment by occupation: 6.6% management, 0.9% professional, 10.2% services, 15.8% sales, 2.9% farming, 14.8% construction, 9.6% production (2006-2010 5-year est.).
Income: Per capita income: $19,835 (2006-2010 5-year est.); Median household income: $34,257 (2006-2010 5-year est.); Average household income: $43,792 (2006-2010 5-year est.); Percent of households with income of $100,000 or more: 5.4% (2006-2010 5-year est.); Poverty rate: 8.6% (2006-2010 5-year est.).
Education: Percent of population age 25 and over with: High school diploma (including GED) or higher: 85.1% (2006-2010 5-year est.); Bachelor's degree or higher: 11.4% (2006-2010 5-year est.); Master's degree or higher: 3.3% (2006-2010 5-year est.).
Housing: Homeownership rate: 83.2% (2010); Median home value: $74,700 (2006-2010 5-year est.); Median contract rent: $373 per month (2006-2010 5-year est.); Median year structure built: 1977 (2006-2010 5-year est.).
Transportation: Commute to work: 83.6% car, 0.0% public transportation, 3.4% walk, 4.9% work from home (2006-2010 5-year est.); Travel time to work: 28.3% less than 15 minutes, 28.7% 15 to 30 minutes, 20.8% 30 to 45 minutes, 9.3% 45 to 60 minutes, 13.0% 60 minutes or more (2006-2010 5-year est.)

Additional Information Contacts
Huntingdon County Chamber of Commerce . . . . (814) 643-1110
http://www.huntingdonchamber.com

SHIRLEYSBURG (borough).
Covers a land area of 0.160 square miles and a water area of 0 square miles. Located at 40.30° N. Lat; 77.88° W. Long. Elevation is 600 feet.
Population: 140 (1990); 140 (2000); 150 (2010); Density: 939.0 persons per square mile (2010); Race: 96.7% White, 0.7% Black, 0.0% Asian, 0.7% American Indian/Alaska Native, 0.0% Native Hawaiian/Other Pacific Islander, 1.9% Other, 0.0% Hispanic of any race (2010); Average household size: 2.42 (2010); Median age: 39.0 (2010); Males per 100 females: 111.3 (2010); Marriage status: 26.6% never married, 50.0% now married, 17.0% widowed, 6.4% divorced (2006-2010 5-year est.); Foreign born: 0.0% (2006-2010 5-year est.); Ancestry (includes multiple ancestries): 41.5% German, 14.4% American, 11.0% Dutch, 9.3% Irish, 6.8% English (2006-2010 5-year est.).
Economy: Single-family building permits issued: 0 (2011); Multi-family building permits issued: 0 (2011); Employment by occupation: 8.7% management, 0.0% professional, 19.6% services, 0.0% sales, 0.0% farming, 17.4% construction, 23.9% production (2006-2010 5-year est.).

Income: Per capita income: $16,719 (2006-2010 5-year est.); Median household income: $32,143 (2006-2010 5-year est.); Average household income: $36,041 (2006-2010 5-year est.); Percent of households with income of $100,000 or more: n/a (2006-2010 5-year est.); Poverty rate: 15.3% (2006-2010 5-year est.).

Education: Percent of population age 25 and over with: High school diploma (including GED) or higher: 76.9% (2006-2010 5-year est.); Bachelor's degree or higher: 12.1% (2006-2010 5-year est.); Master's degree or higher: 0.0% (2006-2010 5-year est.).

Housing: Homeownership rate: 72.6% (2010); Median home value: $55,000 (2006-2010 5-year est.); Median contract rent: n/a per month (2006-2010 5-year est.); Median year structure built: before 1940 (2006-2010 5-year est.).

Transportation: Commute to work: 82.6% car, 0.0% public transportation, 0.0% walk, 0.0% work from home (2006-2010 5-year est.); Travel time to work: 41.3% less than 15 minutes, 26.1% 15 to 30 minutes, 26.1% 30 to 45 minutes, 0.0% 45 to 60 minutes, 6.5% 60 minutes or more (2006-2010 5-year est.)

SMITHFIELD (township). Covers a land area of 5.502 square miles and a water area of 0.101 square miles. Located at 40.48° N. Lat; 78.03° W. Long.

Population: 4,181 (1990); 4,466 (2000); 4,390 (2010); Density: 797.8 persons per square mile (2010); Race: 48.5% White, 43.2% Black, 0.4% Asian, 0.0% American Indian/Alaska Native, 0.0% Native Hawaiian/Other Pacific Islander, 7.9% Other, 8.0% Hispanic of any race (2010); Average household size: 2.11 (2010); Median age: 37.8 (2010); Males per 100 females: 581.7 (2010); Marriage status: 26.8% never married, 52.6% now married, 2.4% widowed, 18.2% divorced (2006-2010 5-year est.); Foreign born: 2.8% (2006-2010 5-year est.); Ancestry (includes multiple ancestries): 12.0% German, 5.9% Irish, 2.6% American, 1.5% Italian, 1.4% English (2006-2010 5-year est.).

Economy: Single-family building permits issued: 1 (2011); Multi-family building permits issued: 0 (2011); Employment by occupation: 5.2% management, 2.8% professional, 12.2% services, 16.5% sales, 3.4% farming, 6.9% construction, 8.2% production (2006-2010 5-year est.).

Income: Per capita income: $16,770 (2006-2010 5-year est.); Median household income: $33,250 (2006-2010 5-year est.); Average household income: $58,538 (2006-2010 5-year est.); Percent of households with income of $100,000 or more: 6.9% (2006-2010 5-year est.); Poverty rate: 12.2% (2006-2010 5-year est.).

Education: Percent of population age 25 and over with: High school diploma (including GED) or higher: 75.2% (2006-2010 5-year est.); Bachelor's degree or higher: 6.5% (2006-2010 5-year est.); Master's degree or higher: 4.1% (2006-2010 5-year est.).

Housing: Homeownership rate: 67.8% (2010); Median home value: $83,000 (2006-2010 5-year est.); Median contract rent: $391 per month (2006-2010 5-year est.); Median year structure built: 1944 (2006-2010 5-year est.).

Transportation: Commute to work: 88.8% car, 0.0% public transportation, 2.6% walk, 3.1% work from home (2006-2010 5-year est.); Travel time to work: 68.9% less than 15 minutes, 13.6% 15 to 30 minutes, 11.8% 30 to 45 minutes, 2.5% 45 to 60 minutes, 3.2% 60 minutes or more (2006-2010 5-year est.)

Additional Information Contacts

Huntingdon County Chamber of Commerce . . . . (814) 643-1110
  http://www.huntingdonchamber.com

SPRINGFIELD (township). Covers a land area of 27.517 square miles and a water area of 0 square miles. Located at 40.15° N. Lat; 77.95° W. Long.

Population: 507 (1990); 612 (2000); 654 (2010); Density: 23.8 persons per square mile (2010); Race: 99.4% White, 0.2% Black, 0.0% Asian, 0.0% American Indian/Alaska Native, 0.0% Native Hawaiian/Other Pacific Islander, 0.4% Other, 1.2% Hispanic of any race (2010); Average household size: 2.45 (2010); Median age: 43.1 (2010); Males per 100 females: 115.8 (2010); Marriage status: 17.2% never married, 70.1% now married, 2.3% widowed, 10.4% divorced (2006-2010 5-year est.); Foreign born: 1.4% (2006-2010 5-year est.); Ancestry (includes multiple ancestries): 46.2% German, 14.9% Irish, 11.1% American, 7.7% English, 2.1% Polish (2006-2010 5-year est.).

Economy: Single-family building permits issued: 1 (2011); Multi-family building permits issued: 0 (2011); Employment by occupation: 10.5% management, 3.2% professional, 8.8% services, 15.5% sales, 2.3% farming, 19.9% construction, 8.8% production (2006-2010 5-year est.).

Income: Per capita income: $27,800 (2006-2010 5-year est.); Median household income: $53,015 (2006-2010 5-year est.); Average household income: $72,637 (2006-2010 5-year est.); Percent of households with income of $100,000 or more: 16.6% (2006-2010 5-year est.); Poverty rate: 4.5% (2006-2010 5-year est.).

Education: Percent of population age 25 and over with: High school diploma (including GED) or higher: 81.7% (2006-2010 5-year est.); Bachelor's degree or higher: 14.6% (2006-2010 5-year est.); Master's degree or higher: 6.7% (2006-2010 5-year est.).

Housing: Homeownership rate: 87.2% (2010); Median home value: $136,900 (2006-2010 5-year est.); Median contract rent: $394 per month (2006-2010 5-year est.); Median year structure built: 1972 (2006-2010 5-year est.).

Transportation: Commute to work: 85.7% car, 0.0% public transportation, 3.8% walk, 1.8% work from home (2006-2010 5-year est.); Travel time to work: 17.3% less than 15 minutes, 34.2% 15 to 30 minutes, 14.9% 30 to 45 minutes, 10.1% 45 to 60 minutes, 23.5% 60 minutes or more (2006-2010 5-year est.)

SPRUCE CREEK (township). Aka Spruce. Covers a land area of 8.464 square miles and a water area of 0.082 square miles. Located at 40.63° N. Lat; 78.14° W. Long. Elevation is 761 feet.

Population: 281 (1990); 263 (2000); 240 (2010); Density: 28.4 persons per square mile (2010); Race: 97.9% White, 0.4% Black, 0.0% Asian, 0.0% American Indian/Alaska Native, 0.8% Native Hawaiian/Other Pacific Islander, 0.9% Other, 0.8% Hispanic of any race (2010); Average household size: 2.20 (2010); Median age: 48.2 (2010); Males per 100 females: 118.2 (2010); Marriage status: 17.0% never married, 62.4% now married, 9.6% widowed, 11.0% divorced (2006-2010 5-year est.); Foreign born: 0.4% (2006-2010 5-year est.); Ancestry (includes multiple ancestries): 60.9% German, 31.6% Irish, 15.4% English, 9.4% Italian, 7.9% Polish (2006-2010 5-year est.).

Economy: Single-family building permits issued: 0 (2011); Multi-family building permits issued: 0 (2011); Employment by occupation: 7.9% management, 1.6% professional, 7.9% services, 11.9% sales, 11.1% farming, 9.5% construction, 8.7% production (2006-2010 5-year est.).

Income: Per capita income: $24,777 (2006-2010 5-year est.); Median household income: $55,500 (2006-2010 5-year est.); Average household income: $58,882 (2006-2010 5-year est.); Percent of households with income of $100,000 or more: 14.3% (2006-2010 5-year est.); Poverty rate: 7.6% (2006-2010 5-year est.).

Education: Percent of population age 25 and over with: High school diploma (including GED) or higher: 92.6% (2006-2010 5-year est.); Bachelor's degree or higher: 27.1% (2006-2010 5-year est.); Master's degree or higher: 7.9% (2006-2010 5-year est.).

Housing: Homeownership rate: 86.3% (2010); Median home value: $131,300 (2006-2010 5-year est.); Median contract rent: $525 per month (2006-2010 5-year est.); Median year structure built: before 1940 (2006-2010 5-year est.).

Transportation: Commute to work: 94.2% car, 0.0% public transportation, 0.0% walk, 4.1% work from home (2006-2010 5-year est.); Travel time to work: 9.5% less than 15 minutes, 33.6% 15 to 30 minutes, 47.4% 30 to 45 minutes, 6.9% 45 to 60 minutes, 2.6% 60 minutes or more (2006-2010 5-year est.)

TELL (township). Covers a land area of 42.646 square miles and a water area of 0 square miles. Located at 40.26° N. Lat; 77.77° W. Long.

Population: 551 (1990); 648 (2000); 662 (2010); Density: 15.5 persons per square mile (2010); Race: 98.6% White, 0.6% Black, 0.2% Asian, 0.2% American Indian/Alaska Native, 0.0% Native Hawaiian/Other Pacific Islander, 0.4% Other, 0.6% Hispanic of any race (2010); Average household size: 2.56 (2010); Median age: 42.5 (2010); Males per 100 females: 108.2 (2010); Marriage status: 20.9% never married, 62.4% now married, 10.4% widowed, 6.3% divorced (2006-2010 5-year est.); Foreign born: 0.6% (2006-2010 5-year est.); Ancestry (includes multiple ancestries): 37.7% German, 16.1% Irish, 15.5% English, 5.7% Italian, 4.7% American (2006-2010 5-year est.).

Economy: Single-family building permits issued: 0 (2011); Multi-family building permits issued: 0 (2011); Employment by occupation: 8.2% management, 0.0% professional, 13.5% services, 15.0% sales, 4.5% farming, 19.9% construction, 18.7% production (2006-2010 5-year est.).

Income: Per capita income: $21,297 (2006-2010 5-year est.); Median household income: $49,167 (2006-2010 5-year est.); Average household income: $54,976 (2006-2010 5-year est.); Percent of households with

income of $100,000 or more: 10.9% (2006-2010 5-year est.); Poverty rate: 11.6% (2006-2010 5-year est.).

Education: Percent of population age 25 and over with: High school diploma (including GED) or higher: 80.0% (2006-2010 5-year est.); Bachelor's degree or higher: 8.5% (2006-2010 5-year est.); Master's degree or higher: 4.3% (2006-2010 5-year est.).

Housing: Homeownership rate: 85.1% (2010); Median home value: $109,600 (2006-2010 5-year est.); Median contract rent: n/a per month (2006-2010 5-year est.); Median year structure built: 1971 (2006-2010 5-year est.).

Transportation: Commute to work: 91.4% car, 0.0% public transportation, 4.1% walk, 2.2% work from home (2006-2010 5-year est.); Travel time to work: 23.0% less than 15 minutes, 30.3% 15 to 30 minutes, 11.9% 30 to 45 minutes, 11.5% 45 to 60 minutes, 23.4% 60 minutes or more (2006-2010 5-year est.)

THREE SPRINGS (borough). Aka Brownsville. Covers a land area of 1.233 square miles and a water area of 0 square miles. Located at 40.20° N. Lat; 77.98° W. Long. Elevation is 738 feet.

Population: 448 (1990); 445 (2000); 444 (2010); Density: 360.1 persons per square mile (2010); Race: 98.4% White, 0.0% Black, 0.2% Asian, 0.0% American Indian/Alaska Native, 0.0% Native Hawaiian/Other Pacific Islander, 1.4% Other, 0.2% Hispanic of any race (2010); Average household size: 2.25 (2010); Median age: 41.8 (2010); Males per 100 females: 88.9 (2010); Marriage status: 18.9% never married, 61.8% now married, 8.3% widowed, 11.0% divorced (2006-2010 5-year est.); Foreign born: 0.0% (2006-2010 5-year est.); Ancestry (includes multiple ancestries): 54.4% German, 10.2% English, 8.1% Italian, 7.8% Irish, 6.5% Dutch (2006-2010 5-year est.).

Economy: Single-family building permits issued: 0 (2011); Multi-family building permits issued: 0 (2011); Employment by occupation: 9.7% management, 0.0% professional, 14.5% services, 12.9% sales, 6.5% farming, 19.4% construction, 16.1% production (2006-2010 5-year est.).

Income: Per capita income: $17,181 (2006-2010 5-year est.); Median household income: $28,125 (2006-2010 5-year est.); Average household income: $37,998 (2006-2010 5-year est.); Percent of households with income of $100,000 or more: 8.8% (2006-2010 5-year est.); Poverty rate: 21.6% (2006-2010 5-year est.).

Education: Percent of population age 25 and over with: High school diploma (including GED) or higher: 79.1% (2006-2010 5-year est.); Bachelor's degree or higher: 7.6% (2006-2010 5-year est.); Master's degree or higher: 0.0% (2006-2010 5-year est.).

School District(s)

Southern Huntingdon County SD (KG-12)

    2010-11 Enrollment: 1,313 . . . . (814) 447-5529

Housing: Homeownership rate: 67.0% (2010); Median home value: $103,700 (2006-2010 5-year est.); Median contract rent: $363 per month (2006-2010 5-year est.); Median year structure built: 1958 (2006-2010 5-year est.).

Transportation: Commute to work: 90.8% car, 0.0% public transportation, 0.0% walk, 2.5% work from home (2006-2010 5-year est.); Travel time to work: 14.7% less than 15 minutes, 8.6% 15 to 30 minutes, 38.8% 30 to 45 minutes, 17.2% 45 to 60 minutes, 20.7% 60 minutes or more (2006-2010 5-year est.)

TODD (township). Covers a land area of 44.419 square miles and a water area of 0.020 square miles. Located at 40.26° N. Lat; 78.11° W. Long. Elevation is 1,132 feet.

Population: 889 (1990); 1,004 (2000); 952 (2010); Density: 21.4 persons per square mile (2010); Race: 96.5% White, 1.8% Black, 0.3% Asian, 0.1% American Indian/Alaska Native, 0.0% Native Hawaiian/Other Pacific Islander, 1.3% Other, 2.0% Hispanic of any race (2010); Average household size: 2.54 (2010); Median age: 44.6 (2010); Males per 100 females: 116.4 (2010); Marriage status: 20.5% never married, 62.9% now married, 8.8% widowed, 7.7% divorced (2006-2010 5-year est.); Foreign born: 0.3% (2006-2010 5-year est.); Ancestry (includes multiple ancestries): 38.9% German, 17.5% English, 16.2% Italian, 8.8% Irish, 8.2% Slovak (2006-2010 5-year est.).

Economy: Single-family building permits issued: 1 (2011); Multi-family building permits issued: 0 (2011); Employment by occupation: 7.0% management, 3.1% professional, 8.0% services, 4.5% sales, 3.5% farming, 18.1% construction, 11.7% production (2006-2010 5-year est.).

Income: Per capita income: $21,989 (2006-2010 5-year est.); Median household income: $46,250 (2006-2010 5-year est.); Average household income: $62,967 (2006-2010 5-year est.); Percent of households with

income of $100,000 or more: 19.0% (2006-2010 5-year est.); Poverty rate: 10.0% (2006-2010 5-year est.).

Education: Percent of population age 25 and over with: High school diploma (including GED) or higher: 84.3% (2006-2010 5-year est.); Bachelor's degree or higher: 4.1% (2006-2010 5-year est.); Master's degree or higher: 0.4% (2006-2010 5-year est.).

Housing: Homeownership rate: 87.0% (2010); Median home value: $127,700 (2006-2010 5-year est.); Median contract rent: $444 per month (2006-2010 5-year est.); Median year structure built: 1976 (2006-2010 5-year est.).

Transportation: Commute to work: 93.4% car, 0.0% public transportation, 3.8% walk, 2.8% work from home (2006-2010 5-year est.); Travel time to work: 9.5% less than 15 minutes, 8.8% 15 to 30 minutes, 43.3% 30 to 45 minutes, 14.4% 45 to 60 minutes, 24.1% 60 minutes or more (2006-2010 5-year est.)

UNION (township). Covers a land area of 39.139 square miles and a water area of 0.154 square miles. Located at 40.38° N. Lat; 77.98° W. Long.

History: Laid out 1849, incorporated 1867.

Population: 992 (1990); 1,005 (2000); 1,029 (2010); Density: 26.3 persons per square mile (2010); Race: 99.6% White, 0.1% Black, 0.1% Asian, 0.0% American Indian/Alaska Native, 0.0% Native Hawaiian/Other Pacific Islander, 0.2% Other, 0.3% Hispanic of any race (2010); Average household size: 2.46 (2010); Median age: 46.1 (2010); Males per 100 females: 105.0 (2010); Marriage status: 14.2% never married, 68.9% now married, 7.3% widowed, 9.6% divorced (2006-2010 5-year est.); Foreign born: 0.4% (2006-2010 5-year est.); Ancestry (includes multiple ancestries): 50.9% German, 21.0% Irish, 7.7% American, 6.3% Italian, 5.9% Dutch (2006-2010 5-year est.).

Economy: Single-family building permits issued: 5 (2011); Multi-family building permits issued: 0 (2011); Employment by occupation: 9.4% management, 2.2% professional, 9.1% services, 17.1% sales, 1.8% farming, 17.8% construction, 8.9% production (2006-2010 5-year est.).

Income: Per capita income: $18,925 (2006-2010 5-year est.); Median household income: $46,458 (2006-2010 5-year est.); Average household income: $51,006 (2006-2010 5-year est.); Percent of households with income of $100,000 or more: 10.0% (2006-2010 5-year est.); Poverty rate: 8.0% (2006-2010 5-year est.).

Education: Percent of population age 25 and over with: High school diploma (including GED) or higher: 86.3% (2006-2010 5-year est.); Bachelor's degree or higher: 10.6% (2006-2010 5-year est.); Master's degree or higher: 3.7% (2006-2010 5-year est.).

Housing: Homeownership rate: 88.3% (2010); Median home value: $97,000 (2006-2010 5-year est.); Median contract rent: n/a per month (2006-2010 5-year est.); Median year structure built: 1977 (2006-2010 5-year est.).

Transportation: Commute to work: 92.0% car, 0.0% public transportation, 0.5% walk, 4.8% work from home (2006-2010 5-year est.); Travel time to work: 19.9% less than 15 minutes, 37.8% 15 to 30 minutes, 12.9% 30 to 45 minutes, 8.1% 45 to 60 minutes, 21.3% 60 minutes or more (2006-2010 5-year est.)

Additional Information Contacts

Huntingdon County Chamber of Commerce . . . . (814) 643-1110
   http://www.huntingdonchamber.com

WALKER (township). Covers a land area of 18.511 square miles and a water area of <.001 square miles. Located at 40.47° N. Lat; 78.12° W. Long.

Population: 1,515 (1990); 1,747 (2000); 1,947 (2010); Density: 105.2 persons per square mile (2010); Race: 98.4% White, 0.2% Black, 0.7% Asian, 0.2% American Indian/Alaska Native, 0.0% Native Hawaiian/Other Pacific Islander, 0.5% Other, 0.5% Hispanic of any race (2010); Average household size: 2.52 (2010); Median age: 44.2 (2010); Males per 100 females: 95.5 (2010); Marriage status: 18.0% never married, 71.5% now married, 5.9% widowed, 4.7% divorced (2006-2010 5-year est.); Foreign born: 0.2% (2006-2010 5-year est.); Ancestry (includes multiple ancestries): 44.4% German, 18.1% Irish, 11.7% English, 8.1% American, 5.5% Scotch-Irish (2006-2010 5-year est.).

Economy: Single-family building permits issued: 4 (2011); Multi-family building permits issued: 0 (2011); Employment by occupation: 8.7% management, 3.8% professional, 7.7% services, 18.4% sales, 5.0% farming, 8.3% construction, 3.9% production (2006-2010 5-year est.).

Income: Per capita income: $26,037 (2006-2010 5-year est.); Median household income: $55,984 (2006-2010 5-year est.); Average household

income: $66,210 (2006-2010 5-year est.); Percent of households with income of $100,000 or more: 16.0% (2006-2010 5-year est.); Poverty rate: 4.8% (2006-2010 5-year est.).

Education: Percent of population age 25 and over with: High school diploma (including GED) or higher: 94.8% (2006-2010 5-year est.); Bachelor's degree or higher: 20.8% (2006-2010 5-year est.); Master's degree or higher: 8.0% (2006-2010 5-year est.).

Housing: Homeownership rate: 86.3% (2010); Median home value: $138,900 (2006-2010 5-year est.); Median contract rent: $432 per month (2006-2010 5-year est.); Median year structure built: 1972 (2006-2010 5-year est.).

Transportation: Commute to work: 93.9% car, 0.6% public transportation, 0.7% walk, 2.7% work from home (2006-2010 5-year est.); Travel time to work: 52.4% less than 15 minutes, 24.0% 15 to 30 minutes, 11.8% 30 to 45 minutes, 8.1% 45 to 60 minutes, 3.7% 60 minutes or more (2006-2010 5-year est.)

Additional Information Contacts

Huntingdon County Chamber of Commerce . . . . (814) 643-1110
  http://www.huntingdonchamber.com

WARRIORS MARK (township). Covers a land area of 29.361 square miles and a water area of 0 square miles. Located at 40.69° N. Lat; 78.15° W. Long. Elevation is 1,089 feet.

Population: 1,362 (1990); 1,635 (2000); 1,796 (2010); Density: 61.2 persons per square mile (2010); Race: 98.9% White, 0.6% Black, 0.0% Asian, 0.1% American Indian/Alaska Native, 0.0% Native Hawaiian/Other Pacific Islander, 0.4% Other, 0.4% Hispanic of any race (2010); Average household size: 2.56 (2010); Median age: 42.4 (2010); Males per 100 females: 96.9 (2010); Marriage status: 20.4% never married, 63.6% now married, 6.9% widowed, 9.1% divorced (2006-2010 5-year est.); Foreign born: 0.3% (2006-2010 5-year est.); Ancestry (includes multiple ancestries): 43.7% German, 22.5% Irish, 7.8% English, 7.6% American, 5.5% Italian (2006-2010 5-year est.).

Economy: Single-family building permits issued: 8 (2011); Multi-family building permits issued: 0 (2011); Employment by occupation: 11.7% management, 7.4% professional, 10.0% services, 15.1% sales, 1.6% farming, 12.5% construction, 6.7% production (2006-2010 5-year est.).

Income: Per capita income: $26,181 (2006-2010 5-year est.); Median household income: $53,472 (2006-2010 5-year est.); Average household income: $64,646 (2006-2010 5-year est.); Percent of households with income of $100,000 or more: 16.8% (2006-2010 5-year est.); Poverty rate: 8.2% (2006-2010 5-year est.).

Education: Percent of population age 25 and over with: High school diploma (including GED) or higher: 93.9% (2006-2010 5-year est.); Bachelor's degree or higher: 24.6% (2006-2010 5-year est.); Master's degree or higher: 9.0% (2006-2010 5-year est.).

Housing: Homeownership rate: 84.2% (2010); Median home value: $161,700 (2006-2010 5-year est.); Median contract rent: $396 per month (2006-2010 5-year est.); Median year structure built: 1973 (2006-2010 5-year est.).

Transportation: Commute to work: 95.7% car, 0.0% public transportation, 1.6% walk, 1.4% work from home (2006-2010 5-year est.); Travel time to work: 15.4% less than 15 minutes, 39.2% 15 to 30 minutes, 34.6% 30 to 45 minutes, 7.5% 45 to 60 minutes, 3.3% 60 minutes or more (2006-2010 5-year est.)

Additional Information Contacts

Tyrone Area Chamber of Commerce . . . . (814) 684-0736
  http://www.tyronechamber.com

WEST (township). Covers a land area of 31.074 square miles and a water area of 0.016 square miles. Located at 40.63° N. Lat; 77.99° W. Long.

Population: 572 (1990); 528 (2000); 571 (2010); Density: 18.4 persons per square mile (2010); Race: 99.5% White, 0.0% Black, 0.2% Asian, 0.0% American Indian/Alaska Native, 0.0% Native Hawaiian/Other Pacific Islander, 0.3% Other, 1.8% Hispanic of any race (2010); Average household size: 2.60 (2010); Median age: 41.6 (2010); Males per 100 females: 98.3 (2010); Marriage status: 18.8% never married, 71.3% now married, 7.9% widowed, 2.1% divorced (2006-2010 5-year est.); Foreign born: 0.9% (2006-2010 5-year est.); Ancestry (includes multiple ancestries): 40.7% German, 15.1% Irish, 14.4% English, 11.9% Scotch-Irish, 8.5% American (2006-2010 5-year est.).

Economy: Single-family building permits issued: 2 (2011); Multi-family building permits issued: 0 (2011); Employment by occupation: 19.2%

management, 2.5% professional, 7.4% services, 13.3% sales, 3.4% farming, 19.7% construction, 13.3% production (2006-2010 5-year est.).

Income: Per capita income: $21,866 (2006-2010 5-year est.); Median household income: $42,969 (2006-2010 5-year est.); Average household income: $53,137 (2006-2010 5-year est.); Percent of households with income of $100,000 or more: 6.7% (2006-2010 5-year est.); Poverty rate: 1.4% (2006-2010 5-year est.).

Education: Percent of population age 25 and over with: High school diploma (including GED) or higher: 86.2% (2006-2010 5-year est.); Bachelor's degree or higher: 15.1% (2006-2010 5-year est.); Master's degree or higher: 3.9% (2006-2010 5-year est.).

Housing: Homeownership rate: 80.0% (2010); Median home value: $109,300 (2006-2010 5-year est.); Median contract rent: $350 per month (2006-2010 5-year est.); Median year structure built: 1955 (2006-2010 5-year est.).

Transportation: Commute to work: 78.3% car, 0.0% public transportation, 1.5% walk, 20.2% work from home (2006-2010 5-year est.); Travel time to work: 5.6% less than 15 minutes, 27.2% 15 to 30 minutes, 51.9% 30 to 45 minutes, 8.6% 45 to 60 minutes, 6.8% 60 minutes or more (2006-2010 5-year est.)

WOOD (township). Covers a land area of 16.452 square miles and a water area of 0 square miles. Located at 40.18° N. Lat; 78.10° W. Long.

Population: 727 (1990); 713 (2000); 708 (2010); Density: 43.0 persons per square mile (2010); Race: 98.3% White, 0.3% Black, 0.3% Asian, 0.1% American Indian/Alaska Native, 0.0% Native Hawaiian/Other Pacific Islander, 1.0% Other, 0.4% Hispanic of any race (2010); Average household size: 2.54 (2010); Median age: 40.6 (2010); Males per 100 females: 93.4 (2010); Marriage status: 25.1% never married, 54.1% now married, 4.3% widowed, 16.5% divorced (2006-2010 5-year est.); Foreign born: 0.0% (2006-2010 5-year est.); Ancestry (includes multiple ancestries): 36.4% German, 10.8% Irish, 7.1% English, 5.6% Italian, 4.2% American (2006-2010 5-year est.).

Economy: Single-family building permits issued: 3 (2011); Multi-family building permits issued: 0 (2011); Employment by occupation: 11.8% management, 0.0% professional, 5.9% services, 5.1% sales, 5.9% farming, 31.6% construction, 20.6% production (2006-2010 5-year est.).

Income: Per capita income: $12,611 (2006-2010 5-year est.); Median household income: $30,132 (2006-2010 5-year est.); Average household income: $32,251 (2006-2010 5-year est.); Percent of households with income of $100,000 or more: n/a (2006-2010 5-year est.); Poverty rate: 27.3% (2006-2010 5-year est.).

Education: Percent of population age 25 and over with: High school diploma (including GED) or higher: 73.9% (2006-2010 5-year est.); Bachelor's degree or higher: 4.0% (2006-2010 5-year est.); Master's degree or higher: 0.9% (2006-2010 5-year est.).

Housing: Homeownership rate: 78.5% (2010); Median home value: $65,400 (2006-2010 5-year est.); Median contract rent: $363 per month (2006-2010 5-year est.); Median year structure built: before 1940 (2006-2010 5-year est.).

Transportation: Commute to work: 92.6% car, 0.0% public transportation, 0.0% walk, 3.7% work from home (2006-2010 5-year est.); Travel time to work: 11.5% less than 15 minutes, 30.5% 15 to 30 minutes, 26.0% 30 to 45 minutes, 6.1% 45 to 60 minutes, 26.0% 60 minutes or more (2006-2010 5-year est.)

Indiana County

Located in west central Pennsylvania; bounded on the south by the Conemaugh River; drained by tributaries of the Allegheny River. Covers a land area of 827.030 square miles, a water area of 7.264 square miles, and is located in the Eastern Time Zone at 40.65° N. Lat., 79.09° W. Long. The county was founded in 1803. County seat is Indiana.

Indiana County is part of the Indiana, PA Micropolitan Statistical Area. The entire metro area includes: Indiana County, PA

Weather Station: Indiana 3 SE   Elevation: 1,102 feet

	Jan	Feb	Mar	Apr	May	Jun	Jul	Aug	Sep	Oct	Nov	Dec
High	36	40	50	62	71	79	82	81	74	63	52	40
Low	20	22	28	37	46	55	59	59	52	41	33	24
Precip	3.4	2.8	4.0	3.9	4.3	4.6	4.9	4.2	4.0	3.1	4.1	3.4
Snow	15.2	10.3	8.6	1.7	tr	0.0	0.0	0.0	0.0	0.2	2.8	9.7

High and Low temperatures in degrees Fahrenheit; Precipitation and Snow in inches

Population: 89,994 (1990); 89,605 (2000); 88,880 (2010); Race: 94.9% White, 2.7% Black, 0.9% Asian, 0.1% American Indian/Alaska Native, 0.0% Native Hawaiian/Other Pacific Islander, 1.4% Other, 1.1% Hispanic of any race (2010); Density: 107.5 persons per square mile (2010); Average household size: 2.39 (2010); Median age: 38.3 (2010); Males per 100 females: 98.9 (2010).

Religion: Six largest groups: 13.9% Catholicism, 10.2% Methodist/Pietist, 4.2% Presbyterian-Reformed, 3.7% Lutheran, 3.7% European Free-Church, 3.6% Non-Denominational (2010)

Economy: Unemployment rate: 8.5% (August 2012); Total civilian labor force: 48,351 (August 2012); Leading industries: 17.4% health care and social assistance; 16.6% retail trade; 11.0% accommodation & food services (2010); Farms: 1,544 totaling 187,711 acres (2007); Companies that employ 500 or more persons: 2 (2010); Companies that employ 100 to 499 persons: 45 (2010); Companies that employ less than 100 persons: 1,884 (2010); Black-owned businesses: n/a (2007); Hispanic-owned businesses: n/a (2007); Asian-owned businesses: n/a (2007); Women-owned businesses: 1,403 (2007); Retail sales per capita: $12,578 (2010). Single-family building permits issued: 31 (2011); Multi-family building permits issued: 42 (2011).

Income: Per capita income: $20,587 (2006-2010 5-year est.); Median household income: $40,225 (2006-2010 5-year est.); Average household income: $51,614 (2006-2010 5-year est.); Percent of households with income of $100,000 or more: 10.3% (2006-2010 5-year est.); Poverty rate: 18.6% (2006-2010 5-year est.); Bankruptcy rate: 1.75% (2011).

Education: Percent of population age 25 and over with: High school diploma (including GED) or higher: 86.7% (2006-2010 5-year est.); Bachelor's degree or higher: 19.2% (2006-2010 5-year est.); Master's degree or higher: 6.9% (2006-2010 5-year est.).

Housing: Homeownership rate: 68.8% (2010); Median home value: $98,200 (2006-2010 5-year est.); Median contract rent: $478 per month (2006-2010 5-year est.); Median year structure built: 1968 (2006-2010 5-year est.)

Health: Birth rate: 99.4 per 10,000 population (2011); Death rate: 97.5 per 10,000 population (2011); Age-adjusted cancer mortality rate: 159.0 deaths per 100,000 population (2009); Number of physicians: 13.6 per 10,000 population (2010); Hospital beds: 18.5 per 10,000 population (2008); Hospital admissions: 928.3 per 10,000 population (2008).

Environment: Air Quality Index: 84.9% good, 13.7% moderate, 1.4% unhealthy for sensitive individuals, 0.0% unhealthy (percent of days in 2011)

Elections: 2012 Presidential election results: 39.8% Obama, 58.6% Romney

National and State Parks: Conemaugh Lake National Recreation Area; Yellow Creek State Park

Additional Information Contacts

Indiana County Government . . . . (724) 465-3805
   http://www.countyofindiana.org
Armstrong County Chamber of Commerce . . . . (724) 543-1305
   http://www.armstrongchamber.org
Indiana County Chamber of Commerce . . . . (724) 465-2511
   http://www.indianapa.com/chamber

Indiana County Communities

ALVERDA (unincorporated postal area)

Zip Code: 15710

Covers a land area of 1.665 square miles and a water area of 0.004 square miles. Located at 40.64° N. Lat; 78.87° W. Long. Elevation is 1,916 feet. Population: 266 (2010); Density: 159.7 persons per square mile (2010); Race: 99.2% White, 0.4% Black, 0.0% Asian, 0.0% American Indian/Alaska Native, 0.0% Native Hawaiian/Other Pacific Islander, 0.4% Other, 0.4% Hispanic of any race (2010); Average household size: 2.32 (2010); Median age: 43.5 (2010); Males per 100 females: 88.7 (2010); Homeownership rate: 82.4% (2010)

ARCADIA (unincorporated postal area)

Zip Code: 15712

Covers a land area of 1.622 square miles and a water area of 0 square miles. Located at 40.79° N. Lat; 78.84° W. Long. Population: 151 (2010); Density: 93.1 persons per square mile (2010); Race: 100.0% White, 0.0% Black, 0.0% Asian, 0.0% American Indian/Alaska Native, 0.0% Native Hawaiian/Other Pacific Islander, 0.0% Other, 0.7% Hispanic of any race (2010); Average household size: 2.60 (2010);

Median age: 43.8 (2010); Males per 100 females: 112.7 (2010); Homeownership rate: 87.9% (2010)

ARMAGH (borough). Covers a land area of 0.057 square miles and a water area of 0 square miles. Located at 40.45° N. Lat; 79.03° W. Long. Elevation is 1,529 feet.

Population: 104 (1990); 131 (2000); 122 (2010); Density: 2,125.7 persons per square mile (2010); Race: 97.5% White, 0.8% Black, 0.0% Asian, 0.8% American Indian/Alaska Native, 0.0% Native Hawaiian/Other Pacific Islander, 0.9% Other, 0.8% Hispanic of any race (2010); Average household size: 2.39 (2010); Median age: 45.0 (2010); Males per 100 females: 84.8 (2010); Marriage status: 23.6% never married, 63.6% now married, 7.3% widowed, 5.5% divorced (2006-2010 5-year est.); Foreign born: 0.0% (2006-2010 5-year est.); Ancestry (includes multiple ancestries): 41.3% German, 34.9% Irish, 19.0% Italian, 12.7% American, 6.3% Scotch-Irish (2006-2010 5-year est.).

Economy: Employment by occupation: 0.0% management, 0.0% professional, 21.1% services, 15.8% sales, 0.0% farming, 10.5% construction, 5.3% production (2006-2010 5-year est.).

Income: Per capita income: $14,844 (2006-2010 5-year est.); Median household income: $38,125 (2006-2010 5-year est.); Average household income: $40,972 (2006-2010 5-year est.); Percent of households with income of $100,000 or more: n/a (2006-2010 5-year est.); Poverty rate: 22.2% (2006-2010 5-year est.).

Education: Percent of population age 25 and over with: High school diploma (including GED) or higher: 89.6% (2006-2010 5-year est.); Bachelor's degree or higher: 0.0% (2006-2010 5-year est.); Master's degree or higher: 0.0% (2006-2010 5-year est.).

School District(s)

United SD (KG-12)
   2010-11 Enrollment: 1,292 . . . . (814) 446-5615

Housing: Homeownership rate: 74.5% (2010); Median home value: $121,900 (2006-2010 5-year est.); Median contract rent: n/a per month (2006-2010 5-year est.); Median year structure built: before 1940 (2006-2010 5-year est.).

Transportation: Commute to work: 88.9% car, 0.0% public transportation, 0.0% walk, 11.1% work from home (2006-2010 5-year est.); Travel time to work: 56.3% less than 15 minutes, 43.8% 15 to 30 minutes, 0.0% 30 to 45 minutes, 0.0% 45 to 60 minutes, 0.0% 60 minutes or more (2006-2010 5-year est.)

ARMSTRONG (township). Covers a land area of 37.601 square miles and a water area of 0.146 square miles. Located at 40.63° N. Lat; 79.28° W. Long.

Population: 3,048 (1990); 3,090 (2000); 2,998 (2010); Density: 79.7 persons per square mile (2010); Race: 98.5% White, 0.3% Black, 0.5% Asian, 0.1% American Indian/Alaska Native, 0.0% Native Hawaiian/Other Pacific Islander, 0.6% Other, 0.1% Hispanic of any race (2010); Average household size: 2.44 (2010); Median age: 45.7 (2010); Males per 100 females: 98.0 (2010); Marriage status: 20.1% never married, 68.5% now married, 4.3% widowed, 7.1% divorced (2006-2010 5-year est.); Foreign born: 1.3% (2006-2010 5-year est.); Ancestry (includes multiple ancestries): 42.9% German, 18.6% Irish, 9.7% English, 7.0% Scotch-Irish, 5.5% Italian (2006-2010 5-year est.).

Economy: Single-family building permits issued: 8 (2011); Multi-family building permits issued: 0 (2011); Employment by occupation: 6.4% management, 5.8% professional, 5.1% services, 21.5% sales, 3.2% farming, 15.0% construction, 9.3% production (2006-2010 5-year est.).

Income: Per capita income: $23,895 (2006-2010 5-year est.); Median household income: $58,214 (2006-2010 5-year est.); Average household income: $60,214 (2006-2010 5-year est.); Percent of households with income of $100,000 or more: 13.7% (2006-2010 5-year est.); Poverty rate: 6.1% (2006-2010 5-year est.).

Education: Percent of population age 25 and over with: High school diploma (including GED) or higher: 89.5% (2006-2010 5-year est.); Bachelor's degree or higher: 23.8% (2006-2010 5-year est.); Master's degree or higher: 7.3% (2006-2010 5-year est.).

Housing: Homeownership rate: 81.4% (2010); Median home value: $111,800 (2006-2010 5-year est.); Median contract rent: $325 per month (2006-2010 5-year est.); Median year structure built: 1979 (2006-2010 5-year est.).

Transportation: Commute to work: 92.0% car, 0.7% public transportation, 1.3% walk, 3.9% work from home (2006-2010 5-year est.); Travel time to work: 30.2% less than 15 minutes, 49.5% 15 to 30 minutes, 6.4% 30 to 45

minutes, 4.6% 45 to 60 minutes, 9.4% 60 minutes or more (2006-2010 5-year est.)

Additional Information Contacts

Armstrong County Chamber of Commerce . . . . (724) 543-1305
http://www.armstrongchamber.org

Armstrong Township . . . . (724) 465-4755
http://www.armstrongtwp.org

AULTMAN (unincorporated postal area)

Zip Code: 15713

Covers a land area of 1.314 square miles and a water area of 0 square miles. Located at 40.56° N. Lat; 79.26° W. Long. Elevation is 1,119 feet.
Population: 294 (2010); Density: 223.6 persons per square mile (2010); Race: 99.0% White, 0.0% Black, 0.3% Asian, 0.0% American Indian/Alaska Native, 0.0% Native Hawaiian/Other Pacific Islander, 0.7% Other, 0.0% Hispanic of any race (2010); Average household size: 2.67 (2010); Median age: 32.9 (2010); Males per 100 females: 87.3 (2010); Homeownership rate: 81.8% (2010)

BANKS (township).

Covers a land area of 31.746 square miles and a water area of 0.120 square miles. Located at 40.85° N. Lat; 78.85° W. Long.

Population: 995 (1990); 997 (2000); 1,018 (2010); Density: 32.1 persons per square mile (2010); Race: 98.9% White, 0.2% Black, 0.0% Asian, 0.5% American Indian/Alaska Native, 0.0% Native Hawaiian/Other Pacific Islander, 0.4% Other, 1.4% Hispanic of any race (2010); Average household size: 2.74 (2010); Median age: 39.4 (2010); Males per 100 females: 102.8 (2010); Marriage status: 22.0% never married, 63.1% now married, 4.4% widowed, 10.5% divorced (2006-2010 5-year est.); Foreign born: 0.8% (2006-2010 5-year est.); Ancestry (includes multiple ancestries): 24.7% German, 21.8% Irish, 9.1% Polish, 6.9% Italian, 6.4% American (2006-2010 5-year est.).
Economy: Employment by occupation: 6.2% management, 1.9% professional, 15.8% services, 18.3% sales, 1.9% farming, 18.9% construction, 6.8% production (2006-2010 5-year est.).
Income: Per capita income: $20,406 (2006-2010 5-year est.); Median household income: $40,430 (2006-2010 5-year est.); Average household income: $50,271 (2006-2010 5-year est.); Percent of households with income of $100,000 or more: 6.3% (2006-2010 5-year est.); Poverty rate: 11.9% (2006-2010 5-year est.).
Education: Percent of population age 25 and over with: High school diploma (including GED) or higher: 78.5% (2006-2010 5-year est.); Bachelor's degree or higher: 7.1% (2006-2010 5-year est.); Master's degree or higher: 3.5% (2006-2010 5-year est.).
Housing: Homeownership rate: 86.5% (2010); Median home value: $76,800 (2006-2010 5-year est.); Median contract rent: $300 per month (2006-2010 5-year est.); Median year structure built: 1965 (2006-2010 5-year est.).
Transportation: Commute to work: 92.2% car, 0.9% public transportation, 0.6% walk, 5.0% work from home (2006-2010 5-year est.); Travel time to work: 8.9% less than 15 minutes, 42.2% 15 to 30 minutes, 21.1% 30 to 45 minutes, 11.9% 45 to 60 minutes, 15.8% 60 minutes or more (2006-2010 5-year est.)

Additional Information Contacts

Indiana County Chamber of Commerce . . . . (724) 465-2511
http://www.indianapa.com/chamber

BEYER (unincorporated postal area)

Zip Code: 16211

Covers a land area of 1.012 square miles and a water area of 0 square miles. Located at 40.79° N. Lat; 79.20° W. Long. Elevation is 1,148 feet.
Population: 104 (2010); Density: 102.7 persons per square mile (2010); Race: 97.1% White, 0.0% Black, 0.0% Asian, 0.0% American Indian/Alaska Native, 0.0% Native Hawaiian/Other Pacific Islander, 2.9% Other, 0.0% Hispanic of any race (2010); Average household size: 2.48 (2010); Median age: 51.0 (2010); Males per 100 females: 116.7 (2010); Homeownership rate: 81.0% (2010)

BLACK LICK (CDP).

Covers a land area of 2.571 square miles and a water area of 0.018 square miles. Located at 40.47° N. Lat; 79.19° W. Long. Elevation is 935 feet.
Population: 1,382 (1990); 1,438 (2000); 1,462 (2010); Density: 568.6 persons per square mile (2010); Race: 95.8% White, 2.5% Black, 0.1% Asian, 0.3% American Indian/Alaska Native, 0.0% Native Hawaiian/Other Pacific Islander, 1.3% Other, 1.8% Hispanic of any race (2010); Average

household size: 2.41 (2010); Median age: 41.4 (2010); Males per 100 females: 90.6 (2010); Marriage status: 29.2% never married, 60.0% now married, 4.9% widowed, 5.9% divorced (2006-2010 5-year est.); Foreign born: 0.0% (2006-2010 5-year est.); Ancestry (includes multiple ancestries): 23.5% Irish, 19.4% Polish, 13.9% German, 4.3% American, 3.4% Slovak (2006-2010 5-year est.).
Economy: Employment by occupation: 3.8% management, 2.3% professional, 15.1% services, 22.6% sales, 2.6% farming, 28.5% construction, 20.6% production (2006-2010 5-year est.).
Income: Per capita income: $18,098 (2006-2010 5-year est.); Median household income: $45,250 (2006-2010 5-year est.); Average household income: $46,218 (2006-2010 5-year est.); Percent of households with income of $100,000 or more: 1.6% (2006-2010 5-year est.); Poverty rate: 29.3% (2006-2010 5-year est.).
Education: Percent of population age 25 and over with: High school diploma (including GED) or higher: 80.4% (2006-2010 5-year est.); Bachelor's degree or higher: 3.9% (2006-2010 5-year est.); Master's degree or higher: 2.3% (2006-2010 5-year est.).
Housing: Homeownership rate: 68.2% (2010); Median home value: $86,400 (2006-2010 5-year est.); Median contract rent: $386 per month (2006-2010 5-year est.); Median year structure built: 1974 (2006-2010 5-year est.).
Transportation: Commute to work: 100.0% car, 0.0% public transportation, 0.0% walk, 0.0% work from home (2006-2010 5-year est.); Travel time to work: 29.7% less than 15 minutes, 50.1% 15 to 30 minutes, 11.9% 30 to 45 minutes, 2.3% 45 to 60 minutes, 6.0% 60 minutes or more (2006-2010 5-year est.)

Additional Information Contacts

Indiana County Chamber of Commerce . . . . (724) 465-2511
http://www.indianapa.com/chamber

BLACK LICK (township).

Covers a land area of 27.327 square miles and a water area of 0.612 square miles. Located at 40.50° N. Lat; 79.25° W. Long. Elevation is 935 feet.
Population: 1,329 (1990); 1,317 (2000); 1,237 (2010); Density: 45.3 persons per square mile (2010); Race: 98.9% White, 0.4% Black, 0.2% Asian, 0.0% American Indian/Alaska Native, 0.0% Native Hawaiian/Other Pacific Islander, 0.5% Other, 0.7% Hispanic of any race (2010); Average household size: 2.43 (2010); Median age: 47.1 (2010); Males per 100 females: 97.9 (2010); Marriage status: 18.9% never married, 66.8% now married, 8.4% widowed, 5.9% divorced (2006-2010 5-year est.); Foreign born: 0.0% (2006-2010 5-year est.); Ancestry (includes multiple ancestries): 34.6% German, 30.3% Irish, 13.4% English, 12.6% Italian, 7.1% Slovak (2006-2010 5-year est.).
Economy: Employment by occupation: 13.2% management, 3.5% professional, 10.5% services, 12.5% sales, 5.4% farming, 18.6% construction, 12.4% production (2006-2010 5-year est.).
Income: Per capita income: $25,800 (2006-2010 5-year est.); Median household income: $49,907 (2006-2010 5-year est.); Average household income: $59,837 (2006-2010 5-year est.); Percent of households with income of $100,000 or more: 17.4% (2006-2010 5-year est.); Poverty rate: 7.5% (2006-2010 5-year est.).
Education: Percent of population age 25 and over with: High school diploma (including GED) or higher: 92.9% (2006-2010 5-year est.); Bachelor's degree or higher: 15.4% (2006-2010 5-year est.); Master's degree or higher: 5.5% (2006-2010 5-year est.).
Housing: Homeownership rate: 85.8% (2010); Median home value: $116,200 (2006-2010 5-year est.); Median contract rent: $449 per month (2006-2010 5-year est.); Median year structure built: 1969 (2006-2010 5-year est.).
Transportation: Commute to work: 90.0% car, 0.0% public transportation, 0.5% walk, 8.9% work from home (2006-2010 5-year est.); Travel time to work: 28.1% less than 15 minutes, 44.8% 15 to 30 minutes, 9.1% 30 to 45 minutes, 8.0% 45 to 60 minutes, 10.1% 60 minutes or more (2006-2010 5-year est.)

Additional Information Contacts

Indiana County Chamber of Commerce . . . . (724) 465-2511
http://www.indianapa.com/chamber

BLAIRSVILLE (borough).

Covers a land area of 1.415 square miles and a water area of 0 square miles. Located at 40.43° N. Lat; 79.26° W. Long. Elevation is 1,017 feet.
Population: 3,595 (1990); 3,607 (2000); 3,412 (2010); Density: 2,412.0 persons per square mile (2010); Race: 95.1% White, 2.3% Black, 0.7% Asian, 0.3% American Indian/Alaska Native, 0.1% Native Hawaiian/Other

Pacific Islander, 1.5% Other, 1.2% Hispanic of any race (2010); Average household size: 2.18 (2010); Median age: 43.2 (2010); Males per 100 females: 97.3 (2010); Marriage status: 29.5% never married, 47.9% now married, 10.4% widowed, 12.3% divorced (2006-2010 5-year est.); Foreign born: 0.5% (2006-2010 5-year est.); Ancestry (includes multiple ancestries): 32.2% German, 22.4% Italian, 14.7% Irish, 12.1% English, 7.3% Polish (2006-2010 5-year est.).

Economy: Single-family building permits issued: 0 (2011); Multi-family building permits issued: 24 (2011); Employment by occupation: 13.3% management, 2.5% professional, 14.3% services, 13.0% sales, 0.5% farming, 11.3% construction, 2.8% production (2006-2010 5-year est.).

Income: Per capita income: $21,314 (2006-2010 5-year est.); Median household income: $35,051 (2006-2010 5-year est.); Average household income: $44,245 (2006-2010 5-year est.); Percent of households with income of $100,000 or more: 8.1% (2006-2010 5-year est.); Poverty rate: 20.1% (2006-2010 5-year est.).

Education: Percent of population age 25 and over with: High school diploma (including GED) or higher: 90.2% (2006-2010 5-year est.); Bachelor's degree or higher: 21.6% (2006-2010 5-year est.); Master's degree or higher: 5.2% (2006-2010 5-year est.).

School District(s)

Blairsville-Saltsburg SD (KG-12)

    2010-11 Enrollment: 1,813 . . . . (724) 459-5500

Two-year College(s)

Wyo Tech-Blairsville (Private, For-profit)

    Fall 2010 Enrollment: 2,308 . . . . (800) 822-8253

Housing: Homeownership rate: 62.7% (2010); Median home value: $89,900 (2006-2010 5-year est.); Median contract rent: $411 per month (2006-2010 5-year est.); Median year structure built: before 1940 (2006-2010 5-year est.).

Safety: Violent crime rate: 52.6 per 10,000 population; Property crime rate: 268.8 per 10,000 population (2011).

Newspapers: Dispatch (Community news)

Transportation: Commute to work: 91.1% car, 0.0% public transportation, 5.1% walk, 2.3% work from home (2006-2010 5-year est.); Travel time to work: 43.0% less than 15 minutes, 28.8% 15 to 30 minutes, 17.1% 30 to 45 minutes, 5.5% 45 to 60 minutes, 5.7% 60 minutes or more (2006-2010 5-year est.)

Additional Information Contacts

Indiana County Chamber of Commerce . . . . (724) 465-2511

    http://www.indianapa.com/chamber

BRUSH VALLEY (township). Covers a land area of 41.385 square miles and a water area of 1.157 square miles. Located at 40.53° N. Lat; 79.06° W. Long. Elevation is 1,444 feet.

Population: 1,808 (1990); 1,881 (2000); 1,858 (2010); Density: 44.9 persons per square mile (2010); Race: 99.1% White, 0.0% Black, 0.1% Asian, 0.1% American Indian/Alaska Native, 0.0% Native Hawaiian/Other Pacific Islander, 0.7% Other, 0.8% Hispanic of any race (2010); Average household size: 2.68 (2010); Median age: 42.2 (2010); Males per 100 females: 103.3 (2010); Marriage status: 17.4% never married, 74.2% now married, 3.1% widowed, 5.4% divorced (2006-2010 5-year est.); Foreign born: 0.0% (2006-2010 5-year est.); Ancestry (includes multiple ancestries): 31.1% German, 18.9% Irish, 10.1% English, 7.8% American, 7.6% Italian (2006-2010 5-year est.).

Economy: Single-family building permits issued: 1 (2011); Multi-family building permits issued: 0 (2011); Employment by occupation: 5.5% management, 2.9% professional, 8.5% services, 19.0% sales, 3.0% farming, 18.4% construction, 8.4% production (2006-2010 5-year est.).

Income: Per capita income: $19,336 (2006-2010 5-year est.); Median household income: $43,426 (2006-2010 5-year est.); Average household income: $51,188 (2006-2010 5-year est.); Percent of households with income of $100,000 or more: 6.9% (2006-2010 5-year est.); Poverty rate: 12.7% (2006-2010 5-year est.).

Education: Percent of population age 25 and over with: High school diploma (including GED) or higher: 87.6% (2006-2010 5-year est.); Bachelor's degree or higher: 11.3% (2006-2010 5-year est.); Master's degree or higher: 3.6% (2006-2010 5-year est.).

Housing: Homeownership rate: 85.6% (2010); Median home value: $97,800 (2006-2010 5-year est.); Median contract rent: $399 per month (2006-2010 5-year est.); Median year structure built: 1973 (2006-2010 5-year est.).

Transportation: Commute to work: 90.9% car, 0.6% public transportation, 2.7% walk, 3.1% work from home (2006-2010 5-year est.); Travel time to work: 13.1% less than 15 minutes, 56.8% 15 to 30 minutes, 17.0% 30 to

45 minutes, 4.2% 45 to 60 minutes, 9.0% 60 minutes or more (2006-2010 5-year est.)

Additional Information Contacts

Brush Valley Regional Chamber of Commerce . . . . (570) 648-4675

    http://www.brushvalleychamber.com

BUFFINGTON (township). Covers a land area of 30.501 square miles and a water area of 0.171 square miles. Located at 40.51° N. Lat; 78.96° W. Long.

Population: 1,220 (1990); 1,275 (2000); 1,328 (2010); Density: 43.5 persons per square mile (2010); Race: 98.6% White, 0.2% Black, 0.2% Asian, 0.4% American Indian/Alaska Native, 0.0% Native Hawaiian/Other Pacific Islander, 0.6% Other, 0.2% Hispanic of any race (2010); Average household size: 2.65 (2010); Median age: 40.6 (2010); Males per 100 females: 101.2 (2010); Marriage status: 23.6% never married, 64.0% now married, 4.4% widowed, 8.0% divorced (2006-2010 5-year est.); Foreign born: 0.2% (2006-2010 5-year est.); Ancestry (includes multiple ancestries): 36.0% German, 19.2% Irish, 12.4% Polish, 7.4% Italian, 5.4% Pennsylvania German (2006-2010 5-year est.).

Economy: Single-family building permits issued: 5 (2011); Multi-family building permits issued: 0 (2011); Employment by occupation: 9.7% management, 0.8% professional, 14.4% services, 21.2% sales, 2.9% farming, 17.1% construction, 10.2% production (2006-2010 5-year est.).

Income: Per capita income: $22,826 (2006-2010 5-year est.); Median household income: $44,500 (2006-2010 5-year est.); Average household income: $60,261 (2006-2010 5-year est.); Percent of households with income of $100,000 or more: 12.5% (2006-2010 5-year est.); Poverty rate: 6.8% (2006-2010 5-year est.).

Education: Percent of population age 25 and over with: High school diploma (including GED) or higher: 82.3% (2006-2010 5-year est.); Bachelor's degree or higher: 9.0% (2006-2010 5-year est.); Master's degree or higher: 2.3% (2006-2010 5-year est.).

Housing: Homeownership rate: 87.0% (2010); Median home value: $116,800 (2006-2010 5-year est.); Median contract rent: $429 per month (2006-2010 5-year est.); Median year structure built: 1978 (2006-2010 5-year est.).

Transportation: Commute to work: 90.9% car, 0.0% public transportation, 2.6% walk, 6.5% work from home (2006-2010 5-year est.); Travel time to work: 16.4% less than 15 minutes, 32.4% 15 to 30 minutes, 30.5% 30 to 45 minutes, 10.0% 45 to 60 minutes, 10.6% 60 minutes or more (2006-2010 5-year est.)

Additional Information Contacts

Indiana County Chamber of Commerce . . . . (724) 465-2511

    http://www.indianapa.com/chamber

BURRELL (township). Covers a land area of 23.876 square miles and a water area of 0.518 square miles. Located at 40.45° N. Lat; 79.21° W. Long.

Population: 3,669 (1990); 3,746 (2000); 4,393 (2010); Density: 184.0 persons per square mile (2010); Race: 94.9% White, 2.9% Black, 0.1% Asian, 0.2% American Indian/Alaska Native, 0.0% Native Hawaiian/Other Pacific Islander, 1.9% Other, 1.7% Hispanic of any race (2010); Average household size: 2.49 (2010); Median age: 37.5 (2010); Males per 100 females: 129.0 (2010); Marriage status: 39.4% never married, 50.4% now married, 5.7% widowed, 4.5% divorced (2006-2010 5-year est.); Foreign born: 0.0% (2006-2010 5-year est.); Ancestry (includes multiple ancestries): 26.9% Irish, 25.6% German, 10.0% Polish, 9.4% Italian, 6.3% Slovak (2006-2010 5-year est.).

Economy: Employment by occupation: 9.8% management, 0.7% professional, 11.1% services, 16.7% sales, 4.0% farming, 21.6% construction, 17.6% production (2006-2010 5-year est.).

Income: Per capita income: $24,925 (2006-2010 5-year est.); Median household income: $46,978 (2006-2010 5-year est.); Average household income: $63,413 (2006-2010 5-year est.); Percent of households with income of $100,000 or more: 16.6% (2006-2010 5-year est.); Poverty rate: 23.7% (2006-2010 5-year est.).

Education: Percent of population age 25 and over with: High school diploma (including GED) or higher: 84.7% (2006-2010 5-year est.); Bachelor's degree or higher: 12.4% (2006-2010 5-year est.); Master's degree or higher: 4.4% (2006-2010 5-year est.).

Housing: Homeownership rate: 64.4% (2010); Median home value: $111,900 (2006-2010 5-year est.); Median contract rent: $435 per month (2006-2010 5-year est.); Median year structure built: 1974 (2006-2010 5-year est.).

Transportation: Commute to work: 96.0% car, 0.1% public transportation, 0.5% walk, 3.4% work from home (2006-2010 5-year est.); Travel time to work: 34.2% less than 15 minutes, 40.2% 15 to 30 minutes, 10.0% 30 to 45 minutes, 8.5% 45 to 60 minutes, 7.1% 60 minutes or more (2006-2010 5-year est.)

Additional Information Contacts
Indiana County Chamber of Commerce . . . . (724) 465-2511
   http://www.indianapa.com/chamber

CANOE (township). Covers a land area of 27.041 square miles and a water area of 0.081 square miles. Located at 40.87° N. Lat; 78.95° W. Long.

Population: 1,915 (1990); 1,670 (2000); 1,505 (2010); Density: 55.7 persons per square mile (2010); Race: 99.3% White, 0.1% Black, 0.1% Asian, 0.4% American Indian/Alaska Native, 0.0% Native Hawaiian/Other Pacific Islander, 0.1% Other, 0.1% Hispanic of any race (2010); Average household size: 2.58 (2010); Median age: 47.5 (2010); Males per 100 females: 115.0 (2010); Marriage status: 24.7% never married, 60.7% now married, 6.7% widowed, 7.9% divorced (2006-2010 5-year est.); Foreign born: 0.0% (2006-2010 5-year est.); Ancestry (includes multiple ancestries): 32.9% German, 22.2% Irish, 10.5% Italian, 8.4% American, 6.4% English (2006-2010 5-year est.).
Economy: Single-family building permits issued: 0 (2011); Multi-family building permits issued: 0 (2011); Employment by occupation: 8.5% management, 1.0% professional, 11.3% services, 16.2% sales, 1.3% farming, 18.8% construction, 12.5% production (2006-2010 5-year est.).
Income: Per capita income: $17,630 (2006-2010 5-year est.); Median household income: $32,500 (2006-2010 5-year est.); Average household income: $42,815 (2006-2010 5-year est.); Percent of households with income of $100,000 or more: 6.2% (2006-2010 5-year est.); Poverty rate: 17.5% (2006-2010 5-year est.).
Education: Percent of population age 25 and over with: High school diploma (including GED) or higher: 83.9% (2006-2010 5-year est.); Bachelor's degree or higher: 4.8% (2006-2010 5-year est.); Master's degree or higher: 0.5% (2006-2010 5-year est.).
Housing: Homeownership rate: 80.0% (2010); Median home value: $70,700 (2006-2010 5-year est.); Median contract rent: $369 per month (2006-2010 5-year est.); Median year structure built: 1942 (2006-2010 5-year est.).
Transportation: Commute to work: 89.6% car, 0.0% public transportation, 8.2% walk, 1.5% work from home (2006-2010 5-year est.); Travel time to work: 34.3% less than 15 minutes, 29.2% 15 to 30 minutes, 13.0% 30 to 45 minutes, 4.0% 45 to 60 minutes, 19.6% 60 minutes or more (2006-2010 5-year est.)

Additional Information Contacts
Punxsutawney Area Chamber of Commerce . . . . (814) 938-7700
   http://www.punxsutawney.com/chamber

CENTER (township). Covers a land area of 40.168 square miles and a water area of 0.447 square miles. Located at 40.54° N. Lat; 79.19° W. Long.

Population: 5,232 (1990); 4,876 (2000); 4,764 (2010); Density: 118.6 persons per square mile (2010); Race: 98.0% White, 0.5% Black, 0.1% Asian, 0.2% American Indian/Alaska Native, 0.0% Native Hawaiian/Other Pacific Islander, 1.2% Other, 0.7% Hispanic of any race (2010); Average household size: 2.38 (2010); Median age: 43.9 (2010); Males per 100 females: 97.8 (2010); Marriage status: 24.8% never married, 56.8% now married, 7.8% widowed, 10.6% divorced (2006-2010 5-year est.); Foreign born: 1.5% (2006-2010 5-year est.); Ancestry (includes multiple ancestries): 29.2% German, 19.1% Irish, 16.3% Italian, 10.3% Polish, 9.5% Slovak (2006-2010 5-year est.).
Economy: Employment by occupation: 7.1% management, 0.5% professional, 10.2% services, 26.6% sales, 6.0% farming, 11.3% construction, 10.2% production (2006-2010 5-year est.).
Income: Per capita income: $19,687 (2006-2010 5-year est.); Median household income: $40,725 (2006-2010 5-year est.); Average household income: $50,760 (2006-2010 5-year est.); Percent of households with income of $100,000 or more: 5.7% (2006-2010 5-year est.); Poverty rate: 14.1% (2006-2010 5-year est.).
Education: Percent of population age 25 and over with: High school diploma (including GED) or higher: 85.3% (2006-2010 5-year est.); Bachelor's degree or higher: 15.4% (2006-2010 5-year est.); Master's degree or higher: 4.1% (2006-2010 5-year est.).
Housing: Homeownership rate: 79.1% (2010); Median home value: $96,300 (2006-2010 5-year est.); Median contract rent: $430 per month

(2006-2010 5-year est.); Median year structure built: 1956 (2006-2010 5-year est.).
Transportation: Commute to work: 89.9% car, 4.4% public transportation, 1.9% walk, 3.7% work from home (2006-2010 5-year est.); Travel time to work: 42.9% less than 15 minutes, 37.6% 15 to 30 minutes, 7.5% 30 to 45 minutes, 8.1% 45 to 60 minutes, 3.8% 60 minutes or more (2006-2010 5-year est.)

Additional Information Contacts
Indiana County Chamber of Commerce . . . . (724) 465-2511
   http://www.indianapa.com/chamber

CHAMBERSVILLE (unincorporated postal area)
Zip Code: 15723
   Covers a land area of 1.049 square miles and a water area of 0.006 square miles. Located at 40.69° N. Lat; 79.15° W. Long. Elevation is 1,096 feet. Population: 46 (2010); Density: 43.8 persons per square mile (2010); Race: 97.8% White, 0.0% Black, 2.2% Asian, 0.0% American Indian/Alaska Native, 0.0% Native Hawaiian/Other Pacific Islander, 0.0% Other, 0.0% Hispanic of any race (2010); Average household size: 1.92 (2010); Median age: 56.5 (2010); Males per 100 females: 130.0 (2010); Homeownership rate: 87.5% (2010)

CHERRY TREE (borough). Covers a land area of 0.520 square miles and a water area of 0.014 square miles. Located at 40.73° N. Lat; 78.81° W. Long. Elevation is 1,385 feet.

Population: 431 (1990); 443 (2000); 364 (2010); Density: 700.1 persons per square mile (2010); Race: 98.9% White, 0.0% Black, 0.3% Asian, 0.0% American Indian/Alaska Native, 0.0% Native Hawaiian/Other Pacific Islander, 0.8% Other, 1.1% Hispanic of any race (2010); Average household size: 2.64 (2010); Median age: 48.5 (2010); Males per 100 females: 106.8 (2010); Marriage status: 22.2% never married, 70.4% now married, 5.9% widowed, 1.5% divorced (2006-2010 5-year est.); Foreign born: 0.0% (2006-2010 5-year est.); Ancestry (includes multiple ancestries): 38.4% German, 21.2% Irish, 16.6% English, 12.3% Polish, 8.9% Italian (2006-2010 5-year est.).
Economy: Employment by occupation: 0.0% management, 4.3% professional, 15.8% services, 12.9% sales, 0.0% farming, 6.5% construction, 9.4% production (2006-2010 5-year est.).
Income: Per capita income: $16,084 (2006-2010 5-year est.); Median household income: $35,313 (2006-2010 5-year est.); Average household income: $39,918 (2006-2010 5-year est.); Percent of households with income of $100,000 or more: 1.4% (2006-2010 5-year est.); Poverty rate: 10.3% (2006-2010 5-year est.).
Education: Percent of population age 25 and over with: High school diploma (including GED) or higher: 82.4% (2006-2010 5-year est.); Bachelor's degree or higher: 7.2% (2006-2010 5-year est.); Master's degree or higher: 0.0% (2006-2010 5-year est.).
Housing: Homeownership rate: 76.1% (2010); Median home value: $73,500 (2006-2010 5-year est.); Median contract rent: $375 per month (2006-2010 5-year est.); Median year structure built: before 1940 (2006-2010 5-year est.).
Safety: Violent crime rate: 0.0 per 10,000 population; Property crime rate: 0.0 per 10,000 population (2011).
Transportation: Commute to work: 95.0% car, 0.0% public transportation, 1.4% walk, 3.6% work from home (2006-2010 5-year est.); Travel time to work: 28.4% less than 15 minutes, 23.1% 15 to 30 minutes, 25.4% 30 to 45 minutes, 10.4% 45 to 60 minutes, 12.7% 60 minutes or more (2006-2010 5-year est.)

CHERRYHILL (township). Covers a land area of 48.646 square miles and a water area of 0.851 square miles. Located at 40.63° N. Lat; 79.01° W. Long.

Population: 2,764 (1990); 2,842 (2000); 2,765 (2010); Density: 56.8 persons per square mile (2010); Race: 98.8% White, 0.3% Black, 0.2% Asian, 0.1% American Indian/Alaska Native, 0.0% Native Hawaiian/Other Pacific Islander, 0.6% Other, 0.6% Hispanic of any race (2010); Average household size: 2.58 (2010); Median age: 43.8 (2010); Males per 100 females: 104.2 (2010); Marriage status: 19.0% never married, 69.8% now married, 4.9% widowed, 6.3% divorced (2006-2010 5-year est.); Foreign born: 0.8% (2006-2010 5-year est.); Ancestry (includes multiple ancestries): 36.4% German, 19.2% Irish, 10.5% English, 9.1% Polish, 6.9% Italian (2006-2010 5-year est.).
Economy: Single-family building permits issued: 0 (2011); Multi-family building permits issued: 0 (2011); Employment by occupation: 5.8%

management, 1.8% professional, 10.8% services, 19.2% sales, 3.2% farming, 18.7% construction, 14.6% production (2006-2010 5-year est.).
Income: Per capita income: $21,891 (2006-2010 5-year est.); Median household income: $56,492 (2006-2010 5-year est.); Average household income: $59,637 (2006-2010 5-year est.); Percent of households with income of $100,000 or more: 11.6% (2006-2010 5-year est.); Poverty rate: 3.9% (2006-2010 5-year est.).
Education: Percent of population age 25 and over with: High school diploma (including GED) or higher: 87.3% (2006-2010 5-year est.); Bachelor's degree or higher: 15.5% (2006-2010 5-year est.); Master's degree or higher: 5.9% (2006-2010 5-year est.).
Housing: Homeownership rate: 80.0% (2010); Median home value: $105,400 (2006-2010 5-year est.); Median contract rent: $357 per month (2006-2010 5-year est.); Median year structure built: 1972 (2006-2010 5-year est.).
Transportation: Commute to work: 92.5% car, 0.0% public transportation, 1.4% walk, 3.4% work from home (2006-2010 5-year est.); Travel time to work: 17.2% less than 15 minutes, 59.6% 15 to 30 minutes, 13.6% 30 to 45 minutes, 5.1% 45 to 60 minutes, 4.6% 60 minutes or more (2006-2010 5-year est.)
Additional Information Contacts
Indiana County Chamber of Commerce . . . . (724) 465-2511
http://www.indianapa.com/chamber

CHEVY CHASE HEIGHTS (CDP). Covers a land area of 1.269
square miles and a water area of 0 square miles. Located at 40.64° N. Lat; 79.15° W. Long. Elevation is 1,437 feet.
Population: 1,535 (1990); 1,511 (2000); 1,502 (2010); Density: 1,184.0 persons per square mile (2010); Race: 86.8% White, 9.0% Black, 0.5% Asian, 0.6% American Indian/Alaska Native, 0.0% Native Hawaiian/Other Pacific Islander, 3.1% Other, 0.7% Hispanic of any race (2010); Average household size: 2.22 (2010); Median age: 41.7 (2010); Males per 100 females: 89.6 (2010); Marriage status: 23.0% never married, 58.1% now married, 8.5% widowed, 10.4% divorced (2006-2010 5-year est.); Foreign born: 1.3% (2006-2010 5-year est.); Ancestry (includes multiple ancestries): 30.6% German, 12.8% Italian, 12.3% Irish, 9.7% English, 6.9% American (2006-2010 5-year est.).
Economy: Employment by occupation: 9.9% management, 1.7% professional, 10.9% services, 23.1% sales, 1.5% farming, 9.4% construction, 2.4% production (2006-2010 5-year est.).
Income: Per capita income: $26,502 (2006-2010 5-year est.); Median household income: $38,333 (2006-2010 5-year est.); Average household income: $56,365 (2006-2010 5-year est.); Percent of households with income of $100,000 or more: 18.2% (2006-2010 5-year est.); Poverty rate: 15.6% (2006-2010 5-year est.).
Education: Percent of population age 25 and over with: High school diploma (including GED) or higher: 86.0% (2006-2010 5-year est.); Bachelor's degree or higher: 30.1% (2006-2010 5-year est.); Master's degree or higher: 17.8% (2006-2010 5-year est.).
Housing: Homeownership rate: 58.1% (2010); Median home value: $99,000 (2006-2010 5-year est.); Median contract rent: $390 per month (2006-2010 5-year est.); Median year structure built: 1975 (2006-2010 5-year est.).
Transportation: Commute to work: 91.7% car, 0.0% public transportation, 3.0% walk, 5.2% work from home (2006-2010 5-year est.); Travel time to work: 57.9% less than 15 minutes, 27.9% 15 to 30 minutes, 11.1% 30 to 45 minutes, 0.0% 45 to 60 minutes, 3.2% 60 minutes or more (2006-2010 5-year est.)
Additional Information Contacts
Indiana County Chamber of Commerce . . . . (724) 465-2511
http://www.indianapa.com/chamber

CLARKSBURG (unincorporated postal area)
Zip Code: 15725
Covers a land area of 29.945 square miles and a water area of 0.584 square miles. Located at 40.51° N. Lat; 79.34° W. Long. Population: 1,446 (2010); Density: 48.3 persons per square mile (2010); Race: 99.0% White, 0.0% Black, 0.0% Asian, 0.1% American Indian/Alaska Native, 0.0% Native Hawaiian/Other Pacific Islander, 0.9% Other, 0.2% Hispanic of any race (2010); Average household size: 2.48 (2010); Median age: 44.2 (2010); Males per 100 females: 106.3 (2010); Homeownership rate: 85.0% (2010)

CLUNE (unincorporated postal area)
Zip Code: 15727

Covers a land area of 1.370 square miles and a water area of 0 square miles. Located at 40.55° N. Lat; 79.30° W. Long. Population: 168 (2010); Density: 122.6 persons per square mile (2010); Race: 95.8% White, 1.2% Black, 0.0% Asian, 0.0% American Indian/Alaska Native, 0.0% Native Hawaiian/Other Pacific Islander, 3.0% Other, 0.0% Hispanic of any race (2010); Average household size: 2.33 (2010); Median age: 32.8 (2010); Males per 100 females: 90.9 (2010); Homeownership rate: 77.8% (2010)

CLYMER (borough). Covers a land area of 0.569 square miles and a
water area of 0.019 square miles. Located at 40.67° N. Lat; 79.01° W. Long. Elevation is 1,250 feet.
Population: 1,499 (1990); 1,547 (2000); 1,357 (2010); Density: 2,383.8 persons per square mile (2010); Race: 98.5% White, 0.5% Black, 0.2% Asian, 0.1% American Indian/Alaska Native, 0.0% Native Hawaiian/Other Pacific Islander, 0.7% Other, 0.5% Hispanic of any race (2010); Average household size: 2.32 (2010); Median age: 40.4 (2010); Males per 100 females: 92.5 (2010); Marriage status: 29.3% never married, 51.1% now married, 12.0% widowed, 7.6% divorced (2006-2010 5-year est.); Foreign born: 0.0% (2006-2010 5-year est.); Ancestry (includes multiple ancestries): 29.5% German, 24.2% Irish, 12.3% Polish, 11.8% English, 10.5% Italian (2006-2010 5-year est.).
Economy: Employment by occupation: 4.7% management, 0.5% professional, 14.3% services, 18.0% sales, 4.3% farming, 13.6% construction, 6.4% production (2006-2010 5-year est.).
Income: Per capita income: $16,222 (2006-2010 5-year est.); Median household income: $32,685 (2006-2010 5-year est.); Average household income: $38,697 (2006-2010 5-year est.); Percent of households with income of $100,000 or more: 1.6% (2006-2010 5-year est.); Poverty rate: 21.2% (2006-2010 5-year est.).
Education: Percent of population age 25 and over with: High school diploma (including GED) or higher: 76.6% (2006-2010 5-year est.); Bachelor's degree or higher: 14.4% (2006-2010 5-year est.); Master's degree or higher: 4.6% (2006-2010 5-year est.).
School District(s)
Penns Manor Area SD (PK-12)
    2010-11 Enrollment: 972. . . . . (724) 254-2666
Housing: Homeownership rate: 65.8% (2010); Median home value: $54,000 (2006-2010 5-year est.); Median contract rent: $396 per month (2006-2010 5-year est.); Median year structure built: before 1940 (2006-2010 5-year est.).
Transportation: Commute to work: 86.9% car, 0.0% public transportation, 9.7% walk, 3.4% work from home (2006-2010 5-year est.); Travel time to work: 29.2% less than 15 minutes, 44.0% 15 to 30 minutes, 15.0% 30 to 45 minutes, 7.3% 45 to 60 minutes, 4.6% 60 minutes or more (2006-2010 5-year est.)
Additional Information Contacts
Indiana County Chamber of Commerce . . . . (724) 465-2511
http://www.indianapa.com/chamber

COMMODORE (CDP). Covers a land area of 0.767 square miles and
a water area of 0.005 square miles. Located at 40.72° N. Lat; 78.93° W. Long. Elevation is 1,421 feet.
Population: 336 (1990); 337 (2000); 331 (2010); Density: 431.7 persons per square mile (2010); Race: 97.3% White, 0.6% Black, 0.0% Asian, 0.3% American Indian/Alaska Native, 0.0% Native Hawaiian/Other Pacific Islander, 1.8% Other, 0.3% Hispanic of any race (2010); Average household size: 2.65 (2010); Median age: 34.5 (2010); Males per 100 females: 97.0 (2010); Marriage status: 14.1% never married, 64.4% now married, 21.5% widowed, 0.0% divorced (2006-2010 5-year est.); Foreign born: 0.0% (2006-2010 5-year est.); Ancestry (includes multiple ancestries): 57.1% German, 31.6% Yugoslavian, 21.5% Irish, 5.6% Hungarian (2006-2010 5-year est.).
Economy: Employment by occupation: 0.0% management, 0.0% professional, 0.0% services, 33.7% sales, 0.0% farming, 17.3% construction, 0.0% production (2006-2010 5-year est.).
Income: Per capita income: $15,622 (2006-2010 5-year est.); Median household income: $22,059 (2006-2010 5-year est.); Average household income: $32,066 (2006-2010 5-year est.); Percent of households with income of $100,000 or more: n/a (2006-2010 5-year est.); Poverty rate: 29.9% (2006-2010 5-year est.).
Education: Percent of population age 25 and over with: High school diploma (including GED) or higher: 100.0% (2006-2010 5-year est.); Bachelor's degree or higher: 11.6% (2006-2010 5-year est.); Master's degree or higher: 0.0% (2006-2010 5-year est.).

School District(s)

Purchase Line SD (KG-12)

   2010-11 Enrollment: 1,035 . . . . (724) 254-4312

Housing: Homeownership rate: 70.4% (2010); Median home value: $24,800 (2006-2010 5-year est.); Median contract rent: $340 per month (2006-2010 5-year est.); Median year structure built: before 1940 (2006-2010 5-year est.).

Transportation: Commute to work: 83.7% car, 0.0% public transportation, 0.0% walk, 0.0% work from home (2006-2010 5-year est.); Travel time to work: 20.2% less than 15 minutes, 16.3% 15 to 30 minutes, 46.2% 30 to 45 minutes, 0.0% 45 to 60 minutes, 17.3% 60 minutes or more (2006-2010 5-year est.)

CONEMAUGH (township). Covers a land area of 33.604 square miles and a water area of 0.914 square miles. Located at 40.51° N. Lat; 79.39° W. Long.

Population: 2,434 (1990); 2,437 (2000); 2,294 (2010); Density: 68.3 persons per square mile (2010); Race: 99.1% White, 0.0% Black, 0.3% Asian, 0.2% American Indian/Alaska Native, 0.0% Native Hawaiian/Other Pacific Islander, 0.4% Other, 0.5% Hispanic of any race (2010); Average household size: 2.42 (2010); Median age: 45.4 (2010); Males per 100 females: 104.1 (2010); Marriage status: 23.4% never married, 57.2% now married, 10.9% widowed, 8.5% divorced (2006-2010 5-year est.); Foreign born: 1.0% (2006-2010 5-year est.); Ancestry (includes multiple ancestries): 31.4% German, 23.7% Irish, 17.2% English, 15.9% Italian, 9.9% Polish (2006-2010 5-year est.).

Economy: Employment by occupation: 7.8% management, 1.3% professional, 13.0% services, 15.1% sales, 1.2% farming, 14.1% construction, 8.7% production (2006-2010 5-year est.).

Income: Per capita income: $21,618 (2006-2010 5-year est.); Median household income: $38,750 (2006-2010 5-year est.); Average household income: $50,144 (2006-2010 5-year est.); Percent of households with income of $100,000 or more: 11.6% (2006-2010 5-year est.); Poverty rate: 12.3% (2006-2010 5-year est.).

Education: Percent of population age 25 and over with: High school diploma (including GED) or higher: 89.1% (2006-2010 5-year est.); Bachelor's degree or higher: 15.4% (2006-2010 5-year est.); Master's degree or higher: 5.5% (2006-2010 5-year est.).

Housing: Homeownership rate: 83.5% (2010); Median home value: $87,800 (2006-2010 5-year est.); Median contract rent: $340 per month (2006-2010 5-year est.); Median year structure built: 1966 (2006-2010 5-year est.).

Transportation: Commute to work: 94.9% car, 0.0% public transportation, 3.7% walk, 1.4% work from home (2006-2010 5-year est.); Travel time to work: 22.7% less than 15 minutes, 37.0% 15 to 30 minutes, 25.1% 30 to 45 minutes, 7.7% 45 to 60 minutes, 7.5% 60 minutes or more (2006-2010 5-year est.)

Additional Information Contacts

Indiana County Chamber of Commerce . . . . (724) 465-2511
   http://www.indianapa.com/chamber

CORAL (CDP). Covers a land area of 0.178 square miles and a water area of 0.003 square miles. Located at 40.50° N. Lat; 79.18° W. Long. Elevation is 1,010 feet.

Population: n/a (1990); n/a (2000); 325 (2010); Density: 1,824.5 persons per square mile (2010); Race: 98.8% White, 0.3% Black, 0.6% Asian, 0.0% American Indian/Alaska Native, 0.0% Native Hawaiian/Other Pacific Islander, 0.3% Other, 0.3% Hispanic of any race (2010); Average household size: 2.15 (2010); Median age: 46.4 (2010); Males per 100 females: 100.6 (2010); Marriage status: 17.2% never married, 51.7% now married, 0.0% widowed, 31.0% divorced (2006-2010 5-year est.); Foreign born: 0.0% (2006-2010 5-year est.); Ancestry (includes multiple ancestries): 33.8% German, 23.2% Irish, 11.6% Polish, 10.9% Italian, 9.3% Canadian (2006-2010 5-year est.).

Economy: Employment by occupation: 0.0% management, 0.0% professional, 27.1% services, 8.4% sales, 14.3% farming, 17.2% construction, 17.2% production (2006-2010 5-year est.).

Income: Per capita income: $21,780 (2006-2010 5-year est.); Median household income: $74,167 (2006-2010 5-year est.); Average household income: $78,413 (2006-2010 5-year est.); Percent of households with income of $100,000 or more: n/a (2006-2010 5-year est.); Poverty rate: 0.0% (2006-2010 5-year est.).

Education: Percent of population age 25 and over with: High school diploma (including GED) or higher: 79.8% (2006-2010 5-year est.);

Bachelor's degree or higher: 21.4% (2006-2010 5-year est.); Master's degree or higher: 21.4% (2006-2010 5-year est.).

Housing: Homeownership rate: 74.9% (2010); Median home value: n/a (2006-2010 5-year est.); Median contract rent: $921 per month (2006-2010 5-year est.); Median year structure built: before 1940 (2006-2010 5-year est.).

Transportation: Commute to work: 100.0% car, 0.0% public transportation, 0.0% walk, 0.0% work from home (2006-2010 5-year est.); Travel time to work: 73.9% less than 15 minutes, 26.1% 15 to 30 minutes, 0.0% 30 to 45 minutes, 0.0% 45 to 60 minutes, 0.0% 60 minutes or more (2006-2010 5-year est.)

CREEKSIDE (borough). Covers a land area of 0.221 square miles and a water area of 0.007 square miles. Located at 40.68° N. Lat; 79.19° W. Long. Elevation is 1,053 feet.

Population: 337 (1990); 323 (2000); 309 (2010); Density: 1,398.0 persons per square mile (2010); Race: 97.4% White, 0.3% Black, 0.0% Asian, 0.0% American Indian/Alaska Native, 0.0% Native Hawaiian/Other Pacific Islander, 2.3% Other, 1.0% Hispanic of any race (2010); Average household size: 2.36 (2010); Median age: 40.1 (2010); Males per 100 females: 99.4 (2010); Marriage status: 38.7% never married, 48.9% now married, 2.7% widowed, 9.6% divorced (2006-2010 5-year est.); Foreign born: 1.1% (2006-2010 5-year est.); Ancestry (includes multiple ancestries): 47.5% German, 23.3% Irish, 14.5% Italian, 14.1% English, 7.9% Scottish (2006-2010 5-year est.).

Economy: Employment by occupation: 3.0% management, 1.0% professional, 18.7% services, 16.3% sales, 8.9% farming, 18.7% construction, 18.2% production (2006-2010 5-year est.).

Income: Per capita income: $16,100 (2006-2010 5-year est.); Median household income: $33,929 (2006-2010 5-year est.); Average household income: $42,037 (2006-2010 5-year est.); Percent of households with income of $100,000 or more: 1.8% (2006-2010 5-year est.); Poverty rate: 33.6% (2006-2010 5-year est.).

Education: Percent of population age 25 and over with: High school diploma (including GED) or higher: 94.0% (2006-2010 5-year est.); Bachelor's degree or higher: 10.9% (2006-2010 5-year est.); Master's degree or higher: 5.6% (2006-2010 5-year est.).

Housing: Homeownership rate: 62.8% (2010); Median home value: $71,000 (2006-2010 5-year est.); Median contract rent: $477 per month (2006-2010 5-year est.); Median year structure built: before 1940 (2006-2010 5-year est.).

Transportation: Commute to work: 89.3% car, 0.0% public transportation, 2.6% walk, 8.2% work from home (2006-2010 5-year est.); Travel time to work: 20.6% less than 15 minutes, 60.6% 15 to 30 minutes, 11.1% 30 to 45 minutes, 1.1% 45 to 60 minutes, 6.7% 60 minutes or more (2006-2010 5-year est.)

DICKSONVILLE (CDP). Covers a land area of 0.902 square miles and a water area of 0.003 square miles. Located at 40.72° N. Lat; 79.01° W. Long. Elevation is 1,280 feet.

Population: 444 (1990); 450 (2000); 467 (2010); Density: 517.6 persons per square mile (2010); Race: 99.1% White, 0.2% Black, 0.0% Asian, 0.0% American Indian/Alaska Native, 0.0% Native Hawaiian/Other Pacific Islander, 0.7% Other, 0.6% Hispanic of any race (2010); Average household size: 2.59 (2010); Median age: 36.6 (2010); Males per 100 females: 103.0 (2010); Marriage status: 52.7% never married, 35.6% now married, 0.0% widowed, 11.8% divorced (2006-2010 5-year est.); Foreign born: 0.0% (2006-2010 5-year est.); Ancestry (includes multiple ancestries): 38.5% German, 35.7% Slovak, 28.8% Polish, 11.1% Ukrainian, 7.7% Irish (2006-2010 5-year est.).

Economy: Employment by occupation: 0.0% management, 0.0% professional, 32.7% services, 24.9% sales, 0.0% farming, 10.0% construction, 13.3% production (2006-2010 5-year est.).

Income: Per capita income: $14,797 (2006-2010 5-year est.); Median household income: $37,813 (2006-2010 5-year est.); Average household income: $35,812 (2006-2010 5-year est.); Percent of households with income of $100,000 or more: n/a (2006-2010 5-year est.); Poverty rate: 16.5% (2006-2010 5-year est.).

Education: Percent of population age 25 and over with: High school diploma (including GED) or higher: 90.9% (2006-2010 5-year est.); Bachelor's degree or higher: 8.1% (2006-2010 5-year est.); Master's degree or higher: 4.0% (2006-2010 5-year est.).

Housing: Homeownership rate: 71.7% (2010); Median home value: $68,500 (2006-2010 5-year est.); Median contract rent: $423 per month

(2006-2010 5-year est.); Median year structure built: before 1940 (2006-2010 5-year est.).

Transportation: Commute to work: 100.0% car, 0.0% public transportation, 0.0% walk, 0.0% work from home (2006-2010 5-year est.); Travel time to work: 17.5% less than 15 minutes, 50.2% 15 to 30 minutes, 28.8% 30 to 45 minutes, 0.0% 45 to 60 minutes, 3.6% 60 minutes or more (2006-2010 5-year est.)

DILLTOWN (unincorporated postal area)
Zip Code: 15929

Covers a land area of 0.577 square miles and a water area of 0.043 square miles. Located at 40.46° N. Lat; 79.00° W. Long. Elevation is 1,352 feet. Population: 75 (2010); Density: 129.8 persons per square mile (2010); Race: 100.0% White, 0.0% Black, 0.0% Asian, 0.0% American Indian/Alaska Native, 0.0% Native Hawaiian/Other Pacific Islander, 0.0% Other, 0.0% Hispanic of any race (2010); Average household size: 2.21 (2010); Median age: 42.8 (2010); Males per 100 females: 87.5 (2010); Homeownership rate: 70.6% (2010)

DIXONVILLE (unincorporated postal area)
Zip Code: 15734

Covers a land area of 1.432 square miles and a water area of 0 square miles. Located at 40.72° N. Lat; 79.00° W. Long. Elevation is 1,280 feet. Population: 322 (2010); Density: 224.8 persons per square mile (2010); Race: 100.0% White, 0.0% Black, 0.0% Asian, 0.0% American Indian/Alaska Native, 0.0% Native Hawaiian/Other Pacific Islander, 0.0% Other, 0.0% Hispanic of any race (2010); Average household size: 2.48 (2010); Median age: 37.0 (2010); Males per 100 females: 102.5 (2010); Homeownership rate: 73.9% (2010)

EAST MAHONING (township). Covers a land area of 31.279 square miles and a water area of 0.093 square miles. Located at 40.79° N. Lat; 79.05° W. Long.

Population: 1,140 (1990); 1,196 (2000); 1,077 (2010); Density: 34.4 persons per square mile (2010); Race: 98.8% White, 0.5% Black, 0.1% Asian, 0.0% American Indian/Alaska Native, 0.0% Native Hawaiian/Other Pacific Islander, 0.6% Other, 0.3% Hispanic of any race (2010); Average household size: 2.64 (2010); Median age: 39.6 (2010); Males per 100 females: 102.8 (2010); Marriage status: 18.6% never married, 65.1% now married, 10.0% widowed, 6.4% divorced (2006-2010 5-year est.); Foreign born: 0.0% (2006-2010 5-year est.); Ancestry (includes multiple ancestries): 41.3% German, 22.6% Irish, 11.2% English, 9.9% Scotch-Irish, 8.2% Dutch (2006-2010 5-year est.).

Economy: Employment by occupation: 9.0% management, 4.0% professional, 7.2% services, 19.2% sales, 0.5% farming, 17.8% construction, 5.5% production (2006-2010 5-year est.).

Income: Per capita income: $18,860 (2006-2010 5-year est.); Median household income: $43,690 (2006-2010 5-year est.); Average household income: $49,233 (2006-2010 5-year est.); Percent of households with income of $100,000 or more: 7.4% (2006-2010 5-year est.); Poverty rate: 13.4% (2006-2010 5-year est.).

Education: Percent of population age 25 and over with: High school diploma (including GED) or higher: 84.4% (2006-2010 5-year est.); Bachelor's degree or higher: 16.9% (2006-2010 5-year est.); Master's degree or higher: 7.5% (2006-2010 5-year est.).

Housing: Homeownership rate: 83.3% (2010); Median home value: $107,500 (2006-2010 5-year est.); Median contract rent: $434 per month (2006-2010 5-year est.); Median year structure built: 1974 (2006-2010 5-year est.).

Transportation: Commute to work: 92.0% car, 0.0% public transportation, 4.6% walk, 1.8% work from home (2006-2010 5-year est.); Travel time to work: 21.9% less than 15 minutes, 23.8% 15 to 30 minutes, 35.9% 30 to 45 minutes, 9.9% 45 to 60 minutes, 8.6% 60 minutes or more (2006-2010 5-year est.)

Additional Information Contacts
Indiana County Chamber of Commerce . . . . (724) 465-2511
http://www.indianapa.com/chamber

EAST WHEATFIELD (township). Covers a land area of 26.884 square miles and a water area of 0.277 square miles. Located at 40.45° N. Lat; 79.01° W. Long.

Population: 2,735 (1990); 2,607 (2000); 2,366 (2010); Density: 88.0 persons per square mile (2010); Race: 98.8% White, 0.1% Black, 0.1% Asian, 0.0% American Indian/Alaska Native, 0.0% Native Hawaiian/Other Pacific Islander, 1.0% Other, 0.6% Hispanic of any race (2010); Average

household size: 2.32 (2010); Median age: 47.5 (2010); Males per 100 females: 99.0 (2010); Marriage status: 23.0% never married, 59.1% now married, 8.7% widowed, 9.2% divorced (2006-2010 5-year est.); Foreign born: 0.0% (2006-2010 5-year est.); Ancestry (includes multiple ancestries): 31.4% German, 19.2% Irish, 8.7% English, 8.5% Polish, 8.1% Italian (2006-2010 5-year est.).

Economy: Employment by occupation: 5.1% management, 1.2% professional, 7.8% services, 18.0% sales, 2.8% farming, 20.4% construction, 12.8% production (2006-2010 5-year est.).

Income: Per capita income: $20,094 (2006-2010 5-year est.); Median household income: $37,742 (2006-2010 5-year est.); Average household income: $44,485 (2006-2010 5-year est.); Percent of households with income of $100,000 or more: 5.7% (2006-2010 5-year est.); Poverty rate: 12.3% (2006-2010 5-year est.).

Education: Percent of population age 25 and over with: High school diploma (including GED) or higher: 86.0% (2006-2010 5-year est.); Bachelor's degree or higher: 12.5% (2006-2010 5-year est.); Master's degree or higher: 4.1% (2006-2010 5-year est.).

Housing: Homeownership rate: 84.4% (2010); Median home value: $87,000 (2006-2010 5-year est.); Median contract rent: $450 per month (2006-2010 5-year est.); Median year structure built: 1968 (2006-2010 5-year est.).

Transportation: Commute to work: 91.1% car, 0.0% public transportation, 4.4% walk, 2.9% work from home (2006-2010 5-year est.); Travel time to work: 16.1% less than 15 minutes, 44.5% 15 to 30 minutes, 31.0% 30 to 45 minutes, 3.0% 45 to 60 minutes, 5.4% 60 minutes or more (2006-2010 5-year est.)

Additional Information Contacts
Indiana County Chamber of Commerce . . . . (724) 465-2511
http://www.indianapa.com/chamber

ERNEST (borough). Covers a land area of 0.230 square miles and a water area of 0.006 square miles. Located at 40.68° N. Lat; 79.17° W. Long. Elevation is 1,184 feet.

Population: 492 (1990); 501 (2000); 462 (2010); Density: 2,011.5 persons per square mile (2010); Race: 97.6% White, 1.7% Black, 0.0% Asian, 0.0% American Indian/Alaska Native, 0.0% Native Hawaiian/Other Pacific Islander, 0.7% Other, 2.2% Hispanic of any race (2010); Average household size: 2.47 (2010); Median age: 32.8 (2010); Males per 100 females: 88.6 (2010); Marriage status: 26.1% never married, 50.0% now married, 8.8% widowed, 15.1% divorced (2006-2010 5-year est.); Foreign born: 0.3% (2006-2010 5-year est.); Ancestry (includes multiple ancestries): 38.6% German, 35.1% Irish, 15.9% Italian, 11.4% Polish, 2.6% Scotch-Irish (2006-2010 5-year est.).

Economy: Employment by occupation: 0.0% management, 0.0% professional, 8.3% services, 18.9% sales, 3.6% farming, 11.2% construction, 6.5% production (2006-2010 5-year est.).

Income: Per capita income: $17,911 (2006-2010 5-year est.); Median household income: $29,500 (2006-2010 5-year est.); Average household income: $36,101 (2006-2010 5-year est.); Percent of households with income of $100,000 or more: n/a (2006-2010 5-year est.); Poverty rate: 15.9% (2006-2010 5-year est.).

Education: Percent of population age 25 and over with: High school diploma (including GED) or higher: 91.8% (2006-2010 5-year est.); Bachelor's degree or higher: 14.2% (2006-2010 5-year est.); Master's degree or higher: 6.5% (2006-2010 5-year est.).

Housing: Homeownership rate: 76.0% (2010); Median home value: $64,900 (2006-2010 5-year est.); Median contract rent: $433 per month (2006-2010 5-year est.); Median year structure built: before 1940 (2006-2010 5-year est.).

Transportation: Commute to work: 93.3% car, 0.0% public transportation, 0.0% walk, 3.7% work from home (2006-2010 5-year est.); Travel time to work: 36.3% less than 15 minutes, 45.2% 15 to 30 minutes, 13.4% 30 to 45 minutes, 3.2% 45 to 60 minutes, 1.9% 60 minutes or more (2006-2010 5-year est.)

GIPSY (unincorporated postal area)
Zip Code: 15741

Covers a land area of 1.754 square miles and a water area of 0.002 square miles. Located at 40.80° N. Lat; 78.89° W. Long. Elevation is 1,562 feet. Population: 83 (2010); Density: 47.3 persons per square mile (2010); Race: 100.0% White, 0.0% Black, 0.0% Asian, 0.0% American Indian/Alaska Native, 0.0% Native Hawaiian/Other Pacific Islander, 0.0% Other, 0.0% Hispanic of any race (2010); Average household size:

2.31 (2010); Median age: 46.5 (2010); Males per 100 females: 118.4 (2010); Homeownership rate: 80.6% (2010)

GLEN CAMPBELL (borough). Covers a land area of 0.931 square miles and a water area of 0 square miles. Located at 40.82° N. Lat; 78.83° W. Long. Elevation is 1,473 feet.
Population: 313 (1990); 306 (2000); 245 (2010); Density: 263.3 persons per square mile (2010); Race: 98.4% White, 0.0% Black, 0.8% Asian, 0.4% American Indian/Alaska Native, 0.0% Native Hawaiian/Other Pacific Islander, 0.4% Other, 0.4% Hispanic of any race (2010); Average household size: 2.63 (2010); Median age: 51.5 (2010); Males per 100 females: 120.7 (2010); Marriage status: 20.5% never married, 67.6% now married, 1.1% widowed, 10.8% divorced (2006-2010 5-year est.); Foreign born: 1.0% (2006-2010 5-year est.); Ancestry (includes multiple ancestries): 44.7% German, 23.1% Irish, 8.5% Dutch, 8.5% Italian, 6.5% English (2006-2010 5-year est.).
Economy: Employment by occupation: 0.0% management, 0.0% professional, 13.4% services, 14.4% sales, 0.0% farming, 30.9% construction, 3.1% production (2006-2010 5-year est.).
Income: Per capita income: $21,019 (2006-2010 5-year est.); Median household income: $50,139 (2006-2010 5-year est.); Average household income: $56,005 (2006-2010 5-year est.); Percent of households with income of $100,000 or more: 9.3% (2006-2010 5-year est.); Poverty rate: 9.0% (2006-2010 5-year est.).
Education: Percent of population age 25 and over with: High school diploma (including GED) or higher: 83.2% (2006-2010 5-year est.); Bachelor's degree or higher: 9.7% (2006-2010 5-year est.); Master's degree or higher: 2.6% (2006-2010 5-year est.).
Housing: Homeownership rate: 81.7% (2010); Median home value: $43,100 (2006-2010 5-year est.); Median contract rent: n/a per month (2006-2010 5-year est.); Median year structure built: before 1940 (2006-2010 5-year est.).
Transportation: Commute to work: 79.1% car, 0.0% public transportation, 10.5% walk, 10.5% work from home (2006-2010 5-year est.); Travel time to work: 24.7% less than 15 minutes, 15.6% 15 to 30 minutes, 20.8% 30 to 45 minutes, 22.1% 45 to 60 minutes, 16.9% 60 minutes or more (2006-2010 5-year est.)

GRACETON (CDP). Covers a land area of 0.121 square miles and a water area of 0 square miles. Located at 40.51° N. Lat; 79.17° W. Long. Elevation is 1,079 feet.
Population: n/a (1990); n/a (2000); 257 (2010); Density: 2,121.2 persons per square mile (2010); Race: 97.3% White, 1.2% Black, 0.4% Asian, 0.0% American Indian/Alaska Native, 0.0% Native Hawaiian/Other Pacific Islander, 1.1% Other, 0.4% Hispanic of any race (2010); Average household size: 2.29 (2010); Median age: 34.9 (2010); Males per 100 females: 78.5 (2010); Marriage status: 31.5% never married, 27.0% now married, 0.0% widowed, 41.4% divorced (2006-2010 5-year est.); Foreign born: 0.0% (2006-2010 5-year est.); Ancestry (includes multiple ancestries): 72.9% English, 52.9% German, 13.9% Dutch, 9.1% Irish, 8.3% Slovak (2006-2010 5-year est.).
Economy: Employment by occupation: 26.3% management, 0.0% professional, 8.8% services, 64.9% sales, 0.0% farming, 0.0% construction, 0.0% production (2006-2010 5-year est.).
Income: Per capita income: $8,564 (2006-2010 5-year est.); Median household income: $26,822 (2006-2010 5-year est.); Average household income: $25,387 (2006-2010 5-year est.); Percent of households with income of $100,000 or more: n/a (2006-2010 5-year est.); Poverty rate: 2.2% (2006-2010 5-year est.).
Education: Percent of population age 25 and over with: High school diploma (including GED) or higher: 94.7% (2006-2010 5-year est.); Bachelor's degree or higher: 0.0% (2006-2010 5-year est.); Master's degree or higher: 0.0% (2006-2010 5-year est.).
Housing: Homeownership rate: 56.4% (2010); Median home value: n/a (2006-2010 5-year est.); Median contract rent: $511 per month (2006-2010 5-year est.); Median year structure built: before 1940 (2006-2010 5-year est.).
Transportation: Commute to work: 71.2% car, 0.0% public transportation, 0.0% walk, 28.8% work from home (2006-2010 5-year est.); Travel time to work: 79.7% less than 15 minutes, 20.3% 15 to 30 minutes, 0.0% 30 to 45 minutes, 0.0% 45 to 60 minutes, 0.0% 60 minutes or more (2006-2010 5-year est.)

GRANT (township). Covers a land area of 26.945 square miles and a water area of 0.059 square miles. Located at 40.78° N. Lat; 78.95° W. Long.
Population: 729 (1990); 696 (2000); 741 (2010); Density: 27.5 persons per square mile (2010); Race: 98.8% White, 0.0% Black, 0.3% Asian, 0.3% American Indian/Alaska Native, 0.0% Native Hawaiian/Other Pacific Islander, 0.6% Other, 1.1% Hispanic of any race (2010); Average household size: 2.38 (2010); Median age: 43.1 (2010); Males per 100 females: 94.5 (2010); Marriage status: 14.1% never married, 65.9% now married, 8.4% widowed, 11.6% divorced (2006-2010 5-year est.); Foreign born: 0.0% (2006-2010 5-year est.); Ancestry (includes multiple ancestries): 35.0% German, 17.8% Irish, 12.3% English, 8.3% Polish, 7.7% Italian (2006-2010 5-year est.).
Economy: Employment by occupation: 6.1% management, 3.3% professional, 12.8% services, 10.3% sales, 4.3% farming, 20.1% construction, 10.6% production (2006-2010 5-year est.).
Income: Per capita income: $18,261 (2006-2010 5-year est.); Median household income: $37,167 (2006-2010 5-year est.); Average household income: $42,484 (2006-2010 5-year est.); Percent of households with income of $100,000 or more: 4.8% (2006-2010 5-year est.); Poverty rate: 6.3% (2006-2010 5-year est.).
Education: Percent of population age 25 and over with: High school diploma (including GED) or higher: 82.2% (2006-2010 5-year est.); Bachelor's degree or higher: 11.0% (2006-2010 5-year est.); Master's degree or higher: 4.4% (2006-2010 5-year est.).
Housing: Homeownership rate: 85.2% (2010); Median home value: $84,600 (2006-2010 5-year est.); Median contract rent: $371 per month (2006-2010 5-year est.); Median year structure built: 1971 (2006-2010 5-year est.).
Transportation: Commute to work: 91.5% car, 0.9% public transportation, 0.0% walk, 6.6% work from home (2006-2010 5-year est.); Travel time to work: 11.7% less than 15 minutes, 31.2% 15 to 30 minutes, 36.9% 30 to 45 minutes, 5.0% 45 to 60 minutes, 15.1% 60 minutes or more (2006-2010 5-year est.)

GREEN (township). Covers a land area of 52.704 square miles and a water area of 0.038 square miles. Located at 40.69° N. Lat; 78.90° W. Long.
Population: 4,095 (1990); 3,995 (2000); 3,839 (2010); Density: 72.8 persons per square mile (2010); Race: 98.5% White, 0.2% Black, 0.1% Asian, 0.1% American Indian/Alaska Native, 0.0% Native Hawaiian/Other Pacific Islander, 1.1% Other, 0.5% Hispanic of any race (2010); Average household size: 2.57 (2010); Median age: 41.5 (2010); Males per 100 females: 103.6 (2010); Marriage status: 26.9% never married, 59.3% now married, 7.3% widowed, 6.5% divorced (2006-2010 5-year est.); Foreign born: 1.3% (2006-2010 5-year est.); Ancestry (includes multiple ancestries): 36.0% German, 15.3% Irish, 12.1% Italian, 9.0% English, 7.6% Polish (2006-2010 5-year est.).
Economy: Single-family building permits issued: 0 (2011); Multi-family building permits issued: 0 (2011); Employment by occupation: 5.3% management, 1.7% professional, 13.3% services, 14.7% sales, 2.8% farming, 15.7% construction, 11.1% production (2006-2010 5-year est.).
Income: Per capita income: $20,360 (2006-2010 5-year est.); Median household income: $39,309 (2006-2010 5-year est.); Average household income: $53,721 (2006-2010 5-year est.); Percent of households with income of $100,000 or more: 6.5% (2006-2010 5-year est.); Poverty rate: 11.1% (2006-2010 5-year est.).
Education: Percent of population age 25 and over with: High school diploma (including GED) or higher: 83.4% (2006-2010 5-year est.); Bachelor's degree or higher: 8.0% (2006-2010 5-year est.); Master's degree or higher: 1.7% (2006-2010 5-year est.).
Housing: Homeownership rate: 82.2% (2010); Median home value: $83,100 (2006-2010 5-year est.); Median contract rent: $416 per month (2006-2010 5-year est.); Median year structure built: 1971 (2006-2010 5-year est.).
Transportation: Commute to work: 93.5% car, 0.0% public transportation, 0.7% walk, 3.1% work from home (2006-2010 5-year est.); Travel time to work: 25.6% less than 15 minutes, 29.4% 15 to 30 minutes, 32.5% 30 to 45 minutes, 4.6% 45 to 60 minutes, 8.0% 60 minutes or more (2006-2010 5-year est.)
Additional Information Contacts
Waynesburg Area Chamber of Commerce . . . . (724) 627-5925
   http://www.waynesburgchamber.com

HEILWOOD (CDP). Covers a land area of 3.801 square miles and a water area of 0.004 square miles. Located at 40.64° N. Lat; 78.86° W. Long. Elevation is 1,755 feet.
Population: 820 (1990); 786 (2000); 711 (2010); Density: 187.1 persons per square mile (2010); Race: 98.9% White, 0.1% Black, 0.0% Asian, 0.0% American Indian/Alaska Native, 0.0% Native Hawaiian/Other Pacific Islander, 1.0% Other, 0.3% Hispanic of any race (2010); Average household size: 2.43 (2010); Median age: 39.4 (2010); Males per 100 females: 97.5 (2010); Marriage status: 27.2% never married, 51.8% now married, 6.2% widowed, 14.8% divorced (2006-2010 5-year est.); Foreign born: 0.0% (2006-2010 5-year est.); Ancestry (includes multiple ancestries): 24.8% Irish, 18.8% German, 17.9% Italian, 9.4% Dutch, 8.7% Polish (2006-2010 5-year est.).
Economy: Employment by occupation: 0.0% management, 0.0% professional, 11.4% services, 26.6% sales, 14.9% farming, 19.4% construction, 9.4% production (2006-2010 5-year est.).
Income: Per capita income: $16,724 (2006-2010 5-year est.); Median household income: $40,833 (2006-2010 5-year est.); Average household income: $41,565 (2006-2010 5-year est.); Percent of households with income of $100,000 or more: n/a (2006-2010 5-year est.); Poverty rate: 27.8% (2006-2010 5-year est.).
Education: Percent of population age 25 and over with: High school diploma (including GED) or higher: 75.5% (2006-2010 5-year est.); Bachelor's degree or higher: 16.7% (2006-2010 5-year est.); Master's degree or higher: 1.6% (2006-2010 5-year est.).
Housing: Homeownership rate: 83.9% (2010); Median home value: $61,500 (2006-2010 5-year est.); Median contract rent: $333 per month (2006-2010 5-year est.); Median year structure built: before 1940 (2006-2010 5-year est.).
Transportation: Commute to work: 88.0% car, 0.0% public transportation, 0.0% walk, 12.0% work from home (2006-2010 5-year est.); Travel time to work: 14.3% less than 15 minutes, 46.7% 15 to 30 minutes, 28.3% 30 to 45 minutes, 0.0% 45 to 60 minutes, 10.7% 60 minutes or more (2006-2010 5-year est.)

HILLSDALE (unincorporated postal area)
Zip Code: 15746
Covers a land area of 1.530 square miles and a water area of 0.006 square miles. Located at 40.75° N. Lat; 78.88° W. Long. Elevation is 1,683 feet. Population: 135 (2010); Density: 88.2 persons per square mile (2010); Race: 99.3% White, 0.0% Black, 0.0% Asian, 0.0% American Indian/Alaska Native, 0.0% Native Hawaiian/Other Pacific Islander, 0.7% Other, 0.7% Hispanic of any race (2010); Average household size: 2.25 (2010); Median age: 46.2 (2010); Males per 100 females: 68.8 (2010); Homeownership rate: 70.0% (2010)

HOME (unincorporated postal area)
Zip Code: 15747
Covers a land area of 30.565 square miles and a water area of 0.040 square miles. Located at 40.77° N. Lat; 79.14° W. Long. Population: 2,027 (2010); Density: 66.3 persons per square mile (2010); Race: 99.9% White, 0.0% Black, 0.0% Asian, 0.0% American Indian/Alaska Native, 0.0% Native Hawaiian/Other Pacific Islander, 0.1% Other, 0.1% Hispanic of any race (2010); Average household size: 2.57 (2010); Median age: 43.2 (2010); Males per 100 females: 97.9 (2010); Homeownership rate: 83.0% (2010)

HOMER CITY (borough). Aka Tide. Covers a land area of 0.552 square miles and a water area of 0.008 square miles. Located at 40.54° N. Lat; 79.16° W. Long. Elevation is 1,030 feet.
Population: 1,834 (1990); 1,844 (2000); 1,707 (2010); Density: 3,091.1 persons per square mile (2010); Race: 98.1% White, 0.4% Black, 0.2% Asian, 0.2% American Indian/Alaska Native, 0.0% Native Hawaiian/Other Pacific Islander, 1.1% Other, 0.3% Hispanic of any race (2010); Average household size: 2.17 (2010); Median age: 44.8 (2010); Males per 100 females: 95.8 (2010); Marriage status: 24.0% never married, 58.7% now married, 9.8% widowed, 7.5% divorced (2006-2010 5-year est.); Foreign born: 0.4% (2006-2010 5-year est.); Ancestry (includes multiple ancestries): 27.7% German, 21.5% Italian, 18.4% Irish, 10.8% English, 10.0% Polish (2006-2010 5-year est.).
Economy: Employment by occupation: 7.7% management, 3.5% professional, 9.3% services, 17.0% sales, 4.7% farming, 14.0% construction, 11.0% production (2006-2010 5-year est.).
Income: Per capita income: $20,882 (2006-2010 5-year est.); Median household income: $39,205 (2006-2010 5-year est.); Average household

income: $46,621 (2006-2010 5-year est.); Percent of households with income of $100,000 or more: 5.5% (2006-2010 5-year est.); Poverty rate: 6.1% (2006-2010 5-year est.).
Education: Percent of population age 25 and over with: High school diploma (including GED) or higher: 91.6% (2006-2010 5-year est.); Bachelor's degree or higher: 17.5% (2006-2010 5-year est.); Master's degree or higher: 4.8% (2006-2010 5-year est.).
School District(s)
Homer-Center SD (KG-12)
   2010-11 Enrollment: 908 . . . . (724) 479-8080
Housing: Homeownership rate: 66.8% (2010); Median home value: $89,700 (2006-2010 5-year est.); Median contract rent: $405 per month (2006-2010 5-year est.); Median year structure built: 1948 (2006-2010 5-year est.).
Safety: Violent crime rate: 23.4 per 10,000 population; Property crime rate: 70.1 per 10,000 population (2011).
Transportation: Commute to work: 91.8% car, 1.0% public transportation, 5.2% walk, 1.2% work from home (2006-2010 5-year est.); Travel time to work: 40.4% less than 15 minutes, 45.5% 15 to 30 minutes, 5.8% 30 to 45 minutes, 2.7% 45 to 60 minutes, 5.5% 60 minutes or more (2006-2010 5-year est.)
Additional Information Contacts
Indiana County Chamber of Commerce . . . . (724) 465-2511
   http://www.indianapa.com/chamber

INDIANA (borough). County seat. Covers a land area of 1.759 square miles and a water area of 0.005 square miles. Located at 40.62° N. Lat; 79.16° W. Long. Elevation is 1,299 feet.
History: Indiana was founded in 1805, when George Clymer of Philadelphia, one of the signers of the Declaration of Independence, donated 250 acres for county buildings. It was probably named for the Territory of Indiana, which Congress formed from the Northwest Territory in 1800.
Population: 15,174 (1990); 14,895 (2000); 13,975 (2010); Density: 7,943.6 persons per square mile (2010); Race: 88.9% White, 6.6% Black, 2.3% Asian, 0.1% American Indian/Alaska Native, 0.0% Native Hawaiian/Other Pacific Islander, 2.1% Other, 2.0% Hispanic of any race (2010); Average household size: 2.23 (2010); Median age: 21.6 (2010); Males per 100 females: 80.9 (2010); Marriage status: 66.2% never married, 24.4% now married, 3.7% widowed, 5.7% divorced (2006-2010 5-year est.); Foreign born: 4.6% (2006-2010 5-year est.); Ancestry (includes multiple ancestries): 32.4% German, 24.8% Irish, 17.8% Italian, 6.8% English, 6.6% Polish (2006-2010 5-year est.).
Economy: Single-family building permits issued: 0 (2011); Multi-family building permits issued: 9 (2011); Employment by occupation: 5.2% management, 4.2% professional, 16.6% services, 20.9% sales, 4.9% farming, 5.7% construction, 5.0% production (2006-2010 5-year est.).
Income: Per capita income: $14,330 (2006-2010 5-year est.); Median household income: $21,729 (2006-2010 5-year est.); Average household income: $37,625 (2006-2010 5-year est.); Percent of households with income of $100,000 or more: 6.8% (2006-2010 5-year est.); Poverty rate: 45.6% (2006-2010 5-year est.).
Taxes: Total city taxes per capita: $192 (2009); City property taxes per capita: $109 (2009).
Education: Percent of population age 25 and over with: High school diploma (including GED) or higher: 95.6% (2006-2010 5-year est.); Bachelor's degree or higher: 39.4% (2006-2010 5-year est.); Master's degree or higher: 16.0% (2006-2010 5-year est.).
School District(s)
Indiana Area SD (KG-12)
   2010-11 Enrollment: 2,769 . . . . (724) 463-8713
Indiana County Technology Center (09-12)
   2010-11 Enrollment: n/a . . . . (724) 349-6700
Four-year College(s)
Indiana University of Pennsylvania-Main Campus (Public)
   Fall 2010 Enrollment: 14,265 . . . . (724) 357-2100
   2011-12 Tuition: In-state $8,362; Out-of-state $18,854
Two-year College(s)
Cambria-Rowe Business College-Indiana (Private, For-profit)
   Fall 2010 Enrollment: 202 . . . . (724) 463-0222
   2011-12 Tuition: In-state $11,205; Out-of-state $11,205
Vocational/Technical School(s)
Indiana County Technology Center (Public)
   Fall 2010 Enrollment: 92 . . . . (724) 349-6700
   2011-12 Tuition: $14,276

Housing: Homeownership rate: 36.5% (2010); Median home value: $94,900 (2006-2010 5-year est.); Median contract rent: $586 per month (2006-2010 5-year est.); Median year structure built: 1951 (2006-2010 5-year est.).
Hospitals: Indiana Regional Medical Center (162 beds)
Safety: Violent crime rate: 134.1 per 10,000 population; Property crime rate: 191.9 per 10,000 population (2011).
Newspapers: The Indiana Gazette (Local news; Circulation 15,578); Pittsburgh Boomers (Local news)
Transportation: Commute to work: 71.9% car, 1.4% public transportation, 22.9% walk, 2.9% work from home (2006-2010 5-year est.); Travel time to work: 67.7% less than 15 minutes, 18.0% 15 to 30 minutes, 7.0% 30 to 45 minutes, 3.2% 45 to 60 minutes, 4.2% 60 minutes or more (2006-2010 5-year est.)
Airports: Indiana County/Jimmy Stewart Field (general aviation)
Additional Information Contacts
Borough of Indiana . . . . (724) 465-2391
　http://www.indianapa.com
Indiana County Chamber of Commerce . . . . (724) 465-2511
　http://www.indianapa.com/chamber

JACKSONVILLE (CDP). Aka Kent. Covers a land area of 6.763 square miles and a water area of 0.013 square miles. Located at 40.57° N. Lat; 79.29° W. Long. Elevation is 1,083 feet.
Population: 728 (1990); 675 (2000); 637 (2010); Density: 94.2 persons per square mile (2010); Race: 98.0% White, 0.6% Black, 0.3% Asian, 0.2% American Indian/Alaska Native, 0.0% Native Hawaiian/Other Pacific Islander, 0.9% Other, 0.2% Hispanic of any race (2010); Average household size: 2.31 (2010); Median age: 39.5 (2010); Males per 100 females: 99.7 (2010); Marriage status: 31.2% never married, 47.7% now married, 11.5% widowed, 9.6% divorced (2006-2010 5-year est.); Foreign born: 0.0% (2006-2010 5-year est.); Ancestry (includes multiple ancestries): 35.7% German, 22.4% Irish, 16.9% Polish, 11.6% Italian, 9.3% Slovak (2006-2010 5-year est.).
Economy: Employment by occupation: 4.5% management, 9.0% professional, 11.5% services, 13.5% sales, 1.7% farming, 14.6% construction, 14.2% production (2006-2010 5-year est.).
Income: Per capita income: $21,767 (2006-2010 5-year est.); Median household income: $42,083 (2006-2010 5-year est.); Average household income: $47,667 (2006-2010 5-year est.); Percent of households with income of $100,000 or more: 7.8% (2006-2010 5-year est.); Poverty rate: 12.1% (2006-2010 5-year est.).
Education: Percent of population age 25 and over with: High school diploma (including GED) or higher: 88.8% (2006-2010 5-year est.); Bachelor's degree or higher: 13.6% (2006-2010 5-year est.); Master's degree or higher: 2.8% (2006-2010 5-year est.).
Housing: Homeownership rate: 77.9% (2010); Median home value: $57,100 (2006-2010 5-year est.); Median contract rent: $508 per month (2006-2010 5-year est.); Median year structure built: before 1940 (2006-2010 5-year est.).
Transportation: Commute to work: 99.7% car, 0.0% public transportation, 0.0% walk, 0.0% work from home (2006-2010 5-year est.); Travel time to work: 9.4% less than 15 minutes, 63.5% 15 to 30 minutes, 15.6% 30 to 45 minutes, 5.6% 45 to 60 minutes, 5.9% 60 minutes or more (2006-2010 5-year est.)

JOSEPHINE (unincorporated postal area)
Zip Code: 15750
　Covers a land area of 0.485 square miles and a water area of 0 square miles. Located at 40.48° N. Lat; 79.18° W. Long. Elevation is 1,030 feet. Population: 245 (2010); Density: 504.5 persons per square mile (2010); Race: 95.9% White, 3.7% Black, 0.0% Asian, 0.0% American Indian/Alaska Native, 0.0% Native Hawaiian/Other Pacific Islander, 0.4% Other, 6.5% Hispanic of any race (2010); Average household size: 2.29 (2010); Median age: 40.3 (2010); Males per 100 females: 100.8 (2010); Homeownership rate: 44.8% (2010)

KENT (unincorporated postal area)
Zip Code: 15752
　Covers a land area of 0.045 square miles and a water area of 0 square miles. Located at 40.54° N. Lat; 79.28° W. Long. Population: 54 (2010); Density: 1,193.9 persons per square mile (2010); Race: 96.3% White, 3.7% Black, 0.0% Asian, 0.0% American Indian/Alaska Native, 0.0% Native Hawaiian/Other Pacific Islander, 0.0% Other, 0.0% Hispanic of any race (2010); Average household size: 2.16 (2010); Median age:

43.0 (2010); Males per 100 females: 63.6 (2010); Homeownership rate: 48.0% (2010)

LUCERNE MINES (CDP). Aka Lucernemines. Covers a land area of 0.835 square miles and a water area of 0.007 square miles. Located at 40.56° N. Lat; 79.15° W. Long. Elevation is 1,148 feet.
Population: 1,074 (1990); 951 (2000); 937 (2010); Density: 1,122.5 persons per square mile (2010); Race: 97.1% White, 0.5% Black, 0.1% Asian, 0.2% American Indian/Alaska Native, 0.0% Native Hawaiian/Other Pacific Islander, 2.1% Other, 0.5% Hispanic of any race (2010); Average household size: 2.32 (2010); Median age: 43.1 (2010); Males per 100 females: 95.2 (2010); Marriage status: 33.3% never married, 48.6% now married, 8.1% widowed, 10.0% divorced (2006-2010 5-year est.); Foreign born: 0.0% (2006-2010 5-year est.); Ancestry (includes multiple ancestries): 26.5% German, 26.1% Irish, 21.3% Italian, 8.2% Slovak, 7.2% Scottish (2006-2010 5-year est.).
Economy: Employment by occupation: 6.5% management, 0.0% professional, 14.4% services, 23.5% sales, 6.7% farming, 18.0% construction, 1.0% production (2006-2010 5-year est.).
Income: Per capita income: $17,947 (2006-2010 5-year est.); Median household income: $33,516 (2006-2010 5-year est.); Average household income: $46,813 (2006-2010 5-year est.); Percent of households with income of $100,000 or more: 2.5% (2006-2010 5-year est.); Poverty rate: 24.8% (2006-2010 5-year est.).
Education: Percent of population age 25 and over with: High school diploma (including GED) or higher: 93.6% (2006-2010 5-year est.); Bachelor's degree or higher: 21.8% (2006-2010 5-year est.); Master's degree or higher: 4.8% (2006-2010 5-year est.).
Housing: Homeownership rate: 81.4% (2010); Median home value: $82,200 (2006-2010 5-year est.); Median contract rent: $360 per month (2006-2010 5-year est.); Median year structure built: before 1940 (2006-2010 5-year est.).
Transportation: Commute to work: 80.0% car, 18.6% public transportation, 1.4% walk, 0.0% work from home (2006-2010 5-year est.); Travel time to work: 56.9% less than 15 minutes, 25.9% 15 to 30 minutes, 3.4% 30 to 45 minutes, 10.5% 45 to 60 minutes, 3.4% 60 minutes or more (2006-2010 5-year est.)

LUCERNEMINES (unincorporated postal area)
Zip Code: 15754
　Covers a land area of 0.432 square miles and a water area of 0 square miles. Located at 40.55° N. Lat; 79.15° W. Long. Population: 502 (2010); Density: 1,160.0 persons per square mile (2010); Race: 95.8% White, 0.8% Black, 0.0% Asian, 0.4% American Indian/Alaska Native, 0.0% Native Hawaiian/Other Pacific Islander, 3.0% Other, 0.6% Hispanic of any race (2010); Average household size: 2.35 (2010); Median age: 44.0 (2010); Males per 100 females: 100.8 (2010); Homeownership rate: 86.9% (2010)

MARION CENTER (borough). Covers a land area of 0.743 square miles and a water area of 0 square miles. Located at 40.77° N. Lat; 79.05° W. Long. Elevation is 1,289 feet.
Population: 476 (1990); 451 (2000); 451 (2010); Density: 606.9 persons per square mile (2010); Race: 98.9% White, 0.4% Black, 0.2% Asian, 0.2% American Indian/Alaska Native, 0.0% Native Hawaiian/Other Pacific Islander, 0.3% Other, 0.0% Hispanic of any race (2010); Average household size: 2.61 (2010); Median age: 33.1 (2010); Males per 100 females: 86.4 (2010); Marriage status: 32.8% never married, 55.5% now married, 1.8% widowed, 9.9% divorced (2006-2010 5-year est.); Foreign born: 0.5% (2006-2010 5-year est.); Ancestry (includes multiple ancestries): 47.3% German, 24.0% Irish, 11.4% Scotch-Irish, 7.8% English, 7.6% Italian (2006-2010 5-year est.).
Economy: Single-family building permits issued: 0 (2011); Multi-family building permits issued: 0 (2011); Employment by occupation: 1.0% management, 0.0% professional, 17.9% services, 19.5% sales, 1.5% farming, 12.3% construction, 10.3% production (2006-2010 5-year est.).
Income: Per capita income: $16,979 (2006-2010 5-year est.); Median household income: $38,942 (2006-2010 5-year est.); Average household income: $43,205 (2006-2010 5-year est.); Percent of households with income of $100,000 or more: 2.4% (2006-2010 5-year est.); Poverty rate: 18.5% (2006-2010 5-year est.).
Education: Percent of population age 25 and over with: High school diploma (including GED) or higher: 88.2% (2006-2010 5-year est.); Bachelor's degree or higher: 15.5% (2006-2010 5-year est.); Master's degree or higher: 0.8% (2006-2010 5-year est.).

School District(s)

Marion Center Area SD (PK-12)

2010-11 Enrollment: 1,480 . . . . (724) 397-5551

Housing: Homeownership rate: 65.3% (2010); Median home value: $70,000 (2006-2010 5-year est.); Median contract rent: $368 per month (2006-2010 5-year est.); Median year structure built: 1964 (2006-2010 5-year est.).

Transportation: Commute to work: 94.6% car, 0.0% public transportation, 2.2% walk, 3.2% work from home (2006-2010 5-year est.); Travel time to work: 31.7% less than 15 minutes, 39.4% 15 to 30 minutes, 23.3% 30 to 45 minutes, 2.8% 45 to 60 minutes, 2.8% 60 minutes or more (2006-2010 5-year est.)

MENTCLE (unincorporated postal area)

Zip Code: 15761

Covers a land area of 1.035 square miles and a water area of 0 square miles. Located at 40.63° N. Lat; 78.88° W. Long. Elevation is 1,768 feet. Population: 111 (2010); Density: 107.2 persons per square mile (2010); Race: 100.0% White, 0.0% Black, 0.0% Asian, 0.0% American Indian/Alaska Native, 0.0% Native Hawaiian/Other Pacific Islander, 0.0% Other, 0.9% Hispanic of any race (2010); Average household size: 2.64 (2010); Median age: 37.5 (2010); Males per 100 females: 94.7 (2010); Homeownership rate: 81.0% (2010).

MONTGOMERY (township).

Covers a land area of 28.657 square miles and a water area of 0.064 square miles. Located at 40.77° N. Lat; 78.86° W. Long.

Population: 1,729 (1990); 1,706 (2000); 1,568 (2010); Density: 54.7 persons per square mile (2010); Race: 98.8% White, 0.5% Black, 0.2% Asian, 0.1% American Indian/Alaska Native, 0.0% Native Hawaiian/Other Pacific Islander, 0.4% Other, 0.3% Hispanic of any race (2010); Average household size: 2.54 (2010); Median age: 46.8 (2010); Males per 100 females: 102.6 (2010); Marriage status: 27.7% never married, 58.2% now married, 10.0% widowed, 4.2% divorced (2006-2010 5-year est.); Foreign born: 0.2% (2006-2010 5-year est.); Ancestry (includes multiple ancestries): 34.1% German, 21.0% Irish, 9.4% Polish, 9.1% Slovak, 7.8% English (2006-2010 5-year est.).

Economy: Employment by occupation: 7.4% management, 1.1% professional, 17.0% services, 14.6% sales, 2.4% farming, 18.2% construction, 5.6% production (2006-2010 5-year est.).

Income: Per capita income: $19,023 (2006-2010 5-year est.); Median household income: $38,281 (2006-2010 5-year est.); Average household income: $50,004 (2006-2010 5-year est.); Percent of households with income of $100,000 or more: 7.5% (2006-2010 5-year est.); Poverty rate: 13.8% (2006-2010 5-year est.).

Education: Percent of population age 25 and over with: High school diploma (including GED) or higher: 80.0% (2006-2010 5-year est.); Bachelor's degree or higher: 5.8% (2006-2010 5-year est.); Master's degree or higher: 0.9% (2006-2010 5-year est.).

Housing: Homeownership rate: 82.8% (2010); Median home value: $71,800 (2006-2010 5-year est.); Median contract rent: $338 per month (2006-2010 5-year est.); Median year structure built: 1971 (2006-2010 5-year est.).

Transportation: Commute to work: 92.9% car, 0.0% public transportation, 0.0% walk, 6.6% work from home (2006-2010 5-year est.); Travel time to work: 19.4% less than 15 minutes, 24.9% 15 to 30 minutes, 29.0% 30 to 45 minutes, 17.8% 45 to 60 minutes, 8.9% 60 minutes or more (2006-2010 5-year est.)

Additional Information Contacts

Indiana County Chamber of Commerce . . . . (724) 465-2511

http://www.indianapa.com/chamber

NORTH MAHONING (township).

Covers a land area of 28.213 square miles and a water area of 0.099 square miles. Located at 40.88° N. Lat; 79.05° W. Long.

Population: 1,254 (1990); 1,383 (2000); 1,428 (2010); Density: 50.6 persons per square mile (2010); Race: 98.7% White, 0.1% Black, 0.0% Asian, 0.1% American Indian/Alaska Native, 0.0% Native Hawaiian/Other Pacific Islander, 1.1% Other, 0.4% Hispanic of any race (2010); Average household size: 2.81 (2010); Median age: 39.5 (2010); Males per 100 females: 97.5 (2010); Marriage status: 21.7% never married, 63.5% now married, 8.8% widowed, 6.0% divorced (2006-2010 5-year est.); Foreign born: 0.5% (2006-2010 5-year est.); Ancestry (includes multiple ancestries): 33.9% German, 18.5% Irish, 8.5% English, 5.4% Pennsylvania German, 5.2% Dutch (2006-2010 5-year est.).

Economy: Employment by occupation: 3.8% management, 0.0% professional, 13.5% services, 9.9% sales, 3.6% farming, 22.1% construction, 15.4% production (2006-2010 5-year est.).

Income: Per capita income: $18,516 (2006-2010 5-year est.); Median household income: $46,328 (2006-2010 5-year est.); Average household income: $48,988 (2006-2010 5-year est.); Percent of households with income of $100,000 or more: 5.1% (2006-2010 5-year est.); Poverty rate: 10.9% (2006-2010 5-year est.).

Education: Percent of population age 25 and over with: High school diploma (including GED) or higher: 74.9% (2006-2010 5-year est.); Bachelor's degree or higher: 8.9% (2006-2010 5-year est.); Master's degree or higher: 2.3% (2006-2010 5-year est.).

Housing: Homeownership rate: 84.0% (2010); Median home value: $117,700 (2006-2010 5-year est.); Median contract rent: $472 per month (2006-2010 5-year est.); Median year structure built: 1972 (2006-2010 5-year est.).

Transportation: Commute to work: 86.3% car, 0.0% public transportation, 3.8% walk, 8.9% work from home (2006-2010 5-year est.); Travel time to work: 26.3% less than 15 minutes, 31.9% 15 to 30 minutes, 15.0% 30 to 45 minutes, 18.8% 45 to 60 minutes, 8.0% 60 minutes or more (2006-2010 5-year est.)

Additional Information Contacts

Punxsutawney Area Chamber of Commerce . . . . (814) 938-7700

http://www.punxsutawney.com

PENN RUN (unincorporated postal area)

Zip Code: 15765

Covers a land area of 37.515 square miles and a water area of 0.617 square miles. Located at 40.59° N. Lat; 78.99° W. Long. Elevation is 1,453 feet. Population: 1,707 (2010); Density: 45.5 persons per square mile (2010); Race: 99.4% White, 0.0% Black, 0.3% Asian, 0.0% American Indian/Alaska Native, 0.0% Native Hawaiian/Other Pacific Islander, 0.3% Other, 0.8% Hispanic of any race (2010); Average household size: 2.52 (2010); Median age: 46.0 (2010); Males per 100 females: 102.7 (2010); Homeownership rate: 78.2% (2010)

PINE (township).

Covers a land area of 31.031 square miles and a water area of 0.023 square miles. Located at 40.59° N. Lat; 78.91° W. Long.

Population: 2,172 (1990); 2,140 (2000); 2,033 (2010); Density: 65.5 persons per square mile (2010); Race: 98.9% White, 0.1% Black, 0.1% Asian, 0.1% American Indian/Alaska Native, 0.0% Native Hawaiian/Other Pacific Islander, 0.8% Other, 0.3% Hispanic of any race (2010); Average household size: 2.51 (2010); Median age: 42.2 (2010); Males per 100 females: 98.0 (2010); Marriage status: 22.1% never married, 63.7% now married, 6.8% widowed, 7.4% divorced (2006-2010 5-year est.); Foreign born: 0.0% (2006-2010 5-year est.); Ancestry (includes multiple ancestries): 34.1% German, 18.3% Irish, 10.2% Italian, 8.2% English, 7.7% Polish (2006-2010 5-year est.).

Economy: Employment by occupation: 5.6% management, 3.7% professional, 11.3% services, 24.9% sales, 9.1% farming, 15.8% construction, 7.2% production (2006-2010 5-year est.).

Income: Per capita income: $19,569 (2006-2010 5-year est.); Median household income: $45,355 (2006-2010 5-year est.); Average household income: $50,675 (2006-2010 5-year est.); Percent of households with income of $100,000 or more: 7.9% (2006-2010 5-year est.); Poverty rate: 17.9% (2006-2010 5-year est.).

Education: Percent of population age 25 and over with: High school diploma (including GED) or higher: 81.1% (2006-2010 5-year est.); Bachelor's degree or higher: 14.5% (2006-2010 5-year est.); Master's degree or higher: 2.2% (2006-2010 5-year est.).

Housing: Homeownership rate: 86.2% (2010); Median home value: $78,400 (2006-2010 5-year est.); Median contract rent: $340 per month (2006-2010 5-year est.); Median year structure built: 1949 (2006-2010 5-year est.).

Transportation: Commute to work: 90.9% car, 0.0% public transportation, 0.8% walk, 8.3% work from home (2006-2010 5-year est.); Travel time to work: 14.3% less than 15 minutes, 41.0% 15 to 30 minutes, 32.4% 30 to 45 minutes, 3.6% 45 to 60 minutes, 8.7% 60 minutes or more (2006-2010 5-year est.)

Additional Information Contacts

Indiana County Chamber of Commerce . . . . (724) 465-2511

http://www.indianapa.com/chamber

PLUMVILLE (borough). Covers a land area of 0.496 square miles and a water area of 0 square miles. Located at 40.79° N. Lat; 79.18° W. Long. Elevation is 1,171 feet.

Population: 390 (1990); 342 (2000); 307 (2010); Density: 619.4 persons per square mile (2010); Race: 98.4% White, 0.3% Black, 0.3% Asian, 0.0% American Indian/Alaska Native, 0.0% Native Hawaiian/Other Pacific Islander, 1.0% Other, 0.3% Hispanic of any race (2010); Average household size: 2.58 (2010); Median age: 36.2 (2010); Males per 100 females: 106.0 (2010); Marriage status: 21.0% never married, 68.5% now married, 6.4% widowed, 4.1% divorced (2006-2010 5-year est.); Foreign born: 2.1% (2006-2010 5-year est.); Ancestry (includes multiple ancestries): 26.8% German, 19.7% Irish, 11.9% English, 10.1% Polish, 6.0% Italian (2006-2010 5-year est.).

Economy: Employment by occupation: 3.3% management, 1.3% professional, 19.6% services, 10.5% sales, 0.7% farming, 22.9% construction, 13.7% production (2006-2010 5-year est.).

Income: Per capita income: $15,871 (2006-2010 5-year est.); Median household income: $37,788 (2006-2010 5-year est.); Average household income: $47,874 (2006-2010 5-year est.); Percent of households with income of $100,000 or more: 6.9% (2006-2010 5-year est.); Poverty rate: 29.8% (2006-2010 5-year est.).

Education: Percent of population age 25 and over with: High school diploma (including GED) or higher: 85.9% (2006-2010 5-year est.); Bachelor's degree or higher: 12.1% (2006-2010 5-year est.); Master's degree or higher: 1.6% (2006-2010 5-year est.).

Housing: Homeownership rate: 81.5% (2010); Median home value: $74,200 (2006-2010 5-year est.); Median contract rent: $420 per month (2006-2010 5-year est.); Median year structure built: before 1940 (2006-2010 5-year est.).

Transportation: Commute to work: 93.0% car, 0.0% public transportation, 5.4% walk, 1.6% work from home (2006-2010 5-year est.); Travel time to work: 21.3% less than 15 minutes, 34.6% 15 to 30 minutes, 29.1% 30 to 45 minutes, 3.1% 45 to 60 minutes, 11.8% 60 minutes or more (2006-2010 5-year est.)

RAYNE (township). Covers a land area of 47.125 square miles and a water area of 0.129 square miles. Located at 40.71° N. Lat; 79.10° W. Long. Elevation is 1,260 feet.

Population: 3,339 (1990); 3,292 (2000); 2,992 (2010); Density: 63.5 persons per square mile (2010); Race: 99.4% White, 0.1% Black, 0.1% Asian, 0.0% American Indian/Alaska Native, 0.0% Native Hawaiian/Other Pacific Islander, 0.4% Other, 0.3% Hispanic of any race (2010); Average household size: 2.45 (2010); Median age: 46.1 (2010); Males per 100 females: 102.3 (2010); Marriage status: 25.3% never married, 64.1% now married, 3.5% widowed, 7.2% divorced (2006-2010 5-year est.); Foreign born: 0.6% (2006-2010 5-year est.); Ancestry (includes multiple ancestries): 38.8% German, 20.4% Irish, 10.7% Slovak, 7.4% English, 6.9% Polish (2006-2010 5-year est.).

Economy: Single-family building permits issued: 3 (2011); Multi-family building permits issued: 0 (2011); Employment by occupation: 8.8% management, 3.5% professional, 6.0% services, 20.6% sales, 4.2% farming, 18.7% construction, 7.1% production (2006-2010 5-year est.).

Income: Per capita income: $25,833 (2006-2010 5-year est.); Median household income: $63,024 (2006-2010 5-year est.); Average household income: $70,898 (2006-2010 5-year est.); Percent of households with income of $100,000 or more: 18.8% (2006-2010 5-year est.); Poverty rate: 9.6% (2006-2010 5-year est.).

Education: Percent of population age 25 and over with: High school diploma (including GED) or higher: 89.4% (2006-2010 5-year est.); Bachelor's degree or higher: 22.6% (2006-2010 5-year est.); Master's degree or higher: 8.9% (2006-2010 5-year est.).

Housing: Homeownership rate: 81.7% (2010); Median home value: $134,900 (2006-2010 5-year est.); Median contract rent: $421 per month (2006-2010 5-year est.); Median year structure built: 1968 (2006-2010 5-year est.).

Transportation: Commute to work: 91.2% car, 0.0% public transportation, 1.3% walk, 6.9% work from home (2006-2010 5-year est.); Travel time to work: 21.7% less than 15 minutes, 50.0% 15 to 30 minutes, 15.2% 30 to 45 minutes, 3.1% 45 to 60 minutes, 10.1% 60 minutes or more (2006-2010 5-year est.).

Additional Information Contacts
Indiana County Chamber of Commerce . . . . (724) 465-2511
  http://www.indianapa.com/chamber

ROBINSON (CDP). Covers a land area of 0.986 square miles and a water area of 0.037 square miles. Located at 40.41° N. Lat; 79.14° W. Long. Elevation is 1,106 feet.

Population: n/a (1990); n/a (2000); 614 (2010); Density: 622.6 persons per square mile (2010); Race: 98.2% White, 0.7% Black, 0.2% Asian, 0.2% American Indian/Alaska Native, 0.0% Native Hawaiian/Other Pacific Islander, 0.7% Other, 1.6% Hispanic of any race (2010); Average household size: 2.41 (2010); Median age: 43.1 (2010); Males per 100 females: 93.7 (2010); Marriage status: 21.4% never married, 60.3% now married, 8.8% widowed, 9.6% divorced (2006-2010 5-year est.); Foreign born: 0.0% (2006-2010 5-year est.); Ancestry (includes multiple ancestries): 38.8% German, 13.7% Irish, 11.6% English, 8.1% Dutch, 3.4% Scottish (2006-2010 5-year est.).

Economy: Employment by occupation: 1.4% management, 0.0% professional, 12.0% services, 5.6% sales, 16.2% farming, 7.7% construction, 15.5% production (2006-2010 5-year est.).

Income: Per capita income: $15,592 (2006-2010 5-year est.); Median household income: $26,250 (2006-2010 5-year est.); Average household income: $35,638 (2006-2010 5-year est.); Percent of households with income of $100,000 or more: 9.4% (2006-2010 5-year est.); Poverty rate: 19.5% (2006-2010 5-year est.).

Education: Percent of population age 25 and over with: High school diploma (including GED) or higher: 73.1% (2006-2010 5-year est.); Bachelor's degree or higher: 2.1% (2006-2010 5-year est.); Master's degree or higher: 0.0% (2006-2010 5-year est.).

Housing: Homeownership rate: 78.0% (2010); Median home value: $54,100 (2006-2010 5-year est.); Median contract rent: $422 per month (2006-2010 5-year est.); Median year structure built: before 1940 (2006-2010 5-year est.).

Transportation: Commute to work: 100.0% car, 0.0% public transportation, 0.0% walk, 0.0% work from home (2006-2010 5-year est.); Travel time to work: 9.2% less than 15 minutes, 36.7% 15 to 30 minutes, 41.7% 30 to 45 minutes, 12.5% 45 to 60 minutes, 0.0% 60 minutes or more (2006-2010 5-year est.).

ROCHESTER MILLS (unincorporated postal area)
Zip Code: 15771

  Covers a land area of 33.435 square miles and a water area of 0.171 square miles. Located at 40.83° N. Lat; 78.98° W. Long. Elevation is 1,319 feet. Population: 991 (2010); Density: 29.6 persons per square mile (2010); Race: 99.0% White, 0.1% Black, 0.1% Asian, 0.1% American Indian/Alaska Native, 0.0% Native Hawaiian/Other Pacific Islander, 0.7% Other, 0.0% Hispanic of any race (2010); Average household size: 2.41 (2010); Median age: 46.7 (2010); Males per 100 females: 95.5 (2010); Homeownership rate: 85.6% (2010)

ROSSITER (CDP). Covers a land area of 1.886 square miles and a water area of <.001 square miles. Located at 40.90° N. Lat; 78.94° W. Long. Elevation is 1,417 feet.

Population: 894 (1990); 790 (2000); 646 (2010); Density: 342.6 persons per square mile (2010); Race: 98.9% White, 0.2% Black, 0.0% Asian, 0.8% American Indian/Alaska Native, 0.0% Native Hawaiian/Other Pacific Islander, 0.1% Other, 0.2% Hispanic of any race (2010); Average household size: 2.70 (2010); Median age: 49.3 (2010); Males per 100 females: 138.4 (2010); Marriage status: 28.1% never married, 56.3% now married, 9.2% widowed, 6.4% divorced (2006-2010 5-year est.); Foreign born: 0.0% (2006-2010 5-year est.); Ancestry (includes multiple ancestries): 26.8% German, 25.2% Irish, 11.3% Italian, 10.1% Slovak, 9.8% American (2006-2010 5-year est.).

Economy: Employment by occupation: 13.4% management, 0.0% professional, 15.5% services, 15.1% sales, 0.0% farming, 17.2% construction, 7.6% production (2006-2010 5-year est.).

Income: Per capita income: $15,290 (2006-2010 5-year est.); Median household income: $29,511 (2006-2010 5-year est.); Average household income: $37,623 (2006-2010 5-year est.); Percent of households with income of $100,000 or more: 2.8% (2006-2010 5-year est.); Poverty rate: 19.8% (2006-2010 5-year est.).

Education: Percent of population age 25 and over with: High school diploma (including GED) or higher: 80.0% (2006-2010 5-year est.); Bachelor's degree or higher: 7.6% (2006-2010 5-year est.); Master's degree or higher: 0.7% (2006-2010 5-year est.).

Housing: Homeownership rate: 69.6% (2010); Median home value: $47,000 (2006-2010 5-year est.); Median contract rent: $387 per month (2006-2010 5-year est.); Median year structure built: before 1940 (2006-2010 5-year est.).

Transportation: Commute to work: 84.2% car, 0.0% public transportation, 15.8% walk, 0.0% work from home (2006-2010 5-year est.); Travel time to work: 42.5% less than 15 minutes, 30.7% 15 to 30 minutes, 9.2% 30 to 45 minutes, 0.9% 45 to 60 minutes, 16.7% 60 minutes or more (2006-2010 5-year est.)

SALTSBURG (borough). Covers a land area of 0.213 square miles and a water area of 0.033 square miles. Located at 40.48° N. Lat; 79.45° W. Long. Elevation is 863 feet.

Population: 1,004 (1990); 955 (2000); 873 (2010); Density: 4,108.2 persons per square mile (2010); Race: 98.6% White, 0.1% Black, 0.0% Asian, 0.0% American Indian/Alaska Native, 0.0% Native Hawaiian/Other Pacific Islander, 1.3% Other, 0.8% Hispanic of any race (2010); Average household size: 2.29 (2010); Median age: 44.1 (2010); Males per 100 females: 93.1 (2010); Marriage status: 23.0% never married, 59.6% now married, 6.4% widowed, 10.9% divorced (2006-2010 5-year est.); Foreign born: 1.3% (2006-2010 5-year est.); Ancestry (includes multiple ancestries): 39.6% German, 24.3% Irish, 15.5% Italian, 14.4% English, 3.6% Polish (2006-2010 5-year est.).

Economy: Employment by occupation: 7.2% management, 3.8% professional, 9.1% services, 15.8% sales, 4.3% farming, 13.2% construction, 8.1% production (2006-2010 5-year est.).

Income: Per capita income: $18,788 (2006-2010 5-year est.); Median household income: $42,500 (2006-2010 5-year est.); Average household income: $45,149 (2006-2010 5-year est.); Percent of households with income of $100,000 or more: 6.3% (2006-2010 5-year est.); Poverty rate: 21.6% (2006-2010 5-year est.).

Education: Percent of population age 25 and over with: High school diploma (including GED) or higher: 90.8% (2006-2010 5-year est.); Bachelor's degree or higher: 17.9% (2006-2010 5-year est.); Master's degree or higher: 5.3% (2006-2010 5-year est.).

School District(s)

Blairsville-Saltsburg SD (KG-12)

   2010-11 Enrollment: 1,813 . . . . (724) 459-5500

Housing: Homeownership rate: 56.0% (2010); Median home value: $88,600 (2006-2010 5-year est.); Median contract rent: $383 per month (2006-2010 5-year est.); Median year structure built: before 1940 (2006-2010 5-year est.).

Safety: Violent crime rate: 0.0 per 10,000 population; Property crime rate: 102.7 per 10,000 population (2011).

Transportation: Commute to work: 86.6% car, 0.7% public transportation, 10.2% walk, 1.2% work from home (2006-2010 5-year est.); Travel time to work: 29.1% less than 15 minutes, 35.8% 15 to 30 minutes, 23.0% 30 to 45 minutes, 4.4% 45 to 60 minutes, 7.7% 60 minutes or more (2006-2010 5-year est.)

SHELOCTA (borough). Covers a land area of 0.104 square miles and a water area of <.001 square miles. Located at 40.66° N. Lat; 79.30° W. Long. Elevation is 988 feet.

Population: 108 (1990); 127 (2000); 130 (2010); Density: 1,249.6 persons per square mile (2010); Race: 93.8% White, 0.0% Black, 0.0% Asian, 0.0% American Indian/Alaska Native, 0.0% Native Hawaiian/Other Pacific Islander, 6.2% Other, 0.0% Hispanic of any race (2010); Average household size: 2.36 (2010); Median age: 35.0 (2010); Males per 100 females: 100.0 (2010); Marriage status: 15.1% never married, 74.2% now married, 2.2% widowed, 8.6% divorced (2006-2010 5-year est.); Foreign born: 5.9% (2006-2010 5-year est.); Ancestry (includes multiple ancestries): 26.3% German, 25.4% Irish, 9.3% Italian, 6.8% Polish, 5.9% Liberian (2006-2010 5-year est.).

Economy: Employment by occupation: 0.0% management, 0.0% professional, 0.0% services, 36.0% sales, 10.0% farming, 6.0% construction, 4.0% production (2006-2010 5-year est.).

Income: Per capita income: $18,795 (2006-2010 5-year est.); Median household income: $47,857 (2006-2010 5-year est.); Average household income: $47,135 (2006-2010 5-year est.); Percent of households with income of $100,000 or more: n/a (2006-2010 5-year est.); Poverty rate: 8.5% (2006-2010 5-year est.).

Education: Percent of population age 25 and over with: High school diploma (including GED) or higher: 93.8% (2006-2010 5-year est.); Bachelor's degree or higher: 9.9% (2006-2010 5-year est.); Master's degree or higher: 1.2% (2006-2010 5-year est.).

Housing: Homeownership rate: 47.2% (2010); Median home value: $82,500 (2006-2010 5-year est.); Median contract rent: $538 per month (2006-2010 5-year est.); Median year structure built: 1957 (2006-2010 5-year est.).

Transportation: Commute to work: 98.0% car, 0.0% public transportation, 0.0% walk, 2.0% work from home (2006-2010 5-year est.); Travel time to work: 20.4% less than 15 minutes, 67.3% 15 to 30 minutes, 4.1% 30 to 45 minutes, 4.1% 45 to 60 minutes, 4.1% 60 minutes or more (2006-2010 5-year est.)

SMICKSBURG (borough). Covers a land area of 0.146 square miles and a water area of 0 square miles. Located at 40.87° N. Lat; 79.17° W. Long. Elevation is 1,178 feet.

Population: 76 (1990); 49 (2000); 46 (2010); Density: 315.1 persons per square mile (2010); Race: 97.8% White, 0.0% Black, 0.0% Asian, 0.0% American Indian/Alaska Native, 0.0% Native Hawaiian/Other Pacific Islander, 2.2% Other, 0.0% Hispanic of any race (2010); Average household size: 2.09 (2010); Median age: 54.0 (2010); Males per 100 females: 84.0 (2010); Marriage status: 0.0% never married, 95.7% now married, 4.3% widowed, 0.0% divorced (2006-2010 5-year est.); Foreign born: 0.0% (2006-2010 5-year est.); Ancestry (includes multiple ancestries): 39.1% German, 21.7% Irish, 13.0% Polish, 8.7% Scottish, 8.7% Italian (2006-2010 5-year est.).

Economy: Employment by occupation: 0.0% management, 0.0% professional, 0.0% services, 20.0% sales, 0.0% farming, 40.0% construction, 40.0% production (2006-2010 5-year est.).

Income: Per capita income: $21,526 (2006-2010 5-year est.); Median household income: $36,250 (2006-2010 5-year est.); Average household income: $41,114 (2006-2010 5-year est.); Percent of households with income of $100,000 or more: n/a (2006-2010 5-year est.); Poverty rate: 0.0% (2006-2010 5-year est.).

Education: Percent of population age 25 and over with: High school diploma (including GED) or higher: 91.3% (2006-2010 5-year est.); Bachelor's degree or higher: 8.7% (2006-2010 5-year est.); Master's degree or higher: 0.0% (2006-2010 5-year est.).

Housing: Homeownership rate: 95.5% (2010); Median home value: $76,400 (2006-2010 5-year est.); Median contract rent: n/a per month (2006-2010 5-year est.); Median year structure built: before 1940 (2006-2010 5-year est.).

Transportation: Commute to work: 50.0% car, 0.0% public transportation, 25.0% walk, 25.0% work from home (2006-2010 5-year est.); Travel time to work: 33.3% less than 15 minutes, 33.3% 15 to 30 minutes, 0.0% 30 to 45 minutes, 0.0% 45 to 60 minutes, 33.3% 60 minutes or more (2006-2010 5-year est.)

SOUTH MAHONING (township). Covers a land area of 28.552 square miles and a water area of 0.045 square miles. Located at 40.81° N. Lat; 79.15° W. Long.

Population: 1,713 (1990); 1,852 (2000); 1,841 (2010); Density: 64.5 persons per square mile (2010); Race: 99.6% White, 0.1% Black, 0.1% Asian, 0.0% American Indian/Alaska Native, 0.0% Native Hawaiian/Other Pacific Islander, 0.2% Other, 0.5% Hispanic of any race (2010); Average household size: 3.04 (2010); Median age: 34.4 (2010); Males per 100 females: 99.9 (2010); Marriage status: 23.8% never married, 67.2% now married, 4.9% widowed, 4.1% divorced (2006-2010 5-year est.); Foreign born: 0.6% (2006-2010 5-year est.); Ancestry (includes multiple ancestries): 33.8% German, 17.1% Irish, 17.0% Pennsylvania German, 16.1% Dutch, 7.6% English (2006-2010 5-year est.).

Economy: Single-family building permits issued: 0 (2011); Multi-family building permits issued: 0 (2011); Employment by occupation: 7.8% management, 2.0% professional, 4.6% services, 18.6% sales, 10.0% farming, 34.3% construction, 13.2% production (2006-2010 5-year est.).

Income: Per capita income: $14,964 (2006-2010 5-year est.); Median household income: $38,542 (2006-2010 5-year est.); Average household income: $45,760 (2006-2010 5-year est.); Percent of households with income of $100,000 or more: 8.0% (2006-2010 5-year est.); Poverty rate: 21.9% (2006-2010 5-year est.).

Education: Percent of population age 25 and over with: High school diploma (including GED) or higher: 73.5% (2006-2010 5-year est.); Bachelor's degree or higher: 9.1% (2006-2010 5-year est.); Master's degree or higher: 1.6% (2006-2010 5-year est.).

Housing: Homeownership rate: 85.6% (2010); Median home value: $111,200 (2006-2010 5-year est.); Median contract rent: $241 per month (2006-2010 5-year est.); Median year structure built: 1972 (2006-2010 5-year est.).

Transportation: Commute to work: 79.2% car, 0.0% public transportation, 6.9% walk, 10.5% work from home (2006-2010 5-year est.); Travel time to work: 19.6% less than 15 minutes, 31.9% 15 to 30 minutes, 25.8% 30 to

45 minutes, 13.2% 45 to 60 minutes, 9.4% 60 minutes or more (2006-2010 5-year est.).

Additional Information Contacts

Indiana County Chamber of Commerce . . . . (724) 465-2511
http://www.indianapa.com/chamber

STARFORD (unincorporated postal area)

Zip Code: 15777

Covers a land area of 1.122 square miles and a water area of 0 square miles. Located at 40.69° N. Lat; 78.96° W. Long. Elevation is 1,352 feet. Population: 170 (2010); Density: 151.5 persons per square mile (2010); Race: 96.5% White, 0.0% Black, 0.0% Asian, 0.0% American Indian/Alaska Native, 0.0% Native Hawaiian/Other Pacific Islander, 3.5% Other, 0.0% Hispanic of any race (2010); Average household size: 2.46 (2010); Median age: 44.0 (2010); Males per 100 females: 86.8 (2010); Homeownership rate: 88.4% (2010)

STRONGSTOWN (unincorporated postal area)

Zip Code: 15957

Covers a land area of 9.479 square miles and a water area of 0.012 square miles. Located at 40.55° N. Lat; 78.90° W. Long. Elevation is 1,886 feet. Population: 755 (2010); Density: 79.6 persons per square mile (2010); Race: 98.1% White, 0.0% Black, 0.4% Asian, 0.3% American Indian/Alaska Native, 0.0% Native Hawaiian/Other Pacific Islander, 1.2% Other, 0.5% Hispanic of any race (2010); Average household size: 2.54 (2010); Median age: 43.6 (2010); Males per 100 females: 96.1 (2010); Homeownership rate: 88.6% (2010)

WASHINGTON (township). Covers a land area of 38.140 square miles and a water area of 0.114 square miles. Located at 40.72° N. Lat; 79.21° W. Long.

Population: 1,861 (1990); 1,805 (2000); 1,808 (2010); Density: 47.4 persons per square mile (2010); Race: 99.3% White, 0.2% Black, 0.1% Asian, 0.0% American Indian/Alaska Native, 0.0% Native Hawaiian/Other Pacific Islander, 0.4% Other, 0.2% Hispanic of any race (2010); Average household size: 2.60 (2010); Median age: 41.1 (2010); Males per 100 females: 104.8 (2010); Marriage status: 21.6% never married, 66.4% now married, 4.6% widowed, 7.4% divorced (2006-2010 5-year est.); Foreign born: 0.5% (2006-2010 5-year est.); Ancestry (includes multiple ancestries): 39.2% German, 21.9% Irish, 10.7% American, 9.7% Italian, 8.7% English (2006-2010 5-year est.).

Economy: Employment by occupation: 8.4% management, 2.3% professional, 10.5% services, 16.3% sales, 2.1% farming, 22.5% construction, 9.5% production (2006-2010 5-year est.).

Income: Per capita income: $22,149 (2006-2010 5-year est.); Median household income: $49,704 (2006-2010 5-year est.); Average household income: $56,571 (2006-2010 5-year est.); Percent of households with income of $100,000 or more: 12.6% (2006-2010 5-year est.); Poverty rate: 12.1% (2006-2010 5-year est.).

Education: Percent of population age 25 and over with: High school diploma (including GED) or higher: 86.6% (2006-2010 5-year est.); Bachelor's degree or higher: 14.1% (2006-2010 5-year est.); Master's degree or higher: 4.6% (2006-2010 5-year est.).

Housing: Homeownership rate: 82.5% (2010); Median home value: $97,800 (2006-2010 5-year est.); Median contract rent: $384 per month (2006-2010 5-year est.); Median year structure built: 1976 (2006-2010 5-year est.).

Transportation: Commute to work: 94.4% car, 0.0% public transportation, 1.4% walk, 3.1% work from home (2006-2010 5-year est.); Travel time to work: 10.7% less than 15 minutes, 44.5% 15 to 30 minutes, 26.8% 30 to 45 minutes, 7.5% 45 to 60 minutes, 10.5% 60 minutes or more (2006-2010 5-year est.)

Additional Information Contacts

Indiana County Chamber of Commerce . . . . (724) 465-2511
http://www.indianapa.com/chamber

WEST MAHONING (township). Covers a land area of 28.936 square miles and a water area of 0.424 square miles. Located at 40.88° N. Lat; 79.17° W. Long.

Population: 1,032 (1990); 1,128 (2000); 1,357 (2010); Density: 46.9 persons per square mile (2010); Race: 99.2% White, 0.0% Black, 0.0% Asian, 0.1% American Indian/Alaska Native, 0.0% Native Hawaiian/Other Pacific Islander, 0.7% Other, 0.5% Hispanic of any race (2010); Average household size: 4.19 (2010); Median age: 18.9 (2010); Males per 100 females: 106.9 (2010); Marriage status: 27.6% never married, 63.0% now

married, 6.9% widowed, 2.5% divorced (2006-2010 5-year est.); Foreign born: 0.0% (2006-2010 5-year est.); Ancestry (includes multiple ancestries): 34.0% Pennsylvania German, 21.1% German, 6.2% Irish, 4.5% Dutch, 3.5% American (2006-2010 5-year est.).

Economy: Employment by occupation: 9.3% management, 0.0% professional, 4.6% services, 14.4% sales, 0.8% farming, 22.7% construction, 4.6% production (2006-2010 5-year est.).

Income: Per capita income: $9,222 (2006-2010 5-year est.); Median household income: $29,808 (2006-2010 5-year est.); Average household income: $38,535 (2006-2010 5-year est.); Percent of households with income of $100,000 or more: 4.7% (2006-2010 5-year est.); Poverty rate: 42.7% (2006-2010 5-year est.).

Education: Percent of population age 25 and over with: High school diploma (including GED) or higher: 56.8% (2006-2010 5-year est.); Bachelor's degree or higher: 3.6% (2006-2010 5-year est.); Master's degree or higher: 0.8% (2006-2010 5-year est.).

Housing: Homeownership rate: 83.6% (2010); Median home value: $93,500 (2006-2010 5-year est.); Median contract rent: $222 per month (2006-2010 5-year est.); Median year structure built: 1976 (2006-2010 5-year est.).

Transportation: Commute to work: 61.7% car, 0.0% public transportation, 13.0% walk, 19.3% work from home (2006-2010 5-year est.); Travel time to work: 30.3% less than 15 minutes, 16.8% 15 to 30 minutes, 20.6% 30 to 45 minutes, 8.4% 45 to 60 minutes, 23.9% 60 minutes or more (2006-2010 5-year est.)

Additional Information Contacts

Indiana County Chamber of Commerce . . . . (724) 465-2511
http://www.indianapa.com/chamber

WEST WHEATFIELD (township). Covers a land area of 31.591 square miles and a water area of 0.299 square miles. Located at 40.43° N. Lat; 79.11° W. Long.

Population: 2,370 (1990); 2,375 (2000); 2,314 (2010); Density: 73.2 persons per square mile (2010); Race: 98.6% White, 0.2% Black, 0.1% Asian, 0.1% American Indian/Alaska Native, 0.0% Native Hawaiian/Other Pacific Islander, 1.0% Other, 0.7% Hispanic of any race (2010); Average household size: 2.55 (2010); Median age: 43.0 (2010); Males per 100 females: 101.7 (2010); Marriage status: 21.0% never married, 66.4% now married, 4.3% widowed, 8.2% divorced (2006-2010 5-year est.); Foreign born: 0.2% (2006-2010 5-year est.); Ancestry (includes multiple ancestries): 38.7% German, 20.7% Irish, 8.3% English, 6.5% Italian, 4.6% Dutch (2006-2010 5-year est.).

Economy: Employment by occupation: 4.1% management, 2.2% professional, 10.2% services, 13.6% sales, 4.8% farming, 11.9% construction, 9.9% production (2006-2010 5-year est.).

Income: Per capita income: $19,517 (2006-2010 5-year est.); Median household income: $41,576 (2006-2010 5-year est.); Average household income: $48,994 (2006-2010 5-year est.); Percent of households with income of $100,000 or more: 11.2% (2006-2010 5-year est.); Poverty rate: 15.7% (2006-2010 5-year est.).

Education: Percent of population age 25 and over with: High school diploma (including GED) or higher: 81.6% (2006-2010 5-year est.); Bachelor's degree or higher: 8.0% (2006-2010 5-year est.); Master's degree or higher: 2.5% (2006-2010 5-year est.).

Housing: Homeownership rate: 86.3% (2010); Median home value: $82,300 (2006-2010 5-year est.); Median contract rent: $375 per month (2006-2010 5-year est.); Median year structure built: 1975 (2006-2010 5-year est.).

Transportation: Commute to work: 95.9% car, 0.9% public transportation, 1.7% walk, 1.2% work from home (2006-2010 5-year est.); Travel time to work: 24.7% less than 15 minutes, 37.5% 15 to 30 minutes, 23.3% 30 to 45 minutes, 9.0% 45 to 60 minutes, 5.4% 60 minutes or more (2006-2010 5-year est.)

Additional Information Contacts

Greater Johnstown Cambria County Chamber of Commerce . . . . (814) 536-5107
http://www.johnstownchamber.com

WHITE (township). Covers a land area of 42.346 square miles and a water area of 0.427 square miles. Located at 40.65° N. Lat; 79.12° W. Long.

Population: 13,788 (1990); 14,034 (2000); 15,821 (2010); Density: 373.6 persons per square mile (2010); Race: 87.9% White, 7.5% Black, 2.2% Asian, 0.2% American Indian/Alaska Native, 0.0% Native Hawaiian/Other Pacific Islander, 2.2% Other, 1.9% Hispanic of any race (2010); Average

household size: 2.09 (2010); Median age: 42.6 (2010); Males per 100 females: 103.1 (2010); Marriage status: 36.6% never married, 46.6% now married, 9.7% widowed, 7.1% divorced (2006-2010 5-year est.); Foreign born: 2.3% (2006-2010 5-year est.); Ancestry (includes multiple ancestries): 26.7% German, 17.5% Irish, 10.5% English, 10.0% Italian, 6.9% Polish (2006-2010 5-year est.).

Economy: Single-family building permits issued: 8 (2011); Multi-family building permits issued: 9 (2011); Employment by occupation: 11.4% management, 3.0% professional, 11.0% services, 16.2% sales, 3.2% farming, 13.0% construction, 7.4% production (2006-2010 5-year est.).

Income: Per capita income: $26,481 (2006-2010 5-year est.); Median household income: $43,294 (2006-2010 5-year est.); Average household income: $61,800 (2006-2010 5-year est.); Percent of households with income of $100,000 or more: 17.1% (2006-2010 5-year est.); Poverty rate: 14.6% (2006-2010 5-year est.).

Education: Percent of population age 25 and over with: High school diploma (including GED) or higher: 88.3% (2006-2010 5-year est.); Bachelor's degree or higher: 30.6% (2006-2010 5-year est.); Master's degree or higher: 13.3% (2006-2010 5-year est.).

Housing: Homeownership rate: 58.1% (2010); Median home value: $139,000 (2006-2010 5-year est.); Median contract rent: $539 per month (2006-2010 5-year est.); Median year structure built: 1978 (2006-2010 5-year est.).

Transportation: Commute to work: 91.7% car, 0.9% public transportation, 3.3% walk, 3.5% work from home (2006-2010 5-year est.); Travel time to work: 59.4% less than 15 minutes, 20.7% 15 to 30 minutes, 7.7% 30 to 45 minutes, 4.7% 45 to 60 minutes, 7.5% 60 minutes or more (2006-2010 5-year est.).

Additional Information Contacts

Indiana County Chamber of Commerce . . . . (724) 465-2511
http://www.indianapa.com/chamber
White Township. . . . . (724) 463-8585
http://www.indianaicecenter.com

YOUNG (township). Covers a land area of 34.777 square miles and a water area of 0.062 square miles. Located at 40.56° N. Lat; 79.35° W. Long.

Population: 1,790 (1990); 1,744 (2000); 1,775 (2010); Density: 51.0 persons per square mile (2010); Race: 98.6% White, 0.3% Black, 0.1% Asian, 0.1% American Indian/Alaska Native, 0.0% Native Hawaiian/Other Pacific Islander, 0.9% Other, 0.1% Hispanic of any race (2010); Average household size: 2.46 (2010); Median age: 39.8 (2010); Males per 100 females: 106.6 (2010); Marriage status: 28.4% never married, 53.2% now married, 7.0% widowed, 11.4% divorced (2006-2010 5-year est.); Foreign born: 0.0% (2006-2010 5-year est.); Ancestry (includes multiple ancestries): 36.1% German, 16.7% Irish, 13.6% Italian, 11.7% Polish, 6.9% English (2006-2010 5-year est.).

Economy: Employment by occupation: 6.1% management, 2.5% professional, 14.7% services, 17.5% sales, 3.1% farming, 18.2% construction, 10.5% production (2006-2010 5-year est.).

Income: Per capita income: $20,358 (2006-2010 5-year est.); Median household income: $45,303 (2006-2010 5-year est.); Average household income: $50,528 (2006-2010 5-year est.); Percent of households with income of $100,000 or more: 8.1% (2006-2010 5-year est.); Poverty rate: 8.7% (2006-2010 5-year est.).

Education: Percent of population age 25 and over with: High school diploma (including GED) or higher: 90.0% (2006-2010 5-year est.); Bachelor's degree or higher: 10.1% (2006-2010 5-year est.); Master's degree or higher: 2.4% (2006-2010 5-year est.).

Housing: Homeownership rate: 80.8% (2010); Median home value: $75,700 (2006-2010 5-year est.); Median contract rent: $378 per month (2006-2010 5-year est.); Median year structure built: 1947 (2006-2010 5-year est.).

Transportation: Commute to work: 98.5% car, 0.0% public transportation, 0.0% walk, 1.4% work from home (2006-2010 5-year est.); Travel time to work: 10.1% less than 15 minutes, 42.3% 15 to 30 minutes, 29.0% 30 to 45 minutes, 7.4% 45 to 60 minutes, 11.2% 60 minutes or more (2006-2010 5-year est.)

Additional Information Contacts

Indiana County Chamber of Commerce . . . . (724) 465-2511
http://www.indianapa.com/chamber

Jefferson County

Located in west central Pennsylvania; bounded on the north by the Clarion River; drained by tributaries of the Allegheny River. Covers a land area of 652.429 square miles, a water area of 4.372 square miles, and is located in the Eastern Time Zone at 41.13° N. Lat, 79.00° W. Long. The county was founded in 1804. County seat is Brookville.

Population: 46,083 (1990); 45,932 (2000); 45,200 (2010); Race: 98.3% White, 0.3% Black, 0.2% Asian, 0.2% American Indian/Alaska Native, 0.0% Native Hawaiian/Other Pacific Islander, 1.0% Other, 0.6% Hispanic of any race (2010); Density: 69.3 persons per square mile (2010); Average household size: 2.39 (2010); Median age: 43.0 (2010); Males per 100 females: 97.4 (2010).

Religion: Six largest groups: 22.9% Catholicism, 15.8% Methodist/Pietist, 4.8% Presbyterian-Reformed, 4.3% Holiness, 2.5% European Free-Church, 2.3% Non-Denominational (2010)

Economy: Unemployment rate: 7.8% (August 2012); Total civilian labor force: 23,780 (August 2012); Leading industries: 26.7% manufacturing; 24.7% health care and social assistance; 14.1% retail trade (2010); Farms: 597 totaling 87,043 acres (2007); Companies that employ 500 or more persons: 0 (2010); Companies that employ 100 to 499 persons: 22 (2010); Companies that employ less than 100 persons: 1,130 (2010); Black-owned businesses: n/a (2007); Hispanic-owned businesses: n/a (2007); Asian-owned businesses: n/a (2007); Women-owned businesses: 1,014 (2007); Retail sales per capita: $9,237 (2010). Single-family building permits issued: 61 (2011); Multi-family building permits issued: 0 (2011).

Income: Per capita income: $20,305 (2006-2010 5-year est.); Median household income: $38,406 (2006-2010 5-year est.); Average household income: $49,252 (2006-2010 5-year est.); Percent of households with income of $100,000 or more: 8.0% (2006-2010 5-year est.); Poverty rate: 13.7% (2006-2010 5-year est.); Bankruptcy rate: 1.91% (2011).

Education: Percent of population age 25 and over with: High school diploma (including GED) or higher: 86.9% (2006-2010 5-year est.); Bachelor's degree or higher: 12.0% (2006-2010 5-year est.); Master's degree or higher: 3.9% (2006-2010 5-year est.).

Housing: Homeownership rate: 74.9% (2010); Median home value: $80,100 (2006-2010 5-year est.); Median contract rent: $370 per month (2006-2010 5-year est.); Median year structure built: 1955 (2006-2010 5-year est.)

Health: Birth rate: 104.9 per 10,000 population (2011); Death rate: 116.7 per 10,000 population (2011); Age-adjusted cancer mortality rate: 188.3 deaths per 100,000 population (2009); Number of physicians: 11.1 per 10,000 population (2010); Hospital beds: 17.4 per 10,000 population (2008); Hospital admissions: 787.0 per 10,000 population (2008).

Elections: 2012 Presidential election results: 26.4% Obama, 72.2% Romney

National and State Parks: Clear Creek State Park; Cook Forest State Park; Kittanning State Forest; State Fish Lands

Additional Information Contacts

Jefferson County Government . . . . (814) 849-1603
http://www.jeffersoncountypa.com

Jefferson County Communities

ANITA (unincorporated postal area)
Zip Code: 15711
Covers a land area of 1.248 square miles and a water area of 0.005 square miles. Located at 41.01° N. Lat; 78.95° W. Long. Elevation is 1,460 feet. Population: 412 (2010); Density: 329.9 persons per square mile (2010); Race: 99.0% White, 0.0% Black, 0.2% Asian, 0.0% American Indian/Alaska Native, 0.0% Native Hawaiian/Other Pacific Islander, 0.8% Other, 0.5% Hispanic of any race (2010); Average household size: 2.44 (2010); Median age: 41.5 (2010); Males per 100 females: 96.2 (2010); Homeownership rate: 76.9% (2010)

BARNETT (township). Covers a land area of 14.582 square miles and a water area of 0.558 square miles. Located at 41.31° N. Lat; 79.15° W. Long.

Population: 269 (1990); 272 (2000); 254 (2010); Density: 17.4 persons per square mile (2010); Race: 99.6% White, 0.0% Black, 0.0% Asian, 0.0% American Indian/Alaska Native, 0.4% Native Hawaiian/Other Pacific Islander, 0.0% Other, 0.0% Hispanic of any race (2010); Average household size: 2.25 (2010); Median age: 48.8 (2010); Males per 100 females: 109.9 (2010); Marriage status: 12.4% never married, 58.9% now married, 6.5% widowed, 22.2% divorced (2006-2010 5-year est.); Foreign

born: 0.0% (2006-2010 5-year est.); Ancestry (includes multiple ancestries): 33.5% Irish, 17.7% German, 13.8% Dutch, 12.3% Italian, 10.8% Hungarian (2006-2010 5-year est.).

Economy: Employment by occupation: 16.0% management, 0.0% professional, 0.0% services, 18.7% sales, 4.0% farming, 8.0% construction, 0.0% production (2006-2010 5-year est.).

Income: Per capita income: $23,856 (2006-2010 5-year est.); Median household income: $41,364 (2006-2010 5-year est.); Average household income: $51,604 (2006-2010 5-year est.); Percent of households with income of $100,000 or more: 12.7% (2006-2010 5-year est.); Poverty rate: 16.3% (2006-2010 5-year est.).

Education: Percent of population age 25 and over with: High school diploma (including GED) or higher: 91.3% (2006-2010 5-year est.); Bachelor's degree or higher: 7.6% (2006-2010 5-year est.); Master's degree or higher: 5.8% (2006-2010 5-year est.).

Housing: Homeownership rate: 88.5% (2010); Median home value: $102,200 (2006-2010 5-year est.); Median contract rent: $450 per month (2006-2010 5-year est.); Median year structure built: 1978 (2006-2010 5-year est.).

Transportation: Commute to work: 81.3% car, 0.0% public transportation, 9.3% walk, 6.7% work from home (2006-2010 5-year est.); Travel time to work: 38.6% less than 15 minutes, 32.9% 15 to 30 minutes, 21.4% 30 to 45 minutes, 4.3% 45 to 60 minutes, 2.9% 60 minutes or more (2006-2010 5-year est.)

BEAVER (township). Covers a land area of 21.206 square miles and a water area of 0.238 square miles. Located at 41.07° N. Lat; 79.17° W. Long.

Population: 551 (1990); 544 (2000); 498 (2010); Density: 23.5 persons per square mile (2010); Race: 99.0% White, 0.4% Black, 0.2% Asian, 0.2% American Indian/Alaska Native, 0.0% Native Hawaiian/Other Pacific Islander, 0.2% Other, 0.8% Hispanic of any race (2010); Average household size: 2.55 (2010); Median age: 42.6 (2010); Males per 100 females: 100.0 (2010); Marriage status: 24.8% never married, 58.6% now married, 7.2% widowed, 9.3% divorced (2006-2010 5-year est.); Foreign born: 0.0% (2006-2010 5-year est.); Ancestry (includes multiple ancestries): 35.4% German, 9.8% Dutch, 8.7% Irish, 8.2% Italian, 3.4% English (2006-2010 5-year est.).

Economy: Employment by occupation: 10.8% management, 1.2% professional, 10.2% services, 22.2% sales, 0.0% farming, 6.6% construction, 5.4% production (2006-2010 5-year est.).

Income: Per capita income: $20,425 (2006-2010 5-year est.); Median household income: $42,708 (2006-2010 5-year est.); Average household income: $48,694 (2006-2010 5-year est.); Percent of households with income of $100,000 or more: 15.0% (2006-2010 5-year est.); Poverty rate: 15.3% (2006-2010 5-year est.).

Education: Percent of population age 25 and over with: High school diploma (including GED) or higher: 83.6% (2006-2010 5-year est.); Bachelor's degree or higher: 22.7% (2006-2010 5-year est.); Master's degree or higher: 4.7% (2006-2010 5-year est.).

Housing: Homeownership rate: 88.2% (2010); Median home value: $75,300 (2006-2010 5-year est.); Median contract rent: n/a per month (2006-2010 5-year est.); Median year structure built: before 1940 (2006-2010 5-year est.).

Transportation: Commute to work: 100.0% car, 0.0% public transportation, 0.0% walk, 0.0% work from home (2006-2010 5-year est.); Travel time to work: 14.2% less than 15 minutes, 64.2% 15 to 30 minutes, 13.6% 30 to 45 minutes, 3.7% 45 to 60 minutes, 4.3% 60 minutes or more (2006-2010 5-year est.)

BELL (township). Covers a land area of 18.581 square miles and a water area of 0.181 square miles. Located at 40.95° N. Lat; 78.93° W. Long.

Population: 2,055 (1990); 2,029 (2000); 2,056 (2010); Density: 110.7 persons per square mile (2010); Race: 98.8% White, 0.0% Black, 0.0% Asian, 0.2% American Indian/Alaska Native, 0.0% Native Hawaiian/Other Pacific Islander, 1.0% Other, 0.1% Hispanic of any race (2010); Average household size: 2.46 (2010); Median age: 45.7 (2010); Males per 100 females: 100.6 (2010); Marriage status: 21.3% never married, 66.9% now married, 6.1% widowed, 5.8% divorced (2006-2010 5-year est.); Foreign born: 0.7% (2006-2010 5-year est.); Ancestry (includes multiple ancestries): 39.3% German, 14.9% Italian, 12.3% Irish, 9.7% American, 7.1% English (2006-2010 5-year est.).

Economy: Employment by occupation: 14.1% management, 2.9% professional, 10.3% services, 15.5% sales, 4.6% farming, 9.4% construction, 5.2% production (2006-2010 5-year est.).

Income: Per capita income: $20,626 (2006-2010 5-year est.); Median household income: $44,590 (2006-2010 5-year est.); Average household income: $53,902 (2006-2010 5-year est.); Percent of households with income of $100,000 or more: 10.2% (2006-2010 5-year est.); Poverty rate: 5.8% (2006-2010 5-year est.).

Education: Percent of population age 25 and over with: High school diploma (including GED) or higher: 94.6% (2006-2010 5-year est.); Bachelor's degree or higher: 12.4% (2006-2010 5-year est.); Master's degree or higher: 2.4% (2006-2010 5-year est.).

Housing: Homeownership rate: 86.5% (2010); Median home value: $87,200 (2006-2010 5-year est.); Median contract rent: $422 per month (2006-2010 5-year est.); Median year structure built: 1966 (2006-2010 5-year est.).

Transportation: Commute to work: 91.5% car, 0.0% public transportation, 2.3% walk, 5.8% work from home (2006-2010 5-year est.); Travel time to work: 44.4% less than 15 minutes, 25.5% 15 to 30 minutes, 11.9% 30 to 45 minutes, 9.6% 45 to 60 minutes, 8.6% 60 minutes or more (2006-2010 5-year est.)

Additional Information Contacts

Punxsutawney Area Chamber of Commerce . . . . (814) 938-7700
http://www.punxsutawney.com

BIG RUN (borough). Covers a land area of 0.691 square miles and a water area of 0.019 square miles. Located at 40.97° N. Lat; 78.88° W. Long. Elevation is 1,286 feet.

Population: 699 (1990); 686 (2000); 624 (2010); Density: 902.5 persons per square mile (2010); Race: 98.6% White, 0.0% Black, 0.0% Asian, 0.6% American Indian/Alaska Native, 0.0% Native Hawaiian/Other Pacific Islander, 0.8% Other, 0.3% Hispanic of any race (2010); Average household size: 2.38 (2010); Median age: 41.4 (2010); Males per 100 females: 105.3 (2010); Marriage status: 29.4% never married, 56.1% now married, 6.8% widowed, 7.7% divorced (2006-2010 5-year est.); Foreign born: 0.0% (2006-2010 5-year est.); Ancestry (includes multiple ancestries): 32.3% German, 14.7% Italian, 11.2% Irish, 9.8% Dutch, 7.6% Polish (2006-2010 5-year est.).

Economy: Employment by occupation: 7.8% management, 0.0% professional, 9.0% services, 12.3% sales, 1.1% farming, 18.7% construction, 10.8% production (2006-2010 5-year est.).

Income: Per capita income: $16,844 (2006-2010 5-year est.); Median household income: $33,125 (2006-2010 5-year est.); Average household income: $41,413 (2006-2010 5-year est.); Percent of households with income of $100,000 or more: 2.5% (2006-2010 5-year est.); Poverty rate: 21.3% (2006-2010 5-year est.).

Education: Percent of population age 25 and over with: High school diploma (including GED) or higher: 79.0% (2006-2010 5-year est.); Bachelor's degree or higher: 9.9% (2006-2010 5-year est.); Master's degree or higher: 1.7% (2006-2010 5-year est.).

Housing: Homeownership rate: 74.0% (2010); Median home value: $53,100 (2006-2010 5-year est.); Median contract rent: $342 per month (2006-2010 5-year est.); Median year structure built: before 1940 (2006-2010 5-year est.).

Transportation: Commute to work: 85.1% car, 0.0% public transportation, 7.3% walk, 2.3% work from home (2006-2010 5-year est.); Travel time to work: 44.5% less than 15 minutes, 32.8% 15 to 30 minutes, 7.0% 30 to 45 minutes, 8.6% 45 to 60 minutes, 7.0% 60 minutes or more (2006-2010 5-year est.)

BROCKWAY (borough). Aka Brockwayville. Covers a land area of 1.144 square miles and a water area of 0.032 square miles. Located at 41.25° N. Lat; 78.79° W. Long. Elevation is 1,467 feet.

History: Settled 1822, incorporated 1883.

Population: 2,230 (1990); 2,182 (2000); 2,072 (2010); Density: 1,810.8 persons per square mile (2010); Race: 98.8% White, 0.1% Black, 0.2% Asian, 0.0% American Indian/Alaska Native, 0.0% Native Hawaiian/Other Pacific Islander, 0.9% Other, 0.3% Hispanic of any race (2010); Average household size: 2.23 (2010); Median age: 43.3 (2010); Males per 100 females: 88.4 (2010); Marriage status: 22.6% never married, 52.6% now married, 12.7% widowed, 12.1% divorced (2006-2010 5-year est.); Foreign born: 1.1% (2006-2010 5-year est.); Ancestry (includes multiple ancestries): 27.8% Italian, 21.7% German, 20.4% Irish, 10.0% English, 9.0% Swedish (2006-2010 5-year est.).

Economy: Employment by occupation: 8.8% management, 2.4% professional, 17.6% services, 13.8% sales, 1.9% farming, 5.4% construction, 6.7% production (2006-2010 5-year est.).

Income: Per capita income: $21,546 (2006-2010 5-year est.); Median household income: $32,169 (2006-2010 5-year est.); Average household income: $46,689 (2006-2010 5-year est.); Percent of households with income of $100,000 or more: 6.4% (2006-2010 5-year est.); Poverty rate: 13.8% (2006-2010 5-year est.).

Taxes: Total city taxes per capita: $278 (2009); City property taxes per capita: $152 (2009).

Education: Percent of population age 25 and over with: High school diploma (including GED) or higher: 90.5% (2006-2010 5-year est.); Bachelor's degree or higher: 14.7% (2006-2010 5-year est.); Master's degree or higher: 3.4% (2006-2010 5-year est.).

School District(s)

Brockway Area SD (KG-12)

   2010-11 Enrollment: 1,033 . . . . (814) 265-8411

Housing: Homeownership rate: 63.5% (2010); Median home value: $75,400 (2006-2010 5-year est.); Median contract rent: $323 per month (2006-2010 5-year est.); Median year structure built: before 1940 (2006-2010 5-year est.).

Safety: Violent crime rate: 9.6 per 10,000 population; Property crime rate: 48.1 per 10,000 population (2011).

Transportation: Commute to work: 90.9% car, 0.0% public transportation, 4.3% walk, 3.9% work from home (2006-2010 5-year est.); Travel time to work: 48.3% less than 15 minutes, 34.8% 15 to 30 minutes, 13.1% 30 to 45 minutes, 1.3% 45 to 60 minutes, 2.5% 60 minutes or more (2006-2010 5-year est.)

Additional Information Contacts

Greater DuBois Chamber of Commerce & Economic Development . . (814) 371-5010

   http://www.duboispachamber.com

BROOKVILLE (borough). County seat. Covers a land area of 3.131 square miles and a water area of 0.091 square miles. Located at 41.16° N. Lat; 79.08° W. Long. Elevation is 1,273 feet.

History: Settled 1801, laid out 1830, incorporated 1843.

Population: 4,162 (1990); 4,230 (2000); 3,924 (2010); Density: 1,253.2 persons per square mile (2010); Race: 97.8% White, 0.4% Black, 0.4% Asian, 0.1% American Indian/Alaska Native, 0.0% Native Hawaiian/Other Pacific Islander, 1.3% Other, 1.1% Hispanic of any race (2010); Average household size: 2.17 (2010); Median age: 44.9 (2010); Males per 100 females: 84.7 (2010); Marriage status: 30.1% never married, 50.6% now married, 9.8% widowed, 9.4% divorced (2006-2010 5-year est.); Foreign born: 1.0% (2006-2010 5-year est.); Ancestry (includes multiple ancestries): 32.5% German, 15.3% Irish, 10.1% Italian, 7.7% English, 7.5% American (2006-2010 5-year est.).

Economy: Employment by occupation: 4.9% management, 2.4% professional, 12.1% services, 12.2% sales, 7.2% farming, 11.6% construction, 7.6% production (2006-2010 5-year est.).

Income: Per capita income: $26,337 (2006-2010 5-year est.); Median household income: $38,578 (2006-2010 5-year est.); Average household income: $57,338 (2006-2010 5-year est.); Percent of households with income of $100,000 or more: 10.8% (2006-2010 5-year est.); Poverty rate: 10.5% (2006-2010 5-year est.).

Education: Percent of population age 25 and over with: High school diploma (including GED) or higher: 92.9% (2006-2010 5-year est.); Bachelor's degree or higher: 22.9% (2006-2010 5-year est.); Master's degree or higher: 9.6% (2006-2010 5-year est.).

School District(s)

Brookville Area SD (KG-12)

   2010-11 Enrollment: 1,610 . . . . (814) 849-8372

Housing: Homeownership rate: 64.9% (2010); Median home value: $91,400 (2006-2010 5-year est.); Median contract rent: $362 per month (2006-2010 5-year est.); Median year structure built: 1949 (2006-2010 5-year est.).

Hospitals: Brookville Hospital (63 beds)

Safety: Violent crime rate: 20.3 per 10,000 population; Property crime rate: 172.7 per 10,000 population (2011).

Newspapers: Jeffersonian Democrat (Community news; Circulation 4,650)

Transportation: Commute to work: 96.7% car, 0.0% public transportation, 2.3% walk, 1.0% work from home (2006-2010 5-year est.); Travel time to work: 67.4% less than 15 minutes, 15.3% 15 to 30 minutes, 10.2% 30 to

45 minutes, 4.0% 45 to 60 minutes, 3.1% 60 minutes or more (2006-2010 5-year est.)

Airports: Dubois Regional (commercial service)

Additional Information Contacts

Brookville Area Chamber of Commerce . . . . (814) 849-8448

   http://www.brookvillechamber.com

CLOVER (township). Covers a land area of 15.943 square miles and a water area of 0.178 square miles. Located at 41.14° N. Lat; 79.18° W. Long.

Population: 523 (1990); 474 (2000); 448 (2010); Density: 28.1 persons per square mile (2010); Race: 99.3% White, 0.0% Black, 0.0% Asian, 0.0% American Indian/Alaska Native, 0.0% Native Hawaiian/Other Pacific Islander, 0.7% Other, 0.7% Hispanic of any race (2010); Average household size: 2.36 (2010); Median age: 46.4 (2010); Males per 100 females: 100.9 (2010); Marriage status: 17.1% never married, 65.5% now married, 6.5% widowed, 10.9% divorced (2006-2010 5-year est.); Foreign born: 0.8% (2006-2010 5-year est.); Ancestry (includes multiple ancestries): 42.3% German, 21.8% Irish, 11.8% English, 8.1% Dutch, 7.3% American (2006-2010 5-year est.).

Economy: Employment by occupation: 7.8% management, 0.0% professional, 9.7% services, 18.0% sales, 3.4% farming, 15.0% construction, 10.7% production (2006-2010 5-year est.).

Income: Per capita income: $23,935 (2006-2010 5-year est.); Median household income: $57,734 (2006-2010 5-year est.); Average household income: $61,577 (2006-2010 5-year est.); Percent of households with income of $100,000 or more: 13.4% (2006-2010 5-year est.); Poverty rate: 4.5% (2006-2010 5-year est.).

Education: Percent of population age 25 and over with: High school diploma (including GED) or higher: 93.6% (2006-2010 5-year est.); Bachelor's degree or higher: 14.2% (2006-2010 5-year est.); Master's degree or higher: 6.8% (2006-2010 5-year est.).

Housing: Homeownership rate: 86.3% (2010); Median home value: $87,100 (2006-2010 5-year est.); Median contract rent: $392 per month (2006-2010 5-year est.); Median year structure built: 1964 (2006-2010 5-year est.).

Transportation: Commute to work: 90.5% car, 0.0% public transportation, 6.5% walk, 3.0% work from home (2006-2010 5-year est.); Travel time to work: 42.1% less than 15 minutes, 35.9% 15 to 30 minutes, 17.4% 30 to 45 minutes, 1.5% 45 to 60 minutes, 3.1% 60 minutes or more (2006-2010 5-year est.)

CORSICA (borough). Covers a land area of 0.403 square miles and a water area of 0 square miles. Located at 41.18° N. Lat; 79.20° W. Long. Elevation is 1,601 feet.

Population: 337 (1990); 354 (2000); 357 (2010); Density: 886.4 persons per square mile (2010); Race: 98.6% White, 0.0% Black, 0.0% Asian, 1.1% American Indian/Alaska Native, 0.0% Native Hawaiian/Other Pacific Islander, 0.3% Other, 0.8% Hispanic of any race (2010); Average household size: 2.45 (2010); Median age: 38.1 (2010); Males per 100 females: 98.3 (2010); Marriage status: 22.5% never married, 61.9% now married, 5.6% widowed, 9.9% divorced (2006-2010 5-year est.); Foreign born: 0.8% (2006-2010 5-year est.); Ancestry (includes multiple ancestries): 33.5% German, 14.5% Irish, 9.9% Dutch, 7.0% Polish, 4.7% French (2006-2010 5-year est.).

Economy: Employment by occupation: 7.4% management, 2.6% professional, 17.5% services, 6.9% sales, 1.6% farming, 14.8% construction, 3.7% production (2006-2010 5-year est.).

Income: Per capita income: $21,232 (2006-2010 5-year est.); Median household income: $41,563 (2006-2010 5-year est.); Average household income: $51,743 (2006-2010 5-year est.); Percent of households with income of $100,000 or more: 7.0% (2006-2010 5-year est.); Poverty rate: 9.2% (2006-2010 5-year est.).

Education: Percent of population age 25 and over with: High school diploma (including GED) or higher: 87.1% (2006-2010 5-year est.); Bachelor's degree or higher: 16.3% (2006-2010 5-year est.); Master's degree or higher: 2.7% (2006-2010 5-year est.).

Housing: Homeownership rate: 67.8% (2010); Median home value: $70,700 (2006-2010 5-year est.); Median contract rent: $296 per month (2006-2010 5-year est.); Median year structure built: before 1940 (2006-2010 5-year est.).

Transportation: Commute to work: 97.9% car, 0.0% public transportation, 2.1% walk, 0.0% work from home (2006-2010 5-year est.); Travel time to work: 32.8% less than 15 minutes, 52.9% 15 to 30 minutes, 4.8% 30 to 45

minutes, 0.0% 45 to 60 minutes, 9.5% 60 minutes or more (2006-2010 5-year est.)

CRENSHAW (CDP). Covers a land area of 1.095 square miles and a water area of 0.021 square miles. Located at 41.25° N. Lat; 78.75° W. Long. Elevation is 1,480 feet.

Population: n/a (1990); n/a (2000); 468 (2010); Density: 427.3 persons per square mile (2010); Race: 98.1% White, 0.0% Black, 1.1% Asian, 0.2% American Indian/Alaska Native, 0.0% Native Hawaiian/Other Pacific Islander, 0.6% Other, 0.4% Hispanic of any race (2010); Average household size: 2.41 (2010); Median age: 46.3 (2010); Males per 100 females: 98.3 (2010); Marriage status: 27.9% never married, 47.0% now married, 12.2% widowed, 12.8% divorced (2006-2010 5-year est.); Foreign born: 1.7% (2006-2010 5-year est.); Ancestry (includes multiple ancestries): 35.8% German, 15.5% Irish, 13.2% Italian, 10.3% American, 7.3% English (2006-2010 5-year est.).

Economy: Employment by occupation: 13.0% management, 0.0% professional, 8.6% services, 6.3% sales, 6.3% farming, 8.2% construction, 12.3% production (2006-2010 5-year est.).

Income: Per capita income: $29,551 (2006-2010 5-year est.); Median household income: $51,250 (2006-2010 5-year est.); Average household income: $73,628 (2006-2010 5-year est.); Percent of households with income of $100,000 or more: 10.1% (2006-2010 5-year est.); Poverty rate: 14.5% (2006-2010 5-year est.).

Education: Percent of population age 25 and over with: High school diploma (including GED) or higher: 89.3% (2006-2010 5-year est.); Bachelor's degree or higher: 14.5% (2006-2010 5-year est.); Master's degree or higher: 0.0% (2006-2010 5-year est.).

Housing: Homeownership rate: 84.0% (2010); Median home value: $60,300 (2006-2010 5-year est.); Median contract rent: $338 per month (2006-2010 5-year est.); Median year structure built: 1956 (2006-2010 5-year est.).

Transportation: Commute to work: 91.4% car, 0.0% public transportation, 7.1% walk, 1.5% work from home (2006-2010 5-year est.); Travel time to work: 52.5% less than 15 minutes, 30.9% 15 to 30 minutes, 12.8% 30 to 45 minutes, 3.8% 45 to 60 minutes, 0.0% 60 minutes or more (2006-2010 5-year est.)

DE LANCEY (unincorporated postal area)

Zip Code: 15733

Covers a land area of 0.397 square miles and a water area of 0.006 square miles. Located at 40.98° N. Lat; 78.95° W. Long. Population: 108 (2010); Density: 271.6 persons per square mile (2010); Race: 100.0% White, 0.0% Black, 0.0% Asian, 0.0% American Indian/Alaska Native, 0.0% Native Hawaiian/Other Pacific Islander, 0.0% Other, 0.0% Hispanic of any race (2010); Average household size: 2.70 (2010); Median age: 37.0 (2010); Males per 100 females: 107.7 (2010); Homeownership rate: 87.5% (2010)

ELDRED (township). Covers a land area of 46.528 square miles and a water area of 0.049 square miles. Located at 41.25° N. Lat; 79.13° W. Long.

Population: 1,197 (1990); 1,277 (2000); 1,226 (2010); Density: 26.3 persons per square mile (2010); Race: 98.9% White, 0.2% Black, 0.1% Asian, 0.3% American Indian/Alaska Native, 0.0% Native Hawaiian/Other Pacific Islander, 0.5% Other, 0.2% Hispanic of any race (2010); Average household size: 2.51 (2010); Median age: 44.8 (2010); Males per 100 females: 106.7 (2010); Marriage status: 16.7% never married, 66.9% now married, 6.4% widowed, 9.9% divorced (2006-2010 5-year est.); Foreign born: 0.2% (2006-2010 5-year est.); Ancestry (includes multiple ancestries): 36.0% German, 21.8% Irish, 9.5% American, 6.1% English, 4.8% Scotch-Irish (2006-2010 5-year est.).

Economy: Employment by occupation: 6.5% management, 3.8% professional, 16.1% services, 17.8% sales, 3.1% farming, 16.8% construction, 8.0% production (2006-2010 5-year est.).

Income: Per capita income: $20,627 (2006-2010 5-year est.); Median household income: $45,000 (2006-2010 5-year est.); Average household income: $50,750 (2006-2010 5-year est.); Percent of households with income of $100,000 or more: 10.9% (2006-2010 5-year est.); Poverty rate: 11.3% (2006-2010 5-year est.).

Education: Percent of population age 25 and over with: High school diploma (including GED) or higher: 88.6% (2006-2010 5-year est.); Bachelor's degree or higher: 9.2% (2006-2010 5-year est.); Master's degree or higher: 3.2% (2006-2010 5-year est.).

Housing: Homeownership rate: 88.9% (2010); Median home value: $102,500 (2006-2010 5-year est.); Median contract rent: $338 per month (2006-2010 5-year est.); Median year structure built: 1970 (2006-2010 5-year est.).

Transportation: Commute to work: 91.6% car, 0.0% public transportation, 1.4% walk, 6.0% work from home (2006-2010 5-year est.); Travel time to work: 28.8% less than 15 minutes, 44.5% 15 to 30 minutes, 15.7% 30 to 45 minutes, 4.2% 45 to 60 minutes, 6.8% 60 minutes or more (2006-2010 5-year est.).

Additional Information Contacts

Brookville Area Chamber of Commerce . . . . (814) 849-8448
    http://www.brookvillechamber.com

FALLS CREEK (borough). Covers a land area of 0.932 square miles and a water area of 0.004 square miles. Located at 41.14° N. Lat; 78.81° W. Long. Elevation is 1,457 feet.

Population: 1,087 (1990); 983 (2000); 1,037 (2010); Density: 1,112.8 persons per square mile (2010); Race: 98.0% White, 0.4% Black, 0.2% Asian, 0.2% American Indian/Alaska Native, 0.0% Native Hawaiian/Other Pacific Islander, 1.2% Other, 1.0% Hispanic of any race (2010); Average household size: 2.29 (2010); Median age: 41.9 (2010); Males per 100 females: 101.0 (2010); Marriage status: 23.2% never married, 58.6% now married, 8.3% widowed, 9.9% divorced (2006-2010 5-year est.); Foreign born: 0.4% (2006-2010 5-year est.); Ancestry (includes multiple ancestries): 29.8% German, 21.9% Irish, 14.4% Italian, 13.9% English, 8.2% Polish (2006-2010 5-year est.).

Economy: Employment by occupation: 8.1% management, 1.1% professional, 14.8% services, 18.5% sales, 3.8% farming, 7.5% construction, 4.2% production (2006-2010 5-year est.).

Income: Per capita income: $16,362 (2006-2010 5-year est.); Median household income: $35,875 (2006-2010 5-year est.); Average household income: $39,796 (2006-2010 5-year est.); Percent of households with income of $100,000 or more: 2.5% (2006-2010 5-year est.); Poverty rate: 16.6% (2006-2010 5-year est.).

Education: Percent of population age 25 and over with: High school diploma (including GED) or higher: 87.8% (2006-2010 5-year est.); Bachelor's degree or higher: 6.9% (2006-2010 5-year est.); Master's degree or higher: 4.1% (2006-2010 5-year est.).

Two-year College(s)

Triangle Tech Inc-Dubois (Private, For-profit)
    Fall 2010 Enrollment: 502 . . . . (814) 371-2090
    2011-12 Tuition: In-state $15,673; Out-of-state $15,673

Housing: Homeownership rate: 70.4% (2010); Median home value: $66,800 (2006-2010 5-year est.); Median contract rent: $402 per month (2006-2010 5-year est.); Median year structure built: 1945 (2006-2010 5-year est.).

Transportation: Commute to work: 95.1% car, 0.0% public transportation, 0.4% walk, 1.5% work from home (2006-2010 5-year est.); Travel time to work: 56.1% less than 15 minutes, 24.5% 15 to 30 minutes, 12.3% 30 to 45 minutes, 4.8% 45 to 60 minutes, 2.3% 60 minutes or more (2006-2010 5-year est.)

GASKILL (township). Covers a land area of 21.375 square miles and a water area of 0.121 square miles. Located at 40.94° N. Lat; 78.86° W. Long.

Population: 674 (1990); 671 (2000); 708 (2010); Density: 33.1 persons per square mile (2010); Race: 97.9% White, 0.0% Black, 0.0% Asian, 0.1% American Indian/Alaska Native, 0.0% Native Hawaiian/Other Pacific Islander, 2.0% Other, 1.0% Hispanic of any race (2010); Average household size: 2.54 (2010); Median age: 42.2 (2010); Males per 100 females: 96.7 (2010); Marriage status: 22.9% never married, 59.9% now married, 5.8% widowed, 11.4% divorced (2006-2010 5-year est.); Foreign born: 0.3% (2006-2010 5-year est.); Ancestry (includes multiple ancestries): 35.8% German, 14.7% English, 14.3% Irish, 9.2% Italian, 5.5% Polish (2006-2010 5-year est.).

Economy: Employment by occupation: 12.1% management, 1.5% professional, 10.0% services, 13.6% sales, 1.5% farming, 7.6% construction, 7.9% production (2006-2010 5-year est.).

Income: Per capita income: $20,171 (2006-2010 5-year est.); Median household income: $40,357 (2006-2010 5-year est.); Average household income: $53,954 (2006-2010 5-year est.); Percent of households with income of $100,000 or more: 14.8% (2006-2010 5-year est.); Poverty rate: 4.3% (2006-2010 5-year est.).

Education: Percent of population age 25 and over with: High school diploma (including GED) or higher: 81.3% (2006-2010 5-year est.);

Bachelor's degree or higher: 9.5% (2006-2010 5-year est.); Master's degree or higher: 1.5% (2006-2010 5-year est.).

Housing: Homeownership rate: 80.9% (2010); Median home value: $112,100 (2006-2010 5-year est.); Median contract rent: $425 per month (2006-2010 5-year est.); Median year structure built: 1973 (2006-2010 5-year est.).

Transportation: Commute to work: 95.2% car, 0.0% public transportation, 1.5% walk, 3.3% work from home (2006-2010 5-year est.); Travel time to work: 24.1% less than 15 minutes, 43.4% 15 to 30 minutes, 18.8% 30 to 45 minutes, 4.1% 45 to 60 minutes, 9.7% 60 minutes or more (2006-2010 5-year est.)

HEATH (township). Covers a land area of 28.848 square miles and a water area of 0.365 square miles. Located at 41.33° N. Lat; 79.02° W. Long.

Population: 109 (1990); 160 (2000); 124 (2010); Density: 4.3 persons per square mile (2010); Race: 99.2% White, 0.0% Black, 0.0% Asian, 0.0% American Indian/Alaska Native, 0.0% Native Hawaiian/Other Pacific Islander, 0.8% Other, 0.8% Hispanic of any race (2010); Average household size: 1.91 (2010); Median age: 54.5 (2010); Males per 100 females: 125.5 (2010); Marriage status: 9.1% never married, 77.7% now married, 3.3% widowed, 9.9% divorced (2006-2010 5-year est.); Foreign born: 0.0% (2006-2010 5-year est.); Ancestry (includes multiple ancestries): 31.6% German, 21.8% English, 15.8% Irish, 10.5% Scotch-Irish, 6.8% Italian (2006-2010 5-year est.).

Economy: Employment by occupation: 0.0% management, 0.0% professional, 0.0% services, 10.5% sales, 0.0% farming, 21.1% construction, 10.5% production (2006-2010 5-year est.).

Income: Per capita income: $20,161 (2006-2010 5-year est.); Median household income: $36,000 (2006-2010 5-year est.); Average household income: $43,437 (2006-2010 5-year est.); Percent of households with income of $100,000 or more: 5.0% (2006-2010 5-year est.); Poverty rate: 1.5% (2006-2010 5-year est.).

Education: Percent of population age 25 and over with: High school diploma (including GED) or higher: 79.8% (2006-2010 5-year est.); Bachelor's degree or higher: 9.2% (2006-2010 5-year est.); Master's degree or higher: 1.7% (2006-2010 5-year est.).

Housing: Homeownership rate: 95.4% (2010); Median home value: $88,600 (2006-2010 5-year est.); Median contract rent: n/a per month (2006-2010 5-year est.); Median year structure built: 1976 (2006-2010 5-year est.).

Transportation: Commute to work: 100.0% car, 0.0% public transportation, 0.0% walk, 0.0% work from home (2006-2010 5-year est.); Travel time to work: 41.2% less than 15 minutes, 35.3% 15 to 30 minutes, 0.0% 30 to 45 minutes, 23.5% 45 to 60 minutes, 0.0% 60 minutes or more (2006-2010 5-year est.)

HENDERSON (township). Covers a land area of 21.940 square miles and a water area of 0.062 square miles. Located at 41.00° N. Lat; 78.85° W. Long.

Population: 1,377 (1990); 1,727 (2000); 1,816 (2010); Density: 82.8 persons per square mile (2010); Race: 97.0% White, 0.0% Black, 0.1% Asian, 0.2% American Indian/Alaska Native, 0.0% Native Hawaiian/Other Pacific Islander, 2.7% Other, 1.2% Hispanic of any race (2010); Average household size: 3.14 (2010); Median age: 30.1 (2010); Males per 100 females: 101.6 (2010); Marriage status: 24.8% never married, 65.7% now married, 5.5% widowed, 4.0% divorced (2006-2010 5-year est.); Foreign born: 0.0% (2006-2010 5-year est.); Ancestry (includes multiple ancestries): 43.7% German, 10.9% Pennsylvania German, 7.4% Irish, 4.9% Dutch, 4.5% Polish (2006-2010 5-year est.).

Economy: Employment by occupation: 9.9% management, 2.0% professional, 7.1% services, 13.4% sales, 2.9% farming, 33.2% construction, 10.8% production (2006-2010 5-year est.).

Income: Per capita income: $16,323 (2006-2010 5-year est.); Median household income: $43,625 (2006-2010 5-year est.); Average household income: $50,500 (2006-2010 5-year est.); Percent of households with income of $100,000 or more: 8.6% (2006-2010 5-year est.); Poverty rate: 18.1% (2006-2010 5-year est.).

Education: Percent of population age 25 and over with: High school diploma (including GED) or higher: 73.4% (2006-2010 5-year est.); Bachelor's degree or higher: 3.4% (2006-2010 5-year est.); Master's degree or higher: 0.7% (2006-2010 5-year est.).

Housing: Homeownership rate: 84.4% (2010); Median home value: $92,900 (2006-2010 5-year est.); Median contract rent: $411 per month

(2006-2010 5-year est.); Median year structure built: 1971 (2006-2010 5-year est.).

Transportation: Commute to work: 86.5% car, 0.0% public transportation, 7.5% walk, 2.3% work from home (2006-2010 5-year est.); Travel time to work: 24.4% less than 15 minutes, 42.2% 15 to 30 minutes, 17.2% 30 to 45 minutes, 8.0% 45 to 60 minutes, 8.3% 60 minutes or more (2006-2010 5-year est.).

Additional Information Contacts

Punxsutawney Area Chamber of Commerce . . . . (814) 938-7700
http://www.punxsutawney.com

KNOX (township). Covers a land area of 31.427 square miles and a water area of 0.129 square miles. Located at 41.10° N. Lat; 79.04° W. Long.

Population: 1,014 (1990); 1,056 (2000); 1,042 (2010); Density: 33.2 persons per square mile (2010); Race: 98.7% White, 0.2% Black, 0.3% Asian, 0.2% American Indian/Alaska Native, 0.0% Native Hawaiian/Other Pacific Islander, 0.6% Other, 0.4% Hispanic of any race (2010); Average household size: 2.38 (2010); Median age: 45.1 (2010); Males per 100 females: 105.9 (2010); Marriage status: 15.2% never married, 68.1% now married, 7.6% widowed, 9.1% divorced (2006-2010 5-year est.); Foreign born: 0.0% (2006-2010 5-year est.); Ancestry (includes multiple ancestries): 33.3% German, 9.1% Irish, 8.9% English, 5.6% Dutch, 4.6% Polish (2006-2010 5-year est.).

Economy: Employment by occupation: 5.0% management, 0.0% professional, 13.0% services, 16.0% sales, 0.9% farming, 17.1% construction, 10.3% production (2006-2010 5-year est.).

Income: Per capita income: $18,512 (2006-2010 5-year est.); Median household income: $35,625 (2006-2010 5-year est.); Average household income: $46,243 (2006-2010 5-year est.); Percent of households with income of $100,000 or more: 6.3% (2006-2010 5-year est.); Poverty rate: 8.1% (2006-2010 5-year est.).

Education: Percent of population age 25 and over with: High school diploma (including GED) or higher: 83.7% (2006-2010 5-year est.); Bachelor's degree or higher: 5.0% (2006-2010 5-year est.); Master's degree or higher: 1.9% (2006-2010 5-year est.).

Housing: Homeownership rate: 87.2% (2010); Median home value: $76,800 (2006-2010 5-year est.); Median contract rent: $320 per month (2006-2010 5-year est.); Median year structure built: 1950 (2006-2010 5-year est.).

Transportation: Commute to work: 94.2% car, 0.0% public transportation, 2.5% walk, 3.2% work from home (2006-2010 5-year est.); Travel time to work: 33.4% less than 15 minutes, 48.9% 15 to 30 minutes, 9.1% 30 to 45 minutes, 5.5% 45 to 60 minutes, 3.1% 60 minutes or more (2006-2010 5-year est.)

Additional Information Contacts

Brookville Area Chamber of Commerce . . . . (814) 849-8448
http://www.brookvillechamber.com

KNOX DALE (unincorporated postal area)
Zip Code: 15847

Covers a land area of 2.715 square miles and a water area of 0.004 square miles. Located at 41.09° N. Lat; 79.03° W. Long. Elevation is 1,690 feet. Population: 255 (2010); Density: 93.9 persons per square mile (2010); Race: 98.0% White, 0.4% Black, 0.4% Asian, 0.4% American Indian/Alaska Native, 0.0% Native Hawaiian/Other Pacific Islander, 0.8% Other, 0.4% Hispanic of any race (2010); Average household size: 2.30 (2010); Median age: 44.5 (2010); Males per 100 females: 100.8 (2010); Homeownership rate: 83.7% (2010)

MCCALMONT (township). Covers a land area of 26.246 square miles and a water area of 0.035 square miles. Located at 41.03° N. Lat; 78.97° W. Long.

Population: 1,006 (1990); 1,068 (2000); 1,082 (2010); Density: 41.2 persons per square mile (2010); Race: 99.4% White, 0.0% Black, 0.1% Asian, 0.0% American Indian/Alaska Native, 0.0% Native Hawaiian/Other Pacific Islander, 0.5% Other, 0.2% Hispanic of any race (2010); Average household size: 2.67 (2010); Median age: 41.0 (2010); Males per 100 females: 96.7 (2010); Marriage status: 26.2% never married, 58.1% now married, 6.6% widowed, 9.0% divorced (2006-2010 5-year est.); Foreign born: 1.6% (2006-2010 5-year est.); Ancestry (includes multiple ancestries): 41.7% German, 12.8% Irish, 7.3% Italian, 5.0% Polish, 4.3% Hungarian (2006-2010 5-year est.).

Economy: Employment by occupation: 4.8% management, 2.0% professional, 13.6% services, 16.1% sales, 0.8% farming, 15.9% construction, 6.5% production (2006-2010 5-year est.).

Income: Per capita income: $17,317 (2006-2010 5-year est.); Median household income: $40,729 (2006-2010 5-year est.); Average household income: $45,930 (2006-2010 5-year est.); Percent of households with income of $100,000 or more: 5.9% (2006-2010 5-year est.); Poverty rate: 14.4% (2006-2010 5-year est.).

Education: Percent of population age 25 and over with: High school diploma (including GED) or higher: 79.4% (2006-2010 5-year est.); Bachelor's degree or higher: 7.1% (2006-2010 5-year est.); Master's degree or higher: 2.1% (2006-2010 5-year est.).

Housing: Homeownership rate: 83.0% (2010); Median home value: $72,200 (2006-2010 5-year est.); Median contract rent: $430 per month (2006-2010 5-year est.); Median year structure built: 1960 (2006-2010 5-year est.).

Transportation: Commute to work: 92.6% car, 0.0% public transportation, 0.0% walk, 6.3% work from home (2006-2010 5-year est.); Travel time to work: 20.7% less than 15 minutes, 41.8% 15 to 30 minutes, 14.9% 30 to 45 minutes, 9.1% 45 to 60 minutes, 13.4% 60 minutes or more (2006-2010 5-year est.)

Additional Information Contacts
Punxsutawney Area Chamber of Commerce . . . . (814) 938-7700
  http://www.punxsutawney.com

OLIVEBURG (unincorporated postal area)

Zip Code: 15764

Covers a land area of 1.698 square miles and a water area of 0.006 square miles. Located at 40.99° N. Lat; 79.02° W. Long. Elevation is 1,604 feet. Population: 163 (2010); Density: 96.0 persons per square mile (2010); Race: 100.0% White, 0.0% Black, 0.0% Asian, 0.0% American Indian/Alaska Native, 0.0% Native Hawaiian/Other Pacific Islander, 0.0% Other, 0.0% Hispanic of any race (2010); Average household size: 2.30 (2010); Median age: 51.5 (2010); Males per 100 females: 129.6 (2010); Homeownership rate: 85.9% (2010)

OLIVER (township). Covers a land area of 30.021 square miles and a water area of 0.094 square miles. Located at 41.02° N. Lat; 79.06° W. Long.

Population: 1,119 (1990); 1,129 (2000); 1,083 (2010); Density: 36.1 persons per square mile (2010); Race: 98.4% White, 0.0% Black, 0.6% Asian, 0.1% American Indian/Alaska Native, 0.0% Native Hawaiian/Other Pacific Islander, 0.9% Other, 0.5% Hispanic of any race (2010); Average household size: 2.44 (2010); Median age: 45.2 (2010); Males per 100 females: 104.7 (2010); Marriage status: 20.4% never married, 66.4% now married, 4.8% widowed, 8.4% divorced (2006-2010 5-year est.); Foreign born: 0.0% (2006-2010 5-year est.); Ancestry (includes multiple ancestries): 46.6% German, 17.0% Irish, 10.6% Dutch, 10.6% American, 6.8% Italian (2006-2010 5-year est.).

Economy: Employment by occupation: 13.0% management, 0.0% professional, 18.4% services, 9.2% sales, 2.0% farming, 19.1% construction, 10.1% production (2006-2010 5-year est.).

Income: Per capita income: $23,816 (2006-2010 5-year est.); Median household income: $44,896 (2006-2010 5-year est.); Average household income: $59,258 (2006-2010 5-year est.); Percent of households with income of $100,000 or more: 12.5% (2006-2010 5-year est.); Poverty rate: 10.9% (2006-2010 5-year est.).

Education: Percent of population age 25 and over with: High school diploma (including GED) or higher: 83.9% (2006-2010 5-year est.); Bachelor's degree or higher: 9.2% (2006-2010 5-year est.); Master's degree or higher: 4.1% (2006-2010 5-year est.).

Housing: Homeownership rate: 85.4% (2010); Median home value: $95,600 (2006-2010 5-year est.); Median contract rent: $391 per month (2006-2010 5-year est.); Median year structure built: 1955 (2006-2010 5-year est.).

Transportation: Commute to work: 91.9% car, 0.0% public transportation, 2.2% walk, 4.7% work from home (2006-2010 5-year est.); Travel time to work: 26.3% less than 15 minutes, 42.7% 15 to 30 minutes, 13.4% 30 to 45 minutes, 6.1% 45 to 60 minutes, 11.5% 60 minutes or more (2006-2010 5-year est.)

Additional Information Contacts
Punxsutawney Area Chamber of Commerce . . . . (814) 938-7700
  http://www.punxsutawney.com

PERRY (township). Covers a land area of 28.428 square miles and a water area of 0.303 square miles. Located at 40.94° N. Lat; 79.06° W. Long.

Population: 1,293 (1990); 1,289 (2000); 1,226 (2010); Density: 43.1 persons per square mile (2010); Race: 99.2% White, 0.3% Black, 0.0% Asian, 0.1% American Indian/Alaska Native, 0.0% Native Hawaiian/Other Pacific Islander, 0.4% Other, 0.3% Hispanic of any race (2010); Average household size: 2.53 (2010); Median age: 43.5 (2010); Males per 100 females: 109.9 (2010); Marriage status: 20.6% never married, 64.7% now married, 7.8% widowed, 6.9% divorced (2006-2010 5-year est.); Foreign born: 0.2% (2006-2010 5-year est.); Ancestry (includes multiple ancestries): 38.3% German, 14.9% Irish, 8.5% English, 7.9% Italian, 7.8% Dutch (2006-2010 5-year est.).

Economy: Employment by occupation: 8.7% management, 0.9% professional, 10.4% services, 13.7% sales, 4.6% farming, 18.8% construction, 7.8% production (2006-2010 5-year est.).

Income: Per capita income: $19,091 (2006-2010 5-year est.); Median household income: $41,750 (2006-2010 5-year est.); Average household income: $50,427 (2006-2010 5-year est.); Percent of households with income of $100,000 or more: 9.3% (2006-2010 5-year est.); Poverty rate: 17.3% (2006-2010 5-year est.).

Education: Percent of population age 25 and over with: High school diploma (including GED) or higher: 85.8% (2006-2010 5-year est.); Bachelor's degree or higher: 9.4% (2006-2010 5-year est.); Master's degree or higher: 3.4% (2006-2010 5-year est.).

Housing: Homeownership rate: 87.6% (2010); Median home value: $86,500 (2006-2010 5-year est.); Median contract rent: $418 per month (2006-2010 5-year est.); Median year structure built: 1971 (2006-2010 5-year est.).

Transportation: Commute to work: 92.0% car, 0.0% public transportation, 0.9% walk, 4.7% work from home (2006-2010 5-year est.); Travel time to work: 35.2% less than 15 minutes, 28.0% 15 to 30 minutes, 10.1% 30 to 45 minutes, 11.3% 45 to 60 minutes, 15.3% 60 minutes or more (2006-2010 5-year est.)

Additional Information Contacts
Brookville Area Chamber of Commerce . . . . (814) 849-8448
  http://www.brookvillechamber.com

PINE CREEK (township). Covers a land area of 28.315 square miles and a water area of 0.283 square miles. Located at 41.15° N. Lat; 79.00° W. Long.

Population: 1,413 (1990); 1,369 (2000); 1,352 (2010); Density: 47.7 persons per square mile (2010); Race: 98.6% White, 0.4% Black, 0.1% Asian, 0.4% American Indian/Alaska Native, 0.0% Native Hawaiian/Other Pacific Islander, 0.5% Other, 0.7% Hispanic of any race (2010); Average household size: 2.18 (2010); Median age: 49.8 (2010); Males per 100 females: 97.1 (2010); Marriage status: 21.6% never married, 52.6% now married, 11.5% widowed, 14.4% divorced (2006-2010 5-year est.); Foreign born: 0.0% (2006-2010 5-year est.); Ancestry (includes multiple ancestries): 37.9% German, 16.3% Irish, 8.4% English, 6.7% Dutch, 5.9% American (2006-2010 5-year est.).

Economy: Employment by occupation: 5.3% management, 1.9% professional, 16.9% services, 16.2% sales, 1.4% farming, 8.3% construction, 9.2% production (2006-2010 5-year est.).

Income: Per capita income: $19,093 (2006-2010 5-year est.); Median household income: $47,027 (2006-2010 5-year est.); Average household income: $47,969 (2006-2010 5-year est.); Percent of households with income of $100,000 or more: 7.8% (2006-2010 5-year est.); Poverty rate: 12.7% (2006-2010 5-year est.).

Education: Percent of population age 25 and over with: High school diploma (including GED) or higher: 85.7% (2006-2010 5-year est.); Bachelor's degree or higher: 7.3% (2006-2010 5-year est.); Master's degree or higher: 1.2% (2006-2010 5-year est.).

Housing: Homeownership rate: 75.0% (2010); Median home value: $88,600 (2006-2010 5-year est.); Median contract rent: $419 per month (2006-2010 5-year est.); Median year structure built: 1950 (2006-2010 5-year est.).

Transportation: Commute to work: 96.6% car, 0.0% public transportation, 0.5% walk, 2.8% work from home (2006-2010 5-year est.); Travel time to work: 60.9% less than 15 minutes, 32.7% 15 to 30 minutes, 4.2% 30 to 45 minutes, 1.5% 45 to 60 minutes, 0.7% 60 minutes or more (2006-2010 5-year est.)

Additional Information Contacts
Brookville Area Chamber of Commerce . . . . (814) 849-8448
  http://www.brookvillechamber.com

POLK (township). Covers a land area of 30.410 square miles and a water area of 0.058 square miles. Located at 41.29° N. Lat; 78.94° W. Long.

Population: 305 (1990); 294 (2000); 265 (2010); Density: 8.7 persons per square mile (2010); Race: 98.9% White, 0.0% Black, 0.0% Asian, 0.0% American Indian/Alaska Native, 0.0% Native Hawaiian/Other Pacific Islander, 1.1% Other, 0.0% Hispanic of any race (2010); Average household size: 2.62 (2010); Median age: 42.4 (2010); Males per 100 females: 102.3 (2010); Marriage status: 30.2% never married, 59.5% now married, 7.3% widowed, 3.1% divorced (2006-2010 5-year est.); Foreign born: 0.0% (2006-2010 5-year est.); Ancestry (includes multiple ancestries): 54.6% German, 25.3% Irish, 17.1% English, 7.8% French, 4.1% Italian (2006-2010 5-year est.).

Economy: Employment by occupation: 4.3% management, 2.9% professional, 17.9% services, 12.1% sales, 13.6% farming, 12.9% construction, 3.6% production (2006-2010 5-year est.).

Income: Per capita income: $18,437 (2006-2010 5-year est.); Median household income: $49,318 (2006-2010 5-year est.); Average household income: $54,413 (2006-2010 5-year est.); Percent of households with income of $100,000 or more: 10.6% (2006-2010 5-year est.); Poverty rate: 17.7% (2006-2010 5-year est.).

Education: Percent of population age 25 and over with: High school diploma (including GED) or higher: 89.6% (2006-2010 5-year est.); Bachelor's degree or higher: 13.9% (2006-2010 5-year est.); Master's degree or higher: 3.5% (2006-2010 5-year est.).

Housing: Homeownership rate: 87.1% (2010); Median home value: $88,600 (2006-2010 5-year est.); Median contract rent: n/a per month (2006-2010 5-year est.); Median year structure built: 1974 (2006-2010 5-year est.).

Transportation: Commute to work: 94.3% car, 0.0% public transportation, 2.9% walk, 2.9% work from home (2006-2010 5-year est.); Travel time to work: 14.7% less than 15 minutes, 49.3% 15 to 30 minutes, 28.7% 30 to 45 minutes, 4.4% 45 to 60 minutes, 2.9% 60 minutes or more (2006-2010 5-year est.)

PORTER (township). Covers a land area of 17.530 square miles and a water area of 0.018 square miles. Located at 40.94° N. Lat; 79.17° W. Long. Elevation is 1,535 feet.

Population: 310 (1990); 282 (2000); 305 (2010); Density: 17.4 persons per square mile (2010); Race: 99.7% White, 0.0% Black, 0.3% Asian, 0.0% American Indian/Alaska Native, 0.0% Native Hawaiian/Other Pacific Islander, 0.0% Other, 0.0% Hispanic of any race (2010); Average household size: 2.77 (2010); Median age: 40.8 (2010); Males per 100 females: 108.9 (2010); Marriage status: 31.8% never married, 53.3% now married, 7.4% widowed, 7.4% divorced (2006-2010 5-year est.); Foreign born: 0.0% (2006-2010 5-year est.); Ancestry (includes multiple ancestries): 50.9% German, 15.8% Dutch, 15.3% Irish, 9.1% American, 6.2% English (2006-2010 5-year est.).

Economy: Employment by occupation: 3.6% management, 3.6% professional, 11.9% services, 22.8% sales, 1.0% farming, 32.1% construction, 4.7% production (2006-2010 5-year est.).

Income: Per capita income: $15,891 (2006-2010 5-year est.); Median household income: $41,250 (2006-2010 5-year est.); Average household income: $43,740 (2006-2010 5-year est.); Percent of households with income of $100,000 or more: 7.5% (2006-2010 5-year est.); Poverty rate: 9.4% (2006-2010 5-year est.).

Education: Percent of population age 25 and over with: High school diploma (including GED) or higher: 80.6% (2006-2010 5-year est.); Bachelor's degree or higher: 7.3% (2006-2010 5-year est.); Master's degree or higher: 0.0% (2006-2010 5-year est.).

Housing: Homeownership rate: 83.7% (2010); Median home value: $91,700 (2006-2010 5-year est.); Median contract rent: $556 per month (2006-2010 5-year est.); Median year structure built: 1965 (2006-2010 5-year est.).

Transportation: Commute to work: 93.2% car, 0.0% public transportation, 6.8% walk, 0.0% work from home (2006-2010 5-year est.); Travel time to work: 25.8% less than 15 minutes, 36.3% 15 to 30 minutes, 8.9% 30 to 45 minutes, 7.4% 45 to 60 minutes, 21.6% 60 minutes or more (2006-2010 5-year est.)

PUNXSUTAWNEY (borough). Covers a land area of 3.353 square miles and a water area of 0.064 square miles. Located at 40.94° N. Lat; 78.97° W. Long. Elevation is 1,227 feet.

History: The first settlement at Punxsutawney was in 1772, when the Reverend John Ettwein, a Moravian missionary, arrived with a band of 241 Christianized Delaware. Swarms of gnats plagued the early settlement. The Delaware called the insects "ponkies", and the village "Ponkis Utenink" or "land of the ponkies," from which the present name evolved.

Population: 6,782 (1990); 6,271 (2000); 5,962 (2010); Density: 1,778.2 persons per square mile (2010); Race: 96.8% White, 1.5% Black, 0.3% Asian, 0.4% American Indian/Alaska Native, 0.0% Native Hawaiian/Other Pacific Islander, 1.0% Other, 0.8% Hispanic of any race (2010); Average household size: 2.13 (2010); Median age: 42.6 (2010); Males per 100 females: 84.5 (2010); Marriage status: 25.7% never married, 47.2% now married, 11.0% widowed, 16.1% divorced (2006-2010 5-year est.); Foreign born: 0.4% (2006-2010 5-year est.); Ancestry (includes multiple ancestries): 34.2% German, 16.2% Italian, 10.7% Irish, 9.4% English, 6.4% American (2006-2010 5-year est.).

Economy: Employment by occupation: 4.4% management, 0.0% professional, 13.4% services, 21.2% sales, 2.8% farming, 12.5% construction, 5.6% production (2006-2010 5-year est.).

Income: Per capita income: $20,701 (2006-2010 5-year est.); Median household income: $28,058 (2006-2010 5-year est.); Average household income: $43,360 (2006-2010 5-year est.); Percent of households with income of $100,000 or more: 6.5% (2006-2010 5-year est.); Poverty rate: 24.8% (2006-2010 5-year est.).

Education: Percent of population age 25 and over with: High school diploma (including GED) or higher: 84.1% (2006-2010 5-year est.); Bachelor's degree or higher: 11.4% (2006-2010 5-year est.); Master's degree or higher: 4.9% (2006-2010 5-year est.).

School District(s)

Punxsutawney Area SD (KG-12)
    2010-11 Enrollment: 2,379 . . . . (814) 938-5151
Punxsutawney Area SD (KG-12)
    2010-11 Enrollment: 2,379 . . . . (814) 938-5151
Punxsutawney Area SD (KG-12)
    2010-11 Enrollment: 2,379 . . . . (814) 938-5151

Housing: Homeownership rate: 55.6% (2010); Median home value: $70,700 (2006-2010 5-year est.); Median contract rent: $367 per month (2006-2010 5-year est.); Median year structure built: 1940 (2006-2010 5-year est.).

Hospitals: Punxsutawney Area Hospital (55 beds)

Safety: Violent crime rate: 30.1 per 10,000 population; Property crime rate: 172.2 per 10,000 population (2011).

Newspapers: Jefferson County Neighbors (Local news; Circulation 7,100); The Punxsutawney Spirit (Local news; Circulation 8,400)

Transportation: Commute to work: 88.2% car, 0.0% public transportation, 9.2% walk, 1.7% work from home (2006-2010 5-year est.); Travel time to work: 62.9% less than 15 minutes, 13.5% 15 to 30 minutes, 11.8% 30 to 45 minutes, 6.1% 45 to 60 minutes, 5.7% 60 minutes or more (2006-2010 5-year est.)

Additional Information Contacts

Borough of Punxsutawney . . . . (814) 938-4480
    http://www.punxsutawney.com
Punxsutawney Area Chamber of Commerce . . . . (814) 938-7700
    http://www.punxsutawney.com

REYNOLDSVILLE (borough). Covers a land area of 1.465 square miles and a water area of 0.028 square miles. Located at 41.09° N. Lat; 78.89° W. Long. Elevation is 1,385 feet.

History: Settled c.1824, laid out 1873.

Population: 2,818 (1990); 2,710 (2000); 2,759 (2010); Density: 1,883.6 persons per square mile (2010); Race: 98.4% White, 0.2% Black, 0.1% Asian, 0.2% American Indian/Alaska Native, 0.0% Native Hawaiian/Other Pacific Islander, 1.1% Other, 1.3% Hispanic of any race (2010); Average household size: 2.36 (2010); Median age: 37.2 (2010); Males per 100 females: 94.0 (2010); Marriage status: 29.0% never married, 50.8% now married, 8.6% widowed, 11.6% divorced (2006-2010 5-year est.); Foreign born: 0.6% (2006-2010 5-year est.); Ancestry (includes multiple ancestries): 32.8% German, 13.3% Irish, 10.8% English, 10.2% Italian, 7.5% Dutch (2006-2010 5-year est.).

Economy: Employment by occupation: 6.4% management, 0.5% professional, 15.9% services, 15.2% sales, 3.0% farming, 15.2% construction, 7.7% production (2006-2010 5-year est.).

Income: Per capita income: $16,003 (2006-2010 5-year est.); Median household income: $37,121 (2006-2010 5-year est.); Average household income: $41,048 (2006-2010 5-year est.); Percent of households with income of $100,000 or more: 4.0% (2006-2010 5-year est.); Poverty rate: 20.8% (2006-2010 5-year est.).

Education: Percent of population age 25 and over with: High school diploma (including GED) or higher: 86.5% (2006-2010 5-year est.); Bachelor's degree or higher: 9.3% (2006-2010 5-year est.); Master's degree or higher: 0.8% (2006-2010 5-year est.).

School District(s)
Dubois Area SD (KG-12)

   2010-11 Enrollment: 4,077 . . . . (814) 371-2700

Jefferson County-Dubois Avts (09-12)

   2010-11 Enrollment: 422 . . . . (814) 653-8265

Vocational/Technical School(s)
Jefferson County Dubois Area Vocational Technical Practical Nursing Program (Public)

   Fall 2010 Enrollment: 57 . . . . (814) 653-8420

   2011-12 Tuition: $12,984

Housing: Homeownership rate: 58.0% (2010); Median home value: $60,000 (2006-2010 5-year est.); Median contract rent: $330 per month (2006-2010 5-year est.); Median year structure built: before 1940 (2006-2010 5-year est.).

Safety: Violent crime rate: 3.6 per 10,000 population; Property crime rate: 72.3 per 10,000 population (2011).

Transportation: Commute to work: 92.2% car, 0.2% public transportation, 3.2% walk, 3.3% work from home (2006-2010 5-year est.); Travel time to work: 30.9% less than 15 minutes, 51.1% 15 to 30 minutes, 11.4% 30 to 45 minutes, 2.7% 45 to 60 minutes, 3.9% 60 minutes or more (2006-2010 5-year est.)

Additional Information Contacts

Greater DuBois Chamber of Commerce & Economic Development . . (814) 371-5010

   http://www.duboispachamber.com

RINGGOLD (township). Covers a land area of 19.140 square miles and a water area of 0.130 square miles. Located at 41.00° N. Lat; 79.17° W. Long. Elevation is 1,483 feet.

Population: 705 (1990); 764 (2000); 741 (2010); Density: 38.7 persons per square mile (2010); Race: 99.5% White, 0.1% Black, 0.1% Asian, 0.0% American Indian/Alaska Native, 0.0% Native Hawaiian/Other Pacific Islander, 0.3% Other, 0.0% Hispanic of any race (2010); Average household size: 2.38 (2010); Median age: 46.9 (2010); Males per 100 females: 116.7 (2010); Marriage status: 17.0% never married, 73.6% now married, 5.4% widowed, 4.0% divorced (2006-2010 5-year est.); Foreign born: 0.0% (2006-2010 5-year est.); Ancestry (includes multiple ancestries): 45.1% German, 12.3% American, 12.0% Irish, 10.3% Dutch, 10.1% English (2006-2010 5-year est.).

Economy: Employment by occupation: 12.0% management, 0.0% professional, 15.5% services, 16.6% sales, 2.6% farming, 16.6% construction, 10.5% production (2006-2010 5-year est.).

Income: Per capita income: $20,871 (2006-2010 5-year est.); Median household income: $38,654 (2006-2010 5-year est.); Average household income: $47,346 (2006-2010 5-year est.); Percent of households with income of $100,000 or more: 7.7% (2006-2010 5-year est.); Poverty rate: 8.9% (2006-2010 5-year est.).

Education: Percent of population age 25 and over with: High school diploma (including GED) or higher: 82.5% (2006-2010 5-year est.); Bachelor's degree or higher: 9.0% (2006-2010 5-year est.); Master's degree or higher: 3.7% (2006-2010 5-year est.).

Housing: Homeownership rate: 85.9% (2010); Median home value: $77,000 (2006-2010 5-year est.); Median contract rent: $367 per month (2006-2010 5-year est.); Median year structure built: 1946 (2006-2010 5-year est.).

Transportation: Commute to work: 92.6% car, 0.0% public transportation, 5.4% walk, 2.1% work from home (2006-2010 5-year est.); Travel time to work: 29.8% less than 15 minutes, 39.2% 15 to 30 minutes, 17.3% 30 to 45 minutes, 8.5% 45 to 60 minutes, 5.2% 60 minutes or more (2006-2010 5-year est.)

ROSE (township). Covers a land area of 19.099 square miles and a water area of 0.134 square miles. Located at 41.14° N. Lat; 79.11° W. Long.

Population: 1,220 (1990); 1,232 (2000); 1,255 (2010); Density: 65.7 persons per square mile (2010); Race: 98.5% White, 0.0% Black, 0.0% Asian, 0.4% American Indian/Alaska Native, 0.1% Native Hawaiian/Other Pacific Islander, 1.0% Other, 0.4% Hispanic of any race (2010); Average household size: 2.58 (2010); Median age: 42.0 (2010); Males per 100 females: 101.1 (2010); Marriage status: 22.8% never married, 63.2% now married, 3.8% widowed, 10.2% divorced (2006-2010 5-year est.); Foreign

born: 0.0% (2006-2010 5-year est.); Ancestry (includes multiple ancestries): 38.7% German, 11.6% Italian, 10.7% Irish, 9.5% English, 8.7% Dutch (2006-2010 5-year est.).

Economy: Employment by occupation: 5.3% management, 0.0% professional, 11.6% services, 11.4% sales, 1.5% farming, 5.5% construction, 7.0% production (2006-2010 5-year est.).

Income: Per capita income: $21,040 (2006-2010 5-year est.); Median household income: $39,821 (2006-2010 5-year est.); Average household income: $53,848 (2006-2010 5-year est.); Percent of households with income of $100,000 or more: 12.2% (2006-2010 5-year est.); Poverty rate: 12.5% (2006-2010 5-year est.).

Education: Percent of population age 25 and over with: High school diploma (including GED) or higher: 86.8% (2006-2010 5-year est.); Bachelor's degree or higher: 19.1% (2006-2010 5-year est.); Master's degree or higher: 2.5% (2006-2010 5-year est.).

Housing: Homeownership rate: 82.9% (2010); Median home value: $91,200 (2006-2010 5-year est.); Median contract rent: $404 per month (2006-2010 5-year est.); Median year structure built: 1954 (2006-2010 5-year est.).

Transportation: Commute to work: 89.8% car, 0.0% public transportation, 1.6% walk, 6.5% work from home (2006-2010 5-year est.); Travel time to work: 67.8% less than 15 minutes, 21.3% 15 to 30 minutes, 8.1% 30 to 45 minutes, 0.6% 45 to 60 minutes, 2.2% 60 minutes or more (2006-2010 5-year est.).

Additional Information Contacts

Brookville Area Chamber of Commerce . . . . (814) 849-8448

   http://www.brookvillechamber.com

SIGEL (unincorporated postal area)

Zip Code: 15860

   Covers a land area of 124.249 square miles and a water area of 0.843 square miles. Located at 41.33° N. Lat; 79.01° W. Long. Population: 1,065 (2010); Density: 8.6 persons per square mile (2010); Race: 98.8% White, 0.1% Black, 0.1% Asian, 0.4% American Indian/Alaska Native, 0.0% Native Hawaiian/Other Pacific Islander, 0.6% Other, 0.4% Hispanic of any race (2010); Average household size: 2.26 (2010); Median age: 50.0 (2010); Males per 100 females: 111.3 (2010); Homeownership rate: 90.7% (2010)

SNYDER (township). Covers a land area of 41.259 square miles and a water area of 0.199 square miles. Located at 41.25° N. Lat; 78.82° W. Long.

Population: 2,512 (1990); 2,432 (2000); 2,547 (2010); Density: 61.7 persons per square mile (2010); Race: 98.4% White, 0.1% Black, 0.3% Asian, 0.1% American Indian/Alaska Native, 0.0% Native Hawaiian/Other Pacific Islander, 1.1% Other, 0.4% Hispanic of any race (2010); Average household size: 2.65 (2010); Median age: 40.1 (2010); Males per 100 females: 104.6 (2010); Marriage status: 25.9% never married, 57.1% now married, 7.4% widowed, 9.6% divorced (2006-2010 5-year est.); Foreign born: 0.4% (2006-2010 5-year est.); Ancestry (includes multiple ancestries): 32.5% German, 16.5% Irish, 12.3% English, 11.7% Italian, 10.7% Swedish (2006-2010 5-year est.).

Economy: Employment by occupation: 9.6% management, 2.2% professional, 7.6% services, 17.4% sales, 5.6% farming, 10.8% construction, 10.9% production (2006-2010 5-year est.).

Income: Per capita income: $23,149 (2006-2010 5-year est.); Median household income: $52,500 (2006-2010 5-year est.); Average household income: $63,015 (2006-2010 5-year est.); Percent of households with income of $100,000 or more: 9.9% (2006-2010 5-year est.); Poverty rate: 7.9% (2006-2010 5-year est.).

Education: Percent of population age 25 and over with: High school diploma (including GED) or higher: 91.9% (2006-2010 5-year est.); Bachelor's degree or higher: 13.1% (2006-2010 5-year est.); Master's degree or higher: 1.9% (2006-2010 5-year est.).

Housing: Homeownership rate: 86.5% (2010); Median home value: $83,800 (2006-2010 5-year est.); Median contract rent: $372 per month (2006-2010 5-year est.); Median year structure built: 1967 (2006-2010 5-year est.).

Transportation: Commute to work: 92.0% car, 0.0% public transportation, 3.2% walk, 4.3% work from home (2006-2010 5-year est.); Travel time to work: 43.0% less than 15 minutes, 40.9% 15 to 30 minutes, 10.6% 30 to 45 minutes, 3.1% 45 to 60 minutes, 2.4% 60 minutes or more (2006-2010 5-year est.)

Additional Information Contacts
Greater DuBois Chamber of Commerce & Economic Development . . (814) 371-5010
http://www.duboispachamber.com

SPRANKLE MILLS (unincorporated postal area)

Zip Code: 15776

Covers a land area of 2.174 square miles and a water area of 0.006 square miles. Located at 41.01° N. Lat; 79.11° W. Long. Elevation is 1,224 feet. Population: 52 (2010); Density: 23.9 persons per square mile (2010); Race: 98.1% White, 0.0% Black, 1.9% Asian, 0.0% American Indian/Alaska Native, 0.0% Native Hawaiian/Other Pacific Islander, 0.0% Other, 0.0% Hispanic of any race (2010); Average household size: 2.26 (2010); Median age: 50.3 (2010); Males per 100 females: 126.1 (2010); Homeownership rate: 91.3% (2010).

STUMP CREEK (unincorporated postal area)

Zip Code: 15863

Covers a land area of 0.671 square miles and a water area of 0 square miles. Located at 41.01° N. Lat; 78.83° W. Long. Elevation is 1,473 feet. Population: 225 (2010); Density: 334.9 persons per square mile (2010); Race: 98.2% White, 0.0% Black, 0.0% Asian, 0.4% American Indian/Alaska Native, 0.0% Native Hawaiian/Other Pacific Islander, 1.4% Other, 0.0% Hispanic of any race (2010); Average household size: 2.34 (2010); Median age: 41.8 (2010); Males per 100 females: 102.7 (2010); Homeownership rate: 83.4% (2010).

SUMMERVILLE (borough). Covers a land area of 0.595 square miles and a water area of 0.025 square miles. Located at 41.12° N. Lat; 79.19° W. Long. Elevation is 1,148 feet.

History: Settled c.1812, incorporated 1887.
Population: 675 (1990); 525 (2000); 528 (2010); Density: 886.7 persons per square mile (2010); Race: 98.7% White, 0.0% Black, 0.0% Asian, 0.4% American Indian/Alaska Native, 0.0% Native Hawaiian/Other Pacific Islander, 0.9% Other, 0.2% Hispanic of any race (2010); Average household size: 2.37 (2010); Median age: 42.8 (2010); Males per 100 females: 107.1 (2010); Marriage status: 26.1% never married, 53.3% now married, 8.1% widowed, 12.6% divorced (2006-2010 5-year est.); Foreign born: 0.0% (2006-2010 5-year est.); Ancestry (includes multiple ancestries): 41.0% German, 18.0% Irish, 9.2% English, 8.4% Welsh, 7.2% Dutch (2006-2010 5-year est.).
Economy: Employment by occupation: 8.0% management, 1.3% professional, 27.3% services, 4.6% sales, 8.8% farming, 15.1% construction, 14.7% production (2006-2010 5-year est.).
Income: Per capita income: $16,211 (2006-2010 5-year est.); Median household income: $33,583 (2006-2010 5-year est.); Average household income: $37,984 (2006-2010 5-year est.); Percent of households with income of $100,000 or more: 1.4% (2006-2010 5-year est.); Poverty rate: 14.8% (2006-2010 5-year est.).
Education: Percent of population age 25 and over with: High school diploma (including GED) or higher: 83.1% (2006-2010 5-year est.); Bachelor's degree or higher: 4.2% (2006-2010 5-year est.); Master's degree or higher: 0.0% (2006-2010 5-year est.).
Housing: Homeownership rate: 71.3% (2010); Median home value: $60,200 (2006-2010 5-year est.); Median contract rent: $320 per month (2006-2010 5-year est.); Median year structure built: before 1940 (2006-2010 5-year est.).
Transportation: Commute to work: 97.4% car, 0.0% public transportation, 1.7% walk, 0.9% work from home (2006-2010 5-year est.); Travel time to work: 46.8% less than 15 minutes, 45.9% 15 to 30 minutes, 7.4% 30 to 45 minutes, 0.0% 45 to 60 minutes, 0.0% 60 minutes or more (2006-2010 5-year est.)

SYKESVILLE (borough). Covers a land area of 1.583 square miles and a water area of 0.007 square miles. Located at 41.04° N. Lat; 78.81° W. Long. Elevation is 1,362 feet.

Population: 1,387 (1990); 1,246 (2000); 1,157 (2010); Density: 730.8 persons per square mile (2010); Race: 98.6% White, 0.3% Black, 0.2% Asian, 0.1% American Indian/Alaska Native, 0.0% Native Hawaiian/Other Pacific Islander, 0.8% Other, 0.6% Hispanic of any race (2010); Average household size: 2.19 (2010); Median age: 41.6 (2010); Males per 100 females: 96.4 (2010); Marriage status: 27.1% never married, 49.4% now married, 11.4% widowed, 12.1% divorced (2006-2010 5-year est.); Foreign born: 0.2% (2006-2010 5-year est.); Ancestry (includes multiple

ancestries): 26.3% German, 19.4% Italian, 13.7% Irish, 12.8% Slovak, 11.7% Polish (2006-2010 5-year est.).
Economy: Employment by occupation: 5.2% management, 2.8% professional, 12.6% services, 14.1% sales, 5.0% farming, 8.4% construction, 9.1% production (2006-2010 5-year est.).
Income: Per capita income: $16,921 (2006-2010 5-year est.); Median household income: $30,147 (2006-2010 5-year est.); Average household income: $37,121 (2006-2010 5-year est.); Percent of households with income of $100,000 or more: 2.9% (2006-2010 5-year est.); Poverty rate: 18.4% (2006-2010 5-year est.).
Education: Percent of population age 25 and over with: High school diploma (including GED) or higher: 79.5% (2006-2010 5-year est.); Bachelor's degree or higher: 10.4% (2006-2010 5-year est.); Master's degree or higher: 5.4% (2006-2010 5-year est.).
Housing: Homeownership rate: 61.5% (2010); Median home value: $56,200 (2006-2010 5-year est.); Median contract rent: $382 per month (2006-2010 5-year est.); Median year structure built: before 1940 (2006-2010 5-year est.).
Safety: Violent crime rate: 0.0 per 10,000 population; Property crime rate: 0.0 per 10,000 population (2011).
Transportation: Commute to work: 87.0% car, 0.0% public transportation, 7.6% walk, 5.3% work from home (2006-2010 5-year est.); Travel time to work: 37.6% less than 15 minutes, 42.5% 15 to 30 minutes, 13.7% 30 to 45 minutes, 3.6% 45 to 60 minutes, 2.6% 60 minutes or more (2006-2010 5-year est.)

Additional Information Contacts
Greater DuBois Chamber of Commerce & Economic Development . . (814) 371-5010
http://www.duboispachamber.com

TIMBLIN (borough). Covers a land area of 0.952 square miles and a water area of 0.003 square miles. Located at 40.97° N. Lat; 79.20° W. Long. Elevation is 1,306 feet.

Population: 165 (1990); 151 (2000); 157 (2010); Density: 164.9 persons per square mile (2010); Race: 98.1% White, 1.3% Black, 0.0% Asian, 0.0% American Indian/Alaska Native, 0.0% Native Hawaiian/Other Pacific Islander, 0.6% Other, 0.6% Hispanic of any race (2010); Average household size: 2.91 (2010); Median age: 36.8 (2010); Males per 100 females: 137.9 (2010); Marriage status: 21.4% never married, 64.1% now married, 2.1% widowed, 12.4% divorced (2006-2010 5-year est.); Foreign born: 0.0% (2006-2010 5-year est.); Ancestry (includes multiple ancestries): 41.4% German, 14.9% Irish, 13.8% Italian, 11.6% Polish, 9.4% American (2006-2010 5-year est.).
Economy: Employment by occupation: 4.2% management, 0.0% professional, 12.5% services, 4.2% sales, 0.0% farming, 27.8% construction, 4.2% production (2006-2010 5-year est.).
Income: Per capita income: $15,702 (2006-2010 5-year est.); Median household income: $52,917 (2006-2010 5-year est.); Average household income: $49,408 (2006-2010 5-year est.); Percent of households with income of $100,000 or more: 5.7% (2006-2010 5-year est.); Poverty rate: 12.2% (2006-2010 5-year est.).
Education: Percent of population age 25 and over with: High school diploma (including GED) or higher: 95.2% (2006-2010 5-year est.); Bachelor's degree or higher: 12.0% (2006-2010 5-year est.); Master's degree or higher: 0.0% (2006-2010 5-year est.).
Housing: Homeownership rate: 83.3% (2010); Median home value: $56,700 (2006-2010 5-year est.); Median contract rent: n/a per month (2006-2010 5-year est.); Median year structure built: before 1940 (2006-2010 5-year est.).
Transportation: Commute to work: 95.8% car, 0.0% public transportation, 4.2% walk, 0.0% work from home (2006-2010 5-year est.); Travel time to work: 26.4% less than 15 minutes, 22.2% 15 to 30 minutes, 40.3% 30 to 45 minutes, 0.0% 45 to 60 minutes, 11.1% 60 minutes or more (2006-2010 5-year est.)

UNION (township). Covers a land area of 17.638 square miles and a water area of 0.015 square miles. Located at 41.19° N. Lat; 79.17° W. Long.

Population: 733 (1990); 816 (2000); 855 (2010); Density: 48.5 persons per square mile (2010); Race: 99.1% White, 0.0% Black, 0.0% Asian, 0.2% American Indian/Alaska Native, 0.0% Native Hawaiian/Other Pacific Islander, 0.7% Other, 0.5% Hispanic of any race (2010); Average household size: 2.39 (2010); Median age: 44.8 (2010); Males per 100 females: 97.0 (2010); Marriage status: 25.5% never married, 56.5% now married, 12.2% widowed, 5.8% divorced (2006-2010 5-year est.); Foreign

born: 0.8% (2006-2010 5-year est.); Ancestry (includes multiple ancestries): 39.7% German, 12.6% English, 12.5% Irish, 8.7% Scotch-Irish, 5.3% Dutch (2006-2010 5-year est.).

Economy: Employment by occupation: 5.0% management, 2.1% professional, 18.8% services, 13.8% sales, 0.6% farming, 16.1% construction, 9.4% production (2006-2010 5-year est.).

Income: Per capita income: $17,741 (2006-2010 5-year est.); Median household income: $36,927 (2006-2010 5-year est.); Average household income: $43,259 (2006-2010 5-year est.); Percent of households with income of $100,000 or more: 8.3% (2006-2010 5-year est.); Poverty rate: 10.4% (2006-2010 5-year est.).

Education: Percent of population age 25 and over with: High school diploma (including GED) or higher: 95.5% (2006-2010 5-year est.); Bachelor's degree or higher: 10.9% (2006-2010 5-year est.); Master's degree or higher: 4.6% (2006-2010 5-year est.).

Housing: Homeownership rate: 82.1% (2010); Median home value: $81,500 (2006-2010 5-year est.); Median contract rent: $375 per month (2006-2010 5-year est.); Median year structure built: 1959 (2006-2010 5-year est.).

Transportation: Commute to work: 95.9% car, 0.0% public transportation, 1.1% walk, 1.1% work from home (2006-2010 5-year est.); Travel time to work: 42.1% less than 15 minutes, 35.5% 15 to 30 minutes, 15.4% 30 to 45 minutes, 5.5% 45 to 60 minutes, 1.5% 60 minutes or more (2006-2010 5-year est.)

VALIER (unincorporated postal area)
Zip Code: 15780

Covers a land area of 1.282 square miles and a water area of <.001 square miles. Located at 40.91° N. Lat; 79.07° W. Long. Population: 148 (2010); Density: 115.4 persons per square mile (2010); Race: 100.0% White, 0.0% Black, 0.0% Asian, 0.0% American Indian/Alaska Native, 0.0% Native Hawaiian/Other Pacific Islander, 0.0% Other, 0.7% Hispanic of any race (2010); Average household size: 2.69 (2010); Median age: 39.5 (2010); Males per 100 females: 97.3 (2010); Homeownership rate: 87.3% (2010)

WALSTON (unincorporated postal area)
Zip Code: 15781

Covers a land area of 1.048 square miles and a water area of 0 square miles. Located at 40.96° N. Lat; 78.98° W. Long. Elevation is 1,335 feet. Population: 94 (2010); Density: 89.7 persons per square mile (2010); Race: 100.0% White, 0.0% Black, 0.0% Asian, 0.0% American Indian/Alaska Native, 0.0% Native Hawaiian/Other Pacific Islander, 0.0% Other, 0.0% Hispanic of any race (2010); Average household size: 2.19 (2010); Median age: 49.5 (2010); Males per 100 females: 108.9 (2010); Homeownership rate: 97.7% (2010)

WARSAW (township).
Covers a land area of 51.284 square miles and a water area of 0.220 square miles. Located at 41.24° N. Lat; 78.98° W. Long. Elevation is 1,719 feet.

Population: 1,213 (1990); 1,346 (2000); 1,424 (2010); Density: 27.8 persons per square mile (2010); Race: 99.1% White, 0.1% Black, 0.0% Asian, 0.3% American Indian/Alaska Native, 0.0% Native Hawaiian/Other Pacific Islander, 0.5% Other, 0.9% Hispanic of any race (2010); Average household size: 2.69 (2010); Median age: 41.3 (2010); Males per 100 females: 105.5 (2010); Marriage status: 22.6% never married, 61.4% now married, 7.4% widowed, 8.6% divorced (2006-2010 5-year est.); Foreign born: 0.5% (2006-2010 5-year est.); Ancestry (includes multiple ancestries): 35.1% German, 14.1% Irish, 12.1% American, 9.8% English, 7.8% Italian (2006-2010 5-year est.).

Economy: Employment by occupation: 5.7% management, 0.0% professional, 12.5% services, 10.0% sales, 3.9% farming, 10.0% construction, 16.2% production (2006-2010 5-year est.).

Income: Per capita income: $17,075 (2006-2010 5-year est.); Median household income: $36,544 (2006-2010 5-year est.); Average household income: $44,656 (2006-2010 5-year est.); Percent of households with income of $100,000 or more: 6.7% (2006-2010 5-year est.); Poverty rate: 9.1% (2006-2010 5-year est.).

Education: Percent of population age 25 and over with: High school diploma (including GED) or higher: 88.3% (2006-2010 5-year est.); Bachelor's degree or higher: 8.4% (2006-2010 5-year est.); Master's degree or higher: 3.5% (2006-2010 5-year est.).

Housing: Homeownership rate: 84.7% (2010); Median home value: $95,000 (2006-2010 5-year est.); Median contract rent: $425 per month

(2006-2010 5-year est.); Median year structure built: 1967 (2006-2010 5-year est.).

Transportation: Commute to work: 93.1% car, 0.9% public transportation, 1.8% walk, 3.2% work from home (2006-2010 5-year est.); Travel time to work: 17.8% less than 15 minutes, 44.1% 15 to 30 minutes, 22.3% 30 to 45 minutes, 5.9% 45 to 60 minutes, 10.0% 60 minutes or more (2006-2010 5-year est.)

Additional Information Contacts
Brookville Area Chamber of Commerce . . . . (814) 849-8448
http://www.brookvillechamber.com

WASHINGTON (township).
Covers a land area of 47.593 square miles and a water area of 0.377 square miles. Located at 41.19° N. Lat; 78.86° W. Long.

Population: 1,939 (1990); 1,931 (2000); 1,926 (2010); Density: 40.5 persons per square mile (2010); Race: 98.5% White, 0.1% Black, 0.4% Asian, 0.2% American Indian/Alaska Native, 0.0% Native Hawaiian/Other Pacific Islander, 0.8% Other, 0.6% Hispanic of any race (2010); Average household size: 2.50 (2010); Median age: 46.2 (2010); Males per 100 females: 107.8 (2010); Marriage status: 22.9% never married, 65.2% now married, 4.8% widowed, 7.1% divorced (2006-2010 5-year est.); Foreign born: 0.2% (2006-2010 5-year est.); Ancestry (includes multiple ancestries): 34.1% German, 16.7% Irish, 14.7% English, 12.9% American, 8.1% Italian (2006-2010 5-year est.).

Economy: Employment by occupation: 9.8% management, 1.4% professional, 7.5% services, 17.3% sales, 2.7% farming, 13.3% construction, 11.8% production (2006-2010 5-year est.).

Income: Per capita income: $19,892 (2006-2010 5-year est.); Median household income: $40,750 (2006-2010 5-year est.); Average household income: $51,223 (2006-2010 5-year est.); Percent of households with income of $100,000 or more: 8.3% (2006-2010 5-year est.); Poverty rate: 7.8% (2006-2010 5-year est.).

Education: Percent of population age 25 and over with: High school diploma (including GED) or higher: 86.3% (2006-2010 5-year est.); Bachelor's degree or higher: 10.3% (2006-2010 5-year est.); Master's degree or higher: 2.0% (2006-2010 5-year est.).

Housing: Homeownership rate: 86.8% (2010); Median home value: $96,400 (2006-2010 5-year est.); Median contract rent: $345 per month (2006-2010 5-year est.); Median year structure built: 1972 (2006-2010 5-year est.).

Transportation: Commute to work: 90.0% car, 1.1% public transportation, 2.0% walk, 5.0% work from home (2006-2010 5-year est.); Travel time to work: 18.8% less than 15 minutes, 65.1% 15 to 30 minutes, 7.8% 30 to 45 minutes, 3.3% 45 to 60 minutes, 5.0% 60 minutes or more (2006-2010 5-year est.)

Additional Information Contacts
Brookville Area Chamber of Commerce . . . . (814) 849-8448
http://www.brookvillechamber.com

WINSLOW (township).
Covers a land area of 45.048 square miles and a water area of 0.262 square miles. Located at 41.05° N. Lat; 78.92° W. Long. Elevation is 1,713 feet.

Population: 2,526 (1990); 2,591 (2000); 2,622 (2010); Density: 58.2 persons per square mile (2010); Race: 99.0% White, 0.2% Black, 0.2% Asian, 0.1% American Indian/Alaska Native, 0.0% Native Hawaiian/Other Pacific Islander, 0.5% Other, 0.3% Hispanic of any race (2010); Average household size: 2.49 (2010); Median age: 45.5 (2010); Males per 100 females: 102.3 (2010); Marriage status: 23.1% never married, 65.4% now married, 6.8% widowed, 4.7% divorced (2006-2010 5-year est.); Foreign born: 0.7% (2006-2010 5-year est.); Ancestry (includes multiple ancestries): 35.6% German, 18.4% Irish, 17.0% English, 14.8% Italian, 12.3% Polish (2006-2010 5-year est.).

Economy: Employment by occupation: 4.6% management, 1.7% professional, 12.0% services, 12.3% sales, 1.7% farming, 23.7% construction, 11.3% production (2006-2010 5-year est.).

Income: Per capita income: $18,405 (2006-2010 5-year est.); Median household income: $38,333 (2006-2010 5-year est.); Average household income: $47,784 (2006-2010 5-year est.); Percent of households with income of $100,000 or more: 6.3% (2006-2010 5-year est.); Poverty rate: 7.7% (2006-2010 5-year est.).

Education: Percent of population age 25 and over with: High school diploma (including GED) or higher: 89.2% (2006-2010 5-year est.); Bachelor's degree or higher: 10.2% (2006-2010 5-year est.); Master's degree or higher: 3.8% (2006-2010 5-year est.).

Housing: Homeownership rate: 87.5% (2010); Median home value: $81,900 (2006-2010 5-year est.); Median contract rent: $413 per month (2006-2010 5-year est.); Median year structure built: 1964 (2006-2010 5-year est.).

Transportation: Commute to work: 97.4% car, 0.0% public transportation, 0.6% walk, 2.1% work from home (2006-2010 5-year est.); Travel time to work: 27.1% less than 15 minutes, 54.6% 15 to 30 minutes, 8.8% 30 to 45 minutes, 6.6% 45 to 60 minutes, 2.9% 60 minutes or more (2006-2010 5-year est.).

Additional Information Contacts

Greater DuBois Chamber of Commerce & Economic Development . . (814) 371-5010
  http://www.duboispachamber.com

WORTHVILLE (borough). Covers a land area of 0.339 square miles and a water area of 0.009 square miles. Located at 41.02° N. Lat; 79.14° W. Long. Elevation is 1,184 feet.

Population: 65 (1990); 85 (2000); 67 (2010); Density: 197.8 persons per square mile (2010); Race: 98.5% White, 0.0% Black, 0.0% Asian, 0.0% American Indian/Alaska Native, 0.0% Native Hawaiian/Other Pacific Islander, 1.5% Other, 1.5% Hispanic of any race (2010); Average household size: 2.23 (2010); Median age: 49.8 (2010); Males per 100 females: 81.1 (2010); Marriage status: 16.7% never married, 77.3% now married, 4.5% widowed, 1.5% divorced (2006-2010 5-year est.); Foreign born: 0.0% (2006-2010 5-year est.); Ancestry (includes multiple ancestries): 30.4% German, 20.3% American, 11.6% English, 10.1% Italian, 5.8% Dutch (2006-2010 5-year est.).

Economy: Employment by occupation: 5.4% management, 0.0% professional, 18.9% services, 0.0% sales, 0.0% farming, 18.9% construction, 10.8% production (2006-2010 5-year est.).

Income: Per capita income: $28,313 (2006-2010 5-year est.); Median household income: $57,500 (2006-2010 5-year est.); Average household income: $63,319 (2006-2010 5-year est.); Percent of households with income of $100,000 or more: 15.6% (2006-2010 5-year est.); Poverty rate: 0.0% (2006-2010 5-year est.).

Education: Percent of population age 25 and over with: High school diploma (including GED) or higher: 91.2% (2006-2010 5-year est.); Bachelor's degree or higher: 19.3% (2006-2010 5-year est.); Master's degree or higher: 12.3% (2006-2010 5-year est.).

Housing: Homeownership rate: 93.4% (2010); Median home value: $81,700 (2006-2010 5-year est.); Median contract rent: n/a per month (2006-2010 5-year est.); Median year structure built: before 1940 (2006-2010 5-year est.).

Transportation: Commute to work: 91.9% car, 0.0% public transportation, 2.7% walk, 5.4% work from home (2006-2010 5-year est.); Travel time to work: 2.9% less than 15 minutes, 82.9% 15 to 30 minutes, 14.3% 30 to 45 minutes, 0.0% 45 to 60 minutes, 0.0% 60 minutes or more (2006-2010 5-year est.)

YOUNG (township). Covers a land area of 15.443 square miles and a water area of 0.081 square miles. Located at 40.96° N. Lat; 79.00° W. Long.

Population: 1,667 (1990); 1,800 (2000); 1,749 (2010); Density: 113.3 persons per square mile (2010); Race: 98.6% White, 0.3% Black, 0.3% Asian, 0.1% American Indian/Alaska Native, 0.0% Native Hawaiian/Other Pacific Islander, 0.7% Other, 0.3% Hispanic of any race (2010); Average household size: 2.43 (2010); Median age: 44.7 (2010); Males per 100 females: 99.4 (2010); Marriage status: 22.7% never married, 60.2% now married, 7.5% widowed, 9.6% divorced (2006-2010 5-year est.); Foreign born: 0.8% (2006-2010 5-year est.); Ancestry (includes multiple ancestries): 32.5% German, 15.8% Irish, 14.5% Italian, 7.0% English, 5.3% American (2006-2010 5-year est.).

Economy: Employment by occupation: 7.8% management, 1.0% professional, 7.5% services, 15.5% sales, 4.2% farming, 9.3% construction, 6.5% production (2006-2010 5-year est.).

Income: Per capita income: $25,570 (2006-2010 5-year est.); Median household income: $43,088 (2006-2010 5-year est.); Average household income: $62,547 (2006-2010 5-year est.); Percent of households with income of $100,000 or more: 12.8% (2006-2010 5-year est.); Poverty rate: 11.4% (2006-2010 5-year est.).

Education: Percent of population age 25 and over with: High school diploma (including GED) or higher: 85.3% (2006-2010 5-year est.); Bachelor's degree or higher: 18.4% (2006-2010 5-year est.); Master's degree or higher: 7.6% (2006-2010 5-year est.).

Housing: Homeownership rate: 85.2% (2010); Median home value: $98,100 (2006-2010 5-year est.); Median contract rent: $410 per month (2006-2010 5-year est.); Median year structure built: 1972 (2006-2010 5-year est.).

Transportation: Commute to work: 94.2% car, 0.0% public transportation, 2.8% walk, 2.4% work from home (2006-2010 5-year est.); Travel time to work: 52.9% less than 15 minutes, 17.9% 15 to 30 minutes, 14.3% 30 to 45 minutes, 7.6% 45 to 60 minutes, 7.3% 60 minutes or more (2006-2010 5-year est.).

Additional Information Contacts

Brookville Area Chamber of Commerce . . . . (814) 849-8448
  http://www.brookvillechamber.com

Juniata County

Located in central Pennsylvania; bounded on the southeast by the Tuscarora Mountains; includes the Blacklog Mountains on the southwest and the Shade Mountains on the northwest; drained by the Juniata River. Covers a land area of 391.350 square miles, a water area of 2.165 square miles, and is located in the Eastern Time Zone at 40.53° N. Lat., 77.40° W. Long. The county was founded in 1831. County seat is Mifflintown.

Population: 20,625 (1990); 22,821 (2000); 24,636 (2010); Race: 96.8% White, 0.6% Black, 0.3% Asian, 0.1% American Indian/Alaska Native, 0.0% Native Hawaiian/Other Pacific Islander, 2.2% Other, 2.5% Hispanic of any race (2010); Density: 63.0 persons per square mile (2010); Average household size: 2.57 (2010); Median age: 40.9 (2010); Males per 100 females: 99.5 (2010).

Religion: Six largest groups: 11.3% Methodist/Pietist, 8.4% Lutheran, 8.0% European Free-Church, 6.3% Hindu, 4.8% Non-Denominational, 3.4% Presbyterian-Reformed (2010)

Economy: Unemployment rate: 7.3% (August 2012); Total civilian labor force: 12,257 (August 2012); Leading industries: 36.2% manufacturing; 12.4% retail trade; 11.9% health care and social assistance (2010); Farms: 788 totaling 97,681 acres (2007); Companies that employ 500 or more persons: 1 (2010); Companies that employ 100 to 499 persons: 6 (2010); Companies that employ less than 100 persons: 458 (2010); Black-owned businesses: n/a (2007); Hispanic-owned businesses: n/a (2007); Asian-owned businesses: n/a (2007); Women-owned businesses: 542 (2007); Retail sales per capita: $8,423 (2010). Single-family building permits issued: 22 (2011); Multi-family building permits issued: 7 (2011).

Income: Per capita income: $20,682 (2006-2010 5-year est.); Median household income: $44,276 (2006-2010 5-year est.); Average household income: $53,805 (2006-2010 5-year est.); Percent of households with income of $100,000 or more: 10.4% (2006-2010 5-year est.); Poverty rate: 8.3% (2006-2010 5-year est.); Bankruptcy rate: 1.84% (2011).

Education: Percent of population age 25 and over with: High school diploma (including GED) or higher: 80.1% (2006-2010 5-year est.); Bachelor's degree or higher: 10.8% (2006-2010 5-year est.); Master's degree or higher: 3.6% (2006-2010 5-year est.).

Housing: Homeownership rate: 76.1% (2010); Median home value: $127,200 (2006-2010 5-year est.); Median contract rent: $405 per month (2006-2010 5-year est.); Median year structure built: 1972 (2006-2010 5-year est.)

Health: Birth rate: 115.6 per 10,000 population (2011); Death rate: 94.3 per 10,000 population (2011); Age-adjusted cancer mortality rate: 179.3 deaths per 100,000 population (2009); Number of physicians: 3.7 per 10,000 population (2010); Hospital beds: 0.0 per 10,000 population (2008); Hospital admissions: 0.0 per 10,000 population (2008).

Elections: 2012 Presidential election results: 26.7% Obama, 72.0% Romney

National and State Parks: Big Spring State Park

Additional Information Contacts

Juniata County Government . . . . (717) 436-8991
  http://www.co.juniata.pa.us

Juniata County Communities

BEALE (township). Covers a land area of 21.886 square miles and a water area of 0 square miles. Located at 40.50° N. Lat; 77.52° W. Long.

Population: 629 (1990); 726 (2000); 830 (2010); Density: 37.9 persons per square mile (2010); Race: 97.2% White, 0.5% Black, 0.1% Asian, 0.1% American Indian/Alaska Native, 0.0% Native Hawaiian/Other Pacific Islander, 2.1% Other, 0.8% Hispanic of any race (2010); Average household size: 2.69 (2010); Median age: 39.4 (2010); Males per 100 females: 101.0 (2010); Marriage status: 20.6% never married, 63.7% now

married, 6.9% widowed, 8.9% divorced (2006-2010 5-year est.); Foreign born: 1.1% (2006-2010 5-year est.); Ancestry (includes multiple ancestries): 43.3% German, 30.8% Irish, 5.8% American, 4.0% Dutch, 3.2% English (2006-2010 5-year est.).

Economy: Single-family building permits issued: 2 (2011); Multi-family building permits issued: 0 (2011); Employment by occupation: 5.6% management, 1.7% professional, 14.6% services, 12.3% sales, 1.3% farming, 15.0% construction, 7.3% production (2006-2010 5-year est.).

Income: Per capita income: $17,332 (2006-2010 5-year est.); Median household income: $41,302 (2006-2010 5-year est.); Average household income: $46,641 (2006-2010 5-year est.); Percent of households with income of $100,000 or more: 1.6% (2006-2010 5-year est.); Poverty rate: 6.9% (2006-2010 5-year est.).

Education: Percent of population age 25 and over with: High school diploma (including GED) or higher: 76.0% (2006-2010 5-year est.); Bachelor's degree or higher: 10.9% (2006-2010 5-year est.); Master's degree or higher: 3.8% (2006-2010 5-year est.).

Housing: Homeownership rate: 89.6% (2010); Median home value: $133,600 (2006-2010 5-year est.); Median contract rent: $467 per month (2006-2010 5-year est.); Median year structure built: 1969 (2006-2010 5-year est.).

Transportation: Commute to work: 91.2% car, 0.0% public transportation, 3.7% walk, 5.1% work from home (2006-2010 5-year est.); Travel time to work: 15.7% less than 15 minutes, 37.1% 15 to 30 minutes, 16.8% 30 to 45 minutes, 8.6% 45 to 60 minutes, 21.8% 60 minutes or more (2006-2010 5-year est.)

DELAWARE (township).

Covers a land area of 29.022 square miles and a water area of 0.593 square miles. Located at 40.59° N. Lat; 77.22° W. Long.

Population: 1,440 (1990); 1,464 (2000); 1,547 (2010); Density: 53.3 persons per square mile (2010); Race: 97.3% White, 0.8% Black, 0.7% Asian, 0.1% American Indian/Alaska Native, 0.0% Native Hawaiian/Other Pacific Islander, 1.1% Other, 1.0% Hispanic of any race (2010); Average household size: 2.54 (2010); Median age: 42.8 (2010); Males per 100 females: 97.1 (2010); Marriage status: 21.1% never married, 64.8% now married, 8.0% widowed, 6.0% divorced (2006-2010 5-year est.); Foreign born: 0.5% (2006-2010 5-year est.); Ancestry (includes multiple ancestries): 44.7% German, 11.4% American, 9.3% Irish, 5.1% Pennsylvania German, 4.8% English (2006-2010 5-year est.).

Economy: Single-family building permits issued: 3 (2011); Multi-family building permits issued: 0 (2011); Employment by occupation: 5.6% management, 2.4% professional, 9.2% services, 13.5% sales, 4.3% farming, 15.1% construction, 12.1% production (2006-2010 5-year est.).

Income: Per capita income: $19,847 (2006-2010 5-year est.); Median household income: $49,063 (2006-2010 5-year est.); Average household income: $55,393 (2006-2010 5-year est.); Percent of households with income of $100,000 or more: 13.1% (2006-2010 5-year est.); Poverty rate: 7.5% (2006-2010 5-year est.).

Education: Percent of population age 25 and over with: High school diploma (including GED) or higher: 85.4% (2006-2010 5-year est.); Bachelor's degree or higher: 10.1% (2006-2010 5-year est.); Master's degree or higher: 2.7% (2006-2010 5-year est.).

Housing: Homeownership rate: 83.7% (2010); Median home value: $132,900 (2006-2010 5-year est.); Median contract rent: $475 per month (2006-2010 5-year est.); Median year structure built: 1971 (2006-2010 5-year est.).

Transportation: Commute to work: 91.3% car, 1.2% public transportation, 2.9% walk, 3.6% work from home (2006-2010 5-year est.); Travel time to work: 37.4% less than 15 minutes, 17.4% 15 to 30 minutes, 16.6% 30 to 45 minutes, 20.9% 45 to 60 minutes, 7.7% 60 minutes or more (2006-2010 5-year est.)

Additional Information Contacts
Juniata River Valley Chamber of Commerce . . . . (717) 248-6713
  http://www.juniatarivervalley.org

EAST RUTHERFORD (CDP).

Covers a land area of 0.376 square miles and a water area of 0 square miles. Located at 40.37° N. Lat; 77.60° W. Long. Elevation is 627 feet.

Population: 178 (1990); 185 (2000); 196 (2010); Density: 521.8 persons per square mile (2010); Race: 100.0% White, 0.0% Black, 0.0% Asian, 0.0% American Indian/Alaska Native, 0.0% Native Hawaiian/Other Pacific Islander, 0.0% Other, 1.0% Hispanic of any race (2010); Average household size: 2.45 (2010); Median age: 34.5 (2010); Males per 100 females: 122.7 (2010); Marriage status: 35.9% never married, 47.0% now

married, 6.0% widowed, 11.1% divorced (2006-2010 5-year est.); Foreign born: 0.0% (2006-2010 5-year est.); Ancestry (includes multiple ancestries): 37.6% German, 10.3% Irish, 4.3% Scotch-Irish, 3.4% Dutch (2006-2010 5-year est.).

Economy: Employment by occupation: 0.0% management, 0.0% professional, 0.0% services, 20.7% sales, 0.0% farming, 0.0% construction, 0.0% production (2006-2010 5-year est.).

Income: Per capita income: $17,821 (2006-2010 5-year est.); Median household income: $19,097 (2006-2010 5-year est.); Average household income: $30,537 (2006-2010 5-year est.); Percent of households with income of $100,000 or more: n/a (2006-2010 5-year est.); Poverty rate: 17.1% (2006-2010 5-year est.).

Education: Percent of population age 25 and over with: High school diploma (including GED) or higher: 71.7% (2006-2010 5-year est.); Bachelor's degree or higher: 10.4% (2006-2010 5-year est.); Master's degree or higher: 0.0% (2006-2010 5-year est.).

Housing: Homeownership rate: 73.8% (2010); Median home value: $64,400 (2006-2010 5-year est.); Median contract rent: $358 per month (2006-2010 5-year est.); Median year structure built: before 1940 (2006-2010 5-year est.).

Transportation: Commute to work: 100.0% car, 0.0% public transportation, 0.0% walk, 0.0% work from home (2006-2010 5-year est.); Travel time to work: 0.0% less than 15 minutes, 27.3% 15 to 30 minutes, 22.7% 30 to 45 minutes, 0.0% 45 to 60 minutes, 50.0% 60 minutes or more (2006-2010 5-year est.)

EAST SALEM (CDP).

Covers a land area of 0.267 square miles and a water area of 0 square miles. Located at 40.61° N. Lat; 77.24° W. Long. Elevation is 614 feet.

Population: n/a (1990); n/a (2000); 186 (2010); Density: 695.9 persons per square mile (2010); Race: 97.3% White, 0.0% Black, 0.5% Asian, 0.5% American Indian/Alaska Native, 0.0% Native Hawaiian/Other Pacific Islander, 1.7% Other, 2.7% Hispanic of any race (2010); Average household size: 2.51 (2010); Median age: 35.0 (2010); Males per 100 females: 93.8 (2010); Marriage status: 8.9% never married, 82.2% now married, 8.9% widowed, 0.0% divorced (2006-2010 5-year est.); Foreign born: 0.0% (2006-2010 5-year est.); Ancestry (includes multiple ancestries): 61.7% German, 28.6% American, 5.3% Scotch-Irish, 5.3% Scottish, 2.3% French (2006-2010 5-year est.).

Economy: Employment by occupation: 8.2% management, 0.0% professional, 11.5% services, 19.7% sales, 3.3% farming, 6.6% construction, 11.5% production (2006-2010 5-year est.).

Income: Per capita income: $20,351 (2006-2010 5-year est.); Median household income: $48,250 (2006-2010 5-year est.); Average household income: $53,173 (2006-2010 5-year est.); Percent of households with income of $100,000 or more: n/a (2006-2010 5-year est.); Poverty rate: 0.0% (2006-2010 5-year est.).

Education: Percent of population age 25 and over with: High school diploma (including GED) or higher: 92.6% (2006-2010 5-year est.); Bachelor's degree or higher: 6.4% (2006-2010 5-year est.); Master's degree or higher: 0.0% (2006-2010 5-year est.).

Housing: Homeownership rate: 63.5% (2010); Median home value: $134,800 (2006-2010 5-year est.); Median contract rent: $308 per month (2006-2010 5-year est.); Median year structure built: 1951 (2006-2010 5-year est.).

Transportation: Commute to work: 90.2% car, 0.0% public transportation, 0.0% walk, 9.8% work from home (2006-2010 5-year est.); Travel time to work: 10.9% less than 15 minutes, 41.8% 15 to 30 minutes, 30.9% 30 to 45 minutes, 7.3% 45 to 60 minutes, 9.1% 60 minutes or more (2006-2010 5-year est.)

EAST WATERFORD (unincorporated postal area)

Zip Code: 17021
  Covers a land area of 52.156 square miles and a water area of 0.010 square miles. Located at 40.33° N. Lat; 77.66° W. Long. Population: 1,088 (2010); Density: 20.9 persons per square mile (2010); Race: 99.1% White, 0.0% Black, 0.1% Asian, 0.0% American Indian/Alaska Native, 0.0% Native Hawaiian/Other Pacific Islander, 0.8% Other, 1.1% Hispanic of any race (2010); Average household size: 2.49 (2010); Median age: 42.0 (2010); Males per 100 females: 116.3 (2010); Homeownership rate: 81.0% (2010)

FAYETTE (township). Covers a land area of 40.037 square miles and a water area of 0 square miles. Located at 40.65° N. Lat; 77.27° W. Long.
Population: 3,002 (1990); 3,252 (2000); 3,478 (2010); Density: 86.9 persons per square mile (2010); Race: 97.6% White, 0.6% Black, 0.2% Asian, 0.1% American Indian/Alaska Native, 0.0% Native Hawaiian/Other Pacific Islander, 1.5% Other, 1.3% Hispanic of any race (2010); Average household size: 2.62 (2010); Median age: 40.9 (2010); Males per 100 females: 100.9 (2010); Marriage status: 22.8% never married, 67.5% now married, 3.0% widowed, 6.7% divorced (2006-2010 5-year est.); Foreign born: 1.8% (2006-2010 5-year est.); Ancestry (includes multiple ancestries): 62.4% German, 11.6% Irish, 9.7% English, 9.3% Swiss, 6.8% Italian (2006-2010 5-year est.).
Economy: Single-family building permits issued: 3 (2011); Multi-family building permits issued: 0 (2011); Employment by occupation: 6.1% management, 1.4% professional, 13.3% services, 14.3% sales, 4.5% farming, 16.5% construction, 3.7% production (2006-2010 5-year est.).
Income: Per capita income: $20,190 (2006-2010 5-year est.); Median household income: $44,349 (2006-2010 5-year est.); Average household income: $56,512 (2006-2010 5-year est.); Percent of households with income of $100,000 or more: 11.2% (2006-2010 5-year est.); Poverty rate: 2.5% (2006-2010 5-year est.).
Education: Percent of population age 25 and over with: High school diploma (including GED) or higher: 77.1% (2006-2010 5-year est.); Bachelor's degree or higher: 9.1% (2006-2010 5-year est.); Master's degree or higher: 1.3% (2006-2010 5-year est.).
Housing: Homeownership rate: 76.1% (2010); Median home value: $136,200 (2006-2010 5-year est.); Median contract rent: $344 per month (2006-2010 5-year est.); Median year structure built: 1975 (2006-2010 5-year est.).
Transportation: Commute to work: 84.3% car, 0.0% public transportation, 6.4% walk, 8.3% work from home (2006-2010 5-year est.); Travel time to work: 28.9% less than 15 minutes, 36.9% 15 to 30 minutes, 10.7% 30 to 45 minutes, 11.4% 45 to 60 minutes, 12.1% 60 minutes or more (2006-2010 5-year est.)
Additional Information Contacts
Juniata River Valley Chamber of Commerce . . . . (717) 248-6713
  http://www.juniatarivervalley.org

FERMANAGH (township). Covers a land area of 32.045 square miles and a water area of 0.444 square miles. Located at 40.62° N. Lat; 77.39° W. Long.
Population: 2,249 (1990); 2,544 (2000); 2,811 (2010); Density: 87.7 persons per square mile (2010); Race: 97.5% White, 0.5% Black, 0.5% Asian, 0.1% American Indian/Alaska Native, 0.0% Native Hawaiian/Other Pacific Islander, 1.4% Other, 2.6% Hispanic of any race (2010); Average household size: 2.31 (2010); Median age: 48.5 (2010); Males per 100 females: 89.9 (2010); Marriage status: 18.2% never married, 67.1% now married, 9.1% widowed, 5.6% divorced (2006-2010 5-year est.); Foreign born: 2.5% (2006-2010 5-year est.); Ancestry (includes multiple ancestries): 42.6% German, 10.9% American, 10.8% Irish, 6.5% English, 4.4% Pennsylvania German (2006-2010 5-year est.).
Economy: Single-family building permits issued: 2 (2011); Multi-family building permits issued: 7 (2011); Employment by occupation: 5.5% management, 3.0% professional, 10.1% services, 18.3% sales, 4.7% farming, 12.4% construction, 4.9% production (2006-2010 5-year est.).
Income: Per capita income: $24,130 (2006-2010 5-year est.); Median household income: $48,591 (2006-2010 5-year est.); Average household income: $60,157 (2006-2010 5-year est.); Percent of households with income of $100,000 or more: 11.1% (2006-2010 5-year est.); Poverty rate: 9.8% (2006-2010 5-year est.).
Education: Percent of population age 25 and over with: High school diploma (including GED) or higher: 82.8% (2006-2010 5-year est.); Bachelor's degree or higher: 9.5% (2006-2010 5-year est.); Master's degree or higher: 3.9% (2006-2010 5-year est.).
Housing: Homeownership rate: 71.2% (2010); Median home value: $145,300 (2006-2010 5-year est.); Median contract rent: $419 per month (2006-2010 5-year est.); Median year structure built: 1975 (2006-2010 5-year est.).
Transportation: Commute to work: 87.6% car, 0.0% public transportation, 4.1% walk, 5.9% work from home (2006-2010 5-year est.); Travel time to work: 38.1% less than 15 minutes, 28.8% 15 to 30 minutes, 6.3% 30 to 45 minutes, 11.7% 45 to 60 minutes, 15.2% 60 minutes or more (2006-2010 5-year est.)

Additional Information Contacts
Juniata River Valley Chamber of Commerce . . . . (717) 248-6713
  http://www.juniatarivervalley.org

GREENWOOD (township). Covers a land area of 19.459 square miles and a water area of 0.001 square miles. Located at 40.63° N. Lat; 77.11° W. Long.
Population: 493 (1990); 548 (2000); 617 (2010); Density: 31.7 persons per square mile (2010); Race: 98.7% White, 0.6% Black, 0.0% Asian, 0.2% American Indian/Alaska Native, 0.0% Native Hawaiian/Other Pacific Islander, 0.5% Other, 1.0% Hispanic of any race (2010); Average household size: 2.73 (2010); Median age: 40.3 (2010); Males per 100 females: 97.1 (2010); Marriage status: 23.3% never married, 61.8% now married, 6.2% widowed, 8.8% divorced (2006-2010 5-year est.); Foreign born: 0.0% (2006-2010 5-year est.); Ancestry (includes multiple ancestries): 52.2% German, 23.1% Irish, 11.8% American, 8.0% English, 3.6% Dutch (2006-2010 5-year est.).
Economy: Single-family building permits issued: 3 (2011); Multi-family building permits issued: 0 (2011); Employment by occupation: 14.7% management, 1.4% professional, 9.6% services, 10.6% sales, 1.8% farming, 28.4% construction, 6.4% production (2006-2010 5-year est.).
Income: Per capita income: $16,361 (2006-2010 5-year est.); Median household income: $32,500 (2006-2010 5-year est.); Average household income: $44,528 (2006-2010 5-year est.); Percent of households with income of $100,000 or more: 7.5% (2006-2010 5-year est.); Poverty rate: 8.2% (2006-2010 5-year est.).
Education: Percent of population age 25 and over with: High school diploma (including GED) or higher: 71.6% (2006-2010 5-year est.); Bachelor's degree or higher: 11.0% (2006-2010 5-year est.); Master's degree or higher: 0.9% (2006-2010 5-year est.).
Housing: Homeownership rate: 83.2% (2010); Median home value: $122,700 (2006-2010 5-year est.); Median contract rent: $417 per month (2006-2010 5-year est.); Median year structure built: 1959 (2006-2010 5-year est.).
Transportation: Commute to work: 77.5% car, 0.0% public transportation, 14.7% walk, 4.6% work from home (2006-2010 5-year est.); Travel time to work: 26.0% less than 15 minutes, 27.9% 15 to 30 minutes, 21.6% 30 to 45 minutes, 11.1% 45 to 60 minutes, 13.5% 60 minutes or more (2006-2010 5-year est.)

HONEY GROVE (unincorporated postal area)
Zip Code: 17035
  Covers a land area of 35.326 square miles and a water area of <.001 square miles. Located at 40.40° N. Lat; 77.58° W. Long. Elevation is 673 feet. Population: 839 (2010); Density: 23.7 persons per square mile (2010); Race: 99.0% White, 0.2% Black, 0.0% Asian, 0.0% American Indian/Alaska Native, 0.0% Native Hawaiian/Other Pacific Islander, 0.8% Other, 0.1% Hispanic of any race (2010); Average household size: 2.49 (2010); Median age: 45.3 (2010); Males per 100 females: 110.3 (2010); Homeownership rate: 88.2% (2010)

LACK (township). Covers a land area of 57.031 square miles and a water area of 0 square miles. Located at 40.36° N. Lat; 77.68° W. Long.
Population: 714 (1990); 750 (2000); 785 (2010); Density: 13.8 persons per square mile (2010); Race: 99.1% White, 0.0% Black, 0.0% Asian, 0.0% American Indian/Alaska Native, 0.0% Native Hawaiian/Other Pacific Islander, 0.9% Other, 1.1% Hispanic of any race (2010); Average household size: 2.49 (2010); Median age: 42.4 (2010); Males per 100 females: 112.2 (2010); Marriage status: 19.3% never married, 70.1% now married, 1.5% widowed, 9.1% divorced (2006-2010 5-year est.); Foreign born: 0.0% (2006-2010 5-year est.); Ancestry (includes multiple ancestries): 45.7% German, 20.5% English, 9.5% American, 9.5% Irish, 7.0% Italian (2006-2010 5-year est.).
Economy: Single-family building permits issued: 1 (2011); Multi-family building permits issued: 0 (2011); Employment by occupation: 21.7% management, 0.9% professional, 12.2% services, 8.3% sales, 0.0% farming, 14.9% construction, 9.8% production (2006-2010 5-year est.).
Income: Per capita income: $18,287 (2006-2010 5-year est.); Median household income: $36,389 (2006-2010 5-year est.); Average household income: $40,647 (2006-2010 5-year est.); Percent of households with income of $100,000 or more: 7.6% (2006-2010 5-year est.); Poverty rate: 23.2% (2006-2010 5-year est.).
Education: Percent of population age 25 and over with: High school diploma (including GED) or higher: 71.8% (2006-2010 5-year est.);

Bachelor's degree or higher: 7.0% (2006-2010 5-year est.); Master's degree or higher: 2.6% (2006-2010 5-year est.).
Housing: Homeownership rate: 83.5% (2010); Median home value: $93,500 (2006-2010 5-year est.); Median contract rent: $402 per month (2006-2010 5-year est.); Median year structure built: 1968 (2006-2010 5-year est.).
Transportation: Commute to work: 85.3% car, 0.0% public transportation, 4.0% walk, 10.7% work from home (2006-2010 5-year est.); Travel time to work: 21.6% less than 15 minutes, 13.4% 15 to 30 minutes, 9.3% 30 to 45 minutes, 23.7% 45 to 60 minutes, 32.0% 60 minutes or more (2006-2010 5-year est.)

MCALISTERVILLE (CDP).
Covers a land area of 1.755 square miles and a water area of 0 square miles. Located at 40.64° N. Lat; 77.27° W. Long. Elevation is 636 feet.
Population: 700 (1990); 765 (2000); 971 (2010); Density: 553.2 persons per square mile (2010); Race: 98.6% White, 0.4% Black, 0.2% Asian, 0.0% American Indian/Alaska Native, 0.0% Native Hawaiian/Other Pacific Islander, 0.8% Other, 0.9% Hispanic of any race (2010); Average household size: 2.35 (2010); Median age: 41.5 (2010); Males per 100 females: 87.1 (2010); Marriage status: 30.2% never married, 63.2% now married, 0.0% widowed, 6.6% divorced (2006-2010 5-year est.); Foreign born: 1.3% (2006-2010 5-year est.); Ancestry (includes multiple ancestries): 73.2% German, 22.7% Irish, 14.9% English, 12.1% Italian, 8.9% Swiss (2006-2010 5-year est.).
Economy: Employment by occupation: 5.2% management, 0.0% professional, 11.9% services, 27.4% sales, 2.4% farming, 11.2% construction, 8.2% production (2006-2010 5-year est.).
Income: Per capita income: $15,108 (2006-2010 5-year est.); Median household income: $34,091 (2006-2010 5-year est.); Average household income: $42,349 (2006-2010 5-year est.); Percent of households with income of $100,000 or more: 3.4% (2006-2010 5-year est.); Poverty rate: 1.5% (2006-2010 5-year est.).
Education: Percent of population age 25 and over with: High school diploma (including GED) or higher: 72.1% (2006-2010 5-year est.); Bachelor's degree or higher: 14.4% (2006-2010 5-year est.); Master's degree or higher: 2.7% (2006-2010 5-year est.).

School District(s)
Juniata County SD (KG-12)
   2010-11 Enrollment: 3,092 . . . . (717) 436-2111
Housing: Homeownership rate: 65.2% (2010); Median home value: $147,200 (2006-2010 5-year est.); Median contract rent: $318 per month (2006-2010 5-year est.); Median year structure built: 1969 (2006-2010 5-year est.).
Transportation: Commute to work: 79.4% car, 0.0% public transportation, 11.7% walk, 9.0% work from home (2006-2010 5-year est.); Travel time to work: 39.2% less than 15 minutes, 22.2% 15 to 30 minutes, 26.6% 30 to 45 minutes, 9.1% 45 to 60 minutes, 3.0% 60 minutes or more (2006-2010 5-year est.)

MEXICO (CDP).
Covers a land area of 1.084 square miles and a water area of 0 square miles. Located at 40.54° N. Lat; 77.36° W. Long. Elevation is 443 feet.
Population: 290 (1990); 279 (2000); 472 (2010); Density: 435.5 persons per square mile (2010); Race: 99.2% White, 0.4% Black, 0.2% Asian, 0.0% American Indian/Alaska Native, 0.2% Native Hawaiian/Other Pacific Islander, 0.0% Other, 1.3% Hispanic of any race (2010); Average household size: 2.52 (2010); Median age: 46.2 (2010); Males per 100 females: 99.2 (2010); Marriage status: 28.7% never married, 60.6% now married, 1.3% widowed, 9.4% divorced (2006-2010 5-year est.); Foreign born: 0.0% (2006-2010 5-year est.); Ancestry (includes multiple ancestries): 57.2% German, 33.8% Irish, 5.4% English, 4.6% American, 4.3% French (2006-2010 5-year est.).
Economy: Employment by occupation: 2.5% management, 0.0% professional, 9.3% services, 24.3% sales, 0.0% farming, 8.5% construction, 6.3% production (2006-2010 5-year est.).
Income: Per capita income: $24,182 (2006-2010 5-year est.); Median household income: $58,935 (2006-2010 5-year est.); Average household income: $66,013 (2006-2010 5-year est.); Percent of households with income of $100,000 or more: 13.8% (2006-2010 5-year est.); Poverty rate: 5.0% (2006-2010 5-year est.).
Education: Percent of population age 25 and over with: High school diploma (including GED) or higher: 89.0% (2006-2010 5-year est.); Bachelor's degree or higher: 2.8% (2006-2010 5-year est.); Master's degree or higher: 2.8% (2006-2010 5-year est.).

Housing: Homeownership rate: 83.9% (2010); Median home value: $104,200 (2006-2010 5-year est.); Median contract rent: n/a per month (2006-2010 5-year est.); Median year structure built: 1954 (2006-2010 5-year est.).
Transportation: Commute to work: 98.4% car, 0.0% public transportation, 1.6% walk, 0.0% work from home (2006-2010 5-year est.); Travel time to work: 51.1% less than 15 minutes, 23.5% 15 to 30 minutes, 9.0% 30 to 45 minutes, 8.5% 45 to 60 minutes, 7.9% 60 minutes or more (2006-2010 5-year est.)

MIFFLIN (borough).
Covers a land area of 0.174 square miles and a water area of 0 square miles. Located at 40.57° N. Lat; 77.40° W. Long. Elevation is 456 feet.
Population: 660 (1990); 627 (2000); 642 (2010); Density: 3,684.6 persons per square mile (2010); Race: 88.8% White, 0.3% Black, 0.0% Asian, 0.3% American Indian/Alaska Native, 0.0% Native Hawaiian/Other Pacific Islander, 10.6% Other, 13.9% Hispanic of any race (2010); Average household size: 2.84 (2010); Median age: 31.7 (2010); Males per 100 females: 99.4 (2010); Marriage status: 29.0% never married, 55.8% now married, 5.1% widowed, 10.1% divorced (2006-2010 5-year est.); Foreign born: 11.4% (2006-2010 5-year est.); Ancestry (includes multiple ancestries): 45.2% German, 8.4% Irish, 6.0% English, 4.2% Swiss, 3.8% American (2006-2010 5-year est.).
Economy: Single-family building permits issued: 0 (2011); Multi-family building permits issued: 0 (2011); Employment by occupation: 1.4% management, 1.4% professional, 3.3% services, 10.0% sales, 0.0% farming, 26.1% construction, 24.2% production (2006-2010 5-year est.).
Income: Per capita income: $16,396 (2006-2010 5-year est.); Median household income: $31,932 (2006-2010 5-year est.); Average household income: $37,927 (2006-2010 5-year est.); Percent of households with income of $100,000 or more: 1.5% (2006-2010 5-year est.); Poverty rate: 21.4% (2006-2010 5-year est.).
Education: Percent of population age 25 and over with: High school diploma (including GED) or higher: 78.2% (2006-2010 5-year est.); Bachelor's degree or higher: 9.4% (2006-2010 5-year est.); Master's degree or higher: 0.9% (2006-2010 5-year est.).

School District(s)
Juniata County SD (KG-12)
   2010-11 Enrollment: 3,092 . . . . (717) 436-2111
Housing: Homeownership rate: 57.1% (2010); Median home value: $78,300 (2006-2010 5-year est.); Median contract rent: $333 per month (2006-2010 5-year est.); Median year structure built: 1956 (2006-2010 5-year est.).
Safety: Violent crime rate: 15.5 per 10,000 population; Property crime rate: 77.6 per 10,000 population (2011).
Transportation: Commute to work: 85.6% car, 0.0% public transportation, 8.0% walk, 4.5% work from home (2006-2010 5-year est.); Travel time to work: 43.2% less than 15 minutes, 11.5% 15 to 30 minutes, 18.2% 30 to 45 minutes, 17.2% 45 to 60 minutes, 9.9% 60 minutes or more (2006-2010 5-year est.)

MIFFLINTOWN (borough).
County seat. Covers a land area of 0.140 square miles and a water area of 0 square miles. Located at 40.57° N. Lat; 77.40° W. Long. Elevation is 469 feet.
History: Laid out 1791, incorporated 1833.
Population: 866 (1990); 861 (2000); 936 (2010); Density: 6,680.6 persons per square mile (2010); Race: 87.4% White, 0.6% Black, 0.4% Asian, 0.7% American Indian/Alaska Native, 0.0% Native Hawaiian/Other Pacific Islander, 10.9% Other, 16.9% Hispanic of any race (2010); Average household size: 2.43 (2010); Median age: 35.1 (2010); Males per 100 females: 104.4 (2010); Marriage status: 22.3% never married, 48.7% now married, 8.7% widowed, 20.3% divorced (2006-2010 5-year est.); Foreign born: 4.3% (2006-2010 5-year est.); Ancestry (includes multiple ancestries): 38.7% German, 19.3% Irish, 6.3% American, 5.3% English, 4.8% Scotch-Irish (2006-2010 5-year est.).
Economy: Single-family building permits issued: 0 (2011); Multi-family building permits issued: 0 (2011); Employment by occupation: 12.4% management, 2.7% professional, 4.1% services, 19.5% sales, 4.6% farming, 19.2% construction, 8.2% production (2006-2010 5-year est.).
Income: Per capita income: $21,447 (2006-2010 5-year est.); Median household income: $43,269 (2006-2010 5-year est.); Average household income: $48,115 (2006-2010 5-year est.); Percent of households with income of $100,000 or more: 7.3% (2006-2010 5-year est.); Poverty rate: 14.1% (2006-2010 5-year est.).

Education: Percent of population age 25 and over with: High school diploma (including GED) or higher: 83.8% (2006-2010 5-year est.); Bachelor's degree or higher: 14.8% (2006-2010 5-year est.); Master's degree or higher: 6.2% (2006-2010 5-year est.).

School District(s)

Juniata County SD (KG-12)
    2010-11 Enrollment: 3,092 . . . . (717) 436-2111

Housing: Homeownership rate: 44.5% (2010); Median home value: $101,200 (2006-2010 5-year est.); Median contract rent: $386 per month (2006-2010 5-year est.); Median year structure built: before 1940 (2006-2010 5-year est.).

Newspapers: Juniata Sentinel (Community news; Circulation 8,050)

Transportation: Commute to work: 91.0% car, 0.0% public transportation, 5.2% walk, 1.1% work from home (2006-2010 5-year est.); Travel time to work: 50.5% less than 15 minutes, 14.3% 15 to 30 minutes, 4.8% 30 to 45 minutes, 13.4% 45 to 60 minutes, 17.0% 60 minutes or more (2006-2010 5-year est.)

MILFORD (township). Covers a land area of 40.051 square miles and a water area of 0.456 square miles. Located at 40.55° N. Lat; 77.47° W. Long.

Population: 1,429 (1990); 1,758 (2000); 2,088 (2010); Density: 52.1 persons per square mile (2010); Race: 96.0% White, 0.6% Black, 0.7% Asian, 0.0% American Indian/Alaska Native, 0.1% Native Hawaiian/Other Pacific Islander, 2.6% Other, 4.1% Hispanic of any race (2010); Average household size: 2.41 (2010); Median age: 44.9 (2010); Males per 100 females: 94.1 (2010); Marriage status: 23.8% never married, 63.1% now married, 6.3% widowed, 6.8% divorced (2006-2010 5-year est.); Foreign born: 0.9% (2006-2010 5-year est.); Ancestry (includes multiple ancestries): 53.2% German, 14.3% Irish, 7.6% English, 6.8% American, 5.2% Scotch-Irish (2006-2010 5-year est.).

Economy: Single-family building permits issued: 3 (2011); Multi-family building permits issued: 0 (2011); Employment by occupation: 10.5% management, 2.7% professional, 10.2% services, 14.1% sales, 3.9% farming, 14.6% construction, 11.5% production (2006-2010 5-year est.).

Income: Per capita income: $20,668 (2006-2010 5-year est.); Median household income: $43,182 (2006-2010 5-year est.); Average household income: $54,081 (2006-2010 5-year est.); Percent of households with income of $100,000 or more: 9.4% (2006-2010 5-year est.); Poverty rate: 14.0% (2006-2010 5-year est.).

Education: Percent of population age 25 and over with: High school diploma (including GED) or higher: 86.4% (2006-2010 5-year est.); Bachelor's degree or higher: 16.6% (2006-2010 5-year est.); Master's degree or higher: 7.4% (2006-2010 5-year est.).

Housing: Homeownership rate: 72.1% (2010); Median home value: $142,100 (2006-2010 5-year est.); Median contract rent: $442 per month (2006-2010 5-year est.); Median year structure built: 1973 (2006-2010 5-year est.).

Transportation: Commute to work: 92.1% car, 0.5% public transportation, 3.3% walk, 3.4% work from home (2006-2010 5-year est.); Travel time to work: 42.1% less than 15 minutes, 22.0% 15 to 30 minutes, 6.2% 30 to 45 minutes, 7.6% 45 to 60 minutes, 22.0% 60 minutes or more (2006-2010 5-year est.)

Additional Information Contacts

Juniata River Valley Chamber of Commerce . . . . (717) 248-6713
    http://www.juniatarivervalley.org

MONROE (township). Covers a land area of 19.892 square miles and a water area of 0 square miles. Located at 40.66° N. Lat; 77.12° W. Long.

Population: 1,800 (1990); 2,042 (2000); 2,237 (2010); Density: 112.5 persons per square mile (2010); Race: 97.6% White, 0.7% Black, 0.3% Asian, 0.0% American Indian/Alaska Native, 0.0% Native Hawaiian/Other Pacific Islander, 1.4% Other, 0.9% Hispanic of any race (2010); Average household size: 2.79 (2010); Median age: 37.4 (2010); Males per 100 females: 98.1 (2010); Marriage status: 25.1% never married, 61.8% now married, 8.1% widowed, 4.9% divorced (2006-2010 5-year est.); Foreign born: 0.7% (2006-2010 5-year est.); Ancestry (includes multiple ancestries): 51.9% German, 8.9% Dutch, 6.9% Irish, 6.3% American, 5.5% English (2006-2010 5-year est.).

Economy: Single-family building permits issued: 0 (2011); Multi-family building permits issued: 0 (2011); Employment by occupation: 9.3% management, 2.7% professional, 9.9% services, 19.2% sales, 0.5% farming, 16.8% construction, 9.7% production (2006-2010 5-year est.).

Income: Per capita income: $21,189 (2006-2010 5-year est.); Median household income: $50,357 (2006-2010 5-year est.); Average household

income: $57,323 (2006-2010 5-year est.); Percent of households with income of $100,000 or more: 12.7% (2006-2010 5-year est.); Poverty rate: 4.3% (2006-2010 5-year est.).

Education: Percent of population age 25 and over with: High school diploma (including GED) or higher: 77.5% (2006-2010 5-year est.); Bachelor's degree or higher: 11.1% (2006-2010 5-year est.); Master's degree or higher: 2.3% (2006-2010 5-year est.).

Housing: Homeownership rate: 78.2% (2010); Median home value: $131,000 (2006-2010 5-year est.); Median contract rent: $404 per month (2006-2010 5-year est.); Median year structure built: 1967 (2006-2010 5-year est.).

Transportation: Commute to work: 92.9% car, 0.9% public transportation, 3.8% walk, 1.7% work from home (2006-2010 5-year est.); Travel time to work: 24.6% less than 15 minutes, 30.8% 15 to 30 minutes, 12.6% 30 to 45 minutes, 14.2% 45 to 60 minutes, 17.8% 60 minutes or more (2006-2010 5-year est.)

Additional Information Contacts

Juniata River Valley Chamber of Commerce . . . . (717) 248-6713
    http://www.juniatarivervalley.org

OAKLAND MILLS (unincorporated postal area)

Zip Code: 17076

    Covers a land area of 0.152 square miles and a water area of 0 square miles. Located at 40.61° N. Lat; 77.31° W. Long. Elevation is 564 feet. Population: 48 (2010); Density: 315.3 persons per square mile (2010); Race: 97.9% White, 0.0% Black, 0.0% Asian, 2.1% American Indian/Alaska Native, 0.0% Native Hawaiian/Other Pacific Islander, 0.0% Other, 0.0% Hispanic of any race (2010); Average household size: 2.67 (2010); Median age: 44.5 (2010); Males per 100 females: 108.7 (2010); Homeownership rate: 72.3% (2010)

PORT ROYAL (borough). Covers a land area of 0.602 square miles and a water area of 0 square miles. Located at 40.53° N. Lat; 77.39° W. Long. Elevation is 472 feet.

Population: 836 (1990); 977 (2000); 925 (2010); Density: 1,536.6 persons per square mile (2010); Race: 95.6% White, 0.1% Black, 0.1% Asian, 0.4% American Indian/Alaska Native, 0.0% Native Hawaiian/Other Pacific Islander, 3.8% Other, 4.0% Hispanic of any race (2010); Average household size: 2.40 (2010); Median age: 39.2 (2010); Males per 100 females: 96.8 (2010); Marriage status: 19.0% never married, 55.1% now married, 9.3% widowed, 16.6% divorced (2006-2010 5-year est.); Foreign born: 4.3% (2006-2010 5-year est.); Ancestry (includes multiple ancestries): 51.1% German, 15.9% Irish, 7.2% American, 5.1% Scotch-Irish, 4.6% English (2006-2010 5-year est.).

Economy: Single-family building permits issued: 0 (2011); Multi-family building permits issued: 0 (2011); Employment by occupation: 6.6% management, 2.0% professional, 15.8% services, 26.7% sales, 3.9% farming, 16.2% construction, 7.9% production (2006-2010 5-year est.).

Income: Per capita income: $19,080 (2006-2010 5-year est.); Median household income: $41,111 (2006-2010 5-year est.); Average household income: $45,612 (2006-2010 5-year est.); Percent of households with income of $100,000 or more: 7.4% (2006-2010 5-year est.); Poverty rate: 11.2% (2006-2010 5-year est.).

Education: Percent of population age 25 and over with: High school diploma (including GED) or higher: 91.4% (2006-2010 5-year est.); Bachelor's degree or higher: 13.3% (2006-2010 5-year est.); Master's degree or higher: 4.0% (2006-2010 5-year est.).

School District(s)

Juniata County SD (KG-12)
    2010-11 Enrollment: 3,092 . . . . (717) 436-2111

Housing: Homeownership rate: 57.5% (2010); Median home value: $96,400 (2006-2010 5-year est.); Median contract rent: $429 per month (2006-2010 5-year est.); Median year structure built: 1962 (2006-2010 5-year est.).

Newspapers: The Times (Local news; Circulation 2,500)

Transportation: Commute to work: 94.1% car, 0.0% public transportation, 2.9% walk, 2.5% work from home (2006-2010 5-year est.); Travel time to work: 33.6% less than 15 minutes, 25.6% 15 to 30 minutes, 7.6% 30 to 45 minutes, 17.6% 45 to 60 minutes, 15.6% 60 minutes or more (2006-2010 5-year est.)

RICHFIELD (CDP). Covers a land area of 1.163 square miles and a water area of 0.002 square miles. Located at 40.68° N. Lat; 77.12° W. Long. Elevation is 656 feet.

Population: 413 (1990); 459 (2000); 549 (2010); Density: 472.2 persons per square mile (2010); Race: 96.7% White, 1.6% Black, 0.5% Asian, 0.2% American Indian/Alaska Native, 0.0% Native Hawaiian/Other Pacific Islander, 1.0% Other, 0.9% Hispanic of any race (2010); Average household size: 2.61 (2010); Median age: 40.7 (2010); Males per 100 females: 84.2 (2010); Marriage status: 25.4% never married, 57.9% now married, 13.8% widowed, 2.9% divorced (2006-2010 5-year est.); Foreign born: 1.3% (2006-2010 5-year est.); Ancestry (includes multiple ancestries): 65.9% German, 7.8% Irish, 5.4% Italian, 4.6% Swiss, 4.4% Dutch (2006-2010 5-year est.).

Economy: Employment by occupation: 4.7% management, 8.5% professional, 9.5% services, 23.7% sales, 2.2% farming, 15.2% construction, 7.6% production (2006-2010 5-year est.).

Income: Per capita income: $23,934 (2006-2010 5-year est.); Median household income: $57,292 (2006-2010 5-year est.); Average household income: $57,985 (2006-2010 5-year est.); Percent of households with income of $100,000 or more: 11.2% (2006-2010 5-year est.); Poverty rate: 2.6% (2006-2010 5-year est.).

Education: Percent of population age 25 and over with: High school diploma (including GED) or higher: 77.4% (2006-2010 5-year est.); Bachelor's degree or higher: 19.0% (2006-2010 5-year est.); Master's degree or higher: 6.3% (2006-2010 5-year est.).

School District(s)

Juniata County SD (KG-12)
   2010-11 Enrollment: 3,092 . . . . (717) 436-2111
Housing: Homeownership rate: 72.1% (2010); Median home value: $90,000 (2006-2010 5-year est.); Median contract rent: $419 per month (2006-2010 5-year est.); Median year structure built: before 1940 (2006-2010 5-year est.).

Transportation: Commute to work: 95.1% car, 3.5% public transportation, 1.4% walk, 0.0% work from home (2006-2010 5-year est.); Travel time to work: 32.3% less than 15 minutes, 26.7% 15 to 30 minutes, 2.1% 30 to 45 minutes, 16.1% 45 to 60 minutes, 22.8% 60 minutes or more (2006-2010 5-year est.)

SPRUCE HILL (township). Covers a land area of 21.753 square miles and a water area of 0 square miles. Located at 40.46° N. Lat; 77.47° W. Long. Elevation is 499 feet.

Population: 694 (1990); 724 (2000); 834 (2010); Density: 38.3 persons per square mile (2010); Race: 92.1% White, 4.4% Black, 0.7% Asian, 0.0% American Indian/Alaska Native, 0.0% Native Hawaiian/Other Pacific Islander, 2.8% Other, 0.7% Hispanic of any race (2010); Average household size: 2.67 (2010); Median age: 42.4 (2010); Males per 100 females: 106.4 (2010); Marriage status: 23.6% never married, 59.5% now married, 6.2% widowed, 10.7% divorced (2006-2010 5-year est.); Foreign born: 0.3% (2006-2010 5-year est.); Ancestry (includes multiple ancestries): 45.8% German, 13.8% Irish, 7.4% English, 7.1% American, 5.7% Pennsylvania German (2006-2010 5-year est.).

Economy: Single-family building permits issued: 2 (2011); Multi-family building permits issued: 0 (2011); Employment by occupation: 8.5% management, 1.4% professional, 4.2% services, 14.2% sales, 7.9% farming, 21.2% construction, 7.9% production (2006-2010 5-year est.).

Income: Per capita income: $21,449 (2006-2010 5-year est.); Median household income: $43,846 (2006-2010 5-year est.); Average household income: $57,241 (2006-2010 5-year est.); Percent of households with income of $100,000 or more: 13.1% (2006-2010 5-year est.); Poverty rate: 9.6% (2006-2010 5-year est.).

Education: Percent of population age 25 and over with: High school diploma (including GED) or higher: 88.3% (2006-2010 5-year est.); Bachelor's degree or higher: 13.8% (2006-2010 5-year est.); Master's degree or higher: 8.1% (2006-2010 5-year est.).

Housing: Homeownership rate: 82.7% (2010); Median home value: $112,500 (2006-2010 5-year est.); Median contract rent: $425 per month (2006-2010 5-year est.); Median year structure built: 1973 (2006-2010 5-year est.).

Transportation: Commute to work: 86.0% car, 0.0% public transportation, 3.4% walk, 9.1% work from home (2006-2010 5-year est.); Travel time to work: 8.5% less than 15 minutes, 33.0% 15 to 30 minutes, 23.6% 30 to 45 minutes, 14.8% 45 to 60 minutes, 20.1% 60 minutes or more (2006-2010 5-year est.)

SUSQUEHANNA (township). Covers a land area of 16.517 square miles and a water area of 0 square miles. Located at 40.63° N. Lat; 77.02° W. Long.

Population: 1,022 (1990); 1,261 (2000); 1,250 (2010); Density: 75.7 persons per square mile (2010); Race: 97.8% White, 0.7% Black, 0.1% Asian, 0.0% American Indian/Alaska Native, 0.0% Native Hawaiian/Other Pacific Islander, 1.4% Other, 0.1% Hispanic of any race (2010); Average household size: 2.71 (2010); Median age: 40.1 (2010); Males per 100 females: 100.3 (2010); Marriage status: 17.7% never married, 70.1% now married, 7.1% widowed, 5.1% divorced (2006-2010 5-year est.); Foreign born: 0.0% (2006-2010 5-year est.); Ancestry (includes multiple ancestries): 43.5% German, 12.4% American, 9.6% Irish, 6.4% Welsh, 5.7% English (2006-2010 5-year est.).

Economy: Single-family building permits issued: 0 (2011); Multi-family building permits issued: 0 (2011); Employment by occupation: 6.2% management, 1.0% professional, 11.3% services, 15.3% sales, 1.6% farming, 17.3% construction, 11.6% production (2006-2010 5-year est.).

Income: Per capita income: $22,683 (2006-2010 5-year est.); Median household income: $52,000 (2006-2010 5-year est.); Average household income: $58,239 (2006-2010 5-year est.); Percent of households with income of $100,000 or more: 14.5% (2006-2010 5-year est.); Poverty rate: 4.5% (2006-2010 5-year est.).

Education: Percent of population age 25 and over with: High school diploma (including GED) or higher: 74.1% (2006-2010 5-year est.); Bachelor's degree or higher: 7.2% (2006-2010 5-year est.); Master's degree or higher: 0.9% (2006-2010 5-year est.).

Housing: Homeownership rate: 89.8% (2010); Median home value: $120,500 (2006-2010 5-year est.); Median contract rent: $490 per month (2006-2010 5-year est.); Median year structure built: 1980 (2006-2010 5-year est.).

Transportation: Commute to work: 94.4% car, 0.5% public transportation, 0.6% walk, 0.9% work from home (2006-2010 5-year est.); Travel time to work: 13.8% less than 15 minutes, 26.9% 15 to 30 minutes, 23.3% 30 to 45 minutes, 17.0% 45 to 60 minutes, 19.0% 60 minutes or more (2006-2010 5-year est.)

Additional Information Contacts

Harrisburg Regional Chamber & CREDC . . . . (717) 232-4099
   http://www.harrisburgregionalchamber.org

THOMPSONTOWN (borough). Covers a land area of 0.326 square miles and a water area of 0 square miles. Located at 40.57° N. Lat; 77.24° W. Long. Elevation is 449 feet.

Population: 582 (1990); 711 (2000); 697 (2010); Density: 2,138.7 persons per square mile (2010); Race: 98.7% White, 0.1% Black, 0.4% Asian, 0.0% American Indian/Alaska Native, 0.0% Native Hawaiian/Other Pacific Islander, 0.8% Other, 0.4% Hispanic of any race (2010); Average household size: 2.05 (2010); Median age: 42.4 (2010); Males per 100 females: 94.7 (2010); Marriage status: 29.9% never married, 46.1% now married, 11.9% widowed, 12.1% divorced (2006-2010 5-year est.); Foreign born: 0.3% (2006-2010 5-year est.); Ancestry (includes multiple ancestries): 42.2% German, 9.3% English, 8.6% Irish, 8.2% European, 6.8% Scottish (2006-2010 5-year est.).

Economy: Single-family building permits issued: 0 (2011); Multi-family building permits issued: 0 (2011); Employment by occupation: 3.6% management, 6.0% professional, 8.6% services, 17.9% sales, 4.8% farming, 11.3% construction, 6.5% production (2006-2010 5-year est.).

Income: Per capita income: $22,372 (2006-2010 5-year est.); Median household income: $35,625 (2006-2010 5-year est.); Average household income: $48,449 (2006-2010 5-year est.); Percent of households with income of $100,000 or more: 10.4% (2006-2010 5-year est.); Poverty rate: 8.0% (2006-2010 5-year est.).

Education: Percent of population age 25 and over with: High school diploma (including GED) or higher: 85.5% (2006-2010 5-year est.); Bachelor's degree or higher: 18.1% (2006-2010 5-year est.); Master's degree or higher: 6.0% (2006-2010 5-year est.).

School District(s)

Juniata County SD (KG-12)
   2010-11 Enrollment: 3,092 . . . . (717) 436-2111
Housing: Homeownership rate: 54.7% (2010); Median home value: $101,600 (2006-2010 5-year est.); Median contract rent: $401 per month (2006-2010 5-year est.); Median year structure built: 1960 (2006-2010 5-year est.).

Transportation: Commute to work: 94.0% car, 0.6% public transportation, 3.6% walk, 1.8% work from home (2006-2010 5-year est.); Travel time to work: 13.5% less than 15 minutes, 26.1% 15 to 30 minutes, 20.2% 30 to

45 minutes, 21.5% 45 to 60 minutes, 18.7% 60 minutes or more (2006-2010 5-year est.)

TURBETT (township). Covers a land area of 16.374 square miles and a water area of 0.146 square miles. Located at 40.50° N. Lat; 77.36° W. Long.

Population: 779 (1990); 819 (2000); 981 (2010); Density: 59.9 persons per square mile (2010); Race: 99.0% White, 0.1% Black, 0.0% Asian, 0.1% American Indian/Alaska Native, 0.0% Native Hawaiian/Other Pacific Islander, 0.8% Other, 0.6% Hispanic of any race (2010); Average household size: 2.66 (2010); Median age: 40.1 (2010); Males per 100 females: 111.4 (2010); Marriage status: 20.1% never married, 56.1% now married, 14.1% widowed, 9.8% divorced (2006-2010 5-year est.); Foreign born: 0.7% (2006-2010 5-year est.); Ancestry (includes multiple ancestries): 44.9% German, 10.8% English, 10.3% Irish, 6.7% Scotch-Irish, 4.3% French (2006-2010 5-year est.).

Economy: Single-family building permits issued: 1 (2011); Multi-family building permits issued: 0 (2011); Employment by occupation: 14.1% management, 2.4% professional, 18.1% services, 14.4% sales, 1.3% farming, 17.3% construction, 9.9% production (2006-2010 5-year est.).

Income: Per capita income: $23,396 (2006-2010 5-year est.); Median household income: $50,000 (2006-2010 5-year est.); Average household income: $58,383 (2006-2010 5-year est.); Percent of households with income of $100,000 or more: 8.2% (2006-2010 5-year est.); Poverty rate: 1.7% (2006-2010 5-year est.).

Education: Percent of population age 25 and over with: High school diploma (including GED) or higher: 83.4% (2006-2010 5-year est.); Bachelor's degree or higher: 12.8% (2006-2010 5-year est.); Master's degree or higher: 6.4% (2006-2010 5-year est.).

Housing: Homeownership rate: 85.1% (2010); Median home value: $116,000 (2006-2010 5-year est.); Median contract rent: $363 per month (2006-2010 5-year est.); Median year structure built: 1976 (2006-2010 5-year est.).

Transportation: Commute to work: 94.2% car, 0.0% public transportation, 0.0% walk, 5.8% work from home (2006-2010 5-year est.); Travel time to work: 30.7% less than 15 minutes, 26.5% 15 to 30 minutes, 17.2% 30 to 45 minutes, 5.9% 45 to 60 minutes, 19.7% 60 minutes or more (2006-2010 5-year est.).

TUSCARORA (township). Covers a land area of 47.214 square miles and a water area of <.001 square miles. Located at 40.43° N. Lat; 77.59° W. Long.

Population: 1,099 (1990); 1,159 (2000); 1,240 (2010); Density: 26.3 persons per square mile (2010); Race: 98.7% White, 0.2% Black, 0.0% Asian, 0.0% American Indian/Alaska Native, 0.0% Native Hawaiian/Other Pacific Islander, 1.1% Other, 0.4% Hispanic of any race (2010); Average household size: 2.48 (2010); Median age: 43.1 (2010); Males per 100 females: 110.5 (2010); Marriage status: 27.2% never married, 63.0% now married, 6.8% widowed, 3.0% divorced (2006-2010 5-year est.); Foreign born: 1.5% (2006-2010 5-year est.); Ancestry (includes multiple ancestries): 33.3% German, 10.7% Irish, 7.6% American, 6.7% English, 5.8% Italian (2006-2010 5-year est.).

Economy: Single-family building permits issued: 1 (2011); Multi-family building permits issued: 0 (2011); Employment by occupation: 7.2% management, 0.0% professional, 11.1% services, 8.4% sales, 5.7% farming, 14.5% construction, 14.9% production (2006-2010 5-year est.).

Income: Per capita income: $15,926 (2006-2010 5-year est.); Median household income: $32,888 (2006-2010 5-year est.); Average household income: $43,852 (2006-2010 5-year est.); Percent of households with income of $100,000 or more: 5.8% (2006-2010 5-year est.); Poverty rate: 9.7% (2006-2010 5-year est.).

Education: Percent of population age 25 and over with: High school diploma (including GED) or higher: 59.8% (2006-2010 5-year est.); Bachelor's degree or higher: 1.8% (2006-2010 5-year est.); Master's degree or higher: 0.0% (2006-2010 5-year est.).

Housing: Homeownership rate: 84.2% (2010); Median home value: $89,100 (2006-2010 5-year est.); Median contract rent: $430 per month (2006-2010 5-year est.); Median year structure built: 1975 (2006-2010 5-year est.).

Transportation: Commute to work: 87.1% car, 0.0% public transportation, 4.9% walk, 1.4% work from home (2006-2010 5-year est.); Travel time to work: 17.4% less than 15 minutes, 32.7% 15 to 30 minutes, 20.5% 30 to 45 minutes, 11.9% 45 to 60 minutes, 17.4% 60 minutes or more (2006-2010 5-year est.)

Additional Information Contacts

Juniata River Valley Chamber of Commerce . . . . (717) 248-6713
http://www.juniatarivervalley.org

WALKER (township). Covers a land area of 28.828 square miles and a water area of 0.523 square miles. Located at 40.56° N. Lat; 77.31° W. Long.

Population: 2,331 (1990); 2,598 (2000); 2,738 (2010); Density: 95.0 persons per square mile (2010); Race: 97.8% White, 0.3% Black, 0.5% Asian, 0.2% American Indian/Alaska Native, 0.0% Native Hawaiian/Other Pacific Islander, 1.2% Other, 2.1% Hispanic of any race (2010); Average household size: 2.89 (2010); Median age: 37.2 (2010); Males per 100 females: 100.7 (2010); Marriage status: 23.8% never married, 66.4% now married, 4.4% widowed, 5.5% divorced (2006-2010 5-year est.); Foreign born: 1.0% (2006-2010 5-year est.); Ancestry (includes multiple ancestries): 49.1% German, 15.2% Irish, 15.2% American, 3.3% English, 3.1% Russian (2006-2010 5-year est.).

Economy: Single-family building permits issued: 1 (2011); Multi-family building permits issued: 0 (2011); Employment by occupation: 8.0% management, 1.1% professional, 7.4% services, 14.1% sales, 1.4% farming, 15.8% construction, 13.4% production (2006-2010 5-year est.).

Income: Per capita income: $20,985 (2006-2010 5-year est.); Median household income: $49,821 (2006-2010 5-year est.); Average household income: $58,299 (2006-2010 5-year est.); Percent of households with income of $100,000 or more: 14.1% (2006-2010 5-year est.); Poverty rate: 7.0% (2006-2010 5-year est.).

Education: Percent of population age 25 and over with: High school diploma (including GED) or higher: 82.0% (2006-2010 5-year est.); Bachelor's degree or higher: 10.9% (2006-2010 5-year est.); Master's degree or higher: 5.0% (2006-2010 5-year est.).

Housing: Homeownership rate: 85.9% (2010); Median home value: $135,000 (2006-2010 5-year est.); Median contract rent: $403 per month (2006-2010 5-year est.); Median year structure built: 1973 (2006-2010 5-year est.).

Transportation: Commute to work: 91.2% car, 0.0% public transportation, 2.1% walk, 3.8% work from home (2006-2010 5-year est.); Travel time to work: 43.2% less than 15 minutes, 22.3% 15 to 30 minutes, 10.7% 30 to 45 minutes, 16.1% 45 to 60 minutes, 7.7% 60 minutes or more (2006-2010 5-year est.)

Additional Information Contacts

Juniata River Valley Chamber of Commerce . . . . (717) 248-6713
http://www.juniatarivervalley.org

Lackawanna County

Located in northeastern Pennsylvania; drained by the Lackawanna and Susquehanna Rivers; includes the Pocono Plateau in the south. Covers a land area of 459.078 square miles, a water area of 5.832 square miles, and is located in the Eastern Time Zone at 41.44° N. Lat., 75.61° W. Long. The county was founded in 1878. County seat is Scranton.

Lackawanna County is part of the Scranton—Wilkes-Barre, PA Metropolitan Statistical Area. The entire metro area includes: Lackawanna County, PA; Luzerne County, PA; Wyoming County, PA

Population: 219,039 (1990); 213,295 (2000); 214,437 (2010); Race: 92.0% White, 2.5% Black, 1.7% Asian, 0.2% American Indian/Alaska Native, 0.0% Native Hawaiian/Other Pacific Islander, 3.6% Other, 5.0% Hispanic of any race (2010); Density: 467.1 persons per square mile (2010); Average household size: 2.37 (2010); Median age: 41.8 (2010); Males per 100 females: 92.6 (2010).

Religion: Six largest groups: 44.8% Catholicism, 5.1% Methodist/Pietist, 2.2% Pentecostal, 2.0% Non-Denominational, 1.7% Presbyterian-Reformed, 1.2% Eastern Liturgical (Orthodox) (2010)

Economy: Unemployment rate: 9.3% (August 2012); Total civilian labor force: 110,508 (August 2012); Leading industries: 23.0% health care and social assistance; 14.0% retail trade; 10.1% manufacturing (2010); Farms: 417 totaling 39,756 acres (2007); Companies that employ 500 or more persons: 19 (2010); Companies that employ 100 to 499 persons: 135 (2010); Companies that employ less than 100 persons: 5,218 (2010); Black-owned businesses: 103 (2007); Hispanic-owned businesses: n/a (2007); Asian-owned businesses: n/a (2007); Women-owned businesses: 3,665 (2007); Retail sales per capita: $14,502 (2010). Single-family building permits issued: 148 (2011); Multi-family building permits issued: 19 (2011).

Income: Per capita income: $24,152 (2006-2010 5-year est.); Median household income: $43,673 (2006-2010 5-year est.); Average household income: $58,722 (2006-2010 5-year est.); Percent of households with income of $100,000 or more: 14.5% (2006-2010 5-year est.); Poverty rate: 13.2% (2006-2010 5-year est.); Bankruptcy rate: 2.40% (2011).

Taxes: Total county taxes per capita: $260 (2009); County property taxes per capita: $252 (2009).

Education: Percent of population age 25 and over with: High school diploma (including GED) or higher: 87.5% (2006-2010 5-year est.); Bachelor's degree or higher: 23.7% (2006-2010 5-year est.); Master's degree or higher: 9.0% (2006-2010 5-year est.).

Housing: Homeownership rate: 65.8% (2010); Median home value: $137,100 (2006-2010 5-year est.); Median contract rent: $486 per month (2006-2010 5-year est.); Median year structure built: 1946 (2006-2010 5-year est.)

Health: Birth rate: 105.6 per 10,000 population (2011); Death rate: 120.6 per 10,000 population (2011); Age-adjusted cancer mortality rate: 196.2 deaths per 100,000 population (2009); Number of physicians: 27.1 per 10,000 population (2010); Hospital beds: 54.3 per 10,000 population (2008); Hospital admissions: 1,913.3 per 10,000 population (2008).

Environment: Air Quality Index: 84.9% good, 15.1% moderate, 0.0% unhealthy for sensitive individuals, 0.0% unhealthy (percent of days in 2011)

Elections: 2012 Presidential election results: 63.1% Obama, 35.8% Romney

National and State Parks: Archbald Pothole State Park; Steamtown National Historic Site

Additional Information Contacts

Lackawanna County Government . . . . (570) 963-6800
   http://www.lackawannacounty.org

Greater Johnstown Cambria County Chamber of Commerce . . . . (570) 342-7711
   http://www.scrantonchamber.com

Lackawanna County Communities

ABINGTON (township). Covers a land area of 4.552 square miles and a water area of 0.008 square miles. Located at 41.52° N. Lat; 75.70° W. Long.

Population: 1,533 (1990); 1,616 (2000); 1,743 (2010); Density: 382.9 persons per square mile (2010); Race: 94.5% White, 0.2% Black, 3.8% Asian, 0.0% American Indian/Alaska Native, 0.0% Native Hawaiian/Other Pacific Islander, 1.5% Other, 2.5% Hispanic of any race (2010); Average household size: 2.72 (2010); Median age: 45.9 (2010); Males per 100 females: 99.0 (2010); Marriage status: 22.5% never married, 67.2% now married, 5.0% widowed, 5.2% divorced (2006-2010 5-year est.); Foreign born: 6.4% (2006-2010 5-year est.); Ancestry (includes multiple ancestries): 31.1% Irish, 28.9% Italian, 24.1% German, 7.8% English, 6.9% Welsh (2006-2010 5-year est.).

Economy: Employment by occupation: 20.5% management, 2.9% professional, 4.7% services, 11.7% sales, 3.5% farming, 8.3% construction, 4.4% production (2006-2010 5-year est.).

Income: Per capita income: $52,653 (2006-2010 5-year est.); Median household income: $122,222 (2006-2010 5-year est.); Average household income: $159,459 (2006-2010 5-year est.); Percent of households with income of $100,000 or more: 61.2% (2006-2010 5-year est.); Poverty rate: 3.4% (2006-2010 5-year est.).

Education: Percent of population age 25 and over with: High school diploma (including GED) or higher: 99.3% (2006-2010 5-year est.); Bachelor's degree or higher: 64.2% (2006-2010 5-year est.); Master's degree or higher: 30.4% (2006-2010 5-year est.).

Housing: Homeownership rate: 92.5% (2010); Median home value: $363,000 (2006-2010 5-year est.); Median contract rent: $670 per month (2006-2010 5-year est.); Median year structure built: 1969 (2006-2010 5-year est.).

Safety: Violent crime rate: 11.4 per 10,000 population; Property crime rate: 114.4 per 10,000 population (2011).

Transportation: Commute to work: 96.1% car, 0.0% public transportation, 0.0% walk, 3.9% work from home (2006-2010 5-year est.); Travel time to work: 28.0% less than 15 minutes, 51.4% 15 to 30 minutes, 11.5% 30 to 45 minutes, 5.5% 45 to 60 minutes, 3.6% 60 minutes or more (2006-2010 5-year est.)

Additional Information Contacts

Greater Scranton Chamber of Commerce . . . . (570) 342-7711
   http://www.scrantonchamber.com

ARCHBALD (borough). Covers a land area of 17.088 square miles and a water area of 0.014 square miles. Located at 41.51° N. Lat; 75.55° W. Long. Elevation is 928 feet.

History: Settled 1831, incorporated 1877.

Population: 6,291 (1990); 6,220 (2000); 6,984 (2010); Density: 408.7 persons per square mile (2010); Race: 96.9% White, 1.1% Black, 0.7% Asian, 0.2% American Indian/Alaska Native, 0.0% Native Hawaiian/Other Pacific Islander, 1.1% Other, 1.1% Hispanic of any race (2010); Average household size: 2.49 (2010); Median age: 42.0 (2010); Males per 100 females: 93.8 (2010); Marriage status: 26.4% never married, 57.7% now married, 7.1% widowed, 8.8% divorced (2006-2010 5-year est.); Foreign born: 2.3% (2006-2010 5-year est.); Ancestry (includes multiple ancestries): 29.7% Irish, 29.0% Italian, 25.6% Polish, 13.6% German, 7.4% English (2006-2010 5-year est.).

Economy: Single-family building permits issued: 17 (2011); Multi-family building permits issued: 0 (2011); Employment by occupation: 11.7% management, 2.8% professional, 10.7% services, 12.8% sales, 4.2% farming, 7.5% construction, 7.9% production (2006-2010 5-year est.).

Income: Per capita income: $23,399 (2006-2010 5-year est.); Median household income: $50,197 (2006-2010 5-year est.); Average household income: $58,670 (2006-2010 5-year est.); Percent of households with income of $100,000 or more: 17.2% (2006-2010 5-year est.); Poverty rate: 12.8% (2006-2010 5-year est.).

Education: Percent of population age 25 and over with: High school diploma (including GED) or higher: 86.8% (2006-2010 5-year est.); Bachelor's degree or higher: 20.9% (2006-2010 5-year est.); Master's degree or higher: 7.3% (2006-2010 5-year est.).

School District(s)

Valley View SD (KG-12)
   2010-11 Enrollment: 2,643 . . . . (570) 876-5080

Housing: Homeownership rate: 79.9% (2010); Median home value: $140,400 (2006-2010 5-year est.); Median contract rent: $500 per month (2006-2010 5-year est.); Median year structure built: 1959 (2006-2010 5-year est.).

Safety: Violent crime rate: 37.1 per 10,000 population; Property crime rate: 40.0 per 10,000 population (2011).

Transportation: Commute to work: 94.5% car, 0.0% public transportation, 0.5% walk, 2.4% work from home (2006-2010 5-year est.); Travel time to work: 30.6% less than 15 minutes, 47.3% 15 to 30 minutes, 10.3% 30 to 45 minutes, 3.8% 45 to 60 minutes, 8.0% 60 minutes or more (2006-2010 5-year est.)

Additional Information Contacts

Borough of Archbald . . . . (570) 876-1800
   http://www.archbaldborough.org

Greater Scranton Chamber of Commerce . . . . (570) 342-7711
   http://www.scrantonchamber.com

BENTON (township). Covers a land area of 24.334 square miles and a water area of 0.632 square miles. Located at 41.61° N. Lat; 75.70° W. Long.

Population: 1,837 (1990); 1,881 (2000); 1,908 (2010); Density: 78.4 persons per square mile (2010); Race: 98.5% White, 0.4% Black, 0.2% Asian, 0.1% American Indian/Alaska Native, 0.0% Native Hawaiian/Other Pacific Islander, 0.8% Other, 0.4% Hispanic of any race (2010); Average household size: 2.48 (2010); Median age: 46.9 (2010); Males per 100 females: 105.4 (2010); Marriage status: 21.8% never married, 64.5% now married, 6.6% widowed, 7.1% divorced (2006-2010 5-year est.); Foreign born: 1.0% (2006-2010 5-year est.); Ancestry (includes multiple ancestries): 25.3% German, 22.3% Irish, 20.3% Polish, 15.9% English, 14.0% Welsh (2006-2010 5-year est.).

Economy: Single-family building permits issued: 4 (2011); Multi-family building permits issued: 0 (2011); Employment by occupation: 15.9% management, 4.0% professional, 10.5% services, 14.2% sales, 5.3% farming, 12.6% construction, 10.7% production (2006-2010 5-year est.).

Income: Per capita income: $28,451 (2006-2010 5-year est.); Median household income: $59,306 (2006-2010 5-year est.); Average household income: $69,165 (2006-2010 5-year est.); Percent of households with income of $100,000 or more: 17.1% (2006-2010 5-year est.); Poverty rate: 4.2% (2006-2010 5-year est.).

Education: Percent of population age 25 and over with: High school diploma (including GED) or higher: 95.9% (2006-2010 5-year est.); Bachelor's degree or higher: 29.4% (2006-2010 5-year est.); Master's degree or higher: 11.4% (2006-2010 5-year est.).

Housing: Homeownership rate: 88.3% (2010); Median home value: $169,100 (2006-2010 5-year est.); Median contract rent: $540 per month

(2006-2010 5-year est.); Median year structure built: 1957 (2006-2010 5-year est.).

Transportation: Commute to work: 87.8% car, 0.0% public transportation, 1.0% walk, 10.8% work from home (2006-2010 5-year est.); Travel time to work: 12.7% less than 15 minutes, 54.9% 15 to 30 minutes, 20.3% 30 to 45 minutes, 6.9% 45 to 60 minutes, 5.3% 60 minutes or more (2006-2010 5-year est.)

Additional Information Contacts

Greater Scranton Chamber of Commerce . . . . (570) 342-7711
http://www.scrantonchamber.com

BIG BASS LAKE (CDP). Covers a land area of 4.131 square miles and a water area of 0.240 square miles. Located at 41.25° N. Lat; 75.48° W. Long.

Population: n/a (1990); n/a (2000); 1,270 (2010); Density: 307.4 persons per square mile (2010); Race: 94.6% White, 2.3% Black, 0.9% Asian, 0.0% American Indian/Alaska Native, 0.0% Native Hawaiian/Other Pacific Islander, 2.2% Other, 5.0% Hispanic of any race (2010); Average household size: 2.31 (2010); Median age: 51.7 (2010); Males per 100 females: 104.8 (2010); Marriage status: 25.5% never married, 59.3% now married, 6.8% widowed, 8.5% divorced (2006-2010 5-year est.); Foreign born: 2.6% (2006-2010 5-year est.); Ancestry (includes multiple ancestries): 31.4% German, 21.9% Irish, 15.0% Italian, 11.3% Polish, 5.8% Hungarian (2006-2010 5-year est.).

Economy: Employment by occupation: 14.3% management, 2.0% professional, 9.3% services, 17.9% sales, 3.7% farming, 10.4% construction, 9.9% production (2006-2010 5-year est.).

Income: Per capita income: $31,089 (2006-2010 5-year est.); Median household income: $63,250 (2006-2010 5-year est.); Average household income: $81,242 (2006-2010 5-year est.); Percent of households with income of $100,000 or more: 27.7% (2006-2010 5-year est.); Poverty rate: 7.0% (2006-2010 5-year est.).

Education: Percent of population age 25 and over with: High school diploma (including GED) or higher: 90.1% (2006-2010 5-year est.); Bachelor's degree or higher: 26.9% (2006-2010 5-year est.); Master's degree or higher: 8.9% (2006-2010 5-year est.).

Housing: Homeownership rate: 88.5% (2010); Median home value: $179,600 (2006-2010 5-year est.); Median contract rent: $1,360 per month (2006-2010 5-year est.); Median year structure built: 1983 (2006-2010 5-year est.).

Transportation: Commute to work: 87.9% car, 3.8% public transportation, 3.4% walk, 4.4% work from home (2006-2010 5-year est.); Travel time to work: 24.9% less than 15 minutes, 29.0% 15 to 30 minutes, 32.6% 30 to 45 minutes, 3.6% 45 to 60 minutes, 10.0% 60 minutes or more (2006-2010 5-year est.)

BLAKELY (borough). Covers a land area of 3.813 square miles and a water area of 0 square miles. Located at 41.49° N. Lat; 75.60° W. Long. Elevation is 810 feet.

History: Incorporated 1867.

Population: 7,222 (1990); 7,027 (2000); 6,564 (2010); Density: 1,721.5 persons per square mile (2010); Race: 96.6% White, 1.0% Black, 0.7% Asian, 0.1% American Indian/Alaska Native, 0.0% Native Hawaiian/Other Pacific Islander, 1.6% Other, 1.8% Hispanic of any race (2010); Average household size: 2.23 (2010); Median age: 47.2 (2010); Males per 100 females: 83.0 (2010); Marriage status: 28.6% never married, 45.6% now married, 13.2% widowed, 12.5% divorced (2006-2010 5-year est.); Foreign born: 4.2% (2006-2010 5-year est.); Ancestry (includes multiple ancestries): 29.5% Italian, 19.9% Irish, 15.9% Polish, 13.6% German, 7.9% Slovak (2006-2010 5-year est.).

Economy: Single-family building permits issued: 0 (2011); Multi-family building permits issued: 0 (2011); Employment by occupation: 5.6% management, 2.0% professional, 10.5% services, 24.0% sales, 6.1% farming, 9.3% construction, 4.0% production (2006-2010 5-year est.).

Income: Per capita income: $23,063 (2006-2010 5-year est.); Median household income: $38,153 (2006-2010 5-year est.); Average household income: $50,380 (2006-2010 5-year est.); Percent of households with income of $100,000 or more: 12.4% (2006-2010 5-year est.); Poverty rate: 12.4% (2006-2010 5-year est.).

Education: Percent of population age 25 and over with: High school diploma (including GED) or higher: 86.7% (2006-2010 5-year est.); Bachelor's degree or higher: 17.4% (2006-2010 5-year est.); Master's degree or higher: 4.4% (2006-2010 5-year est.).

Housing: Homeownership rate: 70.6% (2010); Median home value: $143,300 (2006-2010 5-year est.); Median contract rent: $535 per month

(2006-2010 5-year est.); Median year structure built: 1946 (2006-2010 5-year est.).

Safety: Violent crime rate: 7.6 per 10,000 population; Property crime rate: 139.7 per 10,000 population (2011).

Transportation: Commute to work: 97.6% car, 0.0% public transportation, 2.0% walk, 0.4% work from home (2006-2010 5-year est.); Travel time to work: 38.7% less than 15 minutes, 49.3% 15 to 30 minutes, 5.8% 30 to 45 minutes, 5.4% 45 to 60 minutes, 0.8% 60 minutes or more (2006-2010 5-year est.)

Additional Information Contacts

Borough of Blakely . . . . (570) 383-3340
http://www.lackawannacounty.org/municipalities.aspx
Greater Scranton Chamber of Commerce . . . . (570) 342-7711
http://www.scrantonchamber.com

CARBONDALE (city). Aka Whites. Covers a land area of 3.243 square miles and a water area of 0 square miles. Located at 41.57° N. Lat; 75.50° W. Long. Elevation is 1,086 feet.

Population: 10,774 (1990); 9,804 (2000); 8,891 (2010); Density: 2,741.6 persons per square mile (2010); Race: 96.3% White, 1.0% Black, 0.4% Asian, 0.2% American Indian/Alaska Native, 0.0% Native Hawaiian/Other Pacific Islander, 2.1% Other, 3.1% Hispanic of any race (2010); Average household size: 2.32 (2010); Median age: 40.9 (2010); Males per 100 females: 88.5 (2010); Marriage status: 28.3% never married, 47.5% now married, 11.2% widowed, 13.0% divorced (2006-2010 5-year est.); Foreign born: 2.0% (2006-2010 5-year est.); Ancestry (includes multiple ancestries): 36.0% Irish, 23.5% German, 22.4% Italian, 14.0% Polish, 9.9% English (2006-2010 5-year est.).

Economy: Single-family building permits issued: 4 (2011); Multi-family building permits issued: 8 (2011); Employment by occupation: 4.7% management, 2.6% professional, 17.0% services, 18.0% sales, 2.1% farming, 7.7% construction, 6.7% production (2006-2010 5-year est.).

Income: Per capita income: $17,511 (2006-2010 5-year est.); Median household income: $33,000 (2006-2010 5-year est.); Average household income: $42,257 (2006-2010 5-year est.); Percent of households with income of $100,000 or more: 6.1% (2006-2010 5-year est.); Poverty rate: 19.9% (2006-2010 5-year est.).

Taxes: Total city taxes per capita: $341 (2009); City property taxes per capita: $121 (2009).

Education: Percent of population age 25 and over with: High school diploma (including GED) or higher: 88.2% (2006-2010 5-year est.); Bachelor's degree or higher: 12.6% (2006-2010 5-year est.); Master's degree or higher: 4.6% (2006-2010 5-year est.).

School District(s)

Carbondale Area SD (PK-12)
    2010-11 Enrollment: 1,561 . . . . (570) 282-2507

Housing: Homeownership rate: 56.6% (2010); Median home value: $90,900 (2006-2010 5-year est.); Median contract rent: $432 per month (2006-2010 5-year est.); Median year structure built: before 1940 (2006-2010 5-year est.).

Hospitals: Marian Community Hospital (104 beds)

Safety: Violent crime rate: 16.8 per 10,000 population; Property crime rate: 173.8 per 10,000 population (2011).

Newspapers: Carbondale News (Community news; Circulation 6,300)

Transportation: Commute to work: 91.1% car, 0.3% public transportation, 5.3% walk, 2.7% work from home (2006-2010 5-year est.); Travel time to work: 45.5% less than 15 minutes, 28.8% 15 to 30 minutes, 16.9% 30 to 45 minutes, 3.8% 45 to 60 minutes, 5.0% 60 minutes or more (2006-2010 5-year est.)

Additional Information Contacts

Greater Scranton Chamber of Commerce . . . . (570) 342-7711
http://www.scrantonchamber.com

CARBONDALE (township). Aka Whites. Covers a land area of 13.789 square miles and a water area of 0.221 square miles. Located at 41.55° N. Lat; 75.51° W. Long. Elevation is 1,086 feet.

History: Terence Powderly, the labor leader, was born here. Incorporated 1851.

Population: 907 (1990); 1,008 (2000); 1,115 (2010); Density: 80.9 persons per square mile (2010); Race: 97.6% White, 1.2% Black, 0.0% Asian, 0.1% American Indian/Alaska Native, 0.0% Native Hawaiian/Other Pacific Islander, 1.1% Other, 2.1% Hispanic of any race (2010); Average household size: 2.42 (2010); Median age: 44.5 (2010); Males per 100 females: 101.6 (2010); Marriage status: 33.4% never married, 44.7% now married, 10.0% widowed, 11.9% divorced (2006-2010 5-year est.); Foreign

born: 0.0% (2006-2010 5-year est.); Ancestry (includes multiple ancestries): 38.0% Irish, 34.7% Polish, 25.4% Italian, 13.1% German, 9.9% English (2006-2010 5-year est.).

Economy: Single-family building permits issued: 3 (2011); Multi-family building permits issued: 0 (2011); Employment by occupation: 10.1% management, 4.7% professional, 12.7% services, 14.7% sales, 4.5% farming, 11.8% construction, 7.4% production (2006-2010 5-year est.).

Income: Per capita income: $25,322 (2006-2010 5-year est.); Median household income: $50,909 (2006-2010 5-year est.); Average household income: $60,547 (2006-2010 5-year est.); Percent of households with income of $100,000 or more: 15.2% (2006-2010 5-year est.); Poverty rate: 3.1% (2006-2010 5-year est.).

Education: Percent of population age 25 and over with: High school diploma (including GED) or higher: 89.8% (2006-2010 5-year est.); Bachelor's degree or higher: 19.3% (2006-2010 5-year est.); Master's degree or higher: 5.2% (2006-2010 5-year est.).

Housing: Homeownership rate: 82.2% (2010); Median home value: $130,500 (2006-2010 5-year est.); Median contract rent: $394 per month (2006-2010 5-year est.); Median year structure built: 1970 (2006-2010 5-year est.).

Hospitals: Marian Community Hospital (104 beds)

Newspapers: Carbondale News (Community news; Circulation 6,300)

Transportation: Commute to work: 92.1% car, 0.0% public transportation, 3.1% walk, 3.1% work from home (2006-2010 5-year est.); Travel time to work: 43.9% less than 15 minutes, 28.4% 15 to 30 minutes, 16.5% 30 to 45 minutes, 3.8% 45 to 60 minutes, 7.4% 60 minutes or more (2006-2010 5-year est.)

Additional Information Contacts

Greater Scranton Chamber of Commerce . . . . (570) 342-7711
   http://www.scrantonchamber.com

CHINCHILLA (CDP). Covers a land area of 2.500 square miles and a water area of 0.080 square miles. Located at 41.49° N. Lat; 75.67° W. Long. Elevation is 1,158 feet.

Population: n/a (1990); n/a (2000); 2,098 (2010); Density: 839.4 persons per square mile (2010); Race: 96.9% White, 0.5% Black, 1.2% Asian, 0.1% American Indian/Alaska Native, 0.1% Native Hawaiian/Other Pacific Islander, 1.2% Other, 1.3% Hispanic of any race (2010); Average household size: 2.39 (2010); Median age: 46.9 (2010); Males per 100 females: 91.4 (2010); Marriage status: 16.2% never married, 66.5% now married, 5.6% widowed, 11.6% divorced (2006-2010 5-year est.); Foreign born: 1.2% (2006-2010 5-year est.); Ancestry (includes multiple ancestries): 30.7% Italian, 29.1% Irish, 28.3% German, 19.4% English, 10.4% Welsh (2006-2010 5-year est.).

Economy: Employment by occupation: 10.0% management, 4.2% professional, 7.9% services, 13.1% sales, 4.4% farming, 6.3% construction, 2.8% production (2006-2010 5-year est.).

Income: Per capita income: $33,592 (2006-2010 5-year est.); Median household income: $56,735 (2006-2010 5-year est.); Average household income: $70,309 (2006-2010 5-year est.); Percent of households with income of $100,000 or more: 21.0% (2006-2010 5-year est.); Poverty rate: 6.4% (2006-2010 5-year est.).

Education: Percent of population age 25 and over with: High school diploma (including GED) or higher: 97.8% (2006-2010 5-year est.); Bachelor's degree or higher: 43.0% (2006-2010 5-year est.); Master's degree or higher: 18.0% (2006-2010 5-year est.).

School District(s)

Abington Heights SD (KG-12)
   2010-11 Enrollment: 3,452 . . . . (570) 586-2511

Housing: Homeownership rate: 81.3% (2010); Median home value: $164,900 (2006-2010 5-year est.); Median contract rent: $472 per month (2006-2010 5-year est.); Median year structure built: 1968 (2006-2010 5-year est.).

Transportation: Commute to work: 98.2% car, 0.0% public transportation, 0.0% walk, 1.8% work from home (2006-2010 5-year est.); Travel time to work: 38.6% less than 15 minutes, 47.0% 15 to 30 minutes, 8.8% 30 to 45 minutes, 4.4% 45 to 60 minutes, 1.3% 60 minutes or more (2006-2010 5-year est.)

CLARKS GREEN (borough). Covers a land area of 0.534 square miles and a water area of 0 square miles. Located at 41.50° N. Lat; 75.70° W. Long. Elevation is 1,289 feet.

Population: 1,441 (1990); 1,630 (2000); 1,476 (2010); Density: 2,766.5 persons per square mile (2010); Race: 96.6% White, 0.7% Black, 2.0% Asian, 0.1% American Indian/Alaska Native, 0.0% Native Hawaiian/Other

Pacific Islander, 0.6% Other, 1.5% Hispanic of any race (2010); Average household size: 2.47 (2010); Median age: 47.0 (2010); Males per 100 females: 95.5 (2010); Marriage status: 25.1% never married, 61.6% now married, 6.0% widowed, 7.3% divorced (2006-2010 5-year est.); Foreign born: 5.8% (2006-2010 5-year est.); Ancestry (includes multiple ancestries): 33.9% Irish, 24.2% German, 17.9% Italian, 10.3% English, 9.1% Polish (2006-2010 5-year est.).

Economy: Single-family building permits issued: 1 (2011); Multi-family building permits issued: 0 (2011); Employment by occupation: 22.4% management, 2.0% professional, 3.9% services, 23.0% sales, 0.9% farming, 1.9% construction, 1.8% production (2006-2010 5-year est.).

Income: Per capita income: $35,284 (2006-2010 5-year est.); Median household income: $81,510 (2006-2010 5-year est.); Average household income: $96,694 (2006-2010 5-year est.); Percent of households with income of $100,000 or more: 32.3% (2006-2010 5-year est.); Poverty rate: 4.3% (2006-2010 5-year est.).

Education: Percent of population age 25 and over with: High school diploma (including GED) or higher: 97.1% (2006-2010 5-year est.); Bachelor's degree or higher: 57.3% (2006-2010 5-year est.); Master's degree or higher: 24.4% (2006-2010 5-year est.).

Housing: Homeownership rate: 88.8% (2010); Median home value: $188,900 (2006-2010 5-year est.); Median contract rent: $605 per month (2006-2010 5-year est.); Median year structure built: 1957 (2006-2010 5-year est.).

Transportation: Commute to work: 92.0% car, 0.0% public transportation, 2.5% walk, 5.2% work from home (2006-2010 5-year est.); Travel time to work: 34.1% less than 15 minutes, 48.2% 15 to 30 minutes, 9.3% 30 to 45 minutes, 4.8% 45 to 60 minutes, 3.6% 60 minutes or more (2006-2010 5-year est.)

Additional Information Contacts

Lower Bucks County Chamber of Commerce . . . . (215) 943-7400
   http://www.lbccc.org

CLARKS SUMMIT (borough). Covers a land area of 1.585 square miles and a water area of 0 square miles. Located at 41.49° N. Lat; 75.71° W. Long. Elevation is 1,302 feet.

History: Settled 1799, incorporated 1911.

Population: 5,433 (1990); 5,126 (2000); 5,116 (2010); Density: 3,227.3 persons per square mile (2010); Race: 97.0% White, 0.7% Black, 1.2% Asian, 0.0% American Indian/Alaska Native, 0.0% Native Hawaiian/Other Pacific Islander, 1.1% Other, 1.4% Hispanic of any race (2010); Average household size: 2.31 (2010); Median age: 45.4 (2010); Males per 100 females: 85.9 (2010); Marriage status: 18.2% never married, 60.0% now married, 11.4% widowed, 10.3% divorced (2006-2010 5-year est.); Foreign born: 4.0% (2006-2010 5-year est.); Ancestry (includes multiple ancestries): 33.5% Irish, 25.2% German, 19.4% Italian, 13.3% English, 11.5% Polish (2006-2010 5-year est.).

Economy: Single-family building permits issued: 2 (2011); Multi-family building permits issued: 0 (2011); Employment by occupation: 15.6% management, 4.2% professional, 3.9% services, 18.9% sales, 4.3% farming, 4.9% construction, 4.0% production (2006-2010 5-year est.).

Income: Per capita income: $39,713 (2006-2010 5-year est.); Median household income: $61,825 (2006-2010 5-year est.); Average household income: $94,005 (2006-2010 5-year est.); Percent of households with income of $100,000 or more: 25.7% (2006-2010 5-year est.); Poverty rate: 3.8% (2006-2010 5-year est.).

Education: Percent of population age 25 and over with: High school diploma (including GED) or higher: 93.9% (2006-2010 5-year est.); Bachelor's degree or higher: 50.8% (2006-2010 5-year est.); Master's degree or higher: 21.0% (2006-2010 5-year est.).

School District(s)

Abington Heights SD (KG-12)
   2010-11 Enrollment: 3,452 . . . . (570) 586-2511

Four-year College(s)

Baptist Bible College and Seminary (Private, Not-for-profit, Baptist)
   Fall 2010 Enrollment: 743 . . . . (570) 586-2400
   2011-12 Tuition: In-state $18,260; Out-of-state $18,260

Housing: Homeownership rate: 73.3% (2010); Median home value: $194,300 (2006-2010 5-year est.); Median contract rent: $406 per month (2006-2010 5-year est.); Median year structure built: 1965 (2006-2010 5-year est.).

Hospitals: Clarks Summit State Hospital (265 beds)

Newspapers: Abington Journal (Community news; Circulation 3,800)

Transportation: Commute to work: 92.2% car, 0.0% public transportation, 1.9% walk, 5.9% work from home (2006-2010 5-year est.); Travel time to

work: 34.2% less than 15 minutes, 45.6% 15 to 30 minutes, 15.9% 30 to 45 minutes, 0.8% 45 to 60 minutes, 3.5% 60 minutes or more (2006-2010 5-year est.)

Additional Information Contacts
Borough of Clarks Summit . . . . (570) 586-9316
  http://www.clarkssummitboro.org
Greater Scranton Chamber of Commerce . . . . (570) 342-7711
  http://www.scrantonchamber.com

CLIFTON (township). Covers a land area of 19.400 square miles and a water area of 0.418 square miles. Located at 41.25° N. Lat; 75.53° W. Long. Elevation is 1,624 feet.

Population: 1,041 (1990); 1,139 (2000); 1,480 (2010); Density: 76.3 persons per square mile (2010); Race: 95.3% White, 1.5% Black, 0.7% Asian, 0.0% American Indian/Alaska Native, 0.0% Native Hawaiian/Other Pacific Islander, 2.5% Other, 4.7% Hispanic of any race (2010); Average household size: 2.36 (2010); Median age: 49.5 (2010); Males per 100 females: 107.6 (2010); Marriage status: 19.4% never married, 61.0% now married, 7.8% widowed, 11.8% divorced (2006-2010 5-year est.); Foreign born: 3.3% (2006-2010 5-year est.); Ancestry (includes multiple ancestries): 33.4% German, 22.8% Irish, 16.4% Italian, 14.5% Polish, 6.3% English (2006-2010 5-year est.).

Economy: Single-family building permits issued: 4 (2011); Multi-family building permits issued: 0 (2011); Employment by occupation: 13.0% management, 1.1% professional, 10.0% services, 16.3% sales, 7.4% farming, 14.0% construction, 7.2% production (2006-2010 5-year est.).

Income: Per capita income: $30,509 (2006-2010 5-year est.); Median household income: $61,625 (2006-2010 5-year est.); Average household income: $73,977 (2006-2010 5-year est.); Percent of households with income of $100,000 or more: 23.2% (2006-2010 5-year est.); Poverty rate: 4.5% (2006-2010 5-year est.).

Education: Percent of population age 25 and over with: High school diploma (including GED) or higher: 92.3% (2006-2010 5-year est.); Bachelor's degree or higher: 23.5% (2006-2010 5-year est.); Master's degree or higher: 8.8% (2006-2010 5-year est.).

Housing: Homeownership rate: 87.4% (2010); Median home value: $169,400 (2006-2010 5-year est.); Median contract rent: $1,300 per month (2006-2010 5-year est.); Median year structure built: 1982 (2006-2010 5-year est.).

Transportation: Commute to work: 91.0% car, 1.8% public transportation, 1.6% walk, 5.6% work from home (2006-2010 5-year est.); Travel time to work: 19.2% less than 15 minutes, 31.5% 15 to 30 minutes, 31.0% 30 to 45 minutes, 4.2% 45 to 60 minutes, 14.1% 60 minutes or more (2006-2010 5-year est.).

Additional Information Contacts
Girard-Lake City Chamber of Commerce . . . . (814) 774-3535
  http://www.girardlakecity.org

COVINGTON (township). Covers a land area of 23.696 square miles and a water area of 0.228 square miles. Located at 41.30° N. Lat; 75.50° W. Long.

Population: 2,055 (1990); 1,994 (2000); 2,284 (2010); Density: 96.4 persons per square mile (2010); Race: 97.0% White, 0.8% Black, 0.6% Asian, 0.1% American Indian/Alaska Native, 0.0% Native Hawaiian/Other Pacific Islander, 1.5% Other, 3.5% Hispanic of any race (2010); Average household size: 2.59 (2010); Median age: 44.7 (2010); Males per 100 females: 100.0 (2010); Marriage status: 21.8% never married, 63.0% now married, 6.2% widowed, 8.9% divorced (2006-2010 5-year est.); Foreign born: 1.9% (2006-2010 5-year est.); Ancestry (includes multiple ancestries): 31.3% German, 21.6% Irish, 18.0% Polish, 16.3% Italian, 10.6% American (2006-2010 5-year est.).

Economy: Single-family building permits issued: 9 (2011); Multi-family building permits issued: 0 (2011); Employment by occupation: 13.2% management, 4.3% professional, 5.6% services, 15.2% sales, 6.1% farming, 14.0% construction, 9.6% production (2006-2010 5-year est.).

Income: Per capita income: $30,538 (2006-2010 5-year est.); Median household income: $63,672 (2006-2010 5-year est.); Average household income: $77,101 (2006-2010 5-year est.); Percent of households with income of $100,000 or more: 24.1% (2006-2010 5-year est.); Poverty rate: 8.1% (2006-2010 5-year est.).

Education: Percent of population age 25 and over with: High school diploma (including GED) or higher: 91.1% (2006-2010 5-year est.); Bachelor's degree or higher: 23.7% (2006-2010 5-year est.); Master's degree or higher: 11.4% (2006-2010 5-year est.).

School District(s)
North Pocono SD (KG-12)
  2010-11 Enrollment: 3,173 . . . . (570) 842-7659
Housing: Homeownership rate: 84.8% (2010); Median home value: $198,200 (2006-2010 5-year est.); Median contract rent: $573 per month (2006-2010 5-year est.); Median year structure built: 1977 (2006-2010 5-year est.).

Transportation: Commute to work: 92.5% car, 0.4% public transportation, 1.9% walk, 3.1% work from home (2006-2010 5-year est.); Travel time to work: 25.8% less than 15 minutes, 49.2% 15 to 30 minutes, 16.4% 30 to 45 minutes, 4.5% 45 to 60 minutes, 4.2% 60 minutes or more (2006-2010 5-year est.).

Additional Information Contacts
Covington Township . . . . (570) 842-8336
  http://www.covingtontwp.org
Greater Scranton Chamber of Commerce . . . . (570) 342-7711
  http://www.scrantonchamber.com

DALTON (borough). Covers a land area of 3.019 square miles and a water area of 0.055 square miles. Located at 41.54° N. Lat; 75.74° W. Long. Elevation is 971 feet.

History: Incorporated c.1890.

Population: 1,396 (1990); 1,294 (2000); 1,234 (2010); Density: 408.7 persons per square mile (2010); Race: 97.6% White, 0.1% Black, 1.3% Asian, 0.2% American Indian/Alaska Native, 0.0% Native Hawaiian/Other Pacific Islander, 0.8% Other, 1.0% Hispanic of any race (2010); Average household size: 2.46 (2010); Median age: 45.5 (2010); Males per 100 females: 99.0 (2010); Marriage status: 21.8% never married, 64.8% now married, 5.4% widowed, 8.0% divorced (2006-2010 5-year est.); Foreign born: 2.5% (2006-2010 5-year est.); Ancestry (includes multiple ancestries): 30.3% Irish, 26.5% German, 19.5% Italian, 15.6% English, 12.1% Welsh (2006-2010 5-year est.).

Economy: Single-family building permits issued: 3 (2011); Multi-family building permits issued: 0 (2011); Employment by occupation: 12.8% management, 3.7% professional, 7.0% services, 14.1% sales, 3.7% farming, 5.8% construction, 3.7% production (2006-2010 5-year est.).

Income: Per capita income: $32,329 (2006-2010 5-year est.); Median household income: $52,083 (2006-2010 5-year est.); Average household income: $78,299 (2006-2010 5-year est.); Percent of households with income of $100,000 or more: 23.9% (2006-2010 5-year est.); Poverty rate: 6.3% (2006-2010 5-year est.).

Education: Percent of population age 25 and over with: High school diploma (including GED) or higher: 96.3% (2006-2010 5-year est.); Bachelor's degree or higher: 46.6% (2006-2010 5-year est.); Master's degree or higher: 23.6% (2006-2010 5-year est.).

School District(s)
Tunkhannock Area SD (KG-12)
  2010-11 Enrollment: 2,818 . . . . (570) 836-3111
Housing: Homeownership rate: 83.9% (2010); Median home value: $175,400 (2006-2010 5-year est.); Median contract rent: $618 per month (2006-2010 5-year est.); Median year structure built: before 1940 (2006-2010 5-year est.).

Safety: Violent crime rate: 32.3 per 10,000 population; Property crime rate: 113.1 per 10,000 population (2011).

Transportation: Commute to work: 94.5% car, 0.0% public transportation, 1.7% walk, 3.3% work from home (2006-2010 5-year est.); Travel time to work: 36.0% less than 15 minutes, 36.9% 15 to 30 minutes, 17.5% 30 to 45 minutes, 3.9% 45 to 60 minutes, 5.7% 60 minutes or more (2006-2010 5-year est.).

Additional Information Contacts
Greater Scranton Chamber of Commerce . . . . (570) 342-7711
  http://www.scrantonchamber.com

DICKSON CITY (borough). Covers a land area of 4.795 square miles and a water area of 0 square miles. Located at 41.47° N. Lat; 75.64° W. Long. Elevation is 768 feet.

History: Founded 1859, incorporated 1875.

Population: 6,276 (1990); 6,205 (2000); 6,070 (2010); Density: 1,265.8 persons per square mile (2010); Race: 95.9% White, 1.0% Black, 0.7% Asian, 0.1% American Indian/Alaska Native, 0.0% Native Hawaiian/Other Pacific Islander, 2.3% Other, 3.8% Hispanic of any race (2010); Average household size: 2.24 (2010); Median age: 42.3 (2010); Males per 100 females: 92.1 (2010); Marriage status: 25.1% never married, 53.4% now married, 9.3% widowed, 12.1% divorced (2006-2010 5-year est.); Foreign born: 2.3% (2006-2010 5-year est.); Ancestry (includes multiple

ancestries): 36.6% Polish, 21.2% Irish, 21.1% Italian, 13.7% German, 7.1% Russian (2006-2010 5-year est.).

Economy: Single-family building permits issued: 4 (2011); Multi-family building permits issued: 0 (2011); Employment by occupation: 5.8% management, 2.7% professional, 8.5% services, 20.2% sales, 6.2% farming, 9.2% construction, 5.6% production (2006-2010 5-year est.).

Income: Per capita income: $25,609 (2006-2010 5-year est.); Median household income: $44,279 (2006-2010 5-year est.); Average household income: $57,362 (2006-2010 5-year est.); Percent of households with income of $100,000 or more: 12.9% (2006-2010 5-year est.); Poverty rate: 11.6% (2006-2010 5-year est.).

Education: Percent of population age 25 and over with: High school diploma (including GED) or higher: 90.5% (2006-2010 5-year est.); Bachelor's degree or higher: 24.7% (2006-2010 5-year est.); Master's degree or higher: 6.4% (2006-2010 5-year est.).

Housing: Homeownership rate: 65.7% (2010); Median home value: $145,400 (2006-2010 5-year est.); Median contract rent: $443 per month (2006-2010 5-year est.); Median year structure built: before 1940 (2006-2010 5-year est.).

Transportation: Commute to work: 95.4% car, 0.5% public transportation, 1.3% walk, 2.4% work from home (2006-2010 5-year est.); Travel time to work: 39.6% less than 15 minutes, 40.2% 15 to 30 minutes, 8.4% 30 to 45 minutes, 4.4% 45 to 60 minutes, 7.3% 60 minutes or more (2006-2010 5-year est.)

Additional Information Contacts

Borough of Dickson City . . . . (570) 489-4758
Greater Scranton Chamber of Commerce . . . . (570) 342-7711
   http://www.scrantonchamber.com

DUNMORE (borough). Covers a land area of 8.918 square miles and a water area of 0.076 square miles. Located at 41.41° N. Lat; 75.61° W. Long. Elevation is 968 feet.

History: Pennsylvania State University— Worthington Scranton (2-year) campus near Scranton corporate limits. Incorporated 1783.

Population: 15,403 (1990); 14,018 (2000); 14,057 (2010); Density: 1,576.2 persons per square mile (2010); Race: 95.2% White, 1.1% Black, 1.8% Asian, 0.1% American Indian/Alaska Native, 0.0% Native Hawaiian/Other Pacific Islander, 1.8% Other, 2.3% Hispanic of any race (2010); Average household size: 2.18 (2010); Median age: 42.1 (2010); Males per 100 females: 84.0 (2010); Marriage status: 32.6% never married, 49.6% now married, 8.7% widowed, 9.2% divorced (2006-2010 5-year est.); Foreign born: 5.1% (2006-2010 5-year est.); Ancestry (includes multiple ancestries): 35.7% Italian, 32.2% Irish, 13.6% German, 10.1% Polish, 5.4% English (2006-2010 5-year est.).

Economy: Single-family building permits issued: 3 (2011); Multi-family building permits issued: 0 (2011); Employment by occupation: 9.6% management, 3.9% professional, 8.2% services, 19.6% sales, 5.1% farming, 6.6% construction, 5.6% production (2006-2010 5-year est.).

Income: Per capita income: $27,842 (2006-2010 5-year est.); Median household income: $44,652 (2006-2010 5-year est.); Average household income: $65,027 (2006-2010 5-year est.); Percent of households with income of $100,000 or more: 16.2% (2006-2010 5-year est.); Poverty rate: 12.5% (2006-2010 5-year est.).

Taxes: Total city taxes per capita: $349 (2009); City property taxes per capita: $193 (2009).

Education: Percent of population age 25 and over with: High school diploma (including GED) or higher: 87.9% (2006-2010 5-year est.); Bachelor's degree or higher: 31.6% (2006-2010 5-year est.); Master's degree or higher: 13.9% (2006-2010 5-year est.).

School District(s)
Dunmore SD (KG-12)
   2010-11 Enrollment: 1,590 . . . . (570) 343-2110

Four-year College(s)
Pennsylvania State University-Penn State Worthington Scranton (Public)
   Fall 2010 Enrollment: 1,305 . . . . (570) 963-2500
   2011-12 Tuition: In-state $12,966; Out-of-state $19,406

Two-year College(s)
ITT Technical Institute-Dunmore (Private, For-profit)
   Fall 2010 Enrollment: 297 . . . . (570) 330-0600
   2011-12 Tuition: In-state $18,048; Out-of-state $18,048

Housing: Homeownership rate: 58.6% (2010); Median home value: $141,200 (2006-2010 5-year est.); Median contract rent: $511 per month (2006-2010 5-year est.); Median year structure built: before 1940 (2006-2010 5-year est.).

Safety: Violent crime rate: 14.9 per 10,000 population; Property crime rate: 93.6 per 10,000 population (2011).

Transportation: Commute to work: 90.1% car, 1.3% public transportation, 4.9% walk, 2.2% work from home (2006-2010 5-year est.); Travel time to work: 50.8% less than 15 minutes, 35.9% 15 to 30 minutes, 8.4% 30 to 45 minutes, 2.4% 45 to 60 minutes, 2.5% 60 minutes or more (2006-2010 5-year est.)

Additional Information Contacts

Borough of Dunmore . . . . (570) 343-7611
   http://www.dunmoreborough.com
Greater Scranton Chamber of Commerce . . . . (570) 342-7711
   http://www.scrantonchamber.com

EAGLE LAKE (CDP). Covers a land area of 2.383 square miles and a water area of 0.136 square miles. Located at 41.28° N. Lat; 75.47° W. Long.

Population: n/a (1990); n/a (2000); 12 (2010); Density: 5.0 persons per square mile (2010); Race: 100.0% White, 0.0% Black, 0.0% Asian, 0.0% American Indian/Alaska Native, 0.0% Native Hawaiian/Other Pacific Islander, 0.0% Other, 0.0% Hispanic of any race (2010); Average household size: 2.40 (2010); Median age: 39.5 (2010); Males per 100 females: 140.0 (2010); Marriage status: 0.0% never married, 100.0% now married, 0.0% widowed, 0.0% divorced (2006-2010 5-year est.); Foreign born: 0.0% (2006-2010 5-year est.); Ancestry (includes multiple ancestries): n/a (2006-2010 5-year est.).

Economy: Employment by occupation: 0.0% management, 100.0% professional, 0.0% services, 0.0% sales, 0.0% farming, 0.0% construction, 0.0% production (2006-2010 5-year est.).

Income: Per capita income: $28,345 (2006-2010 5-year est.); Median household income: $43,295 (2006-2010 5-year est.); Average household income: n/a (2006-2010 5-year est.); Percent of households with income of $100,000 or more: n/a (2006-2010 5-year est.); Poverty rate: 0.0% (2006-2010 5-year est.).

Education: Percent of population age 25 and over with: High school diploma (including GED) or higher: 100.0% (2006-2010 5-year est.); Bachelor's degree or higher: 0.0% (2006-2010 5-year est.); Master's degree or higher: 0.0% (2006-2010 5-year est.).

Housing: Homeownership rate: 100.0% (2010); Median home value: $117,000 (2006-2010 5-year est.); Median contract rent: n/a per month (2006-2010 5-year est.); Median year structure built: 1975 (2006-2010 5-year est.).

Transportation: Commute to work: 100.0% car, 0.0% public transportation, 0.0% walk, 0.0% work from home (2006-2010 5-year est.); Travel time to work: 100.0% less than 15 minutes, 0.0% 15 to 30 minutes, 0.0% 30 to 45 minutes, 0.0% 45 to 60 minutes, 0.0% 60 minutes or more (2006-2010 5-year est.)

ELMHURST (township). Covers a land area of 1.844 square miles and a water area of 0.091 square miles. Located at 41.38° N. Lat; 75.55° W. Long. Elevation is 1,375 feet.

History: Former borough reverted to township status, 1941.

Population: 834 (1990); 838 (2000); 894 (2010); Density: 484.7 persons per square mile (2010); Race: 98.4% White, 0.3% Black, 0.1% Asian, 0.0% American Indian/Alaska Native, 0.0% Native Hawaiian/Other Pacific Islander, 1.2% Other, 1.1% Hispanic of any race (2010); Average household size: 2.39 (2010); Median age: 50.2 (2010); Males per 100 females: 79.2 (2010); Marriage status: 12.5% never married, 47.7% now married, 35.8% widowed, 3.9% divorced (2006-2010 5-year est.); Foreign born: 0.9% (2006-2010 5-year est.); Ancestry (includes multiple ancestries): 29.6% German, 24.9% Italian, 17.5% Irish, 15.9% Polish, 10.9% English (2006-2010 5-year est.).

Economy: Single-family building permits issued: 0 (2011); Multi-family building permits issued: 0 (2011); Employment by occupation: 16.3% management, 1.4% professional, 6.9% services, 16.3% sales, 3.4% farming, 12.3% construction, 7.2% production (2006-2010 5-year est.).

Income: Per capita income: $22,070 (2006-2010 5-year est.); Median household income: $39,821 (2006-2010 5-year est.); Average household income: $56,481 (2006-2010 5-year est.); Percent of households with income of $100,000 or more: 16.0% (2006-2010 5-year est.); Poverty rate: 4.5% (2006-2010 5-year est.).

Education: Percent of population age 25 and over with: High school diploma (including GED) or higher: 81.1% (2006-2010 5-year est.); Bachelor's degree or higher: 20.9% (2006-2010 5-year est.); Master's degree or higher: 9.9% (2006-2010 5-year est.).

Housing: Homeownership rate: 73.3% (2010); Median home value: $167,300 (2006-2010 5-year est.); Median contract rent: n/a per month (2006-2010 5-year est.); Median year structure built: 1971 (2006-2010 5-year est.).

Transportation: Commute to work: 93.1% car, 0.0% public transportation, 1.2% walk, 4.5% work from home (2006-2010 5-year est.); Travel time to work: 28.1% less than 15 minutes, 57.2% 15 to 30 minutes, 7.2% 30 to 45 minutes, 3.8% 45 to 60 minutes, 3.8% 60 minutes or more (2006-2010 5-year est.)

FELL (township).

Covers a land area of 15.271 square miles and a water area of 0.077 square miles. Located at 41.60° N. Lat; 75.50° W. Long.

Population: 2,331 (1990); 2,331 (2000); 2,178 (2010); Density: 142.6 persons per square mile (2010); Race: 96.6% White, 0.7% Black, 0.3% Asian, 0.2% American Indian/Alaska Native, 0.0% Native Hawaiian/Other Pacific Islander, 2.2% Other, 3.0% Hispanic of any race (2010); Average household size: 2.35 (2010); Median age: 41.7 (2010); Males per 100 females: 97.1 (2010); Marriage status: 27.9% never married, 56.8% now married, 7.6% widowed, 7.7% divorced (2006-2010 5-year est.); Foreign born: 1.3% (2006-2010 5-year est.); Ancestry (includes multiple ancestries): 25.6% Polish, 25.5% Italian, 25.1% Irish, 14.6% German, 9.6% English (2006-2010 5-year est.).

Economy: Single-family building permits issued: 3 (2011); Multi-family building permits issued: 0 (2011); Employment by occupation: 8.1% management, 1.7% professional, 18.0% services, 13.7% sales, 8.0% farming, 9.3% construction, 7.2% production (2006-2010 5-year est.).

Income: Per capita income: $21,772 (2006-2010 5-year est.); Median household income: $37,727 (2006-2010 5-year est.); Average household income: $52,383 (2006-2010 5-year est.); Percent of households with income of $100,000 or more: 9.6% (2006-2010 5-year est.); Poverty rate: 11.0% (2006-2010 5-year est.).

Taxes: Total city taxes per capita: $183 (2009); City property taxes per capita: $75 (2009).

Education: Percent of population age 25 and over with: High school diploma (including GED) or higher: 86.4% (2006-2010 5-year est.); Bachelor's degree or higher: 9.5% (2006-2010 5-year est.); Master's degree or higher: 3.1% (2006-2010 5-year est.).

Housing: Homeownership rate: 71.6% (2010); Median home value: $90,800 (2006-2010 5-year est.); Median contract rent: $477 per month (2006-2010 5-year est.); Median year structure built: 1944 (2006-2010 5-year est.).

Transportation: Commute to work: 94.7% car, 0.0% public transportation, 3.3% walk, 1.4% work from home (2006-2010 5-year est.); Travel time to work: 44.3% less than 15 minutes, 32.4% 15 to 30 minutes, 15.4% 30 to 45 minutes, 4.4% 45 to 60 minutes, 3.5% 60 minutes or more (2006-2010 5-year est.)

Additional Information Contacts

Greater Scranton Chamber of Commerce . . . . (570) 342-7711
http://www.scrantonchamber.com

FLEETVILLE (unincorporated postal area)

Zip Code: 18420

Covers a land area of 0.280 square miles and a water area of 0 square miles. Located at 41.60° N. Lat; 75.71° W. Long. Elevation is 1,250 feet.
Population: 57 (2010); Density: 203.2 persons per square mile (2010); Race: 96.5% White, 1.8% Black, 0.0% Asian, 0.0% American Indian/Alaska Native, 0.0% Native Hawaiian/Other Pacific Islander, 1.7% Other, 0.0% Hispanic of any race (2010); Average household size: 2.85 (2010); Median age: 26.5 (2010); Males per 100 females: 103.6 (2010); Homeownership rate: 60.0% (2010)

GLENBURN (CDP).

Covers a land area of 1.753 square miles and a water area of 0.045 square miles. Located at 41.52° N. Lat; 75.72° W. Long. Elevation is 1,165 feet.
Population: 1,215 (1990); 1,212 (2000); 953 (2010); Density: 543.6 persons per square mile (2010); Race: 95.3% White, 0.6% Black, 1.2% Asian, 0.1% American Indian/Alaska Native, 0.0% Native Hawaiian/Other Pacific Islander, 2.8% Other, 2.7% Hispanic of any race (2010); Average household size: 2.48 (2010); Median age: 47.3 (2010); Males per 100 females: 96.5 (2010); Marriage status: 28.0% never married, 61.0% now married, 5.7% widowed, 5.2% divorced (2006-2010 5-year est.); Foreign born: 4.3% (2006-2010 5-year est.); Ancestry (includes multiple ancestries): 40.2% Irish, 30.7% Italian, 18.4% German, 10.7% Polish, 6.5% Welsh (2006-2010 5-year est.).

Economy: Employment by occupation: 16.3% management, 3.3% professional, 9.6% services, 12.7% sales, 0.4% farming, 9.6% construction, 3.5% production (2006-2010 5-year est.).

Income: Per capita income: $39,687 (2006-2010 5-year est.); Median household income: $70,000 (2006-2010 5-year est.); Average household income: $115,701 (2006-2010 5-year est.); Percent of households with income of $100,000 or more: 35.6% (2006-2010 5-year est.); Poverty rate: 4.5% (2006-2010 5-year est.).

Education: Percent of population age 25 and over with: High school diploma (including GED) or higher: 96.5% (2006-2010 5-year est.); Bachelor's degree or higher: 49.0% (2006-2010 5-year est.); Master's degree or higher: 20.8% (2006-2010 5-year est.).

Housing: Homeownership rate: 88.6% (2010); Median home value: $196,800 (2006-2010 5-year est.); Median contract rent: $667 per month (2006-2010 5-year est.); Median year structure built: 1969 (2006-2010 5-year est.).

Transportation: Commute to work: 94.3% car, 0.0% public transportation, 0.4% walk, 5.3% work from home (2006-2010 5-year est.); Travel time to work: 24.1% less than 15 minutes, 43.2% 15 to 30 minutes, 27.2% 30 to 45 minutes, 4.0% 45 to 60 minutes, 1.6% 60 minutes or more (2006-2010 5-year est.)

GLENBURN (township).

Covers a land area of 4.642 square miles and a water area of 0.149 square miles. Located at 41.51° N. Lat; 75.75° W. Long. Elevation is 1,165 feet.
Population: 1,215 (1990); 1,212 (2000); 1,246 (2010); Density: 268.4 persons per square mile (2010); Race: 95.1% White, 1.0% Black, 1.4% Asian, 0.1% American Indian/Alaska Native, 0.0% Native Hawaiian/Other Pacific Islander, 2.4% Other, 2.2% Hispanic of any race (2010); Average household size: 2.50 (2010); Median age: 46.3 (2010); Males per 100 females: 101.0 (2010); Marriage status: 27.2% never married, 61.7% now married, 5.1% widowed, 6.0% divorced (2006-2010 5-year est.); Foreign born: 4.2% (2006-2010 5-year est.); Ancestry (includes multiple ancestries): 36.2% Irish, 30.0% Italian, 19.7% German, 9.6% English, 8.6% Polish (2006-2010 5-year est.).

Economy: Single-family building permits issued: 0 (2011); Multi-family building permits issued: 0 (2011); Employment by occupation: 17.6% management, 3.3% professional, 8.9% services, 12.2% sales, 1.3% farming, 8.3% construction, 3.1% production (2006-2010 5-year est.).

Income: Per capita income: $37,469 (2006-2010 5-year est.); Median household income: $66,528 (2006-2010 5-year est.); Average household income: $104,751 (2006-2010 5-year est.); Percent of households with income of $100,000 or more: 33.0% (2006-2010 5-year est.); Poverty rate: 5.1% (2006-2010 5-year est.).

Education: Percent of population age 25 and over with: High school diploma (including GED) or higher: 97.2% (2006-2010 5-year est.); Bachelor's degree or higher: 46.8% (2006-2010 5-year est.); Master's degree or higher: 21.0% (2006-2010 5-year est.).

Housing: Homeownership rate: 89.3% (2010); Median home value: $208,200 (2006-2010 5-year est.); Median contract rent: $592 per month (2006-2010 5-year est.); Median year structure built: 1973 (2006-2010 5-year est.).

Transportation: Commute to work: 94.1% car, 0.0% public transportation, 0.3% walk, 5.5% work from home (2006-2010 5-year est.); Travel time to work: 25.8% less than 15 minutes, 42.3% 15 to 30 minutes, 25.0% 30 to 45 minutes, 5.2% 45 to 60 minutes, 1.7% 60 minutes or more (2006-2010 5-year est.)

Additional Information Contacts

Greater Scranton Chamber of Commerce . . . . (570) 342-7711
http://www.scrantonchamber.com

GREENFIELD (township).

Covers a land area of 20.933 square miles and a water area of 0.606 square miles. Located at 41.61° N. Lat; 75.59° W. Long.
Population: 1,743 (1990); 1,990 (2000); 2,105 (2010); Density: 100.6 persons per square mile (2010); Race: 98.5% White, 0.5% Black, 0.2% Asian, 0.1% American Indian/Alaska Native, 0.0% Native Hawaiian/Other Pacific Islander, 0.7% Other, 0.7% Hispanic of any race (2010); Average household size: 2.54 (2010); Median age: 43.8 (2010); Males per 100 females: 103.6 (2010); Marriage status: 21.0% never married, 60.7% now married, 7.8% widowed, 10.6% divorced (2006-2010 5-year est.); Foreign born: 0.4% (2006-2010 5-year est.); Ancestry (includes multiple ancestries): 25.9% Polish, 24.6% Irish, 24.2% Italian, 17.0% English, 13.2% German (2006-2010 5-year est.).

Economy: Single-family building permits issued: 0 (2011); Multi-family building permits issued: 0 (2011); Employment by occupation: 12.9% management, 4.1% professional, 8.2% services, 18.4% sales, 2.6% farming, 13.7% construction, 7.9% production (2006-2010 5-year est.).
Income: Per capita income: $27,795 (2006-2010 5-year est.); Median household income: $62,386 (2006-2010 5-year est.); Average household income: $72,181 (2006-2010 5-year est.); Percent of households with income of $100,000 or more: 28.5% (2006-2010 5-year est.); Poverty rate: 6.7% (2006-2010 5-year est.).
Education: Percent of population age 25 and over with: High school diploma (including GED) or higher: 92.7% (2006-2010 5-year est.); Bachelor's degree or higher: 24.7% (2006-2010 5-year est.); Master's degree or higher: 6.9% (2006-2010 5-year est.).
Housing: Homeownership rate: 87.9% (2010); Median home value: $198,500 (2006-2010 5-year est.); Median contract rent: $472 per month (2006-2010 5-year est.); Median year structure built: 1977 (2006-2010 5-year est.).
Transportation: Commute to work: 96.2% car, 0.0% public transportation, 0.0% walk, 3.0% work from home (2006-2010 5-year est.); Travel time to work: 21.5% less than 15 minutes, 32.4% 15 to 30 minutes, 28.1% 30 to 45 minutes, 11.5% 45 to 60 minutes, 6.5% 60 minutes or more (2006-2010 5-year est.).
Additional Information Contacts
Greater Scranton Chamber of Commerce . . . . (570) 342-7711
    http://www.scrantonchamber.com

JEFFERSON (township). Covers a land area of 33.550 square miles and a water area of 0.378 square miles. Located at 41.45° N. Lat; 75.49° W. Long.
Population: 3,474 (1990); 3,592 (2000); 3,731 (2010); Density: 111.2 persons per square mile (2010); Race: 98.1% White, 0.6% Black, 0.3% Asian, 0.2% American Indian/Alaska Native, 0.0% Native Hawaiian/Other Pacific Islander, 0.8% Other, 1.5% Hispanic of any race (2010); Average household size: 2.56 (2010); Median age: 45.3 (2010); Males per 100 females: 101.9 (2010); Marriage status: 21.9% never married, 67.3% now married, 5.7% widowed, 5.1% divorced (2006-2010 5-year est.); Foreign born: 0.6% (2006-2010 5-year est.); Ancestry (includes multiple ancestries): 26.6% Italian, 26.4% German, 20.8% Polish, 17.3% Irish, 10.4% English (2006-2010 5-year est.).
Economy: Single-family building permits issued: 3 (2011); Multi-family building permits issued: 0 (2011); Employment by occupation: 11.3% management, 4.2% professional, 6.3% services, 14.1% sales, 2.4% farming, 17.7% construction, 4.8% production (2006-2010 5-year est.).
Income: Per capita income: $26,920 (2006-2010 5-year est.); Median household income: $55,603 (2006-2010 5-year est.); Average household income: $73,177 (2006-2010 5-year est.); Percent of households with income of $100,000 or more: 18.9% (2006-2010 5-year est.); Poverty rate: 2.7% (2006-2010 5-year est.).
Education: Percent of population age 25 and over with: High school diploma (including GED) or higher: 85.3% (2006-2010 5-year est.); Bachelor's degree or higher: 26.2% (2006-2010 5-year est.); Master's degree or higher: 13.5% (2006-2010 5-year est.).
Housing: Homeownership rate: 88.6% (2010); Median home value: $175,800 (2006-2010 5-year est.); Median contract rent: $462 per month (2006-2010 5-year est.); Median year structure built: 1974 (2006-2010 5-year est.).
Transportation: Commute to work: 91.9% car, 0.8% public transportation, 1.6% walk, 5.6% work from home (2006-2010 5-year est.); Travel time to work: 14.2% less than 15 minutes, 52.4% 15 to 30 minutes, 26.2% 30 to 45 minutes, 2.7% 45 to 60 minutes, 4.5% 60 minutes or more (2006-2010 5-year est.).
Additional Information Contacts
Greater Scranton Chamber of Commerce . . . . (570) 342-7711
    http://www.scrantonchamber.com

JERMYN (borough). Covers a land area of 0.792 square miles and a water area of 0 square miles. Located at 41.53° N. Lat; 75.55° W. Long. Elevation is 965 feet.
History: Former anthracite-coal center. Incorporated 1870.
Population: 2,263 (1990); 2,287 (2000); 2,169 (2010); Density: 2,737.3 persons per square mile (2010); Race: 96.8% White, 1.1% Black, 0.4% Asian, 0.3% American Indian/Alaska Native, 0.0% Native Hawaiian/Other Pacific Islander, 1.4% Other, 2.1% Hispanic of any race (2010); Average household size: 2.27 (2010); Median age: 42.1 (2010); Males per 100 females: 92.5 (2010); Marriage status: 33.2% never married, 47.9% now

married, 8.7% widowed, 10.2% divorced (2006-2010 5-year est.); Foreign born: 0.9% (2006-2010 5-year est.); Ancestry (includes multiple ancestries): 27.1% Irish, 26.3% Italian, 21.6% Polish, 16.2% English, 11.7% German (2006-2010 5-year est.).
Economy: Single-family building permits issued: 0 (2011); Multi-family building permits issued: 0 (2011); Employment by occupation: 5.5% management, 2.1% professional, 15.7% services, 19.5% sales, 3.0% farming, 4.4% construction, 4.7% production (2006-2010 5-year est.).
Income: Per capita income: $22,195 (2006-2010 5-year est.); Median household income: $40,167 (2006-2010 5-year est.); Average household income: $49,140 (2006-2010 5-year est.); Percent of households with income of $100,000 or more: 5.8% (2006-2010 5-year est.); Poverty rate: 14.9% (2006-2010 5-year est.).
Education: Percent of population age 25 and over with: High school diploma (including GED) or higher: 93.9% (2006-2010 5-year est.); Bachelor's degree or higher: 15.0% (2006-2010 5-year est.); Master's degree or higher: 4.6% (2006-2010 5-year est.).

School District(s)
Lakeland SD (KG-12)
    2010-11 Enrollment: 1,619 . . . . (570) 254-9485
Housing: Homeownership rate: 68.1% (2010); Median home value: $117,500 (2006-2010 5-year est.); Median contract rent: $429 per month (2006-2010 5-year est.); Median year structure built: before 1940 (2006-2010 5-year est.).
Safety: Violent crime rate: 105.7 per 10,000 population; Property crime rate: 271.1 per 10,000 population (2011).
Transportation: Commute to work: 95.4% car, 2.3% public transportation, 1.8% walk, 0.6% work from home (2006-2010 5-year est.); Travel time to work: 34.4% less than 15 minutes, 38.6% 15 to 30 minutes, 20.9% 30 to 45 minutes, 1.3% 45 to 60 minutes, 4.8% 60 minutes or more (2006-2010 5-year est.).
Additional Information Contacts
Greater Scranton Chamber of Commerce . . . . (570) 342-7711
    http://www.scrantonchamber.com

JESSUP (borough). Aka Winton. Covers a land area of 6.737 square miles and a water area of 0.049 square miles. Located at 41.45° N. Lat; 75.54° W. Long. Elevation is 974 feet.
Population: 4,605 (1990); 4,718 (2000); 4,676 (2010); Density: 694.1 persons per square mile (2010); Race: 96.9% White, 0.8% Black, 0.4% Asian, 0.2% American Indian/Alaska Native, 0.0% Native Hawaiian/Other Pacific Islander, 1.7% Other, 1.9% Hispanic of any race (2010); Average household size: 2.33 (2010); Median age: 42.5 (2010); Males per 100 females: 88.8 (2010); Marriage status: 31.5% never married, 49.5% now married, 9.3% widowed, 9.7% divorced (2006-2010 5-year est.); Foreign born: 3.0% (2006-2010 5-year est.); Ancestry (includes multiple ancestries): 37.6% Italian, 30.1% Polish, 18.7% Irish, 11.1% German, 8.9% English (2006-2010 5-year est.).
Economy: Single-family building permits issued: 1 (2011); Multi-family building permits issued: 0 (2011); Employment by occupation: 1.2% management, 3.9% professional, 7.4% services, 21.9% sales, 3.8% farming, 5.3% construction, 3.1% production (2006-2010 5-year est.).
Income: Per capita income: $23,973 (2006-2010 5-year est.); Median household income: $42,434 (2006-2010 5-year est.); Average household income: $56,076 (2006-2010 5-year est.); Percent of households with income of $100,000 or more: 10.3% (2006-2010 5-year est.); Poverty rate: 14.9% (2006-2010 5-year est.).
Education: Percent of population age 25 and over with: High school diploma (including GED) or higher: 92.5% (2006-2010 5-year est.); Bachelor's degree or higher: 21.7% (2006-2010 5-year est.); Master's degree or higher: 5.7% (2006-2010 5-year est.).
Housing: Homeownership rate: 72.1% (2010); Median home value: $113,600 (2006-2010 5-year est.); Median contract rent: $435 per month (2006-2010 5-year est.); Median year structure built: before 1940 (2006-2010 5-year est.).
Transportation: Commute to work: 97.6% car, 0.0% public transportation, 0.5% walk, 1.9% work from home (2006-2010 5-year est.); Travel time to work: 38.5% less than 15 minutes, 49.0% 15 to 30 minutes, 7.0% 30 to 45 minutes, 3.7% 45 to 60 minutes, 1.9% 60 minutes or more (2006-2010 5-year est.)
Additional Information Contacts
Greater Johnstown Cambria County Chamber of Commerce . . . . (570) 342-7711
    http://www.scrantonchamber.com

LA PLUME (township). Covers a land area of 2.434 square miles and a water area of 0.003 square miles. Located at 41.56° N. Lat; 75.77° W. Long. Elevation is 889 feet.

Population: 660 (1990); 603 (2000); 602 (2010); Density: 247.3 persons per square mile (2010); Race: 97.2% White, 0.5% Black, 0.8% Asian, 0.2% American Indian/Alaska Native, 0.0% Native Hawaiian/Other Pacific Islander, 1.3% Other, 0.8% Hispanic of any race (2010); Average household size: 2.37 (2010); Median age: 42.0 (2010); Males per 100 females: 86.4 (2010); Marriage status: 19.6% never married, 58.3% now married, 6.4% widowed, 15.7% divorced (2006-2010 5-year est.); Foreign born: 0.4% (2006-2010 5-year est.); Ancestry (includes multiple ancestries): 35.6% German, 30.3% Irish, 28.1% Polish, 16.2% English, 12.3% Welsh (2006-2010 5-year est.).

Economy: Single-family building permits issued: 0 (2011); Multi-family building permits issued: 0 (2011); Employment by occupation: 14.4% management, 0.0% professional, 7.9% services, 21.3% sales, 3.7% farming, 16.1% construction, 7.7% production (2006-2010 5-year est.).

Income: Per capita income: $20,000 (2006-2010 5-year est.); Median household income: $35,859 (2006-2010 5-year est.); Average household income: $45,015 (2006-2010 5-year est.); Percent of households with income of $100,000 or more: 12.3% (2006-2010 5-year est.); Poverty rate: 23.0% (2006-2010 5-year est.).

Education: Percent of population age 25 and over with: High school diploma (including GED) or higher: 78.3% (2006-2010 5-year est.); Bachelor's degree or higher: 20.5% (2006-2010 5-year est.); Master's degree or higher: 5.8% (2006-2010 5-year est.).

Four-year College(s)

Keystone College (Private, Not-for-profit)

    Fall 2010 Enrollment: 1,846 . . . . (570) 945-8000

    2011-12 Tuition: In-state $19,620; Out-of-state $19,620

Housing: Homeownership rate: 80.7% (2010); Median home value: $117,500 (2006-2010 5-year est.); Median contract rent: $450 per month (2006-2010 5-year est.); Median year structure built: before 1940 (2006-2010 5-year est.).

Transportation: Commute to work: 85.9% car, 0.0% public transportation, 7.2% walk, 6.9% work from home (2006-2010 5-year est.); Travel time to work: 28.7% less than 15 minutes, 41.5% 15 to 30 minutes, 21.8% 30 to 45 minutes, 1.1% 45 to 60 minutes, 6.9% 60 minutes or more (2006-2010 5-year est.)

MADISON (township). Covers a land area of 16.949 square miles and a water area of 0.105 square miles. Located at 41.35° N. Lat; 75.47° W. Long.

Population: 2,207 (1990); 2,542 (2000); 2,750 (2010); Density: 162.3 persons per square mile (2010); Race: 98.4% White, 0.4% Black, 0.5% Asian, 0.0% American Indian/Alaska Native, 0.0% Native Hawaiian/Other Pacific Islander, 0.7% Other, 0.7% Hispanic of any race (2010); Average household size: 2.68 (2010); Median age: 42.1 (2010); Males per 100 females: 96.3 (2010); Marriage status: 17.7% never married, 72.2% now married, 4.1% widowed, 6.0% divorced (2006-2010 5-year est.); Foreign born: 0.7% (2006-2010 5-year est.); Ancestry (includes multiple ancestries): 33.9% German, 24.0% Italian, 23.6% Irish, 19.4% Polish, 11.3% English (2006-2010 5-year est.).

Economy: Single-family building permits issued: 4 (2011); Multi-family building permits issued: 0 (2011); Employment by occupation: 11.1% management, 2.7% professional, 10.8% services, 15.0% sales, 1.9% farming, 16.1% construction, 9.1% production (2006-2010 5-year est.).

Income: Per capita income: $22,014 (2006-2010 5-year est.); Median household income: $50,592 (2006-2010 5-year est.); Average household income: $58,220 (2006-2010 5-year est.); Percent of households with income of $100,000 or more: 18.3% (2006-2010 5-year est.); Poverty rate: 10.7% (2006-2010 5-year est.).

Education: Percent of population age 25 and over with: High school diploma (including GED) or higher: 88.1% (2006-2010 5-year est.); Bachelor's degree or higher: 16.1% (2006-2010 5-year est.); Master's degree or higher: 8.1% (2006-2010 5-year est.).

Housing: Homeownership rate: 90.2% (2010); Median home value: $181,000 (2006-2010 5-year est.); Median contract rent: $611 per month (2006-2010 5-year est.); Median year structure built: 1981 (2006-2010 5-year est.).

Transportation: Commute to work: 94.5% car, 0.7% public transportation, 0.0% walk, 4.8% work from home (2006-2010 5-year est.); Travel time to work: 25.2% less than 15 minutes, 37.6% 15 to 30 minutes, 24.8% 30 to 45 minutes, 7.9% 45 to 60 minutes, 4.5% 60 minutes or more (2006-2010 5-year est.)

Additional Information Contacts

Greater Scranton Chamber of Commerce . . . . (570) 342-7711

    http://www.scrantonchamber.com

MAYFIELD (borough). Covers a land area of 2.446 square miles and a water area of <.001 square miles. Located at 41.54° N. Lat; 75.53° W. Long. Elevation is 968 feet.

History: Former anthracite-coal center. Founded c.1840.

Population: 1,890 (1990); 1,756 (2000); 1,807 (2010); Density: 738.6 persons per square mile (2010); Race: 97.7% White, 0.8% Black, 0.4% Asian, 0.1% American Indian/Alaska Native, 0.0% Native Hawaiian/Other Pacific Islander, 1.0% Other, 1.1% Hispanic of any race (2010); Average household size: 2.45 (2010); Median age: 41.6 (2010); Males per 100 females: 98.4 (2010); Marriage status: 26.7% never married, 57.4% now married, 10.8% widowed, 5.0% divorced (2006-2010 5-year est.); Foreign born: 2.3% (2006-2010 5-year est.); Ancestry (includes multiple ancestries): 32.1% Italian, 31.4% Polish, 25.7% Irish, 13.4% Russian, 9.7% German (2006-2010 5-year est.).

Economy: Single-family building permits issued: 1 (2011); Multi-family building permits issued: 0 (2011); Employment by occupation: 8.0% management, 2.7% professional, 15.8% services, 14.2% sales, 3.3% farming, 8.5% construction, 9.6% production (2006-2010 5-year est.).

Income: Per capita income: $23,496 (2006-2010 5-year est.); Median household income: $39,786 (2006-2010 5-year est.); Average household income: $53,965 (2006-2010 5-year est.); Percent of households with income of $100,000 or more: 13.6% (2006-2010 5-year est.); Poverty rate: 11.0% (2006-2010 5-year est.).

Education: Percent of population age 25 and over with: High school diploma (including GED) or higher: 90.6% (2006-2010 5-year est.); Bachelor's degree or higher: 23.5% (2006-2010 5-year est.); Master's degree or higher: 6.4% (2006-2010 5-year est.).

School District(s)

Lakeland SD (KG-12)

    2010-11 Enrollment: 1,619 . . . . (570) 254-9485

Housing: Homeownership rate: 78.5% (2010); Median home value: $117,300 (2006-2010 5-year est.); Median contract rent: $430 per month (2006-2010 5-year est.); Median year structure built: before 1940 (2006-2010 5-year est.).

Safety: Violent crime rate: 5.5 per 10,000 population; Property crime rate: 49.6 per 10,000 population (2011).

Transportation: Commute to work: 93.7% car, 0.3% public transportation, 2.4% walk, 2.6% work from home (2006-2010 5-year est.); Travel time to work: 34.2% less than 15 minutes, 45.1% 15 to 30 minutes, 15.2% 30 to 45 minutes, 1.0% 45 to 60 minutes, 4.4% 60 minutes or more (2006-2010 5-year est.)

Additional Information Contacts

Greater Pittston Chamber of Commerce . . . . (570) 655-1424

    http://www.pittstonchamber.org

MOOSIC (borough). Covers a land area of 6.476 square miles and a water area of 0.048 square miles. Located at 41.36° N. Lat; 75.70° W. Long. Elevation is 640 feet.

Population: 5,328 (1990); 5,575 (2000); 5,719 (2010); Density: 883.1 persons per square mile (2010); Race: 95.3% White, 1.0% Black, 1.8% Asian, 0.1% American Indian/Alaska Native, 0.0% Native Hawaiian/Other Pacific Islander, 1.8% Other, 3.7% Hispanic of any race (2010); Average household size: 2.41 (2010); Median age: 44.4 (2010); Males per 100 females: 93.9 (2010); Marriage status: 29.6% never married, 59.2% now married, 5.8% widowed, 5.4% divorced (2006-2010 5-year est.); Foreign born: 2.0% (2006-2010 5-year est.); Ancestry (includes multiple ancestries): 31.7% Italian, 29.0% Polish, 22.6% Irish, 14.8% German, 7.2% Welsh (2006-2010 5-year est.).

Economy: Single-family building permits issued: 14 (2011); Multi-family building permits issued: 0 (2011); Employment by occupation: 10.0% management, 6.3% professional, 11.9% services, 19.1% sales, 8.3% farming, 7.6% construction, 6.4% production (2006-2010 5-year est.).

Income: Per capita income: $31,354 (2006-2010 5-year est.); Median household income: $57,826 (2006-2010 5-year est.); Average household income: $74,541 (2006-2010 5-year est.); Percent of households with income of $100,000 or more: 19.5% (2006-2010 5-year est.); Poverty rate: 10.6% (2006-2010 5-year est.).

Education: Percent of population age 25 and over with: High school diploma (including GED) or higher: 92.5% (2006-2010 5-year est.); Bachelor's degree or higher: 27.9% (2006-2010 5-year est.); Master's degree or higher: 8.4% (2006-2010 5-year est.).

School District(s)

Riverside SD (KG-12)

   2010-11 Enrollment: 1,556 . . . . (570) 562-2121

Vocational/Technical School(s)

Empire Beauty School-Wyoming Valley (Private, For-profit)

   Fall 2010 Enrollment: 335 . . . . (800) 223-3271

   2011-12 Tuition: $14,490

Housing: Homeownership rate: 78.0% (2010); Median home value: $151,500 (2006-2010 5-year est.); Median contract rent: $596 per month (2006-2010 5-year est.); Median year structure built: 1968 (2006-2010 5-year est.).

Safety: Violent crime rate: 57.5 per 10,000 population; Property crime rate: 463.7 per 10,000 population (2011).

Transportation: Commute to work: 92.8% car, 0.0% public transportation, 4.2% walk, 2.5% work from home (2006-2010 5-year est.); Travel time to work: 43.5% less than 15 minutes, 41.0% 15 to 30 minutes, 10.0% 30 to 45 minutes, 2.2% 45 to 60 minutes, 3.4% 60 minutes or more (2006-2010 5-year est.)

Additional Information Contacts

Borough of Moosic . . . . (570) 457-5480

   http://www.moosic.boroughs.org

Greater Northeast Chamber of Commerce . . . . (570) 457-1130

   http://www.gnecc.com

MOSCOW (borough). Covers a land area of 2.849 square miles and a water area of 0.003 square miles. Located at 41.34° N. Lat; 75.53° W. Long. Elevation is 1,562 feet.

History: Settled 1830.

Population: 1,527 (1990); 1,883 (2000); 2,026 (2010); Density: 711.2 persons per square mile (2010); Race: 97.9% White, 0.3% Black, 0.9% Asian, 0.0% American Indian/Alaska Native, 0.0% Native Hawaiian/Other Pacific Islander, 0.9% Other, 1.7% Hispanic of any race (2010); Average household size: 2.70 (2010); Median age: 41.9 (2010); Males per 100 females: 101.0 (2010); Marriage status: 25.4% never married, 61.1% now married, 6.5% widowed, 7.0% divorced (2006-2010 5-year est.); Foreign born: 3.8% (2006-2010 5-year est.); Ancestry (includes multiple ancestries): 29.0% Irish, 25.5% German, 24.9% Italian, 14.8% Polish, 10.3% English (2006-2010 5-year est.).

Economy: Single-family building permits issued: 0 (2011); Multi-family building permits issued: 0 (2011); Employment by occupation: 11.2% management, 4.9% professional, 8.4% services, 13.0% sales, 3.1% farming, 8.6% construction, 8.8% production (2006-2010 5-year est.).

Income: Per capita income: $32,888 (2006-2010 5-year est.); Median household income: $58,686 (2006-2010 5-year est.); Average household income: $85,577 (2006-2010 5-year est.); Percent of households with income of $100,000 or more: 27.2% (2006-2010 5-year est.); Poverty rate: 5.2% (2006-2010 5-year est.).

Education: Percent of population age 25 and over with: High school diploma (including GED) or higher: 90.2% (2006-2010 5-year est.); Bachelor's degree or higher: 34.2% (2006-2010 5-year est.); Master's degree or higher: 14.8% (2006-2010 5-year est.).

School District(s)

North Pocono SD (KG-12)

   2010-11 Enrollment: 3,173 . . . . (570) 842-7659

Housing: Homeownership rate: 77.6% (2010); Median home value: $217,300 (2006-2010 5-year est.); Median contract rent: $625 per month (2006-2010 5-year est.); Median year structure built: 1963 (2006-2010 5-year est.).

Safety: Violent crime rate: 9.8 per 10,000 population; Property crime rate: 103.3 per 10,000 population (2011).

Newspapers: Villager (Community news; Circulation 5,500)

Transportation: Commute to work: 93.2% car, 0.5% public transportation, 1.8% walk, 4.1% work from home (2006-2010 5-year est.); Travel time to work: 30.8% less than 15 minutes, 44.1% 15 to 30 minutes, 16.4% 30 to 45 minutes, 2.8% 45 to 60 minutes, 5.9% 60 minutes or more (2006-2010 5-year est.)

Additional Information Contacts

Greater Northeast Chamber of Commerce . . . . (570) 457-1130

   http://www.gnecc.com

MOUNT COBB (CDP). Covers a land area of 7.141 square miles and a water area of 0.158 square miles. Located at 41.43° N. Lat; 75.50° W. Long. Elevation is 1,663 feet.

Population: 2,081 (1990); 2,140 (2000); 1,799 (2010); Density: 251.9 persons per square mile (2010); Race: 98.5% White, 0.3% Black, 0.4%

Asian, 0.1% American Indian/Alaska Native, 0.0% Native Hawaiian/Other Pacific Islander, 0.7% Other, 0.8% Hispanic of any race (2010); Average household size: 2.58 (2010); Median age: 44.6 (2010); Males per 100 females: 102.4 (2010); Marriage status: 20.6% never married, 65.6% now married, 4.4% widowed, 9.4% divorced (2006-2010 5-year est.); Foreign born: 0.6% (2006-2010 5-year est.); Ancestry (includes multiple ancestries): 30.8% Polish, 29.8% Irish, 23.4% Italian, 22.0% German, 10.3% Slovak (2006-2010 5-year est.).

Economy: Employment by occupation: 15.3% management, 2.7% professional, 6.2% services, 17.3% sales, 4.1% farming, 21.9% construction, 8.2% production (2006-2010 5-year est.).

Income: Per capita income: $30,694 (2006-2010 5-year est.); Median household income: $56,512 (2006-2010 5-year est.); Average household income: $82,538 (2006-2010 5-year est.); Percent of households with income of $100,000 or more: 23.7% (2006-2010 5-year est.); Poverty rate: 3.8% (2006-2010 5-year est.).

Education: Percent of population age 25 and over with: High school diploma (including GED) or higher: 91.4% (2006-2010 5-year est.); Bachelor's degree or higher: 31.5% (2006-2010 5-year est.); Master's degree or higher: 10.0% (2006-2010 5-year est.).

Housing: Homeownership rate: 90.4% (2010); Median home value: $188,500 (2006-2010 5-year est.); Median contract rent: $483 per month (2006-2010 5-year est.); Median year structure built: 1975 (2006-2010 5-year est.).

Transportation: Commute to work: 88.8% car, 1.4% public transportation, 0.9% walk, 8.8% work from home (2006-2010 5-year est.); Travel time to work: 21.1% less than 15 minutes, 43.6% 15 to 30 minutes, 29.5% 30 to 45 minutes, 1.6% 45 to 60 minutes, 4.3% 60 minutes or more (2006-2010 5-year est.)

Additional Information Contacts

Greater Scranton Chamber of Commerce . . . . (570) 342-7711

   http://www.scrantonchamber.com

NEWTON (township). Covers a land area of 22.266 square miles and a water area of 0.234 square miles. Located at 41.45° N. Lat; 75.76° W. Long.

Population: 2,843 (1990); 2,699 (2000); 2,846 (2010); Density: 127.8 persons per square mile (2010); Race: 98.2% White, 0.5% Black, 0.5% Asian, 0.0% American Indian/Alaska Native, 0.0% Native Hawaiian/Other Pacific Islander, 0.8% Other, 0.9% Hispanic of any race (2010); Average household size: 2.72 (2010); Median age: 44.7 (2010); Males per 100 females: 102.7 (2010); Marriage status: 22.9% never married, 62.0% now married, 6.4% widowed, 8.7% divorced (2006-2010 5-year est.); Foreign born: 2.0% (2006-2010 5-year est.); Ancestry (includes multiple ancestries): 27.2% Irish, 25.6% German, 17.9% Italian, 17.8% Polish, 14.1% Welsh (2006-2010 5-year est.).

Economy: Single-family building permits issued: 4 (2011); Multi-family building permits issued: 0 (2011); Employment by occupation: 12.2% management, 5.6% professional, 13.1% services, 16.1% sales, 3.7% farming, 9.8% construction, 5.6% production (2006-2010 5-year est.).

Income: Per capita income: $35,264 (2006-2010 5-year est.); Median household income: $66,940 (2006-2010 5-year est.); Average household income: $98,209 (2006-2010 5-year est.); Percent of households with income of $100,000 or more: 25.8% (2006-2010 5-year est.); Poverty rate: 5.0% (2006-2010 5-year est.).

Education: Percent of population age 25 and over with: High school diploma (including GED) or higher: 90.5% (2006-2010 5-year est.); Bachelor's degree or higher: 29.6% (2006-2010 5-year est.); Master's degree or higher: 14.0% (2006-2010 5-year est.).

Housing: Homeownership rate: 86.4% (2010); Median home value: $207,900 (2006-2010 5-year est.); Median contract rent: $478 per month (2006-2010 5-year est.); Median year structure built: 1972 (2006-2010 5-year est.).

Safety: Violent crime rate: 7.0 per 10,000 population; Property crime rate: 14.0 per 10,000 population (2011).

Transportation: Commute to work: 94.8% car, 0.0% public transportation, 1.3% walk, 3.9% work from home (2006-2010 5-year est.); Travel time to work: 25.4% less than 15 minutes, 44.5% 15 to 30 minutes, 21.3% 30 to 45 minutes, 3.2% 45 to 60 minutes, 5.6% 60 minutes or more (2006-2010 5-year est.)

Additional Information Contacts

Greater Scranton Chamber of Commerce . . . . (570) 342-7711

   http://www.scrantonchamber.com

NORTH ABINGTON (township). Covers a land area of 9.292 square miles and a water area of 0.013 square miles. Located at 41.56° N. Lat; 75.69° W. Long.
Population: 691 (1990); 782 (2000); 703 (2010); Density: 75.7 persons per square mile (2010); Race: 96.2% White, 0.3% Black, 1.6% Asian, 0.6% American Indian/Alaska Native, 0.0% Native Hawaiian/Other Pacific Islander, 1.3% Other, 1.8% Hispanic of any race (2010); Average household size: 2.80 (2010); Median age: 42.3 (2010); Males per 100 females: 99.7 (2010); Marriage status: 18.2% never married, 73.7% now married, 3.5% widowed, 4.6% divorced (2006-2010 5-year est.); Foreign born: 0.5% (2006-2010 5-year est.); Ancestry (includes multiple ancestries): 26.1% Polish, 24.0% Irish, 24.0% Italian, 21.9% German, 9.5% English (2006-2010 5-year est.).
Economy: Single-family building permits issued: 0 (2011); Multi-family building permits issued: 0 (2011); Employment by occupation: 23.5% management, 5.6% professional, 8.1% services, 22.1% sales, 5.0% farming, 4.5% construction, 0.3% production (2006-2010 5-year est.).
Income: Per capita income: $38,892 (2006-2010 5-year est.); Median household income: $83,750 (2006-2010 5-year est.); Average household income: $109,987 (2006-2010 5-year est.); Percent of households with income of $100,000 or more: 41.1% (2006-2010 5-year est.); Poverty rate: 2.6% (2006-2010 5-year est.).
Education: Percent of population age 25 and over with: High school diploma (including GED) or higher: 94.9% (2006-2010 5-year est.); Bachelor's degree or higher: 42.3% (2006-2010 5-year est.); Master's degree or higher: 20.1% (2006-2010 5-year est.).
Housing: Homeownership rate: 91.3% (2010); Median home value: $209,200 (2006-2010 5-year est.); Median contract rent: n/a per month (2006-2010 5-year est.); Median year structure built: 1971 (2006-2010 5-year est.).
Transportation: Commute to work: 83.8% car, 0.0% public transportation, 1.7% walk, 14.0% work from home (2006-2010 5-year est.); Travel time to work: 31.8% less than 15 minutes, 51.3% 15 to 30 minutes, 12.3% 30 to 45 minutes, 4.0% 45 to 60 minutes, 0.7% 60 minutes or more (2006-2010 5-year est.)

OLD FORGE (borough). Covers a land area of 3.415 square miles and a water area of 0 square miles. Located at 41.37° N. Lat; 75.74° W. Long. Elevation is 738 feet.
History: Settled 1798, incorporated 1895.
Population: 8,845 (1990); 8,798 (2000); 8,313 (2010); Density: 2,434.5 persons per square mile (2010); Race: 96.9% White, 1.0% Black, 0.7% Asian, 0.1% American Indian/Alaska Native, 0.0% Native Hawaiian/Other Pacific Islander, 1.3% Other, 2.8% Hispanic of any race (2010); Average household size: 2.23 (2010); Median age: 45.1 (2010); Males per 100 females: 89.1 (2010); Marriage status: 26.1% never married, 57.7% now married, 7.9% widowed, 8.3% divorced (2006-2010 5-year est.); Foreign born: 2.0% (2006-2010 5-year est.); Ancestry (includes multiple ancestries): 41.3% Italian, 22.6% Polish, 21.8% Irish, 13.2% German, 8.6% Russian (2006-2010 5-year est.).
Economy: Single-family building permits issued: 1 (2011); Multi-family building permits issued: 4 (2011); Employment by occupation: 8.5% management, 4.0% professional, 7.3% services, 18.3% sales, 5.2% farming, 8.2% construction, 7.7% production (2006-2010 5-year est.).
Income: Per capita income: $26,557 (2006-2010 5-year est.); Median household income: $49,688 (2006-2010 5-year est.); Average household income: $59,647 (2006-2010 5-year est.); Percent of households with income of $100,000 or more: 13.0% (2006-2010 5-year est.); Poverty rate: 8.7% (2006-2010 5-year est.).
Education: Percent of population age 25 and over with: High school diploma (including GED) or higher: 88.8% (2006-2010 5-year est.); Bachelor's degree or higher: 24.3% (2006-2010 5-year est.); Master's degree or higher: 9.8% (2006-2010 5-year est.).

School District(s)
Old Forge SD (KG-12)
   2010-11 Enrollment: 988 . . . . (570) 457-6721
Housing: Homeownership rate: 68.4% (2010); Median home value: $137,000 (2006-2010 5-year est.); Median contract rent: $484 per month (2006-2010 5-year est.); Median year structure built: 1952 (2006-2010 5-year est.).
Safety: Violent crime rate: 3.6 per 10,000 population; Property crime rate: 128.3 per 10,000 population (2011).
Transportation: Commute to work: 94.6% car, 1.6% public transportation, 1.9% walk, 2.0% work from home (2006-2010 5-year est.); Travel time to work: 40.7% less than 15 minutes, 42.3% 15 to 30 minutes, 13.6% 30 to 45 minutes, 1.6% 45 to 60 minutes, 1.9% 60 minutes or more (2006-2010 5-year est.)
Additional Information Contacts
Borough of Old Forge . . . . (570) 457-8852
   http://oldforgeborough.com
Greater Northeast Chamber of Commerce . . . . (570) 457-1130
   http://www.gnecc.com

OLYPHANT (borough). Covers a land area of 5.437 square miles and a water area of 0.064 square miles. Located at 41.45° N. Lat; 75.58° W. Long. Elevation is 784 feet.
History: Settled 1858, incorporated 1877.
Population: 5,222 (1990); 4,978 (2000); 5,151 (2010); Density: 947.4 persons per square mile (2010); Race: 96.2% White, 1.6% Black, 0.3% Asian, 0.1% American Indian/Alaska Native, 0.0% Native Hawaiian/Other Pacific Islander, 1.8% Other, 3.4% Hispanic of any race (2010); Average household size: 2.22 (2010); Median age: 42.6 (2010); Males per 100 females: 91.9 (2010); Marriage status: 24.9% never married, 55.5% now married, 6.7% widowed, 12.9% divorced (2006-2010 5-year est.); Foreign born: 0.8% (2006-2010 5-year est.); Ancestry (includes multiple ancestries): 24.1% Polish, 23.1% Irish, 17.7% Italian, 11.0% Welsh, 9.1% German (2006-2010 5-year est.).
Economy: Single-family building permits issued: 6 (2011); Multi-family building permits issued: 0 (2011); Employment by occupation: 5.1% management, 2.2% professional, 11.4% services, 22.9% sales, 5.1% farming, 4.8% construction, 5.5% production (2006-2010 5-year est.).
Income: Per capita income: $21,154 (2006-2010 5-year est.); Median household income: $48,361 (2006-2010 5-year est.); Average household income: $51,737 (2006-2010 5-year est.); Percent of households with income of $100,000 or more: 10.9% (2006-2010 5-year est.); Poverty rate: 15.4% (2006-2010 5-year est.).
Education: Percent of population age 25 and over with: High school diploma (including GED) or higher: 85.8% (2006-2010 5-year est.); Bachelor's degree or higher: 16.1% (2006-2010 5-year est.); Master's degree or higher: 3.4% (2006-2010 5-year est.).
Housing: Homeownership rate: 63.9% (2010); Median home value: $121,100 (2006-2010 5-year est.); Median contract rent: $472 per month (2006-2010 5-year est.); Median year structure built: 1946 (2006-2010 5-year est.).
Safety: Violent crime rate: 5.8 per 10,000 population; Property crime rate: 65.8 per 10,000 population (2011).
Transportation: Commute to work: 96.4% car, 1.4% public transportation, 1.2% walk, 1.0% work from home (2006-2010 5-year est.); Travel time to work: 40.9% less than 15 minutes, 43.2% 15 to 30 minutes, 11.7% 30 to 45 minutes, 3.1% 45 to 60 minutes, 1.2% 60 minutes or more (2006-2010 5-year est.)
Additional Information Contacts
Greater Scranton Chamber of Commerce . . . . (570) 342-7711
   http://www.scrantonchamber.com

PECKVILLE (unincorporated postal area)
Zip Code: 18452
   Covers a land area of 1.966 square miles and a water area of 0 square miles. Located at 41.48° N. Lat; 75.59° W. Long. Elevation is 830 feet. Population: 4,802 (2010); Density: 2,441.3 persons per square mile (2010); Race: 96.5% White, 1.1% Black, 0.7% Asian, 0.2% American Indian/Alaska Native, 0.0% Native Hawaiian/Other Pacific Islander, 1.5% Other, 2.0% Hispanic of any race (2010); Average household size: 2.21 (2010); Median age: 47.3 (2010); Males per 100 females: 85.7 (2010); Homeownership rate: 71.0% (2010)

RANSOM (township). Covers a land area of 17.699 square miles and a water area of 0.323 square miles. Located at 41.40° N. Lat; 75.77° W. Long. Elevation is 623 feet.
Population: 1,608 (1990); 1,429 (2000); 1,420 (2010); Density: 80.2 persons per square mile (2010); Race: 97.3% White, 1.1% Black, 0.4% Asian, 0.0% American Indian/Alaska Native, 0.0% Native Hawaiian/Other Pacific Islander, 1.2% Other, 0.4% Hispanic of any race (2010); Average household size: 2.52 (2010); Median age: 45.4 (2010); Males per 100 females: 100.8 (2010); Marriage status: 28.4% never married, 55.9% now married, 6.7% widowed, 9.0% divorced (2006-2010 5-year est.); Foreign born: 1.1% (2006-2010 5-year est.); Ancestry (includes multiple ancestries): 29.4% German, 18.6% Irish, 17.0% Italian, 15.2% Polish, 13.7% English (2006-2010 5-year est.).

Economy: Single-family building permits issued: 0 (2011); Multi-family building permits issued: 0 (2011); Employment by occupation: 9.5% management, 2.9% professional, 12.2% services, 12.3% sales, 2.4% farming, 13.5% construction, 7.8% production (2006-2010 5-year est.).
Income: Per capita income: $24,403 (2006-2010 5-year est.); Median household income: $52,448 (2006-2010 5-year est.); Average household income: $63,292 (2006-2010 5-year est.); Percent of households with income of $100,000 or more: 16.4% (2006-2010 5-year est.); Poverty rate: 8.1% (2006-2010 5-year est.).
Education: Percent of population age 25 and over with: High school diploma (including GED) or higher: 91.5% (2006-2010 5-year est.); Bachelor's degree or higher: 14.2% (2006-2010 5-year est.); Master's degree or higher: 7.0% (2006-2010 5-year est.).
Housing: Homeownership rate: 85.0% (2010); Median home value: $171,800 (2006-2010 5-year est.); Median contract rent: $590 per month (2006-2010 5-year est.); Median year structure built: 1973 (2006-2010 5-year est.).
Transportation: Commute to work: 90.3% car, 1.0% public transportation, 2.2% walk, 3.8% work from home (2006-2010 5-year est.); Travel time to work: 19.0% less than 15 minutes, 50.3% 15 to 30 minutes, 20.5% 30 to 45 minutes, 4.4% 45 to 60 minutes, 5.9% 60 minutes or more (2006-2010 5-year est.)

Additional Information Contacts
Greater Scranton Chamber of Commerce . . . . (570) 342-7711
    http://www.scrantonchamber.com

ROARING BROOK (township). Covers a land area of 21.416 square miles and a water area of 0.452 square miles. Located at 41.38° N. Lat; 75.58° W. Long.
Population: 1,930 (1990); 1,637 (2000); 1,907 (2010); Density: 89.0 persons per square mile (2010); Race: 98.0% White, 0.5% Black, 0.7% Asian, 0.0% American Indian/Alaska Native, 0.1% Native Hawaiian/Other Pacific Islander, 0.7% Other, 1.0% Hispanic of any race (2010); Average household size: 2.61 (2010); Median age: 44.5 (2010); Males per 100 females: 101.8 (2010); Marriage status: 19.2% never married, 64.7% now married, 8.2% widowed, 8.0% divorced (2006-2010 5-year est.); Foreign born: 3.7% (2006-2010 5-year est.); Ancestry (includes multiple ancestries): 33.8% Irish, 27.7% Italian, 25.7% German, 17.8% Polish, 8.2% Welsh (2006-2010 5-year est.).
Economy: Single-family building permits issued: 12 (2011); Multi-family building permits issued: 0 (2011); Employment by occupation: 11.9% management, 6.5% professional, 10.1% services, 12.4% sales, 3.9% farming, 10.0% construction, 8.7% production (2006-2010 5-year est.).
Income: Per capita income: $30,132 (2006-2010 5-year est.); Median household income: $69,583 (2006-2010 5-year est.); Average household income: $75,745 (2006-2010 5-year est.); Percent of households with income of $100,000 or more: 24.5% (2006-2010 5-year est.); Poverty rate: 3.5% (2006-2010 5-year est.).
Education: Percent of population age 25 and over with: High school diploma (including GED) or higher: 95.6% (2006-2010 5-year est.); Bachelor's degree or higher: 35.6% (2006-2010 5-year est.); Master's degree or higher: 17.0% (2006-2010 5-year est.).
Housing: Homeownership rate: 94.7% (2010); Median home value: $199,300 (2006-2010 5-year est.); Median contract rent: $575 per month (2006-2010 5-year est.); Median year structure built: 1971 (2006-2010 5-year est.).
Transportation: Commute to work: 92.2% car, 2.1% public transportation, 0.0% walk, 5.7% work from home (2006-2010 5-year est.); Travel time to work: 25.6% less than 15 minutes, 46.7% 15 to 30 minutes, 19.0% 30 to 45 minutes, 3.0% 45 to 60 minutes, 5.8% 60 minutes or more (2006-2010 5-year est.)

Additional Information Contacts
Greater Scranton Chamber of Commerce . . . . (570) 342-7711
    http://www.scrantonchamber.com

SCOTT (township). Covers a land area of 27.204 square miles and a water area of 0.369 square miles. Located at 41.54° N. Lat; 75.63° W. Long. Elevation is 1,145 feet.
Population: 5,350 (1990); 4,931 (2000); 4,905 (2010); Density: 180.3 persons per square mile (2010); Race: 97.5% White, 0.5% Black, 0.5% Asian, 0.1% American Indian/Alaska Native, 0.0% Native Hawaiian/Other Pacific Islander, 1.4% Other, 1.0% Hispanic of any race (2010); Average household size: 2.48 (2010); Median age: 46.5 (2010); Males per 100 females: 101.1 (2010); Marriage status: 23.3% never married, 61.5% now married, 5.7% widowed, 9.6% divorced (2006-2010 5-year est.); Foreign

born: 3.7% (2006-2010 5-year est.); Ancestry (includes multiple ancestries): 25.1% Polish, 24.4% Irish, 16.9% Italian, 16.4% German, 9.6% Welsh (2006-2010 5-year est.).
Economy: Single-family building permits issued: 11 (2011); Multi-family building permits issued: 0 (2011); Employment by occupation: 12.7% management, 7.4% professional, 12.1% services, 11.6% sales, 4.8% farming, 5.6% construction, 6.0% production (2006-2010 5-year est.).
Income: Per capita income: $31,557 (2006-2010 5-year est.); Median household income: $53,520 (2006-2010 5-year est.); Average household income: $71,007 (2006-2010 5-year est.); Percent of households with income of $100,000 or more: 24.7% (2006-2010 5-year est.); Poverty rate: 6.1% (2006-2010 5-year est.).
Education: Percent of population age 25 and over with: High school diploma (including GED) or higher: 92.0% (2006-2010 5-year est.); Bachelor's degree or higher: 26.8% (2006-2010 5-year est.); Master's degree or higher: 11.3% (2006-2010 5-year est.).
Housing: Homeownership rate: 85.9% (2010); Median home value: $184,800 (2006-2010 5-year est.); Median contract rent: $499 per month (2006-2010 5-year est.); Median year structure built: 1969 (2006-2010 5-year est.).
Safety: Violent crime rate: 8.1 per 10,000 population; Property crime rate: 36.6 per 10,000 population (2011).
Transportation: Commute to work: 86.4% car, 0.4% public transportation, 2.6% walk, 10.2% work from home (2006-2010 5-year est.); Travel time to work: 28.3% less than 15 minutes, 51.9% 15 to 30 minutes, 9.5% 30 to 45 minutes, 6.3% 45 to 60 minutes, 4.0% 60 minutes or more (2006-2010 5-year est.)

Additional Information Contacts
Greater Scranton Chamber of Commerce . . . . (570) 342-7711
    http://www.scrantonchamber.com

SCRANTON (city). County seat. Covers a land area of 25.309 square miles and a water area of 0.229 square miles. Located at 41.40° N. Lat; 75.67° W. Long. Elevation is 755 feet.
History: Until 1771, the Munsee people, under Chief Capoose, lived in the Scranton area. About the middle of the 18th century, other settlers arrived. Ebenezer and Benjamin Slocum, who came about 1800, named the settlement Unionville. In 1816, they changed the name to Slocum Hollow. In 1840 two other brothers, George and Selden Scranton, arrived from New Jersey. They organized the firm of Scranton, Grant, and Company, and built a forge. In 1845, the Scrantons named the place Harrison in honor of President William Henry Harrison. A post office was established in 1850, under the name Scrantonia. It was soon simplified to Scranton. Iron, coal mines, and the railroad insured Scranton's growth.
Population: 81,805 (1990); 76,415 (2000); 76,089 (2010); Density: 3,006.4 persons per square mile (2010); Race: 84.1% White, 5.5% Black, 3.0% Asian, 0.2% American Indian/Alaska Native, 0.0% Native Hawaiian/Other Pacific Islander, 7.2% Other, 9.9% Hispanic of any race (2010); Average household size: 2.35 (2010); Median age: 37.9 (2010); Males per 100 females: 92.9 (2010); Marriage status: 39.0% never married, 41.6% now married, 9.7% widowed, 9.8% divorced (2006-2010 5-year est.); Foreign born: 6.2% (2006-2010 5-year est.); Ancestry (includes multiple ancestries): 30.6% Irish, 21.1% Italian, 19.1% German, 14.4% Polish, 6.0% Welsh (2006-2010 5-year est.).
Economy: Unemployment rate: 10.0% (August 2012); Total civilian labor force: 37,533 (August 2012); Single-family building permits issued: 14 (2011); Multi-family building permits issued: 0 (2011); Employment by occupation: 7.5% management, 2.0% professional, 13.5% services, 19.5% sales, 4.4% farming, 7.9% construction, 6.7% production (2006-2010 5-year est.).
Income: Per capita income: $19,068 (2006-2010 5-year est.); Median household income: $35,606 (2006-2010 5-year est.); Average household income: $46,619 (2006-2010 5-year est.); Percent of households with income of $100,000 or more: 9.1% (2006-2010 5-year est.); Poverty rate: 18.8% (2006-2010 5-year est.).
Taxes: Total city taxes per capita: $642 (2009); City property taxes per capita: $197 (2009).
Education: Percent of population age 25 and over with: High school diploma (including GED) or higher: 83.1% (2006-2010 5-year est.); Bachelor's degree or higher: 18.6% (2006-2010 5-year est.); Master's degree or higher: 6.6% (2006-2010 5-year est.).

School District(s)
Ctc of Lackawanna County (10-12)
    2010-11 Enrollment: n/a . . . . (570) 346-8471

Scranton SD (PK-12)
    2010-11 Enrollment: 9,679 . . . . (570) 348-3400
Four-year College(s)
Marywood University (Private, Not-for-profit, Roman Catholic)
    Fall 2010 Enrollment: 3,226 . . . . (570) 348-6211
    2011-12 Tuition: In-state $28,175; Out-of-state $28,175
The Commonwealth Medical College (Private, Not-for-profit)
    Fall 2010 Enrollment: 419 . . . . (570) 504-7000
University of Scranton (Private, Not-for-profit, Roman Catholic)
    Fall 2010 Enrollment: 5,570 . . . . (570) 941-7400
    2011-12 Tuition: In-state $35,992; Out-of-state $35,992
Yeshivath Beth Moshe (Private, Not-for-profit, Jewish)
    Fall 2010 Enrollment: 77 . . . . (570) 346-1747
    2011-12 Tuition: In-state $7,600; Out-of-state $7,600
Two-year College(s)
Fortis Institute-Scranton (Private, For-profit)
    Fall 2010 Enrollment: 303 . . . . (570) 558-1818
    2011-12 Tuition: In-state $24,190; Out-of-state $24,190
Johnson College (Private, Not-for-profit)
    Fall 2010 Enrollment: 464 . . . . (570) 342-6404
    2011-12 Tuition: In-state $16,462; Out-of-state $16,462
Lackawanna College (Private, Not-for-profit)
    Fall 2010 Enrollment: 1,462 . . . . (570) 961-7810
    2011-12 Tuition: In-state $11,780; Out-of-state $11,780
Vocational/Technical School(s)
Career Technology Center of Lackawanna County (Public)
    Fall 2010 Enrollment: 169 . . . . (570) 346-8728
    2011-12 Tuition: $10,325
Housing: Homeownership rate: 51.3% (2010); Median home value: $106,300 (2006-2010 5-year est.); Median contract rent: $474 per month (2006-2010 5-year est.); Median year structure built: before 1940 (2006-2010 5-year est.).
Hospitals: Allied Services Rehabilitation Hospital (117 beds); Community Medical Center (299 beds); Mercy Hospital (373 beds); Moses Taylor Hospital (224 beds)
Safety: Violent crime rate: 29.6 per 10,000 population; Property crime rate: 334.9 per 10,000 population (2011).
Newspapers: The Catholic Light (Regional news; Circulation 48,500); Rola Boza (Local news; Circulation 6,000); The Scranton Times (Local news; Circulation 28,991); Straz (Local news; Circulation 10,500); Suburban Weekly (Community news; Circulation 7,000); The Sunday Times (Community news); Triboro Banner (Community news; Circulation 6,000); The Tribune (Local news; Circulation 72,550); The Valley Advantage (Community news)
Transportation: Commute to work: 87.9% car, 2.5% public transportation, 7.3% walk, 1.4% work from home (2006-2010 5-year est.); Travel time to work: 49.2% less than 15 minutes, 34.7% 15 to 30 minutes, 9.9% 30 to 45 minutes, 2.6% 45 to 60 minutes, 3.6% 60 minutes or more (2006-2010 5-year est.)
Airports: Wilkes-Barre/Scranton International (primary service)
Additional Information Contacts
City of Scranton . . . . (570) 348-4100
    http://www.scrantonpa.gov
Greater Scranton Chamber of Commerce . . . . (570) 342-7711
    http://www.scrantonchamber.com

SIMPSON (CDP). Covers a land area of 0.883 square miles and a water area of 0.006 square miles. Located at 41.60° N. Lat; 75.48° W. Long. Elevation is 1,138 feet.
Population: n/a (1990); n/a (2000); 1,275 (2010); Density: 1,443.8 persons per square mile (2010); Race: 95.5% White, 0.9% Black, 0.5% Asian, 0.4% American Indian/Alaska Native, 0.0% Native Hawaiian/Other Pacific Islander, 2.7% Other, 3.4% Hispanic of any race (2010); Average household size: 2.24 (2010); Median age: 40.3 (2010); Males per 100 females: 100.8 (2010); Marriage status: 33.2% never married, 50.6% now married, 7.2% widowed, 9.0% divorced (2006-2010 5-year est.); Foreign born: 2.0% (2006-2010 5-year est.); Ancestry (includes multiple ancestries): 27.5% Polish, 22.7% Irish, 21.2% Italian, 11.6% German, 10.3% English (2006-2010 5-year est.).
Economy: Employment by occupation: 6.9% management, 2.9% professional, 15.6% services, 15.9% sales, 5.9% farming, 9.2% construction, 8.7% production (2006-2010 5-year est.).
Income: Per capita income: $16,889 (2006-2010 5-year est.); Median household income: $34,188 (2006-2010 5-year est.); Average household income: $40,351 (2006-2010 5-year est.); Percent of households with

income of $100,000 or more: 4.1% (2006-2010 5-year est.); Poverty rate: 13.6% (2006-2010 5-year est.).
Education: Percent of population age 25 and over with: High school diploma (including GED) or higher: 86.4% (2006-2010 5-year est.); Bachelor's degree or higher: 10.7% (2006-2010 5-year est.); Master's degree or higher: 3.0% (2006-2010 5-year est.).
School District(s)
Fell CS (KG-09)
    2010-11 Enrollment: 159 . . . . (570) 282-5199
Housing: Homeownership rate: 60.1% (2010); Median home value: $86,200 (2006-2010 5-year est.); Median contract rent: $470 per month (2006-2010 5-year est.); Median year structure built: before 1940 (2006-2010 5-year est.).
Transportation: Commute to work: 94.5% car, 0.0% public transportation, 4.8% walk, 0.7% work from home (2006-2010 5-year est.); Travel time to work: 44.6% less than 15 minutes, 35.8% 15 to 30 minutes, 15.2% 30 to 45 minutes, 3.0% 45 to 60 minutes, 1.3% 60 minutes or more (2006-2010 5-year est.)

SOUTH ABINGTON (township). Covers a land area of 9.111 square miles and a water area of 0.138 square miles. Located at 41.49° N. Lat; 75.69° W. Long.
History: South Abington Township was created in 1867 when the larger Abington region was split into north and south parcels. The boroughs of Clarks Summit and Clarks Green (which are surrounded by South Abington) were later carved out of this southern region of the Abingtons. The town is sometimes referenced to as Chinchilla.
Population: 6,539 (1990); 8,638 (2000); 9,073 (2010); Density: 995.8 persons per square mile (2010); Race: 93.6% White, 1.3% Black, 3.4% Asian, 0.1% American Indian/Alaska Native, 0.0% Native Hawaiian/Other Pacific Islander, 1.6% Other, 1.9% Hispanic of any race (2010); Average household size: 2.51 (2010); Median age: 42.2 (2010); Males per 100 females: 91.0 (2010); Marriage status: 25.4% never married, 52.8% now married, 13.9% widowed, 8.0% divorced (2006-2010 5-year est.); Foreign born: 8.0% (2006-2010 5-year est.); Ancestry (includes multiple ancestries): 23.7% Irish, 20.5% German, 16.4% Italian, 13.4% Polish, 10.8% English (2006-2010 5-year est.).
Economy: Single-family building permits issued: 7 (2011); Multi-family building permits issued: 4 (2011); Employment by occupation: 14.8% management, 5.8% professional, 5.3% services, 13.6% sales, 3.1% farming, 5.2% construction, 4.2% production (2006-2010 5-year est.).
Income: Per capita income: $32,935 (2006-2010 5-year est.); Median household income: $75,703 (2006-2010 5-year est.); Average household income: $93,730 (2006-2010 5-year est.); Percent of households with income of $100,000 or more: 39.2% (2006-2010 5-year est.); Poverty rate: 2.8% (2006-2010 5-year est.).
Education: Percent of population age 25 and over with: High school diploma (including GED) or higher: 92.1% (2006-2010 5-year est.); Bachelor's degree or higher: 45.3% (2006-2010 5-year est.); Master's degree or higher: 21.8% (2006-2010 5-year est.).
Housing: Homeownership rate: 76.5% (2010); Median home value: $212,400 (2006-2010 5-year est.); Median contract rent: $877 per month (2006-2010 5-year est.); Median year structure built: 1979 (2006-2010 5-year est.).
Safety: Violent crime rate: 0.0 per 10,000 population; Property crime rate: 101.1 per 10,000 population (2011).
Transportation: Commute to work: 94.3% car, 0.0% public transportation, 2.6% walk, 2.6% work from home (2006-2010 5-year est.); Travel time to work: 30.1% less than 15 minutes, 49.2% 15 to 30 minutes, 13.5% 30 to 45 minutes, 4.5% 45 to 60 minutes, 2.8% 60 minutes or more (2006-2010 5-year est.)
Additional Information Contacts
Greater Scranton Chamber of Commerce . . . . (570) 342-7711
    http://www.scrantonchamber.com
South Abington Township . . . . (570) 586-2111
    http://134.198.33.115/southabington

SPRING BROOK (township). Covers a land area of 34.323 square miles and a water area of 0.597 square miles. Located at 41.31° N. Lat; 75.63° W. Long. Elevation is 1,621 feet.
Population: 2,097 (1990); 2,367 (2000); 2,768 (2010); Density: 80.6 persons per square mile (2010); Race: 97.4% White, 0.4% Black, 0.7% Asian, 0.1% American Indian/Alaska Native, 0.0% Native Hawaiian/Other Pacific Islander, 1.4% Other, 1.6% Hispanic of any race (2010); Average household size: 2.54 (2010); Median age: 43.2 (2010); Males per 100

females: 100.7 (2010); Marriage status: 23.3% never married, 64.0% now married, 7.6% widowed, 5.1% divorced (2006-2010 5-year est.); Foreign born: 2.5% (2006-2010 5-year est.); Ancestry (includes multiple ancestries): 33.1% German, 28.6% Italian, 26.5% Irish, 18.1% Polish, 6.6% Welsh (2006-2010 5-year est.).

Economy: Single-family building permits issued: 4 (2011); Multi-family building permits issued: 0 (2011); Employment by occupation: 9.8% management, 5.8% professional, 4.8% services, 25.1% sales, 2.2% farming, 8.2% construction, 8.0% production (2006-2010 5-year est.).

Income: Per capita income: $26,934 (2006-2010 5-year est.); Median household income: $74,821 (2006-2010 5-year est.); Average household income: $71,630 (2006-2010 5-year est.); Percent of households with income of $100,000 or more: 22.1% (2006-2010 5-year est.); Poverty rate: 1.5% (2006-2010 5-year est.).

Education: Percent of population age 25 and over with: High school diploma (including GED) or higher: 89.1% (2006-2010 5-year est.); Bachelor's degree or higher: 20.8% (2006-2010 5-year est.); Master's degree or higher: 6.4% (2006-2010 5-year est.).

Housing: Homeownership rate: 84.0% (2010); Median home value: $178,100 (2006-2010 5-year est.); Median contract rent: $527 per month (2006-2010 5-year est.); Median year structure built: 1976 (2006-2010 5-year est.).

Transportation: Commute to work: 94.7% car, 0.0% public transportation, 0.5% walk, 4.8% work from home (2006-2010 5-year est.); Travel time to work: 20.7% less than 15 minutes, 54.3% 15 to 30 minutes, 10.2% 30 to 45 minutes, 7.5% 45 to 60 minutes, 7.3% 60 minutes or more (2006-2010 5-year est.)

Additional Information Contacts
Greater Scranton Chamber of Commerce . . . . (570) 342-7711
   http://www.scrantonchamber.com

TAYLOR (borough). Covers a land area of 5.202 square miles and a water area of 0 square miles. Located at 41.40° N. Lat; 75.71° W. Long. Elevation is 722 feet.

History: Anthracite Museum to North. Settled c.1800.

Population: 6,941 (1990); 6,475 (2000); 6,263 (2010); Density: 1,204.0 persons per square mile (2010); Race: 94.5% White, 1.0% Black, 0.6% Asian, 0.1% American Indian/Alaska Native, 0.0% Native Hawaiian/Other Pacific Islander, 3.8% Other, 5.3% Hispanic of any race (2010); Average household size: 2.33 (2010); Median age: 44.6 (2010); Males per 100 females: 89.7 (2010); Marriage status: 30.6% never married, 48.4% now married, 10.8% widowed, 10.2% divorced (2006-2010 5-year est.); Foreign born: 0.0% (2006-2010 5-year est.); Ancestry (includes multiple ancestries): 27.2% Polish, 22.4% Italian, 20.4% German, 20.3% Irish, 10.9% English (2006-2010 5-year est.).

Economy: Single-family building permits issued: 3 (2011); Multi-family building permits issued: 3 (2011); Employment by occupation: 6.3% management, 2.2% professional, 11.4% services, 20.4% sales, 8.1% farming, 6.2% construction, 6.4% production (2006-2010 5-year est.).

Income: Per capita income: $19,807 (2006-2010 5-year est.); Median household income: $36,903 (2006-2010 5-year est.); Average household income: $44,462 (2006-2010 5-year est.); Percent of households with income of $100,000 or more: 5.5% (2006-2010 5-year est.); Poverty rate: 16.8% (2006-2010 5-year est.).

Education: Percent of population age 25 and over with: High school diploma (including GED) or higher: 86.4% (2006-2010 5-year est.); Bachelor's degree or higher: 14.8% (2006-2010 5-year est.); Master's degree or higher: 5.6% (2006-2010 5-year est.).

School District(s)
Riverside SD (KG-12)
   2010-11 Enrollment: 1,556 . . . . (570) 562-2121

Housing: Homeownership rate: 65.3% (2010); Median home value: $100,400 (2006-2010 5-year est.); Median contract rent: $486 per month (2006-2010 5-year est.); Median year structure built: 1942 (2006-2010 5-year est.).

Safety: Violent crime rate: 50.9 per 10,000 population; Property crime rate: 291.3 per 10,000 population (2011).

Transportation: Commute to work: 93.3% car, 0.9% public transportation, 2.2% walk, 1.9% work from home (2006-2010 5-year est.); Travel time to work: 40.2% less than 15 minutes, 43.1% 15 to 30 minutes, 6.7% 30 to 45 minutes, 4.1% 45 to 60 minutes, 5.9% 60 minutes or more (2006-2010 5-year est.)

Additional Information Contacts
Borough of Taylor . . . . (570) 562-1400
   http://www.taylorborough.com

Greater Scranton Chamber of Commerce . . . . (570) 342-7711
   http://www.scrantonchamber.com

THORNHURST (township). Covers a land area of 22.883 square miles and a water area of 0.236 square miles. Located at 41.21° N. Lat; 75.61° W. Long. Elevation is 1,545 feet.

Population: 486 (1990); 798 (2000); 1,085 (2010); Density: 47.4 persons per square mile (2010); Race: 95.9% White, 1.3% Black, 0.7% Asian, 0.2% American Indian/Alaska Native, 0.0% Native Hawaiian/Other Pacific Islander, 1.9% Other, 3.6% Hispanic of any race (2010); Average household size: 2.52 (2010); Median age: 42.5 (2010); Males per 100 females: 106.7 (2010); Marriage status: 33.4% never married, 50.4% now married, 4.0% widowed, 12.2% divorced (2006-2010 5-year est.); Foreign born: 3.5% (2006-2010 5-year est.); Ancestry (includes multiple ancestries): 19.7% Irish, 19.0% Polish, 16.1% German, 12.4% American, 11.2% Italian (2006-2010 5-year est.).

Economy: Single-family building permits issued: 1 (2011); Multi-family building permits issued: 0 (2011); Employment by occupation: 14.8% management, 1.4% professional, 8.7% services, 13.4% sales, 5.3% farming, 14.0% construction, 10.9% production (2006-2010 5-year est.).

Income: Per capita income: $26,859 (2006-2010 5-year est.); Median household income: $47,083 (2006-2010 5-year est.); Average household income: $65,610 (2006-2010 5-year est.); Percent of households with income of $100,000 or more: 17.2% (2006-2010 5-year est.); Poverty rate: 12.3% (2006-2010 5-year est.).

Education: Percent of population age 25 and over with: High school diploma (including GED) or higher: 88.7% (2006-2010 5-year est.); Bachelor's degree or higher: 17.3% (2006-2010 5-year est.); Master's degree or higher: 4.7% (2006-2010 5-year est.).

Housing: Homeownership rate: 89.8% (2010); Median home value: $148,700 (2006-2010 5-year est.); Median contract rent: $772 per month (2006-2010 5-year est.); Median year structure built: 1985 (2006-2010 5-year est.).

Transportation: Commute to work: 93.3% car, 0.8% public transportation, 2.0% walk, 3.9% work from home (2006-2010 5-year est.); Travel time to work: 2.1% less than 15 minutes, 32.5% 15 to 30 minutes, 36.9% 30 to 45 minutes, 6.8% 45 to 60 minutes, 21.7% 60 minutes or more (2006-2010 5-year est.)

Additional Information Contacts
Greater Scranton Chamber of Commerce . . . . (570) 342-7711
   http://www.scrantonchamber.com

THROOP (borough). Covers a land area of 4.968 square miles and a water area of 0 square miles. Located at 41.44° N. Lat; 75.59° W. Long. Elevation is 846 feet.

History: Formerly an anthracite coal-mining center.

Population: 4,070 (1990); 4,010 (2000); 4,088 (2010); Density: 822.9 persons per square mile (2010); Race: 96.0% White, 1.2% Black, 0.6% Asian, 0.2% American Indian/Alaska Native, 0.0% Native Hawaiian/Other Pacific Islander, 2.0% Other, 2.0% Hispanic of any race (2010); Average household size: 2.30 (2010); Median age: 42.4 (2010); Males per 100 females: 92.0 (2010); Marriage status: 34.1% never married, 46.7% now married, 9.6% widowed, 9.5% divorced (2006-2010 5-year est.); Foreign born: 0.6% (2006-2010 5-year est.); Ancestry (includes multiple ancestries): 35.9% Polish, 33.4% Italian, 16.3% Irish, 12.5% German, 10.0% Russian (2006-2010 5-year est.).

Economy: Single-family building permits issued: 4 (2011); Multi-family building permits issued: 0 (2011); Employment by occupation: 6.0% management, 2.6% professional, 11.3% services, 16.9% sales, 5.5% farming, 7.2% construction, 11.3% production (2006-2010 5-year est.).

Income: Per capita income: $20,576 (2006-2010 5-year est.); Median household income: $40,081 (2006-2010 5-year est.); Average household income: $47,352 (2006-2010 5-year est.); Percent of households with income of $100,000 or more: 7.9% (2006-2010 5-year est.); Poverty rate: 15.9% (2006-2010 5-year est.).

Education: Percent of population age 25 and over with: High school diploma (including GED) or higher: 87.0% (2006-2010 5-year est.); Bachelor's degree or higher: 17.6% (2006-2010 5-year est.); Master's degree or higher: 3.8% (2006-2010 5-year est.).

School District(s)
Mid Valley SD (KG-12)
   2010-11 Enrollment: 1,767 . . . . (570) 307-1108

Housing: Homeownership rate: 71.7% (2010); Median home value: $114,900 (2006-2010 5-year est.); Median contract rent: $497 per month

(2006-2010 5-year est.); Median year structure built: before 1940 (2006-2010 5-year est.).
Safety: Violent crime rate: 24.4 per 10,000 population; Property crime rate: 139.0 per 10,000 population (2011).
Transportation: Commute to work: 92.6% car, 0.0% public transportation, 3.7% walk, 3.7% work from home (2006-2010 5-year est.); Travel time to work: 50.1% less than 15 minutes, 32.2% 15 to 30 minutes, 12.5% 30 to 45 minutes, 2.3% 45 to 60 minutes, 2.8% 60 minutes or more (2006-2010 5-year est.)
Additional Information Contacts
Greater Scranton Chamber of Commerce . . . . (570) 342-7711
  http://www.scrantonchamber.com

VANDLING (borough). Covers a land area of 1.313 square miles and a water area of <.001 square miles. Located at 41.63° N. Lat; 75.47° W. Long. Elevation is 1,614 feet.
Population: 645 (1990); 738 (2000); 751 (2010); Density: 572.0 persons per square mile (2010); Race: 96.0% White, 1.3% Black, 0.3% Asian, 0.7% American Indian/Alaska Native, 0.0% Native Hawaiian/Other Pacific Islander, 1.7% Other, 2.1% Hispanic of any race (2010); Average household size: 2.43 (2010); Median age: 42.5 (2010); Males per 100 females: 93.6 (2010); Marriage status: 29.2% never married, 49.5% now married, 9.6% widowed, 11.7% divorced (2006-2010 5-year est.); Foreign born: 0.5% (2006-2010 5-year est.); Ancestry (includes multiple ancestries): 28.7% Italian, 26.3% Irish, 14.0% Polish, 12.3% Slovak, 10.0% English (2006-2010 5-year est.).
Economy: Single-family building permits issued: 0 (2011); Multi-family building permits issued: 0 (2011); Employment by occupation: 9.5% management, 4.8% professional, 12.9% services, 10.5% sales, 1.0% farming, 7.1% construction, 5.4% production (2006-2010 5-year est.).
Income: Per capita income: $24,272 (2006-2010 5-year est.); Median household income: $40,208 (2006-2010 5-year est.); Average household income: $49,060 (2006-2010 5-year est.); Percent of households with income of $100,000 or more: 9.1% (2006-2010 5-year est.); Poverty rate: 13.0% (2006-2010 5-year est.).
Education: Percent of population age 25 and over with: High school diploma (including GED) or higher: 86.8% (2006-2010 5-year est.); Bachelor's degree or higher: 16.2% (2006-2010 5-year est.); Master's degree or higher: 7.8% (2006-2010 5-year est.).
Housing: Homeownership rate: 74.7% (2010); Median home value: $127,800 (2006-2010 5-year est.); Median contract rent: $368 per month (2006-2010 5-year est.); Median year structure built: 1949 (2006-2010 5-year est.).
Safety: Violent crime rate: 0.0 per 10,000 population; Property crime rate: 26.6 per 10,000 population (2011).
Transportation: Commute to work: 96.2% car, 0.0% public transportation, 3.1% walk, 0.7% work from home (2006-2010 5-year est.); Travel time to work: 39.0% less than 15 minutes, 25.1% 15 to 30 minutes, 22.0% 30 to 45 minutes, 5.9% 45 to 60 minutes, 8.0% 60 minutes or more (2006-2010 5-year est.)

WAVERLY (CDP). Covers a land area of 1.567 square miles and a water area of 0.001 square miles. Located at 41.53° N. Lat; 75.70° W. Long. Elevation is 1,283 feet.
Population: n/a (1990); n/a (2000); 604 (2010); Density: 385.6 persons per square mile (2010); Race: 98.0% White, 0.5% Black, 0.5% Asian, 0.0% American Indian/Alaska Native, 0.0% Native Hawaiian/Other Pacific Islander, 1.0% Other, 2.3% Hispanic of any race (2010); Average household size: 2.67 (2010); Median age: 47.5 (2010); Males per 100 females: 91.7 (2010); Marriage status: 33.9% never married, 61.0% now married, 2.3% widowed, 2.8% divorced (2006-2010 5-year est.); Foreign born: 2.3% (2006-2010 5-year est.); Ancestry (includes multiple ancestries): 40.3% German, 27.7% Italian, 26.4% Irish, 14.5% Welsh, 11.9% Russian (2006-2010 5-year est.).
Economy: Employment by occupation: 19.5% management, 0.0% professional, 6.6% services, 15.4% sales, 5.5% farming, 13.6% construction, 6.3% production (2006-2010 5-year est.).
Income: Per capita income: $54,185 (2006-2010 5-year est.); Median household income: $124,167 (2006-2010 5-year est.); Average household income: $161,859 (2006-2010 5-year est.); Percent of households with income of $100,000 or more: 58.4% (2006-2010 5-year est.); Poverty rate: 6.0% (2006-2010 5-year est.).
Education: Percent of population age 25 and over with: High school diploma (including GED) or higher: 100.0% (2006-2010 5-year est.);

Bachelor's degree or higher: 61.8% (2006-2010 5-year est.); Master's degree or higher: 25.2% (2006-2010 5-year est.).
School District(s)
Abington Heights SD (KG-12)
  2010-11 Enrollment: 3,452 . . . . (570) 586-2511
Housing: Homeownership rate: 88.5% (2010); Median home value: $366,700 (2006-2010 5-year est.); Median contract rent: n/a per month (2006-2010 5-year est.); Median year structure built: before 1940 (2006-2010 5-year est.).
Transportation: Commute to work: 94.5% car, 0.0% public transportation, 0.0% walk, 5.5% work from home (2006-2010 5-year est.); Travel time to work: 37.4% less than 15 minutes, 52.1% 15 to 30 minutes, 1.6% 30 to 45 minutes, 8.9% 45 to 60 minutes, 0.0% 60 minutes or more (2006-2010 5-year est.)

WEST ABINGTON (township). Covers a land area of 5.550 square miles and a water area of 0.015 square miles. Located at 41.52° N. Lat; 75.77° W. Long.
Population: 281 (1990); 311 (2000); 250 (2010); Density: 45.0 persons per square mile (2010); Race: 99.2% White, 0.0% Black, 0.0% Asian, 0.0% American Indian/Alaska Native, 0.0% Native Hawaiian/Other Pacific Islander, 0.8% Other, 0.0% Hispanic of any race (2010); Average household size: 2.23 (2010); Median age: 49.2 (2010); Males per 100 females: 100.0 (2010); Marriage status: 20.5% never married, 58.9% now married, 10.8% widowed, 9.7% divorced (2006-2010 5-year est.); Foreign born: 0.0% (2006-2010 5-year est.); Ancestry (includes multiple ancestries): 29.8% German, 20.2% Polish, 17.9% Irish, 13.3% English, 8.3% Lithuanian (2006-2010 5-year est.).
Economy: Single-family building permits issued: 0 (2011); Multi-family building permits issued: 0 (2011); Employment by occupation: 11.6% management, 5.0% professional, 9.1% services, 11.6% sales, 3.3% farming, 9.9% construction, 5.0% production (2006-2010 5-year est.).
Income: Per capita income: $28,089 (2006-2010 5-year est.); Median household income: $46,875 (2006-2010 5-year est.); Average household income: $61,821 (2006-2010 5-year est.); Percent of households with income of $100,000 or more: 14.4% (2006-2010 5-year est.); Poverty rate: 9.2% (2006-2010 5-year est.).
Education: Percent of population age 25 and over with: High school diploma (including GED) or higher: 94.5% (2006-2010 5-year est.); Bachelor's degree or higher: 30.9% (2006-2010 5-year est.); Master's degree or higher: 10.5% (2006-2010 5-year est.).
Housing: Homeownership rate: 87.5% (2010); Median home value: $180,200 (2006-2010 5-year est.); Median contract rent: n/a per month (2006-2010 5-year est.); Median year structure built: 1964 (2006-2010 5-year est.).
Transportation: Commute to work: 94.1% car, 0.0% public transportation, 1.7% walk, 4.2% work from home (2006-2010 5-year est.); Travel time to work: 16.7% less than 15 minutes, 45.6% 15 to 30 minutes, 25.4% 30 to 45 minutes, 6.1% 45 to 60 minutes, 6.1% 60 minutes or more (2006-2010 5-year est.)

Lancaster County

Located in southeastern Pennsylvania; bounded on the west by the Susquehanna River. Covers a land area of 943.810 square miles, a water area of 39.993 square miles, and is located in the Eastern Time Zone at 40.04° N. Lat., 76.25° W. Long. The county was founded in 1729. County seat is Lancaster.

Lancaster County is part of the Lancaster, PA Metropolitan Statistical Area. The entire metro area includes: Lancaster County, PA

Weather Station: Lancaster 2 NE Filt Plant   Elevation: 270 feet

	Jan	Feb	Mar	Apr	May	Jun	Jul	Aug	Sep	Oct	Nov	Dec
High	38	42	51	63	73	81	85	84	77	65	54	43
Low	22	24	31	41	50	60	64	63	55	43	35	27
Precip	2.9	2.4	3.4	3.4	3.9	4.1	4.4	3.2	4.4	3.9	3.6	3.2
Snow	6.5	6.1	2.1	0.4	0.0	0.0	0.0	0.0	0.0	0.0	0.4	2.9

High and Low temperatures in degrees Fahrenheit; Precipitation and Snow in inches

Weather Station: Landisville 2 NW   Elevation: 359 feet

	Jan	Feb	Mar	Apr	May	Jun	Jul	Aug	Sep	Oct	Nov	Dec
High	39	42	52	64	74	82	86	85	78	66	55	43
Low	21	23	30	39	49	59	62	61	53	42	34	25
Precip	2.8	2.4	3.4	3.5	4.1	4.1	4.6	3.6	4.2	3.6	3.7	3.1
Snow	8.0	7.5	3.8	0.5	0.0	0.0	0.0	0.0	0.0	0.0	0.6	3.9

High and Low temperatures in degrees Fahrenheit; Precipitation and Snow in inches

Weather Station: Octoraro Lake | | | | | | | Elevation: 259 feet

	Jan	Feb	Mar	Apr	May	Jun	Jul	Aug	Sep	Oct	Nov	Dec
High	40	44	53	65	75	83	87	86	78	67	55	44
Low	20	22	29	38	48	57	62	61	53	41	33	24
Precip	3.3	2.7	3.9	3.8	4.1	3.9	4.1	3.9	4.8	3.7	3.7	3.7
Snow	4.1	6.2	1.2	0.2	0.0	0.0	0.0	0.0	0.0	0.0	0.3	2.5

High and Low temperatures in degrees Fahrenheit; Precipitation and Snow in inches

Population: 422,822 (1990); 470,658 (2000); 519,445 (2010); Race: 88.6% White, 3.7% Black, 1.9% Asian, 0.2% American Indian/Alaska Native, 0.0% Native Hawaiian/Other Pacific Islander, 5.6% Other, 8.6% Hispanic of any race (2010); Density: 550.4 persons per square mile (2010); Average household size: 2.62 (2010); Median age: 38.2 (2010); Males per 100 females: 95.6 (2010).
Religion: Six largest groups: 10.3% European Free-Church, 9.9% Catholicism, 8.3% Non-Denominational, 6.9% Methodist/Pietist, 4.4% Lutheran, 4.1% Presbyterian-Reformed (2010)
Economy: Unemployment rate: 6.8% (August 2012); Total civilian labor force: 274,381 (August 2012); Leading industries: 16.4% health care and social assistance; 16.4% manufacturing; 14.7% retail trade (2010); Farms: 5,462 totaling 425,336 acres (2007); Companies that employ 500 or more persons: 30 (2010); Companies that employ 100 to 499 persons: 293 (2010); Companies that employ less than 100 persons: 11,720 (2010); Black-owned businesses: 743 (2007); Hispanic-owned businesses: 901 (2007); Asian-owned businesses: 1,005 (2007); Women-owned businesses: 11,942 (2007); Retail sales per capita: $13,675 (2010). Single-family building permits issued: 731 (2011); Multi-family building permits issued: 473 (2011).
Income: Per capita income: $25,854 (2006-2010 5-year est.); Median household income: $54,765 (2006-2010 5-year est.); Average household income: $68,049 (2006-2010 5-year est.); Percent of households with income of $100,000 or more: 18.4% (2006-2010 5-year est.); Poverty rate: 9.7% (2006-2010 5-year est.); Bankruptcy rate: 2.03% (2011).
Taxes: Total county taxes per capita: $205 (2009); County property taxes per capita: $205 (2009).
Education: Percent of population age 25 and over with: High school diploma (including GED) or higher: 82.3% (2006-2010 5-year est.); Bachelor's degree or higher: 23.3% (2006-2010 5-year est.); Master's degree or higher: 7.8% (2006-2010 5-year est.).
Housing: Homeownership rate: 68.6% (2010); Median home value: $184,400 (2006-2010 5-year est.); Median contract rent: $648 per month (2006-2010 5-year est.); Median year structure built: 1972 (2006-2010 5-year est.)
Health: Birth rate: 136.4 per 10,000 population (2011); Death rate: 86.2 per 10,000 population (2011); Age-adjusted cancer mortality rate: 172.4 deaths per 100,000 population (2009); Number of physicians: 21.0 per 10,000 population (2010); Hospital beds: 22.1 per 10,000 population (2008); Hospital admissions: 1,057.5 per 10,000 population (2008).
Environment: Air Quality Index: 57.8% good, 38.6% moderate, 3.6% unhealthy for sensitive individuals, 0.0% unhealthy (percent of days in 2011)
Elections: 2012 Presidential election results: 39.7% Obama, 58.9% Romney
National and State Parks: Susquehannock State Park
Additional Information Contacts
Lancaster County Government . . . . (717) 299-8000
  http://www.co.lancaster.pa.us
Southern Lancaster County Chamber of Commerce . . . . . (610) 608-1240
  http://www.southernlancasterchamber.com
Southern Lancaster County Chamber of Commerce . . . . . (717) 786-1911
  http://www.southernlancasterchamber.com

Lancaster County Communities

ADAMSTOWN (borough). Covers a land area of 1.380 square miles and a water area of 0.007 square miles. Located at 40.24° N. Lat; 76.07° W. Long. Elevation is 472 feet.
History: Settled 1739.
Population: 1,108 (1990); 1,203 (2000); 1,789 (2010); Density: 1,296.6 persons per square mile (2010); Race: 92.3% White, 1.1% Black, 4.4% Asian, 0.3% American Indian/Alaska Native, 0.1% Native Hawaiian/Other Pacific Islander, 1.8% Other, 1.7% Hispanic of any race (2010); Average household size: 2.54 (2010); Median age: 37.5 (2010); Males per 100 females: 102.1 (2010); Marriage status: 20.8% never married, 65.0% now

married, 5.4% widowed, 8.8% divorced (2006-2010 5-year est.); Foreign born: 2.1% (2006-2010 5-year est.); Ancestry (includes multiple ancestries): 62.4% German, 17.9% Italian, 9.2% Irish, 5.8% Dutch, 4.9% English (2006-2010 5-year est.).
Economy: Single-family building permits issued: 1 (2011); Multi-family building permits issued: 0 (2011); Employment by occupation: 10.8% management, 4.1% professional, 5.5% services, 20.5% sales, 4.3% farming, 10.6% construction, 5.7% production (2006-2010 5-year est.).
Income: Per capita income: $23,902 (2006-2010 5-year est.); Median household income: $57,308 (2006-2010 5-year est.); Average household income: $61,751 (2006-2010 5-year est.); Percent of households with income of $100,000 or more: 15.4% (2006-2010 5-year est.); Poverty rate: 2.8% (2006-2010 5-year est.).
Education: Percent of population age 25 and over with: High school diploma (including GED) or higher: 90.2% (2006-2010 5-year est.); Bachelor's degree or higher: 26.7% (2006-2010 5-year est.); Master's degree or higher: 11.9% (2006-2010 5-year est.).
School District(s)
Cocalico SD (PK-12)
  2010-11 Enrollment: 3,295 . . . . (717) 336-1413
Housing: Homeownership rate: 73.6% (2010); Median home value: $223,800 (2006-2010 5-year est.); Median contract rent: $563 per month (2006-2010 5-year est.); Median year structure built: 1970 (2006-2010 5-year est.).
Safety: Violent crime rate: 16.7 per 10,000 population; Property crime rate: 150.4 per 10,000 population (2011).
Transportation: Commute to work: 89.2% car, 0.0% public transportation, 6.2% walk, 4.7% work from home (2006-2010 5-year est.); Travel time to work: 39.1% less than 15 minutes, 37.1% 15 to 30 minutes, 13.5% 30 to 45 minutes, 3.6% 45 to 60 minutes, 6.6% 60 minutes or more (2006-2010 5-year est.)
Additional Information Contacts
Ephrata Area Chamber of Commerce . . . . (717) 738-9010
  http://www.ephrata-area.org

AKRON (borough). Covers a land area of 1.222 square miles and a water area of 0.006 square miles. Located at 40.16° N. Lat; 76.20° W. Long. Elevation is 522 feet.
History: Covered bridges in area. Incorporated 1884.
Population: 4,157 (1990); 4,046 (2000); 3,876 (2010); Density: 3,171.9 persons per square mile (2010); Race: 94.7% White, 1.2% Black, 1.5% Asian, 0.2% American Indian/Alaska Native, 0.0% Native Hawaiian/Other Pacific Islander, 2.4% Other, 3.9% Hispanic of any race (2010); Average household size: 2.37 (2010); Median age: 42.4 (2010); Males per 100 females: 91.9 (2010); Marriage status: 22.6% never married, 58.7% now married, 6.9% widowed, 11.8% divorced (2006-2010 5-year est.); Foreign born: 1.5% (2006-2010 5-year est.); Ancestry (includes multiple ancestries): 52.4% German, 12.8% American, 10.5% English, 10.4% Irish, 7.1% Italian (2006-2010 5-year est.).
Economy: Single-family building permits issued: 6 (2011); Multi-family building permits issued: 0 (2011); Employment by occupation: 12.3% management, 4.2% professional, 10.6% services, 19.1% sales, 6.3% farming, 12.7% construction, 7.1% production (2006-2010 5-year est.).
Income: Per capita income: $26,389 (2006-2010 5-year est.); Median household income: $51,618 (2006-2010 5-year est.); Average household income: $58,645 (2006-2010 5-year est.); Percent of households with income of $100,000 or more: 12.1% (2006-2010 5-year est.); Poverty rate: 2.7% (2006-2010 5-year est.).
Education: Percent of population age 25 and over with: High school diploma (including GED) or higher: 86.7% (2006-2010 5-year est.); Bachelor's degree or higher: 23.3% (2006-2010 5-year est.); Master's degree or higher: 6.1% (2006-2010 5-year est.).
School District(s)
Ephrata Area SD (KG-12)
  2010-11 Enrollment: 4,127 . . . . (717) 721-1513
Housing: Homeownership rate: 65.3% (2010); Median home value: $176,100 (2006-2010 5-year est.); Median contract rent: $636 per month (2006-2010 5-year est.); Median year structure built: 1968 (2006-2010 5-year est.).
Safety: Violent crime rate: 5.1 per 10,000 population; Property crime rate: 77.2 per 10,000 population (2011).
Transportation: Commute to work: 92.8% car, 0.0% public transportation, 1.4% walk, 5.4% work from home (2006-2010 5-year est.); Travel time to work: 32.9% less than 15 minutes, 45.3% 15 to 30 minutes, 15.7% 30 to

45 minutes, 2.1% 45 to 60 minutes, 4.0% 60 minutes or more (2006-2010 5-year est.)

Additional Information Contacts

Ephrata Area Chamber of Commerce . . . . (717) 738-9010
  http://www.ephrata-area.org

BAINBRIDGE (CDP). Covers a land area of 2.280 square miles and a water area of 0.019 square miles. Located at 40.09° N. Lat; 76.66° W. Long. Elevation is 308 feet.

Population: n/a (1990); n/a (2000); 1,355 (2010); Density: 594.2 persons per square mile (2010); Race: 97.0% White, 1.1% Black, 0.2% Asian, 0.2% American Indian/Alaska Native, 0.1% Native Hawaiian/Other Pacific Islander, 1.4% Other, 1.6% Hispanic of any race (2010); Average household size: 2.72 (2010); Median age: 35.0 (2010); Males per 100 females: 101.3 (2010); Marriage status: 18.9% never married, 67.8% now married, 3.7% widowed, 9.6% divorced (2006-2010 5-year est.); Foreign born: 6.3% (2006-2010 5-year est.); Ancestry (includes multiple ancestries): 41.3% German, 11.9% English, 11.2% Italian, 10.2% Irish, 7.6% American (2006-2010 5-year est.).

Economy: Employment by occupation: 16.5% management, 0.8% professional, 8.6% services, 12.6% sales, 3.4% farming, 11.9% construction, 5.8% production (2006-2010 5-year est.).

Income: Per capita income: $30,700 (2006-2010 5-year est.); Median household income: $56,875 (2006-2010 5-year est.); Average household income: $74,428 (2006-2010 5-year est.); Percent of households with income of $100,000 or more: 17.3% (2006-2010 5-year est.); Poverty rate: 3.2% (2006-2010 5-year est.).

Education: Percent of population age 25 and over with: High school diploma (including GED) or higher: 85.2% (2006-2010 5-year est.); Bachelor's degree or higher: 14.4% (2006-2010 5-year est.); Master's degree or higher: 2.1% (2006-2010 5-year est.).

School District(s)

Elizabethtown Area SD (KG-12)
  2010-11 Enrollment: 3,989 . . . . (717) 367-1521

Housing: Homeownership rate: 80.1% (2010); Median home value: $162,600 (2006-2010 5-year est.); Median contract rent: $427 per month (2006-2010 5-year est.); Median year structure built: 1980 (2006-2010 5-year est.).

Transportation: Commute to work: 98.2% car, 0.0% public transportation, 0.0% walk, 0.9% work from home (2006-2010 5-year est.); Travel time to work: 27.6% less than 15 minutes, 38.0% 15 to 30 minutes, 21.0% 30 to 45 minutes, 4.2% 45 to 60 minutes, 9.2% 60 minutes or more (2006-2010 5-year est.)

BART (township). Covers a land area of 16.395 square miles and a water area of 0.055 square miles. Located at 39.92° N. Lat; 76.07° W. Long.

Population: 3,064 (1990); 3,003 (2000); 3,094 (2010); Density: 188.7 persons per square mile (2010); Race: 98.7% White, 0.5% Black, 0.1% Asian, 0.1% American Indian/Alaska Native, 0.0% Native Hawaiian/Other Pacific Islander, 0.6% Other, 0.9% Hispanic of any race (2010); Average household size: 3.59 (2010); Median age: 27.7 (2010); Males per 100 females: 102.6 (2010); Marriage status: 29.5% never married, 64.0% now married, 3.9% widowed, 2.6% divorced (2006-2010 5-year est.); Foreign born: 1.5% (2006-2010 5-year est.); Ancestry (includes multiple ancestries): 30.8% German, 22.4% Pennsylvania German, 10.3% American, 6.4% Irish, 4.5% English (2006-2010 5-year est.).

Economy: Single-family building permits issued: 3 (2011); Multi-family building permits issued: 4 (2011); Employment by occupation: 14.0% management, 0.5% professional, 4.5% services, 19.4% sales, 1.2% farming, 23.5% construction, 8.2% production (2006-2010 5-year est.).

Income: Per capita income: $16,475 (2006-2010 5-year est.); Median household income: $50,089 (2006-2010 5-year est.); Average household income: $61,603 (2006-2010 5-year est.); Percent of households with income of $100,000 or more: 12.8% (2006-2010 5-year est.); Poverty rate: 9.0% (2006-2010 5-year est.).

Education: Percent of population age 25 and over with: High school diploma (including GED) or higher: 50.8% (2006-2010 5-year est.); Bachelor's degree or higher: 6.7% (2006-2010 5-year est.); Master's degree or higher: 1.7% (2006-2010 5-year est.).

Housing: Homeownership rate: 72.3% (2010); Median home value: $237,300 (2006-2010 5-year est.); Median contract rent: $598 per month (2006-2010 5-year est.); Median year structure built: 1971 (2006-2010 5-year est.).

Transportation: Commute to work: 71.1% car, 0.0% public transportation, 11.2% walk, 9.5% work from home (2006-2010 5-year est.); Travel time to work: 30.6% less than 15 minutes, 22.6% 15 to 30 minutes, 26.3% 30 to 45 minutes, 5.1% 45 to 60 minutes, 15.4% 60 minutes or more (2006-2010 5-year est.)

Additional Information Contacts

Southern Lancaster County Chamber of Commerce . . . . . (717) 786-1911
  http://www.southernlancasterchamber.com

BIRD-IN-HAND (CDP). Covers a land area of 0.618 square miles and a water area of 0.003 square miles. Located at 40.04° N. Lat; 76.19° W. Long. Elevation is 358 feet.

Population: n/a (1990); n/a (2000); 402 (2010); Density: 650.5 persons per square mile (2010); Race: 94.5% White, 2.0% Black, 1.7% Asian, 0.0% American Indian/Alaska Native, 0.0% Native Hawaiian/Other Pacific Islander, 1.8% Other, 5.7% Hispanic of any race (2010); Average household size: 3.22 (2010); Median age: 32.0 (2010); Males per 100 females: 115.0 (2010); Marriage status: 30.7% never married, 57.0% now married, 7.0% widowed, 5.3% divorced (2006-2010 5-year est.); Foreign born: 0.0% (2006-2010 5-year est.); Ancestry (includes multiple ancestries): 39.5% Dutch, 36.9% German, 12.4% Irish, 8.8% American, 4.6% Hungarian (2006-2010 5-year est.).

Economy: Employment by occupation: 8.4% management, 0.0% professional, 0.0% services, 18.6% sales, 0.0% farming, 28.7% construction, 24.6% production (2006-2010 5-year est.).

Income: Per capita income: $24,458 (2006-2010 5-year est.); Median household income: $77,014 (2006-2010 5-year est.); Average household income: $75,129 (2006-2010 5-year est.); Percent of households with income of $100,000 or more: 29.7% (2006-2010 5-year est.); Poverty rate: 0.0% (2006-2010 5-year est.).

Education: Percent of population age 25 and over with: High school diploma (including GED) or higher: 76.6% (2006-2010 5-year est.); Bachelor's degree or higher: 0.0% (2006-2010 5-year est.); Master's degree or higher: 0.0% (2006-2010 5-year est.).

Housing: Homeownership rate: 56.8% (2010); Median home value: $281,300 (2006-2010 5-year est.); Median contract rent: $804 per month (2006-2010 5-year est.); Median year structure built: 1956 (2006-2010 5-year est.).

Transportation: Commute to work: 100.0% car, 0.0% public transportation, 0.0% walk, 0.0% work from home (2006-2010 5-year est.); Travel time to work: 24.0% less than 15 minutes, 54.5% 15 to 30 minutes, 9.6% 30 to 45 minutes, 12.0% 45 to 60 minutes, 0.0% 60 minutes or more (2006-2010 5-year est.)

BLUE BALL (CDP). Covers a land area of 1.194 square miles and a water area of 0.001 square miles. Located at 40.11° N. Lat; 76.05° W. Long. Elevation is 440 feet.

Population: n/a (1990); n/a (2000); 1,031 (2010); Density: 863.5 persons per square mile (2010); Race: 94.3% White, 0.6% Black, 3.1% Asian, 0.5% American Indian/Alaska Native, 0.0% Native Hawaiian/Other Pacific Islander, 1.5% Other, 1.5% Hispanic of any race (2010); Average household size: 2.69 (2010); Median age: 33.2 (2010); Males per 100 females: 103.4 (2010); Marriage status: 16.6% never married, 77.9% now married, 3.8% widowed, 1.7% divorced (2006-2010 5-year est.); Foreign born: 4.3% (2006-2010 5-year est.); Ancestry (includes multiple ancestries): 49.5% German, 18.6% Swiss, 16.7% Irish, 14.5% American, 10.1% Welsh (2006-2010 5-year est.).

Economy: Employment by occupation: 11.3% management, 0.0% professional, 12.6% services, 9.9% sales, 11.5% farming, 14.6% construction, 8.4% production (2006-2010 5-year est.).

Income: Per capita income: $20,850 (2006-2010 5-year est.); Median household income: $48,582 (2006-2010 5-year est.); Average household income: $59,254 (2006-2010 5-year est.); Percent of households with income of $100,000 or more: 10.1% (2006-2010 5-year est.); Poverty rate: 7.0% (2006-2010 5-year est.).

Education: Percent of population age 25 and over with: High school diploma (including GED) or higher: 83.1% (2006-2010 5-year est.); Bachelor's degree or higher: 16.7% (2006-2010 5-year est.); Master's degree or higher: 0.0% (2006-2010 5-year est.).

Housing: Homeownership rate: 61.6% (2010); Median home value: $204,100 (2006-2010 5-year est.); Median contract rent: $1,075 per month (2006-2010 5-year est.); Median year structure built: 1974 (2006-2010 5-year est.).

Transportation: Commute to work: 93.2% car, 0.0% public transportation, 3.0% walk, 3.8% work from home (2006-2010 5-year est.); Travel time to

work: 49.1% less than 15 minutes, 13.4% 15 to 30 minutes, 16.0% 30 to 45 minutes, 3.5% 45 to 60 minutes, 18.0% 60 minutes or more (2006-2010 5-year est.)

BOWMANSVILLE (CDP). Covers a land area of 1.837 square miles and a water area of 0.049 square miles. Located at 40.20° N. Lat; 76.02° W. Long. Elevation is 433 feet.

Population: n/a (1990); n/a (2000); 2,077 (2010); Density: 1,130.4 persons per square mile (2010); Race: 97.0% White, 0.5% Black, 1.0% Asian, 0.2% American Indian/Alaska Native, 0.1% Native Hawaiian/Other Pacific Islander, 1.2% Other, 1.9% Hispanic of any race (2010); Average household size: 2.86 (2010); Median age: 37.9 (2010); Males per 100 females: 103.4 (2010); Marriage status: 25.2% never married, 66.0% now married, 4.0% widowed, 4.8% divorced (2006-2010 5-year est.); Foreign born: 1.9% (2006-2010 5-year est.); Ancestry (includes multiple ancestries): 51.1% German, 12.1% American, 11.1% Irish, 10.4% Italian, 6.5% Dutch (2006-2010 5-year est.).

Economy: Employment by occupation: 6.8% management, 4.8% professional, 9.9% services, 23.0% sales, 0.0% farming, 13.2% construction, 20.3% production (2006-2010 5-year est.).

Income: Per capita income: $21,883 (2006-2010 5-year est.); Median household income: $54,917 (2006-2010 5-year est.); Average household income: $60,115 (2006-2010 5-year est.); Percent of households with income of $100,000 or more: 10.3% (2006-2010 5-year est.); Poverty rate: 0.0% (2006-2010 5-year est.).

Education: Percent of population age 25 and over with: High school diploma (including GED) or higher: 77.1% (2006-2010 5-year est.); Bachelor's degree or higher: 14.7% (2006-2010 5-year est.); Master's degree or higher: 4.5% (2006-2010 5-year est.).

Housing: Homeownership rate: 85.9% (2010); Median home value: $195,300 (2006-2010 5-year est.); Median contract rent: $569 per month (2006-2010 5-year est.); Median year structure built: 1989 (2006-2010 5-year est.).

Transportation: Commute to work: 91.5% car, 0.0% public transportation, 1.9% walk, 3.5% work from home (2006-2010 5-year est.); Travel time to work: 44.6% less than 15 minutes, 29.5% 15 to 30 minutes, 13.4% 30 to 45 minutes, 2.9% 45 to 60 minutes, 9.6% 60 minutes or more (2006-2010 5-year est.)

BRECKNOCK (township). Covers a land area of 24.647 square miles and a water area of 0.220 square miles. Located at 40.20° N. Lat; 76.03° W. Long.

Population: 5,186 (1990); 6,699 (2000); 7,199 (2010); Density: 292.1 persons per square mile (2010); Race: 97.2% White, 0.3% Black, 1.3% Asian, 0.1% American Indian/Alaska Native, 0.0% Native Hawaiian/Other Pacific Islander, 1.1% Other, 1.5% Hispanic of any race (2010); Average household size: 3.05 (2010); Median age: 36.6 (2010); Males per 100 females: 102.3 (2010); Marriage status: 28.9% never married, 63.1% now married, 4.4% widowed, 3.6% divorced (2006-2010 5-year est.); Foreign born: 2.1% (2006-2010 5-year est.); Ancestry (includes multiple ancestries): 42.9% German, 14.4% Swiss, 10.5% American, 6.7% Irish, 6.2% English (2006-2010 5-year est.).

Economy: Single-family building permits issued: 17 (2011); Multi-family building permits issued: 0 (2011); Employment by occupation: 9.1% management, 2.2% professional, 9.8% services, 19.0% sales, 5.5% farming, 15.6% construction, 10.4% production (2006-2010 5-year est.).

Income: Per capita income: $25,168 (2006-2010 5-year est.); Median household income: $58,847 (2006-2010 5-year est.); Average household income: $75,880 (2006-2010 5-year est.); Percent of households with income of $100,000 or more: 16.3% (2006-2010 5-year est.); Poverty rate: 3.4% (2006-2010 5-year est.).

Education: Percent of population age 25 and over with: High school diploma (including GED) or higher: 71.7% (2006-2010 5-year est.); Bachelor's degree or higher: 12.6% (2006-2010 5-year est.); Master's degree or higher: 2.8% (2006-2010 5-year est.).

Housing: Homeownership rate: 83.8% (2010); Median home value: $210,500 (2006-2010 5-year est.); Median contract rent: $545 per month (2006-2010 5-year est.); Median year structure built: 1984 (2006-2010 5-year est.).

Transportation: Commute to work: 89.2% car, 0.0% public transportation, 0.9% walk, 5.4% work from home (2006-2010 5-year est.); Travel time to work: 36.0% less than 15 minutes, 35.9% 15 to 30 minutes, 17.2% 30 to 45 minutes, 2.9% 45 to 60 minutes, 8.1% 60 minutes or more (2006-2010 5-year est.)

Additional Information Contacts
Brecknock Township . . . . (717) 445-5933
http://brecknocktownship.us
Ephrata Area Chamber of Commerce . . . . (717) 738-9010
http://www.ephrata-area.org

BRICKERVILLE (CDP). Covers a land area of 2.170 square miles and a water area of 0.018 square miles. Located at 40.23° N. Lat; 76.29° W. Long. Elevation is 538 feet.

Population: 1,268 (1990); 1,287 (2000); 1,309 (2010); Density: 603.3 persons per square mile (2010); Race: 97.4% White, 1.1% Black, 0.2% Asian, 0.0% American Indian/Alaska Native, 0.0% Native Hawaiian/Other Pacific Islander, 1.3% Other, 1.4% Hispanic of any race (2010); Average household size: 2.92 (2010); Median age: 38.5 (2010); Males per 100 females: 98.6 (2010); Marriage status: 18.3% never married, 78.4% now married, 3.3% widowed, 0.0% divorced (2006-2010 5-year est.); Foreign born: 2.8% (2006-2010 5-year est.); Ancestry (includes multiple ancestries): 61.8% German, 13.4% Irish, 9.1% American, 7.5% Italian, 6.9% Swiss (2006-2010 5-year est.).

Economy: Employment by occupation: 11.8% management, 2.6% professional, 7.0% services, 10.0% sales, 1.6% farming, 14.1% construction, 13.5% production (2006-2010 5-year est.).

Income: Per capita income: $25,042 (2006-2010 5-year est.); Median household income: $68,892 (2006-2010 5-year est.); Average household income: $76,008 (2006-2010 5-year est.); Percent of households with income of $100,000 or more: 21.2% (2006-2010 5-year est.); Poverty rate: 7.7% (2006-2010 5-year est.).

Education: Percent of population age 25 and over with: High school diploma (including GED) or higher: 87.4% (2006-2010 5-year est.); Bachelor's degree or higher: 20.4% (2006-2010 5-year est.); Master's degree or higher: 7.3% (2006-2010 5-year est.).

Housing: Homeownership rate: 86.4% (2010); Median home value: $198,100 (2006-2010 5-year est.); Median contract rent: $705 per month (2006-2010 5-year est.); Median year structure built: 1981 (2006-2010 5-year est.).

Transportation: Commute to work: 94.8% car, 0.0% public transportation, 0.0% walk, 3.9% work from home (2006-2010 5-year est.); Travel time to work: 25.1% less than 15 minutes, 42.3% 15 to 30 minutes, 32.6% 30 to 45 minutes, 0.0% 45 to 60 minutes, 0.0% 60 minutes or more (2006-2010 5-year est.)

Additional Information Contacts
Ephrata Area Chamber of Commerce . . . . (717) 738-9010
http://www.ephrata-area.org

BROWNSTOWN (CDP). Covers a land area of 2.486 square miles and a water area of 0.049 square miles. Located at 40.13° N. Lat; 76.22° W. Long. Elevation is 351 feet.

Population: n/a (1990); n/a (2000); 2,816 (2010); Density: 1,132.7 persons per square mile (2010); Race: 94.6% White, 0.4% Black, 2.5% Asian, 0.0% American Indian/Alaska Native, 0.0% Native Hawaiian/Other Pacific Islander, 2.5% Other, 3.2% Hispanic of any race (2010); Average household size: 2.89 (2010); Median age: 40.2 (2010); Males per 100 females: 101.4 (2010); Marriage status: 19.8% never married, 74.3% now married, 2.9% widowed, 3.0% divorced (2006-2010 5-year est.); Foreign born: 4.4% (2006-2010 5-year est.); Ancestry (includes multiple ancestries): 48.6% German, 8.0% English, 7.9% Italian, 5.9% Swiss, 5.8% Irish (2006-2010 5-year est.).

Economy: Employment by occupation: 9.9% management, 2.6% professional, 5.0% services, 16.2% sales, 4.1% farming, 13.3% construction, 9.6% production (2006-2010 5-year est.).

Income: Per capita income: $29,039 (2006-2010 5-year est.); Median household income: $74,922 (2006-2010 5-year est.); Average household income: $89,229 (2006-2010 5-year est.); Percent of households with income of $100,000 or more: 32.3% (2006-2010 5-year est.); Poverty rate: 2.1% (2006-2010 5-year est.).

Education: Percent of population age 25 and over with: High school diploma (including GED) or higher: 78.3% (2006-2010 5-year est.); Bachelor's degree or higher: 24.3% (2006-2010 5-year est.); Master's degree or higher: 8.4% (2006-2010 5-year est.).

School District(s)
Conestoga Valley SD (KG-12)
    2010-11 Enrollment: 4,016 . . . . (717) 397-2421
Lancaster County CTC (10-12)
    2010-11 Enrollment: n/a . . . . (717) 464-7050

Housing: Homeownership rate: 87.7% (2010); Median home value: $203,200 (2006-2010 5-year est.); Median contract rent: $904 per month (2006-2010 5-year est.); Median year structure built: 1981 (2006-2010 5-year est.).

Transportation: Commute to work: 91.9% car, 0.0% public transportation, 0.0% walk, 8.1% work from home (2006-2010 5-year est.); Travel time to work: 24.8% less than 15 minutes, 55.1% 15 to 30 minutes, 15.4% 30 to 45 minutes, 1.1% 45 to 60 minutes, 3.6% 60 minutes or more (2006-2010 5-year est.)

CAERNARVON (township). Covers a land area of 22.957 square miles and a water area of 0.118 square miles. Located at 40.14° N. Lat; 75.95° W. Long.

Population: 3,946 (1990); 4,278 (2000); 4,748 (2010); Density: 206.8 persons per square mile (2010); Race: 98.1% White, 0.6% Black, 0.4% Asian, 0.1% American Indian/Alaska Native, 0.0% Native Hawaiian/Other Pacific Islander, 0.8% Other, 1.2% Hispanic of any race (2010); Average household size: 3.17 (2010); Median age: 37.7 (2010); Males per 100 females: 96.2 (2010); Marriage status: 29.8% never married, 61.6% now married, 3.3% widowed, 5.3% divorced (2006-2010 5-year est.); Foreign born: 1.0% (2006-2010 5-year est.); Ancestry (includes multiple ancestries): 36.3% German, 10.4% American, 10.0% Irish, 9.2% Swiss, 8.5% English (2006-2010 5-year est.).

Economy: Single-family building permits issued: 4 (2011); Multi-family building permits issued: 0 (2011); Employment by occupation: 11.1% management, 2.4% professional, 11.9% services, 13.9% sales, 1.4% farming, 16.3% construction, 14.7% production (2006-2010 5-year est.).

Income: Per capita income: $22,249 (2006-2010 5-year est.); Median household income: $59,907 (2006-2010 5-year est.); Average household income: $69,760 (2006-2010 5-year est.); Percent of households with income of $100,000 or more: 18.4% (2006-2010 5-year est.); Poverty rate: 10.1% (2006-2010 5-year est.).

Education: Percent of population age 25 and over with: High school diploma (including GED) or higher: 67.6% (2006-2010 5-year est.); Bachelor's degree or higher: 13.1% (2006-2010 5-year est.); Master's degree or higher: 5.4% (2006-2010 5-year est.).

Housing: Homeownership rate: 76.6% (2010); Median home value: $236,400 (2006-2010 5-year est.); Median contract rent: $579 per month (2006-2010 5-year est.); Median year structure built: 1978 (2006-2010 5-year est.).

Transportation: Commute to work: 76.7% car, 0.6% public transportation, 3.1% walk, 8.9% work from home (2006-2010 5-year est.); Travel time to work: 36.8% less than 15 minutes, 34.0% 15 to 30 minutes, 14.2% 30 to 45 minutes, 7.9% 45 to 60 minutes, 7.1% 60 minutes or more (2006-2010 5-year est.)

Additional Information Contacts
Caernarvon Township . . . . (717) 445-4244
  http://www.caernarvontwp.org
Ephrata Area Chamber of Commerce . . . . (717) 738-9010
  http://www.ephrata-area.org

CHRISTIANA (borough). Covers a land area of 0.527 square miles and a water area of 0.004 square miles. Located at 39.95° N. Lat; 76.00° W. Long. Elevation is 476 feet.

History: Settled 1691, laid out 1833, incorporated 1894.

Population: 1,045 (1990); 1,124 (2000); 1,168 (2010); Density: 2,215.2 persons per square mile (2010); Race: 90.9% White, 6.0% Black, 0.3% Asian, 0.2% American Indian/Alaska Native, 0.1% Native Hawaiian/Other Pacific Islander, 2.5% Other, 6.8% Hispanic of any race (2010); Average household size: 2.71 (2010); Median age: 38.2 (2010); Males per 100 females: 78.6 (2010); Marriage status: 18.2% never married, 47.3% now married, 22.8% widowed, 11.8% divorced (2006-2010 5-year est.); Foreign born: 0.8% (2006-2010 5-year est.); Ancestry (includes multiple ancestries): 27.0% German, 13.5% Italian, 10.8% Irish, 7.2% English, 5.3% American (2006-2010 5-year est.).

Economy: Single-family building permits issued: 0 (2011); Multi-family building permits issued: 0 (2011); Employment by occupation: 5.8% management, 2.7% professional, 8.8% services, 19.4% sales, 8.5% farming, 11.5% construction, 8.5% production (2006-2010 5-year est.).

Income: Per capita income: $20,764 (2006-2010 5-year est.); Median household income: $54,896 (2006-2010 5-year est.); Average household income: $59,229 (2006-2010 5-year est.); Percent of households with income of $100,000 or more: 11.4% (2006-2010 5-year est.); Poverty rate: 14.7% (2006-2010 5-year est.).

Education: Percent of population age 25 and over with: High school diploma (including GED) or higher: 77.5% (2006-2010 5-year est.); Bachelor's degree or higher: 8.6% (2006-2010 5-year est.); Master's degree or higher: 3.2% (2006-2010 5-year est.).

School District(s)
Solanco SD (KG-12)
  2010-11 Enrollment: 3,742 . . . . (717) 786-8401

Housing: Homeownership rate: 63.1% (2010); Median home value: $175,000 (2006-2010 5-year est.); Median contract rent: $620 per month (2006-2010 5-year est.); Median year structure built: before 1940 (2006-2010 5-year est.).

Safety: Violent crime rate: 34.1 per 10,000 population; Property crime rate: 136.5 per 10,000 population (2011).

Transportation: Commute to work: 93.7% car, 0.0% public transportation, 2.1% walk, 1.9% work from home (2006-2010 5-year est.); Travel time to work: 38.8% less than 15 minutes, 16.1% 15 to 30 minutes, 25.1% 30 to 45 minutes, 12.4% 45 to 60 minutes, 7.5% 60 minutes or more (2006-2010 5-year est.)

Additional Information Contacts
Beaver County Chamber of Commerce . . . . (724) 775-3944
  http://beavercountychamber.com

CHURCHTOWN (CDP). Covers a land area of 1.885 square miles and a water area of 0.014 square miles. Located at 40.14° N. Lat; 75.96° W. Long. Elevation is 564 feet.

Population: n/a (1990); n/a (2000); 470 (2010); Density: 249.4 persons per square mile (2010); Race: 98.5% White, 0.0% Black, 0.0% Asian, 1.1% American Indian/Alaska Native, 0.0% Native Hawaiian/Other Pacific Islander, 0.4% Other, 0.6% Hispanic of any race (2010); Average household size: 3.18 (2010); Median age: 33.1 (2010); Males per 100 females: 96.7 (2010); Marriage status: 32.0% never married, 52.6% now married, 3.8% widowed, 11.7% divorced (2006-2010 5-year est.); Foreign born: 0.0% (2006-2010 5-year est.); Ancestry (includes multiple ancestries): 29.7% English, 29.7% German, 20.9% Polish, 14.1% Irish, 8.3% Pennsylvania German (2006-2010 5-year est.).

Economy: Employment by occupation: 10.6% management, 0.0% professional, 21.7% services, 5.8% sales, 0.0% farming, 5.3% construction, 11.1% production (2006-2010 5-year est.).

Income: Per capita income: $26,151 (2006-2010 5-year est.); Median household income: $53,977 (2006-2010 5-year est.); Average household income: $68,080 (2006-2010 5-year est.); Percent of households with income of $100,000 or more: 32.2% (2006-2010 5-year est.); Poverty rate: 30.2% (2006-2010 5-year est.).

Education: Percent of population age 25 and over with: High school diploma (including GED) or higher: 77.9% (2006-2010 5-year est.); Bachelor's degree or higher: 21.0% (2006-2010 5-year est.); Master's degree or higher: 16.9% (2006-2010 5-year est.).

Housing: Homeownership rate: 77.7% (2010); Median home value: $198,500 (2006-2010 5-year est.); Median contract rent: $773 per month (2006-2010 5-year est.); Median year structure built: before 1940 (2006-2010 5-year est.).

Transportation: Commute to work: 83.1% car, 0.0% public transportation, 10.6% walk, 6.3% work from home (2006-2010 5-year est.); Travel time to work: 53.1% less than 15 minutes, 23.7% 15 to 30 minutes, 23.2% 30 to 45 minutes, 0.0% 45 to 60 minutes, 0.0% 60 minutes or more (2006-2010 5-year est.)

CLAY (CDP). Covers a land area of 2.231 square miles and a water area of 0.011 square miles. Located at 40.22° N. Lat; 76.24° W. Long. Elevation is 354 feet.

Population: n/a (1990); n/a (2000); 1,559 (2010); Density: 698.9 persons per square mile (2010); Race: 94.5% White, 0.3% Black, 2.8% Asian, 0.3% American Indian/Alaska Native, 0.0% Native Hawaiian/Other Pacific Islander, 2.1% Other, 2.6% Hispanic of any race (2010); Average household size: 2.57 (2010); Median age: 43.3 (2010); Males per 100 females: 99.4 (2010); Marriage status: 13.3% never married, 75.6% now married, 4.4% widowed, 6.6% divorced (2006-2010 5-year est.); Foreign born: 0.7% (2006-2010 5-year est.); Ancestry (includes multiple ancestries): 47.6% German, 11.4% Irish, 8.9% American, 5.8% Swiss, 3.8% English (2006-2010 5-year est.).

Economy: Employment by occupation: 17.7% management, 1.7% professional, 3.1% services, 18.0% sales, 3.4% farming, 11.0% construction, 6.3% production (2006-2010 5-year est.).

Income: Per capita income: $26,917 (2006-2010 5-year est.); Median household income: $57,727 (2006-2010 5-year est.); Average household

income: $70,185 (2006-2010 5-year est.); Percent of households with income of $100,000 or more: 17.6% (2006-2010 5-year est.); Poverty rate: 20.4% (2006-2010 5-year est.).

Education: Percent of population age 25 and over with: High school diploma (including GED) or higher: 74.5% (2006-2010 5-year est.); Bachelor's degree or higher: 23.4% (2006-2010 5-year est.); Master's degree or higher: 9.5% (2006-2010 5-year est.).

Housing: Homeownership rate: 88.1% (2010); Median home value: $90,700 (2006-2010 5-year est.); Median contract rent: $824 per month (2006-2010 5-year est.); Median year structure built: 1986 (2006-2010 5-year est.).

Transportation: Commute to work: 95.5% car, 0.0% public transportation, 0.0% walk, 1.2% work from home (2006-2010 5-year est.); Travel time to work: 30.6% less than 15 minutes, 39.1% 15 to 30 minutes, 24.3% 30 to 45 minutes, 4.4% 45 to 60 minutes, 1.7% 60 minutes or more (2006-2010 5-year est.)

CLAY (township). Covers a land area of 21.950 square miles and a water area of 0.794 square miles. Located at 40.24° N. Lat; 76.24° W. Long. Elevation is 354 feet.

Population: 5,052 (1990); 5,173 (2000); 6,308 (2010); Density: 287.4 persons per square mile (2010); Race: 95.6% White, 0.5% Black, 1.6% Asian, 0.2% American Indian/Alaska Native, 0.0% Native Hawaiian/Other Pacific Islander, 2.1% Other, 2.4% Hispanic of any race (2010); Average household size: 2.84 (2010); Median age: 39.9 (2010); Males per 100 females: 100.8 (2010); Marriage status: 17.5% never married, 72.9% now married, 3.9% widowed, 5.7% divorced (2006-2010 5-year est.); Foreign born: 3.4% (2006-2010 5-year est.); Ancestry (includes multiple ancestries): 44.5% German, 12.5% Irish, 10.1% American, 7.0% Swiss, 7.0% English (2006-2010 5-year est.).

Economy: Single-family building permits issued: 1 (2011); Multi-family building permits issued: 14 (2011); Employment by occupation: 12.8% management, 2.7% professional, 5.8% services, 18.3% sales, 2.7% farming, 14.4% construction, 9.5% production (2006-2010 5-year est.).

Income: Per capita income: $28,439 (2006-2010 5-year est.); Median household income: $64,648 (2006-2010 5-year est.); Average household income: $78,066 (2006-2010 5-year est.); Percent of households with income of $100,000 or more: 21.9% (2006-2010 5-year est.); Poverty rate: 9.5% (2006-2010 5-year est.).

Education: Percent of population age 25 and over with: High school diploma (including GED) or higher: 76.4% (2006-2010 5-year est.); Bachelor's degree or higher: 19.2% (2006-2010 5-year est.); Master's degree or higher: 5.6% (2006-2010 5-year est.).

Housing: Homeownership rate: 85.4% (2010); Median home value: $197,500 (2006-2010 5-year est.); Median contract rent: $536 per month (2006-2010 5-year est.); Median year structure built: 1984 (2006-2010 5-year est.).

Transportation: Commute to work: 94.1% car, 0.0% public transportation, 0.9% walk, 3.9% work from home (2006-2010 5-year est.); Travel time to work: 31.1% less than 15 minutes, 36.2% 15 to 30 minutes, 25.5% 30 to 45 minutes, 4.0% 45 to 60 minutes, 3.2% 60 minutes or more (2006-2010 5-year est.)

Additional Information Contacts

Clay Township. . . . . (717) 733-9675
Ephrata Area Chamber of Commerce . . . . (717) 738-9010
  http://www.ephrata-area.org

COLERAIN (township). Covers a land area of 28.351 square miles and a water area of 0.667 square miles. Located at 39.86° N. Lat; 76.07° W. Long.

Population: 2,867 (1990); 3,261 (2000); 3,635 (2010); Density: 128.2 persons per square mile (2010); Race: 96.5% White, 0.8% Black, 0.6% Asian, 0.1% American Indian/Alaska Native, 0.1% Native Hawaiian/Other Pacific Islander, 1.9% Other, 2.2% Hispanic of any race (2010); Average household size: 3.42 (2010); Median age: 30.9 (2010); Males per 100 females: 103.5 (2010); Marriage status: 22.0% never married, 68.2% now married, 3.4% widowed, 6.4% divorced (2006-2010 5-year est.); Foreign born: 0.5% (2006-2010 5-year est.); Ancestry (includes multiple ancestries): 24.3% German, 17.8% Pennsylvania German, 13.3% Irish, 8.4% American, 8.2% English (2006-2010 5-year est.).

Economy: Single-family building permits issued: 7 (2011); Multi-family building permits issued: 0 (2011); Employment by occupation: 15.4% management, 2.8% professional, 12.8% services, 13.3% sales, 3.1% farming, 18.0% construction, 7.6% production (2006-2010 5-year est.).

Income: Per capita income: $21,501 (2006-2010 5-year est.); Median household income: $55,841 (2006-2010 5-year est.); Average household income: $64,243 (2006-2010 5-year est.); Percent of households with income of $100,000 or more: 11.9% (2006-2010 5-year est.); Poverty rate: 9.1% (2006-2010 5-year est.).

Education: Percent of population age 25 and over with: High school diploma (including GED) or higher: 67.7% (2006-2010 5-year est.); Bachelor's degree or higher: 14.1% (2006-2010 5-year est.); Master's degree or higher: 6.1% (2006-2010 5-year est.).

Housing: Homeownership rate: 79.1% (2010); Median home value: $270,000 (2006-2010 5-year est.); Median contract rent: $513 per month (2006-2010 5-year est.); Median year structure built: 1978 (2006-2010 5-year est.).

Transportation: Commute to work: 76.0% car, 0.0% public transportation, 9.3% walk, 12.1% work from home (2006-2010 5-year est.); Travel time to work: 39.4% less than 15 minutes, 19.8% 15 to 30 minutes, 21.5% 30 to 45 minutes, 10.9% 45 to 60 minutes, 8.3% 60 minutes or more (2006-2010 5-year est.)

Additional Information Contacts

Southern Lancaster County Chamber of Commerce . . . . . (717) 786-1911
  http://www.southernlancasterchamber.com

COLUMBIA (borough). Covers a land area of 2.414 square miles and a water area of 0.008 square miles. Located at 40.03° N. Lat; 76.50° W. Long. Elevation is 302 feet.

History: Wrights Ferry Mansion (1738). Two covered bridges to Northeast on Chickies Creek. Settled 1730, laid out 1788, incorporated 1814.

Population: 10,632 (1990); 10,311 (2000); 10,400 (2010); Density: 4,308.4 persons per square mile (2010); Race: 87.1% White, 5.1% Black, 0.6% Asian, 0.2% American Indian/Alaska Native, 0.0% Native Hawaiian/Other Pacific Islander, 7.0% Other, 9.0% Hispanic of any race (2010); Average household size: 2.37 (2010); Median age: 38.9 (2010); Males per 100 females: 93.4 (2010); Marriage status: 30.1% never married, 48.9% now married, 7.8% widowed, 13.3% divorced (2006-2010 5-year est.); Foreign born: 4.2% (2006-2010 5-year est.); Ancestry (includes multiple ancestries): 36.7% German, 9.3% American, 9.1% Irish, 5.9% English, 5.5% Italian (2006-2010 5-year est.).

Economy: Single-family building permits issued: 0 (2011); Multi-family building permits issued: 0 (2011); Employment by occupation: 5.9% management, 1.3% professional, 15.7% services, 18.3% sales, 5.2% farming, 11.4% construction, 12.2% production (2006-2010 5-year est.).

Income: Per capita income: $18,542 (2006-2010 5-year est.); Median household income: $37,119 (2006-2010 5-year est.); Average household income: $44,819 (2006-2010 5-year est.); Percent of households with income of $100,000 or more: 7.3% (2006-2010 5-year est.); Poverty rate: 24.6% (2006-2010 5-year est.).

Education: Percent of population age 25 and over with: High school diploma (including GED) or higher: 79.3% (2006-2010 5-year est.); Bachelor's degree or higher: 9.7% (2006-2010 5-year est.); Master's degree or higher: 1.2% (2006-2010 5-year est.).

School District(s)

Columbia Borough SD (KG-12)
  2010-11 Enrollment: 1,359 . . . . (717) 684-2283

Two-year College(s)

NAWCC School of Horology (Private, Not-for-profit)
  Fall 2010 Enrollment: 38 . . . . (717) 684-8261

Housing: Homeownership rate: 56.6% (2010); Median home value: $97,200 (2006-2010 5-year est.); Median contract rent: $509 per month (2006-2010 5-year est.); Median year structure built: before 1940 (2006-2010 5-year est.).

Hospitals: Lancaster General Hospital-Susquehanna (55 beds)

Safety: Violent crime rate: 22.0 per 10,000 population; Property crime rate: 305.8 per 10,000 population (2011).

Newspapers: Columbia Ledger (Community news; Circulation 3,500)

Transportation: Commute to work: 90.0% car, 1.6% public transportation, 5.3% walk, 1.4% work from home (2006-2010 5-year est.); Travel time to work: 26.4% less than 15 minutes, 46.0% 15 to 30 minutes, 17.1% 30 to 45 minutes, 5.7% 45 to 60 minutes, 4.7% 60 minutes or more (2006-2010 5-year est.)

Additional Information Contacts

Borough of Columbia . . . . (717) 684-2467
  http://psabcontent.com/columbiapa/content/index.php
Susquehanna Valley Chamber of Commerce . . . . (717) 684-5249
  http://www.parivertowns.com

CONESTOGA

CONESTOGA (CDP). Covers a land area of 2.080 square miles and a water area of 0.005 square miles. Located at 39.94° N. Lat; 76.34° W. Long. Elevation is 495 feet.

Population: n/a (1990); n/a (2000); 1,258 (2010); Density: 604.7 persons per square mile (2010); Race: 97.3% White, 0.3% Black, 1.2% Asian, 0.0% American Indian/Alaska Native, 0.0% Native Hawaiian/Other Pacific Islander, 1.2% Other, 1.7% Hispanic of any race (2010); Average household size: 2.71 (2010); Median age: 39.9 (2010); Males per 100 females: 107.2 (2010); Marriage status: 24.1% never married, 56.1% now married, 3.8% widowed, 16.0% divorced (2006-2010 5-year est.); Foreign born: 5.1% (2006-2010 5-year est.); Ancestry (includes multiple ancestries): 48.7% German, 12.9% Irish, 9.2% American, 6.2% European, 5.9% English (2006-2010 5-year est.).

Economy: Employment by occupation: 4.2% management, 2.9% professional, 11.2% services, 16.3% sales, 2.9% farming, 12.2% construction, 4.7% production (2006-2010 5-year est.).

Income: Per capita income: $30,327 (2006-2010 5-year est.); Median household income: $57,100 (2006-2010 5-year est.); Average household income: $77,780 (2006-2010 5-year est.); Percent of households with income of $100,000 or more: 16.9% (2006-2010 5-year est.); Poverty rate: 6.3% (2006-2010 5-year est.).

Education: Percent of population age 25 and over with: High school diploma (including GED) or higher: 89.9% (2006-2010 5-year est.); Bachelor's degree or higher: 25.1% (2006-2010 5-year est.); Master's degree or higher: 17.3% (2006-2010 5-year est.).

School District(s)

Penn Manor SD (KG-12)
    2010-11 Enrollment: 5,169 . . . . (717) 872-9500

Housing: Homeownership rate: 80.4% (2010); Median home value: $188,700 (2006-2010 5-year est.); Median contract rent: $551 per month (2006-2010 5-year est.); Median year structure built: 1964 (2006-2010 5-year est.).

Transportation: Commute to work: 91.4% car, 0.0% public transportation, 1.0% walk, 7.6% work from home (2006-2010 5-year est.); Travel time to work: 16.3% less than 15 minutes, 55.7% 15 to 30 minutes, 19.3% 30 to 45 minutes, 2.2% 45 to 60 minutes, 6.5% 60 minutes or more (2006-2010 5-year est.)

CONESTOGA

CONESTOGA (township). Covers a land area of 14.639 square miles and a water area of 1.938 square miles. Located at 39.94° N. Lat; 76.36° W. Long. Elevation is 495 feet.

History: Once site of Native American village. Gave its name to Conestoga wagon, developed in this region before the American Revolution.

Population: 3,527 (1990); 3,749 (2000); 3,776 (2010); Density: 257.9 persons per square mile (2010); Race: 97.3% White, 0.7% Black, 0.6% Asian, 0.2% American Indian/Alaska Native, 0.0% Native Hawaiian/Other Pacific Islander, 1.2% Other, 2.1% Hispanic of any race (2010); Average household size: 2.65 (2010); Median age: 42.1 (2010); Males per 100 females: 105.3 (2010); Marriage status: 20.0% never married, 64.5% now married, 5.0% widowed, 10.5% divorced (2006-2010 5-year est.); Foreign born: 4.0% (2006-2010 5-year est.); Ancestry (includes multiple ancestries): 46.6% German, 17.1% Irish, 7.5% American, 5.6% Italian, 4.7% English (2006-2010 5-year est.).

Economy: Single-family building permits issued: 9 (2011); Multi-family building permits issued: 0 (2011); Employment by occupation: 8.2% management, 2.9% professional, 10.4% services, 13.5% sales, 2.3% farming, 13.8% construction, 6.8% production (2006-2010 5-year est.).

Income: Per capita income: $28,964 (2006-2010 5-year est.); Median household income: $64,821 (2006-2010 5-year est.); Average household income: $76,449 (2006-2010 5-year est.); Percent of households with income of $100,000 or more: 19.0% (2006-2010 5-year est.); Poverty rate: 3.1% (2006-2010 5-year est.).

Education: Percent of population age 25 and over with: High school diploma (including GED) or higher: 90.7% (2006-2010 5-year est.); Bachelor's degree or higher: 23.6% (2006-2010 5-year est.); Master's degree or higher: 9.8% (2006-2010 5-year est.).

Housing: Homeownership rate: 83.6% (2010); Median home value: $190,800 (2006-2010 5-year est.); Median contract rent: $610 per month (2006-2010 5-year est.); Median year structure built: 1972 (2006-2010 5-year est.).

Transportation: Commute to work: 91.1% car, 0.0% public transportation, 1.5% walk, 5.8% work from home (2006-2010 5-year est.); Travel time to work: 18.0% less than 15 minutes, 48.9% 15 to 30 minutes, 20.5% 30 to

45 minutes, 5.4% 45 to 60 minutes, 7.3% 60 minutes or more (2006-2010 5-year est.)

Additional Information Contacts

Lancaster Chamber of Commerce & Industry . . . . (717) 397-3531
    http://www.lancasterchamber.com

CONOY

CONOY (township). Covers a land area of 14.556 square miles and a water area of 3.891 square miles. Located at 40.11° N. Lat; 76.67° W. Long.

Population: 2,687 (1990); 3,067 (2000); 3,194 (2010); Density: 219.4 persons per square mile (2010); Race: 97.8% White, 0.7% Black, 0.1% Asian, 0.2% American Indian/Alaska Native, 0.0% Native Hawaiian/Other Pacific Islander, 1.2% Other, 1.6% Hispanic of any race (2010); Average household size: 2.68 (2010); Median age: 39.8 (2010); Males per 100 females: 105.1 (2010); Marriage status: 23.8% never married, 63.6% now married, 4.4% widowed, 8.2% divorced (2006-2010 5-year est.); Foreign born: 4.1% (2006-2010 5-year est.); Ancestry (includes multiple ancestries): 41.8% German, 10.2% English, 8.5% American, 8.5% Italian, 8.4% Irish (2006-2010 5-year est.).

Economy: Single-family building permits issued: 0 (2011); Multi-family building permits issued: 0 (2011); Employment by occupation: 13.0% management, 2.2% professional, 8.8% services, 15.5% sales, 4.6% farming, 13.0% construction, 10.2% production (2006-2010 5-year est.).

Income: Per capita income: $31,084 (2006-2010 5-year est.); Median household income: $65,811 (2006-2010 5-year est.); Average household income: $78,027 (2006-2010 5-year est.); Percent of households with income of $100,000 or more: 22.9% (2006-2010 5-year est.); Poverty rate: 2.9% (2006-2010 5-year est.).

Education: Percent of population age 25 and over with: High school diploma (including GED) or higher: 87.5% (2006-2010 5-year est.); Bachelor's degree or higher: 15.2% (2006-2010 5-year est.); Master's degree or higher: 6.6% (2006-2010 5-year est.).

Housing: Homeownership rate: 85.2% (2010); Median home value: $174,100 (2006-2010 5-year est.); Median contract rent: $439 per month (2006-2010 5-year est.); Median year structure built: 1980 (2006-2010 5-year est.).

Safety: Violent crime rate: 12.5 per 10,000 population; Property crime rate: 121.7 per 10,000 population (2011).

Transportation: Commute to work: 94.1% car, 0.4% public transportation, 0.0% walk, 3.5% work from home (2006-2010 5-year est.); Travel time to work: 26.1% less than 15 minutes, 39.6% 15 to 30 minutes, 23.8% 30 to 45 minutes, 4.6% 45 to 60 minutes, 5.9% 60 minutes or more (2006-2010 5-year est.)

Additional Information Contacts

Elizabethtown Area Chamber of Commerce . . . . (717) 361-7188
    http://www.elizabethtowncoc.com

DENVER

DENVER (borough). Covers a land area of 1.278 square miles and a water area of 0.019 square miles. Located at 40.23° N. Lat; 76.14° W. Long. Elevation is 420 feet.

History: Settled 1863, incorporated 1990.

Population: 2,843 (1990); 3,332 (2000); 3,861 (2010); Density: 3,020.9 persons per square mile (2010); Race: 94.4% White, 0.8% Black, 1.5% Asian, 0.3% American Indian/Alaska Native, 0.0% Native Hawaiian/Other Pacific Islander, 3.0% Other, 4.2% Hispanic of any race (2010); Average household size: 2.64 (2010); Median age: 38.4 (2010); Males per 100 females: 92.7 (2010); Marriage status: 24.0% never married, 62.2% now married, 7.4% widowed, 6.5% divorced (2006-2010 5-year est.); Foreign born: 1.7% (2006-2010 5-year est.); Ancestry (includes multiple ancestries): 54.2% German, 11.7% Irish, 9.6% American, 8.2% English, 4.9% Italian (2006-2010 5-year est.).

Economy: Single-family building permits issued: 0 (2011); Multi-family building permits issued: 0 (2011); Employment by occupation: 10.7% management, 3.1% professional, 12.5% services, 15.1% sales, 3.6% farming, 9.5% construction, 6.9% production (2006-2010 5-year est.).

Income: Per capita income: $24,022 (2006-2010 5-year est.); Median household income: $59,280 (2006-2010 5-year est.); Average household income: $62,447 (2006-2010 5-year est.); Percent of households with income of $100,000 or more: 10.7% (2006-2010 5-year est.); Poverty rate: 1.6% (2006-2010 5-year est.).

Education: Percent of population age 25 and over with: High school diploma (including GED) or higher: 83.4% (2006-2010 5-year est.); Bachelor's degree or higher: 18.0% (2006-2010 5-year est.); Master's degree or higher: 5.2% (2006-2010 5-year est.).

School District(s)

Cocalico SD (PK-12)

    2010-11 Enrollment: 3,295 . . . . (717) 336-1413

Eastern Lancaster County SD (KG-12)

    2010-11 Enrollment: 3,111 . . . . (717) 354-1500

Housing: Homeownership rate: 72.1% (2010); Median home value: $162,200 (2006-2010 5-year est.); Median contract rent: $619 per month (2006-2010 5-year est.); Median year structure built: 1963 (2006-2010 5-year est.).

Safety: Violent crime rate: 25.8 per 10,000 population; Property crime rate: 77.5 per 10,000 population (2011).

Transportation: Commute to work: 97.8% car, 0.0% public transportation, 1.2% walk, 1.0% work from home (2006-2010 5-year est.); Travel time to work: 48.5% less than 15 minutes, 19.3% 15 to 30 minutes, 19.7% 30 to 45 minutes, 3.8% 45 to 60 minutes, 8.6% 60 minutes or more (2006-2010 5-year est.).

Additional Information Contacts

Ephrata Area Chamber of Commerce . . . . (717) 738-9010

    http://www.ephrata-area.org

DRUMORE (township). Aka Fishing Creek. Covers a land area of 24.033 square miles and a water area of 4.937 square miles. Located at 39.81° N. Lat; 76.25° W. Long. Elevation is 118 feet.

Population: 2,114 (1990); 2,243 (2000); 2,560 (2010); Density: 106.5 persons per square mile (2010); Race: 98.2% White, 0.2% Black, 0.1% Asian, 0.3% American Indian/Alaska Native, 0.0% Native Hawaiian/Other Pacific Islander, 1.2% Other, 1.7% Hispanic of any race (2010); Average household size: 3.21 (2010); Median age: 33.0 (2010); Males per 100 females: 107.6 (2010); Marriage status: 20.7% never married, 67.8% now married, 4.7% widowed, 6.8% divorced (2006-2010 5-year est.); Foreign born: 1.8% (2006-2010 5-year est.); Ancestry (includes multiple ancestries): 33.0% German, 12.5% American, 10.1% Irish, 9.0% English, 6.3% Pennsylvania German (2006-2010 5-year est.).

Economy: Single-family building permits issued: 3 (2011); Multi-family building permits issued: 0 (2011); Employment by occupation: 16.9% management, 2.3% professional, 11.8% services, 10.1% sales, 2.9% farming, 14.8% construction, 6.3% production (2006-2010 5-year est.).

Income: Per capita income: $21,134 (2006-2010 5-year est.); Median household income: $58,250 (2006-2010 5-year est.); Average household income: $70,194 (2006-2010 5-year est.); Percent of households with income of $100,000 or more: 20.9% (2006-2010 5-year est.); Poverty rate: 16.7% (2006-2010 5-year est.).

Education: Percent of population age 25 and over with: High school diploma (including GED) or higher: 74.8% (2006-2010 5-year est.); Bachelor's degree or higher: 13.0% (2006-2010 5-year est.); Master's degree or higher: 5.1% (2006-2010 5-year est.).

Housing: Homeownership rate: 77.2% (2010); Median home value: $219,400 (2006-2010 5-year est.); Median contract rent: $538 per month (2006-2010 5-year est.); Median year structure built: 1977 (2006-2010 5-year est.).

Transportation: Commute to work: 78.2% car, 0.0% public transportation, 6.8% walk, 13.6% work from home (2006-2010 5-year est.); Travel time to work: 26.0% less than 15 minutes, 23.7% 15 to 30 minutes, 29.0% 30 to 45 minutes, 9.3% 45 to 60 minutes, 11.9% 60 minutes or more (2006-2010 5-year est.)

Additional Information Contacts

Southern Lancaster County Chamber of Commerce . . . . . (717) 786-1911

    http://www.southernlancasterchamber.com

EARL (township). Covers a land area of 21.959 square miles and a water area of 0.141 square miles. Located at 40.11° N. Lat; 76.10° W. Long.

Population: 5,522 (1990); 6,183 (2000); 7,024 (2010); Density: 319.9 persons per square mile (2010); Race: 97.5% White, 0.7% Black, 0.9% Asian, 0.0% American Indian/Alaska Native, 0.0% Native Hawaiian/Other Pacific Islander, 0.9% Other, 1.8% Hispanic of any race (2010); Average household size: 2.89 (2010); Median age: 39.3 (2010); Males per 100 females: 90.7 (2010); Marriage status: 20.8% never married, 69.1% now married, 5.7% widowed, 4.4% divorced (2006-2010 5-year est.); Foreign born: 2.3% (2006-2010 5-year est.); Ancestry (includes multiple ancestries): 32.6% German, 14.4% Pennsylvania German, 11.4% American, 9.0% Swiss, 5.6% English (2006-2010 5-year est.).

Economy: Single-family building permits issued: 5 (2011); Multi-family building permits issued: 6 (2011); Employment by occupation: 17.7%

management, 0.5% professional, 9.5% services, 14.5% sales, 6.2% farming, 19.5% construction, 12.1% production (2006-2010 5-year est.).

Income: Per capita income: $22,754 (2006-2010 5-year est.); Median household income: $48,949 (2006-2010 5-year est.); Average household income: $63,353 (2006-2010 5-year est.); Percent of households with income of $100,000 or more: 15.0% (2006-2010 5-year est.); Poverty rate: 8.0% (2006-2010 5-year est.).

Education: Percent of population age 25 and over with: High school diploma (including GED) or higher: 50.8% (2006-2010 5-year est.); Bachelor's degree or higher: 12.7% (2006-2010 5-year est.); Master's degree or higher: 3.3% (2006-2010 5-year est.).

Housing: Homeownership rate: 62.8% (2010); Median home value: $210,700 (2006-2010 5-year est.); Median contract rent: $891 per month (2006-2010 5-year est.); Median year structure built: 1977 (2006-2010 5-year est.).

Safety: Violent crime rate: 0.0 per 10,000 population; Property crime rate: 44.0 per 10,000 population (2011).

Transportation: Commute to work: 72.9% car, 0.3% public transportation, 4.0% walk, 17.5% work from home (2006-2010 5-year est.); Travel time to work: 55.0% less than 15 minutes, 22.4% 15 to 30 minutes, 11.7% 30 to 45 minutes, 2.0% 45 to 60 minutes, 8.9% 60 minutes or more (2006-2010 5-year est.)

Additional Information Contacts

Earl Township . . . . (717) 354-0773

    http://www.earltownship.com

Ephrata Area Chamber of Commerce . . . . (717) 738-9010

    http://www.ephrata-area.org

EAST COCALICO (township). Covers a land area of 20.428 square miles and a water area of 0.163 square miles. Located at 40.22° N. Lat; 76.11° W. Long.

Population: 7,828 (1990); 9,954 (2000); 10,310 (2010); Density: 504.7 persons per square mile (2010); Race: 95.7% White, 0.9% Black, 2.1% Asian, 0.1% American Indian/Alaska Native, 0.0% Native Hawaiian/Other Pacific Islander, 1.2% Other, 1.8% Hispanic of any race (2010); Average household size: 2.74 (2010); Median age: 39.3 (2010); Males per 100 females: 99.5 (2010); Marriage status: 21.9% never married, 66.5% now married, 4.7% widowed, 6.9% divorced (2006-2010 5-year est.); Foreign born: 2.4% (2006-2010 5-year est.); Ancestry (includes multiple ancestries): 45.9% German, 9.5% American, 8.7% English, 8.6% Irish, 5.6% Swiss (2006-2010 5-year est.).

Economy: Single-family building permits issued: 5 (2011); Multi-family building permits issued: 0 (2011); Employment by occupation: 9.9% management, 2.7% professional, 8.6% services, 13.3% sales, 6.7% farming, 14.9% construction, 12.3% production (2006-2010 5-year est.).

Income: Per capita income: $26,203 (2006-2010 5-year est.); Median household income: $60,410 (2006-2010 5-year est.); Average household income: $73,162 (2006-2010 5-year est.); Percent of households with income of $100,000 or more: 22.9% (2006-2010 5-year est.); Poverty rate: 4.9% (2006-2010 5-year est.).

Taxes: Total city taxes per capita: $261 (2009); City property taxes per capita: $114 (2009).

Education: Percent of population age 25 and over with: High school diploma (including GED) or higher: 79.2% (2006-2010 5-year est.); Bachelor's degree or higher: 19.3% (2006-2010 5-year est.); Master's degree or higher: 7.4% (2006-2010 5-year est.).

Housing: Homeownership rate: 80.5% (2010); Median home value: $184,000 (2006-2010 5-year est.); Median contract rent: $573 per month (2006-2010 5-year est.); Median year structure built: 1984 (2006-2010 5-year est.).

Safety: Violent crime rate: 7.7 per 10,000 population; Property crime rate: 116.0 per 10,000 population (2011).

Transportation: Commute to work: 91.9% car, 1.0% public transportation, 1.5% walk, 4.2% work from home (2006-2010 5-year est.); Travel time to work: 33.8% less than 15 minutes, 35.5% 15 to 30 minutes, 16.3% 30 to 45 minutes, 7.0% 45 to 60 minutes, 7.3% 60 minutes or more (2006-2010 5-year est.)

Additional Information Contacts

East Cocalico Township . . . . (717) 336-1720

    http://www.co.lancaster.pa.us/eastcocalicotwp/site/default.asp

Ephrata Area Chamber of Commerce . . . . (717) 738-9010

    http://www.ephrata-area.org

EAST DONEGAL (township). Covers a land area of 21.432 square miles and a water area of 2.325 square miles. Located at 40.08° N. Lat; 76.57° W. Long.
Population: 4,577 (1990); 5,405 (2000); 7,755 (2010); Density: 361.8 persons per square mile (2010); Race: 94.8% White, 1.8% Black, 0.8% Asian, 0.1% American Indian/Alaska Native, 0.1% Native Hawaiian/Other Pacific Islander, 2.4% Other, 3.2% Hispanic of any race (2010); Average household size: 2.70 (2010); Median age: 36.4 (2010); Males per 100 females: 101.7 (2010); Marriage status: 22.1% never married, 67.3% now married, 2.5% widowed, 8.1% divorced (2006-2010 5-year est.); Foreign born: 4.2% (2006-2010 5-year est.); Ancestry (includes multiple ancestries): 42.2% German, 14.9% Irish, 11.4% American, 10.0% Italian, 6.0% English (2006-2010 5-year est.).
Economy: Single-family building permits issued: 33 (2011); Multi-family building permits issued: 0 (2011); Employment by occupation: 12.5% management, 4.4% professional, 7.5% services, 16.0% sales, 2.6% farming, 10.0% construction, 8.3% production (2006-2010 5-year est.).
Income: Per capita income: $24,953 (2006-2010 5-year est.); Median household income: $63,292 (2006-2010 5-year est.); Average household income: $69,326 (2006-2010 5-year est.); Percent of households with income of $100,000 or more: 16.7% (2006-2010 5-year est.); Poverty rate: 8.8% (2006-2010 5-year est.).
Education: Percent of population age 25 and over with: High school diploma (including GED) or higher: 87.4% (2006-2010 5-year est.); Bachelor's degree or higher: 20.0% (2006-2010 5-year est.); Master's degree or higher: 5.0% (2006-2010 5-year est.).
Housing: Homeownership rate: 76.4% (2010); Median home value: $183,600 (2006-2010 5-year est.); Median contract rent: $724 per month (2006-2010 5-year est.); Median year structure built: 1981 (2006-2010 5-year est.).
Transportation: Commute to work: 96.9% car, 0.3% public transportation, 0.0% walk, 1.8% work from home (2006-2010 5-year est.); Travel time to work: 23.1% less than 15 minutes, 38.8% 15 to 30 minutes, 28.8% 30 to 45 minutes, 4.1% 45 to 60 minutes, 5.3% 60 minutes or more (2006-2010 5-year est.)
Additional Information Contacts
East Donegal Township . . . . (717) 426-3167
  http://www.eastdonegaltwp.com
Mount Joy Chamber of Commerce . . . . (717) 653-0773
  http://mountjoychamber.com

EAST DRUMORE (township). Covers a land area of 23.134 square miles and a water area of 0.083 square miles. Located at 39.85° N. Lat; 76.18° W. Long.
Population: 3,225 (1990); 3,535 (2000); 3,791 (2010); Density: 163.9 persons per square mile (2010); Race: 97.6% White, 0.4% Black, 0.2% Asian, 0.1% American Indian/Alaska Native, 0.2% Native Hawaiian/Other Pacific Islander, 1.5% Other, 1.6% Hispanic of any race (2010); Average household size: 2.72 (2010); Median age: 42.0 (2010); Males per 100 females: 90.1 (2010); Marriage status: 24.9% never married, 62.7% now married, 6.7% widowed, 5.7% divorced (2006-2010 5-year est.); Foreign born: 1.1% (2006-2010 5-year est.); Ancestry (includes multiple ancestries): 34.3% German, 18.9% Irish, 11.1% American, 9.1% English, 7.3% Polish (2006-2010 5-year est.).
Economy: Single-family building permits issued: 5 (2011); Multi-family building permits issued: 0 (2011); Employment by occupation: 15.0% management, 2.5% professional, 8.6% services, 11.0% sales, 3.9% farming, 16.7% construction, 10.8% production (2006-2010 5-year est.).
Income: Per capita income: $23,026 (2006-2010 5-year est.); Median household income: $61,699 (2006-2010 5-year est.); Average household income: $68,798 (2006-2010 5-year est.); Percent of households with income of $100,000 or more: 23.9% (2006-2010 5-year est.); Poverty rate: 6.4% (2006-2010 5-year est.).
Education: Percent of population age 25 and over with: High school diploma (including GED) or higher: 83.8% (2006-2010 5-year est.); Bachelor's degree or higher: 18.5% (2006-2010 5-year est.); Master's degree or higher: 4.9% (2006-2010 5-year est.).
Housing: Homeownership rate: 67.7% (2010); Median home value: $214,800 (2006-2010 5-year est.); Median contract rent: $708 per month (2006-2010 5-year est.); Median year structure built: 1975 (2006-2010 5-year est.).
Transportation: Commute to work: 86.7% car, 0.3% public transportation, 3.6% walk, 7.4% work from home (2006-2010 5-year est.); Travel time to work: 33.7% less than 15 minutes, 25.9% 15 to 30 minutes, 18.6% 30 to

45 minutes, 10.7% 45 to 60 minutes, 11.1% 60 minutes or more (2006-2010 5-year est.)
Additional Information Contacts
Southern Lancaster County Chamber of Commerce . . . . . (717) 786-1911
  http://www.southernlancasterchamber.com

EAST EARL (CDP). Covers a land area of 0.940 square miles and a water area of 0.003 square miles. Located at 40.11° N. Lat; 76.03° W. Long. Elevation is 509 feet.
Population: n/a (1990); n/a (2000); 1,144 (2010); Density: 1,216.6 persons per square mile (2010); Race: 96.4% White, 0.7% Black, 1.3% Asian, 0.2% American Indian/Alaska Native, 0.0% Native Hawaiian/Other Pacific Islander, 1.4% Other, 2.8% Hispanic of any race (2010); Average household size: 3.01 (2010); Median age: 39.7 (2010); Males per 100 females: 95.9 (2010); Marriage status: 9.9% never married, 87.1% now married, 0.0% widowed, 3.0% divorced (2006-2010 5-year est.); Foreign born: 2.4% (2006-2010 5-year est.); Ancestry (includes multiple ancestries): 27.5% German, 21.2% American, 12.5% European, 10.5% Polish, 10.5% Irish (2006-2010 5-year est.).
Economy: Employment by occupation: 7.7% management, 0.0% professional, 8.0% services, 22.9% sales, 0.0% farming, 7.4% construction, 5.1% production (2006-2010 5-year est.).
Income: Per capita income: $22,119 (2006-2010 5-year est.); Median household income: $69,141 (2006-2010 5-year est.); Average household income: $77,087 (2006-2010 5-year est.); Percent of households with income of $100,000 or more: 26.2% (2006-2010 5-year est.); Poverty rate: 0.0% (2006-2010 5-year est.).
Education: Percent of population age 25 and over with: High school diploma (including GED) or higher: 77.4% (2006-2010 5-year est.); Bachelor's degree or higher: 18.2% (2006-2010 5-year est.); Master's degree or higher: 4.6% (2006-2010 5-year est.).
School District(s)
Eastern Lancaster County SD (KG-12)
  2010-11 Enrollment: 3,111 . . . . (717) 354-1500
Housing: Homeownership rate: 86.6% (2010); Median home value: $235,600 (2006-2010 5-year est.); Median contract rent: $1,008 per month (2006-2010 5-year est.); Median year structure built: 1977 (2006-2010 5-year est.).
Transportation: Commute to work: 83.5% car, 0.0% public transportation, 0.0% walk, 13.7% work from home (2006-2010 5-year est.); Travel time to work: 35.6% less than 15 minutes, 16.8% 15 to 30 minutes, 28.2% 30 to 45 minutes, 17.5% 45 to 60 minutes, 2.0% 60 minutes or more (2006-2010 5-year est.)

EAST EARL (township). Covers a land area of 24.545 square miles and a water area of 0.201 square miles. Located at 40.13° N. Lat; 76.03° W. Long. Elevation is 509 feet.
Population: 5,502 (1990); 5,723 (2000); 6,507 (2010); Density: 265.1 persons per square mile (2010); Race: 96.4% White, 0.8% Black, 1.1% Asian, 0.2% American Indian/Alaska Native, 0.0% Native Hawaiian/Other Pacific Islander, 1.5% Other, 2.0% Hispanic of any race (2010); Average household size: 3.15 (2010); Median age: 33.9 (2010); Males per 100 females: 101.0 (2010); Marriage status: 17.1% never married, 76.3% now married, 3.5% widowed, 3.0% divorced (2006-2010 5-year est.); Foreign born: 1.9% (2006-2010 5-year est.); Ancestry (includes multiple ancestries): 41.5% German, 16.9% American, 13.2% Swiss, 8.6% Irish, 3.9% European (2006-2010 5-year est.).
Economy: Single-family building permits issued: 15 (2011); Multi-family building permits issued: 0 (2011); Employment by occupation: 13.0% management, 2.1% professional, 10.9% services, 16.2% sales, 5.7% farming, 12.7% construction, 8.8% production (2006-2010 5-year est.).
Income: Per capita income: $23,893 (2006-2010 5-year est.); Median household income: $60,227 (2006-2010 5-year est.); Average household income: $75,528 (2006-2010 5-year est.); Percent of households with income of $100,000 or more: 21.0% (2006-2010 5-year est.); Poverty rate: 3.9% (2006-2010 5-year est.).
Education: Percent of population age 25 and over with: High school diploma (including GED) or higher: 65.7% (2006-2010 5-year est.); Bachelor's degree or higher: 13.0% (2006-2010 5-year est.); Master's degree or higher: 3.5% (2006-2010 5-year est.).
Housing: Homeownership rate: 76.3% (2010); Median home value: $225,800 (2006-2010 5-year est.); Median contract rent: $613 per month (2006-2010 5-year est.); Median year structure built: 1974 (2006-2010 5-year est.).

Safety: Violent crime rate: 4.6 per 10,000 population; Property crime rate: 121.0 per 10,000 population (2011).

Transportation: Commute to work: 78.2% car, 0.0% public transportation, 1.8% walk, 13.4% work from home (2006-2010 5-year est.); Travel time to work: 39.1% less than 15 minutes, 26.1% 15 to 30 minutes, 16.1% 30 to 45 minutes, 10.0% 45 to 60 minutes, 8.6% 60 minutes or more (2006-2010 5-year est.)

Additional Information Contacts

East Earl Township . . . . (717) 354-5593
Ephrata Area Chamber of Commerce . . . . (717) 738-9010
http://www.ephrata-area.org

EAST HEMPFIELD (township). Covers a land area of 21.069 square miles and a water area of 0.093 square miles. Located at 40.08° N. Lat; 76.38° W. Long.

Population: 18,559 (1990); 21,399 (2000); 23,522 (2010); Density: 1,116.4 persons per square mile (2010); Race: 88.8% White, 2.8% Black, 3.5% Asian, 0.1% American Indian/Alaska Native, 0.0% Native Hawaiian/Other Pacific Islander, 4.8% Other, 6.9% Hispanic of any race (2010); Average household size: 2.43 (2010); Median age: 44.2 (2010); Males per 100 females: 94.9 (2010); Marriage status: 23.0% never married, 64.4% now married, 6.0% widowed, 6.6% divorced (2006-2010 5-year est.); Foreign born: 4.7% (2006-2010 5-year est.); Ancestry (includes multiple ancestries): 40.6% German, 17.0% Irish, 12.2% English, 8.2% Italian, 4.6% American (2006-2010 5-year est.).

Economy: Single-family building permits issued: 70 (2011); Multi-family building permits issued: 0 (2011); Employment by occupation: 15.0% management, 4.1% professional, 8.1% services, 13.7% sales, 5.0% farming, 4.8% construction, 4.0% production (2006-2010 5-year est.).

Income: Per capita income: $37,294 (2006-2010 5-year est.); Median household income: $69,265 (2006-2010 5-year est.); Average household income: $90,494 (2006-2010 5-year est.); Percent of households with income of $100,000 or more: 30.3% (2006-2010 5-year est.); Poverty rate: 5.9% (2006-2010 5-year est.).

Taxes: Total city taxes per capita: $344 (2009); City property taxes per capita: $118 (2009).

Education: Percent of population age 25 and over with: High school diploma (including GED) or higher: 93.4% (2006-2010 5-year est.); Bachelor's degree or higher: 42.5% (2006-2010 5-year est.); Master's degree or higher: 16.1% (2006-2010 5-year est.).

Housing: Homeownership rate: 71.7% (2010); Median home value: $229,100 (2006-2010 5-year est.); Median contract rent: $801 per month (2006-2010 5-year est.); Median year structure built: 1978 (2006-2010 5-year est.).

Safety: Violent crime rate: 8.1 per 10,000 population; Property crime rate: 201.7 per 10,000 population (2011).

Transportation: Commute to work: 92.4% car, 0.5% public transportation, 1.0% walk, 5.9% work from home (2006-2010 5-year est.); Travel time to work: 35.9% less than 15 minutes, 42.8% 15 to 30 minutes, 13.3% 30 to 45 minutes, 4.4% 45 to 60 minutes, 3.6% 60 minutes or more (2006-2010 5-year est.)

Additional Information Contacts

East Hempfield Township . . . . (717) 898-3100
http://www.easthempfield.org
Lancaster Chamber of Commerce & Industry . . . . (717) 397-3531
http://www.lancasterchamber.com

EAST LAMPETER (township). Covers a land area of 19.657 square miles and a water area of 0.289 square miles. Located at 40.04° N. Lat; 76.21° W. Long.

Population: 12,022 (1990); 13,556 (2000); 16,424 (2010); Density: 835.5 persons per square mile (2010); Race: 85.6% White, 4.7% Black, 4.1% Asian, 0.2% American Indian/Alaska Native, 0.0% Native Hawaiian/Other Pacific Islander, 5.4% Other, 9.1% Hispanic of any race (2010); Average household size: 2.55 (2010); Median age: 38.2 (2010); Males per 100 females: 95.3 (2010); Marriage status: 29.0% never married, 60.1% now married, 5.4% widowed, 5.5% divorced (2006-2010 5-year est.); Foreign born: 7.3% (2006-2010 5-year est.); Ancestry (includes multiple ancestries): 37.6% German, 13.7% Irish, 8.1% English, 6.6% American, 6.3% Italian (2006-2010 5-year est.).

Economy: Single-family building permits issued: 15 (2011); Multi-family building permits issued: 57 (2011); Employment by occupation: 10.7% management, 3.8% professional, 9.8% services, 16.3% sales, 4.4% farming, 10.1% construction, 7.4% production (2006-2010 5-year est.).

Income: Per capita income: $28,228 (2006-2010 5-year est.); Median household income: $52,033 (2006-2010 5-year est.); Average household income: $69,663 (2006-2010 5-year est.); Percent of households with income of $100,000 or more: 17.5% (2006-2010 5-year est.); Poverty rate: 8.8% (2006-2010 5-year est.).

Education: Percent of population age 25 and over with: High school diploma (including GED) or higher: 82.9% (2006-2010 5-year est.); Bachelor's degree or higher: 24.2% (2006-2010 5-year est.); Master's degree or higher: 7.7% (2006-2010 5-year est.).

Housing: Homeownership rate: 58.9% (2010); Median home value: $190,200 (2006-2010 5-year est.); Median contract rent: $777 per month (2006-2010 5-year est.); Median year structure built: 1975 (2006-2010 5-year est.).

Safety: Violent crime rate: 14.6 per 10,000 population; Property crime rate: 517.1 per 10,000 population (2011).

Transportation: Commute to work: 90.5% car, 1.2% public transportation, 1.8% walk, 4.5% work from home (2006-2010 5-year est.); Travel time to work: 41.2% less than 15 minutes, 38.1% 15 to 30 minutes, 10.0% 30 to 45 minutes, 5.9% 45 to 60 minutes, 4.9% 60 minutes or more (2006-2010 5-year est.)

Additional Information Contacts

East Lampeter Township . . . . (717) 299-8000
http://www.co.lancaster.pa.us
Lancaster Chamber of Commerce & Industry . . . . (717) 397-3531
http://www.lancasterchamber.com

EAST PETERSBURG (borough). Covers a land area of 1.208 square miles and a water area of 0.001 square miles. Located at 40.10° N. Lat; 76.35° W. Long. Elevation is 371 feet.

History: Incorporated 1946.

Population: 4,375 (1990); 4,450 (2000); 4,506 (2010); Density: 3,730.5 persons per square mile (2010); Race: 89.9% White, 3.3% Black, 1.2% Asian, 0.2% American Indian/Alaska Native, 0.0% Native Hawaiian/Other Pacific Islander, 5.4% Other, 6.9% Hispanic of any race (2010); Average household size: 2.59 (2010); Median age: 39.8 (2010); Males per 100 females: 94.6 (2010); Marriage status: 25.9% never married, 61.3% now married, 3.8% widowed, 9.1% divorced (2006-2010 5-year est.); Foreign born: 5.1% (2006-2010 5-year est.); Ancestry (includes multiple ancestries): 41.4% German, 19.2% Irish, 10.8% English, 7.2% American, 5.9% Italian (2006-2010 5-year est.).

Economy: Single-family building permits issued: 0 (2011); Multi-family building permits issued: 0 (2011); Employment by occupation: 11.1% management, 5.6% professional, 6.3% services, 20.5% sales, 5.6% farming, 6.7% construction, 7.7% production (2006-2010 5-year est.).

Income: Per capita income: $26,522 (2006-2010 5-year est.); Median household income: $55,074 (2006-2010 5-year est.); Average household income: $69,814 (2006-2010 5-year est.); Percent of households with income of $100,000 or more: 22.1% (2006-2010 5-year est.); Poverty rate: 8.3% (2006-2010 5-year est.).

Education: Percent of population age 25 and over with: High school diploma (including GED) or higher: 88.4% (2006-2010 5-year est.); Bachelor's degree or higher: 25.4% (2006-2010 5-year est.); Master's degree or higher: 7.3% (2006-2010 5-year est.).

School District(s)

Hempfield SD (KG-12)
    2010-11 Enrollment: 7,002 . . . . (717) 898-5560

Housing: Homeownership rate: 82.7% (2010); Median home value: $161,800 (2006-2010 5-year est.); Median contract rent: $692 per month (2006-2010 5-year est.); Median year structure built: 1967 (2006-2010 5-year est.).

Safety: Violent crime rate: 2.2 per 10,000 population; Property crime rate: 84.1 per 10,000 population (2011).

Transportation: Commute to work: 91.6% car, 0.5% public transportation, 3.5% walk, 1.6% work from home (2006-2010 5-year est.); Travel time to work: 48.2% less than 15 minutes, 36.3% 15 to 30 minutes, 7.9% 30 to 45 minutes, 4.5% 45 to 60 minutes, 3.2% 60 minutes or more (2006-2010 5-year est.)

Additional Information Contacts

Lancaster Chamber of Commerce & Industry . . . . (717) 397-3531
http://www.lancasterchamber.com

EDEN (township). Covers a land area of 12.534 square miles and a water area of 0.032 square miles. Located at 39.92° N. Lat; 76.14° W. Long. Elevation is 335 feet.

Population: 1,857 (1990); 1,856 (2000); 2,094 (2010); Density: 167.1 persons per square mile (2010); Race: 98.1% White, 0.2% Black, 0.6% Asian, 0.0% American Indian/Alaska Native, 0.0% Native Hawaiian/Other Pacific Islander, 1.1% Other, 1.3% Hispanic of any race (2010); Average household size: 3.24 (2010); Median age: 30.2 (2010); Males per 100 females: 103.5 (2010); Marriage status: 20.8% never married, 69.8% now married, 3.9% widowed, 5.6% divorced (2006-2010 5-year est.); Foreign born: 0.2% (2006-2010 5-year est.); Ancestry (includes multiple ancestries): 41.9% German, 8.5% American, 7.5% Irish, 5.8% Swiss, 5.7% Pennsylvania German (2006-2010 5-year est.).

Economy: Single-family building permits issued: 4 (2011); Multi-family building permits issued: 0 (2011); Employment by occupation: 20.9% management, 1.2% professional, 6.8% services, 16.2% sales, 3.4% farming, 13.3% construction, 10.5% production (2006-2010 5-year est.).

Income: Per capita income: $20,055 (2006-2010 5-year est.); Median household income: $54,375 (2006-2010 5-year est.); Average household income: $58,906 (2006-2010 5-year est.); Percent of households with income of $100,000 or more: 11.6% (2006-2010 5-year est.); Poverty rate: 12.6% (2006-2010 5-year est.).

Education: Percent of population age 25 and over with: High school diploma (including GED) or higher: 67.3% (2006-2010 5-year est.); Bachelor's degree or higher: 11.3% (2006-2010 5-year est.); Master's degree or higher: 3.0% (2006-2010 5-year est.).

Housing: Homeownership rate: 78.2% (2010); Median home value: $221,300 (2006-2010 5-year est.); Median contract rent: $587 per month (2006-2010 5-year est.); Median year structure built: 1978 (2006-2010 5-year est.).

Transportation: Commute to work: 74.1% car, 0.0% public transportation, 6.9% walk, 15.3% work from home (2006-2010 5-year est.); Travel time to work: 38.9% less than 15 minutes, 19.6% 15 to 30 minutes, 19.1% 30 to 45 minutes, 11.8% 45 to 60 minutes, 10.6% 60 minutes or more (2006-2010 5-year est.)

Additional Information Contacts
Ephrata Area Chamber of Commerce . . . . (717) 738-9010
　http://www.ephrata-area.org

ELIZABETH (township). Covers a land area of 17.392 square miles and a water area of 0.281 square miles. Located at 40.22° N. Lat; 76.31° W. Long.

History: Laid out 1751, incorporated 1827.

Population: 3,689 (1990); 3,833 (2000); 3,886 (2010); Density: 223.4 persons per square mile (2010); Race: 97.8% White, 0.6% Black, 0.4% Asian, 0.1% American Indian/Alaska Native, 0.0% Native Hawaiian/Other Pacific Islander, 1.1% Other, 0.8% Hispanic of any race (2010); Average household size: 2.82 (2010); Median age: 39.5 (2010); Males per 100 females: 102.4 (2010); Marriage status: 18.4% never married, 73.5% now married, 3.8% widowed, 4.4% divorced (2006-2010 5-year est.); Foreign born: 1.2% (2006-2010 5-year est.); Ancestry (includes multiple ancestries): 58.2% German, 10.5% American, 9.7% Irish, 5.8% Swiss, 5.4% Italian (2006-2010 5-year est.).

Economy: Single-family building permits issued: 7 (2011); Multi-family building permits issued: 0 (2011); Employment by occupation: 11.0% management, 3.2% professional, 7.7% services, 16.6% sales, 4.6% farming, 15.6% construction, 9.9% production (2006-2010 5-year est.).

Income: Per capita income: $25,170 (2006-2010 5-year est.); Median household income: $64,167 (2006-2010 5-year est.); Average household income: $73,258 (2006-2010 5-year est.); Percent of households with income of $100,000 or more: 24.3% (2006-2010 5-year est.); Poverty rate: 6.2% (2006-2010 5-year est.).

Education: Percent of population age 25 and over with: High school diploma (including GED) or higher: 83.4% (2006-2010 5-year est.); Bachelor's degree or higher: 22.4% (2006-2010 5-year est.); Master's degree or higher: 7.1% (2006-2010 5-year est.).

Housing: Homeownership rate: 85.1% (2010); Median home value: $212,200 (2006-2010 5-year est.); Median contract rent: $573 per month (2006-2010 5-year est.); Median year structure built: 1980 (2006-2010 5-year est.).

Transportation: Commute to work: 95.3% car, 0.0% public transportation, 0.0% walk, 4.3% work from home (2006-2010 5-year est.); Travel time to work: 33.2% less than 15 minutes, 41.4% 15 to 30 minutes, 21.3% 30 to 45 minutes, 4.0% 45 to 60 minutes, 0.0% 60 minutes or more (2006-2010 5-year est.)

Additional Information Contacts
Elizabeth Township . . . . (717) 626-4302
　http://www.elizabethtownship.org
Lancaster Chamber of Commerce & Industry . . . . (717) 397-3531
　http://www.lancasterchamber.com

ELIZABETHTOWN (borough). Covers a land area of 2.641 square miles and a water area of 0.017 square miles. Located at 40.15° N. Lat; 76.60° W. Long. Elevation is 446 feet.

Population: 9,947 (1990); 11,887 (2000); 11,545 (2010); Density: 4,370.7 persons per square mile (2010); Race: 94.8% White, 1.2% Black, 1.1% Asian, 0.2% American Indian/Alaska Native, 0.1% Native Hawaiian/Other Pacific Islander, 2.6% Other, 3.3% Hispanic of any race (2010); Average household size: 2.33 (2010); Median age: 32.3 (2010); Males per 100 females: 87.1 (2010); Marriage status: 38.2% never married, 41.3% now married, 10.2% widowed, 10.3% divorced (2006-2010 5-year est.); Foreign born: 2.4% (2006-2010 5-year est.); Ancestry (includes multiple ancestries): 45.9% German, 11.8% Irish, 8.4% English, 7.5% American, 5.7% Italian (2006-2010 5-year est.).

Economy: Single-family building permits issued: 1 (2011); Multi-family building permits issued: 0 (2011); Employment by occupation: 10.2% management, 2.8% professional, 12.2% services, 19.5% sales, 3.6% farming, 8.5% construction, 6.7% production (2006-2010 5-year est.).

Income: Per capita income: $19,883 (2006-2010 5-year est.); Median household income: $48,135 (2006-2010 5-year est.); Average household income: $51,759 (2006-2010 5-year est.); Percent of households with income of $100,000 or more: 10.7% (2006-2010 5-year est.); Poverty rate: 11.2% (2006-2010 5-year est.).

Education: Percent of population age 25 and over with: High school diploma (including GED) or higher: 87.6% (2006-2010 5-year est.); Bachelor's degree or higher: 24.8% (2006-2010 5-year est.); Master's degree or higher: 8.7% (2006-2010 5-year est.).

School District(s)
Elizabethtown Area SD (KG-12)
　2010-11 Enrollment: 3,989 . . . . (717) 367-1521
Lower Dauphin SD (KG-12)
　2010-11 Enrollment: 3,832 . . . . (717) 566-5300
Four-year College(s)
Elizabethtown College (Private, Not-for-profit, Church of Brethren)
　Fall 2010 Enrollment: 2,305 . . . . (717) 361-1000
　2011-12 Tuition: In-state $34,830; Out-of-state $34,830

Housing: Homeownership rate: 57.6% (2010); Median home value: $161,900 (2006-2010 5-year est.); Median contract rent: $571 per month (2006-2010 5-year est.); Median year structure built: 1960 (2006-2010 5-year est.).

Safety: Violent crime rate: 10.4 per 10,000 population; Property crime rate: 201.2 per 10,000 population (2011).

Newspapers: Elizabethtown Chronicle (Community news; Circulation 3,300)

Transportation: Commute to work: 83.5% car, 0.7% public transportation, 10.9% walk, 3.9% work from home (2006-2010 5-year est.); Travel time to work: 39.7% less than 15 minutes, 34.5% 15 to 30 minutes, 19.5% 30 to 45 minutes, 4.3% 45 to 60 minutes, 2.1% 60 minutes or more (2006-2010 5-year est.); Amtrak: train service available.

Additional Information Contacts
Borough of Elizabethtown . . . . (717) 367-1700
　http://www.etownonline.com
Elizabethtown Area Chamber of Commerce . . . . (717) 361-7188
　http://www.elizabethtowncoc.com

EPHRATA (borough). Covers a land area of 3.418 square miles and a water area of 0.043 square miles. Located at 40.18° N. Lat; 76.18° W. Long. Elevation is 361 feet.

History: Ephrata's history dates from the day in 1732 when Johann Konrad Beissel took up his residence along Cocalico Creek in a hut he shared with the hermit Emanuel Eckerlin, who later became Brother Elimelech of the Cloisters. Driven from his native Germany by persecution, Beissel had fled to Germantown in Pennsylvania in 1720. He left that community to seek solitude, but his partisans soon settled near him. The community was named Ephrata in 1738. In 1735 the Society of the Solitary, one of the oldest non-Catholic monastic bodies in North America, was formed. Although it owes its origin to the Cloisters, the town has led a separate existence from that of the monastic community. While the latter was declining, Ephrata was growing. It became a borough in 1891, when the life of the Cloisters was almost done.

Population: 12,275 (1990); 13,213 (2000); 13,394 (2010); Density: 3,918.5 persons per square mile (2010); Race: 94.0% White, 1.0% Black, 1.3% Asian, 0.2% American Indian/Alaska Native, 0.0% Native Hawaiian/Other Pacific Islander, 3.5% Other, 5.2% Hispanic of any race (2010); Average household size: 2.41 (2010); Median age: 36.8 (2010); Males per 100 females: 94.6 (2010); Marriage status: 27.6% never married, 56.5% now married, 6.0% widowed, 9.9% divorced (2006-2010 5-year est.); Foreign born: 7.6% (2006-2010 5-year est.); Ancestry (includes multiple ancestries): 42.8% German, 10.3% Irish, 8.6% American, 5.4% Italian, 5.2% English (2006-2010 5-year est.).
Economy: Single-family building permits issued: 1 (2011); Multi-family building permits issued: 46 (2011); Employment by occupation: 8.5% management, 2.2% professional, 10.5% services, 16.1% sales, 3.4% farming, 10.2% construction, 9.4% production (2006-2010 5-year est.).
Income: Per capita income: $23,264 (2006-2010 5-year est.); Median household income: $45,065 (2006-2010 5-year est.); Average household income: $53,999 (2006-2010 5-year est.); Percent of households with income of $100,000 or more: 11.4% (2006-2010 5-year est.); Poverty rate: 7.1% (2006-2010 5-year est.).
Taxes: Total city taxes per capita: $251 (2009); City property taxes per capita: $95 (2009).
Education: Percent of population age 25 and over with: High school diploma (including GED) or higher: 82.4% (2006-2010 5-year est.); Bachelor's degree or higher: 18.1% (2006-2010 5-year est.); Master's degree or higher: 6.6% (2006-2010 5-year est.).

School District(s)

Ephrata Area SD (KG-12)
 2010-11 Enrollment: 4,127 . . . . (717) 721-1513
Housing: Homeownership rate: 61.4% (2010); Median home value: $150,900 (2006-2010 5-year est.); Median contract rent: $574 per month (2006-2010 5-year est.); Median year structure built: 1965 (2006-2010 5-year est.).
Hospitals: Ephrata Community Hospital (133 beds)
Safety: Violent crime rate: 17.9 per 10,000 population; Property crime rate: 201.7 per 10,000 population (2011).
Newspapers: Ephrata Review (Community news; Circulation 9,054); The Shopping News of Lancaster County (Community news; Circulation 35,500)
Transportation: Commute to work: 88.4% car, 0.7% public transportation, 5.5% walk, 2.2% work from home (2006-2010 5-year est.); Travel time to work: 38.8% less than 15 minutes, 33.8% 15 to 30 minutes, 18.9% 30 to 45 minutes, 4.1% 45 to 60 minutes, 4.4% 60 minutes or more (2006-2010 5-year est.)
Additional Information Contacts
Borough of Ephrata . . . . (717) 738-9222
 http://www.ephrataboro.org
Ephrata Area Chamber of Commerce . . . . (717) 738-9010
 http://www.ephrata-area.org

EPHRATA (township). Covers a land area of 16.244 square miles and a water area of 0.189 square miles. Located at 40.16° N. Lat; 76.13° W. Long. Elevation is 361 feet.
History: A noted religious community was founded (c.1732) here by Seventh-day Baptists under the leadership of Johann Conrad Beissel. This austere colony, the Ephrata Cloisters, is a state historic site.
Population: 6,677 (1990); 8,026 (2000); 9,400 (2010); Density: 578.7 persons per square mile (2010); Race: 94.8% White, 1.0% Black, 1.9% Asian, 0.1% American Indian/Alaska Native, 0.0% Native Hawaiian/Other Pacific Islander, 2.2% Other, 3.1% Hispanic of any race (2010); Average household size: 2.71 (2010); Median age: 39.0 (2010); Males per 100 females: 94.9 (2010); Marriage status: 25.1% never married, 59.5% now married, 7.3% widowed, 8.0% divorced (2006-2010 5-year est.); Foreign born: 3.1% (2006-2010 5-year est.); Ancestry (includes multiple ancestries): 41.9% German, 8.5% Swiss, 8.5% Irish, 8.4% American, 7.0% English (2006-2010 5-year est.).
Economy: Single-family building permits issued: 29 (2011); Multi-family building permits issued: 57 (2011); Employment by occupation: 13.6% management, 4.3% professional, 7.7% services, 16.2% sales, 2.8% farming, 13.3% construction, 10.6% production (2006-2010 5-year est.).
Income: Per capita income: $27,580 (2006-2010 5-year est.); Median household income: $63,800 (2006-2010 5-year est.); Average household income: $77,226 (2006-2010 5-year est.); Percent of households with income of $100,000 or more: 22.8% (2006-2010 5-year est.); Poverty rate: 4.3% (2006-2010 5-year est.).

Education: Percent of population age 25 and over with: High school diploma (including GED) or higher: 75.4% (2006-2010 5-year est.); Bachelor's degree or higher: 20.8% (2006-2010 5-year est.); Master's degree or higher: 7.0% (2006-2010 5-year est.).
Housing: Homeownership rate: 74.0% (2010); Median home value: $201,200 (2006-2010 5-year est.); Median contract rent: $751 per month (2006-2010 5-year est.); Median year structure built: 1985 (2006-2010 5-year est.).
Hospitals: Ephrata Community Hospital (133 beds)
Safety: Violent crime rate: 7.4 per 10,000 population; Property crime rate: 171.8 per 10,000 population (2011).
Newspapers: Ephrata Review (Community news; Circulation 9,054); The Shopping News of Lancaster County (Community news; Circulation 35,500)
Transportation: Commute to work: 88.7% car, 0.1% public transportation, 3.5% walk, 4.5% work from home (2006-2010 5-year est.); Travel time to work: 36.0% less than 15 minutes, 38.3% 15 to 30 minutes, 14.4% 30 to 45 minutes, 4.8% 45 to 60 minutes, 6.5% 60 minutes or more (2006-2010 5-year est.)
Additional Information Contacts
Ephrata Area Chamber of Commerce . . . . (717) 738-9010
 http://www.ephrata-area.org
Ephrata Township . . . . (717) 733-1044
 http://www.ephratatownship.org

FALMOUTH (CDP). Covers a land area of 0.986 square miles and a water area of <.001 square miles. Located at 40.13° N. Lat; 76.71° W. Long. Elevation is 358 feet.
Population: n/a (1990); n/a (2000); 420 (2010); Density: 425.9 persons per square mile (2010); Race: 99.3% White, 0.0% Black, 0.0% Asian, 0.2% American Indian/Alaska Native, 0.0% Native Hawaiian/Other Pacific Islander, 0.5% Other, 1.4% Hispanic of any race (2010); Average household size: 2.66 (2010); Median age: 41.8 (2010); Males per 100 females: 97.2 (2010); Marriage status: 26.2% never married, 55.2% now married, 9.8% widowed, 8.7% divorced (2006-2010 5-year est.); Foreign born: 0.0% (2006-2010 5-year est.); Ancestry (includes multiple ancestries): 43.7% German, 13.3% Irish, 11.0% Italian, 8.5% English, 8.5% American (2006-2010 5-year est.).
Economy: Employment by occupation: 5.2% management, 3.6% professional, 11.7% services, 13.7% sales, 4.4% farming, 17.7% construction, 19.4% production (2006-2010 5-year est.).
Income: Per capita income: $25,986 (2006-2010 5-year est.); Median household income: $62,604 (2006-2010 5-year est.); Average household income: $70,086 (2006-2010 5-year est.); Percent of households with income of $100,000 or more: 13.0% (2006-2010 5-year est.); Poverty rate: 4.8% (2006-2010 5-year est.).
Education: Percent of population age 25 and over with: High school diploma (including GED) or higher: 81.6% (2006-2010 5-year est.); Bachelor's degree or higher: 10.1% (2006-2010 5-year est.); Master's degree or higher: 5.6% (2006-2010 5-year est.).
Housing: Homeownership rate: 89.9% (2010); Median home value: $177,900 (2006-2010 5-year est.); Median contract rent: n/a per month (2006-2010 5-year est.); Median year structure built: 1976 (2006-2010 5-year est.).
Transportation: Commute to work: 97.4% car, 0.0% public transportation, 0.0% walk, 2.6% work from home (2006-2010 5-year est.); Travel time to work: 23.1% less than 15 minutes, 56.4% 15 to 30 minutes, 20.4% 30 to 45 minutes, 0.0% 45 to 60 minutes, 0.0% 60 minutes or more (2006-2010 5-year est.)

FARMERSVILLE (CDP). Covers a land area of 2.554 square miles and a water area of 0.001 square miles. Located at 40.12° N. Lat; 76.15° W. Long. Elevation is 364 feet.
Population: n/a (1990); n/a (2000); 991 (2010); Density: 388.0 persons per square mile (2010); Race: 99.1% White, 0.1% Black, 0.0% Asian, 0.2% American Indian/Alaska Native, 0.0% Native Hawaiian/Other Pacific Islander, 0.6% Other, 1.0% Hispanic of any race (2010); Average household size: 2.55 (2010); Median age: 54.9 (2010); Males per 100 females: 77.0 (2010); Marriage status: 34.4% never married, 43.2% now married, 20.7% widowed, 1.7% divorced (2006-2010 5-year est.); Foreign born: 0.5% (2006-2010 5-year est.); Ancestry (includes multiple ancestries): 31.1% Pennsylvania German, 27.7% German, 9.6% Swedish, 8.4% American, 4.5% Swiss (2006-2010 5-year est.).

Economy: Employment by occupation: 16.6% management, 9.2% professional, 2.9% services, 5.4% sales, 0.0% farming, 29.9% construction, 18.2% production (2006-2010 5-year est.).

Income: Per capita income: $14,769 (2006-2010 5-year est.); Median household income: $32,407 (2006-2010 5-year est.); Average household income: $52,846 (2006-2010 5-year est.); Percent of households with income of $100,000 or more: 6.8% (2006-2010 5-year est.); Poverty rate: 15.5% (2006-2010 5-year est.).

Education: Percent of population age 25 and over with: High school diploma (including GED) or higher: 45.2% (2006-2010 5-year est.); Bachelor's degree or higher: 10.2% (2006-2010 5-year est.); Master's degree or higher: 3.8% (2006-2010 5-year est.).

Housing: Homeownership rate: 48.7% (2010); Median home value: $340,000 (2006-2010 5-year est.); Median contract rent: $717 per month (2006-2010 5-year est.); Median year structure built: 1963 (2006-2010 5-year est.).

Transportation: Commute to work: 61.8% car, 0.0% public transportation, 7.9% walk, 20.0% work from home (2006-2010 5-year est.); Travel time to work: 71.3% less than 15 minutes, 28.7% 15 to 30 minutes, 0.0% 30 to 45 minutes, 0.0% 45 to 60 minutes, 0.0% 60 minutes or more (2006-2010 5-year est.)

FIVEPOINTVILLE (CDP). Covers a land area of 1.233 square miles and a water area of 0.028 square miles. Located at 40.18° N. Lat; 76.06° W. Long. Elevation is 459 feet.

Population: n/a (1990); n/a (2000); 1,156 (2010); Density: 937.2 persons per square mile (2010); Race: 97.3% White, 0.1% Black, 1.3% Asian, 0.0% American Indian/Alaska Native, 0.0% Native Hawaiian/Other Pacific Islander, 1.3% Other, 2.0% Hispanic of any race (2010); Average household size: 3.05 (2010); Median age: 36.0 (2010); Males per 100 females: 100.0 (2010); Marriage status: 37.1% never married, 59.8% now married, 3.1% widowed, 0.0% divorced (2006-2010 5-year est.); Foreign born: 8.3% (2006-2010 5-year est.); Ancestry (includes multiple ancestries): 37.5% German, 11.6% American, 7.3% English, 6.7% Swiss, 6.7% Irish (2006-2010 5-year est.).

Economy: Employment by occupation: 8.7% management, 0.0% professional, 8.4% services, 12.1% sales, 15.0% farming, 15.2% construction, 1.5% production (2006-2010 5-year est.).

Income: Per capita income: $23,083 (2006-2010 5-year est.); Median household income: $54,306 (2006-2010 5-year est.); Average household income: $68,420 (2006-2010 5-year est.); Percent of households with income of $100,000 or more: 6.7% (2006-2010 5-year est.); Poverty rate: 2.1% (2006-2010 5-year est.).

Education: Percent of population age 25 and over with: High school diploma (including GED) or higher: 85.5% (2006-2010 5-year est.); Bachelor's degree or higher: 18.0% (2006-2010 5-year est.); Master's degree or higher: 3.9% (2006-2010 5-year est.).

Housing: Homeownership rate: 80.5% (2010); Median home value: $198,600 (2006-2010 5-year est.); Median contract rent: $468 per month (2006-2010 5-year est.); Median year structure built: 1989 (2006-2010 5-year est.).

Transportation: Commute to work: 91.8% car, 0.0% public transportation, 0.0% walk, 6.6% work from home (2006-2010 5-year est.); Travel time to work: 27.5% less than 15 minutes, 29.3% 15 to 30 minutes, 30.2% 30 to 45 minutes, 3.9% 45 to 60 minutes, 9.1% 60 minutes or more (2006-2010 5-year est.)

FULTON (township). Covers a land area of 25.789 square miles and a water area of 3.442 square miles. Located at 39.76° N. Lat; 76.19° W. Long.

Population: 2,688 (1990); 2,826 (2000); 3,074 (2010); Density: 119.2 persons per square mile (2010); Race: 96.7% White, 1.5% Black, 0.1% Asian, 0.2% American Indian/Alaska Native, 0.0% Native Hawaiian/Other Pacific Islander, 1.5% Other, 2.1% Hispanic of any race (2010); Average household size: 2.98 (2010); Median age: 35.7 (2010); Males per 100 females: 101.2 (2010); Marriage status: 25.3% never married, 57.7% now married, 5.6% widowed, 11.4% divorced (2006-2010 5-year est.); Foreign born: 0.7% (2006-2010 5-year est.); Ancestry (includes multiple ancestries): 32.4% German, 17.7% Irish, 14.2% American, 10.7% English, 7.3% Italian (2006-2010 5-year est.).

Economy: Single-family building permits issued: 2 (2011); Multi-family building permits issued: 0 (2011); Employment by occupation: 14.3% management, 2.6% professional, 12.7% services, 21.3% sales, 1.8% farming, 15.3% construction, 12.2% production (2006-2010 5-year est.).

Income: Per capita income: $21,598 (2006-2010 5-year est.); Median household income: $48,669 (2006-2010 5-year est.); Average household income: $59,282 (2006-2010 5-year est.); Percent of households with income of $100,000 or more: 12.6% (2006-2010 5-year est.); Poverty rate: 6.7% (2006-2010 5-year est.).

Education: Percent of population age 25 and over with: High school diploma (including GED) or higher: 76.5% (2006-2010 5-year est.); Bachelor's degree or higher: 12.1% (2006-2010 5-year est.); Master's degree or higher: 4.2% (2006-2010 5-year est.).

Housing: Homeownership rate: 76.2% (2010); Median home value: $182,600 (2006-2010 5-year est.); Median contract rent: $512 per month (2006-2010 5-year est.); Median year structure built: 1978 (2006-2010 5-year est.).

Transportation: Commute to work: 85.0% car, 1.0% public transportation, 3.6% walk, 9.1% work from home (2006-2010 5-year est.); Travel time to work: 16.8% less than 15 minutes, 31.9% 15 to 30 minutes, 26.9% 30 to 45 minutes, 10.1% 45 to 60 minutes, 14.2% 60 minutes or more (2006-2010 5-year est.)

Additional Information Contacts

Fulton County Chamber of Commerce and Tourism . . . . . . (717) 485-4064
http://www.fultoncountypa.com

GAP (CDP). Covers a land area of 2.812 square miles and a water area of 0.003 square miles. Located at 39.99° N. Lat; 76.02° W. Long. Elevation is 545 feet.

History: Nickel deposits (formerly mined) are Southwest.

Population: 1,370 (1990); 1,611 (2000); 1,931 (2010); Density: 686.7 persons per square mile (2010); Race: 94.1% White, 1.5% Black, 1.6% Asian, 0.1% American Indian/Alaska Native, 0.0% Native Hawaiian/Other Pacific Islander, 2.7% Other, 2.5% Hispanic of any race (2010); Average household size: 2.92 (2010); Median age: 37.8 (2010); Males per 100 females: 104.6 (2010); Marriage status: 11.7% never married, 77.7% now married, 8.1% widowed, 2.5% divorced (2006-2010 5-year est.); Foreign born: 2.3% (2006-2010 5-year est.); Ancestry (includes multiple ancestries): 37.6% German, 13.8% Pennsylvania German, 9.9% Irish, 8.3% American, 8.3% English (2006-2010 5-year est.).

Economy: Employment by occupation: 15.8% management, 0.0% professional, 8.9% services, 26.4% sales, 5.6% farming, 9.3% construction, 2.3% production (2006-2010 5-year est.).

Income: Per capita income: $24,795 (2006-2010 5-year est.); Median household income: $47,837 (2006-2010 5-year est.); Average household income: $62,421 (2006-2010 5-year est.); Percent of households with income of $100,000 or more: 19.7% (2006-2010 5-year est.); Poverty rate: 8.9% (2006-2010 5-year est.).

Education: Percent of population age 25 and over with: High school diploma (including GED) or higher: 76.8% (2006-2010 5-year est.); Bachelor's degree or higher: 16.2% (2006-2010 5-year est.); Master's degree or higher: 6.4% (2006-2010 5-year est.).

School District(s)

Pequea Valley SD (KG-12)
    2010-11 Enrollment: 1,734 . . . . (717) 768-5530

Housing: Homeownership rate: 73.7% (2010); Median home value: $254,500 (2006-2010 5-year est.); Median contract rent: $525 per month (2006-2010 5-year est.); Median year structure built: 1963 (2006-2010 5-year est.).

Transportation: Commute to work: 97.7% car, 0.0% public transportation, 1.2% walk, 1.2% work from home (2006-2010 5-year est.); Travel time to work: 28.5% less than 15 minutes, 40.6% 15 to 30 minutes, 18.4% 30 to 45 minutes, 4.7% 45 to 60 minutes, 7.8% 60 minutes or more (2006-2010 5-year est.)

Additional Information Contacts

Southern Lancaster County Chamber of Commerce . . . . . (717) 786-1911
http://www.southernlancasterchamber.com

GEORGETOWN (CDP). Covers a land area of 4.075 square miles and a water area of 0.007 square miles. Located at 39.94° N. Lat; 76.08° W. Long. Elevation is 673 feet.

Population: n/a (1990); n/a (2000); 1,022 (2010); Density: 250.8 persons per square mile (2010); Race: 99.7% White, 0.1% Black, 0.1% Asian, 0.1% American Indian/Alaska Native, 0.0% Native Hawaiian/Other Pacific Islander, 0.0% Other, 1.6% Hispanic of any race (2010); Average household size: 3.33 (2010); Median age: 30.5 (2010); Males per 100 females: 102.8 (2010); Marriage status: 34.3% never married, 56.8% now married, 5.8% widowed, 3.0% divorced (2006-2010 5-year est.); Foreign born: 4.5% (2006-2010 5-year est.); Ancestry (includes multiple

ancestries): 23.7% German, 11.3% Pennsylvania German, 8.9% American, 8.2% European, 6.9% English (2006-2010 5-year est.).
Economy: Employment by occupation: 11.7% management, 1.3% professional, 5.3% services, 19.6% sales, 0.9% farming, 34.8% construction, 1.1% production (2006-2010 5-year est.).
Income: Per capita income: $16,760 (2006-2010 5-year est.); Median household income: $48,813 (2006-2010 5-year est.); Average household income: $56,466 (2006-2010 5-year est.); Percent of households with income of $100,000 or more: 7.7% (2006-2010 5-year est.); Poverty rate: 12.2% (2006-2010 5-year est.).
Education: Percent of population age 25 and over with: High school diploma (including GED) or higher: 49.4% (2006-2010 5-year est.); Bachelor's degree or higher: 9.4% (2006-2010 5-year est.); Master's degree or higher: 3.0% (2006-2010 5-year est.).
Housing: Homeownership rate: 72.6% (2010); Median home value: $252,500 (2006-2010 5-year est.); Median contract rent: $588 per month (2006-2010 5-year est.); Median year structure built: 1973 (2006-2010 5-year est.).
Transportation: Commute to work: 79.2% car, 0.0% public transportation, 6.0% walk, 8.0% work from home (2006-2010 5-year est.); Travel time to work: 26.0% less than 15 minutes, 18.2% 15 to 30 minutes, 43.4% 30 to 45 minutes, 2.7% 45 to 60 minutes, 9.7% 60 minutes or more (2006-2010 5-year est.)

GOODVILLE (CDP). Covers a land area of 1.541 square miles and a water area of 0.002 square miles. Located at 40.13° N. Lat; 76.00° W. Long. Elevation is 535 feet.
Population: n/a (1990); n/a (2000); 482 (2010); Density: 312.7 persons per square mile (2010); Race: 94.2% White, 1.5% Black, 0.6% Asian, 0.0% American Indian/Alaska Native, 0.0% Native Hawaiian/Other Pacific Islander, 3.7% Other, 2.9% Hispanic of any race (2010); Average household size: 3.17 (2010); Median age: 29.3 (2010); Males per 100 females: 93.6 (2010); Marriage status: 0.0% never married, 100.0% now married, 0.0% widowed, 0.0% divorced (2006-2010 5-year est.); Foreign born: 0.0% (2006-2010 5-year est.); Ancestry (includes multiple ancestries): 61.9% German, 30.4% Swiss, 9.7% Swedish, 5.8% Danish, 4.7% Italian (2006-2010 5-year est.).
Economy: Employment by occupation: 0.0% management, 23.8% professional, 0.0% services, 0.0% sales, 0.0% farming, 31.7% construction, 19.0% production (2006-2010 5-year est.).
Income: Per capita income: $11,396 (2006-2010 5-year est.); Median household income: $55,563 (2006-2010 5-year est.); Average household income: $46,406 (2006-2010 5-year est.); Percent of households with income of $100,000 or more: n/a (2006-2010 5-year est.); Poverty rate: 22.6% (2006-2010 5-year est.).
Education: Percent of population age 25 and over with: High school diploma (including GED) or higher: 51.8% (2006-2010 5-year est.); Bachelor's degree or higher: 17.6% (2006-2010 5-year est.); Master's degree or higher: 0.0% (2006-2010 5-year est.).
Housing: Homeownership rate: 56.0% (2010); Median home value: $231,700 (2006-2010 5-year est.); Median contract rent: n/a per month (2006-2010 5-year est.); Median year structure built: 1942 (2006-2010 5-year est.).
Transportation: Commute to work: 100.0% car, 0.0% public transportation, 0.0% walk, 0.0% work from home (2006-2010 5-year est.); Travel time to work: 25.4% less than 15 minutes, 31.7% 15 to 30 minutes, 42.9% 30 to 45 minutes, 0.0% 45 to 60 minutes, 0.0% 60 minutes or more (2006-2010 5-year est.)

GORDONVILLE (CDP). Covers a land area of 0.950 square miles and a water area of 0 square miles. Located at 40.02° N. Lat; 76.14° W. Long. Elevation is 400 feet.
Population: n/a (1990); n/a (2000); 508 (2010); Density: 535.0 persons per square mile (2010); Race: 95.9% White, 2.2% Black, 0.0% Asian, 0.0% American Indian/Alaska Native, 0.0% Native Hawaiian/Other Pacific Islander, 1.9% Other, 2.0% Hispanic of any race (2010); Average household size: 2.45 (2010); Median age: 39.0 (2010); Males per 100 females: 100.8 (2010); Marriage status: 30.4% never married, 53.8% now married, 8.1% widowed, 7.7% divorced (2006-2010 5-year est.); Foreign born: 0.0% (2006-2010 5-year est.); Ancestry (includes multiple ancestries): 29.8% German, 21.3% Swedish, 16.6% American, 5.0% Irish, 3.2% Welsh (2006-2010 5-year est.).
Economy: Employment by occupation: 7.5% management, 0.0% professional, 17.1% services, 16.3% sales, 0.0% farming, 15.5% construction, 7.9% production (2006-2010 5-year est.).

Income: Per capita income: $11,576 (2006-2010 5-year est.); Median household income: $31,458 (2006-2010 5-year est.); Average household income: $37,489 (2006-2010 5-year est.); Percent of households with income of $100,000 or more: 3.7% (2006-2010 5-year est.); Poverty rate: 30.1% (2006-2010 5-year est.).
Education: Percent of population age 25 and over with: High school diploma (including GED) or higher: 63.8% (2006-2010 5-year est.); Bachelor's degree or higher: 6.0% (2006-2010 5-year est.); Master's degree or higher: 2.4% (2006-2010 5-year est.).
Housing: Homeownership rate: 63.2% (2010); Median home value: $62,000 (2006-2010 5-year est.); Median contract rent: $679 per month (2006-2010 5-year est.); Median year structure built: 1976 (2006-2010 5-year est.).
Transportation: Commute to work: 75.4% car, 0.0% public transportation, 3.6% walk, 7.1% work from home (2006-2010 5-year est.); Travel time to work: 16.2% less than 15 minutes, 66.7% 15 to 30 minutes, 13.7% 30 to 45 minutes, 0.0% 45 to 60 minutes, 3.4% 60 minutes or more (2006-2010 5-year est.)

HOLTWOOD (unincorporated postal area)
Zip Code: 17532
Covers a land area of 21.199 square miles and a water area of 2.779 square miles. Located at 39.85° N. Lat; 76.28° W. Long. Population: 3,381 (2010); Density: 159.5 persons per square mile (2010); Race: 98.4% White, 0.1% Black, 0.1% Asian, 0.3% American Indian/Alaska Native, 0.0% Native Hawaiian/Other Pacific Islander, 1.1% Other, 1.6% Hispanic of any race (2010); Average household size: 2.85 (2010); Median age: 39.3 (2010); Males per 100 females: 103.8 (2010); Homeownership rate: 86.0% (2010)

HOPELAND (CDP). Covers a land area of 0.660 square miles and a water area of 0.010 square miles. Located at 40.23° N. Lat; 76.26° W. Long. Elevation is 400 feet.
Population: n/a (1990); n/a (2000); 738 (2010); Density: 1,119.0 persons per square mile (2010); Race: 95.1% White, 0.9% Black, 1.4% Asian, 0.0% American Indian/Alaska Native, 0.0% Native Hawaiian/Other Pacific Islander, 2.6% Other, 1.8% Hispanic of any race (2010); Average household size: 2.88 (2010); Median age: 38.4 (2010); Males per 100 females: 106.7 (2010); Marriage status: 23.9% never married, 67.1% now married, 0.0% widowed, 9.0% divorced (2006-2010 5-year est.); Foreign born: 0.0% (2006-2010 5-year est.); Ancestry (includes multiple ancestries): 58.4% German, 22.0% American, 9.0% Irish, 8.6% Dutch, 8.4% Italian (2006-2010 5-year est.).
Economy: Employment by occupation: 15.5% management, 0.0% professional, 8.0% services, 19.7% sales, 0.0% farming, 17.9% construction, 13.9% production (2006-2010 5-year est.).
Income: Per capita income: $31,250 (2006-2010 5-year est.); Median household income: $71,058 (2006-2010 5-year est.); Average household income: $84,166 (2006-2010 5-year est.); Percent of households with income of $100,000 or more: 28.2% (2006-2010 5-year est.); Poverty rate: 2.0% (2006-2010 5-year est.).
Education: Percent of population age 25 and over with: High school diploma (including GED) or higher: 70.6% (2006-2010 5-year est.); Bachelor's degree or higher: 12.2% (2006-2010 5-year est.); Master's degree or higher: 2.1% (2006-2010 5-year est.).
Housing: Homeownership rate: 82.0% (2010); Median home value: $205,100 (2006-2010 5-year est.); Median contract rent: $384 per month (2006-2010 5-year est.); Median year structure built: 1987 (2006-2010 5-year est.).
Transportation: Commute to work: 100.0% car, 0.0% public transportation, 0.0% walk, 0.0% work from home (2006-2010 5-year est.); Travel time to work: 22.9% less than 15 minutes, 40.5% 15 to 30 minutes, 28.3% 30 to 45 minutes, 8.3% 45 to 60 minutes, 0.0% 60 minutes or more (2006-2010 5-year est.)

INTERCOURSE (CDP). Covers a land area of 2.108 square miles and a water area of <.001 square miles. Located at 40.04° N. Lat; 76.11° W. Long. Elevation is 436 feet.
Population: n/a (1990); n/a (2000); 1,274 (2010); Density: 604.2 persons per square mile (2010); Race: 97.7% White, 0.4% Black, 1.2% Asian, 0.0% American Indian/Alaska Native, 0.2% Native Hawaiian/Other Pacific Islander, 0.5% Other, 1.6% Hispanic of any race (2010); Average household size: 2.76 (2010); Median age: 40.6 (2010); Males per 100 females: 91.9 (2010); Marriage status: 20.7% never married, 70.1% now married, 7.9% widowed, 1.4% divorced (2006-2010 5-year est.); Foreign

born: 1.2% (2006-2010 5-year est.); Ancestry (includes multiple ancestries): 53.7% German, 13.5% Irish, 6.5% Dutch, 6.0% Swiss, 5.7% English (2006-2010 5-year est.).

Economy: Employment by occupation: 11.2% management, 4.7% professional, 14.7% services, 6.8% sales, 2.3% farming, 16.0% construction, 13.7% production (2006-2010 5-year est.).

Income: Per capita income: $29,602 (2006-2010 5-year est.); Median household income: $63,895 (2006-2010 5-year est.); Average household income: $67,085 (2006-2010 5-year est.); Percent of households with income of $100,000 or more: 22.8% (2006-2010 5-year est.); Poverty rate: 0.0% (2006-2010 5-year est.).

Education: Percent of population age 25 and over with: High school diploma (including GED) or higher: 64.1% (2006-2010 5-year est.); Bachelor's degree or higher: 9.8% (2006-2010 5-year est.); Master's degree or higher: 5.9% (2006-2010 5-year est.).

Housing: Homeownership rate: 65.6% (2010); Median home value: $219,300 (2006-2010 5-year est.); Median contract rent: $615 per month (2006-2010 5-year est.); Median year structure built: 1969 (2006-2010 5-year est.).

Transportation: Commute to work: 85.3% car, 0.0% public transportation, 7.0% walk, 7.6% work from home (2006-2010 5-year est.); Travel time to work: 47.5% less than 15 minutes, 20.1% 15 to 30 minutes, 17.4% 30 to 45 minutes, 9.3% 45 to 60 minutes, 5.7% 60 minutes or more (2006-2010 5-year est.)

KINZERS (unincorporated postal area)
Zip Code: 17535

Covers a land area of 10.837 square miles and a water area of 0.072 square miles. Located at 39.98° N. Lat; 76.02° W. Long. Population: 2,458 (2010); Density: 226.8 persons per square mile (2010); Race: 94.3% White, 1.8% Black, 0.9% Asian, 0.1% American Indian/Alaska Native, 0.2% Native Hawaiian/Other Pacific Islander, 2.7% Other, 3.3% Hispanic of any race (2010); Average household size: 3.54 (2010); Median age: 27.4 (2010); Males per 100 females: 104.2 (2010); Homeownership rate: 62.7% (2010)

KIRKWOOD (CDP). Covers a land area of 2.222 square miles and a water area of 0.004 square miles. Located at 39.85° N. Lat; 76.08° W. Long. Elevation is 518 feet.

Population: n/a (1990); n/a (2000); 396 (2010); Density: 178.2 persons per square mile (2010); Race: 98.2% White, 0.0% Black, 0.0% Asian, 0.3% American Indian/Alaska Native, 0.3% Native Hawaiian/Other Pacific Islander, 1.2% Other, 4.3% Hispanic of any race (2010); Average household size: 3.30 (2010); Median age: 27.8 (2010); Males per 100 females: 115.2 (2010); Marriage status: 33.6% never married, 66.4% now married, 0.0% widowed, 0.0% divorced (2006-2010 5-year est.); Foreign born: 3.9% (2006-2010 5-year est.); Ancestry (includes multiple ancestries): 49.2% Pennsylvania German, 29.4% German, 9.0% Swiss, 4.2% American, 4.2% Irish (2006-2010 5-year est.).

Economy: Employment by occupation: 23.2% management, 4.3% professional, 0.0% services, 15.2% sales, 17.4% farming, 47.8% construction, 15.2% production (2006-2010 5-year est.).

Income: Per capita income: $26,803 (2006-2010 5-year est.); Median household income: $73,750 (2006-2010 5-year est.); Average household income: $108,652 (2006-2010 5-year est.); Percent of households with income of $100,000 or more: 36.0% (2006-2010 5-year est.); Poverty rate: 0.0% (2006-2010 5-year est.).

Education: Percent of population age 25 and over with: High school diploma (including GED) or higher: 54.6% (2006-2010 5-year est.); Bachelor's degree or higher: 10.9% (2006-2010 5-year est.); Master's degree or higher: 3.4% (2006-2010 5-year est.).

Housing: Homeownership rate: 61.6% (2010); Median home value: $217,900 (2006-2010 5-year est.); Median contract rent: n/a per month (2006-2010 5-year est.); Median year structure built: 1974 (2006-2010 5-year est.).

Transportation: Commute to work: 56.8% car, 0.0% public transportation, 38.6% walk, 4.5% work from home (2006-2010 5-year est.); Travel time to work: 76.2% less than 15 minutes, 9.5% 15 to 30 minutes, 4.0% 30 to 45 minutes, 0.0% 45 to 60 minutes, 10.3% 60 minutes or more (2006-2010 5-year est.)

LAMPETER (CDP). Covers a land area of 1.717 square miles and a water area of 0.001 square miles. Located at 39.99° N. Lat; 76.25° W. Long. Elevation is 407 feet.

Population: n/a (1990); n/a (2000); 1,669 (2010); Density: 972.3 persons per square mile (2010); Race: 92.9% White, 1.5% Black, 1.4% Asian, 0.1% American Indian/Alaska Native, 0.0% Native Hawaiian/Other Pacific Islander, 4.1% Other, 5.9% Hispanic of any race (2010); Average household size: 2.80 (2010); Median age: 34.0 (2010); Males per 100 females: 99.6 (2010); Marriage status: 19.4% never married, 69.8% now married, 1.3% widowed, 9.5% divorced (2006-2010 5-year est.); Foreign born: 0.9% (2006-2010 5-year est.); Ancestry (includes multiple ancestries): 46.5% German, 19.4% American, 18.6% English, 6.9% Irish, 5.0% Scottish (2006-2010 5-year est.).

Economy: Employment by occupation: 13.2% management, 0.0% professional, 11.6% services, 10.2% sales, 1.5% farming, 13.9% construction, 6.2% production (2006-2010 5-year est.).

Income: Per capita income: $24,874 (2006-2010 5-year est.); Median household income: $67,679 (2006-2010 5-year est.); Average household income: $66,774 (2006-2010 5-year est.); Percent of households with income of $100,000 or more: 24.3% (2006-2010 5-year est.); Poverty rate: 3.1% (2006-2010 5-year est.).

Education: Percent of population age 25 and over with: High school diploma (including GED) or higher: 85.3% (2006-2010 5-year est.); Bachelor's degree or higher: 26.0% (2006-2010 5-year est.); Master's degree or higher: 4.4% (2006-2010 5-year est.).

School District(s)
Lampeter-Strasburg SD (KG-12)
    2010-11 Enrollment: 3,168 . . . . (717) 464-3311

Housing: Homeownership rate: 61.8% (2010); Median home value: $220,600 (2006-2010 5-year est.); Median contract rent: $739 per month (2006-2010 5-year est.); Median year structure built: 1960 (2006-2010 5-year est.).

Transportation: Commute to work: 96.4% car, 0.0% public transportation, 0.0% walk, 1.4% work from home (2006-2010 5-year est.); Travel time to work: 35.4% less than 15 minutes, 43.3% 15 to 30 minutes, 7.2% 30 to 45 minutes, 6.0% 45 to 60 minutes, 8.1% 60 minutes or more (2006-2010 5-year est.)

LANCASTER (city). County seat. Covers a land area of 7.226 square miles and a water area of 0.128 square miles. Located at 40.04° N. Lat; 76.30° W. Long. Elevation is 361 feet.

History: Lancaster was laid out in 1730, a year after it was designated the seat of Lancaster County. Both county and town were named by John Wright, chief magistrate, for his home shire of Lancaster, England. The town was incorporated as a borough in 1742. Meanwhile, the provincial government had laid out the King's Highway from Penn Square to Compassville. This was the greatest factor in Lancaster's early growth. The road later became the Philadelphia and Lancaster Turnpike. By 1751 the town was known for its manufacture of farm implements and guns. Lancaster played decisive roles in both the French and Indian War and in the Revolution. Lancaster became a city in 1818.

Population: 56,188 (1990); 56,348 (2000); 59,322 (2010); Density: 8,210.0 persons per square mile (2010); Race: 55.2% White, 16.3% Black, 3.0% Asian, 0.7% American Indian/Alaska Native, 0.1% Native Hawaiian/Other Pacific Islander, 24.7% Other, 39.3% Hispanic of any race (2010); Average household size: 2.58 (2010); Median age: 30.5 (2010); Males per 100 females: 98.7 (2010); Marriage status: 46.3% never married, 36.8% now married, 5.0% widowed, 11.9% divorced (2006-2010 5-year est.); Foreign born: 9.8% (2006-2010 5-year est.); Ancestry (includes multiple ancestries): 20.1% German, 8.3% Irish, 5.1% English, 4.2% Italian, 2.4% American (2006-2010 5-year est.).

Economy: Unemployment rate: 9.7% (August 2012); Total civilian labor force: 28,223 (August 2012); Single-family building permits issued: 8 (2011); Multi-family building permits issued: 0 (2011); Employment by occupation: 6.1% management, 1.3% professional, 13.0% services, 17.0% sales, 5.6% farming, 8.5% construction, 9.2% production (2006-2010 5-year est.).

Income: Per capita income: $15,768 (2006-2010 5-year est.); Median household income: $32,737 (2006-2010 5-year est.); Average household income: $40,846 (2006-2010 5-year est.); Percent of households with income of $100,000 or more: 5.8% (2006-2010 5-year est.); Poverty rate: 27.6% (2006-2010 5-year est.).

Taxes: Total city taxes per capita: $485 (2009); City property taxes per capita: $319 (2009).

Education: Percent of population age 25 and over with: High school diploma (including GED) or higher: 73.7% (2006-2010 5-year est.); Bachelor's degree or higher: 16.4% (2006-2010 5-year est.); Master's degree or higher: 5.4% (2006-2010 5-year est.).

School District(s)

Conestoga Valley SD (KG-12)
    2010-11 Enrollment: 4,016 . . . . (717) 397-2421
Hempfield SD (KG-12)
    2010-11 Enrollment: 7,002 . . . . (717) 898-5560
La Academia-The Partnership Charter School (06-12)
    2010-11 Enrollment: 127 . . . . (717) 295-7763
Lancaster County Academy (-)
    2010-11 Enrollment: n/a . . . . (717) 295-2499
Lancaster SD (PK-12)
    2010-11 Enrollment: 10,972 . . . . (717) 291-6121
Manheim Township SD (KG-12)
    2010-11 Enrollment: 5,911 . . . . (717) 569-8231
Penn Manor SD (KG-12)
    2010-11 Enrollment: 5,169 . . . . (717) 872-9500

Four-year College(s)

Franklin and Marshall College (Private, Not-for-profit)
    Fall 2010 Enrollment: 2,517 . . . . (717) 291-3911
    2011-12 Tuition: In-state $42,610; Out-of-state $42,610
Lancaster Bible College (Private, Not-for-profit)
    Fall 2010 Enrollment: 876 . . . . (717) 569-7071
    2011-12 Tuition: In-state $17,160; Out-of-state $17,160
Lancaster General College of Nursing & Health Sciences (Private, Not-for-profit)
    Fall 2010 Enrollment: 809 . . . . (717) 544-4912
    2011-12 Tuition: In-state $17,860; Out-of-state $17,860
Lancaster Theological Seminary (Private, Not-for-profit, United Church of Christ)
    Fall 2010 Enrollment: 104 . . . . (717) 393-0654
Pennsylvania College of Art and Design (Private, Not-for-profit)
    Fall 2010 Enrollment: 263 . . . . (717) 396-7833
    2011-12 Tuition: In-state $18,980; Out-of-state $18,980

Two-year College(s)

Consolidated School of Business-Lancaster (Private, For-profit)
    Fall 2010 Enrollment: 159 . . . . (717) 394-6211
Thaddeus Stevens College of Technology (Public)
    Fall 2010 Enrollment: 937 . . . . (717) 299-7730
    2011-12 Tuition: In-state $6,830; Out-of-state $6,830

Vocational/Technical School(s)

Empire Beauty School-Lancaster (Private, For-profit)
    Fall 2010 Enrollment: 265 . . . . (800) 223-3271
    2011-12 Tuition: $14,490
Lancaster School of Cosmetology (Private, For-profit)
    Fall 2010 Enrollment: 131 . . . . (717) 299-0200
    2011-12 Tuition: $11,900

Housing: Homeownership rate: 43.9% (2010); Median home value: $94,900 (2006-2010 5-year est.); Median contract rent: $568 per month (2006-2010 5-year est.); Median year structure built: before 1940 (2006-2010 5-year est.).

Hospitals: Lancaster General Hospital (640 beds); Regional Medical Center (268 beds)

Safety: Violent crime rate: 84.7 per 10,000 population; Property crime rate: 506.5 per 10,000 population (2011).

Newspapers: Intelligencer Journal (Local news; Circulation 100,060); La Voz Hispana (Community news; Circulation 60,800); Lancaster New Era (Local news; Circulation 100,060); Sunday News (Community news; Circulation 100,060); This Weekend - Lancaster New Era (Circulation 43,000)

Transportation: Commute to work: 76.8% car, 6.2% public transportation, 11.4% walk, 3.3% work from home (2006-2010 5-year est.); Travel time to work: 38.9% less than 15 minutes, 41.1% 15 to 30 minutes, 12.1% 30 to 45 minutes, 4.3% 45 to 60 minutes, 3.5% 60 minutes or more (2006-2010 5-year est.); Amtrak: train service available.

Airports: Lancaster (commercial service)

Additional Information Contacts

City of Lancaster . . . . (717) 291-4711
    http://www.cityoflancasterpa.com
Lancaster Chamber of Commerce & Industry . . . . (717) 397-3531
    http://www.lancasterchamber.com

LANCASTER (township). Covers a land area of 5.852 square miles and a water area of 0.202 square miles. Located at 40.02° N. Lat; 76.32° W. Long. Elevation is 361 feet.

History: Settled by German Mennonites c.1709. The famous Conestoga wagon was developed here. Borough of Lancaster laid out in 1730, one of the first inland cities in the country. A munitions center during the Revolution, it was briefly (1777) a meeting place of the Continental Congress and served as state capital for more than 10 years. Robert Fulton born nearby. Wheatland, home of President James Buchanan to west (builtin 1828; a national historic site). Incorporated as a city 1818.

Population: 12,580 (1990); 13,944 (2000); 16,149 (2010); Density: 2,759.5 persons per square mile (2010); Race: 75.4% White, 9.7% Black, 2.6% Asian, 0.5% American Indian/Alaska Native, 0.0% Native Hawaiian/Other Pacific Islander, 11.8% Other, 19.3% Hispanic of any race (2010); Average household size: 2.37 (2010); Median age: 38.9 (2010); Males per 100 females: 90.1 (2010); Marriage status: 30.2% never married, 53.1% now married, 8.6% widowed, 8.0% divorced (2006-2010 5-year est.); Foreign born: 6.5% (2006-2010 5-year est.); Ancestry (includes multiple ancestries): 30.7% German, 11.4% Irish, 9.1% Italian, 9.0% English, 4.0% American (2006-2010 5-year est.).

Economy: Single-family building permits issued: 94 (2011); Multi-family building permits issued: 52 (2011); Employment by occupation: 9.2% management, 2.6% professional, 12.1% services, 14.3% sales, 5.9% farming, 6.2% construction, 6.9% production (2006-2010 5-year est.).

Income: Per capita income: $29,737 (2006-2010 5-year est.); Median household income: $52,090 (2006-2010 5-year est.); Average household income: $68,120 (2006-2010 5-year est.); Percent of households with income of $100,000 or more: 16.0% (2006-2010 5-year est.); Poverty rate: 12.4% (2006-2010 5-year est.).

Education: Percent of population age 25 and over with: High school diploma (including GED) or higher: 86.8% (2006-2010 5-year est.); Bachelor's degree or higher: 33.3% (2006-2010 5-year est.); Master's degree or higher: 10.8% (2006-2010 5-year est.).

Four-year College(s)

Franklin and Marshall College (Private, Not-for-profit)
    Fall 2010 Enrollment: 2,517 . . . . (717) 291-3911
    2011-12 Tuition: In-state $42,610; Out-of-state $42,610
Lancaster Bible College (Private, Not-for-profit)
    Fall 2010 Enrollment: 876 . . . . (717) 569-7071
    2011-12 Tuition: In-state $17,160; Out-of-state $17,160
Lancaster General College of Nursing & Health Sciences (Private, Not-for-profit)
    Fall 2010 Enrollment: 809 . . . . (717) 544-4912
    2011-12 Tuition: In-state $17,860; Out-of-state $17,860
Lancaster Theological Seminary (Private, Not-for-profit, United Church of Christ)
    Fall 2010 Enrollment: 104 . . . . (717) 393-0654
Pennsylvania College of Art and Design (Private, Not-for-profit)
    Fall 2010 Enrollment: 263 . . . . (717) 396-7833
    2011-12 Tuition: In-state $18,980; Out-of-state $18,980

Two-year College(s)

Consolidated School of Business-Lancaster (Private, For-profit)
    Fall 2010 Enrollment: 159 . . . . (717) 394-6211
Thaddeus Stevens College of Technology (Public)
    Fall 2010 Enrollment: 937 . . . . (717) 299-7730
    2011-12 Tuition: In-state $6,830; Out-of-state $6,830

Vocational/Technical School(s)

Empire Beauty School-Lancaster (Private, For-profit)
    Fall 2010 Enrollment: 265 . . . . (800) 223-3271
    2011-12 Tuition: $14,490
Lancaster School of Cosmetology (Private, For-profit)
    Fall 2010 Enrollment: 131 . . . . (717) 299-0200
    2011-12 Tuition: $11,900

Housing: Homeownership rate: 59.7% (2010); Median home value: $164,500 (2006-2010 5-year est.); Median contract rent: $753 per month (2006-2010 5-year est.); Median year structure built: 1965 (2006-2010 5-year est.).

Hospitals: Lancaster General Hospital (640 beds); Regional Medical Center (268 beds)

Safety: Violent crime rate: 10.5 per 10,000 population; Property crime rate: 369.1 per 10,000 population (2011).

Newspapers: Intelligencer Journal (Local news; Circulation 100,060); La Voz Hispana (Community news; Circulation 60,800); Lancaster New Era (Local news; Circulation 100,060); Sunday News (Community news;

Circulation 100,060); This Weekend - Lancaster New Era (Circulation 43,000)

Transportation: Commute to work: 92.2% car, 2.2% public transportation, 1.8% walk, 3.0% work from home (2006-2010 5-year est.); Travel time to work: 38.0% less than 15 minutes, 43.5% 15 to 30 minutes, 11.8% 30 to 45 minutes, 3.6% 45 to 60 minutes, 3.0% 60 minutes or more (2006-2010 5-year est.); Amtrak: train service available.

Airports: Lancaster (commercial service)

Additional Information Contacts

Ephrata Area Chamber of Commerce . . . . (717) 738-9010
  http://www.ephrata-area.org
Lancaster Township . . . . (717) 291-1213
  http://www.twp.lancaster.pa.us

LANDISVILLE (CDP). Covers a land area of 1.276 square miles and a water area of 0.004 square miles. Located at 40.09° N. Lat; 76.41° W. Long. Elevation is 407 feet.

Population: n/a (1990); n/a (2000); 1,893 (2010); Density: 1,483.4 persons per square mile (2010); Race: 93.7% White, 1.5% Black, 2.1% Asian, 0.2% American Indian/Alaska Native, 0.0% Native Hawaiian/Other Pacific Islander, 2.5% Other, 4.4% Hispanic of any race (2010); Average household size: 2.63 (2010); Median age: 43.0 (2010); Males per 100 females: 101.8 (2010); Marriage status: 18.9% never married, 68.8% now married, 5.4% widowed, 6.9% divorced (2006-2010 5-year est.); Foreign born: 1.4% (2006-2010 5-year est.); Ancestry (includes multiple ancestries): 37.3% German, 33.8% Irish, 8.2% English, 6.5% Italian, 5.4% American (2006-2010 5-year est.).

Economy: Employment by occupation: 15.3% management, 3.8% professional, 9.3% services, 17.3% sales, 3.0% farming, 3.0% construction, 4.1% production (2006-2010 5-year est.).

Income: Per capita income: $39,479 (2006-2010 5-year est.); Median household income: $89,766 (2006-2010 5-year est.); Average household income: $104,417 (2006-2010 5-year est.); Percent of households with income of $100,000 or more: 39.4% (2006-2010 5-year est.); Poverty rate: 5.6% (2006-2010 5-year est.).

Education: Percent of population age 25 and over with: High school diploma (including GED) or higher: 93.3% (2006-2010 5-year est.); Bachelor's degree or higher: 47.7% (2006-2010 5-year est.); Master's degree or higher: 18.7% (2006-2010 5-year est.).

School District(s)

Hempfield SD (KG-12)
  2010-11 Enrollment: 7,002 . . . . (717) 898-5560

Housing: Homeownership rate: 86.1% (2010); Median home value: $232,500 (2006-2010 5-year est.); Median contract rent: $521 per month (2006-2010 5-year est.); Median year structure built: 1980 (2006-2010 5-year est.).

Transportation: Commute to work: 92.1% car, 0.0% public transportation, 1.7% walk, 6.1% work from home (2006-2010 5-year est.); Travel time to work: 43.5% less than 15 minutes, 44.1% 15 to 30 minutes, 7.5% 30 to 45 minutes, 3.1% 45 to 60 minutes, 1.8% 60 minutes or more (2006-2010 5-year est.)

LEACOCK (township). Covers a land area of 20.552 square miles and a water area of 0.076 square miles. Located at 40.04° N. Lat; 76.12° W. Long. Elevation is 423 feet.

Population: 4,668 (1990); 4,878 (2000); 5,220 (2010); Density: 254.0 persons per square mile (2010); Race: 97.8% White, 0.5% Black, 0.4% Asian, 0.3% American Indian/Alaska Native, 0.1% Native Hawaiian/Other Pacific Islander, 0.9% Other, 1.4% Hispanic of any race (2010); Average household size: 3.42 (2010); Median age: 27.4 (2010); Males per 100 females: 98.2 (2010); Marriage status: 27.1% never married, 66.2% now married, 5.1% widowed, 1.6% divorced (2006-2010 5-year est.); Foreign born: 1.0% (2006-2010 5-year est.); Ancestry (includes multiple ancestries): 37.9% German, 10.3% Swiss, 8.4% American, 7.7% Pennsylvania German, 3.8% Irish (2006-2010 5-year est.).

Economy: Single-family building permits issued: 7 (2011); Multi-family building permits issued: 0 (2011); Employment by occupation: 12.9% management, 1.1% professional, 14.5% services, 8.6% sales, 2.5% farming, 25.8% construction, 11.7% production (2006-2010 5-year est.).

Income: Per capita income: $19,317 (2006-2010 5-year est.); Median household income: $52,214 (2006-2010 5-year est.); Average household income: $64,912 (2006-2010 5-year est.); Percent of households with income of $100,000 or more: 18.5% (2006-2010 5-year est.); Poverty rate: 10.4% (2006-2010 5-year est.).

Education: Percent of population age 25 and over with: High school diploma (including GED) or higher: 44.0% (2006-2010 5-year est.); Bachelor's degree or higher: 9.7% (2006-2010 5-year est.); Master's degree or higher: 6.7% (2006-2010 5-year est.).

Housing: Homeownership rate: 63.5% (2010); Median home value: $227,500 (2006-2010 5-year est.); Median contract rent: $649 per month (2006-2010 5-year est.); Median year structure built: 1967 (2006-2010 5-year est.).

Transportation: Commute to work: 63.8% car, 0.0% public transportation, 9.2% walk, 13.5% work from home (2006-2010 5-year est.); Travel time to work: 40.6% less than 15 minutes, 30.4% 15 to 30 minutes, 15.4% 30 to 45 minutes, 6.3% 45 to 60 minutes, 7.3% 60 minutes or more (2006-2010 5-year est.)

Additional Information Contacts

Lancaster Chamber of Commerce & Industry . . . . (717) 397-3531
  http://www.lancasterchamber.com
Leacock Township . . . . (717) 768-8585
  http://www.leacocktwp.com

LEOLA (CDP). Covers a land area of 6.011 square miles and a water area of 0.009 square miles. Located at 40.09° N. Lat; 76.19° W. Long. Elevation is 430 feet.

Population: n/a (1990); n/a (2000); 7,214 (2010); Density: 1,200.0 persons per square mile (2010); Race: 89.8% White, 1.6% Black, 4.8% Asian, 0.2% American Indian/Alaska Native, 0.1% Native Hawaiian/Other Pacific Islander, 3.5% Other, 7.5% Hispanic of any race (2010); Average household size: 2.75 (2010); Median age: 37.8 (2010); Males per 100 females: 96.2 (2010); Marriage status: 28.3% never married, 60.1% now married, 3.7% widowed, 7.8% divorced (2006-2010 5-year est.); Foreign born: 8.4% (2006-2010 5-year est.); Ancestry (includes multiple ancestries): 36.4% German, 13.7% Irish, 9.8% American, 6.1% Italian, 5.5% English (2006-2010 5-year est.).

Economy: Employment by occupation: 10.7% management, 2.5% professional, 10.9% services, 16.4% sales, 4.1% farming, 9.5% construction, 12.1% production (2006-2010 5-year est.).

Income: Per capita income: $23,628 (2006-2010 5-year est.); Median household income: $56,051 (2006-2010 5-year est.); Average household income: $64,578 (2006-2010 5-year est.); Percent of households with income of $100,000 or more: 20.4% (2006-2010 5-year est.); Poverty rate: 8.0% (2006-2010 5-year est.).

Education: Percent of population age 25 and over with: High school diploma (including GED) or higher: 83.1% (2006-2010 5-year est.); Bachelor's degree or higher: 18.7% (2006-2010 5-year est.); Master's degree or higher: 6.6% (2006-2010 5-year est.).

School District(s)

Conestoga Valley SD (KG-12)
  2010-11 Enrollment: 4,016 . . . . (717) 397-2421

Housing: Homeownership rate: 65.1% (2010); Median home value: $185,400 (2006-2010 5-year est.); Median contract rent: $723 per month (2006-2010 5-year est.); Median year structure built: 1974 (2006-2010 5-year est.).

Transportation: Commute to work: 93.6% car, 0.0% public transportation, 2.9% walk, 3.0% work from home (2006-2010 5-year est.); Travel time to work: 32.3% less than 15 minutes, 47.6% 15 to 30 minutes, 12.7% 30 to 45 minutes, 4.0% 45 to 60 minutes, 3.4% 60 minutes or more (2006-2010 5-year est.)

LITITZ (borough). Covers a land area of 2.310 square miles and a water area of 0.003 square miles. Located at 40.15° N. Lat; 76.30° W. Long. Elevation is 384 feet.

History: Settled c.1740 by Moravians, laid out 1757, incorporated 1759.

Population: 8,280 (1990); 9,029 (2000); 9,369 (2010); Density: 4,055.7 persons per square mile (2010); Race: 94.5% White, 1.3% Black, 1.2% Asian, 0.2% American Indian/Alaska Native, 0.0% Native Hawaiian/Other Pacific Islander, 2.8% Other, 3.7% Hispanic of any race (2010); Average household size: 2.27 (2010); Median age: 43.1 (2010); Males per 100 females: 85.1 (2010); Marriage status: 23.2% never married, 55.5% now married, 11.1% widowed, 10.2% divorced (2006-2010 5-year est.); Foreign born: 0.8% (2006-2010 5-year est.); Ancestry (includes multiple ancestries): 46.1% German, 8.5% Irish, 7.3% English, 5.8% Italian, 5.7% American (2006-2010 5-year est.).

Economy: Single-family building permits issued: 0 (2011); Multi-family building permits issued: 0 (2011); Employment by occupation: 8.9% management, 3.5% professional, 8.1% services, 17.8% sales, 5.9% farming, 6.8% construction, 7.5% production (2006-2010 5-year est.).

Income: Per capita income: $27,496 (2006-2010 5-year est.); Median household income: $50,089 (2006-2010 5-year est.); Average household income: $64,863 (2006-2010 5-year est.); Percent of households with income of $100,000 or more: 14.9% (2006-2010 5-year est.); Poverty rate: 7.6% (2006-2010 5-year est.).

Education: Percent of population age 25 and over with: High school diploma (including GED) or higher: 89.4% (2006-2010 5-year est.); Bachelor's degree or higher: 26.1% (2006-2010 5-year est.); Master's degree or higher: 9.7% (2006-2010 5-year est.).

School District(s)

Manheim Township SD (KG-12)

   2010-11 Enrollment: 5,911 . . . . (717) 569-8231

Warwick SD (KG-12)

   2010-11 Enrollment: 4,477 . . . . (717) 626-3734

Housing: Homeownership rate: 61.6% (2010); Median home value: $174,200 (2006-2010 5-year est.); Median contract rent: $699 per month (2006-2010 5-year est.); Median year structure built: 1966 (2006-2010 5-year est.).

Hospitals: Heart of Lancaster Regional Medical Center (154 beds)

Safety: Violent crime rate: 5.3 per 10,000 population; Property crime rate: 103.2 per 10,000 population (2011).

Newspapers: Record Express (Community news; Circulation 7,800)

Transportation: Commute to work: 90.2% car, 1.5% public transportation, 2.2% walk, 5.6% work from home (2006-2010 5-year est.); Travel time to work: 30.4% less than 15 minutes, 47.8% 15 to 30 minutes, 14.4% 30 to 45 minutes, 3.0% 45 to 60 minutes, 4.4% 60 minutes or more (2006-2010 5-year est.)

Additional Information Contacts

Borough of Lititz . . . . (717) 626-2044

   http://www.co.lancaster.pa.us/lititz/site/default.asp

Lancaster Chamber of Commerce & Industry . . . . (717) 397-3531

   http://www.lancasterchamber.com

LITTLE BRITAIN (CDP). Covers a land area of 1.449 square miles and a water area of 0.003 square miles. Located at 39.78° N. Lat; 76.11° W. Long. Elevation is 453 feet.

Population: n/a (1990); n/a (2000); 372 (2010); Density: 256.7 persons per square mile (2010); Race: 96.5% White, 1.1% Black, 0.5% Asian, 0.0% American Indian/Alaska Native, 0.0% Native Hawaiian/Other Pacific Islander, 1.9% Other, 1.1% Hispanic of any race (2010); Average household size: 3.18 (2010); Median age: 42.8 (2010); Males per 100 females: 100.0 (2010); Marriage status: 21.3% never married, 71.6% now married, 0.0% widowed, 7.1% divorced (2006-2010 5-year est.); Foreign born: 0.0% (2006-2010 5-year est.); Ancestry (includes multiple ancestries): 37.0% English, 27.9% Irish, 27.4% German, 10.0% Dutch, 6.4% Welsh (2006-2010 5-year est.).

Economy: Employment by occupation: 0.0% management, 29.3% professional, 12.1% services, 13.1% sales, 0.0% farming, 0.0% construction, 11.1% production (2006-2010 5-year est.).

Income: Per capita income: $29,127 (2006-2010 5-year est.); Median household income: $97,981 (2006-2010 5-year est.); Average household income: $81,172 (2006-2010 5-year est.); Percent of households with income of $100,000 or more: 36.7% (2006-2010 5-year est.); Poverty rate: 13.2% (2006-2010 5-year est.).

Education: Percent of population age 25 and over with: High school diploma (including GED) or higher: 86.6% (2006-2010 5-year est.); Bachelor's degree or higher: 17.4% (2006-2010 5-year est.); Master's degree or higher: 0.0% (2006-2010 5-year est.).

Housing: Homeownership rate: 90.6% (2010); Median home value: $245,800 (2006-2010 5-year est.); Median contract rent: n/a per month (2006-2010 5-year est.); Median year structure built: 1991 (2006-2010 5-year est.).

Transportation: Commute to work: 100.0% car, 0.0% public transportation, 0.0% walk, 0.0% work from home (2006-2010 5-year est.); Travel time to work: 13.1% less than 15 minutes, 10.1% 15 to 30 minutes, 41.4% 30 to 45 minutes, 12.1% 45 to 60 minutes, 23.2% 60 minutes or more (2006-2010 5-year est.)

LITTLE BRITAIN (township). Covers a land area of 27.241 square miles and a water area of 0.296 square miles. Located at 39.79° N. Lat; 76.11° W. Long. Elevation is 453 feet.

Population: 2,701 (1990); 3,514 (2000); 4,106 (2010); Density: 150.7 persons per square mile (2010); Race: 97.3% White, 0.6% Black, 0.3% Asian, 0.1% American Indian/Alaska Native, 0.0% Native Hawaiian/Other Pacific Islander, 1.7% Other, 2.4% Hispanic of any race (2010); Average

household size: 3.12 (2010); Median age: 35.9 (2010); Males per 100 females: 100.9 (2010); Marriage status: 24.4% never married, 68.0% now married, 1.9% widowed, 5.6% divorced (2006-2010 5-year est.); Foreign born: 1.4% (2006-2010 5-year est.); Ancestry (includes multiple ancestries): 42.2% German, 15.4% Irish, 14.7% English, 6.5% American, 5.7% Pennsylvania German (2006-2010 5-year est.).

Economy: Single-family building permits issued: 8 (2011); Multi-family building permits issued: 0 (2011); Employment by occupation: 18.5% management, 4.1% professional, 16.9% services, 11.1% sales, 2.5% farming, 17.8% construction, 6.4% production (2006-2010 5-year est.).

Income: Per capita income: $25,991 (2006-2010 5-year est.); Median household income: $61,153 (2006-2010 5-year est.); Average household income: $88,814 (2006-2010 5-year est.); Percent of households with income of $100,000 or more: 25.5% (2006-2010 5-year est.); Poverty rate: 9.9% (2006-2010 5-year est.).

Taxes: Total city taxes per capita: $144 (2009); City property taxes per capita: $23 (2009).

Education: Percent of population age 25 and over with: High school diploma (including GED) or higher: 74.5% (2006-2010 5-year est.); Bachelor's degree or higher: 10.2% (2006-2010 5-year est.); Master's degree or higher: 2.4% (2006-2010 5-year est.).

Housing: Homeownership rate: 84.4% (2010); Median home value: $267,500 (2006-2010 5-year est.); Median contract rent: $847 per month (2006-2010 5-year est.); Median year structure built: 1978 (2006-2010 5-year est.).

Transportation: Commute to work: 83.8% car, 0.0% public transportation, 7.0% walk, 6.9% work from home (2006-2010 5-year est.); Travel time to work: 33.0% less than 15 minutes, 17.8% 15 to 30 minutes, 24.2% 30 to 45 minutes, 11.1% 45 to 60 minutes, 13.9% 60 minutes or more (2006-2010 5-year est.)

Additional Information Contacts

Little Britain Township . . . . (717) 529-2373

   http://www.littlebritain.org

Southern Lancaster County Chamber of Commerce . . . . . (717) 786-1911

   http://www.southernlancasterchamber.com

MANHEIM (borough). Covers a land area of 1.383 square miles and a water area of 0.017 square miles. Located at 40.16° N. Lat; 76.40° W. Long. Elevation is 410 feet.

History: Settled 1716, laid out c.1760 by H. W. Stiegel, who probably produced the first flint glass in America here. Incorporated 1848.

Population: 4,900 (1990); 4,784 (2000); 4,858 (2010); Density: 3,511.7 persons per square mile (2010); Race: 95.0% White, 0.9% Black, 1.1% Asian, 0.1% American Indian/Alaska Native, 0.0% Native Hawaiian/Other Pacific Islander, 2.9% Other, 3.4% Hispanic of any race (2010); Average household size: 2.40 (2010); Median age: 39.0 (2010); Males per 100 females: 97.7 (2010); Marriage status: 28.8% never married, 54.4% now married, 6.1% widowed, 10.6% divorced (2006-2010 5-year est.); Foreign born: 0.3% (2006-2010 5-year est.); Ancestry (includes multiple ancestries): 45.4% German, 14.4% Irish, 11.3% American, 8.8% English, 5.3% Italian (2006-2010 5-year est.).

Economy: Single-family building permits issued: 0 (2011); Multi-family building permits issued: 0 (2011); Employment by occupation: 6.1% management, 2.5% professional, 10.2% services, 16.5% sales, 4.9% farming, 14.8% construction, 8.0% production (2006-2010 5-year est.).

Income: Per capita income: $24,163 (2006-2010 5-year est.); Median household income: $52,095 (2006-2010 5-year est.); Average household income: $60,490 (2006-2010 5-year est.); Percent of households with income of $100,000 or more: 17.9% (2006-2010 5-year est.); Poverty rate: 7.5% (2006-2010 5-year est.).

Education: Percent of population age 25 and over with: High school diploma (including GED) or higher: 87.5% (2006-2010 5-year est.); Bachelor's degree or higher: 14.3% (2006-2010 5-year est.); Master's degree or higher: 4.7% (2006-2010 5-year est.).

School District(s)

Manheim Central SD (KG-12)

   2010-11 Enrollment: 2,947 . . . . (717) 665-3422

Housing: Homeownership rate: 67.0% (2010); Median home value: $145,100 (2006-2010 5-year est.); Median contract rent: $583 per month (2006-2010 5-year est.); Median year structure built: 1952 (2006-2010 5-year est.).

Safety: Violent crime rate: 12.3 per 10,000 population; Property crime rate: 248.3 per 10,000 population (2011).

Transportation: Commute to work: 87.5% car, 1.6% public transportation, 4.2% walk, 3.4% work from home (2006-2010 5-year est.); Travel time to

work: 31.3% less than 15 minutes, 42.1% 15 to 30 minutes, 16.0% 30 to 45 minutes, 2.4% 45 to 60 minutes, 8.2% 60 minutes or more (2006-2010 5-year est.)

Additional Information Contacts

Manheim Area Chamber of Commerce . . . . (717) 665-6330
  http://manheimchamber.com/wp

MANHEIM (township). Covers a land area of 23.857 square miles and a water area of 0.215 square miles. Located at 40.09° N. Lat; 76.30° W. Long. Elevation is 410 feet.

Population: 28,823 (1990); 33,697 (2000); 38,133 (2010); Density: 1,598.4 persons per square mile (2010); Race: 87.6% White, 3.0% Black, 5.0% Asian, 0.1% American Indian/Alaska Native, 0.0% Native Hawaiian/Other Pacific Islander, 4.3% Other, 6.6% Hispanic of any race (2010); Average household size: 2.44 (2010); Median age: 44.0 (2010); Males per 100 females: 89.1 (2010); Marriage status: 21.9% never married, 61.8% now married, 8.3% widowed, 8.1% divorced (2006-2010 5-year est.); Foreign born: 7.8% (2006-2010 5-year est.); Ancestry (includes multiple ancestries): 36.7% German, 13.6% Irish, 12.5% English, 6.5% Italian, 4.9% American (2006-2010 5-year est.).

Economy: Unemployment rate: 6.5% (August 2012); Total civilian labor force: 19,471 (August 2012); Single-family building permits issued: 79 (2011); Multi-family building permits issued: 0 (2011); Employment by occupation: 15.4% management, 4.9% professional, 7.1% services, 15.5% sales, 3.4% farming, 7.4% construction, 4.8% production (2006-2010 5-year est.).

Income: Per capita income: $37,307 (2006-2010 5-year est.); Median household income: $66,031 (2006-2010 5-year est.); Average household income: $92,533 (2006-2010 5-year est.); Percent of households with income of $100,000 or more: 29.4% (2006-2010 5-year est.); Poverty rate: 5.7% (2006-2010 5-year est.).

Education: Percent of population age 25 and over with: High school diploma (including GED) or higher: 92.0% (2006-2010 5-year est.); Bachelor's degree or higher: 42.7% (2006-2010 5-year est.); Master's degree or higher: 15.8% (2006-2010 5-year est.).

Housing: Homeownership rate: 71.7% (2010); Median home value: $222,700 (2006-2010 5-year est.); Median contract rent: $816 per month (2006-2010 5-year est.); Median year structure built: 1975 (2006-2010 5-year est.).

Safety: Violent crime rate: 8.6 per 10,000 population; Property crime rate: 228.5 per 10,000 population (2011).

Transportation: Commute to work: 92.2% car, 1.1% public transportation, 0.9% walk, 4.6% work from home (2006-2010 5-year est.); Travel time to work: 39.6% less than 15 minutes, 39.4% 15 to 30 minutes, 12.0% 30 to 45 minutes, 4.0% 45 to 60 minutes, 5.0% 60 minutes or more (2006-2010 5-year est.)

Additional Information Contacts

Manheim Area Chamber of Commerce . . . . (717) 665-6330
  http://manheimchamber.com/wp
Manheim Township . . . . (717) 569-6406
  http://www.manheimtownship.org

MANOR (township). Covers a land area of 38.333 square miles and a water area of 10.285 square miles. Located at 39.98° N. Lat; 76.42° W. Long.

Population: 14,157 (1990); 16,498 (2000); 19,612 (2010); Density: 511.6 persons per square mile (2010); Race: 91.8% White, 2.6% Black, 1.7% Asian, 0.2% American Indian/Alaska Native, 0.0% Native Hawaiian/Other Pacific Islander, 3.7% Other, 6.3% Hispanic of any race (2010); Average household size: 2.46 (2010); Median age: 41.4 (2010); Males per 100 females: 93.2 (2010); Marriage status: 25.2% never married, 60.8% now married, 5.4% widowed, 8.7% divorced (2006-2010 5-year est.); Foreign born: 5.0% (2006-2010 5-year est.); Ancestry (includes multiple ancestries): 45.9% German, 12.9% Irish, 10.5% English, 8.3% Italian, 7.7% American (2006-2010 5-year est.).

Economy: Single-family building permits issued: 34 (2011); Multi-family building permits issued: 28 (2011); Employment by occupation: 9.7% management, 3.8% professional, 8.2% services, 15.7% sales, 5.2% farming, 9.6% construction, 7.5% production (2006-2010 5-year est.).

Income: Per capita income: $28,179 (2006-2010 5-year est.); Median household income: $58,607 (2006-2010 5-year est.); Average household income: $69,363 (2006-2010 5-year est.); Percent of households with income of $100,000 or more: 17.9% (2006-2010 5-year est.); Poverty rate: 4.0% (2006-2010 5-year est.).

Education: Percent of population age 25 and over with: High school diploma (including GED) or higher: 88.4% (2006-2010 5-year est.); Bachelor's degree or higher: 26.1% (2006-2010 5-year est.); Master's degree or higher: 7.6% (2006-2010 5-year est.).

Housing: Homeownership rate: 76.0% (2010); Median home value: $172,600 (2006-2010 5-year est.); Median contract rent: $706 per month (2006-2010 5-year est.); Median year structure built: 1980 (2006-2010 5-year est.).

Safety: Violent crime rate: 4.6 per 10,000 population; Property crime rate: 118.9 per 10,000 population (2011).

Transportation: Commute to work: 93.8% car, 0.4% public transportation, 1.1% walk, 2.5% work from home (2006-2010 5-year est.); Travel time to work: 31.6% less than 15 minutes, 44.4% 15 to 30 minutes, 14.9% 30 to 45 minutes, 3.6% 45 to 60 minutes, 5.4% 60 minutes or more (2006-2010 5-year est.)

Additional Information Contacts

Manor Township . . . . (717) 397-4769
  http://www.manortwp.org
Southern Lancaster County Chamber of Commerce . . . . . (610) 608-1240
  http://www.southernlancasterchamber.com

MARIETTA (borough). Covers a land area of 0.747 square miles and a water area of 0.007 square miles. Located at 40.06° N. Lat; 76.55° W. Long. Elevation is 276 feet.

History: Settled 1718, incorporated 1812.

Population: 2,778 (1990); 2,689 (2000); 2,588 (2010); Density: 3,465.3 persons per square mile (2010); Race: 94.2% White, 2.3% Black, 0.2% Asian, 0.4% American Indian/Alaska Native, 0.0% Native Hawaiian/Other Pacific Islander, 2.9% Other, 4.4% Hispanic of any race (2010); Average household size: 2.37 (2010); Median age: 39.0 (2010); Males per 100 females: 98.5 (2010); Marriage status: 32.4% never married, 48.3% now married, 6.5% widowed, 12.9% divorced (2006-2010 5-year est.); Foreign born: 0.3% (2006-2010 5-year est.); Ancestry (includes multiple ancestries): 45.1% German, 17.9% Irish, 10.0% American, 9.2% English, 6.1% Italian (2006-2010 5-year est.).

Economy: Single-family building permits issued: 3 (2011); Multi-family building permits issued: 0 (2011); Employment by occupation: 4.0% management, 3.9% professional, 8.0% services, 12.7% sales, 4.1% farming, 8.5% construction, 10.1% production (2006-2010 5-year est.).

Income: Per capita income: $23,088 (2006-2010 5-year est.); Median household income: $42,955 (2006-2010 5-year est.); Average household income: $54,513 (2006-2010 5-year est.); Percent of households with income of $100,000 or more: 11.3% (2006-2010 5-year est.); Poverty rate: 10.1% (2006-2010 5-year est.).

Education: Percent of population age 25 and over with: High school diploma (including GED) or higher: 85.0% (2006-2010 5-year est.); Bachelor's degree or higher: 15.2% (2006-2010 5-year est.); Master's degree or higher: 6.9% (2006-2010 5-year est.).

School District(s)

Donegal SD (KG-12)
  2010-11 Enrollment: 2,815 . . . . (717) 492-1302

Housing: Homeownership rate: 67.4% (2010); Median home value: $115,600 (2006-2010 5-year est.); Median contract rent: $568 per month (2006-2010 5-year est.); Median year structure built: before 1940 (2006-2010 5-year est.).

Safety: Violent crime rate: 7.7 per 10,000 population; Property crime rate: 211.9 per 10,000 population (2011).

Transportation: Commute to work: 94.6% car, 0.4% public transportation, 1.3% walk, 3.7% work from home (2006-2010 5-year est.); Travel time to work: 21.6% less than 15 minutes, 52.7% 15 to 30 minutes, 20.6% 30 to 45 minutes, 3.5% 45 to 60 minutes, 1.7% 60 minutes or more (2006-2010 5-year est.)

Additional Information Contacts

Susquehanna Valley Chamber of Commerce . . . . (717) 684-5249
  http://www.parivertowns.com

MARTIC (township). Covers a land area of 29.033 square miles and a water area of 3.587 square miles. Located at 39.87° N. Lat; 76.32° W. Long.

Population: 4,362 (1990); 4,990 (2000); 5,190 (2010); Density: 178.8 persons per square mile (2010); Race: 98.5% White, 0.2% Black, 0.1% Asian, 0.2% American Indian/Alaska Native, 0.0% Native Hawaiian/Other Pacific Islander, 1.0% Other, 1.7% Hispanic of any race (2010); Average household size: 2.83 (2010); Median age: 40.2 (2010); Males per 100 females: 103.3 (2010); Marriage status: 22.4% never married, 64.6% now

married, 6.0% widowed, 7.1% divorced (2006-2010 5-year est.); Foreign born: 0.7% (2006-2010 5-year est.); Ancestry (includes multiple ancestries): 45.3% German, 11.0% Irish, 8.3% American, 6.5% English, 6.3% Italian (2006-2010 5-year est.).

Economy: Single-family building permits issued: 6 (2011); Multi-family building permits issued: 0 (2011); Employment by occupation: 11.1% management, 5.3% professional, 8.0% services, 14.3% sales, 2.8% farming, 15.2% construction, 10.3% production (2006-2010 5-year est.).

Income: Per capita income: $23,358 (2006-2010 5-year est.); Median household income: $57,620 (2006-2010 5-year est.); Average household income: $66,464 (2006-2010 5-year est.); Percent of households with income of $100,000 or more: 19.6% (2006-2010 5-year est.); Poverty rate: 8.4% (2006-2010 5-year est.).

Education: Percent of population age 25 and over with: High school diploma (including GED) or higher: 79.7% (2006-2010 5-year est.); Bachelor's degree or higher: 13.7% (2006-2010 5-year est.); Master's degree or higher: 6.9% (2006-2010 5-year est.).

Housing: Homeownership rate: 87.7% (2010); Median home value: $177,700 (2006-2010 5-year est.); Median contract rent: $428 per month (2006-2010 5-year est.); Median year structure built: 1976 (2006-2010 5-year est.).

Transportation: Commute to work: 89.8% car, 0.0% public transportation, 2.2% walk, 6.7% work from home (2006-2010 5-year est.); Travel time to work: 10.6% less than 15 minutes, 30.9% 15 to 30 minutes, 39.0% 30 to 45 minutes, 10.1% 45 to 60 minutes, 9.4% 60 minutes or more (2006-2010 5-year est.)

Additional Information Contacts
Lancaster Chamber of Commerce & Industry . . . . (717) 397-3531
  http://www.lancasterchamber.com

MAYTOWN (CDP). Covers a land area of 3.680 square miles and a water area of 0.001 square miles. Located at 40.08° N. Lat; 76.57° W. Long. Elevation is 407 feet.

Population: 1,720 (1990); 2,604 (2000); 3,824 (2010); Density: 1,039.2 persons per square mile (2010); Race: 94.3% White, 1.7% Black, 0.7% Asian, 0.1% American Indian/Alaska Native, 0.1% Native Hawaiian/Other Pacific Islander, 3.1% Other, 3.7% Hispanic of any race (2010); Average household size: 2.82 (2010); Median age: 34.2 (2010); Males per 100 females: 98.1 (2010); Marriage status: 24.2% never married, 68.6% now married, 1.4% widowed, 5.8% divorced (2006-2010 5-year est.); Foreign born: 5.2% (2006-2010 5-year est.); Ancestry (includes multiple ancestries): 33.3% German, 16.7% Italian, 15.9% Irish, 9.8% American, 8.1% English (2006-2010 5-year est.).

Economy: Employment by occupation: 14.5% management, 5.3% professional, 8.5% services, 16.4% sales, 0.6% farming, 8.3% construction, 8.9% production (2006-2010 5-year est.).

Income: Per capita income: $24,162 (2006-2010 5-year est.); Median household income: $64,962 (2006-2010 5-year est.); Average household income: $73,845 (2006-2010 5-year est.); Percent of households with income of $100,000 or more: 21.7% (2006-2010 5-year est.); Poverty rate: 9.9% (2006-2010 5-year est.).

Education: Percent of population age 25 and over with: High school diploma (including GED) or higher: 85.4% (2006-2010 5-year est.); Bachelor's degree or higher: 19.2% (2006-2010 5-year est.); Master's degree or higher: 4.0% (2006-2010 5-year est.).

School District(s)
Donegal SD (KG-12)
  2010-11 Enrollment: 2,815 . . . . (717) 492-1302

Housing: Homeownership rate: 81.6% (2010); Median home value: $184,100 (2006-2010 5-year est.); Median contract rent: $667 per month (2006-2010 5-year est.); Median year structure built: 1994 (2006-2010 5-year est.).

Transportation: Commute to work: 98.1% car, 0.0% public transportation, 0.0% walk, 1.9% work from home (2006-2010 5-year est.); Travel time to work: 17.2% less than 15 minutes, 38.6% 15 to 30 minutes, 35.5% 30 to 45 minutes, 2.3% 45 to 60 minutes, 6.4% 60 minutes or more (2006-2010 5-year est.)

Additional Information Contacts
Susquehanna Valley Chamber of Commerce . . . . (717) 684-5249
  http://www.parivertowns.com

MILLERSVILLE (borough). Covers a land area of 1.944 square miles and a water area of 0.008 square miles. Located at 40.01° N. Lat; 76.35° W. Long. Elevation is 325 feet.

History: Seat of Millersville University of Pennsylvania. Incorporated 1932.

Population: 8,110 (1990); 7,774 (2000); 8,168 (2010); Density: 4,200.9 persons per square mile (2010); Race: 90.9% White, 5.0% Black, 1.2% Asian, 0.2% American Indian/Alaska Native, 0.1% Native Hawaiian/Other Pacific Islander, 2.6% Other, 4.3% Hispanic of any race (2010); Average household size: 2.29 (2010); Median age: 22.1 (2010); Males per 100 females: 86.7 (2010); Marriage status: 59.8% never married, 28.4% now married, 6.4% widowed, 5.4% divorced (2006-2010 5-year est.); Foreign born: 3.5% (2006-2010 5-year est.); Ancestry (includes multiple ancestries): 44.1% German, 15.7% Irish, 8.4% Italian, 8.1% English, 5.7% Polish (2006-2010 5-year est.).

Economy: Single-family building permits issued: 0 (2011); Multi-family building permits issued: 16 (2011); Employment by occupation: 6.4% management, 2.1% professional, 12.8% services, 20.8% sales, 5.7% farming, 8.5% construction, 3.9% production (2006-2010 5-year est.).

Income: Per capita income: $17,053 (2006-2010 5-year est.); Median household income: $40,529 (2006-2010 5-year est.); Average household income: $50,337 (2006-2010 5-year est.); Percent of households with income of $100,000 or more: 8.3% (2006-2010 5-year est.); Poverty rate: 21.7% (2006-2010 5-year est.).

Education: Percent of population age 25 and over with: High school diploma (including GED) or higher: 87.5% (2006-2010 5-year est.); Bachelor's degree or higher: 31.3% (2006-2010 5-year est.); Master's degree or higher: 10.8% (2006-2010 5-year est.).

School District(s)
Penn Manor SD (KG-12)
  2010-11 Enrollment: 5,169 . . . . (717) 872-9500

Four-year College(s)
Millersville University of Pennsylvania (Public)
  Fall 2010 Enrollment: 8,163 . . . . (717) 872-3024
  2011-12 Tuition: In-state $8,361; Out-of-state $17,899

Housing: Homeownership rate: 58.8% (2010); Median home value: $169,100 (2006-2010 5-year est.); Median contract rent: $762 per month (2006-2010 5-year est.); Median year structure built: 1963 (2006-2010 5-year est.).

Safety: Violent crime rate: 20.7 per 10,000 population; Property crime rate: 108.6 per 10,000 population (2011).

Transportation: Commute to work: 83.6% car, 0.9% public transportation, 9.1% walk, 4.9% work from home (2006-2010 5-year est.); Travel time to work: 35.9% less than 15 minutes, 44.6% 15 to 30 minutes, 10.5% 30 to 45 minutes, 2.8% 45 to 60 minutes, 6.1% 60 minutes or more (2006-2010 5-year est.)

Additional Information Contacts
Borough of Millersville . . . . (717) 872-4645
  http://www.millersvilleborough.org
Lancaster Chamber of Commerce & Industry . . . . (717) 397-3531
  http://www.lancasterchamber.com

MOUNT JOY (borough). Covers a land area of 2.411 square miles and a water area of 0.016 square miles. Located at 40.11° N. Lat; 76.51° W. Long. Elevation is 381 feet.

Population: 6,371 (1990); 6,765 (2000); 7,410 (2010); Density: 3,073.7 persons per square mile (2010); Race: 91.9% White, 2.5% Black, 0.8% Asian, 0.3% American Indian/Alaska Native, 0.1% Native Hawaiian/Other Pacific Islander, 4.4% Other, 7.4% Hispanic of any race (2010); Average household size: 2.36 (2010); Median age: 38.0 (2010); Males per 100 females: 95.7 (2010); Marriage status: 26.1% never married, 58.7% now married, 5.2% widowed, 10.1% divorced (2006-2010 5-year est.); Foreign born: 2.4% (2006-2010 5-year est.); Ancestry (includes multiple ancestries): 48.2% German, 10.1% Irish, 7.8% American, 7.1% English, 4.5% Italian (2006-2010 5-year est.).

Economy: Single-family building permits issued: 23 (2011); Multi-family building permits issued: 63 (2011); Employment by occupation: 10.4% management, 2.9% professional, 8.4% services, 13.7% sales, 3.7% farming, 9.3% construction, 9.3% production (2006-2010 5-year est.).

Income: Per capita income: $28,146 (2006-2010 5-year est.); Median household income: $54,206 (2006-2010 5-year est.); Average household income: $67,314 (2006-2010 5-year est.); Percent of households with income of $100,000 or more: 17.5% (2006-2010 5-year est.); Poverty rate: 6.6% (2006-2010 5-year est.).

Education: Percent of population age 25 and over with: High school diploma (including GED) or higher: 91.6% (2006-2010 5-year est.); Bachelor's degree or higher: 18.7% (2006-2010 5-year est.); Master's degree or higher: 4.8% (2006-2010 5-year est.).

School District(s)

Donegal SD (KG-12)

2010-11 Enrollment: 2,815 . . . . (717) 492-1302

Hempfield SD (KG-12)

2010-11 Enrollment: 7,002 . . . . (717) 898-5560

Lancaster County CTC (10-12)

2010-11 Enrollment: n/a . . . . (717) 464-7050

Housing: Homeownership rate: 61.8% (2010); Median home value: $155,300 (2006-2010 5-year est.); Median contract rent: $598 per month (2006-2010 5-year est.); Median year structure built: 1956 (2006-2010 5-year est.).

Safety: Violent crime rate: 21.5 per 10,000 population; Property crime rate: 182.9 per 10,000 population (2011).

Newspapers: Camp Hill Shopper (Community news; Circulation 55,208); Columbia-Wrightsville Merchandiser (Local news; Circulation 10,044); Downingtown/Exton Community Courier (Community news; Circulation 34,321); East Shore Shopper (Community news; Circulation 39,000); Elizabethtown-Mount Joy Merchandiser (Community news; Circulation 17,232); Gap Community Courier (Community news; Circulation 16,674); Gap/Oxford Community Courier (Local news; Circulation 16,674); Hempfield-Mountville Merchandiser (Local news; Circulation 12,706); Hershey/Hummelstown Community Courier (Local news; Circulation 22,095); Lititz/Manheim Merchandiser (Community news; Circulation 18,051); Mechanicsburg Shopper (Community news; Circulation 29,800); Middletown Shopper (Community news; Circulation 10,067); Millersville Advertiser (Local news; Circulation 14,000); Morgantown/Honeybrook Comm. Courier (Community news; Circulation 12,181); New Holland Penny Saver (Community news; Circulation 12,400); Phoenixville Community Courier (Local news; Circulation 27,850); Quarryville Advertiser (Community news; Circulation 9,800); Royersford/Phoenixville Community Courier (Community news; Circulation 27,850); Thorndale Community Courier (Community news; Circulation 60,000); The Willow Street Advertiser (Community news; Circulation 8,631); York West Community Courier (Community news; Circulation 27,000)

Transportation: Commute to work: 93.8% car, 0.7% public transportation, 3.8% walk, 1.5% work from home (2006-2010 5-year est.); Travel time to work: 31.1% less than 15 minutes, 45.3% 15 to 30 minutes, 19.0% 30 to 45 minutes, 3.0% 45 to 60 minutes, 1.6% 60 minutes or more (2006-2010 5-year est.); Amtrak: train service available.

Additional Information Contacts

Borough of Mount Joy . . . . (717) 367-8917

http://www.mtjoytwp.org

Mount Joy Chamber of Commerce . . . . (717) 653-0773

http://mountjoychamber.com

MOUNT JOY (township). Covers a land area of 27.838 square miles and a water area of 0.179 square miles. Located at 40.17° N. Lat; 76.55° W. Long. Elevation is 381 feet.

History: Covered bridges in area. Settled 1768, laid out 1812, incorporated 1851.

Population: 6,235 (1990); 7,944 (2000); 9,873 (2010); Density: 354.7 persons per square mile (2010); Race: 95.3% White, 1.1% Black, 1.0% Asian, 0.1% American Indian/Alaska Native, 0.0% Native Hawaiian/Other Pacific Islander, 2.5% Other, 2.9% Hispanic of any race (2010); Average household size: 2.73 (2010); Median age: 37.4 (2010); Males per 100 females: 96.3 (2010); Marriage status: 25.4% never married, 62.7% now married, 4.4% widowed, 7.5% divorced (2006-2010 5-year est.); Foreign born: 2.5% (2006-2010 5-year est.); Ancestry (includes multiple ancestries): 47.3% German, 13.2% Irish, 9.4% American, 6.7% Italian, 6.0% English (2006-2010 5-year est.).

Economy: Single-family building permits issued: 10 (2011); Multi-family building permits issued: 68 (2011); Employment by occupation: 11.1% management, 5.1% professional, 8.1% services, 18.6% sales, 3.1% farming, 8.9% construction, 6.6% production (2006-2010 5-year est.).

Income: Per capita income: $30,676 (2006-2010 5-year est.); Median household income: $65,705 (2006-2010 5-year est.); Average household income: $77,899 (2006-2010 5-year est.); Percent of households with income of $100,000 or more: 20.6% (2006-2010 5-year est.); Poverty rate: 9.5% (2006-2010 5-year est.).

Education: Percent of population age 25 and over with: High school diploma (including GED) or higher: 92.4% (2006-2010 5-year est.); Bachelor's degree or higher: 31.9% (2006-2010 5-year est.); Master's degree or higher: 9.3% (2006-2010 5-year est.).

Housing: Homeownership rate: 77.8% (2010); Median home value: $181,000 (2006-2010 5-year est.); Median contract rent: $875 per month

---

(2006-2010 5-year est.); Median year structure built: 1988 (2006-2010 5-year est.).

Newspapers: Camp Hill Shopper (Community news; Circulation 55,208); Columbia-Wrightsville Merchandiser (Local news; Circulation 10,044); Downingtown/Exton Community Courier (Community news; Circulation 34,321); East Shore Shopper (Community news; Circulation 39,000); Elizabethtown-Mount Joy Merchandiser (Community news; Circulation 17,232); Gap Community Courier (Community news; Circulation 16,674); Gap/Oxford Community Courier (Local news; Circulation 16,674); Hempfield-Mountville Merchandiser (Local news; Circulation 12,706); Hershey/Hummelstown Community Courier (Local news; Circulation 22,095); Lititz/Manheim Merchandiser (Community news; Circulation 18,051); Mechanicsburg Shopper (Community news; Circulation 29,800); Middletown Shopper (Community news; Circulation 10,067); Millersville Advertiser (Local news; Circulation 14,000); Morgantown/Honeybrook Comm. Courier (Community news; Circulation 12,181); New Holland Penny Saver (Community news; Circulation 12,400); Phoenixville Community Courier (Local news; Circulation 27,850); Quarryville Advertiser (Community news; Circulation 9,800); Royersford/Phoenixville Community Courier (Community news; Circulation 27,850); Thorndale Community Courier (Community news; Circulation 60,000); The Willow Street Advertiser (Community news; Circulation 8,631); York West Community Courier (Community news; Circulation 27,000)

Transportation: Commute to work: 91.3% car, 0.6% public transportation, 3.5% walk, 4.4% work from home (2006-2010 5-year est.); Travel time to work: 30.8% less than 15 minutes, 40.9% 15 to 30 minutes, 20.4% 30 to 45 minutes, 5.3% 45 to 60 minutes, 2.5% 60 minutes or more (2006-2010 5-year est.); Amtrak: train service available.

Additional Information Contacts

Mount Joy Chamber of Commerce . . . . (717) 653-0773

http://mountjoychamber.com

Mount Joy Township . . . . (717) 367-8917

http://www.mtjoytwp.org

MOUNTVILLE (borough). Covers a land area of 0.861 square miles and a water area of 0.001 square miles. Located at 40.04° N. Lat; 76.43° W. Long. Elevation is 443 feet.

History: Laid out 1814.

Population: 1,977 (1990); 2,444 (2000); 2,802 (2010); Density: 3,255.3 persons per square mile (2010); Race: 90.0% White, 3.9% Black, 2.3% Asian, 0.1% American Indian/Alaska Native, 0.0% Native Hawaiian/Other Pacific Islander, 3.7% Other, 5.2% Hispanic of any race (2010); Average household size: 2.19 (2010); Median age: 45.1 (2010); Males per 100 females: 90.9 (2010); Marriage status: 27.4% never married, 51.8% now married, 5.5% widowed, 15.3% divorced (2006-2010 5-year est.); Foreign born: 5.7% (2006-2010 5-year est.); Ancestry (includes multiple ancestries): 48.1% German, 12.5% Irish, 12.0% English, 4.7% Italian, 3.8% Scotch-Irish (2006-2010 5-year est.).

Economy: Single-family building permits issued: 8 (2011); Multi-family building permits issued: 0 (2011); Employment by occupation: 8.6% management, 4.5% professional, 8.7% services, 12.6% sales, 7.8% farming, 12.1% construction, 8.0% production (2006-2010 5-year est.).

Income: Per capita income: $27,096 (2006-2010 5-year est.); Median household income: $48,250 (2006-2010 5-year est.); Average household income: $59,551 (2006-2010 5-year est.); Percent of households with income of $100,000 or more: 13.7% (2006-2010 5-year est.); Poverty rate: 6.1% (2006-2010 5-year est.).

Education: Percent of population age 25 and over with: High school diploma (including GED) or higher: 91.5% (2006-2010 5-year est.); Bachelor's degree or higher: 22.0% (2006-2010 5-year est.); Master's degree or higher: 7.5% (2006-2010 5-year est.).

School District(s)

Hempfield SD (KG-12)

2010-11 Enrollment: 7,002 . . . . (717) 898-5560

Housing: Homeownership rate: 68.4% (2010); Median home value: $171,700 (2006-2010 5-year est.); Median contract rent: $579 per month (2006-2010 5-year est.); Median year structure built: 1980 (2006-2010 5-year est.).

Safety: Violent crime rate: 14.2 per 10,000 population; Property crime rate: 167.2 per 10,000 population (2011).

Transportation: Commute to work: 96.1% car, 1.7% public transportation, 1.3% walk, 0.0% work from home (2006-2010 5-year est.); Travel time to work: 35.5% less than 15 minutes, 44.4% 15 to 30 minutes, 11.7% 30 to 45 minutes, 4.7% 45 to 60 minutes, 3.6% 60 minutes or more (2006-2010 5-year est.)

Additional Information Contacts
Susquehanna Valley Chamber of Commerce . . . . (717) 684-5249
http://www.parivertowns.com

NARVON (unincorporated postal area)

Zip Code: 17555

Covers a land area of 34.918 square miles and a water area of 0.198 square miles. Located at 40.12° N. Lat; 75.95° W. Long. Elevation is 771 feet. Population: 7,525 (2010); Density: 215.5 persons per square mile (2010); Race: 97.9% White, 0.5% Black, 0.4% Asian, 0.1% American Indian/Alaska Native, 0.0% Native Hawaiian/Other Pacific Islander, 1.1% Other, 1.0% Hispanic of any race (2010); Average household size: 3.34 (2010); Median age: 33.2 (2010); Males per 100 females: 99.9 (2010); Homeownership rate: 82.0% (2010)

NEW HOLLAND (borough). Covers a land area of 1.943 square miles and a water area of <.001 square miles. Located at 40.10° N. Lat; 76.09° W. Long. Elevation is 492 feet.

History: Settled 1728, incorporated 1895.

Population: 4,477 (1990); 5,092 (2000); 5,378 (2010); Density: 2,767.6 persons per square mile (2010); Race: 88.0% White, 3.1% Black, 3.1% Asian, 0.3% American Indian/Alaska Native, 0.0% Native Hawaiian/Other Pacific Islander, 5.5% Other, 8.2% Hispanic of any race (2010); Average household size: 2.41 (2010); Median age: 42.3 (2010); Males per 100 females: 93.3 (2010); Marriage status: 27.1% never married, 57.9% now married, 7.1% widowed, 7.9% divorced (2006-2010 5-year est.); Foreign born: 8.4% (2006-2010 5-year est.); Ancestry (includes multiple ancestries): 40.8% German, 12.6% Irish, 8.5% English, 6.4% Haitian, 5.4% American (2006-2010 5-year est.).

Economy: Single-family building permits issued: 1 (2011); Multi-family building permits issued: 0 (2011); Employment by occupation: 13.0% management, 2.8% professional, 11.0% services, 14.1% sales, 4.3% farming, 8.7% construction, 10.5% production (2006-2010 5-year est.).

Income: Per capita income: $25,554 (2006-2010 5-year est.); Median household income: $51,932 (2006-2010 5-year est.); Average household income: $60,056 (2006-2010 5-year est.); Percent of households with income of $100,000 or more: 11.6% (2006-2010 5-year est.); Poverty rate: 9.4% (2006-2010 5-year est.).

Education: Percent of population age 25 and over with: High school diploma (including GED) or higher: 88.8% (2006-2010 5-year est.); Bachelor's degree or higher: 20.7% (2006-2010 5-year est.); Master's degree or higher: 5.8% (2006-2010 5-year est.).

School District(s)

Eastern Lancaster County SD (KG-12)
  2010-11 Enrollment: 3,111 . . . . (717) 354-1500

Housing: Homeownership rate: 65.4% (2010); Median home value: $173,100 (2006-2010 5-year est.); Median contract rent: $622 per month (2006-2010 5-year est.); Median year structure built: 1961 (2006-2010 5-year est.).

Safety: Violent crime rate: 14.8 per 10,000 population; Property crime rate: 137.2 per 10,000 population (2011).

Transportation: Commute to work: 92.0% car, 1.9% public transportation, 2.2% walk, 2.4% work from home (2006-2010 5-year est.); Travel time to work: 43.8% less than 15 minutes, 32.9% 15 to 30 minutes, 14.7% 30 to 45 minutes, 2.8% 45 to 60 minutes, 5.8% 60 minutes or more (2006-2010 5-year est.)

Additional Information Contacts
Borough of New Holland . . . . (717) 354-4567
  http://www.co.lancaster.pa.us/newholland/site/default.asp
Ephrata Area Chamber of Commerce . . . . (717) 738-9010
  http://www.ephrata-area.org

NEW PROVIDENCE (unincorporated postal area)

Zip Code: 17560

Covers a land area of 16.052 square miles and a water area of 0.098 square miles. Located at 39.91° N. Lat; 76.22° W. Long. Elevation is 384 feet. Population: 5,118 (2010); Density: 318.8 persons per square mile (2010); Race: 97.5% White, 0.7% Black, 0.2% Asian, 0.2% American Indian/Alaska Native, 0.1% Native Hawaiian/Other Pacific Islander, 1.3% Other, 2.0% Hispanic of any race (2010); Average household size: 2.71 (2010); Median age: 42.6 (2010); Males per 100 females: 97.5 (2010); Homeownership rate: 85.3% (2010)

PARADISE (CDP). Covers a land area of 1.164 square miles and a water area of 0.018 square miles. Located at 40.01° N. Lat; 76.12° W. Long. Elevation is 364 feet.

Population: 1,043 (1990); 1,028 (2000); 1,129 (2010); Density: 969.7 persons per square mile (2010); Race: 93.7% White, 1.3% Black, 0.2% Asian, 0.0% American Indian/Alaska Native, 0.0% Native Hawaiian/Other Pacific Islander, 4.8% Other, 5.0% Hispanic of any race (2010); Average household size: 2.82 (2010); Median age: 33.2 (2010); Males per 100 females: 100.5 (2010); Marriage status: 34.2% never married, 51.6% now married, 3.2% widowed, 11.0% divorced (2006-2010 5-year est.); Foreign born: 0.0% (2006-2010 5-year est.); Ancestry (includes multiple ancestries): 38.4% German, 18.9% Irish, 15.3% American, 6.1% Polish, 5.5% Italian (2006-2010 5-year est.).

Economy: Employment by occupation: 3.8% management, 9.6% professional, 8.1% services, 20.3% sales, 3.1% farming, 17.9% construction, 12.7% production (2006-2010 5-year est.).

Income: Per capita income: $22,923 (2006-2010 5-year est.); Median household income: $64,375 (2006-2010 5-year est.); Average household income: $68,781 (2006-2010 5-year est.); Percent of households with income of $100,000 or more: 21.8% (2006-2010 5-year est.); Poverty rate: 9.0% (2006-2010 5-year est.).

Education: Percent of population age 25 and over with: High school diploma (including GED) or higher: 83.1% (2006-2010 5-year est.); Bachelor's degree or higher: 16.3% (2006-2010 5-year est.); Master's degree or higher: 3.5% (2006-2010 5-year est.).

School District(s)

Pequea Valley SD (KG-12)
  2010-11 Enrollment: 1,734 . . . . (717) 768-5530

Housing: Homeownership rate: 61.6% (2010); Median home value: $188,900 (2006-2010 5-year est.); Median contract rent: $811 per month (2006-2010 5-year est.); Median year structure built: before 1940 (2006-2010 5-year est.).

Transportation: Commute to work: 93.3% car, 0.0% public transportation, 4.2% walk, 0.0% work from home (2006-2010 5-year est.); Travel time to work: 24.4% less than 15 minutes, 32.3% 15 to 30 minutes, 16.1% 30 to 45 minutes, 20.4% 45 to 60 minutes, 6.9% 60 minutes or more (2006-2010 5-year est.)

Additional Information Contacts
Southern Lancaster County Chamber of Commerce . . . . . (717) 786-1911
  http://www.southernlancasterchamber.com

PARADISE (township). Covers a land area of 18.597 square miles and a water area of 0.109 square miles. Located at 39.99° N. Lat; 76.10° W. Long. Elevation is 364 feet.

Population: 4,212 (1990); 4,698 (2000); 5,131 (2010); Density: 275.9 persons per square mile (2010); Race: 96.1% White, 1.0% Black, 0.2% Asian, 0.1% American Indian/Alaska Native, 0.0% Native Hawaiian/Other Pacific Islander, 2.6% Other, 2.8% Hispanic of any race (2010); Average household size: 3.11 (2010); Median age: 31.7 (2010); Males per 100 females: 103.0 (2010); Marriage status: 24.4% never married, 64.4% now married, 6.1% widowed, 5.0% divorced (2006-2010 5-year est.); Foreign born: 0.2% (2006-2010 5-year est.); Ancestry (includes multiple ancestries): 36.4% German, 12.6% American, 10.9% Pennsylvania German, 9.5% Irish, 8.2% English (2006-2010 5-year est.).

Economy: Single-family building permits issued: 9 (2011); Multi-family building permits issued: 0 (2011); Employment by occupation: 10.2% management, 4.3% professional, 8.0% services, 13.4% sales, 2.5% farming, 22.1% construction, 9.1% production (2006-2010 5-year est.).

Income: Per capita income: $21,791 (2006-2010 5-year est.); Median household income: $52,686 (2006-2010 5-year est.); Average household income: $67,075 (2006-2010 5-year est.); Percent of households with income of $100,000 or more: 15.1% (2006-2010 5-year est.); Poverty rate: 12.4% (2006-2010 5-year est.).

Education: Percent of population age 25 and over with: High school diploma (including GED) or higher: 58.2% (2006-2010 5-year est.); Bachelor's degree or higher: 10.4% (2006-2010 5-year est.); Master's degree or higher: 2.7% (2006-2010 5-year est.).

Housing: Homeownership rate: 66.3% (2010); Median home value: $220,300 (2006-2010 5-year est.); Median contract rent: $673 per month (2006-2010 5-year est.); Median year structure built: 1966 (2006-2010 5-year est.).

Transportation: Commute to work: 76.8% car, 0.0% public transportation, 2.1% walk, 14.8% work from home (2006-2010 5-year est.); Travel time to work: 29.9% less than 15 minutes, 36.2% 15 to 30 minutes, 12.5% 30 to

45 minutes, 9.2% 45 to 60 minutes, 12.1% 60 minutes or more (2006-2010 5-year est.)

Additional Information Contacts

Southern Lancaster County Chamber of Commerce ..... (717) 786-1911
http://www.southernlancasterchamber.com

PENN (township). Covers a land area of 29.583 square miles and a water area of 0.129 square miles. Located at 40.19° N. Lat; 76.38° W. Long.

Population: 6,842 (1990); 7,312 (2000); 8,789 (2010); Density: 297.1 persons per square mile (2010); Race: 95.9% White, 1.0% Black, 1.3% Asian, 0.1% American Indian/Alaska Native, 0.0% Native Hawaiian/Other Pacific Islander, 1.7% Other, 2.3% Hispanic of any race (2010); Average household size: 2.59 (2010); Median age: 42.6 (2010); Males per 100 females: 97.7 (2010); Marriage status: 16.6% never married, 66.4% now married, 8.0% widowed, 9.0% divorced (2006-2010 5-year est.); Foreign born: 5.3% (2006-2010 5-year est.); Ancestry (includes multiple ancestries): 49.0% German, 8.2% American, 7.5% Irish, 7.1% Swiss, 6.6% English (2006-2010 5-year est.).

Economy: Single-family building permits issued: 28 (2011); Multi-family building permits issued: 0 (2011); Employment by occupation: 9.7% management, 4.4% professional, 8.5% services, 21.4% sales, 2.6% farming, 12.6% construction, 12.3% production (2006-2010 5-year est.).

Income: Per capita income: $23,797 (2006-2010 5-year est.); Median household income: $56,838 (2006-2010 5-year est.); Average household income: $60,620 (2006-2010 5-year est.); Percent of households with income of $100,000 or more: 12.4% (2006-2010 5-year est.); Poverty rate: 4.5% (2006-2010 5-year est.).

Education: Percent of population age 25 and over with: High school diploma (including GED) or higher: 81.5% (2006-2010 5-year est.); Bachelor's degree or higher: 17.0% (2006-2010 5-year est.); Master's degree or higher: 5.2% (2006-2010 5-year est.).

Housing: Homeownership rate: 77.0% (2010); Median home value: $186,900 (2006-2010 5-year est.); Median contract rent: $828 per month (2006-2010 5-year est.); Median year structure built: 1980 (2006-2010 5-year est.).

Transportation: Commute to work: 86.0% car, 0.0% public transportation, 3.8% walk, 8.0% work from home (2006-2010 5-year est.); Travel time to work: 34.1% less than 15 minutes, 40.1% 15 to 30 minutes, 15.8% 30 to 45 minutes, 4.5% 45 to 60 minutes, 5.5% 60 minutes or more (2006-2010 5-year est.)

Additional Information Contacts

Lancaster Chamber of Commerce & Industry .... (717) 397-3531
http://www.lancasterchamber.com

Penn Township .... (717) 665-4508
http://www.penn.co.lancaster.pa.us

PENRYN (CDP). Covers a land area of 1.887 square miles and a water area of 0.013 square miles. Located at 40.20° N. Lat; 76.37° W. Long. Elevation is 584 feet.

Population: n/a (1990); n/a (2000); 1,024 (2010); Density: 542.6 persons per square mile (2010); Race: 96.6% White, 0.4% Black, 0.4% Asian, 0.1% American Indian/Alaska Native, 0.0% Native Hawaiian/Other Pacific Islander, 2.5% Other, 1.9% Hispanic of any race (2010); Average household size: 2.75 (2010); Median age: 41.4 (2010); Males per 100 females: 105.2 (2010); Marriage status: 15.3% never married, 76.8% now married, 2.9% widowed, 5.1% divorced (2006-2010 5-year est.); Foreign born: 9.6% (2006-2010 5-year est.); Ancestry (includes multiple ancestries): 45.6% German, 10.0% American, 8.3% Swiss, 7.0% Irish, 6.5% Italian (2006-2010 5-year est.).

Economy: Employment by occupation: 7.6% management, 7.0% professional, 13.5% services, 15.1% sales, 0.0% farming, 15.1% construction, 16.6% production (2006-2010 5-year est.).

Income: Per capita income: $24,465 (2006-2010 5-year est.); Median household income: $59,875 (2006-2010 5-year est.); Average household income: $75,302 (2006-2010 5-year est.); Percent of households with income of $100,000 or more: 14.7% (2006-2010 5-year est.); Poverty rate: 0.0% (2006-2010 5-year est.).

Education: Percent of population age 25 and over with: High school diploma (including GED) or higher: 85.1% (2006-2010 5-year est.); Bachelor's degree or higher: 29.9% (2006-2010 5-year est.); Master's degree or higher: 4.7% (2006-2010 5-year est.).

Housing: Homeownership rate: 83.9% (2010); Median home value: $184,900 (2006-2010 5-year est.); Median contract rent: n/a per month

(2006-2010 5-year est.); Median year structure built: 1977 (2006-2010 5-year est.).

Transportation: Commute to work: 95.4% car, 0.0% public transportation, 0.0% walk, 4.6% work from home (2006-2010 5-year est.); Travel time to work: 24.9% less than 15 minutes, 49.4% 15 to 30 minutes, 22.9% 30 to 45 minutes, 0.0% 45 to 60 minutes, 2.8% 60 minutes or more (2006-2010 5-year est.).

PEQUEA (township). Covers a land area of 13.424 square miles and a water area of 0.184 square miles. Located at 39.97° N. Lat; 76.30° W. Long. Elevation is 171 feet.

Population: 4,455 (1990); 4,358 (2000); 4,605 (2010); Density: 343.0 persons per square mile (2010); Race: 95.9% White, 1.2% Black, 0.7% Asian, 0.2% American Indian/Alaska Native, 0.0% Native Hawaiian/Other Pacific Islander, 2.0% Other, 2.7% Hispanic of any race (2010); Average household size: 2.74 (2010); Median age: 42.2 (2010); Males per 100 females: 97.4 (2010); Marriage status: 16.3% never married, 73.9% now married, 4.0% widowed, 5.8% divorced (2006-2010 5-year est.); Foreign born: 1.9% (2006-2010 5-year est.); Ancestry (includes multiple ancestries): 49.7% German, 21.1% Irish, 10.9% English, 6.1% Italian, 5.3% Swiss (2006-2010 5-year est.).

Economy: Single-family building permits issued: 1 (2011); Multi-family building permits issued: 0 (2011); Employment by occupation: 8.1% management, 0.7% professional, 6.2% services, 22.6% sales, 3.8% farming, 12.6% construction, 7.6% production (2006-2010 5-year est.).

Income: Per capita income: $32,882 (2006-2010 5-year est.); Median household income: $65,617 (2006-2010 5-year est.); Average household income: $85,068 (2006-2010 5-year est.); Percent of households with income of $100,000 or more: 18.6% (2006-2010 5-year est.); Poverty rate: 7.5% (2006-2010 5-year est.).

Education: Percent of population age 25 and over with: High school diploma (including GED) or higher: 88.9% (2006-2010 5-year est.); Bachelor's degree or higher: 16.2% (2006-2010 5-year est.); Master's degree or higher: 6.5% (2006-2010 5-year est.).

School District(s)

Penn Manor SD (KG-12)
2010-11 Enrollment: 5,169 .... (717) 872-9500

Housing: Homeownership rate: 82.9% (2010); Median home value: $191,900 (2006-2010 5-year est.); Median contract rent: $571 per month (2006-2010 5-year est.); Median year structure built: 1968 (2006-2010 5-year est.).

Transportation: Commute to work: 94.7% car, 1.2% public transportation, 0.8% walk, 1.7% work from home (2006-2010 5-year est.); Travel time to work: 23.0% less than 15 minutes, 47.7% 15 to 30 minutes, 12.3% 30 to 45 minutes, 9.3% 45 to 60 minutes, 7.6% 60 minutes or more (2006-2010 5-year est.)

Additional Information Contacts

Lancaster Chamber of Commerce & Industry .... (717) 397-3531
http://www.lancasterchamber.com

PROVIDENCE (township). Covers a land area of 19.876 square miles and a water area of 0.133 square miles. Located at 39.91° N. Lat; 76.23° W. Long.

Population: 6,071 (1990); 6,651 (2000); 6,897 (2010); Density: 347.0 persons per square mile (2010); Race: 97.5% White, 0.7% Black, 0.2% Asian, 0.3% American Indian/Alaska Native, 0.1% Native Hawaiian/Other Pacific Islander, 1.2% Other, 2.0% Hispanic of any race (2010); Average household size: 2.71 (2010); Median age: 42.3 (2010); Males per 100 females: 98.4 (2010); Marriage status: 23.5% never married, 62.8% now married, 5.3% widowed, 8.3% divorced (2006-2010 5-year est.); Foreign born: 1.3% (2006-2010 5-year est.); Ancestry (includes multiple ancestries): 45.3% German, 13.9% Irish, 11.8% American, 10.0% English, 4.4% Polish (2006-2010 5-year est.).

Economy: Single-family building permits issued: 7 (2011); Multi-family building permits issued: 0 (2011); Employment by occupation: 3.5% management, 3.5% professional, 12.5% services, 19.2% sales, 5.1% farming, 15.5% construction, 8.4% production (2006-2010 5-year est.).

Income: Per capita income: $22,742 (2006-2010 5-year est.); Median household income: $51,667 (2006-2010 5-year est.); Average household income: $59,360 (2006-2010 5-year est.); Percent of households with income of $100,000 or more: 15.8% (2006-2010 5-year est.); Poverty rate: 4.1% (2006-2010 5-year est.).

Education: Percent of population age 25 and over with: High school diploma (including GED) or higher: 83.3% (2006-2010 5-year est.);

Bachelor's degree or higher: 8.6% (2006-2010 5-year est.); Master's degree or higher: 2.7% (2006-2010 5-year est.).
Housing: Homeownership rate: 83.8% (2010); Median home value: $184,100 (2006-2010 5-year est.); Median contract rent: $538 per month (2006-2010 5-year est.); Median year structure built: 1979 (2006-2010 5-year est.).
Transportation: Commute to work: 94.6% car, 0.4% public transportation, 0.8% walk, 1.3% work from home (2006-2010 5-year est.); Travel time to work: 24.5% less than 15 minutes, 32.9% 15 to 30 minutes, 25.8% 30 to 45 minutes, 10.5% 45 to 60 minutes, 6.4% 60 minutes or more (2006-2010 5-year est.)
Additional Information Contacts
Providence Township . . . . (717) 786-7596
    http://www.co.lancaster.pa.us/providencetwp/site/default.asp
Southern Lancaster County Chamber of Commerce . . . . . (717) 786-1911
    http://www.southernlancasterchamber.com

QUARRYVILLE (borough). Covers a land area of 1.291 square miles and a water area of 0.020 square miles. Located at 39.90° N. Lat; 76.16° W. Long. Elevation is 512 feet.
History: Settled 1791, incorporated 1892.
Population: 1,642 (1990); 1,994 (2000); 2,576 (2010); Density: 1,995.0 persons per square mile (2010); Race: 94.1% White, 1.2% Black, 0.6% Asian, 0.2% American Indian/Alaska Native, 0.2% Native Hawaiian/Other Pacific Islander, 3.7% Other, 4.7% Hispanic of any race (2010); Average household size: 2.53 (2010); Median age: 34.9 (2010); Males per 100 females: 93.1 (2010); Marriage status: 22.4% never married, 59.6% now married, 5.0% widowed, 13.0% divorced (2006-2010 5-year est.); Foreign born: 4.8% (2006-2010 5-year est.); Ancestry (includes multiple ancestries): 37.0% German, 16.4% Irish, 12.8% English, 10.3% American, 6.5% Italian (2006-2010 5-year est.).
Economy: Single-family building permits issued: 10 (2011); Multi-family building permits issued: 0 (2011); Employment by occupation: 7.5% management, 5.1% professional, 11.4% services, 19.9% sales, 2.6% farming, 8.8% construction, 6.8% production (2006-2010 5-year est.).
Income: Per capita income: $27,072 (2006-2010 5-year est.); Median household income: $53,837 (2006-2010 5-year est.); Average household income: $65,603 (2006-2010 5-year est.); Percent of households with income of $100,000 or more: 16.2% (2006-2010 5-year est.); Poverty rate: 11.3% (2006-2010 5-year est.).
Education: Percent of population age 25 and over with: High school diploma (including GED) or higher: 83.1% (2006-2010 5-year est.); Bachelor's degree or higher: 18.3% (2006-2010 5-year est.); Master's degree or higher: 3.2% (2006-2010 5-year est.).
School District(s)
Solanco SD (KG-12)
    2010-11 Enrollment: 3,742 . . . . (717) 786-8401
Housing: Homeownership rate: 61.1% (2010); Median home value: $192,600 (2006-2010 5-year est.); Median contract rent: $575 per month (2006-2010 5-year est.); Median year structure built: 1968 (2006-2010 5-year est.).
Safety: Violent crime rate: 50.3 per 10,000 population; Property crime rate: 232.2 per 10,000 population (2011).
Newspapers: Parkesburg Post-Christiana Ledger (Local news; Circulation 3,500); Solanco Sun Ledger (Local news; Circulation 4,600)
Transportation: Commute to work: 83.1% car, 0.0% public transportation, 2.6% walk, 7.2% work from home (2006-2010 5-year est.); Travel time to work: 31.9% less than 15 minutes, 24.2% 15 to 30 minutes, 17.5% 30 to 45 minutes, 19.1% 45 to 60 minutes, 7.3% 60 minutes or more (2006-2010 5-year est.)
Additional Information Contacts
Southern Lancaster County Chamber of Commerce . . . . . (717) 786-1911
    http://www.southernlancasterchamber.com

RAPHO (township). Covers a land area of 47.423 square miles and a water area of 0.352 square miles. Located at 40.16° N. Lat; 76.46° W. Long.
Population: 8,256 (1990); 8,578 (2000); 10,442 (2010); Density: 220.2 persons per square mile (2010); Race: 96.4% White, 0.8% Black, 1.1% Asian, 0.1% American Indian/Alaska Native, 0.0% Native Hawaiian/Other Pacific Islander, 1.6% Other, 2.3% Hispanic of any race (2010); Average household size: 2.58 (2010); Median age: 43.3 (2010); Males per 100 females: 101.7 (2010); Marriage status: 20.8% never married, 68.9% now married, 4.5% widowed, 5.8% divorced (2006-2010 5-year est.); Foreign born: 1.3% (2006-2010 5-year est.); Ancestry (includes multiple

ancestries): 42.8% German, 12.5% American, 8.2% Irish, 6.5% English, 6.4% Pennsylvania German (2006-2010 5-year est.).
Economy: Single-family building permits issued: 46 (2011); Multi-family building permits issued: 0 (2011); Employment by occupation: 12.2% management, 3.5% professional, 9.5% services, 13.5% sales, 3.7% farming, 13.1% construction, 9.3% production (2006-2010 5-year est.).
Income: Per capita income: $27,760 (2006-2010 5-year est.); Median household income: $63,266 (2006-2010 5-year est.); Average household income: $73,017 (2006-2010 5-year est.); Percent of households with income of $100,000 or more: 21.0% (2006-2010 5-year est.); Poverty rate: 9.2% (2006-2010 5-year est.).
Education: Percent of population age 25 and over with: High school diploma (including GED) or higher: 84.1% (2006-2010 5-year est.); Bachelor's degree or higher: 22.7% (2006-2010 5-year est.); Master's degree or higher: 8.0% (2006-2010 5-year est.).
Housing: Homeownership rate: 80.4% (2010); Median home value: $187,300 (2006-2010 5-year est.); Median contract rent: $841 per month (2006-2010 5-year est.); Median year structure built: 1980 (2006-2010 5-year est.).
Transportation: Commute to work: 88.0% car, 0.8% public transportation, 2.6% walk, 7.6% work from home (2006-2010 5-year est.); Travel time to work: 32.3% less than 15 minutes, 43.6% 15 to 30 minutes, 18.1% 30 to 45 minutes, 3.3% 45 to 60 minutes, 2.7% 60 minutes or more (2006-2010 5-year est.)
Additional Information Contacts
Mount Joy Chamber of Commerce . . . . (717) 653-0773
    http://mountjoychamber.com
Rapho Township . . . . (717) 665-3827
    http://www.raphotownship.com

REAMSTOWN (CDP). Covers a land area of 2.257 square miles and a water area of 0.013 square miles. Located at 40.21° N. Lat; 76.12° W. Long. Elevation is 387 feet.
Population: 2,649 (1990); 3,498 (2000); 3,361 (2010); Density: 1,489.1 persons per square mile (2010); Race: 95.9% White, 0.7% Black, 2.0% Asian, 0.2% American Indian/Alaska Native, 0.0% Native Hawaiian/Other Pacific Islander, 1.2% Other, 1.9% Hispanic of any race (2010); Average household size: 2.72 (2010); Median age: 40.1 (2010); Males per 100 females: 99.7 (2010); Marriage status: 22.5% never married, 71.0% now married, 4.0% widowed, 2.5% divorced (2006-2010 5-year est.); Foreign born: 1.8% (2006-2010 5-year est.); Ancestry (includes multiple ancestries): 50.7% German, 11.9% Irish, 7.6% English, 5.4% Swiss, 5.0% American (2006-2010 5-year est.).
Economy: Employment by occupation: 8.8% management, 4.0% professional, 7.4% services, 16.3% sales, 5.3% farming, 9.9% construction, 13.7% production (2006-2010 5-year est.).
Income: Per capita income: $26,706 (2006-2010 5-year est.); Median household income: $65,915 (2006-2010 5-year est.); Average household income: $79,216 (2006-2010 5-year est.); Percent of households with income of $100,000 or more: 24.0% (2006-2010 5-year est.); Poverty rate: 0.8% (2006-2010 5-year est.).
Education: Percent of population age 25 and over with: High school diploma (including GED) or higher: 90.8% (2006-2010 5-year est.); Bachelor's degree or higher: 18.0% (2006-2010 5-year est.); Master's degree or higher: 7.2% (2006-2010 5-year est.).
School District(s)
Cocalico SD (PK-12)
    2010-11 Enrollment: 3,295 . . . . (717) 336-1413
Housing: Homeownership rate: 76.4% (2010); Median home value: $193,200 (2006-2010 5-year est.); Median contract rent: $553 per month (2006-2010 5-year est.); Median year structure built: 1980 (2006-2010 5-year est.).
Transportation: Commute to work: 92.7% car, 1.0% public transportation, 3.3% walk, 2.3% work from home (2006-2010 5-year est.); Travel time to work: 35.2% less than 15 minutes, 33.5% 15 to 30 minutes, 16.5% 30 to 45 minutes, 6.1% 45 to 60 minutes, 8.8% 60 minutes or more (2006-2010 5-year est.)
Additional Information Contacts
Ephrata Area Chamber of Commerce . . . . (717) 738-9010
    http://www.ephrata-area.org

REFTON (CDP). Covers a land area of 1.199 square miles and a water area of 0.022 square miles. Located at 39.95° N. Lat; 76.24° W. Long. Elevation is 410 feet.
Population: n/a (1990); n/a (2000); 298 (2010); Density: 248.4 persons per square mile (2010); Race: 99.7% White, 0.0% Black, 0.3% Asian, 0.0% American Indian/Alaska Native, 0.0% Native Hawaiian/Other Pacific Islander, 0.0% Other, 1.3% Hispanic of any race (2010); Average household size: 2.81 (2010); Median age: 42.3 (2010); Males per 100 females: 114.4 (2010); Marriage status: 37.6% never married, 52.0% now married, 0.0% widowed, 10.4% divorced (2006-2010 5-year est.); Foreign born: 0.0% (2006-2010 5-year est.); Ancestry (includes multiple ancestries): 42.1% German, 10.5% Scottish, 5.7% Lithuanian, 5.7% Irish, 5.7% French (2006-2010 5-year est.).
Economy: Employment by occupation: 0.0% management, 0.0% professional, 0.0% services, 16.4% sales, 0.0% farming, 0.0% construction, 0.0% production (2006-2010 5-year est.).
Income: Per capita income: $21,285 (2006-2010 5-year est.); Median household income: $56,389 (2006-2010 5-year est.); Average household income: $68,853 (2006-2010 5-year est.); Percent of households with income of $100,000 or more: 37.5% (2006-2010 5-year est.); Poverty rate: 12.1% (2006-2010 5-year est.).
Education: Percent of population age 25 and over with: High school diploma (including GED) or higher: 59.3% (2006-2010 5-year est.); Bachelor's degree or higher: 22.2% (2006-2010 5-year est.); Master's degree or higher: 11.1% (2006-2010 5-year est.).
Housing: Homeownership rate: 83.0% (2010); Median home value: $181,300 (2006-2010 5-year est.); Median contract rent: n/a per month (2006-2010 5-year est.); Median year structure built: 1971 (2006-2010 5-year est.).
Transportation: Commute to work: 100.0% car, 0.0% public transportation, 0.0% walk, 0.0% work from home (2006-2010 5-year est.); Travel time to work: 50.7% less than 15 minutes, 49.3% 15 to 30 minutes, 0.0% 30 to 45 minutes, 0.0% 45 to 60 minutes, 0.0% 60 minutes or more (2006-2010 5-year est.)

REINHOLDS (CDP). Covers a land area of 0.921 square miles and a water area of 0.004 square miles. Located at 40.27° N. Lat; 76.12° W. Long. Elevation is 463 feet.
Population: n/a (1990); n/a (2000); 1,803 (2010); Density: 1,958.5 persons per square mile (2010); Race: 94.6% White, 1.3% Black, 0.9% Asian, 0.2% American Indian/Alaska Native, 0.0% Native Hawaiian/Other Pacific Islander, 3.0% Other, 2.3% Hispanic of any race (2010); Average household size: 3.00 (2010); Median age: 33.5 (2010); Males per 100 females: 98.6 (2010); Marriage status: 33.7% never married, 55.9% now married, 3.7% widowed, 6.7% divorced (2006-2010 5-year est.); Foreign born: 6.8% (2006-2010 5-year est.); Ancestry (includes multiple ancestries): 34.9% German, 8.5% Irish, 7.6% American, 7.4% English, 7.2% Italian (2006-2010 5-year est.).
Economy: Employment by occupation: 7.4% management, 1.0% professional, 7.8% services, 20.3% sales, 3.5% farming, 19.9% construction, 10.7% production (2006-2010 5-year est.).
Income: Per capita income: $21,609 (2006-2010 5-year est.); Median household income: $62,656 (2006-2010 5-year est.); Average household income: $65,704 (2006-2010 5-year est.); Percent of households with income of $100,000 or more: 5.5% (2006-2010 5-year est.); Poverty rate: 7.0% (2006-2010 5-year est.).
Education: Percent of population age 25 and over with: High school diploma (including GED) or higher: 86.7% (2006-2010 5-year est.); Bachelor's degree or higher: 4.4% (2006-2010 5-year est.); Master's degree or higher: 1.0% (2006-2010 5-year est.).
Housing: Homeownership rate: 88.0% (2010); Median home value: $171,000 (2006-2010 5-year est.); Median contract rent: $629 per month (2006-2010 5-year est.); Median year structure built: 1992 (2006-2010 5-year est.).
Transportation: Commute to work: 96.6% car, 0.0% public transportation, 0.0% walk, 2.4% work from home (2006-2010 5-year est.); Travel time to work: 25.4% less than 15 minutes, 44.6% 15 to 30 minutes, 19.5% 30 to 45 minutes, 5.7% 45 to 60 minutes, 4.8% 60 minutes or more (2006-2010 5-year est.)

RHEEMS (CDP). Covers a land area of 1.179 square miles and a water area of 0.002 square miles. Located at 40.13° N. Lat; 76.57° W. Long. Elevation is 433 feet.
Population: 1,044 (1990); 1,557 (2000); 1,598 (2010); Density: 1,355.3 persons per square mile (2010); Race: 97.2% White, 0.6% Black, 0.9%

Asian, 0.0% American Indian/Alaska Native, 0.0% Native Hawaiian/Other Pacific Islander, 1.3% Other, 2.1% Hispanic of any race (2010); Average household size: 2.74 (2010); Median age: 42.0 (2010); Males per 100 females: 96.8 (2010); Marriage status: 13.4% never married, 72.3% now married, 7.4% widowed, 6.9% divorced (2006-2010 5-year est.); Foreign born: 3.3% (2006-2010 5-year est.); Ancestry (includes multiple ancestries): 42.8% German, 14.6% Italian, 10.0% Irish, 9.6% American, 6.5% Austrian (2006-2010 5-year est.).
Economy: Employment by occupation: 5.7% management, 7.2% professional, 7.5% services, 15.6% sales, 4.7% farming, 9.9% construction, 15.6% production (2006-2010 5-year est.).
Income: Per capita income: $28,514 (2006-2010 5-year est.); Median household income: $70,179 (2006-2010 5-year est.); Average household income: $73,481 (2006-2010 5-year est.); Percent of households with income of $100,000 or more: 27.7% (2006-2010 5-year est.); Poverty rate: 10.7% (2006-2010 5-year est.).
Education: Percent of population age 25 and over with: High school diploma (including GED) or higher: 93.3% (2006-2010 5-year est.); Bachelor's degree or higher: 30.6% (2006-2010 5-year est.); Master's degree or higher: 10.3% (2006-2010 5-year est.).

School District(s)
Elizabethtown Area SD (KG-12)
   2010-11 Enrollment: 3,989 . . . . (717) 367-1521
Housing: Homeownership rate: 78.9% (2010); Median home value: $158,300 (2006-2010 5-year est.); Median contract rent: $559 per month (2006-2010 5-year est.); Median year structure built: 1972 (2006-2010 5-year est.).
Transportation: Commute to work: 95.2% car, 1.8% public transportation, 1.7% walk, 0.0% work from home (2006-2010 5-year est.); Travel time to work: 41.6% less than 15 minutes, 37.7% 15 to 30 minutes, 13.2% 30 to 45 minutes, 7.4% 45 to 60 minutes, 0.0% 60 minutes or more (2006-2010 5-year est.)
Additional Information Contacts
Lancaster Chamber of Commerce & Industry . . . . (717) 397-3531
   http://www.lancasterchamber.com

RONKS (CDP). Covers a land area of 0.665 square miles and a water area of <.001 square miles. Located at 40.03° N. Lat; 76.18° W. Long. Elevation is 377 feet.
Population: n/a (1990); n/a (2000); 362 (2010); Density: 544.4 persons per square mile (2010); Race: 96.4% White, 1.9% Black, 0.0% Asian, 0.0% American Indian/Alaska Native, 0.0% Native Hawaiian/Other Pacific Islander, 1.7% Other, 3.0% Hispanic of any race (2010); Average household size: 2.55 (2010); Median age: 35.9 (2010); Males per 100 females: 97.8 (2010); Marriage status: 47.4% never married, 39.1% now married, 9.0% widowed, 4.5% divorced (2006-2010 5-year est.); Foreign born: 0.0% (2006-2010 5-year est.); Ancestry (includes multiple ancestries): 37.2% Pennsylvania German, 10.2% German, 10.2% European, 9.8% Italian, 6.8% English (2006-2010 5-year est.).
Economy: Employment by occupation: 11.6% management, 0.0% professional, 24.6% services, 13.0% sales, 7.2% farming, 12.6% construction, 0.0% production (2006-2010 5-year est.).
Income: Per capita income: $35,315 (2006-2010 5-year est.); Median household income: $55,046 (2006-2010 5-year est.); Average household income: $72,339 (2006-2010 5-year est.); Percent of households with income of $100,000 or more: 29.8% (2006-2010 5-year est.); Poverty rate: 0.0% (2006-2010 5-year est.).
Education: Percent of population age 25 and over with: High school diploma (including GED) or higher: 47.1% (2006-2010 5-year est.); Bachelor's degree or higher: 6.6% (2006-2010 5-year est.); Master's degree or higher: 6.6% (2006-2010 5-year est.).
Housing: Homeownership rate: 50.0% (2010); Median home value: $180,400 (2006-2010 5-year est.); Median contract rent: $508 per month (2006-2010 5-year est.); Median year structure built: 1964 (2006-2010 5-year est.).
Transportation: Commute to work: 85.0% car, 0.0% public transportation, 0.0% walk, 0.0% work from home (2006-2010 5-year est.); Travel time to work: 62.8% less than 15 minutes, 13.0% 15 to 30 minutes, 0.0% 30 to 45 minutes, 0.0% 45 to 60 minutes, 24.2% 60 minutes or more (2006-2010 5-year est.)

ROTHSVILLE (CDP). Covers a land area of 2.464 square miles and a water area of 0.017 square miles. Located at 40.15° N. Lat; 76.25° W. Long. Elevation is 492 feet.

Population: 2,076 (1990); 3,017 (2000); 3,044 (2010); Density: 1,235.2 persons per square mile (2010); Race: 94.2% White, 1.1% Black, 1.1% Asian, 0.0% American Indian/Alaska Native, 0.0% Native Hawaiian/Other Pacific Islander, 3.6% Other, 5.2% Hispanic of any race (2010); Average household size: 2.82 (2010); Median age: 38.8 (2010); Males per 100 females: 102.5 (2010); Marriage status: 17.0% never married, 70.3% now married, 2.6% widowed, 10.1% divorced (2006-2010 5-year est.); Foreign born: 1.5% (2006-2010 5-year est.); Ancestry (includes multiple ancestries): 41.1% German, 10.2% Irish, 10.0% American, 8.7% Italian, 6.3% Polish (2006-2010 5-year est.).

Economy: Employment by occupation: 21.3% management, 1.4% professional, 8.0% services, 12.5% sales, 6.5% farming, 9.5% construction, 10.5% production (2006-2010 5-year est.).

Income: Per capita income: $36,162 (2006-2010 5-year est.); Median household income: $70,640 (2006-2010 5-year est.); Average household income: $103,696 (2006-2010 5-year est.); Percent of households with income of $100,000 or more: 34.4% (2006-2010 5-year est.); Poverty rate: 2.1% (2006-2010 5-year est.).

Education: Percent of population age 25 and over with: High school diploma (including GED) or higher: 91.9% (2006-2010 5-year est.); Bachelor's degree or higher: 30.8% (2006-2010 5-year est.); Master's degree or higher: 10.5% (2006-2010 5-year est.).

Housing: Homeownership rate: 79.6% (2010); Median home value: $187,500 (2006-2010 5-year est.); Median contract rent: $775 per month (2006-2010 5-year est.); Median year structure built: 1988 (2006-2010 5-year est.).

Transportation: Commute to work: 93.9% car, 0.0% public transportation, 0.0% walk, 6.1% work from home (2006-2010 5-year est.); Travel time to work: 29.1% less than 15 minutes, 52.2% 15 to 30 minutes, 15.8% 30 to 45 minutes, 0.6% 45 to 60 minutes, 2.4% 60 minutes or more (2006-2010 5-year est.)

Additional Information Contacts
Lancaster Chamber of Commerce & Industry . . . . (717) 397-3531
  http://www.lancasterchamber.com

SADSBURY (township). Covers a land area of 19.559 square miles and a water area of 0.101 square miles. Located at 39.94° N. Lat; 76.02° W. Long.

Population: 2,640 (1990); 3,025 (2000); 3,395 (2010); Density: 173.6 persons per square mile (2010); Race: 97.8% White, 0.4% Black, 0.2% Asian, 0.0% American Indian/Alaska Native, 0.0% Native Hawaiian/Other Pacific Islander, 1.6% Other, 1.1% Hispanic of any race (2010); Average household size: 3.53 (2010); Median age: 28.9 (2010); Males per 100 females: 101.2 (2010); Marriage status: 23.5% never married, 68.7% now married, 3.9% widowed, 4.0% divorced (2006-2010 5-year est.); Foreign born: 1.0% (2006-2010 5-year est.); Ancestry (includes multiple ancestries): 33.8% German, 11.0% American, 11.0% English, 10.7% Irish, 9.7% Pennsylvania German (2006-2010 5-year est.).

Economy: Single-family building permits issued: 4 (2011); Multi-family building permits issued: 0 (2011); Employment by occupation: 17.8% management, 2.1% professional, 11.4% services, 13.5% sales, 4.0% farming, 17.8% construction, 9.5% production (2006-2010 5-year est.).

Income: Per capita income: $22,834 (2006-2010 5-year est.); Median household income: $58,333 (2006-2010 5-year est.); Average household income: $73,248 (2006-2010 5-year est.); Percent of households with income of $100,000 or more: 20.0% (2006-2010 5-year est.); Poverty rate: 9.8% (2006-2010 5-year est.).

Education: Percent of population age 25 and over with: High school diploma (including GED) or higher: 72.7% (2006-2010 5-year est.); Bachelor's degree or higher: 14.4% (2006-2010 5-year est.); Master's degree or higher: 4.7% (2006-2010 5-year est.).

Housing: Homeownership rate: 81.2% (2010); Median home value: $251,500 (2006-2010 5-year est.); Median contract rent: $656 per month (2006-2010 5-year est.); Median year structure built: 1976 (2006-2010 5-year est.).

Transportation: Commute to work: 82.1% car, 0.0% public transportation, 2.9% walk, 11.7% work from home (2006-2010 5-year est.); Travel time to work: 38.3% less than 15 minutes, 29.6% 15 to 30 minutes, 18.8% 30 to 45 minutes, 6.0% 45 to 60 minutes, 7.3% 60 minutes or more (2006-2010 5-year est.)

Additional Information Contacts
Lancaster Chamber of Commerce & Industry . . . . (717) 397-3531
  http://www.lancasterchamber.com

SALISBURY (township). Covers a land area of 41.758 square miles and a water area of 0.190 square miles. Located at 40.04° N. Lat; 76.00° W. Long.

Population: 8,527 (1990); 10,012 (2000); 11,062 (2010); Density: 264.9 persons per square mile (2010); Race: 96.8% White, 1.1% Black, 0.4% Asian, 0.1% American Indian/Alaska Native, 0.0% Native Hawaiian/Other Pacific Islander, 1.6% Other, 1.9% Hispanic of any race (2010); Average household size: 3.37 (2010); Median age: 30.0 (2010); Males per 100 females: 103.9 (2010); Marriage status: 29.6% never married, 62.2% now married, 4.2% widowed, 4.0% divorced (2006-2010 5-year est.); Foreign born: 0.5% (2006-2010 5-year est.); Ancestry (includes multiple ancestries): 36.7% German, 14.0% Pennsylvania German, 10.9% American, 8.2% Irish, 7.3% English (2006-2010 5-year est.).

Economy: Single-family building permits issued: 19 (2011); Multi-family building permits issued: 0 (2011); Employment by occupation: 14.9% management, 1.2% professional, 8.7% services, 13.3% sales, 2.6% farming, 22.6% construction, 9.8% production (2006-2010 5-year est.).

Income: Per capita income: $20,821 (2006-2010 5-year est.); Median household income: $61,987 (2006-2010 5-year est.); Average household income: $71,959 (2006-2010 5-year est.); Percent of households with income of $100,000 or more: 25.3% (2006-2010 5-year est.); Poverty rate: 9.3% (2006-2010 5-year est.).

Education: Percent of population age 25 and over with: High school diploma (including GED) or higher: 63.4% (2006-2010 5-year est.); Bachelor's degree or higher: 13.1% (2006-2010 5-year est.); Master's degree or higher: 2.8% (2006-2010 5-year est.).

Housing: Homeownership rate: 75.4% (2010); Median home value: $240,400 (2006-2010 5-year est.); Median contract rent: $500 per month (2006-2010 5-year est.); Median year structure built: 1977 (2006-2010 5-year est.).

Transportation: Commute to work: 78.4% car, 0.9% public transportation, 6.1% walk, 11.9% work from home (2006-2010 5-year est.); Travel time to work: 37.6% less than 15 minutes, 32.1% 15 to 30 minutes, 15.8% 30 to 45 minutes, 5.0% 45 to 60 minutes, 9.5% 60 minutes or more (2006-2010 5-year est.)

Additional Information Contacts
Lancaster Chamber of Commerce & Industry . . . . (717) 397-3531
  http://www.lancasterchamber.com
Salisbury Township . . . . (717) 768-8059
  http://www.salisburytownship.org

SALUNGA (CDP). Covers a land area of 1.799 square miles and a water area of <.001 square miles. Located at 40.09° N. Lat; 76.43° W. Long. Elevation is 407 feet.

Population: n/a (1990); n/a (2000); 2,695 (2010); Density: 1,498.1 persons per square mile (2010); Race: 93.8% White, 2.2% Black, 1.6% Asian, 0.2% American Indian/Alaska Native, 0.0% Native Hawaiian/Other Pacific Islander, 2.2% Other, 3.9% Hispanic of any race (2010); Average household size: 2.57 (2010); Median age: 43.8 (2010); Males per 100 females: 98.6 (2010); Marriage status: 27.0% never married, 63.6% now married, 3.7% widowed, 5.7% divorced (2006-2010 5-year est.); Foreign born: 0.9% (2006-2010 5-year est.); Ancestry (includes multiple ancestries): 41.5% German, 13.1% English, 12.6% Irish, 10.2% American, 5.0% Italian (2006-2010 5-year est.).

Economy: Employment by occupation: 7.6% management, 3.5% professional, 10.2% services, 19.6% sales, 5.3% farming, 7.4% construction, 5.1% production (2006-2010 5-year est.).

Income: Per capita income: $28,983 (2006-2010 5-year est.); Median household income: $73,256 (2006-2010 5-year est.); Average household income: $78,964 (2006-2010 5-year est.); Percent of households with income of $100,000 or more: 22.4% (2006-2010 5-year est.); Poverty rate: 3.8% (2006-2010 5-year est.).

Education: Percent of population age 25 and over with: High school diploma (including GED) or higher: 94.9% (2006-2010 5-year est.); Bachelor's degree or higher: 28.8% (2006-2010 5-year est.); Master's degree or higher: 7.1% (2006-2010 5-year est.).

Housing: Homeownership rate: 83.2% (2010); Median home value: $206,900 (2006-2010 5-year est.); Median contract rent: $539 per month (2006-2010 5-year est.); Median year structure built: 1968 (2006-2010 5-year est.).

Transportation: Commute to work: 90.3% car, 1.0% public transportation, 4.3% walk, 3.0% work from home (2006-2010 5-year est.); Travel time to work: 36.5% less than 15 minutes, 42.1% 15 to 30 minutes, 14.1% 30 to 45 minutes, 4.1% 45 to 60 minutes, 3.3% 60 minutes or more (2006-2010 5-year est.)

SCHOENECK (CDP).
Covers a land area of 3.088 square miles and a water area of 0.030 square miles. Located at 40.24° N. Lat; 76.17° W. Long. Elevation is 561 feet.

Population: n/a (1990); n/a (2000); 1,056 (2010); Density: 342.0 persons per square mile (2010); Race: 98.7% White, 0.2% Black, 0.4% Asian, 0.0% American Indian/Alaska Native, 0.0% Native Hawaiian/Other Pacific Islander, 0.7% Other, 1.8% Hispanic of any race (2010); Average household size: 3.17 (2010); Median age: 31.6 (2010); Males per 100 females: 94.1 (2010); Marriage status: 38.5% never married, 51.9% now married, 4.4% widowed, 5.2% divorced (2006-2010 5-year est.); Foreign born: 6.5% (2006-2010 5-year est.); Ancestry (includes multiple ancestries): 52.1% German, 12.3% Swiss, 11.5% American, 9.6% Russian, 9.4% Irish (2006-2010 5-year est.).

Economy: Employment by occupation: 5.7% management, 0.0% professional, 10.4% services, 11.7% sales, 12.8% farming, 30.8% construction, 9.9% production (2006-2010 5-year est.).

Income: Per capita income: $21,829 (2006-2010 5-year est.); Median household income: $54,135 (2006-2010 5-year est.); Average household income: $62,816 (2006-2010 5-year est.); Percent of households with income of $100,000 or more: 14.6% (2006-2010 5-year est.); Poverty rate: 14.2% (2006-2010 5-year est.).

Education: Percent of population age 25 and over with: High school diploma (including GED) or higher: 76.2% (2006-2010 5-year est.); Bachelor's degree or higher: 7.1% (2006-2010 5-year est.); Master's degree or higher: 0.0% (2006-2010 5-year est.).

Housing: Homeownership rate: 80.8% (2010); Median home value: $203,000 (2006-2010 5-year est.); Median contract rent: $660 per month (2006-2010 5-year est.); Median year structure built: 1941 (2006-2010 5-year est.).

Transportation: Commute to work: 97.4% car, 0.0% public transportation, 0.0% walk, 2.6% work from home (2006-2010 5-year est.); Travel time to work: 33.8% less than 15 minutes, 41.6% 15 to 30 minutes, 12.6% 30 to 45 minutes, 0.0% 45 to 60 minutes, 12.1% 60 minutes or more (2006-2010 5-year est.)

SMOKETOWN (CDP).
Covers a land area of 0.573 square miles and a water area of 0.015 square miles. Located at 40.04° N. Lat; 76.20° W. Long. Elevation is 358 feet.

Population: n/a (1990); n/a (2000); 357 (2010); Density: 623.0 persons per square mile (2010); Race: 95.8% White, 2.5% Black, 0.6% Asian, 0.0% American Indian/Alaska Native, 0.0% Native Hawaiian/Other Pacific Islander, 1.1% Other, 7.8% Hispanic of any race (2010); Average household size: 2.55 (2010); Median age: 43.1 (2010); Males per 100 females: 86.9 (2010); Marriage status: 22.8% never married, 77.2% now married, 0.0% widowed, 0.0% divorced (2006-2010 5-year est.); Foreign born: 7.2% (2006-2010 5-year est.); Ancestry (includes multiple ancestries): 28.9% German, 22.8% Scotch-Irish, 22.0% American, 9.0% Swiss, 7.2% Romanian (2006-2010 5-year est.).

Economy: Employment by occupation: 0.0% management, 0.0% professional, 23.5% services, 11.7% sales, 0.0% farming, 18.4% construction, 10.1% production (2006-2010 5-year est.).

Income: Per capita income: $24,504 (2006-2010 5-year est.); Median household income: $50,859 (2006-2010 5-year est.); Average household income: $56,728 (2006-2010 5-year est.); Percent of households with income of $100,000 or more: 16.6% (2006-2010 5-year est.); Poverty rate: 1.6% (2006-2010 5-year est.).

Education: Percent of population age 25 and over with: High school diploma (including GED) or higher: 83.8% (2006-2010 5-year est.); Bachelor's degree or higher: 23.7% (2006-2010 5-year est.); Master's degree or higher: 15.8% (2006-2010 5-year est.).

Housing: Homeownership rate: 66.4% (2010); Median home value: $165,800 (2006-2010 5-year est.); Median contract rent: n/a per month (2006-2010 5-year est.); Median year structure built: 1970 (2006-2010 5-year est.).

Transportation: Commute to work: 89.2% car, 0.0% public transportation, 0.0% walk, 10.8% work from home (2006-2010 5-year est.); Travel time to work: 0.0% less than 15 minutes, 89.5% 15 to 30 minutes, 10.5% 30 to 45 minutes, 0.0% 45 to 60 minutes, 0.0% 60 minutes or more (2006-2010 5-year est.)

SOUDERSBURG (CDP).
Covers a land area of 1.149 square miles and a water area of 0.014 square miles. Located at 40.02° N. Lat; 76.15° W. Long. Elevation is 377 feet.

Population: n/a (1990); n/a (2000); 540 (2010); Density: 470.2 persons per square mile (2010); Race: 87.0% White, 2.2% Black, 3.7% Asian, 0.2% American Indian/Alaska Native, 0.2% Native Hawaiian/Other Pacific Islander, 6.7% Other, 6.3% Hispanic of any race (2010); Average household size: 2.55 (2010); Median age: 36.4 (2010); Males per 100 females: 100.0 (2010); Marriage status: 10.0% never married, 73.6% now married, 5.7% widowed, 10.8% divorced (2006-2010 5-year est.); Foreign born: 0.0% (2006-2010 5-year est.); Ancestry (includes multiple ancestries): 37.8% German, 19.4% Irish, 19.2% English, 15.0% Swiss, 3.0% Finnish (2006-2010 5-year est.).

Economy: Employment by occupation: 0.0% management, 0.0% professional, 18.0% services, 23.5% sales, 5.2% farming, 21.8% construction, 6.9% production (2006-2010 5-year est.).

Income: Per capita income: $33,856 (2006-2010 5-year est.); Median household income: $65,813 (2006-2010 5-year est.); Average household income: $68,233 (2006-2010 5-year est.); Percent of households with income of $100,000 or more: 24.9% (2006-2010 5-year est.); Poverty rate: 9.5% (2006-2010 5-year est.).

Education: Percent of population age 25 and over with: High school diploma (including GED) or higher: 93.7% (2006-2010 5-year est.); Bachelor's degree or higher: 25.3% (2006-2010 5-year est.); Master's degree or higher: 17.6% (2006-2010 5-year est.).

Housing: Homeownership rate: 49.5% (2010); Median home value: $229,500 (2006-2010 5-year est.); Median contract rent: $533 per month (2006-2010 5-year est.); Median year structure built: 1955 (2006-2010 5-year est.).

Transportation: Commute to work: 77.5% car, 5.2% public transportation, 4.8% walk, 5.5% work from home (2006-2010 5-year est.); Travel time to work: 45.4% less than 15 minutes, 19.8% 15 to 30 minutes, 18.7% 30 to 45 minutes, 11.4% 45 to 60 minutes, 4.8% 60 minutes or more (2006-2010 5-year est.)

STEVENS (CDP).
Covers a land area of 1.557 square miles and a water area of <.001 square miles. Located at 40.22° N. Lat; 76.17° W. Long. Elevation is 381 feet.

Population: n/a (1990); n/a (2000); 612 (2010); Density: 393.0 persons per square mile (2010); Race: 96.7% White, 0.0% Black, 2.5% Asian, 0.2% American Indian/Alaska Native, 0.0% Native Hawaiian/Other Pacific Islander, 0.6% Other, 1.6% Hispanic of any race (2010); Average household size: 2.81 (2010); Median age: 36.7 (2010); Males per 100 females: 95.5 (2010); Marriage status: 21.3% never married, 65.2% now married, 1.4% widowed, 12.1% divorced (2006-2010 5-year est.); Foreign born: 2.5% (2006-2010 5-year est.); Ancestry (includes multiple ancestries): 35.7% American, 28.4% German, 15.6% English, 12.4% Polish, 6.3% Dutch (2006-2010 5-year est.).

Economy: Employment by occupation: 3.9% management, 5.3% professional, 24.7% services, 16.1% sales, 2.2% farming, 22.4% construction, 8.3% production (2006-2010 5-year est.).

Income: Per capita income: $15,670 (2006-2010 5-year est.); Median household income: $26,790 (2006-2010 5-year est.); Average household income: $48,710 (2006-2010 5-year est.); Percent of households with income of $100,000 or more: 12.4% (2006-2010 5-year est.); Poverty rate: 9.8% (2006-2010 5-year est.).

Education: Percent of population age 25 and over with: High school diploma (including GED) or higher: 65.6% (2006-2010 5-year est.); Bachelor's degree or higher: 4.2% (2006-2010 5-year est.); Master's degree or higher: 0.0% (2006-2010 5-year est.).

School District(s)
Cocalico SD (PK-12)
    2010-11 Enrollment: 3,295 . . . . (717) 336-1413

Housing: Homeownership rate: 77.5% (2010); Median home value: $116,800 (2006-2010 5-year est.); Median contract rent: $399 per month (2006-2010 5-year est.); Median year structure built: 1984 (2006-2010 5-year est.).

Transportation: Commute to work: 71.2% car, 3.3% public transportation, 2.8% walk, 18.3% work from home (2006-2010 5-year est.); Travel time to work: 50.5% less than 15 minutes, 19.3% 15 to 30 minutes, 4.4% 30 to 45 minutes, 17.3% 45 to 60 minutes, 8.5% 60 minutes or more (2006-2010 5-year est.)

STRASBURG (borough). Covers a land area of 0.958 square miles and a water area of 0.003 square miles. Located at 39.98° N. Lat; 76.19° W. Long. Elevation is 469 feet.
Population: 2,578 (1990); 2,800 (2000); 2,809 (2010); Density: 2,933.1 persons per square mile (2010); Race: 96.0% White, 0.7% Black, 0.7% Asian, 0.0% American Indian/Alaska Native, 0.1% Native Hawaiian/Other Pacific Islander, 2.5% Other, 2.6% Hispanic of any race (2010); Average household size: 2.50 (2010); Median age: 40.3 (2010); Males per 100 females: 93.3 (2010); Marriage status: 23.0% never married, 62.4% now married, 4.9% widowed, 9.7% divorced (2006-2010 5-year est.); Foreign born: 3.5% (2006-2010 5-year est.); Ancestry (includes multiple ancestries): 38.6% German, 17.5% Irish, 9.9% English, 8.7% Italian, 7.3% Scotch-Irish (2006-2010 5-year est.).
Economy: Single-family building permits issued: 4 (2011); Multi-family building permits issued: 0 (2011); Employment by occupation: 10.8% management, 2.5% professional, 7.8% services, 25.0% sales, 3.5% farming, 13.1% construction, 4.6% production (2006-2010 5-year est.).
Income: Per capita income: $25,475 (2006-2010 5-year est.); Median household income: $62,031 (2006-2010 5-year est.); Average household income: $67,193 (2006-2010 5-year est.); Percent of households with income of $100,000 or more: 19.6% (2006-2010 5-year est.); Poverty rate: 5.8% (2006-2010 5-year est.).
Taxes: Total city taxes per capita: $287 (2009); City property taxes per capita: $126 (2009).
Education: Percent of population age 25 and over with: High school diploma (including GED) or higher: 90.8% (2006-2010 5-year est.); Bachelor's degree or higher: 25.3% (2006-2010 5-year est.); Master's degree or higher: 6.1% (2006-2010 5-year est.).

School District(s)
Lampeter-Strasburg SD (KG-12)
    2010-11 Enrollment: 3,168 . . . . (717) 464-3311
Housing: Homeownership rate: 71.2% (2010); Median home value: $210,400 (2006-2010 5-year est.); Median contract rent: $611 per month (2006-2010 5-year est.); Median year structure built: 1965 (2006-2010 5-year est.).
Safety: Violent crime rate: 3.5 per 10,000 population; Property crime rate: 92.3 per 10,000 population (2011).
Newspapers: Strasburg Weekly News (Community news; Circulation 825)
Transportation: Commute to work: 94.3% car, 0.0% public transportation, 0.4% walk, 3.6% work from home (2006-2010 5-year est.); Travel time to work: 34.7% less than 15 minutes, 40.8% 15 to 30 minutes, 13.0% 30 to 45 minutes, 8.4% 45 to 60 minutes, 3.1% 60 minutes or more (2006-2010 5-year est.)
Additional Information Contacts
Southern Lancaster County Chamber of Commerce . . . . . (717) 786-1911
  http://www.southernlancasterchamber.com

STRASBURG (township). Covers a land area of 19.979 square miles and a water area of 0.160 square miles. Located at 39.96° N. Lat; 76.19° W. Long. Elevation is 469 feet.
History: Railroad Museum. Covered bridges to West, on Pequea Creek. Settled c.1733, incorporated 1816.
Population: 3,678 (1990); 4,021 (2000); 4,182 (2010); Density: 209.3 persons per square mile (2010); Race: 98.0% White, 0.2% Black, 0.6% Asian, 0.0% American Indian/Alaska Native, 0.0% Native Hawaiian/Other Pacific Islander, 1.2% Other, 1.5% Hispanic of any race (2010); Average household size: 3.21 (2010); Median age: 34.1 (2010); Males per 100 females: 103.2 (2010); Marriage status: 26.6% never married, 64.7% now married, 3.8% widowed, 4.8% divorced (2006-2010 5-year est.); Foreign born: 3.2% (2006-2010 5-year est.); Ancestry (includes multiple ancestries): 48.4% German, 9.8% American, 7.1% English, 5.0% Italian, 4.9% Irish (2006-2010 5-year est.).
Economy: Single-family building permits issued: 3 (2011); Multi-family building permits issued: 0 (2011); Employment by occupation: 16.6% management, 1.8% professional, 9.3% services, 11.5% sales, 3.3% farming, 19.6% construction, 5.0% production (2006-2010 5-year est.).
Income: Per capita income: $23,048 (2006-2010 5-year est.); Median household income: $62,885 (2006-2010 5-year est.); Average household income: $77,105 (2006-2010 5-year est.); Percent of households with income of $100,000 or more: 25.6% (2006-2010 5-year est.); Poverty rate: 8.9% (2006-2010 5-year est.).
Education: Percent of population age 25 and over with: High school diploma (including GED) or higher: 79.7% (2006-2010 5-year est.); Bachelor's degree or higher: 19.9% (2006-2010 5-year est.); Master's degree or higher: 4.8% (2006-2010 5-year est.).

Housing: Homeownership rate: 81.3% (2010); Median home value: $240,100 (2006-2010 5-year est.); Median contract rent: $727 per month (2006-2010 5-year est.); Median year structure built: 1967 (2006-2010 5-year est.).
Newspapers: Strasburg Weekly News (Community news; Circulation 825)
Transportation: Commute to work: 78.9% car, 0.6% public transportation, 7.6% walk, 10.3% work from home (2006-2010 5-year est.); Travel time to work: 30.3% less than 15 minutes, 38.8% 15 to 30 minutes, 23.5% 30 to 45 minutes, 3.6% 45 to 60 minutes, 3.9% 60 minutes or more (2006-2010 5-year est.)
Additional Information Contacts
Southern Lancaster County Chamber of Commerce . . . . . (717) 786-1911
  http://www.southernlancasterchamber.com

SWARTZVILLE (CDP). Covers a land area of 1.458 square miles and a water area of 0.007 square miles. Located at 40.23° N. Lat; 76.08° W. Long. Elevation is 561 feet.
Population: n/a (1990); n/a (2000); 2,283 (2010); Density: 1,566.3 persons per square mile (2010); Race: 92.5% White, 1.5% Black, 4.4% Asian, 0.0% American Indian/Alaska Native, 0.1% Native Hawaiian/Other Pacific Islander, 1.5% Other, 1.8% Hispanic of any race (2010); Average household size: 2.61 (2010); Median age: 40.8 (2010); Males per 100 females: 99.2 (2010); Marriage status: 25.6% never married, 63.7% now married, 3.2% widowed, 7.5% divorced (2006-2010 5-year est.); Foreign born: 4.5% (2006-2010 5-year est.); Ancestry (includes multiple ancestries): 49.1% German, 11.1% English, 9.2% Italian, 7.2% American, 6.4% European (2006-2010 5-year est.).
Economy: Employment by occupation: 14.0% management, 2.0% professional, 8.9% services, 7.3% sales, 7.6% farming, 11.2% construction, 10.0% production (2006-2010 5-year est.).
Income: Per capita income: $28,248 (2006-2010 5-year est.); Median household income: $67,986 (2006-2010 5-year est.); Average household income: $79,925 (2006-2010 5-year est.); Percent of households with income of $100,000 or more: 29.1% (2006-2010 5-year est.); Poverty rate: 1.2% (2006-2010 5-year est.).
Education: Percent of population age 25 and over with: High school diploma (including GED) or higher: 84.9% (2006-2010 5-year est.); Bachelor's degree or higher: 26.2% (2006-2010 5-year est.); Master's degree or higher: 10.5% (2006-2010 5-year est.).
Housing: Homeownership rate: 85.7% (2010); Median home value: $175,900 (2006-2010 5-year est.); Median contract rent: $688 per month (2006-2010 5-year est.); Median year structure built: 1992 (2006-2010 5-year est.).
Transportation: Commute to work: 97.7% car, 1.0% public transportation, 0.0% walk, 1.3% work from home (2006-2010 5-year est.); Travel time to work: 23.5% less than 15 minutes, 41.0% 15 to 30 minutes, 15.7% 30 to 45 minutes, 9.6% 45 to 60 minutes, 10.3% 60 minutes or more (2006-2010 5-year est.)

TERRE HILL (borough). Covers a land area of 0.454 square miles and a water area of <.001 square miles. Located at 40.16° N. Lat; 76.05° W. Long. Elevation is 541 feet.
Population: 1,282 (1990); 1,237 (2000); 1,295 (2010); Density: 2,850.1 persons per square mile (2010); Race: 96.6% White, 0.7% Black, 1.4% Asian, 0.2% American Indian/Alaska Native, 0.0% Native Hawaiian/Other Pacific Islander, 1.1% Other, 2.1% Hispanic of any race (2010); Average household size: 2.67 (2010); Median age: 38.2 (2010); Males per 100 females: 105.2 (2010); Marriage status: 18.4% never married, 72.5% now married, 7.1% widowed, 2.1% divorced (2006-2010 5-year est.); Foreign born: 1.6% (2006-2010 5-year est.); Ancestry (includes multiple ancestries): 58.9% German, 13.8% Swiss, 12.1% Irish, 4.0% English, 2.5% Italian (2006-2010 5-year est.).
Economy: Single-family building permits issued: 5 (2011); Multi-family building permits issued: 0 (2011); Employment by occupation: 6.5% management, 4.0% professional, 4.3% services, 21.2% sales, 4.3% farming, 20.1% construction, 15.0% production (2006-2010 5-year est.).
Income: Per capita income: $23,453 (2006-2010 5-year est.); Median household income: $45,000 (2006-2010 5-year est.); Average household income: $55,266 (2006-2010 5-year est.); Percent of households with income of $100,000 or more: 16.5% (2006-2010 5-year est.); Poverty rate: 8.9% (2006-2010 5-year est.).
Education: Percent of population age 25 and over with: High school diploma (including GED) or higher: 76.7% (2006-2010 5-year est.); Bachelor's degree or higher: 8.7% (2006-2010 5-year est.); Master's degree or higher: 0.9% (2006-2010 5-year est.).

Housing: Homeownership rate: 71.4% (2010); Median home value: $180,200 (2006-2010 5-year est.); Median contract rent: $604 per month (2006-2010 5-year est.); Median year structure built: 1954 (2006-2010 5-year est.).

Transportation: Commute to work: 88.1% car, 0.0% public transportation, 2.6% walk, 8.8% work from home (2006-2010 5-year est.); Travel time to work: 55.2% less than 15 minutes, 18.5% 15 to 30 minutes, 9.4% 30 to 45 minutes, 12.0% 45 to 60 minutes, 4.8% 60 minutes or more (2006-2010 5-year est.).

Additional Information Contacts
Ephrata Area Chamber of Commerce . . . . (717) 738-9010
  http://www.ephrata-area.org

UPPER LEACOCK (township). Covers a land area of 18.119 square miles and a water area of 0.123 square miles. Located at 40.08° N. Lat; 76.18° W. Long.

Population: 7,254 (1990); 8,229 (2000); 8,708 (2010); Density: 480.6 persons per square mile (2010); Race: 91.6% White, 1.5% Black, 3.8% Asian, 0.1% American Indian/Alaska Native, 0.0% Native Hawaiian/Other Pacific Islander, 3.0% Other, 6.2% Hispanic of any race (2010); Average household size: 2.97 (2010); Median age: 33.5 (2010); Males per 100 females: 96.8 (2010); Marriage status: 28.6% never married, 60.8% now married, 3.9% widowed, 6.8% divorced (2006-2010 5-year est.); Foreign born: 6.1% (2006-2010 5-year est.); Ancestry (includes multiple ancestries): 36.2% German, 9.5% American, 8.4% Irish, 6.3% Pennsylvania German, 5.4% English (2006-2010 5-year est.).

Economy: Single-family building permits issued: 8 (2011); Multi-family building permits issued: 4 (2011); Employment by occupation: 14.7% management, 1.8% professional, 9.4% services, 14.0% sales, 4.3% farming, 13.8% construction, 11.5% production (2006-2010 5-year est.).

Income: Per capita income: $23,176 (2006-2010 5-year est.); Median household income: $57,857 (2006-2010 5-year est.); Average household income: $70,907 (2006-2010 5-year est.); Percent of households with income of $100,000 or more: 22.7% (2006-2010 5-year est.); Poverty rate: 7.9% (2006-2010 5-year est.).

Education: Percent of population age 25 and over with: High school diploma (including GED) or higher: 70.4% (2006-2010 5-year est.); Bachelor's degree or higher: 17.7% (2006-2010 5-year est.); Master's degree or higher: 6.3% (2006-2010 5-year est.).

Housing: Homeownership rate: 61.5% (2010); Median home value: $197,300 (2006-2010 5-year est.); Median contract rent: $721 per month (2006-2010 5-year est.); Median year structure built: 1968 (2006-2010 5-year est.).

Safety: Violent crime rate: 4.6 per 10,000 population; Property crime rate: 117.9 per 10,000 population (2011).

Transportation: Commute to work: 81.3% car, 0.0% public transportation, 3.5% walk, 11.0% work from home (2006-2010 5-year est.); Travel time to work: 35.9% less than 15 minutes, 42.5% 15 to 30 minutes, 12.5% 30 to 45 minutes, 3.4% 45 to 60 minutes, 5.7% 60 minutes or more (2006-2010 5-year est.)

Additional Information Contacts
Lancaster Chamber of Commerce & Industry . . . . (717) 397-3531
  http://www.lancasterchamber.com
Upper Leacock Township . . . . (717) 656-9755
  http://www.ultwp.com

WAKEFIELD (CDP). Covers a land area of 1.704 square miles and a water area of 0.008 square miles. Located at 39.78° N. Lat; 76.18° W. Long. Elevation is 390 feet.

Population: n/a (1990); n/a (2000); 609 (2010); Density: 357.3 persons per square mile (2010); Race: 95.9% White, 1.3% Black, 0.2% Asian, 0.2% American Indian/Alaska Native, 0.0% Native Hawaiian/Other Pacific Islander, 2.4% Other, 4.6% Hispanic of any race (2010); Average household size: 2.82 (2010); Median age: 37.4 (2010); Males per 100 females: 103.0 (2010); Marriage status: 31.5% never married, 56.6% now married, 4.7% widowed, 7.2% divorced (2006-2010 5-year est.); Foreign born: 0.0% (2006-2010 5-year est.); Ancestry (includes multiple ancestries): 26.8% German, 23.6% Irish, 22.5% American, 22.2% English, 2.6% Scotch-Irish (2006-2010 5-year est.).

Economy: Employment by occupation: 19.8% management, 7.3% professional, 10.5% services, 17.4% sales, 7.3% farming, 23.5% construction, 21.9% production (2006-2010 5-year est.).

Income: Per capita income: $21,196 (2006-2010 5-year est.); Median household income: $65,104 (2006-2010 5-year est.); Average household income: $62,727 (2006-2010 5-year est.); Percent of households with

income of $100,000 or more: 12.1% (2006-2010 5-year est.); Poverty rate: 4.5% (2006-2010 5-year est.).

Education: Percent of population age 25 and over with: High school diploma (including GED) or higher: 68.1% (2006-2010 5-year est.); Bachelor's degree or higher: 11.0% (2006-2010 5-year est.); Master's degree or higher: 1.8% (2006-2010 5-year est.).

Housing: Homeownership rate: 76.4% (2010); Median home value: $198,300 (2006-2010 5-year est.); Median contract rent: $647 per month (2006-2010 5-year est.); Median year structure built: 1981 (2006-2010 5-year est.).

Transportation: Commute to work: 70.5% car, 5.6% public transportation, 0.0% walk, 20.5% work from home (2006-2010 5-year est.); Travel time to work: 12.9% less than 15 minutes, 25.8% 15 to 30 minutes, 36.0% 30 to 45 minutes, 17.7% 45 to 60 minutes, 7.5% 60 minutes or more (2006-2010 5-year est.)

WARWICK (township). Covers a land area of 19.777 square miles and a water area of 0.150 square miles. Located at 40.16° N. Lat; 76.28° W. Long. Elevation is 397 feet.

Population: 11,509 (1990); 15,475 (2000); 17,783 (2010); Density: 899.2 persons per square mile (2010); Race: 95.7% White, 1.2% Black, 1.0% Asian, 0.2% American Indian/Alaska Native, 0.0% Native Hawaiian/Other Pacific Islander, 1.9% Other, 2.9% Hispanic of any race (2010); Average household size: 2.64 (2010); Median age: 40.3 (2010); Males per 100 females: 95.9 (2010); Marriage status: 20.5% never married, 66.8% now married, 4.1% widowed, 8.6% divorced (2006-2010 5-year est.); Foreign born: 2.9% (2006-2010 5-year est.); Ancestry (includes multiple ancestries): 44.8% German, 12.4% Irish, 9.2% American, 7.5% Italian, 6.8% English (2006-2010 5-year est.).

Economy: Single-family building permits issued: 3 (2011); Multi-family building permits issued: 0 (2011); Employment by occupation: 12.5% management, 5.4% professional, 8.0% services, 17.3% sales, 4.7% farming, 8.7% construction, 7.4% production (2006-2010 5-year est.).

Income: Per capita income: $30,551 (2006-2010 5-year est.); Median household income: $69,378 (2006-2010 5-year est.); Average household income: $81,791 (2006-2010 5-year est.); Percent of households with income of $100,000 or more: 27.4% (2006-2010 5-year est.); Poverty rate: 2.5% (2006-2010 5-year est.).

Education: Percent of population age 25 and over with: High school diploma (including GED) or higher: 90.5% (2006-2010 5-year est.); Bachelor's degree or higher: 28.5% (2006-2010 5-year est.); Master's degree or higher: 9.4% (2006-2010 5-year est.).

Housing: Homeownership rate: 76.7% (2010); Median home value: $198,000 (2006-2010 5-year est.); Median contract rent: $887 per month (2006-2010 5-year est.); Median year structure built: 1987 (2006-2010 5-year est.).

Transportation: Commute to work: 94.5% car, 0.3% public transportation, 1.3% walk, 3.8% work from home (2006-2010 5-year est.); Travel time to work: 32.4% less than 15 minutes, 40.7% 15 to 30 minutes, 16.1% 30 to 45 minutes, 5.0% 45 to 60 minutes, 5.9% 60 minutes or more (2006-2010 5-year est.)

Additional Information Contacts
Lancaster Chamber of Commerce & Industry . . . . (717) 397-3531
  http://www.lancasterchamber.com
Warwick Township . . . . (717) 626-8900
  http://www.warwicktownship.org

WASHINGTON BORO (CDP). Covers a land area of 1.927 square miles and a water area of 0.002 square miles. Located at 40.01° N. Lat; 76.47° W. Long. Elevation is 285 feet.

Population: n/a (1990); n/a (2000); 729 (2010); Density: 378.3 persons per square mile (2010); Race: 98.5% White, 0.3% Black, 0.4% Asian, 0.0% American Indian/Alaska Native, 0.0% Native Hawaiian/Other Pacific Islander, 0.8% Other, 1.4% Hispanic of any race (2010); Average household size: 2.59 (2010); Median age: 43.3 (2010); Males per 100 females: 100.3 (2010); Marriage status: 30.8% never married, 54.7% now married, 5.9% widowed, 8.6% divorced (2006-2010 5-year est.); Foreign born: 2.5% (2006-2010 5-year est.); Ancestry (includes multiple ancestries): 56.1% German, 17.2% Irish, 13.7% English, 9.8% American, 8.4% Swiss (2006-2010 5-year est.).

Economy: Employment by occupation: 4.1% management, 0.0% professional, 5.6% services, 23.1% sales, 5.2% farming, 29.5% construction, 10.7% production (2006-2010 5-year est.).

Income: Per capita income: $27,161 (2006-2010 5-year est.); Median household income: $61,023 (2006-2010 5-year est.); Average household

income: $72,519 (2006-2010 5-year est.); Percent of households with income of $100,000 or more: 16.9% (2006-2010 5-year est.); Poverty rate: 6.4% (2006-2010 5-year est.).

Education: Percent of population age 25 and over with: High school diploma (including GED) or higher: 84.7% (2006-2010 5-year est.); Bachelor's degree or higher: 17.3% (2006-2010 5-year est.); Master's degree or higher: 3.7% (2006-2010 5-year est.).

School District(s)

Penn Manor SD (KG-12)

    2010-11 Enrollment: 5,169 . . . . (717) 872-9500

Housing: Homeownership rate: 89.0% (2010); Median home value: $161,500 (2006-2010 5-year est.); Median contract rent: $675 per month (2006-2010 5-year est.); Median year structure built: before 1940 (2006-2010 5-year est.).

Transportation: Commute to work: 94.6% car, 0.0% public transportation, 0.0% walk, 2.5% work from home (2006-2010 5-year est.); Travel time to work: 22.8% less than 15 minutes, 53.7% 15 to 30 minutes, 23.5% 30 to 45 minutes, 0.0% 45 to 60 minutes, 0.0% 60 minutes or more (2006-2010 5-year est.)

WEST COCALICO (township). Covers a land area of 27.316 square miles and a water area of 0.292 square miles. Located at 40.26° N. Lat; 76.16° W. Long.

Population: 5,529 (1990); 6,967 (2000); 7,280 (2010); Density: 266.5 persons per square mile (2010); Race: 97.5% White, 0.5% Black, 0.5% Asian, 0.1% American Indian/Alaska Native, 0.0% Native Hawaiian/Other Pacific Islander, 1.4% Other, 1.4% Hispanic of any race (2010); Average household size: 2.96 (2010); Median age: 36.7 (2010); Males per 100 females: 99.3 (2010); Marriage status: 25.6% never married, 64.1% now married, 4.4% widowed, 5.9% divorced (2006-2010 5-year est.); Foreign born: 2.8% (2006-2010 5-year est.); Ancestry (includes multiple ancestries): 42.3% German, 15.0% American, 7.3% Irish, 5.1% English, 5.0% Swiss (2006-2010 5-year est.).

Economy: Single-family building permits issued: 3 (2011); Multi-family building permits issued: 0 (2011); Employment by occupation: 9.0% management, 3.0% professional, 8.7% services, 16.5% sales, 3.7% farming, 23.9% construction, 10.8% production (2006-2010 5-year est.).

Income: Per capita income: $22,107 (2006-2010 5-year est.); Median household income: $57,951 (2006-2010 5-year est.); Average household income: $64,728 (2006-2010 5-year est.); Percent of households with income of $100,000 or more: 15.5% (2006-2010 5-year est.); Poverty rate: 4.7% (2006-2010 5-year est.).

Education: Percent of population age 25 and over with: High school diploma (including GED) or higher: 70.7% (2006-2010 5-year est.); Bachelor's degree or higher: 6.7% (2006-2010 5-year est.); Master's degree or higher: 1.9% (2006-2010 5-year est.).

Housing: Homeownership rate: 86.2% (2010); Median home value: $192,800 (2006-2010 5-year est.); Median contract rent: $589 per month (2006-2010 5-year est.); Median year structure built: 1977 (2006-2010 5-year est.).

Safety: Violent crime rate: 5.5 per 10,000 population; Property crime rate: 91.7 per 10,000 population (2011).

Transportation: Commute to work: 94.3% car, 0.4% public transportation, 1.6% walk, 3.0% work from home (2006-2010 5-year est.); Travel time to work: 32.2% less than 15 minutes, 42.6% 15 to 30 minutes, 17.3% 30 to 45 minutes, 3.6% 45 to 60 minutes, 4.2% 60 minutes or more (2006-2010 5-year est.)

Additional Information Contacts

Ephrata Area Chamber of Commerce. . . . . (717) 738-9010
    http://www.ephrata-area.org
West Cocalico Township. . . . . (717) 336-8720
    http://www.co.lancaster.pa.us/west_cocalico/site/default.asp

---

WEST DONEGAL (township). Covers a land area of 15.788 square miles and a water area of 0.074 square miles. Located at 40.13° N. Lat; 76.62° W. Long.

Population: 5,536 (1990); 6,539 (2000); 8,260 (2010); Density: 523.2 persons per square mile (2010); Race: 97.5% White, 0.7% Black, 0.7% Asian, 0.0% American Indian/Alaska Native, 0.0% Native Hawaiian/Other Pacific Islander, 1.1% Other, 1.5% Hispanic of any race (2010); Average household size: 2.44 (2010); Median age: 47.5 (2010); Males per 100 females: 90.5 (2010); Marriage status: 13.4% never married, 75.1% now married, 8.9% widowed, 2.6% divorced (2006-2010 5-year est.); Foreign born: 2.1% (2006-2010 5-year est.); Ancestry (includes multiple

ancestries): 41.3% German, 11.5% English, 9.3% American, 9.2% Irish, 8.1% Italian (2006-2010 5-year est.).

Economy: Single-family building permits issued: 7 (2011); Multi-family building permits issued: 40 (2011); Employment by occupation: 13.3% management, 3.9% professional, 8.2% services, 14.7% sales, 3.9% farming, 12.1% construction, 13.8% production (2006-2010 5-year est.).

Income: Per capita income: $28,520 (2006-2010 5-year est.); Median household income: $65,115 (2006-2010 5-year est.); Average household income: $72,627 (2006-2010 5-year est.); Percent of households with income of $100,000 or more: 23.3% (2006-2010 5-year est.); Poverty rate: 5.9% (2006-2010 5-year est.).

Education: Percent of population age 25 and over with: High school diploma (including GED) or higher: 92.5% (2006-2010 5-year est.); Bachelor's degree or higher: 27.3% (2006-2010 5-year est.); Master's degree or higher: 11.0% (2006-2010 5-year est.).

Housing: Homeownership rate: 68.8% (2010); Median home value: $178,900 (2006-2010 5-year est.); Median contract rent: $1,619 per month (2006-2010 5-year est.); Median year structure built: 1984 (2006-2010 5-year est.).

Transportation: Commute to work: 93.9% car, 1.4% public transportation, 2.5% walk, 1.8% work from home (2006-2010 5-year est.); Travel time to work: 36.8% less than 15 minutes, 33.4% 15 to 30 minutes, 18.8% 30 to 45 minutes, 9.7% 45 to 60 minutes, 1.4% 60 minutes or more (2006-2010 5-year est.)

Additional Information Contacts

Elizabethtown Area Chamber of Commerce. . . . . (717) 361-7188
    http://www.elizabethtowncoc.com
West Donegal Township . . . . (717) 367-7178
    http://www.co.lancaster.pa.us/westdonegaltwp/site/default.asp

---

WEST EARL (township). Covers a land area of 17.749 square miles and a water area of 0.192 square miles. Located at 40.13° N. Lat; 76.17° W. Long.

Population: 6,434 (1990); 6,766 (2000); 7,868 (2010); Density: 443.3 persons per square mile (2010); Race: 95.2% White, 0.8% Black, 2.2% Asian, 0.1% American Indian/Alaska Native, 0.0% Native Hawaiian/Other Pacific Islander, 1.7% Other, 2.9% Hispanic of any race (2010); Average household size: 2.94 (2010); Median age: 37.1 (2010); Males per 100 females: 94.9 (2010); Marriage status: 24.0% never married, 65.9% now married, 7.0% widowed, 3.2% divorced (2006-2010 5-year est.); Foreign born: 3.1% (2006-2010 5-year est.); Ancestry (includes multiple ancestries): 41.9% German, 10.9% Irish, 8.9% American, 8.2% Pennsylvania German, 7.0% Swiss (2006-2010 5-year est.).

Economy: Single-family building permits issued: 7 (2011); Multi-family building permits issued: 0 (2011); Employment by occupation: 12.5% management, 3.0% professional, 6.9% services, 15.7% sales, 2.9% farming, 15.5% construction, 10.2% production (2006-2010 5-year est.).

Income: Per capita income: $23,050 (2006-2010 5-year est.); Median household income: $56,542 (2006-2010 5-year est.); Average household income: $70,486 (2006-2010 5-year est.); Percent of households with income of $100,000 or more: 20.6% (2006-2010 5-year est.); Poverty rate: 8.0% (2006-2010 5-year est.).

Education: Percent of population age 25 and over with: High school diploma (including GED) or higher: 69.4% (2006-2010 5-year est.); Bachelor's degree or higher: 16.0% (2006-2010 5-year est.); Master's degree or higher: 5.7% (2006-2010 5-year est.).

Housing: Homeownership rate: 79.5% (2010); Median home value: $177,000 (2006-2010 5-year est.); Median contract rent: $602 per month (2006-2010 5-year est.); Median year structure built: 1979 (2006-2010 5-year est.).

Safety: Violent crime rate: 13.9 per 10,000 population; Property crime rate: 70.9 per 10,000 population (2011).

Transportation: Commute to work: 86.4% car, 0.0% public transportation, 1.8% walk, 8.0% work from home (2006-2010 5-year est.); Travel time to work: 33.1% less than 15 minutes, 49.0% 15 to 30 minutes, 11.8% 30 to 45 minutes, 2.0% 45 to 60 minutes, 4.1% 60 minutes or more (2006-2010 5-year est.)

Additional Information Contacts

Ephrata Area Chamber of Commerce. . . . . (717) 738-9010
    http://www.ephrata-area.org
West Earl Township . . . . (717) 859-3201
    http://www.co.lancaster.pa.us/west_earl

WEST HEMPFIELD (township). Covers a land area of 18.454 square miles and a water area of 2.574 square miles. Located at 40.06° N. Lat; 76.47° W. Long.

Population: 12,984 (1990); 15,128 (2000); 16,153 (2010); Density: 875.3 persons per square mile (2010); Race: 91.1% White, 2.8% Black, 2.1% Asian, 0.2% American Indian/Alaska Native, 0.0% Native Hawaiian/Other Pacific Islander, 3.8% Other, 6.8% Hispanic of any race (2010); Average household size: 2.67 (2010); Median age: 40.2 (2010); Males per 100 females: 95.5 (2010); Marriage status: 24.7% never married, 62.6% now married, 5.2% widowed, 7.5% divorced (2006-2010 5-year est.); Foreign born: 3.0% (2006-2010 5-year est.); Ancestry (includes multiple ancestries): 43.5% German, 14.3% Irish, 9.4% English, 6.4% American, 6.0% Italian (2006-2010 5-year est.).

Economy: Single-family building permits issued: 18 (2011); Multi-family building permits issued: 0 (2011); Employment by occupation: 10.6% management, 4.0% professional, 8.3% services, 18.8% sales, 4.2% farming, 7.7% construction, 7.6% production (2006-2010 5-year est.).

Income: Per capita income: $29,007 (2006-2010 5-year est.); Median household income: $67,666 (2006-2010 5-year est.); Average household income: $75,388 (2006-2010 5-year est.); Percent of households with income of $100,000 or more: 25.8% (2006-2010 5-year est.); Poverty rate: 4.8% (2006-2010 5-year est.).

Education: Percent of population age 25 and over with: High school diploma (including GED) or higher: 90.6% (2006-2010 5-year est.); Bachelor's degree or higher: 26.4% (2006-2010 5-year est.); Master's degree or higher: 6.1% (2006-2010 5-year est.).

Housing: Homeownership rate: 82.2% (2010); Median home value: $187,800 (2006-2010 5-year est.); Median contract rent: $601 per month (2006-2010 5-year est.); Median year structure built: 1981 (2006-2010 5-year est.).

Safety: Violent crime rate: 9.9 per 10,000 population; Property crime rate: 170.3 per 10,000 population (2011).

Transportation: Commute to work: 93.0% car, 0.3% public transportation, 2.5% walk, 3.6% work from home (2006-2010 5-year est.); Travel time to work: 33.5% less than 15 minutes, 48.4% 15 to 30 minutes, 11.5% 30 to 45 minutes, 4.1% 45 to 60 minutes, 2.4% 60 minutes or more (2006-2010 5-year est.)

Additional Information Contacts
Susquehanna Valley Chamber of Commerce . . . . (717) 684-5249
    http://www.parivertowns.com
West Hempfield Township . . . . (717) 285-5554
    http://www.twp.west-hempfield.pa.us

WEST LAMPETER (township). Covers a land area of 16.395 square miles and a water area of 0.222 square miles. Located at 39.99° N. Lat; 76.26° W. Long. Elevation is 295 feet.

Population: 9,815 (1990); 13,145 (2000); 15,209 (2010); Density: 927.6 persons per square mile (2010); Race: 95.4% White, 0.9% Black, 1.4% Asian, 0.1% American Indian/Alaska Native, 0.0% Native Hawaiian/Other Pacific Islander, 2.2% Other, 3.1% Hispanic of any race (2010); Average household size: 2.37 (2010); Median age: 48.3 (2010); Males per 100 females: 88.9 (2010); Marriage status: 18.4% never married, 67.1% now married, 9.0% widowed, 5.5% divorced (2006-2010 5-year est.); Foreign born: 1.8% (2006-2010 5-year est.); Ancestry (includes multiple ancestries): 43.2% German, 14.2% Irish, 12.9% English, 9.6% Italian, 9.5% American (2006-2010 5-year est.).

Economy: Single-family building permits issued: 25 (2011); Multi-family building permits issued: 18 (2011); Employment by occupation: 15.4% management, 2.1% professional, 7.4% services, 15.6% sales, 4.1% farming, 8.8% construction, 4.5% production (2006-2010 5-year est.).

Income: Per capita income: $32,516 (2006-2010 5-year est.); Median household income: $64,315 (2006-2010 5-year est.); Average household income: $78,105 (2006-2010 5-year est.); Percent of households with income of $100,000 or more: 26.5% (2006-2010 5-year est.); Poverty rate: 3.3% (2006-2010 5-year est.).

Taxes: Total city taxes per capita: $202 (2009); City property taxes per capita: $43 (2009).

Education: Percent of population age 25 and over with: High school diploma (including GED) or higher: 91.3% (2006-2010 5-year est.); Bachelor's degree or higher: 35.2% (2006-2010 5-year est.); Master's degree or higher: 13.1% (2006-2010 5-year est.).

Housing: Homeownership rate: 66.8% (2010); Median home value: $231,400 (2006-2010 5-year est.); Median contract rent: $1,533 per month (2006-2010 5-year est.); Median year structure built: 1985 (2006-2010 5-year est.).

Safety: Violent crime rate: 5.2 per 10,000 population; Property crime rate: 118.6 per 10,000 population (2011).

Transportation: Commute to work: 94.0% car, 0.4% public transportation, 0.8% walk, 4.1% work from home (2006-2010 5-year est.); Travel time to work: 34.5% less than 15 minutes, 40.0% 15 to 30 minutes, 12.7% 30 to 45 minutes, 5.7% 45 to 60 minutes, 7.2% 60 minutes or more (2006-2010 5-year est.)

Additional Information Contacts
Lancaster Chamber of Commerce & Industry . . . . (717) 397-3531
    http://www.lancasterchamber.com
West Lampeter Township . . . . (717) 464-3731
    http://www.westlampeter.com

WILLOW STREET (CDP). Covers a land area of 5.434 square miles and a water area of 0.019 square miles. Located at 39.98° N. Lat; 76.27° W. Long. Elevation is 482 feet.

History: Covered bridges in area.

Population: 5,800 (1990); 7,258 (2000); 7,578 (2010); Density: 1,394.5 persons per square mile (2010); Race: 96.5% White, 0.9% Black, 0.9% Asian, 0.1% American Indian/Alaska Native, 0.0% Native Hawaiian/Other Pacific Islander, 1.6% Other, 2.5% Hispanic of any race (2010); Average household size: 2.07 (2010); Median age: 58.6 (2010); Males per 100 females: 80.6 (2010); Marriage status: 15.9% never married, 67.2% now married, 12.0% widowed, 4.9% divorced (2006-2010 5-year est.); Foreign born: 2.4% (2006-2010 5-year est.); Ancestry (includes multiple ancestries): 44.4% German, 16.5% Irish, 13.2% English, 6.4% Italian, 6.4% American (2006-2010 5-year est.).

Economy: Employment by occupation: 11.9% management, 0.8% professional, 12.2% services, 18.7% sales, 5.4% farming, 7.6% construction, 3.9% production (2006-2010 5-year est.).

Income: Per capita income: $31,629 (2006-2010 5-year est.); Median household income: $57,630 (2006-2010 5-year est.); Average household income: $67,525 (2006-2010 5-year est.); Percent of households with income of $100,000 or more: 19.6% (2006-2010 5-year est.); Poverty rate: 6.9% (2006-2010 5-year est.).

Education: Percent of population age 25 and over with: High school diploma (including GED) or higher: 93.1% (2006-2010 5-year est.); Bachelor's degree or higher: 30.1% (2006-2010 5-year est.); Master's degree or higher: 11.9% (2006-2010 5-year est.).

School District(s)
Lancaster County CTC (10-12)
    2010-11 Enrollment: n/a . . . . (717) 464-7050
Penn Manor SD (KG-12)
    2010-11 Enrollment: 5,169 . . . . (717) 872-9500
Vocational/Technical School(s)
Lancaster County Career and Technology Center (Public)
    Fall 2010 Enrollment: 453 . . . . (717) 464-7050
    2011-12 Tuition: $10,854

Housing: Homeownership rate: 52.0% (2010); Median home value: $202,800 (2006-2010 5-year est.); Median contract rent: $1,782 per month (2006-2010 5-year est.); Median year structure built: 1984 (2006-2010 5-year est.).

Transportation: Commute to work: 95.2% car, 0.6% public transportation, 0.7% walk, 2.8% work from home (2006-2010 5-year est.); Travel time to work: 31.8% less than 15 minutes, 33.6% 15 to 30 minutes, 18.9% 30 to 45 minutes, 9.4% 45 to 60 minutes, 6.2% 60 minutes or more (2006-2010 5-year est.)

Additional Information Contacts
Southern Lancaster County Chamber of Commerce . . . . . (717) 786-1911
    http://www.southernlancasterchamber.com

WITMER (CDP). Covers a land area of 1.243 square miles and a water area of 0.001 square miles. Located at 40.05° N. Lat; 76.21° W. Long. Elevation is 400 feet.

Population: n/a (1990); n/a (2000); 492 (2010); Density: 395.8 persons per square mile (2010); Race: 94.5% White, 1.0% Black, 2.2% Asian, 0.2% American Indian/Alaska Native, 0.0% Native Hawaiian/Other Pacific Islander, 2.1% Other, 2.2% Hispanic of any race (2010); Average household size: 2.96 (2010); Median age: 34.9 (2010); Males per 100 females: 90.7 (2010); Marriage status: 37.4% never married, 56.8% now married, 0.0% widowed, 5.8% divorced (2006-2010 5-year est.); Foreign born: 0.0% (2006-2010 5-year est.); Ancestry (includes multiple ancestries): 57.5% German, 13.9% Pennsylvania German, 13.0% Swiss, 11.8% American, 5.9% Welsh (2006-2010 5-year est.).

Economy: Employment by occupation: 0.0% management, 0.0% professional, 0.0% services, 16.5% sales, 5.7% farming, 39.7% construction, 11.9% production (2006-2010 5-year est.).

Income: Per capita income: $18,106 (2006-2010 5-year est.); Median household income: $36,023 (2006-2010 5-year est.); Average household income: $53,574 (2006-2010 5-year est.); Percent of households with income of $100,000 or more: 16.1% (2006-2010 5-year est.); Poverty rate: 47.4% (2006-2010 5-year est.).

Education: Percent of population age 25 and over with: High school diploma (including GED) or higher: 71.2% (2006-2010 5-year est.); Bachelor's degree or higher: 9.0% (2006-2010 5-year est.); Master's degree or higher: 9.0% (2006-2010 5-year est.).

Housing: Homeownership rate: 65.4% (2010); Median home value: $222,600 (2006-2010 5-year est.); Median contract rent: $777 per month (2006-2010 5-year est.); Median year structure built: 1960 (2006-2010 5-year est.)

Transportation: Commute to work: 71.6% car, 0.0% public transportation, 0.0% walk, 0.0% work from home (2006-2010 5-year est.); Travel time to work: 67.0% less than 15 minutes, 27.3% 15 to 30 minutes, 5.7% 30 to 45 minutes, 0.0% 45 to 60 minutes, 0.0% 60 minutes or more (2006-2010 5-year est.)

Lawrence County

Located in western Pennsylvania; bounded on the west by Ohio; drained by the Shenango, Mahoning, and Beaver Rivers. Covers a land area of 358.175 square miles, a water area of 4.540 square miles, and is located in the Eastern Time Zone at 40.99° N. Lat., 80.33° W. Long. The county was founded in 1849. County seat is New Castle.

Lawrence County is part of the New Castle, PA Micropolitan Statistical Area. The entire metro area includes: Lawrence County, PA

Weather Station: New Castle 1 N										Elevation: 825 feet	
	Jan	Feb	Mar	Apr	May	Jun	Jul	Aug	Sep	Oct	Nov	Dec
High	36	39	48	62	72	80	84	83	76	65	53	40
Low	19	20	26	35	45	54	59	58	51	40	32	23
Precip	2.5	2.1	3.0	3.3	3.7	4.0	4.7	3.7	3.7	2.9	3.2	2.8
Snow	9.2	5.6	3.9	0.6	0.0	0.0	0.0	0.0	0.0	tr	0.9	5.2

High and Low temperatures in degrees Fahrenheit; Precipitation and Snow in inches

Population: 96,246 (1990); 94,643 (2000); 91,108 (2010); Race: 93.8% White, 3.8% Black, 0.4% Asian, 0.1% American Indian/Alaska Native, 0.0% Native Hawaiian/Other Pacific Islander, 1.9% Other, 1.0% Hispanic of any race (2010); Density: 254.4 persons per square mile (2010); Average household size: 2.39 (2010); Median age: 43.6 (2010); Males per 100 females: 93.0 (2010).

Religion: Six largest groups: 27.6% Catholicism, 9.6% Presbyterian-Reformed, 5.2% Methodist/Pietist, 5.1% Non-Denominational, 2.1% Holiness, 1.8% Pentecostal (2010)

Economy: Unemployment rate: 8.3% (August 2012); Total civilian labor force: 43,403 (August 2012); Leading industries: 22.3% health care and social assistance; 13.6% manufacturing; 13.2% retail trade (2010); Farms: 708 totaling 92,391 acres (2007); Companies that employ 500 or more persons: 2 (2010); Companies that employ 100 to 499 persons: 37 (2010); Companies that employ less than 100 persons: 1,974 (2010); Black-owned businesses: n/a (2007); Hispanic-owned businesses: n/a (2007); Asian-owned businesses: n/a (2007); Women-owned businesses: 1,767 (2007); Retail sales per capita: $10,575 (2010). Single-family building permits issued: 33 (2011); Multi-family building permits issued: 2 (2011).

Income: Per capita income: $21,467 (2006-2010 5-year est.); Median household income: $42,570 (2006-2010 5-year est.); Average household income: $52,739 (2006-2010 5-year est.); Percent of households with income of $100,000 or more: 11.2% (2006-2010 5-year est.); Poverty rate: 12.7% (2006-2010 5-year est.); Bankruptcy rate: 3.44% (2011).

Taxes: Total county taxes per capita: $203 (2009); County property taxes per capita: $201 (2009).

Education: Percent of population age 25 and over with: High school diploma (including GED) or higher: 86.5% (2006-2010 5-year est.); Bachelor's degree or higher: 18.6% (2006-2010 5-year est.); Master's degree or higher: 5.8% (2006-2010 5-year est.).

Housing: Homeownership rate: 75.3% (2010); Median home value: $92,600 (2006-2010 5-year est.); Median contract rent: $441 per month (2006-2010 5-year est.); Median year structure built: 1954 (2006-2010 5-year est.)

Health: Birth rate: 103.8 per 10,000 population (2011); Death rate: 121.8 per 10,000 population (2011); Age-adjusted cancer mortality rate: 211.0 deaths per 100,000 population (2009); Number of physicians: 12.7 per 10,000 population (2010); Hospital beds: 38.8 per 10,000 population (2008); Hospital admissions: 1,555.5 per 10,000 population (2008).

Environment: Air Quality Index: 91.2% good, 8.5% moderate, 0.3% unhealthy for sensitive individuals, 0.0% unhealthy (percent of days in 2011)

Elections: 2012 Presidential election results: 44.9% Obama, 53.9% Romney

National and State Parks: McConnells Mill State Park

Additional Information Contacts

Lawrence County Government . . . . (724) 658-2541
  http://www.co.lawrence.pa.us
Lawrence County Chamber of Commerce . . . . (724) 654-5593
  http://www.lawrencecountychamber.org

Lawrence County Communities

BESSEMER (borough). Aka Walford. Covers a land area of 1.654 square miles and a water area of 0.076 square miles. Located at 40.98° N. Lat; 80.49° W. Long. Elevation is 1,083 feet.

History: Incorporated c.1910.

Population: 1,235 (1990); 1,172 (2000); 1,111 (2010); Density: 671.7 persons per square mile (2010); Race: 98.3% White, 0.1% Black, 0.4% Asian, 0.0% American Indian/Alaska Native, 0.0% Native Hawaiian/Other Pacific Islander, 1.2% Other, 0.6% Hispanic of any race (2010); Average household size: 2.39 (2010); Median age: 43.2 (2010); Males per 100 females: 92.5 (2010); Marriage status: 26.8% never married, 55.0% now married, 7.2% widowed, 11.1% divorced (2006-2010 5-year est.); Foreign born: 1.4% (2006-2010 5-year est.); Ancestry (includes multiple ancestries): 24.0% German, 22.5% Italian, 17.8% Irish, 9.1% English, 8.3% Polish (2006-2010 5-year est.).

Economy: Single-family building permits issued: 0 (2011); Multi-family building permits issued: 0 (2011); Employment by occupation: 2.1% management, 0.6% professional, 12.1% services, 19.5% sales, 6.2% farming, 9.8% construction, 9.5% production (2006-2010 5-year est.).

Income: Per capita income: $18,431 (2006-2010 5-year est.); Median household income: $32,400 (2006-2010 5-year est.); Average household income: $42,970 (2006-2010 5-year est.); Percent of households with income of $100,000 or more: 3.6% (2006-2010 5-year est.); Poverty rate: 10.9% (2006-2010 5-year est.).

Education: Percent of population age 25 and over with: High school diploma (including GED) or higher: 84.5% (2006-2010 5-year est.); Bachelor's degree or higher: 10.6% (2006-2010 5-year est.); Master's degree or higher: 3.6% (2006-2010 5-year est.).

School District(s)

Mohawk Area SD (KG-12)
  2010-11 Enrollment: 1,516 . . . . (724) 667-7723

Housing: Homeownership rate: 79.4% (2010); Median home value: $84,500 (2006-2010 5-year est.); Median contract rent: $440 per month (2006-2010 5-year est.); Median year structure built: 1942 (2006-2010 5-year est.).

Safety: Violent crime rate: 0.0 per 10,000 population; Property crime rate: 0.0 per 10,000 population (2011).

Transportation: Commute to work: 97.7% car, 0.0% public transportation, 0.0% walk, 1.5% work from home (2006-2010 5-year est.); Travel time to work: 26.4% less than 15 minutes, 46.9% 15 to 30 minutes, 20.3% 30 to 45 minutes, 2.9% 45 to 60 minutes, 3.5% 60 minutes or more (2006-2010 5-year est.)

Additional Information Contacts

Lawrence County Chamber of Commerce . . . . (724) 654-5593
  http://www.lawrencecountychamber.org

CHEWTON (CDP). Covers a land area of 1.494 square miles and a water area of 0.016 square miles. Located at 40.90° N. Lat; 80.32° W. Long. Elevation is 896 feet.

Population: n/a (1990); n/a (2000); 488 (2010); Density: 326.6 persons per square mile (2010); Race: 98.6% White, 0.4% Black, 0.4% Asian, 0.0% American Indian/Alaska Native, 0.0% Native Hawaiian/Other Pacific Islander, 0.6% Other, 0.8% Hispanic of any race (2010); Average household size: 2.33 (2010); Median age: 44.4 (2010); Males per 100 females: 95.2 (2010); Marriage status: 13.7% never married, 46.0% now married, 18.5% widowed, 21.8% divorced (2006-2010 5-year est.); Foreign born: 0.0% (2006-2010 5-year est.); Ancestry (includes multiple

ancestries): 22.1% American, 18.8% German, 11.2% Irish, 10.7% English, 8.3% Polish (2006-2010 5-year est.).
Economy: Employment by occupation: 14.8% management, 3.2% professional, 7.9% services, 3.2% sales, 0.0% farming, 8.5% construction, 5.8% production (2006-2010 5-year est.).
Income: Per capita income: $19,479 (2006-2010 5-year est.); Median household income: $38,056 (2006-2010 5-year est.); Average household income: $48,174 (2006-2010 5-year est.); Percent of households with income of $100,000 or more: 10.0% (2006-2010 5-year est.); Poverty rate: 0.0% (2006-2010 5-year est.).
Education: Percent of population age 25 and over with: High school diploma (including GED) or higher: 83.5% (2006-2010 5-year est.); Bachelor's degree or higher: 15.8% (2006-2010 5-year est.); Master's degree or higher: 0.0% (2006-2010 5-year est.).
Housing: Homeownership rate: 83.2% (2010); Median home value: $85,600 (2006-2010 5-year est.); Median contract rent: n/a per month (2006-2010 5-year est.); Median year structure built: 1941 (2006-2010 5-year est.).
Transportation: Commute to work: 97.4% car, 0.0% public transportation, 0.0% walk, 0.0% work from home (2006-2010 5-year est.); Travel time to work: 52.4% less than 15 minutes, 22.8% 15 to 30 minutes, 0.0% 30 to 45 minutes, 15.9% 45 to 60 minutes, 9.0% 60 minutes or more (2006-2010 5-year est.)

EDINBURG (unincorporated postal area)
Zip Code: 16116
Covers a land area of 26.422 square miles and a water area of 0.636 square miles. Located at 41.04° N. Lat; 80.44° W. Long. Elevation is 801 feet. Population: 3,074 (2010); Density: 116.3 persons per square mile (2010); Race: 98.5% White, 0.2% Black, 0.4% Asian, 0.1% American Indian/Alaska Native, 0.0% Native Hawaiian/Other Pacific Islander, 0.8% Other, 0.8% Hispanic of any race (2010); Average household size: 2.38 (2010); Median age: 45.6 (2010); Males per 100 females: 92.1 (2010); Homeownership rate: 85.8% (2010)

ELLPORT (borough). Covers a land area of 0.429 square miles and a water area of 0.034 square miles. Located at 40.86° N. Lat; 80.26° W. Long. Elevation is 892 feet.
Population: 1,243 (1990); 1,148 (2000); 1,180 (2010); Density: 2,751.9 persons per square mile (2010); Race: 97.8% White, 0.3% Black, 0.4% Asian, 0.0% American Indian/Alaska Native, 0.0% Native Hawaiian/Other Pacific Islander, 1.5% Other, 1.4% Hispanic of any race (2010); Average household size: 2.45 (2010); Median age: 42.6 (2010); Males per 100 females: 94.1 (2010); Marriage status: 24.2% never married, 50.9% now married, 13.3% widowed, 11.6% divorced (2006-2010 5-year est.); Foreign born: 1.8% (2006-2010 5-year est.); Ancestry (includes multiple ancestries): 38.2% German, 28.5% Italian, 13.7% Irish, 11.3% English, 9.8% Polish (2006-2010 5-year est.).
Economy: Single-family building permits issued: 0 (2011); Multi-family building permits issued: 0 (2011); Employment by occupation: 7.7% management, 4.4% professional, 9.9% services, 12.6% sales, 1.8% farming, 11.4% construction, 6.7% production (2006-2010 5-year est.).
Income: Per capita income: $19,805 (2006-2010 5-year est.); Median household income: $39,191 (2006-2010 5-year est.); Average household income: $46,372 (2006-2010 5-year est.); Percent of households with income of $100,000 or more: 6.1% (2006-2010 5-year est.); Poverty rate: 8.1% (2006-2010 5-year est.).
Education: Percent of population age 25 and over with: High school diploma (including GED) or higher: 86.8% (2006-2010 5-year est.); Bachelor's degree or higher: 14.4% (2006-2010 5-year est.); Master's degree or higher: 2.2% (2006-2010 5-year est.).
Housing: Homeownership rate: 84.2% (2010); Median home value: $101,500 (2006-2010 5-year est.); Median contract rent: $446 per month (2006-2010 5-year est.); Median year structure built: 1951 (2006-2010 5-year est.).
Transportation: Commute to work: 94.6% car, 0.9% public transportation, 2.5% walk, 1.4% work from home (2006-2010 5-year est.); Travel time to work: 33.6% less than 15 minutes, 22.8% 15 to 30 minutes, 24.9% 30 to 45 minutes, 7.5% 45 to 60 minutes, 11.2% 60 minutes or more (2006-2010 5-year est.)
Additional Information Contacts
Ellwood City Chamber of Commerce . . . . (724) 758-5501
http://ellwoodchamber.org

ELLWOOD CITY (borough). Covers a land area of 2.324 square miles and a water area of 0.034 square miles. Located at 40.86° N. Lat; 80.28° W. Long. Elevation is 886 feet.
Population: 8,657 (1990); 8,688 (2000); 7,921 (2010); Density: 3,408.3 persons per square mile (2010); Race: 97.0% White, 1.1% Black, 0.3% Asian, 0.1% American Indian/Alaska Native, 0.0% Native Hawaiian/Other Pacific Islander, 1.5% Other, 1.3% Hispanic of any race (2010); Average household size: 2.25 (2010); Median age: 42.0 (2010); Males per 100 females: 88.6 (2010); Marriage status: 26.6% never married, 52.0% now married, 11.4% widowed, 10.0% divorced (2006-2010 5-year est.); Foreign born: 2.8% (2006-2010 5-year est.); Ancestry (includes multiple ancestries): 35.5% Italian, 32.4% German, 15.9% Irish, 10.8% Polish, 8.7% English (2006-2010 5-year est.).
Economy: Single-family building permits issued: 0 (2011); Multi-family building permits issued: 0 (2011); Employment by occupation: 7.2% management, 2.0% professional, 15.9% services, 13.5% sales, 5.4% farming, 6.0% construction, 5.1% production (2006-2010 5-year est.).
Income: Per capita income: $21,232 (2006-2010 5-year est.); Median household income: $39,024 (2006-2010 5-year est.); Average household income: $49,199 (2006-2010 5-year est.); Percent of households with income of $100,000 or more: 11.4% (2006-2010 5-year est.); Poverty rate: 17.8% (2006-2010 5-year est.).
Taxes: Total city taxes per capita: $271 (2009); City property taxes per capita: $163 (2009).
Education: Percent of population age 25 and over with: High school diploma (including GED) or higher: 90.0% (2006-2010 5-year est.); Bachelor's degree or higher: 19.0% (2006-2010 5-year est.); Master's degree or higher: 4.4% (2006-2010 5-year est.).
School District(s)
Ellwood City Area SD (KG-12)
2010-11 Enrollment: 1,939 . . . . (724) 752-1591
Riverside Beaver County SD (KG-12)
2010-11 Enrollment: 1,575 . . . . (724) 758-7512
Housing: Homeownership rate: 65.5% (2010); Median home value: $85,000 (2006-2010 5-year est.); Median contract rent: $435 per month (2006-2010 5-year est.); Median year structure built: 1942 (2006-2010 5-year est.).
Hospitals: Ellwood City Hospital (95 beds)
Safety: Violent crime rate: 37.8 per 10,000 population; Property crime rate: 305.8 per 10,000 population (2011).
Newspapers: Ellwood City Ledger (Local news; Circulation 6,300); South County News (Community news; Circulation 8,100); Valley Tribune (Community news; Circulation 21,000)
Transportation: Commute to work: 93.6% car, 0.3% public transportation, 4.6% walk, 1.1% work from home (2006-2010 5-year est.); Travel time to work: 43.4% less than 15 minutes, 21.4% 15 to 30 minutes, 21.0% 30 to 45 minutes, 6.3% 45 to 60 minutes, 7.9% 60 minutes or more (2006-2010 5-year est.)
Additional Information Contacts
Borough of Ellwood City . . . . (724) 752-5552
http://ellwoodcity.org
Ellwood City Chamber of Commerce . . . . (724) 758-5501
http://ellwoodchamber.org

ENON VALLEY (borough). Aka Enon. Covers a land area of 0.489 square miles and a water area of 0.007 square miles. Located at 40.86° N. Lat; 80.46° W. Long. Elevation is 991 feet.
Population: 355 (1990); 387 (2000); 306 (2010); Density: 625.8 persons per square mile (2010); Race: 99.7% White, 0.0% Black, 0.0% Asian, 0.0% American Indian/Alaska Native, 0.0% Native Hawaiian/Other Pacific Islander, 0.3% Other, 1.0% Hispanic of any race (2010); Average household size: 2.51 (2010); Median age: 40.1 (2010); Males per 100 females: 100.0 (2010); Marriage status: 27.6% never married, 53.9% now married, 9.1% widowed, 9.4% divorced (2006-2010 5-year est.); Foreign born: 0.0% (2006-2010 5-year est.); Ancestry (includes multiple ancestries): 35.2% German, 22.8% English, 22.5% Irish, 10.7% Italian, 6.5% Scotch-Irish (2006-2010 5-year est.).
Economy: Single-family building permits issued: 0 (2011); Multi-family building permits issued: 0 (2011); Employment by occupation: 9.0% management, 0.0% professional, 11.5% services, 17.9% sales, 0.0% farming, 15.4% construction, 5.8% production (2006-2010 5-year est.).
Income: Per capita income: $22,142 (2006-2010 5-year est.); Median household income: $41,607 (2006-2010 5-year est.); Average household income: $51,970 (2006-2010 5-year est.); Percent of households with

income of $100,000 or more: 8.9% (2006-2010 5-year est.); Poverty rate: 16.9% (2006-2010 5-year est.).

Education: Percent of population age 25 and over with: High school diploma (including GED) or higher: 86.5% (2006-2010 5-year est.); Bachelor's degree or higher: 15.5% (2006-2010 5-year est.); Master's degree or higher: 1.2% (2006-2010 5-year est.).

Housing: Homeownership rate: 78.7% (2010); Median home value: $85,000 (2006-2010 5-year est.); Median contract rent: $479 per month (2006-2010 5-year est.); Median year structure built: 1942 (2006-2010 5-year est.).

Transportation: Commute to work: 88.9% car, 2.0% public transportation, 0.0% walk, 7.2% work from home (2006-2010 5-year est.); Travel time to work: 23.2% less than 15 minutes, 43.7% 15 to 30 minutes, 22.5% 30 to 45 minutes, 1.4% 45 to 60 minutes, 9.2% 60 minutes or more (2006-2010 5-year est.)

FRIZZLEBURG (CDP). Covers a land area of 2.803 square miles and a water area of 0.012 square miles. Located at 41.07° N. Lat; 80.44° W. Long. Elevation is 1,076 feet.

Population: n/a (1990); n/a (2000); 602 (2010); Density: 214.8 persons per square mile (2010); Race: 96.5% White, 1.0% Black, 0.0% Asian, 0.0% American Indian/Alaska Native, 0.0% Native Hawaiian/Other Pacific Islander, 2.5% Other, 0.8% Hispanic of any race (2010); Average household size: 2.43 (2010); Median age: 41.1 (2010); Males per 100 females: 91.7 (2010); Marriage status: 21.5% never married, 68.3% now married, 4.6% widowed, 5.6% divorced (2006-2010 5-year est.); Foreign born: 0.0% (2006-2010 5-year est.); Ancestry (includes multiple ancestries): 48.2% German, 32.7% Irish, 22.8% Italian, 12.1% Scotch-Irish, 11.3% English (2006-2010 5-year est.).

Economy: Employment by occupation: 6.3% management, 0.0% professional, 22.0% services, 2.8% sales, 0.0% farming, 10.5% construction, 8.4% production (2006-2010 5-year est.).

Income: Per capita income: $16,500 (2006-2010 5-year est.); Median household income: $25,931 (2006-2010 5-year est.); Average household income: $31,693 (2006-2010 5-year est.); Percent of households with income of $100,000 or more: n/a (2006-2010 5-year est.); Poverty rate: 29.1% (2006-2010 5-year est.).

Education: Percent of population age 25 and over with: High school diploma (including GED) or higher: 94.0% (2006-2010 5-year est.); Bachelor's degree or higher: 10.5% (2006-2010 5-year est.); Master's degree or higher: 0.0% (2006-2010 5-year est.).

Housing: Homeownership rate: 88.7% (2010); Median home value: $36,800 (2006-2010 5-year est.); Median contract rent: $511 per month (2006-2010 5-year est.); Median year structure built: 1968 (2006-2010 5-year est.).

Transportation: Commute to work: 87.5% car, 0.0% public transportation, 8.7% walk, 3.8% work from home (2006-2010 5-year est.); Travel time to work: 30.4% less than 15 minutes, 67.4% 15 to 30 minutes, 0.0% 30 to 45 minutes, 2.2% 45 to 60 minutes, 0.0% 60 minutes or more (2006-2010 5-year est.)

HICKORY (township). Covers a land area of 15.841 square miles and a water area of 0.091 square miles. Located at 41.04° N. Lat; 80.29° W. Long.

Population: 2,317 (1990); 2,356 (2000); 2,470 (2010); Density: 155.9 persons per square mile (2010); Race: 98.4% White, 0.4% Black, 0.4% Asian, 0.1% American Indian/Alaska Native, 0.0% Native Hawaiian/Other Pacific Islander, 0.7% Other, 0.5% Hispanic of any race (2010); Average household size: 2.45 (2010); Median age: 46.0 (2010); Males per 100 females: 96.7 (2010); Marriage status: 23.6% never married, 62.1% now married, 5.9% widowed, 8.4% divorced (2006-2010 5-year est.); Foreign born: 0.6% (2006-2010 5-year est.); Ancestry (includes multiple ancestries): 27.3% German, 26.6% Italian, 19.8% Irish, 9.4% English, 9.1% Polish (2006-2010 5-year est.).

Economy: Single-family building permits issued: 1 (2011); Multi-family building permits issued: 2 (2011); Employment by occupation: 5.0% management, 1.6% professional, 9.5% services, 21.7% sales, 4.5% farming, 12.8% construction, 9.0% production (2006-2010 5-year est.).

Income: Per capita income: $22,358 (2006-2010 5-year est.); Median household income: $48,277 (2006-2010 5-year est.); Average household income: $58,003 (2006-2010 5-year est.); Percent of households with income of $100,000 or more: 15.0% (2006-2010 5-year est.); Poverty rate: 8.9% (2006-2010 5-year est.).

Education: Percent of population age 25 and over with: High school diploma (including GED) or higher: 92.4% (2006-2010 5-year est.);

Bachelor's degree or higher: 19.7% (2006-2010 5-year est.); Master's degree or higher: 5.4% (2006-2010 5-year est.).

Housing: Homeownership rate: 83.6% (2010); Median home value: $118,200 (2006-2010 5-year est.); Median contract rent: $456 per month (2006-2010 5-year est.); Median year structure built: 1963 (2006-2010 5-year est.).

Transportation: Commute to work: 94.4% car, 0.0% public transportation, 1.7% walk, 2.5% work from home (2006-2010 5-year est.); Travel time to work: 41.1% less than 15 minutes, 32.2% 15 to 30 minutes, 15.1% 30 to 45 minutes, 6.2% 45 to 60 minutes, 5.5% 60 minutes or more (2006-2010 5-year est.)

Additional Information Contacts

Washington County Chamber of Commerce . . . . (724) 225-3010
  http://www.washcochamber.com

HILLSVILLE (unincorporated postal area)
Zip Code: 16132

Covers a land area of 1.767 square miles and a water area of 0.239 square miles. Located at 41.00° N. Lat; 80.50° W. Long. Elevation is 1,135 feet. Population: 355 (2010); Density: 200.9 persons per square mile (2010); Race: 99.4% White, 0.0% Black, 0.0% Asian, 0.6% American Indian/Alaska Native, 0.0% Native Hawaiian/Other Pacific Islander, 0.0% Other, 0.8% Hispanic of any race (2010); Average household size: 2.29 (2010); Median age: 43.4 (2010); Males per 100 females: 100.6 (2010); Homeownership rate: 80.0% (2010)

LITTLE BEAVER (township). Covers a land area of 20.371 square miles and a water area of 0.133 square miles. Located at 40.87° N. Lat; 80.47° W. Long.

Population: 1,251 (1990); 1,310 (2000); 1,411 (2010); Density: 69.3 persons per square mile (2010); Race: 98.2% White, 0.4% Black, 0.3% Asian, 0.0% American Indian/Alaska Native, 0.0% Native Hawaiian/Other Pacific Islander, 1.1% Other, 0.2% Hispanic of any race (2010); Average household size: 2.69 (2010); Median age: 42.4 (2010); Males per 100 females: 102.7 (2010); Marriage status: 27.9% never married, 58.7% now married, 9.4% widowed, 3.9% divorced (2006-2010 5-year est.); Foreign born: 0.4% (2006-2010 5-year est.); Ancestry (includes multiple ancestries): 26.4% German, 16.1% Irish, 11.8% English, 8.1% Scotch-Irish, 6.8% Polish (2006-2010 5-year est.).

Economy: Single-family building permits issued: 1 (2011); Multi-family building permits issued: 0 (2011); Employment by occupation: 4.7% management, 1.2% professional, 12.3% services, 11.5% sales, 0.8% farming, 19.9% construction, 12.1% production (2006-2010 5-year est.).

Income: Per capita income: $20,129 (2006-2010 5-year est.); Median household income: $43,317 (2006-2010 5-year est.); Average household income: $51,228 (2006-2010 5-year est.); Percent of households with income of $100,000 or more: 8.4% (2006-2010 5-year est.); Poverty rate: 5.3% (2006-2010 5-year est.).

Education: Percent of population age 25 and over with: High school diploma (including GED) or higher: 83.4% (2006-2010 5-year est.); Bachelor's degree or higher: 8.2% (2006-2010 5-year est.); Master's degree or higher: 1.1% (2006-2010 5-year est.).

Housing: Homeownership rate: 83.4% (2010); Median home value: $100,000 (2006-2010 5-year est.); Median contract rent: $318 per month (2006-2010 5-year est.); Median year structure built: 1971 (2006-2010 5-year est.).

Safety: Violent crime rate: 0.0 per 10,000 population; Property crime rate: 0.0 per 10,000 population (2011).

Transportation: Commute to work: 93.3% car, 1.6% public transportation, 1.8% walk, 0.6% work from home (2006-2010 5-year est.); Travel time to work: 17.3% less than 15 minutes, 31.1% 15 to 30 minutes, 32.1% 30 to 45 minutes, 14.9% 45 to 60 minutes, 4.6% 60 minutes or more (2006-2010 5-year est.)

Additional Information Contacts

Ellwood City Area Chamber of Commerce . . . . (724) 758-5501
  http://ellwoodchamber.org

MAHONING (township). Covers a land area of 23.909 square miles and a water area of 0.793 square miles. Located at 41.03° N. Lat; 80.48° W. Long.

Population: 3,560 (1990); 3,447 (2000); 3,083 (2010); Density: 128.9 persons per square mile (2010); Race: 98.9% White, 0.1% Black, 0.3% Asian, 0.1% American Indian/Alaska Native, 0.0% Native Hawaiian/Other Pacific Islander, 0.6% Other, 0.6% Hispanic of any race (2010); Average household size: 2.39 (2010); Median age: 44.8 (2010); Males per 100

females: 93.2 (2010); Marriage status: 23.4% never married, 56.0% now married, 10.2% widowed, 10.4% divorced (2006-2010 5-year est.); Foreign born: 0.0% (2006-2010 5-year est.); Ancestry (includes multiple ancestries): 40.0% German, 24.6% Italian, 19.5% Irish, 8.8% Scotch-Irish, 7.9% English (2006-2010 5-year est.).

Economy: Single-family building permits issued: 2 (2011); Multi-family building permits issued: 0 (2011); Employment by occupation: 4.9% management, 2.7% professional, 12.4% services, 13.6% sales, 6.1% farming, 11.5% construction, 11.0% production (2006-2010 5-year est.).

Income: Per capita income: $22,002 (2006-2010 5-year est.); Median household income: $34,847 (2006-2010 5-year est.); Average household income: $51,959 (2006-2010 5-year est.); Percent of households with income of $100,000 or more: 12.4% (2006-2010 5-year est.); Poverty rate: 14.8% (2006-2010 5-year est.).

Education: Percent of population age 25 and over with: High school diploma (including GED) or higher: 86.1% (2006-2010 5-year est.); Bachelor's degree or higher: 16.6% (2006-2010 5-year est.); Master's degree or higher: 5.2% (2006-2010 5-year est.).

Housing: Homeownership rate: 84.5% (2010); Median home value: $85,700 (2006-2010 5-year est.); Median contract rent: $420 per month (2006-2010 5-year est.); Median year structure built: 1963 (2006-2010 5-year est.).

Safety: Violent crime rate: 12.9 per 10,000 population; Property crime rate: 148.7 per 10,000 population (2011).

Transportation: Commute to work: 93.5% car, 0.7% public transportation, 0.7% walk, 4.3% work from home (2006-2010 5-year est.); Travel time to work: 28.3% less than 15 minutes, 45.1% 15 to 30 minutes, 20.4% 30 to 45 minutes, 2.7% 45 to 60 minutes, 3.6% 60 minutes or more (2006-2010 5-year est.)

Additional Information Contacts
Lawrence County Chamber of Commerce . . . . (724) 654-5593
  http://www.lawrencecountychamber.org

NESHANNOCK (township). Covers a land area of 17.235 square miles and a water area of 0.187 square miles. Located at 41.05° N. Lat; 80.35° W. Long.

Population: 8,373 (1990); 9,216 (2000); 9,609 (2010); Density: 557.5 persons per square mile (2010); Race: 96.6% White, 1.0% Black, 1.1% Asian, 0.1% American Indian/Alaska Native, 0.0% Native Hawaiian/Other Pacific Islander, 1.2% Other, 1.1% Hispanic of any race (2010); Average household size: 2.29 (2010); Median age: 49.1 (2010); Males per 100 females: 87.8 (2010); Marriage status: 18.6% never married, 63.1% now married, 11.1% widowed, 7.1% divorced (2006-2010 5-year est.); Foreign born: 3.0% (2006-2010 5-year est.); Ancestry (includes multiple ancestries): 35.4% Italian, 20.7% German, 19.0% Irish, 10.3% Polish, 9.8% English (2006-2010 5-year est.).

Economy: Single-family building permits issued: 9 (2011); Multi-family building permits issued: 0 (2011); Employment by occupation: 12.5% management, 2.1% professional, 10.3% services, 13.2% sales, 4.6% farming, 4.1% construction, 2.2% production (2006-2010 5-year est.).

Income: Per capita income: $32,741 (2006-2010 5-year est.); Median household income: $51,528 (2006-2010 5-year est.); Average household income: $73,109 (2006-2010 5-year est.); Percent of households with income of $100,000 or more: 22.1% (2006-2010 5-year est.); Poverty rate: 4.5% (2006-2010 5-year est.).

Education: Percent of population age 25 and over with: High school diploma (including GED) or higher: 93.6% (2006-2010 5-year est.); Bachelor's degree or higher: 33.4% (2006-2010 5-year est.); Master's degree or higher: 9.8% (2006-2010 5-year est.).

Housing: Homeownership rate: 80.2% (2010); Median home value: $153,600 (2006-2010 5-year est.); Median contract rent: $588 per month (2006-2010 5-year est.); Median year structure built: 1966 (2006-2010 5-year est.).

Transportation: Commute to work: 95.1% car, 1.0% public transportation, 0.9% walk, 3.0% work from home (2006-2010 5-year est.); Travel time to work: 50.2% less than 15 minutes, 25.7% 15 to 30 minutes, 9.0% 30 to 45 minutes, 6.6% 45 to 60 minutes, 8.6% 60 minutes or more (2006-2010 5-year est.)

Additional Information Contacts
Lawrence County Chamber of Commerce . . . . (724) 654-5593
  http://www.lawrencecountychamber.org
Neshannock Township . . . . (724) 658-6062
  http://www.neshannock.org

NEW BEAVER (borough). Aka Big Beaver Township. Covers a land area of 14.449 square miles and a water area of 0.119 square miles. Located at 40.88° N. Lat; 80.38° W. Long. Elevation is 1,207 feet.

Population: 1,736 (1990); 1,677 (2000); 1,502 (2010); Density: 103.9 persons per square mile (2010); Race: 98.2% White, 0.8% Black, 0.2% Asian, 0.1% American Indian/Alaska Native, 0.0% Native Hawaiian/Other Pacific Islander, 0.7% Other, 0.4% Hispanic of any race (2010); Average household size: 2.31 (2010); Median age: 46.9 (2010); Males per 100 females: 100.5 (2010); Marriage status: 26.3% never married, 51.8% now married, 9.3% widowed, 12.5% divorced (2006-2010 5-year est.); Foreign born: 1.6% (2006-2010 5-year est.); Ancestry (includes multiple ancestries): 37.9% German, 23.0% Italian, 18.2% Irish, 11.0% English, 9.9% Scotch-Irish (2006-2010 5-year est.).

Economy: Single-family building permits issued: 0 (2011); Multi-family building permits issued: 0 (2011); Employment by occupation: 8.7% management, 1.7% professional, 8.1% services, 24.7% sales, 3.2% farming, 15.1% construction, 11.5% production (2006-2010 5-year est.).

Income: Per capita income: $20,511 (2006-2010 5-year est.); Median household income: $31,932 (2006-2010 5-year est.); Average household income: $45,621 (2006-2010 5-year est.); Percent of households with income of $100,000 or more: 9.7% (2006-2010 5-year est.); Poverty rate: 15.8% (2006-2010 5-year est.).

Education: Percent of population age 25 and over with: High school diploma (including GED) or higher: 82.1% (2006-2010 5-year est.); Bachelor's degree or higher: 8.4% (2006-2010 5-year est.); Master's degree or higher: 2.2% (2006-2010 5-year est.).

Housing: Homeownership rate: 82.0% (2010); Median home value: $101,600 (2006-2010 5-year est.); Median contract rent: $360 per month (2006-2010 5-year est.); Median year structure built: 1973 (2006-2010 5-year est.).

Safety: Violent crime rate: 6.6 per 10,000 population; Property crime rate: 39.8 per 10,000 population (2011).

Transportation: Commute to work: 89.7% car, 0.4% public transportation, 5.2% walk, 3.9% work from home (2006-2010 5-year est.); Travel time to work: 22.5% less than 15 minutes, 35.3% 15 to 30 minutes, 26.5% 30 to 45 minutes, 10.1% 45 to 60 minutes, 5.6% 60 minutes or more (2006-2010 5-year est.)

Additional Information Contacts
Beaver County Chamber of Commerce . . . . (724) 775-3944
  http://www.beavercountychamber.com

NEW BEDFORD (CDP). Covers a land area of 2.552 square miles and a water area of 0.004 square miles. Located at 41.09° N. Lat; 80.49° W. Long. Elevation is 1,145 feet.

Population: n/a (1990); n/a (2000); 925 (2010); Density: 362.5 persons per square mile (2010); Race: 99.0% White, 0.4% Black, 0.1% Asian, 0.0% American Indian/Alaska Native, 0.0% Native Hawaiian/Other Pacific Islander, 0.5% Other, 1.0% Hispanic of any race (2010); Average household size: 2.32 (2010); Median age: 47.8 (2010); Males per 100 females: 98.1 (2010); Marriage status: 14.5% never married, 55.5% now married, 15.8% widowed, 14.3% divorced (2006-2010 5-year est.); Foreign born: 0.0% (2006-2010 5-year est.); Ancestry (includes multiple ancestries): 35.5% German, 22.7% English, 13.0% Scotch-Irish, 10.9% American, 10.3% Irish (2006-2010 5-year est.).

Economy: Employment by occupation: 4.9% management, 7.0% professional, 15.2% services, 13.7% sales, 3.7% farming, 19.5% construction, 7.6% production (2006-2010 5-year est.).

Income: Per capita income: $29,148 (2006-2010 5-year est.); Median household income: $46,667 (2006-2010 5-year est.); Average household income: $59,833 (2006-2010 5-year est.); Percent of households with income of $100,000 or more: 15.2% (2006-2010 5-year est.); Poverty rate: 5.1% (2006-2010 5-year est.).

Education: Percent of population age 25 and over with: High school diploma (including GED) or higher: 94.6% (2006-2010 5-year est.); Bachelor's degree or higher: 27.1% (2006-2010 5-year est.); Master's degree or higher: 8.0% (2006-2010 5-year est.).

Housing: Homeownership rate: 88.8% (2010); Median home value: $93,800 (2006-2010 5-year est.); Median contract rent: n/a per month (2006-2010 5-year est.); Median year structure built: 1953 (2006-2010 5-year est.).

Transportation: Commute to work: 89.3% car, 0.0% public transportation, 0.0% walk, 6.1% work from home (2006-2010 5-year est.); Travel time to work: 18.2% less than 15 minutes, 56.2% 15 to 30 minutes, 21.4% 30 to 45 minutes, 0.0% 45 to 60 minutes, 4.2% 60 minutes or more (2006-2010 5-year est.)

NEW CASTLE (city). County seat. Covers a land area of 8.307 square miles and a water area of 0.227 square miles. Located at 41.00° N. Lat; 80.35° W. Long. Elevation is 853 feet.

History: The site of New Castle became the capital of the Delawares of western Pennsylvania after Colonel John Armstrong destroyed Kittanning in 1756. In resurveying "donation lands" set aside for Revolutionary soldiers, John Stewart discovered and settled on an unassigned 50-acre tract. He built a charcoal furnace to make pig iron from local ore, and named the spot for Newcastle upon Tyne, the English industrial city, which he desired to duplicate. The Erie Extension Canal, completed in 1833, stimulated settlement. In 1859 New Castle became a city.

Population: 28,334 (1990); 26,309 (2000); 23,273 (2010); Density: 2,801.5 persons per square mile (2010); Race: 83.2% White, 12.2% Black, 0.4% Asian, 0.1% American Indian/Alaska Native, 0.0% Native Hawaiian/Other Pacific Islander, 4.1% Other, 1.6% Hispanic of any race (2010); Average household size: 2.30 (2010); Median age: 40.8 (2010); Males per 100 females: 90.1 (2010); Marriage status: 30.0% never married, 48.6% now married, 9.9% widowed, 11.5% divorced (2006-2010 5-year est.); Foreign born: 1.4% (2006-2010 5-year est.); Ancestry (includes multiple ancestries): 31.2% Italian, 20.7% German, 15.8% Irish, 8.2% Polish, 7.1% English (2006-2010 5-year est.).

Economy: Unemployment rate: 10.9% (August 2012); Total civilian labor force: 9,883 (August 2012); Single-family building permits issued: 1 (2011); Multi-family building permits issued: 0 (2011); Employment by occupation: 6.7% management, 2.4% professional, 13.3% services, 21.1% sales, 6.1% farming, 5.8% construction, 5.6% production (2006-2010 5-year est.).

Income: Per capita income: $16,756 (2006-2010 5-year est.); Median household income: $30,690 (2006-2010 5-year est.); Average household income: $39,791 (2006-2010 5-year est.); Percent of households with income of $100,000 or more: 4.0% (2006-2010 5-year est.); Poverty rate: 21.2% (2006-2010 5-year est.).

Taxes: Total city taxes per capita: $408 (2009); City property taxes per capita: $218 (2009).

Education: Percent of population age 25 and over with: High school diploma (including GED) or higher: 80.5% (2006-2010 5-year est.); Bachelor's degree or higher: 13.8% (2006-2010 5-year est.); Master's degree or higher: 4.4% (2006-2010 5-year est.).

School District(s)

Laurel SD (KG-12)
    2010-11 Enrollment: 1,354 . . . . (724) 658-8940
Lawrence County CTC (10-12)
    2010-11 Enrollment: 357. (724) 658-3583
Neshannock Township SD (KG-12)
    2010-11 Enrollment: 1,326 . . . . (724) 658-4793
New Castle Area SD (KG-12)
    2010-11 Enrollment: 3,307 . . . . (724) 656-4756
New Castle Youth Dev Ctr (UG-UG)
    2010-11 Enrollment: 105. (724) 656-7330
Shenango Area SD (KG-12)
    2010-11 Enrollment: 1,260 . . . . (724) 658-7287
Union Area SD (KG-12)
    2010-11 Enrollment: 832. (724) 658-4775

Two-year College(s)

Erie Business Center-New Castle (Private, For-profit)
    Fall 2010 Enrollment: 93 . . . . (724) 658-9066
    2011-12 Tuition: In-state $6,350; Out-of-state $6,350
Jameson Health System (Private, Not-for-profit)
    Fall 2010 Enrollment: 89 . . . . (724) 658-9001

Vocational/Technical School(s)

Lawrence County Career and Technical Center-Practical Nursing Program (Public)
    Fall 2010 Enrollment: 176 . . . . (724) 658-3583
    2011-12 Tuition: $10,200
New Castle School of Beauty Culture (Private, For-profit)
    Fall 2010 Enrollment: 89 . . . . (724) 287-0708
    2011-12 Tuition: $13,800

Housing: Homeownership rate: 60.8% (2010); Median home value: $56,600 (2006-2010 5-year est.); Median contract rent: $410 per month (2006-2010 5-year est.); Median year structure built: before 1940 (2006-2010 5-year est.).

Hospitals: Jameson Memorial Hospital (230 beds)

Newspapers: New Castle News (Local news; Circulation 17,422); Vindicator - New Castle Bureau (Local news)

Transportation: Commute to work: 90.2% car, 2.2% public transportation, 3.6% walk, 1.6% work from home (2006-2010 5-year est.); Travel time to work: 51.4% less than 15 minutes, 26.8% 15 to 30 minutes, 10.8% 30 to 45 minutes, 5.1% 45 to 60 minutes, 5.9% 60 minutes or more (2006-2010 5-year est.)

Airports: New Castle Municipal (general aviation)

Additional Information Contacts
City of New Castle. . . . . (724) 658-5698
    http://www.newcastlepa.org
Lawrence County Chamber of Commerce . . . . (724) 654-5593
    http://www.lawrencecountychamber.org

NEW CASTLE NORTHWEST (CDP). Covers a land area of 0.870 square miles and a water area of 0.003 square miles. Located at 41.02° N. Lat; 80.36° W. Long.

Population: 1,515 (1990); 1,535 (2000); 1,413 (2010); Density: 1,624.2 persons per square mile (2010); Race: 96.1% White, 1.6% Black, 1.1% Asian, 0.1% American Indian/Alaska Native, 0.0% Native Hawaiian/Other Pacific Islander, 1.1% Other, 2.4% Hispanic of any race (2010); Average household size: 2.11 (2010); Median age: 50.7 (2010); Males per 100 females: 81.9 (2010); Marriage status: 21.8% never married, 55.4% now married, 12.5% widowed, 10.3% divorced (2006-2010 5-year est.); Foreign born: 0.9% (2006-2010 5-year est.); Ancestry (includes multiple ancestries): 40.9% Italian, 27.1% German, 15.1% Irish, 11.4% Polish, 8.3% English (2006-2010 5-year est.).

Economy: Employment by occupation: 11.7% management, 0.0% professional, 6.4% services, 22.9% sales, 5.9% farming, 0.0% construction, 0.0% production (2006-2010 5-year est.).

Income: Per capita income: $26,327 (2006-2010 5-year est.); Median household income: $40,170 (2006-2010 5-year est.); Average household income: $50,730 (2006-2010 5-year est.); Percent of households with income of $100,000 or more: 11.6% (2006-2010 5-year est.); Poverty rate: 7.4% (2006-2010 5-year est.).

Education: Percent of population age 25 and over with: High school diploma (including GED) or higher: 88.5% (2006-2010 5-year est.); Bachelor's degree or higher: 30.8% (2006-2010 5-year est.); Master's degree or higher: 12.5% (2006-2010 5-year est.).

Housing: Homeownership rate: 76.6% (2010); Median home value: $93,100 (2006-2010 5-year est.); Median contract rent: $563 per month (2006-2010 5-year est.); Median year structure built: 1952 (2006-2010 5-year est.).

Transportation: Commute to work: 91.2% car, 1.8% public transportation, 4.5% walk, 2.5% work from home (2006-2010 5-year est.); Travel time to work: 66.4% less than 15 minutes, 8.3% 15 to 30 minutes, 15.3% 30 to 45 minutes, 0.0% 45 to 60 minutes, 10.0% 60 minutes or more (2006-2010 5-year est.)

Additional Information Contacts
Lawrence County Chamber of Commerce . . . . (724) 654-5593
    http://www.lawrencecountychamber.org

NEW WILMINGTON (borough). Covers a land area of 1.063 square miles and a water area of 0.027 square miles. Located at 41.12° N. Lat; 80.33° W. Long. Elevation is 1,047 feet.

Population: 2,706 (1990); 2,452 (2000); 2,466 (2010); Density: 2,319.5 persons per square mile (2010); Race: 97.3% White, 1.2% Black, 0.4% Asian, 0.1% American Indian/Alaska Native, 0.0% Native Hawaiian/Other Pacific Islander, 1.0% Other, 0.9% Hispanic of any race (2010); Average household size: 2.21 (2010); Median age: 21.7 (2010); Males per 100 females: 74.6 (2010); Marriage status: 64.9% never married, 25.2% now married, 7.5% widowed, 2.4% divorced (2006-2010 5-year est.); Foreign born: 2.6% (2006-2010 5-year est.); Ancestry (includes multiple ancestries): 34.2% German, 18.2% Irish, 17.5% Italian, 10.1% English, 7.1% Scotch-Irish (2006-2010 5-year est.).

Economy: Single-family building permits issued: 0 (2011); Multi-family building permits issued: 0 (2011); Employment by occupation: 9.9% management, 1.4% professional, 23.0% services, 20.0% sales, 1.1% farming, 3.0% construction, 1.8% production (2006-2010 5-year est.).

Income: Per capita income: $14,993 (2006-2010 5-year est.); Median household income: $48,269 (2006-2010 5-year est.); Average household income: $59,088 (2006-2010 5-year est.); Percent of households with income of $100,000 or more: 14.0% (2006-2010 5-year est.); Poverty rate: 9.7% (2006-2010 5-year est.).

Education: Percent of population age 25 and over with: High school diploma (including GED) or higher: 91.8% (2006-2010 5-year est.); Bachelor's degree or higher: 51.3% (2006-2010 5-year est.); Master's degree or higher: 27.9% (2006-2010 5-year est.).

School District(s)

Wilmington Area SD (KG-12)

   2010-11 Enrollment: 1,386 . . . . (724) 656-8866

Four-year College(s)

Westminster College (Private, Not-for-profit, Presbyterian Church (USA))

   Fall 2010 Enrollment: 1,703 . . . . (724) 946-8761

   2011-12 Tuition: In-state $30,510; Out-of-state $30,510

Housing: Homeownership rate: 56.7% (2010); Median home value: $156,400 (2006-2010 5-year est.); Median contract rent: $560 per month (2006-2010 5-year est.); Median year structure built: 1951 (2006-2010 5-year est.).

Newspapers: The Globe-Leader (National news; Circulation 2,000)

Transportation: Commute to work: 56.2% car, 0.4% public transportation, 37.5% walk, 5.7% work from home (2006-2010 5-year est.); Travel time to work: 60.7% less than 15 minutes, 25.3% 15 to 30 minutes, 8.0% 30 to 45 minutes, 2.7% 45 to 60 minutes, 3.3% 60 minutes or more (2006-2010 5-year est.)

Additional Information Contacts

Mercer Area Chamber of Commerce . . . . (724) 662-4185

   http://www.mercerareachamber.com

NORTH BEAVER (township). Covers a land area of 42.361 square miles and a water area of 0.682 square miles. Located at 40.95° N. Lat; 80.45° W. Long.

Population: 3,943 (1990); 4,022 (2000); 4,121 (2010); Density: 97.3 persons per square mile (2010); Race: 99.0% White, 0.1% Black, 0.3% Asian, 0.0% American Indian/Alaska Native, 0.0% Native Hawaiian/Other Pacific Islander, 0.6% Other, 0.4% Hispanic of any race (2010); Average household size: 2.59 (2010); Median age: 44.1 (2010); Males per 100 females: 100.7 (2010); Marriage status: 23.0% never married, 64.6% now married, 6.4% widowed, 5.9% divorced (2006-2010 5-year est.); Foreign born: 1.5% (2006-2010 5-year est.); Ancestry (includes multiple ancestries): 31.3% German, 23.0% Italian, 13.7% Irish, 11.7% English, 8.8% Scotch-Irish (2006-2010 5-year est.).

Economy: Single-family building permits issued: 0 (2011); Multi-family building permits issued: 0 (2011); Employment by occupation: 12.2% management, 1.9% professional, 8.6% services, 13.8% sales, 2.7% farming, 11.3% construction, 5.4% production (2006-2010 5-year est.).

Income: Per capita income: $26,465 (2006-2010 5-year est.); Median household income: $62,649 (2006-2010 5-year est.); Average household income: $71,450 (2006-2010 5-year est.); Percent of households with income of $100,000 or more: 21.5% (2006-2010 5-year est.); Poverty rate: 4.8% (2006-2010 5-year est.).

Education: Percent of population age 25 and over with: High school diploma (including GED) or higher: 93.2% (2006-2010 5-year est.); Bachelor's degree or higher: 18.1% (2006-2010 5-year est.); Master's degree or higher: 5.2% (2006-2010 5-year est.).

Housing: Homeownership rate: 86.9% (2010); Median home value: $127,800 (2006-2010 5-year est.); Median contract rent: $435 per month (2006-2010 5-year est.); Median year structure built: 1964 (2006-2010 5-year est.).

Transportation: Commute to work: 96.7% car, 0.0% public transportation, 1.9% walk, 1.5% work from home (2006-2010 5-year est.); Travel time to work: 26.4% less than 15 minutes, 36.7% 15 to 30 minutes, 22.1% 30 to 45 minutes, 4.7% 45 to 60 minutes, 10.1% 60 minutes or more (2006-2010 5-year est.).

Additional Information Contacts

Beaver Area Chamber of Commerce . . . . (724) 773-6504

   http://beaverareachamber.com

OAKLAND (CDP). Covers a land area of 0.918 square miles and a water area of 0.014 square miles. Located at 40.99° N. Lat; 80.37° W. Long. Elevation is 1,115 feet.

Population: 1,766 (1990); 1,516 (2000); 1,569 (2010); Density: 1,709.9 persons per square mile (2010); Race: 89.1% White, 7.0% Black, 0.5% Asian, 0.0% American Indian/Alaska Native, 0.0% Native Hawaiian/Other Pacific Islander, 3.4% Other, 1.3% Hispanic of any race (2010); Average household size: 2.52 (2010); Median age: 39.9 (2010); Males per 100 females: 95.4 (2010); Marriage status: 26.4% never married, 53.2% now married, 8.9% widowed, 11.5% divorced (2006-2010 5-year est.); Foreign born: 0.5% (2006-2010 5-year est.); Ancestry (includes multiple ancestries): 41.1% Italian, 23.7% Irish, 22.7% Polish, 21.8% German, 5.5% Scotch-Irish (2006-2010 5-year est.).

Economy: Employment by occupation: 0.9% management, 6.0% professional, 9.4% services, 5.7% sales, 6.1% farming, 10.5% construction, 8.6% production (2006-2010 5-year est.).

Income: Per capita income: $17,719 (2006-2010 5-year est.); Median household income: $41,250 (2006-2010 5-year est.); Average household income: $50,422 (2006-2010 5-year est.); Percent of households with income of $100,000 or more: 4.8% (2006-2010 5-year est.); Poverty rate: 10.2% (2006-2010 5-year est.).

Education: Percent of population age 25 and over with: High school diploma (including GED) or higher: 86.3% (2006-2010 5-year est.); Bachelor's degree or higher: 11.3% (2006-2010 5-year est.); Master's degree or higher: 0.8% (2006-2010 5-year est.).

Housing: Homeownership rate: 80.1% (2010); Median home value: $73,400 (2006-2010 5-year est.); Median contract rent: $493 per month (2006-2010 5-year est.); Median year structure built: 1955 (2006-2010 5-year est.).

Transportation: Commute to work: 94.9% car, 1.7% public transportation, 1.9% walk, 1.5% work from home (2006-2010 5-year est.); Travel time to work: 41.1% less than 15 minutes, 36.4% 15 to 30 minutes, 7.9% 30 to 45 minutes, 3.2% 45 to 60 minutes, 11.4% 60 minutes or more (2006-2010 5-year est.)

Additional Information Contacts

Lawrence County Chamber of Commerce . . . . (724) 654-5593

   http://www.lawrencecountychamber.org

OAKWOOD (CDP). Aka New Castle West. Covers a land area of 2.626 square miles and a water area of 0.054 square miles. Located at 41.01° N. Lat; 80.38° W. Long. Elevation is 1,040 feet.

Population: 2,541 (1990); 2,249 (2000); 2,270 (2010); Density: 864.3 persons per square mile (2010); Race: 91.7% White, 5.8% Black, 0.2% Asian, 0.0% American Indian/Alaska Native, 0.0% Native Hawaiian/Other Pacific Islander, 2.3% Other, 1.0% Hispanic of any race (2010); Average household size: 2.38 (2010); Median age: 48.0 (2010); Males per 100 females: 92.7 (2010); Marriage status: 18.3% never married, 53.3% now married, 10.3% widowed, 18.1% divorced (2006-2010 5-year est.); Foreign born: 0.6% (2006-2010 5-year est.); Ancestry (includes multiple ancestries): 28.7% Italian, 22.1% German, 21.9% Irish, 9.0% English, 7.6% Polish (2006-2010 5-year est.).

Economy: Employment by occupation: 6.5% management, 0.0% professional, 12.8% services, 31.8% sales, 4.9% farming, 7.6% construction, 9.6% production (2006-2010 5-year est.).

Income: Per capita income: $20,855 (2006-2010 5-year est.); Median household income: $42,339 (2006-2010 5-year est.); Average household income: $46,006 (2006-2010 5-year est.); Percent of households with income of $100,000 or more: 9.4% (2006-2010 5-year est.); Poverty rate: 9.3% (2006-2010 5-year est.).

Education: Percent of population age 25 and over with: High school diploma (including GED) or higher: 82.9% (2006-2010 5-year est.); Bachelor's degree or higher: 9.2% (2006-2010 5-year est.); Master's degree or higher: 2.8% (2006-2010 5-year est.).

Housing: Homeownership rate: 84.5% (2010); Median home value: $77,600 (2006-2010 5-year est.); Median contract rent: $470 per month (2006-2010 5-year est.); Median year structure built: 1955 (2006-2010 5-year est.).

Transportation: Commute to work: 97.2% car, 0.9% public transportation, 1.9% walk, 0.0% work from home (2006-2010 5-year est.); Travel time to work: 37.7% less than 15 minutes, 32.2% 15 to 30 minutes, 11.6% 30 to 45 minutes, 14.5% 45 to 60 minutes, 4.0% 60 minutes or more (2006-2010 5-year est.)

Additional Information Contacts

Lawrence County Chamber of Commerce . . . . (724) 654-5593

   http://www.lawrencecountychamber.org

PERRY (township). Covers a land area of 18.376 square miles and a water area of 0.196 square miles. Located at 40.89° N. Lat; 80.21° W. Long.

Population: 1,841 (1990); 1,930 (2000); 1,938 (2010); Density: 105.5 persons per square mile (2010); Race: 98.0% White, 0.5% Black, 0.2% Asian, 0.1% American Indian/Alaska Native, 0.0% Native Hawaiian/Other Pacific Islander, 1.2% Other, 0.6% Hispanic of any race (2010); Average household size: 2.52 (2010); Median age: 45.8 (2010); Males per 100 females: 98.4 (2010); Marriage status: 17.5% never married, 71.3% now married, 4.9% widowed, 6.4% divorced (2006-2010 5-year est.); Foreign born: 1.0% (2006-2010 5-year est.); Ancestry (includes multiple

ancestries): 42.5% German, 24.6% Irish, 19.5% Italian, 15.0% English, 5.0% American (2006-2010 5-year est.).

Economy: Single-family building permits issued: 1 (2011); Multi-family building permits issued: 0 (2011); Employment by occupation: 4.5% management, 4.1% professional, 9.1% services, 17.4% sales, 4.3% farming, 7.7% construction, 13.9% production (2006-2010 5-year est.).

Income: Per capita income: $21,316 (2006-2010 5-year est.); Median household income: $46,442 (2006-2010 5-year est.); Average household income: $52,382 (2006-2010 5-year est.); Percent of households with income of $100,000 or more: 7.5% (2006-2010 5-year est.); Poverty rate: 4.0% (2006-2010 5-year est.).

Education: Percent of population age 25 and over with: High school diploma (including GED) or higher: 86.5% (2006-2010 5-year est.); Bachelor's degree or higher: 13.2% (2006-2010 5-year est.); Master's degree or higher: 6.5% (2006-2010 5-year est.).

Housing: Homeownership rate: 89.1% (2010); Median home value: $115,900 (2006-2010 5-year est.); Median contract rent: $481 per month (2006-2010 5-year est.); Median year structure built: 1960 (2006-2010 5-year est.).

Transportation: Commute to work: 92.9% car, 1.3% public transportation, 0.0% walk, 5.8% work from home (2006-2010 5-year est.); Travel time to work: 26.6% less than 15 minutes, 38.8% 15 to 30 minutes, 20.6% 30 to 45 minutes, 11.6% 45 to 60 minutes, 2.5% 60 minutes or more (2006-2010 5-year est.).

Additional Information Contacts

Ellwood City Area Chamber of Commerce . . . . (724) 758-5501
  http://ellwoodchamber.org

PLAIN GROVE (township). Covers a land area of 17.812 square miles and a water area of 0.118 square miles. Located at 41.08° N. Lat; 80.15° W. Long. Elevation is 1,165 feet.

Population: 791 (1990); 854 (2000); 813 (2010); Density: 45.6 persons per square mile (2010); Race: 98.5% White, 0.1% Black, 0.1% Asian, 0.0% American Indian/Alaska Native, 0.2% Native Hawaiian/Other Pacific Islander, 1.1% Other, 1.5% Hispanic of any race (2010); Average household size: 2.51 (2010); Median age: 41.6 (2010); Males per 100 females: 100.2 (2010); Marriage status: 23.8% never married, 56.7% now married, 9.4% widowed, 10.1% divorced (2006-2010 5-year est.); Foreign born: 2.6% (2006-2010 5-year est.); Ancestry (includes multiple ancestries): 39.8% German, 24.5% Irish, 10.1% English, 8.5% Scotch-Irish, 8.2% Italian (2006-2010 5-year est.).

Economy: Single-family building permits issued: 2 (2011); Multi-family building permits issued: 0 (2011); Employment by occupation: 9.9% management, 4.6% professional, 6.8% services, 11.8% sales, 2.5% farming, 22.9% construction, 11.8% production (2006-2010 5-year est.).

Income: Per capita income: $19,452 (2006-2010 5-year est.); Median household income: $40,208 (2006-2010 5-year est.); Average household income: $46,566 (2006-2010 5-year est.); Percent of households with income of $100,000 or more: 6.3% (2006-2010 5-year est.); Poverty rate: 16.9% (2006-2010 5-year est.).

Education: Percent of population age 25 and over with: High school diploma (including GED) or higher: 82.2% (2006-2010 5-year est.); Bachelor's degree or higher: 14.9% (2006-2010 5-year est.); Master's degree or higher: 3.5% (2006-2010 5-year est.).

Housing: Homeownership rate: 86.5% (2010); Median home value: $132,600 (2006-2010 5-year est.); Median contract rent: $427 per month (2006-2010 5-year est.); Median year structure built: 1974 (2006-2010 5-year est.).

Transportation: Commute to work: 83.1% car, 0.0% public transportation, 5.6% walk, 5.3% work from home (2006-2010 5-year est.); Travel time to work: 30.0% less than 15 minutes, 40.9% 15 to 30 minutes, 17.5% 30 to 45 minutes, 4.3% 45 to 60 minutes, 7.3% 60 minutes or more (2006-2010 5-year est.)

PULASKI (township). Covers a land area of 30.677 square miles and a water area of 0.245 square miles. Located at 41.10° N. Lat; 80.45° W. Long. Elevation is 853 feet.

Population: 3,469 (1990); 3,658 (2000); 3,452 (2010); Density: 112.5 persons per square mile (2010); Race: 98.5% White, 0.4% Black, 0.1% Asian, 0.1% American Indian/Alaska Native, 0.0% Native Hawaiian/Other Pacific Islander, 0.9% Other, 0.8% Hispanic of any race (2010); Average household size: 2.50 (2010); Median age: 44.7 (2010); Males per 100 females: 95.9 (2010); Marriage status: 20.8% never married, 63.7% now married, 9.1% widowed, 6.4% divorced (2006-2010 5-year est.); Foreign born: 0.3% (2006-2010 5-year est.); Ancestry (includes multiple

ancestries): 38.1% German, 15.3% Irish, 14.0% English, 13.4% Italian, 6.0% Slovak (2006-2010 5-year est.).

Economy: Single-family building permits issued: 0 (2011); Multi-family building permits issued: 0 (2011); Employment by occupation: 8.1% management, 3.5% professional, 21.3% services, 13.3% sales, 2.3% farming, 11.6% construction, 8.6% production (2006-2010 5-year est.).

Income: Per capita income: $22,785 (2006-2010 5-year est.); Median household income: $46,167 (2006-2010 5-year est.); Average household income: $52,881 (2006-2010 5-year est.); Percent of households with income of $100,000 or more: 10.0% (2006-2010 5-year est.); Poverty rate: 7.2% (2006-2010 5-year est.).

Education: Percent of population age 25 and over with: High school diploma (including GED) or higher: 90.5% (2006-2010 5-year est.); Bachelor's degree or higher: 14.9% (2006-2010 5-year est.); Master's degree or higher: 4.4% (2006-2010 5-year est.).

School District(s)

Wilmington Area SD (KG-12)
  2010-11 Enrollment: 1,386 . . . . (724) 656-8866

Two-year College(s)

New Castle School of Trades (Private, For-profit)
  Fall 2010 Enrollment: 600 . . . . (724) 964-8811

Housing: Homeownership rate: 84.9% (2010); Median home value: $88,000 (2006-2010 5-year est.); Median contract rent: $505 per month (2006-2010 5-year est.); Median year structure built: 1964 (2006-2010 5-year est.).

Safety: Violent crime rate: 11.6 per 10,000 population; Property crime rate: 106.8 per 10,000 population (2011).

Transportation: Commute to work: 88.8% car, 0.0% public transportation, 4.2% walk, 4.8% work from home (2006-2010 5-year est.); Travel time to work: 24.0% less than 15 minutes, 55.8% 15 to 30 minutes, 13.0% 30 to 45 minutes, 4.7% 45 to 60 minutes, 2.5% 60 minutes or more (2006-2010 5-year est.)

Additional Information Contacts

Lawrence County Chamber of Commerce . . . . (724) 654-5593
  http://www.lawrencecountychamber.org

S.N.P.J. (borough). Covers a land area of 0.749 square miles and a water area of 0.028 square miles. Located at 40.93° N. Lat; 80.50° W. Long.

Population: 12 (1990); n/a (2000); 19 (2010); Density: 25.4 persons per square mile (2010); Race: 100.0% White, 0.0% Black, 0.0% Asian, 0.0% American Indian/Alaska Native, 0.0% Native Hawaiian/Other Pacific Islander, 0.0% Other, 0.0% Hispanic of any race (2010); Average household size: 2.38 (2010); Median age: 53.3 (2010); Males per 100 females: 90.0 (2010); Marriage status: n/a never married, n/a now married, n/a widowed, n/a divorced (2006-2010 5-year est.); Foreign born: n/a (2006-2010 5-year est.); Ancestry (includes multiple ancestries): n/a (2006-2010 5-year est.).

Economy: Employment by occupation: n/a management, n/a professional, n/a services, n/a sales, n/a farming, n/a construction, n/a production (2006-2010 5-year est.).

Income: Per capita income: n/a (2006-2010 5-year est.); Median household income: n/a (2006-2010 5-year est.); Average household income: n/a (2006-2010 5-year est.); Percent of households with income of $100,000 or more: n/a (2006-2010 5-year est.); Poverty rate: n/a (2006-2010 5-year est.).

Education: Percent of population age 25 and over with: High school diploma (including GED) or higher: n/a (2006-2010 5-year est.); Bachelor's degree or higher: n/a (2006-2010 5-year est.); Master's degree or higher: n/a (2006-2010 5-year est.).

Housing: Homeownership rate: 75.0% (2010); Median home value: n/a (2006-2010 5-year est.); Median contract rent: n/a per month (2006-2010 5-year est.); Median year structure built: n/a (2006-2010 5-year est.).

Transportation: Commute to work: n/a car, n/a public transportation, n/a walk, n/a work from home (2006-2010 5-year est.); Travel time to work: n/a less than 15 minutes, n/a 15 to 30 minutes, n/a 30 to 45 minutes, n/a 45 to 60 minutes, n/a 60 minutes or more (2006-2010 5-year est.)

SCOTT (township). Covers a land area of 20.004 square miles and a water area of 0.231 square miles. Located at 41.03° N. Lat; 80.22° W. Long.

Population: 2,200 (1990); 2,235 (2000); 2,347 (2010); Density: 117.3 persons per square mile (2010); Race: 99.1% White, 0.1% Black, 0.3% Asian, 0.0% American Indian/Alaska Native, 0.0% Native Hawaiian/Other Pacific Islander, 0.5% Other, 0.3% Hispanic of any race (2010); Average

household size: 2.66 (2010); Median age: 42.3 (2010); Males per 100 females: 98.1 (2010); Marriage status: 22.8% never married, 59.6% now married, 7.9% widowed, 9.8% divorced (2006-2010 5-year est.); Foreign born: 0.2% (2006-2010 5-year est.); Ancestry (includes multiple ancestries): 43.0% German, 18.8% Irish, 15.1% Polish, 14.4% English, 11.2% Italian (2006-2010 5-year est.).

Economy: Single-family building permits issued: 1 (2011); Multi-family building permits issued: 0 (2011); Employment by occupation: 8.4% management, 1.8% professional, 8.2% services, 15.3% sales, 3.6% farming, 11.2% construction, 8.0% production (2006-2010 5-year est.).

Income: Per capita income: $24,526 (2006-2010 5-year est.); Median household income: $56,375 (2006-2010 5-year est.); Average household income: $67,477 (2006-2010 5-year est.); Percent of households with income of $100,000 or more: 21.5% (2006-2010 5-year est.); Poverty rate: 6.6% (2006-2010 5-year est.).

Education: Percent of population age 25 and over with: High school diploma (including GED) or higher: 88.0% (2006-2010 5-year est.); Bachelor's degree or higher: 20.3% (2006-2010 5-year est.); Master's degree or higher: 7.4% (2006-2010 5-year est.).

Housing: Homeownership rate: 87.8% (2010); Median home value: $128,900 (2006-2010 5-year est.); Median contract rent: $448 per month (2006-2010 5-year est.); Median year structure built: 1974 (2006-2010 5-year est.).

Transportation: Commute to work: 89.2% car, 0.3% public transportation, 2.1% walk, 6.6% work from home (2006-2010 5-year est.); Travel time to work: 25.4% less than 15 minutes, 45.3% 15 to 30 minutes, 16.9% 30 to 45 minutes, 5.8% 45 to 60 minutes, 6.6% 60 minutes or more (2006-2010 5-year est.)

Additional Information Contacts

Lawrence County Chamber of Commerce . . . . (724) 654-5593
  http://www.lawrencecountychamber.org

SHENANGO (township). Covers a land area of 24.431 square miles and a water area of 0.077 square miles. Located at 40.95° N. Lat; 80.30° W. Long.

Population: 7,243 (1990); 7,633 (2000); 7,479 (2010); Density: 306.1 persons per square mile (2010); Race: 98.4% White, 0.7% Black, 0.1% Asian, 0.0% American Indian/Alaska Native, 0.0% Native Hawaiian/Other Pacific Islander, 0.8% Other, 0.5% Hispanic of any race (2010); Average household size: 2.48 (2010); Median age: 44.5 (2010); Males per 100 females: 98.6 (2010); Marriage status: 26.5% never married, 59.6% now married, 6.4% widowed, 7.6% divorced (2006-2010 5-year est.); Foreign born: 1.9% (2006-2010 5-year est.); Ancestry (includes multiple ancestries): 30.1% Italian, 27.1% German, 18.2% Irish, 9.0% English, 8.0% Polish (2006-2010 5-year est.).

Economy: Single-family building permits issued: 10 (2011); Multi-family building permits issued: 0 (2011); Employment by occupation: 11.6% management, 2.1% professional, 8.0% services, 16.0% sales, 3.8% farming, 9.0% construction, 7.1% production (2006-2010 5-year est.).

Income: Per capita income: $23,604 (2006-2010 5-year est.); Median household income: $51,353 (2006-2010 5-year est.); Average household income: $60,759 (2006-2010 5-year est.); Percent of households with income of $100,000 or more: 16.3% (2006-2010 5-year est.); Poverty rate: 10.0% (2006-2010 5-year est.).

Education: Percent of population age 25 and over with: High school diploma (including GED) or higher: 85.7% (2006-2010 5-year est.); Bachelor's degree or higher: 22.4% (2006-2010 5-year est.); Master's degree or higher: 7.7% (2006-2010 5-year est.).

Housing: Homeownership rate: 85.3% (2010); Median home value: $121,900 (2006-2010 5-year est.); Median contract rent: $423 per month (2006-2010 5-year est.); Median year structure built: 1960 (2006-2010 5-year est.).

Safety: Violent crime rate: 17.3 per 10,000 population; Property crime rate: 283.9 per 10,000 population (2011).

Transportation: Commute to work: 96.4% car, 0.0% public transportation, 1.5% walk, 1.5% work from home (2006-2010 5-year est.); Travel time to work: 38.0% less than 15 minutes, 38.8% 15 to 30 minutes, 10.0% 30 to 45 minutes, 9.0% 45 to 60 minutes, 4.1% 60 minutes or more (2006-2010 5-year est.)

Additional Information Contacts

Lawrence County Chamber of Commerce . . . . (724) 654-5593
  http://www.lawrencecountychamber.org
Shenango Township . . . . (724) 528-9571
  http://www.mcc.co.mercer.pa.us/TOWNSHIP/shenango.htm

SLIPPERY ROCK (township). Covers a land area of 29.852 square miles and a water area of 0.213 square miles. Located at 40.96° N. Lat; 80.22° W. Long.

Population: 3,140 (1990); 3,179 (2000); 3,283 (2010); Density: 110.0 persons per square mile (2010); Race: 99.0% White, 0.2% Black, 0.2% Asian, 0.0% American Indian/Alaska Native, 0.1% Native Hawaiian/Other Pacific Islander, 0.5% Other, 0.5% Hispanic of any race (2010); Average household size: 2.57 (2010); Median age: 43.3 (2010); Males per 100 females: 99.8 (2010); Marriage status: 21.0% never married, 65.4% now married, 4.6% widowed, 9.0% divorced (2006-2010 5-year est.); Foreign born: 1.7% (2006-2010 5-year est.); Ancestry (includes multiple ancestries): 29.1% German, 17.2% Irish, 14.2% English, 11.3% Polish, 10.8% Italian (2006-2010 5-year est.).

Economy: Single-family building permits issued: 0 (2011); Multi-family building permits issued: 0 (2011); Employment by occupation: 8.3% management, 4.1% professional, 9.3% services, 19.6% sales, 2.1% farming, 15.9% construction, 7.4% production (2006-2010 5-year est.).

Income: Per capita income: $21,008 (2006-2010 5-year est.); Median household income: $46,492 (2006-2010 5-year est.); Average household income: $55,406 (2006-2010 5-year est.); Percent of households with income of $100,000 or more: 11.8% (2006-2010 5-year est.); Poverty rate: 9.0% (2006-2010 5-year est.).

Education: Percent of population age 25 and over with: High school diploma (including GED) or higher: 89.1% (2006-2010 5-year est.); Bachelor's degree or higher: 16.3% (2006-2010 5-year est.); Master's degree or higher: 3.9% (2006-2010 5-year est.).

Housing: Homeownership rate: 86.1% (2010); Median home value: $131,300 (2006-2010 5-year est.); Median contract rent: $439 per month (2006-2010 5-year est.); Median year structure built: 1975 (2006-2010 5-year est.).

Transportation: Commute to work: 93.9% car, 0.0% public transportation, 2.2% walk, 3.9% work from home (2006-2010 5-year est.); Travel time to work: 22.4% less than 15 minutes, 42.5% 15 to 30 minutes, 23.4% 30 to 45 minutes, 9.6% 45 to 60 minutes, 2.2% 60 minutes or more (2006-2010 5-year est.)

Additional Information Contacts

Butler County Chamber of Commerce . . . . (724) 283-2222
  http://www.butlercountychamber.com

SOUTH NEW CASTLE (borough). Covers a land area of 0.324 square miles and a water area of 0 square miles. Located at 40.97° N. Lat; 80.35° W. Long. Elevation is 997 feet.

Population: 805 (1990); 808 (2000); 709 (2010); Density: 2,186.9 persons per square mile (2010); Race: 97.3% White, 1.3% Black, 0.3% Asian, 0.1% American Indian/Alaska Native, 0.0% Native Hawaiian/Other Pacific Islander, 1.0% Other, 0.6% Hispanic of any race (2010); Average household size: 2.54 (2010); Median age: 43.1 (2010); Males per 100 females: 97.5 (2010); Marriage status: 20.8% never married, 59.6% now married, 11.5% widowed, 8.1% divorced (2006-2010 5-year est.); Foreign born: 1.2% (2006-2010 5-year est.); Ancestry (includes multiple ancestries): 35.3% German, 31.9% Irish, 21.6% Italian, 11.9% Polish, 5.5% English (2006-2010 5-year est.).

Economy: Single-family building permits issued: 0 (2011); Multi-family building permits issued: 0 (2011); Employment by occupation: 1.1% management, 3.7% professional, 16.2% services, 16.5% sales, 0.7% farming, 11.4% construction, 9.2% production (2006-2010 5-year est.).

Income: Per capita income: $17,278 (2006-2010 5-year est.); Median household income: $41,042 (2006-2010 5-year est.); Average household income: $45,559 (2006-2010 5-year est.); Percent of households with income of $100,000 or more: 7.4% (2006-2010 5-year est.); Poverty rate: 18.8% (2006-2010 5-year est.).

Education: Percent of population age 25 and over with: High school diploma (including GED) or higher: 82.7% (2006-2010 5-year est.); Bachelor's degree or higher: 8.2% (2006-2010 5-year est.); Master's degree or higher: 3.3% (2006-2010 5-year est.).

Housing: Homeownership rate: 84.2% (2010); Median home value: $67,800 (2006-2010 5-year est.); Median contract rent: $344 per month (2006-2010 5-year est.); Median year structure built: 1944 (2006-2010 5-year est.).

Transportation: Commute to work: 97.8% car, 0.0% public transportation, 2.2% walk, 0.0% work from home (2006-2010 5-year est.); Travel time to work: 55.5% less than 15 minutes, 23.2% 15 to 30 minutes, 9.2% 30 to 45 minutes, 6.3% 45 to 60 minutes, 5.9% 60 minutes or more (2006-2010 5-year est.)

TAYLOR (township). Covers a land area of 5.213 square miles and a water area of 0.271 square miles. Located at 40.95° N. Lat; 80.36° W. Long.

Population: 1,326 (1990); 1,198 (2000); 1,052 (2010); Density: 201.8 persons per square mile (2010); Race: 98.3% White, 0.9% Black, 0.0% Asian, 0.0% American Indian/Alaska Native, 0.0% Native Hawaiian/Other Pacific Islander, 0.8% Other, 0.5% Hispanic of any race (2010); Average household size: 2.13 (2010); Median age: 52.1 (2010); Males per 100 females: 90.9 (2010); Marriage status: 29.1% never married, 54.0% now married, 6.5% widowed, 10.3% divorced (2006-2010 5-year est.); Foreign born: 1.5% (2006-2010 5-year est.); Ancestry (includes multiple ancestries): 33.3% Italian, 22.7% German, 12.0% Irish, 9.6% Polish, 4.4% English (2006-2010 5-year est.).

Economy: Single-family building permits issued: 0 (2011); Multi-family building permits issued: 0 (2011); Employment by occupation: 5.5% management, 1.8% professional, 11.1% services, 21.6% sales, 5.0% farming, 3.2% construction, 3.4% production (2006-2010 5-year est.).

Income: Per capita income: $17,859 (2006-2010 5-year est.); Median household income: $39,688 (2006-2010 5-year est.); Average household income: $41,797 (2006-2010 5-year est.); Percent of households with income of $100,000 or more: 4.4% (2006-2010 5-year est.); Poverty rate: 24.7% (2006-2010 5-year est.).

Education: Percent of population age 25 and over with: High school diploma (including GED) or higher: 81.9% (2006-2010 5-year est.); Bachelor's degree or higher: 6.7% (2006-2010 5-year est.); Master's degree or higher: 0.0% (2006-2010 5-year est.).

Housing: Homeownership rate: 77.0% (2010); Median home value: $77,300 (2006-2010 5-year est.); Median contract rent: $383 per month (2006-2010 5-year est.); Median year structure built: 1963 (2006-2010 5-year est.).

Transportation: Commute to work: 95.2% car, 1.6% public transportation, 0.0% walk, 1.6% work from home (2006-2010 5-year est.); Travel time to work: 43.3% less than 15 minutes, 35.7% 15 to 30 minutes, 8.2% 30 to 45 minutes, 9.3% 45 to 60 minutes, 3.5% 60 minutes or more (2006-2010 5-year est.)

Additional Information Contacts

Lawrence County Chamber of Commerce . . . . (724) 654-5593
    http://www.lawrencecountychamber.org

UNION (township). Covers a land area of 9.517 square miles and a water area of 0.098 square miles. Located at 41.01° N. Lat; 80.39° W. Long.

Population: 5,581 (1990); 5,103 (2000); 5,190 (2010); Density: 545.4 persons per square mile (2010); Race: 92.1% White, 5.3% Black, 0.3% Asian, 0.0% American Indian/Alaska Native, 0.0% Native Hawaiian/Other Pacific Islander, 2.3% Other, 1.1% Hispanic of any race (2010); Average household size: 2.35 (2010); Median age: 46.8 (2010); Males per 100 females: 92.0 (2010); Marriage status: 22.2% never married, 55.1% now married, 10.5% widowed, 12.2% divorced (2006-2010 5-year est.); Foreign born: 0.4% (2006-2010 5-year est.); Ancestry (includes multiple ancestries): 36.1% Italian, 24.0% German, 21.2% Irish, 14.4% Polish, 8.1% English (2006-2010 5-year est.).

Economy: Single-family building permits issued: 2 (2011); Multi-family building permits issued: 0 (2011); Employment by occupation: 5.8% management, 5.1% professional, 12.8% services, 20.2% sales, 4.3% farming, 8.7% construction, 8.3% production (2006-2010 5-year est.).

Income: Per capita income: $20,564 (2006-2010 5-year est.); Median household income: $41,378 (2006-2010 5-year est.); Average household income: $47,961 (2006-2010 5-year est.); Percent of households with income of $100,000 or more: 9.0% (2006-2010 5-year est.); Poverty rate: 9.6% (2006-2010 5-year est.).

Education: Percent of population age 25 and over with: High school diploma (including GED) or higher: 85.3% (2006-2010 5-year est.); Bachelor's degree or higher: 13.3% (2006-2010 5-year est.); Master's degree or higher: 4.1% (2006-2010 5-year est.).

Housing: Homeownership rate: 80.3% (2010); Median home value: $80,300 (2006-2010 5-year est.); Median contract rent: $569 per month (2006-2010 5-year est.); Median year structure built: 1958 (2006-2010 5-year est.).

Safety: Violent crime rate: 19.2 per 10,000 population; Property crime rate: 424.4 per 10,000 population (2011).

Transportation: Commute to work: 96.0% car, 1.0% public transportation, 2.4% walk, 0.6% work from home (2006-2010 5-year est.); Travel time to work: 43.7% less than 15 minutes, 32.2% 15 to 30 minutes, 9.6% 30 to 45

minutes, 8.0% 45 to 60 minutes, 6.5% 60 minutes or more (2006-2010 5-year est.)

Additional Information Contacts

Lawrence County Chamber of Commerce . . . . (724) 654-5593
    http://www.lawrencecountychamber.org
Union Township. . . . . (724) 658-7921

VILLA MARIA (unincorporated postal area)

Zip Code: 16155

Covers a land area of 0.677 square miles and a water area of 0 square miles. Located at 41.06° N. Lat; 80.51° W. Long. Elevation is 1,089 feet. Population: 103 (2010); Density: 152.1 persons per square mile (2010); Race: 100.0% White, 0.0% Black, 0.0% Asian, 0.0% American Indian/Alaska Native, 0.0% Native Hawaiian/Other Pacific Islander, 0.0% Other, 0.0% Hispanic of any race (2010); Average household size: 1.34 (2010); Median age: 80.4 (2010); Males per 100 females: 22.6 (2010); Homeownership rate: 12.2% (2010)

VOLANT (borough). Covers a land area of 0.112 square miles and a water area of 0.009 square miles. Located at 41.11° N. Lat; 80.26° W. Long. Elevation is 1,033 feet.

History: Covered bridges to Southwest.

Population: 152 (1990); 113 (2000); 168 (2010); Density: 1,495.5 persons per square mile (2010); Race: 99.4% White, 0.0% Black, 0.0% Asian, 0.0% American Indian/Alaska Native, 0.0% Native Hawaiian/Other Pacific Islander, 0.6% Other, 1.2% Hispanic of any race (2010); Average household size: 2.51 (2010); Median age: 37.0 (2010); Males per 100 females: 84.6 (2010); Marriage status: 17.3% never married, 61.8% now married, 8.2% widowed, 12.7% divorced (2006-2010 5-year est.); Foreign born: 0.0% (2006-2010 5-year est.); Ancestry (includes multiple ancestries): 37.2% German, 19.8% Irish, 12.2% Scotch-Irish, 11.6% English, 11.6% Dutch (2006-2010 5-year est.).

Economy: Single-family building permits issued: 0 (2011); Multi-family building permits issued: 0 (2011); Employment by occupation: 3.2% management, 0.0% professional, 17.5% services, 31.7% sales, 3.2% farming, 9.5% construction, 0.0% production (2006-2010 5-year est.).

Income: Per capita income: $11,912 (2006-2010 5-year est.); Median household income: $35,000 (2006-2010 5-year est.); Average household income: $33,053 (2006-2010 5-year est.); Percent of households with income of $100,000 or more: n/a (2006-2010 5-year est.); Poverty rate: 43.6% (2006-2010 5-year est.).

Education: Percent of population age 25 and over with: High school diploma (including GED) or higher: 97.7% (2006-2010 5-year est.); Bachelor's degree or higher: 19.5% (2006-2010 5-year est.); Master's degree or higher: 6.9% (2006-2010 5-year est.).

School District(s)

Wilmington Area SD (KG-12)
    2010-11 Enrollment: 1,386 . . . . (724) 656-8866

Housing: Homeownership rate: 61.2% (2010); Median home value: $76,700 (2006-2010 5-year est.); Median contract rent: $521 per month (2006-2010 5-year est.); Median year structure built: before 1940 (2006-2010 5-year est.).

Transportation: Commute to work: 76.2% car, 0.0% public transportation, 14.3% walk, 9.5% work from home (2006-2010 5-year est.); Travel time to work: 43.9% less than 15 minutes, 36.8% 15 to 30 minutes, 5.3% 30 to 45 minutes, 14.0% 45 to 60 minutes, 0.0% 60 minutes or more (2006-2010 5-year est.)

WAMPUM (borough). Covers a land area of 0.985 square miles and a water area of 0.046 square miles. Located at 40.89° N. Lat; 80.34° W. Long. Elevation is 761 feet.

History: Settled 1796, incorporated 1876.

Population: 666 (1990); 678 (2000); 717 (2010); Density: 728.3 persons per square mile (2010); Race: 94.3% White, 1.8% Black, 0.1% Asian, 0.6% American Indian/Alaska Native, 0.0% Native Hawaiian/Other Pacific Islander, 3.2% Other, 3.1% Hispanic of any race (2010); Average household size: 2.37 (2010); Median age: 42.6 (2010); Males per 100 females: 92.2 (2010); Marriage status: 29.7% never married, 50.8% now married, 9.8% widowed, 9.8% divorced (2006-2010 5-year est.); Foreign born: 1.1% (2006-2010 5-year est.); Ancestry (includes multiple ancestries): 44.9% German, 20.7% Irish, 20.6% Italian, 9.4% Scotch-Irish, 5.5% English (2006-2010 5-year est.).

Economy: Single-family building permits issued: 0 (2011); Multi-family building permits issued: 0 (2011); Employment by occupation: 7.7%

management, 0.8% professional, 12.9% services, 12.9% sales, 2.2% farming, 15.7% construction, 10.7% production (2006-2010 5-year est.).

Income: Per capita income: $19,194 (2006-2010 5-year est.); Median household income: $44,659 (2006-2010 5-year est.); Average household income: $48,475 (2006-2010 5-year est.); Percent of households with income of $100,000 or more: 8.1% (2006-2010 5-year est.); Poverty rate: 20.5% (2006-2010 5-year est.).

Education: Percent of population age 25 and over with: High school diploma (including GED) or higher: 94.4% (2006-2010 5-year est.); Bachelor's degree or higher: 14.6% (2006-2010 5-year est.); Master's degree or higher: 2.1% (2006-2010 5-year est.).

Housing: Homeownership rate: 66.2% (2010); Median home value: $82,200 (2006-2010 5-year est.); Median contract rent: $383 per month (2006-2010 5-year est.); Median year structure built: 1949 (2006-2010 5-year est.).

Safety: Violent crime rate: 0.0 per 10,000 population; Property crime rate: 111.3 per 10,000 population (2011).

Transportation: Commute to work: 87.1% car, 0.8% public transportation, 8.3% walk, 0.8% work from home (2006-2010 5-year est.); Travel time to work: 23.6% less than 15 minutes, 40.8% 15 to 30 minutes, 24.2% 30 to 45 minutes, 5.6% 45 to 60 minutes, 5.8% 60 minutes or more (2006-2010 5-year est.)

WASHINGTON (township).

Covers a land area of 16.167 square miles and a water area of 0.192 square miles. Located at 41.08° N. Lat; 80.22° W. Long.

Population: 671 (1990); 714 (2000); 799 (2010); Density: 49.4 persons per square mile (2010); Race: 99.5% White, 0.0% Black, 0.0% Asian, 0.0% American Indian/Alaska Native, 0.0% Native Hawaiian/Other Pacific Islander, 0.5% Other, 0.8% Hispanic of any race (2010); Average household size: 2.66 (2010); Median age: 43.1 (2010); Males per 100 females: 104.9 (2010); Marriage status: 24.9% never married, 65.7% now married, 2.8% widowed, 6.6% divorced (2006-2010 5-year est.); Foreign born: 1.4% (2006-2010 5-year est.); Ancestry (includes multiple ancestries): 24.2% German, 17.9% Irish, 9.8% Italian, 9.4% American, 9.3% Scotch-Irish (2006-2010 5-year est.).

Economy: Employment by occupation: 10.6% management, 2.3% professional, 10.8% services, 20.3% sales, 3.3% farming, 19.0% construction, 5.2% production (2006-2010 5-year est.).

Income: Per capita income: $22,628 (2006-2010 5-year est.); Median household income: $55,662 (2006-2010 5-year est.); Average household income: $61,691 (2006-2010 5-year est.); Percent of households with income of $100,000 or more: 13.2% (2006-2010 5-year est.); Poverty rate: 9.3% (2006-2010 5-year est.).

Education: Percent of population age 25 and over with: High school diploma (including GED) or higher: 92.0% (2006-2010 5-year est.); Bachelor's degree or higher: 20.5% (2006-2010 5-year est.); Master's degree or higher: 7.2% (2006-2010 5-year est.).

Housing: Homeownership rate: 85.0% (2010); Median home value: $143,400 (2006-2010 5-year est.); Median contract rent: $547 per month (2006-2010 5-year est.); Median year structure built: 1974 (2006-2010 5-year est.).

Transportation: Commute to work: 88.3% car, 0.0% public transportation, 6.4% walk, 5.3% work from home (2006-2010 5-year est.); Travel time to work: 33.7% less than 15 minutes, 41.6% 15 to 30 minutes, 17.4% 30 to 45 minutes, 2.6% 45 to 60 minutes, 4.7% 60 minutes or more (2006-2010 5-year est.)

WAYNE (township).

Covers a land area of 16.114 square miles and a water area of 0.224 square miles. Located at 40.89° N. Lat; 80.28° W. Long.

Population: 2,791 (1990); 2,328 (2000); 2,606 (2010); Density: 161.7 persons per square mile (2010); Race: 97.1% White, 0.7% Black, 0.9% Asian, 0.1% American Indian/Alaska Native, 0.0% Native Hawaiian/Other Pacific Islander, 1.2% Other, 1.3% Hispanic of any race (2010); Average household size: 2.47 (2010); Median age: 47.0 (2010); Males per 100 females: 98.2 (2010); Marriage status: 24.3% never married, 54.2% now married, 10.8% widowed, 10.7% divorced (2006-2010 5-year est.); Foreign born: 0.7% (2006-2010 5-year est.); Ancestry (includes multiple ancestries): 35.5% German, 22.0% Italian, 10.3% Irish, 10.0% English, 7.1% Polish (2006-2010 5-year est.).

Economy: Single-family building permits issued: 1 (2011); Multi-family building permits issued: 0 (2011); Employment by occupation: 8.6% management, 1.9% professional, 8.8% services, 12.2% sales, 3.1% farming, 13.1% construction, 14.1% production (2006-2010 5-year est.).

Income: Per capita income: $21,144 (2006-2010 5-year est.); Median household income: $46,111 (2006-2010 5-year est.); Average household income: $55,914 (2006-2010 5-year est.); Percent of households with income of $100,000 or more: 9.3% (2006-2010 5-year est.); Poverty rate: 3.8% (2006-2010 5-year est.).

Education: Percent of population age 25 and over with: High school diploma (including GED) or higher: 81.3% (2006-2010 5-year est.); Bachelor's degree or higher: 11.1% (2006-2010 5-year est.); Master's degree or higher: 2.6% (2006-2010 5-year est.).

Housing: Homeownership rate: 88.3% (2010); Median home value: $97,800 (2006-2010 5-year est.); Median contract rent: $412 per month (2006-2010 5-year est.); Median year structure built: 1955 (2006-2010 5-year est.).

Transportation: Commute to work: 94.1% car, 0.9% public transportation, 1.9% walk, 1.3% work from home (2006-2010 5-year est.); Travel time to work: 39.4% less than 15 minutes, 23.6% 15 to 30 minutes, 13.4% 30 to 45 minutes, 12.9% 45 to 60 minutes, 10.6% 60 minutes or more (2006-2010 5-year est.)

Additional Information Contacts

Lawrence County Chamber of Commerce . . . . (724) 654-5593
http://www.lawrencecountychamber.org

WEST PITTSBURG (CDP).

Covers a land area of 0.686 square miles and a water area of 0 square miles. Located at 40.93° N. Lat; 80.36° W. Long. Elevation is 860 feet.

Population: n/a (1990); n/a (2000); 808 (2010); Density: 1,177.9 persons per square mile (2010); Race: 98.5% White, 0.6% Black, 0.0% Asian, 0.0% American Indian/Alaska Native, 0.0% Native Hawaiian/Other Pacific Islander, 0.9% Other, 0.6% Hispanic of any race (2010); Average household size: 2.17 (2010); Median age: 50.8 (2010); Males per 100 females: 96.6 (2010); Marriage status: 25.8% never married, 59.9% now married, 7.0% widowed, 7.2% divorced (2006-2010 5-year est.); Foreign born: 2.1% (2006-2010 5-year est.); Ancestry (includes multiple ancestries): 37.4% Italian, 17.9% German, 9.8% Irish, 8.2% Polish, 4.5% Scotch-Irish (2006-2010 5-year est.).

Economy: Employment by occupation: 2.9% management, 0.0% professional, 15.0% services, 25.0% sales, 6.1% farming, 4.3% construction, 2.9% production (2006-2010 5-year est.).

Income: Per capita income: $18,572 (2006-2010 5-year est.); Median household income: $45,078 (2006-2010 5-year est.); Average household income: $44,853 (2006-2010 5-year est.); Percent of households with income of $100,000 or more: 2.9% (2006-2010 5-year est.); Poverty rate: 18.5% (2006-2010 5-year est.).

Education: Percent of population age 25 and over with: High school diploma (including GED) or higher: 79.8% (2006-2010 5-year est.); Bachelor's degree or higher: 6.6% (2006-2010 5-year est.); Master's degree or higher: 0.0% (2006-2010 5-year est.).

Housing: Homeownership rate: 76.9% (2010); Median home value: $76,400 (2006-2010 5-year est.); Median contract rent: $320 per month (2006-2010 5-year est.); Median year structure built: 1959 (2006-2010 5-year est.).

Transportation: Commute to work: 95.6% car, 0.0% public transportation, 0.0% walk, 2.2% work from home (2006-2010 5-year est.); Travel time to work: 42.7% less than 15 minutes, 40.1% 15 to 30 minutes, 9.7% 30 to 45 minutes, 4.9% 45 to 60 minutes, 2.6% 60 minutes or more (2006-2010 5-year est.)

WILMINGTON (township).

Covers a land area of 19.732 square miles and a water area of 0.182 square miles. Located at 41.11° N. Lat; 80.32° W. Long.

History: Westminister College. Covered bridge to Southeast; Amish Town Farm to North. Incorporated 1863.

Population: 2,467 (1990); 2,760 (2000); 2,715 (2010); Density: 137.6 persons per square mile (2010); Race: 98.7% White, 0.1% Black, 0.7% Asian, 0.0% American Indian/Alaska Native, 0.0% Native Hawaiian/Other Pacific Islander, 0.5% Other, 0.4% Hispanic of any race (2010); Average household size: 2.83 (2010); Median age: 39.0 (2010); Males per 100 females: 102.6 (2010); Marriage status: 29.8% never married, 56.6% now married, 5.2% widowed, 8.4% divorced (2006-2010 5-year est.); Foreign born: 0.9% (2006-2010 5-year est.); Ancestry (includes multiple ancestries): 37.5% German, 15.6% Irish, 10.2% English, 8.0% Scotch-Irish, 8.0% Dutch (2006-2010 5-year est.).

Economy: Single-family building permits issued: 2 (2011); Multi-family building permits issued: 0 (2011); Employment by occupation: 9.0%

management, 4.7% professional, 11.9% services, 10.7% sales, 4.7% farming, 13.2% construction, 3.3% production (2006-2010 5-year est.).
Income: Per capita income: $22,059 (2006-2010 5-year est.); Median household income: $49,036 (2006-2010 5-year est.); Average household income: $63,533 (2006-2010 5-year est.); Percent of households with income of $100,000 or more: 16.2% (2006-2010 5-year est.); Poverty rate: 8.7% (2006-2010 5-year est.).
Education: Percent of population age 25 and over with: High school diploma (including GED) or higher: 87.0% (2006-2010 5-year est.); Bachelor's degree or higher: 30.0% (2006-2010 5-year est.); Master's degree or higher: 11.7% (2006-2010 5-year est.).
Housing: Homeownership rate: 78.8% (2010); Median home value: $148,700 (2006-2010 5-year est.); Median contract rent: $561 per month (2006-2010 5-year est.); Median year structure built: 1972 (2006-2010 5-year est.).
Transportation: Commute to work: 89.0% car, 1.1% public transportation, 3.0% walk, 6.3% work from home (2006-2010 5-year est.); Travel time to work: 31.8% less than 15 minutes, 35.1% 15 to 30 minutes, 21.2% 30 to 45 minutes, 4.6% 45 to 60 minutes, 7.3% 60 minutes or more (2006-2010 5-year est.)
Additional Information Contacts
Lawrence County Chamber of Commerce . . . . (724) 654-5593
http://www.lawrencecountychamber.org

Lebanon County

Located in southeast central Pennsylvania; drained by Swatara Creek; includes Blue Mountain in the north, and Lebanon Valley in the south. Covers a land area of 361.833 square miles, a water area of 0.666 square miles, and is located in the Eastern Time Zone at 40.37° N. Lat., 76.46° W. Long. The county was founded in 1815. County seat is Lebanon.

Lebanon County is part of the Lebanon, PA Metropolitan Statistical Area. The entire metro area includes: Lebanon County, PA

Weather Station: Lebanon 2 W | | | | | | | | | Elevation: 450 feet

	Jan	Feb	Mar	Apr	May	Jun	Jul	Aug	Sep	Oct	Nov	Dec
High	37	41	50	62	72	80	84	83	75	64	53	41
Low	21	23	29	39	49	58	62	61	53	42	33	25
Precip	2.7	2.4	3.2	3.7	4.1	4.2	4.5	3.6	3.8	3.5	3.5	3.2
Snow	7.6	6.3	3.2	0.2	0.0	0.0	0.0	0.0	0.0	tr	0.6	4.0

High and Low temperatures in degrees Fahrenheit; Precipitation and Snow in inches

Population: 113,744 (1990); 120,327 (2000); 133,568 (2010); Race: 91.0% White, 2.2% Black, 1.1% Asian, 0.2% American Indian/Alaska Native, 0.0% Native Hawaiian/Other Pacific Islander, 5.5% Other, 9.3% Hispanic of any race (2010); Density: 369.1 persons per square mile (2010); Average household size: 2.49 (2010); Median age: 41.0 (2010); Males per 100 females: 95.3 (2010).
Religion: Six largest groups: 11.9% Methodist/Pietist, 9.1% Catholicism, 6.0% Lutheran, 5.9% Presbyterian-Reformed, 3.3% Non-Denominational, 3.3% European Free-Church (2010)
Economy: Unemployment rate: 6.9% (August 2012); Total civilian labor force: 74,438 (August 2012); Leading industries: 20.4% manufacturing; 17.5% health care and social assistance; 15.1% retail trade (2010); Farms: 1,193 totaling 113,486 acres (2007); Companies that employ 500 or more persons: 9 (2010); Companies that employ 100 to 499 persons: 62 (2010); Companies that employ less than 100 persons: 2,570 (2010); Black-owned businesses: n/a (2007); Hispanic-owned businesses: n/a (2007); Asian-owned businesses: 160 (2007); Women-owned businesses: 2,379 (2007); Retail sales per capita: $12,877 (2010). Single-family building permits issued: 159 (2011); Multi-family building permits issued: 16 (2011).
Income: Per capita income: $25,525 (2006-2010 5-year est.); Median household income: $52,356 (2006-2010 5-year est.); Average household income: $63,795 (2006-2010 5-year est.); Percent of households with income of $100,000 or more: 16.1% (2006-2010 5-year est.); Poverty rate: 8.9% (2006-2010 5-year est.); Bankruptcy rate: 2.66% (2011).
Taxes: Total county taxes per capita: $143 (2009); County property taxes per capita: $141 (2009).
Education: Percent of population age 25 and over with: High school diploma (including GED) or higher: 84.4% (2006-2010 5-year est.); Bachelor's degree or higher: 18.3% (2006-2010 5-year est.); Master's degree or higher: 6.1% (2006-2010 5-year est.).
Housing: Homeownership rate: 72.0% (2010); Median home value: $155,900 (2006-2010 5-year est.); Median contract rent: $534 per month

(2006-2010 5-year est.); Median year structure built: 1967 (2006-2010 5-year est.)
Health: Birth rate: 120.7 per 10,000 population (2011); Death rate: 103.1 per 10,000 population (2011); Age-adjusted cancer mortality rate: 180.5 deaths per 100,000 population (2009); Number of physicians: 22.5 per 10,000 population (2010); Hospital beds: 37.4 per 10,000 population (2008); Hospital admissions: 1,233.7 per 10,000 population (2008).
Environment: Air Quality Index: 71.6% good, 25.8% moderate, 2.6% unhealthy for sensitive individuals, 0.0% unhealthy (percent of days in 2011)
Elections: 2012 Presidential election results: 35.2% Obama, 63.4% Romney
National and State Parks: Memorial Lake State Park; Swatara State Park
Additional Information Contacts
Lebanon County Government . . . . (717) 274-2801
http://www.lebcounty.org

Lebanon County Communities

ANNVILLE (cdp/township). Covers a land area of 1.613 square miles and a water area of 0.009 square miles. Located at 40.33° N. Lat; 76.51° W. Long. Elevation is 420 feet.
Population: 4,300 (1990); 4,518 (2000); 4,767 (2010); Density: 2,955.3 persons per square mile (2010); Race: 94.4% White, 1.5% Black, 1.4% Asian, 0.1% American Indian/Alaska Native, 0.1% Native Hawaiian/Other Pacific Islander, 2.5% Other, 3.8% Hispanic of any race (2010); Average household size: 2.25 (2010); Median age: 26.6 (2010); Males per 100 females: 87.4 (2010); Marriage status: 54.5% never married, 32.1% now married, 7.0% widowed, 6.3% divorced (2006-2010 5-year est.); Foreign born: 4.7% (2006-2010 5-year est.); Ancestry (includes multiple ancestries): 27.4% German, 11.4% Irish, 8.0% Italian, 4.1% Polish, 4.0% English (2006-2010 5-year est.).
Economy: Employment by occupation: 6.9% management, 2.0% professional, 20.5% services, 19.9% sales, 6.4% farming, 3.1% construction, 3.9% production (2006-2010 5-year est.).
Income: Per capita income: $18,298 (2006-2010 5-year est.); Median household income: $53,500 (2006-2010 5-year est.); Average household income: $64,277 (2006-2010 5-year est.); Percent of households with income of $100,000 or more: 21.4% (2006-2010 5-year est.); Poverty rate: 11.4% (2006-2010 5-year est.).
Education: Percent of population age 25 and over with: High school diploma (including GED) or higher: 87.8% (2006-2010 5-year est.); Bachelor's degree or higher: 20.8% (2006-2010 5-year est.); Master's degree or higher: 6.1% (2006-2010 5-year est.).
School District(s)
Annville-Cleona SD (KG-12)
   2010-11 Enrollment: 1,562 . . . . (717) 867-7600
Housing: Homeownership rate: 58.9% (2010); Median home value: $143,500 (2006-2010 5-year est.); Median contract rent: $495 per month (2006-2010 5-year est.); Median year structure built: 1950 (2006-2010 5-year est.).
Safety: Violent crime rate: 2.1 per 10,000 population; Property crime rate: 154.7 per 10,000 population (2011).
Transportation: Commute to work: 84.9% car, 0.0% public transportation, 9.4% walk, 1.9% work from home (2006-2010 5-year est.); Travel time to work: 42.3% less than 15 minutes, 34.1% 15 to 30 minutes, 16.3% 30 to 45 minutes, 5.9% 45 to 60 minutes, 1.4% 60 minutes or more (2006-2010 5-year est.)

AVON (CDP). Covers a land area of 1.388 square miles and a water area of 0 square miles. Located at 40.34° N. Lat; 76.38° W. Long. Elevation is 479 feet.
Population: 2,644 (1990); 2,856 (2000); 1,667 (2010); Density: 1,201.1 persons per square mile (2010); Race: 94.8% White, 1.4% Black, 0.5% Asian, 0.0% American Indian/Alaska Native, 0.1% Native Hawaiian/Other Pacific Islander, 3.2% Other, 7.6% Hispanic of any race (2010); Average household size: 2.58 (2010); Median age: 41.2 (2010); Males per 100 females: 97.0 (2010); Marriage status: 20.0% never married, 61.7% now married, 7.7% widowed, 10.6% divorced (2006-2010 5-year est.); Foreign born: 6.7% (2006-2010 5-year est.); Ancestry (includes multiple ancestries): 49.4% German, 13.1% Italian, 11.8% Irish, 7.1% American, 4.8% Polish (2006-2010 5-year est.).

Economy: Employment by occupation: 13.2% management, 3.0% professional, 20.3% services, 17.6% sales, 2.3% farming, 9.1% construction, 10.3% production (2006-2010 5-year est.).

Income: Per capita income: $24,452 (2006-2010 5-year est.); Median household income: $59,083 (2006-2010 5-year est.); Average household income: $65,229 (2006-2010 5-year est.); Percent of households with income of $100,000 or more: 17.3% (2006-2010 5-year est.); Poverty rate: 3.2% (2006-2010 5-year est.).

Education: Percent of population age 25 and over with: High school diploma (including GED) or higher: 85.3% (2006-2010 5-year est.); Bachelor's degree or higher: 11.7% (2006-2010 5-year est.); Master's degree or higher: 2.7% (2006-2010 5-year est.).

Housing: Homeownership rate: 79.5% (2010); Median home value: $123,700 (2006-2010 5-year est.); Median contract rent: $513 per month (2006-2010 5-year est.); Median year structure built: 1964 (2006-2010 5-year est.).

Transportation: Commute to work: 86.4% car, 1.0% public transportation, 8.5% walk, 4.1% work from home (2006-2010 5-year est.); Travel time to work: 36.9% less than 15 minutes, 29.0% 15 to 30 minutes, 21.9% 30 to 45 minutes, 11.0% 45 to 60 minutes, 1.2% 60 minutes or more (2006-2010 5-year est.)

Additional Information Contacts

Lebanon Valley Chamber of Commerce . . . . (717) 273-3727
  http://www.lvchamber.org

BETHEL (township). Covers a land area of 34.585 square miles and a water area of 0.027 square miles. Located at 40.45° N. Lat; 76.42° W. Long.

Population: 4,343 (1990); 4,526 (2000); 5,007 (2010); Density: 144.8 persons per square mile (2010); Race: 96.6% White, 0.9% Black, 0.5% Asian, 0.1% American Indian/Alaska Native, 0.1% Native Hawaiian/Other Pacific Islander, 1.8% Other, 2.2% Hispanic of any race (2010); Average household size: 2.73 (2010); Median age: 40.2 (2010); Males per 100 females: 102.8 (2010); Marriage status: 24.9% never married, 56.6% now married, 3.5% widowed, 15.0% divorced (2006-2010 5-year est.); Foreign born: 0.4% (2006-2010 5-year est.); Ancestry (includes multiple ancestries): 43.9% German, 10.4% American, 9.4% Irish, 6.1% Pennsylvania German, 5.0% Italian (2006-2010 5-year est.).

Economy: Single-family building permits issued: 6 (2011); Multi-family building permits issued: 0 (2011); Employment by occupation: 9.1% management, 2.3% professional, 9.8% services, 15.6% sales, 7.0% farming, 15.6% construction, 7.5% production (2006-2010 5-year est.).

Income: Per capita income: $24,573 (2006-2010 5-year est.); Median household income: $55,330 (2006-2010 5-year est.); Average household income: $67,247 (2006-2010 5-year est.); Percent of households with income of $100,000 or more: 16.2% (2006-2010 5-year est.); Poverty rate: 7.5% (2006-2010 5-year est.).

Education: Percent of population age 25 and over with: High school diploma (including GED) or higher: 77.3% (2006-2010 5-year est.); Bachelor's degree or higher: 8.3% (2006-2010 5-year est.); Master's degree or higher: 4.4% (2006-2010 5-year est.).

Housing: Homeownership rate: 82.9% (2010); Median home value: $153,800 (2006-2010 5-year est.); Median contract rent: $573 per month (2006-2010 5-year est.); Median year structure built: 1973 (2006-2010 5-year est.).

Transportation: Commute to work: 94.9% car, 0.0% public transportation, 2.3% walk, 2.3% work from home (2006-2010 5-year est.); Travel time to work: 28.1% less than 15 minutes, 40.8% 15 to 30 minutes, 20.2% 30 to 45 minutes, 5.3% 45 to 60 minutes, 5.5% 60 minutes or more (2006-2010 5-year est.)

Additional Information Contacts

Lebanon Valley Chamber of Commerce . . . . (717) 273-3727
  http://www.lvchamber.org

CAMPBELLTOWN (CDP). Covers a land area of 2.929 square miles and a water area of 0 square miles. Located at 40.28° N. Lat; 76.58° W. Long. Elevation is 449 feet.

Population: 1,451 (1990); 2,415 (2000); 3,616 (2010); Density: 1,234.7 persons per square mile (2010); Race: 95.0% White, 1.0% Black, 2.3% Asian, 0.1% American Indian/Alaska Native, 0.0% Native Hawaiian/Other Pacific Islander, 1.6% Other, 2.3% Hispanic of any race (2010); Average household size: 2.58 (2010); Median age: 40.6 (2010); Males per 100 females: 92.2 (2010); Marriage status: 18.2% never married, 66.7% now married, 9.7% widowed, 5.4% divorced (2006-2010 5-year est.); Foreign born: 4.9% (2006-2010 5-year est.); Ancestry (includes multiple

ancestries): 48.8% German, 25.9% Irish, 13.3% English, 6.3% Pennsylvania German, 5.9% Italian (2006-2010 5-year est.).

Economy: Employment by occupation: 12.0% management, 4.8% professional, 7.7% services, 10.5% sales, 0.4% farming, 7.1% construction, 8.6% production (2006-2010 5-year est.).

Income: Per capita income: $28,515 (2006-2010 5-year est.); Median household income: $76,779 (2006-2010 5-year est.); Average household income: $83,102 (2006-2010 5-year est.); Percent of households with income of $100,000 or more: 31.7% (2006-2010 5-year est.); Poverty rate: 0.0% (2006-2010 5-year est.).

Education: Percent of population age 25 and over with: High school diploma (including GED) or higher: 94.0% (2006-2010 5-year est.); Bachelor's degree or higher: 31.3% (2006-2010 5-year est.); Master's degree or higher: 13.2% (2006-2010 5-year est.).

Housing: Homeownership rate: 79.7% (2010); Median home value: $193,400 (2006-2010 5-year est.); Median contract rent: $579 per month (2006-2010 5-year est.); Median year structure built: 1992 (2006-2010 5-year est.).

Transportation: Commute to work: 94.0% car, 0.7% public transportation, 2.9% walk, 1.7% work from home (2006-2010 5-year est.); Travel time to work: 30.7% less than 15 minutes, 38.3% 15 to 30 minutes, 21.7% 30 to 45 minutes, 4.0% 45 to 60 minutes, 5.2% 60 minutes or more (2006-2010 5-year est.)

Additional Information Contacts

Hershey Partnership Chamber of Commerce . . . . (717) 298-1359
  http://www.hersheypartnership.com

CLEONA (borough). Covers a land area of 0.839 square miles and a water area of 0 square miles. Located at 40.34° N. Lat; 76.48° W. Long. Elevation is 443 feet.

Population: 2,322 (1990); 2,148 (2000); 2,080 (2010); Density: 2,478.3 persons per square mile (2010); Race: 95.4% White, 1.0% Black, 1.0% Asian, 0.3% American Indian/Alaska Native, 0.0% Native Hawaiian/Other Pacific Islander, 2.3% Other, 3.1% Hispanic of any race (2010); Average household size: 2.41 (2010); Median age: 40.2 (2010); Males per 100 females: 97.0 (2010); Marriage status: 20.0% never married, 65.3% now married, 7.2% widowed, 7.5% divorced (2006-2010 5-year est.); Foreign born: 1.5% (2006-2010 5-year est.); Ancestry (includes multiple ancestries): 58.0% German, 11.4% Irish, 8.3% American, 6.4% Italian, 4.1% Pennsylvania German (2006-2010 5-year est.).

Economy: Employment by occupation: 8.4% management, 3.4% professional, 10.2% services, 18.5% sales, 5.7% farming, 9.8% construction, 6.7% production (2006-2010 5-year est.).

Income: Per capita income: $24,042 (2006-2010 5-year est.); Median household income: $57,660 (2006-2010 5-year est.); Average household income: $58,003 (2006-2010 5-year est.); Percent of households with income of $100,000 or more: 10.1% (2006-2010 5-year est.); Poverty rate: 3.7% (2006-2010 5-year est.).

Education: Percent of population age 25 and over with: High school diploma (including GED) or higher: 90.7% (2006-2010 5-year est.); Bachelor's degree or higher: 18.8% (2006-2010 5-year est.); Master's degree or higher: 4.3% (2006-2010 5-year est.).

School District(s)

Annville-Cleona SD (KG-12)
  2010-11 Enrollment: 1,562 . . . . (717) 867-7600

Housing: Homeownership rate: 78.0% (2010); Median home value: $142,300 (2006-2010 5-year est.); Median contract rent: $577 per month (2006-2010 5-year est.); Median year structure built: 1951 (2006-2010 5-year est.).

Safety: Violent crime rate: 0.0 per 10,000 population; Property crime rate: 76.7 per 10,000 population (2011).

Transportation: Commute to work: 95.1% car, 0.0% public transportation, 2.8% walk, 2.1% work from home (2006-2010 5-year est.); Travel time to work: 31.9% less than 15 minutes, 35.2% 15 to 30 minutes, 19.3% 30 to 45 minutes, 9.3% 45 to 60 minutes, 4.2% 60 minutes or more (2006-2010 5-year est.)

Additional Information Contacts

Lebanon Valley Chamber of Commerce . . . . (717) 273-3727
  http://www.lvchamber.org

COLD SPRING (township). Covers a land area of 24.810 square miles and a water area of 0.009 square miles. Located at 40.50° N. Lat; 76.60° W. Long.

Population: 42 (1990); 49 (2000); 52 (2010); Density: 2.1 persons per square mile (2010); Race: 100.0% White, 0.0% Black, 0.0% Asian, 0.0%

American Indian/Alaska Native, 0.0% Native Hawaiian/Other Pacific Islander, 0.0% Other, 0.0% Hispanic of any race (2010); Average household size: 2.48 (2010); Median age: 48.0 (2010); Males per 100 females: 136.4 (2010); Marriage status: 0.0% never married, 0.0% now married, 0.0% widowed, 100.0% divorced (2006-2010 5-year est.); Foreign born: 0.0% (2006-2010 5-year est.); Ancestry (includes multiple ancestries): 100.0% Irish, 100.0% German (2006-2010 5-year est.).

Economy: Employment by occupation: 0.0% management, 0.0% professional, 0.0% services, 0.0% sales, 0.0% farming, 0.0% construction, 100.0% production (2006-2010 5-year est.).

Income: Per capita income: $-1 (2006-2010 5-year est.); Median household income: n/a (2006-2010 5-year est.); Average household income: n/a (2006-2010 5-year est.); Percent of households with income of $100,000 or more: n/a (2006-2010 5-year est.); Poverty rate: 0.0% (2006-2010 5-year est.).

Education: Percent of population age 25 and over with: High school diploma (including GED) or higher: 100.0% (2006-2010 5-year est.); Bachelor's degree or higher: 100.0% (2006-2010 5-year est.); Master's degree or higher: 0.0% (2006-2010 5-year est.).

Housing: Homeownership rate: 80.9% (2010); Median home value: n/a (2006-2010 5-year est.); Median contract rent: n/a per month (2006-2010 5-year est.); Median year structure built: 1962 (2006-2010 5-year est.).

Transportation: Commute to work: 100.0% car, 0.0% public transportation, 0.0% walk, 0.0% work from home (2006-2010 5-year est.); Travel time to work: 0.0% less than 15 minutes, 100.0% 15 to 30 minutes, 0.0% 30 to 45 minutes, 0.0% 45 to 60 minutes, 0.0% 60 minutes or more (2006-2010 5-year est.)

CORNWALL (borough).
Covers a land area of 9.703 square miles and a water area of 0.054 square miles. Located at 40.26° N. Lat; 76.41° W. Long. Elevation is 620 feet.

History: Rich deposits of magnetite (mining stopped in 1972). Cornwall Iron Furnace historical site, operated 1742-1883. Incorporated 1926.

Population: 3,172 (1990); 3,486 (2000); 4,112 (2010); Density: 423.8 persons per square mile (2010); Race: 97.5% White, 0.6% Black, 0.9% Asian, 0.0% American Indian/Alaska Native, 0.0% Native Hawaiian/Other Pacific Islander, 1.0% Other, 1.8% Hispanic of any race (2010); Average household size: 2.24 (2010); Median age: 52.4 (2010); Males per 100 females: 87.4 (2010); Marriage status: 14.1% never married, 69.1% now married, 10.5% widowed, 6.4% divorced (2006-2010 5-year est.); Foreign born: 4.2% (2006-2010 5-year est.); Ancestry (includes multiple ancestries): 46.2% German, 12.4% Irish, 10.6% English, 6.6% Italian, 5.5% American (2006-2010 5-year est.).

Economy: Employment by occupation: 14.1% management, 1.7% professional, 7.8% services, 14.0% sales, 3.9% farming, 6.7% construction, 5.7% production (2006-2010 5-year est.).

Income: Per capita income: $38,195 (2006-2010 5-year est.); Median household income: $68,872 (2006-2010 5-year est.); Average household income: $87,141 (2006-2010 5-year est.); Percent of households with income of $100,000 or more: 28.8% (2006-2010 5-year est.); Poverty rate: 2.8% (2006-2010 5-year est.).

Education: Percent of population age 25 and over with: High school diploma (including GED) or higher: 92.3% (2006-2010 5-year est.); Bachelor's degree or higher: 35.2% (2006-2010 5-year est.); Master's degree or higher: 14.5% (2006-2010 5-year est.).

School District(s)
Cornwall-Lebanon SD (KG-12)
    2010-11 Enrollment: 4,650 . . . . (717) 272-2031

Housing: Homeownership rate: 79.5% (2010); Median home value: $213,900 (2006-2010 5-year est.); Median contract rent: $1,608 per month (2006-2010 5-year est.); Median year structure built: 1983 (2006-2010 5-year est.).

Safety: Violent crime rate: 2.4 per 10,000 population; Property crime rate: 2.4 per 10,000 population (2011).

Transportation: Commute to work: 92.3% car, 0.0% public transportation, 0.5% walk, 5.9% work from home (2006-2010 5-year est.); Travel time to work: 33.2% less than 15 minutes, 29.6% 15 to 30 minutes, 26.0% 30 to 45 minutes, 5.2% 45 to 60 minutes, 6.0% 60 minutes or more (2006-2010 5-year est.)

Additional Information Contacts
Lebanon Valley Chamber of Commerce . . . . (717) 273-3727
    http://www.lvchamber.org

EAST HANOVER (township).
Covers a land area of 32.460 square miles and a water area of 0.170 square miles. Located at 40.41° N. Lat; 76.59° W. Long. Elevation is 453 feet.

Population: 3,058 (1990); 2,858 (2000); 2,801 (2010); Density: 86.3 persons per square mile (2010); Race: 93.6% White, 1.7% Black, 1.1% Asian, 0.2% American Indian/Alaska Native, 0.0% Native Hawaiian/Other Pacific Islander, 3.4% Other, 5.1% Hispanic of any race (2010); Average household size: 2.49 (2010); Median age: 43.5 (2010); Males per 100 females: 103.4 (2010); Marriage status: 27.0% never married, 57.2% now married, 7.6% widowed, 8.2% divorced (2006-2010 5-year est.); Foreign born: 2.8% (2006-2010 5-year est.); Ancestry (includes multiple ancestries): 47.4% German, 9.7% Irish, 8.7% English, 6.2% Pennsylvania German, 6.1% American (2006-2010 5-year est.).

Economy: Employment by occupation: 9.1% management, 2.4% professional, 7.5% services, 18.8% sales, 4.9% farming, 17.1% construction, 16.5% production (2006-2010 5-year est.).

Income: Per capita income: $24,007 (2006-2010 5-year est.); Median household income: $57,381 (2006-2010 5-year est.); Average household income: $61,623 (2006-2010 5-year est.); Percent of households with income of $100,000 or more: 12.1% (2006-2010 5-year est.); Poverty rate: 1.4% (2006-2010 5-year est.).

Education: Percent of population age 25 and over with: High school diploma (including GED) or higher: 83.3% (2006-2010 5-year est.); Bachelor's degree or higher: 13.4% (2006-2010 5-year est.); Master's degree or higher: 3.2% (2006-2010 5-year est.).

School District(s)
Northern Lebanon SD (KG-12)
    2010-11 Enrollment: 2,386 . . . . (717) 865-2117

Housing: Homeownership rate: 80.3% (2010); Median home value: $182,800 (2006-2010 5-year est.); Median contract rent: $546 per month (2006-2010 5-year est.); Median year structure built: 1973 (2006-2010 5-year est.).

Transportation: Commute to work: 92.9% car, 1.3% public transportation, 1.7% walk, 2.9% work from home (2006-2010 5-year est.); Travel time to work: 29.9% less than 15 minutes, 43.4% 15 to 30 minutes, 21.5% 30 to 45 minutes, 3.2% 45 to 60 minutes, 2.0% 60 minutes or more (2006-2010 5-year est.)

Additional Information Contacts
Lebanon Valley Chamber of Commerce . . . . (717) 273-3727
    http://www.lvchamber.org

FORT INDIANTOWN GAP (CDP).
Covers a land area of 19.305 square miles and a water area of 0.166 square miles. Located at 40.45° N. Lat; 76.59° W. Long. Elevation is 571 feet.

Population: 299 (1990); 85 (2000); 143 (2010); Density: 7.4 persons per square mile (2010); Race: 97.9% White, 0.7% Black, 0.0% Asian, 0.0% American Indian/Alaska Native, 0.0% Native Hawaiian/Other Pacific Islander, 1.4% Other, 0.0% Hispanic of any race (2010); Average household size: 2.50 (2010); Median age: 46.8 (2010); Males per 100 females: 104.3 (2010); Marriage status: 2.5% never married, 78.3% now married, 0.0% widowed, 19.2% divorced (2006-2010 5-year est.); Foreign born: 0.0% (2006-2010 5-year est.); Ancestry (includes multiple ancestries): 41.7% German, 25.8% Pennsylvania German, 21.7% Irish, 11.7% English, 5.8% Italian (2006-2010 5-year est.).

Economy: Employment by occupation: 0.0% management, 0.0% professional, 3.0% services, 9.9% sales, 30.7% farming, 22.8% construction, 30.7% production (2006-2010 5-year est.).

Income: Per capita income: $34,687 (2006-2010 5-year est.); Median household income: $61,532 (2006-2010 5-year est.); Average household income: $59,463 (2006-2010 5-year est.); Percent of households with income of $100,000 or more: n/a (2006-2010 5-year est.); Poverty rate: 0.0% (2006-2010 5-year est.).

Education: Percent of population age 25 and over with: High school diploma (including GED) or higher: 81.2% (2006-2010 5-year est.); Bachelor's degree or higher: 0.0% (2006-2010 5-year est.); Master's degree or higher: 0.0% (2006-2010 5-year est.).

Housing: Homeownership rate: 56.3% (2010); Median home value: $47,600 (2006-2010 5-year est.); Median contract rent: n/a per month (2006-2010 5-year est.); Median year structure built: 1988 (2006-2010 5-year est.).

Transportation: Commute to work: 100.0% car, 0.0% public transportation, 0.0% walk, 0.0% work from home (2006-2010 5-year est.); Travel time to work: 53.5% less than 15 minutes, 33.7% 15 to 30 minutes, 5.9% 30 to 45 minutes, 6.9% 45 to 60 minutes, 0.0% 60 minutes or more (2006-2010 5-year est.)

FREDERICKSBURG (CDP). Covers a land area of 1.918 square miles and a water area of 0 square miles. Located at 40.44° N. Lat; 76.44° W. Long. Elevation is 476 feet.

History: Appalachian Trail passes to North, on Blue Mt. ridge.

Population: 872 (1990); 987 (2000); 1,357 (2010); Density: 707.4 persons per square mile (2010); Race: 95.2% White, 1.8% Black, 1.1% Asian, 0.0% American Indian/Alaska Native, 0.1% Native Hawaiian/Other Pacific Islander, 1.8% Other, 2.1% Hispanic of any race (2010); Average household size: 2.49 (2010); Median age: 40.4 (2010); Males per 100 females: 100.7 (2010); Marriage status: 21.4% never married, 69.3% now married, 1.9% widowed, 7.4% divorced (2006-2010 5-year est.); Foreign born: 1.7% (2006-2010 5-year est.); Ancestry (includes multiple ancestries): 50.8% German, 9.6% Irish, 7.4% Dutch, 4.9% West Indian, 4.3% English (2006-2010 5-year est.).

Economy: Employment by occupation: 6.2% management, 4.1% professional, 15.1% services, 17.6% sales, 6.7% farming, 11.9% construction, 11.0% production (2006-2010 5-year est.).

Income: Per capita income: $24,127 (2006-2010 5-year est.); Median household income: $58,512 (2006-2010 5-year est.); Average household income: $67,563 (2006-2010 5-year est.); Percent of households with income of $100,000 or more: 17.6% (2006-2010 5-year est.); Poverty rate: 3.4% (2006-2010 5-year est.).

Education: Percent of population age 25 and over with: High school diploma (including GED) or higher: 77.6% (2006-2010 5-year est.); Bachelor's degree or higher: 13.9% (2006-2010 5-year est.); Master's degree or higher: 7.4% (2006-2010 5-year est.).

School District(s)

Northern Lebanon SD (KG-12)

    2010-11 Enrollment: 2,386 . . . . (717) 865-2117

Housing: Homeownership rate: 76.8% (2010); Median home value: $128,000 (2006-2010 5-year est.); Median contract rent: $574 per month (2006-2010 5-year est.); Median year structure built: 1959 (2006-2010 5-year est.).

Transportation: Commute to work: 91.7% car, 0.0% public transportation, 8.3% walk, 0.0% work from home (2006-2010 5-year est.); Travel time to work: 38.4% less than 15 minutes, 29.9% 15 to 30 minutes, 23.4% 30 to 45 minutes, 6.2% 45 to 60 minutes, 2.1% 60 minutes or more (2006-2010 5-year est.)

Additional Information Contacts

Lebanon Valley Chamber of Commerce . . . . (717) 273-3727
    http://www.lvchamber.org

HEBRON (CDP). Covers a land area of 0.200 square miles and a water area of 0 square miles. Located at 40.34° N. Lat; 76.40° W. Long. Elevation is 509 feet.

Population: n/a (1990); n/a (2000); 1,305 (2010); Density: 6,524.1 persons per square mile (2010); Race: 84.8% White, 5.7% Black, 0.5% Asian, 0.4% American Indian/Alaska Native, 0.0% Native Hawaiian/Other Pacific Islander, 8.6% Other, 13.9% Hispanic of any race (2010); Average household size: 2.52 (2010); Median age: 42.1 (2010); Males per 100 females: 123.5 (2010); Marriage status: 39.9% never married, 31.3% now married, 15.7% widowed, 13.1% divorced (2006-2010 5-year est.); Foreign born: 0.6% (2006-2010 5-year est.); Ancestry (includes multiple ancestries): 14.2% German, 4.6% Irish, 3.9% Italian, 3.8% Dutch, 3.4% American (2006-2010 5-year est.).

Economy: Employment by occupation: 19.0% management, 0.0% professional, 10.3% services, 20.3% sales, 4.5% farming, 9.0% construction, 5.8% production (2006-2010 5-year est.).

Income: Per capita income: $16,748 (2006-2010 5-year est.); Median household income: $71,250 (2006-2010 5-year est.); Average household income: $67,266 (2006-2010 5-year est.); Percent of households with income of $100,000 or more: 6.2% (2006-2010 5-year est.); Poverty rate: 0.0% (2006-2010 5-year est.).

Education: Percent of population age 25 and over with: High school diploma (including GED) or higher: 61.8% (2006-2010 5-year est.); Bachelor's degree or higher: 5.4% (2006-2010 5-year est.); Master's degree or higher: 2.8% (2006-2010 5-year est.).

Housing: Homeownership rate: 71.3% (2010); Median home value: $98,700 (2006-2010 5-year est.); Median contract rent: $585 per month (2006-2010 5-year est.); Median year structure built: 1943 (2006-2010 5-year est.).

Transportation: Commute to work: 96.9% car, 0.0% public transportation, 0.0% walk, 3.1% work from home (2006-2010 5-year est.); Travel time to work: 34.8% less than 15 minutes, 29.7% 15 to 30 minutes, 15.0% 30 to

45 minutes, 20.4% 45 to 60 minutes, 0.0% 60 minutes or more (2006-2010 5-year est.)

HEIDELBERG (township). Covers a land area of 24.237 square miles and a water area of 0.010 square miles. Located at 40.29° N. Lat; 76.29° W. Long.

Population: 3,797 (1990); 3,832 (2000); 4,069 (2010); Density: 167.9 persons per square mile (2010); Race: 98.2% White, 0.4% Black, 0.4% Asian, 0.0% American Indian/Alaska Native, 0.0% Native Hawaiian/Other Pacific Islander, 1.0% Other, 0.9% Hispanic of any race (2010); Average household size: 2.96 (2010); Median age: 36.8 (2010); Males per 100 females: 103.5 (2010); Marriage status: 22.4% never married, 70.2% now married, 5.1% widowed, 2.3% divorced (2006-2010 5-year est.); Foreign born: 0.2% (2006-2010 5-year est.); Ancestry (includes multiple ancestries): 51.4% German, 11.3% Swiss, 6.7% Irish, 6.3% Italian, 6.3% English (2006-2010 5-year est.).

Economy: Employment by occupation: 8.8% management, 1.7% professional, 7.0% services, 12.1% sales, 2.3% farming, 14.2% construction, 14.0% production (2006-2010 5-year est.).

Income: Per capita income: $20,600 (2006-2010 5-year est.); Median household income: $56,797 (2006-2010 5-year est.); Average household income: $61,957 (2006-2010 5-year est.); Percent of households with income of $100,000 or more: 16.8% (2006-2010 5-year est.); Poverty rate: 8.6% (2006-2010 5-year est.).

Education: Percent of population age 25 and over with: High school diploma (including GED) or higher: 79.4% (2006-2010 5-year est.); Bachelor's degree or higher: 10.6% (2006-2010 5-year est.); Master's degree or higher: 4.8% (2006-2010 5-year est.).

Housing: Homeownership rate: 82.7% (2010); Median home value: $198,600 (2006-2010 5-year est.); Median contract rent: $527 per month (2006-2010 5-year est.); Median year structure built: 1960 (2006-2010 5-year est.).

Transportation: Commute to work: 86.9% car, 0.0% public transportation, 4.5% walk, 7.4% work from home (2006-2010 5-year est.); Travel time to work: 36.7% less than 15 minutes, 36.9% 15 to 30 minutes, 19.7% 30 to 45 minutes, 4.4% 45 to 60 minutes, 2.3% 60 minutes or more (2006-2010 5-year est.)

Additional Information Contacts

Lebanon Valley Chamber of Commerce . . . . (717) 273-3727
    http://www.lvchamber.org

JACKSON (township). Covers a land area of 24.056 square miles and a water area of 0.077 square miles. Located at 40.38° N. Lat; 76.33° W. Long.

Population: 5,732 (1990); 6,338 (2000); 8,163 (2010); Density: 339.3 persons per square mile (2010); Race: 97.7% White, 0.6% Black, 0.6% Asian, 0.1% American Indian/Alaska Native, 0.0% Native Hawaiian/Other Pacific Islander, 1.0% Other, 1.6% Hispanic of any race (2010); Average household size: 2.58 (2010); Median age: 43.8 (2010); Males per 100 females: 92.6 (2010); Marriage status: 14.5% never married, 70.5% now married, 8.6% widowed, 6.3% divorced (2006-2010 5-year est.); Foreign born: 1.2% (2006-2010 5-year est.); Ancestry (includes multiple ancestries): 45.9% German, 8.7% American, 7.4% Italian, 7.2% Irish, 5.9% English (2006-2010 5-year est.).

Economy: Single-family building permits issued: 19 (2011); Multi-family building permits issued: 4 (2011); Employment by occupation: 8.0% management, 1.5% professional, 10.2% services, 14.6% sales, 3.9% farming, 12.5% construction, 12.7% production (2006-2010 5-year est.).

Income: Per capita income: $29,147 (2006-2010 5-year est.); Median household income: $56,000 (2006-2010 5-year est.); Average household income: $72,664 (2006-2010 5-year est.); Percent of households with income of $100,000 or more: 17.5% (2006-2010 5-year est.); Poverty rate: 5.3% (2006-2010 5-year est.).

Taxes: Total city taxes per capita: $137 (2009); City property taxes per capita: $21 (2009).

Education: Percent of population age 25 and over with: High school diploma (including GED) or higher: 79.7% (2006-2010 5-year est.); Bachelor's degree or higher: 15.2% (2006-2010 5-year est.); Master's degree or higher: 5.3% (2006-2010 5-year est.).

Housing: Homeownership rate: 86.6% (2010); Median home value: $166,300 (2006-2010 5-year est.); Median contract rent: $620 per month (2006-2010 5-year est.); Median year structure built: 1979 (2006-2010 5-year est.).

Transportation: Commute to work: 90.9% car, 0.0% public transportation, 2.9% walk, 3.9% work from home (2006-2010 5-year est.); Travel time to

work: 32.5% less than 15 minutes, 38.6% 15 to 30 minutes, 13.9% 30 to 45 minutes, 8.0% 45 to 60 minutes, 6.9% 60 minutes or more (2006-2010 5-year est.)

Additional Information Contacts

Jackson Township............................... (717) 866-4771
  http://www.jacksontownship-pa.gov
Lebanon Valley Chamber of Commerce .... (717) 273-3727
  http://www.lvchamber.org

JONESTOWN (borough).
Covers a land area of 0.634 square miles and a water area of 0 square miles. Located at 40.41° N. Lat; 76.48° W. Long. Elevation is 482 feet.

History: Appalachian Trail passes to North on Blue Mt. ridge.

Population: 931 (1990); 1,028 (2000); 1,905 (2010); Density: 3,003.7 persons per square mile (2010); Race: 93.2% White, 1.9% Black, 1.1% Asian, 0.0% American Indian/Alaska Native, 0.0% Native Hawaiian/Other Pacific Islander, 3.8% Other, 5.6% Hispanic of any race (2010); Average household size: 2.70 (2010); Median age: 32.4 (2010); Males per 100 females: 105.3 (2010); Marriage status: 27.5% never married, 50.4% now married, 9.0% widowed, 13.1% divorced (2006-2010 5-year est.); Foreign born: 2.1% (2006-2010 5-year est.); Ancestry (includes multiple ancestries): 53.1% German, 18.6% Irish, 8.2% Pennsylvania German, 7.5% English, 5.9% American (2006-2010 5-year est.).

Economy: Employment by occupation: 9.4% management, 0.4% professional, 7.4% services, 16.1% sales, 3.5% farming, 12.2% construction, 9.4% production (2006-2010 5-year est.).

Income: Per capita income: $22,752 (2006-2010 5-year est.); Median household income: $48,125 (2006-2010 5-year est.); Average household income: $55,809 (2006-2010 5-year est.); Percent of households with income of $100,000 or more: 11.1% (2006-2010 5-year est.); Poverty rate: 7.6% (2006-2010 5-year est.).

Education: Percent of population age 25 and over with: High school diploma (including GED) or higher: 82.9% (2006-2010 5-year est.); Bachelor's degree or higher: 16.2% (2006-2010 5-year est.); Master's degree or higher: 4.1% (2006-2010 5-year est.).

School District(s)
Northern Lebanon SD (KG-12)
  2010-11 Enrollment: 2,386 .... (717) 865-2117

Housing: Homeownership rate: 73.6% (2010); Median home value: $156,500 (2006-2010 5-year est.); Median contract rent: $488 per month (2006-2010 5-year est.); Median year structure built: 1947 (2006-2010 5-year est.).

Transportation: Commute to work: 93.7% car, 0.0% public transportation, 4.1% walk, 1.3% work from home (2006-2010 5-year est.); Travel time to work: 31.6% less than 15 minutes, 33.4% 15 to 30 minutes, 21.1% 30 to 45 minutes, 10.3% 45 to 60 minutes, 3.6% 60 minutes or more (2006-2010 5-year est.)

Additional Information Contacts

Borough of Jonestown .... (717) 861-5414
  http://www.jonestownpa.org
Hershey Partnership Chamber of Commerce .... (717) 298-1359
  http://www.hersheypartnership.com

KLEINFELTERSVILLE (unincorporated postal area)
Zip Code: 17039

Covers a land area of 0.600 square miles and a water area of 0.009 square miles. Located at 40.29° N. Lat; 76.24° W. Long. Elevation is 581 feet. Population: 37 (2010); Density: 61.6 persons per square mile (2010); Race: 94.6% White, 5.4% Black, 0.0% Asian, 0.0% American Indian/Alaska Native, 0.0% Native Hawaiian/Other Pacific Islander, 0.0% Other, 5.4% Hispanic of any race (2010); Average household size: 2.85 (2010); Median age: 45.5 (2010); Males per 100 females: 105.6 (2010); Homeownership rate: 69.2% (2010)

LAWN (unincorporated postal area)
Zip Code: 17041

Covers a land area of 0.562 square miles and a water area of 0 square miles. Located at 40.21° N. Lat; 76.53° W. Long. Elevation is 479 feet. Population: 213 (2010); Density: 378.5 persons per square mile (2010); Race: 97.7% White, 0.0% Black, 1.4% Asian, 0.0% American Indian/Alaska Native, 0.0% Native Hawaiian/Other Pacific Islander, 0.9% Other, 0.0% Hispanic of any race (2010); Average household size: 2.84 (2010); Median age: 36.6 (2010); Males per 100 females: 117.3 (2010); Homeownership rate: 90.7% (2010)

LEBANON (city).
County seat. Covers a land area of 4.167 square miles and a water area of 0 square miles. Located at 40.34° N. Lat; 76.42° W. Long. Elevation is 469 feet.

History: Laid out in 1756 by George Steitz, the settlement at Lebanon was first known as Steitztown. Cedar trees growing in the vicinity may have reminded the Moravian settlers of the biblical "cedars of Lebanon," and thus inspired its name. The community was incorporated as a borough in 1821 and chartered as a city in 1868. Much of its industrial wealth was derived from iron works and rolling mills.

Population: 24,787 (1990); 24,461 (2000); 25,477 (2010); Density: 6,113.5 persons per square mile (2010); Race: 74.1% White, 5.9% Black, 1.1% Asian, 0.5% American Indian/Alaska Native, 0.0% Native Hawaiian/Other Pacific Islander, 18.4% Other, 32.1% Hispanic of any race (2010); Average household size: 2.42 (2010); Median age: 35.6 (2010); Males per 100 females: 93.7 (2010); Marriage status: 37.0% never married, 39.2% now married, 8.6% widowed, 15.2% divorced (2006-2010 5-year est.); Foreign born: 4.5% (2006-2010 5-year est.); Ancestry (includes multiple ancestries): 32.5% German, 11.7% Irish, 5.8% Italian, 4.0% Pennsylvania German, 3.8% American (2006-2010 5-year est.).

Economy: Unemployment rate: 9.4% (August 2012); Total civilian labor force: 13,151 (August 2012); Single-family building permits issued: 1 (2011); Multi-family building permits issued: 0 (2011); Employment by occupation: 7.1% management, 1.9% professional, 14.1% services, 17.0% sales, 6.6% farming, 7.0% construction, 7.9% production (2006-2010 5-year est.).

Income: Per capita income: $18,539 (2006-2010 5-year est.); Median household income: $33,840 (2006-2010 5-year est.); Average household income: $42,408 (2006-2010 5-year est.); Percent of households with income of $100,000 or more: 5.6% (2006-2010 5-year est.); Poverty rate: 22.9% (2006-2010 5-year est.).

Taxes: Total city taxes per capita: $255 (2009); City property taxes per capita: $87 (2009).

Education: Percent of population age 25 and over with: High school diploma (including GED) or higher: 76.2% (2006-2010 5-year est.); Bachelor's degree or higher: 9.1% (2006-2010 5-year est.); Master's degree or higher: 3.1% (2006-2010 5-year est.).

School District(s)
Cornwall-Lebanon SD (KG-12)
  2010-11 Enrollment: 4,650 .... (717) 272-2031
Lebanon County CTC (07-12)
  2010-11 Enrollment: n/a .... (717) 273-8551
Lebanon SD (PK-12)
  2010-11 Enrollment: 4,586 .... (717) 273-9391

Vocational/Technical School(s)
Empire Beauty School-Lebanon (Private, For-profit)
  Fall 2010 Enrollment: 107 .... (800) 223-3271
  2011-12 Tuition: $14,490
Lebanon County Area Vocational Technical School (Public)
  Fall 2010 Enrollment: 190 .... (717) 273-4401
  2011-12 Tuition: $10,500

Housing: Homeownership rate: 45.7% (2010); Median home value: $86,300 (2006-2010 5-year est.); Median contract rent: $470 per month (2006-2010 5-year est.); Median year structure built: 1945 (2006-2010 5-year est.).

Safety: Violent crime rate: 34.0 per 10,000 population; Property crime rate: 251.6 per 10,000 population (2011).

Newspapers: Area Merchandiser Dauphin Schuylkill Edition (Community news; Circulation 17,644); Area Merchandiser Gettysburg Edition (Community news; Circulation 19,673); Area Merchandiser Greater Reading Zone 1 Edition (Community news; Circulation 97,403); Area Merchandiser Hanover Edition (Community news; Circulation 36,822); Area Merchandiser Hershey Edition (Community news; Circulation 27,577); Area Merchandiser Lebanon Edition (Community news; Circulation 33,752); Area Merchandiser Myerstown Edition (Community news; Circulation 20,654); Area Merchandiser Northern Adams York Edition (Community news; Circulation 20,233); The Lebanon Daily News (Local news; Circulation 20,349); Lebanon Valley Review (Community news; Circulation 12,700); Palm Advertiser (Community news; Circulation 27,500); The Patriot-News - Lebanon Bureau (Local news)

Transportation: Commute to work: 89.1% car, 1.1% public transportation, 7.5% walk, 1.6% work from home (2006-2010 5-year est.); Travel time to work: 41.0% less than 15 minutes, 31.9% 15 to 30 minutes, 14.5% 30 to 45 minutes, 7.8% 45 to 60 minutes, 4.9% 60 minutes or more (2006-2010 5-year est.)

Additional Information Contacts

City of Lebanon . . . . (717) 273-6711
   http://www.lebanonpa.org
Lebanon Valley Chamber of Commerce . . . . (717) 273-3727
   http://www.lvchamber.org

LEBANON SOUTH (CDP). Covers a land area of 0.785 square miles and a water area of 0.003 square miles. Located at 40.33° N. Lat; 76.41° W. Long.

Population: 1,817 (1990); 2,145 (2000); 2,270 (2010); Density: 2,891.0 persons per square mile (2010); Race: 94.1% White, 0.9% Black, 1.5% Asian, 0.2% American Indian/Alaska Native, 0.0% Native Hawaiian/Other Pacific Islander, 3.3% Other, 4.2% Hispanic of any race (2010); Average household size: 2.23 (2010); Median age: 48.6 (2010); Males per 100 females: 89.3 (2010); Marriage status: 15.3% never married, 66.2% now married, 6.6% widowed, 12.0% divorced (2006-2010 5-year est.); Foreign born: 2.5% (2006-2010 5-year est.); Ancestry (includes multiple ancestries): 52.9% German, 13.5% English, 9.9% American, 8.4% Irish, 4.5% Dutch (2006-2010 5-year est.).

Economy: Employment by occupation: 5.4% management, 6.6% professional, 12.3% services, 15.6% sales, 1.5% farming, 13.7% construction, 13.0% production (2006-2010 5-year est.).

Income: Per capita income: $31,379 (2006-2010 5-year est.); Median household income: $56,133 (2006-2010 5-year est.); Average household income: $68,546 (2006-2010 5-year est.); Percent of households with income of $100,000 or more: 21.1% (2006-2010 5-year est.); Poverty rate: 5.2% (2006-2010 5-year est.).

Education: Percent of population age 25 and over with: High school diploma (including GED) or higher: 91.8% (2006-2010 5-year est.); Bachelor's degree or higher: 19.0% (2006-2010 5-year est.); Master's degree or higher: 4.7% (2006-2010 5-year est.).

Housing: Homeownership rate: 84.5% (2010); Median home value: $137,800 (2006-2010 5-year est.); Median contract rent: $542 per month (2006-2010 5-year est.); Median year structure built: 1957 (2006-2010 5-year est.).

Transportation: Commute to work: 96.2% car, 0.0% public transportation, 0.0% walk, 0.9% work from home (2006-2010 5-year est.); Travel time to work: 45.8% less than 15 minutes, 19.6% 15 to 30 minutes, 22.0% 30 to 45 minutes, 9.4% 45 to 60 minutes, 3.1% 60 minutes or more (2006-2010 5-year est.)

Additional Information Contacts

Lebanon Valley Chamber of Commerce . . . . (717) 273-3727
   http://www.lvchamber.org

MILLCREEK (township). Covers a land area of 20.427 square miles and a water area of 0.009 square miles. Located at 40.33° N. Lat; 76.21° W. Long.

Population: 2,687 (1990); 2,921 (2000); 3,892 (2010); Density: 190.5 persons per square mile (2010); Race: 97.7% White, 0.5% Black, 0.4% Asian, 0.1% American Indian/Alaska Native, 0.0% Native Hawaiian/Other Pacific Islander, 1.3% Other, 2.3% Hispanic of any race (2010); Average household size: 2.79 (2010); Median age: 36.9 (2010); Males per 100 females: 101.2 (2010); Marriage status: 20.7% never married, 62.3% now married, 7.7% widowed, 9.3% divorced (2006-2010 5-year est.); Foreign born: 3.7% (2006-2010 5-year est.); Ancestry (includes multiple ancestries): 42.0% German, 10.7% Irish, 7.2% American, 7.1% English, 6.9% Pennsylvania German (2006-2010 5-year est.).

Economy: Employment by occupation: 10.1% management, 1.4% professional, 11.3% services, 13.7% sales, 4.4% farming, 13.3% construction, 11.6% production (2006-2010 5-year est.).

Income: Per capita income: $22,919 (2006-2010 5-year est.); Median household income: $56,786 (2006-2010 5-year est.); Average household income: $65,945 (2006-2010 5-year est.); Percent of households with income of $100,000 or more: 12.5% (2006-2010 5-year est.); Poverty rate: 6.6% (2006-2010 5-year est.).

Education: Percent of population age 25 and over with: High school diploma (including GED) or higher: 78.9% (2006-2010 5-year est.); Bachelor's degree or higher: 11.4% (2006-2010 5-year est.); Master's degree or higher: 2.6% (2006-2010 5-year est.).

Housing: Homeownership rate: 83.4% (2010); Median home value: $171,100 (2006-2010 5-year est.); Median contract rent: $525 per month (2006-2010 5-year est.); Median year structure built: 1975 (2006-2010 5-year est.).

Safety: Violent crime rate: 12.8 per 10,000 population; Property crime rate: 130.6 per 10,000 population (2011).

Transportation: Commute to work: 89.4% car, 0.0% public transportation, 4.0% walk, 5.0% work from home (2006-2010 5-year est.); Travel time to work: 30.8% less than 15 minutes, 28.2% 15 to 30 minutes, 23.9% 30 to 45 minutes, 8.3% 45 to 60 minutes, 8.8% 60 minutes or more (2006-2010 5-year est.)

Additional Information Contacts

Ephrata Area Chamber of Commerce . . . . (717) 738-9010
   http://www.ephrata-area.org

MOUNT GRETNA (borough). Covers a land area of 0.144 square miles and a water area of 0 square miles. Located at 40.25° N. Lat; 76.47° W. Long. Elevation is 673 feet.

Population: 300 (1990); 242 (2000); 196 (2010); Density: 1,359.7 persons per square mile (2010); Race: 99.0% White, 0.0% Black, 0.0% Asian, 0.0% American Indian/Alaska Native, 0.0% Native Hawaiian/Other Pacific Islander, 1.0% Other, 0.5% Hispanic of any race (2010); Average household size: 1.87 (2010); Median age: 59.8 (2010); Males per 100 females: 106.3 (2010); Marriage status: 4.1% never married, 77.0% now married, 3.4% widowed, 15.5% divorced (2006-2010 5-year est.); Foreign born: 5.9% (2006-2010 5-year est.); Ancestry (includes multiple ancestries): 48.0% German, 32.2% Irish, 23.0% English, 6.6% Scotch-Irish, 5.9% Swiss (2006-2010 5-year est.).

Economy: Single-family building permits issued: 0 (2011); Multi-family building permits issued: 0 (2011); Employment by occupation: 29.4% management, 11.8% professional, 0.0% services, 17.6% sales, 2.5% farming, 3.4% construction, 0.0% production (2006-2010 5-year est.).

Income: Per capita income: $57,546 (2006-2010 5-year est.); Median household income: $88,571 (2006-2010 5-year est.); Average household income: $94,550 (2006-2010 5-year est.); Percent of households with income of $100,000 or more: 36.5% (2006-2010 5-year est.); Poverty rate: 0.0% (2006-2010 5-year est.).

Education: Percent of population age 25 and over with: High school diploma (including GED) or higher: 89.2% (2006-2010 5-year est.); Bachelor's degree or higher: 41.9% (2006-2010 5-year est.); Master's degree or higher: 29.7% (2006-2010 5-year est.).

Housing: Homeownership rate: 91.4% (2010); Median home value: $288,800 (2006-2010 5-year est.); Median contract rent: n/a per month (2006-2010 5-year est.); Median year structure built: before 1940 (2006-2010 5-year est.).

Hospitals: Philhaven Behavioral Healthcare Services (83 beds)

Safety: Violent crime rate: 0.0 per 10,000 population; Property crime rate: 0.0 per 10,000 population (2011).

Transportation: Commute to work: 71.3% car, 0.0% public transportation, 16.5% walk, 8.7% work from home (2006-2010 5-year est.); Travel time to work: 37.1% less than 15 minutes, 23.8% 15 to 30 minutes, 11.4% 30 to 45 minutes, 21.0% 45 to 60 minutes, 6.7% 60 minutes or more (2006-2010 5-year est.)

MOUNT GRETNA HEIGHTS (CDP). Covers a land area of 0.123 square miles and a water area of 0 square miles. Located at 40.25° N. Lat; 76.47° W. Long. Elevation is 722 feet.

Population: 445 (1990); 360 (2000); 323 (2010); Density: 2,620.8 persons per square mile (2010); Race: 98.1% White, 0.0% Black, 0.6% Asian, 0.0% American Indian/Alaska Native, 0.0% Native Hawaiian/Other Pacific Islander, 1.3% Other, 3.1% Hispanic of any race (2010); Average household size: 1.99 (2010); Median age: 54.4 (2010); Males per 100 females: 87.8 (2010); Marriage status: 13.4% never married, 65.2% now married, 14.0% widowed, 7.3% divorced (2006-2010 5-year est.); Foreign born: 0.0% (2006-2010 5-year est.); Ancestry (includes multiple ancestries): 32.9% English, 23.8% German, 17.7% Scottish, 17.1% Russian, 14.6% Irish (2006-2010 5-year est.).

Economy: Employment by occupation: 16.9% management, 0.0% professional, 6.5% services, 0.0% sales, 0.0% farming, 0.0% construction, 0.0% production (2006-2010 5-year est.).

Income: Per capita income: $44,055 (2006-2010 5-year est.); Median household income: $59,556 (2006-2010 5-year est.); Average household income: $78,586 (2006-2010 5-year est.); Percent of households with income of $100,000 or more: 24.1% (2006-2010 5-year est.); Poverty rate: 0.0% (2006-2010 5-year est.).

Education: Percent of population age 25 and over with: High school diploma (including GED) or higher: 100.0% (2006-2010 5-year est.); Bachelor's degree or higher: 54.2% (2006-2010 5-year est.); Master's degree or higher: 26.8% (2006-2010 5-year est.).

Housing: Homeownership rate: 87.1% (2010); Median home value: $280,000 (2006-2010 5-year est.); Median contract rent: n/a per month

(2006-2010 5-year est.); Median year structure built: before 1940 (2006-2010 5-year est.).
Transportation: Commute to work: 100.0% car, 0.0% public transportation, 0.0% walk, 0.0% work from home (2006-2010 5-year est.); Travel time to work: 20.8% less than 15 minutes, 70.1% 15 to 30 minutes, 9.1% 30 to 45 minutes, 0.0% 45 to 60 minutes, 0.0% 60 minutes or more (2006-2010 5-year est.)

MYERSTOWN (borough). Covers a land area of 0.856 square miles and a water area of 0 square miles. Located at 40.37° N. Lat; 76.31° W. Long. Elevation is 479 feet.

History: Laid out 1768, incorporated c.1910.
Population: 3,236 (1990); 3,171 (2000); 3,062 (2010); Density: 3,575.2 persons per square mile (2010); Race: 96.6% White, 1.0% Black, 0.6% Asian, 0.1% American Indian/Alaska Native, 0.0% Native Hawaiian/Other Pacific Islander, 1.7% Other, 2.4% Hispanic of any race (2010); Average household size: 2.37 (2010); Median age: 38.6 (2010); Males per 100 females: 88.7 (2010); Marriage status: 28.7% never married, 46.4% now married, 11.5% widowed, 13.3% divorced (2006-2010 5-year est.); Foreign born: 1.2% (2006-2010 5-year est.); Ancestry (includes multiple ancestries): 52.8% German, 12.8% American, 9.7% Irish, 9.1% English, 7.0% Italian (2006-2010 5-year est.).
Economy: Employment by occupation: 6.4% management, 1.3% professional, 19.3% services, 14.5% sales, 5.3% farming, 14.2% construction, 10.3% production (2006-2010 5-year est.).
Income: Per capita income: $20,320 (2006-2010 5-year est.); Median household income: $39,567 (2006-2010 5-year est.); Average household income: $48,880 (2006-2010 5-year est.); Percent of households with income of $100,000 or more: 9.0% (2006-2010 5-year est.); Poverty rate: 12.1% (2006-2010 5-year est.).
Education: Percent of population age 25 and over with: High school diploma (including GED) or higher: 85.9% (2006-2010 5-year est.); Bachelor's degree or higher: 14.3% (2006-2010 5-year est.); Master's degree or higher: 3.8% (2006-2010 5-year est.).

School District(s)
Eastern Lebanon County SD (KG-12)
    2010-11 Enrollment: 2,452 . . . . (717) 866-7117

Four-year College(s)
Evangelical Theological Seminary (Private, Not-for-profit, Evangelical Congregational Church)
    Fall 2010 Enrollment: 97 . . . . (717) 866-5775
Housing: Homeownership rate: 54.9% (2010); Median home value: $133,500 (2006-2010 5-year est.); Median contract rent: $516 per month (2006-2010 5-year est.); Median year structure built: 1953 (2006-2010 5-year est.).
Safety: Violent crime rate: 45.6 per 10,000 population; Property crime rate: 136.7 per 10,000 population (2011).
Transportation: Commute to work: 91.8% car, 0.0% public transportation, 5.5% walk, 1.6% work from home (2006-2010 5-year est.); Travel time to work: 29.1% less than 15 minutes, 33.6% 15 to 30 minutes, 23.5% 30 to 45 minutes, 9.5% 45 to 60 minutes, 4.4% 60 minutes or more (2006-2010 5-year est.)

Additional Information Contacts
Lebanon Valley Chamber of Commerce . . . . (717) 273-3727
    http://www.lvchamber.org

NEWMANSTOWN (CDP). Covers a land area of 2.200 square miles and a water area of 0 square miles. Located at 40.35° N. Lat; 76.21° W. Long. Elevation is 486 feet.

Population: 1,410 (1990); 1,536 (2000); 2,478 (2010); Density: 1,126.5 persons per square mile (2010); Race: 97.2% White, 0.8% Black, 0.4% Asian, 0.0% American Indian/Alaska Native, 0.0% Native Hawaiian/Other Pacific Islander, 1.6% Other, 3.0% Hispanic of any race (2010); Average household size: 2.62 (2010); Median age: 37.7 (2010); Males per 100 females: 101.1 (2010); Marriage status: 21.3% never married, 58.8% now married, 8.3% widowed, 11.6% divorced (2006-2010 5-year est.); Foreign born: 4.6% (2006-2010 5-year est.); Ancestry (includes multiple ancestries): 39.8% German, 13.5% Irish, 7.3% American, 6.5% English, 6.2% Italian (2006-2010 5-year est.).
Economy: Employment by occupation: 5.1% management, 1.1% professional, 12.0% services, 13.6% sales, 4.7% farming, 12.5% construction, 12.9% production (2006-2010 5-year est.).
Income: Per capita income: $23,157 (2006-2010 5-year est.); Median household income: $56,000 (2006-2010 5-year est.); Average household income: $63,904 (2006-2010 5-year est.); Percent of households with

income of $100,000 or more: 11.9% (2006-2010 5-year est.); Poverty rate: 6.6% (2006-2010 5-year est.).
Education: Percent of population age 25 and over with: High school diploma (including GED) or higher: 83.3% (2006-2010 5-year est.); Bachelor's degree or higher: 12.5% (2006-2010 5-year est.); Master's degree or higher: 1.9% (2006-2010 5-year est.).
Housing: Homeownership rate: 83.2% (2010); Median home value: $150,900 (2006-2010 5-year est.); Median contract rent: $525 per month (2006-2010 5-year est.); Median year structure built: 1974 (2006-2010 5-year est.).
Transportation: Commute to work: 94.1% car, 0.0% public transportation, 1.6% walk, 2.0% work from home (2006-2010 5-year est.); Travel time to work: 31.3% less than 15 minutes, 27.4% 15 to 30 minutes, 22.3% 30 to 45 minutes, 10.6% 45 to 60 minutes, 8.5% 60 minutes or more (2006-2010 5-year est.)

Additional Information Contacts
Ephrata Area Chamber of Commerce . . . . (717) 738-9010
    http://www.ephrata-area.org

NORTH ANNVILLE (township). Covers a land area of 17.252 square miles and a water area of 0.038 square miles. Located at 40.36° N. Lat; 76.54° W. Long.

Population: 2,435 (1990); 2,279 (2000); 2,381 (2010); Density: 138.0 persons per square mile (2010); Race: 98.6% White, 0.2% Black, 0.2% Asian, 0.0% American Indian/Alaska Native, 0.0% Native Hawaiian/Other Pacific Islander, 1.0% Other, 1.0% Hispanic of any race (2010); Average household size: 2.47 (2010); Median age: 47.3 (2010); Males per 100 females: 93.1 (2010); Marriage status: 25.3% never married, 61.8% now married, 7.3% widowed, 5.5% divorced (2006-2010 5-year est.); Foreign born: 1.0% (2006-2010 5-year est.); Ancestry (includes multiple ancestries): 61.9% German, 9.6% Irish, 7.5% American, 5.9% Swiss, 5.7% Italian (2006-2010 5-year est.).
Economy: Employment by occupation: 11.1% management, 2.2% professional, 12.4% services, 16.9% sales, 3.3% farming, 19.6% construction, 12.3% production (2006-2010 5-year est.).
Income: Per capita income: $26,304 (2006-2010 5-year est.); Median household income: $57,986 (2006-2010 5-year est.); Average household income: $66,296 (2006-2010 5-year est.); Percent of households with income of $100,000 or more: 15.3% (2006-2010 5-year est.); Poverty rate: 3.5% (2006-2010 5-year est.).
Education: Percent of population age 25 and over with: High school diploma (including GED) or higher: 88.6% (2006-2010 5-year est.); Bachelor's degree or higher: 13.4% (2006-2010 5-year est.); Master's degree or higher: 3.1% (2006-2010 5-year est.).
Housing: Homeownership rate: 77.5% (2010); Median home value: $165,200 (2006-2010 5-year est.); Median contract rent: $525 per month (2006-2010 5-year est.); Median year structure built: 1963 (2006-2010 5-year est.).
Transportation: Commute to work: 87.4% car, 1.0% public transportation, 5.1% walk, 3.8% work from home (2006-2010 5-year est.); Travel time to work: 30.3% less than 15 minutes, 44.4% 15 to 30 minutes, 14.7% 30 to 45 minutes, 5.3% 45 to 60 minutes, 5.3% 60 minutes or more (2006-2010 5-year est.)

Additional Information Contacts
Lebanon Valley Chamber of Commerce . . . . (717) 273-3727
    http://www.lvchamber.org

NORTH CORNWALL (township). Covers a land area of 9.498 square miles and a water area of 0 square miles. Located at 40.31° N. Lat; 76.45° W. Long. Elevation is 561 feet.

Population: 4,926 (1990); 6,403 (2000); 7,553 (2010); Density: 795.2 persons per square mile (2010); Race: 87.3% White, 4.1% Black, 2.8% Asian, 0.2% American Indian/Alaska Native, 0.0% Native Hawaiian/Other Pacific Islander, 5.6% Other, 10.9% Hispanic of any race (2010); Average household size: 2.53 (2010); Median age: 41.3 (2010); Males per 100 females: 92.1 (2010); Marriage status: 21.0% never married, 60.3% now married, 7.5% widowed, 11.1% divorced (2006-2010 5-year est.); Foreign born: 4.3% (2006-2010 5-year est.); Ancestry (includes multiple ancestries): 43.2% German, 8.2% Irish, 7.2% American, 6.9% Italian, 5.8% English (2006-2010 5-year est.).
Economy: Employment by occupation: 13.2% management, 5.4% professional, 8.9% services, 14.8% sales, 3.1% farming, 4.6% construction, 6.4% production (2006-2010 5-year est.).
Income: Per capita income: $32,227 (2006-2010 5-year est.); Median household income: $56,391 (2006-2010 5-year est.); Average household

income: $79,143 (2006-2010 5-year est.); Percent of households with income of $100,000 or more: 20.1% (2006-2010 5-year est.); Poverty rate: 5.4% (2006-2010 5-year est.).

Education: Percent of population age 25 and over with: High school diploma (including GED) or higher: 90.9% (2006-2010 5-year est.); Bachelor's degree or higher: 26.1% (2006-2010 5-year est.); Master's degree or higher: 9.4% (2006-2010 5-year est.).

Housing: Homeownership rate: 66.6% (2010); Median home value: $171,800 (2006-2010 5-year est.); Median contract rent: $638 per month (2006-2010 5-year est.); Median year structure built: 1977 (2006-2010 5-year est.).

Safety: Violent crime rate: 22.4 per 10,000 population; Property crime rate: 273.2 per 10,000 population (2011).

Transportation: Commute to work: 97.0% car, 0.2% public transportation, 0.6% walk, 1.9% work from home (2006-2010 5-year est.); Travel time to work: 42.9% less than 15 minutes, 28.8% 15 to 30 minutes, 16.0% 30 to 45 minutes, 9.1% 45 to 60 minutes, 3.2% 60 minutes or more (2006-2010 5-year est.)

Additional Information Contacts
Lebanon Valley Chamber of Commerce . . . . (717) 273-3727
  http://www.lvchamber.org
North Cornwall Township . . . . (717) 273-9200
  http://www.geocities.com/northcornwalltownship

NORTH LEBANON (township). Covers a land area of 16.748 square miles and a water area of 0.124 square miles. Located at 40.37° N. Lat; 76.42° W. Long.

Population: 9,741 (1990); 10,629 (2000); 11,429 (2010); Density: 682.4 persons per square mile (2010); Race: 92.3% White, 1.7% Black, 1.4% Asian, 0.1% American Indian/Alaska Native, 0.0% Native Hawaiian/Other Pacific Islander, 4.5% Other, 8.0% Hispanic of any race (2010); Average household size: 2.55 (2010); Median age: 44.1 (2010); Males per 100 females: 96.2 (2010); Marriage status: 19.8% never married, 64.1% now married, 7.9% widowed, 8.1% divorced (2006-2010 5-year est.); Foreign born: 4.7% (2006-2010 5-year est.); Ancestry (includes multiple ancestries): 42.9% German, 10.1% Irish, 8.0% American, 7.5% Italian, 3.9% English (2006-2010 5-year est.).

Economy: Employment by occupation: 6.0% management, 4.1% professional, 11.0% services, 20.2% sales, 3.4% farming, 9.3% construction, 10.4% production (2006-2010 5-year est.).

Income: Per capita income: $25,542 (2006-2010 5-year est.); Median household income: $57,987 (2006-2010 5-year est.); Average household income: $66,853 (2006-2010 5-year est.); Percent of households with income of $100,000 or more: 13.5% (2006-2010 5-year est.); Poverty rate: 5.8% (2006-2010 5-year est.).

Education: Percent of population age 25 and over with: High school diploma (including GED) or higher: 83.6% (2006-2010 5-year est.); Bachelor's degree or higher: 16.1% (2006-2010 5-year est.); Master's degree or higher: 3.7% (2006-2010 5-year est.).

Housing: Homeownership rate: 85.3% (2010); Median home value: $156,200 (2006-2010 5-year est.); Median contract rent: $665 per month (2006-2010 5-year est.); Median year structure built: 1977 (2006-2010 5-year est.).

Safety: Violent crime rate: 11.3 per 10,000 population; Property crime rate: 246.0 per 10,000 population (2011).

Transportation: Commute to work: 94.6% car, 0.9% public transportation, 1.9% walk, 2.0% work from home (2006-2010 5-year est.); Travel time to work: 31.9% less than 15 minutes, 35.6% 15 to 30 minutes, 16.2% 30 to 45 minutes, 10.9% 45 to 60 minutes, 5.5% 60 minutes or more (2006-2010 5-year est.)

Additional Information Contacts
Lebanon Valley Chamber of Commerce . . . . (717) 273-3727
  http://www.lvchamber.org
North Lebanon Township . . . . (717) 273-7132
  http://www.twp.northlebanon.pa.us

NORTH LONDONDERRY (township). Covers a land area of 10.760 square miles and a water area of 0.006 square miles. Located at 40.32° N. Lat; 76.58° W. Long.

Population: 5,848 (1990); 6,771 (2000); 8,068 (2010); Density: 749.8 persons per square mile (2010); Race: 96.5% White, 0.7% Black, 1.6% Asian, 0.1% American Indian/Alaska Native, 0.0% Native Hawaiian/Other Pacific Islander, 1.1% Other, 1.5% Hispanic of any race (2010); Average household size: 2.41 (2010); Median age: 48.0 (2010); Males per 100 females: 89.3 (2010); Marriage status: 16.8% never married, 66.3% now

married, 9.5% widowed, 7.4% divorced (2006-2010 5-year est.); Foreign born: 3.0% (2006-2010 5-year est.); Ancestry (includes multiple ancestries): 48.9% German, 14.5% Irish, 8.7% English, 7.6% Italian, 5.5% Polish (2006-2010 5-year est.).

Economy: Employment by occupation: 23.0% management, 4.2% professional, 10.4% services, 17.5% sales, 1.5% farming, 3.3% construction, 3.5% production (2006-2010 5-year est.).

Income: Per capita income: $34,108 (2006-2010 5-year est.); Median household income: $67,875 (2006-2010 5-year est.); Average household income: $80,251 (2006-2010 5-year est.); Percent of households with income of $100,000 or more: 29.0% (2006-2010 5-year est.); Poverty rate: 2.3% (2006-2010 5-year est.).

Education: Percent of population age 25 and over with: High school diploma (including GED) or higher: 92.1% (2006-2010 5-year est.); Bachelor's degree or higher: 34.5% (2006-2010 5-year est.); Master's degree or higher: 8.9% (2006-2010 5-year est.).

Housing: Homeownership rate: 85.6% (2010); Median home value: $191,400 (2006-2010 5-year est.); Median contract rent: $582 per month (2006-2010 5-year est.); Median year structure built: 1983 (2006-2010 5-year est.).

Safety: Violent crime rate: 2.5 per 10,000 population; Property crime rate: 128.5 per 10,000 population (2011).

Transportation: Commute to work: 97.1% car, 0.4% public transportation, 0.3% walk, 1.5% work from home (2006-2010 5-year est.); Travel time to work: 37.0% less than 15 minutes, 34.6% 15 to 30 minutes, 20.0% 30 to 45 minutes, 5.4% 45 to 60 minutes, 3.0% 60 minutes or more (2006-2010 5-year est.)

Additional Information Contacts
Lebanon Valley Chamber of Commerce . . . . (717) 273-3727
  http://www.lvchamber.org
North Londonderry Township . . . . (717) 838-1373
  http://www.nlondtwp.com

ONO (unincorporated postal area)
Zip Code: 17077

Covers a land area of 0.003 square miles and a water area of 0 square miles. Located at 40.40° N. Lat; 76.53° W. Long. Elevation is 512 feet. Population: 46 (2010); Density: 12,820.5 persons per square mile (2010); Race: 97.8% White, 0.0% Black, 0.0% Asian, 0.0% American Indian/Alaska Native, 0.0% Native Hawaiian/Other Pacific Islander, 2.2% Other, 2.2% Hispanic of any race (2010); Average household size: 2.88 (2010); Median age: 24.0 (2010); Males per 100 females: 58.6 (2010); Homeownership rate: 31.3% (2010)

PALMYRA (borough). Covers a land area of 1.926 square miles and a water area of 0 square miles. Located at 40.31° N. Lat; 76.59° W. Long. Elevation is 456 feet.

History: Settled 1749, incorporated 1913.

Population: 6,910 (1990); 7,096 (2000); 7,320 (2010); Density: 3,801.5 persons per square mile (2010); Race: 95.2% White, 1.0% Black, 1.6% Asian, 0.2% American Indian/Alaska Native, 0.0% Native Hawaiian/Other Pacific Islander, 2.0% Other, 3.0% Hispanic of any race (2010); Average household size: 2.23 (2010); Median age: 40.2 (2010); Males per 100 females: 91.7 (2010); Marriage status: 21.8% never married, 56.9% now married, 5.8% widowed, 15.5% divorced (2006-2010 5-year est.); Foreign born: 1.7% (2006-2010 5-year est.); Ancestry (includes multiple ancestries): 47.7% German, 16.6% Irish, 8.6% Italian, 7.6% American, 6.8% English (2006-2010 5-year est.).

Economy: Employment by occupation: 9.1% management, 1.5% professional, 9.3% services, 20.1% sales, 6.3% farming, 7.0% construction, 7.3% production (2006-2010 5-year est.).

Income: Per capita income: $26,798 (2006-2010 5-year est.); Median household income: $46,881 (2006-2010 5-year est.); Average household income: $58,337 (2006-2010 5-year est.); Percent of households with income of $100,000 or more: 11.6% (2006-2010 5-year est.); Poverty rate: 6.7% (2006-2010 5-year est.).

Taxes: Total city taxes per capita: $277 (2009); City property taxes per capita: $140 (2009).

Education: Percent of population age 25 and over with: High school diploma (including GED) or higher: 88.0% (2006-2010 5-year est.); Bachelor's degree or higher: 21.0% (2006-2010 5-year est.); Master's degree or higher: 7.3% (2006-2010 5-year est.).

School District(s)
Palmyra Area SD (KG-12)
  2010-11 Enrollment: 3,248 . . . . (717) 838-3144

Housing: Homeownership rate: 57.9% (2010); Median home value: $141,000 (2006-2010 5-year est.); Median contract rent: $539 per month (2006-2010 5-year est.); Median year structure built: 1954 (2006-2010 5-year est.).

Safety: Violent crime rate: 12.3 per 10,000 population; Property crime rate: 183.8 per 10,000 population (2011).

Transportation: Commute to work: 95.5% car, 0.0% public transportation, 3.4% walk, 0.3% work from home (2006-2010 5-year est.); Travel time to work: 29.4% less than 15 minutes, 40.8% 15 to 30 minutes, 23.3% 30 to 45 minutes, 4.1% 45 to 60 minutes, 2.4% 60 minutes or more (2006-2010 5-year est.).

Additional Information Contacts

Borough of Palmyra. . . . . (717) 838-6361
  http://psabcontent.com/palmyraborough/content/index.php
Lebanon Valley Chamber of Commerce . . . . (717) 273-3727
  http://www.lvchamber.org

PLEASANT HILL (CDP). Covers a land area of 0.744 square miles and a water area of 0.006 square miles. Located at 40.34° N. Lat; 76.45° W. Long. Elevation is 456 feet.

Population: 1,659 (1990); 2,301 (2000); 2,643 (2010); Density: 3,550.8 persons per square mile (2010); Race: 78.8% White, 7.0% Black, 2.9% Asian, 0.5% American Indian/Alaska Native, 0.0% Native Hawaiian/Other Pacific Islander, 10.8% Other, 21.6% Hispanic of any race (2010); Average household size: 2.54 (2010); Median age: 31.6 (2010); Males per 100 females: 86.9 (2010); Marriage status: 23.4% never married, 56.3% now married, 5.7% widowed, 14.6% divorced (2006-2010 5-year est.); Foreign born: 6.1% (2006-2010 5-year est.); Ancestry (includes multiple ancestries): 42.8% German, 7.0% American, 6.6% Irish, 5.8% French, 4.6% Hungarian (2006-2010 5-year est.).

Economy: Employment by occupation: 8.2% management, 4.0% professional, 11.9% services, 11.6% sales, 1.4% farming, 5.1% construction, 13.4% production (2006-2010 5-year est.).

Income: Per capita income: $22,437 (2006-2010 5-year est.); Median household income: $44,846 (2006-2010 5-year est.); Average household income: $55,590 (2006-2010 5-year est.); Percent of households with income of $100,000 or more: 5.1% (2006-2010 5-year est.); Poverty rate: 11.0% (2006-2010 5-year est.).

Education: Percent of population age 25 and over with: High school diploma (including GED) or higher: 88.6% (2006-2010 5-year est.); Bachelor's degree or higher: 16.3% (2006-2010 5-year est.); Master's degree or higher: 5.1% (2006-2010 5-year est.).

Housing: Homeownership rate: 58.3% (2010); Median home value: $100,900 (2006-2010 5-year est.); Median contract rent: $600 per month (2006-2010 5-year est.); Median year structure built: 1982 (2006-2010 5-year est.).

Transportation: Commute to work: 97.2% car, 0.5% public transportation, 1.4% walk, 0.0% work from home (2006-2010 5-year est.); Travel time to work: 39.9% less than 15 minutes, 33.2% 15 to 30 minutes, 17.6% 30 to 45 minutes, 6.8% 45 to 60 minutes, 2.6% 60 minutes or more (2006-2010 5-year est.).

Additional Information Contacts

Lebanon Valley Chamber of Commerce . . . . (717) 273-3727
  http://www.lvchamber.org

QUENTIN (CDP). Aka Bismarck. Covers a land area of 0.637 square miles and a water area of 0 square miles. Located at 40.28° N. Lat; 76.44° W. Long. Elevation is 558 feet.

Population: 517 (1990); 529 (2000); 594 (2010); Density: 932.1 persons per square mile (2010); Race: 96.6% White, 0.2% Black, 0.5% Asian, 0.2% American Indian/Alaska Native, 0.0% Native Hawaiian/Other Pacific Islander, 2.5% Other, 2.5% Hispanic of any race (2010); Average household size: 2.27 (2010); Median age: 40.5 (2010); Males per 100 females: 87.4 (2010); Marriage status: 21.6% never married, 59.0% now married, 8.1% widowed, 11.4% divorced (2006-2010 5-year est.); Foreign born: 3.7% (2006-2010 5-year est.); Ancestry (includes multiple ancestries): 60.0% German, 20.3% Irish, 9.3% Italian, 4.1% Pennsylvania German, 3.7% English (2006-2010 5-year est.).

Economy: Employment by occupation: 9.2% management, 7.0% professional, 13.7% services, 22.9% sales, 5.4% farming, 11.6% construction, 3.0% production (2006-2010 5-year est.).

Income: Per capita income: $33,545 (2006-2010 5-year est.); Median household income: $54,306 (2006-2010 5-year est.); Average household income: $63,737 (2006-2010 5-year est.); Percent of households with income of $100,000 or more: 25.7% (2006-2010 5-year est.); Poverty rate: 7.0% (2006-2010 5-year est.).

Education: Percent of population age 25 and over with: High school diploma (including GED) or higher: 95.1% (2006-2010 5-year est.); Bachelor's degree or higher: 16.8% (2006-2010 5-year est.); Master's degree or higher: 4.4% (2006-2010 5-year est.).

Housing: Homeownership rate: 83.2% (2010); Median home value: $133,100 (2006-2010 5-year est.); Median contract rent: $596 per month (2006-2010 5-year est.); Median year structure built: 1957 (2006-2010 5-year est.).

Transportation: Commute to work: 98.2% car, 0.0% public transportation, 0.0% walk, 1.8% work from home (2006-2010 5-year est.); Travel time to work: 45.3% less than 15 minutes, 34.3% 15 to 30 minutes, 14.0% 30 to 45 minutes, 4.6% 45 to 60 minutes, 1.8% 60 minutes or more (2006-2010 5-year est.).

RICHLAND (borough). Covers a land area of 1.386 square miles and a water area of 0 square miles. Located at 40.36° N. Lat; 76.26° W. Long. Elevation is 492 feet.

History: Incorporated 1906.

Population: 1,457 (1990); 1,508 (2000); 1,519 (2010); Density: 1,095.7 persons per square mile (2010); Race: 97.3% White, 0.3% Black, 0.1% Asian, 0.1% American Indian/Alaska Native, 0.0% Native Hawaiian/Other Pacific Islander, 2.2% Other, 3.0% Hispanic of any race (2010); Average household size: 2.50 (2010); Median age: 39.4 (2010); Males per 100 females: 102.8 (2010); Marriage status: 20.0% never married, 64.0% now married, 6.7% widowed, 9.3% divorced (2006-2010 5-year est.); Foreign born: 0.5% (2006-2010 5-year est.); Ancestry (includes multiple ancestries): 59.3% German, 8.6% Irish, 8.5% American, 7.0% Pennsylvania German, 4.0% Italian (2006-2010 5-year est.).

Economy: Employment by occupation: 5.6% management, 1.0% professional, 11.8% services, 17.6% sales, 1.9% farming, 13.2% construction, 13.2% production (2006-2010 5-year est.).

Income: Per capita income: $25,612 (2006-2010 5-year est.); Median household income: $52,716 (2006-2010 5-year est.); Average household income: $60,183 (2006-2010 5-year est.); Percent of households with income of $100,000 or more: 6.9% (2006-2010 5-year est.); Poverty rate: 3.2% (2006-2010 5-year est.).

Education: Percent of population age 25 and over with: High school diploma (including GED) or higher: 88.3% (2006-2010 5-year est.); Bachelor's degree or higher: 11.3% (2006-2010 5-year est.); Master's degree or higher: 2.4% (2006-2010 5-year est.).

School District(s)

Eastern Lebanon County SD (KG-12)
    2010-11 Enrollment: 2,452 . . . . (717) 866-7117

Housing: Homeownership rate: 82.5% (2010); Median home value: $150,100 (2006-2010 5-year est.); Median contract rent: $499 per month (2006-2010 5-year est.); Median year structure built: 1954 (2006-2010 5-year est.).

Transportation: Commute to work: 92.6% car, 0.0% public transportation, 3.1% walk, 3.1% work from home (2006-2010 5-year est.); Travel time to work: 30.5% less than 15 minutes, 37.4% 15 to 30 minutes, 16.7% 30 to 45 minutes, 9.7% 45 to 60 minutes, 5.7% 60 minutes or more (2006-2010 5-year est.).

Additional Information Contacts

Lebanon Valley Chamber of Commerce . . . . (717) 273-3727
  http://www.lvchamber.org

SAND HILL (CDP). Covers a land area of 1.007 square miles and a water area of 0 square miles. Located at 40.36° N. Lat; 76.42° W. Long. Elevation is 614 feet.

Population: 2,247 (1990); 2,345 (2000); 2,496 (2010); Density: 2,477.5 persons per square mile (2010); Race: 93.9% White, 1.0% Black, 1.4% Asian, 0.1% American Indian/Alaska Native, 0.0% Native Hawaiian/Other Pacific Islander, 3.6% Other, 5.9% Hispanic of any race (2010); Average household size: 2.58 (2010); Median age: 45.3 (2010); Males per 100 females: 100.0 (2010); Marriage status: 20.9% never married, 66.4% now married, 6.7% widowed, 6.0% divorced (2006-2010 5-year est.); Foreign born: 2.2% (2006-2010 5-year est.); Ancestry (includes multiple ancestries): 43.1% German, 12.1% Irish, 9.5% Pennsylvania German, 8.5% American, 8.0% Italian (2006-2010 5-year est.).

Economy: Employment by occupation: 5.0% management, 0.8% professional, 6.8% services, 24.0% sales, 1.4% farming, 7.6% construction, 8.6% production (2006-2010 5-year est.).

Income: Per capita income: $28,865 (2006-2010 5-year est.); Median household income: $57,578 (2006-2010 5-year est.); Average household income: $68,803 (2006-2010 5-year est.); Percent of households with income of $100,000 or more: 12.6% (2006-2010 5-year est.); Poverty rate: 2.5% (2006-2010 5-year est.).

Education: Percent of population age 25 and over with: High school diploma (including GED) or higher: 85.2% (2006-2010 5-year est.); Bachelor's degree or higher: 14.4% (2006-2010 5-year est.); Master's degree or higher: 4.2% (2006-2010 5-year est.).

Housing: Homeownership rate: 89.6% (2010); Median home value: $155,200 (2006-2010 5-year est.); Median contract rent: $492 per month (2006-2010 5-year est.); Median year structure built: 1979 (2006-2010 5-year est.).

Transportation: Commute to work: 97.3% car, 0.0% public transportation, 0.0% walk, 1.4% work from home (2006-2010 5-year est.); Travel time to work: 39.0% less than 15 minutes, 22.0% 15 to 30 minutes, 22.2% 30 to 45 minutes, 11.7% 45 to 60 minutes, 5.0% 60 minutes or more (2006-2010 5-year est.)

Additional Information Contacts

Lebanon Valley Chamber of Commerce . . . . (717) 273-3727
http://www.lvchamber.org

SCHAEFFERSTOWN (CDP). Covers a land area of 2.685 square miles and a water area of 0 square miles. Located at 40.30° N. Lat; 76.29° W. Long. Elevation is 577 feet.

Population: 1,171 (1990); 984 (2000); 941 (2010); Density: 350.5 persons per square mile (2010); Race: 96.9% White, 0.5% Black, 0.5% Asian, 0.0% American Indian/Alaska Native, 0.1% Native Hawaiian/Other Pacific Islander, 2.0% Other, 2.0% Hispanic of any race (2010); Average household size: 2.64 (2010); Median age: 39.7 (2010); Males per 100 females: 96.0 (2010); Marriage status: 22.4% never married, 71.8% now married, 4.3% widowed, 1.5% divorced (2006-2010 5-year est.); Foreign born: 1.2% (2006-2010 5-year est.); Ancestry (includes multiple ancestries): 63.7% German, 10.8% Irish, 9.3% Slovak, 6.5% American, 6.2% Polish (2006-2010 5-year est.).

Economy: Employment by occupation: 7.8% management, 3.8% professional, 7.2% services, 0.9% sales, 4.9% farming, 11.9% construction, 11.0% production (2006-2010 5-year est.).

Income: Per capita income: $29,080 (2006-2010 5-year est.); Median household income: $48,958 (2006-2010 5-year est.); Average household income: $59,105 (2006-2010 5-year est.); Percent of households with income of $100,000 or more: 11.4% (2006-2010 5-year est.); Poverty rate: 3.4% (2006-2010 5-year est.).

Education: Percent of population age 25 and over with: High school diploma (including GED) or higher: 88.2% (2006-2010 5-year est.); Bachelor's degree or higher: 8.8% (2006-2010 5-year est.); Master's degree or higher: 1.4% (2006-2010 5-year est.).

Housing: Homeownership rate: 76.5% (2010); Median home value: $182,300 (2006-2010 5-year est.); Median contract rent: n/a per month (2006-2010 5-year est.); Median year structure built: before 1940 (2006-2010 5-year est.).

Transportation: Commute to work: 79.4% car, 0.0% public transportation, 13.3% walk, 7.2% work from home (2006-2010 5-year est.); Travel time to work: 23.1% less than 15 minutes, 33.8% 15 to 30 minutes, 35.6% 30 to 45 minutes, 7.5% 45 to 60 minutes, 0.0% 60 minutes or more (2006-2010 5-year est.)

SOUTH ANNVILLE (township). Covers a land area of 19.469 square miles and a water area of 0 square miles. Located at 40.29° N. Lat; 76.52° W. Long.

Population: 2,996 (1990); 2,946 (2000); 2,850 (2010); Density: 146.4 persons per square mile (2010); Race: 97.6% White, 0.7% Black, 0.5% Asian, 0.0% American Indian/Alaska Native, 0.0% Native Hawaiian/Other Pacific Islander, 1.2% Other, 2.5% Hispanic of any race (2010); Average household size: 2.57 (2010); Median age: 45.5 (2010); Males per 100 females: 99.2 (2010); Marriage status: 22.1% never married, 66.1% now married, 4.5% widowed, 7.3% divorced (2006-2010 5-year est.); Foreign born: 2.2% (2006-2010 5-year est.); Ancestry (includes multiple ancestries): 53.9% German, 13.0% Irish, 6.9% English, 6.3% Italian, 4.8% American (2006-2010 5-year est.).

Economy: Employment by occupation: 12.8% management, 1.3% professional, 12.7% services, 16.9% sales, 3.3% farming, 10.7% construction, 11.5% production (2006-2010 5-year est.).

Income: Per capita income: $27,830 (2006-2010 5-year est.); Median household income: $62,417 (2006-2010 5-year est.); Average household

income: $71,759 (2006-2010 5-year est.); Percent of households with income of $100,000 or more: 24.3% (2006-2010 5-year est.); Poverty rate: 7.1% (2006-2010 5-year est.).

Education: Percent of population age 25 and over with: High school diploma (including GED) or higher: 88.1% (2006-2010 5-year est.); Bachelor's degree or higher: 23.7% (2006-2010 5-year est.); Master's degree or higher: 6.6% (2006-2010 5-year est.).

Housing: Homeownership rate: 88.7% (2010); Median home value: $177,900 (2006-2010 5-year est.); Median contract rent: $601 per month (2006-2010 5-year est.); Median year structure built: 1974 (2006-2010 5-year est.).

Transportation: Commute to work: 94.1% car, 0.0% public transportation, 2.1% walk, 3.8% work from home (2006-2010 5-year est.); Travel time to work: 33.4% less than 15 minutes, 44.8% 15 to 30 minutes, 14.6% 30 to 45 minutes, 3.8% 45 to 60 minutes, 3.4% 60 minutes or more (2006-2010 5-year est.)

Additional Information Contacts

Lebanon Valley Chamber of Commerce . . . . (717) 273-3727
http://www.lvchamber.org

SOUTH LEBANON (township). Covers a land area of 21.673 square miles and a water area of 0.069 square miles. Located at 40.31° N. Lat; 76.38° W. Long. Elevation is 512 feet.

Population: 7,491 (1990); 8,383 (2000); 9,463 (2010); Density: 436.6 persons per square mile (2010); Race: 92.6% White, 2.3% Black, 0.9% Asian, 0.2% American Indian/Alaska Native, 0.0% Native Hawaiian/Other Pacific Islander, 4.0% Other, 6.1% Hispanic of any race (2010); Average household size: 2.51 (2010); Median age: 44.6 (2010); Males per 100 females: 97.9 (2010); Marriage status: 22.8% never married, 60.3% now married, 8.3% widowed, 8.6% divorced (2006-2010 5-year est.); Foreign born: 2.4% (2006-2010 5-year est.); Ancestry (includes multiple ancestries): 37.3% German, 10.4% Irish, 7.8% English, 6.9% American, 6.1% Italian (2006-2010 5-year est.).

Economy: Employment by occupation: 11.2% management, 4.9% professional, 13.4% services, 15.8% sales, 1.9% farming, 9.9% construction, 8.7% production (2006-2010 5-year est.).

Income: Per capita income: $28,315 (2006-2010 5-year est.); Median household income: $67,783 (2006-2010 5-year est.); Average household income: $75,207 (2006-2010 5-year est.); Percent of households with income of $100,000 or more: 24.7% (2006-2010 5-year est.); Poverty rate: 4.6% (2006-2010 5-year est.).

Education: Percent of population age 25 and over with: High school diploma (including GED) or higher: 85.9% (2006-2010 5-year est.); Bachelor's degree or higher: 20.2% (2006-2010 5-year est.); Master's degree or higher: 7.1% (2006-2010 5-year est.).

Housing: Homeownership rate: 82.6% (2010); Median home value: $159,600 (2006-2010 5-year est.); Median contract rent: $653 per month (2006-2010 5-year est.); Median year structure built: 1969 (2006-2010 5-year est.).

Safety: Violent crime rate: 2.1 per 10,000 population; Property crime rate: 82.2 per 10,000 population (2011).

Transportation: Commute to work: 93.3% car, 0.4% public transportation, 1.9% walk, 3.6% work from home (2006-2010 5-year est.); Travel time to work: 39.0% less than 15 minutes, 24.1% 15 to 30 minutes, 22.2% 30 to 45 minutes, 10.8% 45 to 60 minutes, 3.9% 60 minutes or more (2006-2010 5-year est.)

Additional Information Contacts

Lebanon Valley Chamber of Commerce . . . . (717) 273-3727
http://www.lvchamber.org
South Lebanon Township . . . . (717) 274-0481
http://www.twp.south-lebanon.pa.us

SOUTH LONDONDERRY (township). Covers a land area of 24.351 square miles and a water area of 0.025 square miles. Located at 40.24° N. Lat; 76.54° W. Long.

Population: 4,299 (1990); 5,458 (2000); 6,991 (2010); Density: 287.1 persons per square mile (2010); Race: 96.2% White, 0.7% Black, 1.7% Asian, 0.1% American Indian/Alaska Native, 0.0% Native Hawaiian/Other Pacific Islander, 1.3% Other, 1.8% Hispanic of any race (2010); Average household size: 2.57 (2010); Median age: 42.3 (2010); Males per 100 females: 96.7 (2010); Marriage status: 16.2% never married, 70.7% now married, 5.9% widowed, 7.2% divorced (2006-2010 5-year est.); Foreign born: 3.7% (2006-2010 5-year est.); Ancestry (includes multiple ancestries): 48.5% German, 18.5% Irish, 12.3% English, 5.5% Pennsylvania German, 5.4% American (2006-2010 5-year est.).

Economy: Single-family building permits issued: 10 (2011); Multi-family building permits issued: 0 (2011); Employment by occupation: 13.3% management, 7.0% professional, 7.6% services, 13.0% sales, 1.9% farming, 9.8% construction, 7.2% production (2006-2010 5-year est.).
Income: Per capita income: $30,045 (2006-2010 5-year est.); Median household income: $75,913 (2006-2010 5-year est.); Average household income: $81,437 (2006-2010 5-year est.); Percent of households with income of $100,000 or more: 34.0% (2006-2010 5-year est.); Poverty rate: 1.2% (2006-2010 5-year est.).
Education: Percent of population age 25 and over with: High school diploma (including GED) or higher: 92.4% (2006-2010 5-year est.); Bachelor's degree or higher: 32.8% (2006-2010 5-year est.); Master's degree or higher: 14.7% (2006-2010 5-year est.).
Housing: Homeownership rate: 85.3% (2010); Median home value: $214,500 (2006-2010 5-year est.); Median contract rent: $755 per month (2006-2010 5-year est.); Median year structure built: 1984 (2006-2010 5-year est.).
Safety: Violent crime rate: 5.7 per 10,000 population; Property crime rate: 101.2 per 10,000 population (2011).
Transportation: Commute to work: 92.4% car, 1.0% public transportation, 2.4% walk, 3.8% work from home (2006-2010 5-year est.); Travel time to work: 25.1% less than 15 minutes, 38.3% 15 to 30 minutes, 23.2% 30 to 45 minutes, 6.6% 45 to 60 minutes, 6.9% 60 minutes or more (2006-2010 5-year est.)
Additional Information Contacts
Lebanon Valley Chamber of Commerce . . . . (717) 273-3727
  http://www.lvchamber.org
South Londonderry Township . . . . (717) 838-5556
  http://www.southlondonderry.org

SWATARA (township). Covers a land area of 21.566 square miles and a water area of 0.006 square miles. Located at 40.43° N. Lat; 76.47° W. Long.
Population: 3,318 (1990); 3,941 (2000); 4,555 (2010); Density: 211.2 persons per square mile (2010); Race: 96.4% White, 0.9% Black, 1.0% Asian, 0.2% American Indian/Alaska Native, 0.1% Native Hawaiian/Other Pacific Islander, 1.4% Other, 2.3% Hispanic of any race (2010); Average household size: 2.63 (2010); Median age: 39.1 (2010); Males per 100 females: 102.4 (2010); Marriage status: 23.1% never married, 63.4% now married, 4.2% widowed, 9.3% divorced (2006-2010 5-year est.); Foreign born: 0.8% (2006-2010 5-year est.); Ancestry (includes multiple ancestries): 57.2% German, 13.4% Irish, 6.1% American, 5.8% Italian, 5.3% English (2006-2010 5-year est.).
Economy: Employment by occupation: 11.4% management, 1.9% professional, 11.5% services, 18.1% sales, 5.3% farming, 14.3% construction, 9.7% production (2006-2010 5-year est.).
Income: Per capita income: $22,611 (2006-2010 5-year est.); Median household income: $53,875 (2006-2010 5-year est.); Average household income: $61,633 (2006-2010 5-year est.); Percent of households with income of $100,000 or more: 15.5% (2006-2010 5-year est.); Poverty rate: 7.3% (2006-2010 5-year est.).
Education: Percent of population age 25 and over with: High school diploma (including GED) or higher: 85.6% (2006-2010 5-year est.); Bachelor's degree or higher: 12.1% (2006-2010 5-year est.); Master's degree or higher: 1.6% (2006-2010 5-year est.).
Housing: Homeownership rate: 85.1% (2010); Median home value: $147,600 (2006-2010 5-year est.); Median contract rent: $536 per month (2006-2010 5-year est.); Median year structure built: 1978 (2006-2010 5-year est.).
Transportation: Commute to work: 92.5% car, 0.0% public transportation, 2.0% walk, 5.4% work from home (2006-2010 5-year est.); Travel time to work: 25.4% less than 15 minutes, 43.4% 15 to 30 minutes, 18.2% 30 to 45 minutes, 9.5% 45 to 60 minutes, 3.5% 60 minutes or more (2006-2010 5-year est.)
Additional Information Contacts
Lebanon Valley Chamber of Commerce . . . . (717) 273-3727
  http://www.lvchamber.org

TIMBER HILLS (CDP). Covers a land area of 0.660 square miles and a water area of 0.022 square miles. Located at 40.24° N. Lat; 76.48° W. Long. Elevation is 653 feet.
Population: 252 (1990); 329 (2000); 360 (2010); Density: 545.1 persons per square mile (2010); Race: 98.3% White, 0.0% Black, 0.0% Asian, 0.0% American Indian/Alaska Native, 0.0% Native Hawaiian/Other Pacific Islander, 1.7% Other, 1.9% Hispanic of any race (2010); Average

household size: 2.09 (2010); Median age: 60.1 (2010); Males per 100 females: 86.5 (2010); Marriage status: 13.5% never married, 86.5% now married, 0.0% widowed, 0.0% divorced (2006-2010 5-year est.); Foreign born: 0.0% (2006-2010 5-year est.); Ancestry (includes multiple ancestries): 50.2% German, 32.1% English, 23.4% Irish, 16.5% Welsh, 10.5% Danish (2006-2010 5-year est.).
Economy: Employment by occupation: 10.4% management, 27.6% professional, 0.0% services, 19.0% sales, 0.0% farming, 8.0% construction, 0.0% production (2006-2010 5-year est.).
Income: Per capita income: $59,763 (2006-2010 5-year est.); Median household income: $116,445 (2006-2010 5-year est.); Average household income: $124,281 (2006-2010 5-year est.); Percent of households with income of $100,000 or more: 81.4% (2006-2010 5-year est.); Poverty rate: 0.0% (2006-2010 5-year est.).
Education: Percent of population age 25 and over with: High school diploma (including GED) or higher: 100.0% (2006-2010 5-year est.); Bachelor's degree or higher: 71.7% (2006-2010 5-year est.); Master's degree or higher: 45.2% (2006-2010 5-year est.).
Housing: Homeownership rate: 82.0% (2010); Median home value: $303,400 (2006-2010 5-year est.); Median contract rent: n/a per month (2006-2010 5-year est.); Median year structure built: 1981 (2006-2010 5-year est.).
Transportation: Commute to work: 80.4% car, 0.0% public transportation, 19.6% walk, 0.0% work from home (2006-2010 5-year est.); Travel time to work: 27.0% less than 15 minutes, 23.9% 15 to 30 minutes, 9.8% 30 to 45 minutes, 31.3% 45 to 60 minutes, 8.0% 60 minutes or more (2006-2010 5-year est.)

UNION (township). Covers a land area of 29.642 square miles and a water area of 0.023 square miles. Located at 40.45° N. Lat; 76.55° W. Long.
Population: 2,716 (1990); 2,590 (2000); 3,099 (2010); Density: 104.5 persons per square mile (2010); Race: 96.7% White, 0.5% Black, 1.1% Asian, 0.1% American Indian/Alaska Native, 0.0% Native Hawaiian/Other Pacific Islander, 1.6% Other, 2.3% Hispanic of any race (2010); Average household size: 2.54 (2010); Median age: 41.9 (2010); Males per 100 females: 104.7 (2010); Marriage status: 23.3% never married, 60.7% now married, 4.4% widowed, 11.6% divorced (2006-2010 5-year est.); Foreign born: 2.1% (2006-2010 5-year est.); Ancestry (includes multiple ancestries): 43.2% German, 11.1% Irish, 8.6% Italian, 7.3% Pennsylvania German, 7.0% American (2006-2010 5-year est.).
Economy: Single-family building permits issued: 2 (2011); Multi-family building permits issued: 0 (2011); Employment by occupation: 5.2% management, 0.5% professional, 8.9% services, 20.4% sales, 1.3% farming, 12.7% construction, 10.4% production (2006-2010 5-year est.).
Income: Per capita income: $24,285 (2006-2010 5-year est.); Median household income: $55,669 (2006-2010 5-year est.); Average household income: $62,673 (2006-2010 5-year est.); Percent of households with income of $100,000 or more: 18.2% (2006-2010 5-year est.); Poverty rate: 6.9% (2006-2010 5-year est.).
Education: Percent of population age 25 and over with: High school diploma (including GED) or higher: 82.6% (2006-2010 5-year est.); Bachelor's degree or higher: 11.9% (2006-2010 5-year est.); Master's degree or higher: 4.8% (2006-2010 5-year est.).
Housing: Homeownership rate: 76.0% (2010); Median home value: $182,500 (2006-2010 5-year est.); Median contract rent: $456 per month (2006-2010 5-year est.); Median year structure built: 1972 (2006-2010 5-year est.).
Transportation: Commute to work: 94.0% car, 0.0% public transportation, 1.5% walk, 3.8% work from home (2006-2010 5-year est.); Travel time to work: 25.4% less than 15 minutes, 39.6% 15 to 30 minutes, 22.3% 30 to 45 minutes, 8.2% 45 to 60 minutes, 4.5% 60 minutes or more (2006-2010 5-year est.)
Additional Information Contacts
Lebanon Valley Chamber of Commerce . . . . (717) 273-3727
  http://www.lvchamber.org

WEST CORNWALL (township). Covers a land area of 8.644 square miles and a water area of 0.003 square miles. Located at 40.27° N. Lat; 76.45° W. Long.
Population: 2,028 (1990); 1,909 (2000); 1,976 (2010); Density: 228.6 persons per square mile (2010); Race: 96.9% White, 0.8% Black, 0.8% Asian, 0.1% American Indian/Alaska Native, 0.0% Native Hawaiian/Other Pacific Islander, 1.4% Other, 2.4% Hispanic of any race (2010); Average household size: 2.14 (2010); Median age: 52.2 (2010); Males per 100

females: 89.5 (2010); Marriage status: 15.6% never married, 66.5% now married, 11.1% widowed, 6.7% divorced (2006-2010 5-year est.); Foreign born: 4.6% (2006-2010 5-year est.); Ancestry (includes multiple ancestries): 48.1% German, 13.8% Irish, 12.7% English, 5.9% Italian, 4.8% American (2006-2010 5-year est.).

Economy: Employment by occupation: 12.0% management, 4.6% professional, 8.3% services, 13.8% sales, 2.1% farming, 10.5% construction, 4.1% production (2006-2010 5-year est.).

Income: Per capita income: $36,150 (2006-2010 5-year est.); Median household income: $59,254 (2006-2010 5-year est.); Average household income: $78,421 (2006-2010 5-year est.); Percent of households with income of $100,000 or more: 25.1% (2006-2010 5-year est.); Poverty rate: 3.2% (2006-2010 5-year est.).

Education: Percent of population age 25 and over with: High school diploma (including GED) or higher: 94.0% (2006-2010 5-year est.); Bachelor's degree or higher: 36.1% (2006-2010 5-year est.); Master's degree or higher: 14.0% (2006-2010 5-year est.).

Housing: Homeownership rate: 89.4% (2010); Median home value: $138,300 (2006-2010 5-year est.); Median contract rent: $545 per month (2006-2010 5-year est.); Median year structure built: 1971 (2006-2010 5-year est.).

Safety: Violent crime rate: 0.0 per 10,000 population; Property crime rate: 15.1 per 10,000 population (2011).

Transportation: Commute to work: 98.6% car, 0.0% public transportation, 0.0% walk, 1.4% work from home (2006-2010 5-year est.); Travel time to work: 36.8% less than 15 minutes, 41.2% 15 to 30 minutes, 18.1% 30 to 45 minutes, 2.6% 45 to 60 minutes, 1.3% 60 minutes or more (2006-2010 5-year est.)

Additional Information Contacts
Lebanon Valley Chamber of Commerce . . . . (717) 273-3727
  http://www.lvchamber.org

WEST LEBANON (township). Covers a land area of 0.387 square miles and a water area of 0.006 square miles. Located at 40.34° N. Lat; 76.45° W. Long. Elevation is 472 feet.

Population: 872 (1990); 836 (2000); 781 (2010); Density: 2,020.4 persons per square mile (2010); Race: 89.8% White, 2.4% Black, 0.8% Asian, 0.0% American Indian/Alaska Native, 0.0% Native Hawaiian/Other Pacific Islander, 7.0% Other, 11.3% Hispanic of any race (2010); Average household size: 2.40 (2010); Median age: 40.0 (2010); Males per 100 females: 103.9 (2010); Marriage status: 26.2% never married, 53.7% now married, 9.6% widowed, 10.5% divorced (2006-2010 5-year est.); Foreign born: 0.4% (2006-2010 5-year est.); Ancestry (includes multiple ancestries): 50.0% German, 14.5% Irish, 7.9% English, 7.8% Pennsylvania German, 5.2% Polish (2006-2010 5-year est.).

Economy: Employment by occupation: 2.8% management, 0.0% professional, 17.4% services, 15.4% sales, 6.1% farming, 5.7% construction, 8.5% production (2006-2010 5-year est.).

Income: Per capita income: $20,030 (2006-2010 5-year est.); Median household income: $48,875 (2006-2010 5-year est.); Average household income: $49,830 (2006-2010 5-year est.); Percent of households with income of $100,000 or more: 3.0% (2006-2010 5-year est.); Poverty rate: 7.9% (2006-2010 5-year est.).

Education: Percent of population age 25 and over with: High school diploma (including GED) or higher: 87.0% (2006-2010 5-year est.); Bachelor's degree or higher: 10.8% (2006-2010 5-year est.); Master's degree or higher: 5.0% (2006-2010 5-year est.).

Housing: Homeownership rate: 71.1% (2010); Median home value: $93,200 (2006-2010 5-year est.); Median contract rent: $498 per month (2006-2010 5-year est.); Median year structure built: 1945 (2006-2010 5-year est.).

Safety: Violent crime rate: 51.1 per 10,000 population; Property crime rate: 1,098.3 per 10,000 population (2011).

Transportation: Commute to work: 93.2% car, 1.0% public transportation, 4.8% walk, 0.4% work from home (2006-2010 5-year est.); Travel time to work: 26.2% less than 15 minutes, 47.4% 15 to 30 minutes, 13.9% 30 to 45 minutes, 8.9% 45 to 60 minutes, 3.5% 60 minutes or more (2006-2010 5-year est.)

Lehigh County

Located in eastern Pennsylvania; drained by the Lehigh River. Covers a land area of 345.166 square miles, a water area of 3.073 square miles, and is located in the Eastern Time Zone at 40.61° N. Lat., 75.59° W. Long. The county was founded in 1812. County seat is Allentown.

Lehigh County is part of the Allentown-Bethlehem-Easton, PA-NJ Metropolitan Statistical Area. The entire metro area includes: Warren County, NJ; Carbon County, PA; Lehigh County, PA; Northampton County, PA

Weather Station: Allentown A-B-E Intl Arpt   Elevation: 390 feet

	Jan	Feb	Mar	Apr	May	Jun	Jul	Aug	Sep	Oct	Nov	Dec
High	36	40	49	61	72	80	85	83	75	64	53	41
Low	21	23	30	40	49	59	64	62	54	42	34	25
Precip	3.0	2.6	3.4	3.6	4.1	4.4	4.7	3.7	4.4	3.8	3.5	3.5
Snow	10.0	10.0	5.5	1.0	tr	tr	0.0	0.0	0.0	tr	0.9	5.4

High and Low temperatures in degrees Fahrenheit; Precipitation and Snow in inches

Population: 291,129 (1990); 312,090 (2000); 349,497 (2010); Race: 79.1% White, 6.1% Black, 2.9% Asian, 0.4% American Indian/Alaska Native, 0.0% Native Hawaiian/Other Pacific Islander, 11.5% Other, 18.8% Hispanic of any race (2010); Density: 1,012.5 persons per square mile (2010); Average household size: 2.54 (2010); Median age: 39.4 (2010); Males per 100 females: 94.0 (2010).

Religion: Six largest groups: 19.5% Catholicism, 8.3% Lutheran, 7.6% Presbyterian-Reformed, 3.2% Hindu, 3.1% Methodist/Pietist, 2.6% Non-Denominational (2010)

Economy: Unemployment rate: 8.8% (August 2012); Total civilian labor force: 185,174 (August 2012); Leading industries: 22.3% health care and social assistance; 12.9% retail trade; 9.5% manufacturing (2010); Farms: 516 totaling 84,643 acres (2007); Companies that employ 500 or more persons: 32 (2010); Companies that employ 100 to 499 persons: 207 (2010); Companies that employ less than 100 persons: 8,171 (2010); Black-owned businesses: 1,257 (2007); Hispanic-owned businesses: 2,263 (2007); Asian-owned businesses: 946 (2007); Women-owned businesses: 8,010 (2007); Retail sales per capita: $15,648 (2007). Single-family building permits issued: 407 (2011); Multi-family building permits issued: 2 (2011).

Income: Per capita income: $27,301 (2006-2010 5-year est.); Median household income: $53,541 (2006-2010 5-year est.); Average household income: $69,406 (2006-2010 5-year est.); Percent of households with income of $100,000 or more: 21.1% (2006-2010 5-year est.); Poverty rate: 11.9% (2006-2010 5-year est.); Bankruptcy rate: 3.15% (2011).

Taxes: Total county taxes per capita: $273 (2009); County property taxes per capita: $272 (2009).

Education: Percent of population age 25 and over with: High school diploma (including GED) or higher: 85.9% (2006-2010 5-year est.); Bachelor's degree or higher: 27.0% (2006-2010 5-year est.); Master's degree or higher: 10.8% (2006-2010 5-year est.).

Housing: Homeownership rate: 67.8% (2010); Median home value: $203,200 (2006-2010 5-year est.); Median contract rent: $708 per month (2006-2010 5-year est.); Median year structure built: 1964 (2006-2010 5-year est.)

Health: Birth rate: 119.5 per 10,000 population (2011); Death rate: 87.5 per 10,000 population (2011); Age-adjusted cancer mortality rate: 174.4 deaths per 100,000 population (2009); Number of physicians: 38.5 per 10,000 population (2010); Hospital beds: 40.4 per 10,000 population (2008); Hospital admissions: 1,821.3 per 10,000 population (2008).

Environment: Air Quality Index: 90.9% good, 7.4% moderate, 1.7% unhealthy for sensitive individuals, 0.0% unhealthy (percent of days in 2011)

Elections: 2012 Presidential election results: 53.2% Obama, 45.5% Romney

Additional Information Contacts
Lehigh County Government . . . . (610) 782-3000
  http://www.lehighcounty.org

Lehigh County Communities

ALBURTIS (borough). Aka New Hensingerville. Covers a land area of 0.707 square miles and a water area of <.001 square miles. Located at 40.51° N. Lat; 75.60° W. Long. Elevation is 453 feet.

Population: 1,415 (1990); 2,117 (2000); 2,361 (2010); Density: 3,339.9 persons per square mile (2010); Race: 93.0% White, 2.0% Black, 1.3% Asian, 0.1% American Indian/Alaska Native, 0.0% Native Hawaiian/Other Pacific Islander, 3.6% Other, 5.5% Hispanic of any race (2010); Average household size: 2.68 (2010); Median age: 34.7 (2010); Males per 100 females: 96.1 (2010); Marriage status: 23.4% never married, 65.8% now married, 2.9% widowed, 7.9% divorced (2006-2010 5-year est.); Foreign born: 0.8% (2006-2010 5-year est.); Ancestry (includes multiple

ancestries): 41.7% German, 16.1% Pennsylvania German, 11.8% Irish, 10.6% Italian, 7.3% English (2006-2010 5-year est.).
Economy: Single-family building permits issued: 0 (2011); Multi-family building permits issued: 0 (2011); Employment by occupation: 12.9% management, 4.0% professional, 9.4% services, 18.4% sales, 4.6% farming, 7.0% construction, 4.1% production (2006-2010 5-year est.).
Income: Per capita income: $27,580 (2006-2010 5-year est.); Median household income: $69,667 (2006-2010 5-year est.); Average household income: $75,404 (2006-2010 5-year est.); Percent of households with income of $100,000 or more: 24.9% (2006-2010 5-year est.); Poverty rate: 6.6% (2006-2010 5-year est.).
Education: Percent of population age 25 and over with: High school diploma (including GED) or higher: 92.5% (2006-2010 5-year est.); Bachelor's degree or higher: 25.1% (2006-2010 5-year est.); Master's degree or higher: 8.1% (2006-2010 5-year est.).

School District(s)
East Penn SD (KG-12)
  2010-11 Enrollment: 8,029 . . . . (610) 966-8300
Housing: Homeownership rate: 83.4% (2010); Median home value: $191,600 (2006-2010 5-year est.); Median contract rent: $914 per month (2006-2010 5-year est.); Median year structure built: 1975 (2006-2010 5-year est.).
Safety: Violent crime rate: 4.2 per 10,000 population; Property crime rate: 80.2 per 10,000 population (2011).
Transportation: Commute to work: 92.8% car, 0.0% public transportation, 0.7% walk, 6.0% work from home (2006-2010 5-year est.); Travel time to work: 22.8% less than 15 minutes, 46.0% 15 to 30 minutes, 19.8% 30 to 45 minutes, 6.2% 45 to 60 minutes, 5.2% 60 minutes or more (2006-2010 5-year est.)
Additional Information Contacts
Greater Lehigh Valley Chamber of Commerce . . . . (610) 841-5800
  http://www.lehighvalleychamber.org

ALLENTOWN (city). Aka Scherersville. County seat. Covers a land area of 17.546 square miles and a water area of 0.478 square miles. Located at 40.59° N. Lat; 75.48° W. Long. Elevation is 338 feet.
History: Immigrants from Germany moved to eastern Pennsylvania as early as 1723, some settling near what is now Allentown. In 1735, William Allen, later chief justice of the State supreme court, acquired a large tract of land in the area from Joseph Turner who, according to early records, had obtained it from Thomas Penn in 1732. A town was laid out in 1762, known as Northampton or Northamptontown. Early growth was slow. The community was incorporated as a borough in 1811. In 1820, the borough's name was changed to honor William Allen. Flood and fire struck the town, but with reconstruction came growth. In 1867, Allentown became a city.
Population: 105,066 (1990); 106,632 (2000); 118,032 (2010); Density: 6,727.1 persons per square mile (2010); Race: 58.5% White, 12.5% Black, 2.2% Asian, 0.8% American Indian/Alaska Native, 0.0% Native Hawaiian/Other Pacific Islander, 26.0% Other, 42.8% Hispanic of any race (2010); Average household size: 2.64 (2010); Median age: 32.7 (2010); Males per 100 females: 93.0 (2010); Marriage status: 39.7% never married, 42.7% now married, 6.8% widowed, 10.7% divorced (2006-2010 5-year est.); Foreign born: 14.0% (2006-2010 5-year est.); Ancestry (includes multiple ancestries): 17.2% German, 7.6% Irish, 6.5% Italian, 3.7% Pennsylvania German, 3.6% English (2006-2010 5-year est.).
Economy: Unemployment rate: 12.1% (August 2012); Total civilian labor force: 58,095 (August 2012); Single-family building permits issued: 31 (2011); Multi-family building permits issued: 0 (2011); Employment by occupation: 6.4% management, 3.4% professional, 12.5% services, 17.9% sales, 4.9% farming, 8.1% construction, 8.3% production (2006-2010 5-year est.).
Income: Per capita income: $18,139 (2006-2010 5-year est.); Median household income: $36,202 (2006-2010 5-year est.); Average household income: $46,815 (2006-2010 5-year est.); Percent of households with income of $100,000 or more: 8.7% (2006-2010 5-year est.); Poverty rate: 24.6% (2006-2010 5-year est.).
Taxes: Total city taxes per capita: $466 (2009); City property taxes per capita: $275 (2009).
Education: Percent of population age 25 and over with: High school diploma (including GED) or higher: 76.2% (2006-2010 5-year est.); Bachelor's degree or higher: 16.6% (2006-2010 5-year est.); Master's degree or higher: 6.1% (2006-2010 5-year est.).

School District(s)
Allentown City SD (PK-12)
  2010-11 Enrollment: 17,637 . . . . (484) 765-4000

Lincoln Leadership Academy Charter School (KG-12)
  2010-11 Enrollment: 312 . . . . (484) 860-3300
Parkland SD (KG-12)
  2010-11 Enrollment: 9,354 . . . . (610) 351-5503
Roberto Clemente CS (06-12)
  2010-11 Enrollment: 307 . . . . (610) 439-5181
Salisbury Township SD (KG-12)
  2010-11 Enrollment: 1,629 . . . . (610) 797-2062

Four-year College(s)
Cedar Crest College (Private, Not-for-profit)
  Fall 2010 Enrollment: 1,390 . . . . (610) 606-4666
  2011-12 Tuition: In-state $30,110; Out-of-state $30,110
Muhlenberg College (Private, Not-for-profit, Evangelical Lutheran Church)
  Fall 2010 Enrollment: 2,822 . . . . (484) 664-3100
  2011-12 Tuition: In-state $39,915; Out-of-state $39,915

Two-year College(s)
Lincoln Technical Institute-Allentown (Private, For-profit)
  Fall 2010 Enrollment: 666 . . . . (610) 398-5300
Pennsylvania School of Business (Private, For-profit)
  Fall 2010 Enrollment: 714 . . . . (610) 841-3333
  2011-12 Tuition: In-state $11,115; Out-of-state $11,115

Vocational/Technical School(s)
International Academy of Medical Reflexology (Private, For-profit)
  Fall 2010 Enrollment: 2 . . . . (267) 424-4549
  2011-12 Tuition: $2,013
Metro Beauty Academy (Private, For-profit)
  Fall 2010 Enrollment: 241 . . . . (610) 398-6227
  2011-12 Tuition: $16,225
The Vision Academy (Private, For-profit)
  Fall 2010 Enrollment: 159 . . . . (610) 437-4626
  2011-12 Tuition: $17,200
Welder Training and Testing Institute (Private, For-profit)
  Fall 2010 Enrollment: 78 . . . . (610) 437-9720
  2011-12 Tuition: $8,625
Housing: Homeownership rate: 48.5% (2010); Median home value: $143,500 (2006-2010 5-year est.); Median contract rent: $676 per month (2006-2010 5-year est.); Median year structure built: 1951 (2006-2010 5-year est.).
Hospitals: Allentown State Hospital (181 beds); Good Shepherd Rehabilitation Hospital (63 beds); Lehigh Valley Hospital (800 beds); Sacred Heart Hospital (243 beds); St. Lukes Hospital-Allentown Campus (124 beds)
Safety: Violent crime rate: 54.6 per 10,000 population; Property crime rate: 386.4 per 10,000 population (2011).
Newspapers: The AD Times (Regional news; Circulation 60,700); East Penn Press (Community news; Circulation 6,500); The Morning Call (Local news; Circulation 149,264); Northhampton Press (Local news; Circulation 647); Northwestern Press (Local news); Parkland Press (Community news; Circulation 5,000); Whitehall Coplay Press (Local news; Circulation 4,500)
Transportation: Commute to work: 86.3% car, 4.9% public transportation, 5.4% walk, 2.3% work from home (2006-2010 5-year est.); Travel time to work: 31.5% less than 15 minutes, 43.3% 15 to 30 minutes, 13.0% 30 to 45 minutes, 5.0% 45 to 60 minutes, 7.2% 60 minutes or more (2006-2010 5-year est.)
Airports: Lehigh Valley International (primary service/small hub)
Additional Information Contacts
City of Allentown . . . . (610) 439-5999
  http://www.allentownpa.gov
Greater Lehigh Valley Chamber of Commerce . . . . (610) 841-5800
  http://www.lehighvalleychamber.org

ANCIENT OAKS (CDP). Covers a land area of 2.424 square miles and a water area of <.001 square miles. Located at 40.54° N. Lat; 75.59° W. Long. Elevation is 394 feet.
Population: 2,663 (1990); 3,161 (2000); 6,661 (2010); Density: 2,748.2 persons per square mile (2010); Race: 86.0% White, 2.6% Black, 8.1% Asian, 0.2% American Indian/Alaska Native, 0.0% Native Hawaiian/Other Pacific Islander, 3.1% Other, 4.8% Hispanic of any race (2010); Average household size: 2.83 (2010); Median age: 39.0 (2010); Males per 100 females: 97.3 (2010); Marriage status: 22.3% never married, 69.1% now married, 3.1% widowed, 5.4% divorced (2006-2010 5-year est.); Foreign born: 9.2% (2006-2010 5-year est.); Ancestry (includes multiple ancestries): 31.6% German, 18.1% Italian, 17.1% Irish, 6.7% English, 6.5% Polish (2006-2010 5-year est.).

Economy: Employment by occupation: 17.3% management, 8.7% professional, 5.9% services, 17.1% sales, 2.6% farming, 2.0% construction, 1.8% production (2006-2010 5-year est.).

Income: Per capita income: $34,816 (2006-2010 5-year est.); Median household income: $94,188 (2006-2010 5-year est.); Average household income: $102,903 (2006-2010 5-year est.); Percent of households with income of $100,000 or more: 47.9% (2006-2010 5-year est.); Poverty rate: 4.3% (2006-2010 5-year est.).

Education: Percent of population age 25 and over with: High school diploma (including GED) or higher: 96.7% (2006-2010 5-year est.); Bachelor's degree or higher: 52.5% (2006-2010 5-year est.); Master's degree or higher: 18.2% (2006-2010 5-year est.).

Housing: Homeownership rate: 87.5% (2010); Median home value: $297,200 (2006-2010 5-year est.); Median contract rent: $1,122 per month (2006-2010 5-year est.); Median year structure built: 1999 (2006-2010 5-year est.).

Transportation: Commute to work: 93.1% car, 0.4% public transportation, 0.0% walk, 5.8% work from home (2006-2010 5-year est.); Travel time to work: 32.4% less than 15 minutes, 32.5% 15 to 30 minutes, 18.4% 30 to 45 minutes, 5.2% 45 to 60 minutes, 11.5% 60 minutes or more (2006-2010 5-year est.).

Additional Information Contacts

Upper Bucks Chamber of Commerce . . . . (215) 536-3211
    http://www.ubcc.org

BREINIGSVILLE (CDP). Covers a land area of 3.220 square miles and a water area of 0.005 square miles. Located at 40.54° N. Lat; 75.63° W. Long. Elevation is 407 feet.

Population: n/a (1990); n/a (2000); 4,138 (2010); Density: 1,285.0 persons per square mile (2010); Race: 79.9% White, 5.2% Black, 11.1% Asian, 0.5% American Indian/Alaska Native, 0.0% Native Hawaiian/Other Pacific Islander, 3.3% Other, 7.1% Hispanic of any race (2010); Average household size: 2.67 (2010); Median age: 34.6 (2010); Males per 100 females: 95.7 (2010); Marriage status: 18.8% never married, 60.2% now married, 8.0% widowed, 13.0% divorced (2006-2010 5-year est.); Foreign born: 12.6% (2006-2010 5-year est.); Ancestry (includes multiple ancestries): 32.2% German, 9.0% Italian, 8.5% Swiss, 8.1% Irish, 7.3% Polish (2006-2010 5-year est.).

Economy: Employment by occupation: 9.5% management, 5.1% professional, 0.8% services, 27.8% sales, 4.2% farming, 5.9% construction, 5.0% production (2006-2010 5-year est.).

Income: Per capita income: $29,516 (2006-2010 5-year est.); Median household income: $56,250 (2006-2010 5-year est.); Average household income: $72,333 (2006-2010 5-year est.); Percent of households with income of $100,000 or more: 23.5% (2006-2010 5-year est.); Poverty rate: 3.0% (2006-2010 5-year est.).

Education: Percent of population age 25 and over with: High school diploma (including GED) or higher: 90.3% (2006-2010 5-year est.); Bachelor's degree or higher: 31.9% (2006-2010 5-year est.); Master's degree or higher: 15.0% (2006-2010 5-year est.).

School District(s)

Parkland SD (KG-12)
    2010-11 Enrollment: 9,354 . . . . (610) 351-5503
Housing: Homeownership rate: 91.3% (2010); Median home value: $79,500 (2006-2010 5-year est.); Median contract rent: $775 per month (2006-2010 5-year est.); Median year structure built: 1992 (2006-2010 5-year est.).

Transportation: Commute to work: 100.0% car, 0.0% public transportation, 0.0% walk, 0.0% work from home (2006-2010 5-year est.); Travel time to work: 31.1% less than 15 minutes, 40.5% 15 to 30 minutes, 11.7% 30 to 45 minutes, 2.5% 45 to 60 minutes, 14.3% 60 minutes or more (2006-2010 5-year est.)

CATASAUQUA (borough). Covers a land area of 1.291 square miles and a water area of 0.038 square miles. Located at 40.65° N. Lat; 75.46° W. Long. Elevation is 312 feet.

History: Incorporated c.1853.

Population: 6,662 (1990); 6,588 (2000); 6,436 (2010); Density: 4,986.1 persons per square mile (2010); Race: 89.0% White, 3.0% Black, 0.6% Asian, 0.1% American Indian/Alaska Native, 0.1% Native Hawaiian/Other Pacific Islander, 7.2% Other, 10.5% Hispanic of any race (2010); Average household size: 2.44 (2010); Median age: 37.9 (2010); Males per 100 females: 93.3 (2010); Marriage status: 34.9% never married, 47.8% now married, 9.6% widowed, 7.6% divorced (2006-2010 5-year est.); Foreign born: 4.9% (2006-2010 5-year est.); Ancestry (includes multiple

ancestries): 28.1% German, 11.4% Pennsylvania German, 10.8% Irish, 8.3% Italian, 7.2% English (2006-2010 5-year est.).

Economy: Single-family building permits issued: 4 (2011); Multi-family building permits issued: 0 (2011); Employment by occupation: 8.1% management, 4.8% professional, 12.3% services, 18.4% sales, 4.7% farming, 10.8% construction, 6.1% production (2006-2010 5-year est.).

Income: Per capita income: $23,540 (2006-2010 5-year est.); Median household income: $53,766 (2006-2010 5-year est.); Average household income: $59,112 (2006-2010 5-year est.); Percent of households with income of $100,000 or more: 10.9% (2006-2010 5-year est.); Poverty rate: 8.4% (2006-2010 5-year est.).

Education: Percent of population age 25 and over with: High school diploma (including GED) or higher: 87.7% (2006-2010 5-year est.); Bachelor's degree or higher: 15.1% (2006-2010 5-year est.); Master's degree or higher: 3.3% (2006-2010 5-year est.).

School District(s)

Catasauqua Area SD (KG-12)
    2010-11 Enrollment: 1,566 . . . . (610) 264-5571
Housing: Homeownership rate: 65.6% (2010); Median home value: $138,900 (2006-2010 5-year est.); Median contract rent: $717 per month (2006-2010 5-year est.); Median year structure built: 1954 (2006-2010 5-year est.).

Safety: Violent crime rate: 10.8 per 10,000 population; Property crime rate: 254.0 per 10,000 population (2011).

Transportation: Commute to work: 94.6% car, 2.8% public transportation, 0.6% walk, 0.6% work from home (2006-2010 5-year est.); Travel time to work: 28.5% less than 15 minutes, 43.3% 15 to 30 minutes, 16.0% 30 to 45 minutes, 5.4% 45 to 60 minutes, 6.7% 60 minutes or more (2006-2010 5-year est.)

Additional Information Contacts

Borough of Catasauqua . . . . (610) 264-0571
    http://catasauquaborough.govoffice.com
Greater Lehigh Valley Chamber of Commerce . . . . (610) 841-5800
    http://www.lehighvalleychamber.org

CEMENTON (CDP). Covers a land area of 0.651 square miles and a water area of 0.026 square miles. Located at 40.69° N. Lat; 75.52° W. Long. Elevation is 315 feet.

Population: n/a (1990); n/a (2000); 1,538 (2010); Density: 2,363.9 persons per square mile (2010); Race: 90.0% White, 2.4% Black, 2.0% Asian, 0.1% American Indian/Alaska Native, 0.0% Native Hawaiian/Other Pacific Islander, 5.5% Other, 6.9% Hispanic of any race (2010); Average household size: 2.53 (2010); Median age: 39.2 (2010); Males per 100 females: 90.6 (2010); Marriage status: 30.6% never married, 54.0% now married, 8.8% widowed, 6.6% divorced (2006-2010 5-year est.); Foreign born: 8.0% (2006-2010 5-year est.); Ancestry (includes multiple ancestries): 26.6% German, 19.4% Italian, 10.8% Slovak, 8.2% Polish, 6.2% Ukrainian (2006-2010 5-year est.).

Economy: Employment by occupation: 5.2% management, 1.5% professional, 11.7% services, 20.5% sales, 2.9% farming, 16.3% construction, 11.1% production (2006-2010 5-year est.).

Income: Per capita income: $21,880 (2006-2010 5-year est.); Median household income: $53,333 (2006-2010 5-year est.); Average household income: $56,218 (2006-2010 5-year est.); Percent of households with income of $100,000 or more: 11.6% (2006-2010 5-year est.); Poverty rate: 12.2% (2006-2010 5-year est.).

Education: Percent of population age 25 and over with: High school diploma (including GED) or higher: 83.3% (2006-2010 5-year est.); Bachelor's degree or higher: 15.6% (2006-2010 5-year est.); Master's degree or higher: 7.5% (2006-2010 5-year est.).

Housing: Homeownership rate: 74.5% (2010); Median home value: $179,400 (2006-2010 5-year est.); Median contract rent: $631 per month (2006-2010 5-year est.); Median year structure built: before 1940 (2006-2010 5-year est.).

Transportation: Commute to work: 96.2% car, 0.0% public transportation, 2.6% walk, 0.0% work from home (2006-2010 5-year est.); Travel time to work: 27.9% less than 15 minutes, 48.2% 15 to 30 minutes, 15.7% 30 to 45 minutes, 3.9% 45 to 60 minutes, 4.3% 60 minutes or more (2006-2010 5-year est.)

CENTER VALLEY (unincorporated postal area)

Zip Code: 18034

Covers a land area of 11.334 square miles and a water area of 0.075 square miles. Located at 40.54° N. Lat; 75.41° W. Long. Elevation is 440 feet. Population: 8,256 (2010); Density: 728.4 persons per square

mile (2010); Race: 92.4% White, 1.4% Black, 4.1% Asian, 0.1% American Indian/Alaska Native, 0.0% Native Hawaiian/Other Pacific Islander, 2.0% Other, 3.5% Hispanic of any race (2010); Average household size: 2.74 (2010); Median age: 36.9 (2010); Males per 100 females: 95.4 (2010); Homeownership rate: 85.3% (2010)

CETRONIA (CDP). Covers a land area of 0.759 square miles and a water area of 0 square miles. Located at 40.59° N. Lat; 75.54° W. Long. Elevation is 328 feet.

Population: n/a (1990); n/a (2000); 2,115 (2010); Density: 2,787.7 persons per square mile (2010); Race: 93.0% White, 2.4% Black, 1.5% Asian, 0.0% American Indian/Alaska Native, 0.0% Native Hawaiian/Other Pacific Islander, 3.1% Other, 5.6% Hispanic of any race (2010); Average household size: 2.36 (2010); Median age: 46.7 (2010); Males per 100 females: 88.3 (2010); Marriage status: 24.7% never married, 52.1% now married, 8.6% widowed, 14.6% divorced (2006-2010 5-year est.); Foreign born: 4.1% (2006-2010 5-year est.); Ancestry (includes multiple ancestries): 32.1% German, 20.3% Irish, 16.3% Italian, 9.7% English, 6.8% Swedish (2006-2010 5-year est.).

Economy: Employment by occupation: 9.6% management, 10.0% professional, 7.9% services, 16.9% sales, 1.6% farming, 3.2% construction, 4.8% production (2006-2010 5-year est.).

Income: Per capita income: $30,544 (2006-2010 5-year est.); Median household income: $56,629 (2006-2010 5-year est.); Average household income: $65,927 (2006-2010 5-year est.); Percent of households with income of $100,000 or more: 18.6% (2006-2010 5-year est.); Poverty rate: 3.9% (2006-2010 5-year est.).

Education: Percent of population age 25 and over with: High school diploma (including GED) or higher: 93.4% (2006-2010 5-year est.); Bachelor's degree or higher: 34.4% (2006-2010 5-year est.); Master's degree or higher: 11.3% (2006-2010 5-year est.).

Housing: Homeownership rate: 87.5% (2010); Median home value: $196,000 (2006-2010 5-year est.); Median contract rent: $1,063 per month (2006-2010 5-year est.); Median year structure built: 1955 (2006-2010 5-year est.).

Transportation: Commute to work: 94.1% car, 0.0% public transportation, 1.2% walk, 4.7% work from home (2006-2010 5-year est.); Travel time to work: 38.6% less than 15 minutes, 46.8% 15 to 30 minutes, 5.1% 30 to 45 minutes, 0.0% 45 to 60 minutes, 9.6% 60 minutes or more (2006-2010 5-year est.)

COOPERSBURG (borough). Covers a land area of 0.933 square miles and a water area of 0.002 square miles. Located at 40.51° N. Lat; 75.39° W. Long. Elevation is 469 feet.

History: Allentown College of St. Francis de Sales to North at Center Valley. Settled 1780 as Fryburg, renamed 1832, incorporated 1879.

Population: 2,534 (1990); 2,582 (2000); 2,386 (2010); Density: 2,557.3 persons per square mile (2010); Race: 95.7% White, 0.6% Black, 1.1% Asian, 0.1% American Indian/Alaska Native, 0.0% Native Hawaiian/Other Pacific Islander, 2.5% Other, 3.5% Hispanic of any race (2010); Average household size: 2.32 (2010); Median age: 45.9 (2010); Males per 100 females: 93.4 (2010); Marriage status: 23.1% never married, 52.8% now married, 12.4% widowed, 11.8% divorced (2006-2010 5-year est.); Foreign born: 2.6% (2006-2010 5-year est.); Ancestry (includes multiple ancestries): 44.9% German, 15.2% Irish, 13.0% Italian, 6.7% English, 6.2% Pennsylvania German (2006-2010 5-year est.).

Economy: Single-family building permits issued: 0 (2011); Multi-family building permits issued: 0 (2011); Employment by occupation: 10.1% management, 5.3% professional, 7.4% services, 17.9% sales, 3.7% farming, 8.2% construction, 4.2% production (2006-2010 5-year est.).

Income: Per capita income: $27,658 (2006-2010 5-year est.); Median household income: $54,063 (2006-2010 5-year est.); Average household income: $66,768 (2006-2010 5-year est.); Percent of households with income of $100,000 or more: 19.6% (2006-2010 5-year est.); Poverty rate: 2.8% (2006-2010 5-year est.).

Taxes: Total city taxes per capita: $410 (2009); City property taxes per capita: $280 (2009).

Education: Percent of population age 25 and over with: High school diploma (including GED) or higher: 85.6% (2006-2010 5-year est.); Bachelor's degree or higher: 22.0% (2006-2010 5-year est.); Master's degree or higher: 7.7% (2006-2010 5-year est.).

School District(s)

Southern Lehigh SD (KG-12)

    2010-11 Enrollment: 3,085 . . . . (610) 282-3121

Housing: Homeownership rate: 66.8% (2010); Median home value: $227,000 (2006-2010 5-year est.); Median contract rent: $591 per month (2006-2010 5-year est.); Median year structure built: 1951 (2006-2010 5-year est.).

Safety: Violent crime rate: 16.7 per 10,000 population; Property crime rate: 71.0 per 10,000 population (2011).

Transportation: Commute to work: 92.2% car, 0.0% public transportation, 3.7% walk, 4.1% work from home (2006-2010 5-year est.); Travel time to work: 34.3% less than 15 minutes, 40.3% 15 to 30 minutes, 15.9% 30 to 45 minutes, 3.3% 45 to 60 minutes, 6.2% 60 minutes or more (2006-2010 5-year est.)

Additional Information Contacts

Upper Bucks Chamber of Commerce . . . . (215) 536-3211
    http://www.ubcc.org

COPLAY (borough). Covers a land area of 0.610 square miles and a water area of 0.017 square miles. Located at 40.67° N. Lat; 75.50° W. Long. Elevation is 404 feet.

History: Cement industry museum at former cement industrial site.

Population: 3,267 (1990); 3,387 (2000); 3,192 (2010); Density: 5,230.2 persons per square mile (2010); Race: 92.5% White, 2.6% Black, 1.0% Asian, 0.3% American Indian/Alaska Native, 0.0% Native Hawaiian/Other Pacific Islander, 3.6% Other, 6.3% Hispanic of any race (2010); Average household size: 2.24 (2010); Median age: 45.3 (2010); Males per 100 females: 86.0 (2010); Marriage status: 28.8% never married, 46.7% now married, 12.5% widowed, 12.0% divorced (2006-2010 5-year est.); Foreign born: 4.2% (2006-2010 5-year est.); Ancestry (includes multiple ancestries): 38.5% German, 9.9% Irish, 9.6% American, 8.8% Austrian, 8.5% Italian (2006-2010 5-year est.).

Economy: Single-family building permits issued: 1 (2011); Multi-family building permits issued: 0 (2011); Employment by occupation: 8.3% management, 2.9% professional, 8.1% services, 22.6% sales, 4.4% farming, 9.2% construction, 8.8% production (2006-2010 5-year est.).

Income: Per capita income: $24,060 (2006-2010 5-year est.); Median household income: $50,023 (2006-2010 5-year est.); Average household income: $54,941 (2006-2010 5-year est.); Percent of households with income of $100,000 or more: 11.4% (2006-2010 5-year est.); Poverty rate: 14.0% (2006-2010 5-year est.).

Education: Percent of population age 25 and over with: High school diploma (including GED) or higher: 80.1% (2006-2010 5-year est.); Bachelor's degree or higher: 13.0% (2006-2010 5-year est.); Master's degree or higher: 4.3% (2006-2010 5-year est.).

School District(s)

Parkland SD (KG-12)

    2010-11 Enrollment: 9,354 . . . . (610) 351-5503

Housing: Homeownership rate: 72.2% (2010); Median home value: $170,400 (2006-2010 5-year est.); Median contract rent: $593 per month (2006-2010 5-year est.); Median year structure built: 1952 (2006-2010 5-year est.).

Safety: Violent crime rate: 3.1 per 10,000 population; Property crime rate: 137.4 per 10,000 population (2011).

Transportation: Commute to work: 91.5% car, 5.0% public transportation, 2.8% walk, 0.7% work from home (2006-2010 5-year est.); Travel time to work: 20.4% less than 15 minutes, 48.5% 15 to 30 minutes, 22.3% 30 to 45 minutes, 3.9% 45 to 60 minutes, 5.0% 60 minutes or more (2006-2010 5-year est.)

Additional Information Contacts

Whitehall Area Chamber of Commerce. . . . . (610) 432-4130
    http://www.waccpa.org

DESALES UNIVERSITY (CDP). Covers a land area of 0.255 square miles and a water area of 0 square miles. Located at 40.54° N. Lat; 75.38° W. Long.

Population: n/a (1990); n/a (2000); 953 (2010); Density: 3,740.4 persons per square mile (2010); Race: 93.8% White, 2.9% Black, 0.6% Asian, 0.0% American Indian/Alaska Native, 0.0% Native Hawaiian/Other Pacific Islander, 2.7% Other, 3.7% Hispanic of any race (2010); Average household size: 0.00 (2010); Median age: 20.1 (2010); Males per 100 females: 88.7 (2010); Marriage status: 100.0% never married, 0.0% now married, 0.0% widowed, 0.0% divorced (2006-2010 5-year est.); Foreign born: 0.0% (2006-2010 5-year est.); Ancestry (includes multiple ancestries): 48.0% German, 44.6% Irish, 32.7% Italian, 9.5% English, 9.2% Polish (2006-2010 5-year est.).

Economy: Employment by occupation: 11.2% management, 0.0% professional, 22.7% services, 15.0% sales, 12.2% farming, 0.7% construction, 1.0% production (2006-2010 5-year est.).
Income: Per capita income: $4,631 (2006-2010 5-year est.); Median household income: n/a (2006-2010 5-year est.); Average household income: n/a (2006-2010 5-year est.); Percent of households with income of $100,000 or more: n/a (2006-2010 5-year est.); Poverty rate: n/a (2006-2010 5-year est.).
Education: Percent of population age 25 and over with: High school diploma (including GED) or higher: 100.0% (2006-2010 5-year est.); Bachelor's degree or higher: 100.0% (2006-2010 5-year est.); Master's degree or higher: 100.0% (2006-2010 5-year est.).
Housing: Homeownership rate: 0.0% (2010); Median home value: n/a (2006-2010 5-year est.); Median contract rent: n/a per month (2006-2010 5-year est.); Median year structure built: n/a (2006-2010 5-year est.).
Transportation: Commute to work: 55.8% car, 0.0% public transportation, 8.7% walk, 35.6% work from home (2006-2010 5-year est.); Travel time to work: 61.1% less than 15 minutes, 19.0% 15 to 30 minutes, 5.1% 30 to 45 minutes, 14.8% 45 to 60 minutes, 0.0% 60 minutes or more (2006-2010 5-year est.)

DORNEYVILLE (CDP).
Covers a land area of 2.003 square miles and a water area of 0.009 square miles. Located at 40.58° N. Lat; 75.52° W. Long. Elevation is 381 feet.
Population: n/a (1990); n/a (2000); 4,406 (2010); Density: 2,199.9 persons per square mile (2010); Race: 91.8% White, 2.6% Black, 3.2% Asian, 0.0% American Indian/Alaska Native, 0.0% Native Hawaiian/Other Pacific Islander, 2.4% Other, 3.6% Hispanic of any race (2010); Average household size: 2.52 (2010); Median age: 49.8 (2010); Males per 100 females: 96.2 (2010); Marriage status: 18.8% never married, 67.9% now married, 9.1% widowed, 4.2% divorced (2006-2010 5-year est.); Foreign born: 5.2% (2006-2010 5-year est.); Ancestry (includes multiple ancestries): 30.0% German, 17.6% Irish, 11.3% Italian, 7.0% Polish, 6.6% English (2006-2010 5-year est.).
Economy: Employment by occupation: 15.6% management, 14.5% professional, 4.0% services, 18.0% sales, 2.3% farming, 5.2% construction, 3.4% production (2006-2010 5-year est.).
Income: Per capita income: $38,932 (2006-2010 5-year est.); Median household income: $75,968 (2006-2010 5-year est.); Average household income: $95,773 (2006-2010 5-year est.); Percent of households with income of $100,000 or more: 35.0% (2006-2010 5-year est.); Poverty rate: 4.4% (2006-2010 5-year est.).
Education: Percent of population age 25 and over with: High school diploma (including GED) or higher: 94.8% (2006-2010 5-year est.); Bachelor's degree or higher: 46.0% (2006-2010 5-year est.); Master's degree or higher: 18.3% (2006-2010 5-year est.).
Housing: Homeownership rate: 92.3% (2010); Median home value: $265,900 (2006-2010 5-year est.); Median contract rent: $753 per month (2006-2010 5-year est.); Median year structure built: 1968 (2006-2010 5-year est.).
Transportation: Commute to work: 89.3% car, 1.8% public transportation, 1.7% walk, 5.7% work from home (2006-2010 5-year est.); Travel time to work: 40.2% less than 15 minutes, 34.9% 15 to 30 minutes, 9.8% 30 to 45 minutes, 4.5% 45 to 60 minutes, 10.7% 60 minutes or more (2006-2010 5-year est.)

EAST TEXAS (unincorporated postal area)
Zip Code: 18046
Covers a land area of 0.018 square miles and a water area of 0 square miles. Located at 40.54° N. Lat; 75.56° W. Long. Elevation is 446 feet.
Population: 64 (2010); Density: 3,507.4 persons per square mile (2010); Race: 95.3% White, 0.0% Black, 1.6% Asian, 0.0% American Indian/Alaska Native, 0.0% Native Hawaiian/Other Pacific Islander, 3.1% Other, 0.0% Hispanic of any race (2010); Average household size: 2.78 (2010); Median age: 37.5 (2010); Males per 100 females: 93.9 (2010); Homeownership rate: 78.3% (2010)

EGYPT (CDP).
Covers a land area of 1.449 square miles and a water area of 0.004 square miles. Located at 40.69° N. Lat; 75.53° W. Long. Elevation is 413 feet.
Population: n/a (1990); n/a (2000); 2,391 (2010); Density: 1,650.0 persons per square mile (2010); Race: 94.2% White, 1.1% Black, 1.5% Asian, 0.0% American Indian/Alaska Native, 0.0% Native Hawaiian/Other Pacific Islander, 3.2% Other, 3.8% Hispanic of any race (2010); Average household size: 2.67 (2010); Median age: 42.5 (2010); Males per 100

females: 94.2 (2010); Marriage status: 28.5% never married, 57.4% now married, 4.9% widowed, 9.3% divorced (2006-2010 5-year est.); Foreign born: 2.6% (2006-2010 5-year est.); Ancestry (includes multiple ancestries): 40.5% German, 13.1% Irish, 8.9% Pennsylvania German, 8.6% Slovak, 8.4% Italian (2006-2010 5-year est.).
Economy: Employment by occupation: 9.3% management, 4.7% professional, 6.5% services, 22.4% sales, 2.4% farming, 8.9% construction, 6.3% production (2006-2010 5-year est.).
Income: Per capita income: $29,849 (2006-2010 5-year est.); Median household income: $71,445 (2006-2010 5-year est.); Average household income: $82,779 (2006-2010 5-year est.); Percent of households with income of $100,000 or more: 33.5% (2006-2010 5-year est.); Poverty rate: 2.4% (2006-2010 5-year est.).
Education: Percent of population age 25 and over with: High school diploma (including GED) or higher: 89.6% (2006-2010 5-year est.); Bachelor's degree or higher: 26.9% (2006-2010 5-year est.); Master's degree or higher: 9.4% (2006-2010 5-year est.).
Housing: Homeownership rate: 88.0% (2010); Median home value: $228,800 (2006-2010 5-year est.); Median contract rent: $710 per month (2006-2010 5-year est.); Median year structure built: 1966 (2006-2010 5-year est.).
Transportation: Commute to work: 91.4% car, 1.8% public transportation, 1.5% walk, 4.7% work from home (2006-2010 5-year est.); Travel time to work: 21.5% less than 15 minutes, 44.5% 15 to 30 minutes, 24.7% 30 to 45 minutes, 2.7% 45 to 60 minutes, 6.6% 60 minutes or more (2006-2010 5-year est.)

EMMAUS (borough).
Aka Emaus. Covers a land area of 2.894 square miles and a water area of 0.004 square miles. Located at 40.54° N. Lat; 75.50° W. Long. Elevation is 446 feet.
History: Bieber Farmhouse (1734) to Northwest. Founded in 1740 by Moravians. Incorporated 1859.
Population: 11,219 (1990); 11,313 (2000); 11,211 (2010); Density: 3,873.6 persons per square mile (2010); Race: 93.4% White, 1.6% Black, 1.5% Asian, 0.2% American Indian/Alaska Native, 0.0% Native Hawaiian/Other Pacific Islander, 3.3% Other, 4.7% Hispanic of any race (2010); Average household size: 2.27 (2010); Median age: 40.3 (2010); Males per 100 females: 92.0 (2010); Marriage status: 27.7% never married, 56.5% now married, 6.6% widowed, 9.2% divorced (2006-2010 5-year est.); Foreign born: 5.1% (2006-2010 5-year est.); Ancestry (includes multiple ancestries): 37.1% German, 19.4% Irish, 10.1% Italian, 8.3% Pennsylvania German, 6.6% English (2006-2010 5-year est.).
Economy: Single-family building permits issued: 0 (2011); Multi-family building permits issued: 0 (2011); Employment by occupation: 9.1% management, 6.5% professional, 7.4% services, 15.6% sales, 2.6% farming, 6.9% construction, 6.5% production (2006-2010 5-year est.).
Income: Per capita income: $27,746 (2006-2010 5-year est.); Median household income: $61,214 (2006-2010 5-year est.); Average household income: $66,649 (2006-2010 5-year est.); Percent of households with income of $100,000 or more: 16.5% (2006-2010 5-year est.); Poverty rate: 2.8% (2006-2010 5-year est.).
Taxes: Total city taxes per capita: $410 (2009); City property taxes per capita: $250 (2009).
Education: Percent of population age 25 and over with: High school diploma (including GED) or higher: 89.9% (2006-2010 5-year est.); Bachelor's degree or higher: 30.5% (2006-2010 5-year est.); Master's degree or higher: 9.7% (2006-2010 5-year est.).

School District(s)
East Penn SD (KG-12)
    2010-11 Enrollment: 8,029 . . . . (610) 966-8300
Seven Generations Charter School (KG-12)
    2010-11 Enrollment: 261. . . . . (610) 421-8844
Housing: Homeownership rate: 63.0% (2010); Median home value: $186,400 (2006-2010 5-year est.); Median contract rent: $808 per month (2006-2010 5-year est.); Median year structure built: 1956 (2006-2010 5-year est.).
Safety: Violent crime rate: 10.7 per 10,000 population; Property crime rate: 208.1 per 10,000 population (2011).
Transportation: Commute to work: 90.7% car, 0.4% public transportation, 3.5% walk, 3.4% work from home (2006-2010 5-year est.); Travel time to work: 37.1% less than 15 minutes, 42.2% 15 to 30 minutes, 12.1% 30 to 45 minutes, 2.6% 45 to 60 minutes, 5.9% 60 minutes or more (2006-2010 5-year est.)

Additional Information Contacts

Borough of Emmaus . . . . (610) 965-9292
  http://www.borough.emmaus.pa.us
Greater Lehigh Valley Chamber of Commerce . . . . (610) 841-5800
  http://www.lehighvalleychamber.org

FOGELSVILLE (unincorporated postal area)

Zip Code: 18051

Covers a land area of 8.361 square miles and a water area of 0.017 square miles. Located at 40.59° N. Lat; 75.66° W. Long. Population: 3,327 (2010); Density: 397.9 persons per square mile (2010); Race: 95.5% White, 0.6% Black, 2.3% Asian, 0.0% American Indian/Alaska Native, 0.1% Native Hawaiian/Other Pacific Islander, 1.5% Other, 3.5% Hispanic of any race (2010); Average household size: 2.70 (2010); Median age: 43.0 (2010); Males per 100 females: 98.6 (2010); Homeownership rate: 87.4% (2010)

FOUNTAIN HILL (borough). Covers a land area of 0.735 square miles and a water area of 0.019 square miles. Located at 40.60° N. Lat; 75.40° W. Long. Elevation is 374 feet.

Population: 4,637 (1990); 4,614 (2000); 4,597 (2010); Density: 6,251.2 persons per square mile (2010); Race: 81.4% White, 6.6% Black, 0.8% Asian, 0.1% American Indian/Alaska Native, 0.0% Native Hawaiian/Other Pacific Islander, 11.1% Other, 22.5% Hispanic of any race (2010); Average household size: 2.31 (2010); Median age: 40.5 (2010); Males per 100 females: 88.4 (2010); Marriage status: 33.6% never married, 43.6% now married, 12.3% widowed, 10.5% divorced (2006-2010 5-year est.); Foreign born: 5.7% (2006-2010 5-year est.); Ancestry (includes multiple ancestries): 19.6% German, 12.6% Irish, 9.7% Italian, 7.0% Polish, 6.5% Hungarian (2006-2010 5-year est.).
Economy: Single-family building permits issued: 0 (2011); Multi-family building permits issued: 0 (2011); Employment by occupation: 8.2% management, 2.9% professional, 15.4% services, 18.3% sales, 6.9% farming, 4.0% construction, 2.1% production (2006-2010 5-year est.).
Income: Per capita income: $23,529 (2006-2010 5-year est.); Median household income: $40,580 (2006-2010 5-year est.); Average household income: $55,003 (2006-2010 5-year est.); Percent of households with income of $100,000 or more: 14.3% (2006-2010 5-year est.); Poverty rate: 8.7% (2006-2010 5-year est.).
Education: Percent of population age 25 and over with: High school diploma (including GED) or higher: 83.0% (2006-2010 5-year est.); Bachelor's degree or higher: 14.2% (2006-2010 5-year est.); Master's degree or higher: 2.8% (2006-2010 5-year est.).
Housing: Homeownership rate: 63.4% (2010); Median home value: $149,000 (2006-2010 5-year est.); Median contract rent: $554 per month (2006-2010 5-year est.); Median year structure built: before 1940 (2006-2010 5-year est.).
Safety: Violent crime rate: 23.9 per 10,000 population; Property crime rate: 271.0 per 10,000 population (2011).
Transportation: Commute to work: 92.1% car, 2.0% public transportation, 3.6% walk, 0.8% work from home (2006-2010 5-year est.); Travel time to work: 33.2% less than 15 minutes, 45.2% 15 to 30 minutes, 12.7% 30 to 45 minutes, 2.9% 45 to 60 minutes, 6.1% 60 minutes or more (2006-2010 5-year est.)
Additional Information Contacts
Whitehall Area Chamber of Commerce. . . . . (610) 432-4130
  http://www.waccpa.org

FULLERTON (CDP). Covers a land area of 3.676 square miles and a water area of 0.038 square miles. Located at 40.63° N. Lat; 75.48° W. Long. Elevation is 371 feet.

Population: 13,139 (1990); 14,268 (2000); 14,925 (2010); Density: 4,060.3 persons per square mile (2010); Race: 75.8% White, 8.6% Black, 5.8% Asian, 0.4% American Indian/Alaska Native, 0.0% Native Hawaiian/Other Pacific Islander, 9.4% Other, 14.6% Hispanic of any race (2010); Average household size: 2.33 (2010); Median age: 39.0 (2010); Males per 100 females: 90.5 (2010); Marriage status: 31.8% never married, 51.3% now married, 6.3% widowed, 10.6% divorced (2006-2010 5-year est.); Foreign born: 18.2% (2006-2010 5-year est.); Ancestry (includes multiple ancestries): 25.1% German, 10.5% Irish, 7.2% Italian, 4.5% English, 3.8% Polish (2006-2010 5-year est.).
Economy: Employment by occupation: 8.1% management, 5.6% professional, 10.0% services, 17.8% sales, 7.8% farming, 7.8% construction, 6.0% production (2006-2010 5-year est.).

Income: Per capita income: $25,099 (2006-2010 5-year est.); Median household income: $51,284 (2006-2010 5-year est.); Average household income: $57,599 (2006-2010 5-year est.); Percent of households with income of $100,000 or more: 12.5% (2006-2010 5-year est.); Poverty rate: 10.4% (2006-2010 5-year est.).
Education: Percent of population age 25 and over with: High school diploma (including GED) or higher: 87.9% (2006-2010 5-year est.); Bachelor's degree or higher: 25.2% (2006-2010 5-year est.); Master's degree or higher: 8.8% (2006-2010 5-year est.).
Housing: Homeownership rate: 52.8% (2010); Median home value: $189,300 (2006-2010 5-year est.); Median contract rent: $802 per month (2006-2010 5-year est.); Median year structure built: 1970 (2006-2010 5-year est.).
Transportation: Commute to work: 90.8% car, 4.2% public transportation, 3.1% walk, 1.7% work from home (2006-2010 5-year est.); Travel time to work: 39.0% less than 15 minutes, 38.1% 15 to 30 minutes, 12.5% 30 to 45 minutes, 2.8% 45 to 60 minutes, 7.6% 60 minutes or more (2006-2010 5-year est.)
Additional Information Contacts
Greater Lehigh Valley Chamber of Commerce . . . . (610) 841-5800
  http://www.lehighvalleychamber.org

GERMANSVILLE (unincorporated postal area)

Zip Code: 18053

Covers a land area of 16.408 square miles and a water area of 0.048 square miles. Located at 40.71° N. Lat; 75.70° W. Long. Elevation is 604 feet. Population: 2,375 (2010); Density: 144.7 persons per square mile (2010); Race: 97.6% White, 0.3% Black, 0.5% Asian, 0.1% American Indian/Alaska Native, 0.0% Native Hawaiian/Other Pacific Islander, 1.5% Other, 2.2% Hispanic of any race (2010); Average household size: 2.72 (2010); Median age: 40.3 (2010); Males per 100 females: 101.4 (2010); Homeownership rate: 85.9% (2010)

HANOVER (township). Covers a land area of 4.206 square miles and a water area of 0.032 square miles. Located at 40.65° N. Lat; 75.44° W. Long.

Population: 2,243 (1990); 1,913 (2000); 1,571 (2010); Density: 373.5 persons per square mile (2010); Race: 78.7% White, 7.6% Black, 4.9% Asian, 0.1% American Indian/Alaska Native, 0.1% Native Hawaiian/Other Pacific Islander, 8.6% Other, 14.6% Hispanic of any race (2010); Average household size: 2.20 (2010); Median age: 38.1 (2010); Males per 100 females: 95.6 (2010); Marriage status: 20.4% never married, 63.9% now married, 5.7% widowed, 10.0% divorced (2006-2010 5-year est.); Foreign born: 9.2% (2006-2010 5-year est.); Ancestry (includes multiple ancestries): 28.0% German, 16.5% Irish, 11.5% Italian, 9.8% English, 8.8% Polish (2006-2010 5-year est.).
Economy: Single-family building permits issued: 0 (2011); Multi-family building permits issued: 0 (2011); Employment by occupation: 11.3% management, 9.7% professional, 14.4% services, 18.4% sales, 3.6% farming, 6.4% construction, 10.0% production (2006-2010 5-year est.).
Income: Per capita income: $23,682 (2006-2010 5-year est.); Median household income: $50,529 (2006-2010 5-year est.); Average household income: $54,490 (2006-2010 5-year est.); Percent of households with income of $100,000 or more: 9.8% (2006-2010 5-year est.); Poverty rate: 11.9% (2006-2010 5-year est.).
Education: Percent of population age 25 and over with: High school diploma (including GED) or higher: 86.4% (2006-2010 5-year est.); Bachelor's degree or higher: 19.8% (2006-2010 5-year est.); Master's degree or higher: 8.7% (2006-2010 5-year est.).
Housing: Homeownership rate: 51.5% (2010); Median home value: $123,300 (2006-2010 5-year est.); Median contract rent: $869 per month (2006-2010 5-year est.); Median year structure built: 1973 (2006-2010 5-year est.).
Transportation: Commute to work: 96.9% car, 0.0% public transportation, 3.1% walk, 0.0% work from home (2006-2010 5-year est.); Travel time to work: 35.1% less than 15 minutes, 47.8% 15 to 30 minutes, 6.7% 30 to 45 minutes, 1.4% 45 to 60 minutes, 9.0% 60 minutes or more (2006-2010 5-year est.)
Additional Information Contacts
Greater Lehigh Valley Chamber of Commerce . . . . (610) 841-5800
  http://www.lehighvalleychamber.org

HEIDELBERG (township).
Covers a land area of 24.645 square miles and a water area of 0.086 square miles. Located at 40.70° N. Lat; 75.70° W. Long.

Population: 3,250 (1990); 3,279 (2000); 3,416 (2010); Density: 138.6 persons per square mile (2010); Race: 97.0% White, 0.4% Black, 0.7% Asian, 0.2% American Indian/Alaska Native, 0.1% Native Hawaiian/Other Pacific Islander, 1.6% Other, 2.4% Hispanic of any race (2010); Average household size: 2.68 (2010); Median age: 41.7 (2010); Males per 100 females: 102.0 (2010); Marriage status: 22.9% never married, 58.9% now married, 6.2% widowed, 12.0% divorced (2006-2010 5-year est.); Foreign born: 2.5% (2006-2010 5-year est.); Ancestry (includes multiple ancestries): 45.8% German, 13.7% Italian, 13.3% Irish, 11.2% Pennsylvania German, 9.0% Polish (2006-2010 5-year est.).

Economy: Single-family building permits issued: 2 (2011); Multi-family building permits issued: 0 (2011); Employment by occupation: 15.6% management, 4.1% professional, 9.4% services, 19.7% sales, 5.7% farming, 13.7% construction, 4.5% production (2006-2010 5-year est.).

Income: Per capita income: $31,503 (2006-2010 5-year est.); Median household income: $73,316 (2006-2010 5-year est.); Average household income: $74,052 (2006-2010 5-year est.); Percent of households with income of $100,000 or more: 17.6% (2006-2010 5-year est.); Poverty rate: 2.5% (2006-2010 5-year est.).

Education: Percent of population age 25 and over with: High school diploma (including GED) or higher: 91.2% (2006-2010 5-year est.); Bachelor's degree or higher: 19.4% (2006-2010 5-year est.); Master's degree or higher: 5.4% (2006-2010 5-year est.).

Housing: Homeownership rate: 86.6% (2010); Median home value: $215,600 (2006-2010 5-year est.); Median contract rent: $737 per month (2006-2010 5-year est.); Median year structure built: 1975 (2006-2010 5-year est.).

Transportation: Commute to work: 90.8% car, 0.0% public transportation, 4.1% walk, 1.7% work from home (2006-2010 5-year est.); Travel time to work: 17.7% less than 15 minutes, 31.3% 15 to 30 minutes, 33.1% 30 to 45 minutes, 11.4% 45 to 60 minutes, 6.5% 60 minutes or more (2006-2010 5-year est.)

Additional Information Contacts
Greater Lehigh Valley Chamber of Commerce . . . . (610) 841-5800
http://www.lehighvalleychamber.org

HOKENDAUQUA (CDP).
Covers a land area of 1.103 square miles and a water area of 0 square miles. Located at 40.66° N. Lat; 75.50° W. Long. Elevation is 367 feet.

Population: 3,413 (1990); 3,411 (2000); 3,378 (2010); Density: 3,063.3 persons per square mile (2010); Race: 92.5% White, 2.9% Black, 1.3% Asian, 0.1% American Indian/Alaska Native, 0.0% Native Hawaiian/Other Pacific Islander, 3.2% Other, 6.2% Hispanic of any race (2010); Average household size: 2.39 (2010); Median age: 46.1 (2010); Males per 100 females: 93.2 (2010); Marriage status: 23.8% never married, 55.7% now married, 10.2% widowed, 10.3% divorced (2006-2010 5-year est.); Foreign born: 4.1% (2006-2010 5-year est.); Ancestry (includes multiple ancestries): 30.5% German, 15.8% Irish, 8.9% Hungarian, 8.5% Italian, 7.4% Slovak (2006-2010 5-year est.).

Economy: Employment by occupation: 10.3% management, 3.6% professional, 8.6% services, 16.8% sales, 6.9% farming, 8.4% construction, 10.0% production (2006-2010 5-year est.).

Income: Per capita income: $26,963 (2006-2010 5-year est.); Median household income: $49,714 (2006-2010 5-year est.); Average household income: $65,702 (2006-2010 5-year est.); Percent of households with income of $100,000 or more: 20.2% (2006-2010 5-year est.); Poverty rate: 2.9% (2006-2010 5-year est.).

Education: Percent of population age 25 and over with: High school diploma (including GED) or higher: 86.6% (2006-2010 5-year est.); Bachelor's degree or higher: 18.3% (2006-2010 5-year est.); Master's degree or higher: 6.7% (2006-2010 5-year est.).

Housing: Homeownership rate: 75.9% (2010); Median home value: $203,100 (2006-2010 5-year est.); Median contract rent: $728 per month (2006-2010 5-year est.); Median year structure built: 1966 (2006-2010 5-year est.).

Transportation: Commute to work: 98.2% car, 0.9% public transportation, 0.0% walk, 1.0% work from home (2006-2010 5-year est.); Travel time to work: 23.2% less than 15 minutes, 55.6% 15 to 30 minutes, 15.2% 30 to 45 minutes, 2.4% 45 to 60 minutes, 3.5% 60 minutes or more (2006-2010 5-year est.)

Additional Information Contacts
Greater Lehigh Valley Chamber of Commerce . . . . (610) 841-5800
http://www.lehighvalleychamber.org

LAURYS STATION (CDP).
Covers a land area of 1.624 square miles and a water area of 0.136 square miles. Located at 40.72° N. Lat; 75.54° W. Long. Elevation is 377 feet.

Population: n/a (1990); n/a (2000); 1,243 (2010); Density: 765.5 persons per square mile (2010); Race: 95.3% White, 1.4% Black, 1.3% Asian, 0.2% American Indian/Alaska Native, 0.0% Native Hawaiian/Other Pacific Islander, 1.8% Other, 4.3% Hispanic of any race (2010); Average household size: 2.73 (2010); Median age: 42.9 (2010); Males per 100 females: 96.1 (2010); Marriage status: 29.5% never married, 57.6% now married, 10.2% widowed, 2.7% divorced (2006-2010 5-year est.); Foreign born: 1.3% (2006-2010 5-year est.); Ancestry (includes multiple ancestries): 35.5% German, 21.2% Irish, 16.4% Polish, 15.8% Italian, 11.7% English (2006-2010 5-year est.).

Economy: Employment by occupation: 6.4% management, 3.5% professional, 6.3% services, 16.5% sales, 0.0% farming, 5.6% construction, 2.2% production (2006-2010 5-year est.).

Income: Per capita income: $37,280 (2006-2010 5-year est.); Median household income: $92,931 (2006-2010 5-year est.); Average household income: $103,494 (2006-2010 5-year est.); Percent of households with income of $100,000 or more: 43.1% (2006-2010 5-year est.); Poverty rate: 15.0% (2006-2010 5-year est.).

Education: Percent of population age 25 and over with: High school diploma (including GED) or higher: 93.2% (2006-2010 5-year est.); Bachelor's degree or higher: 38.8% (2006-2010 5-year est.); Master's degree or higher: 14.7% (2006-2010 5-year est.).

Housing: Homeownership rate: 91.7% (2010); Median home value: $300,000 (2006-2010 5-year est.); Median contract rent: n/a per month (2006-2010 5-year est.); Median year structure built: 1987 (2006-2010 5-year est.).

Transportation: Commute to work: 87.2% car, 2.2% public transportation, 4.3% walk, 4.5% work from home (2006-2010 5-year est.); Travel time to work: 12.4% less than 15 minutes, 47.3% 15 to 30 minutes, 32.8% 30 to 45 minutes, 5.1% 45 to 60 minutes, 2.5% 60 minutes or more (2006-2010 5-year est.)

LOWER MACUNGIE (township).
Covers a land area of 22.350 square miles and a water area of 0.112 square miles. Located at 40.53° N. Lat; 75.57° W. Long.

Population: 16,832 (1990); 19,220 (2000); 30,633 (2010); Density: 1,370.6 persons per square mile (2010); Race: 87.4% White, 3.3% Black, 6.0% Asian, 0.1% American Indian/Alaska Native, 0.0% Native Hawaiian/Other Pacific Islander, 3.2% Other, 5.0% Hispanic of any race (2010); Average household size: 2.65 (2010); Median age: 41.0 (2010); Males per 100 females: 93.7 (2010); Marriage status: 19.2% never married, 67.2% now married, 6.3% widowed, 7.3% divorced (2006-2010 5-year est.); Foreign born: 8.5% (2006-2010 5-year est.); Ancestry (includes multiple ancestries): 32.6% German, 17.4% Irish, 14.8% Italian, 8.0% English, 5.3% Polish (2006-2010 5-year est.).

Economy: Unemployment rate: 5.6% (August 2012); Total civilian labor force: 16,950 (August 2012); Single-family building permits issued: 52 (2011); Multi-family building permits issued: 0 (2011); Employment by occupation: 17.4% management, 7.8% professional, 5.9% services, 15.3% sales, 3.0% farming, 3.6% construction, 3.5% production (2006-2010 5-year est.).

Income: Per capita income: $38,688 (2006-2010 5-year est.); Median household income: $80,344 (2006-2010 5-year est.); Average household income: $100,009 (2006-2010 5-year est.); Percent of households with income of $100,000 or more: 40.0% (2006-2010 5-year est.); Poverty rate: 4.5% (2006-2010 5-year est.).

Education: Percent of population age 25 and over with: High school diploma (including GED) or higher: 93.6% (2006-2010 5-year est.); Bachelor's degree or higher: 47.9% (2006-2010 5-year est.); Master's degree or higher: 21.6% (2006-2010 5-year est.).

Housing: Homeownership rate: 88.2% (2010); Median home value: $280,000 (2006-2010 5-year est.); Median contract rent: $1,060 per month (2006-2010 5-year est.); Median year structure built: 1991 (2006-2010 5-year est.).

Transportation: Commute to work: 93.3% car, 0.5% public transportation, 0.1% walk, 5.6% work from home (2006-2010 5-year est.); Travel time to work: 32.7% less than 15 minutes, 37.2% 15 to 30 minutes, 15.0% 30 to

45 minutes, 4.9% 45 to 60 minutes, 10.1% 60 minutes or more (2006-2010 5-year est.)

Additional Information Contacts

Greater Lehigh Valley Chamber of Commerce . . . . (610) 841-5800
   http://www.lehighvalleychamber.org

Lower Macungie Township . . . . (610) 966-4343
   http://www.lowermac.org

LOWER MILFORD (township). Covers a land area of 19.695 square miles and a water area of 0.024 square miles. Located at 40.47° N. Lat; 75.48° W. Long.

History: Lower Milford Township was incorporated in 1853 when the area was separated form Upper Milford Township. Prior to 1738, both Upper and Lower Milford Townships were part of Milford Township, Bucks County.

Population: 3,299 (1990); 3,617 (2000); 3,775 (2010); Density: 191.7 persons per square mile (2010); Race: 97.0% White, 0.4% Black, 0.9% Asian, 0.3% American Indian/Alaska Native, 0.0% Native Hawaiian/Other Pacific Islander, 1.4% Other, 1.4% Hispanic of any race (2010); Average household size: 2.77 (2010); Median age: 45.0 (2010); Males per 100 females: 102.8 (2010); Marriage status: 19.3% never married, 66.8% now married, 8.1% widowed, 5.8% divorced (2006-2010 5-year est.); Foreign born: 1.3% (2006-2010 5-year est.); Ancestry (includes multiple ancestries): 44.2% German, 15.3% Irish, 12.4% Italian, 10.1% English, 8.2% American (2006-2010 5-year est.).

Economy: Single-family building permits issued: 2 (2011); Multi-family building permits issued: 0 (2011); Employment by occupation: 9.7% management, 3.7% professional, 8.0% services, 12.8% sales, 5.6% farming, 11.7% construction, 9.4% production (2006-2010 5-year est.).

Income: Per capita income: $31,805 (2006-2010 5-year est.); Median household income: $70,904 (2006-2010 5-year est.); Average household income: $81,622 (2006-2010 5-year est.); Percent of households with income of $100,000 or more: 28.8% (2006-2010 5-year est.); Poverty rate: 2.6% (2006-2010 5-year est.).

Education: Percent of population age 25 and over with: High school diploma (including GED) or higher: 89.3% (2006-2010 5-year est.); Bachelor's degree or higher: 30.8% (2006-2010 5-year est.); Master's degree or higher: 11.1% (2006-2010 5-year est.).

Housing: Homeownership rate: 91.0% (2010); Median home value: $294,000 (2006-2010 5-year est.); Median contract rent: $686 per month (2006-2010 5-year est.); Median year structure built: 1970 (2006-2010 5-year est.).

Transportation: Commute to work: 96.0% car, 0.8% public transportation, 0.4% walk, 2.3% work from home (2006-2010 5-year est.); Travel time to work: 16.4% less than 15 minutes, 43.2% 15 to 30 minutes, 28.9% 30 to 45 minutes, 4.9% 45 to 60 minutes, 6.6% 60 minutes or more (2006-2010 5-year est.)

Additional Information Contacts

Lower Milford Township . . . . (610) 967-4949
   http://lowermilford.net

Upper Bucks Chamber of Commerce . . . . (215) 536-3211
   http://www.ubcc.org

LOWHILL (township). Covers a land area of 14.014 square miles and a water area of 0.107 square miles. Located at 40.64° N. Lat; 75.67° W. Long.

Population: 1,595 (1990); 1,869 (2000); 2,173 (2010); Density: 155.1 persons per square mile (2010); Race: 96.9% White, 0.8% Black, 0.6% Asian, 0.0% American Indian/Alaska Native, 0.0% Native Hawaiian/Other Pacific Islander, 1.7% Other, 1.3% Hispanic of any race (2010); Average household size: 2.69 (2010); Median age: 45.6 (2010); Males per 100 females: 97.9 (2010); Marriage status: 19.5% never married, 69.3% now married, 5.3% widowed, 5.9% divorced (2006-2010 5-year est.); Foreign born: 3.4% (2006-2010 5-year est.); Ancestry (includes multiple ancestries): 32.2% German, 12.7% Irish, 11.2% Italian, 6.6% Pennsylvania German, 6.5% English (2006-2010 5-year est.).

Economy: Single-family building permits issued: 3 (2011); Multi-family building permits issued: 0 (2011); Employment by occupation: 18.1% management, 5.5% professional, 5.9% services, 15.3% sales, 2.8% farming, 10.3% construction, 7.7% production (2006-2010 5-year est.).

Income: Per capita income: $39,983 (2006-2010 5-year est.); Median household income: $90,446 (2006-2010 5-year est.); Average household income: $107,058 (2006-2010 5-year est.); Percent of households with income of $100,000 or more: 42.0% (2006-2010 5-year est.); Poverty rate: 4.5% (2006-2010 5-year est.).

Education: Percent of population age 25 and over with: High school diploma (including GED) or higher: 90.6% (2006-2010 5-year est.); Bachelor's degree or higher: 38.5% (2006-2010 5-year est.); Master's degree or higher: 14.1% (2006-2010 5-year est.).

Housing: Homeownership rate: 90.2% (2010); Median home value: $297,400 (2006-2010 5-year est.); Median contract rent: $531 per month (2006-2010 5-year est.); Median year structure built: 1979 (2006-2010 5-year est.).

Transportation: Commute to work: 92.2% car, 0.6% public transportation, 0.5% walk, 4.7% work from home (2006-2010 5-year est.); Travel time to work: 14.0% less than 15 minutes, 47.6% 15 to 30 minutes, 24.0% 30 to 45 minutes, 5.5% 45 to 60 minutes, 8.9% 60 minutes or more (2006-2010 5-year est.)

Additional Information Contacts

Greater Lehigh Valley Chamber of Commerce . . . . (610) 841-5800
   http://www.lehighvalleychamber.org

LYNN (township). Covers a land area of 41.241 square miles and a water area of 0.302 square miles. Located at 40.66° N. Lat; 75.78° W. Long.

Population: 3,220 (1990); 3,849 (2000); 4,229 (2010); Density: 102.5 persons per square mile (2010); Race: 97.1% White, 0.6% Black, 0.4% Asian, 0.2% American Indian/Alaska Native, 0.1% Native Hawaiian/Other Pacific Islander, 1.6% Other, 2.8% Hispanic of any race (2010); Average household size: 2.63 (2010); Median age: 41.6 (2010); Males per 100 females: 100.9 (2010); Marriage status: 20.6% never married, 65.5% now married, 7.1% widowed, 6.8% divorced (2006-2010 5-year est.); Foreign born: 0.6% (2006-2010 5-year est.); Ancestry (includes multiple ancestries): 41.8% German, 13.3% Irish, 11.6% Pennsylvania German, 8.8% Italian, 8.5% English (2006-2010 5-year est.).

Economy: Single-family building permits issued: 6 (2011); Multi-family building permits issued: 0 (2011); Employment by occupation: 12.7% management, 6.5% professional, 7.0% services, 13.1% sales, 3.7% farming, 11.4% construction, 4.4% production (2006-2010 5-year est.).

Income: Per capita income: $30,471 (2006-2010 5-year est.); Median household income: $76,219 (2006-2010 5-year est.); Average household income: $77,550 (2006-2010 5-year est.); Percent of households with income of $100,000 or more: 32.6% (2006-2010 5-year est.); Poverty rate: 2.5% (2006-2010 5-year est.).

Education: Percent of population age 25 and over with: High school diploma (including GED) or higher: 92.5% (2006-2010 5-year est.); Bachelor's degree or higher: 29.5% (2006-2010 5-year est.); Master's degree or higher: 9.3% (2006-2010 5-year est.).

Housing: Homeownership rate: 84.2% (2010); Median home value: $244,200 (2006-2010 5-year est.); Median contract rent: $838 per month (2006-2010 5-year est.); Median year structure built: 1975 (2006-2010 5-year est.).

Transportation: Commute to work: 92.3% car, 0.0% public transportation, 1.1% walk, 6.6% work from home (2006-2010 5-year est.); Travel time to work: 12.6% less than 15 minutes, 43.0% 15 to 30 minutes, 26.3% 30 to 45 minutes, 11.6% 45 to 60 minutes, 6.5% 60 minutes or more (2006-2010 5-year est.)

Additional Information Contacts

Northeast Berks Chamber of Commerce . . . . (610) 683-8860
   http://www.northeastberkschamber.com

MACUNGIE (borough). Covers a land area of 0.989 square miles and a water area of <.001 square miles. Located at 40.52° N. Lat; 75.55° W. Long. Elevation is 390 feet.

Population: 2,597 (1990); 3,039 (2000); 3,074 (2010); Density: 3,107.9 persons per square mile (2010); Race: 92.1% White, 1.8% Black, 1.8% Asian, 0.2% American Indian/Alaska Native, 0.0% Native Hawaiian/Other Pacific Islander, 4.1% Other, 5.2% Hispanic of any race (2010); Average household size: 2.21 (2010); Median age: 41.3 (2010); Males per 100 females: 86.6 (2010); Marriage status: 23.4% never married, 54.0% now married, 9.3% widowed, 13.3% divorced (2006-2010 5-year est.); Foreign born: 3.8% (2006-2010 5-year est.); Ancestry (includes multiple ancestries): 35.9% German, 15.4% Irish, 8.6% Italian, 7.9% Pennsylvania German, 7.4% English (2006-2010 5-year est.).

Economy: Single-family building permits issued: 0 (2011); Multi-family building permits issued: 0 (2011); Employment by occupation: 7.5% management, 6.8% professional, 8.5% services, 18.0% sales, 7.1% farming, 8.1% construction, 7.6% production (2006-2010 5-year est.).

Income: Per capita income: $32,424 (2006-2010 5-year est.); Median household income: $56,387 (2006-2010 5-year est.); Average household

income: $70,247 (2006-2010 5-year est.); Percent of households with income of $100,000 or more: 20.0% (2006-2010 5-year est.); Poverty rate: 4.6% (2006-2010 5-year est.).

Education: Percent of population age 25 and over with: High school diploma (including GED) or higher: 92.5% (2006-2010 5-year est.); Bachelor's degree or higher: 25.2% (2006-2010 5-year est.); Master's degree or higher: 13.2% (2006-2010 5-year est.).

School District(s)

East Penn SD (KG-12)

   2010-11 Enrollment: 8,029 . . . . (610) 966-8300

Housing: Homeownership rate: 58.4% (2010); Median home value: $191,100 (2006-2010 5-year est.); Median contract rent: $834 per month (2006-2010 5-year est.); Median year structure built: 1977 (2006-2010 5-year est.).

Safety: Violent crime rate: 16.2 per 10,000 population; Property crime rate: 48.6 per 10,000 population (2011).

Transportation: Commute to work: 95.9% car, 0.7% public transportation, 0.5% walk, 2.8% work from home (2006-2010 5-year est.); Travel time to work: 21.0% less than 15 minutes, 47.8% 15 to 30 minutes, 23.8% 30 to 45 minutes, 2.3% 45 to 60 minutes, 5.1% 60 minutes or more (2006-2010 5-year est.)

Additional Information Contacts

Greater Lehigh Valley Chamber of Commerce . . . . (610) 841-5800

   http://www.lehighvalleychamber.org

NEW TRIPOLI (CDP). Covers a land area of 0.925 square miles and a water area of 0.002 square miles. Located at 40.67° N. Lat; 75.75° W. Long. Elevation is 581 feet.

Population: n/a (1990); n/a (2000); 898 (2010); Density: 971.0 persons per square mile (2010); Race: 95.1% White, 1.7% Black, 0.1% Asian, 0.2% American Indian/Alaska Native, 0.2% Native Hawaiian/Other Pacific Islander, 2.7% Other, 5.2% Hispanic of any race (2010); Average household size: 2.61 (2010); Median age: 33.4 (2010); Males per 100 females: 96.9 (2010); Marriage status: 25.3% never married, 46.4% now married, 10.9% widowed, 17.4% divorced (2006-2010 5-year est.); Foreign born: 0.0% (2006-2010 5-year est.); Ancestry (includes multiple ancestries): 28.9% German, 18.6% Polish, 18.6% Italian, 14.4% Irish, 9.3% Pennsylvania German (2006-2010 5-year est.).

Economy: Employment by occupation: 6.6% management, 6.2% professional, 2.8% services, 15.5% sales, 5.8% farming, 8.6% construction, 2.8% production (2006-2010 5-year est.).

Income: Per capita income: $31,255 (2006-2010 5-year est.); Median household income: $78,973 (2006-2010 5-year est.); Average household income: $74,374 (2006-2010 5-year est.); Percent of households with income of $100,000 or more: 25.1% (2006-2010 5-year est.); Poverty rate: 4.9% (2006-2010 5-year est.).

Education: Percent of population age 25 and over with: High school diploma (including GED) or higher: 92.2% (2006-2010 5-year est.); Bachelor's degree or higher: 34.2% (2006-2010 5-year est.); Master's degree or higher: 12.1% (2006-2010 5-year est.).

School District(s)

Northwestern Lehigh SD (KG-12)

   2010-11 Enrollment: 2,337 . . . . (610) 298-8661

Housing: Homeownership rate: 72.1% (2010); Median home value: $167,600 (2006-2010 5-year est.); Median contract rent: n/a per month (2006-2010 5-year est.); Median year structure built: 1991 (2006-2010 5-year est.).

Transportation: Commute to work: 100.0% car, 0.0% public transportation, 0.0% walk, 0.0% work from home (2006-2010 5-year est.); Travel time to work: 14.8% less than 15 minutes, 41.9% 15 to 30 minutes, 19.3% 30 to 45 minutes, 10.7% 45 to 60 minutes, 13.3% 60 minutes or more (2006-2010 5-year est.)

NORTH WHITEHALL (township). Covers a land area of 28.062 square miles and a water area of 0.489 square miles. Located at 40.68° N. Lat; 75.58° W. Long.

Population: 10,806 (1990); 14,731 (2000); 15,703 (2010); Density: 559.6 persons per square mile (2010); Race: 94.7% White, 1.5% Black, 1.3% Asian, 0.1% American Indian/Alaska Native, 0.0% Native Hawaiian/Other Pacific Islander, 2.4% Other, 3.7% Hispanic of any race (2010); Average household size: 2.68 (2010); Median age: 43.3 (2010); Males per 100 females: 98.7 (2010); Marriage status: 21.9% never married, 65.4% now married, 5.7% widowed, 7.0% divorced (2006-2010 5-year est.); Foreign born: 3.6% (2006-2010 5-year est.); Ancestry (includes multiple

ancestries): 38.8% German, 13.1% Irish, 13.0% Italian, 10.0% Pennsylvania German, 8.3% Polish (2006-2010 5-year est.).

Economy: Single-family building permits issued: 22 (2011); Multi-family building permits issued: 0 (2011); Employment by occupation: 11.8% management, 4.3% professional, 7.6% services, 17.6% sales, 3.0% farming, 7.8% construction, 4.4% production (2006-2010 5-year est.).

Income: Per capita income: $33,761 (2006-2010 5-year est.); Median household income: $72,953 (2006-2010 5-year est.); Average household income: $90,443 (2006-2010 5-year est.); Percent of households with income of $100,000 or more: 34.9% (2006-2010 5-year est.); Poverty rate: 4.4% (2006-2010 5-year est.).

Education: Percent of population age 25 and over with: High school diploma (including GED) or higher: 92.0% (2006-2010 5-year est.); Bachelor's degree or higher: 32.9% (2006-2010 5-year est.); Master's degree or higher: 14.0% (2006-2010 5-year est.).

Housing: Homeownership rate: 87.0% (2010); Median home value: $261,700 (2006-2010 5-year est.); Median contract rent: $703 per month (2006-2010 5-year est.); Median year structure built: 1981 (2006-2010 5-year est.).

Transportation: Commute to work: 94.6% car, 0.7% public transportation, 0.9% walk, 2.7% work from home (2006-2010 5-year est.); Travel time to work: 25.2% less than 15 minutes, 43.7% 15 to 30 minutes, 20.2% 30 to 45 minutes, 4.2% 45 to 60 minutes, 6.8% 60 minutes or more (2006-2010 5-year est.)

Additional Information Contacts

Greater Lehigh Valley Chamber of Commerce . . . . (610) 841-5800

   http://www.lehighvalleychamber.org

North Whitehall Township . . . . (610) 799-3411

   http://www.northwhitehall.org

OLD ZIONSVILLE (unincorporated postal area)

Zip Code: 18068

   Covers a land area of 0.004 square miles and a water area of 0 square miles. Located at 40.48° N. Lat; 75.52° W. Long. Elevation is 778 feet. Population: 42 (2010); Density: 10,390.9 persons per square mile (2010); Race: 97.6% White, 0.0% Black, 0.0% Asian, 0.0% American Indian/Alaska Native, 0.0% Native Hawaiian/Other Pacific Islander, 2.4% Other, 0.0% Hispanic of any race (2010); Average household size: 2.47 (2010); Median age: 29.5 (2010); Males per 100 females: 90.9 (2010); Homeownership rate: 47.0% (2010)

OREFIELD (unincorporated postal area)

Zip Code: 18069

   Covers a land area of 13.817 square miles and a water area of 0.099 square miles. Located at 40.62° N. Lat; 75.61° W. Long. Elevation is 453 feet. Population: 8,017 (2010); Density: 580.2 persons per square mile (2010); Race: 89.0% White, 2.6% Black, 5.6% Asian, 0.2% American Indian/Alaska Native, 0.0% Native Hawaiian/Other Pacific Islander, 2.6% Other, 4.0% Hispanic of any race (2010); Average household size: 2.75 (2010); Median age: 42.1 (2010); Males per 100 females: 101.5 (2010); Homeownership rate: 90.6% (2010)

SALISBURY (township). Covers a land area of 11.172 square miles and a water area of 0.101 square miles. Located at 40.60° N. Lat; 75.43° W. Long.

Population: 13,688 (1990); 13,498 (2000); 13,505 (2010); Density: 1,208.8 persons per square mile (2010); Race: 91.4% White, 2.9% Black, 1.6% Asian, 0.0% American Indian/Alaska Native, 0.0% Native Hawaiian/Other Pacific Islander, 4.1% Other, 6.7% Hispanic of any race (2010); Average household size: 2.47 (2010); Median age: 46.8 (2010); Males per 100 females: 99.1 (2010); Marriage status: 22.3% never married, 61.6% now married, 8.4% widowed, 7.6% divorced (2006-2010 5-year est.); Foreign born: 5.7% (2006-2010 5-year est.); Ancestry (includes multiple ancestries): 34.2% German, 15.7% Irish, 9.6% Italian, 6.5% Polish, 6.1% English (2006-2010 5-year est.).

Economy: Single-family building permits issued: 1 (2011); Multi-family building permits issued: 0 (2011); Employment by occupation: 13.5% management, 6.9% professional, 7.6% services, 17.9% sales, 2.1% farming, 10.2% construction, 6.4% production (2006-2010 5-year est.).

Income: Per capita income: $36,880 (2006-2010 5-year est.); Median household income: $67,470 (2006-2010 5-year est.); Average household income: $91,135 (2006-2010 5-year est.); Percent of households with income of $100,000 or more: 29.8% (2006-2010 5-year est.); Poverty rate: 3.9% (2006-2010 5-year est.).

Education: Percent of population age 25 and over with: High school diploma (including GED) or higher: 91.0% (2006-2010 5-year est.); Bachelor's degree or higher: 27.7% (2006-2010 5-year est.); Master's degree or higher: 11.8% (2006-2010 5-year est.).

Housing: Homeownership rate: 84.7% (2010); Median home value: $222,300 (2006-2010 5-year est.); Median contract rent: $838 per month (2006-2010 5-year est.); Median year structure built: 1967 (2006-2010 5-year est.).

Safety: Violent crime rate: 4.4 per 10,000 population; Property crime rate: 218.5 per 10,000 population (2011).

Transportation: Commute to work: 94.1% car, 0.3% public transportation, 0.7% walk, 3.5% work from home (2006-2010 5-year est.); Travel time to work: 31.5% less than 15 minutes, 43.1% 15 to 30 minutes, 13.1% 30 to 45 minutes, 3.5% 45 to 60 minutes, 8.8% 60 minutes or more (2006-2010 5-year est.)

Additional Information Contacts

Greater Lehigh Valley Chamber of Commerce . . . . (610) 841-5800
  http://www.lehighvalleychamber.org
Salisbury Township . . . . (610) 797-4000
  http://www.salisburytownshippa.org

SCHNECKSVILLE (CDP). Covers a land area of 2.690 square miles and a water area of 0.009 square miles. Located at 40.67° N. Lat; 75.61° W. Long. Elevation is 663 feet.

Population: 1,810 (1990); 1,989 (2000); 2,935 (2010); Density: 1,091.1 persons per square mile (2010); Race: 95.8% White, 0.9% Black, 1.4% Asian, 0.1% American Indian/Alaska Native, 0.0% Native Hawaiian/Other Pacific Islander, 1.8% Other, 2.9% Hispanic of any race (2010); Average household size: 2.47 (2010); Median age: 43.4 (2010); Males per 100 females: 89.8 (2010); Marriage status: 23.2% never married, 62.0% now married, 4.7% widowed, 10.1% divorced (2006-2010 5-year est.); Foreign born: 4.3% (2006-2010 5-year est.); Ancestry (includes multiple ancestries): 30.3% German, 16.3% Italian, 12.6% Irish, 9.3% Pennsylvania German, 7.3% English (2006-2010 5-year est.).

Economy: Employment by occupation: 11.8% management, 5.7% professional, 5.4% services, 17.7% sales, 2.6% farming, 6.3% construction, 6.7% production (2006-2010 5-year est.).

Income: Per capita income: $34,673 (2006-2010 5-year est.); Median household income: $63,080 (2006-2010 5-year est.); Average household income: $82,299 (2006-2010 5-year est.); Percent of households with income of $100,000 or more: 28.9% (2006-2010 5-year est.); Poverty rate: 1.9% (2006-2010 5-year est.).

Education: Percent of population age 25 and over with: High school diploma (including GED) or higher: 91.2% (2006-2010 5-year est.); Bachelor's degree or higher: 44.4% (2006-2010 5-year est.); Master's degree or higher: 20.5% (2006-2010 5-year est.).

School District(s)

Lehigh Career & Technical Institute (09-12)
  2010-11 Enrollment: 2,624 . . . . (610) 799-1323
Parkland SD (KG-12)
  2010-11 Enrollment: 9,354 . . . . (610) 351-5503

Two-year College(s)

Lehigh Carbon Community College (Public)
  Fall 2010 Enrollment: 4,917 . . . . (610) 799-2121
  2011-12 Tuition: In-state $6,240; Out-of-state $9,240

Housing: Homeownership rate: 72.6% (2010); Median home value: $261,900 (2006-2010 5-year est.); Median contract rent: $690 per month (2006-2010 5-year est.); Median year structure built: 1979 (2006-2010 5-year est.).

Transportation: Commute to work: 94.7% car, 1.6% public transportation, 0.8% walk, 1.8% work from home (2006-2010 5-year est.); Travel time to work: 20.4% less than 15 minutes, 42.7% 15 to 30 minutes, 22.3% 30 to 45 minutes, 5.3% 45 to 60 minutes, 9.4% 60 minutes or more (2006-2010 5-year est.)

Additional Information Contacts

Greater Lehigh Valley Chamber of Commerce . . . . (610) 841-5800
  http://www.lehighvalleychamber.org

SLATEDALE (CDP). Covers a land area of 0.297 square miles and a water area of 0.002 square miles. Located at 40.74° N. Lat; 75.66° W. Long. Elevation is 505 feet.

Population: n/a (1990); n/a (2000); 455 (2010); Density: 1,533.3 persons per square mile (2010); Race: 98.5% White, 0.0% Black, 1.1% Asian, 0.0% American Indian/Alaska Native, 0.0% Native Hawaiian/Other Pacific Islander, 0.4% Other, 1.1% Hispanic of any race (2010); Average

household size: 2.60 (2010); Median age: 40.3 (2010); Males per 100 females: 99.6 (2010); Marriage status: 43.5% never married, 51.1% now married, 5.4% widowed, 0.0% divorced (2006-2010 5-year est.); Foreign born: 0.0% (2006-2010 5-year est.); Ancestry (includes multiple ancestries): 38.4% Pennsylvania German, 36.6% German, 28.5% Dutch, 16.7% Hungarian, 15.1% Scottish (2006-2010 5-year est.).

Economy: Employment by occupation: 0.0% management, 0.0% professional, 10.4% services, 21.4% sales, 7.4% farming, 11.9% construction, 9.8% production (2006-2010 5-year est.).

Income: Per capita income: $24,823 (2006-2010 5-year est.); Median household income: $71,629 (2006-2010 5-year est.); Average household income: $61,354 (2006-2010 5-year est.); Percent of households with income of $100,000 or more: 10.3% (2006-2010 5-year est.); Poverty rate: 11.6% (2006-2010 5-year est.).

Education: Percent of population age 25 and over with: High school diploma (including GED) or higher: 85.2% (2006-2010 5-year est.); Bachelor's degree or higher: 7.6% (2006-2010 5-year est.); Master's degree or higher: 0.0% (2006-2010 5-year est.).

Housing: Homeownership rate: 79.5% (2010); Median home value: $173,700 (2006-2010 5-year est.); Median contract rent: $499 per month (2006-2010 5-year est.); Median year structure built: before 1940 (2006-2010 5-year est.).

Transportation: Commute to work: 100.0% car, 0.0% public transportation, 0.0% walk, 0.0% work from home (2006-2010 5-year est.); Travel time to work: 19.3% less than 15 minutes, 19.3% 15 to 30 minutes, 54.0% 30 to 45 minutes, 0.0% 45 to 60 minutes, 7.4% 60 minutes or more (2006-2010 5-year est.)

SLATINGTON (borough). Covers a land area of 1.321 square miles and a water area of 0.057 square miles. Located at 40.75° N. Lat; 75.61° W. Long. Elevation is 495 feet.

History: Appalachian Trail on Blue Mt. ridge, to North. Settled 1737, incorporated 1864.

Population: 4,678 (1990); 4,434 (2000); 4,232 (2010); Density: 3,204.1 persons per square mile (2010); Race: 94.1% White, 1.6% Black, 0.5% Asian, 0.4% American Indian/Alaska Native, 0.0% Native Hawaiian/Other Pacific Islander, 3.4% Other, 5.2% Hispanic of any race (2010); Average household size: 2.40 (2010); Median age: 39.2 (2010); Males per 100 females: 92.3 (2010); Marriage status: 28.0% never married, 54.8% now married, 6.7% widowed, 10.5% divorced (2006-2010 5-year est.); Foreign born: 1.5% (2006-2010 5-year est.); Ancestry (includes multiple ancestries): 35.9% German, 12.4% Irish, 9.4% Italian, 9.2% Pennsylvania German, 8.3% Dutch (2006-2010 5-year est.).

Economy: Single-family building permits issued: 0 (2011); Multi-family building permits issued: 0 (2011); Employment by occupation: 9.0% management, 2.6% professional, 9.0% services, 16.8% sales, 5.2% farming, 15.2% construction, 12.4% production (2006-2010 5-year est.).

Income: Per capita income: $22,113 (2006-2010 5-year est.); Median household income: $41,083 (2006-2010 5-year est.); Average household income: $54,223 (2006-2010 5-year est.); Percent of households with income of $100,000 or more: 16.0% (2006-2010 5-year est.); Poverty rate: 15.9% (2006-2010 5-year est.).

Education: Percent of population age 25 and over with: High school diploma (including GED) or higher: 88.5% (2006-2010 5-year est.); Bachelor's degree or higher: 12.5% (2006-2010 5-year est.); Master's degree or higher: 4.5% (2006-2010 5-year est.).

School District(s)

Northern Lehigh SD (KG-12)
  2010-11 Enrollment: 1,885 . . . . (610) 767-9800

Housing: Homeownership rate: 58.5% (2010); Median home value: $141,700 (2006-2010 5-year est.); Median contract rent: $571 per month (2006-2010 5-year est.); Median year structure built: 1941 (2006-2010 5-year est.).

Safety: Violent crime rate: 9.4 per 10,000 population; Property crime rate: 195.5 per 10,000 population (2011).

Transportation: Commute to work: 94.5% car, 0.8% public transportation, 0.9% walk, 3.8% work from home (2006-2010 5-year est.); Travel time to work: 16.8% less than 15 minutes, 28.9% 15 to 30 minutes, 40.6% 30 to 45 minutes, 7.3% 45 to 60 minutes, 6.4% 60 minutes or more (2006-2010 5-year est.)

Additional Information Contacts

Lehighton Chamber of Commerce . . . . (610) 377-2191
  http://lehigtonareacouncil.org

SOUTH WHITEHALL (township). Covers a land area of 17.079 square miles and a water area of 0.170 square miles. Located at 40.62° N. Lat; 75.55° W. Long.

Population: 18,125 (1990); 18,028 (2000); 19,180 (2010); Density: 1,123.0 persons per square mile (2010); Race: 89.8% White, 2.8% Black, 4.7% Asian, 0.1% American Indian/Alaska Native, 0.0% Native Hawaiian/Other Pacific Islander, 2.6% Other, 4.7% Hispanic of any race (2010); Average household size: 2.38 (2010); Median age: 47.4 (2010); Males per 100 females: 89.6 (2010); Marriage status: 21.1% never married, 58.3% now married, 10.2% widowed, 10.4% divorced (2006-2010 5-year est.); Foreign born: 8.0% (2006-2010 5-year est.); Ancestry (includes multiple ancestries): 28.9% German, 15.4% Irish, 12.7% Italian, 5.9% English, 5.9% Pennsylvania German (2006-2010 5-year est.).

Economy: Single-family building permits issued: 18 (2011); Multi-family building permits issued: 0 (2011); Employment by occupation: 13.6% management, 6.8% professional, 6.6% services, 18.2% sales, 2.2% farming, 5.9% construction, 5.3% production (2006-2010 5-year est.).

Income: Per capita income: $36,274 (2006-2010 5-year est.); Median household income: $64,854 (2006-2010 5-year est.); Average household income: $88,208 (2006-2010 5-year est.); Percent of households with income of $100,000 or more: 27.5% (2006-2010 5-year est.); Poverty rate: 3.8% (2006-2010 5-year est.).

Education: Percent of population age 25 and over with: High school diploma (including GED) or higher: 91.2% (2006-2010 5-year est.); Bachelor's degree or higher: 38.7% (2006-2010 5-year est.); Master's degree or higher: 16.9% (2006-2010 5-year est.).

Housing: Homeownership rate: 81.3% (2010); Median home value: $234,400 (2006-2010 5-year est.); Median contract rent: $709 per month (2006-2010 5-year est.); Median year structure built: 1970 (2006-2010 5-year est.).

Safety: Violent crime rate: 10.4 per 10,000 population; Property crime rate: 399.1 per 10,000 population (2011).

Transportation: Commute to work: 93.7% car, 0.3% public transportation, 1.4% walk, 4.4% work from home (2006-2010 5-year est.); Travel time to work: 36.1% less than 15 minutes, 45.5% 15 to 30 minutes, 7.0% 30 to 45 minutes, 3.3% 45 to 60 minutes, 8.1% 60 minutes or more (2006-2010 5-year est.).

Additional Information Contacts

South Whitehall Township . . . . (610) 398-0401
    http://www.southwhitehall.com
Whitehall Area Chamber of Commerce . . . . (610) 432-4130
    http://www.waccpa.org

STILES (CDP). Covers a land area of 0.215 square miles and a water area of <.001 square miles. Located at 40.67° N. Lat; 75.51° W. Long. Elevation is 358 feet.

Population: n/a (1990); n/a (2000); 1,113 (2010); Density: 5,175.7 persons per square mile (2010); Race: 88.4% White, 3.1% Black, 2.4% Asian, 0.4% American Indian/Alaska Native, 0.0% Native Hawaiian/Other Pacific Islander, 5.7% Other, 9.3% Hispanic of any race (2010); Average household size: 2.68 (2010); Median age: 41.8 (2010); Males per 100 females: 92.6 (2010); Marriage status: 19.8% never married, 61.9% now married, 13.2% widowed, 5.1% divorced (2006-2010 5-year est.); Foreign born: 12.8% (2006-2010 5-year est.); Ancestry (includes multiple ancestries): 48.1% German, 26.3% Polish, 7.9% Italian, 7.4% Irish, 7.0% Austrian (2006-2010 5-year est.).

Economy: Employment by occupation: 0.0% management, 4.2% professional, 9.7% services, 37.4% sales, 3.8% farming, 7.8% construction, 0.0% production (2006-2010 5-year est.).

Income: Per capita income: $23,869 (2006-2010 5-year est.); Median household income: $55,531 (2006-2010 5-year est.); Average household income: $57,382 (2006-2010 5-year est.); Percent of households with income of $100,000 or more: 10.1% (2006-2010 5-year est.); Poverty rate: 4.2% (2006-2010 5-year est.).

Education: Percent of population age 25 and over with: High school diploma (including GED) or higher: 88.0% (2006-2010 5-year est.); Bachelor's degree or higher: 17.1% (2006-2010 5-year est.); Master's degree or higher: 6.4% (2006-2010 5-year est.).

Housing: Homeownership rate: 88.2% (2010); Median home value: $201,600 (2006-2010 5-year est.); Median contract rent: $1,082 per month (2006-2010 5-year est.); Median year structure built: 1965 (2006-2010 5-year est.).

Transportation: Commute to work: 97.5% car, 0.0% public transportation, 0.0% walk, 2.5% work from home (2006-2010 5-year est.); Travel time to work: 25.7% less than 15 minutes, 54.5% 15 to 30 minutes, 7.8% 30 to 45

minutes, 0.0% 45 to 60 minutes, 12.1% 60 minutes or more (2006-2010 5-year est.)

TREXLERTOWN (CDP). Covers a land area of 2.228 square miles and a water area of 0.033 square miles. Located at 40.56° N. Lat; 75.59° W. Long. Elevation is 400 feet.

Population: n/a (1990); n/a (2000); 1,988 (2010); Density: 892.1 persons per square mile (2010); Race: 83.4% White, 4.2% Black, 8.1% Asian, 0.1% American Indian/Alaska Native, 0.0% Native Hawaiian/Other Pacific Islander, 4.2% Other, 4.8% Hispanic of any race (2010); Average household size: 2.21 (2010); Median age: 36.5 (2010); Males per 100 females: 91.7 (2010); Marriage status: 23.7% never married, 57.4% now married, 10.4% widowed, 8.6% divorced (2006-2010 5-year est.); Foreign born: 22.4% (2006-2010 5-year est.); Ancestry (includes multiple ancestries): 34.3% German, 11.3% Italian, 7.3% Irish, 7.0% Pennsylvania German, 6.0% English (2006-2010 5-year est.).

Economy: Employment by occupation: 4.4% management, 11.3% professional, 2.5% services, 12.8% sales, 4.3% farming, 3.3% construction, 4.3% production (2006-2010 5-year est.).

Income: Per capita income: $29,290 (2006-2010 5-year est.); Median household income: $60,476 (2006-2010 5-year est.); Average household income: $71,325 (2006-2010 5-year est.); Percent of households with income of $100,000 or more: 26.0% (2006-2010 5-year est.); Poverty rate: 8.5% (2006-2010 5-year est.).

Education: Percent of population age 25 and over with: High school diploma (including GED) or higher: 83.5% (2006-2010 5-year est.); Bachelor's degree or higher: 38.3% (2006-2010 5-year est.); Master's degree or higher: 16.0% (2006-2010 5-year est.).

Housing: Homeownership rate: 47.7% (2010); Median home value: $211,400 (2006-2010 5-year est.); Median contract rent: $1,175 per month (2006-2010 5-year est.); Median year structure built: 1997 (2006-2010 5-year est.).

Transportation: Commute to work: 92.4% car, 0.0% public transportation, 2.0% walk, 5.6% work from home (2006-2010 5-year est.); Travel time to work: 52.6% less than 15 minutes, 25.6% 15 to 30 minutes, 15.0% 30 to 45 minutes, 4.1% 45 to 60 minutes, 2.8% 60 minutes or more (2006-2010 5-year est.)

UPPER MACUNGIE (township). Covers a land area of 26.069 square miles and a water area of 0.193 square miles. Located at 40.57° N. Lat; 75.62° W. Long.

Population: 8,744 (1990); 13,895 (2000); 20,063 (2010); Density: 769.6 persons per square mile (2010); Race: 85.0% White, 2.7% Black, 9.0% Asian, 0.1% American Indian/Alaska Native, 0.0% Native Hawaiian/Other Pacific Islander, 3.2% Other, 4.9% Hispanic of any race (2010); Average household size: 2.71 (2010); Median age: 39.1 (2010); Males per 100 females: 97.2 (2010); Marriage status: 20.5% never married, 67.3% now married, 5.6% widowed, 6.6% divorced (2006-2010 5-year est.); Foreign born: 10.8% (2006-2010 5-year est.); Ancestry (includes multiple ancestries): 32.7% German, 15.9% Irish, 14.5% Italian, 7.6% English, 6.3% Polish (2006-2010 5-year est.).

Economy: Single-family building permits issued: 104 (2011); Multi-family building permits issued: 0 (2011); Employment by occupation: 17.9% management, 10.0% professional, 2.6% services, 13.8% sales, 3.6% farming, 4.5% construction, 3.4% production (2006-2010 5-year est.).

Income: Per capita income: $36,465 (2006-2010 5-year est.); Median household income: $90,188 (2006-2010 5-year est.); Average household income: $100,480 (2006-2010 5-year est.); Percent of households with income of $100,000 or more: 44.0% (2006-2010 5-year est.); Poverty rate: 3.5% (2006-2010 5-year est.).

Taxes: Total city taxes per capita: $357 (2009); City property taxes per capita: $65 (2009).

Education: Percent of population age 25 and over with: High school diploma (including GED) or higher: 92.8% (2006-2010 5-year est.); Bachelor's degree or higher: 43.8% (2006-2010 5-year est.); Master's degree or higher: 19.9% (2006-2010 5-year est.).

Housing: Homeownership rate: 81.6% (2010); Median home value: $292,600 (2006-2010 5-year est.); Median contract rent: $1,048 per month (2006-2010 5-year est.); Median year structure built: 1992 (2006-2010 5-year est.).

Transportation: Commute to work: 94.0% car, 0.3% public transportation, 2.1% walk, 3.3% work from home (2006-2010 5-year est.); Travel time to work: 35.9% less than 15 minutes, 40.6% 15 to 30 minutes, 11.3% 30 to 45 minutes, 2.9% 45 to 60 minutes, 9.4% 60 minutes or more (2006-2010 5-year est.)

Additional Information Contacts

Northeast Berks Chamber of Commerce . . . . (610) 683-8860
    http://www.northeastberkschamber.com
Upper Macungie Township . . . . (610) 395-4892
    http://www.uppermac.org

UPPER MILFORD (township). Covers a land area of 17.956 square miles and a water area of 0.053 square miles. Located at 40.49° N. Lat; 75.52° W. Long.

Population: 6,280 (1990); 6,889 (2000); 7,292 (2010); Density: 406.1 persons per square mile (2010); Race: 96.6% White, 0.4% Black, 1.2% Asian, 0.1% American Indian/Alaska Native, 0.1% Native Hawaiian/Other Pacific Islander, 1.6% Other, 2.3% Hispanic of any race (2010); Average household size: 2.61 (2010); Median age: 46.3 (2010); Males per 100 females: 101.1 (2010); Marriage status: 28.2% never married, 59.6% now married, 4.9% widowed, 7.3% divorced (2006-2010 5-year est.); Foreign born: 0.7% (2006-2010 5-year est.); Ancestry (includes multiple ancestries): 39.9% German, 12.4% Pennsylvania German, 11.4% Irish, 8.8% Polish, 7.9% Italian (2006-2010 5-year est.).

Economy: Single-family building permits issued: 10 (2011); Multi-family building permits issued: 0 (2011); Employment by occupation: 8.7% management, 4.2% professional, 9.6% services, 15.3% sales, 4.6% farming, 13.7% construction, 7.0% production (2006-2010 5-year est.).

Income: Per capita income: $31,446 (2006-2010 5-year est.); Median household income: $65,589 (2006-2010 5-year est.); Average household income: $84,411 (2006-2010 5-year est.); Percent of households with income of $100,000 or more: 28.8% (2006-2010 5-year est.); Poverty rate: 6.9% (2006-2010 5-year est.).

Education: Percent of population age 25 and over with: High school diploma (including GED) or higher: 92.0% (2006-2010 5-year est.); Bachelor's degree or higher: 25.2% (2006-2010 5-year est.); Master's degree or higher: 8.4% (2006-2010 5-year est.).

Housing: Homeownership rate: 90.6% (2010); Median home value: $287,300 (2006-2010 5-year est.); Median contract rent: $776 per month (2006-2010 5-year est.); Median year structure built: 1971 (2006-2010 5-year est.).

Transportation: Commute to work: 93.9% car, 0.0% public transportation, 2.5% walk, 3.6% work from home (2006-2010 5-year est.); Travel time to work: 26.2% less than 15 minutes, 42.9% 15 to 30 minutes, 18.0% 30 to 45 minutes, 7.0% 45 to 60 minutes, 5.8% 60 minutes or more (2006-2010 5-year est.)

Additional Information Contacts

Upper Bucks Chamber of Commerce . . . . (215) 536-3211
    http://www.ubcc.org
Upper Milford Township . . . . (610) 966-3223
    http://www.uppermilford.net

UPPER SAUCON (township). Covers a land area of 24.461 square miles and a water area of 0.151 square miles. Located at 40.54° N. Lat; 75.41° W. Long.

Population: 9,671 (1990); 11,939 (2000); 14,808 (2010); Density: 605.4 persons per square mile (2010); Race: 93.6% White, 1.2% Black, 3.3% Asian, 0.1% American Indian/Alaska Native, 0.1% Native Hawaiian/Other Pacific Islander, 1.7% Other, 3.1% Hispanic of any race (2010); Average household size: 2.74 (2010); Median age: 41.1 (2010); Males per 100 females: 98.0 (2010); Marriage status: 31.9% never married, 60.1% now married, 4.4% widowed, 3.6% divorced (2006-2010 5-year est.); Foreign born: 4.9% (2006-2010 5-year est.); Ancestry (includes multiple ancestries): 41.1% German, 21.6% Irish, 14.9% Italian, 9.2% English, 6.1% Polish (2006-2010 5-year est.).

Economy: Single-family building permits issued: 112 (2011); Multi-family building permits issued: 2 (2011); Employment by occupation: 17.6% management, 4.6% professional, 11.3% services, 13.1% sales, 4.0% farming, 7.7% construction, 5.6% production (2006-2010 5-year est.).

Income: Per capita income: $37,644 (2006-2010 5-year est.); Median household income: $95,107 (2006-2010 5-year est.); Average household income: $116,837 (2006-2010 5-year est.); Percent of households with income of $100,000 or more: 46.5% (2006-2010 5-year est.); Poverty rate: 2.6% (2006-2010 5-year est.).

Education: Percent of population age 25 and over with: High school diploma (including GED) or higher: 93.2% (2006-2010 5-year est.); Bachelor's degree or higher: 43.7% (2006-2010 5-year est.); Master's degree or higher: 19.8% (2006-2010 5-year est.).

Housing: Homeownership rate: 89.5% (2010); Median home value: $299,800 (2006-2010 5-year est.); Median contract rent: $641 per month

(2006-2010 5-year est.); Median year structure built: 1975 (2006-2010 5-year est.).

Safety: Violent crime rate: 4.7 per 10,000 population; Property crime rate: 136.7 per 10,000 population (2011).

Transportation: Commute to work: 86.7% car, 0.0% public transportation, 2.2% walk, 10.8% work from home (2006-2010 5-year est.); Travel time to work: 27.6% less than 15 minutes, 42.1% 15 to 30 minutes, 12.1% 30 to 45 minutes, 8.8% 45 to 60 minutes, 9.5% 60 minutes or more (2006-2010 5-year est.)

Additional Information Contacts

Upper Bucks Chamber of Commerce . . . . (215) 536-3211
    http://www.ubcc.org
Upper Saucon Township . . . . (610) 282-1171
    http://www.uppersaucon.org

WASHINGTON (township). Covers a land area of 23.554 square miles and a water area of 0.184 square miles. Located at 40.74° N. Lat; 75.64° W. Long.

Population: 6,374 (1990); 6,588 (2000); 6,624 (2010); Density: 281.2 persons per square mile (2010); Race: 98.0% White, 0.4% Black, 0.4% Asian, 0.2% American Indian/Alaska Native, 0.0% Native Hawaiian/Other Pacific Islander, 1.0% Other, 1.8% Hispanic of any race (2010); Average household size: 2.50 (2010); Median age: 45.3 (2010); Males per 100 females: 102.9 (2010); Marriage status: 25.6% never married, 65.3% now married, 5.0% widowed, 4.1% divorced (2006-2010 5-year est.); Foreign born: 0.9% (2006-2010 5-year est.); Ancestry (includes multiple ancestries): 43.8% German, 18.7% Pennsylvania German, 9.7% Irish, 8.4% Italian, 6.1% American (2006-2010 5-year est.).

Economy: Single-family building permits issued: 6 (2011); Multi-family building permits issued: 0 (2011); Employment by occupation: 12.5% management, 2.7% professional, 9.0% services, 17.6% sales, 3.1% farming, 14.8% construction, 10.6% production (2006-2010 5-year est.).

Income: Per capita income: $26,228 (2006-2010 5-year est.); Median household income: $67,411 (2006-2010 5-year est.); Average household income: $67,850 (2006-2010 5-year est.); Percent of households with income of $100,000 or more: 20.7% (2006-2010 5-year est.); Poverty rate: 7.8% (2006-2010 5-year est.).

Education: Percent of population age 25 and over with: High school diploma (including GED) or higher: 85.4% (2006-2010 5-year est.); Bachelor's degree or higher: 15.5% (2006-2010 5-year est.); Master's degree or higher: 4.9% (2006-2010 5-year est.).

Housing: Homeownership rate: 90.3% (2010); Median home value: $209,600 (2006-2010 5-year est.); Median contract rent: $573 per month (2006-2010 5-year est.); Median year structure built: 1977 (2006-2010 5-year est.).

Transportation: Commute to work: 95.5% car, 0.0% public transportation, 0.7% walk, 3.1% work from home (2006-2010 5-year est.); Travel time to work: 17.9% less than 15 minutes, 32.6% 15 to 30 minutes, 34.3% 30 to 45 minutes, 6.2% 45 to 60 minutes, 9.0% 60 minutes or more (2006-2010 5-year est.)

Additional Information Contacts

Greater Lehigh Valley Chamber of Commerce . . . . (610) 841-5800
    http://www.lehighvalleychamber.org
Washington Township . . . . (610) 767-8108

WEISENBERG (township). Covers a land area of 26.771 square miles and a water area of 0.052 square miles. Located at 40.60° N. Lat; 75.71° W. Long. Elevation is 564 feet.

Population: 3,266 (1990); 4,144 (2000); 4,923 (2010); Density: 183.9 persons per square mile (2010); Race: 97.4% White, 0.5% Black, 0.5% Asian, 0.1% American Indian/Alaska Native, 0.1% Native Hawaiian/Other Pacific Islander, 1.4% Other, 2.4% Hispanic of any race (2010); Average household size: 2.78 (2010); Median age: 43.6 (2010); Males per 100 females: 105.9 (2010); Marriage status: 15.5% never married, 74.0% now married, 3.4% widowed, 7.1% divorced (2006-2010 5-year est.); Foreign born: 2.4% (2006-2010 5-year est.); Ancestry (includes multiple ancestries): 46.3% German, 18.8% Italian, 9.1% Irish, 6.8% Polish, 6.7% Pennsylvania German (2006-2010 5-year est.).

Economy: Single-family building permits issued: 8 (2011); Multi-family building permits issued: 0 (2011); Employment by occupation: 17.1% management, 8.7% professional, 5.3% services, 12.4% sales, 2.7% farming, 9.7% construction, 8.7% production (2006-2010 5-year est.).

Income: Per capita income: $36,429 (2006-2010 5-year est.); Median household income: $73,924 (2006-2010 5-year est.); Average household income: $94,619 (2006-2010 5-year est.); Percent of households with

income of $100,000 or more: 34.9% (2006-2010 5-year est.); Poverty rate: 2.0% (2006-2010 5-year est.).

Education: Percent of population age 25 and over with: High school diploma (including GED) or higher: 94.3% (2006-2010 5-year est.); Bachelor's degree or higher: 35.7% (2006-2010 5-year est.); Master's degree or higher: 13.5% (2006-2010 5-year est.).

Housing: Homeownership rate: 92.5% (2010); Median home value: $336,100 (2006-2010 5-year est.); Median contract rent: $684 per month (2006-2010 5-year est.); Median year structure built: 1991 (2006-2010 5-year est.).

Transportation: Commute to work: 94.7% car, 2.3% public transportation, 1.0% walk, 1.7% work from home (2006-2010 5-year est.); Travel time to work: 20.7% less than 15 minutes, 47.2% 15 to 30 minutes, 22.6% 30 to 45 minutes, 1.4% 45 to 60 minutes, 8.2% 60 minutes or more (2006-2010 5-year est.)

Additional Information Contacts

Northeast Berks Chamber of Commerce . . . . (610) 683-8860
    http://www.northeastberkschamber.com

WESCOSVILLE (CDP). Covers a land area of 2.740 square miles and a water area of 0.004 square miles. Located at 40.56° N. Lat; 75.55° W. Long. Elevation is 413 feet.

Population: n/a (1990); n/a (2000); 5,872 (2010); Density: 2,142.7 persons per square mile (2010); Race: 86.3% White, 3.0% Black, 7.2% Asian, 0.2% American Indian/Alaska Native, 0.0% Native Hawaiian/Other Pacific Islander, 3.3% Other, 5.1% Hispanic of any race (2010); Average household size: 2.69 (2010); Median age: 42.3 (2010); Males per 100 females: 92.3 (2010); Marriage status: 22.5% never married, 66.4% now married, 5.2% widowed, 5.9% divorced (2006-2010 5-year est.); Foreign born: 7.4% (2006-2010 5-year est.); Ancestry (includes multiple ancestries): 30.1% German, 18.0% Irish, 15.0% Italian, 8.0% Polish, 6.0% English (2006-2010 5-year est.).

Economy: Employment by occupation: 14.0% management, 7.4% professional, 8.3% services, 12.4% sales, 4.0% farming, 2.9% construction, 2.0% production (2006-2010 5-year est.).

Income: Per capita income: $36,507 (2006-2010 5-year est.); Median household income: $84,773 (2006-2010 5-year est.); Average household income: $101,791 (2006-2010 5-year est.); Percent of households with income of $100,000 or more: 42.5% (2006-2010 5-year est.); Poverty rate: 4.6% (2006-2010 5-year est.).

Education: Percent of population age 25 and over with: High school diploma (including GED) or higher: 91.2% (2006-2010 5-year est.); Bachelor's degree or higher: 47.7% (2006-2010 5-year est.); Master's degree or higher: 25.8% (2006-2010 5-year est.).

School District(s)

East Penn SD (KG-12)
    2010-11 Enrollment: 8,029 . . . . (610) 966-8300

Housing: Homeownership rate: 86.6% (2010); Median home value: $304,100 (2006-2010 5-year est.); Median contract rent: $1,028 per month (2006-2010 5-year est.); Median year structure built: 1983 (2006-2010 5-year est.).

Transportation: Commute to work: 91.1% car, 1.0% public transportation, 0.6% walk, 7.3% work from home (2006-2010 5-year est.); Travel time to work: 40.6% less than 15 minutes, 38.3% 15 to 30 minutes, 9.4% 30 to 45 minutes, 3.7% 45 to 60 minutes, 8.1% 60 minutes or more (2006-2010 5-year est.)

WHITEHALL (township). Aka Fullerton. Covers a land area of 12.567 square miles and a water area of 0.301 square miles. Located at 40.66° N. Lat; 75.50° W. Long.

Population: 22,794 (1990); 24,896 (2000); 26,738 (2010); Density: 2,127.7 persons per square mile (2010); Race: 82.9% White, 5.7% Black, 4.1% Asian, 0.3% American Indian/Alaska Native, 0.0% Native Hawaiian/Other Pacific Islander, 7.0% Other, 10.7% Hispanic of any race (2010); Average household size: 2.40 (2010); Median age: 41.6 (2010); Males per 100 females: 90.6 (2010); Marriage status: 28.7% never married, 54.2% now married, 7.6% widowed, 9.5% divorced (2006-2010 5-year est.); Foreign born: 13.3% (2006-2010 5-year est.); Ancestry (includes multiple ancestries): 28.8% German, 10.4% Irish, 8.3% Italian, 5.5% Polish, 4.5% Slovak (2006-2010 5-year est.).

Economy: Unemployment rate: 8.3% (August 2012); Total civilian labor force: 14,908 (August 2012); Single-family building permits issued: 25 (2011); Multi-family building permits issued: 0 (2011); Employment by occupation: 8.8% management, 4.9% professional, 9.5% services, 18.3%

sales, 6.1% farming, 8.6% construction, 6.7% production (2006-2010 5-year est.).

Income: Per capita income: $26,253 (2006-2010 5-year est.); Median household income: $52,200 (2006-2010 5-year est.); Average household income: $62,651 (2006-2010 5-year est.); Percent of households with income of $100,000 or more: 16.7% (2006-2010 5-year est.); Poverty rate: 8.0% (2006-2010 5-year est.).

Education: Percent of population age 25 and over with: High school diploma (including GED) or higher: 87.4% (2006-2010 5-year est.); Bachelor's degree or higher: 24.1% (2006-2010 5-year est.); Master's degree or higher: 8.6% (2006-2010 5-year est.).

School District(s)

Whitehall-Coplay SD (KG-12)
    2010-11 Enrollment: 4,175 . . . . (610) 439-1431

Vocational/Technical School(s)

Empire Beauty School-Lehigh Valley (Private, For-profit)
    Fall 2010 Enrollment: 342 . . . . (800) 223-3271
    2011-12 Tuition: $14,490

Housing: Homeownership rate: 63.9% (2010); Median home value: $195,300 (2006-2010 5-year est.); Median contract rent: $794 per month (2006-2010 5-year est.); Median year structure built: 1968 (2006-2010 5-year est.).

Safety: Violent crime rate: 13.0 per 10,000 population; Property crime rate: 542.8 per 10,000 population (2011).

Transportation: Commute to work: 92.3% car, 2.9% public transportation, 2.3% walk, 2.1% work from home (2006-2010 5-year est.); Travel time to work: 34.2% less than 15 minutes, 42.0% 15 to 30 minutes, 14.0% 30 to 45 minutes, 2.9% 45 to 60 minutes, 6.9% 60 minutes or more (2006-2010 5-year est.)

Additional Information Contacts

Greater Lehigh Valley Chamber of Commerce . . . . (610) 841-5800
    http://www.lehighvalleychamber.org
Whitehall Township . . . . (610) 437-5524
    http://www.whitehalltownship.com

ZIONSVILLE (unincorporated postal area)

Zip Code: 18092

    Covers a land area of 14.963 square miles and a water area of 0.035 square miles. Located at 40.46° N. Lat; 75.51° W. Long. Elevation is 617 feet. Population: 3,223 (2010); Density: 215.4 persons per square mile (2010); Race: 97.1% White, 0.3% Black, 1.1% Asian, 0.2% American Indian/Alaska Native, 0.0% Native Hawaiian/Other Pacific Islander, 1.3% Other, 1.6% Hispanic of any race (2010); Average household size: 2.65 (2010); Median age: 46.6 (2010); Males per 100 females: 103.2 (2010); Homeownership rate: 90.0% (2010)

Luzerne County

Located in east central Pennsylvania; drained by the Susquehanna and Lehigh Rivers; includes the Wyoming Valley. Covers a land area of 890.332 square miles, a water area of 15.932 square miles, and is located in the Eastern Time Zone at 41.17° N. Lat., 75.98° W. Long. The county was founded in 1786. County seat is Wilkes-Barre.

Luzerne County is part of the Scranton—Wilkes-Barre, PA Metropolitan Statistical Area. The entire metro area includes: Lackawanna County, PA; Luzerne County, PA; Wyoming County, PA

Weather Station: Wilkes-Barre Scranton Arpt										Elevation: 930 feet	
	Jan	Feb	Mar	Apr	May	Jun	Jul	Aug	Sep	Oct	Nov	Dec
High	34	37	46	59	70	78	82	80	73	61	50	38
Low	19	21	28	39	48	57	62	60	53	42	34	24
Precip	2.3	2.1	2.6	3.3	3.5	4.1	3.8	3.4	4.0	3.3	3.2	2.6
Snow	na	na	na	na	na	na	na	na	na	na	na	na

High and Low temperatures in degrees Fahrenheit; Precipitation and Snow in inches

Population: 328,149 (1990); 319,250 (2000); 320,918 (2010); Race: 90.7% White, 3.4% Black, 1.0% Asian, 0.2% American Indian/Alaska Native, 0.0% Native Hawaiian/Other Pacific Islander, 4.7% Other, 6.7% Hispanic of any race (2010); Density: 360.4 persons per square mile (2010); Average household size: 2.34 (2010); Median age: 42.5 (2010); Males per 100 females: 95.6 (2010).

Religion: Six largest groups: 43.0% Catholicism, 4.4% Methodist/Pietist, 3.1% Lutheran, 1.9% Presbyterian-Reformed, 1.3% Non-Denominational, 1.0% Pentecostal (2010)

Economy: Unemployment rate: 9.9% (August 2012); Total civilian labor force: 165,666 (August 2012); Leading industries: 19.7% health care and social assistance; 15.1% retail trade; 13.2% manufacturing (2010); Farms: 610 totaling 66,577 acres (2007); Companies that employ 500 or more persons: 20 (2010); Companies that employ 100 to 499 persons: 200 (2010); Companies that employ less than 100 persons: 7,106 (2010); Black-owned businesses: 231 (2007); Hispanic-owned businesses: 624 (2007); Asian-owned businesses: 431 (2007); Women-owned businesses: 5,332 (2007); Retail sales per capita: $14,238 (2010). Single-family building permits issued: 191 (2011); Multi-family building permits issued: 9 (2011).

Income: Per capita income: $23,245 (2006-2010 5-year est.); Median household income: $42,224 (2006-2010 5-year est.); Average household income: $55,064 (2006-2010 5-year est.); Percent of households with income of $100,000 or more: 12.4% (2006-2010 5-year est.); Poverty rate: 13.7% (2006-2010 5-year est.); Bankruptcy rate: 2.33% (2011).

Taxes: Total county taxes per capita: $242 (2009); County property taxes per capita: $235 (2009).

Education: Percent of population age 25 and over with: High school diploma (including GED) or higher: 87.0% (2006-2010 5-year est.); Bachelor's degree or higher: 20.2% (2006-2010 5-year est.); Master's degree or higher: 7.3% (2006-2010 5-year est.).

Housing: Homeownership rate: 68.0% (2010); Median home value: $113,300 (2006-2010 5-year est.); Median contract rent: $451 per month (2006-2010 5-year est.); Median year structure built: 1949 (2006-2010 5-year est.)

Health: Birth rate: 96.8 per 10,000 population (2011); Death rate: 124.5 per 10,000 population (2011); Age-adjusted cancer mortality rate: 195.1 deaths per 100,000 population (2009); Number of physicians: 23.2 per 10,000 population (2010); Hospital beds: 42.4 per 10,000 population (2008); Hospital admissions: 1,597.6 per 10,000 population (2008).

Environment: Air Quality Index: 97.3% good, 2.7% moderate, 0.0% unhealthy for sensitive individuals, 0.0% unhealthy (percent of days in 2011)

Elections: 2012 Presidential election results: 51.7% Obama, 46.9% Romney

National and State Parks: Frances Slocum State Park; Ricketts Glen State Park

Additional Information Contacts
Luzerne County Government . . . . (570) 825-1500
  http://www.luzernecounty.org

Luzerne County Communities

ASHLEY (borough). Covers a land area of 0.924 square miles and a water area of 0 square miles. Located at 41.21° N. Lat; 75.90° W. Long. Elevation is 689 feet.

History: Settled 1810, incorporated 1870.

Population: 3,291 (1990); 2,866 (2000); 2,790 (2010); Density: 3,018.2 persons per square mile (2010); Race: 95.2% White, 2.1% Black, 0.3% Asian, 0.0% American Indian/Alaska Native, 0.0% Native Hawaiian/Other Pacific Islander, 2.4% Other, 2.4% Hispanic of any race (2010); Average household size: 2.24 (2010); Median age: 42.6 (2010); Males per 100 females: 99.6 (2010); Marriage status: 28.3% never married, 51.0% now married, 7.5% widowed, 13.2% divorced (2006-2010 5-year est.); Foreign born: 1.0% (2006-2010 5-year est.); Ancestry (includes multiple ancestries): 35.3% Polish, 23.0% Italian, 19.2% Irish, 12.6% Slovak, 9.0% German (2006-2010 5-year est.).

Economy: Single-family building permits issued: 2 (2011); Multi-family building permits issued: 0 (2011); Employment by occupation: 8.7% management, 3.3% professional, 13.0% services, 18.1% sales, 1.3% farming, 11.6% construction, 9.2% production (2006-2010 5-year est.).

Income: Per capita income: $19,216 (2006-2010 5-year est.); Median household income: $37,545 (2006-2010 5-year est.); Average household income: $44,566 (2006-2010 5-year est.); Percent of households with income of $100,000 or more: 8.8% (2006-2010 5-year est.); Poverty rate: 20.2% (2006-2010 5-year est.).

Education: Percent of population age 25 and over with: High school diploma (including GED) or higher: 87.4% (2006-2010 5-year est.); Bachelor's degree or higher: 6.6% (2006-2010 5-year est.); Master's degree or higher: 2.2% (2006-2010 5-year est.).

Housing: Homeownership rate: 70.0% (2010); Median home value: $75,700 (2006-2010 5-year est.); Median contract rent: $468 per month (2006-2010 5-year est.); Median year structure built: before 1940 (2006-2010 5-year est.).

Transportation: Commute to work: 92.4% car, 2.8% public transportation, 0.8% walk, 1.5% work from home (2006-2010 5-year est.); Travel time to work: 50.5% less than 15 minutes, 30.1% 15 to 30 minutes, 10.5% 30 to 45 minutes, 3.0% 45 to 60 minutes, 5.9% 60 minutes or more (2006-2010 5-year est.)

Additional Information Contacts
Ephrata Area Chamber of Commerce . . . . (717) 738-9010
  http://www.ephrata-area.org

AVOCA (borough). Covers a land area of 1.032 square miles and a water area of 0 square miles. Located at 41.34° N. Lat; 75.74° W. Long. Elevation is 814 feet.

History: Incorporated 1889.

Population: 2,833 (1990); 2,851 (2000); 2,661 (2010); Density: 2,578.8 persons per square mile (2010); Race: 97.8% White, 0.7% Black, 0.3% Asian, 0.0% American Indian/Alaska Native, 0.0% Native Hawaiian/Other Pacific Islander, 1.2% Other, 1.8% Hispanic of any race (2010); Average household size: 2.36 (2010); Median age: 43.6 (2010); Males per 100 females: 100.2 (2010); Marriage status: 25.0% never married, 62.5% now married, 6.4% widowed, 6.2% divorced (2006-2010 5-year est.); Foreign born: 0.7% (2006-2010 5-year est.); Ancestry (includes multiple ancestries): 36.2% Polish, 30.4% Irish, 26.7% Italian, 15.1% German, 6.4% Russian (2006-2010 5-year est.).

Economy: Employment by occupation: 3.0% management, 3.2% professional, 10.8% services, 18.9% sales, 11.5% farming, 8.1% construction, 4.7% production (2006-2010 5-year est.).

Income: Per capita income: $23,318 (2006-2010 5-year est.); Median household income: $45,094 (2006-2010 5-year est.); Average household income: $53,575 (2006-2010 5-year est.); Percent of households with income of $100,000 or more: 7.0% (2006-2010 5-year est.); Poverty rate: 2.0% (2006-2010 5-year est.).

Education: Percent of population age 25 and over with: High school diploma (including GED) or higher: 91.9% (2006-2010 5-year est.); Bachelor's degree or higher: 12.9% (2006-2010 5-year est.); Master's degree or higher: 2.3% (2006-2010 5-year est.).

Housing: Homeownership rate: 73.9% (2010); Median home value: $93,700 (2006-2010 5-year est.); Median contract rent: $464 per month (2006-2010 5-year est.); Median year structure built: before 1940 (2006-2010 5-year est.).

Transportation: Commute to work: 92.7% car, 0.0% public transportation, 3.4% walk, 3.3% work from home (2006-2010 5-year est.); Travel time to work: 39.9% less than 15 minutes, 42.9% 15 to 30 minutes, 10.9% 30 to 45 minutes, 3.9% 45 to 60 minutes, 2.2% 60 minutes or more (2006-2010 5-year est.)

Additional Information Contacts
Greater Northeast Chamber of Commerce . . . . (570) 457-1130
  http://www.gnecc.com

BEAR CREEK (township). Aka Bear Creek Village. Covers a land area of 66.475 square miles and a water area of 1.479 square miles. Located at 41.20° N. Lat; 75.72° W. Long.

Population: 2,444 (1990); 2,580 (2000); 2,774 (2010); Density: 41.7 persons per square mile (2010); Race: 98.1% White, 0.5% Black, 0.5% Asian, 0.1% American Indian/Alaska Native, 0.0% Native Hawaiian/Other Pacific Islander, 0.8% Other, 0.8% Hispanic of any race (2010); Average household size: 2.45 (2010); Median age: 45.4 (2010); Males per 100 females: 107.0 (2010); Marriage status: 19.2% never married, 69.3% now married, 4.7% widowed, 6.8% divorced (2006-2010 5-year est.); Foreign born: 1.9% (2006-2010 5-year est.); Ancestry (includes multiple ancestries): 32.7% Polish, 26.4% Irish, 23.5% German, 16.8% Italian, 9.5% Russian (2006-2010 5-year est.).

Economy: Single-family building permits issued: 1 (2011); Multi-family building permits issued: 0 (2011); Employment by occupation: 15.3% management, 5.3% professional, 14.5% services, 11.9% sales, 3.2% farming, 9.4% construction, 4.2% production (2006-2010 5-year est.).

Income: Per capita income: $26,731 (2006-2010 5-year est.); Median household income: $57,609 (2006-2010 5-year est.); Average household income: $69,040 (2006-2010 5-year est.); Percent of households with income of $100,000 or more: 20.6% (2006-2010 5-year est.); Poverty rate: 7.2% (2006-2010 5-year est.).

Education: Percent of population age 25 and over with: High school diploma (including GED) or higher: 92.1% (2006-2010 5-year est.); Bachelor's degree or higher: 30.8% (2006-2010 5-year est.); Master's degree or higher: 8.2% (2006-2010 5-year est.).

Housing: Homeownership rate: 91.3% (2010); Median home value: $168,400 (2006-2010 5-year est.); Median contract rent: $778 per month (2006-2010 5-year est.); Median year structure built: 1973 (2006-2010 5-year est.).

Transportation: Commute to work: 97.2% car, 0.0% public transportation, 0.0% walk, 2.3% work from home (2006-2010 5-year est.); Travel time to work: 23.1% less than 15 minutes, 40.6% 15 to 30 minutes, 21.7% 30 to 45 minutes, 4.7% 45 to 60 minutes, 9.8% 60 minutes or more (2006-2010 5-year est.).

Additional Information Contacts
Greater Scranton Chamber of Commerce . . . . (570) 342-7711
  http://www.scrantonchamber.com

BEAR CREEK VILLAGE (borough). Aka Bear Creek. Covers a land area of 1.937 square miles and a water area of 0.099 square miles. Located at 41.18° N. Lat; 75.75° W. Long. Elevation is 1,526 feet.

Population: 274 (1990); 284 (2000); 257 (2010); Density: 132.6 persons per square mile (2010); Race: 98.4% White, 0.0% Black, 0.4% Asian, 0.8% American Indian/Alaska Native, 0.0% Native Hawaiian/Other Pacific Islander, 0.4% Other, 0.0% Hispanic of any race (2010); Average household size: 2.16 (2010); Median age: 54.9 (2010); Males per 100 females: 96.2 (2010); Marriage status: 13.7% never married, 79.0% now married, 2.7% widowed, 4.6% divorced (2006-2010 5-year est.); Foreign born: 2.3% (2006-2010 5-year est.); Ancestry (includes multiple ancestries): 33.7% Irish, 26.4% German, 25.6% English, 14.0% Polish, 13.2% Italian (2006-2010 5-year est.).

Economy: Single-family building permits issued: 0 (2011); Multi-family building permits issued: 0 (2011); Employment by occupation: 25.2% management, 0.0% professional, 0.0% services, 17.0% sales, 0.0% farming, 1.5% construction, 4.4% production (2006-2010 5-year est.).

Income: Per capita income: $61,234 (2006-2010 5-year est.); Median household income: $112,083 (2006-2010 5-year est.); Average household income: $154,507 (2006-2010 5-year est.); Percent of households with income of $100,000 or more: 54.8% (2006-2010 5-year est.); Poverty rate: 0.0% (2006-2010 5-year est.).

Education: Percent of population age 25 and over with: High school diploma (including GED) or higher: 96.0% (2006-2010 5-year est.); Bachelor's degree or higher: 61.2% (2006-2010 5-year est.); Master's degree or higher: 27.4% (2006-2010 5-year est.).

Housing: Homeownership rate: 90.7% (2010); Median home value: $371,900 (2006-2010 5-year est.); Median contract rent: $592 per month (2006-2010 5-year est.); Median year structure built: 1974 (2006-2010 5-year est.).

Transportation: Commute to work: 90.2% car, 0.0% public transportation, 2.3% walk, 6.0% work from home (2006-2010 5-year est.); Travel time to work: 5.6% less than 15 minutes, 83.2% 15 to 30 minutes, 8.0% 30 to 45 minutes, 0.0% 45 to 60 minutes, 3.2% 60 minutes or more (2006-2010 5-year est.).

BEECH MOUNTAIN LAKES (CDP). Covers a land area of 2.144 square miles and a water area of 0.231 square miles. Located at 41.04° N. Lat; 75.93° W. Long.

Population: n/a (1990); n/a (2000); 2,022 (2010); Density: 942.9 persons per square mile (2010); Race: 94.0% White, 1.9% Black, 0.9% Asian, 0.1% American Indian/Alaska Native, 0.0% Native Hawaiian/Other Pacific Islander, 3.1% Other, 3.5% Hispanic of any race (2010); Average household size: 2.54 (2010); Median age: 40.5 (2010); Males per 100 females: 100.8 (2010); Marriage status: 23.9% never married, 60.7% now married, 4.4% widowed, 11.0% divorced (2006-2010 5-year est.); Foreign born: 8.1% (2006-2010 5-year est.); Ancestry (includes multiple ancestries): 34.8% Italian, 21.2% Polish, 14.8% Irish, 9.7% German, 6.6% Norwegian (2006-2010 5-year est.).

Economy: Employment by occupation: 14.5% management, 6.8% professional, 6.5% services, 8.6% sales, 10.3% farming, 2.9% construction, 1.7% production (2006-2010 5-year est.).

Income: Per capita income: $31,461 (2006-2010 5-year est.); Median household income: $71,798 (2006-2010 5-year est.); Average household income: $77,192 (2006-2010 5-year est.); Percent of households with income of $100,000 or more: 22.8% (2006-2010 5-year est.); Poverty rate: 4.9% (2006-2010 5-year est.).

Education: Percent of population age 25 and over with: High school diploma (including GED) or higher: 96.7% (2006-2010 5-year est.); Bachelor's degree or higher: 40.2% (2006-2010 5-year est.); Master's degree or higher: 14.8% (2006-2010 5-year est.).

Housing: Homeownership rate: 93.2% (2010); Median home value: $157,000 (2006-2010 5-year est.); Median contract rent: $888 per month (2006-2010 5-year est.); Median year structure built: 1998 (2006-2010 5-year est.).

Transportation: Commute to work: 92.7% car, 1.6% public transportation, 0.0% walk, 1.5% work from home (2006-2010 5-year est.); Travel time to work: 14.3% less than 15 minutes, 48.9% 15 to 30 minutes, 20.3% 30 to 45 minutes, 5.8% 45 to 60 minutes, 10.7% 60 minutes or more (2006-2010 5-year est.).

BLACK CREEK (township). Covers a land area of 24.398 square miles and a water area of 0.096 square miles. Located at 40.97° N. Lat; 76.16° W. Long.

Population: 1,887 (1990); 2,132 (2000); 2,016 (2010); Density: 82.6 persons per square mile (2010); Race: 98.3% White, 0.3% Black, 0.2% Asian, 0.0% American Indian/Alaska Native, 0.1% Native Hawaiian/Other Pacific Islander, 1.1% Other, 0.6% Hispanic of any race (2010); Average household size: 2.30 (2010); Median age: 46.9 (2010); Males per 100 females: 104.3 (2010); Marriage status: 19.2% never married, 63.7% now married, 9.7% widowed, 7.4% divorced (2006-2010 5-year est.); Foreign born: 2.3% (2006-2010 5-year est.); Ancestry (includes multiple ancestries): 36.7% German, 29.9% Irish, 17.9% Polish, 11.8% Italian, 7.9% Dutch (2006-2010 5-year est.).

Economy: Single-family building permits issued: 6 (2011); Multi-family building permits issued: 0 (2011); Employment by occupation: 6.8% management, 0.0% professional, 10.2% services, 17.2% sales, 4.1% farming, 14.2% construction, 8.4% production (2006-2010 5-year est.).

Income: Per capita income: $23,743 (2006-2010 5-year est.); Median household income: $39,922 (2006-2010 5-year est.); Average household income: $53,928 (2006-2010 5-year est.); Percent of households with income of $100,000 or more: 11.1% (2006-2010 5-year est.); Poverty rate: 8.9% (2006-2010 5-year est.).

Education: Percent of population age 25 and over with: High school diploma (including GED) or higher: 83.2% (2006-2010 5-year est.); Bachelor's degree or higher: 14.1% (2006-2010 5-year est.); Master's degree or higher: 3.3% (2006-2010 5-year est.).

Housing: Homeownership rate: 82.3% (2010); Median home value: $127,300 (2006-2010 5-year est.); Median contract rent: $377 per month (2006-2010 5-year est.); Median year structure built: 1957 (2006-2010 5-year est.).

Transportation: Commute to work: 88.0% car, 0.0% public transportation, 5.0% walk, 7.1% work from home (2006-2010 5-year est.); Travel time to work: 21.5% less than 15 minutes, 51.3% 15 to 30 minutes, 17.5% 30 to 45 minutes, 6.2% 45 to 60 minutes, 3.5% 60 minutes or more (2006-2010 5-year est.).

Additional Information Contacts
Southern Chester County Chamber of Commerce . . . . (610) 444-0774
  http://www.scccc.com

BROWNTOWN (CDP). Covers a land area of 0.463 square miles and a water area of 0 square miles. Located at 41.31° N. Lat; 75.78° W. Long. Elevation is 705 feet.

Population: n/a (1990); n/a (2000); 1,418 (2010); Density: 3,062.1 persons per square mile (2010); Race: 98.4% White, 0.4% Black, 0.0% Asian, 0.1% American Indian/Alaska Native, 0.0% Native Hawaiian/Other Pacific Islander, 1.1% Other, 1.5% Hispanic of any race (2010); Average household size: 2.27 (2010); Median age: 47.3 (2010); Males per 100 females: 92.1 (2010); Marriage status: 25.5% never married, 50.0% now married, 13.4% widowed, 11.1% divorced (2006-2010 5-year est.); Foreign born: 1.6% (2006-2010 5-year est.); Ancestry (includes multiple ancestries): 45.9% Italian, 31.4% Polish, 17.5% Irish, 12.9% German, 10.9% Lithuanian (2006-2010 5-year est.).

Economy: Employment by occupation: 9.7% management, 0.0% professional, 12.2% services, 16.9% sales, 0.0% farming, 6.8% construction, 8.9% production (2006-2010 5-year est.).

Income: Per capita income: $22,890 (2006-2010 5-year est.); Median household income: $43,636 (2006-2010 5-year est.); Average household income: $50,346 (2006-2010 5-year est.); Percent of households with income of $100,000 or more: 11.6% (2006-2010 5-year est.); Poverty rate: 12.2% (2006-2010 5-year est.).

Education: Percent of population age 25 and over with: High school diploma (including GED) or higher: 94.1% (2006-2010 5-year est.); Bachelor's degree or higher: 21.5% (2006-2010 5-year est.); Master's degree or higher: 7.6% (2006-2010 5-year est.).

Housing: Homeownership rate: 79.1% (2010); Median home value: $95,700 (2006-2010 5-year est.); Median contract rent: $441 per month (2006-2010 5-year est.); Median year structure built: 1942 (2006-2010 5-year est.).

Transportation: Commute to work: 90.2% car, 0.0% public transportation, 6.2% walk, 1.5% work from home (2006-2010 5-year est.); Travel time to work: 31.8% less than 15 minutes, 41.9% 15 to 30 minutes, 10.7% 30 to 45 minutes, 7.8% 45 to 60 minutes, 7.8% 60 minutes or more (2006-2010 5-year est.)

BUCK (township). Covers a land area of 16.754 square miles and a water area of 0.051 square miles. Located at 41.17° N. Lat; 75.65° W. Long.

Population: 378 (1990); 396 (2000); 435 (2010); Density: 26.0 persons per square mile (2010); Race: 97.0% White, 1.6% Black, 0.7% Asian, 0.2% American Indian/Alaska Native, 0.0% Native Hawaiian/Other Pacific Islander, 0.5% Other, 0.2% Hispanic of any race (2010); Average household size: 2.44 (2010); Median age: 45.7 (2010); Males per 100 females: 111.2 (2010); Marriage status: 10.4% never married, 65.1% now married, 6.6% widowed, 17.8% divorced (2006-2010 5-year est.); Foreign born: 3.6% (2006-2010 5-year est.); Ancestry (includes multiple ancestries): 20.9% German, 19.9% Italian, 12.3% Polish, 6.3% Irish, 3.6% Scottish (2006-2010 5-year est.).

Economy: Single-family building permits issued: 2 (2011); Multi-family building permits issued: 0 (2011); Employment by occupation: 19.5% management, 3.1% professional, 10.9% services, 22.7% sales, 0.0% farming, 9.4% construction, 5.5% production (2006-2010 5-year est.).

Income: Per capita income: $21,764 (2006-2010 5-year est.); Median household income: $41,696 (2006-2010 5-year est.); Average household income: $52,002 (2006-2010 5-year est.); Percent of households with income of $100,000 or more: 13.2% (2006-2010 5-year est.); Poverty rate: 2.6% (2006-2010 5-year est.).

Education: Percent of population age 25 and over with: High school diploma (including GED) or higher: 92.9% (2006-2010 5-year est.); Bachelor's degree or higher: 10.7% (2006-2010 5-year est.); Master's degree or higher: 4.9% (2006-2010 5-year est.).

Housing: Homeownership rate: 88.2% (2010); Median home value: $155,400 (2006-2010 5-year est.); Median contract rent: $711 per month (2006-2010 5-year est.); Median year structure built: 1964 (2006-2010 5-year est.).

Transportation: Commute to work: 100.0% car, 0.0% public transportation, 0.0% walk, 0.0% work from home (2006-2010 5-year est.); Travel time to work: 8.1% less than 15 minutes, 50.4% 15 to 30 minutes, 17.1% 30 to 45 minutes, 8.1% 45 to 60 minutes, 16.3% 60 minutes or more (2006-2010 5-year est.)

BUTLER (township). Covers a land area of 33.361 square miles and a water area of 0.251 square miles. Located at 41.04° N. Lat; 75.97° W. Long.

Population: 6,051 (1990); 7,166 (2000); 9,221 (2010); Density: 276.4 persons per square mile (2010); Race: 92.1% White, 4.5% Black, 1.1% Asian, 0.2% American Indian/Alaska Native, 0.0% Native Hawaiian/Other Pacific Islander, 2.1% Other, 2.9% Hispanic of any race (2010); Average household size: 2.44 (2010); Median age: 43.0 (2010); Males per 100 females: 99.8 (2010); Marriage status: 20.3% never married, 65.1% now married, 6.1% widowed, 8.5% divorced (2006-2010 5-year est.); Foreign born: 5.7% (2006-2010 5-year est.); Ancestry (includes multiple ancestries): 29.7% Italian, 23.6% German, 21.3% Irish, 18.1% Polish, 7.7% Slovak (2006-2010 5-year est.).

Economy: Single-family building permits issued: 26 (2011); Multi-family building permits issued: 0 (2011); Employment by occupation: 14.3% management, 3.7% professional, 11.4% services, 16.7% sales, 6.1% farming, 8.7% construction, 6.5% production (2006-2010 5-year est.).

Income: Per capita income: $27,519 (2006-2010 5-year est.); Median household income: $56,090 (2006-2010 5-year est.); Average household income: $68,055 (2006-2010 5-year est.); Percent of households with income of $100,000 or more: 17.5% (2006-2010 5-year est.); Poverty rate: 7.3% (2006-2010 5-year est.).

Education: Percent of population age 25 and over with: High school diploma (including GED) or higher: 96.1% (2006-2010 5-year est.); Bachelor's degree or higher: 26.2% (2006-2010 5-year est.); Master's degree or higher: 9.7% (2006-2010 5-year est.).

Housing: Homeownership rate: 84.5% (2010); Median home value: $158,700 (2006-2010 5-year est.); Median contract rent: $555 per month

(2006-2010 5-year est.); Median year structure built: 1985 (2006-2010 5-year est.).

Safety: Violent crime rate: 43.2 per 10,000 population; Property crime rate: 131.9 per 10,000 population (2011).

Transportation: Commute to work: 92.7% car, 0.6% public transportation, 1.3% walk, 4.0% work from home (2006-2010 5-year est.); Travel time to work: 19.0% less than 15 minutes, 55.5% 15 to 30 minutes, 14.8% 30 to 45 minutes, 4.4% 45 to 60 minutes, 6.3% 60 minutes or more (2006-2010 5-year est.)

Additional Information Contacts

Butler Township. . . . . (570) 788-3547
  http://www.butler-township.com
Greater Hazelton Chamber of Commerce. . . . . (570) 455-1509
  http://www.hazletonchamber.org

CHASE (CDP). Covers a land area of 2.289 square miles and a water area of 0.003 square miles. Located at 41.28° N. Lat; 75.97° W. Long. Elevation is 1,066 feet.

Population: n/a (1990); n/a (2000); 978 (2010); Density: 427.2 persons per square mile (2010); Race: 97.8% White, 0.3% Black, 0.9% Asian, 0.0% American Indian/Alaska Native, 0.0% Native Hawaiian/Other Pacific Islander, 1.0% Other, 1.1% Hispanic of any race (2010); Average household size: 2.53 (2010); Median age: 45.5 (2010); Males per 100 females: 96.4 (2010); Marriage status: 20.1% never married, 61.7% now married, 9.7% widowed, 8.4% divorced (2006-2010 5-year est.); Foreign born: 1.9% (2006-2010 5-year est.); Ancestry (includes multiple ancestries): 31.9% Polish, 24.1% Irish, 23.8% German, 18.2% Slovak, 11.0% Welsh (2006-2010 5-year est.).

Economy: Employment by occupation: 13.2% management, 1.2% professional, 6.1% services, 20.6% sales, 5.8% farming, 7.8% construction, 5.5% production (2006-2010 5-year est.).

Income: Per capita income: $34,617 (2006-2010 5-year est.); Median household income: $86,042 (2006-2010 5-year est.); Average household income: $94,170 (2006-2010 5-year est.); Percent of households with income of $100,000 or more: 37.9% (2006-2010 5-year est.); Poverty rate: 0.5% (2006-2010 5-year est.).

Education: Percent of population age 25 and over with: High school diploma (including GED) or higher: 95.0% (2006-2010 5-year est.); Bachelor's degree or higher: 30.6% (2006-2010 5-year est.); Master's degree or higher: 11.6% (2006-2010 5-year est.).

Housing: Homeownership rate: 89.4% (2010); Median home value: $186,600 (2006-2010 5-year est.); Median contract rent: $393 per month (2006-2010 5-year est.); Median year structure built: 1973 (2006-2010 5-year est.).

Transportation: Commute to work: 97.2% car, 0.0% public transportation, 1.2% walk, 0.0% work from home (2006-2010 5-year est.); Travel time to work: 24.7% less than 15 minutes, 54.9% 15 to 30 minutes, 6.1% 30 to 45 minutes, 9.4% 45 to 60 minutes, 4.9% 60 minutes or more (2006-2010 5-year est.)

CONYNGHAM (borough). Covers a land area of 1.021 square miles and a water area of 0 square miles. Located at 40.99° N. Lat; 76.06° W. Long. Elevation is 951 feet.

Population: 2,060 (1990); 1,958 (2000); 1,914 (2010); Density: 1,874.7 persons per square mile (2010); Race: 97.4% White, 0.5% Black, 0.9% Asian, 0.1% American Indian/Alaska Native, 0.0% Native Hawaiian/Other Pacific Islander, 1.1% Other, 2.0% Hispanic of any race (2010); Average household size: 2.29 (2010); Median age: 48.5 (2010); Males per 100 females: 94.5 (2010); Marriage status: 21.4% never married, 57.4% now married, 6.4% widowed, 14.7% divorced (2006-2010 5-year est.); Foreign born: 2.7% (2006-2010 5-year est.); Ancestry (includes multiple ancestries): 25.6% Italian, 23.7% German, 22.6% Polish, 16.0% Irish, 8.1% English (2006-2010 5-year est.).

Economy: Single-family building permits issued: 0 (2011); Multi-family building permits issued: 0 (2011); Employment by occupation: 5.5% management, 1.4% professional, 4.9% services, 18.9% sales, 7.6% farming, 4.3% construction, 2.9% production (2006-2010 5-year est.).

Income: Per capita income: $41,968 (2006-2010 5-year est.); Median household income: $62,708 (2006-2010 5-year est.); Average household income: $90,847 (2006-2010 5-year est.); Percent of households with income of $100,000 or more: 34.6% (2006-2010 5-year est.); Poverty rate: 6.1% (2006-2010 5-year est.).

Education: Percent of population age 25 and over with: High school diploma (including GED) or higher: 96.7% (2006-2010 5-year est.);

Bachelor's degree or higher: 37.5% (2006-2010 5-year est.); Master's degree or higher: 19.1% (2006-2010 5-year est.).

Housing: Homeownership rate: 79.0% (2010); Median home value: $165,500 (2006-2010 5-year est.); Median contract rent: $654 per month (2006-2010 5-year est.); Median year structure built: 1961 (2006-2010 5-year est.).

Safety: Violent crime rate: 0.0 per 10,000 population; Property crime rate: 62.5 per 10,000 population (2011).

Transportation: Commute to work: 99.0% car, 0.0% public transportation, 0.0% walk, 0.7% work from home (2006-2010 5-year est.); Travel time to work: 27.6% less than 15 minutes, 42.6% 15 to 30 minutes, 16.7% 30 to 45 minutes, 3.6% 45 to 60 minutes, 9.4% 60 minutes or more (2006-2010 5-year est.)

Additional Information Contacts

Greater Hazelton Chamber of Commerce . . . . (570) 455-1509
http://www.hazletonchamber.org

CONYNGHAM (township). Covers a land area of 16.003 square miles and a water area of 0.973 square miles. Located at 41.14° N. Lat; 76.11° W. Long. Elevation is 951 feet.

Population: 1,406 (1990); 1,385 (2000); 1,453 (2010); Density: 90.8 persons per square mile (2010); Race: 95.8% White, 0.5% Black, 0.8% Asian, 0.3% American Indian/Alaska Native, 0.2% Native Hawaiian/Other Pacific Islander, 2.4% Other, 1.9% Hispanic of any race (2010); Average household size: 2.31 (2010); Median age: 42.8 (2010); Males per 100 females: 96.9 (2010); Marriage status: 23.8% never married, 55.2% now married, 10.3% widowed, 10.8% divorced (2006-2010 5-year est.); Foreign born: 1.4% (2006-2010 5-year est.); Ancestry (includes multiple ancestries): 34.6% German, 29.9% Polish, 12.7% Irish, 11.3% Italian, 5.6% Pennsylvania German (2006-2010 5-year est.).

Economy: Employment by occupation: 5.6% management, 1.4% professional, 18.7% services, 15.0% sales, 3.9% farming, 11.9% construction, 11.4% production (2006-2010 5-year est.).

Income: Per capita income: $21,995 (2006-2010 5-year est.); Median household income: $44,583 (2006-2010 5-year est.); Average household income: $50,165 (2006-2010 5-year est.); Percent of households with income of $100,000 or more: 8.4% (2006-2010 5-year est.); Poverty rate: 10.5% (2006-2010 5-year est.).

Education: Percent of population age 25 and over with: High school diploma (including GED) or higher: 82.7% (2006-2010 5-year est.); Bachelor's degree or higher: 10.4% (2006-2010 5-year est.); Master's degree or higher: 3.2% (2006-2010 5-year est.).

Housing: Homeownership rate: 75.2% (2010); Median home value: $72,600 (2006-2010 5-year est.); Median contract rent: $401 per month (2006-2010 5-year est.); Median year structure built: 1941 (2006-2010 5-year est.).

Transportation: Commute to work: 92.2% car, 1.8% public transportation, 0.5% walk, 5.0% work from home (2006-2010 5-year est.); Travel time to work: 9.1% less than 15 minutes, 39.6% 15 to 30 minutes, 34.2% 30 to 45 minutes, 6.8% 45 to 60 minutes, 10.3% 60 minutes or more (2006-2010 5-year est.)

Additional Information Contacts

Greater Hazelton Chamber of Commerce . . . . (570) 455-1509
http://www.hazletonchamber.org

COURTDALE (borough). Covers a land area of 1.006 square miles and a water area of 0 square miles. Located at 41.28° N. Lat; 75.91° W. Long. Elevation is 738 feet.

History: Incorporated 1897.

Population: 784 (1990); 791 (2000); 732 (2010); Density: 727.6 persons per square mile (2010); Race: 99.0% White, 0.3% Black, 0.0% Asian, 0.0% American Indian/Alaska Native, 0.0% Native Hawaiian/Other Pacific Islander, 0.7% Other, 1.2% Hispanic of any race (2010); Average household size: 2.35 (2010); Median age: 45.8 (2010); Males per 100 females: 93.1 (2010); Marriage status: 23.1% never married, 63.3% now married, 9.2% widowed, 4.4% divorced (2006-2010 5-year est.); Foreign born: 0.4% (2006-2010 5-year est.); Ancestry (includes multiple ancestries): 30.4% Polish, 29.1% Irish, 13.2% German, 13.0% Welsh, 10.8% Italian (2006-2010 5-year est.).

Economy: Employment by occupation: 4.1% management, 0.0% professional, 2.3% services, 22.5% sales, 1.8% farming, 8.5% construction, 11.7% production (2006-2010 5-year est.).

Income: Per capita income: $20,905 (2006-2010 5-year est.); Median household income: $50,221 (2006-2010 5-year est.); Average household income: $49,429 (2006-2010 5-year est.); Percent of households with

income of $100,000 or more: 3.2% (2006-2010 5-year est.); Poverty rate: 6.2% (2006-2010 5-year est.).

Education: Percent of population age 25 and over with: High school diploma (including GED) or higher: 86.7% (2006-2010 5-year est.); Bachelor's degree or higher: 10.1% (2006-2010 5-year est.); Master's degree or higher: 2.2% (2006-2010 5-year est.).

Housing: Homeownership rate: 81.6% (2010); Median home value: $105,500 (2006-2010 5-year est.); Median contract rent: $709 per month (2006-2010 5-year est.); Median year structure built: 1951 (2006-2010 5-year est.).

Transportation: Commute to work: 98.5% car, 0.0% public transportation, 0.6% walk, 0.9% work from home (2006-2010 5-year est.); Travel time to work: 35.4% less than 15 minutes, 46.4% 15 to 30 minutes, 11.9% 30 to 45 minutes, 4.2% 45 to 60 minutes, 2.1% 60 minutes or more (2006-2010 5-year est.)

DALLAS (borough). Covers a land area of 2.321 square miles and a water area of 0.093 square miles. Located at 41.33° N. Lat; 75.97° W. Long. Elevation is 1,129 feet.

Population: 2,546 (1990); 2,557 (2000); 2,804 (2010); Density: 1,208.2 persons per square mile (2010); Race: 97.0% White, 0.7% Black, 1.4% Asian, 0.0% American Indian/Alaska Native, 0.0% Native Hawaiian/Other Pacific Islander, 0.9% Other, 0.9% Hispanic of any race (2010); Average household size: 2.44 (2010); Median age: 42.1 (2010); Males per 100 females: 89.5 (2010); Marriage status: 32.8% never married, 54.6% now married, 5.6% widowed, 7.0% divorced (2006-2010 5-year est.); Foreign born: 2.4% (2006-2010 5-year est.); Ancestry (includes multiple ancestries): 25.2% German, 22.4% Irish, 18.1% Polish, 16.9% Italian, 15.6% English (2006-2010 5-year est.).

Economy: Single-family building permits issued: 1 (2011); Multi-family building permits issued: 0 (2011); Employment by occupation: 12.6% management, 1.3% professional, 11.0% services, 13.0% sales, 5.7% farming, 6.9% construction, 3.7% production (2006-2010 5-year est.).

Income: Per capita income: $34,323 (2006-2010 5-year est.); Median household income: $60,625 (2006-2010 5-year est.); Average household income: $82,181 (2006-2010 5-year est.); Percent of households with income of $100,000 or more: 26.2% (2006-2010 5-year est.); Poverty rate: 10.1% (2006-2010 5-year est.).

Education: Percent of population age 25 and over with: High school diploma (including GED) or higher: 97.0% (2006-2010 5-year est.); Bachelor's degree or higher: 51.1% (2006-2010 5-year est.); Master's degree or higher: 23.6% (2006-2010 5-year est.).

School District(s)

Dallas SD (KG-12)
    2010-11 Enrollment: 2,745 . . . . (570) 675-5201
Lake-Lehman SD (KG-12)
    2010-11 Enrollment: 2,080 . . . . (570) 675-2165

Four-year College(s)

Misericordia University (Private, Not-for-profit, Roman Catholic)
    Fall 2010 Enrollment: 2,452 . . . . (570) 674-6400
    2011-12 Tuition: In-state $25,990; Out-of-state $25,990

Housing: Homeownership rate: 80.6% (2010); Median home value: $165,400 (2006-2010 5-year est.); Median contract rent: $601 per month (2006-2010 5-year est.); Median year structure built: 1958 (2006-2010 5-year est.).

Safety: Violent crime rate: 3.6 per 10,000 population; Property crime rate: 106.6 per 10,000 population (2011).

Transportation: Commute to work: 93.6% car, 0.0% public transportation, 1.4% walk, 5.0% work from home (2006-2010 5-year est.); Travel time to work: 31.8% less than 15 minutes, 40.3% 15 to 30 minutes, 17.2% 30 to 45 minutes, 7.0% 45 to 60 minutes, 3.8% 60 minutes or more (2006-2010 5-year est.)

Additional Information Contacts

Greater Northeast Chamber of Commerce . . . . (570) 457-1130
http://www.gnecc.com

DALLAS (township). Covers a land area of 18.523 square miles and a water area of 0.204 square miles. Located at 41.36° N. Lat; 75.97° W. Long. Elevation is 1,129 feet.

History: Incorporated 1879.

Population: 7,675 (1990); 8,179 (2000); 8,994 (2010); Density: 485.6 persons per square mile (2010); Race: 97.9% White, 0.3% Black, 0.9% Asian, 0.1% American Indian/Alaska Native, 0.0% Native Hawaiian/Other Pacific Islander, 0.8% Other, 1.0% Hispanic of any race (2010); Average household size: 2.33 (2010); Median age: 44.3 (2010); Males per 100

females: 80.7 (2010); Marriage status: 26.4% never married, 50.5% now married, 14.8% widowed, 8.3% divorced (2006-2010 5-year est.); Foreign born: 2.5% (2006-2010 5-year est.); Ancestry (includes multiple ancestries): 22.5% German, 18.4% Polish, 18.3% Irish, 13.8% Italian, 9.8% English (2006-2010 5-year est.).

Economy: Single-family building permits issued: 21 (2011); Multi-family building permits issued: 0 (2011); Employment by occupation: 10.8% management, 3.5% professional, 11.4% services, 14.6% sales, 1.5% farming, 7.8% construction, 6.6% production (2006-2010 5-year est.).

Income: Per capita income: $27,377 (2006-2010 5-year est.); Median household income: $50,868 (2006-2010 5-year est.); Average household income: $67,021 (2006-2010 5-year est.); Percent of households with income of $100,000 or more: 18.9% (2006-2010 5-year est.); Poverty rate: 8.2% (2006-2010 5-year est.).

Taxes: Total city taxes per capita: $200 (2009); City property taxes per capita: $41 (2009).

Education: Percent of population age 25 and over with: High school diploma (including GED) or higher: 85.6% (2006-2010 5-year est.); Bachelor's degree or higher: 32.1% (2006-2010 5-year est.); Master's degree or higher: 10.4% (2006-2010 5-year est.).

Four-year College(s)

Misericordia University (Private, Not-for-profit, Roman Catholic)
Fall 2010 Enrollment: 2,452 . . . . (570) 674-6400
2011-12 Tuition: In-state $25,990; Out-of-state $25,990

Housing: Homeownership rate: 74.4% (2010); Median home value: $161,800 (2006-2010 5-year est.); Median contract rent: $468 per month (2006-2010 5-year est.); Median year structure built: 1970 (2006-2010 5-year est.).

Safety: Violent crime rate: 3.3 per 10,000 population; Property crime rate: 73.1 per 10,000 population (2011).

Transportation: Commute to work: 95.0% car, 0.0% public transportation, 3.1% walk, 1.6% work from home (2006-2010 5-year est.); Travel time to work: 35.7% less than 15 minutes, 37.6% 15 to 30 minutes, 15.3% 30 to 45 minutes, 5.8% 45 to 60 minutes, 5.7% 60 minutes or more (2006-2010 5-year est.)

Additional Information Contacts

Dallas Township . . . . (570) 674-2008
http://www.dallastownship.com
Greater Northeast Chamber of Commerce . . . . (570) 457-1130
http://www.gnecc.com

DENNISON (township).
Covers a land area of 35.428 square miles and a water area of 0.132 square miles. Located at 41.10° N. Lat; 75.84° W. Long.

Population: 685 (1990); 908 (2000); 1,125 (2010); Density: 31.8 persons per square mile (2010); Race: 98.0% White, 0.4% Black, 0.1% Asian, 0.0% American Indian/Alaska Native, 0.0% Native Hawaiian/Other Pacific Islander, 1.5% Other, 2.0% Hispanic of any race (2010); Average household size: 2.57 (2010); Median age: 43.7 (2010); Males per 100 females: 107.2 (2010); Marriage status: 23.5% never married, 65.7% now married, 5.9% widowed, 4.9% divorced (2006-2010 5-year est.); Foreign born: 6.7% (2006-2010 5-year est.); Ancestry (includes multiple ancestries): 31.1% German, 21.1% Irish, 14.6% Polish, 13.6% Italian, 6.5% American (2006-2010 5-year est.).

Economy: Single-family building permits issued: 0 (2011); Multi-family building permits issued: 0 (2011); Employment by occupation: 13.6% management, 2.0% professional, 9.8% services, 17.7% sales, 5.6% farming, 12.5% construction, 2.4% production (2006-2010 5-year est.).

Income: Per capita income: $24,322 (2006-2010 5-year est.); Median household income: $56,964 (2006-2010 5-year est.); Average household income: $65,726 (2006-2010 5-year est.); Percent of households with income of $100,000 or more: 21.8% (2006-2010 5-year est.); Poverty rate: 12.0% (2006-2010 5-year est.).

Education: Percent of population age 25 and over with: High school diploma (including GED) or higher: 90.0% (2006-2010 5-year est.); Bachelor's degree or higher: 18.0% (2006-2010 5-year est.); Master's degree or higher: 2.0% (2006-2010 5-year est.).

Housing: Homeownership rate: 89.3% (2010); Median home value: $162,100 (2006-2010 5-year est.); Median contract rent: $652 per month (2006-2010 5-year est.); Median year structure built: 1977 (2006-2010 5-year est.).

Transportation: Commute to work: 97.4% car, 0.0% public transportation, 0.0% walk, 2.0% work from home (2006-2010 5-year est.); Travel time to work: 18.2% less than 15 minutes, 35.3% 15 to 30 minutes, 29.2% 30 to

45 minutes, 4.8% 45 to 60 minutes, 12.5% 60 minutes or more (2006-2010 5-year est.)

Additional Information Contacts

Greater Hazleton Chamber of Commerce . . . . (570) 455-1509
http://www.hazletonchamber.org

DORRANCE (township).
Covers a land area of 24.198 square miles and a water area of 0.167 square miles. Located at 41.11° N. Lat; 75.99° W. Long. Elevation is 1,125 feet.

Population: 1,767 (1990); 2,109 (2000); 2,188 (2010); Density: 90.4 persons per square mile (2010); Race: 98.4% White, 0.4% Black, 0.2% Asian, 0.1% American Indian/Alaska Native, 0.0% Native Hawaiian/Other Pacific Islander, 0.9% Other, 0.4% Hispanic of any race (2010); Average household size: 2.66 (2010); Median age: 44.0 (2010); Males per 100 females: 105.1 (2010); Marriage status: 15.3% never married, 70.4% now married, 5.4% widowed, 8.9% divorced (2006-2010 5-year est.); Foreign born: 0.0% (2006-2010 5-year est.); Ancestry (includes multiple ancestries): 30.3% German, 26.6% Polish, 15.1% Irish, 12.6% Italian, 9.1% English (2006-2010 5-year est.).

Economy: Single-family building permits issued: 1 (2011); Multi-family building permits issued: 0 (2011); Employment by occupation: 6.1% management, 3.6% professional, 12.2% services, 14.5% sales, 2.5% farming, 10.2% construction, 13.5% production (2006-2010 5-year est.).

Income: Per capita income: $27,797 (2006-2010 5-year est.); Median household income: $57,102 (2006-2010 5-year est.); Average household income: $68,226 (2006-2010 5-year est.); Percent of households with income of $100,000 or more: 15.5% (2006-2010 5-year est.); Poverty rate: 2.9% (2006-2010 5-year est.).

Education: Percent of population age 25 and over with: High school diploma (including GED) or higher: 94.2% (2006-2010 5-year est.); Bachelor's degree or higher: 21.5% (2006-2010 5-year est.); Master's degree or higher: 6.5% (2006-2010 5-year est.).

Housing: Homeownership rate: 90.5% (2010); Median home value: $158,200 (2006-2010 5-year est.); Median contract rent: $479 per month (2006-2010 5-year est.); Median year structure built: 1979 (2006-2010 5-year est.).

Transportation: Commute to work: 95.9% car, 0.4% public transportation, 1.0% walk, 2.6% work from home (2006-2010 5-year est.); Travel time to work: 16.7% less than 15 minutes, 57.5% 15 to 30 minutes, 20.7% 30 to 45 minutes, 2.2% 45 to 60 minutes, 2.8% 60 minutes or more (2006-2010 5-year est.)

Additional Information Contacts

Greater Hazleton Chamber of Commerce . . . . (570) 455-1509
http://www.hazletonchamber.org

DRIFTON (unincorporated postal area)
Zip Code: 18221

Covers a land area of 1.976 square miles and a water area of 0 square miles. Located at 41.00° N. Lat; 75.91° W. Long. Elevation is 1,667 feet. Population: 389 (2010); Density: 196.8 persons per square mile (2010); Race: 97.2% White, 0.0% Black, 0.3% Asian, 0.5% American Indian/Alaska Native, 0.0% Native Hawaiian/Other Pacific Islander, 2.0% Other, 1.3% Hispanic of any race (2010); Average household size: 2.49 (2010); Median age: 45.5 (2010); Males per 100 females: 104.7 (2010); Homeownership rate: 90.4% (2010)

DRUMS (unincorporated postal area)
Zip Code: 18222

Covers a land area of 37.549 square miles and a water area of 0.251 square miles. Located at 41.03° N. Lat; 76.00° W. Long. Elevation is 1,102 feet. Population: 9,020 (2010); Density: 240.2 persons per square mile (2010); Race: 91.9% White, 4.6% Black, 1.2% Asian, 0.2% American Indian/Alaska Native, 0.0% Native Hawaiian/Other Pacific Islander, 2.1% Other, 3.0% Hispanic of any race (2010); Average household size: 2.46 (2010); Median age: 42.7 (2010); Males per 100 females: 100.0 (2010); Homeownership rate: 86.2% (2010)

DUPONT (borough).
Covers a land area of 1.518 square miles and a water area of 0 square miles. Located at 41.32° N. Lat; 75.74° W. Long. Elevation is 725 feet.

History: Former anthracite coal mining area. Incorporated 1917.

Population: 3,026 (1990); 2,719 (2000); 2,711 (2010); Density: 1,785.6 persons per square mile (2010); Race: 97.9% White, 0.5% Black, 0.6% Asian, 0.2% American Indian/Alaska Native, 0.0% Native Hawaiian/Other Pacific Islander, 0.8% Other, 1.1% Hispanic of any race (2010); Average

household size: 2.22 (2010); Median age: 45.6 (2010); Males per 100 females: 92.8 (2010); Marriage status: 27.8% never married, 52.5% now married, 12.1% widowed, 7.6% divorced (2006-2010 5-year est.); Foreign born: 0.9% (2006-2010 5-year est.); Ancestry (includes multiple ancestries): 48.8% Polish, 20.3% Italian, 20.1% Irish, 9.5% German, 9.3% Welsh (2006-2010 5-year est.).

Economy: Employment by occupation: 6.8% management, 0.6% professional, 3.1% services, 21.9% sales, 6.0% farming, 9.7% construction, 7.9% production (2006-2010 5-year est.).

Income: Per capita income: $25,169 (2006-2010 5-year est.); Median household income: $45,996 (2006-2010 5-year est.); Average household income: $55,560 (2006-2010 5-year est.); Percent of households with income of $100,000 or more: 8.8% (2006-2010 5-year est.); Poverty rate: 3.0% (2006-2010 5-year est.).

Education: Percent of population age 25 and over with: High school diploma (including GED) or higher: 85.5% (2006-2010 5-year est.); Bachelor's degree or higher: 21.2% (2006-2010 5-year est.); Master's degree or higher: 9.0% (2006-2010 5-year est.).

School District(s)

Pittston Area SD (KG-12)
   2010-11 Enrollment: 3,364 . . . . (570) 654-2271

Housing: Homeownership rate: 73.2% (2010); Median home value: $95,200 (2006-2010 5-year est.); Median contract rent: $471 per month (2006-2010 5-year est.); Median year structure built: before 1940 (2006-2010 5-year est.).

Transportation: Commute to work: 96.1% car, 0.0% public transportation, 1.6% walk, 1.4% work from home (2006-2010 5-year est.); Travel time to work: 32.5% less than 15 minutes, 59.9% 15 to 30 minutes, 3.9% 30 to 45 minutes, 0.0% 45 to 60 minutes, 3.7% 60 minutes or more (2006-2010 5-year est.)

Additional Information Contacts

Borough of Dupont . . . . (570) 655-6216
   http://www.dupontpa.info
Greater Northeast Chamber of Commerce . . . . (570) 457-1130
   http://www.gnecc.com

DURYEA (borough). Covers a land area of 5.548 square miles and a water area of 0.191 square miles. Located at 41.36° N. Lat; 75.77° W. Long. Elevation is 705 feet.

History: Former anthracite coal center. Incorporated 1891.

Population: 4,869 (1990); 4,634 (2000); 4,917 (2010); Density: 886.3 persons per square mile (2010); Race: 97.8% White, 0.4% Black, 0.7% Asian, 0.1% American Indian/Alaska Native, 0.0% Native Hawaiian/Other Pacific Islander, 1.0% Other, 1.9% Hispanic of any race (2010); Average household size: 2.32 (2010); Median age: 43.0 (2010); Males per 100 females: 92.4 (2010); Marriage status: 25.6% never married, 56.9% now married, 7.8% widowed, 9.7% divorced (2006-2010 5-year est.); Foreign born: 3.3% (2006-2010 5-year est.); Ancestry (includes multiple ancestries): 41.5% Polish, 25.1% Italian, 23.7% Irish, 11.3% German, 5.8% English (2006-2010 5-year est.).

Economy: Employment by occupation: 12.9% management, 2.6% professional, 4.8% services, 23.8% sales, 6.4% farming, 5.2% construction, 7.2% production (2006-2010 5-year est.).

Income: Per capita income: $24,777 (2006-2010 5-year est.); Median household income: $45,114 (2006-2010 5-year est.); Average household income: $55,351 (2006-2010 5-year est.); Percent of households with income of $100,000 or more: 13.3% (2006-2010 5-year est.); Poverty rate: 9.1% (2006-2010 5-year est.).

Education: Percent of population age 25 and over with: High school diploma (including GED) or higher: 90.8% (2006-2010 5-year est.); Bachelor's degree or higher: 28.7% (2006-2010 5-year est.); Master's degree or higher: 14.9% (2006-2010 5-year est.).

Housing: Homeownership rate: 72.8% (2010); Median home value: $109,600 (2006-2010 5-year est.); Median contract rent: $433 per month (2006-2010 5-year est.); Median year structure built: before 1940 (2006-2010 5-year est.).

Safety: Violent crime rate: 4.1 per 10,000 population; Property crime rate: 231.1 per 10,000 population (2011).

Transportation: Commute to work: 97.2% car, 0.0% public transportation, 1.7% walk, 0.6% work from home (2006-2010 5-year est.); Travel time to work: 34.8% less than 15 minutes, 47.5% 15 to 30 minutes, 9.1% 30 to 45 minutes, 4.4% 45 to 60 minutes, 4.2% 60 minutes or more (2006-2010 5-year est.)

Additional Information Contacts

Greater Scranton Chamber of Commerce . . . . (570) 342-7711
   http://www.scrantonchamber.com

EAST BERWICK (CDP). Covers a land area of 0.861 square miles and a water area of 0.167 square miles. Located at 41.07° N. Lat; 76.22° W. Long. Elevation is 584 feet.

Population: 2,128 (1990); 1,998 (2000); 2,007 (2010); Density: 2,330.7 persons per square mile (2010); Race: 96.5% White, 0.2% Black, 0.6% Asian, 0.1% American Indian/Alaska Native, 0.0% Native Hawaiian/Other Pacific Islander, 2.6% Other, 3.4% Hispanic of any race (2010); Average household size: 2.40 (2010); Median age: 45.8 (2010); Males per 100 females: 87.2 (2010); Marriage status: 23.2% never married, 57.8% now married, 11.0% widowed, 8.0% divorced (2006-2010 5-year est.); Foreign born: 2.4% (2006-2010 5-year est.); Ancestry (includes multiple ancestries): 25.9% German, 15.4% Italian, 14.1% Polish, 13.4% Irish, 8.1% American (2006-2010 5-year est.).

Economy: Employment by occupation: 12.4% management, 3.2% professional, 16.4% services, 13.3% sales, 3.9% farming, 12.5% construction, 10.3% production (2006-2010 5-year est.).

Income: Per capita income: $23,209 (2006-2010 5-year est.); Median household income: $44,340 (2006-2010 5-year est.); Average household income: $63,007 (2006-2010 5-year est.); Percent of households with income of $100,000 or more: 20.8% (2006-2010 5-year est.); Poverty rate: 13.5% (2006-2010 5-year est.).

Education: Percent of population age 25 and over with: High school diploma (including GED) or higher: 91.2% (2006-2010 5-year est.); Bachelor's degree or higher: 23.6% (2006-2010 5-year est.); Master's degree or higher: 4.0% (2006-2010 5-year est.).

Housing: Homeownership rate: 84.0% (2010); Median home value: $126,600 (2006-2010 5-year est.); Median contract rent: $385 per month (2006-2010 5-year est.); Median year structure built: 1961 (2006-2010 5-year est.).

Transportation: Commute to work: 95.8% car, 0.0% public transportation, 2.5% walk, 1.7% work from home (2006-2010 5-year est.); Travel time to work: 50.6% less than 15 minutes, 24.7% 15 to 30 minutes, 18.9% 30 to 45 minutes, 3.8% 45 to 60 minutes, 2.1% 60 minutes or more (2006-2010 5-year est.)

Additional Information Contacts

Columbia Montour Chamber of Commerce . . . . (570) 784-2522
   http://www.bloomsburg.org

EBERVALE (unincorporated postal area)

Zip Code: 18223
   Covers a land area of 1.247 square miles and a water area of 0 square miles. Located at 40.98° N. Lat; 75.95° W. Long. Population: 115 (2010); Density: 92.2 persons per square mile (2010); Race: 98.3% White, 0.0% Black, 0.0% Asian, 0.0% American Indian/Alaska Native, 0.0% Native Hawaiian/Other Pacific Islander, 1.7% Other, 0.0% Hispanic of any race (2010); Average household size: 1.92 (2010); Median age: 52.3 (2010); Males per 100 females: 113.0 (2010); Homeownership rate: 83.4% (2010)

EDWARDSVILLE (borough). Covers a land area of 1.158 square miles and a water area of 0.035 square miles. Located at 41.26° N. Lat; 75.91° W. Long. Elevation is 702 feet.

History: Incorporated 1884.

Population: 5,399 (1990); 4,984 (2000); 4,816 (2010); Density: 4,157.2 persons per square mile (2010); Race: 89.1% White, 5.2% Black, 0.8% Asian, 0.4% American Indian/Alaska Native, 0.0% Native Hawaiian/Other Pacific Islander, 4.5% Other, 5.4% Hispanic of any race (2010); Average household size: 2.16 (2010); Median age: 36.3 (2010); Males per 100 females: 81.7 (2010); Marriage status: 40.9% never married, 33.5% now married, 12.9% widowed, 12.7% divorced (2006-2010 5-year est.); Foreign born: 3.9% (2006-2010 5-year est.); Ancestry (includes multiple ancestries): 22.1% Irish, 21.5% Polish, 18.6% Italian, 16.7% German, 8.9% Russian (2006-2010 5-year est.).

Economy: Single-family building permits issued: 0 (2011); Multi-family building permits issued: 0 (2011); Employment by occupation: 6.7% management, 1.3% professional, 12.8% services, 16.1% sales, 4.1% farming, 8.8% construction, 7.3% production (2006-2010 5-year est.).

Income: Per capita income: $17,510 (2006-2010 5-year est.); Median household income: $28,402 (2006-2010 5-year est.); Average household income: $35,104 (2006-2010 5-year est.); Percent of households with

income of $100,000 or more: 3.0% (2006-2010 5-year est.); Poverty rate: 28.1% (2006-2010 5-year est.).

Education: Percent of population age 25 and over with: High school diploma (including GED) or higher: 82.7% (2006-2010 5-year est.); Bachelor's degree or higher: 18.1% (2006-2010 5-year est.); Master's degree or higher: 8.0% (2006-2010 5-year est.).

Housing: Homeownership rate: 36.9% (2010); Median home value: $86,100 (2006-2010 5-year est.); Median contract rent: $428 per month (2006-2010 5-year est.); Median year structure built: 1946 (2006-2010 5-year est.).

Safety: Violent crime rate: 64.2 per 10,000 population; Property crime rate: 362.2 per 10,000 population (2011).

Transportation: Commute to work: 91.9% car, 0.0% public transportation, 5.7% walk, 0.9% work from home (2006-2010 5-year est.); Travel time to work: 46.7% less than 15 minutes, 36.9% 15 to 30 minutes, 12.8% 30 to 45 minutes, 1.4% 45 to 60 minutes, 2.2% 60 minutes or more (2006-2010 5-year est.)

Additional Information Contacts

South Valley Chamber of Commerce . . . . (570) 735-6990
  http://www.southvalleychamber.com

EXETER (borough). Covers a land area of 4.673 square miles and a water area of 0.326 square miles. Located at 41.33° N. Lat; 75.82° W. Long. Elevation is 564 feet.

Population: 5,691 (1990); 5,955 (2000); 5,652 (2010); Density: 1,209.5 persons per square mile (2010); Race: 97.2% White, 1.2% Black, 0.5% Asian, 0.1% American Indian/Alaska Native, 0.0% Native Hawaiian/Other Pacific Islander, 1.0% Other, 1.1% Hispanic of any race (2010); Average household size: 2.25 (2010); Median age: 44.4 (2010); Males per 100 females: 87.6 (2010); Marriage status: 28.1% never married, 50.7% now married, 11.2% widowed, 10.0% divorced (2006-2010 5-year est.); Foreign born: 0.7% (2006-2010 5-year est.); Ancestry (includes multiple ancestries): 34.1% Italian, 24.4% Irish, 19.8% Polish, 10.5% German, 8.3% English (2006-2010 5-year est.).

Economy: Single-family building permits issued: 2 (2011); Multi-family building permits issued: 0 (2011); Employment by occupation: 8.6% management, 2.8% professional, 8.6% services, 26.6% sales, 4.8% farming, 6.2% construction, 5.1% production (2006-2010 5-year est.).

Income: Per capita income: $22,894 (2006-2010 5-year est.); Median household income: $44,000 (2006-2010 5-year est.); Average household income: $54,274 (2006-2010 5-year est.); Percent of households with income of $100,000 or more: 12.5% (2006-2010 5-year est.); Poverty rate: 17.8% (2006-2010 5-year est.).

Education: Percent of population age 25 and over with: High school diploma (including GED) or higher: 88.6% (2006-2010 5-year est.); Bachelor's degree or higher: 21.0% (2006-2010 5-year est.); Master's degree or higher: 8.1% (2006-2010 5-year est.).

School District(s)

Wyoming Area SD (KG-12)
  2010-11 Enrollment: 2,536 . . . . (570) 655-3733

Housing: Homeownership rate: 72.0% (2010); Median home value: $111,100 (2006-2010 5-year est.); Median contract rent: $435 per month (2006-2010 5-year est.); Median year structure built: 1962 (2006-2010 5-year est.).

Safety: Violent crime rate: 21.2 per 10,000 population; Property crime rate: 243.4 per 10,000 population (2011).

Transportation: Commute to work: 95.0% car, 0.4% public transportation, 0.5% walk, 3.7% work from home (2006-2010 5-year est.); Travel time to work: 32.6% less than 15 minutes, 43.8% 15 to 30 minutes, 20.5% 30 to 45 minutes, 1.0% 45 to 60 minutes, 2.0% 60 minutes or more (2006-2010 5-year est.)

Additional Information Contacts

Borough of Exeter . . . . (610) 779-5660
  http://www.co.berks.pa.us/exeter
Greater Northeast Chamber of Commerce . . . . (570) 457-1130
  http://www.gnecc.com

EXETER (township). Covers a land area of 12.995 square miles and a water area of 0.480 square miles. Located at 41.38° N. Lat; 75.84° W. Long. Elevation is 564 feet.

History: Settled 1790, incorporated 1884.

Population: 2,457 (1990); 2,557 (2000); 2,378 (2010); Density: 183.0 persons per square mile (2010); Race: 99.3% White, 0.2% Black, 0.1% Asian, 0.0% American Indian/Alaska Native, 0.0% Native Hawaiian/Other Pacific Islander, 0.4% Other, 0.5% Hispanic of any race (2010); Average

household size: 2.66 (2010); Median age: 44.6 (2010); Males per 100 females: 104.3 (2010); Marriage status: 25.3% never married, 64.7% now married, 6.5% widowed, 3.4% divorced (2006-2010 5-year est.); Foreign born: 0.3% (2006-2010 5-year est.); Ancestry (includes multiple ancestries): 21.8% Polish, 17.4% Italian, 16.5% German, 16.0% Irish, 10.0% Slovak (2006-2010 5-year est.).

Economy: Single-family building permits issued: 3 (2011); Multi-family building permits issued: 0 (2011); Employment by occupation: 6.6% management, 1.4% professional, 4.3% services, 21.3% sales, 3.4% farming, 13.6% construction, 10.7% production (2006-2010 5-year est.).

Income: Per capita income: $29,140 (2006-2010 5-year est.); Median household income: $62,000 (2006-2010 5-year est.); Average household income: $79,116 (2006-2010 5-year est.); Percent of households with income of $100,000 or more: 16.0% (2006-2010 5-year est.); Poverty rate: 3.3% (2006-2010 5-year est.).

Education: Percent of population age 25 and over with: High school diploma (including GED) or higher: 91.8% (2006-2010 5-year est.); Bachelor's degree or higher: 16.0% (2006-2010 5-year est.); Master's degree or higher: 4.0% (2006-2010 5-year est.).

Housing: Homeownership rate: 89.7% (2010); Median home value: $135,900 (2006-2010 5-year est.); Median contract rent: $463 per month (2006-2010 5-year est.); Median year structure built: 1971 (2006-2010 5-year est.).

Transportation: Commute to work: 98.0% car, 0.0% public transportation, 0.0% walk, 1.5% work from home (2006-2010 5-year est.); Travel time to work: 17.8% less than 15 minutes, 34.1% 15 to 30 minutes, 40.9% 30 to 45 minutes, 2.5% 45 to 60 minutes, 4.7% 60 minutes or more (2006-2010 5-year est.)

Additional Information Contacts

Greater Northeast Chamber of Commerce . . . . (570) 457-1130
  http://www.gnecc.com

FAIRMOUNT (township). Covers a land area of 45.711 square miles and a water area of 0.496 square miles. Located at 41.29° N. Lat; 76.26° W. Long.

Population: 1,215 (1990); 1,226 (2000); 1,276 (2010); Density: 27.9 persons per square mile (2010); Race: 98.2% White, 0.2% Black, 0.1% Asian, 0.2% American Indian/Alaska Native, 0.0% Native Hawaiian/Other Pacific Islander, 1.3% Other, 2.8% Hispanic of any race (2010); Average household size: 2.49 (2010); Median age: 43.0 (2010); Males per 100 females: 104.2 (2010); Marriage status: 22.1% never married, 60.5% now married, 9.1% widowed, 8.3% divorced (2006-2010 5-year est.); Foreign born: 0.2% (2006-2010 5-year est.); Ancestry (includes multiple ancestries): 31.9% German, 19.8% Polish, 14.6% Irish, 11.9% English, 6.9% Welsh (2006-2010 5-year est.).

Economy: Employment by occupation: 5.5% management, 2.0% professional, 13.0% services, 15.1% sales, 4.5% farming, 19.8% construction, 6.3% production (2006-2010 5-year est.).

Income: Per capita income: $22,054 (2006-2010 5-year est.); Median household income: $51,597 (2006-2010 5-year est.); Average household income: $55,411 (2006-2010 5-year est.); Percent of households with income of $100,000 or more: 11.8% (2006-2010 5-year est.); Poverty rate: 9.9% (2006-2010 5-year est.).

Education: Percent of population age 25 and over with: High school diploma (including GED) or higher: 87.7% (2006-2010 5-year est.); Bachelor's degree or higher: 18.9% (2006-2010 5-year est.); Master's degree or higher: 3.8% (2006-2010 5-year est.).

Housing: Homeownership rate: 85.9% (2010); Median home value: $155,300 (2006-2010 5-year est.); Median contract rent: $275 per month (2006-2010 5-year est.); Median year structure built: 1973 (2006-2010 5-year est.).

Transportation: Commute to work: 97.1% car, 0.0% public transportation, 0.9% walk, 2.1% work from home (2006-2010 5-year est.); Travel time to work: 9.0% less than 15 minutes, 27.0% 15 to 30 minutes, 35.8% 30 to 45 minutes, 16.9% 45 to 60 minutes, 11.3% 60 minutes or more (2006-2010 5-year est.)

Additional Information Contacts

Greater Philadelphia Chamber of Commerce . . . . (215) 545-1234
  http://www.greaterphilachamber.com

FAIRVIEW (township). Covers a land area of 9.434 square miles and a water area of 0.009 square miles. Located at 41.16° N. Lat; 75.86° W. Long. Elevation is 1,598 feet.

Population: 3,014 (1990); 3,995 (2000); 4,520 (2010); Density: 479.1 persons per square mile (2010); Race: 94.4% White, 1.0% Black, 2.8%

Asian, 0.0% American Indian/Alaska Native, 0.0% Native Hawaiian/Other Pacific Islander, 1.8% Other, 1.9% Hispanic of any race (2010); Average household size: 2.72 (2010); Median age: 41.6 (2010); Males per 100 females: 94.0 (2010); Marriage status: 25.7% never married, 63.8% now married, 6.7% widowed, 3.8% divorced (2006-2010 5-year est.); Foreign born: 7.3% (2006-2010 5-year est.); Ancestry (includes multiple ancestries): 25.2% Irish, 22.7% German, 19.5% Polish, 16.0% Italian, 7.3% English (2006-2010 5-year est.).

Economy: Single-family building permits issued: 2 (2011); Multi-family building permits issued: 0 (2011); Employment by occupation: 21.8% management, 4.3% professional, 11.0% services, 16.1% sales, 4.4% farming, 4.0% construction, 2.4% production (2006-2010 5-year est.).

Income: Per capita income: $35,884 (2006-2010 5-year est.); Median household income: $83,090 (2006-2010 5-year est.); Average household income: $96,840 (2006-2010 5-year est.); Percent of households with income of $100,000 or more: 37.6% (2006-2010 5-year est.); Poverty rate: 7.2% (2006-2010 5-year est.).

Education: Percent of population age 25 and over with: High school diploma (including GED) or higher: 96.0% (2006-2010 5-year est.); Bachelor's degree or higher: 39.3% (2006-2010 5-year est.); Master's degree or higher: 19.4% (2006-2010 5-year est.).

Housing: Homeownership rate: 85.5% (2010); Median home value: $225,100 (2006-2010 5-year est.); Median contract rent: $352 per month (2006-2010 5-year est.); Median year structure built: 1976 (2006-2010 5-year est.).

Transportation: Commute to work: 92.6% car, 0.0% public transportation, 3.5% walk, 3.3% work from home (2006-2010 5-year est.); Travel time to work: 31.9% less than 15 minutes, 42.7% 15 to 30 minutes, 12.3% 30 to 45 minutes, 6.0% 45 to 60 minutes, 7.0% 60 minutes or more (2006-2010 5-year est.).

Additional Information Contacts
South Valley Chamber of Commerce . . . . (570) 735-6990
  http://www.southvalleychamber.com

FORTY FORT (borough). Covers a land area of 1.313 square miles and a water area of 0.261 square miles. Located at 41.28° N. Lat; 75.87° W. Long. Elevation is 551 feet.

History: Settled 1772 on site of Colonial fort in the Wyoming Valley. Settlers made last stand here in Wyoming Valley massacre, 1778.

Population: 5,049 (1990); 4,579 (2000); 4,214 (2010); Density: 3,209.1 persons per square mile (2010); Race: 97.0% White, 1.0% Black, 0.8% Asian, 0.0% American Indian/Alaska Native, 0.0% Native Hawaiian/Other Pacific Islander, 1.2% Other, 1.4% Hispanic of any race (2010); Average household size: 2.22 (2010); Median age: 43.2 (2010); Males per 100 females: 87.1 (2010); Marriage status: 31.3% never married, 47.6% now married, 8.0% widowed, 13.2% divorced (2006-2010 5-year est.); Foreign born: 0.4% (2006-2010 5-year est.); Ancestry (includes multiple ancestries): 31.0% Irish, 22.6% Italian, 19.9% German, 17.2% Polish, 12.9% English (2006-2010 5-year est.).

Economy: Single-family building permits issued: 0 (2011); Multi-family building permits issued: 0 (2011); Employment by occupation: 10.1% management, 4.1% professional, 10.4% services, 26.7% sales, 2.5% farming, 4.3% construction, 4.4% production (2006-2010 5-year est.).

Income: Per capita income: $26,502 (2006-2010 5-year est.); Median household income: $57,400 (2006-2010 5-year est.); Average household income: $61,304 (2006-2010 5-year est.); Percent of households with income of $100,000 or more: 17.4% (2006-2010 5-year est.); Poverty rate: 10.2% (2006-2010 5-year est.).

Education: Percent of population age 25 and over with: High school diploma (including GED) or higher: 95.0% (2006-2010 5-year est.); Bachelor's degree or higher: 32.0% (2006-2010 5-year est.); Master's degree or higher: 11.7% (2006-2010 5-year est.).

School District(s)
Wyoming Valley West SD (KG-12)
  2010-11 Enrollment: 4,855 . . . . (570) 288-6551

Two-year College(s)
Fortis Institute-Forty Fort (Private, For-profit)
  Fall 2010 Enrollment: 321 . . . . (570) 288-8400
  2011-12 Tuition: In-state $13,575; Out-of-state $13,575

Housing: Homeownership rate: 69.5% (2010); Median home value: $131,100 (2006-2010 5-year est.); Median contract rent: $526 per month (2006-2010 5-year est.); Median year structure built: before 1940 (2006-2010 5-year est.).

Safety: Violent crime rate: 4.7 per 10,000 population; Property crime rate: 362.0 per 10,000 population (2011).

Transportation: Commute to work: 95.6% car, 0.6% public transportation, 1.9% walk, 1.3% work from home (2006-2010 5-year est.); Travel time to work: 52.5% less than 15 minutes, 32.5% 15 to 30 minutes, 7.0% 30 to 45 minutes, 3.5% 45 to 60 minutes, 4.5% 60 minutes or more (2006-2010 5-year est.).

Additional Information Contacts
Greater Northeast Chamber of Commerce . . . . (570) 457-1130
  http://www.gnecc.com

FOSTER (township). Covers a land area of 44.870 square miles and a water area of 0.286 square miles. Located at 41.01° N. Lat; 75.86° W. Long.

Population: 3,499 (1990); 3,323 (2000); 3,467 (2010); Density: 77.3 persons per square mile (2010); Race: 96.9% White, 1.2% Black, 0.2% Asian, 0.3% American Indian/Alaska Native, 0.0% Native Hawaiian/Other Pacific Islander, 1.4% Other, 2.8% Hispanic of any race (2010); Average household size: 2.27 (2010); Median age: 47.8 (2010); Males per 100 females: 106.4 (2010); Marriage status: 31.5% never married, 51.2% now married, 7.3% widowed, 10.0% divorced (2006-2010 5-year est.); Foreign born: 0.8% (2006-2010 5-year est.); Ancestry (includes multiple ancestries): 29.4% Italian, 21.3% Polish, 20.1% German, 14.1% Irish, 9.2% Greek (2006-2010 5-year est.).

Economy: Single-family building permits issued: 1 (2011); Multi-family building permits issued: 0 (2011); Employment by occupation: 7.3% management, 3.0% professional, 16.1% services, 14.3% sales, 3.1% farming, 16.0% construction, 10.5% production (2006-2010 5-year est.).

Income: Per capita income: $19,461 (2006-2010 5-year est.); Median household income: $37,431 (2006-2010 5-year est.); Average household income: $46,150 (2006-2010 5-year est.); Percent of households with income of $100,000 or more: 6.5% (2006-2010 5-year est.); Poverty rate: 22.1% (2006-2010 5-year est.).

Education: Percent of population age 25 and over with: High school diploma (including GED) or higher: 82.2% (2006-2010 5-year est.); Bachelor's degree or higher: 10.5% (2006-2010 5-year est.); Master's degree or higher: 2.1% (2006-2010 5-year est.).

Housing: Homeownership rate: 87.3% (2010); Median home value: $94,900 (2006-2010 5-year est.); Median contract rent: $402 per month (2006-2010 5-year est.); Median year structure built: 1974 (2006-2010 5-year est.).

Transportation: Commute to work: 96.2% car, 0.0% public transportation, 3.1% walk, 0.0% work from home (2006-2010 5-year est.); Travel time to work: 17.4% less than 15 minutes, 39.4% 15 to 30 minutes, 24.0% 30 to 45 minutes, 7.9% 45 to 60 minutes, 11.3% 60 minutes or more (2006-2010 5-year est.).

Additional Information Contacts
Greater Hazelton Chamber of Commerce . . . . (570) 455-1509
  http://www.hazletonchamber.org

FRANKLIN (township). Covers a land area of 12.698 square miles and a water area of 0.351 square miles. Located at 41.39° N. Lat; 75.90° W. Long.

Population: 1,385 (1990); 1,601 (2000); 1,757 (2010); Density: 138.4 persons per square mile (2010); Race: 98.0% White, 0.3% Black, 0.4% Asian, 0.2% American Indian/Alaska Native, 0.1% Native Hawaiian/Other Pacific Islander, 1.0% Other, 0.6% Hispanic of any race (2010); Average household size: 2.53 (2010); Median age: 44.5 (2010); Males per 100 females: 103.4 (2010); Marriage status: 23.5% never married, 63.3% now married, 6.6% widowed, 6.5% divorced (2006-2010 5-year est.); Foreign born: 0.3% (2006-2010 5-year est.); Ancestry (includes multiple ancestries): 26.2% German, 26.0% Polish, 23.7% Irish, 15.4% Italian, 11.6% English (2006-2010 5-year est.).

Economy: Single-family building permits issued: 1 (2011); Multi-family building permits issued: 0 (2011); Employment by occupation: 8.1% management, 8.1% professional, 8.1% services, 18.5% sales, 5.2% farming, 14.9% construction, 10.0% production (2006-2010 5-year est.).

Income: Per capita income: $23,191 (2006-2010 5-year est.); Median household income: $55,263 (2006-2010 5-year est.); Average household income: $60,507 (2006-2010 5-year est.); Percent of households with income of $100,000 or more: 15.8% (2006-2010 5-year est.); Poverty rate: 9.4% (2006-2010 5-year est.).

Education: Percent of population age 25 and over with: High school diploma (including GED) or higher: 97.1% (2006-2010 5-year est.); Bachelor's degree or higher: 17.1% (2006-2010 5-year est.); Master's degree or higher: 6.0% (2006-2010 5-year est.).

Housing: Homeownership rate: 91.0% (2010); Median home value: $163,100 (2006-2010 5-year est.); Median contract rent: $427 per month (2006-2010 5-year est.); Median year structure built: 1972 (2006-2010 5-year est.).

Transportation: Commute to work: 94.8% car, 0.0% public transportation, 1.3% walk, 3.0% work from home (2006-2010 5-year est.); Travel time to work: 18.3% less than 15 minutes, 47.0% 15 to 30 minutes, 22.3% 30 to 45 minutes, 7.1% 45 to 60 minutes, 5.3% 60 minutes or more (2006-2010 5-year est.).

Additional Information Contacts

Greater Northeast Chamber of Commerce . . . . (570) 457-1130
    http://www.gnecc.com

FREELAND (borough). Covers a land area of 0.673 square miles and a water area of 0 square miles. Located at 41.02° N. Lat; 75.90° W. Long. Elevation is 1,864 feet.

History: Eckley Miners' Village, 19th-century coal-mining town, to South. Laid out 1868, incorporated 1876.

Population: 3,909 (1990); 3,643 (2000); 3,531 (2010); Density: 5,248.6 persons per square mile (2010); Race: 95.8% White, 0.6% Black, 0.5% Asian, 0.1% American Indian/Alaska Native, 0.0% Native Hawaiian/Other Pacific Islander, 3.0% Other, 5.8% Hispanic of any race (2010); Average household size: 2.34 (2010); Median age: 40.1 (2010); Males per 100 females: 93.0 (2010); Marriage status: 32.9% never married, 43.6% now married, 11.3% widowed, 12.2% divorced (2006-2010 5-year est.); Foreign born: 2.3% (2006-2010 5-year est.); Ancestry (includes multiple ancestries): 24.2% German, 20.3% Irish, 18.5% Italian, 17.3% Polish, 7.9% Slovak (2006-2010 5-year est.).

Economy: Single-family building permits issued: 0 (2011); Multi-family building permits issued: 0 (2011); Employment by occupation: 5.6% management, 4.9% professional, 14.1% services, 17.2% sales, 4.1% farming, 6.8% construction, 7.0% production (2006-2010 5-year est.).

Income: Per capita income: $20,695 (2006-2010 5-year est.); Median household income: $34,591 (2006-2010 5-year est.); Average household income: $43,973 (2006-2010 5-year est.); Percent of households with income of $100,000 or more: 7.1% (2006-2010 5-year est.); Poverty rate: 15.0% (2006-2010 5-year est.).

Education: Percent of population age 25 and over with: High school diploma (including GED) or higher: 89.6% (2006-2010 5-year est.); Bachelor's degree or higher: 16.3% (2006-2010 5-year est.); Master's degree or higher: 3.6% (2006-2010 5-year est.).

School District(s)

Hazleton Area SD (PK-12)
    2010-11 Enrollment: 10,301 . . . . (570) 459-3111

Housing: Homeownership rate: 63.7% (2010); Median home value: $86,100 (2006-2010 5-year est.); Median contract rent: $450 per month (2006-2010 5-year est.); Median year structure built: before 1940 (2006-2010 5-year est.).

Transportation: Commute to work: 93.5% car, 0.7% public transportation, 2.8% walk, 3.0% work from home (2006-2010 5-year est.); Travel time to work: 29.2% less than 15 minutes, 43.0% 15 to 30 minutes, 22.3% 30 to 45 minutes, 5.5% 45 to 60 minutes, 0.0% 60 minutes or more (2006-2010 5-year est.).

Additional Information Contacts

Greater Hazleton Chamber of Commerce. . . . . (570) 455-1509
    http://www.hazletonchamber.org

GEORGETOWN (CDP). Covers a land area of 0.749 square miles and a water area of 0 square miles. Located at 41.23° N. Lat; 75.87° W. Long. Elevation is 699 feet.

Population: n/a (1990); n/a (2000); 1,640 (2010); Density: 2,190.1 persons per square mile (2010); Race: 96.7% White, 1.1% Black, 0.8% Asian, 0.1% American Indian/Alaska Native, 0.0% Native Hawaiian/Other Pacific Islander, 1.3% Other, 1.5% Hispanic of any race (2010); Average household size: 2.16 (2010); Median age: 45.9 (2010); Males per 100 females: 96.9 (2010); Marriage status: 38.9% never married, 38.9% now married, 6.1% widowed, 16.1% divorced (2006-2010 5-year est.); Foreign born: 4.3% (2006-2010 5-year est.); Ancestry (includes multiple ancestries): 41.7% Polish, 30.3% Irish, 21.0% German, 11.8% Italian, 6.5% Syrian (2006-2010 5-year est.).

Economy: Employment by occupation: 8.6% management, 1.4% professional, 9.6% services, 26.0% sales, 8.3% farming, 11.4% construction, 7.9% production (2006-2010 5-year est.).

Income: Per capita income: $18,921 (2006-2010 5-year est.); Median household income: $35,250 (2006-2010 5-year est.); Average household

income: $40,871 (2006-2010 5-year est.); Percent of households with income of $100,000 or more: 4.8% (2006-2010 5-year est.); Poverty rate: 9.4% (2006-2010 5-year est.).

Education: Percent of population age 25 and over with: High school diploma (including GED) or higher: 83.5% (2006-2010 5-year est.); Bachelor's degree or higher: 13.7% (2006-2010 5-year est.); Master's degree or higher: 2.7% (2006-2010 5-year est.).

Housing: Homeownership rate: 73.5% (2010); Median home value: $85,500 (2006-2010 5-year est.); Median contract rent: $345 per month (2006-2010 5-year est.); Median year structure built: before 1940 (2006-2010 5-year est.).

Transportation: Commute to work: 95.9% car, 2.4% public transportation, 1.1% walk, 0.6% work from home (2006-2010 5-year est.); Travel time to work: 47.6% less than 15 minutes, 38.8% 15 to 30 minutes, 7.6% 30 to 45 minutes, 2.6% 45 to 60 minutes, 3.4% 60 minutes or more (2006-2010 5-year est.)

GLEN LYON (CDP). Covers a land area of 3.311 square miles and a water area of 0.087 square miles. Located at 41.18° N. Lat; 76.09° W. Long. Elevation is 676 feet.

Population: 2,108 (1990); 1,881 (2000); 1,873 (2010); Density: 565.7 persons per square mile (2010); Race: 95.1% White, 2.0% Black, 0.2% Asian, 0.0% American Indian/Alaska Native, 0.0% Native Hawaiian/Other Pacific Islander, 2.7% Other, 3.2% Hispanic of any race (2010); Average household size: 2.43 (2010); Median age: 37.0 (2010); Males per 100 females: 94.5 (2010); Marriage status: 39.4% never married, 38.4% now married, 7.8% widowed, 14.4% divorced (2006-2010 5-year est.); Foreign born: 2.0% (2006-2010 5-year est.); Ancestry (includes multiple ancestries): 40.4% Polish, 15.9% German, 15.2% Irish, 6.8% Welsh, 5.5% English (2006-2010 5-year est.).

Economy: Employment by occupation: 1.4% management, 0.0% professional, 7.5% services, 17.7% sales, 4.8% farming, 22.2% construction, 13.8% production (2006-2010 5-year est.).

Income: Per capita income: $17,230 (2006-2010 5-year est.); Median household income: $29,674 (2006-2010 5-year est.); Average household income: $36,457 (2006-2010 5-year est.); Percent of households with income of $100,000 or more: 4.6% (2006-2010 5-year est.); Poverty rate: 30.3% (2006-2010 5-year est.).

Education: Percent of population age 25 and over with: High school diploma (including GED) or higher: 80.2% (2006-2010 5-year est.); Bachelor's degree or higher: 5.2% (2006-2010 5-year est.); Master's degree or higher: 1.8% (2006-2010 5-year est.).

Housing: Homeownership rate: 57.5% (2010); Median home value: $70,000 (2006-2010 5-year est.); Median contract rent: $417 per month (2006-2010 5-year est.); Median year structure built: before 1940 (2006-2010 5-year est.).

Transportation: Commute to work: 97.6% car, 1.2% public transportation, 0.0% walk, 0.0% work from home (2006-2010 5-year est.); Travel time to work: 17.3% less than 15 minutes, 37.7% 15 to 30 minutes, 33.8% 30 to 45 minutes, 5.7% 45 to 60 minutes, 5.5% 60 minutes or more (2006-2010 5-year est.)

Additional Information Contacts

South Valley Chamber of Commerce . . . . (570) 735-6990
    http://www.southvalleychamber.com

HANOVER (township). Covers a land area of 18.866 square miles and a water area of 0.349 square miles. Located at 41.20° N. Lat; 75.94° W. Long. Elevation is 669 feet.

Population: 11,979 (1990); 11,488 (2000); 11,076 (2010); Density: 587.1 persons per square mile (2010); Race: 93.5% White, 3.2% Black, 0.6% Asian, 0.1% American Indian/Alaska Native, 0.0% Native Hawaiian/Other Pacific Islander, 2.6% Other, 2.9% Hispanic of any race (2010); Average household size: 2.25 (2010); Median age: 42.8 (2010); Males per 100 females: 86.8 (2010); Marriage status: 29.9% never married, 47.8% now married, 11.7% widowed, 10.7% divorced (2006-2010 5-year est.); Foreign born: 1.3% (2006-2010 5-year est.); Ancestry (includes multiple ancestries): 30.4% Polish, 23.3% Irish, 15.8% Italian, 14.3% German, 8.0% Welsh (2006-2010 5-year est.).

Economy: Single-family building permits issued: 4 (2011); Multi-family building permits issued: 0 (2011); Employment by occupation: 9.6% management, 1.6% professional, 11.9% services, 20.3% sales, 5.7% farming, 6.8% construction, 6.4% production (2006-2010 5-year est.).

Income: Per capita income: $21,999 (2006-2010 5-year est.); Median household income: $37,521 (2006-2010 5-year est.); Average household income: $49,259 (2006-2010 5-year est.); Percent of households with

income of $100,000 or more: 9.3% (2006-2010 5-year est.); Poverty rate: 14.3% (2006-2010 5-year est.).

Education: Percent of population age 25 and over with: High school diploma (including GED) or higher: 86.0% (2006-2010 5-year est.); Bachelor's degree or higher: 16.3% (2006-2010 5-year est.); Master's degree or higher: 5.1% (2006-2010 5-year est.).

School District(s)

Hanover Area SD (KG-12)

  2010-11 Enrollment: 2,000 . . . . (570) 831-2313

Housing: Homeownership rate: 64.8% (2010); Median home value: $91,900 (2006-2010 5-year est.); Median contract rent: $398 per month (2006-2010 5-year est.); Median year structure built: 1945 (2006-2010 5-year est.).

Safety: Violent crime rate: 9.0 per 10,000 population; Property crime rate: 167.4 per 10,000 population (2011).

Transportation: Commute to work: 95.9% car, 0.2% public transportation, 2.6% walk, 0.3% work from home (2006-2010 5-year est.); Travel time to work: 45.2% less than 15 minutes, 36.5% 15 to 30 minutes, 8.9% 30 to 45 minutes, 3.3% 45 to 60 minutes, 6.1% 60 minutes or more (2006-2010 5-year est.)

Additional Information Contacts

Hanover Township . . . . (570) 825-8522

  http://www.hanovertownship.org

South Valley Chamber of Commerce . . . . (570) 735-6990

  http://www.southvalleychamber.com

HARLEIGH (CDP). Covers a land area of 0.570 square miles and a water area of 0 square miles. Located at 40.99° N. Lat; 75.97° W. Long. Elevation is 1,535 feet.

Population: n/a (1990); n/a (2000); 1,104 (2010); Density: 1,937.8 persons per square mile (2010); Race: 95.1% White, 0.8% Black, 1.5% Asian, 0.4% American Indian/Alaska Native, 0.0% Native Hawaiian/Other Pacific Islander, 2.2% Other, 3.2% Hispanic of any race (2010); Average household size: 2.46 (2010); Median age: 49.0 (2010); Males per 100 females: 98.9 (2010); Marriage status: 30.4% never married, 58.8% now married, 8.5% widowed, 2.3% divorced (2006-2010 5-year est.); Foreign born: 3.2% (2006-2010 5-year est.); Ancestry (includes multiple ancestries): 27.5% Italian, 16.1% Irish, 14.8% Polish, 14.5% Slovak, 10.9% German (2006-2010 5-year est.).

Economy: Employment by occupation: 13.0% management, 0.0% professional, 4.9% services, 19.6% sales, 6.3% farming, 1.8% construction, 11.3% production (2006-2010 5-year est.).

Income: Per capita income: $32,462 (2006-2010 5-year est.); Median household income: $60,833 (2006-2010 5-year est.); Average household income: $69,527 (2006-2010 5-year est.); Percent of households with income of $100,000 or more: 21.3% (2006-2010 5-year est.); Poverty rate: 12.0% (2006-2010 5-year est.).

Education: Percent of population age 25 and over with: High school diploma (including GED) or higher: 95.1% (2006-2010 5-year est.); Bachelor's degree or higher: 24.8% (2006-2010 5-year est.); Master's degree or higher: 11.5% (2006-2010 5-year est.).

Housing: Homeownership rate: 94.2% (2010); Median home value: $193,100 (2006-2010 5-year est.); Median contract rent: n/a per month (2006-2010 5-year est.); Median year structure built: 1993 (2006-2010 5-year est.).

Transportation: Commute to work: 92.3% car, 0.0% public transportation, 2.7% walk, 5.0% work from home (2006-2010 5-year est.); Travel time to work: 25.3% less than 15 minutes, 43.4% 15 to 30 minutes, 7.0% 30 to 45 minutes, 20.1% 45 to 60 minutes, 4.1% 60 minutes or more (2006-2010 5-year est.)

HARVEYS LAKE (borough). Covers a land area of 5.160 square miles and a water area of 1.016 square miles. Located at 41.36° N. Lat; 76.04° W. Long. Elevation is 1,319 feet.

Population: 2,851 (1990); 2,888 (2000); 2,791 (2010); Density: 540.9 persons per square mile (2010); Race: 97.7% White, 0.2% Black, 0.5% Asian, 0.1% American Indian/Alaska Native, 0.0% Native Hawaiian/Other Pacific Islander, 1.5% Other, 0.6% Hispanic of any race (2010); Average household size: 2.30 (2010); Median age: 45.7 (2010); Males per 100 females: 102.2 (2010); Marriage status: 25.0% never married, 55.5% now married, 6.9% widowed, 12.5% divorced (2006-2010 5-year est.); Foreign born: 3.7% (2006-2010 5-year est.); Ancestry (includes multiple ancestries): 28.5% German, 18.0% Irish, 17.3% Polish, 12.8% Welsh, 10.5% English (2006-2010 5-year est.).

Economy: Single-family building permits issued: 5 (2011); Multi-family building permits issued: 0 (2011); Employment by occupation: 9.8% management, 5.0% professional, 12.8% services, 15.3% sales, 1.7% farming, 12.6% construction, 8.6% production (2006-2010 5-year est.).

Income: Per capita income: $29,669 (2006-2010 5-year est.); Median household income: $55,650 (2006-2010 5-year est.); Average household income: $67,216 (2006-2010 5-year est.); Percent of households with income of $100,000 or more: 19.3% (2006-2010 5-year est.); Poverty rate: 9.5% (2006-2010 5-year est.).

Taxes: Total city taxes per capita: $211 (2009); City property taxes per capita: $87 (2009).

Education: Percent of population age 25 and over with: High school diploma (including GED) or higher: 90.2% (2006-2010 5-year est.); Bachelor's degree or higher: 31.3% (2006-2010 5-year est.); Master's degree or higher: 11.0% (2006-2010 5-year est.).

School District(s)

Lake-Lehman SD (KG-12)

  2010-11 Enrollment: 2,080 . . . . (570) 675-2165

Housing: Homeownership rate: 80.6% (2010); Median home value: $154,000 (2006-2010 5-year est.); Median contract rent: $477 per month (2006-2010 5-year est.); Median year structure built: 1953 (2006-2010 5-year est.).

Safety: Violent crime rate: 3.6 per 10,000 population; Property crime rate: 157.1 per 10,000 population (2011).

Transportation: Commute to work: 95.3% car, 0.0% public transportation, 0.5% walk, 2.8% work from home (2006-2010 5-year est.); Travel time to work: 14.0% less than 15 minutes, 27.4% 15 to 30 minutes, 39.4% 30 to 45 minutes, 7.8% 45 to 60 minutes, 11.4% 60 minutes or more (2006-2010 5-year est.)

Additional Information Contacts

Greater Scranton Chamber of Commerce . . . . (570) 342-7711

  http://www.scrantonchamber.com

HAZLE (township). Covers a land area of 45.070 square miles and a water area of 0.266 square miles. Located at 40.96° N. Lat; 76.01° W. Long.

History: Incorporated 1889.

Population: 9,334 (1990); 9,000 (2000); 9,549 (2010); Density: 211.9 persons per square mile (2010); Race: 92.2% White, 1.0% Black, 0.8% Asian, 0.3% American Indian/Alaska Native, 0.0% Native Hawaiian/Other Pacific Islander, 5.7% Other, 8.9% Hispanic of any race (2010); Average household size: 2.28 (2010); Median age: 47.9 (2010); Males per 100 females: 93.4 (2010); Marriage status: 28.7% never married, 51.4% now married, 11.1% widowed, 8.8% divorced (2006-2010 5-year est.); Foreign born: 2.6% (2006-2010 5-year est.); Ancestry (includes multiple ancestries): 24.6% Italian, 20.1% Polish, 20.0% German, 19.9% Irish, 11.2% Slovak (2006-2010 5-year est.).

Economy: Single-family building permits issued: 16 (2011); Multi-family building permits issued: 0 (2011); Employment by occupation: 10.8% management, 1.7% professional, 10.1% services, 19.3% sales, 3.7% farming, 9.2% construction, 11.6% production (2006-2010 5-year est.).

Income: Per capita income: $22,614 (2006-2010 5-year est.); Median household income: $39,552 (2006-2010 5-year est.); Average household income: $50,683 (2006-2010 5-year est.); Percent of households with income of $100,000 or more: 8.2% (2006-2010 5-year est.); Poverty rate: 11.8% (2006-2010 5-year est.).

Education: Percent of population age 25 and over with: High school diploma (including GED) or higher: 87.2% (2006-2010 5-year est.); Bachelor's degree or higher: 12.4% (2006-2010 5-year est.); Master's degree or higher: 4.9% (2006-2010 5-year est.).

Housing: Homeownership rate: 76.8% (2010); Median home value: $123,800 (2006-2010 5-year est.); Median contract rent: $423 per month (2006-2010 5-year est.); Median year structure built: 1972 (2006-2010 5-year est.).

Transportation: Commute to work: 92.8% car, 1.0% public transportation, 3.8% walk, 2.0% work from home (2006-2010 5-year est.); Travel time to work: 39.0% less than 15 minutes, 39.3% 15 to 30 minutes, 12.8% 30 to 45 minutes, 4.0% 45 to 60 minutes, 4.9% 60 minutes or more (2006-2010 5-year est.)

Additional Information Contacts

Greater Hazleton Chamber of Commerce . . . . (570) 455-1509

  http://www.hazletonchamber.org

Hazle Township . . . . (570) 636-5745

  http://www.hazletownship.com

HAZLETON (city). Covers a land area of 6.011 square miles and a water area of 0 square miles. Located at 40.95° N. Lat; 75.97° W. Long. Elevation is 1,657 feet.

History: Once a major anthracite-coal-producing region. Settled c.1809. Named by German settlers for the hazel bushes that grew in the swamp called Haselschwamm. The settlement increased in size and development after coal was discovered nearby in 1826. Coal production reached its peak during the first half of the 20th century, but declined afterward. Eckley Miners' Village, 19th-century mining town, to east. Incorporated as a borough 1856, as a city 1892.

Population: 24,730 (1990); 23,329 (2000); 25,340 (2010); Density: 4,215.4 persons per square mile (2010); Race: 69.4% White, 4.0% Black, 0.8% Asian, 0.4% American Indian/Alaska Native, 0.0% Native Hawaiian/Other Pacific Islander, 25.4% Other, 37.3% Hispanic of any race (2010); Average household size: 2.54 (2010); Median age: 37.6 (2010); Males per 100 females: 93.6 (2010); Marriage status: 33.5% never married, 46.1% now married, 9.3% widowed, 11.1% divorced (2006-2010 5-year est.); Foreign born: 19.9% (2006-2010 5-year est.); Ancestry (includes multiple ancestries): 20.2% Italian, 13.0% Polish, 12.6% German, 10.3% Irish, 8.2% Slovak (2006-2010 5-year est.).

Economy: Unemployment rate: 14.7% (August 2012); Total civilian labor force: 12,697 (August 2012); Single-family building permits issued: 0 (2011); Multi-family building permits issued: 0 (2011); Employment by occupation: 4.1% management, 1.4% professional, 12.0% services, 15.9% sales, 4.5% farming, 8.5% construction, 12.4% production (2006-2010 5-year est.).

Income: Per capita income: $18,215 (2006-2010 5-year est.); Median household income: $32,169 (2006-2010 5-year est.); Average household income: $43,556 (2006-2010 5-year est.); Percent of households with income of $100,000 or more: 6.1% (2006-2010 5-year est.); Poverty rate: 20.1% (2006-2010 5-year est.).

Taxes: Total city taxes per capita: $283 (2009); City property taxes per capita: $74 (2009).

Education: Percent of population age 25 and over with: High school diploma (including GED) or higher: 77.7% (2006-2010 5-year est.); Bachelor's degree or higher: 11.8% (2006-2010 5-year est.); Master's degree or higher: 3.6% (2006-2010 5-year est.).

School District(s)

Hazleton Area Career Center (09-12)
     2010-11 Enrollment: n/a . . . . (570) 459-3221
Hazleton Area SD (PK-12)
     2010-11 Enrollment: 10,301 . . . . (570) 459-3111

Four-year College(s)

Pennsylvania State University-Penn State Hazleton (Public)
     Fall 2010 Enrollment: 1,313 . . . . (570) 450-3000
     2011-12 Tuition: In-state $13,048; Out-of-state $19,488

Vocational/Technical School(s)

Hazleton Area Career Center (Public)
     Fall 2010 Enrollment: 103 . . . . (570) 459-3221
     2011-12 Tuition: $10,500
Jolie Hair And Beauty Academy-Hazleton (Private, For-profit)
     Fall 2010 Enrollment: 38 . . . . (570) 459-5501
     2011-12 Tuition: $14,800

Housing: Homeownership rate: 53.4% (2010); Median home value: $93,300 (2006-2010 5-year est.); Median contract rent: $476 per month (2006-2010 5-year est.); Median year structure built: 1942 (2006-2010 5-year est.).

Hospitals: Hazleton General Hospital (160 beds)

Safety: Violent crime rate: 46.0 per 10,000 population; Property crime rate: 177.4 per 10,000 population (2011).

Newspapers: Standard-Speaker (Regional news; Circulation 20,662)

Transportation: Commute to work: 90.3% car, 1.4% public transportation, 4.9% walk, 1.3% work from home (2006-2010 5-year est.); Travel time to work: 42.3% less than 15 minutes, 38.9% 15 to 30 minutes, 10.2% 30 to 45 minutes, 3.0% 45 to 60 minutes, 5.5% 60 minutes or more (2006-2010 5-year est.)

Airports: Hazleton Municipal (general aviation)

Additional Information Contacts

City of Hazleton . . . . (570) 459-4910
     http://www.hazletoncity.org
Greater Hazleton Chamber of Commerce . . . . (570) 455-1509
     http://www.hazletonchamber.org

HICKORY HILLS (CDP). Covers a land area of 1.403 square miles and a water area of 0.008 square miles. Located at 41.03° N. Lat; 75.82° W. Long. Elevation is 1,381 feet.

Population: n/a (1990); n/a (2000); 562 (2010); Density: 400.5 persons per square mile (2010); Race: 95.4% White, 1.4% Black, 0.2% Asian, 0.5% American Indian/Alaska Native, 0.0% Native Hawaiian/Other Pacific Islander, 2.5% Other, 4.6% Hispanic of any race (2010); Average household size: 2.21 (2010); Median age: 47.7 (2010); Males per 100 females: 105.1 (2010); Marriage status: 10.8% never married, 65.2% now married, 5.1% widowed, 18.9% divorced (2006-2010 5-year est.); Foreign born: 5.2% (2006-2010 5-year est.); Ancestry (includes multiple ancestries): 20.2% German, 17.2% Polish, 15.5% American, 15.3% Italian, 14.0% Irish (2006-2010 5-year est.).

Economy: Employment by occupation: 2.2% management, 0.0% professional, 26.2% services, 6.1% sales, 0.0% farming, 8.2% construction, 0.0% production (2006-2010 5-year est.).

Income: Per capita income: $25,168 (2006-2010 5-year est.); Median household income: $36,563 (2006-2010 5-year est.); Average household income: $45,193 (2006-2010 5-year est.); Percent of households with income of $100,000 or more: 12.3% (2006-2010 5-year est.); Poverty rate: 5.8% (2006-2010 5-year est.).

Education: Percent of population age 25 and over with: High school diploma (including GED) or higher: 76.9% (2006-2010 5-year est.); Bachelor's degree or higher: 14.5% (2006-2010 5-year est.); Master's degree or higher: 4.4% (2006-2010 5-year est.).

Housing: Homeownership rate: 89.0% (2010); Median home value: $92,100 (2006-2010 5-year est.); Median contract rent: n/a per month (2006-2010 5-year est.); Median year structure built: 1985 (2006-2010 5-year est.).

Transportation: Commute to work: 100.0% car, 0.0% public transportation, 0.0% walk, 0.0% work from home (2006-2010 5-year est.); Travel time to work: 12.9% less than 15 minutes, 21.1% 15 to 30 minutes, 46.6% 30 to 45 minutes, 3.9% 45 to 60 minutes, 15.4% 60 minutes or more (2006-2010 5-year est.)

HILLDALE (CDP). Covers a land area of 0.853 square miles and a water area of 0 square miles. Located at 41.29° N. Lat; 75.84° W. Long. Elevation is 597 feet.

Population: n/a (1990); n/a (2000); 1,246 (2010); Density: 1,461.1 persons per square mile (2010); Race: 97.9% White, 0.0% Black, 0.6% Asian, 0.0% American Indian/Alaska Native, 0.0% Native Hawaiian/Other Pacific Islander, 1.5% Other, 1.4% Hispanic of any race (2010); Average household size: 2.29 (2010); Median age: 52.1 (2010); Males per 100 females: 95.9 (2010); Marriage status: 26.6% never married, 62.1% now married, 6.4% widowed, 5.0% divorced (2006-2010 5-year est.); Foreign born: 4.0% (2006-2010 5-year est.); Ancestry (includes multiple ancestries): 30.9% Italian, 25.2% Polish, 14.4% Irish, 10.8% German, 10.0% Slovak (2006-2010 5-year est.).

Economy: Employment by occupation: 20.3% management, 1.8% professional, 5.2% services, 30.6% sales, 4.8% farming, 7.0% construction, 6.5% production (2006-2010 5-year est.).

Income: Per capita income: $28,389 (2006-2010 5-year est.); Median household income: $55,500 (2006-2010 5-year est.); Average household income: $66,158 (2006-2010 5-year est.); Percent of households with income of $100,000 or more: 20.9% (2006-2010 5-year est.); Poverty rate: 5.0% (2006-2010 5-year est.).

Education: Percent of population age 25 and over with: High school diploma (including GED) or higher: 89.6% (2006-2010 5-year est.); Bachelor's degree or higher: 25.4% (2006-2010 5-year est.); Master's degree or higher: 6.3% (2006-2010 5-year est.).

Housing: Homeownership rate: 84.9% (2010); Median home value: $161,800 (2006-2010 5-year est.); Median contract rent: $428 per month (2006-2010 5-year est.); Median year structure built: 1974 (2006-2010 5-year est.).

Transportation: Commute to work: 92.6% car, 0.0% public transportation, 6.0% walk, 0.0% work from home (2006-2010 5-year est.); Travel time to work: 41.2% less than 15 minutes, 43.2% 15 to 30 minutes, 10.5% 30 to 45 minutes, 0.0% 45 to 60 minutes, 5.1% 60 minutes or more (2006-2010 5-year est.)

HOLLENBACK (township). Covers a land area of 15.159 square miles and a water area of 0 square miles. Located at 41.07° N. Lat; 76.08° W. Long.

Population: 1,301 (1990); 1,243 (2000); 1,196 (2010); Density: 78.9 persons per square mile (2010); Race: 97.5% White, 0.6% Black, 0.2%

Asian, 0.0% American Indian/Alaska Native, 0.0% Native Hawaiian/Other Pacific Islander, 1.7% Other, 1.2% Hispanic of any race (2010); Average household size: 2.58 (2010); Median age: 45.1 (2010); Males per 100 females: 99.7 (2010); Marriage status: 26.3% never married, 62.6% now married, 4.5% widowed, 6.6% divorced (2006-2010 5-year est.); Foreign born: 0.0% (2006-2010 5-year est.); Ancestry (includes multiple ancestries): 40.9% German, 14.0% Irish, 12.6% Polish, 12.2% English, 9.5% Italian (2006-2010 5-year est.).

Economy: Single-family building permits issued: 1 (2011); Multi-family building permits issued: 0 (2011); Employment by occupation: 6.6% management, 5.4% professional, 2.2% services, 21.7% sales, 4.5% farming, 13.6% construction, 11.5% production (2006-2010 5-year est.).

Income: Per capita income: $23,032 (2006-2010 5-year est.); Median household income: $49,489 (2006-2010 5-year est.); Average household income: $60,788 (2006-2010 5-year est.); Percent of households with income of $100,000 or more: 17.4% (2006-2010 5-year est.); Poverty rate: 6.3% (2006-2010 5-year est.).

Education: Percent of population age 25 and over with: High school diploma (including GED) or higher: 91.3% (2006-2010 5-year est.); Bachelor's degree or higher: 17.7% (2006-2010 5-year est.); Master's degree or higher: 5.8% (2006-2010 5-year est.).

Housing: Homeownership rate: 88.6% (2010); Median home value: $153,100 (2006-2010 5-year est.); Median contract rent: $325 per month (2006-2010 5-year est.); Median year structure built: 1977 (2006-2010 5-year est.).

Transportation: Commute to work: 95.8% car, 0.0% public transportation, 1.6% walk, 2.6% work from home (2006-2010 5-year est.); Travel time to work: 12.2% less than 15 minutes, 49.2% 15 to 30 minutes, 25.2% 30 to 45 minutes, 8.3% 45 to 60 minutes, 5.1% 60 minutes or more (2006-2010 5-year est.)

HUDSON (CDP). Covers a land area of 0.378 square miles and a water area of 0 square miles. Located at 41.28° N. Lat; 75.83° W. Long. Elevation is 627 feet.

Population: n/a (1990); n/a (2000); 1,443 (2010); Density: 3,822.1 persons per square mile (2010); Race: 98.0% White, 0.8% Black, 0.3% Asian, 0.1% American Indian/Alaska Native, 0.0% Native Hawaiian/Other Pacific Islander, 0.8% Other, 0.7% Hispanic of any race (2010); Average household size: 2.22 (2010); Median age: 47.2 (2010); Males per 100 females: 90.4 (2010); Marriage status: 19.0% never married, 65.6% now married, 8.7% widowed, 6.6% divorced (2006-2010 5-year est.); Foreign born: 0.0% (2006-2010 5-year est.); Ancestry (includes multiple ancestries): 29.7% Polish, 22.9% English, 14.9% Slovak, 10.8% Italian, 10.1% Irish (2006-2010 5-year est.).

Economy: Employment by occupation: 14.4% management, 0.0% professional, 7.7% services, 25.2% sales, 0.0% farming, 8.9% construction, 6.5% production (2006-2010 5-year est.).

Income: Per capita income: $27,745 (2006-2010 5-year est.); Median household income: $65,215 (2006-2010 5-year est.); Average household income: $62,592 (2006-2010 5-year est.); Percent of households with income of $100,000 or more: 14.3% (2006-2010 5-year est.); Poverty rate: 2.4% (2006-2010 5-year est.).

Education: Percent of population age 25 and over with: High school diploma (including GED) or higher: 90.3% (2006-2010 5-year est.); Bachelor's degree or higher: 24.5% (2006-2010 5-year est.); Master's degree or higher: 2.8% (2006-2010 5-year est.).

Housing: Homeownership rate: 72.5% (2010); Median home value: $147,900 (2006-2010 5-year est.); Median contract rent: $408 per month (2006-2010 5-year est.); Median year structure built: 1951 (2006-2010 5-year est.).

Transportation: Commute to work: 91.5% car, 0.0% public transportation, 0.0% walk, 8.5% work from home (2006-2010 5-year est.); Travel time to work: 48.0% less than 15 minutes, 32.7% 15 to 30 minutes, 1.6% 30 to 45 minutes, 5.8% 45 to 60 minutes, 11.8% 60 minutes or more (2006-2010 5-year est.)

HUGHESTOWN (borough). Covers a land area of 0.912 square miles and a water area of 0 square miles. Located at 41.33° N. Lat; 75.77° W. Long. Elevation is 774 feet.

History: Incorporated 1879.

Population: 1,734 (1990); 1,541 (2000); 1,392 (2010); Density: 1,527.1 persons per square mile (2010); Race: 98.4% White, 0.1% Black, 0.1% Asian, 0.6% American Indian/Alaska Native, 0.0% Native Hawaiian/Other Pacific Islander, 0.8% Other, 1.8% Hispanic of any race (2010); Average household size: 2.28 (2010); Median age: 46.8 (2010); Males per 100

females: 94.7 (2010); Marriage status: 24.3% never married, 53.3% now married, 12.1% widowed, 10.3% divorced (2006-2010 5-year est.); Foreign born: 1.1% (2006-2010 5-year est.); Ancestry (includes multiple ancestries): 41.4% Italian, 35.2% Irish, 22.0% Polish, 12.2% German, 9.5% English (2006-2010 5-year est.).

Economy: Employment by occupation: 14.6% management, 3.6% professional, 10.5% services, 20.2% sales, 6.3% farming, 5.1% construction, 5.1% production (2006-2010 5-year est.).

Income: Per capita income: $29,053 (2006-2010 5-year est.); Median household income: $52,298 (2006-2010 5-year est.); Average household income: $67,944 (2006-2010 5-year est.); Percent of households with income of $100,000 or more: 21.9% (2006-2010 5-year est.); Poverty rate: 6.9% (2006-2010 5-year est.).

Education: Percent of population age 25 and over with: High school diploma (including GED) or higher: 89.4% (2006-2010 5-year est.); Bachelor's degree or higher: 22.4% (2006-2010 5-year est.); Master's degree or higher: 9.6% (2006-2010 5-year est.).

Housing: Homeownership rate: 82.9% (2010); Median home value: $121,300 (2006-2010 5-year est.); Median contract rent: $460 per month (2006-2010 5-year est.); Median year structure built: 1945 (2006-2010 5-year est.).

Transportation: Commute to work: 94.8% car, 0.3% public transportation, 0.8% walk, 4.2% work from home (2006-2010 5-year est.); Travel time to work: 40.6% less than 15 minutes, 40.1% 15 to 30 minutes, 9.8% 30 to 45 minutes, 4.8% 45 to 60 minutes, 4.7% 60 minutes or more (2006-2010 5-year est.)

Additional Information Contacts

Greater Pittston Chamber of Commerce . . . . (570) 655-1424
http://www.pittstonchamber.org

HUNLOCK (township). Covers a land area of 20.638 square miles and a water area of 0.244 square miles. Located at 41.23° N. Lat; 76.10° W. Long. Elevation is 686 feet.

Population: 2,578 (1990); 2,568 (2000); 2,443 (2010); Density: 118.4 persons per square mile (2010); Race: 98.2% White, 0.3% Black, 0.4% Asian, 0.0% American Indian/Alaska Native, 0.0% Native Hawaiian/Other Pacific Islander, 1.1% Other, 0.6% Hispanic of any race (2010); Average household size: 2.64 (2010); Median age: 44.6 (2010); Males per 100 females: 103.9 (2010); Marriage status: 25.7% never married, 61.8% now married, 5.9% widowed, 6.7% divorced (2006-2010 5-year est.); Foreign born: 0.7% (2006-2010 5-year est.); Ancestry (includes multiple ancestries): 30.3% German, 22.1% Polish, 15.7% Irish, 12.6% English, 8.4% Dutch (2006-2010 5-year est.).

Economy: Employment by occupation: 4.5% management, 1.1% professional, 11.6% services, 19.5% sales, 8.5% farming, 19.1% construction, 9.2% production (2006-2010 5-year est.).

Income: Per capita income: $23,098 (2006-2010 5-year est.); Median household income: $51,818 (2006-2010 5-year est.); Average household income: $62,765 (2006-2010 5-year est.); Percent of households with income of $100,000 or more: 20.0% (2006-2010 5-year est.); Poverty rate: 10.3% (2006-2010 5-year est.).

Education: Percent of population age 25 and over with: High school diploma (including GED) or higher: 81.6% (2006-2010 5-year est.); Bachelor's degree or higher: 12.7% (2006-2010 5-year est.); Master's degree or higher: 3.7% (2006-2010 5-year est.).

Housing: Homeownership rate: 89.0% (2010); Median home value: $130,800 (2006-2010 5-year est.); Median contract rent: $442 per month (2006-2010 5-year est.); Median year structure built: 1965 (2006-2010 5-year est.).

Transportation: Commute to work: 97.2% car, 0.0% public transportation, 1.5% walk, 1.3% work from home (2006-2010 5-year est.); Travel time to work: 12.0% less than 15 minutes, 34.9% 15 to 30 minutes, 37.1% 30 to 45 minutes, 10.4% 45 to 60 minutes, 5.7% 60 minutes or more (2006-2010 5-year est.)

Additional Information Contacts

South Valley Chamber of Commerce . . . . (570) 735-6990
http://www.southvalleychamber.com

HUNLOCK CREEK (unincorporated postal area)
Zip Code: 18621

Covers a land area of 44.446 square miles and a water area of 1.520 square miles. Located at 41.24° N. Lat; 76.09° W. Long. Elevation is 528 feet. Population: 6,248 (2010); Density: 140.6 persons per square mile (2010); Race: 87.4% White, 9.2% Black, 0.3% Asian, 0.1% American Indian/Alaska Native, 0.0% Native Hawaiian/Other Pacific

Islander, 3.0% Other, 2.8% Hispanic of any race (2010); Average household size: 2.58 (2010); Median age: 41.8 (2010); Males per 100 females: 145.9 (2010); Homeownership rate: 87.8% (2010)

HUNTINGTON (township). Covers a land area of 28.477 square miles and a water area of 0.244 square miles. Located at 41.18° N. Lat; 76.25° W. Long.

Population: 1,905 (1990); 2,104 (2000); 2,244 (2010); Density: 78.8 persons per square mile (2010); Race: 98.9% White, 0.1% Black, 0.3% Asian, 0.0% American Indian/Alaska Native, 0.0% Native Hawaiian/Other Pacific Islander, 0.7% Other, 1.2% Hispanic of any race (2010); Average household size: 2.56 (2010); Median age: 44.2 (2010); Males per 100 females: 97.7 (2010); Marriage status: 24.8% never married, 53.8% now married, 11.6% widowed, 9.8% divorced (2006-2010 5-year est.); Foreign born: 0.7% (2006-2010 5-year est.); Ancestry (includes multiple ancestries): 29.4% German, 23.2% Polish, 14.6% Irish, 9.5% Italian, 8.9% English (2006-2010 5-year est.).
Economy: Employment by occupation: 5.8% management, 2.9% professional, 9.5% services, 18.7% sales, 2.1% farming, 13.9% construction, 10.5% production (2006-2010 5-year est.).
Income: Per capita income: $20,824 (2006-2010 5-year est.); Median household income: $50,581 (2006-2010 5-year est.); Average household income: $54,208 (2006-2010 5-year est.); Percent of households with income of $100,000 or more: 10.2% (2006-2010 5-year est.); Poverty rate: 5.5% (2006-2010 5-year est.).
Education: Percent of population age 25 and over with: High school diploma (including GED) or higher: 86.9% (2006-2010 5-year est.); Bachelor's degree or higher: 13.3% (2006-2010 5-year est.); Master's degree or higher: 3.5% (2006-2010 5-year est.).
Housing: Homeownership rate: 87.5% (2010); Median home value: $129,100 (2006-2010 5-year est.); Median contract rent: $462 per month (2006-2010 5-year est.); Median year structure built: 1968 (2006-2010 5-year est.).
Transportation: Commute to work: 94.5% car, 0.4% public transportation, 2.3% walk, 2.5% work from home (2006-2010 5-year est.); Travel time to work: 10.9% less than 15 minutes, 26.8% 15 to 30 minutes, 41.9% 30 to 45 minutes, 10.0% 45 to 60 minutes, 10.4% 60 minutes or more (2006-2010 5-year est.)
Additional Information Contacts
Huntingdon County Chamber of Commerce . . . . (814) 643-1110
http://www.huntingdonchamber.com

HUNTINGTON MILLS (unincorporated postal area)
Zip Code: 18622
Covers a land area of 3.672 square miles and a water area of 0.012 square miles. Located at 41.20° N. Lat; 76.27° W. Long. Population: 257 (2010); Density: 70.0 persons per square mile (2010); Race: 99.2% White, 0.0% Black, 0.0% Asian, 0.0% American Indian/Alaska Native, 0.0% Native Hawaiian/Other Pacific Islander, 0.8% Other, 0.8% Hispanic of any race (2010); Average household size: 2.47 (2010); Median age: 45.6 (2010); Males per 100 females: 114.2 (2010); Homeownership rate: 84.6% (2010)

INKERMAN (CDP). Covers a land area of 0.738 square miles and a water area of 0 square miles. Located at 41.30° N. Lat; 75.82° W. Long. Elevation is 791 feet.

Population: n/a (1990); n/a (2000); 1,819 (2010); Density: 2,463.4 persons per square mile (2010); Race: 98.0% White, 0.8% Black, 0.5% Asian, 0.0% American Indian/Alaska Native, 0.0% Native Hawaiian/Other Pacific Islander, 0.7% Other, 1.2% Hispanic of any race (2010); Average household size: 2.00 (2010); Median age: 56.0 (2010); Males per 100 females: 75.6 (2010); Marriage status: 20.6% never married, 44.3% now married, 29.4% widowed, 5.6% divorced (2006-2010 5-year est.); Foreign born: 0.7% (2006-2010 5-year est.); Ancestry (includes multiple ancestries): 21.5% Polish, 19.8% Italian, 18.3% Irish, 17.2% German, 11.9% English (2006-2010 5-year est.).
Economy: Employment by occupation: 9.8% management, 1.2% professional, 5.8% services, 19.6% sales, 1.8% farming, 8.0% construction, 6.7% production (2006-2010 5-year est.).
Income: Per capita income: $21,710 (2006-2010 5-year est.); Median household income: $43,750 (2006-2010 5-year est.); Average household income: $51,361 (2006-2010 5-year est.); Percent of households with income of $100,000 or more: 9.5% (2006-2010 5-year est.); Poverty rate: 7.0% (2006-2010 5-year est.).

Education: Percent of population age 25 and over with: High school diploma (including GED) or higher: 83.5% (2006-2010 5-year est.); Bachelor's degree or higher: 20.9% (2006-2010 5-year est.); Master's degree or higher: 8.6% (2006-2010 5-year est.).
Housing: Homeownership rate: 57.3% (2010); Median home value: $48,500 (2006-2010 5-year est.); Median contract rent: $498 per month (2006-2010 5-year est.); Median year structure built: 1994 (2006-2010 5-year est.).
Transportation: Commute to work: 93.5% car, 1.6% public transportation, 0.0% walk, 1.2% work from home (2006-2010 5-year est.); Travel time to work: 12.0% less than 15 minutes, 76.2% 15 to 30 minutes, 7.8% 30 to 45 minutes, 1.7% 45 to 60 minutes, 2.4% 60 minutes or more (2006-2010 5-year est.)

JACKSON (township). Covers a land area of 13.292 square miles and a water area of 0.085 square miles. Located at 41.28° N. Lat; 75.98° W. Long.

Population: 5,114 (1990); 4,453 (2000); 4,646 (2010); Density: 349.5 persons per square mile (2010); Race: 70.8% White, 25.0% Black, 1.2% Asian, 0.1% American Indian/Alaska Native, 0.0% Native Hawaiian/Other Pacific Islander, 2.9% Other, 5.0% Hispanic of any race (2010); Average household size: 2.60 (2010); Median age: 41.7 (2010); Males per 100 females: 257.9 (2010); Marriage status: 33.5% never married, 52.0% now married, 5.4% widowed, 9.0% divorced (2006-2010 5-year est.); Foreign born: 1.2% (2006-2010 5-year est.); Ancestry (includes multiple ancestries): 16.1% Polish, 14.8% Irish, 14.3% German, 8.4% Slovak, 7.8% English (2006-2010 5-year est.).
Economy: Single-family building permits issued: 0 (2011); Multi-family building permits issued: 0 (2011); Employment by occupation: 15.9% management, 1.1% professional, 9.5% services, 15.7% sales, 4.4% farming, 7.6% construction, 3.9% production (2006-2010 5-year est.).
Income: Per capita income: $28,020 (2006-2010 5-year est.); Median household income: $72,569 (2006-2010 5-year est.); Average household income: $105,610 (2006-2010 5-year est.); Percent of households with income of $100,000 or more: 34.9% (2006-2010 5-year est.); Poverty rate: 1.6% (2006-2010 5-year est.).
Education: Percent of population age 25 and over with: High school diploma (including GED) or higher: 81.3% (2006-2010 5-year est.); Bachelor's degree or higher: 20.8% (2006-2010 5-year est.); Master's degree or higher: 10.2% (2006-2010 5-year est.).
Housing: Homeownership rate: 91.6% (2010); Median home value: $210,400 (2006-2010 5-year est.); Median contract rent: $456 per month (2006-2010 5-year est.); Median year structure built: 1971 (2006-2010 5-year est.).
Safety: Violent crime rate: 12.9 per 10,000 population; Property crime rate: 21.5 per 10,000 population (2011).
Transportation: Commute to work: 97.2% car, 0.0% public transportation, 1.4% walk, 0.2% work from home (2006-2010 5-year est.); Travel time to work: 27.5% less than 15 minutes, 56.4% 15 to 30 minutes, 5.6% 30 to 45 minutes, 8.2% 45 to 60 minutes, 2.4% 60 minutes or more (2006-2010 5-year est.)
Additional Information Contacts
Greater Pittston Chamber of Commerce . . . . (570) 655-1424
http://www.pittstonchamber.org

JEDDO (borough). Covers a land area of 0.282 square miles and a water area of 0 square miles. Located at 40.99° N. Lat; 75.90° W. Long. Elevation is 1,640 feet.

History: Former anthracite coal-mining area.
Population: 124 (1990); 144 (2000); 98 (2010); Density: 347.2 persons per square mile (2010); Race: 100.0% White, 0.0% Black, 0.0% Asian, 0.0% American Indian/Alaska Native, 0.0% Native Hawaiian/Other Pacific Islander, 0.0% Other, 3.1% Hispanic of any race (2010); Average household size: 2.28 (2010); Median age: 39.0 (2010); Males per 100 females: 84.9 (2010); Marriage status: 11.6% never married, 60.5% now married, 14.0% widowed, 14.0% divorced (2006-2010 5-year est.); Foreign born: 2.8% (2006-2010 5-year est.); Ancestry (includes multiple ancestries): 40.7% Slovak, 19.4% Irish, 13.0% Pennsylvania German, 8.3% English, 7.4% Italian (2006-2010 5-year est.).
Economy: Employment by occupation: 0.0% management, 0.0% professional, 18.5% services, 11.1% sales, 11.1% farming, 5.6% construction, 7.4% production (2006-2010 5-year est.).
Income: Per capita income: $23,889 (2006-2010 5-year est.); Median household income: $60,208 (2006-2010 5-year est.); Average household income: $54,238 (2006-2010 5-year est.); Percent of households with

income of $100,000 or more: n/a (2006-2010 5-year est.); Poverty rate: 27.8% (2006-2010 5-year est.).

Education: Percent of population age 25 and over with: High school diploma (including GED) or higher: 89.9% (2006-2010 5-year est.); Bachelor's degree or higher: 12.7% (2006-2010 5-year est.); Master's degree or higher: 12.7% (2006-2010 5-year est.).

Housing: Homeownership rate: 83.7% (2010); Median home value: $75,600 (2006-2010 5-year est.); Median contract rent: $500 per month (2006-2010 5-year est.); Median year structure built: before 1940 (2006-2010 5-year est.).

Transportation: Commute to work: 100.0% car, 0.0% public transportation, 0.0% walk, 0.0% work from home (2006-2010 5-year est.); Travel time to work: 22.0% less than 15 minutes, 48.0% 15 to 30 minutes, 24.0% 30 to 45 minutes, 6.0% 45 to 60 minutes, 0.0% 60 minutes or more (2006-2010 5-year est.)

JENKINS (township). Covers a land area of 13.694 square miles and a water area of 0.288 square miles. Located at 41.28° N. Lat; 75.75° W. Long.

Population: 4,571 (1990); 4,584 (2000); 4,442 (2010); Density: 324.4 persons per square mile (2010); Race: 98.1% White, 0.7% Black, 0.3% Asian, 0.0% American Indian/Alaska Native, 0.0% Native Hawaiian/Other Pacific Islander, 0.9% Other, 1.3% Hispanic of any race (2010); Average household size: 2.27 (2010); Median age: 49.3 (2010); Males per 100 females: 86.6 (2010); Marriage status: 22.6% never married, 54.5% now married, 17.8% widowed, 5.1% divorced (2006-2010 5-year est.); Foreign born: 1.2% (2006-2010 5-year est.); Ancestry (includes multiple ancestries): 28.1% Italian, 24.0% Polish, 24.0% Irish, 17.0% German, 7.3% Lithuanian (2006-2010 5-year est.).

Economy: Single-family building permits issued: 13 (2011); Multi-family building permits issued: 0 (2011); Employment by occupation: 12.4% management, 2.1% professional, 5.2% services, 19.8% sales, 4.3% farming, 5.9% construction, 5.6% production (2006-2010 5-year est.).

Income: Per capita income: $24,170 (2006-2010 5-year est.); Median household income: $50,286 (2006-2010 5-year est.); Average household income: $62,323 (2006-2010 5-year est.); Percent of households with income of $100,000 or more: 11.6% (2006-2010 5-year est.); Poverty rate: 4.7% (2006-2010 5-year est.).

Education: Percent of population age 25 and over with: High school diploma (including GED) or higher: 86.2% (2006-2010 5-year est.); Bachelor's degree or higher: 21.0% (2006-2010 5-year est.); Master's degree or higher: 10.2% (2006-2010 5-year est.).

Housing: Homeownership rate: 73.2% (2010); Median home value: $108,100 (2006-2010 5-year est.); Median contract rent: $519 per month (2006-2010 5-year est.); Median year structure built: 1974 (2006-2010 5-year est.).

Safety: Violent crime rate: 20.2 per 10,000 population; Property crime rate: 347.8 per 10,000 population (2011).

Transportation: Commute to work: 97.0% car, 0.6% public transportation, 0.0% walk, 1.0% work from home (2006-2010 5-year est.); Travel time to work: 22.3% less than 15 minutes, 64.8% 15 to 30 minutes, 10.8% 30 to 45 minutes, 0.6% 45 to 60 minutes, 1.5% 60 minutes or more (2006-2010 5-year est.)

Additional Information Contacts
Greater Pittston Chamber of Commerce . . . . (570) 655-1424
  http://www.pittstonchamber.org

KINGSTON (borough). Aka Westmoore. Covers a land area of 2.128 square miles and a water area of 0.080 square miles. Located at 41.26° N. Lat; 75.89° W. Long. Elevation is 538 feet.

Population: 14,507 (1990); 13,855 (2000); 13,182 (2010); Density: 6,195.1 persons per square mile (2010); Race: 91.8% White, 3.2% Black, 2.4% Asian, 0.1% American Indian/Alaska Native, 0.0% Native Hawaiian/Other Pacific Islander, 2.5% Other, 3.2% Hispanic of any race (2010); Average household size: 2.13 (2010); Median age: 42.7 (2010); Males per 100 females: 89.8 (2010); Marriage status: 31.8% never married, 43.0% now married, 12.5% widowed, 12.7% divorced (2006-2010 5-year est.); Foreign born: 2.9% (2006-2010 5-year est.); Ancestry (includes multiple ancestries): 23.3% Irish, 19.7% Polish, 14.4% German, 10.5% Italian, 8.4% English (2006-2010 5-year est.).

Economy: Single-family building permits issued: 0 (2011); Multi-family building permits issued: 0 (2011); Employment by occupation: 9.4% management, 2.5% professional, 7.0% services, 19.6% sales, 5.3% farming, 4.6% construction, 3.9% production (2006-2010 5-year est.).

Income: Per capita income: $26,579 (2006-2010 5-year est.); Median household income: $40,208 (2006-2010 5-year est.); Average household income: $55,570 (2006-2010 5-year est.); Percent of households with income of $100,000 or more: 12.1% (2006-2010 5-year est.); Poverty rate: 8.7% (2006-2010 5-year est.).

Taxes: Total city taxes per capita: $415 (2009); City property taxes per capita: $66 (2009).

Education: Percent of population age 25 and over with: High school diploma (including GED) or higher: 89.8% (2006-2010 5-year est.); Bachelor's degree or higher: 29.8% (2006-2010 5-year est.); Master's degree or higher: 11.1% (2006-2010 5-year est.).

School District(s)
West Side CTC (09-12)
  2010-11 Enrollment: 579 . . . . (570) 288-8493
Wyoming Valley West SD (KG-12)
  2010-11 Enrollment: 4,855 . . . . (570) 288-6551

Housing: Homeownership rate: 51.5% (2010); Median home value: $120,700 (2006-2010 5-year est.); Median contract rent: $469 per month (2006-2010 5-year est.); Median year structure built: 1941 (2006-2010 5-year est.).

Hospitals: First Hospital Wyoming Valley (96 beds)

Safety: Violent crime rate: 22.7 per 10,000 population; Property crime rate: 286.6 per 10,000 population (2011).

Transportation: Commute to work: 87.6% car, 2.8% public transportation, 6.0% walk, 1.7% work from home (2006-2010 5-year est.); Travel time to work: 50.5% less than 15 minutes, 29.7% 15 to 30 minutes, 9.0% 30 to 45 minutes, 5.6% 45 to 60 minutes, 5.1% 60 minutes or more (2006-2010 5-year est.)

Additional Information Contacts
Borough of Kingston . . . . (570) 288-4576
  http://www.kingstonpa.org
Greater Northeast Chamber of Commerce . . . . (570) 457-1130
  http://www.gnecc.com

KINGSTON (township). Aka Westmoore. Covers a land area of 13.654 square miles and a water area of 0.260 square miles. Located at 41.32° N. Lat; 75.91° W. Long. Elevation is 538 feet.

History: Settled 1769, incorporated 1857.

Population: 6,763 (1990); 7,145 (2000); 6,999 (2010); Density: 512.6 persons per square mile (2010); Race: 97.5% White, 0.6% Black, 0.9% Asian, 0.0% American Indian/Alaska Native, 0.0% Native Hawaiian/Other Pacific Islander, 1.0% Other, 0.7% Hispanic of any race (2010); Average household size: 2.48 (2010); Median age: 45.1 (2010); Males per 100 females: 96.3 (2010); Marriage status: 20.4% never married, 67.1% now married, 5.4% widowed, 7.1% divorced (2006-2010 5-year est.); Foreign born: 1.2% (2006-2010 5-year est.); Ancestry (includes multiple ancestries): 22.8% Irish, 22.3% Polish, 21.1% German, 16.7% Italian, 9.9% English (2006-2010 5-year est.).

Economy: Single-family building permits issued: 5 (2011); Multi-family building permits issued: 0 (2011); Employment by occupation: 11.0% management, 3.5% professional, 9.8% services, 16.1% sales, 4.9% farming, 6.6% construction, 2.5% production (2006-2010 5-year est.).

Income: Per capita income: $38,223 (2006-2010 5-year est.); Median household income: $61,069 (2006-2010 5-year est.); Average household income: $93,734 (2006-2010 5-year est.); Percent of households with income of $100,000 or more: 27.0% (2006-2010 5-year est.); Poverty rate: 3.5% (2006-2010 5-year est.).

Education: Percent of population age 25 and over with: High school diploma (including GED) or higher: 96.2% (2006-2010 5-year est.); Bachelor's degree or higher: 38.6% (2006-2010 5-year est.); Master's degree or higher: 15.8% (2006-2010 5-year est.).

Housing: Homeownership rate: 86.1% (2010); Median home value: $159,500 (2006-2010 5-year est.); Median contract rent: $446 per month (2006-2010 5-year est.); Median year structure built: 1970 (2006-2010 5-year est.).

Hospitals: First Hospital Wyoming Valley (96 beds)

Safety: Violent crime rate: 18.5 per 10,000 population; Property crime rate: 88.3 per 10,000 population (2011).

Transportation: Commute to work: 96.4% car, 0.0% public transportation, 1.4% walk, 1.8% work from home (2006-2010 5-year est.); Travel time to work: 23.7% less than 15 minutes, 53.9% 15 to 30 minutes, 17.8% 30 to 45 minutes, 1.3% 45 to 60 minutes, 3.4% 60 minutes or more (2006-2010 5-year est.)

Additional Information Contacts

Greater Northeast Chamber of Commerce . . . . (570) 457-1130
　http://www.gnecc.com
Kingston Township . . . . (570) 696-3809
　http://www.kingstontownship.com

LAFLIN (borough). Covers a land area of 1.350 square miles and a water area of 0 square miles. Located at 41.29° N. Lat; 75.79° W. Long. Elevation is 728 feet.

Population: 1,498 (1990); 1,502 (2000); 1,487 (2010); Density: 1,101.7 persons per square mile (2010); Race: 94.8% White, 0.0% Black, 5.0% Asian, 0.0% American Indian/Alaska Native, 0.0% Native Hawaiian/Other Pacific Islander, 0.2% Other, 0.5% Hispanic of any race (2010); Average household size: 2.36 (2010); Median age: 47.6 (2010); Males per 100 females: 89.2 (2010); Marriage status: 18.1% never married, 68.4% now married, 6.4% widowed, 7.2% divorced (2006-2010 5-year est.); Foreign born: 5.6% (2006-2010 5-year est.); Ancestry (includes multiple ancestries): 28.7% Italian, 27.6% Polish, 19.7% Irish, 9.8% German, 7.7% Russian (2006-2010 5-year est.).

Economy: Single-family building permits issued: 0 (2011); Multi-family building permits issued: 0 (2011); Employment by occupation: 14.5% management, 5.0% professional, 9.1% services, 13.8% sales, 2.2% farming, 5.5% construction, 1.3% production (2006-2010 5-year est.).

Income: Per capita income: $34,460 (2006-2010 5-year est.); Median household income: $67,379 (2006-2010 5-year est.); Average household income: $83,900 (2006-2010 5-year est.); Percent of households with income of $100,000 or more: 30.8% (2006-2010 5-year est.); Poverty rate: 2.6% (2006-2010 5-year est.).

Education: Percent of population age 25 and over with: High school diploma (including GED) or higher: 96.4% (2006-2010 5-year est.); Bachelor's degree or higher: 47.8% (2006-2010 5-year est.); Master's degree or higher: 23.8% (2006-2010 5-year est.).

Housing: Homeownership rate: 92.7% (2010); Median home value: $175,800 (2006-2010 5-year est.); Median contract rent: $543 per month (2006-2010 5-year est.); Median year structure built: 1974 (2006-2010 5-year est.).

Safety: Violent crime rate: 33.5 per 10,000 population; Property crime rate: 241.3 per 10,000 population (2011).

Transportation: Commute to work: 92.5% car, 0.3% public transportation, 2.9% walk, 4.0% work from home (2006-2010 5-year est.); Travel time to work: 34.2% less than 15 minutes, 51.6% 15 to 30 minutes, 10.0% 30 to 45 minutes, 1.6% 45 to 60 minutes, 2.6% 60 minutes or more (2006-2010 5-year est.)

Additional Information Contacts

Borough of Laflin . . . . (570) 654-3323
　http://www.laflinboro.com
Greater Northeast Chamber of Commerce . . . . (570) 457-1130
　http://www.gnecc.com

LAKE (township). Covers a land area of 26.670 square miles and a water area of 0.019 square miles. Located at 41.34° N. Lat; 76.09° W. Long. Elevation is 1,263 feet.

Population: 1,944 (1990); 2,110 (2000); 2,049 (2010); Density: 76.8 persons per square mile (2010); Race: 98.3% White, 0.0% Black, 0.2% Asian, 0.0% American Indian/Alaska Native, 0.0% Native Hawaiian/Other Pacific Islander, 1.5% Other, 0.8% Hispanic of any race (2010); Average household size: 2.53 (2010); Median age: 43.8 (2010); Males per 100 females: 100.5 (2010); Marriage status: 22.2% never married, 63.6% now married, 6.2% widowed, 8.0% divorced (2006-2010 5-year est.); Foreign born: 1.2% (2006-2010 5-year est.); Ancestry (includes multiple ancestries): 27.6% German, 20.0% Irish, 13.3% English, 12.6% Polish, 11.5% Italian (2006-2010 5-year est.).

Economy: Employment by occupation: 8.2% management, 1.9% professional, 13.2% services, 16.3% sales, 3.6% farming, 8.6% construction, 6.2% production (2006-2010 5-year est.).

Income: Per capita income: $24,820 (2006-2010 5-year est.); Median household income: $58,646 (2006-2010 5-year est.); Average household income: $64,510 (2006-2010 5-year est.); Percent of households with income of $100,000 or more: 18.5% (2006-2010 5-year est.); Poverty rate: 10.5% (2006-2010 5-year est.).

Education: Percent of population age 25 and over with: High school diploma (including GED) or higher: 88.1% (2006-2010 5-year est.); Bachelor's degree or higher: 12.6% (2006-2010 5-year est.); Master's degree or higher: 3.6% (2006-2010 5-year est.).

Housing: Homeownership rate: 85.8% (2010); Median home value: $151,900 (2006-2010 5-year est.); Median contract rent: $434 per month (2006-2010 5-year est.); Median year structure built: 1979 (2006-2010 5-year est.).

Transportation: Commute to work: 94.6% car, 0.0% public transportation, 0.0% walk, 5.4% work from home (2006-2010 5-year est.); Travel time to work: 19.1% less than 15 minutes, 35.0% 15 to 30 minutes, 26.9% 30 to 45 minutes, 14.3% 45 to 60 minutes, 4.7% 60 minutes or more (2006-2010 5-year est.)

Additional Information Contacts

Greater Pittston Chamber of Commerce . . . . (570) 655-1424
　http://www.pittstonchamber.org

LARKSVILLE (borough). Covers a land area of 4.701 square miles and a water area of 0.158 square miles. Located at 41.26° N. Lat; 75.93° W. Long. Elevation is 548 feet.

History: Incorporated 1909.

Population: 4,696 (1990); 4,694 (2000); 4,480 (2010); Density: 952.9 persons per square mile (2010); Race: 96.9% White, 0.8% Black, 0.6% Asian, 0.1% American Indian/Alaska Native, 0.0% Native Hawaiian/Other Pacific Islander, 1.6% Other, 1.7% Hispanic of any race (2010); Average household size: 2.47 (2010); Median age: 44.3 (2010); Males per 100 females: 95.5 (2010); Marriage status: 33.1% never married, 54.3% now married, 7.5% widowed, 5.1% divorced (2006-2010 5-year est.); Foreign born: 1.1% (2006-2010 5-year est.); Ancestry (includes multiple ancestries): 35.9% Polish, 23.0% Irish, 13.3% German, 10.7% Slovak, 8.8% Italian (2006-2010 5-year est.).

Economy: Single-family building permits issued: 1 (2011); Multi-family building permits issued: 0 (2011); Employment by occupation: 4.2% management, 1.3% professional, 10.8% services, 22.9% sales, 4.8% farming, 11.9% construction, 9.1% production (2006-2010 5-year est.).

Income: Per capita income: $22,517 (2006-2010 5-year est.); Median household income: $36,354 (2006-2010 5-year est.); Average household income: $53,749 (2006-2010 5-year est.); Percent of households with income of $100,000 or more: 18.3% (2006-2010 5-year est.); Poverty rate: 13.7% (2006-2010 5-year est.).

Education: Percent of population age 25 and over with: High school diploma (including GED) or higher: 86.1% (2006-2010 5-year est.); Bachelor's degree or higher: 14.9% (2006-2010 5-year est.); Master's degree or higher: 4.4% (2006-2010 5-year est.).

School District(s)

Wyoming Valley West SD (KG-12)
　2010-11 Enrollment: 4,855 . . . . (570) 288-6551

Housing: Homeownership rate: 76.1% (2010); Median home value: $98,400 (2006-2010 5-year est.); Median contract rent: $487 per month (2006-2010 5-year est.); Median year structure built: 1950 (2006-2010 5-year est.).

Safety: Violent crime rate: 11.1 per 10,000 population; Property crime rate: 198.0 per 10,000 population (2011).

Transportation: Commute to work: 96.3% car, 1.2% public transportation, 0.6% walk, 0.5% work from home (2006-2010 5-year est.); Travel time to work: 30.7% less than 15 minutes, 51.0% 15 to 30 minutes, 11.8% 30 to 45 minutes, 1.8% 45 to 60 minutes, 4.7% 60 minutes or more (2006-2010 5-year est.)

Additional Information Contacts

South Valley Chamber of Commerce . . . . (570) 735-6990
　http://www.southvalleychamber.com

LATTIMER (CDP). Covers a land area of 0.229 square miles and a water area of 0 square miles. Located at 40.99° N. Lat; 75.96° W. Long. Elevation is 1,637 feet.

Population: n/a (1990); n/a (2000); 554 (2010); Density: 2,416.3 persons per square mile (2010); Race: 96.2% White, 2.0% Black, 0.2% Asian, 0.0% American Indian/Alaska Native, 0.0% Native Hawaiian/Other Pacific Islander, 1.6% Other, 1.6% Hispanic of any race (2010); Average household size: 2.45 (2010); Median age: 45.7 (2010); Males per 100 females: 91.7 (2010); Marriage status: 10.8% never married, 70.0% now married, 11.7% widowed, 7.5% divorced (2006-2010 5-year est.); Foreign born: 11.3% (2006-2010 5-year est.); Ancestry (includes multiple ancestries): 40.8% Italian, 25.8% Slovak, 11.3% German, 10.0% Irish, 7.8% Polish (2006-2010 5-year est.).

Economy: Employment by occupation: 6.3% management, 0.0% professional, 4.5% services, 5.7% sales, 10.8% farming, 22.7% construction, 12.5% production (2006-2010 5-year est.).

Income: Per capita income: $26,368 (2006-2010 5-year est.); Median household income: $42,031 (2006-2010 5-year est.); Average household income: $49,120 (2006-2010 5-year est.); Percent of households with income of $100,000 or more: 4.8% (2006-2010 5-year est.); Poverty rate: 3.0% (2006-2010 5-year est.).

Education: Percent of population age 25 and over with: High school diploma (including GED) or higher: 91.5% (2006-2010 5-year est.); Bachelor's degree or higher: 17.3% (2006-2010 5-year est.); Master's degree or higher: 7.9% (2006-2010 5-year est.).

Housing: Homeownership rate: 87.4% (2010); Median home value: $105,000 (2006-2010 5-year est.); Median contract rent: n/a per month (2006-2010 5-year est.); Median year structure built: 1983 (2006-2010 5-year est.).

Transportation: Commute to work: 100.0% car, 0.0% public transportation, 0.0% walk, 0.0% work from home (2006-2010 5-year est.); Travel time to work: 47.2% less than 15 minutes, 4.5% 15 to 30 minutes, 17.0% 30 to 45 minutes, 4.0% 45 to 60 minutes, 27.3% 60 minutes or more (2006-2010 5-year est.)

LATTIMER MINES (unincorporated postal area)
Zip Code: 18234

Covers a land area of 0.258 square miles and a water area of 0 square miles. Located at 40.99° N. Lat; 75.96° W. Long. Population: 401 (2010); Density: 1,549.0 persons per square mile (2010); Race: 96.0% White, 2.2% Black, 0.2% Asian, 0.0% American Indian/Alaska Native, 0.0% Native Hawaiian/Other Pacific Islander, 1.6% Other, 2.0% Hispanic of any race (2010); Average household size: 2.35 (2010); Median age: 45.1 (2010); Males per 100 females: 77.4 (2010); Homeownership rate: 84.4% (2010)

LAUREL RUN (borough). Covers a land area of 5.186 square miles and a water area of 0 square miles. Located at 41.22° N. Lat; 75.84° W. Long. Elevation is 892 feet.

Population: 708 (1990); 723 (2000); 500 (2010); Density: 96.4 persons per square mile (2010); Race: 99.0% White, 0.2% Black, 0.4% Asian, 0.0% American Indian/Alaska Native, 0.0% Native Hawaiian/Other Pacific Islander, 0.4% Other, 0.8% Hispanic of any race (2010); Average household size: 2.13 (2010); Median age: 48.1 (2010); Males per 100 females: 105.8 (2010); Marriage status: 26.6% never married, 50.2% now married, 9.7% widowed, 13.4% divorced (2006-2010 5-year est.); Foreign born: 0.0% (2006-2010 5-year est.); Ancestry (includes multiple ancestries): 37.3% Polish, 22.0% German, 19.6% Irish, 11.4% Russian, 10.0% Italian (2006-2010 5-year est.).

Economy: Single-family building permits issued: 2 (2011); Multi-family building permits issued: 0 (2011); Employment by occupation: 2.8% management, 2.0% professional, 6.8% services, 19.7% sales, 0.8% farming, 15.3% construction, 10.8% production (2006-2010 5-year est.).

Income: Per capita income: $22,592 (2006-2010 5-year est.); Median household income: $41,346 (2006-2010 5-year est.); Average household income: $48,055 (2006-2010 5-year est.); Percent of households with income of $100,000 or more: 7.1% (2006-2010 5-year est.); Poverty rate: 11.7% (2006-2010 5-year est.).

Education: Percent of population age 25 and over with: High school diploma (including GED) or higher: 85.0% (2006-2010 5-year est.); Bachelor's degree or higher: 17.9% (2006-2010 5-year est.); Master's degree or higher: 6.3% (2006-2010 5-year est.).

Housing: Homeownership rate: 92.4% (2010); Median home value: $56,100 (2006-2010 5-year est.); Median contract rent: $350 per month (2006-2010 5-year est.); Median year structure built: 1977 (2006-2010 5-year est.).

Transportation: Commute to work: 92.2% car, 0.0% public transportation, 3.3% walk, 4.5% work from home (2006-2010 5-year est.); Travel time to work: 26.9% less than 15 minutes, 53.4% 15 to 30 minutes, 11.1% 30 to 45 minutes, 6.0% 45 to 60 minutes, 2.6% 60 minutes or more (2006-2010 5-year est.)

LEHMAN (township). Covers a land area of 21.939 square miles and a water area of 1.269 square miles. Located at 41.30° N. Lat; 76.04° W. Long. Elevation is 1,312 feet.

Population: 3,076 (1990); 3,206 (2000); 3,508 (2010); Density: 159.9 persons per square mile (2010); Race: 97.9% White, 0.5% Black, 0.2% Asian, 0.3% American Indian/Alaska Native, 0.0% Native Hawaiian/Other Pacific Islander, 1.1% Other, 0.5% Hispanic of any race (2010); Average household size: 2.55 (2010); Median age: 44.0 (2010); Males per 100 females: 99.5 (2010); Marriage status: 22.8% never married, 64.6% now

married, 7.6% widowed, 5.0% divorced (2006-2010 5-year est.); Foreign born: 5.4% (2006-2010 5-year est.); Ancestry (includes multiple ancestries): 26.1% Polish, 22.0% German, 19.9% Irish, 12.3% English, 8.4% Italian (2006-2010 5-year est.).

Economy: Single-family building permits issued: 5 (2011); Multi-family building permits issued: 0 (2011); Employment by occupation: 10.8% management, 3.4% professional, 11.1% services, 10.4% sales, 3.3% farming, 10.2% construction, 5.6% production (2006-2010 5-year est.).

Income: Per capita income: $29,721 (2006-2010 5-year est.); Median household income: $55,488 (2006-2010 5-year est.); Average household income: $77,352 (2006-2010 5-year est.); Percent of households with income of $100,000 or more: 22.8% (2006-2010 5-year est.); Poverty rate: 14.7% (2006-2010 5-year est.).

Education: Percent of population age 25 and over with: High school diploma (including GED) or higher: 91.5% (2006-2010 5-year est.); Bachelor's degree or higher: 22.7% (2006-2010 5-year est.); Master's degree or higher: 10.2% (2006-2010 5-year est.).

School District(s)

Lake-Lehman SD (KG-12)
    2010-11 Enrollment: 2,080 . . . . (570) 675-2165

Four-year College(s)

Pennsylvania State University-Penn State Wilkes-Barre (Public)
    Fall 2010 Enrollment: 712 . . . . (570) 675-2171
    2011-12 Tuition: In-state $12,994; Out-of-state $19,434

Housing: Homeownership rate: 86.5% (2010); Median home value: $147,300 (2006-2010 5-year est.); Median contract rent: $513 per month (2006-2010 5-year est.); Median year structure built: 1961 (2006-2010 5-year est.).

Safety: Violent crime rate: 0.0 per 10,000 population; Property crime rate: 0.0 per 10,000 population (2011).

Transportation: Commute to work: 95.7% car, 0.0% public transportation, 1.1% walk, 3.0% work from home (2006-2010 5-year est.); Travel time to work: 25.2% less than 15 minutes, 45.6% 15 to 30 minutes, 18.1% 30 to 45 minutes, 5.8% 45 to 60 minutes, 5.3% 60 minutes or more (2006-2010 5-year est.)

Additional Information Contacts

Greater Northeast Chamber of Commerce . . . . (570) 457-1130
    http://www.gnecc.com

LUZERNE (borough). Covers a land area of 0.689 square miles and a water area of 0 square miles. Located at 41.29° N. Lat; 75.90° W. Long. Elevation is 610 feet.

History: Incorporated 1882.

Population: 3,206 (1990); 2,952 (2000); 2,845 (2010); Density: 4,126.2 persons per square mile (2010); Race: 97.6% White, 0.6% Black, 0.2% Asian, 0.2% American Indian/Alaska Native, 0.0% Native Hawaiian/Other Pacific Islander, 1.4% Other, 2.1% Hispanic of any race (2010); Average household size: 2.07 (2010); Median age: 44.2 (2010); Males per 100 females: 93.4 (2010); Marriage status: 38.8% never married, 39.7% now married, 11.0% widowed, 10.4% divorced (2006-2010 5-year est.); Foreign born: 0.8% (2006-2010 5-year est.); Ancestry (includes multiple ancestries): 25.2% Polish, 23.5% Italian, 18.3% Irish, 9.9% Lithuanian, 8.6% German (2006-2010 5-year est.).

Economy: Employment by occupation: 1.1% management, 0.6% professional, 9.9% services, 16.1% sales, 2.0% farming, 13.6% construction, 12.1% production (2006-2010 5-year est.).

Income: Per capita income: $17,750 (2006-2010 5-year est.); Median household income: $31,339 (2006-2010 5-year est.); Average household income: $38,330 (2006-2010 5-year est.); Percent of households with income of $100,000 or more: 4.2% (2006-2010 5-year est.); Poverty rate: 24.1% (2006-2010 5-year est.).

Education: Percent of population age 25 and over with: High school diploma (including GED) or higher: 85.2% (2006-2010 5-year est.); Bachelor's degree or higher: 12.4% (2006-2010 5-year est.); Master's degree or higher: 3.8% (2006-2010 5-year est.).

Housing: Homeownership rate: 56.9% (2010); Median home value: $82,600 (2006-2010 5-year est.); Median contract rent: $451 per month (2006-2010 5-year est.); Median year structure built: before 1940 (2006-2010 5-year est.).

Safety: Violent crime rate: 35.0 per 10,000 population; Property crime rate: 424.0 per 10,000 population (2011).

Transportation: Commute to work: 91.8% car, 1.1% public transportation, 3.4% walk, 1.2% work from home (2006-2010 5-year est.); Travel time to work: 53.1% less than 15 minutes, 31.9% 15 to 30 minutes, 10.0% 30 to

45 minutes, 0.9% 45 to 60 minutes, 4.0% 60 minutes or more (2006-2010 5-year est.)
Additional Information Contacts
Greater Hazelton Chamber of Commerce . . . . (570) 455-1509
  http://www.hazletonchamber.org

MILNESVILLE (unincorporated postal area)
Zip Code: 18239
  Covers a land area of 0.269 square miles and a water area of 0 square miles. Located at 40.98° N. Lat; 75.98° W. Long. Elevation is 1,608 feet.
Population: 232 (2010); Density: 861.4 persons per square mile (2010); Race: 97.4% White, 0.0% Black, 0.4% Asian, 0.0% American Indian/Alaska Native, 0.0% Native Hawaiian/Other Pacific Islander, 2.2% Other, 4.7% Hispanic of any race (2010); Average household size: 2.15 (2010); Median age: 49.4 (2010); Males per 100 females: 112.8 (2010); Homeownership rate: 77.8% (2010)

MOCANAQUA (CDP). Covers a land area of 0.496 square miles and a water area of 0.052 square miles. Located at 41.14° N. Lat; 76.13° W. Long. Elevation is 554 feet.
Population: n/a (1990); n/a (2000); 646 (2010); Density: 1,303.5 persons per square mile (2010); Race: 93.7% White, 0.8% Black, 0.9% Asian, 0.6% American Indian/Alaska Native, 0.0% Native Hawaiian/Other Pacific Islander, 4.0% Other, 2.0% Hispanic of any race (2010); Average household size: 2.19 (2010); Median age: 42.5 (2010); Males per 100 females: 90.6 (2010); Marriage status: 25.8% never married, 50.2% now married, 13.1% widowed, 10.8% divorced (2006-2010 5-year est.); Foreign born: 3.2% (2006-2010 5-year est.); Ancestry (includes multiple ancestries): 28.5% Polish, 22.6% German, 21.9% Italian, 10.7% Irish, 6.8% American (2006-2010 5-year est.).
Economy: Employment by occupation: 8.9% management, 1.2% professional, 15.5% services, 20.9% sales, 6.2% farming, 4.3% construction, 1.2% production (2006-2010 5-year est.).
Income: Per capita income: $23,506 (2006-2010 5-year est.); Median household income: $40,469 (2006-2010 5-year est.); Average household income: $47,081 (2006-2010 5-year est.); Percent of households with income of $100,000 or more: 9.5% (2006-2010 5-year est.); Poverty rate: 8.2% (2006-2010 5-year est.).
Education: Percent of population age 25 and over with: High school diploma (including GED) or higher: 85.4% (2006-2010 5-year est.); Bachelor's degree or higher: 15.8% (2006-2010 5-year est.); Master's degree or higher: 5.9% (2006-2010 5-year est.).
Housing: Homeownership rate: 63.7% (2010); Median home value: $68,000 (2006-2010 5-year est.); Median contract rent: $412 per month (2006-2010 5-year est.); Median year structure built: before 1940 (2006-2010 5-year est.).
Transportation: Commute to work: 90.7% car, 4.3% public transportation, 1.2% walk, 2.7% work from home (2006-2010 5-year est.); Travel time to work: 12.0% less than 15 minutes, 25.1% 15 to 30 minutes, 40.6% 30 to 45 minutes, 10.0% 45 to 60 minutes, 12.4% 60 minutes or more (2006-2010 5-year est.)

MOUNTAIN TOP (CDP). Covers a land area of 15.043 square miles and a water area of 0 square miles. Located at 41.14° N. Lat; 75.90° W. Long. Elevation is 1,565 feet.
History: Founded 1788.
Population: 12,540 (1990); 15,269 (2000); 10,982 (2010); Density: 730.0 persons per square mile (2010); Race: 93.7% White, 0.8% Black, 3.6% Asian, 0.1% American Indian/Alaska Native, 0.0% Native Hawaiian/Other Pacific Islander, 1.8% Other, 2.2% Hispanic of any race (2010); Average household size: 2.62 (2010); Median age: 43.5 (2010); Males per 100 females: 92.8 (2010); Marriage status: 20.9% never married, 66.9% now married, 6.8% widowed, 5.4% divorced (2006-2010 5-year est.); Foreign born: 5.0% (2006-2010 5-year est.); Ancestry (includes multiple ancestries): 23.4% German, 22.0% Polish, 21.7% Irish, 14.3% Italian, 9.4% English (2006-2010 5-year est.).
Economy: Employment by occupation: 15.8% management, 5.0% professional, 8.8% services, 14.1% sales, 3.8% farming, 4.3% construction, 3.8% production (2006-2010 5-year est.).
Income: Per capita income: $33,352 (2006-2010 5-year est.); Median household income: $78,183 (2006-2010 5-year est.); Average household income: $89,115 (2006-2010 5-year est.); Percent of households with income of $100,000 or more: 30.6% (2006-2010 5-year est.); Poverty rate: 4.5% (2006-2010 5-year est.).

Education: Percent of population age 25 and over with: High school diploma (including GED) or higher: 94.4% (2006-2010 5-year est.); Bachelor's degree or higher: 37.7% (2006-2010 5-year est.); Master's degree or higher: 18.2% (2006-2010 5-year est.).
School District(s)
Crestwood SD (KG-12)
  2010-11 Enrollment: 3,029 . . . . (570) 474-6888
Crestwood SD (KG-12)
  2010-11 Enrollment: 3,029 . . . . (570) 474-6888
Housing: Homeownership rate: 87.6% (2010); Median home value: $189,100 (2006-2010 5-year est.); Median contract rent: $384 per month (2006-2010 5-year est.); Median year structure built: 1980 (2006-2010 5-year est.).
Newspapers: Mountaintop Eagle (Community news; Circulation 2,800)
Transportation: Commute to work: 94.7% car, 0.0% public transportation, 2.2% walk, 2.8% work from home (2006-2010 5-year est.); Travel time to work: 23.5% less than 15 minutes, 43.1% 15 to 30 minutes, 17.2% 30 to 45 minutes, 7.5% 45 to 60 minutes, 8.7% 60 minutes or more (2006-2010 5-year est.)
Additional Information Contacts
Greater Hazelton Chamber of Commerce . . . . (570) 455-1509
  http://www.hazletonchamber.org

NANTICOKE (city). Covers a land area of 3.456 square miles and a water area of 0.088 square miles. Located at 41.20° N. Lat; 76.00° W. Long. Elevation is 568 feet.
History: Formerly the heart of a major anthracite-coal-mining region, but production has declined. Founded 1793, incorporated as a city 1926.
Population: 12,267 (1990); 10,955 (2000); 10,465 (2010); Density: 3,028.0 persons per square mile (2010); Race: 95.9% White, 1.6% Black, 0.4% Asian, 0.1% American Indian/Alaska Native, 0.0% Native Hawaiian/Other Pacific Islander, 2.0% Other, 2.6% Hispanic of any race (2010); Average household size: 2.20 (2010); Median age: 42.6 (2010); Males per 100 females: 91.5 (2010); Marriage status: 34.2% never married, 43.7% now married, 11.5% widowed, 10.6% divorced (2006-2010 5-year est.); Foreign born: 1.4% (2006-2010 5-year est.); Ancestry (includes multiple ancestries): 41.8% Polish, 19.0% German, 12.3% Irish, 7.8% Italian, 6.2% English (2006-2010 5-year est.).
Economy: Single-family building permits issued: 0 (2011); Multi-family building permits issued: 0 (2011); Employment by occupation: 5.4% management, 1.8% professional, 14.1% services, 19.6% sales, 4.7% farming, 10.2% construction, 9.1% production (2006-2010 5-year est.).
Income: Per capita income: $20,269 (2006-2010 5-year est.); Median household income: $36,656 (2006-2010 5-year est.); Average household income: $44,357 (2006-2010 5-year est.); Percent of households with income of $100,000 or more: 6.2% (2006-2010 5-year est.); Poverty rate: 16.4% (2006-2010 5-year est.).
Education: Percent of population age 25 and over with: High school diploma (including GED) or higher: 82.6% (2006-2010 5-year est.); Bachelor's degree or higher: 13.2% (2006-2010 5-year est.); Master's degree or higher: 3.5% (2006-2010 5-year est.).
School District(s)
Greater Nanticoke Area SD (KG-12)
  2010-11 Enrollment: 2,244 . . . . (570) 735-1270
Two-year College(s)
Luzerne County Community College (Public)
  Fall 2010 Enrollment: 5,249 . . . . (570) 740-0200
  2011-12 Tuition: In-state $6,000; Out-of-state $8,820
Housing: Homeownership rate: 57.9% (2010); Median home value: $80,800 (2006-2010 5-year est.); Median contract rent: $390 per month (2006-2010 5-year est.); Median year structure built: before 1940 (2006-2010 5-year est.).
Hospitals: Mercy SpecialCare Hospital (68 beds)
Safety: Violent crime rate: 31.4 per 10,000 population; Property crime rate: 346.7 per 10,000 population (2011).
Transportation: Commute to work: 91.3% car, 2.3% public transportation, 3.4% walk, 2.3% work from home (2006-2010 5-year est.); Travel time to work: 28.2% less than 15 minutes, 45.9% 15 to 30 minutes, 16.0% 30 to 45 minutes, 3.4% 45 to 60 minutes, 6.4% 60 minutes or more (2006-2010 5-year est.)
Additional Information Contacts
City of Nanticoke . . . . (570) 735-2800
  http://www.nanticokecity.com
South Valley Chamber of Commerce . . . . (570) 375-6990
  http://www.southvalleychamber.com

NESCOPECK (borough). Covers a land area of 1.026 square miles and a water area of 0 square miles. Located at 41.05° N. Lat; 76.21° W. Long. Elevation is 512 feet.

Population: 1,651 (1990); 1,528 (2000); 1,583 (2010); Density: 1,543.5 persons per square mile (2010); Race: 98.6% White, 0.3% Black, 0.3% Asian, 0.1% American Indian/Alaska Native, 0.0% Native Hawaiian/Other Pacific Islander, 0.7% Other, 2.2% Hispanic of any race (2010); Average household size: 2.30 (2010); Median age: 40.4 (2010); Males per 100 females: 90.5 (2010); Marriage status: 26.2% never married, 52.3% now married, 12.1% widowed, 9.4% divorced (2006-2010 5-year est.); Foreign born: 1.4% (2006-2010 5-year est.); Ancestry (includes multiple ancestries): 40.3% German, 11.4% Irish, 11.3% Pennsylvania German, 11.2% Italian, 8.7% Polish (2006-2010 5-year est.).

Economy: Single-family building permits issued: 0 (2011); Multi-family building permits issued: 0 (2011); Employment by occupation: 5.1% management, 2.0% professional, 15.9% services, 16.2% sales, 2.1% farming, 11.4% construction, 13.8% production (2006-2010 5-year est.).

Income: Per capita income: $19,178 (2006-2010 5-year est.); Median household income: $37,794 (2006-2010 5-year est.); Average household income: $44,734 (2006-2010 5-year est.); Percent of households with income of $100,000 or more: 4.6% (2006-2010 5-year est.); Poverty rate: 9.7% (2006-2010 5-year est.).

Education: Percent of population age 25 and over with: High school diploma (including GED) or higher: 85.9% (2006-2010 5-year est.); Bachelor's degree or higher: 11.6% (2006-2010 5-year est.); Master's degree or higher: 2.8% (2006-2010 5-year est.).

School District(s)

Berwick Area SD (KG-12)
    2010-11 Enrollment: 3,014 . . . . (570) 759-6400

Housing: Homeownership rate: 60.5% (2010); Median home value: $91,500 (2006-2010 5-year est.); Median contract rent: $454 per month (2006-2010 5-year est.); Median year structure built: before 1940 (2006-2010 5-year est.).

Safety: Violent crime rate: 0.0 per 10,000 population; Property crime rate: 56.7 per 10,000 population (2011).

Transportation: Commute to work: 94.0% car, 0.0% public transportation, 2.0% walk, 4.0% work from home (2006-2010 5-year est.); Travel time to work: 45.0% less than 15 minutes, 20.3% 15 to 30 minutes, 19.8% 30 to 45 minutes, 7.0% 45 to 60 minutes, 7.9% 60 minutes or more (2006-2010 5-year est.)

Additional Information Contacts

Columbia Montour Chamber of Commerce. . . . . (570) 784-2522
    http://www.bloomsburg.org

NESCOPECK (township). Covers a land area of 17.984 square miles and a water area of 0.675 square miles. Located at 41.04° N. Lat; 76.16° W. Long. Elevation is 512 feet.

History: Settled 1786, incorporated 1896.

Population: 1,072 (1990); 1,096 (2000); 1,155 (2010); Density: 64.2 persons per square mile (2010); Race: 98.0% White, 0.2% Black, 0.3% Asian, 0.3% American Indian/Alaska Native, 0.0% Native Hawaiian/Other Pacific Islander, 1.2% Other, 0.8% Hispanic of any race (2010); Average household size: 2.60 (2010); Median age: 44.1 (2010); Males per 100 females: 101.9 (2010); Marriage status: 24.1% never married, 62.5% now married, 5.2% widowed, 8.2% divorced (2006-2010 5-year est.); Foreign born: 0.4% (2006-2010 5-year est.); Ancestry (includes multiple ancestries): 39.2% German, 15.3% Irish, 10.9% English, 9.6% Italian, 9.5% Dutch (2006-2010 5-year est.).

Economy: Single-family building permits issued: 0 (2011); Multi-family building permits issued: 0 (2011); Employment by occupation: 9.0% management, 1.3% professional, 6.1% services, 15.2% sales, 5.2% farming, 15.2% construction, 14.2% production (2006-2010 5-year est.).

Income: Per capita income: $20,098 (2006-2010 5-year est.); Median household income: $48,750 (2006-2010 5-year est.); Average household income: $56,637 (2006-2010 5-year est.); Percent of households with income of $100,000 or more: 11.2% (2006-2010 5-year est.); Poverty rate: 8.3% (2006-2010 5-year est.).

Education: Percent of population age 25 and over with: High school diploma (including GED) or higher: 87.6% (2006-2010 5-year est.); Bachelor's degree or higher: 11.9% (2006-2010 5-year est.); Master's degree or higher: 6.2% (2006-2010 5-year est.).

Housing: Homeownership rate: 91.2% (2010); Median home value: $130,000 (2006-2010 5-year est.); Median contract rent: $439 per month (2006-2010 5-year est.); Median year structure built: 1979 (2006-2010 5-year est.).

Transportation: Commute to work: 96.6% car, 0.0% public transportation, 0.9% walk, 1.9% work from home (2006-2010 5-year est.); Travel time to work: 16.0% less than 15 minutes, 56.5% 15 to 30 minutes, 15.5% 30 to 45 minutes, 7.2% 45 to 60 minutes, 4.8% 60 minutes or more (2006-2010 5-year est.)

NEW COLUMBUS (borough). Covers a land area of 3.065 square miles and a water area of 0 square miles. Located at 41.17° N. Lat; 76.29° W. Long. Elevation is 991 feet.

Population: 228 (1990); 215 (2000); 227 (2010); Density: 74.1 persons per square mile (2010); Race: 100.0% White, 0.0% Black, 0.0% Asian, 0.0% American Indian/Alaska Native, 0.0% Native Hawaiian/Other Pacific Islander, 0.0% Other, 0.9% Hispanic of any race (2010); Average household size: 2.49 (2010); Median age: 38.1 (2010); Males per 100 females: 90.8 (2010); Marriage status: 20.8% never married, 72.8% now married, 5.8% widowed, 0.6% divorced (2006-2010 5-year est.); Foreign born: 6.2% (2006-2010 5-year est.); Ancestry (includes multiple ancestries): 18.7% Polish, 18.2% German, 14.7% Irish, 12.9% English, 10.2% Pennsylvania German (2006-2010 5-year est.).

Economy: Employment by occupation: 3.2% management, 0.0% professional, 31.6% services, 15.8% sales, 4.2% farming, 30.5% construction, 18.9% production (2006-2010 5-year est.).

Income: Per capita income: $18,362 (2006-2010 5-year est.); Median household income: $37,679 (2006-2010 5-year est.); Average household income: $48,102 (2006-2010 5-year est.); Percent of households with income of $100,000 or more: 6.2% (2006-2010 5-year est.); Poverty rate: 19.6% (2006-2010 5-year est.).

Education: Percent of population age 25 and over with: High school diploma (including GED) or higher: 73.3% (2006-2010 5-year est.); Bachelor's degree or higher: 8.7% (2006-2010 5-year est.); Master's degree or higher: 3.3% (2006-2010 5-year est.).

Housing: Homeownership rate: 72.6% (2010); Median home value: $140,600 (2006-2010 5-year est.); Median contract rent: $611 per month (2006-2010 5-year est.); Median year structure built: before 1940 (2006-2010 5-year est.).

Transportation: Commute to work: 87.4% car, 0.0% public transportation, 0.0% walk, 12.6% work from home (2006-2010 5-year est.); Travel time to work: 12.0% less than 15 minutes, 34.9% 15 to 30 minutes, 14.5% 30 to 45 minutes, 28.9% 45 to 60 minutes, 9.6% 60 minutes or more (2006-2010 5-year est.)

NEWPORT (township). Covers a land area of 16.759 square miles and a water area of 0.428 square miles. Located at 41.18° N. Lat; 76.05° W. Long.

Population: 4,593 (1990); 5,006 (2000); 5,374 (2010); Density: 320.7 persons per square mile (2010); Race: 84.6% White, 11.4% Black, 0.3% Asian, 0.1% American Indian/Alaska Native, 0.0% Native Hawaiian/Other Pacific Islander, 3.6% Other, 4.3% Hispanic of any race (2010); Average household size: 2.37 (2010); Median age: 39.7 (2010); Males per 100 females: 140.9 (2010); Marriage status: 34.1% never married, 45.6% now married, 8.0% widowed, 12.3% divorced (2006-2010 5-year est.); Foreign born: 2.4% (2006-2010 5-year est.); Ancestry (includes multiple ancestries): 37.9% Polish, 16.3% Irish, 16.2% German, 10.7% Welsh, 6.5% Italian (2006-2010 5-year est.).

Economy: Employment by occupation: 5.5% management, 1.0% professional, 6.5% services, 18.5% sales, 7.4% farming, 13.9% construction, 12.1% production (2006-2010 5-year est.).

Income: Per capita income: $17,508 (2006-2010 5-year est.); Median household income: $39,361 (2006-2010 5-year est.); Average household income: $45,317 (2006-2010 5-year est.); Percent of households with income of $100,000 or more: 8.3% (2006-2010 5-year est.); Poverty rate: 17.4% (2006-2010 5-year est.).

Education: Percent of population age 25 and over with: High school diploma (including GED) or higher: 84.1% (2006-2010 5-year est.); Bachelor's degree or higher: 10.4% (2006-2010 5-year est.); Master's degree or higher: 4.9% (2006-2010 5-year est.).

Housing: Homeownership rate: 69.8% (2010); Median home value: $90,100 (2006-2010 5-year est.); Median contract rent: $429 per month (2006-2010 5-year est.); Median year structure built: before 1940 (2006-2010 5-year est.).

Safety: Violent crime rate: 29.7 per 10,000 population; Property crime rate: 16.7 per 10,000 population (2011).

Transportation: Commute to work: 97.5% car, 1.1% public transportation, 0.5% walk, 0.4% work from home (2006-2010 5-year est.); Travel time to work: 25.4% less than 15 minutes, 40.1% 15 to 30 minutes, 25.9% 30 to

45 minutes, 2.8% 45 to 60 minutes, 5.7% 60 minutes or more (2006-2010 5-year est.)
Additional Information Contacts
Newport Township. . . . . (570) 735-4735
   http://www.luzernecounty.org/living/municipalities/newport_township
South Valley Chamber of Commerce . . . . (570) 735-6990
   http://www.southvalleychamber.com

NUANGOLA (borough). Covers a land area of 1.052 square miles and a water area of 0.158 square miles. Located at 41.16° N. Lat; 75.98° W. Long. Elevation is 1,234 feet.
Population: 701 (1990); 671 (2000); 679 (2010); Density: 645.6 persons per square mile (2010); Race: 99.0% White, 0.0% Black, 0.9% Asian, 0.1% American Indian/Alaska Native, 0.0% Native Hawaiian/Other Pacific Islander, 0.0% Other, 0.1% Hispanic of any race (2010); Average household size: 2.47 (2010); Median age: 45.5 (2010); Males per 100 females: 96.8 (2010); Marriage status: 25.9% never married, 62.3% now married, 6.1% widowed, 5.7% divorced (2006-2010 5-year est.); Foreign born: 1.2% (2006-2010 5-year est.); Ancestry (includes multiple ancestries): 37.1% Polish, 25.2% Irish, 20.2% German, 16.9% Italian, 7.8% Welsh (2006-2010 5-year est.).
Economy: Single-family building permits issued: 0 (2011); Multi-family building permits issued: 0 (2011); Employment by occupation: 11.5% management, 4.9% professional, 14.4% services, 13.3% sales, 2.0% farming, 12.2% construction, 9.5% production (2006-2010 5-year est.).
Income: Per capita income: $26,240 (2006-2010 5-year est.); Median household income: $64,231 (2006-2010 5-year est.); Average household income: $74,657 (2006-2010 5-year est.); Percent of households with income of $100,000 or more: 25.0% (2006-2010 5-year est.); Poverty rate: 5.8% (2006-2010 5-year est.).
Education: Percent of population age 25 and over with: High school diploma (including GED) or higher: 89.3% (2006-2010 5-year est.); Bachelor's degree or higher: 35.0% (2006-2010 5-year est.); Master's degree or higher: 15.6% (2006-2010 5-year est.).
Housing: Homeownership rate: 91.6% (2010); Median home value: $158,800 (2006-2010 5-year est.); Median contract rent: $625 per month (2006-2010 5-year est.); Median year structure built: 1954 (2006-2010 5-year est.).
Transportation: Commute to work: 94.4% car, 0.7% public transportation, 0.0% walk, 4.0% work from home (2006-2010 5-year est.); Travel time to work: 17.4% less than 15 minutes, 59.5% 15 to 30 minutes, 10.2% 30 to 45 minutes, 8.6% 45 to 60 minutes, 4.2% 60 minutes or more (2006-2010 5-year est.)

PARDEESVILLE (CDP). Covers a land area of 0.653 square miles and a water area of 0 square miles. Located at 41.00° N. Lat; 75.97° W. Long. Elevation is 1,670 feet.
Population: n/a (1990); n/a (2000); 572 (2010); Density: 875.5 persons per square mile (2010); Race: 97.7% White, 0.0% Black, 1.0% Asian, 0.0% American Indian/Alaska Native, 0.0% Native Hawaiian/Other Pacific Islander, 1.3% Other, 0.7% Hispanic of any race (2010); Average household size: 2.39 (2010); Median age: 43.0 (2010); Males per 100 females: 122.6 (2010); Marriage status: 27.6% never married, 53.4% now married, 1.4% widowed, 17.6% divorced (2006-2010 5-year est.); Foreign born: 7.2% (2006-2010 5-year est.); Ancestry (includes multiple ancestries): 43.5% Italian, 25.9% Polish, 15.9% Slovak, 15.7% Irish, 13.0% German (2006-2010 5-year est.).
Economy: Employment by occupation: 0.0% management, 5.0% professional, 17.6% services, 21.8% sales, 4.6% farming, 10.5% construction, 7.1% production (2006-2010 5-year est.).
Income: Per capita income: $19,491 (2006-2010 5-year est.); Median household income: $45,054 (2006-2010 5-year est.); Average household income: $37,568 (2006-2010 5-year est.); Percent of households with income of $100,000 or more: n/a (2006-2010 5-year est.); Poverty rate: 28.4% (2006-2010 5-year est.).
Education: Percent of population age 25 and over with: High school diploma (including GED) or higher: 97.7% (2006-2010 5-year est.); Bachelor's degree or higher: 10.5% (2006-2010 5-year est.); Master's degree or higher: 6.9% (2006-2010 5-year est.).
Housing: Homeownership rate: 72.8% (2010); Median home value: $117,400 (2006-2010 5-year est.); Median contract rent: $586 per month (2006-2010 5-year est.); Median year structure built: 1969 (2006-2010 5-year est.).
Transportation: Commute to work: 100.0% car, 0.0% public transportation, 0.0% walk, 0.0% work from home (2006-2010 5-year est.);

Travel time to work: 26.5% less than 15 minutes, 58.0% 15 to 30 minutes, 15.5% 30 to 45 minutes, 0.0% 45 to 60 minutes, 0.0% 60 minutes or more (2006-2010 5-year est.)

PENN LAKE PARK (borough). Covers a land area of 1.551 square miles and a water area of 0.083 square miles. Located at 41.12° N. Lat; 75.77° W. Long. Elevation is 1,339 feet.
Population: 242 (1990); 269 (2000); 308 (2010); Density: 198.5 persons per square mile (2010); Race: 98.1% White, 0.0% Black, 0.0% Asian, 0.3% American Indian/Alaska Native, 0.0% Native Hawaiian/Other Pacific Islander, 0.6% Other, 0.0% Hispanic of any race (2010); Average household size: 2.18 (2010); Median age: 53.3 (2010); Males per 100 females: 92.5 (2010); Marriage status: 20.4% never married, 54.1% now married, 3.8% widowed, 21.7% divorced (2006-2010 5-year est.); Foreign born: 0.6% (2006-2010 5-year est.); Ancestry (includes multiple ancestries): 20.6% German, 17.4% Italian, 15.3% Irish, 10.9% Polish, 8.3% English (2006-2010 5-year est.).
Economy: Single-family building permits issued: 0 (2011); Multi-family building permits issued: 0 (2011); Employment by occupation: 19.8% management, 0.0% professional, 4.4% services, 22.0% sales, 2.7% farming, 6.0% construction, 3.3% production (2006-2010 5-year est.).
Income: Per capita income: $26,950 (2006-2010 5-year est.); Median household income: $43,611 (2006-2010 5-year est.); Average household income: $56,238 (2006-2010 5-year est.); Percent of households with income of $100,000 or more: 14.6% (2006-2010 5-year est.); Poverty rate: 16.5% (2006-2010 5-year est.).
Education: Percent of population age 25 and over with: High school diploma (including GED) or higher: 89.3% (2006-2010 5-year est.); Bachelor's degree or higher: 26.3% (2006-2010 5-year est.); Master's degree or higher: 2.8% (2006-2010 5-year est.).
Housing: Homeownership rate: 95.0% (2010); Median home value: $162,500 (2006-2010 5-year est.); Median contract rent: $1,038 per month (2006-2010 5-year est.); Median year structure built: 1968 (2006-2010 5-year est.).
Transportation: Commute to work: 100.0% car, 0.0% public transportation, 0.0% walk, 0.0% work from home (2006-2010 5-year est.); Travel time to work: 5.7% less than 15 minutes, 46.6% 15 to 30 minutes, 35.2% 30 to 45 minutes, 12.5% 45 to 60 minutes, 0.0% 60 minutes or more (2006-2010 5-year est.)

PIKES CREEK (CDP). Covers a land area of 1.263 square miles and a water area of 0 square miles. Located at 41.31° N. Lat; 76.10° W. Long. Elevation is 1,171 feet.
Population: n/a (1990); n/a (2000); 269 (2010); Density: 212.9 persons per square mile (2010); Race: 98.5% White, 0.0% Black, 0.4% Asian, 0.0% American Indian/Alaska Native, 0.0% Native Hawaiian/Other Pacific Islander, 1.1% Other, 1.9% Hispanic of any race (2010); Average household size: 2.32 (2010); Median age: 46.9 (2010); Males per 100 females: 100.7 (2010); Marriage status: 24.2% never married, 55.8% now married, 15.8% widowed, 4.2% divorced (2006-2010 5-year est.); Foreign born: 0.0% (2006-2010 5-year est.); Ancestry (includes multiple ancestries): 33.1% German, 20.1% Polish, 15.8% Irish, 12.9% French, 10.1% English (2006-2010 5-year est.).
Economy: Employment by occupation: 6.0% management, 1.7% professional, 17.9% services, 16.2% sales, 2.6% farming, 7.7% construction, 8.5% production (2006-2010 5-year est.).
Income: Per capita income: $22,440 (2006-2010 5-year est.); Median household income: $33,182 (2006-2010 5-year est.); Average household income: $51,502 (2006-2010 5-year est.); Percent of households with income of $100,000 or more: 13.9% (2006-2010 5-year est.); Poverty rate: 21.9% (2006-2010 5-year est.).
Education: Percent of population age 25 and over with: High school diploma (including GED) or higher: 82.5% (2006-2010 5-year est.); Bachelor's degree or higher: 11.3% (2006-2010 5-year est.); Master's degree or higher: 2.4% (2006-2010 5-year est.).
Housing: Homeownership rate: 70.7% (2010); Median home value: $169,400 (2006-2010 5-year est.); Median contract rent: $656 per month (2006-2010 5-year est.); Median year structure built: 1977 (2006-2010 5-year est.).
Transportation: Commute to work: 100.0% car, 0.0% public transportation, 0.0% walk, 0.0% work from home (2006-2010 5-year est.); Travel time to work: 7.7% less than 15 minutes, 47.0% 15 to 30 minutes, 45.3% 30 to 45 minutes, 0.0% 45 to 60 minutes, 0.0% 60 minutes or more (2006-2010 5-year est.)

PITTSTON (city). Covers a land area of 1.551 square miles and a water area of 0.155 square miles. Located at 41.33° N. Lat; 75.79° W. Long. Elevation is 587 feet.

Population: 9,389 (1990); 8,104 (2000); 7,739 (2010); Density: 4,989.8 persons per square mile (2010); Race: 95.0% White, 1.9% Black, 0.5% Asian, 0.2% American Indian/Alaska Native, 0.0% Native Hawaiian/Other Pacific Islander, 2.4% Other, 2.7% Hispanic of any race (2010); Average household size: 2.20 (2010); Median age: 41.0 (2010); Males per 100 females: 87.9 (2010); Marriage status: 35.3% never married, 35.6% now married, 13.0% widowed, 16.1% divorced (2006-2010 5-year est.); Foreign born: 1.6% (2006-2010 5-year est.); Ancestry (includes multiple ancestries): 33.4% Italian, 29.9% Irish, 21.0% Polish, 15.0% German, 5.8% English (2006-2010 5-year est.).

Economy: Single-family building permits issued: 3 (2011); Multi-family building permits issued: 0 (2011); Employment by occupation: 6.3% management, 1.5% professional, 13.3% services, 17.8% sales, 7.7% farming, 9.1% construction, 7.7% production (2006-2010 5-year est.).

Income: Per capita income: $17,655 (2006-2010 5-year est.); Median household income: $32,446 (2006-2010 5-year est.); Average household income: $39,249 (2006-2010 5-year est.); Percent of households with income of $100,000 or more: 3.7% (2006-2010 5-year est.); Poverty rate: 14.8% (2006-2010 5-year est.).

Education: Percent of population age 25 and over with: High school diploma (including GED) or higher: 81.4% (2006-2010 5-year est.); Bachelor's degree or higher: 15.6% (2006-2010 5-year est.); Master's degree or higher: 4.0% (2006-2010 5-year est.).

School District(s)

Pittston Area SD (KG-12)
    2010-11 Enrollment: 3,364 . . . . (570) 654-2271
Wyoming Area SD (KG-12)
    2010-11 Enrollment: 2,536 . . . . (570) 655-3733

Housing: Homeownership rate: 53.7% (2010); Median home value: $86,400 (2006-2010 5-year est.); Median contract rent: $421 per month (2006-2010 5-year est.); Median year structure built: before 1940 (2006-2010 5-year est.).

Newspapers: The Sunday Dispatch (Community news)

Transportation: Commute to work: 89.1% car, 2.0% public transportation, 5.7% walk, 2.6% work from home (2006-2010 5-year est.); Travel time to work: 34.0% less than 15 minutes, 47.9% 15 to 30 minutes, 8.0% 30 to 45 minutes, 4.8% 45 to 60 minutes, 5.3% 60 minutes or more (2006-2010 5-year est.)

Additional Information Contacts

City of Pittston . . . . (570) 654-0513
    http://www.pittstoncity.org
Greater Pittston Chamber of Commerce . . . . (570) 655-1424
    http://www.pittstonchamber.org

PITTSTON (township). Covers a land area of 13.767 square miles and a water area of 0.021 square miles. Located at 41.30° N. Lat; 75.71° W. Long. Elevation is 587 feet.

History: Settled c.1770 by the Susquehanna Company of Connecticut, incorporated 1894 as a city.

Population: 2,747 (1990); 3,450 (2000); 3,368 (2010); Density: 244.6 persons per square mile (2010); Race: 97.2% White, 1.5% Black, 0.3% Asian, 0.0% American Indian/Alaska Native, 0.0% Native Hawaiian/Other Pacific Islander, 1.0% Other, 0.9% Hispanic of any race (2010); Average household size: 2.47 (2010); Median age: 43.9 (2010); Males per 100 females: 100.0 (2010); Marriage status: 26.6% never married, 55.2% now married, 10.6% widowed, 7.5% divorced (2006-2010 5-year est.); Foreign born: 1.3% (2006-2010 5-year est.); Ancestry (includes multiple ancestries): 37.8% Polish, 33.1% Italian, 27.1% Irish, 17.3% German, 8.0% Lithuanian (2006-2010 5-year est.).

Economy: Single-family building permits issued: 0 (2011); Multi-family building permits issued: 0 (2011); Employment by occupation: 10.1% management, 0.0% professional, 13.5% services, 16.8% sales, 3.6% farming, 9.9% construction, 8.1% production (2006-2010 5-year est.).

Income: Per capita income: $26,858 (2006-2010 5-year est.); Median household income: $54,112 (2006-2010 5-year est.); Average household income: $66,807 (2006-2010 5-year est.); Percent of households with income of $100,000 or more: 12.7% (2006-2010 5-year est.); Poverty rate: 9.7% (2006-2010 5-year est.).

Education: Percent of population age 25 and over with: High school diploma (including GED) or higher: 89.8% (2006-2010 5-year est.); Bachelor's degree or higher: 20.2% (2006-2010 5-year est.); Master's degree or higher: 8.5% (2006-2010 5-year est.).

Housing: Homeownership rate: 84.3% (2010); Median home value: $126,900 (2006-2010 5-year est.); Median contract rent: $430 per month (2006-2010 5-year est.); Median year structure built: 1965 (2006-2010 5-year est.).

Newspapers: The Sunday Dispatch (Community news)

Transportation: Commute to work: 95.9% car, 0.0% public transportation, 2.6% walk, 0.6% work from home (2006-2010 5-year est.); Travel time to work: 29.1% less than 15 minutes, 43.4% 15 to 30 minutes, 12.4% 30 to 45 minutes, 6.1% 45 to 60 minutes, 9.0% 60 minutes or more (2006-2010 5-year est.)

Additional Information Contacts

Greater Pittston Chamber of Commerce . . . . (570) 655-1424
    http://www.pittstonchamber.org

PLAINS (CDP). Covers a land area of 1.279 square miles and a water area of 0 square miles. Located at 41.28° N. Lat; 75.85° W. Long. Elevation is 656 feet.

Population: n/a (1990); n/a (2000); 4,335 (2010); Density: 3,390.1 persons per square mile (2010); Race: 96.0% White, 1.1% Black, 0.9% Asian, 0.1% American Indian/Alaska Native, 0.0% Native Hawaiian/Other Pacific Islander, 1.9% Other, 1.9% Hispanic of any race (2010); Average household size: 2.16 (2010); Median age: 45.4 (2010); Males per 100 females: 89.5 (2010); Marriage status: 28.0% never married, 49.2% now married, 14.8% widowed, 8.0% divorced (2006-2010 5-year est.); Foreign born: 3.1% (2006-2010 5-year est.); Ancestry (includes multiple ancestries): 28.6% Polish, 23.7% Italian, 20.2% Irish, 15.7% German, 7.9% English (2006-2010 5-year est.).

Economy: Employment by occupation: 9.3% management, 5.0% professional, 9.7% services, 18.7% sales, 4.8% farming, 7.1% construction, 7.1% production (2006-2010 5-year est.).

Income: Per capita income: $28,430 (2006-2010 5-year est.); Median household income: $40,509 (2006-2010 5-year est.); Average household income: $60,576 (2006-2010 5-year est.); Percent of households with income of $100,000 or more: 14.0% (2006-2010 5-year est.); Poverty rate: 10.2% (2006-2010 5-year est.).

Education: Percent of population age 25 and over with: High school diploma (including GED) or higher: 90.9% (2006-2010 5-year est.); Bachelor's degree or higher: 24.4% (2006-2010 5-year est.); Master's degree or higher: 5.8% (2006-2010 5-year est.).

School District(s)

Wilkes-Barre Area SD (KG-12)
    2010-11 Enrollment: 6,997 . . . . (570) 826-7182

Housing: Homeownership rate: 69.2% (2010); Median home value: $89,100 (2006-2010 5-year est.); Median contract rent: $444 per month (2006-2010 5-year est.); Median year structure built: before 1940 (2006-2010 5-year est.).

Transportation: Commute to work: 92.0% car, 0.8% public transportation, 4.3% walk, 1.7% work from home (2006-2010 5-year est.); Travel time to work: 48.7% less than 15 minutes, 32.5% 15 to 30 minutes, 6.6% 30 to 45 minutes, 5.3% 45 to 60 minutes, 7.0% 60 minutes or more (2006-2010 5-year est.)

PLAINS (township). Covers a land area of 12.907 square miles and a water area of 0.256 square miles. Located at 41.27° N. Lat; 75.82° W. Long. Elevation is 656 feet.

Population: 11,339 (1990); 10,906 (2000); 9,961 (2010); Density: 771.8 persons per square mile (2010); Race: 95.9% White, 1.3% Black, 1.4% Asian, 0.1% American Indian/Alaska Native, 0.0% Native Hawaiian/Other Pacific Islander, 1.3% Other, 1.4% Hispanic of any race (2010); Average household size: 2.19 (2010); Median age: 47.5 (2010); Males per 100 females: 91.4 (2010); Marriage status: 25.6% never married, 54.5% now married, 11.7% widowed, 8.2% divorced (2006-2010 5-year est.); Foreign born: 2.7% (2006-2010 5-year est.); Ancestry (includes multiple ancestries): 30.5% Polish, 19.6% Irish, 19.4% Italian, 15.8% German, 9.9% English (2006-2010 5-year est.).

Economy: Single-family building permits issued: 0 (2011); Multi-family building permits issued: 0 (2011); Employment by occupation: 12.1% management, 3.9% professional, 8.2% services, 21.1% sales, 3.7% farming, 6.5% construction, 5.8% production (2006-2010 5-year est.).

Income: Per capita income: $27,265 (2006-2010 5-year est.); Median household income: $50,093 (2006-2010 5-year est.); Average household income: $61,667 (2006-2010 5-year est.); Percent of households with income of $100,000 or more: 14.2% (2006-2010 5-year est.); Poverty rate: 8.5% (2006-2010 5-year est.).

Education: Percent of population age 25 and over with: High school diploma (including GED) or higher: 89.6% (2006-2010 5-year est.); Bachelor's degree or higher: 25.6% (2006-2010 5-year est.); Master's degree or higher: 6.3% (2006-2010 5-year est.).

Housing: Homeownership rate: 69.5% (2010); Median home value: $113,100 (2006-2010 5-year est.); Median contract rent: $459 per month (2006-2010 5-year est.); Median year structure built: 1961 (2006-2010 5-year est.).

Safety: Violent crime rate: 17.0 per 10,000 population; Property crime rate: 210.1 per 10,000 population (2011).

Transportation: Commute to work: 93.4% car, 0.3% public transportation, 2.7% walk, 2.9% work from home (2006-2010 5-year est.); Travel time to work: 47.1% less than 15 minutes, 36.7% 15 to 30 minutes, 6.5% 30 to 45 minutes, 3.7% 45 to 60 minutes, 6.0% 60 minutes or more (2006-2010 5-year est.)

Additional Information Contacts

Greater Pittston Chamber of Commerce . . . . (570) 655-1424
http://www.pittstonchamber.org

Plains Township . . . . (570) 829-3439
http://www.luzernecounty.org/living/municipalities/plains_township

PLYMOUTH (borough). Covers a land area of 1.097 square miles and a water area of 0.087 square miles. Located at 41.24° N. Lat; 75.95° W. Long. Elevation is 525 feet.

Population: 7,134 (1990); 6,507 (2000); 5,951 (2010); Density: 5,423.1 persons per square mile (2010); Race: 92.1% White, 4.3% Black, 0.5% Asian, 0.2% American Indian/Alaska Native, 0.0% Native Hawaiian/Other Pacific Islander, 2.9% Other, 3.3% Hispanic of any race (2010); Average household size: 2.31 (2010); Median age: 39.1 (2010); Males per 100 females: 90.1 (2010); Marriage status: 36.6% never married, 40.7% now married, 10.3% widowed, 12.4% divorced (2006-2010 5-year est.); Foreign born: 1.6% (2006-2010 5-year est.); Ancestry (includes multiple ancestries): 34.6% Polish, 19.0% Irish, 14.2% German, 9.5% Welsh, 7.2% Italian (2006-2010 5-year est.).

Economy: Single-family building permits issued: 0 (2011); Multi-family building permits issued: 0 (2011); Employment by occupation: 3.4% management, 1.6% professional, 16.5% services, 21.8% sales, 6.4% farming, 8.0% construction, 10.3% production (2006-2010 5-year est.).

Income: Per capita income: $16,441 (2006-2010 5-year est.); Median household income: $29,972 (2006-2010 5-year est.); Average household income: $36,348 (2006-2010 5-year est.); Percent of households with income of $100,000 or more: 3.2% (2006-2010 5-year est.); Poverty rate: 24.0% (2006-2010 5-year est.).

Education: Percent of population age 25 and over with: High school diploma (including GED) or higher: 80.9% (2006-2010 5-year est.); Bachelor's degree or higher: 11.1% (2006-2010 5-year est.); Master's degree or higher: 4.0% (2006-2010 5-year est.).

School District(s)

Wyoming Valley West SD (KG-12)
2010-11 Enrollment: 4,855 . . . . (570) 288-6551

Housing: Homeownership rate: 52.8% (2010); Median home value: $82,600 (2006-2010 5-year est.); Median contract rent: $430 per month (2006-2010 5-year est.); Median year structure built: before 1940 (2006-2010 5-year est.).

Safety: Violent crime rate: 73.7 per 10,000 population; Property crime rate: 345.1 per 10,000 population (2011).

Transportation: Commute to work: 94.5% car, 1.1% public transportation, 1.2% walk, 2.8% work from home (2006-2010 5-year est.); Travel time to work: 27.7% less than 15 minutes, 52.7% 15 to 30 minutes, 11.7% 30 to 45 minutes, 2.0% 45 to 60 minutes, 5.9% 60 minutes or more (2006-2010 5-year est.)

Additional Information Contacts

Borough of Plymouth. . . . . (570) 779-1011
http://www.luzernecounty.org/living/municipalities/plymouth_borough

South Valley Chamber of Commerce . . . . (570) 735-6990
http://www.southvalleychamber.com

PLYMOUTH (township). Covers a land area of 15.925 square miles and a water area of 0.502 square miles. Located at 41.24° N. Lat; 76.03° W. Long. Elevation is 525 feet.

History: Incorporated 1866.

Population: 1,999 (1990); 2,097 (2000); 1,812 (2010); Density: 113.8 persons per square mile (2010); Race: 98.6% White, 0.4% Black, 0.0% Asian, 0.1% American Indian/Alaska Native, 0.0% Native Hawaiian/Other Pacific Islander, 0.9% Other, 0.9% Hispanic of any race (2010); Average

household size: 2.32 (2010); Median age: 45.6 (2010); Males per 100 females: 101.3 (2010); Marriage status: 25.0% never married, 58.1% now married, 8.6% widowed, 8.3% divorced (2006-2010 5-year est.); Foreign born: 0.6% (2006-2010 5-year est.); Ancestry (includes multiple ancestries): 38.3% Polish, 24.4% German, 18.9% Irish, 12.6% Slovak, 9.8% Welsh (2006-2010 5-year est.).

Economy: Single-family building permits issued: 3 (2011); Multi-family building permits issued: 0 (2011); Employment by occupation: 11.1% management, 2.8% professional, 10.9% services, 13.9% sales, 3.9% farming, 7.8% construction, 3.5% production (2006-2010 5-year est.).

Income: Per capita income: $27,905 (2006-2010 5-year est.); Median household income: $49,886 (2006-2010 5-year est.); Average household income: $59,517 (2006-2010 5-year est.); Percent of households with income of $100,000 or more: 17.7% (2006-2010 5-year est.); Poverty rate: 6.9% (2006-2010 5-year est.).

Education: Percent of population age 25 and over with: High school diploma (including GED) or higher: 82.5% (2006-2010 5-year est.); Bachelor's degree or higher: 19.5% (2006-2010 5-year est.); Master's degree or higher: 7.9% (2006-2010 5-year est.).

Housing: Homeownership rate: 83.2% (2010); Median home value: $105,800 (2006-2010 5-year est.); Median contract rent: $414 per month (2006-2010 5-year est.); Median year structure built: 1953 (2006-2010 5-year est.).

Transportation: Commute to work: 97.4% car, 0.6% public transportation, 0.0% walk, 2.0% work from home (2006-2010 5-year est.); Travel time to work: 21.3% less than 15 minutes, 41.5% 15 to 30 minutes, 24.7% 30 to 45 minutes, 3.5% 45 to 60 minutes, 8.9% 60 minutes or more (2006-2010 5-year est.)

Additional Information Contacts

South Valley Chamber of Commerce . . . . (570) 735-6990
http://www.southvalleychamber.com

PRINGLE (borough). Covers a land area of 0.465 square miles and a water area of 0 square miles. Located at 41.28° N. Lat; 75.90° W. Long. Elevation is 636 feet.

History: Incorporated 1914.

Population: 1,161 (1990); 991 (2000); 979 (2010); Density: 2,104.6 persons per square mile (2010); Race: 98.1% White, 0.3% Black, 0.2% Asian, 0.0% American Indian/Alaska Native, 0.0% Native Hawaiian/Other Pacific Islander, 1.4% Other, 1.8% Hispanic of any race (2010); Average household size: 2.34 (2010); Median age: 46.0 (2010); Males per 100 females: 90.5 (2010); Marriage status: 31.8% never married, 44.2% now married, 9.2% widowed, 14.8% divorced (2006-2010 5-year est.); Foreign born: 0.6% (2006-2010 5-year est.); Ancestry (includes multiple ancestries): 36.4% Polish, 16.7% Irish, 13.2% German, 12.3% Slovak, 11.0% Italian (2006-2010 5-year est.).

Economy: Single-family building permits issued: 0 (2011); Multi-family building permits issued: 0 (2011); Employment by occupation: 4.7% management, 3.0% professional, 7.7% services, 30.7% sales, 3.5% farming, 10.0% construction, 6.5% production (2006-2010 5-year est.).

Income: Per capita income: $21,644 (2006-2010 5-year est.); Median household income: $45,060 (2006-2010 5-year est.); Average household income: $52,139 (2006-2010 5-year est.); Percent of households with income of $100,000 or more: 11.5% (2006-2010 5-year est.); Poverty rate: 5.0% (2006-2010 5-year est.).

Education: Percent of population age 25 and over with: High school diploma (including GED) or higher: 87.3% (2006-2010 5-year est.); Bachelor's degree or higher: 13.0% (2006-2010 5-year est.); Master's degree or higher: 3.6% (2006-2010 5-year est.).

Housing: Homeownership rate: 76.2% (2010); Median home value: $96,400 (2006-2010 5-year est.); Median contract rent: $408 per month (2006-2010 5-year est.); Median year structure built: before 1940 (2006-2010 5-year est.).

Safety: Violent crime rate: 20.4 per 10,000 population; Property crime rate: 621.2 per 10,000 population (2011).

Transportation: Commute to work: 96.9% car, 1.8% public transportation, 1.2% walk, 0.0% work from home (2006-2010 5-year est.); Travel time to work: 46.6% less than 15 minutes, 38.6% 15 to 30 minutes, 10.5% 30 to 45 minutes, 3.7% 45 to 60 minutes, 0.6% 60 minutes or more (2006-2010 5-year est.)

RICE (township). Covers a land area of 10.925 square miles and a water area of 0.250 square miles. Located at 41.16° N. Lat; 75.92° W. Long.

Population: 1,918 (1990); 2,460 (2000); 3,335 (2010); Density: 305.3 persons per square mile (2010); Race: 92.9% White, 1.5% Black, 3.2%

Asian, 0.1% American Indian/Alaska Native, 0.0% Native Hawaiian/Other Pacific Islander, 2.3% Other, 2.3% Hispanic of any race (2010); Average household size: 2.71 (2010); Median age: 40.1 (2010); Males per 100 females: 95.1 (2010); Marriage status: 23.3% never married, 66.3% now married, 4.5% widowed, 5.9% divorced (2006-2010 5-year est.); Foreign born: 1.8% (2006-2010 5-year est.); Ancestry (includes multiple ancestries): 29.4% Polish, 24.8% German, 20.0% Irish, 16.6% Italian, 9.9% English (2006-2010 5-year est.).

Economy: Single-family building permits issued: 23 (2011); Multi-family building permits issued: 0 (2011); Employment by occupation: 13.0% management, 4.8% professional, 9.8% services, 14.1% sales, 2.2% farming, 5.3% construction, 5.3% production (2006-2010 5-year est.).

Income: Per capita income: $31,773 (2006-2010 5-year est.); Median household income: $76,384 (2006-2010 5-year est.); Average household income: $87,921 (2006-2010 5-year est.); Percent of households with income of $100,000 or more: 36.3% (2006-2010 5-year est.); Poverty rate: 0.4% (2006-2010 5-year est.).

Education: Percent of population age 25 and over with: High school diploma (including GED) or higher: 93.8% (2006-2010 5-year est.); Bachelor's degree or higher: 36.1% (2006-2010 5-year est.); Master's degree or higher: 17.5% (2006-2010 5-year est.).

Housing: Homeownership rate: 94.0% (2010); Median home value: $178,800 (2006-2010 5-year est.); Median contract rent: n/a per month (2006-2010 5-year est.); Median year structure built: 1991 (2006-2010 5-year est.).

Safety: Violent crime rate: 0.0 per 10,000 population; Property crime rate: 23.9 per 10,000 population (2011).

Transportation: Commute to work: 95.1% car, 0.4% public transportation, 1.8% walk, 2.7% work from home (2006-2010 5-year est.); Travel time to work: 17.8% less than 15 minutes, 44.3% 15 to 30 minutes, 23.7% 30 to 45 minutes, 6.5% 45 to 60 minutes, 7.7% 60 minutes or more (2006-2010 5-year est.)

Additional Information Contacts
South Valley Chamber of Commerce . . . . (570) 735-6990
  http://www.southvalleychamber.com

ROCK GLEN (unincorporated postal area)
Zip Code: 18246
  Covers a land area of 2.121 square miles and a water area of 0 square miles. Located at 40.95° N. Lat; 76.19° W. Long. Elevation is 850 feet. Population: 143 (2010); Density: 67.4 persons per square mile (2010); Race: 99.3% White, 0.0% Black, 0.7% Asian, 0.0% American Indian/Alaska Native, 0.0% Native Hawaiian/Other Pacific Islander, 0.0% Other, 0.0% Hispanic of any race (2010); Average household size: 2.34 (2010); Median age: 42.3 (2010); Males per 100 females: 90.7 (2010); Homeownership rate: 93.4% (2010)

ROSS (township). Covers a land area of 43.416 square miles and a water area of 0.510 square miles. Located at 41.30° N. Lat; 76.18° W. Long.
Population: 2,543 (1990); 2,742 (2000); 2,937 (2010); Density: 67.6 persons per square mile (2010); Race: 98.4% White, 0.0% Black, 0.4% Asian, 0.1% American Indian/Alaska Native, 0.0% Native Hawaiian/Other Pacific Islander, 1.1% Other, 1.0% Hispanic of any race (2010); Average household size: 2.60 (2010); Median age: 42.7 (2010); Males per 100 females: 101.0 (2010); Marriage status: 24.1% never married, 57.9% now married, 8.6% widowed, 9.3% divorced (2006-2010 5-year est.); Foreign born: 0.2% (2006-2010 5-year est.); Ancestry (includes multiple ancestries): 27.4% German, 21.7% Polish, 16.7% Irish, 15.3% English, 11.7% Italian (2006-2010 5-year est.).

Economy: Employment by occupation: 15.7% management, 3.4% professional, 6.6% services, 16.0% sales, 3.4% farming, 13.5% construction, 8.3% production (2006-2010 5-year est.).

Income: Per capita income: $22,679 (2006-2010 5-year est.); Median household income: $50,313 (2006-2010 5-year est.); Average household income: $58,270 (2006-2010 5-year est.); Percent of households with income of $100,000 or more: 12.2% (2006-2010 5-year est.); Poverty rate: 14.7% (2006-2010 5-year est.).

Education: Percent of population age 25 and over with: High school diploma (including GED) or higher: 87.0% (2006-2010 5-year est.); Bachelor's degree or higher: 15.7% (2006-2010 5-year est.); Master's degree or higher: 5.9% (2006-2010 5-year est.).

Housing: Homeownership rate: 87.8% (2010); Median home value: $155,300 (2006-2010 5-year est.); Median contract rent: $341 per month

(2006-2010 5-year est.); Median year structure built: 1972 (2006-2010 5-year est.).

Transportation: Commute to work: 94.5% car, 0.0% public transportation, 1.7% walk, 3.4% work from home (2006-2010 5-year est.); Travel time to work: 8.1% less than 15 minutes, 28.0% 15 to 30 minutes, 41.5% 30 to 45 minutes, 12.2% 45 to 60 minutes, 10.2% 60 minutes or more (2006-2010 5-year est.)

Additional Information Contacts
Greater Pittston Chamber of Commerce . . . . (570) 655-1424
  http://www.pittstonchamber.org

SALEM (township). Covers a land area of 28.990 square miles and a water area of 1,003 square miles. Located at 41.11° N. Lat; 76.18° W. Long.
Population: 4,580 (1990); 4,269 (2000); 4,254 (2010); Density: 146.7 persons per square mile (2010); Race: 96.6% White, 0.5% Black, 0.7% Asian, 0.1% American Indian/Alaska Native, 0.0% Native Hawaiian/Other Pacific Islander, 2.1% Other, 2.3% Hispanic of any race (2010); Average household size: 2.31 (2010); Median age: 47.8 (2010); Males per 100 females: 91.6 (2010); Marriage status: 19.8% never married, 58.8% now married, 10.2% widowed, 11.2% divorced (2006-2010 5-year est.); Foreign born: 1.6% (2006-2010 5-year est.); Ancestry (includes multiple ancestries): 31.1% German, 16.3% Irish, 13.2% Polish, 11.7% Italian, 8.3% Dutch (2006-2010 5-year est.).

Economy: Single-family building permits issued: 1 (2011); Multi-family building permits issued: 0 (2011); Employment by occupation: 9.9% management, 4.5% professional, 10.0% services, 16.3% sales, 4.3% farming, 10.0% construction, 12.6% production (2006-2010 5-year est.).

Income: Per capita income: $21,743 (2006-2010 5-year est.); Median household income: $38,618 (2006-2010 5-year est.); Average household income: $52,237 (2006-2010 5-year est.); Percent of households with income of $100,000 or more: 16.1% (2006-2010 5-year est.); Poverty rate: 13.0% (2006-2010 5-year est.).

Education: Percent of population age 25 and over with: High school diploma (including GED) or higher: 84.0% (2006-2010 5-year est.); Bachelor's degree or higher: 14.3% (2006-2010 5-year est.); Master's degree or higher: 2.0% (2006-2010 5-year est.).

Housing: Homeownership rate: 79.7% (2010); Median home value: $126,900 (2006-2010 5-year est.); Median contract rent: $454 per month (2006-2010 5-year est.); Median year structure built: 1965 (2006-2010 5-year est.).

Safety: Violent crime rate: 16.4 per 10,000 population; Property crime rate: 121.8 per 10,000 population (2011).

Transportation: Commute to work: 95.6% car, 0.0% public transportation, 2.6% walk, 1.9% work from home (2006-2010 5-year est.); Travel time to work: 42.1% less than 15 minutes, 28.7% 15 to 30 minutes, 19.0% 30 to 45 minutes, 6.2% 45 to 60 minutes, 4.0% 60 minutes or more (2006-2010 5-year est.)

Additional Information Contacts
Greater Hazleton Chamber of Commerce . . . . (570) 455-1509
  http://www.hazletonchamber.org

SHAVERTOWN (CDP). Covers a land area of 1.218 square miles and a water area of 0 square miles. Located at 41.32° N. Lat; 75.94° W. Long. Elevation is 1,027 feet.
Population: n/a (1990); n/a (2000); 2,019 (2010); Density: 1,658.0 persons per square mile (2010); Race: 97.5% White, 0.6% Black, 1.0% Asian, 0.0% American Indian/Alaska Native, 0.0% Native Hawaiian/Other Pacific Islander, 0.9% Other, 0.9% Hispanic of any race (2010); Average household size: 2.30 (2010); Median age: 46.9 (2010); Males per 100 females: 96.0 (2010); Marriage status: 20.8% never married, 64.4% now married, 6.4% widowed, 8.5% divorced (2006-2010 5-year est.); Foreign born: 1.5% (2006-2010 5-year est.); Ancestry (includes multiple ancestries): 23.6% Irish, 19.7% German, 17.1% Polish, 15.3% Italian, 14.7% English (2006-2010 5-year est.).

Economy: Employment by occupation: 15.0% management, 1.2% professional, 9.9% services, 21.1% sales, 1.3% farming, 9.6% construction, 4.0% production (2006-2010 5-year est.).

Income: Per capita income: $27,864 (2006-2010 5-year est.); Median household income: $47,582 (2006-2010 5-year est.); Average household income: $62,016 (2006-2010 5-year est.); Percent of households with income of $100,000 or more: 20.3% (2006-2010 5-year est.); Poverty rate: 2.1% (2006-2010 5-year est.).

Education: Percent of population age 25 and over with: High school diploma (including GED) or higher: 99.3% (2006-2010 5-year est.);

Bachelor's degree or higher: 25.8% (2006-2010 5-year est.); Master's degree or higher: 8.9% (2006-2010 5-year est.).
Housing: Homeownership rate: 84.1% (2010); Median home value: $152,400 (2006-2010 5-year est.); Median contract rent: $525 per month (2006-2010 5-year est.); Median year structure built: 1952 (2006-2010 5-year est.).
Transportation: Commute to work: 93.6% car, 0.0% public transportation, 3.0% walk, 3.3% work from home (2006-2010 5-year est.); Travel time to work: 25.5% less than 15 minutes, 48.0% 15 to 30 minutes, 23.9% 30 to 45 minutes, 0.0% 45 to 60 minutes, 2.7% 60 minutes or more (2006-2010 5-year est.)

SHEATOWN (CDP). Covers a land area of 0.515 square miles and a water area of 0 square miles. Located at 41.19° N. Lat; 76.02° W. Long. Elevation is 663 feet.
Population: n/a (1990); n/a (2000); 671 (2010); Density: 1,301.7 persons per square mile (2010); Race: 98.1% White, 1.3% Black, 0.3% Asian, 0.0% American Indian/Alaska Native, 0.0% Native Hawaiian/Other Pacific Islander, 0.3% Other, 1.3% Hispanic of any race (2010); Average household size: 2.15 (2010); Median age: 53.7 (2010); Males per 100 females: 78.0 (2010); Marriage status: 25.7% never married, 48.2% now married, 12.4% widowed, 13.7% divorced (2006-2010 5-year est.); Foreign born: 1.4% (2006-2010 5-year est.); Ancestry (includes multiple ancestries): 43.4% Polish, 30.9% German, 28.1% Irish, 14.5% Italian, 7.1% Pennsylvania German (2006-2010 5-year est.).
Economy: Employment by occupation: 3.7% management, 0.0% professional, 0.0% services, 12.9% sales, 7.7% farming, 15.1% construction, 33.6% production (2006-2010 5-year est.).
Income: Per capita income: $25,828 (2006-2010 5-year est.); Median household income: $50,903 (2006-2010 5-year est.); Average household income: $62,731 (2006-2010 5-year est.); Percent of households with income of $100,000 or more: 18.9% (2006-2010 5-year est.); Poverty rate: 3.6% (2006-2010 5-year est.).
Education: Percent of population age 25 and over with: High school diploma (including GED) or higher: 88.7% (2006-2010 5-year est.); Bachelor's degree or higher: 12.1% (2006-2010 5-year est.); Master's degree or higher: 0.0% (2006-2010 5-year est.).
Housing: Homeownership rate: 74.6% (2010); Median home value: $92,300 (2006-2010 5-year est.); Median contract rent: $490 per month (2006-2010 5-year est.); Median year structure built: 1944 (2006-2010 5-year est.).
Transportation: Commute to work: 95.6% car, 4.4% public transportation, 0.0% walk, 0.0% work from home (2006-2010 5-year est.); Travel time to work: 36.9% less than 15 minutes, 34.3% 15 to 30 minutes, 24.4% 30 to 45 minutes, 0.0% 45 to 60 minutes, 4.4% 60 minutes or more (2006-2010 5-year est.)

SHICKSHINNY (borough). Covers a land area of 0.452 square miles and a water area of 0.047 square miles. Located at 41.15° N. Lat; 76.15° W. Long. Elevation is 515 feet.
History: Incorporated 1861.
Population: 985 (1990); 959 (2000); 838 (2010); Density: 1,854.3 persons per square mile (2010); Race: 97.9% White, 0.1% Black, 0.0% Asian, 0.5% American Indian/Alaska Native, 0.0% Native Hawaiian/Other Pacific Islander, 1.5% Other, 1.0% Hispanic of any race (2010); Average household size: 2.26 (2010); Median age: 43.3 (2010); Males per 100 females: 93.5 (2010); Marriage status: 30.4% never married, 48.2% now married, 7.2% widowed, 14.2% divorced (2006-2010 5-year est.); Foreign born: 1.2% (2006-2010 5-year est.); Ancestry (includes multiple ancestries): 34.1% German, 16.5% English, 16.0% Polish, 15.8% Irish, 11.4% Dutch (2006-2010 5-year est.).
Economy: Single-family building permits issued: 0 (2011); Multi-family building permits issued: 0 (2011); Employment by occupation: 6.4% management, 0.9% professional, 11.0% services, 22.6% sales, 7.8% farming, 2.9% construction, 4.6% production (2006-2010 5-year est.).
Income: Per capita income: $16,732 (2006-2010 5-year est.); Median household income: $34,615 (2006-2010 5-year est.); Average household income: $43,359 (2006-2010 5-year est.); Percent of households with income of $100,000 or more: 4.9% (2006-2010 5-year est.); Poverty rate: 18.4% (2006-2010 5-year est.).
Education: Percent of population age 25 and over with: High school diploma (including GED) or higher: 82.9% (2006-2010 5-year est.); Bachelor's degree or higher: 5.2% (2006-2010 5-year est.); Master's degree or higher: 0.3% (2006-2010 5-year est.).

School District(s)
Northwest Area SD (KG-12)
  2010-11 Enrollment: 1,219 . . . . (570) 542-4126
Housing: Homeownership rate: 56.9% (2010); Median home value: $69,200 (2006-2010 5-year est.); Median contract rent: $325 per month (2006-2010 5-year est.); Median year structure built: before 1940 (2006-2010 5-year est.).
Hospitals: Clear Brook Lodge (46 beds)
Transportation: Commute to work: 91.3% car, 0.0% public transportation, 8.1% walk, 0.6% work from home (2006-2010 5-year est.); Travel time to work: 23.9% less than 15 minutes, 37.0% 15 to 30 minutes, 19.4% 30 to 45 minutes, 15.5% 45 to 60 minutes, 4.2% 60 minutes or more (2006-2010 5-year est.)

SILKWORTH (CDP). Covers a land area of 3.388 square miles and a water area of 0.419 square miles. Located at 41.28° N. Lat; 76.07° W. Long. Elevation is 1,214 feet.
Population: n/a (1990); n/a (2000); 820 (2010); Density: 242.0 persons per square mile (2010); Race: 97.3% White, 0.5% Black, 0.1% Asian, 0.1% American Indian/Alaska Native, 0.0% Native Hawaiian/Other Pacific Islander, 2.0% Other, 1.0% Hispanic of any race (2010); Average household size: 2.46 (2010); Median age: 43.3 (2010); Males per 100 females: 99.0 (2010); Marriage status: 15.5% never married, 68.2% now married, 8.8% widowed, 7.5% divorced (2006-2010 5-year est.); Foreign born: 0.0% (2006-2010 5-year est.); Ancestry (includes multiple ancestries): 29.4% Polish, 19.8% Irish, 15.8% Slovak, 11.3% English, 11.3% Italian (2006-2010 5-year est.).
Economy: Employment by occupation: 13.2% management, 3.1% professional, 10.1% services, 1.6% sales, 7.4% farming, 21.7% construction, 7.4% production (2006-2010 5-year est.).
Income: Per capita income: $18,227 (2006-2010 5-year est.); Median household income: $41,216 (2006-2010 5-year est.); Average household income: $45,793 (2006-2010 5-year est.); Percent of households with income of $100,000 or more: 1.9% (2006-2010 5-year est.); Poverty rate: 28.9% (2006-2010 5-year est.).
Education: Percent of population age 25 and over with: High school diploma (including GED) or higher: 87.1% (2006-2010 5-year est.); Bachelor's degree or higher: 11.4% (2006-2010 5-year est.); Master's degree or higher: 7.6% (2006-2010 5-year est.).
Housing: Homeownership rate: 85.9% (2010); Median home value: $111,800 (2006-2010 5-year est.); Median contract rent: n/a per month (2006-2010 5-year est.); Median year structure built: 1965 (2006-2010 5-year est.).
Transportation: Commute to work: 98.4% car, 0.0% public transportation, 0.0% walk, 0.0% work from home (2006-2010 5-year est.); Travel time to work: 7.4% less than 15 minutes, 58.9% 15 to 30 minutes, 17.1% 30 to 45 minutes, 0.0% 45 to 60 minutes, 16.7% 60 minutes or more (2006-2010 5-year est.)

SLOCUM (township). Covers a land area of 9.650 square miles and a water area of 0.368 square miles. Located at 41.14° N. Lat; 76.03° W. Long. Elevation is 1,145 feet.
Population: 1,159 (1990); 1,112 (2000); 1,115 (2010); Density: 115.5 persons per square mile (2010); Race: 99.1% White, 0.3% Black, 0.1% Asian, 0.1% American Indian/Alaska Native, 0.0% Native Hawaiian/Other Pacific Islander, 0.4% Other, 0.5% Hispanic of any race (2010); Average household size: 2.48 (2010); Median age: 44.9 (2010); Males per 100 females: 98.0 (2010); Marriage status: 26.5% never married, 60.0% now married, 5.4% widowed, 8.0% divorced (2006-2010 5-year est.); Foreign born: 0.0% (2006-2010 5-year est.); Ancestry (includes multiple ancestries): 36.3% German, 31.2% Polish, 12.4% Irish, 11.9% Italian, 9.5% English (2006-2010 5-year est.).
Economy: Single-family building permits issued: 0 (2011); Multi-family building permits issued: 0 (2011); Employment by occupation: 13.7% management, 0.6% professional, 9.8% services, 4.4% sales, 3.3% farming, 12.7% construction, 7.7% production (2006-2010 5-year est.).
Income: Per capita income: $25,269 (2006-2010 5-year est.); Median household income: $52,644 (2006-2010 5-year est.); Average household income: $58,710 (2006-2010 5-year est.); Percent of households with income of $100,000 or more: 14.0% (2006-2010 5-year est.); Poverty rate: 2.4% (2006-2010 5-year est.).
Education: Percent of population age 25 and over with: High school diploma (including GED) or higher: 89.0% (2006-2010 5-year est.); Bachelor's degree or higher: 20.1% (2006-2010 5-year est.); Master's degree or higher: 6.5% (2006-2010 5-year est.).

Housing: Homeownership rate: 89.1% (2010); Median home value: $147,600 (2006-2010 5-year est.); Median contract rent: $406 per month (2006-2010 5-year est.); Median year structure built: 1968 (2006-2010 5-year est.).

Transportation: Commute to work: 97.3% car, 0.0% public transportation, 0.0% walk, 1.4% work from home (2006-2010 5-year est.); Travel time to work: 15.1% less than 15 minutes, 51.9% 15 to 30 minutes, 27.8% 30 to 45 minutes, 2.2% 45 to 60 minutes, 3.1% 60 minutes or more (2006-2010 5-year est.).

Additional Information Contacts

South Valley Chamber of Commerce . . . . (570) 735-6990
http://www.southvalleychamber.com

SUGAR NOTCH (borough). Covers a land area of 1.081 square miles and a water area of 0 square miles. Located at 41.19° N. Lat; 75.93° W. Long. Elevation is 719 feet.

History: Incorporated 1867.

Population: 1,115 (1990); 1,023 (2000); 989 (2010); Density: 914.9 persons per square mile (2010); Race: 98.0% White, 0.3% Black, 0.1% Asian, 0.2% American Indian/Alaska Native, 0.0% Native Hawaiian/Other Pacific Islander, 1.4% Other, 2.1% Hispanic of any race (2010); Average household size: 2.41 (2010); Median age: 40.7 (2010); Males per 100 females: 106.0 (2010); Marriage status: 38.6% never married, 43.2% now married, 7.8% widowed, 10.4% divorced (2006-2010 5-year est.); Foreign born: 1.0% (2006-2010 5-year est.); Ancestry (includes multiple ancestries): 36.8% Polish, 35.4% Irish, 13.8% German, 13.1% Italian, 6.2% Welsh (2006-2010 5-year est.).

Economy: Single-family building permits issued: 0 (2011); Multi-family building permits issued: 0 (2011); Employment by occupation: 4.5% management, 1.1% professional, 9.2% services, 24.4% sales, 8.5% farming, 9.0% construction, 6.8% production (2006-2010 5-year est.).

Income: Per capita income: $22,516 (2006-2010 5-year est.); Median household income: $40,313 (2006-2010 5-year est.); Average household income: $57,542 (2006-2010 5-year est.); Percent of households with income of $100,000 or more: 11.1% (2006-2010 5-year est.); Poverty rate: 16.1% (2006-2010 5-year est.).

Education: Percent of population age 25 and over with: High school diploma (including GED) or higher: 83.9% (2006-2010 5-year est.); Bachelor's degree or higher: 17.3% (2006-2010 5-year est.); Master's degree or higher: 5.5% (2006-2010 5-year est.).

Housing: Homeownership rate: 70.2% (2010); Median home value: $77,700 (2006-2010 5-year est.); Median contract rent: $431 per month (2006-2010 5-year est.); Median year structure built: before 1940 (2006-2010 5-year est.).

Safety: Violent crime rate: 0.0 per 10,000 population; Property crime rate: 30.2 per 10,000 population (2011).

Transportation: Commute to work: 93.6% car, 0.0% public transportation, 4.4% walk, 0.0% work from home (2006-2010 5-year est.); Travel time to work: 36.5% less than 15 minutes, 42.3% 15 to 30 minutes, 12.9% 30 to 45 minutes, 5.2% 45 to 60 minutes, 3.1% 60 minutes or more (2006-2010 5-year est.)

SUGARLOAF (township). Aka Tomhicken. Covers a land area of 22.454 square miles and a water area of 0.016 square miles. Located at 41.00° N. Lat; 76.09° W. Long.

Population: 3,553 (1990); 3,652 (2000); 4,211 (2010); Density: 187.5 persons per square mile (2010); Race: 95.1% White, 1.7% Black, 1.5% Asian, 0.0% American Indian/Alaska Native, 0.0% Native Hawaiian/Other Pacific Islander, 1.7% Other, 2.8% Hispanic of any race (2010); Average household size: 2.51 (2010); Median age: 42.3 (2010); Males per 100 females: 101.9 (2010); Marriage status: 41.0% never married, 47.3% now married, 6.9% widowed, 4.8% divorced (2006-2010 5-year est.); Foreign born: 2.4% (2006-2010 5-year est.); Ancestry (includes multiple ancestries): 25.3% German, 22.7% Italian, 17.1% Irish, 16.2% Polish, 10.0% Slovak (2006-2010 5-year est.).

Economy: Single-family building permits issued: 3 (2011); Multi-family building permits issued: 0 (2011); Employment by occupation: 8.8% management, 1.7% professional, 9.9% services, 15.0% sales, 5.3% farming, 14.1% construction, 8.1% production (2006-2010 5-year est.).

Income: Per capita income: $22,798 (2006-2010 5-year est.); Median household income: $58,468 (2006-2010 5-year est.); Average household income: $71,159 (2006-2010 5-year est.); Percent of households with income of $100,000 or more: 22.2% (2006-2010 5-year est.); Poverty rate: 7.0% (2006-2010 5-year est.).

Education: Percent of population age 25 and over with: High school diploma (including GED) or higher: 92.6% (2006-2010 5-year est.); Bachelor's degree or higher: 31.0% (2006-2010 5-year est.); Master's degree or higher: 14.9% (2006-2010 5-year est.).

School District(s)

Hazleton Area SD (PK-12)
   2010-11 Enrollment: 10,301 . . . . (570) 459-3111

Housing: Homeownership rate: 89.6% (2010); Median home value: $181,600 (2006-2010 5-year est.); Median contract rent: $950 per month (2006-2010 5-year est.); Median year structure built: 1974 (2006-2010 5-year est.).

Safety: Violent crime rate: 2.4 per 10,000 population; Property crime rate: 0.0 per 10,000 population (2011).

Transportation: Commute to work: 89.8% car, 0.0% public transportation, 5.2% walk, 4.5% work from home (2006-2010 5-year est.); Travel time to work: 37.0% less than 15 minutes, 44.7% 15 to 30 minutes, 13.6% 30 to 45 minutes, 3.0% 45 to 60 minutes, 1.6% 60 minutes or more (2006-2010 5-year est.)

Additional Information Contacts

Greater Hazleton Chamber of Commerce . . . . (570) 455-1509
http://www.hazletonchamber.org

SWEET VALLEY (unincorporated postal area)
Zip Code: 18656

Covers a land area of 52.100 square miles and a water area of 0.538 square miles. Located at 41.33° N. Lat; 76.18° W. Long. Population: 2,195 (2010); Density: 42.1 persons per square mile (2010); Race: 98.0% White, 0.1% Black, 0.4% Asian, 0.1% American Indian/Alaska Native, 0.0% Native Hawaiian/Other Pacific Islander, 1.4% Other, 1.7% Hispanic of any race (2010); Average household size: 2.56 (2010); Median age: 42.1 (2010); Males per 100 females: 102.9 (2010); Homeownership rate: 86.8% (2010)

SWOYERSVILLE (borough). Aka Swoyerville. Covers a land area of 2.125 square miles and a water area of 0 square miles. Located at 41.30° N. Lat; 75.88° W. Long. Elevation is 554 feet.

History: Incorporated 1888.

Population: 5,630 (1990); 5,157 (2000); 5,062 (2010); Density: 2,382.4 persons per square mile (2010); Race: 98.2% White, 0.5% Black, 0.3% Asian, 0.1% American Indian/Alaska Native, 0.0% Native Hawaiian/Other Pacific Islander, 0.9% Other, 1.0% Hispanic of any race (2010); Average household size: 2.24 (2010); Median age: 45.6 (2010); Males per 100 females: 92.8 (2010); Marriage status: 33.8% never married, 41.8% now married, 11.5% widowed, 13.0% divorced (2006-2010 5-year est.); Foreign born: 0.9% (2006-2010 5-year est.); Ancestry (includes multiple ancestries): 36.9% Polish, 18.5% Irish, 14.5% Italian, 12.7% Slovak, 9.9% German (2006-2010 5-year est.).

Economy: Single-family building permits issued: 0 (2011); Multi-family building permits issued: 4 (2011); Employment by occupation: 10.5% management, 2.4% professional, 8.3% services, 17.7% sales, 2.5% farming, 7.8% construction, 5.5% production (2006-2010 5-year est.).

Income: Per capita income: $25,438 (2006-2010 5-year est.); Median household income: $49,063 (2006-2010 5-year est.); Average household income: $56,135 (2006-2010 5-year est.); Percent of households with income of $100,000 or more: 14.0% (2006-2010 5-year est.); Poverty rate: 9.0% (2006-2010 5-year est.).

Education: Percent of population age 25 and over with: High school diploma (including GED) or higher: 88.3% (2006-2010 5-year est.); Bachelor's degree or higher: 22.2% (2006-2010 5-year est.); Master's degree or higher: 7.5% (2006-2010 5-year est.).

Housing: Homeownership rate: 78.0% (2010); Median home value: $107,100 (2006-2010 5-year est.); Median contract rent: $379 per month (2006-2010 5-year est.); Median year structure built: 1944 (2006-2010 5-year est.).

Safety: Violent crime rate: 9.8 per 10,000 population; Property crime rate: 204.8 per 10,000 population (2011).

Transportation: Commute to work: 98.2% car, 1.4% public transportation, 0.0% walk, 0.4% work from home (2006-2010 5-year est.); Travel time to work: 30.1% less than 15 minutes, 51.8% 15 to 30 minutes, 7.8% 30 to 45 minutes, 2.0% 45 to 60 minutes, 8.3% 60 minutes or more (2006-2010 5-year est.)

Additional Information Contacts

Borough of Swoyersville . . . . (570) 288-6581
http://www.luzernecounty.org/living/municipalities/swoyersville_borough

Greater Pittston Chamber of Commerce . . . . (570) 655-1424
http://www.pittstonchamber.org

SYBERTSVILLE (unincorporated postal area)
Zip Code: 18251

Covers a land area of 0.106 square miles and a water area of 0 square miles. Located at 41.00° N. Lat; 76.07° W. Long. Elevation is 899 feet. Population: 46 (2010); Density: 433.2 persons per square mile (2010); Race: 100.0% White, 0.0% Black, 0.0% Asian, 0.0% American Indian/Alaska Native, 0.0% Native Hawaiian/Other Pacific Islander, 0.0% Other, 2.2% Hispanic of any race (2010); Average household size: 2.09 (2010); Median age: 43.5 (2010); Males per 100 females: 91.7 (2010); Homeownership rate: 54.5% (2010)

TRUCKSVILLE (CDP). Covers a land area of 1.737 square miles and a water area of 0 square miles. Located at 41.31° N. Lat; 75.93° W. Long. Elevation is 883 feet.
Population: n/a (1990); n/a (2000); 2,152 (2010); Density: 1,238.6 persons per square mile (2010); Race: 97.4% White, 0.8% Black, 0.5% Asian, 0.0% American Indian/Alaska Native, 0.0% Native Hawaiian/Other Pacific Islander, 1.3% Other, 0.7% Hispanic of any race (2010); Average household size: 2.44 (2010); Median age: 43.2 (2010); Males per 100 females: 92.5 (2010); Marriage status: 19.6% never married, 67.9% now married, 6.2% widowed, 6.3% divorced (2006-2010 5-year est.); Foreign born: 2.1% (2006-2010 5-year est.); Ancestry (includes multiple ancestries): 29.9% Polish, 19.2% German, 14.3% Irish, 13.8% Italian, 9.2% Welsh (2006-2010 5-year est.).
Economy: Employment by occupation: 10.4% management, 4.1% professional, 7.8% services, 18.0% sales, 4.0% farming, 6.4% construction, 0.0% production (2006-2010 5-year est.).
Income: Per capita income: $39,644 (2006-2010 5-year est.); Median household income: $67,991 (2006-2010 5-year est.); Average household income: $93,699 (2006-2010 5-year est.); Percent of households with income of $100,000 or more: 13.8% (2006-2010 5-year est.); Poverty rate: 3.1% (2006-2010 5-year est.).
Education: Percent of population age 25 and over with: High school diploma (including GED) or higher: 93.9% (2006-2010 5-year est.); Bachelor's degree or higher: 38.4% (2006-2010 5-year est.); Master's degree or higher: 14.6% (2006-2010 5-year est.).
Housing: Homeownership rate: 78.6% (2010); Median home value: $150,300 (2006-2010 5-year est.); Median contract rent: $352 per month (2006-2010 5-year est.); Median year structure built: 1956 (2006-2010 5-year est.).
Transportation: Commute to work: 96.8% car, 0.0% public transportation, 2.0% walk, 0.0% work from home (2006-2010 5-year est.); Travel time to work: 21.5% less than 15 minutes, 57.7% 15 to 30 minutes, 14.1% 30 to 45 minutes, 0.0% 45 to 60 minutes, 6.7% 60 minutes or more (2006-2010 5-year est.)

UNION (township). Covers a land area of 19.679 square miles and a water area of 0.377 square miles. Located at 41.20° N. Lat; 76.15° W. Long.
Population: 1,954 (1990); 2,100 (2000); 2,042 (2010); Density: 103.8 persons per square mile (2010); Race: 98.3% White, 0.3% Black, 0.3% Asian, 0.0% American Indian/Alaska Native, 0.0% Native Hawaiian/Other Pacific Islander, 1.1% Other, 0.8% Hispanic of any race (2010); Average household size: 2.55 (2010); Median age: 44.7 (2010); Males per 100 females: 98.8 (2010); Marriage status: 24.2% never married, 63.3% now married, 7.6% widowed, 4.9% divorced (2006-2010 5-year est.); Foreign born: 0.5% (2006-2010 5-year est.); Ancestry (includes multiple ancestries): 29.5% German, 21.5% Irish, 18.2% Polish, 11.9% English, 11.6% Italian (2006-2010 5-year est.).
Economy: Employment by occupation: 5.8% management, 6.2% professional, 11.6% services, 15.1% sales, 2.8% farming, 9.9% construction, 8.0% production (2006-2010 5-year est.).
Income: Per capita income: $23,421 (2006-2010 5-year est.); Median household income: $62,917 (2006-2010 5-year est.); Average household income: $64,552 (2006-2010 5-year est.); Percent of households with income of $100,000 or more: 17.9% (2006-2010 5-year est.); Poverty rate: 11.0% (2006-2010 5-year est.).
Education: Percent of population age 25 and over with: High school diploma (including GED) or higher: 88.0% (2006-2010 5-year est.); Bachelor's degree or higher: 15.0% (2006-2010 5-year est.); Master's degree or higher: 4.7% (2006-2010 5-year est.).

Housing: Homeownership rate: 88.9% (2010); Median home value: $125,400 (2006-2010 5-year est.); Median contract rent: $505 per month (2006-2010 5-year est.); Median year structure built: 1973 (2006-2010 5-year est.).
Transportation: Commute to work: 97.8% car, 0.0% public transportation, 1.5% walk, 0.7% work from home (2006-2010 5-year est.); Travel time to work: 20.6% less than 15 minutes, 31.2% 15 to 30 minutes, 32.4% 30 to 45 minutes, 6.6% 45 to 60 minutes, 9.3% 60 minutes or more (2006-2010 5-year est.)
Additional Information Contacts
Greater Pittston Chamber of Commerce . . . . (570) 655-1424
http://www.pittstonchamber.org

UPPER EXETER (CDP). Covers a land area of 1.966 square miles and a water area of 0.092 square miles. Located at 41.40° N. Lat; 75.85° W. Long. Elevation is 594 feet.
Population: n/a (1990); n/a (2000); 707 (2010); Density: 359.5 persons per square mile (2010); Race: 99.6% White, 0.3% Black, 0.0% Asian, 0.0% American Indian/Alaska Native, 0.0% Native Hawaiian/Other Pacific Islander, 0.1% Other, 1.0% Hispanic of any race (2010); Average household size: 2.81 (2010); Median age: 46.2 (2010); Males per 100 females: 103.2 (2010); Marriage status: 19.5% never married, 75.5% now married, 5.0% widowed, 0.0% divorced (2006-2010 5-year est.); Foreign born: 0.9% (2006-2010 5-year est.); Ancestry (includes multiple ancestries): 28.6% Polish, 19.4% Irish, 18.0% Italian, 14.2% German, 12.5% American (2006-2010 5-year est.).
Economy: Employment by occupation: 7.1% management, 3.9% professional, 0.0% services, 15.9% sales, 3.0% farming, 14.4% construction, 10.5% production (2006-2010 5-year est.).
Income: Per capita income: $27,292 (2006-2010 5-year est.); Median household income: $73,000 (2006-2010 5-year est.); Average household income: $84,718 (2006-2010 5-year est.); Percent of households with income of $100,000 or more: 27.9% (2006-2010 5-year est.); Poverty rate: 1.5% (2006-2010 5-year est.).
Education: Percent of population age 25 and over with: High school diploma (including GED) or higher: 92.3% (2006-2010 5-year est.); Bachelor's degree or higher: 16.2% (2006-2010 5-year est.); Master's degree or higher: 5.0% (2006-2010 5-year est.).
Housing: Homeownership rate: 94.8% (2010); Median home value: $163,100 (2006-2010 5-year est.); Median contract rent: n/a per month (2006-2010 5-year est.); Median year structure built: 1973 (2006-2010 5-year est.).
Transportation: Commute to work: 98.1% car, 0.0% public transportation, 0.0% walk, 1.9% work from home (2006-2010 5-year est.); Travel time to work: 13.6% less than 15 minutes, 25.2% 15 to 30 minutes, 51.6% 30 to 45 minutes, 2.8% 45 to 60 minutes, 6.8% 60 minutes or more (2006-2010 5-year est.)

WANAMIE (CDP). Covers a land area of 0.981 square miles and a water area of <.001 square miles. Located at 41.17° N. Lat; 76.04° W. Long. Elevation is 676 feet.
Population: n/a (1990); n/a (2000); 612 (2010); Density: 623.7 persons per square mile (2010); Race: 97.4% White, 0.7% Black, 0.5% Asian, 0.0% American Indian/Alaska Native, 0.0% Native Hawaiian/Other Pacific Islander, 1.4% Other, 1.6% Hispanic of any race (2010); Average household size: 2.53 (2010); Median age: 41.4 (2010); Males per 100 females: 90.7 (2010); Marriage status: 40.1% never married, 43.4% now married, 2.5% widowed, 14.0% divorced (2006-2010 5-year est.); Foreign born: 0.0% (2006-2010 5-year est.); Ancestry (includes multiple ancestries): 36.7% Polish, 30.7% Irish, 24.3% German, 16.7% Italian, 13.2% American (2006-2010 5-year est.).
Economy: Employment by occupation: 5.2% management, 0.0% professional, 13.6% services, 16.7% sales, 11.7% farming, 11.3% construction, 8.0% production (2006-2010 5-year est.).
Income: Per capita income: $22,594 (2006-2010 5-year est.); Median household income: $58,036 (2006-2010 5-year est.); Average household income: $59,924 (2006-2010 5-year est.); Percent of households with income of $100,000 or more: 12.6% (2006-2010 5-year est.); Poverty rate: 3.5% (2006-2010 5-year est.).
Education: Percent of population age 25 and over with: High school diploma (including GED) or higher: 88.0% (2006-2010 5-year est.); Bachelor's degree or higher: 15.4% (2006-2010 5-year est.); Master's degree or higher: 2.0% (2006-2010 5-year est.).
Housing: Homeownership rate: 81.8% (2010); Median home value: $58,800 (2006-2010 5-year est.); Median contract rent: $500 per month

(2006-2010 5-year est.); Median year structure built: before 1940 (2006-2010 5-year est.).

Transportation: Commute to work: 100.0% car, 0.0% public transportation, 0.0% walk, 0.0% work from home (2006-2010 5-year est.); Travel time to work: 20.3% less than 15 minutes, 55.9% 15 to 30 minutes, 15.7% 30 to 45 minutes, 2.4% 45 to 60 minutes, 5.7% 60 minutes or more (2006-2010 5-year est.)

WAPWALLOPEN (unincorporated postal area)

Zip Code: 18660

Covers a land area of 42.492 square miles and a water area of 1.520 square miles. Located at 41.09° N. Lat; 76.06° W. Long. Elevation is 541 feet. Population: 3,702 (2010); Density: 87.1 persons per square mile (2010); Race: 98.1% White, 0.3% Black, 0.3% Asian, 0.1% American Indian/Alaska Native, 0.1% Native Hawaiian/Other Pacific Islander, 1.1% Other, 0.8% Hispanic of any race (2010); Average household size: 2.54 (2010); Median age: 44.3 (2010); Males per 100 females: 101.9 (2010); Homeownership rate: 88.4% (2010)

WARRIOR RUN (borough). Aka Peely. Covers a land area of 0.749 square miles and a water area of 0 square miles. Located at 41.19° N. Lat; 75.95° W. Long. Elevation is 709 feet.

History: Incorporated 1895.

Population: 656 (1990); 624 (2000); 584 (2010); Density: 779.9 persons per square mile (2010); Race: 97.4% White, 0.0% Black, 0.2% Asian, 0.0% American Indian/Alaska Native, 0.0% Native Hawaiian/Other Pacific Islander, 2.4% Other, 1.5% Hispanic of any race (2010); Average household size: 2.45 (2010); Median age: 41.2 (2010); Males per 100 females: 91.5 (2010); Marriage status: 35.6% never married, 44.0% now married, 10.9% widowed, 9.5% divorced (2006-2010 5-year est.); Foreign born: 0.8% (2006-2010 5-year est.); Ancestry (includes multiple ancestries): 39.1% Polish, 24.1% Irish, 17.6% German, 10.6% Welsh, 10.6% Italian (2006-2010 5-year est.).

Economy: Employment by occupation: 4.3% management, 2.0% professional, 13.1% services, 19.0% sales, 2.3% farming, 12.8% construction, 11.8% production (2006-2010 5-year est.).

Income: Per capita income: $18,417 (2006-2010 5-year est.); Median household income: $42,000 (2006-2010 5-year est.); Average household income: $46,734 (2006-2010 5-year est.); Percent of households with income of $100,000 or more: 4.9% (2006-2010 5-year est.); Poverty rate: 6.9% (2006-2010 5-year est.).

Education: Percent of population age 25 and over with: High school diploma (including GED) or higher: 86.2% (2006-2010 5-year est.); Bachelor's degree or higher: 8.0% (2006-2010 5-year est.); Master's degree or higher: 1.1% (2006-2010 5-year est.).

Housing: Homeownership rate: 75.2% (2010); Median home value: $77,000 (2006-2010 5-year est.); Median contract rent: $425 per month (2006-2010 5-year est.); Median year structure built: before 1940 (2006-2010 5-year est.).

Transportation: Commute to work: 93.8% car, 1.0% public transportation, 2.0% walk, 3.3% work from home (2006-2010 5-year est.); Travel time to work: 37.7% less than 15 minutes, 44.4% 15 to 30 minutes, 11.8% 30 to 45 minutes, 1.7% 45 to 60 minutes, 4.4% 60 minutes or more (2006-2010 5-year est.)

WEST HAZLETON (borough). Covers a land area of 1.499 square miles and a water area of 0 square miles. Located at 40.97° N. Lat; 76.01° W. Long. Elevation is 1,699 feet.

Population: 4,125 (1990); 3,542 (2000); 4,594 (2010); Density: 3,065.1 persons per square mile (2010); Race: 71.9% White, 3.1% Black, 0.3% Asian, 0.4% American Indian/Alaska Native, 0.1% Native Hawaiian/Other Pacific Islander, 24.2% Other, 35.4% Hispanic of any race (2010); Average household size: 2.55 (2010); Median age: 35.9 (2010); Males per 100 females: 96.8 (2010); Marriage status: 35.5% never married, 46.3% now married, 8.6% widowed, 9.5% divorced (2006-2010 5-year est.); Foreign born: 22.5% (2006-2010 5-year est.); Ancestry (includes multiple ancestries): 17.1% Italian, 13.9% Polish, 11.5% Irish, 10.3% German, 5.2% Slovak (2006-2010 5-year est.).

Economy: Single-family building permits issued: 0 (2011); Multi-family building permits issued: 0 (2011); Employment by occupation: 5.8% management, 0.4% professional, 10.4% services, 17.1% sales, 3.9% farming, 6.7% construction, 19.1% production (2006-2010 5-year est.).

Income: Per capita income: $14,809 (2006-2010 5-year est.); Median household income: $35,946 (2006-2010 5-year est.); Average household income: $37,914 (2006-2010 5-year est.); Percent of households with income of $100,000 or more: 1.5% (2006-2010 5-year est.); Poverty rate: 28.0% (2006-2010 5-year est.).

Education: Percent of population age 25 and over with: High school diploma (including GED) or higher: 83.7% (2006-2010 5-year est.); Bachelor's degree or higher: 7.4% (2006-2010 5-year est.); Master's degree or higher: 2.2% (2006-2010 5-year est.).

School District(s)

Hazleton Area SD (PK-12)

    2010-11 Enrollment: 10,301 . . . . (570) 459-3111

Housing: Homeownership rate: 54.9% (2010); Median home value: $92,500 (2006-2010 5-year est.); Median contract rent: $473 per month (2006-2010 5-year est.); Median year structure built: 1944 (2006-2010 5-year est.).

Safety: Violent crime rate: 54.2 per 10,000 population; Property crime rate: 423.1 per 10,000 population (2011).

Transportation: Commute to work: 88.8% car, 0.6% public transportation, 9.5% walk, 0.0% work from home (2006-2010 5-year est.); Travel time to work: 58.8% less than 15 minutes, 28.3% 15 to 30 minutes, 7.0% 30 to 45 minutes, 2.0% 45 to 60 minutes, 4.0% 60 minutes or more (2006-2010 5-year est.)

Additional Information Contacts

Greater Hazleton Chamber of Commerce . . . . (570) 455-1509

    http://www.hazletonchamber.org

WEST NANTICOKE (CDP). Covers a land area of 0.591 square miles and a water area of 0.123 square miles. Located at 41.22° N. Lat; 76.01° W. Long. Elevation is 522 feet.

Population: n/a (1990); n/a (2000); 749 (2010); Density: 1,266.9 persons per square mile (2010); Race: 97.5% White, 0.3% Black, 0.0% Asian, 0.1% American Indian/Alaska Native, 0.0% Native Hawaiian/Other Pacific Islander, 2.1% Other, 1.9% Hispanic of any race (2010); Average household size: 2.28 (2010); Median age: 45.2 (2010); Males per 100 females: 96.6 (2010); Marriage status: 26.9% never married, 47.2% now married, 17.3% widowed, 8.5% divorced (2006-2010 5-year est.); Foreign born: 0.0% (2006-2010 5-year est.); Ancestry (includes multiple ancestries): 42.1% Polish, 31.8% German, 19.9% Irish, 8.8% Slovak, 5.0% American (2006-2010 5-year est.).

Economy: Employment by occupation: 6.7% management, 2.4% professional, 4.7% services, 26.5% sales, 6.3% farming, 7.9% construction, 2.0% production (2006-2010 5-year est.).

Income: Per capita income: $25,209 (2006-2010 5-year est.); Median household income: $46,500 (2006-2010 5-year est.); Average household income: $53,018 (2006-2010 5-year est.); Percent of households with income of $100,000 or more: 11.4% (2006-2010 5-year est.); Poverty rate: 6.4% (2006-2010 5-year est.).

Education: Percent of population age 25 and over with: High school diploma (including GED) or higher: 85.2% (2006-2010 5-year est.); Bachelor's degree or higher: 17.5% (2006-2010 5-year est.); Master's degree or higher: 5.2% (2006-2010 5-year est.).

Housing: Homeownership rate: 79.5% (2010); Median home value: $83,500 (2006-2010 5-year est.); Median contract rent: $420 per month (2006-2010 5-year est.); Median year structure built: before 1940 (2006-2010 5-year est.).

Transportation: Commute to work: 98.0% car, 0.0% public transportation, 0.0% walk, 2.0% work from home (2006-2010 5-year est.); Travel time to work: 24.3% less than 15 minutes, 44.4% 15 to 30 minutes, 21.8% 30 to 45 minutes, 2.9% 45 to 60 minutes, 6.6% 60 minutes or more (2006-2010 5-year est.)

WEST PITTSTON (borough). Covers a land area of 0.820 square miles and a water area of 0.146 square miles. Located at 41.33° N. Lat; 75.80° W. Long. Elevation is 545 feet.

History: Incorporated 1857.

Population: 5,590 (1990); 5,072 (2000); 4,868 (2010); Density: 5,937.2 persons per square mile (2010); Race: 97.3% White, 0.8% Black, 0.4% Asian, 0.0% American Indian/Alaska Native, 0.0% Native Hawaiian/Other Pacific Islander, 1.5% Other, 1.5% Hispanic of any race (2010); Average household size: 2.22 (2010); Median age: 43.8 (2010); Males per 100 females: 88.2 (2010); Marriage status: 28.6% never married, 49.5% now married, 9.3% widowed, 12.6% divorced (2006-2010 5-year est.); Foreign born: 1.0% (2006-2010 5-year est.); Ancestry (includes multiple ancestries): 35.5% Italian, 23.6% Irish, 22.3% Polish, 18.2% German, 9.0% English (2006-2010 5-year est.).

Economy: Single-family building permits issued: 1 (2011); Multi-family building permits issued: 0 (2011); Employment by occupation: 9.0%

management, 4.1% professional, 9.4% services, 17.5% sales, 4.6% farming, 7.4% construction, 7.2% production (2006-2010 5-year est.).
Income: Per capita income: $31,100 (2006-2010 5-year est.); Median household income: $45,722 (2006-2010 5-year est.); Average household income: $64,698 (2006-2010 5-year est.); Percent of households with income of $100,000 or more: 16.2% (2006-2010 5-year est.); Poverty rate: 6.2% (2006-2010 5-year est.).
Education: Percent of population age 25 and over with: High school diploma (including GED) or higher: 91.4% (2006-2010 5-year est.); Bachelor's degree or higher: 25.1% (2006-2010 5-year est.); Master's degree or higher: 10.3% (2006-2010 5-year est.).

School District(s)

Wyoming Area SD (KG-12)
   2010-11 Enrollment: 2,536 . . . . (570) 655-3733
Housing: Homeownership rate: 62.1% (2010); Median home value: $124,700 (2006-2010 5-year est.); Median contract rent: $475 per month (2006-2010 5-year est.); Median year structure built: before 1940 (2006-2010 5-year est.).
Safety: Violent crime rate: 16.4 per 10,000 population; Property crime rate: 325.6 per 10,000 population (2011).
Transportation: Commute to work: 90.6% car, 0.0% public transportation, 0.7% walk, 6.0% work from home (2006-2010 5-year est.); Travel time to work: 37.2% less than 15 minutes, 47.8% 15 to 30 minutes, 8.7% 30 to 45 minutes, 3.0% 45 to 60 minutes, 3.3% 60 minutes or more (2006-2010 5-year est.)

Additional Information Contacts

Borough of West Pittston . . . . (570) 655-7782
   http://www.luzernecounty.org/living/municipalities/west_pittston_borough
Greater Pittston Chamber of Commerce . . . . (570) 655-1424
   http://www.pittstonchamber.org

WEST WYOMING (borough). Covers a land area of 3.619 square miles and a water area of 0 square miles. Located at 41.32° N. Lat; 75.86° W. Long. Elevation is 594 feet.

Population: 3,117 (1990); 2,833 (2000); 2,725 (2010); Density: 752.9 persons per square mile (2010); Race: 98.8% White, 0.3% Black, 0.1% Asian, 0.0% American Indian/Alaska Native, 0.2% Native Hawaiian/Other Pacific Islander, 0.6% Other, 0.6% Hispanic of any race (2010); Average household size: 2.33 (2010); Median age: 46.0 (2010); Males per 100 females: 91.6 (2010); Marriage status: 19.9% never married, 61.3% now married, 8.8% widowed, 9.9% divorced (2006-2010 5-year est.); Foreign born: 0.5% (2006-2010 5-year est.); Ancestry (includes multiple ancestries): 29.1% Italian, 28.7% Polish, 18.0% Irish, 13.1% German, 11.3% Slovak (2006-2010 5-year est.).
Economy: Single-family building permits issued: 1 (2011); Multi-family building permits issued: 0 (2011); Employment by occupation: 8.8% management, 1.4% professional, 4.9% services, 25.8% sales, 2.4% farming, 9.9% construction, 5.5% production (2006-2010 5-year est.).
Income: Per capita income: $28,244 (2006-2010 5-year est.); Median household income: $54,861 (2006-2010 5-year est.); Average household income: $65,651 (2006-2010 5-year est.); Percent of households with income of $100,000 or more: 21.5% (2006-2010 5-year est.); Poverty rate: 6.7% (2006-2010 5-year est.).
Education: Percent of population age 25 and over with: High school diploma (including GED) or higher: 92.0% (2006-2010 5-year est.); Bachelor's degree or higher: 25.3% (2006-2010 5-year est.); Master's degree or higher: 5.7% (2006-2010 5-year est.).
Housing: Homeownership rate: 83.1% (2010); Median home value: $120,000 (2006-2010 5-year est.); Median contract rent: $447 per month (2006-2010 5-year est.); Median year structure built: 1953 (2006-2010 5-year est.).
Transportation: Commute to work: 97.9% car, 0.0% public transportation, 0.6% walk, 1.5% work from home (2006-2010 5-year est.); Travel time to work: 39.5% less than 15 minutes, 42.8% 15 to 30 minutes, 12.2% 30 to 45 minutes, 2.3% 45 to 60 minutes, 3.1% 60 minutes or more (2006-2010 5-year est.)

Additional Information Contacts

Wyoming County Chamber of Commerce . . . . (570) 836-7755
   http://www.wyccc.com

WESTON (CDP). Covers a land area of 0.424 square miles and a water area of 0 square miles. Located at 40.94° N. Lat; 76.14° W. Long. Elevation is 1,135 feet.

Population: n/a (1990); n/a (2000); 321 (2010); Density: 757.3 persons per square mile (2010); Race: 96.9% White, 0.6% Black, 0.0% Asian,

0.3% American Indian/Alaska Native, 0.0% Native Hawaiian/Other Pacific Islander, 2.2% Other, 0.3% Hispanic of any race (2010); Average household size: 2.24 (2010); Median age: 47.8 (2010); Males per 100 females: 108.4 (2010); Marriage status: 10.9% never married, 72.6% now married, 13.5% widowed, 2.9% divorced (2006-2010 5-year est.); Foreign born: 0.0% (2006-2010 5-year est.); Ancestry (includes multiple ancestries): 42.9% German, 38.9% Irish, 14.9% Italian, 14.6% Slovak, 13.1% Lithuanian (2006-2010 5-year est.).
Economy: Employment by occupation: 0.0% management, 0.0% professional, 8.9% services, 28.5% sales, 0.0% farming, 12.2% construction, 0.0% production (2006-2010 5-year est.).
Income: Per capita income: $23,992 (2006-2010 5-year est.); Median household income: $43,929 (2006-2010 5-year est.); Average household income: $58,831 (2006-2010 5-year est.); Percent of households with income of $100,000 or more: 5.7% (2006-2010 5-year est.); Poverty rate: 24.3% (2006-2010 5-year est.).
Education: Percent of population age 25 and over with: High school diploma (including GED) or higher: 81.8% (2006-2010 5-year est.); Bachelor's degree or higher: 0.0% (2006-2010 5-year est.); Master's degree or higher: 0.0% (2006-2010 5-year est.).
Housing: Homeownership rate: 80.5% (2010); Median home value: $86,000 (2006-2010 5-year est.); Median contract rent: n/a per month (2006-2010 5-year est.); Median year structure built: before 1940 (2006-2010 5-year est.).
Transportation: Commute to work: 91.1% car, 0.0% public transportation, 8.9% walk, 0.0% work from home (2006-2010 5-year est.); Travel time to work: 16.3% less than 15 minutes, 50.4% 15 to 30 minutes, 26.8% 30 to 45 minutes, 0.0% 45 to 60 minutes, 6.5% 60 minutes or more (2006-2010 5-year est.)

WHITE HAVEN (borough). Covers a land area of 1.219 square miles and a water area of 0.027 square miles. Located at 41.06° N. Lat; 75.79° W. Long. Elevation is 1,148 feet.

History: Incorporated c.1853.
Population: 1,132 (1990); 1,182 (2000); 1,097 (2010); Density: 900.1 persons per square mile (2010); Race: 97.6% White, 0.5% Black, 0.7% Asian, 0.3% American Indian/Alaska Native, 0.0% Native Hawaiian/Other Pacific Islander, 0.9% Other, 3.2% Hispanic of any race (2010); Average household size: 2.34 (2010); Median age: 42.0 (2010); Males per 100 females: 85.3 (2010); Marriage status: 20.9% never married, 60.5% now married, 8.6% widowed, 10.0% divorced (2006-2010 5-year est.); Foreign born: 2.6% (2006-2010 5-year est.); Ancestry (includes multiple ancestries): 27.8% German, 21.6% Polish, 17.6% Irish, 11.8% Italian, 8.1% English (2006-2010 5-year est.).
Economy: Single-family building permits issued: 2 (2011); Multi-family building permits issued: 0 (2011); Employment by occupation: 6.9% management, 3.6% professional, 9.9% services, 20.9% sales, 7.3% farming, 9.5% construction, 6.7% production (2006-2010 5-year est.).
Income: Per capita income: $23,217 (2006-2010 5-year est.); Median household income: $44,821 (2006-2010 5-year est.); Average household income: $52,906 (2006-2010 5-year est.); Percent of households with income of $100,000 or more: 13.5% (2006-2010 5-year est.); Poverty rate: 8.6% (2006-2010 5-year est.).
Education: Percent of population age 25 and over with: High school diploma (including GED) or higher: 89.3% (2006-2010 5-year est.); Bachelor's degree or higher: 17.7% (2006-2010 5-year est.); Master's degree or higher: 5.7% (2006-2010 5-year est.).

School District(s)

Youth Forestry Camp #2 (07-12)
   2010-11 Enrollment: 30 . . . . (570) 443-7031
Housing: Homeownership rate: 76.2% (2010); Median home value: $107,600 (2006-2010 5-year est.); Median contract rent: $547 per month (2006-2010 5-year est.); Median year structure built: 1941 (2006-2010 5-year est.).
Safety: Violent crime rate: 9.1 per 10,000 population; Property crime rate: 54.5 per 10,000 population (2011).
Newspapers: The Herald (Local news; Circulation 70,000); Journal Valley Views (Local news; Circulation 6,500); Journal of the Pocono Plateau (Local news; Circulation 14,000); Journal-Mountaintop (Local news; Circulation 4,000); The White Haven Journal-Herald (Community news; Circulation 1,500)
Transportation: Commute to work: 92.3% car, 0.0% public transportation, 5.2% walk, 1.5% work from home (2006-2010 5-year est.); Travel time to work: 32.6% less than 15 minutes, 24.5% 15 to 30 minutes, 27.7% 30 to

45 minutes, 8.2% 45 to 60 minutes, 7.0% 60 minutes or more (2006-2010 5-year est.)

Additional Information Contacts

Greater White Haven Chamber of Commerce . . . . (800) 315-2621
   http://www.whitehavenchamber.org

WILKES-BARRE (city). County seat. Covers a land area of 6.980 square miles and a water area of 0.329 square miles. Located at 41.25° N. Lat; 75.88° W. Long. Elevation is 535 feet.

History: Wilkes-Barre was a strategic point in the long conflict between Pennsylvania and Connecticut over the Wyoming Valley lands. In the summer of 1769 John Durkee, verteran of the French and Indian War, came to the Wyoming Valley with a small band of settlers from Connecticut. He built Fort Durkee and laid out Wilkes-Barre, naming it for two members of the British Parliament, John Wilkes and Colonel Isaac Barre, who were supporters of the American Colonies. After a long period of disagreement and confusion, Connecticut formally released all its claims in the valley about 1800. Wilkes-Barre was incorporated as a borough in 1806, and began a gradual change from a farming center to an industrial one. It was made a city in 1898.

Population: 47,444 (1990); 43,123 (2000); 41,498 (2010); Density: 5,945.0 persons per square mile (2010); Race: 79.2% White, 10.9% Black, 1.4% Asian, 0.3% American Indian/Alaska Native, 0.0% Native Hawaiian/Other Pacific Islander, 8.2% Other, 11.3% Hispanic of any race (2010); Average household size: 2.28 (2010); Median age: 36.5 (2010); Males per 100 females: 95.6 (2010); Marriage status: 44.5% never married, 36.5% now married, 9.3% widowed, 9.6% divorced (2006-2010 5-year est.); Foreign born: 4.6% (2006-2010 5-year est.); Ancestry (includes multiple ancestries): 21.8% Irish, 19.4% Polish, 17.8% German, 12.3% Italian, 5.6% Welsh (2006-2010 5-year est.).

Economy: Unemployment rate: 11.5% (August 2012); Total civilian labor force: 20,040 (August 2012); Single-family building permits issued: 1 (2011); Multi-family building permits issued: 0 (2011); Employment by occupation: 7.2% management, 1.9% professional, 14.5% services, 20.6% sales, 5.6% farming, 5.6% construction, 6.8% production (2006-2010 5-year est.).

Income: Per capita income: $16,712 (2006-2010 5-year est.); Median household income: $29,518 (2006-2010 5-year est.); Average household income: $39,379 (2006-2010 5-year est.); Percent of households with income of $100,000 or more: 6.0% (2006-2010 5-year est.); Poverty rate: 25.4% (2006-2010 5-year est.).

Taxes: Total city taxes per capita: $513 (2009); City property taxes per capita: $161 (2009).

Education: Percent of population age 25 and over with: High school diploma (including GED) or higher: 83.5% (2006-2010 5-year est.); Bachelor's degree or higher: 14.5% (2006-2010 5-year est.); Master's degree or higher: 4.7% (2006-2010 5-year est.).

School District(s)

Bear Creek Community CS (KG-08)
   2010-11 Enrollment: 420 . . . . (570) 820-4070
Wilkes-Barre Area CTC (09-12)
   2010-11 Enrollment: n/a . . . . (570) 822-4131
Wilkes-Barre Area SD (KG-12)
   2010-11 Enrollment: 6,997 . . . . (570) 826-7182
Wilkes-Barre Area SD (KG-12)
   2010-11 Enrollment: 6,997 . . . . (570) 826-7182

Four-year College(s)

King's College (Private, Not-for-profit, Roman Catholic)
   Fall 2010 Enrollment: 2,505 . . . . (570) 208-5900
   2011-12 Tuition: In-state $27,680; Out-of-state $27,680
Wilkes University (Private, Not-for-profit)
   Fall 2010 Enrollment: 4,671 . . . . (570) 408-5000
   2011-12 Tuition: In-state $28,210; Out-of-state $28,210

Vocational/Technical School(s)

CDE Careeer Institute (Private, For-profit)
   Fall 2010 Enrollment: 94 . . . . (570) 823-3891
   2011-12 Tuition: $11,369
Jolie Hair and Beauty Academy of Wilkes-Barre (Private, For-profit)
   Fall 2010 Enrollment: 277 . . . . (570) 825-8363
   2011-12 Tuition: $14,800
Wilkes-Barre Area Career and Technical Center Practical Nursing (Public)
   Fall 2010 Enrollment: 188 . . . . (570) 822-6539
   2011-12 Tuition: $9,338

Housing: Homeownership rate: 48.9% (2010); Median home value: $77,700 (2006-2010 5-year est.); Median contract rent: $444 per month

(2006-2010 5-year est.); Median year structure built: before 1940 (2006-2010 5-year est.).

Hospitals: Clear Brook Manor (50 beds); Geisinger Wyoming Valley Medical Center (177 beds); Geisinger Wyoming Valley Medical center (177 beds); John Heinz Institute of Rehabilitation Medicine (94 beds); Wilkes Barre General Hospital (519 beds); Wilkes-Barre Veterans Affairs Medical Center

Safety: Violent crime rate: 51.2 per 10,000 population; Property crime rate: 356.2 per 10,000 population (2011).

Newspapers: The Citizens' Voice (Local news; Circulation 33,032); Dallas Post (Community news; Circulation 3,000); Times Leader (Local news; Circulation 51,573); The Weekender (Local news)

Transportation: Commute to work: 85.7% car, 3.3% public transportation, 7.9% walk, 2.1% work from home (2006-2010 5-year est.); Travel time to work: 51.2% less than 15 minutes, 32.9% 15 to 30 minutes, 8.9% 30 to 45 minutes, 2.8% 45 to 60 minutes, 4.3% 60 minutes or more (2006-2010 5-year est.)

Airports: Wilkes-Barre/Scranton International (primary service)

Additional Information Contacts

City of Wilkes-Barre . . . . (570) 208-4117
   http://www.wilkes-barre.pa.us
Greater Scranton Chamber of Commerce . . . . (570) 342-7711
   http://www.scrantonchamber.com

WILKES-BARRE (township). Covers a land area of 2.864 square miles and a water area of 0 square miles. Located at 41.23° N. Lat; 75.86° W. Long. Elevation is 535 feet.

History: Named for John Wilkes and Isaac Barre, defenders of the colonies before Parliament. The settlement was burned in 1778 by the British and Native Americans and again burned in 1784. Wilkes University, King's College, College Misericordia, and Pennsylvania State University, Nesbitt Campus are here. The Swetland Homestead (early 1800s) is of historical interest. Area severely damaged by the flooding of the Susquehanna in 1972. Settled 1769, Incorporated as a city 1871.

Population: 3,469 (1990); 3,235 (2000); 2,967 (2010); Density: 1,036.0 persons per square mile (2010); Race: 88.5% White, 3.2% Black, 6.4% Asian, 0.0% American Indian/Alaska Native, 0.0% Native Hawaiian/Other Pacific Islander, 1.9% Other, 2.0% Hispanic of any race (2010); Average household size: 2.08 (2010); Median age: 44.9 (2010); Males per 100 females: 96.5 (2010); Marriage status: 38.4% never married, 43.5% now married, 5.8% widowed, 12.3% divorced (2006-2010 5-year est.); Foreign born: 8.5% (2006-2010 5-year est.); Ancestry (includes multiple ancestries): 33.2% Polish, 24.2% Irish, 16.7% German, 8.3% Italian, 4.2% Slovak (2006-2010 5-year est.).

Economy: Single-family building permits issued: 0 (2011); Multi-family building permits issued: 0 (2011); Employment by occupation: 11.6% management, 3.5% professional, 6.9% services, 22.4% sales, 6.1% farming, 10.6% construction, 7.1% production (2006-2010 5-year est.).

Income: Per capita income: $21,809 (2006-2010 5-year est.); Median household income: $38,494 (2006-2010 5-year est.); Average household income: $45,045 (2006-2010 5-year est.); Percent of households with income of $100,000 or more: 8.3% (2006-2010 5-year est.); Poverty rate: 12.0% (2006-2010 5-year est.).

Education: Percent of population age 25 and over with: High school diploma (including GED) or higher: 87.6% (2006-2010 5-year est.); Bachelor's degree or higher: 22.6% (2006-2010 5-year est.); Master's degree or higher: 3.9% (2006-2010 5-year est.).

Four-year College(s)

King's College (Private, Not-for-profit, Roman Catholic)
   Fall 2010 Enrollment: 2,505 . . . . (570) 208-5900
   2011-12 Tuition: In-state $27,680; Out-of-state $27,680
Wilkes University (Private, Not-for-profit)
   Fall 2010 Enrollment: 4,671 . . . . (570) 408-5000
   2011-12 Tuition: In-state $28,210; Out-of-state $28,210

Vocational/Technical School(s)

CDE Careeer Institute (Private, For-profit)
   Fall 2010 Enrollment: 94 . . . . (570) 823-3891
   2011-12 Tuition: $11,369
Jolie Hair and Beauty Academy of Wilkes-Barre (Private, For-profit)
   Fall 2010 Enrollment: 277 . . . . (570) 825-8363
   2011-12 Tuition: $14,800
Wilkes-Barre Area Career and Technical Center Practical Nursing (Public)
   Fall 2010 Enrollment: 188 . . . . (570) 822-6539
   2011-12 Tuition: $9,338

Housing: Homeownership rate: 56.5% (2010); Median home value: $83,700 (2006-2010 5-year est.); Median contract rent: $703 per month (2006-2010 5-year est.); Median year structure built: 1946 (2006-2010 5-year est.).

Hospitals: Clear Brook Manor (50 beds); Geisinger Wyoming Valley Medical Center (177 beds); Geisinger Wyoming Valley Medical Center (177 beds); John Heinz Institute of Rehabilitation Medicine (94 beds); Wilkes Barre General Hospital (519 beds); Wilkes-Barre Veterans Affairs Medical Center

Safety: Violent crime rate: 50.4 per 10,000 population; Property crime rate: 2,187.5 per 10,000 population (2011).

Newspapers: The Citizens' Voice (Local news; Circulation 33,032); Dallas Post (Community news; Circulation 3,000); Times Leader (Local news; Circulation 51,573); The Weekender (Local news)

Transportation: Commute to work: 94.3% car, 1.4% public transportation, 2.5% walk, 1.8% work from home (2006-2010 5-year est.); Travel time to work: 45.3% less than 15 minutes, 38.6% 15 to 30 minutes, 9.5% 30 to 45 minutes, 2.9% 45 to 60 minutes, 3.7% 60 minutes or more (2006-2010 5-year est.)

Airports: Wilkes-Barre/Scranton International (primary service)

Additional Information Contacts

Greater Scranton Chamber of Commerce . . . . (570) 342-7711
　http://www.scrantonchamber.com

WRIGHT (township). Covers a land area of 13.310 square miles and a water area of 0.005 square miles. Located at 41.12° N. Lat; 75.90° W. Long.

Population: 4,682 (1990); 5,593 (2000); 5,651 (2010); Density: 424.6 persons per square mile (2010); Race: 93.8% White, 0.8% Black, 3.8% Asian, 0.1% American Indian/Alaska Native, 0.0% Native Hawaiian/Other Pacific Islander, 1.5% Other, 2.0% Hispanic of any race (2010); Average household size: 2.58 (2010); Median age: 46.1 (2010); Males per 100 females: 93.3 (2010); Marriage status: 17.9% never married, 69.7% now married, 7.5% widowed, 5.0% divorced (2006-2010 5-year est.); Foreign born: 3.1% (2006-2010 5-year est.); Ancestry (includes multiple ancestries): 25.0% German, 22.2% Polish, 21.4% Irish, 13.5% Italian, 10.6% English (2006-2010 5-year est.).

Economy: Single-family building permits issued: 5 (2011); Multi-family building permits issued: 0 (2011); Employment by occupation: 13.1% management, 4.8% professional, 5.8% services, 14.5% sales, 3.0% farming, 5.6% construction, 4.7% production (2006-2010 5-year est.).

Income: Per capita income: $31,847 (2006-2010 5-year est.); Median household income: $74,590 (2006-2010 5-year est.); Average household income: $86,977 (2006-2010 5-year est.); Percent of households with income of $100,000 or more: 27.9% (2006-2010 5-year est.); Poverty rate: 3.1% (2006-2010 5-year est.).

Education: Percent of population age 25 and over with: High school diploma (including GED) or higher: 93.7% (2006-2010 5-year est.); Bachelor's degree or higher: 36.5% (2006-2010 5-year est.); Master's degree or higher: 17.0% (2006-2010 5-year est.).

Housing: Homeownership rate: 88.0% (2010); Median home value: $184,100 (2006-2010 5-year est.); Median contract rent: $553 per month (2006-2010 5-year est.); Median year structure built: 1977 (2006-2010 5-year est.).

Safety: Violent crime rate: 3.5 per 10,000 population; Property crime rate: 164.1 per 10,000 population (2011).

Transportation: Commute to work: 96.8% car, 0.0% public transportation, 0.8% walk, 2.4% work from home (2006-2010 5-year est.); Travel time to work: 18.5% less than 15 minutes, 43.7% 15 to 30 minutes, 18.7% 30 to 45 minutes, 7.2% 45 to 60 minutes, 11.9% 60 minutes or more (2006-2010 5-year est.)

Additional Information Contacts

Greater Scranton Chamber of Commerce . . . . (570) 342-7711
　http://www.scrantonchamber.com
Wright Township . . . . (570) 474-9067
　http://www.luzernecounty.org/living/municipalities/wright_township

WYOMING (borough). Covers a land area of 1.437 square miles and a water area of 0.147 square miles. Located at 41.31° N. Lat; 75.84° W. Long. Elevation is 564 feet.

History: Incorporated 1898.

Population: 3,255 (1990); 3,221 (2000); 3,073 (2010); Density: 2,138.2 persons per square mile (2010); Race: 97.3% White, 0.8% Black, 0.5% Asian, 0.3% American Indian/Alaska Native, 0.1% Native Hawaiian/Other Pacific Islander, 1.0% Other, 0.9% Hispanic of any race (2010); Average

household size: 2.12 (2010); Median age: 44.9 (2010); Males per 100 females: 85.6 (2010); Marriage status: 29.0% never married, 42.8% now married, 13.4% widowed, 14.8% divorced (2006-2010 5-year est.); Foreign born: 3.0% (2006-2010 5-year est.); Ancestry (includes multiple ancestries): 24.1% Italian, 23.9% Irish, 22.3% German, 19.7% Polish, 8.1% Slovak (2006-2010 5-year est.).

Economy: Single-family building permits issued: 0 (2011); Multi-family building permits issued: 0 (2011); Employment by occupation: 7.6% management, 2.9% professional, 12.2% services, 19.5% sales, 3.5% farming, 5.4% construction, 2.8% production (2006-2010 5-year est.).

Income: Per capita income: $26,198 (2006-2010 5-year est.); Median household income: $40,234 (2006-2010 5-year est.); Average household income: $50,887 (2006-2010 5-year est.); Percent of households with income of $100,000 or more: 10.4% (2006-2010 5-year est.); Poverty rate: 15.1% (2006-2010 5-year est.).

Education: Percent of population age 25 and over with: High school diploma (including GED) or higher: 90.3% (2006-2010 5-year est.); Bachelor's degree or higher: 23.5% (2006-2010 5-year est.); Master's degree or higher: 7.9% (2006-2010 5-year est.).

School District(s)

Wyoming Area SD (KG-12)
　2010-11 Enrollment: 2,536 . . . . (570) 655-3733

Housing: Homeownership rate: 59.2% (2010); Median home value: $121,600 (2006-2010 5-year est.); Median contract rent: $470 per month (2006-2010 5-year est.); Median year structure built: before 1940 (2006-2010 5-year est.).

Safety: Violent crime rate: 13.0 per 10,000 population; Property crime rate: 266.0 per 10,000 population (2011).

Transportation: Commute to work: 96.3% car, 0.6% public transportation, 1.5% walk, 1.6% work from home (2006-2010 5-year est.); Travel time to work: 33.2% less than 15 minutes, 45.6% 15 to 30 minutes, 13.7% 30 to 45 minutes, 2.7% 45 to 60 minutes, 4.8% 60 minutes or more (2006-2010 5-year est.)

Additional Information Contacts

Wyoming County Chamber of Commerce. . . . . (570) 836-7755
　http://www.wyccc.com

YATESVILLE (borough). Covers a land area of 0.609 square miles and a water area of 0 square miles. Located at 41.30° N. Lat; 75.78° W. Long. Elevation is 755 feet.

Population: 506 (1990); 649 (2000); 607 (2010); Density: 997.3 persons per square mile (2010); Race: 97.4% White, 0.8% Black, 1.0% Asian, 0.0% American Indian/Alaska Native, 0.0% Native Hawaiian/Other Pacific Islander, 0.8% Other, 0.5% Hispanic of any race (2010); Average household size: 2.54 (2010); Median age: 46.5 (2010); Males per 100 females: 83.9 (2010); Marriage status: 22.3% never married, 58.7% now married, 12.3% widowed, 6.7% divorced (2006-2010 5-year est.); Foreign born: 5.2% (2006-2010 5-year est.); Ancestry (includes multiple ancestries): 51.9% Italian, 22.8% Polish, 22.8% Irish, 17.1% German, 10.7% Russian (2006-2010 5-year est.).

Economy: Employment by occupation: 21.7% management, 3.1% professional, 6.3% services, 13.6% sales, 9.4% farming, 2.8% construction, 4.9% production (2006-2010 5-year est.).

Income: Per capita income: $32,994 (2006-2010 5-year est.); Median household income: $57,750 (2006-2010 5-year est.); Average household income: $83,399 (2006-2010 5-year est.); Percent of households with income of $100,000 or more: 30.8% (2006-2010 5-year est.); Poverty rate: 8.2% (2006-2010 5-year est.).

Education: Percent of population age 25 and over with: High school diploma (including GED) or higher: 94.2% (2006-2010 5-year est.); Bachelor's degree or higher: 33.4% (2006-2010 5-year est.); Master's degree or higher: 16.5% (2006-2010 5-year est.).

Housing: Homeownership rate: 84.5% (2010); Median home value: $132,800 (2006-2010 5-year est.); Median contract rent: n/a per month (2006-2010 5-year est.); Median year structure built: 1976 (2006-2010 5-year est.).

Transportation: Commute to work: 94.0% car, 0.0% public transportation, 2.1% walk, 0.7% work from home (2006-2010 5-year est.); Travel time to work: 36.3% less than 15 minutes, 45.9% 15 to 30 minutes, 12.8% 30 to 45 minutes, 1.1% 45 to 60 minutes, 3.9% 60 minutes or more (2006-2010 5-year est.)

Lycoming County

Located in north central Pennsylvania; drained by the West Branch of the Susquehanna River. Covers a land area of 1,228.594 square miles, a water area of 15.241 square miles, and is located in the Eastern Time Zone at 41.34° N. Lat., 77.06° W. Long. The county was founded in 1795. County seat is Williamsport.

Lycoming County is part of the Williamsport, PA Metropolitan Statistical Area. The entire metro area includes: Lycoming County, PA

Weather Station: Williamsport-Lycoming County   Elevation: 520 feet

	Jan	Feb	Mar	Apr	May	Jun	Jul	Aug	Sep	Oct	Nov	Dec
High	35	39	48	61	72	80	84	82	74	62	50	39
Low	19	21	28	39	48	57	62	61	53	42	33	24
Precip	2.6	2.3	3.1	3.4	3.6	3.9	4.3	3.8	4.0	3.4	3.7	2.8
Snow	11.1	8.1	7.1	1.1	tr	tr	tr	tr	0.0	0.1	2.1	7.0

High and Low temperatures in degrees Fahrenheit; Precipitation and Snow in inches

Population: 118,710 (1990); 120,044 (2000); 116,111 (2010); Race: 92.6% White, 4.5% Black, 0.6% Asian, 0.2% American Indian/Alaska Native, 0.0% Native Hawaiian/Other Pacific Islander, 2.1% Other, 1.3% Hispanic of any race (2010); Density: 94.5 persons per square mile (2010); Average household size: 2.37 (2010); Median age: 41.1 (2010); Males per 100 females: 95.9 (2010).
Religion: Six largest groups: 15.9% Catholicism, 11.8% Methodist/Pietist, 6.4% Lutheran, 3.9% Baptist, 3.1% Non-Denominational, 2.1% Holiness (2010)
Economy: Unemployment rate: 8.1% (August 2012); Total civilian labor force: 63,026 (August 2012); Leading industries: 19.5% manufacturing; 18.4% health care and social assistance; 16.1% retail trade (2010); Farms: 1,211 totaling 160,456 acres (2007); Companies that employ 500 or more persons: 4 (2010); Companies that employ 100 to 499 persons: 71 (2010); Companies that employ less than 100 persons: 2,778 (2010); Black-owned businesses: n/a (2007); Hispanic-owned businesses: 99 (2007); Asian-owned businesses: 139 (2007); Women-owned businesses: 2,507 (2007); Retail sales per capita: $15,822 (2010). Single-family building permits issued: 76 (2011); Multi-family building permits issued: 80 (2011).
Income: Per capita income: $21,802 (2006-2010 5-year est.); Median household income: $42,689 (2006-2010 5-year est.); Average household income: $53,383 (2006-2010 5-year est.); Percent of households with income of $100,000 or more: 11.1% (2006-2010 5-year est.); Poverty rate: 14.4% (2006-2010 5-year est.); Bankruptcy rate: 1.52% (2011).
Taxes: Total county taxes per capita: $223 (2009); County property taxes per capita: $218 (2009).
Education: Percent of population age 25 and over with: High school diploma (including GED) or higher: 85.9% (2006-2010 5-year est.); Bachelor's degree or higher: 18.8% (2006-2010 5-year est.); Master's degree or higher: 6.2% (2006-2010 5-year est.).
Housing: Homeownership rate: 68.1% (2010); Median home value: $119,200 (2006-2010 5-year est.); Median contract rent: $479 per month (2006-2010 5-year est.); Median year structure built: 1956 (2006-2010 5-year est.)
Health: Birth rate: 103.5 per 10,000 population (2011); Death rate: 109.9 per 10,000 population (2011); Age-adjusted cancer mortality rate: 180.9 deaths per 100,000 population (2009); Number of physicians: 21.4 per 10,000 population (2010); Hospital beds: 37.2 per 10,000 population (2008); Hospital admissions: 1,192.6 per 10,000 population (2008).
Environment: Air Quality Index: 96.8% good, 3.2% moderate, 0.0% unhealthy for sensitive individuals, 0.0% unhealthy (percent of days in 2011)
Elections: 2012 Presidential election results: 32.7% Obama, 66.0% Romney
National and State Parks: Little Pine State Park; Loyalsock State Game Farm; Susquehanna State Park; Tiadaghton State Forest; Upper Pine Bottom State Park
Additional Information Contacts
Lycoming County Government . . . . (570) 327-2200
  http://www.lyco.org

Lycoming County Communities

ANTHONY (township). Covers a land area of 15.561 square miles and a water area of 0.034 square miles. Located at 41.29° N. Lat; 77.17° W. Long.
Population: 727 (1990); 904 (2000); 865 (2010); Density: 55.6 persons per square mile (2010); Race: 98.7% White, 0.2% Black, 0.2% Asian, 0.0% American Indian/Alaska Native, 0.0% Native Hawaiian/Other Pacific Islander, 0.9% Other, 0.6% Hispanic of any race (2010); Average household size: 2.69 (2010); Median age: 44.9 (2010); Males per 100 females: 100.2 (2010); Marriage status: 18.6% never married, 70.3% now married, 4.4% widowed, 6.8% divorced (2006-2010 5-year est.); Foreign born: 0.0% (2006-2010 5-year est.); Ancestry (includes multiple ancestries): 51.7% German, 12.1% American, 9.6% Irish, 9.1% English, 8.5% Dutch (2006-2010 5-year est.).
Economy: Single-family building permits issued: 5 (2011); Multi-family building permits issued: 0 (2011); Employment by occupation: 9.4% management, 4.0% professional, 5.4% services, 18.2% sales, 6.6% farming, 13.0% construction, 6.8% production (2006-2010 5-year est.).
Income: Per capita income: $26,874 (2006-2010 5-year est.); Median household income: $54,688 (2006-2010 5-year est.); Average household income: $71,290 (2006-2010 5-year est.); Percent of households with income of $100,000 or more: 20.0% (2006-2010 5-year est.); Poverty rate: 5.7% (2006-2010 5-year est.).
Education: Percent of population age 25 and over with: High school diploma (including GED) or higher: 88.2% (2006-2010 5-year est.); Bachelor's degree or higher: 16.1% (2006-2010 5-year est.); Master's degree or higher: 5.7% (2006-2010 5-year est.).
Housing: Homeownership rate: 89.4% (2010); Median home value: $158,700 (2006-2010 5-year est.); Median contract rent: $616 per month (2006-2010 5-year est.); Median year structure built: 1975 (2006-2010 5-year est.).
Transportation: Commute to work: 95.3% car, 0.0% public transportation, 1.6% walk, 3.1% work from home (2006-2010 5-year est.); Travel time to work: 21.4% less than 15 minutes, 55.1% 15 to 30 minutes, 20.1% 30 to 45 minutes, 1.7% 45 to 60 minutes, 1.7% 60 minutes or more (2006-2010 5-year est.)

ARMSTRONG (township). Covers a land area of 24.744 square miles and a water area of 0.761 square miles. Located at 41.19° N. Lat; 77.02° W. Long.
Population: 754 (1990); 717 (2000); 681 (2010); Density: 27.5 persons per square mile (2010); Race: 98.5% White, 0.0% Black, 0.7% Asian, 0.0% American Indian/Alaska Native, 0.0% Native Hawaiian/Other Pacific Islander, 0.8% Other, 1.2% Hispanic of any race (2010); Average household size: 2.43 (2010); Median age: 45.4 (2010); Males per 100 females: 109.5 (2010); Marriage status: 18.3% never married, 55.6% now married, 9.7% widowed, 16.4% divorced (2006-2010 5-year est.); Foreign born: 1.5% (2006-2010 5-year est.); Ancestry (includes multiple ancestries): 39.7% German, 12.8% Irish, 9.3% Italian, 9.0% Dutch, 7.9% Pennsylvania German (2006-2010 5-year est.).
Economy: Single-family building permits issued: 3 (2011); Multi-family building permits issued: 0 (2011); Employment by occupation: 3.4% management, 0.6% professional, 11.5% services, 15.5% sales, 2.2% farming, 18.6% construction, 16.4% production (2006-2010 5-year est.).
Income: Per capita income: $25,275 (2006-2010 5-year est.); Median household income: $32,125 (2006-2010 5-year est.); Average household income: $58,405 (2006-2010 5-year est.); Percent of households with income of $100,000 or more: 12.0% (2006-2010 5-year est.); Poverty rate: 22.3% (2006-2010 5-year est.).
Education: Percent of population age 25 and over with: High school diploma (including GED) or higher: 74.0% (2006-2010 5-year est.); Bachelor's degree or higher: 14.2% (2006-2010 5-year est.); Master's degree or higher: 7.7% (2006-2010 5-year est.).
Housing: Homeownership rate: 84.3% (2010); Median home value: $116,100 (2006-2010 5-year est.); Median contract rent: $249 per month (2006-2010 5-year est.); Median year structure built: 1961 (2006-2010 5-year est.).
Transportation: Commute to work: 92.8% car, 2.3% public transportation, 3.6% walk, 1.3% work from home (2006-2010 5-year est.); Travel time to work: 38.1% less than 15 minutes, 39.1% 15 to 30 minutes, 10.9% 30 to 45 minutes, 3.3% 45 to 60 minutes, 8.6% 60 minutes or more (2006-2010 5-year est.)

BASTRESS (township). Covers a land area of 9.416 square miles and a water area of 0.007 square miles. Located at 41.19° N. Lat; 77.11° W. Long. Elevation is 1,181 feet.

Population: 513 (1990); 574 (2000); 546 (2010); Density: 58.0 persons per square mile (2010); Race: 98.5% White, 0.5% Black, 0.2% Asian, 0.7% American Indian/Alaska Native, 0.0% Native Hawaiian/Other Pacific Islander, 0.1% Other, 0.7% Hispanic of any race (2010); Average household size: 2.69 (2010); Median age: 45.7 (2010); Males per 100 females: 92.9 (2010); Marriage status: 17.6% never married, 72.5% now married, 4.3% widowed, 5.5% divorced (2006-2010 5-year est.); Foreign born: 0.5% (2006-2010 5-year est.); Ancestry (includes multiple ancestries): 59.8% German, 9.0% Irish, 6.9% Polish, 6.9% Dutch, 4.8% Italian (2006-2010 5-year est.).

Economy: Single-family building permits issued: 4 (2011); Multi-family building permits issued: 0 (2011); Employment by occupation: 4.4% management, 4.4% professional, 5.5% services, 11.0% sales, 3.8% farming, 15.9% construction, 15.4% production (2006-2010 5-year est.).

Income: Per capita income: $27,341 (2006-2010 5-year est.); Median household income: $49,205 (2006-2010 5-year est.); Average household income: $61,188 (2006-2010 5-year est.); Percent of households with income of $100,000 or more: 11.1% (2006-2010 5-year est.); Poverty rate: 1.0% (2006-2010 5-year est.).

Education: Percent of population age 25 and over with: High school diploma (including GED) or higher: 84.2% (2006-2010 5-year est.); Bachelor's degree or higher: 13.9% (2006-2010 5-year est.); Master's degree or higher: 6.1% (2006-2010 5-year est.).

Housing: Homeownership rate: 87.7% (2010); Median home value: $169,000 (2006-2010 5-year est.); Median contract rent: n/a per month (2006-2010 5-year est.); Median year structure built: 1970 (2006-2010 5-year est.).

Transportation: Commute to work: 96.1% car, 0.0% public transportation, 1.1% walk, 2.2% work from home (2006-2010 5-year est.); Travel time to work: 2.8% less than 15 minutes, 61.9% 15 to 30 minutes, 26.7% 30 to 45 minutes, 6.3% 45 to 60 minutes, 2.3% 60 minutes or more (2006-2010 5-year est.)

BRADY (township). Covers a land area of 8.842 square miles and a water area of 0.210 square miles. Located at 41.17° N. Lat; 76.94° W. Long.

Population: 822 (1990); 494 (2000); 521 (2010); Density: 58.9 persons per square mile (2010); Race: 98.5% White, 0.0% Black, 0.4% Asian, 0.0% American Indian/Alaska Native, 0.0% Native Hawaiian/Other Pacific Islander, 1.1% Other, 0.4% Hispanic of any race (2010); Average household size: 2.67 (2010); Median age: 42.9 (2010); Males per 100 females: 113.5 (2010); Marriage status: 24.3% never married, 61.3% now married, 3.1% widowed, 11.2% divorced (2006-2010 5-year est.); Foreign born: 1.3% (2006-2010 5-year est.); Ancestry (includes multiple ancestries): 40.5% German, 21.1% Irish, 13.5% American, 8.5% Pennsylvania German, 6.8% English (2006-2010 5-year est.).

Economy: Single-family building permits issued: 2 (2011); Multi-family building permits issued: 0 (2011); Employment by occupation: 9.3% management, 3.1% professional, 5.4% services, 13.6% sales, 4.7% farming, 21.7% construction, 22.9% production (2006-2010 5-year est.).

Income: Per capita income: $22,651 (2006-2010 5-year est.); Median household income: $47,250 (2006-2010 5-year est.); Average household income: $55,912 (2006-2010 5-year est.); Percent of households with income of $100,000 or more: 8.3% (2006-2010 5-year est.); Poverty rate: 16.6% (2006-2010 5-year est.).

Education: Percent of population age 25 and over with: High school diploma (including GED) or higher: 85.1% (2006-2010 5-year est.); Bachelor's degree or higher: 11.8% (2006-2010 5-year est.); Master's degree or higher: 3.4% (2006-2010 5-year est.).

Housing: Homeownership rate: 92.8% (2010); Median home value: $124,700 (2006-2010 5-year est.); Median contract rent: $575 per month (2006-2010 5-year est.); Median year structure built: 1978 (2006-2010 5-year est.).

Transportation: Commute to work: 94.1% car, 1.3% public transportation, 1.7% walk, 0.0% work from home (2006-2010 5-year est.); Travel time to work: 29.5% less than 15 minutes, 50.2% 15 to 30 minutes, 10.5% 30 to 45 minutes, 2.5% 45 to 60 minutes, 7.2% 60 minutes or more (2006-2010 5-year est.)

BROWN (township). Covers a land area of 73.343 square miles and a water area of 0.687 square miles. Located at 41.51° N. Lat; 77.50° W. Long.

Population: 102 (1990); 111 (2000); 96 (2010); Density: 1.3 persons per square mile (2010); Race: 99.0% White, 0.0% Black, 0.0% Asian, 1.0% American Indian/Alaska Native, 0.0% Native Hawaiian/Other Pacific Islander, 0.0% Other, 1.0% Hispanic of any race (2010); Average household size: 2.00 (2010); Median age: 58.5 (2010); Males per 100 females: 146.2 (2010); Marriage status: 6.7% never married, 76.7% now married, 3.3% widowed, 13.3% divorced (2006-2010 5-year est.); Foreign born: 0.0% (2006-2010 5-year est.); Ancestry (includes multiple ancestries): 32.3% German, 24.2% English, 16.1% Polish, 14.5% Irish, 9.7% Pennsylvania German (2006-2010 5-year est.).

Economy: Single-family building permits issued: 0 (2011); Multi-family building permits issued: 0 (2011); Employment by occupation: 57.6% management, 0.0% professional, 9.1% services, 6.1% sales, 12.1% farming, 9.1% construction, 0.0% production (2006-2010 5-year est.).

Income: Per capita income: $31,715 (2006-2010 5-year est.); Median household income: $37,500 (2006-2010 5-year est.); Average household income: $53,403 (2006-2010 5-year est.); Percent of households with income of $100,000 or more: 13.9% (2006-2010 5-year est.); Poverty rate: 0.0% (2006-2010 5-year est.).

Education: Percent of population age 25 and over with: High school diploma (including GED) or higher: 83.3% (2006-2010 5-year est.); Bachelor's degree or higher: 16.7% (2006-2010 5-year est.); Master's degree or higher: 5.0% (2006-2010 5-year est.).

Housing: Homeownership rate: 89.6% (2010); Median home value: $162,500 (2006-2010 5-year est.); Median contract rent: n/a per month (2006-2010 5-year est.); Median year structure built: 1967 (2006-2010 5-year est.).

Transportation: Commute to work: 50.0% car, 0.0% public transportation, 43.3% walk, 6.7% work from home (2006-2010 5-year est.); Travel time to work: 67.9% less than 15 minutes, 0.0% 15 to 30 minutes, 14.3% 30 to 45 minutes, 0.0% 45 to 60 minutes, 17.9% 60 minutes or more (2006-2010 5-year est.)

CASCADE (township). Covers a land area of 39.205 square miles and a water area of 0.322 square miles. Located at 41.46° N. Lat; 76.87° W. Long.

Population: 382 (1990); 419 (2000); 413 (2010); Density: 10.5 persons per square mile (2010); Race: 98.3% White, 1.0% Black, 0.5% Asian, 0.0% American Indian/Alaska Native, 0.0% Native Hawaiian/Other Pacific Islander, 0.2% Other, 0.0% Hispanic of any race (2010); Average household size: 2.39 (2010); Median age: 49.0 (2010); Males per 100 females: 99.5 (2010); Marriage status: 17.3% never married, 76.7% now married, 2.0% widowed, 4.0% divorced (2006-2010 5-year est.); Foreign born: 4.5% (2006-2010 5-year est.); Ancestry (includes multiple ancestries): 41.3% German, 30.2% Irish, 12.5% Italian, 9.3% English, 5.9% Austrian (2006-2010 5-year est.).

Economy: Single-family building permits issued: 0 (2011); Multi-family building permits issued: 0 (2011); Employment by occupation: 11.4% management, 4.5% professional, 5.0% services, 21.4% sales, 0.0% farming, 19.5% construction, 4.5% production (2006-2010 5-year est.).

Income: Per capita income: $20,634 (2006-2010 5-year est.); Median household income: $57,500 (2006-2010 5-year est.); Average household income: $60,822 (2006-2010 5-year est.); Percent of households with income of $100,000 or more: 10.0% (2006-2010 5-year est.); Poverty rate: 0.9% (2006-2010 5-year est.).

Education: Percent of population age 25 and over with: High school diploma (including GED) or higher: 92.3% (2006-2010 5-year est.); Bachelor's degree or higher: 23.5% (2006-2010 5-year est.); Master's degree or higher: 4.6% (2006-2010 5-year est.).

Housing: Homeownership rate: 87.8% (2010); Median home value: $148,400 (2006-2010 5-year est.); Median contract rent: $392 per month (2006-2010 5-year est.); Median year structure built: 1971 (2006-2010 5-year est.).

Transportation: Commute to work: 95.8% car, 0.0% public transportation, 4.2% walk, 0.0% work from home (2006-2010 5-year est.); Travel time to work: 7.4% less than 15 minutes, 28.2% 15 to 30 minutes, 49.1% 30 to 45 minutes, 5.6% 45 to 60 minutes, 9.7% 60 minutes or more (2006-2010 5-year est.)

CEDAR RUN (unincorporated postal area)
Zip Code: 17727

Covers a land area of 106.884 square miles and a water area of 0.697 square miles. Located at 41.51° N. Lat; 77.49° W. Long. Population: 72 (2010); Density: 0.7 persons per square mile (2010); Race: 100.0% White, 0.0% Black, 0.0% Asian, 0.0% American Indian/Alaska Native, 0.0% Native Hawaiian/Other Pacific Islander, 0.0% Other, 0.0% Hispanic of any race (2010); Average household size: 1.95 (2010); Median age: 58.0 (2010); Males per 100 females: 132.3 (2010); Homeownership rate: 91.9% (2010)

CLINTON (township). Covers a land area of 27.422 square miles and a water area of 0.916 square miles. Located at 41.20° N. Lat; 76.90° W. Long.

Population: 3,086 (1990); 3,947 (2000); 3,708 (2010); Density: 135.2 persons per square mile (2010); Race: 82.6% White, 14.6% Black, 0.2% Asian, 0.1% American Indian/Alaska Native, 0.0% Native Hawaiian/Other Pacific Islander, 2.5% Other, 2.4% Hispanic of any race (2010); Average household size: 2.50 (2010); Median age: 39.3 (2010); Males per 100 females: 41.3 (2010); Marriage status: 23.1% never married, 53.6% now married, 6.7% widowed, 16.6% divorced (2006-2010 5-year est.); Foreign born: 1.3% (2006-2010 5-year est.); Ancestry (includes multiple ancestries): 28.4% German, 8.2% Italian, 7.6% American, 6.0% Irish, 4.3% Pennsylvania German (2006-2010 5-year est.)

Economy: Single-family building permits issued: 1 (2011); Multi-family building permits issued: 0 (2011); Employment by occupation: 5.4% management, 1.1% professional, 8.9% services, 20.3% sales, 2.6% farming, 8.9% construction, 10.7% production (2006-2010 5-year est.).

Income: Per capita income: $15,844 (2006-2010 5-year est.); Median household income: $46,089 (2006-2010 5-year est.); Average household income: $52,086 (2006-2010 5-year est.); Percent of households with income of $100,000 or more: 7.5% (2006-2010 5-year est.); Poverty rate: 14.9% (2006-2010 5-year est.).

Education: Percent of population age 25 and over with: High school diploma (including GED) or higher: 75.8% (2006-2010 5-year est.); Bachelor's degree or higher: 9.8% (2006-2010 5-year est.); Master's degree or higher: 2.9% (2006-2010 5-year est.).

Housing: Homeownership rate: 79.9% (2010); Median home value: $120,000 (2006-2010 5-year est.); Median contract rent: $395 per month (2006-2010 5-year est.); Median year structure built: 1965 (2006-2010 5-year est.).

Transportation: Commute to work: 92.2% car, 0.7% public transportation, 2.9% walk, 2.8% work from home (2006-2010 5-year est.); Travel time to work: 35.5% less than 15 minutes, 51.3% 15 to 30 minutes, 8.4% 30 to 45 minutes, 2.1% 45 to 60 minutes, 2.7% 60 minutes or more (2006-2010 5-year est.)

Additional Information Contacts

Williamsport/Lycoming Chamber of Commerce . . . . (570) 326-1971
http://www.williamsport.org

COGAN HOUSE (township). Covers a land area of 69.918 square miles and a water area of 0.068 square miles. Located at 41.40° N. Lat; 77.14° W. Long.

Population: 807 (1990); 974 (2000); 955 (2010); Density: 13.7 persons per square mile (2010); Race: 98.8% White, 0.1% Black, 0.1% Asian, 0.0% American Indian/Alaska Native, 0.0% Native Hawaiian/Other Pacific Islander, 1.0% Other, 1.0% Hispanic of any race (2010); Average household size: 2.64 (2010); Median age: 43.8 (2010); Males per 100 females: 104.1 (2010); Marriage status: 28.5% never married, 59.3% now married, 5.7% widowed, 6.5% divorced (2006-2010 5-year est.); Foreign born: 0.8% (2006-2010 5-year est.); Ancestry (includes multiple ancestries): 52.6% German, 15.2% Irish, 11.4% English, 6.2% French, 6.0% Dutch (2006-2010 5-year est.).

Economy: Single-family building permits issued: 0 (2011); Multi-family building permits issued: 0 (2011); Employment by occupation: 9.8% management, 1.0% professional, 10.3% services, 16.4% sales, 0.7% farming, 19.8% construction, 13.4% production (2006-2010 5-year est.).

Income: Per capita income: $18,497 (2006-2010 5-year est.); Median household income: $41,103 (2006-2010 5-year est.); Average household income: $48,778 (2006-2010 5-year est.); Percent of households with income of $100,000 or more: 8.6% (2006-2010 5-year est.); Poverty rate: 14.0% (2006-2010 5-year est.).

Education: Percent of population age 25 and over with: High school diploma (including GED) or higher: 83.6% (2006-2010 5-year est.); Bachelor's degree or higher: 14.4% (2006-2010 5-year est.); Master's degree or higher: 3.5% (2006-2010 5-year est.).

Housing: Homeownership rate: 90.9% (2010); Median home value: $116,600 (2006-2010 5-year est.); Median contract rent: $428 per month (2006-2010 5-year est.); Median year structure built: 1975 (2006-2010 5-year est.).

Transportation: Commute to work: 94.8% car, 0.0% public transportation, 2.7% walk, 2.5% work from home (2006-2010 5-year est.); Travel time to work: 20.0% less than 15 minutes, 27.8% 15 to 30 minutes, 39.0% 30 to 45 minutes, 7.1% 45 to 60 minutes, 6.1% 60 minutes or more (2006-2010 5-year est.).

COGAN STATION (unincorporated postal area)
Zip Code: 17728

Covers a land area of 47.476 square miles and a water area of 0.272 square miles. Located at 41.33° N. Lat; 77.07° W. Long. Population: 5,120 (2010); Density: 107.8 persons per square mile (2010); Race: 97.9% White, 0.4% Black, 0.6% Asian, 0.2% American Indian/Alaska Native, 0.1% Native Hawaiian/Other Pacific Islander, 0.8% Other, 0.8% Hispanic of any race (2010); Average household size: 2.49 (2010); Median age: 46.2 (2010); Males per 100 females: 104.3 (2010); Homeownership rate: 86.5% (2010)

CUMMINGS (township). Covers a land area of 69.371 square miles and a water area of 0.621 square miles. Located at 41.35° N. Lat; 77.33° W. Long.

Population: 334 (1990); 355 (2000); 273 (2010); Density: 3.9 persons per square mile (2010); Race: 99.6% White, 0.0% Black, 0.0% Asian, 0.0% American Indian/Alaska Native, 0.0% Native Hawaiian/Other Pacific Islander, 0.4% Other, 0.4% Hispanic of any race (2010); Average household size: 2.17 (2010); Median age: 53.7 (2010); Males per 100 females: 100.7 (2010); Marriage status: 12.4% never married, 62.8% now married, 5.0% widowed, 19.7% divorced (2006-2010 5-year est.); Foreign born: 0.0% (2006-2010 5-year est.); Ancestry (includes multiple ancestries): 32.4% German, 15.1% American, 14.8% Irish, 13.0% Italian, 8.5% English (2006-2010 5-year est.).

Economy: Single-family building permits issued: 0 (2011); Multi-family building permits issued: 0 (2011); Employment by occupation: 7.0% management, 7.0% professional, 15.8% services, 11.4% sales, 0.0% farming, 4.4% construction, 7.9% production (2006-2010 5-year est.).

Income: Per capita income: $18,972 (2006-2010 5-year est.); Median household income: $35,714 (2006-2010 5-year est.); Average household income: $47,036 (2006-2010 5-year est.); Percent of households with income of $100,000 or more: 11.0% (2006-2010 5-year est.); Poverty rate: 13.4% (2006-2010 5-year est.).

Education: Percent of population age 25 and over with: High school diploma (including GED) or higher: 82.2% (2006-2010 5-year est.); Bachelor's degree or higher: 19.4% (2006-2010 5-year est.); Master's degree or higher: 8.4% (2006-2010 5-year est.).

Housing: Homeownership rate: 85.7% (2010); Median home value: $146,400 (2006-2010 5-year est.); Median contract rent: $493 per month (2006-2010 5-year est.); Median year structure built: 1964 (2006-2010 5-year est.).

Transportation: Commute to work: 85.2% car, 0.0% public transportation, 13.9% walk, 0.0% work from home (2006-2010 5-year est.); Travel time to work: 25.0% less than 15 minutes, 18.5% 15 to 30 minutes, 31.5% 30 to 45 minutes, 9.3% 45 to 60 minutes, 15.7% 60 minutes or more (2006-2010 5-year est.)

DUBOISTOWN (borough). Covers a land area of 0.552 square miles and a water area of 0.127 square miles. Located at 41.22° N. Lat; 77.04° W. Long. Elevation is 531 feet.

History: Settled 1773, incorporated 1878.

Population: 1,123 (1990); 1,280 (2000); 1,205 (2010); Density: 2,181.4 persons per square mile (2010); Race: 98.7% White, 0.1% Black, 0.4% Asian, 0.1% American Indian/Alaska Native, 0.0% Native Hawaiian/Other Pacific Islander, 0.7% Other, 0.8% Hispanic of any race (2010); Average household size: 2.31 (2010); Median age: 45.2 (2010); Males per 100 females: 94.4 (2010); Marriage status: 22.3% never married, 63.2% now married, 6.9% widowed, 7.5% divorced (2006-2010 5-year est.); Foreign born: 0.6% (2006-2010 5-year est.); Ancestry (includes multiple ancestries): 46.6% German, 13.9% Irish, 12.1% Italian, 9.0% English, 8.9% Polish (2006-2010 5-year est.).

Economy: Single-family building permits issued: 0 (2011); Multi-family building permits issued: 0 (2011); Employment by occupation: 8.5% management, 2.7% professional, 12.8% services, 18.1% sales, 5.3% farming, 9.1% construction, 7.8% production (2006-2010 5-year est.).

Income: Per capita income: $21,297 (2006-2010 5-year est.); Median household income: $46,354 (2006-2010 5-year est.); Average household income: $51,873 (2006-2010 5-year est.); Percent of households with income of $100,000 or more: 9.7% (2006-2010 5-year est.); Poverty rate: 8.0% (2006-2010 5-year est.).

Education: Percent of population age 25 and over with: High school diploma (including GED) or higher: 86.9% (2006-2010 5-year est.); Bachelor's degree or higher: 12.1% (2006-2010 5-year est.); Master's degree or higher: 3.5% (2006-2010 5-year est.).

Housing: Homeownership rate: 76.8% (2010); Median home value: $107,100 (2006-2010 5-year est.); Median contract rent: $564 per month (2006-2010 5-year est.); Median year structure built: 1950 (2006-2010 5-year est.).

Transportation: Commute to work: 96.5% car, 0.7% public transportation, 0.8% walk, 0.0% work from home (2006-2010 5-year est.); Travel time to work: 64.7% less than 15 minutes, 22.2% 15 to 30 minutes, 10.0% 30 to 45 minutes, 0.3% 45 to 60 minutes, 2.7% 60 minutes or more (2006-2010 5-year est.)

Additional Information Contacts
Williamsport/Lycoming Chamber of Commerce . . . . (570) 326-1971
http://williamsport.org

ELDRED (township). Covers a land area of 14.233 square miles and a water area of 0.110 square miles. Located at 41.32° N. Lat; 76.97° W. Long.

Population: 2,055 (1990); 2,178 (2000); 2,122 (2010); Density: 149.1 persons per square mile (2010); Race: 98.1% White, 0.3% Black, 0.4% Asian, 0.1% American Indian/Alaska Native, 0.0% Native Hawaiian/Other Pacific Islander, 1.1% Other, 0.5% Hispanic of any race (2010); Average household size: 2.65 (2010); Median age: 44.9 (2010); Males per 100 females: 99.2 (2010); Marriage status: 17.9% never married, 68.9% now married, 4.2% widowed, 9.0% divorced (2006-2010 5-year est.); Foreign born: 0.4% (2006-2010 5-year est.); Ancestry (includes multiple ancestries): 42.8% German, 14.8% Irish, 10.4% English, 10.0% American, 9.9% Italian (2006-2010 5-year est.).

Economy: Single-family building permits issued: 1 (2011); Multi-family building permits issued: 0 (2011); Employment by occupation: 8.5% management, 3.4% professional, 7.7% services, 19.4% sales, 4.5% farming, 13.6% construction, 7.8% production (2006-2010 5-year est.).

Income: Per capita income: $26,583 (2006-2010 5-year est.); Median household income: $60,438 (2006-2010 5-year est.); Average household income: $69,022 (2006-2010 5-year est.); Percent of households with income of $100,000 or more: 20.3% (2006-2010 5-year est.); Poverty rate: 3.1% (2006-2010 5-year est.).

Education: Percent of population age 25 and over with: High school diploma (including GED) or higher: 94.3% (2006-2010 5-year est.); Bachelor's degree or higher: 23.0% (2006-2010 5-year est.); Master's degree or higher: 6.3% (2006-2010 5-year est.).

Housing: Homeownership rate: 93.6% (2010); Median home value: $176,500 (2006-2010 5-year est.); Median contract rent: $522 per month (2006-2010 5-year est.); Median year structure built: 1978 (2006-2010 5-year est.).

Transportation: Commute to work: 92.9% car, 0.0% public transportation, 1.6% walk, 5.3% work from home (2006-2010 5-year est.); Travel time to work: 22.3% less than 15 minutes, 63.2% 15 to 30 minutes, 8.5% 30 to 45 minutes, 3.4% 45 to 60 minutes, 2.7% 60 minutes or more (2006-2010 5-year est.)

Additional Information Contacts
Williamsport/Lycoming Chamber of Commerce . . . . (570) 326-1971
http://www.williamsport.org

FAIRFIELD (township). Covers a land area of 12.135 square miles and a water area of 0.219 square miles. Located at 41.26° N. Lat; 76.88° W. Long.

Population: 2,580 (1990); 2,659 (2000); 2,792 (2010); Density: 230.1 persons per square mile (2010); Race: 97.9% White, 0.5% Black, 0.5% Asian, 0.3% American Indian/Alaska Native, 0.0% Native Hawaiian/Other Pacific Islander, 0.8% Other, 0.6% Hispanic of any race (2010); Average household size: 2.43 (2010); Median age: 45.4 (2010); Males per 100 females: 99.3 (2010); Marriage status: 20.4% never married, 66.6% now married, 4.6% widowed, 8.5% divorced (2006-2010 5-year est.); Foreign born: 2.1% (2006-2010 5-year est.); Ancestry (includes multiple ancestries): 51.6% German, 16.7% Irish, 11.8% English, 8.4% Italian, 5.6% Polish (2006-2010 5-year est.).

Economy: Single-family building permits issued: 2 (2011); Multi-family building permits issued: 0 (2011); Employment by occupation: 6.6% management, 5.9% professional, 7.6% services, 17.6% sales, 6.8% farming, 10.7% construction, 10.8% production (2006-2010 5-year est.).

Income: Per capita income: $32,328 (2006-2010 5-year est.); Median household income: $60,100 (2006-2010 5-year est.); Average household income: $76,292 (2006-2010 5-year est.); Percent of households with income of $100,000 or more: 24.3% (2006-2010 5-year est.); Poverty rate: 3.3% (2006-2010 5-year est.).

Education: Percent of population age 25 and over with: High school diploma (including GED) or higher: 94.7% (2006-2010 5-year est.); Bachelor's degree or higher: 33.6% (2006-2010 5-year est.); Master's degree or higher: 10.8% (2006-2010 5-year est.).

Housing: Homeownership rate: 86.2% (2010); Median home value: $163,400 (2006-2010 5-year est.); Median contract rent: $1,095 per month (2006-2010 5-year est.); Median year structure built: 1980 (2006-2010 5-year est.).

Transportation: Commute to work: 93.8% car, 0.4% public transportation, 0.6% walk, 1.7% work from home (2006-2010 5-year est.); Travel time to work: 37.5% less than 15 minutes, 49.2% 15 to 30 minutes, 6.7% 30 to 45 minutes, 2.4% 45 to 60 minutes, 4.3% 60 minutes or more (2006-2010 5-year est.)

Additional Information Contacts
Williamsport/Lycoming Chamber of Commerce . . . . (570) 326-1971
http://www.williamsport.org

FAXON (CDP). Covers a land area of 0.473 square miles and a water area of 0 square miles. Located at 41.26° N. Lat; 76.98° W. Long. Elevation is 522 feet.

Population: n/a (1990); n/a (2000); 1,395 (2010); Density: 2,948.0 persons per square mile (2010); Race: 96.8% White, 1.3% Black, 1.1% Asian, 0.1% American Indian/Alaska Native, 0.0% Native Hawaiian/Other Pacific Islander, 0.7% Other, 0.9% Hispanic of any race (2010); Average household size: 2.24 (2010); Median age: 48.8 (2010); Males per 100 females: 96.5 (2010); Marriage status: 15.3% never married, 64.3% now married, 9.3% widowed, 11.0% divorced (2006-2010 5-year est.); Foreign born: 3.9% (2006-2010 5-year est.); Ancestry (includes multiple ancestries): 42.5% German, 22.5% Irish, 12.5% Italian, 8.2% Dutch, 8.2% English (2006-2010 5-year est.).

Economy: Employment by occupation: 20.5% management, 2.3% professional, 1.4% services, 9.8% sales, 2.0% farming, 9.2% construction, 5.4% production (2006-2010 5-year est.).

Income: Per capita income: $26,550 (2006-2010 5-year est.); Median household income: $51,473 (2006-2010 5-year est.); Average household income: $60,162 (2006-2010 5-year est.); Percent of households with income of $100,000 or more: 14.9% (2006-2010 5-year est.); Poverty rate: 10.2% (2006-2010 5-year est.).

Education: Percent of population age 25 and over with: High school diploma (including GED) or higher: 89.1% (2006-2010 5-year est.); Bachelor's degree or higher: 28.5% (2006-2010 5-year est.); Master's degree or higher: 11.4% (2006-2010 5-year est.).

Housing: Homeownership rate: 77.7% (2010); Median home value: $150,000 (2006-2010 5-year est.); Median contract rent: $657 per month (2006-2010 5-year est.); Median year structure built: 1954 (2006-2010 5-year est.).

Transportation: Commute to work: 91.6% car, 0.0% public transportation, 1.9% walk, 6.5% work from home (2006-2010 5-year est.); Travel time to work: 61.6% less than 15 minutes, 38.4% 15 to 30 minutes, 0.0% 30 to 45 minutes, 0.0% 45 to 60 minutes, 0.0% 60 minutes or more (2006-2010 5-year est.)

FRANKLIN (township). Covers a land area of 23.913 square miles and a water area of 0.135 square miles. Located at 41.23° N. Lat; 76.59° W. Long.

Population: 901 (1990); 915 (2000); 933 (2010); Density: 39.0 persons per square mile (2010); Race: 99.0% White, 0.0% Black, 0.1% Asian, 0.4% American Indian/Alaska Native, 0.0% Native Hawaiian/Other Pacific Islander, 0.5% Other, 0.0% Hispanic of any race (2010); Average household size: 2.56 (2010); Median age: 42.6 (2010); Males per 100 females: 102.4 (2010); Marriage status: 18.6% never married, 70.7% now married, 4.5% widowed, 6.2% divorced (2006-2010 5-year est.); Foreign born: 0.3% (2006-2010 5-year est.); Ancestry (includes multiple ancestries): 43.3% German, 14.8% American, 12.3% Irish, 9.6% English, 6.0% Polish (2006-2010 5-year est.).

Economy: Single-family building permits issued: 0 (2011); Multi-family building permits issued: 0 (2011); Employment by occupation: 5.5% management, 2.1% professional, 10.3% services, 16.8% sales, 2.9% farming, 16.8% construction, 10.9% production (2006-2010 5-year est.).
Income: Per capita income: $19,973 (2006-2010 5-year est.); Median household income: $54,044 (2006-2010 5-year est.); Average household income: $56,847 (2006-2010 5-year est.); Percent of households with income of $100,000 or more: 7.5% (2006-2010 5-year est.); Poverty rate: 10.2% (2006-2010 5-year est.).
Education: Percent of population age 25 and over with: High school diploma (including GED) or higher: 86.9% (2006-2010 5-year est.); Bachelor's degree or higher: 9.0% (2006-2010 5-year est.); Master's degree or higher: 3.8% (2006-2010 5-year est.).
Housing: Homeownership rate: 82.8% (2010); Median home value: $137,200 (2006-2010 5-year est.); Median contract rent: $418 per month (2006-2010 5-year est.); Median year structure built: 1971 (2006-2010 5-year est.).
Transportation: Commute to work: 98.1% car, 0.6% public transportation, 0.0% walk, 1.3% work from home (2006-2010 5-year est.); Travel time to work: 7.8% less than 15 minutes, 47.5% 15 to 30 minutes, 25.7% 30 to 45 minutes, 12.4% 45 to 60 minutes, 6.5% 60 minutes or more (2006-2010 5-year est.)

GAMBLE (township). Covers a land area of 44.963 square miles and a water area of 0.813 square miles. Located at 41.37° N. Lat; 76.95° W. Long.
Population: 744 (1990); 854 (2000); 756 (2010); Density: 16.8 persons per square mile (2010); Race: 99.3% White, 0.0% Black, 0.1% Asian, 0.1% American Indian/Alaska Native, 0.0% Native Hawaiian/Other Pacific Islander, 0.5% Other, 0.0% Hispanic of any race (2010); Average household size: 2.45 (2010); Median age: 47.5 (2010); Males per 100 females: 106.0 (2010); Marriage status: 19.6% never married, 64.3% now married, 7.1% widowed, 9.0% divorced (2006-2010 5-year est.); Foreign born: 1.7% (2006-2010 5-year est.); Ancestry (includes multiple ancestries): 40.4% German, 20.3% Irish, 11.3% English, 9.5% American, 7.9% Italian (2006-2010 5-year est.).
Economy: Single-family building permits issued: 2 (2011); Multi-family building permits issued: 0 (2011); Employment by occupation: 13.7% management, 3.9% professional, 10.0% services, 10.0% sales, 2.7% farming, 14.4% construction, 11.2% production (2006-2010 5-year est.).
Income: Per capita income: $24,000 (2006-2010 5-year est.); Median household income: $51,250 (2006-2010 5-year est.); Average household income: $60,177 (2006-2010 5-year est.); Percent of households with income of $100,000 or more: 14.2% (2006-2010 5-year est.); Poverty rate: 6.1% (2006-2010 5-year est.).
Education: Percent of population age 25 and over with: High school diploma (including GED) or higher: 88.2% (2006-2010 5-year est.); Bachelor's degree or higher: 19.7% (2006-2010 5-year est.); Master's degree or higher: 6.6% (2006-2010 5-year est.).
Housing: Homeownership rate: 89.9% (2010); Median home value: $147,400 (2006-2010 5-year est.); Median contract rent: $397 per month (2006-2010 5-year est.); Median year structure built: 1976 (2006-2010 5-year est.).
Transportation: Commute to work: 90.7% car, 0.7% public transportation, 5.3% walk, 2.3% work from home (2006-2010 5-year est.); Travel time to work: 9.7% less than 15 minutes, 52.4% 15 to 30 minutes, 29.9% 30 to 45 minutes, 4.5% 45 to 60 minutes, 3.6% 60 minutes or more (2006-2010 5-year est.)

GARDEN VIEW (CDP). Covers a land area of 1.063 square miles and a water area of 0.023 square miles. Located at 41.26° N. Lat; 77.05° W. Long. Elevation is 548 feet.
Population: 2,687 (1990); 2,679 (2000); 2,503 (2010); Density: 2,353.9 persons per square mile (2010); Race: 96.3% White, 1.4% Black, 0.7% Asian, 0.2% American Indian/Alaska Native, 0.0% Native Hawaiian/Other Pacific Islander, 1.4% Other, 1.0% Hispanic of any race (2010); Average household size: 2.19 (2010); Median age: 47.5 (2010); Males per 100 females: 94.3 (2010); Marriage status: 26.0% never married, 57.8% now married, 6.3% widowed, 9.9% divorced (2006-2010 5-year est.); Foreign born: 4.0% (2006-2010 5-year est.); Ancestry (includes multiple ancestries): 35.4% German, 21.1% Irish, 12.2% Italian, 9.8% English, 6.5% Dutch (2006-2010 5-year est.).
Economy: Employment by occupation: 5.3% management, 1.2% professional, 12.2% services, 13.9% sales, 1.7% farming, 9.2% construction, 17.7% production (2006-2010 5-year est.).

Income: Per capita income: $21,061 (2006-2010 5-year est.); Median household income: $40,962 (2006-2010 5-year est.); Average household income: $47,255 (2006-2010 5-year est.); Percent of households with income of $100,000 or more: 4.4% (2006-2010 5-year est.); Poverty rate: 2.6% (2006-2010 5-year est.).
Education: Percent of population age 25 and over with: High school diploma (including GED) or higher: 83.6% (2006-2010 5-year est.); Bachelor's degree or higher: 13.0% (2006-2010 5-year est.); Master's degree or higher: 4.0% (2006-2010 5-year est.).
Housing: Homeownership rate: 69.1% (2010); Median home value: $104,400 (2006-2010 5-year est.); Median contract rent: $469 per month (2006-2010 5-year est.); Median year structure built: 1966 (2006-2010 5-year est.).
Transportation: Commute to work: 86.0% car, 0.0% public transportation, 3.8% walk, 5.0% work from home (2006-2010 5-year est.); Travel time to work: 50.2% less than 15 minutes, 32.4% 15 to 30 minutes, 12.2% 30 to 45 minutes, 3.3% 45 to 60 minutes, 1.9% 60 minutes or more (2006-2010 5-year est.)
Additional Information Contacts
Butler County Chamber of Commerce . . . . (724) 283-2222
  http://www.butlercountychamber.com

HEPBURN (township). Covers a land area of 16.668 square miles and a water area of 0.097 square miles. Located at 41.32° N. Lat; 77.03° W. Long.
Population: 2,834 (1990); 2,836 (2000); 2,762 (2010); Density: 165.7 persons per square mile (2010); Race: 97.5% White, 0.7% Black, 0.8% Asian, 0.2% American Indian/Alaska Native, 0.1% Native Hawaiian/Other Pacific Islander, 0.7% Other, 0.9% Hispanic of any race (2010); Average household size: 2.49 (2010); Median age: 47.2 (2010); Males per 100 females: 101.9 (2010); Marriage status: 22.1% never married, 71.0% now married, 2.0% widowed, 4.9% divorced (2006-2010 5-year est.); Foreign born: 2.6% (2006-2010 5-year est.); Ancestry (includes multiple ancestries): 43.4% German, 15.5% Italian, 10.8% American, 8.9% Irish, 7.3% English (2006-2010 5-year est.).
Economy: Single-family building permits issued: 3 (2011); Multi-family building permits issued: 0 (2011); Employment by occupation: 8.9% management, 1.6% professional, 2.7% services, 20.7% sales, 5.0% farming, 16.3% construction, 11.3% production (2006-2010 5-year est.).
Income: Per capita income: $26,924 (2006-2010 5-year est.); Median household income: $56,008 (2006-2010 5-year est.); Average household income: $70,668 (2006-2010 5-year est.); Percent of households with income of $100,000 or more: 15.8% (2006-2010 5-year est.); Poverty rate: 2.3% (2006-2010 5-year est.).
Education: Percent of population age 25 and over with: High school diploma (including GED) or higher: 89.9% (2006-2010 5-year est.); Bachelor's degree or higher: 19.6% (2006-2010 5-year est.); Master's degree or higher: 2.8% (2006-2010 5-year est.).
Housing: Homeownership rate: 87.1% (2010); Median home value: $133,100 (2006-2010 5-year est.); Median contract rent: $393 per month (2006-2010 5-year est.); Median year structure built: 1975 (2006-2010 5-year est.).
Transportation: Commute to work: 95.2% car, 0.0% public transportation, 0.0% walk, 3.5% work from home (2006-2010 5-year est.); Travel time to work: 38.5% less than 15 minutes, 52.7% 15 to 30 minutes, 7.0% 30 to 45 minutes, 0.0% 45 to 60 minutes, 1.8% 60 minutes or more (2006-2010 5-year est.)
Additional Information Contacts
Williamsport/Lycoming Chamber of Commerce . . . . (570) 326-1971
  http://www.williamsport.org

HUGHESVILLE (borough). Covers a land area of 0.645 square miles and a water area of 0 square miles. Located at 41.24° N. Lat; 76.73° W. Long. Elevation is 581 feet.
History: Laid out 1816, incorporated 1852.
Population: 2,049 (1990); 2,220 (2000); 2,128 (2010); Density: 3,299.8 persons per square mile (2010); Race: 97.6% White, 0.5% Black, 0.4% Asian, 0.2% American Indian/Alaska Native, 0.0% Native Hawaiian/Other Pacific Islander, 1.3% Other, 0.9% Hispanic of any race (2010); Average household size: 2.21 (2010); Median age: 41.8 (2010); Males per 100 females: 87.3 (2010); Marriage status: 25.4% never married, 53.7% now married, 10.7% widowed, 10.3% divorced (2006-2010 5-year est.); Foreign born: 1.4% (2006-2010 5-year est.); Ancestry (includes multiple ancestries): 43.0% German, 11.4% English, 11.4% Irish, 7.4% American, 7.2% Italian (2006-2010 5-year est.).

Economy: Single-family building permits issued: 1 (2011); Multi-family building permits issued: 0 (2011); Employment by occupation: 6.4% management, 3.0% professional, 6.6% services, 20.7% sales, 4.7% farming, 9.3% construction, 9.3% production (2006-2010 5-year est.).
Income: Per capita income: $21,110 (2006-2010 5-year est.); Median household income: $38,672 (2006-2010 5-year est.); Average household income: $48,847 (2006-2010 5-year est.); Percent of households with income of $100,000 or more: 8.5% (2006-2010 5-year est.); Poverty rate: 10.3% (2006-2010 5-year est.).
Education: Percent of population age 25 and over with: High school diploma (including GED) or higher: 88.4% (2006-2010 5-year est.); Bachelor's degree or higher: 18.9% (2006-2010 5-year est.); Master's degree or higher: 6.0% (2006-2010 5-year est.).

School District(s)

East Lycoming SD (PK-12)
   2010-11 Enrollment: 1,682 . . . . (570) 584-2131
Lycoming CTC (10-12)
   2010-11 Enrollment: n/a . . . . (570) 584-2300
Housing: Homeownership rate: 59.2% (2010); Median home value: $107,300 (2006-2010 5-year est.); Median contract rent: $385 per month (2006-2010 5-year est.); Median year structure built: before 1940 (2006-2010 5-year est.).
Safety: Violent crime rate: 32.8 per 10,000 population; Property crime rate: 309.1 per 10,000 population (2011).
Newspapers: East Lycoming Shopper and News (Community news; Circulation 18,700)
Transportation: Commute to work: 90.8% car, 0.6% public transportation, 3.5% walk, 5.0% work from home (2006-2010 5-year est.); Travel time to work: 32.1% less than 15 minutes, 38.9% 15 to 30 minutes, 20.3% 30 to 45 minutes, 5.5% 45 to 60 minutes, 3.3% 60 minutes or more (2006-2010 5-year est.)

Additional Information Contacts

Williamsport/Lycoming Chamber of Commerce . . . . (570) 326-1971
  http://www.williamsport.org

JACKSON (township). Covers a land area of 37.044 square miles and a water area of 0.212 square miles. Located at 41.51° N. Lat; 77.11° W. Long.
Population: 421 (1990); 414 (2000); 396 (2010); Density: 10.7 persons per square mile (2010); Race: 99.5% White, 0.0% Black, 0.0% Asian, 0.0% American Indian/Alaska Native, 0.0% Native Hawaiian/Other Pacific Islander, 0.5% Other, 0.3% Hispanic of any race (2010); Average household size: 2.54 (2010); Median age: 46.7 (2010); Males per 100 females: 105.2 (2010); Marriage status: 23.4% never married, 64.9% now married, 7.1% widowed, 4.6% divorced (2006-2010 5-year est.); Foreign born: 1.1% (2006-2010 5-year est.); Ancestry (includes multiple ancestries): 50.0% German, 14.4% Irish, 12.3% English, 8.9% Scottish, 5.5% Italian (2006-2010 5-year est.).
Economy: Single-family building permits issued: 0 (2011); Multi-family building permits issued: 0 (2011); Employment by occupation: 6.7% management, 1.7% professional, 7.9% services, 19.2% sales, 2.9% farming, 15.8% construction, 7.1% production (2006-2010 5-year est.).
Income: Per capita income: $21,006 (2006-2010 5-year est.); Median household income: $50,588 (2006-2010 5-year est.); Average household income: $53,376 (2006-2010 5-year est.); Percent of households with income of $100,000 or more: 7.4% (2006-2010 5-year est.); Poverty rate: 18.5% (2006-2010 5-year est.).
Education: Percent of population age 25 and over with: High school diploma (including GED) or higher: 92.6% (2006-2010 5-year est.); Bachelor's degree or higher: 12.2% (2006-2010 5-year est.); Master's degree or higher: 4.1% (2006-2010 5-year est.).
Housing: Homeownership rate: 92.9% (2010); Median home value: $154,300 (2006-2010 5-year est.); Median contract rent: $439 per month (2006-2010 5-year est.); Median year structure built: 1965 (2006-2010 5-year est.).
Transportation: Commute to work: 91.1% car, 0.0% public transportation, 1.3% walk, 1.7% work from home (2006-2010 5-year est.); Travel time to work: 28.1% less than 15 minutes, 13.4% 15 to 30 minutes, 43.7% 30 to 45 minutes, 9.5% 45 to 60 minutes, 5.2% 60 minutes or more (2006-2010 5-year est.)

JERSEY MILLS (unincorporated postal area)
Zip Code: 17739
  Covers a land area of 12.542 square miles and a water area of 0.140 square miles. Located at 41.39° N. Lat; 77.40° W. Long. Elevation is

650 feet. Population: 32 (2010); Density: 2.6 persons per square mile (2010); Race: 100.0% White, 0.0% Black, 0.0% Asian, 0.0% American Indian/Alaska Native, 0.0% Native Hawaiian/Other Pacific Islander, 0.0% Other, 0.0% Hispanic of any race (2010); Average household size: 1.60 (2010); Median age: 63.0 (2010); Males per 100 females: 77.8 (2010); Homeownership rate: 85.0% (2010)

JERSEY SHORE (borough). Aka Tombs Run. Covers a land area of 1.158 square miles and a water area of 0.024 square miles. Located at 41.20° N. Lat; 77.27° W. Long. Elevation is 604 feet.
History: Settled 1785, incorporated 1826.
Population: 4,353 (1990); 4,482 (2000); 4,361 (2010); Density: 3,766.7 persons per square mile (2010); Race: 97.9% White, 0.8% Black, 0.2% Asian, 0.1% American Indian/Alaska Native, 0.1% Native Hawaiian/Other Pacific Islander, 0.9% Other, 0.6% Hispanic of any race (2010); Average household size: 2.49 (2010); Median age: 35.1 (2010); Males per 100 females: 89.0 (2010); Marriage status: 37.4% never married, 46.9% now married, 5.8% widowed, 9.9% divorced (2006-2010 5-year est.); Foreign born: 0.4% (2006-2010 5-year est.); Ancestry (includes multiple ancestries): 43.1% German, 10.8% Italian, 6.4% English, 6.3% Irish, 5.1% Dutch (2006-2010 5-year est.).
Economy: Single-family building permits issued: 0 (2011); Multi-family building permits issued: 0 (2011); Employment by occupation: 4.2% management, 1.4% professional, 5.0% services, 22.0% sales, 4.1% farming, 8.8% construction, 10.3% production (2006-2010 5-year est.).
Income: Per capita income: $17,888 (2006-2010 5-year est.); Median household income: $43,694 (2006-2010 5-year est.); Average household income: $46,118 (2006-2010 5-year est.); Percent of households with income of $100,000 or more: 8.4% (2006-2010 5-year est.); Poverty rate: 21.6% (2006-2010 5-year est.).
Education: Percent of population age 25 and over with: High school diploma (including GED) or higher: 82.8% (2006-2010 5-year est.); Bachelor's degree or higher: 14.7% (2006-2010 5-year est.); Master's degree or higher: 3.5% (2006-2010 5-year est.).

School District(s)

Jersey Shore Area SD (KG-12)
   2010-11 Enrollment: 2,762 . . . . (570) 398-1561
Housing: Homeownership rate: 53.8% (2010); Median home value: $90,900 (2006-2010 5-year est.); Median contract rent: $461 per month (2006-2010 5-year est.); Median year structure built: before 1940 (2006-2010 5-year est.).
Hospitals: Jersey Shore Hospital (49 beds)
Transportation: Commute to work: 93.5% car, 0.0% public transportation, 1.7% walk, 1.8% work from home (2006-2010 5-year est.); Travel time to work: 33.9% less than 15 minutes, 49.4% 15 to 30 minutes, 9.2% 30 to 45 minutes, 2.0% 45 to 60 minutes, 5.4% 60 minutes or more (2006-2010 5-year est.)

Additional Information Contacts

Williamsport/Lycoming Chamber of Commerce . . . . (570) 326-1971
  http://www.williamsport.org

JORDAN (township). Covers a land area of 20.893 square miles and a water area of 0.034 square miles. Located at 41.24° N. Lat; 76.53° W. Long.
Population: 871 (1990); 878 (2000); 863 (2010); Density: 41.3 persons per square mile (2010); Race: 99.7% White, 0.1% Black, 0.1% Asian, 0.0% American Indian/Alaska Native, 0.0% Native Hawaiian/Other Pacific Islander, 0.1% Other, 0.3% Hispanic of any race (2010); Average household size: 2.49 (2010); Median age: 42.3 (2010); Males per 100 females: 108.0 (2010); Marriage status: 23.0% never married, 62.8% now married, 6.1% widowed, 8.2% divorced (2006-2010 5-year est.); Foreign born: 0.0% (2006-2010 5-year est.); Ancestry (includes multiple ancestries): 45.7% German, 16.0% American, 12.4% Irish, 8.5% English, 5.4% Italian (2006-2010 5-year est.).
Economy: Single-family building permits issued: 1 (2011); Multi-family building permits issued: 0 (2011); Employment by occupation: 10.5% management, 3.1% professional, 8.2% services, 17.3% sales, 2.4% farming, 24.1% construction, 9.9% production (2006-2010 5-year est.).
Income: Per capita income: $21,269 (2006-2010 5-year est.); Median household income: $37,083 (2006-2010 5-year est.); Average household income: $52,497 (2006-2010 5-year est.); Percent of households with income of $100,000 or more: 11.0% (2006-2010 5-year est.); Poverty rate: 17.8% (2006-2010 5-year est.).
Education: Percent of population age 25 and over with: High school diploma (including GED) or higher: 81.5% (2006-2010 5-year est.);

Bachelor's degree or higher: 13.0% (2006-2010 5-year est.); Master's degree or higher: 6.3% (2006-2010 5-year est.).

Housing: Homeownership rate: 80.3% (2010); Median home value: $112,500 (2006-2010 5-year est.); Median contract rent: $369 per month (2006-2010 5-year est.); Median year structure built: 1974 (2006-2010 5-year est.).

Transportation: Commute to work: 90.4% car, 0.0% public transportation, 1.1% walk, 7.5% work from home (2006-2010 5-year est.); Travel time to work: 10.4% less than 15 minutes, 25.5% 15 to 30 minutes, 36.3% 30 to 45 minutes, 12.0% 45 to 60 minutes, 15.8% 60 minutes or more (2006-2010 5-year est.)

KENMAR (CDP). Covers a land area of 2.048 square miles and a water area of 0.008 square miles. Located at 41.25° N. Lat; 76.95° W. Long. Elevation is 551 feet.

Population: n/a (1990); n/a (2000); 4,124 (2010); Density: 2,013.2 persons per square mile (2010); Race: 90.4% White, 5.1% Black, 1.3% Asian, 0.1% American Indian/Alaska Native, 0.1% Native Hawaiian/Other Pacific Islander, 3.0% Other, 1.8% Hispanic of any race (2010); Average household size: 2.07 (2010); Median age: 49.0 (2010); Males per 100 females: 74.5 (2010); Marriage status: 15.3% never married, 53.5% now married, 18.2% widowed, 13.0% divorced (2006-2010 5-year est.); Foreign born: 4.0% (2006-2010 5-year est.); Ancestry (includes multiple ancestries): 32.7% German, 21.5% Irish, 15.9% English, 12.4% Italian, 7.7% American (2006-2010 5-year est.).

Economy: Employment by occupation: 10.7% management, 4.3% professional, 6.8% services, 26.1% sales, 5.0% farming, 6.6% construction, 2.1% production (2006-2010 5-year est.).

Income: Per capita income: $23,009 (2006-2010 5-year est.); Median household income: $35,285 (2006-2010 5-year est.); Average household income: $46,611 (2006-2010 5-year est.); Percent of households with income of $100,000 or more: 7.5% (2006-2010 5-year est.); Poverty rate: 12.5% (2006-2010 5-year est.).

Education: Percent of population age 25 and over with: High school diploma (including GED) or higher: 91.3% (2006-2010 5-year est.); Bachelor's degree or higher: 23.5% (2006-2010 5-year est.); Master's degree or higher: 7.1% (2006-2010 5-year est.).

Housing: Homeownership rate: 65.3% (2010); Median home value: $132,900 (2006-2010 5-year est.); Median contract rent: $461 per month (2006-2010 5-year est.); Median year structure built: 1963 (2006-2010 5-year est.).

Transportation: Commute to work: 88.5% car, 0.0% public transportation, 4.7% walk, 5.9% work from home (2006-2010 5-year est.); Travel time to work: 67.2% less than 15 minutes, 19.5% 15 to 30 minutes, 5.4% 30 to 45 minutes, 4.0% 45 to 60 minutes, 3.9% 60 minutes or more (2006-2010 5-year est.)

LAIRDSVILLE (unincorporated postal area)

Zip Code: 17742

Covers a land area of 0.076 square miles and a water area of 0.003 square miles. Located at 41.23° N. Lat; 76.60° W. Long. Elevation is 748 feet. Population: 39 (2010); Density: 513.0 persons per square mile (2010); Race: 97.4% White, 0.0% Black, 0.0% Asian, 0.0% American Indian/Alaska Native, 0.0% Native Hawaiian/Other Pacific Islander, 2.6% Other, 0.0% Hispanic of any race (2010); Average household size: 2.05 (2010); Median age: 49.8 (2010); Males per 100 females: 69.6 (2010); Homeownership rate: 68.4% (2010)

LEWIS (township). Covers a land area of 37.091 square miles and a water area of 0.351 square miles. Located at 41.42° N. Lat; 77.05° W. Long.

Population: 1,194 (1990); 1,139 (2000); 987 (2010); Density: 26.6 persons per square mile (2010); Race: 98.7% White, 0.4% Black, 0.0% Asian, 0.0% American Indian/Alaska Native, 0.0% Native Hawaiian/Other Pacific Islander, 0.9% Other, 1.2% Hispanic of any race (2010); Average household size: 2.36 (2010); Median age: 46.1 (2010); Males per 100 females: 113.2 (2010); Marriage status: 22.8% never married, 58.6% now married, 7.6% widowed, 11.0% divorced (2006-2010 5-year est.); Foreign born: 0.5% (2006-2010 5-year est.); Ancestry (includes multiple ancestries): 57.6% German, 14.8% Irish, 11.4% English, 5.0% Dutch, 4.7% Italian (2006-2010 5-year est.).

Economy: Single-family building permits issued: 0 (2011); Multi-family building permits issued: 0 (2011); Employment by occupation: 2.8% management, 2.2% professional, 12.1% services, 15.7% sales, 2.2% farming, 15.5% construction, 19.4% production (2006-2010 5-year est.).

Income: Per capita income: $16,045 (2006-2010 5-year est.); Median household income: $41,250 (2006-2010 5-year est.); Average household income: $44,555 (2006-2010 5-year est.); Percent of households with income of $100,000 or more: 3.8% (2006-2010 5-year est.); Poverty rate: 21.7% (2006-2010 5-year est.).

Education: Percent of population age 25 and over with: High school diploma (including GED) or higher: 85.8% (2006-2010 5-year est.); Bachelor's degree or higher: 10.3% (2006-2010 5-year est.); Master's degree or higher: 3.6% (2006-2010 5-year est.).

Housing: Homeownership rate: 76.0% (2010); Median home value: $108,300 (2006-2010 5-year est.); Median contract rent: $443 per month (2006-2010 5-year est.); Median year structure built: 1967 (2006-2010 5-year est.).

Transportation: Commute to work: 94.4% car, 0.0% public transportation, 3.5% walk, 1.4% work from home (2006-2010 5-year est.); Travel time to work: 16.9% less than 15 minutes, 58.9% 15 to 30 minutes, 16.9% 30 to 45 minutes, 4.0% 45 to 60 minutes, 3.3% 60 minutes or more (2006-2010 5-year est.)

Additional Information Contacts

Williamsport/Lycoming Chamber of Commerce . . . . (570) 326-1971
http://www.williamsport.org

LIMESTONE (township). Covers a land area of 33.618 square miles and a water area of 0.127 square miles. Located at 41.14° N. Lat; 77.16° W. Long.

Population: 1,893 (1990); 2,136 (2000); 2,019 (2010); Density: 60.1 persons per square mile (2010); Race: 99.1% White, 0.0% Black, 0.2% Asian, 0.2% American Indian/Alaska Native, 0.0% Native Hawaiian/Other Pacific Islander, 0.5% Other, 0.7% Hispanic of any race (2010); Average household size: 2.84 (2010); Median age: 40.4 (2010); Males per 100 females: 106.4 (2010); Marriage status: 19.7% never married, 69.3% now married, 3.7% widowed, 7.2% divorced (2006-2010 5-year est.); Foreign born: 0.4% (2006-2010 5-year est.); Ancestry (includes multiple ancestries): 57.7% German, 10.2% Irish, 9.3% American, 7.0% Italian, 5.2% English (2006-2010 5-year est.).

Economy: Single-family building permits issued: 0 (2011); Multi-family building permits issued: 0 (2011); Employment by occupation: 13.1% management, 1.4% professional, 9.8% services, 15.5% sales, 5.0% farming, 13.1% construction, 12.1% production (2006-2010 5-year est.).

Income: Per capita income: $23,272 (2006-2010 5-year est.); Median household income: $59,811 (2006-2010 5-year est.); Average household income: $67,687 (2006-2010 5-year est.); Percent of households with income of $100,000 or more: 16.0% (2006-2010 5-year est.); Poverty rate: 3.2% (2006-2010 5-year est.).

Education: Percent of population age 25 and over with: High school diploma (including GED) or higher: 88.0% (2006-2010 5-year est.); Bachelor's degree or higher: 16.0% (2006-2010 5-year est.); Master's degree or higher: 3.7% (2006-2010 5-year est.).

Housing: Homeownership rate: 89.3% (2010); Median home value: $151,700 (2006-2010 5-year est.); Median contract rent: $363 per month (2006-2010 5-year est.); Median year structure built: 1974 (2006-2010 5-year est.).

Transportation: Commute to work: 91.4% car, 0.0% public transportation, 3.9% walk, 3.7% work from home (2006-2010 5-year est.); Travel time to work: 10.9% less than 15 minutes, 52.8% 15 to 30 minutes, 26.6% 30 to 45 minutes, 2.8% 45 to 60 minutes, 6.8% 60 minutes or more (2006-2010 5-year est.)

Additional Information Contacts

Williamsport/Lycoming Chamber of Commerce . . . . (570) 326-1971
http://www.williamsport.org

LINDEN (unincorporated postal area)

Zip Code: 17744

Covers a land area of 23.934 square miles and a water area of 0.596 square miles. Located at 41.24° N. Lat; 77.15° W. Long. Population: 3,175 (2010); Density: 132.7 persons per square mile (2010); Race: 97.4% White, 0.4% Black, 0.5% Asian, 0.3% American Indian/Alaska Native, 0.1% Native Hawaiian/Other Pacific Islander, 1.3% Other, 1.2% Hispanic of any race (2010); Average household size: 2.49 (2010); Median age: 45.0 (2010); Males per 100 females: 103.3 (2010); Homeownership rate: 82.9% (2010)

LOYALSOCK (township). Covers a land area of 21.151 square miles and a water area of 0.344 square miles. Located at 41.27° N. Lat; 76.98° W. Long.

Population: 10,644 (1990); 10,876 (2000); 11,026 (2010); Density: 521.3 persons per square mile (2010); Race: 93.8% White, 2.8% Black, 1.4% Asian, 0.1% American Indian/Alaska Native, 0.0% Native Hawaiian/Other Pacific Islander, 1.9% Other, 1.2% Hispanic of any race (2010); Average household size: 2.18 (2010); Median age: 50.0 (2010); Males per 100 females: 86.6 (2010); Marriage status: 15.6% never married, 57.9% now married, 17.4% widowed, 9.1% divorced (2006-2010 5-year est.); Foreign born: 3.6% (2006-2010 5-year est.); Ancestry (includes multiple ancestries): 37.0% German, 18.3% Irish, 12.2% Italian, 10.7% English, 6.2% American (2006-2010 5-year est.).

Economy: Single-family building permits issued: 11 (2011); Multi-family building permits issued: 48 (2011); Employment by occupation: 15.0% management, 2.9% professional, 6.1% services, 18.7% sales, 4.0% farming, 7.9% construction, 5.2% production (2006-2010 5-year est.).

Income: Per capita income: $26,688 (2006-2010 5-year est.); Median household income: $45,440 (2006-2010 5-year est.); Average household income: $59,302 (2006-2010 5-year est.); Percent of households with income of $100,000 or more: 14.7% (2006-2010 5-year est.); Poverty rate: 10.1% (2006-2010 5-year est.).

Education: Percent of population age 25 and over with: High school diploma (including GED) or higher: 88.9% (2006-2010 5-year est.); Bachelor's degree or higher: 26.5% (2006-2010 5-year est.); Master's degree or higher: 8.7% (2006-2010 5-year est.).

Housing: Homeownership rate: 69.1% (2010); Median home value: $149,300 (2006-2010 5-year est.); Median contract rent: $600 per month (2006-2010 5-year est.); Median year structure built: 1967 (2006-2010 5-year est.).

Transportation: Commute to work: 93.4% car, 0.0% public transportation, 2.6% walk, 3.3% work from home (2006-2010 5-year est.); Travel time to work: 60.6% less than 15 minutes, 30.8% 15 to 30 minutes, 4.4% 30 to 45 minutes, 1.4% 45 to 60 minutes, 2.8% 60 minutes or more (2006-2010 5-year est.)

Additional Information Contacts
Loyalsock Township . . . . (570) 323-6151
   http://www.loyalsocktownshipbos.com
Williamsport/Lycoming Chamber of Commerce . . . . (570) 326-1971
   http://www.williamsport.org

LYCOMING (township). Covers a land area of 15.175 square miles and a water area of 0.108 square miles. Located at 41.31° N. Lat; 77.10° W. Long.

Population: 1,939 (1990); 1,606 (2000); 1,478 (2010); Density: 97.4 persons per square mile (2010); Race: 98.0% White, 0.1% Black, 0.4% Asian, 0.2% American Indian/Alaska Native, 0.0% Native Hawaiian/Other Pacific Islander, 1.3% Other, 0.6% Hispanic of any race (2010); Average household size: 2.42 (2010); Median age: 46.4 (2010); Males per 100 females: 104.1 (2010); Marriage status: 21.0% never married, 64.3% now married, 5.2% widowed, 9.5% divorced (2006-2010 5-year est.); Foreign born: 1.1% (2006-2010 5-year est.); Ancestry (includes multiple ancestries): 46.2% German, 14.6% Irish, 10.6% English, 8.3% Italian, 4.1% French (2006-2010 5-year est.).

Economy: Single-family building permits issued: 3 (2011); Multi-family building permits issued: 0 (2011); Employment by occupation: 6.1% management, 1.3% professional, 12.1% services, 17.0% sales, 5.8% farming, 13.8% construction, 8.7% production (2006-2010 5-year est.).

Income: Per capita income: $24,804 (2006-2010 5-year est.); Median household income: $51,615 (2006-2010 5-year est.); Average household income: $61,853 (2006-2010 5-year est.); Percent of households with income of $100,000 or more: 10.5% (2006-2010 5-year est.); Poverty rate: 6.4% (2006-2010 5-year est.).

Education: Percent of population age 25 and over with: High school diploma (including GED) or higher: 86.8% (2006-2010 5-year est.); Bachelor's degree or higher: 9.3% (2006-2010 5-year est.); Master's degree or higher: 3.7% (2006-2010 5-year est.).

Housing: Homeownership rate: 85.3% (2010); Median home value: $115,400 (2006-2010 5-year est.); Median contract rent: $456 per month (2006-2010 5-year est.); Median year structure built: 1966 (2006-2010 5-year est.).

Transportation: Commute to work: 95.0% car, 0.5% public transportation, 2.4% walk, 1.2% work from home (2006-2010 5-year est.); Travel time to work: 22.0% less than 15 minutes, 60.3% 15 to 30 minutes, 9.7% 30 to 45

minutes, 2.6% 45 to 60 minutes, 5.4% 60 minutes or more (2006-2010 5-year est.)

Additional Information Contacts
Williamsport/Lycoming Chamber of Commerce . . . . (570) 326-1971
   http://www.williamsport.org

MCHENRY (township). Covers a land area of 76.221 square miles and a water area of 0.478 square miles. Located at 41.40° N. Lat; 77.45° W. Long.

Population: 246 (1990); 145 (2000); 143 (2010); Density: 1.9 persons per square mile (2010); Race: 96.5% White, 0.0% Black, 0.0% Asian, 2.1% American Indian/Alaska Native, 0.0% Native Hawaiian/Other Pacific Islander, 1.4% Other, 1.4% Hispanic of any race (2010); Average household size: 2.01 (2010); Median age: 55.4 (2010); Males per 100 females: 107.2 (2010); Marriage status: 18.7% never married, 55.6% now married, 11.1% widowed, 14.6% divorced (2006-2010 5-year est.); Foreign born: 0.0% (2006-2010 5-year est.); Ancestry (includes multiple ancestries): 52.6% German, 40.7% Irish, 11.0% Italian, 10.0% Pennsylvania German, 9.6% English (2006-2010 5-year est.).

Economy: Single-family building permits issued: 0 (2011); Multi-family building permits issued: 0 (2011); Employment by occupation: 2.5% management, 3.8% professional, 20.0% services, 11.3% sales, 0.0% farming, 7.5% construction, 5.0% production (2006-2010 5-year est.).

Income: Per capita income: $16,647 (2006-2010 5-year est.); Median household income: $28,929 (2006-2010 5-year est.); Average household income: $34,331 (2006-2010 5-year est.); Percent of households with income of $100,000 or more: 2.9% (2006-2010 5-year est.); Poverty rate: 35.9% (2006-2010 5-year est.).

Education: Percent of population age 25 and over with: High school diploma (including GED) or higher: 89.9% (2006-2010 5-year est.); Bachelor's degree or higher: 8.2% (2006-2010 5-year est.); Master's degree or higher: 5.7% (2006-2010 5-year est.).

Housing: Homeownership rate: 87.3% (2010); Median home value: $131,300 (2006-2010 5-year est.); Median contract rent: $429 per month (2006-2010 5-year est.); Median year structure built: 1959 (2006-2010 5-year est.).

Transportation: Commute to work: 100.0% car, 0.0% public transportation, 0.0% walk, 0.0% work from home (2006-2010 5-year est.); Travel time to work: 27.0% less than 15 minutes, 4.1% 15 to 30 minutes, 45.9% 30 to 45 minutes, 21.6% 45 to 60 minutes, 1.4% 60 minutes or more (2006-2010 5-year est.)

MCINTYRE (township). Covers a land area of 46.604 square miles and a water area of 0.856 square miles. Located at 41.51° N. Lat; 76.98° W. Long.

Population: 588 (1990); 539 (2000); 520 (2010); Density: 11.2 persons per square mile (2010); Race: 97.5% White, 0.4% Black, 0.2% Asian, 0.4% American Indian/Alaska Native, 0.0% Native Hawaiian/Other Pacific Islander, 1.5% Other, 0.0% Hispanic of any race (2010); Average household size: 2.56 (2010); Median age: 41.3 (2010); Males per 100 females: 96.2 (2010); Marriage status: 25.1% never married, 55.4% now married, 5.0% widowed, 14.5% divorced (2006-2010 5-year est.); Foreign born: 0.0% (2006-2010 5-year est.); Ancestry (includes multiple ancestries): 40.7% German, 27.6% Irish, 12.2% American, 9.6% English, 6.7% Hungarian (2006-2010 5-year est.).

Economy: Single-family building permits issued: 0 (2011); Multi-family building permits issued: 0 (2011); Employment by occupation: 3.8% management, 0.0% professional, 16.8% services, 12.5% sales, 2.7% farming, 14.1% construction, 9.8% production (2006-2010 5-year est.).

Income: Per capita income: $14,121 (2006-2010 5-year est.); Median household income: $33,026 (2006-2010 5-year est.); Average household income: $34,523 (2006-2010 5-year est.); Percent of households with income of $100,000 or more: 2.5% (2006-2010 5-year est.); Poverty rate: 23.8% (2006-2010 5-year est.).

Education: Percent of population age 25 and over with: High school diploma (including GED) or higher: 82.9% (2006-2010 5-year est.); Bachelor's degree or higher: 6.8% (2006-2010 5-year est.); Master's degree or higher: 2.8% (2006-2010 5-year est.).

Housing: Homeownership rate: 82.7% (2010); Median home value: $83,800 (2006-2010 5-year est.); Median contract rent: $369 per month (2006-2010 5-year est.); Median year structure built: 1961 (2006-2010 5-year est.).

Transportation: Commute to work: 86.4% car, 0.0% public transportation, 11.9% walk, 1.7% work from home (2006-2010 5-year est.); Travel time to work: 27.7% less than 15 minutes, 24.3% 15 to 30 minutes, 44.5% 30 to

45 minutes, 0.0% 45 to 60 minutes, 3.5% 60 minutes or more (2006-2010 5-year est.)

MCNETT (township). Covers a land area of 33.543 square miles and a water area of 0.374 square miles. Located at 41.55° N. Lat; 76.86° W. Long.

Population: 200 (1990); 211 (2000); 174 (2010); Density: 5.2 persons per square mile (2010); Race: 100.0% White, 0.0% Black, 0.0% Asian, 0.0% American Indian/Alaska Native, 0.0% Native Hawaiian/Other Pacific Islander, 0.0% Other, 0.6% Hispanic of any race (2010); Average household size: 2.38 (2010); Median age: 48.7 (2010); Males per 100 females: 109.6 (2010); Marriage status: 15.3% never married, 58.8% now married, 11.8% widowed, 14.1% divorced (2006-2010 5-year est.); Foreign born: 0.0% (2006-2010 5-year est.); Ancestry (includes multiple ancestries): 24.7% Irish, 20.6% Italian, 14.4% German, 10.3% English, 8.2% Dutch (2006-2010 5-year est.).

Economy: Single-family building permits issued: 0 (2011); Multi-family building permits issued: 0 (2011); Employment by occupation: 12.5% management, 4.2% professional, 12.5% services, 12.5% sales, 0.0% farming, 0.0% construction, 0.0% production (2006-2010 5-year est.).

Income: Per capita income: $18,068 (2006-2010 5-year est.); Median household income: $30,469 (2006-2010 5-year est.); Average household income: $37,136 (2006-2010 5-year est.); Percent of households with income of $100,000 or more: 10.6% (2006-2010 5-year est.); Poverty rate: 13.8% (2006-2010 5-year est.).

Education: Percent of population age 25 and over with: High school diploma (including GED) or higher: 88.0% (2006-2010 5-year est.); Bachelor's degree or higher: 17.3% (2006-2010 5-year est.); Master's degree or higher: 0.0% (2006-2010 5-year est.).

Housing: Homeownership rate: 82.2% (2010); Median home value: $95,000 (2006-2010 5-year est.); Median contract rent: $242 per month (2006-2010 5-year est.); Median year structure built: 1960 (2006-2010 5-year est.).

Transportation: Commute to work: 100.0% car, 0.0% public transportation, 0.0% walk, 0.0% work from home (2006-2010 5-year est.); Travel time to work: 13.6% less than 15 minutes, 40.9% 15 to 30 minutes, 13.6% 30 to 45 minutes, 9.1% 45 to 60 minutes, 22.7% 60 minutes or more (2006-2010 5-year est.)

MIFFLIN (township). Covers a land area of 27.702 square miles and a water area of 0.115 square miles. Located at 41.30° N. Lat; 77.25° W. Long.

Population: 1,110 (1990); 1,145 (2000); 1,070 (2010); Density: 38.6 persons per square mile (2010); Race: 98.2% White, 0.3% Black, 0.0% Asian, 0.4% American Indian/Alaska Native, 0.0% Native Hawaiian/Other Pacific Islander, 1.1% Other, 0.3% Hispanic of any race (2010); Average household size: 2.44 (2010); Median age: 44.3 (2010); Males per 100 females: 99.6 (2010); Marriage status: 21.2% never married, 65.4% now married, 3.4% widowed, 10.1% divorced (2006-2010 5-year est.); Foreign born: 0.9% (2006-2010 5-year est.); Ancestry (includes multiple ancestries): 48.7% German, 9.8% Irish, 9.3% English, 8.9% American, 7.6% Italian (2006-2010 5-year est.).

Economy: Single-family building permits issued: 1 (2011); Multi-family building permits issued: 0 (2011); Employment by occupation: 9.1% management, 1.4% professional, 7.7% services, 19.2% sales, 1.6% farming, 12.7% construction, 10.4% production (2006-2010 5-year est.).

Income: Per capita income: $22,891 (2006-2010 5-year est.); Median household income: $46,719 (2006-2010 5-year est.); Average household income: $56,956 (2006-2010 5-year est.); Percent of households with income of $100,000 or more: 13.2% (2006-2010 5-year est.); Poverty rate: 9.1% (2006-2010 5-year est.).

Education: Percent of population age 25 and over with: High school diploma (including GED) or higher: 84.3% (2006-2010 5-year est.); Bachelor's degree or higher: 12.9% (2006-2010 5-year est.); Master's degree or higher: 4.7% (2006-2010 5-year est.).

Housing: Homeownership rate: 87.2% (2010); Median home value: $121,000 (2006-2010 5-year est.); Median contract rent: $475 per month (2006-2010 5-year est.); Median year structure built: 1977 (2006-2010 5-year est.).

Transportation: Commute to work: 93.8% car, 0.0% public transportation, 0.4% walk, 3.8% work from home (2006-2010 5-year est.); Travel time to work: 17.9% less than 15 minutes, 54.6% 15 to 30 minutes, 17.9% 30 to 45 minutes, 1.9% 45 to 60 minutes, 7.8% 60 minutes or more (2006-2010 5-year est.)

Additional Information Contacts
Williamsport/Lycoming Chamber of Commerce . . . . (570) 326-1971
    http://www.williamsport.org

MILL CREEK (township). Covers a land area of 11.409 square miles and a water area of 0.017 square miles. Located at 41.30° N. Lat; 76.79° W. Long.

Population: 477 (1990); 572 (2000); 604 (2010); Density: 52.9 persons per square mile (2010); Race: 97.7% White, 0.3% Black, 0.0% Asian, 0.5% American Indian/Alaska Native, 0.3% Native Hawaiian/Other Pacific Islander, 1.2% Other, 1.3% Hispanic of any race (2010); Average household size: 2.70 (2010); Median age: 43.1 (2010); Males per 100 females: 106.8 (2010); Marriage status: 14.8% never married, 77.2% now married, 3.7% widowed, 4.3% divorced (2006-2010 5-year est.); Foreign born: 0.3% (2006-2010 5-year est.); Ancestry (includes multiple ancestries): 43.4% German, 13.3% American, 10.5% English, 8.9% Irish, 7.5% Italian (2006-2010 5-year est.).

Economy: Single-family building permits issued: 0 (2011); Multi-family building permits issued: 0 (2011); Employment by occupation: 8.6% management, 3.8% professional, 8.0% services, 19.1% sales, 2.2% farming, 10.5% construction, 12.1% production (2006-2010 5-year est.).

Income: Per capita income: $22,416 (2006-2010 5-year est.); Median household income: $61,250 (2006-2010 5-year est.); Average household income: $62,248 (2006-2010 5-year est.); Percent of households with income of $100,000 or more: 11.4% (2006-2010 5-year est.); Poverty rate: 8.8% (2006-2010 5-year est.).

Education: Percent of population age 25 and over with: High school diploma (including GED) or higher: 89.8% (2006-2010 5-year est.); Bachelor's degree or higher: 18.6% (2006-2010 5-year est.); Master's degree or higher: 5.7% (2006-2010 5-year est.).

Housing: Homeownership rate: 89.7% (2010); Median home value: $159,000 (2006-2010 5-year est.); Median contract rent: $392 per month (2006-2010 5-year est.); Median year structure built: 1976 (2006-2010 5-year est.).

Transportation: Commute to work: 98.1% car, 0.0% public transportation, 0.0% walk, 0.6% work from home (2006-2010 5-year est.); Travel time to work: 7.8% less than 15 minutes, 51.5% 15 to 30 minutes, 31.9% 30 to 45 minutes, 2.6% 45 to 60 minutes, 6.2% 60 minutes or more (2006-2010 5-year est.)

MONTGOMERY (borough). Covers a land area of 0.547 square miles and a water area of 0.005 square miles. Located at 41.17° N. Lat; 76.87° W. Long. Elevation is 509 feet.

History: Settled 1778, Incorporated 1887.

Population: 1,631 (1990); 1,695 (2000); 1,579 (2010); Density: 2,888.6 persons per square mile (2010); Race: 95.9% White, 1.2% Black, 0.1% Asian, 0.3% American Indian/Alaska Native, 0.0% Native Hawaiian/Other Pacific Islander, 2.5% Other, 2.1% Hispanic of any race (2010); Average household size: 2.66 (2010); Median age: 33.7 (2010); Males per 100 females: 93.3 (2010); Marriage status: 34.8% never married, 50.6% now married, 5.0% widowed, 9.6% divorced (2006-2010 5-year est.); Foreign born: 1.6% (2006-2010 5-year est.); Ancestry (includes multiple ancestries): 48.4% German, 14.6% Irish, 8.6% Dutch, 5.9% American, 5.6% English (2006-2010 5-year est.).

Economy: Single-family building permits issued: 0 (2011); Multi-family building permits issued: 0 (2011); Employment by occupation: 5.2% management, 2.2% professional, 10.2% services, 18.1% sales, 4.6% farming, 7.8% construction, 11.2% production (2006-2010 5-year est.).

Income: Per capita income: $19,288 (2006-2010 5-year est.); Median household income: $40,417 (2006-2010 5-year est.); Average household income: $49,761 (2006-2010 5-year est.); Percent of households with income of $100,000 or more: 6.7% (2006-2010 5-year est.); Poverty rate: 14.3% (2006-2010 5-year est.).

Education: Percent of population age 25 and over with: High school diploma (including GED) or higher: 89.7% (2006-2010 5-year est.); Bachelor's degree or higher: 14.0% (2006-2010 5-year est.); Master's degree or higher: 3.5% (2006-2010 5-year est.).

School District(s)
Montgomery Area SD (KG-12)
    2010-11 Enrollment: 915. . . . . (570) 547-1608
Housing: Homeownership rate: 59.5% (2010); Median home value: $82,100 (2006-2010 5-year est.); Median contract rent: $428 per month (2006-2010 5-year est.); Median year structure built: before 1940 (2006-2010 5-year est.).

Safety: Violent crime rate: 12.6 per 10,000 population; Property crime rate: 221.0 per 10,000 population (2011).

Transportation: Commute to work: 94.9% car, 0.0% public transportation, 2.5% walk, 1.7% work from home (2006-2010 5-year est.); Travel time to work: 33.7% less than 15 minutes, 49.2% 15 to 30 minutes, 9.7% 30 to 45 minutes, 3.4% 45 to 60 minutes, 4.0% 60 minutes or more (2006-2010 5-year est.)

Additional Information Contacts

Williamsport/Lycoming Chamber of Commerce . . . . (570) 326-1971
   http://www.williamsport.org

MONTOURSVILLE (borough). Covers a land area of 3.608 square miles and a water area of 0.574 square miles. Located at 41.25° N. Lat; 76.92° W. Long. Elevation is 538 feet.

History: Settled 1807, laid out 1820, incorporated 1850.

Population: 4,983 (1990); 4,777 (2000); 4,615 (2010); Density: 1,279.2 persons per square mile (2010); Race: 97.3% White, 0.4% Black, 0.7% Asian, 0.1% American Indian/Alaska Native, 0.0% Native Hawaiian/Other Pacific Islander, 1.5% Other, 1.3% Hispanic of any race (2010); Average household size: 2.22 (2010); Median age: 44.7 (2010); Males per 100 females: 90.9 (2010); Marriage status: 23.2% never married, 56.3% now married, 7.7% widowed, 12.9% divorced (2006-2010 5-year est.); Foreign born: 1.7% (2006-2010 5-year est.); Ancestry (includes multiple ancestries): 48.4% German, 10.4% Irish, 9.5% Italian, 7.5% English, 6.2% Polish (2006-2010 5-year est.).

Economy: Single-family building permits issued: 1 (2011); Multi-family building permits issued: 0 (2011); Employment by occupation: 11.3% management, 2.5% professional, 11.1% services, 23.1% sales, 4.1% farming, 7.6% construction, 3.2% production (2006-2010 5-year est.).

Income: Per capita income: $23,980 (2006-2010 5-year est.); Median household income: $44,146 (2006-2010 5-year est.); Average household income: $51,664 (2006-2010 5-year est.); Percent of households with income of $100,000 or more: 7.3% (2006-2010 5-year est.); Poverty rate: 10.0% (2006-2010 5-year est.).

Education: Percent of population age 25 and over with: High school diploma (including GED) or higher: 93.4% (2006-2010 5-year est.); Bachelor's degree or higher: 27.6% (2006-2010 5-year est.); Master's degree or higher: 8.2% (2006-2010 5-year est.).

School District(s)

Loyalsock Township SD (KG-12)
   2010-11 Enrollment: 1,417 . . . . (570) 326-6508
Montoursville Area SD (KG-12)
   2010-11 Enrollment: 1,956 . . . . (570) 368-2491

Housing: Homeownership rate: 67.5% (2010); Median home value: $123,400 (2006-2010 5-year est.); Median contract rent: $573 per month (2006-2010 5-year est.); Median year structure built: 1955 (2006-2010 5-year est.).

Safety: Violent crime rate: 0.0 per 10,000 population; Property crime rate: 21.6 per 10,000 population (2011).

Transportation: Commute to work: 94.5% car, 0.5% public transportation, 2.8% walk, 1.7% work from home (2006-2010 5-year est.); Travel time to work: 64.4% less than 15 minutes, 28.9% 15 to 30 minutes, 4.3% 30 to 45 minutes, 1.5% 45 to 60 minutes, 1.0% 60 minutes or more (2006-2010 5-year est.)

Additional Information Contacts

Williamsport/Lycoming Chamber of Commerce . . . . (570) 326-1971
   http://www.williamsport.org

MORELAND (township). Covers a land area of 23.914 square miles and a water area of 0.133 square miles. Located at 41.19° N. Lat; 76.65° W. Long. Elevation is 686 feet.

Population: 997 (1990); 1,036 (2000); 943 (2010); Density: 39.4 persons per square mile (2010); Race: 99.5% White, 0.1% Black, 0.1% Asian, 0.1% American Indian/Alaska Native, 0.0% Native Hawaiian/Other Pacific Islander, 0.2% Other, 0.3% Hispanic of any race (2010); Average household size: 2.51 (2010); Median age: 47.2 (2010); Males per 100 females: 105.0 (2010); Marriage status: 20.8% never married, 62.0% now married, 8.2% widowed, 9.0% divorced (2006-2010 5-year est.); Foreign born: 0.2% (2006-2010 5-year est.); Ancestry (includes multiple ancestries): 51.7% German, 13.2% American, 9.1% Irish, 9.0% Dutch, 6.9% English (2006-2010 5-year est.).

Economy: Single-family building permits issued: 1 (2011); Multi-family building permits issued: 0 (2011); Employment by occupation: 9.1% management, 1.5% professional, 6.5% services, 24.4% sales, 4.3% farming, 15.3% construction, 17.0% production (2006-2010 5-year est.).

Income: Per capita income: $24,412 (2006-2010 5-year est.); Median household income: $55,357 (2006-2010 5-year est.); Average household income: $59,005 (2006-2010 5-year est.); Percent of households with income of $100,000 or more: 12.9% (2006-2010 5-year est.); Poverty rate: 5.0% (2006-2010 5-year est.).

Education: Percent of population age 25 and over with: High school diploma (including GED) or higher: 80.9% (2006-2010 5-year est.); Bachelor's degree or higher: 14.0% (2006-2010 5-year est.); Master's degree or higher: 2.3% (2006-2010 5-year est.).

Housing: Homeownership rate: 92.0% (2010); Median home value: $145,300 (2006-2010 5-year est.); Median contract rent: $300 per month (2006-2010 5-year est.); Median year structure built: 1976 (2006-2010 5-year est.).

Transportation: Commute to work: 92.5% car, 0.0% public transportation, 3.7% walk, 3.9% work from home (2006-2010 5-year est.); Travel time to work: 25.5% less than 15 minutes, 44.3% 15 to 30 minutes, 18.8% 30 to 45 minutes, 4.4% 45 to 60 minutes, 7.0% 60 minutes or more (2006-2010 5-year est.)

Additional Information Contacts

Williamsport/Lycoming Chamber of Commerce . . . . (570) 326-1971
   http://www.williamsport.org

MUNCY (borough). Covers a land area of 0.844 square miles and a water area of 0 square miles. Located at 41.20° N. Lat; 76.79° W. Long. Elevation is 499 feet.

History: Laid out 1797, Incorporated 1826.

Population: 2,702 (1990); 2,663 (2000); 2,477 (2010); Density: 2,935.3 persons per square mile (2010); Race: 97.0% White, 0.2% Black, 1.0% Asian, 0.4% American Indian/Alaska Native, 0.0% Native Hawaiian/Other Pacific Islander, 1.4% Other, 1.7% Hispanic of any race (2010); Average household size: 2.36 (2010); Median age: 39.4 (2010); Males per 100 females: 89.8 (2010); Marriage status: 25.7% never married, 54.1% now married, 6.4% widowed, 13.8% divorced (2006-2010 5-year est.); Foreign born: 0.8% (2006-2010 5-year est.); Ancestry (includes multiple ancestries): 47.0% German, 14.0% Irish, 12.2% English, 5.1% American, 4.2% Italian (2006-2010 5-year est.).

Economy: Single-family building permits issued: 1 (2011); Multi-family building permits issued: 0 (2011); Employment by occupation: 6.7% management, 4.7% professional, 11.7% services, 17.9% sales, 6.8% farming, 7.7% construction, 6.3% production (2006-2010 5-year est.).

Income: Per capita income: $23,103 (2006-2010 5-year est.); Median household income: $40,188 (2006-2010 5-year est.); Average household income: $51,907 (2006-2010 5-year est.); Percent of households with income of $100,000 or more: 11.7% (2006-2010 5-year est.); Poverty rate: 12.1% (2006-2010 5-year est.).

Education: Percent of population age 25 and over with: High school diploma (including GED) or higher: 89.6% (2006-2010 5-year est.); Bachelor's degree or higher: 24.7% (2006-2010 5-year est.); Master's degree or higher: 7.9% (2006-2010 5-year est.).

School District(s)

Muncy SD (KG-12)
   2010-11 Enrollment: 997 . . . . (570) 546-3125

Housing: Homeownership rate: 64.4% (2010); Median home value: $109,200 (2006-2010 5-year est.); Median contract rent: $511 per month (2006-2010 5-year est.); Median year structure built: before 1940 (2006-2010 5-year est.).

Hospitals: Muncy Valley Hospital (139 beds)

Safety: Violent crime rate: 0.0 per 10,000 population; Property crime rate: 0.0 per 10,000 population (2011).

Newspapers: Luminary (Community news; Circulation 1,500)

Transportation: Commute to work: 94.8% car, 0.0% public transportation, 2.2% walk, 2.7% work from home (2006-2010 5-year est.); Travel time to work: 46.1% less than 15 minutes, 33.1% 15 to 30 minutes, 15.5% 30 to 45 minutes, 5.0% 45 to 60 minutes, 0.3% 60 minutes or more (2006-2010 5-year est.)

Additional Information Contacts

Williamsport/Lycoming Chamber of Commerce . . . . (570) 326-1971
   http://www.williamsport.org

MUNCY (township). Covers a land area of 15.484 square miles and a water area of 0.224 square miles. Located at 41.25° N. Lat; 76.81° W. Long. Elevation is 499 feet.

Population: 1,050 (1990); 1,059 (2000); 1,089 (2010); Density: 70.3 persons per square mile (2010); Race: 97.2% White, 0.2% Black, 0.2% Asian, 0.4% American Indian/Alaska Native, 0.0% Native Hawaiian/Other

Pacific Islander, 2.0% Other, 1.8% Hispanic of any race (2010); Average household size: 2.46 (2010); Median age: 43.9 (2010); Males per 100 females: 93.4 (2010); Marriage status: 19.8% never married, 64.8% now married, 6.2% widowed, 9.2% divorced (2006-2010 5-year est.); Foreign born: 1.3% (2006-2010 5-year est.); Ancestry (includes multiple ancestries): 43.5% German, 19.1% Irish, 8.7% English, 6.4% American, 3.8% Polish (2006-2010 5-year est.).

Economy: Single-family building permits issued: 2 (2011); Multi-family building permits issued: 0 (2011); Employment by occupation: 8.6% management, 3.1% professional, 14.0% services, 16.8% sales, 5.1% farming, 10.4% construction, 3.9% production (2006-2010 5-year est.).

Income: Per capita income: $21,919 (2006-2010 5-year est.); Median household income: $46,016 (2006-2010 5-year est.); Average household income: $54,762 (2006-2010 5-year est.); Percent of households with income of $100,000 or more: 13.8% (2006-2010 5-year est.); Poverty rate: 2.5% (2006-2010 5-year est.).

Education: Percent of population age 25 and over with: High school diploma (including GED) or higher: 87.9% (2006-2010 5-year est.); Bachelor's degree or higher: 16.1% (2006-2010 5-year est.); Master's degree or higher: 5.2% (2006-2010 5-year est.).

Housing: Homeownership rate: 79.8% (2010); Median home value: $152,800 (2006-2010 5-year est.); Median contract rent: $431 per month (2006-2010 5-year est.); Median year structure built: 1973 (2006-2010 5-year est.).

Hospitals: Muncy Valley Hospital (139 beds)

Newspapers: Luminary (Community news; Circulation 1,500)

Transportation: Commute to work: 90.3% car, 0.0% public transportation, 3.5% walk, 2.7% work from home (2006-2010 5-year est.); Travel time to work: 43.8% less than 15 minutes, 41.7% 15 to 30 minutes, 12.1% 30 to 45 minutes, 0.3% 45 to 60 minutes, 2.1% 60 minutes or more (2006-2010 5-year est.)

MUNCY CREEK (township). Covers a land area of 19.920 square miles and a water area of 0.693 square miles. Located at 41.20° N. Lat; 76.76° W. Long.

Population: 3,401 (1990); 3,487 (2000); 3,474 (2010); Density: 174.4 persons per square mile (2010); Race: 98.2% White, 0.3% Black, 0.3% Asian, 0.1% American Indian/Alaska Native, 0.0% Native Hawaiian/Other Pacific Islander, 1.1% Other, 0.8% Hispanic of any race (2010); Average household size: 2.38 (2010); Median age: 46.0 (2010); Males per 100 females: 93.1 (2010); Marriage status: 23.3% never married, 55.6% now married, 11.2% widowed, 10.0% divorced (2006-2010 5-year est.); Foreign born: 0.8% (2006-2010 5-year est.); Ancestry (includes multiple ancestries): 46.2% German, 13.8% Irish, 13.1% English, 9.9% American, 4.4% Italian (2006-2010 5-year est.).

Economy: Single-family building permits issued: 8 (2011); Multi-family building permits issued: 0 (2011); Employment by occupation: 8.5% management, 3.9% professional, 10.8% services, 20.0% sales, 1.6% farming, 12.1% construction, 13.7% production (2006-2010 5-year est.).

Income: Per capita income: $22,356 (2006-2010 5-year est.); Median household income: $41,172 (2006-2010 5-year est.); Average household income: $51,949 (2006-2010 5-year est.); Percent of households with income of $100,000 or more: 12.0% (2006-2010 5-year est.); Poverty rate: 5.2% (2006-2010 5-year est.).

Education: Percent of population age 25 and over with: High school diploma (including GED) or higher: 82.2% (2006-2010 5-year est.); Bachelor's degree or higher: 18.5% (2006-2010 5-year est.); Master's degree or higher: 6.8% (2006-2010 5-year est.).

Housing: Homeownership rate: 81.1% (2010); Median home value: $96,300 (2006-2010 5-year est.); Median contract rent: $449 per month (2006-2010 5-year est.); Median year structure built: 1976 (2006-2010 5-year est.).

Transportation: Commute to work: 94.4% car, 0.0% public transportation, 3.8% walk, 1.8% work from home (2006-2010 5-year est.); Travel time to work: 35.4% less than 15 minutes, 36.1% 15 to 30 minutes, 13.9% 30 to 45 minutes, 11.0% 45 to 60 minutes, 3.5% 60 minutes or more (2006-2010 5-year est.)

Additional Information Contacts

Williamsport/Lycoming Chamber of Commerce . . . . (570) 326-1971
http://www.williamsport.org

NIPPENOSE (township). Covers a land area of 10.983 square miles and a water area of 0.534 square miles. Located at 41.19° N. Lat; 77.21° W. Long.

Population: 742 (1990); 729 (2000); 709 (2010); Density: 64.6 persons per square mile (2010); Race: 99.3% White, 0.0% Black, 0.6% Asian, 0.1% American Indian/Alaska Native, 0.0% Native Hawaiian/Other Pacific Islander, 0.0% Other, 0.7% Hispanic of any race (2010); Average household size: 2.51 (2010); Median age: 42.3 (2010); Males per 100 females: 102.6 (2010); Marriage status: 20.2% never married, 60.9% now married, 8.6% widowed, 10.4% divorced (2006-2010 5-year est.); Foreign born: 0.0% (2006-2010 5-year est.); Ancestry (includes multiple ancestries): 50.4% German, 10.3% Irish, 7.8% Italian, 6.2% American, 5.7% Dutch (2006-2010 5-year est.).

Economy: Single-family building permits issued: 0 (2011); Multi-family building permits issued: 0 (2011); Employment by occupation: 8.3% management, 1.2% professional, 4.8% services, 25.0% sales, 0.9% farming, 11.6% construction, 11.9% production (2006-2010 5-year est.).

Income: Per capita income: $23,211 (2006-2010 5-year est.); Median household income: $49,583 (2006-2010 5-year est.); Average household income: $58,629 (2006-2010 5-year est.); Percent of households with income of $100,000 or more: 9.2% (2006-2010 5-year est.); Poverty rate: 13.0% (2006-2010 5-year est.).

Education: Percent of population age 25 and over with: High school diploma (including GED) or higher: 79.9% (2006-2010 5-year est.); Bachelor's degree or higher: 12.0% (2006-2010 5-year est.); Master's degree or higher: 4.4% (2006-2010 5-year est.).

Housing: Homeownership rate: 82.3% (2010); Median home value: $92,100 (2006-2010 5-year est.); Median contract rent: $352 per month (2006-2010 5-year est.); Median year structure built: 1972 (2006-2010 5-year est.).

Transportation: Commute to work: 100.0% car, 0.0% public transportation, 0.0% walk, 0.0% work from home (2006-2010 5-year est.); Travel time to work: 21.9% less than 15 minutes, 54.4% 15 to 30 minutes, 18.1% 30 to 45 minutes, 3.4% 45 to 60 minutes, 2.2% 60 minutes or more (2006-2010 5-year est.)

OLD LYCOMING (township). Covers a land area of 9.385 square miles and a water area of 0.057 square miles. Located at 41.26° N. Lat; 77.07° W. Long.

Population: 5,335 (1990); 5,508 (2000); 4,938 (2010); Density: 526.2 persons per square mile (2010); Race: 96.8% White, 1.2% Black, 0.9% Asian, 0.2% American Indian/Alaska Native, 0.0% Native Hawaiian/Other Pacific Islander, 0.9% Other, 0.5% Hispanic of any race (2010); Average household size: 2.30 (2010); Median age: 48.2 (2010); Males per 100 females: 98.8 (2010); Marriage status: 21.9% never married, 63.4% now married, 5.6% widowed, 9.1% divorced (2006-2010 5-year est.); Foreign born: 2.5% (2006-2010 5-year est.); Ancestry (includes multiple ancestries): 46.8% German, 18.0% Irish, 12.6% Italian, 9.7% English, 7.7% Polish (2006-2010 5-year est.).

Economy: Single-family building permits issued: 1 (2011); Multi-family building permits issued: 22 (2011); Employment by occupation: 8.5% management, 2.1% professional, 11.2% services, 14.6% sales, 4.3% farming, 10.8% construction, 13.0% production (2006-2010 5-year est.).

Income: Per capita income: $23,916 (2006-2010 5-year est.); Median household income: $46,750 (2006-2010 5-year est.); Average household income: $55,204 (2006-2010 5-year est.); Percent of households with income of $100,000 or more: 11.6% (2006-2010 5-year est.); Poverty rate: 4.1% (2006-2010 5-year est.).

Education: Percent of population age 25 and over with: High school diploma (including GED) or higher: 87.8% (2006-2010 5-year est.); Bachelor's degree or higher: 16.6% (2006-2010 5-year est.); Master's degree or higher: 5.9% (2006-2010 5-year est.).

Housing: Homeownership rate: 80.6% (2010); Median home value: $115,800 (2006-2010 5-year est.); Median contract rent: $461 per month (2006-2010 5-year est.); Median year structure built: 1966 (2006-2010 5-year est.).

Safety: Violent crime rate: 4.0 per 10,000 population; Property crime rate: 252.3 per 10,000 population (2011).

Transportation: Commute to work: 91.5% car, 0.0% public transportation, 2.0% walk, 3.9% work from home (2006-2010 5-year est.); Travel time to work: 44.1% less than 15 minutes, 39.1% 15 to 30 minutes, 11.1% 30 to 45 minutes, 3.8% 45 to 60 minutes, 2.0% 60 minutes or more (2006-2010 5-year est.)

Additional Information Contacts
Old Lycoming Township . . . . (570) 322-6906
  http://www.oldlycomingtwp.org
Williamsport/Lycoming Chamber of Commerce . . . . (570) 326-1971
  http://www.williamsport.org

OVAL (CDP). Covers a land area of 1.096 square miles and a water
area of 0 square miles. Located at 41.15° N. Lat; 77.17° W. Long.
Elevation is 810 feet.
Population: n/a (1990); n/a (2000); 361 (2010); Density: 329.5 persons
per square mile (2010); Race: 99.4% White, 0.0% Black, 0.3% Asian,
0.3% American Indian/Alaska Native, 0.0% Native Hawaiian/Other Pacific
Islander, 0.0% Other, 0.0% Hispanic of any race (2010); Average
household size: 2.58 (2010); Median age: 44.2 (2010); Males per 100
females: 106.3 (2010); Marriage status: 18.6% never married, 67.4% now
married, 8.1% widowed, 6.0% divorced (2006-2010 5-year est.); Foreign
born: 2.4% (2006-2010 5-year est.); Ancestry (includes multiple
ancestries): 56.0% German, 13.3% American, 7.4% English, 7.4% Italian,
6.4% Dutch (2006-2010 5-year est.).
Economy: Employment by occupation: 16.7% management, 0.0%
professional, 2.8% services, 17.2% sales, 0.0% farming, 12.8%
construction, 10.0% production (2006-2010 5-year est.).
Income: Per capita income: $24,213 (2006-2010 5-year est.); Median
household income: $44,489 (2006-2010 5-year est.); Average household
income: $60,576 (2006-2010 5-year est.); Percent of households with
income of $100,000 or more: 14.8% (2006-2010 5-year est.); Poverty rate:
4.2% (2006-2010 5-year est.).
Education: Percent of population age 25 and over with: High school
diploma (including GED) or higher: 90.6% (2006-2010 5-year est.);
Bachelor's degree or higher: 17.1% (2006-2010 5-year est.); Master's
degree or higher: 3.0% (2006-2010 5-year est.).
Housing: Homeownership rate: 94.3% (2010); Median home value:
$131,600 (2006-2010 5-year est.); Median contract rent: n/a per month
(2006-2010 5-year est.); Median year structure built: 1972 (2006-2010
5-year est.).
Transportation: Commute to work: 92.8% car, 0.0% public transportation,
4.4% walk, 2.8% work from home (2006-2010 5-year est.); Travel time to
work: 11.4% less than 15 minutes, 51.4% 15 to 30 minutes, 33.7% 30 to
45 minutes, 1.7% 45 to 60 minutes, 1.7% 60 minutes or more (2006-2010
5-year est.)

PENN (township). Covers a land area of 26.280 square miles and a
water area of 0.307 square miles. Located at 41.28° N. Lat; 76.64° W.
Long.
Population: 788 (1990); 900 (2000); 960 (2010); Density: 36.5 persons
per square mile (2010); Race: 98.1% White, 0.7% Black, 0.1% Asian,
0.1% American Indian/Alaska Native, 0.0% Native Hawaiian/Other Pacific
Islander, 1.0% Other, 0.5% Hispanic of any race (2010); Average
household size: 2.55 (2010); Median age: 43.7 (2010); Males per 100
females: 115.2 (2010); Marriage status: 18.8% never married, 67.4% now
married, 4.2% widowed, 9.6% divorced (2006-2010 5-year est.); Foreign
born: 0.7% (2006-2010 5-year est.); Ancestry (includes multiple
ancestries): 44.8% German, 15.9% American, 9.1% English, 8.1% Irish,
4.0% Dutch (2006-2010 5-year est.).
Economy: Single-family building permits issued: 3 (2011); Multi-family
building permits issued: 0 (2011); Employment by occupation: 7.5%
management, 0.7% professional, 9.1% services, 17.9% sales, 2.2%
farming, 19.2% construction, 16.2% production (2006-2010 5-year est.).
Income: Per capita income: $23,487 (2006-2010 5-year est.); Median
household income: $53,854 (2006-2010 5-year est.); Average household
income: $59,618 (2006-2010 5-year est.); Percent of households with
income of $100,000 or more: 13.6% (2006-2010 5-year est.); Poverty rate:
6.6% (2006-2010 5-year est.).
Education: Percent of population age 25 and over with: High school
diploma (including GED) or higher: 87.8% (2006-2010 5-year est.);
Bachelor's degree or higher: 11.6% (2006-2010 5-year est.); Master's
degree or higher: 4.8% (2006-2010 5-year est.).
Housing: Homeownership rate: 90.2% (2010); Median home value:
$139,900 (2006-2010 5-year est.); Median contract rent: $538 per month
(2006-2010 5-year est.); Median year structure built: 1977 (2006-2010
5-year est.).
Transportation: Commute to work: 91.6% car, 0.0% public transportation,
1.8% walk, 5.2% work from home (2006-2010 5-year est.); Travel time to
work: 18.7% less than 15 minutes, 46.8% 15 to 30 minutes, 18.2% 30 to

45 minutes, 9.4% 45 to 60 minutes, 7.0% 60 minutes or more (2006-2010
5-year est.)

PIATT (township). Covers a land area of 9.772 square miles and a water
area of 0.320 square miles. Located at 41.23° N. Lat; 77.21° W. Long.
Population: 1,097 (1990); 1,259 (2000); 1,180 (2010); Density: 120.8
persons per square mile (2010); Race: 96.9% White, 0.5% Black, 0.2%
Asian, 0.6% American Indian/Alaska Native, 0.3% Native Hawaiian/Other
Pacific Islander, 1.5% Other, 1.3% Hispanic of any race (2010); Average
household size: 2.71 (2010); Median age: 40.7 (2010); Males per 100
females: 102.1 (2010); Marriage status: 25.4% never married, 58.1% now
married, 7.9% widowed, 8.6% divorced (2006-2010 5-year est.); Foreign
born: 1.9% (2006-2010 5-year est.); Ancestry (includes multiple
ancestries): 43.4% German, 9.2% Irish, 9.1% American, 7.3% Italian, 5.5%
English (2006-2010 5-year est.).
Economy: Single-family building permits issued: 1 (2011); Multi-family
building permits issued: 0 (2011); Employment by occupation: 4.6%
management, 2.0% professional, 8.8% services, 14.6% sales, 2.1%
farming, 15.9% construction, 16.8% production (2006-2010 5-year est.).
Income: Per capita income: $24,313 (2006-2010 5-year est.); Median
household income: $51,563 (2006-2010 5-year est.); Average household
income: $65,884 (2006-2010 5-year est.); Percent of households with
income of $100,000 or more: 12.6% (2006-2010 5-year est.); Poverty rate:
6.2% (2006-2010 5-year est.).
Education: Percent of population age 25 and over with: High school
diploma (including GED) or higher: 84.5% (2006-2010 5-year est.);
Bachelor's degree or higher: 11.3% (2006-2010 5-year est.); Master's
degree or higher: 5.1% (2006-2010 5-year est.).
Housing: Homeownership rate: 77.9% (2010); Median home value:
$121,900 (2006-2010 5-year est.); Median contract rent: $532 per month
(2006-2010 5-year est.); Median year structure built: 1973 (2006-2010
5-year est.).
Transportation: Commute to work: 93.6% car, 0.0% public transportation,
3.5% walk, 1.3% work from home (2006-2010 5-year est.); Travel time to
work: 29.3% less than 15 minutes, 49.1% 15 to 30 minutes, 11.1% 30 to
45 minutes, 2.0% 45 to 60 minutes, 8.5% 60 minutes or more (2006-2010
5-year est.)
Additional Information Contacts
Williamsport/Lycoming Chamber of Commerce . . . . (570) 326-1971
  http://www.williamsport.org

PICTURE ROCKS (borough). Covers a land area of 0.974 square
miles and a water area of 0.027 square miles. Located at 41.28° N. Lat;
76.71° W. Long. Elevation is 646 feet.
Population: 660 (1990); 693 (2000); 678 (2010); Density: 695.8 persons
per square mile (2010); Race: 97.2% White, 1.5% Black, 0.4% Asian,
0.4% American Indian/Alaska Native, 0.0% Native Hawaiian/Other Pacific
Islander, 0.5% Other, 0.1% Hispanic of any race (2010); Average
household size: 2.53 (2010); Median age: 40.8 (2010); Males per 100
females: 96.0 (2010); Marriage status: 23.5% never married, 68.4% now
married, 3.5% widowed, 4.6% divorced (2006-2010 5-year est.); Foreign
born: 0.0% (2006-2010 5-year est.); Ancestry (includes multiple
ancestries): 43.8% German, 16.1% English, 14.8% Polish, 13.7% Irish,
9.7% Italian (2006-2010 5-year est.).
Economy: Single-family building permits issued: 0 (2011); Multi-family
building permits issued: 0 (2011); Employment by occupation: 5.5%
management, 1.2% professional, 8.2% services, 16.4% sales, 6.6%
farming, 9.0% construction, 3.1% production (2006-2010 5-year est.).
Income: Per capita income: $21,747 (2006-2010 5-year est.); Median
household income: $49,444 (2006-2010 5-year est.); Average household
income: $57,810 (2006-2010 5-year est.); Percent of households with
income of $100,000 or more: 17.7% (2006-2010 5-year est.); Poverty rate:
10.7% (2006-2010 5-year est.).
Education: Percent of population age 25 and over with: High school
diploma (including GED) or higher: 85.3% (2006-2010 5-year est.);
Bachelor's degree or higher: 29.7% (2006-2010 5-year est.); Master's
degree or higher: 9.4% (2006-2010 5-year est.).
School District(s)
East Lycoming SD (PK-12)
  2010-11 Enrollment: 1,682 . . . . (570) 584-2131
Housing: Homeownership rate: 80.6% (2010); Median home value:
$121,400 (2006-2010 5-year est.); Median contract rent: $456 per month
(2006-2010 5-year est.); Median year structure built: 1954 (2006-2010
5-year est.).

Transportation: Commute to work: 90.4% car, 0.0% public transportation, 9.6% walk, 0.0% work from home (2006-2010 5-year est.); Travel time to work: 35.0% less than 15 minutes, 48.3% 15 to 30 minutes, 10.8% 30 to 45 minutes, 1.3% 45 to 60 minutes, 4.6% 60 minutes or more (2006-2010 5-year est.)

PINE (township). Covers a land area of 74.743 square miles and a water area of 0.328 square miles. Located at 41.48° N. Lat; 77.27° W. Long.
Population: 290 (1990); 329 (2000); 294 (2010); Density: 3.9 persons per square mile (2010); Race: 98.0% White, 0.3% Black, 0.3% Asian, 0.0% American Indian/Alaska Native, 0.0% Native Hawaiian/Other Pacific Islander, 1.4% Other, 0.0% Hispanic of any race (2010); Average household size: 2.28 (2010); Median age: 52.0 (2010); Males per 100 females: 111.5 (2010); Marriage status: 15.3% never married, 72.5% now married, 5.3% widowed, 6.9% divorced (2006-2010 5-year est.); Foreign born: 2.0% (2006-2010 5-year est.); Ancestry (includes multiple ancestries): 48.8% German, 15.8% Irish, 11.8% English, 11.1% Swiss, 6.1% Italian (2006-2010 5-year est.).
Economy: Single-family building permits issued: 0 (2011); Multi-family building permits issued: 0 (2011); Employment by occupation: 4.5% management, 2.7% professional, 15.5% services, 14.5% sales, 0.0% farming, 25.5% construction, 10.9% production (2006-2010 5-year est.).
Income: Per capita income: $20,674 (2006-2010 5-year est.); Median household income: $38,333 (2006-2010 5-year est.); Average household income: $46,205 (2006-2010 5-year est.); Percent of households with income of $100,000 or more: 3.8% (2006-2010 5-year est.); Poverty rate: 5.1% (2006-2010 5-year est.).
Education: Percent of population age 25 and over with: High school diploma (including GED) or higher: 76.4% (2006-2010 5-year est.); Bachelor's degree or higher: 9.9% (2006-2010 5-year est.); Master's degree or higher: 1.7% (2006-2010 5-year est.).
Housing: Homeownership rate: 83.8% (2010); Median home value: $156,600 (2006-2010 5-year est.); Median contract rent: $400 per month (2006-2010 5-year est.); Median year structure built: 1965 (2006-2010 5-year est.).
Transportation: Commute to work: 100.0% car, 0.0% public transportation, 0.0% walk, 0.0% work from home (2006-2010 5-year est.); Travel time to work: 36.4% less than 15 minutes, 16.8% 15 to 30 minutes, 16.8% 30 to 45 minutes, 10.3% 45 to 60 minutes, 19.6% 60 minutes or more (2006-2010 5-year est.)

PLUNKETTS CREEK (township). Covers a land area of 53.549 square miles and a water area of 0.526 square miles. Located at 41.37° N. Lat; 76.81° W. Long.
Population: 905 (1990); 771 (2000); 684 (2010); Density: 12.8 persons per square mile (2010); Race: 98.0% White, 0.1% Black, 0.1% Asian, 0.4% American Indian/Alaska Native, 0.0% Native Hawaiian/Other Pacific Islander, 1.4% Other, 2.0% Hispanic of any race (2010); Average household size: 2.30 (2010); Median age: 46.5 (2010); Males per 100 females: 103.0 (2010); Marriage status: 21.5% never married, 58.4% now married, 8.7% widowed, 11.4% divorced (2006-2010 5-year est.); Foreign born: 2.2% (2006-2010 5-year est.); Ancestry (includes multiple ancestries): 42.1% German, 12.9% Irish, 11.8% American, 9.3% Dutch, 8.7% English (2006-2010 5-year est.).
Economy: Single-family building permits issued: 1 (2011); Multi-family building permits issued: 0 (2011); Employment by occupation: 15.2% management, 1.0% professional, 6.3% services, 19.9% sales, 2.0% farming, 19.2% construction, 12.6% production (2006-2010 5-year est.).
Income: Per capita income: $28,457 (2006-2010 5-year est.); Median household income: $50,694 (2006-2010 5-year est.); Average household income: $66,429 (2006-2010 5-year est.); Percent of households with income of $100,000 or more: 14.3% (2006-2010 5-year est.); Poverty rate: 11.8% (2006-2010 5-year est.).
Education: Percent of population age 25 and over with: High school diploma (including GED) or higher: 89.9% (2006-2010 5-year est.); Bachelor's degree or higher: 20.9% (2006-2010 5-year est.); Master's degree or higher: 8.0% (2006-2010 5-year est.).
Housing: Homeownership rate: 84.8% (2010); Median home value: $148,000 (2006-2010 5-year est.); Median contract rent: $510 per month (2006-2010 5-year est.); Median year structure built: 1957 (2006-2010 5-year est.).
Transportation: Commute to work: 96.9% car, 0.0% public transportation, 0.0% walk, 1.4% work from home (2006-2010 5-year est.); Travel time to work: 6.6% less than 15 minutes, 60.6% 15 to 30 minutes, 21.1% 30 to 45

minutes, 6.6% 45 to 60 minutes, 5.2% 60 minutes or more (2006-2010 5-year est.)

PORTER (township). Covers a land area of 7.606 square miles and a water area of 0.297 square miles. Located at 41.21° N. Lat; 77.28° W. Long.
Population: 1,441 (1990); 1,633 (2000); 1,601 (2010); Density: 210.5 persons per square mile (2010); Race: 98.4% White, 0.7% Black, 0.6% Asian, 0.0% American Indian/Alaska Native, 0.0% Native Hawaiian/Other Pacific Islander, 0.3% Other, 0.2% Hispanic of any race (2010); Average household size: 2.38 (2010); Median age: 45.8 (2010); Males per 100 females: 96.2 (2010); Marriage status: 22.2% never married, 62.5% now married, 7.3% widowed, 8.0% divorced (2006-2010 5-year est.); Foreign born: 1.2% (2006-2010 5-year est.); Ancestry (includes multiple ancestries): 46.7% German, 13.4% Irish, 8.9% American, 7.8% English, 7.2% Italian (2006-2010 5-year est.).
Economy: Single-family building permits issued: 1 (2011); Multi-family building permits issued: 0 (2011); Employment by occupation: 5.0% management, 2.4% professional, 7.1% services, 15.1% sales, 2.2% farming, 13.0% construction, 8.8% production (2006-2010 5-year est.).
Income: Per capita income: $23,652 (2006-2010 5-year est.); Median household income: $48,533 (2006-2010 5-year est.); Average household income: $55,151 (2006-2010 5-year est.); Percent of households with income of $100,000 or more: 9.4% (2006-2010 5-year est.); Poverty rate: 6.9% (2006-2010 5-year est.).
Education: Percent of population age 25 and over with: High school diploma (including GED) or higher: 81.2% (2006-2010 5-year est.); Bachelor's degree or higher: 16.6% (2006-2010 5-year est.); Master's degree or higher: 7.2% (2006-2010 5-year est.).
Housing: Homeownership rate: 75.9% (2010); Median home value: $132,800 (2006-2010 5-year est.); Median contract rent: $414 per month (2006-2010 5-year est.); Median year structure built: 1973 (2006-2010 5-year est.).
Transportation: Commute to work: 92.3% car, 1.1% public transportation, 2.5% walk, 3.8% work from home (2006-2010 5-year est.); Travel time to work: 39.5% less than 15 minutes, 35.1% 15 to 30 minutes, 11.2% 30 to 45 minutes, 5.7% 45 to 60 minutes, 8.5% 60 minutes or more (2006-2010 5-year est.)
Additional Information Contacts
Williamsport/Lycoming Chamber of Commerce . . . . (570) 326-1971
    http://www.williamsport.org

RALSTON (unincorporated postal area)
Zip Code: 17763
    Covers a land area of 24.825 square miles and a water area of 0.541 square miles. Located at 41.50° N. Lat; 76.97° W. Long. Elevation is 853 feet. Population: 309 (2010); Density: 12.4 persons per square mile (2010); Race: 98.7% White, 0.6% Black, 0.0% Asian, 0.0% American Indian/Alaska Native, 0.0% Native Hawaiian/Other Pacific Islander, 0.7% Other, 0.0% Hispanic of any race (2010); Average household size: 2.49 (2010); Median age: 40.9 (2010); Males per 100 females: 91.9 (2010); Homeownership rate: 79.9% (2010)

SALLADASBURG (borough). Covers a land area of 0.777 square miles and a water area of 0.013 square miles. Located at 41.28° N. Lat; 77.23° W. Long. Elevation is 666 feet.
Population: 301 (1990); 260 (2000); 238 (2010); Density: 306.1 persons per square mile (2010); Race: 96.6% White, 2.1% Black, 0.8% Asian, 0.0% American Indian/Alaska Native, 0.0% Native Hawaiian/Other Pacific Islander, 0.5% Other, 0.4% Hispanic of any race (2010); Average household size: 2.16 (2010); Median age: 42.8 (2010); Males per 100 females: 95.1 (2010); Marriage status: 25.0% never married, 66.5% now married, 3.2% widowed, 5.3% divorced (2006-2010 5-year est.); Foreign born: 0.0% (2006-2010 5-year est.); Ancestry (includes multiple ancestries): 36.7% German, 15.6% American, 13.9% Irish, 13.9% Scotch-Irish, 5.1% English (2006-2010 5-year est.).
Economy: Single-family building permits issued: 0 (2011); Multi-family building permits issued: 0 (2011); Employment by occupation: 8.3% management, 0.9% professional, 3.7% services, 6.4% sales, 7.3% farming, 17.4% construction, 8.3% production (2006-2010 5-year est.).
Income: Per capita income: $18,777 (2006-2010 5-year est.); Median household income: $41,932 (2006-2010 5-year est.); Average household income: $50,908 (2006-2010 5-year est.); Percent of households with income of $100,000 or more: 9.2% (2006-2010 5-year est.); Poverty rate: 14.8% (2006-2010 5-year est.).

Education: Percent of population age 25 and over with: High school diploma (including GED) or higher: 86.8% (2006-2010 5-year est.); Bachelor's degree or higher: 12.5% (2006-2010 5-year est.); Master's degree or higher: 2.9% (2006-2010 5-year est.).
Housing: Homeownership rate: 66.3% (2010); Median home value: $86,100 (2006-2010 5-year est.); Median contract rent: $510 per month (2006-2010 5-year est.); Median year structure built: before 1940 (2006-2010 5-year est.).
Transportation: Commute to work: 91.7% car, 0.0% public transportation, 6.4% walk, 1.8% work from home (2006-2010 5-year est.); Travel time to work: 8.4% less than 15 minutes, 51.4% 15 to 30 minutes, 37.4% 30 to 45 minutes, 0.0% 45 to 60 minutes, 2.8% 60 minutes or more (2006-2010 5-year est.)

SHREWSBURY (township). Covers a land area of 18.657 square miles and a water area of 0.091 square miles. Located at 41.32° N. Lat; 76.68° W. Long.

Population: 402 (1990); 433 (2000); 409 (2010); Density: 21.9 persons per square mile (2010); Race: 99.5% White, 0.2% Black, 0.0% Asian, 0.0% American Indian/Alaska Native, 0.0% Native Hawaiian/Other Pacific Islander, 0.3% Other, 0.0% Hispanic of any race (2010); Average household size: 2.36 (2010); Median age: 46.0 (2010); Males per 100 females: 94.8 (2010); Marriage status: 18.5% never married, 69.4% now married, 7.3% widowed, 4.8% divorced (2006-2010 5-year est.); Foreign born: 1.0% (2006-2010 5-year est.); Ancestry (includes multiple ancestries): 45.8% German, 19.5% Irish, 9.5% American, 8.5% English, 6.7% Dutch (2006-2010 5-year est.).
Economy: Single-family building permits issued: 0 (2011); Multi-family building permits issued: 0 (2011); Employment by occupation: 3.5% management, 2.3% professional, 4.7% services, 16.9% sales, 2.3% farming, 12.2% construction, 15.1% production (2006-2010 5-year est.).
Income: Per capita income: $20,543 (2006-2010 5-year est.); Median household income: $40,714 (2006-2010 5-year est.); Average household income: $49,707 (2006-2010 5-year est.); Percent of households with income of $100,000 or more: 8.0% (2006-2010 5-year est.); Poverty rate: 7.2% (2006-2010 5-year est.).
Education: Percent of population age 25 and over with: High school diploma (including GED) or higher: 83.0% (2006-2010 5-year est.); Bachelor's degree or higher: 21.9% (2006-2010 5-year est.); Master's degree or higher: 3.8% (2006-2010 5-year est.).
Housing: Homeownership rate: 82.7% (2010); Median home value: $98,500 (2006-2010 5-year est.); Median contract rent: $400 per month (2006-2010 5-year est.); Median year structure built: 1963 (2006-2010 5-year est.).
Transportation: Commute to work: 94.2% car, 1.2% public transportation, 2.9% walk, 0.0% work from home (2006-2010 5-year est.); Travel time to work: 13.4% less than 15 minutes, 37.2% 15 to 30 minutes, 36.6% 30 to 45 minutes, 7.6% 45 to 60 minutes, 5.2% 60 minutes or more (2006-2010 5-year est.)

SOUTH WILLIAMSPORT (borough). Covers a land area of 1.887 square miles and a water area of 0.275 square miles. Located at 41.23° N. Lat; 77.00° W. Long. Elevation is 522 feet.

Population: 6,496 (1990); 6,412 (2000); 6,379 (2010); Density: 3,381.2 persons per square mile (2010); Race: 97.5% White, 0.9% Black, 0.2% Asian, 0.1% American Indian/Alaska Native, 0.0% Native Hawaiian/Other Pacific Islander, 1.3% Other, 0.7% Hispanic of any race (2010); Average household size: 2.31 (2010); Median age: 39.9 (2010); Males per 100 females: 94.9 (2010); Marriage status: 34.9% never married, 49.0% now married, 7.1% widowed, 9.1% divorced (2006-2010 5-year est.); Foreign born: 1.1% (2006-2010 5-year est.); Ancestry (includes multiple ancestries): 51.3% German, 20.3% Irish, 10.3% English, 8.6% Italian, 6.7% Polish (2006-2010 5-year est.).
Economy: Single-family building permits issued: 1 (2011); Multi-family building permits issued: 0 (2011); Employment by occupation: 5.4% management, 7.7% professional, 10.3% services, 20.5% sales, 6.4% farming, 6.1% construction, 5.8% production (2006-2010 5-year est.).
Income: Per capita income: $22,063 (2006-2010 5-year est.); Median household income: $48,713 (2006-2010 5-year est.); Average household income: $53,368 (2006-2010 5-year est.); Percent of households with income of $100,000 or more: 11.3% (2006-2010 5-year est.); Poverty rate: 13.7% (2006-2010 5-year est.).
Education: Percent of population age 25 and over with: High school diploma (including GED) or higher: 86.7% (2006-2010 5-year est.);

Bachelor's degree or higher: 22.3% (2006-2010 5-year est.); Master's degree or higher: 5.5% (2006-2010 5-year est.).
School District(s)
South Williamsport Area SD (KG-12)
   2010-11 Enrollment: 1,325 . . . . (570) 327-1581
Housing: Homeownership rate: 65.3% (2010); Median home value: $107,200 (2006-2010 5-year est.); Median contract rent: $573 per month (2006-2010 5-year est.); Median year structure built: 1945 (2006-2010 5-year est.).
Safety: Violent crime rate: 45.3 per 10,000 population; Property crime rate: 189.1 per 10,000 population (2011).
Transportation: Commute to work: 90.8% car, 1.9% public transportation, 3.5% walk, 1.5% work from home (2006-2010 5-year est.); Travel time to work: 61.3% less than 15 minutes, 21.8% 15 to 30 minutes, 10.7% 30 to 45 minutes, 2.5% 45 to 60 minutes, 3.6% 60 minutes or more (2006-2010 5-year est.)
Additional Information Contacts
Borough of South Williamsport . . . . (570) 327-8152
  http://www.southwilliamsport.net
Williamsport/Lycoming Chamber of Commerce . . . . (570) 326-1971
  http://www.williamsport.org

SUSQUEHANNA (township). Covers a land area of 6.567 square miles and a water area of 0.612 square miles. Located at 41.21° N. Lat; 77.13° W. Long.

Population: 1,046 (1990); 993 (2000); 1,000 (2010); Density: 152.3 persons per square mile (2010); Race: 97.7% White, 0.5% Black, 0.6% Asian, 0.0% American Indian/Alaska Native, 0.0% Native Hawaiian/Other Pacific Islander, 1.2% Other, 0.8% Hispanic of any race (2010); Average household size: 2.41 (2010); Median age: 46.8 (2010); Males per 100 females: 99.6 (2010); Marriage status: 24.9% never married, 58.5% now married, 8.5% widowed, 8.0% divorced (2006-2010 5-year est.); Foreign born: 0.5% (2006-2010 5-year est.); Ancestry (includes multiple ancestries): 64.1% German, 17.4% Irish, 7.2% Italian, 5.8% American, 5.6% Dutch (2006-2010 5-year est.).
Economy: Single-family building permits issued: 0 (2011); Multi-family building permits issued: 0 (2011); Employment by occupation: 5.7% management, 3.6% professional, 11.6% services, 15.2% sales, 4.6% farming, 8.8% construction, 8.8% production (2006-2010 5-year est.).
Income: Per capita income: $23,468 (2006-2010 5-year est.); Median household income: $47,961 (2006-2010 5-year est.); Average household income: $56,227 (2006-2010 5-year est.); Percent of households with income of $100,000 or more: 8.3% (2006-2010 5-year est.); Poverty rate: 5.0% (2006-2010 5-year est.).
Education: Percent of population age 25 and over with: High school diploma (including GED) or higher: 86.8% (2006-2010 5-year est.); Bachelor's degree or higher: 16.9% (2006-2010 5-year est.); Master's degree or higher: 7.0% (2006-2010 5-year est.).
Housing: Homeownership rate: 88.7% (2010); Median home value: $117,900 (2006-2010 5-year est.); Median contract rent: $523 per month (2006-2010 5-year est.); Median year structure built: 1964 (2006-2010 5-year est.).
Transportation: Commute to work: 92.0% car, 0.9% public transportation, 2.8% walk, 4.3% work from home (2006-2010 5-year est.); Travel time to work: 24.0% less than 15 minutes, 57.8% 15 to 30 minutes, 9.4% 30 to 45 minutes, 4.5% 45 to 60 minutes, 4.3% 60 minutes or more (2006-2010 5-year est.)

TROUT RUN (unincorporated postal area)
Zip Code: 17771
  Covers a land area of 215.793 square miles and a water area of 1.802 square miles. Located at 41.43° N. Lat; 77.03° W. Long. Population: 3,158 (2010); Density: 14.6 persons per square mile (2010); Race: 98.8% White, 0.2% Black, 0.2% Asian, 0.1% American Indian/Alaska Native, 0.0% Native Hawaiian/Other Pacific Islander, 0.7% Other, 0.5% Hispanic of any race (2010); Average household size: 2.50 (2010); Median age: 45.6 (2010); Males per 100 females: 104.3 (2010); Homeownership rate: 86.4% (2010)

UNITYVILLE (unincorporated postal area)
Zip Code: 17774
  Covers a land area of 47.671 square miles and a water area of 0.140 square miles. Located at 41.28° N. Lat; 76.53° W. Long. Population: 1,277 (2010); Density: 26.8 persons per square mile (2010); Race: 99.5% White, 0.1% Black, 0.1% Asian, 0.2% American Indian/Alaska

Native, 0.0% Native Hawaiian/Other Pacific Islander, 0.1% Other, 0.3% Hispanic of any race (2010); Average household size: 2.51 (2010); Median age: 42.6 (2010); Males per 100 females: 105.3 (2010); Homeownership rate: 82.9% (2010)

UPPER FAIRFIELD (township). Covers a land area of 17.963 square miles and a water area of 0.156 square miles. Located at 41.31° N. Lat; 76.87° W. Long.

Population: 1,774 (1990); 1,854 (2000); 1,823 (2010); Density: 101.5 persons per square mile (2010); Race: 97.6% White, 0.7% Black, 0.2% Asian, 0.1% American Indian/Alaska Native, 0.1% Native Hawaiian/Other Pacific Islander, 1.3% Other, 0.3% Hispanic of any race (2010); Average household size: 2.54 (2010); Median age: 45.2 (2010); Males per 100 females: 102.1 (2010); Marriage status: 18.6% never married, 69.4% now married, 5.4% widowed, 6.6% divorced (2006-2010 5-year est.); Foreign born: 0.3% (2006-2010 5-year est.); Ancestry (includes multiple ancestries): 47.0% German, 14.1% Irish, 12.6% English, 11.1% American, 6.1% Italian (2006-2010 5-year est.).

Economy: Single-family building permits issued: 2 (2011); Multi-family building permits issued: 0 (2011); Employment by occupation: 6.9% management, 1.9% professional, 6.1% services, 19.8% sales, 6.0% farming, 8.5% construction, 6.8% production (2006-2010 5-year est.).

Income: Per capita income: $25,040 (2006-2010 5-year est.); Median household income: $54,609 (2006-2010 5-year est.); Average household income: $62,784 (2006-2010 5-year est.); Percent of households with income of $100,000 or more: 16.3% (2006-2010 5-year est.); Poverty rate: 8.2% (2006-2010 5-year est.).

Taxes: Total city taxes per capita: $110 (2009); City property taxes per capita: $6 (2009).

Education: Percent of population age 25 and over with: High school diploma (including GED) or higher: 87.9% (2006-2010 5-year est.); Bachelor's degree or higher: 18.3% (2006-2010 5-year est.); Master's degree or higher: 4.8% (2006-2010 5-year est.).

Housing: Homeownership rate: 88.9% (2010); Median home value: $151,800 (2006-2010 5-year est.); Median contract rent: $438 per month (2006-2010 5-year est.); Median year structure built: 1975 (2006-2010 5-year est.).

Transportation: Commute to work: 92.6% car, 0.0% public transportation, 1.7% walk, 4.3% work from home (2006-2010 5-year est.); Travel time to work: 18.2% less than 15 minutes, 60.0% 15 to 30 minutes, 14.6% 30 to 45 minutes, 3.2% 45 to 60 minutes, 4.0% 60 minutes or more (2006-2010 5-year est.)

Additional Information Contacts

Williamsport/Lycoming Chamber of Commerce . . . . (570) 326-1971
    http://www.williamsport.org

WASHINGTON (township). Covers a land area of 48.219 square miles and a water area of 0.108 square miles. Located at 41.12° N. Lat; 77.05° W. Long.

Population: 1,552 (1990); 1,613 (2000); 1,619 (2010); Density: 33.6 persons per square mile (2010); Race: 97.2% White, 1.1% Black, 0.4% Asian, 0.2% American Indian/Alaska Native, 0.0% Native Hawaiian/Other Pacific Islander, 1.1% Other, 0.9% Hispanic of any race (2010); Average household size: 2.84 (2010); Median age: 41.8 (2010); Males per 100 females: 100.9 (2010); Marriage status: 22.7% never married, 68.5% now married, 3.8% widowed, 5.1% divorced (2006-2010 5-year est.); Foreign born: 0.8% (2006-2010 5-year est.); Ancestry (includes multiple ancestries): 46.2% German, 12.2% Irish, 7.7% American, 5.9% English, 4.9% Dutch (2006-2010 5-year est.).

Economy: Single-family building permits issued: 4 (2011); Multi-family building permits issued: 0 (2011); Employment by occupation: 11.3% management, 2.7% professional, 10.3% services, 16.6% sales, 1.4% farming, 17.3% construction, 11.4% production (2006-2010 5-year est.).

Income: Per capita income: $22,447 (2006-2010 5-year est.); Median household income: $50,972 (2006-2010 5-year est.); Average household income: $60,062 (2006-2010 5-year est.); Percent of households with income of $100,000 or more: 13.5% (2006-2010 5-year est.); Poverty rate: 9.1% (2006-2010 5-year est.).

Education: Percent of population age 25 and over with: High school diploma (including GED) or higher: 89.5% (2006-2010 5-year est.); Bachelor's degree or higher: 13.6% (2006-2010 5-year est.); Master's degree or higher: 2.3% (2006-2010 5-year est.).

Housing: Homeownership rate: 87.8% (2010); Median home value: $138,000 (2006-2010 5-year est.); Median contract rent: $514 per month

(2006-2010 5-year est.); Median year structure built: 1973 (2006-2010 5-year est.).

Transportation: Commute to work: 93.5% car, 0.0% public transportation, 1.2% walk, 3.8% work from home (2006-2010 5-year est.); Travel time to work: 22.0% less than 15 minutes, 52.2% 15 to 30 minutes, 16.7% 30 to 45 minutes, 3.8% 45 to 60 minutes, 5.4% 60 minutes or more (2006-2010 5-year est.)

Additional Information Contacts

Williamsport/Lycoming Chamber of Commerce . . . . (570) 326-1971
    http://www.williamsport.org

WATERVILLE (unincorporated postal area)
Zip Code: 17776

Covers a land area of 87.515 square miles and a water area of 0.828 square miles. Located at 41.41° N. Lat; 77.29° W. Long. Population: 295 (2010); Density: 3.4 persons per square mile (2010); Race: 99.0% White, 0.3% Black, 0.0% Asian, 0.0% American Indian/Alaska Native, 0.0% Native Hawaiian/Other Pacific Islander, 0.7% Other, 0.3% Hispanic of any race (2010); Average household size: 2.17 (2010); Median age: 54.3 (2010); Males per 100 females: 106.3 (2010); Homeownership rate: 85.3% (2010)

WATSON (township). Covers a land area of 23.034 square miles and a water area of 0.389 square miles. Located at 41.26° N. Lat; 77.35° W. Long.

Population: 565 (1990); 550 (2000); 537 (2010); Density: 23.3 persons per square mile (2010); Race: 99.3% White, 0.0% Black, 0.0% Asian, 0.0% American Indian/Alaska Native, 0.0% Native Hawaiian/Other Pacific Islander, 0.7% Other, 0.4% Hispanic of any race (2010); Average household size: 2.45 (2010); Median age: 47.2 (2010); Males per 100 females: 111.4 (2010); Marriage status: 19.7% never married, 66.9% now married, 6.1% widowed, 7.3% divorced (2006-2010 5-year est.); Foreign born: 0.6% (2006-2010 5-year est.); Ancestry (includes multiple ancestries): 32.3% German, 20.1% English, 17.4% Irish, 11.8% Polish, 5.5% American (2006-2010 5-year est.).

Economy: Single-family building permits issued: 4 (2011); Multi-family building permits issued: 0 (2011); Employment by occupation: 9.8% management, 0.0% professional, 6.2% services, 16.3% sales, 2.2% farming, 15.9% construction, 6.5% production (2006-2010 5-year est.).

Income: Per capita income: $31,936 (2006-2010 5-year est.); Median household income: $61,250 (2006-2010 5-year est.); Average household income: $78,776 (2006-2010 5-year est.); Percent of households with income of $100,000 or more: 20.5% (2006-2010 5-year est.); Poverty rate: 1.8% (2006-2010 5-year est.).

Education: Percent of population age 25 and over with: High school diploma (including GED) or higher: 93.0% (2006-2010 5-year est.); Bachelor's degree or higher: 14.5% (2006-2010 5-year est.); Master's degree or higher: 5.6% (2006-2010 5-year est.).

Housing: Homeownership rate: 90.9% (2010); Median home value: $168,000 (2006-2010 5-year est.); Median contract rent: $341 per month (2006-2010 5-year est.); Median year structure built: 1971 (2006-2010 5-year est.).

Transportation: Commute to work: 97.0% car, 0.0% public transportation, 0.0% walk, 2.2% work from home (2006-2010 5-year est.); Travel time to work: 10.9% less than 15 minutes, 54.0% 15 to 30 minutes, 24.2% 30 to 45 minutes, 2.6% 45 to 60 minutes, 8.3% 60 minutes or more (2006-2010 5-year est.)

Additional Information Contacts

Watson Township . . . . (570) 398-7829
    http://www.watsontwp.org

WILLIAMSPORT (city). County seat. Covers a land area of 8.731 square miles and a water area of 0.696 square miles. Located at 41.24° N. Lat; 77.04° W. Long. Elevation is 518 feet.

History: The site of Williamsport was once occupied by a village named French Margaret's Town for the daughter of Madame Montour. Other settlers arrived in the 1770s, and the town was laid out about 1796. The settlement was known as William's Port for a boatman, William Russell, who had discovered and used a convenient landing place on the river. The designation eventually became a single word. Peter J. McGovern Little League Museum is here. Incorporated 1886.

Population: 31,933 (1990); 30,706 (2000); 29,381 (2010); Density: 3,365.1 persons per square mile (2010); Race: 80.8% White, 13.5% Black, 0.7% Asian, 0.2% American Indian/Alaska Native, 0.0% Native Hawaiian/Other Pacific Islander, 4.8% Other, 2.6% Hispanic of any race

(2010); Average household size: 2.27 (2010); Median age: 29.7 (2010); Males per 100 females: 104.4 (2010); Marriage status: 45.7% never married, 36.4% now married, 6.7% widowed, 11.1% divorced (2006-2010 5-year est.); Foreign born: 1.3% (2006-2010 5-year est.); Ancestry (includes multiple ancestries): 30.8% German, 16.0% Irish, 11.4% Italian, 7.2% English, 6.1% Polish (2006-2010 5-year est.).

Economy: Unemployment rate: 9.3% (August 2012); Total civilian labor force: 15,089 (August 2012); Single-family building permits issued: 0 (2011); Multi-family building permits issued: 10 (2011); Employment by occupation: 6.2% management, 2.1% professional, 13.8% services, 15.5% sales, 5.7% farming, 7.1% construction, 8.2% production (2006-2010 5-year est.).

Income: Per capita income: $17,446 (2006-2010 5-year est.); Median household income: $27,138 (2006-2010 5-year est.); Average household income: $42,476 (2006-2010 5-year est.); Percent of households with income of $100,000 or more: 7.4% (2006-2010 5-year est.); Poverty rate: 28.2% (2006-2010 5-year est.).

Education: Percent of population age 25 and over with: High school diploma (including GED) or higher: 82.0% (2006-2010 5-year est.); Bachelor's degree or higher: 18.3% (2006-2010 5-year est.); Master's degree or higher: 7.1% (2006-2010 5-year est.).

School District(s)

Jersey Shore Area SD (KG-12)
  2010-11 Enrollment: 2,762 . . . . (570) 398-1561
Loyalsock Township SD (KG-12)
  2010-11 Enrollment: 1,417 . . . . (570) 326-6508
Williamsport Area SD (KG-12)
  2010-11 Enrollment: 5,427 . . . . (570) 327-5500

Four-year College(s)

Lycoming College (Private, Not-for-profit, United Methodist)
  Fall 2010 Enrollment: 1,375 . . . . (570) 321-4000
  2011-12 Tuition: In-state $31,818; Out-of-state $31,818
Pennsylvania College of Technology (Public)
  Fall 2010 Enrollment: 5,784 . . . . (570) 326-3761
  2011-12 Tuition: In-state $13,590; Out-of-state $17,010

Two-year College(s)

Newport Business Institute-Williamsport (Private, For-profit)
  Fall 2010 Enrollment: 114 . . . . (570) 326-2869
  2011-12 Tuition: In-state $11,250; Out-of-state $11,250

Vocational/Technical School(s)

Barone Beauty Academy (Private, For-profit)
  Fall 2010 Enrollment: 34 . . . . (570) 326-7534
  2011-12 Tuition: $16,600
Empire Beauty School-Williamsport (Private, For-profit)
  Fall 2010 Enrollment: 109 . . . . (800) 223-3271
  2011-12 Tuition: $14,490

Housing: Homeownership rate: 41.9% (2010); Median home value: $86,700 (2006-2010 5-year est.); Median contract rent: $463 per month (2006-2010 5-year est.); Median year structure built: before 1940 (2006-2010 5-year est.).

Hospitals: Divine Providence Hospital (31 beds); Williamsport Hospital & Medical Center (238 beds)

Safety: Violent crime rate: 33.9 per 10,000 population; Property crime rate: 425.4 per 10,000 population (2011).

Newspapers: Food - Williamsport Sun-Gazette (Circulation 33,520); Williamsport Sun-Gazette (Local news; Circulation 31,730)

Transportation: Commute to work: 80.0% car, 4.7% public transportation, 10.8% walk, 2.8% work from home (2006-2010 5-year est.); Travel time to work: 57.2% less than 15 minutes, 31.6% 15 to 30 minutes, 6.1% 30 to 45 minutes, 1.8% 45 to 60 minutes, 3.3% 60 minutes or more (2006-2010 5-year est.).

Airports: Williamsport Regional (primary service)

Additional Information Contacts
City of Williamsport . . . . (570) 327-7500
  http://www.cityofwilliamsport.org
Williamsport/Lycoming Chamber of Commerce . . . . (570) 326-1971
  http://www.williamsport.org

WOLF (township). Covers a land area of 19.629 square miles and a water area of 0.148 square miles. Located at 41.26° N. Lat; 76.73° W. Long.

Population: 2,603 (1990); 2,707 (2000); 2,907 (2010); Density: 148.1 persons per square mile (2010); Race: 98.0% White, 0.3% Black, 0.3% Asian, 0.1% American Indian/Alaska Native, 0.0% Native Hawaiian/Other Pacific Islander, 1.3% Other, 0.7% Hispanic of any race (2010); Average

household size: 2.51 (2010); Median age: 43.6 (2010); Males per 100 females: 97.6 (2010); Marriage status: 23.1% never married, 61.2% now married, 6.8% widowed, 9.0% divorced (2006-2010 5-year est.); Foreign born: 2.1% (2006-2010 5-year est.); Ancestry (includes multiple ancestries): 42.5% German, 16.1% Irish, 8.6% English, 6.1% American, 5.3% Italian (2006-2010 5-year est.).

Economy: Single-family building permits issued: 5 (2011); Multi-family building permits issued: 0 (2011); Employment by occupation: 6.5% management, 3.3% professional, 11.5% services, 15.8% sales, 4.6% farming, 8.6% construction, 10.8% production (2006-2010 5-year est.).

Income: Per capita income: $26,092 (2006-2010 5-year est.); Median household income: $52,929 (2006-2010 5-year est.); Average household income: $66,896 (2006-2010 5-year est.); Percent of households with income of $100,000 or more: 13.1% (2006-2010 5-year est.); Poverty rate: 12.5% (2006-2010 5-year est.).

Education: Percent of population age 25 and over with: High school diploma (including GED) or higher: 87.1% (2006-2010 5-year est.); Bachelor's degree or higher: 17.1% (2006-2010 5-year est.); Master's degree or higher: 8.4% (2006-2010 5-year est.).

Housing: Homeownership rate: 89.5% (2010); Median home value: $141,000 (2006-2010 5-year est.); Median contract rent: $432 per month (2006-2010 5-year est.); Median year structure built: 1979 (2006-2010 5-year est.).

Transportation: Commute to work: 89.7% car, 0.0% public transportation, 1.1% walk, 5.4% work from home (2006-2010 5-year est.); Travel time to work: 26.4% less than 15 minutes, 43.2% 15 to 30 minutes, 18.2% 30 to 45 minutes, 6.6% 45 to 60 minutes, 5.6% 60 minutes or more (2006-2010 5-year est.)

Additional Information Contacts
Williamsport/Lycoming Chamber of Commerce . . . . (570) 326-1971
  http://www.williamsport.org

WOODWARD (township). Covers a land area of 12.983 square miles and a water area of 0.560 square miles. Located at 41.24° N. Lat; 77.15° W. Long.

Population: 2,267 (1990); 2,397 (2000); 2,200 (2010); Density: 169.5 persons per square mile (2010); Race: 97.4% White, 0.4% Black, 0.6% Asian, 0.3% American Indian/Alaska Native, 0.0% Native Hawaiian/Other Pacific Islander, 1.3% Other, 1.3% Hispanic of any race (2010); Average household size: 2.41 (2010); Median age: 46.3 (2010); Males per 100 females: 102.0 (2010); Marriage status: 23.3% never married, 63.2% now married, 3.4% widowed, 10.1% divorced (2006-2010 5-year est.); Foreign born: 0.2% (2006-2010 5-year est.); Ancestry (includes multiple ancestries): 41.2% German, 17.4% Irish, 9.4% American, 8.8% Italian, 8.3% English (2006-2010 5-year est.).

Economy: Single-family building permits issued: 0 (2011); Multi-family building permits issued: 0 (2011); Employment by occupation: 10.4% management, 0.0% professional, 12.8% services, 16.9% sales, 1.8% farming, 15.1% construction, 7.5% production (2006-2010 5-year est.).

Income: Per capita income: $20,532 (2006-2010 5-year est.); Median household income: $43,702 (2006-2010 5-year est.); Average household income: $51,675 (2006-2010 5-year est.); Percent of households with income of $100,000 or more: 12.1% (2006-2010 5-year est.); Poverty rate: 18.4% (2006-2010 5-year est.).

Education: Percent of population age 25 and over with: High school diploma (including GED) or higher: 85.6% (2006-2010 5-year est.); Bachelor's degree or higher: 13.6% (2006-2010 5-year est.); Master's degree or higher: 5.6% (2006-2010 5-year est.).

Housing: Homeownership rate: 84.1% (2010); Median home value: $111,400 (2006-2010 5-year est.); Median contract rent: $493 per month (2006-2010 5-year est.); Median year structure built: 1972 (2006-2010 5-year est.).

Transportation: Commute to work: 95.7% car, 0.8% public transportation, 1.8% walk, 0.5% work from home (2006-2010 5-year est.); Travel time to work: 32.7% less than 15 minutes, 50.6% 15 to 30 minutes, 9.2% 30 to 45 minutes, 3.1% 45 to 60 minutes, 4.4% 60 minutes or more (2006-2010 5-year est.).

Additional Information Contacts
Williamsport/Lycoming Chamber of Commerce . . . . (570) 326-1971
  http://www.williamsport.org

McKean County

Located in northern Pennsylvania; bounded on the north by New York; plateau area, drained by the Allegheny River. Covers a land area of

979.197 square miles, a water area of 5.022 square miles, and is located in the Eastern Time Zone at 41.81° N. Lat., 78.57° W. Long. The county was founded in 1804. County seat is Smethport.

McKean County is part of the Bradford, PA Micropolitan Statistical Area. The entire metro area includes: McKean County, PA

Weather Station: Bradford 4 SW Res 5   Elevation: 1,691 feet

	Jan	Feb	Mar	Apr	May	Jun	Jul	Aug	Sep	Oct	Nov	Dec
High	30	33	42	56	67	75	79	77	70	58	46	34
Low	12	13	20	32	41	50	54	53	46	35	28	18
Precip	3.1	2.5	3.4	3.8	4.3	5.3	4.9	4.6	4.4	4.0	4.0	3.7
Snow	18.0	13.5	10.8	2.2	0.1	0.0	0.0	0.0	0.0	0.5	7.5	19.5

High and Low temperatures in degrees Fahrenheit; Precipitation and Snow in inches

Weather Station: Bradford Regional Arpt   Elevation: 2,117 feet

	Jan	Feb	Mar	Apr	May	Jun	Jul	Aug	Sep	Oct	Nov	Dec
High	28	31	41	55	65	73	77	75	68	56	45	32
Low	14	15	22	33	41	50	54	53	46	36	30	18
Precip	2.8	2.4	3.5	3.6	4.1	5.1	4.4	4.3	3.9	3.4	3.7	3.6
Snow	na	na	na	na	na	na	na	na	na	na	na	na

High and Low temperatures in degrees Fahrenheit; Precipitation and Snow in inches

Weather Station: Kane 1 NNE   Elevation: 1,750 feet

	Jan	Feb	Mar	Apr	May	Jun	Jul	Aug	Sep	Oct	Nov	Dec
High	30	33	42	55	66	74	78	77	69	57	45	34
Low	12	12	19	30	38	48	52	51	44	34	27	18
Precip	3.3	2.6	3.5	3.9	4.3	4.8	4.6	4.5	4.1	3.6	4.0	3.7
Snow	24.3	17.8	14.2	2.8	0.2	0.0	0.0	0.0	tr	1.0	8.4	21.5

High and Low temperatures in degrees Fahrenheit; Precipitation and Snow in inches

Population: 47,131 (1990); 45,936 (2000); 43,450 (2010); Race: 95.9% White, 2.4% Black, 0.4% Asian, 0.2% American Indian/Alaska Native, 0.0% Native Hawaiian/Other Pacific Islander, 1.1% Other, 1.7% Hispanic of any race (2010); Density: 44.4 persons per square mile (2010); Average household size: 2.34 (2010); Median age: 41.5 (2010); Males per 100 females: 104.1 (2010).

Religion: Six largest groups: 18.4% Catholicism, 10.6% Methodist/Pietist, 7.3% Holiness, 4.3% Lutheran, 1.9% Baptist, 1.9% Presbyterian-Reformed (2010)

Economy: Unemployment rate: 8.3% (August 2012); Total civilian labor force: 21,874 (August 2012); Leading industries: 23.5% manufacturing; 20.8% health care and social assistance; 13.4% retail trade (2010); Farms: 313 totaling 41,466 acres (2007); Companies that employ 500 or more persons: 1 (2010); Companies that employ 100 to 499 persons: 21 (2010); Companies that employ less than 100 persons: 1,046 (2010); Black-owned businesses: n/a (2007); Hispanic-owned businesses: n/a (2007); Asian-owned businesses: n/a (2007); Women-owned businesses: 652 (2007); Retail sales per capita: $8,861 (2010). Single-family building permits issued: 21 (2011); Multi-family building permits issued: 0 (2011).

Income: Per capita income: $21,022 (2006-2010 5-year est.); Median household income: $40,097 (2006-2010 5-year est.); Average household income: $50,443 (2006-2010 5-year est.); Percent of households with income of $100,000 or more: 8.2% (2006-2010 5-year est.); Poverty rate: 13.9% (2006-2010 5-year est.); Bankruptcy rate: 1.66% (2011).

Education: Percent of population age 25 and over with: High school diploma (including GED) or higher: 88.3% (2006-2010 5-year est.); Bachelor's degree or higher: 15.6% (2006-2010 5-year est.); Master's degree or higher: 5.5% (2006-2010 5-year est.).

Housing: Homeownership rate: 73.5% (2010); Median home value: $72,300 (2006-2010 5-year est.); Median contract rent: $418 per month (2006-2010 5-year est.); Median year structure built: 1949 (2006-2010 5-year est.)

Health: Birth rate: 107.6 per 10,000 population (2011); Death rate: 119.6 per 10,000 population (2011); Age-adjusted cancer mortality rate: 195.9 deaths per 100,000 population (2009); Number of physicians: 12.4 per 10,000 population (2010); Hospital beds: 49.3 per 10,000 population (2008); Hospital admissions: 1,232.4 per 10,000 population (2008).

Elections: 2012 Presidential election results: 35.0% Obama, 63.2% Romney

National and State Parks: Kinzua Bridge State Park; Susquehanna State Forest

Additional Information Contacts
McKean County Government . . . . (814) 887-3200
http://www.mckeancountypa.org

McKean County Communities

ANNIN (township). Covers a land area of 33.312 square miles and a water area of 0.120 square miles. Located at 41.89° N. Lat; 78.29° W. Long.

Population: 805 (1990); 835 (2000); 694 (2010); Density: 20.8 persons per square mile (2010); Race: 98.6% White, 0.3% Black, 0.3% Asian, 0.0% American Indian/Alaska Native, 0.0% Native Hawaiian/Other Pacific Islander, 0.8% Other, 0.4% Hispanic of any race (2010); Average household size: 2.48 (2010); Median age: 44.8 (2010); Males per 100 females: 102.3 (2010); Marriage status: 23.9% never married, 60.2% now married, 8.1% widowed, 7.8% divorced (2006-2010 5-year est.); Foreign born: 2.4% (2006-2010 5-year est.); Ancestry (includes multiple ancestries): 25.1% German, 14.3% Irish, 9.7% American, 8.9% English, 7.1% Italian (2006-2010 5-year est.).

Economy: Single-family building permits issued: 2 (2011); Multi-family building permits issued: 0 (2011); Employment by occupation: 4.6% management, 6.2% professional, 15.4% services, 11.8% sales, 2.9% farming, 16.0% construction, 8.5% production (2006-2010 5-year est.).

Income: Per capita income: $18,670 (2006-2010 5-year est.); Median household income: $37,917 (2006-2010 5-year est.); Average household income: $45,436 (2006-2010 5-year est.); Percent of households with income of $100,000 or more: 10.3% (2006-2010 5-year est.); Poverty rate: 23.1% (2006-2010 5-year est.).

Education: Percent of population age 25 and over with: High school diploma (including GED) or higher: 79.2% (2006-2010 5-year est.); Bachelor's degree or higher: 11.2% (2006-2010 5-year est.); Master's degree or higher: 4.8% (2006-2010 5-year est.).

Housing: Homeownership rate: 79.2% (2010); Median home value: $79,300 (2006-2010 5-year est.); Median contract rent: $403 per month (2006-2010 5-year est.); Median year structure built: 1974 (2006-2010 5-year est.).

Transportation: Commute to work: 98.7% car, 0.0% public transportation, 0.0% walk, 1.3% work from home (2006-2010 5-year est.); Travel time to work: 34.7% less than 15 minutes, 25.9% 15 to 30 minutes, 25.9% 30 to 45 minutes, 8.8% 45 to 60 minutes, 4.7% 60 minutes or more (2006-2010 5-year est.)

BRADFORD (city). Covers a land area of 3.349 square miles and a water area of 0.073 square miles. Located at 41.96° N. Lat; 78.64° W. Long. Elevation is 1,440 feet.

History: Bradford was a cluster of dwellings until oil was discovered in the mid-1870's. Bradford grew and, in 1879, it was incorporated as a city.

Population: 9,646 (1990); 9,175 (2000); 8,770 (2010); Density: 2,619.1 persons per square mile (2010); Race: 96.3% White, 1.0% Black, 0.7% Asian, 0.4% American Indian/Alaska Native, 0.0% Native Hawaiian/Other Pacific Islander, 1.6% Other, 1.4% Hispanic of any race (2010); Average household size: 2.29 (2010); Median age: 37.5 (2010); Males per 100 females: 92.9 (2010); Marriage status: 32.0% never married, 43.9% now married, 9.1% widowed, 15.0% divorced (2006-2010 5-year est.); Foreign born: 0.9% (2006-2010 5-year est.); Ancestry (includes multiple ancestries): 28.3% German, 20.4% Italian, 15.7% Irish, 10.2% English, 7.2% Polish (2006-2010 5-year est.).

Economy: Single-family building permits issued: 0 (2011); Multi-family building permits issued: 0 (2011); Employment by occupation: 10.2% management, 1.1% professional, 16.7% services, 17.5% sales, 1.8% farming, 9.1% construction, 7.2% production (2006-2010 5-year est.).

Income: Per capita income: $17,561 (2006-2010 5-year est.); Median household income: $32,406 (2006-2010 5-year est.); Average household income: $39,850 (2006-2010 5-year est.); Percent of households with income of $100,000 or more: 3.8% (2006-2010 5-year est.); Poverty rate: 21.8% (2006-2010 5-year est.).

Education: Percent of population age 25 and over with: High school diploma (including GED) or higher: 85.0% (2006-2010 5-year est.); Bachelor's degree or higher: 15.5% (2006-2010 5-year est.); Master's degree or higher: 5.8% (2006-2010 5-year est.).

School District(s)
Bradford Area SD (PK-12)
   2010-11 Enrollment: 2,654 . . . . (814) 362-3841

Four-year College(s)
University of Pittsburgh-Bradford (Public)
   Fall 2010 Enrollment: 1,533 . . . . (814) 362-7500
   2011-12 Tuition: In-state $12,496; Out-of-state $22,688

Housing: Homeownership rate: 51.8% (2010); Median home value: $54,800 (2006-2010 5-year est.); Median contract rent: $436 per month (2006-2010 5-year est.); Median year structure built: before 1940 (2006-2010 5-year est.).
Hospitals: Bradford Regional Medical Center (127 beds)
Safety: Violent crime rate: 53.4 per 10,000 population; Property crime rate: 433.1 per 10,000 population (2011).
Newspapers: The Bradford Era (Regional news; Circulation 13,000); Bradford Journal (Community news; Circulation 5,500); McKean County Miner (Community news; Circulation 1,200)
Transportation: Commute to work: 85.0% car, 0.2% public transportation, 11.1% walk, 2.3% work from home (2006-2010 5-year est.); Travel time to work: 70.4% less than 15 minutes, 20.0% 15 to 30 minutes, 5.4% 30 to 45 minutes, 1.2% 45 to 60 minutes, 3.0% 60 minutes or more (2006-2010 5-year est.)
Airports: Bradford Regional (commercial service)
Additional Information Contacts
Bradford Area Chamber of Commerce . . . . (814) 368-7115
   http://www.bradfordchamber.com
City of Bradford . . . . (814) 362-3884
   http://www.bradfordpa.com

BRADFORD (township). Covers a land area of 56.090 square miles and a water area of 0.354 square miles. Located at 41.92° N. Lat; 78.69° W. Long. Elevation is 1,440 feet.
History: The growth of the city was initiated by the discovery of oil (c.1871), which has been eclipsed by diverse manufacturing. Seat of University of Pittsburgh-Bradford Campus. Settled c.1823, Incorporated as a city 1879.
Population: 5,065 (1990); 4,816 (2000); 4,805 (2010); Density: 85.7 persons per square mile (2010); Race: 96.6% White, 1.5% Black, 1.0% Asian, 0.2% American Indian/Alaska Native, 0.0% Native Hawaiian/Other Pacific Islander, 0.7% Other, 0.9% Hispanic of any race (2010); Average household size: 2.29 (2010); Median age: 41.1 (2010); Males per 100 females: 94.1 (2010); Marriage status: 26.5% never married, 52.1% now married, 10.4% widowed, 11.1% divorced (2006-2010 5-year est.); Foreign born: 1.1% (2006-2010 5-year est.); Ancestry (includes multiple ancestries): 38.8% German, 22.7% Irish, 16.5% Italian, 9.3% English, 7.0% Swedish (2006-2010 5-year est.).
Economy: Single-family building permits issued: 2 (2011); Multi-family building permits issued: 0 (2011); Employment by occupation: 10.2% management, 1.8% professional, 10.9% services, 10.9% sales, 3.6% farming, 8.4% construction, 7.5% production (2006-2010 5-year est.).
Income: Per capita income: $25,336 (2006-2010 5-year est.); Median household income: $48,068 (2006-2010 5-year est.); Average household income: $62,831 (2006-2010 5-year est.); Percent of households with income of $100,000 or more: 14.4% (2006-2010 5-year est.); Poverty rate: 4.1% (2006-2010 5-year est.).
Education: Percent of population age 25 and over with: High school diploma (including GED) or higher: 94.6% (2006-2010 5-year est.); Bachelor's degree or higher: 26.3% (2006-2010 5-year est.); Master's degree or higher: 10.0% (2006-2010 5-year est.).
Four-year College(s)
University of Pittsburgh-Bradford (Public)
   Fall 2010 Enrollment: 1,533 . . . . (814) 362-7500
   2011-12 Tuition: In-state $12,496; Out-of-state $22,688
Housing: Homeownership rate: 87.0% (2010); Median home value: $90,400 (2006-2010 5-year est.); Median contract rent: $557 per month (2006-2010 5-year est.); Median year structure built: 1954 (2006-2010 5-year est.).
Hospitals: Bradford Regional Medical Center (127 beds)
Safety: Violent crime rate: 20.7 per 10,000 population; Property crime rate: 53.9 per 10,000 population (2011).
Newspapers: The Bradford Era (Regional news; Circulation 13,000); Bradford Journal (Community news; Circulation 5,500); McKean County Miner (Community news; Circulation 1,200)
Transportation: Commute to work: 95.6% car, 0.0% public transportation, 1.3% walk, 3.1% work from home (2006-2010 5-year est.); Travel time to work: 60.1% less than 15 minutes, 26.3% 15 to 30 minutes, 8.6% 30 to 45 minutes, 1.1% 45 to 60 minutes, 3.8% 60 minutes or more (2006-2010 5-year est.)
Airports: Bradford Regional (commercial service)
Additional Information Contacts
Bradford Area Chamber of Commerce . . . . (814) 368-7115
   http://www.bradfordchamber.com

Bradford Township . . . . (814) 368-3564
   http://bradfordtwpmckeancnty.jimdo.com

CERES (township). Covers a land area of 40.670 square miles and a water area of 0.166 square miles. Located at 41.96° N. Lat; 78.26° W. Long.
Population: 981 (1990); 1,003 (2000); 905 (2010); Density: 22.3 persons per square mile (2010); Race: 97.2% White, 0.1% Black, 0.2% Asian, 0.0% American Indian/Alaska Native, 0.0% Native Hawaiian/Other Pacific Islander, 2.5% Other, 0.3% Hispanic of any race (2010); Average household size: 2.48 (2010); Median age: 43.3 (2010); Males per 100 females: 105.2 (2010); Marriage status: 22.1% never married, 59.5% now married, 9.7% widowed, 8.7% divorced (2006-2010 5-year est.); Foreign born: 0.2% (2006-2010 5-year est.); Ancestry (includes multiple ancestries): 29.0% German, 24.3% Irish, 14.7% English, 5.5% Italian, 3.8% American (2006-2010 5-year est.).
Economy: Single-family building permits issued: 0 (2011); Multi-family building permits issued: 0 (2011); Employment by occupation: 8.4% management, 0.9% professional, 7.8% services, 18.6% sales, 4.1% farming, 16.3% construction, 15.7% production (2006-2010 5-year est.).
Income: Per capita income: $18,454 (2006-2010 5-year est.); Median household income: $40,109 (2006-2010 5-year est.); Average household income: $43,640 (2006-2010 5-year est.); Percent of households with income of $100,000 or more: 1.8% (2006-2010 5-year est.); Poverty rate: 7.7% (2006-2010 5-year est.).
Education: Percent of population age 25 and over with: High school diploma (including GED) or higher: 86.8% (2006-2010 5-year est.); Bachelor's degree or higher: 10.5% (2006-2010 5-year est.); Master's degree or higher: 2.9% (2006-2010 5-year est.).
Housing: Homeownership rate: 82.2% (2010); Median home value: $69,500 (2006-2010 5-year est.); Median contract rent: $440 per month (2006-2010 5-year est.); Median year structure built: 1973 (2006-2010 5-year est.).
Transportation: Commute to work: 88.9% car, 0.9% public transportation, 9.4% walk, 0.9% work from home (2006-2010 5-year est.); Travel time to work: 16.3% less than 15 minutes, 43.2% 15 to 30 minutes, 31.4% 30 to 45 minutes, 9.2% 45 to 60 minutes, 0.0% 60 minutes or more (2006-2010 5-year est.)

CORYDON (township). Covers a land area of 72.980 square miles and a water area of 0.461 square miles. Located at 41.94° N. Lat; 78.87° W. Long.
Population: 319 (1990); 301 (2000); 275 (2010); Density: 3.8 persons per square mile (2010); Race: 100.0% White, 0.0% Black, 0.0% Asian, 0.0% American Indian/Alaska Native, 0.0% Native Hawaiian/Other Pacific Islander, 0.0% Other, 1.5% Hispanic of any race (2010); Average household size: 2.17 (2010); Median age: 53.1 (2010); Males per 100 females: 131.1 (2010); Marriage status: 16.8% never married, 69.6% now married, 2.5% widowed, 11.1% divorced (2006-2010 5-year est.); Foreign born: 0.0% (2006-2010 5-year est.); Ancestry (includes multiple ancestries): 33.1% German, 18.8% English, 15.9% Irish, 6.8% Italian, 6.5% American (2006-2010 5-year est.).
Economy: Single-family building permits issued: 1 (2011); Multi-family building permits issued: 0 (2011); Employment by occupation: 10.9% management, 1.1% professional, 6.3% services, 16.6% sales, 4.0% farming, 8.0% construction, 3.4% production (2006-2010 5-year est.).
Income: Per capita income: $26,783 (2006-2010 5-year est.); Median household income: $55,714 (2006-2010 5-year est.); Average household income: $56,758 (2006-2010 5-year est.); Percent of households with income of $100,000 or more: 4.9% (2006-2010 5-year est.); Poverty rate: 7.1% (2006-2010 5-year est.).
Education: Percent of population age 25 and over with: High school diploma (including GED) or higher: 93.8% (2006-2010 5-year est.); Bachelor's degree or higher: 14.7% (2006-2010 5-year est.); Master's degree or higher: 4.6% (2006-2010 5-year est.).
Housing: Homeownership rate: 89.0% (2010); Median home value: $90,000 (2006-2010 5-year est.); Median contract rent: n/a per month (2006-2010 5-year est.); Median year structure built: 1976 (2006-2010 5-year est.).
Transportation: Commute to work: 94.0% car, 0.0% public transportation, 1.8% walk, 4.2% work from home (2006-2010 5-year est.); Travel time to work: 2.5% less than 15 minutes, 50.9% 15 to 30 minutes, 31.1% 30 to 45 minutes, 14.3% 45 to 60 minutes, 1.2% 60 minutes or more (2006-2010 5-year est.)

CROSBY (unincorporated postal area)

Zip Code: 16724

Covers a land area of 2.251 square miles and a water area of 0.013 square miles. Located at 41.73° N. Lat; 78.36° W. Long. Elevation is 1,509 feet. Population: 143 (2010); Density: 63.5 persons per square mile (2010); Race: 98.6% White, 0.0% Black, 0.0% Asian, 0.7% American Indian/Alaska Native, 0.0% Native Hawaiian/Other Pacific Islander, 0.7% Other, 0.0% Hispanic of any race (2010); Average household size: 2.31 (2010); Median age: 40.8 (2010); Males per 100 females: 116.7 (2010); Homeownership rate: 80.7% (2010)

CUSTER CITY (unincorporated postal area)

Zip Code: 16725

Covers a land area of 0.437 square miles and a water area of 0.007 square miles. Located at 41.90° N. Lat; 78.65° W. Long. Elevation is 1,512 feet. Population: 166 (2010); Density: 379.4 persons per square mile (2010); Race: 99.4% White, 0.0% Black, 0.0% Asian, 0.0% American Indian/Alaska Native, 0.0% Native Hawaiian/Other Pacific Islander, 0.6% Other, 0.6% Hispanic of any race (2010); Average household size: 2.36 (2010); Median age: 41.5 (2010); Males per 100 females: 93.0 (2010); Homeownership rate: 76.1% (2010)

CYCLONE (unincorporated postal area)

Zip Code: 16726

Covers a land area of 25.467 square miles and a water area of 0.004 square miles. Located at 41.81° N. Lat; 78.57° W. Long. Elevation is 2,211 feet. Population: 542 (2010); Density: 21.3 persons per square mile (2010); Race: 99.6% White, 0.0% Black, 0.4% Asian, 0.0% American Indian/Alaska Native, 0.0% Native Hawaiian/Other Pacific Islander, 0.0% Other, 0.6% Hispanic of any race (2010); Average household size: 2.56 (2010); Median age: 43.6 (2010); Males per 100 females: 120.3 (2010); Homeownership rate: 87.7% (2010)

DERRICK CITY (unincorporated postal area)

Zip Code: 16727

Covers a land area of 4.310 square miles and a water area of 0 square miles. Located at 41.98° N. Lat; 78.53° W. Long. Population: 211 (2010); Density: 49.0 persons per square mile (2010); Race: 98.1% White, 0.0% Black, 0.5% Asian, 0.0% American Indian/Alaska Native, 0.0% Native Hawaiian/Other Pacific Islander, 1.4% Other, 0.0% Hispanic of any race (2010); Average household size: 2.45 (2010); Median age: 41.1 (2010); Males per 100 females: 95.4 (2010); Homeownership rate: 88.4% (2010)

DUKE CENTER (unincorporated postal area)

Zip Code: 16729

Covers a land area of 13.848 square miles and a water area of 0.006 square miles. Located at 41.96° N. Lat; 78.47° W. Long. Elevation is 1,575 feet. Population: 761 (2010); Density: 55.0 persons per square mile (2010); Race: 98.6% White, 0.1% Black, 0.3% Asian, 0.1% American Indian/Alaska Native, 0.0% Native Hawaiian/Other Pacific Islander, 0.9% Other, 0.4% Hispanic of any race (2010); Average household size: 2.42 (2010); Median age: 43.8 (2010); Males per 100 females: 98.2 (2010); Homeownership rate: 83.8% (2010)

EAST SMETHPORT (unincorporated postal area)

Zip Code: 16730

Covers a land area of 0.584 square miles and a water area of 0.014 square miles. Located at 41.81° N. Lat; 78.42° W. Long. Elevation is 1,512 feet. Population: 121 (2010); Density: 206.8 persons per square mile (2010); Race: 100.0% White, 0.0% Black, 0.0% Asian, 0.0% American Indian/Alaska Native, 0.0% Native Hawaiian/Other Pacific Islander, 0.0% Other, 0.0% Hispanic of any race (2010); Average household size: 2.20 (2010); Median age: 45.8 (2010); Males per 100 females: 89.1 (2010); Homeownership rate: 81.8% (2010)

ELDRED (borough). Covers a land area of 0.820 square miles and a water area of 0.030 square miles. Located at 41.96° N. Lat; 78.38° W. Long. Elevation is 1,440 feet.

Population: 869 (1990); 858 (2000); 825 (2010); Density: 1,006.0 persons per square mile (2010); Race: 96.5% White, 0.1% Black, 0.2% Asian, 0.1% American Indian/Alaska Native, 0.0% Native Hawaiian/Other Pacific Islander, 3.1% Other, 2.4% Hispanic of any race (2010); Average household size: 2.39 (2010); Median age: 37.2 (2010); Males per 100 females: 87.9 (2010); Marriage status: 23.6% never married, 48.9% now married, 10.2% widowed, 17.3% divorced (2006-2010 5-year est.); Foreign born: 0.6% (2006-2010 5-year est.); Ancestry (includes multiple ancestries): 38.6% German, 25.9% Irish, 19.3% English, 11.1% Italian, 5.7% Dutch (2006-2010 5-year est.).

Economy: Single-family building permits issued: 0 (2011); Multi-family building permits issued: 0 (2011); Employment by occupation: 4.2% management, 2.6% professional, 12.2% services, 9.1% sales, 1.6% farming, 15.4% construction, 15.9% production (2006-2010 5-year est.).

Income: Per capita income: $15,624 (2006-2010 5-year est.); Median household income: $35,385 (2006-2010 5-year est.); Average household income: $40,877 (2006-2010 5-year est.); Percent of households with income of $100,000 or more: 5.7% (2006-2010 5-year est.); Poverty rate: 21.2% (2006-2010 5-year est.).

Education: Percent of population age 25 and over with: High school diploma (including GED) or higher: 85.3% (2006-2010 5-year est.); Bachelor's degree or higher: 8.8% (2006-2010 5-year est.); Master's degree or higher: 4.0% (2006-2010 5-year est.).

School District(s)

Otto-Eldred SD (PK-12)

   2010-11 Enrollment: 701 . . . . (814) 966-3214

Housing: Homeownership rate: 68.4% (2010); Median home value: $50,800 (2006-2010 5-year est.); Median contract rent: $385 per month (2006-2010 5-year est.); Median year structure built: 1940 (2006-2010 5-year est.).

Transportation: Commute to work: 80.5% car, 2.3% public transportation, 13.3% walk, 1.3% work from home (2006-2010 5-year est.); Travel time to work: 33.0% less than 15 minutes, 48.3% 15 to 30 minutes, 12.1% 30 to 45 minutes, 5.3% 45 to 60 minutes, 1.3% 60 minutes or more (2006-2010 5-year est.)

ELDRED (township). Covers a land area of 38.737 square miles and a water area of 0.504 square miles. Located at 41.94° N. Lat; 78.40° W. Long. Elevation is 1,440 feet.

History: Incorporated 1880.

Population: 1,768 (1990); 1,696 (2000); 1,592 (2010); Density: 41.1 persons per square mile (2010); Race: 98.8% White, 0.1% Black, 0.2% Asian, 0.4% American Indian/Alaska Native, 0.0% Native Hawaiian/Other Pacific Islander, 0.5% Other, 0.7% Hispanic of any race (2010); Average household size: 2.51 (2010); Median age: 44.0 (2010); Males per 100 females: 101.3 (2010); Marriage status: 21.6% never married, 62.8% now married, 4.7% widowed, 10.9% divorced (2006-2010 5-year est.); Foreign born: 0.0% (2006-2010 5-year est.); Ancestry (includes multiple ancestries): 26.6% German, 19.6% Irish, 12.7% English, 10.2% Italian, 7.1% American (2006-2010 5-year est.).

Economy: Single-family building permits issued: 7 (2011); Multi-family building permits issued: 0 (2011); Employment by occupation: 5.6% management, 3.3% professional, 4.9% services, 18.8% sales, 5.2% farming, 13.3% construction, 14.4% production (2006-2010 5-year est.).

Income: Per capita income: $20,108 (2006-2010 5-year est.); Median household income: $44,844 (2006-2010 5-year est.); Average household income: $49,637 (2006-2010 5-year est.); Percent of households with income of $100,000 or more: 9.9% (2006-2010 5-year est.); Poverty rate: 12.0% (2006-2010 5-year est.).

Education: Percent of population age 25 and over with: High school diploma (including GED) or higher: 88.3% (2006-2010 5-year est.); Bachelor's degree or higher: 12.5% (2006-2010 5-year est.); Master's degree or higher: 5.6% (2006-2010 5-year est.).

Housing: Homeownership rate: 87.4% (2010); Median home value: $79,800 (2006-2010 5-year est.); Median contract rent: $409 per month (2006-2010 5-year est.); Median year structure built: 1967 (2006-2010 5-year est.).

Transportation: Commute to work: 93.3% car, 0.0% public transportation, 0.0% walk, 5.2% work from home (2006-2010 5-year est.); Travel time to work: 18.6% less than 15 minutes, 38.6% 15 to 30 minutes, 31.5% 30 to 45 minutes, 3.5% 45 to 60 minutes, 7.8% 60 minutes or more (2006-2010 5-year est.)

Additional Information Contacts

Bradford Area Chamber of Commerce . . . . (814) 368-7115

   http://www.bradfordchamber.com

FOSTER (township). Covers a land area of 46.904 square miles and a water area of 0.055 square miles. Located at 41.96° N. Lat; 78.62° W. Long.

Population: 4,670 (1990); 4,566 (2000); 4,316 (2010); Density: 92.0 persons per square mile (2010); Race: 98.3% White, 0.2% Black, 0.5%

Asian, 0.3% American Indian/Alaska Native, 0.0% Native Hawaiian/Other Pacific Islander, 0.7% Other, 0.8% Hispanic of any race (2010); Average household size: 2.34 (2010); Median age: 44.8 (2010); Males per 100 females: 98.3 (2010); Marriage status: 25.4% never married, 59.1% now married, 5.2% widowed, 10.3% divorced (2006-2010 5-year est.); Foreign born: 0.9% (2006-2010 5-year est.); Ancestry (includes multiple ancestries): 33.7% German, 16.6% Irish, 12.5% Italian, 10.0% English, 8.4% American (2006-2010 5-year est.).

Economy: Single-family building permits issued: 3 (2011); Multi-family building permits issued: 0 (2011); Employment by occupation: 12.5% management, 2.0% professional, 15.6% services, 15.7% sales, 4.6% farming, 8.9% construction, 7.2% production (2006-2010 5-year est.).

Income: Per capita income: $29,663 (2006-2010 5-year est.); Median household income: $43,083 (2006-2010 5-year est.); Average household income: $69,613 (2006-2010 5-year est.); Percent of households with income of $100,000 or more: 10.6% (2006-2010 5-year est.); Poverty rate: 8.3% (2006-2010 5-year est.).

Education: Percent of population age 25 and over with: High school diploma (including GED) or higher: 95.2% (2006-2010 5-year est.); Bachelor's degree or higher: 19.3% (2006-2010 5-year est.); Master's degree or higher: 7.6% (2006-2010 5-year est.).

Housing: Homeownership rate: 83.2% (2010); Median home value: $69,100 (2006-2010 5-year est.); Median contract rent: $453 per month (2006-2010 5-year est.); Median year structure built: 1951 (2006-2010 5-year est.).

Safety: Violent crime rate: 9.2 per 10,000 population; Property crime rate: 122.4 per 10,000 population (2011).

Transportation: Commute to work: 96.0% car, 0.0% public transportation, 1.8% walk, 1.8% work from home (2006-2010 5-year est.); Travel time to work: 44.7% less than 15 minutes, 38.9% 15 to 30 minutes, 12.2% 30 to 45 minutes, 2.1% 45 to 60 minutes, 2.0% 60 minutes or more (2006-2010 5-year est.)

Additional Information Contacts

Bradford Area Chamber of Commerce . . . . (814) 368-7115
http://www.bradfordchamber.com

FOSTER BROOK (CDP). Covers a land area of 3.153 square miles and a water area of 0.018 square miles. Located at 41.98° N. Lat; 78.60° W. Long. Elevation is 1,437 feet.

Population: n/a (1990); n/a (2000); 1,251 (2010); Density: 396.7 persons per square mile (2010); Race: 98.1% White, 0.2% Black, 0.6% Asian, 0.7% American Indian/Alaska Native, 0.0% Native Hawaiian/Other Pacific Islander, 0.4% Other, 1.0% Hispanic of any race (2010); Average household size: 2.30 (2010); Median age: 42.5 (2010); Males per 100 females: 101.4 (2010); Marriage status: 28.9% never married, 55.9% now married, 5.1% widowed, 10.0% divorced (2006-2010 5-year est.); Foreign born: 0.8% (2006-2010 5-year est.); Ancestry (includes multiple ancestries): 22.2% German, 19.8% Italian, 13.0% Irish, 11.3% English, 10.0% American (2006-2010 5-year est.).

Economy: Employment by occupation: 8.7% management, 1.3% professional, 19.3% services, 8.5% sales, 5.8% farming, 6.6% construction, 7.3% production (2006-2010 5-year est.).

Income: Per capita income: $18,960 (2006-2010 5-year est.); Median household income: $36,875 (2006-2010 5-year est.); Average household income: $45,019 (2006-2010 5-year est.); Percent of households with income of $100,000 or more: 5.1% (2006-2010 5-year est.); Poverty rate: 21.4% (2006-2010 5-year est.).

Education: Percent of population age 25 and over with: High school diploma (including GED) or higher: 97.5% (2006-2010 5-year est.); Bachelor's degree or higher: 19.5% (2006-2010 5-year est.); Master's degree or higher: 3.8% (2006-2010 5-year est.).

Housing: Homeownership rate: 80.7% (2010); Median home value: $66,900 (2006-2010 5-year est.); Median contract rent: $485 per month (2006-2010 5-year est.); Median year structure built: 1949 (2006-2010 5-year est.).

Transportation: Commute to work: 93.1% car, 0.0% public transportation, 5.8% walk, 1.0% work from home (2006-2010 5-year est.); Travel time to work: 45.6% less than 15 minutes, 35.5% 15 to 30 minutes, 13.1% 30 to 45 minutes, 4.7% 45 to 60 minutes, 1.1% 60 minutes or more (2006-2010 5-year est.)

GIFFORD (unincorporated postal area)

Zip Code: 16732

Covers a land area of 6.595 square miles and a water area of 0 square miles. Located at 41.85° N. Lat; 78.61° W. Long. Elevation is 2,244 feet.

Population: 293 (2010); Density: 44.4 persons per square mile (2010); Race: 99.3% White, 0.0% Black, 0.3% Asian, 0.0% American Indian/Alaska Native, 0.0% Native Hawaiian/Other Pacific Islander, 0.4% Other, 0.3% Hispanic of any race (2010); Average household size: 2.33 (2010); Median age: 47.9 (2010); Males per 100 females: 95.3 (2010); Homeownership rate: 88.9% (2010)

HAMILTON (township). Covers a land area of 72.529 square miles and a water area of 1.949 square miles. Located at 41.79° N. Lat; 78.89° W. Long.

Population: 612 (1990); 637 (2000); 543 (2010); Density: 7.5 persons per square mile (2010); Race: 99.1% White, 0.2% Black, 0.0% Asian, 0.0% American Indian/Alaska Native, 0.0% Native Hawaiian/Other Pacific Islander, 0.7% Other, 0.0% Hispanic of any race (2010); Average household size: 2.23 (2010); Median age: 47.2 (2010); Males per 100 females: 104.9 (2010); Marriage status: 29.0% never married, 53.9% now married, 10.1% widowed, 7.0% divorced (2006-2010 5-year est.); Foreign born: 0.0% (2006-2010 5-year est.); Ancestry (includes multiple ancestries): 33.8% German, 21.3% Irish, 15.1% English, 13.3% Swedish, 10.2% Italian (2006-2010 5-year est.).

Economy: Single-family building permits issued: 0 (2011); Multi-family building permits issued: 0 (2011); Employment by occupation: 13.6% management, 0.0% professional, 9.7% services, 13.6% sales, 0.0% farming, 16.5% construction, 8.5% production (2006-2010 5-year est.).

Income: Per capita income: $16,663 (2006-2010 5-year est.); Median household income: $34,375 (2006-2010 5-year est.); Average household income: $39,388 (2006-2010 5-year est.); Percent of households with income of $100,000 or more: 5.5% (2006-2010 5-year est.); Poverty rate: 10.2% (2006-2010 5-year est.).

Education: Percent of population age 25 and over with: High school diploma (including GED) or higher: 84.1% (2006-2010 5-year est.); Bachelor's degree or higher: 5.1% (2006-2010 5-year est.); Master's degree or higher: 2.3% (2006-2010 5-year est.).

Housing: Homeownership rate: 89.8% (2010); Median home value: $51,700 (2006-2010 5-year est.); Median contract rent: $420 per month (2006-2010 5-year est.); Median year structure built: 1955 (2006-2010 5-year est.).

Transportation: Commute to work: 89.0% car, 0.0% public transportation, 4.2% walk, 6.8% work from home (2006-2010 5-year est.); Travel time to work: 25.9% less than 15 minutes, 28.2% 15 to 30 minutes, 23.6% 30 to 45 minutes, 11.8% 45 to 60 minutes, 10.5% 60 minutes or more (2006-2010 5-year est.)

HAMLIN (township). Covers a land area of 64.186 square miles and a water area of 0.064 square miles. Located at 41.74° N. Lat; 78.57° W. Long.

Population: 822 (1990); 819 (2000); 734 (2010); Density: 11.4 persons per square mile (2010); Race: 99.0% White, 0.0% Black, 0.3% Asian, 0.0% American Indian/Alaska Native, 0.0% Native Hawaiian/Other Pacific Islander, 0.7% Other, 0.0% Hispanic of any race (2010); Average household size: 2.22 (2010); Median age: 46.9 (2010); Males per 100 females: 114.0 (2010); Marriage status: 20.7% never married, 55.6% now married, 11.0% widowed, 12.8% divorced (2006-2010 5-year est.); Foreign born: 1.0% (2006-2010 5-year est.); Ancestry (includes multiple ancestries): 35.4% German, 17.1% Swedish, 15.0% Irish, 14.1% English, 9.0% American (2006-2010 5-year est.).

Economy: Single-family building permits issued: 0 (2011); Multi-family building permits issued: 0 (2011); Employment by occupation: 12.3% management, 0.8% professional, 10.7% services, 18.6% sales, 2.0% farming, 19.4% construction, 9.5% production (2006-2010 5-year est.).

Income: Per capita income: $22,090 (2006-2010 5-year est.); Median household income: $44,625 (2006-2010 5-year est.); Average household income: $47,699 (2006-2010 5-year est.); Percent of households with income of $100,000 or more: 7.5% (2006-2010 5-year est.); Poverty rate: 12.0% (2006-2010 5-year est.).

Education: Percent of population age 25 and over with: High school diploma (including GED) or higher: 86.3% (2006-2010 5-year est.); Bachelor's degree or higher: 18.1% (2006-2010 5-year est.); Master's degree or higher: 4.6% (2006-2010 5-year est.).

School District(s)

Western Wayne SD (PK-12)

2010-11 Enrollment: 2,251 . . . . (570) 937-4270

Housing: Homeownership rate: 87.3% (2010); Median home value: $75,300 (2006-2010 5-year est.); Median contract rent: $350 per month

(2006-2010 5-year est.); Median year structure built: 1963 (2006-2010 5-year est.).

Transportation: Commute to work: 91.2% car, 0.0% public transportation, 5.2% walk, 2.0% work from home (2006-2010 5-year est.); Travel time to work: 29.9% less than 15 minutes, 33.2% 15 to 30 minutes, 16.4% 30 to 45 minutes, 19.3% 45 to 60 minutes, 1.2% 60 minutes or more (2006-2010 5-year est.).

HAZEL HURST (unincorporated postal area)

Zip Code: 16733

Covers a land area of 11.470 square miles and a water area of 0.002 square miles. Located at 41.69° N. Lat; 78.58° W. Long. Elevation is 1,726 feet. Population: 222 (2010); Density: 19.4 persons per square mile (2010); Race: 98.2% White, 0.0% Black, 0.9% Asian, 0.0% American Indian/Alaska Native, 0.0% Native Hawaiian/Other Pacific Islander, 0.9% Other, 0.0% Hispanic of any race (2010); Average household size: 2.18 (2010); Median age: 45.0 (2010); Males per 100 females: 109.4 (2010); Homeownership rate: 79.4% (2010)

KANE (borough). Covers a land area of 1.568 square miles and a water area of <.001 square miles. Located at 41.66° N. Lat; 78.81° W. Long. Elevation is 2,024 feet.

History: Laid out 1860.

Population: 4,590 (1990); 4,126 (2000); 3,730 (2010); Density: 2,378.8 persons per square mile (2010); Race: 98.0% White, 0.3% Black, 0.5% Asian, 0.1% American Indian/Alaska Native, 0.0% Native Hawaiian/Other Pacific Islander, 1.1% Other, 0.7% Hispanic of any race (2010); Average household size: 2.27 (2010); Median age: 42.5 (2010); Males per 100 females: 88.8 (2010); Marriage status: 27.3% never married, 51.4% now married, 9.6% widowed, 11.6% divorced (2006-2010 5-year est.); Foreign born: 0.2% (2006-2010 5-year est.); Ancestry (includes multiple ancestries): 35.2% German, 14.4% Swedish, 9.2% English, 9.0% Italian, 8.6% Irish (2006-2010 5-year est.).

Economy: Single-family building permits issued: 1 (2011); Multi-family building permits issued: 0 (2011); Employment by occupation: 8.1% management, 0.6% professional, 9.9% services, 17.1% sales, 2.7% farming, 12.3% construction, 7.8% production (2006-2010 5-year est.).

Income: Per capita income: $16,971 (2006-2010 5-year est.); Median household income: $35,427 (2006-2010 5-year est.); Average household income: $40,346 (2006-2010 5-year est.); Percent of households with income of $100,000 or more: 4.3% (2006-2010 5-year est.); Poverty rate: 18.0% (2006-2010 5-year est.).

Taxes: Total city taxes per capita: $215 (2009); City property taxes per capita: $116 (2009).

Education: Percent of population age 25 and over with: High school diploma (including GED) or higher: 82.1% (2006-2010 5-year est.); Bachelor's degree or higher: 11.0% (2006-2010 5-year est.); Master's degree or higher: 3.2% (2006-2010 5-year est.).

School District(s)

Kane Area SD (KG-12)

2010-11 Enrollment: 1,184 . . . . (814) 837-9570

Housing: Homeownership rate: 64.5% (2010); Median home value: $60,400 (2006-2010 5-year est.); Median contract rent: $370 per month (2006-2010 5-year est.); Median year structure built: before 1940 (2006-2010 5-year est.).

Hospitals: Kane Community Hospital (38 beds)

Newspapers: Kane Republican (Local news; Circulation 2,750)

Transportation: Commute to work: 88.5% car, 0.0% public transportation, 6.9% walk, 4.0% work from home (2006-2010 5-year est.); Travel time to work: 56.0% less than 15 minutes, 13.5% 15 to 30 minutes, 17.5% 30 to 45 minutes, 7.9% 45 to 60 minutes, 5.1% 60 minutes or more (2006-2010 5-year est.)

Additional Information Contacts

Borough of Kane . . . . (814) 837-9240
Kane Area Chamber of Commerce . . . . (814) 837-6565
  http://www.kanepa.com

KEATING (township). Covers a land area of 97.894 square miles and a water area of 0.314 square miles. Located at 41.83° N. Lat; 78.50° W. Long.

Population: 3,070 (1990); 3,087 (2000); 3,021 (2010); Density: 30.9 persons per square mile (2010); Race: 98.5% White, 0.7% Black, 0.2% Asian, 0.1% American Indian/Alaska Native, 0.0% Native Hawaiian/Other Pacific Islander, 0.5% Other, 0.8% Hispanic of any race (2010); Average household size: 2.57 (2010); Median age: 43.0 (2010); Males per 100

females: 104.8 (2010); Marriage status: 16.4% never married, 64.5% now married, 12.0% widowed, 7.2% divorced (2006-2010 5-year est.); Foreign born: 0.0% (2006-2010 5-year est.); Ancestry (includes multiple ancestries): 23.3% German, 16.3% Irish, 12.1% American, 10.9% Swedish, 8.8% Italian (2006-2010 5-year est.).

Economy: Single-family building permits issued: 3 (2011); Multi-family building permits issued: 0 (2011); Employment by occupation: 10.1% management, 6.5% professional, 8.3% services, 11.5% sales, 0.8% farming, 13.0% construction, 7.1% production (2006-2010 5-year est.).

Income: Per capita income: $22,310 (2006-2010 5-year est.); Median household income: $53,205 (2006-2010 5-year est.); Average household income: $60,047 (2006-2010 5-year est.); Percent of households with income of $100,000 or more: 11.4% (2006-2010 5-year est.); Poverty rate: 7.9% (2006-2010 5-year est.).

Education: Percent of population age 25 and over with: High school diploma (including GED) or higher: 84.2% (2006-2010 5-year est.); Bachelor's degree or higher: 10.9% (2006-2010 5-year est.); Master's degree or higher: 2.9% (2006-2010 5-year est.).

Housing: Homeownership rate: 85.7% (2010); Median home value: $77,900 (2006-2010 5-year est.); Median contract rent: $439 per month (2006-2010 5-year est.); Median year structure built: 1954 (2006-2010 5-year est.).

Transportation: Commute to work: 86.9% car, 0.0% public transportation, 3.6% walk, 7.5% work from home (2006-2010 5-year est.); Travel time to work: 32.7% less than 15 minutes, 45.6% 15 to 30 minutes, 12.2% 30 to 45 minutes, 3.6% 45 to 60 minutes, 5.9% 60 minutes or more (2006-2010 5-year est.)

Additional Information Contacts

Cameron County Chamber of Commerce . . . . (814) 486-4314
  http://www.cameroncountychamber.org

LAFAYETTE (township). Covers a land area of 71.408 square miles and a water area of 0.089 square miles. Located at 41.81° N. Lat; 78.68° W. Long. Elevation is 2,142 feet.

Population: 2,106 (1990); 2,337 (2000); 2,350 (2010); Density: 32.9 persons per square mile (2010); Race: 63.7% White, 35.1% Black, 0.3% Asian, 0.2% American Indian/Alaska Native, 0.0% Native Hawaiian/Other Pacific Islander, 0.7% Other, 16.9% Hispanic of any race (2010); Average household size: 2.20 (2010); Median age: 37.0 (2010); Males per 100 females: 441.5 (2010); Marriage status: 45.8% never married, 38.8% now married, 2.6% widowed, 12.8% divorced (2006-2010 5-year est.); Foreign born: 7.3% (2006-2010 5-year est.); Ancestry (includes multiple ancestries): 16.6% German, 11.2% Irish, 8.3% Italian, 5.1% English, 3.9% Swedish (2006-2010 5-year est.).

Economy: Single-family building permits issued: 0 (2011); Multi-family building permits issued: 0 (2011); Employment by occupation: 12.8% management, 3.2% professional, 10.2% services, 15.8% sales, 2.6% farming, 9.8% construction, 10.9% production (2006-2010 5-year est.).

Income: Per capita income: $19,078 (2006-2010 5-year est.); Median household income: $44,000 (2006-2010 5-year est.); Average household income: $51,677 (2006-2010 5-year est.); Percent of households with income of $100,000 or more: 9.1% (2006-2010 5-year est.); Poverty rate: 10.1% (2006-2010 5-year est.).

Education: Percent of population age 25 and over with: High school diploma (including GED) or higher: 84.5% (2006-2010 5-year est.); Bachelor's degree or higher: 8.5% (2006-2010 5-year est.); Master's degree or higher: 2.9% (2006-2010 5-year est.).

Housing: Homeownership rate: 84.7% (2010); Median home value: $69,100 (2006-2010 5-year est.); Median contract rent: $403 per month (2006-2010 5-year est.); Median year structure built: 1970 (2006-2010 5-year est.).

Transportation: Commute to work: 96.5% car, 0.0% public transportation, 1.3% walk, 0.7% work from home (2006-2010 5-year est.); Travel time to work: 15.7% less than 15 minutes, 56.5% 15 to 30 minutes, 13.5% 30 to 45 minutes, 12.6% 45 to 60 minutes, 1.8% 60 minutes or more (2006-2010 5-year est.)

Additional Information Contacts

Bradford Area Chamber of Commerce . . . . (814) 368-7115
  http://www.bradfordchamber.com

LEWIS RUN (borough). Covers a land area of 1.743 square miles and a water area of 0.011 square miles. Located at 41.87° N. Lat; 78.65° W. Long. Elevation is 1,552 feet.

Population: 578 (1990); 577 (2000); 617 (2010); Density: 354.0 persons per square mile (2010); Race: 97.4% White, 0.2% Black, 0.0% Asian,

0.0% American Indian/Alaska Native, 0.0% Native Hawaiian/Other Pacific Islander, 2.4% Other, 0.6% Hispanic of any race (2010); Average household size: 2.23 (2010); Median age: 44.3 (2010); Males per 100 females: 96.5 (2010); Marriage status: 16.2% never married, 57.8% now married, 11.9% widowed, 14.2% divorced (2006-2010 5-year est.); Foreign born: 1.6% (2006-2010 5-year est.); Ancestry (includes multiple ancestries): 24.2% Italian, 22.6% German, 16.6% Irish, 10.2% English, 10.0% Swedish (2006-2010 5-year est.).

Economy: Single-family building permits issued: 0 (2011); Multi-family building permits issued: 0 (2011); Employment by occupation: 6.0% management, 2.8% professional, 7.8% services, 16.0% sales, 9.6% farming, 15.3% construction, 5.3% production (2006-2010 5-year est.).

Income: Per capita income: $19,351 (2006-2010 5-year est.); Median household income: $38,333 (2006-2010 5-year est.); Average household income: $44,061 (2006-2010 5-year est.); Percent of households with income of $100,000 or more: 4.5% (2006-2010 5-year est.); Poverty rate: 5.8% (2006-2010 5-year est.).

Education: Percent of population age 25 and over with: High school diploma (including GED) or higher: 92.6% (2006-2010 5-year est.); Bachelor's degree or higher: 16.5% (2006-2010 5-year est.); Master's degree or higher: 2.4% (2006-2010 5-year est.).

Housing: Homeownership rate: 74.7% (2010); Median home value: $63,700 (2006-2010 5-year est.); Median contract rent: $474 per month (2006-2010 5-year est.); Median year structure built: 1948 (2006-2010 5-year est.).

Transportation: Commute to work: 98.9% car, 0.0% public transportation, 0.0% walk, 1.1% work from home (2006-2010 5-year est.); Travel time to work: 32.0% less than 15 minutes, 48.5% 15 to 30 minutes, 14.3% 30 to 45 minutes, 2.6% 45 to 60 minutes, 2.6% 60 minutes or more (2006-2010 5-year est.)

LIBERTY (township).
Covers a land area of 83.343 square miles and a water area of 0.385 square miles. Located at 41.77° N. Lat; 78.29° W. Long. Elevation is 1,640 feet.

Population: 1,764 (1990); 1,726 (2000); 1,612 (2010); Density: 19.3 persons per square mile (2010); Race: 98.8% White, 0.2% Black, 0.1% Asian, 0.2% American Indian/Alaska Native, 0.0% Native Hawaiian/Other Pacific Islander, 0.7% Other, 0.6% Hispanic of any race (2010); Average household size: 2.40 (2010); Median age: 44.7 (2010); Males per 100 females: 103.3 (2010); Marriage status: 20.9% never married, 60.9% now married, 7.5% widowed, 10.8% divorced (2006-2010 5-year est.); Foreign born: 0.6% (2006-2010 5-year est.); Ancestry (includes multiple ancestries): 28.5% German, 21.9% Irish, 15.3% English, 8.6% Swedish, 6.8% American (2006-2010 5-year est.).

Economy: Single-family building permits issued: 2 (2011); Multi-family building permits issued: 0 (2011); Employment by occupation: 6.1% management, 2.2% professional, 11.9% services, 15.3% sales, 4.5% farming, 14.0% construction, 12.7% production (2006-2010 5-year est.).

Income: Per capita income: $19,525 (2006-2010 5-year est.); Median household income: $38,750 (2006-2010 5-year est.); Average household income: $48,592 (2006-2010 5-year est.); Percent of households with income of $100,000 or more: 11.9% (2006-2010 5-year est.); Poverty rate: 21.5% (2006-2010 5-year est.).

Education: Percent of population age 25 and over with: High school diploma (including GED) or higher: 87.0% (2006-2010 5-year est.); Bachelor's degree or higher: 12.7% (2006-2010 5-year est.); Master's degree or higher: 4.0% (2006-2010 5-year est.).

Housing: Homeownership rate: 81.1% (2010); Median home value: $88,000 (2006-2010 5-year est.); Median contract rent: $458 per month (2006-2010 5-year est.); Median year structure built: 1971 (2006-2010 5-year est.).

Transportation: Commute to work: 91.1% car, 0.6% public transportation, 0.4% walk, 7.3% work from home (2006-2010 5-year est.); Travel time to work: 46.7% less than 15 minutes, 21.9% 15 to 30 minutes, 24.2% 30 to 45 minutes, 5.4% 45 to 60 minutes, 1.9% 60 minutes or more (2006-2010 5-year est.)

Additional Information Contacts
Smethport Area Chamber of Commerce . . . . (814) 887-4134
    http://www.smethportchamber.com

LUDLOW (unincorporated postal area)
Zip Code: 16333
    Covers a land area of 6.551 square miles and a water area of <.001 square miles. Located at 41.69° N. Lat; 78.91° W. Long. Elevation is 1,591 feet. Population: 240 (2010); Density: 36.6 persons per square

mile (2010); Race: 99.2% White, 0.0% Black, 0.0% Asian, 0.0% American Indian/Alaska Native, 0.0% Native Hawaiian/Other Pacific Islander, 0.8% Other, 0.0% Hispanic of any race (2010); Average household size: 2.29 (2010); Median age: 48.3 (2010); Males per 100 females: 98.3 (2010); Homeownership rate: 89.5% (2010)

MOUNT JEWETT (borough).
Covers a land area of 2.340 square miles and a water area of 0.024 square miles. Located at 41.73° N. Lat; 78.64° W. Long. Elevation is 2,231 feet.

History: Kinzua Bridge State Park (bridge originally built of iron 1882, rebuilt 1900 of steel; 301 feet high, 2,110 feet long; on abandoned RR line); Settled c.1838, incorporated 1893.

Population: 1,029 (1990); 1,070 (2000); 919 (2010); Density: 392.7 persons per square mile (2010); Race: 99.1% White, 0.0% Black, 0.0% Asian, 0.3% American Indian/Alaska Native, 0.0% Native Hawaiian/Other Pacific Islander, 0.6% Other, 1.0% Hispanic of any race (2010); Average household size: 2.34 (2010); Median age: 40.9 (2010); Males per 100 females: 99.8 (2010); Marriage status: 25.9% never married, 56.5% now married, 6.9% widowed, 10.6% divorced (2006-2010 5-year est.); Foreign born: 0.0% (2006-2010 5-year est.); Ancestry (includes multiple ancestries): 27.6% German, 20.2% Swedish, 19.8% Irish, 10.4% Italian, 9.5% English (2006-2010 5-year est.).

Economy: Single-family building permits issued: 0 (2011); Multi-family building permits issued: 0 (2011); Employment by occupation: 11.2% management, 1.3% professional, 11.7% services, 19.6% sales, 1.0% farming, 19.4% construction, 12.5% production (2006-2010 5-year est.).

Income: Per capita income: $21,323 (2006-2010 5-year est.); Median household income: $46,629 (2006-2010 5-year est.); Average household income: $53,692 (2006-2010 5-year est.); Percent of households with income of $100,000 or more: 10.5% (2006-2010 5-year est.); Poverty rate: 10.6% (2006-2010 5-year est.).

Education: Percent of population age 25 and over with: High school diploma (including GED) or higher: 95.6% (2006-2010 5-year est.); Bachelor's degree or higher: 14.1% (2006-2010 5-year est.); Master's degree or higher: 3.7% (2006-2010 5-year est.).

Housing: Homeownership rate: 76.0% (2010); Median home value: $64,100 (2006-2010 5-year est.); Median contract rent: $347 per month (2006-2010 5-year est.); Median year structure built: before 1940 (2006-2010 5-year est.).

Safety: Violent crime rate: 43.4 per 10,000 population; Property crime rate: 65.1 per 10,000 population (2011).

Transportation: Commute to work: 92.4% car, 0.0% public transportation, 4.2% walk, 3.4% work from home (2006-2010 5-year est.); Travel time to work: 26.0% less than 15 minutes, 38.2% 15 to 30 minutes, 25.7% 30 to 45 minutes, 6.0% 45 to 60 minutes, 4.1% 60 minutes or more (2006-2010 5-year est.)

NORWICH (township).
Covers a land area of 95.330 square miles and a water area of 0.203 square miles. Located at 41.67° N. Lat; 78.35° W. Long. Elevation is 1,627 feet.

Population: 593 (1990); 633 (2000); 583 (2010); Density: 6.1 persons per square mile (2010); Race: 98.6% White, 0.3% Black, 0.0% Asian, 0.2% American Indian/Alaska Native, 0.0% Native Hawaiian/Other Pacific Islander, 0.9% Other, 0.2% Hispanic of any race (2010); Average household size: 2.46 (2010); Median age: 44.6 (2010); Males per 100 females: 120.0 (2010); Marriage status: 29.1% never married, 49.4% now married, 5.1% widowed, 16.5% divorced (2006-2010 5-year est.); Foreign born: 0.0% (2006-2010 5-year est.); Ancestry (includes multiple ancestries): 26.2% German, 23.7% Irish, 14.2% Swedish, 10.8% Italian, 8.7% English (2006-2010 5-year est.).

Economy: Single-family building permits issued: 0 (2011); Multi-family building permits issued: 0 (2011); Employment by occupation: 2.4% management, 2.9% professional, 15.0% services, 13.8% sales, 7.1% farming, 15.3% construction, 8.8% production (2006-2010 5-year est.).

Income: Per capita income: $20,106 (2006-2010 5-year est.); Median household income: $35,147 (2006-2010 5-year est.); Average household income: $44,319 (2006-2010 5-year est.); Percent of households with income of $100,000 or more: 7.7% (2006-2010 5-year est.); Poverty rate: 19.1% (2006-2010 5-year est.).

Education: Percent of population age 25 and over with: High school diploma (including GED) or higher: 90.0% (2006-2010 5-year est.); Bachelor's degree or higher: 15.7% (2006-2010 5-year est.); Master's degree or higher: 2.8% (2006-2010 5-year est.).

Housing: Homeownership rate: 89.4% (2010); Median home value: $84,400 (2006-2010 5-year est.); Median contract rent: $363 per month

(2006-2010 5-year est.); Median year structure built: 1952 (2006-2010 5-year est.).

Transportation: Commute to work: 93.6% car, 0.0% public transportation, 0.0% walk, 6.4% work from home (2006-2010 5-year est.); Travel time to work: 20.8% less than 15 minutes, 36.9% 15 to 30 minutes, 28.7% 30 to 45 minutes, 11.3% 45 to 60 minutes, 2.4% 60 minutes or more (2006-2010 5-year est.)

OTTO (township). Covers a land area of 34.396 square miles and a water area of 0.035 square miles. Located at 41.94° N. Lat; 78.48° W. Long.

Population: 1,820 (1990); 1,738 (2000); 1,556 (2010); Density: 45.2 persons per square mile (2010); Race: 98.3% White, 0.1% Black, 0.2% Asian, 0.5% American Indian/Alaska Native, 0.0% Native Hawaiian/Other Pacific Islander, 0.9% Other, 0.5% Hispanic of any race (2010); Average household size: 2.49 (2010); Median age: 42.7 (2010); Males per 100 females: 101.0 (2010); Marriage status: 25.5% never married, 61.4% now married, 5.5% widowed, 7.5% divorced (2006-2010 5-year est.); Foreign born: 0.0% (2006-2010 5-year est.); Ancestry (includes multiple ancestries): 28.1% German, 17.7% English, 14.8% Irish, 6.6% Swedish, 5.9% Scotch-Irish (2006-2010 5-year est.).

Economy: Single-family building permits issued: 0 (2011); Multi-family building permits issued: 0 (2011); Employment by occupation: 7.6% management, 1.7% professional, 16.8% services, 12.8% sales, 0.8% farming, 9.0% construction, 11.1% production (2006-2010 5-year est.).

Income: Per capita income: $20,518 (2006-2010 5-year est.); Median household income: $41,020 (2006-2010 5-year est.); Average household income: $51,554 (2006-2010 5-year est.); Percent of households with income of $100,000 or more: 9.6% (2006-2010 5-year est.); Poverty rate: 19.1% (2006-2010 5-year est.).

Education: Percent of population age 25 and over with: High school diploma (including GED) or higher: 87.6% (2006-2010 5-year est.); Bachelor's degree or higher: 14.8% (2006-2010 5-year est.); Master's degree or higher: 5.1% (2006-2010 5-year est.).

Housing: Homeownership rate: 83.8% (2010); Median home value: $63,800 (2006-2010 5-year est.); Median contract rent: $375 per month (2006-2010 5-year est.); Median year structure built: 1948 (2006-2010 5-year est.).

Transportation: Commute to work: 98.4% car, 0.0% public transportation, 0.5% walk, 1.1% work from home (2006-2010 5-year est.); Travel time to work: 15.6% less than 15 minutes, 63.2% 15 to 30 minutes, 18.0% 30 to 45 minutes, 1.5% 45 to 60 minutes, 1.9% 60 minutes or more (2006-2010 5-year est.)

Additional Information Contacts

Bradford Area Chamber of Commerce . . . . (814) 368-7115
http://www.bradfordchamber.com

PORT ALLEGANY (borough). Covers a land area of 1.807 square miles and a water area of 0.024 square miles. Located at 41.82° N. Lat; 78.28° W. Long. Elevation is 1,483 feet.

History: Lumber center in 1830s. Settled c.1816, incorporated 1882.

Population: 2,391 (1990); 2,355 (2000); 2,157 (2010); Density: 1,193.9 persons per square mile (2010); Race: 98.3% White, 0.1% Black, 0.1% Asian, 0.2% American Indian/Alaska Native, 0.0% Native Hawaiian/Other Pacific Islander, 1.3% Other, 0.8% Hispanic of any race (2010); Average household size: 2.40 (2010); Median age: 38.7 (2010); Males per 100 females: 92.9 (2010); Marriage status: 26.3% never married, 50.7% now married, 8.1% widowed, 15.0% divorced (2006-2010 5-year est.); Foreign born: 0.1% (2006-2010 5-year est.); Ancestry (includes multiple ancestries): 31.9% German, 18.2% Irish, 13.6% English, 9.8% Italian, 7.2% Swedish (2006-2010 5-year est.).

Economy: Single-family building permits issued: 0 (2011); Multi-family building permits issued: 0 (2011); Employment by occupation: 6.4% management, 2.4% professional, 16.2% services, 19.8% sales, 0.0% farming, 8.4% construction, 6.4% production (2006-2010 5-year est.).

Income: Per capita income: $20,725 (2006-2010 5-year est.); Median household income: $40,861 (2006-2010 5-year est.); Average household income: $48,218 (2006-2010 5-year est.); Percent of households with income of $100,000 or more: 7.2% (2006-2010 5-year est.); Poverty rate: 13.7% (2006-2010 5-year est.).

Education: Percent of population age 25 and over with: High school diploma (including GED) or higher: 94.4% (2006-2010 5-year est.); Bachelor's degree or higher: 21.0% (2006-2010 5-year est.); Master's degree or higher: 7.3% (2006-2010 5-year est.).

School District(s)

Port Allegany SD (KG-12)
  2010-11 Enrollment: 946 . . . . (814) 642-2596
Seneca Highlands Avts (10-12)
  2010-11 Enrollment: n/a . . . . (814) 642-2573

Housing: Homeownership rate: 64.1% (2010); Median home value: $77,000 (2006-2010 5-year est.); Median contract rent: $397 per month (2006-2010 5-year est.); Median year structure built: 1948 (2006-2010 5-year est.).

Safety: Violent crime rate: 9.2 per 10,000 population; Property crime rate: 203.3 per 10,000 population (2011).

Transportation: Commute to work: 85.4% car, 0.0% public transportation, 7.3% walk, 4.1% work from home (2006-2010 5-year est.); Travel time to work: 57.0% less than 15 minutes, 18.9% 15 to 30 minutes, 14.7% 30 to 45 minutes, 6.3% 45 to 60 minutes, 3.0% 60 minutes or more (2006-2010 5-year est.)

Additional Information Contacts

Coudersport Area Chamber of Commerce . . . . (814) 274-8165
http://www.coudersport.org

REW (CDP). Covers a land area of 0.962 square miles and a water area of 0 square miles. Located at 41.90° N. Lat; 78.54° W. Long. Elevation is 2,254 feet.

Population: n/a (1990); n/a (2000); 199 (2010); Density: 206.9 persons per square mile (2010); Race: 99.5% White, 0.0% Black, 0.0% Asian, 0.0% American Indian/Alaska Native, 0.0% Native Hawaiian/Other Pacific Islander, 0.5% Other, 0.0% Hispanic of any race (2010); Average household size: 2.40 (2010); Median age: 45.8 (2010); Males per 100 females: 109.5 (2010); Marriage status: 6.5% never married, 86.5% now married, 0.0% widowed, 7.1% divorced (2006-2010 5-year est.); Foreign born: 0.0% (2006-2010 5-year est.); Ancestry (includes multiple ancestries): 52.0% German, 27.7% Irish, 6.2% Polish (2006-2010 5-year est.).

Economy: Employment by occupation: 10.4% management, 0.0% professional, 30.2% services, 16.0% sales, 0.0% farming, 16.0% construction, 16.0% production (2006-2010 5-year est.).

Income: Per capita income: $33,607 (2006-2010 5-year est.); Median household income: $72,852 (2006-2010 5-year est.); Average household income: $78,157 (2006-2010 5-year est.); Percent of households with income of $100,000 or more: 14.3% (2006-2010 5-year est.); Poverty rate: 0.0% (2006-2010 5-year est.).

Education: Percent of population age 25 and over with: High school diploma (including GED) or higher: 100.0% (2006-2010 5-year est.); Bachelor's degree or higher: 27.9% (2006-2010 5-year est.); Master's degree or higher: 7.4% (2006-2010 5-year est.).

Housing: Homeownership rate: 84.3% (2010); Median home value: $63,800 (2006-2010 5-year est.); Median contract rent: n/a per month (2006-2010 5-year est.); Median year structure built: before 1940 (2006-2010 5-year est.).

Transportation: Commute to work: 100.0% car, 0.0% public transportation, 0.0% walk, 0.0% work from home (2006-2010 5-year est.); Travel time to work: 0.0% less than 15 minutes, 51.9% 15 to 30 minutes, 30.2% 30 to 45 minutes, 0.0% 45 to 60 minutes, 17.9% 60 minutes or more (2006-2010 5-year est.)

RIXFORD (unincorporated postal area)

Zip Code: 16745

  Covers a land area of 11.207 square miles and a water area of 0.017 square miles. Located at 41.92° N. Lat; 78.48° W. Long. Elevation is 1,598 feet. Population: 611 (2010); Density: 54.5 persons per square mile (2010); Race: 97.5% White, 0.2% Black, 0.2% Asian, 1.1% American Indian/Alaska Native, 0.0% Native Hawaiian/Other Pacific Islander, 1.0% Other, 0.8% Hispanic of any race (2010); Average household size: 2.60 (2010); Median age: 40.5 (2010); Males per 100 females: 110.0 (2010); Homeownership rate: 84.2% (2010)

SERGEANT (township). Covers a land area of 80.117 square miles and a water area of 0.066 square miles. Located at 41.67° N. Lat; 78.57° W. Long. Elevation is 1,709 feet.

Population: 154 (1990); 176 (2000); 141 (2010); Density: 1.8 persons per square mile (2010); Race: 98.6% White, 0.0% Black, 0.0% Asian, 0.0% American Indian/Alaska Native, 0.0% Native Hawaiian/Other Pacific Islander, 1.4% Other, 0.0% Hispanic of any race (2010); Average household size: 2.17 (2010); Median age: 51.9 (2010); Males per 100 females: 101.4 (2010); Marriage status: 26.2% never married, 53.0% now

married, 7.4% widowed, 13.4% divorced (2006-2010 5-year est.); Foreign born: 0.0% (2006-2010 5-year est.); Ancestry (includes multiple ancestries): 46.1% German, 26.9% Swedish, 18.0% English, 9.6% Irish, 6.6% Dutch (2006-2010 5-year est.).

Economy: Single-family building permits issued: 0 (2011); Multi-family building permits issued: 0 (2011); Employment by occupation: 7.5% management, 0.0% professional, 10.4% services, 17.9% sales, 7.5% farming, 20.9% construction, 11.9% production (2006-2010 5-year est.).

Income: Per capita income: $20,816 (2006-2010 5-year est.); Median household income: $45,313 (2006-2010 5-year est.); Average household income: $48,790 (2006-2010 5-year est.); Percent of households with income of $100,000 or more: 6.8% (2006-2010 5-year est.); Poverty rate: 14.2% (2006-2010 5-year est.).

Education: Percent of population age 25 and over with: High school diploma (including GED) or higher: 84.3% (2006-2010 5-year est.); Bachelor's degree or higher: 3.5% (2006-2010 5-year est.); Master's degree or higher: 0.9% (2006-2010 5-year est.).

Housing: Homeownership rate: 87.7% (2010); Median home value: $30,800 (2006-2010 5-year est.); Median contract rent: n/a per month (2006-2010 5-year est.); Median year structure built: 1956 (2006-2010 5-year est.).

Transportation: Commute to work: 100.0% car, 0.0% public transportation, 0.0% walk, 0.0% work from home (2006-2010 5-year est.); Travel time to work: 7.5% less than 15 minutes, 29.9% 15 to 30 minutes, 32.8% 30 to 45 minutes, 16.4% 45 to 60 minutes, 13.4% 60 minutes or more (2006-2010 5-year est.)

SMETHPORT (borough). County seat. Covers a land area of 1.637 square miles and a water area of 0.047 square miles. Located at 41.81° N. Lat; 78.44° W. Long. Elevation is 1,558 feet.

History: Laid out 1807, incorporated 1853.

Population: 1,734 (1990); 1,684 (2000); 1,655 (2010); Density: 1,010.6 persons per square mile (2010); Race: 98.4% White, 0.0% Black, 0.5% Asian, 0.0% American Indian/Alaska Native, 0.0% Native Hawaiian/Other Pacific Islander, 1.1% Other, 1.4% Hispanic of any race (2010); Average household size: 2.24 (2010); Median age: 44.1 (2010); Males per 100 females: 86.4 (2010); Marriage status: 25.3% never married, 51.2% now married, 10.3% widowed, 13.2% divorced (2006-2010 5-year est.); Foreign born: 0.3% (2006-2010 5-year est.); Ancestry (includes multiple ancestries): 32.0% German, 26.7% Irish, 14.4% English, 12.8% Italian, 7.4% Swedish (2006-2010 5-year est.).

Economy: Single-family building permits issued: 0 (2011); Multi-family building permits issued: 0 (2011); Employment by occupation: 13.9% management, 3.5% professional, 14.9% services, 11.7% sales, 1.6% farming, 10.3% construction, 6.8% production (2006-2010 5-year est.).

Income: Per capita income: $20,509 (2006-2010 5-year est.); Median household income: $35,074 (2006-2010 5-year est.); Average household income: $46,098 (2006-2010 5-year est.); Percent of households with income of $100,000 or more: 6.7% (2006-2010 5-year est.); Poverty rate: 15.2% (2006-2010 5-year est.).

Education: Percent of population age 25 and over with: High school diploma (including GED) or higher: 90.7% (2006-2010 5-year est.); Bachelor's degree or higher: 18.1% (2006-2010 5-year est.); Master's degree or higher: 7.0% (2006-2010 5-year est.).

School District(s)

Smethport Area SD (PK-12)

    2010-11 Enrollment: 944 . . . . (814) 887-5543

Housing: Homeownership rate: 65.5% (2010); Median home value: $71,800 (2006-2010 5-year est.); Median contract rent: $385 per month (2006-2010 5-year est.); Median year structure built: 1943 (2006-2010 5-year est.).

Transportation: Commute to work: 80.5% car, 0.0% public transportation, 13.1% walk, 4.9% work from home (2006-2010 5-year est.); Travel time to work: 47.4% less than 15 minutes, 26.1% 15 to 30 minutes, 22.2% 30 to 45 minutes, 3.5% 45 to 60 minutes, 0.7% 60 minutes or more (2006-2010 5-year est.)

Additional Information Contacts

Smethport Area Chamber of Commerce . . . . (814) 887-4134

    http://www.smethportchamber.com

TURTLEPOINT (unincorporated postal area)

Zip Code: 16750

    Covers a land area of 19.288 square miles and a water area of 0.080 square miles. Located at 41.88° N. Lat; 78.29° W. Long. Elevation is 1,470 feet. Population: 417 (2010); Density: 21.6 persons per square

mile (2010); Race: 97.6% White, 0.5% Black, 0.5% Asian, 0.0% American Indian/Alaska Native, 0.0% Native Hawaiian/Other Pacific Islander, 1.4% Other, 0.7% Hispanic of any race (2010); Average household size: 2.62 (2010); Median age: 42.4 (2010); Males per 100 females: 98.6 (2010); Homeownership rate: 78.7% (2010)

WETMORE (township). Covers a land area of 78.037 square miles and a water area of 0.047 square miles. Located at 41.67° N. Lat; 78.83° W. Long. Elevation is 1,788 feet.

Population: 1,745 (1990); 1,721 (2000); 1,650 (2010); Density: 21.1 persons per square mile (2010); Race: 98.9% White, 0.2% Black, 0.2% Asian, 0.4% American Indian/Alaska Native, 0.0% Native Hawaiian/Other Pacific Islander, 0.3% Other, 0.2% Hispanic of any race (2010); Average household size: 2.37 (2010); Median age: 46.3 (2010); Males per 100 females: 110.5 (2010); Marriage status: 24.2% never married, 59.2% now married, 8.3% widowed, 8.2% divorced (2006-2010 5-year est.); Foreign born: 0.2% (2006-2010 5-year est.); Ancestry (includes multiple ancestries): 31.0% German, 28.3% Swedish, 17.3% Irish, 15.0% Italian, 9.7% Polish (2006-2010 5-year est.).

Economy: Single-family building permits issued: 0 (2011); Multi-family building permits issued: 0 (2011); Employment by occupation: 7.0% management, 3.4% professional, 14.4% services, 9.6% sales, 0.8% farming, 17.4% construction, 8.1% production (2006-2010 5-year est.).

Income: Per capita income: $24,056 (2006-2010 5-year est.); Median household income: $47,132 (2006-2010 5-year est.); Average household income: $57,278 (2006-2010 5-year est.); Percent of households with income of $100,000 or more: 13.4% (2006-2010 5-year est.); Poverty rate: 7.9% (2006-2010 5-year est.).

Education: Percent of population age 25 and over with: High school diploma (including GED) or higher: 91.5% (2006-2010 5-year est.); Bachelor's degree or higher: 20.4% (2006-2010 5-year est.); Master's degree or higher: 8.0% (2006-2010 5-year est.).

Housing: Homeownership rate: 88.5% (2010); Median home value: $97,200 (2006-2010 5-year est.); Median contract rent: $433 per month (2006-2010 5-year est.); Median year structure built: 1961 (2006-2010 5-year est.).

Transportation: Commute to work: 94.8% car, 0.0% public transportation, 1.9% walk, 2.9% work from home (2006-2010 5-year est.); Travel time to work: 50.0% less than 15 minutes, 21.0% 15 to 30 minutes, 14.5% 30 to 45 minutes, 8.8% 45 to 60 minutes, 5.7% 60 minutes or more (2006-2010 5-year est.)

Additional Information Contacts

Kane Chamber of Commerce . . . . (814) 837-6565

    http://www.kanepa.com

Mercer County

Located in northwestern Pennsylvania; bounded on the west by Ohio; drained by the Shenango River and tributaries of the Allegheny River. Covers a land area of 672.575 square miles, a water area of 10.030 square miles, and is located in the Eastern Time Zone at 41.30° N. Lat., 80.25° W. Long. The county was founded in 1800. County seat is Mercer.

Mercer County is part of the Youngstown-Warren-Boardman, OH-PA Metropolitan Statistical Area. The entire metro area includes: Mahoning County, OH; Trumbull County, OH; Mercer County, PA

Weather Station: Mercer   Elevation: 1,220 feet

	Jan	Feb	Mar	Apr	May	Jun	Jul	Aug	Sep	Oct	Nov	Dec
High	35	38	48	61	70	78	82	81	74	62	50	39
Low	16	18	25	35	45	53	57	56	49	38	31	22
Precip	2.9	2.5	3.2	3.6	3.8	4.5	4.7	3.9	4.0	2.9	3.5	3.3
Snow	13.3	9.6	7.9	2.3	tr	0.0	0.0	0.0	0.0	0.2	3.6	9.8

High and Low temperatures in degrees Fahrenheit; Precipitation and Snow in inches

Population: 121,003 (1990); 120,293 (2000); 116,638 (2010); Race: 91.6% White, 5.8% Black, 0.6% Asian, 0.1% American Indian/Alaska Native, 0.0% Native Hawaiian/Other Pacific Islander, 1.9% Other, 1.1% Hispanic of any race (2010); Density: 173.4 persons per square mile (2010); Average household size: 2.37 (2010); Median age: 42.8 (2010); Males per 100 females: 95.9 (2010).

Religion: Six largest groups: 24.2% Catholicism, 8.1% Presbyterian-Reformed, 7.7% Methodist/Pietist, 3.8% Holiness, 2.6% Non-Denominational, 2.5% Baptist (2010)

Economy: Unemployment rate: 8.8% (August 2012); Total civilian labor force: 54,798 (August 2012); Leading industries: 24.7% health care and

social assistance; 16.4% manufacturing; 16.3% retail trade (2010); Farms: 1,210 totaling 171,860 acres (2007); Companies that employ 500 or more persons: 7 (2010); Companies that employ 100 to 499 persons: 62 (2010); Companies that employ less than 100 persons: 2,715 (2010); Black-owned businesses: n/a (2007); Hispanic-owned businesses: 48 (2007); Asian-owned businesses: n/a (2007); Women-owned businesses: 2,478 (2007); Retail sales per capita: $16,519 (2010). Single-family building permits issued: 86 (2011); Multi-family building permits issued: 0 (2011).
Income: Per capita income: $21,765 (2006-2010 5-year est.); Median household income: $42,573 (2006-2010 5-year est.); Average household income: $53,892 (2006-2010 5-year est.); Percent of households with income of $100,000 or more: 10.9% (2006-2010 5-year est.); Poverty rate: 13.2% (2006-2010 5-year est.); Bankruptcy rate: 2.97% (2011).
Taxes: Total county taxes per capita: $204 (2009); County property taxes per capita: $204 (2009).
Education: Percent of population age 25 and over with: High school diploma (including GED) or higher: 87.1% (2006-2010 5-year est.); Bachelor's degree or higher: 19.0% (2006-2010 5-year est.); Master's degree or higher: 6.2% (2006-2010 5-year est.).
Housing: Homeownership rate: 73.1% (2010); Median home value: $101,700 (2006-2010 5-year est.); Median contract rent: $430 per month (2006-2010 5-year est.); Median year structure built: 1958 (2006-2010 5-year est.)
Health: Birth rate: 95.6 per 10,000 population (2011); Death rate: 121.6 per 10,000 population (2011); Age-adjusted cancer mortality rate: 214.4 deaths per 100,000 population (2009); Number of physicians: 20.8 per 10,000 population (2010); Hospital beds: 47.0 per 10,000 population (2008); Hospital admissions: 1,909.1 per 10,000 population (2008).
Environment: Air Quality Index: 77.8% good, 21.1% moderate, 1.1% unhealthy for sensitive individuals, 0.0% unhealthy (percent of days in 2011)
Elections: 2012 Presidential election results: 47.7% Obama, 50.9% Romney
National and State Parks: Maurice K Goddard State Park
Additional Information Contacts
Mercer County Government . . . . (724) 662-3800
  http://www.mcc.co.mercer.pa.us

Mercer County Communities

CARLTON (unincorporated postal area)
Zip Code: 16311
  Covers a land area of 14.684 square miles and a water area of 0.121 square miles. Located at 41.46° N. Lat; 80.04° W. Long. Elevation is 1,056 feet. Population: 564 (2010); Density: 38.4 persons per square mile (2010); Race: 99.1% White, 0.0% Black, 0.0% Asian, 0.4% American Indian/Alaska Native, 0.0% Native Hawaiian/Other Pacific Islander, 0.5% Other, 1.4% Hispanic of any race (2010); Average household size: 2.38 (2010); Median age: 42.5 (2010); Males per 100 females: 103.6 (2010); Homeownership rate: 85.2% (2010)

CLARK (borough). Aka Clarksville. Covers a land area of 3.011 square miles and a water area of 0.610 square miles. Located at 41.29° N. Lat; 80.40° W. Long. Elevation is 896 feet.
Population: 610 (1990); 633 (2000); 640 (2010); Density: 212.6 persons per square mile (2010); Race: 98.4% White, 0.2% Black, 0.0% Asian, 0.0% American Indian/Alaska Native, 0.0% Native Hawaiian/Other Pacific Islander, 1.4% Other, 0.5% Hispanic of any race (2010); Average household size: 2.67 (2010); Median age: 44.7 (2010); Males per 100 females: 102.5 (2010); Marriage status: 20.5% never married, 68.9% now married, 4.8% widowed, 5.8% divorced (2006-2010 5-year est.); Foreign born: 0.0% (2006-2010 5-year est.); Ancestry (includes multiple ancestries): 29.7% German, 18.3% Irish, 15.5% Italian, 10.3% Polish, 9.3% Slovak (2006-2010 5-year est.).
Economy: Single-family building permits issued: 0 (2011); Multi-family building permits issued: 0 (2011); Employment by occupation: 9.3% management, 2.5% professional, 6.8% services, 18.6% sales, 1.4% farming, 17.1% construction, 16.4% production (2006-2010 5-year est.).
Income: Per capita income: $28,946 (2006-2010 5-year est.); Median household income: $67,875 (2006-2010 5-year est.); Average household income: $76,392 (2006-2010 5-year est.); Percent of households with income of $100,000 or more: 22.7% (2006-2010 5-year est.); Poverty rate: 8.2% (2006-2010 5-year est.).
Education: Percent of population age 25 and over with: High school diploma (including GED) or higher: 86.4% (2006-2010 5-year est.);

Bachelor's degree or higher: 22.7% (2006-2010 5-year est.); Master's degree or higher: 10.7% (2006-2010 5-year est.).
Housing: Homeownership rate: 90.9% (2010); Median home value: $159,800 (2006-2010 5-year est.); Median contract rent: n/a per month (2006-2010 5-year est.); Median year structure built: 1970 (2006-2010 5-year est.).
Transportation: Commute to work: 93.4% car, 0.0% public transportation, 1.8% walk, 1.5% work from home (2006-2010 5-year est.); Travel time to work: 29.6% less than 15 minutes, 48.7% 15 to 30 minutes, 11.2% 30 to 45 minutes, 7.1% 45 to 60 minutes, 3.4% 60 minutes or more (2006-2010 5-year est.)

CLARKS MILLS (unincorporated postal area)
Zip Code: 16114
  Covers a land area of 10.148 square miles and a water area of 0.164 square miles. Located at 41.40° N. Lat; 80.18° W. Long. Elevation is 1,171 feet. Population: 606 (2010); Density: 59.7 persons per square mile (2010); Race: 98.2% White, 0.2% Black, 0.8% Asian, 0.3% American Indian/Alaska Native, 0.0% Native Hawaiian/Other Pacific Islander, 0.5% Other, 0.2% Hispanic of any race (2010); Average household size: 2.71 (2010); Median age: 41.2 (2010); Males per 100 females: 104.7 (2010); Homeownership rate: 88.4% (2010)

COOLSPRING (township). Covers a land area of 18.772 square miles and a water area of 0.321 square miles. Located at 41.28° N. Lat; 80.22° W. Long.
Population: 2,140 (1990); 2,287 (2000); 2,278 (2010); Density: 121.4 persons per square mile (2010); Race: 98.2% White, 0.3% Black, 0.5% Asian, 0.0% American Indian/Alaska Native, 0.0% Native Hawaiian/Other Pacific Islander, 1.0% Other, 0.5% Hispanic of any race (2010); Average household size: 2.36 (2010); Median age: 48.2 (2010); Males per 100 females: 91.3 (2010); Marriage status: 28.3% never married, 52.3% now married, 11.2% widowed, 8.2% divorced (2006-2010 5-year est.); Foreign born: 0.0% (2006-2010 5-year est.); Ancestry (includes multiple ancestries): 27.5% German, 19.6% Irish, 10.8% English, 7.5% American, 6.2% Italian (2006-2010 5-year est.).
Economy: Single-family building permits issued: 2 (2011); Multi-family building permits issued: 0 (2011); Employment by occupation: 4.8% management, 3.0% professional, 14.1% services, 13.8% sales, 0.8% farming, 9.9% construction, 4.5% production (2006-2010 5-year est.).
Income: Per capita income: $22,082 (2006-2010 5-year est.); Median household income: $45,781 (2006-2010 5-year est.); Average household income: $53,653 (2006-2010 5-year est.); Percent of households with income of $100,000 or more: 14.4% (2006-2010 5-year est.); Poverty rate: 12.7% (2006-2010 5-year est.).
Education: Percent of population age 25 and over with: High school diploma (including GED) or higher: 84.6% (2006-2010 5-year est.); Bachelor's degree or higher: 15.5% (2006-2010 5-year est.); Master's degree or higher: 3.9% (2006-2010 5-year est.).
Housing: Homeownership rate: 82.6% (2010); Median home value: $132,100 (2006-2010 5-year est.); Median contract rent: $399 per month (2006-2010 5-year est.); Median year structure built: 1977 (2006-2010 5-year est.).
Transportation: Commute to work: 96.2% car, 0.0% public transportation, 0.0% walk, 3.1% work from home (2006-2010 5-year est.); Travel time to work: 28.9% less than 15 minutes, 41.2% 15 to 30 minutes, 18.5% 30 to 45 minutes, 5.1% 45 to 60 minutes, 6.4% 60 minutes or more (2006-2010 5-year est.)
Additional Information Contacts
Brookville Area Chamber of Commerce . . . . (814) 849-8448
  http://www.brookvillechamber.com

DEER CREEK (township). Covers a land area of 14.546 square miles and a water area of 0.305 square miles. Located at 41.46° N. Lat; 80.13° W. Long.
Population: 513 (1990); 465 (2000); 502 (2010); Density: 34.5 persons per square mile (2010); Race: 99.0% White, 0.0% Black, 0.2% Asian, 0.2% American Indian/Alaska Native, 0.0% Native Hawaiian/Other Pacific Islander, 0.6% Other, 0.2% Hispanic of any race (2010); Average household size: 2.64 (2010); Median age: 46.0 (2010); Males per 100 females: 99.2 (2010); Marriage status: 24.6% never married, 66.7% now married, 5.6% widowed, 3.2% divorced (2006-2010 5-year est.); Foreign born: 1.4% (2006-2010 5-year est.); Ancestry (includes multiple ancestries): 46.8% German, 13.2% Polish, 8.9% American, 7.5% Irish, 7.0% English (2006-2010 5-year est.).

Economy: Single-family building permits issued: 0 (2011); Multi-family building permits issued: 0 (2011); Employment by occupation: 4.9% management, 2.2% professional, 13.4% services, 12.9% sales, 4.0% farming, 13.8% construction, 6.7% production (2006-2010 5-year est.).
Income: Per capita income: $17,484 (2006-2010 5-year est.); Median household income: $43,500 (2006-2010 5-year est.); Average household income: $50,641 (2006-2010 5-year est.); Percent of households with income of $100,000 or more: 10.1% (2006-2010 5-year est.); Poverty rate: 4.4% (2006-2010 5-year est.).
Education: Percent of population age 25 and over with: High school diploma (including GED) or higher: 77.4% (2006-2010 5-year est.); Bachelor's degree or higher: 6.6% (2006-2010 5-year est.); Master's degree or higher: 2.3% (2006-2010 5-year est.).
Housing: Homeownership rate: 91.6% (2010); Median home value: $119,800 (2006-2010 5-year est.); Median contract rent: $400 per month (2006-2010 5-year est.); Median year structure built: 1971 (2006-2010 5-year est.).
Transportation: Commute to work: 86.9% car, 0.0% public transportation, 0.9% walk, 9.0% work from home (2006-2010 5-year est.); Travel time to work: 24.3% less than 15 minutes, 29.7% 15 to 30 minutes, 23.3% 30 to 45 minutes, 5.9% 45 to 60 minutes, 16.8% 60 minutes or more (2006-2010 5-year est.)

DELAWARE (township). Covers a land area of 32.682 square miles and a water area of 0.357 square miles. Located at 41.32° N. Lat; 80.32° W. Long.
Population: 2,064 (1990); 2,159 (2000); 2,291 (2010); Density: 70.1 persons per square mile (2010); Race: 97.9% White, 0.7% Black, 0.1% Asian, 0.2% American Indian/Alaska Native, 0.0% Native Hawaiian/Other Pacific Islander, 1.1% Other, 0.4% Hispanic of any race (2010); Average household size: 2.56 (2010); Median age: 46.4 (2010); Males per 100 females: 104.9 (2010); Marriage status: 25.3% never married, 64.2% now married, 3.7% widowed, 6.8% divorced (2006-2010 5-year est.); Foreign born: 0.9% (2006-2010 5-year est.); Ancestry (includes multiple ancestries): 44.2% German, 16.8% Irish, 11.6% English, 9.8% Italian, 8.4% American (2006-2010 5-year est.).
Economy: Single-family building permits issued: 1 (2011); Multi-family building permits issued: 0 (2011); Employment by occupation: 8.0% management, 1.5% professional, 19.5% services, 14.0% sales, 2.5% farming, 12.2% construction, 4.6% production (2006-2010 5-year est.).
Income: Per capita income: $25,350 (2006-2010 5-year est.); Median household income: $58,397 (2006-2010 5-year est.); Average household income: $71,340 (2006-2010 5-year est.); Percent of households with income of $100,000 or more: 18.2% (2006-2010 5-year est.); Poverty rate: 6.7% (2006-2010 5-year est.).
Education: Percent of population age 25 and over with: High school diploma (including GED) or higher: 92.7% (2006-2010 5-year est.); Bachelor's degree or higher: 12.5% (2006-2010 5-year est.); Master's degree or higher: 5.5% (2006-2010 5-year est.).
Housing: Homeownership rate: 90.0% (2010); Median home value: $133,600 (2006-2010 5-year est.); Median contract rent: $428 per month (2006-2010 5-year est.); Median year structure built: 1972 (2006-2010 5-year est.).
Transportation: Commute to work: 93.2% car, 0.4% public transportation, 1.2% walk, 4.7% work from home (2006-2010 5-year est.); Travel time to work: 33.3% less than 15 minutes, 44.1% 15 to 30 minutes, 14.9% 30 to 45 minutes, 1.7% 45 to 60 minutes, 6.1% 60 minutes or more (2006-2010 5-year est.).
Additional Information Contacts
Mercer Area Chamber of Commerce . . . . (724) 662-4185
  http://www.mercerareachamber.com

EAST LACKAWANNOCK (township). Covers a land area of 21.404 square miles and a water area of 0.017 square miles. Located at 41.20° N. Lat; 80.27° W. Long.
Population: 1,630 (1990); 1,701 (2000); 1,682 (2010); Density: 78.6 persons per square mile (2010); Race: 98.3% White, 0.7% Black, 0.4% Asian, 0.0% American Indian/Alaska Native, 0.0% Native Hawaiian/Other Pacific Islander, 0.6% Other, 0.5% Hispanic of any race (2010); Average household size: 2.57 (2010); Median age: 44.7 (2010); Males per 100 females: 96.7 (2010); Marriage status: 18.8% never married, 63.0% now married, 8.5% widowed, 9.7% divorced (2006-2010 5-year est.); Foreign born: 2.2% (2006-2010 5-year est.); Ancestry (includes multiple ancestries): 34.9% German, 17.3% Irish, 10.7% English, 6.8% Italian, 6.2% Polish (2006-2010 5-year est.).

Economy: Single-family building permits issued: 2 (2011); Multi-family building permits issued: 0 (2011); Employment by occupation: 9.4% management, 3.4% professional, 10.2% services, 15.4% sales, 4.5% farming, 11.0% construction, 7.7% production (2006-2010 5-year est.).
Income: Per capita income: $20,428 (2006-2010 5-year est.); Median household income: $45,909 (2006-2010 5-year est.); Average household income: $54,724 (2006-2010 5-year est.); Percent of households with income of $100,000 or more: 13.3% (2006-2010 5-year est.); Poverty rate: 14.7% (2006-2010 5-year est.).
Education: Percent of population age 25 and over with: High school diploma (including GED) or higher: 81.8% (2006-2010 5-year est.); Bachelor's degree or higher: 20.0% (2006-2010 5-year est.); Master's degree or higher: 5.9% (2006-2010 5-year est.).
Housing: Homeownership rate: 89.7% (2010); Median home value: $121,300 (2006-2010 5-year est.); Median contract rent: $259 per month (2006-2010 5-year est.); Median year structure built: 1972 (2006-2010 5-year est.).
Transportation: Commute to work: 91.4% car, 0.0% public transportation, 0.6% walk, 5.7% work from home (2006-2010 5-year est.); Travel time to work: 35.7% less than 15 minutes, 32.0% 15 to 30 minutes, 21.3% 30 to 45 minutes, 4.8% 45 to 60 minutes, 6.2% 60 minutes or more (2006-2010 5-year est.).
Additional Information Contacts
Mercer Area Chamber of Commerce . . . . (724) 662-4185
  http://www.mercerareachamber.com

FAIRVIEW (township). Covers a land area of 18.538 square miles and a water area of 0.007 square miles. Located at 41.34° N. Lat; 80.22° W. Long. Elevation is 1,293 feet.
Population: 910 (1990); 1,036 (2000); 1,085 (2010); Density: 58.5 persons per square mile (2010); Race: 99.7% White, 0.1% Black, 0.0% Asian, 0.0% American Indian/Alaska Native, 0.0% Native Hawaiian/Other Pacific Islander, 0.2% Other, 0.4% Hispanic of any race (2010); Average household size: 2.99 (2010); Median age: 36.8 (2010); Males per 100 females: 108.7 (2010); Marriage status: 24.2% never married, 62.7% now married, 4.4% widowed, 8.7% divorced (2006-2010 5-year est.); Foreign born: 0.5% (2006-2010 5-year est.); Ancestry (includes multiple ancestries): 23.0% German, 20.3% Irish, 14.5% Pennsylvania German, 10.3% English, 8.4% Czech (2006-2010 5-year est.).
Economy: Single-family building permits issued: 1 (2011); Multi-family building permits issued: 0 (2011); Employment by occupation: 16.5% management, 2.0% professional, 6.9% services, 17.9% sales, 2.0% farming, 12.8% construction, 3.2% production (2006-2010 5-year est.).
Income: Per capita income: $17,574 (2006-2010 5-year est.); Median household income: $51,250 (2006-2010 5-year est.); Average household income: $55,178 (2006-2010 5-year est.); Percent of households with income of $100,000 or more: 10.2% (2006-2010 5-year est.); Poverty rate: 28.8% (2006-2010 5-year est.).
Education: Percent of population age 25 and over with: High school diploma (including GED) or higher: 81.0% (2006-2010 5-year est.); Bachelor's degree or higher: 11.8% (2006-2010 5-year est.); Master's degree or higher: 3.4% (2006-2010 5-year est.).
Housing: Homeownership rate: 84.5% (2010); Median home value: $111,800 (2006-2010 5-year est.); Median contract rent: $248 per month (2006-2010 5-year est.); Median year structure built: 1972 (2006-2010 5-year est.).
Transportation: Commute to work: 84.7% car, 0.0% public transportation, 2.7% walk, 7.4% work from home (2006-2010 5-year est.); Travel time to work: 23.2% less than 15 minutes, 38.9% 15 to 30 minutes, 21.3% 30 to 45 minutes, 9.1% 45 to 60 minutes, 7.5% 60 minutes or more (2006-2010 5-year est.).
Additional Information Contacts
Mercer Area Chamber of Commerce . . . . (724) 662-4185
  http://www.mercerareachamber.com

FARRELL (city). Covers a land area of 2.289 square miles and a water area of 0 square miles. Located at 41.21° N. Lat; 80.50° W. Long. Elevation is 978 feet.
History: Steel and iron works industries have declined. Incorporated 1901.
Population: 6,844 (1990); 6,050 (2000); 5,111 (2010); Density: 2,232.9 persons per square mile (2010); Race: 45.4% White, 48.8% Black, 0.2% Asian, 0.2% American Indian/Alaska Native, 0.0% Native Hawaiian/Other Pacific Islander, 5.4% Other, 1.4% Hispanic of any race (2010); Average household size: 2.25 (2010); Median age: 40.9 (2010); Males per 100 females: 84.4 (2010); Marriage status: 38.8% never married, 40.6% now

married, 10.6% widowed, 9.9% divorced (2006-2010 5-year est.); Foreign born: 0.9% (2006-2010 5-year est.); Ancestry (includes multiple ancestries): 12.6% Italian, 9.9% German, 8.7% Irish, 5.5% Polish, 4.4% Slovak (2006-2010 5-year est.).

Economy: Single-family building permits issued: 0 (2011); Multi-family building permits issued: 0 (2011); Employment by occupation: 1.8% management, 1.6% professional, 12.7% services, 15.3% sales, 1.0% farming, 9.6% construction, 7.6% production (2006-2010 5-year est.).

Income: Per capita income: $16,139 (2006-2010 5-year est.); Median household income: $28,058 (2006-2010 5-year est.); Average household income: $36,535 (2006-2010 5-year est.); Percent of households with income of $100,000 or more: 5.0% (2006-2010 5-year est.); Poverty rate: 29.6% (2006-2010 5-year est.).

Education: Percent of population age 25 and over with: High school diploma (including GED) or higher: 84.5% (2006-2010 5-year est.); Bachelor's degree or higher: 14.2% (2006-2010 5-year est.); Master's degree or higher: 3.6% (2006-2010 5-year est.).

School District(s)

Farrell Area SD (PK-12)

    2010-11 Enrollment: 801 . . . . (724) 346-6585

Housing: Homeownership rate: 58.5% (2010); Median home value: $59,700 (2006-2010 5-year est.); Median contract rent: $369 per month (2006-2010 5-year est.); Median year structure built: 1951 (2006-2010 5-year est.).

Hospitals: UPMC Horizon (118 beds)

Transportation: Commute to work: 93.4% car, 0.0% public transportation, 0.7% walk, 5.9% work from home (2006-2010 5-year est.); Travel time to work: 54.1% less than 15 minutes, 30.2% 15 to 30 minutes, 12.1% 30 to 45 minutes, 0.7% 45 to 60 minutes, 3.0% 60 minutes or more (2006-2010 5-year est.)

Additional Information Contacts

City of Farrell . . . . (724) 983-2703
    http://www.cityoffarrell.com
Shenango Valley Chamber of Commerce . . . . (724) 981-5880
    http://www.svchamber.com

FINDLEY (township). Covers a land area of 21.223 square miles and a water area of 0.034 square miles. Located at 41.20° N. Lat; 80.17° W. Long.

Population: 2,284 (1990); 2,305 (2000); 2,910 (2010); Density: 137.1 persons per square mile (2010); Race: 77.7% White, 18.0% Black, 0.4% Asian, 0.0% American Indian/Alaska Native, 0.0% Native Hawaiian/Other Pacific Islander, 3.9% Other, 4.2% Hispanic of any race (2010); Average household size: 2.42 (2010); Median age: 42.4 (2010); Males per 100 females: 316.3 (2010); Marriage status: 33.6% never married, 48.9% now married, 3.4% widowed, 14.1% divorced (2006-2010 5-year est.); Foreign born: 0.7% (2006-2010 5-year est.); Ancestry (includes multiple ancestries): 29.1% German, 11.5% Irish, 7.6% English, 5.8% Italian, 4.4% Scotch-Irish (2006-2010 5-year est.).

Economy: Single-family building permits issued: 3 (2011); Multi-family building permits issued: 0 (2011); Employment by occupation: 6.2% management, 2.1% professional, 11.6% services, 12.1% sales, 3.4% farming, 16.2% construction, 7.7% production (2006-2010 5-year est.).

Income: Per capita income: $15,527 (2006-2010 5-year est.); Median household income: $46,779 (2006-2010 5-year est.); Average household income: $57,497 (2006-2010 5-year est.); Percent of households with income of $100,000 or more: 9.8% (2006-2010 5-year est.); Poverty rate: 11.1% (2006-2010 5-year est.).

Education: Percent of population age 25 and over with: High school diploma (including GED) or higher: 84.8% (2006-2010 5-year est.); Bachelor's degree or higher: 13.1% (2006-2010 5-year est.); Master's degree or higher: 4.0% (2006-2010 5-year est.).

Housing: Homeownership rate: 85.1% (2010); Median home value: $102,100 (2006-2010 5-year est.); Median contract rent: $424 per month (2006-2010 5-year est.); Median year structure built: 1972 (2006-2010 5-year est.).

Transportation: Commute to work: 95.3% car, 0.3% public transportation, 1.0% walk, 2.0% work from home (2006-2010 5-year est.); Travel time to work: 39.5% less than 15 minutes, 32.3% 15 to 30 minutes, 16.6% 30 to 45 minutes, 6.1% 45 to 60 minutes, 5.6% 60 minutes or more (2006-2010 5-year est.)

Additional Information Contacts

Mercer Area Chamber of Commerce . . . . (724) 662-4185
    http://www.mercerareachamber.com

FREDONIA (borough). Covers a land area of 0.357 square miles and a water area of 0 square miles. Located at 41.32° N. Lat; 80.26° W. Long. Elevation is 1,188 feet.

Population: 683 (1990); 652 (2000); 502 (2010); Density: 1,406.1 persons per square mile (2010); Race: 97.0% White, 0.0% Black, 0.2% Asian, 0.6% American Indian/Alaska Native, 0.0% Native Hawaiian/Other Pacific Islander, 2.2% Other, 2.0% Hispanic of any race (2010); Average household size: 2.21 (2010); Median age: 43.9 (2010); Males per 100 females: 94.6 (2010); Marriage status: 27.2% never married, 51.9% now married, 6.9% widowed, 14.0% divorced (2006-2010 5-year est.); Foreign born: 0.0% (2006-2010 5-year est.); Ancestry (includes multiple ancestries): 32.8% German, 20.8% Irish, 13.3% American, 12.7% Scotch-Irish, 10.2% English (2006-2010 5-year est.).

Economy: Single-family building permits issued: 0 (2011); Multi-family building permits issued: 0 (2011); Employment by occupation: 0.0% management, 1.4% professional, 14.9% services, 14.5% sales, 0.5% farming, 1.8% construction, 6.8% production (2006-2010 5-year est.).

Income: Per capita income: $18,953 (2006-2010 5-year est.); Median household income: $37,679 (2006-2010 5-year est.); Average household income: $38,537 (2006-2010 5-year est.); Percent of households with income of $100,000 or more: 1.6% (2006-2010 5-year est.); Poverty rate: 21.4% (2006-2010 5-year est.).

Education: Percent of population age 25 and over with: High school diploma (including GED) or higher: 92.7% (2006-2010 5-year est.); Bachelor's degree or higher: 10.5% (2006-2010 5-year est.); Master's degree or higher: 2.4% (2006-2010 5-year est.).

Housing: Homeownership rate: 63.9% (2010); Median home value: $77,200 (2006-2010 5-year est.); Median contract rent: $304 per month (2006-2010 5-year est.); Median year structure built: before 1940 (2006-2010 5-year est.).

Transportation: Commute to work: 96.8% car, 0.0% public transportation, 3.2% walk, 0.0% work from home (2006-2010 5-year est.); Travel time to work: 28.6% less than 15 minutes, 34.6% 15 to 30 minutes, 21.7% 30 to 45 minutes, 3.2% 45 to 60 minutes, 12.0% 60 minutes or more (2006-2010 5-year est.)

FRENCH CREEK (township). Covers a land area of 20.724 square miles and a water area of 0.134 square miles. Located at 41.46° N. Lat; 80.04° W. Long.

Population: 789 (1990); 764 (2000); 771 (2010); Density: 37.2 persons per square mile (2010); Race: 99.0% White, 0.4% Black, 0.0% Asian, 0.3% American Indian/Alaska Native, 0.0% Native Hawaiian/Other Pacific Islander, 0.3% Other, 1.2% Hispanic of any race (2010); Average household size: 2.49 (2010); Median age: 43.5 (2010); Males per 100 females: 106.7 (2010); Marriage status: 15.7% never married, 69.2% now married, 5.9% widowed, 9.2% divorced (2006-2010 5-year est.); Foreign born: 0.0% (2006-2010 5-year est.); Ancestry (includes multiple ancestries): 33.4% German, 17.0% English, 15.5% Irish, 12.2% American, 8.4% Polish (2006-2010 5-year est.).

Economy: Single-family building permits issued: 2 (2011); Multi-family building permits issued: 0 (2011); Employment by occupation: 1.1% management, 2.5% professional, 11.0% services, 15.6% sales, 4.6% farming, 10.6% construction, 8.2% production (2006-2010 5-year est.).

Income: Per capita income: $19,400 (2006-2010 5-year est.); Median household income: $44,861 (2006-2010 5-year est.); Average household income: $49,187 (2006-2010 5-year est.); Percent of households with income of $100,000 or more: 3.9% (2006-2010 5-year est.); Poverty rate: 9.1% (2006-2010 5-year est.).

Education: Percent of population age 25 and over with: High school diploma (including GED) or higher: 86.4% (2006-2010 5-year est.); Bachelor's degree or higher: 10.5% (2006-2010 5-year est.); Master's degree or higher: 0.7% (2006-2010 5-year est.).

Housing: Homeownership rate: 87.1% (2010); Median home value: $102,800 (2006-2010 5-year est.); Median contract rent: $343 per month (2006-2010 5-year est.); Median year structure built: 1977 (2006-2010 5-year est.).

Transportation: Commute to work: 95.7% car, 0.0% public transportation, 0.7% walk, 2.5% work from home (2006-2010 5-year est.); Travel time to work: 23.4% less than 15 minutes, 42.4% 15 to 30 minutes, 16.7% 30 to 45 minutes, 13.4% 45 to 60 minutes, 4.1% 60 minutes or more (2006-2010 5-year est.)

GREENE (township). Covers a land area of 21.829 square miles and a water area of 0.017 square miles. Located at 41.46° N. Lat; 80.45° W. Long.

Population: 1,247 (1990); 1,153 (2000); 1,091 (2010); Density: 50.0 persons per square mile (2010); Race: 99.5% White, 0.0% Black, 0.0% Asian, 0.2% American Indian/Alaska Native, 0.0% Native Hawaiian/Other Pacific Islander, 0.3% Other, 0.4% Hispanic of any race (2010); Average household size: 2.53 (2010); Median age: 47.0 (2010); Males per 100 females: 102.4 (2010); Marriage status: 17.1% never married, 72.8% now married, 4.3% widowed, 5.8% divorced (2006-2010 5-year est.); Foreign born: 0.8% (2006-2010 5-year est.); Ancestry (includes multiple ancestries): 28.3% German, 16.8% Irish, 16.8% English, 10.2% American, 6.2% Scotch-Irish (2006-2010 5-year est.).

Economy: Single-family building permits issued: 0 (2011); Multi-family building permits issued: 0 (2011); Employment by occupation: 6.2% management, 2.1% professional, 16.5% services, 12.4% sales, 2.5% farming, 15.7% construction, 7.6% production (2006-2010 5-year est.).

Income: Per capita income: $21,236 (2006-2010 5-year est.); Median household income: $46,542 (2006-2010 5-year est.); Average household income: $57,566 (2006-2010 5-year est.); Percent of households with income of $100,000 or more: 11.7% (2006-2010 5-year est.); Poverty rate: 8.9% (2006-2010 5-year est.).

Education: Percent of population age 25 and over with: High school diploma (including GED) or higher: 82.0% (2006-2010 5-year est.); Bachelor's degree or higher: 18.3% (2006-2010 5-year est.); Master's degree or higher: 5.6% (2006-2010 5-year est.).

Housing: Homeownership rate: 89.7% (2010); Median home value: $111,100 (2006-2010 5-year est.); Median contract rent: $431 per month (2006-2010 5-year est.); Median year structure built: 1967 (2006-2010 5-year est.).

Transportation: Commute to work: 90.4% car, 0.0% public transportation, 0.8% walk, 5.5% work from home (2006-2010 5-year est.); Travel time to work: 29.4% less than 15 minutes, 32.7% 15 to 30 minutes, 20.5% 30 to 45 minutes, 6.0% 45 to 60 minutes, 11.4% 60 minutes or more (2006-2010 5-year est.)

Additional Information Contacts

Mercer Area Chamber of Commerce . . . . (724) 662-4185
  http://www.mercerareachamber.com

GREENVILLE (borough). Covers a land area of 1.887 square miles and a water area of 0 square miles. Located at 41.41° N. Lat; 80.38° W. Long. Elevation is 945 feet.

History: Seat of Thiel College. Settled c.1796, laid out 1798, incorporated 1837.

Population: 6,734 (1990); 6,380 (2000); 5,919 (2010); Density: 3,137.2 persons per square mile (2010); Race: 95.2% White, 1.7% Black, 1.5% Asian, 0.1% American Indian/Alaska Native, 0.1% Native Hawaiian/Other Pacific Islander, 1.4% Other, 1.5% Hispanic of any race (2010); Average household size: 2.29 (2010); Median age: 33.1 (2010); Males per 100 females: 92.4 (2010); Marriage status: 38.6% never married, 42.2% now married, 6.7% widowed, 12.5% divorced (2006-2010 5-year est.); Foreign born: 5.8% (2006-2010 5-year est.); Ancestry (includes multiple ancestries): 27.2% German, 15.9% Irish, 12.3% English, 8.9% Italian, 4.6% Dutch (2006-2010 5-year est.).

Economy: Single-family building permits issued: 0 (2011); Multi-family building permits issued: 0 (2011); Employment by occupation: 2.4% management, 0.0% professional, 16.3% services, 22.3% sales, 3.3% farming, 10.3% construction, 6.9% production (2006-2010 5-year est.).

Income: Per capita income: $16,556 (2006-2010 5-year est.); Median household income: $32,545 (2006-2010 5-year est.); Average household income: $42,341 (2006-2010 5-year est.); Percent of households with income of $100,000 or more: 3.6% (2006-2010 5-year est.); Poverty rate: 22.7% (2006-2010 5-year est.).

Education: Percent of population age 25 and over with: High school diploma (including GED) or higher: 82.4% (2006-2010 5-year est.); Bachelor's degree or higher: 16.6% (2006-2010 5-year est.); Master's degree or higher: 7.5% (2006-2010 5-year est.).

School District(s)

Greenville Area SD (KG-12)
  2010-11 Enrollment: 1,453 . . . . (724) 588-2500
Keystone Education Center CS (07-12)
  2010-11 Enrollment: 272 . . . . (724) 588-2511
Reynolds SD (KG-12)
  2010-11 Enrollment: 1,253 . . . . (724) 646-5500

Four-year College(s)

Thiel College (Private, Not-for-profit, Evangelical Lutheran Church)
  Fall 2010 Enrollment: 1,016 . . . . (724) 589-2000
  2011-12 Tuition: In-state $24,856; Out-of-state $24,856

Housing: Homeownership rate: 58.0% (2010); Median home value: $76,700 (2006-2010 5-year est.); Median contract rent: $433 per month (2006-2010 5-year est.); Median year structure built: before 1940 (2006-2010 5-year est.).

Hospitals: UPMC Horizon-Greenville (218 beds)

Safety: Violent crime rate: 28.6 per 10,000 population; Property crime rate: 293.0 per 10,000 population (2011).

Newspapers: Greenville Record-Argus (Local news; Circulation 5,557)

Transportation: Commute to work: 73.4% car, 0.8% public transportation, 13.3% walk, 9.2% work from home (2006-2010 5-year est.); Travel time to work: 50.7% less than 15 minutes, 25.6% 15 to 30 minutes, 13.9% 30 to 45 minutes, 5.0% 45 to 60 minutes, 4.8% 60 minutes or more (2006-2010 5-year est.)

Additional Information Contacts

Borough of Greenville . . . . (724) 588-4193
  http://www.greenvilleborough.com
Greenville Area Chamber of Commerce . . . . (724) 588-7150
  http://www.greenvillechamber-pa.com

GROVE CITY (borough). Covers a land area of 2.692 square miles and a water area of 0.006 square miles. Located at 41.16° N. Lat; 80.09° W. Long. Elevation is 1,270 feet.

History: Settled 1798, laid out 1844, incorporated 1883.

Population: 8,240 (1990); 8,024 (2000); 8,322 (2010); Density: 3,091.1 persons per square mile (2010); Race: 96.0% White, 1.3% Black, 1.4% Asian, 0.2% American Indian/Alaska Native, 0.0% Native Hawaiian/Other Pacific Islander, 1.1% Other, 1.1% Hispanic of any race (2010); Average household size: 2.25 (2010); Median age: 24.7 (2010); Males per 100 females: 88.9 (2010); Marriage status: 57.8% never married, 30.5% now married, 6.5% widowed, 5.2% divorced (2006-2010 5-year est.); Foreign born: 1.4% (2006-2010 5-year est.); Ancestry (includes multiple ancestries): 34.2% German, 17.8% Irish, 12.2% English, 11.8% Italian, 6.9% Scotch-Irish (2006-2010 5-year est.).

Economy: Single-family building permits issued: 0 (2011); Multi-family building permits issued: 0 (2011); Employment by occupation: 9.8% management, 1.9% professional, 17.9% services, 18.8% sales, 2.8% farming, 4.7% construction, 2.4% production (2006-2010 5-year est.).

Income: Per capita income: $15,297 (2006-2010 5-year est.); Median household income: $44,671 (2006-2010 5-year est.); Average household income: $52,078 (2006-2010 5-year est.); Percent of households with income of $100,000 or more: 9.8% (2006-2010 5-year est.); Poverty rate: 10.0% (2006-2010 5-year est.).

Education: Percent of population age 25 and over with: High school diploma (including GED) or higher: 90.6% (2006-2010 5-year est.); Bachelor's degree or higher: 30.9% (2006-2010 5-year est.); Master's degree or higher: 13.2% (2006-2010 5-year est.).

School District(s)

Grove City Area SD (KG-12)
  2010-11 Enrollment: 2,626 . . . . (724) 458-6733

Four-year College(s)

Grove City College (Private, Not-for-profit, Presbyterian Church (USA))
  Fall 2010 Enrollment: 2,585 . . . . (724) 458-2000
  2011-12 Tuition: In-state $13,598; Out-of-state $13,598

Housing: Homeownership rate: 60.9% (2010); Median home value: $107,300 (2006-2010 5-year est.); Median contract rent: $501 per month (2006-2010 5-year est.); Median year structure built: 1946 (2006-2010 5-year est.).

Hospitals: Grove City Medical Center (111 beds); United Community Hospital

Safety: Violent crime rate: 6.0 per 10,000 population; Property crime rate: 110.2 per 10,000 population (2011).

Newspapers: Allied News (Community news; Circulation 15,000)

Transportation: Commute to work: 66.6% car, 0.0% public transportation, 8.6% walk, 23.9% work from home (2006-2010 5-year est.); Travel time to work: 55.4% less than 15 minutes, 20.9% 15 to 30 minutes, 8.5% 30 to 45 minutes, 9.8% 45 to 60 minutes, 5.3% 60 minutes or more (2006-2010 5-year est.)

Additional Information Contacts

Borough of Grove City . . . . (724) 458-7060
  http://grovecityonline.com

Grove City Area Chamber of Commerce. . . . . (724) 458-6410
http://www.shopgrovecity.com

HADLEY (unincorporated postal area)
Zip Code: 16130
Covers a land area of 30.945 square miles and a water area of 0.502 square miles. Located at 41.44° N. Lat; 80.22° W. Long. Elevation is 1,056 feet. Population: 2,023 (2010); Density: 65.4 persons per square mile (2010); Race: 98.4% White, 0.7% Black, 0.0% Asian, 0.0% American Indian/Alaska Native, 0.0% Native Hawaiian/Other Pacific Islander, 0.9% Other, 0.2% Hispanic of any race (2010); Average household size: 2.42 (2010); Median age: 46.8 (2010); Males per 100 females: 101.7 (2010); Homeownership rate: 86.0% (2010)

HEMPFIELD (township). Covers a land area of 14.151 square miles and a water area of 0.029 square miles. Located at 41.39° N. Lat; 80.36° W. Long.
Population: 3,826 (1990); 4,004 (2000); 3,741 (2010); Density: 264.4 persons per square mile (2010); Race: 98.0% White, 0.3% Black, 0.9% Asian, 0.2% American Indian/Alaska Native, 0.0% Native Hawaiian/Other Pacific Islander, 0.6% Other, 0.9% Hispanic of any race (2010); Average household size: 2.34 (2010); Median age: 49.9 (2010); Males per 100 females: 92.0 (2010); Marriage status: 11.3% never married, 69.8% now married, 11.5% widowed, 7.4% divorced (2006-2010 5-year est.); Foreign born: 4.1% (2006-2010 5-year est.); Ancestry (includes multiple ancestries): 23.7% German, 13.1% Irish, 11.0% English, 10.8% Italian, 8.4% Polish (2006-2010 5-year est.).
Economy: Single-family building permits issued: 3 (2011); Multi-family building permits issued: 0 (2011); Employment by occupation: 16.1% management, 0.0% professional, 16.1% services, 12.8% sales, 3.9% farming, 5.6% construction, 4.1% production (2006-2010 5-year est.).
Income: Per capita income: $24,846 (2006-2010 5-year est.); Median household income: $43,462 (2006-2010 5-year est.); Average household income: $55,971 (2006-2010 5-year est.); Percent of households with income of $100,000 or more: 12.2% (2006-2010 5-year est.); Poverty rate: 6.0% (2006-2010 5-year est.).
Education: Percent of population age 25 and over with: High school diploma (including GED) or higher: 89.3% (2006-2010 5-year est.); Bachelor's degree or higher: 22.9% (2006-2010 5-year est.); Master's degree or higher: 10.4% (2006-2010 5-year est.).
Housing: Homeownership rate: 81.4% (2010); Median home value: $114,100 (2006-2010 5-year est.); Median contract rent: $559 per month (2006-2010 5-year est.); Median year structure built: 1958 (2006-2010 5-year est.).
Transportation: Commute to work: 97.9% car, 0.0% public transportation, 0.0% walk, 2.1% work from home (2006-2010 5-year est.); Travel time to work: 61.6% less than 15 minutes, 20.9% 15 to 30 minutes, 9.4% 30 to 45 minutes, 3.3% 45 to 60 minutes, 4.8% 60 minutes or more (2006-2010 5-year est.)
Additional Information Contacts
Mercer Area Chamber of Commerce . . . . (724) 662-4185
http://www.mercerareachamber.com

HERMITAGE (city). Covers a land area of 29.235 square miles and a water area of 0.090 square miles. Located at 41.23° N. Lat; 80.44° W. Long. Elevation is 1,076 feet.
History: Formerly a township.
Population: 15,183 (1990); 16,157 (2000); 16,220 (2010); Density: 554.8 persons per square mile (2010); Race: 93.3% White, 3.8% Black, 1.2% Asian, 0.1% American Indian/Alaska Native, 0.0% Native Hawaiian/Other Pacific Islander, 1.6% Other, 1.0% Hispanic of any race (2010); Average household size: 2.21 (2010); Median age: 48.8 (2010); Males per 100 females: 85.6 (2010); Marriage status: 16.8% never married, 62.0% now married, 11.5% widowed, 9.7% divorced (2006-2010 5-year est.); Foreign born: 2.6% (2006-2010 5-year est.); Ancestry (includes multiple ancestries): 33.0% German, 19.8% Italian, 15.8% Irish, 10.2% English, 8.7% Slovak (2006-2010 5-year est.).
Economy: Single-family building permits issued: 9 (2011); Multi-family building permits issued: 0 (2011); Employment by occupation: 13.0% management, 3.7% professional, 9.9% services, 18.5% sales, 2.5% farming, 7.1% construction, 4.8% production (2006-2010 5-year est.).
Income: Per capita income: $29,807 (2006-2010 5-year est.); Median household income: $49,320 (2006-2010 5-year est.); Average household income: $64,381 (2006-2010 5-year est.); Percent of households with income of $100,000 or more: 15.3% (2006-2010 5-year est.); Poverty rate: 5.5% (2006-2010 5-year est.).
Taxes: Total city taxes per capita: $526 (2009); City property taxes per capita: $86 (2009).
Education: Percent of population age 25 and over with: High school diploma (including GED) or higher: 90.9% (2006-2010 5-year est.); Bachelor's degree or higher: 27.6% (2006-2010 5-year est.); Master's degree or higher: 6.7% (2006-2010 5-year est.).
School District(s)
Hermitage SD (KG-12)
    2010-11 Enrollment: 2,086 . . . . (724) 981-8750
Housing: Homeownership rate: 70.7% (2010); Median home value: $129,000 (2006-2010 5-year est.); Median contract rent: $545 per month (2006-2010 5-year est.); Median year structure built: 1965 (2006-2010 5-year est.).
Safety: Violent crime rate: 19.1 per 10,000 population; Property crime rate: 314.0 per 10,000 population (2011).
Transportation: Commute to work: 94.5% car, 0.0% public transportation, 1.0% walk, 3.7% work from home (2006-2010 5-year est.); Travel time to work: 53.6% less than 15 minutes, 28.0% 15 to 30 minutes, 9.5% 30 to 45 minutes, 4.3% 45 to 60 minutes, 4.6% 60 minutes or more (2006-2010 5-year est.)
Additional Information Contacts
City of Hermitage. . . . . (724) 981-0800
http://www.hermitage.net
Shenango Valley Chamber of Commerce. . . . . (724) 981-5880
http://www.svchamber.com

JACKSON (township). Covers a land area of 17.507 square miles and a water area of 0.197 square miles. Located at 41.25° N. Lat; 80.16° W. Long.
Population: 1,089 (1990); 1,206 (2000); 1,273 (2010); Density: 72.7 persons per square mile (2010); Race: 98.7% White, 0.3% Black, 0.1% Asian, 0.2% American Indian/Alaska Native, 0.0% Native Hawaiian/Other Pacific Islander, 0.7% Other, 0.5% Hispanic of any race (2010); Average household size: 2.49 (2010); Median age: 48.2 (2010); Males per 100 females: 97.4 (2010); Marriage status: 16.8% never married, 74.5% now married, 5.2% widowed, 3.5% divorced (2006-2010 5-year est.); Foreign born: 0.0% (2006-2010 5-year est.); Ancestry (includes multiple ancestries): 40.6% German, 23.8% Irish, 10.9% English, 8.8% Italian, 7.0% American (2006-2010 5-year est.).
Economy: Single-family building permits issued: 0 (2011); Multi-family building permits issued: 0 (2011); Employment by occupation: 12.8% management, 0.5% professional, 5.7% services, 19.2% sales, 6.2% farming, 13.9% construction, 7.6% production (2006-2010 5-year est.).
Income: Per capita income: $36,308 (2006-2010 5-year est.); Median household income: $60,000 (2006-2010 5-year est.); Average household income: $94,026 (2006-2010 5-year est.); Percent of households with income of $100,000 or more: 21.0% (2006-2010 5-year est.); Poverty rate: 2.7% (2006-2010 5-year est.).
Education: Percent of population age 25 and over with: High school diploma (including GED) or higher: 90.0% (2006-2010 5-year est.); Bachelor's degree or higher: 22.8% (2006-2010 5-year est.); Master's degree or higher: 8.8% (2006-2010 5-year est.).
Housing: Homeownership rate: 91.2% (2010); Median home value: $142,300 (2006-2010 5-year est.); Median contract rent: $446 per month (2006-2010 5-year est.); Median year structure built: 1974 (2006-2010 5-year est.).
Transportation: Commute to work: 89.7% car, 0.0% public transportation, 1.7% walk, 7.5% work from home (2006-2010 5-year est.); Travel time to work: 23.1% less than 15 minutes, 36.7% 15 to 30 minutes, 21.1% 30 to 45 minutes, 10.3% 45 to 60 minutes, 8.8% 60 minutes or more (2006-2010 5-year est.)
Additional Information Contacts
Mercer Area Chamber of Commerce . . . . (724) 662-4185
http://www.mercerareachamber.com

JACKSON CENTER (borough). Covers a land area of 1.138 square miles and a water area of 0 square miles. Located at 41.27° N. Lat; 80.14° W. Long. Elevation is 1,319 feet.
Population: 244 (1990); 221 (2000); 224 (2010); Density: 196.8 persons per square mile (2010); Race: 100.0% White, 0.0% Black, 0.0% Asian, 0.0% American Indian/Alaska Native, 0.0% Native Hawaiian/Other Pacific Islander, 0.0% Other, 0.0% Hispanic of any race (2010); Average household size: 2.80 (2010); Median age: 35.0 (2010); Males per 100

females: 96.5 (2010); Marriage status: 11.6% never married, 64.6% now married, 10.4% widowed, 13.4% divorced (2006-2010 5-year est.); Foreign born: 2.0% (2006-2010 5-year est.); Ancestry (includes multiple ancestries): 35.8% German, 28.9% Irish, 7.8% Dutch, 6.9% English, 6.4% French (2006-2010 5-year est.).

Economy: Single-family building permits issued: 0 (2011); Multi-family building permits issued: 0 (2011); Employment by occupation: 9.2% management, 0.0% professional, 17.3% services, 4.1% sales, 9.2% farming, 7.1% construction, 6.1% production (2006-2010 5-year est.).

Income: Per capita income: $18,024 (2006-2010 5-year est.); Median household income: $40,750 (2006-2010 5-year est.); Average household income: $42,813 (2006-2010 5-year est.); Percent of households with income of $100,000 or more: 3.4% (2006-2010 5-year est.); Poverty rate: 11.3% (2006-2010 5-year est.).

Education: Percent of population age 25 and over with: High school diploma (including GED) or higher: 80.4% (2006-2010 5-year est.); Bachelor's degree or higher: 11.1% (2006-2010 5-year est.); Master's degree or higher: 3.9% (2006-2010 5-year est.).

Housing: Homeownership rate: 78.8% (2010); Median home value: $76,800 (2006-2010 5-year est.); Median contract rent: $392 per month (2006-2010 5-year est.); Median year structure built: 1957 (2006-2010 5-year est.).

Transportation: Commute to work: 84.8% car, 0.0% public transportation, 7.6% walk, 0.0% work from home (2006-2010 5-year est.); Travel time to work: 26.1% less than 15 minutes, 41.3% 15 to 30 minutes, 18.5% 30 to 45 minutes, 6.5% 45 to 60 minutes, 7.6% 60 minutes or more (2006-2010 5-year est.)

JAMESTOWN (borough). Covers a land area of 0.833 square miles and a water area of 0.005 square miles. Located at 41.48° N. Lat; 80.44° W. Long. Elevation is 991 feet.

Population: 761 (1990); 636 (2000); 617 (2010); Density: 740.5 persons per square mile (2010); Race: 99.2% White, 0.0% Black, 0.3% Asian, 0.0% American Indian/Alaska Native, 0.3% Native Hawaiian/Other Pacific Islander, 0.2% Other, 0.2% Hispanic of any race (2010); Average household size: 2.39 (2010); Median age: 44.5 (2010); Males per 100 females: 94.0 (2010); Marriage status: 31.5% never married, 51.9% now married, 6.1% widowed, 10.5% divorced (2006-2010 5-year est.); Foreign born: 0.0% (2006-2010 5-year est.); Ancestry (includes multiple ancestries): 43.8% German, 19.2% English, 13.7% Irish, 8.6% Scotch-Irish, 5.8% Dutch (2006-2010 5-year est.).

Economy: Single-family building permits issued: 0 (2011); Multi-family building permits issued: 0 (2011); Employment by occupation: 4.7% management, 2.2% professional, 22.5% services, 14.1% sales, 3.1% farming, 1.9% construction, 5.0% production (2006-2010 5-year est.).

Income: Per capita income: $18,844 (2006-2010 5-year est.); Median household income: $38,750 (2006-2010 5-year est.); Average household income: $48,669 (2006-2010 5-year est.); Percent of households with income of $100,000 or more: 8.5% (2006-2010 5-year est.); Poverty rate: 12.0% (2006-2010 5-year est.).

Education: Percent of population age 25 and over with: High school diploma (including GED) or higher: 88.2% (2006-2010 5-year est.); Bachelor's degree or higher: 9.8% (2006-2010 5-year est.); Master's degree or higher: 4.8% (2006-2010 5-year est.).

School District(s)

Jamestown Area SD (KG-12)
    2010-11 Enrollment: 562 . . . . (724) 932-5557
Jamestown Area SD (KG-12)
    2010-11 Enrollment: 562 . . . . (724) 932-5557

Housing: Homeownership rate: 76.0% (2010); Median home value: $76,300 (2006-2010 5-year est.); Median contract rent: $413 per month (2006-2010 5-year est.); Median year structure built: before 1940 (2006-2010 5-year est.).

Safety: Violent crime rate: 0.0 per 10,000 population; Property crime rate: 113.1 per 10,000 population (2011).

Transportation: Commute to work: 93.2% car, 0.0% public transportation, 3.2% walk, 3.5% work from home (2006-2010 5-year est.); Travel time to work: 49.8% less than 15 minutes, 27.1% 15 to 30 minutes, 11.4% 30 to 45 minutes, 9.7% 45 to 60 minutes, 2.0% 60 minutes or more (2006-2010 5-year est.)

JEFFERSON (township). Covers a land area of 24.666 square miles and a water area of 0.770 square miles. Located at 41.26° N. Lat; 80.33° W. Long.

Population: 2,069 (1990); 2,416 (2000); 1,880 (2010); Density: 76.2 persons per square mile (2010); Race: 98.0% White, 0.2% Black, 0.4% Asian, 0.3% American Indian/Alaska Native, 0.0% Native Hawaiian/Other Pacific Islander, 1.1% Other, 0.3% Hispanic of any race (2010); Average household size: 2.41 (2010); Median age: 46.5 (2010); Males per 100 females: 106.6 (2010); Marriage status: 26.8% never married, 58.8% now married, 3.3% widowed, 11.0% divorced (2006-2010 5-year est.); Foreign born: 1.3% (2006-2010 5-year est.); Ancestry (includes multiple ancestries): 31.6% German, 12.9% Irish, 11.3% Italian, 11.0% English, 5.3% Slovak (2006-2010 5-year est.).

Economy: Single-family building permits issued: 3 (2011); Multi-family building permits issued: 0 (2011); Employment by occupation: 8.2% management, 1.3% professional, 12.4% services, 22.4% sales, 3.1% farming, 15.2% construction, 7.0% production (2006-2010 5-year est.).

Income: Per capita income: $22,014 (2006-2010 5-year est.); Median household income: $45,994 (2006-2010 5-year est.); Average household income: $55,041 (2006-2010 5-year est.); Percent of households with income of $100,000 or more: 10.3% (2006-2010 5-year est.); Poverty rate: 14.8% (2006-2010 5-year est.).

Education: Percent of population age 25 and over with: High school diploma (including GED) or higher: 87.1% (2006-2010 5-year est.); Bachelor's degree or higher: 13.4% (2006-2010 5-year est.); Master's degree or higher: 2.8% (2006-2010 5-year est.).

Housing: Homeownership rate: 90.7% (2010); Median home value: $115,400 (2006-2010 5-year est.); Median contract rent: $428 per month (2006-2010 5-year est.); Median year structure built: 1976 (2006-2010 5-year est.).

Safety: Violent crime rate: 5.3 per 10,000 population; Property crime rate: 90.1 per 10,000 population (2011).

Transportation: Commute to work: 93.6% car, 0.0% public transportation, 0.8% walk, 5.6% work from home (2006-2010 5-year est.); Travel time to work: 19.5% less than 15 minutes, 58.8% 15 to 30 minutes, 9.2% 30 to 45 minutes, 6.1% 45 to 60 minutes, 6.4% 60 minutes or more (2006-2010 5-year est.)

Additional Information Contacts

Mercer Area Chamber of Commerce . . . . (724) 662-4185
    http://www.mercerareachamber.com

LACKAWANNOCK (township). Covers a land area of 20.867 square miles and a water area of 0.008 square miles. Located at 41.20° N. Lat; 80.35° W. Long.

Population: 2,706 (1990); 2,561 (2000); 2,662 (2010); Density: 127.6 persons per square mile (2010); Race: 97.6% White, 0.8% Black, 0.2% Asian, 0.3% American Indian/Alaska Native, 0.0% Native Hawaiian/Other Pacific Islander, 1.1% Other, 1.2% Hispanic of any race (2010); Average household size: 2.70 (2010); Median age: 40.3 (2010); Males per 100 females: 99.8 (2010); Marriage status: 22.6% never married, 63.6% now married, 6.7% widowed, 7.0% divorced (2006-2010 5-year est.); Foreign born: 3.0% (2006-2010 5-year est.); Ancestry (includes multiple ancestries): 24.1% German, 13.0% Irish, 11.7% Pennsylvania German, 8.9% English, 7.2% Italian (2006-2010 5-year est.).

Economy: Single-family building permits issued: 5 (2011); Multi-family building permits issued: 0 (2011); Employment by occupation: 3.1% management, 2.2% professional, 10.1% services, 11.2% sales, 0.0% farming, 7.9% construction, 4.9% production (2006-2010 5-year est.).

Income: Per capita income: $17,673 (2006-2010 5-year est.); Median household income: $48,891 (2006-2010 5-year est.); Average household income: $53,931 (2006-2010 5-year est.); Percent of households with income of $100,000 or more: 9.8% (2006-2010 5-year est.); Poverty rate: 14.5% (2006-2010 5-year est.).

Education: Percent of population age 25 and over with: High school diploma (including GED) or higher: 79.3% (2006-2010 5-year est.); Bachelor's degree or higher: 14.2% (2006-2010 5-year est.); Master's degree or higher: 3.3% (2006-2010 5-year est.).

Housing: Homeownership rate: 86.6% (2010); Median home value: $128,100 (2006-2010 5-year est.); Median contract rent: $444 per month (2006-2010 5-year est.); Median year structure built: 1975 (2006-2010 5-year est.).

Transportation: Commute to work: 86.6% car, 0.0% public transportation, 7.4% walk, 3.7% work from home (2006-2010 5-year est.); Travel time to work: 28.3% less than 15 minutes, 56.6% 15 to 30 minutes, 9.7% 30 to 45

minutes, 2.8% 45 to 60 minutes, 2.6% 60 minutes or more (2006-2010 5-year est.)

Additional Information Contacts

Mercer Area Chamber of Commerce .... (724) 662-4185
http://www.mercerareachamber.com

LAKE (township). Covers a land area of 16.385 square miles and a water area of 0.140 square miles. Located at 41.34° N. Lat; 80.14° W. Long.

Population: 651 (1990); 706 (2000); 780 (2010); Density: 47.6 persons per square mile (2010); Race: 99.5% White, 0.0% Black, 0.1% Asian, 0.1% American Indian/Alaska Native, 0.0% Native Hawaiian/Other Pacific Islander, 0.3% Other, 0.4% Hispanic of any race (2010); Average household size: 2.87 (2010); Median age: 35.2 (2010); Males per 100 females: 101.6 (2010); Marriage status: 28.4% never married, 58.8% now married, 3.1% widowed, 9.7% divorced (2006-2010 5-year est.); Foreign born: 1.0% (2006-2010 5-year est.); Ancestry (includes multiple ancestries): 20.3% Pennsylvania German, 20.2% German, 19.1% English, 14.9% Irish, 9.1% Italian (2006-2010 5-year est.).

Economy: Single-family building permits issued: 0 (2011); Multi-family building permits issued: 0 (2011); Employment by occupation: 10.7% management, 7.0% professional, 10.1% services, 12.8% sales, 1.8% farming, 14.0% construction, 5.8% production (2006-2010 5-year est.).

Income: Per capita income: $20,191 (2006-2010 5-year est.); Median household income: $37,115 (2006-2010 5-year est.); Average household income: $58,699 (2006-2010 5-year est.); Percent of households with income of $100,000 or more: 10.9% (2006-2010 5-year est.); Poverty rate: 29.5% (2006-2010 5-year est.).

Education: Percent of population age 25 and over with: High school diploma (including GED) or higher: 76.6% (2006-2010 5-year est.); Bachelor's degree or higher: 13.8% (2006-2010 5-year est.); Master's degree or higher: 3.3% (2006-2010 5-year est.).

Housing: Homeownership rate: 79.5% (2010); Median home value: $129,800 (2006-2010 5-year est.); Median contract rent: $400 per month (2006-2010 5-year est.); Median year structure built: 1979 (2006-2010 5-year est.).

Transportation: Commute to work: 79.4% car, 0.0% public transportation, 1.9% walk, 10.1% work from home (2006-2010 5-year est.); Travel time to work: 21.8% less than 15 minutes, 31.3% 15 to 30 minutes, 30.3% 30 to 45 minutes, 4.9% 45 to 60 minutes, 11.6% 60 minutes or more (2006-2010 5-year est.)

LAKE LATONKA (CDP). Covers a land area of 2.355 square miles and a water area of 0.406 square miles. Located at 41.28° N. Lat; 80.18° W. Long.

Population: n/a (1990); n/a (2000); 1,012 (2010); Density: 429.7 persons per square mile (2010); Race: 98.9% White, 0.2% Black, 0.2% Asian, 0.1% American Indian/Alaska Native, 0.0% Native Hawaiian/Other Pacific Islander, 0.6% Other, 0.5% Hispanic of any race (2010); Average household size: 2.43 (2010); Median age: 50.2 (2010); Males per 100 females: 94.6 (2010); Marriage status: 15.0% never married, 75.7% now married, 4.4% widowed, 4.8% divorced (2006-2010 5-year est.); Foreign born: 0.0% (2006-2010 5-year est.); Ancestry (includes multiple ancestries): 37.8% German, 21.1% Irish, 14.7% English, 8.4% Italian, 7.3% Scotch-Irish (2006-2010 5-year est.).

Economy: Employment by occupation: 18.6% management, 3.2% professional, 6.7% services, 15.2% sales, 2.4% farming, 6.9% construction, 1.1% production (2006-2010 5-year est.).

Income: Per capita income: $42,177 (2006-2010 5-year est.); Median household income: $67,778 (2006-2010 5-year est.); Average household income: $100,147 (2006-2010 5-year est.); Percent of households with income of $100,000 or more: 33.0% (2006-2010 5-year est.); Poverty rate: 4.8% (2006-2010 5-year est.).

Education: Percent of population age 25 and over with: High school diploma (including GED) or higher: 94.7% (2006-2010 5-year est.); Bachelor's degree or higher: 42.3% (2006-2010 5-year est.); Master's degree or higher: 14.8% (2006-2010 5-year est.).

Housing: Homeownership rate: 97.1% (2010); Median home value: $189,100 (2006-2010 5-year est.); Median contract rent: n/a per month (2006-2010 5-year est.); Median year structure built: 1982 (2006-2010 5-year est.).

Transportation: Commute to work: 91.2% car, 0.0% public transportation, 0.0% walk, 6.6% work from home (2006-2010 5-year est.); Travel time to work: 23.3% less than 15 minutes, 34.7% 15 to 30 minutes, 19.3% 30 to

45 minutes, 11.6% 45 to 60 minutes, 11.1% 60 minutes or more (2006-2010 5-year est.)

LIBERTY (township). Covers a land area of 14.762 square miles and a water area of 0.077 square miles. Located at 41.11° N. Lat; 80.11° W. Long.

Population: 1,223 (1990); 1,276 (2000); 1,414 (2010); Density: 95.8 persons per square mile (2010); Race: 99.2% White, 0.0% Black, 0.1% Asian, 0.0% American Indian/Alaska Native, 0.0% Native Hawaiian/Other Pacific Islander, 0.7% Other, 0.3% Hispanic of any race (2010); Average household size: 2.61 (2010); Median age: 44.7 (2010); Males per 100 females: 104.3 (2010); Marriage status: 18.1% never married, 68.3% now married, 4.9% widowed, 8.7% divorced (2006-2010 5-year est.); Foreign born: 0.0% (2006-2010 5-year est.); Ancestry (includes multiple ancestries): 38.3% German, 18.1% Irish, 17.0% English, 10.8% Scotch-Irish, 9.7% Italian (2006-2010 5-year est.).

Economy: Single-family building permits issued: 3 (2011); Multi-family building permits issued: 0 (2011); Employment by occupation: 13.7% management, 3.7% professional, 10.6% services, 9.4% sales, 5.1% farming, 7.9% construction, 4.1% production (2006-2010 5-year est.).

Income: Per capita income: $24,026 (2006-2010 5-year est.); Median household income: $56,875 (2006-2010 5-year est.); Average household income: $64,090 (2006-2010 5-year est.); Percent of households with income of $100,000 or more: 17.6% (2006-2010 5-year est.); Poverty rate: 8.6% (2006-2010 5-year est.).

Education: Percent of population age 25 and over with: High school diploma (including GED) or higher: 86.7% (2006-2010 5-year est.); Bachelor's degree or higher: 27.2% (2006-2010 5-year est.); Master's degree or higher: 11.3% (2006-2010 5-year est.).

Housing: Homeownership rate: 89.1% (2010); Median home value: $142,900 (2006-2010 5-year est.); Median contract rent: $504 per month (2006-2010 5-year est.); Median year structure built: 1974 (2006-2010 5-year est.).

Transportation: Commute to work: 91.8% car, 0.0% public transportation, 0.0% walk, 5.2% work from home (2006-2010 5-year est.); Travel time to work: 42.4% less than 15 minutes, 24.8% 15 to 30 minutes, 21.2% 30 to 45 minutes, 5.6% 45 to 60 minutes, 5.9% 60 minutes or more (2006-2010 5-year est.)

Additional Information Contacts

Mercer Area Chamber of Commerce .... (724) 662-4185
http://www.mercerareachamber.com

MERCER (borough). County seat. Covers a land area of 1.139 square miles and a water area of 0.002 square miles. Located at 41.23° N. Lat; 80.24° W. Long. Elevation is 1,296 feet.

History: Settled 1795, laid out 1803, incorporated 1814.

Population: 2,420 (1990); 2,391 (2000); 2,002 (2010); Density: 1,757.9 persons per square mile (2010); Race: 97.1% White, 1.0% Black, 0.4% Asian, 0.1% American Indian/Alaska Native, 0.0% Native Hawaiian/Other Pacific Islander, 1.4% Other, 0.8% Hispanic of any race (2010); Average household size: 2.21 (2010); Median age: 39.4 (2010); Males per 100 females: 87.3 (2010); Marriage status: 23.3% never married, 52.1% now married, 8.7% widowed, 15.8% divorced (2006-2010 5-year est.); Foreign born: 0.6% (2006-2010 5-year est.); Ancestry (includes multiple ancestries): 25.9% German, 21.0% Irish, 13.4% English, 12.1% American, 11.2% Italian (2006-2010 5-year est.).

Economy: Single-family building permits issued: 0 (2011); Multi-family building permits issued: 0 (2011); Employment by occupation: 7.4% management, 5.1% professional, 16.6% services, 22.2% sales, 1.3% farming, 8.4% construction, 5.7% production (2006-2010 5-year est.).

Income: Per capita income: $23,526 (2006-2010 5-year est.); Median household income: $42,375 (2006-2010 5-year est.); Average household income: $49,776 (2006-2010 5-year est.); Percent of households with income of $100,000 or more: 7.4% (2006-2010 5-year est.); Poverty rate: 11.9% (2006-2010 5-year est.).

Education: Percent of population age 25 and over with: High school diploma (including GED) or higher: 88.2% (2006-2010 5-year est.); Bachelor's degree or higher: 17.9% (2006-2010 5-year est.); Master's degree or higher: 3.6% (2006-2010 5-year est.).

School District(s)

Mercer Area SD (KG-12)
    2010-11 Enrollment: 1,314 .... (724) 662-5100
Mercer County Career Center (10-12)
    2010-11 Enrollment: n/a .... (724) 662-3000

Vocational/Technical School(s)

Mercer County Career Center (Public)

Fall 2010 Enrollment: 87 . . . . (724) 662-3000

2011-12 Tuition: $10,900

Housing: Homeownership rate: 54.4% (2010); Median home value: $101,900 (2006-2010 5-year est.); Median contract rent: $381 per month (2006-2010 5-year est.); Median year structure built: 1943 (2006-2010 5-year est.).

Safety: Violent crime rate: 29.9 per 10,000 population; Property crime rate: 59.8 per 10,000 population (2011).

Transportation: Commute to work: 91.0% car, 0.0% public transportation, 4.5% walk, 3.6% work from home (2006-2010 5-year est.); Travel time to work: 39.8% less than 15 minutes, 35.2% 15 to 30 minutes, 17.4% 30 to 45 minutes, 1.9% 45 to 60 minutes, 5.7% 60 minutes or more (2006-2010 5-year est.).

Additional Information Contacts

Mercer Area Chamber of Commerce . . . . (724) 662-4185

http://www.mercerareachamber.com

MILL CREEK (township). Covers a land area of 18.993 square miles and a water area of 0.393 square miles. Located at 41.40° N. Lat; 80.04° W. Long.

Population: 604 (1990); 639 (2000); 721 (2010); Density: 38.0 persons per square mile (2010); Race: 99.3% White, 0.1% Black, 0.0% Asian, 0.1% American Indian/Alaska Native, 0.0% Native Hawaiian/Other Pacific Islander, 0.5% Other, 0.4% Hispanic of any race (2010); Average household size: 2.39 (2010); Median age: 45.0 (2010); Males per 100 females: 103.7 (2010); Marriage status: 17.0% never married, 61.5% now married, 6.2% widowed, 15.3% divorced (2006-2010 5-year est.); Foreign born: 2.5% (2006-2010 5-year est.); Ancestry (includes multiple ancestries): 41.3% German, 18.8% Irish, 9.8% English, 9.3% American, 6.6% Italian (2006-2010 5-year est.).

Economy: Employment by occupation: 6.1% management, 1.0% professional, 11.8% services, 16.2% sales, 3.7% farming, 19.2% construction, 11.1% production (2006-2010 5-year est.).

Income: Per capita income: $22,810 (2006-2010 5-year est.); Median household income: $45,469 (2006-2010 5-year est.); Average household income: $50,766 (2006-2010 5-year est.); Percent of households with income of $100,000 or more: 5.0% (2006-2010 5-year est.); Poverty rate: 5.7% (2006-2010 5-year est.).

Education: Percent of population age 25 and over with: High school diploma (including GED) or higher: 88.0% (2006-2010 5-year est.); Bachelor's degree or higher: 16.9% (2006-2010 5-year est.); Master's degree or higher: 4.3% (2006-2010 5-year est.).

Housing: Homeownership rate: 92.4% (2010); Median home value: $115,500 (2006-2010 5-year est.); Median contract rent: $242 per month (2006-2010 5-year est.); Median year structure built: 1971 (2006-2010 5-year est.).

Transportation: Commute to work: 84.0% car, 3.1% public transportation, 3.4% walk, 6.5% work from home (2006-2010 5-year est.); Travel time to work: 23.4% less than 15 minutes, 37.6% 15 to 30 minutes, 25.2% 30 to 45 minutes, 5.1% 45 to 60 minutes, 8.8% 60 minutes or more (2006-2010 5-year est.).

NEW LEBANON (borough). Covers a land area of 1.273 square miles and a water area of 0.005 square miles. Located at 41.42° N. Lat; 80.08° W. Long. Elevation is 1,401 feet.

Population: 209 (1990); 205 (2000); 188 (2010); Density: 147.7 persons per square mile (2010); Race: 96.8% White, 0.5% Black, 0.0% Asian, 0.0% American Indian/Alaska Native, 0.0% Native Hawaiian/Other Pacific Islander, 2.7% Other, 0.5% Hispanic of any race (2010); Average household size: 2.47 (2010); Median age: 39.8 (2010); Males per 100 females: 93.8 (2010); Marriage status: 18.4% never married, 67.0% now married, 4.3% widowed, 10.3% divorced (2006-2010 5-year est.); Foreign born: 0.0% (2006-2010 5-year est.); Ancestry (includes multiple ancestries): 34.4% German, 14.4% Irish, 10.0% English, 5.2% Scotch-Irish, 4.4% Dutch (2006-2010 5-year est.).

Economy: Single-family building permits issued: 0 (2011); Multi-family building permits issued: 0 (2011); Employment by occupation: 5.9% management, 7.1% professional, 16.5% services, 17.6% sales, 0.0% farming, 11.8% construction, 11.8% production (2006-2010 5-year est.).

Income: Per capita income: $15,282 (2006-2010 5-year est.); Median household income: $34,375 (2006-2010 5-year est.); Average household income: $44,170 (2006-2010 5-year est.); Percent of households with income of $100,000 or more: 3.5% (2006-2010 5-year est.); Poverty rate: 19.2% (2006-2010 5-year est.).

Education: Percent of population age 25 and over with: High school diploma (including GED) or higher: 76.6% (2006-2010 5-year est.); Bachelor's degree or higher: 3.6% (2006-2010 5-year est.); Master's degree or higher: 0.0% (2006-2010 5-year est.).

Housing: Homeownership rate: 94.7% (2010); Median home value: $53,100 (2006-2010 5-year est.); Median contract rent: $225 per month (2006-2010 5-year est.); Median year structure built: 1973 (2006-2010 5-year est.).

Transportation: Commute to work: 92.9% car, 0.0% public transportation, 3.5% walk, 3.5% work from home (2006-2010 5-year est.); Travel time to work: 7.3% less than 15 minutes, 46.3% 15 to 30 minutes, 22.0% 30 to 45 minutes, 17.1% 45 to 60 minutes, 7.3% 60 minutes or more (2006-2010 5-year est.)

NEW VERNON (township). Covers a land area of 14.932 square miles and a water area of 1.405 square miles. Located at 41.40° N. Lat; 80.15° W. Long. Elevation is 1,257 feet.

Population: 493 (1990); 524 (2000); 504 (2010); Density: 33.8 persons per square mile (2010); Race: 98.2% White, 0.2% Black, 0.6% Asian, 0.2% American Indian/Alaska Native, 0.0% Native Hawaiian/Other Pacific Islander, 0.8% Other, 0.0% Hispanic of any race (2010); Average household size: 2.53 (2010); Median age: 45.3 (2010); Males per 100 females: 102.4 (2010); Marriage status: 20.6% never married, 66.8% now married, 5.4% widowed, 7.2% divorced (2006-2010 5-year est.); Foreign born: 1.2% (2006-2010 5-year est.); Ancestry (includes multiple ancestries): 36.3% German, 27.4% Irish, 17.5% English, 7.6% American, 4.1% Scotch-Irish (2006-2010 5-year est.).

Economy: Single-family building permits issued: 5 (2011); Multi-family building permits issued: 0 (2011); Employment by occupation: 11.1% management, 1.3% professional, 11.9% services, 11.1% sales, 2.6% farming, 10.2% construction, 19.1% production (2006-2010 5-year est.).

Income: Per capita income: $20,660 (2006-2010 5-year est.); Median household income: $49,167 (2006-2010 5-year est.); Average household income: $54,388 (2006-2010 5-year est.); Percent of households with income of $100,000 or more: 11.7% (2006-2010 5-year est.); Poverty rate: 11.8% (2006-2010 5-year est.).

Education: Percent of population age 25 and over with: High school diploma (including GED) or higher: 86.8% (2006-2010 5-year est.); Bachelor's degree or higher: 16.5% (2006-2010 5-year est.); Master's degree or higher: 2.1% (2006-2010 5-year est.).

Housing: Homeownership rate: 85.9% (2010); Median home value: $107,400 (2006-2010 5-year est.); Median contract rent: $342 per month (2006-2010 5-year est.); Median year structure built: 1981 (2006-2010 5-year est.).

Transportation: Commute to work: 89.9% car, 1.3% public transportation, 3.9% walk, 4.8% work from home (2006-2010 5-year est.); Travel time to work: 31.3% less than 15 minutes, 27.2% 15 to 30 minutes, 18.4% 30 to 45 minutes, 12.0% 45 to 60 minutes, 11.1% 60 minutes or more (2006-2010 5-year est.)

OTTER CREEK (township). Covers a land area of 11.816 square miles and a water area of 0.004 square miles. Located at 41.39° N. Lat; 80.29° W. Long.

Population: 583 (1990); 611 (2000); 589 (2010); Density: 49.8 persons per square mile (2010); Race: 97.8% White, 0.8% Black, 0.0% Asian, 0.0% American Indian/Alaska Native, 0.0% Native Hawaiian/Other Pacific Islander, 1.4% Other, 0.7% Hispanic of any race (2010); Average household size: 2.62 (2010); Median age: 44.0 (2010); Males per 100 females: 109.6 (2010); Marriage status: 15.2% never married, 66.0% now married, 3.3% widowed, 15.6% divorced (2006-2010 5-year est.); Foreign born: 0.0% (2006-2010 5-year est.); Ancestry (includes multiple ancestries): 45.7% German, 17.1% Irish, 7.3% English, 6.5% American, 6.3% Dutch (2006-2010 5-year est.).

Economy: Single-family building permits issued: 0 (2011); Multi-family building permits issued: 0 (2011); Employment by occupation: 16.0% management, 0.0% professional, 8.0% services, 9.1% sales, 3.4% farming, 5.7% construction, 12.9% production (2006-2010 5-year est.).

Income: Per capita income: $19,775 (2006-2010 5-year est.); Median household income: $48,571 (2006-2010 5-year est.); Average household income: $50,027 (2006-2010 5-year est.); Percent of households with income of $100,000 or more: 9.7% (2006-2010 5-year est.); Poverty rate: 16.5% (2006-2010 5-year est.).

Education: Percent of population age 25 and over with: High school diploma (including GED) or higher: 83.1% (2006-2010 5-year est.); Bachelor's degree or higher: 7.8% (2006-2010 5-year est.); Master's degree or higher: 1.0% (2006-2010 5-year est.).

Housing: Homeownership rate: 84.8% (2010); Median home value: $119,000 (2006-2010 5-year est.); Median contract rent: $375 per month (2006-2010 5-year est.); Median year structure built: 1973 (2006-2010 5-year est.).

Transportation: Commute to work: 87.7% car, 0.0% public transportation, 0.8% walk, 8.8% work from home (2006-2010 5-year est.); Travel time to work: 25.7% less than 15 minutes, 41.8% 15 to 30 minutes, 28.3% 30 to 45 minutes, 1.7% 45 to 60 minutes, 2.5% 60 minutes or more (2006-2010 5-year est.)

PERRY (township). Covers a land area of 17.999 square miles and a water area of 0.009 square miles. Located at 41.39° N. Lat; 80.22° W. Long.

Population: 1,468 (1990); 1,471 (2000); 1,453 (2010); Density: 80.7 persons per square mile (2010); Race: 98.9% White, 0.1% Black, 0.4% Asian, 0.1% American Indian/Alaska Native, 0.0% Native Hawaiian/Other Pacific Islander, 0.5% Other, 0.3% Hispanic of any race (2010); Average household size: 2.47 (2010); Median age: 47.2 (2010); Males per 100 females: 103.8 (2010); Marriage status: 22.6% never married, 59.4% now married, 7.6% widowed, 10.5% divorced (2006-2010 5-year est.); Foreign born: 0.2% (2006-2010 5-year est.); Ancestry (includes multiple ancestries): 42.9% German, 17.1% Irish, 15.4% English, 7.5% American, 7.2% Scotch-Irish (2006-2010 5-year est.).

Economy: Single-family building permits issued: 1 (2011); Multi-family building permits issued: 0 (2011); Employment by occupation: 9.4% management, 1.6% professional, 10.9% services, 17.4% sales, 1.6% farming, 9.4% construction, 9.6% production (2006-2010 5-year est.).

Income: Per capita income: $19,442 (2006-2010 5-year est.); Median household income: $44,185 (2006-2010 5-year est.); Average household income: $50,722 (2006-2010 5-year est.); Percent of households with income of $100,000 or more: 9.2% (2006-2010 5-year est.); Poverty rate: 11.1% (2006-2010 5-year est.).

Education: Percent of population age 25 and over with: High school diploma (including GED) or higher: 90.2% (2006-2010 5-year est.); Bachelor's degree or higher: 9.4% (2006-2010 5-year est.); Master's degree or higher: 3.4% (2006-2010 5-year est.).

Housing: Homeownership rate: 88.5% (2010); Median home value: $90,600 (2006-2010 5-year est.); Median contract rent: $425 per month (2006-2010 5-year est.); Median year structure built: 1971 (2006-2010 5-year est.).

Transportation: Commute to work: 86.1% car, 0.7% public transportation, 1.8% walk, 9.8% work from home (2006-2010 5-year est.); Travel time to work: 23.7% less than 15 minutes, 38.5% 15 to 30 minutes, 22.5% 30 to 45 minutes, 7.9% 45 to 60 minutes, 7.4% 60 minutes or more (2006-2010 5-year est.)

Additional Information Contacts
Mercer Area Chamber of Commerce . . . . (724) 662-4185
  http://www.mercerareachamber.com

PINE (township). Covers a land area of 25.410 square miles and a water area of 0.268 square miles. Located at 41.17° N. Lat; 80.06° W. Long.
Population: 4,193 (1990); 4,493 (2000); 5,150 (2010); Density: 202.7 persons per square mile (2010); Race: 91.0% White, 6.4% Black, 0.9% Asian, 0.0% American Indian/Alaska Native, 0.0% Native Hawaiian/Other Pacific Islander, 1.7% Other, 1.6% Hispanic of any race (2010); Average household size: 2.46 (2010); Median age: 43.0 (2010); Males per 100 females: 111.2 (2010); Marriage status: 23.1% never married, 61.0% now married, 9.8% widowed, 6.1% divorced (2006-2010 5-year est.); Foreign born: 2.8% (2006-2010 5-year est.); Ancestry (includes multiple ancestries): 34.0% German, 19.9% Irish, 14.1% English, 9.1% Italian, 6.9% Scotch-Irish (2006-2010 5-year est.).
Economy: Single-family building permits issued: 13 (2011); Multi-family building permits issued: 0 (2011); Employment by occupation: 15.5% management, 3.9% professional, 6.0% services, 13.6% sales, 3.4% farming, 5.0% construction, 3.8% production (2006-2010 5-year est.).
Income: Per capita income: $23,427 (2006-2010 5-year est.); Median household income: $53,383 (2006-2010 5-year est.); Average household income: $66,436 (2006-2010 5-year est.); Percent of households with income of $100,000 or more: 16.6% (2006-2010 5-year est.); Poverty rate: 6.7% (2006-2010 5-year est.).

Education: Percent of population age 25 and over with: High school diploma (including GED) or higher: 85.6% (2006-2010 5-year est.); Bachelor's degree or higher: 28.7% (2006-2010 5-year est.); Master's degree or higher: 12.1% (2006-2010 5-year est.).

Housing: Homeownership rate: 82.3% (2010); Median home value: $156,100 (2006-2010 5-year est.); Median contract rent: $493 per month (2006-2010 5-year est.); Median year structure built: 1983 (2006-2010 5-year est.).

Transportation: Commute to work: 96.0% car, 0.6% public transportation, 0.0% walk, 2.8% work from home (2006-2010 5-year est.); Travel time to work: 58.0% less than 15 minutes, 17.0% 15 to 30 minutes, 14.7% 30 to 45 minutes, 5.5% 45 to 60 minutes, 4.8% 60 minutes or more (2006-2010 5-year est.)

Additional Information Contacts
Mercer Area Chamber of Commerce . . . . (724) 662-4185
  http://www.mercerareachamber.com

PYMATUNING (township). Covers a land area of 16.157 square miles and a water area of 1.561 square miles. Located at 41.33° N. Lat; 80.42° W. Long.
Population: 3,736 (1990); 3,782 (2000); 3,281 (2010); Density: 203.1 persons per square mile (2010); Race: 97.0% White, 0.9% Black, 0.4% Asian, 0.1% American Indian/Alaska Native, 0.0% Native Hawaiian/Other Pacific Islander, 1.6% Other, 0.8% Hispanic of any race (2010); Average household size: 2.45 (2010); Median age: 41.7 (2010); Males per 100 females: 93.6 (2010); Marriage status: 21.7% never married, 52.3% now married, 9.6% widowed, 16.5% divorced (2006-2010 5-year est.); Foreign born: 0.0% (2006-2010 5-year est.); Ancestry (includes multiple ancestries): 35.1% German, 22.0% English, 18.7% Irish, 9.3% Italian, 8.9% American (2006-2010 5-year est.).
Economy: Single-family building permits issued: 3 (2011); Multi-family building permits issued: 0 (2011); Employment by occupation: 5.6% management, 1.0% professional, 12.6% services, 22.2% sales, 5.9% farming, 7.4% construction, 7.3% production (2006-2010 5-year est.).
Income: Per capita income: $20,170 (2006-2010 5-year est.); Median household income: $32,663 (2006-2010 5-year est.); Average household income: $43,558 (2006-2010 5-year est.); Percent of households with income of $100,000 or more: 8.5% (2006-2010 5-year est.); Poverty rate: 16.2% (2006-2010 5-year est.).
Education: Percent of population age 25 and over with: High school diploma (including GED) or higher: 81.1% (2006-2010 5-year est.); Bachelor's degree or higher: 10.2% (2006-2010 5-year est.); Master's degree or higher: 2.6% (2006-2010 5-year est.).
Housing: Homeownership rate: 74.3% (2010); Median home value: $82,800 (2006-2010 5-year est.); Median contract rent: $139 per month (2006-2010 5-year est.); Median year structure built: 1972 (2006-2010 5-year est.).
Safety: Violent crime rate: 15.2 per 10,000 population; Property crime rate: 440.6 per 10,000 population (2011).
Transportation: Commute to work: 100.0% car, 0.0% public transportation, 0.0% walk, 0.0% work from home (2006-2010 5-year est.); Travel time to work: 24.7% less than 15 minutes, 53.1% 15 to 30 minutes, 9.2% 30 to 45 minutes, 6.8% 45 to 60 minutes, 6.2% 60 minutes or more (2006-2010 5-year est.)
Additional Information Contacts
Shenango Valley Chamber of Commerce . . . . (724) 981-5880
  http://www.svchamber.com

REYNOLDS HEIGHTS (CDP). Covers a land area of 2.898 square miles and a water area of 0.005 square miles. Located at 41.34° N. Lat; 80.40° W. Long. Elevation is 1,073 feet.
Population: n/a (1990); n/a (2000); 2,061 (2010); Density: 711.3 persons per square mile (2010); Race: 96.5% White, 1.3% Black, 0.1% Asian, 0.0% American Indian/Alaska Native, 0.0% Native Hawaiian/Other Pacific Islander, 2.1% Other, 0.7% Hispanic of any race (2010); Average household size: 2.43 (2010); Median age: 37.9 (2010); Males per 100 females: 85.5 (2010); Marriage status: 25.9% never married, 44.4% now married, 9.5% widowed, 20.2% divorced (2006-2010 5-year est.); Foreign born: 0.0% (2006-2010 5-year est.); Ancestry (includes multiple ancestries): 39.9% German, 21.1% English, 14.3% Irish, 6.7% Italian, 5.8% American (2006-2010 5-year est.).
Economy: Employment by occupation: 6.6% management, 0.0% professional, 14.6% services, 19.8% sales, 6.8% farming, 10.0% construction, 10.3% production (2006-2010 5-year est.).

Income: Per capita income: $18,561 (2006-2010 5-year est.); Median household income: $30,526 (2006-2010 5-year est.); Average household income: $39,179 (2006-2010 5-year est.); Percent of households with income of $100,000 or more: 7.3% (2006-2010 5-year est.); Poverty rate: 17.2% (2006-2010 5-year est.).

Education: Percent of population age 25 and over with: High school diploma (including GED) or higher: 80.9% (2006-2010 5-year est.); Bachelor's degree or higher: 11.3% (2006-2010 5-year est.); Master's degree or higher: 3.1% (2006-2010 5-year est.).

Housing: Homeownership rate: 66.4% (2010); Median home value: $76,800 (2006-2010 5-year est.); Median contract rent: <$101 per month (2006-2010 5-year est.); Median year structure built: 1973 (2006-2010 5-year est.).

Transportation: Commute to work: 100.0% car, 0.0% public transportation, 0.0% walk, 0.0% work from home (2006-2010 5-year est.); Travel time to work: 23.6% less than 15 minutes, 55.0% 15 to 30 minutes, 13.4% 30 to 45 minutes, 4.1% 45 to 60 minutes, 4.0% 60 minutes or more (2006-2010 5-year est.)

SALEM (township). Aka Leechs Corners. Covers a land area of 13.363 square miles and a water area of 0.027 square miles. Located at 41.45° N. Lat; 80.30° W. Long. Elevation is 991 feet.

Population: 678 (1990); 769 (2000); 754 (2010); Density: 56.4 persons per square mile (2010); Race: 96.4% White, 1.7% Black, 0.1% Asian, 0.0% American Indian/Alaska Native, 0.0% Native Hawaiian/Other Pacific Islander, 1.8% Other, 0.9% Hispanic of any race (2010); Average household size: 2.66 (2010); Median age: 43.4 (2010); Males per 100 females: 95.8 (2010); Marriage status: 19.0% never married, 64.8% now married, 7.0% widowed, 9.2% divorced (2006-2010 5-year est.); Foreign born: 1.1% (2006-2010 5-year est.); Ancestry (includes multiple ancestries): 36.9% German, 19.5% Irish, 12.9% English, 9.4% Pennsylvania German, 6.0% American (2006-2010 5-year est.).

Economy: Single-family building permits issued: 2 (2011); Multi-family building permits issued: 0 (2011); Employment by occupation: 7.7% management, 2.7% professional, 14.7% services, 14.7% sales, 4.1% farming, 15.9% construction, 10.9% production (2006-2010 5-year est.).

Income: Per capita income: $21,377 (2006-2010 5-year est.); Median household income: $48,833 (2006-2010 5-year est.); Average household income: $54,534 (2006-2010 5-year est.); Percent of households with income of $100,000 or more: 8.9% (2006-2010 5-year est.); Poverty rate: 9.0% (2006-2010 5-year est.).

Education: Percent of population age 25 and over with: High school diploma (including GED) or higher: 91.4% (2006-2010 5-year est.); Bachelor's degree or higher: 14.0% (2006-2010 5-year est.); Master's degree or higher: 4.1% (2006-2010 5-year est.).

Housing: Homeownership rate: 85.8% (2010); Median home value: $122,600 (2006-2010 5-year est.); Median contract rent: $300 per month (2006-2010 5-year est.); Median year structure built: 1976 (2006-2010 5-year est.).

Transportation: Commute to work: 90.1% car, 0.0% public transportation, 4.5% walk, 3.6% work from home (2006-2010 5-year est.); Travel time to work: 26.0% less than 15 minutes, 39.9% 15 to 30 minutes, 13.9% 30 to 45 minutes, 10.2% 45 to 60 minutes, 9.9% 60 minutes or more (2006-2010 5-year est.)

SANDY CREEK (township). Covers a land area of 15.787 square miles and a water area of 0.255 square miles. Located at 41.45° N. Lat; 80.22° W. Long.

Population: 817 (1990); 848 (2000); 795 (2010); Density: 50.4 persons per square mile (2010); Race: 98.6% White, 0.3% Black, 0.1% Asian, 0.0% American Indian/Alaska Native, 0.0% Native Hawaiian/Other Pacific Islander, 1.0% Other, 0.1% Hispanic of any race (2010); Average household size: 2.48 (2010); Median age: 43.9 (2010); Males per 100 females: 103.3 (2010); Marriage status: 24.5% never married, 59.8% now married, 3.7% widowed, 12.0% divorced (2006-2010 5-year est.); Foreign born: 0.0% (2006-2010 5-year est.); Ancestry (includes multiple ancestries): 36.5% German, 24.3% Irish, 17.5% English, 6.9% Italian, 6.8% American (2006-2010 5-year est.).

Economy: Single-family building permits issued: 0 (2011); Multi-family building permits issued: 0 (2011); Employment by occupation: 9.4% management, 1.1% professional, 9.4% services, 9.7% sales, 0.0% farming, 17.1% construction, 5.4% production (2006-2010 5-year est.).

Income: Per capita income: $20,607 (2006-2010 5-year est.); Median household income: $43,500 (2006-2010 5-year est.); Average household income: $50,311 (2006-2010 5-year est.); Percent of households with

income of $100,000 or more: 10.2% (2006-2010 5-year est.); Poverty rate: 10.3% (2006-2010 5-year est.).

Education: Percent of population age 25 and over with: High school diploma (including GED) or higher: 86.2% (2006-2010 5-year est.); Bachelor's degree or higher: 10.4% (2006-2010 5-year est.); Master's degree or higher: 1.1% (2006-2010 5-year est.).

Housing: Homeownership rate: 86.6% (2010); Median home value: $100,800 (2006-2010 5-year est.); Median contract rent: $366 per month (2006-2010 5-year est.); Median year structure built: 1967 (2006-2010 5-year est.).

Transportation: Commute to work: 92.8% car, 0.0% public transportation, 0.0% walk, 7.2% work from home (2006-2010 5-year est.); Travel time to work: 23.8% less than 15 minutes, 39.4% 15 to 30 minutes, 15.0% 30 to 45 minutes, 5.9% 45 to 60 minutes, 15.9% 60 minutes or more (2006-2010 5-year est.)

SANDY LAKE (borough). Covers a land area of 0.832 square miles and a water area of 0 square miles. Located at 41.35° N. Lat; 80.08° W. Long. Elevation is 1,158 feet.

Population: 713 (1990); 743 (2000); 659 (2010); Density: 791.9 persons per square mile (2010); Race: 97.6% White, 0.6% Black, 0.3% Asian, 0.2% American Indian/Alaska Native, 0.0% Native Hawaiian/Other Pacific Islander, 1.3% Other, 0.3% Hispanic of any race (2010); Average household size: 2.41 (2010); Median age: 37.3 (2010); Males per 100 females: 89.4 (2010); Marriage status: 27.0% never married, 61.1% now married, 4.3% widowed, 7.6% divorced (2006-2010 5-year est.); Foreign born: 1.0% (2006-2010 5-year est.); Ancestry (includes multiple ancestries): 33.9% German, 19.8% Irish, 19.3% English, 9.2% American, 8.2% Italian (2006-2010 5-year est.).

Economy: Single-family building permits issued: 1 (2011); Multi-family building permits issued: 0 (2011); Employment by occupation: 7.5% management, 5.6% professional, 11.5% services, 15.1% sales, 0.0% farming, 9.9% construction, 6.7% production (2006-2010 5-year est.).

Income: Per capita income: $21,451 (2006-2010 5-year est.); Median household income: $46,136 (2006-2010 5-year est.); Average household income: $52,865 (2006-2010 5-year est.); Percent of households with income of $100,000 or more: 6.3% (2006-2010 5-year est.); Poverty rate: 21.3% (2006-2010 5-year est.).

Education: Percent of population age 25 and over with: High school diploma (including GED) or higher: 93.0% (2006-2010 5-year est.); Bachelor's degree or higher: 22.2% (2006-2010 5-year est.); Master's degree or higher: 7.0% (2006-2010 5-year est.).

Housing: Homeownership rate: 66.1% (2010); Median home value: $95,500 (2006-2010 5-year est.); Median contract rent: $293 per month (2006-2010 5-year est.); Median year structure built: 1955 (2006-2010 5-year est.).

Transportation: Commute to work: 89.4% car, 4.1% public transportation, 2.9% walk, 2.4% work from home (2006-2010 5-year est.); Travel time to work: 31.0% less than 15 minutes, 33.1% 15 to 30 minutes, 20.1% 30 to 45 minutes, 5.9% 45 to 60 minutes, 10.0% 60 minutes or more (2006-2010 5-year est.)

SANDY LAKE (township). Covers a land area of 24.379 square miles and a water area of 0.252 square miles. Located at 41.34° N. Lat; 80.05° W. Long. Elevation is 1,158 feet.

Population: 1,170 (1990); 1,248 (2000); 1,226 (2010); Density: 50.3 persons per square mile (2010); Race: 98.6% White, 0.2% Black, 0.5% Asian, 0.2% American Indian/Alaska Native, 0.0% Native Hawaiian/Other Pacific Islander, 0.5% Other, 0.7% Hispanic of any race (2010); Average household size: 2.49 (2010); Median age: 45.8 (2010); Males per 100 females: 95.5 (2010); Marriage status: 21.2% never married, 67.0% now married, 5.7% widowed, 6.1% divorced (2006-2010 5-year est.); Foreign born: 1.1% (2006-2010 5-year est.); Ancestry (includes multiple ancestries): 27.4% German, 16.8% Irish, 14.0% English, 10.3% Italian, 5.9% American (2006-2010 5-year est.).

Economy: Single-family building permits issued: 3 (2011); Multi-family building permits issued: 0 (2011); Employment by occupation: 3.6% management, 3.6% professional, 8.4% services, 21.0% sales, 5.7% farming, 9.7% construction, 4.5% production (2006-2010 5-year est.).

Income: Per capita income: $20,488 (2006-2010 5-year est.); Median household income: $45,724 (2006-2010 5-year est.); Average household income: $53,530 (2006-2010 5-year est.); Percent of households with income of $100,000 or more: 11.3% (2006-2010 5-year est.); Poverty rate: 15.1% (2006-2010 5-year est.).

Education: Percent of population age 25 and over with: High school diploma (including GED) or higher: 91.9% (2006-2010 5-year est.); Bachelor's degree or higher: 14.0% (2006-2010 5-year est.); Master's degree or higher: 6.5% (2006-2010 5-year est.).

Housing: Homeownership rate: 86.2% (2010); Median home value: $117,400 (2006-2010 5-year est.); Median contract rent: $450 per month (2006-2010 5-year est.); Median year structure built: 1971 (2006-2010 5-year est.).

Transportation: Commute to work: 93.9% car, 0.5% public transportation, 0.9% walk, 3.2% work from home (2006-2010 5-year est.); Travel time to work: 26.8% less than 15 minutes, 39.3% 15 to 30 minutes, 21.6% 30 to 45 minutes, 5.4% 45 to 60 minutes, 6.9% 60 minutes or more (2006-2010 5-year est.)

Additional Information Contacts

Mercer Area Chamber of Commerce . . . . (724) 662-4185
   http://www.mercerareachamber.com

SHARON (city). Covers a land area of 3.770 square miles and a water area of 0 square miles. Located at 41.23° N. Lat; 80.50° W. Long. Elevation is 1,001 feet.

History: A mill, erected on the banks of the Shenango River in 1802, became the nucleus of a settlement that was named, probably, by some Bible-reading pioneer who likened its flat topography to the plain of Sharon in Palestine. Completion of the Lake Erie extension of the Pennsylvania Canal in 1844 attracted the Sharon Furnace, and after the advent of the railroad the town began to grow industrially. A large Italian settlement dates from about 1885

Population: 17,476 (1990); 16,328 (2000); 14,038 (2010); Density: 3,724.0 persons per square mile (2010); Race: 80.4% White, 14.6% Black, 0.5% Asian, 0.2% American Indian/Alaska Native, 0.0% Native Hawaiian/Other Pacific Islander, 4.3% Other, 1.8% Hispanic of any race (2010); Average household size: 2.29 (2010); Median age: 39.8 (2010); Males per 100 females: 88.8 (2010); Marriage status: 29.7% never married, 48.0% now married, 8.1% widowed, 14.3% divorced (2006-2010 5-year est.); Foreign born: 1.4% (2006-2010 5-year est.); Ancestry (includes multiple ancestries): 30.6% German, 16.2% Irish, 15.9% Italian, 6.8% English, 6.0% Polish (2006-2010 5-year est.).

Economy: Single-family building permits issued: 0 (2011); Multi-family building permits issued: 0 (2011); Employment by occupation: 6.8% management, 2.2% professional, 14.9% services, 19.1% sales, 3.8% farming, 5.6% construction, 4.3% production (2006-2010 5-year est.).

Income: Per capita income: $17,596 (2006-2010 5-year est.); Median household income: $29,411 (2006-2010 5-year est.); Average household income: $39,305 (2006-2010 5-year est.); Percent of households with income of $100,000 or more: 6.3% (2006-2010 5-year est.); Poverty rate: 23.8% (2006-2010 5-year est.).

Education: Percent of population age 25 and over with: High school diploma (including GED) or higher: 86.9% (2006-2010 5-year est.); Bachelor's degree or higher: 15.6% (2006-2010 5-year est.); Master's degree or higher: 6.0% (2006-2010 5-year est.).

School District(s)

Sharon City SD (KG-12)
   2010-11 Enrollment: 2,099 . . . . (724) 983-4000

Four-year College(s)

Pennsylvania State University-Penn State Shenango (Public)
   Fall 2010 Enrollment: 588 . . . . (724) 983-2803
   2011-12 Tuition: In-state $12,994; Out-of-state $19,434

Two-year College(s)

Laurel Technical Institute (Private, For-profit)
   Fall 2010 Enrollment: 470 . . . . (724) 983-0700
   2011-12 Tuition: In-state $9,079; Out-of-state $9,079

Vocational/Technical School(s)

Sharon Regional Health System School of Nursing (Private, Not-for-profit)
   Fall 2010 Enrollment: 81 . . . . (724) 983-3988

Housing: Homeownership rate: 57.2% (2010); Median home value: $65,200 (2006-2010 5-year est.); Median contract rent: $393 per month (2006-2010 5-year est.); Median year structure built: 1941 (2006-2010 5-year est.).

Hospitals: Sharon Regional Health System (240 beds)

Safety: Violent crime rate: 60.4 per 10,000 population; Property crime rate: 409.0 per 10,000 population (2011).

Newspapers: The Herald (Local news; Circulation 20,907)

Transportation: Commute to work: 94.1% car, 0.0% public transportation, 2.5% walk, 2.2% work from home (2006-2010 5-year est.); Travel time to work: 61.3% less than 15 minutes, 23.0% 15 to 30 minutes, 11.3% 30 to 45 minutes, 2.1% 45 to 60 minutes, 2.3% 60 minutes or more (2006-2010 5-year est.)

Additional Information Contacts

City of Sharon . . . . (724) 983-3232
   http://www.cityofsharon.net
Shenango Valley Chamber of Commerce . . . . (724) 981-5880
   http://www.svchamber.com

SHARPSVILLE (borough). Covers a land area of 1.391 square miles and a water area of 0.012 square miles. Located at 41.26° N. Lat; 80.48° W. Long. Elevation is 1,030 feet.

History: Settled 1798, incorporated 1874.

Population: 4,729 (1990); 4,500 (2000); 4,415 (2010); Density: 3,174.0 persons per square mile (2010); Race: 95.3% White, 2.2% Black, 0.5% Asian, 0.1% American Indian/Alaska Native, 0.0% Native Hawaiian/Other Pacific Islander, 1.9% Other, 0.8% Hispanic of any race (2010); Average household size: 2.35 (2010); Median age: 40.4 (2010); Males per 100 females: 91.7 (2010); Marriage status: 25.7% never married, 60.5% now married, 6.5% widowed, 7.3% divorced (2006-2010 5-year est.); Foreign born: 1.4% (2006-2010 5-year est.); Ancestry (includes multiple ancestries): 34.0% German, 26.7% Italian, 17.5% Irish, 11.3% English, 7.9% Polish (2006-2010 5-year est.).

Economy: Single-family building permits issued: 0 (2011); Multi-family building permits issued: 0 (2011); Employment by occupation: 4.2% management, 2.3% professional, 11.9% services, 17.3% sales, 5.0% farming, 5.7% construction, 7.8% production (2006-2010 5-year est.).

Income: Per capita income: $21,529 (2006-2010 5-year est.); Median household income: $46,294 (2006-2010 5-year est.); Average household income: $52,620 (2006-2010 5-year est.); Percent of households with income of $100,000 or more: 13.0% (2006-2010 5-year est.); Poverty rate: 10.8% (2006-2010 5-year est.).

Education: Percent of population age 25 and over with: High school diploma (including GED) or higher: 90.1% (2006-2010 5-year est.); Bachelor's degree or higher: 19.8% (2006-2010 5-year est.); Master's degree or higher: 5.3% (2006-2010 5-year est.).

School District(s)

Sharpsville Area SD (KG-12)
   2010-11 Enrollment: 1,336 . . . . (724) 962-7874

Housing: Homeownership rate: 65.9% (2010); Median home value: $82,200 (2006-2010 5-year est.); Median contract rent: $474 per month (2006-2010 5-year est.); Median year structure built: 1945 (2006-2010 5-year est.).

Safety: Violent crime rate: 72.3 per 10,000 population; Property crime rate: 167.1 per 10,000 population (2011).

Transportation: Commute to work: 95.3% car, 0.0% public transportation, 1.7% walk, 2.9% work from home (2006-2010 5-year est.); Travel time to work: 54.0% less than 15 minutes, 25.3% 15 to 30 minutes, 12.1% 30 to 45 minutes, 3.9% 45 to 60 minutes, 4.6% 60 minutes or more (2006-2010 5-year est.)

Additional Information Contacts

Mercer Area Chamber of Commerce . . . . (724) 662-4185
   http://www.mercerareachamber.com

SHEAKLEYVILLE (borough). Covers a land area of 0.196 square miles and a water area of 0 square miles. Located at 41.44° N. Lat; 80.21° W. Long. Elevation is 1,283 feet.

Population: 134 (1990); 164 (2000); 142 (2010); Density: 723.2 persons per square mile (2010); Race: 100.0% White, 0.0% Black, 0.0% Asian, 0.0% American Indian/Alaska Native, 0.0% Native Hawaiian/Other Pacific Islander, 0.0% Other, 0.0% Hispanic of any race (2010); Average household size: 2.22 (2010); Median age: 44.7 (2010); Males per 100 females: 108.8 (2010); Marriage status: 33.3% never married, 43.0% now married, 8.9% widowed, 14.8% divorced (2006-2010 5-year est.); Foreign born: 0.0% (2006-2010 5-year est.); Ancestry (includes multiple ancestries): 32.7% German, 19.0% English, 11.1% Irish, 10.5% Hungarian, 5.9% Italian (2006-2010 5-year est.).

Economy: Employment by occupation: 9.4% management, 3.8% professional, 10.4% services, 6.6% sales, 6.6% farming, 9.4% construction, 11.3% production (2006-2010 5-year est.).

Income: Per capita income: $27,312 (2006-2010 5-year est.); Median household income: $51,250 (2006-2010 5-year est.); Average household income: $57,319 (2006-2010 5-year est.); Percent of households with income of $100,000 or more: 5.6% (2006-2010 5-year est.); Poverty rate: 1.3% (2006-2010 5-year est.).

Education: Percent of population age 25 and over with: High school diploma (including GED) or higher: 92.2% (2006-2010 5-year est.); Bachelor's degree or higher: 11.3% (2006-2010 5-year est.); Master's degree or higher: 7.8% (2006-2010 5-year est.).

Housing: Homeownership rate: 71.9% (2010); Median home value: $76,400 (2006-2010 5-year est.); Median contract rent: $384 per month (2006-2010 5-year est.); Median year structure built: 1940 (2006-2010 5-year est.).

Transportation: Commute to work: 85.7% car, 0.0% public transportation, 3.1% walk, 3.1% work from home (2006-2010 5-year est.); Travel time to work: 42.1% less than 15 minutes, 30.5% 15 to 30 minutes, 22.1% 30 to 45 minutes, 3.2% 45 to 60 minutes, 2.1% 60 minutes or more (2006-2010 5-year est.)

SHENANGO (township). Covers a land area of 30.241 square miles and a water area of 0.056 square miles. Located at 41.15° N. Lat; 80.46° W. Long. Elevation is 978 feet.

Population: 4,339 (1990); 4,037 (2000); 3,929 (2010); Density: 129.9 persons per square mile (2010); Race: 97.3% White, 1.3% Black, 0.3% Asian, 0.1% American Indian/Alaska Native, 0.0% Native Hawaiian/Other Pacific Islander, 1.0% Other, 0.6% Hispanic of any race (2010); Average household size: 2.42 (2010); Median age: 45.9 (2010); Males per 100 females: 99.0 (2010); Marriage status: 20.1% never married, 63.9% now married, 4.4% widowed, 11.6% divorced (2006-2010 5-year est.); Foreign born: 1.4% (2006-2010 5-year est.); Ancestry (includes multiple ancestries): 28.2% German, 24.9% Italian, 20.2% Irish, 10.8% Polish, 9.8% Welsh (2006-2010 5-year est.).

Economy: Single-family building permits issued: 0 (2011); Multi-family building permits issued: 0 (2011); Employment by occupation: 4.9% management, 0.7% professional, 11.9% services, 15.9% sales, 1.6% farming, 11.2% construction, 3.5% production (2006-2010 5-year est.).

Income: Per capita income: $25,884 (2006-2010 5-year est.); Median household income: $48,333 (2006-2010 5-year est.); Average household income: $62,565 (2006-2010 5-year est.); Percent of households with income of $100,000 or more: 12.2% (2006-2010 5-year est.); Poverty rate: 9.8% (2006-2010 5-year est.).

Education: Percent of population age 25 and over with: High school diploma (including GED) or higher: 86.2% (2006-2010 5-year est.); Bachelor's degree or higher: 18.4% (2006-2010 5-year est.); Master's degree or higher: 6.1% (2006-2010 5-year est.).

Housing: Homeownership rate: 83.0% (2010); Median home value: $129,400 (2006-2010 5-year est.); Median contract rent: $500 per month (2006-2010 5-year est.); Median year structure built: 1971 (2006-2010 5-year est.).

Transportation: Commute to work: 95.8% car, 0.0% public transportation, 0.0% walk, 4.2% work from home (2006-2010 5-year est.); Travel time to work: 40.2% less than 15 minutes, 42.2% 15 to 30 minutes, 15.1% 30 to 45 minutes, 0.9% 45 to 60 minutes, 1.6% 60 minutes or more (2006-2010 5-year est.)

Additional Information Contacts

Mercer Area Chamber of Commerce . . . . (724) 662-4185
    http://www.mercerareachamber.com

SOUTH PYMATUNING (township). Covers a land area of 19.563 square miles and a water area of 2.063 square miles. Located at 41.32° N. Lat; 80.49° W. Long.

Population: 2,775 (1990); 2,857 (2000); 2,695 (2010); Density: 137.8 persons per square mile (2010); Race: 97.6% White, 0.9% Black, 0.3% Asian, 0.0% American Indian/Alaska Native, 0.0% Native Hawaiian/Other Pacific Islander, 1.2% Other, 0.3% Hispanic of any race (2010); Average household size: 2.43 (2010); Median age: 46.3 (2010); Males per 100 females: 94.0 (2010); Marriage status: 16.9% never married, 67.0% now married, 8.1% widowed, 8.0% divorced (2006-2010 5-year est.); Foreign born: 0.6% (2006-2010 5-year est.); Ancestry (includes multiple ancestries): 28.2% German, 24.8% Italian, 19.1% Irish, 12.1% Slovak, 9.4% English (2006-2010 5-year est.).

Economy: Single-family building permits issued: 0 (2011); Multi-family building permits issued: 0 (2011); Employment by occupation: 13.3% management, 3.2% professional, 7.8% services, 17.8% sales, 0.6% farming, 10.3% construction, 5.6% production (2006-2010 5-year est.).

Income: Per capita income: $25,185 (2006-2010 5-year est.); Median household income: $50,750 (2006-2010 5-year est.); Average household income: $61,215 (2006-2010 5-year est.); Percent of households with income of $100,000 or more: 16.8% (2006-2010 5-year est.); Poverty rate: 4.3% (2006-2010 5-year est.).

Education: Percent of population age 25 and over with: High school diploma (including GED) or higher: 91.1% (2006-2010 5-year est.); Bachelor's degree or higher: 19.4% (2006-2010 5-year est.); Master's degree or higher: 4.9% (2006-2010 5-year est.).

Housing: Homeownership rate: 87.1% (2010); Median home value: $118,400 (2006-2010 5-year est.); Median contract rent: $425 per month (2006-2010 5-year est.); Median year structure built: 1962 (2006-2010 5-year est.).

Safety: Violent crime rate: 11.1 per 10,000 population; Property crime rate: 85.1 per 10,000 population (2011).

Transportation: Commute to work: 95.0% car, 0.0% public transportation, 1.2% walk, 3.4% work from home (2006-2010 5-year est.); Travel time to work: 38.7% less than 15 minutes, 40.8% 15 to 30 minutes, 10.0% 30 to 45 minutes, 5.7% 45 to 60 minutes, 4.9% 60 minutes or more (2006-2010 5-year est.)

Additional Information Contacts

Shenango Valley Chamber of Commerce . . . . (724) 981-5880
    http://www.svchamber.com

SPRINGFIELD (township). Covers a land area of 27.364 square miles and a water area of 0.143 square miles. Located at 41.15° N. Lat; 80.20° W. Long.

Population: 1,892 (1990); 1,972 (2000); 1,981 (2010); Density: 72.4 persons per square mile (2010); Race: 98.5% White, 0.8% Black, 0.2% Asian, 0.2% American Indian/Alaska Native, 0.0% Native Hawaiian/Other Pacific Islander, 0.3% Other, 0.8% Hispanic of any race (2010); Average household size: 2.66 (2010); Median age: 41.3 (2010); Males per 100 females: 105.9 (2010); Marriage status: 20.5% never married, 65.8% now married, 5.5% widowed, 8.1% divorced (2006-2010 5-year est.); Foreign born: 0.6% (2006-2010 5-year est.); Ancestry (includes multiple ancestries): 35.1% German, 16.7% Irish, 11.3% Italian, 10.2% English, 7.9% American (2006-2010 5-year est.).

Economy: Single-family building permits issued: 5 (2011); Multi-family building permits issued: 0 (2011); Employment by occupation: 8.6% management, 2.0% professional, 9.8% services, 15.6% sales, 2.1% farming, 14.7% construction, 6.2% production (2006-2010 5-year est.).

Income: Per capita income: $26,896 (2006-2010 5-year est.); Median household income: $53,354 (2006-2010 5-year est.); Average household income: $69,138 (2006-2010 5-year est.); Percent of households with income of $100,000 or more: 18.7% (2006-2010 5-year est.); Poverty rate: 9.9% (2006-2010 5-year est.).

Education: Percent of population age 25 and over with: High school diploma (including GED) or higher: 84.1% (2006-2010 5-year est.); Bachelor's degree or higher: 21.4% (2006-2010 5-year est.); Master's degree or higher: 9.8% (2006-2010 5-year est.).

Housing: Homeownership rate: 85.9% (2010); Median home value: $133,700 (2006-2010 5-year est.); Median contract rent: $421 per month (2006-2010 5-year est.); Median year structure built: 1963 (2006-2010 5-year est.).

Transportation: Commute to work: 90.1% car, 0.0% public transportation, 1.0% walk, 8.5% work from home (2006-2010 5-year est.); Travel time to work: 31.0% less than 15 minutes, 35.0% 15 to 30 minutes, 20.5% 30 to 45 minutes, 9.8% 45 to 60 minutes, 3.7% 60 minutes or more (2006-2010 5-year est.)

Additional Information Contacts

Mercer Area Chamber of Commerce . . . . (724) 662-4185
    http://www.mercerareachamber.com
Springfield Township . . . . (724) 748-4999
    http://www.mcrpc.com/SPRINGFIELD/index.htm

STONEBORO (borough). Covers a land area of 2.834 square miles and a water area of 0.104 square miles. Located at 41.33° N. Lat; 80.12° W. Long. Elevation is 1,178 feet.

History: Incorporated 1866.

Population: 1,091 (1990); 1,104 (2000); 1,051 (2010); Density: 370.9 persons per square mile (2010); Race: 98.3% White, 0.0% Black, 0.2% Asian, 0.1% American Indian/Alaska Native, 0.0% Native Hawaiian/Other Pacific Islander, 1.4% Other, 0.8% Hispanic of any race (2010); Average household size: 2.24 (2010); Median age: 42.8 (2010); Males per 100 females: 95.0 (2010); Marriage status: 23.4% never married, 54.7% now married, 8.8% widowed, 13.2% divorced (2006-2010 5-year est.); Foreign born: 0.0% (2006-2010 5-year est.); Ancestry (includes multiple ancestries): 36.2% German, 23.9% Irish, 14.6% English, 9.9% Italian, 7.3% American (2006-2010 5-year est.).

Economy: Single-family building permits issued: 0 (2011); Multi-family building permits issued: 0 (2011); Employment by occupation: 5.0% management, 1.5% professional, 14.5% services, 20.3% sales, 3.1% farming, 12.4% construction, 4.4% production (2006-2010 5-year est.).
Income: Per capita income: $20,894 (2006-2010 5-year est.); Median household income: $41,750 (2006-2010 5-year est.); Average household income: $47,789 (2006-2010 5-year est.); Percent of households with income of $100,000 or more: 5.3% (2006-2010 5-year est.); Poverty rate: 6.7% (2006-2010 5-year est.).
Education: Percent of population age 25 and over with: High school diploma (including GED) or higher: 90.7% (2006-2010 5-year est.); Bachelor's degree or higher: 15.0% (2006-2010 5-year est.); Master's degree or higher: 4.0% (2006-2010 5-year est.).

School District(s)

Lakeview SD (PK-12)
   2010-11 Enrollment: 1,260 . . . . (724) 376-7911
Housing: Homeownership rate: 69.1% (2010); Median home value: $82,500 (2006-2010 5-year est.); Median contract rent: $362 per month (2006-2010 5-year est.); Median year structure built: 1940 (2006-2010 5-year est.).
Transportation: Commute to work: 96.1% car, 0.6% public transportation, 1.6% walk, 1.8% work from home (2006-2010 5-year est.); Travel time to work: 17.1% less than 15 minutes, 43.5% 15 to 30 minutes, 24.7% 30 to 45 minutes, 7.8% 45 to 60 minutes, 7.0% 60 minutes or more (2006-2010 5-year est.)

SUGAR GROVE (township). Covers a land area of 12.391 square miles and a water area of 0.007 square miles. Located at 41.46° N. Lat; 80.35° W. Long.

Population: 987 (1990); 909 (2000); 971 (2010); Density: 78.4 persons per square mile (2010); Race: 97.3% White, 0.6% Black, 0.8% Asian, 0.4% American Indian/Alaska Native, 0.0% Native Hawaiian/Other Pacific Islander, 0.9% Other, 0.6% Hispanic of any race (2010); Average household size: 2.46 (2010); Median age: 47.5 (2010); Males per 100 females: 96.6 (2010); Marriage status: 25.9% never married, 60.4% now married, 6.1% widowed, 7.6% divorced (2006-2010 5-year est.); Foreign born: 0.4% (2006-2010 5-year est.); Ancestry (includes multiple ancestries): 35.1% German, 14.3% Irish, 13.3% Pennsylvania German, 13.0% English, 5.9% Polish (2006-2010 5-year est.).
Economy: Single-family building permits issued: 0 (2011); Multi-family building permits issued: 0 (2011); Employment by occupation: 5.2% management, 1.3% professional, 12.8% services, 14.6% sales, 5.7% farming, 8.2% construction, 10.0% production (2006-2010 5-year est.).
Income: Per capita income: $20,248 (2006-2010 5-year est.); Median household income: $49,280 (2006-2010 5-year est.); Average household income: $54,919 (2006-2010 5-year est.); Percent of households with income of $100,000 or more: 7.9% (2006-2010 5-year est.); Poverty rate: 13.6% (2006-2010 5-year est.).
Education: Percent of population age 25 and over with: High school diploma (including GED) or higher: 86.3% (2006-2010 5-year est.); Bachelor's degree or higher: 8.3% (2006-2010 5-year est.); Master's degree or higher: 1.6% (2006-2010 5-year est.).
Housing: Homeownership rate: 88.8% (2010); Median home value: $94,700 (2006-2010 5-year est.); Median contract rent: $507 per month (2006-2010 5-year est.); Median year structure built: 1967 (2006-2010 5-year est.).
Transportation: Commute to work: 86.9% car, 0.4% public transportation, 0.8% walk, 8.7% work from home (2006-2010 5-year est.); Travel time to work: 40.3% less than 15 minutes, 34.5% 15 to 30 minutes, 9.5% 30 to 45 minutes, 6.9% 45 to 60 minutes, 8.7% 60 minutes or more (2006-2010 5-year est.)

TRANSFER (unincorporated postal area)

Zip Code: 16154
   Covers a land area of 26.047 square miles and a water area of 2.758 square miles. Located at 41.32° N. Lat; 80.42° W. Long. Elevation is 1,007 feet. Population: 2,492 (2010); Density: 95.7 persons per square mile (2010); Race: 97.8% White, 0.6% Black, 0.5% Asian, 0.1% American Indian/Alaska Native, 0.0% Native Hawaiian/Other Pacific Islander, 1.0% Other, 0.8% Hispanic of any race (2010); Average household size: 2.45 (2010); Median age: 45.8 (2010); Males per 100 females: 105.8 (2010); Homeownership rate: 87.9% (2010)

WEST MIDDLESEX (borough). Covers a land area of 0.845 square miles and a water area of <.001 square miles. Located at 41.17° N. Lat; 80.46° W. Long. Elevation is 869 feet.

History: Settled 1821, laid out 1836, incorporated 1864.
Population: 982 (1990); 929 (2000); 863 (2010); Density: 1,020.8 persons per square mile (2010); Race: 96.9% White, 1.2% Black, 0.3% Asian, 0.0% American Indian/Alaska Native, 0.0% Native Hawaiian/Other Pacific Islander, 1.6% Other, 0.3% Hispanic of any race (2010); Average household size: 2.35 (2010); Median age: 43.3 (2010); Males per 100 females: 94.4 (2010); Marriage status: 23.4% never married, 54.4% now married, 9.2% widowed, 13.0% divorced (2006-2010 5-year est.); Foreign born: 1.2% (2006-2010 5-year est.); Ancestry (includes multiple ancestries): 47.9% German, 14.6% Irish, 14.4% Italian, 12.2% English, 7.4% Slovak (2006-2010 5-year est.).
Economy: Single-family building permits issued: 1 (2011); Multi-family building permits issued: 0 (2011); Employment by occupation: 5.9% management, 3.1% professional, 10.1% services, 17.8% sales, 2.1% farming, 7.7% construction, 4.9% production (2006-2010 5-year est.).
Income: Per capita income: $24,469 (2006-2010 5-year est.); Median household income: $47,500 (2006-2010 5-year est.); Average household income: $57,634 (2006-2010 5-year est.); Percent of households with income of $100,000 or more: 7.9% (2006-2010 5-year est.); Poverty rate: 9.0% (2006-2010 5-year est.).
Education: Percent of population age 25 and over with: High school diploma (including GED) or higher: 91.0% (2006-2010 5-year est.); Bachelor's degree or higher: 18.7% (2006-2010 5-year est.); Master's degree or higher: 8.4% (2006-2010 5-year est.).

School District(s)

West Middlesex Area SD (KG-12)
   2010-11 Enrollment: 1,125 . . . . (724) 634-3030
Housing: Homeownership rate: 74.5% (2010); Median home value: $91,000 (2006-2010 5-year est.); Median contract rent: $509 per month (2006-2010 5-year est.); Median year structure built: 1951 (2006-2010 5-year est.).
Transportation: Commute to work: 89.1% car, 0.7% public transportation, 2.1% walk, 4.3% work from home (2006-2010 5-year est.); Travel time to work: 56.0% less than 15 minutes, 31.1% 15 to 30 minutes, 4.9% 30 to 45 minutes, 0.7% 45 to 60 minutes, 7.2% 60 minutes or more (2006-2010 5-year est.)

WEST SALEM (township). Covers a land area of 36.882 square miles and a water area of 0.010 square miles. Located at 41.40° N. Lat; 80.45° W. Long.

Population: 3,547 (1990); 3,565 (2000); 3,538 (2010); Density: 95.9 persons per square mile (2010); Race: 98.3% White, 0.7% Black, 0.2% Asian, 0.0% American Indian/Alaska Native, 0.0% Native Hawaiian/Other Pacific Islander, 0.8% Other, 0.5% Hispanic of any race (2010); Average household size: 2.28 (2010); Median age: 50.8 (2010); Males per 100 females: 92.2 (2010); Marriage status: 16.4% never married, 59.7% now married, 15.3% widowed, 8.6% divorced (2006-2010 5-year est.); Foreign born: 0.0% (2006-2010 5-year est.); Ancestry (includes multiple ancestries): 34.3% German, 27.2% Irish, 12.9% English, 10.5% American, 7.9% Polish (2006-2010 5-year est.).
Economy: Single-family building permits issued: 8 (2011); Multi-family building permits issued: 0 (2011); Employment by occupation: 5.1% management, 0.0% professional, 17.4% services, 10.0% sales, 1.8% farming, 17.4% construction, 11.5% production (2006-2010 5-year est.).
Income: Per capita income: $23,051 (2006-2010 5-year est.); Median household income: $47,367 (2006-2010 5-year est.); Average household income: $56,159 (2006-2010 5-year est.); Percent of households with income of $100,000 or more: 10.0% (2006-2010 5-year est.); Poverty rate: 10.9% (2006-2010 5-year est.).
Education: Percent of population age 25 and over with: High school diploma (including GED) or higher: 83.2% (2006-2010 5-year est.); Bachelor's degree or higher: 12.0% (2006-2010 5-year est.); Master's degree or higher: 3.8% (2006-2010 5-year est.).
Housing: Homeownership rate: 78.4% (2010); Median home value: $95,100 (2006-2010 5-year est.); Median contract rent: $655 per month (2006-2010 5-year est.); Median year structure built: 1959 (2006-2010 5-year est.).
Safety: Violent crime rate: 2.8 per 10,000 population; Property crime rate: 118.3 per 10,000 population (2011).
Transportation: Commute to work: 94.3% car, 0.0% public transportation, 0.0% walk, 5.7% work from home (2006-2010 5-year est.); Travel time to work: 31.6% less than 15 minutes, 45.4% 15 to 30 minutes, 14.4% 30 to

45 minutes, 2.3% 45 to 60 minutes, 6.2% 60 minutes or more (2006-2010 5-year est.)

Additional Information Contacts

Mercer Area Chamber of Commerce . . . . (724) 662-4185
http://www.mercerareachamber.com

WHEATLAND (borough). Covers a land area of 0.864 square miles and a water area of 0 square miles. Located at 41.20° N. Lat; 80.50° W. Long. Elevation is 869 feet.

History: Settled 1812, incorporated 1872.

Population: 791 (1990); 748 (2000); 632 (2010); Density: 731.4 persons per square mile (2010); Race: 76.9% White, 17.7% Black, 0.3% Asian, 0.2% American Indian/Alaska Native, 0.0% Native Hawaiian/Other Pacific Islander, 4.9% Other, 2.5% Hispanic of any race (2010); Average household size: 2.01 (2010); Median age: 48.1 (2010); Males per 100 females: 84.8 (2010); Marriage status: 22.1% never married, 63.6% now married, 8.5% widowed, 5.8% divorced (2006-2010 5-year est.); Foreign born: 0.6% (2006-2010 5-year est.); Ancestry (includes multiple ancestries): 26.5% German, 20.1% Irish, 12.7% Polish, 7.8% Italian, 6.4% Slovak (2006-2010 5-year est.).

Economy: Single-family building permits issued: 0 (2011); Multi-family building permits issued: 0 (2011); Employment by occupation: 5.5% management, 0.0% professional, 28.3% services, 12.6% sales, 9.1% farming, 2.0% construction, 6.3% production (2006-2010 5-year est.).

Income: Per capita income: $16,297 (2006-2010 5-year est.); Median household income: $33,365 (2006-2010 5-year est.); Average household income: $35,112 (2006-2010 5-year est.); Percent of households with income of $100,000 or more: 1.0% (2006-2010 5-year est.); Poverty rate: 14.5% (2006-2010 5-year est.).

Education: Percent of population age 25 and over with: High school diploma (including GED) or higher: 86.9% (2006-2010 5-year est.); Bachelor's degree or higher: 11.3% (2006-2010 5-year est.); Master's degree or higher: 2.3% (2006-2010 5-year est.).

Housing: Homeownership rate: 66.6% (2010); Median home value: $45,800 (2006-2010 5-year est.); Median contract rent: $419 per month (2006-2010 5-year est.); Median year structure built: 1954 (2006-2010 5-year est.).

Transportation: Commute to work: 94.6% car, 1.2% public transportation, 0.0% walk, 2.5% work from home (2006-2010 5-year est.); Travel time to work: 58.5% less than 15 minutes, 28.8% 15 to 30 minutes, 5.9% 30 to 45 minutes, 5.5% 45 to 60 minutes, 1.3% 60 minutes or more (2006-2010 5-year est.)

WILMINGTON (township). Covers a land area of 13.045 square miles and a water area of 0.014 square miles. Located at 41.15° N. Lat; 80.32° W. Long.

Population: 1,177 (1990); 1,105 (2000); 1,415 (2010); Density: 108.5 persons per square mile (2010); Race: 98.9% White, 0.4% Black, 0.1% Asian, 0.0% American Indian/Alaska Native, 0.0% Native Hawaiian/Other Pacific Islander, 0.6% Other, 1.1% Hispanic of any race (2010); Average household size: 2.82 (2010); Median age: 36.6 (2010); Males per 100 females: 88.2 (2010); Marriage status: 21.2% never married, 70.2% now married, 6.0% widowed, 2.5% divorced (2006-2010 5-year est.); Foreign born: 0.5% (2006-2010 5-year est.); Ancestry (includes multiple ancestries): 27.3% German, 14.3% English, 14.1% Pennsylvania German, 11.0% Italian, 8.6% Irish (2006-2010 5-year est.).

Economy: Single-family building permits issued: 0 (2011); Multi-family building permits issued: 0 (2011); Employment by occupation: 7.8% management, 0.4% professional, 8.8% services, 20.1% sales, 2.5% farming, 13.6% construction, 8.5% production (2006-2010 5-year est.).

Income: Per capita income: $25,163 (2006-2010 5-year est.); Median household income: $53,839 (2006-2010 5-year est.); Average household income: $74,305 (2006-2010 5-year est.); Percent of households with income of $100,000 or more: 17.8% (2006-2010 5-year est.); Poverty rate: 11.5% (2006-2010 5-year est.).

Education: Percent of population age 25 and over with: High school diploma (including GED) or higher: 81.8% (2006-2010 5-year est.); Bachelor's degree or higher: 24.7% (2006-2010 5-year est.); Master's degree or higher: 10.0% (2006-2010 5-year est.).

Housing: Homeownership rate: 81.9% (2010); Median home value: $156,800 (2006-2010 5-year est.); Median contract rent: $473 per month (2006-2010 5-year est.); Median year structure built: 1978 (2006-2010 5-year est.).

Transportation: Commute to work: 80.9% car, 0.0% public transportation, 5.3% walk, 6.2% work from home (2006-2010 5-year est.); Travel time to

work: 32.3% less than 15 minutes, 35.7% 15 to 30 minutes, 22.3% 30 to 45 minutes, 2.6% 45 to 60 minutes, 7.0% 60 minutes or more (2006-2010 5-year est.)

Additional Information Contacts

Mercer Area Chamber of Commerce . . . . (724) 662-4185
http://www.mercerareachamber.com

WOLF CREEK (township). Covers a land area of 16.931 square miles and a water area of 0.145 square miles. Located at 41.21° N. Lat; 80.06° W. Long.

Population: 653 (1990); 729 (2000); 832 (2010); Density: 49.1 persons per square mile (2010); Race: 97.1% White, 0.6% Black, 0.1% Asian, 0.6% American Indian/Alaska Native, 0.0% Native Hawaiian/Other Pacific Islander, 1.6% Other, 1.2% Hispanic of any race (2010); Average household size: 2.65 (2010); Median age: 41.9 (2010); Males per 100 females: 96.7 (2010); Marriage status: 18.7% never married, 72.0% now married, 3.4% widowed, 5.9% divorced (2006-2010 5-year est.); Foreign born: 0.0% (2006-2010 5-year est.); Ancestry (includes multiple ancestries): 31.6% German, 16.9% Irish, 10.8% Scotch-Irish, 9.0% Polish, 8.2% American (2006-2010 5-year est.).

Economy: Single-family building permits issued: 6 (2011); Multi-family building permits issued: 0 (2011); Employment by occupation: 10.4% management, 2.2% professional, 12.6% services, 11.5% sales, 5.5% farming, 13.7% construction, 6.0% production (2006-2010 5-year est.).

Income: Per capita income: $25,681 (2006-2010 5-year est.); Median household income: $52,440 (2006-2010 5-year est.); Average household income: $66,160 (2006-2010 5-year est.); Percent of households with income of $100,000 or more: 15.8% (2006-2010 5-year est.); Poverty rate: 4.4% (2006-2010 5-year est.).

Education: Percent of population age 25 and over with: High school diploma (including GED) or higher: 92.0% (2006-2010 5-year est.); Bachelor's degree or higher: 22.8% (2006-2010 5-year est.); Master's degree or higher: 5.3% (2006-2010 5-year est.).

Housing: Homeownership rate: 88.6% (2010); Median home value: $128,600 (2006-2010 5-year est.); Median contract rent: $517 per month (2006-2010 5-year est.); Median year structure built: 1972 (2006-2010 5-year est.).

Transportation: Commute to work: 89.1% car, 0.6% public transportation, 0.0% walk, 8.6% work from home (2006-2010 5-year est.); Travel time to work: 29.3% less than 15 minutes, 47.0% 15 to 30 minutes, 8.5% 30 to 45 minutes, 4.6% 45 to 60 minutes, 10.7% 60 minutes or more (2006-2010 5-year est.)

WORTH (township). Covers a land area of 24.679 square miles and a water area of 0.174 square miles. Located at 41.27° N. Lat; 80.05° W. Long.

Population: 906 (1990); 830 (2000); 899 (2010); Density: 36.4 persons per square mile (2010); Race: 98.6% White, 0.7% Black, 0.1% Asian, 0.0% American Indian/Alaska Native, 0.0% Native Hawaiian/Other Pacific Islander, 0.6% Other, 0.3% Hispanic of any race (2010); Average household size: 2.52 (2010); Median age: 45.0 (2010); Males per 100 females: 95.9 (2010); Marriage status: 14.1% never married, 73.1% now married, 3.0% widowed, 9.8% divorced (2006-2010 5-year est.); Foreign born: 0.9% (2006-2010 5-year est.); Ancestry (includes multiple ancestries): 39.5% German, 19.6% Irish, 15.8% English, 12.3% American, 10.0% Scotch-Irish (2006-2010 5-year est.).

Economy: Single-family building permits issued: 4 (2011); Multi-family building permits issued: 0 (2011); Employment by occupation: 11.8% management, 2.4% professional, 9.9% services, 17.6% sales, 0.7% farming, 15.4% construction, 8.7% production (2006-2010 5-year est.).

Income: Per capita income: $24,300 (2006-2010 5-year est.); Median household income: $51,250 (2006-2010 5-year est.); Average household income: $54,052 (2006-2010 5-year est.); Percent of households with income of $100,000 or more: 8.2% (2006-2010 5-year est.); Poverty rate: 3.7% (2006-2010 5-year est.).

Education: Percent of population age 25 and over with: High school diploma (including GED) or higher: 89.4% (2006-2010 5-year est.); Bachelor's degree or higher: 12.7% (2006-2010 5-year est.); Master's degree or higher: 3.0% (2006-2010 5-year est.).

Housing: Homeownership rate: 84.6% (2010); Median home value: $117,500 (2006-2010 5-year est.); Median contract rent: $448 per month (2006-2010 5-year est.); Median year structure built: 1972 (2006-2010 5-year est.).

Transportation: Commute to work: 93.1% car, 0.0% public transportation, 0.5% walk, 3.1% work from home (2006-2010 5-year est.); Travel time to

work: 23.8% less than 15 minutes, 36.9% 15 to 30 minutes, 20.1% 30 to 45 minutes, 9.8% 45 to 60 minutes, 9.3% 60 minutes or more (2006-2010 5-year est.)

Mifflin County

Located in central Pennsylvania; crossed by the Jacks Mountains; drained by the Juniata River. Covers a land area of 411.031 square miles, a water area of 3.685 square miles, and is located in the Eastern Time Zone at 40.61° N. Lat., 77.62° W. Long. The county was founded in 1789. County seat is Lewistown.

Mifflin County is part of the Lewistown, PA Micropolitan Statistical Area. The entire metro area includes: Mifflin County, PA

Weather Station: Lewistown   Elevation: 459 feet

	Jan	Feb	Mar	Apr	May	Jun	Jul	Aug	Sep	Oct	Nov	Dec
High	37	40	49	62	72	80	84	83	75	64	52	40
Low	20	22	28	38	48	57	61	60	53	41	33	25
Precip	2.6	2.3	3.4	3.4	4.2	4.2	4.0	3.4	3.8	3.3	3.5	2.9
Snow	9.0	6.3	5.4	0.3	0.0	0.0	0.0	0.0	0.0	tr	0.5	4.6

High and Low temperatures in degrees Fahrenheit; Precipitation and Snow in inches

Population: 46,196 (1990); 46,486 (2000); 46,682 (2010); Race: 97.5% White, 0.6% Black, 0.4% Asian, 0.1% American Indian/Alaska Native, 0.0% Native Hawaiian/Other Pacific Islander, 1.4% Other, 1.1% Hispanic of any race (2010); Density: 113.6 persons per square mile (2010); Average household size: 2.46 (2010); Median age: 42.5 (2010); Males per 100 females: 95.8 (2010).
Religion: Six largest groups: 13.4% European Free-Church, 11.4% Methodist/Pietist, 6.2% Lutheran, 6.1% Non-Denominational, 3.1% Presbyterian-Reformed, 3.0% Holiness (2010)
Economy: Unemployment rate: 8.2% (August 2012); Total civilian labor force: 22,723 (August 2012); Leading industries: 28.0% manufacturing; 24.8% health care and social assistance; 15.7% retail trade (2010); Farms: 1,024 totaling 94,133 acres (2007); Companies that employ 500 or more persons: 2 (2010); Companies that employ 100 to 499 persons: 15 (2010); Companies that employ less than 100 persons: 915 (2010); Black-owned businesses: n/a (2007); Hispanic-owned businesses: n/a (2007); Asian-owned businesses: n/a (2007); Women-owned businesses: 963 (2007); Retail sales per capita: $11,789 (2010). Single-family building permits issued: 24 (2011); Multi-family building permits issued: 31 (2011).
Income: Per capita income: $19,085 (2006-2010 5-year est.); Median household income: $37,539 (2006-2010 5-year est.); Average household income: $46,107 (2006-2010 5-year est.); Percent of households with income of $100,000 or more: 6.4% (2006-2010 5-year est.); Poverty rate: 13.9% (2006-2010 5-year est.); Bankruptcy rate: 2.41% (2011).
Education: Percent of population age 25 and over with: High school diploma (including GED) or higher: 80.8% (2006-2010 5-year est.); Bachelor's degree or higher: 11.1% (2006-2010 5-year est.); Master's degree or higher: 3.9% (2006-2010 5-year est.).
Housing: Homeownership rate: 72.6% (2010); Median home value: $92,500 (2006-2010 5-year est.); Median contract rent: $384 per month (2006-2010 5-year est.); Median year structure built: 1958 (2006-2010 5-year est.).
Health: Birth rate: 119.5 per 10,000 population (2011); Death rate: 105.4 per 10,000 population (2011); Age-adjusted cancer mortality rate: 171.1 deaths per 100,000 population (2009); Number of physicians: 11.6 per 10,000 population (2010); Hospital beds: 26.8 per 10,000 population (2008); Hospital admissions: 1,300.3 per 10,000 population (2008).
Elections: 2012 Presidential election results: 26.1% Obama, 72.9% Romney
National and State Parks: Reeds Gap State Park
Additional Information Contacts
Mifflin County Government . . . . (717) 248-6733
   http://www.co.mifflin.pa.us

Mifflin County Communities

ALFARATA (CDP). Covers a land area of 0.559 square miles and a water area of 0 square miles. Located at 40.66° N. Lat; 77.46° W. Long. Elevation is 591 feet.
Population: n/a (1990); n/a (2000); 149 (2010); Density: 266.5 persons per square mile (2010); Race: 99.3% White, 0.0% Black, 0.0% Asian, 0.7% American Indian/Alaska Native, 0.0% Native Hawaiian/Other Pacific Islander, 0.0% Other, 0.0% Hispanic of any race (2010); Average

household size: 2.53 (2010); Median age: 43.3 (2010); Males per 100 females: 104.1 (2010); Marriage status: 6.5% never married, 80.5% now married, 13.0% widowed, 0.0% divorced (2006-2010 5-year est.); Foreign born: 0.0% (2006-2010 5-year est.); Ancestry (includes multiple ancestries): 38.8% German, 35.9% English, 13.2% American, 4.0% Scotch-Irish (2006-2010 5-year est.).
Economy: Employment by occupation: 0.0% management, 0.0% professional, 23.1% services, 21.2% sales, 0.0% farming, 28.8% construction, 0.0% production (2006-2010 5-year est.).
Income: Per capita income: $12,681 (2006-2010 5-year est.); Median household income: $46,833 (2006-2010 5-year est.); Average household income: $56,288 (2006-2010 5-year est.); Percent of households with income of $100,000 or more: n/a (2006-2010 5-year est.); Poverty rate: 0.0% (2006-2010 5-year est.).
Education: Percent of population age 25 and over with: High school diploma (including GED) or higher: 87.3% (2006-2010 5-year est.); Bachelor's degree or higher: 10.0% (2006-2010 5-year est.); Master's degree or higher: 0.0% (2006-2010 5-year est.).
Housing: Homeownership rate: 77.9% (2010); Median home value: $95,800 (2006-2010 5-year est.); Median contract rent: n/a per month (2006-2010 5-year est.); Median year structure built: before 1940 (2006-2010 5-year est.).
Transportation: Commute to work: 100.0% car, 0.0% public transportation, 0.0% walk, 0.0% work from home (2006-2010 5-year est.); Travel time to work: 50.0% less than 15 minutes, 19.2% 15 to 30 minutes, 19.2% 30 to 45 minutes, 11.5% 45 to 60 minutes, 0.0% 60 minutes or more (2006-2010 5-year est.)

ALLENSVILLE (CDP). Covers a land area of 1.967 square miles and a water area of <.001 square miles. Located at 40.53° N. Lat; 77.81° W. Long. Elevation is 968 feet.
Population: n/a (1990); n/a (2000); 503 (2010); Density: 255.8 persons per square mile (2010); Race: 98.6% White, 0.8% Black, 0.0% Asian, 0.0% American Indian/Alaska Native, 0.0% Native Hawaiian/Other Pacific Islander, 0.6% Other, 0.0% Hispanic of any race (2010); Average household size: 3.27 (2010); Median age: 29.9 (2010); Males per 100 females: 91.3 (2010); Marriage status: 34.0% never married, 57.3% now married, 8.7% widowed, 0.0% divorced (2006-2010 5-year est.); Foreign born: 0.0% (2006-2010 5-year est.); Ancestry (includes multiple ancestries): 50.1% German, 18.7% Swiss, 7.0% American, 5.2% Irish, 3.3% Swedish (2006-2010 5-year est.).
Economy: Employment by occupation: 16.1% management, 1.9% professional, 12.3% services, 7.1% sales, 2.6% farming, 23.2% construction, 6.5% production (2006-2010 5-year est.).
Income: Per capita income: $15,714 (2006-2010 5-year est.); Median household income: $39,773 (2006-2010 5-year est.); Average household income: $47,329 (2006-2010 5-year est.); Percent of households with income of $100,000 or more: 3.3% (2006-2010 5-year est.); Poverty rate: 16.2% (2006-2010 5-year est.).
Education: Percent of population age 25 and over with: High school diploma (including GED) or higher: 71.2% (2006-2010 5-year est.); Bachelor's degree or higher: 5.3% (2006-2010 5-year est.); Master's degree or higher: 2.7% (2006-2010 5-year est.).
Housing: Homeownership rate: 76.0% (2010); Median home value: $125,300 (2006-2010 5-year est.); Median contract rent: $370 per month (2006-2010 5-year est.); Median year structure built: before 1940 (2006-2010 5-year est.).
Transportation: Commute to work: 77.4% car, 0.0% public transportation, 9.0% walk, 13.5% work from home (2006-2010 5-year est.); Travel time to work: 34.3% less than 15 minutes, 37.3% 15 to 30 minutes, 7.5% 30 to 45 minutes, 5.2% 45 to 60 minutes, 15.7% 60 minutes or more (2006-2010 5-year est.)

ARMAGH (township). Covers a land area of 92.838 square miles and a water area of 0.323 square miles. Located at 40.76° N. Lat; 77.48° W. Long.
Population: 3,627 (1990); 3,988 (2000); 3,863 (2010); Density: 41.6 persons per square mile (2010); Race: 98.7% White, 0.1% Black, 0.3% Asian, 0.1% American Indian/Alaska Native, 0.0% Native Hawaiian/Other Pacific Islander, 0.8% Other, 0.2% Hispanic of any race (2010); Average household size: 2.52 (2010); Median age: 41.8 (2010); Males per 100 females: 101.4 (2010); Marriage status: 22.7% never married, 58.9% now married, 10.4% widowed, 8.0% divorced (2006-2010 5-year est.); Foreign born: 0.0% (2006-2010 5-year est.); Ancestry (includes multiple

ancestries): 42.0% German, 13.1% Irish, 9.5% Dutch, 9.4% English, 5.8% American (2006-2010 5-year est.).

Economy: Single-family building permits issued: 2 (2011); Multi-family building permits issued: 0 (2011); Employment by occupation: 10.3% management, 1.7% professional, 14.3% services, 7.9% sales, 2.4% farming, 12.9% construction, 13.2% production (2006-2010 5-year est.).

Income: Per capita income: $19,655 (2006-2010 5-year est.); Median household income: $41,169 (2006-2010 5-year est.); Average household income: $48,304 (2006-2010 5-year est.); Percent of households with income of $100,000 or more: 5.7% (2006-2010 5-year est.); Poverty rate: 13.7% (2006-2010 5-year est.).

Education: Percent of population age 25 and over with: High school diploma (including GED) or higher: 80.9% (2006-2010 5-year est.); Bachelor's degree or higher: 4.2% (2006-2010 5-year est.); Master's degree or higher: 1.7% (2006-2010 5-year est.).

Housing: Homeownership rate: 80.2% (2010); Median home value: $86,500 (2006-2010 5-year est.); Median contract rent: $365 per month (2006-2010 5-year est.); Median year structure built: 1963 (2006-2010 5-year est.).

Transportation: Commute to work: 94.8% car, 0.0% public transportation, 2.1% walk, 1.4% work from home (2006-2010 5-year est.); Travel time to work: 33.5% less than 15 minutes, 39.2% 15 to 30 minutes, 14.4% 30 to 45 minutes, 7.1% 45 to 60 minutes, 5.7% 60 minutes or more (2006-2010 5-year est.).

Additional Information Contacts

Greater Johnstown Cambria County Chamber of Commerce . . . . (814) 536-5107

　http://www.johnstownchamber.com

ATKINSON MILLS (CDP). Covers a land area of 1.019 square miles and a water area of 0.001 square miles. Located at 40.45° N. Lat; 77.80° W. Long. Elevation is 784 feet.

Population: n/a (1990); n/a (2000); 174 (2010); Density: 170.7 persons per square mile (2010); Race: 98.3% White, 0.0% Black, 0.0% Asian, 0.0% American Indian/Alaska Native, 1.7% Native Hawaiian/Other Pacific Islander, 0.0% Other, 0.0% Hispanic of any race (2010); Average household size: 2.85 (2010); Median age: 38.3 (2010); Males per 100 females: 93.3 (2010); Marriage status: 19.2% never married, 76.2% now married, 0.0% widowed, 4.6% divorced (2006-2010 5-year est.); Foreign born: 0.0% (2006-2010 5-year est.); Ancestry (includes multiple ancestries): 38.2% German, 21.1% American, 17.2% Irish, 10.3% Italian, 10.3% Dutch (2006-2010 5-year est.).

Economy: Employment by occupation: 5.8% management, 0.0% professional, 13.6% services, 0.0% sales, 0.0% farming, 5.8% construction, 31.1% production (2006-2010 5-year est.).

Income: Per capita income: $21,656 (2006-2010 5-year est.); Median household income: $62,857 (2006-2010 5-year est.); Average household income: $60,654 (2006-2010 5-year est.); Percent of households with income of $100,000 or more: 6.8% (2006-2010 5-year est.); Poverty rate: 2.6% (2006-2010 5-year est.).

Education: Percent of population age 25 and over with: High school diploma (including GED) or higher: 100.0% (2006-2010 5-year est.); Bachelor's degree or higher: 7.1% (2006-2010 5-year est.); Master's degree or higher: 0.0% (2006-2010 5-year est.).

Housing: Homeownership rate: 95.1% (2010); Median home value: $94,000 (2006-2010 5-year est.); Median contract rent: n/a per month (2006-2010 5-year est.); Median year structure built: 1973 (2006-2010 5-year est.).

Transportation: Commute to work: 100.0% car, 0.0% public transportation, 0.0% walk, 0.0% work from home (2006-2010 5-year est.); Travel time to work: 10.7% less than 15 minutes, 33.0% 15 to 30 minutes, 52.4% 30 to 45 minutes, 0.0% 45 to 60 minutes, 3.9% 60 minutes or more (2006-2010 5-year est.)

BARRVILLE (CDP). Covers a land area of 0.704 square miles and a water area of <.001 square miles. Located at 40.67° N. Lat; 77.68° W. Long. Elevation is 883 feet.

Population: n/a (1990); n/a (2000); 160 (2010); Density: 227.1 persons per square mile (2010); Race: 98.8% White, 0.6% Black, 0.6% Asian, 0.0% American Indian/Alaska Native, 0.0% Native Hawaiian/Other Pacific Islander, 0.0% Other, 0.0% Hispanic of any race (2010); Average household size: 3.56 (2010); Median age: 25.0 (2010); Males per 100 females: 97.5 (2010); Marriage status: 0.0% never married, 68.2% now married, 20.2% widowed, 11.6% divorced (2006-2010 5-year est.); Foreign born: 0.0% (2006-2010 5-year est.); Ancestry (includes multiple

ancestries): 28.7% Dutch, 13.2% English, 9.3% American, 7.0% German, 6.2% Scottish (2006-2010 5-year est.).

Economy: Employment by occupation: 0.0% management, 0.0% professional, 0.0% services, 30.7% sales, 0.0% farming, 0.0% construction, 0.0% production (2006-2010 5-year est.).

Income: Per capita income: $17,405 (2006-2010 5-year est.); Median household income: $38,750 (2006-2010 5-year est.); Average household income: $32,332 (2006-2010 5-year est.); Percent of households with income of $100,000 or more: n/a (2006-2010 5-year est.); Poverty rate: 0.0% (2006-2010 5-year est.).

Education: Percent of population age 25 and over with: High school diploma (including GED) or higher: 50.0% (2006-2010 5-year est.); Bachelor's degree or higher: 0.0% (2006-2010 5-year est.); Master's degree or higher: 0.0% (2006-2010 5-year est.).

Housing: Homeownership rate: 84.5% (2010); Median home value: $78,100 (2006-2010 5-year est.); Median contract rent: n/a per month (2006-2010 5-year est.); Median year structure built: before 1940 (2006-2010 5-year est.).

Transportation: Commute to work: 100.0% car, 0.0% public transportation, 0.0% walk, 0.0% work from home (2006-2010 5-year est.); Travel time to work: 20.0% less than 15 minutes, 26.7% 15 to 30 minutes, 53.3% 30 to 45 minutes, 0.0% 45 to 60 minutes, 0.0% 60 minutes or more (2006-2010 5-year est.)

BELLEVILLE (CDP). Covers a land area of 1.996 square miles and a water area of <.001 square miles. Located at 40.61° N. Lat; 77.72° W. Long. Elevation is 797 feet.

Population: 1,523 (1990); 1,386 (2000); 1,827 (2010); Density: 915.4 persons per square mile (2010); Race: 99.1% White, 0.1% Black, 0.0% Asian, 0.1% American Indian/Alaska Native, 0.0% Native Hawaiian/Other Pacific Islander, 0.7% Other, 1.6% Hispanic of any race (2010); Average household size: 2.14 (2010); Median age: 54.4 (2010); Males per 100 females: 84.2 (2010); Marriage status: 16.1% never married, 67.6% now married, 10.6% widowed, 5.8% divorced (2006-2010 5-year est.); Foreign born: 0.9% (2006-2010 5-year est.); Ancestry (includes multiple ancestries): 36.4% German, 13.4% Irish, 13.3% American, 7.7% English, 3.9% Swiss (2006-2010 5-year est.).

Economy: Employment by occupation: 5.4% management, 1.0% professional, 13.3% services, 11.7% sales, 1.5% farming, 9.1% construction, 7.9% production (2006-2010 5-year est.).

Income: Per capita income: $19,068 (2006-2010 5-year est.); Median household income: $28,398 (2006-2010 5-year est.); Average household income: $43,768 (2006-2010 5-year est.); Percent of households with income of $100,000 or more: 5.7% (2006-2010 5-year est.); Poverty rate: 15.2% (2006-2010 5-year est.).

Education: Percent of population age 25 and over with: High school diploma (including GED) or higher: 77.8% (2006-2010 5-year est.); Bachelor's degree or higher: 11.0% (2006-2010 5-year est.); Master's degree or higher: 2.7% (2006-2010 5-year est.).

School District(s)

Mifflin County SD (KG-12)

　2010-11 Enrollment: 5,472 . . . . (717) 248-0148

Housing: Homeownership rate: 69.2% (2010); Median home value: $91,900 (2006-2010 5-year est.); Median contract rent: $296 per month (2006-2010 5-year est.); Median year structure built: 1959 (2006-2010 5-year est.).

Transportation: Commute to work: 90.6% car, 0.0% public transportation, 6.1% walk, 3.2% work from home (2006-2010 5-year est.); Travel time to work: 36.3% less than 15 minutes, 37.7% 15 to 30 minutes, 15.7% 30 to 45 minutes, 5.1% 45 to 60 minutes, 5.3% 60 minutes or more (2006-2010 5-year est.)

Additional Information Contacts

Juniata River Valley Chamber of Commerce . . . . (717) 248-6713

　http://www.juniatarivervalley.org

BRATTON (township). Covers a land area of 32.786 square miles and a water area of 0.465 square miles. Located at 40.49° N. Lat; 77.67° W. Long.

Population: 1,427 (1990); 1,259 (2000); 1,317 (2010); Density: 40.2 persons per square mile (2010); Race: 98.5% White, 0.2% Black, 0.0% Asian, 0.1% American Indian/Alaska Native, 0.0% Native Hawaiian/Other Pacific Islander, 1.2% Other, 0.5% Hispanic of any race (2010); Average household size: 2.57 (2010); Median age: 44.1 (2010); Males per 100 females: 103.6 (2010); Marriage status: 19.7% never married, 62.8% now married, 8.8% widowed, 8.7% divorced (2006-2010 5-year est.); Foreign

born: 1.7% (2006-2010 5-year est.); Ancestry (includes multiple ancestries): 41.6% German, 13.5% Irish, 11.0% American, 8.1% English, 5.0% Dutch (2006-2010 5-year est.).

Economy: Single-family building permits issued: 0 (2011); Multi-family building permits issued: 0 (2011); Employment by occupation: 10.0% management, 1.2% professional, 14.6% services, 12.0% sales, 4.7% farming, 13.8% construction, 11.6% production (2006-2010 5-year est.).

Income: Per capita income: $17,594 (2006-2010 5-year est.); Median household income: $40,469 (2006-2010 5-year est.); Average household income: $45,766 (2006-2010 5-year est.); Percent of households with income of $100,000 or more: 4.7% (2006-2010 5-year est.); Poverty rate: 12.5% (2006-2010 5-year est.).

Education: Percent of population age 25 and over with: High school diploma (including GED) or higher: 78.5% (2006-2010 5-year est.); Bachelor's degree or higher: 9.8% (2006-2010 5-year est.); Master's degree or higher: 3.2% (2006-2010 5-year est.).

Housing: Homeownership rate: 86.7% (2010); Median home value: $97,400 (2006-2010 5-year est.); Median contract rent: $267 per month (2006-2010 5-year est.); Median year structure built: 1949 (2006-2010 5-year est.).

Transportation: Commute to work: 86.3% car, 0.0% public transportation, 5.7% walk, 6.2% work from home (2006-2010 5-year est.); Travel time to work: 24.1% less than 15 minutes, 43.9% 15 to 30 minutes, 20.3% 30 to 45 minutes, 3.5% 45 to 60 minutes, 8.2% 60 minutes or more (2006-2010 5-year est.)

Additional Information Contacts
Juniata River Valley Chamber of Commerce . . . . (717) 248-6713
   http://www.juniatarivervalley.org

BROWN (township). Covers a land area of 32.820 square miles and a water area of 0.102 square miles. Located at 40.67° N. Lat; 77.65° W. Long.

Population: 3,320 (1990); 3,852 (2000); 4,053 (2010); Density: 123.5 persons per square mile (2010); Race: 98.7% White, 0.2% Black, 0.5% Asian, 0.1% American Indian/Alaska Native, 0.0% Native Hawaiian/Other Pacific Islander, 0.5% Other, 0.4% Hispanic of any race (2010); Average household size: 2.57 (2010); Median age: 42.1 (2010); Males per 100 females: 97.0 (2010); Marriage status: 23.8% never married, 58.5% now married, 11.2% widowed, 6.5% divorced (2006-2010 5-year est.); Foreign born: 1.2% (2006-2010 5-year est.); Ancestry (includes multiple ancestries): 36.7% German, 9.2% Irish, 7.2% American, 6.3% English, 6.1% Pennsylvania German (2006-2010 5-year est.).

Economy: Single-family building permits issued: 3 (2011); Multi-family building permits issued: 0 (2011); Employment by occupation: 10.4% management, 2.0% professional, 8.9% services, 9.1% sales, 2.9% farming, 7.2% construction, 6.1% production (2006-2010 5-year est.).

Income: Per capita income: $23,001 (2006-2010 5-year est.); Median household income: $46,338 (2006-2010 5-year est.); Average household income: $56,748 (2006-2010 5-year est.); Percent of households with income of $100,000 or more: 13.9% (2006-2010 5-year est.); Poverty rate: 12.7% (2006-2010 5-year est.).

Education: Percent of population age 25 and over with: High school diploma (including GED) or higher: 83.2% (2006-2010 5-year est.); Bachelor's degree or higher: 17.2% (2006-2010 5-year est.); Master's degree or higher: 7.2% (2006-2010 5-year est.).

Housing: Homeownership rate: 79.2% (2010); Median home value: $151,400 (2006-2010 5-year est.); Median contract rent: $532 per month (2006-2010 5-year est.); Median year structure built: 1967 (2006-2010 5-year est.).

Transportation: Commute to work: 87.9% car, 0.7% public transportation, 4.4% walk, 4.0% work from home (2006-2010 5-year est.); Travel time to work: 49.5% less than 15 minutes, 30.2% 15 to 30 minutes, 13.0% 30 to 45 minutes, 2.7% 45 to 60 minutes, 4.6% 60 minutes or more (2006-2010 5-year est.)

Additional Information Contacts
Brown Township . . . . (717) 667-2531
   http://www.browntownshipmc.info/Pages/Home.aspx
Wellsboro Area Chamber of Commerce . . . . (570) 724-1926
   http://www.wellsboropa.com

BURNHAM (borough). Covers a land area of 1.052 square miles and a water area of 0.014 square miles. Located at 40.63° N. Lat; 77.56° W. Long. Elevation is 561 feet.

History: Settled 1795, incorporated 1911.

Population: 2,197 (1990); 2,144 (2000); 2,054 (2010); Density: 1,951.7 persons per square mile (2010); Race: 98.0% White, 0.4% Black, 0.2% Asian, 0.0% American Indian/Alaska Native, 0.0% Native Hawaiian/Other Pacific Islander, 1.4% Other, 1.5% Hispanic of any race (2010); Average household size: 2.37 (2010); Median age: 40.4 (2010); Males per 100 females: 98.1 (2010); Marriage status: 26.4% never married, 50.5% now married, 11.0% widowed, 12.1% divorced (2006-2010 5-year est.); Foreign born: 0.3% (2006-2010 5-year est.); Ancestry (includes multiple ancestries): 43.3% German, 13.7% Irish, 10.1% American, 6.5% English, 5.1% Dutch (2006-2010 5-year est.).

Economy: Single-family building permits issued: 1 (2011); Multi-family building permits issued: 0 (2011); Employment by occupation: 3.0% management, 3.6% professional, 20.2% services, 16.8% sales, 4.2% farming, 7.6% construction, 7.0% production (2006-2010 5-year est.).

Income: Per capita income: $18,929 (2006-2010 5-year est.); Median household income: $36,411 (2006-2010 5-year est.); Average household income: $42,523 (2006-2010 5-year est.); Percent of households with income of $100,000 or more: 2.5% (2006-2010 5-year est.); Poverty rate: 9.5% (2006-2010 5-year est.).

Education: Percent of population age 25 and over with: High school diploma (including GED) or higher: 86.2% (2006-2010 5-year est.); Bachelor's degree or higher: 7.8% (2006-2010 5-year est.); Master's degree or higher: 2.4% (2006-2010 5-year est.).

Housing: Homeownership rate: 70.7% (2010); Median home value: $75,800 (2006-2010 5-year est.); Median contract rent: $409 per month (2006-2010 5-year est.); Median year structure built: 1945 (2006-2010 5-year est.).

Transportation: Commute to work: 94.0% car, 0.0% public transportation, 4.5% walk, 0.9% work from home (2006-2010 5-year est.); Travel time to work: 48.0% less than 15 minutes, 34.0% 15 to 30 minutes, 7.8% 30 to 45 minutes, 2.5% 45 to 60 minutes, 7.8% 60 minutes or more (2006-2010 5-year est.)

Additional Information Contacts
Juniata River Valley Chamber of Commerce . . . . (717) 248-6713
   http://www.juniatarivervalley.org

CEDAR CREST (CDP). Covers a land area of 0.217 square miles and a water area of 0 square miles. Located at 40.40° N. Lat; 77.89° W. Long.

Population: n/a (1990); n/a (2000); 195 (2010); Density: 896.9 persons per square mile (2010); Race: 97.4% White, 0.0% Black, 0.0% Asian, 0.0% American Indian/Alaska Native, 0.0% Native Hawaiian/Other Pacific Islander, 2.6% Other, 1.0% Hispanic of any race (2010); Average household size: 2.38 (2010); Median age: 40.8 (2010); Males per 100 females: 109.7 (2010); Marriage status: 24.7% never married, 53.4% now married, 8.1% widowed, 13.9% divorced (2006-2010 5-year est.); Foreign born: 2.3% (2006-2010 5-year est.); Ancestry (includes multiple ancestries): 43.6% German, 14.7% Dutch, 14.3% American, 6.2% Scottish, 5.8% Irish (2006-2010 5-year est.).

Economy: Employment by occupation: 0.0% management, 0.0% professional, 16.9% services, 6.7% sales, 0.0% farming, 6.7% construction, 28.1% production (2006-2010 5-year est.).

Income: Per capita income: $14,758 (2006-2010 5-year est.); Median household income: $29,107 (2006-2010 5-year est.); Average household income: $36,607 (2006-2010 5-year est.); Percent of households with income of $100,000 or more: 9.3% (2006-2010 5-year est.); Poverty rate: 28.2% (2006-2010 5-year est.).

Education: Percent of population age 25 and over with: High school diploma (including GED) or higher: 84.0% (2006-2010 5-year est.); Bachelor's degree or higher: 6.6% (2006-2010 5-year est.); Master's degree or higher: 3.3% (2006-2010 5-year est.).

Housing: Homeownership rate: 74.3% (2010); Median home value: $43,000 (2006-2010 5-year est.); Median contract rent: n/a per month (2006-2010 5-year est.); Median year structure built: 1973 (2006-2010 5-year est.).

Transportation: Commute to work: 87.6% car, 0.0% public transportation, 5.6% walk, 0.0% work from home (2006-2010 5-year est.); Travel time to work: 49.4% less than 15 minutes, 43.8% 15 to 30 minutes, 0.0% 30 to 45 minutes, 0.0% 45 to 60 minutes, 6.7% 60 minutes or more (2006-2010 5-year est.)

CHURCH HILL (CDP). Covers a land area of 1.385 square miles and a water area of 0 square miles. Located at 40.69° N. Lat; 77.59° W. Long. Elevation is 784 feet.

Population: n/a (1990); n/a (2000); 1,627 (2010); Density: 1,174.3 persons per square mile (2010); Race: 98.5% White, 0.2% Black, 0.7% Asian, 0.2% American Indian/Alaska Native, 0.1% Native Hawaiian/Other Pacific Islander, 0.3% Other, 0.6% Hispanic of any race (2010); Average household size: 2.25 (2010); Median age: 48.3 (2010); Males per 100 females: 91.6 (2010); Marriage status: 14.0% never married, 59.0% now married, 16.1% widowed, 10.9% divorced (2006-2010 5-year est.); Foreign born: 1.7% (2006-2010 5-year est.); Ancestry (includes multiple ancestries): 31.5% German, 9.0% Italian, 7.8% American, 7.4% Irish, 7.2% English (2006-2010 5-year est.).

Economy: Employment by occupation: 18.3% management, 3.1% professional, 14.0% services, 5.7% sales, 2.7% farming, 1.5% construction, 4.6% production (2006-2010 5-year est.).

Income: Per capita income: $25,259 (2006-2010 5-year est.); Median household income: $50,063 (2006-2010 5-year est.); Average household income: $59,005 (2006-2010 5-year est.); Percent of households with income of $100,000 or more: 18.2% (2006-2010 5-year est.); Poverty rate: 8.2% (2006-2010 5-year est.).

Education: Percent of population age 25 and over with: High school diploma (including GED) or higher: 86.3% (2006-2010 5-year est.); Bachelor's degree or higher: 20.8% (2006-2010 5-year est.); Master's degree or higher: 10.3% (2006-2010 5-year est.).

Housing: Homeownership rate: 87.2% (2010); Median home value: $143,700 (2006-2010 5-year est.); Median contract rent: n/a per month (2006-2010 5-year est.); Median year structure built: 1982 (2006-2010 5-year est.).

Transportation: Commute to work: 92.8% car, 1.6% public transportation, 4.4% walk, 0.0% work from home (2006-2010 5-year est.); Travel time to work: 39.7% less than 15 minutes, 33.3% 15 to 30 minutes, 11.0% 30 to 45 minutes, 5.7% 45 to 60 minutes, 10.3% 60 minutes or more (2006-2010 5-year est.).

DECATUR (township). Covers a land area of 45.076 square miles and a water area of 0.095 square miles. Located at 40.70° N. Lat; 77.41° W. Long. Elevation is 679 feet.

Population: 2,792 (1990); 3,021 (2000); 3,137 (2010); Density: 69.6 persons per square mile (2010); Race: 97.8% White, 0.7% Black, 0.2% Asian, 0.1% American Indian/Alaska Native, 0.0% Native Hawaiian/Other Pacific Islander, 1.2% Other, 0.5% Hispanic of any race (2010); Average household size: 2.68 (2010); Median age: 42.2 (2010); Males per 100 females: 106.9 (2010); Marriage status: 24.1% never married, 60.5% now married, 7.3% widowed, 8.2% divorced (2006-2010 5-year est.); Foreign born: 0.0% (2006-2010 5-year est.); Ancestry (includes multiple ancestries): 45.6% German, 13.9% American, 12.2% Irish, 6.3% English, 4.5% Italian (2006-2010 5-year est.).

Economy: Single-family building permits issued: 1 (2011); Multi-family building permits issued: 0 (2011); Employment by occupation: 8.2% management, 2.0% professional, 12.5% services, 10.6% sales, 3.0% farming, 15.1% construction, 15.5% production (2006-2010 5-year est.).

Income: Per capita income: $17,688 (2006-2010 5-year est.); Median household income: $44,241 (2006-2010 5-year est.); Average household income: $48,849 (2006-2010 5-year est.); Percent of households with income of $100,000 or more: 6.3% (2006-2010 5-year est.); Poverty rate: 9.1% (2006-2010 5-year est.).

Education: Percent of population age 25 and over with: High school diploma (including GED) or higher: 81.0% (2006-2010 5-year est.); Bachelor's degree or higher: 6.8% (2006-2010 5-year est.); Master's degree or higher: 1.4% (2006-2010 5-year est.).

Housing: Homeownership rate: 84.8% (2010); Median home value: $106,300 (2006-2010 5-year est.); Median contract rent: $430 per month (2006-2010 5-year est.); Median year structure built: 1976 (2006-2010 5-year est.).

Transportation: Commute to work: 94.7% car, 0.0% public transportation, 0.8% walk, 3.4% work from home (2006-2010 5-year est.); Travel time to work: 19.5% less than 15 minutes, 45.9% 15 to 30 minutes, 14.5% 30 to 45 minutes, 15.1% 45 to 60 minutes, 5.1% 60 minutes or more (2006-2010 5-year est.).

Additional Information Contacts
Juniata River Valley Chamber of Commerce . . . . (717) 248-6713
   http://www.juniatarivervalley.org

DERRY (township). Covers a land area of 30.721 square miles and a water area of 0.274 square miles. Located at 40.64° N. Lat; 77.53° W. Long.

Population: 7,593 (1990); 7,256 (2000); 7,339 (2010); Density: 238.9 persons per square mile (2010); Race: 97.6% White, 0.6% Black, 0.8% Asian, 0.1% American Indian/Alaska Native, 0.0% Native Hawaiian/Other Pacific Islander, 0.9% Other, 0.7% Hispanic of any race (2010); Average household size: 2.36 (2010); Median age: 46.9 (2010); Males per 100 females: 92.4 (2010); Marriage status: 20.9% never married, 57.5% now married, 11.9% widowed, 9.7% divorced (2006-2010 5-year est.); Foreign born: 0.5% (2006-2010 5-year est.); Ancestry (includes multiple ancestries): 42.8% German, 14.9% Irish, 11.5% American, 10.7% English, 5.9% Dutch (2006-2010 5-year est.).

Economy: Single-family building permits issued: 7 (2011); Multi-family building permits issued: 0 (2011); Employment by occupation: 10.6% management, 2.2% professional, 13.1% services, 16.1% sales, 2.4% farming, 9.2% construction, 8.4% production (2006-2010 5-year est.).

Income: Per capita income: $22,927 (2006-2010 5-year est.); Median household income: $39,934 (2006-2010 5-year est.); Average household income: $51,879 (2006-2010 5-year est.); Percent of households with income of $100,000 or more: 9.8% (2006-2010 5-year est.); Poverty rate: 6.9% (2006-2010 5-year est.).

Education: Percent of population age 25 and over with: High school diploma (including GED) or higher: 86.2% (2006-2010 5-year est.); Bachelor's degree or higher: 15.4% (2006-2010 5-year est.); Master's degree or higher: 6.3% (2006-2010 5-year est.).

Housing: Homeownership rate: 80.5% (2010); Median home value: $97,300 (2006-2010 5-year est.); Median contract rent: $390 per month (2006-2010 5-year est.); Median year structure built: 1961 (2006-2010 5-year est.).

Transportation: Commute to work: 95.0% car, 0.5% public transportation, 1.5% walk, 2.7% work from home (2006-2010 5-year est.); Travel time to work: 53.0% less than 15 minutes, 25.2% 15 to 30 minutes, 9.9% 30 to 45 minutes, 5.8% 45 to 60 minutes, 6.2% 60 minutes or more (2006-2010 5-year est.)

Additional Information Contacts
Derry Township . . . . (717) 248-8151
   http://www.co.mifflin.pa.us/mif-derry
Juniata River Valley Chamber of Commerce . . . . (717) 248-6713
   http://www.juniatarivervalley.org

GRANVILLE (CDP). Covers a land area of 1.326 square miles and a water area of <.001 square miles. Located at 40.55° N. Lat; 77.62° W. Long. Elevation is 499 feet.

Population: n/a (1990); n/a (2000); 440 (2010); Density: 331.7 persons per square mile (2010); Race: 97.0% White, 1.6% Black, 0.0% Asian, 0.0% American Indian/Alaska Native, 0.2% Native Hawaiian/Other Pacific Islander, 1.2% Other, 0.0% Hispanic of any race (2010); Average household size: 2.49 (2010); Median age: 50.6 (2010); Males per 100 females: 98.2 (2010); Marriage status: 11.4% never married, 65.5% now married, 14.2% widowed, 8.9% divorced (2006-2010 5-year est.); Foreign born: 0.0% (2006-2010 5-year est.); Ancestry (includes multiple ancestries): 50.0% German, 46.9% Irish, 6.5% European, 5.6% Dutch, 3.9% Scotch-Irish (2006-2010 5-year est.).

Economy: Employment by occupation: 0.0% management, 0.0% professional, 28.2% services, 13.9% sales, 0.0% farming, 34.3% construction, 28.2% production (2006-2010 5-year est.).

Income: Per capita income: $21,184 (2006-2010 5-year est.); Median household income: $29,865 (2006-2010 5-year est.); Average household income: $38,585 (2006-2010 5-year est.); Percent of households with income of $100,000 or more: n/a (2006-2010 5-year est.); Poverty rate: 3.7% (2006-2010 5-year est.).

Education: Percent of population age 25 and over with: High school diploma (including GED) or higher: 91.7% (2006-2010 5-year est.); Bachelor's degree or higher: 0.0% (2006-2010 5-year est.); Master's degree or higher: 0.0% (2006-2010 5-year est.).

Housing: Homeownership rate: 84.5% (2010); Median home value: $95,600 (2006-2010 5-year est.); Median contract rent: n/a per month (2006-2010 5-year est.); Median year structure built: 1970 (2006-2010 5-year est.).

Transportation: Commute to work: 93.9% car, 0.0% public transportation, 0.0% walk, 6.1% work from home (2006-2010 5-year est.); Travel time to work: 23.5% less than 15 minutes, 6.9% 15 to 30 minutes, 53.5% 30 to 45 minutes, 9.2% 45 to 60 minutes, 6.9% 60 minutes or more (2006-2010 5-year est.)

GRANVILLE (township). Covers a land area of 40.229 square miles and a water area of 0.917 square miles. Located at 40.58° N. Lat; 77.61° W. Long. Elevation is 499 feet.

Population: 5,128 (1990); 4,895 (2000); 5,104 (2010); Density: 126.9 persons per square mile (2010); Race: 97.6% White, 0.6% Black, 0.5% Asian, 0.1% American Indian/Alaska Native, 0.0% Native Hawaiian/Other Pacific Islander, 1.2% Other, 0.7% Hispanic of any race (2010); Average household size: 2.39 (2010); Median age: 46.9 (2010); Males per 100 females: 101.6 (2010); Marriage status: 26.8% never married, 56.9% now married, 8.0% widowed, 8.2% divorced (2006-2010 5-year est.); Foreign born: 0.4% (2006-2010 5-year est.); Ancestry (includes multiple ancestries): 40.1% German, 14.7% Irish, 11.3% American, 6.5% English, 4.9% Scotch-Irish (2006-2010 5-year est.).

Economy: Single-family building permits issued: 2 (2011); Multi-family building permits issued: 0 (2011); Employment by occupation: 4.8% management, 2.6% professional, 10.4% services, 20.6% sales, 0.5% farming, 13.0% construction, 10.1% production (2006-2010 5-year est.).

Income: Per capita income: $18,763 (2006-2010 5-year est.); Median household income: $36,800 (2006-2010 5-year est.); Average household income: $43,525 (2006-2010 5-year est.); Percent of households with income of $100,000 or more: 2.0% (2006-2010 5-year est.); Poverty rate: 5.0% (2006-2010 5-year est.).

Education: Percent of population age 25 and over with: High school diploma (including GED) or higher: 81.9% (2006-2010 5-year est.); Bachelor's degree or higher: 10.7% (2006-2010 5-year est.); Master's degree or higher: 5.0% (2006-2010 5-year est.).

Housing: Homeownership rate: 78.3% (2010); Median home value: $93,800 (2006-2010 5-year est.); Median contract rent: $408 per month (2006-2010 5-year est.); Median year structure built: 1971 (2006-2010 5-year est.).

Safety: Violent crime rate: 7.8 per 10,000 population; Property crime rate: 240.2 per 10,000 population (2011).

Transportation: Commute to work: 94.4% car, 0.0% public transportation, 1.3% walk, 3.8% work from home (2006-2010 5-year est.); Travel time to work: 43.7% less than 15 minutes, 28.2% 15 to 30 minutes, 12.5% 30 to 45 minutes, 10.7% 45 to 60 minutes, 5.0% 60 minutes or more (2006-2010 5-year est.)

Additional Information Contacts
Juniata River Valley Chamber of Commerce . . . . (717) 248-6713
    http://www.juniatarivervalley.org

HIGHLAND PARK (CDP). Covers a land area of 0.740 square miles and a water area of 0 square miles. Located at 40.62° N. Lat; 77.57° W. Long. Elevation is 568 feet.

Population: 1,583 (1990); 1,446 (2000); 1,380 (2010); Density: 1,864.6 persons per square mile (2010); Race: 97.5% White, 0.4% Black, 0.9% Asian, 0.0% American Indian/Alaska Native, 0.0% Native Hawaiian/Other Pacific Islander, 1.2% Other, 1.2% Hispanic of any race (2010); Average household size: 2.16 (2010); Median age: 51.1 (2010); Males per 100 females: 78.1 (2010); Marriage status: 13.3% never married, 64.4% now married, 12.6% widowed, 9.7% divorced (2006-2010 5-year est.); Foreign born: 0.0% (2006-2010 5-year est.); Ancestry (includes multiple ancestries): 46.3% German, 19.4% English, 17.5% Irish, 11.8% Dutch, 10.7% American (2006-2010 5-year est.).

Economy: Employment by occupation: 9.6% management, 6.3% professional, 22.0% services, 17.4% sales, 6.3% farming, 2.6% construction, 6.3% production (2006-2010 5-year est.).

Income: Per capita income: $20,330 (2006-2010 5-year est.); Median household income: $37,115 (2006-2010 5-year est.); Average household income: $47,583 (2006-2010 5-year est.); Percent of households with income of $100,000 or more: 10.3% (2006-2010 5-year est.); Poverty rate: 7.7% (2006-2010 5-year est.).

Education: Percent of population age 25 and over with: High school diploma (including GED) or higher: 81.4% (2006-2010 5-year est.); Bachelor's degree or higher: 22.1% (2006-2010 5-year est.); Master's degree or higher: 9.6% (2006-2010 5-year est.).

Housing: Homeownership rate: 65.2% (2010); Median home value: $99,300 (2006-2010 5-year est.); Median contract rent: $339 per month (2006-2010 5-year est.); Median year structure built: 1955 (2006-2010 5-year est.).

Transportation: Commute to work: 87.1% car, 0.0% public transportation, 3.6% walk, 9.4% work from home (2006-2010 5-year est.); Travel time to work: 65.3% less than 15 minutes, 17.2% 15 to 30 minutes, 6.7% 30 to 45 minutes, 3.4% 45 to 60 minutes, 7.4% 60 minutes or more (2006-2010 5-year est.)

Additional Information Contacts
Juniata River Valley Chamber of Commerce . . . . (717) 248-6713
    http://www.juniatarivervalley.org

JUNIATA TERRACE (borough). Covers a land area of 0.168 square miles and a water area of 0 square miles. Located at 40.59° N. Lat; 77.58° W. Long. Elevation is 554 feet.

Population: 556 (1990); 502 (2000); 542 (2010); Density: 3,230.1 persons per square mile (2010); Race: 98.0% White, 0.0% Black, 0.2% Asian, 0.4% American Indian/Alaska Native, 0.0% Native Hawaiian/Other Pacific Islander, 1.4% Other, 1.5% Hispanic of any race (2010); Average household size: 2.28 (2010); Median age: 35.0 (2010); Males per 100 females: 92.2 (2010); Marriage status: 20.9% never married, 43.7% now married, 11.3% widowed, 24.1% divorced (2006-2010 5-year est.); Foreign born: 0.6% (2006-2010 5-year est.); Ancestry (includes multiple ancestries): 30.3% German, 19.9% Irish, 11.6% English, 9.8% American, 5.4% Italian (2006-2010 5-year est.).

Economy: Employment by occupation: 2.7% management, 0.0% professional, 9.3% services, 15.5% sales, 4.4% farming, 4.0% construction, 18.1% production (2006-2010 5-year est.).

Income: Per capita income: $17,884 (2006-2010 5-year est.); Median household income: $29,491 (2006-2010 5-year est.); Average household income: $35,062 (2006-2010 5-year est.); Percent of households with income of $100,000 or more: n/a (2006-2010 5-year est.); Poverty rate: 5.2% (2006-2010 5-year est.).

Taxes: Total city taxes per capita: $174 (2009); City property taxes per capita: $86 (2009).

Education: Percent of population age 25 and over with: High school diploma (including GED) or higher: 91.2% (2006-2010 5-year est.); Bachelor's degree or higher: 8.2% (2006-2010 5-year est.); Master's degree or higher: 5.6% (2006-2010 5-year est.).

Housing: Homeownership rate: 63.5% (2010); Median home value: $46,600 (2006-2010 5-year est.); Median contract rent: $437 per month (2006-2010 5-year est.); Median year structure built: before 1940 (2006-2010 5-year est.).

Transportation: Commute to work: 94.4% car, 0.0% public transportation, 0.0% walk, 0.0% work from home (2006-2010 5-year est.); Travel time to work: 69.6% less than 15 minutes, 17.8% 15 to 30 minutes, 8.9% 30 to 45 minutes, 0.0% 45 to 60 minutes, 3.7% 60 minutes or more (2006-2010 5-year est.)

KISTLER (borough). Covers a land area of 0.253 square miles and a water area of 0 square miles. Located at 40.38° N. Lat; 77.87° W. Long. Elevation is 564 feet.

Population: 314 (1990); 344 (2000); 320 (2010); Density: 1,266.7 persons per square mile (2010); Race: 94.1% White, 2.2% Black, 0.3% Asian, 0.6% American Indian/Alaska Native, 0.0% Native Hawaiian/Other Pacific Islander, 2.8% Other, 4.1% Hispanic of any race (2010); Average household size: 2.52 (2010); Median age: 38.9 (2010); Males per 100 females: 96.3 (2010); Marriage status: 37.3% never married, 46.0% now married, 3.1% widowed, 13.6% divorced (2006-2010 5-year est.); Foreign born: 0.5% (2006-2010 5-year est.); Ancestry (includes multiple ancestries): 25.0% German, 10.3% Irish, 4.2% Italian, 3.7% English, 2.4% Scotch-Irish (2006-2010 5-year est.).

Economy: Employment by occupation: 3.7% management, 0.7% professional, 11.2% services, 16.4% sales, 2.2% farming, 16.4% construction, 8.2% production (2006-2010 5-year est.).

Income: Per capita income: $13,348 (2006-2010 5-year est.); Median household income: $25,341 (2006-2010 5-year est.); Average household income: $34,451 (2006-2010 5-year est.); Percent of households with income of $100,000 or more: 3.2% (2006-2010 5-year est.); Poverty rate: 40.0% (2006-2010 5-year est.).

Education: Percent of population age 25 and over with: High school diploma (including GED) or higher: 67.0% (2006-2010 5-year est.); Bachelor's degree or higher: 9.6% (2006-2010 5-year est.); Master's degree or higher: 2.2% (2006-2010 5-year est.).

Housing: Homeownership rate: 78.7% (2010); Median home value: $53,400 (2006-2010 5-year est.); Median contract rent: $375 per month (2006-2010 5-year est.); Median year structure built: 1945 (2006-2010 5-year est.).

Transportation: Commute to work: 95.3% car, 0.0% public transportation, 1.6% walk, 1.6% work from home (2006-2010 5-year est.); Travel time to work: 27.8% less than 15 minutes, 30.2% 15 to 30 minutes, 11.9% 30 to 45 minutes, 4.0% 45 to 60 minutes, 26.2% 60 minutes or more (2006-2010 5-year est.)

LEWISTOWN (borough). County seat. Covers a land area of 2.030 square miles and a water area of 0.020 square miles. Located at 40.60° N. Lat; 77.57° W. Long. Elevation is 492 feet.

History: Lewistown was laid out in 1790.

Population: 9,341 (1990); 8,998 (2000); 8,338 (2010); Density: 4,106.7 persons per square mile (2010); Race: 95.2% White, 1.5% Black, 0.3% Asian, 0.3% American Indian/Alaska Native, 0.0% Native Hawaiian/Other Pacific Islander, 2.7% Other, 3.1% Hispanic of any race (2010); Average household size: 2.21 (2010); Median age: 39.6 (2010); Males per 100 females: 89.5 (2010); Marriage status: 30.4% never married, 45.2% now married, 9.0% widowed, 15.4% divorced (2006-2010 5-year est.); Foreign born: 0.7% (2006-2010 5-year est.); Ancestry (includes multiple ancestries): 37.4% German, 17.0% Irish, 8.8% American, 6.7% English, 6.2% Italian (2006-2010 5-year est.).

Economy: Single-family building permits issued: 1 (2011); Multi-family building permits issued: 31 (2011); Employment by occupation: 3.4% management, 0.9% professional, 13.8% services, 13.4% sales, 4.8% farming, 7.9% construction, 10.4% production (2006-2010 5-year est.).

Income: Per capita income: $16,447 (2006-2010 5-year est.); Median household income: $26,584 (2006-2010 5-year est.); Average household income: $35,618 (2006-2010 5-year est.); Percent of households with income of $100,000 or more: 2.7% (2006-2010 5-year est.); Poverty rate: 27.4% (2006-2010 5-year est.).

Education: Percent of population age 25 and over with: High school diploma (including GED) or higher: 81.1% (2006-2010 5-year est.); Bachelor's degree or higher: 11.5% (2006-2010 5-year est.); Master's degree or higher: 2.7% (2006-2010 5-year est.).

School District(s)

Mifflin County SD (KG-12)

    2010-11 Enrollment: 5,472 . . . . (717) 248-0148

Mifflin-Juniata CTC (10-12)

    2010-11 Enrollment: n/a . . . . (717) 248-3933

Two-year College(s)

Lewistown Hospital School of Nursing (Private, Not-for-profit)

    Fall 2010 Enrollment: 25 . . . . (717) 242-7930

Vocational/Technical School(s)

Mifflin-Juniata Career and Technology Center (Public)

    Fall 2010 Enrollment: 81 . . . . (717) 248-3933

    2011-12 Tuition: $11,625

Housing: Homeownership rate: 46.0% (2010); Median home value: $69,800 (2006-2010 5-year est.); Median contract rent: $384 per month (2006-2010 5-year est.); Median year structure built: before 1940 (2006-2010 5-year est.).

Hospitals: Lewistown Hospital (139 beds)

Newspapers: The Sentinel (Community news; Circulation 13,737)

Transportation: Commute to work: 90.2% car, 0.6% public transportation, 6.5% walk, 0.4% work from home (2006-2010 5-year est.); Travel time to work: 61.8% less than 15 minutes, 17.2% 15 to 30 minutes, 7.4% 30 to 45 minutes, 6.2% 45 to 60 minutes, 7.4% 60 minutes or more (2006-2010 5-year est.); Amtrak: train service available.

Additional Information Contacts

Borough of Lewistown . . . . (717) 447-0086

Juniata River Valley Chamber of Commerce . . . . (717) 248-6713

  http://www.juniatarivervalley.org

LONGFELLOW (CDP). Covers a land area of 0.644 square miles and a water area of <.001 square miles. Located at 40.51° N. Lat; 77.67° W. Long. Elevation is 558 feet.

Population: n/a (1990); n/a (2000); 215 (2010); Density: 333.8 persons per square mile (2010); Race: 100.0% White, 0.0% Black, 0.0% Asian, 0.0% American Indian/Alaska Native, 0.0% Native Hawaiian/Other Pacific Islander, 0.0% Other, 0.0% Hispanic of any race (2010); Average household size: 2.39 (2010); Median age: 48.9 (2010); Males per 100 females: 93.7 (2010); Marriage status: 12.8% never married, 69.1% now married, 8.1% widowed, 10.1% divorced (2006-2010 5-year est.); Foreign born: 0.0% (2006-2010 5-year est.); Ancestry (includes multiple ancestries): 30.2% German, 17.5% English, 15.3% Dutch, 7.9% Polish, 7.9% Irish (2006-2010 5-year est.).

Economy: Employment by occupation: 3.5% management, 3.5% professional, 14.0% services, 7.0% sales, 4.7% farming, 17.4% construction, 15.1% production (2006-2010 5-year est.).

Income: Per capita income: $19,408 (2006-2010 5-year est.); Median household income: $44,167 (2006-2010 5-year est.); Average household income: $51,572 (2006-2010 5-year est.); Percent of households with

income of $100,000 or more: 4.4% (2006-2010 5-year est.); Poverty rate: 7.0% (2006-2010 5-year est.).

Education: Percent of population age 25 and over with: High school diploma (including GED) or higher: 76.9% (2006-2010 5-year est.); Bachelor's degree or higher: 6.2% (2006-2010 5-year est.); Master's degree or higher: 0.0% (2006-2010 5-year est.).

Housing: Homeownership rate: 94.5% (2010); Median home value: $86,700 (2006-2010 5-year est.); Median contract rent: n/a per month (2006-2010 5-year est.); Median year structure built: 1972 (2006-2010 5-year est.).

Transportation: Commute to work: 92.8% car, 0.0% public transportation, 3.6% walk, 0.0% work from home (2006-2010 5-year est.); Travel time to work: 9.6% less than 15 minutes, 56.6% 15 to 30 minutes, 26.5% 30 to 45 minutes, 3.6% 45 to 60 minutes, 3.6% 60 minutes or more (2006-2010 5-year est.)

LUMBER CITY (CDP). Covers a land area of 0.186 square miles and a water area of <.001 square miles. Located at 40.66° N. Lat; 77.60° W. Long. Elevation is 604 feet.

Population: n/a (1990); n/a (2000); 255 (2010); Density: 1,369.3 persons per square mile (2010); Race: 99.6% White, 0.0% Black, 0.0% Asian, 0.0% American Indian/Alaska Native, 0.0% Native Hawaiian/Other Pacific Islander, 0.4% Other, 1.2% Hispanic of any race (2010); Average household size: 2.38 (2010); Median age: 44.2 (2010); Males per 100 females: 112.5 (2010); Marriage status: 22.0% never married, 65.6% now married, 4.4% widowed, 7.9% divorced (2006-2010 5-year est.); Foreign born: 0.0% (2006-2010 5-year est.); Ancestry (includes multiple ancestries): 29.1% German, 25.1% Dutch, 23.3% Irish, 18.5% Scottish, 7.9% Pennsylvania German (2006-2010 5-year est.).

Economy: Employment by occupation: 0.0% management, 0.0% professional, 16.5% services, 0.0% sales, 0.0% farming, 0.0% construction, 20.0% production (2006-2010 5-year est.).

Income: Per capita income: $24,433 (2006-2010 5-year est.); Median household income: $47,059 (2006-2010 5-year est.); Average household income: $43,659 (2006-2010 5-year est.); Percent of households with income of $100,000 or more: n/a (2006-2010 5-year est.); Poverty rate: 4.4% (2006-2010 5-year est.).

Education: Percent of population age 25 and over with: High school diploma (including GED) or higher: 76.7% (2006-2010 5-year est.); Bachelor's degree or higher: 18.5% (2006-2010 5-year est.); Master's degree or higher: 0.0% (2006-2010 5-year est.).

Housing: Homeownership rate: 86.0% (2010); Median home value: $61,800 (2006-2010 5-year est.); Median contract rent: n/a per month (2006-2010 5-year est.); Median year structure built: 1950 (2006-2010 5-year est.).

Transportation: Commute to work: 100.0% car, 0.0% public transportation, 0.0% walk, 0.0% work from home (2006-2010 5-year est.); Travel time to work: 30.6% less than 15 minutes, 69.4% 15 to 30 minutes, 0.0% 30 to 45 minutes, 0.0% 45 to 60 minutes, 0.0% 60 minutes or more (2006-2010 5-year est.)

MAITLAND (CDP). Covers a land area of 1.439 square miles and a water area of 0.003 square miles. Located at 40.62° N. Lat; 77.50° W. Long. Elevation is 545 feet.

Population: n/a (1990); n/a (2000); 357 (2010); Density: 248.1 persons per square mile (2010); Race: 97.5% White, 0.8% Black, 0.0% Asian, 0.3% American Indian/Alaska Native, 0.0% Native Hawaiian/Other Pacific Islander, 1.4% Other, 0.0% Hispanic of any race (2010); Average household size: 2.51 (2010); Median age: 44.9 (2010); Males per 100 females: 98.3 (2010); Marriage status: 11.9% never married, 70.6% now married, 17.5% widowed, 0.0% divorced (2006-2010 5-year est.); Foreign born: 0.0% (2006-2010 5-year est.); Ancestry (includes multiple ancestries): 46.3% German, 29.8% Irish, 15.4% Dutch, 8.0% Welsh, 8.0% Italian (2006-2010 5-year est.).

Economy: Employment by occupation: 23.3% management, 0.0% professional, 14.2% services, 12.5% sales, 12.5% farming, 0.0% construction, 0.0% production (2006-2010 5-year est.).

Income: Per capita income: $19,684 (2006-2010 5-year est.); Median household income: $22,411 (2006-2010 5-year est.); Average household income: $43,764 (2006-2010 5-year est.); Percent of households with income of $100,000 or more: 18.1% (2006-2010 5-year est.); Poverty rate: 0.0% (2006-2010 5-year est.).

Education: Percent of population age 25 and over with: High school diploma (including GED) or higher: 83.1% (2006-2010 5-year est.);

Bachelor's degree or higher: 25.6% (2006-2010 5-year est.); Master's degree or higher: 8.1% (2006-2010 5-year est.).

Housing: Homeownership rate: 84.5% (2010); Median home value: $108,400 (2006-2010 5-year est.); Median contract rent: n/a per month (2006-2010 5-year est.); Median year structure built: 1947 (2006-2010 5-year est.).

Transportation: Commute to work: 87.5% car, 0.0% public transportation, 0.0% walk, 12.5% work from home (2006-2010 5-year est.); Travel time to work: 14.3% less than 15 minutes, 57.1% 15 to 30 minutes, 0.0% 30 to 45 minutes, 0.0% 45 to 60 minutes, 28.6% 60 minutes or more (2006-2010 5-year est.)

MATTAWANA (CDP). Covers a land area of 0.781 square miles and a water area of <.001 square miles. Located at 40.50° N. Lat; 77.73° W. Long. Elevation is 554 feet.

Population: n/a (1990); n/a (2000); 276 (2010); Density: 353.2 persons per square mile (2010); Race: 98.2% White, 0.4% Black, 0.0% Asian, 0.0% American Indian/Alaska Native, 0.0% Native Hawaiian/Other Pacific Islander, 1.4% Other, 0.0% Hispanic of any race (2010); Average household size: 2.60 (2010); Median age: 37.9 (2010); Males per 100 females: 102.9 (2010); Marriage status: 23.0% never married, 63.2% now married, 10.9% widowed, 2.9% divorced (2006-2010 5-year est.); Foreign born: 0.0% (2006-2010 5-year est.); Ancestry (includes multiple ancestries): 55.8% German, 13.7% Irish, 10.6% Italian, 10.3% English, 6.5% European (2006-2010 5-year est.).

Economy: Employment by occupation: 15.1% management, 2.3% professional, 18.6% services, 7.6% sales, 7.6% farming, 7.0% construction, 7.6% production (2006-2010 5-year est.).

Income: Per capita income: $18,383 (2006-2010 5-year est.); Median household income: $33,542 (2006-2010 5-year est.); Average household income: $43,798 (2006-2010 5-year est.); Percent of households with income of $100,000 or more: 8.2% (2006-2010 5-year est.); Poverty rate: 2.1% (2006-2010 5-year est.).

Education: Percent of population age 25 and over with: High school diploma (including GED) or higher: 84.4% (2006-2010 5-year est.); Bachelor's degree or higher: 23.6% (2006-2010 5-year est.); Master's degree or higher: 7.5% (2006-2010 5-year est.).

Housing: Homeownership rate: 75.4% (2010); Median home value: $111,500 (2006-2010 5-year est.); Median contract rent: $234 per month (2006-2010 5-year est.); Median year structure built: before 1940 (2006-2010 5-year est.).

Transportation: Commute to work: 79.6% car, 0.0% public transportation, 16.7% walk, 3.7% work from home (2006-2010 5-year est.); Travel time to work: 31.4% less than 15 minutes, 49.4% 15 to 30 minutes, 12.2% 30 to 45 minutes, 4.5% 45 to 60 minutes, 2.6% 60 minutes or more (2006-2010 5-year est.)

MCVEYTOWN (borough). Covers a land area of 0.095 square miles and a water area of 0.011 square miles. Located at 40.50° N. Lat; 77.74° W. Long. Elevation is 515 feet.

Population: 409 (1990); 405 (2000); 342 (2010); Density: 3,586.1 persons per square mile (2010); Race: 97.7% White, 0.3% Black, 0.0% Asian, 0.0% American Indian/Alaska Native, 0.0% Native Hawaiian/Other Pacific Islander, 2.0% Other, 1.8% Hispanic of any race (2010); Average household size: 2.24 (2010); Median age: 48.0 (2010); Males per 100 females: 84.9 (2010); Marriage status: 17.6% never married, 55.0% now married, 16.6% widowed, 10.7% divorced (2006-2010 5-year est.); Foreign born: 0.0% (2006-2010 5-year est.); Ancestry (includes multiple ancestries): 47.7% German, 22.7% Irish, 10.3% American, 9.4% Scotch-Irish, 4.8% English (2006-2010 5-year est.).

Economy: Single-family building permits issued: 0 (2011); Multi-family building permits issued: 0 (2011); Employment by occupation: 18.6% management, 0.0% professional, 10.3% services, 9.7% sales, 1.4% farming, 6.2% construction, 20.7% production (2006-2010 5-year est.).

Income: Per capita income: $19,807 (2006-2010 5-year est.); Median household income: $38,125 (2006-2010 5-year est.); Average household income: $42,475 (2006-2010 5-year est.); Percent of households with income of $100,000 or more: 3.9% (2006-2010 5-year est.); Poverty rate: 22.7% (2006-2010 5-year est.).

Education: Percent of population age 25 and over with: High school diploma (including GED) or higher: 93.1% (2006-2010 5-year est.); Bachelor's degree or higher: 14.5% (2006-2010 5-year est.); Master's degree or higher: 3.4% (2006-2010 5-year est.).

School District(s)

Mifflin County SD (KG-12)

   2010-11 Enrollment: 5,472 . . . . (717) 248-0148

Housing: Homeownership rate: 75.9% (2010); Median home value: $84,700 (2006-2010 5-year est.); Median contract rent: $403 per month (2006-2010 5-year est.); Median year structure built: before 1940 (2006-2010 5-year est.).

Transportation: Commute to work: 88.7% car, 0.0% public transportation, 7.0% walk, 0.0% work from home (2006-2010 5-year est.); Travel time to work: 21.1% less than 15 minutes, 53.5% 15 to 30 minutes, 12.0% 30 to 45 minutes, 2.8% 45 to 60 minutes, 10.6% 60 minutes or more (2006-2010 5-year est.)

MENNO (township). Covers a land area of 23.689 square miles and a water area of 0.010 square miles. Located at 40.56° N. Lat; 77.79° W. Long. Elevation is 935 feet.

Population: 1,637 (1990); 1,763 (2000); 1,883 (2010); Density: 79.5 persons per square mile (2010); Race: 98.7% White, 0.5% Black, 0.2% Asian, 0.0% American Indian/Alaska Native, 0.0% Native Hawaiian/Other Pacific Islander, 0.6% Other, 0.2% Hispanic of any race (2010); Average household size: 3.64 (2010); Median age: 25.6 (2010); Males per 100 females: 94.1 (2010); Marriage status: 29.6% never married, 65.3% now married, 4.5% widowed, 0.6% divorced (2006-2010 5-year est.); Foreign born: 0.5% (2006-2010 5-year est.); Ancestry (includes multiple ancestries): 40.1% German, 15.9% Pennsylvania German, 8.9% Swiss, 7.9% American, 2.7% English (2006-2010 5-year est.).

Economy: Single-family building permits issued: 0 (2011); Multi-family building permits issued: 0 (2011); Employment by occupation: 19.5% management, 3.1% professional, 10.8% services, 10.8% sales, 2.3% farming, 18.5% construction, 7.6% production (2006-2010 5-year est.).

Income: Per capita income: $13,759 (2006-2010 5-year est.); Median household income: $42,500 (2006-2010 5-year est.); Average household income: $54,570 (2006-2010 5-year est.); Percent of households with income of $100,000 or more: 9.6% (2006-2010 5-year est.); Poverty rate: 26.9% (2006-2010 5-year est.).

Education: Percent of population age 25 and over with: High school diploma (including GED) or higher: 51.5% (2006-2010 5-year est.); Bachelor's degree or higher: 6.7% (2006-2010 5-year est.); Master's degree or higher: 1.8% (2006-2010 5-year est.).

Housing: Homeownership rate: 78.4% (2010); Median home value: $147,800 (2006-2010 5-year est.); Median contract rent: $370 per month (2006-2010 5-year est.); Median year structure built: 1959 (2006-2010 5-year est.).

Transportation: Commute to work: 75.5% car, 0.0% public transportation, 8.2% walk, 15.8% work from home (2006-2010 5-year est.); Travel time to work: 46.9% less than 15 minutes, 33.9% 15 to 30 minutes, 7.7% 30 to 45 minutes, 2.2% 45 to 60 minutes, 9.3% 60 minutes or more (2006-2010 5-year est.)

Additional Information Contacts

Juniata River Valley Chamber of Commerce . . . . (717) 248-6713
   http://www.juniatarivervalley.org

MILROY (CDP). Covers a land area of 1.009 square miles and a water area of 0.003 square miles. Located at 40.72° N. Lat; 77.59° W. Long. Elevation is 778 feet.

Population: 1,456 (1990); 1,386 (2000); 1,498 (2010); Density: 1,484.4 persons per square mile (2010); Race: 98.0% White, 0.1% Black, 0.5% Asian, 0.1% American Indian/Alaska Native, 0.0% Native Hawaiian/Other Pacific Islander, 1.3% Other, 0.5% Hispanic of any race (2010); Average household size: 2.24 (2010); Median age: 43.2 (2010); Males per 100 females: 97.9 (2010); Marriage status: 26.0% never married, 57.3% now married, 10.9% widowed, 5.8% divorced (2006-2010 5-year est.); Foreign born: 0.0% (2006-2010 5-year est.); Ancestry (includes multiple ancestries): 37.5% German, 18.3% Irish, 14.4% Dutch, 14.3% English, 6.9% American (2006-2010 5-year est.).

Economy: Employment by occupation: 10.0% management, 4.3% professional, 12.1% services, 5.0% sales, 0.0% farming, 20.9% construction, 16.7% production (2006-2010 5-year est.).

Income: Per capita income: $21,794 (2006-2010 5-year est.); Median household income: $43,209 (2006-2010 5-year est.); Average household income: $47,333 (2006-2010 5-year est.); Percent of households with income of $100,000 or more: 8.5% (2006-2010 5-year est.); Poverty rate: 7.5% (2006-2010 5-year est.).

Education: Percent of population age 25 and over with: High school diploma (including GED) or higher: 85.3% (2006-2010 5-year est.);

Bachelor's degree or higher: 3.6% (2006-2010 5-year est.); Master's degree or higher: 1.0% (2006-2010 5-year est.).

School District(s)

Mifflin County SD (KG-12)

   2010-11 Enrollment: 5,472 . . . . (717) 248-0148

Housing: Homeownership rate: 72.4% (2010); Median home value: $82,300 (2006-2010 5-year est.); Median contract rent: $385 per month (2006-2010 5-year est.); Median year structure built: 1958 (2006-2010 5-year est.).

Transportation: Commute to work: 93.2% car, 0.0% public transportation, 2.4% walk, 1.8% work from home (2006-2010 5-year est.); Travel time to work: 39.5% less than 15 minutes, 39.3% 15 to 30 minutes, 18.9% 30 to 45 minutes, 1.0% 45 to 60 minutes, 1.3% 60 minutes or more (2006-2010 5-year est.)

Additional Information Contacts

Juniata River Valley Chamber of Commerce . . . . (717) 248-6713
   http://www.juniatarivervalley.org

NEWTON HAMILTON (borough). Covers a land area of 0.155 square miles and a water area of 0.030 square miles. Located at 40.39° N. Lat; 77.84° W. Long. Elevation is 548 feet.

Population: 287 (1990); 272 (2000); 205 (2010); Density: 1,323.2 persons per square mile (2010); Race: 97.1% White, 1.0% Black, 0.0% Asian, 0.0% American Indian/Alaska Native, 0.0% Native Hawaiian/Other Pacific Islander, 1.9% Other, 2.4% Hispanic of any race (2010); Average household size: 2.41 (2010); Median age: 41.8 (2010); Males per 100 females: 88.1 (2010); Marriage status: 23.8% never married, 51.7% now married, 4.8% widowed, 19.7% divorced (2006-2010 5-year est.); Foreign born: 1.6% (2006-2010 5-year est.); Ancestry (includes multiple ancestries): 47.3% German, 17.2% Irish, 10.2% American, 4.3% English, 2.7% Dutch (2006-2010 5-year est.).

Economy: Single-family building permits issued: 0 (2011); Multi-family building permits issued: 0 (2011); Employment by occupation: 7.1% management, 0.0% professional, 10.7% services, 14.3% sales, 0.0% farming, 6.0% construction, 19.0% production (2006-2010 5-year est.).

Income: Per capita income: $17,124 (2006-2010 5-year est.); Median household income: $43,889 (2006-2010 5-year est.); Average household income: $42,623 (2006-2010 5-year est.); Percent of households with income of $100,000 or more: 10.0% (2006-2010 5-year est.); Poverty rate: 12.9% (2006-2010 5-year est.).

Education: Percent of population age 25 and over with: High school diploma (including GED) or higher: 86.7% (2006-2010 5-year est.); Bachelor's degree or higher: 1.6% (2006-2010 5-year est.); Master's degree or higher: 1.6% (2006-2010 5-year est.).

Housing: Homeownership rate: 75.3% (2010); Median home value: $59,000 (2006-2010 5-year est.); Median contract rent: $428 per month (2006-2010 5-year est.); Median year structure built: before 1940 (2006-2010 5-year est.).

Transportation: Commute to work: 84.5% car, 0.0% public transportation, 11.9% walk, 0.0% work from home (2006-2010 5-year est.); Travel time to work: 26.2% less than 15 minutes, 51.2% 15 to 30 minutes, 15.5% 30 to 45 minutes, 0.0% 45 to 60 minutes, 7.1% 60 minutes or more (2006-2010 5-year est.)

OLIVER (township). Covers a land area of 34.987 square miles and a water area of 0.506 square miles. Located at 40.52° N. Lat; 77.73° W. Long.

Population: 1,783 (1990); 2,060 (2000); 2,175 (2010); Density: 62.2 persons per square mile (2010); Race: 98.3% White, 0.3% Black, 0.3% Asian, 0.0% American Indian/Alaska Native, 0.0% Native Hawaiian/Other Pacific Islander, 1.1% Other, 0.7% Hispanic of any race (2010); Average household size: 2.55 (2010); Median age: 42.7 (2010); Males per 100 females: 99.0 (2010); Marriage status: 17.8% never married, 67.2% now married, 7.8% widowed, 7.3% divorced (2006-2010 5-year est.); Foreign born: 0.3% (2006-2010 5-year est.); Ancestry (includes multiple ancestries): 37.2% German, 15.7% American, 11.8% Irish, 4.4% Dutch, 4.4% English (2006-2010 5-year est.).

Economy: Single-family building permits issued: 4 (2011); Multi-family building permits issued: 0 (2011); Employment by occupation: 8.1% management, 4.4% professional, 6.1% services, 15.3% sales, 2.5% farming, 12.8% construction, 13.6% production (2006-2010 5-year est.).

Income: Per capita income: $20,489 (2006-2010 5-year est.); Median household income: $40,104 (2006-2010 5-year est.); Average household income: $48,701 (2006-2010 5-year est.); Percent of households with

income of $100,000 or more: 7.1% (2006-2010 5-year est.); Poverty rate: 6.0% (2006-2010 5-year est.).

Education: Percent of population age 25 and over with: High school diploma (including GED) or higher: 83.9% (2006-2010 5-year est.); Bachelor's degree or higher: 10.0% (2006-2010 5-year est.); Master's degree or higher: 3.3% (2006-2010 5-year est.).

Housing: Homeownership rate: 81.7% (2010); Median home value: $100,400 (2006-2010 5-year est.); Median contract rent: $330 per month (2006-2010 5-year est.); Median year structure built: 1973 (2006-2010 5-year est.).

Transportation: Commute to work: 89.8% car, 0.0% public transportation, 4.6% walk, 4.6% work from home (2006-2010 5-year est.); Travel time to work: 27.4% less than 15 minutes, 46.1% 15 to 30 minutes, 14.9% 30 to 45 minutes, 5.6% 45 to 60 minutes, 5.9% 60 minutes or more (2006-2010 5-year est.)

Additional Information Contacts

Juniata River Valley Chamber of Commerce . . . . (717) 248-6713
   http://www.juniatarivervalley.org

POTLICKER FLATS (CDP). Covers a land area of 0.171 square miles and a water area of <.001 square miles. Located at 40.73° N. Lat; 77.61° W. Long.

Population: n/a (1990); n/a (2000); 172 (2010); Density: 1,003.9 persons per square mile (2010); Race: 99.4% White, 0.6% Black, 0.0% Asian, 0.0% American Indian/Alaska Native, 0.0% Native Hawaiian/Other Pacific Islander, 0.0% Other, 0.0% Hispanic of any race (2010); Average household size: 1.95 (2010); Median age: 54.3 (2010); Males per 100 females: 117.7 (2010); Marriage status: 3.6% never married, 89.3% now married, 7.1% widowed, 0.0% divorced (2006-2010 5-year est.); Foreign born: 0.0% (2006-2010 5-year est.); Ancestry (includes multiple ancestries): 52.3% German, 17.0% French, 12.0% Ukrainian, 10.2% Scottish, 2.5% American (2006-2010 5-year est.).

Economy: Employment by occupation: 23.4% management, 0.0% professional, 31.9% services, 0.0% sales, 0.0% farming, 0.0% construction, 0.0% production (2006-2010 5-year est.).

Income: Per capita income: $11,162 (2006-2010 5-year est.); Median household income: $22,500 (2006-2010 5-year est.); Average household income: $27,746 (2006-2010 5-year est.); Percent of households with income of $100,000 or more: n/a (2006-2010 5-year est.); Poverty rate: 43.1% (2006-2010 5-year est.).

Education: Percent of population age 25 and over with: High school diploma (including GED) or higher: 87.8% (2006-2010 5-year est.); Bachelor's degree or higher: 6.1% (2006-2010 5-year est.); Master's degree or higher: 0.0% (2006-2010 5-year est.).

Housing: Homeownership rate: 73.8% (2010); Median home value: $83,100 (2006-2010 5-year est.); Median contract rent: n/a per month (2006-2010 5-year est.); Median year structure built: 1951 (2006-2010 5-year est.).

Transportation: Commute to work: 100.0% car, 0.0% public transportation, 0.0% walk, 0.0% work from home (2006-2010 5-year est.); Travel time to work: 46.8% less than 15 minutes, 53.2% 15 to 30 minutes, 0.0% 30 to 45 minutes, 0.0% 45 to 60 minutes, 0.0% 60 minutes or more (2006-2010 5-year est.)

REEDSVILLE (CDP). Covers a land area of 0.663 square miles and a water area of 0.022 square miles. Located at 40.66° N. Lat; 77.59° W. Long. Elevation is 594 feet.

Population: 880 (1990); 858 (2000); 641 (2010); Density: 966.7 persons per square mile (2010); Race: 98.9% White, 0.5% Black, 0.2% Asian, 0.2% American Indian/Alaska Native, 0.0% Native Hawaiian/Other Pacific Islander, 0.2% Other, 0.0% Hispanic of any race (2010); Average household size: 2.41 (2010); Median age: 40.2 (2010); Males per 100 females: 97.8 (2010); Marriage status: 31.4% never married, 57.0% now married, 8.7% widowed, 2.9% divorced (2006-2010 5-year est.); Foreign born: 0.0% (2006-2010 5-year est.); Ancestry (includes multiple ancestries): 57.5% German, 13.3% American, 10.1% English, 6.9% Croatian, 6.7% Irish (2006-2010 5-year est.).

Economy: Employment by occupation: 11.2% management, 4.7% professional, 11.6% services, 21.7% sales, 7.8% farming, 5.8% construction, 5.0% production (2006-2010 5-year est.).

Income: Per capita income: $24,478 (2006-2010 5-year est.); Median household income: $53,984 (2006-2010 5-year est.); Average household income: $50,412 (2006-2010 5-year est.); Percent of households with income of $100,000 or more: n/a (2006-2010 5-year est.); Poverty rate: 8.0% (2006-2010 5-year est.).

Education: Percent of population age 25 and over with: High school diploma (including GED) or higher: 96.1% (2006-2010 5-year est.); Bachelor's degree or higher: 10.1% (2006-2010 5-year est.); Master's degree or higher: 10.1% (2006-2010 5-year est.).

School District(s)

Mifflin County SD (KG-12)

   2010-11 Enrollment: 5,472 . . . . (717) 248-0148

Housing: Homeownership rate: 68.8% (2010); Median home value: $111,700 (2006-2010 5-year est.); Median contract rent: $349 per month (2006-2010 5-year est.); Median year structure built: 1954 (2006-2010 5-year est.).

Transportation: Commute to work: 96.9% car, 0.0% public transportation, 0.0% walk, 0.0% work from home (2006-2010 5-year est.); Travel time to work: 67.1% less than 15 minutes, 13.2% 15 to 30 minutes, 19.8% 30 to 45 minutes, 0.0% 45 to 60 minutes, 0.0% 60 minutes or more (2006-2010 5-year est.)

SIGLERVILLE (CDP). Covers a land area of 0.119 square miles and a water area of 0 square miles. Located at 40.74° N. Lat; 77.53° W. Long. Elevation is 751 feet.

Population: n/a (1990); n/a (2000); 106 (2010); Density: 893.1 persons per square mile (2010); Race: 95.3% White, 0.0% Black, 1.9% Asian, 0.0% American Indian/Alaska Native, 0.0% Native Hawaiian/Other Pacific Islander, 2.8% Other, 0.0% Hispanic of any race (2010); Average household size: 2.36 (2010); Median age: 47.3 (2010); Males per 100 females: 92.7 (2010); Marriage status: 48.0% never married, 13.3% now married, 20.0% widowed, 18.7% divorced (2006-2010 5-year est.); Foreign born: 0.0% (2006-2010 5-year est.); Ancestry (includes multiple ancestries): 35.3% Dutch, 29.4% English (2006-2010 5-year est.).

Economy: Employment by occupation: 0.0% management, 0.0% professional, 0.0% services, 20.0% sales, 20.0% farming, 0.0% construction, 28.0% production (2006-2010 5-year est.).

Income: Per capita income: $24,787 (2006-2010 5-year est.); Median household income: $47,578 (2006-2010 5-year est.); Average household income: $41,869 (2006-2010 5-year est.); Percent of households with income of $100,000 or more: n/a (2006-2010 5-year est.); Poverty rate: 0.0% (2006-2010 5-year est.).

Education: Percent of population age 25 and over with: High school diploma (including GED) or higher: 61.5% (2006-2010 5-year est.); Bachelor's degree or higher: 0.0% (2006-2010 5-year est.); Master's degree or higher: 0.0% (2006-2010 5-year est.).

Housing: Homeownership rate: 95.5% (2010); Median home value: $65,300 (2006-2010 5-year est.); Median contract rent: n/a per month (2006-2010 5-year est.); Median year structure built: before 1940 (2006-2010 5-year est.).

Transportation: Commute to work: 100.0% car, 0.0% public transportation, 0.0% walk, 0.0% work from home (2006-2010 5-year est.); Travel time to work: 48.0% less than 15 minutes, 20.0% 15 to 30 minutes, 0.0% 30 to 45 minutes, 0.0% 45 to 60 minutes, 32.0% 60 minutes or more (2006-2010 5-year est.)

STRODES MILLS (CDP). Covers a land area of 1.896 square miles and a water area of <.001 square miles. Located at 40.54° N. Lat; 77.68° W. Long. Elevation is 561 feet.

Population: n/a (1990); n/a (2000); 757 (2010); Density: 399.4 persons per square mile (2010); Race: 98.9% White, 0.3% Black, 0.1% Asian, 0.0% American Indian/Alaska Native, 0.0% Native Hawaiian/Other Pacific Islander, 0.7% Other, 0.5% Hispanic of any race (2010); Average household size: 2.41 (2010); Median age: 43.8 (2010); Males per 100 females: 100.8 (2010); Marriage status: 13.7% never married, 72.3% now married, 9.8% widowed, 4.1% divorced (2006-2010 5-year est.); Foreign born: 1.2% (2006-2010 5-year est.); Ancestry (includes multiple ancestries): 42.8% German, 18.2% Irish, 10.6% American, 10.2% Dutch, 4.3% Scottish (2006-2010 5-year est.).

Economy: Employment by occupation: 0.0% management, 3.0% professional, 6.0% services, 25.8% sales, 0.0% farming, 10.1% construction, 13.1% production (2006-2010 5-year est.).

Income: Per capita income: $15,979 (2006-2010 5-year est.); Median household income: $37,845 (2006-2010 5-year est.); Average household income: $37,070 (2006-2010 5-year est.); Percent of households with income of $100,000 or more: n/a (2006-2010 5-year est.); Poverty rate: 3.3% (2006-2010 5-year est.).

Education: Percent of population age 25 and over with: High school diploma (including GED) or higher: 71.1% (2006-2010 5-year est.);

Bachelor's degree or higher: 1.0% (2006-2010 5-year est.); Master's degree or higher: 1.0% (2006-2010 5-year est.).

Housing: Homeownership rate: 84.1% (2010); Median home value: $84,800 (2006-2010 5-year est.); Median contract rent: $517 per month (2006-2010 5-year est.); Median year structure built: 1973 (2006-2010 5-year est.).

Transportation: Commute to work: 89.9% car, 0.0% public transportation, 10.1% walk, 0.0% work from home (2006-2010 5-year est.); Travel time to work: 38.6% less than 15 minutes, 35.6% 15 to 30 minutes, 11.2% 30 to 45 minutes, 14.6% 45 to 60 minutes, 0.0% 60 minutes or more (2006-2010 5-year est.)

UNION (township). Covers a land area of 25.462 square miles and a water area of 0.040 square miles. Located at 40.62° N. Lat; 77.72° W. Long.

Population: 3,265 (1990); 3,313 (2000); 3,460 (2010); Density: 135.9 persons per square mile (2010); Race: 97.8% White, 0.6% Black, 0.1% Asian, 0.1% American Indian/Alaska Native, 0.0% Native Hawaiian/Other Pacific Islander, 1.4% Other, 1.3% Hispanic of any race (2010); Average household size: 2.66 (2010); Median age: 41.5 (2010); Males per 100 females: 90.0 (2010); Marriage status: 16.6% never married, 68.4% now married, 9.7% widowed, 5.2% divorced (2006-2010 5-year est.); Foreign born: 0.8% (2006-2010 5-year est.); Ancestry (includes multiple ancestries): 34.9% German, 15.1% American, 9.8% Irish, 9.4% Pennsylvania German, 7.0% Swiss (2006-2010 5-year est.).

Economy: Single-family building permits issued: 2 (2011); Multi-family building permits issued: 0 (2011); Employment by occupation: 11.3% management, 1.0% professional, 10.5% services, 8.6% sales, 2.5% farming, 15.8% construction, 5.6% production (2006-2010 5-year est.).

Income: Per capita income: $17,725 (2006-2010 5-year est.); Median household income: $31,700 (2006-2010 5-year est.); Average household income: $46,486 (2006-2010 5-year est.); Percent of households with income of $100,000 or more: 7.6% (2006-2010 5-year est.); Poverty rate: 15.1% (2006-2010 5-year est.).

Education: Percent of population age 25 and over with: High school diploma (including GED) or higher: 69.5% (2006-2010 5-year est.); Bachelor's degree or higher: 10.4% (2006-2010 5-year est.); Master's degree or higher: 2.3% (2006-2010 5-year est.).

Housing: Homeownership rate: 73.0% (2010); Median home value: $104,700 (2006-2010 5-year est.); Median contract rent: $231 per month (2006-2010 5-year est.); Median year structure built: 1966 (2006-2010 5-year est.).

Transportation: Commute to work: 83.2% car, 0.0% public transportation, 7.6% walk, 7.1% work from home (2006-2010 5-year est.); Travel time to work: 39.0% less than 15 minutes, 29.8% 15 to 30 minutes, 15.5% 30 to 45 minutes, 9.5% 45 to 60 minutes, 6.3% 60 minutes or more (2006-2010 5-year est.)

Additional Information Contacts

Juniata River Valley Chamber of Commerce . . . . (717) 248-6713

   http://www.juniatarivervalley.org

WAGNER (CDP). Covers a land area of 0.790 square miles and a water area of <.001 square miles. Located at 40.68° N. Lat; 77.39° W. Long. Elevation is 669 feet.

Population: n/a (1990); n/a (2000); 128 (2010); Density: 162.0 persons per square mile (2010); Race: 100.0% White, 0.0% Black, 0.0% Asian, 0.0% American Indian/Alaska Native, 0.0% Native Hawaiian/Other Pacific Islander, 0.0% Other, 0.0% Hispanic of any race (2010); Average household size: 2.78 (2010); Median age: 40.5 (2010); Males per 100 females: 128.6 (2010); Marriage status: 14.4% never married, 63.1% now married, 22.5% widowed, 0.0% divorced (2006-2010 5-year est.); Foreign born: 0.0% (2006-2010 5-year est.); Ancestry (includes multiple ancestries): 33.6% German, 23.8% American, 11.5% English, 5.7% Dutch, 4.9% Scotch-Irish (2006-2010 5-year est.).

Economy: Income: Per capita income: $23,916 (2006-2010 5-year est.); Median household income: $36,250 (2006-2010 5-year est.); Average household income: $54,122 (2006-2010 5-year est.); Percent of households with income of $100,000 or more: 14.8% (2006-2010 5-year est.); Poverty rate: 3.3% (2006-2010 5-year est.).

Education: Percent of population age 25 and over with: High school diploma (including GED) or higher: 74.3% (2006-2010 5-year est.); Bachelor's degree or higher: 0.0% (2006-2010 5-year est.); Master's degree or higher: 0.0% (2006-2010 5-year est.).

Housing: Homeownership rate: 86.9% (2010); Median home value: $132,100 (2006-2010 5-year est.); Median contract rent: n/a per month

(2006-2010 5-year est.); Median year structure built: 1965 (2006-2010 5-year est.).

Transportation: Commute to work: 80.0% car, 0.0% public transportation, 0.0% walk, 0.0% work from home (2006-2010 5-year est.); Travel time to work: 0.0% less than 15 minutes, 83.3% 15 to 30 minutes, 0.0% 30 to 45 minutes, 0.0% 45 to 60 minutes, 16.7% 60 minutes or more (2006-2010 5-year est.)

WAYNE (township). Covers a land area of 48.671 square miles and a water area of 0.878 square miles. Located at 40.42° N. Lat; 77.82° W. Long.

Population: 2,520 (1990); 2,414 (2000); 2,550 (2010); Density: 52.4 persons per square mile (2010); Race: 98.6% White, 0.2% Black, 0.2% Asian, 0.0% American Indian/Alaska Native, 0.1% Native Hawaiian/Other Pacific Islander, 0.9% Other, 0.7% Hispanic of any race (2010); Average household size: 2.52 (2010); Median age: 44.4 (2010); Males per 100 females: 96.9 (2010); Marriage status: 21.3% never married, 64.9% now married, 5.2% widowed, 8.6% divorced (2006-2010 5-year est.); Foreign born: 0.2% (2006-2010 5-year est.); Ancestry (includes multiple ancestries): 35.9% German, 12.6% American, 11.2% English, 8.0% Irish, 4.0% Dutch (2006-2010 5-year est.).

Economy: Single-family building permits issued: 1 (2011); Multi-family building permits issued: 0 (2011); Employment by occupation: 9.2% management, 0.9% professional, 10.8% services, 12.9% sales, 2.1% farming, 15.4% construction, 18.6% production (2006-2010 5-year est.).

Income: Per capita income: $19,186 (2006-2010 5-year est.); Median household income: $41,419 (2006-2010 5-year est.); Average household income: $52,581 (2006-2010 5-year est.); Percent of households with income of $100,000 or more: 11.4% (2006-2010 5-year est.); Poverty rate: 9.4% (2006-2010 5-year est.).

Education: Percent of population age 25 and over with: High school diploma (including GED) or higher: 77.8% (2006-2010 5-year est.); Bachelor's degree or higher: 11.0% (2006-2010 5-year est.); Master's degree or higher: 4.9% (2006-2010 5-year est.).

Housing: Homeownership rate: 84.8% (2010); Median home value: $96,200 (2006-2010 5-year est.); Median contract rent: $375 per month (2006-2010 5-year est.); Median year structure built: 1975 (2006-2010 5-year est.).

Transportation: Commute to work: 93.3% car, 0.0% public transportation, 4.0% walk, 1.2% work from home (2006-2010 5-year est.); Travel time to work: 29.3% less than 15 minutes, 38.3% 15 to 30 minutes, 22.0% 30 to 45 minutes, 3.9% 45 to 60 minutes, 6.5% 60 minutes or more (2006-2010 5-year est.)

Additional Information Contacts

Juniata River Valley Chamber of Commerce . . . . (717) 248-6713
   http://www.juniatarivervalley.org

YEAGERTOWN (CDP). Covers a land area of 0.449 square miles and a water area of 0.012 square miles. Located at 40.64° N. Lat; 77.58° W. Long. Elevation is 581 feet.

Population: 1,165 (1990); 1,035 (2000); 1,050 (2010); Density: 2,337.3 persons per square mile (2010); Race: 98.3% White, 0.9% Black, 0.4% Asian, 0.0% American Indian/Alaska Native, 0.0% Native Hawaiian/Other Pacific Islander, 0.4% Other, 1.0% Hispanic of any race (2010); Average household size: 2.43 (2010); Median age: 39.6 (2010); Males per 100 females: 98.5 (2010); Marriage status: 42.0% never married, 43.3% now married, 5.6% widowed, 9.2% divorced (2006-2010 5-year est.); Foreign born: 2.5% (2006-2010 5-year est.); Ancestry (includes multiple ancestries): 61.2% German, 18.1% Irish, 6.5% English, 4.5% Italian, 3.8% American (2006-2010 5-year est.).

Economy: Employment by occupation: 11.7% management, 7.8% professional, 2.8% services, 30.0% sales, 0.0% farming, 6.6% construction, 10.7% production (2006-2010 5-year est.).

Income: Per capita income: $18,340 (2006-2010 5-year est.); Median household income: $37,799 (2006-2010 5-year est.); Average household income: $39,141 (2006-2010 5-year est.); Percent of households with income of $100,000 or more: n/a (2006-2010 5-year est.); Poverty rate: 15.9% (2006-2010 5-year est.).

Education: Percent of population age 25 and over with: High school diploma (including GED) or higher: 95.7% (2006-2010 5-year est.); Bachelor's degree or higher: 5.7% (2006-2010 5-year est.); Master's degree or higher: 0.0% (2006-2010 5-year est.).

Housing: Homeownership rate: 71.3% (2010); Median home value: $79,500 (2006-2010 5-year est.); Median contract rent: $407 per month

(2006-2010 5-year est.); Median year structure built: 1944 (2006-2010 5-year est.).

Newspapers: County Observer (Community news; Circulation 5,200)

Transportation: Commute to work: 100.0% car, 0.0% public transportation, 0.0% walk, 0.0% work from home (2006-2010 5-year est.); Travel time to work: 77.3% less than 15 minutes, 5.0% 15 to 30 minutes, 8.5% 30 to 45 minutes, 9.3% 45 to 60 minutes, 0.0% 60 minutes or more (2006-2010 5-year est.)

Monroe County

Located in eastern Pennsylvania; bounded on the east by the Delaware River and the New Jersey border; includes the Pocono Plateau in the west, and ridges of the Kittstinny Mountains in the east. Covers a land area of 608.285 square miles, a water area of 8.973 square miles, and is located in the Eastern Time Zone at 41.06° N. Lat., 75.33° W. Long. The county was founded in 1836. County seat is Stroudsburg.

Monroe County is part of the East Stroudsburg, PA Micropolitan Statistical Area. The entire metro area includes: Monroe County, PA

Weather Station: Stroudsburg — Elevation: 459 feet

	Jan	Feb	Mar	Apr	May	Jun	Jul	Aug	Sep	Oct	Nov	Dec
High	37	40	50	63	73	81	86	84	76	64	52	41
Low	19	20	27	37	47	56	61	59	52	40	32	23
Precip	3.4	3.0	3.7	4.1	4.4	4.6	4.8	4.5	5.0	4.7	4.2	4.0
Snow	11.4	10.3	7.3	1.5	0.0	0.0	0.0	0.0	0.0	tr	1.9	7.9

High and Low temperatures in degrees Fahrenheit; Precipitation and Snow in inches

Population: 95,796 (1990); 138,687 (2000); 169,842 (2010); Race: 77.2% White, 13.2% Black, 2.1% Asian, 0.3% American Indian/Alaska Native, 0.0% Native Hawaiian/Other Pacific Islander, 7.2% Other, 13.1% Hispanic of any race (2010); Density: 279.2 persons per square mile (2010); Average household size: 2.72 (2010); Median age: 40.3 (2010); Males per 100 females: 97.5 (2010).

Religion: Six largest groups: 24.5% Catholicism, 5.7% Pentecostal, 3.8% Methodist/Pietist, 3.5% Lutheran, 1.7% Presbyterian-Reformed, 1.7% Non-Denominational (2010)

Economy: Unemployment rate: 9.9% (August 2012); Total civilian labor force: 84,545 (August 2012); Leading industries: 20.1% retail trade; 17.0% accommodation & food services; 13.5% health care and social assistance (2010); Farms: 349 totaling 29,165 acres (2007); Companies that employ 500 or more persons: 8 (2010); Companies that employ 100 to 499 persons: 48 (2010); Companies that employ less than 100 persons: 3,352 (2010); Black-owned businesses: 833 (2007); Hispanic-owned businesses: n/a (2007); Asian-owned businesses: 470 (2007); Women-owned businesses: 3,553 (2007); Retail sales per capita: $14,716 (2010). Single-family building permits issued: 197 (2011); Multi-family building permits issued: 0 (2011).

Income: Per capita income: $24,824 (2006-2010 5-year est.); Median household income: $56,733 (2006-2010 5-year est.); Average household income: $68,449 (2006-2010 5-year est.); Percent of households with income of $100,000 or more: 21.0% (2006-2010 5-year est.); Poverty rate: 10.4% (2006-2010 5-year est.); Bankruptcy rate: 5.28% (2011).

Taxes: Total county taxes per capita: $187 (2009); County property taxes per capita: $187 (2009).

Education: Percent of population age 25 and over with: High school diploma (including GED) or higher: 88.7% (2006-2010 5-year est.); Bachelor's degree or higher: 23.8% (2006-2010 5-year est.); Master's degree or higher: 7.9% (2006-2010 5-year est.).

Housing: Homeownership rate: 78.6% (2010); Median home value: $206,400 (2006-2010 5-year est.); Median contract rent: $755 per month (2006-2010 5-year est.); Median year structure built: 1982 (2006-2010 5-year est.)

Health: Birth rate: 90.7 per 10,000 population (2011); Death rate: 80.1 per 10,000 population (2011); Age-adjusted cancer mortality rate: 203.9 deaths per 100,000 population (2009); Number of physicians: 13.4 per 10,000 population (2010); Hospital beds: 14.0 per 10,000 population (2008); Hospital admissions: 772.7 per 10,000 population (2008).

Environment: Air Quality Index: 93.6% good, 6.4% moderate, 0.0% unhealthy for sensitive individuals, 0.0% unhealthy (percent of days in 2011)

Elections: 2012 Presidential election results: 56.0% Obama, 42.7% Romney

National and State Parks: Big Pocono State Park; Delaware State Forest; Gouldsboro State Park

Additional Information Contacts

Monroe County Government . . . . (570) 420-3450
   http://www.co.monroe.pa.us

Monroe County Communities

ARLINGTON HEIGHTS (CDP). Covers a land area of 5.364 square miles and a water area of 0.012 square miles. Located at 41.00° N. Lat; 75.21° W. Long. Elevation is 509 feet.
Population: 4,768 (1990); 5,132 (2000); 6,333 (2010); Density: 1,180.6 persons per square mile (2010); Race: 77.9% White, 9.6% Black, 4.4% Asian, 0.2% American Indian/Alaska Native, 0.0% Native Hawaiian/Other Pacific Islander, 7.9% Other, 12.7% Hispanic of any race (2010); Average household size: 2.58 (2010); Median age: 41.7 (2010); Males per 100 females: 93.3 (2010); Marriage status: 24.1% never married, 57.0% now married, 9.9% widowed, 9.0% divorced (2006-2010 5-year est.); Foreign born: 13.6% (2006-2010 5-year est.); Ancestry (includes multiple ancestries): 20.8% Italian, 15.5% German, 10.7% Irish, 7.4% English, 4.0% Polish (2006-2010 5-year est.).
Economy: Employment by occupation: 11.5% management, 3.7% professional, 15.5% services, 18.3% sales, 3.1% farming, 6.7% construction, 1.1% production (2006-2010 5-year est.).
Income: Per capita income: $25,070 (2006-2010 5-year est.); Median household income: $55,159 (2006-2010 5-year est.); Average household income: $62,816 (2006-2010 5-year est.); Percent of households with income of $100,000 or more: 18.8% (2006-2010 5-year est.); Poverty rate: 5.0% (2006-2010 5-year est.).
Education: Percent of population age 25 and over with: High school diploma (including GED) or higher: 82.0% (2006-2010 5-year est.); Bachelor's degree or higher: 26.2% (2006-2010 5-year est.); Master's degree or higher: 9.4% (2006-2010 5-year est.).
Housing: Homeownership rate: 73.8% (2010); Median home value: $228,800 (2006-2010 5-year est.); Median contract rent: $784 per month (2006-2010 5-year est.); Median year structure built: 1972 (2006-2010 5-year est.).
Transportation: Commute to work: 86.8% car, 8.7% public transportation, 2.6% walk, 1.2% work from home (2006-2010 5-year est.); Travel time to work: 44.9% less than 15 minutes, 20.3% 15 to 30 minutes, 9.6% 30 to 45 minutes, 4.9% 45 to 60 minutes, 20.3% 60 minutes or more (2006-2010 5-year est.)
Additional Information Contacts
Greater Pocono Chamber of Commerce . . . . (570) 421-4433
   http://www.greaterpoconochamber.com/newindex.cfm?

BARRETT (township). Covers a land area of 52.378 square miles and a water area of 0.612 square miles. Located at 41.21° N. Lat; 75.24° W. Long.
Population: 3,183 (1990); 3,880 (2000); 4,225 (2010); Density: 80.7 persons per square mile (2010); Race: 91.4% White, 3.9% Black, 0.9% Asian, 0.1% American Indian/Alaska Native, 0.1% Native Hawaiian/Other Pacific Islander, 3.6% Other, 5.2% Hispanic of any race (2010); Average household size: 2.30 (2010); Median age: 45.8 (2010); Males per 100 females: 97.3 (2010); Marriage status: 34.6% never married, 49.1% now married, 5.1% widowed, 11.1% divorced (2006-2010 5-year est.); Foreign born: 5.7% (2006-2010 5-year est.); Ancestry (includes multiple ancestries): 29.2% German, 22.1% Irish, 19.3% Italian, 14.3% English, 8.0% Polish (2006-2010 5-year est.).
Economy: Single-family building permits issued: 2 (2011); Multi-family building permits issued: 0 (2011); Employment by occupation: 18.2% management, 4.9% professional, 11.5% services, 13.9% sales, 0.0% farming, 10.0% construction, 7.2% production (2006-2010 5-year est.).
Income: Per capita income: $23,605 (2006-2010 5-year est.); Median household income: $48,932 (2006-2010 5-year est.); Average household income: $58,259 (2006-2010 5-year est.); Percent of households with income of $100,000 or more: 10.1% (2006-2010 5-year est.); Poverty rate: 10.1% (2006-2010 5-year est.).
Education: Percent of population age 25 and over with: High school diploma (including GED) or higher: 94.1% (2006-2010 5-year est.); Bachelor's degree or higher: 29.2% (2006-2010 5-year est.); Master's degree or higher: 6.7% (2006-2010 5-year est.).
Housing: Homeownership rate: 68.6% (2010); Median home value: $231,600 (2006-2010 5-year est.); Median contract rent: $643 per month (2006-2010 5-year est.); Median year structure built: 1959 (2006-2010 5-year est.).

Transportation: Commute to work: 85.7% car, 1.7% public transportation, 5.9% walk, 4.6% work from home (2006-2010 5-year est.); Travel time to work: 30.9% less than 15 minutes, 27.0% 15 to 30 minutes, 20.4% 30 to 45 minutes, 7.0% 45 to 60 minutes, 14.7% 60 minutes or more (2006-2010 5-year est.)
Additional Information Contacts
Barrett Township . . . . (570) 595-2602
   http://www.barrett.monroe.pa.us
Greater Pocono Chamber of Commerce . . . . (570) 421-4433
   http://www.greaterpoconochamber.com/newindex.cfm?

BARTONSVILLE (unincorporated postal area)
Zip Code: 18321
   Covers a land area of 2.740 square miles and a water area of 0.037 square miles. Located at 41.02° N. Lat; 75.28° W. Long. Elevation is 768 feet. Population: 1,711 (2010); Density: 624.3 persons per square mile (2010); Race: 84.6% White, 8.0% Black, 2.0% Asian, 0.2% American Indian/Alaska Native, 0.0% Native Hawaiian/Other Pacific Islander, 5.2% Other, 10.1% Hispanic of any race (2010); Average household size: 2.65 (2010); Median age: 43.7 (2010); Males per 100 females: 103.2 (2010); Homeownership rate: 80.1% (2010)

BLAKESLEE (unincorporated postal area)
Zip Code: 18610
   Covers a land area of 30.169 square miles and a water area of 0.290 square miles. Located at 41.06° N. Lat; 75.54° W. Long. Population: 5,008 (2010); Density: 166.0 persons per square mile (2010); Race: 73.0% White, 17.8% Black, 1.3% Asian, 0.3% American Indian/Alaska Native, 0.0% Native Hawaiian/Other Pacific Islander, 7.6% Other, 13.9% Hispanic of any race (2010); Average household size: 2.80 (2010); Median age: 40.9 (2010); Males per 100 females: 99.9 (2010); Homeownership rate: 89.0% (2010)

BRODHEADSVILLE (CDP). Covers a land area of 4.271 square miles and a water area of 0.047 square miles. Located at 40.93° N. Lat; 75.40° W. Long. Elevation is 745 feet.
History: Appalachian Trail passes to South on Blue Mt. ridge.
Population: 1,389 (1990); 1,637 (2000); 1,800 (2010); Density: 421.4 persons per square mile (2010); Race: 88.6% White, 6.6% Black, 0.9% Asian, 0.4% American Indian/Alaska Native, 0.0% Native Hawaiian/Other Pacific Islander, 3.5% Other, 7.6% Hispanic of any race (2010); Average household size: 2.70 (2010); Median age: 43.1 (2010); Males per 100 females: 97.4 (2010); Marriage status: 22.8% never married, 56.0% now married, 12.2% widowed, 9.0% divorced (2006-2010 5-year est.); Foreign born: 7.3% (2006-2010 5-year est.); Ancestry (includes multiple ancestries): 34.6% Italian, 26.7% German, 15.6% Irish, 11.9% English, 6.9% Polish (2006-2010 5-year est.).
Economy: Employment by occupation: 8.9% management, 0.0% professional, 7.5% services, 21.7% sales, 1.2% farming, 11.4% construction, 4.3% production (2006-2010 5-year est.).
Income: Per capita income: $30,448 (2006-2010 5-year est.); Median household income: $47,102 (2006-2010 5-year est.); Average household income: $79,042 (2006-2010 5-year est.); Percent of households with income of $100,000 or more: 29.5% (2006-2010 5-year est.); Poverty rate: 6.7% (2006-2010 5-year est.).
Education: Percent of population age 25 and over with: High school diploma (including GED) or higher: 88.2% (2006-2010 5-year est.); Bachelor's degree or higher: 18.1% (2006-2010 5-year est.); Master's degree or higher: 9.9% (2006-2010 5-year est.).
School District(s)
Pleasant Valley SD (KG-12)
   2010-11 Enrollment: 5,786 . . . . (570) 402-1000
Housing: Homeownership rate: 76.1% (2010); Median home value: $237,400 (2006-2010 5-year est.); Median contract rent: $847 per month (2006-2010 5-year est.); Median year structure built: 1983 (2006-2010 5-year est.).
Transportation: Commute to work: 92.6% car, 1.3% public transportation, 1.9% walk, 4.2% work from home (2006-2010 5-year est.); Travel time to work: 25.7% less than 15 minutes, 31.5% 15 to 30 minutes, 30.5% 30 to 45 minutes, 1.3% 45 to 60 minutes, 11.0% 60 minutes or more (2006-2010 5-year est.)
Additional Information Contacts
Slate Belt Chamber of Commerce . . . . (610) 588-1000
   http://www.slatebeltchamber.org

BUCK HILL FALLS (unincorporated postal area)
Zip Code: 18323

Covers a land area of 1.859 square miles and a water area of 0 square miles. Located at 41.19° N. Lat; 75.27° W. Long. Elevation is 1,302 feet. Population: 275 (2010); Density: 147.9 persons per square mile (2010); Race: 98.2% White, 0.4% Black, 0.7% Asian, 0.0% American Indian/Alaska Native, 0.0% Native Hawaiian/Other Pacific Islander, 0.7% Other, 0.7% Hispanic of any race (2010); Average household size: 2.18 (2010); Median age: 54.0 (2010); Males per 100 females: 100.7 (2010); Homeownership rate: 89.7% (2010)

CANADENSIS (unincorporated postal area)
Zip Code: 18325

Covers a land area of 43.034 square miles and a water area of 0.692 square miles. Located at 41.20° N. Lat; 75.22° W. Long. Population: 2,465 (2010); Density: 57.3 persons per square mile (2010); Race: 91.4% White, 4.0% Black, 0.6% Asian, 0.2% American Indian/Alaska Native, 0.2% Native Hawaiian/Other Pacific Islander, 3.6% Other, 4.8% Hispanic of any race (2010); Average household size: 2.35 (2010); Median age: 46.4 (2010); Males per 100 females: 102.2 (2010); Homeownership rate: 80.0% (2010)

CHESTNUTHILL (township). Covers a land area of 37.384 square miles and a water area of 0.139 square miles. Located at 40.95° N. Lat; 75.43° W. Long.
Population: 8,946 (1990); 14,418 (2000); 17,156 (2010); Density: 458.9 persons per square mile (2010); Race: 84.1% White, 8.8% Black, 1.3% Asian, 0.3% American Indian/Alaska Native, 0.0% Native Hawaiian/Other Pacific Islander, 5.5% Other, 10.7% Hispanic of any race (2010); Average household size: 2.87 (2010); Median age: 41.1 (2010); Males per 100 females: 98.7 (2010); Marriage status: 26.8% never married, 59.4% now married, 6.2% widowed, 7.6% divorced (2006-2010 5-year est.); Foreign born: 7.9% (2006-2010 5-year est.); Ancestry (includes multiple ancestries): 26.5% German, 20.2% Italian, 17.4% Irish, 9.0% Polish, 8.1% English (2006-2010 5-year est.).
Economy: Single-family building permits issued: 2 (2011); Multi-family building permits issued: 0 (2011); Employment by occupation: 10.2% management, 4.4% professional, 9.3% services, 15.3% sales, 3.1% farming, 11.1% construction, 6.0% production (2006-2010 5-year est.).
Income: Per capita income: $24,242 (2006-2010 5-year est.); Median household income: $55,853 (2006-2010 5-year est.); Average household income: $68,228 (2006-2010 5-year est.); Percent of households with income of $100,000 or more: 20.6% (2006-2010 5-year est.); Poverty rate: 8.0% (2006-2010 5-year est.).
Taxes: Total city taxes per capita: $152 (2009); City property taxes per capita: $40 (2009).
Education: Percent of population age 25 and over with: High school diploma (including GED) or higher: 87.4% (2006-2010 5-year est.); Bachelor's degree or higher: 22.3% (2006-2010 5-year est.); Master's degree or higher: 8.7% (2006-2010 5-year est.).
Housing: Homeownership rate: 85.9% (2010); Median home value: $225,900 (2006-2010 5-year est.); Median contract rent: $739 per month (2006-2010 5-year est.); Median year structure built: 1986 (2006-2010 5-year est.).
Transportation: Commute to work: 93.4% car, 3.3% public transportation, 0.9% walk, 2.1% work from home (2006-2010 5-year est.); Travel time to work: 14.4% less than 15 minutes, 23.7% 15 to 30 minutes, 26.5% 30 to 45 minutes, 10.0% 45 to 60 minutes, 25.5% 60 minutes or more (2006-2010 5-year est.)
Additional Information Contacts
Chestnuthill Township . . . . (570) 992-7247
  http://www.chestnuthilltwp-pa.gov
Greater Pocono Chamber of Commerce . . . . (570) 421-4433
  http://www.greaterpoconochamber.com/newindex.cfm?

COOLBAUGH (township). Covers a land area of 86.205 square miles and a water area of 1.772 square miles. Located at 41.19° N. Lat; 75.45° W. Long. Elevation is 505 feet.
Population: 6,764 (1990); 15,205 (2000); 20,564 (2010); Density: 238.5 persons per square mile (2010); Race: 56.4% White, 27.8% Black, 1.8% Asian, 0.7% American Indian/Alaska Native, 0.1% Native Hawaiian/Other Pacific Islander, 13.2% Other, 23.3% Hispanic of any race (2010); Average household size: 2.95 (2010); Median age: 37.4 (2010); Males per 100 females: 95.6 (2010); Marriage status: 30.4% never married, 54.6% now married, 5.0% widowed, 10.0% divorced (2006-2010 5-year est.); Foreign

born: 10.9% (2006-2010 5-year est.); Ancestry (includes multiple ancestries): 11.9% Irish, 11.5% Italian, 11.5% German, 6.3% Polish, 4.0% English (2006-2010 5-year est.).
Economy: Single-family building permits issued: 46 (2011); Multi-family building permits issued: 0 (2011); Employment by occupation: 6.9% management, 2.9% professional, 16.6% services, 20.7% sales, 6.8% farming, 9.5% construction, 6.8% production (2006-2010 5-year est.).
Income: Per capita income: $20,327 (2006-2010 5-year est.); Median household income: $54,290 (2006-2010 5-year est.); Average household income: $59,536 (2006-2010 5-year est.); Percent of households with income of $100,000 or more: 13.5% (2006-2010 5-year est.); Poverty rate: 15.6% (2006-2010 5-year est.).
Education: Percent of population age 25 and over with: High school diploma (including GED) or higher: 88.1% (2006-2010 5-year est.); Bachelor's degree or higher: 20.0% (2006-2010 5-year est.); Master's degree or higher: 5.1% (2006-2010 5-year est.).
Housing: Homeownership rate: 80.2% (2010); Median home value: $155,000 (2006-2010 5-year est.); Median contract rent: $737 per month (2006-2010 5-year est.); Median year structure built: 1986 (2006-2010 5-year est.).
Transportation: Commute to work: 88.2% car, 7.1% public transportation, 0.2% walk, 3.1% work from home (2006-2010 5-year est.); Travel time to work: 17.4% less than 15 minutes, 30.3% 15 to 30 minutes, 16.0% 30 to 45 minutes, 3.6% 45 to 60 minutes, 32.8% 60 minutes or more (2006-2010 5-year est.)
Additional Information Contacts
Coolbaugh Township . . . . (570) 894-8490
  http://www.coolbaughtwp.org
Greater Scranton Chamber of Commerce . . . . (570) 342-7711
  http://www.scrantonchamber.com

CRESCO (unincorporated postal area)
Zip Code: 18326

Covers a land area of 33.303 square miles and a water area of 0.073 square miles. Located at 41.16° N. Lat; 75.25° W. Long. Elevation is 1,184 feet. Population: 4,152 (2010); Density: 124.7 persons per square mile (2010); Race: 90.5% White, 4.6% Black, 1.1% Asian, 0.3% American Indian/Alaska Native, 0.0% Native Hawaiian/Other Pacific Islander, 3.5% Other, 6.3% Hispanic of any race (2010); Average household size: 2.48 (2010); Median age: 44.4 (2010); Males per 100 females: 93.6 (2010); Homeownership rate: 74.6% (2010)

DELAWARE WATER GAP (borough). Aka Water Gap. Covers a land area of 1.930 square miles and a water area of 0.133 square miles. Located at 40.97° N. Lat; 75.13° W. Long. Elevation is 509 feet.
History: Appalachian Trail passes through town and crosses river here.
Population: 733 (1990); 744 (2000); 746 (2010); Density: 386.5 persons per square mile (2010); Race: 85.5% White, 7.2% Black, 3.9% Asian, 0.1% American Indian/Alaska Native, 0.1% Native Hawaiian/Other Pacific Islander, 3.2% Other, 7.2% Hispanic of any race (2010); Average household size: 2.13 (2010); Median age: 42.1 (2010); Males per 100 females: 108.4 (2010); Marriage status: 35.0% never married, 47.0% now married, 7.4% widowed, 10.6% divorced (2006-2010 5-year est.); Foreign born: 10.3% (2006-2010 5-year est.); Ancestry (includes multiple ancestries): 25.2% Irish, 23.0% Italian, 21.9% German, 12.5% Polish, 9.3% English (2006-2010 5-year est.).
Economy: Single-family building permits issued: 0 (2011); Multi-family building permits issued: 0 (2011); Employment by occupation: 10.3% management, 5.3% professional, 8.4% services, 15.6% sales, 5.0% farming, 17.5% construction, 8.2% production (2006-2010 5-year est.).
Income: Per capita income: $29,702 (2006-2010 5-year est.); Median household income: $44,375 (2006-2010 5-year est.); Average household income: $73,676 (2006-2010 5-year est.); Percent of households with income of $100,000 or more: 22.3% (2006-2010 5-year est.); Poverty rate: 12.6% (2006-2010 5-year est.).
Education: Percent of population age 25 and over with: High school diploma (including GED) or higher: 84.7% (2006-2010 5-year est.); Bachelor's degree or higher: 27.6% (2006-2010 5-year est.); Master's degree or higher: 7.1% (2006-2010 5-year est.).
Housing: Homeownership rate: 47.6% (2010); Median home value: $227,700 (2006-2010 5-year est.); Median contract rent: $894 per month (2006-2010 5-year est.); Median year structure built: before 1940 (2006-2010 5-year est.).
Safety: Violent crime rate: 0.0 per 10,000 population; Property crime rate: 0.0 per 10,000 population (2011).

Transportation: Commute to work: 90.8% car, 2.8% public transportation, 3.8% walk, 2.8% work from home (2006-2010 5-year est.); Travel time to work: 36.8% less than 15 minutes, 24.2% 15 to 30 minutes, 6.7% 30 to 45 minutes, 13.6% 45 to 60 minutes, 18.8% 60 minutes or more (2006-2010 5-year est.)

EAST STROUDSBURG (borough). Covers a land area of 2.844 square miles and a water area of 0.016 square miles. Located at 41.00° N. Lat; 75.18° W. Long. Elevation is 430 feet.

History: Appalachian Trail passes to South. Settled 1737, Incorporated 1870.

Population: 8,773 (1990); 9,888 (2000); 9,840 (2010); Density: 3,459.7 persons per square mile (2010); Race: 79.2% White, 11.1% Black, 2.5% Asian, 0.2% American Indian/Alaska Native, 0.0% Native Hawaiian/Other Pacific Islander, 7.0% Other, 11.8% Hispanic of any race (2010); Average household size: 2.38 (2010); Median age: 25.6 (2010); Males per 100 females: 86.2 (2010); Marriage status: 59.4% never married, 27.3% now married, 5.2% widowed, 8.0% divorced (2006-2010 5-year est.); Foreign born: 6.7% (2006-2010 5-year est.); Ancestry (includes multiple ancestries): 26.9% Irish, 24.3% German, 21.0% Italian, 8.8% Polish, 6.1% English (2006-2010 5-year est.).

Economy: Single-family building permits issued: 1 (2011); Multi-family building permits issued: 0 (2011); Employment by occupation: 8.6% management, 3.7% professional, 14.2% services, 23.1% sales, 4.4% farming, 3.2% construction, 3.6% production (2006-2010 5-year est.).

Income: Per capita income: $18,678 (2006-2010 5-year est.); Median household income: $45,536 (2006-2010 5-year est.); Average household income: $60,441 (2006-2010 5-year est.); Percent of households with income of $100,000 or more: 19.2% (2006-2010 5-year est.); Poverty rate: 17.8% (2006-2010 5-year est.).

Education: Percent of population age 25 and over with: High school diploma (including GED) or higher: 88.9% (2006-2010 5-year est.); Bachelor's degree or higher: 29.8% (2006-2010 5-year est.); Master's degree or higher: 12.5% (2006-2010 5-year est.).

School District(s)
East Stroudsburg Area SD (KG-12)
　　2010-11 Enrollment: 7,851 . . . . (570) 424-8500

Four-year College(s)
East Stroudsburg University of Pennsylvania (Public)
　　Fall 2010 Enrollment: 6,891 . . . . (570) 422-3211
　　2011-12 Tuition: In-state $8,351; Out-of-state $17,889

Housing: Homeownership rate: 46.5% (2010); Median home value: $212,700 (2006-2010 5-year est.); Median contract rent: $763 per month (2006-2010 5-year est.); Median year structure built: 1964 (2006-2010 5-year est.).

Hospitals: Pocono Medical Center (192 beds)

Newspapers: The Pocono Shopper (Community news; Circulation 28,000)

Transportation: Commute to work: 80.8% car, 2.2% public transportation, 10.7% walk, 3.9% work from home (2006-2010 5-year est.); Travel time to work: 52.7% less than 15 minutes, 15.4% 15 to 30 minutes, 7.2% 30 to 45 minutes, 10.9% 45 to 60 minutes, 13.8% 60 minutes or more (2006-2010 5-year est.)

Additional Information Contacts
Borough of East Stroudsburg . . . . (570) 421-8300
　　http://eastburg.org
Greater Pocono Chamber of Commerce. . . . . (570) 421-4433
　　http://www.poconochamber.net

EFFORT (CDP). Covers a land area of 5.046 square miles and a water area of 0.014 square miles. Located at 40.94° N. Lat; 75.44° W. Long. Elevation is 774 feet.

Population: n/a (1990); n/a (2000); 2,269 (2010); Density: 449.7 persons per square mile (2010); Race: 85.4% White, 6.6% Black, 1.9% Asian, 0.1% American Indian/Alaska Native, 0.0% Native Hawaiian/Other Pacific Islander, 6.0% Other, 9.9% Hispanic of any race (2010); Average household size: 2.94 (2010); Median age: 40.0 (2010); Males per 100 females: 97.6 (2010); Marriage status: 29.8% never married, 51.5% now married, 4.7% widowed, 14.0% divorced (2006-2010 5-year est.); Foreign born: 7.9% (2006-2010 5-year est.); Ancestry (includes multiple ancestries): 15.6% German, 13.7% Irish, 12.8% Italian, 12.0% Polish, 9.4% Dutch (2006-2010 5-year est.).

Economy: Employment by occupation: 10.9% management, 2.7% professional, 20.9% services, 22.9% sales, 2.4% farming, 0.0% construction, 2.5% production (2006-2010 5-year est.).

Income: Per capita income: $23,757 (2006-2010 5-year est.); Median household income: $56,581 (2006-2010 5-year est.); Average household income: $63,420 (2006-2010 5-year est.); Percent of households with income of $100,000 or more: 12.5% (2006-2010 5-year est.); Poverty rate: 7.7% (2006-2010 5-year est.).

Education: Percent of population age 25 and over with: High school diploma (including GED) or higher: 91.4% (2006-2010 5-year est.); Bachelor's degree or higher: 24.8% (2006-2010 5-year est.); Master's degree or higher: 9.9% (2006-2010 5-year est.).

Housing: Homeownership rate: 84.4% (2010); Median home value: $203,500 (2006-2010 5-year est.); Median contract rent: $727 per month (2006-2010 5-year est.); Median year structure built: 1983 (2006-2010 5-year est.).

Transportation: Commute to work: 92.1% car, 6.9% public transportation, 0.0% walk, 1.0% work from home (2006-2010 5-year est.); Travel time to work: 9.5% less than 15 minutes, 27.0% 15 to 30 minutes, 20.5% 30 to 45 minutes, 10.1% 45 to 60 minutes, 32.9% 60 minutes or more (2006-2010 5-year est.)

ELDRED (township). Covers a land area of 24.502 square miles and a water area of 0.005 square miles. Located at 40.86° N. Lat; 75.45° W. Long.

Population: 2,228 (1990); 2,665 (2000); 2,910 (2010); Density: 118.8 persons per square mile (2010); Race: 94.0% White, 3.1% Black, 0.3% Asian, 0.0% American Indian/Alaska Native, 0.0% Native Hawaiian/Other Pacific Islander, 2.6% Other, 2.9% Hispanic of any race (2010); Average household size: 2.61 (2010); Median age: 43.8 (2010); Males per 100 females: 96.9 (2010); Marriage status: 20.9% never married, 64.9% now married, 6.2% widowed, 8.0% divorced (2006-2010 5-year est.); Foreign born: 4.6% (2006-2010 5-year est.); Ancestry (includes multiple ancestries): 43.3% German, 14.4% Irish, 12.5% English, 10.1% Polish, 8.5% Italian (2006-2010 5-year est.).

Economy: Single-family building permits issued: 4 (2011); Multi-family building permits issued: 0 (2011); Employment by occupation: 9.7% management, 3.2% professional, 3.2% services, 14.9% sales, 1.8% farming, 20.0% construction, 15.2% production (2006-2010 5-year est.).

Income: Per capita income: $24,782 (2006-2010 5-year est.); Median household income: $56,250 (2006-2010 5-year est.); Average household income: $62,287 (2006-2010 5-year est.); Percent of households with income of $100,000 or more: 16.6% (2006-2010 5-year est.); Poverty rate: 5.3% (2006-2010 5-year est.).

Education: Percent of population age 25 and over with: High school diploma (including GED) or higher: 83.9% (2006-2010 5-year est.); Bachelor's degree or higher: 17.4% (2006-2010 5-year est.); Master's degree or higher: 2.9% (2006-2010 5-year est.).

Housing: Homeownership rate: 82.4% (2010); Median home value: $193,100 (2006-2010 5-year est.); Median contract rent: $729 per month (2006-2010 5-year est.); Median year structure built: 1976 (2006-2010 5-year est.).

Transportation: Commute to work: 94.8% car, 1.1% public transportation, 0.0% walk, 4.1% work from home (2006-2010 5-year est.); Travel time to work: 20.4% less than 15 minutes, 22.0% 15 to 30 minutes, 32.7% 30 to 45 minutes, 13.4% 45 to 60 minutes, 11.4% 60 minutes or more (2006-2010 5-year est.)

Additional Information Contacts
Greater Lehigh Valley Chamber of Commerce . . . . (610) 841-5800
　　http://www.lehighvalleychamber.org

EMERALD LAKES (CDP). Covers a land area of 2.959 square miles and a water area of 0.224 square miles. Located at 41.08° N. Lat; 75.41° W. Long. Elevation is 2,011 feet.

Population: n/a (1990); n/a (2000); 2,886 (2010); Density: 975.4 persons per square mile (2010); Race: 60.5% White, 24.3% Black, 2.8% Asian, 0.7% American Indian/Alaska Native, 0.0% Native Hawaiian/Other Pacific Islander, 11.7% Other, 24.2% Hispanic of any race (2010); Average household size: 2.98 (2010); Median age: 37.5 (2010); Males per 100 females: 99.6 (2010); Marriage status: 20.8% never married, 67.5% now married, 6.1% widowed, 5.6% divorced (2006-2010 5-year est.); Foreign born: 7.7% (2006-2010 5-year est.); Ancestry (includes multiple ancestries): 20.2% German, 16.8% Italian, 5.8% Irish, 4.4% Polish, 4.1% Pennsylvania German (2006-2010 5-year est.).

Economy: Employment by occupation: 1.6% management, 1.0% professional, 19.2% services, 29.0% sales, 2.7% farming, 16.5% construction, 9.4% production (2006-2010 5-year est.).

Income: Per capita income: $19,424 (2006-2010 5-year est.); Median household income: $45,892 (2006-2010 5-year est.); Average household income: $58,951 (2006-2010 5-year est.); Percent of households with income of $100,000 or more: 16.2% (2006-2010 5-year est.); Poverty rate: 4.7% (2006-2010 5-year est.).

Education: Percent of population age 25 and over with: High school diploma (including GED) or higher: 90.2% (2006-2010 5-year est.); Bachelor's degree or higher: 11.4% (2006-2010 5-year est.); Master's degree or higher: 3.9% (2006-2010 5-year est.).

Housing: Homeownership rate: 89.6% (2010); Median home value: $179,000 (2006-2010 5-year est.); Median contract rent: $1,307 per month (2006-2010 5-year est.); Median year structure built: 1989 (2006-2010 5-year est.).

Transportation: Commute to work: 92.9% car, 2.5% public transportation, 0.9% walk, 2.9% work from home (2006-2010 5-year est.); Travel time to work: 9.3% less than 15 minutes, 31.7% 15 to 30 minutes, 10.9% 30 to 45 minutes, 12.7% 45 to 60 minutes, 35.5% 60 minutes or more (2006-2010 5-year est.)

GILBERT (unincorporated postal area)
Zip Code: 18331

Covers a land area of 3.426 square miles and a water area of 0.009 square miles. Located at 40.90° N. Lat; 75.44° W. Long. Elevation is 712 feet. Population: 867 (2010); Density: 253.0 persons per square mile (2010); Race: 93.0% White, 2.3% Black, 1.0% Asian, 0.0% American Indian/Alaska Native, 0.0% Native Hawaiian/Other Pacific Islander, 3.7% Other, 6.5% Hispanic of any race (2010); Average household size: 2.59 (2010); Median age: 42.6 (2010); Males per 100 females: 104.5 (2010); Homeownership rate: 73.6% (2010)

HAMILTON (township). Covers a land area of 38.326 square miles and a water area of 0.181 square miles. Located at 40.94° N. Lat; 75.28° W. Long.

Population: 6,668 (1990); 8,235 (2000); 9,083 (2010); Density: 237.0 persons per square mile (2010); Race: 90.7% White, 4.6% Black, 1.7% Asian, 0.2% American Indian/Alaska Native, 0.0% Native Hawaiian/Other Pacific Islander, 2.8% Other, 5.5% Hispanic of any race (2010); Average household size: 2.60 (2010); Median age: 44.0 (2010); Males per 100 females: 102.4 (2010); Marriage status: 21.2% never married, 61.2% now married, 7.8% widowed, 9.8% divorced (2006-2010 5-year est.); Foreign born: 7.0% (2006-2010 5-year est.); Ancestry (includes multiple ancestries): 30.2% German, 18.9% Italian, 18.9% Irish, 11.6% Polish, 8.3% English (2006-2010 5-year est.).

Economy: Single-family building permits issued: 4 (2011); Multi-family building permits issued: 0 (2011); Employment by occupation: 12.6% management, 2.3% professional, 12.1% services, 13.9% sales, 2.6% farming, 12.7% construction, 7.6% production (2006-2010 5-year est.).

Income: Per capita income: $29,966 (2006-2010 5-year est.); Median household income: $65,248 (2006-2010 5-year est.); Average household income: $82,199 (2006-2010 5-year est.); Percent of households with income of $100,000 or more: 29.5% (2006-2010 5-year est.); Poverty rate: 5.7% (2006-2010 5-year est.).

Education: Percent of population age 25 and over with: High school diploma (including GED) or higher: 87.4% (2006-2010 5-year est.); Bachelor's degree or higher: 26.0% (2006-2010 5-year est.); Master's degree or higher: 10.6% (2006-2010 5-year est.).

Housing: Homeownership rate: 79.5% (2010); Median home value: $228,200 (2006-2010 5-year est.); Median contract rent: $717 per month (2006-2010 5-year est.); Median year structure built: 1974 (2006-2010 5-year est.).

Transportation: Commute to work: 90.8% car, 1.8% public transportation, 1.3% walk, 5.8% work from home (2006-2010 5-year est.); Travel time to work: 31.4% less than 15 minutes, 27.3% 15 to 30 minutes, 17.6% 30 to 45 minutes, 10.9% 45 to 60 minutes, 12.8% 60 minutes or more (2006-2010 5-year est.)

Additional Information Contacts

Greater Pocono Chamber of Commerce . . . . (570) 421-4433
    http://www.greaterpoconochamber.com/newindex.cfm?
Hamilton Township . . . . (570) 992-7020
    http://www.hamiltontwp.org

HENRYVILLE (unincorporated postal area)
Zip Code: 18332

Covers a land area of 13.911 square miles and a water area of 0.085 square miles. Located at 41.09° N. Lat; 75.26° W. Long. Population:

3,085 (2010); Density: 221.8 persons per square mile (2010); Race: 75.3% White, 13.9% Black, 1.4% Asian, 0.5% American Indian/Alaska Native, 0.0% Native Hawaiian/Other Pacific Islander, 8.9% Other, 15.3% Hispanic of any race (2010); Average household size: 2.81 (2010); Median age: 38.2 (2010); Males per 100 females: 98.9 (2010); Homeownership rate: 82.3% (2010)

INDIAN MOUNTAIN LAKE (CDP). Covers a land area of 6.357 square miles and a water area of 0.087 square miles. Located at 41.00° N. Lat; 75.51° W. Long. Elevation is 1,801 feet.

Population: n/a (1990); n/a (2000); 4,372 (2010); Density: 687.8 persons per square mile (2010); Race: 77.6% White, 14.2% Black, 1.8% Asian, 0.3% American Indian/Alaska Native, 0.0% Native Hawaiian/Other Pacific Islander, 6.1% Other, 14.1% Hispanic of any race (2010); Average household size: 2.78 (2010); Median age: 39.8 (2010); Males per 100 females: 100.4 (2010); Marriage status: 34.1% never married, 54.5% now married, 2.1% widowed, 9.2% divorced (2006-2010 5-year est.); Foreign born: 3.9% (2006-2010 5-year est.); Ancestry (includes multiple ancestries): 22.2% Irish, 17.8% Italian, 16.7% German, 6.8% Polish, 6.7% American (2006-2010 5-year est.).

Economy: Employment by occupation: 13.4% management, 2.3% professional, 8.9% services, 18.2% sales, 3.9% farming, 9.9% construction, 8.1% production (2006-2010 5-year est.).

Income: Per capita income: $21,432 (2006-2010 5-year est.); Median household income: $54,266 (2006-2010 5-year est.); Average household income: $61,871 (2006-2010 5-year est.); Percent of households with income of $100,000 or more: 12.1% (2006-2010 5-year est.); Poverty rate: 4.3% (2006-2010 5-year est.).

Education: Percent of population age 25 and over with: High school diploma (including GED) or higher: 87.7% (2006-2010 5-year est.); Bachelor's degree or higher: 18.6% (2006-2010 5-year est.); Master's degree or higher: 8.4% (2006-2010 5-year est.).

Housing: Homeownership rate: 88.0% (2010); Median home value: $169,000 (2006-2010 5-year est.); Median contract rent: $930 per month (2006-2010 5-year est.); Median year structure built: 1985 (2006-2010 5-year est.).

Transportation: Commute to work: 92.2% car, 7.0% public transportation, 0.8% walk, 0.0% work from home (2006-2010 5-year est.); Travel time to work: 11.8% less than 15 minutes, 23.4% 15 to 30 minutes, 20.4% 30 to 45 minutes, 12.2% 45 to 60 minutes, 32.2% 60 minutes or more (2006-2010 5-year est.)

JACKSON (township). Covers a land area of 29.478 square miles and a water area of 0.417 square miles. Located at 41.01° N. Lat; 75.36° W. Long. Elevation is 715 feet.

Population: 3,757 (1990); 5,979 (2000); 7,033 (2010); Density: 238.6 persons per square mile (2010); Race: 83.4% White, 9.7% Black, 1.8% Asian, 0.3% American Indian/Alaska Native, 0.0% Native Hawaiian/Other Pacific Islander, 4.8% Other, 10.1% Hispanic of any race (2010); Average household size: 2.75 (2010); Median age: 43.6 (2010); Males per 100 females: 96.9 (2010); Marriage status: 23.3% never married, 64.5% now married, 4.5% widowed, 7.7% divorced (2006-2010 5-year est.); Foreign born: 8.9% (2006-2010 5-year est.); Ancestry (includes multiple ancestries): 31.8% German, 19.2% Italian, 18.7% Irish, 10.8% Polish, 8.1% English (2006-2010 5-year est.).

Economy: Single-family building permits issued: 5 (2011); Multi-family building permits issued: 0 (2011); Employment by occupation: 13.9% management, 4.9% professional, 7.6% services, 23.4% sales, 1.3% farming, 11.3% construction, 5.5% production (2006-2010 5-year est.).

Income: Per capita income: $28,086 (2006-2010 5-year est.); Median household income: $61,267 (2006-2010 5-year est.); Average household income: $76,870 (2006-2010 5-year est.); Percent of households with income of $100,000 or more: 34.9% (2006-2010 5-year est.); Poverty rate: 6.6% (2006-2010 5-year est.).

Education: Percent of population age 25 and over with: High school diploma (including GED) or higher: 86.9% (2006-2010 5-year est.); Bachelor's degree or higher: 24.8% (2006-2010 5-year est.); Master's degree or higher: 7.2% (2006-2010 5-year est.).

Housing: Homeownership rate: 85.6% (2010); Median home value: $231,100 (2006-2010 5-year est.); Median contract rent: $763 per month (2006-2010 5-year est.); Median year structure built: 1985 (2006-2010 5-year est.).

Transportation: Commute to work: 86.2% car, 8.6% public transportation, 0.0% walk, 3.8% work from home (2006-2010 5-year est.); Travel time to work: 14.0% less than 15 minutes, 40.2% 15 to 30 minutes, 11.2% 30 to

45 minutes, 4.2% 45 to 60 minutes, 30.5% 60 minutes or more (2006-2010 5-year est.)

Additional Information Contacts

Greater Pocono Chamber of Commerce . . . . (570) 421-4433
http://www.greaterpoconochamber.com/newindex.cfm?

Jackson Township . . . . (570) 629-0153
http://jacksontownship.info

KRESGEVILLE (unincorporated postal area)

Zip Code: 18333

Covers a land area of 2.148 square miles and a water area of 0.006 square miles. Located at 40.90° N. Lat; 75.49° W. Long. Elevation is 676 feet. Population: 712 (2010); Density: 331.5 persons per square mile (2010); Race: 93.0% White, 4.1% Black, 0.8% Asian, 0.4% American Indian/Alaska Native, 0.0% Native Hawaiian/Other Pacific Islander, 1.7% Other, 8.7% Hispanic of any race (2010); Average household size: 2.88 (2010); Median age: 43.5 (2010); Males per 100 females: 93.5 (2010); Homeownership rate: 82.8% (2010)

KUNKLETOWN (unincorporated postal area)

Zip Code: 18058

Covers a land area of 51.648 square miles and a water area of 0.547 square miles. Located at 40.88° N. Lat; 75.49° W. Long. Population: 9,464 (2010); Density: 183.2 persons per square mile (2010); Race: 92.7% White, 3.3% Black, 0.5% Asian, 0.1% American Indian/Alaska Native, 0.1% Native Hawaiian/Other Pacific Islander, 3.3% Other, 5.3% Hispanic of any race (2010); Average household size: 2.65 (2010); Median age: 42.5 (2010); Males per 100 females: 100.9 (2010); Homeownership rate: 86.3% (2010)

LONG POND (unincorporated postal area)

Zip Code: 18334

Covers a land area of 21.792 square miles and a water area of 0.241 square miles. Located at 41.05° N. Lat; 75.43° W. Long. Population: 4,156 (2010); Density: 190.7 persons per square mile (2010); Race: 67.4% White, 18.9% Black, 2.2% Asian, 0.6% American Indian/Alaska Native, 0.0% Native Hawaiian/Other Pacific Islander, 10.9% Other, 20.2% Hispanic of any race (2010); Average household size: 2.84 (2010); Median age: 39.2 (2010); Males per 100 females: 101.8 (2010); Homeownership rate: 88.2% (2010)

MARSHALLS CREEK (unincorporated postal area)

Zip Code: 18335

Covers a land area of 0.897 square miles and a water area of 0.016 square miles. Located at 41.06° N. Lat; 75.10° W. Long. Population: 672 (2010); Density: 748.4 persons per square mile (2010); Race: 57.6% White, 28.1% Black, 6.3% Asian, 0.9% American Indian/Alaska Native, 0.0% Native Hawaiian/Other Pacific Islander, 7.1% Other, 15.3% Hispanic of any race (2010); Average household size: 2.77 (2010); Median age: 40.4 (2010); Males per 100 females: 98.2 (2010); Homeownership rate: 87.2% (2010)

MIDDLE SMITHFIELD (township). Covers a land area of 53.125 square miles and a water area of 1.214 square miles. Located at 41.11° N. Lat; 75.11° W. Long.

Population: 6,541 (1990); 11,495 (2000); 15,997 (2010); Density: 301.1 persons per square mile (2010); Race: 71.4% White, 17.4% Black, 3.1% Asian, 0.3% American Indian/Alaska Native, 0.0% Native Hawaiian/Other Pacific Islander, 7.8% Other, 17.3% Hispanic of any race (2010); Average household size: 2.86 (2010); Median age: 39.7 (2010); Males per 100 females: 100.7 (2010); Marriage status: 28.8% never married, 59.8% now married, 4.7% widowed, 6.7% divorced (2006-2010 5-year est.); Foreign born: 13.9% (2006-2010 5-year est.); Ancestry (includes multiple ancestries): 19.2% German, 14.1% Irish, 13.4% Italian, 6.9% English, 4.5% American (2006-2010 5-year est.).

Economy: Single-family building permits issued: 24 (2011); Multi-family building permits issued: 0 (2011); Employment by occupation: 13.2% management, 4.7% professional, 7.3% services, 13.9% sales, 5.3% farming, 9.0% construction, 8.0% production (2006-2010 5-year est.).

Income: Per capita income: $22,564 (2006-2010 5-year est.); Median household income: $59,639 (2006-2010 5-year est.); Average household income: $66,998 (2006-2010 5-year est.); Percent of households with income of $100,000 or more: 21.0% (2006-2010 5-year est.); Poverty rate: 9.7% (2006-2010 5-year est.).

Taxes: Total city taxes per capita: $127 (2009); City property taxes per capita: $37 (2009).

Education: Percent of population age 25 and over with: High school diploma (including GED) or higher: 89.6% (2006-2010 5-year est.); Bachelor's degree or higher: 23.3% (2006-2010 5-year est.); Master's degree or higher: 6.1% (2006-2010 5-year est.).

Housing: Homeownership rate: 86.4% (2010); Median home value: $187,600 (2006-2010 5-year est.); Median contract rent: $868 per month (2006-2010 5-year est.); Median year structure built: 1986 (2006-2010 5-year est.).

Transportation: Commute to work: 87.6% car, 10.7% public transportation, 0.2% walk, 1.3% work from home (2006-2010 5-year est.); Travel time to work: 11.1% less than 15 minutes, 36.2% 15 to 30 minutes, 9.4% 30 to 45 minutes, 8.8% 45 to 60 minutes, 34.5% 60 minutes or more (2006-2010 5-year est.)

Additional Information Contacts

Greater Pocono Chamber of Commerce . . . . (570) 421-4433
http://www.greaterpoconochamber.com/newindex.cfm?

Middle Smithfield Township . . . . (570) 223-8920
http://www.middlesmithfieldtownship.com

MOUNT POCONO (borough). Covers a land area of 3.454 square miles and a water area of 0.003 square miles. Located at 41.12° N. Lat; 75.36° W. Long. Elevation is 1,844 feet.

Population: 1,806 (1990); 2,742 (2000); 3,170 (2010); Density: 917.8 persons per square mile (2010); Race: 66.7% White, 19.9% Black, 2.5% Asian, 0.7% American Indian/Alaska Native, 0.1% Native Hawaiian/Other Pacific Islander, 10.1% Other, 17.7% Hispanic of any race (2010); Average household size: 2.58 (2010); Median age: 39.0 (2010); Males per 100 females: 92.4 (2010); Marriage status: 31.7% never married, 51.9% now married, 5.4% widowed, 11.0% divorced (2006-2010 5-year est.); Foreign born: 9.5% (2006-2010 5-year est.); Ancestry (includes multiple ancestries): 22.3% Irish, 19.0% German, 12.0% Italian, 6.7% Polish, 6.0% English (2006-2010 5-year est.).

Economy: Single-family building permits issued: 1 (2011); Multi-family building permits issued: 0 (2011); Employment by occupation: 10.9% management, 6.1% professional, 9.4% services, 12.9% sales, 2.7% farming, 9.9% construction, 10.4% production (2006-2010 5-year est.).

Income: Per capita income: $21,555 (2006-2010 5-year est.); Median household income: $39,682 (2006-2010 5-year est.); Average household income: $54,510 (2006-2010 5-year est.); Percent of households with income of $100,000 or more: 12.9% (2006-2010 5-year est.); Poverty rate: 15.4% (2006-2010 5-year est.).

Taxes: Total city taxes per capita: $492 (2009); City property taxes per capita: $355 (2009).

Education: Percent of population age 25 and over with: High school diploma (including GED) or higher: 88.1% (2006-2010 5-year est.); Bachelor's degree or higher: 21.4% (2006-2010 5-year est.); Master's degree or higher: 3.9% (2006-2010 5-year est.).

Housing: Homeownership rate: 60.8% (2010); Median home value: $204,800 (2006-2010 5-year est.); Median contract rent: $668 per month (2006-2010 5-year est.); Median year structure built: 1975 (2006-2010 5-year est.).

Transportation: Commute to work: 91.2% car, 4.7% public transportation, 4.1% walk, 0.0% work from home (2006-2010 5-year est.); Travel time to work: 28.3% less than 15 minutes, 39.6% 15 to 30 minutes, 17.7% 30 to 45 minutes, 2.7% 45 to 60 minutes, 11.8% 60 minutes or more (2006-2010 5-year est.)

Airports: Pocono Mountains Municipal (general aviation)

Additional Information Contacts

Greater Pocono Chamber of Commerce . . . . (570) 421-4433
http://www.greaterpoconochamber.com/newindex.cfm?

MOUNTAINHOME (CDP). Aka Mountain Home. Covers a land area of 1.895 square miles and a water area of 0 square miles. Located at 41.18° N. Lat; 75.26° W. Long. Elevation is 1,234 feet.

Population: 1,076 (1990); 1,169 (2000); 1,182 (2010); Density: 623.8 persons per square mile (2010); Race: 91.7% White, 2.9% Black, 0.8% Asian, 0.3% American Indian/Alaska Native, 0.1% Native Hawaiian/Other Pacific Islander, 4.2% Other, 4.8% Hispanic of any race (2010); Average household size: 2.42 (2010); Median age: 43.3 (2010); Males per 100 females: 93.8 (2010); Marriage status: 42.8% never married, 48.0% now married, 5.6% widowed, 3.5% divorced (2006-2010 5-year est.); Foreign born: 5.6% (2006-2010 5-year est.); Ancestry (includes multiple

ancestries): 36.2% German, 29.4% Irish, 22.7% Italian, 6.5% Swiss, 5.8% Polish (2006-2010 5-year est.).

Economy: Employment by occupation: 16.2% management, 7.8% professional, 13.4% services, 7.3% sales, 0.0% farming, 9.2% construction, 9.6% production (2006-2010 5-year est.).

Income: Per capita income: $25,399 (2006-2010 5-year est.); Median household income: $59,397 (2006-2010 5-year est.); Average household income: $59,511 (2006-2010 5-year est.); Percent of households with income of $100,000 or more: 10.1% (2006-2010 5-year est.); Poverty rate: 10.7% (2006-2010 5-year est.).

Education: Percent of population age 25 and over with: High school diploma (including GED) or higher: 96.3% (2006-2010 5-year est.); Bachelor's degree or higher: 22.2% (2006-2010 5-year est.); Master's degree or higher: 5.6% (2006-2010 5-year est.).

Housing: Homeownership rate: 75.3% (2010); Median home value: $219,500 (2006-2010 5-year est.); Median contract rent: $548 per month (2006-2010 5-year est.); Median year structure built: 1957 (2006-2010 5-year est.).

Transportation: Commute to work: 82.5% car, 0.0% public transportation, 0.0% walk, 15.0% work from home (2006-2010 5-year est.); Travel time to work: 29.5% less than 15 minutes, 28.0% 15 to 30 minutes, 28.5% 30 to 45 minutes, 8.5% 45 to 60 minutes, 5.5% 60 minutes or more (2006-2010 5-year est.).

Additional Information Contacts

Greater Pocono Chamber of Commerce. . . . . (570) 421-4433
    http://www.greaterpoconochamber.com/newindex.cfm?

PARADISE (township). Covers a land area of 21.290 square miles and a water area of 0.094 square miles. Located at 41.11° N. Lat; 75.28° W. Long.

Population: 2,270 (1990); 2,671 (2000); 3,186 (2010); Density: 149.6 persons per square mile (2010); Race: 82.5% White, 10.1% Black, 1.1% Asian, 0.5% American Indian/Alaska Native, 0.1% Native Hawaiian/Other Pacific Islander, 5.7% Other, 10.3% Hispanic of any race (2010); Average household size: 2.64 (2010); Median age: 42.5 (2010); Males per 100 females: 95.2 (2010); Marriage status: 25.4% never married, 58.1% now married, 4.6% widowed, 11.9% divorced (2006-2010 5-year est.); Foreign born: 3.8% (2006-2010 5-year est.); Ancestry (includes multiple ancestries): 37.5% German, 25.3% Italian, 18.7% Irish, 13.0% English, 6.8% Polish (2006-2010 5-year est.).

Economy: Single-family building permits issued: 1 (2011); Multi-family building permits issued: 0 (2011); Employment by occupation: 10.7% management, 1.3% professional, 11.5% services, 21.0% sales, 4.1% farming, 5.5% construction, 4.1% production (2006-2010 5-year est.).

Income: Per capita income: $29,961 (2006-2010 5-year est.); Median household income: $63,162 (2006-2010 5-year est.); Average household income: $76,464 (2006-2010 5-year est.); Percent of households with income of $100,000 or more: 25.5% (2006-2010 5-year est.); Poverty rate: 7.8% (2006-2010 5-year est.).

Education: Percent of population age 25 and over with: High school diploma (including GED) or higher: 86.7% (2006-2010 5-year est.); Bachelor's degree or higher: 30.2% (2006-2010 5-year est.); Master's degree or higher: 5.7% (2006-2010 5-year est.).

Housing: Homeownership rate: 82.0% (2010); Median home value: $213,900 (2006-2010 5-year est.); Median contract rent: $687 per month (2006-2010 5-year est.); Median year structure built: 1966 (2006-2010 5-year est.).

Transportation: Commute to work: 87.7% car, 1.6% public transportation, 1.4% walk, 7.2% work from home (2006-2010 5-year est.); Travel time to work: 29.1% less than 15 minutes, 37.8% 15 to 30 minutes, 6.0% 30 to 45 minutes, 9.2% 45 to 60 minutes, 17.9% 60 minutes or more (2006-2010 5-year est.)

Additional Information Contacts

Greater Pocono Chamber of Commerce. . . . . (570) 421-4433
    http://www.greaterpoconochamber.com/newindex.cfm?
Paradise Township . . . . (570) 595-9880
    http://www.paradisetownship.com

PENN ESTATES (CDP). Covers a land area of 2.021 square miles and a water area of 0.038 square miles. Located at 41.03° N. Lat; 75.24° W. Long.

Population: n/a (1990); n/a (2000); 4,493 (2010); Density: 2,223.4 persons per square mile (2010); Race: 49.5% White, 30.0% Black, 3.3% Asian, 0.5% American Indian/Alaska Native, 0.0% Native Hawaiian/Other Pacific Islander, 16.7% Other, 26.6% Hispanic of any race (2010); Average

household size: 3.27 (2010); Median age: 34.9 (2010); Males per 100 females: 94.1 (2010); Marriage status: 22.0% never married, 62.6% now married, 5.0% widowed, 10.4% divorced (2006-2010 5-year est.); Foreign born: 10.1% (2006-2010 5-year est.); Ancestry (includes multiple ancestries): 20.6% Italian, 18.7% Irish, 14.2% German, 5.0% English, 3.9% Jamaican (2006-2010 5-year est.).

Economy: Employment by occupation: 6.5% management, 5.4% professional, 8.0% services, 27.8% sales, 5.5% farming, 1.7% construction, 5.8% production (2006-2010 5-year est.).

Income: Per capita income: $27,668 (2006-2010 5-year est.); Median household income: $64,459 (2006-2010 5-year est.); Average household income: $84,631 (2006-2010 5-year est.); Percent of households with income of $100,000 or more: 25.2% (2006-2010 5-year est.); Poverty rate: 0.9% (2006-2010 5-year est.).

Education: Percent of population age 25 and over with: High school diploma (including GED) or higher: 93.0% (2006-2010 5-year est.); Bachelor's degree or higher: 21.9% (2006-2010 5-year est.); Master's degree or higher: 0.0% (2006-2010 5-year est.).

Housing: Homeownership rate: 89.9% (2010); Median home value: $191,200 (2006-2010 5-year est.); Median contract rent: $1,019 per month (2006-2010 5-year est.); Median year structure built: 1987 (2006-2010 5-year est.).

Transportation: Commute to work: 88.5% car, 7.5% public transportation, 0.0% walk, 2.6% work from home (2006-2010 5-year est.); Travel time to work: 12.7% less than 15 minutes, 25.5% 15 to 30 minutes, 11.2% 30 to 45 minutes, 6.8% 45 to 60 minutes, 43.9% 60 minutes or more (2006-2010 5-year est.)

POCONO (township). Covers a land area of 34.240 square miles and a water area of 0.185 square miles. Located at 41.05° N. Lat; 75.31° W. Long.

Population: 7,529 (1990); 9,607 (2000); 11,065 (2010); Density: 323.2 persons per square mile (2010); Race: 78.9% White, 11.2% Black, 2.4% Asian, 0.1% American Indian/Alaska Native, 0.1% Native Hawaiian/Other Pacific Islander, 7.3% Other, 11.4% Hispanic of any race (2010); Average household size: 2.71 (2010); Median age: 42.0 (2010); Males per 100 females: 100.0 (2010); Marriage status: 26.5% never married, 55.1% now married, 5.5% widowed, 12.9% divorced (2006-2010 5-year est.); Foreign born: 6.3% (2006-2010 5-year est.); Ancestry (includes multiple ancestries): 24.1% German, 21.2% Italian, 19.4% Irish, 8.5% Polish, 8.4% English (2006-2010 5-year est.).

Economy: Single-family building permits issued: 12 (2011); Multi-family building permits issued: 0 (2011); Employment by occupation: 10.2% management, 5.0% professional, 8.6% services, 22.1% sales, 3.5% farming, 8.6% construction, 5.4% production (2006-2010 5-year est.).

Income: Per capita income: $30,885 (2006-2010 5-year est.); Median household income: $55,488 (2006-2010 5-year est.); Average household income: $76,974 (2006-2010 5-year est.); Percent of households with income of $100,000 or more: 23.7% (2006-2010 5-year est.); Poverty rate: 13.0% (2006-2010 5-year est.).

Education: Percent of population age 25 and over with: High school diploma (including GED) or higher: 91.9% (2006-2010 5-year est.); Bachelor's degree or higher: 27.9% (2006-2010 5-year est.); Master's degree or higher: 9.0% (2006-2010 5-year est.).

Housing: Homeownership rate: 81.8% (2010); Median home value: $219,900 (2006-2010 5-year est.); Median contract rent: $674 per month (2006-2010 5-year est.); Median year structure built: 1980 (2006-2010 5-year est.).

Safety: Violent crime rate: 22.5 per 10,000 population; Property crime rate: 295.5 per 10,000 population (2011).

Transportation: Commute to work: 91.4% car, 3.0% public transportation, 2.4% walk, 3.1% work from home (2006-2010 5-year est.); Travel time to work: 32.3% less than 15 minutes, 27.9% 15 to 30 minutes, 8.4% 30 to 45 minutes, 10.0% 45 to 60 minutes, 21.3% 60 minutes or more (2006-2010 5-year est.)

Additional Information Contacts

Greater Pocono Chamber of Commerce. . . . . (570) 421-4433
    http://www.greaterpoconochamber.com/newindex.cfm?
Pocono Township . . . . (570) 629-1922
    http://www.poconotownship.org

POCONO LAKE (unincorporated postal area)
Zip Code: 18347
    Covers a land area of 27.034 square miles and a water area of 1.335 square miles. Located at 41.13° N. Lat; 75.56° W. Long. Population:

3,364 (2010); Density: 124.4 persons per square mile (2010); Race: 94.4% White, 1.8% Black, 0.6% Asian, 0.2% American Indian/Alaska Native, 0.0% Native Hawaiian/Other Pacific Islander, 3.0% Other, 6.8% Hispanic of any race (2010); Average household size: 2.30 (2010); Median age: 50.0 (2010); Males per 100 females: 102.8 (2010); Homeownership rate: 88.0% (2010)

POCONO MANOR (unincorporated postal area)
Zip Code: 18349

Covers a land area of 1.402 square miles and a water area of <.001 square miles. Located at 41.10° N. Lat; 75.36° W. Long. Elevation is 1,706 feet. Population: 132 (2010); Density: 94.1 persons per square mile (2010); Race: 91.7% White, 6.1% Black, 0.0% Asian, 0.0% American Indian/Alaska Native, 0.0% Native Hawaiian/Other Pacific Islander, 2.2% Other, 3.8% Hispanic of any race (2010); Average household size: 2.44 (2010); Median age: 50.5 (2010); Males per 100 females: 94.1 (2010); Homeownership rate: 90.7% (2010)

POCONO PINES (CDP). Aka Naomi Pines. Covers a land area of 4.073 square miles and a water area of 0.476 square miles. Located at 41.12° N. Lat; 75.45° W. Long. Elevation is 1,804 feet.

Population: 812 (1990); 1,013 (2000); 1,409 (2010); Density: 345.9 persons per square mile (2010); Race: 91.3% White, 3.1% Black, 0.8% Asian, 0.3% American Indian/Alaska Native, 0.0% Native Hawaiian/Other Pacific Islander, 4.5% Other, 7.0% Hispanic of any race (2010); Average household size: 2.21 (2010); Median age: 52.9 (2010); Males per 100 females: 100.1 (2010); Marriage status: 27.1% never married, 48.4% now married, 11.8% widowed, 12.8% divorced (2006-2010 5-year est.); Foreign born: 6.4% (2006-2010 5-year est.); Ancestry (includes multiple ancestries): 43.3% German, 20.1% English, 15.2% Italian, 5.0% American, 3.6% Norwegian (2006-2010 5-year est.).
Economy: Employment by occupation: 22.8% management, 4.0% professional, 9.2% services, 9.6% sales, 8.1% farming, 16.5% construction, 16.5% production (2006-2010 5-year est.).
Income: Per capita income: $30,030 (2006-2010 5-year est.); Median household income: $41,868 (2006-2010 5-year est.); Average household income: $64,773 (2006-2010 5-year est.); Percent of households with income of $100,000 or more: 19.8% (2006-2010 5-year est.); Poverty rate: 36.9% (2006-2010 5-year est.).
Education: Percent of population age 25 and over with: High school diploma (including GED) or higher: 95.8% (2006-2010 5-year est.); Bachelor's degree or higher: 30.4% (2006-2010 5-year est.); Master's degree or higher: 16.6% (2006-2010 5-year est.).

School District(s)
Pocono Mountain SD (KG-12)
   2010-11 Enrollment: 10,693 . . . . (570) 839-7121
Housing: Homeownership rate: 84.5% (2010); Median home value: $273,200 (2006-2010 5-year est.); Median contract rent: $982 per month (2006-2010 5-year est.); Median year structure built: 1982 (2006-2010 5-year est.).
Transportation: Commute to work: 85.2% car, 8.5% public transportation, 2.5% walk, 3.8% work from home (2006-2010 5-year est.); Travel time to work: 31.0% less than 15 minutes, 25.8% 15 to 30 minutes, 13.3% 30 to 45 minutes, 1.3% 45 to 60 minutes, 28.6% 60 minutes or more (2006-2010 5-year est.)
Additional Information Contacts
Greater Scranton Chamber of Commerce . . . . (570) 342-7711
   http://www.scrantonchamber.com

POCONO SUMMIT (unincorporated postal area)
Zip Code: 18346

Covers a land area of 11.036 square miles and a water area of 0.719 square miles. Located at 41.14° N. Lat; 75.42° W. Long. Elevation is 1,818 feet. Population: 2,964 (2010); Density: 268.6 persons per square mile (2010); Race: 66.9% White, 18.7% Black, 2.8% Asian, 0.6% American Indian/Alaska Native, 0.1% Native Hawaiian/Other Pacific Islander, 10.9% Other, 19.9% Hispanic of any race (2010); Average household size: 2.87 (2010); Median age: 38.4 (2010); Males per 100 females: 104.0 (2010); Homeownership rate: 87.4% (2010)

POLK (township). Covers a land area of 30.793 square miles and a water area of 0.388 square miles. Located at 40.93° N. Lat; 75.50° W. Long.

Population: 4,471 (1990); 6,533 (2000); 7,874 (2010); Density: 255.7 persons per square mile (2010); Race: 91.3% White, 4.1% Black, 0.7%

Asian, 0.2% American Indian/Alaska Native, 0.1% Native Hawaiian/Other Pacific Islander, 3.6% Other, 7.1% Hispanic of any race (2010); Average household size: 2.73 (2010); Median age: 41.6 (2010); Males per 100 females: 100.5 (2010); Marriage status: 22.6% never married, 60.0% now married, 7.6% widowed, 9.7% divorced (2006-2010 5-year est.); Foreign born: 6.0% (2006-2010 5-year est.); Ancestry (includes multiple ancestries): 23.5% German, 20.5% Irish, 16.5% Italian, 6.2% English, 6.0% American (2006-2010 5-year est.).
Economy: Single-family building permits issued: 2 (2011); Multi-family building permits issued: 0 (2011); Employment by occupation: 13.8% management, 1.0% professional, 13.6% services, 15.9% sales, 4.3% farming, 14.2% construction, 7.1% production (2006-2010 5-year est.).
Income: Per capita income: $24,824 (2006-2010 5-year est.); Median household income: $62,361 (2006-2010 5-year est.); Average household income: $66,950 (2006-2010 5-year est.); Percent of households with income of $100,000 or more: 19.4% (2006-2010 5-year est.); Poverty rate: 6.1% (2006-2010 5-year est.).
Education: Percent of population age 25 and over with: High school diploma (including GED) or higher: 85.5% (2006-2010 5-year est.); Bachelor's degree or higher: 14.5% (2006-2010 5-year est.); Master's degree or higher: 3.4% (2006-2010 5-year est.).
Housing: Homeownership rate: 85.8% (2010); Median home value: $198,400 (2006-2010 5-year est.); Median contract rent: $843 per month (2006-2010 5-year est.); Median year structure built: 1979 (2006-2010 5-year est.).
Transportation: Commute to work: 86.7% car, 4.1% public transportation, 1.8% walk, 6.5% work from home (2006-2010 5-year est.); Travel time to work: 15.7% less than 15 minutes, 15.7% 15 to 30 minutes, 25.1% 30 to 45 minutes, 20.9% 45 to 60 minutes, 22.6% 60 minutes or more (2006-2010 5-year est.)
Additional Information Contacts
Lehighton Chamber of Commerce . . . . (610) 377-2191
   http://lehigtonareacouncil.org
Polk Township . . . . (610) 681-5376

PRICE (township). Covers a land area of 25.023 square miles and a water area of 0.162 square miles. Located at 41.12° N. Lat; 75.20° W. Long.

Population: 1,436 (1990); 2,649 (2000); 3,573 (2010); Density: 142.8 persons per square mile (2010); Race: 79.3% White, 12.0% Black, 1.6% Asian, 0.3% American Indian/Alaska Native, 0.0% Native Hawaiian/Other Pacific Islander, 6.8% Other, 12.6% Hispanic of any race (2010); Average household size: 2.76 (2010); Median age: 40.2 (2010); Males per 100 females: 105.5 (2010); Marriage status: 29.0% never married, 57.6% now married, 6.4% widowed, 7.0% divorced (2006-2010 5-year est.); Foreign born: 13.4% (2006-2010 5-year est.); Ancestry (includes multiple ancestries): 24.9% German, 18.0% Irish, 14.9% Italian, 7.2% English, 5.3% Other Subsaharan African (2006-2010 5-year est.).
Economy: Single-family building permits issued: 10 (2011); Multi-family building permits issued: 0 (2011); Employment by occupation: 10.5% management, 5.9% professional, 4.1% services, 15.2% sales, 2.7% farming, 10.1% construction, 5.7% production (2006-2010 5-year est.).
Income: Per capita income: $27,995 (2006-2010 5-year est.); Median household income: $73,933 (2006-2010 5-year est.); Average household income: $76,237 (2006-2010 5-year est.); Percent of households with income of $100,000 or more: 24.7% (2006-2010 5-year est.); Poverty rate: 11.9% (2006-2010 5-year est.).
Education: Percent of population age 25 and over with: High school diploma (including GED) or higher: 88.8% (2006-2010 5-year est.); Bachelor's degree or higher: 26.5% (2006-2010 5-year est.); Master's degree or higher: 10.8% (2006-2010 5-year est.).
Housing: Homeownership rate: 86.0% (2010); Median home value: $230,200 (2006-2010 5-year est.); Median contract rent: $782 per month (2006-2010 5-year est.); Median year structure built: 1986 (2006-2010 5-year est.).
Transportation: Commute to work: 86.5% car, 5.2% public transportation, 0.0% walk, 7.3% work from home (2006-2010 5-year est.); Travel time to work: 5.9% less than 15 minutes, 40.7% 15 to 30 minutes, 9.7% 30 to 45 minutes, 3.7% 45 to 60 minutes, 40.0% 60 minutes or more (2006-2010 5-year est.)
Additional Information Contacts
Greater Pocono Chamber of Commerce . . . . (570) 421-4433
   http://www.greaterpoconochamber.com/newindex.cfm?

REEDERS (unincorporated postal area)
Zip Code: 18352

Covers a land area of 3.757 square miles and a water area of 0.266 square miles. Located at 41.00° N. Lat; 75.35° W. Long. Population: 1,098 (2010); Density: 292.2 persons per square mile (2010); Race: 86.2% White, 8.0% Black, 1.1% Asian, 0.1% American Indian/Alaska Native, 0.0% Native Hawaiian/Other Pacific Islander, 4.6% Other, 8.9% Hispanic of any race (2010); Average household size: 2.61 (2010); Median age: 44.4 (2010); Males per 100 females: 98.9 (2010); Homeownership rate: 82.9% (2010)

ROSS (township).
Covers a land area of 22.897 square miles and a water area of 0.035 square miles. Located at 40.88° N. Lat; 75.36° W. Long.

Population: 3,696 (1990); 5,435 (2000); 5,940 (2010); Density: 259.4 persons per square mile (2010); Race: 93.7% White, 2.9% Black, 0.8% Asian, 0.3% American Indian/Alaska Native, 0.0% Native Hawaiian/Other Pacific Islander, 2.3% Other, 4.7% Hispanic of any race (2010); Average household size: 2.82 (2010); Median age: 43.2 (2010); Males per 100 females: 101.4 (2010); Marriage status: 28.3% never married, 62.3% now married, 4.3% widowed, 5.1% divorced (2006-2010 5-year est.); Foreign born: 4.6% (2006-2010 5-year est.); Ancestry (includes multiple ancestries): 33.6% German, 18.9% Italian, 17.6% Irish, 10.1% English, 8.2% Pennsylvania German (2006-2010 5-year est.).

Economy: Single-family building permits issued: 2 (2011); Multi-family building permits issued: 0 (2011); Employment by occupation: 6.7% management, 3.7% professional, 8.4% services, 17.9% sales, 5.3% farming, 20.9% construction, 10.6% production (2006-2010 5-year est.).

Income: Per capita income: $26,412 (2006-2010 5-year est.); Median household income: $67,319 (2006-2010 5-year est.); Average household income: $73,211 (2006-2010 5-year est.); Percent of households with income of $100,000 or more: 22.9% (2006-2010 5-year est.); Poverty rate: 7.3% (2006-2010 5-year est.).

Education: Percent of population age 25 and over with: High school diploma (including GED) or higher: 89.5% (2006-2010 5-year est.); Bachelor's degree or higher: 18.5% (2006-2010 5-year est.); Master's degree or higher: 5.3% (2006-2010 5-year est.).

Housing: Homeownership rate: 89.4% (2010); Median home value: $217,900 (2006-2010 5-year est.); Median contract rent: $603 per month (2006-2010 5-year est.); Median year structure built: 1984 (2006-2010 5-year est.).

Transportation: Commute to work: 94.7% car, 0.5% public transportation, 2.3% walk, 2.5% work from home (2006-2010 5-year est.); Travel time to work: 16.4% less than 15 minutes, 33.3% 15 to 30 minutes, 30.9% 30 to 45 minutes, 6.5% 45 to 60 minutes, 12.8% 60 minutes or more (2006-2010 5-year est.).

Additional Information Contacts

Ross Township . . . . (570) 992-4990
   http://www.rosstwp.com
Slate Belt Chamber of Commerce. (610) 588-1000
   http://www.slatebeltchamber.org

SAYLORSBURG (CDP).
Covers a land area of 1.206 square miles and a water area of 0.059 square miles. Located at 40.90° N. Lat; 75.32° W. Long. Elevation is 669 feet.

Population: n/a (1990); n/a (2000); 1,126 (2010); Density: 934.0 persons per square mile (2010); Race: 95.2% White, 2.0% Black, 0.6% Asian, 0.3% American Indian/Alaska Native, 0.0% Native Hawaiian/Other Pacific Islander, 1.9% Other, 3.6% Hispanic of any race (2010); Average household size: 2.35 (2010); Median age: 43.6 (2010); Males per 100 females: 104.0 (2010); Marriage status: 29.4% never married, 52.2% now married, 1.3% widowed, 17.1% divorced (2006-2010 5-year est.); Foreign born: 5.2% (2006-2010 5-year est.); Ancestry (includes multiple ancestries): 34.8% German, 23.2% Irish, 15.5% Italian, 10.4% Polish, 8.3% Pennsylvania German (2006-2010 5-year est.).

Economy: Employment by occupation: 8.0% management, 1.6% professional, 25.0% services, 2.7% sales, 1.6% farming, 19.0% construction, 17.3% production (2006-2010 5-year est.).

Income: Per capita income: $18,734 (2006-2010 5-year est.); Median household income: $46,927 (2006-2010 5-year est.); Average household income: $54,677 (2006-2010 5-year est.); Percent of households with income of $100,000 or more: 8.3% (2006-2010 5-year est.); Poverty rate: 13.5% (2006-2010 5-year est.).

Education: Percent of population age 25 and over with: High school diploma (including GED) or higher: 80.2% (2006-2010 5-year est.);

Bachelor's degree or higher: 13.6% (2006-2010 5-year est.); Master's degree or higher: 2.2% (2006-2010 5-year est.).

Housing: Homeownership rate: 65.0% (2010); Median home value: $140,500 (2006-2010 5-year est.); Median contract rent: $731 per month (2006-2010 5-year est.); Median year structure built: 1960 (2006-2010 5-year est.).

Transportation: Commute to work: 94.8% car, 0.0% public transportation, 2.4% walk, 2.8% work from home (2006-2010 5-year est.); Travel time to work: 28.1% less than 15 minutes, 27.1% 15 to 30 minutes, 28.1% 30 to 45 minutes, 8.8% 45 to 60 minutes, 8.0% 60 minutes or more (2006-2010 5-year est.)

SCIOTA (unincorporated postal area)
Zip Code: 18354

Covers a land area of 3.385 square miles and a water area of 0.013 square miles. Located at 40.92° N. Lat; 75.32° W. Long. Elevation is 561 feet. Population: 951 (2010); Density: 280.9 persons per square mile (2010); Race: 91.8% White, 3.7% Black, 1.1% Asian, 0.5% American Indian/Alaska Native, 0.0% Native Hawaiian/Other Pacific Islander, 2.9% Other, 6.1% Hispanic of any race (2010); Average household size: 2.63 (2010); Median age: 42.6 (2010); Males per 100 females: 98.1 (2010); Homeownership rate: 83.4% (2010)

SCOTRUN (unincorporated postal area)
Zip Code: 18355

Covers a land area of 7.154 square miles and a water area of 0.052 square miles. Located at 41.07° N. Lat; 75.35° W. Long. Population: 1,492 (2010); Density: 208.5 persons per square mile (2010); Race: 80.4% White, 9.7% Black, 2.7% Asian, 0.2% American Indian/Alaska Native, 0.1% Native Hawaiian/Other Pacific Islander, 6.9% Other, 9.9% Hispanic of any race (2010); Average household size: 2.55 (2010); Median age: 42.1 (2010); Males per 100 females: 105.5 (2010); Homeownership rate: 82.1% (2010)

SHAWNEE ON DELAWARE (unincorporated postal area)
Zip Code: 18356

Covers a land area of 0.650 square miles and a water area of 0 square miles. Located at 41.01° N. Lat; 75.11° W. Long. Population: 136 (2010); Density: 209.1 persons per square mile (2010); Race: 92.6% White, 5.9% Black, 1.5% Asian, 0.0% American Indian/Alaska Native, 0.0% Native Hawaiian/Other Pacific Islander, 0.0% Other, 13.2% Hispanic of any race (2010); Average household size: 2.57 (2010); Median age: 47.5 (2010); Males per 100 females: 100.0 (2010); Homeownership rate: 64.2% (2010)

SIERRA VIEW (CDP).
Covers a land area of 5.060 square miles and a water area of 0 square miles. Located at 40.99° N. Lat; 75.43° W. Long.

Population: n/a (1990); n/a (2000); 4,813 (2010); Density: 951.2 persons per square mile (2010); Race: 73.5% White, 17.2% Black, 1.4% Asian, 0.3% American Indian/Alaska Native, 0.0% Native Hawaiian/Other Pacific Islander, 7.6% Other, 15.7% Hispanic of any race (2010); Average household size: 3.10 (2010); Median age: 39.1 (2010); Males per 100 females: 102.1 (2010); Marriage status: 24.3% never married, 64.0% now married, 4.5% widowed, 7.3% divorced (2006-2010 5-year est.); Foreign born: 12.8% (2006-2010 5-year est.); Ancestry (includes multiple ancestries): 21.4% German, 15.2% Irish, 13.0% Italian, 8.3% Polish, 7.1% English (2006-2010 5-year est.).

Economy: Employment by occupation: 9.3% management, 12.9% professional, 6.5% services, 10.6% sales, 2.9% farming, 9.7% construction, 10.5% production (2006-2010 5-year est.).

Income: Per capita income: $24,109 (2006-2010 5-year est.); Median household income: $66,793 (2006-2010 5-year est.); Average household income: $76,865 (2006-2010 5-year est.); Percent of households with income of $100,000 or more: 30.7% (2006-2010 5-year est.); Poverty rate: 7.0% (2006-2010 5-year est.).

Education: Percent of population age 25 and over with: High school diploma (including GED) or higher: 89.7% (2006-2010 5-year est.); Bachelor's degree or higher: 21.7% (2006-2010 5-year est.); Master's degree or higher: 4.3% (2006-2010 5-year est.).

Housing: Homeownership rate: 93.1% (2010); Median home value: $209,300 (2006-2010 5-year est.); Median contract rent: $614 per month (2006-2010 5-year est.); Median year structure built: 1992 (2006-2010 5-year est.).

Transportation: Commute to work: 93.7% car, 3.7% public transportation, 0.0% walk, 1.8% work from home (2006-2010 5-year est.); Travel time to

work: 9.8% less than 15 minutes, 24.5% 15 to 30 minutes, 18.0% 30 to 45 minutes, 14.4% 45 to 60 minutes, 33.3% 60 minutes or more (2006-2010 5-year est.)

SKYTOP (unincorporated postal area)
Zip Code: 18357

Covers a land area of 3.984 square miles and a water area of 0.165 square miles. Located at 41.23° N. Lat; 75.21° W. Long. Elevation is 1,562 feet. Population: 104 (2010); Density: 26.1 persons per square mile (2010); Race: 85.6% White, 7.7% Black, 1.0% Asian, 0.0% American Indian/Alaska Native, 0.0% Native Hawaiian/Other Pacific Islander, 5.7% Other, 11.5% Hispanic of any race (2010); Average household size: 1.46 (2010); Median age: 53.5 (2010); Males per 100 females: 103.9 (2010); Homeownership rate: 38.1% (2010)

SMITHFIELD (township). Covers a land area of 22.900 square miles and a water area of 0.648 square miles. Located at 41.02° N. Lat; 75.14° W. Long.

Population: 4,691 (1990); 5,672 (2000); 7,357 (2010); Density: 321.3 persons per square mile (2010); Race: 78.3% White, 11.7% Black, 2.9% Asian, 0.3% American Indian/Alaska Native, 0.1% Native Hawaiian/Other Pacific Islander, 6.7% Other, 12.9% Hispanic of any race (2010); Average household size: 2.67 (2010); Median age: 38.8 (2010); Males per 100 females: 96.7 (2010); Marriage status: 29.0% never married, 60.2% now married, 3.5% widowed, 7.3% divorced (2006-2010 5-year est.); Foreign born: 13.0% (2006-2010 5-year est.); Ancestry (includes multiple ancestries): 20.4% German, 13.9% Irish, 8.2% Italian, 6.0% Polish, 4.8% French (2006-2010 5-year est.).
Economy: Single-family building permits issued: 27 (2011); Multi-family building permits issued: 0 (2011); Employment by occupation: 10.4% management, 2.7% professional, 6.4% services, 17.7% sales, 3.1% farming, 10.7% construction, 7.3% production (2006-2010 5-year est.).
Income: Per capita income: $24,134 (2006-2010 5-year est.); Median household income: $49,842 (2006-2010 5-year est.); Average household income: $66,662 (2006-2010 5-year est.); Percent of households with income of $100,000 or more: 22.4% (2006-2010 5-year est.); Poverty rate: 9.8% (2006-2010 5-year est.).
Education: Percent of population age 25 and over with: High school diploma (including GED) or higher: 88.9% (2006-2010 5-year est.); Bachelor's degree or higher: 29.7% (2006-2010 5-year est.); Master's degree or higher: 14.1% (2006-2010 5-year est.).
Housing: Homeownership rate: 74.7% (2010); Median home value: $224,500 (2006-2010 5-year est.); Median contract rent: $714 per month (2006-2010 5-year est.); Median year structure built: 1981 (2006-2010 5-year est.).
Transportation: Commute to work: 82.1% car, 7.9% public transportation, 4.9% walk, 2.8% work from home (2006-2010 5-year est.); Travel time to work: 32.7% less than 15 minutes, 21.4% 15 to 30 minutes, 8.3% 30 to 45 minutes, 4.8% 45 to 60 minutes, 32.8% 60 minutes or more (2006-2010 5-year est.)

Additional Information Contacts
Greater Pocono Chamber of Commerce . . . . (570) 421-4433
  http://www.greaterpoconochamber.com/newindex.cfm?
Smithfield Township . . . . (570) 421-6931
  http://smithfieldtownship.com

STROUD (township). Covers a land area of 31.053 square miles and a water area of 0.263 square miles. Located at 41.00° N. Lat; 75.22° W. Long.

Population: 10,614 (1990); 13,978 (2000); 19,213 (2010); Density: 618.7 persons per square mile (2010); Race: 70.8% White, 16.4% Black, 3.6% Asian, 0.3% American Indian/Alaska Native, 0.0% Native Hawaiian/Other Pacific Islander, 8.9% Other, 15.2% Hispanic of any race (2010); Average household size: 2.81 (2010); Median age: 40.2 (2010); Males per 100 females: 95.0 (2010); Marriage status: 22.6% never married, 61.2% now married, 7.5% widowed, 8.7% divorced (2006-2010 5-year est.); Foreign born: 13.5% (2006-2010 5-year est.); Ancestry (includes multiple ancestries): 19.8% German, 16.9% Italian, 14.9% Irish, 7.5% English, 3.3% Polish (2006-2010 5-year est.).
Economy: Single-family building permits issued: 12 (2011); Multi-family building permits issued: 0 (2011); Employment by occupation: 12.4% management, 4.1% professional, 10.0% services, 19.0% sales, 4.1% farming, 5.8% construction, 4.2% production (2006-2010 5-year est.).
Income: Per capita income: $30,256 (2006-2010 5-year est.); Median household income: $65,747 (2006-2010 5-year est.); Average household

income: $80,401 (2006-2010 5-year est.); Percent of households with income of $100,000 or more: 27.8% (2006-2010 5-year est.); Poverty rate: 3.7% (2006-2010 5-year est.).
Education: Percent of population age 25 and over with: High school diploma (including GED) or higher: 89.3% (2006-2010 5-year est.); Bachelor's degree or higher: 28.2% (2006-2010 5-year est.); Master's degree or higher: 10.3% (2006-2010 5-year est.).
Housing: Homeownership rate: 81.0% (2010); Median home value: $229,600 (2006-2010 5-year est.); Median contract rent: $743 per month (2006-2010 5-year est.); Median year structure built: 1980 (2006-2010 5-year est.).
Transportation: Commute to work: 85.8% car, 7.9% public transportation, 1.9% walk, 3.2% work from home (2006-2010 5-year est.); Travel time to work: 35.3% less than 15 minutes, 23.8% 15 to 30 minutes, 8.6% 30 to 45 minutes, 5.6% 45 to 60 minutes, 26.7% 60 minutes or more (2006-2010 5-year est.)

Additional Information Contacts
Greater Pocono Chamber of Commerce . . . . (570) 421-4433
  http://www.greaterpoconochamber.com/newindex.cfm?
Stroud Township . . . . (570) 421-3362
  http://www.township.stroud.pa.us

STROUDSBURG (borough). County seat. Covers a land area of 1.725 square miles and a water area of 0.017 square miles. Located at 40.98° N. Lat; 75.20° W. Long. Elevation is 433 feet.

History: Appalachian Trail passes to south. Settled 1738, Incorporated 1815.
Population: 5,312 (1990); 5,756 (2000); 5,567 (2010); Density: 3,227.9 persons per square mile (2010); Race: 77.3% White, 11.2% Black, 1.9% Asian, 0.4% American Indian/Alaska Native, 0.0% Native Hawaiian/Other Pacific Islander, 9.2% Other, 14.3% Hispanic of any race (2010); Average household size: 2.30 (2010); Median age: 34.3 (2010); Males per 100 females: 90.7 (2010); Marriage status: 37.4% never married, 47.7% now married, 5.0% widowed, 9.9% divorced (2006-2010 5-year est.); Foreign born: 12.0% (2006-2010 5-year est.); Ancestry (includes multiple ancestries): 22.1% German, 19.8% Irish, 17.3% Italian, 9.1% English, 5.9% Polish (2006-2010 5-year est.).
Economy: Single-family building permits issued: 1 (2011); Multi-family building permits issued: 0 (2011); Employment by occupation: 10.5% management, 3.1% professional, 9.5% services, 20.2% sales, 3.0% farming, 3.4% construction, 3.9% production (2006-2010 5-year est.).
Income: Per capita income: $20,595 (2006-2010 5-year est.); Median household income: $34,405 (2006-2010 5-year est.); Average household income: $52,702 (2006-2010 5-year est.); Percent of households with income of $100,000 or more: 17.6% (2006-2010 5-year est.); Poverty rate: 26.0% (2006-2010 5-year est.).
Education: Percent of population age 25 and over with: High school diploma (including GED) or higher: 87.2% (2006-2010 5-year est.); Bachelor's degree or higher: 30.6% (2006-2010 5-year est.); Master's degree or higher: 10.5% (2006-2010 5-year est.).

School District(s)
Stroudsburg Area SD (KG-12)
  2010-11 Enrollment: 5,568 . . . . (570) 421-1990
Vocational/Technical School(s)
Stroudsburg School of Cosmetology (Private, For-profit)
  Fall 2010 Enrollment: 63 . . . . (570) 421-3387
  2011-12 Tuition: $15,300
Housing: Homeownership rate: 36.9% (2010); Median home value: $206,000 (2006-2010 5-year est.); Median contract rent: $797 per month (2006-2010 5-year est.); Median year structure built: 1942 (2006-2010 5-year est.).
Newspapers: Pocono Record (Local news; Circulation 24,801)
Transportation: Commute to work: 87.2% car, 0.6% public transportation, 8.5% walk, 3.2% work from home (2006-2010 5-year est.); Travel time to work: 50.9% less than 15 minutes, 26.9% 15 to 30 minutes, 8.2% 30 to 45 minutes, 4.0% 45 to 60 minutes, 10.1% 60 minutes or more (2006-2010 5-year est.)

Additional Information Contacts
Borough of Stroudsburg . . . . (570) 421-5444
  http://www.borough.stroudsburg.pa.us
Greater Pocono Chamber of Commerce . . . . (570) 421-4433
  http://www.greaterpoconochamber.com/newindex.cfm?

SUN VALLEY (CDP). Covers a land area of 2.872 square miles and a water area of 0.013 square miles. Located at 40.98° N. Lat; 75.47° W. Long. Elevation is 1,184 feet.

Population: n/a (1990); n/a (2000); 2,399 (2010); Density: 835.2 persons per square mile (2010); Race: 84.7% White, 8.2% Black, 0.5% Asian, 0.2% American Indian/Alaska Native, 0.0% Native Hawaiian/Other Pacific Islander, 6.4% Other, 10.7% Hispanic of any race (2010); Average household size: 2.81 (2010); Median age: 39.9 (2010); Males per 100 females: 99.9 (2010); Marriage status: 21.5% never married, 68.9% now married, 4.9% widowed, 4.7% divorced (2006-2010 5-year est.); Foreign born: 6.6% (2006-2010 5-year est.); Ancestry (includes multiple ancestries): 19.7% Irish, 17.8% German, 15.7% Italian, 9.5% English, 7.2% Jordanian (2006-2010 5-year est.).

Economy: Employment by occupation: 14.4% management, 4.2% professional, 9.1% services, 15.6% sales, 5.2% farming, 18.0% construction, 0.8% production (2006-2010 5-year est.).

Income: Per capita income: $16,941 (2006-2010 5-year est.); Median household income: $36,906 (2006-2010 5-year est.); Average household income: $45,162 (2006-2010 5-year est.); Percent of households with income of $100,000 or more: 6.2% (2006-2010 5-year est.); Poverty rate: 22.3% (2006-2010 5-year est.).

Education: Percent of population age 25 and over with: High school diploma (including GED) or higher: 82.8% (2006-2010 5-year est.); Bachelor's degree or higher: 17.6% (2006-2010 5-year est.); Master's degree or higher: 5.1% (2006-2010 5-year est.).

Housing: Homeownership rate: 87.4% (2010); Median home value: $200,500 (2006-2010 5-year est.); Median contract rent: $779 per month (2006-2010 5-year est.); Median year structure built: 1986 (2006-2010 5-year est.).

Transportation: Commute to work: 92.1% car, 6.3% public transportation, 0.0% walk, 1.5% work from home (2006-2010 5-year est.); Travel time to work: 17.8% less than 15 minutes, 18.3% 15 to 30 minutes, 20.7% 30 to 45 minutes, 13.6% 45 to 60 minutes, 29.6% 60 minutes or more (2006-2010 5-year est.)

SWIFTWATER (unincorporated postal area)

Zip Code: 18370

Covers a land area of 5.212 square miles and a water area of 0.036 square miles. Located at 41.09° N. Lat; 75.33° W. Long. Elevation is 1,181 feet. Population: 1,096 (2010); Density: 210.3 persons per square mile (2010); Race: 83.9% White, 7.2% Black, 1.6% Asian, 0.1% American Indian/Alaska Native, 0.9% Native Hawaiian/Other Pacific Islander, 6.3% Other, 11.0% Hispanic of any race (2010); Average household size: 2.48 (2010); Median age: 45.3 (2010); Males per 100 females: 103.7 (2010); Homeownership rate: 83.1% (2010)

TANNERSVILLE (unincorporated postal area)

Zip Code: 18372

Covers a land area of 8.832 square miles and a water area of 0.010 square miles. Located at 41.04° N. Lat; 75.33° W. Long. Elevation is 883 feet. Population: 3,210 (2010); Density: 363.4 persons per square mile (2010); Race: 75.1% White, 13.2% Black, 3.8% Asian, 0.3% American Indian/Alaska Native, 0.1% Native Hawaiian/Other Pacific Islander, 7.5% Other, 11.7% Hispanic of any race (2010); Average household size: 2.78 (2010); Median age: 40.0 (2010); Males per 100 females: 101.0 (2010); Homeownership rate: 78.9% (2010)

TOBYHANNA (township). Covers a land area of 50.191 square miles and a water area of 2.399 square miles. Located at 41.11° N. Lat; 75.52° W. Long.

Population: 4,310 (1990); 6,152 (2000); 8,554 (2010); Density: 170.4 persons per square mile (2010); Race: 81.8% White, 10.0% Black, 1.4% Asian, 0.5% American Indian/Alaska Native, 0.0% Native Hawaiian/Other Pacific Islander, 6.3% Other, 11.8% Hispanic of any race (2010); Average household size: 2.49 (2010); Median age: 45.3 (2010); Males per 100 females: 102.3 (2010); Marriage status: 24.8% never married, 58.7% now married, 6.3% widowed, 10.1% divorced (2006-2010 5-year est.); Foreign born: 4.3% (2006-2010 5-year est.); Ancestry (includes multiple ancestries): 26.6% German, 26.0% Italian, 13.9% Irish, 7.7% Polish, 7.6% English (2006-2010 5-year est.).

Economy: Single-family building permits issued: 30 (2011); Multi-family building permits issued: 0 (2011); Employment by occupation: 11.5% management, 3.5% professional, 15.5% services, 24.3% sales, 3.4% farming, 10.9% construction, 8.7% production (2006-2010 5-year est.).

Income: Per capita income: $23,109 (2006-2010 5-year est.); Median household income: $47,760 (2006-2010 5-year est.); Average household income: $61,547 (2006-2010 5-year est.); Percent of households with income of $100,000 or more: 13.5% (2006-2010 5-year est.); Poverty rate: 12.3% (2006-2010 5-year est.).

Education: Percent of population age 25 and over with: High school diploma (including GED) or higher: 92.6% (2006-2010 5-year est.); Bachelor's degree or higher: 17.7% (2006-2010 5-year est.); Master's degree or higher: 8.0% (2006-2010 5-year est.).

School District(s)

Pocono Mountain Charter School (KG-12)

    2010-11 Enrollment: 329 . . . . (570) 894-5108

Pocono Mountain SD (KG-12)

    2010-11 Enrollment: 10,693 . . . . (570) 839-7121

Housing: Homeownership rate: 86.6% (2010); Median home value: $193,100 (2006-2010 5-year est.); Median contract rent: $1,003 per month (2006-2010 5-year est.); Median year structure built: 1980 (2006-2010 5-year est.).

Transportation: Commute to work: 87.4% car, 2.3% public transportation, 5.7% walk, 4.3% work from home (2006-2010 5-year est.); Travel time to work: 29.9% less than 15 minutes, 25.1% 15 to 30 minutes, 17.2% 30 to 45 minutes, 4.8% 45 to 60 minutes, 23.0% 60 minutes or more (2006-2010 5-year est.)

Additional Information Contacts

Greater Scranton Chamber of Commerce . . . . (570) 342-7711

    http://www.scrantonchamber.com

Tobyhanna Township . . . . (570) 646-1212

    http://www.tobyhannatownship.org

TUNKHANNOCK (township). Covers a land area of 38.546 square miles and a water area of 0.289 square miles. Located at 41.04° N. Lat; 75.49° W. Long.

Population: 2,068 (1990); 4,983 (2000); 6,789 (2010); Density: 176.1 persons per square mile (2010); Race: 71.6% White, 18.0% Black, 1.9% Asian, 0.3% American Indian/Alaska Native, 0.0% Native Hawaiian/Other Pacific Islander, 8.2% Other, 15.5% Hispanic of any race (2010); Average household size: 2.88 (2010); Median age: 39.8 (2010); Males per 100 females: 101.0 (2010); Marriage status: 32.0% never married, 51.6% now married, 5.9% widowed, 10.5% divorced (2006-2010 5-year est.); Foreign born: 10.2% (2006-2010 5-year est.); Ancestry (includes multiple ancestries): 20.5% German, 14.8% Irish, 10.6% Italian, 5.9% Polish, 3.9% American (2006-2010 5-year est.).

Economy: Single-family building permits issued: 11 (2011); Multi-family building permits issued: 0 (2011); Employment by occupation: 8.6% management, 6.9% professional, 7.3% services, 15.8% sales, 5.2% farming, 16.0% construction, 10.0% production (2006-2010 5-year est.).

Income: Per capita income: $21,298 (2006-2010 5-year est.); Median household income: $47,039 (2006-2010 5-year est.); Average household income: $60,612 (2006-2010 5-year est.); Percent of households with income of $100,000 or more: 16.9% (2006-2010 5-year est.); Poverty rate: 12.0% (2006-2010 5-year est.).

Education: Percent of population age 25 and over with: High school diploma (including GED) or higher: 86.9% (2006-2010 5-year est.); Bachelor's degree or higher: 15.9% (2006-2010 5-year est.); Master's degree or higher: 5.6% (2006-2010 5-year est.).

Housing: Homeownership rate: 89.2% (2010); Median home value: $172,900 (2006-2010 5-year est.); Median contract rent: $638 per month (2006-2010 5-year est.); Median year structure built: 1989 (2006-2010 5-year est.).

Transportation: Commute to work: 90.5% car, 6.7% public transportation, 0.6% walk, 2.2% work from home (2006-2010 5-year est.); Travel time to work: 8.2% less than 15 minutes, 25.4% 15 to 30 minutes, 14.5% 30 to 45 minutes, 14.5% 45 to 60 minutes, 37.3% 60 minutes or more (2006-2010 5-year est.)

Additional Information Contacts

Greater Pocono Chamber of Commerce . . . . (570) 421-4433

    http://www.greaterpoconochamber.com/newindex.cfm?

Tunkhannock Township . . . . (570) 646-3008

    http://www.longpondpa.com

Montgomery County

Located in southeastern Pennsylvania; drained by the Schuylkill River. Covers a land area of 483.040 square miles, a water area of 4.155 square

miles, and is located in the Eastern Time Zone at 40.21° N. Lat., 75.37° W. Long. The county was founded in 1784. County seat is Norristown.

Montgomery County is part of the Philadelphia-Camden-Wilmington, PA-NJ-DE-MD Metropolitan Statistical Area. The entire metro area includes: Camden, NJ Metropolitan Division (Burlington County, NJ; Camden County, NJ; Gloucester County, NJ); Philadelphia, PA Metropolitan Division (Bucks County, PA; Chester County, PA; Delaware County, PA; Montgomery County, PA; Philadelphia County, PA); Wilmington, DE-MD-NJ Metropolitan Division (New Castle County, DE; Cecil County, MD; Salem County, NJ)

Weather Station: Graterford 1 E										Elevation: 240 feet		
	Jan	Feb	Mar	Apr	May	Jun	Jul	Aug	Sep	Oct	Nov	Dec
High	38	41	50	61	71	81	85	83	77	66	55	43
Low	19	21	28	38	47	57	62	59	51	39	32	23
Precip	3.0	2.1	3.5	4.0	4.1	3.9	4.4	4.2	4.5	3.8	3.7	3.6
Snow	2.9	4.3	0.9	0.3	0.0	0.0	0.0	0.0	0.0	0.0	0.2	1.9

High and Low temperatures in degrees Fahrenheit; Precipitation and Snow in inches

Population: 678,111 (1990); 750,097 (2000); 799,874 (2010); Race: 81.1% White, 8.7% Black, 6.4% Asian, 0.1% American Indian/Alaska Native, 0.0% Native Hawaiian/Other Pacific Islander, 3.7% Other, 4.3% Hispanic of any race (2010); Density: 1,655.9 persons per square mile (2010); Average household size: 2.53 (2010); Median age: 40.6 (2010); Males per 100 females: 94.2 (2010).

Religion: Six largest groups: 37.7% Catholicism, 4.7% Lutheran, 4.3% Judaism, 3.7% Presbyterian-Reformed, 3.2% Non-Denominational, 2.1% Baptist (2010)

Economy: Unemployment rate: 7.1% (August 2012); Total civilian labor force: 435,496 (August 2012); Leading industries: 15.3% health care and social assistance; 12.0% retail trade; 9.9% professional, scientific & technical services (2010); Farms: 719 totaling 41,908 acres (2007); Companies that employ 500 or more persons: 85 (2010); Companies that employ 100 to 499 persons: 657 (2010); Companies that employ less than 100 persons: 25,056 (2010); Black-owned businesses: 2,779 (2007); Hispanic-owned businesses: n/a (2007); Asian-owned businesses: 3,922 (2007); Women-owned businesses: 21,954 (2007); Retail sales per capita: $19,117 (2010). Single-family building permits issued: 668 (2011); Multi-family building permits issued: 241 (2011).

Income: Per capita income: $40,076 (2006-2010 5-year est.); Median household income: $76,380 (2006-2010 5-year est.); Average household income: $101,910 (2006-2010 5-year est.); Percent of households with income of $100,000 or more: 36.3% (2006-2010 5-year est.); Poverty rate: 5.6% (2006-2010 5-year est.); Bankruptcy rate: 2.18% (2011).

Taxes: Total county taxes per capita: $205 (2009); County property taxes per capita: $200 (2009).

Education: Percent of population age 25 and over with: High school diploma (including GED) or higher: 92.6% (2006-2010 5-year est.); Bachelor's degree or higher: 44.2% (2006-2010 5-year est.); Master's degree or higher: 18.5% (2006-2010 5-year est.).

Housing: Homeownership rate: 73.1% (2010); Median home value: $297,200 (2006-2010 5-year est.); Median contract rent: $897 per month (2006-2010 5-year est.); Median year structure built: 1965 (2006-2010 5-year est.)

Health: Birth rate: 113.5 per 10,000 population (2011); Death rate: 88.4 per 10,000 population (2011); Age-adjusted cancer mortality rate: 178.0 deaths per 100,000 population (2009); Number of physicians: 63.3 per 10,000 population (2010); Hospital beds: 45.9 per 10,000 population (2008); Hospital admissions: 1,950.0 per 10,000 population (2008).

Environment: Air Quality Index: 71.8% good, 26.3% moderate, 1.9% unhealthy for sensitive individuals, 0.0% unhealthy (percent of days in 2011)

Elections: 2012 Presidential election results: 56.5% Obama, 42.4% Romney

National and State Parks: Eastern State Game Farm; Evansburg State Park; Evansburg State Park; Fort Washington State Park; Fort Washington State Park; Graeme State Park; Valley Forge National Historical Park

Additional Information Contacts

Montgomery County Government . . . . (610) 278-3000
   http://www2.montcopa.org
Eastern Montgomery County Chamber of Commerce . . . . (215) 887-5122
   http://www.emccc.org
Montgomery County Chamber of Commerce . . . . (610) 278-3000
   http://www.montcopa.org/montco/site/default.asp

Montgomery County Chamber of Commerce . . . . (610) 265-1776
   http://www.montgomerycountychamber.org
TriCounty Area Chamber of Commerce . . . . (610) 326-2900
   http://www.tricountyareachamber.com

Montgomery County Communities

ABINGTON (township). Covers a land area of 15.510 square miles and a water area of <.001 square miles. Located at 40.11° N. Lat; 75.12° W. Long. Elevation is 341 feet.

History: Abington was founded in 1714.

Population: 56,322 (1990); 56,103 (2000); 55,310 (2010); Density: 3,566.2 persons per square mile (2010); Race: 79.7% White, 12.4% Black, 4.9% Asian, 0.1% American Indian/Alaska Native, 0.0% Native Hawaiian/Other Pacific Islander, 2.9% Other, 3.2% Hispanic of any race (2010); Average household size: 2.55 (2010); Median age: 42.8 (2010); Males per 100 females: 90.5 (2010); Marriage status: 27.5% never married, 57.1% now married, 8.3% widowed, 7.1% divorced (2006-2010 5-year est.); Foreign born: 8.3% (2006-2010 5-year est.); Ancestry (includes multiple ancestries): 25.5% Irish, 22.4% German, 13.8% Italian, 8.8% English, 7.3% Polish (2006-2010 5-year est.).

Economy: Unemployment rate: 7.2% (August 2012); Total civilian labor force: 29,491 (August 2012); Single-family building permits issued: 5 (2011); Multi-family building permits issued: 0 (2011); Employment by occupation: 13.7% management, 5.1% professional, 6.3% services, 17.7% sales, 4.6% farming, 7.7% construction, 4.0% production (2006-2010 5-year est.).

Income: Per capita income: $38,663 (2006-2010 5-year est.); Median household income: $75,542 (2006-2010 5-year est.); Average household income: $98,724 (2006-2010 5-year est.); Percent of households with income of $100,000 or more: 34.7% (2006-2010 5-year est.); Poverty rate: 4.4% (2006-2010 5-year est.).

Taxes: Total city taxes per capita: $538 (2009); City property taxes per capita: $220 (2009).

Education: Percent of population age 25 and over with: High school diploma (including GED) or higher: 93.1% (2006-2010 5-year est.); Bachelor's degree or higher: 42.1% (2006-2010 5-year est.); Master's degree or higher: 17.7% (2006-2010 5-year est.).

School District(s)

Abington SD (KG-12)
   2010-11 Enrollment: 7,465 . . . . (215) 884-4700

Four-year College(s)

Pennsylvania State University-Penn State Abington (Public)
   Fall 2010 Enrollment: 3,418 . . . . (215) 881-7300
   2011-12 Tuition: In-state $13,102; Out-of-state $19,542

Housing: Homeownership rate: 78.2% (2010); Median home value: $268,400 (2006-2010 5-year est.); Median contract rent: $903 per month (2006-2010 5-year est.); Median year structure built: 1955 (2006-2010 5-year est.).

Hospitals: Abington Memorial Hospital (508 beds)

Safety: Violent crime rate: 15.1 per 10,000 population; Property crime rate: 213.4 per 10,000 population (2011).

Newspapers: Willow Grove Life (Local news; Circulation 12,000)

Transportation: Commute to work: 87.7% car, 7.1% public transportation, 1.9% walk, 3.0% work from home (2006-2010 5-year est.); Travel time to work: 28.5% less than 15 minutes, 28.6% 15 to 30 minutes, 22.3% 30 to 45 minutes, 11.4% 45 to 60 minutes, 9.2% 60 minutes or more (2006-2010 5-year est.)

Additional Information Contacts

Abington Township . . . . (267) 536-1000
   http://www.abington.org
Eastern Montgomery County Chamber of Commerce . . . . (215) 887-5122
   http://www.emccc.org

AMBLER (borough). Covers a land area of 0.852 square miles and a water area of 0 square miles. Located at 40.16° N. Lat; 75.22° W. Long. Elevation is 213 feet.

History: Incorporated 1888.

Population: 6,609 (1990); 6,426 (2000); 6,417 (2010); Density: 7,529.6 persons per square mile (2010); Race: 76.5% White, 12.8% Black, 3.8% Asian, 0.2% American Indian/Alaska Native, 0.3% Native Hawaiian/Other Pacific Islander, 6.4% Other, 7.9% Hispanic of any race (2010); Average household size: 2.40 (2010); Median age: 36.8 (2010); Males per 100 females: 90.9 (2010); Marriage status: 30.7% never married, 49.5% now married, 10.5% widowed, 9.3% divorced (2006-2010 5-year est.); Foreign

born: 14.4% (2006-2010 5-year est.); Ancestry (includes multiple ancestries): 22.1% Italian, 20.2% German, 18.4% Irish, 12.7% English, 3.6% Polish (2006-2010 5-year est.).

Economy: Single-family building permits issued: 1 (2011); Multi-family building permits issued: 0 (2011); Employment by occupation: 10.2% management, 6.2% professional, 9.4% services, 14.1% sales, 3.0% farming, 12.1% construction, 5.7% production (2006-2010 5-year est.).

Income: Per capita income: $31,673 (2006-2010 5-year est.); Median household income: $57,340 (2006-2010 5-year est.); Average household income: $72,553 (2006-2010 5-year est.); Percent of households with income of $100,000 or more: 20.4% (2006-2010 5-year est.); Poverty rate: 8.1% (2006-2010 5-year est.).

Education: Percent of population age 25 and over with: High school diploma (including GED) or higher: 88.9% (2006-2010 5-year est.); Bachelor's degree or higher: 33.4% (2006-2010 5-year est.); Master's degree or higher: 13.7% (2006-2010 5-year est.).

School District(s)
Hatboro-Horsham SD (KG-12)
   2010-11 Enrollment: 5,105 . . . . (215) 420-5000
Wissahickon SD (KG-12)
   2010-11 Enrollment: 4,472 . . . . (215) 619-8000

Vocational/Technical School(s)
Magnolia School (Private, For-profit)
   Fall 2010 Enrollment: 230 . . . . (215) 643-5994
   2011-12 Tuition: $17,200

Housing: Homeownership rate: 53.9% (2010); Median home value: $247,200 (2006-2010 5-year est.); Median contract rent: $844 per month (2006-2010 5-year est.); Median year structure built: 1951 (2006-2010 5-year est.).

Hospitals: Horsham Clinic (146 beds)

Safety: Violent crime rate: 20.2 per 10,000 population; Property crime rate: 228.4 per 10,000 population (2011).

Transportation: Commute to work: 88.2% car, 4.4% public transportation, 3.8% walk, 1.5% work from home (2006-2010 5-year est.); Travel time to work: 28.9% less than 15 minutes, 39.7% 15 to 30 minutes, 18.5% 30 to 45 minutes, 9.9% 45 to 60 minutes, 3.0% 60 minutes or more (2006-2010 5-year est.).

Airports: Wings Field (general aviation)

Additional Information Contacts
Borough of Ambler . . . . (215) 646-1000
   http://www.boroughofambler.com
Eastern Montgomery County Chamber of Commerce . . . . (215) 887-5122
   http://www.emccc.org

ARCADIA UNIVERSITY (CDP).
Covers a land area of 0.083 square miles and a water area of 0 square miles. Located at 40.09° N. Lat; 75.17° W. Long.

Population: n/a (1990); n/a (2000); 595 (2010); Density: 7,181.0 persons per square mile (2010); Race: 83.9% White, 8.2% Black, 3.7% Asian, 0.2% American Indian/Alaska Native, 0.2% Native Hawaiian/Other Pacific Islander, 3.8% Other, 7.2% Hispanic of any race (2010); Average household size: 0.00 (2010); Median age: 19.5 (2010); Males per 100 females: 39.0 (2010); Marriage status: 100.0% never married, 0.0% now married, 0.0% widowed, 0.0% divorced (2006-2010 5-year est.); Foreign born: 1.8% (2006-2010 5-year est.); Ancestry (includes multiple ancestries): 27.1% Irish, 21.0% Italian, 19.8% Polish, 15.6% German, 10.2% English (2006-2010 5-year est.).

Economy: Employment by occupation: 4.2% management, 0.0% professional, 17.1% services, 52.7% sales, 10.4% farming, 0.0% construction, 6.5% production (2006-2010 5-year est.).

Income: Per capita income: $3,448 (2006-2010 5-year est.); Median household income: n/a (2006-2010 5-year est.); Average household income: n/a (2006-2010 5-year est.); Percent of households with income of $100,000 or more: n/a (2006-2010 5-year est.); Poverty rate: n/a (2006-2010 5-year est.).

Education: Percent of population age 25 and over with: High school diploma (including GED) or higher: 100.0% (2006-2010 5-year est.); Bachelor's degree or higher: 100.0% (2006-2010 5-year est.); Master's degree or higher: 50.0% (2006-2010 5-year est.).

Housing: Homeownership rate: 0.0% (2010); Median home value: n/a (2006-2010 5-year est.); Median contract rent: n/a per month (2006-2010 5-year est.); Median year structure built: n/a (2006-2010 5-year est.).

Transportation: Commute to work: 11.6% car, 12.1% public transportation, 76.3% walk, 0.0% work from home (2006-2010 5-year est.); Travel time to work: 81.9% less than 15 minutes, 13.8% 15 to 30 minutes,

4.2% 30 to 45 minutes, 0.0% 45 to 60 minutes, 0.0% 60 minutes or more (2006-2010 5-year est.)

ARDMORE (CDP).
Covers a land area of 1.970 square miles and a water area of 0 square miles. Located at 40.00° N. Lat; 75.29° W. Long. Elevation is 351 feet.

History: Named for a town in Ireland. Settled c.1800.

Population: 12,641 (1990); 12,616 (2000); 12,455 (2010); Density: 6,321.6 persons per square mile (2010); Race: 79.3% White, 12.9% Black, 4.1% Asian, 0.1% American Indian/Alaska Native, 0.1% Native Hawaiian/Other Pacific Islander, 3.5% Other, 4.0% Hispanic of any race (2010); Average household size: 2.26 (2010); Median age: 40.4 (2010); Males per 100 females: 87.5 (2010); Marriage status: 38.5% never married, 46.3% now married, 6.1% widowed, 9.2% divorced (2006-2010 5-year est.); Foreign born: 12.7% (2006-2010 5-year est.); Ancestry (includes multiple ancestries): 20.7% Irish, 20.4% German, 15.6% Italian, 10.5% English, 3.7% Russian (2006-2010 5-year est.).

Economy: Employment by occupation: 15.7% management, 6.9% professional, 5.1% services, 12.5% sales, 3.4% farming, 3.6% construction, 2.1% production (2006-2010 5-year est.).

Income: Per capita income: $48,177 (2006-2010 5-year est.); Median household income: $67,829 (2006-2010 5-year est.); Average household income: $106,343 (2006-2010 5-year est.); Percent of households with income of $100,000 or more: 35.5% (2006-2010 5-year est.); Poverty rate: 8.5% (2006-2010 5-year est.).

Education: Percent of population age 25 and over with: High school diploma (including GED) or higher: 95.2% (2006-2010 5-year est.); Bachelor's degree or higher: 60.6% (2006-2010 5-year est.); Master's degree or higher: 32.8% (2006-2010 5-year est.).

School District(s)
Haverford Township SD (KG-12)
   2010-11 Enrollment: 5,622 . . . . (610) 853-5900
Lower Merion SD (KG-12)
   2010-11 Enrollment: 7,212 . . . . (610) 645-1800

Housing: Homeownership rate: 63.9% (2010); Median home value: $291,300 (2006-2010 5-year est.); Median contract rent: $986 per month (2006-2010 5-year est.); Median year structure built: 1943 (2006-2010 5-year est.).

Newspapers: Main Line Times (Community news; Circulation 10,000)

Transportation: Commute to work: 73.3% car, 13.0% public transportation, 6.5% walk, 6.1% work from home (2006-2010 5-year est.); Travel time to work: 25.7% less than 15 minutes, 28.7% 15 to 30 minutes, 26.6% 30 to 45 minutes, 11.8% 45 to 60 minutes, 7.3% 60 minutes or more (2006-2010 5-year est.); Amtrak: train service available.

Additional Information Contacts
Greater Philadelphia Chamber of Commerce . . . . (215) 545-1234
   http://www.greaterphilachamber.com

AUDUBON (CDP).
Covers a land area of 4.583 square miles and a water area of 0.013 square miles. Located at 40.13° N. Lat; 75.43° W. Long. Elevation is 194 feet.

History: Valley Forge National Historical Park to South.

Population: 6,328 (1990); 6,549 (2000); 8,433 (2010); Density: 1,840.2 persons per square mile (2010); Race: 79.5% White, 5.2% Black, 13.4% Asian, 0.0% American Indian/Alaska Native, 0.0% Native Hawaiian/Other Pacific Islander, 1.9% Other, 2.3% Hispanic of any race (2010); Average household size: 2.47 (2010); Median age: 42.7 (2010); Males per 100 females: 98.7 (2010); Marriage status: 18.3% never married, 66.4% now married, 9.4% widowed, 5.9% divorced (2006-2010 5-year est.); Foreign born: 14.1% (2006-2010 5-year est.); Ancestry (includes multiple ancestries): 22.7% Irish, 20.9% German, 19.5% Italian, 8.2% English, 7.4% American (2006-2010 5-year est.).

Economy: Employment by occupation: 16.1% management, 15.3% professional, 7.0% services, 17.3% sales, 1.7% farming, 3.0% construction, 2.9% production (2006-2010 5-year est.).

Income: Per capita income: $39,827 (2006-2010 5-year est.); Median household income: $82,803 (2006-2010 5-year est.); Average household income: $104,472 (2006-2010 5-year est.); Percent of households with income of $100,000 or more: 38.3% (2006-2010 5-year est.); Poverty rate: 1.1% (2006-2010 5-year est.).

Education: Percent of population age 25 and over with: High school diploma (including GED) or higher: 95.4% (2006-2010 5-year est.); Bachelor's degree or higher: 52.7% (2006-2010 5-year est.); Master's degree or higher: 24.4% (2006-2010 5-year est.).

School District(s)

Methacton SD (KG-12)

    2010-11 Enrollment: 5,289 . . . . (610) 489-5000

Housing: Homeownership rate: 67.0% (2010); Median home value: $341,100 (2006-2010 5-year est.); Median contract rent: $1,152 per month (2006-2010 5-year est.); Median year structure built: 1976 (2006-2010 5-year est.).

Transportation: Commute to work: 90.5% car, 2.4% public transportation, 1.5% walk, 3.5% work from home (2006-2010 5-year est.); Travel time to work: 32.9% less than 15 minutes, 31.9% 15 to 30 minutes, 17.9% 30 to 45 minutes, 9.1% 45 to 60 minutes, 8.1% 60 minutes or more (2006-2010 5-year est.)

Additional Information Contacts

Greater Philadelphia Chamber of Commerce . . . . (215) 545-1234

    http://www.greaterphilachamber.com

BALA CYNWYD (unincorporated postal area)

Zip Code: 19004

    Covers a land area of 2.763 square miles and a water area of 0.007 square miles. Located at 40.00° N. Lat; 75.23° W. Long. Population: 9,416 (2010); Density: 3,407.4 persons per square mile (2010); Race: 87.8% White, 3.5% Black, 6.0% Asian, 0.1% American Indian/Alaska Native, 0.0% Native Hawaiian/Other Pacific Islander, 2.6% Other, 2.7% Hispanic of any race (2010); Average household size: 2.49 (2010); Median age: 43.5 (2010); Males per 100 females: 93.5 (2010); Homeownership rate: 80.8% (2010)

BLUE BELL (CDP). Covers a land area of 5.389 square miles and a water area of 0 square miles. Located at 40.15° N. Lat; 75.27° W. Long. Elevation is 358 feet.

History: Blue Bell was originally known as Pigeontown, Pennsylvania, after the large flocks of the now-extinct passenger pigeons that once gathered there. The town was renamed in 1840 after the historically prominent Blue Bell Inn.

Population: 6,091 (1990); 6,395 (2000); 6,067 (2010); Density: 1,125.7 persons per square mile (2010); Race: 87.8% White, 2.9% Black, 8.1% Asian, 0.0% American Indian/Alaska Native, 0.0% Native Hawaiian/Other Pacific Islander, 1.2% Other, 1.5% Hispanic of any race (2010); Average household size: 2.49 (2010); Median age: 46.8 (2010); Males per 100 females: 91.2 (2010); Marriage status: 19.4% never married, 68.2% now married, 5.4% widowed, 6.9% divorced (2006-2010 5-year est.); Foreign born: 8.7% (2006-2010 5-year est.); Ancestry (includes multiple ancestries): 28.1% Irish, 18.2% German, 14.6% Italian, 11.8% Polish, 10.2% English (2006-2010 5-year est.).

Economy: Employment by occupation: 20.7% management, 7.0% professional, 3.4% services, 13.8% sales, 4.2% farming, 3.1% construction, 1.1% production (2006-2010 5-year est.).

Income: Per capita income: $57,970 (2006-2010 5-year est.); Median household income: $118,446 (2006-2010 5-year est.); Average household income: $145,710 (2006-2010 5-year est.); Percent of households with income of $100,000 or more: 59.9% (2006-2010 5-year est.); Poverty rate: 1.2% (2006-2010 5-year est.).

Education: Percent of population age 25 and over with: High school diploma (including GED) or higher: 98.0% (2006-2010 5-year est.); Bachelor's degree or higher: 64.0% (2006-2010 5-year est.); Master's degree or higher: 26.4% (2006-2010 5-year est.).

School District(s)

Wissahickon SD (KG-12)

    2010-11 Enrollment: 4,472 . . . . (215) 619-8000

Four-year College(s)

Theological Seminary of the Reformed Episcopal Church (Private, Not-for-profit, Episcopal Church- Reformed)

    Fall 2010 Enrollment: n/a . . . . (610) 292-9852

Two-year College(s)

Montgomery County Community College-Central Campus (Public)

    Fall 2010 Enrollment: 7,339 . . . . (215) 641-6300

    2011-12 Tuition: In-state $7,140; Out-of-state $10,530

Housing: Homeownership rate: 88.2% (2010); Median home value: $443,200 (2006-2010 5-year est.); Median contract rent: $1,708 per month (2006-2010 5-year est.); Median year structure built: 1981 (2006-2010 5-year est.).

Transportation: Commute to work: 86.8% car, 4.3% public transportation, 1.8% walk, 6.9% work from home (2006-2010 5-year est.); Travel time to work: 30.2% less than 15 minutes, 26.2% 15 to 30 minutes, 25.9% 30 to

45 minutes, 10.7% 45 to 60 minutes, 7.0% 60 minutes or more (2006-2010 5-year est.)

Additional Information Contacts

Greater Hatboro Chamber of Commerce . . . . (215) 956-9540

    http://hatborochamber.org

BRIDGEPORT (borough). Covers a land area of 0.659 square miles and a water area of 0.053 square miles. Located at 40.10° N. Lat; 75.34° W. Long. Elevation is 92 feet.

History: Settled 1829, incorporated 1851.

Population: 4,195 (1990); 4,371 (2000); 4,554 (2010); Density: 6,909.2 persons per square mile (2010); Race: 79.8% White, 7.9% Black, 2.8% Asian, 0.3% American Indian/Alaska Native, 0.0% Native Hawaiian/Other Pacific Islander, 9.2% Other, 12.8% Hispanic of any race (2010); Average household size: 2.26 (2010); Median age: 33.7 (2010); Males per 100 females: 101.0 (2010); Marriage status: 51.0% never married, 28.2% now married, 8.4% widowed, 12.4% divorced (2006-2010 5-year est.); Foreign born: 5.1% (2006-2010 5-year est.); Ancestry (includes multiple ancestries): 25.1% German, 24.7% Italian, 21.6% Irish, 12.8% Polish, 7.1% English (2006-2010 5-year est.).

Economy: Single-family building permits issued: 0 (2011); Multi-family building permits issued: 0 (2011); Employment by occupation: 12.9% management, 6.0% professional, 14.0% services, 20.0% sales, 4.2% farming, 10.2% construction, 7.5% production (2006-2010 5-year est.).

Income: Per capita income: $27,158 (2006-2010 5-year est.); Median household income: $39,472 (2006-2010 5-year est.); Average household income: $56,657 (2006-2010 5-year est.); Percent of households with income of $100,000 or more: 16.8% (2006-2010 5-year est.); Poverty rate: 15.2% (2006-2010 5-year est.).

Education: Percent of population age 25 and over with: High school diploma (including GED) or higher: 84.9% (2006-2010 5-year est.); Bachelor's degree or higher: 26.9% (2006-2010 5-year est.); Master's degree or higher: 8.0% (2006-2010 5-year est.).

School District(s)

Upper Merion Area SD (KG-12)

    2010-11 Enrollment: 3,791 . . . . (610) 205-6400

Housing: Homeownership rate: 47.7% (2010); Median home value: $196,600 (2006-2010 5-year est.); Median contract rent: $674 per month (2006-2010 5-year est.); Median year structure built: 1950 (2006-2010 5-year est.).

Safety: Violent crime rate: 19.7 per 10,000 population; Property crime rate: 323.9 per 10,000 population (2011).

Transportation: Commute to work: 87.3% car, 9.3% public transportation, 1.9% walk, 1.5% work from home (2006-2010 5-year est.); Travel time to work: 39.8% less than 15 minutes, 35.8% 15 to 30 minutes, 12.9% 30 to 45 minutes, 7.2% 45 to 60 minutes, 4.4% 60 minutes or more (2006-2010 5-year est.)

Additional Information Contacts

Borough of Bridgeport . . . . (610) 272-1811

    http://www.boroughofbridgeport.com

Main Line Chamber of Commerce . . . . (610) 687-6232

    http://www.mlcc.org

BRYN ATHYN (borough). Covers a land area of 1.931 square miles and a water area of 0 square miles. Located at 40.14° N. Lat; 75.07° W. Long. Elevation is 236 feet.

History: Swedenborgian cathedral located here.

Population: 1,081 (1990); 1,351 (2000); 1,375 (2010); Density: 712.0 persons per square mile (2010); Race: 92.5% White, 2.7% Black, 2.5% Asian, 0.0% American Indian/Alaska Native, 0.1% Native Hawaiian/Other Pacific Islander, 2.2% Other, 1.2% Hispanic of any race (2010); Average household size: 2.82 (2010); Median age: 36.0 (2010); Males per 100 females: 95.0 (2010); Marriage status: 41.8% never married, 48.7% now married, 5.0% widowed, 4.5% divorced (2006-2010 5-year est.); Foreign born: 8.4% (2006-2010 5-year est.); Ancestry (includes multiple ancestries): 28.7% German, 17.9% English, 13.8% Scottish, 9.0% Irish, 9.0% Swedish (2006-2010 5-year est.).

Economy: Single-family building permits issued: 0 (2011); Multi-family building permits issued: 0 (2011); Employment by occupation: 19.0% management, 2.6% professional, 8.1% services, 10.7% sales, 4.9% farming, 7.6% construction, 5.7% production (2006-2010 5-year est.).

Income: Per capita income: $27,790 (2006-2010 5-year est.); Median household income: $82,232 (2006-2010 5-year est.); Average household income: $104,324 (2006-2010 5-year est.); Percent of households with

income of $100,000 or more: 33.3% (2006-2010 5-year est.); Poverty rate: 1.4% (2006-2010 5-year est.).

Education: Percent of population age 25 and over with: High school diploma (including GED) or higher: 97.7% (2006-2010 5-year est.); Bachelor's degree or higher: 57.7% (2006-2010 5-year est.); Master's degree or higher: 21.6% (2006-2010 5-year est.).

Four-year College(s)

Bryn Athyn College of the New Church (Private, Not-for-profit, Other (none of the above))

    Fall 2010 Enrollment: 232 . . . . (267) 502-2543
    2011-12 Tuition: In-state $16,074; Out-of-state $16,074

Housing: Homeownership rate: 69.2% (2010); Median home value: $477,900 (2006-2010 5-year est.); Median contract rent: $1,165 per month (2006-2010 5-year est.); Median year structure built: 1953 (2006-2010 5-year est.).

Transportation: Commute to work: 56.0% car, 1.0% public transportation, 27.1% walk, 14.7% work from home (2006-2010 5-year est.); Travel time to work: 66.2% less than 15 minutes, 18.8% 15 to 30 minutes, 7.6% 30 to 45 minutes, 2.4% 45 to 60 minutes, 5.0% 60 minutes or more (2006-2010 5-year est.)

Additional Information Contacts

Eastern Montgomery County Chamber of Commerce . . . . (215) 887-5122
    http://www.emccc.org

BRYN MAWR (CDP). Covers a land area of 0.634 square miles and a water area of 0 square miles. Located at 40.02° N. Lat; 75.32° W. Long. Elevation is 420 feet.

History: Seat of Bryn Mawr College, opened in 1885 by the Society of Friends.

Population: 3,271 (1990); 4,382 (2000); 3,779 (2010); Density: 5,961.1 persons per square mile (2010); Race: 74.0% White, 10.5% Black, 10.7% Asian, 0.0% American Indian/Alaska Native, 0.1% Native Hawaiian/Other Pacific Islander, 4.7% Other, 4.9% Hispanic of any race (2010); Average household size: 2.00 (2010); Median age: 23.5 (2010); Males per 100 females: 49.4 (2010); Marriage status: 71.0% never married, 19.2% now married, 5.1% widowed, 4.7% divorced (2006-2010 5-year est.); Foreign born: 13.1% (2006-2010 5-year est.); Ancestry (includes multiple ancestries): 17.0% Irish, 12.6% English, 12.1% Italian, 11.9% German, 4.7% Polish (2006-2010 5-year est.).

Economy: Employment by occupation: 5.5% management, 8.6% professional, 27.3% services, 20.6% sales, 1.0% farming, 4.1% construction, 2.2% production (2006-2010 5-year est.).

Income: Per capita income: $28,213 (2006-2010 5-year est.); Median household income: $48,000 (2006-2010 5-year est.); Average household income: $74,813 (2006-2010 5-year est.); Percent of households with income of $100,000 or more: 18.2% (2006-2010 5-year est.); Poverty rate: 20.0% (2006-2010 5-year est.).

Education: Percent of population age 25 and over with: High school diploma (including GED) or higher: 93.5% (2006-2010 5-year est.); Bachelor's degree or higher: 68.2% (2006-2010 5-year est.); Master's degree or higher: 34.5% (2006-2010 5-year est.).

School District(s)

Haverford Township SD (KG-12)

    2010-11 Enrollment: 5,622 . . . . (610) 853-5900

Radnor Township SD (KG-12)

    2010-11 Enrollment: 3,584 . . . . (610) 688-8100

Four-year College(s)

American College (Private, Not-for-profit)

    Fall 2010 Enrollment: 218 . . . . (610) 526-1000

Bryn Mawr College (Private, Not-for-profit)

    Fall 2010 Enrollment: 1,753 . . . . (610) 526-5000
    2011-12 Tuition: In-state $40,824; Out-of-state $40,824

Rosemont College (Private, Not-for-profit, Roman Catholic)

    Fall 2010 Enrollment: 720 . . . . (610) 527-0200
    2011-12 Tuition: In-state $29,050; Out-of-state $29,050

Two-year College(s)

Harcum College (Private, Not-for-profit)

    Fall 2010 Enrollment: 1,200 . . . . (610) 525-4100
    2011-12 Tuition: In-state $19,880; Out-of-state $19,880

Housing: Homeownership rate: 35.6% (2010); Median home value: $276,600 (2006-2010 5-year est.); Median contract rent: $996 per month (2006-2010 5-year est.); Median year structure built: 1948 (2006-2010 5-year est.).

Hospitals: Bryn Mawr Hospital (307 beds)

Transportation: Commute to work: 47.5% car, 10.4% public transportation, 34.4% walk, 7.4% work from home (2006-2010 5-year est.); Travel time to work: 50.6% less than 15 minutes, 22.4% 15 to 30 minutes, 13.5% 30 to 45 minutes, 7.6% 45 to 60 minutes, 5.9% 60 minutes or more (2006-2010 5-year est.)

Additional Information Contacts

Main Line Chamber of Commerce . . . . (610) 687-6232
    http://www.mlcc.org

CHELTENHAM (township). Aka Cheltenham Township. Covers a land area of 9.044 square miles and a water area of 0.002 square miles. Located at 40.08° N. Lat; 75.14° W. Long. Elevation is 128 feet.

History: Seat of Tyler School of Art (Temple University).

Population: 34,923 (1990); 36,875 (2000); 36,793 (2010); Density: 4,068.2 persons per square mile (2010); Race: 57.4% White, 31.1% Black, 7.7% Asian, 0.2% American Indian/Alaska Native, 0.0% Native Hawaiian/Other Pacific Islander, 3.6% Other, 3.9% Hispanic of any race (2010); Average household size: 2.44 (2010); Median age: 40.0 (2010); Males per 100 females: 83.4 (2010); Marriage status: 33.1% never married, 50.8% now married, 7.0% widowed, 9.1% divorced (2006-2010 5-year est.); Foreign born: 12.4% (2006-2010 5-year est.); Ancestry (includes multiple ancestries): 14.9% Irish, 12.0% German, 8.0% Italian, 6.7% Russian, 6.4% English (2006-2010 5-year est.).

Economy: Unemployment rate: 8.2% (August 2012); Total civilian labor force: 19,534 (August 2012); Single-family building permits issued: 4 (2011); Multi-family building permits issued: 0 (2011); Employment by occupation: 17.7% management, 6.4% professional, 6.9% services, 16.6% sales, 3.0% farming, 4.1% construction, 2.7% production (2006-2010 5-year est.).

Income: Per capita income: $39,879 (2006-2010 5-year est.); Median household income: $72,584 (2006-2010 5-year est.); Average household income: $96,548 (2006-2010 5-year est.); Percent of households with income of $100,000 or more: 35.7% (2006-2010 5-year est.); Poverty rate: 6.7% (2006-2010 5-year est.).

Taxes: Total city taxes per capita: $596 (2009); City property taxes per capita: $362 (2009).

Education: Percent of population age 25 and over with: High school diploma (including GED) or higher: 94.5% (2006-2010 5-year est.); Bachelor's degree or higher: 52.6% (2006-2010 5-year est.); Master's degree or higher: 26.0% (2006-2010 5-year est.).

School District(s)

Cheltenham Township SD (KG-12)

    2010-11 Enrollment: 4,445 . . . . (215) 886-9500

Housing: Homeownership rate: 63.0% (2010); Median home value: $293,000 (2006-2010 5-year est.); Median contract rent: $889 per month (2006-2010 5-year est.); Median year structure built: 1951 (2006-2010 5-year est.).

Safety: Violent crime rate: 20.6 per 10,000 population; Property crime rate: 278.0 per 10,000 population (2011).

Transportation: Commute to work: 80.9% car, 10.5% public transportation, 4.0% walk, 3.7% work from home (2006-2010 5-year est.); Travel time to work: 20.3% less than 15 minutes, 29.6% 15 to 30 minutes, 30.2% 30 to 45 minutes, 11.1% 45 to 60 minutes, 8.7% 60 minutes or more (2006-2010 5-year est.)

Additional Information Contacts

Cheltenham Township . . . . (215) 887-1000
    http://www.cheltenhamtownship.org

Eastern Montgomery County Chamber of Commerce . . . . (215) 887-5122
    http://www.emccc.org

COLLEGEVILLE (borough). Aka Ironbridge. Covers a land area of 1.572 square miles and a water area of 0.040 square miles. Located at 40.19° N. Lat; 75.46° W. Long. Elevation is 151 feet.

History: Ursinus College to East.

Population: 4,227 (1990); 8,032 (2000); 5,089 (2010); Density: 3,237.6 persons per square mile (2010); Race: 89.4% White, 4.0% Black, 3.8% Asian, 0.2% American Indian/Alaska Native, 0.0% Native Hawaiian/Other Pacific Islander, 2.6% Other, 2.4% Hispanic of any race (2010); Average household size: 2.58 (2010); Median age: 22.7 (2010); Males per 100 females: 92.0 (2010); Marriage status: 48.7% never married, 40.4% now married, 3.5% widowed, 7.4% divorced (2006-2010 5-year est.); Foreign born: 4.1% (2006-2010 5-year est.); Ancestry (includes multiple ancestries): 27.0% German, 20.4% Irish, 16.9% Italian, 10.7% English, 7.4% Polish (2006-2010 5-year est.).

Economy: Single-family building permits issued: 8 (2011); Multi-family building permits issued: 2 (2011); Employment by occupation: 20.0% management, 10.2% professional, 5.2% services, 17.9% sales, 3.6% farming, 6.9% construction, 3.1% production (2006-2010 5-year est.).
Income: Per capita income: $29,029 (2006-2010 5-year est.); Median household income: $104,830 (2006-2010 5-year est.); Average household income: $112,830 (2006-2010 5-year est.); Percent of households with income of $100,000 or more: 52.9% (2006-2010 5-year est.); Poverty rate: 2.9% (2006-2010 5-year est.).
Education: Percent of population age 25 and over with: High school diploma (including GED) or higher: 91.8% (2006-2010 5-year est.); Bachelor's degree or higher: 46.5% (2006-2010 5-year est.); Master's degree or higher: 20.2% (2006-2010 5-year est.).

School District(s)
Methacton SD (KG-12)
　　2010-11 Enrollment: 5,289 . . . . (610) 489-5000
Perkiomen Valley SD (KG-12)
　　2010-11 Enrollment: 5,899 . . . . (610) 489-8506

Four-year College(s)
Ursinus College (Private, Not-for-profit)
　　Fall 2010 Enrollment: 1,794 . . . . (610) 409-3000
　　2011-12 Tuition: In-state $41,820; Out-of-state $41,820

Housing: Homeownership rate: 72.5% (2010); Median home value: $331,300 (2006-2010 5-year est.); Median contract rent: $891 per month (2006-2010 5-year est.); Median year structure built: 1978 (2006-2010 5-year est.).
Safety: Violent crime rate: 3.9 per 10,000 population; Property crime rate: 150.8 per 10,000 population (2011).
Transportation: Commute to work: 73.8% car, 1.1% public transportation, 19.7% walk, 4.8% work from home (2006-2010 5-year est.); Travel time to work: 39.4% less than 15 minutes, 21.7% 15 to 30 minutes, 20.4% 30 to 45 minutes, 9.7% 45 to 60 minutes, 8.8% 60 minutes or more (2006-2010 5-year est.)

Additional Information Contacts
Borough of Collegeville . . . . (610) 489-9208
　　http://www.collegeville-pa.gov
Perkiomen Valley Chamber of Commerce . . . . (610) 489-6660
　　http://perkiomenvalleychamber.org

COLMAR (unincorporated postal area)
Zip Code: 18915
　　Covers a land area of 1.052 square miles and a water area of 0 square miles. Located at 40.27° N. Lat; 75.25° W. Long. Elevation is 315 feet.
　　Population: 1,063 (2010); Density: 1,009.6 persons per square mile (2010); Race: 76.5% White, 3.5% Black, 16.9% Asian, 0.6% American Indian/Alaska Native, 0.2% Native Hawaiian/Other Pacific Islander, 2.3% Other, 4.8% Hispanic of any race (2010); Average household size: 2.83 (2010); Median age: 41.6 (2010); Males per 100 females: 101.7 (2010); Homeownership rate: 87.2% (2010)

CONSHOHOCKEN (borough). Covers a land area of 0.998 square miles and a water area of 0.036 square miles. Located at 40.08° N. Lat; 75.30° W. Long. Elevation is 207 feet.
History: Incorporated 1850.
Population: 8,064 (1990); 7,589 (2000); 7,833 (2010); Density: 7,850.6 persons per square mile (2010); Race: 88.7% White, 6.5% Black, 1.8% Asian, 0.1% American Indian/Alaska Native, 0.0% Native Hawaiian/Other Pacific Islander, 2.9% Other, 3.5% Hispanic of any race (2010); Average household size: 2.05 (2010); Median age: 32.7 (2010); Males per 100 females: 99.8 (2010); Marriage status: 51.5% never married, 34.6% now married, 6.0% widowed, 7.9% divorced (2006-2010 5-year est.); Foreign born: 4.6% (2006-2010 5-year est.); Ancestry (includes multiple ancestries): 30.8% Irish, 26.3% Italian, 19.2% German, 12.7% Polish, 7.6% English (2006-2010 5-year est.).
Economy: Single-family building permits issued: 6 (2011); Multi-family building permits issued: 0 (2011); Employment by occupation: 15.4% management, 5.4% professional, 11.1% services, 12.4% sales, 2.3% farming, 6.5% construction, 4.9% production (2006-2010 5-year est.).
Income: Per capita income: $38,126 (2006-2010 5-year est.); Median household income: $63,839 (2006-2010 5-year est.); Average household income: $74,765 (2006-2010 5-year est.); Percent of households with income of $100,000 or more: 27.7% (2006-2010 5-year est.); Poverty rate: 6.1% (2006-2010 5-year est.).
Education: Percent of population age 25 and over with: High school diploma (including GED) or higher: 92.8% (2006-2010 5-year est.);

Bachelor's degree or higher: 44.2% (2006-2010 5-year est.); Master's degree or higher: 12.3% (2006-2010 5-year est.).

School District(s)
Colonial SD (KG-12)
　　2010-11 Enrollment: 4,662 . . . . (610) 834-1670

Housing: Homeownership rate: 56.7% (2010); Median home value: $239,300 (2006-2010 5-year est.); Median contract rent: $912 per month (2006-2010 5-year est.); Median year structure built: 1948 (2006-2010 5-year est.).
Safety: Violent crime rate: 25.5 per 10,000 population; Property crime rate: 169.3 per 10,000 population (2011).
Newspapers: The Philadelphia Inquirer - Pennsylvania Suburban Bureau (Local news); The Recorder (Local news; Circulation 5,000)
Transportation: Commute to work: 84.2% car, 5.3% public transportation, 6.6% walk, 1.9% work from home (2006-2010 5-year est.); Travel time to work: 28.1% less than 15 minutes, 39.3% 15 to 30 minutes, 23.1% 30 to 45 minutes, 6.6% 45 to 60 minutes, 3.0% 60 minutes or more (2006-2010 5-year est.)

Additional Information Contacts
Borough of Conshohocken . . . . (610) 828-1092
　　http://www.conshohocken.boroughs.org
Main Line Chamber of Commerce . . . . (610) 687-6232
　　http://www.mlcc.org

DOUGLASS (township). Covers a land area of 15.294 square miles and a water area of 0.003 square miles. Located at 40.34° N. Lat; 75.60° W. Long.
Population: 7,048 (1990); 9,104 (2000); 10,195 (2010); Density: 666.6 persons per square mile (2010); Race: 96.0% White, 1.0% Black, 1.1% Asian, 0.3% American Indian/Alaska Native, 0.0% Native Hawaiian/Other Pacific Islander, 1.6% Other, 1.8% Hispanic of any race (2010); Average household size: 2.82 (2010); Median age: 40.4 (2010); Males per 100 females: 97.2 (2010); Marriage status: 23.7% never married, 58.5% now married, 8.3% widowed, 9.5% divorced (2006-2010 5-year est.); Foreign born: 2.4% (2006-2010 5-year est.); Ancestry (includes multiple ancestries): 37.6% German, 21.8% Irish, 13.4% Italian, 9.0% Polish, 8.7% English (2006-2010 5-year est.).
Economy: Single-family building permits issued: 13 (2011); Multi-family building permits issued: 0 (2011); Employment by occupation: 12.0% management, 6.5% professional, 8.1% services, 17.3% sales, 5.2% farming, 8.4% construction, 5.6% production (2006-2010 5-year est.).
Income: Per capita income: $29,731 (2006-2010 5-year est.); Median household income: $69,178 (2006-2010 5-year est.); Average household income: $81,041 (2006-2010 5-year est.); Percent of households with income of $100,000 or more: 27.3% (2006-2010 5-year est.); Poverty rate: 6.4% (2006-2010 5-year est.).
Education: Percent of population age 25 and over with: High school diploma (including GED) or higher: 90.2% (2006-2010 5-year est.); Bachelor's degree or higher: 29.9% (2006-2010 5-year est.); Master's degree or higher: 11.3% (2006-2010 5-year est.).
Housing: Homeownership rate: 82.4% (2010); Median home value: $268,600 (2006-2010 5-year est.); Median contract rent: $624 per month (2006-2010 5-year est.); Median year structure built: 1979 (2006-2010 5-year est.).
Safety: Violent crime rate: 34.2 per 10,000 population; Property crime rate: 140.8 per 10,000 population (2011).
Transportation: Commute to work: 94.3% car, 0.4% public transportation, 1.4% walk, 3.2% work from home (2006-2010 5-year est.); Travel time to work: 24.7% less than 15 minutes, 22.8% 15 to 30 minutes, 20.9% 30 to 45 minutes, 19.7% 45 to 60 minutes, 12.0% 60 minutes or more (2006-2010 5-year est.)

Additional Information Contacts
Douglass Township . . . . (610) 367-6062
　　http://www.douglasstownship.org
TriCounty Area Chamber of Commerce . . . . (610) 326-2900
　　http://tricountyareachamber.com

DRESHER (unincorporated postal area)
Zip Code: 19025
　　Covers a land area of 2.997 square miles and a water area of 0 square miles. Located at 40.14° N. Lat; 75.16° W. Long. Elevation is 203 feet.
　　Population: 5,395 (2010); Density: 1,799.8 persons per square mile (2010); Race: 83.4% White, 5.1% Black, 10.2% Asian, 0.1% American Indian/Alaska Native, 0.0% Native Hawaiian/Other Pacific Islander, 1.2% Other, 1.4% Hispanic of any race (2010); Average household size:

2.73 (2010); Median age: 46.1 (2010); Males per 100 females: 93.4 (2010); Homeownership rate: 86.7% (2010)

EAGLEVILLE (CDP). Covers a land area of 1.616 square miles and a water area of 0 square miles. Located at 40.16° N. Lat; 75.41° W. Long. Elevation is 433 feet.

Population: 3,637 (1990); 4,458 (2000); 4,800 (2010); Density: 2,971.2 persons per square mile (2010); Race: 68.8% White, 22.4% Black, 5.5% Asian, 0.1% American Indian/Alaska Native, 0.0% Native Hawaiian/Other Pacific Islander, 3.2% Other, 4.1% Hispanic of any race (2010); Average household size: 2.63 (2010); Median age: 34.8 (2010); Males per 100 females: 167.6 (2010); Marriage status: 53.8% never married, 32.9% now married, 2.1% widowed, 11.1% divorced (2006-2010 5-year est.); Foreign born: 9.8% (2006-2010 5-year est.); Ancestry (includes multiple ancestries): 21.0% Irish, 20.4% Italian, 16.2% German, 10.1% American, 5.9% English (2006-2010 5-year est.).

Economy: Employment by occupation: 18.0% management, 11.1% professional, 13.0% services, 20.2% sales, 6.8% farming, 3.6% construction, 4.8% production (2006-2010 5-year est.).

Income: Per capita income: $24,850 (2006-2010 5-year est.); Median household income: $64,444 (2006-2010 5-year est.); Average household income: $87,756 (2006-2010 5-year est.); Percent of households with income of $100,000 or more: 32.4% (2006-2010 5-year est.); Poverty rate: 8.2% (2006-2010 5-year est.).

Education: Percent of population age 25 and over with: High school diploma (including GED) or higher: 84.7% (2006-2010 5-year est.); Bachelor's degree or higher: 17.9% (2006-2010 5-year est.); Master's degree or higher: 5.6% (2006-2010 5-year est.).

School District(s)

Methacton SD (KG-12)

   2010-11 Enrollment: 5,289 . . . . (610) 489-5000

Housing: Homeownership rate: 59.4% (2010); Median home value: $362,000 (2006-2010 5-year est.); Median contract rent: $927 per month (2006-2010 5-year est.); Median year structure built: 1976 (2006-2010 5-year est.).

Hospitals: Eagleville Hospital (350 beds)

Transportation: Commute to work: 88.4% car, 2.3% public transportation, 3.3% walk, 4.6% work from home (2006-2010 5-year est.); Travel time to work: 25.2% less than 15 minutes, 35.6% 15 to 30 minutes, 20.3% 30 to 45 minutes, 6.1% 45 to 60 minutes, 12.7% 60 minutes or more (2006-2010 5-year est.)

Additional Information Contacts

Main Line Chamber of Commerce . . . . (610) 687-6232

   http://www.mlcc.org

EAST GREENVILLE (borough). Covers a land area of 0.531 square miles and a water area of 0 square miles. Located at 40.41° N. Lat; 75.51° W. Long. Elevation is 400 feet.

History: Settled 1850, incorporated 1875.

Population: 3,117 (1990); 3,103 (2000); 2,951 (2010); Density: 5,553.7 persons per square mile (2010); Race: 93.7% White, 2.3% Black, 1.0% Asian, 0.1% American Indian/Alaska Native, 0.0% Native Hawaiian/Other Pacific Islander, 2.9% Other, 3.3% Hispanic of any race (2010); Average household size: 2.64 (2010); Median age: 33.0 (2010); Males per 100 females: 97.7 (2010); Marriage status: 26.1% never married, 61.3% now married, 6.8% widowed, 5.8% divorced (2006-2010 5-year est.); Foreign born: 3.8% (2006-2010 5-year est.); Ancestry (includes multiple ancestries): 47.2% German, 18.2% Irish, 13.9% Italian, 7.2% English, 5.1% Pennsylvania German (2006-2010 5-year est.).

Economy: Single-family building permits issued: 0 (2011); Multi-family building permits issued: 0 (2011); Employment by occupation: 4.5% management, 3.3% professional, 12.3% services, 22.8% sales, 5.7% farming, 12.9% construction, 6.9% production (2006-2010 5-year est.).

Income: Per capita income: $25,845 (2006-2010 5-year est.); Median household income: $59,250 (2006-2010 5-year est.); Average household income: $67,498 (2006-2010 5-year est.); Percent of households with income of $100,000 or more: 13.6% (2006-2010 5-year est.); Poverty rate: 11.9% (2006-2010 5-year est.).

Education: Percent of population age 25 and over with: High school diploma (including GED) or higher: 83.9% (2006-2010 5-year est.); Bachelor's degree or higher: 11.7% (2006-2010 5-year est.); Master's degree or higher: 3.2% (2006-2010 5-year est.).

School District(s)

Upper Perkiomen SD (KG-12)

   2010-11 Enrollment: 3,187 . . . . (215) 679-7961

Housing: Homeownership rate: 66.2% (2010); Median home value: $172,800 (2006-2010 5-year est.); Median contract rent: $699 per month (2006-2010 5-year est.); Median year structure built: 1955 (2006-2010 5-year est.).

Transportation: Commute to work: 92.8% car, 0.0% public transportation, 3.6% walk, 1.4% work from home (2006-2010 5-year est.); Travel time to work: 25.7% less than 15 minutes, 32.9% 15 to 30 minutes, 25.0% 30 to 45 minutes, 13.1% 45 to 60 minutes, 3.2% 60 minutes or more (2006-2010 5-year est.)

Additional Information Contacts

Upper Bucks Chamber of Commerce . . . . (215) 536-3211

   http://www.ubcc.org

EAST NORRITON (township). Covers a land area of 6.053 square miles and a water area of 0.011 square miles. Located at 40.15° N. Lat; 75.34° W. Long. Elevation is 253 feet.

Population: 13,324 (1990); 13,211 (2000); 13,590 (2010); Density: 2,245.2 persons per square mile (2010); Race: 82.0% White, 9.0% Black, 6.3% Asian, 0.1% American Indian/Alaska Native, 0.0% Native Hawaiian/Other Pacific Islander, 2.6% Other, 3.2% Hispanic of any race (2010); Average household size: 2.33 (2010); Median age: 45.6 (2010); Males per 100 females: 92.5 (2010); Marriage status: 28.1% never married, 57.9% now married, 8.1% widowed, 6.0% divorced (2006-2010 5-year est.); Foreign born: 7.9% (2006-2010 5-year est.); Ancestry (includes multiple ancestries): 26.0% Irish, 25.1% Italian, 23.0% German, 9.7% English, 7.1% Polish (2006-2010 5-year est.).

Economy: Single-family building permits issued: 21 (2011); Multi-family building permits issued: 26 (2011); Employment by occupation: 14.6% management, 10.3% professional, 6.9% services, 17.0% sales, 3.1% farming, 4.6% construction, 3.1% production (2006-2010 5-year est.).

Income: Per capita income: $36,839 (2006-2010 5-year est.); Median household income: $73,019 (2006-2010 5-year est.); Average household income: $87,480 (2006-2010 5-year est.); Percent of households with income of $100,000 or more: 30.9% (2006-2010 5-year est.); Poverty rate: 6.2% (2006-2010 5-year est.).

Education: Percent of population age 25 and over with: High school diploma (including GED) or higher: 93.1% (2006-2010 5-year est.); Bachelor's degree or higher: 36.9% (2006-2010 5-year est.); Master's degree or higher: 11.6% (2006-2010 5-year est.).

Housing: Homeownership rate: 74.8% (2010); Median home value: $280,400 (2006-2010 5-year est.); Median contract rent: $1,071 per month (2006-2010 5-year est.); Median year structure built: 1969 (2006-2010 5-year est.).

Safety: Violent crime rate: 6.6 per 10,000 population; Property crime rate: 221.5 per 10,000 population (2011).

Transportation: Commute to work: 92.7% car, 2.6% public transportation, 0.9% walk, 3.6% work from home (2006-2010 5-year est.); Travel time to work: 22.9% less than 15 minutes, 32.9% 15 to 30 minutes, 25.3% 30 to 45 minutes, 11.4% 45 to 60 minutes, 7.6% 60 minutes or more (2006-2010 5-year est.)

Additional Information Contacts

East Norriton Township . . . . (610) 275-2800

   http://www.eastnorritontwp.org

Main Line Chamber of Commerce . . . . (610) 687-6232

   http://www.mlcc.org

ELKINS PARK (unincorporated postal area)

Zip Code: 19027

   Covers a land area of 3.952 square miles and a water area of 0.001 square miles. Located at 40.07° N. Lat; 75.12° W. Long. Elevation is 157 feet. Population: 19,067 (2010); Density: 4,823.6 persons per square mile (2010); Race: 54.1% White, 34.0% Black, 7.9% Asian, 0.3% American Indian/Alaska Native, 0.1% Native Hawaiian/Other Pacific Islander, 3.6% Other, 3.6% Hispanic of any race (2010); Average household size: 2.37 (2010); Median age: 41.9 (2010); Males per 100 females: 85.4 (2010); Homeownership rate: 63.2% (2010)

EVANSBURG (CDP). Covers a land area of 1.505 square miles and a water area of 0 square miles. Located at 40.19° N. Lat; 75.43° W. Long. Elevation is 203 feet.

Population: 1,047 (1990); 1,536 (2000); 2,129 (2010); Density: 1,414.6 persons per square mile (2010); Race: 82.8% White, 2.7% Black, 12.6% Asian, 0.1% American Indian/Alaska Native, 0.0% Native Hawaiian/Other Pacific Islander, 1.8% Other, 2.5% Hispanic of any race (2010); Average household size: 2.82 (2010); Median age: 39.5 (2010); Males per 100

females: 97.3 (2010); Marriage status: 26.7% never married, 64.7% now married, 3.7% widowed, 4.9% divorced (2006-2010 5-year est.); Foreign born: 12.5% (2006-2010 5-year est.); Ancestry (includes multiple ancestries): 26.9% German, 23.9% Irish, 22.2% Italian, 12.0% English, 4.4% French (2006-2010 5-year est.).

Economy: Employment by occupation: 16.5% management, 17.6% professional, 4.7% services, 7.6% sales, 3.3% farming, 8.5% construction, 4.6% production (2006-2010 5-year est.).

Income: Per capita income: $37,318 (2006-2010 5-year est.); Median household income: $106,979 (2006-2010 5-year est.); Average household income: $106,766 (2006-2010 5-year est.); Percent of households with income of $100,000 or more: 51.3% (2006-2010 5-year est.); Poverty rate: 1.3% (2006-2010 5-year est.).

Education: Percent of population age 25 and over with: High school diploma (including GED) or higher: 97.5% (2006-2010 5-year est.); Bachelor's degree or higher: 48.8% (2006-2010 5-year est.); Master's degree or higher: 25.2% (2006-2010 5-year est.).

Housing: Homeownership rate: 85.7% (2010); Median home value: $317,700 (2006-2010 5-year est.); Median contract rent: $750 per month (2006-2010 5-year est.); Median year structure built: 1991 (2006-2010 5-year est.).

Transportation: Commute to work: 94.0% car, 5.0% public transportation, 0.0% walk, 1.0% work from home (2006-2010 5-year est.); Travel time to work: 16.2% less than 15 minutes, 27.2% 15 to 30 minutes, 26.8% 30 to 45 minutes, 11.5% 45 to 60 minutes, 18.3% 60 minutes or more (2006-2010 5-year est.)

Additional Information Contacts
Perkiomen Valley Chamber of Commerce . . . . (610) 489-6660
http://perkiomenvalleychamber.org

FLOURTOWN (CDP). Covers a land area of 1.411 square miles and a water area of 0.002 square miles. Located at 40.11° N. Lat; 75.21° W. Long. Elevation is 187 feet.

History: An ample flow of water found in the Wissahickon Creek and its tributaries supported at least three local mills. It was from this industry that Flourtown took its name.

Population: 4,823 (1990); 4,669 (2000); 4,538 (2010); Density: 3,215.1 persons per square mile (2010); Race: 90.6% White, 5.3% Black, 2.1% Asian, 0.1% American Indian/Alaska Native, 0.0% Native Hawaiian/Other Pacific Islander, 1.9% Other, 1.8% Hispanic of any race (2010); Average household size: 2.64 (2010); Median age: 42.9 (2010); Males per 100 females: 93.8 (2010); Marriage status: 24.4% never married, 64.0% now married, 6.2% widowed, 5.4% divorced (2006-2010 5-year est.); Foreign born: 5.5% (2006-2010 5-year est.); Ancestry (includes multiple ancestries): 27.6% Irish, 21.1% German, 16.2% Italian, 14.9% English, 6.5% Polish (2006-2010 5-year est.).

Economy: Employment by occupation: 19.4% management, 3.8% professional, 6.3% services, 14.6% sales, 1.9% farming, 6.5% construction, 2.1% production (2006-2010 5-year est.).

Income: Per capita income: $46,865 (2006-2010 5-year est.); Median household income: $99,216 (2006-2010 5-year est.); Average household income: $120,657 (2006-2010 5-year est.); Percent of households with income of $100,000 or more: 48.8% (2006-2010 5-year est.); Poverty rate: 1.0% (2006-2010 5-year est.).

Education: Percent of population age 25 and over with: High school diploma (including GED) or higher: 97.0% (2006-2010 5-year est.); Bachelor's degree or higher: 56.6% (2006-2010 5-year est.); Master's degree or higher: 25.3% (2006-2010 5-year est.).

School District(s)
Springfield Township SD (KG-12)
    2010-11 Enrollment: 2,133 . . . . (215) 233-6000

Housing: Homeownership rate: 86.5% (2010); Median home value: $345,200 (2006-2010 5-year est.); Median contract rent: $1,226 per month (2006-2010 5-year est.); Median year structure built: 1953 (2006-2010 5-year est.).

Transportation: Commute to work: 86.2% car, 3.2% public transportation, 2.0% walk, 7.4% work from home (2006-2010 5-year est.); Travel time to work: 19.3% less than 15 minutes, 36.2% 15 to 30 minutes, 27.3% 30 to 45 minutes, 9.9% 45 to 60 minutes, 7.3% 60 minutes or more (2006-2010 5-year est.)

Additional Information Contacts
Eastern Montgomery County Chamber of Commerce . . . . (215) 887-5122
http://www.emccc.org

FORT WASHINGTON (CDP). Covers a land area of 3.252 square miles and a water area of 0 square miles. Located at 40.14° N. Lat; 75.19° W. Long. Elevation is 233 feet.

History: Fort Washington State Park to Southwest, with remains of Revolutionary fortifications. Childventure Museum; Hope Lodge, 18th-century Georgian mansion; Highlands Mansion and Gardens.

Population: 3,699 (1990); 3,680 (2000); 5,446 (2010); Density: 1,674.4 persons per square mile (2010); Race: 87.5% White, 4.5% Black, 6.2% Asian, 0.1% American Indian/Alaska Native, 0.0% Native Hawaiian/Other Pacific Islander, 1.7% Other, 1.8% Hispanic of any race (2010); Average household size: 2.69 (2010); Median age: 44.3 (2010); Males per 100 females: 96.7 (2010); Marriage status: 24.3% never married, 63.8% now married, 5.0% widowed, 6.9% divorced (2006-2010 5-year est.); Foreign born: 6.7% (2006-2010 5-year est.); Ancestry (includes multiple ancestries): 24.5% German, 22.3% Irish, 16.3% English, 13.7% Italian, 9.3% Russian (2006-2010 5-year est.).

Economy: Employment by occupation: 17.1% management, 6.7% professional, 4.0% services, 15.1% sales, 1.6% farming, 3.8% construction, 2.6% production (2006-2010 5-year est.).

Income: Per capita income: $50,555 (2006-2010 5-year est.); Median household income: $108,194 (2006-2010 5-year est.); Average household income: $143,675 (2006-2010 5-year est.); Percent of households with income of $100,000 or more: 54.2% (2006-2010 5-year est.); Poverty rate: 1.3% (2006-2010 5-year est.).

Education: Percent of population age 25 and over with: High school diploma (including GED) or higher: 96.6% (2006-2010 5-year est.); Bachelor's degree or higher: 67.3% (2006-2010 5-year est.); Master's degree or higher: 36.0% (2006-2010 5-year est.).

School District(s)
Upper Dublin SD (KG-12)
    2010-11 Enrollment: 4,270 . . . . (215) 643-8800

Four-year College(s)
DeVry University's Keller Graduate School of Management-Pennsylvania (Private, For-profit)
    Fall 2010 Enrollment: 438 . . . . (215) 591-5700
DeVry University-Pennsylvania (Private, For-profit)
    Fall 2010 Enrollment: 1,965 . . . . (215) 591-5700
    2011-12 Tuition: In-state $15,188; Out-of-state $15,188

Housing: Homeownership rate: 88.1% (2010); Median home value: $447,600 (2006-2010 5-year est.); Median contract rent: $1,354 per month (2006-2010 5-year est.); Median year structure built: 1972 (2006-2010 5-year est.).

Newspapers: The Ambler Gazette (Community news; Circulation 10,511); Central Bucks Life (Community news; Circulation 21,681); The Colonial (Local news; Circulation 4,700); Glenside News (Community news; Circulation 2,883); Montgomery Life (Community news); North Penn Life (Community news; Circulation 21,681); Public Spirit (Local news; Circulation 11,195); Springfield Sun (Community news; Circulation 2,681); Times Chronicle (Community news; Circulation 7,275); Willow Grove Guide (Community news; Circulation 2,000)

Transportation: Commute to work: 84.1% car, 7.9% public transportation, 1.6% walk, 6.3% work from home (2006-2010 5-year est.); Travel time to work: 20.0% less than 15 minutes, 33.9% 15 to 30 minutes, 27.0% 30 to 45 minutes, 12.6% 45 to 60 minutes, 6.4% 60 minutes or more (2006-2010 5-year est.)

Additional Information Contacts
Eastern Montgomery County Chamber of Commerce . . . . (215) 887-5122
http://www.emccc.org

FRANCONIA (township). Covers a land area of 13.833 square miles and a water area of 0.020 square miles. Located at 40.30° N. Lat; 75.36° W. Long. Elevation is 397 feet.

Population: 7,231 (1990); 11,523 (2000); 13,064 (2010); Density: 944.4 persons per square mile (2010); Race: 93.2% White, 1.6% Black, 3.3% Asian, 0.2% American Indian/Alaska Native, 0.0% Native Hawaiian/Other Pacific Islander, 1.7% Other, 1.8% Hispanic of any race (2010); Average household size: 2.70 (2010); Median age: 45.2 (2010); Males per 100 females: 92.9 (2010); Marriage status: 17.4% never married, 69.2% now married, 8.6% widowed, 4.8% divorced (2006-2010 5-year est.); Foreign born: 2.9% (2006-2010 5-year est.); Ancestry (includes multiple ancestries): 42.1% German, 16.1% Irish, 10.4% English, 8.0% Italian, 6.8% Polish (2006-2010 5-year est.).

Economy: Single-family building permits issued: 13 (2011); Multi-family building permits issued: 0 (2011); Employment by occupation: 14.4%

management, 7.1% professional, 5.8% services, 18.9% sales, 5.7% farming, 9.9% construction, 6.2% production (2006-2010 5-year est.).
Income: Per capita income: $34,682 (2006-2010 5-year est.); Median household income: $80,533 (2006-2010 5-year est.); Average household income: $92,393 (2006-2010 5-year est.); Percent of households with income of $100,000 or more: 35.7% (2006-2010 5-year est.); Poverty rate: 2.4% (2006-2010 5-year est.).
Education: Percent of population age 25 and over with: High school diploma (including GED) or higher: 92.5% (2006-2010 5-year est.); Bachelor's degree or higher: 34.8% (2006-2010 5-year est.); Master's degree or higher: 12.1% (2006-2010 5-year est.).
Housing: Homeownership rate: 85.3% (2010); Median home value: $311,900 (2006-2010 5-year est.); Median contract rent: $1,035 per month (2006-2010 5-year est.); Median year structure built: 1985 (2006-2010 5-year est.).
Safety: Violent crime rate: 5.3 per 10,000 population; Property crime rate: 64.1 per 10,000 population (2011).
Transportation: Commute to work: 92.4% car, 0.9% public transportation, 0.9% walk, 5.4% work from home (2006-2010 5-year est.); Travel time to work: 35.2% less than 15 minutes, 28.9% 15 to 30 minutes, 20.1% 30 to 45 minutes, 9.0% 45 to 60 minutes, 6.7% 60 minutes or more (2006-2010 5-year est.)
Additional Information Contacts
Franconia Township . . . . (215) 723-1137
    http://www.franconiatownship.org
Indian Valley Chamber of Commerce . . . . (215) 723-9472
    http://indianvalleychamber.com

FREDERICK (unincorporated postal area)
Zip Code: 19435
    Covers a land area of 0.776 square miles and a water area of 0 square miles. Located at 40.32° N. Lat; 75.56° W. Long. Population: 100 (2010); Density: 128.8 persons per square mile (2010); Race: 95.0% White, 1.0% Black, 0.0% Asian, 0.0% American Indian/Alaska Native, 0.0% Native Hawaiian/Other Pacific Islander, 4.0% Other, 3.0% Hispanic of any race (2010); Average household size: 2.50 (2010); Median age: 48.0 (2010); Males per 100 females: 81.8 (2010); Homeownership rate: 95.0% (2010)

GILBERTSVILLE (CDP). Covers a land area of 3.346 square miles and a water area of 0.001 square miles. Located at 40.32° N. Lat; 75.61° W. Long. Elevation is 338 feet.
Population: 3,994 (1990); 4,242 (2000); 4,832 (2010); Density: 1,443.9 persons per square mile (2010); Race: 95.7% White, 1.4% Black, 1.1% Asian, 0.2% American Indian/Alaska Native, 0.0% Native Hawaiian/Other Pacific Islander, 1.6% Other, 2.4% Hispanic of any race (2010); Average household size: 2.65 (2010); Median age: 39.8 (2010); Males per 100 females: 94.2 (2010); Marriage status: 25.8% never married, 51.7% now married, 10.1% widowed, 12.4% divorced (2006-2010 5-year est.); Foreign born: 1.7% (2006-2010 5-year est.); Ancestry (includes multiple ancestries): 35.3% German, 22.7% Irish, 14.9% Italian, 9.2% English, 8.0% Polish (2006-2010 5-year est.).
Economy: Employment by occupation: 13.5% management, 5.1% professional, 7.9% services, 18.9% sales, 3.0% farming, 8.5% construction, 5.6% production (2006-2010 5-year est.).
Income: Per capita income: $27,557 (2006-2010 5-year est.); Median household income: $60,145 (2006-2010 5-year est.); Average household income: $66,823 (2006-2010 5-year est.); Percent of households with income of $100,000 or more: 18.6% (2006-2010 5-year est.); Poverty rate: 9.4% (2006-2010 5-year est.).
Education: Percent of population age 25 and over with: High school diploma (including GED) or higher: 92.1% (2006-2010 5-year est.); Bachelor's degree or higher: 29.2% (2006-2010 5-year est.); Master's degree or higher: 11.8% (2006-2010 5-year est.).
School District(s)
Boyertown Area SD (KG-12)
    2010-11 Enrollment: 7,099 . . . . (610) 367-6031
Housing: Homeownership rate: 73.5% (2010); Median home value: $249,200 (2006-2010 5-year est.); Median contract rent: $644 per month (2006-2010 5-year est.); Median year structure built: 1975 (2006-2010 5-year est.).
Transportation: Commute to work: 93.5% car, 0.0% public transportation, 2.8% walk, 2.4% work from home (2006-2010 5-year est.); Travel time to work: 30.1% less than 15 minutes, 20.8% 15 to 30 minutes, 20.5% 30 to

45 minutes, 17.9% 45 to 60 minutes, 10.7% 60 minutes or more (2006-2010 5-year est.)
Additional Information Contacts
TriCounty Area Chamber of Commerce . . . . (610) 326-2900
    http://www.tricountyareachamber.com

GLADWYNE (unincorporated postal area)
Zip Code: 19035
    Covers a land area of 4.760 square miles and a water area of 0.111 square miles. Located at 40.05° N. Lat; 75.27° W. Long. Population: 3,780 (2010); Density: 794.1 persons per square mile (2010); Race: 93.8% White, 1.3% Black, 3.6% Asian, 0.0% American Indian/Alaska Native, 0.0% Native Hawaiian/Other Pacific Islander, 1.3% Other, 1.9% Hispanic of any race (2010); Average household size: 2.54 (2010); Median age: 49.3 (2010); Males per 100 females: 87.2 (2010); Homeownership rate: 83.5% (2010)

GLENSIDE (CDP). Covers a land area of 1.281 square miles and a water area of 0 square miles. Located at 40.10° N. Lat; 75.15° W. Long. Elevation is 262 feet.
History: Seat of Beaver College, and Reconstructionist and Rabbinical College.
Population: 8,704 (1990); 7,914 (2000); 8,384 (2010); Density: 6,547.3 persons per square mile (2010); Race: 87.1% White, 7.2% Black, 2.8% Asian, 0.2% American Indian/Alaska Native, 0.0% Native Hawaiian/Other Pacific Islander, 2.7% Other, 2.9% Hispanic of any race (2010); Average household size: 2.57 (2010); Median age: 33.8 (2010); Males per 100 females: 83.0 (2010); Marriage status: 26.1% never married, 55.8% now married, 5.6% widowed, 12.5% divorced (2006-2010 5-year est.); Foreign born: 6.5% (2006-2010 5-year est.); Ancestry (includes multiple ancestries): 37.1% Irish, 24.8% German, 14.4% Italian, 12.0% English, 4.5% Polish (2006-2010 5-year est.).
Economy: Employment by occupation: 15.0% management, 5.5% professional, 5.3% services, 15.4% sales, 2.8% farming, 9.6% construction, 4.0% production (2006-2010 5-year est.).
Income: Per capita income: $34,644 (2006-2010 5-year est.); Median household income: $68,629 (2006-2010 5-year est.); Average household income: $82,872 (2006-2010 5-year est.); Percent of households with income of $100,000 or more: 28.3% (2006-2010 5-year est.); Poverty rate: 5.3% (2006-2010 5-year est.).
Education: Percent of population age 25 and over with: High school diploma (including GED) or higher: 95.9% (2006-2010 5-year est.); Bachelor's degree or higher: 48.4% (2006-2010 5-year est.); Master's degree or higher: 18.9% (2006-2010 5-year est.).
School District(s)
Abington SD (KG-12)
    2010-11 Enrollment: 7,465 . . . . (215) 884-4700
Four-year College(s)
Arcadia University (Private, Not-for-profit, Presbyterian Church (USA))
    Fall 2010 Enrollment: 3,859 . . . . (215) 572-2900
    2011-12 Tuition: In-state $34,150; Out-of-state $34,150
Westminster Theological Seminary (Private, Not-for-profit, Other Protestant)
    Fall 2010 Enrollment: 400 . . . . (215) 887-5511
Won Institute of Graduate Studies (Private, Not-for-profit)
    Fall 2010 Enrollment: 56 . . . . (215) 884-8942
Two-year College(s)
Antonelli Institute (Private, For-profit)
    Fall 2010 Enrollment: 194 . . . . (215) 836-2222
    2011-12 Tuition: In-state $19,730; Out-of-state $19,730
Vocational/Technical School(s)
Princeton Information Technology Center (Private, For-profit)
    Fall 2010 Enrollment: 272 . . . . (215) 576-5650
    2011-12 Tuition: $18,900
Housing: Homeownership rate: 66.6% (2010); Median home value: $274,400 (2006-2010 5-year est.); Median contract rent: $810 per month (2006-2010 5-year est.); Median year structure built: before 1940 (2006-2010 5-year est.).
Transportation: Commute to work: 83.0% car, 9.1% public transportation, 3.4% walk, 4.2% work from home (2006-2010 5-year est.); Travel time to work: 29.0% less than 15 minutes, 26.1% 15 to 30 minutes, 29.3% 30 to 45 minutes, 8.8% 45 to 60 minutes, 6.8% 60 minutes or more (2006-2010 5-year est.)

Additional Information Contacts
Greater Glenside Chamber of Commerce . . . . (215) 500-4080
  http://glensidechamber.org

GREEN LANE (borough). Covers a land area of 0.331 square miles and a water area of 0.008 square miles. Located at 40.34° N. Lat; 75.47° W. Long. Elevation is 246 feet.
Population: 438 (1990); 584 (2000); 508 (2010); Density: 1,535.7 persons per square mile (2010); Race: 97.4% White, 2.0% Black, 0.2% Asian, 0.4% American Indian/Alaska Native, 0.0% Native Hawaiian/Other Pacific Islander, 0.0% Other, 1.0% Hispanic of any race (2010); Average household size: 2.41 (2010); Median age: 45.0 (2010); Males per 100 females: 94.6 (2010); Marriage status: 35.9% never married, 53.0% now married, 4.1% widowed, 6.9% divorced (2006-2010 5-year est.); Foreign born: 3.2% (2006-2010 5-year est.); Ancestry (includes multiple ancestries): 49.2% German, 14.9% Irish, 11.5% Swiss, 7.4% English, 7.0% Italian (2006-2010 5-year est.).
Economy: Single-family building permits issued: 0 (2011); Multi-family building permits issued: 0 (2011); Employment by occupation: 9.8% management, 3.4% professional, 7.5% services, 21.1% sales, 5.6% farming, 13.2% construction, 13.2% production (2006-2010 5-year est.).
Income: Per capita income: $24,344 (2006-2010 5-year est.); Median household income: $52,212 (2006-2010 5-year est.); Average household income: $66,719 (2006-2010 5-year est.); Percent of households with income of $100,000 or more: 20.8% (2006-2010 5-year est.); Poverty rate: 13.4% (2006-2010 5-year est.).
Education: Percent of population age 25 and over with: High school diploma (including GED) or higher: 94.5% (2006-2010 5-year est.); Bachelor's degree or higher: 26.0% (2006-2010 5-year est.); Master's degree or higher: 4.8% (2006-2010 5-year est.).
School District(s)
Upper Perkiomen SD (KG-12)
  2010-11 Enrollment: 3,187 . . . . (215) 679-7961
Housing: Homeownership rate: 66.4% (2010); Median home value: $193,800 (2006-2010 5-year est.); Median contract rent: $660 per month (2006-2010 5-year est.); Median year structure built: 1945 (2006-2010 5-year est.).
Transportation: Commute to work: 89.3% car, 0.0% public transportation, 3.8% walk, 5.7% work from home (2006-2010 5-year est.); Travel time to work: 18.3% less than 15 minutes, 46.3% 15 to 30 minutes, 18.7% 30 to 45 minutes, 8.5% 45 to 60 minutes, 8.1% 60 minutes or more (2006-2010 5-year est.)

GWYNEDD (unincorporated postal area)
Zip Code: 19436
  Covers a land area of 0.350 square miles and a water area of 0 square miles. Located at 40.20° N. Lat; 75.24° W. Long. Population: 640 (2010); Density: 1,825.2 persons per square mile (2010); Race: 96.4% White, 1.3% Black, 2.0% Asian, 0.0% American Indian/Alaska Native, 0.0% Native Hawaiian/Other Pacific Islander, 0.3% Other, 1.3% Hispanic of any race (2010); Average household size: 1.63 (2010); Median age: 80.9 (2010); Males per 100 females: 57.6 (2010); Homeownership rate: 21.8% (2010)

GWYNEDD VALLEY (unincorporated postal area)
Zip Code: 19437
  Covers a land area of 1.092 square miles and a water area of 0 square miles. Located at 40.18° N. Lat; 75.25° W. Long. Elevation is 272 feet. Population: 757 (2010); Density: 692.7 persons per square mile (2010); Race: 90.5% White, 0.9% Black, 7.3% Asian, 0.0% American Indian/Alaska Native, 0.0% Native Hawaiian/Other Pacific Islander, 1.3% Other, 0.5% Hispanic of any race (2010); Average household size: 2.78 (2010); Median age: 50.7 (2010); Males per 100 females: 96.1 (2010); Homeownership rate: 96.3% (2010)

HALFWAY HOUSE (CDP). Covers a land area of 2.048 square miles and a water area of 0 square miles. Located at 40.28° N. Lat; 75.64° W. Long. Elevation is 384 feet.
Population: 1,415 (1990); 1,823 (2000); 2,881 (2010); Density: 1,406.4 persons per square mile (2010); Race: 86.3% White, 8.1% Black, 2.8% Asian, 0.2% American Indian/Alaska Native, 0.1% Native Hawaiian/Other Pacific Islander, 2.5% Other, 2.8% Hispanic of any race (2010); Average household size: 2.84 (2010); Median age: 35.3 (2010); Males per 100 females: 101.9 (2010); Marriage status: 22.9% never married, 70.5% now married, 3.1% widowed, 3.5% divorced (2006-2010 5-year est.); Foreign

born: 4.4% (2006-2010 5-year est.); Ancestry (includes multiple ancestries): 29.3% German, 18.8% Italian, 18.7% Irish, 8.5% Pennsylvania German, 8.5% Polish (2006-2010 5-year est.).
Economy: Employment by occupation: 4.0% management, 9.8% professional, 6.7% services, 15.8% sales, 7.3% farming, 13.9% construction, 4.5% production (2006-2010 5-year est.).
Income: Per capita income: $29,613 (2006-2010 5-year est.); Median household income: $82,672 (2006-2010 5-year est.); Average household income: $89,120 (2006-2010 5-year est.); Percent of households with income of $100,000 or more: 31.9% (2006-2010 5-year est.); Poverty rate: 0.3% (2006-2010 5-year est.).
Education: Percent of population age 25 and over with: High school diploma (including GED) or higher: 89.6% (2006-2010 5-year est.); Bachelor's degree or higher: 27.8% (2006-2010 5-year est.); Master's degree or higher: 9.1% (2006-2010 5-year est.).
Housing: Homeownership rate: 89.3% (2010); Median home value: $240,900 (2006-2010 5-year est.); Median contract rent: $897 per month (2006-2010 5-year est.); Median year structure built: 1990 (2006-2010 5-year est.).
Transportation: Commute to work: 96.2% car, 2.6% public transportation, 1.2% walk, 0.0% work from home (2006-2010 5-year est.); Travel time to work: 21.1% less than 15 minutes, 14.7% 15 to 30 minutes, 21.6% 30 to 45 minutes, 20.8% 45 to 60 minutes, 21.7% 60 minutes or more (2006-2010 5-year est.)
Additional Information Contacts
TriCounty Area Chamber of Commerce . . . . (610) 326-2900
  http://tricountyareachamber.com

HARLEYSVILLE (CDP). Covers a land area of 4.175 square miles and a water area of 0.003 square miles. Located at 40.28° N. Lat; 75.39° W. Long. Elevation is 259 feet.
Population: 7,456 (1990); 8,795 (2000); 9,286 (2010); Density: 2,224.4 persons per square mile (2010); Race: 92.0% White, 2.6% Black, 3.5% Asian, 0.1% American Indian/Alaska Native, 0.0% Native Hawaiian/Other Pacific Islander, 1.8% Other, 2.4% Hispanic of any race (2010); Average household size: 2.51 (2010); Median age: 41.4 (2010); Males per 100 females: 90.6 (2010); Marriage status: 24.7% never married, 57.5% now married, 9.1% widowed, 8.6% divorced (2006-2010 5-year est.); Foreign born: 4.5% (2006-2010 5-year est.); Ancestry (includes multiple ancestries): 40.4% German, 27.4% Irish, 16.3% Italian, 9.4% English, 7.0% Polish (2006-2010 5-year est.).
Economy: Employment by occupation: 13.5% management, 7.1% professional, 5.5% services, 14.1% sales, 6.3% farming, 6.5% construction, 5.1% production (2006-2010 5-year est.).
Income: Per capita income: $36,296 (2006-2010 5-year est.); Median household income: $76,563 (2006-2010 5-year est.); Average household income: $92,895 (2006-2010 5-year est.); Percent of households with income of $100,000 or more: 35.1% (2006-2010 5-year est.); Poverty rate: 2.1% (2006-2010 5-year est.).
Education: Percent of population age 25 and over with: High school diploma (including GED) or higher: 91.9% (2006-2010 5-year est.); Bachelor's degree or higher: 38.3% (2006-2010 5-year est.); Master's degree or higher: 16.0% (2006-2010 5-year est.).
School District(s)
North Penn SD (KG-12)
  2010-11 Enrollment: 12,698 . . . . (215) 368-0400
Souderton Area SD (KG-12)
  2010-11 Enrollment: 6,739 . . . . (215) 723-6061
Housing: Homeownership rate: 64.6% (2010); Median home value: $290,600 (2006-2010 5-year est.); Median contract rent: $999 per month (2006-2010 5-year est.); Median year structure built: 1983 (2006-2010 5-year est.).
Transportation: Commute to work: 90.6% car, 1.4% public transportation, 3.3% walk, 3.8% work from home (2006-2010 5-year est.); Travel time to work: 22.8% less than 15 minutes, 31.7% 15 to 30 minutes, 24.1% 30 to 45 minutes, 11.2% 45 to 60 minutes, 10.3% 60 minutes or more (2006-2010 5-year est.)
Additional Information Contacts
Indian Valley Chamber of Commerce . . . . (215) 723-9472
  http://indianvalleychamber.com

HATBORO (borough). Covers a land area of 1.422 square miles and a water area of 0 square miles. Located at 40.18° N. Lat; 75.11° W. Long. Elevation is 226 feet.
History: Settled in early 18th century, incorporated 1871.

Population: 7,443 (1990); 7,393 (2000); 7,360 (2010); Density: 5,176.7 persons per square mile (2010); Race: 92.4% White, 2.7% Black, 1.6% Asian, 0.3% American Indian/Alaska Native, 0.0% Native Hawaiian/Other Pacific Islander, 3.0% Other, 4.3% Hispanic of any race (2010); Average household size: 2.42 (2010); Median age: 38.9 (2010); Males per 100 females: 93.6 (2010); Marriage status: 27.6% never married, 54.9% now married, 6.6% widowed, 11.0% divorced (2006-2010 5-year est.); Foreign born: 4.0% (2006-2010 5-year est.); Ancestry (includes multiple ancestries): 36.6% German, 27.6% Irish, 15.6% English, 14.9% Italian, 4.3% Polish (2006-2010 5-year est.).

Economy: Single-family building permits issued: 0 (2011); Multi-family building permits issued: 0 (2011); Employment by occupation: 10.9% management, 7.0% professional, 9.3% services, 16.6% sales, 6.4% farming, 8.7% construction, 5.4% production (2006-2010 5-year est.).

Income: Per capita income: $30,577 (2006-2010 5-year est.); Median household income: $66,211 (2006-2010 5-year est.); Average household income: $74,624 (2006-2010 5-year est.); Percent of households with income of $100,000 or more: 22.8% (2006-2010 5-year est.); Poverty rate: 4.8% (2006-2010 5-year est.).

Education: Percent of population age 25 and over with: High school diploma (including GED) or higher: 91.1% (2006-2010 5-year est.); Bachelor's degree or higher: 29.1% (2006-2010 5-year est.); Master's degree or higher: 9.8% (2006-2010 5-year est.).

School District(s)

Hatboro-Horsham SD (KG-12)
   2010-11 Enrollment: 5,105 . . . . (215) 420-5000
Upper Moreland Township SD (KG-12)
   2010-11 Enrollment: 3,063 . . . . (215) 659-6800

Housing: Homeownership rate: 64.4% (2010); Median home value: $256,400 (2006-2010 5-year est.); Median contract rent: $798 per month (2006-2010 5-year est.); Median year structure built: 1954 (2006-2010 5-year est.).

Safety: Violent crime rate: 20.3 per 10,000 population; Property crime rate: 128.7 per 10,000 population (2011).

Transportation: Commute to work: 86.7% car, 6.6% public transportation, 1.8% walk, 3.4% work from home (2006-2010 5-year est.); Travel time to work: 27.7% less than 15 minutes, 30.8% 15 to 30 minutes, 22.0% 30 to 45 minutes, 12.7% 45 to 60 minutes, 6.8% 60 minutes or more (2006-2010 5-year est.)

Additional Information Contacts

Borough of Hatboro . . . . (215) 443-9100
   http://www.hatborogov.com
Greater Hatboro Chamber of Commerce . . . . (215) 956-9540
   http://hatborochamber.org

HATFIELD (borough). Covers a land area of 0.642 square miles and a water area of 0 square miles. Located at 40.28° N. Lat; 75.30° W. Long. Elevation is 331 feet.

Population: 2,650 (1990); 2,605 (2000); 3,290 (2010); Density: 5,122.6 persons per square mile (2010); Race: 66.6% White, 4.1% Black, 23.5% Asian, 0.1% American Indian/Alaska Native, 0.0% Native Hawaiian/Other Pacific Islander, 5.7% Other, 6.8% Hispanic of any race (2010); Average household size: 2.59 (2010); Median age: 36.3 (2010); Males per 100 females: 104.7 (2010); Marriage status: 30.9% never married, 55.3% now married, 3.8% widowed, 9.9% divorced (2006-2010 5-year est.); Foreign born: 22.8% (2006-2010 5-year est.); Ancestry (includes multiple ancestries): 29.8% German, 18.3% Irish, 9.4% Italian, 7.7% Polish, 7.5% English (2006-2010 5-year est.).

Economy: Single-family building permits issued: 0 (2011); Multi-family building permits issued: 0 (2011); Employment by occupation: 8.1% management, 7.3% professional, 8.0% services, 14.9% sales, 6.4% farming, 12.3% construction, 10.6% production (2006-2010 5-year est.).

Income: Per capita income: $29,756 (2006-2010 5-year est.); Median household income: $62,025 (2006-2010 5-year est.); Average household income: $68,545 (2006-2010 5-year est.); Percent of households with income of $100,000 or more: 19.1% (2006-2010 5-year est.); Poverty rate: 9.1% (2006-2010 5-year est.).

Taxes: Total city taxes per capita: $211 (2009); City property taxes per capita: $32 (2009).

Education: Percent of population age 25 and over with: High school diploma (including GED) or higher: 90.9% (2006-2010 5-year est.); Bachelor's degree or higher: 30.3% (2006-2010 5-year est.); Master's degree or higher: 11.7% (2006-2010 5-year est.).

School District(s)

North Penn SD (KG-12)
   2010-11 Enrollment: 12,698 . . . . (215) 368-0400

Four-year College(s)

Biblical Theological Seminary (Private, Not-for-profit, Interdenominational)
   Fall 2010 Enrollment: 227 . . . . (215) 368-5000

Housing: Homeownership rate: 52.4% (2010); Median home value: $255,300 (2006-2010 5-year est.); Median contract rent: $736 per month (2006-2010 5-year est.); Median year structure built: 1959 (2006-2010 5-year est.).

Transportation: Commute to work: 91.4% car, 3.0% public transportation, 1.9% walk, 2.8% work from home (2006-2010 5-year est.); Travel time to work: 27.0% less than 15 minutes, 35.3% 15 to 30 minutes, 16.8% 30 to 45 minutes, 10.3% 45 to 60 minutes, 10.7% 60 minutes or more (2006-2010 5-year est.)

Additional Information Contacts

Borough of Hatfield . . . . (215) 855-0781
   http://www.hatfieldborough.com
Hatfield Chamber of Commerce . . . . (215) 855-3335
   http://www.hatfieldchamber.com

HATFIELD (township). Covers a land area of 9.938 square miles and a water area of 0 square miles. Located at 40.28° N. Lat; 75.29° W. Long. Elevation is 331 feet.

History: Settled 1860, incorporated 1898.

Population: 15,357 (1990); 16,712 (2000); 17,249 (2010); Density: 1,735.7 persons per square mile (2010); Race: 75.6% White, 4.5% Black, 16.3% Asian, 0.2% American Indian/Alaska Native, 0.1% Native Hawaiian/Other Pacific Islander, 3.3% Other, 3.8% Hispanic of any race (2010); Average household size: 2.63 (2010); Median age: 40.6 (2010); Males per 100 females: 99.4 (2010); Marriage status: 27.6% never married, 61.0% now married, 4.6% widowed, 6.8% divorced (2006-2010 5-year est.); Foreign born: 16.7% (2006-2010 5-year est.); Ancestry (includes multiple ancestries): 25.1% German, 19.8% Irish, 13.7% Italian, 8.9% English, 7.6% Polish (2006-2010 5-year est.).

Economy: Single-family building permits issued: 10 (2011); Multi-family building permits issued: 60 (2011); Employment by occupation: 12.0% management, 8.8% professional, 7.3% services, 14.9% sales, 5.2% farming, 7.5% construction, 7.1% production (2006-2010 5-year est.).

Income: Per capita income: $29,965 (2006-2010 5-year est.); Median household income: $63,483 (2006-2010 5-year est.); Average household income: $76,850 (2006-2010 5-year est.); Percent of households with income of $100,000 or more: 26.7% (2006-2010 5-year est.); Poverty rate: 6.2% (2006-2010 5-year est.).

Education: Percent of population age 25 and over with: High school diploma (including GED) or higher: 89.2% (2006-2010 5-year est.); Bachelor's degree or higher: 34.6% (2006-2010 5-year est.); Master's degree or higher: 9.5% (2006-2010 5-year est.).

Four-year College(s)

Biblical Theological Seminary (Private, Not-for-profit, Interdenominational)
   Fall 2010 Enrollment: 227 . . . . (215) 368-5000

Housing: Homeownership rate: 67.7% (2010); Median home value: $282,500 (2006-2010 5-year est.); Median contract rent: $887 per month (2006-2010 5-year est.); Median year structure built: 1975 (2006-2010 5-year est.).

Safety: Violent crime rate: 15.5 per 10,000 population; Property crime rate: 173.3 per 10,000 population (2011).

Transportation: Commute to work: 94.2% car, 1.4% public transportation, 0.3% walk, 2.7% work from home (2006-2010 5-year est.); Travel time to work: 26.8% less than 15 minutes, 36.6% 15 to 30 minutes, 16.5% 30 to 45 minutes, 9.9% 45 to 60 minutes, 10.1% 60 minutes or more (2006-2010 5-year est.)

Additional Information Contacts

Hatfield Chamber of Commerce . . . . (215) 855-3335
   http://www.hatfieldchamber.com
Hatfield Township . . . . (215) 855-0900
   http://www.hatfieldtownship.org

HORSHAM (CDP). Covers a land area of 5.470 square miles and a water area of 0 square miles. Located at 40.18° N. Lat; 75.14° W. Long. Elevation is 249 feet.

Population: 15,047 (1990); 14,779 (2000); 14,842 (2010); Density: 2,713.4 persons per square mile (2010); Race: 86.5% White, 4.7% Black, 5.8% Asian, 0.2% American Indian/Alaska Native, 0.1% Native Hawaiian/Other Pacific Islander, 2.7% Other, 3.5% Hispanic of any race

(2010); Average household size: 2.50 (2010); Median age: 40.3 (2010); Males per 100 females: 93.2 (2010); Marriage status: 30.4% never married, 54.2% now married, 5.6% widowed, 9.7% divorced (2006-2010 5-year est.); Foreign born: 9.5% (2006-2010 5-year est.); Ancestry (includes multiple ancestries): 31.3% German, 29.3% Irish, 13.5% Italian, 13.3% English, 8.8% Polish (2006-2010 5-year est.).

Economy: Employment by occupation: 13.3% management, 6.5% professional, 6.8% services, 16.7% sales, 3.7% farming, 8.6% construction, 6.3% production (2006-2010 5-year est.).

Income: Per capita income: $31,464 (2006-2010 5-year est.); Median household income: $65,593 (2006-2010 5-year est.); Average household income: $77,827 (2006-2010 5-year est.); Percent of households with income of $100,000 or more: 25.8% (2006-2010 5-year est.); Poverty rate: 5.3% (2006-2010 5-year est.).

Education: Percent of population age 25 and over with: High school diploma (including GED) or higher: 92.1% (2006-2010 5-year est.); Bachelor's degree or higher: 38.4% (2006-2010 5-year est.); Master's degree or higher: 13.9% (2006-2010 5-year est.).

School District(s)
Hatboro-Horsham SD (KG-12)
    2010-11 Enrollment: 5,105 . . . . (215) 420-5000

Housing: Homeownership rate: 71.8% (2010); Median home value: $267,000 (2006-2010 5-year est.); Median contract rent: $903 per month (2006-2010 5-year est.); Median year structure built: 1973 (2006-2010 5-year est.).

Newspapers: Bucks County Tribune (Community news; Circulation 16,300); Far Northeast Citizen-Sentinel (Community news; Circulation 14,000); Montgomery County Progress (Community news; Circulation 17,251); Sunday Bucks County Telegraph (Community news; Circulation 7,476)

Transportation: Commute to work: 91.1% car, 3.4% public transportation, 1.9% walk, 3.0% work from home (2006-2010 5-year est.); Travel time to work: 28.9% less than 15 minutes, 31.2% 15 to 30 minutes, 22.7% 30 to 45 minutes, 8.8% 45 to 60 minutes, 8.4% 60 minutes or more (2006-2010 5-year est.)

Additional Information Contacts
Greater Horsham Chamber of Commerce . . . . (215) 360-2968
    http://www.horshamchamberofcommerce.com

HORSHAM (township). Covers a land area of 17.322 square miles and a water area of 0 square miles. Located at 40.20° N. Lat; 75.17° W. Long. Elevation is 249 feet.

Population: 21,900 (1990); 24,232 (2000); 26,147 (2010); Density: 1,509.5 persons per square mile (2010); Race: 86.0% White, 4.3% Black, 7.2% Asian, 0.1% American Indian/Alaska Native, 0.0% Native Hawaiian/Other Pacific Islander, 2.4% Other, 2.9% Hispanic of any race (2010); Average household size: 2.67 (2010); Median age: 40.5 (2010); Males per 100 females: 94.6 (2010); Marriage status: 29.3% never married, 57.8% now married, 4.6% widowed, 8.3% divorced (2006-2010 5-year est.); Foreign born: 9.9% (2006-2010 5-year est.); Ancestry (includes multiple ancestries): 28.6% Irish, 28.5% German, 16.5% Italian, 12.2% English, 8.0% Polish (2006-2010 5-year est.).

Economy: Unemployment rate: 6.7% (August 2012); Total civilian labor force: 14,942 (August 2012); Single-family building permits issued: 7 (2011); Multi-family building permits issued: 2 (2011); Employment by occupation: 17.8% management, 6.8% professional, 5.6% services, 15.1% sales, 3.7% farming, 6.8% construction, 4.7% production (2006-2010 5-year est.).

Income: Per capita income: $41,429 (2006-2010 5-year est.); Median household income: $81,888 (2006-2010 5-year est.); Average household income: $109,401 (2006-2010 5-year est.); Percent of households with income of $100,000 or more: 37.6% (2006-2010 5-year est.); Poverty rate: 4.6% (2006-2010 5-year est.).

Taxes: Total city taxes per capita: $423 (2009); City property taxes per capita: $91 (2009).

Education: Percent of population age 25 and over with: High school diploma (including GED) or higher: 94.0% (2006-2010 5-year est.); Bachelor's degree or higher: 45.8% (2006-2010 5-year est.); Master's degree or higher: 17.7% (2006-2010 5-year est.).

Housing: Homeownership rate: 75.3% (2010); Median home value: $330,600 (2006-2010 5-year est.); Median contract rent: $940 per month (2006-2010 5-year est.); Median year structure built: 1977 (2006-2010 5-year est.).

Safety: Violent crime rate: 7.6 per 10,000 population; Property crime rate: 114.4 per 10,000 population (2011).

Newspapers: Bucks County Tribune (Community news; Circulation 16,300); Far Northeast Citizen-Sentinel (Community news; Circulation 14,000); Montgomery County Progress (Community news; Circulation 17,251); Sunday Bucks County Telegraph (Community news; Circulation 7,476)

Transportation: Commute to work: 88.9% car, 4.0% public transportation, 2.4% walk, 4.0% work from home (2006-2010 5-year est.); Travel time to work: 25.3% less than 15 minutes, 32.3% 15 to 30 minutes, 23.4% 30 to 45 minutes, 9.8% 45 to 60 minutes, 9.2% 60 minutes or more (2006-2010 5-year est.)

Additional Information Contacts
Greater Horsham Chamber of Commerce . . . . (215) 360-2968
    http://www.horshamchamberofcommerce.com
Horsham Township . . . . (215) 643-3131
    http://www.horsham.org

HUNTINGDON VALLEY (unincorporated postal area)
Zip Code: 19006

Covers a land area of 12.838 square miles and a water area of 0 square miles. Located at 40.15° N. Lat; 75.03° W. Long. Population: 21,423 (2010); Density: 1,668.6 persons per square mile (2010); Race: 88.4% White, 1.3% Black, 8.2% Asian, 0.1% American Indian/Alaska Native, 0.0% Native Hawaiian/Other Pacific Islander, 2.0% Other, 2.3% Hispanic of any race (2010); Average household size: 2.65 (2010); Median age: 46.6 (2010); Males per 100 females: 90.9 (2010); Homeownership rate: 78.9% (2010)

JENKINTOWN (borough). Covers a land area of 0.580 square miles and a water area of 0 square miles. Located at 40.10° N. Lat; 75.13° W. Long. Elevation is 322 feet.

History: Seat of Beaver College to West (Glenside). Only synagogue designed by Frank Lloyd Wright is here. Settled 1750, incorporated 1874.

Population: 4,574 (1990); 4,478 (2000); 4,422 (2010); Density: 7,628.3 persons per square mile (2010); Race: 90.2% White, 5.7% Black, 2.0% Asian, 0.0% American Indian/Alaska Native, 0.0% Native Hawaiian/Other Pacific Islander, 2.1% Other, 3.0% Hispanic of any race (2010); Average household size: 2.19 (2010); Median age: 43.6 (2010); Males per 100 females: 81.5 (2010); Marriage status: 27.4% never married, 51.4% now married, 10.1% widowed, 11.1% divorced (2006-2010 5-year est.); Foreign born: 6.6% (2006-2010 5-year est.); Ancestry (includes multiple ancestries): 26.5% Irish, 18.7% German, 14.0% Italian, 9.2% English, 5.1% Scottish (2006-2010 5-year est.).

Economy: Single-family building permits issued: 0 (2011); Multi-family building permits issued: 0 (2011); Employment by occupation: 17.3% management, 6.2% professional, 6.3% services, 16.0% sales, 3.9% farming, 3.8% construction, 2.2% production (2006-2010 5-year est.).

Income: Per capita income: $38,250 (2006-2010 5-year est.); Median household income: $63,780 (2006-2010 5-year est.); Average household income: $84,715 (2006-2010 5-year est.); Percent of households with income of $100,000 or more: 29.7% (2006-2010 5-year est.); Poverty rate: 4.6% (2006-2010 5-year est.).

Education: Percent of population age 25 and over with: High school diploma (including GED) or higher: 95.9% (2006-2010 5-year est.); Bachelor's degree or higher: 53.0% (2006-2010 5-year est.); Master's degree or higher: 23.1% (2006-2010 5-year est.).

School District(s)
Jenkintown SD (KG-12)
    2010-11 Enrollment: 622 . . . . (215) 885-3722

Two-year College(s)
Manor College (Private, Not-for-profit, Other (none of the above))
    Fall 2010 Enrollment: 655 . . . . (215) 885-2360
    2011-12 Tuition: In-state $13,816; Out-of-state $13,816

Housing: Homeownership rate: 66.6% (2010); Median home value: $226,500 (2006-2010 5-year est.); Median contract rent: $802 per month (2006-2010 5-year est.); Median year structure built: before 1940 (2006-2010 5-year est.).

Hospitals: Holy Redeemer Hospital and Medical Center (249 beds)

Safety: Violent crime rate: 4.5 per 10,000 population; Property crime rate: 94.7 per 10,000 population (2011).

Transportation: Commute to work: 73.6% car, 14.5% public transportation, 9.6% walk, 1.7% work from home (2006-2010 5-year est.); Travel time to work: 23.5% less than 15 minutes, 26.7% 15 to 30 minutes, 21.1% 30 to 45 minutes, 16.5% 45 to 60 minutes, 12.2% 60 minutes or more (2006-2010 5-year est.)

Additional Information Contacts
Borough of Jenkintown . . . . (215) 885-0700
  http://www.jenkintownboro.com
Eastern Montgomery County Chamber of Commerce . . . . (215) 887-5122
  http://www.emccc.org

KING OF PRUSSIA (CDP). Covers a land area of 8.486 square
miles and a water area of 0.151 square miles. Located at 40.10° N. Lat;
75.38° W. Long. Elevation is 200 feet.
History: Named for a local tavern. Unincorporated city. Villanova
University is nearby. Valley Forge National Park, to northwest, contains the
Freedom Foundation national shrine that honors medal recipients from
U.S. wars. Revolutionary War Museum to southeast.
Population: 18,406 (1990); 18,511 (2000); 19,936 (2010); Density:
2,349.2 persons per square mile (2010); Race: 71.8% White, 5.7% Black,
18.6% Asian, 0.3% American Indian/Alaska Native, 0.0% Native
Hawaiian/Other Pacific Islander, 3.6% Other, 4.2% Hispanic of any race
(2010); Average household size: 2.31 (2010); Median age: 37.8 (2010);
Males per 100 females: 98.9 (2010); Marriage status: 31.6% never
married, 54.3% now married, 6.6% widowed, 7.5% divorced (2006-2010
5-year est.); Foreign born: 21.8% (2006-2010 5-year est.); Ancestry
(includes multiple ancestries): 20.7% Irish, 18.0% German, 17.4% Italian,
7.6% Polish, 6.2% English (2006-2010 5-year est.).
Economy: Employment by occupation: 16.5% management, 14.5%
professional, 5.1% services, 15.9% sales, 3.2% farming, 3.9%
construction, 4.3% production (2006-2010 5-year est.).
Income: Per capita income: $38,780 (2006-2010 5-year est.); Median
household income: $72,357 (2006-2010 5-year est.); Average household
income: $85,694 (2006-2010 5-year est.); Percent of households with
income of $100,000 or more: 32.6% (2006-2010 5-year est.); Poverty rate:
4.1% (2006-2010 5-year est.).
Education: Percent of population age 25 and over with: High school
diploma (including GED) or higher: 94.9% (2006-2010 5-year est.);
Bachelor's degree or higher: 52.8% (2006-2010 5-year est.); Master's
degree or higher: 24.3% (2006-2010 5-year est.).

School District(s)
Upper Merion Area SD (KG-12)
  2010-11 Enrollment: 3,791 . . . . (610) 205-6400

Two-year College(s)
ITT Technical Institute-King of Prussia (Private, For-profit)
  Fall 2010 Enrollment: 535 . . . . (610) 491-8004
  2011-12 Tuition: In-state $18,048; Out-of-state $18,048

Vocational/Technical School(s)
Cortiva Institute-Pennsylvania School of Muscle Therapy (Private,
For-profit)
  Fall 2010 Enrollment: 300 . . . . (610) 666-9060
  2011-12 Tuition: $9,900
Housing: Homeownership rate: 59.0% (2010); Median home value:
$310,100 (2006-2010 5-year est.); Median contract rent: $1,012 per month
(2006-2010 5-year est.); Median year structure built: 1968 (2006-2010
5-year est.).
Newspapers: Main Line Midweek (Community news; Circulation 74,271)
Transportation: Commute to work: 89.1% car, 4.5% public transportation,
2.7% walk, 3.3% work from home (2006-2010 5-year est.); Travel time to
work: 31.4% less than 15 minutes, 34.1% 15 to 30 minutes, 19.3% 30 to
45 minutes, 7.5% 45 to 60 minutes, 7.7% 60 minutes or more (2006-2010
5-year est.)
Additional Information Contacts
Greater Philadelphia Chamber of Commerce . . . . (215) 545-1234
  http://www.greaterphilachamber.com/about

KULPSVILLE (CDP). Covers a land area of 3.414 square miles and a
water area of 0 square miles. Located at 40.24° N. Lat; 75.34° W. Long.
Elevation is 289 feet.
Population: 5,444 (1990); 8,005 (2000); 8,194 (2010); Density: 2,400.0
persons per square mile (2010); Race: 84.9% White, 4.6% Black, 8.0%
Asian, 0.1% American Indian/Alaska Native, 0.0% Native Hawaiian/Other
Pacific Islander, 2.4% Other, 2.3% Hispanic of any race (2010); Average
household size: 2.37 (2010); Median age: 43.0 (2010); Males per 100
females: 83.7 (2010); Marriage status: 21.8% never married, 63.2% now
married, 8.2% widowed, 6.8% divorced (2006-2010 5-year est.); Foreign
born: 9.7% (2006-2010 5-year est.); Ancestry (includes multiple
ancestries): 25.6% Irish, 24.5% German, 18.9% Italian, 11.9% English,
6.1% American (2006-2010 5-year est.).

Economy: Employment by occupation: 19.1% management, 8.5%
professional, 6.3% services, 15.3% sales, 4.2% farming, 3.8%
construction, 6.1% production (2006-2010 5-year est.).
Income: Per capita income: $39,892 (2006-2010 5-year est.); Median
household income: $77,688 (2006-2010 5-year est.); Average household
income: $92,093 (2006-2010 5-year est.); Percent of households with
income of $100,000 or more: 36.2% (2006-2010 5-year est.); Poverty rate:
1.6% (2006-2010 5-year est.).
Education: Percent of population age 25 and over with: High school
diploma (including GED) or higher: 94.9% (2006-2010 5-year est.);
Bachelor's degree or higher: 44.4% (2006-2010 5-year est.); Master's
degree or higher: 14.7% (2006-2010 5-year est.).
Housing: Homeownership rate: 78.3% (2010); Median home value:
$251,300 (2006-2010 5-year est.); Median contract rent: $875 per month
(2006-2010 5-year est.); Median year structure built: 1985 (2006-2010
5-year est.).
Transportation: Commute to work: 93.1% car, 3.7% public transportation,
0.0% walk, 2.9% work from home (2006-2010 5-year est.); Travel time to
work: 19.5% less than 15 minutes, 28.3% 15 to 30 minutes, 29.0% 30 to
45 minutes, 11.8% 45 to 60 minutes, 11.4% 60 minutes or more
(2006-2010 5-year est.)
Additional Information Contacts
Indian Valley Chamber of Commerce . . . . (215) 723-9472
  http://indianvalleychamber.com

LAFAYETTE HILL (unincorporated postal area)
Zip Code: 19444
  Covers a land area of 4.844 square miles and a water area of 0 square
  miles. Located at 40.08° N. Lat; 75.25° W. Long. Population: 10,519
  (2010); Density: 2,171.5 persons per square mile (2010); Race: 90.7%
  White, 4.0% Black, 3.7% Asian, 0.1% American Indian/Alaska Native,
  0.0% Native Hawaiian/Other Pacific Islander, 1.5% Other, 1.4%
  Hispanic of any race (2010); Average household size: 2.41 (2010);
  Median age: 44.7 (2010); Males per 100 females: 88.6 (2010);
  Homeownership rate: 76.2% (2010)

LANSDALE (borough). Covers a land area of 2.993 square miles and
a water area of 0 square miles. Located at 40.24° N. Lat; 75.28° W. Long.
Elevation is 358 feet.
History: Named for Philip Lansdale Fox, a railroad surveyor. The Jenkins
House here dates from 1702. Incorporated 1872.
Population: 16,362 (1990); 16,071 (2000); 16,269 (2010); Density:
5,436.5 persons per square mile (2010); Race: 75.9% White, 5.9% Black,
13.3% Asian, 0.2% American Indian/Alaska Native, 0.1% Native
Hawaiian/Other Pacific Islander, 4.6% Other, 5.0% Hispanic of any race
(2010); Average household size: 2.39 (2010); Median age: 38.1 (2010);
Males per 100 females: 95.1 (2010); Marriage status: 31.9% never
married, 50.3% now married, 8.0% widowed, 9.8% divorced (2006-2010
5-year est.); Foreign born: 16.4% (2006-2010 5-year est.); Ancestry
(includes multiple ancestries): 25.8% German, 21.2% Irish, 11.8% Italian,
9.4% English, 8.7% Polish (2006-2010 5-year est.).
Economy: Single-family building permits issued: 21 (2011); Multi-family
building permits issued: 0 (2011); Employment by occupation: 8.4%
management, 4.5% professional, 11.0% services, 19.9% sales, 5.1%
farming, 7.6% construction, 7.5% production (2006-2010 5-year est.).
Income: Per capita income: $27,872 (2006-2010 5-year est.); Median
household income: $56,378 (2006-2010 5-year est.); Average household
income: $66,528 (2006-2010 5-year est.); Percent of households with
income of $100,000 or more: 17.1% (2006-2010 5-year est.); Poverty rate:
9.4% (2006-2010 5-year est.).
Taxes: Total city taxes per capita: $284 (2009); City property taxes per
capita: $98 (2009).
Education: Percent of population age 25 and over with: High school
diploma (including GED) or higher: 86.0% (2006-2010 5-year est.);
Bachelor's degree or higher: 28.2% (2006-2010 5-year est.); Master's
degree or higher: 8.4% (2006-2010 5-year est.).

School District(s)
Methacton SD (KG-12)
  2010-11 Enrollment: 5,289 . . . . (610) 489-5000
North Montco Tech Career Center (09-12)
  2010-11 Enrollment: 1,078 . . . . (215) 368-1177
North Penn SD (KG-12)
  2010-11 Enrollment: 12,698 . . . . (215) 368-0400

Four-year College(s)

Calvary Baptist Theological Seminary (Private, Not-for-profit, Baptist)
  Fall 2010 Enrollment: 51 . . . . (215) 368-7538

Vocational/Technical School(s)

Lansdale School of Cosmetology Inc (Private, For-profit)
  Fall 2010 Enrollment: 122 . . . . (215) 362-2322
  2011-12 Tuition: $14,075

Housing: Homeownership rate: 55.8% (2010); Median home value: $228,000 (2006-2010 5-year est.); Median contract rent: $807 per month (2006-2010 5-year est.); Median year structure built: 1956 (2006-2010 5-year est.).

Hospitals: Central Montgomery Medical Center (125 beds)

Safety: Violent crime rate: 13.5 per 10,000 population; Property crime rate: 194.2 per 10,000 population (2011).

Newspapers: The Reporter (Local news; Circulation 14,243)

Transportation: Commute to work: 89.2% car, 4.2% public transportation, 2.8% walk, 2.2% work from home (2006-2010 5-year est.); Travel time to work: 28.8% less than 15 minutes, 34.0% 15 to 30 minutes, 18.6% 30 to 45 minutes, 8.6% 45 to 60 minutes, 10.0% 60 minutes or more (2006-2010 5-year est.)

Additional Information Contacts

Borough of Lansdale . . . . (215) 368-1691
  http://www.lansdale.org
PennSuburban Chamber of Commerce . . . . (215) 362-9200
  http://www.pennsuburban.org

LIMERICK (township). Covers a land area of 22.507 square miles and a water area of 0.203 square miles. Located at 40.23° N. Lat; 75.53° W. Long. Elevation is 292 feet.

Population: 6,691 (1990); 13,534 (2000); 18,074 (2010); Density: 803.0 persons per square mile (2010); Race: 91.5% White, 3.4% Black, 3.2% Asian, 0.1% American Indian/Alaska Native, 0.0% Native Hawaiian/Other Pacific Islander, 1.8% Other, 1.8% Hispanic of any race (2010); Average household size: 2.62 (2010); Median age: 39.0 (2010); Males per 100 females: 94.7 (2010); Marriage status: 23.9% never married, 62.6% now married, 5.0% widowed, 8.6% divorced (2006-2010 5-year est.); Foreign born: 5.9% (2006-2010 5-year est.); Ancestry (includes multiple ancestries): 28.8% German, 25.7% Irish, 22.9% Italian, 11.5% Polish, 10.9% English (2006-2010 5-year est.).

Economy: Single-family building permits issued: 25 (2011); Multi-family building permits issued: 0 (2011); Employment by occupation: 16.5% management, 7.7% professional, 8.9% services, 18.0% sales, 5.5% farming, 6.1% construction, 4.3% production (2006-2010 5-year est.).

Income: Per capita income: $34,672 (2006-2010 5-year est.); Median household income: $76,682 (2006-2010 5-year est.); Average household income: $89,198 (2006-2010 5-year est.); Percent of households with income of $100,000 or more: 38.6% (2006-2010 5-year est.); Poverty rate: 4.9% (2006-2010 5-year est.).

Education: Percent of population age 25 and over with: High school diploma (including GED) or higher: 93.3% (2006-2010 5-year est.); Bachelor's degree or higher: 37.2% (2006-2010 5-year est.); Master's degree or higher: 12.1% (2006-2010 5-year est.).

School District(s)

Spring-Ford Area SD (KG-12)
  2010-11 Enrollment: 7,730 . . . . (610) 705-6000
Western Montgomery CTC (10-12)
  2010-11 Enrollment: n/a . . . . (610) 489-7272

Housing: Homeownership rate: 80.3% (2010); Median home value: $293,900 (2006-2010 5-year est.); Median contract rent: $1,054 per month (2006-2010 5-year est.); Median year structure built: 1994 (2006-2010 5-year est.).

Safety: Violent crime rate: 5.5 per 10,000 population; Property crime rate: 238.8 per 10,000 population (2011).

Transportation: Commute to work: 91.9% car, 1.0% public transportation, 1.5% walk, 4.5% work from home (2006-2010 5-year est.); Travel time to work: 23.5% less than 15 minutes, 24.4% 15 to 30 minutes, 28.5% 30 to 45 minutes, 12.7% 45 to 60 minutes, 10.9% 60 minutes or more (2006-2010 5-year est.)

Additional Information Contacts

Limerick Township. . . . . (610) 495-6432
  http://www.limerickpa.org
Spring-Ford Chamber of Commerce . . . . (610) 489-7200
  http://www.springfordchamber.com

LOWER FREDERICK (township). Covers a land area of 8.009 square miles and a water area of 0.117 square miles. Located at 40.28° N. Lat; 75.49° W. Long.

Population: 3,398 (1990); 4,795 (2000); 4,840 (2010); Density: 604.3 persons per square mile (2010); Race: 94.3% White, 2.0% Black, 1.4% Asian, 0.3% American Indian/Alaska Native, 0.0% Native Hawaiian/Other Pacific Islander, 2.0% Other, 3.0% Hispanic of any race (2010); Average household size: 2.64 (2010); Median age: 39.3 (2010); Males per 100 females: 97.0 (2010); Marriage status: 24.4% never married, 61.2% now married, 3.3% widowed, 11.1% divorced (2006-2010 5-year est.); Foreign born: 3.2% (2006-2010 5-year est.); Ancestry (includes multiple ancestries): 35.7% German, 22.5% Irish, 16.3% Italian, 7.9% English, 7.7% Polish (2006-2010 5-year est.).

Economy: Single-family building permits issued: 1 (2011); Multi-family building permits issued: 0 (2011); Employment by occupation: 12.3% management, 7.4% professional, 9.2% services, 19.2% sales, 4.8% farming, 9.9% construction, 2.2% production (2006-2010 5-year est.).

Income: Per capita income: $32,272 (2006-2010 5-year est.); Median household income: $80,030 (2006-2010 5-year est.); Average household income: $83,174 (2006-2010 5-year est.); Percent of households with income of $100,000 or more: 28.9% (2006-2010 5-year est.); Poverty rate: 3.5% (2006-2010 5-year est.).

Education: Percent of population age 25 and over with: High school diploma (including GED) or higher: 90.9% (2006-2010 5-year est.); Bachelor's degree or higher: 33.9% (2006-2010 5-year est.); Master's degree or higher: 13.5% (2006-2010 5-year est.).

Housing: Homeownership rate: 88.2% (2010); Median home value: $247,100 (2006-2010 5-year est.); Median contract rent: $929 per month (2006-2010 5-year est.); Median year structure built: 1983 (2006-2010 5-year est.).

Safety: Violent crime rate: 4.1 per 10,000 population; Property crime rate: 43.3 per 10,000 population (2011).

Transportation: Commute to work: 91.0% car, 0.5% public transportation, 4.3% walk, 4.2% work from home (2006-2010 5-year est.); Travel time to work: 14.3% less than 15 minutes, 25.4% 15 to 30 minutes, 32.6% 30 to 45 minutes, 13.6% 45 to 60 minutes, 14.1% 60 minutes or more (2006-2010 5-year est.)

Additional Information Contacts

Lower Frederick Township . . . . (610) 287-8857
  http://www.lowerfrederick.org
TriCounty Area Chamber of Commerce . . . . (610) 326-2900
  http://tricountyareachamber.com

LOWER GWYNEDD (township). Covers a land area of 9.303 square miles and a water area of 0.008 square miles. Located at 40.19° N. Lat; 75.24° W. Long.

History: The town, part of Pennsylvania's Welsh Tract, is named after the county of Gwynedd in Wales. However, local residents use the English pronunciation.

Population: 9,958 (1990); 10,422 (2000); 11,405 (2010); Density: 1,225.9 persons per square mile (2010); Race: 84.0% White, 6.9% Black, 7.1% Asian, 0.1% American Indian/Alaska Native, 0.0% Native Hawaiian/Other Pacific Islander, 1.9% Other, 1.9% Hispanic of any race (2010); Average household size: 2.36 (2010); Median age: 49.2 (2010); Males per 100 females: 84.4 (2010); Marriage status: 22.1% never married, 57.6% now married, 15.3% widowed, 5.0% divorced (2006-2010 5-year est.); Foreign born: 9.3% (2006-2010 5-year est.); Ancestry (includes multiple ancestries): 22.9% German, 19.2% Irish, 16.1% English, 10.7% Italian, 5.4% Russian (2006-2010 5-year est.).

Economy: Single-family building permits issued: 15 (2011); Multi-family building permits issued: 0 (2011); Employment by occupation: 21.0% management, 7.7% professional, 3.9% services, 13.6% sales, 3.2% farming, 2.6% construction, 1.9% production (2006-2010 5-year est.).

Income: Per capita income: $56,457 (2006-2010 5-year est.); Median household income: $96,513 (2006-2010 5-year est.); Average household income: $143,677 (2006-2010 5-year est.); Percent of households with income of $100,000 or more: 49.1% (2006-2010 5-year est.); Poverty rate: 3.7% (2006-2010 5-year est.).

Taxes: Total city taxes per capita: $551 (2009); City property taxes per capita: $131 (2009).

Education: Percent of population age 25 and over with: High school diploma (including GED) or higher: 97.2% (2006-2010 5-year est.); Bachelor's degree or higher: 65.3% (2006-2010 5-year est.); Master's degree or higher: 30.0% (2006-2010 5-year est.).

Housing: Homeownership rate: 73.2% (2010); Median home value: $481,700 (2006-2010 5-year est.); Median contract rent: $1,655 per month (2006-2010 5-year est.); Median year structure built: 1977 (2006-2010 5-year est.).

Safety: Violent crime rate: 8.7 per 10,000 population; Property crime rate: 172.2 per 10,000 population (2011).

Transportation: Commute to work: 87.3% car, 4.0% public transportation, 1.6% walk, 6.4% work from home (2006-2010 5-year est.); Travel time to work: 21.7% less than 15 minutes, 29.3% 15 to 30 minutes, 26.4% 30 to 45 minutes, 12.2% 45 to 60 minutes, 10.4% 60 minutes or more (2006-2010 5-year est.)

Additional Information Contacts

Greater Hatboro Chamber of Commerce . . . . (215) 956-9540
  http://hatborochamber.org
Lower Gwynedd Township . . . . (215) 646-5302
  http://www.lowergwynedd.org

LOWER MERION (township). Covers a land area of 23.671 square miles and a water area of 0.161 square miles. Located at 40.03° N. Lat; 75.28° W. Long.

History: Seat of Rosemont College.

Population: 58,003 (1990); 59,850 (2000); 57,825 (2010); Density: 2,442.9 persons per square mile (2010); Race: 85.7% White, 5.6% Black, 6.0% Asian, 0.1% American Indian/Alaska Native, 0.0% Native Hawaiian/Other Pacific Islander, 2.6% Other, 3.0% Hispanic of any race (2010); Average household size: 2.43 (2010); Median age: 43.4 (2010); Males per 100 females: 85.3 (2010); Marriage status: 28.7% never married, 58.6% now married, 5.9% widowed, 6.8% divorced (2006-2010 5-year est.); Foreign born: 11.5% (2006-2010 5-year est.); Ancestry (includes multiple ancestries): 15.4% Irish, 13.9% German, 10.8% Russian, 9.5% English, 9.4% Italian (2006-2010 5-year est.).

Economy: Unemployment rate: 5.6% (August 2012); Total civilian labor force: 28,833 (August 2012); Single-family building permits issued: 28 (2011); Multi-family building permits issued: 0 (2011); Employment by occupation: 18.7% management, 5.8% professional, 6.0% services, 12.2% sales, 2.5% farming, 1.8% construction, 1.5% production (2006-2010 5-year est.).

Income: Per capita income: $73,031 (2006-2010 5-year est.); Median household income: $111,165 (2006-2010 5-year est.); Average household income: $184,975 (2006-2010 5-year est.); Percent of households with income of $100,000 or more: 54.6% (2006-2010 5-year est.); Poverty rate: 5.4% (2006-2010 5-year est.).

Taxes: Total city taxes per capita: $753 (2009); City property taxes per capita: $473 (2009).

Education: Percent of population age 25 and over with: High school diploma (including GED) or higher: 97.8% (2006-2010 5-year est.); Bachelor's degree or higher: 73.1% (2006-2010 5-year est.); Master's degree or higher: 43.4% (2006-2010 5-year est.).

Housing: Homeownership rate: 76.3% (2010); Median home value: $551,100 (2006-2010 5-year est.); Median contract rent: $1,106 per month (2006-2010 5-year est.); Median year structure built: 1953 (2006-2010 5-year est.).

Safety: Violent crime rate: 9.0 per 10,000 population; Property crime rate: 176.9 per 10,000 population (2011).

Transportation: Commute to work: 73.1% car, 10.0% public transportation, 7.7% walk, 8.3% work from home (2006-2010 5-year est.); Travel time to work: 26.0% less than 15 minutes, 33.6% 15 to 30 minutes, 26.6% 30 to 45 minutes, 9.1% 45 to 60 minutes, 4.8% 60 minutes or more (2006-2010 5-year est.)

Additional Information Contacts

Lower Merion Township . . . . (611) 649-4000
  http://www.lowermerion.org
Main Line Chamber of Commerce . . . . (610) 687-6232
  http://www.mlcc.org

LOWER MORELAND (township). Covers a land area of 7.281 square miles and a water area of 0 square miles. Located at 40.12° N. Lat; 75.07° W. Long.

History: William Penn presented the tract of land around present day Lower Moreland Township to Nicholas More in 1682. At the time, the area was referred to as the "Manor of Mooreland".

Population: 11,768 (1990); 11,281 (2000); 12,982 (2010); Density: 1,783.0 persons per square mile (2010); Race: 88.2% White, 1.0% Black, 8.9% Asian, 0.1% American Indian/Alaska Native, 0.1% Native Hawaiian/Other Pacific Islander, 1.7% Other, 1.8% Hispanic of any race

(2010); Average household size: 2.82 (2010); Median age: 45.1 (2010); Males per 100 females: 92.0 (2010); Marriage status: 23.1% never married, 66.5% now married, 7.5% widowed, 2.9% divorced (2006-2010 5-year est.); Foreign born: 17.1% (2006-2010 5-year est.); Ancestry (includes multiple ancestries): 17.7% Irish, 15.7% Italian, 15.7% German, 12.7% Russian, 9.3% English (2006-2010 5-year est.).

Economy: Single-family building permits issued: 3 (2011); Multi-family building permits issued: 0 (2011); Employment by occupation: 21.2% management, 4.6% professional, 5.2% services, 14.1% sales, 7.0% farming, 7.0% construction, 4.0% production (2006-2010 5-year est.).

Income: Per capita income: $40,159 (2006-2010 5-year est.); Median household income: $91,611 (2006-2010 5-year est.); Average household income: $116,521 (2006-2010 5-year est.); Percent of households with income of $100,000 or more: 47.5% (2006-2010 5-year est.); Poverty rate: 5.9% (2006-2010 5-year est.).

Education: Percent of population age 25 and over with: High school diploma (including GED) or higher: 94.0% (2006-2010 5-year est.); Bachelor's degree or higher: 50.5% (2006-2010 5-year est.); Master's degree or higher: 22.5% (2006-2010 5-year est.).

Housing: Homeownership rate: 86.8% (2010); Median home value: $424,300 (2006-2010 5-year est.); Median contract rent: $606 per month (2006-2010 5-year est.); Median year structure built: 1965 (2006-2010 5-year est.).

Safety: Violent crime rate: 3.1 per 10,000 population; Property crime rate: 135.1 per 10,000 population (2011).

Transportation: Commute to work: 83.3% car, 7.5% public transportation, 1.5% walk, 6.1% work from home (2006-2010 5-year est.); Travel time to work: 25.8% less than 15 minutes, 30.8% 15 to 30 minutes, 19.7% 30 to 45 minutes, 12.5% 45 to 60 minutes, 11.2% 60 minutes or more (2006-2010 5-year est.)

Additional Information Contacts

Greater Hatboro Chamber of Commerce . . . . (215) 956-9540
  http://hatborochamber.org
Lower Moreland Township . . . . (215) 947-3100
  http://www.lowermoreland.org

LOWER POTTSGROVE (township). Covers a land area of 7.920 square miles and a water area of 0.116 square miles. Located at 40.25° N. Lat; 75.59° W. Long.

Population: 8,808 (1990); 11,213 (2000); 12,059 (2010); Density: 1,522.5 persons per square mile (2010); Race: 85.3% White, 10.1% Black, 1.6% Asian, 0.1% American Indian/Alaska Native, 0.1% Native Hawaiian/Other Pacific Islander, 2.8% Other, 2.7% Hispanic of any race (2010); Average household size: 2.65 (2010); Median age: 39.2 (2010); Males per 100 females: 92.1 (2010); Marriage status: 25.1% never married, 61.2% now married, 6.8% widowed, 6.8% divorced (2006-2010 5-year est.); Foreign born: 3.5% (2006-2010 5-year est.); Ancestry (includes multiple ancestries): 31.7% German, 21.0% Irish, 18.2% Italian, 10.3% English, 6.6% Polish (2006-2010 5-year est.).

Economy: Single-family building permits issued: 3 (2011); Multi-family building permits issued: 0 (2011); Employment by occupation: 12.8% management, 8.8% professional, 5.3% services, 18.5% sales, 4.3% farming, 8.6% construction, 4.9% production (2006-2010 5-year est.).

Income: Per capita income: $32,507 (2006-2010 5-year est.); Median household income: $76,213 (2006-2010 5-year est.); Average household income: $85,397 (2006-2010 5-year est.); Percent of households with income of $100,000 or more: 29.7% (2006-2010 5-year est.); Poverty rate: 9.2% (2006-2010 5-year est.).

Education: Percent of population age 25 and over with: High school diploma (including GED) or higher: 93.1% (2006-2010 5-year est.); Bachelor's degree or higher: 31.9% (2006-2010 5-year est.); Master's degree or higher: 9.3% (2006-2010 5-year est.).

Housing: Homeownership rate: 83.1% (2010); Median home value: $216,200 (2006-2010 5-year est.); Median contract rent: $689 per month (2006-2010 5-year est.); Median year structure built: 1982 (2006-2010 5-year est.).

Safety: Violent crime rate: 15.7 per 10,000 population; Property crime rate: 230.6 per 10,000 population (2011).

Transportation: Commute to work: 95.5% car, 0.3% public transportation, 0.5% walk, 3.7% work from home (2006-2010 5-year est.); Travel time to work: 23.8% less than 15 minutes, 25.0% 15 to 30 minutes, 24.4% 30 to 45 minutes, 11.3% 45 to 60 minutes, 15.6% 60 minutes or more (2006-2010 5-year est.)

Additional Information Contacts

Lower Pottsgrove Township . . . . (610) 323-0436
  http://www.lowerpottsgrove.org
TriCounty Area Chamber of Commerce . . . . (610) 326-2900
  http://tricountyareachamber.com

LOWER PROVIDENCE (township). Covers a land area of 15.249
square miles and a water area of 0.209 square miles. Located at 40.15° N.
Lat; 75.42° W. Long.

Population: 19,351 (1990); 22,390 (2000); 25,436 (2010); Density:
1,668.1 persons per square mile (2010); Race: 81.0% White, 7.1% Black,
9.7% Asian, 0.1% American Indian/Alaska Native, 0.0% Native
Hawaiian/Other Pacific Islander, 2.1% Other, 2.9% Hispanic of any race
(2010); Average household size: 2.66 (2010); Median age: 40.8 (2010);
Males per 100 females: 108.6 (2010); Marriage status: 28.0% never
married, 59.0% now married, 5.7% widowed, 7.2% divorced (2006-2010
5-year est.); Foreign born: 10.9% (2006-2010 5-year est.); Ancestry
(includes multiple ancestries): 24.7% Italian, 23.6% Irish, 22.3% German,
7.9% English, 6.6% Polish (2006-2010 5-year est.).
Economy: Unemployment rate: 7.0% (August 2012); Total civilian labor
force: 13,159 (August 2012); Single-family building permits issued: 8
(2011); Multi-family building permits issued: 0 (2011); Employment by
occupation: 17.3% management, 12.5% professional, 6.2% services,
16.9% sales, 2.9% farming, 5.4% construction, 3.8% production
(2006-2010 5-year est.).
Income: Per capita income: $36,828 (2006-2010 5-year est.); Median
household income: $88,964 (2006-2010 5-year est.); Average household
income: $106,153 (2006-2010 5-year est.); Percent of households with
income of $100,000 or more: 43.2% (2006-2010 5-year est.); Poverty rate:
2.9% (2006-2010 5-year est.).
Taxes: Total city taxes per capita: $311 (2009); City property taxes per
capita: $93 (2009).
Education: Percent of population age 25 and over with: High school
diploma (including GED) or higher: 91.4% (2006-2010 5-year est.);
Bachelor's degree or higher: 43.3% (2006-2010 5-year est.); Master's
degree or higher: 18.2% (2006-2010 5-year est.).
Housing: Homeownership rate: 77.2% (2010); Median home value:
$331,200 (2006-2010 5-year est.); Median contract rent: $1,030 per month
(2006-2010 5-year est.); Median year structure built: 1974 (2006-2010
5-year est.).
Safety: Violent crime rate: 16.5 per 10,000 population; Property crime rate:
105.0 per 10,000 population (2011).
Transportation: Commute to work: 90.0% car, 3.2% public transportation,
1.7% walk, 4.1% work from home (2006-2010 5-year est.); Travel time to
work: 24.6% less than 15 minutes, 33.6% 15 to 30 minutes, 23.4% 30 to
45 minutes, 8.6% 45 to 60 minutes, 9.8% 60 minutes or more (2006-2010
5-year est.)

Additional Information Contacts

Lower Providence Township . . . . (610) 539-8020
  http://www.lowerprovidence.org
Montgomery County Chamber of Commerce . . . . (610) 265-1776
  http://www.montgomerycountychamber.org

LOWER SALFORD (township). Covers a land area of 14.442
square miles and a water area of 0.051 square miles. Located at 40.26° N.
Lat; 75.40° W. Long.

History: The area now known as Lower Salford, Upper Salford, Salford
and Marlborough Township was originally one municipality known as
Salford Township. As this area was too large to govern, and with most of
the early settlers located in the lower section of the township, a resident
named Jacob Reiff, acting on behalf of his neighbors, submitted a petition
to the Philadelphia County officials to create what is now Lower Salford
Township.
Population: 10,728 (1990); 12,893 (2000); 14,959 (2010); Density:
1,035.8 persons per square mile (2010); Race: 90.6% White, 2.9% Black,
4.4% Asian, 0.1% American Indian/Alaska Native, 0.0% Native
Hawaiian/Other Pacific Islander, 2.0% Other, 2.6% Hispanic of any race
(2010); Average household size: 2.73 (2010); Median age: 40.2 (2010);
Males per 100 females: 93.6 (2010); Marriage status: 23.7% never
married, 64.8% now married, 4.7% widowed, 6.8% divorced (2006-2010
5-year est.); Foreign born: 5.1% (2006-2010 5-year est.); Ancestry
(includes multiple ancestries): 37.4% German, 25.9% Irish, 16.9% Italian,
9.4% English, 6.4% Polish (2006-2010 5-year est.).
Economy: Single-family building permits issued: 28 (2011); Multi-family
building permits issued: 0 (2011); Employment by occupation: 16.4%

management, 6.7% professional, 5.1% services, 14.1% sales, 4.5%
farming, 6.4% construction, 4.5% production (2006-2010 5-year est.).
Income: Per capita income: $40,869 (2006-2010 5-year est.); Median
household income: $92,589 (2006-2010 5-year est.); Average household
income: $112,182 (2006-2010 5-year est.); Percent of households with
income of $100,000 or more: 45.5% (2006-2010 5-year est.); Poverty rate:
2.5% (2006-2010 5-year est.).
Taxes: Total city taxes per capita: $388 (2009); City property taxes per
capita: $135 (2009).
Education: Percent of population age 25 and over with: High school
diploma (including GED) or higher: 94.5% (2006-2010 5-year est.);
Bachelor's degree or higher: 46.0% (2006-2010 5-year est.); Master's
degree or higher: 17.4% (2006-2010 5-year est.).
Housing: Homeownership rate: 75.5% (2010); Median home value:
$343,600 (2006-2010 5-year est.); Median contract rent: $857 per month
(2006-2010 5-year est.); Median year structure built: 1983 (2006-2010
5-year est.).
Safety: Violent crime rate: 4.7 per 10,000 population; Property crime rate:
54.0 per 10,000 population (2011).
Transportation: Commute to work: 91.3% car, 1.4% public transportation,
2.2% walk, 3.6% work from home (2006-2010 5-year est.); Travel time to
work: 21.7% less than 15 minutes, 29.3% 15 to 30 minutes, 25.7% 30 to
45 minutes, 11.4% 45 to 60 minutes, 11.9% 60 minutes or more
(2006-2010 5-year est.)

Additional Information Contacts

Indian Valley Chamber of Commerce . . . . (215) 723-9472
  http://indianvalleychamber.com
Lower Salford Township . . . . (215) 256-8087
  http://www.lowersalfordtownship.org

MAPLE GLEN (CDP). Aka Mapleglen. Covers a land area of 3.119
square miles and a water area of 0 square miles. Located at 40.18° N. Lat;
75.18° W. Long. Elevation is 374 feet.

History: Maple Glen is adjacent to the Willow Grove Naval Air
Stationhome to the 111th Fighter Wing, an Air Combat Command gained
unit of the Air National Guard operating the A-10 Thunderbolt II.The area
was part of the Welsh Tract — an area of Pennsylvania settled by Quakers
from Wales.
Population: 5,881 (1990); 7,042 (2000); 6,742 (2010); Density: 2,161.7
persons per square mile (2010); Race: 87.2% White, 2.7% Black, 8.6%
Asian, 0.1% American Indian/Alaska Native, 0.0% Native Hawaiian/Other
Pacific Islander, 1.4% Other, 2.0% Hispanic of any race (2010); Average
household size: 2.87 (2010); Median age: 42.3 (2010); Males per 100
females: 95.9 (2010); Marriage status: 25.9% never married, 66.3% now
married, 2.1% widowed, 5.7% divorced (2006-2010 5-year est.); Foreign
born: 11.0% (2006-2010 5-year est.); Ancestry (includes multiple
ancestries): 28.9% Irish, 24.1% German, 18.4% Italian, 9.7% English,
9.2% Polish (2006-2010 5-year est.).
Economy: Employment by occupation: 23.5% management, 5.5%
professional, 3.3% services, 11.7% sales, 2.3% farming, 5.5%
construction, 2.3% production (2006-2010 5-year est.).
Income: Per capita income: $45,405 (2006-2010 5-year est.); Median
household income: $113,194 (2006-2010 5-year est.); Average household
income: $133,373 (2006-2010 5-year est.); Percent of households with
income of $100,000 or more: 56.7% (2006-2010 5-year est.); Poverty rate:
2.0% (2006-2010 5-year est.).
Education: Percent of population age 25 and over with: High school
diploma (including GED) or higher: 98.3% (2006-2010 5-year est.);
Bachelor's degree or higher: 56.3% (2006-2010 5-year est.); Master's
degree or higher: 20.5% (2006-2010 5-year est.).

School District(s)

Upper Dublin SD (KG-12)
  2010-11 Enrollment: 4,270 . . . . (215) 643-8800
Housing: Homeownership rate: 92.6% (2010); Median home value:
$388,600 (2006-2010 5-year est.); Median contract rent: $1,341 per month
(2006-2010 5-year est.); Median year structure built: 1982 (2006-2010
5-year est.).
Transportation: Commute to work: 92.3% car, 4.1% public transportation,
0.3% walk, 3.3% work from home (2006-2010 5-year est.); Travel time to
work: 18.8% less than 15 minutes, 27.2% 15 to 30 minutes, 31.9% 30 to
45 minutes, 11.1% 45 to 60 minutes, 11.0% 60 minutes or more
(2006-2010 5-year est.)

Additional Information Contacts

Greater Hatboro Chamber of Commerce . . . . (215) 956-9540
  http://hatborochamber.org

MARLBOROUGH (township). Covers a land area of 12.223 square miles and a water area of 0.152 square miles. Located at 40.36° N. Lat; 75.45° W. Long.
Population: 3,120 (1990); 3,104 (2000); 3,178 (2010); Density: 260.0 persons per square mile (2010); Race: 97.4% White, 1.0% Black, 0.2% Asian, 0.2% American Indian/Alaska Native, 0.0% Native Hawaiian/Other Pacific Islander, 1.2% Other, 1.2% Hispanic of any race (2010); Average household size: 2.48 (2010); Median age: 45.2 (2010); Males per 100 females: 101.0 (2010); Marriage status: 18.7% never married, 69.2% now married, 5.2% widowed, 6.8% divorced (2006-2010 5-year est.); Foreign born: 1.4% (2006-2010 5-year est.); Ancestry (includes multiple ancestries): 40.5% German, 21.0% Irish, 9.6% English, 6.8% American, 5.0% Pennsylvania German (2006-2010 5-year est.).
Economy: Single-family building permits issued: 11 (2011); Multi-family building permits issued: 0 (2011); Employment by occupation: 13.0% management, 4.8% professional, 12.3% services, 17.8% sales, 2.5% farming, 11.7% construction, 7.2% production (2006-2010 5-year est.).
Income: Per capita income: $32,115 (2006-2010 5-year est.); Median household income: $73,787 (2006-2010 5-year est.); Average household income: $93,441 (2006-2010 5-year est.); Percent of households with income of $100,000 or more: 32.3% (2006-2010 5-year est.); Poverty rate: 6.7% (2006-2010 5-year est.).
Education: Percent of population age 25 and over with: High school diploma (including GED) or higher: 89.2% (2006-2010 5-year est.); Bachelor's degree or higher: 16.9% (2006-2010 5-year est.); Master's degree or higher: 4.9% (2006-2010 5-year est.).
Housing: Homeownership rate: 88.0% (2010); Median home value: $303,800 (2006-2010 5-year est.); Median contract rent: $1,031 per month (2006-2010 5-year est.); Median year structure built: 1969 (2006-2010 5-year est.).
Safety: Violent crime rate: 12.5 per 10,000 population; Property crime rate: 91.0 per 10,000 population (2011).
Transportation: Commute to work: 93.5% car, 0.0% public transportation, 3.0% walk, 2.3% work from home (2006-2010 5-year est.); Travel time to work: 18.9% less than 15 minutes, 37.0% 15 to 30 minutes, 26.3% 30 to 45 minutes, 6.8% 45 to 60 minutes, 11.0% 60 minutes or more (2006-2010 5-year est.)
Additional Information Contacts
Upper Bucks Chamber of Commerce . . . . (215) 536-3211
   http://www.ubcc.org

MERION STATION (unincorporated postal area)
Zip Code: 19066
   Covers a land area of 1.364 square miles and a water area of 0 square miles. Located at 40.00° N. Lat; 75.24° W. Long. Population: 5,864 (2010); Density: 4,296.8 persons per square mile (2010); Race: 92.2% White, 2.2% Black, 3.7% Asian, 0.1% American Indian/Alaska Native, 0.0% Native Hawaiian/Other Pacific Islander, 1.8% Other, 2.6% Hispanic of any race (2010); Average household size: 2.84 (2010); Median age: 40.0 (2010); Males per 100 females: 90.0 (2010); Homeownership rate: 93.4% (2010)

MONT CLARE (unincorporated postal area)
Zip Code: 19453
   Covers a land area of 0.658 square miles and a water area of 0.047 square miles. Located at 40.14° N. Lat; 75.49° W. Long. Elevation is 184 feet. Population: 1,483 (2010); Density: 2,251.3 persons per square mile (2010); Race: 91.9% White, 4.0% Black, 1.8% Asian, 0.4% American Indian/Alaska Native, 0.0% Native Hawaiian/Other Pacific Islander, 1.9% Other, 2.0% Hispanic of any race (2010); Average household size: 2.06 (2010); Median age: 41.0 (2010); Males per 100 females: 90.6 (2010); Homeownership rate: 76.7% (2010)

MONTGOMERY (township). Covers a land area of 10.630 square miles and a water area of <.001 square miles. Located at 40.25° N. Lat; 75.23° W. Long.
History: Much of Montgomery Township's development is suburban in character, with newer tract houses and strip shopping centers. Homes in Montgomery Township have North Wales and Lansdale (even though Lansdale Borough is distinct from Montgomery Township, parts of the Township are still listed as Lansdale) addresses.
Population: 12,175 (1990); 22,025 (2000); 24,790 (2010); Density: 2,332.2 persons per square mile (2010); Race: 76.7% White, 4.6% Black, 16.6% Asian, 0.1% American Indian/Alaska Native, 0.0% Native Hawaiian/Other Pacific Islander, 2.0% Other, 2.2% Hispanic of any race

(2010); Average household size: 2.68 (2010); Median age: 41.3 (2010); Males per 100 females: 92.5 (2010); Marriage status: 24.7% never married, 63.2% now married, 6.0% widowed, 6.1% divorced (2006-2010 5-year est.); Foreign born: 14.0% (2006-2010 5-year est.); Ancestry (includes multiple ancestries): 26.6% Irish, 21.2% German, 17.4% Italian, 8.4% English, 5.4% Polish (2006-2010 5-year est.).
Economy: Single-family building permits issued: 133 (2011); Multi-family building permits issued: 0 (2011); Employment by occupation: 19.2% management, 7.5% professional, 4.9% services, 15.3% sales, 3.5% farming, 3.7% construction, 3.3% production (2006-2010 5-year est.).
Income: Per capita income: $40,891 (2006-2010 5-year est.); Median household income: $86,875 (2006-2010 5-year est.); Average household income: $110,773 (2006-2010 5-year est.); Percent of households with income of $100,000 or more: 44.7% (2006-2010 5-year est.); Poverty rate: 2.0% (2006-2010 5-year est.).
Education: Percent of population age 25 and over with: High school diploma (including GED) or higher: 95.5% (2006-2010 5-year est.); Bachelor's degree or higher: 55.1% (2006-2010 5-year est.); Master's degree or higher: 22.8% (2006-2010 5-year est.).
Housing: Homeownership rate: 90.8% (2010); Median home value: $332,800 (2006-2010 5-year est.); Median contract rent: $1,271 per month (2006-2010 5-year est.); Median year structure built: 1990 (2006-2010 5-year est.).
Safety: Violent crime rate: 2.4 per 10,000 population; Property crime rate: 206.7 per 10,000 population (2011).
Transportation: Commute to work: 90.0% car, 3.9% public transportation, 1.6% walk, 3.7% work from home (2006-2010 5-year est.); Travel time to work: 20.4% less than 15 minutes, 33.1% 15 to 30 minutes, 21.1% 30 to 45 minutes, 12.0% 45 to 60 minutes, 13.4% 60 minutes or more (2006-2010 5-year est.)
Additional Information Contacts
Eastern Montgomery County Chamber of Commerce . . . . (215) 887-5122
   http://www.emccc.org
Montgomery Township . . . . (215) 393-6900
   http://www.montgomerytwp.org

MONTGOMERYVILLE (CDP). Covers a land area of 4.755 square miles and a water area of 0 square miles. Located at 40.25° N. Lat; 75.24° W. Long. Elevation is 456 feet.
History: Winfield Scott Hancock, U.S. Army officer in the American Civil War was a resident of Montgomeryville.
Population: 9,114 (1990); 12,031 (2000); 12,624 (2010); Density: 2,654.8 persons per square mile (2010); Race: 79.0% White, 4.5% Black, 14.6% Asian, 0.1% American Indian/Alaska Native, 0.0% Native Hawaiian/Other Pacific Islander, 1.8% Other, 2.3% Hispanic of any race (2010); Average household size: 2.78 (2010); Median age: 40.1 (2010); Males per 100 females: 96.0 (2010); Marriage status: 25.1% never married, 65.1% now married, 4.2% widowed, 5.6% divorced (2006-2010 5-year est.); Foreign born: 13.7% (2006-2010 5-year est.); Ancestry (includes multiple ancestries): 27.7% Irish, 21.7% German, 18.1% Italian, 6.8% English, 4.6% Polish (2006-2010 5-year est.).
Economy: Employment by occupation: 18.3% management, 6.8% professional, 4.1% services, 15.8% sales, 3.8% farming, 4.1% construction, 4.3% production (2006-2010 5-year est.).
Income: Per capita income: $37,911 (2006-2010 5-year est.); Median household income: $95,614 (2006-2010 5-year est.); Average household income: $110,515 (2006-2010 5-year est.); Percent of households with income of $100,000 or more: 48.1% (2006-2010 5-year est.); Poverty rate: 1.9% (2006-2010 5-year est.).
Education: Percent of population age 25 and over with: High school diploma (including GED) or higher: 95.8% (2006-2010 5-year est.); Bachelor's degree or higher: 52.9% (2006-2010 5-year est.); Master's degree or higher: 21.6% (2006-2010 5-year est.).
Housing: Homeownership rate: 93.3% (2010); Median home value: $324,100 (2006-2010 5-year est.); Median contract rent: $1,157 per month (2006-2010 5-year est.); Median year structure built: 1986 (2006-2010 5-year est.).
Transportation: Commute to work: 91.8% car, 3.5% public transportation, 2.1% walk, 1.9% work from home (2006-2010 5-year est.); Travel time to work: 21.9% less than 15 minutes, 33.7% 15 to 30 minutes, 19.2% 30 to 45 minutes, 12.9% 45 to 60 minutes, 12.3% 60 minutes or more (2006-2010 5-year est.)
Additional Information Contacts
Hatfield Chamber of Commerce . . . . (215) 855-3335
   http://www.hatfieldchamber.com

NARBERTH (borough). Covers a land area of 0.503 square miles and a water area of 0 square miles. Located at 40.01° N. Lat; 75.26° W. Long. Elevation is 312 feet.

History: Settled 1860, incorporated 1895.

Population: 4,278 (1990); 4,233 (2000); 4,282 (2010); Density: 8,514.3 persons per square mile (2010); Race: 90.4% White, 1.9% Black, 4.4% Asian, 0.0% American Indian/Alaska Native, 0.1% Native Hawaiian/Other Pacific Islander, 3.2% Other, 2.4% Hispanic of any race (2010); Average household size: 2.29 (2010); Median age: 39.6 (2010); Males per 100 females: 87.6 (2010); Marriage status: 38.2% never married, 48.4% now married, 2.9% widowed, 10.5% divorced (2006-2010 5-year est.); Foreign born: 6.7% (2006-2010 5-year est.); Ancestry (includes multiple ancestries): 38.3% Irish, 20.9% Italian, 15.0% German, 9.3% English, 4.9% Scottish (2006-2010 5-year est.).

Economy: Single-family building permits issued: 0 (2011); Multi-family building permits issued: 0 (2011); Employment by occupation: 14.2% management, 7.4% professional, 4.7% services, 14.2% sales, 2.0% farming, 1.0% construction, 0.9% production (2006-2010 5-year est.).

Income: Per capita income: $40,632 (2006-2010 5-year est.); Median household income: $78,040 (2006-2010 5-year est.); Average household income: $96,037 (2006-2010 5-year est.); Percent of households with income of $100,000 or more: 35.9% (2006-2010 5-year est.); Poverty rate: 1.8% (2006-2010 5-year est.).

Education: Percent of population age 25 and over with: High school diploma (including GED) or higher: 96.6% (2006-2010 5-year est.); Bachelor's degree or higher: 62.4% (2006-2010 5-year est.); Master's degree or higher: 37.0% (2006-2010 5-year est.).

School District(s)

Lower Merion SD (KG-12)

    2010-11 Enrollment: 7,212 . . . . (610) 645-1800

Housing: Homeownership rate: 60.8% (2010); Median home value: $399,100 (2006-2010 5-year est.); Median contract rent: $1,012 per month (2006-2010 5-year est.); Median year structure built: before 1940 (2006-2010 5-year est.).

Safety: Violent crime rate: 14.0 per 10,000 population; Property crime rate: 100.1 per 10,000 population (2011).

Newspapers: City Line News (Community news; Circulation 40,000)

Transportation: Commute to work: 65.4% car, 21.3% public transportation, 5.8% walk, 5.4% work from home (2006-2010 5-year est.); Travel time to work: 23.6% less than 15 minutes, 41.6% 15 to 30 minutes, 24.1% 30 to 45 minutes, 6.6% 45 to 60 minutes, 4.0% 60 minutes or more (2006-2010 5-year est.)

Additional Information Contacts

Borough of Narberth . . . . (610) 664-2840

    http://www.narberthborough.com

Main Line Chamber of Commerce . . . . (610) 687-6232

    http://www.mlcc.org

NEW HANOVER (township). Covers a land area of 21.681 square miles and a water area of <.001 square miles. Located at 40.31° N. Lat; 75.56° W. Long. Elevation is 256 feet.

Population: 5,956 (1990); 7,369 (2000); 10,939 (2010); Density: 504.5 persons per square mile (2010); Race: 95.3% White, 1.2% Black, 2.0% Asian, 0.1% American Indian/Alaska Native, 0.0% Native Hawaiian/Other Pacific Islander, 1.4% Other, 1.6% Hispanic of any race (2010); Average household size: 2.88 (2010); Median age: 40.1 (2010); Males per 100 females: 98.6 (2010); Marriage status: 19.2% never married, 74.0% now married, 3.3% widowed, 3.5% divorced (2006-2010 5-year est.); Foreign born: 2.0% (2006-2010 5-year est.); Ancestry (includes multiple ancestries): 39.0% German, 26.1% Irish, 17.1% Italian, 10.9% English, 6.7% Polish (2006-2010 5-year est.).

Economy: Single-family building permits issued: 66 (2011); Multi-family building permits issued: 0 (2011); Employment by occupation: 14.7% management, 10.0% professional, 5.6% services, 16.0% sales, 4.6% farming, 9.7% construction, 4.0% production (2006-2010 5-year est.).

Income: Per capita income: $34,293 (2006-2010 5-year est.); Median household income: $88,581 (2006-2010 5-year est.); Average household income: $98,615 (2006-2010 5-year est.); Percent of households with income of $100,000 or more: 43.9% (2006-2010 5-year est.); Poverty rate: 1.5% (2006-2010 5-year est.).

Taxes: Total city taxes per capita: $331 (2009); City property taxes per capita: $108 (2009).

Education: Percent of population age 25 and over with: High school diploma (including GED) or higher: 91.1% (2006-2010 5-year est.);

Bachelor's degree or higher: 34.5% (2006-2010 5-year est.); Master's degree or higher: 7.5% (2006-2010 5-year est.).

Housing: Homeownership rate: 94.5% (2010); Median home value: $295,100 (2006-2010 5-year est.); Median contract rent: $856 per month (2006-2010 5-year est.); Median year structure built: 1987 (2006-2010 5-year est.).

Safety: Violent crime rate: 3.6 per 10,000 population; Property crime rate: 82.0 per 10,000 population (2011).

Transportation: Commute to work: 94.0% car, 0.3% public transportation, 0.9% walk, 4.3% work from home (2006-2010 5-year est.); Travel time to work: 19.3% less than 15 minutes, 26.7% 15 to 30 minutes, 22.5% 30 to 45 minutes, 17.7% 45 to 60 minutes, 13.8% 60 minutes or more (2006-2010 5-year est.)

Additional Information Contacts

New Hanover Township . . . . (610) 323-1008

    http://www.newhanover-pa.org

TriCounty Area Chamber of Commerce . . . . (610) 326-2900

    http://tricountyareachamber.com

NORRISTOWN (borough). Aka Mogeetown. County seat. Covers a land area of 3.519 square miles and a water area of 0.089 square miles. Located at 40.12° N. Lat; 75.34° W. Long. Elevation is 157 feet.

History: The borough is named for Isaac Norris (1671—1735), a Quaker merchant and a mayor of Philadelphia, who in 1704 bought a large tract of land here from his friend William Penn. Gen. Winfield Scott Hancock, a commander during the Civil War and Democratic candidate for president in 1880, was born in Norristown and is buried here. Valley Forge National Historical Park to west.

Population: 30,749 (1990); 31,282 (2000); 34,324 (2010); Density: 9,752.9 persons per square mile (2010); Race: 40.9% White, 35.9% Black, 2.1% Asian, 0.4% American Indian/Alaska Native, 0.1% Native Hawaiian/Other Pacific Islander, 20.6% Other, 28.3% Hispanic of any race (2010); Average household size: 2.79 (2010); Median age: 31.2 (2010); Males per 100 females: 99.3 (2010); Marriage status: 45.3% never married, 39.7% now married, 6.3% widowed, 8.7% divorced (2006-2010 5-year est.); Foreign born: 19.3% (2006-2010 5-year est.); Ancestry (includes multiple ancestries): 13.5% Italian, 11.7% Irish, 9.1% German, 4.2% American, 3.6% Polish (2006-2010 5-year est.).

Economy: Unemployment rate: 8.8% (August 2012); Total civilian labor force: 17,650 (August 2012); Single-family building permits issued: 0 (2011); Multi-family building permits issued: 6 (2011); Employment by occupation: 8.2% management, 2.5% professional, 11.8% services, 16.2% sales, 5.1% farming, 10.5% construction, 5.5% production (2006-2010 5-year est.).

Income: Per capita income: $20,123 (2006-2010 5-year est.); Median household income: $43,551 (2006-2010 5-year est.); Average household income: $52,464 (2006-2010 5-year est.); Percent of households with income of $100,000 or more: 10.8% (2006-2010 5-year est.); Poverty rate: 18.0% (2006-2010 5-year est.).

Taxes: Total city taxes per capita: $650 (2009); City property taxes per capita: $331 (2009).

Education: Percent of population age 25 and over with: High school diploma (including GED) or higher: 77.2% (2006-2010 5-year est.); Bachelor's degree or higher: 16.2% (2006-2010 5-year est.); Master's degree or higher: 5.7% (2006-2010 5-year est.).

School District(s)

Methacton SD (KG-12)

    2010-11 Enrollment: 5,289 . . . . (610) 489-5000

Norristown Area SD (KG-12)

    2010-11 Enrollment: 6,821 . . . . (610) 630-5000

Pennsylvania Virtual CS (KG-12)

    2010-11 Enrollment: 3,353 . . . . (610) 275-8501

Vocational/Technical School(s)

Star Career Academy-Norristown (Private, For-profit)

    Fall 2010 Enrollment: 53 . . . . (610) 783-7827

    2011-12 Tuition: $14,675

Housing: Homeownership rate: 41.5% (2010); Median home value: $153,100 (2006-2010 5-year est.); Median contract rent: $789 per month (2006-2010 5-year est.); Median year structure built: 1944 (2006-2010 5-year est.).

Hospitals: Eagleville Hospital & Riverside Care (350 beds); Montgomery County Emergency Service (73 beds); Montgomery Hospital Medical Center (210 beds); Norristown State Hospital (442 beds); Suburban General Hospital (140 beds); Valley Forge Medical Center & Hospital (78 beds)

Safety: Violent crime rate: 106.6 per 10,000 population; Property crime rate: 289.5 per 10,000 population (2011).
Newspapers: Times Herald (Local news; Circulation 25,721)
Transportation: Commute to work: 76.2% car, 10.4% public transportation, 9.5% walk, 1.3% work from home (2006-2010 5-year est.); Travel time to work: 27.4% less than 15 minutes, 40.4% 15 to 30 minutes, 20.5% 30 to 45 minutes, 5.8% 45 to 60 minutes, 5.9% 60 minutes or more (2006-2010 5-year est.)
Additional Information Contacts
Borough of Norristown. . . . . (610) 270-0420
   http://www.norristown.org
Montgomery County Chamber of Commerce . . . . (610) 278-3000
   http://www.montcopa.org/montco/site/default.asp

NORTH WALES (borough). Covers a land area of 0.587 square miles and a water area of 0 square miles. Located at 40.21° N. Lat; 75.27° W. Long. Elevation is 367 feet.

History: Settled 1850, laid out 1867, incorporated 1869.
Population: 3,802 (1990); 3,342 (2000); 3,229 (2010); Density: 5,499.2 persons per square mile (2010); Race: 87.7% White, 5.1% Black, 2.5% Asian, 0.1% American Indian/Alaska Native, 0.0% Native Hawaiian/Other Pacific Islander, 4.6% Other, 3.8% Hispanic of any race (2010); Average household size: 2.50 (2010); Median age: 39.3 (2010); Males per 100 females: 101.8 (2010); Marriage status: 21.3% never married, 61.7% now married, 5.0% widowed, 11.9% divorced (2006-2010 5-year est.); Foreign born: 1.8% (2006-2010 5-year est.); Ancestry (includes multiple ancestries): 41.0% German, 34.1% Irish, 18.1% Italian, 10.0% English, 5.3% Polish (2006-2010 5-year est.).
Economy: Single-family building permits issued: 0 (2011); Multi-family building permits issued: 0 (2011); Employment by occupation: 16.8% management, 1.4% professional, 7.9% services, 14.6% sales, 8.1% farming, 14.9% construction, 9.5% production (2006-2010 5-year est.).
Income: Per capita income: $30,124 (2006-2010 5-year est.); Median household income: $62,000 (2006-2010 5-year est.); Average household income: $70,311 (2006-2010 5-year est.); Percent of households with income of $100,000 or more: 25.1% (2006-2010 5-year est.); Poverty rate: 4.3% (2006-2010 5-year est.).
Education: Percent of population age 25 and over with: High school diploma (including GED) or higher: 95.3% (2006-2010 5-year est.); Bachelor's degree or higher: 36.5% (2006-2010 5-year est.); Master's degree or higher: 13.0% (2006-2010 5-year est.).
School District(s)
North Penn SD (KG-12)
   2010-11 Enrollment: 12,698 . . . . (215) 368-0400
Two-year College(s)
Lansdale School of Business (Private, For-profit)
   Fall 2010 Enrollment: 418 . . . . (215) 699-5700
   2011-12 Tuition: In-state $8,550; Out-of-state $8,550
Housing: Homeownership rate: 70.4% (2010); Median home value: $252,500 (2006-2010 5-year est.); Median contract rent: $835 per month (2006-2010 5-year est.); Median year structure built: 1946 (2006-2010 5-year est.).
Safety: Violent crime rate: 15.4 per 10,000 population; Property crime rate: 206.9 per 10,000 population (2011).
Transportation: Commute to work: 84.9% car, 3.8% public transportation, 5.6% walk, 4.8% work from home (2006-2010 5-year est.); Travel time to work: 27.5% less than 15 minutes, 29.5% 15 to 30 minutes, 18.0% 30 to 45 minutes, 15.9% 45 to 60 minutes, 9.1% 60 minutes or more (2006-2010 5-year est.)
Additional Information Contacts
PennSuburban Chamber of Commerce . . . . (215) 362-9200
   http://www.pennsuburban.org

OAKS (unincorporated postal area)
Zip Code: 19456
   Covers a land area of 0.409 square miles and a water area of 0.012 square miles. Located at 40.13° N. Lat; 75.46° W. Long. Elevation is 121 feet. Population: 737 (2010); Density: 1,798.7 persons per square mile (2010); Race: 88.5% White, 2.4% Black, 6.4% Asian, 0.1% American Indian/Alaska Native, 0.0% Native Hawaiian/Other Pacific Islander, 2.6% Other, 1.6% Hispanic of any race (2010); Average household size: 2.70 (2010); Median age: 40.6 (2010); Males per 100 females: 97.6 (2010); Homeownership rate: 85.0% (2010)

ORELAND (CDP). Covers a land area of 1.462 square miles and a water area of 0 square miles. Located at 40.11° N. Lat; 75.18° W. Long. Elevation is 259 feet.

Population: 5,830 (1990); 5,509 (2000); 5,678 (2010); Density: 3,883.5 persons per square mile (2010); Race: 79.7% White, 14.6% Black, 2.7% Asian, 0.1% American Indian/Alaska Native, 0.0% Native Hawaiian/Other Pacific Islander, 2.9% Other, 2.4% Hispanic of any race (2010); Average household size: 2.65 (2010); Median age: 39.6 (2010); Males per 100 females: 91.0 (2010); Marriage status: 29.4% never married, 58.1% now married, 5.5% widowed, 7.0% divorced (2006-2010 5-year est.); Foreign born: 3.7% (2006-2010 5-year est.); Ancestry (includes multiple ancestries): 35.3% Irish, 24.4% German, 24.0% Italian, 10.0% English, 4.1% Polish (2006-2010 5-year est.).
Economy: Employment by occupation: 17.2% management, 4.4% professional, 5.2% services, 17.6% sales, 6.2% farming, 3.4% construction, 4.3% production (2006-2010 5-year est.).
Income: Per capita income: $35,903 (2006-2010 5-year est.); Median household income: $78,244 (2006-2010 5-year est.); Average household income: $91,933 (2006-2010 5-year est.); Percent of households with income of $100,000 or more: 35.8% (2006-2010 5-year est.); Poverty rate: 3.9% (2006-2010 5-year est.).
Education: Percent of population age 25 and over with: High school diploma (including GED) or higher: 95.8% (2006-2010 5-year est.); Bachelor's degree or higher: 40.2% (2006-2010 5-year est.); Master's degree or higher: 16.1% (2006-2010 5-year est.).
School District(s)
Springfield Township SD (KG-12)
   2010-11 Enrollment: 2,133 . . . . (215) 233-6000
Housing: Homeownership rate: 80.9% (2010); Median home value: $292,000 (2006-2010 5-year est.); Median contract rent: $776 per month (2006-2010 5-year est.); Median year structure built: 1950 (2006-2010 5-year est.).
Transportation: Commute to work: 83.8% car, 10.3% public transportation, 1.2% walk, 4.5% work from home (2006-2010 5-year est.); Travel time to work: 23.0% less than 15 minutes, 32.6% 15 to 30 minutes, 20.7% 30 to 45 minutes, 12.7% 45 to 60 minutes, 11.0% 60 minutes or more (2006-2010 5-year est.)
Additional Information Contacts
Eastern Montgomery County Chamber of Commerce . . . . (215) 887-5122
   http://www.emccc.org

PALM (unincorporated postal area)
Zip Code: 18070
   Covers a land area of 2.383 square miles and a water area of <.001 square miles. Located at 40.43° N. Lat; 75.53° W. Long. Elevation is 374 feet. Population: 739 (2010); Density: 310.0 persons per square mile (2010); Race: 98.9% White, 0.0% Black, 0.8% Asian, 0.1% American Indian/Alaska Native, 0.0% Native Hawaiian/Other Pacific Islander, 0.2% Other, 0.7% Hispanic of any race (2010); Average household size: 2.54 (2010); Median age: 44.1 (2010); Males per 100 females: 106.4 (2010); Homeownership rate: 84.9% (2010)

PENN WYNNE (CDP). Covers a land area of 1.063 square miles and a water area of 0 square miles. Located at 39.99° N. Lat; 75.27° W. Long. Elevation is 217 feet.

History: The Penn Wynne area was first known as the Green Hill Zone plantation. It was established in the 17th century by the Welsh Quaker, Thomas Lloyd. In the early 1900s, the land was subdivided and developed. There are two sections to Penn Wynne, the southern section of homes, which are primarily twin homes and were built from the early 1920s to the mid-1940s.
Population: 5,807 (1990); 5,382 (2000); 5,697 (2010); Density: 5,358.3 persons per square mile (2010); Race: 81.0% White, 7.2% Black, 9.5% Asian, 0.0% American Indian/Alaska Native, 0.0% Native Hawaiian/Other Pacific Islander, 2.3% Other, 2.8% Hispanic of any race (2010); Average household size: 2.44 (2010); Median age: 46.0 (2010); Males per 100 females: 85.3 (2010); Marriage status: 22.0% never married, 61.9% now married, 10.3% widowed, 5.8% divorced (2006-2010 5-year est.); Foreign born: 15.1% (2006-2010 5-year est.); Ancestry (includes multiple ancestries): 12.7% German, 11.3% Irish, 10.6% Russian, 9.8% Italian, 8.3% Polish (2006-2010 5-year est.).
Economy: Employment by occupation: 17.3% management, 8.6% professional, 6.8% services, 9.2% sales, 2.1% farming, 1.7% construction, 1.5% production (2006-2010 5-year est.).

Income: Per capita income: $45,591 (2006-2010 5-year est.); Median household income: $95,938 (2006-2010 5-year est.); Average household income: $119,907 (2006-2010 5-year est.); Percent of households with income of $100,000 or more: 47.9% (2006-2010 5-year est.); Poverty rate: 3.4% (2006-2010 5-year est.).

Education: Percent of population age 25 and over with: High school diploma (including GED) or higher: 95.5% (2006-2010 5-year est.); Bachelor's degree or higher: 67.1% (2006-2010 5-year est.); Master's degree or higher: 42.1% (2006-2010 5-year est.).

Housing: Homeownership rate: 92.5% (2010); Median home value: $347,800 (2006-2010 5-year est.); Median contract rent: $956 per month (2006-2010 5-year est.); Median year structure built: 1952 (2006-2010 5-year est.).

Transportation: Commute to work: 80.5% car, 12.4% public transportation, 1.2% walk, 5.2% work from home (2006-2010 5-year est.); Travel time to work: 15.7% less than 15 minutes, 33.3% 15 to 30 minutes, 30.2% 30 to 45 minutes, 14.2% 45 to 60 minutes, 6.6% 60 minutes or more (2006-2010 5-year est.)

Additional Information Contacts
Greater Philadelphia Chamber of Commerce . . . . (215) 545-1234
    http://www.greaterphilachamber.com

PENNSBURG (borough). Aka Pennsburg-East Greenville. Covers a land area of 0.801 square miles and a water area of <.001 square miles. Located at 40.39° N. Lat; 75.50° W. Long. Elevation is 384 feet.

History: Settled 1840, incorporated 1887.

Population: 2,460 (1990); 2,732 (2000); 3,843 (2010); Density: 4,798.7 persons per square mile (2010); Race: 90.0% White, 2.0% Black, 5.2% Asian, 0.1% American Indian/Alaska Native, 0.1% Native Hawaiian/Other Pacific Islander, 2.6% Other, 4.1% Hispanic of any race (2010); Average household size: 2.70 (2010); Median age: 33.1 (2010); Males per 100 females: 102.6 (2010); Marriage status: 24.4% never married, 57.7% now married, 7.6% widowed, 10.4% divorced (2006-2010 5-year est.); Foreign born: 3.0% (2006-2010 5-year est.); Ancestry (includes multiple ancestries): 37.8% German, 19.2% Irish, 11.8% Italian, 10.3% English, 8.1% Pennsylvania German (2006-2010 5-year est.).

Economy: Single-family building permits issued: 0 (2011); Multi-family building permits issued: 0 (2011); Employment by occupation: 5.7% management, 4.7% professional, 5.8% services, 16.5% sales, 3.6% farming, 9.3% construction, 11.5% production (2006-2010 5-year est.).

Income: Per capita income: $24,306 (2006-2010 5-year est.); Median household income: $58,083 (2006-2010 5-year est.); Average household income: $66,596 (2006-2010 5-year est.); Percent of households with income of $100,000 or more: 21.9% (2006-2010 5-year est.); Poverty rate: 5.2% (2006-2010 5-year est.).

Education: Percent of population age 25 and over with: High school diploma (including GED) or higher: 87.7% (2006-2010 5-year est.); Bachelor's degree or higher: 24.3% (2006-2010 5-year est.); Master's degree or higher: 7.0% (2006-2010 5-year est.).

School District(s)
Upper Perkiomen SD (KG-12)
    2010-11 Enrollment: 3,187 . . . . (215) 679-7961
Housing: Homeownership rate: 67.8% (2010); Median home value: $202,000 (2006-2010 5-year est.); Median contract rent: $675 per month (2006-2010 5-year est.); Median year structure built: 1968 (2006-2010 5-year est.).

Transportation: Commute to work: 93.4% car, 0.3% public transportation, 4.7% walk, 1.1% work from home (2006-2010 5-year est.); Travel time to work: 23.7% less than 15 minutes, 25.7% 15 to 30 minutes, 27.1% 30 to 45 minutes, 10.4% 45 to 60 minutes, 13.1% 60 minutes or more (2006-2010 5-year est.)

Additional Information Contacts
Upper Bucks Chamber of Commerce . . . . (215) 536-3211
    http://www.ubcc.org

PERKIOMEN (township). Covers a land area of 4.855 square miles and a water area of 0.078 square miles. Located at 40.24° N. Lat; 75.47° W. Long. Elevation is 115 feet.

Population: 3,155 (1990); 7,093 (2000); 9,139 (2010); Density: 1,882.3 persons per square mile (2010); Race: 88.1% White, 4.1% Black, 5.2% Asian, 0.0% American Indian/Alaska Native, 0.0% Native Hawaiian/Other Pacific Islander, 2.6% Other, 2.9% Hispanic of any race (2010); Average household size: 3.00 (2010); Median age: 35.5 (2010); Males per 100 females: 98.9 (2010); Marriage status: 19.1% never married, 69.9% now married, 3.6% widowed, 7.4% divorced (2006-2010 5-year est.); Foreign

born: 6.8% (2006-2010 5-year est.); Ancestry (includes multiple ancestries): 30.9% Irish, 30.1% German, 17.9% Italian, 13.6% English, 7.3% Polish (2006-2010 5-year est.).

Economy: Single-family building permits issued: 0 (2011); Multi-family building permits issued: 0 (2011); Employment by occupation: 19.9% management, 8.3% professional, 6.3% services, 14.3% sales, 2.9% farming, 7.6% construction, 2.9% production (2006-2010 5-year est.).

Income: Per capita income: $36,362 (2006-2010 5-year est.); Median household income: $100,495 (2006-2010 5-year est.); Average household income: $103,628 (2006-2010 5-year est.); Percent of households with income of $100,000 or more: 50.4% (2006-2010 5-year est.); Poverty rate: 2.4% (2006-2010 5-year est.).

Education: Percent of population age 25 and over with: High school diploma (including GED) or higher: 95.3% (2006-2010 5-year est.); Bachelor's degree or higher: 46.3% (2006-2010 5-year est.); Master's degree or higher: 16.4% (2006-2010 5-year est.).

Housing: Homeownership rate: 90.3% (2010); Median home value: $294,000 (2006-2010 5-year est.); Median contract rent: $926 per month (2006-2010 5-year est.); Median year structure built: 1992 (2006-2010 5-year est.).

Transportation: Commute to work: 91.5% car, 1.7% public transportation, 1.9% walk, 4.9% work from home (2006-2010 5-year est.); Travel time to work: 18.4% less than 15 minutes, 23.6% 15 to 30 minutes, 26.1% 30 to 45 minutes, 16.5% 45 to 60 minutes, 15.5% 60 minutes or more (2006-2010 5-year est.)

Additional Information Contacts
Perkiomen Township . . . . (610) 489-4034
    http://www.perkiomentownship.org
Perkiomen Valley Chamber of Commerce . . . . (610) 489-6660
    http://perkiomenvalleychamber.org

PERKIOMENVILLE (unincorporated postal area)
Zip Code: 18074
    Covers a land area of 18.886 square miles and a water area of 0.119 square miles. Located at 40.31° N. Lat; 75.51° W. Long. Elevation is 200 feet. Population: 5,775 (2010); Density: 305.8 persons per square mile (2010); Race: 96.6% White, 1.2% Black, 0.7% Asian, 0.1% American Indian/Alaska Native, 0.1% Native Hawaiian/Other Pacific Islander, 1.3% Other, 1.9% Hispanic of any race (2010); Average household size: 2.65 (2010); Median age: 42.3 (2010); Males per 100 females: 101.7 (2010); Homeownership rate: 92.1% (2010)

PLYMOUTH (township). Covers a land area of 8.391 square miles and a water area of 0.099 square miles. Located at 40.11° N. Lat; 75.30° W. Long.

History: Has old meetinghouse built 1710-1712, rebuilt 1867.

Population: 15,958 (1990); 16,045 (2000); 16,525 (2010); Density: 1,969.4 persons per square mile (2010); Race: 83.1% White, 7.0% Black, 7.2% Asian, 0.1% American Indian/Alaska Native, 0.0% Native Hawaiian/Other Pacific Islander, 2.6% Other, 2.6% Hispanic of any race (2010); Average household size: 2.41 (2010); Median age: 41.3 (2010); Males per 100 females: 97.2 (2010); Marriage status: 29.4% never married, 54.3% now married, 6.9% widowed, 9.4% divorced (2006-2010 5-year est.); Foreign born: 8.1% (2006-2010 5-year est.); Ancestry (includes multiple ancestries): 26.9% Irish, 24.5% Italian, 22.9% German, 8.7% Polish, 8.1% English (2006-2010 5-year est.).

Economy: Single-family building permits issued: 4 (2011); Multi-family building permits issued: 0 (2011); Employment by occupation: 19.1% management, 6.4% professional, 5.2% services, 17.0% sales, 5.2% farming, 5.0% construction, 3.5% production (2006-2010 5-year est.).

Income: Per capita income: $36,890 (2006-2010 5-year est.); Median household income: $68,598 (2006-2010 5-year est.); Average household income: $87,918 (2006-2010 5-year est.); Percent of households with income of $100,000 or more: 30.6% (2006-2010 5-year est.); Poverty rate: 4.2% (2006-2010 5-year est.).

Education: Percent of population age 25 and over with: High school diploma (including GED) or higher: 91.6% (2006-2010 5-year est.); Bachelor's degree or higher: 41.4% (2006-2010 5-year est.); Master's degree or higher: 15.7% (2006-2010 5-year est.).

Housing: Homeownership rate: 70.5% (2010); Median home value: $294,900 (2006-2010 5-year est.); Median contract rent: $1,010 per month (2006-2010 5-year est.); Median year structure built: 1964 (2006-2010 5-year est.).

Safety: Violent crime rate: 16.3 per 10,000 population; Property crime rate: 339.0 per 10,000 population (2011).

Transportation: Commute to work: 89.1% car, 4.1% public transportation, 2.5% walk, 3.1% work from home (2006-2010 5-year est.); Travel time to work: 29.8% less than 15 minutes, 32.6% 15 to 30 minutes, 23.9% 30 to 45 minutes, 7.4% 45 to 60 minutes, 6.3% 60 minutes or more (2006-2010 5-year est.)

Additional Information Contacts
Eastern Montgomery County Chamber of Commerce . . . . (215) 887-5122
  http://www.emccc.org
Plymouth Township. . . . . (610) 277-4100
  http://www.plymouthtownship.org

PLYMOUTH MEETING (CDP). Covers a land area of 3.769 square miles and a water area of 0 square miles. Located at 40.11° N. Lat; 75.28° W. Long. Elevation is 184 feet.

History: The area known today as Plymouth Meeting was laid out by William Penn on May 5, 1686. Among early industries in Plymouth meeting was the Hickorytown Forge operated by the Wood family and was engaged in the manufacture of nails.

Population: 6,241 (1990); 5,593 (2000); 6,177 (2010); Density: 1,638.8 persons per square mile (2010); Race: 83.4% White, 6.2% Black, 8.4% Asian, 0.0% American Indian/Alaska Native, 0.0% Native Hawaiian/Other Pacific Islander, 2.0% Other, 2.1% Hispanic of any race (2010); Average household size: 2.41 (2010); Median age: 42.4 (2010); Males per 100 females: 94.0 (2010); Marriage status: 26.9% never married, 56.3% now married, 6.4% widowed, 10.4% divorced (2006-2010 5-year est.); Foreign born: 7.7% (2006-2010 5-year est.); Ancestry (includes multiple ancestries): 28.8% Irish, 22.5% Italian, 18.3% German, 10.2% Polish, 7.1% Russian (2006-2010 5-year est.).

Economy: Employment by occupation: 21.7% management, 5.3% professional, 4.6% services, 20.3% sales, 3.6% farming, 3.4% construction, 1.6% production (2006-2010 5-year est.).

Income: Per capita income: $37,554 (2006-2010 5-year est.); Median household income: $69,732 (2006-2010 5-year est.); Average household income: $88,922 (2006-2010 5-year est.); Percent of households with income of $100,000 or more: 31.1% (2006-2010 5-year est.); Poverty rate: 5.9% (2006-2010 5-year est.).

Education: Percent of population age 25 and over with: High school diploma (including GED) or higher: 94.3% (2006-2010 5-year est.); Bachelor's degree or higher: 46.7% (2006-2010 5-year est.); Master's degree or higher: 22.1% (2006-2010 5-year est.).

School District(s)
Central Montco Technical High School (10-12)
  2010-11 Enrollment: n/a . . . . (610) 277-2301
Colonial SD (KG-12)
  2010-11 Enrollment: 4,662 . . . . (610) 834-1670

Housing: Homeownership rate: 70.8% (2010); Median home value: $305,500 (2006-2010 5-year est.); Median contract rent: $1,175 per month (2006-2010 5-year est.); Median year structure built: 1964 (2006-2010 5-year est.).

Transportation: Commute to work: 87.8% car, 4.5% public transportation, 1.4% walk, 4.9% work from home (2006-2010 5-year est.); Travel time to work: 25.5% less than 15 minutes, 34.5% 15 to 30 minutes, 22.9% 30 to 45 minutes, 10.8% 45 to 60 minutes, 6.3% 60 minutes or more (2006-2010 5-year est.)

Additional Information Contacts
Eastern Montgomery County Chamber of Commerce . . . . (215) 887-5122
  http://www.emccc.org

POTTSGROVE (CDP). Covers a land area of 2.752 square miles and a water area of 0 square miles. Located at 40.26° N. Lat; 75.61° W. Long. Elevation is 256 feet.

Population: 3,122 (1990); 3,266 (2000); 3,469 (2010); Density: 1,260.6 persons per square mile (2010); Race: 94.6% White, 3.1% Black, 0.9% Asian, 0.0% American Indian/Alaska Native, 0.0% Native Hawaiian/Other Pacific Islander, 1.4% Other, 1.8% Hispanic of any race (2010); Average household size: 2.70 (2010); Median age: 44.3 (2010); Males per 100 females: 95.8 (2010); Marriage status: 20.0% never married, 69.4% now married, 5.2% widowed, 5.4% divorced (2006-2010 5-year est.); Foreign born: 3.2% (2006-2010 5-year est.); Ancestry (includes multiple ancestries): 40.1% German, 24.6% Irish, 20.2% Italian, 12.0% English, 9.2% Polish (2006-2010 5-year est.).

Economy: Employment by occupation: 15.0% management, 5.8% professional, 3.3% services, 14.9% sales, 3.7% farming, 10.0% construction, 5.1% production (2006-2010 5-year est.).

Income: Per capita income: $39,162 (2006-2010 5-year est.); Median household income: $94,628 (2006-2010 5-year est.); Average household income: $102,995 (2006-2010 5-year est.); Percent of households with income of $100,000 or more: 42.4% (2006-2010 5-year est.); Poverty rate: 2.1% (2006-2010 5-year est.).

Education: Percent of population age 25 and over with: High school diploma (including GED) or higher: 94.8% (2006-2010 5-year est.); Bachelor's degree or higher: 41.4% (2006-2010 5-year est.); Master's degree or higher: 14.7% (2006-2010 5-year est.).

Housing: Homeownership rate: 94.8% (2010); Median home value: $241,300 (2006-2010 5-year est.); Median contract rent: $624 per month (2006-2010 5-year est.); Median year structure built: 1964 (2006-2010 5-year est.).

Transportation: Commute to work: 95.8% car, 0.0% public transportation, 0.5% walk, 3.7% work from home (2006-2010 5-year est.); Travel time to work: 28.7% less than 15 minutes, 24.0% 15 to 30 minutes, 20.1% 30 to 45 minutes, 10.3% 45 to 60 minutes, 16.8% 60 minutes or more (2006-2010 5-year est.)

Additional Information Contacts
TriCounty Area Chamber of Commerce . . . . (610) 326-2900
  http://www.tricountyareachamber.com

POTTSTOWN (borough). Covers a land area of 4.888 square miles and a water area of 0.076 square miles. Located at 40.25° N. Lat; 75.64° W. Long. Elevation is 151 feet.

History: Named for John Potts, an ironmaster who laid out the town in 1754. The state's first ironworks were established here in 1715. The Hill School, a preparatory school, is here. Other points of interest are Pottsgrove Manor, the home of John Potts (1754), colonial ironmaster and the community's planner and Hopewell Furnace National Historic Site. Settled c.1700. Incorporated 1815.

Population: 21,831 (1990); 21,859 (2000); 22,377 (2010); Density: 4,578.3 persons per square mile (2010); Race: 72.1% White, 19.5% Black, 0.9% Asian, 0.3% American Indian/Alaska Native, 0.1% Native Hawaiian/Other Pacific Islander, 7.1% Other, 8.0% Hispanic of any race (2010); Average household size: 2.36 (2010); Median age: 36.1 (2010); Males per 100 females: 92.1 (2010); Marriage status: 34.6% never married, 43.2% now married, 7.7% widowed, 14.5% divorced (2006-2010 5-year est.); Foreign born: 2.4% (2006-2010 5-year est.); Ancestry (includes multiple ancestries): 25.0% German, 17.3% Irish, 11.9% Italian, 8.6% English, 7.3% Polish (2006-2010 5-year est.).

Economy: Single-family building permits issued: 2 (2011); Multi-family building permits issued: 0 (2011); Employment by occupation: 7.1% management, 4.2% professional, 12.7% services, 20.0% sales, 3.3% farming, 8.7% construction, 8.0% production (2006-2010 5-year est.).

Income: Per capita income: $22,648 (2006-2010 5-year est.); Median household income: $43,311 (2006-2010 5-year est.); Average household income: $52,181 (2006-2010 5-year est.); Percent of households with income of $100,000 or more: 11.0% (2006-2010 5-year est.); Poverty rate: 14.9% (2006-2010 5-year est.).

Education: Percent of population age 25 and over with: High school diploma (including GED) or higher: 84.1% (2006-2010 5-year est.); Bachelor's degree or higher: 17.3% (2006-2010 5-year est.); Master's degree or higher: 4.1% (2006-2010 5-year est.).

School District(s)
Owen J Roberts SD (KG-12)
  2010-11 Enrollment: 5,026 . . . . (610) 469-5100
Pottsgrove SD (KG-12)
  2010-11 Enrollment: 3,342 . . . . (610) 327-2277
Pottstown SD (KG-12)
  2010-11 Enrollment: 3,097 . . . . (610) 323-8200

Two-year College(s)
Montgomery County Community College-West Campus (Public)
  Fall 2010 Enrollment: 2,042 . . . . (610) 718-1800
  2011-12 Tuition: In-state $7,140; Out-of-state $10,530

Vocational/Technical School(s)
Antonelli Medical and Professional Institute (Private, For-profit)
  Fall 2010 Enrollment: 179 . . . . (610) 323-7270
  2011-12 Tuition: $9,200

Housing: Homeownership rate: 55.3% (2010); Median home value: $142,100 (2006-2010 5-year est.); Median contract rent: $627 per month (2006-2010 5-year est.); Median year structure built: 1944 (2006-2010 5-year est.).

Hospitals: Pottstown Memorial Medical Center (299 beds)

Safety: Violent crime rate: 84.6 per 10,000 population; Property crime rate: 474.9 per 10,000 population (2011).
Newspapers: The Mercury (Local news; Circulation 23,618); Tri-County Market Place (Local news; Circulation 12,000)
Transportation: Commute to work: 87.9% car, 2.3% public transportation, 5.5% walk, 2.4% work from home (2006-2010 5-year est.); Travel time to work: 32.4% less than 15 minutes, 32.0% 15 to 30 minutes, 19.6% 30 to 45 minutes, 8.0% 45 to 60 minutes, 8.0% 60 minutes or more (2006-2010 5-year est.)
Airports: Pottstown Limerick (general aviation)
Additional Information Contacts
Borough of Pottstown . . . . (610) 970-6500
  http://www.pottstown.org
TriCounty Area Chamber of Commerce . . . . (610) 326-2900
  http://www.tricountyareachamber.com

RED HILL (borough). Covers a land area of 0.677 square miles and a water area of 0 square miles. Located at 40.38° N. Lat; 75.48° W. Long. Elevation is 381 feet.
Population: 1,794 (1990); 2,196 (2000); 2,383 (2010); Density: 3,521.4 persons per square mile (2010); Race: 96.4% White, 1.4% Black, 0.7% Asian, 0.0% American Indian/Alaska Native, 0.0% Native Hawaiian/Other Pacific Islander, 1.5% Other, 2.1% Hispanic of any race (2010); Average household size: 2.17 (2010); Median age: 45.9 (2010); Males per 100 females: 88.2 (2010); Marriage status: 21.0% never married, 57.3% now married, 12.6% widowed, 9.2% divorced (2006-2010 5-year est.); Foreign born: 2.1% (2006-2010 5-year est.); Ancestry (includes multiple ancestries): 37.5% German, 20.5% Irish, 12.0% English, 11.8% Italian, 6.3% Polish (2006-2010 5-year est.).
Economy: Single-family building permits issued: 0 (2011); Multi-family building permits issued: 0 (2011); Employment by occupation: 10.0% management, 2.1% professional, 6.6% services, 15.0% sales, 3.5% farming, 16.2% construction, 14.1% production (2006-2010 5-year est.).
Income: Per capita income: $26,518 (2006-2010 5-year est.); Median household income: $56,364 (2006-2010 5-year est.); Average household income: $61,826 (2006-2010 5-year est.); Percent of households with income of $100,000 or more: 14.3% (2006-2010 5-year est.); Poverty rate: 6.0% (2006-2010 5-year est.).
Education: Percent of population age 25 and over with: High school diploma (including GED) or higher: 82.2% (2006-2010 5-year est.); Bachelor's degree or higher: 20.2% (2006-2010 5-year est.); Master's degree or higher: 4.9% (2006-2010 5-year est.).
Housing: Homeownership rate: 67.9% (2010); Median home value: $178,900 (2006-2010 5-year est.); Median contract rent: $546 per month (2006-2010 5-year est.); Median year structure built: 1978 (2006-2010 5-year est.).
Newspapers: Hearthstone Town and Country (Local news; Circulation 5,000)
Transportation: Commute to work: 96.1% car, 0.0% public transportation, 1.4% walk, 2.2% work from home (2006-2010 5-year est.); Travel time to work: 16.7% less than 15 minutes, 35.8% 15 to 30 minutes, 24.3% 30 to 45 minutes, 14.1% 45 to 60 minutes, 9.1% 60 minutes or more (2006-2010 5-year est.)
Additional Information Contacts
Upper Bucks Chamber of Commerce . . . . (215) 536-3211
  http://www.ubcc.org

ROCKLEDGE (borough). Covers a land area of 0.348 square miles and a water area of 0 square miles. Located at 40.08° N. Lat; 75.09° W. Long. Elevation is 243 feet.
History: Settled 1880, incorporated 1893.
Population: 2,679 (1990); 2,577 (2000); 2,543 (2010); Density: 7,313.5 persons per square mile (2010); Race: 95.8% White, 0.4% Black, 1.2% Asian, 0.0% American Indian/Alaska Native, 0.0% Native Hawaiian/Other Pacific Islander, 2.6% Other, 2.0% Hispanic of any race (2010); Average household size: 2.42 (2010); Median age: 42.1 (2010); Males per 100 females: 98.8 (2010); Marriage status: 35.0% never married, 51.8% now married, 6.5% widowed, 6.7% divorced (2006-2010 5-year est.); Foreign born: 7.7% (2006-2010 5-year est.); Ancestry (includes multiple ancestries): 42.0% Irish, 24.4% German, 20.8% Italian, 8.1% Polish, 6.5% English (2006-2010 5-year est.).
Economy: Single-family building permits issued: 0 (2011); Multi-family building permits issued: 0 (2011); Employment by occupation: 8.7% management, 3.3% professional, 10.5% services, 19.7% sales, 4.1% farming, 15.4% construction, 7.1% production (2006-2010 5-year est.).

Income: Per capita income: $28,368 (2006-2010 5-year est.); Median household income: $66,146 (2006-2010 5-year est.); Average household income: $73,434 (2006-2010 5-year est.); Percent of households with income of $100,000 or more: 26.5% (2006-2010 5-year est.); Poverty rate: 1.9% (2006-2010 5-year est.).
Taxes: Total city taxes per capita: $354 (2009); City property taxes per capita: $196 (2009).
Education: Percent of population age 25 and over with: High school diploma (including GED) or higher: 91.8% (2006-2010 5-year est.); Bachelor's degree or higher: 25.9% (2006-2010 5-year est.); Master's degree or higher: 11.2% (2006-2010 5-year est.).
Housing: Homeownership rate: 65.7% (2010); Median home value: $253,800 (2006-2010 5-year est.); Median contract rent: $730 per month (2006-2010 5-year est.); Median year structure built: 1940 (2006-2010 5-year est.).
Safety: Violent crime rate: 47.0 per 10,000 population; Property crime rate: 188.2 per 10,000 population (2011).
Transportation: Commute to work: 86.6% car, 5.7% public transportation, 4.7% walk, 1.8% work from home (2006-2010 5-year est.); Travel time to work: 23.6% less than 15 minutes, 33.1% 15 to 30 minutes, 26.3% 30 to 45 minutes, 8.9% 45 to 60 minutes, 8.2% 60 minutes or more (2006-2010 5-year est.)
Additional Information Contacts
Eastern Montgomery County Chamber of Commerce . . . . (215) 887-5122
  http://www.emccc.org

ROYERSFORD (borough). Covers a land area of 0.780 square miles and a water area of 0.043 square miles. Located at 40.19° N. Lat; 75.54° W. Long. Elevation is 207 feet.
History: Settled 1839, incorporated 1879.
Population: 4,458 (1990); 4,246 (2000); 4,752 (2010); Density: 6,091.6 persons per square mile (2010); Race: 89.7% White, 5.1% Black, 1.7% Asian, 0.2% American Indian/Alaska Native, 0.0% Native Hawaiian/Other Pacific Islander, 3.3% Other, 4.2% Hispanic of any race (2010); Average household size: 2.22 (2010); Median age: 35.7 (2010); Males per 100 females: 97.8 (2010); Marriage status: 33.1% never married, 41.5% now married, 11.7% widowed, 13.7% divorced (2006-2010 5-year est.); Foreign born: 6.9% (2006-2010 5-year est.); Ancestry (includes multiple ancestries): 27.4% German, 27.1% Irish, 11.4% Italian, 11.1% English, 6.8% Polish (2006-2010 5-year est.).
Economy: Single-family building permits issued: 0 (2011); Multi-family building permits issued: 0 (2011); Employment by occupation: 9.4% management, 5.7% professional, 10.9% services, 20.2% sales, 3.4% farming, 9.0% construction, 6.3% production (2006-2010 5-year est.).
Income: Per capita income: $27,797 (2006-2010 5-year est.); Median household income: $49,924 (2006-2010 5-year est.); Average household income: $61,147 (2006-2010 5-year est.); Percent of households with income of $100,000 or more: 15.2% (2006-2010 5-year est.); Poverty rate: 4.1% (2006-2010 5-year est.).
Education: Percent of population age 25 and over with: High school diploma (including GED) or higher: 90.3% (2006-2010 5-year est.); Bachelor's degree or higher: 25.4% (2006-2010 5-year est.); Master's degree or higher: 6.8% (2006-2010 5-year est.).
School District(s)
Spring-Ford Area SD (KG-12)
    2010-11 Enrollment: 7,730 . . . . (610) 705-6000
Housing: Homeownership rate: 50.1% (2010); Median home value: $181,600 (2006-2010 5-year est.); Median contract rent: $706 per month (2006-2010 5-year est.); Median year structure built: 1943 (2006-2010 5-year est.).
Safety: Violent crime rate: 14.7 per 10,000 population; Property crime rate: 186.7 per 10,000 population (2011).
Newspapers: Spring-Ford Reporter (Community news; Circulation 3,524); Spring/Ford Reporter (Community news; Circulation 3,524); Valley Item (Community news; Circulation 3,524)
Transportation: Commute to work: 92.9% car, 0.7% public transportation, 6.0% walk, 0.4% work from home (2006-2010 5-year est.); Travel time to work: 26.1% less than 15 minutes, 34.2% 15 to 30 minutes, 19.7% 30 to 45 minutes, 9.5% 45 to 60 minutes, 10.6% 60 minutes or more (2006-2010 5-year est.)
Additional Information Contacts
Spring-Ford Chamber of Commerce . . . . (610) 489-7200
  http://www.springfordchamber.com

SALFORD (township). Covers a land area of 9.813 square miles and a water area of 0.022 square miles. Located at 40.34° N. Lat; 75.40° W. Long. Elevation is 190 feet.

Population: 2,216 (1990); 2,363 (2000); 2,504 (2010); Density: 255.2 persons per square mile (2010); Race: 96.8% White, 0.8% Black, 1.0% Asian, 0.2% American Indian/Alaska Native, 0.0% Native Hawaiian/Other Pacific Islander, 1.2% Other, 1.3% Hispanic of any race (2010); Average household size: 2.82 (2010); Median age: 44.9 (2010); Males per 100 females: 108.3 (2010); Marriage status: 21.2% never married, 67.1% now married, 6.4% widowed, 5.3% divorced (2006-2010 5-year est.); Foreign born: 4.3% (2006-2010 5-year est.); Ancestry (includes multiple ancestries): 45.8% German, 19.5% Irish, 12.7% English, 7.6% Italian, 7.0% Polish (2006-2010 5-year est.).

Economy: Single-family building permits issued: 48 (2011); Multi-family building permits issued: 0 (2011); Employment by occupation: 14.7% management, 4.2% professional, 9.6% services, 16.7% sales, 2.8% farming, 12.8% construction, 7.7% production (2006-2010 5-year est.).

Income: Per capita income: $36,503 (2006-2010 5-year est.); Median household income: $85,602 (2006-2010 5-year est.); Average household income: $98,998 (2006-2010 5-year est.); Percent of households with income of $100,000 or more: 36.7% (2006-2010 5-year est.); Poverty rate: 3.3% (2006-2010 5-year est.).

Education: Percent of population age 25 and over with: High school diploma (including GED) or higher: 92.9% (2006-2010 5-year est.); Bachelor's degree or higher: 30.8% (2006-2010 5-year est.); Master's degree or higher: 10.6% (2006-2010 5-year est.).

Housing: Homeownership rate: 89.6% (2010); Median home value: $387,400 (2006-2010 5-year est.); Median contract rent: $722 per month (2006-2010 5-year est.); Median year structure built: 1973 (2006-2010 5-year est.).

Transportation: Commute to work: 86.8% car, 0.0% public transportation, 2.8% walk, 8.4% work from home (2006-2010 5-year est.); Travel time to work: 21.7% less than 15 minutes, 48.4% 15 to 30 minutes, 18.5% 30 to 45 minutes, 8.9% 45 to 60 minutes, 2.6% 60 minutes or more (2006-2010 5-year est.)

Additional Information Contacts
Indian Valley Chamber of Commerce . . . . (215) 723-9472
   http://indianvalleychamber.com

SANATOGA (CDP). Covers a land area of 3.377 square miles and a water area of 0.008 square miles. Located at 40.25° N. Lat; 75.59° W. Long. Elevation is 236 feet.

Population: 5,534 (1990); 7,734 (2000); 8,378 (2010); Density: 2,481.0 persons per square mile (2010); Race: 81.2% White, 13.3% Black, 1.9% Asian, 0.1% American Indian/Alaska Native, 0.1% Native Hawaiian/Other Pacific Islander, 3.4% Other, 3.1% Hispanic of any race (2010); Average household size: 2.63 (2010); Median age: 37.3 (2010); Males per 100 females: 90.1 (2010); Marriage status: 27.2% never married, 57.4% now married, 7.7% widowed, 7.6% divorced (2006-2010 5-year est.); Foreign born: 3.7% (2006-2010 5-year est.); Ancestry (includes multiple ancestries): 27.6% German, 19.7% Irish, 17.7% Italian, 9.9% English, 5.7% Polish (2006-2010 5-year est.).

Economy: Employment by occupation: 11.4% management, 10.4% professional, 6.2% services, 19.9% sales, 4.8% farming, 7.9% construction, 4.7% production (2006-2010 5-year est.).

Income: Per capita income: $29,612 (2006-2010 5-year est.); Median household income: $68,750 (2006-2010 5-year est.); Average household income: $77,472 (2006-2010 5-year est.); Percent of households with income of $100,000 or more: 24.0% (2006-2010 5-year est.); Poverty rate: 12.4% (2006-2010 5-year est.).

Education: Percent of population age 25 and over with: High school diploma (including GED) or higher: 92.2% (2006-2010 5-year est.); Bachelor's degree or higher: 27.7% (2006-2010 5-year est.); Master's degree or higher: 7.0% (2006-2010 5-year est.).

Housing: Homeownership rate: 78.1% (2010); Median home value: $197,200 (2006-2010 5-year est.); Median contract rent: $728 per month (2006-2010 5-year est.); Median year structure built: 1988 (2006-2010 5-year est.).

Transportation: Commute to work: 95.4% car, 0.5% public transportation, 0.5% walk, 3.6% work from home (2006-2010 5-year est.); Travel time to work: 20.7% less than 15 minutes, 25.3% 15 to 30 minutes, 26.9% 30 to 45 minutes, 11.9% 45 to 60 minutes, 15.2% 60 minutes or more (2006-2010 5-year est.)

Additional Information Contacts
Spring-Ford Chamber of Commerce . . . . (610) 489-7200
   http://www.springfordchamber.com

SASSAMANSVILLE (unincorporated postal area)
Zip Code: 19472

   Covers a land area of 0.168 square miles and a water area of 0 square miles. Located at 40.33° N. Lat; 75.57° W. Long. Elevation is 341 feet. Population: 74 (2010); Density: 439.0 persons per square mile (2010); Race: 91.9% White, 1.4% Black, 0.0% Asian, 0.0% American Indian/Alaska Native, 0.0% Native Hawaiian/Other Pacific Islander, 6.7% Other, 0.0% Hispanic of any race (2010); Average household size: 2.47 (2010); Median age: 40.5 (2010); Males per 100 females: 89.7 (2010); Homeownership rate: 63.3% (2010)

SCHWENKSVILLE (borough). Covers a land area of 0.412 square miles and a water area of 0.008 square miles. Located at 40.26° N. Lat; 75.47° W. Long. Elevation is 148 feet.

History: Sunrise Mill Historic Site to Northwest; Pennypacker Mill Historic Site to Southeast.

Population: 1,329 (1990); 1,693 (2000); 1,385 (2010); Density: 3,358.8 persons per square mile (2010); Race: 94.9% White, 2.5% Black, 0.7% Asian, 0.1% American Indian/Alaska Native, 0.1% Native Hawaiian/Other Pacific Islander, 1.7% Other, 2.7% Hispanic of any race (2010); Average household size: 2.06 (2010); Median age: 41.2 (2010); Males per 100 females: 93.4 (2010); Marriage status: 23.2% never married, 51.2% now married, 7.0% widowed, 18.6% divorced (2006-2010 5-year est.); Foreign born: 6.3% (2006-2010 5-year est.); Ancestry (includes multiple ancestries): 40.6% German, 17.1% Italian, 16.0% Irish, 9.6% English, 3.6% Welsh (2006-2010 5-year est.).

Economy: Single-family building permits issued: 0 (2011); Multi-family building permits issued: 0 (2011); Employment by occupation: 7.3% management, 3.9% professional, 11.4% services, 20.3% sales, 4.8% farming, 8.8% construction, 8.9% production (2006-2010 5-year est.).

Income: Per capita income: $27,726 (2006-2010 5-year est.); Median household income: $47,697 (2006-2010 5-year est.); Average household income: $55,312 (2006-2010 5-year est.); Percent of households with income of $100,000 or more: 12.7% (2006-2010 5-year est.); Poverty rate: 6.1% (2006-2010 5-year est.).

Education: Percent of population age 25 and over with: High school diploma (including GED) or higher: 90.8% (2006-2010 5-year est.); Bachelor's degree or higher: 23.3% (2006-2010 5-year est.); Master's degree or higher: 5.0% (2006-2010 5-year est.).

School District(s)
Perkiomen Valley SD (KG-12)
   2010-11 Enrollment: 5,899 . . . . (610) 489-8506

Housing: Homeownership rate: 62.3% (2010); Median home value: $144,800 (2006-2010 5-year est.); Median contract rent: $699 per month (2006-2010 5-year est.); Median year structure built: 1972 (2006-2010 5-year est.).

Transportation: Commute to work: 94.9% car, 0.0% public transportation, 1.6% walk, 1.3% work from home (2006-2010 5-year est.); Travel time to work: 16.6% less than 15 minutes, 41.4% 15 to 30 minutes, 13.8% 30 to 45 minutes, 15.5% 45 to 60 minutes, 12.6% 60 minutes or more (2006-2010 5-year est.)

Additional Information Contacts
Phoenixville Area Chamber of Commerce . . . . (610) 933-3070
   http://www.phoenixvillechamber.org

SKIPPACK (CDP). Covers a land area of 2.523 square miles and a water area of 0.006 square miles. Located at 40.22° N. Lat; 75.40° W. Long. Elevation is 184 feet.

Population: 2,042 (1990); 2,889 (2000); 3,758 (2010); Density: 1,489.4 persons per square mile (2010); Race: 90.8% White, 2.0% Black, 5.1% Asian, 0.0% American Indian/Alaska Native, 0.0% Native Hawaiian/Other Pacific Islander, 2.1% Other, 2.2% Hispanic of any race (2010); Average household size: 2.61 (2010); Median age: 39.7 (2010); Males per 100 females: 90.7 (2010); Marriage status: 23.0% never married, 59.1% now married, 5.0% widowed, 12.9% divorced (2006-2010 5-year est.); Foreign born: 4.6% (2006-2010 5-year est.); Ancestry (includes multiple ancestries): 32.0% German, 29.7% Irish, 18.3% Italian, 13.1% English, 6.4% Polish (2006-2010 5-year est.).

Economy: Employment by occupation: 14.3% management, 9.9% professional, 11.5% services, 13.1% sales, 3.0% farming, 5.9% construction, 5.2% production (2006-2010 5-year est.).

Income: Per capita income: $43,631 (2006-2010 5-year est.); Median household income: $95,472 (2006-2010 5-year est.); Average household income: $114,682 (2006-2010 5-year est.); Percent of households with income of $100,000 or more: 46.6% (2006-2010 5-year est.); Poverty rate: 1.3% (2006-2010 5-year est.).

Education: Percent of population age 25 and over with: High school diploma (including GED) or higher: 96.9% (2006-2010 5-year est.); Bachelor's degree or higher: 47.7% (2006-2010 5-year est.); Master's degree or higher: 11.9% (2006-2010 5-year est.).

Housing: Homeownership rate: 87.6% (2010); Median home value: $314,100 (2006-2010 5-year est.); Median contract rent: $869 per month (2006-2010 5-year est.); Median year structure built: 1989 (2006-2010 5-year est.).

Transportation: Commute to work: 89.8% car, 2.1% public transportation, 2.6% walk, 5.5% work from home (2006-2010 5-year est.); Travel time to work: 14.3% less than 15 minutes, 39.2% 15 to 30 minutes, 30.2% 30 to 45 minutes, 9.7% 45 to 60 minutes, 6.7% 60 minutes or more (2006-2010 5-year est.)

Additional Information Contacts

Perkiomen Valley Chamber of Commerce . . . . (610) 489-6660
  http://perkiomenvalleychamber.org

SKIPPACK (township). Covers a land area of 13.837 square miles and a water area of 0.127 square miles. Located at 40.22° N. Lat; 75.42° W. Long. Elevation is 184 feet.

History: General Washington, his officers, and army of 11,000 camped in Skippack on two occasions.

Population: 8,790 (1990); 6,516 (2000); 13,715 (2010); Density: 991.2 persons per square mile (2010); Race: 75.0% White, 16.6% Black, 3.6% Asian, 0.1% American Indian/Alaska Native, 0.0% Native Hawaiian/Other Pacific Islander, 4.7% Other, 4.7% Hispanic of any race (2010); Average household size: 2.76 (2010); Median age: 39.4 (2010); Males per 100 females: 159.2 (2010); Marriage status: 27.8% never married, 58.2% now married, 3.8% widowed, 10.2% divorced (2006-2010 5-year est.); Foreign born: 4.0% (2006-2010 5-year est.); Ancestry (includes multiple ancestries): 22.6% Irish, 21.3% German, 13.0% Italian, 8.9% English, 6.1% Polish (2006-2010 5-year est.).

Economy: Single-family building permits issued: 14 (2011); Multi-family building permits issued: 0 (2011); Employment by occupation: 19.1% management, 10.8% professional, 8.5% services, 14.3% sales, 4.0% farming, 7.5% construction, 4.7% production (2006-2010 5-year est.).

Income: Per capita income: $35,811 (2006-2010 5-year est.); Median household income: $102,233 (2006-2010 5-year est.); Average household income: $122,006 (2006-2010 5-year est.); Percent of households with income of $100,000 or more: 52.7% (2006-2010 5-year est.); Poverty rate: 3.6% (2006-2010 5-year est.).

Education: Percent of population age 25 and over with: High school diploma (including GED) or higher: 87.4% (2006-2010 5-year est.); Bachelor's degree or higher: 37.9% (2006-2010 5-year est.); Master's degree or higher: 11.6% (2006-2010 5-year est.).

Housing: Homeownership rate: 89.5% (2010); Median home value: $349,900 (2006-2010 5-year est.); Median contract rent: $894 per month (2006-2010 5-year est.); Median year structure built: 1994 (2006-2010 5-year est.).

Transportation: Commute to work: 92.2% car, 1.5% public transportation, 1.2% walk, 4.8% work from home (2006-2010 5-year est.); Travel time to work: 11.2% less than 15 minutes, 35.0% 15 to 30 minutes, 30.7% 30 to 45 minutes, 13.0% 45 to 60 minutes, 10.0% 60 minutes or more (2006-2010 5-year est.)

Additional Information Contacts

Perkiomen Valley Chamber of Commerce . . . . (610) 489-6660
  http://perkiomenvalleychamber.org
Skippack Township . . . . (610) 454-0909
  http://skippacktownship.org

SOUDERTON (borough). Covers a land area of 1.121 square miles and a water area of 0 square miles. Located at 40.31° N. Lat; 75.32° W. Long. Elevation is 420 feet.

History: Settled 1860, incorporated 1887.

Population: 5,957 (1990); 6,730 (2000); 6,618 (2010); Density: 5,901.6 persons per square mile (2010); Race: 85.6% White, 2.5% Black, 4.7% Asian, 0.3% American Indian/Alaska Native, 0.0% Native Hawaiian/Other Pacific Islander, 6.9% Other, 11.5% Hispanic of any race (2010); Average household size: 2.50 (2010); Median age: 36.8 (2010); Males per 100 females: 97.2 (2010); Marriage status: 29.4% never married, 53.1% now

married, 9.4% widowed, 8.1% divorced (2006-2010 5-year est.); Foreign born: 7.8% (2006-2010 5-year est.); Ancestry (includes multiple ancestries): 38.2% German, 18.8% Irish, 10.8% Italian, 8.7% English, 5.6% Polish (2006-2010 5-year est.).

Economy: Single-family building permits issued: 0 (2011); Multi-family building permits issued: 0 (2011); Employment by occupation: 11.5% management, 5.2% professional, 9.7% services, 18.3% sales, 3.8% farming, 8.1% construction, 6.2% production (2006-2010 5-year est.).

Income: Per capita income: $27,513 (2006-2010 5-year est.); Median household income: $53,250 (2006-2010 5-year est.); Average household income: $66,031 (2006-2010 5-year est.); Percent of households with income of $100,000 or more: 20.3% (2006-2010 5-year est.); Poverty rate: 6.3% (2006-2010 5-year est.).

Education: Percent of population age 25 and over with: High school diploma (including GED) or higher: 84.4% (2006-2010 5-year est.); Bachelor's degree or higher: 24.4% (2006-2010 5-year est.); Master's degree or higher: 7.8% (2006-2010 5-year est.).

School District(s)

Souderton Area SD (KG-12)
  2010-11 Enrollment: 6,739 . . . . (215) 723-6061
Souderton CS Collaborative (KG-08)
  2010-11 Enrollment: 163 . . . . (215) 721-4560

Housing: Homeownership rate: 58.6% (2010); Median home value: $232,900 (2006-2010 5-year est.); Median contract rent: $701 per month (2006-2010 5-year est.); Median year structure built: 1955 (2006-2010 5-year est.).

Safety: Violent crime rate: 28.6 per 10,000 population; Property crime rate: 93.4 per 10,000 population (2011).

Newspapers: News-Herald (Community news; Circulation 5,000); Souderton Independent (Local news; Circulation 6,328)

Transportation: Commute to work: 91.1% car, 1.3% public transportation, 3.5% walk, 2.8% work from home (2006-2010 5-year est.); Travel time to work: 32.9% less than 15 minutes, 29.2% 15 to 30 minutes, 16.3% 30 to 45 minutes, 11.2% 45 to 60 minutes, 10.5% 60 minutes or more (2006-2010 5-year est.)

Additional Information Contacts

Borough of Souderton . . . . (215) 723-4371
  http://www.soudertonborough.org
Indian Valley Chamber of Commerce . . . . (215) 723-9472
  http://indianvalleychamber.com

SPRING HOUSE (CDP). Covers a land area of 2.614 square miles and a water area of 0.005 square miles. Located at 40.18° N. Lat; 75.22° W. Long. Elevation is 285 feet.

History: Seat of Gwynedd Mercere College.

Population: 2,782 (1990); 3,290 (2000); 3,804 (2010); Density: 1,455.3 persons per square mile (2010); Race: 88.6% White, 2.3% Black, 7.8% Asian, 0.0% American Indian/Alaska Native, 0.0% Native Hawaiian/Other Pacific Islander, 1.3% Other, 1.8% Hispanic of any race (2010); Average household size: 2.34 (2010); Median age: 51.9 (2010); Males per 100 females: 81.7 (2010); Marriage status: 14.6% never married, 63.3% now married, 16.1% widowed, 5.9% divorced (2006-2010 5-year est.); Foreign born: 12.2% (2006-2010 5-year est.); Ancestry (includes multiple ancestries): 26.2% German, 17.7% English, 17.3% Irish, 11.0% Italian, 6.7% Polish (2006-2010 5-year est.).

Economy: Employment by occupation: 27.0% management, 7.6% professional, 4.6% services, 11.0% sales, 2.6% farming, 0.8% construction, 0.0% production (2006-2010 5-year est.).

Income: Per capita income: $61,978 (2006-2010 5-year est.); Median household income: $112,917 (2006-2010 5-year est.); Average household income: $159,740 (2006-2010 5-year est.); Percent of households with income of $100,000 or more: 55.2% (2006-2010 5-year est.); Poverty rate: 1.0% (2006-2010 5-year est.).

Education: Percent of population age 25 and over with: High school diploma (including GED) or higher: 95.1% (2006-2010 5-year est.); Bachelor's degree or higher: 65.4% (2006-2010 5-year est.); Master's degree or higher: 28.7% (2006-2010 5-year est.).

Housing: Homeownership rate: 77.0% (2010); Median home value: $476,000 (2006-2010 5-year est.); Median contract rent: $1,924 per month (2006-2010 5-year est.); Median year structure built: 1984 (2006-2010 5-year est.).

Transportation: Commute to work: 85.1% car, 4.1% public transportation, 1.2% walk, 8.1% work from home (2006-2010 5-year est.); Travel time to work: 17.4% less than 15 minutes, 29.9% 15 to 30 minutes, 27.5% 30 to

45 minutes, 15.3% 45 to 60 minutes, 9.8% 60 minutes or more (2006-2010 5-year est.).

Additional Information Contacts
Greater Hatboro Chamber of Commerce . . . . (215) 956-9540
  http://hatborochamber.org

SPRING MOUNT (CDP). Covers a land area of 0.669 square miles and a water area of 0.006 square miles. Located at 40.27° N. Lat; 75.47° W. Long. Elevation is 154 feet.

Population: 1,263 (1990); 2,205 (2000); 2,259 (2010); Density: 3,375.2 persons per square mile (2010); Race: 93.0% White, 3.1% Black, 1.2% Asian, 0.4% American Indian/Alaska Native, 0.0% Native Hawaiian/Other Pacific Islander, 2.3% Other, 3.2% Hispanic of any race (2010); Average household size: 2.55 (2010); Median age: 35.3 (2010); Males per 100 females: 91.8 (2010); Marriage status: 24.6% never married, 59.0% now married, 1.4% widowed, 15.0% divorced (2006-2010 5-year est.); Foreign born: 3.4% (2006-2010 5-year est.); Ancestry (includes multiple ancestries): 33.5% German, 20.1% Italian, 19.6% Irish, 8.9% Polish, 7.2% English (2006-2010 5-year est.).

Economy: Employment by occupation: 12.9% management, 6.3% professional, 11.9% services, 16.3% sales, 8.1% farming, 9.0% construction, 2.8% production (2006-2010 5-year est.).

Income: Per capita income: $32,314 (2006-2010 5-year est.); Median household income: $64,000 (2006-2010 5-year est.); Average household income: $73,500 (2006-2010 5-year est.); Percent of households with income of $100,000 or more: 23.0% (2006-2010 5-year est.); Poverty rate: 1.8% (2006-2010 5-year est.).

Education: Percent of population age 25 and over with: High school diploma (including GED) or higher: 95.6% (2006-2010 5-year est.); Bachelor's degree or higher: 34.1% (2006-2010 5-year est.); Master's degree or higher: 12.0% (2006-2010 5-year est.).

Housing: Homeownership rate: 89.0% (2010); Median home value: $218,100 (2006-2010 5-year est.); Median contract rent: $988 per month (2006-2010 5-year est.); Median year structure built: 1985 (2006-2010 5-year est.).

Transportation: Commute to work: 89.2% car, 1.0% public transportation, 7.5% walk, 2.3% work from home (2006-2010 5-year est.); Travel time to work: 14.4% less than 15 minutes, 18.1% 15 to 30 minutes, 40.8% 30 to 45 minutes, 11.2% 45 to 60 minutes, 15.4% 60 minutes or more (2006-2010 5-year est.)

Additional Information Contacts
Spring-Ford Chamber of Commerce . . . . (610) 489-7200
  http://www.springfordchamber.com

SPRINGFIELD (township). Covers a land area of 6.780 square miles and a water area of 0.012 square miles. Located at 40.10° N. Lat; 75.20° W. Long.

History: Springfield Township was William Penn's gift to his first wife, Gulielma Maria Springett Penn. "Gulielma Maria Penn's Mannor of Springfield" was first designated on a map in 1681 and this date is prominently displayed on the Township Seal. The first reference to "Springfield Township" occurred in 1718.

Population: 19,612 (1990); 19,533 (2000); 19,418 (2010); Density: 2,863.9 persons per square mile (2010); Race: 83.6% White, 11.1% Black, 2.8% Asian, 0.1% American Indian/Alaska Native, 0.0% Native Hawaiian/Other Pacific Islander, 2.4% Other, 2.4% Hispanic of any race (2010); Average household size: 2.45 (2010); Median age: 45.3 (2010); Males per 100 females: 86.5 (2010); Marriage status: 29.4% never married, 54.9% now married, 9.3% widowed, 6.4% divorced (2006-2010 5-year est.); Foreign born: 5.1% (2006-2010 5-year est.); Ancestry (includes multiple ancestries): 31.2% Irish, 21.2% German, 16.6% Italian, 11.9% English, 5.1% Polish (2006-2010 5-year est.).

Economy: Single-family building permits issued: 2 (2011); Multi-family building permits issued: 0 (2011); Employment by occupation: 18.6% management, 4.7% professional, 5.9% services, 15.1% sales, 2.7% farming, 6.6% construction, 3.0% production (2006-2010 5-year est.).

Income: Per capita income: $42,937 (2006-2010 5-year est.); Median household income: $94,732 (2006-2010 5-year est.); Average household income: $113,456 (2006-2010 5-year est.); Percent of households with income of $100,000 or more: 45.9% (2006-2010 5-year est.); Poverty rate: 6.1% (2006-2010 5-year est.).

Taxes: Total city taxes per capita: $462 (2009); City property taxes per capita: $225 (2009).

Education: Percent of population age 25 and over with: High school diploma (including GED) or higher: 94.1% (2006-2010 5-year est.);

Bachelor's degree or higher: 51.4% (2006-2010 5-year est.); Master's degree or higher: 23.9% (2006-2010 5-year est.).

School District(s)
Springfield Township SD (KG-12)
  2010-11 Enrollment: 2,133 . . . . (215) 233-6000

Housing: Homeownership rate: 80.1% (2010); Median home value: $327,100 (2006-2010 5-year est.); Median contract rent: $1,048 per month (2006-2010 5-year est.); Median year structure built: 1954 (2006-2010 5-year est.).

Safety: Violent crime rate: 18.5 per 10,000 population; Property crime rate: 94.5 per 10,000 population (2011).

Transportation: Commute to work: 81.6% car, 7.7% public transportation, 2.2% walk, 7.6% work from home (2006-2010 5-year est.); Travel time to work: 20.3% less than 15 minutes, 33.0% 15 to 30 minutes, 27.2% 30 to 45 minutes, 10.9% 45 to 60 minutes, 8.6% 60 minutes or more (2006-2010 5-year est.)

Additional Information Contacts
Montgomery County Chamber of Commerce . . . . (610) 265-1776
  http://www.montgomerycountychamber.org
Springfield Township . . . . (215) 836-7600
  http://www.springfield-montco.org

STOWE (CDP). Covers a land area of 1.420 square miles and a water area of 0.029 square miles. Located at 40.25° N. Lat; 75.68° W. Long. Elevation is 197 feet.

Population: 3,598 (1990); 3,585 (2000); 3,695 (2010); Density: 2,601.9 persons per square mile (2010); Race: 85.4% White, 9.7% Black, 0.6% Asian, 0.3% American Indian/Alaska Native, 0.0% Native Hawaiian/Other Pacific Islander, 4.0% Other, 3.3% Hispanic of any race (2010); Average household size: 2.54 (2010); Median age: 37.3 (2010); Males per 100 females: 94.6 (2010); Marriage status: 35.0% never married, 51.8% now married, 5.4% widowed, 7.8% divorced (2006-2010 5-year est.); Foreign born: 1.5% (2006-2010 5-year est.); Ancestry (includes multiple ancestries): 45.3% German, 14.0% Italian, 12.7% Irish, 10.9% Polish, 6.5% English (2006-2010 5-year est.).

Economy: Employment by occupation: 5.5% management, 4.6% professional, 13.0% services, 18.0% sales, 6.4% farming, 12.7% construction, 10.1% production (2006-2010 5-year est.).

Income: Per capita income: $23,437 (2006-2010 5-year est.); Median household income: $51,448 (2006-2010 5-year est.); Average household income: $57,205 (2006-2010 5-year est.); Percent of households with income of $100,000 or more: 12.5% (2006-2010 5-year est.); Poverty rate: 11.2% (2006-2010 5-year est.).

Education: Percent of population age 25 and over with: High school diploma (including GED) or higher: 84.2% (2006-2010 5-year est.); Bachelor's degree or higher: 12.2% (2006-2010 5-year est.); Master's degree or higher: 2.4% (2006-2010 5-year est.).

School District(s)
Pottsgrove SD (KG-12)
  2010-11 Enrollment: 3,342 . . . . (610) 327-2277

Housing: Homeownership rate: 66.7% (2010); Median home value: $160,800 (2006-2010 5-year est.); Median contract rent: $811 per month (2006-2010 5-year est.); Median year structure built: 1956 (2006-2010 5-year est.).

Transportation: Commute to work: 96.7% car, 0.0% public transportation, 2.1% walk, 0.0% work from home (2006-2010 5-year est.); Travel time to work: 32.7% less than 15 minutes, 18.8% 15 to 30 minutes, 24.2% 30 to 45 minutes, 11.3% 45 to 60 minutes, 13.0% 60 minutes or more (2006-2010 5-year est.)

Additional Information Contacts
TriCounty Area Chamber of Commerce . . . . (610) 326-2900
  http://www.tricountyareachamber.com

TELFORD (borough). Covers a land area of 1.023 square miles and a water area of <.001 square miles. Located at 40.33° N. Lat; 75.33° W. Long. Elevation is 443 feet.

Population: 4,238 (1990); 4,680 (2000); 4,872 (2010); Density: 4,764.5 persons per square mile (2010); Race: 86.7% White, 2.6% Black, 5.6% Asian, 0.1% American Indian/Alaska Native, 0.1% Native Hawaiian/Other Pacific Islander, 4.9% Other, 8.0% Hispanic of any race (2010); Average household size: 2.33 (2010); Median age: 40.4 (2010); Males per 100 females: 87.5 (2010); Marriage status: 27.6% never married, 50.7% now married, 14.1% widowed, 7.5% divorced (2006-2010 5-year est.); Foreign born: 7.1% (2006-2010 5-year est.); Ancestry (includes multiple

ancestries): 31.2% German, 22.5% Irish, 12.8% Italian, 9.7% English, 6.0% Polish (2006-2010 5-year est.).

Economy: Single-family building permits issued: 1 (2011); Multi-family building permits issued: 0 (2011); Employment by occupation: 8.5% management, 7.0% professional, 10.5% services, 19.2% sales, 3.5% farming, 7.9% construction, 7.2% production (2006-2010 5-year est.).

Income: Per capita income: $33,038 (2006-2010 5-year est.); Median household income: $57,335 (2006-2010 5-year est.); Average household income: $80,251 (2006-2010 5-year est.); Percent of households with income of $100,000 or more: 15.8% (2006-2010 5-year est.); Poverty rate: 8.4% (2006-2010 5-year est.).

Education: Percent of population age 25 and over with: High school diploma (including GED) or higher: 80.6% (2006-2010 5-year est.); Bachelor's degree or higher: 27.2% (2006-2010 5-year est.); Master's degree or higher: 6.1% (2006-2010 5-year est.).

School District(s)

Souderton Area SD (KG-12)

    2010-11 Enrollment: 6,739 . . . . (215) 723-6061

Housing: Homeownership rate: 56.4% (2010); Median home value: $235,400 (2006-2010 5-year est.); Median contract rent: $704 per month (2006-2010 5-year est.); Median year structure built: 1971 (2006-2010 5-year est.).

Safety: Violent crime rate: 30.7 per 10,000 population; Property crime rate: 139.1 per 10,000 population (2011).

Transportation: Commute to work: 94.1% car, 1.3% public transportation, 1.8% walk, 1.9% work from home (2006-2010 5-year est.); Travel time to work: 36.7% less than 15 minutes, 27.2% 15 to 30 minutes, 21.1% 30 to 45 minutes, 9.4% 45 to 60 minutes, 5.6% 60 minutes or more (2006-2010 5-year est.)

Additional Information Contacts

Indian Valley Chamber of Commerce . . . . (215) 723-9472
    http://indianvalleychamber.com

TOWAMENCIN (township). Covers a land area of 9.682 square miles and a water area of 0 square miles. Located at 40.24° N. Lat; 75.34° W. Long.

History: The first settlers arrived in Towamencin Township around the turn of the 18th century. The first grant of land in Towamencin Township was in 1703 from William Penn's Commissioners to Benjamin Furley on June 8.

Population: 14,167 (1990); 17,597 (2000); 17,578 (2010); Density: 1,815.6 persons per square mile (2010); Race: 85.1% White, 4.1% Black, 8.4% Asian, 0.1% American Indian/Alaska Native, 0.0% Native Hawaiian/Other Pacific Islander, 2.3% Other, 2.5% Hispanic of any race (2010); Average household size: 2.40 (2010); Median age: 43.8 (2010); Males per 100 females: 88.2 (2010); Marriage status: 24.8% never married, 61.2% now married, 7.2% widowed, 6.9% divorced (2006-2010 5-year est.); Foreign born: 10.4% (2006-2010 5-year est.); Ancestry (includes multiple ancestries): 27.7% German, 25.4% Irish, 17.0% Italian, 12.1% English, 5.3% Polish (2006-2010 5-year est.).

Economy: Single-family building permits issued: 2 (2011); Multi-family building permits issued: 120 (2011); Employment by occupation: 18.3% management, 8.7% professional, 5.4% services, 16.7% sales, 4.7% farming, 4.3% construction, 5.5% production (2006-2010 5-year est.).

Income: Per capita income: $38,773 (2006-2010 5-year est.); Median household income: $75,128 (2006-2010 5-year est.); Average household income: $93,480 (2006-2010 5-year est.); Percent of households with income of $100,000 or more: 36.7% (2006-2010 5-year est.); Poverty rate: 4.9% (2006-2010 5-year est.).

Education: Percent of population age 25 and over with: High school diploma (including GED) or higher: 93.9% (2006-2010 5-year est.); Bachelor's degree or higher: 43.9% (2006-2010 5-year est.); Master's degree or higher: 14.8% (2006-2010 5-year est.).

Housing: Homeownership rate: 72.1% (2010); Median home value: $301,900 (2006-2010 5-year est.); Median contract rent: $933 per month (2006-2010 5-year est.); Median year structure built: 1979 (2006-2010 5-year est.).

Safety: Violent crime rate: 12.5 per 10,000 population; Property crime rate: 98.1 per 10,000 population (2011).

Transportation: Commute to work: 92.6% car, 2.4% public transportation, 0.8% walk, 3.6% work from home (2006-2010 5-year est.); Travel time to work: 22.8% less than 15 minutes, 29.8% 15 to 30 minutes, 26.7% 30 to 45 minutes, 11.0% 45 to 60 minutes, 9.7% 60 minutes or more (2006-2010 5-year est.)

Additional Information Contacts

Indian Valley Chamber of Commerce . . . . (215) 723-9472
    http://indianvalleychamber.com
Towamencin Township . . . . (215) 368-7602
    http://www.towamencin.org

TRAPPE (borough). Covers a land area of 2.061 square miles and a water area of 0 square miles. Located at 40.20° N. Lat; 75.48° W. Long. Elevation is 289 feet.

History: Oldest Lutheran church (1743) in America here.

Population: 2,115 (1990); 3,210 (2000); 3,509 (2010); Density: 1,702.6 persons per square mile (2010); Race: 89.2% White, 3.2% Black, 4.5% Asian, 0.3% American Indian/Alaska Native, 0.0% Native Hawaiian/Other Pacific Islander, 2.8% Other, 2.7% Hispanic of any race (2010); Average household size: 2.59 (2010); Median age: 37.7 (2010); Males per 100 females: 100.1 (2010); Marriage status: 26.7% never married, 60.9% now married, 4.1% widowed, 8.3% divorced (2006-2010 5-year est.); Foreign born: 7.9% (2006-2010 5-year est.); Ancestry (includes multiple ancestries): 24.7% German, 20.1% Irish, 17.7% Italian, 10.5% English, 9.3% Polish (2006-2010 5-year est.).

Economy: Single-family building permits issued: 0 (2011); Multi-family building permits issued: 0 (2011); Employment by occupation: 18.7% management, 9.8% professional, 7.0% services, 19.3% sales, 3.1% farming, 6.2% construction, 6.1% production (2006-2010 5-year est.).

Income: Per capita income: $34,825 (2006-2010 5-year est.); Median household income: $73,935 (2006-2010 5-year est.); Average household income: $88,879 (2006-2010 5-year est.); Percent of households with income of $100,000 or more: 33.7% (2006-2010 5-year est.); Poverty rate: 8.2% (2006-2010 5-year est.).

Education: Percent of population age 25 and over with: High school diploma (including GED) or higher: 93.5% (2006-2010 5-year est.); Bachelor's degree or higher: 41.2% (2006-2010 5-year est.); Master's degree or higher: 11.7% (2006-2010 5-year est.).

School District(s)

Perkiomen Valley SD (KG-12)

    2010-11 Enrollment: 5,899 . . . . (610) 489-8506

Housing: Homeownership rate: 81.0% (2010); Median home value: $269,200 (2006-2010 5-year est.); Median contract rent: $891 per month (2006-2010 5-year est.); Median year structure built: 1990 (2006-2010 5-year est.).

Transportation: Commute to work: 92.4% car, 0.6% public transportation, 3.8% walk, 2.4% work from home (2006-2010 5-year est.); Travel time to work: 18.0% less than 15 minutes, 33.4% 15 to 30 minutes, 30.6% 30 to 45 minutes, 8.6% 45 to 60 minutes, 9.3% 60 minutes or more (2006-2010 5-year est.)

Additional Information Contacts

Perkiomen Valley Chamber of Commerce . . . . (610) 489-6660
    http://perkiomenvalleychamber.org

TROOPER (CDP). Covers a land area of 2.385 square miles and a water area of 0 square miles. Located at 40.15° N. Lat; 75.40° W. Long. Elevation is 377 feet.

Population: 5,137 (1990); 6,061 (2000); 5,744 (2010); Density: 2,408.8 persons per square mile (2010); Race: 88.9% White, 2.2% Black, 6.8% Asian, 0.1% American Indian/Alaska Native, 0.0% Native Hawaiian/Other Pacific Islander, 2.0% Other, 3.2% Hispanic of any race (2010); Average household size: 2.86 (2010); Median age: 42.6 (2010); Males per 100 females: 98.1 (2010); Marriage status: 24.8% never married, 64.3% now married, 4.3% widowed, 6.6% divorced (2006-2010 5-year est.); Foreign born: 8.5% (2006-2010 5-year est.); Ancestry (includes multiple ancestries): 28.6% Italian, 24.5% German, 21.3% Irish, 8.8% English, 8.5% Polish (2006-2010 5-year est.).

Economy: Employment by occupation: 16.9% management, 9.2% professional, 4.9% services, 17.5% sales, 3.0% farming, 9.6% construction, 5.9% production (2006-2010 5-year est.).

Income: Per capita income: $37,530 (2006-2010 5-year est.); Median household income: $88,065 (2006-2010 5-year est.); Average household income: $106,434 (2006-2010 5-year est.); Percent of households with income of $100,000 or more: 42.1% (2006-2010 5-year est.); Poverty rate: 4.6% (2006-2010 5-year est.).

Education: Percent of population age 25 and over with: High school diploma (including GED) or higher: 89.2% (2006-2010 5-year est.); Bachelor's degree or higher: 43.1% (2006-2010 5-year est.); Master's degree or higher: 18.4% (2006-2010 5-year est.).

Housing: Homeownership rate: 90.3% (2010); Median home value: $296,900 (2006-2010 5-year est.); Median contract rent: $824 per month (2006-2010 5-year est.); Median year structure built: 1965 (2006-2010 5-year est.).

Transportation: Commute to work: 90.5% car, 2.4% public transportation, 1.6% walk, 4.8% work from home (2006-2010 5-year est.); Travel time to work: 21.9% less than 15 minutes, 37.6% 15 to 30 minutes, 25.1% 30 to 45 minutes, 9.3% 45 to 60 minutes, 6.2% 60 minutes or more (2006-2010 5-year est.).

Additional Information Contacts

Phoenixville Area Chamber of Commerce . . . . (610) 933-3070
http://www.phoenixvillechamber.org

UPPER DUBLIN (township). Covers a land area of 13.230 square miles and a water area of 0.030 square miles. Located at 40.15° N. Lat; 75.18° W. Long.

Population: 24,028 (1990); 25,878 (2000); 25,569 (2010); Density: 1,932.7 persons per square mile (2010); Race: 83.0% White, 6.6% Black, 8.5% Asian, 0.1% American Indian/Alaska Native, 0.0% Native Hawaiian/Other Pacific Islander, 1.8% Other, 1.8% Hispanic of any race (2010); Average household size: 2.69 (2010); Median age: 43.9 (2010); Males per 100 females: 94.6 (2010); Marriage status: 24.1% never married, 64.3% now married, 6.0% widowed, 5.6% divorced (2006-2010 5-year est.); Foreign born: 9.6% (2006-2010 5-year est.); Ancestry (includes multiple ancestries): 21.0% German, 20.7% Irish, 14.4% Italian, 10.6% English, 8.3% Russian (2006-2010 5-year est.).

Economy: Unemployment rate: 6.0% (August 2012); Total civilian labor force: 13,224 (August 2012); Single-family building permits issued: 6 (2011); Multi-family building permits issued: 16 (2011); Employment by occupation: 18.5% management, 8.3% professional, 3.5% services, 14.1% sales, 2.3% farming, 4.0% construction, 3.0% production (2006-2010 5-year est.).

Income: Per capita income: $49,085 (2006-2010 5-year est.); Median household income: $107,285 (2006-2010 5-year est.); Average household income: $137,363 (2006-2010 5-year est.); Percent of households with income of $100,000 or more: 54.7% (2006-2010 5-year est.); Poverty rate: 3.5% (2006-2010 5-year est.).

Taxes: Total city taxes per capita: $701 (2009); City property taxes per capita: $371 (2009).

Education: Percent of population age 25 and over with: High school diploma (including GED) or higher: 97.3% (2006-2010 5-year est.); Bachelor's degree or higher: 62.2% (2006-2010 5-year est.); Master's degree or higher: 28.7% (2006-2010 5-year est.).

Housing: Homeownership rate: 86.8% (2010); Median home value: $406,500 (2006-2010 5-year est.); Median contract rent: $1,201 per month (2006-2010 5-year est.); Median year structure built: 1971 (2006-2010 5-year est.).

Safety: Violent crime rate: 9.7 per 10,000 population; Property crime rate: 95.5 per 10,000 population (2011).

Transportation: Commute to work: 86.1% car, 7.8% public transportation, 0.9% walk, 4.8% work from home (2006-2010 5-year est.); Travel time to work: 23.2% less than 15 minutes, 30.6% 15 to 30 minutes, 24.7% 30 to 45 minutes, 12.3% 45 to 60 minutes, 9.1% 60 minutes or more (2006-2010 5-year est.)

Additional Information Contacts

Eastern Montgomery County Chamber of Commerce . . . . (215) 887-5122
http://www.emccc.org
Upper Dublin Township . . . . (215) 643-1600
http://www.upperdublin.net

UPPER FREDERICK (township). Covers a land area of 9.944 square miles and a water area of 0.149 square miles. Located at 40.31° N. Lat; 75.51° W. Long.

Population: 2,165 (1990); 3,141 (2000); 3,523 (2010); Density: 354.3 persons per square mile (2010); Race: 96.1% White, 1.5% Black, 0.6% Asian, 0.1% American Indian/Alaska Native, 0.1% Native Hawaiian/Other Pacific Islander, 1.6% Other, 2.0% Hispanic of any race (2010); Average household size: 2.51 (2010); Median age: 40.7 (2010); Males per 100 females: 94.4 (2010); Marriage status: 21.3% never married, 63.1% now married, 7.9% widowed, 7.7% divorced (2006-2010 5-year est.); Foreign born: 1.2% (2006-2010 5-year est.); Ancestry (includes multiple ancestries): 44.5% German, 24.4% Irish, 13.2% English, 10.6% Italian, 9.4% Polish (2006-2010 5-year est.).

Economy: Single-family building permits issued: 1 (2011); Multi-family building permits issued: 0 (2011); Employment by occupation: 13.2%

management, 6.3% professional, 7.2% services, 14.4% sales, 2.6% farming, 11.7% construction, 8.3% production (2006-2010 5-year est.).

Income: Per capita income: $32,593 (2006-2010 5-year est.); Median household income: $75,625 (2006-2010 5-year est.); Average household income: $87,263 (2006-2010 5-year est.); Percent of households with income of $100,000 or more: 30.4% (2006-2010 5-year est.); Poverty rate: 5.0% (2006-2010 5-year est.).

Education: Percent of population age 25 and over with: High school diploma (including GED) or higher: 92.9% (2006-2010 5-year est.); Bachelor's degree or higher: 31.2% (2006-2010 5-year est.); Master's degree or higher: 11.5% (2006-2010 5-year est.).

Housing: Homeownership rate: 80.9% (2010); Median home value: $248,400 (2006-2010 5-year est.); Median contract rent: $818 per month (2006-2010 5-year est.); Median year structure built: 1987 (2006-2010 5-year est.).

Transportation: Commute to work: 93.9% car, 0.0% public transportation, 0.8% walk, 3.9% work from home (2006-2010 5-year est.); Travel time to work: 12.2% less than 15 minutes, 32.6% 15 to 30 minutes, 31.0% 30 to 45 minutes, 13.5% 45 to 60 minutes, 10.6% 60 minutes or more (2006-2010 5-year est.)

Additional Information Contacts

TriCounty Area Chamber of Commerce . . . . (610) 326-2900
http://tricountyareachamber.com

UPPER GWYNEDD (township). Covers a land area of 8.126 square miles and a water area of 0.002 square miles. Located at 40.21° N. Lat; 75.29° W. Long.

History: The township is so named because it was originally settled largely by migrants from Gwynedd and other parts of north Wales in the 17th and 18th Centuries. For several generations the main language used in the township was Welsh.

Population: 12,197 (1990); 14,243 (2000); 15,552 (2010); Density: 1,913.8 persons per square mile (2010); Race: 81.1% White, 4.2% Black, 12.3% Asian, 0.0% American Indian/Alaska Native, 0.0% Native Hawaiian/Other Pacific Islander, 2.4% Other, 2.2% Hispanic of any race (2010); Average household size: 2.45 (2010); Median age: 44.6 (2010); Males per 100 females: 90.1 (2010); Marriage status: 22.0% never married, 64.6% now married, 5.4% widowed, 8.0% divorced (2006-2010 5-year est.); Foreign born: 12.7% (2006-2010 5-year est.); Ancestry (includes multiple ancestries): 30.0% German, 26.6% Irish, 15.4% Italian, 9.5% English, 8.0% Polish (2006-2010 5-year est.).

Economy: Single-family building permits issued: 19 (2011); Multi-family building permits issued: 0 (2011); Employment by occupation: 19.4% management, 11.8% professional, 5.0% services, 14.1% sales, 5.3% farming, 4.4% construction, 3.0% production (2006-2010 5-year est.).

Income: Per capita income: $46,198 (2006-2010 5-year est.); Median household income: $94,613 (2006-2010 5-year est.); Average household income: $110,341 (2006-2010 5-year est.); Percent of households with income of $100,000 or more: 47.6% (2006-2010 5-year est.); Poverty rate: 2.5% (2006-2010 5-year est.).

Education: Percent of population age 25 and over with: High school diploma (including GED) or higher: 95.3% (2006-2010 5-year est.); Bachelor's degree or higher: 55.0% (2006-2010 5-year est.); Master's degree or higher: 19.3% (2006-2010 5-year est.).

Housing: Homeownership rate: 76.8% (2010); Median home value: $325,800 (2006-2010 5-year est.); Median contract rent: $1,343 per month (2006-2010 5-year est.); Median year structure built: 1981 (2006-2010 5-year est.).

Safety: Violent crime rate: 7.1 per 10,000 population; Property crime rate: 79.5 per 10,000 population (2011).

Transportation: Commute to work: 89.0% car, 4.5% public transportation, 0.9% walk, 5.5% work from home (2006-2010 5-year est.); Travel time to work: 26.4% less than 15 minutes, 32.5% 15 to 30 minutes, 18.6% 30 to 45 minutes, 10.1% 45 to 60 minutes, 12.3% 60 minutes or more (2006-2010 5-year est.)

Additional Information Contacts

Hatfield Chamber of Commerce . . . . (215) 855-3335
http://www.hatfieldchamber.com
Upper Gwynedd Township . . . . (215) 699-7777
http://www.uppergwynedd.org

UPPER HANOVER

UPPER HANOVER (township). Covers a land area of 20.236 square miles and a water area of 0.937 square miles. Located at 40.39° N. Lat; 75.51° W. Long.

Population: 4,604 (1990); 4,885 (2000); 6,464 (2010); Density: 319.4 persons per square mile (2010); Race: 95.7% White, 1.5% Black, 1.5% Asian, 0.0% American Indian/Alaska Native, 0.1% Native Hawaiian/Other Pacific Islander, 1.2% Other, 1.8% Hispanic of any race (2010); Average household size: 2.75 (2010); Median age: 42.4 (2010); Males per 100 females: 99.8 (2010); Marriage status: 18.7% never married, 67.9% now married, 4.8% widowed, 8.6% divorced (2006-2010 5-year est.); Foreign born: 2.6% (2006-2010 5-year est.); Ancestry (includes multiple ancestries): 47.4% German, 21.8% Irish, 16.3% Italian, 10.8% English, 5.8% American (2006-2010 5-year est.).

Economy: Single-family building permits issued: 31 (2011); Multi-family building permits issued: 0 (2011); Employment by occupation: 11.7% management, 7.8% professional, 7.0% services, 16.7% sales, 2.7% farming, 11.2% construction, 10.5% production (2006-2010 5-year est.).

Income: Per capita income: $34,170 (2006-2010 5-year est.); Median household income: $75,078 (2006-2010 5-year est.); Average household income: $91,911 (2006-2010 5-year est.); Percent of households with income of $100,000 or more: 31.8% (2006-2010 5-year est.); Poverty rate: 3.7% (2006-2010 5-year est.).

Education: Percent of population age 25 and over with: High school diploma (including GED) or higher: 94.0% (2006-2010 5-year est.); Bachelor's degree or higher: 25.0% (2006-2010 5-year est.); Master's degree or higher: 9.1% (2006-2010 5-year est.).

Housing: Homeownership rate: 91.9% (2010); Median home value: $286,700 (2006-2010 5-year est.); Median contract rent: $1,040 per month (2006-2010 5-year est.); Median year structure built: 1976 (2006-2010 5-year est.).

Transportation: Commute to work: 94.7% car, 0.0% public transportation, 2.4% walk, 2.0% work from home (2006-2010 5-year est.); Travel time to work: 20.5% less than 15 minutes, 30.6% 15 to 30 minutes, 27.6% 30 to 45 minutes, 13.2% 45 to 60 minutes, 8.1% 60 minutes or more (2006-2010 5-year est.)

Additional Information Contacts

Upper Bucks Chamber of Commerce . . . . (215) 536-3211
    http://www.ubcc.org
Upper Hanover Township . . . . (215) 679-4401
    http://upperhanovertownship.org

UPPER MERION

UPPER MERION (township). Covers a land area of 16.955 square miles and a water area of 0.317 square miles. Located at 40.09° N. Lat; 75.38° W. Long.

Population: 25,819 (1990); 26,863 (2000); 28,395 (2010); Density: 1,674.7 persons per square mile (2010); Race: 76.0% White, 5.5% Black, 14.7% Asian, 0.2% American Indian/Alaska Native, 0.0% Native Hawaiian/Other Pacific Islander, 3.6% Other, 3.9% Hispanic of any race (2010); Average household size: 2.35 (2010); Median age: 39.4 (2010); Males per 100 females: 98.9 (2010); Marriage status: 29.6% never married, 56.3% now married, 6.4% widowed, 7.7% divorced (2006-2010 5-year est.); Foreign born: 18.1% (2006-2010 5-year est.); Ancestry (includes multiple ancestries): 21.5% Irish, 18.5% German, 18.1% Italian, 8.3% Polish, 7.9% English (2006-2010 5-year est.).

Economy: Unemployment rate: 5.6% (August 2012); Total civilian labor force: 17,218 (August 2012); Single-family building permits issued: 3 (2011); Multi-family building permits issued: 0 (2011); Employment by occupation: 17.4% management, 12.6% professional, 5.1% services, 15.6% sales, 3.1% farming, 4.4% construction, 3.9% production (2006-2010 5-year est.).

Income: Per capita income: $44,063 (2006-2010 5-year est.); Median household income: $77,955 (2006-2010 5-year est.); Average household income: $100,157 (2006-2010 5-year est.); Percent of households with income of $100,000 or more: 38.2% (2006-2010 5-year est.); Poverty rate: 4.6% (2006-2010 5-year est.).

Taxes: Total city taxes per capita: $830 (2009); City property taxes per capita: $224 (2009).

Education: Percent of population age 25 and over with: High school diploma (including GED) or higher: 95.0% (2006-2010 5-year est.); Bachelor's degree or higher: 54.5% (2006-2010 5-year est.); Master's degree or higher: 25.2% (2006-2010 5-year est.).

Housing: Homeownership rate: 67.2% (2010); Median home value: $324,200 (2006-2010 5-year est.); Median contract rent: $1,010 per month (2006-2010 5-year est.); Median year structure built: 1968 (2006-2010 5-year est.).

Safety: Violent crime rate: 8.4 per 10,000 population; Property crime rate: 498.8 per 10,000 population (2011).

Transportation: Commute to work: 88.8% car, 4.8% public transportation, 2.4% walk, 3.5% work from home (2006-2010 5-year est.); Travel time to work: 30.2% less than 15 minutes, 35.0% 15 to 30 minutes, 19.1% 30 to 45 minutes, 8.5% 45 to 60 minutes, 7.2% 60 minutes or more (2006-2010 5-year est.)

Additional Information Contacts

Main Line Chamber of Commerce . . . . (610) 687-6232
    http://www.mlcc.org
Upper Merion Township . . . . (615) 265-2600
    http://www.umtownship.org

UPPER MORELAND

UPPER MORELAND (township). Covers a land area of 7.972 square miles and a water area of 0.005 square miles. Located at 40.16° N. Lat; 75.10° W. Long.

Population: 25,252 (1990); 24,993 (2000); 24,015 (2010); Density: 3,012.3 persons per square mile (2010); Race: 87.0% White, 5.1% Black, 4.4% Asian, 0.2% American Indian/Alaska Native, 0.1% Native Hawaiian/Other Pacific Islander, 3.2% Other, 3.6% Hispanic of any race (2010); Average household size: 2.39 (2010); Median age: 41.2 (2010); Males per 100 females: 94.9 (2010); Marriage status: 28.6% never married, 54.4% now married, 8.4% widowed, 8.6% divorced (2006-2010 5-year est.); Foreign born: 6.4% (2006-2010 5-year est.); Ancestry (includes multiple ancestries): 30.9% Irish, 28.1% German, 15.8% Italian, 12.5% English, 5.5% Polish (2006-2010 5-year est.).

Economy: Unemployment rate: 7.2% (August 2012); Total civilian labor force: 13,324 (August 2012); Single-family building permits issued: 3 (2011); Multi-family building permits issued: 0 (2011); Employment by occupation: 13.2% management, 4.3% professional, 9.3% services, 17.4% sales, 4.7% farming, 8.9% construction, 5.3% production (2006-2010 5-year est.).

Income: Per capita income: $32,075 (2006-2010 5-year est.); Median household income: $63,167 (2006-2010 5-year est.); Average household income: $73,918 (2006-2010 5-year est.); Percent of households with income of $100,000 or more: 24.2% (2006-2010 5-year est.); Poverty rate: 4.2% (2006-2010 5-year est.).

Education: Percent of population age 25 and over with: High school diploma (including GED) or higher: 93.3% (2006-2010 5-year est.); Bachelor's degree or higher: 32.7% (2006-2010 5-year est.); Master's degree or higher: 10.2% (2006-2010 5-year est.).

Housing: Homeownership rate: 62.4% (2010); Median home value: $264,800 (2006-2010 5-year est.); Median contract rent: $895 per month (2006-2010 5-year est.); Median year structure built: 1959 (2006-2010 5-year est.).

Safety: Violent crime rate: 4.6 per 10,000 population; Property crime rate: 204.6 per 10,000 population (2011).

Transportation: Commute to work: 89.2% car, 3.7% public transportation, 3.0% walk, 3.1% work from home (2006-2010 5-year est.); Travel time to work: 29.8% less than 15 minutes, 35.2% 15 to 30 minutes, 18.7% 30 to 45 minutes, 9.1% 45 to 60 minutes, 7.1% 60 minutes or more (2006-2010 5-year est.)

Additional Information Contacts

Eastern Montgomery County Chamber of Commerce . . . . (215) 887-5122
    http://www.emccc.org
Upper Moreland Township . . . . (215) 659-3100
    http://www.uppermoreland.org

UPPER POTTSGROVE

UPPER POTTSGROVE (township). Covers a land area of 5.051 square miles and a water area of <.001 square miles. Located at 40.28° N. Lat; 75.64° W. Long.

Population: 3,315 (1990); 4,102 (2000); 5,315 (2010); Density: 1,052.3 persons per square mile (2010); Race: 89.1% White, 5.8% Black, 2.4% Asian, 0.2% American Indian/Alaska Native, 0.1% Native Hawaiian/Other Pacific Islander, 2.4% Other, 2.7% Hispanic of any race (2010); Average household size: 2.86 (2010); Median age: 38.0 (2010); Males per 100 females: 100.9 (2010); Marriage status: 23.4% never married, 67.6% now married, 3.6% widowed, 5.4% divorced (2006-2010 5-year est.); Foreign born: 4.0% (2006-2010 5-year est.); Ancestry (includes multiple ancestries): 32.8% German, 22.9% Irish, 16.2% Italian, 11.4% Polish, 7.3% Pennsylvania German (2006-2010 5-year est.).

Economy: Single-family building permits issued: 1 (2011); Multi-family building permits issued: 0 (2011); Employment by occupation: 13.6% management, 8.4% professional, 5.9% services, 14.6% sales, 4.8% farming, 10.4% construction, 5.1% production (2006-2010 5-year est.).

Income: Per capita income: $32,060 (2006-2010 5-year est.); Median household income: $86,322 (2006-2010 5-year est.); Average household income: $91,823 (2006-2010 5-year est.); Percent of households with income of $100,000 or more: 40.0% (2006-2010 5-year est.); Poverty rate: 0.6% (2006-2010 5-year est.).

Taxes: Total city taxes per capita: $423 (2009); City property taxes per capita: $161 (2009).

Education: Percent of population age 25 and over with: High school diploma (including GED) or higher: 90.0% (2006-2010 5-year est.); Bachelor's degree or higher: 27.5% (2006-2010 5-year est.); Master's degree or higher: 8.2% (2006-2010 5-year est.).

Housing: Homeownership rate: 90.2% (2010); Median home value: $240,000 (2006-2010 5-year est.); Median contract rent: $922 per month (2006-2010 5-year est.); Median year structure built: 1982 (2006-2010 5-year est.).

Safety: Violent crime rate: 13.1 per 10,000 population; Property crime rate: 118.2 per 10,000 population (2011).

Transportation: Commute to work: 96.4% car, 1.3% public transportation, 0.6% walk, 1.7% work from home (2006-2010 5-year est.); Travel time to work: 24.3% less than 15 minutes, 20.4% 15 to 30 minutes, 17.8% 30 to 45 minutes, 15.3% 45 to 60 minutes, 22.0% 60 minutes or more (2006-2010 5-year est.)

Additional Information Contacts

TriCounty Area Chamber of Commerce . . . . (610) 326-2900
   http://tricountyareachamber.com
Upper Pottsgrove Township . . . . (610) 323-8675
   http://www.upperpottsgrovetownship.org

UPPER PROVIDENCE (township). Covers a land area of 17.809 square miles and a water area of 0.356 square miles. Located at 40.17° N. Lat; 75.48° W. Long.

History: Upper Providence Township was established in 1805 by the division of the former Providence Township along the Perkiomen Creek. In 1896, the Burroughs of Collegeville and Trappe were created from northeastern portions of the township, yielding the present township boundaries.

Population: 9,722 (1990); 15,398 (2000); 21,219 (2010); Density: 1,191.5 persons per square mile (2010); Race: 86.6% White, 3.5% Black, 7.9% Asian, 0.1% American Indian/Alaska Native, 0.0% Native Hawaiian/Other Pacific Islander, 1.9% Other, 2.2% Hispanic of any race (2010); Average household size: 2.82 (2010); Median age: 38.7 (2010); Males per 100 females: 93.9 (2010); Marriage status: 22.8% never married, 64.7% now married, 6.2% widowed, 6.2% divorced (2006-2010 5-year est.); Foreign born: 7.6% (2006-2010 5-year est.); Ancestry (includes multiple ancestries): 28.2% German, 25.4% Irish, 21.3% Italian, 10.5% English, 8.9% Polish (2006-2010 5-year est.).

Economy: Single-family building permits issued: 36 (2011); Multi-family building permits issued: 0 (2011); Employment by occupation: 23.5% management, 9.3% professional, 4.3% services, 14.5% sales, 3.6% farming, 4.2% construction, 2.1% production (2006-2010 5-year est.).

Income: Per capita income: $44,946 (2006-2010 5-year est.); Median household income: $107,438 (2006-2010 5-year est.); Average household income: $126,445 (2006-2010 5-year est.); Percent of households with income of $100,000 or more: 53.6% (2006-2010 5-year est.); Poverty rate: 2.4% (2006-2010 5-year est.).

Taxes: Total city taxes per capita: $468 (2009); City property taxes per capita: $3 (2009).

Education: Percent of population age 25 and over with: High school diploma (including GED) or higher: 95.4% (2006-2010 5-year est.); Bachelor's degree or higher: 51.5% (2006-2010 5-year est.); Master's degree or higher: 19.0% (2006-2010 5-year est.).

Housing: Homeownership rate: 89.7% (2010); Median home value: $331,500 (2006-2010 5-year est.); Median contract rent: $910 per month (2006-2010 5-year est.); Median year structure built: 1990 (2006-2010 5-year est.).

Safety: Violent crime rate: 3.8 per 10,000 population; Property crime rate: 140.0 per 10,000 population (2011).

Transportation: Commute to work: 91.6% car, 1.2% public transportation, 1.9% walk, 4.4% work from home (2006-2010 5-year est.); Travel time to work: 22.4% less than 15 minutes, 27.7% 15 to 30 minutes, 25.2% 30 to 45 minutes, 14.1% 45 to 60 minutes, 10.5% 60 minutes or more (2006-2010 5-year est.)

Additional Information Contacts

Perkiomen Valley Chamber of Commerce . . . . (610) 489-6660
   http://perkiomenvalleychamber.org

Upper Providence Township . . . . (610) 933-9179
   http://www.uprov-montco.org

UPPER SALFORD (township). Covers a land area of 9.025 square miles and a water area of 0.054 square miles. Located at 40.30° N. Lat; 75.45° W. Long.

Population: 2,719 (1990); 3,024 (2000); 3,299 (2010); Density: 365.6 persons per square mile (2010); Race: 96.0% White, 1.4% Black, 1.0% Asian, 0.0% American Indian/Alaska Native, 0.0% Native Hawaiian/Other Pacific Islander, 1.6% Other, 1.8% Hispanic of any race (2010); Average household size: 2.82 (2010); Median age: 43.7 (2010); Males per 100 females: 103.4 (2010); Marriage status: 24.7% never married, 65.7% now married, 3.1% widowed, 6.5% divorced (2006-2010 5-year est.); Foreign born: 2.1% (2006-2010 5-year est.); Ancestry (includes multiple ancestries): 49.8% German, 14.7% Irish, 12.1% English, 11.0% Italian, 8.9% Polish (2006-2010 5-year est.).

Economy: Single-family building permits issued: 2 (2011); Multi-family building permits issued: 0 (2011); Employment by occupation: 11.5% management, 4.9% professional, 6.1% services, 18.6% sales, 3.6% farming, 12.8% construction, 6.9% production (2006-2010 5-year est.).

Income: Per capita income: $34,387 (2006-2010 5-year est.); Median household income: $89,432 (2006-2010 5-year est.); Average household income: $105,832 (2006-2010 5-year est.); Percent of households with income of $100,000 or more: 40.4% (2006-2010 5-year est.); Poverty rate: 2.0% (2006-2010 5-year est.).

Education: Percent of population age 25 and over with: High school diploma (including GED) or higher: 92.7% (2006-2010 5-year est.); Bachelor's degree or higher: 35.0% (2006-2010 5-year est.); Master's degree or higher: 10.3% (2006-2010 5-year est.).

Housing: Homeownership rate: 87.8% (2010); Median home value: $355,200 (2006-2010 5-year est.); Median contract rent: $977 per month (2006-2010 5-year est.); Median year structure built: 1969 (2006-2010 5-year est.).

Transportation: Commute to work: 93.8% car, 0.3% public transportation, 1.1% walk, 4.5% work from home (2006-2010 5-year est.); Travel time to work: 19.6% less than 15 minutes, 42.1% 15 to 30 minutes, 21.1% 30 to 45 minutes, 7.8% 45 to 60 minutes, 9.5% 60 minutes or more (2006-2010 5-year est.)

Additional Information Contacts

Indian Valley Chamber of Commerce . . . . (215) 723-9472
   http://indianvalleychamber.com

WEST CONSHOHOCKEN (borough). Covers a land area of 0.859 square miles and a water area of 0.040 square miles. Located at 40.07° N. Lat; 75.32° W. Long. Elevation is 213 feet.

History: Settled 1850, incorporated 1874.

Population: 1,294 (1990); 1,446 (2000); 1,320 (2010); Density: 1,536.6 persons per square mile (2010); Race: 90.1% White, 3.6% Black, 3.3% Asian, 0.5% American Indian/Alaska Native, 0.0% Native Hawaiian/Other Pacific Islander, 2.5% Other, 3.6% Hispanic of any race (2010); Average household size: 2.25 (2010); Median age: 34.2 (2010); Males per 100 females: 112.6 (2010); Marriage status: 48.5% never married, 40.4% now married, 4.7% widowed, 6.3% divorced (2006-2010 5-year est.); Foreign born: 4.6% (2006-2010 5-year est.); Ancestry (includes multiple ancestries): 33.9% Irish, 25.3% Italian, 16.9% German, 16.2% Polish, 8.8% English (2006-2010 5-year est.).

Economy: Single-family building permits issued: 3 (2011); Multi-family building permits issued: 0 (2011); Employment by occupation: 16.2% management, 5.6% professional, 9.2% services, 15.0% sales, 3.0% farming, 5.6% construction, 2.5% production (2006-2010 5-year est.).

Income: Per capita income: $46,490 (2006-2010 5-year est.); Median household income: $87,768 (2006-2010 5-year est.); Average household income: $108,567 (2006-2010 5-year est.); Percent of households with income of $100,000 or more: 38.4% (2006-2010 5-year est.); Poverty rate: 10.6% (2006-2010 5-year est.).

Education: Percent of population age 25 and over with: High school diploma (including GED) or higher: 93.2% (2006-2010 5-year est.); Bachelor's degree or higher: 51.2% (2006-2010 5-year est.); Master's degree or higher: 17.8% (2006-2010 5-year est.).

Housing: Homeownership rate: 71.7% (2010); Median home value: $309,400 (2006-2010 5-year est.); Median contract rent: $1,125 per month (2006-2010 5-year est.); Median year structure built: 1945 (2006-2010 5-year est.).

Transportation: Commute to work: 88.4% car, 4.3% public transportation, 2.0% walk, 5.3% work from home (2006-2010 5-year est.); Travel time to

work: 27.7% less than 15 minutes, 38.9% 15 to 30 minutes, 23.9% 30 to 45 minutes, 5.5% 45 to 60 minutes, 4.0% 60 minutes or more (2006-2010 5-year est.)

Additional Information Contacts
Main Line Chamber of Commerce . . . . (610) 687-6232
    http://www.mlcc.org

WEST NORRITON (township). Covers a land area of 5.887 square miles and a water area of 0.334 square miles. Located at 40.13° N. Lat; 75.38° W. Long. Elevation is 233 feet.

History: Valley Forge National Historical Park to Southwest.

Population: 15,209 (1990); 14,901 (2000); 15,663 (2010); Density: 2,660.5 persons per square mile (2010); Race: 83.0% White, 9.0% Black, 5.2% Asian, 0.1% American Indian/Alaska Native, 0.1% Native Hawaiian/Other Pacific Islander, 2.6% Other, 3.1% Hispanic of any race (2010); Average household size: 2.10 (2010); Median age: 42.0 (2010); Males per 100 females: 94.0 (2010); Marriage status: 29.1% never married, 51.7% now married, 7.3% widowed, 11.9% divorced (2006-2010 5-year est.); Foreign born: 5.3% (2006-2010 5-year est.); Ancestry (includes multiple ancestries): 27.5% Italian, 27.0% Irish, 23.0% German, 8.4% Polish, 8.2% English (2006-2010 5-year est.).

Economy: Single-family building permits issued: 0 (2011); Multi-family building permits issued: 0 (2011); Employment by occupation: 16.6% management, 8.6% professional, 6.4% services, 18.0% sales, 6.1% farming, 6.4% construction, 4.2% production (2006-2010 5-year est.).

Income: Per capita income: $37,658 (2006-2010 5-year est.); Median household income: $63,750 (2006-2010 5-year est.); Average household income: $76,857 (2006-2010 5-year est.); Percent of households with income of $100,000 or more: 27.1% (2006-2010 5-year est.); Poverty rate: 4.2% (2006-2010 5-year est.).

Education: Percent of population age 25 and over with: High school diploma (including GED) or higher: 93.8% (2006-2010 5-year est.); Bachelor's degree or higher: 40.0% (2006-2010 5-year est.); Master's degree or higher: 15.6% (2006-2010 5-year est.).

Housing: Homeownership rate: 69.8% (2010); Median home value: $229,100 (2006-2010 5-year est.); Median contract rent: $949 per month (2006-2010 5-year est.); Median year structure built: 1975 (2006-2010 5-year est.).

Safety: Violent crime rate: 17.2 per 10,000 population; Property crime rate: 174.4 per 10,000 population (2011).

Transportation: Commute to work: 95.5% car, 1.6% public transportation, 0.9% walk, 1.5% work from home (2006-2010 5-year est.); Travel time to work: 22.3% less than 15 minutes, 43.9% 15 to 30 minutes, 20.8% 30 to 45 minutes, 7.5% 45 to 60 minutes, 5.6% 60 minutes or more (2006-2010 5-year est.)

Additional Information Contacts
Montgomery County Chamber of Commerce . . . . (610) 265-1776
    http://www.montgomerycountychamber.org
West Norriton Township . . . . (610) 631-0450
    http://www.westnorritontwp.org

WEST POTTSGROVE (township). Covers a land area of 2.324 square miles and a water area of 0.029 square miles. Located at 40.25° N. Lat; 75.68° W. Long. Elevation is 259 feet.

Population: 3,829 (1990); 3,815 (2000); 3,874 (2010); Density: 1,666.7 persons per square mile (2010); Race: 85.8% White, 9.5% Black, 0.6% Asian, 0.3% American Indian/Alaska Native, 0.0% Native Hawaiian/Other Pacific Islander, 3.8% Other, 3.3% Hispanic of any race (2010); Average household size: 2.54 (2010); Median age: 37.3 (2010); Males per 100 females: 94.0 (2010); Marriage status: 37.6% never married, 49.6% now married, 5.0% widowed, 7.8% divorced (2006-2010 5-year est.); Foreign born: 1.4% (2006-2010 5-year est.); Ancestry (includes multiple ancestries): 45.5% German, 13.6% Italian, 12.9% Irish, 10.2% Polish, 6.7% English (2006-2010 5-year est.).

Economy: Single-family building permits issued: 0 (2011); Multi-family building permits issued: 0 (2011); Employment by occupation: 5.1% management, 5.1% professional, 14.1% services, 17.4% sales, 5.9% farming, 13.8% construction, 10.6% production (2006-2010 5-year est.).

Income: Per capita income: $23,477 (2006-2010 5-year est.); Median household income: $52,500 (2006-2010 5-year est.); Average household income: $57,346 (2006-2010 5-year est.); Percent of households with income of $100,000 or more: 11.7% (2006-2010 5-year est.); Poverty rate: 11.1% (2006-2010 5-year est.).

Education: Percent of population age 25 and over with: High school diploma (including GED) or higher: 84.1% (2006-2010 5-year est.);

Bachelor's degree or higher: 11.7% (2006-2010 5-year est.); Master's degree or higher: 2.5% (2006-2010 5-year est.).

Housing: Homeownership rate: 67.0% (2010); Median home value: $159,000 (2006-2010 5-year est.); Median contract rent: $811 per month (2006-2010 5-year est.); Median year structure built: 1956 (2006-2010 5-year est.).

Safety: Violent crime rate: 28.3 per 10,000 population; Property crime rate: 380.9 per 10,000 population (2011).

Transportation: Commute to work: 97.0% car, 0.0% public transportation, 1.9% walk, 0.0% work from home (2006-2010 5-year est.); Travel time to work: 34.4% less than 15 minutes, 18.3% 15 to 30 minutes, 24.9% 30 to 45 minutes, 10.4% 45 to 60 minutes, 12.0% 60 minutes or more (2006-2010 5-year est.)

Additional Information Contacts
TriCounty Area Chamber of Commerce . . . . (610) 326-2900
    http://tricountyareachamber.com

WHITEMARSH (township). Covers a land area of 14.592 square miles and a water area of 0.141 square miles. Located at 40.10° N. Lat; 75.24° W. Long. Elevation is 184 feet.

History: Whitemarsh was originally inhabited by the Lenni Lenape tribe of Native Americans. Whitemarsh Township was incorporated in 1704 as part of Philadelphia County and was one of the 28 original communities that comprised Montgomery County when it was erected in 1784.

Population: 14,863 (1990); 16,702 (2000); 17,349 (2010); Density: 1,189.0 persons per square mile (2010); Race: 90.7% White, 3.5% Black, 4.2% Asian, 0.1% American Indian/Alaska Native, 0.0% Native Hawaiian/Other Pacific Islander, 1.5% Other, 1.7% Hispanic of any race (2010); Average household size: 2.52 (2010); Median age: 42.6 (2010); Males per 100 females: 93.0 (2010); Marriage status: 28.4% never married, 58.5% now married, 5.7% widowed, 7.4% divorced (2006-2010 5-year est.); Foreign born: 6.0% (2006-2010 5-year est.); Ancestry (includes multiple ancestries): 25.6% Irish, 19.3% German, 16.3% Italian, 11.4% Polish, 11.0% English (2006-2010 5-year est.).

Economy: Single-family building permits issued: 2 (2011); Multi-family building permits issued: 0 (2011); Employment by occupation: 19.6% management, 5.9% professional, 5.8% services, 15.3% sales, 2.3% farming, 3.9% construction, 1.7% production (2006-2010 5-year est.).

Income: Per capita income: $51,760 (2006-2010 5-year est.); Median household income: $102,316 (2006-2010 5-year est.); Average household income: $136,639 (2006-2010 5-year est.); Percent of households with income of $100,000 or more: 51.7% (2006-2010 5-year est.); Poverty rate: 6.5% (2006-2010 5-year est.).

Taxes: Total city taxes per capita: $770 (2009); City property taxes per capita: $194 (2009).

Education: Percent of population age 25 and over with: High school diploma (including GED) or higher: 96.4% (2006-2010 5-year est.); Bachelor's degree or higher: 62.0% (2006-2010 5-year est.); Master's degree or higher: 29.8% (2006-2010 5-year est.).

Housing: Homeownership rate: 77.8% (2010); Median home value: $376,900 (2006-2010 5-year est.); Median contract rent: $1,239 per month (2006-2010 5-year est.); Median year structure built: 1967 (2006-2010 5-year est.).

Safety: Violent crime rate: 6.3 per 10,000 population; Property crime rate: 121.2 per 10,000 population (2011).

Transportation: Commute to work: 86.9% car, 4.0% public transportation, 4.2% walk, 4.3% work from home (2006-2010 5-year est.); Travel time to work: 21.8% less than 15 minutes, 33.1% 15 to 30 minutes, 26.3% 30 to 45 minutes, 11.8% 45 to 60 minutes, 7.0% 60 minutes or more (2006-2010 5-year est.)

Additional Information Contacts
Eastern Montgomery County Chamber of Commerce . . . . (215) 887-5122
    http://www.emccc.org
Whitemarsh Township . . . . (610) 825-3535
    http://www.whitemarshtwp.org

WHITPAIN (township). Covers a land area of 12.846 square miles and a water area of 0.006 square miles. Located at 40.16° N. Lat; 75.28° W. Long.

History: Richard Whitpaine, a London butcher, purchased a 4500 acre (18 km²) tract of land as part of William Penn's "Holy Experiment". His 16-year old son, Zechariah, travelled to Pennsylvania on the ship "The Welcome" with Penn in 1682 to settle his father's properties and escape persecution of his Quaker beliefs.

Population: 15,673 (1990); 18,562 (2000); 18,875 (2010); Density: 1,469.4 persons per square mile (2010); Race: 81.9% White, 5.2% Black, 10.9% Asian, 0.1% American Indian/Alaska Native, 0.0% Native Hawaiian/Other Pacific Islander, 1.9% Other, 2.6% Hispanic of any race (2010); Average household size: 2.51 (2010); Median age: 45.0 (2010); Males per 100 females: 91.1 (2010); Marriage status: 21.5% never married, 65.5% now married, 7.9% widowed, 5.1% divorced (2006-2010 5-year est.); Foreign born: 10.7% (2006-2010 5-year est.); Ancestry (includes multiple ancestries): 22.4% Irish, 20.5% German, 15.7% Italian, 10.4% English, 7.2% Polish (2006-2010 5-year est.).
Economy: Single-family building permits issued: 22 (2011); Multi-family building permits issued: 0 (2011); Employment by occupation: 20.2% management, 9.8% professional, 3.8% services, 15.1% sales, 2.8% farming, 3.3% construction, 2.7% production (2006-2010 5-year est.).
Income: Per capita income: $57,557 (2006-2010 5-year est.); Median household income: $108,180 (2006-2010 5-year est.); Average household income: $143,140 (2006-2010 5-year est.); Percent of households with income of $100,000 or more: 53.6% (2006-2010 5-year est.); Poverty rate: 2.2% (2006-2010 5-year est.).
Taxes: Total city taxes per capita: $601 (2009); City property taxes per capita: $239 (2009).
Education: Percent of population age 25 and over with: High school diploma (including GED) or higher: 96.3% (2006-2010 5-year est.); Bachelor's degree or higher: 59.1% (2006-2010 5-year est.); Master's degree or higher: 26.3% (2006-2010 5-year est.).
Housing: Homeownership rate: 77.3% (2010); Median home value: $432,200 (2006-2010 5-year est.); Median contract rent: $1,477 per month (2006-2010 5-year est.); Median year structure built: 1982 (2006-2010 5-year est.).
Safety: Violent crime rate: 9.5 per 10,000 population; Property crime rate: 137.8 per 10,000 population (2011).
Transportation: Commute to work: 89.1% car, 4.5% public transportation, 1.0% walk, 4.9% work from home (2006-2010 5-year est.); Travel time to work: 22.4% less than 15 minutes, 32.2% 15 to 30 minutes, 23.8% 30 to 45 minutes, 12.0% 45 to 60 minutes, 9.6% 60 minutes or more (2006-2010 5-year est.)
Additional Information Contacts
Main Line Chamber of Commerce . . . . (610) 687-6232
   http://www.mlcc.org
Whitpain Township . . . . (610) 277-2400
   http://www.whitpaintownship.org

WILLOW GROVE (CDP).

Covers a land area of 3.659 square miles and a water area of 0.005 square miles. Located at 40.15° N. Lat; 75.12° W. Long. Elevation is 269 feet.
Population: 16,325 (1990); 16,234 (2000); 15,726 (2010); Density: 4,297.3 persons per square mile (2010); Race: 83.3% White, 8.2% Black, 4.9% Asian, 0.2% American Indian/Alaska Native, 0.0% Native Hawaiian/Other Pacific Islander, 3.4% Other, 3.5% Hispanic of any race (2010); Average household size: 2.43 (2010); Median age: 40.1 (2010); Males per 100 females: 93.8 (2010); Marriage status: 28.8% never married, 53.7% now married, 7.6% widowed, 9.9% divorced (2006-2010 5-year est.); Foreign born: 6.3% (2006-2010 5-year est.); Ancestry (includes multiple ancestries): 28.5% Irish, 25.6% German, 17.9% Italian, 11.8% English, 6.1% Polish (2006-2010 5-year est.).
Economy: Employment by occupation: 14.1% management, 4.5% professional, 8.7% services, 20.0% sales, 6.3% farming, 8.2% construction, 4.7% production (2006-2010 5-year est.).
Income: Per capita income: $29,996 (2006-2010 5-year est.); Median household income: $65,884 (2006-2010 5-year est.); Average household income: $71,788 (2006-2010 5-year est.); Percent of households with income of $100,000 or more: 23.0% (2006-2010 5-year est.); Poverty rate: 4.0% (2006-2010 5-year est.).
Education: Percent of population age 25 and over with: High school diploma (including GED) or higher: 93.6% (2006-2010 5-year est.); Bachelor's degree or higher: 34.1% (2006-2010 5-year est.); Master's degree or higher: 10.4% (2006-2010 5-year est.).
School District(s)
Abington SD (KG-12)
   2010-11 Enrollment: 7,465 . . . . (215) 884-4700
Eastern Center for Arts & Technology (10-12)
   2010-11 Enrollment: n/a . . . . (215) 784-4800
Upper Dublin SD (KG-12)
   2010-11 Enrollment: 4,270 . . . . (215) 643-8800

Upper Moreland Township SD (KG-12)
   2010-11 Enrollment: 3,063 . . . . (215) 659-6800
Four-year College(s)
Bethel Seminary of the East (Private, Not-for-profit, Baptist)
   Fall 2010 Enrollment: 41 . . . . (215) 659-1000
Two-year College(s)
Abington Memorial Hospital Dixon School of Nursing (Private, Not-for-profit)
   Fall 2010 Enrollment: 304 . . . . (215) 481-5500
Vocational/Technical School(s)
Eastern Center for Arts and Technology (Public)
   Fall 2010 Enrollment: 123 . . . . (215) 784-4800
   2011-12 Tuition: $12,000
Housing: Homeownership rate: 65.3% (2010); Median home value: $254,600 (2006-2010 5-year est.); Median contract rent: $917 per month (2006-2010 5-year est.); Median year structure built: 1957 (2006-2010 5-year est.).
Transportation: Commute to work: 88.0% car, 4.3% public transportation, 3.8% walk, 3.3% work from home (2006-2010 5-year est.); Travel time to work: 30.8% less than 15 minutes, 33.4% 15 to 30 minutes, 18.3% 30 to 45 minutes, 9.4% 45 to 60 minutes, 8.2% 60 minutes or more (2006-2010 5-year est.)
Airports: Willow Grove NAS Jrb (general aviation)
Additional Information Contacts
Eastern Montgomery County Chamber of Commerce . . . . (215) 887-5122
   http://www.emccc.org

WORCESTER (township).

Aka Center Point. Covers a land area of 16.220 square miles and a water area of 0.008 square miles. Located at 40.19° N. Lat; 75.35° W. Long. Elevation is 233 feet.
History: Shortly after the Civil War in 1865, the town now known as Woodway was founded by a war veteran by the name of Burl Kendrick who purchased 320 acres on the eastern side of present day Woodway.
Population: 4,686 (1990); 7,789 (2000); 9,750 (2010); Density: 601.1 persons per square mile (2010); Race: 85.3% White, 2.8% Black, 10.3% Asian, 0.0% American Indian/Alaska Native, 0.0% Native Hawaiian/Other Pacific Islander, 1.6% Other, 1.6% Hispanic of any race (2010); Average household size: 2.71 (2010); Median age: 44.0 (2010); Males per 100 females: 92.5 (2010); Marriage status: 19.2% never married, 67.5% now married, 5.7% widowed, 7.6% divorced (2006-2010 5-year est.); Foreign born: 8.8% (2006-2010 5-year est.); Ancestry (includes multiple ancestries): 25.9% Irish, 24.0% German, 22.1% Italian, 10.5% English, 8.5% Polish (2006-2010 5-year est.).
Economy: Single-family building permits issued: 36 (2011); Multi-family building permits issued: 9 (2011); Employment by occupation: 22.6% management, 7.2% professional, 6.3% services, 15.0% sales, 1.8% farming, 9.4% construction, 5.1% production (2006-2010 5-year est.).
Income: Per capita income: $55,180 (2006-2010 5-year est.); Median household income: $105,930 (2006-2010 5-year est.); Average household income: $142,138 (2006-2010 5-year est.); Percent of households with income of $100,000 or more: 51.7% (2006-2010 5-year est.); Poverty rate: 1.7% (2006-2010 5-year est.).
Education: Percent of population age 25 and over with: High school diploma (including GED) or higher: 95.9% (2006-2010 5-year est.); Bachelor's degree or higher: 53.3% (2006-2010 5-year est.); Master's degree or higher: 20.2% (2006-2010 5-year est.).
Housing: Homeownership rate: 85.0% (2010); Median home value: $435,100 (2006-2010 5-year est.); Median contract rent: $1,204 per month (2006-2010 5-year est.); Median year structure built: 1990 (2006-2010 5-year est.).
Transportation: Commute to work: 89.5% car, 0.9% public transportation, 0.4% walk, 8.6% work from home (2006-2010 5-year est.); Travel time to work: 20.5% less than 15 minutes, 37.5% 15 to 30 minutes, 24.0% 30 to 45 minutes, 6.9% 45 to 60 minutes, 11.1% 60 minutes or more (2006-2010 5-year est.)
Additional Information Contacts
Montgomery County Chamber of Commerce . . . . (610) 265-1776
   http://www.montgomerycountychamber.org
Worcester Township . . . . (610) 584-1410
   http://www.worcestertwp.com

WOXHALL (CDP). Covers a land area of 2.448 square miles and a water area of 0.015 square miles. Located at 40.31° N. Lat; 75.45° W. Long. Elevation is 410 feet.
Population: n/a (1990); n/a (2000); 1,318 (2010); Density: 538.3 persons per square mile (2010); Race: 95.9% White, 1.3% Black, 0.8% Asian, 0.0% American Indian/Alaska Native, 0.0% Native Hawaiian/Other Pacific Islander, 2.0% Other, 2.0% Hispanic of any race (2010); Average household size: 2.97 (2010); Median age: 41.2 (2010); Males per 100 females: 99.4 (2010); Marriage status: 26.5% never married, 67.2% now married, 1.2% widowed, 5.1% divorced (2006-2010 5-year est.); Foreign born: 0.0% (2006-2010 5-year est.); Ancestry (includes multiple ancestries): 60.6% German, 13.7% English, 11.0% Irish, 8.8% Polish, 3.7% French (2006-2010 5-year est.).
Economy: Employment by occupation: 15.1% management, 5.2% professional, 3.8% services, 21.4% sales, 2.1% farming, 13.2% construction, 11.3% production (2006-2010 5-year est.).
Income: Per capita income: $34,009 (2006-2010 5-year est.); Median household income: $91,136 (2006-2010 5-year est.); Average household income: $106,961 (2006-2010 5-year est.); Percent of households with income of $100,000 or more: 43.0% (2006-2010 5-year est.); Poverty rate: 0.4% (2006-2010 5-year est.).
Education: Percent of population age 25 and over with: High school diploma (including GED) or higher: 96.1% (2006-2010 5-year est.); Bachelor's degree or higher: 36.3% (2006-2010 5-year est.); Master's degree or higher: 8.1% (2006-2010 5-year est.).
Housing: Homeownership rate: 89.8% (2010); Median home value: $365,300 (2006-2010 5-year est.); Median contract rent: $975 per month (2006-2010 5-year est.); Median year structure built: 1978 (2006-2010 5-year est.).
Transportation: Commute to work: 92.5% car, 0.9% public transportation, 0.0% walk, 6.6% work from home (2006-2010 5-year est.); Travel time to work: 9.9% less than 15 minutes, 38.8% 15 to 30 minutes, 27.7% 30 to 45 minutes, 7.6% 45 to 60 minutes, 16.0% 60 minutes or more (2006-2010 5-year est.)

WYNCOTE (CDP). Covers a land area of 0.820 square miles and a water area of 0 square miles. Located at 40.09° N. Lat; 75.15° W. Long. Elevation is 285 feet.
Population: 2,960 (1990); 3,046 (2000); 3,044 (2010); Density: 3,711.8 persons per square mile (2010); Race: 79.7% White, 13.6% Black, 3.9% Asian, 0.3% American Indian/Alaska Native, 0.1% Native Hawaiian/Other Pacific Islander, 2.4% Other, 2.8% Hispanic of any race (2010); Average household size: 2.34 (2010); Median age: 52.2 (2010); Males per 100 females: 74.9 (2010); Marriage status: 16.0% never married, 56.6% now married, 17.6% widowed, 9.8% divorced (2006-2010 5-year est.); Foreign born: 5.6% (2006-2010 5-year est.); Ancestry (includes multiple ancestries): 21.6% German, 16.3% Irish, 14.7% English, 14.3% Russian, 9.4% Polish (2006-2010 5-year est.).
Economy: Employment by occupation: 15.6% management, 10.1% professional, 4.4% services, 16.8% sales, 1.2% farming, 2.7% construction, 1.0% production (2006-2010 5-year est.).
Income: Per capita income: $47,869 (2006-2010 5-year est.); Median household income: $104,611 (2006-2010 5-year est.); Average household income: $125,640 (2006-2010 5-year est.); Percent of households with income of $100,000 or more: 55.2% (2006-2010 5-year est.); Poverty rate: 8.2% (2006-2010 5-year est.).
Education: Percent of population age 25 and over with: High school diploma (including GED) or higher: 92.2% (2006-2010 5-year est.); Bachelor's degree or higher: 56.4% (2006-2010 5-year est.); Master's degree or higher: 29.6% (2006-2010 5-year est.).
School District(s)
Cheltenham Township SD (KG-12)
    2010-11 Enrollment: 4,445 . . . . (215) 886-9500
Four-year College(s)
Reconstructionist Rabbinical College (Private, Not-for-profit, Jewish)
    Fall 2010 Enrollment: 41 . . . . (215) 576-0800
Housing: Homeownership rate: 62.0% (2010); Median home value: $375,200 (2006-2010 5-year est.); Median contract rent: $1,226 per month (2006-2010 5-year est.); Median year structure built: before 1940 (2006-2010 5-year est.).
Transportation: Commute to work: 73.1% car, 10.9% public transportation, 0.0% walk, 12.2% work from home (2006-2010 5-year est.); Travel time to work: 12.9% less than 15 minutes, 35.4% 15 to 30 minutes, 37.7% 30 to 45 minutes, 8.5% 45 to 60 minutes, 5.6% 60 minutes or more (2006-2010 5-year est.)

Additional Information Contacts
Eastern Montgomery County Chamber of Commerce . . . . (215) 887-5122
    http://www.emccc.org

WYNDMOOR (CDP). Covers a land area of 1.645 square miles and a water area of 0 square miles. Located at 40.09° N. Lat; 75.19° W. Long. Elevation is 420 feet.
History: Wyndmoor, originally called "Tedyuscung", is the subject of many Native American legends. It is believed the original Native American name did not translate to the English language and it was renamed "Windmoor", referencing the winds blowing through the valleys and over the rolling hills.
Population: 5,682 (1990); 5,601 (2000); 5,498 (2010); Density: 3,341.5 persons per square mile (2010); Race: 75.1% White, 18.8% Black, 3.3% Asian, 0.2% American Indian/Alaska Native, 0.0% Native Hawaiian/Other Pacific Islander, 2.6% Other, 2.5% Hispanic of any race (2010); Average household size: 2.43 (2010); Median age: 48.5 (2010); Males per 100 females: 83.9 (2010); Marriage status: 23.2% never married, 55.5% now married, 13.8% widowed, 7.4% divorced (2006-2010 5-year est.); Foreign born: 5.5% (2006-2010 5-year est.); Ancestry (includes multiple ancestries): 18.9% German, 18.6% Irish, 13.8% Italian, 10.9% English, 5.0% Polish (2006-2010 5-year est.).
Economy: Employment by occupation: 15.8% management, 5.9% professional, 5.9% services, 11.5% sales, 2.8% farming, 6.8% construction, 3.3% production (2006-2010 5-year est.).
Income: Per capita income: $43,879 (2006-2010 5-year est.); Median household income: $100,553 (2006-2010 5-year est.); Average household income: $126,491 (2006-2010 5-year est.); Percent of households with income of $100,000 or more: 50.7% (2006-2010 5-year est.); Poverty rate: 4.7% (2006-2010 5-year est.).
Education: Percent of population age 25 and over with: High school diploma (including GED) or higher: 91.9% (2006-2010 5-year est.); Bachelor's degree or higher: 50.6% (2006-2010 5-year est.); Master's degree or higher: 27.6% (2006-2010 5-year est.).
Housing: Homeownership rate: 85.7% (2010); Median home value: $328,800 (2006-2010 5-year est.); Median contract rent: $1,394 per month (2006-2010 5-year est.); Median year structure built: 1953 (2006-2010 5-year est.).
Hospitals: Chestnut Hill Rehabilitation Hospital (99 beds)
Transportation: Commute to work: 75.2% car, 10.5% public transportation, 3.4% walk, 9.4% work from home (2006-2010 5-year est.); Travel time to work: 22.2% less than 15 minutes, 28.6% 15 to 30 minutes, 32.6% 30 to 45 minutes, 10.6% 45 to 60 minutes, 6.1% 60 minutes or more (2006-2010 5-year est.)
Additional Information Contacts
Montgomery County Chamber of Commerce . . . . (610) 265-1776
    http://www.montgomerycountychamber.org

WYNNEWOOD (unincorporated postal area)
Zip Code: 19096
    Covers a land area of 3.503 square miles and a water area of 0 square miles. Located at 39.99° N. Lat; 75.27° W. Long. Elevation is 295 feet. Population: 13,572 (2010); Density: 3,873.4 persons per square mile (2010); Race: 84.9% White, 4.4% Black, 8.6% Asian, 0.0% American Indian/Alaska Native, 0.0% Native Hawaiian/Other Pacific Islander, 2.1% Other, 2.6% Hispanic of any race (2010); Average household size: 2.44 (2010); Median age: 45.5 (2010); Males per 100 females: 87.3 (2010); Homeownership rate: 80.6% (2010)

ZIEGLERVILLE (unincorporated postal area)
Zip Code: 19492
    Covers a land area of 1.174 square miles and a water area of 0 square miles. Located at 40.28° N. Lat; 75.49° W. Long. Population: 717 (2010); Density: 610.7 persons per square mile (2010); Race: 95.4% White, 0.8% Black, 0.8% Asian, 0.0% American Indian/Alaska Native, 0.0% Native Hawaiian/Other Pacific Islander, 3.0% Other, 3.8% Hispanic of any race (2010); Average household size: 1.95 (2010); Median age: 56.6 (2010); Males per 100 females: 73.2 (2010); Homeownership rate: 38.4% (2010)

Montour County

Located in central Pennsylvania; drained by the Susquehanna River. Covers a land area of 130.242 square miles, a water area of 2.088 square miles, and is located in the Eastern Time Zone at 41.03° N. Lat., 76.67° W. Long. The county was founded in 1850. County seat is Danville.

Montour County is part of the Bloomsburg-Berwick, PA Micropolitan Statistical Area. The entire metro area includes: Columbia County, PA; Montour County, PA

Population: 17,735 (1990); 18,236 (2000); 18,267 (2010); Race: 95.3% White, 1.4% Black, 1.8% Asian, 0.1% American Indian/Alaska Native, 0.0% Native Hawaiian/Other Pacific Islander, 1.4% Other, 1.8% Hispanic of any race (2010); Density: 140.3 persons per square mile (2010); Average household size: 2.36 (2010); Median age: 43.9 (2010); Males per 100 females: 92.6 (2010).
Religion: Six largest groups: 16.1% Catholicism, 10.0% Lutheran, 7.4% Presbyterian-Reformed, 4.4% Methodist/Pietist, 2.4% European Free-Church, 1.1% Baptist (2010)
Economy: Unemployment rate: 6.5% (August 2012); Total civilian labor force: 9,429 (August 2012); Leading industries: 52.9% health care and social assistance; 5.7% retail trade; 5.4% accommodation & food services (2010); Farms: 583 totaling 50,252 acres (2007); Companies that employ 500 or more persons: 4 (2010); Companies that employ 100 to 499 persons: 13 (2010); Companies that employ less than 100 persons: 399 (2010); Black-owned businesses: n/a (2007); Hispanic-owned businesses: n/a (2007); Asian-owned businesses: n/a (2007); Women-owned businesses: n/a (2007); Retail sales per capita: $14,861 (2010). Single-family building permits issued: 24 (2011); Multi-family building permits issued: 0 (2011).
Income: Per capita income: $26,124 (2006-2010 5-year est.); Median household income: $45,255 (2006-2010 5-year est.); Average household income: $63,309 (2006-2010 5-year est.); Percent of households with income of $100,000 or more: 15.1% (2006-2010 5-year est.); Poverty rate: 11.0% (2006-2010 5-year est.); Bankruptcy rate: 1.09% (2011).
Education: Percent of population age 25 and over with: High school diploma (including GED) or higher: 87.5% (2006-2010 5-year est.); Bachelor's degree or higher: 25.0% (2006-2010 5-year est.); Master's degree or higher: 11.5% (2006-2010 5-year est.).
Housing: Homeownership rate: 71.9% (2010); Median home value: $143,900 (2006-2010 5-year est.); Median contract rent: $500 per month (2006-2010 5-year est.); Median year structure built: 1970 (2006-2010 5-year est.)
Health: Birth rate: 114.8 per 10,000 population (2011); Death rate: 123.5 per 10,000 population (2011); Age-adjusted cancer mortality rate: 169.9 deaths per 100,000 population (2009); Number of physicians: 372.8 per 10,000 population (2010); Hospital beds: 359.8 per 10,000 population (2008); Hospital admissions: 13,643.1 per 10,000 population (2008).
Elections: 2012 Presidential election results: 38.9% Obama, 59.5% Romney
Additional Information Contacts
Montour County Government . . . . (570) 271-3000
  http://www.montourco.org

Montour County Communities

ANTHONY (township). Covers a land area of 25.904 square miles and a water area of 0.344 square miles. Located at 41.13° N. Lat; 76.69° W. Long.
Population: 1,287 (1990); 1,388 (2000); 1,501 (2010); Density: 57.9 persons per square mile (2010); Race: 98.9% White, 0.4% Black, 0.0% Asian, 0.1% American Indian/Alaska Native, 0.0% Native Hawaiian/Other Pacific Islander, 0.6% Other, 0.1% Hispanic of any race (2010); Average household size: 2.84 (2010); Median age: 41.0 (2010); Males per 100 females: 102.0 (2010); Marriage status: 16.9% never married, 73.3% now married, 3.2% widowed, 6.6% divorced (2006-2010 5-year est.); Foreign born: 0.3% (2006-2010 5-year est.); Ancestry (includes multiple ancestries): 38.8% German, 15.2% Pennsylvania German, 8.0% American, 7.4% English, 7.2% Irish (2006-2010 5-year est.).
Economy: Employment by occupation: 6.6% management, 1.9% professional, 9.9% services, 15.4% sales, 0.9% farming, 17.1% construction, 9.4% production (2006-2010 5-year est.).
Income: Per capita income: $20,672 (2006-2010 5-year est.); Median household income: $47,578 (2006-2010 5-year est.); Average household income: $55,849 (2006-2010 5-year est.); Percent of households with income of $100,000 or more: 11.9% (2006-2010 5-year est.); Poverty rate: 16.8% (2006-2010 5-year est.).
Education: Percent of population age 25 and over with: High school diploma (including GED) or higher: 77.6% (2006-2010 5-year est.); Bachelor's degree or higher: 8.4% (2006-2010 5-year est.); Master's degree or higher: 2.9% (2006-2010 5-year est.).

Housing: Homeownership rate: 90.2% (2010); Median home value: $139,300 (2006-2010 5-year est.); Median contract rent: $583 per month (2006-2010 5-year est.); Median year structure built: 1973 (2006-2010 5-year est.).
Transportation: Commute to work: 90.7% car, 0.0% public transportation, 1.2% walk, 4.2% work from home (2006-2010 5-year est.); Travel time to work: 19.7% less than 15 minutes, 51.7% 15 to 30 minutes, 15.7% 30 to 45 minutes, 4.3% 45 to 60 minutes, 8.7% 60 minutes or more (2006-2010 5-year est.)
Additional Information Contacts
Greater Philadelphia Chamber of Commerce . . . . (215) 545-1234
  http://www.greaterphilachamber.com

COOPER (township). Covers a land area of 6.874 square miles and a water area of 0.329 square miles. Located at 40.96° N. Lat; 76.54° W. Long.
Population: 934 (1990); 966 (2000); 932 (2010); Density: 135.6 persons per square mile (2010); Race: 98.9% White, 0.0% Black, 0.4% Asian, 0.2% American Indian/Alaska Native, 0.0% Native Hawaiian/Other Pacific Islander, 0.5% Other, 0.6% Hispanic of any race (2010); Average household size: 2.25 (2010); Median age: 50.2 (2010); Males per 100 females: 97.5 (2010); Marriage status: 21.8% never married, 57.4% now married, 8.2% widowed, 12.6% divorced (2006-2010 5-year est.); Foreign born: 1.5% (2006-2010 5-year est.); Ancestry (includes multiple ancestries): 51.7% German, 11.6% Irish, 9.6% English, 6.9% American, 6.7% Dutch (2006-2010 5-year est.).
Economy: Employment by occupation: 6.7% management, 3.4% professional, 13.3% services, 17.7% sales, 1.8% farming, 8.9% construction, 6.0% production (2006-2010 5-year est.).
Income: Per capita income: $27,235 (2006-2010 5-year est.); Median household income: $48,125 (2006-2010 5-year est.); Average household income: $58,076 (2006-2010 5-year est.); Percent of households with income of $100,000 or more: 13.6% (2006-2010 5-year est.); Poverty rate: 7.7% (2006-2010 5-year est.).
Education: Percent of population age 25 and over with: High school diploma (including GED) or higher: 88.7% (2006-2010 5-year est.); Bachelor's degree or higher: 20.1% (2006-2010 5-year est.); Master's degree or higher: 7.5% (2006-2010 5-year est.).
Housing: Homeownership rate: 88.2% (2010); Median home value: $105,100 (2006-2010 5-year est.); Median contract rent: $342 per month (2006-2010 5-year est.); Median year structure built: 1979 (2006-2010 5-year est.)
Transportation: Commute to work: 96.7% car, 0.0% public transportation, 1.6% walk, 1.6% work from home (2006-2010 5-year est.); Travel time to work: 51.5% less than 15 minutes, 27.8% 15 to 30 minutes, 13.4% 30 to 45 minutes, 2.7% 45 to 60 minutes, 4.6% 60 minutes or more (2006-2010 5-year est.)

DANVILLE (borough). County seat. Covers a land area of 1.555 square miles and a water area of 0.018 square miles. Located at 40.96° N. Lat; 76.61° W. Long. Elevation is 486 feet.
History: Laid out 1790, incorporated 1849.
Population: 5,165 (1990); 4,897 (2000); 4,699 (2010); Density: 3,020.9 persons per square mile (2010); Race: 93.8% White, 1.1% Black, 2.3% Asian, 0.2% American Indian/Alaska Native, 0.0% Native Hawaiian/Other Pacific Islander, 2.6% Other, 3.7% Hispanic of any race (2010); Average household size: 2.07 (2010); Median age: 37.2 (2010); Males per 100 females: 85.8 (2010); Marriage status: 33.7% never married, 43.9% now married, 10.6% widowed, 11.8% divorced (2006-2010 5-year est.); Foreign born: 8.3% (2006-2010 5-year est.); Ancestry (includes multiple ancestries): 32.7% German, 14.5% Irish, 10.9% American, 8.7% English, 5.9% Dutch (2006-2010 5-year est.).
Economy: Single-family building permits issued: 0 (2011); Multi-family building permits issued: 0 (2011); Employment by occupation: 5.5% management, 1.5% professional, 20.5% services, 6.1% sales, 4.4% farming, 5.0% construction, 5.5% production (2006-2010 5-year est.).
Income: Per capita income: $20,207 (2006-2010 5-year est.); Median household income: $34,250 (2006-2010 5-year est.); Average household income: $43,134 (2006-2010 5-year est.); Percent of households with income of $100,000 or more: 6.6% (2006-2010 5-year est.); Poverty rate: 17.1% (2006-2010 5-year est.).
Education: Percent of population age 25 and over with: High school diploma (including GED) or higher: 85.9% (2006-2010 5-year est.); Bachelor's degree or higher: 21.6% (2006-2010 5-year est.); Master's degree or higher: 9.0% (2006-2010 5-year est.).

School District(s)

Danville Area SD (PK-12)
2010-11 Enrollment: 2,431 .... (570) 271-3268
Danville Area SD (PK-12)
2010-11 Enrollment: 2,431 .... (570) 271-3268
Danville Ctr Adolescent Female (09-12)
2010-11 Enrollment: 29 .... (570) 271-4751
North Central Secure Treatment Unit (09-12)
2010-11 Enrollment: 77 .... (570) 271-4710

Housing: Homeownership rate: 47.8% (2010); Median home value: $93,800 (2006-2010 5-year est.); Median contract rent: $493 per month (2006-2010 5-year est.); Median year structure built: before 1940 (2006-2010 5-year est.).

Hospitals: Geisinger Medical Center (403 beds)

Safety: Violent crime rate: 38.2 per 10,000 population; Property crime rate: 263.0 per 10,000 population (2011).

Newspapers: The Danville News (Local news; Circulation 4,300)

Transportation: Commute to work: 87.5% car, 0.0% public transportation, 11.3% walk, 0.6% work from home (2006-2010 5-year est.); Travel time to work: 57.7% less than 15 minutes, 22.7% 15 to 30 minutes, 12.9% 30 to 45 minutes, 1.9% 45 to 60 minutes, 4.8% 60 minutes or more (2006-2010 5-year est.)

Additional Information Contacts

Borough of Danville .... (570) 275-3091
http://www.danvilleboro.org
Columbia Montour Chamber of Commerce .... (570) 784-2522
http://www.bloomsburg.org

DERRY (township). Covers a land area of 16.064 square miles and a water area of 0.301 square miles. Located at 41.05° N. Lat; 76.64° W. Long.

Population: 1,264 (1990); 1,215 (2000); 1,130 (2010); Density: 70.3 persons per square mile (2010); Race: 97.7% White, 0.4% Black, 0.3% Asian, 0.2% American Indian/Alaska Native, 0.0% Native Hawaiian/Other Pacific Islander, 1.4% Other, 0.4% Hispanic of any race (2010); Average household size: 2.55 (2010); Median age: 41.8 (2010); Males per 100 females: 97.2 (2010); Marriage status: 20.4% never married, 66.9% now married, 4.1% widowed, 8.6% divorced (2006-2010 5-year est.); Foreign born: 1.2% (2006-2010 5-year est.); Ancestry (includes multiple ancestries): 36.0% German, 13.7% English, 6.7% Irish, 5.6% Dutch, 5.1% American (2006-2010 5-year est.).

Economy: Single-family building permits issued: 6 (2011); Multi-family building permits issued: 0 (2011); Employment by occupation: 10.3% management, 3.2% professional, 12.9% services, 17.1% sales, 4.8% farming, 10.3% construction, 6.7% production (2006-2010 5-year est.).

Income: Per capita income: $22,438 (2006-2010 5-year est.); Median household income: $39,125 (2006-2010 5-year est.); Average household income: $55,171 (2006-2010 5-year est.); Percent of households with income of $100,000 or more: 9.1% (2006-2010 5-year est.); Poverty rate: 18.1% (2006-2010 5-year est.).

Education: Percent of population age 25 and over with: High school diploma (including GED) or higher: 78.8% (2006-2010 5-year est.); Bachelor's degree or higher: 7.8% (2006-2010 5-year est.); Master's degree or higher: 2.2% (2006-2010 5-year est.).

Housing: Homeownership rate: 85.7% (2010); Median home value: $109,100 (2006-2010 5-year est.); Median contract rent: $433 per month (2006-2010 5-year est.); Median year structure built: 1978 (2006-2010 5-year est.).

Transportation: Commute to work: 86.7% car, 0.0% public transportation, 3.2% walk, 6.3% work from home (2006-2010 5-year est.); Travel time to work: 44.6% less than 15 minutes, 38.9% 15 to 30 minutes, 14.9% 30 to 45 minutes, 0.7% 45 to 60 minutes, 1.0% 60 minutes or more (2006-2010 5-year est.)

Additional Information Contacts

Columbia Montour Chamber of Commerce .... (570) 784-2522
http://www.bloomsburg.org

LIBERTY (township). Covers a land area of 27.311 square miles and a water area of 0.136 square miles. Located at 40.99° N. Lat; 76.72° W. Long.

Population: 1,376 (1990); 1,476 (2000); 1,584 (2010); Density: 58.0 persons per square mile (2010); Race: 98.0% White, 0.5% Black, 0.6% Asian, 0.0% American Indian/Alaska Native, 0.0% Native Hawaiian/Other Pacific Islander, 0.9% Other, 0.1% Hispanic of any race (2010); Average household size: 2.58 (2010); Median age: 45.1 (2010); Males per 100

females: 105.4 (2010); Marriage status: 16.0% never married, 75.3% now married, 4.0% widowed, 4.7% divorced (2006-2010 5-year est.); Foreign born: 0.9% (2006-2010 5-year est.); Ancestry (includes multiple ancestries): 39.4% German, 8.9% Irish, 8.5% American, 8.3% English, 5.8% Pennsylvania German (2006-2010 5-year est.).

Economy: Employment by occupation: 9.2% management, 2.1% professional, 11.7% services, 12.5% sales, 2.9% farming, 17.9% construction, 12.7% production (2006-2010 5-year est.).

Income: Per capita income: $29,013 (2006-2010 5-year est.); Median household income: $61,111 (2006-2010 5-year est.); Average household income: $70,210 (2006-2010 5-year est.); Percent of households with income of $100,000 or more: 21.8% (2006-2010 5-year est.); Poverty rate: 3.7% (2006-2010 5-year est.).

Education: Percent of population age 25 and over with: High school diploma (including GED) or higher: 91.8% (2006-2010 5-year est.); Bachelor's degree or higher: 18.1% (2006-2010 5-year est.); Master's degree or higher: 8.2% (2006-2010 5-year est.).

Housing: Homeownership rate: 87.3% (2010); Median home value: $171,500 (2006-2010 5-year est.); Median contract rent: $420 per month (2006-2010 5-year est.); Median year structure built: 1975 (2006-2010 5-year est.).

Transportation: Commute to work: 93.7% car, 0.0% public transportation, 0.4% walk, 5.9% work from home (2006-2010 5-year est.); Travel time to work: 27.3% less than 15 minutes, 48.5% 15 to 30 minutes, 16.6% 30 to 45 minutes, 6.1% 45 to 60 minutes, 1.4% 60 minutes or more (2006-2010 5-year est.)

Additional Information Contacts

Columbia Montour Chamber of Commerce .... (570) 784-2522
http://www.bloomsburg.org

LIMESTONE (township). Covers a land area of 13.349 square miles and a water area of 0.033 square miles. Located at 41.06° N. Lat; 76.73° W. Long.

Population: 787 (1990); 1,004 (2000); 1,066 (2010); Density: 79.9 persons per square mile (2010); Race: 98.8% White, 0.0% Black, 0.4% Asian, 0.0% American Indian/Alaska Native, 0.0% Native Hawaiian/Other Pacific Islander, 0.8% Other, 0.1% Hispanic of any race (2010); Average household size: 2.90 (2010); Median age: 40.1 (2010); Males per 100 females: 109.0 (2010); Marriage status: 21.6% never married, 71.1% now married, 3.6% widowed, 3.7% divorced (2006-2010 5-year est.); Foreign born: 0.7% (2006-2010 5-year est.); Ancestry (includes multiple ancestries): 36.2% German, 6.9% Italian, 6.6% Irish, 5.8% American, 5.6% European (2006-2010 5-year est.).

Economy: Single-family building permits issued: 0 (2011); Multi-family building permits issued: 0 (2011); Employment by occupation: 7.3% management, 2.0% professional, 7.3% services, 11.5% sales, 3.8% farming, 18.3% construction, 4.3% production (2006-2010 5-year est.).

Income: Per capita income: $19,802 (2006-2010 5-year est.); Median household income: $51,618 (2006-2010 5-year est.); Average household income: $64,488 (2006-2010 5-year est.); Percent of households with income of $100,000 or more: 20.1% (2006-2010 5-year est.); Poverty rate: 8.2% (2006-2010 5-year est.).

Education: Percent of population age 25 and over with: High school diploma (including GED) or higher: 82.3% (2006-2010 5-year est.); Bachelor's degree or higher: 13.1% (2006-2010 5-year est.); Master's degree or higher: 5.9% (2006-2010 5-year est.).

Housing: Homeownership rate: 90.0% (2010); Median home value: $163,900 (2006-2010 5-year est.); Median contract rent: $425 per month (2006-2010 5-year est.); Median year structure built: 1976 (2006-2010 5-year est.).

Transportation: Commute to work: 90.0% car, 0.0% public transportation, 3.0% walk, 6.3% work from home (2006-2010 5-year est.); Travel time to work: 19.5% less than 15 minutes, 50.8% 15 to 30 minutes, 21.9% 30 to 45 minutes, 2.9% 45 to 60 minutes, 4.8% 60 minutes or more (2006-2010 5-year est.)

Additional Information Contacts

Columbia Montour Chamber of Commerce .... (570) 784-2522
http://www.bloomsburg.org

MAHONING (township). Covers a land area of 8.202 square miles and a water area of 0.672 square miles. Located at 40.96° N. Lat; 76.60° W. Long.

Population: 4,067 (1990); 4,263 (2000); 4,171 (2010); Density: 508.5 persons per square mile (2010); Race: 91.3% White, 3.5% Black, 4.0% Asian, 0.0% American Indian/Alaska Native, 0.0% Native Hawaiian/Other

Pacific Islander, 1.2% Other, 2.4% Hispanic of any race (2010); Average household size: 2.20 (2010); Median age: 50.2 (2010); Males per 100 females: 80.4 (2010); Marriage status: 25.2% never married, 49.6% now married, 13.5% widowed, 11.7% divorced (2006-2010 5-year est.); Foreign born: 6.2% (2006-2010 5-year est.); Ancestry (includes multiple ancestries): 29.9% German, 16.0% English, 13.3% Irish, 8.1% Italian, 3.7% Polish (2006-2010 5-year est.).

Economy: Single-family building permits issued: 8 (2011); Multi-family building permits issued: 0 (2011); Employment by occupation: 10.9% management, 4.1% professional, 9.5% services, 15.6% sales, 2.4% farming, 3.6% construction, 3.2% production (2006-2010 5-year est.).

Income: Per capita income: $34,139 (2006-2010 5-year est.); Median household income: $51,550 (2006-2010 5-year est.); Average household income: $82,957 (2006-2010 5-year est.); Percent of households with income of $100,000 or more: 20.4% (2006-2010 5-year est.); Poverty rate: 8.4% (2006-2010 5-year est.).

Education: Percent of population age 25 and over with: High school diploma (including GED) or higher: 93.1% (2006-2010 5-year est.); Bachelor's degree or higher: 44.5% (2006-2010 5-year est.); Master's degree or higher: 23.5% (2006-2010 5-year est.).

Housing: Homeownership rate: 70.7% (2010); Median home value: $172,200 (2006-2010 5-year est.); Median contract rent: $563 per month (2006-2010 5-year est.); Median year structure built: 1976 (2006-2010 5-year est.).

Safety: Violent crime rate: 21.5 per 10,000 population; Property crime rate: 52.6 per 10,000 population (2011).

Transportation: Commute to work: 90.0% car, 0.0% public transportation, 6.5% walk, 2.7% work from home (2006-2010 5-year est.); Travel time to work: 63.0% less than 15 minutes, 22.8% 15 to 30 minutes, 9.2% 30 to 45 minutes, 1.6% 45 to 60 minutes, 3.4% 60 minutes or more (2006-2010 5-year est.)

Additional Information Contacts
Columbia Montour Chamber of Commerce. . . . . (570) 784-2522
http://www.bloomsburg.org

MAYBERRY (township). Covers a land area of 7.038 square miles and a water area of 0.208 square miles. Located at 40.92° N. Lat; 76.54° W. Long.

Population: 207 (1990); 244 (2000); 250 (2010); Density: 35.5 persons per square mile (2010); Race: 93.2% White, 3.6% Black, 0.0% Asian, 0.0% American Indian/Alaska Native, 0.0% Native Hawaiian/Other Pacific Islander, 3.2% Other, 2.4% Hispanic of any race (2010); Average household size: 2.36 (2010); Median age: 46.3 (2010); Males per 100 females: 106.6 (2010); Marriage status: 18.1% never married, 67.5% now married, 8.2% widowed, 6.2% divorced (2006-2010 5-year est.); Foreign born: 4.9% (2006-2010 5-year est.); Ancestry (includes multiple ancestries): 26.6% German, 14.8% English, 13.5% Polish, 7.9% Irish, 7.2% American (2006-2010 5-year est.).

Economy: Employment by occupation: 10.5% management, 0.0% professional, 8.1% services, 9.3% sales, 2.3% farming, 12.8% construction, 0.0% production (2006-2010 5-year est.).

Income: Per capita income: $20,801 (2006-2010 5-year est.); Median household income: $55,938 (2006-2010 5-year est.); Average household income: $62,979 (2006-2010 5-year est.); Percent of households with income of $100,000 or more: 19.8% (2006-2010 5-year est.); Poverty rate: 3.9% (2006-2010 5-year est.).

Education: Percent of population age 25 and over with: High school diploma (including GED) or higher: 75.9% (2006-2010 5-year est.); Bachelor's degree or higher: 12.0% (2006-2010 5-year est.); Master's degree or higher: 5.1% (2006-2010 5-year est.).

Housing: Homeownership rate: 85.8% (2010); Median home value: $189,600 (2006-2010 5-year est.); Median contract rent: $663 per month (2006-2010 5-year est.); Median year structure built: 1971 (2006-2010 5-year est.).

Transportation: Commute to work: 90.5% car, 0.0% public transportation, 0.0% walk, 9.5% work from home (2006-2010 5-year est.); Travel time to work: 26.3% less than 15 minutes, 39.5% 15 to 30 minutes, 11.8% 30 to 45 minutes, 0.0% 45 to 60 minutes, 22.4% 60 minutes or more (2006-2010 5-year est.)

VALLEY (township). Covers a land area of 16.191 square miles and a water area of 0.036 square miles. Located at 41.01° N. Lat; 76.63° W. Long.

Population: 2,010 (1990); 2,093 (2000); 2,158 (2010); Density: 133.3 persons per square mile (2010); Race: 96.5% White, 1.3% Black, 1.3%

Asian, 0.0% American Indian/Alaska Native, 0.0% Native Hawaiian/Other Pacific Islander, 0.9% Other, 1.2% Hispanic of any race (2010); Average household size: 2.57 (2010); Median age: 45.7 (2010); Males per 100 females: 101.3 (2010); Marriage status: 15.6% never married, 72.8% now married, 5.1% widowed, 6.5% divorced (2006-2010 5-year est.); Foreign born: 1.6% (2006-2010 5-year est.); Ancestry (includes multiple ancestries): 41.4% German, 13.3% English, 11.1% Irish, 8.0% Polish, 6.4% Dutch (2006-2010 5-year est.).

Economy: Single-family building permits issued: 2 (2011); Multi-family building permits issued: 0 (2011); Employment by occupation: 9.2% management, 7.0% professional, 11.4% services, 11.9% sales, 2.4% farming, 6.0% construction, 4.7% production (2006-2010 5-year est.).

Income: Per capita income: $32,503 (2006-2010 5-year est.); Median household income: $67,390 (2006-2010 5-year est.); Average household income: $83,781 (2006-2010 5-year est.); Percent of households with income of $100,000 or more: 22.7% (2006-2010 5-year est.); Poverty rate: 2.5% (2006-2010 5-year est.).

Education: Percent of population age 25 and over with: High school diploma (including GED) or higher: 91.4% (2006-2010 5-year est.); Bachelor's degree or higher: 31.3% (2006-2010 5-year est.); Master's degree or higher: 12.5% (2006-2010 5-year est.).

Housing: Homeownership rate: 88.3% (2010); Median home value: $166,400 (2006-2010 5-year est.); Median contract rent: $346 per month (2006-2010 5-year est.); Median year structure built: 1978 (2006-2010 5-year est.).

Transportation: Commute to work: 94.6% car, 0.0% public transportation, 0.0% walk, 4.3% work from home (2006-2010 5-year est.); Travel time to work: 52.2% less than 15 minutes, 30.5% 15 to 30 minutes, 10.8% 30 to 45 minutes, 3.3% 45 to 60 minutes, 3.2% 60 minutes or more (2006-2010 5-year est.)

Additional Information Contacts
Greater Susquehanna Valley Chamber of Commerce . . . . (570) 743-4100
http://www.gsvcc.org

WASHINGTONVILLE (borough). Covers a land area of 0.054 square miles and a water area of 0 square miles. Located at 41.05° N. Lat; 76.67° W. Long. Elevation is 541 feet.

Population: 228 (1990); 201 (2000); 273 (2010); Density: 5,015.9 persons per square mile (2010); Race: 98.5% White, 0.0% Black, 0.4% Asian, 0.0% American Indian/Alaska Native, 0.0% Native Hawaiian/Other Pacific Islander, 1.1% Other, 0.0% Hispanic of any race (2010); Average household size: 2.49 (2010); Median age: 33.5 (2010); Males per 100 females: 105.3 (2010); Marriage status: 23.6% never married, 51.6% now married, 9.3% widowed, 15.4% divorced (2006-2010 5-year est.); Foreign born: 3.6% (2006-2010 5-year est.); Ancestry (includes multiple ancestries): 69.3% German, 12.9% Irish, 8.9% English, 5.3% Pennsylvania German, 4.9% Dutch (2006-2010 5-year est.).

Economy: Employment by occupation: 5.2% management, 3.9% professional, 7.8% services, 22.1% sales, 0.0% farming, 24.7% construction, 11.7% production (2006-2010 5-year est.).

Income: Per capita income: $15,655 (2006-2010 5-year est.); Median household income: $29,375 (2006-2010 5-year est.); Average household income: $39,733 (2006-2010 5-year est.); Percent of households with income of $100,000 or more: 11.1% (2006-2010 5-year est.); Poverty rate: 18.2% (2006-2010 5-year est.).

Education: Percent of population age 25 and over with: High school diploma (including GED) or higher: 81.5% (2006-2010 5-year est.); Bachelor's degree or higher: 9.9% (2006-2010 5-year est.); Master's degree or higher: 6.0% (2006-2010 5-year est.).

Housing: Homeownership rate: 44.2% (2010); Median home value: $101,700 (2006-2010 5-year est.); Median contract rent: $425 per month (2006-2010 5-year est.); Median year structure built: before 1940 (2006-2010 5-year est.).

Transportation: Commute to work: 94.8% car, 0.0% public transportation, 5.2% walk, 0.0% work from home (2006-2010 5-year est.); Travel time to work: 40.3% less than 15 minutes, 33.8% 15 to 30 minutes, 26.0% 30 to 45 minutes, 0.0% 45 to 60 minutes, 0.0% 60 minutes or more (2006-2010 5-year est.)

WEST HEMLOCK (township). Covers a land area of 7.699 square miles and a water area of 0.010 square miles. Located at 41.03° N. Lat; 76.59° W. Long.

Population: 410 (1990); 489 (2000); 503 (2010); Density: 65.3 persons per square mile (2010); Race: 97.4% White, 0.4% Black, 0.0% Asian, 0.0% American Indian/Alaska Native, 0.0% Native Hawaiian/Other Pacific

Islander, 2.2% Other, 1.2% Hispanic of any race (2010); Average household size: 2.68 (2010); Median age: 42.2 (2010); Males per 100 females: 103.6 (2010); Marriage status: 17.4% never married, 73.6% now married, 2.7% widowed, 6.3% divorced (2006-2010 5-year est.); Foreign born: 0.0% (2006-2010 5-year est.); Ancestry (includes multiple ancestries): 43.2% German, 16.8% Italian, 11.0% American, 9.6% English, 9.0% Irish (2006-2010 5-year est.).

Economy: Single-family building permits issued: 1 (2011); Multi-family building permits issued: 0 (2011); Employment by occupation: 11.5% management, 9.1% professional, 11.8% services, 12.8% sales, 4.7% farming, 9.8% construction, 5.1% production (2006-2010 5-year est.).

Income: Per capita income: $25,865 (2006-2010 5-year est.); Median household income: $67,083 (2006-2010 5-year est.); Average household income: $74,128 (2006-2010 5-year est.); Percent of households with income of $100,000 or more: 30.5% (2006-2010 5-year est.); Poverty rate: 4.4% (2006-2010 5-year est.).

Education: Percent of population age 25 and over with: High school diploma (including GED) or higher: 91.4% (2006-2010 5-year est.); Bachelor's degree or higher: 26.7% (2006-2010 5-year est.); Master's degree or higher: 12.8% (2006-2010 5-year est.).

Housing: Homeownership rate: 93.1% (2010); Median home value: $161,900 (2006-2010 5-year est.); Median contract rent: n/a per month (2006-2010 5-year est.); Median year structure built: 1986 (2006-2010 5-year est.).

Transportation: Commute to work: 92.9% car, 0.0% public transportation, 0.7% walk, 6.4% work from home (2006-2010 5-year est.); Travel time to work: 34.3% less than 15 minutes, 38.9% 15 to 30 minutes, 18.5% 30 to 45 minutes, 5.7% 45 to 60 minutes, 2.6% 60 minutes or more (2006-2010 5-year est.)

Northampton County

Located in eastern Pennsylvania; bounded on the east by the Delaware River and the New Jersey border, and on the northwest by the Lehigh River; includes Blue Mountain on the north border. Covers a land area of 369.671 square miles, a water area of 7.725 square miles, and is located in the Eastern Time Zone at 40.75° N. Lat., 75.31° W. Long. The county was founded in 1752. County seat is Easton.

Northampton County is part of the Allentown-Bethlehem-Easton, PA-NJ Metropolitan Statistical Area. The entire metro area includes: Warren County, NJ; Carbon County, PA; Lehigh County, PA; Northampton County, PA

Population: 247,111 (1990); 267,066 (2000); 297,735 (2010); Race: 86.3% White, 5.0% Black, 2.4% Asian, 0.2% American Indian/Alaska Native, 0.0% Native Hawaiian/Other Pacific Islander, 6.1% Other, 10.5% Hispanic of any race (2010); Density: 805.4 persons per square mile (2010); Average household size: 2.53 (2010); Median age: 40.9 (2010); Males per 100 females: 95.4 (2010).

Religion: Six largest groups: 27.4% Catholicism, 8.5% Lutheran, 5.7% Presbyterian-Reformed, 4.3% Methodist/Pietist, 1.8% Non-Denominational, 1.4% Holiness (2010)

Economy: Unemployment rate: 8.7% (August 2012); Total civilian labor force: 156,444 (August 2012); Leading industries: 14.7% retail trade; 13.8% health care and social assistance; 12.2% manufacturing (2010); Farms: 486 totaling 68,252 acres (2007); Companies that employ 500 or more persons: 17 (2010); Companies that employ 100 to 499 persons: 128 (2010); Companies that employ less than 100 persons: 6,083 (2010); Black-owned businesses: 672 (2007); Hispanic-owned businesses: 905 (2007); Asian-owned businesses: n/a (2007); Women-owned businesses: 5,955 (2007); Retail sales per capita: $10,955 (2010). Single-family building permits issued: 369 (2011); Multi-family building permits issued: 67 (2011).

Income: Per capita income: $28,362 (2006-2010 5-year est.); Median household income: $58,762 (2006-2010 5-year est.); Average household income: $73,073 (2006-2010 5-year est.); Percent of households with income of $100,000 or more: 23.0% (2006-2010 5-year est.); Poverty rate: 8.8% (2006-2010 5-year est.); Bankruptcy rate: 3.23% (2011).

Taxes: Total county taxes per capita: $279 (2009); County property taxes per capita: $275 (2009).

Education: Percent of population age 25 and over with: High school diploma (including GED) or higher: 87.0% (2006-2010 5-year est.); Bachelor's degree or higher: 26.3% (2006-2010 5-year est.); Master's degree or higher: 9.5% (2006-2010 5-year est.).

Housing: Homeownership rate: 72.8% (2010); Median home value: $220,800 (2006-2010 5-year est.); Median contract rent: $693 per month (2006-2010 5-year est.); Median year structure built: 1964 (2006-2010 5-year est.)

Health: Birth rate: 99.7 per 10,000 population (2011); Death rate: 90.1 per 10,000 population (2011); Age-adjusted cancer mortality rate: 182.3 deaths per 100,000 population (2009); Number of physicians: 31.6 per 10,000 population (2010); Hospital beds: 29.1 per 10,000 population (2008); Hospital admissions: 1,595.7 per 10,000 population (2008).

Environment: Air Quality Index: 58.4% good, 38.9% moderate, 2.7% unhealthy for sensitive individuals, 0.0% unhealthy (percent of days in 2011)

Elections: 2012 Presidential election results: 51.7% Obama, 47.1% Romney

National and State Parks: Jacobsburg State Park

Additional Information Contacts

Northampton County Government . . . . (610) 559-3000
   http://www.northamptoncounty.org

Northampton County Communities

ACKERMANVILLE (CDP). Covers a land area of 1.370 square miles and a water area of 0.006 square miles. Located at 40.83° N. Lat; 75.23° W. Long. Elevation is 486 feet.

Population: n/a (1990); n/a (2000); 610 (2010); Density: 445.4 persons per square mile (2010); Race: 98.2% White, 0.5% Black, 0.2% Asian, 1.0% American Indian/Alaska Native, 0.0% Native Hawaiian/Other Pacific Islander, 0.1% Other, 2.5% Hispanic of any race (2010); Average household size: 2.65 (2010); Median age: 44.4 (2010); Males per 100 females: 92.4 (2010); Marriage status: 30.9% never married, 64.3% now married, 2.2% widowed, 2.6% divorced (2006-2010 5-year est.); Foreign born: 1.4% (2006-2010 5-year est.); Ancestry (includes multiple ancestries): 49.2% German, 14.7% English, 9.2% French, 8.3% Italian, 8.1% Swedish (2006-2010 5-year est.).

Economy: Employment by occupation: 9.0% management, 6.8% professional, 13.3% services, 23.2% sales, 0.0% farming, 9.0% construction, 9.0% production (2006-2010 5-year est.).

Income: Per capita income: $29,423 (2006-2010 5-year est.); Median household income: $73,295 (2006-2010 5-year est.); Average household income: $69,300 (2006-2010 5-year est.); Percent of households with income of $100,000 or more: 31.1% (2006-2010 5-year est.); Poverty rate: 12.2% (2006-2010 5-year est.).

Education: Percent of population age 25 and over with: High school diploma (including GED) or higher: 85.1% (2006-2010 5-year est.); Bachelor's degree or higher: 14.1% (2006-2010 5-year est.); Master's degree or higher: 6.0% (2006-2010 5-year est.).

Housing: Homeownership rate: 88.7% (2010); Median home value: $283,300 (2006-2010 5-year est.); Median contract rent: n/a per month (2006-2010 5-year est.); Median year structure built: 1966 (2006-2010 5-year est.)

Transportation: Commute to work: 90.5% car, 0.0% public transportation, 6.3% walk, 3.2% work from home (2006-2010 5-year est.); Travel time to work: 33.4% less than 15 minutes, 40.7% 15 to 30 minutes, 10.2% 30 to 45 minutes, 12.1% 45 to 60 minutes, 3.6% 60 minutes or more (2006-2010 5-year est.)

ALLEN (township). Covers a land area of 10.839 square miles and a water area of 0.322 square miles. Located at 40.71° N. Lat; 75.49° W. Long.

Population: 2,626 (1990); 2,630 (2000); 4,269 (2010); Density: 393.9 persons per square mile (2010); Race: 93.6% White, 2.0% Black, 1.9% Asian, 0.1% American Indian/Alaska Native, 0.0% Native Hawaiian/Other Pacific Islander, 2.4% Other, 4.7% Hispanic of any race (2010); Average household size: 2.53 (2010); Median age: 43.9 (2010); Males per 100 females: 92.6 (2010); Marriage status: 17.3% never married, 69.2% now married, 5.5% widowed, 8.0% divorced (2006-2010 5-year est.); Foreign born: 5.1% (2006-2010 5-year est.); Ancestry (includes multiple ancestries): 35.5% German, 13.1% Italian, 11.0% Pennsylvania German, 9.8% Irish, 7.1% Polish (2006-2010 5-year est.).

Economy: Single-family building permits issued: 40 (2011); Multi-family building permits issued: 0 (2011); Employment by occupation: 10.7% management, 6.8% professional, 8.2% services, 19.3% sales, 4.7% farming, 9.3% construction, 7.2% production (2006-2010 5-year est.).

Income: Per capita income: $32,880 (2006-2010 5-year est.); Median household income: $72,230 (2006-2010 5-year est.); Average household

income: $84,205 (2006-2010 5-year est.); Percent of households with income of $100,000 or more: 27.7% (2006-2010 5-year est.); Poverty rate: 1.2% (2006-2010 5-year est.).

Education: Percent of population age 25 and over with: High school diploma (including GED) or higher: 90.2% (2006-2010 5-year est.); Bachelor's degree or higher: 28.3% (2006-2010 5-year est.); Master's degree or higher: 11.2% (2006-2010 5-year est.).

Housing: Homeownership rate: 94.0% (2010); Median home value: $229,800 (2006-2010 5-year est.); Median contract rent: $1,680 per month (2006-2010 5-year est.); Median year structure built: 1994 (2006-2010 5-year est.).

Transportation: Commute to work: 94.9% car, 0.5% public transportation, 0.6% walk, 3.3% work from home (2006-2010 5-year est.); Travel time to work: 19.8% less than 15 minutes, 52.8% 15 to 30 minutes, 16.5% 30 to 45 minutes, 1.3% 45 to 60 minutes, 9.6% 60 minutes or more (2006-2010 5-year est.)

Additional Information Contacts

Allen Township . . . . (610) 262-7012
   http://www.allentownship.org
Greater Lehigh Valley Chamber of Commerce . . . . (610) 841-5800
   http://www.lehighvalleychamber.org

BANGOR (borough). Covers a land area of 1.504 square miles and a water area of 0.033 square miles. Located at 40.87° N. Lat; 75.21° W. Long. Elevation is 518 feet.

History: Founded 1773, incorporated 1875.

Population: 5,389 (1990); 5,319 (2000); 5,273 (2010); Density: 3,505.4 persons per square mile (2010); Race: 94.9% White, 1.2% Black, 0.2% Asian, 0.1% American Indian/Alaska Native, 0.0% Native Hawaiian/Other Pacific Islander, 3.6% Other, 5.0% Hispanic of any race (2010); Average household size: 2.54 (2010); Median age: 36.9 (2010); Males per 100 females: 95.7 (2010); Marriage status: 30.2% never married, 47.7% now married, 8.0% widowed, 14.1% divorced (2006-2010 5-year est.); Foreign born: 6.0% (2006-2010 5-year est.); Ancestry (includes multiple ancestries): 28.3% German, 20.3% Italian, 14.9% Irish, 12.1% English, 7.7% Pennsylvania German (2006-2010 5-year est.).

Economy: Single-family building permits issued: 2 (2011); Multi-family building permits issued: 0 (2011); Employment by occupation: 6.3% management, 1.2% professional, 12.6% services, 20.3% sales, 2.9% farming, 21.4% construction, 16.3% production (2006-2010 5-year est.).

Income: Per capita income: $21,884 (2006-2010 5-year est.); Median household income: $50,887 (2006-2010 5-year est.); Average household income: $55,289 (2006-2010 5-year est.); Percent of households with income of $100,000 or more: 11.8% (2006-2010 5-year est.); Poverty rate: 12.9% (2006-2010 5-year est.).

Education: Percent of population age 25 and over with: High school diploma (including GED) or higher: 80.1% (2006-2010 5-year est.); Bachelor's degree or higher: 17.3% (2006-2010 5-year est.); Master's degree or higher: 5.6% (2006-2010 5-year est.).

School District(s)

Bangor Area SD (KG-12)
   2010-11 Enrollment: 3,320 . . . . (610) 588-2163

Housing: Homeownership rate: 59.3% (2010); Median home value: $152,800 (2006-2010 5-year est.); Median contract rent: $622 per month (2006-2010 5-year est.); Median year structure built: before 1940 (2006-2010 5-year est.).

Safety: Violent crime rate: 35.9 per 10,000 population; Property crime rate: 240.1 per 10,000 population (2011).

Transportation: Commute to work: 93.3% car, 0.8% public transportation, 2.6% walk, 3.2% work from home (2006-2010 5-year est.); Travel time to work: 17.9% less than 15 minutes, 31.1% 15 to 30 minutes, 23.2% 30 to 45 minutes, 15.4% 45 to 60 minutes, 12.4% 60 minutes or more (2006-2010 5-year est.)

Additional Information Contacts

Borough of Bangor . . . . (610) 599-3000

http://www.northamptoncounty.org/countyguide/cwp/view.asp?a=1546&Q=622975
Slate Belt Chamber of Commerce. . . . . (610) 588-1000
   http://www.slatebeltchamber.org

BATH (borough). Covers a land area of 0.903 square miles and a water area of 0.009 square miles. Located at 40.73° N. Lat; 75.39° W. Long. Elevation is 423 feet.

History: Laid out 1816, incorporated 1856.

Population: 2,358 (1990); 2,678 (2000); 2,693 (2010); Density: 2,983.5 persons per square mile (2010); Race: 92.6% White, 2.9% Black, 1.0% Asian, 0.3% American Indian/Alaska Native, 0.0% Native Hawaiian/Other Pacific Islander, 3.2% Other, 6.6% Hispanic of any race (2010); Average household size: 2.51 (2010); Median age: 37.6 (2010); Males per 100 females: 92.9 (2010); Marriage status: 26.0% never married, 52.5% now married, 11.8% widowed, 9.7% divorced (2006-2010 5-year est.); Foreign born: 2.5% (2006-2010 5-year est.); Ancestry (includes multiple ancestries): 27.6% German, 18.8% Irish, 14.5% Pennsylvania German, 11.6% Italian, 7.4% American (2006-2010 5-year est.).

Economy: Single-family building permits issued: 0 (2011); Multi-family building permits issued: 0 (2011); Employment by occupation: 5.8% management, 2.0% professional, 15.8% services, 17.3% sales, 4.5% farming, 9.1% construction, 7.9% production (2006-2010 5-year est.).

Income: Per capita income: $22,414 (2006-2010 5-year est.); Median household income: $45,915 (2006-2010 5-year est.); Average household income: $56,692 (2006-2010 5-year est.); Percent of households with income of $100,000 or more: 16.2% (2006-2010 5-year est.); Poverty rate: 14.3% (2006-2010 5-year est.).

Education: Percent of population age 25 and over with: High school diploma (including GED) or higher: 82.6% (2006-2010 5-year est.); Bachelor's degree or higher: 15.7% (2006-2010 5-year est.); Master's degree or higher: 4.1% (2006-2010 5-year est.).

School District(s)

Northampton Area SD (KG-12)
   2010-11 Enrollment: 5,632 . . . . (610) 262-7811

Housing: Homeownership rate: 56.7% (2010); Median home value: $174,600 (2006-2010 5-year est.); Median contract rent: $638 per month (2006-2010 5-year est.); Median year structure built: 1960 (2006-2010 5-year est.).

Newspapers: Home News (Community news; Circulation 4,800)

Transportation: Commute to work: 89.7% car, 0.0% public transportation, 7.6% walk, 2.3% work from home (2006-2010 5-year est.); Travel time to work: 29.7% less than 15 minutes, 45.7% 15 to 30 minutes, 13.0% 30 to 45 minutes, 7.9% 45 to 60 minutes, 3.8% 60 minutes or more (2006-2010 5-year est.)

Additional Information Contacts

Nazareth Area Chamber of Commerce . . . . (610) 759-9188
   http://nazarethchamber.com

BELFAST (CDP). Covers a land area of 1.131 square miles and a water area of 0.003 square miles. Located at 40.78° N. Lat; 75.28° W. Long. Elevation is 525 feet.

Population: 1,102 (1990); 1,301 (2000); 1,257 (2010); Density: 1,111.9 persons per square mile (2010); Race: 97.4% White, 0.8% Black, 0.8% Asian, 0.1% American Indian/Alaska Native, 0.0% Native Hawaiian/Other Pacific Islander, 0.9% Other, 2.7% Hispanic of any race (2010); Average household size: 2.53 (2010); Median age: 47.3 (2010); Males per 100 females: 100.8 (2010); Marriage status: 29.5% never married, 58.9% now married, 8.9% widowed, 2.8% divorced (2006-2010 5-year est.); Foreign born: 2.7% (2006-2010 5-year est.); Ancestry (includes multiple ancestries): 41.6% German, 23.7% Irish, 18.0% Italian, 15.2% Polish, 11.4% English (2006-2010 5-year est.).

Economy: Employment by occupation: 8.4% management, 2.4% professional, 1.9% services, 33.4% sales, 2.1% farming, 4.0% construction, 1.6% production (2006-2010 5-year est.).

Income: Per capita income: $27,379 (2006-2010 5-year est.); Median household income: $63,203 (2006-2010 5-year est.); Average household income: $72,593 (2006-2010 5-year est.); Percent of households with income of $100,000 or more: 16.1% (2006-2010 5-year est.); Poverty rate: 6.3% (2006-2010 5-year est.).

Education: Percent of population age 25 and over with: High school diploma (including GED) or higher: 88.6% (2006-2010 5-year est.); Bachelor's degree or higher: 20.1% (2006-2010 5-year est.); Master's degree or higher: 2.4% (2006-2010 5-year est.).

Housing: Homeownership rate: 86.0% (2010); Median home value: $200,500 (2006-2010 5-year est.); Median contract rent: $676 per month (2006-2010 5-year est.); Median year structure built: 1974 (2006-2010 5-year est.).

Transportation: Commute to work: 87.6% car, 0.0% public transportation, 0.0% walk, 12.4% work from home (2006-2010 5-year est.); Travel time to work: 24.9% less than 15 minutes, 31.7% 15 to 30 minutes, 24.7% 30 to 45 minutes, 0.0% 45 to 60 minutes, 18.8% 60 minutes or more (2006-2010 5-year est.)

Additional Information Contacts

Slate Belt Chamber of Commerce. . . . . (610) 588-1000
http://www.slatebeltchamber.org

BETHLEHEM (city). Covers a land area of 19.102 square miles and a water area of 0.350 square miles. Located at 40.63° N. Lat; 75.37° W. Long. Elevation is 358 feet.

History: A Moravian group that fled religious persecution in Europe settled in Bethlehem in 1740. The town gained its name from a Christmas carol which said, "Not Jerusalem, rather Bethlehem gave us that which maketh life rich." The settlement was a music center from its very beginning, with many premiere concerts. Bethlehem served as a hospital for the wounded during the Revolutionary War. In 1829, the Lehigh Canal opened, and a new group of people arrived. Bridges were built, and buildings erected. South Bethlehem was established. The two were combined as Bethlehem in 1917.

Population: 71,428 (1990); 71,329 (2000); 74,982 (2010); Density: 3,925.4 persons per square mile (2010); Race: 76.4% White, 6.9% Black, 2.9% Asian, 0.3% American Indian/Alaska Native, 0.0% Native Hawaiian/Other Pacific Islander, 13.5% Other, 24.4% Hispanic of any race (2010); Average household size: 2.34 (2010); Median age: 35.7 (2010); Males per 100 females: 92.5 (2010); Marriage status: 41.0% never married, 41.5% now married, 7.4% widowed, 10.1% divorced (2006-2010 5-year est.); Foreign born: 6.9% (2006-2010 5-year est.); Ancestry (includes multiple ancestries): 22.7% German, 14.1% Irish, 11.1% Italian, 6.1% English, 5.0% Polish (2006-2010 5-year est.).

Economy: Unemployment rate: 9.6% (August 2012); Total civilian labor force: 36,696 (August 2012); Single-family building permits issued: 18 (2011); Multi-family building permits issued: 2 (2011); Employment by occupation: 8.6% management, 3.9% professional, 12.1% services, 18.2% sales, 5.0% farming, 7.0% construction, 6.5% production (2006-2010 5-year est.).

Income: Per capita income: $23,042 (2006-2010 5-year est.); Median household income: $44,310 (2006-2010 5-year est.); Average household income: $56,206 (2006-2010 5-year est.); Percent of households with income of $100,000 or more: 13.1% (2006-2010 5-year est.); Poverty rate: 16.8% (2006-2010 5-year est.).

Taxes: Total city taxes per capita: $451 (2009); City property taxes per capita: $264 (2009).

Education: Percent of population age 25 and over with: High school diploma (including GED) or higher: 84.1% (2006-2010 5-year est.); Bachelor's degree or higher: 26.6% (2006-2010 5-year est.); Master's degree or higher: 10.9% (2006-2010 5-year est.).

School District(s)

Bethlehem Area SD (KG-12)
   2010-11 Enrollment: 14,959 . . . . (610) 861-0500
Bethlehem Area SD (KG-12)
   2010-11 Enrollment: 14,959 . . . . (610) 861-0500
Bethlehem Avts (09-12)
   2010-11 Enrollment: n/a . . . . (610) 866-8013
Lehigh Valley Academy Regional CS (KG-12)
   2010-11 Enrollment: 973. . . . . (610) 866-9660
Lehigh Valley CHS for Performing Arts (09-12)
   2010-11 Enrollment: 451. . . . . (610) 868-2971
Lehigh Valley Dual Language Charter School (KG-08)
   2010-11 Enrollment: 236. . . . . (610) 868-7800
Southern Lehigh SD (KG-12)
   2010-11 Enrollment: 3,085 . . . . (610) 282-3121
Vitalistic Therapeutic CS of the Lehigh Valley (PK-12)
   2010-11 Enrollment: 122. . . . . (610) 861-7570

Four-year College(s)

International Institute for Restorative Practices (Private, Not-for-profit)
   Fall 2010 Enrollment: 49. . . . . (610) 807-9221
Lehigh University (Private, Not-for-profit)
   Fall 2010 Enrollment: 6,481 . . . . (610) 758-3000
   2011-12 Tuition: In-state $40,960; Out-of-state $40,960
Moravian College and Moravian Theological Seminary (Private, Not-for-profit, Moravian Church)
   Fall 2010 Enrollment: 1,932 . . . . (610) 861-1360
   2011-12 Tuition: In-state $33,446; Out-of-state $33,446

Two-year College(s)

Northampton County Area Community College (Public)
   Fall 2010 Enrollment: 7,539 . . . . (610) 861-5300
   2011-12 Tuition: In-state $7,500; Out-of-state $11,130

St Lukes Hospital School of Nursing (Private, Not-for-profit)
   Fall 2010 Enrollment: 218. . . . . (610) 954-3401
Triangle Tech Inc-Bethlehem (Private, For-profit)
   Fall 2010 Enrollment: 207. . . . . (610) 691-1300
   2011-12 Tuition: In-state $15,754; Out-of-state $15,754

Housing: Homeownership rate: 53.6% (2010); Median home value: $175,900 (2006-2010 5-year est.); Median contract rent: $705 per month (2006-2010 5-year est.); Median year structure built: 1955 (2006-2010 5-year est.).

Hospitals: Lehigh Valley Hospital - Muhlenberg (148 beds); St. Luke's Hospital (436 beds)

Safety: Violent crime rate: 29.1 per 10,000 population; Property crime rate: 247.5 per 10,000 population (2011).

Newspapers: The Morning Call - Bethlehem Bureau (Local news)

Transportation: Commute to work: 88.4% car, 2.8% public transportation, 5.0% walk, 2.6% work from home (2006-2010 5-year est.); Travel time to work: 39.6% less than 15 minutes, 36.7% 15 to 30 minutes, 11.7% 30 to 45 minutes, 3.8% 45 to 60 minutes, 8.2% 60 minutes or more (2006-2010 5-year est.)

Additional Information Contacts

City of Bethlehem . . . . (610) 865-7000
http://www.bethlehem-pa.gov
Greater Lehigh Valley Chamber of Commerce . . . . (610) 841-5800
http://www.lehighvalleychamber.org

BETHLEHEM (township). Covers a land area of 14.384 square miles and a water area of 0.172 square miles. Located at 40.66° N. Lat; 75.31° W. Long. Elevation is 358 feet.

History: Settled 1740—1741 by Moravians. During the Revolutionary War a community building was used as a hospital for Continental soldiers. Points of interest include the Central Moravian Church (c.1803), the Schnitz House (1749), and other early Moravian buildings; historic 18th-century industrial area. Seat of Lehigh University and Moravian College. Moravian Museum. Incorporated 1845 as a borough, as a city 1917.

Population: 16,425 (1990); 21,171 (2000); 23,730 (2010); Density: 1,649.8 persons per square mile (2010); Race: 86.7% White, 4.7% Black, 4.4% Asian, 0.2% American Indian/Alaska Native, 0.1% Native Hawaiian/Other Pacific Islander, 3.9% Other, 7.9% Hispanic of any race (2010); Average household size: 2.64 (2010); Median age: 43.9 (2010); Males per 100 females: 94.0 (2010); Marriage status: 21.6% never married, 64.6% now married, 7.4% widowed, 6.4% divorced (2006-2010 5-year est.); Foreign born: 12.0% (2006-2010 5-year est.); Ancestry (includes multiple ancestries): 25.3% German, 19.5% Italian, 15.1% Irish, 6.3% Polish, 5.9% English (2006-2010 5-year est.).

Economy: Single-family building permits issued: 20 (2011); Multi-family building permits issued: 0 (2011); Employment by occupation: 13.6% management, 6.5% professional, 7.7% services, 16.8% sales, 2.9% farming, 6.3% construction, 5.9% production (2006-2010 5-year est.).

Income: Per capita income: $34,313 (2006-2010 5-year est.); Median household income: $71,743 (2006-2010 5-year est.); Average household income: $90,845 (2006-2010 5-year est.); Percent of households with income of $100,000 or more: 34.4% (2006-2010 5-year est.); Poverty rate: 3.0% (2006-2010 5-year est.).

Education: Percent of population age 25 and over with: High school diploma (including GED) or higher: 91.1% (2006-2010 5-year est.); Bachelor's degree or higher: 35.9% (2006-2010 5-year est.); Master's degree or higher: 13.0% (2006-2010 5-year est.).

Four-year College(s)

International Institute for Restorative Practices (Private, Not-for-profit)
   Fall 2010 Enrollment: 49. . . . . (610) 807-9221
Lehigh University (Private, Not-for-profit)
   Fall 2010 Enrollment: 6,481 . . . . (610) 758-3000
   2011-12 Tuition: In-state $40,960; Out-of-state $40,960
Moravian College and Moravian Theological Seminary (Private, Not-for-profit, Moravian Church)
   Fall 2010 Enrollment: 1,932 . . . . (610) 861-1360
   2011-12 Tuition: In-state $33,446; Out-of-state $33,446

Two-year College(s)

Northampton County Area Community College (Public)
   Fall 2010 Enrollment: 7,539 . . . . (610) 861-5300
   2011-12 Tuition: In-state $7,500; Out-of-state $11,130
St Lukes Hospital School of Nursing (Private, Not-for-profit)
   Fall 2010 Enrollment: 218. . . . . (610) 954-3401

Triangle Tech Inc-Bethlehem (Private, For-profit)
Fall 2010 Enrollment: 207 . . . . (610) 691-1300
2011-12 Tuition: In-state $15,754; Out-of-state $15,754
Housing: Homeownership rate: 86.3% (2010); Median home value:
$267,100 (2006-2010 5-year est.); Median contract rent: $792 per month
(2006-2010 5-year est.); Median year structure built: 1982 (2006-2010
5-year est.).
Hospitals: Lehigh Valley Hospital - Muhlenberg (148 beds); St. Luke's
Hospital (436 beds)
Safety: Violent crime rate: 5.0 per 10,000 population; Property crime rate:
171.8 per 10,000 population (2011).
Newspapers: The Morning Call - Bethlehem Bureau (Local news)
Transportation: Commute to work: 93.4% car, 1.6% public transportation,
0.7% walk, 3.5% work from home (2006-2010 5-year est.); Travel time to
work: 27.7% less than 15 minutes, 36.6% 15 to 30 minutes, 14.3% 30 to
45 minutes, 5.2% 45 to 60 minutes, 16.2% 60 minutes or more (2006-2010
5-year est.)
Additional Information Contacts
Bethlehem Township . . . . (610) 814-6440
http://www.bethlehemtwp.com
Greater Lehigh Valley Chamber of Commerce . . . . (610) 841-5800
http://www.lehighvalleychamber.org

BUSHKILL (township). Covers a land area of 24.891 square miles and
a water area of 0.360 square miles. Located at 40.80° N. Lat; 75.33° W.
Long.
Population: 5,502 (1990); 6,982 (2000); 8,178 (2010); Density: 328.6
persons per square mile (2010); Race: 96.8% White, 0.7% Black, 0.9%
Asian, 0.1% American Indian/Alaska Native, 0.0% Native Hawaiian/Other
Pacific Islander, 1.5% Other, 2.0% Hispanic of any race (2010); Average
household size: 2.89 (2010); Median age: 43.8 (2010); Males per 100
females: 101.4 (2010); Marriage status: 24.0% never married, 65.3% now
married, 3.8% widowed, 6.9% divorced (2006-2010 5-year est.); Foreign
born: 3.5% (2006-2010 5-year est.); Ancestry (includes multiple
ancestries): 37.1% German, 13.5% Irish, 12.6% Italian, 10.9% Polish,
8.8% English (2006-2010 5-year est.)
Economy: Single-family building permits issued: 15 (2011); Multi-family
building permits issued: 0 (2011); Employment by occupation: 14.2%
management, 5.8% professional, 8.1% services, 17.7% sales, 3.2%
farming, 7.3% construction, 7.0% production (2006-2010 5-year est.).
Income: Per capita income: $30,831 (2006-2010 5-year est.); Median
household income: $77,766 (2006-2010 5-year est.); Average household
income: $89,405 (2006-2010 5-year est.); Percent of households with
income of $100,000 or more: 33.3% (2006-2010 5-year est.); Poverty rate:
4.4% (2006-2010 5-year est.).
Education: Percent of population age 25 and over with: High school
diploma (including GED) or higher: 91.8% (2006-2010 5-year est.);
Bachelor's degree or higher: 28.0% (2006-2010 5-year est.); Master's
degree or higher: 9.0% (2006-2010 5-year est.).
Housing: Homeownership rate: 93.2% (2010); Median home value:
$289,600 (2006-2010 5-year est.); Median contract rent: $670 per month
(2006-2010 5-year est.); Median year structure built: 1981 (2006-2010
5-year est.).
Safety: Violent crime rate: 15.8 per 10,000 population; Property crime rate:
98.7 per 10,000 population (2011).
Transportation: Commute to work: 95.2% car, 0.0% public transportation,
1.0% walk, 3.3% work from home (2006-2010 5-year est.); Travel time to
work: 23.9% less than 15 minutes, 34.4% 15 to 30 minutes, 21.9% 30 to
45 minutes, 8.8% 45 to 60 minutes, 11.1% 60 minutes or more (2006-2010
5-year est.)
Additional Information Contacts
Bushkill Township . . . . (610) 759-1250
http://www.bushkilltownship.com
Slate Belt Chamber of Commerce. . . . . (570) 421-4433
http://www.slatebeltchamber.org

CHAPMAN (borough). Aka Chapman Quarries. Covers a land area of
0.330 square miles and a water area of 0.028 square miles. Located at
40.76° N. Lat; 75.40° W. Long. Elevation is 705 feet.
Population: 254 (1990); 234 (2000); 199 (2010); Density: 603.8 persons
per square mile (2010); Race: 98.0% White, 0.5% Black, 0.0% Asian,
0.5% American Indian/Alaska Native, 0.0% Native Hawaiian/Other Pacific
Islander, 1.0% Other, 1.5% Hispanic of any race (2010); Average
household size: 2.37 (2010); Median age: 43.8 (2010); Males per 100
females: 101.0 (2010); Marriage status: 9.2% never married, 69.3% now

married, 4.3% widowed, 17.2% divorced (2006-2010 5-year est.); Foreign
born: 1.7% (2006-2010 5-year est.); Ancestry (includes multiple
ancestries): 34.5% German, 24.4% Irish, 19.3% Italian, 18.5% Polish,
10.9% English (2006-2010 5-year est.).
Economy: Employment by occupation: 12.9% management, 5.0%
professional, 5.9% services, 13.9% sales, 7.9% farming, 13.9%
construction, 10.9% production (2006-2010 5-year est.).
Income: Per capita income: $24,950 (2006-2010 5-year est.); Median
household income: $69,531 (2006-2010 5-year est.); Average household
income: $67,779 (2006-2010 5-year est.); Percent of households with
income of $100,000 or more: 19.1% (2006-2010 5-year est.); Poverty rate:
1.3% (2006-2010 5-year est.).
Education: Percent of population age 25 and over with: High school
diploma (including GED) or higher: 79.2% (2006-2010 5-year est.);
Bachelor's degree or higher: 28.3% (2006-2010 5-year est.); Master's
degree or higher: 3.8% (2006-2010 5-year est.).
Housing: Homeownership rate: 67.8% (2010); Median home value:
$147,200 (2006-2010 5-year est.); Median contract rent: $831 per month
(2006-2010 5-year est.); Median year structure built: before 1940
(2006-2010 5-year est.).
Transportation: Commute to work: 99.0% car, 0.0% public transportation,
1.0% walk, 0.0% work from home (2006-2010 5-year est.); Travel time to
work: 15.2% less than 15 minutes, 44.4% 15 to 30 minutes, 18.2% 30 to
45 minutes, 4.0% 45 to 60 minutes, 18.2% 60 minutes or more (2006-2010
5-year est.)

CHERRYVILLE (CDP). Covers a land area of 2.621 square miles
and a water area of 0.007 square miles. Located at 40.76° N. Lat; 75.53°
W. Long. Elevation is 725 feet.
Population: n/a (1990); n/a (2000); 1,580 (2010); Density: 602.9 persons
per square mile (2010); Race: 96.5% White, 0.9% Black, 1.5% Asian,
0.0% American Indian/Alaska Native, 0.0% Native Hawaiian/Other Pacific
Islander, 1.1% Other, 3.1% Hispanic of any race (2010); Average
household size: 2.70 (2010); Median age: 45.2 (2010); Males per 100
females: 102.3 (2010); Marriage status: 15.8% never married, 76.1% now
married, 2.1% widowed, 6.1% divorced (2006-2010 5-year est.); Foreign
born: 5.7% (2006-2010 5-year est.); Ancestry (includes multiple
ancestries): 49.1% German, 12.4% Irish, 12.1% Italian, 10.9%
Pennsylvania German, 8.0% Ukrainian (2006-2010 5-year est.).
Economy: Employment by occupation: 11.9% management, 4.4%
professional, 4.3% services, 18.1% sales, 6.9% farming, 6.4%
construction, 6.4% production (2006-2010 5-year est.).
Income: Per capita income: $35,271 (2006-2010 5-year est.); Median
household income: $74,069 (2006-2010 5-year est.); Average household
income: $86,242 (2006-2010 5-year est.); Percent of households with
income of $100,000 or more: 33.7% (2006-2010 5-year est.); Poverty rate:
3.3% (2006-2010 5-year est.).
Education: Percent of population age 25 and over with: High school
diploma (including GED) or higher: 89.3% (2006-2010 5-year est.);
Bachelor's degree or higher: 32.0% (2006-2010 5-year est.); Master's
degree or higher: 13.2% (2006-2010 5-year est.).
Housing: Homeownership rate: 92.6% (2010); Median home value:
$243,300 (2006-2010 5-year est.); Median contract rent: n/a per month
(2006-2010 5-year est.); Median year structure built: 1975 (2006-2010
5-year est.).
Transportation: Commute to work: 98.3% car, 0.0% public transportation,
0.0% walk, 1.7% work from home (2006-2010 5-year est.); Travel time to
work: 10.2% less than 15 minutes, 24.6% 15 to 30 minutes, 46.9% 30 to
45 minutes, 10.0% 45 to 60 minutes, 8.3% 60 minutes or more (2006-2010
5-year est.)

DANIELSVILLE (unincorporated postal area)
Zip Code: 18038
Covers a land area of 12.988 square miles and a water area of 0.289
square miles. Located at 40.79° N. Lat; 75.48° W. Long. Elevation is
682 feet. Population: 3,091 (2010); Density: 238.0 persons per square
mile (2010); Race: 97.8% White, 0.4% Black, 0.4% Asian, 0.1%
American Indian/Alaska Native, 0.0% Native Hawaiian/Other Pacific
Islander, 1.3% Other, 1.2% Hispanic of any race (2010); Average
household size: 2.68 (2010); Median age: 43.9 (2010); Males per 100
females: 103.0 (2010); Homeownership rate: 89.9% (2010)

EAST ALLEN (township). Covers a land area of 14.580 square miles and a water area of 0.093 square miles. Located at 40.71° N. Lat; 75.43° W. Long.

Population: 4,572 (1990); 4,903 (2000); 4,903 (2010); Density: 336.3 persons per square mile (2010); Race: 96.8% White, 0.9% Black, 0.9% Asian, 0.0% American Indian/Alaska Native, 0.0% Native Hawaiian/Other Pacific Islander, 1.4% Other, 3.2% Hispanic of any race (2010); Average household size: 2.52 (2010); Median age: 48.0 (2010); Males per 100 females: 101.9 (2010); Marriage status: 20.6% never married, 66.4% now married, 6.3% widowed, 6.7% divorced (2006-2010 5-year est.); Foreign born: 5.3% (2006-2010 5-year est.); Ancestry (includes multiple ancestries): 39.2% German, 17.9% Irish, 12.4% Italian, 9.0% English, 7.0% Hungarian (2006-2010 5-year est.).

Economy: Single-family building permits issued: 2 (2011); Multi-family building permits issued: 0 (2011); Employment by occupation: 9.8% management, 7.5% professional, 6.4% services, 16.6% sales, 4.4% farming, 7.6% construction, 4.5% production (2006-2010 5-year est.).

Income: Per capita income: $29,478 (2006-2010 5-year est.); Median household income: $69,375 (2006-2010 5-year est.); Average household income: $78,378 (2006-2010 5-year est.); Percent of households with income of $100,000 or more: 30.5% (2006-2010 5-year est.); Poverty rate: 2.8% (2006-2010 5-year est.).

Education: Percent of population age 25 and over with: High school diploma (including GED) or higher: 88.3% (2006-2010 5-year est.); Bachelor's degree or higher: 25.3% (2006-2010 5-year est.); Master's degree or higher: 7.4% (2006-2010 5-year est.).

Housing: Homeownership rate: 92.6% (2010); Median home value: $223,000 (2006-2010 5-year est.); Median contract rent: $592 per month (2006-2010 5-year est.); Median year structure built: 1981 (2006-2010 5-year est.).

Transportation: Commute to work: 94.5% car, 0.0% public transportation, 2.6% walk, 2.6% work from home (2006-2010 5-year est.); Travel time to work: 27.9% less than 15 minutes, 49.0% 15 to 30 minutes, 12.1% 30 to 45 minutes, 3.6% 45 to 60 minutes, 7.5% 60 minutes or more (2006-2010 5-year est.)

Additional Information Contacts
Greater Lehigh Valley Chamber of Commerce . . . . (610) 841-5800
http://www.lehighvalleychamber.org

EAST BANGOR (borough). Covers a land area of 0.819 square miles and a water area of 0.106 square miles. Located at 40.88° N. Lat; 75.19° W. Long. Elevation is 699 feet.

Population: 1,082 (1990); 979 (2000); 1,172 (2010); Density: 1,431.1 persons per square mile (2010); Race: 96.8% White, 0.1% Black, 0.3% Asian, 0.0% American Indian/Alaska Native, 0.0% Native Hawaiian/Other Pacific Islander, 2.8% Other, 5.5% Hispanic of any race (2010); Average household size: 2.76 (2010); Median age: 35.9 (2010); Males per 100 females: 92.4 (2010); Marriage status: 22.1% never married, 61.4% now married, 8.6% widowed, 7.9% divorced (2006-2010 5-year est.); Foreign born: 1.2% (2006-2010 5-year est.); Ancestry (includes multiple ancestries): 39.2% German, 29.4% Irish, 17.1% Italian, 15.5% English, 10.1% American (2006-2010 5-year est.).

Economy: Single-family building permits issued: 0 (2011); Multi-family building permits issued: 38 (2011); Employment by occupation: 10.7% management, 1.8% professional, 16.1% services, 18.9% sales, 2.5% farming, 12.6% construction, 7.7% production (2006-2010 5-year est.).

Income: Per capita income: $21,830 (2006-2010 5-year est.); Median household income: $55,208 (2006-2010 5-year est.); Average household income: $65,234 (2006-2010 5-year est.); Percent of households with income of $100,000 or more: 18.1% (2006-2010 5-year est.); Poverty rate: 13.5% (2006-2010 5-year est.).

Education: Percent of population age 25 and over with: High school diploma (including GED) or higher: 77.5% (2006-2010 5-year est.); Bachelor's degree or higher: 11.5% (2006-2010 5-year est.); Master's degree or higher: 3.1% (2006-2010 5-year est.).

Housing: Homeownership rate: 64.4% (2010); Median home value: $164,800 (2006-2010 5-year est.); Median contract rent: $704 per month (2006-2010 5-year est.); Median year structure built: before 1940 (2006-2010 5-year est.).

Safety: Violent crime rate: 0.0 per 10,000 population; Property crime rate: 59.5 per 10,000 population (2011).

Transportation: Commute to work: 93.0% car, 1.6% public transportation, 1.6% walk, 3.2% work from home (2006-2010 5-year est.); Travel time to work: 20.9% less than 15 minutes, 20.1% 15 to 30 minutes, 25.9% 30 to

45 minutes, 6.7% 45 to 60 minutes, 26.4% 60 minutes or more (2006-2010 5-year est.)

Additional Information Contacts
Slate Belt Chamber of Commerce . . . . (610) 588-1000
http://www.slatebeltchamber.org

EASTLAWN GARDENS (CDP). Covers a land area of 1.632 square miles and a water area of 0.019 square miles. Located at 40.75° N. Lat; 75.29° W. Long. Elevation is 469 feet.

Population: 1,977 (1990); 2,832 (2000); 3,307 (2010); Density: 2,026.4 persons per square mile (2010); Race: 95.0% White, 1.1% Black, 1.5% Asian, 0.1% American Indian/Alaska Native, 0.0% Native Hawaiian/Other Pacific Islander, 2.3% Other, 3.1% Hispanic of any race (2010); Average household size: 2.78 (2010); Median age: 41.0 (2010); Males per 100 females: 93.6 (2010); Marriage status: 22.0% never married, 63.3% now married, 5.7% widowed, 8.9% divorced (2006-2010 5-year est.); Foreign born: 5.0% (2006-2010 5-year est.); Ancestry (includes multiple ancestries): 46.3% German, 18.7% Italian, 12.8% Irish, 9.4% English, 7.0% Polish (2006-2010 5-year est.).

Economy: Employment by occupation: 18.5% management, 3.5% professional, 6.1% services, 20.7% sales, 2.4% farming, 3.8% construction, 4.6% production (2006-2010 5-year est.).

Income: Per capita income: $35,044 (2006-2010 5-year est.); Median household income: $83,725 (2006-2010 5-year est.); Average household income: $96,436 (2006-2010 5-year est.); Percent of households with income of $100,000 or more: 32.4% (2006-2010 5-year est.); Poverty rate: 4.2% (2006-2010 5-year est.).

Education: Percent of population age 25 and over with: High school diploma (including GED) or higher: 92.4% (2006-2010 5-year est.); Bachelor's degree or higher: 30.0% (2006-2010 5-year est.); Master's degree or higher: 7.1% (2006-2010 5-year est.).

Housing: Homeownership rate: 85.7% (2010); Median home value: $250,300 (2006-2010 5-year est.); Median contract rent: $730 per month (2006-2010 5-year est.); Median year structure built: 1976 (2006-2010 5-year est.).

Transportation: Commute to work: 96.8% car, 0.0% public transportation, 1.0% walk, 2.2% work from home (2006-2010 5-year est.); Travel time to work: 25.2% less than 15 minutes, 39.5% 15 to 30 minutes, 20.6% 30 to 45 minutes, 3.5% 45 to 60 minutes, 11.2% 60 minutes or more (2006-2010 5-year est.)

Additional Information Contacts
Nazareth Area Chamber of Commerce . . . . (610) 759-9188
http://nazarethchamber.com

EASTON (city). Aka Seipsville. County seat. Covers a land area of 4.072 square miles and a water area of 0.616 square miles. Located at 40.69° N. Lat; 75.22° W. Long. Elevation is 318 feet.

History: The area of Easton was surveyed for a town in 1750, under the instructions of Thomas Penn. The town was named Easton, at the proprietor's wish, for the Northamptonshire estate (Easton-Weston) of Lord Pomfret, Penn's father-in-law. As early as 1752, Easton became a county seat, and by 1755 a combined church and schoolhouse had been erected. The town's location at a crossroads of traffic brought rapid development and growth. In 1789 it was incorporated as a borough and in 1887 it became a city.

Population: 26,276 (1990); 26,263 (2000); 26,800 (2010); Density: 6,581.7 persons per square mile (2010); Race: 67.2% White, 16.8% Black, 2.4% Asian, 0.4% American Indian/Alaska Native, 0.1% Native Hawaiian/Other Pacific Islander, 13.1% Other, 19.9% Hispanic of any race (2010); Average household size: 2.55 (2010); Median age: 31.9 (2010); Males per 100 females: 101.5 (2010); Marriage status: 46.2% never married, 37.3% now married, 5.5% widowed, 11.1% divorced (2006-2010 5-year est.); Foreign born: 9.1% (2006-2010 5-year est.); Ancestry (includes multiple ancestries): 21.7% German, 13.6% Italian, 12.8% Irish, 5.6% English, 5.3% American (2006-2010 5-year est.).

Economy: Unemployment rate: 10.6% (August 2012); Total civilian labor force: 13,242 (August 2012); Single-family building permits issued: 43 (2011); Multi-family building permits issued: 15 (2011); Employment by occupation: 7.1% management, 2.1% professional, 15.0% services, 15.8% sales, 4.2% farming, 9.3% construction, 8.5% production (2006-2010 5-year est.).

Income: Per capita income: $18,899 (2006-2010 5-year est.); Median household income: $38,613 (2006-2010 5-year est.); Average household income: $51,634 (2006-2010 5-year est.); Percent of households with

income of $100,000 or more: 11.2% (2006-2010 5-year est.); Poverty rate: 20.3% (2006-2010 5-year est.).

Taxes: Total city taxes per capita: $475 (2009); City property taxes per capita: $334 (2009).

Education: Percent of population age 25 and over with: High school diploma (including GED) or higher: 77.3% (2006-2010 5-year est.); Bachelor's degree or higher: 16.8% (2006-2010 5-year est.); Master's degree or higher: 6.0% (2006-2010 5-year est.).

School District(s)

Bethlehem Area SD (KG-12)
    2010-11 Enrollment: 14,959 . . . . (610) 861-0500
Career Institute of Technology (10-12)
    2010-11 Enrollment: n/a . . . . (610) 258-2857
Easton Area SD (KG-12)
    2010-11 Enrollment: 9,010 . . . . (610) 250-2400
Wilson Area SD (KG-12)
    2010-11 Enrollment: 2,215 . . . . (484) 373-6000

Four-year College(s)

Lafayette College (Private, Not-for-profit, Presbyterian Church (USA))
    Fall 2010 Enrollment: 2,537 . . . . (610) 330-5000
    2011-12 Tuition: In-state $41,358; Out-of-state $41,358

Housing: Homeownership rate: 46.5% (2010); Median home value: $139,200 (2006-2010 5-year est.); Median contract rent: $660 per month (2006-2010 5-year est.); Median year structure built: before 1940 (2006-2010 5-year est.).

Hospitals: Easton Hospital (233 beds)

Safety: Violent crime rate: 35.7 per 10,000 population; Property crime rate: 309.5 per 10,000 population (2011).

Newspapers: The Express-Times (Community news; Circulation 50,268); The Morning Call - Easton Bureau (Regional news)

Transportation: Commute to work: 86.4% car, 3.8% public transportation, 4.3% walk, 4.6% work from home (2006-2010 5-year est.); Travel time to work: 28.6% less than 15 minutes, 34.4% 15 to 30 minutes, 16.1% 30 to 45 minutes, 8.3% 45 to 60 minutes, 12.6% 60 minutes or more (2006-2010 5-year est.)

Additional Information Contacts

City of Easton . . . . (610) 250-6600
    http://easton-pa.com
Greater Lehigh Valley Chamber of Commerce . . . . (610) 841-5800
    http://www.lehighvalleychamber.org

FORKS (township). Covers a land area of 12.109 square miles and a water area of 0.169 square miles. Located at 40.73° N. Lat; 75.23° W. Long.

Population: 5,923 (1990); 8,419 (2000); 14,721 (2010); Density: 1,215.7 persons per square mile (2010); Race: 84.6% White, 7.0% Black, 4.3% Asian, 0.1% American Indian/Alaska Native, 0.0% Native Hawaiian/Other Pacific Islander, 4.0% Other, 7.2% Hispanic of any race (2010); Average household size: 2.72 (2010); Median age: 40.7 (2010); Males per 100 females: 93.0 (2010); Marriage status: 17.3% never married, 67.6% now married, 7.5% widowed, 7.7% divorced (2006-2010 5-year est.); Foreign born: 9.7% (2006-2010 5-year est.); Ancestry (includes multiple ancestries): 23.7% German, 21.4% Italian, 20.2% Irish, 8.1% English, 7.5% Polish (2006-2010 5-year est.).

Economy: Single-family building permits issued: 27 (2011); Multi-family building permits issued: 0 (2011); Employment by occupation: 23.1% management, 6.6% professional, 6.7% services, 14.0% sales, 2.3% farming, 7.4% construction, 6.9% production (2006-2010 5-year est.).

Income: Per capita income: $37,099 (2006-2010 5-year est.); Median household income: $85,967 (2006-2010 5-year est.); Average household income: $97,161 (2006-2010 5-year est.); Percent of households with income of $100,000 or more: 42.4% (2006-2010 5-year est.); Poverty rate: 1.4% (2006-2010 5-year est.).

Education: Percent of population age 25 and over with: High school diploma (including GED) or higher: 94.5% (2006-2010 5-year est.); Bachelor's degree or higher: 39.6% (2006-2010 5-year est.); Master's degree or higher: 14.9% (2006-2010 5-year est.).

Housing: Homeownership rate: 89.7% (2010); Median home value: $289,400 (2006-2010 5-year est.); Median contract rent: $1,003 per month (2006-2010 5-year est.); Median year structure built: 1996 (2006-2010 5-year est.).

Safety: Violent crime rate: 2.0 per 10,000 population; Property crime rate: 108.3 per 10,000 population (2011).

Transportation: Commute to work: 90.2% car, 1.4% public transportation, 1.6% walk, 6.4% work from home (2006-2010 5-year est.); Travel time to

work: 22.7% less than 15 minutes, 22.2% 15 to 30 minutes, 15.1% 30 to 45 minutes, 8.5% 45 to 60 minutes, 31.5% 60 minutes or more (2006-2010 5-year est.)

Additional Information Contacts

Forks Township . . . . (610) 252-0785
    http://www.forkstownship.org
Greater Lehigh Valley Chamber of Commerce . . . . (610) 841-5800
    http://www.lehighvalleychamber.org

FREEMANSBURG (borough). Covers a land area of 0.697 square miles and a water area of 0.047 square miles. Located at 40.63° N. Lat; 75.34° W. Long. Elevation is 318 feet.

History: Settled c.1760, incorporated 1856.

Population: 1,946 (1990); 1,897 (2000); 2,636 (2010); Density: 3,779.3 persons per square mile (2010); Race: 70.6% White, 13.6% Black, 0.8% Asian, 0.5% American Indian/Alaska Native, 0.0% Native Hawaiian/Other Pacific Islander, 14.5% Other, 24.0% Hispanic of any race (2010); Average household size: 2.72 (2010); Median age: 34.1 (2010); Males per 100 females: 99.5 (2010); Marriage status: 31.9% never married, 53.1% now married, 4.2% widowed, 10.9% divorced (2006-2010 5-year est.); Foreign born: 13.6% (2006-2010 5-year est.); Ancestry (includes multiple ancestries): 17.6% German, 12.3% Italian, 10.4% Irish, 4.4% English, 3.3% Polish (2006-2010 5-year est.).

Economy: Single-family building permits issued: 0 (2011); Multi-family building permits issued: 0 (2011); Employment by occupation: 8.2% management, 2.7% professional, 13.9% services, 18.7% sales, 3.1% farming, 10.8% construction, 8.1% production (2006-2010 5-year est.).

Income: Per capita income: $20,920 (2006-2010 5-year est.); Median household income: $57,986 (2006-2010 5-year est.); Average household income: $64,847 (2006-2010 5-year est.); Percent of households with income of $100,000 or more: 13.2% (2006-2010 5-year est.); Poverty rate: 13.1% (2006-2010 5-year est.).

Education: Percent of population age 25 and over with: High school diploma (including GED) or higher: 82.6% (2006-2010 5-year est.); Bachelor's degree or higher: 14.6% (2006-2010 5-year est.); Master's degree or higher: 3.1% (2006-2010 5-year est.).

School District(s)

Bethlehem Area SD (KG-12)
    2010-11 Enrollment: 14,959 . . . . (610) 861-0500

Housing: Homeownership rate: 68.0% (2010); Median home value: $167,500 (2006-2010 5-year est.); Median contract rent: $900 per month (2006-2010 5-year est.); Median year structure built: 1959 (2006-2010 5-year est.).

Safety: Violent crime rate: 3.8 per 10,000 population; Property crime rate: 211.8 per 10,000 population (2011).

Transportation: Commute to work: 95.3% car, 2.8% public transportation, 0.0% walk, 1.9% work from home (2006-2010 5-year est.); Travel time to work: 31.2% less than 15 minutes, 35.2% 15 to 30 minutes, 14.4% 30 to 45 minutes, 4.0% 45 to 60 minutes, 15.3% 60 minutes or more (2006-2010 5-year est.)

Additional Information Contacts

Greater Lehigh Valley Chamber of Commerce . . . . (610) 841-5800
    http://www.lehighvalleychamber.org

GLENDON (borough). Covers a land area of 0.615 square miles and a water area of <.001 square miles. Located at 40.66° N. Lat; 75.24° W. Long. Elevation is 230 feet.

Population: 395 (1990); 367 (2000); 440 (2010); Density: 715.2 persons per square mile (2010); Race: 79.8% White, 10.5% Black, 4.3% Asian, 0.2% American Indian/Alaska Native, 0.0% Native Hawaiian/Other Pacific Islander, 5.2% Other, 6.1% Hispanic of any race (2010); Average household size: 2.72 (2010); Median age: 33.2 (2010); Males per 100 females: 117.8 (2010); Marriage status: 24.2% never married, 58.2% now married, 5.6% widowed, 11.9% divorced (2006-2010 5-year est.); Foreign born: 1.4% (2006-2010 5-year est.); Ancestry (includes multiple ancestries): 30.8% German, 22.3% Italian, 13.1% Irish, 7.4% English, 6.8% Slovak (2006-2010 5-year est.).

Economy: Single-family building permits issued: 0 (2011); Multi-family building permits issued: 0 (2011); Employment by occupation: 6.3% management, 2.9% professional, 10.9% services, 24.6% sales, 0.0% farming, 9.1% construction, 5.7% production (2006-2010 5-year est.).

Income: Per capita income: $25,839 (2006-2010 5-year est.); Median household income: $57,604 (2006-2010 5-year est.); Average household income: $68,032 (2006-2010 5-year est.); Percent of households with

income of $100,000 or more: 10.8% (2006-2010 5-year est.); Poverty rate: 13.4% (2006-2010 5-year est.).

Education: Percent of population age 25 and over with: High school diploma (including GED) or higher: 86.6% (2006-2010 5-year est.); Bachelor's degree or higher: 8.9% (2006-2010 5-year est.); Master's degree or higher: 3.3% (2006-2010 5-year est.).

Housing: Homeownership rate: 83.8% (2010); Median home value: $171,300 (2006-2010 5-year est.); Median contract rent: $925 per month (2006-2010 5-year est.); Median year structure built: before 1940 (2006-2010 5-year est.).

Transportation: Commute to work: 90.0% car, 0.6% public transportation, 1.2% walk, 6.5% work from home (2006-2010 5-year est.); Travel time to work: 30.2% less than 15 minutes, 36.5% 15 to 30 minutes, 13.2% 30 to 45 minutes, 13.8% 45 to 60 minutes, 6.3% 60 minutes or more (2006-2010 5-year est.)

HANOVER (township). Covers a land area of 6.553 square miles and a water area of 0.022 square miles. Located at 40.67° N. Lat; 75.40° W. Long. Elevation is 387 feet.

History: Established in 1798, Hanover Township is a beautiful residential community with many excellent recreational facilities and community based activities.The European settlers called the area "The Barrens" or "The Dry Lands".

Population: 7,176 (1990); 9,563 (2000); 10,866 (2010); Density: 1,658.2 persons per square mile (2010); Race: 87.1% White, 2.7% Black, 6.5% Asian, 0.0% American Indian/Alaska Native, 0.0% Native Hawaiian/Other Pacific Islander, 3.7% Other, 4.8% Hispanic of any race (2010); Average household size: 2.56 (2010); Median age: 45.9 (2010); Males per 100 females: 93.0 (2010); Marriage status: 18.5% never married, 65.8% now married, 8.9% widowed, 6.9% divorced (2006-2010 5-year est.); Foreign born: 12.3% (2006-2010 5-year est.); Ancestry (includes multiple ancestries): 26.1% German, 18.7% Irish, 13.7% Italian, 9.2% English, 4.5% Hungarian (2006-2010 5-year est.).

Economy: Single-family building permits issued: 24 (2011); Multi-family building permits issued: 8 (2011); Employment by occupation: 18.5% management, 5.6% professional, 4.8% services, 14.0% sales, 4.6% farming, 5.3% construction, 6.3% production (2006-2010 5-year est.).

Income: Per capita income: $38,980 (2006-2010 5-year est.); Median household income: $90,523 (2006-2010 5-year est.); Average household income: $103,094 (2006-2010 5-year est.); Percent of households with income of $100,000 or more: 43.3% (2006-2010 5-year est.); Poverty rate: 0.7% (2006-2010 5-year est.).

Education: Percent of population age 25 and over with: High school diploma (including GED) or higher: 95.9% (2006-2010 5-year est.); Bachelor's degree or higher: 51.9% (2006-2010 5-year est.); Master's degree or higher: 22.4% (2006-2010 5-year est.).

Housing: Homeownership rate: 83.0% (2010); Median home value: $320,800 (2006-2010 5-year est.); Median contract rent: $1,129 per month (2006-2010 5-year est.); Median year structure built: 1987 (2006-2010 5-year est.).

Transportation: Commute to work: 96.2% car, 0.4% public transportation, 0.9% walk, 2.4% work from home (2006-2010 5-year est.); Travel time to work: 37.6% less than 15 minutes, 40.4% 15 to 30 minutes, 8.8% 30 to 45 minutes, 3.4% 45 to 60 minutes, 9.8% 60 minutes or more (2006-2010 5-year est.)

Additional Information Contacts

Hanover Township . . . . (610) 866-1140
  http://hanovertwp-nc.org
Slate Belt Chamber of Commerce . . . . (610) 588-1000
  http://www.slatebeltchamber.org

HELLERTOWN (borough). Covers a land area of 1.312 square miles and a water area of 0.004 square miles. Located at 40.58° N. Lat; 75.34° W. Long. Elevation is 289 feet.

History: Campus of Lehigh University to Northwest. Settled c.1740, incorporated 1872.

Population: 5,662 (1990); 5,606 (2000); 5,898 (2010); Density: 4,496.7 persons per square mile (2010); Race: 95.3% White, 1.3% Black, 0.8% Asian, 0.1% American Indian/Alaska Native, 0.0% Native Hawaiian/Other Pacific Islander, 2.5% Other, 4.5% Hispanic of any race (2010); Average household size: 2.26 (2010); Median age: 42.2 (2010); Males per 100 females: 88.0 (2010); Marriage status: 25.6% never married, 54.8% now married, 8.3% widowed, 11.3% divorced (2006-2010 5-year est.); Foreign born: 2.1% (2006-2010 5-year est.); Ancestry (includes multiple

ancestries): 37.4% German, 15.8% Irish, 10.9% Italian, 9.2% Polish, 5.7% Pennsylvania German (2006-2010 5-year est.).

Economy: Single-family building permits issued: 0 (2011); Multi-family building permits issued: 0 (2011); Employment by occupation: 9.0% management, 2.9% professional, 10.9% services, 18.8% sales, 2.3% farming, 12.3% construction, 6.5% production (2006-2010 5-year est.).

Income: Per capita income: $27,827 (2006-2010 5-year est.); Median household income: $48,771 (2006-2010 5-year est.); Average household income: $64,335 (2006-2010 5-year est.); Percent of households with income of $100,000 or more: 14.1% (2006-2010 5-year est.); Poverty rate: 4.9% (2006-2010 5-year est.).

Education: Percent of population age 25 and over with: High school diploma (including GED) or higher: 87.1% (2006-2010 5-year est.); Bachelor's degree or higher: 24.7% (2006-2010 5-year est.); Master's degree or higher: 9.4% (2006-2010 5-year est.).

School District(s)

Saucon Valley SD (PK-12)
  2010-11 Enrollment: 2,380 . . . . (610) 838-7026

Housing: Homeownership rate: 68.3% (2010); Median home value: $189,500 (2006-2010 5-year est.); Median contract rent: $743 per month (2006-2010 5-year est.); Median year structure built: 1950 (2006-2010 5-year est.).

Newspapers: Valley Voice (Community news; Circulation 3,700)

Transportation: Commute to work: 91.3% car, 0.8% public transportation, 3.1% walk, 4.1% work from home (2006-2010 5-year est.); Travel time to work: 24.8% less than 15 minutes, 40.1% 15 to 30 minutes, 20.2% 30 to 45 minutes, 7.0% 45 to 60 minutes, 7.9% 60 minutes or more (2006-2010 5-year est.)

Additional Information Contacts

Borough of Hellertown. . . . . (610) 838-7041
  http://www.hellertown.boroughs.org
Greater Lehigh Valley Chamber of Commerce . . . . (610) 841-5800
  http://www.lehighvalleychamber.org

LEHIGH (township). Covers a land area of 29.277 square miles and a water area of 0.575 square miles. Located at 40.76° N. Lat; 75.54° W. Long.

Population: 9,278 (1990); 9,728 (2000); 10,526 (2010); Density: 359.5 persons per square mile (2010); Race: 98.0% White, 0.5% Black, 0.5% Asian, 0.1% American Indian/Alaska Native, 0.0% Native Hawaiian/Other Pacific Islander, 0.9% Other, 1.6% Hispanic of any race (2010); Average household size: 2.53 (2010); Median age: 46.4 (2010); Males per 100 females: 100.8 (2010); Marriage status: 20.7% never married, 65.2% now married, 6.2% widowed, 7.9% divorced (2006-2010 5-year est.); Foreign born: 2.2% (2006-2010 5-year est.); Ancestry (includes multiple ancestries): 38.5% German, 15.6% Pennsylvania German, 10.5% Irish, 8.8% Italian, 7.8% American (2006-2010 5-year est.).

Economy: Single-family building permits issued: 0 (2011); Multi-family building permits issued: 0 (2011); Employment by occupation: 9.2% management, 2.7% professional, 7.4% services, 18.9% sales, 3.1% farming, 14.4% construction, 12.6% production (2006-2010 5-year est.).

Income: Per capita income: $29,552 (2006-2010 5-year est.); Median household income: $67,698 (2006-2010 5-year est.); Average household income: $73,050 (2006-2010 5-year est.); Percent of households with income of $100,000 or more: 25.1% (2006-2010 5-year est.); Poverty rate: 3.5% (2006-2010 5-year est.).

Education: Percent of population age 25 and over with: High school diploma (including GED) or higher: 87.3% (2006-2010 5-year est.); Bachelor's degree or higher: 17.6% (2006-2010 5-year est.); Master's degree or higher: 5.5% (2006-2010 5-year est.).

Housing: Homeownership rate: 91.9% (2010); Median home value: $212,400 (2006-2010 5-year est.); Median contract rent: $492 per month (2006-2010 5-year est.); Median year structure built: 1977 (2006-2010 5-year est.).

Safety: Violent crime rate: 22.7 per 10,000 population; Property crime rate: 95.6 per 10,000 population (2011).

Transportation: Commute to work: 95.0% car, 0.4% public transportation, 0.7% walk, 3.2% work from home (2006-2010 5-year est.); Travel time to work: 13.8% less than 15 minutes, 35.9% 15 to 30 minutes, 36.2% 30 to 45 minutes, 6.3% 45 to 60 minutes, 7.7% 60 minutes or more (2006-2010 5-year est.)

Additional Information Contacts

Greater Lehigh Valley Chamber of Commerce . . . . (610) 841-5800
  http://www.lehighvalleychamber.org
Lehigh Township. . . . . (610) 767-6771

LOWER MOUNT BETHEL (township). Covers a land area of 23.819 square miles and a water area of 0.765 square miles. Located at 40.80° N. Lat; 75.16° W. Long.

Population: 3,187 (1990); 3,228 (2000); 3,101 (2010); Density: 130.2 persons per square mile (2010); Race: 97.5% White, 1.0% Black, 0.4% Asian, 0.1% American Indian/Alaska Native, 0.1% Native Hawaiian/Other Pacific Islander, 0.9% Other, 1.9% Hispanic of any race (2010); Average household size: 2.47 (2010); Median age: 46.1 (2010); Males per 100 females: 101.9 (2010); Marriage status: 20.3% never married, 64.9% now married, 7.0% widowed, 7.8% divorced (2006-2010 5-year est.); Foreign born: 1.2% (2006-2010 5-year est.); Ancestry (includes multiple ancestries): 29.8% German, 15.8% Italian, 14.4% Irish, 11.3% English, 8.5% Dutch (2006-2010 5-year est.).

Economy: Single-family building permits issued: 1 (2011); Multi-family building permits issued: 0 (2011); Employment by occupation: 9.3% management, 1.5% professional, 11.9% services, 15.8% sales, 1.6% farming, 17.1% construction, 13.6% production (2006-2010 5-year est.).

Income: Per capita income: $29,125 (2006-2010 5-year est.); Median household income: $62,449 (2006-2010 5-year est.); Average household income: $72,065 (2006-2010 5-year est.); Percent of households with income of $100,000 or more: 21.5% (2006-2010 5-year est.); Poverty rate: 5.5% (2006-2010 5-year est.).

Education: Percent of population age 25 and over with: High school diploma (including GED) or higher: 86.7% (2006-2010 5-year est.); Bachelor's degree or higher: 14.5% (2006-2010 5-year est.); Master's degree or higher: 2.5% (2006-2010 5-year est.).

Housing: Homeownership rate: 82.1% (2010); Median home value: $235,200 (2006-2010 5-year est.); Median contract rent: $573 per month (2006-2010 5-year est.); Median year structure built: 1965 (2006-2010 5-year est.).

Transportation: Commute to work: 90.7% car, 0.8% public transportation, 3.3% walk, 4.5% work from home (2006-2010 5-year est.); Travel time to work: 15.3% less than 15 minutes, 36.0% 15 to 30 minutes, 20.3% 30 to 45 minutes, 5.4% 45 to 60 minutes, 23.0% 60 minutes or more (2006-2010 5-year est.)

Additional Information Contacts
Greater Lehigh Valley Chamber of Commerce . . . . (610) 841-5800
  http://www.lehighvalleychamber.org

LOWER NAZARETH (township). Covers a land area of 13.326 square miles and a water area of 0.091 square miles. Located at 40.71° N. Lat; 75.32° W. Long.

History: It was originally part of the "Walking Purchase" of 1737. Purchased from William Penn, this area was originally known as "The Drylands". This 83 hundred-acre section was once thought to be doomed and was termed, "Barren". There was very little forest land as the Indians had burned all of the vegetation to drive the game into the open to hunt.

Population: 4,483 (1990); 5,259 (2000); 5,674 (2010); Density: 425.8 persons per square mile (2010); Race: 93.6% White, 1.4% Black, 3.0% Asian, 0.0% American Indian/Alaska Native, 0.0% Native Hawaiian/Other Pacific Islander, 2.0% Other, 3.0% Hispanic of any race (2010); Average household size: 2.80 (2010); Median age: 44.4 (2010); Males per 100 females: 96.5 (2010); Marriage status: 20.4% never married, 70.1% now married, 4.6% widowed, 4.9% divorced (2006-2010 5-year est.); Foreign born: 4.5% (2006-2010 5-year est.); Ancestry (includes multiple ancestries): 39.3% German, 17.5% Irish, 17.5% Italian, 13.5% English, 6.6% American (2006-2010 5-year est.).

Economy: Single-family building permits issued: 2 (2011); Multi-family building permits issued: 4 (2011); Employment by occupation: 18.8% management, 4.8% professional, 8.2% services, 20.4% sales, 2.4% farming, 9.5% construction, 7.3% production (2006-2010 5-year est.).

Income: Per capita income: $37,930 (2006-2010 5-year est.); Median household income: $86,379 (2006-2010 5-year est.); Average household income: $104,398 (2006-2010 5-year est.); Percent of households with income of $100,000 or more: 41.6% (2006-2010 5-year est.); Poverty rate: 1.4% (2006-2010 5-year est.).

Education: Percent of population age 25 and over with: High school diploma (including GED) or higher: 94.0% (2006-2010 5-year est.); Bachelor's degree or higher: 37.7% (2006-2010 5-year est.); Master's degree or higher: 13.5% (2006-2010 5-year est.).

Housing: Homeownership rate: 91.2% (2010); Median home value: $319,300 (2006-2010 5-year est.); Median contract rent: $852 per month (2006-2010 5-year est.); Median year structure built: 1978 (2006-2010 5-year est.).

Transportation: Commute to work: 90.6% car, 0.0% public transportation, 2.1% walk, 6.4% work from home (2006-2010 5-year est.); Travel time to work: 37.8% less than 15 minutes, 35.2% 15 to 30 minutes, 12.7% 30 to 45 minutes, 4.5% 45 to 60 minutes, 9.8% 60 minutes or more (2006-2010 5-year est.)

Additional Information Contacts
Lower Nazareth Township . . . . (610) 759-7434
  http://www.lowernazareth.com
Nazareth Area Chamber of Commerce . . . . (610) 759-9188
  http://nazarethchamber.com

LOWER SAUCON (township). Covers a land area of 24.269 square miles and a water area of 0.241 square miles. Located at 40.59° N. Lat; 75.30° W. Long. Elevation is 338 feet.

Population: 8,448 (1990); 9,884 (2000); 10,772 (2010); Density: 443.9 persons per square mile (2010); Race: 95.0% White, 1.1% Black, 1.9% Asian, 0.2% American Indian/Alaska Native, 0.0% Native Hawaiian/Other Pacific Islander, 1.8% Other, 3.8% Hispanic of any race (2010); Average household size: 2.60 (2010); Median age: 45.9 (2010); Males per 100 females: 99.9 (2010); Marriage status: 23.7% never married, 64.5% now married, 5.5% widowed, 6.2% divorced (2006-2010 5-year est.); Foreign born: 3.3% (2006-2010 5-year est.); Ancestry (includes multiple ancestries): 29.1% German, 18.5% Irish, 12.8% Italian, 12.1% English, 7.0% Pennsylvania German (2006-2010 5-year est.).

Economy: Single-family building permits issued: 6 (2011); Multi-family building permits issued: 0 (2011); Employment by occupation: 16.4% management, 3.2% professional, 6.1% services, 16.0% sales, 5.1% farming, 7.9% construction, 5.6% production (2006-2010 5-year est.).

Income: Per capita income: $43,404 (2006-2010 5-year est.); Median household income: $85,408 (2006-2010 5-year est.); Average household income: $116,878 (2006-2010 5-year est.); Percent of households with income of $100,000 or more: 39.1% (2006-2010 5-year est.); Poverty rate: 3.2% (2006-2010 5-year est.).

Education: Percent of population age 25 and over with: High school diploma (including GED) or higher: 90.6% (2006-2010 5-year est.); Bachelor's degree or higher: 39.7% (2006-2010 5-year est.); Master's degree or higher: 15.1% (2006-2010 5-year est.).

Housing: Homeownership rate: 90.1% (2010); Median home value: $305,300 (2006-2010 5-year est.); Median contract rent: $778 per month (2006-2010 5-year est.); Median year structure built: 1974 (2006-2010 5-year est.).

Safety: Violent crime rate: 19.4 per 10,000 population; Property crime rate: 88.8 per 10,000 population (2011).

Transportation: Commute to work: 89.9% car, 1.7% public transportation, 0.9% walk, 7.3% work from home (2006-2010 5-year est.); Travel time to work: 23.3% less than 15 minutes, 41.1% 15 to 30 minutes, 17.7% 30 to 45 minutes, 6.6% 45 to 60 minutes, 11.3% 60 minutes or more (2006-2010 5-year est.)

Additional Information Contacts
Greater Lehigh Valley Chamber of Commerce . . . . (610) 841-5800
  http://www.lehighvalleychamber.org
Lower Saucon Township . . . . (610) 865-3291
  http://www.lowersaucontownship.org

MARTINS CREEK (CDP). Covers a land area of 0.816 square miles and a water area of 0.006 square miles. Located at 40.78° N. Lat; 75.19° W. Long. Elevation is 272 feet.

Population: n/a (1990); n/a (2000); 631 (2010); Density: 773.3 persons per square mile (2010); Race: 97.8% White, 0.5% Black, 0.3% Asian, 0.0% American Indian/Alaska Native, 0.0% Native Hawaiian/Other Pacific Islander, 1.4% Other, 1.1% Hispanic of any race (2010); Average household size: 2.25 (2010); Median age: 49.7 (2010); Males per 100 females: 91.2 (2010); Marriage status: 15.7% never married, 68.0% now married, 9.5% widowed, 6.7% divorced (2006-2010 5-year est.); Foreign born: 0.0% (2006-2010 5-year est.); Ancestry (includes multiple ancestries): 28.0% Hungarian, 21.6% Irish, 18.8% Italian, 17.8% Greek, 15.9% German (2006-2010 5-year est.).

Economy: Employment by occupation: 5.1% management, 3.0% professional, 14.8% services, 13.3% sales, 0.0% farming, 19.6% construction, 17.2% production (2006-2010 5-year est.).

Income: Per capita income: $31,344 (2006-2010 5-year est.); Median household income: $62,500 (2006-2010 5-year est.); Average household income: $61,523 (2006-2010 5-year est.); Percent of households with income of $100,000 or more: n/a (2006-2010 5-year est.); Poverty rate: 0.0% (2006-2010 5-year est.).

Education: Percent of population age 25 and over with: High school diploma (including GED) or higher: 84.9% (2006-2010 5-year est.); Bachelor's degree or higher: 6.8% (2006-2010 5-year est.); Master's degree or higher: 0.0% (2006-2010 5-year est.).
Housing: Homeownership rate: 75.0% (2010); Median home value: $236,100 (2006-2010 5-year est.); Median contract rent: $754 per month (2006-2010 5-year est.); Median year structure built: 1942 (2006-2010 5-year est.).
Transportation: Commute to work: 84.3% car, 0.0% public transportation, 5.3% walk, 6.6% work from home (2006-2010 5-year est.); Travel time to work: 17.2% less than 15 minutes, 28.3% 15 to 30 minutes, 12.8% 30 to 45 minutes, 5.7% 45 to 60 minutes, 36.0% 60 minutes or more (2006-2010 5-year est.)

MIDDLETOWN (CDP). Covers a land area of 2.620 square miles and a water area of 0.005 square miles. Located at 40.64° N. Lat; 75.32° W. Long. Elevation is 276 feet.
Population: 6,742 (1990); 7,378 (2000); 7,441 (2010); Density: 2,839.9 persons per square mile (2010); Race: 89.3% White, 3.9% Black, 1.6% Asian, 0.1% American Indian/Alaska Native, 0.0% Native Hawaiian/Other Pacific Islander, 5.1% Other, 9.6% Hispanic of any race (2010); Average household size: 2.64 (2010); Median age: 44.0 (2010); Males per 100 females: 96.7 (2010); Marriage status: 23.3% never married, 64.3% now married, 6.5% widowed, 5.9% divorced (2006-2010 5-year est.); Foreign born: 8.4% (2006-2010 5-year est.); Ancestry (includes multiple ancestries): 26.1% German, 17.2% Italian, 12.3% Irish, 9.9% Hungarian, 6.1% Polish (2006-2010 5-year est.).
Economy: Employment by occupation: 10.6% management, 4.8% professional, 12.4% services, 16.3% sales, 2.5% farming, 8.1% construction, 7.8% production (2006-2010 5-year est.).
Income: Per capita income: $30,192 (2006-2010 5-year est.); Median household income: $61,230 (2006-2010 5-year est.); Average household income: $77,184 (2006-2010 5-year est.); Percent of households with income of $100,000 or more: 27.1% (2006-2010 5-year est.); Poverty rate: 4.7% (2006-2010 5-year est.).
Education: Percent of population age 25 and over with: High school diploma (including GED) or higher: 87.8% (2006-2010 5-year est.); Bachelor's degree or higher: 25.5% (2006-2010 5-year est.); Master's degree or higher: 6.3% (2006-2010 5-year est.).
Housing: Homeownership rate: 89.2% (2010); Median home value: $230,100 (2006-2010 5-year est.); Median contract rent: $766 per month (2006-2010 5-year est.); Median year structure built: 1968 (2006-2010 5-year est.).
Transportation: Commute to work: 96.7% car, 0.3% public transportation, 0.4% walk, 2.3% work from home (2006-2010 5-year est.); Travel time to work: 27.1% less than 15 minutes, 37.3% 15 to 30 minutes, 15.6% 30 to 45 minutes, 3.7% 45 to 60 minutes, 16.3% 60 minutes or more (2006-2010 5-year est.)
Additional Information Contacts
Greater Lehigh Valley Chamber of Commerce . . . . (610) 841-5800
http://www.lehighvalleychamber.org

MOORE (township). Covers a land area of 37.157 square miles and a water area of 0.421 square miles. Located at 40.78° N. Lat; 75.42° W. Long.
Population: 8,439 (1990); 8,673 (2000); 9,198 (2010); Density: 247.5 persons per square mile (2010); Race: 97.2% White, 0.8% Black, 0.5% Asian, 0.1% American Indian/Alaska Native, 0.0% Native Hawaiian/Other Pacific Islander, 1.4% Other, 2.0% Hispanic of any race (2010); Average household size: 2.54 (2010); Median age: 46.5 (2010); Males per 100 females: 101.4 (2010); Marriage status: 17.8% never married, 67.1% now married, 7.3% widowed, 7.9% divorced (2006-2010 5-year est.); Foreign born: 3.7% (2006-2010 5-year est.); Ancestry (includes multiple ancestries): 38.3% German, 11.1% Irish, 10.0% Pennsylvania German, 8.8% Italian, 6.5% English (2006-2010 5-year est.).
Economy: Single-family building permits issued: 14 (2011); Multi-family building permits issued: 0 (2011); Employment by occupation: 11.3% management, 4.2% professional, 7.5% services, 20.1% sales, 3.8% farming, 12.7% construction, 8.4% production (2006-2010 5-year est.).
Income: Per capita income: $28,013 (2006-2010 5-year est.); Median household income: $66,312 (2006-2010 5-year est.); Average household income: $73,021 (2006-2010 5-year est.); Percent of households with income of $100,000 or more: 24.1% (2006-2010 5-year est.); Poverty rate: 4.7% (2006-2010 5-year est.).

Education: Percent of population age 25 and over with: High school diploma (including GED) or higher: 85.5% (2006-2010 5-year est.); Bachelor's degree or higher: 14.3% (2006-2010 5-year est.); Master's degree or higher: 5.0% (2006-2010 5-year est.).
Housing: Homeownership rate: 91.2% (2010); Median home value: $235,100 (2006-2010 5-year est.); Median contract rent: $696 per month (2006-2010 5-year est.); Median year structure built: 1977 (2006-2010 5-year est.).
Safety: Violent crime rate: 4.3 per 10,000 population; Property crime rate: 66.1 per 10,000 population (2011).
Transportation: Commute to work: 90.3% car, 0.3% public transportation, 1.0% walk, 7.5% work from home (2006-2010 5-year est.); Travel time to work: 19.3% less than 15 minutes, 45.8% 15 to 30 minutes, 23.9% 30 to 45 minutes, 4.7% 45 to 60 minutes, 6.3% 60 minutes or more (2006-2010 5-year est.)
Additional Information Contacts
Greater Lehigh Valley Chamber of Commerce . . . . (610) 841-5800
http://www.lehighvalleychamber.org
Moore Township . . . . (610) 759-9449

MOUNT BETHEL (unincorporated postal area)
Zip Code: 18343
Covers a land area of 22.207 square miles and a water area of 0.964 square miles. Located at 40.89° N. Lat; 75.11° W. Long. Elevation is 525 feet. Population: 3,982 (2010); Density: 179.3 persons per square mile (2010); Race: 92.6% White, 3.5% Black, 1.4% Asian, 0.3% American Indian/Alaska Native, 0.0% Native Hawaiian/Other Pacific Islander, 2.2% Other, 4.7% Hispanic of any race (2010); Average household size: 2.60 (2010); Median age: 44.6 (2010); Males per 100 females: 98.0 (2010); Homeownership rate: 81.2% (2010)

NAZARETH (borough). Covers a land area of 1.628 square miles and a water area of 0.041 square miles. Located at 40.74° N. Lat; 75.31° W. Long. Elevation is 492 feet.
History: Settled c.1740, incorporated 1863.
Population: 5,713 (1990); 6,023 (2000); 5,746 (2010); Density: 3,528.8 persons per square mile (2010); Race: 96.6% White, 0.9% Black, 0.7% Asian, 0.2% American Indian/Alaska Native, 0.0% Native Hawaiian/Other Pacific Islander, 1.6% Other, 2.7% Hispanic of any race (2010); Average household size: 2.08 (2010); Median age: 43.9 (2010); Males per 100 females: 85.5 (2010); Marriage status: 27.5% never married, 53.0% now married, 9.8% widowed, 9.7% divorced (2006-2010 5-year est.); Foreign born: 2.5% (2006-2010 5-year est.); Ancestry (includes multiple ancestries): 43.7% German, 13.8% Italian, 11.5% Irish, 7.8% American, 7.6% English (2006-2010 5-year est.).
Economy: Single-family building permits issued: 1 (2011); Multi-family building permits issued: 0 (2011); Employment by occupation: 8.5% management, 2.1% professional, 9.4% services, 15.6% sales, 5.2% farming, 10.6% construction, 9.4% production (2006-2010 5-year est.).
Income: Per capita income: $29,294 (2006-2010 5-year est.); Median household income: $59,554 (2006-2010 5-year est.); Average household income: $65,208 (2006-2010 5-year est.); Percent of households with income of $100,000 or more: 18.1% (2006-2010 5-year est.); Poverty rate: 5.1% (2006-2010 5-year est.).
Education: Percent of population age 25 and over with: High school diploma (including GED) or higher: 85.7% (2006-2010 5-year est.); Bachelor's degree or higher: 26.8% (2006-2010 5-year est.); Master's degree or higher: 8.4% (2006-2010 5-year est.).
School District(s)
Nazareth Area SD (KG-12)
2010-11 Enrollment: 4,675 . . . . (610) 759-1170
Pen Argyl Area SD (KG-12)
2010-11 Enrollment: 1,814 . . . . (610) 863-3191
Housing: Homeownership rate: 48.1% (2010); Median home value: $192,200 (2006-2010 5-year est.); Median contract rent: $690 per month (2006-2010 5-year est.); Median year structure built: before 1940 (2006-2010 5-year est.).
Safety: Violent crime rate: 46.8 per 10,000 population; Property crime rate: 142.3 per 10,000 population (2011).
Transportation: Commute to work: 95.2% car, 0.0% public transportation, 3.3% walk, 1.0% work from home (2006-2010 5-year est.); Travel time to work: 32.0% less than 15 minutes, 41.6% 15 to 30 minutes, 17.3% 30 to 45 minutes, 2.9% 45 to 60 minutes, 6.1% 60 minutes or more (2006-2010 5-year est.)

Additional Information Contacts
Borough of Nazareth . . . . (610) 759-0202
  http://www.nazarethborough.com
Nazareth Area Chamber of Commerce . . . . (610) 759-9188
  http://nazarethchamber.com

NORTH CATASAUQUA (borough).
Covers a land area of 0.717 square miles and a water area of 0.022 square miles. Located at 40.66° N. Lat; 75.47° W. Long. Elevation is 367 feet.

Population: 2,867 (1990); 2,814 (2000); 2,849 (2010); Density: 3,973.4 persons per square mile (2010); Race: 95.2% White, 1.2% Black, 0.9% Asian, 0.1% American Indian/Alaska Native, 0.0% Native Hawaiian/Other Pacific Islander, 2.6% Other, 5.2% Hispanic of any race (2010); Average household size: 2.41 (2010); Median age: 42.6 (2010); Males per 100 females: 97.2 (2010); Marriage status: 23.2% never married, 59.1% now married, 8.2% widowed, 9.5% divorced (2006-2010 5-year est.); Foreign born: 2.9% (2006-2010 5-year est.); Ancestry (includes multiple ancestries): 52.5% German, 13.7% Irish, 9.6% Polish, 8.7% Slovak, 8.4% English (2006-2010 5-year est.).

Economy: Single-family building permits issued: 0 (2011); Multi-family building permits issued: 0 (2011); Employment by occupation: 8.1% management, 3.9% professional, 5.5% services, 15.1% sales, 5.6% farming, 5.5% construction, 9.9% production (2006-2010 5-year est.).

Income: Per capita income: $27,494 (2006-2010 5-year est.); Median household income: $55,500 (2006-2010 5-year est.); Average household income: $61,675 (2006-2010 5-year est.); Percent of households with income of $100,000 or more: 12.5% (2006-2010 5-year est.); Poverty rate: 1.8% (2006-2010 5-year est.).

Education: Percent of population age 25 and over with: High school diploma (including GED) or higher: 93.7% (2006-2010 5-year est.); Bachelor's degree or higher: 19.4% (2006-2010 5-year est.); Master's degree or higher: 4.9% (2006-2010 5-year est.).

Housing: Homeownership rate: 75.0% (2010); Median home value: $177,000 (2006-2010 5-year est.); Median contract rent: $583 per month (2006-2010 5-year est.); Median year structure built: 1946 (2006-2010 5-year est.).

Safety: Violent crime rate: 10.5 per 10,000 population; Property crime rate: 80.5 per 10,000 population (2011).

Transportation: Commute to work: 97.8% car, 0.0% public transportation, 1.0% walk, 0.7% work from home (2006-2010 5-year est.); Travel time to work: 34.0% less than 15 minutes, 50.0% 15 to 30 minutes, 10.4% 30 to 45 minutes, 2.5% 45 to 60 minutes, 3.0% 60 minutes or more (2006-2010 5-year est.)

Additional Information Contacts
Whitehall Area Chamber of Commerce . . . . (610) 432-4130
  http://www.waccpa.org

NORTHAMPTON (borough).
Covers a land area of 2.462 square miles and a water area of 0.148 square miles. Located at 40.69° N. Lat; 75.49° W. Long. Elevation is 325 feet.

History: Mary Immaculate Missionary College to North. Settled c.1763; incorporated 1901.

Population: 8,717 (1990); 9,405 (2000); 9,926 (2010); Density: 4,032.0 persons per square mile (2010); Race: 95.2% White, 1.7% Black, 0.7% Asian, 0.2% American Indian/Alaska Native, 0.0% Native Hawaiian/Other Pacific Islander, 2.2% Other, 3.5% Hispanic of any race (2010); Average household size: 2.36 (2010); Median age: 40.8 (2010); Males per 100 females: 94.1 (2010); Marriage status: 25.2% never married, 55.6% now married, 8.8% widowed, 10.3% divorced (2006-2010 5-year est.); Foreign born: 4.8% (2006-2010 5-year est.); Ancestry (includes multiple ancestries): 40.2% German, 16.1% Irish, 12.3% Italian, 10.2% Polish, 6.8% Slovak (2006-2010 5-year est.).

Economy: Single-family building permits issued: 16 (2011); Multi-family building permits issued: 0 (2011); Employment by occupation: 9.8% management, 4.0% professional, 10.5% services, 20.2% sales, 4.8% farming, 10.5% construction, 6.1% production (2006-2010 5-year est.).

Income: Per capita income: $26,480 (2006-2010 5-year est.); Median household income: $52,941 (2006-2010 5-year est.); Average household income: $63,301 (2006-2010 5-year est.); Percent of households with income of $100,000 or more: 16.7% (2006-2010 5-year est.); Poverty rate: 8.6% (2006-2010 5-year est.).

Education: Percent of population age 25 and over with: High school diploma (including GED) or higher: 84.1% (2006-2010 5-year est.); Bachelor's degree or higher: 20.7% (2006-2010 5-year est.); Master's degree or higher: 6.9% (2006-2010 5-year est.).

Catasauqua Area SD (KG-12)
  2010-11 Enrollment: 1,566 . . . . (610) 264-5571
Northampton Area SD (KG-12)
  2010-11 Enrollment: 5,632 . . . . (610) 262-7811

Housing: Homeownership rate: 71.1% (2010); Median home value: $170,000 (2006-2010 5-year est.); Median contract rent: $575 per month (2006-2010 5-year est.); Median year structure built: 1948 (2006-2010 5-year est.).

Safety: Violent crime rate: 6.0 per 10,000 population; Property crime rate: 155.7 per 10,000 population (2011).

Transportation: Commute to work: 94.3% car, 0.6% public transportation, 1.1% walk, 3.2% work from home (2006-2010 5-year est.); Travel time to work: 18.3% less than 15 minutes, 48.0% 15 to 30 minutes, 27.0% 30 to 45 minutes, 2.2% 45 to 60 minutes, 4.4% 60 minutes or more (2006-2010 5-year est.)

Additional Information Contacts
Borough of Northampton . . . . (610) 262-2576
  http://www.northamptonboro.com
Greater Lehigh Valley Chamber of Commerce . . . . (610) 841-5800
  http://www.lehighvalleychamber.org

OLD ORCHARD (CDP).
Aka Wilden. Covers a land area of 0.693 square miles and a water area of 0 square miles. Located at 40.66° N. Lat; 75.26° W. Long. Elevation is 410 feet.

Population: 2,598 (1990); 2,443 (2000); 2,434 (2010); Density: 3,514.7 persons per square mile (2010); Race: 93.8% White, 1.6% Black, 1.2% Asian, 0.1% American Indian/Alaska Native, 0.0% Native Hawaiian/Other Pacific Islander, 3.3% Other, 3.6% Hispanic of any race (2010); Average household size: 2.63 (2010); Median age: 47.4 (2010); Males per 100 females: 96.4 (2010); Marriage status: 16.5% never married, 64.6% now married, 6.8% widowed, 12.1% divorced (2006-2010 5-year est.); Foreign born: 7.0% (2006-2010 5-year est.); Ancestry (includes multiple ancestries): 34.1% German, 18.7% Irish, 17.1% Italian, 11.0% English, 5.2% Dutch (2006-2010 5-year est.).

Economy: Employment by occupation: 6.4% management, 8.6% professional, 3.9% services, 14.0% sales, 2.4% farming, 9.5% construction, 4.6% production (2006-2010 5-year est.).

Income: Per capita income: $34,847 (2006-2010 5-year est.); Median household income: $87,434 (2006-2010 5-year est.); Average household income: $92,435 (2006-2010 5-year est.); Percent of households with income of $100,000 or more: 40.0% (2006-2010 5-year est.); Poverty rate: 1.5% (2006-2010 5-year est.).

Education: Percent of population age 25 and over with: High school diploma (including GED) or higher: 91.6% (2006-2010 5-year est.); Bachelor's degree or higher: 26.8% (2006-2010 5-year est.); Master's degree or higher: 9.4% (2006-2010 5-year est.).

Housing: Homeownership rate: 96.9% (2010); Median home value: $264,600 (2006-2010 5-year est.); Median contract rent: $1,175 per month (2006-2010 5-year est.); Median year structure built: 1963 (2006-2010 5-year est.).

Transportation: Commute to work: 95.1% car, 0.0% public transportation, 0.0% walk, 2.6% work from home (2006-2010 5-year est.); Travel time to work: 25.3% less than 15 minutes, 41.1% 15 to 30 minutes, 14.4% 30 to 45 minutes, 5.7% 45 to 60 minutes, 13.6% 60 minutes or more (2006-2010 5-year est.)

Additional Information Contacts
Greater Lehigh Valley Chamber of Commerce . . . . (610) 841-5800
  http://www.lehighvalleychamber.org

PALMER (township).
Covers a land area of 10.754 square miles and a water area of 0.092 square miles. Located at 40.70° N. Lat; 75.26° W. Long.

Population: 14,965 (1990); 16,809 (2000); 20,691 (2010); Density: 1,923.9 persons per square mile (2010); Race: 86.5% White, 5.3% Black, 4.1% Asian, 0.2% American Indian/Alaska Native, 0.0% Native Hawaiian/Other Pacific Islander, 3.9% Other, 6.1% Hispanic of any race (2010); Average household size: 2.53 (2010); Median age: 44.9 (2010); Males per 100 females: 92.0 (2010); Marriage status: 18.9% never married, 63.0% now married, 8.1% widowed, 9.9% divorced (2006-2010 5-year est.); Foreign born: 7.6% (2006-2010 5-year est.); Ancestry (includes multiple ancestries): 26.5% German, 21.6% Italian, 16.0% Irish, 9.4% English, 6.5% Polish (2006-2010 5-year est.).

Economy: Single-family building permits issued: 51 (2011); Multi-family building permits issued: 0 (2011); Employment by occupation: 10.5%

management, 5.4% professional, 7.8% services, 17.2% sales, 3.6% farming, 7.0% construction, 5.5% production (2006-2010 5-year est.).
Income: Per capita income: $31,652 (2006-2010 5-year est.); Median household income: $67,545 (2006-2010 5-year est.); Average household income: $77,899 (2006-2010 5-year est.); Percent of households with income of $100,000 or more: 27.2% (2006-2010 5-year est.); Poverty rate: 2.9% (2006-2010 5-year est.).
Taxes: Total city taxes per capita: $430 (2009); City property taxes per capita: $174 (2009).
Education: Percent of population age 25 and over with: High school diploma (including GED) or higher: 91.1% (2006-2010 5-year est.); Bachelor's degree or higher: 29.7% (2006-2010 5-year est.); Master's degree or higher: 10.2% (2006-2010 5-year est.).
Housing: Homeownership rate: 86.7% (2010); Median home value: $239,800 (2006-2010 5-year est.); Median contract rent: $836 per month (2006-2010 5-year est.); Median year structure built: 1972 (2006-2010 5-year est.).
Safety: Violent crime rate: 5.8 per 10,000 population; Property crime rate: 193.2 per 10,000 population (2011).
Transportation: Commute to work: 94.3% car, 1.0% public transportation, 0.8% walk, 3.3% work from home (2006-2010 5-year est.); Travel time to work: 32.0% less than 15 minutes, 32.6% 15 to 30 minutes, 14.6% 30 to 45 minutes, 4.7% 45 to 60 minutes, 16.1% 60 minutes or more (2006-2010 5-year est.)

Additional Information Contacts
Greater Lehigh Valley Chamber of Commerce . . . . (610) 841-5800
    http://www.lehighvalleychamber.org
Palmer Township. . . . . (610) 253-7191
    http://www.palmertwp.com

PALMER HEIGHTS (CDP). Covers a land area of 1.197 square miles and a water area of <.001 square miles. Located at 40.69° N. Lat; 75.27° W. Long. Elevation is 364 feet.
Population: 3,960 (1990); 3,612 (2000); 3,762 (2010); Density: 3,142.8 persons per square mile (2010); Race: 90.5% White, 4.1% Black, 1.3% Asian, 0.2% American Indian/Alaska Native, 0.0% Native Hawaiian/Other Pacific Islander, 3.9% Other, 6.6% Hispanic of any race (2010); Average household size: 2.49 (2010); Median age: 49.0 (2010); Males per 100 females: 89.7 (2010); Marriage status: 19.0% never married, 61.4% now married, 11.1% widowed, 8.5% divorced (2006-2010 5-year est.); Foreign born: 4.5% (2006-2010 5-year est.); Ancestry (includes multiple ancestries): 28.1% German, 24.7% Italian, 14.9% Irish, 8.9% English, 4.9% American (2006-2010 5-year est.).
Economy: Employment by occupation: 9.3% management, 4.0% professional, 10.4% services, 13.5% sales, 3.2% farming, 8.7% construction, 8.3% production (2006-2010 5-year est.).
Income: Per capita income: $28,337 (2006-2010 5-year est.); Median household income: $64,274 (2006-2010 5-year est.); Average household income: $69,190 (2006-2010 5-year est.); Percent of households with income of $100,000 or more: 22.1% (2006-2010 5-year est.); Poverty rate: 0.8% (2006-2010 5-year est.).
Education: Percent of population age 25 and over with: High school diploma (including GED) or higher: 90.0% (2006-2010 5-year est.); Bachelor's degree or higher: 23.8% (2006-2010 5-year est.); Master's degree or higher: 7.1% (2006-2010 5-year est.).
Housing: Homeownership rate: 92.4% (2010); Median home value: $225,500 (2006-2010 5-year est.); Median contract rent: $1,042 per month (2006-2010 5-year est.); Median year structure built: 1959 (2006-2010 5-year est.).
Transportation: Commute to work: 98.9% car, 0.0% public transportation, 0.0% walk, 0.5% work from home (2006-2010 5-year est.); Travel time to work: 34.9% less than 15 minutes, 40.6% 15 to 30 minutes, 11.9% 30 to 45 minutes, 3.6% 45 to 60 minutes, 8.9% 60 minutes or more (2006-2010 5-year est.)

Additional Information Contacts
Greater Lehigh Valley Chamber of Commerce . . . . (610) 841-5800
    http://www.lehighvalleychamber.org

PEN ARGYL (borough). Covers a land area of 1.342 square miles and a water area of 0.052 square miles. Located at 40.87° N. Lat; 75.25° W. Long. Elevation is 830 feet.
History: Appalachian Trail passes to North on Kittatinny Mt. Founded 1868, incorporated 1882.
Population: 3,492 (1990); 3,615 (2000); 3,595 (2010); Density: 2,678.1 persons per square mile (2010); Race: 96.1% White, 1.1% Black, 0.4%

Asian, 0.2% American Indian/Alaska Native, 0.0% Native Hawaiian/Other Pacific Islander, 2.2% Other, 4.0% Hispanic of any race (2010); Average household size: 2.56 (2010); Median age: 37.6 (2010); Males per 100 females: 90.3 (2010); Marriage status: 29.5% never married, 49.6% now married, 6.9% widowed, 13.9% divorced (2006-2010 5-year est.); Foreign born: 0.7% (2006-2010 5-year est.); Ancestry (includes multiple ancestries): 36.9% German, 25.6% Italian, 15.2% English, 10.2% Irish, 9.8% American (2006-2010 5-year est.).
Economy: Single-family building permits issued: 0 (2011); Multi-family building permits issued: 0 (2011); Employment by occupation: 8.9% management, 3.2% professional, 12.4% services, 14.1% sales, 0.3% farming, 12.8% construction, 13.6% production (2006-2010 5-year est.).
Income: Per capita income: $24,945 (2006-2010 5-year est.); Median household income: $52,500 (2006-2010 5-year est.); Average household income: $61,693 (2006-2010 5-year est.); Percent of households with income of $100,000 or more: 17.2% (2006-2010 5-year est.); Poverty rate: 17.4% (2006-2010 5-year est.).
Education: Percent of population age 25 and over with: High school diploma (including GED) or higher: 86.6% (2006-2010 5-year est.); Bachelor's degree or higher: 14.4% (2006-2010 5-year est.); Master's degree or higher: 4.3% (2006-2010 5-year est.).
School District(s)
Pen Argyl Area SD (KG-12)
    2010-11 Enrollment: 1,814 . . . . (610) 863-3191
Housing: Homeownership rate: 65.9% (2010); Median home value: $146,000 (2006-2010 5-year est.); Median contract rent: $624 per month (2006-2010 5-year est.); Median year structure built: before 1940 (2006-2010 5-year est.).
Safety: Violent crime rate: 0.0 per 10,000 population; Property crime rate: 138.7 per 10,000 population (2011).
Transportation: Commute to work: 94.3% car, 0.3% public transportation, 2.5% walk, 2.9% work from home (2006-2010 5-year est.); Travel time to work: 27.1% less than 15 minutes, 32.7% 15 to 30 minutes, 24.5% 30 to 45 minutes, 7.3% 45 to 60 minutes, 8.4% 60 minutes or more (2006-2010 5-year est.)
Additional Information Contacts
Borough of Pen Argyl . . . . (610) 863-4119
    http://www.penargylborough.com
Slate Belt Chamber of Commerce. . . . . (610) 588-1000
    http://www.slatebeltchamber.org

PLAINFIELD (township). Covers a land area of 24.758 square miles and a water area of 0.222 square miles. Located at 40.82° N. Lat; 75.26° W. Long.
Population: 5,444 (1990); 5,668 (2000); 6,138 (2010); Density: 247.9 persons per square mile (2010); Race: 97.6% White, 0.8% Black, 0.4% Asian, 0.1% American Indian/Alaska Native, 0.0% Native Hawaiian/Other Pacific Islander, 1.1% Other, 2.2% Hispanic of any race (2010); Average household size: 2.61 (2010); Median age: 45.5 (2010); Males per 100 females: 97.8 (2010); Marriage status: 22.1% never married, 63.6% now married, 7.9% widowed, 6.4% divorced (2006-2010 5-year est.); Foreign born: 2.3% (2006-2010 5-year est.); Ancestry (includes multiple ancestries): 38.9% German, 21.5% Italian, 20.1% Irish, 10.0% English, 9.2% Pennsylvania German (2006-2010 5-year est.).
Economy: Single-family building permits issued: 7 (2011); Multi-family building permits issued: 0 (2011); Employment by occupation: 7.1% management, 4.4% professional, 9.6% services, 18.6% sales, 3.0% farming, 8.8% construction, 6.1% production (2006-2010 5-year est.).
Income: Per capita income: $26,481 (2006-2010 5-year est.); Median household income: $63,665 (2006-2010 5-year est.); Average household income: $70,701 (2006-2010 5-year est.); Percent of households with income of $100,000 or more: 22.4% (2006-2010 5-year est.); Poverty rate: 6.2% (2006-2010 5-year est.).
Education: Percent of population age 25 and over with: High school diploma (including GED) or higher: 86.4% (2006-2010 5-year est.); Bachelor's degree or higher: 20.4% (2006-2010 5-year est.); Master's degree or higher: 5.4% (2006-2010 5-year est.).
Housing: Homeownership rate: 83.6% (2010); Median home value: $239,200 (2006-2010 5-year est.); Median contract rent: $697 per month (2006-2010 5-year est.); Median year structure built: 1970 (2006-2010 5-year est.).
Safety: Violent crime rate: 1.6 per 10,000 population; Property crime rate: 92.6 per 10,000 population (2011).
Transportation: Commute to work: 93.6% car, 0.0% public transportation, 1.4% walk, 5.0% work from home (2006-2010 5-year est.); Travel time to

work: 26.9% less than 15 minutes, 36.2% 15 to 30 minutes, 22.3% 30 to 45 minutes, 3.9% 45 to 60 minutes, 10.6% 60 minutes or more (2006-2010 5-year est.)

Additional Information Contacts

Greater Carlisle Area Chamber of Commerce . . . . (717) 243-4515
   http://carlislechamber.org

Plainfield Township . . . . (610) 759-6944
   http://twp.plainfield.pa.us

PORTLAND (borough). Covers a land area of 0.491 square miles and a water area of 0.075 square miles. Located at 40.92° N. Lat; 75.10° W. Long. Elevation is 292 feet.

History: Delaware Water Gap National Recreation Area to North, includes Slateford Farm, 10-room, 19th-century farmhouse and slate quarry site.

Population: 516 (1990); 579 (2000); 519 (2010); Density: 1,057.9 persons per square mile (2010); Race: 92.3% White, 3.5% Black, 0.8% Asian, 0.8% American Indian/Alaska Native, 0.0% Native Hawaiian/Other Pacific Islander, 2.6% Other, 3.3% Hispanic of any race (2010); Average household size: 2.33 (2010); Median age: 44.6 (2010); Males per 100 females: 101.2 (2010); Marriage status: 27.4% never married, 53.3% now married, 8.3% widowed, 11.0% divorced (2006-2010 5-year est.); Foreign born: 2.0% (2006-2010 5-year est.); Ancestry (includes multiple ancestries): 37.8% German, 21.4% Irish, 16.2% English, 16.0% American, 8.1% Italian (2006-2010 5-year est.).

Economy: Single-family building permits issued: 1 (2011); Multi-family building permits issued: 0 (2011); Employment by occupation: 16.8% management, 1.0% professional, 14.7% services, 14.7% sales, 0.0% farming, 3.0% construction, 7.6% production (2006-2010 5-year est.).

Income: Per capita income: $22,372 (2006-2010 5-year est.); Median household income: $50,114 (2006-2010 5-year est.); Average household income: $53,915 (2006-2010 5-year est.); Percent of households with income of $100,000 or more: 9.6% (2006-2010 5-year est.); Poverty rate: 9.7% (2006-2010 5-year est.).

Education: Percent of population age 25 and over with: High school diploma (including GED) or higher: 93.2% (2006-2010 5-year est.); Bachelor's degree or higher: 17.2% (2006-2010 5-year est.); Master's degree or higher: 2.8% (2006-2010 5-year est.).

Housing: Homeownership rate: 64.2% (2010); Median home value: $219,400 (2006-2010 5-year est.); Median contract rent: $671 per month (2006-2010 5-year est.); Median year structure built: before 1940 (2006-2010 5-year est.).

Safety: Violent crime rate: 0.0 per 10,000 population; Property crime rate: 38.4 per 10,000 population (2011).

Transportation: Commute to work: 92.1% car, 0.0% public transportation, 0.0% walk, 7.9% work from home (2006-2010 5-year est.); Travel time to work: 6.9% less than 15 minutes, 33.9% 15 to 30 minutes, 28.7% 30 to 45 minutes, 24.1% 45 to 60 minutes, 6.3% 60 minutes or more (2006-2010 5-year est.)

RAUBSVILLE (CDP). Covers a land area of 1.591 square miles and a water area of 0.108 square miles. Located at 40.63° N. Lat; 75.21° W. Long. Elevation is 174 feet.

Population: n/a (1990); n/a (2000); 1,088 (2010); Density: 683.7 persons per square mile (2010); Race: 90.0% White, 4.1% Black, 3.5% Asian, 0.0% American Indian/Alaska Native, 0.0% Native Hawaiian/Other Pacific Islander, 2.4% Other, 2.6% Hispanic of any race (2010); Average household size: 2.60 (2010); Median age: 44.8 (2010); Males per 100 females: 98.5 (2010); Marriage status: 19.1% never married, 76.4% now married, 1.4% widowed, 3.1% divorced (2006-2010 5-year est.); Foreign born: 0.0% (2006-2010 5-year est.); Ancestry (includes multiple ancestries): 38.3% German, 30.7% Irish, 14.6% English, 14.2% Polish, 12.7% Italian (2006-2010 5-year est.).

Economy: Employment by occupation: 7.1% management, 8.9% professional, 5.2% services, 16.8% sales, 2.0% farming, 8.0% construction, 3.9% production (2006-2010 5-year est.).

Income: Per capita income: $44,443 (2006-2010 5-year est.); Median household income: $98,197 (2006-2010 5-year est.); Average household income: $119,858 (2006-2010 5-year est.); Percent of households with income of $100,000 or more: 41.5% (2006-2010 5-year est.); Poverty rate: 10.6% (2006-2010 5-year est.).

Education: Percent of population age 25 and over with: High school diploma (including GED) or higher: 95.8% (2006-2010 5-year est.); Bachelor's degree or higher: 25.8% (2006-2010 5-year est.); Master's degree or higher: 10.1% (2006-2010 5-year est.).

Housing: Homeownership rate: 87.4% (2010); Median home value: $240,900 (2006-2010 5-year est.); Median contract rent: $661 per month (2006-2010 5-year est.); Median year structure built: 1974 (2006-2010 5-year est.).

Transportation: Commute to work: 86.9% car, 0.0% public transportation, 0.0% walk, 13.1% work from home (2006-2010 5-year est.); Travel time to work: 19.6% less than 15 minutes, 29.3% 15 to 30 minutes, 21.0% 30 to 45 minutes, 10.3% 45 to 60 minutes, 19.7% 60 minutes or more (2006-2010 5-year est.)

ROSETO (borough). Covers a land area of 0.614 square miles and a water area of 0.006 square miles. Located at 40.88° N. Lat; 75.22° W. Long. Elevation is 702 feet.

History: Appalachian Trail passes to North. Incorporated 1910.

Population: 1,555 (1990); 1,653 (2000); 1,567 (2010); Density: 2,552.3 persons per square mile (2010); Race: 96.9% White, 1.0% Black, 0.5% Asian, 0.1% American Indian/Alaska Native, 0.0% Native Hawaiian/Other Pacific Islander, 1.5% Other, 2.7% Hispanic of any race (2010); Average household size: 2.46 (2010); Median age: 41.6 (2010); Males per 100 females: 96.6 (2010); Marriage status: 25.2% never married, 56.4% now married, 9.9% widowed, 8.6% divorced (2006-2010 5-year est.); Foreign born: 5.3% (2006-2010 5-year est.); Ancestry (includes multiple ancestries): 39.5% Italian, 26.9% German, 8.7% Irish, 6.6% English, 5.8% Portuguese (2006-2010 5-year est.).

Economy: Single-family building permits issued: 0 (2011); Multi-family building permits issued: 0 (2011); Employment by occupation: 10.1% management, 2.7% professional, 10.1% services, 18.1% sales, 3.8% farming, 14.6% construction, 11.5% production (2006-2010 5-year est.).

Income: Per capita income: $26,209 (2006-2010 5-year est.); Median household income: $54,167 (2006-2010 5-year est.); Average household income: $60,263 (2006-2010 5-year est.); Percent of households with income of $100,000 or more: 11.4% (2006-2010 5-year est.); Poverty rate: 10.8% (2006-2010 5-year est.).

Education: Percent of population age 25 and over with: High school diploma (including GED) or higher: 84.8% (2006-2010 5-year est.); Bachelor's degree or higher: 16.0% (2006-2010 5-year est.); Master's degree or higher: 3.5% (2006-2010 5-year est.).

Housing: Homeownership rate: 73.2% (2010); Median home value: $177,300 (2006-2010 5-year est.); Median contract rent: $623 per month (2006-2010 5-year est.); Median year structure built: 1945 (2006-2010 5-year est.).

Safety: Violent crime rate: 12.7 per 10,000 population; Property crime rate: 178.1 per 10,000 population (2011).

Transportation: Commute to work: 94.2% car, 1.4% public transportation, 2.5% walk, 1.9% work from home (2006-2010 5-year est.); Travel time to work: 24.9% less than 15 minutes, 29.6% 15 to 30 minutes, 26.2% 30 to 45 minutes, 10.0% 45 to 60 minutes, 9.3% 60 minutes or more (2006-2010 5-year est.)

Additional Information Contacts

Slate Belt Chamber of Commerce. (610) 588-1000
   http://www.slatebeltchamber.org

STOCKERTOWN (borough). Covers a land area of 0.969 square miles and a water area of 0.029 square miles. Located at 40.75° N. Lat; 75.26° W. Long. Elevation is 358 feet.

Population: 641 (1990); 687 (2000); 927 (2010); Density: 956.7 persons per square mile (2010); Race: 97.7% White, 0.3% Black, 0.5% Asian, 0.2% American Indian/Alaska Native, 0.0% Native Hawaiian/Other Pacific Islander, 1.3% Other, 3.0% Hispanic of any race (2010); Average household size: 2.67 (2010); Median age: 36.8 (2010); Males per 100 females: 98.1 (2010); Marriage status: 24.7% never married, 54.0% now married, 6.4% widowed, 14.9% divorced (2006-2010 5-year est.); Foreign born: 1.6% (2006-2010 5-year est.); Ancestry (includes multiple ancestries): 49.3% German, 28.6% Italian, 17.7% Irish, 8.1% English, 5.9% American (2006-2010 5-year est.).

Economy: Single-family building permits issued: 1 (2011); Multi-family building permits issued: 0 (2011); Employment by occupation: 4.7% management, 2.1% professional, 8.3% services, 18.4% sales, 1.9% farming, 12.6% construction, 13.2% production (2006-2010 5-year est.).

Income: Per capita income: $23,586 (2006-2010 5-year est.); Median household income: $58,036 (2006-2010 5-year est.); Average household income: $62,545 (2006-2010 5-year est.); Percent of households with income of $100,000 or more: 14.3% (2006-2010 5-year est.); Poverty rate: 7.6% (2006-2010 5-year est.).

Education: Percent of population age 25 and over with: High school diploma (including GED) or higher: 89.1% (2006-2010 5-year est.); Bachelor's degree or higher: 21.1% (2006-2010 5-year est.); Master's degree or higher: 6.5% (2006-2010 5-year est.).

Housing: Homeownership rate: 72.3% (2010); Median home value: $214,900 (2006-2010 5-year est.); Median contract rent: $767 per month (2006-2010 5-year est.); Median year structure built: 1952 (2006-2010 5-year est.).

Transportation: Commute to work: 89.4% car, 0.0% public transportation, 1.5% walk, 9.1% work from home (2006-2010 5-year est.); Travel time to work: 42.2% less than 15 minutes, 27.9% 15 to 30 minutes, 11.4% 30 to 45 minutes, 4.1% 45 to 60 minutes, 14.3% 60 minutes or more (2006-2010 5-year est.)

TATAMY (borough). Covers a land area of 0.553 square miles and a water area of 0.015 square miles. Located at 40.74° N. Lat; 75.25° W. Long. Elevation is 394 feet.

Population: 873 (1990); 930 (2000); 1,203 (2010); Density: 2,176.2 persons per square mile (2010); Race: 91.5% White, 3.7% Black, 2.2% Asian, 0.0% American Indian/Alaska Native, 0.0% Native Hawaiian/Other Pacific Islander, 2.6% Other, 4.3% Hispanic of any race (2010); Average household size: 2.78 (2010); Median age: 39.5 (2010); Males per 100 females: 99.5 (2010); Marriage status: 25.7% never married, 60.4% now married, 6.5% widowed, 7.4% divorced (2006-2010 5-year est.); Foreign born: 0.0% (2006-2010 5-year est.); Ancestry (includes multiple ancestries): 37.1% German, 19.0% Irish, 15.7% Italian, 12.1% Polish, 10.6% Pennsylvania German (2006-2010 5-year est.).

Economy: Single-family building permits issued: 0 (2011); Multi-family building permits issued: 0 (2011); Employment by occupation: 10.5% management, 9.0% professional, 5.9% services, 17.6% sales, 10.8% farming, 7.2% construction, 6.2% production (2006-2010 5-year est.).

Income: Per capita income: $28,899 (2006-2010 5-year est.); Median household income: $67,031 (2006-2010 5-year est.); Average household income: $73,894 (2006-2010 5-year est.); Percent of households with income of $100,000 or more: 20.8% (2006-2010 5-year est.); Poverty rate: 6.2% (2006-2010 5-year est.).

Education: Percent of population age 25 and over with: High school diploma (including GED) or higher: 93.9% (2006-2010 5-year est.); Bachelor's degree or higher: 21.7% (2006-2010 5-year est.); Master's degree or higher: 9.9% (2006-2010 5-year est.).

Housing: Homeownership rate: 82.9% (2010); Median home value: $227,000 (2006-2010 5-year est.); Median contract rent: $643 per month (2006-2010 5-year est.); Median year structure built: 1966 (2006-2010 5-year est.).

Safety: Violent crime rate: 0.0 per 10,000 population; Property crime rate: 49.7 per 10,000 population (2011).

Transportation: Commute to work: 96.9% car, 0.0% public transportation, 0.8% walk, 2.3% work from home (2006-2010 5-year est.); Travel time to work: 30.5% less than 15 minutes, 35.6% 15 to 30 minutes, 14.1% 30 to 45 minutes, 7.0% 45 to 60 minutes, 12.7% 60 minutes or more (2006-2010 5-year est.)

Additional Information Contacts
Greater Lehigh Valley Chamber of Commerce . . . . (610) 841-5800
  http://www.lehighvalleychamber.org

TREICHLERS (unincorporated postal area)
Zip Code: 18086

Covers a land area of 0.475 square miles and a water area of 0.002 square miles. Located at 40.73° N. Lat; 75.54° W. Long. Elevation is 384 feet. Population: 398 (2010); Density: 837.7 persons per square mile (2010); Race: 96.5% White, 1.5% Black, 0.0% Asian, 0.3% American Indian/Alaska Native, 0.0% Native Hawaiian/Other Pacific Islander, 1.7% Other, 1.3% Hispanic of any race (2010); Average household size: 2.49 (2010); Median age: 48.0 (2010); Males per 100 females: 105.2 (2010); Homeownership rate: 91.3% (2010)

UPPER MOUNT BETHEL (township). Covers a land area of 42.409 square miles and a water area of 1.826 square miles. Located at 40.90° N. Lat; 75.14° W. Long.

Population: 5,377 (1990); 6,063 (2000); 6,706 (2010); Density: 158.1 persons per square mile (2010); Race: 94.2% White, 2.4% Black, 1.2% Asian, 0.2% American Indian/Alaska Native, 0.0% Native Hawaiian/Other Pacific Islander, 2.0% Other, 3.5% Hispanic of any race (2010); Average household size: 2.60 (2010); Median age: 45.4 (2010); Males per 100 females: 100.4 (2010); Marriage status: 22.8% never married, 59.2% now

married, 7.5% widowed, 10.5% divorced (2006-2010 5-year est.); Foreign born: 3.2% (2006-2010 5-year est.); Ancestry (includes multiple ancestries): 30.9% German, 17.5% Italian, 15.7% Irish, 11.1% English, 9.6% American (2006-2010 5-year est.).

Economy: Single-family building permits issued: 36 (2011); Multi-family building permits issued: 0 (2011); Employment by occupation: 10.1% management, 7.1% professional, 5.5% services, 22.2% sales, 0.8% farming, 10.2% construction, 5.6% production (2006-2010 5-year est.).

Income: Per capita income: $28,980 (2006-2010 5-year est.); Median household income: $60,320 (2006-2010 5-year est.); Average household income: $74,688 (2006-2010 5-year est.); Percent of households with income of $100,000 or more: 25.0% (2006-2010 5-year est.); Poverty rate: 2.4% (2006-2010 5-year est.).

Education: Percent of population age 25 and over with: High school diploma (including GED) or higher: 85.6% (2006-2010 5-year est.); Bachelor's degree or higher: 18.5% (2006-2010 5-year est.); Master's degree or higher: 6.7% (2006-2010 5-year est.).

Housing: Homeownership rate: 82.6% (2010); Median home value: $230,000 (2006-2010 5-year est.); Median contract rent: $638 per month (2006-2010 5-year est.); Median year structure built: 1972 (2006-2010 5-year est.).

Transportation: Commute to work: 86.9% car, 0.2% public transportation, 0.4% walk, 12.5% work from home (2006-2010 5-year est.); Travel time to work: 23.1% less than 15 minutes, 25.7% 15 to 30 minutes, 23.8% 30 to 45 minutes, 8.8% 45 to 60 minutes, 18.6% 60 minutes or more (2006-2010 5-year est.)

Additional Information Contacts
Slate Belt Chamber of Commerce . . . . (610) 588-1000
  http://www.slatebeltchamber.org
Upper Mount Bethel Township . . . . (570) 897-6127
  http://www.uppermtbethel.org

UPPER NAZARETH (township). Covers a land area of 7.233 square miles and a water area of 0.101 square miles. Located at 40.74° N. Lat; 75.33° W. Long.

Population: 3,402 (1990); 4,426 (2000); 6,231 (2010); Density: 861.4 persons per square mile (2010); Race: 93.1% White, 2.2% Black, 1.9% Asian, 0.1% American Indian/Alaska Native, 0.0% Native Hawaiian/Other Pacific Islander, 2.7% Other, 3.9% Hispanic of any race (2010); Average household size: 2.87 (2010); Median age: 42.2 (2010); Males per 100 females: 86.3 (2010); Marriage status: 21.2% never married, 54.7% now married, 14.8% widowed, 9.2% divorced (2006-2010 5-year est.); Foreign born: 5.1% (2006-2010 5-year est.); Ancestry (includes multiple ancestries): 38.2% German, 14.6% Italian, 13.9% Irish, 10.9% English, 5.3% Polish (2006-2010 5-year est.).

Economy: Single-family building permits issued: 23 (2011); Multi-family building permits issued: 0 (2011); Employment by occupation: 16.2% management, 4.0% professional, 6.6% services, 18.0% sales, 2.8% farming, 7.2% construction, 7.0% production (2006-2010 5-year est.).

Income: Per capita income: $30,886 (2006-2010 5-year est.); Median household income: $83,833 (2006-2010 5-year est.); Average household income: $92,394 (2006-2010 5-year est.); Percent of households with income of $100,000 or more: 33.7% (2006-2010 5-year est.); Poverty rate: 4.2% (2006-2010 5-year est.).

Education: Percent of population age 25 and over with: High school diploma (including GED) or higher: 82.3% (2006-2010 5-year est.); Bachelor's degree or higher: 22.8% (2006-2010 5-year est.); Master's degree or higher: 5.8% (2006-2010 5-year est.).

Housing: Homeownership rate: 88.1% (2010); Median home value: $256,600 (2006-2010 5-year est.); Median contract rent: $733 per month (2006-2010 5-year est.); Median year structure built: 1983 (2006-2010 5-year est.).

Transportation: Commute to work: 97.3% car, 0.0% public transportation, 0.7% walk, 1.5% work from home (2006-2010 5-year est.); Travel time to work: 21.5% less than 15 minutes, 37.3% 15 to 30 minutes, 19.9% 30 to 45 minutes, 5.4% 45 to 60 minutes, 15.9% 60 minutes or more (2006-2010 5-year est.)

Additional Information Contacts
Nazareth Area Chamber of Commerce . . . . (610) 759-9188
  http://nazarethchamber.com

WALNUTPORT (borough). Covers a land area of 0.721 square miles and a water area of 0.080 square miles. Located at 40.75° N. Lat; 75.60° W. Long. Elevation is 381 feet.

History: Appalachian Trail passes to North, on Blue Mt. ridge. Incorporated 1909.

Population: 2,073 (1990); 2,043 (2000); 2,070 (2010); Density: 2,871.1 persons per square mile (2010); Race: 94.8% White, 0.9% Black, 0.8% Asian, 0.4% American Indian/Alaska Native, 0.0% Native Hawaiian/Other Pacific Islander, 3.1% Other, 3.3% Hispanic of any race (2010); Average household size: 2.50 (2010); Median age: 41.8 (2010); Males per 100 females: 92.7 (2010); Marriage status: 26.2% never married, 53.4% now married, 10.6% widowed, 9.7% divorced (2006-2010 5-year est.); Foreign born: 0.3% (2006-2010 5-year est.); Ancestry (includes multiple ancestries): 30.4% German, 11.2% Pennsylvania German, 8.9% Irish, 8.9% Italian, 8.4% Welsh (2006-2010 5-year est.).

Economy: Single-family building permits issued: 0 (2011); Multi-family building permits issued: 0 (2011); Employment by occupation: 8.4% management, 2.9% professional, 12.0% services, 24.1% sales, 2.8% farming, 13.0% construction, 7.9% production (2006-2010 5-year est.).

Income: Per capita income: $20,880 (2006-2010 5-year est.); Median household income: $44,449 (2006-2010 5-year est.); Average household income: $51,274 (2006-2010 5-year est.); Percent of households with income of $100,000 or more: 12.2% (2006-2010 5-year est.); Poverty rate: 10.4% (2006-2010 5-year est.).

Education: Percent of population age 25 and over with: High school diploma (including GED) or higher: 77.4% (2006-2010 5-year est.); Bachelor's degree or higher: 7.0% (2006-2010 5-year est.); Master's degree or higher: 2.4% (2006-2010 5-year est.).

School District(s)

Northampton Area SD (KG-12)

    2010-11 Enrollment: 5,632 . . . . (610) 262-7811

Housing: Homeownership rate: 77.8% (2010); Median home value: $174,700 (2006-2010 5-year est.); Median contract rent: $624 per month (2006-2010 5-year est.); Median year structure built: 1964 (2006-2010 5-year est.).

Safety: Violent crime rate: 4.8 per 10,000 population; Property crime rate: 91.5 per 10,000 population (2011).

Transportation: Commute to work: 93.5% car, 0.0% public transportation, 2.4% walk, 1.2% work from home (2006-2010 5-year est.); Travel time to work: 22.2% less than 15 minutes, 27.5% 15 to 30 minutes, 34.4% 30 to 45 minutes, 8.3% 45 to 60 minutes, 7.6% 60 minutes or more (2006-2010 5-year est.)

Additional Information Contacts

Greater Lehigh Valley Chamber of Commerce . . . . (610) 841-5800
   http://www.lehighvalleychamber.org

WASHINGTON (township). Covers a land area of 17.789 square miles and a water area of 0.176 square miles. Located at 40.85° N. Lat; 75.19° W. Long.

Population: 3,784 (1990); 4,152 (2000); 5,122 (2010); Density: 287.9 persons per square mile (2010); Race: 97.4% White, 0.8% Black, 0.4% Asian, 0.2% American Indian/Alaska Native, 0.0% Native Hawaiian/Other Pacific Islander, 1.2% Other, 2.4% Hispanic of any race (2010); Average household size: 2.61 (2010); Median age: 45.1 (2010); Males per 100 females: 94.3 (2010); Marriage status: 25.5% never married, 57.0% now married, 9.6% widowed, 7.9% divorced (2006-2010 5-year est.); Foreign born: 1.8% (2006-2010 5-year est.); Ancestry (includes multiple ancestries): 32.1% German, 23.6% Italian, 14.9% English, 12.3% Irish, 7.5% Polish (2006-2010 5-year est.).

Economy: Single-family building permits issued: 5 (2011); Multi-family building permits issued: 0 (2011); Employment by occupation: 12.5% management, 2.4% professional, 13.9% services, 14.6% sales, 4.4% farming, 7.3% construction, 7.6% production (2006-2010 5-year est.).

Income: Per capita income: $27,443 (2006-2010 5-year est.); Median household income: $60,517 (2006-2010 5-year est.); Average household income: $71,820 (2006-2010 5-year est.); Percent of households with income of $100,000 or more: 25.1% (2006-2010 5-year est.); Poverty rate: 6.7% (2006-2010 5-year est.).

Education: Percent of population age 25 and over with: High school diploma (including GED) or higher: 89.7% (2006-2010 5-year est.); Bachelor's degree or higher: 21.0% (2006-2010 5-year est.); Master's degree or higher: 4.9% (2006-2010 5-year est.).

Housing: Homeownership rate: 83.8% (2010); Median home value: $244,600 (2006-2010 5-year est.); Median contract rent: $606 per month

(2006-2010 5-year est.); Median year structure built: 1970 (2006-2010 5-year est.).

Safety: Violent crime rate: 3.9 per 10,000 population; Property crime rate: 107.0 per 10,000 population (2011).

Transportation: Commute to work: 92.7% car, 0.0% public transportation, 1.1% walk, 5.4% work from home (2006-2010 5-year est.); Travel time to work: 29.4% less than 15 minutes, 30.1% 15 to 30 minutes, 19.3% 30 to 45 minutes, 10.7% 45 to 60 minutes, 10.5% 60 minutes or more (2006-2010 5-year est.)

Additional Information Contacts

Greater Lehigh Valley Chamber of Commerce . . . . (610) 841-5800
   http://www.lehighvalleychamber.org

WEST EASTON (borough). Covers a land area of 0.305 square miles and a water area of 0.031 square miles. Located at 40.68° N. Lat; 75.24° W. Long. Elevation is 269 feet.

History: Incorporated 1890.

Population: 1,163 (1990); 1,152 (2000); 1,257 (2010); Density: 4,117.0 persons per square mile (2010); Race: 90.6% White, 4.6% Black, 0.7% Asian, 0.4% American Indian/Alaska Native, 0.0% Native Hawaiian/Other Pacific Islander, 3.7% Other, 8.4% Hispanic of any race (2010); Average household size: 2.57 (2010); Median age: 39.9 (2010); Males per 100 females: 99.2 (2010); Marriage status: 37.8% never married, 46.2% now married, 6.1% widowed, 9.8% divorced (2006-2010 5-year est.); Foreign born: 2.2% (2006-2010 5-year est.); Ancestry (includes multiple ancestries): 33.3% German, 27.2% Italian, 16.1% Irish, 7.6% Pennsylvania German, 6.1% English (2006-2010 5-year est.).

Economy: Single-family building permits issued: 0 (2011); Multi-family building permits issued: 0 (2011); Employment by occupation: 3.6% management, 2.4% professional, 10.9% services, 19.4% sales, 7.0% farming, 11.0% construction, 8.3% production (2006-2010 5-year est.).

Income: Per capita income: $23,045 (2006-2010 5-year est.); Median household income: $55,357 (2006-2010 5-year est.); Average household income: $62,212 (2006-2010 5-year est.); Percent of households with income of $100,000 or more: 16.1% (2006-2010 5-year est.); Poverty rate: 10.2% (2006-2010 5-year est.).

Education: Percent of population age 25 and over with: High school diploma (including GED) or higher: 90.3% (2006-2010 5-year est.); Bachelor's degree or higher: 9.7% (2006-2010 5-year est.); Master's degree or higher: 0.8% (2006-2010 5-year est.).

Housing: Homeownership rate: 69.7% (2010); Median home value: $151,400 (2006-2010 5-year est.); Median contract rent: $836 per month (2006-2010 5-year est.); Median year structure built: before 1940 (2006-2010 5-year est.).

Transportation: Commute to work: 93.3% car, 1.0% public transportation, 2.4% walk, 2.4% work from home (2006-2010 5-year est.); Travel time to work: 30.7% less than 15 minutes, 38.8% 15 to 30 minutes, 18.2% 30 to 45 minutes, 6.3% 45 to 60 minutes, 6.0% 60 minutes or more (2006-2010 5-year est.)

Additional Information Contacts

Borough of West Easton . . . . (610) 252-6651
   http://www.westeastonborough.com

Greater Lehigh Valley Chamber of Commerce . . . . (610) 841-5800
   http://www.lehighvalleychamber.org

WILLIAMS (township). Covers a land area of 18.170 square miles and a water area of 0.451 square miles. Located at 40.63° N. Lat; 75.23° W. Long.

Population: 3,976 (1990); 4,470 (2000); 5,884 (2010); Density: 323.8 persons per square mile (2010); Race: 92.6% White, 2.8% Black, 3.0% Asian, 0.1% American Indian/Alaska Native, 0.0% Native Hawaiian/Other Pacific Islander, 1.5% Other, 2.3% Hispanic of any race (2010); Average household size: 2.49 (2010); Median age: 46.2 (2010); Males per 100 females: 100.1 (2010); Marriage status: 19.5% never married, 72.8% now married, 3.6% widowed, 4.1% divorced (2006-2010 5-year est.); Foreign born: 6.9% (2006-2010 5-year est.); Ancestry (includes multiple ancestries): 34.1% German, 20.3% Italian, 14.8% Irish, 9.5% English, 9.4% Polish (2006-2010 5-year est.).

Economy: Single-family building permits issued: 10 (2011); Multi-family building permits issued: 0 (2011); Employment by occupation: 12.4% management, 8.4% professional, 10.2% services, 12.3% sales, 1.9% farming, 8.5% construction, 7.6% production (2006-2010 5-year est.).

Income: Per capita income: $42,943 (2006-2010 5-year est.); Median household income: $87,266 (2006-2010 5-year est.); Average household income: $109,827 (2006-2010 5-year est.); Percent of households with

income of $100,000 or more: 40.8% (2006-2010 5-year est.); Poverty rate: 4.5% (2006-2010 5-year est.).

Education: Percent of population age 25 and over with: High school diploma (including GED) or higher: 92.0% (2006-2010 5-year est.); Bachelor's degree or higher: 33.2% (2006-2010 5-year est.); Master's degree or higher: 12.6% (2006-2010 5-year est.).

Housing: Homeownership rate: 85.4% (2010); Median home value: $283,700 (2006-2010 5-year est.); Median contract rent: $1,250 per month (2006-2010 5-year est.); Median year structure built: 1982 (2006-2010 5-year est.).

Transportation: Commute to work: 91.5% car, 0.5% public transportation, 1.3% walk, 5.7% work from home (2006-2010 5-year est.); Travel time to work: 20.7% less than 15 minutes, 29.4% 15 to 30 minutes, 18.8% 30 to 45 minutes, 11.1% 45 to 60 minutes, 19.9% 60 minutes or more (2006-2010 5-year est.)

Additional Information Contacts
Greater Lehigh Valley Chamber of Commerce . . . . (610) 841-5800
   http://www.lehighvalleychamber.org

WILSON (borough). Covers a land area of 1.160 square miles and a water area of 0.005 square miles. Located at 40.68° N. Lat; 75.24° W. Long. Elevation is 384 feet.

History: Incorporated 1920.

Population: 7,830 (1990); 7,682 (2000); 7,896 (2010); Density: 6,809.2 persons per square mile (2010); Race: 84.1% White, 6.5% Black, 2.1% Asian, 0.2% American Indian/Alaska Native, 0.0% Native Hawaiian/Other Pacific Islander, 7.1% Other, 10.6% Hispanic of any race (2010); Average household size: 2.53 (2010); Median age: 35.5 (2010); Males per 100 females: 89.5 (2010); Marriage status: 29.5% never married, 47.6% now married, 6.8% widowed, 16.1% divorced (2006-2010 5-year est.); Foreign born: 4.7% (2006-2010 5-year est.); Ancestry (includes multiple ancestries): 37.8% German, 17.9% Italian, 14.2% Irish, 10.4% English, 6.1% Pennsylvania German (2006-2010 5-year est.).

Economy: Single-family building permits issued: 0 (2011); Multi-family building permits issued: 0 (2011); Employment by occupation: 4.9% management, 2.4% professional, 14.5% services, 24.6% sales, 4.3% farming, 6.0% construction, 6.1% production (2006-2010 5-year est.).

Income: Per capita income: $22,459 (2006-2010 5-year est.); Median household income: $45,028 (2006-2010 5-year est.); Average household income: $52,741 (2006-2010 5-year est.); Percent of households with income of $100,000 or more: 7.3% (2006-2010 5-year est.); Poverty rate: 11.6% (2006-2010 5-year est.).

Education: Percent of population age 25 and over with: High school diploma (including GED) or higher: 87.7% (2006-2010 5-year est.); Bachelor's degree or higher: 12.9% (2006-2010 5-year est.); Master's degree or higher: 5.0% (2006-2010 5-year est.).

Housing: Homeownership rate: 60.5% (2010); Median home value: $138,400 (2006-2010 5-year est.); Median contract rent: $689 per month (2006-2010 5-year est.); Median year structure built: before 1940 (2006-2010 5-year est.).

Transportation: Commute to work: 91.7% car, 2.0% public transportation, 4.4% walk, 1.6% work from home (2006-2010 5-year est.); Travel time to work: 34.3% less than 15 minutes, 32.6% 15 to 30 minutes, 15.9% 30 to 45 minutes, 7.4% 45 to 60 minutes, 9.8% 60 minutes or more (2006-2010 5-year est.)

Additional Information Contacts
Borough of Wilson . . . . (610) 258-6142
   http://www.wilsonborough.org
Greater Lehigh Valley Chamber of Commerce . . . . (610) 841-5800
   http://www.lehighvalleychamber.org

WIND GAP (borough). Aka Windgap. Covers a land area of 1.337 square miles and a water area of 0.029 square miles. Located at 40.85° N. Lat; 75.29° W. Long. Elevation is 755 feet.

History: Appalachian Trail passes to North on Blue Mt. ridge and Northeast on Kittantinny Mountain. Incorporated 1893.

Population: 2,741 (1990); 2,812 (2000); 2,720 (2010); Density: 2,034.0 persons per square mile (2010); Race: 95.7% White, 1.0% Black, 0.6% Asian, 0.1% American Indian/Alaska Native, 0.0% Native Hawaiian/Other Pacific Islander, 2.6% Other, 3.2% Hispanic of any race (2010); Average household size: 2.21 (2010); Median age: 42.7 (2010); Males per 100 females: 93.2 (2010); Marriage status: 20.6% never married, 56.6% now married, 9.9% widowed, 13.0% divorced (2006-2010 5-year est.); Foreign born: 8.2% (2006-2010 5-year est.); Ancestry (includes multiple

ancestries): 33.2% German, 21.8% Italian, 12.3% Irish, 10.7% English, 8.6% Dutch (2006-2010 5-year est.).

Economy: Single-family building permits issued: 4 (2011); Multi-family building permits issued: 0 (2011); Employment by occupation: 4.3% management, 5.2% professional, 7.9% services, 15.4% sales, 3.7% farming, 6.7% construction, 16.4% production (2006-2010 5-year est.).

Income: Per capita income: $24,525 (2006-2010 5-year est.); Median household income: $48,658 (2006-2010 5-year est.); Average household income: $53,452 (2006-2010 5-year est.); Percent of households with income of $100,000 or more: 9.0% (2006-2010 5-year est.); Poverty rate: 5.1% (2006-2010 5-year est.).

Education: Percent of population age 25 and over with: High school diploma (including GED) or higher: 80.2% (2006-2010 5-year est.); Bachelor's degree or higher: 19.6% (2006-2010 5-year est.); Master's degree or higher: 6.3% (2006-2010 5-year est.).

Housing: Homeownership rate: 48.7% (2010); Median home value: $165,000 (2006-2010 5-year est.); Median contract rent: $626 per month (2006-2010 5-year est.); Median year structure built: 1961 (2006-2010 5-year est.).

Safety: Violent crime rate: 18.3 per 10,000 population; Property crime rate: 190.5 per 10,000 population (2011).

Transportation: Commute to work: 95.6% car, 0.0% public transportation, 0.0% walk, 3.8% work from home (2006-2010 5-year est.); Travel time to work: 18.7% less than 15 minutes, 49.3% 15 to 30 minutes, 18.5% 30 to 45 minutes, 5.2% 45 to 60 minutes, 8.4% 60 minutes or more (2006-2010 5-year est.)

Additional Information Contacts
Borough of Wind Gap . . . . (610) 698-4582
   http://www.windgap-pa.gov
Slate Belt Chamber of Commerce . . . . (610) 588-1000
   http://www.slatebeltchamber.org

Northumberland County

Located in east central Pennsylvania; drained by the Susquehanna River and its West Branch. Covers a land area of 458.368 square miles, a water area of 19.157 square miles, and is located in the Eastern Time Zone at 40.85° N. Lat., 76.71° W. Long. The county was founded in 1772. County seat is Sunbury.

Northumberland County is part of the Sunbury, PA Micropolitan Statistical Area. The entire metro area includes: Northumberland County, PA

Population: 96,771 (1990); 94,556 (2000); 94,528 (2010); Race: 95.4% White, 2.0% Black, 0.4% Asian, 0.2% American Indian/Alaska Native, 0.0% Native Hawaiian/Other Pacific Islander, 2.0% Other, 2.4% Hispanic of any race (2010); Density: 206.2 persons per square mile (2010); Average household size: 2.32 (2010); Median age: 43.4 (2010); Males per 100 females: 99.7 (2010).

Religion: Six largest groups: 15.4% Catholicism, 9.2% Lutheran, 8.6% Methodist/Pietist, 5.5% Presbyterian-Reformed, 5.0% Holiness, 2.1% Non-Denominational (2010)

Economy: Unemployment rate: 8.6% (August 2012); Total civilian labor force: 48,065 (August 2012); Leading industries: 19.5% manufacturing; 18.8% health care and social assistance; 13.9% retail trade (2010); Farms: 936 totaling 147,660 acres (2007); Companies that employ 500 or more persons: 3 (2010); Companies that employ 100 to 499 persons: 31 (2010); Companies that employ less than 100 persons: 1,646 (2010); Black-owned businesses: n/a (2007); Hispanic-owned businesses: n/a (2007); Asian-owned businesses: 76 (2007); Women-owned businesses: 1,568 (2007); Retail sales per capita: $7,679 (2010). Single-family building permits issued: 53 (2011); Multi-family building permits issued: 2 (2011).

Income: Per capita income: $20,654 (2006-2010 5-year est.); Median household income: $38,387 (2006-2010 5-year est.); Average household income: $48,670 (2006-2010 5-year est.); Percent of households with income of $100,000 or more: 8.7% (2006-2010 5-year est.); Poverty rate: 14.9% (2006-2010 5-year est.); Bankruptcy rate: 2.34% (2011).

Education: Percent of population age 25 and over with: High school diploma (including GED) or higher: 84.2% (2006-2010 5-year est.); Bachelor's degree or higher: 13.5% (2006-2010 5-year est.); Master's degree or higher: 4.4% (2006-2010 5-year est.).

Housing: Homeownership rate: 72.5% (2010); Median home value: $93,500 (2006-2010 5-year est.); Median contract rent: $393 per month (2006-2010 5-year est.); Median year structure built: 1944 (2006-2010 5-year est.)

Health: Birth rate: 102.9 per 10,000 population (2011); Death rate: 115.5 per 10,000 population (2011); Age-adjusted cancer mortality rate: 183.9 deaths per 100,000 population (2009); Number of physicians: 8.0 per 10,000 population (2010); Hospital beds: 20.9 per 10,000 population (2008); Hospital admissions: 681.0 per 10,000 population (2008).

Elections: 2012 Presidential election results: 39.3% Obama, 58.8% Romney

National and State Parks: Milton State Park; Shikellamy State Park

Additional Information Contacts

Northumberland County Government . . . . (570) 988-4100
  http://www.northumberlandco.org

Northumberland County Communities

ATLAS (CDP). Covers a land area of 0.250 square miles and a water area of 0 square miles. Located at 40.80° N. Lat; 76.43° W. Long. Elevation is 1,129 feet.

Population: n/a (1990); n/a (2000); 809 (2010); Density: 3,232.5 persons per square mile (2010); Race: 97.7% White, 1.7% Black, 0.0% Asian, 0.0% American Indian/Alaska Native, 0.0% Native Hawaiian/Other Pacific Islander, 0.6% Other, 1.1% Hispanic of any race (2010); Average household size: 2.19 (2010); Median age: 46.5 (2010); Males per 100 females: 100.2 (2010); Marriage status: 22.8% never married, 60.0% now married, 8.9% widowed, 8.3% divorced (2006-2010 5-year est.); Foreign born: 0.0% (2006-2010 5-year est.); Ancestry (includes multiple ancestries): 30.9% Polish, 17.5% Italian, 12.9% German, 12.2% Irish, 5.5% American (2006-2010 5-year est.).

Economy: Employment by occupation: 6.6% management, 0.0% professional, 13.4% services, 23.9% sales, 1.3% farming, 5.8% construction, 8.9% production (2006-2010 5-year est.).

Income: Per capita income: $19,831 (2006-2010 5-year est.); Median household income: $39,321 (2006-2010 5-year est.); Average household income: $46,277 (2006-2010 5-year est.); Percent of households with income of $100,000 or more: 7.4% (2006-2010 5-year est.); Poverty rate: 12.4% (2006-2010 5-year est.).

Education: Percent of population age 25 and over with: High school diploma (including GED) or higher: 82.6% (2006-2010 5-year est.); Bachelor's degree or higher: 9.2% (2006-2010 5-year est.); Master's degree or higher: 3.9% (2006-2010 5-year est.).

Housing: Homeownership rate: 77.2% (2010); Median home value: $50,600 (2006-2010 5-year est.); Median contract rent: $387 per month (2006-2010 5-year est.); Median year structure built: before 1940 (2006-2010 5-year est.).

Transportation: Commute to work: 95.7% car, 0.0% public transportation, 0.0% walk, 4.3% work from home (2006-2010 5-year est.); Travel time to work: 47.1% less than 15 minutes, 33.3% 15 to 30 minutes, 7.6% 30 to 45 minutes, 8.1% 45 to 60 minutes, 3.9% 60 minutes or more (2006-2010 5-year est.)

COAL (township). Covers a land area of 26.361 square miles and a water area of 0.098 square miles. Located at 40.78° N. Lat; 76.52° W. Long.

Population: 9,922 (1990); 10,628 (2000); 10,383 (2010); Density: 393.9 persons per square mile (2010); Race: 87.2% White, 10.2% Black, 0.2% Asian, 0.2% American Indian/Alaska Native, 0.0% Native Hawaiian/Other Pacific Islander, 2.2% Other, 2.5% Hispanic of any race (2010); Average household size: 2.22 (2010); Median age: 41.8 (2010); Males per 100 females: 143.2 (2010); Marriage status: 31.2% never married, 48.1% now married, 8.9% widowed, 11.9% divorced (2006-2010 5-year est.); Foreign born: 0.6% (2006-2010 5-year est.); Ancestry (includes multiple ancestries): 23.4% Polish, 17.6% German, 11.1% Italian, 10.3% Irish, 8.7% Dutch (2006-2010 5-year est.).

Economy: Single-family building permits issued: 1 (2011); Multi-family building permits issued: 0 (2011); Employment by occupation: 5.5% management, 2.7% professional, 12.3% services, 17.2% sales, 4.3% farming, 11.9% construction, 6.6% production (2006-2010 5-year est.).

Income: Per capita income: $15,421 (2006-2010 5-year est.); Median household income: $30,939 (2006-2010 5-year est.); Average household income: $39,107 (2006-2010 5-year est.); Percent of households with income of $100,000 or more: 4.7% (2006-2010 5-year est.); Poverty rate: 17.7% (2006-2010 5-year est.).

Education: Percent of population age 25 and over with: High school diploma (including GED) or higher: 78.6% (2006-2010 5-year est.); Bachelor's degree or higher: 10.5% (2006-2010 5-year est.); Master's degree or higher: 3.0% (2006-2010 5-year est.).

School District(s)

Northumberland County CTC (11-12)
  2010-11 Enrollment: n/a . . . . (570) 644-0304
Shamokin Area SD (KG-12)
  2010-11 Enrollment: 2,578 . . . . (570) 648-5752

Housing: Homeownership rate: 78.8% (2010); Median home value: $53,700 (2006-2010 5-year est.); Median contract rent: $323 per month (2006-2010 5-year est.); Median year structure built: before 1940 (2006-2010 5-year est.).

Safety: Violent crime rate: 24.0 per 10,000 population; Property crime rate: 183.4 per 10,000 population (2011).

Transportation: Commute to work: 92.4% car, 0.2% public transportation, 3.6% walk, 2.0% work from home (2006-2010 5-year est.); Travel time to work: 39.1% less than 15 minutes, 25.5% 15 to 30 minutes, 20.5% 30 to 45 minutes, 8.0% 45 to 60 minutes, 6.8% 60 minutes or more (2006-2010 5-year est.)

Additional Information Contacts

Brush Valley Regional Chamber of Commerce . . . . (570) 648-4675
  http://www.brushvalleychamber.com
Coal Township . . . . (570) 644-0971

DALMATIA (CDP). Covers a land area of 0.733 square miles and a water area of 0.052 square miles. Located at 40.65° N. Lat; 76.90° W. Long. Elevation is 413 feet.

Population: n/a (1990); n/a (2000); 488 (2010); Density: 665.9 persons per square mile (2010); Race: 96.5% White, 0.8% Black, 0.0% Asian, 0.2% American Indian/Alaska Native, 0.0% Native Hawaiian/Other Pacific Islander, 2.5% Other, 0.8% Hispanic of any race (2010); Average household size: 2.36 (2010); Median age: 44.1 (2010); Males per 100 females: 95.2 (2010); Marriage status: 26.4% never married, 56.3% now married, 6.0% widowed, 11.3% divorced (2006-2010 5-year est.); Foreign born: 0.0% (2006-2010 5-year est.); Ancestry (includes multiple ancestries): 81.9% German, 5.5% Polish, 2.3% Italian, 1.9% French, 1.6% Slovak (2006-2010 5-year est.).

Economy: Employment by occupation: 3.9% management, 9.8% professional, 2.8% services, 25.6% sales, 2.5% farming, 1.4% construction, 2.1% production (2006-2010 5-year est.).

Income: Per capita income: $20,181 (2006-2010 5-year est.); Median household income: $43,813 (2006-2010 5-year est.); Average household income: $55,083 (2006-2010 5-year est.); Percent of households with income of $100,000 or more: 11.5% (2006-2010 5-year est.); Poverty rate: 18.1% (2006-2010 5-year est.).

Education: Percent of population age 25 and over with: High school diploma (including GED) or higher: 82.1% (2006-2010 5-year est.); Bachelor's degree or higher: 9.7% (2006-2010 5-year est.); Master's degree or higher: 4.9% (2006-2010 5-year est.).

School District(s)

Line Mountain SD (KG-12)
  2010-11 Enrollment: 1,250 . . . . (570) 758-2640

Housing: Homeownership rate: 71.0% (2010); Median home value: $87,000 (2006-2010 5-year est.); Median contract rent: $450 per month (2006-2010 5-year est.); Median year structure built: 1952 (2006-2010 5-year est.).

Transportation: Commute to work: 98.6% car, 0.0% public transportation, 1.4% walk, 0.0% work from home (2006-2010 5-year est.); Travel time to work: 15.1% less than 15 minutes, 47.7% 15 to 30 minutes, 14.0% 30 to 45 minutes, 11.6% 45 to 60 minutes, 11.6% 60 minutes or more (2006-2010 5-year est.)

DELAWARE (township). Covers a land area of 30.321 square miles and a water area of 1.051 square miles. Located at 41.12° N. Lat; 76.84° W. Long.

Population: 4,018 (1990); 4,341 (2000); 4,489 (2010); Density: 148.1 persons per square mile (2010); Race: 98.0% White, 0.8% Black, 0.3% Asian, 0.2% American Indian/Alaska Native, 0.0% Native Hawaiian/Other Pacific Islander, 0.7% Other, 1.0% Hispanic of any race (2010); Average household size: 2.45 (2010); Median age: 44.4 (2010); Males per 100 females: 97.0 (2010); Marriage status: 22.8% never married, 60.7% now married, 5.8% widowed, 10.8% divorced (2006-2010 5-year est.); Foreign born: 0.0% (2006-2010 5-year est.); Ancestry (includes multiple ancestries): 43.8% German, 16.7% Irish, 13.5% American, 7.4% Italian, 6.3% English (2006-2010 5-year est.).

Economy: Single-family building permits issued: 1 (2011); Multi-family building permits issued: 0 (2011); Employment by occupation: 12.2%

management, 2.6% professional, 12.3% services, 13.5% sales, 5.3% farming, 14.4% construction, 10.4% production (2006-2010 5-year est.).

Income: Per capita income: $21,092 (2006-2010 5-year est.); Median household income: $45,063 (2006-2010 5-year est.); Average household income: $56,742 (2006-2010 5-year est.); Percent of households with income of $100,000 or more: 10.8% (2006-2010 5-year est.); Poverty rate: 14.6% (2006-2010 5-year est.).

Education: Percent of population age 25 and over with: High school diploma (including GED) or higher: 78.4% (2006-2010 5-year est.); Bachelor's degree or higher: 9.4% (2006-2010 5-year est.); Master's degree or higher: 2.1% (2006-2010 5-year est.).

Housing: Homeownership rate: 83.4% (2010); Median home value: $136,400 (2006-2010 5-year est.); Median contract rent: $409 per month (2006-2010 5-year est.); Median year structure built: 1978 (2006-2010 5-year est.).

Transportation: Commute to work: 86.7% car, 0.0% public transportation, 0.0% walk, 8.4% work from home (2006-2010 5-year est.); Travel time to work: 25.0% less than 15 minutes, 49.1% 15 to 30 minutes, 14.4% 30 to 45 minutes, 1.8% 45 to 60 minutes, 9.6% 60 minutes or more (2006-2010 5-year est.)

Additional Information Contacts

Williamsport/Lycoming Chamber of Commerce . . . . (570) 326-1971
http://www.williamsport.org

DEWART (CDP). Covers a land area of 2.038 square miles and a water area of 0 square miles. Located at 41.11° N. Lat; 76.87° W. Long. Elevation is 486 feet.

Population: n/a (1990); n/a (2000); 1,471 (2010); Density: 721.9 persons per square mile (2010); Race: 97.8% White, 0.7% Black, 0.3% Asian, 0.0% American Indian/Alaska Native, 0.0% Native Hawaiian/Other Pacific Islander, 1.2% Other, 1.3% Hispanic of any race (2010); Average household size: 2.43 (2010); Median age: 42.6 (2010); Males per 100 females: 95.1 (2010); Marriage status: 24.4% never married, 63.6% now married, 4.0% widowed, 8.0% divorced (2006-2010 5-year est.); Foreign born: 0.0% (2006-2010 5-year est.); Ancestry (includes multiple ancestries): 39.9% German, 23.5% Irish, 17.7% American, 15.8% Italian, 6.0% English (2006-2010 5-year est.).

Economy: Employment by occupation: 15.5% management, 6.1% professional, 11.0% services, 10.6% sales, 6.0% farming, 11.4% construction, 8.2% production (2006-2010 5-year est.).

Income: Per capita income: $24,371 (2006-2010 5-year est.); Median household income: $51,098 (2006-2010 5-year est.); Average household income: $61,918 (2006-2010 5-year est.); Percent of households with income of $100,000 or more: 14.5% (2006-2010 5-year est.); Poverty rate: 2.6% (2006-2010 5-year est.).

Education: Percent of population age 25 and over with: High school diploma (including GED) or higher: 89.8% (2006-2010 5-year est.); Bachelor's degree or higher: 11.6% (2006-2010 5-year est.); Master's degree or higher: 1.3% (2006-2010 5-year est.).

Housing: Homeownership rate: 84.4% (2010); Median home value: $121,200 (2006-2010 5-year est.); Median contract rent: $560 per month (2006-2010 5-year est.); Median year structure built: 1971 (2006-2010 5-year est.).

Transportation: Commute to work: 98.8% car, 0.0% public transportation, 0.0% walk, 1.2% work from home (2006-2010 5-year est.); Travel time to work: 21.7% less than 15 minutes, 48.3% 15 to 30 minutes, 13.1% 30 to 45 minutes, 4.1% 45 to 60 minutes, 12.8% 60 minutes or more (2006-2010 5-year est.)

DORNSIFE (unincorporated postal area)
Zip Code: 17823

Covers a land area of 34.335 square miles and a water area of 0.107 square miles. Located at 40.74° N. Lat; 76.77° W. Long. Elevation is 495 feet. Population: 1,273 (2010); Density: 37.1 persons per square mile (2010); Race: 99.1% White, 0.1% Black, 0.1% Asian, 0.1% American Indian/Alaska Native, 0.1% Native Hawaiian/Other Pacific Islander, 0.5% Other, 0.6% Hispanic of any race (2010); Average household size: 2.69 (2010); Median age: 41.9 (2010); Males per 100 females: 103.7 (2010); Homeownership rate: 81.8% (2010)

EAST CAMERON (township). Covers a land area of 12.013 square miles and a water area of 0.151 square miles. Located at 40.75° N. Lat; 76.52° W. Long.

Population: 646 (1990); 686 (2000); 748 (2010); Density: 62.3 persons per square mile (2010); Race: 97.5% White, 0.1% Black, 0.3% Asian,

0.7% American Indian/Alaska Native, 0.0% Native Hawaiian/Other Pacific Islander, 1.4% Other, 0.1% Hispanic of any race (2010); Average household size: 2.40 (2010); Median age: 48.2 (2010); Males per 100 females: 103.8 (2010); Marriage status: 13.8% never married, 72.3% now married, 5.8% widowed, 8.0% divorced (2006-2010 5-year est.); Foreign born: 0.6% (2006-2010 5-year est.); Ancestry (includes multiple ancestries): 44.4% German, 10.8% Irish, 10.3% Dutch, 9.7% Polish, 8.4% English (2006-2010 5-year est.).

Economy: Employment by occupation: 8.1% management, 1.1% professional, 7.0% services, 14.8% sales, 1.4% farming, 19.3% construction, 14.8% production (2006-2010 5-year est.).

Income: Per capita income: $24,035 (2006-2010 5-year est.); Median household income: $49,821 (2006-2010 5-year est.); Average household income: $54,640 (2006-2010 5-year est.); Percent of households with income of $100,000 or more: 10.4% (2006-2010 5-year est.); Poverty rate: 11.0% (2006-2010 5-year est.).

Education: Percent of population age 25 and over with: High school diploma (including GED) or higher: 84.1% (2006-2010 5-year est.); Bachelor's degree or higher: 11.9% (2006-2010 5-year est.); Master's degree or higher: 4.9% (2006-2010 5-year est.).

Housing: Homeownership rate: 90.1% (2010); Median home value: $96,400 (2006-2010 5-year est.); Median contract rent: n/a per month (2006-2010 5-year est.); Median year structure built: 1967 (2006-2010 5-year est.).

Transportation: Commute to work: 88.9% car, 0.0% public transportation, 3.4% walk, 7.7% work from home (2006-2010 5-year est.); Travel time to work: 22.5% less than 15 minutes, 28.7% 15 to 30 minutes, 27.2% 30 to 45 minutes, 14.5% 45 to 60 minutes, 7.1% 60 minutes or more (2006-2010 5-year est.)

EAST CHILLISQUAQUE (township). Covers a land area of 8.026 square miles and a water area of 0.045 square miles. Located at 40.99° N. Lat; 76.79° W. Long.

Population: 679 (1990); 664 (2000); 668 (2010); Density: 83.2 persons per square mile (2010); Race: 99.1% White, 0.0% Black, 0.1% Asian, 0.0% American Indian/Alaska Native, 0.0% Native Hawaiian/Other Pacific Islander, 0.8% Other, 0.3% Hispanic of any race (2010); Average household size: 2.52 (2010); Median age: 46.4 (2010); Males per 100 females: 106.2 (2010); Marriage status: 16.4% never married, 69.7% now married, 3.6% widowed, 10.3% divorced (2006-2010 5-year est.); Foreign born: 0.0% (2006-2010 5-year est.); Ancestry (includes multiple ancestries): 47.4% German, 17.6% English, 13.3% Irish, 9.2% Dutch, 9.0% American (2006-2010 5-year est.).

Economy: Single-family building permits issued: 0 (2011); Multi-family building permits issued: 0 (2011); Employment by occupation: 13.2% management, 2.8% professional, 6.7% services, 14.5% sales, 2.6% farming, 16.1% construction, 24.9% production (2006-2010 5-year est.).

Income: Per capita income: $38,492 (2006-2010 5-year est.); Median household income: $48,819 (2006-2010 5-year est.); Average household income: $88,069 (2006-2010 5-year est.); Percent of households with income of $100,000 or more: 15.9% (2006-2010 5-year est.); Poverty rate: 20.6% (2006-2010 5-year est.).

Education: Percent of population age 25 and over with: High school diploma (including GED) or higher: 84.7% (2006-2010 5-year est.); Bachelor's degree or higher: 14.0% (2006-2010 5-year est.); Master's degree or higher: 5.7% (2006-2010 5-year est.).

Housing: Homeownership rate: 84.2% (2010); Median home value: $131,000 (2006-2010 5-year est.); Median contract rent: $444 per month (2006-2010 5-year est.); Median year structure built: before 1940 (2006-2010 5-year est.).

Transportation: Commute to work: 86.3% car, 1.6% public transportation, 2.6% walk, 8.8% work from home (2006-2010 5-year est.); Travel time to work: 27.3% less than 15 minutes, 45.5% 15 to 30 minutes, 24.4% 30 to 45 minutes, 0.0% 45 to 60 minutes, 2.8% 60 minutes or more (2006-2010 5-year est.)

EDGEWOOD (CDP). Covers a land area of 0.502 square miles and a water area of 0 square miles. Located at 40.79° N. Lat; 76.58° W. Long. Elevation is 794 feet.

Population: 3,055 (1990); 2,619 (2000); 2,384 (2010); Density: 4,747.1 persons per square mile (2010); Race: 97.8% White, 0.4% Black, 0.4% Asian, 0.1% American Indian/Alaska Native, 0.0% Native Hawaiian/Other Pacific Islander, 1.3% Other, 1.3% Hispanic of any race (2010); Average household size: 2.15 (2010); Median age: 45.9 (2010); Males per 100 females: 90.7 (2010); Marriage status: 27.9% never married, 48.3% now

married, 10.7% widowed, 13.1% divorced (2006-2010 5-year est.); Foreign born: 0.0% (2006-2010 5-year est.); Ancestry (includes multiple ancestries): 28.5% German, 25.3% Polish, 18.0% Italian, 16.2% Irish, 11.8% Dutch (2006-2010 5-year est.).

Economy: Employment by occupation: 2.8% management, 5.2% professional, 14.2% services, 15.0% sales, 6.4% farming, 14.0% construction, 5.5% production (2006-2010 5-year est.).

Income: Per capita income: $18,397 (2006-2010 5-year est.); Median household income: $28,868 (2006-2010 5-year est.); Average household income: $38,128 (2006-2010 5-year est.); Percent of households with income of $100,000 or more: 5.9% (2006-2010 5-year est.); Poverty rate: 22.8% (2006-2010 5-year est.).

Education: Percent of population age 25 and over with: High school diploma (including GED) or higher: 89.8% (2006-2010 5-year est.); Bachelor's degree or higher: 12.3% (2006-2010 5-year est.); Master's degree or higher: 4.1% (2006-2010 5-year est.).

Housing: Homeownership rate: 74.2% (2010); Median home value: $46,000 (2006-2010 5-year est.); Median contract rent: $287 per month (2006-2010 5-year est.); Median year structure built: before 1940 (2006-2010 5-year est.).

Transportation: Commute to work: 91.8% car, 0.7% public transportation, 2.4% walk, 1.7% work from home (2006-2010 5-year est.); Travel time to work: 40.0% less than 15 minutes, 22.9% 15 to 30 minutes, 21.1% 30 to 45 minutes, 8.7% 45 to 60 minutes, 7.3% 60 minutes or more (2006-2010 5-year est.)

Additional Information Contacts

Brush Valley Regional Chamber of Commerce . . . . (570) 648-4675
   http://www.brushvalleychamber.com

ELYSBURG (CDP).
Covers a land area of 2.916 square miles and a water area of 0 square miles. Located at 40.87° N. Lat; 76.55° W. Long. Elevation is 587 feet.

Population: 1,890 (1990); 2,067 (2000); 2,194 (2010); Density: 752.4 persons per square mile (2010); Race: 98.0% White, 0.5% Black, 0.7% Asian, 0.2% American Indian/Alaska Native, 0.0% Native Hawaiian/Other Pacific Islander, 0.6% Other, 1.0% Hispanic of any race (2010); Average household size: 2.26 (2010); Median age: 47.4 (2010); Males per 100 females: 87.4 (2010); Marriage status: 20.6% never married, 59.0% now married, 7.3% widowed, 13.2% divorced (2006-2010 5-year est.); Foreign born: 2.6% (2006-2010 5-year est.); Ancestry (includes multiple ancestries): 43.6% German, 20.4% Polish, 14.3% Irish, 9.6% Dutch, 8.8% Italian (2006-2010 5-year est.).

Economy: Employment by occupation: 11.3% management, 1.0% professional, 4.7% services, 12.1% sales, 3.3% farming, 7.4% construction, 12.7% production (2006-2010 5-year est.).

Income: Per capita income: $26,712 (2006-2010 5-year est.); Median household income: $44,228 (2006-2010 5-year est.); Average household income: $57,464 (2006-2010 5-year est.); Percent of households with income of $100,000 or more: 22.8% (2006-2010 5-year est.); Poverty rate: 14.9% (2006-2010 5-year est.).

Education: Percent of population age 25 and over with: High school diploma (including GED) or higher: 91.5% (2006-2010 5-year est.); Bachelor's degree or higher: 33.8% (2006-2010 5-year est.); Master's degree or higher: 13.2% (2006-2010 5-year est.).

Housing: Homeownership rate: 78.6% (2010); Median home value: $160,300 (2006-2010 5-year est.); Median contract rent: $459 per month (2006-2010 5-year est.); Median year structure built: 1982 (2006-2010 5-year est.).

Transportation: Commute to work: 93.0% car, 0.0% public transportation, 0.0% walk, 3.9% work from home (2006-2010 5-year est.); Travel time to work: 30.7% less than 15 minutes, 41.4% 15 to 30 minutes, 11.8% 30 to 45 minutes, 10.7% 45 to 60 minutes, 5.3% 60 minutes or more (2006-2010 5-year est.)

Additional Information Contacts

Columbia Montour Chamber of Commerce . . . . (570) 784-2522
   http://www.bloomsburg.org

FAIRVIEW-FERNDALE (CDP).
Covers a land area of 0.895 square miles and a water area of 0.003 square miles. Located at 40.78° N. Lat; 76.58° W. Long.

Population: 2,559 (1990); 2,411 (2000); 2,139 (2010); Density: 2,389.7 persons per square mile (2010); Race: 98.6% White, 0.5% Black, 0.0% Asian, 0.1% American Indian/Alaska Native, 0.0% Native Hawaiian/Other Pacific Islander, 0.8% Other, 1.1% Hispanic of any race (2010); Average household size: 2.19 (2010); Median age: 45.5 (2010); Males per 100

females: 96.6 (2010); Marriage status: 23.7% never married, 53.6% now married, 9.3% widowed, 13.5% divorced (2006-2010 5-year est.); Foreign born: 0.0% (2006-2010 5-year est.); Ancestry (includes multiple ancestries): 25.2% Polish, 20.5% German, 16.4% Dutch, 12.0% Italian, 11.3% Irish (2006-2010 5-year est.).

Economy: Employment by occupation: 7.8% management, 1.4% professional, 10.1% services, 15.3% sales, 4.8% farming, 10.5% construction, 4.0% production (2006-2010 5-year est.).

Income: Per capita income: $16,873 (2006-2010 5-year est.); Median household income: $27,092 (2006-2010 5-year est.); Average household income: $35,109 (2006-2010 5-year est.); Percent of households with income of $100,000 or more: 2.0% (2006-2010 5-year est.); Poverty rate: 16.8% (2006-2010 5-year est.).

Education: Percent of population age 25 and over with: High school diploma (including GED) or higher: 78.8% (2006-2010 5-year est.); Bachelor's degree or higher: 8.4% (2006-2010 5-year est.); Master's degree or higher: 1.9% (2006-2010 5-year est.).

Housing: Homeownership rate: 80.7% (2010); Median home value: $59,500 (2006-2010 5-year est.); Median contract rent: $338 per month (2006-2010 5-year est.); Median year structure built: before 1940 (2006-2010 5-year est.).

Transportation: Commute to work: 92.6% car, 0.0% public transportation, 1.9% walk, 5.5% work from home (2006-2010 5-year est.); Travel time to work: 41.1% less than 15 minutes, 20.9% 15 to 30 minutes, 23.9% 30 to 45 minutes, 9.0% 45 to 60 minutes, 5.0% 60 minutes or more (2006-2010 5-year est.)

Additional Information Contacts

Brush Valley Regional Chamber of Commerce . . . . (570) 648-4675
   http://www.brushvalleychamber.com

HERNDON (borough).
Covers a land area of 0.880 square miles and a water area of 0.992 square miles. Located at 40.71° N. Lat; 76.85° W. Long. Elevation is 463 feet.

Population: 422 (1990); 383 (2000); 324 (2010); Density: 368.1 persons per square mile (2010); Race: 95.4% White, 3.4% Black, 0.3% Asian, 0.3% American Indian/Alaska Native, 0.0% Native Hawaiian/Other Pacific Islander, 0.6% Other, 0.0% Hispanic of any race (2010); Average household size: 2.38 (2010); Median age: 37.4 (2010); Males per 100 females: 101.2 (2010); Marriage status: 12.5% never married, 76.9% now married, 4.4% widowed, 6.2% divorced (2006-2010 5-year est.); Foreign born: 0.9% (2006-2010 5-year est.); Ancestry (includes multiple ancestries): 73.8% German, 5.1% English, 4.8% Polish, 1.8% Ukrainian, 1.8% French (2006-2010 5-year est.).

Economy: Single-family building permits issued: 0 (2011); Multi-family building permits issued: 0 (2011); Employment by occupation: 2.8% management, 5.7% professional, 5.0% services, 32.6% sales, 0.0% farming, 7.8% construction, 9.9% production (2006-2010 5-year est.).

Income: Per capita income: $21,392 (2006-2010 5-year est.); Median household income: $41,563 (2006-2010 5-year est.); Average household income: $47,774 (2006-2010 5-year est.); Percent of households with income of $100,000 or more: 5.4% (2006-2010 5-year est.); Poverty rate: 9.0% (2006-2010 5-year est.).

Education: Percent of population age 25 and over with: High school diploma (including GED) or higher: 89.4% (2006-2010 5-year est.); Bachelor's degree or higher: 11.8% (2006-2010 5-year est.); Master's degree or higher: 3.5% (2006-2010 5-year est.).

School District(s)

Line Mountain SD (KG-12)
   2010-11 Enrollment: 1,250 . . . . (570) 758-2640

Housing: Homeownership rate: 72.8% (2010); Median home value: $82,500 (2006-2010 5-year est.); Median contract rent: $336 per month (2006-2010 5-year est.); Median year structure built: before 1940 (2006-2010 5-year est.).

Transportation: Commute to work: 94.3% car, 0.0% public transportation, 0.0% walk, 5.7% work from home (2006-2010 5-year est.); Travel time to work: 8.3% less than 15 minutes, 37.6% 15 to 30 minutes, 29.3% 30 to 45 minutes, 16.5% 45 to 60 minutes, 8.3% 60 minutes or more (2006-2010 5-year est.)

JACKSON (township).
Covers a land area of 12.588 square miles and a water area of 1.567 square miles. Located at 40.72° N. Lat; 76.82° W. Long.

Population: 845 (1990); 928 (2000); 875 (2010); Density: 69.5 persons per square mile (2010); Race: 98.5% White, 0.3% Black, 0.0% Asian, 0.5% American Indian/Alaska Native, 0.0% Native Hawaiian/Other Pacific

Islander, 0.7% Other, 1.0% Hispanic of any race (2010); Average household size: 2.52 (2010); Median age: 45.4 (2010); Males per 100 females: 104.9 (2010); Marriage status: 20.2% never married, 67.7% now married, 6.6% widowed, 5.5% divorced (2006-2010 5-year est.); Foreign born: 0.5% (2006-2010 5-year est.); Ancestry (includes multiple ancestries): 60.9% German, 9.2% English, 5.1% Irish, 4.5% Pennsylvania German, 3.7% American (2006-2010 5-year est.).

Economy: Single-family building permits issued: 5 (2011); Multi-family building permits issued: 0 (2011); Employment by occupation: 6.0% management, 2.2% professional, 7.2% services, 21.9% sales, 1.4% farming, 14.5% construction, 13.0% production (2006-2010 5-year est.).

Income: Per capita income: $22,926 (2006-2010 5-year est.); Median household income: $42,188 (2006-2010 5-year est.); Average household income: $60,484 (2006-2010 5-year est.); Percent of households with income of $100,000 or more: 17.8% (2006-2010 5-year est.); Poverty rate: 6.4% (2006-2010 5-year est.).

Education: Percent of population age 25 and over with: High school diploma (including GED) or higher: 91.3% (2006-2010 5-year est.); Bachelor's degree or higher: 13.3% (2006-2010 5-year est.); Master's degree or higher: 2.3% (2006-2010 5-year est.).

Housing: Homeownership rate: 87.9% (2010); Median home value: $125,200 (2006-2010 5-year est.); Median contract rent: $433 per month (2006-2010 5-year est.); Median year structure built: 1956 (2006-2010 5-year est.).

Transportation: Commute to work: 91.3% car, 1.0% public transportation, 1.5% walk, 3.3% work from home (2006-2010 5-year est.); Travel time to work: 19.6% less than 15 minutes, 35.4% 15 to 30 minutes, 18.1% 30 to 45 minutes, 17.6% 45 to 60 minutes, 9.3% 60 minutes or more (2006-2010 5-year est.)

JORDAN (township). Covers a land area of 17.192 square miles and a water area of 0.070 square miles. Located at 40.67° N. Lat; 76.75° W. Long.

Population: 847 (1990); 761 (2000); 794 (2010); Density: 46.2 persons per square mile (2010); Race: 99.1% White, 0.1% Black, 0.0% Asian, 0.0% American Indian/Alaska Native, 0.0% Native Hawaiian/Other Pacific Islander, 0.8% Other, 0.6% Hispanic of any race (2010); Average household size: 2.50 (2010); Median age: 45.8 (2010); Males per 100 females: 101.5 (2010); Marriage status: 14.9% never married, 73.4% now married, 5.8% widowed, 5.8% divorced (2006-2010 5-year est.); Foreign born: 2.7% (2006-2010 5-year est.); Ancestry (includes multiple ancestries): 51.8% German, 9.8% Dutch, 5.7% Italian, 5.3% Irish, 4.6% Polish (2006-2010 5-year est.).

Economy: Single-family building permits issued: 1 (2011); Multi-family building permits issued: 0 (2011); Employment by occupation: 12.3% management, 1.9% professional, 8.8% services, 15.3% sales, 5.0% farming, 20.7% construction, 11.1% production (2006-2010 5-year est.).

Income: Per capita income: $22,538 (2006-2010 5-year est.); Median household income: $41,563 (2006-2010 5-year est.); Average household income: $49,681 (2006-2010 5-year est.); Percent of households with income of $100,000 or more: 10.4% (2006-2010 5-year est.); Poverty rate: 9.8% (2006-2010 5-year est.).

Education: Percent of population age 25 and over with: High school diploma (including GED) or higher: 81.9% (2006-2010 5-year est.); Bachelor's degree or higher: 7.2% (2006-2010 5-year est.); Master's degree or higher: 2.5% (2006-2010 5-year est.).

Housing: Homeownership rate: 85.5% (2010); Median home value: $148,400 (2006-2010 5-year est.); Median contract rent: $398 per month (2006-2010 5-year est.); Median year structure built: 1963 (2006-2010 5-year est.).

Transportation: Commute to work: 82.4% car, 0.0% public transportation, 4.3% walk, 8.6% work from home (2006-2010 5-year est.); Travel time to work: 38.2% less than 15 minutes, 22.3% 15 to 30 minutes, 17.6% 30 to 45 minutes, 9.0% 45 to 60 minutes, 12.9% 60 minutes or more (2006-2010 5-year est.)

KAPP HEIGHTS (CDP). Covers a land area of 0.350 square miles and a water area of 0 square miles. Located at 40.90° N. Lat; 76.81° W. Long. Elevation is 577 feet.

Population: n/a (1990); n/a (2000); 863 (2010); Density: 2,465.8 persons per square mile (2010); Race: 93.6% White, 2.8% Black, 0.7% Asian, 0.2% American Indian/Alaska Native, 0.0% Native Hawaiian/Other Pacific Islander, 2.7% Other, 1.9% Hispanic of any race (2010); Average household size: 2.36 (2010); Median age: 43.0 (2010); Males per 100 females: 95.7 (2010); Marriage status: 33.7% never married, 44.4% now

married, 8.3% widowed, 13.6% divorced (2006-2010 5-year est.); Foreign born: 1.0% (2006-2010 5-year est.); Ancestry (includes multiple ancestries): 38.8% German, 14.3% American, 10.0% English, 8.6% Irish, 4.9% Pennsylvania German (2006-2010 5-year est.).

Economy: Employment by occupation: 0.0% management, 3.8% professional, 21.5% services, 20.6% sales, 2.6% farming, 12.5% construction, 13.7% production (2006-2010 5-year est.).

Income: Per capita income: $19,721 (2006-2010 5-year est.); Median household income: $38,750 (2006-2010 5-year est.); Average household income: $46,311 (2006-2010 5-year est.); Percent of households with income of $100,000 or more: 3.7% (2006-2010 5-year est.); Poverty rate: 7.9% (2006-2010 5-year est.).

Education: Percent of population age 25 and over with: High school diploma (including GED) or higher: 65.7% (2006-2010 5-year est.); Bachelor's degree or higher: 3.7% (2006-2010 5-year est.); Master's degree or higher: 0.0% (2006-2010 5-year est.).

Housing: Homeownership rate: 77.5% (2010); Median home value: $75,800 (2006-2010 5-year est.); Median contract rent: $414 per month (2006-2010 5-year est.); Median year structure built: 1967 (2006-2010 5-year est.).

Transportation: Commute to work: 100.0% car, 0.0% public transportation, 0.0% walk, 0.0% work from home (2006-2010 5-year est.); Travel time to work: 39.0% less than 15 minutes, 45.6% 15 to 30 minutes, 13.4% 30 to 45 minutes, 0.0% 45 to 60 minutes, 2.0% 60 minutes or more (2006-2010 5-year est.)

KULPMONT (borough). Covers a land area of 0.960 square miles and a water area of 0 square miles. Located at 40.80° N. Lat; 76.47° W. Long. Elevation is 1,122 feet.

History: Settled 1905, incorporated 1916.

Population: 3,233 (1990); 2,985 (2000); 2,924 (2010); Density: 3,046.1 persons per square mile (2010); Race: 97.5% White, 0.4% Black, 0.5% Asian, 0.0% American Indian/Alaska Native, 0.0% Native Hawaiian/Other Pacific Islander, 1.6% Other, 1.4% Hispanic of any race (2010); Average household size: 2.17 (2010); Median age: 46.1 (2010); Males per 100 females: 95.1 (2010); Marriage status: 25.5% never married, 52.5% now married, 12.0% widowed, 10.0% divorced (2006-2010 5-year est.); Foreign born: 3.8% (2006-2010 5-year est.); Ancestry (includes multiple ancestries): 30.2% Polish, 21.3% Italian, 13.0% German, 7.7% Irish, 6.4% Dutch (2006-2010 5-year est.).

Economy: Single-family building permits issued: 0 (2011); Multi-family building permits issued: 0 (2011); Employment by occupation: 7.9% management, 2.9% professional, 9.4% services, 12.4% sales, 5.2% farming, 17.2% construction, 13.9% production (2006-2010 5-year est.).

Income: Per capita income: $20,218 (2006-2010 5-year est.); Median household income: $33,889 (2006-2010 5-year est.); Average household income: $47,846 (2006-2010 5-year est.); Percent of households with income of $100,000 or more: 10.8% (2006-2010 5-year est.); Poverty rate: 19.2% (2006-2010 5-year est.).

Education: Percent of population age 25 and over with: High school diploma (including GED) or higher: 86.3% (2006-2010 5-year est.); Bachelor's degree or higher: 11.7% (2006-2010 5-year est.); Master's degree or higher: 3.9% (2006-2010 5-year est.).

Housing: Homeownership rate: 73.7% (2010); Median home value: $78,700 (2006-2010 5-year est.); Median contract rent: $349 per month (2006-2010 5-year est.); Median year structure built: before 1940 (2006-2010 5-year est.).

Safety: Violent crime rate: 61.4 per 10,000 population; Property crime rate: 71.6 per 10,000 population (2011).

Transportation: Commute to work: 93.1% car, 1.2% public transportation, 4.7% walk, 0.0% work from home (2006-2010 5-year est.); Travel time to work: 34.0% less than 15 minutes, 30.2% 15 to 30 minutes, 13.6% 30 to 45 minutes, 10.1% 45 to 60 minutes, 12.1% 60 minutes or more (2006-2010 5-year est.)

Additional Information Contacts

Brush Valley Regional Chamber of Commerce . . . . (570) 648-4675
http://www.brushvalleychamber.com

LECK KILL (unincorporated postal area)

Zip Code: 17836

Covers a land area of 4.094 square miles and a water area of 0.006 square miles. Located at 40.71° N. Lat; 76.60° W. Long. Elevation is 764 feet. Population: 266 (2010); Density: 65.0 persons per square mile (2010); Race: 99.2% White, 0.4% Black, 0.0% Asian, 0.0% American Indian/Alaska Native, 0.0% Native Hawaiian/Other Pacific Islander,

0.4% Other, 0.4% Hispanic of any race (2010); Average household size: 2.44 (2010); Median age: 45.2 (2010); Males per 100 females: 104.6 (2010); Homeownership rate: 91.8% (2010)

LEWIS (township). Covers a land area of 26.394 square miles and a water area of 0.013 square miles. Located at 41.11° N. Lat; 76.77° W. Long.

Population: 1,881 (1990); 1,862 (2000); 1,915 (2010); Density: 72.6 persons per square mile (2010); Race: 98.8% White, 0.2% Black, 0.2% Asian, 0.0% American Indian/Alaska Native, 0.0% Native Hawaiian/Other Pacific Islander, 0.8% Other, 0.4% Hispanic of any race (2010); Average household size: 2.84 (2010); Median age: 43.2 (2010); Males per 100 females: 103.9 (2010); Marriage status: 16.6% never married, 68.2% now married, 6.2% widowed, 8.9% divorced (2006-2010 5-year est.); Foreign born: 0.9% (2006-2010 5-year est.); Ancestry (includes multiple ancestries): 44.6% German, 19.4% Pennsylvania German, 8.8% Irish, 7.9% Swiss, 7.6% English (2006-2010 5-year est.).

Economy: Single-family building permits issued: 1 (2011); Multi-family building permits issued: 0 (2011); Employment by occupation: 8.5% management, 3.4% professional, 8.2% services, 19.4% sales, 1.8% farming, 13.2% construction, 11.4% production (2006-2010 5-year est.).

Income: Per capita income: $26,155 (2006-2010 5-year est.); Median household income: $51,979 (2006-2010 5-year est.); Average household income: $73,625 (2006-2010 5-year est.); Percent of households with income of $100,000 or more: 18.7% (2006-2010 5-year est.); Poverty rate: 13.6% (2006-2010 5-year est.).

Education: Percent of population age 25 and over with: High school diploma (including GED) or higher: 82.9% (2006-2010 5-year est.); Bachelor's degree or higher: 10.6% (2006-2010 5-year est.); Master's degree or higher: 2.5% (2006-2010 5-year est.).

Housing: Homeownership rate: 90.0% (2010); Median home value: $169,600 (2006-2010 5-year est.); Median contract rent: $481 per month (2006-2010 5-year est.); Median year structure built: 1972 (2006-2010 5-year est.).

Transportation: Commute to work: 89.3% car, 0.0% public transportation, 3.8% walk, 5.8% work from home (2006-2010 5-year est.); Travel time to work: 27.1% less than 15 minutes, 50.7% 15 to 30 minutes, 15.0% 30 to 45 minutes, 4.8% 45 to 60 minutes, 2.4% 60 minutes or more (2006-2010 5-year est.)

Additional Information Contacts

Williamsport/Lycoming Chamber of Commerce . . . . (570) 326-1971
  http://www.williamsport.org

LITTLE MAHANOY (township). Covers a land area of 10.399 square miles and a water area of 0.099 square miles. Located at 40.75° N. Lat; 76.77° W. Long.

Population: 432 (1990); 435 (2000); 479 (2010); Density: 46.1 persons per square mile (2010); Race: 98.5% White, 0.6% Black, 0.6% Asian, 0.0% American Indian/Alaska Native, 0.0% Native Hawaiian/Other Pacific Islander, 0.3% Other, 1.3% Hispanic of any race (2010); Average household size: 2.82 (2010); Median age: 40.9 (2010); Males per 100 females: 115.8 (2010); Marriage status: 23.6% never married, 68.6% now married, 4.4% widowed, 3.3% divorced (2006-2010 5-year est.); Foreign born: 0.0% (2006-2010 5-year est.); Ancestry (includes multiple ancestries): 56.4% German, 4.5% Polish, 4.2% Irish, 3.1% Slovak, 2.8% Pennsylvania German (2006-2010 5-year est.).

Economy: Single-family building permits issued: 0 (2011); Multi-family building permits issued: 0 (2011); Employment by occupation: 2.2% management, 0.0% professional, 16.9% services, 9.6% sales, 3.7% farming, 8.8% construction, 10.3% production (2006-2010 5-year est.).

Income: Per capita income: $16,859 (2006-2010 5-year est.); Median household income: $48,056 (2006-2010 5-year est.); Average household income: $49,869 (2006-2010 5-year est.); Percent of households with income of $100,000 or more: 6.8% (2006-2010 5-year est.); Poverty rate: 12.1% (2006-2010 5-year est.).

Education: Percent of population age 25 and over with: High school diploma (including GED) or higher: 89.0% (2006-2010 5-year est.); Bachelor's degree or higher: 3.2% (2006-2010 5-year est.); Master's degree or higher: 0.9% (2006-2010 5-year est.).

Housing: Homeownership rate: 78.3% (2010); Median home value: $108,300 (2006-2010 5-year est.); Median contract rent: $700 per month (2006-2010 5-year est.); Median year structure built: 1947 (2006-2010 5-year est.).

Transportation: Commute to work: 98.5% car, 0.0% public transportation, 0.0% walk, 1.5% work from home (2006-2010 5-year est.); Travel time to

work: 23.9% less than 15 minutes, 47.0% 15 to 30 minutes, 12.7% 30 to 45 minutes, 7.5% 45 to 60 minutes, 9.0% 60 minutes or more (2006-2010 5-year est.)

LOCUST GAP (unincorporated postal area)
Zip Code: 17840

  Covers a land area of 2.491 square miles and a water area of 0 square miles. Located at 40.77° N. Lat; 76.43° W. Long. Elevation is 1,191 feet. Population: 533 (2010); Density: 214.0 persons per square mile (2010); Race: 98.1% White, 0.2% Black, 0.6% Asian, 0.0% American Indian/Alaska Native, 0.4% Native Hawaiian/Other Pacific Islander, 0.7% Other, 0.6% Hispanic of any race (2010); Average household size: 2.56 (2010); Median age: 43.1 (2010); Males per 100 females: 101.9 (2010); Homeownership rate: 83.7% (2010)

LOWER AUGUSTA (township). Covers a land area of 19.198 square miles and a water area of 2.190 square miles. Located at 40.78° N. Lat; 76.81° W. Long.

Population: 1,024 (1990); 1,079 (2000); 1,064 (2010); Density: 55.4 persons per square mile (2010); Race: 98.2% White, 0.3% Black, 0.4% Asian, 0.1% American Indian/Alaska Native, 0.0% Native Hawaiian/Other Pacific Islander, 1.0% Other, 0.8% Hispanic of any race (2010); Average household size: 2.46 (2010); Median age: 46.7 (2010); Males per 100 females: 101.9 (2010); Marriage status: 10.6% never married, 78.8% now married, 6.4% widowed, 4.2% divorced (2006-2010 5-year est.); Foreign born: 0.0% (2006-2010 5-year est.); Ancestry (includes multiple ancestries): 52.1% German, 7.1% Polish, 6.2% English, 5.7% Irish, 5.7% Dutch (2006-2010 5-year est.).

Economy: Single-family building permits issued: 0 (2011); Multi-family building permits issued: 0 (2011); Employment by occupation: 6.9% management, 6.7% professional, 8.1% services, 21.4% sales, 3.9% farming, 12.9% construction, 9.3% production (2006-2010 5-year est.).

Income: Per capita income: $23,328 (2006-2010 5-year est.); Median household income: $49,712 (2006-2010 5-year est.); Average household income: $55,329 (2006-2010 5-year est.); Percent of households with income of $100,000 or more: 12.5% (2006-2010 5-year est.); Poverty rate: 4.2% (2006-2010 5-year est.).

Education: Percent of population age 25 and over with: High school diploma (including GED) or higher: 88.6% (2006-2010 5-year est.); Bachelor's degree or higher: 8.8% (2006-2010 5-year est.); Master's degree or higher: 3.4% (2006-2010 5-year est.).

Housing: Homeownership rate: 88.1% (2010); Median home value: $141,900 (2006-2010 5-year est.); Median contract rent: $350 per month (2006-2010 5-year est.); Median year structure built: 1977 (2006-2010 5-year est.).

Transportation: Commute to work: 95.1% car, 0.0% public transportation, 0.6% walk, 3.7% work from home (2006-2010 5-year est.); Travel time to work: 19.5% less than 15 minutes, 52.5% 15 to 30 minutes, 20.0% 30 to 45 minutes, 3.8% 45 to 60 minutes, 4.2% 60 minutes or more (2006-2010 5-year est.)

Additional Information Contacts

Central PA Chamber of Commerce. . . . . (570) 742-7341
  http://www.centralpachamber.com/index.php

LOWER MAHANOY (township). Covers a land area of 21.940 square miles and a water area of 3.664 square miles. Located at 40.65° N. Lat; 76.88° W. Long.

Population: 1,669 (1990); 1,586 (2000); 1,709 (2010); Density: 77.9 persons per square mile (2010); Race: 98.4% White, 0.2% Black, 0.1% Asian, 0.1% American Indian/Alaska Native, 0.0% Native Hawaiian/Other Pacific Islander, 1.2% Other, 0.8% Hispanic of any race (2010); Average household size: 2.45 (2010); Median age: 44.6 (2010); Males per 100 females: 100.8 (2010); Marriage status: 19.5% never married, 65.7% now married, 7.1% widowed, 7.7% divorced (2006-2010 5-year est.); Foreign born: 0.0% (2006-2010 5-year est.); Ancestry (includes multiple ancestries): 77.4% German, 5.7% English, 5.1% Irish, 4.3% Italian, 3.1% Polish (2006-2010 5-year est.).

Economy: Single-family building permits issued: 4 (2011); Multi-family building permits issued: 0 (2011); Employment by occupation: 8.0% management, 4.6% professional, 8.3% services, 20.1% sales, 2.7% farming, 9.1% construction, 8.3% production (2006-2010 5-year est.).

Income: Per capita income: $25,457 (2006-2010 5-year est.); Median household income: $50,430 (2006-2010 5-year est.); Average household income: $64,733 (2006-2010 5-year est.); Percent of households with

income of $100,000 or more: 14.9% (2006-2010 5-year est.); Poverty rate: 11.3% (2006-2010 5-year est.).

Education: Percent of population age 25 and over with: High school diploma (including GED) or higher: 86.1% (2006-2010 5-year est.); Bachelor's degree or higher: 10.4% (2006-2010 5-year est.); Master's degree or higher: 3.7% (2006-2010 5-year est.).

Housing: Homeownership rate: 79.6% (2010); Median home value: $122,800 (2006-2010 5-year est.); Median contract rent: $425 per month (2006-2010 5-year est.); Median year structure built: 1957 (2006-2010 5-year est.).

Transportation: Commute to work: 94.6% car, 0.0% public transportation, 2.0% walk, 1.9% work from home (2006-2010 5-year est.); Travel time to work: 26.1% less than 15 minutes, 36.9% 15 to 30 minutes, 14.7% 30 to 45 minutes, 11.2% 45 to 60 minutes, 11.1% 60 minutes or more (2006-2010 5-year est.)

Additional Information Contacts
Harrisburg Regional Chamber & CREDC . . . . (717) 232-4099
  http://www.harrisburgregionalchamber.org

MARION HEIGHTS (borough). Aka Keiser. Covers a land area of 0.201 square miles and a water area of 0 square miles. Located at 40.80° N. Lat; 76.46° W. Long. Elevation is 1,371 feet.

Population: 857 (1990); 735 (2000); 611 (2010); Density: 3,040.9 persons per square mile (2010); Race: 99.3% White, 0.0% Black, 0.2% Asian, 0.0% American Indian/Alaska Native, 0.0% Native Hawaiian/Other Pacific Islander, 0.5% Other, 0.7% Hispanic of any race (2010); Average household size: 2.20 (2010); Median age: 48.3 (2010); Males per 100 females: 95.8 (2010); Marriage status: 27.1% never married, 47.7% now married, 16.8% widowed, 8.4% divorced (2006-2010 5-year est.); Foreign born: 0.3% (2006-2010 5-year est.); Ancestry (includes multiple ancestries): 29.2% Polish, 23.4% German, 15.1% Italian, 11.9% Irish, 10.8% Ukrainian (2006-2010 5-year est.).

Economy: Employment by occupation: 13.0% management, 1.1% professional, 16.2% services, 11.3% sales, 0.7% farming, 10.9% construction, 8.1% production (2006-2010 5-year est.).

Income: Per capita income: $20,086 (2006-2010 5-year est.); Median household income: $32,130 (2006-2010 5-year est.); Average household income: $41,384 (2006-2010 5-year est.); Percent of households with income of $100,000 or more: 3.1% (2006-2010 5-year est.); Poverty rate: 3.1% (2006-2010 5-year est.).

Education: Percent of population age 25 and over with: High school diploma (including GED) or higher: 83.1% (2006-2010 5-year est.); Bachelor's degree or higher: 12.2% (2006-2010 5-year est.); Master's degree or higher: 1.6% (2006-2010 5-year est.).

Housing: Homeownership rate: 89.2% (2010); Median home value: $58,400 (2006-2010 5-year est.); Median contract rent: $419 per month (2006-2010 5-year est.); Median year structure built: before 1940 (2006-2010 5-year est.).

Transportation: Commute to work: 94.6% car, 0.0% public transportation, 3.6% walk, 1.8% work from home (2006-2010 5-year est.); Travel time to work: 31.6% less than 15 minutes, 33.5% 15 to 30 minutes, 14.9% 30 to 45 minutes, 3.6% 45 to 60 minutes, 16.4% 60 minutes or more (2006-2010 5-year est.)

MARSHALLTON (CDP). Covers a land area of 0.868 square miles and a water area of 0.018 square miles. Located at 40.79° N. Lat; 76.54° W. Long. Elevation is 883 feet.

Population: 1,482 (1990); 1,437 (2000); 1,441 (2010); Density: 1,661.0 persons per square mile (2010); Race: 98.1% White, 0.1% Black, 0.2% Asian, 0.8% American Indian/Alaska Native, 0.0% Native Hawaiian/Other Pacific Islander, 0.8% Other, 0.8% Hispanic of any race (2010); Average household size: 2.33 (2010); Median age: 43.0 (2010); Males per 100 females: 95.0 (2010); Marriage status: 23.8% never married, 58.8% now married, 6.3% widowed, 11.1% divorced (2006-2010 5-year est.); Foreign born: 1.0% (2006-2010 5-year est.); Ancestry (includes multiple ancestries): 46.1% Polish, 22.6% German, 17.4% Italian, 9.4% Irish, 6.1% Dutch (2006-2010 5-year est.).

Economy: Employment by occupation: 6.8% management, 0.0% professional, 8.3% services, 24.7% sales, 4.5% farming, 9.3% construction, 9.2% production (2006-2010 5-year est.).

Income: Per capita income: $15,857 (2006-2010 5-year est.); Median household income: $32,011 (2006-2010 5-year est.); Average household income: $38,984 (2006-2010 5-year est.); Percent of households with income of $100,000 or more: 3.5% (2006-2010 5-year est.); Poverty rate: 16.2% (2006-2010 5-year est.).

Education: Percent of population age 25 and over with: High school diploma (including GED) or higher: 81.1% (2006-2010 5-year est.); Bachelor's degree or higher: 12.9% (2006-2010 5-year est.); Master's degree or higher: 0.6% (2006-2010 5-year est.).

Housing: Homeownership rate: 78.1% (2010); Median home value: $45,400 (2006-2010 5-year est.); Median contract rent: $238 per month (2006-2010 5-year est.); Median year structure built: before 1940 (2006-2010 5-year est.).

Transportation: Commute to work: 91.4% car, 0.0% public transportation, 5.3% walk, 0.0% work from home (2006-2010 5-year est.); Travel time to work: 34.5% less than 15 minutes, 27.2% 15 to 30 minutes, 24.1% 30 to 45 minutes, 8.3% 45 to 60 minutes, 5.9% 60 minutes or more (2006-2010 5-year est.)

Additional Information Contacts
Greater West Chester Chamber of Commerce . . . . (610) 696-4046
  http://www.gwcc.org

MCEWENSVILLE (borough). Covers a land area of 0.117 square miles and a water area of 0 square miles. Located at 41.07° N. Lat; 76.82° W. Long. Elevation is 538 feet.

Population: 273 (1990); 314 (2000); 279 (2010); Density: 2,385.1 persons per square mile (2010); Race: 95.3% White, 3.2% Black, 0.4% Asian, 0.0% American Indian/Alaska Native, 0.0% Native Hawaiian/Other Pacific Islander, 1.1% Other, 0.0% Hispanic of any race (2010); Average household size: 2.61 (2010); Median age: 38.8 (2010); Males per 100 females: 108.2 (2010); Marriage status: 17.5% never married, 65.1% now married, 5.3% widowed, 12.2% divorced (2006-2010 5-year est.); Foreign born: 0.0% (2006-2010 5-year est.); Ancestry (includes multiple ancestries): 50.9% German, 11.2% American, 10.8% Irish, 6.5% Scotch-Irish, 4.7% French (2006-2010 5-year est.).

Economy: Single-family building permits issued: 0 (2011); Multi-family building permits issued: 0 (2011); Employment by occupation: 9.3% management, 0.0% professional, 10.3% services, 25.2% sales, 0.0% farming, 9.3% construction, 11.2% production (2006-2010 5-year est.).

Income: Per capita income: $23,087 (2006-2010 5-year est.); Median household income: $50,417 (2006-2010 5-year est.); Average household income: $52,345 (2006-2010 5-year est.); Percent of households with income of $100,000 or more: 10.4% (2006-2010 5-year est.); Poverty rate: 6.0% (2006-2010 5-year est.).

Education: Percent of population age 25 and over with: High school diploma (including GED) or higher: 87.4% (2006-2010 5-year est.); Bachelor's degree or higher: 18.0% (2006-2010 5-year est.); Master's degree or higher: 2.4% (2006-2010 5-year est.).

Housing: Homeownership rate: 70.1% (2010); Median home value: $129,000 (2006-2010 5-year est.); Median contract rent: $394 per month (2006-2010 5-year est.); Median year structure built: 1961 (2006-2010 5-year est.).

Transportation: Commute to work: 94.1% car, 0.0% public transportation, 0.0% walk, 5.9% work from home (2006-2010 5-year est.); Travel time to work: 27.1% less than 15 minutes, 59.4% 15 to 30 minutes, 5.2% 30 to 45 minutes, 2.1% 45 to 60 minutes, 6.3% 60 minutes or more (2006-2010 5-year est.)

MILTON (borough). Covers a land area of 3.432 square miles and a water area of 0.296 square miles. Located at 41.01° N. Lat; 76.85° W. Long. Elevation is 505 feet.

History: Laid out 1792, incorporated 1817.

Population: 6,744 (1990); 6,650 (2000); 7,042 (2010); Density: 2,051.9 persons per square mile (2010); Race: 91.1% White, 2.9% Black, 0.7% Asian, 0.2% American Indian/Alaska Native, 0.0% Native Hawaiian/Other Pacific Islander, 5.1% Other, 6.2% Hispanic of any race (2010); Average household size: 2.32 (2010); Median age: 39.9 (2010); Males per 100 females: 94.3 (2010); Marriage status: 25.5% never married, 51.4% now married, 9.4% widowed, 13.7% divorced (2006-2010 5-year est.); Foreign born: 3.4% (2006-2010 5-year est.); Ancestry (includes multiple ancestries): 43.3% German, 11.4% Irish, 9.6% American, 5.9% English, 4.7% Italian (2006-2010 5-year est.).

Economy: Single-family building permits issued: 4 (2011); Multi-family building permits issued: 0 (2011); Employment by occupation: 4.9% management, 0.8% professional, 15.7% services, 18.6% sales, 3.6% farming, 7.2% construction, 8.9% production (2006-2010 5-year est.).

Income: Per capita income: $17,491 (2006-2010 5-year est.); Median household income: $36,509 (2006-2010 5-year est.); Average household income: $40,487 (2006-2010 5-year est.); Percent of households with

income of $100,000 or more: 4.4% (2006-2010 5-year est.); Poverty rate: 24.4% (2006-2010 5-year est.).

Education: Percent of population age 25 and over with: High school diploma (including GED) or higher: 86.9% (2006-2010 5-year est.); Bachelor's degree or higher: 13.0% (2006-2010 5-year est.); Master's degree or higher: 3.5% (2006-2010 5-year est.).

School District(s)

Milton Area SD (KG-12)

   2010-11 Enrollment: 2,283 . . . . (570) 742-7614

Housing: Homeownership rate: 54.3% (2010); Median home value: $108,100 (2006-2010 5-year est.); Median contract rent: $435 per month (2006-2010 5-year est.); Median year structure built: 1950 (2006-2010 5-year est.).

Newspapers: Lewisburg Daily Journal (Local news; Circulation 5,000); Standard-Journal (Local news; Circulation 5,000)

Transportation: Commute to work: 95.7% car, 0.0% public transportation, 0.9% walk, 2.7% work from home (2006-2010 5-year est.); Travel time to work: 45.5% less than 15 minutes, 34.5% 15 to 30 minutes, 12.1% 30 to 45 minutes, 4.5% 45 to 60 minutes, 3.4% 60 minutes or more (2006-2010 5-year est.)

Additional Information Contacts

Borough of Milton . . . . (570) 742-8759
   http://www.miltonpa.org
Central PA Chamber of Commerce. . . . . (570) 742-7341
   http://www.centralpachamber.com/index.php

MONTANDON (CDP). Covers a land area of 0.887 square miles and a water area of 0 square miles. Located at 40.97° N. Lat; 76.85° W. Long. Elevation is 472 feet.

Population: n/a (1990); n/a (2000); 903 (2010); Density: 1,017.9 persons per square mile (2010); Race: 97.9% White, 0.8% Black, 0.2% Asian, 0.0% American Indian/Alaska Native, 0.0% Native Hawaiian/Other Pacific Islander, 1.1% Other, 1.3% Hispanic of any race (2010); Average household size: 2.31 (2010); Median age: 43.9 (2010); Males per 100 females: 103.8 (2010); Marriage status: 23.3% never married, 56.1% now married, 5.7% widowed, 14.9% divorced (2006-2010 5-year est.); Foreign born: 2.2% (2006-2010 5-year est.); Ancestry (includes multiple ancestries): 48.7% German, 11.7% English, 10.7% French, 9.8% American, 9.3% Irish (2006-2010 5-year est.).

Economy: Employment by occupation: 0.0% management, 2.6% professional, 20.0% services, 14.8% sales, 2.8% farming, 12.3% construction, 13.6% production (2006-2010 5-year est.).

Income: Per capita income: $17,486 (2006-2010 5-year est.); Median household income: $32,650 (2006-2010 5-year est.); Average household income: $44,440 (2006-2010 5-year est.); Percent of households with income of $100,000 or more: 8.0% (2006-2010 5-year est.); Poverty rate: 7.2% (2006-2010 5-year est.).

Education: Percent of population age 25 and over with: High school diploma (including GED) or higher: 83.9% (2006-2010 5-year est.); Bachelor's degree or higher: 13.9% (2006-2010 5-year est.); Master's degree or higher: 5.4% (2006-2010 5-year est.).

School District(s)

Milton Area SD (KG-12)

   2010-11 Enrollment: 2,283 . . . . (570) 742-7614

Housing: Homeownership rate: 76.7% (2010); Median home value: $107,900 (2006-2010 5-year est.); Median contract rent: $395 per month (2006-2010 5-year est.); Median year structure built: 1975 (2006-2010 5-year est.).

Transportation: Commute to work: 97.1% car, 0.0% public transportation, 0.0% walk, 0.0% work from home (2006-2010 5-year est.); Travel time to work: 53.6% less than 15 minutes, 32.5% 15 to 30 minutes, 10.8% 30 to 45 minutes, 3.1% 45 to 60 minutes, 0.0% 60 minutes or more (2006-2010 5-year est.)

MOUNT CARMEL (borough). Covers a land area of 0.657 square miles and a water area of 0 square miles. Located at 40.80° N. Lat; 76.41° W. Long. Elevation is 1,102 feet.

Population: 7,196 (1990); 6,390 (2000); 5,893 (2010); Density: 8,975.0 persons per square mile (2010); Race: 97.3% White, 0.6% Black, 0.4% Asian, 0.2% American Indian/Alaska Native, 0.0% Native Hawaiian/Other Pacific Islander, 1.5% Other, 1.5% Hispanic of any race (2010); Average household size: 2.16 (2010); Median age: 44.0 (2010); Males per 100 females: 92.9 (2010); Marriage status: 25.8% never married, 52.1% now married, 10.6% widowed, 11.4% divorced (2006-2010 5-year est.); Foreign born: 3.2% (2006-2010 5-year est.); Ancestry (includes multiple

ancestries): 24.6% Polish, 20.9% German, 16.3% Irish, 15.3% Italian, 10.9% Dutch (2006-2010 5-year est.).

Economy: Single-family building permits issued: 0 (2011); Multi-family building permits issued: 0 (2011); Employment by occupation: 4.6% management, 0.7% professional, 7.0% services, 22.4% sales, 6.2% farming, 11.6% construction, 3.8% production (2006-2010 5-year est.).

Income: Per capita income: $18,675 (2006-2010 5-year est.); Median household income: $31,433 (2006-2010 5-year est.); Average household income: $39,481 (2006-2010 5-year est.); Percent of households with income of $100,000 or more: 3.7% (2006-2010 5-year est.); Poverty rate: 18.1% (2006-2010 5-year est.).

Education: Percent of population age 25 and over with: High school diploma (including GED) or higher: 85.3% (2006-2010 5-year est.); Bachelor's degree or higher: 12.4% (2006-2010 5-year est.); Master's degree or higher: 4.5% (2006-2010 5-year est.).

School District(s)

Mount Carmel Area SD (PK-12)

   2010-11 Enrollment: 1,615 . . . . (570) 339-1500

Housing: Homeownership rate: 69.7% (2010); Median home value: $46,100 (2006-2010 5-year est.); Median contract rent: $321 per month (2006-2010 5-year est.); Median year structure built: before 1940 (2006-2010 5-year est.).

Safety: Violent crime rate: 15.2 per 10,000 population; Property crime rate: 196.2 per 10,000 population (2011).

Transportation: Commute to work: 89.5% car, 0.0% public transportation, 8.2% walk, 1.9% work from home (2006-2010 5-year est.); Travel time to work: 37.3% less than 15 minutes, 21.4% 15 to 30 minutes, 17.2% 30 to 45 minutes, 7.7% 45 to 60 minutes, 16.4% 60 minutes or more (2006-2010 5-year est.)

Additional Information Contacts

Borough of Mount Carmel . . . . (570) 339-4486
   http://www.joeba.com/main.html
Columbia Montour Chamber of Commerce. . . . . (570) 784-2522
   http://www.bloomsburg.org

MOUNT CARMEL (township). Covers a land area of 21.346 square miles and a water area of 0.181 square miles. Located at 40.79° N. Lat; 76.44° W. Long. Elevation is 1,102 feet.

History: Laid out 1835, incorporated 1864.

Population: 2,659 (1990); 2,701 (2000); 3,139 (2010); Density: 147.1 persons per square mile (2010); Race: 98.4% White, 0.6% Black, 0.3% Asian, 0.0% American Indian/Alaska Native, 0.1% Native Hawaiian/Other Pacific Islander, 0.6% Other, 0.7% Hispanic of any race (2010); Average household size: 2.24 (2010); Median age: 48.6 (2010); Males per 100 females: 93.5 (2010); Marriage status: 23.4% never married, 56.1% now married, 11.4% widowed, 9.0% divorced (2006-2010 5-year est.); Foreign born: 1.8% (2006-2010 5-year est.); Ancestry (includes multiple ancestries): 28.2% Polish, 21.2% German, 16.8% Irish, 15.7% Italian, 6.3% Dutch (2006-2010 5-year est.).

Economy: Single-family building permits issued: 0 (2011); Multi-family building permits issued: 0 (2011); Employment by occupation: 7.3% management, 2.0% professional, 10.0% services, 18.8% sales, 3.2% farming, 8.9% construction, 8.0% production (2006-2010 5-year est.).

Income: Per capita income: $21,119 (2006-2010 5-year est.); Median household income: $42,704 (2006-2010 5-year est.); Average household income: $50,801 (2006-2010 5-year est.); Percent of households with income of $100,000 or more: 11.3% (2006-2010 5-year est.); Poverty rate: 15.2% (2006-2010 5-year est.).

Education: Percent of population age 25 and over with: High school diploma (including GED) or higher: 83.1% (2006-2010 5-year est.); Bachelor's degree or higher: 14.0% (2006-2010 5-year est.); Master's degree or higher: 6.6% (2006-2010 5-year est.).

Housing: Homeownership rate: 81.8% (2010); Median home value: $55,800 (2006-2010 5-year est.); Median contract rent: $343 per month (2006-2010 5-year est.); Median year structure built: before 1940 (2006-2010 5-year est.).

Safety: Violent crime rate: 50.8 per 10,000 population; Property crime rate: 44.5 per 10,000 population (2011).

Transportation: Commute to work: 97.0% car, 0.0% public transportation, 1.8% walk, 1.2% work from home (2006-2010 5-year est.); Travel time to work: 38.1% less than 15 minutes, 31.7% 15 to 30 minutes, 15.4% 30 to 45 minutes, 7.0% 45 to 60 minutes, 7.7% 60 minutes or more (2006-2010 5-year est.)

Additional Information Contacts
Brush Valley Regional Chamber of Commerce . . . . (570) 648-4675
  http://www.brushvalleychamber.com

NORTHUMBERLAND (borough). Covers a land area of 1.507 square miles and a water area of 0.001 square miles. Located at 40.90° N. Lat; 76.79° W. Long. Elevation is 505 feet.

History: Dr. Joseph Priestley lived here 1794-1804. Laid out c.1775, incorporated 1828.

Population: 3,860 (1990); 3,714 (2000); 3,804 (2010); Density: 2,524.4 persons per square mile (2010); Race: 96.2% White, 1.0% Black, 0.3% Asian, 0.2% American Indian/Alaska Native, 0.0% Native Hawaiian/Other Pacific Islander, 2.3% Other, 2.6% Hispanic of any race (2010); Average household size: 2.23 (2010); Median age: 41.8 (2010); Males per 100 females: 91.8 (2010); Marriage status: 29.8% never married, 46.1% now married, 7.8% widowed, 16.4% divorced (2006-2010 5-year est.); Foreign born: 0.9% (2006-2010 5-year est.); Ancestry (includes multiple ancestries): 43.7% German, 10.9% Irish, 10.8% Dutch, 9.2% American, 6.8% Polish (2006-2010 5-year est.).

Economy: Single-family building permits issued: 1 (2011); Multi-family building permits issued: 0 (2011); Employment by occupation: 4.5% management, 0.5% professional, 12.8% services, 17.0% sales, 2.0% farming, 10.6% construction, 3.5% production (2006-2010 5-year est.).

Income: Per capita income: $23,574 (2006-2010 5-year est.); Median household income: $42,188 (2006-2010 5-year est.); Average household income: $51,132 (2006-2010 5-year est.); Percent of households with income of $100,000 or more: 12.1% (2006-2010 5-year est.); Poverty rate: 16.0% (2006-2010 5-year est.).

Education: Percent of population age 25 and over with: High school diploma (including GED) or higher: 90.0% (2006-2010 5-year est.); Bachelor's degree or higher: 22.8% (2006-2010 5-year est.); Master's degree or higher: 9.3% (2006-2010 5-year est.).

School District(s)
Shikellamy SD (KG-12)
  2010-11 Enrollment: 2,917 . . . . (570) 286-3721

Housing: Homeownership rate: 64.6% (2010); Median home value: $108,300 (2006-2010 5-year est.); Median contract rent: $430 per month (2006-2010 5-year est.); Median year structure built: 1945 (2006-2010 5-year est.).

Safety: Violent crime rate: 2.6 per 10,000 population; Property crime rate: 162.5 per 10,000 population (2011).

Transportation: Commute to work: 92.9% car, 0.0% public transportation, 2.6% walk, 0.9% work from home (2006-2010 5-year est.); Travel time to work: 37.2% less than 15 minutes, 38.4% 15 to 30 minutes, 15.9% 30 to 45 minutes, 2.0% 45 to 60 minutes, 6.6% 60 minutes or more (2006-2010 5-year est.)

Additional Information Contacts
Borough of Northumberland . . . . (570) 473-3414
  http://www.northumberlandborough.com
Greater Susquehanna Valley Chamber of Commerce . . . . (570) 743-4100
  http://www.gsvcc.org

PAXINOS (unincorporated postal area)
Zip Code: 17860

Covers a land area of 26.397 square miles and a water area of 0.105 square miles. Located at 40.86° N. Lat; 76.61° W. Long. Elevation is 561 feet. Population: 1,994 (2010); Density: 75.5 persons per square mile (2010); Race: 98.3% White, 0.6% Black, 0.5% Asian, 0.1% American Indian/Alaska Native, 0.0% Native Hawaiian/Other Pacific Islander, 0.5% Other, 0.5% Hispanic of any race (2010); Average household size: 2.51 (2010); Median age: 46.9 (2010); Males per 100 females: 107.5 (2010); Homeownership rate: 89.9% (2010)

POINT (township). Covers a land area of 25.175 square miles and a water area of 2.307 square miles. Located at 40.93° N. Lat; 76.77° W. Long.

Population: 3,466 (1990); 3,722 (2000); 3,685 (2010); Density: 146.4 persons per square mile (2010); Race: 97.2% White, 0.9% Black, 0.3% Asian, 0.1% American Indian/Alaska Native, 0.0% Native Hawaiian/Other Pacific Islander, 1.5% Other, 1.4% Hispanic of any race (2010); Average household size: 2.28 (2010); Median age: 48.6 (2010); Males per 100 females: 95.2 (2010); Marriage status: 20.0% never married, 58.9% now married, 12.2% widowed, 8.9% divorced (2006-2010 5-year est.); Foreign born: 0.4% (2006-2010 5-year est.); Ancestry (includes multiple

ancestries): 40.7% German, 11.3% Irish, 10.0% American, 8.2% Polish, 6.6% English (2006-2010 5-year est.).

Economy: Single-family building permits issued: 15 (2011); Multi-family building permits issued: 0 (2011); Employment by occupation: 4.9% management, 2.9% professional, 12.4% services, 18.2% sales, 3.2% farming, 6.8% construction, 7.4% production (2006-2010 5-year est.).

Income: Per capita income: $24,430 (2006-2010 5-year est.); Median household income: $48,100 (2006-2010 5-year est.); Average household income: $57,725 (2006-2010 5-year est.); Percent of households with income of $100,000 or more: 12.5% (2006-2010 5-year est.); Poverty rate: 9.8% (2006-2010 5-year est.).

Education: Percent of population age 25 and over with: High school diploma (including GED) or higher: 87.9% (2006-2010 5-year est.); Bachelor's degree or higher: 21.9% (2006-2010 5-year est.); Master's degree or higher: 4.8% (2006-2010 5-year est.).

Housing: Homeownership rate: 83.1% (2010); Median home value: $124,600 (2006-2010 5-year est.); Median contract rent: $458 per month (2006-2010 5-year est.); Median year structure built: 1974 (2006-2010 5-year est.).

Safety: Violent crime rate: 24.3 per 10,000 population; Property crime rate: 124.4 per 10,000 population (2011).

Transportation: Commute to work: 96.6% car, 0.0% public transportation, 0.4% walk, 1.2% work from home (2006-2010 5-year est.); Travel time to work: 33.3% less than 15 minutes, 49.3% 15 to 30 minutes, 11.9% 30 to 45 minutes, 4.1% 45 to 60 minutes, 1.4% 60 minutes or more (2006-2010 5-year est.)

Additional Information Contacts
Greater Susquehanna Valley Chamber of Commerce . . . . (570) 743-4100
  http://www.gsvcc.org

POTTS GROVE (unincorporated postal area)
Zip Code: 17865

Covers a land area of 0.155 square miles and a water area of 0 square miles. Located at 40.99° N. Lat; 76.78° W. Long. Elevation is 489 feet. Population: 92 (2010); Density: 591.6 persons per square mile (2010); Race: 100.0% White, 0.0% Black, 0.0% Asian, 0.0% American Indian/Alaska Native, 0.0% Native Hawaiian/Other Pacific Islander, 0.0% Other, 0.0% Hispanic of any race (2010); Average household size: 2.56 (2010); Median age: 43.8 (2010); Males per 100 females: 124.4 (2010); Homeownership rate: 77.8% (2010)

RALPHO (township). Covers a land area of 18.464 square miles and a water area of 0.040 square miles. Located at 40.85° N. Lat; 76.56° W. Long.

Population: 3,625 (1990); 3,764 (2000); 4,321 (2010); Density: 234.0 persons per square mile (2010); Race: 98.4% White, 0.3% Black, 0.5% Asian, 0.1% American Indian/Alaska Native, 0.0% Native Hawaiian/Other Pacific Islander, 0.7% Other, 0.8% Hispanic of any race (2010); Average household size: 2.40 (2010); Median age: 46.5 (2010); Males per 100 females: 93.7 (2010); Marriage status: 16.7% never married, 68.9% now married, 5.4% widowed, 9.0% divorced (2006-2010 5-year est.); Foreign born: 1.5% (2006-2010 5-year est.); Ancestry (includes multiple ancestries): 39.7% German, 21.0% Polish, 12.3% Irish, 8.7% Italian, 7.0% American (2006-2010 5-year est.).

Economy: Single-family building permits issued: 3 (2011); Multi-family building permits issued: 0 (2011); Employment by occupation: 11.1% management, 1.9% professional, 3.7% services, 14.1% sales, 3.2% farming, 6.3% construction, 9.5% production (2006-2010 5-year est.).

Income: Per capita income: $31,606 (2006-2010 5-year est.); Median household income: $56,224 (2006-2010 5-year est.); Average household income: $71,942 (2006-2010 5-year est.); Percent of households with income of $100,000 or more: 23.2% (2006-2010 5-year est.); Poverty rate: 7.7% (2006-2010 5-year est.).

Education: Percent of population age 25 and over with: High school diploma (including GED) or higher: 92.2% (2006-2010 5-year est.); Bachelor's degree or higher: 28.9% (2006-2010 5-year est.); Master's degree or higher: 13.3% (2006-2010 5-year est.).

Housing: Homeownership rate: 85.3% (2010); Median home value: $162,300 (2006-2010 5-year est.); Median contract rent: $463 per month (2006-2010 5-year est.); Median year structure built: 1978 (2006-2010 5-year est.).

Transportation: Commute to work: 94.6% car, 0.0% public transportation, 0.6% walk, 3.3% work from home (2006-2010 5-year est.); Travel time to work: 32.7% less than 15 minutes, 46.7% 15 to 30 minutes, 12.2% 30 to

45 minutes, 5.8% 45 to 60 minutes, 2.6% 60 minutes or more (2006-2010 5-year est.).

Additional Information Contacts

Brush Valley Regional Chamber of Commerce . . . . (570) 648-4675
  http://www.brushvalleychamber.com

RANSHAW (CDP). Covers a land area of 0.123 square miles and a water area of 0 square miles. Located at 40.79° N. Lat; 76.52° W. Long. Elevation is 856 feet.

Population: n/a (1990); n/a (2000); 510 (2010); Density: 4,152.1 persons per square mile (2010); Race: 98.4% White, 0.2% Black, 0.4% Asian, 0.2% American Indian/Alaska Native, 0.0% Native Hawaiian/Other Pacific Islander, 0.8% Other, 2.5% Hispanic of any race (2010); Average household size: 2.19 (2010); Median age: 43.0 (2010); Males per 100 females: 99.2 (2010); Marriage status: 28.0% never married, 51.8% now married, 7.9% widowed, 12.3% divorced (2006-2010 5-year est.); Foreign born: 0.0% (2006-2010 5-year est.); Ancestry (includes multiple ancestries): 36.5% Polish, 16.2% Italian, 13.7% German, 12.6% Irish, 5.2% Welsh (2006-2010 5-year est.).

Economy: Employment by occupation: 3.6% management, 4.3% professional, 12.9% services, 9.4% sales, 0.0% farming, 19.8% construction, 14.7% production (2006-2010 5-year est.).

Income: Per capita income: $19,819 (2006-2010 5-year est.); Median household income: $32,235 (2006-2010 5-year est.); Average household income: $43,060 (2006-2010 5-year est.); Percent of households with income of $100,000 or more: 11.1% (2006-2010 5-year est.); Poverty rate: 19.4% (2006-2010 5-year est.).

Education: Percent of population age 25 and over with: High school diploma (including GED) or higher: 77.7% (2006-2010 5-year est.); Bachelor's degree or higher: 9.7% (2006-2010 5-year est.); Master's degree or higher: 2.8% (2006-2010 5-year est.).

Housing: Homeownership rate: 74.3% (2010); Median home value: $52,600 (2006-2010 5-year est.); Median contract rent: $345 per month (2006-2010 5-year est.); Median year structure built: before 1940 (2006-2010 5-year est.).

Transportation: Commute to work: 87.2% car, 0.0% public transportation, 12.8% walk, 0.0% work from home (2006-2010 5-year est.); Travel time to work: 35.3% less than 15 minutes, 23.3% 15 to 30 minutes, 15.4% 30 to 45 minutes, 9.0% 45 to 60 minutes, 16.9% 60 minutes or more (2006-2010 5-year est.).

REBUCK (unincorporated postal area)

Zip Code: 17867

Covers a land area of 3.551 square miles and a water area of 0 square miles. Located at 40.71° N. Lat; 76.68° W. Long. Elevation is 558 feet. Population: 169 (2010); Density: 47.6 persons per square mile (2010); Race: 97.0% White, 0.0% Black, 0.6% Asian, 0.0% American Indian/Alaska Native, 0.0% Native Hawaiian/Other Pacific Islander, 2.4% Other, 0.6% Hispanic of any race (2010); Average household size: 2.41 (2010); Median age: 43.2 (2010); Males per 100 females: 85.7 (2010); Homeownership rate: 78.6% (2010)

RIVERSIDE (borough). Aka South Danville. Covers a land area of 4.832 square miles and a water area of 0.509 square miles. Located at 40.95° N. Lat; 76.64° W. Long. Elevation is 499 feet.

Population: 1,991 (1990); 1,861 (2000); 1,932 (2010); Density: 399.8 persons per square mile (2010); Race: 97.4% White, 0.5% Black, 1.1% Asian, 0.1% American Indian/Alaska Native, 0.1% Native Hawaiian/Other Pacific Islander, 0.8% Other, 1.0% Hispanic of any race (2010); Average household size: 2.40 (2010); Median age: 44.8 (2010); Males per 100 females: 92.4 (2010); Marriage status: 12.5% never married, 69.6% now married, 9.3% widowed, 8.5% divorced (2006-2010 5-year est.); Foreign born: 1.6% (2006-2010 5-year est.); Ancestry (includes multiple ancestries): 47.7% German, 19.8% Irish, 8.5% Polish, 7.5% English, 7.4% Dutch (2006-2010 5-year est.).

Economy: Single-family building permits issued: 1 (2011); Multi-family building permits issued: 0 (2011); Employment by occupation: 11.7% management, 3.3% professional, 9.7% services, 14.1% sales, 3.1% farming, 4.3% construction, 5.0% production (2006-2010 5-year est.).

Income: Per capita income: $28,763 (2006-2010 5-year est.); Median household income: $54,522 (2006-2010 5-year est.); Average household income: $65,223 (2006-2010 5-year est.); Percent of households with income of $100,000 or more: 15.2% (2006-2010 5-year est.); Poverty rate: 5.3% (2006-2010 5-year est.).

Education: Percent of population age 25 and over with: High school diploma (including GED) or higher: 95.6% (2006-2010 5-year est.); Bachelor's degree or higher: 30.4% (2006-2010 5-year est.); Master's degree or higher: 14.1% (2006-2010 5-year est.).

School District(s)

Danville Area SD (PK-12)
  2010-11 Enrollment: 2,431 . . . . (570) 271-3268

Housing: Homeownership rate: 87.7% (2010); Median home value: $150,000 (2006-2010 5-year est.); Median contract rent: $520 per month (2006-2010 5-year est.); Median year structure built: 1960 (2006-2010 5-year est.).

Safety: Violent crime rate: 5.2 per 10,000 population; Property crime rate: 118.7 per 10,000 population (2011).

Transportation: Commute to work: 94.9% car, 0.0% public transportation, 1.3% walk, 3.8% work from home (2006-2010 5-year est.); Travel time to work: 52.6% less than 15 minutes, 29.2% 15 to 30 minutes, 13.3% 30 to 45 minutes, 3.8% 45 to 60 minutes, 1.0% 60 minutes or more (2006-2010 5-year est.).

Additional Information Contacts

Borough of Riverside . . . . (570) 275-1751
  http://www.riversideborough.org
Columbia Montour Chamber of Commerce . . . . (570) 784-2522
  http://columbiamontourchamber.com

ROCKEFELLER (township). Covers a land area of 20.340 square miles and a water area of 0.018 square miles. Located at 40.82° N. Lat; 76.73° W. Long.

Population: 2,029 (1990); 2,221 (2000); 2,273 (2010); Density: 111.7 persons per square mile (2010); Race: 98.7% White, 0.5% Black, 0.0% Asian, 0.1% American Indian/Alaska Native, 0.0% Native Hawaiian/Other Pacific Islander, 0.7% Other, 0.9% Hispanic of any race (2010); Average household size: 2.52 (2010); Median age: 46.5 (2010); Males per 100 females: 100.6 (2010); Marriage status: 17.7% never married, 70.4% now married, 3.2% widowed, 8.7% divorced (2006-2010 5-year est.); Foreign born: 0.3% (2006-2010 5-year est.); Ancestry (includes multiple ancestries): 58.9% German, 12.2% Irish, 6.0% Dutch, 5.8% Italian, 4.4% American (2006-2010 5-year est.).

Economy: Single-family building permits issued: 2 (2011); Multi-family building permits issued: 0 (2011); Employment by occupation: 9.2% management, 3.1% professional, 5.6% services, 16.2% sales, 3.4% farming, 8.9% construction, 6.9% production (2006-2010 5-year est.).

Income: Per capita income: $21,585 (2006-2010 5-year est.); Median household income: $44,914 (2006-2010 5-year est.); Average household income: $54,584 (2006-2010 5-year est.); Percent of households with income of $100,000 or more: 9.3% (2006-2010 5-year est.); Poverty rate: 1.5% (2006-2010 5-year est.).

Education: Percent of population age 25 and over with: High school diploma (including GED) or higher: 87.5% (2006-2010 5-year est.); Bachelor's degree or higher: 11.7% (2006-2010 5-year est.); Master's degree or higher: 2.2% (2006-2010 5-year est.).

Housing: Homeownership rate: 89.7% (2010); Median home value: $133,600 (2006-2010 5-year est.); Median contract rent: $442 per month (2006-2010 5-year est.); Median year structure built: 1973 (2006-2010 5-year est.).

Transportation: Commute to work: 92.9% car, 0.0% public transportation, 2.4% walk, 2.9% work from home (2006-2010 5-year est.); Travel time to work: 12.7% less than 15 minutes, 50.9% 15 to 30 minutes, 28.4% 30 to 45 minutes, 3.3% 45 to 60 minutes, 4.7% 60 minutes or more (2006-2010 5-year est.).

Additional Information Contacts

Central PA Chamber of Commerce . . . . (570) 742-7341
  http://www.centralpachamber.com/index.php

RUSH (township). Covers a land area of 26.636 square miles and a water area of 0.637 square miles. Located at 40.91° N. Lat; 76.62° W. Long.

Population: 1,097 (1990); 1,189 (2000); 1,122 (2010); Density: 42.1 persons per square mile (2010); Race: 97.6% White, 0.8% Black, 0.5% Asian, 0.0% American Indian/Alaska Native, 0.0% Native Hawaiian/Other Pacific Islander, 1.1% Other, 0.9% Hispanic of any race (2010); Average household size: 2.58 (2010); Median age: 43.6 (2010); Males per 100 females: 98.6 (2010); Marriage status: 16.2% never married, 71.9% now married, 4.2% widowed, 7.7% divorced (2006-2010 5-year est.); Foreign born: 0.8% (2006-2010 5-year est.); Ancestry (includes multiple

ancestries): 38.5% German, 12.8% American, 11.1% English, 9.1% Irish, 6.1% Dutch (2006-2010 5-year est.).

Economy: Single-family building permits issued: 0 (2011); Multi-family building permits issued: 0 (2011); Employment by occupation: 16.8% management, 1.3% professional, 11.8% services, 8.2% sales, 1.6% farming, 14.7% construction, 10.2% production (2006-2010 5-year est.).

Income: Per capita income: $30,110 (2006-2010 5-year est.); Median household income: $57,625 (2006-2010 5-year est.); Average household income: $75,177 (2006-2010 5-year est.); Percent of households with income of $100,000 or more: 19.3% (2006-2010 5-year est.); Poverty rate: 8.1% (2006-2010 5-year est.).

Education: Percent of population age 25 and over with: High school diploma (including GED) or higher: 84.1% (2006-2010 5-year est.); Bachelor's degree or higher: 16.6% (2006-2010 5-year est.); Master's degree or higher: 5.5% (2006-2010 5-year est.).

Housing: Homeownership rate: 88.1% (2010); Median home value: $165,500 (2006-2010 5-year est.); Median contract rent: $418 per month (2006-2010 5-year est.); Median year structure built: 1971 (2006-2010 5-year est.).

Transportation: Commute to work: 90.1% car, 0.0% public transportation, 5.7% walk, 3.9% work from home (2006-2010 5-year est.); Travel time to work: 35.4% less than 15 minutes, 48.1% 15 to 30 minutes, 10.0% 30 to 45 minutes, 3.6% 45 to 60 minutes, 3.0% 60 minutes or more (2006-2010 5-year est.)

Additional Information Contacts

Greater Susquehanna Valley Chamber of Commerce . . . . (570) 743-4100
  http://www.gsvcc.org

SHAMOKIN (city). Aka Luke. Covers a land area of 0.834 square miles and a water area of 0 square miles. Located at 40.79° N. Lat; 76.55° W. Long. Elevation is 722 feet.

Population: 9,184 (1990); 8,009 (2000); 7,374 (2010); Density: 8,841.6 persons per square mile (2010); Race: 96.8% White, 0.6% Black, 0.4% Asian, 0.1% American Indian/Alaska Native, 0.0% Native Hawaiian/Other Pacific Islander, 2.1% Other, 2.6% Hispanic of any race (2010); Average household size: 2.21 (2010); Median age: 39.3 (2010); Males per 100 females: 88.5 (2010); Marriage status: 30.4% never married, 43.5% now married, 12.1% widowed, 13.9% divorced (2006-2010 5-year est.); Foreign born: 0.6% (2006-2010 5-year est.); Ancestry (includes multiple ancestries): 29.7% German, 17.3% Polish, 15.5% Irish, 14.1% Italian, 8.7% Dutch (2006-2010 5-year est.).

Economy: Single-family building permits issued: 0 (2011); Multi-family building permits issued: 0 (2011); Employment by occupation: 4.2% management, 0.3% professional, 18.7% services, 17.1% sales, 2.4% farming, 9.5% construction, 4.9% production (2006-2010 5-year est.).

Income: Per capita income: $16,842 (2006-2010 5-year est.); Median household income: $27,210 (2006-2010 5-year est.); Average household income: $36,368 (2006-2010 5-year est.); Percent of households with income of $100,000 or more: 4.6% (2006-2010 5-year est.); Poverty rate: 20.0% (2006-2010 5-year est.).

Education: Percent of population age 25 and over with: High school diploma (including GED) or higher: 83.8% (2006-2010 5-year est.); Bachelor's degree or higher: 10.6% (2006-2010 5-year est.); Master's degree or higher: 3.3% (2006-2010 5-year est.).

School District(s)

Shamokin Area SD (KG-12)
  2010-11 Enrollment: 2,578 . . . . (570) 648-5752

Housing: Homeownership rate: 58.6% (2010); Median home value: $41,500 (2006-2010 5-year est.); Median contract rent: $317 per month (2006-2010 5-year est.); Median year structure built: before 1940 (2006-2010 5-year est.).

Safety: Violent crime rate: 4.1 per 10,000 population; Property crime rate: 82.5 per 10,000 population (2011).

Newspapers: The News-Item (Community news; Circulation 10,030)

Transportation: Commute to work: 88.9% car, 0.4% public transportation, 5.9% walk, 1.4% work from home (2006-2010 5-year est.); Travel time to work: 37.4% less than 15 minutes, 22.2% 15 to 30 minutes, 23.2% 30 to 45 minutes, 9.8% 45 to 60 minutes, 7.3% 60 minutes or more (2006-2010 5-year est.)

Additional Information Contacts

Brush Valley Regional Chamber of Commerce . . . . (570) 648-4675
  http://www.brushvalleychamber.com
City of Shamokin . . . . (570) 644-0876
  http://www.shamokincity.org

SHAMOKIN (township). Aka Luke. Covers a land area of 30.901 square miles and a water area of 0.214 square miles. Located at 40.84° N. Lat; 76.64° W. Long. Elevation is 722 feet.

History: Settled c.1835, incorporated 1864.

Population: 1,697 (1990); 2,159 (2000); 2,407 (2010); Density: 77.9 persons per square mile (2010); Race: 98.5% White, 0.5% Black, 0.3% Asian, 0.1% American Indian/Alaska Native, 0.0% Native Hawaiian/Other Pacific Islander, 0.6% Other, 0.5% Hispanic of any race (2010); Average household size: 2.52 (2010); Median age: 44.5 (2010); Males per 100 females: 108.4 (2010); Marriage status: 19.4% never married, 70.2% now married, 4.8% widowed, 5.7% divorced (2006-2010 5-year est.); Foreign born: 0.4% (2006-2010 5-year est.); Ancestry (includes multiple ancestries): 36.6% German, 19.9% Polish, 16.3% Irish, 10.8% Dutch, 10.1% Italian (2006-2010 5-year est.).

Economy: Single-family building permits issued: 3 (2011); Multi-family building permits issued: 0 (2011); Employment by occupation: 4.7% management, 2.1% professional, 9.1% services, 18.0% sales, 2.0% farming, 15.1% construction, 11.3% production (2006-2010 5-year est.).

Income: Per capita income: $22,369 (2006-2010 5-year est.); Median household income: $52,000 (2006-2010 5-year est.); Average household income: $59,123 (2006-2010 5-year est.); Percent of households with income of $100,000 or more: 11.8% (2006-2010 5-year est.); Poverty rate: 10.9% (2006-2010 5-year est.).

Education: Percent of population age 25 and over with: High school diploma (including GED) or higher: 87.0% (2006-2010 5-year est.); Bachelor's degree or higher: 12.8% (2006-2010 5-year est.); Master's degree or higher: 1.7% (2006-2010 5-year est.).

Housing: Homeownership rate: 88.8% (2010); Median home value: $125,600 (2006-2010 5-year est.); Median contract rent: $217 per month (2006-2010 5-year est.); Median year structure built: 1972 (2006-2010 5-year est.).

Newspapers: The News-Item (Community news; Circulation 10,030)

Transportation: Commute to work: 92.1% car, 0.0% public transportation, 3.4% walk, 2.3% work from home (2006-2010 5-year est.); Travel time to work: 17.5% less than 15 minutes, 44.5% 15 to 30 minutes, 26.0% 30 to 45 minutes, 6.4% 45 to 60 minutes, 5.6% 60 minutes or more (2006-2010 5-year est.)

Additional Information Contacts

Brush Valley Regional Chamber of Commerce . . . . (570) 648-4675
  http://www.brushvalleychamber.com

SNYDERTOWN (borough). Covers a land area of 3.451 square miles and a water area of 0.056 square miles. Located at 40.87° N. Lat; 76.68° W. Long. Elevation is 531 feet.

Population: 416 (1990); 357 (2000); 339 (2010); Density: 98.2 persons per square mile (2010); Race: 97.9% White, 0.3% Black, 0.3% Asian, 0.0% American Indian/Alaska Native, 0.0% Native Hawaiian/Other Pacific Islander, 1.5% Other, 0.9% Hispanic of any race (2010); Average household size: 2.35 (2010); Median age: 47.7 (2010); Males per 100 females: 114.6 (2010); Marriage status: 16.8% never married, 66.5% now married, 3.6% widowed, 13.2% divorced (2006-2010 5-year est.); Foreign born: 1.2% (2006-2010 5-year est.); Ancestry (includes multiple ancestries): 41.7% German, 19.4% Italian, 17.5% Polish, 9.9% Dutch, 9.5% Irish (2006-2010 5-year est.).

Economy: Single-family building permits issued: 0 (2011); Multi-family building permits issued: 0 (2011); Employment by occupation: 2.4% management, 0.0% professional, 23.0% services, 19.0% sales, 1.6% farming, 4.0% construction, 9.5% production (2006-2010 5-year est.).

Income: Per capita income: $23,952 (2006-2010 5-year est.); Median household income: $61,500 (2006-2010 5-year est.); Average household income: $63,633 (2006-2010 5-year est.); Percent of households with income of $100,000 or more: 16.7% (2006-2010 5-year est.); Poverty rate: 3.6% (2006-2010 5-year est.).

Education: Percent of population age 25 and over with: High school diploma (including GED) or higher: 96.2% (2006-2010 5-year est.); Bachelor's degree or higher: 22.2% (2006-2010 5-year est.); Master's degree or higher: 4.3% (2006-2010 5-year est.).

Housing: Homeownership rate: 90.3% (2010); Median home value: $142,000 (2006-2010 5-year est.); Median contract rent: n/a per month (2006-2010 5-year est.); Median year structure built: 1954 (2006-2010 5-year est.).

Transportation: Commute to work: 87.8% car, 0.0% public transportation, 1.7% walk, 7.8% work from home (2006-2010 5-year est.); Travel time to work: 19.8% less than 15 minutes, 53.8% 15 to 30 minutes, 20.8% 30 to

45 minutes, 1.9% 45 to 60 minutes, 3.8% 60 minutes or more (2006-2010 5-year est.)

STRONG (CDP). Covers a land area of 0.042 square miles and a water area of 0 square miles. Located at 40.80° N. Lat; 76.44° W. Long. Elevation is 1,056 feet.

Population: n/a (1990); n/a (2000); 147 (2010); Density: 3,503.1 persons per square mile (2010); Race: 99.3% White, 0.0% Black, 0.0% Asian, 0.0% American Indian/Alaska Native, 0.0% Native Hawaiian/Other Pacific Islander, 0.7% Other, 0.7% Hispanic of any race (2010); Average household size: 2.33 (2010); Median age: 44.3 (2010); Males per 100 females: 75.0 (2010); Marriage status: 31.5% never married, 45.8% now married, 22.7% widowed, 0.0% divorced (2006-2010 5-year est.); Foreign born: 0.0% (2006-2010 5-year est.); Ancestry (includes multiple ancestries): 37.5% Italian, 28.7% German, 18.7% Polish, 15.1% Irish, 4.8% Dutch (2006-2010 5-year est.).
Economy: Employment by occupation: 0.0% management, 0.0% professional, 0.0% services, 39.2% sales, 0.0% farming, 4.1% construction, 9.3% production (2006-2010 5-year est.).
Income: Per capita income: $26,580 (2006-2010 5-year est.); Median household income: $70,066 (2006-2010 5-year est.); Average household income: $61,128 (2006-2010 5-year est.); Percent of households with income of $100,000 or more: 29.4% (2006-2010 5-year est.); Poverty rate: 7.2% (2006-2010 5-year est.).
Education: Percent of population age 25 and over with: High school diploma (including GED) or higher: 96.3% (2006-2010 5-year est.); Bachelor's degree or higher: 23.2% (2006-2010 5-year est.); Master's degree or higher: 12.6% (2006-2010 5-year est.).
Housing: Homeownership rate: 85.7% (2010); Median home value: $42,300 (2006-2010 5-year est.); Median contract rent: n/a per month (2006-2010 5-year est.); Median year structure built: before 1940 (2006-2010 5-year est.).
Transportation: Commute to work: 91.4% car, 0.0% public transportation, 8.6% walk, 0.0% work from home (2006-2010 5-year est.); Travel time to work: 45.2% less than 15 minutes, 0.0% 15 to 30 minutes, 41.9% 30 to 45 minutes, 0.0% 45 to 60 minutes, 12.9% 60 minutes or more (2006-2010 5-year est.)

SUNBURY (city). County seat. Covers a land area of 2.062 square miles and a water area of 0.101 square miles. Located at 40.86° N. Lat; 76.79° W. Long. Elevation is 466 feet.

History: Sunbury was once the central site of Shamokin, a cluster of three Native American villages. Eventually they abandoned the site and Governor Richard Penn ordered a town laid out. In Sunbury, Thomas Edison built and operated the first three-wire central station incandescent electric lighting plant in the world.
Population: 11,591 (1990); 10,610 (2000); 9,905 (2010); Density: 4,802.7 persons per square mile (2010); Race: 91.0% White, 2.8% Black, 0.3% Asian, 0.3% American Indian/Alaska Native, 0.0% Native Hawaiian/Other Pacific Islander, 5.6% Other, 6.7% Hispanic of any race (2010); Average household size: 2.25 (2010); Median age: 38.9 (2010); Males per 100 females: 90.7 (2010); Marriage status: 32.4% never married, 43.1% now married, 9.1% widowed, 15.3% divorced (2006-2010 5-year est.); Foreign born: 1.2% (2006-2010 5-year est.); Ancestry (includes multiple ancestries): 33.7% German, 10.5% Irish, 10.2% American, 8.5% Italian, 6.4% English (2006-2010 5-year est.).
Economy: Single-family building permits issued: 0 (2011); Multi-family building permits issued: 0 (2011); Employment by occupation: 3.0% management, 0.7% professional, 19.0% services, 16.1% sales, 4.3% farming, 7.2% construction, 8.7% production (2006-2010 5-year est.).
Income: Per capita income: $15,594 (2006-2010 5-year est.); Median household income: $28,143 (2006-2010 5-year est.); Average household income: $34,168 (2006-2010 5-year est.); Percent of households with income of $100,000 or more: 2.3% (2006-2010 5-year est.); Poverty rate: 22.2% (2006-2010 5-year est.).
Education: Percent of population age 25 and over with: High school diploma (including GED) or higher: 75.4% (2006-2010 5-year est.); Bachelor's degree or higher: 7.9% (2006-2010 5-year est.); Master's degree or higher: 2.4% (2006-2010 5-year est.).

School District(s)
Shikellamy SD (KG-12)
 2010-11 Enrollment: 2,917 . . . . (570) 286-3721
Shikellamy SD (KG-12)
 2010-11 Enrollment: 2,917 . . . . (570) 286-3721

Two-year College(s)
Triangle Tech Inc-Sunbury (Private, For-profit)
 Fall 2010 Enrollment: 250 . . . . (570) 988-0700
 2011-12 Tuition: In-state $15,754; Out-of-state $15,754
Vocational/Technical School(s)
Central Susquehanna Intermediate Unit LPN Career (Public)
 Fall 2010 Enrollment: 122 . . . . (570) 768-4960
 2011-12 Tuition: $14,566
Housing: Homeownership rate: 45.1% (2010); Median home value: $68,700 (2006-2010 5-year est.); Median contract rent: $409 per month (2006-2010 5-year est.); Median year structure built: before 1940 (2006-2010 5-year est.).
Hospitals: Sunbury Community Hospital (123 beds)
Safety: Violent crime rate: 106.7 per 10,000 population; Property crime rate: 347.2 per 10,000 population (2011).
Newspapers: The Daily Item (Local news; Circulation 25,735)
Transportation: Commute to work: 87.4% car, 0.0% public transportation, 8.6% walk, 1.0% work from home (2006-2010 5-year est.); Travel time to work: 42.0% less than 15 minutes, 36.4% 15 to 30 minutes, 13.2% 30 to 45 minutes, 2.5% 45 to 60 minutes, 5.9% 60 minutes or more (2006-2010 5-year est.)
Additional Information Contacts
City of Sunbury . . . . (570) 286-7820
 http://www.cityofsunbury.com
Greater Susquehanna Valley Chamber of Commerce . . . . (570) 743-4100
 http://www.gsvcc.org

THARPTOWN (UNIONTOWN) (CDP). Covers a land area of 0.098 square miles and a water area of 0.009 square miles. Located at 40.80° N. Lat; 76.57° W. Long.

Population: n/a (1990); n/a (2000); 498 (2010); Density: 5,102.7 persons per square mile (2010); Race: 99.0% White, 0.0% Black, 0.4% Asian, 0.0% American Indian/Alaska Native, 0.0% Native Hawaiian/Other Pacific Islander, 0.6% Other, 0.6% Hispanic of any race (2010); Average household size: 2.13 (2010); Median age: 47.0 (2010); Males per 100 females: 91.5 (2010); Marriage status: 36.6% never married, 24.2% now married, 20.2% widowed, 19.0% divorced (2006-2010 5-year est.); Foreign born: 0.0% (2006-2010 5-year est.); Ancestry (includes multiple ancestries): 37.0% German, 30.9% Polish, 17.2% American, 15.2% Dutch, 14.5% Irish (2006-2010 5-year est.).
Economy: Employment by occupation: 7.1% management, 0.0% professional, 12.9% services, 31.4% sales, 0.0% farming, 0.0% construction, 0.0% production (2006-2010 5-year est.).
Income: Per capita income: $16,208 (2006-2010 5-year est.); Median household income: $28,942 (2006-2010 5-year est.); Average household income: $33,399 (2006-2010 5-year est.); Percent of households with income of $100,000 or more: n/a (2006-2010 5-year est.); Poverty rate: 19.4% (2006-2010 5-year est.).
Education: Percent of population age 25 and over with: High school diploma (including GED) or higher: 82.3% (2006-2010 5-year est.); Bachelor's degree or higher: 6.8% (2006-2010 5-year est.); Master's degree or higher: 0.0% (2006-2010 5-year est.).
Housing: Homeownership rate: 77.3% (2010); Median home value: $58,700 (2006-2010 5-year est.); Median contract rent: $405 per month (2006-2010 5-year est.); Median year structure built: 1941 (2006-2010 5-year est.).
Transportation: Commute to work: 100.0% car, 0.0% public transportation, 0.0% walk, 0.0% work from home (2006-2010 5-year est.); Travel time to work: 32.9% less than 15 minutes, 60.0% 15 to 30 minutes, 7.1% 30 to 45 minutes, 0.0% 45 to 60 minutes, 0.0% 60 minutes or more (2006-2010 5-year est.)

TREVORTON (CDP). Covers a land area of 4.270 square miles and a water area of 0 square miles. Located at 40.78° N. Lat; 76.67° W. Long. Elevation is 840 feet.

Population: 2,067 (1990); 2,010 (2000); 1,834 (2010); Density: 429.5 persons per square mile (2010); Race: 98.5% White, 0.1% Black, 0.5% Asian, 0.1% American Indian/Alaska Native, 0.0% Native Hawaiian/Other Pacific Islander, 0.8% Other, 0.5% Hispanic of any race (2010); Average household size: 2.33 (2010); Median age: 41.7 (2010); Males per 100 females: 94.5 (2010); Marriage status: 23.5% never married, 54.0% now married, 11.6% widowed, 10.9% divorced (2006-2010 5-year est.); Foreign born: 0.8% (2006-2010 5-year est.); Ancestry (includes multiple ancestries): 37.1% German, 12.7% Dutch, 10.8% Polish, 7.7% Irish, 7.3% American (2006-2010 5-year est.).

Economy: Employment by occupation: 3.8% management, 1.6% professional, 16.8% services, 12.8% sales, 5.6% farming, 14.1% construction, 13.2% production (2006-2010 5-year est.).

Income: Per capita income: $18,417 (2006-2010 5-year est.); Median household income: $30,208 (2006-2010 5-year est.); Average household income: $42,626 (2006-2010 5-year est.); Percent of households with income of $100,000 or more: 4.6% (2006-2010 5-year est.); Poverty rate: 16.8% (2006-2010 5-year est.).

Education: Percent of population age 25 and over with: High school diploma (including GED) or higher: 82.6% (2006-2010 5-year est.); Bachelor's degree or higher: 8.1% (2006-2010 5-year est.); Master's degree or higher: 2.1% (2006-2010 5-year est.).

School District(s)

Line Mountain SD (KG-12)

    2010-11 Enrollment: 1,250 . . . . (570) 758-2640

Housing: Homeownership rate: 80.0% (2010); Median home value: $69,300 (2006-2010 5-year est.); Median contract rent: $344 per month (2006-2010 5-year est.); Median year structure built: 1942 (2006-2010 5-year est.).

Transportation: Commute to work: 92.1% car, 0.5% public transportation, 4.1% walk, 3.3% work from home (2006-2010 5-year est.); Travel time to work: 18.5% less than 15 minutes, 40.2% 15 to 30 minutes, 19.4% 30 to 45 minutes, 9.2% 45 to 60 minutes, 12.7% 60 minutes or more (2006-2010 5-year est.).

Additional Information Contacts

Brush Valley Regional Chamber of Commerce . . . . (570) 648-4675
    http://www.brushvalleychamber.com

TURBOT (township). Covers a land area of 13.842 square miles and a water area of 0.235 square miles. Located at 41.03° N. Lat; 76.80° W. Long.

Population: 1,645 (1990); 1,677 (2000); 1,806 (2010); Density: 130.5 persons per square mile (2010); Race: 97.2% White, 0.5% Black, 0.0% Asian, 0.0% American Indian/Alaska Native, 0.0% Native Hawaiian/Other Pacific Islander, 2.3% Other, 2.2% Hispanic of any race (2010); Average household size: 2.38 (2010); Median age: 46.5 (2010); Males per 100 females: 98.5 (2010); Marriage status: 16.6% never married, 67.9% now married, 7.6% widowed, 7.9% divorced (2006-2010 5-year est.); Foreign born: 1.3% (2006-2010 5-year est.); Ancestry (includes multiple ancestries): 38.8% German, 12.8% American, 10.4% Irish, 7.2% English, 5.0% Dutch (2006-2010 5-year est.).

Economy: Single-family building permits issued: 3 (2011); Multi-family building permits issued: 0 (2011); Employment by occupation: 13.2% management, 1.9% professional, 12.8% services, 18.3% sales, 2.5% farming, 6.5% construction, 4.9% production (2006-2010 5-year est.).

Income: Per capita income: $27,143 (2006-2010 5-year est.); Median household income: $57,016 (2006-2010 5-year est.); Average household income: $69,630 (2006-2010 5-year est.); Percent of households with income of $100,000 or more: 19.2% (2006-2010 5-year est.); Poverty rate: 4.4% (2006-2010 5-year est.).

Education: Percent of population age 25 and over with: High school diploma (including GED) or higher: 85.6% (2006-2010 5-year est.); Bachelor's degree or higher: 19.2% (2006-2010 5-year est.); Master's degree or higher: 7.6% (2006-2010 5-year est.).

Housing: Homeownership rate: 87.6% (2010); Median home value: $157,600 (2006-2010 5-year est.); Median contract rent: $406 per month (2006-2010 5-year est.); Median year structure built: 1966 (2006-2010 5-year est.).

Transportation: Commute to work: 91.6% car, 0.0% public transportation, 1.8% walk, 4.4% work from home (2006-2010 5-year est.); Travel time to work: 47.4% less than 15 minutes, 33.1% 15 to 30 minutes, 12.2% 30 to 45 minutes, 3.3% 45 to 60 minutes, 4.1% 60 minutes or more (2006-2010 5-year est.)

Additional Information Contacts

Central PA Chamber of Commerce . . . . (570) 742-7341
    http://www.centralpachamber.com/index.php

TURBOTVILLE (borough). Covers a land area of 0.449 square miles and a water area of 0 square miles. Located at 41.10° N. Lat; 76.77° W. Long. Elevation is 584 feet.

Population: 675 (1990); 691 (2000); 705 (2010); Density: 1,569.7 persons per square mile (2010); Race: 97.9% White, 1.0% Black, 0.0% Asian, 0.1% American Indian/Alaska Native, 0.0% Native Hawaiian/Other Pacific Islander, 1.0% Other, 1.4% Hispanic of any race (2010); Average household size: 2.47 (2010); Median age: 37.9 (2010); Males per 100

females: 98.0 (2010); Marriage status: 29.0% never married, 60.2% now married, 5.7% widowed, 5.1% divorced (2006-2010 5-year est.); Foreign born: 0.4% (2006-2010 5-year est.); Ancestry (includes multiple ancestries): 57.7% German, 8.3% Irish, 6.1% Dutch, 6.0% Italian, 4.7% Polish (2006-2010 5-year est.).

Economy: Single-family building permits issued: 0 (2011); Multi-family building permits issued: 0 (2011); Employment by occupation: 4.1% management, 3.4% professional, 12.3% services, 22.8% sales, 4.5% farming, 13.1% construction, 10.5% production (2006-2010 5-year est.).

Income: Per capita income: $23,768 (2006-2010 5-year est.); Median household income: $56,136 (2006-2010 5-year est.); Average household income: $61,333 (2006-2010 5-year est.); Percent of households with income of $100,000 or more: 13.6% (2006-2010 5-year est.); Poverty rate: 8.6% (2006-2010 5-year est.).

Education: Percent of population age 25 and over with: High school diploma (including GED) or higher: 91.0% (2006-2010 5-year est.); Bachelor's degree or higher: 13.0% (2006-2010 5-year est.); Master's degree or higher: 6.2% (2006-2010 5-year est.).

School District(s)

Warrior Run SD (KG-12)

    2010-11 Enrollment: 1,636 . . . . (570) 649-5138

Housing: Homeownership rate: 72.1% (2010); Median home value: $102,000 (2006-2010 5-year est.); Median contract rent: $412 per month (2006-2010 5-year est.); Median year structure built: before 1940 (2006-2010 5-year est.).

Transportation: Commute to work: 90.5% car, 0.0% public transportation, 6.2% walk, 1.7% work from home (2006-2010 5-year est.); Travel time to work: 33.9% less than 15 minutes, 39.0% 15 to 30 minutes, 18.7% 30 to 45 minutes, 6.1% 45 to 60 minutes, 2.4% 60 minutes or more (2006-2010 5-year est.)

UPPER AUGUSTA (township). Covers a land area of 19.546 square miles and a water area of 3.102 square miles. Located at 40.87° N. Lat; 76.76° W. Long.

Population: 2,681 (1990); 2,556 (2000); 2,586 (2010); Density: 132.3 persons per square mile (2010); Race: 98.3% White, 0.4% Black, 0.4% Asian, 0.2% American Indian/Alaska Native, 0.0% Native Hawaiian/Other Pacific Islander, 0.7% Other, 2.1% Hispanic of any race (2010); Average household size: 2.43 (2010); Median age: 47.7 (2010); Males per 100 females: 100.8 (2010); Marriage status: 21.6% never married, 62.2% now married, 9.4% widowed, 6.8% divorced (2006-2010 5-year est.); Foreign born: 0.6% (2006-2010 5-year est.); Ancestry (includes multiple ancestries): 53.1% German, 11.0% Irish, 7.7% Polish, 5.2% English, 5.0% Italian (2006-2010 5-year est.).

Economy: Single-family building permits issued: 1 (2011); Multi-family building permits issued: 0 (2011); Employment by occupation: 10.3% management, 0.4% professional, 10.0% services, 12.0% sales, 7.1% farming, 6.7% construction, 4.1% production (2006-2010 5-year est.).

Income: Per capita income: $27,050 (2006-2010 5-year est.); Median household income: $49,594 (2006-2010 5-year est.); Average household income: $62,594 (2006-2010 5-year est.); Percent of households with income of $100,000 or more: 11.7% (2006-2010 5-year est.); Poverty rate: 10.3% (2006-2010 5-year est.).

Education: Percent of population age 25 and over with: High school diploma (including GED) or higher: 87.7% (2006-2010 5-year est.); Bachelor's degree or higher: 16.7% (2006-2010 5-year est.); Master's degree or higher: 5.1% (2006-2010 5-year est.).

Housing: Homeownership rate: 89.2% (2010); Median home value: $118,300 (2006-2010 5-year est.); Median contract rent: $450 per month (2006-2010 5-year est.); Median year structure built: 1958 (2006-2010 5-year est.).

Transportation: Commute to work: 96.9% car, 0.0% public transportation, 0.5% walk, 2.0% work from home (2006-2010 5-year est.); Travel time to work: 23.2% less than 15 minutes, 47.2% 15 to 30 minutes, 13.4% 30 to 45 minutes, 6.2% 45 to 60 minutes, 10.1% 60 minutes or more (2006-2010 5-year est.)

Additional Information Contacts

Central PA Chamber of Commerce . . . . (570) 742-7341
    http://www.centralpachamber.com/index.php

UPPER MAHANOY (township). Covers a land area of 23.337 square miles and a water area of 0.022 square miles. Located at 40.71° N. Lat; 76.63° W. Long.

Population: 621 (1990); 599 (2000); 796 (2010); Density: 34.1 persons per square mile (2010); Race: 99.7% White, 0.1% Black, 0.0% Asian,

0.0% American Indian/Alaska Native, 0.0% Native Hawaiian/Other Pacific Islander, 0.2% Other, 0.1% Hispanic of any race (2010); Average household size: 2.54 (2010); Median age: 45.1 (2010); Males per 100 females: 99.5 (2010); Marriage status: 19.2% never married, 72.2% now married, 3.1% widowed, 5.5% divorced (2006-2010 5-year est.); Foreign born: 0.0% (2006-2010 5-year est.); Ancestry (includes multiple ancestries): 75.6% German, 7.2% Polish, 5.4% Pennsylvania German, 5.2% English, 4.0% Irish (2006-2010 5-year est.).

Economy: Single-family building permits issued: 0 (2011); Multi-family building permits issued: 0 (2011); Employment by occupation: 8.0% management, 0.7% professional, 6.9% services, 8.0% sales, 2.9% farming, 17.5% construction, 10.5% production (2006-2010 5-year est.).

Income: Per capita income: $19,897 (2006-2010 5-year est.); Median household income: $39,091 (2006-2010 5-year est.); Average household income: $52,113 (2006-2010 5-year est.); Percent of households with income of $100,000 or more: 13.4% (2006-2010 5-year est.); Poverty rate: 11.8% (2006-2010 5-year est.).

Education: Percent of population age 25 and over with: High school diploma (including GED) or higher: 92.8% (2006-2010 5-year est.); Bachelor's degree or higher: 10.8% (2006-2010 5-year est.); Master's degree or higher: 2.2% (2006-2010 5-year est.).

Housing: Homeownership rate: 88.5% (2010); Median home value: $123,700 (2006-2010 5-year est.); Median contract rent: $475 per month (2006-2010 5-year est.); Median year structure built: before 1940 (2006-2010 5-year est.).

Transportation: Commute to work: 83.6% car, 0.0% public transportation, 10.2% walk, 6.2% work from home (2006-2010 5-year est.); Travel time to work: 32.6% less than 15 minutes, 30.6% 15 to 30 minutes, 20.5% 30 to 45 minutes, 8.1% 45 to 60 minutes, 8.1% 60 minutes or more (2006-2010 5-year est.)

WASHINGTON (township). Covers a land area of 18.091 square miles and a water area of 0.012 square miles. Located at 40.71° N. Lat; 76.73° W. Long.

Population: 620 (1990); 660 (2000); 746 (2010); Density: 41.2 persons per square mile (2010); Race: 98.0% White, 0.1% Black, 0.1% Asian, 0.1% American Indian/Alaska Native, 0.1% Native Hawaiian/Other Pacific Islander, 1.6% Other, 1.1% Hispanic of any race (2010); Average household size: 2.67 (2010); Median age: 41.4 (2010); Males per 100 females: 97.9 (2010); Marriage status: 14.2% never married, 69.0% now married, 6.0% widowed, 10.8% divorced (2006-2010 5-year est.); Foreign born: 1.5% (2006-2010 5-year est.); Ancestry (includes multiple ancestries): 66.0% German, 7.2% Dutch, 5.0% Italian, 4.2% Hungarian, 3.3% Pennsylvania German (2006-2010 5-year est.).

Economy: Single-family building permits issued: 0 (2011); Multi-family building permits issued: 0 (2011); Employment by occupation: 12.1% management, 0.0% professional, 9.1% services, 21.2% sales, 8.6% farming, 18.0% construction, 11.5% production (2006-2010 5-year est.).

Income: Per capita income: $23,836 (2006-2010 5-year est.); Median household income: $43,906 (2006-2010 5-year est.); Average household income: $55,318 (2006-2010 5-year est.); Percent of households with income of $100,000 or more: 12.1% (2006-2010 5-year est.); Poverty rate: 2.7% (2006-2010 5-year est.).

Education: Percent of population age 25 and over with: High school diploma (including GED) or higher: 84.1% (2006-2010 5-year est.); Bachelor's degree or higher: 5.1% (2006-2010 5-year est.); Master's degree or higher: 4.4% (2006-2010 5-year est.).

Housing: Homeownership rate: 81.4% (2010); Median home value: $128,500 (2006-2010 5-year est.); Median contract rent: $328 per month (2006-2010 5-year est.); Median year structure built: 1970 (2006-2010 5-year est.).

Transportation: Commute to work: 92.3% car, 0.0% public transportation, 0.0% walk, 7.7% work from home (2006-2010 5-year est.); Travel time to work: 11.0% less than 15 minutes, 43.1% 15 to 30 minutes, 35.1% 30 to 45 minutes, 4.7% 45 to 60 minutes, 6.0% 60 minutes or more (2006-2010 5-year est.)

WATSONTOWN (borough). Covers a land area of 0.674 square miles and a water area of 0.223 square miles. Located at 41.08° N. Lat; 76.86° W. Long. Elevation is 476 feet.

History: Laid out 1794, incorporated 1867.

Population: 2,310 (1990); 2,255 (2000); 2,351 (2010); Density: 3,489.1 persons per square mile (2010); Race: 97.0% White, 0.6% Black, 0.8% Asian, 0.3% American Indian/Alaska Native, 0.0% Native Hawaiian/Other Pacific Islander, 1.3% Other, 1.1% Hispanic of any race (2010); Average

household size: 2.22 (2010); Median age: 42.0 (2010); Males per 100 females: 90.2 (2010); Marriage status: 24.8% never married, 50.1% now married, 11.8% widowed, 13.3% divorced (2006-2010 5-year est.); Foreign born: 0.0% (2006-2010 5-year est.); Ancestry (includes multiple ancestries): 49.7% German, 11.8% American, 7.8% Irish, 6.9% Dutch, 3.6% English (2006-2010 5-year est.).

Economy: Single-family building permits issued: 4 (2011); Multi-family building permits issued: 2 (2011); Employment by occupation: 3.7% management, 2.7% professional, 12.9% services, 20.7% sales, 5.0% farming, 4.7% construction, 8.4% production (2006-2010 5-year est.).

Income: Per capita income: $19,573 (2006-2010 5-year est.); Median household income: $39,458 (2006-2010 5-year est.); Average household income: $46,086 (2006-2010 5-year est.); Percent of households with income of $100,000 or more: 5.5% (2006-2010 5-year est.); Poverty rate: 10.9% (2006-2010 5-year est.).

Education: Percent of population age 25 and over with: High school diploma (including GED) or higher: 90.0% (2006-2010 5-year est.); Bachelor's degree or higher: 13.7% (2006-2010 5-year est.); Master's degree or higher: 4.0% (2006-2010 5-year est.).

School District(s)

Warrior Run SD (KG-12)

   2010-11 Enrollment: 1,636 . . . . (570) 649-5138

Housing: Homeownership rate: 52.9% (2010); Median home value: $108,300 (2006-2010 5-year est.); Median contract rent: $424 per month (2006-2010 5-year est.); Median year structure built: 1941 (2006-2010 5-year est.).

Safety: Violent crime rate: 25.4 per 10,000 population; Property crime rate: 279.9 per 10,000 population (2011).

Transportation: Commute to work: 84.8% car, 0.0% public transportation, 9.8% walk, 3.1% work from home (2006-2010 5-year est.); Travel time to work: 41.4% less than 15 minutes, 38.5% 15 to 30 minutes, 15.3% 30 to 45 minutes, 3.5% 45 to 60 minutes, 1.3% 60 minutes or more (2006-2010 5-year est.)

Additional Information Contacts

Central PA Chamber of Commerce. . . . . (570) 742-7341
   http://www.centralpachamber.com/index.php

WEST CAMERON (township). Covers a land area of 11.727 square miles and a water area of 0.162 square miles. Located at 40.75° N. Lat; 76.66° W. Long. Elevation is 974 feet.

Population: 527 (1990); 517 (2000); 541 (2010); Density: 46.1 persons per square mile (2010); Race: 98.2% White, 0.4% Black, 0.0% Asian, 0.0% American Indian/Alaska Native, 0.0% Native Hawaiian/Other Pacific Islander, 1.4% Other, 2.0% Hispanic of any race (2010); Average household size: 2.63 (2010); Median age: 41.8 (2010); Males per 100 females: 104.2 (2010); Marriage status: 28.5% never married, 58.6% now married, 4.1% widowed, 8.7% divorced (2006-2010 5-year est.); Foreign born: 0.0% (2006-2010 5-year est.); Ancestry (includes multiple ancestries): 33.5% German, 17.3% Dutch, 11.5% Polish, 10.9% Pennsylvania German, 9.6% American (2006-2010 5-year est.).

Economy: Employment by occupation: 5.3% management, 0.0% professional, 13.4% services, 11.2% sales, 5.9% farming, 9.6% construction, 9.0% production (2006-2010 5-year est.).

Income: Per capita income: $22,218 (2006-2010 5-year est.); Median household income: $42,656 (2006-2010 5-year est.); Average household income: $54,248 (2006-2010 5-year est.); Percent of households with income of $100,000 or more: 14.2% (2006-2010 5-year est.); Poverty rate: 4.1% (2006-2010 5-year est.).

Education: Percent of population age 25 and over with: High school diploma (including GED) or higher: 83.3% (2006-2010 5-year est.); Bachelor's degree or higher: 13.5% (2006-2010 5-year est.); Master's degree or higher: 1.5% (2006-2010 5-year est.).

Housing: Homeownership rate: 92.2% (2010); Median home value: $108,200 (2006-2010 5-year est.); Median contract rent: $184 per month (2006-2010 5-year est.); Median year structure built: 1945 (2006-2010 5-year est.).

Transportation: Commute to work: 96.2% car, 0.0% public transportation, 0.0% walk, 2.9% work from home (2006-2010 5-year est.); Travel time to work: 8.9% less than 15 minutes, 44.9% 15 to 30 minutes, 27.1% 30 to 45 minutes, 11.6% 45 to 60 minutes, 7.6% 60 minutes or more (2006-2010 5-year est.)

WEST CHILLISQUAQUE (township). Covers a land area of 12.889 square miles and a water area of 1.081 square miles. Located at 40.97° N. Lat; 76.84° W. Long.

Population: 3,322 (1990); 2,846 (2000); 2,627 (2010); Density: 203.8 persons per square mile (2010); Race: 97.5% White, 1.0% Black, 0.2% Asian, 0.0% American Indian/Alaska Native, 0.0% Native Hawaiian/Other Pacific Islander, 1.3% Other, 1.4% Hispanic of any race (2010); Average household size: 2.28 (2010); Median age: 46.6 (2010); Males per 100 females: 100.7 (2010); Marriage status: 19.9% never married, 59.3% now married, 9.9% widowed, 10.9% divorced (2006-2010 5-year est.); Foreign born: 0.9% (2006-2010 5-year est.); Ancestry (includes multiple ancestries): 48.3% German, 8.1% American, 7.9% English, 7.8% French, 7.7% Irish (2006-2010 5-year est.).

Economy: Single-family building permits issued: 2 (2011); Multi-family building permits issued: 0 (2011); Employment by occupation: 1.8% management, 1.1% professional, 18.2% services, 15.0% sales, 2.9% farming, 14.9% construction, 19.1% production (2006-2010 5-year est.).

Income: Per capita income: $19,004 (2006-2010 5-year est.); Median household income: $34,808 (2006-2010 5-year est.); Average household income: $45,457 (2006-2010 5-year est.); Percent of households with income of $100,000 or more: 5.1% (2006-2010 5-year est.); Poverty rate: 7.2% (2006-2010 5-year est.).

Education: Percent of population age 25 and over with: High school diploma (including GED) or higher: 78.8% (2006-2010 5-year est.); Bachelor's degree or higher: 11.9% (2006-2010 5-year est.); Master's degree or higher: 2.5% (2006-2010 5-year est.).

Housing: Homeownership rate: 82.4% (2010); Median home value: $90,800 (2006-2010 5-year est.); Median contract rent: $391 per month (2006-2010 5-year est.); Median year structure built: 1978 (2006-2010 5-year est.).

Transportation: Commute to work: 91.8% car, 0.6% public transportation, 0.0% walk, 3.3% work from home (2006-2010 5-year est.); Travel time to work: 42.6% less than 15 minutes, 30.6% 15 to 30 minutes, 18.7% 30 to 45 minutes, 6.7% 45 to 60 minutes, 1.4% 60 minutes or more (2006-2010 5-year est.)

Additional Information Contacts
Central PA Chamber of Commerce . . . . (570) 742-7341
  http://www.centralpachamber.com/index.php

ZERBE (township). Covers a land area of 11.582 square miles and a water area of 0.021 square miles. Located at 40.78° N. Lat; 76.66° W. Long.

Population: 2,067 (1990); 2,021 (2000); 1,872 (2010); Density: 161.6 persons per square mile (2010); Race: 98.3% White, 0.1% Black, 0.5% Asian, 0.1% American Indian/Alaska Native, 0.0% Native Hawaiian/Other Pacific Islander, 1.0% Other, 0.5% Hispanic of any race (2010); Average household size: 2.33 (2010); Median age: 41.4 (2010); Males per 100 females: 94.6 (2010); Marriage status: 23.5% never married, 54.0% now married, 11.6% widowed, 10.9% divorced (2006-2010 5-year est.); Foreign born: 0.8% (2006-2010 5-year est.); Ancestry (includes multiple ancestries): 37.1% German, 12.7% Dutch, 10.8% Polish, 7.7% Irish, 7.3% American (2006-2010 5-year est.).

Economy: Single-family building permits issued: 0 (2011); Multi-family building permits issued: 0 (2011); Employment by occupation: 3.8% management, 1.6% professional, 16.8% services, 12.8% sales, 5.6% farming, 14.1% construction, 13.2% production (2006-2010 5-year est.).

Income: Per capita income: $18,417 (2006-2010 5-year est.); Median household income: $30,208 (2006-2010 5-year est.); Average household income: $42,626 (2006-2010 5-year est.); Percent of households with income of $100,000 or more: 4.6% (2006-2010 5-year est.); Poverty rate: 16.8% (2006-2010 5-year est.).

Education: Percent of population age 25 and over with: High school diploma (including GED) or higher: 82.6% (2006-2010 5-year est.); Bachelor's degree or higher: 8.1% (2006-2010 5-year est.); Master's degree or higher: 2.1% (2006-2010 5-year est.).

Housing: Homeownership rate: 78.8% (2010); Median home value: $69,300 (2006-2010 5-year est.); Median contract rent: $344 per month (2006-2010 5-year est.); Median year structure built: 1942 (2006-2010 5-year est.).

Safety: Violent crime rate: 0.0 per 10,000 population; Property crime rate: 21.3 per 10,000 population (2011).

Transportation: Commute to work: 92.1% car, 0.5% public transportation, 4.1% walk, 3.3% work from home (2006-2010 5-year est.); Travel time to work: 18.5% less than 15 minutes, 40.2% 15 to 30 minutes, 19.4% 30 to

45 minutes, 9.2% 45 to 60 minutes, 12.7% 60 minutes or more (2006-2010 5-year est.)

Additional Information Contacts
Brush Valley Regional Chamber of Commerce . . . . (570) 648-4675
  http://www.brushvalleychamber.com

Perry County

Located in south central Pennsylvania; mountainous area, bounded on the east by the Susquehanna River; drained by the Juniata River; includes the Tuscarora and Blue Mountains. Covers a land area of 551.445 square miles, a water area of 4.092 square miles, and is located in the Eastern Time Zone at 40.40° N. Lat., 77.27° W. Long. The county was founded in 1820. County seat is Bloomfield.

Perry County is part of the Harrisburg-Carlisle, PA Metropolitan Statistical Area. The entire metro area includes: Cumberland County, PA; Dauphin County, PA; Perry County, PA

Population: 41,172 (1990); 43,602 (2000); 45,969 (2010); Race: 97.4% White, 0.6% Black, 0.4% Asian, 0.2% American Indian/Alaska Native, 0.0% Native Hawaiian/Other Pacific Islander, 1.4% Other, 1.3% Hispanic of any race (2010); Density: 83.4 persons per square mile (2010); Average household size: 2.53 (2010); Median age: 41.1 (2010); Males per 100 females: 100.6 (2010).

Religion: Six largest groups: 11.9% Methodist/Pietist, 5.8% Presbyterian-Reformed, 5.6% Lutheran, 4.4% Catholicism, 2.5% Non-Denominational, 2.2% Pentecostal (2010)

Economy: Unemployment rate: 7.9% (August 2012); Total civilian labor force: 24,823 (August 2012); Leading industries: 21.2% retail trade; 15.2% transportation & warehousing; 14.8% health care and social assistance (2010); Farms: 1,002 totaling 144,375 acres (2007); Companies that employ 500 or more persons: 1 (2010); Companies that employ 100 to 499 persons: 6 (2010); Companies that employ less than 100 persons: 789 (2010); Black-owned businesses: n/a (2007); Hispanic-owned businesses: n/a (2007); Asian-owned businesses: n/a (2007); Women-owned businesses: 889 (2007); Retail sales per capita: $6,753 (2010). Single-family building permits issued: 76 (2011); Multi-family building permits issued: 0 (2011).

Income: Per capita income: $23,701 (2006-2010 5-year est.); Median household income: $52,659 (2006-2010 5-year est.); Average household income: $60,447 (2006-2010 5-year est.); Percent of households with income of $100,000 or more: 14.3% (2006-2010 5-year est.); Poverty rate: 9.1% (2006-2010 5-year est.); Bankruptcy rate: 2.70% (2011).

Education: Percent of population age 25 and over with: High school diploma (including GED) or higher: 85.4% (2006-2010 5-year est.); Bachelor's degree or higher: 14.0% (2006-2010 5-year est.); Master's degree or higher: 4.3% (2006-2010 5-year est.).

Housing: Homeownership rate: 79.4% (2010); Median home value: $144,800 (2006-2010 5-year est.); Median contract rent: $485 per month (2006-2010 5-year est.); Median year structure built: 1972 (2006-2010 5-year est.)

Health: Birth rate: 117.3 per 10,000 population (2011); Death rate: 88.6 per 10,000 population (2011); Age-adjusted cancer mortality rate: 216.5 deaths per 100,000 population (2009); Number of physicians: 4.6 per 10,000 population (2010); Hospital beds: 0.0 per 10,000 population (2008); Hospital admissions: 0.0 per 10,000 population (2008).

Environment: Air Quality Index: 93.3% good, 6.4% moderate, 0.3% unhealthy for sensitive individuals, 0.0% unhealthy (percent of days in 2011)

Elections: 2012 Presidential election results: 29.8% Obama, 68.6% Romney

National and State Parks: Fowler Hollow State Park; Little Buffalo State Park; Tuscarora State Forest

Additional Information Contacts
Perry County Government . . . . (717) 582-2131
  http://www.perryco.org
Perry County Chamber of Commerce . . . . (717) 582-4523
  http://www.perrycountychamber.org

Perry County Communities

BLAIN (borough). Covers a land area of 0.318 square miles and a water area of 0 square miles. Located at 40.34° N. Lat; 77.51° W. Long. Elevation is 715 feet.

History: Covered bridges in area.

Population: 266 (1990); 252 (2000); 263 (2010); Density: 828.3 persons per square mile (2010); Race: 99.2% White, 0.0% Black, 0.0% Asian, 0.0% American Indian/Alaska Native, 0.0% Native Hawaiian/Other Pacific Islander, 0.8% Other, 0.0% Hispanic of any race (2010); Average household size: 2.80 (2010); Median age: 39.4 (2010); Males per 100 females: 97.7 (2010); Marriage status: 26.7% never married, 62.8% now married, 4.7% widowed, 5.8% divorced (2006-2010 5-year est.); Foreign born: 0.0% (2006-2010 5-year est.); Ancestry (includes multiple ancestries): 45.2% German, 10.1% Irish, 6.5% Italian, 6.5% Scotch-Irish, 5.5% Dutch (2006-2010 5-year est.).

Economy: Employment by occupation: 6.3% management, 0.0% professional, 6.3% services, 16.8% sales, 7.4% farming, 14.7% construction, 9.5% production (2006-2010 5-year est.).

Income: Per capita income: $18,616 (2006-2010 5-year est.); Median household income: $47,222 (2006-2010 5-year est.); Average household income: $51,403 (2006-2010 5-year est.); Percent of households with income of $100,000 or more: 9.7% (2006-2010 5-year est.); Poverty rate: 3.5% (2006-2010 5-year est.).

Education: Percent of population age 25 and over with: High school diploma (including GED) or higher: 85.0% (2006-2010 5-year est.); Bachelor's degree or higher: 3.0% (2006-2010 5-year est.); Master's degree or higher: 1.5% (2006-2010 5-year est.).

School District(s)
West Perry SD (KG-12)

    2010-11 Enrollment: 2,689 . . . . (717) 789-3934

Housing: Homeownership rate: 77.7% (2010); Median home value: $86,700 (2006-2010 5-year est.); Median contract rent: $670 per month (2006-2010 5-year est.); Median year structure built: before 1940 (2006-2010 5-year est.).

Transportation: Commute to work: 85.9% car, 0.0% public transportation, 9.8% walk, 4.3% work from home (2006-2010 5-year est.); Travel time to work: 20.5% less than 15 minutes, 6.8% 15 to 30 minutes, 21.6% 30 to 45 minutes, 25.0% 45 to 60 minutes, 26.1% 60 minutes or more (2006-2010 5-year est.)

BLOOMFIELD (borough). Aka New Bloomfield. County seat. Covers a land area of 0.611 square miles and a water area of 0 square miles. Located at 40.42° N. Lat; 77.19° W. Long.

History: Appalachian Trail passes to Southeast. Laid out c.1824.

Population: 911 (1990); 1,077 (2000); 1,247 (2010); Density: 2,042.1 persons per square mile (2010); Race: 95.0% White, 1.9% Black, 1.7% Asian, 0.1% American Indian/Alaska Native, 0.0% Native Hawaiian/Other Pacific Islander, 1.3% Other, 1.3% Hispanic of any race (2010); Average household size: 2.27 (2010); Median age: 38.0 (2010); Males per 100 females: 99.5 (2010); Marriage status: 26.6% never married, 53.1% now married, 11.4% widowed, 9.0% divorced (2006-2010 5-year est.); Foreign born: 0.7% (2006-2010 5-year est.); Ancestry (includes multiple ancestries): 48.2% German, 18.3% Irish, 9.2% English, 5.1% Scottish, 3.9% American (2006-2010 5-year est.).

Economy: Employment by occupation: 12.0% management, 2.4% professional, 11.1% services, 24.3% sales, 1.5% farming, 13.1% construction, 6.9% production (2006-2010 5-year est.).

Income: Per capita income: $21,916 (2006-2010 5-year est.); Median household income: $54,545 (2006-2010 5-year est.); Average household income: $67,044 (2006-2010 5-year est.); Percent of households with income of $100,000 or more: 14.8% (2006-2010 5-year est.); Poverty rate: 2.6% (2006-2010 5-year est.).

Education: Percent of population age 25 and over with: High school diploma (including GED) or higher: 81.7% (2006-2010 5-year est.); Bachelor's degree or higher: 20.4% (2006-2010 5-year est.); Master's degree or higher: 8.6% (2006-2010 5-year est.).

Housing: Homeownership rate: 62.5% (2010); Median home value: $146,600 (2006-2010 5-year est.); Median contract rent: $530 per month (2006-2010 5-year est.); Median year structure built: before 1940 (2006-2010 5-year est.).

Transportation: Commute to work: 87.0% car, 0.5% public transportation, 5.3% walk, 6.4% work from home (2006-2010 5-year est.); Travel time to work: 29.6% less than 15 minutes, 8.8% 15 to 30 minutes, 34.1% 30 to 45

minutes, 17.9% 45 to 60 minutes, 9.6% 60 minutes or more (2006-2010 5-year est.)

Additional Information Contacts

Perry County Chamber of Commerce . . . . (717) 582-4523
    http://www.perrycountychamber.org

BUFFALO (township). Covers a land area of 20.104 square miles and a water area of 0.068 square miles. Located at 40.51° N. Lat; 77.04° W. Long.

Population: 1,080 (1990); 1,128 (2000); 1,219 (2010); Density: 60.6 persons per square mile (2010); Race: 98.6% White, 0.3% Black, 0.1% Asian, 0.2% American Indian/Alaska Native, 0.1% Native Hawaiian/Other Pacific Islander, 0.7% Other, 0.6% Hispanic of any race (2010); Average household size: 2.53 (2010); Median age: 43.9 (2010); Males per 100 females: 102.2 (2010); Marriage status: 18.8% never married, 69.1% now married, 5.3% widowed, 6.8% divorced (2006-2010 5-year est.); Foreign born: 0.0% (2006-2010 5-year est.); Ancestry (includes multiple ancestries): 52.1% German, 13.2% Irish, 11.3% American, 7.0% English, 5.6% Italian (2006-2010 5-year est.).

Economy: Employment by occupation: 7.8% management, 5.6% professional, 5.8% services, 17.0% sales, 4.4% farming, 16.8% construction, 9.8% production (2006-2010 5-year est.).

Income: Per capita income: $30,633 (2006-2010 5-year est.); Median household income: $63,438 (2006-2010 5-year est.); Average household income: $74,576 (2006-2010 5-year est.); Percent of households with income of $100,000 or more: 22.0% (2006-2010 5-year est.); Poverty rate: 3.9% (2006-2010 5-year est.).

Education: Percent of population age 25 and over with: High school diploma (including GED) or higher: 88.3% (2006-2010 5-year est.); Bachelor's degree or higher: 15.9% (2006-2010 5-year est.); Master's degree or higher: 6.8% (2006-2010 5-year est.).

Housing: Homeownership rate: 89.0% (2010); Median home value: $157,500 (2006-2010 5-year est.); Median contract rent: $465 per month (2006-2010 5-year est.); Median year structure built: 1975 (2006-2010 5-year est.).

Transportation: Commute to work: 97.6% car, 0.0% public transportation, 0.0% walk, 2.4% work from home (2006-2010 5-year est.); Travel time to work: 13.1% less than 15 minutes, 21.5% 15 to 30 minutes, 37.5% 30 to 45 minutes, 19.7% 45 to 60 minutes, 8.2% 60 minutes or more (2006-2010 5-year est.)

Additional Information Contacts

Perry County Chamber of Commerce . . . . (717) 582-4523
    http://www.perrycountychamber.org

CARROLL (township). Covers a land area of 34.274 square miles and a water area of 0.263 square miles. Located at 40.35° N. Lat; 77.18° W. Long.

Population: 4,597 (1990); 5,095 (2000); 5,269 (2010); Density: 153.7 persons per square mile (2010); Race: 97.7% White, 0.2% Black, 0.3% Asian, 0.2% American Indian/Alaska Native, 0.0% Native Hawaiian/Other Pacific Islander, 1.6% Other, 1.4% Hispanic of any race (2010); Average household size: 2.55 (2010); Median age: 40.7 (2010); Males per 100 females: 102.3 (2010); Marriage status: 17.8% never married, 67.5% now married, 4.0% widowed, 10.7% divorced (2006-2010 5-year est.); Foreign born: 0.8% (2006-2010 5-year est.); Ancestry (includes multiple ancestries): 45.7% German, 16.5% Irish, 13.8% American, 5.9% English, 5.9% Italian (2006-2010 5-year est.).

Economy: Employment by occupation: 7.7% management, 4.8% professional, 8.5% services, 20.0% sales, 4.8% farming, 19.4% construction, 13.9% production (2006-2010 5-year est.).

Income: Per capita income: $25,189 (2006-2010 5-year est.); Median household income: $57,727 (2006-2010 5-year est.); Average household income: $65,156 (2006-2010 5-year est.); Percent of households with income of $100,000 or more: 13.8% (2006-2010 5-year est.); Poverty rate: 10.1% (2006-2010 5-year est.).

Education: Percent of population age 25 and over with: High school diploma (including GED) or higher: 86.2% (2006-2010 5-year est.); Bachelor's degree or higher: 13.4% (2006-2010 5-year est.); Master's degree or higher: 4.2% (2006-2010 5-year est.).

Housing: Homeownership rate: 86.1% (2010); Median home value: $155,800 (2006-2010 5-year est.); Median contract rent: $559 per month (2006-2010 5-year est.); Median year structure built: 1989 (2006-2010 5-year est.).

Transportation: Commute to work: 95.4% car, 0.9% public transportation, 0.0% walk, 3.1% work from home (2006-2010 5-year est.); Travel time to

work: 7.9% less than 15 minutes, 32.1% 15 to 30 minutes, 48.9% 30 to 45 minutes, 8.2% 45 to 60 minutes, 2.9% 60 minutes or more (2006-2010 5-year est.)

Additional Information Contacts

Carroll Township . . . . (717) 582-8200
  http://carrolltwp.org

Perry County Chamber of Commerce . . . . (717) 582-4523
  http://www.perrycountychamber.org

CENTRE (township). Covers a land area of 30.022 square miles and a water area of 0.106 square miles. Located at 40.40° N. Lat; 77.24° W. Long. Elevation is 620 feet.

Population: 2,155 (1990); 2,209 (2000); 2,491 (2010); Density: 83.0 persons per square mile (2010); Race: 98.1% White, 0.7% Black, 0.2% Asian, 0.3% American Indian/Alaska Native, 0.0% Native Hawaiian/Other Pacific Islander, 0.7% Other, 1.3% Hispanic of any race (2010); Average household size: 2.60 (2010); Median age: 42.0 (2010); Males per 100 females: 111.8 (2010); Marriage status: 27.5% never married, 64.3% now married, 1.5% widowed, 6.7% divorced (2006-2010 5-year est.); Foreign born: 0.7% (2006-2010 5-year est.); Ancestry (includes multiple ancestries): 54.7% German, 11.2% Irish, 7.9% American, 5.9% Dutch, 5.0% Italian (2006-2010 5-year est.).

Economy: Employment by occupation: 7.7% management, 1.7% professional, 12.0% services, 14.9% sales, 2.0% farming, 17.8% construction, 17.8% production (2006-2010 5-year est.).

Income: Per capita income: $25,155 (2006-2010 5-year est.); Median household income: $60,987 (2006-2010 5-year est.); Average household income: $66,640 (2006-2010 5-year est.); Percent of households with income of $100,000 or more: 15.9% (2006-2010 5-year est.); Poverty rate: 1.3% (2006-2010 5-year est.).

Education: Percent of population age 25 and over with: High school diploma (including GED) or higher: 93.0% (2006-2010 5-year est.); Bachelor's degree or higher: 13.4% (2006-2010 5-year est.); Master's degree or higher: 3.3% (2006-2010 5-year est.).

Housing: Homeownership rate: 86.8% (2010); Median home value: $147,700 (2006-2010 5-year est.); Median contract rent: $469 per month (2006-2010 5-year est.); Median year structure built: 1981 (2006-2010 5-year est.).

Transportation: Commute to work: 94.1% car, 0.0% public transportation, 1.4% walk, 4.0% work from home (2006-2010 5-year est.); Travel time to work: 13.8% less than 15 minutes, 18.5% 15 to 30 minutes, 33.9% 30 to 45 minutes, 27.6% 45 to 60 minutes, 6.1% 60 minutes or more (2006-2010 5-year est.)

Additional Information Contacts

Perry County Chamber of Commerce . . . . (717) 582-4523
  http://www.perrycountychamber.org

DUNCANNON (borough). Covers a land area of 0.407 square miles and a water area of 0 square miles. Located at 40.40° N. Lat; 77.03° W. Long. Elevation is 351 feet.

History: Appalachian Trail descends from Peters Mt. ridge (Susquehanna River flows through gap in mountain) to cross both rivers, passes through to West. Incorporated 1844.

Population: 1,450 (1990); 1,508 (2000); 1,522 (2010); Density: 3,738.6 persons per square mile (2010); Race: 97.2% White, 0.9% Black, 0.3% Asian, 0.1% American Indian/Alaska Native, 0.0% Native Hawaiian/Other Pacific Islander, 1.5% Other, 2.4% Hispanic of any race (2010); Average household size: 2.33 (2010); Median age: 37.8 (2010); Males per 100 females: 91.0 (2010); Marriage status: 30.4% never married, 49.3% now married, 8.9% widowed, 11.4% divorced (2006-2010 5-year est.); Foreign born: 0.0% (2006-2010 5-year est.); Ancestry (includes multiple ancestries): 47.5% German, 21.8% Irish, 8.9% American, 7.1% English, 6.8% Scotch-Irish (2006-2010 5-year est.).

Economy: Single-family building permits issued: 1 (2011); Multi-family building permits issued: 0 (2011); Employment by occupation: 12.0% management, 3.4% professional, 11.1% services, 18.5% sales, 7.7% farming, 8.0% construction, 3.7% production (2006-2010 5-year est.).

Income: Per capita income: $23,054 (2006-2010 5-year est.); Median household income: $40,170 (2006-2010 5-year est.); Average household income: $50,104 (2006-2010 5-year est.); Percent of households with income of $100,000 or more: 8.1% (2006-2010 5-year est.); Poverty rate: 9.3% (2006-2010 5-year est.).

Education: Percent of population age 25 and over with: High school diploma (including GED) or higher: 84.6% (2006-2010 5-year est.);

Bachelor's degree or higher: 9.3% (2006-2010 5-year est.); Master's degree or higher: 2.3% (2006-2010 5-year est.).

School District(s)

Susquenita SD (KG-12)
  2010-11 Enrollment: 1,873 . . . . (717) 957-6000

Housing: Homeownership rate: 51.9% (2010); Median home value: $102,200 (2006-2010 5-year est.); Median contract rent: $470 per month (2006-2010 5-year est.); Median year structure built: before 1940 (2006-2010 5-year est.).

Transportation: Commute to work: 93.1% car, 0.3% public transportation, 1.2% walk, 3.8% work from home (2006-2010 5-year est.); Travel time to work: 23.3% less than 15 minutes, 28.3% 15 to 30 minutes, 34.5% 30 to 45 minutes, 9.9% 45 to 60 minutes, 4.1% 60 minutes or more (2006-2010 5-year est.)

Additional Information Contacts

Perry County Chamber of Commerce . . . . (717) 582-4523
  http://www.perrycountychamber.org

ELLIOTTSBURG (unincorporated postal area)

Zip Code: 17024

Covers a land area of 31.573 square miles and a water area of 0.033 square miles. Located at 40.40° N. Lat; 77.30° W. Long. Elevation is 640 feet. Population: 1,893 (2010); Density: 60.0 persons per square mile (2010); Race: 97.9% White, 0.3% Black, 0.1% Asian, 0.3% American Indian/Alaska Native, 0.0% Native Hawaiian/Other Pacific Islander, 1.4% Other, 0.3% Hispanic of any race (2010); Average household size: 2.68 (2010); Median age: 40.1 (2010); Males per 100 females: 97.6 (2010); Homeownership rate: 83.7% (2010)

GREENWOOD (township). Covers a land area of 25.062 square miles and a water area of 0.283 square miles. Located at 40.56° N. Lat; 77.11° W. Long.

Population: 943 (1990); 1,010 (2000); 998 (2010); Density: 39.8 persons per square mile (2010); Race: 97.2% White, 1.0% Black, 0.2% Asian, 0.0% American Indian/Alaska Native, 0.0% Native Hawaiian/Other Pacific Islander, 1.6% Other, 0.7% Hispanic of any race (2010); Average household size: 2.51 (2010); Median age: 43.8 (2010); Males per 100 females: 103.3 (2010); Marriage status: 20.1% never married, 64.6% now married, 9.0% widowed, 6.3% divorced (2006-2010 5-year est.); Foreign born: 0.5% (2006-2010 5-year est.); Ancestry (includes multiple ancestries): 49.4% German, 18.5% Irish, 7.9% American, 5.3% Scotch-Irish, 3.9% Italian (2006-2010 5-year est.).

Economy: Employment by occupation: 11.4% management, 5.6% professional, 10.7% services, 15.8% sales, 1.6% farming, 21.2% construction, 17.8% production (2006-2010 5-year est.).

Income: Per capita income: $24,711 (2006-2010 5-year est.); Median household income: $50,188 (2006-2010 5-year est.); Average household income: $55,983 (2006-2010 5-year est.); Percent of households with income of $100,000 or more: 10.5% (2006-2010 5-year est.); Poverty rate: 6.4% (2006-2010 5-year est.).

Education: Percent of population age 25 and over with: High school diploma (including GED) or higher: 95.8% (2006-2010 5-year est.); Bachelor's degree or higher: 17.5% (2006-2010 5-year est.); Master's degree or higher: 5.7% (2006-2010 5-year est.).

Housing: Homeownership rate: 84.9% (2010); Median home value: $146,000 (2006-2010 5-year est.); Median contract rent: $393 per month (2006-2010 5-year est.); Median year structure built: 1971 (2006-2010 5-year est.).

Transportation: Commute to work: 88.0% car, 0.9% public transportation, 2.7% walk, 6.3% work from home (2006-2010 5-year est.); Travel time to work: 25.4% less than 15 minutes, 17.9% 15 to 30 minutes, 23.7% 30 to 45 minutes, 26.3% 45 to 60 minutes, 6.8% 60 minutes or more (2006-2010 5-year est.)

Additional Information Contacts

Perry County Chamber of Commerce . . . . (717) 582-4523
  http://www.perrycountychamber.org

HOWE (township). Covers a land area of 8.114 square miles and a water area of 0.421 square miles. Located at 40.50° N. Lat; 77.09° W. Long.

Population: 459 (1990); 493 (2000); 393 (2010); Density: 48.4 persons per square mile (2010); Race: 98.5% White, 0.0% Black, 0.0% Asian, 0.0% American Indian/Alaska Native, 0.0% Native Hawaiian/Other Pacific Islander, 1.5% Other, 0.8% Hispanic of any race (2010); Average household size: 2.22 (2010); Median age: 47.9 (2010); Males per 100

females: 109.0 (2010); Marriage status: 17.4% never married, 54.2% now married, 9.4% widowed, 19.0% divorced (2006-2010 5-year est.); Foreign born: 3.1% (2006-2010 5-year est.); Ancestry (includes multiple ancestries): 47.6% German, 21.0% Irish, 13.1% English, 7.6% Swiss, 6.4% American (2006-2010 5-year est.).

Economy: Employment by occupation: 6.3% management, 1.2% professional, 10.6% services, 19.7% sales, 2.4% farming, 16.5% construction, 16.9% production (2006-2010 5-year est.).

Income: Per capita income: $28,141 (2006-2010 5-year est.); Median household income: $50,625 (2006-2010 5-year est.); Average household income: $61,371 (2006-2010 5-year est.); Percent of households with income of $100,000 or more: 14.4% (2006-2010 5-year est.); Poverty rate: 4.8% (2006-2010 5-year est.).

Education: Percent of population age 25 and over with: High school diploma (including GED) or higher: 95.1% (2006-2010 5-year est.); Bachelor's degree or higher: 13.2% (2006-2010 5-year est.); Master's degree or higher: 4.0% (2006-2010 5-year est.).

Housing: Homeownership rate: 77.4% (2010); Median home value: $121,900 (2006-2010 5-year est.); Median contract rent: $492 per month (2006-2010 5-year est.); Median year structure built: 1963 (2006-2010 5-year est.).

Transportation: Commute to work: 86.9% car, 0.0% public transportation, 8.0% walk, 4.4% work from home (2006-2010 5-year est.); Travel time to work: 20.8% less than 15 minutes, 26.7% 15 to 30 minutes, 19.2% 30 to 45 minutes, 29.2% 45 to 60 minutes, 4.2% 60 minutes or more (2006-2010 5-year est.)

ICKESBURG (unincorporated postal area)

Zip Code: 17037

Covers a land area of 24.683 square miles and a water area of 0.041 square miles. Located at 40.43° N. Lat; 77.42° W. Long. Population: 1,126 (2010); Density: 45.6 persons per square mile (2010); Race: 97.9% White, 0.1% Black, 0.1% Asian, 0.2% American Indian/Alaska Native, 0.1% Native Hawaiian/Other Pacific Islander, 1.6% Other, 1.7% Hispanic of any race (2010); Average household size: 2.83 (2010); Median age: 37.4 (2010); Males per 100 females: 112.1 (2010); Homeownership rate: 82.9% (2010)

JACKSON (township). Covers a land area of 37.166 square miles and a water area of 0.146 square miles. Located at 40.31° N. Lat; 77.51° W. Long.

Population: 489 (1990); 525 (2000); 547 (2010); Density: 14.7 persons per square mile (2010); Race: 98.9% White, 0.0% Black, 0.0% Asian, 0.0% American Indian/Alaska Native, 0.7% Native Hawaiian/Other Pacific Islander, 0.4% Other, 2.4% Hispanic of any race (2010); Average household size: 2.93 (2010); Median age: 34.3 (2010); Males per 100 females: 104.1 (2010); Marriage status: 18.6% never married, 71.6% now married, 6.4% widowed, 3.4% divorced (2006-2010 5-year est.); Foreign born: 1.3% (2006-2010 5-year est.); Ancestry (includes multiple ancestries): 64.8% German, 8.3% Irish, 3.4% American, 3.2% European, 2.3% Scotch-Irish (2006-2010 5-year est.).

Economy: Employment by occupation: 9.8% management, 3.8% professional, 13.6% services, 7.6% sales, 2.2% farming, 28.3% construction, 0.0% production (2006-2010 5-year est.).

Income: Per capita income: $16,321 (2006-2010 5-year est.); Median household income: $41,944 (2006-2010 5-year est.); Average household income: $48,787 (2006-2010 5-year est.); Percent of households with income of $100,000 or more: 5.6% (2006-2010 5-year est.); Poverty rate: 7.9% (2006-2010 5-year est.).

Education: Percent of population age 25 and over with: High school diploma (including GED) or higher: 72.3% (2006-2010 5-year est.); Bachelor's degree or higher: 4.7% (2006-2010 5-year est.); Master's degree or higher: 0.7% (2006-2010 5-year est.).

Housing: Homeownership rate: 78.6% (2010); Median home value: $161,000 (2006-2010 5-year est.); Median contract rent: $429 per month (2006-2010 5-year est.); Median year structure built: 1965 (2006-2010 5-year est.).

Transportation: Commute to work: 80.8% car, 0.0% public transportation, 0.0% walk, 15.9% work from home (2006-2010 5-year est.); Travel time to work: 9.8% less than 15 minutes, 14.4% 15 to 30 minutes, 9.8% 30 to 45 minutes, 37.3% 45 to 60 minutes, 28.8% 60 minutes or more (2006-2010 5-year est.)

JUNIATA (township). Covers a land area of 20.877 square miles and a water area of 0.233 square miles. Located at 40.47° N. Lat; 77.22° W. Long.

Population: 1,278 (1990); 1,359 (2000); 1,412 (2010); Density: 67.6 persons per square mile (2010); Race: 98.9% White, 0.0% Black, 0.1% Asian, 0.1% American Indian/Alaska Native, 0.1% Native Hawaiian/Other Pacific Islander, 0.8% Other, 1.0% Hispanic of any race (2010); Average household size: 2.58 (2010); Median age: 44.3 (2010); Males per 100 females: 98.0 (2010); Marriage status: 19.2% never married, 72.1% now married, 3.1% widowed, 5.7% divorced (2006-2010 5-year est.); Foreign born: 0.7% (2006-2010 5-year est.); Ancestry (includes multiple ancestries): 42.1% German, 13.0% Italian, 12.1% Irish, 10.8% English, 9.1% American (2006-2010 5-year est.).

Economy: Employment by occupation: 9.9% management, 8.3% professional, 7.0% services, 17.0% sales, 3.3% farming, 8.7% construction, 7.7% production (2006-2010 5-year est.).

Income: Per capita income: $24,080 (2006-2010 5-year est.); Median household income: $60,761 (2006-2010 5-year est.); Average household income: $63,913 (2006-2010 5-year est.); Percent of households with income of $100,000 or more: 19.3% (2006-2010 5-year est.); Poverty rate: 12.9% (2006-2010 5-year est.).

Education: Percent of population age 25 and over with: High school diploma (including GED) or higher: 87.4% (2006-2010 5-year est.); Bachelor's degree or higher: 19.3% (2006-2010 5-year est.); Master's degree or higher: 4.8% (2006-2010 5-year est.).

Housing: Homeownership rate: 91.1% (2010); Median home value: $168,800 (2006-2010 5-year est.); Median contract rent: $511 per month (2006-2010 5-year est.); Median year structure built: 1979 (2006-2010 5-year est.).

Transportation: Commute to work: 88.8% car, 1.2% public transportation, 2.1% walk, 7.9% work from home (2006-2010 5-year est.); Travel time to work: 13.3% less than 15 minutes, 15.8% 15 to 30 minutes, 14.1% 30 to 45 minutes, 44.2% 45 to 60 minutes, 12.6% 60 minutes or more (2006-2010 5-year est.)

Additional Information Contacts

Perry County Chamber of Commerce . . . . (717) 582-4523
http://www.perrycountychamber.org

LANDISBURG (borough). Covers a land area of 0.070 square miles and a water area of 0 square miles. Located at 40.34° N. Lat; 77.31° W. Long. Elevation is 581 feet.

Population: 178 (1990); 195 (2000); 218 (2010); Density: 3,132.5 persons per square mile (2010); Race: 92.7% White, 0.9% Black, 0.0% Asian, 0.5% American Indian/Alaska Native, 0.0% Native Hawaiian/Other Pacific Islander, 5.9% Other, 6.0% Hispanic of any race (2010); Average household size: 2.53 (2010); Median age: 32.5 (2010); Males per 100 females: 98.2 (2010); Marriage status: 20.0% never married, 54.8% now married, 12.3% widowed, 12.9% divorced (2006-2010 5-year est.); Foreign born: 8.3% (2006-2010 5-year est.); Ancestry (includes multiple ancestries): 31.1% German, 18.1% Irish, 7.3% American, 7.3% Pennsylvania German, 7.3% European (2006-2010 5-year est.).

Economy: Employment by occupation: 10.0% management, 2.7% professional, 1.8% services, 20.9% sales, 0.0% farming, 18.2% construction, 13.6% production (2006-2010 5-year est.).

Income: Per capita income: $25,694 (2006-2010 5-year est.); Median household income: $60,625 (2006-2010 5-year est.); Average household income: $59,590 (2006-2010 5-year est.); Percent of households with income of $100,000 or more: 3.6% (2006-2010 5-year est.); Poverty rate: 2.6% (2006-2010 5-year est.).

Education: Percent of population age 25 and over with: High school diploma (including GED) or higher: 76.6% (2006-2010 5-year est.); Bachelor's degree or higher: 3.1% (2006-2010 5-year est.); Master's degree or higher: 0.0% (2006-2010 5-year est.).

Housing: Homeownership rate: 60.4% (2010); Median home value: $142,200 (2006-2010 5-year est.); Median contract rent: $425 per month (2006-2010 5-year est.); Median year structure built: before 1940 (2006-2010 5-year est.).

Transportation: Commute to work: 80.4% car, 0.0% public transportation, 6.9% walk, 12.7% work from home (2006-2010 5-year est.); Travel time to work: 20.2% less than 15 minutes, 3.4% 15 to 30 minutes, 36.0% 30 to 45 minutes, 28.1% 45 to 60 minutes, 12.4% 60 minutes or more (2006-2010 5-year est.)

LIVERPOOL (borough). Covers a land area of 0.881 square miles and a water area of <.001 square miles. Located at 40.57° N. Lat; 76.99° W. Long. Elevation is 400 feet.

Population: 934 (1990); 876 (2000); 955 (2010); Density: 1,084.6 persons per square mile (2010); Race: 96.3% White, 0.5% Black, 1.0% Asian, 0.1% American Indian/Alaska Native, 0.2% Native Hawaiian/Other Pacific Islander, 1.9% Other, 0.6% Hispanic of any race (2010); Average household size: 2.18 (2010); Median age: 40.2 (2010); Males per 100 females: 89.5 (2010); Marriage status: 17.0% never married, 52.6% now married, 17.1% widowed, 13.3% divorced (2006-2010 5-year est.); Foreign born: 0.9% (2006-2010 5-year est.); Ancestry (includes multiple ancestries): 55.5% German, 8.9% Irish, 6.0% American, 5.6% English, 5.3% Dutch (2006-2010 5-year est.).

Economy: Employment by occupation: 4.1% management, 4.6% professional, 12.2% services, 22.7% sales, 1.8% farming, 12.2% construction, 5.6% production (2006-2010 5-year est.).

Income: Per capita income: $20,317 (2006-2010 5-year est.); Median household income: $37,552 (2006-2010 5-year est.); Average household income: $42,880 (2006-2010 5-year est.); Percent of households with income of $100,000 or more: 3.1% (2006-2010 5-year est.); Poverty rate: 8.2% (2006-2010 5-year est.).

Education: Percent of population age 25 and over with: High school diploma (including GED) or higher: 78.1% (2006-2010 5-year est.); Bachelor's degree or higher: 10.6% (2006-2010 5-year est.); Master's degree or higher: 1.9% (2006-2010 5-year est.).

School District(s)

Juniata County SD (KG-12)

    2010-11 Enrollment: 3,092 . . . . (717) 436-2111

Housing: Homeownership rate: 55.2% (2010); Median home value: $130,600 (2006-2010 5-year est.); Median contract rent: $424 per month (2006-2010 5-year est.); Median year structure built: 1957 (2006-2010 5-year est.).

Transportation: Commute to work: 92.6% car, 0.0% public transportation, 6.6% walk, 0.8% work from home (2006-2010 5-year est.); Travel time to work: 12.6% less than 15 minutes, 23.3% 15 to 30 minutes, 25.4% 30 to 45 minutes, 27.3% 45 to 60 minutes, 11.5% 60 minutes or more (2006-2010 5-year est.)

LIVERPOOL (township). Covers a land area of 20.912 square miles and a water area of 0.029 square miles. Located at 40.58° N. Lat; 77.02° W. Long. Elevation is 400 feet.

Population: 915 (1990); 966 (2000); 1,057 (2010); Density: 50.5 persons per square mile (2010); Race: 98.3% White, 0.2% Black, 0.3% Asian, 0.0% American Indian/Alaska Native, 0.0% Native Hawaiian/Other Pacific Islander, 1.2% Other, 0.8% Hispanic of any race (2010); Average household size: 2.60 (2010); Median age: 42.2 (2010); Males per 100 females: 112.7 (2010); Marriage status: 14.1% never married, 76.7% now married, 5.2% widowed, 4.0% divorced (2006-2010 5-year est.); Foreign born: 1.2% (2006-2010 5-year est.); Ancestry (includes multiple ancestries): 47.4% German, 11.2% Irish, 8.8% American, 7.0% Italian, 5.1% English (2006-2010 5-year est.).

Economy: Employment by occupation: 10.1% management, 6.0% professional, 12.9% services, 10.6% sales, 3.4% farming, 15.8% construction, 6.9% production (2006-2010 5-year est.).

Income: Per capita income: $27,013 (2006-2010 5-year est.); Median household income: $66,250 (2006-2010 5-year est.); Average household income: $70,371 (2006-2010 5-year est.); Percent of households with income of $100,000 or more: 22.4% (2006-2010 5-year est.); Poverty rate: 2.6% (2006-2010 5-year est.).

Education: Percent of population age 25 and over with: High school diploma (including GED) or higher: 91.0% (2006-2010 5-year est.); Bachelor's degree or higher: 13.7% (2006-2010 5-year est.); Master's degree or higher: 4.5% (2006-2010 5-year est.).

School District(s)

Juniata County SD (KG-12)

    2010-11 Enrollment: 3,092 . . . . (717) 436-2111

Housing: Homeownership rate: 86.2% (2010); Median home value: $143,900 (2006-2010 5-year est.); Median contract rent: $381 per month (2006-2010 5-year est.); Median year structure built: 1975 (2006-2010 5-year est.).

Transportation: Commute to work: 89.1% car, 0.0% public transportation, 1.8% walk, 7.1% work from home (2006-2010 5-year est.); Travel time to work: 20.2% less than 15 minutes, 18.4% 15 to 30 minutes, 23.9% 30 to 45 minutes, 29.4% 45 to 60 minutes, 8.1% 60 minutes or more (2006-2010 5-year est.)

Additional Information Contacts

Harrisburg Regional Chamber & CREDC . . . . (717) 232-4099

    http://www.harrisburgregionalchamber.org

LOYSVILLE (unincorporated postal area)

Zip Code: 17047

    Covers a land area of 46.053 square miles and a water area of 0.231 square miles. Located at 40.37° N. Lat; 77.42° W. Long. Population: 2,526 (2010); Density: 54.8 persons per square mile (2010); Race: 95.2% White, 2.9% Black, 0.1% Asian, 0.1% American Indian/Alaska Native, 0.0% Native Hawaiian/Other Pacific Islander, 1.7% Other, 1.1% Hispanic of any race (2010); Average household size: 2.72 (2010); Median age: 34.7 (2010); Males per 100 females: 108.6 (2010); Homeownership rate: 74.5% (2010)

MARYSVILLE (borough). Covers a land area of 2.335 square miles and a water area of 0.004 square miles. Located at 40.34° N. Lat; 76.93° W. Long. Elevation is 374 feet.

History: Appalachian Trail passes to West and North. Laid out 1861, incorporated 1866.

Population: 2,425 (1990); 2,306 (2000); 2,534 (2010); Density: 1,085.2 persons per square mile (2010); Race: 95.5% White, 1.2% Black, 0.5% Asian, 0.0% American Indian/Alaska Native, 0.1% Native Hawaiian/Other Pacific Islander, 2.7% Other, 2.4% Hispanic of any race (2010); Average household size: 2.23 (2010); Median age: 39.6 (2010); Males per 100 females: 92.4 (2010); Marriage status: 29.2% never married, 49.5% now married, 8.2% widowed, 13.1% divorced (2006-2010 5-year est.); Foreign born: 2.8% (2006-2010 5-year est.); Ancestry (includes multiple ancestries): 44.7% German, 15.8% Irish, 7.4% English, 5.2% Italian, 4.8% American (2006-2010 5-year est.).

Economy: Employment by occupation: 11.4% management, 4.1% professional, 13.9% services, 18.8% sales, 3.7% farming, 7.8% construction, 10.1% production (2006-2010 5-year est.).

Income: Per capita income: $23,918 (2006-2010 5-year est.); Median household income: $44,888 (2006-2010 5-year est.); Average household income: $52,501 (2006-2010 5-year est.); Percent of households with income of $100,000 or more: 8.7% (2006-2010 5-year est.); Poverty rate: 10.0% (2006-2010 5-year est.).

Education: Percent of population age 25 and over with: High school diploma (including GED) or higher: 90.1% (2006-2010 5-year est.); Bachelor's degree or higher: 19.4% (2006-2010 5-year est.); Master's degree or higher: 6.7% (2006-2010 5-year est.).

Housing: Homeownership rate: 72.8% (2010); Median home value: $123,600 (2006-2010 5-year est.); Median contract rent: $501 per month (2006-2010 5-year est.); Median year structure built: 1948 (2006-2010 5-year est.).

Safety: Violent crime rate: 0.0 per 10,000 population; Property crime rate: 129.8 per 10,000 population (2011).

Transportation: Commute to work: 95.1% car, 0.0% public transportation, 0.5% walk, 3.1% work from home (2006-2010 5-year est.); Travel time to work: 20.0% less than 15 minutes, 59.1% 15 to 30 minutes, 15.4% 30 to 45 minutes, 4.3% 45 to 60 minutes, 1.2% 60 minutes or more (2006-2010 5-year est.)

Additional Information Contacts

Perry County Chamber of Commerce . . . . (717) 582-4523

    http://www.perrycountychamber.org

MILLER (township). Covers a land area of 12.458 square miles and a water area of 0.395 square miles. Located at 40.46° N. Lat; 77.07° W. Long.

Population: 894 (1990); 953 (2000); 1,098 (2010); Density: 88.1 persons per square mile (2010); Race: 99.1% White, 0.4% Black, 0.0% Asian, 0.0% American Indian/Alaska Native, 0.0% Native Hawaiian/Other Pacific Islander, 0.5% Other, 1.0% Hispanic of any race (2010); Average household size: 2.69 (2010); Median age: 39.9 (2010); Males per 100 females: 108.7 (2010); Marriage status: 23.9% never married, 53.0% now married, 5.6% widowed, 17.4% divorced (2006-2010 5-year est.); Foreign born: 0.0% (2006-2010 5-year est.); Ancestry (includes multiple ancestries): 40.0% German, 12.4% Irish, 9.9% Italian, 7.1% English, 5.2% American (2006-2010 5-year est.).

Economy: Employment by occupation: 7.8% management, 2.0% professional, 12.7% services, 19.2% sales, 1.3% farming, 13.7% construction, 10.6% production (2006-2010 5-year est.).

Income: Per capita income: $16,919 (2006-2010 5-year est.); Median household income: $33,875 (2006-2010 5-year est.); Average household

income: $44,682 (2006-2010 5-year est.); Percent of households with income of $100,000 or more: 7.4% (2006-2010 5-year est.); Poverty rate: 24.6% (2006-2010 5-year est.).

Education: Percent of population age 25 and over with: High school diploma (including GED) or higher: 77.8% (2006-2010 5-year est.); Bachelor's degree or higher: 10.6% (2006-2010 5-year est.); Master's degree or higher: 2.5% (2006-2010 5-year est.).

Housing: Homeownership rate: 85.0% (2010); Median home value: $119,300 (2006-2010 5-year est.); Median contract rent: $573 per month (2006-2010 5-year est.); Median year structure built: 1980 (2006-2010 5-year est.).

Transportation: Commute to work: 87.7% car, 0.0% public transportation, 4.3% walk, 7.9% work from home (2006-2010 5-year est.); Travel time to work: 13.9% less than 15 minutes, 24.4% 15 to 30 minutes, 36.1% 30 to 45 minutes, 16.9% 45 to 60 minutes, 8.6% 60 minutes or more (2006-2010 5-year est.)

Additional Information Contacts

Perry County Chamber of Commerce . . . . (717) 582-4523
   http://www.perrycountychamber.org

MILLERSTOWN (borough). Covers a land area of 0.845 square miles and a water area of 0.074 square miles. Located at 40.56° N. Lat; 77.15° W. Long. Elevation is 436 feet.

Population: 646 (1990); 679 (2000); 673 (2010); Density: 796.2 persons per square mile (2010); Race: 97.5% White, 0.0% Black, 0.3% Asian, 0.4% American Indian/Alaska Native, 0.1% Native Hawaiian/Other Pacific Islander, 1.7% Other, 2.1% Hispanic of any race (2010); Average household size: 2.66 (2010); Median age: 39.8 (2010); Males per 100 females: 96.2 (2010); Marriage status: 18.4% never married, 71.5% now married, 3.4% widowed, 6.8% divorced (2006-2010 5-year est.); Foreign born: 0.8% (2006-2010 5-year est.); Ancestry (includes multiple ancestries): 63.1% German, 26.5% Irish, 6.7% Scotch-Irish, 4.6% English, 3.9% American (2006-2010 5-year est.).

Economy: Employment by occupation: 14.7% management, 4.6% professional, 7.4% services, 9.4% sales, 1.0% farming, 14.5% construction, 7.4% production (2006-2010 5-year est.).

Income: Per capita income: $22,870 (2006-2010 5-year est.); Median household income: $55,625 (2006-2010 5-year est.); Average household income: $65,576 (2006-2010 5-year est.); Percent of households with income of $100,000 or more: 15.7% (2006-2010 5-year est.); Poverty rate: 3.9% (2006-2010 5-year est.).

Education: Percent of population age 25 and over with: High school diploma (including GED) or higher: 94.3% (2006-2010 5-year est.); Bachelor's degree or higher: 25.8% (2006-2010 5-year est.); Master's degree or higher: 12.2% (2006-2010 5-year est.).

School District(s)

Greenwood SD (KG-12)
   2010-11 Enrollment: 815. . . . . (717) 589-3117

Housing: Homeownership rate: 85.8% (2010); Median home value: $136,300 (2006-2010 5-year est.); Median contract rent: $502 per month (2006-2010 5-year est.); Median year structure built: before 1940 (2006-2010 5-year est.).

Transportation: Commute to work: 88.0% car, 0.0% public transportation, 7.7% walk, 3.6% work from home (2006-2010 5-year est.); Travel time to work: 29.7% less than 15 minutes, 13.5% 15 to 30 minutes, 19.6% 30 to 45 minutes, 27.9% 45 to 60 minutes, 9.3% 60 minutes or more (2006-2010 5-year est.)

NEW BLOOMFIELD (unincorporated postal area)

Zip Code: 17068

Covers a land area of 33.580 square miles and a water area of 0.104 square miles. Located at 40.41° N. Lat; 77.17° W. Long. Elevation is 673 feet. Population: 4,298 (2010); Density: 128.0 persons per square mile (2010); Race: 97.2% White, 1.0% Black, 0.6% Asian, 0.1% American Indian/Alaska Native, 0.0% Native Hawaiian/Other Pacific Islander, 1.1% Other, 1.3% Hispanic of any race (2010); Average household size: 2.48 (2010); Median age: 41.2 (2010); Males per 100 females: 105.7 (2010); Homeownership rate: 81.5% (2010)

NEW BUFFALO (borough). Covers a land area of 0.059 square miles and a water area of 0 square miles. Located at 40.45° N. Lat; 76.97° W. Long. Elevation is 371 feet.

Population: 145 (1990); 123 (2000); 129 (2010); Density: 2,179.2 persons per square mile (2010); Race: 96.1% White, 2.3% Black, 0.0% Asian, 0.0% American Indian/Alaska Native, 0.0% Native Hawaiian/Other Pacific

Islander, 1.6% Other, 0.8% Hispanic of any race (2010); Average household size: 2.15 (2010); Median age: 39.8 (2010); Males per 100 females: 87.0 (2010); Marriage status: 18.1% never married, 63.8% now married, 13.8% widowed, 4.3% divorced (2006-2010 5-year est.); Foreign born: 0.0% (2006-2010 5-year est.); Ancestry (includes multiple ancestries): 44.3% German, 10.7% American, 9.8% Irish, 7.4% Scotch-Irish, 7.4% Norwegian (2006-2010 5-year est.).

Economy: Employment by occupation: 4.8% management, 4.8% professional, 7.9% services, 17.5% sales, 11.1% farming, 27.0% construction, 9.5% production (2006-2010 5-year est.).

Income: Per capita income: $20,638 (2006-2010 5-year est.); Median household income: $44,375 (2006-2010 5-year est.); Average household income: $49,635 (2006-2010 5-year est.); Percent of households with income of $100,000 or more: 10.4% (2006-2010 5-year est.); Poverty rate: 4.9% (2006-2010 5-year est.).

Education: Percent of population age 25 and over with: High school diploma (including GED) or higher: 90.9% (2006-2010 5-year est.); Bachelor's degree or higher: 6.5% (2006-2010 5-year est.); Master's degree or higher: 0.0% (2006-2010 5-year est.).

Housing: Homeownership rate: 55.0% (2010); Median home value: $131,300 (2006-2010 5-year est.); Median contract rent: $433 per month (2006-2010 5-year est.); Median year structure built: before 1940 (2006-2010 5-year est.).

Transportation: Commute to work: 88.1% car, 0.0% public transportation, 6.8% walk, 5.1% work from home (2006-2010 5-year est.); Travel time to work: 37.5% less than 15 minutes, 17.9% 15 to 30 minutes, 28.6% 30 to 45 minutes, 10.7% 45 to 60 minutes, 5.4% 60 minutes or more (2006-2010 5-year est.)

NEW GERMANTOWN (unincorporated postal area)

Zip Code: 17071

Covers a land area of 8.320 square miles and a water area of 0.004 square miles. Located at 40.29° N. Lat; 77.60° W. Long. Elevation is 748 feet. Population: 108 (2010); Density: 13.0 persons per square mile (2010); Race: 97.2% White, 1.9% Black, 0.0% Asian, 0.0% American Indian/Alaska Native, 0.0% Native Hawaiian/Other Pacific Islander, 0.9% Other, 2.8% Hispanic of any race (2010); Average household size: 2.25 (2010); Median age: 47.0 (2010); Males per 100 females: 129.8 (2010); Homeownership rate: 81.2% (2010)

NEWPORT (borough). Covers a land area of 0.301 square miles and a water area of 0.038 square miles. Located at 40.48° N. Lat; 77.13° W. Long. Elevation is 390 feet.

History: Settled 1789, laid out 1814, incorporated 1840.

Population: 1,568 (1990); 1,506 (2000); 1,574 (2010); Density: 5,226.7 persons per square mile (2010); Race: 97.5% White, 0.8% Black, 0.1% Asian, 0.2% American Indian/Alaska Native, 0.0% Native Hawaiian/Other Pacific Islander, 1.4% Other, 1.3% Hispanic of any race (2010); Average household size: 2.41 (2010); Median age: 33.7 (2010); Males per 100 females: 89.6 (2010); Marriage status: 31.2% never married, 50.0% now married, 8.2% widowed, 10.7% divorced (2006-2010 5-year est.); Foreign born: 2.4% (2006-2010 5-year est.); Ancestry (includes multiple ancestries): 39.6% German, 15.4% Irish, 10.2% American, 5.6% English, 4.9% Italian (2006-2010 5-year est.).

Economy: Employment by occupation: 4.4% management, 6.1% professional, 13.4% services, 18.2% sales, 4.9% farming, 12.7% construction, 10.3% production (2006-2010 5-year est.).

Income: Per capita income: $18,105 (2006-2010 5-year est.); Median household income: $38,000 (2006-2010 5-year est.); Average household income: $44,530 (2006-2010 5-year est.); Percent of households with income of $100,000 or more: 5.0% (2006-2010 5-year est.); Poverty rate: 21.1% (2006-2010 5-year est.).

Education: Percent of population age 25 and over with: High school diploma (including GED) or higher: 84.1% (2006-2010 5-year est.); Bachelor's degree or higher: 12.7% (2006-2010 5-year est.); Master's degree or higher: 3.8% (2006-2010 5-year est.).

School District(s)

Newport SD (KG-12)
   2010-11 Enrollment: 1,165 . . . . (717) 567-3806

Housing: Homeownership rate: 48.4% (2010); Median home value: $88,900 (2006-2010 5-year est.); Median contract rent: $454 per month (2006-2010 5-year est.); Median year structure built: before 1940 (2006-2010 5-year est.).

Safety: Violent crime rate: 6.3 per 10,000 population; Property crime rate: 6.3 per 10,000 population (2011).

Transportation: Commute to work: 89.4% car, 1.7% public transportation, 7.6% walk, 1.1% work from home (2006-2010 5-year est.); Travel time to work: 23.2% less than 15 minutes, 14.4% 15 to 30 minutes, 33.0% 30 to 45 minutes, 22.9% 45 to 60 minutes, 6.6% 60 minutes or more (2006-2010 5-year est.)

Additional Information Contacts
Perry County Chamber of Commerce . . . . (717) 582-4523
  http://www.perrycountychamber.org

NORTHEAST MADISON (township). Covers a land area of 25.765 square miles and a water area of 0.041 square miles. Located at 40.39° N. Lat; 77.46° W. Long.

Population: 674 (1990); 856 (2000); 786 (2010); Density: 30.5 persons per square mile (2010); Race: 98.0% White, 0.1% Black, 0.0% Asian, 0.1% American Indian/Alaska Native, 0.1% Native Hawaiian/Other Pacific Islander, 1.7% Other, 2.0% Hispanic of any race (2010); Average household size: 2.67 (2010); Median age: 40.3 (2010); Males per 100 females: 107.4 (2010); Marriage status: 30.6% never married, 62.1% now married, 1.5% widowed, 5.8% divorced (2006-2010 5-year est.); Foreign born: 0.0% (2006-2010 5-year est.); Ancestry (includes multiple ancestries): 51.9% German, 15.8% American, 8.4% Scotch-Irish, 4.9% English, 4.9% Irish (2006-2010 5-year est.).

Economy: Employment by occupation: 16.1% management, 1.8% professional, 3.6% services, 15.2% sales, 6.9% farming, 20.1% construction, 4.9% production (2006-2010 5-year est.).

Income: Per capita income: $19,265 (2006-2010 5-year est.); Median household income: $53,750 (2006-2010 5-year est.); Average household income: $61,723 (2006-2010 5-year est.); Percent of households with income of $100,000 or more: 21.5% (2006-2010 5-year est.); Poverty rate: 20.8% (2006-2010 5-year est.).

Education: Percent of population age 25 and over with: High school diploma (including GED) or higher: 68.4% (2006-2010 5-year est.); Bachelor's degree or higher: 8.2% (2006-2010 5-year est.); Master's degree or higher: 6.0% (2006-2010 5-year est.).

Housing: Homeownership rate: 79.9% (2010); Median home value: $147,100 (2006-2010 5-year est.); Median contract rent: $661 per month (2006-2010 5-year est.); Median year structure built: 1972 (2006-2010 5-year est.).

Transportation: Commute to work: 69.6% car, 0.0% public transportation, 5.9% walk, 23.4% work from home (2006-2010 5-year est.); Travel time to work: 30.9% less than 15 minutes, 8.5% 15 to 30 minutes, 15.6% 30 to 45 minutes, 16.5% 45 to 60 minutes, 28.5% 60 minutes or more (2006-2010 5-year est.)

OLIVER (township). Covers a land area of 8.234 square miles and a water area of 0.301 square miles. Located at 40.49° N. Lat; 77.14° W. Long.

Population: 2,039 (1990); 2,061 (2000); 1,931 (2010); Density: 234.5 persons per square mile (2010); Race: 96.4% White, 1.0% Black, 0.4% Asian, 0.6% American Indian/Alaska Native, 0.1% Native Hawaiian/Other Pacific Islander, 1.5% Other, 1.4% Hispanic of any race (2010); Average household size: 2.42 (2010); Median age: 41.7 (2010); Males per 100 females: 88.8 (2010); Marriage status: 28.4% never married, 50.7% now married, 6.9% widowed, 14.0% divorced (2006-2010 5-year est.); Foreign born: 1.4% (2006-2010 5-year est.); Ancestry (includes multiple ancestries): 42.2% German, 11.2% Irish, 10.4% American, 3.6% English, 2.5% Italian (2006-2010 5-year est.).

Economy: Employment by occupation: 8.8% management, 2.1% professional, 10.5% services, 20.7% sales, 4.6% farming, 18.6% construction, 10.1% production (2006-2010 5-year est.).

Income: Per capita income: $20,720 (2006-2010 5-year est.); Median household income: $43,750 (2006-2010 5-year est.); Average household income: $50,512 (2006-2010 5-year est.); Percent of households with income of $100,000 or more: 6.4% (2006-2010 5-year est.); Poverty rate: 16.3% (2006-2010 5-year est.).

Education: Percent of population age 25 and over with: High school diploma (including GED) or higher: 75.3% (2006-2010 5-year est.); Bachelor's degree or higher: 9.2% (2006-2010 5-year est.); Master's degree or higher: 2.2% (2006-2010 5-year est.).

Housing: Homeownership rate: 70.1% (2010); Median home value: $117,900 (2006-2010 5-year est.); Median contract rent: $415 per month (2006-2010 5-year est.); Median year structure built: 1973 (2006-2010 5-year est.).

Transportation: Commute to work: 92.3% car, 0.0% public transportation, 2.6% walk, 4.6% work from home (2006-2010 5-year est.); Travel time to

work: 29.4% less than 15 minutes, 12.3% 15 to 30 minutes, 32.9% 30 to 45 minutes, 19.3% 45 to 60 minutes, 6.1% 60 minutes or more (2006-2010 5-year est.)

Additional Information Contacts
Perry County Chamber of Commerce . . . . (717) 582-4523
  http://www.perrycountychamber.org

PENN (township). Covers a land area of 21.189 square miles and a water area of 0.289 square miles. Located at 40.35° N. Lat; 77.05° W. Long.

Population: 3,283 (1990); 3,013 (2000); 3,225 (2010); Density: 152.2 persons per square mile (2010); Race: 97.2% White, 1.0% Black, 0.2% Asian, 0.1% American Indian/Alaska Native, 0.0% Native Hawaiian/Other Pacific Islander, 1.5% Other, 1.6% Hispanic of any race (2010); Average household size: 2.45 (2010); Median age: 43.4 (2010); Males per 100 females: 94.7 (2010); Marriage status: 26.9% never married, 53.8% now married, 7.2% widowed, 12.0% divorced (2006-2010 5-year est.); Foreign born: 0.0% (2006-2010 5-year est.); Ancestry (includes multiple ancestries): 40.7% German, 22.5% Irish, 6.0% English, 4.7% American, 3.6% Italian (2006-2010 5-year est.).

Economy: Single-family building permits issued: 4 (2011); Multi-family building permits issued: 0 (2011); Employment by occupation: 9.4% management, 4.0% professional, 11.2% services, 20.4% sales, 11.3% farming, 11.5% construction, 9.2% production (2006-2010 5-year est.).

Income: Per capita income: $25,235 (2006-2010 5-year est.); Median household income: $49,522 (2006-2010 5-year est.); Average household income: $61,933 (2006-2010 5-year est.); Percent of households with income of $100,000 or more: 23.2% (2006-2010 5-year est.); Poverty rate: 8.6% (2006-2010 5-year est.).

Education: Percent of population age 25 and over with: High school diploma (including GED) or higher: 82.9% (2006-2010 5-year est.); Bachelor's degree or higher: 11.7% (2006-2010 5-year est.); Master's degree or higher: 1.7% (2006-2010 5-year est.).

Housing: Homeownership rate: 74.1% (2010); Median home value: $136,400 (2006-2010 5-year est.); Median contract rent: $549 per month (2006-2010 5-year est.); Median year structure built: 1972 (2006-2010 5-year est.).

Safety: Violent crime rate: 0.0 per 10,000 population; Property crime rate: 151.5 per 10,000 population (2011).

Transportation: Commute to work: 98.1% car, 0.0% public transportation, 0.0% walk, 1.2% work from home (2006-2010 5-year est.); Travel time to work: 14.0% less than 15 minutes, 30.2% 15 to 30 minutes, 38.9% 30 to 45 minutes, 10.9% 45 to 60 minutes, 5.9% 60 minutes or more (2006-2010 5-year est.)

Additional Information Contacts
Perry County Chamber of Commerce . . . . (717) 582-4523
  http://www.perrycountychamber.org

RYE (township). Covers a land area of 25.716 square miles and a water area of 0.011 square miles. Located at 40.32° N. Lat; 77.04° W. Long.

Population: 2,136 (1990); 2,327 (2000); 2,364 (2010); Density: 91.9 persons per square mile (2010); Race: 98.1% White, 0.3% Black, 0.2% Asian, 0.1% American Indian/Alaska Native, 0.1% Native Hawaiian/Other Pacific Islander, 1.2% Other, 0.9% Hispanic of any race (2010); Average household size: 2.60 (2010); Median age: 46.0 (2010); Males per 100 females: 100.7 (2010); Marriage status: 23.1% never married, 63.8% now married, 5.9% widowed, 7.3% divorced (2006-2010 5-year est.); Foreign born: 0.3% (2006-2010 5-year est.); Ancestry (includes multiple ancestries): 46.9% German, 8.6% American, 7.9% English, 6.7% Irish, 4.6% Welsh (2006-2010 5-year est.).

Economy: Single-family building permits issued: 1 (2011); Multi-family building permits issued: 0 (2011); Employment by occupation: 4.4% management, 6.7% professional, 6.1% services, 23.1% sales, 1.5% farming, 15.6% construction, 12.0% production (2006-2010 5-year est.).

Income: Per capita income: $29,636 (2006-2010 5-year est.); Median household income: $70,179 (2006-2010 5-year est.); Average household income: $77,919 (2006-2010 5-year est.); Percent of households with income of $100,000 or more: 24.7% (2006-2010 5-year est.); Poverty rate: 1.4% (2006-2010 5-year est.).

Education: Percent of population age 25 and over with: High school diploma (including GED) or higher: 90.6% (2006-2010 5-year est.); Bachelor's degree or higher: 16.9% (2006-2010 5-year est.); Master's degree or higher: 4.6% (2006-2010 5-year est.).

Housing: Homeownership rate: 94.3% (2010); Median home value: $169,800 (2006-2010 5-year est.); Median contract rent: $1,268 per month

(2006-2010 5-year est.); Median year structure built: 1979 (2006-2010 5-year est.).

Transportation: Commute to work: 95.3% car, 1.0% public transportation, 0.5% walk, 2.9% work from home (2006-2010 5-year est.); Travel time to work: 9.9% less than 15 minutes, 53.7% 15 to 30 minutes, 28.3% 30 to 45 minutes, 4.5% 45 to 60 minutes, 3.6% 60 minutes or more (2006-2010 5-year est.)

Additional Information Contacts

Harrisburg Regional Chamber & CREDC . . . . (717) 232-4099
  http://www.harrisburgregionalchamber.org
Rye Township . . . . (717) 957-2348
  http://www.ryetwp.com

SAVILLE (township).
Covers a land area of 45.925 square miles and a water area of 0.066 square miles. Located at 40.44° N. Lat; 77.35° W. Long. Elevation is 728 feet.

Population: 1,818 (1990); 2,204 (2000); 2,502 (2010); Density: 54.5 persons per square mile (2010); Race: 97.6% White, 0.0% Black, 0.6% Asian, 0.2% American Indian/Alaska Native, 0.0% Native Hawaiian/Other Pacific Islander, 1.6% Other, 0.5% Hispanic of any race (2010); Average household size: 2.84 (2010); Median age: 37.5 (2010); Males per 100 females: 105.6 (2010); Marriage status: 21.3% never married, 64.5% now married, 3.5% widowed, 10.7% divorced (2006-2010 5-year est.); Foreign born: 1.6% (2006-2010 5-year est.); Ancestry (includes multiple ancestries): 37.5% German, 16.0% Irish, 12.0% American, 7.1% English, 4.3% Pennsylvania German (2006-2010 5-year est.).

Economy: Employment by occupation: 12.4% management, 0.2% professional, 9.6% services, 17.5% sales, 5.0% farming, 14.5% construction, 5.5% production (2006-2010 5-year est.).

Income: Per capita income: $19,819 (2006-2010 5-year est.); Median household income: $54,708 (2006-2010 5-year est.); Average household income: $59,153 (2006-2010 5-year est.); Percent of households with income of $100,000 or more: 12.3% (2006-2010 5-year est.); Poverty rate: 10.7% (2006-2010 5-year est.).

Education: Percent of population age 25 and over with: High school diploma (including GED) or higher: 83.6% (2006-2010 5-year est.); Bachelor's degree or higher: 12.2% (2006-2010 5-year est.); Master's degree or higher: 4.3% (2006-2010 5-year est.).

Housing: Homeownership rate: 84.3% (2010); Median home value: $153,800 (2006-2010 5-year est.); Median contract rent: $508 per month (2006-2010 5-year est.); Median year structure built: 1977 (2006-2010 5-year est.).

Transportation: Commute to work: 85.2% car, 0.3% public transportation, 6.1% walk, 8.1% work from home (2006-2010 5-year est.); Travel time to work: 19.0% less than 15 minutes, 13.7% 15 to 30 minutes, 15.7% 30 to 45 minutes, 28.9% 45 to 60 minutes, 22.7% 60 minutes or more (2006-2010 5-year est.)

Additional Information Contacts

Juniata River Valley Chamber of Commerce . . . . (717) 248-6713
  http://www.juniatarivervalley.org

SHERMANS DALE (unincorporated postal area)
Zip Code: 17090

Covers a land area of 33.838 square miles and a water area of 0.262 square miles. Located at 40.31° N. Lat; 77.18° W. Long. Elevation is 469 feet. Population: 5,216 (2010); Density: 154.1 persons per square mile (2010); Race: 97.7% White, 0.3% Black, 0.3% Asian, 0.2% American Indian/Alaska Native, 0.0% Native Hawaiian/Other Pacific Islander, 1.5% Other, 1.4% Hispanic of any race (2010); Average household size: 2.55 (2010); Median age: 40.2 (2010); Males per 100 females: 102.7 (2010); Homeownership rate: 85.8% (2010)

SOUTHWEST MADISON (township).
Covers a land area of 27.358 square miles and a water area of 0.175 square miles. Located at 40.34° N. Lat; 77.43° W. Long.

Population: 745 (1990); 856 (2000); 999 (2010); Density: 36.5 persons per square mile (2010); Race: 96.8% White, 0.2% Black, 0.1% Asian, 0.2% American Indian/Alaska Native, 0.0% Native Hawaiian/Other Pacific Islander, 2.7% Other, 1.5% Hispanic of any race (2010); Average household size: 2.98 (2010); Median age: 33.4 (2010); Males per 100 females: 103.0 (2010); Marriage status: 22.6% never married, 56.5% now married, 12.1% widowed, 8.8% divorced (2006-2010 5-year est.); Foreign born: 1.4% (2006-2010 5-year est.); Ancestry (includes multiple ancestries): 45.6% German, 18.0% Irish, 10.0% American, 5.2% Scotch-Irish, 4.1% Dutch (2006-2010 5-year est.).

Economy: Employment by occupation: 8.8% management, 2.4% professional, 13.8% services, 16.0% sales, 8.5% farming, 17.0% construction, 8.8% production (2006-2010 5-year est.).

Income: Per capita income: $20,004 (2006-2010 5-year est.); Median household income: $43,750 (2006-2010 5-year est.); Average household income: $50,914 (2006-2010 5-year est.); Percent of households with income of $100,000 or more: 9.9% (2006-2010 5-year est.); Poverty rate: 13.8% (2006-2010 5-year est.).

Education: Percent of population age 25 and over with: High school diploma (including GED) or higher: 82.6% (2006-2010 5-year est.); Bachelor's degree or higher: 10.9% (2006-2010 5-year est.); Master's degree or higher: 0.8% (2006-2010 5-year est.).

Housing: Homeownership rate: 83.2% (2010); Median home value: $163,000 (2006-2010 5-year est.); Median contract rent: $575 per month (2006-2010 5-year est.); Median year structure built: 1950 (2006-2010 5-year est.).

Transportation: Commute to work: 91.4% car, 1.4% public transportation, 2.0% walk, 5.2% work from home (2006-2010 5-year est.); Travel time to work: 26.3% less than 15 minutes, 13.6% 15 to 30 minutes, 17.8% 30 to 45 minutes, 19.0% 45 to 60 minutes, 23.3% 60 minutes or more (2006-2010 5-year est.)

SPRING (township).
Covers a land area of 28.638 square miles and a water area of 0.176 square miles. Located at 40.34° N. Lat; 77.26° W. Long.

Population: 1,665 (1990); 2,021 (2000); 2,208 (2010); Density: 77.1 persons per square mile (2010); Race: 97.6% White, 0.5% Black, 0.2% Asian, 0.3% American Indian/Alaska Native, 0.0% Native Hawaiian/Other Pacific Islander, 1.4% Other, 1.0% Hispanic of any race (2010); Average household size: 2.63 (2010); Median age: 40.9 (2010); Males per 100 females: 99.8 (2010); Marriage status: 20.0% never married, 69.1% now married, 2.2% widowed, 8.7% divorced (2006-2010 5-year est.); Foreign born: 2.0% (2006-2010 5-year est.); Ancestry (includes multiple ancestries): 43.1% German, 14.0% Irish, 9.8% American, 4.6% English, 3.4% Italian (2006-2010 5-year est.).

Economy: Employment by occupation: 8.0% management, 3.6% professional, 7.8% services, 16.5% sales, 3.6% farming, 17.4% construction, 13.4% production (2006-2010 5-year est.).

Income: Per capita income: $22,748 (2006-2010 5-year est.); Median household income: $56,172 (2006-2010 5-year est.); Average household income: $60,916 (2006-2010 5-year est.); Percent of households with income of $100,000 or more: 13.1% (2006-2010 5-year est.); Poverty rate: 7.6% (2006-2010 5-year est.).

Education: Percent of population age 25 and over with: High school diploma (including GED) or higher: 88.4% (2006-2010 5-year est.); Bachelor's degree or higher: 15.9% (2006-2010 5-year est.); Master's degree or higher: 4.6% (2006-2010 5-year est.).

Housing: Homeownership rate: 86.5% (2010); Median home value: $166,000 (2006-2010 5-year est.); Median contract rent: $516 per month (2006-2010 5-year est.); Median year structure built: 1977 (2006-2010 5-year est.).

Transportation: Commute to work: 90.2% car, 0.0% public transportation, 1.2% walk, 6.8% work from home (2006-2010 5-year est.); Travel time to work: 17.9% less than 15 minutes, 24.8% 15 to 30 minutes, 31.0% 30 to 45 minutes, 17.2% 45 to 60 minutes, 9.2% 60 minutes or more (2006-2010 5-year est.)

Additional Information Contacts

Perry County Chamber of Commerce . . . . (717) 582-4523
  http://www.perrycountychamber.org

TOBOYNE (township).
Covers a land area of 56.132 square miles and a water area of 0.090 square miles. Located at 40.23° N. Lat; 77.65° W. Long.

Population: 455 (1990); 494 (2000); 443 (2010); Density: 7.9 persons per square mile (2010); Race: 98.2% White, 0.7% Black, 0.2% Asian, 0.0% American Indian/Alaska Native, 0.0% Native Hawaiian/Other Pacific Islander, 0.9% Other, 0.7% Hispanic of any race (2010); Average household size: 2.34 (2010); Median age: 48.9 (2010); Males per 100 females: 119.3 (2010); Marriage status: 28.4% never married, 55.8% now married, 5.9% widowed, 10.0% divorced (2006-2010 5-year est.); Foreign born: 1.4% (2006-2010 5-year est.); Ancestry (includes multiple ancestries): 53.7% German, 16.4% Irish, 15.2% Pennsylvania German, 4.3% American, 2.9% Welsh (2006-2010 5-year est.).

Economy: Employment by occupation: 2.5% management, 11.2% professional, 5.6% services, 14.3% sales, 1.9% farming, 34.8% construction, 13.0% production (2006-2010 5-year est.).
Income: Per capita income: $20,094 (2006-2010 5-year est.); Median household income: $37,500 (2006-2010 5-year est.); Average household income: $49,309 (2006-2010 5-year est.); Percent of households with income of $100,000 or more: 11.5% (2006-2010 5-year est.); Poverty rate: 5.2% (2006-2010 5-year est.).
Education: Percent of population age 25 and over with: High school diploma (including GED) or higher: 65.2% (2006-2010 5-year est.); Bachelor's degree or higher: 0.6% (2006-2010 5-year est.); Master's degree or higher: 0.6% (2006-2010 5-year est.).
Housing: Homeownership rate: 85.9% (2010); Median home value: $94,000 (2006-2010 5-year est.); Median contract rent: n/a per month (2006-2010 5-year est.); Median year structure built: 1966 (2006-2010 5-year est.).
Transportation: Commute to work: 78.9% car, 0.0% public transportation, 0.0% walk, 21.1% work from home (2006-2010 5-year est.); Travel time to work: 5.5% less than 15 minutes, 11.0% 15 to 30 minutes, 7.1% 30 to 45 minutes, 36.2% 45 to 60 minutes, 40.2% 60 minutes or more (2006-2010 5-year est.)

TUSCARORA (township). Covers a land area of 29.324 square miles and a water area of 0.207 square miles. Located at 40.50° N. Lat; 77.25° W. Long.
Population: 1,034 (1990); 1,122 (2000); 1,189 (2010); Density: 40.5 persons per square mile (2010); Race: 97.2% White, 0.2% Black, 0.7% Asian, 0.4% American Indian/Alaska Native, 0.0% Native Hawaiian/Other Pacific Islander, 1.5% Other, 1.9% Hispanic of any race (2010); Average household size: 2.57 (2010); Median age: 42.7 (2010); Males per 100 females: 101.5 (2010); Marriage status: 21.7% never married, 60.6% now married, 6.6% widowed, 11.1% divorced (2006-2010 5-year est.); Foreign born: 0.8% (2006-2010 5-year est.); Ancestry (includes multiple ancestries): 49.7% German, 13.9% American, 13.2% Irish, 4.6% Swedish, 3.8% English (2006-2010 5-year est.).
Economy: Employment by occupation: 9.6% management, 6.5% professional, 11.0% services, 15.1% sales, 3.3% farming, 9.6% construction, 3.7% production (2006-2010 5-year est.).
Income: Per capita income: $23,145 (2006-2010 5-year est.); Median household income: $45,536 (2006-2010 5-year est.); Average household income: $55,362 (2006-2010 5-year est.); Percent of households with income of $100,000 or more: 10.5% (2006-2010 5-year est.); Poverty rate: 9.4% (2006-2010 5-year est.).
Education: Percent of population age 25 and over with: High school diploma (including GED) or higher: 77.6% (2006-2010 5-year est.); Bachelor's degree or higher: 12.5% (2006-2010 5-year est.); Master's degree or higher: 0.9% (2006-2010 5-year est.).
Housing: Homeownership rate: 87.5% (2010); Median home value: $135,600 (2006-2010 5-year est.); Median contract rent: $535 per month (2006-2010 5-year est.); Median year structure built: 1966 (2006-2010 5-year est.).
Transportation: Commute to work: 92.5% car, 0.4% public transportation, 1.0% walk, 5.4% work from home (2006-2010 5-year est.); Travel time to work: 11.0% less than 15 minutes, 27.8% 15 to 30 minutes, 13.2% 30 to 45 minutes, 27.1% 45 to 60 minutes, 20.9% 60 minutes or more (2006-2010 5-year est.)
Additional Information Contacts
Perry County Chamber of Commerce . . . . (717) 582-4523
    http://www.perrycountychamber.org

TYRONE (township). Covers a land area of 35.670 square miles and a water area of 0.208 square miles. Located at 40.30° N. Lat; 77.36° W. Long.
Population: 1,741 (1990); 1,863 (2000); 2,124 (2010); Density: 59.5 persons per square mile (2010); Race: 95.1% White, 3.4% Black, 0.2% Asian, 0.0% American Indian/Alaska Native, 0.0% Native Hawaiian/Other Pacific Islander, 1.3% Other, 1.0% Hispanic of any race (2010); Average household size: 2.55 (2010); Median age: 38.9 (2010); Males per 100 females: 111.6 (2010); Marriage status: 27.9% never married, 54.7% now married, 9.4% widowed, 8.0% divorced (2006-2010 5-year est.); Foreign born: 0.3% (2006-2010 5-year est.); Ancestry (includes multiple ancestries): 44.0% German, 11.1% Irish, 9.2% English, 5.3% Pennsylvania German, 4.8% American (2006-2010 5-year est.).

Economy: Employment by occupation: 10.5% management, 2.6% professional, 9.0% services, 15.4% sales, 4.4% farming, 12.2% construction, 2.5% production (2006-2010 5-year est.).
Income: Per capita income: $20,410 (2006-2010 5-year est.); Median household income: $45,096 (2006-2010 5-year est.); Average household income: $56,092 (2006-2010 5-year est.); Percent of households with income of $100,000 or more: 13.0% (2006-2010 5-year est.); Poverty rate: 17.4% (2006-2010 5-year est.).
Education: Percent of population age 25 and over with: High school diploma (including GED) or higher: 81.9% (2006-2010 5-year est.); Bachelor's degree or higher: 10.3% (2006-2010 5-year est.); Master's degree or higher: 3.1% (2006-2010 5-year est.).
Housing: Homeownership rate: 73.5% (2010); Median home value: $142,900 (2006-2010 5-year est.); Median contract rent: $544 per month (2006-2010 5-year est.); Median year structure built: 1970 (2006-2010 5-year est.).
Transportation: Commute to work: 86.8% car, 0.0% public transportation, 5.3% walk, 5.8% work from home (2006-2010 5-year est.); Travel time to work: 21.3% less than 15 minutes, 15.5% 15 to 30 minutes, 39.5% 30 to 45 minutes, 18.0% 45 to 60 minutes, 5.6% 60 minutes or more (2006-2010 5-year est.).
Additional Information Contacts
Greater Carlisle Area Chamber of Commerce . . . . (717) 243-4515
    http://carlislechamber.org

WATTS (township). Covers a land area of 11.877 square miles and a water area of 0.296 square miles. Located at 40.46° N. Lat; 76.99° W. Long.
Population: 1,152 (1990); 1,196 (2000); 1,265 (2010); Density: 106.5 persons per square mile (2010); Race: 98.8% White, 0.1% Black, 0.2% Asian, 0.1% American Indian/Alaska Native, 0.0% Native Hawaiian/Other Pacific Islander, 0.8% Other, 1.1% Hispanic of any race (2010); Average household size: 2.49 (2010); Median age: 43.5 (2010); Males per 100 females: 106.0 (2010); Marriage status: 16.1% never married, 66.4% now married, 7.6% widowed, 9.9% divorced (2006-2010 5-year est.); Foreign born: 0.9% (2006-2010 5-year est.); Ancestry (includes multiple ancestries): 50.8% German, 11.8% Irish, 8.0% Italian, 4.8% American, 4.4% Scotch-Irish (2006-2010 5-year est.).
Economy: Employment by occupation: 5.4% management, 1.5% professional, 4.7% services, 26.8% sales, 5.4% farming, 19.1% construction, 11.0% production (2006-2010 5-year est.).
Income: Per capita income: $24,982 (2006-2010 5-year est.); Median household income: $55,192 (2006-2010 5-year est.); Average household income: $61,584 (2006-2010 5-year est.); Percent of households with income of $100,000 or more: 15.6% (2006-2010 5-year est.); Poverty rate: 7.3% (2006-2010 5-year est.).
Education: Percent of population age 25 and over with: High school diploma (including GED) or higher: 85.1% (2006-2010 5-year est.); Bachelor's degree or higher: 12.5% (2006-2010 5-year est.); Master's degree or higher: 8.5% (2006-2010 5-year est.).
Housing: Homeownership rate: 77.9% (2010); Median home value: $162,500 (2006-2010 5-year est.); Median contract rent: $540 per month (2006-2010 5-year est.); Median year structure built: 1975 (2006-2010 5-year est.).
Transportation: Commute to work: 92.2% car, 0.0% public transportation, 2.0% walk, 4.7% work from home (2006-2010 5-year est.); Travel time to work: 17.9% less than 15 minutes, 18.9% 15 to 30 minutes, 46.8% 30 to 45 minutes, 13.0% 45 to 60 minutes, 3.4% 60 minutes or more (2006-2010 5-year est.)
Additional Information Contacts
Harrisburg Regional Chamber & CREDC . . . . (717) 232-4099
    http://www.harrisburgregionalchamber.org

WHEATFIELD (township). Covers a land area of 20.804 square miles and a water area of 0.173 square miles. Located at 40.40° N. Lat; 77.10° W. Long.
Population: 3,097 (1990); 3,329 (2000); 3,334 (2010); Density: 160.3 persons per square mile (2010); Race: 98.1% White, 0.1% Black, 0.7% Asian, 0.1% American Indian/Alaska Native, 0.0% Native Hawaiian/Other Pacific Islander, 1.0% Other, 0.8% Hispanic of any race (2010); Average household size: 2.65 (2010); Median age: 42.4 (2010); Males per 100 females: 101.1 (2010); Marriage status: 20.0% never married, 67.9% now married, 5.8% widowed, 6.3% divorced (2006-2010 5-year est.); Foreign born: 0.3% (2006-2010 5-year est.); Ancestry (includes multiple

ancestries): 56.0% German, 17.1% Irish, 9.1% English, 7.6% Italian, 6.6% American (2006-2010 5-year est.).

Economy: Single-family building permits issued: 4 (2011); Multi-family building permits issued: 0 (2011); Employment by occupation: 9.5% management, 5.8% professional, 3.1% services, 29.7% sales, 2.7% farming, 8.2% construction, 4.1% production (2006-2010 5-year est.).

Income: Per capita income: $27,236 (2006-2010 5-year est.); Median household income: $66,731 (2006-2010 5-year est.); Average household income: $68,131 (2006-2010 5-year est.); Percent of households with income of $100,000 or more: 17.4% (2006-2010 5-year est.); Poverty rate: 3.6% (2006-2010 5-year est.).

Education: Percent of population age 25 and over with: High school diploma (including GED) or higher: 89.3% (2006-2010 5-year est.); Bachelor's degree or higher: 18.7% (2006-2010 5-year est.); Master's degree or higher: 4.5% (2006-2010 5-year est.).

Housing: Homeownership rate: 91.8% (2010); Median home value: $148,100 (2006-2010 5-year est.); Median contract rent: n/a per month (2006-2010 5-year est.); Median year structure built: 1978 (2006-2010 5-year est.).

Transportation: Commute to work: 94.4% car, 0.0% public transportation, 0.0% walk, 5.6% work from home (2006-2010 5-year est.); Travel time to work: 11.2% less than 15 minutes, 18.7% 15 to 30 minutes, 46.4% 30 to 45 minutes, 17.4% 45 to 60 minutes, 6.2% 60 minutes or more (2006-2010 5-year est.)

Additional Information Contacts

Perry County Chamber of Commerce . . . . (717) 582-4523
http://www.perrycountychamber.org

Philadelphia County

Located in southeastern Pennsylvania, on the Delaware River, at the mouth of the Schuylkill River. Consolidated with the City of Philadelphia in 1854. All remaining county functions were assumed by the city in 1952. The county is coterminous with the City of Philadelphia. Covers a land area of 134.101 square miles, a water area of 8.606 square miles, and is located in the Eastern Time Zone at 40.01° N. Lat., 75.13° W. Long. The county was founded in 1682. County seat is Philadelphia.

Philadelphia County is part of the Philadelphia-Camden-Wilmington, PA-NJ-DE-MD Metropolitan Statistical Area. The entire metro area includes: Camden, NJ Metropolitan Division (Burlington County, NJ; Camden County, NJ; Gloucester County, NJ); Philadelphia, PA Metropolitan Division (Bucks County, PA; Chester County, PA; Delaware County, PA; Montgomery County, PA; Philadelphia County, PA); Wilmington, DE-MD-NJ Metropolitan Division (New Castle County, DE; Cecil County, MD; Salem County, NJ)

Weather Station: Philadelphia Int'l Arpt										Elevation: 4 feet	
	Jan	Feb	Mar	Apr	May	Jun	Jul	Aug	Sep	Oct	Nov	Dec
High	40	44	52	64	74	82	87	85	78	67	56	45
Low	25	27	34	44	54	63	69	68	60	48	39	30
Precip	3.0	2.5	3.8	3.6	3.7	3.4	4.4	3.5	3.8	3.2	3.0	3.5
Snow	5.4	6.6	3.0	0.5	tr	tr	tr	0.0	0.0	tr	0.4	3.0

High and Low temperatures in degrees Fahrenheit; Precipitation and Snow in inches

Economy: Unemployment rate: 11.5% (August 2012); Total civilian labor force: 655,604 (August 2012); Leading industries: 25.5% health care and social assistance; 13.0% educational services; 9.1% accommodation & food services (2010); Farms: 17 totaling 262 acres (2007); Companies that employ 500 or more persons: 115 (2010); Companies that employ 100 to 499 persons: 705 (2010); Companies that employ less than 100 persons: 26,113 (2010); Black-owned businesses: 19,835 (2007); Hispanic-owned businesses: 6,877 (2007); Asian-owned businesses: 8,494 (2007); Women-owned businesses: 28,022 (2007); Retail sales per capita: $7,831 (2010). Single-family building permits issued: 445 (2011); Multi-family building permits issued: 1,107 (2011).

Income: Per capita income: $21,117 (2006-2010 5-year est.); Median household income: $36,251 (2006-2010 5-year est.); Average household income: $51,060 (2006-2010 5-year est.); Percent of households with income of $100,000 or more: 11.9% (2006-2010 5-year est.); Poverty rate: 25.1% (2006-2010 5-year est.); Bankruptcy rate: 2.04% (2011).

Education: Percent of population age 25 and over with: High school diploma (including GED) or higher: 79.4% (2006-2010 5-year est.); Bachelor's degree or higher: 22.2% (2006-2010 5-year est.); Master's degree or higher: 9.3% (2006-2010 5-year est.).

Housing: Homeownership rate: 54.1% (2010); Median home value: $135,200 (2006-2010 5-year est.); Median contract rent: $656 per month (2006-2010 5-year est.); Median year structure built: 1946 (2006-2010 5-year est.)

Health: Birth rate: 152.0 per 10,000 population (2011); Death rate: 94.2 per 10,000 population (2011); Age-adjusted cancer mortality rate: 220.3 deaths per 100,000 population (2009); Number of physicians: 56.0 per 10,000 population (2010); Hospital beds: 51.7 per 10,000 population (2008); Hospital admissions: 2,352.1 per 10,000 population (2008).

Environment: Air Quality Index: 55.1% good, 41.6% moderate, 3.3% unhealthy for sensitive individuals, 0.0% unhealthy (percent of days in 2011)

Elections: 2012 Presidential election results: 85.3% Obama, 14.0% Romney

National and State Parks: Benjamin Franklin National Memorial; Edgar Allan Poe National Historic Site; Gloria Dei-Old Swedes Church National Historic Site; Independence Mall State Park; Independence National Historical Park; Thaddeus Kosciuszko National Memorial

Religion: Six largest groups: 24.8% Catholicism, 8.6% Baptist, 3.2% Non-Denominational, 2.6% Muslim Estimate, 1.4% Methodist/Pietist, 1.1% Presbyterian-Reformed (2010)

History: People had already settled in the Philadelphia area, but the city itself came into being when the Quaker colonizer, William Penn, acquired the Pennsylvania grant from Charles II in 1681. Philadelphia grew and prospered. In 1723, a young printer, Benjamin Franklin appeared. Among other accomplishments, Franklin published "Poor Richard's Almanac," helped to found what later became the University of Pennsylvania, and conducted his famous kite experiment. Philadelphia became the center of the newly forming American independence movement. The Continental Congress adopted the Declaration of Independence here. In 1777, Philadelphia had its first Fourth of July celebration, honoring the new American flag. Philadelphia remained the state capital until 1799, and was the seat of the national government from 1775 to 1789, and again from 1790 to 1800. Consolidated with Philadelphia County in 1854.

Population: 1,585,577 (1990); 1,517,550 (2000); 1,526,006 (2010); Density: 11,379.5 persons per square mile (2010); Race: 41.0% White, 43.4% Black, 6.3% Asian, 0.5% American Indian/Alaska Native, 0.0% Native Hawaiian/Other Pacific Islander, 8.8% Other, 12.3% Hispanic of any race (2010); Average household size: 2.45 (2010); Median age: 33.5 (2010); Males per 100 females: 89.3 (2010); Marriage status: 49.2% never married, 34.3% now married, 7.7% widowed, 8.7% divorced (2006-2010 5-year est.); Foreign born: 11.5% (2006-2010 5-year est.); Ancestry (includes multiple ancestries): 13.0% Irish, 8.3% Italian, 8.2% German, 3.9% Polish, 3.1% English (2006-2010 5-year est.).

Employment by occupation: 8.6% management, 3.4% professional, 12.4% services, 17.9% sales, 5.1% farming, 6.2% construction, 5.2% production (2006-2010 5-year est.).

Taxes: Total city taxes per capita: $1,901 (2009); City property taxes per capita: $276 (2009).

School District(s)

Ad Prima CS (KG-08)
    2010-11 Enrollment: 329 . . . . (610) 617-9121
Alliance for Progress CS (KG-06)
    2010-11 Enrollment: 328 . . . . (215) 232-4892
Antonia Pantoja Community Charter School (KG-08)
    2010-11 Enrollment: 735 . . . . (215) 455-1300
Arise Academy Charter High School (UG-UG)
    2010-11 Enrollment: 214 . . . . (215) 563-1656
Aspira Bilingual Cyber Charter School (KG-12)
    2010-11 Enrollment: n/a . . . . (215) 455-1300
Belmont Academy Charter School (PK-KG)
    2010-11 Enrollment: 106 . . . . (215) 386-5768
Belmont Charter School (01-08)
    2010-11 Enrollment: 445 . . . . (215) 823-8208
Boys Latin of Philadelphia CS (09-12)
    2010-11 Enrollment: 463 . . . . (215) 387-5149
Charter High School for Architecture and Design (09-12)
    2010-11 Enrollment: 606 . . . . (215) 351-2900
Christopher Columbus CS (KG-08)
    2010-11 Enrollment: 769 . . . . (215) 925-7400
Community Academy of Philadelphia CS (KG-12)
    2010-11 Enrollment: 1,213 . . . . (215) 533-6700
Delaware Valley CHS (09-12)
    2010-11 Enrollment: 633 . . . . (215) 455-2550

Discovery Charter School (KG-08)
2010-11 Enrollment: 612 . . . . (215) 879-8182
Eastern University Academy Charter School (07-12)
2010-11 Enrollment: 237 . . . . (215) 769-3131
Esperanza Academy Charter High School (09-12)
2010-11 Enrollment: 727 . . . . (215) 457-3667
Eugenio Maria De Hostos CS (KG-07)
2010-11 Enrollment: 350 . . . . (215) 455-2300
First Phila CS for Literacy (KG-08)
2010-11 Enrollment: 735 . . . . (215) 743-3100
Folk Arts-Cultural Treasures CS (KG-08)
2010-11 Enrollment: 453 . . . . (215) 569-2600
Franklin Towne CHS (09-12)
2010-11 Enrollment: 966 . . . . (215) 289-5000
Franklin Towne Charter Elementary School (03-06)
2010-11 Enrollment: 343 . . . . (215) 289-5000
Freire CS (09-12)
2010-11 Enrollment: 504 . . . . (215) 557-8555
Global Leadership Academy CS (KG-08)
2010-11 Enrollment: 592 . . . . (215) 477-6672
Green Woods CS (KG-08)
2010-11 Enrollment: 216 . . . . (215) 482-6337
Hardy Williams Academy CS (KG-08)
2010-11 Enrollment: 828 . . . . (215) 724-2343
Hope CS (09-12)
2010-11 Enrollment: 401 . . . . (267) 336-2730
Imani Education Circle CS (KG-08)
2010-11 Enrollment: 451 . . . . (215) 713-9240
Imhotep Institute CHS (09-12)
2010-11 Enrollment: 538 . . . . (215) 438-4140
Independence CS (KG-08)
2010-11 Enrollment: 775 . . . . (215) 238-8000
John B. Stetson Charter School (05-08)
2010-11 Enrollment: 645 . . . . (215) 455-1300
Khepera CS (KG-08)
2010-11 Enrollment: 425 . . . . (215) 843-1700
Kipp Philadelphia Charter School (05-09)
2010-11 Enrollment: 521 . . . . (215) 227-1728
Kipp West Philadelphia Preparatory Charter School (05-08)
2010-11 Enrollment: 184 . . . . (215) 294-2973
Laboratory CS (KG-08)
2010-11 Enrollment: 395 . . . . (610) 617-9121
Mariana Bracetti Academy CS (06-12)
2010-11 Enrollment: 1,105 . . . . (215) 291-4436
Maritime Academy Charter School (05-12)
2010-11 Enrollment: 762 . . . . (215) 535-4555
Mast Community Charter School (KG-12)
2010-11 Enrollment: 1,244 . . . . (267) 348-1100
Mastery CS-Pickett Campus (07-11)
2010-11 Enrollment: 574 . . . . (215) 866-9000
Mastery CS-Shoemaker Campus (07-12)
2010-11 Enrollment: 676 . . . . (267) 296-7111
Mastery CS-Thomas Campus (07-12)
2010-11 Enrollment: 609 . . . . (267) 236-0036
Mastery Charter High School (06-12)
2010-11 Enrollment: 519 . . . . (215) 922-1902
Mastery Charter School Harrity Campus (KG-08)
2010-11 Enrollment: 801 . . . . (215) 866-9000
Mastery Charter School Mann Campus (KG-05)
2010-11 Enrollment: 426 . . . . (717) 866-9000
Mastery Charter School Smedley Campus (KG-05)
2010-11 Enrollment: 588 . . . . (215) 866-9000
Math Civics and Sciences CS (01-12)
2010-11 Enrollment: 916 . . . . (215) 923-4880
Multi-Cultural Academy CS (09-12)
2010-11 Enrollment: 217 . . . . (215) 457-6666
New Foundations CS (KG-09)
2010-11 Enrollment: 683 . . . . (215) 624-8100
New Media Technology CS (05-12)
2010-11 Enrollment: 450 . . . . (267) 286-6900
Northwood Academy CS (KG-08)
2010-11 Enrollment: 753 . . . . (215) 289-5606
Pan American Academy CS (KG-06)
2010-11 Enrollment: 413 . . . . (215) 763-8870
People for People CS (KG-08)
2010-11 Enrollment: 529 . . . . (215) 763-7060

Philadelphia Academy CS (KG-12)
2010-11 Enrollment: 1,189 . . . . (215) 676-8320
Philadelphia City SD (PK-12)
2010-11 Enrollment: 166,233 . . . . (215) 400-4000
Philadelphia Electrical & Tech CHS (09-12)
2010-11 Enrollment: 607 . . . . (267) 514-1823
Philadelphia Harambee Inst CS (KG-08)
2010-11 Enrollment: 453 . . . . (215) 472-8770
Philadelphia Montessori CS (PK-06)
2010-11 Enrollment: 145 . . . . (215) 365-4011
Philadelphia Performing Arts CS (PK-08)
2010-11 Enrollment: 617 . . . . (215) 551-4000
Planet Abacus CS (KG-07)
2010-11 Enrollment: 379 . . . . (610) 617-9121
Preparatory CS of Mathematics Science Tech (09-12)
2010-11 Enrollment: 603 . . . . (215) 334-6144
Richard Allen Preparatory CS (05-08)
2010-11 Enrollment: 416 . . . . (215) 878-1544
Russell Byers CS (KG-06)
2010-11 Enrollment: 417 . . . . (215) 972-1700
Sankofa Freedom Academy Charter School (KG-10)
2010-11 Enrollment: 400 . . . . (215) 288-2001
Southwest Leadership Academy CS (KG-06)
2010-11 Enrollment: 348 . . . . (215) 729-1939
Tacony Academy Charter School (KG-12)
2010-11 Enrollment: 561 . . . . (215) 742-5100
Truebright Science Academy CS (07-12)
2010-11 Enrollment: 350 . . . . (215) 225-3437
Universal Bluford Charter School (KG-06)
2010-11 Enrollment: 557 . . . . (215) 732-6518
Universal Daroff Charter School (KG-08)
2010-11 Enrollment: 616 . . . . (215) 732-6518
Universal Institute CS (KG-08)
2010-11 Enrollment: 647 . . . . (215) 732-7988
Wakisha CS (06-08)
2010-11 Enrollment: 331 . . . . (267) 940-4800
Walter D Palmer Leadership Learning Partners CS (PK-12)
2010-11 Enrollment: 860 . . . . (215) 627-9482
West Oak Lane CS (KG-08)
2010-11 Enrollment: 735 . . . . (215) 927-7995
West Philadelphia Achievement CES (KG-05)
2010-11 Enrollment: 417 . . . . (215) 476-6471
Wissahickon CS (KG-08)
2010-11 Enrollment: 419 . . . . (267) 338-1020
World Communications CS (06-12)
2010-11 Enrollment: 510 . . . . (215) 735-3198
Young Scholars CS (06-08)
2010-11 Enrollment: 238 . . . . (215) 232-9727
Young Scholars Frederick Douglas Charter School (KG-08)
2010-11 Enrollment: 655 . . . . (267) 443-0673
Youth Build Philadelphia CS (12-12)
2010-11 Enrollment: 243 . . . . (215) 627-8671

Four-year College(s)

Academy of Vocal Arts (Private, Not-for-profit)
Fall 2010 Enrollment: 28 . . . . (215) 735-1685
Chestnut Hill College (Private, Not-for-profit, Roman Catholic)
Fall 2010 Enrollment: 1,970 . . . . (215) 248-7000
2011-12 Tuition: In-state $29,200; Out-of-state $29,200
Curtis Institute of Music (Private, Not-for-profit)
Fall 2010 Enrollment: 128 . . . . (215) 893-5252
2011-12 Tuition: In-state $2,300; Out-of-state $2,300
Drexel University (Private, Not-for-profit)
Fall 2010 Enrollment: 20,907 . . . . (215) 895-2000
2011-12 Tuition: In-state $34,505; Out-of-state $34,505
Holy Family University (Private, Not-for-profit, Roman Catholic)
Fall 2010 Enrollment: 2,428 . . . . (215) 637-7700
2011-12 Tuition: In-state $24,640; Out-of-state $24,640
La Salle University (Private, Not-for-profit, Roman Catholic)
Fall 2010 Enrollment: 5,483 . . . . (215) 951-1000
2011-12 Tuition: In-state $35,240; Out-of-state $35,240
Lutheran Theological Seminary at Philadelphia (Private, Not-for-profit, Evangelical Lutheran Church)
Fall 2010 Enrollment: 176 . . . . (215) 248-4616

Moore College of Art and Design (Private, Not-for-profit)
    Fall 2010 Enrollment: 522 . . . . (215) 568-4515
    2011-12 Tuition: In-state $31,478; Out-of-state $31,478
Peirce College (Private, Not-for-profit)
    Fall 2010 Enrollment: 1,387 . . . . (888) 467-3472
    2011-12 Tuition: In-state $15,900; Out-of-state $15,900
Pennsylvania Academy of the Fine Arts (Private, Not-for-profit)
    Fall 2010 Enrollment: 384 . . . . (215) 972-7600
    2011-12 Tuition: In-state $27,210; Out-of-state $27,210
Philadelphia College of Osteopathic Medicine (Private, Not-for-profit)
    Fall 2010 Enrollment: 3,305 . . . . (215) 871-6770
Philadelphia University (Private, Not-for-profit)
    Fall 2010 Enrollment: 3,688 . . . . (215) 951-2700
    2011-12 Tuition: In-state $30,546; Out-of-state $30,546
Saint Joseph's University (Private, Not-for-profit, Roman Catholic)
    Fall 2010 Enrollment: 6,647 . . . . (610) 660-1000
    2011-12 Tuition: In-state $36,640; Out-of-state $36,640
Talmudical Yeshiva of Philadelphia (Private, Not-for-profit, Jewish)
    Fall 2010 Enrollment: 116 . . . . (215) 473-1212
    2011-12 Tuition: In-state $8,100; Out-of-state $8,100
Temple University (Public)
    Fall 2010 Enrollment: 34,376 . . . . (215) 204-7000
    2011-12 Tuition: In-state $13,596; Out-of-state $23,422
The Art Institute of Philadelphia (Private, For-profit)
    Fall 2010 Enrollment: 3,039 . . . . (800) 275-2474
    2011-12 Tuition: In-state $18,120; Out-of-state $18,120
The Restaurant School at Walnut Hill College (Private, For-profit)
    Fall 2010 Enrollment: 282 . . . . (215) 222-4200
    2011-12 Tuition: In-state $22,575; Out-of-state $22,575
The University of the Arts (Private, Not-for-profit)
    Fall 2010 Enrollment: 2,492 . . . . (215) 717-6000
    2011-12 Tuition: In-state $33,500; Out-of-state $33,500
Thomas Jefferson University (Private, Not-for-profit)
    Fall 2010 Enrollment: 3,025 . . . . (215) 955-6000
University of Pennsylvania (Private, Not-for-profit)
    Fall 2010 Enrollment: 24,609 . . . . (215) 898-5000
    2011-12 Tuition: In-state $42,098; Out-of-state $42,098
University of the Sciences (Private, Not-for-profit)
    Fall 2010 Enrollment: 3,381 . . . . (215) 596-8800
    2011-12 Tuition: In-state $32,148; Out-of-state $32,148

Two-year College(s)
Aria Health School of Nursing (Private, Not-for-profit)
    Fall 2010 Enrollment: 219 . . . . (215) 831-6740
    2011-12 Tuition: In-state $12,130; Out-of-state $12,130
Aviation Institute of Maintenance-Philadelphia (Private, For-profit)
    Fall 2010 Enrollment: 435 . . . . (215) 676-7700
    2011-12 Tuition: In-state $13,447; Out-of-state $13,447
CHI Institute-Philadelphia (Private, For-profit)
    Fall 2010 Enrollment: 1,550 . . . . (215) 612-6600
Community College of Philadelphia (Public)
    Fall 2010 Enrollment: 16,090 . . . . (215) 751-8000
    2011-12 Tuition: In-state $8,760; Out-of-state $12,900
Hussian School of Art (Private, For-profit)
    Fall 2010 Enrollment: 161 . . . . (215) 574-9600
    2011-12 Tuition: In-state $14,550; Out-of-state $14,550
Jna Institute of Culinary Arts (Private, For-profit)
    Fall 2010 Enrollment: 86 . . . . (215) 468-8800
    2011-12 Tuition: In-state $10,075; Out-of-state $10,075
Lincoln Technical Institute-Center City Philadelphia (Private, For-profit)
    Fall 2010 Enrollment: 910 . . . . (215) 382-1553
Lincoln Technical Institute-Northeast Philadelphia (Private, For-profit)
    Fall 2010 Enrollment: 409 . . . . (215) 969-0869
Lincoln Technical Institute-Philadelphia (Private, For-profit)
    Fall 2010 Enrollment: 640 . . . . (215) 335-0800
Metropolitan Career Center Computer Technology Institute (Private, Not-for-profit)
    Fall 2010 Enrollment: 157 . . . . (267) 763-1008
    2011-12 Tuition: In-state $24,194; Out-of-state $24,194
National Massage Therapy Institute (Private, For-profit)
    Fall 2010 Enrollment: 556 . . . . (800) 264-9845
Northeastern Hospital School of Nursing (Private, Not-for-profit)
    Fall 2010 Enrollment: 55 . . . . (215) 926-3145
Orleans Technical Institute (Private, Not-for-profit)
    Fall 2010 Enrollment: 756 . . . . (215) 728-4400

Roxborough Memorial Hospital School of Nursing (Private, For-profit)
    Fall 2010 Enrollment: 125 . . . . (215) 487-4344
Thompson Institute (Private, For-profit)
    Fall 2010 Enrollment: 1,386 . . . . (215) 594-4000

Vocational/Technical School(s)
DPT Business School (Private, For-profit)
    Fall 2010 Enrollment: 1,346 . . . . (215) 673-2275
    2011-12 Tuition: $5,800
Empire Beauty School-Center City Philadelphia (Private, For-profit)
    Fall 2010 Enrollment: 864 . . . . (800) 223-3271
    2011-12 Tuition: $16,380
Empire Beauty School-NE Philadelphia (Private, For-profit)
    Fall 2010 Enrollment: 406 . . . . (800) 223-3271
    2011-12 Tuition: $15,120
International Beauty Academy (Private, For-profit)
    Fall 2010 Enrollment: 41 . . . . (215) 288-9080
    2011-12 Tuition: $14,050
Jean Madeline Aveda Institute (Private, For-profit)
    Fall 2010 Enrollment: 330 . . . . (267) 295-7221
    2011-12 Tuition: $17,280
L T International Beauty School (Private, For-profit)
    Fall 2010 Enrollment: 92 . . . . (215) 922-4478
    2011-12 Tuition: $10,575
Prism Career Institute-Philadelphia (Private, For-profit)
    Fall 2010 Enrollment: 487 . . . . (215) 331-4600
    2011-12 Tuition: $24,990
Star Career Academy-Philadelphia (Private, For-profit)
    Fall 2010 Enrollment: 698 . . . . (215) 969-5877
    2011-12 Tuition: $13,221

Hospitals: Albert Einstein Medical Center (987 beds); Aria Health - Frankford Campus; Belmont Center for Comprehensive Treatment (147 beds); Chestnut Hill Hospital (200 beds); Children's Hospital of Philadelphia (430 beds); Eastern Regional Medical Center (22 beds); Fairmount Behavioral Health System (180 beds); Fox Chase Cancer Center (100 beds); Frankford Hospital (239 beds); Friends Hospital (192 beds); Girard Medical Center (168 beds); Hahnemann University Hospital (496 beds); Hospital of the University of Pennsylvania (725 beds); Jeanes Hospital (197 beds); Kensington Hospital (45 beds); Magee Rehabilitation Hospital (96 beds); Mercy Hospital of Philadelphia (266 beds); Moss Rehab (147 beds); Nazareth Hospital/Franciscan Health System (347 beds); North Philadelphia Health System - St. Joseph Division (172 beds); Northeastern Hospital (187 beds); Pennsylvania Hospital (515 beds); Philadelphia VA Medical Center (145 beds); Presbyterian Medical Center (344 beds); Roxborough Memorial Hospital (165 beds); Shriners Hospital for Children (59 beds); St. Agnes Medical Center (259 beds); St. Christophers Hospital-Children (183 beds); Temple University Hospital (514 beds); Temple University Hospital - Episcopal Campus (617 beds); Thomas Jefferson University Hospital (957 beds); Wills Eye Hospital (115 beds)

Safety: Violent crime rate: 119.3 per 10,000 population; Property crime rate: 389.4 per 10,000 population (2011).

Newspapers: Al Dia (Local news; Circulation 50,000); America-The Ukrainian Catholic Newspaper (National news; Circulation 5,000); America/Ukrainian Catholic Newspaper (Local news; Circulation 5,000); Brazilian News Week (Local news; Circulation 10,000); Bridesburg Bulletin (Community news; Circulation 6,500); Bridesburg Star (Community news; Circulation 4,000); Bustleton/Somertown News Gleaner (Local news; Circulation 18,130); The Catholic Standard & Times (Regional news; Circulation 71,962); Chestnut Hill Local (Regional news; Circulation 9,400); Community Focus/Enfoque Communal (Local news; Circulation 25,000); El Sol Latino (Local news; Circulation 25,000); The Evening Bulletin (Local news; Circulation 11,000); The Fallser (Community news; Circulation 7,500); Fishtown Star (Community news; Circulation 12,000); Frankford News Gleaner (Community news; Circulation 18,130); Germantown Courier (Community news; Circulation 15,000); Inside Magazine (Local news; Circulation 50,000); Juniata News (Community news; Circulation 10,000); Mayfair News Gleaner (Community news; Circulation 20,256); Metro - Philadelphia Edition (Regional news; Circulation 154,000); Mount Airy Times/Express (Community news; Circulation 14,000); News Gleaner (Community news; Circulation 13,155); News Gleaner, Frankford Edition (Community news; Circulation 18,130); The Northeast Breeze (Community news; Circulation 22,400); Northeast News Gleaner (Community news; Circulation 10,120); Philadelphia City Paper (Local news; Circulation 94,000); Philadelphia Daily News (Local news; Circulation 112,601); The Philadelphia Inquirer - Bucks County Bureau; The Philadelphia Inquirer

(Local news; Circulation 688,670); Philadelphia New Observer (Local news; Circulation 80,000); The Philadelphia Public Record (Local news; Circulation 39,000); Philadelphia Sunday Sun (Local news); The Philadelphia Tribune (Local news; Circulation 20,545); Philadelphia Weekly (Local news; Circulation 135,000); The Review (Local news; Circulation 1,100); South Philadelphia Review (Community news; Circulation 72,000); South Philadelphia Review (Community news; Circulation 26,550); University City Review (Community news); Weekend - The Philadelphia Inquirer (Regional news); The Weekly Press (Community news)

Transportation: Commute to work: 60.1% car, 26.2% public transportation, 8.4% walk, 2.6% work from home (2006-2010 5-year est.); Travel time to work: 16.1% less than 15 minutes, 32.7% 15 to 30 minutes, 26.9% 30 to 45 minutes, 11.8% 45 to 60 minutes, 12.5% 60 minutes or more (2006-2010 5-year est.); Amtrak: train service available.

Airports: Northeast Philadelphia (general aviation); Penn's Landing (general aviation); Philadelphia International (primary service/large hub)

Additional Information Contacts
City of Philadelphia . . . . (215) 686-1776
   http://www.phila.gov
Greater Philadelphia Chamber of Commerce . . . . (215) 545-1234
   http://www.greaterphilachamber.com

Pike County

Located in northeastern Pennsylvania; bounded on the east by the Delaware River and the New Jersey border. Covers a land area of 544.961 square miles, a water area of 21.889 square miles, and is located in the Eastern Time Zone at 41.33° N. Lat., 75.03° W. Long. The county was founded in 1814. County seat is Milford.

Pike County is part of the New York-Northern New Jersey-Long Island, NY-NJ-PA Metropolitan Statistical Area. The entire metro area includes: Edison-New Brunswick, NJ Metropolitan Division (Middlesex County, NJ; Monmouth County, NJ; Ocean County, NJ; Somerset County, NJ); Nassau-Suffolk, NY Metropolitan Division (Nassau County, NY; Suffolk County, NY); New York-White Plains-Wayne, NY-NJ Metropolitan Division (Bergen County, NJ; Hudson County, NJ; Passaic County, NJ; Bronx County, NY; Kings County, NY; New York County, NY; Putnam County, NY; Queens County, NY; Richmond County, NY; Rockland County, NY; Westchester County, NY); Newark-Union, NJ-PA Metropolitan Division (Essex County, NJ; Hunterdon County, NJ; Morris County, NJ; Sussex County, NJ; Union County, NJ; Pike County, PA)

Weather Station: Hawley 1 E   Elevation: 890 feet

	Jan	Feb	Mar	Apr	May	Jun	Jul	Aug	Sep	Oct	Nov	Dec
High	33	36	45	57	69	76	80	79	72	61	50	37
Low	13	15	23	33	43	52	57	56	48	36	29	19
Precip	2.9	2.6	3.1	3.8	3.8	4.4	3.8	3.5	4.0	3.6	3.4	3.1
Snow	12.2	9.6	8.1	2.4	0.0	0.0	0.0	0.0	0.0	tr	1.5	10.0

High and Low temperatures in degrees Fahrenheit; Precipitation and Snow in inches

Weather Station: Matamoras   Elevation: 419 feet

	Jan	Feb	Mar	Apr	May	Jun	Jul	Aug	Sep	Oct	Nov	Dec
High	35	39	47	60	71	78	82	81	74	62	51	39
Low	16	18	25	35	45	54	59	58	51	39	31	22
Precip	2.9	2.7	3.5	3.9	3.8	4.6	4.0	3.8	4.6	4.1	3.4	3.6
Snow	11.0	7.9	7.3	1.7	tr	0.0	0.0	0.0	0.0	tr	1.2	8.1

High and Low temperatures in degrees Fahrenheit; Precipitation and Snow in inches

Population: 28,007 (1990); 46,302 (2000); 57,369 (2010); Race: 88.6% White, 5.8% Black, 1.0% Asian, 0.3% American Indian/Alaska Native, 0.0% Native Hawaiian/Other Pacific Islander, 4.3% Other, 9.0% Hispanic of any race (2010); Density: 105.3 persons per square mile (2010); Average household size: 2.59 (2010); Median age: 43.7 (2010); Males per 100 females: 100.0 (2010).

Religion: Six largest groups: 21.8% Catholicism, 3.5% Methodist/Pietist, 2.1% Lutheran, 1.6% Non-Denominational, 0.6% Presbyterian-Reformed, 0.4% Episcopalianism/Anglicanism (2010)

Economy: Unemployment rate: 9.7% (August 2012); Total civilian labor force: 26,746 (August 2012); Leading industries: 24.9% retail trade; 22.4% accommodation & food services; 12.2% other services (except public administration) (2010); Farms: 54 totaling 27,569 acres (2007); Companies that employ 500 or more persons: 1 (2010); Companies that employ 100 to 499 persons: 10 (2010); Companies that employ less than 100 persons: 876 (2010); Black-owned businesses: 227 (2007); Hispanic-owned

businesses: 143 (2007); Asian-owned businesses: n/a (2007); Women-owned businesses: 1,255 (2007); Retail sales per capita: $6,197 (2010). Single-family building permits issued: 102 (2011); Multi-family building permits issued: 6 (2011).

Income: Per capita income: $27,564 (2006-2010 5-year est.); Median household income: $56,843 (2006-2010 5-year est.); Average household income: $70,510 (2006-2010 5-year est.); Percent of households with income of $100,000 or more: 17.9% (2006-2010 5-year est.); Poverty rate: 8.7% (2006-2010 5-year est.); Bankruptcy rate: 6.10% (2011).

Education: Percent of population age 25 and over with: High school diploma (including GED) or higher: 91.5% (2006-2010 5-year est.); Bachelor's degree or higher: 23.3% (2006-2010 5-year est.); Master's degree or higher: 7.9% (2006-2010 5-year est.).

Housing: Homeownership rate: 85.8% (2010); Median home value: $217,900 (2006-2010 5-year est.); Median contract rent: $811 per month (2006-2010 5-year est.); Median year structure built: 1983 (2006-2010 5-year est.)

Health: Birth rate: 83.2 per 10,000 population (2011); Death rate: 74.1 per 10,000 population (2011); Age-adjusted cancer mortality rate: 162.4 deaths per 100,000 population (2009); Number of physicians: 8.2 per 10,000 population (2010); Hospital beds: 0.0 per 10,000 population (2008); Hospital admissions: 0.0 per 10,000 population (2008).

Elections: 2012 Presidential election results: 43.8% Obama, 54.9% Romney

National and State Parks: Delaware Water Gap National Recreation Area; George W Childs State Park; Promised Land State Park

Additional Information Contacts
Pike County Government . . . . (570) 296-7613
   http://www.pikepa.org
Pike County Chamber of Commerce. . . . . (570) 296-8700
   http://www.pikechamber.com

Pike County Communities

BIRCHWOOD LAKES (CDP). Covers a land area of 1.247 square miles and a water area of 0.201 square miles. Located at 41.25° N. Lat; 74.91° W. Long. Elevation is 1,129 feet.

Population: n/a (1990); n/a (2000); 1,386 (2010); Density: 1,111.6 persons per square mile (2010); Race: 96.3% White, 1.5% Black, 0.4% Asian, 0.0% American Indian/Alaska Native, 0.0% Native Hawaiian/Other Pacific Islander, 1.8% Other, 6.0% Hispanic of any race (2010); Average household size: 2.62 (2010); Median age: 39.4 (2010); Males per 100 females: 98.9 (2010); Marriage status: 31.5% never married, 55.1% now married, 2.2% widowed, 11.3% divorced (2006-2010 5-year est.); Foreign born: 2.5% (2006-2010 5-year est.); Ancestry (includes multiple ancestries): 35.8% German, 30.7% Italian, 21.8% Irish, 11.0% American, 6.0% Polish (2006-2010 5-year est.).

Economy: Employment by occupation: 3.0% management, 3.1% professional, 18.3% services, 26.6% sales, 0.0% farming, 15.1% construction, 15.5% production (2006-2010 5-year est.).

Income: Per capita income: $18,738 (2006-2010 5-year est.); Median household income: $43,813 (2006-2010 5-year est.); Average household income: $50,399 (2006-2010 5-year est.); Percent of households with income of $100,000 or more: 8.7% (2006-2010 5-year est.); Poverty rate: 6.7% (2006-2010 5-year est.).

Education: Percent of population age 25 and over with: High school diploma (including GED) or higher: 93.0% (2006-2010 5-year est.); Bachelor's degree or higher: 1.3% (2006-2010 5-year est.); Master's degree or higher: 0.0% (2006-2010 5-year est.).

Housing: Homeownership rate: 88.5% (2010); Median home value: $152,300 (2006-2010 5-year est.); Median contract rent: $854 per month (2006-2010 5-year est.); Median year structure built: 1975 (2006-2010 5-year est.).

Transportation: Commute to work: 92.9% car, 4.9% public transportation, 0.0% walk, 2.3% work from home (2006-2010 5-year est.); Travel time to work: 26.5% less than 15 minutes, 10.6% 15 to 30 minutes, 17.3% 30 to 45 minutes, 12.9% 45 to 60 minutes, 32.8% 60 minutes or more (2006-2010 5-year est.)

BLOOMING GROVE (township). Covers a land area of 74.831 square miles and a water area of 2.156 square miles. Located at 41.36° N. Lat; 75.10° W. Long. Elevation is 1,437 feet.

Population: 2,022 (1990); 3,621 (2000); 4,819 (2010); Density: 64.4 persons per square mile (2010); Race: 91.8% White, 3.5% Black, 1.1% Asian, 0.2% American Indian/Alaska Native, 0.0% Native Hawaiian/Other

Pacific Islander, 3.4% Other, 5.4% Hispanic of any race (2010); Average household size: 2.44 (2010); Median age: 47.5 (2010); Males per 100 females: 112.3 (2010); Marriage status: 21.9% never married, 61.4% now married, 8.8% widowed, 7.8% divorced (2006-2010 5-year est.); Foreign born: 10.9% (2006-2010 5-year est.); Ancestry (includes multiple ancestries): 27.2% German, 21.8% Irish, 16.3% Italian, 12.2% Polish, 8.0% English (2006-2010 5-year est.).

Economy: Single-family building permits issued: 5 (2011); Multi-family building permits issued: 0 (2011); Employment by occupation: 12.0% management, 7.1% professional, 15.2% services, 9.8% sales, 2.3% farming, 11.8% construction, 7.4% production (2006-2010 5-year est.).

Income: Per capita income: $27,510 (2006-2010 5-year est.); Median household income: $50,119 (2006-2010 5-year est.); Average household income: $68,018 (2006-2010 5-year est.); Percent of households with income of $100,000 or more: 16.2% (2006-2010 5-year est.); Poverty rate: 8.8% (2006-2010 5-year est.).

Education: Percent of population age 25 and over with: High school diploma (including GED) or higher: 88.3% (2006-2010 5-year est.); Bachelor's degree or higher: 27.6% (2006-2010 5-year est.); Master's degree or higher: 10.4% (2006-2010 5-year est.).

Housing: Homeownership rate: 87.5% (2010); Median home value: $248,000 (2006-2010 5-year est.); Median contract rent: $855 per month (2006-2010 5-year est.); Median year structure built: 1980 (2006-2010 5-year est.).

Transportation: Commute to work: 85.1% car, 3.2% public transportation, 2.6% walk, 6.6% work from home (2006-2010 5-year est.); Travel time to work: 34.7% less than 15 minutes, 27.8% 15 to 30 minutes, 13.6% 30 to 45 minutes, 4.9% 45 to 60 minutes, 18.9% 60 minutes or more (2006-2010 5-year est.).

Additional Information Contacts
Blooming Grove Township . . . . (570) 775-6461
  http://www.bloominggrovetownship.com
Pike County Chamber of Commerce. . . . . (570) 296-8700
  http://www.pikechamber.com

CONASHAUGH LAKES (CDP). Covers a land area of 2.617 square miles and a water area of 0.081 square miles. Located at 41.30° N. Lat; 74.99° W. Long.

Population: n/a (1990); n/a (2000); 1,294 (2010); Density: 494.5 persons per square mile (2010); Race: 84.3% White, 8.0% Black, 1.4% Asian, 1.1% American Indian/Alaska Native, 0.4% Native Hawaiian/Other Pacific Islander, 4.8% Other, 11.4% Hispanic of any race (2010); Average household size: 3.09 (2010); Median age: 38.5 (2010); Males per 100 females: 95.5 (2010); Marriage status: 32.4% never married, 57.8% now married, 1.6% widowed, 8.2% divorced (2006-2010 5-year est.); Foreign born: 28.2% (2006-2010 5-year est.); Ancestry (includes multiple ancestries): 10.1% Irish, 10.1% American, 9.1% Italian, 7.7% Polish, 5.5% German (2006-2010 5-year est.).

Economy: Employment by occupation: 4.7% management, 0.0% professional, 7.3% services, 23.0% sales, 14.7% farming, 2.4% construction, 14.4% production (2006-2010 5-year est.).

Income: Per capita income: $28,313 (2006-2010 5-year est.); Median household income: $63,066 (2006-2010 5-year est.); Average household income: $81,092 (2006-2010 5-year est.); Percent of households with income of $100,000 or more: 19.5% (2006-2010 5-year est.); Poverty rate: 1.6% (2006-2010 5-year est.).

Education: Percent of population age 25 and over with: High school diploma (including GED) or higher: 92.2% (2006-2010 5-year est.); Bachelor's degree or higher: 33.1% (2006-2010 5-year est.); Master's degree or higher: 15.9% (2006-2010 5-year est.).

Housing: Homeownership rate: 96.2% (2010); Median home value: $241,400 (2006-2010 5-year est.); Median contract rent: n/a per month (2006-2010 5-year est.); Median year structure built: 2000 (2006-2010 5-year est.).

Transportation: Commute to work: 88.5% car, 0.0% public transportation, 11.5% walk, 0.0% work from home (2006-2010 5-year est.); Travel time to work: 9.9% less than 15 minutes, 23.3% 15 to 30 minutes, 13.6% 30 to 45 minutes, 14.9% 45 to 60 minutes, 38.2% 60 minutes or more (2006-2010 5-year est.)

DELAWARE (township). Covers a land area of 43.716 square miles and a water area of 1.759 square miles. Located at 41.24° N. Lat; 74.93° W. Long. Elevation is 354 feet.

Population: 3,527 (1990); 6,319 (2000); 7,396 (2010); Density: 169.2 persons per square mile (2010); Race: 94.0% White, 2.9% Black, 0.7%

Asian, 0.1% American Indian/Alaska Native, 0.0% Native Hawaiian/Other Pacific Islander, 2.3% Other, 7.0% Hispanic of any race (2010); Average household size: 2.66 (2010); Median age: 41.2 (2010); Males per 100 females: 102.1 (2010); Marriage status: 24.3% never married, 57.4% now married, 5.9% widowed, 12.3% divorced (2006-2010 5-year est.); Foreign born: 7.3% (2006-2010 5-year est.); Ancestry (includes multiple ancestries): 29.8% Italian, 25.6% German, 21.0% Irish, 7.8% English, 6.3% Polish (2006-2010 5-year est.).

Economy: Single-family building permits issued: 3 (2011); Multi-family building permits issued: 0 (2011); Employment by occupation: 5.6% management, 4.3% professional, 11.4% services, 19.0% sales, 2.9% farming, 14.8% construction, 10.1% production (2006-2010 5-year est.).

Income: Per capita income: $23,108 (2006-2010 5-year est.); Median household income: $56,721 (2006-2010 5-year est.); Average household income: $60,897 (2006-2010 5-year est.); Percent of households with income of $100,000 or more: 12.9% (2006-2010 5-year est.); Poverty rate: 8.1% (2006-2010 5-year est.).

Education: Percent of population age 25 and over with: High school diploma (including GED) or higher: 92.4% (2006-2010 5-year est.); Bachelor's degree or higher: 16.2% (2006-2010 5-year est.); Master's degree or higher: 2.4% (2006-2010 5-year est.).

Housing: Homeownership rate: 89.8% (2010); Median home value: $184,200 (2006-2010 5-year est.); Median contract rent: $908 per month (2006-2010 5-year est.); Median year structure built: 1981 (2006-2010 5-year est.).

Transportation: Commute to work: 91.2% car, 2.0% public transportation, 2.5% walk, 4.0% work from home (2006-2010 5-year est.); Travel time to work: 19.2% less than 15 minutes, 19.1% 15 to 30 minutes, 17.3% 30 to 45 minutes, 12.6% 45 to 60 minutes, 31.8% 60 minutes or more (2006-2010 5-year est.)

Additional Information Contacts
Delaware Township. . . . . (570) 828-2347
  http://www.delawaretownshippa.gov
Pike County Chamber of Commerce. . . . . (570) 296-8700
  http://www.pikechamber.com

DINGMAN (township). Covers a land area of 58.188 square miles and a water area of 1.862 square miles. Located at 41.32° N. Lat; 74.93° W. Long.

Population: 4,591 (1990); 8,788 (2000); 11,926 (2010); Density: 205.0 persons per square mile (2010); Race: 91.7% White, 3.4% Black, 0.8% Asian, 0.3% American Indian/Alaska Native, 0.1% Native Hawaiian/Other Pacific Islander, 3.7% Other, 8.8% Hispanic of any race (2010); Average household size: 2.85 (2010); Median age: 41.1 (2010); Males per 100 females: 99.8 (2010); Marriage status: 23.9% never married, 61.1% now married, 5.3% widowed, 9.7% divorced (2006-2010 5-year est.); Foreign born: 5.0% (2006-2010 5-year est.); Ancestry (includes multiple ancestries): 25.0% Italian, 23.6% German, 22.9% Irish, 12.2% English, 10.3% Polish (2006-2010 5-year est.).

Economy: Single-family building permits issued: 22 (2011); Multi-family building permits issued: 0 (2011); Employment by occupation: 11.8% management, 2.4% professional, 12.9% services, 16.3% sales, 5.4% farming, 10.8% construction, 6.9% production (2006-2010 5-year est.).

Income: Per capita income: $28,709 (2006-2010 5-year est.); Median household income: $69,239 (2006-2010 5-year est.); Average household income: $80,143 (2006-2010 5-year est.); Percent of households with income of $100,000 or more: 25.4% (2006-2010 5-year est.); Poverty rate: 7.2% (2006-2010 5-year est.).

Education: Percent of population age 25 and over with: High school diploma (including GED) or higher: 93.8% (2006-2010 5-year est.); Bachelor's degree or higher: 25.6% (2006-2010 5-year est.); Master's degree or higher: 8.1% (2006-2010 5-year est.).

Housing: Homeownership rate: 92.1% (2010); Median home value: $250,800 (2006-2010 5-year est.); Median contract rent: $1,051 per month (2006-2010 5-year est.); Median year structure built: 1988 (2006-2010 5-year est.).

Transportation: Commute to work: 92.8% car, 1.5% public transportation, 1.8% walk, 3.8% work from home (2006-2010 5-year est.); Travel time to work: 20.4% less than 15 minutes, 18.6% 15 to 30 minutes, 16.4% 30 to 45 minutes, 12.0% 45 to 60 minutes, 32.6% 60 minutes or more (2006-2010 5-year est.)

Additional Information Contacts
Dingman Township . . . . (570) 296-8455
  http://www.angelfire.com/pa5/dingmantownship

Pike County Chamber of Commerce.................. (570) 296-8700
http://www.pikechamber.com

DINGMANS FERRY (unincorporated postal area)

Zip Code: 18328

Covers a land area of 83.289 square miles and a water area of 3.472 square miles. Located at 41.22° N. Lat; 74.97° W. Long. Population: 7,759 (2010); Density: 93.2 persons per square mile (2010); Race: 93.6% White, 3.1% Black, 0.8% Asian, 0.1% American Indian/Alaska Native, 0.0% Native Hawaiian/Other Pacific Islander, 2.4% Other, 7.4% Hispanic of any race (2010); Average household size: 2.64 (2010); Median age: 41.1 (2010); Males per 100 females: 102.7 (2010); Homeownership rate: 89.7% (2010)

FAWN LAKE FOREST (CDP). Covers a land area of 2.552 square miles and a water area of 0.433 square miles. Located at 41.52° N. Lat; 75.05° W. Long. Elevation is 1,293 feet.

Population: n/a (1990); n/a (2000); 755 (2010); Density: 295.8 persons per square mile (2010); Race: 93.4% White, 4.2% Black, 0.5% Asian, 0.1% American Indian/Alaska Native, 0.0% Native Hawaiian/Other Pacific Islander, 1.8% Other, 3.3% Hispanic of any race (2010); Average household size: 2.30 (2010); Median age: 53.6 (2010); Males per 100 females: 109.1 (2010); Marriage status: 17.9% never married, 69.5% now married, 4.2% widowed, 8.4% divorced (2006-2010 5-year est.); Foreign born: 6.4% (2006-2010 5-year est.); Ancestry (includes multiple ancestries): 28.9% Italian, 24.6% German, 24.2% Irish, 15.9% Polish, 5.8% Russian (2006-2010 5-year est.).
Economy: Employment by occupation: 10.3% management, 12.1% professional, 6.4% services, 23.4% sales, 0.0% farming, 18.8% construction, 5.0% production (2006-2010 5-year est.).
Income: Per capita income: $29,869 (2006-2010 5-year est.); Median household income: $46,875 (2006-2010 5-year est.); Average household income: $58,402 (2006-2010 5-year est.); Percent of households with income of $100,000 or more: 5.1% (2006-2010 5-year est.); Poverty rate: 3.6% (2006-2010 5-year est.).
Education: Percent of population age 25 and over with: High school diploma (including GED) or higher: 84.3% (2006-2010 5-year est.); Bachelor's degree or higher: 14.5% (2006-2010 5-year est.); Master's degree or higher: 7.0% (2006-2010 5-year est.).
Housing: Homeownership rate: 91.8% (2010); Median home value: $202,500 (2006-2010 5-year est.); Median contract rent: $876 per month (2006-2010 5-year est.); Median year structure built: 1983 (2006-2010 5-year est.).
Transportation: Commute to work: 74.3% car, 13.1% public transportation, 3.4% walk, 9.3% work from home (2006-2010 5-year est.); Travel time to work: 25.9% less than 15 minutes, 38.7% 15 to 30 minutes, 0.0% 30 to 45 minutes, 7.8% 45 to 60 minutes, 27.6% 60 minutes or more (2006-2010 5-year est.)

GOLD KEY LAKE (CDP). Covers a land area of 2.277 square miles and a water area of 0.254 square miles. Located at 41.31° N. Lat; 74.94° W. Long. Elevation is 1,375 feet.

Population: n/a (1990); n/a (2000); 1,830 (2010); Density: 803.8 persons per square mile (2010); Race: 93.2% White, 3.9% Black, 0.4% Asian, 0.4% American Indian/Alaska Native, 0.2% Native Hawaiian/Other Pacific Islander, 1.9% Other, 10.4% Hispanic of any race (2010); Average household size: 2.75 (2010); Median age: 39.0 (2010); Males per 100 females: 100.4 (2010); Marriage status: 32.6% never married, 56.3% now married, 2.9% widowed, 8.2% divorced (2006-2010 5-year est.); Foreign born: 2.9% (2006-2010 5-year est.); Ancestry (includes multiple ancestries): 38.0% Italian, 23.6% Irish, 21.4% German, 17.9% English, 8.9% Dutch (2006-2010 5-year est.).
Economy: Employment by occupation: 7.6% management, 0.0% professional, 21.9% services, 15.7% sales, 2.5% farming, 12.2% construction, 7.1% production (2006-2010 5-year est.).
Income: Per capita income: $24,858 (2006-2010 5-year est.); Median household income: $66,591 (2006-2010 5-year est.); Average household income: $82,355 (2006-2010 5-year est.); Percent of households with income of $100,000 or more: 20.4% (2006-2010 5-year est.); Poverty rate: 10.1% (2006-2010 5-year est.).
Education: Percent of population age 25 and over with: High school diploma (including GED) or higher: 82.6% (2006-2010 5-year est.); Bachelor's degree or higher: 19.3% (2006-2010 5-year est.); Master's degree or higher: 4.1% (2006-2010 5-year est.).

Housing: Homeownership rate: 93.3% (2010); Median home value: $188,400 (2006-2010 5-year est.); Median contract rent: n/a per month (2006-2010 5-year est.); Median year structure built: 1982 (2006-2010 5-year est.).
Transportation: Commute to work: 92.9% car, 2.0% public transportation, 2.6% walk, 1.7% work from home (2006-2010 5-year est.); Travel time to work: 27.4% less than 15 minutes, 15.9% 15 to 30 minutes, 11.5% 30 to 45 minutes, 10.3% 45 to 60 minutes, 35.0% 60 minutes or more (2006-2010 5-year est.)

GREELEY (unincorporated postal area)

Zip Code: 18425

Covers a land area of 22.462 square miles and a water area of 0.554 square miles. Located at 41.43° N. Lat; 75.04° W. Long. Elevation is 1,102 feet. Population: 1,354 (2010); Density: 60.3 persons per square mile (2010); Race: 93.6% White, 1.9% Black, 0.4% Asian, 0.3% American Indian/Alaska Native, 0.0% Native Hawaiian/Other Pacific Islander, 3.8% Other, 4.9% Hispanic of any race (2010); Average household size: 2.50 (2010); Median age: 44.5 (2010); Males per 100 females: 102.4 (2010); Homeownership rate: 81.0% (2010)

GREENE (township). Covers a land area of 59.862 square miles and a water area of 2.184 square miles. Located at 41.30° N. Lat; 75.25° W. Long.

Population: 2,097 (1990); 3,149 (2000); 3,956 (2010); Density: 66.1 persons per square mile (2010); Race: 96.0% White, 1.0% Black, 0.3% Asian, 0.4% American Indian/Alaska Native, 0.0% Native Hawaiian/Other Pacific Islander, 2.3% Other, 3.9% Hispanic of any race (2010); Average household size: 2.42 (2010); Median age: 46.4 (2010); Males per 100 females: 98.4 (2010); Marriage status: 27.1% never married, 59.3% now married, 4.3% widowed, 9.3% divorced (2006-2010 5-year est.); Foreign born: 4.4% (2006-2010 5-year est.); Ancestry (includes multiple ancestries): 30.1% German, 20.5% Irish, 16.3% Italian, 8.5% English, 8.0% Polish (2006-2010 5-year est.).
Economy: Single-family building permits issued: 6 (2011); Multi-family building permits issued: 0 (2011); Employment by occupation: 11.7% management, 2.9% professional, 11.4% services, 21.7% sales, 2.7% farming, 19.7% construction, 7.4% production (2006-2010 5-year est.).
Income: Per capita income: $26,534 (2006-2010 5-year est.); Median household income: $42,369 (2006-2010 5-year est.); Average household income: $69,313 (2006-2010 5-year est.); Percent of households with income of $100,000 or more: 18.1% (2006-2010 5-year est.); Poverty rate: 17.0% (2006-2010 5-year est.).
Education: Percent of population age 25 and over with: High school diploma (including GED) or higher: 85.7% (2006-2010 5-year est.); Bachelor's degree or higher: 16.5% (2006-2010 5-year est.); Master's degree or higher: 6.9% (2006-2010 5-year est.).
Housing: Homeownership rate: 85.6% (2010); Median home value: $193,900 (2006-2010 5-year est.); Median contract rent: $597 per month (2006-2010 5-year est.); Median year structure built: 1980 (2006-2010 5-year est.).
Transportation: Commute to work: 87.0% car, 1.6% public transportation, 4.5% walk, 4.7% work from home (2006-2010 5-year est.); Travel time to work: 30.8% less than 15 minutes, 30.0% 15 to 30 minutes, 22.4% 30 to 45 minutes, 6.0% 45 to 60 minutes, 10.8% 60 minutes or more (2006-2010 5-year est.)

Additional Information Contacts

Pike County Chamber of Commerce.................. (570) 296-8700
http://www.pikechamber.com

GREENTOWN (unincorporated postal area)

Zip Code: 18426

Covers a land area of 59.133 square miles and a water area of 3.009 square miles. Located at 41.32° N. Lat; 75.23° W. Long. Population: 4,526 (2010); Density: 76.5 persons per square mile (2010); Race: 96.2% White, 1.1% Black, 0.4% Asian, 0.4% American Indian/Alaska Native, 0.0% Native Hawaiian/Other Pacific Islander, 1.9% Other, 3.9% Hispanic of any race (2010); Average household size: 2.38 (2010); Median age: 47.5 (2010); Males per 100 females: 98.3 (2010); Homeownership rate: 85.0% (2010)

HEMLOCK FARMS (CDP). Covers a land area of 7.706 square miles and a water area of 0.447 square miles. Located at 41.32° N. Lat; 75.05° W. Long. Elevation is 1,355 feet.

Population: n/a (1990); n/a (2000); 3,271 (2010); Density: 424.5 persons per square mile (2010); Race: 93.5% White, 2.2% Black, 1.0% Asian, 0.1% American Indian/Alaska Native, 0.0% Native Hawaiian/Other Pacific Islander, 3.2% Other, 5.4% Hispanic of any race (2010); Average household size: 2.42 (2010); Median age: 52.3 (2010); Males per 100 females: 97.5 (2010); Marriage status: 15.4% never married, 66.7% now married, 9.3% widowed, 8.6% divorced (2006-2010 5-year est.); Foreign born: 7.5% (2006-2010 5-year est.); Ancestry (includes multiple ancestries): 25.6% Italian, 25.6% Irish, 20.7% German, 15.9% Polish, 7.0% Russian (2006-2010 5-year est.).

Economy: Employment by occupation: 10.1% management, 5.5% professional, 19.5% services, 12.4% sales, 2.8% farming, 10.6% construction, 5.4% production (2006-2010 5-year est.).

Income: Per capita income: $29,672 (2006-2010 5-year est.); Median household income: $52,931 (2006-2010 5-year est.); Average household income: $69,889 (2006-2010 5-year est.); Percent of households with income of $100,000 or more: 15.6% (2006-2010 5-year est.); Poverty rate: 8.0% (2006-2010 5-year est.).

Education: Percent of population age 25 and over with: High school diploma (including GED) or higher: 96.8% (2006-2010 5-year est.); Bachelor's degree or higher: 28.5% (2006-2010 5-year est.); Master's degree or higher: 12.4% (2006-2010 5-year est.).

Housing: Homeownership rate: 90.8% (2010); Median home value: $241,900 (2006-2010 5-year est.); Median contract rent: $887 per month (2006-2010 5-year est.); Median year structure built: 1980 (2006-2010 5-year est.).

Transportation: Commute to work: 91.0% car, 1.9% public transportation, 1.1% walk, 2.0% work from home (2006-2010 5-year est.); Travel time to work: 40.3% less than 15 minutes, 29.4% 15 to 30 minutes, 16.3% 30 to 45 minutes, 2.7% 45 to 60 minutes, 11.3% 60 minutes or more (2006-2010 5-year est.).

LACKAWAXEN (township). Covers a land area of 78.441 square miles and a water area of 2.800 square miles. Located at 41.49° N. Lat; 75.07° W. Long. Elevation is 633 feet.

Population: 2,832 (1990); 4,154 (2000); 4,994 (2010); Density: 63.7 persons per square mile (2010); Race: 94.2% White, 2.7% Black, 0.6% Asian, 0.2% American Indian/Alaska Native, 0.1% Native Hawaiian/Other Pacific Islander, 2.2% Other, 4.2% Hispanic of any race (2010); Average household size: 2.38 (2010); Median age: 48.8 (2010); Males per 100 females: 101.2 (2010); Marriage status: 22.8% never married, 63.7% now married, 5.0% widowed, 8.5% divorced (2006-2010 5-year est.); Foreign born: 5.1% (2006-2010 5-year est.); Ancestry (includes multiple ancestries): 27.5% Italian, 26.0% German, 24.7% Irish, 11.8% Polish, 9.6% English (2006-2010 5-year est.).

Economy: Single-family building permits issued: 36 (2011); Multi-family building permits issued: 0 (2011); Employment by occupation: 12.5% management, 2.9% professional, 10.4% services, 12.2% sales, 3.2% farming, 18.6% construction, 10.8% production (2006-2010 5-year est.).

Income: Per capita income: $28,410 (2006-2010 5-year est.); Median household income: $47,642 (2006-2010 5-year est.); Average household income: $65,161 (2006-2010 5-year est.); Percent of households with income of $100,000 or more: 15.6% (2006-2010 5-year est.); Poverty rate: 7.2% (2006-2010 5-year est.).

Education: Percent of population age 25 and over with: High school diploma (including GED) or higher: 89.7% (2006-2010 5-year est.); Bachelor's degree or higher: 19.6% (2006-2010 5-year est.); Master's degree or higher: 8.5% (2006-2010 5-year est.).

Housing: Homeownership rate: 85.7% (2010); Median home value: $205,000 (2006-2010 5-year est.); Median contract rent: $830 per month (2006-2010 5-year est.); Median year structure built: 1983 (2006-2010 5-year est.).

Transportation: Commute to work: 82.8% car, 2.9% public transportation, 4.7% walk, 9.3% work from home (2006-2010 5-year est.); Travel time to work: 28.8% less than 15 minutes, 37.8% 15 to 30 minutes, 12.6% 30 to 45 minutes, 5.3% 45 to 60 minutes, 15.5% 60 minutes or more (2006-2010 5-year est.).

Additional Information Contacts

Lackawaxen Township . . . . (570) 685-7288
  http://www.lackawaxen.org
Pike County Chamber of Commerce. . . . . (570) 296-8700
  http://www.pikechamber.com

LEHMAN (township). Covers a land area of 48.941 square miles and a water area of 1.437 square miles. Located at 41.15° N. Lat; 74.99° W. Long.

Population: 3,096 (1990); 7,515 (2000); 10,663 (2010); Density: 217.9 persons per square mile (2010); Race: 66.2% White, 20.7% Black, 2.1% Asian, 0.5% American Indian/Alaska Native, 0.0% Native Hawaiian/Other Pacific Islander, 10.5% Other, 22.0% Hispanic of any race (2010); Average household size: 2.94 (2010); Median age: 38.5 (2010); Males per 100 females: 98.0 (2010); Marriage status: 24.3% never married, 58.8% now married, 5.4% widowed, 11.5% divorced (2006-2010 5-year est.); Foreign born: 7.9% (2006-2010 5-year est.); Ancestry (includes multiple ancestries): 18.7% Italian, 14.3% German, 13.6% Irish, 4.4% English, 3.7% American (2006-2010 5-year est.).

Economy: Single-family building permits issued: 9 (2011); Multi-family building permits issued: 0 (2011); Employment by occupation: 14.5% management, 3.8% professional, 12.7% services, 16.3% sales, 5.9% farming, 9.7% construction, 9.4% production (2006-2010 5-year est.).

Income: Per capita income: $23,822 (2006-2010 5-year est.); Median household income: $55,744 (2006-2010 5-year est.); Average household income: $64,981 (2006-2010 5-year est.); Percent of households with income of $100,000 or more: 9.5% (2006-2010 5-year est.); Poverty rate: 11.3% (2006-2010 5-year est.).

Education: Percent of population age 25 and over with: High school diploma (including GED) or higher: 90.4% (2006-2010 5-year est.); Bachelor's degree or higher: 21.4% (2006-2010 5-year est.); Master's degree or higher: 6.2% (2006-2010 5-year est.).

Housing: Homeownership rate: 87.3% (2010); Median home value: $175,500 (2006-2010 5-year est.); Median contract rent: $841 per month (2006-2010 5-year est.); Median year structure built: 1988 (2006-2010 5-year est.).

Transportation: Commute to work: 91.3% car, 6.4% public transportation, 0.0% walk, 2.1% work from home (2006-2010 5-year est.); Travel time to work: 6.6% less than 15 minutes, 20.2% 15 to 30 minutes, 21.0% 30 to 45 minutes, 8.0% 45 to 60 minutes, 44.2% 60 minutes or more (2006-2010 5-year est.)

Additional Information Contacts

Lehman Township . . . . (570) 588-9365
  http://lehmantownship.com
Pike County Chamber of Commerce. . . . . (570) 296-8700
  http://www.pikechamber.com

MASTHOPE (CDP). Covers a land area of 5.230 square miles and a water area of 0.225 square miles. Located at 41.52° N. Lat; 75.03° W. Long. Elevation is 692 feet.

Population: n/a (1990); n/a (2000); 685 (2010); Density: 131.0 persons per square mile (2010); Race: 92.7% White, 4.8% Black, 0.3% Asian, 0.7% American Indian/Alaska Native, 0.1% Native Hawaiian/Other Pacific Islander, 1.4% Other, 8.8% Hispanic of any race (2010); Average household size: 2.38 (2010); Median age: 51.0 (2010); Males per 100 females: 105.1 (2010); Marriage status: 51.0% never married, 38.6% now married, 3.7% widowed, 6.7% divorced (2006-2010 5-year est.); Foreign born: 7.1% (2006-2010 5-year est.); Ancestry (includes multiple ancestries): 46.5% Italian, 21.8% Irish, 17.4% English, 12.3% German, 5.9% Canadian (2006-2010 5-year est.).

Economy: Employment by occupation: 4.7% management, 6.1% professional, 17.3% services, 0.0% sales, 0.0% farming, 31.8% construction, 7.0% production (2006-2010 5-year est.).

Income: Per capita income: $21,082 (2006-2010 5-year est.); Median household income: $51,667 (2006-2010 5-year est.); Average household income: $55,685 (2006-2010 5-year est.); Percent of households with income of $100,000 or more: 11.1% (2006-2010 5-year est.); Poverty rate: 0.0% (2006-2010 5-year est.).

Education: Percent of population age 25 and over with: High school diploma (including GED) or higher: 100.0% (2006-2010 5-year est.); Bachelor's degree or higher: 39.3% (2006-2010 5-year est.); Master's degree or higher: 19.2% (2006-2010 5-year est.).

Housing: Homeownership rate: 91.0% (2010); Median home value: $148,100 (2006-2010 5-year est.); Median contract rent: $832 per month (2006-2010 5-year est.); Median year structure built: 1986 (2006-2010 5-year est.).

Transportation: Commute to work: 87.7% car, 0.0% public transportation, 0.0% walk, 12.3% work from home (2006-2010 5-year est.); Travel time to work: 61.0% less than 15 minutes, 17.7% 15 to 30 minutes, 0.0% 30 to 45 minutes, 6.1% 45 to 60 minutes, 15.2% 60 minutes or more (2006-2010 5-year est.)

MATAMORAS (borough). Covers a land area of 0.684 square miles and a water area of 0.090 square miles. Located at 41.37° N. Lat; 74.70° W. Long. Elevation is 430 feet.

Population: 1,934 (1990); 2,312 (2000); 2,469 (2010); Density: 3,611.5 persons per square mile (2010); Race: 93.3% White, 1.4% Black, 1.8% Asian, 0.3% American Indian/Alaska Native, 0.0% Native Hawaiian/Other Pacific Islander, 3.2% Other, 5.5% Hispanic of any race (2010); Average household size: 2.59 (2010); Median age: 39.1 (2010); Males per 100 females: 90.2 (2010); Marriage status: 27.8% never married, 45.8% now married, 10.2% widowed, 16.2% divorced (2006-2010 5-year est.); Foreign born: 2.9% (2006-2010 5-year est.); Ancestry (includes multiple ancestries): 29.4% Italian, 28.9% Irish, 25.0% German, 11.7% English, 9.1% Ukrainian (2006-2010 5-year est.).

Economy: Single-family building permits issued: 2 (2011); Multi-family building permits issued: 0 (2011); Employment by occupation: 10.1% management, 3.0% professional, 11.1% services, 20.4% sales, 3.2% farming, 9.6% construction, 3.5% production (2006-2010 5-year est.).

Income: Per capita income: $26,113 (2006-2010 5-year est.); Median household income: $50,298 (2006-2010 5-year est.); Average household income: $61,986 (2006-2010 5-year est.); Percent of households with income of $100,000 or more: 19.1% (2006-2010 5-year est.); Poverty rate: 6.7% (2006-2010 5-year est.).

Education: Percent of population age 25 and over with: High school diploma (including GED) or higher: 83.3% (2006-2010 5-year est.); Bachelor's degree or higher: 24.4% (2006-2010 5-year est.); Master's degree or higher: 7.4% (2006-2010 5-year est.).

Housing: Homeownership rate: 68.3% (2010); Median home value: $194,500 (2006-2010 5-year est.); Median contract rent: $709 per month (2006-2010 5-year est.); Median year structure built: 1945 (2006-2010 5-year est.).

Transportation: Commute to work: 91.9% car, 0.0% public transportation, 3.0% walk, 2.8% work from home (2006-2010 5-year est.); Travel time to work: 40.6% less than 15 minutes, 18.3% 15 to 30 minutes, 15.0% 30 to 45 minutes, 8.1% 45 to 60 minutes, 18.0% 60 minutes or more (2006-2010 5-year est.).

Additional Information Contacts

Pike County Chamber of Commerce . . . . (570) 296-8700
    http://www.pikechamber.com

MILFORD (borough). County seat. Covers a land area of 0.469 square miles and a water area of 0.031 square miles. Located at 41.32° N. Lat; 74.80° W. Long. Elevation is 492 feet.

Population: 1,064 (1990); 1,104 (2000); 1,021 (2010); Density: 2,177.3 persons per square mile (2010); Race: 95.2% White, 0.6% Black, 0.5% Asian, 0.5% American Indian/Alaska Native, 0.0% Native Hawaiian/Other Pacific Islander, 3.2% Other, 5.5% Hispanic of any race (2010); Average household size: 2.01 (2010); Median age: 48.3 (2010); Males per 100 females: 87.3 (2010); Marriage status: 30.1% never married, 43.2% now married, 10.9% widowed, 15.8% divorced (2006-2010 5-year est.); Foreign born: 7.5% (2006-2010 5-year est.); Ancestry (includes multiple ancestries): 35.4% Irish, 34.3% German, 17.3% Italian, 13.8% English, 7.3% Polish (2006-2010 5-year est.).

Economy: Single-family building permits issued: 0 (2011); Multi-family building permits issued: 0 (2011); Employment by occupation: 16.0% management, 2.7% professional, 13.6% services, 20.4% sales, 3.3% farming, 8.0% construction, 3.7% production (2006-2010 5-year est.).

Income: Per capita income: $40,228 (2006-2010 5-year est.); Median household income: $40,458 (2006-2010 5-year est.); Average household income: $84,738 (2006-2010 5-year est.); Percent of households with income of $100,000 or more: 25.3% (2006-2010 5-year est.); Poverty rate: 11.1% (2006-2010 5-year est.).

Education: Percent of population age 25 and over with: High school diploma (including GED) or higher: 95.5% (2006-2010 5-year est.); Bachelor's degree or higher: 35.9% (2006-2010 5-year est.); Master's degree or higher: 12.9% (2006-2010 5-year est.).

School District(s)

Delaware Valley SD (PK-12)
    2010-11 Enrollment: 5,327 . . . . (570) 296-1800

Housing: Homeownership rate: 51.3% (2010); Median home value: $377,900 (2006-2010 5-year est.); Median contract rent: $679 per month (2006-2010 5-year est.); Median year structure built: before 1940 (2006-2010 5-year est.).

Safety: Violent crime rate: 9.8 per 10,000 population; Property crime rate: 312.5 per 10,000 population (2011).

Newspapers: Pike County Dispatch (Community news; Circulation 6,700)

Transportation: Commute to work: 80.5% car, 2.3% public transportation, 9.4% walk, 7.8% work from home (2006-2010 5-year est.); Travel time to work: 47.0% less than 15 minutes, 26.1% 15 to 30 minutes, 12.3% 30 to 45 minutes, 3.9% 45 to 60 minutes, 10.7% 60 minutes or more (2006-2010 5-year est.).

Additional Information Contacts

Pike County Chamber of Commerce . . . . (570) 296-8700
    http://www.pikechamber.com

MILFORD (township). Covers a land area of 13.014 square miles and a water area of 0.149 square miles. Located at 41.36° N. Lat; 74.84° W. Long. Elevation is 492 feet.

History: Settled 1733.

Population: 1,036 (1990); 1,292 (2000); 1,530 (2010); Density: 117.6 persons per square mile (2010); Race: 94.6% White, 1.0% Black, 1.6% Asian, 0.5% American Indian/Alaska Native, 0.1% Native Hawaiian/Other Pacific Islander, 2.2% Other, 5.2% Hispanic of any race (2010); Average household size: 2.46 (2010); Median age: 48.4 (2010); Males per 100 females: 95.7 (2010); Marriage status: 20.9% never married, 64.5% now married, 5.7% widowed, 8.9% divorced (2006-2010 5-year est.); Foreign born: 4.2% (2006-2010 5-year est.); Ancestry (includes multiple ancestries): 32.3% German, 28.3% Irish, 21.2% Italian, 10.6% English, 10.6% Polish (2006-2010 5-year est.).

Economy: Single-family building permits issued: 2 (2011); Multi-family building permits issued: 0 (2011); Employment by occupation: 11.8% management, 3.7% professional, 5.8% services, 19.6% sales, 5.5% farming, 9.8% construction, 4.7% production (2006-2010 5-year est.).

Income: Per capita income: $37,111 (2006-2010 5-year est.); Median household income: $79,327 (2006-2010 5-year est.); Average household income: $90,242 (2006-2010 5-year est.); Percent of households with income of $100,000 or more: 34.6% (2006-2010 5-year est.); Poverty rate: 2.4% (2006-2010 5-year est.).

Education: Percent of population age 25 and over with: High school diploma (including GED) or higher: 95.4% (2006-2010 5-year est.); Bachelor's degree or higher: 37.5% (2006-2010 5-year est.); Master's degree or higher: 17.6% (2006-2010 5-year est.).

Housing: Homeownership rate: 81.2% (2010); Median home value: $281,100 (2006-2010 5-year est.); Median contract rent: $816 per month (2006-2010 5-year est.); Median year structure built: 1984 (2006-2010 5-year est.).

Newspapers: Pike County Dispatch (Community news; Circulation 6,700)

Transportation: Commute to work: 89.5% car, 1.3% public transportation, 1.5% walk, 7.7% work from home (2006-2010 5-year est.); Travel time to work: 41.9% less than 15 minutes, 20.4% 15 to 30 minutes, 15.1% 30 to 45 minutes, 6.8% 45 to 60 minutes, 15.9% 60 minutes or more (2006-2010 5-year est.).

Additional Information Contacts

Milford Township . . . . (215) 536-2090
    http://www.milfordtownship.org
Pike County Chamber of Commerce . . . . (570) 296-8700
    http://www.pikechamber.com

MILLRIFT (unincorporated postal area)

Zip Code: 18340

    Covers a land area of 3.101 square miles and a water area of 0.272 square miles. Located at 41.41° N. Lat; 74.76° W. Long. Population: 174 (2010); Density: 56.1 persons per square mile (2010); Race: 98.3% White, 0.6% Black, 0.0% Asian, 0.0% American Indian/Alaska Native, 0.0% Native Hawaiian/Other Pacific Islander, 1.1% Other, 4.6% Hispanic of any race (2010); Average household size: 2.85 (2010); Median age: 46.0 (2010); Males per 100 females: 102.3 (2010); Homeownership rate: 93.5% (2010)

PALMYRA (township). Covers a land area of 34.142 square miles and a water area of 5.407 square miles. Located at 41.40° N. Lat; 75.22° W. Long.

Population: 1,976 (1990); 3,145 (2000); 3,312 (2010); Density: 97.0 persons per square mile (2010); Race: 97.3% White, 0.8% Black, 0.7% Asian, 0.3% American Indian/Alaska Native, 0.0% Native Hawaiian/Other Pacific Islander, 0.9% Other, 2.7% Hispanic of any race (2010); Average household size: 2.28 (2010); Median age: 51.1 (2010); Males per 100 females: 100.0 (2010); Marriage status: 20.1% never married, 67.0% now married, 4.3% widowed, 8.5% divorced (2006-2010 5-year est.); Foreign born: 3.2% (2006-2010 5-year est.); Ancestry (includes multiple

ancestries): 33.9% German, 24.5% Italian, 21.1% Irish, 17.1% English, 8.6% Polish (2006-2010 5-year est.).

Economy: Single-family building permits issued: 13 (2011); Multi-family building permits issued: 0 (2011); Employment by occupation: 5.9% management, 2.3% professional, 7.2% services, 14.2% sales, 3.0% farming, 23.0% construction, 6.6% production (2006-2010 5-year est.).

Income: Per capita income: $30,346 (2006-2010 5-year est.); Median household income: $58,942 (2006-2010 5-year est.); Average household income: $69,236 (2006-2010 5-year est.); Percent of households with income of $100,000 or more: 17.8% (2006-2010 5-year est.); Poverty rate: 4.8% (2006-2010 5-year est.).

Education: Percent of population age 25 and over with: High school diploma (including GED) or higher: 97.5% (2006-2010 5-year est.); Bachelor's degree or higher: 29.7% (2006-2010 5-year est.); Master's degree or higher: 10.1% (2006-2010 5-year est.).

Housing: Homeownership rate: 88.2% (2010); Median home value: $250,400 (2006-2010 5-year est.); Median contract rent: $724 per month (2006-2010 5-year est.); Median year structure built: 1977 (2006-2010 5-year est.).

Transportation: Commute to work: 89.1% car, 0.0% public transportation, 7.3% walk, 3.6% work from home (2006-2010 5-year est.); Travel time to work: 28.9% less than 15 minutes, 27.9% 15 to 30 minutes, 15.1% 30 to 45 minutes, 4.0% 45 to 60 minutes, 24.1% 60 minutes or more (2006-2010 5-year est.)

Additional Information Contacts

Pike County Chamber of Commerce. . . . . (570) 296-8700
  http://www.pikechamber.com

PINE RIDGE (CDP). Covers a land area of 2.372 square miles and a water area of 0.015 square miles. Located at 41.14° N. Lat; 74.99° W. Long.

Population: n/a (1990); n/a (2000); 2,707 (2010); Density: 1,141.2 persons per square mile (2010); Race: 57.0% White, 26.6% Black, 1.7% Asian, 0.4% American Indian/Alaska Native, 0.0% Native Hawaiian/Other Pacific Islander, 14.3% Other, 23.7% Hispanic of any race (2010); Average household size: 3.12 (2010); Median age: 37.0 (2010); Males per 100 females: 97.4 (2010); Marriage status: 16.6% never married, 66.0% now married, 7.7% widowed, 9.7% divorced (2006-2010 5-year est.); Foreign born: 8.9% (2006-2010 5-year est.); Ancestry (includes multiple ancestries): 21.5% Italian, 13.2% German, 11.4% Irish, 7.9% African, 3.7% Romanian (2006-2010 5-year est.).

Economy: Employment by occupation: 9.0% management, 3.6% professional, 17.3% services, 20.3% sales, 5.7% farming, 7.7% construction, 9.3% production (2006-2010 5-year est.).

Income: Per capita income: $22,463 (2006-2010 5-year est.); Median household income: $60,172 (2006-2010 5-year est.); Average household income: $62,063 (2006-2010 5-year est.); Percent of households with income of $100,000 or more: 11.8% (2006-2010 5-year est.); Poverty rate: 16.0% (2006-2010 5-year est.).

Education: Percent of population age 25 and over with: High school diploma (including GED) or higher: 89.2% (2006-2010 5-year est.); Bachelor's degree or higher: 19.8% (2006-2010 5-year est.); Master's degree or higher: 4.5% (2006-2010 5-year est.).

Housing: Homeownership rate: 91.8% (2010); Median home value: $168,300 (2006-2010 5-year est.); Median contract rent: $936 per month (2006-2010 5-year est.); Median year structure built: 1987 (2006-2010 5-year est.).

Transportation: Commute to work: 93.2% car, 6.8% public transportation, 0.0% walk, 0.0% work from home (2006-2010 5-year est.); Travel time to work: 2.5% less than 15 minutes, 25.8% 15 to 30 minutes, 17.0% 30 to 45 minutes, 14.8% 45 to 60 minutes, 39.8% 60 minutes or more (2006-2010 5-year est.)

POCONO MOUNTAIN LAKE ESTATES (CDP). Covers a land area of 2.127 square miles and a water area of 0.025 square miles. Located at 41.16° N. Lat; 74.97° W. Long. Elevation is 1,001 feet.

Population: n/a (1990); n/a (2000); 842 (2010); Density: 395.8 persons per square mile (2010); Race: 84.8% White, 5.6% Black, 2.3% Asian, 0.8% American Indian/Alaska Native, 0.0% Native Hawaiian/Other Pacific Islander, 6.5% Other, 13.5% Hispanic of any race (2010); Average household size: 2.65 (2010); Median age: 44.0 (2010); Males per 100 females: 102.9 (2010); Marriage status: 26.3% never married, 57.9% now married, 9.4% widowed, 6.3% divorced (2006-2010 5-year est.); Foreign born: 3.7% (2006-2010 5-year est.); Ancestry (includes multiple

ancestries): 38.5% Italian, 23.0% German, 19.3% Irish, 13.2% English, 11.3% Dutch (2006-2010 5-year est.).

Economy: Employment by occupation: 11.7% management, 2.5% professional, 1.3% services, 19.6% sales, 0.0% farming, 7.4% construction, 7.9% production (2006-2010 5-year est.).

Income: Per capita income: $27,312 (2006-2010 5-year est.); Median household income: $63,594 (2006-2010 5-year est.); Average household income: $70,171 (2006-2010 5-year est.); Percent of households with income of $100,000 or more: 14.3% (2006-2010 5-year est.); Poverty rate: 7.9% (2006-2010 5-year est.).

Education: Percent of population age 25 and over with: High school diploma (including GED) or higher: 79.4% (2006-2010 5-year est.); Bachelor's degree or higher: 16.2% (2006-2010 5-year est.); Master's degree or higher: 5.2% (2006-2010 5-year est.).

Housing: Homeownership rate: 91.8% (2010); Median home value: $206,800 (2006-2010 5-year est.); Median contract rent: $398 per month (2006-2010 5-year est.); Median year structure built: 1989 (2006-2010 5-year est.).

Transportation: Commute to work: 91.0% car, 5.2% public transportation, 0.0% walk, 2.1% work from home (2006-2010 5-year est.); Travel time to work: 1.6% less than 15 minutes, 22.1% 15 to 30 minutes, 21.1% 30 to 45 minutes, 2.1% 45 to 60 minutes, 53.2% 60 minutes or more (2006-2010 5-year est.)

POCONO RANCH LANDS (CDP). Covers a land area of 2.008 square miles and a water area of <.001 square miles. Located at 41.18° N. Lat; 74.97° W. Long.

Population: n/a (1990); n/a (2000); 1,062 (2010); Density: 528.9 persons per square mile (2010); Race: 77.1% White, 11.1% Black, 0.8% Asian, 0.2% American Indian/Alaska Native, 0.0% Native Hawaiian/Other Pacific Islander, 10.8% Other, 19.0% Hispanic of any race (2010); Average household size: 3.06 (2010); Median age: 35.6 (2010); Males per 100 females: 101.5 (2010); Marriage status: 28.4% never married, 57.3% now married, 2.8% widowed, 11.5% divorced (2006-2010 5-year est.); Foreign born: 0.0% (2006-2010 5-year est.); Ancestry (includes multiple ancestries): 43.5% German, 20.2% Italian, 20.1% Irish, 6.7% Dutch, 5.0% English (2006-2010 5-year est.).

Economy: Employment by occupation: 25.7% management, 0.0% professional, 0.0% services, 26.7% sales, 7.4% farming, 3.7% construction, 3.7% production (2006-2010 5-year est.).

Income: Per capita income: $18,031 (2006-2010 5-year est.); Median household income: $48,006 (2006-2010 5-year est.); Average household income: $42,270 (2006-2010 5-year est.); Percent of households with income of $100,000 or more: 3.4% (2006-2010 5-year est.); Poverty rate: 25.3% (2006-2010 5-year est.).

Education: Percent of population age 25 and over with: High school diploma (including GED) or higher: 94.2% (2006-2010 5-year est.); Bachelor's degree or higher: 12.0% (2006-2010 5-year est.); Master's degree or higher: 3.7% (2006-2010 5-year est.).

Housing: Homeownership rate: 83.3% (2010); Median home value: $157,500 (2006-2010 5-year est.); Median contract rent: $644 per month (2006-2010 5-year est.); Median year structure built: 1991 (2006-2010 5-year est.).

Transportation: Commute to work: 94.4% car, 5.6% public transportation, 0.0% walk, 0.0% work from home (2006-2010 5-year est.); Travel time to work: 0.0% less than 15 minutes, 34.7% 15 to 30 minutes, 37.0% 30 to 45 minutes, 0.0% 45 to 60 minutes, 28.3% 60 minutes or more (2006-2010 5-year est.)

POCONO WOODLAND LAKES (CDP). Covers a land area of 6.238 square miles and a water area of 0.081 square miles. Located at 41.32° N. Lat; 74.89° W. Long.

Population: n/a (1990); n/a (2000); 3,209 (2010); Density: 514.5 persons per square mile (2010); Race: 92.4% White, 2.9% Black, 0.8% Asian, 0.2% American Indian/Alaska Native, 0.0% Native Hawaiian/Other Pacific Islander, 3.7% Other, 7.1% Hispanic of any race (2010); Average household size: 2.94 (2010); Median age: 41.1 (2010); Males per 100 females: 97.5 (2010); Marriage status: 19.8% never married, 67.3% now married, 4.7% widowed, 8.1% divorced (2006-2010 5-year est.); Foreign born: 5.0% (2006-2010 5-year est.); Ancestry (includes multiple ancestries): 29.9% German, 22.6% Irish, 21.5% Italian, 14.1% English, 9.9% Polish (2006-2010 5-year est.).

Economy: Employment by occupation: 18.3% management, 1.9% professional, 8.4% services, 16.1% sales, 11.0% farming, 12.3% construction, 6.2% production (2006-2010 5-year est.).

Income: Per capita income: $34,921 (2006-2010 5-year est.); Median household income: $81,420 (2006-2010 5-year est.); Average household income: $88,642 (2006-2010 5-year est.); Percent of households with income of $100,000 or more: 33.5% (2006-2010 5-year est.); Poverty rate: 1.3% (2006-2010 5-year est.).

Education: Percent of population age 25 and over with: High school diploma (including GED) or higher: 97.0% (2006-2010 5-year est.); Bachelor's degree or higher: 27.3% (2006-2010 5-year est.); Master's degree or higher: 4.8% (2006-2010 5-year est.).

Housing: Homeownership rate: 96.7% (2010); Median home value: $239,100 (2006-2010 5-year est.); Median contract rent: n/a per month (2006-2010 5-year est.); Median year structure built: 1993 (2006-2010 5-year est.).

Transportation: Commute to work: 90.5% car, 1.1% public transportation, 0.0% walk, 8.4% work from home (2006-2010 5-year est.); Travel time to work: 16.3% less than 15 minutes, 18.6% 15 to 30 minutes, 12.9% 30 to 45 minutes, 9.8% 45 to 60 minutes, 42.4% 60 minutes or more (2006-2010 5-year est.)

PORTER (township). Covers a land area of 58.540 square miles and a water area of 1.989 square miles. Located at 41.22° N. Lat; 75.07° W. Long.

Population: 163 (1990); 385 (2000); 485 (2010); Density: 8.3 persons per square mile (2010); Race: 91.5% White, 3.3% Black, 1.4% Asian, 0.0% American Indian/Alaska Native, 0.0% Native Hawaiian/Other Pacific Islander, 3.8% Other, 5.6% Hispanic of any race (2010); Average household size: 2.30 (2010); Median age: 52.2 (2010); Males per 100 females: 112.7 (2010); Marriage status: 12.8% never married, 77.0% now married, 1.5% widowed, 8.8% divorced (2006-2010 5-year est.); Foreign born: 4.1% (2006-2010 5-year est.); Ancestry (includes multiple ancestries): 34.2% Irish, 30.4% Italian, 19.2% Polish, 11.5% Dutch, 7.7% German (2006-2010 5-year est.).

Economy: Single-family building permits issued: 2 (2011); Multi-family building permits issued: 0 (2011); Employment by occupation: 16.4% management, 1.6% professional, 9.8% services, 20.5% sales, 2.5% farming, 9.8% construction, 9.8% production (2006-2010 5-year est.).

Income: Per capita income: $31,619 (2006-2010 5-year est.); Median household income: $82,656 (2006-2010 5-year est.); Average household income: $84,421 (2006-2010 5-year est.); Percent of households with income of $100,000 or more: 23.2% (2006-2010 5-year est.); Poverty rate: 3.8% (2006-2010 5-year est.).

Education: Percent of population age 25 and over with: High school diploma (including GED) or higher: 94.8% (2006-2010 5-year est.); Bachelor's degree or higher: 16.5% (2006-2010 5-year est.); Master's degree or higher: 5.2% (2006-2010 5-year est.).

Housing: Homeownership rate: 85.8% (2010); Median home value: $266,700 (2006-2010 5-year est.); Median contract rent: n/a per month (2006-2010 5-year est.); Median year structure built: 1966 (2006-2010 5-year est.).

Transportation: Commute to work: 66.7% car, 0.0% public transportation, 3.5% walk, 29.8% work from home (2006-2010 5-year est.); Travel time to work: 16.3% less than 15 minutes, 10.0% 15 to 30 minutes, 30.0% 30 to 45 minutes, 7.5% 45 to 60 minutes, 36.3% 60 minutes or more (2006-2010 5-year est.)

ROWLAND (unincorporated postal area)
Zip Code: 18457

Covers a land area of 0.480 square miles and a water area of 0.015 square miles. Located at 41.47° N. Lat; 75.04° W. Long. Elevation is 692 feet. Population: 82 (2010); Density: 170.6 persons per square mile (2010); Race: 98.8% White, 1.2% Black, 0.0% Asian, 0.0% American Indian/Alaska Native, 0.0% Native Hawaiian/Other Pacific Islander, 0.0% Other, 6.1% Hispanic of any race (2010); Average household size: 2.56 (2010); Median age: 41.0 (2010); Males per 100 females: 121.6 (2010); Homeownership rate: 71.9% (2010)

SAW CREEK (CDP). Covers a land area of 3.186 square miles and a water area of 0.022 square miles. Located at 41.12° N. Lat; 75.05° W. Long. Elevation is 741 feet.

Population: n/a (1990); n/a (2000); 4,016 (2010); Density: 1,260.4 persons per square mile (2010); Race: 59.0% White, 27.2% Black, 3.1% Asian, 0.7% American Indian/Alaska Native, 0.0% Native Hawaiian/Other Pacific Islander, 10.0% Other, 23.9% Hispanic of any race (2010); Average household size: 2.88 (2010); Median age: 38.2 (2010); Males per 100 females: 94.0 (2010); Marriage status: 31.8% never married, 56.6% now

married, 2.3% widowed, 9.3% divorced (2006-2010 5-year est.); Foreign born: 8.7% (2006-2010 5-year est.); Ancestry (includes multiple ancestries): 12.5% Irish, 12.0% Italian, 4.5% German, 3.1% Polish, 3.1% American (2006-2010 5-year est.).

Economy: Employment by occupation: 16.1% management, 6.7% professional, 11.6% services, 11.8% sales, 7.0% farming, 7.9% construction, 7.1% production (2006-2010 5-year est.).

Income: Per capita income: $25,679 (2006-2010 5-year est.); Median household income: $60,815 (2006-2010 5-year est.); Average household income: $77,721 (2006-2010 5-year est.); Percent of households with income of $100,000 or more: 11.6% (2006-2010 5-year est.); Poverty rate: 8.2% (2006-2010 5-year est.).

Education: Percent of population age 25 and over with: High school diploma (including GED) or higher: 94.2% (2006-2010 5-year est.); Bachelor's degree or higher: 24.9% (2006-2010 5-year est.); Master's degree or higher: 7.9% (2006-2010 5-year est.).

Housing: Homeownership rate: 82.9% (2010); Median home value: $178,300 (2006-2010 5-year est.); Median contract rent: $922 per month (2006-2010 5-year est.); Median year structure built: 1987 (2006-2010 5-year est.).

Transportation: Commute to work: 89.7% car, 8.1% public transportation, 0.0% walk, 2.2% work from home (2006-2010 5-year est.); Travel time to work: 10.3% less than 15 minutes, 15.6% 15 to 30 minutes, 16.8% 30 to 45 minutes, 11.7% 45 to 60 minutes, 45.6% 60 minutes or more (2006-2010 5-year est.)

SHOHOLA (township). Covers a land area of 45.290 square miles and a water area of 1.408 square miles. Located at 41.42° N. Lat; 74.91° W. Long. Elevation is 646 feet.

Population: 1,586 (1990); 2,088 (2000); 2,475 (2010); Density: 54.6 persons per square mile (2010); Race: 96.0% White, 0.9% Black, 0.4% Asian, 0.2% American Indian/Alaska Native, 0.0% Native Hawaiian/Other Pacific Islander, 2.5% Other, 4.9% Hispanic of any race (2010); Average household size: 2.40 (2010); Median age: 45.8 (2010); Males per 100 females: 107.8 (2010); Marriage status: 24.1% never married, 60.6% now married, 5.3% widowed, 10.0% divorced (2006-2010 5-year est.); Foreign born: 8.8% (2006-2010 5-year est.); Ancestry (includes multiple ancestries): 36.9% German, 31.9% Irish, 18.6% Italian, 12.3% English, 4.1% Polish (2006-2010 5-year est.).

Economy: Single-family building permits issued: 1 (2011); Multi-family building permits issued: 0 (2011); Employment by occupation: 9.4% management, 2.9% professional, 6.7% services, 14.3% sales, 3.8% farming, 21.8% construction, 6.0% production (2006-2010 5-year est.).

Income: Per capita income: $29,612 (2006-2010 5-year est.); Median household income: $52,950 (2006-2010 5-year est.); Average household income: $72,518 (2006-2010 5-year est.); Percent of households with income of $100,000 or more: 20.5% (2006-2010 5-year est.); Poverty rate: 5.2% (2006-2010 5-year est.).

Education: Percent of population age 25 and over with: High school diploma (including GED) or higher: 91.7% (2006-2010 5-year est.); Bachelor's degree or higher: 24.0% (2006-2010 5-year est.); Master's degree or higher: 9.4% (2006-2010 5-year est.).

School District(s)

Delaware Valley SD (PK-12)
    2010-11 Enrollment: 5,327 . . . . (570) 296-1800

Housing: Homeownership rate: 85.4% (2010); Median home value: $243,500 (2006-2010 5-year est.); Median contract rent: $617 per month (2006-2010 5-year est.); Median year structure built: 1976 (2006-2010 5-year est.).

Safety: Violent crime rate: 0.0 per 10,000 population; Property crime rate: 132.9 per 10,000 population (2011).

Transportation: Commute to work: 92.0% car, 1.7% public transportation, 4.8% walk, 1.5% work from home (2006-2010 5-year est.); Travel time to work: 23.5% less than 15 minutes, 30.1% 15 to 30 minutes, 15.3% 30 to 45 minutes, 11.5% 45 to 60 minutes, 19.6% 60 minutes or more (2006-2010 5-year est.)

Additional Information Contacts
Pike County Chamber of Commerce. . . . . (570) 296-8700
    http://www.pikechamber.com

SUNRISE LAKE (CDP). Covers a land area of 1.829 square miles and a water area of 0.137 square miles. Located at 41.31° N. Lat; 74.96° W. Long. Elevation is 1,467 feet.

Population: n/a (1990); n/a (2000); 1,387 (2010); Density: 758.2 persons per square mile (2010); Race: 92.7% White, 3.0% Black, 0.5% Asian,

0.1% American Indian/Alaska Native, 0.0% Native Hawaiian/Other Pacific Islander, 3.7% Other, 9.3% Hispanic of any race (2010); Average household size: 2.90 (2010); Median age: 38.8 (2010); Males per 100 females: 107.9 (2010); Marriage status: 30.1% never married, 50.5% now married, 5.1% widowed, 14.3% divorced (2006-2010 5-year est.); Foreign born: 4.4% (2006-2010 5-year est.); Ancestry (includes multiple ancestries): 45.9% Irish, 30.1% German, 13.6% Italian, 12.5% English, 7.9% Polish (2006-2010 5-year est.).

Economy: Employment by occupation: 7.7% management, 0.0% professional, 18.1% services, 20.9% sales, 0.0% farming, 6.6% construction, 11.1% production (2006-2010 5-year est.).

Income: Per capita income: $26,036 (2006-2010 5-year est.); Median household income: $77,686 (2006-2010 5-year est.); Average household income: $81,016 (2006-2010 5-year est.); Percent of households with income of $100,000 or more: 15.2% (2006-2010 5-year est.); Poverty rate: 9.7% (2006-2010 5-year est.).

Education: Percent of population age 25 and over with: High school diploma (including GED) or higher: 93.0% (2006-2010 5-year est.); Bachelor's degree or higher: 13.5% (2006-2010 5-year est.); Master's degree or higher: 4.7% (2006-2010 5-year est.).

Housing: Homeownership rate: 92.1% (2010); Median home value: $179,800 (2006-2010 5-year est.); Median contract rent: n/a per month (2006-2010 5-year est.); Median year structure built: 1986 (2006-2010 5-year est.).

Transportation: Commute to work: 97.2% car, 0.0% public transportation, 0.0% walk, 2.8% work from home (2006-2010 5-year est.); Travel time to work: 15.1% less than 15 minutes, 14.2% 15 to 30 minutes, 27.0% 30 to 45 minutes, 12.4% 45 to 60 minutes, 31.3% 60 minutes or more (2006-2010 5-year est.)

TAFTON (unincorporated postal area)
Zip Code: 18464

Covers a land area of 12.034 square miles and a water area of 0.249 square miles. Located at 41.40° N. Lat; 75.17° W. Long. Elevation is 1,532 feet. Population: 1,193 (2010); Density: 99.1 persons per square mile (2010); Race: 96.4% White, 0.7% Black, 0.8% Asian, 0.5% American Indian/Alaska Native, 0.0% Native Hawaiian/Other Pacific Islander, 1.6% Other, 2.8% Hispanic of any race (2010); Average household size: 2.37 (2010); Median age: 49.0 (2010); Males per 100 females: 94.6 (2010); Homeownership rate: 89.7% (2010)

TAMIMENT (unincorporated postal area)
Zip Code: 18371

Covers a land area of 3.530 square miles and a water area of 0.132 square miles. Located at 41.15° N. Lat; 75.04° W. Long. Population: 747 (2010); Density: 211.6 persons per square mile (2010); Race: 57.0% White, 26.4% Black, 1.7% Asian, 0.7% American Indian/Alaska Native, 0.0% Native Hawaiian/Other Pacific Islander, 14.2% Other, 28.9% Hispanic of any race (2010); Average household size: 3.10 (2010); Median age: 37.7 (2010); Males per 100 females: 108.7 (2010); Homeownership rate: 90.9% (2010)

WESTFALL (township). Covers a land area of 28.844 square miles and a water area of 0.617 square miles. Located at 41.40° N. Lat; 74.77° W. Long.

Population: 2,083 (1990); 2,430 (2000); 2,323 (2010); Density: 80.5 persons per square mile (2010); Race: 95.3% White, 1.2% Black, 0.7% Asian, 0.6% American Indian/Alaska Native, 0.0% Native Hawaiian/Other Pacific Islander, 2.2% Other, 5.3% Hispanic of any race (2010); Average household size: 2.23 (2010); Median age: 49.9 (2010); Males per 100 females: 90.1 (2010); Marriage status: 24.9% never married, 55.6% now married, 11.5% widowed, 7.9% divorced (2006-2010 5-year est.); Foreign born: 5.2% (2006-2010 5-year est.); Ancestry (includes multiple ancestries): 35.6% Irish, 34.3% German, 16.8% English, 13.2% Italian, 7.5% Polish (2006-2010 5-year est.).

Economy: Single-family building permits issued: 1 (2011); Multi-family building permits issued: 6 (2011); Employment by occupation: 14.6% management, 3.6% professional, 7.2% services, 16.2% sales, 3.5% farming, 10.2% construction, 5.6% production (2006-2010 5-year est.).

Income: Per capita income: $33,675 (2006-2010 5-year est.); Median household income: $47,188 (2006-2010 5-year est.); Average household income: $79,675 (2006-2010 5-year est.); Percent of households with income of $100,000 or more: 16.8% (2006-2010 5-year est.); Poverty rate: 11.0% (2006-2010 5-year est.).

Education: Percent of population age 25 and over with: High school diploma (including GED) or higher: 94.8% (2006-2010 5-year est.); Bachelor's degree or higher: 24.1% (2006-2010 5-year est.); Master's degree or higher: 11.3% (2006-2010 5-year est.).

Housing: Homeownership rate: 73.4% (2010); Median home value: $233,500 (2006-2010 5-year est.); Median contract rent: $700 per month (2006-2010 5-year est.); Median year structure built: 1977 (2006-2010 5-year est.).

Transportation: Commute to work: 88.7% car, 3.9% public transportation, 1.9% walk, 4.8% work from home (2006-2010 5-year est.); Travel time to work: 35.4% less than 15 minutes, 13.5% 15 to 30 minutes, 24.4% 30 to 45 minutes, 6.5% 45 to 60 minutes, 20.1% 60 minutes or more (2006-2010 5-year est.)

Additional Information Contacts
Pike County Chamber of Commerce . . . . (570) 296-8700
http://www.pikechamber.com

Potter County

Located in northern Pennsylvania; bounded on the north by New York; drained by the Allegheny River. Covers a land area of 1,081.323 square miles, a water area of 0.216 square miles, and is located in the Eastern Time Zone at 41.75° N. Lat., 77.89° W. Long. The county was founded in 1804. County seat is Coudersport.

Population: 16,717 (1990); 18,080 (2000); 17,457 (2010); Race: 98.1% White, 0.4% Black, 0.3% Asian, 0.3% American Indian/Alaska Native, 0.0% Native Hawaiian/Other Pacific Islander, 0.9% Other, 1.0% Hispanic of any race (2010); Density: 16.1 persons per square mile (2010); Average household size: 2.39 (2010); Median age: 44.9 (2010); Males per 100 females: 99.9 (2010).

Religion: Six largest groups: 10.7% Catholicism, 6.7% Methodist/Pietist, 5.6% Non-Denominational, 4.0% Holiness, 3.1% Lutheran, 1.8% Baptist (2010)

Economy: Unemployment rate: 9.4% (August 2012); Total civilian labor force: 8,076 (August 2012); Leading industries: 21.4% health care and social assistance; 16.5% manufacturing; 12.8% retail trade (2010); Farms: 378 totaling 88,457 acres (2007); Companies that employ 500 or more persons: 1 (2010); Companies that employ 100 to 499 persons: 7 (2010); Companies that employ less than 100 persons: 370 (2010); Black-owned businesses: n/a (2007); Hispanic-owned businesses: n/a (2007); Asian-owned businesses: n/a (2007); Women-owned businesses: 467 (2007); Retail sales per capita: $9,477 (2010). Single-family building permits issued: 16 (2011); Multi-family building permits issued: 0 (2011).

Income: Per capita income: $20,594 (2006-2010 5-year est.); Median household income: $39,196 (2006-2010 5-year est.); Average household income: $50,302 (2006-2010 5-year est.); Percent of households with income of $100,000 or more: 8.8% (2006-2010 5-year est.); Poverty rate: 14.8% (2006-2010 5-year est.); Bankruptcy rate: 1.49% (2011).

Education: Percent of population age 25 and over with: High school diploma (including GED) or higher: 85.5% (2006-2010 5-year est.); Bachelor's degree or higher: 12.4% (2006-2010 5-year est.); Master's degree or higher: 4.0% (2006-2010 5-year est.).

Housing: Homeownership rate: 76.4% (2010); Median home value: $89,600 (2006-2010 5-year est.); Median contract rent: $435 per month (2006-2010 5-year est.); Median year structure built: 1966 (2006-2010 5-year est.)

Health: Birth rate: 105.4 per 10,000 population (2011); Death rate: 118.0 per 10,000 population (2011); Age-adjusted cancer mortality rate: 192.3 deaths per 100,000 population (2009); Number of physicians: 12.6 per 10,000 population (2010); Hospital beds: 55.7 per 10,000 population (2008); Hospital admissions: 1,361.8 per 10,000 population (2008).

Elections: 2012 Presidential election results: 26.2% Obama, 72.2% Romney

National and State Parks: Cherry Springs State Park; Denton Hill State Park; Lyman Run State Park; Ole Bull State Park; Ole Bull State Park; Patterson State Park; Prouty Place State Park; Susquehannock State Forest

Additional Information Contacts
Potter County Government . . . . (814) 274-8290
http://www.pottercountypa.net

Potter County Communities

ABBOTT (township). Covers a land area of 69.977 square miles and a water area of 0 square miles. Located at 41.61° N. Lat; 77.71° W. Long. Elevation is 1,371 feet.

Population: 173 (1990); 226 (2000); 242 (2010); Density: 3.5 persons per square mile (2010); Race: 97.9% White, 0.4% Black, 0.0% Asian, 0.4% American Indian/Alaska Native, 0.0% Native Hawaiian/Other Pacific Islander, 1.3% Other, 0.0% Hispanic of any race (2010); Average household size: 2.14 (2010); Median age: 54.4 (2010); Males per 100 females: 112.3 (2010); Marriage status: 26.4% never married, 62.3% now married, 1.7% widowed, 9.6% divorced (2006-2010 5-year est.); Foreign born: 0.0% (2006-2010 5-year est.); Ancestry (includes multiple ancestries): 50.7% German, 12.7% Italian, 8.8% American, 8.5% English, 7.4% Irish (2006-2010 5-year est.).

Economy: Single-family building permits issued: 0 (2011); Multi-family building permits issued: 0 (2011); Employment by occupation: 6.8% management, 5.3% professional, 8.3% services, 24.2% sales, 1.5% farming, 27.3% construction, 12.1% production (2006-2010 5-year est.).

Income: Per capita income: $18,246 (2006-2010 5-year est.); Median household income: $41,667 (2006-2010 5-year est.); Average household income: $44,422 (2006-2010 5-year est.); Percent of households with income of $100,000 or more: 4.3% (2006-2010 5-year est.); Poverty rate: 12.3% (2006-2010 5-year est.).

Education: Percent of population age 25 and over with: High school diploma (including GED) or higher: 83.2% (2006-2010 5-year est.); Bachelor's degree or higher: 19.4% (2006-2010 5-year est.); Master's degree or higher: 11.7% (2006-2010 5-year est.).

Housing: Homeownership rate: 85.0% (2010); Median home value: $119,300 (2006-2010 5-year est.); Median contract rent: $475 per month (2006-2010 5-year est.); Median year structure built: 1957 (2006-2010 5-year est.).

Transportation: Commute to work: 79.2% car, 0.0% public transportation, 7.7% walk, 13.1% work from home (2006-2010 5-year est.); Travel time to work: 31.0% less than 15 minutes, 23.0% 15 to 30 minutes, 18.6% 30 to 45 minutes, 12.4% 45 to 60 minutes, 15.0% 60 minutes or more (2006-2010 5-year est.)

ALLEGANY (township). Covers a land area of 40.513 square miles and a water area of 0.019 square miles. Located at 41.87° N. Lat; 77.90° W. Long.

Population: 413 (1990); 402 (2000); 422 (2010); Density: 10.4 persons per square mile (2010); Race: 99.1% White, 0.0% Black, 0.0% Asian, 0.5% American Indian/Alaska Native, 0.0% Native Hawaiian/Other Pacific Islander, 0.4% Other, 0.7% Hispanic of any race (2010); Average household size: 2.45 (2010); Median age: 47.2 (2010); Males per 100 females: 117.5 (2010); Marriage status: 13.2% never married, 71.1% now married, 5.6% widowed, 10.2% divorced (2006-2010 5-year est.); Foreign born: 0.5% (2006-2010 5-year est.); Ancestry (includes multiple ancestries): 27.5% German, 15.5% English, 14.4% Irish, 13.9% American, 4.4% Dutch (2006-2010 5-year est.).

Economy: Single-family building permits issued: 1 (2011); Multi-family building permits issued: 0 (2011); Employment by occupation: 9.8% management, 2.4% professional, 10.4% services, 19.5% sales, 10.4% farming, 14.0% construction, 5.5% production (2006-2010 5-year est.).

Income: Per capita income: $23,099 (2006-2010 5-year est.); Median household income: $43,906 (2006-2010 5-year est.); Average household income: $55,748 (2006-2010 5-year est.); Percent of households with income of $100,000 or more: 14.6% (2006-2010 5-year est.); Poverty rate: 12.5% (2006-2010 5-year est.).

Education: Percent of population age 25 and over with: High school diploma (including GED) or higher: 91.4% (2006-2010 5-year est.); Bachelor's degree or higher: 9.0% (2006-2010 5-year est.); Master's degree or higher: 4.3% (2006-2010 5-year est.).

Housing: Homeownership rate: 85.5% (2010); Median home value: $119,700 (2006-2010 5-year est.); Median contract rent: $325 per month (2006-2010 5-year est.); Median year structure built: 1974 (2006-2010 5-year est.).

Transportation: Commute to work: 94.2% car, 0.0% public transportation, 1.3% walk, 4.5% work from home (2006-2010 5-year est.); Travel time to work: 35.6% less than 15 minutes, 36.2% 15 to 30 minutes, 15.4% 30 to 45 minutes, 7.4% 45 to 60 minutes, 5.4% 60 minutes or more (2006-2010 5-year est.)

AUSTIN (borough). Aka Hull. Covers a land area of 4.041 square miles and a water area of 0 square miles. Located at 41.64° N. Lat; 78.09° W. Long. Elevation is 1,348 feet.

Population: 569 (1990); 623 (2000); 562 (2010); Density: 139.1 persons per square mile (2010); Race: 100.0% White, 0.0% Black, 0.0% Asian, 0.0% American Indian/Alaska Native, 0.0% Native Hawaiian/Other Pacific Islander, 0.0% Other, 0.0% Hispanic of any race (2010); Average household size: 2.43 (2010); Median age: 38.8 (2010); Males per 100 females: 105.9 (2010); Marriage status: 27.7% never married, 48.6% now married, 8.6% widowed, 15.2% divorced (2006-2010 5-year est.); Foreign born: 0.5% (2006-2010 5-year est.); Ancestry (includes multiple ancestries): 25.0% German, 15.8% Irish, 12.6% English, 12.0% Polish, 10.2% American (2006-2010 5-year est.).

Economy: Single-family building permits issued: 0 (2011); Multi-family building permits issued: 0 (2011); Employment by occupation: 2.7% management, 7.1% professional, 15.6% services, 12.0% sales, 2.7% farming, 8.9% construction, 11.1% production (2006-2010 5-year est.).

Income: Per capita income: $15,478 (2006-2010 5-year est.); Median household income: $25,417 (2006-2010 5-year est.); Average household income: $38,148 (2006-2010 5-year est.); Percent of households with income of $100,000 or more: 7.1% (2006-2010 5-year est.); Poverty rate: 18.9% (2006-2010 5-year est.).

Education: Percent of population age 25 and over with: High school diploma (including GED) or higher: 87.6% (2006-2010 5-year est.); Bachelor's degree or higher: 8.3% (2006-2010 5-year est.); Master's degree or higher: 0.7% (2006-2010 5-year est.).

School District(s)

Austin Area SD (PK-12)
   2010-11 Enrollment: 198 . . . . (814) 647-8603

Housing: Homeownership rate: 71.0% (2010); Median home value: $46,200 (2006-2010 5-year est.); Median contract rent: $423 per month (2006-2010 5-year est.); Median year structure built: 1968 (2006-2010 5-year est.).

Transportation: Commute to work: 87.6% car, 0.0% public transportation, 2.7% walk, 9.8% work from home (2006-2010 5-year est.); Travel time to work: 21.2% less than 15 minutes, 46.8% 15 to 30 minutes, 31.0% 30 to 45 minutes, 0.0% 45 to 60 minutes, 1.0% 60 minutes or more (2006-2010 5-year est.).

BINGHAM (township). Covers a land area of 35.730 square miles and a water area of 0.008 square miles. Located at 41.96° N. Lat; 77.81° W. Long.

Population: 557 (1990); 687 (2000); 684 (2010); Density: 19.1 persons per square mile (2010); Race: 98.7% White, 0.1% Black, 0.0% Asian, 0.1% American Indian/Alaska Native, 0.0% Native Hawaiian/Other Pacific Islander, 1.1% Other, 0.9% Hispanic of any race (2010); Average household size: 2.85 (2010); Median age: 41.1 (2010); Males per 100 females: 110.5 (2010); Marriage status: 24.4% never married, 60.7% now married, 7.9% widowed, 7.1% divorced (2006-2010 5-year est.); Foreign born: 0.0% (2006-2010 5-year est.); Ancestry (includes multiple ancestries): 22.0% German, 17.4% Swiss, 16.5% English, 14.1% Irish, 7.5% American (2006-2010 5-year est.).

Economy: Single-family building permits issued: 0 (2011); Multi-family building permits issued: 0 (2011); Employment by occupation: 13.3% management, 5.8% professional, 2.2% services, 14.4% sales, 7.6% farming, 23.7% construction, 6.8% production (2006-2010 5-year est.).

Income: Per capita income: $17,029 (2006-2010 5-year est.); Median household income: $35,000 (2006-2010 5-year est.); Average household income: $49,615 (2006-2010 5-year est.); Percent of households with income of $100,000 or more: 10.8% (2006-2010 5-year est.); Poverty rate: 47.8% (2006-2010 5-year est.).

Education: Percent of population age 25 and over with: High school diploma (including GED) or higher: 70.8% (2006-2010 5-year est.); Bachelor's degree or higher: 12.2% (2006-2010 5-year est.); Master's degree or higher: 4.3% (2006-2010 5-year est.).

Housing: Homeownership rate: 85.4% (2010); Median home value: $110,900 (2006-2010 5-year est.); Median contract rent: $413 per month (2006-2010 5-year est.); Median year structure built: 1974 (2006-2010 5-year est.).

Transportation: Commute to work: 71.6% car, 0.0% public transportation, 3.6% walk, 23.6% work from home (2006-2010 5-year est.); Travel time to work: 19.0% less than 15 minutes, 24.3% 15 to 30 minutes, 26.2% 30 to 45 minutes, 13.8% 45 to 60 minutes, 16.7% 60 minutes or more (2006-2010 5-year est.)

CLARA (township). Covers a land area of 19.644 square miles and a water area of 0 square miles. Located at 41.87° N. Lat; 78.12° W. Long. Elevation is 1,647 feet.

Population: 133 (1990); 168 (2000); 199 (2010); Density: 10.1 persons per square mile (2010); Race: 99.0% White, 0.0% Black, 0.0% Asian, 0.0% American Indian/Alaska Native, 0.0% Native Hawaiian/Other Pacific Islander, 1.0% Other, 0.0% Hispanic of any race (2010); Average household size: 2.37 (2010); Median age: 46.6 (2010); Males per 100 females: 97.0 (2010); Marriage status: 18.3% never married, 63.9% now married, 7.1% widowed, 10.7% divorced (2006-2010 5-year est.); Foreign born: 1.5% (2006-2010 5-year est.); Ancestry (includes multiple ancestries): 22.3% German, 18.8% Irish, 15.2% American, 13.7% English, 12.2% Dutch (2006-2010 5-year est.).

Economy: Single-family building permits issued: 0 (2011); Multi-family building permits issued: 0 (2011); Employment by occupation: 5.0% management, 5.0% professional, 12.9% services, 14.9% sales, 0.0% farming, 18.8% construction, 16.8% production (2006-2010 5-year est.).

Income: Per capita income: $20,290 (2006-2010 5-year est.); Median household income: $43,750 (2006-2010 5-year est.); Average household income: $50,212 (2006-2010 5-year est.); Percent of households with income of $100,000 or more: 7.3% (2006-2010 5-year est.); Poverty rate: 4.1% (2006-2010 5-year est.).

Education: Percent of population age 25 and over with: High school diploma (including GED) or higher: 80.6% (2006-2010 5-year est.); Bachelor's degree or higher: 17.4% (2006-2010 5-year est.); Master's degree or higher: 9.7% (2006-2010 5-year est.).

Housing: Homeownership rate: 88.1% (2010); Median home value: $75,800 (2006-2010 5-year est.); Median contract rent: $342 per month (2006-2010 5-year est.); Median year structure built: 1973 (2006-2010 5-year est.).

Transportation: Commute to work: 95.0% car, 0.0% public transportation, 3.0% walk, 2.0% work from home (2006-2010 5-year est.); Travel time to work: 22.2% less than 15 minutes, 57.6% 15 to 30 minutes, 7.1% 30 to 45 minutes, 9.1% 45 to 60 minutes, 4.0% 60 minutes or more (2006-2010 5-year est.)

COUDERSPORT (borough). County seat. Covers a land area of 5.634 square miles and a water area of 0 square miles. Located at 41.78° N. Lat; 78.02° W. Long. Elevation is 1,647 feet.

History: John Keating, Irish soldier of fortune and manager of the Ceres Land Company which had acquired 300,000 acres in the area, gave 50-acre homesteads to each of the first 50 settlers. At Keating's suggestion, Coudersport was named for Jean Samuel Couderc, of the Amsterdam banking firm that had managed the interests of those exiled Frenchmen of Asylum who had invested in the Ceres Land Company.

Population: 2,854 (1990); 2,650 (2000); 2,546 (2010); Density: 451.9 persons per square mile (2010); Race: 97.6% White, 0.5% Black, 0.4% Asian, 0.3% American Indian/Alaska Native, 0.0% Native Hawaiian/Other Pacific Islander, 1.2% Other, 1.6% Hispanic of any race (2010); Average household size: 2.23 (2010); Median age: 40.3 (2010); Males per 100 females: 90.1 (2010); Marriage status: 29.3% never married, 47.0% now married, 9.9% widowed, 13.7% divorced (2006-2010 5-year est.); Foreign born: 1.1% (2006-2010 5-year est.); Ancestry (includes multiple ancestries): 39.4% German, 21.6% Irish, 7.6% English, 5.4% American, 3.9% Polish (2006-2010 5-year est.).

Economy: Single-family building permits issued: 0 (2011); Multi-family building permits issued: 0 (2011); Employment by occupation: 14.6% management, 7.2% professional, 7.6% services, 16.9% sales, 3.2% farming, 6.9% construction, 3.8% production (2006-2010 5-year est.).

Income: Per capita income: $22,116 (2006-2010 5-year est.); Median household income: $36,891 (2006-2010 5-year est.); Average household income: $52,786 (2006-2010 5-year est.); Percent of households with income of $100,000 or more: 12.0% (2006-2010 5-year est.); Poverty rate: 9.8% (2006-2010 5-year est.).

Education: Percent of population age 25 and over with: High school diploma (including GED) or higher: 87.9% (2006-2010 5-year est.); Bachelor's degree or higher: 19.2% (2006-2010 5-year est.); Master's degree or higher: 5.4% (2006-2010 5-year est.).

School District(s)

Coudersport Area SD (KG-12)
    2010-11 Enrollment: 865. . . . . (814) 274-9480

Housing: Homeownership rate: 58.8% (2010); Median home value: $81,300 (2006-2010 5-year est.); Median contract rent: $482 per month (2006-2010 5-year est.); Median year structure built: 1943 (2006-2010 5-year est.).

Hospitals: Charles Cole Memorial Hospital (140 beds)

Newspapers: Potter Leader-Enterprise (Community news; Circulation 10,200); Reporter-Argus (Community news; Circulation 3,000)

Transportation: Commute to work: 84.4% car, 0.8% public transportation, 10.8% walk, 2.6% work from home (2006-2010 5-year est.); Travel time to work: 74.9% less than 15 minutes, 12.0% 15 to 30 minutes, 3.8% 30 to 45 minutes, 1.4% 45 to 60 minutes, 7.8% 60 minutes or more (2006-2010 5-year est.)

Additional Information Contacts

Coudersport Area Chamber of Commerce . . . . (814) 274-8165
    http://www.coudersport.org

CROSS FORK (unincorporated postal area)

Zip Code: 17729

Covers a land area of 109.210 square miles and a water area of 0.052 square miles. Located at 41.51° N. Lat; 77.73° W. Long. Population: 159 (2010); Density: 1.5 persons per square mile (2010); Race: 99.4% White, 0.0% Black, 0.0% Asian, 0.6% American Indian/Alaska Native, 0.0% Native Hawaiian/Other Pacific Islander, 0.0% Other, 0.0% Hispanic of any race (2010); Average household size: 1.77 (2010); Median age: 58.9 (2010); Males per 100 females: 117.8 (2010); Homeownership rate: 91.1% (2010)

EULALIA (township). Covers a land area of 31.120 square miles and a water area of 0 square miles. Located at 41.76° N. Lat; 78.06° W. Long.

Population: 686 (1990); 941 (2000); 889 (2010); Density: 28.6 persons per square mile (2010); Race: 97.5% White, 0.1% Black, 1.5% Asian, 0.0% American Indian/Alaska Native, 0.0% Native Hawaiian/Other Pacific Islander, 0.9% Other, 0.2% Hispanic of any race (2010); Average household size: 2.50 (2010); Median age: 49.6 (2010); Males per 100 females: 86.8 (2010); Marriage status: 16.3% never married, 64.9% now married, 12.3% widowed, 6.5% divorced (2006-2010 5-year est.); Foreign born: 1.5% (2006-2010 5-year est.); Ancestry (includes multiple ancestries): 30.0% German, 14.7% Irish, 11.1% English, 9.4% American, 5.4% French (2006-2010 5-year est.).

Economy: Single-family building permits issued: 0 (2011); Multi-family building permits issued: 0 (2011); Employment by occupation: 13.1% management, 4.4% professional, 11.5% services, 14.8% sales, 3.8% farming, 6.6% construction, 7.1% production (2006-2010 5-year est.).

Income: Per capita income: $31,121 (2006-2010 5-year est.); Median household income: $56,103 (2006-2010 5-year est.); Average household income: $79,114 (2006-2010 5-year est.); Percent of households with income of $100,000 or more: 19.9% (2006-2010 5-year est.); Poverty rate: 4.2% (2006-2010 5-year est.).

Education: Percent of population age 25 and over with: High school diploma (including GED) or higher: 90.6% (2006-2010 5-year est.); Bachelor's degree or higher: 28.5% (2006-2010 5-year est.); Master's degree or higher: 10.4% (2006-2010 5-year est.).

Housing: Homeownership rate: 84.5% (2010); Median home value: $162,500 (2006-2010 5-year est.); Median contract rent: $571 per month (2006-2010 5-year est.); Median year structure built: 1983 (2006-2010 5-year est.).

Transportation: Commute to work: 96.3% car, 1.1% public transportation, 2.0% walk, 0.0% work from home (2006-2010 5-year est.); Travel time to work: 69.3% less than 15 minutes, 16.7% 15 to 30 minutes, 7.5% 30 to 45 minutes, 0.0% 45 to 60 minutes, 6.6% 60 minutes or more (2006-2010 5-year est.)

GALETON (borough). Covers a land area of 1.271 square miles and a water area of 0.024 square miles. Located at 41.73° N. Lat; 77.64° W. Long. Elevation is 1,319 feet.

History: Incorporated 1896.

Population: 1,370 (1990); 1,325 (2000); 1,149 (2010); Density: 904.1 persons per square mile (2010); Race: 97.0% White, 0.9% Black, 0.4% Asian, 0.0% American Indian/Alaska Native, 0.0% Native Hawaiian/Other Pacific Islander, 1.7% Other, 1.0% Hispanic of any race (2010); Average household size: 2.34 (2010); Median age: 42.8 (2010); Males per 100 females: 94.1 (2010); Marriage status: 26.4% never married, 51.2% now married, 10.3% widowed, 12.1% divorced (2006-2010 5-year est.); Foreign born: 1.7% (2006-2010 5-year est.); Ancestry (includes multiple ancestries): 29.3% German, 11.6% English, 10.3% Irish, 9.9% Italian, 8.5% American (2006-2010 5-year est.).

Economy: Single-family building permits issued: 0 (2011); Multi-family building permits issued: 0 (2011); Employment by occupation: 5.1%

management, 5.9% professional, 16.0% services, 15.6% sales, 3.8% farming, 5.7% construction, 8.1% production (2006-2010 5-year est.).
Income: Per capita income: $16,804 (2006-2010 5-year est.); Median household income: $33,478 (2006-2010 5-year est.); Average household income: $39,514 (2006-2010 5-year est.); Percent of households with income of $100,000 or more: 2.3% (2006-2010 5-year est.); Poverty rate: 20.2% (2006-2010 5-year est.).
Education: Percent of population age 25 and over with: High school diploma (including GED) or higher: 84.0% (2006-2010 5-year est.); Bachelor's degree or higher: 6.3% (2006-2010 5-year est.); Master's degree or higher: 2.5% (2006-2010 5-year est.).

School District(s)

Galeton Area SD (PK-12)
    2010-11 Enrollment: 368. . . . . (814) 435-6571
Housing: Homeownership rate: 65.9% (2010); Median home value: $65,300 (2006-2010 5-year est.); Median contract rent: $468 per month (2006-2010 5-year est.); Median year structure built: before 1940 (2006-2010 5-year est.).
Transportation: Commute to work: 94.4% car, 0.0% public transportation, 2.5% walk, 2.5% work from home (2006-2010 5-year est.); Travel time to work: 51.6% less than 15 minutes, 17.5% 15 to 30 minutes, 20.3% 30 to 45 minutes, 6.6% 45 to 60 minutes, 4.0% 60 minutes or more (2006-2010 5-year est.)
Additional Information Contacts
Galeton Area Chamber of Commerce . . . . (814) 435-8737
    http://visitgaleton.com

GENESEE (township). Covers a land area of 35.733 square miles and a water area of 0.009 square miles. Located at 41.96° N. Lat; 77.91° W. Long. Elevation is 1,627 feet.
Population: 803 (1990); 789 (2000); 799 (2010); Density: 22.4 persons per square mile (2010); Race: 97.7% White, 0.4% Black, 0.1% Asian, 0.4% American Indian/Alaska Native, 0.0% Native Hawaiian/Other Pacific Islander, 1.4% Other, 1.6% Hispanic of any race (2010); Average household size: 2.42 (2010); Median age: 40.7 (2010); Males per 100 females: 107.5 (2010); Marriage status: 26.3% never married, 58.2% now married, 6.4% widowed, 9.1% divorced (2006-2010 5-year est.); Foreign born: 0.7% (2006-2010 5-year est.); Ancestry (includes multiple ancestries): 24.4% German, 16.6% English, 11.6% Irish, 8.8% Italian, 6.3% American (2006-2010 5-year est.).
Economy: Single-family building permits issued: 0 (2011); Multi-family building permits issued: 0 (2011); Employment by occupation: 9.2% management, 1.4% professional, 12.7% services, 13.3% sales, 3.2% farming, 8.9% construction, 3.2% production (2006-2010 5-year est.).
Income: Per capita income: $19,171 (2006-2010 5-year est.); Median household income: $36,250 (2006-2010 5-year est.); Average household income: $45,608 (2006-2010 5-year est.); Percent of households with income of $100,000 or more: 8.2% (2006-2010 5-year est.); Poverty rate: 18.1% (2006-2010 5-year est.).
Education: Percent of population age 25 and over with: High school diploma (including GED) or higher: 82.5% (2006-2010 5-year est.); Bachelor's degree or higher: 8.3% (2006-2010 5-year est.); Master's degree or higher: 3.2% (2006-2010 5-year est.).
Housing: Homeownership rate: 70.0% (2010); Median home value: $76,700 (2006-2010 5-year est.); Median contract rent: $416 per month (2006-2010 5-year est.); Median year structure built: 1957 (2006-2010 5-year est.).
Transportation: Commute to work: 92.8% car, 0.0% public transportation, 2.4% walk, 3.0% work from home (2006-2010 5-year est.); Travel time to work: 17.3% less than 15 minutes, 51.9% 15 to 30 minutes, 19.4% 30 to 45 minutes, 7.4% 45 to 60 minutes, 4.0% 60 minutes or more (2006-2010 5-year est.)

HARRISON (township). Covers a land area of 36.413 square miles and a water area of 0.007 square miles. Located at 41.96° N. Lat; 77.67° W. Long. Elevation is 2,277 feet.
Population: 1,129 (1990); 1,093 (2000); 1,037 (2010); Density: 28.5 persons per square mile (2010); Race: 97.3% White, 1.0% Black, 0.3% Asian, 0.2% American Indian/Alaska Native, 0.0% Native Hawaiian/Other Pacific Islander, 1.2% Other, 1.0% Hispanic of any race (2010); Average household size: 2.41 (2010); Median age: 46.1 (2010); Males per 100 females: 105.8 (2010); Marriage status: 20.1% never married, 64.7% now married, 7.3% widowed, 7.9% divorced (2006-2010 5-year est.); Foreign born: 1.3% (2006-2010 5-year est.); Ancestry (includes multiple

ancestries): 23.8% German, 12.3% Irish, 10.4% English, 10.3% Italian, 9.6% American (2006-2010 5-year est.).
Economy: Single-family building permits issued: 1 (2011); Multi-family building permits issued: 0 (2011); Employment by occupation: 6.1% management, 0.9% professional, 13.5% services, 11.4% sales, 4.3% farming, 28.5% construction, 13.0% production (2006-2010 5-year est.).
Income: Per capita income: $21,424 (2006-2010 5-year est.); Median household income: $34,583 (2006-2010 5-year est.); Average household income: $56,870 (2006-2010 5-year est.); Percent of households with income of $100,000 or more: 11.4% (2006-2010 5-year est.); Poverty rate: 11.5% (2006-2010 5-year est.).
Education: Percent of population age 25 and over with: High school diploma (including GED) or higher: 83.2% (2006-2010 5-year est.); Bachelor's degree or higher: 3.6% (2006-2010 5-year est.); Master's degree or higher: 1.7% (2006-2010 5-year est.).
Housing: Homeownership rate: 81.8% (2010); Median home value: $86,300 (2006-2010 5-year est.); Median contract rent: $558 per month (2006-2010 5-year est.); Median year structure built: 1963 (2006-2010 5-year est.).
Transportation: Commute to work: 77.1% car, 0.0% public transportation, 14.0% walk, 6.4% work from home (2006-2010 5-year est.); Travel time to work: 39.4% less than 15 minutes, 15.4% 15 to 30 minutes, 22.2% 30 to 45 minutes, 10.3% 45 to 60 minutes, 12.7% 60 minutes or more (2006-2010 5-year est.)
Additional Information Contacts
Coudersport Area Chamber of Commerce . . . . (814) 274-8165
    http://www.coudersport.org

HARRISON VALLEY (unincorporated postal area)
Zip Code: 16927
    Covers a land area of 18.881 square miles and a water area of 0 square miles. Located at 41.95° N. Lat; 77.65° W. Long. Population: 651 (2010); Density: 34.5 persons per square mile (2010); Race: 96.2% White, 1.4% Black, 0.3% Asian, 0.3% American Indian/Alaska Native, 0.0% Native Hawaiian/Other Pacific Islander, 1.8% Other, 1.1% Hispanic of any race (2010); Average household size: 2.45 (2010); Median age: 43.9 (2010); Males per 100 females: 112.1 (2010); Homeownership rate: 78.6% (2010)

HEBRON (township). Covers a land area of 43.743 square miles and a water area of 0.002 square miles. Located at 41.87° N. Lat; 78.03° W. Long. Elevation is 2,096 feet.
Population: 525 (1990); 622 (2000); 589 (2010); Density: 13.5 persons per square mile (2010); Race: 98.3% White, 0.0% Black, 0.0% Asian, 0.5% American Indian/Alaska Native, 0.0% Native Hawaiian/Other Pacific Islander, 1.2% Other, 1.0% Hispanic of any race (2010); Average household size: 2.44 (2010); Median age: 47.3 (2010); Males per 100 females: 104.5 (2010); Marriage status: 21.7% never married, 65.4% now married, 3.3% widowed, 9.5% divorced (2006-2010 5-year est.); Foreign born: 1.8% (2006-2010 5-year est.); Ancestry (includes multiple ancestries): 31.6% German, 20.6% English, 11.7% Irish, 11.1% American, 11.1% Italian (2006-2010 5-year est.).
Economy: Single-family building permits issued: 3 (2011); Multi-family building permits issued: 0 (2011); Employment by occupation: 11.1% management, 0.0% professional, 7.8% services, 13.5% sales, 3.6% farming, 13.8% construction, 12.3% production (2006-2010 5-year est.).
Income: Per capita income: $21,630 (2006-2010 5-year est.); Median household income: $46,429 (2006-2010 5-year est.); Average household income: $53,586 (2006-2010 5-year est.); Percent of households with income of $100,000 or more: 8.2% (2006-2010 5-year est.); Poverty rate: 7.1% (2006-2010 5-year est.).
Taxes: Total city taxes per capita: $123 (2009); City property taxes per capita: $53 (2009).
Education: Percent of population age 25 and over with: High school diploma (including GED) or higher: 86.2% (2006-2010 5-year est.); Bachelor's degree or higher: 15.2% (2006-2010 5-year est.); Master's degree or higher: 3.9% (2006-2010 5-year est.).
Housing: Homeownership rate: 85.1% (2010); Median home value: $110,300 (2006-2010 5-year est.); Median contract rent: $713 per month (2006-2010 5-year est.); Median year structure built: 1975 (2006-2010 5-year est.).
Transportation: Commute to work: 88.2% car, 0.0% public transportation, 2.5% walk, 5.6% work from home (2006-2010 5-year est.); Travel time to work: 23.6% less than 15 minutes, 56.7% 15 to 30 minutes, 9.8% 30 to 45

minutes, 3.0% 45 to 60 minutes, 6.9% 60 minutes or more (2006-2010 5-year est.)

HECTOR (township). Covers a land area of 41.113 square miles and a water area of <.001 square miles. Located at 41.87° N. Lat; 77.68° W. Long. Elevation is 2,103 feet.

Population: 336 (1990); 453 (2000); 386 (2010); Density: 9.4 persons per square mile (2010); Race: 99.0% White, 0.3% Black, 0.3% Asian, 0.0% American Indian/Alaska Native, 0.0% Native Hawaiian/Other Pacific Islander, 0.4% Other, 0.0% Hispanic of any race (2010); Average household size: 2.44 (2010); Median age: 47.5 (2010); Males per 100 females: 100.0 (2010); Marriage status: 19.6% never married, 56.8% now married, 10.4% widowed, 13.2% divorced (2006-2010 5-year est.); Foreign born: 0.6% (2006-2010 5-year est.); Ancestry (includes multiple ancestries): 34.1% German, 11.8% Irish, 9.4% American, 8.8% Italian, 8.5% English (2006-2010 5-year est.).
Economy: Single-family building permits issued: 0 (2011); Multi-family building permits issued: 0 (2011); Employment by occupation: 10.4% management, 0.0% professional, 4.8% services, 16.0% sales, 0.0% farming, 20.0% construction, 13.6% production (2006-2010 5-year est.).
Income: Per capita income: $19,146 (2006-2010 5-year est.); Median household income: $36,111 (2006-2010 5-year est.); Average household income: $42,241 (2006-2010 5-year est.); Percent of households with income of $100,000 or more: 5.2% (2006-2010 5-year est.); Poverty rate: 14.3% (2006-2010 5-year est.).
Education: Percent of population age 25 and over with: High school diploma (including GED) or higher: 76.3% (2006-2010 5-year est.); Bachelor's degree or higher: 12.6% (2006-2010 5-year est.); Master's degree or higher: 5.5% (2006-2010 5-year est.).
Housing: Homeownership rate: 84.8% (2010); Median home value: $108,600 (2006-2010 5-year est.); Median contract rent: $310 per month (2006-2010 5-year est.); Median year structure built: 1975 (2006-2010 5-year est.).
Transportation: Commute to work: 94.4% car, 0.0% public transportation, 1.6% walk, 1.6% work from home (2006-2010 5-year est.); Travel time to work: 35.8% less than 15 minutes, 29.3% 15 to 30 minutes, 14.6% 30 to 45 minutes, 12.2% 45 to 60 minutes, 8.1% 60 minutes or more (2006-2010 5-year est.)

HOMER (township). Covers a land area of 31.997 square miles and a water area of 0 square miles. Located at 41.69° N. Lat; 78.02° W. Long.

Population: 216 (1990); 390 (2000); 437 (2010); Density: 13.7 persons per square mile (2010); Race: 97.0% White, 1.6% Black, 0.2% Asian, 0.0% American Indian/Alaska Native, 0.0% Native Hawaiian/Other Pacific Islander, 1.2% Other, 1.1% Hispanic of any race (2010); Average household size: 2.57 (2010); Median age: 40.7 (2010); Males per 100 females: 103.3 (2010); Marriage status: 22.4% never married, 65.1% now married, 1.4% widowed, 11.1% divorced (2006-2010 5-year est.); Foreign born: 0.7% (2006-2010 5-year est.); Ancestry (includes multiple ancestries): 33.6% German, 25.7% Irish, 13.1% English, 12.2% Italian, 8.4% French (2006-2010 5-year est.).
Economy: Single-family building permits issued: 0 (2011); Multi-family building permits issued: 0 (2011); Employment by occupation: 4.7% management, 7.1% professional, 10.3% services, 25.3% sales, 4.3% farming, 5.9% construction, 4.7% production (2006-2010 5-year est.).
Income: Per capita income: $31,945 (2006-2010 5-year est.); Median household income: $76,103 (2006-2010 5-year est.); Average household income: $87,927 (2006-2010 5-year est.); Percent of households with income of $100,000 or more: 32.4% (2006-2010 5-year est.); Poverty rate: 5.2% (2006-2010 5-year est.).
Education: Percent of population age 25 and over with: High school diploma (including GED) or higher: 97.6% (2006-2010 5-year est.); Bachelor's degree or higher: 28.7% (2006-2010 5-year est.); Master's degree or higher: 10.8% (2006-2010 5-year est.).
Housing: Homeownership rate: 87.0% (2010); Median home value: $146,400 (2006-2010 5-year est.); Median contract rent: $378 per month (2006-2010 5-year est.); Median year structure built: 1981 (2006-2010 5-year est.).
Transportation: Commute to work: 90.9% car, 0.0% public transportation, 3.2% walk, 4.3% work from home (2006-2010 5-year est.); Travel time to work: 53.7% less than 15 minutes, 25.6% 15 to 30 minutes, 9.5% 30 to 45 minutes, 2.9% 45 to 60 minutes, 8.3% 60 minutes or more (2006-2010 5-year est.)

KEATING (township). Covers a land area of 41.548 square miles and a water area of 0 square miles. Located at 41.69° N. Lat; 78.14° W. Long.

Population: 304 (1990); 307 (2000); 312 (2010); Density: 7.5 persons per square mile (2010); Race: 97.4% White, 0.0% Black, 0.0% Asian, 0.0% American Indian/Alaska Native, 0.0% Native Hawaiian/Other Pacific Islander, 2.6% Other, 0.3% Hispanic of any race (2010); Average household size: 2.00 (2010); Median age: 56.4 (2010); Males per 100 females: 109.4 (2010); Marriage status: 9.0% never married, 61.9% now married, 12.2% widowed, 16.9% divorced (2006-2010 5-year est.); Foreign born: 0.0% (2006-2010 5-year est.); Ancestry (includes multiple ancestries): 27.9% German, 21.1% English, 15.2% Irish, 5.9% French, 5.4% Italian (2006-2010 5-year est.).
Economy: Single-family building permits issued: 0 (2011); Multi-family building permits issued: 0 (2011); Employment by occupation: 8.1% management, 1.8% professional, 8.1% services, 17.1% sales, 7.2% farming, 11.7% construction, 12.6% production (2006-2010 5-year est.).
Income: Per capita income: $25,824 (2006-2010 5-year est.); Median household income: $40,000 (2006-2010 5-year est.); Average household income: $46,503 (2006-2010 5-year est.); Percent of households with income of $100,000 or more: 6.3% (2006-2010 5-year est.); Poverty rate: 10.0% (2006-2010 5-year est.).
Education: Percent of population age 25 and over with: High school diploma (including GED) or higher: 89.0% (2006-2010 5-year est.); Bachelor's degree or higher: 9.9% (2006-2010 5-year est.); Master's degree or higher: 2.2% (2006-2010 5-year est.).
Housing: Homeownership rate: 93.6% (2010); Median home value: $110,500 (2006-2010 5-year est.); Median contract rent: n/a per month (2006-2010 5-year est.); Median year structure built: 1968 (2006-2010 5-year est.).
Transportation: Commute to work: 94.4% car, 0.0% public transportation, 1.9% walk, 3.7% work from home (2006-2010 5-year est.); Travel time to work: 3.8% less than 15 minutes, 51.0% 15 to 30 minutes, 32.7% 30 to 45 minutes, 0.0% 45 to 60 minutes, 12.5% 60 minutes or more (2006-2010 5-year est.)

MILLS (unincorporated postal area)
Zip Code: 16937

Covers a land area of 7.338 square miles and a water area of 0.004 square miles. Located at 41.96° N. Lat; 77.71° W. Long. Population: 172 (2010); Density: 23.4 persons per square mile (2010); Race: 100.0% White, 0.0% Black, 0.0% Asian, 0.0% American Indian/Alaska Native, 0.0% Native Hawaiian/Other Pacific Islander, 0.0% Other, 1.2% Hispanic of any race (2010); Average household size: 2.61 (2010); Median age: 44.8 (2010); Males per 100 females: 102.4 (2010); Homeownership rate: 83.3% (2010)

OSWAYO (borough). Covers a land area of 1.380 square miles and a water area of 0 square miles. Located at 41.92° N. Lat; 78.02° W. Long. Elevation is 1,699 feet.

Population: 156 (1990); 159 (2000); 139 (2010); Density: 100.7 persons per square mile (2010); Race: 97.1% White, 0.0% Black, 0.0% Asian, 0.7% American Indian/Alaska Native, 0.0% Native Hawaiian/Other Pacific Islander, 2.2% Other, 0.0% Hispanic of any race (2010); Average household size: 2.73 (2010); Median age: 39.9 (2010); Males per 100 females: 104.4 (2010); Marriage status: 12.4% never married, 77.5% now married, 3.4% widowed, 6.7% divorced (2006-2010 5-year est.); Foreign born: 0.0% (2006-2010 5-year est.); Ancestry (includes multiple ancestries): 36.3% German, 21.0% American, 11.3% Irish, 10.5% Italian, 5.6% English (2006-2010 5-year est.).
Economy: Single-family building permits issued: 0 (2011); Multi-family building permits issued: 0 (2011); Employment by occupation: 10.9% management, 9.1% professional, 5.5% services, 16.4% sales, 0.0% farming, 20.0% construction, 9.1% production (2006-2010 5-year est.).
Income: Per capita income: $14,114 (2006-2010 5-year est.); Median household income: $31,000 (2006-2010 5-year est.); Average household income: $41,164 (2006-2010 5-year est.); Percent of households with income of $100,000 or more: n/a (2006-2010 5-year est.); Poverty rate: 25.8% (2006-2010 5-year est.).
Education: Percent of population age 25 and over with: High school diploma (including GED) or higher: 78.7% (2006-2010 5-year est.); Bachelor's degree or higher: 5.3% (2006-2010 5-year est.); Master's degree or higher: 0.0% (2006-2010 5-year est.).
Housing: Homeownership rate: 88.3% (2010); Median home value: $84,300 (2006-2010 5-year est.); Median contract rent: $375 per month

(2006-2010 5-year est.); Median year structure built: before 1940 (2006-2010 5-year est.).

Transportation: Commute to work: 92.3% car, 0.0% public transportation, 0.0% walk, 7.7% work from home (2006-2010 5-year est.); Travel time to work: 12.5% less than 15 minutes, 50.0% 15 to 30 minutes, 22.9% 30 to 45 minutes, 0.0% 45 to 60 minutes, 14.6% 60 minutes or more (2006-2010 5-year est.)

OSWAYO (township). Covers a land area of 37.257 square miles and a water area of 0.017 square miles. Located at 41.95° N. Lat; 78.01° W. Long. Elevation is 1,699 feet.

Population: 214 (1990); 251 (2000); 278 (2010); Density: 7.5 persons per square mile (2010); Race: 97.8% White, 0.0% Black, 0.0% Asian, 0.0% American Indian/Alaska Native, 0.0% Native Hawaiian/Other Pacific Islander, 2.2% Other, 1.8% Hispanic of any race (2010); Average household size: 2.55 (2010); Median age: 44.0 (2010); Males per 100 females: 97.2 (2010); Marriage status: 12.5% never married, 59.6% now married, 6.6% widowed, 21.3% divorced (2006-2010 5-year est.); Foreign born: 0.0% (2006-2010 5-year est.); Ancestry (includes multiple ancestries): 43.4% German, 36.2% Irish, 19.1% Polish, 14.5% English, 7.2% Italian (2006-2010 5-year est.).

Economy: Single-family building permits issued: 1 (2011); Multi-family building permits issued: 0 (2011); Employment by occupation: 12.1% management, 0.0% professional, 19.7% services, 15.2% sales, 9.1% farming, 19.7% construction, 12.1% production (2006-2010 5-year est.).

Income: Per capita income: $20,111 (2006-2010 5-year est.); Median household income: $33,750 (2006-2010 5-year est.); Average household income: $45,454 (2006-2010 5-year est.); Percent of households with income of $100,000 or more: 6.9% (2006-2010 5-year est.); Poverty rate: 9.2% (2006-2010 5-year est.).

Education: Percent of population age 25 and over with: High school diploma (including GED) or higher: 86.8% (2006-2010 5-year est.); Bachelor's degree or higher: 2.3% (2006-2010 5-year est.); Master's degree or higher: 0.0% (2006-2010 5-year est.).

Housing: Homeownership rate: 87.1% (2010); Median home value: $115,000 (2006-2010 5-year est.); Median contract rent: n/a per month (2006-2010 5-year est.); Median year structure built: 1973 (2006-2010 5-year est.).

Transportation: Commute to work: 90.9% car, 0.0% public transportation, 0.0% walk, 6.1% work from home (2006-2010 5-year est.); Travel time to work: 25.8% less than 15 minutes, 21.0% 15 to 30 minutes, 37.1% 30 to 45 minutes, 12.9% 45 to 60 minutes, 3.2% 60 minutes or more (2006-2010 5-year est.)

PIKE (township). Covers a land area of 36.620 square miles and a water area of 0 square miles. Located at 41.77° N. Lat; 77.67° W. Long.

Population: 252 (1990); 292 (2000); 324 (2010); Density: 8.8 persons per square mile (2010); Race: 98.5% White, 0.0% Black, 0.3% Asian, 0.3% American Indian/Alaska Native, 0.0% Native Hawaiian/Other Pacific Islander, 0.9% Other, 0.0% Hispanic of any race (2010); Average household size: 2.27 (2010); Median age: 51.1 (2010); Males per 100 females: 96.4 (2010); Marriage status: 17.9% never married, 66.1% now married, 9.2% widowed, 6.9% divorced (2006-2010 5-year est.); Foreign born: 0.7% (2006-2010 5-year est.); Ancestry (includes multiple ancestries): 27.5% English, 22.7% German, 12.7% Irish, 12.0% Polish, 9.6% Italian (2006-2010 5-year est.).

Economy: Single-family building permits issued: 0 (2011); Multi-family building permits issued: 0 (2011); Employment by occupation: 14.5% management, 0.0% professional, 15.4% services, 15.4% sales, 0.0% farming, 17.1% construction, 1.7% production (2006-2010 5-year est.).

Income: Per capita income: $17,435 (2006-2010 5-year est.); Median household income: $43,375 (2006-2010 5-year est.); Average household income: $41,178 (2006-2010 5-year est.); Percent of households with income of $100,000 or more: 4.1% (2006-2010 5-year est.); Poverty rate: 23.4% (2006-2010 5-year est.).

Education: Percent of population age 25 and over with: High school diploma (including GED) or higher: 85.4% (2006-2010 5-year est.); Bachelor's degree or higher: 8.1% (2006-2010 5-year est.); Master's degree or higher: 2.0% (2006-2010 5-year est.).

Housing: Homeownership rate: 77.0% (2010); Median home value: $154,500 (2006-2010 5-year est.); Median contract rent: $453 per month (2006-2010 5-year est.); Median year structure built: 1969 (2006-2010 5-year est.).

Transportation: Commute to work: 93.0% car, 0.0% public transportation, 0.0% walk, 7.0% work from home (2006-2010 5-year est.); Travel time to

work: 32.7% less than 15 minutes, 42.1% 15 to 30 minutes, 12.1% 30 to 45 minutes, 12.1% 45 to 60 minutes, 0.9% 60 minutes or more (2006-2010 5-year est.)

PLEASANT VALLEY (township). Covers a land area of 19.617 square miles and a water area of 0 square miles. Located at 41.87° N. Lat; 78.18° W. Long.

Population: 78 (1990); 80 (2000); 86 (2010); Density: 4.4 persons per square mile (2010); Race: 97.7% White, 0.0% Black, 0.0% Asian, 0.0% American Indian/Alaska Native, 0.0% Native Hawaiian/Other Pacific Islander, 2.3% Other, 2.3% Hispanic of any race (2010); Average household size: 2.39 (2010); Median age: 41.5 (2010); Males per 100 females: 120.5 (2010); Marriage status: 4.1% never married, 91.9% now married, 4.1% widowed, 0.0% divorced (2006-2010 5-year est.); Foreign born: 0.0% (2006-2010 5-year est.); Ancestry (includes multiple ancestries): 31.0% English, 30.0% Irish, 28.0% German, 10.0% Dutch, 7.0% American (2006-2010 5-year est.).

Economy: Single-family building permits issued: 0 (2011); Multi-family building permits issued: 0 (2011); Employment by occupation: 4.7% management, 0.0% professional, 11.6% services, 7.0% sales, 0.0% farming, 30.2% construction, 20.9% production (2006-2010 5-year est.).

Income: Per capita income: $16,176 (2006-2010 5-year est.); Median household income: $35,000 (2006-2010 5-year est.); Average household income: $41,180 (2006-2010 5-year est.); Percent of households with income of $100,000 or more: n/a (2006-2010 5-year est.); Poverty rate: 14.0% (2006-2010 5-year est.).

Education: Percent of population age 25 and over with: High school diploma (including GED) or higher: 93.1% (2006-2010 5-year est.); Bachelor's degree or higher: 23.6% (2006-2010 5-year est.); Master's degree or higher: 6.9% (2006-2010 5-year est.).

Housing: Homeownership rate: 80.6% (2010); Median home value: $100,000 (2006-2010 5-year est.); Median contract rent: $475 per month (2006-2010 5-year est.); Median year structure built: 1961 (2006-2010 5-year est.).

Transportation: Commute to work: 95.3% car, 0.0% public transportation, 0.0% walk, 4.7% work from home (2006-2010 5-year est.); Travel time to work: 9.8% less than 15 minutes, 26.8% 15 to 30 minutes, 36.6% 30 to 45 minutes, 22.0% 45 to 60 minutes, 4.9% 60 minutes or more (2006-2010 5-year est.)

PORTAGE (township). Covers a land area of 37.535 square miles and a water area of 0 square miles. Located at 41.60° N. Lat; 78.13° W. Long.

Population: 176 (1990); 223 (2000); 228 (2010); Density: 6.1 persons per square mile (2010); Race: 99.1% White, 0.0% Black, 0.4% Asian, 0.0% American Indian/Alaska Native, 0.0% Native Hawaiian/Other Pacific Islander, 0.5% Other, 0.0% Hispanic of any race (2010); Average household size: 2.43 (2010); Median age: 48.1 (2010); Males per 100 females: 94.9 (2010); Marriage status: 21.1% never married, 69.6% now married, 5.2% widowed, 4.1% divorced (2006-2010 5-year est.); Foreign born: 0.0% (2006-2010 5-year est.); Ancestry (includes multiple ancestries): 53.8% German, 17.9% Irish, 10.8% Swedish, 10.8% English, 3.3% Scottish (2006-2010 5-year est.).

Economy: Single-family building permits issued: 2 (2011); Multi-family building permits issued: 0 (2011); Employment by occupation: 4.4% management, 5.9% professional, 20.6% services, 11.8% sales, 5.9% farming, 11.8% construction, 25.0% production (2006-2010 5-year est.).

Income: Per capita income: $21,542 (2006-2010 5-year est.); Median household income: $45,625 (2006-2010 5-year est.); Average household income: $48,175 (2006-2010 5-year est.); Percent of households with income of $100,000 or more: 2.1% (2006-2010 5-year est.); Poverty rate: 17.5% (2006-2010 5-year est.).

Education: Percent of population age 25 and over with: High school diploma (including GED) or higher: 98.9% (2006-2010 5-year est.); Bachelor's degree or higher: 8.0% (2006-2010 5-year est.); Master's degree or higher: 0.0% (2006-2010 5-year est.).

Housing: Homeownership rate: 86.2% (2010); Median home value: $88,900 (2006-2010 5-year est.); Median contract rent: <$101 per month (2006-2010 5-year est.); Median year structure built: 1969 (2006-2010 5-year est.).

Transportation: Commute to work: 91.2% car, 0.0% public transportation, 1.5% walk, 7.4% work from home (2006-2010 5-year est.); Travel time to work: 23.8% less than 15 minutes, 44.4% 15 to 30 minutes, 22.2% 30 to 45 minutes, 4.8% 45 to 60 minutes, 4.8% 60 minutes or more (2006-2010 5-year est.)

ROULETTE (CDP). Covers a land area of 1.722 square miles and a water area of 0 square miles. Located at 41.78° N. Lat; 78.16° W. Long. Elevation is 1,529 feet.

Population: n/a (1990); n/a (2000); 779 (2010); Density: 452.5 persons per square mile (2010); Race: 99.2% White, 0.4% Black, 0.0% Asian, 0.4% American Indian/Alaska Native, 0.0% Native Hawaiian/Other Pacific Islander, 0.0% Other, 2.1% Hispanic of any race (2010); Average household size: 2.40 (2010); Median age: 44.1 (2010); Males per 100 females: 97.7 (2010); Marriage status: 21.5% never married, 65.6% now married, 4.0% widowed, 9.0% divorced (2006-2010 5-year est.); Foreign born: 0.0% (2006-2010 5-year est.); Ancestry (includes multiple ancestries): 26.6% German, 9.2% Irish, 8.9% American, 7.6% English, 5.3% French (2006-2010 5-year est.).

Economy: Employment by occupation: 3.1% management, 2.7% professional, 16.1% services, 14.9% sales, 2.9% farming, 16.1% construction, 16.1% production (2006-2010 5-year est.).

Income: Per capita income: $16,158 (2006-2010 5-year est.); Median household income: $42,361 (2006-2010 5-year est.); Average household income: $42,533 (2006-2010 5-year est.); Percent of households with income of $100,000 or more: 1.3% (2006-2010 5-year est.); Poverty rate: 17.2% (2006-2010 5-year est.).

Education: Percent of population age 25 and over with: High school diploma (including GED) or higher: 85.4% (2006-2010 5-year est.); Bachelor's degree or higher: 3.1% (2006-2010 5-year est.); Master's degree or higher: 0.0% (2006-2010 5-year est.).

Housing: Homeownership rate: 71.6% (2010); Median home value: $60,900 (2006-2010 5-year est.); Median contract rent: $441 per month (2006-2010 5-year est.); Median year structure built: 1947 (2006-2010 5-year est.).

Transportation: Commute to work: 91.2% car, 0.0% public transportation, 6.6% walk, 2.2% work from home (2006-2010 5-year est.); Travel time to work: 31.9% less than 15 minutes, 41.6% 15 to 30 minutes, 8.2% 30 to 45 minutes, 9.5% 45 to 60 minutes, 8.7% 60 minutes or more (2006-2010 5-year est.)

ROULETTE (township). Covers a land area of 32.620 square miles and a water area of <.001 square miles. Located at 41.78° N. Lat; 78.14° W. Long. Elevation is 1,529 feet.

Population: 1,266 (1990); 1,348 (2000); 1,197 (2010); Density: 36.7 persons per square mile (2010); Race: 99.0% White, 0.4% Black, 0.0% Asian, 0.3% American Indian/Alaska Native, 0.0% Native Hawaiian/Other Pacific Islander, 0.3% Other, 1.8% Hispanic of any race (2010); Average household size: 2.38 (2010); Median age: 45.7 (2010); Males per 100 females: 103.6 (2010); Marriage status: 20.6% never married, 66.2% now married, 5.1% widowed, 8.0% divorced (2006-2010 5-year est.); Foreign born: 0.2% (2006-2010 5-year est.); Ancestry (includes multiple ancestries): 26.1% German, 13.0% English, 9.9% Irish, 7.2% American, 5.4% French (2006-2010 5-year est.).

Economy: Single-family building permits issued: 2 (2011); Multi-family building permits issued: 0 (2011); Employment by occupation: 5.0% management, 1.8% professional, 14.2% services, 12.7% sales, 3.0% farming, 15.3% construction, 17.8% production (2006-2010 5-year est.).

Income: Per capita income: $18,210 (2006-2010 5-year est.); Median household income: $43,672 (2006-2010 5-year est.); Average household income: $47,133 (2006-2010 5-year est.); Percent of households with income of $100,000 or more: 4.5% (2006-2010 5-year est.); Poverty rate: 13.8% (2006-2010 5-year est.).

Education: Percent of population age 25 and over with: High school diploma (including GED) or higher: 88.6% (2006-2010 5-year est.); Bachelor's degree or higher: 7.1% (2006-2010 5-year est.); Master's degree or higher: 1.5% (2006-2010 5-year est.).

Housing: Homeownership rate: 76.5% (2010); Median home value: $69,900 (2006-2010 5-year est.); Median contract rent: $443 per month (2006-2010 5-year est.); Median year structure built: 1957 (2006-2010 5-year est.).

Transportation: Commute to work: 92.5% car, 0.0% public transportation, 4.6% walk, 2.9% work from home (2006-2010 5-year est.); Travel time to work: 32.1% less than 15 minutes, 44.7% 15 to 30 minutes, 7.3% 30 to 45 minutes, 8.0% 45 to 60 minutes, 7.9% 60 minutes or more (2006-2010 5-year est.).

Additional Information Contacts

Coudersport Area Chamber of Commerce . . . . (814) 274-8165
  http://www.coudersport.org

SHARON (township). Covers a land area of 34.039 square miles and a water area of 0.026 square miles. Located at 41.96° N. Lat; 78.14° W. Long.

Population: 841 (1990); 907 (2000); 866 (2010); Density: 25.4 persons per square mile (2010); Race: 98.8% White, 0.3% Black, 0.1% Asian, 0.5% American Indian/Alaska Native, 0.0% Native Hawaiian/Other Pacific Islander, 0.3% Other, 1.7% Hispanic of any race (2010); Average household size: 2.48 (2010); Median age: 43.7 (2010); Males per 100 females: 95.0 (2010); Marriage status: 24.2% never married, 63.0% now married, 6.3% widowed, 6.6% divorced (2006-2010 5-year est.); Foreign born: 0.4% (2006-2010 5-year est.); Ancestry (includes multiple ancestries): 28.3% German, 18.1% English, 12.1% Irish, 5.2% American, 4.6% Scotch-Irish (2006-2010 5-year est.).

Economy: Single-family building permits issued: 0 (2011); Multi-family building permits issued: 0 (2011); Employment by occupation: 5.2% management, 2.4% professional, 20.1% services, 22.5% sales, 1.4% farming, 9.3% construction, 9.0% production (2006-2010 5-year est.).

Income: Per capita income: $18,255 (2006-2010 5-year est.); Median household income: $33,988 (2006-2010 5-year est.); Average household income: $45,458 (2006-2010 5-year est.); Percent of households with income of $100,000 or more: 6.7% (2006-2010 5-year est.); Poverty rate: 13.7% (2006-2010 5-year est.).

Education: Percent of population age 25 and over with: High school diploma (including GED) or higher: 79.0% (2006-2010 5-year est.); Bachelor's degree or higher: 10.2% (2006-2010 5-year est.); Master's degree or higher: 4.4% (2006-2010 5-year est.).

Housing: Homeownership rate: 90.8% (2010); Median home value: $74,000 (2006-2010 5-year est.); Median contract rent: $248 per month (2006-2010 5-year est.); Median year structure built: 1964 (2006-2010 5-year est.).

Transportation: Commute to work: 90.7% car, 0.0% public transportation, 1.0% walk, 8.3% work from home (2006-2010 5-year est.); Travel time to work: 43.8% less than 15 minutes, 24.2% 15 to 30 minutes, 22.3% 30 to 45 minutes, 3.4% 45 to 60 minutes, 6.4% 60 minutes or more (2006-2010 5-year est.)

SHINGLEHOUSE (borough). Covers a land area of 2.094 square miles and a water area of 0.002 square miles. Located at 41.97° N. Lat; 78.19° W. Long. Elevation is 1,489 feet.

History: Settled 1808, incorporated 1902.

Population: 1,243 (1990); 1,250 (2000); 1,127 (2010); Density: 538.2 persons per square mile (2010); Race: 98.8% White, 0.0% Black, 0.3% Asian, 0.5% American Indian/Alaska Native, 0.0% Native Hawaiian/Other Pacific Islander, 0.4% Other, 1.0% Hispanic of any race (2010); Average household size: 2.33 (2010); Median age: 41.6 (2010); Males per 100 females: 98.1 (2010); Marriage status: 27.4% never married, 50.4% now married, 11.2% widowed, 10.9% divorced (2006-2010 5-year est.); Foreign born: 2.2% (2006-2010 5-year est.); Ancestry (includes multiple ancestries): 28.1% German, 25.8% English, 23.7% Irish, 4.1% Italian, 3.9% Polish (2006-2010 5-year est.).

Economy: Single-family building permits issued: 0 (2011); Multi-family building permits issued: 0 (2011); Employment by occupation: 9.9% management, 2.4% professional, 10.1% services, 17.9% sales, 0.0% farming, 7.5% construction, 11.1% production (2006-2010 5-year est.).

Income: Per capita income: $17,643 (2006-2010 5-year est.); Median household income: $30,139 (2006-2010 5-year est.); Average household income: $40,217 (2006-2010 5-year est.); Percent of households with income of $100,000 or more: 4.8% (2006-2010 5-year est.); Poverty rate: 22.3% (2006-2010 5-year est.).

Education: Percent of population age 25 and over with: High school diploma (including GED) or higher: 85.5% (2006-2010 5-year est.); Bachelor's degree or higher: 6.2% (2006-2010 5-year est.); Master's degree or higher: 1.2% (2006-2010 5-year est.).

School District(s)

Oswayo Valley SD (PK-12)
  2010-11 Enrollment: 537 . . . . (814) 697-7175

Housing: Homeownership rate: 66.7% (2010); Median home value: $75,500 (2006-2010 5-year est.); Median contract rent: $392 per month (2006-2010 5-year est.); Median year structure built: 1945 (2006-2010 5-year est.).

Safety: Violent crime rate: 8.8 per 10,000 population; Property crime rate: 26.5 per 10,000 population (2011).

Transportation: Commute to work: 89.2% car, 0.0% public pennsportation, 8.6% walk, 2.2% work from home (2006-2010 5-year est.); Travel time to work: 28.7% less than 15 minutes, 31.1% 15 to 30 minutes, 34.8% 30 to

45 minutes, 5.4% 45 to 60 minutes, 0.0% 60 minutes or more (2006-2010 5-year est.)

Additional Information Contacts

Coudersport Area Chamber of Commerce . . . . (814) 274-8165
    http://www.coudersport.org

STEWARDSON (township). Covers a land area of 74.064 square miles and a water area of <.001 square miles. Located at 41.51° N. Lat; 77.74° W. Long.

Population: 66 (1990); 74 (2000); 74 (2010); Density: 1.0 persons per square mile (2010); Race: 100.0% White, 0.0% Black, 0.0% Asian, 0.0% American Indian/Alaska Native, 0.0% Native Hawaiian/Other Pacific Islander, 0.0% Other, 0.0% Hispanic of any race (2010); Average household size: 1.68 (2010); Median age: 60.5 (2010); Males per 100 females: 117.6 (2010); Marriage status: 27.3% never married, 54.5% now married, 18.2% widowed, 0.0% divorced (2006-2010 5-year est.); Foreign born: 0.0% (2006-2010 5-year est.); Ancestry (includes multiple ancestries): 45.5% German, 18.2% English, 18.2% French, 15.2% Swedish, 15.2% Irish (2006-2010 5-year est.).

Economy: Single-family building permits issued: 0 (2011); Multi-family building permits issued: 0 (2011); Employment by occupation: 0.0% management, 0.0% professional, 15.8% services, 26.3% sales, 10.5% farming, 0.0% construction, 10.5% production (2006-2010 5-year est.).

Income: Per capita income: $17,455 (2006-2010 5-year est.); Median household income: $25,938 (2006-2010 5-year est.); Average household income: $31,732 (2006-2010 5-year est.); Percent of households with income of $100,000 or more: 10.5% (2006-2010 5-year est.); Poverty rate: 21.2% (2006-2010 5-year est.).

Education: Percent of population age 25 and over with: High school diploma (including GED) or higher: 93.3% (2006-2010 5-year est.); Bachelor's degree or higher: 0.0% (2006-2010 5-year est.); Master's degree or higher: 0.0% (2006-2010 5-year est.).

Housing: Homeownership rate: 90.9% (2010); Median home value: $147,900 (2006-2010 5-year est.); Median contract rent: n/a per month (2006-2010 5-year est.); Median year structure built: 1952 (2006-2010 5-year est.).

Transportation: Commute to work: 70.6% car, 0.0% public transportation, 5.9% walk, 23.5% work from home (2006-2010 5-year est.); Travel time to work: 69.2% less than 15 minutes, 15.4% 15 to 30 minutes, 0.0% 30 to 45 minutes, 0.0% 45 to 60 minutes, 15.4% 60 minutes or more (2006-2010 5-year est.)

SUMMIT (township). Covers a land area of 49.233 square miles and a water area of 0 square miles. Located at 41.68° N. Lat; 77.90° W. Long.

Population: 115 (1990); 112 (2000); 188 (2010); Density: 3.8 persons per square mile (2010); Race: 100.0% White, 0.0% Black, 0.0% Asian, 0.0% American Indian/Alaska Native, 0.0% Native Hawaiian/Other Pacific Islander, 0.0% Other, 0.5% Hispanic of any race (2010); Average household size: 2.61 (2010); Median age: 46.0 (2010); Males per 100 females: 106.6 (2010); Marriage status: 12.7% never married, 63.7% now married, 15.7% widowed, 7.8% divorced (2006-2010 5-year est.); Foreign born: 0.0% (2006-2010 5-year est.); Ancestry (includes multiple ancestries): 31.9% German, 19.0% Irish, 18.1% Italian, 15.5% Polish, 6.9% English (2006-2010 5-year est.).

Economy: Single-family building permits issued: 0 (2011); Multi-family building permits issued: 0 (2011); Employment by occupation: 12.5% management, 7.8% professional, 0.0% services, 21.9% sales, 4.7% farming, 6.3% construction, 4.7% production (2006-2010 5-year est.).

Income: Per capita income: $24,505 (2006-2010 5-year est.); Median household income: $40,833 (2006-2010 5-year est.); Average household income: $52,287 (2006-2010 5-year est.); Percent of households with income of $100,000 or more: 11.1% (2006-2010 5-year est.); Poverty rate: 0.0% (2006-2010 5-year est.).

Education: Percent of population age 25 and over with: High school diploma (including GED) or higher: 84.7% (2006-2010 5-year est.); Bachelor's degree or higher: 23.5% (2006-2010 5-year est.); Master's degree or higher: 4.1% (2006-2010 5-year est.).

Housing: Homeownership rate: 90.3% (2010); Median home value: $142,900 (2006-2010 5-year est.); Median contract rent: n/a per month (2006-2010 5-year est.); Median year structure built: 1973 (2006-2010 5-year est.).

Transportation: Commute to work: 89.7% car, 0.0% public transportation, 0.0% walk, 5.2% work from home (2006-2010 5-year est.); Travel time to work: 10.9% less than 15 minutes, 45.5% 15 to 30 minutes, 32.7% 30 to

45 minutes, 0.0% 45 to 60 minutes, 10.9% 60 minutes or more (2006-2010 5-year est.)

SWEDEN (township). Covers a land area of 33.822 square miles and a water area of 0.014 square miles. Located at 41.77° N. Lat; 77.92° W. Long. Elevation is 2,306 feet.

Population: 581 (1990); 775 (2000); 872 (2010); Density: 25.8 persons per square mile (2010); Race: 97.7% White, 0.2% Black, 0.2% Asian, 0.6% American Indian/Alaska Native, 0.0% Native Hawaiian/Other Pacific Islander, 1.3% Other, 2.1% Hispanic of any race (2010); Average household size: 2.51 (2010); Median age: 41.6 (2010); Males per 100 females: 115.3 (2010); Marriage status: 21.2% never married, 66.8% now married, 4.4% widowed, 7.6% divorced (2006-2010 5-year est.); Foreign born: 0.8% (2006-2010 5-year est.); Ancestry (includes multiple ancestries): 31.4% German, 14.8% Polish, 9.7% English, 7.2% Italian, 6.8% American (2006-2010 5-year est.).

Economy: Single-family building permits issued: 0 (2011); Multi-family building permits issued: 0 (2011); Employment by occupation: 17.0% management, 9.6% professional, 6.6% services, 11.0% sales, 0.5% farming, 12.4% construction, 6.6% production (2006-2010 5-year est.).

Income: Per capita income: $24,171 (2006-2010 5-year est.); Median household income: $56,875 (2006-2010 5-year est.); Average household income: $65,491 (2006-2010 5-year est.); Percent of households with income of $100,000 or more: 10.0% (2006-2010 5-year est.); Poverty rate: 4.9% (2006-2010 5-year est.).

Education: Percent of population age 25 and over with: High school diploma (including GED) or higher: 91.8% (2006-2010 5-year est.); Bachelor's degree or higher: 17.0% (2006-2010 5-year est.); Master's degree or higher: 6.8% (2006-2010 5-year est.).

Housing: Homeownership rate: 81.6% (2010); Median home value: $133,600 (2006-2010 5-year est.); Median contract rent: $703 per month (2006-2010 5-year est.); Median year structure built: 1979 (2006-2010 5-year est.).

Transportation: Commute to work: 81.8% car, 0.0% public transportation, 8.0% walk, 10.2% work from home (2006-2010 5-year est.); Travel time to work: 57.9% less than 15 minutes, 25.3% 15 to 30 minutes, 7.3% 30 to 45 minutes, 5.1% 45 to 60 minutes, 4.4% 60 minutes or more (2006-2010 5-year est.).

SWEDEN VALLEY (CDP). Covers a land area of 1.029 square miles and a water area of 0 square miles. Located at 41.76° N. Lat; 77.95° W. Long. Elevation is 1,795 feet.

Population: n/a (1990); n/a (2000); 223 (2010); Density: 216.7 persons per square mile (2010); Race: 97.3% White, 0.0% Black, 0.4% Asian, 1.8% American Indian/Alaska Native, 0.0% Native Hawaiian/Other Pacific Islander, 0.5% Other, 2.7% Hispanic of any race (2010); Average household size: 2.42 (2010); Median age: 37.2 (2010); Males per 100 females: 108.4 (2010); Marriage status: 19.0% never married, 71.3% now married, 6.9% widowed, 2.9% divorced (2006-2010 5-year est.); Foreign born: 1.8% (2006-2010 5-year est.); Ancestry (includes multiple ancestries): 12.3% Italian, 11.9% German, 8.1% American, 8.1% Polish, 6.7% French (2006-2010 5-year est.).

Economy: Employment by occupation: 0.0% management, 12.4% professional, 6.7% services, 12.4% sales, 0.0% farming, 11.2% construction, 3.4% production (2006-2010 5-year est.).

Income: Per capita income: $16,562 (2006-2010 5-year est.); Median household income: $41,691 (2006-2010 5-year est.); Average household income: $55,758 (2006-2010 5-year est.); Percent of households with income of $100,000 or more: 6.0% (2006-2010 5-year est.); Poverty rate: 4.9% (2006-2010 5-year est.).

Education: Percent of population age 25 and over with: High school diploma (including GED) or higher: 95.9% (2006-2010 5-year est.); Bachelor's degree or higher: 10.2% (2006-2010 5-year est.); Master's degree or higher: 2.7% (2006-2010 5-year est.).

Housing: Homeownership rate: 61.9% (2010); Median home value: $108,000 (2006-2010 5-year est.); Median contract rent: $383 per month (2006-2010 5-year est.); Median year structure built: 1955 (2006-2010 5-year est.).

Transportation: Commute to work: 93.3% car, 0.0% public transportation, 6.7% walk, 0.0% work from home (2006-2010 5-year est.); Travel time to work: 60.7% less than 15 minutes, 25.8% 15 to 30 minutes, 2.2% 30 to 45 minutes, 7.9% 45 to 60 minutes, 3.4% 60 minutes or more (2006-2010 5-year est.)

SYLVANIA (township). Covers a land area of 29.676 square miles and a water area of 0 square miles. Located at 41.61° N. Lat; 78.01° W. Long.
Population: 80 (1990); 61 (2000); 77 (2010); Density: 2.6 persons per square mile (2010); Race: 100.0% White, 0.0% Black, 0.0% Asian, 0.0% American Indian/Alaska Native, 0.0% Native Hawaiian/Other Pacific Islander, 0.0% Other, 1.3% Hispanic of any race (2010); Average household size: 2.26 (2010); Median age: 52.2 (2010); Males per 100 females: 108.1 (2010); Marriage status: 28.6% never married, 46.8% now married, 2.6% widowed, 22.1% divorced (2006-2010 5-year est.); Foreign born: 0.0% (2006-2010 5-year est.); Ancestry (includes multiple ancestries): 20.7% German, 18.4% Polish, 14.9% English, 13.8% Irish, 10.3% Scottish (2006-2010 5-year est.).
Economy: Single-family building permits issued: 0 (2011); Multi-family building permits issued: 0 (2011); Employment by occupation: 0.0% management, 0.0% professional, 9.4% services, 6.3% sales, 15.6% farming, 6.3% construction, 25.0% production (2006-2010 5-year est.).
Income: Per capita income: $23,153 (2006-2010 5-year est.); Median household income: $35,893 (2006-2010 5-year est.); Average household income: $41,835 (2006-2010 5-year est.); Percent of households with income of $100,000 or more: 5.9% (2006-2010 5-year est.); Poverty rate: 23.0% (2006-2010 5-year est.).
Education: Percent of population age 25 and over with: High school diploma (including GED) or higher: 90.5% (2006-2010 5-year est.); Bachelor's degree or higher: 4.1% (2006-2010 5-year est.); Master's degree or higher: 0.0% (2006-2010 5-year est.).
Housing: Homeownership rate: 82.4% (2010); Median home value: $87,500 (2006-2010 5-year est.); Median contract rent: $388 per month (2006-2010 5-year est.); Median year structure built: 1974 (2006-2010 5-year est.).
Transportation: Commute to work: 81.3% car, 0.0% public transportation, 0.0% walk, 18.8% work from home (2006-2010 5-year est.); Travel time to work: 19.2% less than 15 minutes, 7.7% 15 to 30 minutes, 42.3% 30 to 45 minutes, 30.8% 45 to 60 minutes, 0.0% 60 minutes or more (2006-2010 5-year est.)

ULYSSES (borough). Aka Lewisville. Covers a land area of 4.054 square miles and a water area of 0 square miles. Located at 41.90° N. Lat; 77.75° W. Long. Elevation is 2,096 feet.
Population: 653 (1990); 684 (2000); 621 (2010); Density: 153.2 persons per square mile (2010); Race: 98.7% White, 0.8% Black, 0.0% Asian, 0.0% American Indian/Alaska Native, 0.0% Native Hawaiian/Other Pacific Islander, 0.5% Other, 0.3% Hispanic of any race (2010); Average household size: 2.48 (2010); Median age: 39.6 (2010); Males per 100 females: 86.5 (2010); Marriage status: 17.9% never married, 65.7% now married, 8.6% widowed, 7.8% divorced (2006-2010 5-year est.); Foreign born: 0.5% (2006-2010 5-year est.); Ancestry (includes multiple ancestries): 28.4% German, 16.3% Irish, 14.1% English, 5.2% Polish, 3.9% French (2006-2010 5-year est.).
Economy: Single-family building permits issued: 0 (2011); Multi-family building permits issued: 0 (2011); Employment by occupation: 3.2% management, 4.0% professional, 13.6% services, 17.2% sales, 4.4% farming, 15.2% construction, 3.2% production (2006-2010 5-year est.).
Income: Per capita income: $15,117 (2006-2010 5-year est.); Median household income: $36,146 (2006-2010 5-year est.); Average household income: $38,192 (2006-2010 5-year est.); Percent of households with income of $100,000 or more: 5.0% (2006-2010 5-year est.); Poverty rate: 25.4% (2006-2010 5-year est.).
Education: Percent of population age 25 and over with: High school diploma (including GED) or higher: 76.2% (2006-2010 5-year est.); Bachelor's degree or higher: 5.0% (2006-2010 5-year est.); Master's degree or higher: 1.2% (2006-2010 5-year est.).
School District(s)
Northern Potter SD (KG-12)
    2010-11 Enrollment: 605. . . . . (814) 848-7506
Housing: Homeownership rate: 66.0% (2010); Median home value: $71,300 (2006-2010 5-year est.); Median contract rent: $305 per month (2006-2010 5-year est.); Median year structure built: 1973 (2006-2010 5-year est.).
Transportation: Commute to work: 79.8% car, 0.0% public transportation, 11.7% walk, 6.5% work from home (2006-2010 5-year est.); Travel time to work: 45.5% less than 15 minutes, 33.8% 15 to 30 minutes, 13.0% 30 to 45 minutes, 3.5% 45 to 60 minutes, 4.3% 60 minutes or more (2006-2010 5-year est.)

ULYSSES (township). Aka Lewisville. Covers a land area of 75.475 square miles and a water area of 0.017 square miles. Located at 41.83° N. Lat; 77.78° W. Long. Elevation is 2,096 feet.
History: Pennsylvania Lumber Museum to South.
Population: 557 (1990); 691 (2000); 635 (2010); Density: 8.4 persons per square mile (2010); Race: 98.3% White, 0.5% Black, 0.2% Asian, 0.6% American Indian/Alaska Native, 0.0% Native Hawaiian/Other Pacific Islander, 0.4% Other, 0.2% Hispanic of any race (2010); Average household size: 2.53 (2010); Median age: 49.0 (2010); Males per 100 females: 99.1 (2010); Marriage status: 20.4% never married, 67.7% now married, 2.4% widowed, 9.4% divorced (2006-2010 5-year est.); Foreign born: 1.1% (2006-2010 5-year est.); Ancestry (includes multiple ancestries): 21.9% German, 16.1% English, 12.3% Irish, 10.0% American, 5.4% European (2006-2010 5-year est.).
Economy: Single-family building permits issued: 3 (2011); Multi-family building permits issued: 0 (2011); Employment by occupation: 10.1% management, 0.0% professional, 14.5% services, 9.4% sales, 0.0% farming, 21.2% construction, 8.8% production (2006-2010 5-year est.).
Income: Per capita income: $21,324 (2006-2010 5-year est.); Median household income: $47,768 (2006-2010 5-year est.); Average household income: $52,326 (2006-2010 5-year est.); Percent of households with income of $100,000 or more: 3.8% (2006-2010 5-year est.); Poverty rate: 11.8% (2006-2010 5-year est.).
Education: Percent of population age 25 and over with: High school diploma (including GED) or higher: 86.6% (2006-2010 5-year est.); Bachelor's degree or higher: 8.6% (2006-2010 5-year est.); Master's degree or higher: 2.6% (2006-2010 5-year est.).
Housing: Homeownership rate: 86.4% (2010); Median home value: $112,500 (2006-2010 5-year est.); Median contract rent: $325 per month (2006-2010 5-year est.); Median year structure built: 1973 (2006-2010 5-year est.).
Transportation: Commute to work: 86.4% car, 0.0% public transportation, 1.1% walk, 9.3% work from home (2006-2010 5-year est.); Travel time to work: 36.6% less than 15 minutes, 35.4% 15 to 30 minutes, 16.1% 30 to 45 minutes, 6.7% 45 to 60 minutes, 5.1% 60 minutes or more (2006-2010 5-year est.)

WEST BRANCH (township). Covers a land area of 62.112 square miles and a water area of 0.067 square miles. Located at 41.69° N. Lat; 77.72° W. Long.
Population: 286 (1990); 392 (2000); 393 (2010); Density: 6.3 persons per square mile (2010); Race: 96.4% White, 0.5% Black, 0.3% Asian, 0.0% American Indian/Alaska Native, 0.0% Native Hawaiian/Other Pacific Islander, 2.8% Other, 1.0% Hispanic of any race (2010); Average household size: 2.12 (2010); Median age: 53.1 (2010); Males per 100 females: 106.8 (2010); Marriage status: 12.8% never married, 72.4% now married, 7.7% widowed, 7.1% divorced (2006-2010 5-year est.); Foreign born: 1.2% (2006-2010 5-year est.); Ancestry (includes multiple ancestries): 46.9% German, 11.8% English, 9.9% Irish, 5.6% American, 4.8% Polish (2006-2010 5-year est.).
Economy: Single-family building permits issued: 3 (2011); Multi-family building permits issued: 0 (2011); Employment by occupation: 9.1% management, 1.7% professional, 16.0% services, 28.0% sales, 0.0% farming, 18.9% construction, 6.3% production (2006-2010 5-year est.).
Income: Per capita income: $24,414 (2006-2010 5-year est.); Median household income: $49,732 (2006-2010 5-year est.); Average household income: $54,784 (2006-2010 5-year est.); Percent of households with income of $100,000 or more: 15.7% (2006-2010 5-year est.); Poverty rate: 6.0% (2006-2010 5-year est.).
Education: Percent of population age 25 and over with: High school diploma (including GED) or higher: 79.2% (2006-2010 5-year est.); Bachelor's degree or higher: 17.1% (2006-2010 5-year est.); Master's degree or higher: 4.0% (2006-2010 5-year est.).
Housing: Homeownership rate: 88.1% (2010); Median home value: $150,500 (2006-2010 5-year est.); Median contract rent: <$101 per month (2006-2010 5-year est.); Median year structure built: 1971 (2006-2010 5-year est.).
Transportation: Commute to work: 86.1% car, 0.0% public transportation, 3.5% walk, 8.1% work from home (2006-2010 5-year est.); Travel time to work: 49.7% less than 15 minutes, 18.2% 15 to 30 minutes, 28.9% 30 to 45 minutes, 1.9% 45 to 60 minutes, 1.3% 60 minutes or more (2006-2010 5-year est.)

WHARTON (township). Covers a land area of 113.250 square miles and a water area of 0.003 square miles. Located at 41.54° N. Lat; 77.94° W. Long. Elevation is 1,102 feet.

Population: 70 (1990); 91 (2000); 99 (2010); Density: 0.9 persons per square mile (2010); Race: 98.0% White, 0.0% Black, 1.0% Asian, 0.0% American Indian/Alaska Native, 0.0% Native Hawaiian/Other Pacific Islander, 1.0% Other, 1.0% Hispanic of any race (2010); Average household size: 1.94 (2010); Median age: 62.3 (2010); Males per 100 females: 120.0 (2010); Marriage status: 20.8% never married, 49.5% now married, 9.9% widowed, 19.8% divorced (2006-2010 5-year est.); Foreign born: 2.0% (2006-2010 5-year est.); Ancestry (includes multiple ancestries): 29.7% German, 20.8% Irish, 14.9% American, 6.9% English, 5.0% Welsh (2006-2010 5-year est.).

Economy: Single-family building permits issued: 0 (2011); Multi-family building permits issued: 0 (2011); Employment by occupation: 12.5% management, 9.4% professional, 28.1% services, 18.8% sales, 0.0% farming, 6.3% construction, 0.0% production (2006-2010 5-year est.).

Income: Per capita income: $18,984 (2006-2010 5-year est.); Median household income: $28,750 (2006-2010 5-year est.); Average household income: $35,452 (2006-2010 5-year est.); Percent of households with income of $100,000 or more: n/a (2006-2010 5-year est.); Poverty rate: 16.8% (2006-2010 5-year est.).

Education: Percent of population age 25 and over with: High school diploma (including GED) or higher: 80.6% (2006-2010 5-year est.); Bachelor's degree or higher: 10.8% (2006-2010 5-year est.); Master's degree or higher: 7.5% (2006-2010 5-year est.).

Housing: Homeownership rate: 94.1% (2010); Median home value: $88,600 (2006-2010 5-year est.); Median contract rent: n/a per month (2006-2010 5-year est.); Median year structure built: 1971 (2006-2010 5-year est.).

Transportation: Commute to work: 92.9% car, 0.0% public transportation, 0.0% walk, 7.1% work from home (2006-2010 5-year est.); Travel time to work: 34.6% less than 15 minutes, 26.9% 15 to 30 minutes, 30.8% 30 to 45 minutes, 7.7% 45 to 60 minutes, 0.0% 60 minutes or more (2006-2010 5-year est.)

Schuylkill County

Located in east central Pennsylvania; mountainous area, drained by the Schuylkill River; includes the Blue Mountains. Covers a land area of 778.634 square miles, a water area of 4.181 square miles, and is located in the Eastern Time Zone at 40.70° N. Lat., 76.22° W. Long. The county was founded in 1811. County seat is Pottsville.

Schuylkill County is part of the Pottsville, PA Micropolitan Statistical Area. The entire metro area includes: Schuylkill County, PA

Population: 152,585 (1990); 150,336 (2000); 148,289 (2010); Race: 94.4% White, 2.7% Black, 0.5% Asian, 0.1% American Indian/Alaska Native, 0.0% Native Hawaiian/Other Pacific Islander, 2.3% Other, 2.8% Hispanic of any race (2010); Density: 190.4 persons per square mile (2010); Average household size: 2.35 (2010); Median age: 43.2 (2010); Males per 100 females: 102.8 (2010).

Religion: Six largest groups: 27.5% Catholicism, 13.0% Lutheran, 7.0% Methodist/Pietist, 7.0% Presbyterian-Reformed, 1.2% Non-Denominational, 1.0% Holiness (2010)

Economy: Unemployment rate: 9.7% (August 2012); Total civilian labor force: 75,440 (August 2012); Leading industries: 22.3% manufacturing; 20.5% health care and social assistance; 14.6% retail trade (2010); Farms: 966 totaling 118,501 acres (2007); Companies that employ 500 or more persons: 7 (2010); Companies that employ 100 to 499 persons: 63 (2010); Companies that employ less than 100 persons: 2,794 (2010); Black-owned businesses: 50 (2007); Hispanic-owned businesses: 76 (2007); Asian-owned businesses: 157 (2007); Women-owned businesses: 2,432 (2007); Retail sales per capita: $10,954 (2010). Single-family building permits issued: 101 (2011); Multi-family building permits issued: 0 (2011).

Income: Per capita income: $21,408 (2006-2010 5-year est.); Median household income: $42,315 (2006-2010 5-year est.); Average household income: $51,618 (2006-2010 5-year est.); Percent of households with income of $100,000 or more: 10.6% (2006-2010 5-year est.); Poverty rate: 11.9% (2006-2010 5-year est.); Bankruptcy rate: 2.23% (2011).

Taxes: Total county taxes per capita: $190 (2009); County property taxes per capita: $189 (2009).

Education: Percent of population age 25 and over with: High school diploma (including GED) or higher: 83.6% (2006-2010 5-year est.);

Bachelor's degree or higher: 13.6% (2006-2010 5-year est.); Master's degree or higher: 5.1% (2006-2010 5-year est.).

Housing: Homeownership rate: 75.6% (2010); Median home value: $88,400 (2006-2010 5-year est.); Median contract rent: $426 per month (2006-2010 5-year est.); Median year structure built: 1940 (2006-2010 5-year est.)

Health: Birth rate: 95.7 per 10,000 population (2011); Death rate: 125.1 per 10,000 population (2011); Age-adjusted cancer mortality rate: 191.6 deaths per 100,000 population (2009); Number of physicians: 14.2 per 10,000 population (2010); Hospital beds: 34.5 per 10,000 population (2008); Hospital admissions: 1,280.5 per 10,000 population (2008).

Elections: 2012 Presidential election results: 42.5% Obama, 55.9% Romney

National and State Parks: Appalachian National Scenic Trail; Locust Lake State Park; Swatara State Park; Tuscarora State Park; Weiser State Forest

Additional Information Contacts

Schuylkill County Government . . . . (570) 622-5570
  http://www.co.schuylkill.pa.us

Schuylkill County Communities

ALTAMONT (CDP). Covers a land area of 0.924 square miles and a water area of 0 square miles. Located at 40.78° N. Lat; 76.22° W. Long. Elevation is 1,549 feet.

Population: 1,292 (1990); 2,689 (2000); 602 (2010); Density: 651.9 persons per square mile (2010); Race: 98.3% White, 0.2% Black, 0.2% Asian, 0.0% American Indian/Alaska Native, 0.0% Native Hawaiian/Other Pacific Islander, 1.3% Other, 1.3% Hispanic of any race (2010); Average household size: 2.12 (2010); Median age: 50.6 (2010); Males per 100 females: 96.1 (2010); Marriage status: 24.0% never married, 55.8% now married, 14.6% widowed, 5.6% divorced (2006-2010 5-year est.); Foreign born: 0.0% (2006-2010 5-year est.); Ancestry (includes multiple ancestries): 32.3% Lithuanian, 21.7% German, 18.0% Polish, 15.2% Ukrainian, 11.6% English (2006-2010 5-year est.).

Economy: Employment by occupation: 16.1% management, 0.0% professional, 9.5% services, 13.6% sales, 9.3% farming, 10.4% construction, 0.0% production (2006-2010 5-year est.).

Income: Per capita income: $24,635 (2006-2010 5-year est.); Median household income: $47,273 (2006-2010 5-year est.); Average household income: $53,378 (2006-2010 5-year est.); Percent of households with income of $100,000 or more: 9.5% (2006-2010 5-year est.); Poverty rate: 7.2% (2006-2010 5-year est.).

Education: Percent of population age 25 and over with: High school diploma (including GED) or higher: 84.3% (2006-2010 5-year est.); Bachelor's degree or higher: 13.0% (2006-2010 5-year est.); Master's degree or higher: 6.7% (2006-2010 5-year est.).

Housing: Homeownership rate: 87.3% (2010); Median home value: $77,100 (2006-2010 5-year est.); Median contract rent: n/a per month (2006-2010 5-year est.); Median year structure built: before 1940 (2006-2010 5-year est.).

Transportation: Commute to work: 92.5% car, 0.0% public transportation, 3.6% walk, 3.9% work from home (2006-2010 5-year est.); Travel time to work: 39.1% less than 15 minutes, 49.9% 15 to 30 minutes, 4.6% 30 to 45 minutes, 0.0% 45 to 60 minutes, 6.4% 60 minutes or more (2006-2010 5-year est.)

Additional Information Contacts

Schuylkill Chamber of Commerce . . . . (570) 622-1942
  http://www.schuylkillchamber.com

ANDREAS (unincorporated postal area)

Zip Code: 18211

Covers a land area of 21.347 square miles and a water area of 0.198 square miles. Located at 40.74° N. Lat; 75.83° W. Long. Population: 1,304 (2010); Density: 61.1 persons per square mile (2010); Race: 98.6% White, 0.3% Black, 0.7% Asian, 0.0% American Indian/Alaska Native, 0.0% Native Hawaiian/Other Pacific Islander, 0.4% Other, 1.5% Hispanic of any race (2010); Average household size: 2.47 (2010); Median age: 46.5 (2010); Males per 100 females: 101.5 (2010); Homeownership rate: 88.6% (2010)

ASHLAND (borough). Aka Big Mine Run. Covers a land area of 1.658 square miles and a water area of 0 square miles. Located at 40.78° N. Lat; 76.35° W. Long. Elevation is 988 feet.

History: Pioneer Tunnel Coal Mine tours; Anthracite Museum. Settled 1845, incorporated 1857.

Population: 3,891 (1990); 3,283 (2000); 2,817 (2010); Density: 1,699.1 persons per square mile (2010); Race: 98.2% White, 0.2% Black, 0.3% Asian, 0.1% American Indian/Alaska Native, 0.0% Native Hawaiian/Other Pacific Islander, 1.2% Other, 1.0% Hispanic of any race (2010); Average household size: 2.17 (2010); Median age: 44.3 (2010); Males per 100 females: 94.5 (2010); Marriage status: 27.9% never married, 48.8% now married, 10.8% widowed, 12.4% divorced (2006-2010 5-year est.); Foreign born: 0.5% (2006-2010 5-year est.); Ancestry (includes multiple ancestries): 37.4% German, 36.4% Irish, 12.0% Dutch, 6.9% Welsh, 6.2% Italian (2006-2010 5-year est.).

Economy: Employment by occupation: 8.8% management, 0.7% professional, 12.2% services, 15.1% sales, 3.1% farming, 10.2% construction, 15.4% production (2006-2010 5-year est.).

Income: Per capita income: $17,872 (2006-2010 5-year est.); Median household income: $35,039 (2006-2010 5-year est.); Average household income: $41,257 (2006-2010 5-year est.); Percent of households with income of $100,000 or more: 5.4% (2006-2010 5-year est.); Poverty rate: 15.2% (2006-2010 5-year est.).

Education: Percent of population age 25 and over with: High school diploma (including GED) or higher: 78.8% (2006-2010 5-year est.); Bachelor's degree or higher: 10.0% (2006-2010 5-year est.); Master's degree or higher: 3.1% (2006-2010 5-year est.).

School District(s)
North Schuylkill SD (PK-12)
   2010-11 Enrollment: 1,912 . . . . (570) 874-0466

Housing: Homeownership rate: 66.8% (2010); Median home value: $40,200 (2006-2010 5-year est.); Median contract rent: $359 per month (2006-2010 5-year est.); Median year structure built: before 1940 (2006-2010 5-year est.).

Hospitals: Saint Catherine Medical Center Fountain Springs (141 beds)

Safety: Violent crime rate: 21.2 per 10,000 population; Property crime rate: 176.9 per 10,000 population (2011).

Transportation: Commute to work: 91.7% car, 0.0% public transportation, 4.8% walk, 2.3% work from home (2006-2010 5-year est.); Travel time to work: 41.4% less than 15 minutes, 28.3% 15 to 30 minutes, 16.5% 30 to 45 minutes, 3.9% 45 to 60 minutes, 9.9% 60 minutes or more (2006-2010 5-year est.)

Additional Information Contacts
Schuylkill Chamber of Commerce . . . . (570) 622-1942
   http://www.schuylkillchamber.com

AUBURN (borough). Covers a land area of 1.623 square miles and a water area of 0.051 square miles. Located at 40.60° N. Lat; 76.10° W. Long. Elevation is 476 feet.

History: Appalachian Trail passes to Southeast on Blue Mt. ridge.

Population: 901 (1990); 839 (2000); 741 (2010); Density: 456.5 persons per square mile (2010); Race: 97.7% White, 0.4% Black, 0.3% Asian, 0.0% American Indian/Alaska Native, 0.0% Native Hawaiian/Other Pacific Islander, 1.6% Other, 1.3% Hispanic of any race (2010); Average household size: 2.44 (2010); Median age: 43.9 (2010); Males per 100 females: 103.6 (2010); Marriage status: 20.9% never married, 55.0% now married, 8.5% widowed, 15.6% divorced (2006-2010 5-year est.); Foreign born: 1.0% (2006-2010 5-year est.); Ancestry (includes multiple ancestries): 59.2% German, 21.0% Irish, 21.0% Dutch, 9.1% Pennsylvania German, 6.7% Polish (2006-2010 5-year est.).

Economy: Employment by occupation: 4.9% management, 8.5% professional, 11.0% services, 9.5% sales, 3.5% farming, 10.2% construction, 14.5% production (2006-2010 5-year est.).

Income: Per capita income: $19,624 (2006-2010 5-year est.); Median household income: $43,819 (2006-2010 5-year est.); Average household income: $50,657 (2006-2010 5-year est.); Percent of households with income of $100,000 or more: 4.8% (2006-2010 5-year est.); Poverty rate: 7.8% (2006-2010 5-year est.).

Education: Percent of population age 25 and over with: High school diploma (including GED) or higher: 70.2% (2006-2010 5-year est.); Bachelor's degree or higher: 9.0% (2006-2010 5-year est.); Master's degree or higher: 3.4% (2006-2010 5-year est.).

Housing: Homeownership rate: 78.0% (2010); Median home value: $88,800 (2006-2010 5-year est.); Median contract rent: $333 per month

(2006-2010 5-year est.); Median year structure built: before 1940 (2006-2010 5-year est.).

Transportation: Commute to work: 97.0% car, 0.0% public transportation, 0.0% walk, 3.0% work from home (2006-2010 5-year est.); Travel time to work: 21.4% less than 15 minutes, 50.8% 15 to 30 minutes, 12.6% 30 to 45 minutes, 12.6% 45 to 60 minutes, 2.7% 60 minutes or more (2006-2010 5-year est.)

BARNESVILLE (unincorporated postal area)
Zip Code: 18214
   Covers a land area of 23.923 square miles and a water area of 0.386 square miles. Located at 40.80° N. Lat; 76.08° W. Long. Population: 2,078 (2010); Density: 86.9 persons per square mile (2010); Race: 99.1% White, 0.0% Black, 0.2% Asian, 0.0% American Indian/Alaska Native, 0.0% Native Hawaiian/Other Pacific Islander, 0.7% Other, 1.4% Hispanic of any race (2010); Average household size: 2.38 (2010); Median age: 46.9 (2010); Males per 100 females: 105.3 (2010); Homeownership rate: 89.1% (2010)

BARRY (township). Covers a land area of 16.780 square miles and a water area of 0.025 square miles. Located at 40.71° N. Lat; 76.40° W. Long.

Population: 845 (1990); 967 (2000); 932 (2010); Density: 55.5 persons per square mile (2010); Race: 99.4% White, 0.1% Black, 0.1% Asian, 0.0% American Indian/Alaska Native, 0.0% Native Hawaiian/Other Pacific Islander, 0.4% Other, 0.9% Hispanic of any race (2010); Average household size: 2.43 (2010); Median age: 46.3 (2010); Males per 100 females: 100.4 (2010); Marriage status: 19.8% never married, 68.4% now married, 4.8% widowed, 7.0% divorced (2006-2010 5-year est.); Foreign born: 1.1% (2006-2010 5-year est.); Ancestry (includes multiple ancestries): 45.7% German, 18.5% Irish, 17.1% Dutch, 10.0% Pennsylvania German, 8.4% Italian (2006-2010 5-year est.).

Economy: Employment by occupation: 10.2% management, 0.6% professional, 12.5% services, 10.8% sales, 2.7% farming, 17.8% construction, 11.4% production (2006-2010 5-year est.).

Income: Per capita income: $24,780 (2006-2010 5-year est.); Median household income: $55,417 (2006-2010 5-year est.); Average household income: $62,311 (2006-2010 5-year est.); Percent of households with income of $100,000 or more: 18.8% (2006-2010 5-year est.); Poverty rate: 7.0% (2006-2010 5-year est.).

Education: Percent of population age 25 and over with: High school diploma (including GED) or higher: 79.6% (2006-2010 5-year est.); Bachelor's degree or higher: 13.3% (2006-2010 5-year est.); Master's degree or higher: 6.9% (2006-2010 5-year est.).

Housing: Homeownership rate: 87.5% (2010); Median home value: $115,800 (2006-2010 5-year est.); Median contract rent: $219 per month (2006-2010 5-year est.); Median year structure built: 1963 (2006-2010 5-year est.).

Transportation: Commute to work: 88.5% car, 0.0% public transportation, 4.6% walk, 5.6% work from home (2006-2010 5-year est.); Travel time to work: 22.5% less than 15 minutes, 39.9% 15 to 30 minutes, 17.6% 30 to 45 minutes, 10.1% 45 to 60 minutes, 9.9% 60 minutes or more (2006-2010 5-year est.)

Additional Information Contacts
Schuylkill Chamber of Commerce . . . . (570) 622-1942
   http://www.schuylkillchamber.com

BEURYS LAKE (CDP). Covers a land area of 0.390 square miles and a water area of 0.015 square miles. Located at 40.72° N. Lat; 76.38° W. Long. Elevation is 974 feet.

Population: 117 (1990); 133 (2000); 124 (2010); Density: 317.6 persons per square mile (2010); Race: 100.0% White, 0.0% Black, 0.0% Asian, 0.0% American Indian/Alaska Native, 0.0% Native Hawaiian/Other Pacific Islander, 0.0% Other, 0.8% Hispanic of any race (2010); Average household size: 2.07 (2010); Median age: 45.0 (2010); Males per 100 females: 103.3 (2010); Marriage status: 21.8% never married, 69.7% now married, 4.2% widowed, 4.2% divorced (2006-2010 5-year est.); Foreign born: 0.0% (2006-2010 5-year est.); Ancestry (includes multiple ancestries): 30.0% Irish, 18.9% German, 9.4% Italian, 9.4% Lithuanian, 7.8% Dutch (2006-2010 5-year est.).

Economy: Employment by occupation: 4.7% management, 0.0% professional, 3.5% services, 16.5% sales, 4.7% farming, 24.7% construction, 15.3% production (2006-2010 5-year est.).

Income: Per capita income: $29,452 (2006-2010 5-year est.); Median household income: $50,781 (2006-2010 5-year est.); Average household

income: $63,954 (2006-2010 5-year est.); Percent of households with income of $100,000 or more: 18.5% (2006-2010 5-year est.); Poverty rate: 22.8% (2006-2010 5-year est.).

Education: Percent of population age 25 and over with: High school diploma (including GED) or higher: 80.3% (2006-2010 5-year est.); Bachelor's degree or higher: 11.8% (2006-2010 5-year est.); Master's degree or higher: 3.1% (2006-2010 5-year est.).

Housing: Homeownership rate: 91.7% (2010); Median home value: $109,600 (2006-2010 5-year est.); Median contract rent: n/a per month (2006-2010 5-year est.); Median year structure built: 1953 (2006-2010 5-year est.).

Transportation: Commute to work: 78.0% car, 0.0% public transportation, 9.8% walk, 12.2% work from home (2006-2010 5-year est.); Travel time to work: 22.2% less than 15 minutes, 48.6% 15 to 30 minutes, 5.6% 30 to 45 minutes, 5.6% 45 to 60 minutes, 18.1% 60 minutes or more (2006-2010 5-year est.)

BLYTHE (township). Covers a land area of 27.588 square miles and a water area of 0.186 square miles. Located at 40.75° N. Lat; 76.10° W. Long.

Population: 1,023 (1990); 905 (2000); 924 (2010); Density: 33.5 persons per square mile (2010); Race: 98.3% White, 0.1% Black, 0.2% Asian, 0.1% American Indian/Alaska Native, 0.0% Native Hawaiian/Other Pacific Islander, 1.3% Other, 1.8% Hispanic of any race (2010); Average household size: 2.41 (2010); Median age: 42.8 (2010); Males per 100 females: 96.6 (2010); Marriage status: 25.0% never married, 51.9% now married, 14.7% widowed, 8.4% divorced (2006-2010 5-year est.); Foreign born: 1.0% (2006-2010 5-year est.); Ancestry (includes multiple ancestries): 29.7% German, 24.3% Polish, 23.7% Irish, 13.0% Lithuanian, 8.0% Italian (2006-2010 5-year est.).

Economy: Single-family building permits issued: 0 (2011); Multi-family building permits issued: 0 (2011); Employment by occupation: 3.5% management, 0.0% professional, 13.6% services, 18.3% sales, 4.3% farming, 14.5% construction, 9.3% production (2006-2010 5-year est.).

Income: Per capita income: $20,826 (2006-2010 5-year est.); Median household income: $33,438 (2006-2010 5-year est.); Average household income: $43,749 (2006-2010 5-year est.); Percent of households with income of $100,000 or more: 6.8% (2006-2010 5-year est.); Poverty rate: 9.9% (2006-2010 5-year est.).

Education: Percent of population age 25 and over with: High school diploma (including GED) or higher: 80.5% (2006-2010 5-year est.); Bachelor's degree or higher: 9.3% (2006-2010 5-year est.); Master's degree or higher: 2.0% (2006-2010 5-year est.).

Housing: Homeownership rate: 77.9% (2010); Median home value: $73,000 (2006-2010 5-year est.); Median contract rent: $443 per month (2006-2010 5-year est.); Median year structure built: before 1940 (2006-2010 5-year est.).

Safety: Violent crime rate: 0.0 per 10,000 population; Property crime rate: 10.8 per 10,000 population (2011).

Transportation: Commute to work: 93.5% car, 0.0% public transportation, 1.2% walk, 4.1% work from home (2006-2010 5-year est.); Travel time to work: 25.9% less than 15 minutes, 38.6% 15 to 30 minutes, 15.1% 30 to 45 minutes, 13.6% 45 to 60 minutes, 6.8% 60 minutes or more (2006-2010 5-year est.)

BRANCH (township). Covers a land area of 11.466 square miles and a water area of 0.076 square miles. Located at 40.67° N. Lat; 76.26° W. Long.

Population: 2,051 (1990); 1,871 (2000); 1,840 (2010); Density: 160.5 persons per square mile (2010); Race: 99.0% White, 0.5% Black, 0.0% Asian, 0.1% American Indian/Alaska Native, 0.0% Native Hawaiian/Other Pacific Islander, 0.4% Other, 0.8% Hispanic of any race (2010); Average household size: 2.42 (2010); Median age: 47.3 (2010); Males per 100 females: 99.1 (2010); Marriage status: 27.0% never married, 57.7% now married, 9.6% widowed, 5.7% divorced (2006-2010 5-year est.); Foreign born: 0.3% (2006-2010 5-year est.); Ancestry (includes multiple ancestries): 26.3% Irish, 21.9% German, 16.2% Polish, 13.5% Lithuanian, 12.6% Italian (2006-2010 5-year est.).

Economy: Single-family building permits issued: 1 (2011); Multi-family building permits issued: 0 (2011); Employment by occupation: 11.0% management, 3.8% professional, 6.5% services, 14.5% sales, 8.1% farming, 12.5% construction, 8.2% production (2006-2010 5-year est.).

Income: Per capita income: $23,541 (2006-2010 5-year est.); Median household income: $47,813 (2006-2010 5-year est.); Average household income: $59,494 (2006-2010 5-year est.); Percent of households with

income of $100,000 or more: 16.7% (2006-2010 5-year est.); Poverty rate: 13.5% (2006-2010 5-year est.).

Education: Percent of population age 25 and over with: High school diploma (including GED) or higher: 89.9% (2006-2010 5-year est.); Bachelor's degree or higher: 17.8% (2006-2010 5-year est.); Master's degree or higher: 6.1% (2006-2010 5-year est.).

Housing: Homeownership rate: 91.2% (2010); Median home value: $126,000 (2006-2010 5-year est.); Median contract rent: $481 per month (2006-2010 5-year est.); Median year structure built: 1959 (2006-2010 5-year est.).

Safety: Violent crime rate: 0.0 per 10,000 population; Property crime rate: 86.7 per 10,000 population (2011).

Transportation: Commute to work: 96.4% car, 0.0% public transportation, 0.4% walk, 3.2% work from home (2006-2010 5-year est.); Travel time to work: 36.2% less than 15 minutes, 34.5% 15 to 30 minutes, 10.5% 30 to 45 minutes, 8.6% 45 to 60 minutes, 10.3% 60 minutes or more (2006-2010 5-year est.)

Additional Information Contacts

Lebanon Valley Chamber of Commerce . . . . (717) 273-3727
http://www.lvchamber.org

BRANCHDALE (CDP). Covers a land area of 0.714 square miles and a water area of 0 square miles. Located at 40.67° N. Lat; 76.32° W. Long. Elevation is 804 feet.

Population: 454 (1990); 436 (2000); 388 (2010); Density: 543.1 persons per square mile (2010); Race: 97.4% White, 0.3% Black, 0.8% Asian, 0.0% American Indian/Alaska Native, 0.0% Native Hawaiian/Other Pacific Islander, 1.5% Other, 1.3% Hispanic of any race (2010); Average household size: 2.26 (2010); Median age: 45.8 (2010); Males per 100 females: 102.1 (2010); Marriage status: 18.8% never married, 71.8% now married, 2.6% widowed, 6.8% divorced (2006-2010 5-year est.); Foreign born: 0.0% (2006-2010 5-year est.); Ancestry (includes multiple ancestries): 41.6% Irish, 24.0% German, 22.5% Polish, 11.8% Pennsylvania German, 11.8% Dutch (2006-2010 5-year est.).

Economy: Employment by occupation: 4.2% management, 0.0% professional, 10.8% services, 28.3% sales, 8.3% farming, 12.5% construction, 8.3% production (2006-2010 5-year est.).

Income: Per capita income: $20,520 (2006-2010 5-year est.); Median household income: $39,063 (2006-2010 5-year est.); Average household income: $43,893 (2006-2010 5-year est.); Percent of households with income of $100,000 or more: 7.5% (2006-2010 5-year est.); Poverty rate: 0.0% (2006-2010 5-year est.).

Education: Percent of population age 25 and over with: High school diploma (including GED) or higher: 78.6% (2006-2010 5-year est.); Bachelor's degree or higher: 1.8% (2006-2010 5-year est.); Master's degree or higher: 0.0% (2006-2010 5-year est.).

Housing: Homeownership rate: 88.9% (2010); Median home value: $53,100 (2006-2010 5-year est.); Median contract rent: n/a per month (2006-2010 5-year est.); Median year structure built: before 1940 (2006-2010 5-year est.).

Transportation: Commute to work: 95.8% car, 0.0% public transportation, 0.0% walk, 4.2% work from home (2006-2010 5-year est.); Travel time to work: 17.4% less than 15 minutes, 50.4% 15 to 30 minutes, 10.4% 30 to 45 minutes, 0.0% 45 to 60 minutes, 21.7% 60 minutes or more (2006-2010 5-year est.)

BRANDONVILLE (CDP). Covers a land area of 1.402 square miles and a water area of 0 square miles. Located at 40.86° N. Lat; 76.17° W. Long. Elevation is 1,211 feet.

Population: 210 (1990); 217 (2000); 197 (2010); Density: 140.5 persons per square mile (2010); Race: 100.0% White, 0.0% Black, 0.0% Asian, 0.0% American Indian/Alaska Native, 0.0% Native Hawaiian/Other Pacific Islander, 0.0% Other, 0.0% Hispanic of any race (2010); Average household size: 2.32 (2010); Median age: 48.5 (2010); Males per 100 females: 105.2 (2010); Marriage status: 24.8% never married, 46.0% now married, 8.7% widowed, 20.5% divorced (2006-2010 5-year est.); Foreign born: 0.0% (2006-2010 5-year est.); Ancestry (includes multiple ancestries): 25.6% Polish, 23.3% Lithuanian, 19.8% German, 17.4% Dutch, 15.1% Irish (2006-2010 5-year est.).

Economy: Employment by occupation: 5.0% management, 6.7% professional, 0.0% services, 5.0% sales, 0.0% farming, 10.0% construction, 25.0% production (2006-2010 5-year est.).

Income: Per capita income: $17,402 (2006-2010 5-year est.); Median household income: $29,375 (2006-2010 5-year est.); Average household income: $36,901 (2006-2010 5-year est.); Percent of households with

income of $100,000 or more: n/a (2006-2010 5-year est.); Poverty rate: 13.1% (2006-2010 5-year est.).

Education: Percent of population age 25 and over with: High school diploma (including GED) or higher: 83.7% (2006-2010 5-year est.); Bachelor's degree or higher: 4.1% (2006-2010 5-year est.); Master's degree or higher: 0.0% (2006-2010 5-year est.).

Housing: Homeownership rate: 83.5% (2010); Median home value: $95,500 (2006-2010 5-year est.); Median contract rent: n/a per month (2006-2010 5-year est.); Median year structure built: 1952 (2006-2010 5-year est.).

Transportation: Commute to work: 100.0% car, 0.0% public transportation, 0.0% walk, 0.0% work from home (2006-2010 5-year est.); Travel time to work: 36.7% less than 15 minutes, 56.7% 15 to 30 minutes, 6.7% 30 to 45 minutes, 0.0% 45 to 60 minutes, 0.0% 60 minutes or more (2006-2010 5-year est.)

BROCKTON (unincorporated postal area)
Zip Code: 17925

Covers a land area of 0.977 square miles and a water area of <.001 square miles. Located at 40.75° N. Lat; 76.06° W. Long. Population: 376 (2010); Density: 384.7 persons per square mile (2010); Race: 99.2% White, 0.0% Black, 0.0% Asian, 0.5% American Indian/Alaska Native, 0.0% Native Hawaiian/Other Pacific Islander, 0.3% Other, 0.8% Hispanic of any race (2010); Average household size: 2.32 (2010); Median age: 46.6 (2010); Males per 100 females: 98.9 (2010); Homeownership rate: 86.4% (2010)

BUCK RUN (CDP). Covers a land area of 0.501 square miles and a water area of 0 square miles. Located at 40.71° N. Lat; 76.32° W. Long. Elevation is 1,388 feet.

Population: 54 (1990); 203 (2000); 176 (2010); Density: 351.2 persons per square mile (2010); Race: 100.0% White, 0.0% Black, 0.0% Asian, 0.0% American Indian/Alaska Native, 0.0% Native Hawaiian/Other Pacific Islander, 0.0% Other, 0.0% Hispanic of any race (2010); Average household size: 2.44 (2010); Median age: 45.8 (2010); Males per 100 females: 102.3 (2010); Marriage status: 12.5% never married, 67.0% now married, 9.8% widowed, 10.7% divorced (2006-2010 5-year est.); Foreign born: 0.0% (2006-2010 5-year est.); Ancestry (includes multiple ancestries): 38.9% Irish, 37.4% Polish, 31.3% German, 7.6% Italian, 6.1% Pennsylvania German (2006-2010 5-year est.).

Economy: Employment by occupation: 6.4% management, 12.8% professional, 12.8% services, 7.7% sales, 0.0% farming, 21.8% construction, 16.7% production (2006-2010 5-year est.).

Income: Per capita income: $24,108 (2006-2010 5-year est.); Median household income: $44,500 (2006-2010 5-year est.); Average household income: $53,863 (2006-2010 5-year est.); Percent of households with income of $100,000 or more: 13.3% (2006-2010 5-year est.); Poverty rate: 1.5% (2006-2010 5-year est.).

Education: Percent of population age 25 and over with: High school diploma (including GED) or higher: 88.0% (2006-2010 5-year est.); Bachelor's degree or higher: 13.0% (2006-2010 5-year est.); Master's degree or higher: 4.3% (2006-2010 5-year est.).

Housing: Homeownership rate: 88.9% (2010); Median home value: $67,200 (2006-2010 5-year est.); Median contract rent: n/a per month (2006-2010 5-year est.); Median year structure built: 1941 (2006-2010 5-year est.).

Transportation: Commute to work: 92.0% car, 0.0% public transportation, 2.7% walk, 2.7% work from home (2006-2010 5-year est.); Travel time to work: 37.0% less than 15 minutes, 32.9% 15 to 30 minutes, 8.2% 30 to 45 minutes, 8.2% 45 to 60 minutes, 13.7% 60 minutes or more (2006-2010 5-year est.)

BUTLER (township). Covers a land area of 26.036 square miles and a water area of 0.033 square miles. Located at 40.77° N. Lat; 76.33° W. Long.

Population: 3,843 (1990); 3,588 (2000); 5,224 (2010); Density: 200.6 persons per square mile (2010); Race: 77.8% White, 16.2% Black, 0.1% Asian, 0.1% American Indian/Alaska Native, 0.0% Native Hawaiian/Other Pacific Islander, 5.8% Other, 6.0% Hispanic of any race (2010); Average household size: 2.37 (2010); Median age: 41.6 (2010); Males per 100 females: 170.7 (2010); Marriage status: 32.0% never married, 51.1% now married, 10.6% widowed, 6.3% divorced (2006-2010 5-year est.); Foreign born: 3.1% (2006-2010 5-year est.); Ancestry (includes multiple ancestries): 26.9% German, 19.8% Irish, 8.4% Polish, 8.2% Italian, 6.9% Dutch (2006-2010 5-year est.).

Economy: Single-family building permits issued: 5 (2011); Multi-family building permits issued: 0 (2011); Employment by occupation: 9.9% management, 1.9% professional, 8.8% services, 15.9% sales, 0.0% farming, 14.6% construction, 9.0% production (2006-2010 5-year est.).

Income: Per capita income: $20,163 (2006-2010 5-year est.); Median household income: $50,270 (2006-2010 5-year est.); Average household income: $59,275 (2006-2010 5-year est.); Percent of households with income of $100,000 or more: 13.0% (2006-2010 5-year est.); Poverty rate: 4.3% (2006-2010 5-year est.).

Education: Percent of population age 25 and over with: High school diploma (including GED) or higher: 83.0% (2006-2010 5-year est.); Bachelor's degree or higher: 11.4% (2006-2010 5-year est.); Master's degree or higher: 4.1% (2006-2010 5-year est.).

Housing: Homeownership rate: 90.7% (2010); Median home value: $116,300 (2006-2010 5-year est.); Median contract rent: $368 per month (2006-2010 5-year est.); Median year structure built: 1942 (2006-2010 5-year est.).

Safety: Violent crime rate: 5.0 per 10,000 population; Property crime rate: 51.6 per 10,000 population (2011).

Transportation: Commute to work: 91.5% car, 0.0% public transportation, 5.8% walk, 2.7% work from home (2006-2010 5-year est.); Travel time to work: 33.8% less than 15 minutes, 42.1% 15 to 30 minutes, 15.8% 30 to 45 minutes, 2.7% 45 to 60 minutes, 5.6% 60 minutes or more (2006-2010 5-year est.)

Additional Information Contacts
Schuylkill Chamber of Commerce . . . . (570) 622-1942
http://www.schuylkillchamber.com

CASS (township). Covers a land area of 14.388 square miles and a water area of 0.047 square miles. Located at 40.72° N. Lat; 76.28° W. Long.

Population: 2,320 (1990); 2,383 (2000); 1,958 (2010); Density: 136.1 persons per square mile (2010); Race: 98.6% White, 0.4% Black, 0.2% Asian, 0.1% American Indian/Alaska Native, 0.0% Native Hawaiian/Other Pacific Islander, 0.7% Other, 0.5% Hispanic of any race (2010); Average household size: 2.41 (2010); Median age: 43.5 (2010); Males per 100 females: 101.6 (2010); Marriage status: 25.2% never married, 58.5% now married, 5.0% widowed, 11.4% divorced (2006-2010 5-year est.); Foreign born: 0.8% (2006-2010 5-year est.); Ancestry (includes multiple ancestries): 27.4% Irish, 20.0% German, 19.5% Ukrainian, 17.5% Polish, 13.6% Italian (2006-2010 5-year est.).

Economy: Employment by occupation: 6.2% management, 3.2% professional, 10.9% services, 11.2% sales, 5.8% farming, 20.0% construction, 9.2% production (2006-2010 5-year est.).

Income: Per capita income: $20,436 (2006-2010 5-year est.); Median household income: $39,868 (2006-2010 5-year est.); Average household income: $47,749 (2006-2010 5-year est.); Percent of households with income of $100,000 or more: 13.0% (2006-2010 5-year est.); Poverty rate: 6.1% (2006-2010 5-year est.).

Education: Percent of population age 25 and over with: High school diploma (including GED) or higher: 86.4% (2006-2010 5-year est.); Bachelor's degree or higher: 14.3% (2006-2010 5-year est.); Master's degree or higher: 3.7% (2006-2010 5-year est.).

Housing: Homeownership rate: 86.6% (2010); Median home value: $74,200 (2006-2010 5-year est.); Median contract rent: $383 per month (2006-2010 5-year est.); Median year structure built: before 1940 (2006-2010 5-year est.).

Safety: Violent crime rate: 25.5 per 10,000 population; Property crime rate: 76.4 per 10,000 population (2011).

Transportation: Commute to work: 97.5% car, 0.0% public transportation, 0.0% walk, 0.8% work from home (2006-2010 5-year est.); Travel time to work: 17.9% less than 15 minutes, 45.6% 15 to 30 minutes, 10.0% 30 to 45 minutes, 10.7% 45 to 60 minutes, 15.8% 60 minutes or more (2006-2010 5-year est.)

Additional Information Contacts
Schuylkill Chamber of Commerce . . . . (570) 622-1942
http://www.schuylkillchamber.com

COALDALE (borough). Covers a land area of 2.175 square miles and a water area of 0 square miles. Located at 40.82° N. Lat; 75.92° W. Long. Elevation is 1,053 feet.

History: Settled 1868, incorporated 1871.

Population: 2,531 (1990); 2,295 (2000); 2,281 (2010); Density: 1,048.5 persons per square mile (2010); Race: 96.1% White, 0.7% Black, 0.7% Asian, 0.1% American Indian/Alaska Native, 0.0% Native Hawaiian/Other

Pacific Islander, 2.4% Other, 3.3% Hispanic of any race (2010); Average household size: 2.32 (2010); Median age: 41.0 (2010); Males per 100 females: 95.3 (2010); Marriage status: 32.1% never married, 44.3% now married, 11.5% widowed, 12.1% divorced (2006-2010 5-year est.); Foreign born: 1.2% (2006-2010 5-year est.); Ancestry (includes multiple ancestries): 26.6% Irish, 26.0% German, 11.7% Slovak, 7.2% Italian, 6.8% Pennsylvania German (2006-2010 5-year est.).

Economy: Single-family building permits issued: 0 (2011); Multi-family building permits issued: 0 (2011); Employment by occupation: 7.0% management, 2.3% professional, 4.5% services, 18.1% sales, 4.2% farming, 17.5% construction, 12.2% production (2006-2010 5-year est.).

Income: Per capita income: $16,976 (2006-2010 5-year est.); Median household income: $30,777 (2006-2010 5-year est.); Average household income: $37,114 (2006-2010 5-year est.); Percent of households with income of $100,000 or more: 2.7% (2006-2010 5-year est.); Poverty rate: 17.5% (2006-2010 5-year est.).

Education: Percent of population age 25 and over with: High school diploma (including GED) or higher: 86.7% (2006-2010 5-year est.); Bachelor's degree or higher: 14.1% (2006-2010 5-year est.); Master's degree or higher: 8.0% (2006-2010 5-year est.).

Housing: Homeownership rate: 73.6% (2010); Median home value: $53,000 (2006-2010 5-year est.); Median contract rent: $387 per month (2006-2010 5-year est.); Median year structure built: before 1940 (2006-2010 5-year est.).

Hospitals: St. Lukes Hospital - Miners Campus (45 beds)

Safety: Violent crime rate: 13.1 per 10,000 population; Property crime rate: 43.7 per 10,000 population (2011).

Transportation: Commute to work: 94.2% car, 0.0% public transportation, 2.5% walk, 2.4% work from home (2006-2010 5-year est.); Travel time to work: 24.6% less than 15 minutes, 38.0% 15 to 30 minutes, 14.7% 30 to 45 minutes, 8.0% 45 to 60 minutes, 14.8% 60 minutes or more (2006-2010 5-year est.)

Additional Information Contacts

Greater Hazelton Chamber of Commerce . . . . (570) 455-1509
   http://www.hazletonchamber.org

CRESSONA (borough). Covers a land area of 0.998 square miles and a water area of 0 square miles. Located at 40.63° N. Lat; 76.19° W. Long. Elevation is 597 feet.

History: Laid out 1847, incorporated 1857.

Population: 1,694 (1990); 1,635 (2000); 1,651 (2010); Density: 1,654.6 persons per square mile (2010); Race: 96.8% White, 0.8% Black, 1.1% Asian, 0.1% American Indian/Alaska Native, 0.0% Native Hawaiian/Other Pacific Islander, 1.2% Other, 1.9% Hispanic of any race (2010); Average household size: 2.51 (2010); Median age: 38.9 (2010); Males per 100 females: 97.3 (2010); Marriage status: 30.7% never married, 53.3% now married, 7.9% widowed, 8.0% divorced (2006-2010 5-year est.); Foreign born: 3.0% (2006-2010 5-year est.); Ancestry (includes multiple ancestries): 36.5% German, 16.4% Irish, 14.0% Dutch, 10.4% Italian, 9.3% Polish (2006-2010 5-year est.).

Economy: Single-family building permits issued: 1 (2011); Multi-family building permits issued: 0 (2011); Employment by occupation: 9.9% management, 1.7% professional, 13.3% services, 13.3% sales, 4.4% farming, 6.6% construction, 7.1% production (2006-2010 5-year est.).

Income: Per capita income: $22,894 (2006-2010 5-year est.); Median household income: $51,250 (2006-2010 5-year est.); Average household income: $57,479 (2006-2010 5-year est.); Percent of households with income of $100,000 or more: 11.4% (2006-2010 5-year est.); Poverty rate: 4.2% (2006-2010 5-year est.).

Education: Percent of population age 25 and over with: High school diploma (including GED) or higher: 91.5% (2006-2010 5-year est.); Bachelor's degree or higher: 14.5% (2006-2010 5-year est.); Master's degree or higher: 5.3% (2006-2010 5-year est.).

School District(s)

Blue Mountain SD (KG-12)
   2010-11 Enrollment: 2,877 . . . . (570) 366-0515

Housing: Homeownership rate: 76.8% (2010); Median home value: $91,900 (2006-2010 5-year est.); Median contract rent: $516 per month (2006-2010 5-year est.); Median year structure built: before 1940 (2006-2010 5-year est.).

Transportation: Commute to work: 92.1% car, 0.0% public transportation, 5.0% walk, 2.1% work from home (2006-2010 5-year est.); Travel time to work: 25.5% less than 15 minutes, 48.4% 15 to 30 minutes, 10.4% 30 to 45 minutes, 9.6% 45 to 60 minutes, 6.1% 60 minutes or more (2006-2010 5-year est.)

Additional Information Contacts

Schuylkill Chamber of Commerce . . . . (570) 622-1942
   http://www.schuylkillchamber.com

CUMBOLA (CDP). Covers a land area of 0.394 square miles and a water area of 0 square miles. Located at 40.71° N. Lat; 76.14° W. Long. Elevation is 709 feet.

Population: n/a (1990); n/a (2000); 443 (2010); Density: 1,123.1 persons per square mile (2010); Race: 96.6% White, 0.2% Black, 0.5% Asian, 0.0% American Indian/Alaska Native, 0.0% Native Hawaiian/Other Pacific Islander, 2.7% Other, 3.2% Hispanic of any race (2010); Average household size: 2.43 (2010); Median age: 39.4 (2010); Males per 100 females: 92.6 (2010); Marriage status: 24.1% never married, 49.3% now married, 12.9% widowed, 13.8% divorced (2006-2010 5-year est.); Foreign born: 1.3% (2006-2010 5-year est.); Ancestry (includes multiple ancestries): 35.8% German, 26.6% Irish, 24.9% Polish, 17.5% Lithuanian, 8.1% Greek (2006-2010 5-year est.).

Economy: Employment by occupation: 2.2% management, 0.0% professional, 18.8% services, 18.8% sales, 2.9% farming, 5.8% construction, 5.8% production (2006-2010 5-year est.).

Income: Per capita income: $17,949 (2006-2010 5-year est.); Median household income: $30,000 (2006-2010 5-year est.); Average household income: $36,559 (2006-2010 5-year est.); Percent of households with income of $100,000 or more: 1.6% (2006-2010 5-year est.); Poverty rate: 12.9% (2006-2010 5-year est.).

Education: Percent of population age 25 and over with: High school diploma (including GED) or higher: 78.1% (2006-2010 5-year est.); Bachelor's degree or higher: 10.8% (2006-2010 5-year est.); Master's degree or higher: 2.0% (2006-2010 5-year est.).

Housing: Homeownership rate: 63.7% (2010); Median home value: $72,600 (2006-2010 5-year est.); Median contract rent: $443 per month (2006-2010 5-year est.); Median year structure built: 1943 (2006-2010 5-year est.).

Transportation: Commute to work: 94.2% car, 0.0% public transportation, 2.9% walk, 2.9% work from home (2006-2010 5-year est.); Travel time to work: 37.3% less than 15 minutes, 23.1% 15 to 30 minutes, 18.7% 30 to 45 minutes, 17.9% 45 to 60 minutes, 3.0% 60 minutes or more (2006-2010 5-year est.)

DEER LAKE (borough). Covers a land area of 0.439 square miles and a water area of 0.032 square miles. Located at 40.62° N. Lat; 76.06° W. Long. Elevation is 492 feet.

History: Appalachian Trail passes to Southeast.

Population: 550 (1990); 528 (2000); 687 (2010); Density: 1,566.5 persons per square mile (2010); Race: 97.2% White, 0.6% Black, 1.0% Asian, 0.3% American Indian/Alaska Native, 0.0% Native Hawaiian/Other Pacific Islander, 0.9% Other, 1.0% Hispanic of any race (2010); Average household size: 2.61 (2010); Median age: 40.1 (2010); Males per 100 females: 114.7 (2010); Marriage status: 21.7% never married, 65.4% now married, 3.1% widowed, 9.8% divorced (2006-2010 5-year est.); Foreign born: 3.1% (2006-2010 5-year est.); Ancestry (includes multiple ancestries): 50.2% German, 23.3% Irish, 8.9% Polish, 8.5% Welsh, 7.4% Austrian (2006-2010 5-year est.).

Economy: Single-family building permits issued: 5 (2011); Multi-family building permits issued: 0 (2011); Employment by occupation: 15.9% management, 5.3% professional, 5.5% services, 16.1% sales, 6.0% farming, 9.9% construction, 6.7% production (2006-2010 5-year est.).

Income: Per capita income: $29,473 (2006-2010 5-year est.); Median household income: $76,346 (2006-2010 5-year est.); Average household income: $79,027 (2006-2010 5-year est.); Percent of households with income of $100,000 or more: 32.3% (2006-2010 5-year est.); Poverty rate: 5.3% (2006-2010 5-year est.).

Education: Percent of population age 25 and over with: High school diploma (including GED) or higher: 95.7% (2006-2010 5-year est.); Bachelor's degree or higher: 22.0% (2006-2010 5-year est.); Master's degree or higher: 9.7% (2006-2010 5-year est.).

Housing: Homeownership rate: 95.5% (2010); Median home value: $174,600 (2006-2010 5-year est.); Median contract rent: n/a per month (2006-2010 5-year est.); Median year structure built: 1974 (2006-2010 5-year est.).

Transportation: Commute to work: 95.9% car, 0.5% public transportation, 2.9% walk, 0.7% work from home (2006-2010 5-year est.); Travel time to work: 29.5% less than 15 minutes, 26.6% 15 to 30 minutes, 25.9% 30 to 45 minutes, 8.0% 45 to 60 minutes, 10.0% 60 minutes or more (2006-2010 5-year est.)

DELANO (CDP). Covers a land area of 0.630 square miles and a water area of 0.004 square miles. Located at 40.84° N. Lat; 76.08° W. Long. Elevation is 1,650 feet.

Population: 425 (1990); 377 (2000); 342 (2010); Density: 543.2 persons per square mile (2010); Race: 99.4% White, 0.0% Black, 0.3% Asian, 0.0% American Indian/Alaska Native, 0.0% Native Hawaiian/Other Pacific Islander, 0.3% Other, 0.6% Hispanic of any race (2010); Average household size: 2.21 (2010); Median age: 46.4 (2010); Males per 100 females: 116.5 (2010); Marriage status: 27.5% never married, 45.3% now married, 15.0% widowed, 12.2% divorced (2006-2010 5-year est.); Foreign born: 0.8% (2006-2010 5-year est.); Ancestry (includes multiple ancestries): 32.4% German, 25.7% Irish, 17.4% Polish, 14.5% Pennsylvania German, 11.0% English (2006-2010 5-year est.).

Economy: Employment by occupation: 4.8% management, 7.5% professional, 10.2% services, 8.2% sales, 0.0% farming, 9.5% construction, 19.0% production (2006-2010 5-year est.).

Income: Per capita income: $17,308 (2006-2010 5-year est.); Median household income: $42,222 (2006-2010 5-year est.); Average household income: $42,858 (2006-2010 5-year est.); Percent of households with income of $100,000 or more: 3.9% (2006-2010 5-year est.); Poverty rate: 6.7% (2006-2010 5-year est.).

Education: Percent of population age 25 and over with: High school diploma (including GED) or higher: 87.1% (2006-2010 5-year est.); Bachelor's degree or higher: 8.6% (2006-2010 5-year est.); Master's degree or higher: 0.0% (2006-2010 5-year est.).

Housing: Homeownership rate: 92.3% (2010); Median home value: $48,400 (2006-2010 5-year est.); Median contract rent: n/a per month (2006-2010 5-year est.); Median year structure built: before 1940 (2006-2010 5-year est.).

Transportation: Commute to work: 98.0% car, 0.0% public transportation, 0.0% walk, 0.0% work from home (2006-2010 5-year est.); Travel time to work: 27.2% less than 15 minutes, 50.3% 15 to 30 minutes, 15.6% 30 to 45 minutes, 2.0% 45 to 60 minutes, 4.8% 60 minutes or more (2006-2010 5-year est.)

DELANO (township). Covers a land area of 8.099 square miles and a water area of 0.004 square miles. Located at 40.85° N. Lat; 76.05° W. Long. Elevation is 1,650 feet.

Population: 551 (1990); 487 (2000); 445 (2010); Density: 54.9 persons per square mile (2010); Race: 99.3% White, 0.0% Black, 0.4% Asian, 0.0% American Indian/Alaska Native, 0.0% Native Hawaiian/Other Pacific Islander, 0.3% Other, 1.1% Hispanic of any race (2010); Average household size: 2.17 (2010); Median age: 46.5 (2010); Males per 100 females: 107.0 (2010); Marriage status: 27.3% never married, 47.6% now married, 15.4% widowed, 9.8% divorced (2006-2010 5-year est.); Foreign born: 0.6% (2006-2010 5-year est.); Ancestry (includes multiple ancestries): 34.8% German, 20.9% Irish, 19.4% Polish, 12.2% Slovak, 10.2% Pennsylvania German (2006-2010 5-year est.).

Economy: Employment by occupation: 3.7% management, 5.9% professional, 9.6% services, 11.2% sales, 0.0% farming, 9.0% construction, 16.5% production (2006-2010 5-year est.).

Income: Per capita income: $16,786 (2006-2010 5-year est.); Median household income: $38,864 (2006-2010 5-year est.); Average household income: $42,172 (2006-2010 5-year est.); Percent of households with income of $100,000 or more: 4.2% (2006-2010 5-year est.); Poverty rate: 18.8% (2006-2010 5-year est.).

Education: Percent of population age 25 and over with: High school diploma (including GED) or higher: 78.4% (2006-2010 5-year est.); Bachelor's degree or higher: 6.0% (2006-2010 5-year est.); Master's degree or higher: 0.0% (2006-2010 5-year est.).

Housing: Homeownership rate: 90.8% (2010); Median home value: $51,400 (2006-2010 5-year est.); Median contract rent: $400 per month (2006-2010 5-year est.); Median year structure built: before 1940 (2006-2010 5-year est.).

Safety: Violent crime rate: 22.4 per 10,000 population; Property crime rate: 22.4 per 10,000 population (2011).

Transportation: Commute to work: 96.8% car, 0.0% public transportation, 1.6% walk, 0.0% work from home (2006-2010 5-year est.); Travel time to work: 23.2% less than 15 minutes, 49.2% 15 to 30 minutes, 17.3% 30 to 45 minutes, 4.9% 45 to 60 minutes, 5.4% 60 minutes or more (2006-2010 5-year est.)

DONALDSON (CDP). Aka Frailey Township. Covers a land area of 0.114 square miles and a water area of 0 square miles. Located at 40.64° N. Lat; 76.41° W. Long. Elevation is 928 feet.

Population: 405 (1990); 325 (2000); 328 (2010); Density: 2,880.1 persons per square mile (2010); Race: 99.7% White, 0.0% Black, 0.0% Asian, 0.3% American Indian/Alaska Native, 0.0% Native Hawaiian/Other Pacific Islander, 0.0% Other, 0.3% Hispanic of any race (2010); Average household size: 2.60 (2010); Median age: 39.2 (2010); Males per 100 females: 97.6 (2010); Marriage status: 27.8% never married, 59.6% now married, 7.6% widowed, 5.0% divorced (2006-2010 5-year est.); Foreign born: 0.0% (2006-2010 5-year est.); Ancestry (includes multiple ancestries): 53.3% German, 24.0% Dutch, 13.3% Irish, 7.7% Pennsylvania German, 6.9% American (2006-2010 5-year est.).

Economy: Employment by occupation: 0.0% management, 3.4% professional, 9.6% services, 24.7% sales, 9.6% farming, 16.9% construction, 10.7% production (2006-2010 5-year est.).

Income: Per capita income: $19,588 (2006-2010 5-year est.); Median household income: $41,667 (2006-2010 5-year est.); Average household income: $49,077 (2006-2010 5-year est.); Percent of households with income of $100,000 or more: 8.2% (2006-2010 5-year est.); Poverty rate: 3.6% (2006-2010 5-year est.).

Education: Percent of population age 25 and over with: High school diploma (including GED) or higher: 79.3% (2006-2010 5-year est.); Bachelor's degree or higher: 2.8% (2006-2010 5-year est.); Master's degree or higher: 0.0% (2006-2010 5-year est.).

Housing: Homeownership rate: 78.6% (2010); Median home value: $65,700 (2006-2010 5-year est.); Median contract rent: $433 per month (2006-2010 5-year est.); Median year structure built: before 1940 (2006-2010 5-year est.).

Transportation: Commute to work: 97.2% car, 0.0% public transportation, 2.8% walk, 0.0% work from home (2006-2010 5-year est.); Travel time to work: 25.0% less than 15 minutes, 26.1% 15 to 30 minutes, 18.2% 30 to 45 minutes, 25.0% 45 to 60 minutes, 5.7% 60 minutes or more (2006-2010 5-year est.)

EAST BRUNSWICK (township). Covers a land area of 30.600 square miles and a water area of 0.020 square miles. Located at 40.68° N. Lat; 75.98° W. Long.

Population: 1,506 (1990); 1,601 (2000); 1,793 (2010); Density: 58.6 persons per square mile (2010); Race: 97.0% White, 0.3% Black, 0.6% Asian, 0.1% American Indian/Alaska Native, 0.0% Native Hawaiian/Other Pacific Islander, 2.0% Other, 2.0% Hispanic of any race (2010); Average household size: 2.50 (2010); Median age: 44.5 (2010); Males per 100 females: 108.5 (2010); Marriage status: 23.6% never married, 63.7% now married, 5.6% widowed, 7.1% divorced (2006-2010 5-year est.); Foreign born: 0.4% (2006-2010 5-year est.); Ancestry (includes multiple ancestries): 43.2% German, 19.0% Irish, 10.6% Pennsylvania German, 7.5% Italian, 7.2% Dutch (2006-2010 5-year est.).

Economy: Employment by occupation: 13.2% management, 3.6% professional, 6.1% services, 23.5% sales, 1.0% farming, 7.5% construction, 4.1% production (2006-2010 5-year est.).

Income: Per capita income: $35,005 (2006-2010 5-year est.); Median household income: $66,823 (2006-2010 5-year est.); Average household income: $88,620 (2006-2010 5-year est.); Percent of households with income of $100,000 or more: 29.4% (2006-2010 5-year est.); Poverty rate: 4.6% (2006-2010 5-year est.).

Education: Percent of population age 25 and over with: High school diploma (including GED) or higher: 89.8% (2006-2010 5-year est.); Bachelor's degree or higher: 26.6% (2006-2010 5-year est.); Master's degree or higher: 9.9% (2006-2010 5-year est.).

Housing: Homeownership rate: 85.1% (2010); Median home value: $199,700 (2006-2010 5-year est.); Median contract rent: $444 per month (2006-2010 5-year est.); Median year structure built: 1970 (2006-2010 5-year est.).

Transportation: Commute to work: 94.0% car, 0.3% public transportation, 3.8% walk, 1.9% work from home (2006-2010 5-year est.); Travel time to work: 24.0% less than 15 minutes, 38.2% 15 to 30 minutes, 21.3% 30 to 45 minutes, 8.9% 45 to 60 minutes, 7.6% 60 minutes or more (2006-2010 5-year est.)

Additional Information Contacts

Tamaqua Area Chamber of Commerce . . . . (570) 668-1880
http://www.tamaqua.net

EAST NORWEGIAN (township). Covers a land area of 4.075 square miles and a water area of 0 square miles. Located at 40.71° N. Lat; 76.16° W. Long.
Population: 991 (1990); 864 (2000); 863 (2010); Density: 211.8 persons per square mile (2010); Race: 99.1% White, 0.0% Black, 0.5% Asian, 0.0% American Indian/Alaska Native, 0.0% Native Hawaiian/Other Pacific Islander, 0.4% Other, 0.1% Hispanic of any race (2010); Average household size: 2.28 (2010); Median age: 45.8 (2010); Males per 100 females: 97.5 (2010); Marriage status: 22.7% never married, 59.2% now married, 9.6% widowed, 8.4% divorced (2006-2010 5-year est.); Foreign born: 0.0% (2006-2010 5-year est.); Ancestry (includes multiple ancestries): 30.6% Irish, 27.7% German, 16.7% Polish, 11.6% Italian, 8.8% Slovak (2006-2010 5-year est.).
Economy: Employment by occupation: 3.4% management, 1.1% professional, 9.2% services, 15.1% sales, 3.9% farming, 13.0% construction, 8.2% production (2006-2010 5-year est.).
Income: Per capita income: $22,561 (2006-2010 5-year est.); Median household income: $49,732 (2006-2010 5-year est.); Average household income: $52,368 (2006-2010 5-year est.); Percent of households with income of $100,000 or more: 10.6% (2006-2010 5-year est.); Poverty rate: 19.2% (2006-2010 5-year est.).
Education: Percent of population age 25 and over with: High school diploma (including GED) or higher: 78.3% (2006-2010 5-year est.); Bachelor's degree or higher: 8.8% (2006-2010 5-year est.); Master's degree or higher: 3.8% (2006-2010 5-year est.).
Housing: Homeownership rate: 85.2% (2010); Median home value: $79,800 (2006-2010 5-year est.); Median contract rent: $520 per month (2006-2010 5-year est.); Median year structure built: 1951 (2006-2010 5-year est.).
Safety: Violent crime rate: 0.0 per 10,000 population; Property crime rate: 0.0 per 10,000 population (2011).
Transportation: Commute to work: 94.9% car, 0.0% public transportation, 1.9% walk, 2.1% work from home (2006-2010 5-year est.); Travel time to work: 42.5% less than 15 minutes, 26.5% 15 to 30 minutes, 15.0% 30 to 45 minutes, 3.8% 45 to 60 minutes, 12.2% 60 minutes or more (2006-2010 5-year est.)

EAST UNION (township). Covers a land area of 25.788 square miles and a water area of 0.030 square miles. Located at 40.89° N. Lat; 76.13° W. Long.
Population: 1,374 (1990); 1,419 (2000); 1,605 (2010); Density: 62.2 persons per square mile (2010); Race: 97.6% White, 0.5% Black, 0.1% Asian, 0.2% American Indian/Alaska Native, 0.0% Native Hawaiian/Other Pacific Islander, 1.6% Other, 1.6% Hispanic of any race (2010); Average household size: 2.33 (2010); Median age: 45.9 (2010); Males per 100 females: 105.0 (2010); Marriage status: 25.1% never married, 51.8% now married, 7.4% widowed, 15.7% divorced (2006-2010 5-year est.); Foreign born: 2.7% (2006-2010 5-year est.); Ancestry (includes multiple ancestries): 20.7% German, 20.3% Polish, 18.4% Italian, 15.0% Irish, 11.0% Pennsylvania German (2006-2010 5-year est.).
Economy: Single-family building permits issued: 9 (2011); Multi-family building permits issued: 0 (2011); Employment by occupation: 3.8% management, 5.5% professional, 9.2% services, 18.5% sales, 2.8% farming, 15.5% construction, 13.8% production (2006-2010 5-year est.).
Income: Per capita income: $21,438 (2006-2010 5-year est.); Median household income: $47,313 (2006-2010 5-year est.); Average household income: $51,209 (2006-2010 5-year est.); Percent of households with income of $100,000 or more: 8.6% (2006-2010 5-year est.); Poverty rate: 12.1% (2006-2010 5-year est.).
Education: Percent of population age 25 and over with: High school diploma (including GED) or higher: 90.0% (2006-2010 5-year est.); Bachelor's degree or higher: 10.2% (2006-2010 5-year est.); Master's degree or higher: 4.4% (2006-2010 5-year est.).
Housing: Homeownership rate: 84.5% (2010); Median home value: $94,700 (2006-2010 5-year est.); Median contract rent: $471 per month (2006-2010 5-year est.); Median year structure built: 1956 (2006-2010 5-year est.).
Transportation: Commute to work: 93.4% car, 0.0% public transportation, 4.5% walk, 2.0% work from home (2006-2010 5-year est.); Travel time to work: 30.8% less than 15 minutes, 41.5% 15 to 30 minutes, 16.4% 30 to 45 minutes, 4.6% 45 to 60 minutes, 6.7% 60 minutes or more (2006-2010 5-year est.)
Additional Information Contacts
Schuylkill Chamber of Commerce . . . . (570) 622-1942
  http://www.schuylkillchamber.com

ELDRED (township). Covers a land area of 22.253 square miles and a water area of 0 square miles. Located at 40.71° N. Lat; 76.49° W. Long.
Population: 736 (1990); 719 (2000); 758 (2010); Density: 34.1 persons per square mile (2010); Race: 97.0% White, 1.2% Black, 0.3% Asian, 0.3% American Indian/Alaska Native, 0.0% Native Hawaiian/Other Pacific Islander, 1.2% Other, 1.5% Hispanic of any race (2010); Average household size: 2.58 (2010); Median age: 45.9 (2010); Males per 100 females: 92.9 (2010); Marriage status: 21.9% never married, 58.9% now married, 10.4% widowed, 8.7% divorced (2006-2010 5-year est.); Foreign born: 0.0% (2006-2010 5-year est.); Ancestry (includes multiple ancestries): 49.7% German, 14.6% Dutch, 11.3% Pennsylvania German, 4.6% American, 3.5% Swedish (2006-2010 5-year est.).
Economy: Employment by occupation: 12.4% management, 1.3% professional, 8.6% services, 9.0% sales, 1.3% farming, 11.6% construction, 12.0% production (2006-2010 5-year est.).
Income: Per capita income: $22,523 (2006-2010 5-year est.); Median household income: $37,344 (2006-2010 5-year est.); Average household income: $49,413 (2006-2010 5-year est.); Percent of households with income of $100,000 or more: 10.1% (2006-2010 5-year est.); Poverty rate: 12.5% (2006-2010 5-year est.).
Education: Percent of population age 25 and over with: High school diploma (including GED) or higher: 83.6% (2006-2010 5-year est.); Bachelor's degree or higher: 10.9% (2006-2010 5-year est.); Master's degree or higher: 5.9% (2006-2010 5-year est.).
Housing: Homeownership rate: 83.4% (2010); Median home value: $145,000 (2006-2010 5-year est.); Median contract rent: $208 per month (2006-2010 5-year est.); Median year structure built: 1960 (2006-2010 5-year est.).
Transportation: Commute to work: 81.1% car, 0.0% public transportation, 2.6% walk, 13.3% work from home (2006-2010 5-year est.); Travel time to work: 20.8% less than 15 minutes, 31.2% 15 to 30 minutes, 19.8% 30 to 45 minutes, 14.4% 45 to 60 minutes, 13.9% 60 minutes or more (2006-2010 5-year est.)

ENGLEWOOD (CDP). Covers a land area of 0.476 square miles and a water area of 0 square miles. Located at 40.78° N. Lat; 76.24° W. Long. Elevation is 1,493 feet.
Population: 583 (1990); 484 (2000); 532 (2010); Density: 1,117.2 persons per square mile (2010); Race: 99.2% White, 0.4% Black, 0.0% Asian, 0.0% American Indian/Alaska Native, 0.0% Native Hawaiian/Other Pacific Islander, 0.4% Other, 0.0% Hispanic of any race (2010); Average household size: 2.36 (2010); Median age: 45.3 (2010); Males per 100 females: 96.3 (2010); Marriage status: 15.8% never married, 58.7% now married, 25.5% widowed, 0.0% divorced (2006-2010 5-year est.); Foreign born: 2.9% (2006-2010 5-year est.); Ancestry (includes multiple ancestries): 49.6% German, 32.1% Irish, 14.6% Dutch, 11.7% Polish, 10.5% Czechoslovakian (2006-2010 5-year est.).
Economy: Employment by occupation: 0.0% management, 0.0% professional, 6.7% services, 7.7% sales, 0.0% farming, 0.0% construction, 5.6% production (2006-2010 5-year est.).
Income: Per capita income: $27,127 (2006-2010 5-year est.); Median household income: $34,118 (2006-2010 5-year est.); Average household income: $57,149 (2006-2010 5-year est.); Percent of households with income of $100,000 or more: 6.1% (2006-2010 5-year est.); Poverty rate: 0.0% (2006-2010 5-year est.).
Education: Percent of population age 25 and over with: High school diploma (including GED) or higher: 96.0% (2006-2010 5-year est.); Bachelor's degree or higher: 21.0% (2006-2010 5-year est.); Master's degree or higher: 7.9% (2006-2010 5-year est.).
Housing: Homeownership rate: 94.7% (2010); Median home value: $124,300 (2006-2010 5-year est.); Median contract rent: n/a per month (2006-2010 5-year est.); Median year structure built: 1955 (2006-2010 5-year est.).
Transportation: Commute to work: 100.0% car, 0.0% public transportation, 0.0% walk, 0.0% work from home (2006-2010 5-year est.); Travel time to work: 37.7% less than 15 minutes, 50.4% 15 to 30 minutes, 12.0% 30 to 45 minutes, 0.0% 45 to 60 minutes, 0.0% 60 minutes or more (2006-2010 5-year est.)

FORESTVILLE (CDP). Covers a land area of 0.869 square miles and a water area of 0 square miles. Located at 40.69° N. Lat; 76.29° W. Long. Elevation is 863 feet.
Population: n/a (1990); n/a (2000); 435 (2010); Density: 500.4 persons per square mile (2010); Race: 99.5% White, 0.0% Black, 0.2% Asian, 0.0% American Indian/Alaska Native, 0.0% Native Hawaiian/Other Pacific

Islander, 0.3% Other, 0.2% Hispanic of any race (2010); Average household size: 2.40 (2010); Median age: 44.2 (2010); Males per 100 females: 94.2 (2010); Marriage status: 30.7% never married, 57.0% now married, 3.4% widowed, 9.0% divorced (2006-2010 5-year est.); Foreign born: 4.1% (2006-2010 5-year est.); Ancestry (includes multiple ancestries): 47.7% Ukrainian, 28.7% Polish, 24.4% Irish, 13.6% Italian, 12.5% German (2006-2010 5-year est.).

Economy: Employment by occupation: 10.9% management, 5.8% professional, 6.5% services, 13.0% sales, 4.3% farming, 9.4% construction, 4.3% production (2006-2010 5-year est.).

Income: Per capita income: $22,712 (2006-2010 5-year est.); Median household income: $37,639 (2006-2010 5-year est.); Average household income: $49,929 (2006-2010 5-year est.); Percent of households with income of $100,000 or more: 10.8% (2006-2010 5-year est.); Poverty rate: 3.5% (2006-2010 5-year est.).

Education: Percent of population age 25 and over with: High school diploma (including GED) or higher: 95.8% (2006-2010 5-year est.); Bachelor's degree or higher: 22.3% (2006-2010 5-year est.); Master's degree or higher: 2.1% (2006-2010 5-year est.).

Housing: Homeownership rate: 86.8% (2010); Median home value: $82,700 (2006-2010 5-year est.); Median contract rent: n/a per month (2006-2010 5-year est.); Median year structure built: 1944 (2006-2010 5-year est.).

Transportation: Commute to work: 100.0% car, 0.0% public transportation, 0.0% walk, 0.0% work from home (2006-2010 5-year est.); Travel time to work: 8.7% less than 15 minutes, 39.1% 15 to 30 minutes, 6.5% 30 to 45 minutes, 5.8% 45 to 60 minutes, 39.9% 60 minutes or more (2006-2010 5-year est.)

FOSTER (township).
Covers a land area of 13.148 square miles and a water area of 0.030 square miles. Located at 40.70° N. Lat; 76.35° W. Long.

Population: 298 (1990); 1,124 (2000); 251 (2010); Density: 19.1 persons per square mile (2010); Race: 100.0% White, 0.0% Black, 0.0% Asian, 0.0% American Indian/Alaska Native, 0.0% Native Hawaiian/Other Pacific Islander, 0.0% Other, 0.0% Hispanic of any race (2010); Average household size: 2.32 (2010); Median age: 46.9 (2010); Males per 100 females: 94.6 (2010); Marriage status: 16.7% never married, 61.1% now married, 13.6% widowed, 8.6% divorced (2006-2010 5-year est.); Foreign born: 0.0% (2006-2010 5-year est.); Ancestry (includes multiple ancestries): 33.7% Irish, 29.8% Polish, 27.1% German, 8.8% Lithuanian, 6.6% Scottish (2006-2010 5-year est.).

Economy: Single-family building permits issued: 0 (2011); Multi-family building permits issued: 0 (2011); Employment by occupation: 4.5% management, 9.1% professional, 10.9% services, 9.1% sales, 0.0% farming, 20.9% construction, 20.9% production (2006-2010 5-year est.).

Income: Per capita income: $23,551 (2006-2010 5-year est.); Median household income: $43,750 (2006-2010 5-year est.); Average household income: $50,699 (2006-2010 5-year est.); Percent of households with income of $100,000 or more: 12.8% (2006-2010 5-year est.); Poverty rate: 2.2% (2006-2010 5-year est.).

Education: Percent of population age 25 and over with: High school diploma (including GED) or higher: 86.5% (2006-2010 5-year est.); Bachelor's degree or higher: 9.0% (2006-2010 5-year est.); Master's degree or higher: 3.0% (2006-2010 5-year est.).

Housing: Homeownership rate: 86.1% (2010); Median home value: $66,100 (2006-2010 5-year est.); Median contract rent: n/a per month (2006-2010 5-year est.); Median year structure built: before 1940 (2006-2010 5-year est.).

Transportation: Commute to work: 94.2% car, 0.0% public transportation, 1.9% walk, 1.9% work from home (2006-2010 5-year est.); Travel time to work: 32.7% less than 15 minutes, 33.7% 15 to 30 minutes, 10.9% 30 to 45 minutes, 7.9% 45 to 60 minutes, 14.9% 60 minutes or more (2006-2010 5-year est.)

Additional Information Contacts
Schuylkill Chamber of Commerce . . . . (570) 622-1942
http://www.schuylkillchamber.com

FOUNTAIN SPRINGS (CDP).
Covers a land area of 0.562 square miles and a water area of 0 square miles. Located at 40.77° N. Lat; 76.33° W. Long. Elevation is 1,056 feet.

Population: 121 (1990); 100 (2000); 278 (2010); Density: 494.9 persons per square mile (2010); Race: 97.1% White, 1.8% Black, 0.0% Asian, 0.4% American Indian/Alaska Native, 0.0% Native Hawaiian/Other Pacific Islander, 0.7% Other, 1.4% Hispanic of any race (2010); Average

household size: 2.09 (2010); Median age: 48.1 (2010); Males per 100 females: 65.5 (2010); Marriage status: 15.2% never married, 69.2% now married, 9.7% widowed, 5.9% divorced (2006-2010 5-year est.); Foreign born: 0.0% (2006-2010 5-year est.); Ancestry (includes multiple ancestries): 33.1% German, 21.2% Polish, 18.9% Irish, 16.9% Italian, 16.1% English (2006-2010 5-year est.).

Economy: Employment by occupation: 23.8% management, 0.0% professional, 0.0% services, 24.9% sales, 0.0% farming, 0.0% construction, 0.0% production (2006-2010 5-year est.).

Income: Per capita income: $29,405 (2006-2010 5-year est.); Median household income: $75,515 (2006-2010 5-year est.); Average household income: $77,144 (2006-2010 5-year est.); Percent of households with income of $100,000 or more: 13.0% (2006-2010 5-year est.); Poverty rate: 0.0% (2006-2010 5-year est.).

Education: Percent of population age 25 and over with: High school diploma (including GED) or higher: 89.7% (2006-2010 5-year est.); Bachelor's degree or higher: 27.1% (2006-2010 5-year est.); Master's degree or higher: 5.5% (2006-2010 5-year est.).

Housing: Homeownership rate: 87.8% (2010); Median home value: $148,000 (2006-2010 5-year est.); Median contract rent: n/a per month (2006-2010 5-year est.); Median year structure built: 1959 (2006-2010 5-year est.).

Transportation: Commute to work: 73.5% car, 0.0% public transportation, 17.5% walk, 9.0% work from home (2006-2010 5-year est.); Travel time to work: 65.1% less than 15 minutes, 25.6% 15 to 30 minutes, 9.3% 30 to 45 minutes, 0.0% 45 to 60 minutes, 0.0% 60 minutes or more (2006-2010 5-year est.)

FRACKVILLE (borough).
Covers a land area of 0.595 square miles and a water area of 0 square miles. Located at 40.78° N. Lat; 76.23° W. Long. Elevation is 1,483 feet.

History: Settled 1852, laid out 1861, incorporated 1876.

Population: 4,700 (1990); 4,361 (2000); 3,805 (2010); Density: 6,399.0 persons per square mile (2010); Race: 97.6% White, 0.3% Black, 0.9% Asian, 0.2% American Indian/Alaska Native, 0.0% Native Hawaiian/Other Pacific Islander, 1.0% Other, 1.1% Hispanic of any race (2010); Average household size: 2.23 (2010); Median age: 44.7 (2010); Males per 100 females: 91.6 (2010); Marriage status: 22.8% never married, 51.4% now married, 14.1% widowed, 11.7% divorced (2006-2010 5-year est.); Foreign born: 2.3% (2006-2010 5-year est.); Ancestry (includes multiple ancestries): 23.6% German, 22.1% Polish, 16.0% Irish, 11.5% Dutch, 10.4% Lithuanian (2006-2010 5-year est.).

Economy: Employment by occupation: 7.8% management, 0.0% professional, 10.8% services, 15.1% sales, 3.7% farming, 6.1% construction, 10.7% production (2006-2010 5-year est.).

Income: Per capita income: $19,577 (2006-2010 5-year est.); Median household income: $38,727 (2006-2010 5-year est.); Average household income: $48,732 (2006-2010 5-year est.); Percent of households with income of $100,000 or more: 8.7% (2006-2010 5-year est.); Poverty rate: 11.0% (2006-2010 5-year est.).

Education: Percent of population age 25 and over with: High school diploma (including GED) or higher: 86.4% (2006-2010 5-year est.); Bachelor's degree or higher: 13.3% (2006-2010 5-year est.); Master's degree or higher: 5.1% (2006-2010 5-year est.).

School District(s)
Schuylkill Technology Centers (10-12)
    2010-11 Enrollment: n/a . . . . (570) 544-4748
Vocational/Technical School(s)
Schuylkill Technology Center (Public)
    Fall 2010 Enrollment: 279 . . . . (570) 874-1034
    2011-12 Tuition: $12,360

Housing: Homeownership rate: 72.4% (2010); Median home value: $68,800 (2006-2010 5-year est.); Median contract rent: $435 per month (2006-2010 5-year est.); Median year structure built: before 1940 (2006-2010 5-year est.).

Safety: Violent crime rate: 15.7 per 10,000 population; Property crime rate: 15.7 per 10,000 population (2011).

Transportation: Commute to work: 97.1% car, 0.5% public transportation, 2.0% walk, 0.5% work from home (2006-2010 5-year est.); Travel time to work: 50.7% less than 15 minutes, 31.2% 15 to 30 minutes, 10.0% 30 to 45 minutes, 4.2% 45 to 60 minutes, 3.9% 60 minutes or more (2006-2010 5-year est.)

Additional Information Contacts
Schuylkill Chamber of Commerce . . . . (570) 622-1942
    http://www.schuylkillchamber.com

FRAILEY (township). Covers a land area of 9.146 square miles and a water area of 0.031 square miles. Located at 40.65° N. Lat; 76.39° W. Long.

Population: 518 (1990); 416 (2000); 429 (2010); Density: 46.9 persons per square mile (2010); Race: 99.8% White, 0.0% Black, 0.0% Asian, 0.2% American Indian/Alaska Native, 0.0% Native Hawaiian/Other Pacific Islander, 0.0% Other, 0.2% Hispanic of any race (2010); Average household size: 2.60 (2010); Median age: 39.3 (2010); Males per 100 females: 100.5 (2010); Marriage status: 31.0% never married, 55.9% now married, 7.6% widowed, 5.5% divorced (2006-2010 5-year est.); Foreign born: 0.0% (2006-2010 5-year est.); Ancestry (includes multiple ancestries): 48.1% German, 20.1% Dutch, 12.8% Irish, 8.8% Pennsylvania German, 8.2% American (2006-2010 5-year est.).

Economy: Employment by occupation: 0.8% management, 3.7% professional, 9.9% services, 21.8% sales, 7.0% farming, 18.1% construction, 9.9% production (2006-2010 5-year est.).

Income: Per capita income: $19,593 (2006-2010 5-year est.); Median household income: $42,500 (2006-2010 5-year est.); Average household income: $48,582 (2006-2010 5-year est.); Percent of households with income of $100,000 or more: 8.3% (2006-2010 5-year est.); Poverty rate: 7.7% (2006-2010 5-year est.).

Education: Percent of population age 25 and over with: High school diploma (including GED) or higher: 79.7% (2006-2010 5-year est.); Bachelor's degree or higher: 4.8% (2006-2010 5-year est.); Master's degree or higher: 1.0% (2006-2010 5-year est.).

Housing: Homeownership rate: 79.4% (2010); Median home value: $66,500 (2006-2010 5-year est.); Median contract rent: $408 per month (2006-2010 5-year est.); Median year structure built: before 1940 (2006-2010 5-year est.).

Transportation: Commute to work: 97.9% car, 0.0% public transportation, 2.1% walk, 0.0% work from home (2006-2010 5-year est.); Travel time to work: 29.4% less than 15 minutes, 26.1% 15 to 30 minutes, 16.8% 30 to 45 minutes, 22.3% 45 to 60 minutes, 5.5% 60 minutes or more (2006-2010 5-year est.)

FRIEDENSBURG (CDP). Covers a land area of 1.578 square miles and a water area of 0 square miles. Located at 40.61° N. Lat; 76.23° W. Long. Elevation is 679 feet.

Population: 770 (1990); 828 (2000); 858 (2010); Density: 543.6 persons per square mile (2010); Race: 98.4% White, 0.1% Black, 0.2% Asian, 0.0% American Indian/Alaska Native, 0.0% Native Hawaiian/Other Pacific Islander, 1.3% Other, 0.8% Hispanic of any race (2010); Average household size: 2.15 (2010); Median age: 45.6 (2010); Males per 100 females: 102.8 (2010); Marriage status: 20.4% never married, 48.0% now married, 16.3% widowed, 15.4% divorced (2006-2010 5-year est.); Foreign born: 0.0% (2006-2010 5-year est.); Ancestry (includes multiple ancestries): 47.6% German, 15.2% Dutch, 12.7% American, 11.8% Italian, 11.8% Irish (2006-2010 5-year est.).

Economy: Employment by occupation: 14.8% management, 3.4% professional, 19.3% services, 23.2% sales, 3.4% farming, 7.7% construction, 2.4% production (2006-2010 5-year est.).

Income: Per capita income: $28,664 (2006-2010 5-year est.); Median household income: $47,222 (2006-2010 5-year est.); Average household income: $60,029 (2006-2010 5-year est.); Percent of households with income of $100,000 or more: 8.0% (2006-2010 5-year est.); Poverty rate: 5.7% (2006-2010 5-year est.).

Education: Percent of population age 25 and over with: High school diploma (including GED) or higher: 78.4% (2006-2010 5-year est.); Bachelor's degree or higher: 7.9% (2006-2010 5-year est.); Master's degree or higher: 5.0% (2006-2010 5-year est.).

School District(s)

Blue Mountain SD (KG-12)

    2010-11 Enrollment: 2,877 . . . . (570) 366-0515

Housing: Homeownership rate: 81.0% (2010); Median home value: $71,600 (2006-2010 5-year est.); Median contract rent: $564 per month (2006-2010 5-year est.); Median year structure built: 1982 (2006-2010 5-year est.).

Transportation: Commute to work: 97.8% car, 0.0% public transportation, 2.2% walk, 0.0% work from home (2006-2010 5-year est.); Travel time to work: 25.3% less than 15 minutes, 36.4% 15 to 30 minutes, 19.3% 30 to 45 minutes, 5.7% 45 to 60 minutes, 13.3% 60 minutes or more (2006-2010 5-year est.)

GILBERTON (borough). Covers a land area of 1.419 square miles and a water area of 0.034 square miles. Located at 40.80° N. Lat; 76.22° W. Long. Elevation is 1,129 feet.

History: Incorporated 1873.

Population: 953 (1990); 867 (2000); 769 (2010); Density: 541.8 persons per square mile (2010); Race: 97.4% White, 0.0% Black, 0.0% Asian, 0.0% American Indian/Alaska Native, 0.0% Native Hawaiian/Other Pacific Islander, 2.6% Other, 2.9% Hispanic of any race (2010); Average household size: 2.36 (2010); Median age: 44.9 (2010); Males per 100 females: 102.4 (2010); Marriage status: 31.2% never married, 38.6% now married, 13.6% widowed, 16.6% divorced (2006-2010 5-year est.); Foreign born: 0.0% (2006-2010 5-year est.); Ancestry (includes multiple ancestries): 38.8% Irish, 28.1% German, 13.4% Ukrainian, 10.0% Lithuanian, 8.9% Polish (2006-2010 5-year est.).

Economy: Employment by occupation: 5.1% management, 0.9% professional, 6.9% services, 18.0% sales, 4.9% farming, 22.9% construction, 13.4% production (2006-2010 5-year est.).

Income: Per capita income: $18,670 (2006-2010 5-year est.); Median household income: $34,018 (2006-2010 5-year est.); Average household income: $41,316 (2006-2010 5-year est.); Percent of households with income of $100,000 or more: 2.1% (2006-2010 5-year est.); Poverty rate: 16.4% (2006-2010 5-year est.).

Education: Percent of population age 25 and over with: High school diploma (including GED) or higher: 81.3% (2006-2010 5-year est.); Bachelor's degree or higher: 5.2% (2006-2010 5-year est.); Master's degree or higher: 0.5% (2006-2010 5-year est.).

Housing: Homeownership rate: 84.6% (2010); Median home value: $26,700 (2006-2010 5-year est.); Median contract rent: $347 per month (2006-2010 5-year est.); Median year structure built: before 1940 (2006-2010 5-year est.).

Transportation: Commute to work: 91.0% car, 0.0% public transportation, 2.7% walk, 6.3% work from home (2006-2010 5-year est.); Travel time to work: 32.2% less than 15 minutes, 22.9% 15 to 30 minutes, 15.6% 30 to 45 minutes, 5.7% 45 to 60 minutes, 23.6% 60 minutes or more (2006-2010 5-year est.)

Additional Information Contacts

Schuylkill Chamber of Commerce . . . . (570) 622-1942

    http://www.schuylkillchamber.com

GIRARDVILLE (borough). Covers a land area of 0.518 square miles and a water area of 0.013 square miles. Located at 40.79° N. Lat; 76.28° W. Long. Elevation is 994 feet.

History: Settled c.1832, incorporated 1872.

Population: 1,881 (1990); 1,742 (2000); 1,519 (2010); Density: 2,934.3 persons per square mile (2010); Race: 97.2% White, 1.2% Black, 0.0% Asian, 0.3% American Indian/Alaska Native, 0.0% Native Hawaiian/Other Pacific Islander, 1.3% Other, 1.6% Hispanic of any race (2010); Average household size: 2.29 (2010); Median age: 42.9 (2010); Males per 100 females: 98.6 (2010); Marriage status: 18.7% never married, 56.9% now married, 14.2% widowed, 10.2% divorced (2006-2010 5-year est.); Foreign born: 0.4% (2006-2010 5-year est.); Ancestry (includes multiple ancestries): 41.4% Irish, 21.3% German, 20.1% Italian, 12.9% Dutch, 12.3% Lithuanian (2006-2010 5-year est.).

Economy: Employment by occupation: 4.8% management, 0.9% professional, 11.3% services, 12.2% sales, 0.9% farming, 15.6% construction, 25.9% production (2006-2010 5-year est.).

Income: Per capita income: $17,196 (2006-2010 5-year est.); Median household income: $31,944 (2006-2010 5-year est.); Average household income: $39,362 (2006-2010 5-year est.); Percent of households with income of $100,000 or more: 3.8% (2006-2010 5-year est.); Poverty rate: 15.0% (2006-2010 5-year est.).

Education: Percent of population age 25 and over with: High school diploma (including GED) or higher: 92.0% (2006-2010 5-year est.); Bachelor's degree or higher: 5.7% (2006-2010 5-year est.); Master's degree or higher: 2.2% (2006-2010 5-year est.).

Housing: Homeownership rate: 75.0% (2010); Median home value: $34,600 (2006-2010 5-year est.); Median contract rent: $324 per month (2006-2010 5-year est.); Median year structure built: before 1940 (2006-2010 5-year est.).

Transportation: Commute to work: 96.1% car, 1.4% public transportation, 1.2% walk, 1.4% work from home (2006-2010 5-year est.); Travel time to work: 36.0% less than 15 minutes, 31.0% 15 to 30 minutes, 13.9% 30 to 45 minutes, 6.0% 45 to 60 minutes, 13.0% 60 minutes or more (2006-2010 5-year est.)

Additional Information Contacts
Schuylkill Chamber of Commerce . . . . (570) 622-1942
   http://www.schuylkillchamber.com

GORDON (borough). Covers a land area of 0.593 square miles and a water area of 0 square miles. Located at 40.75° N. Lat; 76.34° W. Long. Elevation is 853 feet.
History: Settled 1856, incorporated 1891.
Population: 768 (1990); 781 (2000); 763 (2010); Density: 1,286.7 persons per square mile (2010); Race: 98.4% White, 0.5% Black, 0.0% Asian, 0.3% American Indian/Alaska Native, 0.0% Native Hawaiian/Other Pacific Islander, 0.8% Other, 2.5% Hispanic of any race (2010); Average household size: 2.37 (2010); Median age: 40.7 (2010); Males per 100 females: 96.1 (2010); Marriage status: 24.9% never married, 53.6% now married, 11.0% widowed, 10.5% divorced (2006-2010 5-year est.); Foreign born: 3.2% (2006-2010 5-year est.); Ancestry (includes multiple ancestries): 48.9% German, 31.2% Irish, 10.8% Polish, 9.2% Italian, 7.2% Dutch (2006-2010 5-year est.).
Economy: Employment by occupation: 13.0% management, 2.2% professional, 7.6% services, 21.1% sales, 2.2% farming, 4.6% construction, 5.4% production (2006-2010 5-year est.).
Income: Per capita income: $20,504 (2006-2010 5-year est.); Median household income: $41,250 (2006-2010 5-year est.); Average household income: $46,504 (2006-2010 5-year est.); Percent of households with income of $100,000 or more: 5.0% (2006-2010 5-year est.); Poverty rate: 13.5% (2006-2010 5-year est.).
Education: Percent of population age 25 and over with: High school diploma (including GED) or higher: 90.9% (2006-2010 5-year est.); Bachelor's degree or higher: 8.9% (2006-2010 5-year est.); Master's degree or higher: 2.5% (2006-2010 5-year est.).
Housing: Homeownership rate: 76.4% (2010); Median home value: $80,800 (2006-2010 5-year est.); Median contract rent: $398 per month (2006-2010 5-year est.); Median year structure built: before 1940 (2006-2010 5-year est.).
Transportation: Commute to work: 94.6% car, 0.0% public transportation, 3.5% walk, 1.9% work from home (2006-2010 5-year est.); Travel time to work: 33.9% less than 15 minutes, 35.6% 15 to 30 minutes, 13.6% 30 to 45 minutes, 10.0% 45 to 60 minutes, 6.9% 60 minutes or more (2006-2010 5-year est.)

GRIER CITY (CDP). Covers a land area of 0.358 square miles and a water area of 0 square miles. Located at 40.83° N. Lat; 76.06° W. Long. Elevation is 1,250 feet.
Population: n/a (1990); n/a (2000); 241 (2010); Density: 673.0 persons per square mile (2010); Race: 100.0% White, 0.0% Black, 0.0% Asian, 0.0% American Indian/Alaska Native, 0.0% Native Hawaiian/Other Pacific Islander, 0.0% Other, 0.8% Hispanic of any race (2010); Average household size: 2.59 (2010); Median age: 41.6 (2010); Males per 100 females: 109.6 (2010); Marriage status: 18.8% never married, 65.9% now married, 15.3% widowed, 0.0% divorced (2006-2010 5-year est.); Foreign born: 0.0% (2006-2010 5-year est.); Ancestry (includes multiple ancestries): 51.8% Polish, 50.0% German, 38.6% Italian, 22.8% Swedish, 14.0% Welsh (2006-2010 5-year est.).
Economy: Employment by occupation: 26.8% management, 0.0% professional, 23.2% services, 0.0% sales, 0.0% farming, 0.0% construction, 0.0% production (2006-2010 5-year est.).
Income: Per capita income: $21,941 (2006-2010 5-year est.); Median household income: $63,654 (2006-2010 5-year est.); Average household income: $56,848 (2006-2010 5-year est.); Percent of households with income of $100,000 or more: n/a (2006-2010 5-year est.); Poverty rate: 0.0% (2006-2010 5-year est.).
Education: Percent of population age 25 and over with: High school diploma (including GED) or higher: 84.7% (2006-2010 5-year est.); Bachelor's degree or higher: 35.3% (2006-2010 5-year est.); Master's degree or higher: 17.6% (2006-2010 5-year est.).
Housing: Homeownership rate: 90.3% (2010); Median home value: $135,000 (2006-2010 5-year est.); Median contract rent: n/a per month (2006-2010 5-year est.); Median year structure built: before 1940 (2006-2010 5-year est.).
Transportation: Commute to work: 100.0% car, 0.0% public transportation, 0.0% walk, 0.0% work from home (2006-2010 5-year est.); Travel time to work: 23.2% less than 15 minutes, 26.8% 15 to 30 minutes, 23.2% 30 to 45 minutes, 0.0% 45 to 60 minutes, 26.8% 60 minutes or more (2006-2010 5-year est.)

HECKSCHERVILLE (CDP). Covers a land area of 0.332 square miles and a water area of 0 square miles. Located at 40.72° N. Lat; 76.27° W. Long. Elevation is 1,007 feet.
Population: 70 (1990); 76 (2000); 220 (2010); Density: 663.6 persons per square mile (2010); Race: 99.1% White, 0.0% Black, 0.0% Asian, 0.0% American Indian/Alaska Native, 0.0% Native Hawaiian/Other Pacific Islander, 0.9% Other, 0.0% Hispanic of any race (2010); Average household size: 2.32 (2010); Median age: 43.9 (2010); Males per 100 females: 111.5 (2010); Marriage status: 22.1% never married, 57.1% now married, 2.6% widowed, 18.2% divorced (2006-2010 5-year est.); Foreign born: 0.0% (2006-2010 5-year est.); Ancestry (includes multiple ancestries): 51.9% Irish, 24.9% German, 12.5% Ukrainian, 9.7% Italian, 9.0% Welsh (2006-2010 5-year est.).
Economy: Employment by occupation: 0.0% management, 0.0% professional, 13.5% services, 5.2% sales, 5.2% farming, 18.8% construction, 13.5% production (2006-2010 5-year est.).
Income: Per capita income: $15,472 (2006-2010 5-year est.); Median household income: $48,750 (2006-2010 5-year est.); Average household income: $40,690 (2006-2010 5-year est.); Percent of households with income of $100,000 or more: n/a (2006-2010 5-year est.); Poverty rate: 6.2% (2006-2010 5-year est.).
Education: Percent of population age 25 and over with: High school diploma (including GED) or higher: 74.7% (2006-2010 5-year est.); Bachelor's degree or higher: 5.6% (2006-2010 5-year est.); Master's degree or higher: 3.0% (2006-2010 5-year est.).
Housing: Homeownership rate: 86.3% (2010); Median home value: $31,300 (2006-2010 5-year est.); Median contract rent: n/a per month (2006-2010 5-year est.); Median year structure built: before 1940 (2006-2010 5-year est.).
Transportation: Commute to work: 100.0% car, 0.0% public transportation, 0.0% walk, 0.0% work from home (2006-2010 5-year est.); Travel time to work: 19.1% less than 15 minutes, 47.2% 15 to 30 minutes, 22.5% 30 to 45 minutes, 11.2% 45 to 60 minutes, 0.0% 60 minutes or more (2006-2010 5-year est.)

HEGINS (CDP). Covers a land area of 1.994 square miles and a water area of 0 square miles. Located at 40.65° N. Lat; 76.49° W. Long. Elevation is 827 feet.
Population: n/a (1990); n/a (2000); 812 (2010); Density: 407.1 persons per square mile (2010); Race: 98.4% White, 0.0% Black, 0.2% Asian, 0.0% American Indian/Alaska Native, 0.0% Native Hawaiian/Other Pacific Islander, 1.4% Other, 1.5% Hispanic of any race (2010); Average household size: 2.27 (2010); Median age: 42.8 (2010); Males per 100 females: 108.7 (2010); Marriage status: 27.7% never married, 60.0% now married, 4.6% widowed, 7.6% divorced (2006-2010 5-year est.); Foreign born: 6.7% (2006-2010 5-year est.); Ancestry (includes multiple ancestries): 46.1% German, 26.8% Dutch, 5.7% Italian, 5.4% Irish, 3.9% Lithuanian (2006-2010 5-year est.).
Economy: Employment by occupation: 4.0% management, 5.6% professional, 8.5% services, 20.9% sales, 0.0% farming, 25.8% construction, 17.1% production (2006-2010 5-year est.).
Income: Per capita income: $23,420 (2006-2010 5-year est.); Median household income: $44,375 (2006-2010 5-year est.); Average household income: $53,479 (2006-2010 5-year est.); Percent of households with income of $100,000 or more: 7.0% (2006-2010 5-year est.); Poverty rate: 5.9% (2006-2010 5-year est.).
Education: Percent of population age 25 and over with: High school diploma (including GED) or higher: 85.3% (2006-2010 5-year est.); Bachelor's degree or higher: 7.6% (2006-2010 5-year est.); Master's degree or higher: 5.3% (2006-2010 5-year est.).
School District(s)
Tri-Valley SD (KG-12)
   2010-11 Enrollment: 871 . . . . (570) 682-9013
Housing: Homeownership rate: 77.6% (2010); Median home value: $100,600 (2006-2010 5-year est.); Median contract rent: $377 per month (2006-2010 5-year est.); Median year structure built: 1950 (2006-2010 5-year est.).
Transportation: Commute to work: 93.9% car, 6.1% public transportation, 0.0% walk, 0.0% work from home (2006-2010 5-year est.); Travel time to work: 30.2% less than 15 minutes, 32.7% 15 to 30 minutes, 21.8% 30 to 45 minutes, 2.3% 45 to 60 minutes, 13.0% 60 minutes or more (2006-2010 5-year est.)

HEGINS (township). Covers a land area of 31.916 square miles and a water area of 0.005 square miles. Located at 40.65° N. Lat; 76.51° W. Long. Elevation is 827 feet.

Population: 3,561 (1990); 3,519 (2000); 3,516 (2010); Density: 110.2 persons per square mile (2010); Race: 98.5% White, 0.1% Black, 0.3% Asian, 0.1% American Indian/Alaska Native, 0.0% Native Hawaiian/Other Pacific Islander, 1.0% Other, 0.7% Hispanic of any race (2010); Average household size: 2.35 (2010); Median age: 44.4 (2010); Males per 100 females: 102.2 (2010); Marriage status: 21.3% never married, 64.2% now married, 7.7% widowed, 6.8% divorced (2006-2010 5-year est.); Foreign born: 1.5% (2006-2010 5-year est.); Ancestry (includes multiple ancestries): 52.3% German, 13.7% Dutch, 9.3% Irish, 8.2% Pennsylvania German, 7.0% American (2006-2010 5-year est.).

Economy: Single-family building permits issued: 7 (2011); Multi-family building permits issued: 0 (2011); Employment by occupation: 4.7% management, 2.8% professional, 12.6% services, 16.4% sales, 0.7% farming, 17.2% construction, 13.1% production (2006-2010 5-year est.).

Income: Per capita income: $24,358 (2006-2010 5-year est.); Median household income: $53,750 (2006-2010 5-year est.); Average household income: $60,113 (2006-2010 5-year est.); Percent of households with income of $100,000 or more: 13.0% (2006-2010 5-year est.); Poverty rate: 2.9% (2006-2010 5-year est.).

Education: Percent of population age 25 and over with: High school diploma (including GED) or higher: 81.8% (2006-2010 5-year est.); Bachelor's degree or higher: 10.7% (2006-2010 5-year est.); Master's degree or higher: 4.8% (2006-2010 5-year est.).

Housing: Homeownership rate: 79.9% (2010); Median home value: $128,200 (2006-2010 5-year est.); Median contract rent: $509 per month (2006-2010 5-year est.); Median year structure built: 1952 (2006-2010 5-year est.).

Transportation: Commute to work: 88.1% car, 1.5% public transportation, 6.3% walk, 3.0% work from home (2006-2010 5-year est.); Travel time to work: 29.6% less than 15 minutes, 25.7% 15 to 30 minutes, 22.4% 30 to 45 minutes, 4.1% 45 to 60 minutes, 18.2% 60 minutes or more (2006-2010 5-year est.)

Additional Information Contacts
Brush Valley Regional Chamber of Commerce . . . . (570) 648-4675
http://www.brushvalleychamber.com

HOMETOWN (CDP). Covers a land area of 1.998 square miles and a water area of 0 square miles. Located at 40.82° N. Lat; 75.99° W. Long. Elevation is 1,129 feet.

Population: 1,491 (1990); 1,399 (2000); 1,349 (2010); Density: 675.2 persons per square mile (2010); Race: 98.4% White, 0.1% Black, 1.1% Asian, 0.0% American Indian/Alaska Native, 0.0% Native Hawaiian/Other Pacific Islander, 0.4% Other, 0.7% Hispanic of any race (2010); Average household size: 2.34 (2010); Median age: 50.8 (2010); Males per 100 females: 91.6 (2010); Marriage status: 30.9% never married, 57.4% now married, 8.6% widowed, 3.1% divorced (2006-2010 5-year est.); Foreign born: 2.0% (2006-2010 5-year est.); Ancestry (includes multiple ancestries): 23.6% German, 20.5% Irish, 16.0% Slovak, 9.9% Polish, 9.7% Italian (2006-2010 5-year est.).

Economy: Employment by occupation: 6.5% management, 1.9% professional, 14.6% services, 6.8% sales, 2.6% farming, 9.9% construction, 8.9% production (2006-2010 5-year est.).

Income: Per capita income: $25,797 (2006-2010 5-year est.); Median household income: $34,125 (2006-2010 5-year est.); Average household income: $56,349 (2006-2010 5-year est.); Percent of households with income of $100,000 or more: 18.5% (2006-2010 5-year est.); Poverty rate: 16.8% (2006-2010 5-year est.).

Education: Percent of population age 25 and over with: High school diploma (including GED) or higher: 89.2% (2006-2010 5-year est.); Bachelor's degree or higher: 28.7% (2006-2010 5-year est.); Master's degree or higher: 10.6% (2006-2010 5-year est.).

Housing: Homeownership rate: 91.7% (2010); Median home value: $132,300 (2006-2010 5-year est.); Median contract rent: $238 per month (2006-2010 5-year est.); Median year structure built: 1968 (2006-2010 5-year est.).

Transportation: Commute to work: 85.0% car, 0.0% public transportation, 10.3% walk, 4.7% work from home (2006-2010 5-year est.); Travel time to work: 30.0% less than 15 minutes, 16.7% 15 to 30 minutes, 26.7% 30 to 45 minutes, 21.8% 45 to 60 minutes, 4.8% 60 minutes or more (2006-2010 5-year est.)

Additional Information Contacts
Tamaqua Area Chamber of Commerce . . . . (570) 668-1880
http://www.tamaqua.net

HUBLEY (township). Covers a land area of 13.323 square miles and a water area of 0 square miles. Located at 40.64° N. Lat; 76.62° W. Long.

Population: 928 (1990); 889 (2000); 854 (2010); Density: 64.1 persons per square mile (2010); Race: 98.7% White, 0.1% Black, 0.2% Asian, 0.1% American Indian/Alaska Native, 0.0% Native Hawaiian/Other Pacific Islander, 0.9% Other, 0.5% Hispanic of any race (2010); Average household size: 2.48 (2010); Median age: 44.3 (2010); Males per 100 females: 97.2 (2010); Marriage status: 26.8% never married, 57.9% now married, 10.2% widowed, 5.1% divorced (2006-2010 5-year est.); Foreign born: 0.0% (2006-2010 5-year est.); Ancestry (includes multiple ancestries): 56.2% German, 13.8% Pennsylvania German, 13.4% Irish, 11.4% Dutch, 4.7% Italian (2006-2010 5-year est.).

Economy: Single-family building permits issued: 0 (2011); Multi-family building permits issued: 0 (2011); Employment by occupation: 12.8% management, 0.9% professional, 8.9% services, 10.5% sales, 3.4% farming, 23.9% construction, 15.7% production (2006-2010 5-year est.).

Income: Per capita income: $27,652 (2006-2010 5-year est.); Median household income: $47,589 (2006-2010 5-year est.); Average household income: $67,326 (2006-2010 5-year est.); Percent of households with income of $100,000 or more: 14.5% (2006-2010 5-year est.); Poverty rate: 5.7% (2006-2010 5-year est.).

Education: Percent of population age 25 and over with: High school diploma (including GED) or higher: 82.3% (2006-2010 5-year est.); Bachelor's degree or higher: 10.0% (2006-2010 5-year est.); Master's degree or higher: 3.6% (2006-2010 5-year est.).

Housing: Homeownership rate: 77.6% (2010); Median home value: $116,800 (2006-2010 5-year est.); Median contract rent: $435 per month (2006-2010 5-year est.); Median year structure built: before 1940 (2006-2010 5-year est.).

Transportation: Commute to work: 87.2% car, 0.0% public transportation, 4.9% walk, 5.1% work from home (2006-2010 5-year est.); Travel time to work: 35.5% less than 15 minutes, 31.6% 15 to 30 minutes, 15.0% 30 to 45 minutes, 3.7% 45 to 60 minutes, 14.2% 60 minutes or more (2006-2010 5-year est.)

KELAYRES (CDP). Covers a land area of 0.115 square miles and a water area of 0 square miles. Located at 40.90° N. Lat; 76.00° W. Long. Elevation is 1,742 feet.

Population: n/a (1990); n/a (2000); 533 (2010); Density: 4,654.5 persons per square mile (2010); Race: 96.8% White, 0.2% Black, 0.6% Asian, 0.0% American Indian/Alaska Native, 0.0% Native Hawaiian/Other Pacific Islander, 2.4% Other, 4.9% Hispanic of any race (2010); Average household size: 2.32 (2010); Median age: 40.9 (2010); Males per 100 females: 95.2 (2010); Marriage status: 23.9% never married, 46.8% now married, 10.9% widowed, 18.3% divorced (2006-2010 5-year est.); Foreign born: 3.6% (2006-2010 5-year est.); Ancestry (includes multiple ancestries): 26.7% Italian, 17.9% Polish, 12.1% German, 11.6% Irish, 10.8% Slovak (2006-2010 5-year est.).

Economy: Employment by occupation: 0.0% management, 0.9% professional, 8.5% services, 24.3% sales, 9.4% farming, 10.2% construction, 17.0% production (2006-2010 5-year est.).

Income: Per capita income: $17,258 (2006-2010 5-year est.); Median household income: $32,283 (2006-2010 5-year est.); Average household income: $39,881 (2006-2010 5-year est.); Percent of households with income of $100,000 or more: 2.8% (2006-2010 5-year est.); Poverty rate: 12.3% (2006-2010 5-year est.).

Education: Percent of population age 25 and over with: High school diploma (including GED) or higher: 82.0% (2006-2010 5-year est.); Bachelor's degree or higher: 10.5% (2006-2010 5-year est.); Master's degree or higher: 0.5% (2006-2010 5-year est.).

Housing: Homeownership rate: 77.4% (2010); Median home value: $92,900 (2006-2010 5-year est.); Median contract rent: $461 per month (2006-2010 5-year est.); Median year structure built: before 1940 (2006-2010 5-year est.).

Transportation: Commute to work: 100.0% car, 0.0% public transportation, 0.0% walk, 0.0% work from home (2006-2010 5-year est.); Travel time to work: 37.6% less than 15 minutes, 44.0% 15 to 30 minutes, 6.0% 30 to 45 minutes, 7.3% 45 to 60 minutes, 5.0% 60 minutes or more (2006-2010 5-year est.)

KLINE (township). Covers a land area of 12.260 square miles and a water area of 0.156 square miles. Located at 40.88° N. Lat; 76.05° W. Long.

Population: 1,722 (1990); 1,591 (2000); 1,438 (2010); Density: 117.3 persons per square mile (2010); Race: 97.9% White, 0.1% Black, 0.4% Asian, 0.1% American Indian/Alaska Native, 0.1% Native Hawaiian/Other Pacific Islander, 1.4% Other, 2.9% Hispanic of any race (2010); Average household size: 2.27 (2010); Median age: 48.0 (2010); Males per 100 females: 98.6 (2010); Marriage status: 24.1% never married, 50.7% now married, 11.9% widowed, 13.3% divorced (2006-2010 5-year est.); Foreign born: 2.1% (2006-2010 5-year est.); Ancestry (includes multiple ancestries): 27.2% Italian, 24.9% Polish, 14.0% Irish, 12.4% German, 12.0% Slovak (2006-2010 5-year est.).

Economy: Single-family building permits issued: 2 (2011); Multi-family building permits issued: 0 (2011); Employment by occupation: 4.3% management, 2.1% professional, 10.3% services, 13.7% sales, 3.1% farming, 11.8% construction, 12.3% production (2006-2010 5-year est.).

Income: Per capita income: $21,690 (2006-2010 5-year est.); Median household income: $40,577 (2006-2010 5-year est.); Average household income: $47,310 (2006-2010 5-year est.); Percent of households with income of $100,000 or more: 5.5% (2006-2010 5-year est.); Poverty rate: 5.9% (2006-2010 5-year est.).

Education: Percent of population age 25 and over with: High school diploma (including GED) or higher: 87.9% (2006-2010 5-year est.); Bachelor's degree or higher: 9.4% (2006-2010 5-year est.); Master's degree or higher: 3.0% (2006-2010 5-year est.).

Housing: Homeownership rate: 84.9% (2010); Median home value: $103,200 (2006-2010 5-year est.); Median contract rent: $476 per month (2006-2010 5-year est.); Median year structure built: 1950 (2006-2010 5-year est.).

Safety: Violent crime rate: 6.9 per 10,000 population; Property crime rate: 311.9 per 10,000 population (2011).

Transportation: Commute to work: 96.7% car, 0.0% public transportation, 2.1% walk, 0.0% work from home (2006-2010 5-year est.); Travel time to work: 25.6% less than 15 minutes, 43.4% 15 to 30 minutes, 11.2% 30 to 45 minutes, 5.8% 45 to 60 minutes, 14.0% 60 minutes or more (2006-2010 5-year est.)

Additional Information Contacts

Greater Hazelton Chamber of Commerce . . . . (570) 455-1509
  http://www.hazletonchamber.org

KLINGERSTOWN (CDP). Covers a land area of 0.491 square miles and a water area of 0 square miles. Located at 40.66° N. Lat; 76.69° W. Long. Elevation is 522 feet.

Population: 109 (1990); 102 (2000); 127 (2010); Density: 258.5 persons per square mile (2010); Race: 98.4% White, 0.0% Black, 0.0% Asian, 0.0% American Indian/Alaska Native, 0.0% Native Hawaiian/Other Pacific Islander, 1.6% Other, 0.0% Hispanic of any race (2010); Average household size: 2.54 (2010); Median age: 36.5 (2010); Males per 100 females: 111.7 (2010); Marriage status: 23.8% never married, 52.4% now married, 20.2% widowed, 3.6% divorced (2006-2010 5-year est.); Foreign born: 0.0% (2006-2010 5-year est.); Ancestry (includes multiple ancestries): 62.3% German, 16.0% Pennsylvania German, 10.4% Irish, 2.8% Canadian, 2.8% Slovak (2006-2010 5-year est.).

Economy: Employment by occupation: 8.1% management, 8.1% professional, 0.0% services, 8.1% sales, 0.0% farming, 54.1% construction, 0.0% production (2006-2010 5-year est.).

Income: Per capita income: $23,584 (2006-2010 5-year est.); Median household income: $42,813 (2006-2010 5-year est.); Average household income: $51,018 (2006-2010 5-year est.); Percent of households with income of $100,000 or more: 10.2% (2006-2010 5-year est.); Poverty rate: 0.0% (2006-2010 5-year est.).

Education: Percent of population age 25 and over with: High school diploma (including GED) or higher: 93.4% (2006-2010 5-year est.); Bachelor's degree or higher: 17.1% (2006-2010 5-year est.); Master's degree or higher: 10.5% (2006-2010 5-year est.).

School District(s)

Tri-Valley SD (KG-12)
    2010-11 Enrollment: 871 . . . . (570) 682-9013

Housing: Homeownership rate: 70.0% (2010); Median home value: $86,900 (2006-2010 5-year est.); Median contract rent: $434 per month (2006-2010 5-year est.); Median year structure built: before 1940 (2006-2010 5-year est.).

Transportation: Commute to work: 64.9% car, 0.0% public transportation, 27.0% walk, 8.1% work from home (2006-2010 5-year est.); Travel time to

work: 47.1% less than 15 minutes, 23.5% 15 to 30 minutes, 0.0% 30 to 45 minutes, 8.8% 45 to 60 minutes, 20.6% 60 minutes or more (2006-2010 5-year est.)

LAKE WYNONAH (CDP). Covers a land area of 3.085 square miles and a water area of 0.299 square miles. Located at 40.59° N. Lat; 76.18° W. Long. Elevation is 745 feet.

Population: 1,041 (1990); 1,961 (2000); 2,640 (2010); Density: 855.9 persons per square mile (2010); Race: 97.3% White, 0.9% Black, 0.5% Asian, 0.0% American Indian/Alaska Native, 0.0% Native Hawaiian/Other Pacific Islander, 1.3% Other, 1.9% Hispanic of any race (2010); Average household size: 2.63 (2010); Median age: 42.4 (2010); Males per 100 females: 105.1 (2010); Marriage status: 17.9% never married, 71.9% now married, 3.7% widowed, 6.5% divorced (2006-2010 5-year est.); Foreign born: 0.9% (2006-2010 5-year est.); Ancestry (includes multiple ancestries): 45.4% German, 22.4% Irish, 14.6% Polish, 8.3% Italian, 6.8% English (2006-2010 5-year est.).

Economy: Employment by occupation: 17.0% management, 3.9% professional, 7.8% services, 13.3% sales, 2.0% farming, 7.0% construction, 4.4% production (2006-2010 5-year est.).

Income: Per capita income: $31,241 (2006-2010 5-year est.); Median household income: $71,522 (2006-2010 5-year est.); Average household income: $81,599 (2006-2010 5-year est.); Percent of households with income of $100,000 or more: 24.3% (2006-2010 5-year est.); Poverty rate: 3.7% (2006-2010 5-year est.).

Education: Percent of population age 25 and over with: High school diploma (including GED) or higher: 94.9% (2006-2010 5-year est.); Bachelor's degree or higher: 30.0% (2006-2010 5-year est.); Master's degree or higher: 13.3% (2006-2010 5-year est.).

Housing: Homeownership rate: 96.9% (2010); Median home value: $177,500 (2006-2010 5-year est.); Median contract rent: n/a per month (2006-2010 5-year est.); Median year structure built: 1992 (2006-2010 5-year est.).

Transportation: Commute to work: 94.2% car, 0.0% public transportation, 1.1% walk, 4.0% work from home (2006-2010 5-year est.); Travel time to work: 14.2% less than 15 minutes, 33.1% 15 to 30 minutes, 22.4% 30 to 45 minutes, 16.5% 45 to 60 minutes, 13.8% 60 minutes or more (2006-2010 5-year est.)

Additional Information Contacts

Schuylkill Chamber of Commerce . . . . (570) 622-1942
  http://www.schuylkillchamber.com

LANDINGVILLE (borough). Covers a land area of 0.858 square miles and a water area of <.001 square miles. Located at 40.62° N. Lat; 76.12° W. Long. Elevation is 499 feet.

Population: 192 (1990); 175 (2000); 159 (2010); Density: 185.3 persons per square mile (2010); Race: 98.1% White, 0.0% Black, 0.0% Asian, 0.6% American Indian/Alaska Native, 0.6% Native Hawaiian/Other Pacific Islander, 0.7% Other, 1.3% Hispanic of any race (2010); Average household size: 2.69 (2010); Median age: 41.9 (2010); Males per 100 females: 80.7 (2010); Marriage status: 26.7% never married, 60.2% now married, 9.9% widowed, 3.1% divorced (2006-2010 5-year est.); Foreign born: 2.6% (2006-2010 5-year est.); Ancestry (includes multiple ancestries): 64.6% German, 28.2% Swedish, 25.1% Dutch, 11.3% Irish, 9.2% Pennsylvania German (2006-2010 5-year est.).

Economy: Employment by occupation: 5.5% management, 0.0% professional, 10.9% services, 11.8% sales, 0.0% farming, 5.5% construction, 14.5% production (2006-2010 5-year est.).

Income: Per capita income: $18,668 (2006-2010 5-year est.); Median household income: $51,500 (2006-2010 5-year est.); Average household income: $48,943 (2006-2010 5-year est.); Percent of households with income of $100,000 or more: 6.6% (2006-2010 5-year est.); Poverty rate: 3.1% (2006-2010 5-year est.).

Education: Percent of population age 25 and over with: High school diploma (including GED) or higher: 80.5% (2006-2010 5-year est.); Bachelor's degree or higher: 21.1% (2006-2010 5-year est.); Master's degree or higher: 14.6% (2006-2010 5-year est.).

Housing: Homeownership rate: 91.5% (2010); Median home value: $138,800 (2006-2010 5-year est.); Median contract rent: $463 per month (2006-2010 5-year est.); Median year structure built: before 1940 (2006-2010 5-year est.).

Transportation: Commute to work: 94.0% car, 0.0% public transportation, 3.0% walk, 3.0% work from home (2006-2010 5-year est.); Travel time to work: 43.3% less than 15 minutes, 40.2% 15 to 30 minutes, 8.2% 30 to 45

minutes, 3.1% 45 to 60 minutes, 5.2% 60 minutes or more (2006-2010 5-year est.)

LAVELLE (CDP). Covers a land area of 1.134 square miles and a water area of 0 square miles. Located at 40.76° N. Lat; 76.39° W. Long. Elevation is 1,027 feet.

Population: n/a (1990); n/a (2000); 742 (2010); Density: 654.3 persons per square mile (2010); Race: 98.9% White, 0.0% Black, 0.1% Asian, 0.1% American Indian/Alaska Native, 0.0% Native Hawaiian/Other Pacific Islander, 0.9% Other, 0.7% Hispanic of any race (2010); Average household size: 2.30 (2010); Median age: 45.8 (2010); Males per 100 females: 89.8 (2010); Marriage status: 9.0% never married, 69.6% now married, 15.8% widowed, 5.6% divorced (2006-2010 5-year est.); Foreign born: 0.0% (2006-2010 5-year est.); Ancestry (includes multiple ancestries): 41.9% German, 26.2% Irish, 14.8% Dutch, 10.6% Welsh, 7.8% Italian (2006-2010 5-year est.).

Economy: Employment by occupation: 14.2% management, 4.4% professional, 11.6% services, 14.5% sales, 0.0% farming, 31.1% construction, 15.7% production (2006-2010 5-year est.).

Income: Per capita income: $23,679 (2006-2010 5-year est.); Median household income: $40,294 (2006-2010 5-year est.); Average household income: $45,768 (2006-2010 5-year est.); Percent of households with income of $100,000 or more: n/a (2006-2010 5-year est.); Poverty rate: 2.7% (2006-2010 5-year est.).

Education: Percent of population age 25 and over with: High school diploma (including GED) or higher: 84.3% (2006-2010 5-year est.); Bachelor's degree or higher: 10.9% (2006-2010 5-year est.); Master's degree or higher: 0.0% (2006-2010 5-year est.).

Housing: Homeownership rate: 90.1% (2010); Median home value: $98,000 (2006-2010 5-year est.); Median contract rent: n/a per month (2006-2010 5-year est.); Median year structure built: before 1940 (2006-2010 5-year est.).

Transportation: Commute to work: 94.5% car, 0.0% public transportation, 0.0% walk, 5.5% work from home (2006-2010 5-year est.); Travel time to work: 13.2% less than 15 minutes, 39.9% 15 to 30 minutes, 23.3% 30 to 45 minutes, 9.3% 45 to 60 minutes, 14.3% 60 minutes or more (2006-2010 5-year est.)

LLEWELLYN (unincorporated postal area)

Zip Code: 17944

Covers a land area of 0.136 square miles and a water area of 0 square miles. Located at 40.67° N. Lat; 76.27° W. Long. Elevation is 751 feet. Population: 205 (2010); Density: 1,496.6 persons per square mile (2010); Race: 95.1% White, 2.4% Black, 0.0% Asian, 0.5% American Indian/Alaska Native, 0.0% Native Hawaiian/Other Pacific Islander, 2.0% Other, 2.0% Hispanic of any race (2010); Average household size: 2.33 (2010); Median age: 41.8 (2010); Males per 100 females: 120.4 (2010); Homeownership rate: 81.8% (2010)

LOST CREEK (unincorporated postal area)

Zip Code: 17946

Covers a land area of 1.911 square miles and a water area of 0.013 square miles. Located at 40.81° N. Lat; 76.25° W. Long. Population: 263 (2010); Density: 137.6 persons per square mile (2010); Race: 94.7% White, 0.0% Black, 0.0% Asian, 0.4% American Indian/Alaska Native, 0.0% Native Hawaiian/Other Pacific Islander, 4.9% Other, 5.3% Hispanic of any race (2010); Average household size: 2.31 (2010); Median age: 45.6 (2010); Males per 100 females: 113.8 (2010); Homeownership rate: 97.4% (2010)

MAHANOY (township). Covers a land area of 21.079 square miles and a water area of 0.192 square miles. Located at 40.82° N. Lat; 76.14° W. Long.

History: Settled 1859, incorporated 1863.

Population: 1,273 (1990); 1,112 (2000); 3,152 (2010); Density: 149.5 persons per square mile (2010); Race: 53.2% White, 38.6% Black, 0.3% Asian, 0.0% American Indian/Alaska Native, 0.0% Native Hawaiian/Other Pacific Islander, 7.9% Other, 9.3% Hispanic of any race (2010); Average household size: 2.15 (2010); Median age: 37.7 (2010); Males per 100 females: 555.3 (2010); Marriage status: 41.5% never married, 39.5% now married, 5.4% widowed, 13.6% divorced (2006-2010 5-year est.); Foreign born: 2.3% (2006-2010 5-year est.); Ancestry (includes multiple ancestries): 8.2% Irish, 7.5% German, 5.2% Polish, 3.7% Italian, 3.3% Lithuanian (2006-2010 5-year est.).

Economy: Employment by occupation: 3.4% management, 1.9% professional, 3.1% services, 13.8% sales, 5.3% farming, 15.9% construction, 15.7% production (2006-2010 5-year est.).

Income: Per capita income: $8,283 (2006-2010 5-year est.); Median household income: $39,087 (2006-2010 5-year est.); Average household income: $43,134 (2006-2010 5-year est.); Percent of households with income of $100,000 or more: 7.2% (2006-2010 5-year est.); Poverty rate: 17.5% (2006-2010 5-year est.).

Education: Percent of population age 25 and over with: High school diploma (including GED) or higher: 63.4% (2006-2010 5-year est.); Bachelor's degree or higher: 6.8% (2006-2010 5-year est.); Master's degree or higher: 3.2% (2006-2010 5-year est.).

Housing: Homeownership rate: 78.6% (2010); Median home value: $51,400 (2006-2010 5-year est.); Median contract rent: $380 per month (2006-2010 5-year est.); Median year structure built: before 1940 (2006-2010 5-year est.).

Safety: Violent crime rate: 0.0 per 10,000 population; Property crime rate: 9.5 per 10,000 population (2011).

Transportation: Commute to work: 97.0% car, 0.0% public transportation, 0.7% walk, 2.2% work from home (2006-2010 5-year est.); Travel time to work: 34.3% less than 15 minutes, 47.7% 15 to 30 minutes, 6.9% 30 to 45 minutes, 0.8% 45 to 60 minutes, 10.4% 60 minutes or more (2006-2010 5-year est.)

Additional Information Contacts

Tamaqua Area Chamber of Commerce . . . . (570) 668-1880
http://www.tamaqua.net

MAHANOY CITY (borough). Covers a land area of 0.510 square miles and a water area of 0 square miles. Located at 40.81° N. Lat; 76.14° W. Long. Elevation is 1,217 feet.

Population: 5,209 (1990); 4,647 (2000); 4,162 (2010); Density: 8,165.6 persons per square mile (2010); Race: 95.3% White, 1.0% Black, 0.3% Asian, 0.3% American Indian/Alaska Native, 0.0% Native Hawaiian/Other Pacific Islander, 3.1% Other, 4.7% Hispanic of any race (2010); Average household size: 2.34 (2010); Median age: 40.6 (2010); Males per 100 females: 90.0 (2010); Marriage status: 29.6% never married, 42.0% now married, 13.7% widowed, 14.7% divorced (2006-2010 5-year est.); Foreign born: 0.9% (2006-2010 5-year est.); Ancestry (includes multiple ancestries): 26.9% German, 25.7% Irish, 22.0% Polish, 13.1% Lithuanian, 8.1% Italian (2006-2010 5-year est.).

Economy: Employment by occupation: 7.6% management, 0.8% professional, 11.5% services, 10.1% sales, 7.0% farming, 7.0% construction, 12.9% production (2006-2010 5-year est.).

Income: Per capita income: $16,601 (2006-2010 5-year est.); Median household income: $26,709 (2006-2010 5-year est.); Average household income: $33,171 (2006-2010 5-year est.); Percent of households with income of $100,000 or more: 1.9% (2006-2010 5-year est.); Poverty rate: 18.6% (2006-2010 5-year est.).

Education: Percent of population age 25 and over with: High school diploma (including GED) or higher: 81.3% (2006-2010 5-year est.); Bachelor's degree or higher: 7.0% (2006-2010 5-year est.); Master's degree or higher: 2.4% (2006-2010 5-year est.).

School District(s)

Mahanoy Area SD (KG-12)
   2010-11 Enrollment: 1,091 . . . . (570) 773-3443

Housing: Homeownership rate: 70.4% (2010); Median home value: $29,900 (2006-2010 5-year est.); Median contract rent: $425 per month (2006-2010 5-year est.); Median year structure built: before 1940 (2006-2010 5-year est.).

Transportation: Commute to work: 96.5% car, 0.0% public transportation, 2.9% walk, 0.0% work from home (2006-2010 5-year est.); Travel time to work: 30.8% less than 15 minutes, 38.9% 15 to 30 minutes, 13.8% 30 to 45 minutes, 7.6% 45 to 60 minutes, 8.8% 60 minutes or more (2006-2010 5-year est.)

Additional Information Contacts

Schuylkill Chamber of Commerce . . . . (570) 622-1942
http://www.schuylkillchamber.com

MAHANOY PLANE (unincorporated postal area)

Zip Code: 17949

Covers a land area of 0.100 square miles and a water area of 0 square miles. Located at 40.79° N. Lat; 76.24° W. Long. Elevation is 1,119 feet. Population: 263 (2010); Density: 2,612.3 persons per square mile (2010); Race: 97.0% White, 0.0% Black, 0.0% Asian, 0.0% American Indian/Alaska Native, 0.0% Native Hawaiian/Other Pacific Islander,

3.0% Other, 4.2% Hispanic of any race (2010); Average household size: 2.44 (2010); Median age: 44.8 (2010); Males per 100 females: 108.7 (2010); Homeownership rate: 83.4% (2010)

MAR LIN (unincorporated postal area)
Zip Code: 17951

Covers a land area of 0.184 square miles and a water area of 0 square miles. Located at 40.67° N. Lat; 76.24° W. Long. Population: 325 (2010); Density: 1,759.1 persons per square mile (2010); Race: 96.3% White, 0.0% Black, 0.3% Asian, 0.0% American Indian/Alaska Native, 0.0% Native Hawaiian/Other Pacific Islander, 3.4% Other, 1.2% Hispanic of any race (2010); Average household size: 2.39 (2010); Median age: 43.6 (2010); Males per 100 females: 94.6 (2010); Homeownership rate: 94.8% (2010)

MARLIN (CDP). Covers a land area of 0.906 square miles and a water area of 0 square miles. Located at 40.69° N. Lat; 76.24° W. Long. Elevation is 738 feet.

Population: 593 (1990); 640 (2000); 661 (2010); Density: 729.3 persons per square mile (2010); Race: 97.4% White, 0.6% Black, 0.2% Asian, 0.0% American Indian/Alaska Native, 0.0% Native Hawaiian/Other Pacific Islander, 1.8% Other, 0.6% Hispanic of any race (2010); Average household size: 2.28 (2010); Median age: 46.0 (2010); Males per 100 females: 87.8 (2010); Marriage status: 14.4% never married, 61.4% now married, 12.9% widowed, 11.2% divorced (2006-2010 5-year est.); Foreign born: 0.0% (2006-2010 5-year est.); Ancestry (includes multiple ancestries): 26.7% German, 19.6% Dutch, 17.6% Irish, 14.7% Italian, 9.2% Ukrainian (2006-2010 5-year est.).
Economy: Employment by occupation: 17.8% management, 0.0% professional, 9.9% services, 12.2% sales, 0.0% farming, 6.1% construction, 3.8% production (2006-2010 5-year est.).
Income: Per capita income: $21,580 (2006-2010 5-year est.); Median household income: $41,563 (2006-2010 5-year est.); Average household income: $53,745 (2006-2010 5-year est.); Percent of households with income of $100,000 or more: 14.8% (2006-2010 5-year est.); Poverty rate: 9.7% (2006-2010 5-year est.).
Education: Percent of population age 25 and over with: High school diploma (including GED) or higher: 79.5% (2006-2010 5-year est.); Bachelor's degree or higher: 17.2% (2006-2010 5-year est.); Master's degree or higher: 4.1% (2006-2010 5-year est.).

School District(s)
Schuylkill Technology Centers (10-12)
    2010-11 Enrollment: n/a . . . . (570) 544-4748
Housing: Homeownership rate: 72.4% (2010); Median home value: $137,500 (2006-2010 5-year est.); Median contract rent: $404 per month (2006-2010 5-year est.); Median year structure built: 1973 (2006-2010 5-year est.).
Transportation: Commute to work: 97.6% car, 0.0% public transportation, 0.0% walk, 2.4% work from home (2006-2010 5-year est.); Travel time to work: 32.5% less than 15 minutes, 43.3% 15 to 30 minutes, 14.8% 30 to 45 minutes, 0.0% 45 to 60 minutes, 9.4% 60 minutes or more (2006-2010 5-year est.)

MARY D (unincorporated postal area)
Zip Code: 17952

Covers a land area of 3.479 square miles and a water area of 0 square miles. Located at 40.75° N. Lat; 76.05° W. Long. Population: 282 (2010); Density: 81.1 persons per square mile (2010); Race: 99.3% White, 0.0% Black, 0.4% Asian, 0.0% American Indian/Alaska Native, 0.0% Native Hawaiian/Other Pacific Islander, 0.3% Other, 1.4% Hispanic of any race (2010); Average household size: 2.10 (2010); Median age: 50.0 (2010); Males per 100 females: 95.8 (2010); Homeownership rate: 87.3% (2010)

MCADOO (borough). Covers a land area of 0.349 square miles and a water area of 0 square miles. Located at 40.90° N. Lat; 75.99° W. Long. Elevation is 1,716 feet.
History: Founded 1880, incorporated 1896.
Population: 2,459 (1990); 2,274 (2000); 2,300 (2010); Density: 6,593.8 persons per square mile (2010); Race: 95.4% White, 0.9% Black, 0.3% Asian, 0.1% American Indian/Alaska Native, 0.0% Native Hawaiian/Other Pacific Islander, 3.3% Other, 8.5% Hispanic of any race (2010); Average household size: 2.33 (2010); Median age: 39.7 (2010); Males per 100 females: 96.6 (2010); Marriage status: 33.7% never married, 44.1% now married, 10.4% widowed, 11.8% divorced (2006-2010 5-year est.); Foreign

born: 2.7% (2006-2010 5-year est.); Ancestry (includes multiple ancestries): 27.3% Polish, 24.5% Italian, 21.1% Irish, 11.5% Slovak, 10.7% German (2006-2010 5-year est.).
Economy: Single-family building permits issued: 0 (2011); Multi-family building permits issued: 0 (2011); Employment by occupation: 8.7% management, 1.6% professional, 10.4% services, 25.8% sales, 5.6% farming, 12.0% construction, 7.1% production (2006-2010 5-year est.).
Income: Per capita income: $17,341 (2006-2010 5-year est.); Median household income: $33,477 (2006-2010 5-year est.); Average household income: $40,048 (2006-2010 5-year est.); Percent of households with income of $100,000 or more: 3.9% (2006-2010 5-year est.); Poverty rate: 14.7% (2006-2010 5-year est.).
Education: Percent of population age 25 and over with: High school diploma (including GED) or higher: 80.8% (2006-2010 5-year est.); Bachelor's degree or higher: 9.8% (2006-2010 5-year est.); Master's degree or higher: 1.8% (2006-2010 5-year est.).

School District(s)
Hazleton Area SD (PK-12)
    2010-11 Enrollment: 10,301 . . . . (570) 459-3111
Housing: Homeownership rate: 64.7% (2010); Median home value: $76,200 (2006-2010 5-year est.); Median contract rent: $467 per month (2006-2010 5-year est.); Median year structure built: before 1940 (2006-2010 5-year est.).
Safety: Violent crime rate: 8.7 per 10,000 population; Property crime rate: 164.7 per 10,000 population (2011).
Transportation: Commute to work: 93.0% car, 2.1% public transportation, 4.9% walk, 0.0% work from home (2006-2010 5-year est.); Travel time to work: 35.2% less than 15 minutes, 39.1% 15 to 30 minutes, 10.6% 30 to 45 minutes, 5.9% 45 to 60 minutes, 9.3% 60 minutes or more (2006-2010 5-year est.)
Additional Information Contacts
Greater Hazleton Chamber of Commerce . . . . (570) 455-1509
    http://www.hazletonchamber.org

MCKEANSBURG (CDP). Covers a land area of 0.338 square miles and a water area of 0 square miles. Located at 40.68° N. Lat; 76.02° W. Long. Elevation is 696 feet.
Population: 149 (1990); 155 (2000); 163 (2010); Density: 481.6 persons per square mile (2010); Race: 95.1% White, 0.0% Black, 0.6% Asian, 0.0% American Indian/Alaska Native, 0.0% Native Hawaiian/Other Pacific Islander, 4.3% Other, 3.7% Hispanic of any race (2010); Average household size: 2.36 (2010); Median age: 40.5 (2010); Males per 100 females: 120.3 (2010); Marriage status: 16.6% never married, 57.9% now married, 14.5% widowed, 11.0% divorced (2006-2010 5-year est.); Foreign born: 0.0% (2006-2010 5-year est.); Ancestry (includes multiple ancestries): 26.2% German, 21.5% Dutch, 20.3% Italian, 14.5% Pennsylvania German, 13.4% American (2006-2010 5-year est.).
Economy: Employment by occupation: 17.9% management, 0.0% professional, 12.8% services, 14.1% sales, 0.0% farming, 5.1% construction, 19.2% production (2006-2010 5-year est.).
Income: Per capita income: $25,652 (2006-2010 5-year est.); Median household income: $46,875 (2006-2010 5-year est.); Average household income: $61,228 (2006-2010 5-year est.); Percent of households with income of $100,000 or more: 29.2% (2006-2010 5-year est.); Poverty rate: 0.0% (2006-2010 5-year est.).
Education: Percent of population age 25 and over with: High school diploma (including GED) or higher: 77.6% (2006-2010 5-year est.); Bachelor's degree or higher: 6.4% (2006-2010 5-year est.); Master's degree or higher: 0.0% (2006-2010 5-year est.).
Housing: Homeownership rate: 71.0% (2010); Median home value: $136,200 (2006-2010 5-year est.); Median contract rent: $432 per month (2006-2010 5-year est.); Median year structure built: 1955 (2006-2010 5-year est.).
Transportation: Commute to work: 100.0% car, 0.0% public transportation, 0.0% walk, 0.0% work from home (2006-2010 5-year est.); Travel time to work: 5.4% less than 15 minutes, 59.5% 15 to 30 minutes, 27.0% 30 to 45 minutes, 8.1% 45 to 60 minutes, 0.0% 60 minutes or more (2006-2010 5-year est.)

MECHANICSVILLE (borough). Covers a land area of 0.326 square miles and a water area of 0 square miles. Located at 40.69° N. Lat; 76.18° W. Long. Elevation is 699 feet.
Population: 540 (1990); 515 (2000); 457 (2010); Density: 1,402.8 persons per square mile (2010); Race: 98.2% White, 0.2% Black, 0.9% Asian, 0.0% American Indian/Alaska Native, 0.0% Native Hawaiian/Other Pacific

Islander, 0.7% Other, 2.4% Hispanic of any race (2010); Average household size: 2.39 (2010); Median age: 46.2 (2010); Males per 100 females: 96.1 (2010); Marriage status: 25.5% never married, 50.4% now married, 12.2% widowed, 11.9% divorced (2006-2010 5-year est.); Foreign born: 1.5% (2006-2010 5-year est.); Ancestry (includes multiple ancestries): 34.9% German, 13.3% Irish, 12.8% Italian, 11.5% Polish, 10.1% Welsh (2006-2010 5-year est.).

Economy: Employment by occupation: 8.0% management, 1.3% professional, 10.7% services, 18.8% sales, 3.1% farming, 7.6% construction, 8.9% production (2006-2010 5-year est.).

Income: Per capita income: $23,222 (2006-2010 5-year est.); Median household income: $47,857 (2006-2010 5-year est.); Average household income: $50,014 (2006-2010 5-year est.); Percent of households with income of $100,000 or more: 6.8% (2006-2010 5-year est.); Poverty rate: 13.0% (2006-2010 5-year est.).

Education: Percent of population age 25 and over with: High school diploma (including GED) or higher: 89.5% (2006-2010 5-year est.); Bachelor's degree or higher: 16.3% (2006-2010 5-year est.); Master's degree or higher: 9.0% (2006-2010 5-year est.).

Housing: Homeownership rate: 92.1% (2010); Median home value: $80,000 (2006-2010 5-year est.); Median contract rent: n/a per month (2006-2010 5-year est.); Median year structure built: 1944 (2006-2010 5-year est.).

Transportation: Commute to work: 91.0% car, 0.0% public transportation, 4.5% walk, 4.5% work from home (2006-2010 5-year est.); Travel time to work: 59.7% less than 15 minutes, 18.5% 15 to 30 minutes, 11.8% 30 to 45 minutes, 1.4% 45 to 60 minutes, 8.5% 60 minutes or more (2006-2010 5-year est.)

MIDDLEPORT (borough). Covers a land area of 0.439 square miles and a water area of 0 square miles. Located at 40.73° N. Lat; 76.09° W. Long. Elevation is 719 feet.

Population: 520 (1990); 458 (2000); 405 (2010); Density: 922.5 persons per square mile (2010); Race: 98.8% White, 1.0% Black, 0.0% Asian, 0.0% American Indian/Alaska Native, 0.0% Native Hawaiian/Other Pacific Islander, 0.2% Other, 0.0% Hispanic of any race (2010); Average household size: 2.20 (2010); Median age: 45.6 (2010); Males per 100 females: 95.7 (2010); Marriage status: 35.8% never married, 38.1% now married, 12.4% widowed, 13.7% divorced (2006-2010 5-year est.); Foreign born: 2.4% (2006-2010 5-year est.); Ancestry (includes multiple ancestries): 31.6% Polish, 26.4% German, 20.4% Irish, 13.8% Lithuanian, 9.7% Slovak (2006-2010 5-year est.).

Economy: Employment by occupation: 1.5% management, 1.5% professional, 5.9% services, 31.0% sales, 11.8% farming, 15.3% construction, 14.8% production (2006-2010 5-year est.).

Income: Per capita income: $17,266 (2006-2010 5-year est.); Median household income: $30,156 (2006-2010 5-year est.); Average household income: $34,134 (2006-2010 5-year est.); Percent of households with income of $100,000 or more: n/a (2006-2010 5-year est.); Poverty rate: 8.3% (2006-2010 5-year est.).

Education: Percent of population age 25 and over with: High school diploma (including GED) or higher: 80.2% (2006-2010 5-year est.); Bachelor's degree or higher: 4.0% (2006-2010 5-year est.); Master's degree or higher: 0.9% (2006-2010 5-year est.).

Housing: Homeownership rate: 70.7% (2010); Median home value: $55,900 (2006-2010 5-year est.); Median contract rent: $477 per month (2006-2010 5-year est.); Median year structure built: before 1940 (2006-2010 5-year est.).

Transportation: Commute to work: 97.9% car, 0.0% public transportation, 2.1% walk, 0.0% work from home (2006-2010 5-year est.); Travel time to work: 14.9% less than 15 minutes, 55.3% 15 to 30 minutes, 16.0% 30 to 45 minutes, 7.4% 45 to 60 minutes, 6.4% 60 minutes or more (2006-2010 5-year est.)

MINERSVILLE (borough). Covers a land area of 0.657 square miles and a water area of 0 square miles. Located at 40.69° N. Lat; 76.26° W. Long. Elevation is 758 feet.

History: Settled c.1793, incorporated 1831.

Population: 4,877 (1990); 4,552 (2000); 4,397 (2010); Density: 6,694.6 persons per square mile (2010); Race: 95.6% White, 1.4% Black, 0.6% Asian, 0.2% American Indian/Alaska Native, 0.0% Native Hawaiian/Other Pacific Islander, 2.2% Other, 2.5% Hispanic of any race (2010); Average household size: 2.21 (2010); Median age: 39.7 (2010); Males per 100 females: 92.0 (2010); Marriage status: 28.3% never married, 51.6% now married, 9.0% widowed, 11.1% divorced (2006-2010 5-year est.); Foreign

born: 0.9% (2006-2010 5-year est.); Ancestry (includes multiple ancestries): 25.4% German, 24.6% Polish, 21.3% Italian, 20.0% Irish, 11.6% Lithuanian (2006-2010 5-year est.).

Economy: Single-family building permits issued: 0 (2011); Multi-family building permits issued: 0 (2011); Employment by occupation: 7.6% management, 2.6% professional, 9.7% services, 17.6% sales, 1.8% farming, 8.0% construction, 3.8% production (2006-2010 5-year est.).

Income: Per capita income: $19,170 (2006-2010 5-year est.); Median household income: $35,116 (2006-2010 5-year est.); Average household income: $42,310 (2006-2010 5-year est.); Percent of households with income of $100,000 or more: 7.1% (2006-2010 5-year est.); Poverty rate: 15.7% (2006-2010 5-year est.).

Education: Percent of population age 25 and over with: High school diploma (including GED) or higher: 86.6% (2006-2010 5-year est.); Bachelor's degree or higher: 15.0% (2006-2010 5-year est.); Master's degree or higher: 4.7% (2006-2010 5-year est.).

School District(s)

Minersville Area SD (KG-12)

   2010-11 Enrollment: 1,243 . . . . (570) 544-4764

Housing: Homeownership rate: 60.7% (2010); Median home value: $61,200 (2006-2010 5-year est.); Median contract rent: $415 per month (2006-2010 5-year est.); Median year structure built: before 1940 (2006-2010 5-year est.).

Safety: Violent crime rate: 11.3 per 10,000 population; Property crime rate: 49.9 per 10,000 population (2011).

Transportation: Commute to work: 91.2% car, 1.4% public transportation, 3.3% walk, 4.1% work from home (2006-2010 5-year est.); Travel time to work: 22.9% less than 15 minutes, 55.9% 15 to 30 minutes, 12.2% 30 to 45 minutes, 3.8% 45 to 60 minutes, 5.2% 60 minutes or more (2006-2010 5-year est.)

Additional Information Contacts

Schuylkill Chamber of Commerce . . . . (570) 622-1942
  http://www.schuylkillchamber.com

MOUNT CARBON (borough). Covers a land area of 0.069 square miles and a water area of 0 square miles. Located at 40.67° N. Lat; 76.19° W. Long. Elevation is 614 feet.

Population: 132 (1990); 87 (2000); 91 (2010); Density: 1,318.8 persons per square mile (2010); Race: 91.2% White, 3.3% Black, 2.2% Asian, 0.0% American Indian/Alaska Native, 0.0% Native Hawaiian/Other Pacific Islander, 3.3% Other, 1.1% Hispanic of any race (2010); Average household size: 2.12 (2010); Median age: 47.5 (2010); Males per 100 females: 97.8 (2010); Marriage status: 41.5% never married, 33.0% now married, 4.3% widowed, 21.3% divorced (2006-2010 5-year est.); Foreign born: 0.0% (2006-2010 5-year est.); Ancestry (includes multiple ancestries): 43.0% Dutch, 29.0% Irish, 24.0% Polish, 20.0% German, 9.0% Italian (2006-2010 5-year est.).

Economy: Employment by occupation: 9.5% management, 0.0% professional, 17.5% services, 15.9% sales, 0.0% farming, 19.0% construction, 14.3% production (2006-2010 5-year est.).

Income: Per capita income: $21,217 (2006-2010 5-year est.); Median household income: $37,857 (2006-2010 5-year est.); Average household income: $40,233 (2006-2010 5-year est.); Percent of households with income of $100,000 or more: n/a (2006-2010 5-year est.); Poverty rate: 9.0% (2006-2010 5-year est.).

Education: Percent of population age 25 and over with: High school diploma (including GED) or higher: 86.1% (2006-2010 5-year est.); Bachelor's degree or higher: 0.0% (2006-2010 5-year est.); Master's degree or higher: 0.0% (2006-2010 5-year est.).

Housing: Homeownership rate: 81.4% (2010); Median home value: $53,300 (2006-2010 5-year est.); Median contract rent: $564 per month (2006-2010 5-year est.); Median year structure built: before 1940 (2006-2010 5-year est.).

Transportation: Commute to work: 92.1% car, 0.0% public transportation, 3.2% walk, 0.0% work from home (2006-2010 5-year est.); Travel time to work: 58.7% less than 15 minutes, 27.0% 15 to 30 minutes, 4.8% 30 to 45 minutes, 7.9% 45 to 60 minutes, 1.6% 60 minutes or more (2006-2010 5-year est.)

MUIR (CDP). Covers a land area of 0.497 square miles and a water area of 0 square miles. Located at 40.59° N. Lat; 76.52° W. Long. Elevation is 850 feet.

Population: n/a (1990); n/a (2000); 451 (2010); Density: 908.2 persons per square mile (2010); Race: 99.3% White, 0.0% Black, 0.0% Asian, 0.0% American Indian/Alaska Native, 0.0% Native Hawaiian/Other Pacific

Islander, 0.7% Other, 0.4% Hispanic of any race (2010); Average household size: 2.48 (2010); Median age: 41.1 (2010); Males per 100 females: 105.9 (2010); Marriage status: 18.4% never married, 68.4% now married, 11.5% widowed, 1.7% divorced (2006-2010 5-year est.); Foreign born: 0.0% (2006-2010 5-year est.); Ancestry (includes multiple ancestries): 53.1% German, 8.4% American, 8.4% Welsh, 7.1% Dutch, 5.0% Pennsylvania German (2006-2010 5-year est.).
Economy: Employment by occupation: 8.8% management, 3.3% professional, 0.0% services, 19.8% sales, 7.7% farming, 14.3% construction, 13.2% production (2006-2010 5-year est.).
Income: Per capita income: $29,430 (2006-2010 5-year est.); Median household income: $49,500 (2006-2010 5-year est.); Average household income: $59,976 (2006-2010 5-year est.); Percent of households with income of $100,000 or more: 8.9% (2006-2010 5-year est.); Poverty rate: 0.0% (2006-2010 5-year est.).
Education: Percent of population age 25 and over with: High school diploma (including GED) or higher: 76.7% (2006-2010 5-year est.); Bachelor's degree or higher: 17.7% (2006-2010 5-year est.); Master's degree or higher: 10.4% (2006-2010 5-year est.).
Housing: Homeownership rate: 89.0% (2010); Median home value: $77,200 (2006-2010 5-year est.); Median contract rent: n/a per month (2006-2010 5-year est.); Median year structure built: before 1940 (2006-2010 5-year est.).
Transportation: Commute to work: 100.0% car, 0.0% public transportation, 0.0% walk, 0.0% work from home (2006-2010 5-year est.); Travel time to work: 23.6% less than 15 minutes, 7.1% 15 to 30 minutes, 15.4% 30 to 45 minutes, 44.0% 45 to 60 minutes, 9.9% 60 minutes or more (2006-2010 5-year est.)

NEW CASTLE (township).
Covers a land area of 12.257 square miles and a water area of 0.201 square miles. Located at 40.74° N. Lat; 76.22° W. Long. Elevation is 1,129 feet.
Population: 567 (1990); 395 (2000); 414 (2010); Density: 33.8 persons per square mile (2010); Race: 99.3% White, 0.2% Black, 0.2% Asian, 0.0% American Indian/Alaska Native, 0.0% Native Hawaiian/Other Pacific Islander, 0.3% Other, 2.2% Hispanic of any race (2010); Average household size: 2.27 (2010); Median age: 43.2 (2010); Males per 100 females: 106.0 (2010); Marriage status: 32.2% never married, 43.3% now married, 9.8% widowed, 14.6% divorced (2006-2010 5-year est.); Foreign born: 0.7% (2006-2010 5-year est.); Ancestry (includes multiple ancestries): 28.5% Polish, 23.2% Irish, 17.8% Italian, 15.1% Dutch, 14.9% German (2006-2010 5-year est.).
Economy: Single-family building permits issued: 0 (2011); Multi-family building permits issued: 0 (2011); Employment by occupation: 1.4% management, 9.8% professional, 7.4% services, 13.5% sales, 6.0% farming, 12.6% construction, 10.2% production (2006-2010 5-year est.).
Income: Per capita income: $20,407 (2006-2010 5-year est.); Median household income: $38,611 (2006-2010 5-year est.); Average household income: $45,962 (2006-2010 5-year est.); Percent of households with income of $100,000 or more: 8.3% (2006-2010 5-year est.); Poverty rate: 4.3% (2006-2010 5-year est.).
Taxes: Total city taxes per capita: $393 (2009); City property taxes per capita: $163 (2009).
Education: Percent of population age 25 and over with: High school diploma (including GED) or higher: 81.9% (2006-2010 5-year est.); Bachelor's degree or higher: 17.2% (2006-2010 5-year est.); Master's degree or higher: 10.3% (2006-2010 5-year est.).
Housing: Homeownership rate: 75.3% (2010); Median home value: $61,800 (2006-2010 5-year est.); Median contract rent: $392 per month (2006-2010 5-year est.); Median year structure built: before 1940 (2006-2010 5-year est.).
Transportation: Commute to work: 95.3% car, 0.0% public transportation, 1.4% walk, 0.9% work from home (2006-2010 5-year est.); Travel time to work: 40.8% less than 15 minutes, 31.9% 15 to 30 minutes, 11.3% 30 to 45 minutes, 6.6% 45 to 60 minutes, 9.4% 60 minutes or more (2006-2010 5-year est.)

NEW PHILADELPHIA (borough).
Covers a land area of 1.505 square miles and a water area of 0 square miles. Located at 40.72° N. Lat; 76.12° W. Long. Elevation is 679 feet.
History: Laid out c.1828, incorporated 1868.
Population: 1,283 (1990); 1,149 (2000); 1,085 (2010); Density: 721.0 persons per square mile (2010); Race: 97.1% White, 0.2% Black, 0.1% Asian, 0.6% American Indian/Alaska Native, 0.4% Native Hawaiian/Other Pacific Islander, 1.6% Other, 1.7% Hispanic of any race (2010); Average

household size: 2.27 (2010); Median age: 44.9 (2010); Males per 100 females: 99.1 (2010); Marriage status: 30.5% never married, 51.3% now married, 9.3% widowed, 8.9% divorced (2006-2010 5-year est.); Foreign born: 0.0% (2006-2010 5-year est.); Ancestry (includes multiple ancestries): 27.1% Lithuanian, 23.5% Irish, 20.9% German, 17.7% Polish, 6.1% Italian (2006-2010 5-year est.).
Economy: Employment by occupation: 6.2% management, 2.4% professional, 12.4% services, 13.0% sales, 1.5% farming, 14.3% construction, 8.2% production (2006-2010 5-year est.).
Income: Per capita income: $20,975 (2006-2010 5-year est.); Median household income: $40,714 (2006-2010 5-year est.); Average household income: $46,582 (2006-2010 5-year est.); Percent of households with income of $100,000 or more: 8.3% (2006-2010 5-year est.); Poverty rate: 17.6% (2006-2010 5-year est.).
Education: Percent of population age 25 and over with: High school diploma (including GED) or higher: 85.1% (2006-2010 5-year est.); Bachelor's degree or higher: 9.3% (2006-2010 5-year est.); Master's degree or higher: 3.4% (2006-2010 5-year est.).
Housing: Homeownership rate: 70.7% (2010); Median home value: $62,600 (2006-2010 5-year est.); Median contract rent: $358 per month (2006-2010 5-year est.); Median year structure built: before 1940 (2006-2010 5-year est.).
Transportation: Commute to work: 97.2% car, 0.0% public transportation, 1.3% walk, 0.9% work from home (2006-2010 5-year est.); Travel time to work: 22.7% less than 15 minutes, 42.4% 15 to 30 minutes, 14.8% 30 to 45 minutes, 6.2% 45 to 60 minutes, 13.9% 60 minutes or more (2006-2010 5-year est.)
Additional Information Contacts
Schuylkill Chamber of Commerce . . . . (570) 622-1942
http://www.schuylkillchamber.com

NEW RINGGOLD (borough).
Covers a land area of 0.799 square miles and a water area of 0 square miles. Located at 40.69° N. Lat; 75.99° W. Long. Elevation is 551 feet.
History: Appalachian Trail passes to Southeast, on Blue Mt. ridge.
Population: 315 (1990); 291 (2000); 276 (2010); Density: 345.5 persons per square mile (2010); Race: 96.4% White, 1.4% Black, 0.0% Asian, 0.7% American Indian/Alaska Native, 0.0% Native Hawaiian/Other Pacific Islander, 1.5% Other, 1.8% Hispanic of any race (2010); Average household size: 2.49 (2010); Median age: 42.0 (2010); Males per 100 females: 106.0 (2010); Marriage status: 21.0% never married, 67.1% now married, 3.3% widowed, 8.6% divorced (2006-2010 5-year est.); Foreign born: 2.6% (2006-2010 5-year est.); Ancestry (includes multiple ancestries): 56.1% German, 23.4% Irish, 12.5% Italian, 12.2% Pennsylvania German, 6.9% Dutch (2006-2010 5-year est.).
Economy: Employment by occupation: 7.1% management, 3.9% professional, 14.9% services, 7.1% sales, 3.9% farming, 17.5% construction, 17.5% production (2006-2010 5-year est.).
Income: Per capita income: $23,408 (2006-2010 5-year est.); Median household income: $50,000 (2006-2010 5-year est.); Average household income: $59,028 (2006-2010 5-year est.); Percent of households with income of $100,000 or more: 20.0% (2006-2010 5-year est.); Poverty rate: 3.6% (2006-2010 5-year est.).
Education: Percent of population age 25 and over with: High school diploma (including GED) or higher: 77.0% (2006-2010 5-year est.); Bachelor's degree or higher: 4.6% (2006-2010 5-year est.); Master's degree or higher: 0.0% (2006-2010 5-year est.).
School District(s)
Tamaqua Area SD (KG-12)
    2010-11 Enrollment: 2,098 . . . . (570) 668-2570
Housing: Homeownership rate: 75.7% (2010); Median home value: $89,100 (2006-2010 5-year est.); Median contract rent: $504 per month (2006-2010 5-year est.); Median year structure built: before 1940 (2006-2010 5-year est.).
Transportation: Commute to work: 98.7% car, 0.0% public transportation, 0.0% walk, 1.3% work from home (2006-2010 5-year est.); Travel time to work: 14.1% less than 15 minutes, 28.9% 15 to 30 minutes, 33.6% 30 to 45 minutes, 10.7% 45 to 60 minutes, 12.8% 60 minutes or more (2006-2010 5-year est.)

NEWTOWN (CDP).
Covers a land area of 0.641 square miles and a water area of 0 square miles. Located at 40.65° N. Lat; 76.35° W. Long. Elevation is 938 feet.
Population: 254 (1990); 244 (2000); 243 (2010); Density: 379.0 persons per square mile (2010); Race: 100.0% White, 0.0% Black, 0.0% Asian,

0.0% American Indian/Alaska Native, 0.0% Native Hawaiian/Other Pacific Islander, 0.0% Other, 0.4% Hispanic of any race (2010); Average household size: 2.48 (2010); Median age: 43.5 (2010); Males per 100 females: 107.7 (2010); Marriage status: 16.7% never married, 67.3% now married, 4.5% widowed, 11.5% divorced (2006-2010 5-year est.); Foreign born: 0.0% (2006-2010 5-year est.); Ancestry (includes multiple ancestries): 47.9% German, 25.2% Irish, 13.4% Dutch, 7.7% Polish, 7.3% Italian (2006-2010 5-year est.).

Economy: Employment by occupation: 2.9% management, 3.4% professional, 4.0% services, 13.1% sales, 1.7% farming, 10.9% construction, 19.4% production (2006-2010 5-year est.).

Income: Per capita income: $21,359 (2006-2010 5-year est.); Median household income: $49,643 (2006-2010 5-year est.); Average household income: $54,773 (2006-2010 5-year est.); Percent of households with income of $100,000 or more: 4.2% (2006-2010 5-year est.); Poverty rate: 1.3% (2006-2010 5-year est.).

Education: Percent of population age 25 and over with: High school diploma (including GED) or higher: 93.0% (2006-2010 5-year est.); Bachelor's degree or higher: 10.9% (2006-2010 5-year est.); Master's degree or higher: 1.7% (2006-2010 5-year est.).

Housing: Homeownership rate: 85.7% (2010); Median home value: $81,300 (2006-2010 5-year est.); Median contract rent: $423 per month (2006-2010 5-year est.); Median year structure built: before 1940 (2006-2010 5-year est.).

Transportation: Commute to work: 95.4% car, 0.0% public transportation, 2.9% walk, 1.7% work from home (2006-2010 5-year est.); Travel time to work: 32.0% less than 15 minutes, 32.0% 15 to 30 minutes, 15.1% 30 to 45 minutes, 5.8% 45 to 60 minutes, 15.1% 60 minutes or more (2006-2010 5-year est.)

NORTH MANHEIM (township). Covers a land area of 20.327 square miles and a water area of 0.089 square miles. Located at 40.66° N. Lat; 76.16° W. Long.

Population: 3,404 (1990); 3,287 (2000); 3,770 (2010); Density: 185.5 persons per square mile (2010); Race: 93.6% White, 3.4% Black, 1.4% Asian, 0.1% American Indian/Alaska Native, 0.0% Native Hawaiian/Other Pacific Islander, 1.5% Other, 1.6% Hispanic of any race (2010); Average household size: 2.48 (2010); Median age: 43.5 (2010); Males per 100 females: 97.7 (2010); Marriage status: 26.9% never married, 54.1% now married, 13.5% widowed, 5.5% divorced (2006-2010 5-year est.); Foreign born: 4.3% (2006-2010 5-year est.); Ancestry (includes multiple ancestries): 34.3% German, 13.3% Irish, 10.2% American, 8.3% English, 6.9% Polish (2006-2010 5-year est.).

Economy: Single-family building permits issued: 7 (2011); Multi-family building permits issued: 0 (2011); Employment by occupation: 13.5% management, 0.9% professional, 10.8% services, 14.8% sales, 3.0% farming, 10.0% construction, 10.4% production (2006-2010 5-year est.).

Income: Per capita income: $25,057 (2006-2010 5-year est.); Median household income: $56,000 (2006-2010 5-year est.); Average household income: $66,752 (2006-2010 5-year est.); Percent of households with income of $100,000 or more: 20.1% (2006-2010 5-year est.); Poverty rate: 4.8% (2006-2010 5-year est.).

Education: Percent of population age 25 and over with: High school diploma (including GED) or higher: 83.5% (2006-2010 5-year est.); Bachelor's degree or higher: 18.3% (2006-2010 5-year est.); Master's degree or higher: 9.1% (2006-2010 5-year est.).

Housing: Homeownership rate: 80.5% (2010); Median home value: $166,000 (2006-2010 5-year est.); Median contract rent: $343 per month (2006-2010 5-year est.); Median year structure built: 1966 (2006-2010 5-year est.).

Transportation: Commute to work: 96.7% car, 0.0% public transportation, 2.7% walk, 0.0% work from home (2006-2010 5-year est.); Travel time to work: 36.6% less than 15 minutes, 33.6% 15 to 30 minutes, 9.1% 30 to 45 minutes, 7.2% 45 to 60 minutes, 13.5% 60 minutes or more (2006-2010 5-year est.)

Additional Information Contacts
Schuylkill Chamber of Commerce . . . . (570) 622-1942
http://www.schuylkillchamber.com

NORTH UNION (township). Covers a land area of 20.723 square miles and a water area of 0.038 square miles. Located at 40.91° N. Lat; 76.20° W. Long.

Population: 1,143 (1990); 1,225 (2000); 1,476 (2010); Density: 71.2 persons per square mile (2010); Race: 98.0% White, 0.3% Black, 0.4% Asian, 0.1% American Indian/Alaska Native, 0.0% Native Hawaiian/Other

Pacific Islander, 1.2% Other, 1.9% Hispanic of any race (2010); Average household size: 2.44 (2010); Median age: 44.1 (2010); Males per 100 females: 104.4 (2010); Marriage status: 23.2% never married, 50.7% now married, 6.2% widowed, 19.9% divorced (2006-2010 5-year est.); Foreign born: 0.8% (2006-2010 5-year est.); Ancestry (includes multiple ancestries): 27.0% German, 18.7% Italian, 16.7% Irish, 12.9% Polish, 7.3% English (2006-2010 5-year est.).

Economy: Employment by occupation: 11.1% management, 2.2% professional, 7.6% services, 17.6% sales, 0.0% farming, 21.4% construction, 17.2% production (2006-2010 5-year est.).

Income: Per capita income: $21,131 (2006-2010 5-year est.); Median household income: $50,195 (2006-2010 5-year est.); Average household income: $51,769 (2006-2010 5-year est.); Percent of households with income of $100,000 or more: 6.3% (2006-2010 5-year est.); Poverty rate: 15.0% (2006-2010 5-year est.).

Education: Percent of population age 25 and over with: High school diploma (including GED) or higher: 82.7% (2006-2010 5-year est.); Bachelor's degree or higher: 11.7% (2006-2010 5-year est.); Master's degree or higher: 3.0% (2006-2010 5-year est.).

Housing: Homeownership rate: 85.0% (2010); Median home value: $109,400 (2006-2010 5-year est.); Median contract rent: $439 per month (2006-2010 5-year est.); Median year structure built: 1973 (2006-2010 5-year est.).

Safety: Violent crime rate: 0.0 per 10,000 population; Property crime rate: 13.5 per 10,000 population (2011).

Transportation: Commute to work: 96.8% car, 0.0% public transportation, 0.8% walk, 2.3% work from home (2006-2010 5-year est.); Travel time to work: 16.3% less than 15 minutes, 50.1% 15 to 30 minutes, 17.1% 30 to 45 minutes, 11.0% 45 to 60 minutes, 5.4% 60 minutes or more (2006-2010 5-year est.)

Additional Information Contacts
Schuylkill Chamber of Commerce . . . . (570) 622-1942
http://www.schuylkillchamber.com

NORWEGIAN (township). Covers a land area of 5.868 square miles and a water area of 0.009 square miles. Located at 40.69° N. Lat; 76.22° W. Long.

Population: 1,938 (1990); 2,172 (2000); 2,310 (2010); Density: 393.7 persons per square mile (2010); Race: 98.2% White, 0.3% Black, 0.5% Asian, 0.0% American Indian/Alaska Native, 0.0% Native Hawaiian/Other Pacific Islander, 1.0% Other, 0.7% Hispanic of any race (2010); Average household size: 2.36 (2010); Median age: 48.1 (2010); Males per 100 females: 93.5 (2010); Marriage status: 20.6% never married, 58.7% now married, 10.5% widowed, 10.3% divorced (2006-2010 5-year est.); Foreign born: 0.3% (2006-2010 5-year est.); Ancestry (includes multiple ancestries): 29.0% Irish, 25.4% German, 14.3% Italian, 12.4% Lithuanian, 10.1% Ukrainian (2006-2010 5-year est.).

Economy: Single-family building permits issued: 0 (2011); Multi-family building permits issued: 0 (2011); Employment by occupation: 15.8% management, 1.9% professional, 4.0% services, 19.2% sales, 1.5% farming, 9.4% construction, 7.7% production (2006-2010 5-year est.).

Income: Per capita income: $23,621 (2006-2010 5-year est.); Median household income: $48,226 (2006-2010 5-year est.); Average household income: $54,890 (2006-2010 5-year est.); Percent of households with income of $100,000 or more: 12.6% (2006-2010 5-year est.); Poverty rate: 5.6% (2006-2010 5-year est.).

Education: Percent of population age 25 and over with: High school diploma (including GED) or higher: 83.9% (2006-2010 5-year est.); Bachelor's degree or higher: 19.6% (2006-2010 5-year est.); Master's degree or higher: 6.4% (2006-2010 5-year est.).

Housing: Homeownership rate: 83.3% (2010); Median home value: $138,500 (2006-2010 5-year est.); Median contract rent: $479 per month (2006-2010 5-year est.); Median year structure built: 1975 (2006-2010 5-year est.).

Transportation: Commute to work: 88.0% car, 1.2% public transportation, 0.6% walk, 10.2% work from home (2006-2010 5-year est.); Travel time to work: 39.2% less than 15 minutes, 29.4% 15 to 30 minutes, 11.6% 30 to 45 minutes, 4.2% 45 to 60 minutes, 15.6% 60 minutes or more (2006-2010 5-year est.)

Additional Information Contacts
Schuylkill Chamber of Commerce . . . . (570) 622-1942
http://www.schuylkillchamber.com

NUREMBERG (CDP). Covers a land area of 0.598 square miles and a water area of 0 square miles. Located at 40.94° N. Lat; 76.17° W. Long. Elevation is 1,161 feet.
Population: 227 (1990); 231 (2000); 434 (2010); Density: 726.1 persons per square mile (2010); Race: 98.6% White, 0.0% Black, 1.2% Asian, 0.0% American Indian/Alaska Native, 0.0% Native Hawaiian/Other Pacific Islander, 0.2% Other, 0.7% Hispanic of any race (2010); Average household size: 2.26 (2010); Median age: 42.4 (2010); Males per 100 females: 103.8 (2010); Marriage status: 23.9% never married, 41.5% now married, 13.5% widowed, 21.1% divorced (2006-2010 5-year est.); Foreign born: 0.0% (2006-2010 5-year est.); Ancestry (includes multiple ancestries): 27.9% German, 21.4% Irish, 20.4% Polish, 15.3% Italian, 10.5% Pennsylvania German (2006-2010 5-year est.).
Economy: Employment by occupation: 10.2% management, 0.0% professional, 17.5% services, 12.0% sales, 0.0% farming, 36.1% construction, 30.1% production (2006-2010 5-year est.).
Income: Per capita income: $19,473 (2006-2010 5-year est.); Median household income: $36,250 (2006-2010 5-year est.); Average household income: $40,472 (2006-2010 5-year est.); Percent of households with income of $100,000 or more: n/a (2006-2010 5-year est.); Poverty rate: 24.1% (2006-2010 5-year est.).
Education: Percent of population age 25 and over with: High school diploma (including GED) or higher: 81.2% (2006-2010 5-year est.); Bachelor's degree or higher: 3.1% (2006-2010 5-year est.); Master's degree or higher: 0.0% (2006-2010 5-year est.).
Housing: Homeownership rate: 72.4% (2010); Median home value: $62,700 (2006-2010 5-year est.); Median contract rent: $423 per month (2006-2010 5-year est.); Median year structure built: before 1940 (2006-2010 5-year est.).
Transportation: Commute to work: 96.8% car, 0.0% public transportation, 0.0% walk, 3.2% work from home (2006-2010 5-year est.); Travel time to work: 4.6% less than 15 minutes, 69.9% 15 to 30 minutes, 3.3% 30 to 45 minutes, 9.2% 45 to 60 minutes, 13.1% 60 minutes or more (2006-2010 5-year est.)

ONEIDA (CDP). Covers a land area of 0.183 square miles and a water area of 0 square miles. Located at 40.91° N. Lat; 76.12° W. Long. Elevation is 1,680 feet.
Population: 212 (1990); 219 (2000); 200 (2010); Density: 1,092.8 persons per square mile (2010); Race: 98.5% White, 0.0% Black, 0.0% Asian, 0.0% American Indian/Alaska Native, 0.0% Native Hawaiian/Other Pacific Islander, 1.5% Other, 0.5% Hispanic of any race (2010); Average household size: 2.06 (2010); Median age: 42.0 (2010); Males per 100 females: 100.0 (2010); Marriage status: 28.3% never married, 39.1% now married, 16.3% widowed, 16.3% divorced (2006-2010 5-year est.); Foreign born: 0.0% (2006-2010 5-year est.); Ancestry (includes multiple ancestries): 28.3% Polish, 25.0% German, 25.0% Irish, 20.7% Italian, 14.7% Pennsylvania German (2006-2010 5-year est.).
Economy: Employment by occupation: 0.0% management, 0.0% professional, 12.6% services, 37.9% sales, 0.0% farming, 20.4% construction, 25.2% production (2006-2010 5-year est.).
Income: Per capita income: $22,313 (2006-2010 5-year est.); Median household income: $29,491 (2006-2010 5-year est.); Average household income: $45,070 (2006-2010 5-year est.); Percent of households with income of $100,000 or more: 13.2% (2006-2010 5-year est.); Poverty rate: 8.7% (2006-2010 5-year est.).
Education: Percent of population age 25 and over with: High school diploma (including GED) or higher: 85.5% (2006-2010 5-year est.); Bachelor's degree or higher: 0.0% (2006-2010 5-year est.); Master's degree or higher: 0.0% (2006-2010 5-year est.).
Housing: Homeownership rate: 83.5% (2010); Median home value: $61,500 (2006-2010 5-year est.); Median contract rent: n/a per month (2006-2010 5-year est.); Median year structure built: before 1940 (2006-2010 5-year est.).
Transportation: Commute to work: 100.0% car, 0.0% public transportation, 0.0% walk, 0.0% work from home (2006-2010 5-year est.); Travel time to work: 50.5% less than 15 minutes, 46.2% 15 to 30 minutes, 3.2% 30 to 45 minutes, 0.0% 45 to 60 minutes, 0.0% 60 minutes or more (2006-2010 5-year est.)

ORWIGSBURG (borough). Covers a land area of 2.170 square miles and a water area of 0 square miles. Located at 40.65° N. Lat; 76.10° W. Long. Elevation is 623 feet.
History: Hawk Mt. Sanctuary and Appalachian Trail to East. Settled 1747, laid out 1796, incorporated 1813.

Population: 2,801 (1990); 3,106 (2000); 3,099 (2010); Density: 1,428.4 persons per square mile (2010); Race: 95.7% White, 1.0% Black, 2.1% Asian, 0.3% American Indian/Alaska Native, 0.0% Native Hawaiian/Other Pacific Islander, 0.9% Other, 1.5% Hispanic of any race (2010); Average household size: 2.30 (2010); Median age: 45.5 (2010); Males per 100 females: 82.6 (2010); Marriage status: 19.6% never married, 57.0% now married, 12.2% widowed, 11.2% divorced (2006-2010 5-year est.); Foreign born: 3.1% (2006-2010 5-year est.); Ancestry (includes multiple ancestries): 37.0% German, 18.6% Irish, 10.7% Italian, 9.5% Polish, 7.1% Pennsylvania German (2006-2010 5-year est.).
Economy: Single-family building permits issued: 1 (2011); Multi-family building permits issued: 0 (2011); Employment by occupation: 11.1% management, 3.5% professional, 11.9% services, 10.7% sales, 2.0% farming, 11.4% construction, 6.4% production (2006-2010 5-year est.).
Income: Per capita income: $26,442 (2006-2010 5-year est.); Median household income: $44,865 (2006-2010 5-year est.); Average household income: $64,084 (2006-2010 5-year est.); Percent of households with income of $100,000 or more: 17.3% (2006-2010 5-year est.); Poverty rate: 5.9% (2006-2010 5-year est.).
Education: Percent of population age 25 and over with: High school diploma (including GED) or higher: 88.4% (2006-2010 5-year est.); Bachelor's degree or higher: 32.0% (2006-2010 5-year est.); Master's degree or higher: 10.6% (2006-2010 5-year est.).

School District(s)
Blue Mountain SD (KG-12)
    2010-11 Enrollment: 2,877 . . . . (570) 366-0515
Housing: Homeownership rate: 72.1% (2010); Median home value: $155,800 (2006-2010 5-year est.); Median contract rent: $452 per month (2006-2010 5-year est.); Median year structure built: 1950 (2006-2010 5-year est.).
Safety: Violent crime rate: 6.4 per 10,000 population; Property crime rate: 164.0 per 10,000 population (2011).
Transportation: Commute to work: 92.8% car, 0.0% public transportation, 3.6% walk, 3.1% work from home (2006-2010 5-year est.); Travel time to work: 37.6% less than 15 minutes, 35.9% 15 to 30 minutes, 18.3% 30 to 45 minutes, 4.8% 45 to 60 minutes, 3.4% 60 minutes or more (2006-2010 5-year est.)
Additional Information Contacts
Schuylkill Chamber of Commerce . . . . (570) 622-1942
    http://www.schuylkillchamber.com

ORWIN (CDP). Covers a land area of 0.615 square miles and a water area of 0 square miles. Located at 40.58° N. Lat; 76.53° W. Long. Elevation is 801 feet.
Population: n/a (1990); n/a (2000); 314 (2010); Density: 510.9 persons per square mile (2010); Race: 100.0% White, 0.0% Black, 0.0% Asian, 0.0% American Indian/Alaska Native, 0.0% Native Hawaiian/Other Pacific Islander, 0.0% Other, 1.0% Hispanic of any race (2010); Average household size: 2.55 (2010); Median age: 41.5 (2010); Males per 100 females: 101.3 (2010); Marriage status: 9.5% never married, 61.5% now married, 12.2% widowed, 16.9% divorced (2006-2010 5-year est.); Foreign born: 0.0% (2006-2010 5-year est.); Ancestry (includes multiple ancestries): 66.1% German, 11.5% Dutch, 4.2% Italian, 3.6% Welsh, 3.0% Irish (2006-2010 5-year est.).
Economy: Employment by occupation: 10.6% management, 0.0% professional, 0.0% services, 39.4% sales, 0.0% farming, 0.0% construction, 24.2% production (2006-2010 5-year est.).
Income: Per capita income: $19,210 (2006-2010 5-year est.); Median household income: $33,125 (2006-2010 5-year est.); Average household income: $42,142 (2006-2010 5-year est.); Percent of households with income of $100,000 or more: n/a (2006-2010 5-year est.); Poverty rate: 0.0% (2006-2010 5-year est.).
Education: Percent of population age 25 and over with: High school diploma (including GED) or higher: 95.5% (2006-2010 5-year est.); Bachelor's degree or higher: 4.5% (2006-2010 5-year est.); Master's degree or higher: 0.0% (2006-2010 5-year est.).
Housing: Homeownership rate: 88.6% (2010); Median home value: $78,100 (2006-2010 5-year est.); Median contract rent: n/a per month (2006-2010 5-year est.); Median year structure built: 1942 (2006-2010 5-year est.).
Transportation: Commute to work: 100.0% car, 0.0% public transportation, 0.0% walk, 0.0% work from home (2006-2010 5-year est.); Travel time to work: 22.7% less than 15 minutes, 37.9% 15 to 30 minutes, 21.2% 30 to 45 minutes, 0.0% 45 to 60 minutes, 18.2% 60 minutes or more (2006-2010 5-year est.)

PALO ALTO (borough). Covers a land area of 1.044 square miles and a water area of 0 square miles. Located at 40.69° N. Lat; 76.17° W. Long. Elevation is 679 feet.

History: Laid out c.1844; incorporated 1854.

Population: 1,192 (1990); 1,052 (2000); 1,032 (2010); Density: 988.2 persons per square mile (2010); Race: 97.6% White, 0.8% Black, 0.7% Asian, 0.0% American Indian/Alaska Native, 0.0% Native Hawaiian/Other Pacific Islander, 0.9% Other, 1.9% Hispanic of any race (2010); Average household size: 2.37 (2010); Median age: 42.7 (2010); Males per 100 females: 99.6 (2010); Marriage status: 27.4% never married, 59.0% now married, 5.7% widowed, 7.9% divorced (2006-2010 5-year est.); Foreign born: 0.6% (2006-2010 5-year est.); Ancestry (includes multiple ancestries): 32.9% German, 30.1% Irish, 18.4% Italian, 11.9% Dutch, 8.2% Polish (2006-2010 5-year est.).

Economy: Employment by occupation: 6.1% management, 0.8% professional, 19.3% services, 14.9% sales, 6.1% farming, 8.8% construction, 9.2% production (2006-2010 5-year est.).

Income: Per capita income: $18,671 (2006-2010 5-year est.); Median household income: $34,375 (2006-2010 5-year est.); Average household income: $45,105 (2006-2010 5-year est.); Percent of households with income of $100,000 or more: 7.0% (2006-2010 5-year est.); Poverty rate: 12.1% (2006-2010 5-year est.).

Education: Percent of population age 25 and over with: High school diploma (including GED) or higher: 84.7% (2006-2010 5-year est.); Bachelor's degree or higher: 6.3% (2006-2010 5-year est.); Master's degree or higher: 2.9% (2006-2010 5-year est.).

Housing: Homeownership rate: 80.9% (2010); Median home value: $73,300 (2006-2010 5-year est.); Median contract rent: $470 per month (2006-2010 5-year est.); Median year structure built: before 1940 (2006-2010 5-year est.).

Transportation: Commute to work: 95.8% car, 1.0% public transportation, 1.6% walk, 1.6% work from home (2006-2010 5-year est.); Travel time to work: 61.9% less than 15 minutes, 23.3% 15 to 30 minutes, 1.6% 30 to 45 minutes, 2.6% 45 to 60 minutes, 10.5% 60 minutes or more (2006-2010 5-year est.)

PARK CREST (CDP). Covers a land area of 0.711 square miles and a water area of <.001 square miles. Located at 40.82° N. Lat; 76.06° W. Long. Elevation is 1,122 feet.

Population: n/a (1990); n/a (2000); 542 (2010); Density: 762.5 persons per square mile (2010); Race: 99.4% White, 0.0% Black, 0.0% Asian, 0.0% American Indian/Alaska Native, 0.0% Native Hawaiian/Other Pacific Islander, 0.6% Other, 2.0% Hispanic of any race (2010); Average household size: 2.32 (2010); Median age: 48.7 (2010); Males per 100 females: 101.5 (2010); Marriage status: 22.5% never married, 52.9% now married, 11.1% widowed, 13.6% divorced (2006-2010 5-year est.); Foreign born: 0.4% (2006-2010 5-year est.); Ancestry (includes multiple ancestries): 31.3% German, 28.0% Irish, 17.8% Polish, 13.3% Lithuanian, 11.6% Slovak (2006-2010 5-year est.).

Economy: Employment by occupation: 5.3% management, 8.2% professional, 6.3% services, 18.2% sales, 0.9% farming, 30.2% construction, 25.2% production (2006-2010 5-year est.).

Income: Per capita income: $28,178 (2006-2010 5-year est.); Median household income: $50,375 (2006-2010 5-year est.); Average household income: $63,183 (2006-2010 5-year est.); Percent of households with income of $100,000 or more: 17.4% (2006-2010 5-year est.); Poverty rate: 4.7% (2006-2010 5-year est.).

Education: Percent of population age 25 and over with: High school diploma (including GED) or higher: 96.4% (2006-2010 5-year est.); Bachelor's degree or higher: 14.9% (2006-2010 5-year est.); Master's degree or higher: 6.0% (2006-2010 5-year est.).

Housing: Homeownership rate: 90.2% (2010); Median home value: $100,400 (2006-2010 5-year est.); Median contract rent: n/a per month (2006-2010 5-year est.); Median year structure built: 1952 (2006-2010 5-year est.).

Transportation: Commute to work: 98.7% car, 0.0% public transportation, 0.0% walk, 0.0% work from home (2006-2010 5-year est.); Travel time to work: 31.5% less than 15 minutes, 40.4% 15 to 30 minutes, 12.1% 30 to 45 minutes, 8.0% 45 to 60 minutes, 8.0% 60 minutes or more (2006-2010 5-year est.)

PINE GROVE (borough). Covers a land area of 1.065 square miles and a water area of 0 square miles. Located at 40.55° N. Lat; 76.39° W. Long. Elevation is 545 feet.

Population: 2,118 (1990); 2,154 (2000); 2,186 (2010); Density: 2,053.3 persons per square mile (2010); Race: 97.0% White, 0.8% Black, 0.3% Asian, 0.1% American Indian/Alaska Native, 0.0% Native Hawaiian/Other Pacific Islander, 1.8% Other, 2.1% Hispanic of any race (2010); Average household size: 2.34 (2010); Median age: 39.3 (2010); Males per 100 females: 100.6 (2010); Marriage status: 25.8% never married, 54.2% now married, 8.6% widowed, 11.3% divorced (2006-2010 5-year est.); Foreign born: 2.0% (2006-2010 5-year est.); Ancestry (includes multiple ancestries): 53.2% German, 10.3% Dutch, 8.7% Italian, 8.6% Irish, 7.4% American (2006-2010 5-year est.).

Economy: Employment by occupation: 6.8% management, 1.5% professional, 13.2% services, 15.0% sales, 4.5% farming, 10.2% construction, 7.4% production (2006-2010 5-year est.).

Income: Per capita income: $23,651 (2006-2010 5-year est.); Median household income: $52,042 (2006-2010 5-year est.); Average household income: $56,234 (2006-2010 5-year est.); Percent of households with income of $100,000 or more: 13.1% (2006-2010 5-year est.); Poverty rate: 7.9% (2006-2010 5-year est.).

Education: Percent of population age 25 and over with: High school diploma (including GED) or higher: 83.3% (2006-2010 5-year est.); Bachelor's degree or higher: 16.5% (2006-2010 5-year est.); Master's degree or higher: 5.1% (2006-2010 5-year est.).

School District(s)

Pine Grove Area SD (PK-12)

    2010-11 Enrollment: 1,677 . . . . (570) 345-2731

Housing: Homeownership rate: 62.1% (2010); Median home value: $89,600 (2006-2010 5-year est.); Median contract rent: $443 per month (2006-2010 5-year est.); Median year structure built: 1947 (2006-2010 5-year est.).

Safety: Violent crime rate: 41.0 per 10,000 population; Property crime rate: 73.0 per 10,000 population (2011).

Transportation: Commute to work: 94.4% car, 0.5% public transportation, 5.0% walk, 0.0% work from home (2006-2010 5-year est.); Travel time to work: 33.3% less than 15 minutes, 26.9% 15 to 30 minutes, 26.2% 30 to 45 minutes, 7.2% 45 to 60 minutes, 6.4% 60 minutes or more (2006-2010 5-year est.)

Additional Information Contacts

Schuylkill Chamber of Commerce . . . . (570) 622-1942

    http://www.schuylkillchamber.com

PINE GROVE (township). Covers a land area of 37.803 square miles and a water area of 0.160 square miles. Located at 40.54° N. Lat; 76.42° W. Long. Elevation is 545 feet.

History: Appalachian Trail passes to South. Settled 1771, laid out 1830, incorporated 1832.

Population: 3,699 (1990); 3,930 (2000); 4,123 (2010); Density: 109.1 persons per square mile (2010); Race: 98.7% White, 0.2% Black, 0.1% Asian, 0.4% American Indian/Alaska Native, 0.0% Native Hawaiian/Other Pacific Islander, 0.6% Other, 0.6% Hispanic of any race (2010); Average household size: 2.45 (2010); Median age: 45.5 (2010); Males per 100 females: 97.1 (2010); Marriage status: 21.2% never married, 66.4% now married, 6.8% widowed, 5.5% divorced (2006-2010 5-year est.); Foreign born: 2.2% (2006-2010 5-year est.); Ancestry (includes multiple ancestries): 57.2% German, 15.8% Irish, 10.6% Dutch, 6.5% American, 5.5% Pennsylvania German (2006-2010 5-year est.).

Economy: Single-family building permits issued: 12 (2011); Multi-family building permits issued: 0 (2011); Employment by occupation: 4.5% management, 4.1% professional, 19.7% services, 10.3% sales, 3.8% farming, 17.1% construction, 10.2% production (2006-2010 5-year est.).

Income: Per capita income: $23,324 (2006-2010 5-year est.); Median household income: $43,971 (2006-2010 5-year est.); Average household income: $58,128 (2006-2010 5-year est.); Percent of households with income of $100,000 or more: 18.3% (2006-2010 5-year est.); Poverty rate: 6.4% (2006-2010 5-year est.).

Education: Percent of population age 25 and over with: High school diploma (including GED) or higher: 86.0% (2006-2010 5-year est.); Bachelor's degree or higher: 12.7% (2006-2010 5-year est.); Master's degree or higher: 3.8% (2006-2010 5-year est.).

Housing: Homeownership rate: 83.7% (2010); Median home value: $133,800 (2006-2010 5-year est.); Median contract rent: $503 per month (2006-2010 5-year est.); Median year structure built: 1967 (2006-2010 5-year est.).

Transportation: Commute to work: 98.2% car, 0.0% public transportation, 0.6% walk, 1.2% work from home (2006-2010 5-year est.); Travel time to work: 30.3% less than 15 minutes, 21.1% 15 to 30 minutes, 28.9% 30 to 45 minutes, 13.8% 45 to 60 minutes, 5.9% 60 minutes or more (2006-2010 5-year est.)

Additional Information Contacts
Schuylkill Chamber of Commerce . . . . (570) 622-1942
http://www.schuylkillchamber.com

PITMAN (unincorporated postal area)
Zip Code: 17964

Covers a land area of 22.904 square miles and a water area of 0.004 square miles. Located at 40.71° N. Lat; 76.50° W. Long. Elevation is 938 feet. Population: 798 (2010); Density: 34.8 persons per square mile (2010); Race: 97.1% White, 1.1% Black, 0.3% Asian, 0.3% American Indian/Alaska Native, 0.0% Native Hawaiian/Other Pacific Islander, 1.2% Other, 1.4% Hispanic of any race (2010); Average household size: 2.57 (2010); Median age: 45.7 (2010); Males per 100 females: 92.3 (2010); Homeownership rate: 83.3% (2010)

PORT CARBON (borough). Covers a land area of 0.754 square miles and a water area of 0 square miles. Located at 40.70° N. Lat; 76.17° W. Long. Elevation is 656 feet.
History: Laid out 1828, incorporated 1852.
Population: 2,134 (1990); 2,019 (2000); 1,889 (2010); Density: 2,504.7 persons per square mile (2010); Race: 96.3% White, 0.8% Black, 0.4% Asian, 0.0% American Indian/Alaska Native, 0.0% Native Hawaiian/Other Pacific Islander, 2.5% Other, 2.2% Hispanic of any race (2010); Average household size: 2.39 (2010); Median age: 40.7 (2010); Males per 100 females: 94.3 (2010); Marriage status: 30.1% never married, 47.4% now married, 9.7% widowed, 12.8% divorced (2006-2010 5-year est.); Foreign born: 0.2% (2006-2010 5-year est.); Ancestry (includes multiple ancestries): 25.5% German, 20.2% Irish, 13.1% Italian, 12.7% Polish, 10.3% Lithuanian (2006-2010 5-year est.).
Economy: Single-family building permits issued: 0 (2011); Multi-family building permits issued: 0 (2011); Employment by occupation: 3.8% management, 1.3% professional, 12.9% services, 24.7% sales, 3.3% farming, 9.6% construction, 7.7% production (2006-2010 5-year est.).
Income: Per capita income: $20,076 (2006-2010 5-year est.); Median household income: $39,423 (2006-2010 5-year est.); Average household income: $42,211 (2006-2010 5-year est.); Percent of households with income of $100,000 or more: 3.1% (2006-2010 5-year est.); Poverty rate: 13.7% (2006-2010 5-year est.).
Education: Percent of population age 25 and over with: High school diploma (including GED) or higher: 84.8% (2006-2010 5-year est.); Bachelor's degree or higher: 6.6% (2006-2010 5-year est.); Master's degree or higher: 3.2% (2006-2010 5-year est.).
Housing: Homeownership rate: 74.8% (2010); Median home value: $72,200 (2006-2010 5-year est.); Median contract rent: $422 per month (2006-2010 5-year est.); Median year structure built: before 1940 (2006-2010 5-year est.).
Safety: Violent crime rate: 5.3 per 10,000 population; Property crime rate: 31.7 per 10,000 population (2011).
Transportation: Commute to work: 92.0% car, 0.7% public transportation, 4.8% walk, 1.6% work from home (2006-2010 5-year est.); Travel time to work: 46.4% less than 15 minutes, 30.8% 15 to 30 minutes, 8.7% 30 to 45 minutes, 6.7% 45 to 60 minutes, 7.5% 60 minutes or more (2006-2010 5-year est.)

Additional Information Contacts
Schuylkill Chamber of Commerce . . . . (570) 622-1942
http://www.schuylkillchamber.com

PORT CLINTON (borough). Covers a land area of 0.762 square miles and a water area of 0.005 square miles. Located at 40.58° N. Lat; 76.03° W. Long. Elevation is 417 feet.
History: Appalachian Trail passes through town from Blue Mt. to cross Schuylkill River.
Population: 328 (1990); 288 (2000); 326 (2010); Density: 428.1 persons per square mile (2010); Race: 98.2% White, 0.0% Black, 0.0% Asian, 0.0% American Indian/Alaska Native, 0.0% Native Hawaiian/Other Pacific Islander, 1.8% Other, 0.9% Hispanic of any race (2010); Average household size: 2.65 (2010); Median age: 37.5 (2010); Males per 100 females: 123.3 (2010); Marriage status: 23.4% never married, 52.8% now married, 9.8% widowed, 14.0% divorced (2006-2010 5-year est.); Foreign born: 0.0% (2006-2010 5-year est.); Ancestry (includes multiple

ancestries): 48.8% German, 24.9% Dutch, 13.1% Irish, 7.9% Pennsylvania German, 5.0% Italian (2006-2010 5-year est.).
Economy: Employment by occupation: 4.9% management, 0.0% professional, 5.6% services, 22.8% sales, 1.9% farming, 16.0% construction, 21.0% production (2006-2010 5-year est.).
Income: Per capita income: $16,443 (2006-2010 5-year est.); Median household income: $37,857 (2006-2010 5-year est.); Average household income: $48,964 (2006-2010 5-year est.); Percent of households with income of $100,000 or more: 10.9% (2006-2010 5-year est.); Poverty rate: 14.4% (2006-2010 5-year est.).
Education: Percent of population age 25 and over with: High school diploma (including GED) or higher: 67.8% (2006-2010 5-year est.); Bachelor's degree or higher: 6.3% (2006-2010 5-year est.); Master's degree or higher: 0.0% (2006-2010 5-year est.).
Housing: Homeownership rate: 69.1% (2010); Median home value: $85,400 (2006-2010 5-year est.); Median contract rent: $608 per month (2006-2010 5-year est.); Median year structure built: before 1940 (2006-2010 5-year est.).
Transportation: Commute to work: 83.8% car, 0.0% public transportation, 6.8% walk, 0.0% work from home (2006-2010 5-year est.); Travel time to work: 26.4% less than 15 minutes, 40.5% 15 to 30 minutes, 23.6% 30 to 45 minutes, 5.4% 45 to 60 minutes, 4.1% 60 minutes or more (2006-2010 5-year est.)

PORTER (township). Covers a land area of 17.985 square miles and a water area of 0.006 square miles. Located at 40.60° N. Lat; 76.51° W. Long.
Population: 2,564 (1990); 2,032 (2000); 2,176 (2010); Density: 121.0 persons per square mile (2010); Race: 98.4% White, 0.4% Black, 0.4% Asian, 0.3% American Indian/Alaska Native, 0.0% Native Hawaiian/Other Pacific Islander, 0.5% Other, 0.6% Hispanic of any race (2010); Average household size: 2.35 (2010); Median age: 44.8 (2010); Males per 100 females: 100.2 (2010); Marriage status: 17.5% never married, 64.5% now married, 9.8% widowed, 8.2% divorced (2006-2010 5-year est.); Foreign born: 1.0% (2006-2010 5-year est.); Ancestry (includes multiple ancestries): 50.1% German, 8.4% Dutch, 8.4% Irish, 8.0% American, 5.8% Welsh (2006-2010 5-year est.).
Economy: Employment by occupation: 5.4% management, 3.6% professional, 8.3% services, 20.3% sales, 5.7% farming, 11.2% construction, 13.8% production (2006-2010 5-year est.).
Income: Per capita income: $26,002 (2006-2010 5-year est.); Median household income: $49,000 (2006-2010 5-year est.); Average household income: $57,226 (2006-2010 5-year est.); Percent of households with income of $100,000 or more: 11.5% (2006-2010 5-year est.); Poverty rate: 8.5% (2006-2010 5-year est.).
Education: Percent of population age 25 and over with: High school diploma (including GED) or higher: 88.8% (2006-2010 5-year est.); Bachelor's degree or higher: 13.8% (2006-2010 5-year est.); Master's degree or higher: 5.4% (2006-2010 5-year est.).
Housing: Homeownership rate: 84.9% (2010); Median home value: $79,100 (2006-2010 5-year est.); Median contract rent: $432 per month (2006-2010 5-year est.); Median year structure built: before 1940 (2006-2010 5-year est.).
Transportation: Commute to work: 96.7% car, 1.3% public transportation, 0.0% walk, 2.0% work from home (2006-2010 5-year est.); Travel time to work: 17.2% less than 15 minutes, 32.0% 15 to 30 minutes, 14.4% 30 to 45 minutes, 24.3% 45 to 60 minutes, 12.1% 60 minutes or more (2006-2010 5-year est.)

Additional Information Contacts
Schuylkill Chamber of Commerce . . . . (570) 622-1942
http://www.schuylkillchamber.com

POTTSVILLE (city). Aka Beckville. County seat. Covers a land area of 4.166 square miles and a water area of 0 square miles. Located at 40.68° N. Lat; 76.21° W. Long. Elevation is 627 feet.
History: Pottsville had its beginnings when John Pott purchased land here in 1806. The rush to the coal fields in the mid-1820's had an impact on John Pott's town. Though Pottsville proved to have no coal, some of the newcomers went to work manufacturing equipment needed in the mines.
Population: 16,603 (1990); 15,549 (2000); 14,324 (2010); Density: 3,438.6 persons per square mile (2010); Race: 93.1% White, 3.1% Black, 0.7% Asian, 0.2% American Indian/Alaska Native, 0.0% Native Hawaiian/Other Pacific Islander, 2.9% Other, 2.5% Hispanic of any race (2010); Average household size: 2.26 (2010); Median age: 41.5 (2010); Males per 100 females: 89.7 (2010); Marriage status: 31.0% never

married, 49.3% now married, 9.3% widowed, 10.4% divorced (2006-2010 5-year est.); Foreign born: 2.1% (2006-2010 5-year est.); Ancestry (includes multiple ancestries): 30.1% German, 24.5% Irish, 13.7% Italian, 10.3% Dutch, 6.8% Polish (2006-2010 5-year est.).

Economy: Single-family building permits issued: 0 (2011); Multi-family building permits issued: 0 (2011); Employment by occupation: 7.0% management, 0.6% professional, 14.2% services, 21.1% sales, 3.8% farming, 8.4% construction, 7.9% production (2006-2010 5-year est.).

Income: Per capita income: $19,095 (2006-2010 5-year est.); Median household income: $31,772 (2006-2010 5-year est.); Average household income: $45,175 (2006-2010 5-year est.); Percent of households with income of $100,000 or more: 8.2% (2006-2010 5-year est.); Poverty rate: 18.7% (2006-2010 5-year est.).

Taxes: Total city taxes per capita: $378 (2009); City property taxes per capita: $180 (2009).

Education: Percent of population age 25 and over with: High school diploma (including GED) or higher: 83.6% (2006-2010 5-year est.); Bachelor's degree or higher: 14.3% (2006-2010 5-year est.); Master's degree or higher: 6.3% (2006-2010 5-year est.).

School District(s)

Pottsville Area SD (KG-12)
  2010-11 Enrollment: 3,034 . . . . (570) 621-2900

Two-year College(s)

McCann School of Business and Technology (Private, For-profit)
  Fall 2010 Enrollment: 3,978 . . . . (570) 622-7622
  2011-12 Tuition: In-state $9,805; Out-of-state $9,805
Schuylkill Health School of Nursing (Private, Not-for-profit)
  Fall 2010 Enrollment: 63 . . . . (570) 621-5035

Vocational/Technical School(s)

Empire Beauty School-Pottsville (Private, For-profit)
  Fall 2010 Enrollment: 102 . . . . (800) 223-3271
  2011-12 Tuition: $14,490

Housing: Homeownership rate: 58.0% (2010); Median home value: $71,900 (2006-2010 5-year est.); Median contract rent: $418 per month (2006-2010 5-year est.); Median year structure built: before 1940 (2006-2010 5-year est.).

Hospitals: Schuylkill Medical Center - East Norwegian Street; Schuylkill Medical Center - South Jackson Street

Safety: Violent crime rate: 41.8 per 10,000 population; Property crime rate: 136.4 per 10,000 population (2011).

Newspapers: Pottsville Republican & Evening Herald (Local news; Circulation 36,668)

Transportation: Commute to work: 89.8% car, 1.2% public transportation, 8.4% walk, 0.3% work from home (2006-2010 5-year est.); Travel time to work: 51.4% less than 15 minutes, 29.0% 15 to 30 minutes, 9.0% 30 to 45 minutes, 4.7% 45 to 60 minutes, 6.0% 60 minutes or more (2006-2010 5-year est.)

Airports: Schuylkill County /Joe Zerbey/ (general aviation)

Additional Information Contacts
City of Pottsville. . . . . (570) 622-1234
  http://www.ci.pottsville.pa.us
Schuylkill Chamber of Commerce . . . . (570) 622-1942
  http://www.schuylkillchamber.com

QUAKAKE (unincorporated postal area)
Zip Code: 18245
  Covers a land area of 3.605 square miles and a water area of 0 square miles. Located at 40.85° N. Lat; 76.03° W. Long. Elevation is 1,280 feet.
  Population: 348 (2010); Density: 96.5 persons per square mile (2010); Race: 99.7% White, 0.0% Black, 0.0% Asian, 0.0% American Indian/Alaska Native, 0.0% Native Hawaiian/Other Pacific Islander, 0.3% Other, 1.7% Hispanic of any race (2010); Average household size: 2.47 (2010); Median age: 47.0 (2010); Males per 100 females: 97.7 (2010); Homeownership rate: 92.2% (2010)

RAVINE (CDP). Covers a land area of 1.091 square miles and a water area of 0 square miles. Located at 40.57° N. Lat; 76.39° W. Long. Elevation is 574 feet.
Population: 634 (1990); 629 (2000); 662 (2010); Density: 606.8 persons per square mile (2010); Race: 97.6% White, 0.9% Black, 0.0% Asian, 0.8% American Indian/Alaska Native, 0.0% Native Hawaiian/Other Pacific Islander, 0.7% Other, 0.3% Hispanic of any race (2010); Average household size: 2.37 (2010); Median age: 41.6 (2010); Males per 100 females: 87.0 (2010); Marriage status: 29.1% never married, 53.2% now married, 11.4% widowed, 6.4% divorced (2006-2010 5-year est.); Foreign

born: 2.2% (2006-2010 5-year est.); Ancestry (includes multiple ancestries): 47.7% German, 19.8% Irish, 17.1% Dutch, 13.2% Pennsylvania German, 7.2% Lithuanian (2006-2010 5-year est.).
Economy: Employment by occupation: 8.3% management, 2.8% professional, 16.2% services, 4.4% sales, 4.4% farming, 7.9% construction, 3.0% production (2006-2010 5-year est.).
Income: Per capita income: $22,388 (2006-2010 5-year est.); Median household income: $41,316 (2006-2010 5-year est.); Average household income: $57,093 (2006-2010 5-year est.); Percent of households with income of $100,000 or more: 25.7% (2006-2010 5-year est.); Poverty rate: 10.5% (2006-2010 5-year est.).
Education: Percent of population age 25 and over with: High school diploma (including GED) or higher: 88.2% (2006-2010 5-year est.); Bachelor's degree or higher: 20.3% (2006-2010 5-year est.); Master's degree or higher: 11.2% (2006-2010 5-year est.).
Housing: Homeownership rate: 76.7% (2010); Median home value: $127,400 (2006-2010 5-year est.); Median contract rent: $352 per month (2006-2010 5-year est.); Median year structure built: 1956 (2006-2010 5-year est.).
Transportation: Commute to work: 98.4% car, 0.0% public transportation, 0.0% walk, 1.6% work from home (2006-2010 5-year est.); Travel time to work: 32.6% less than 15 minutes, 11.7% 15 to 30 minutes, 29.3% 30 to 45 minutes, 20.2% 45 to 60 minutes, 6.1% 60 minutes or more (2006-2010 5-year est.)

REILLY (township). Covers a land area of 15.630 square miles and a water area of 0.024 square miles. Located at 40.65° N. Lat; 76.33° W. Long.
Population: 835 (1990); 802 (2000); 726 (2010); Density: 46.4 persons per square mile (2010); Race: 98.6% White, 0.1% Black, 0.4% Asian, 0.0% American Indian/Alaska Native, 0.0% Native Hawaiian/Other Pacific Islander, 0.9% Other, 0.8% Hispanic of any race (2010); Average household size: 2.34 (2010); Median age: 45.5 (2010); Males per 100 females: 106.3 (2010); Marriage status: 15.4% never married, 69.6% now married, 4.0% widowed, 10.9% divorced (2006-2010 5-year est.); Foreign born: 0.0% (2006-2010 5-year est.); Ancestry (includes multiple ancestries): 37.0% German, 34.3% Irish, 12.9% Dutch, 11.6% Polish, 6.3% Pennsylvania German (2006-2010 5-year est.).
Economy: Employment by occupation: 2.7% management, 5.4% professional, 6.8% services, 16.5% sales, 3.5% farming, 13.2% construction, 14.6% production (2006-2010 5-year est.).
Income: Per capita income: $23,480 (2006-2010 5-year est.); Median household income: $46,711 (2006-2010 5-year est.); Average household income: $52,981 (2006-2010 5-year est.); Percent of households with income of $100,000 or more: 9.3% (2006-2010 5-year est.); Poverty rate: 1.7% (2006-2010 5-year est.).
Education: Percent of population age 25 and over with: High school diploma (including GED) or higher: 86.6% (2006-2010 5-year est.); Bachelor's degree or higher: 5.8% (2006-2010 5-year est.); Master's degree or higher: 1.5% (2006-2010 5-year est.).
Housing: Homeownership rate: 88.7% (2010); Median home value: $67,100 (2006-2010 5-year est.); Median contract rent: $423 per month (2006-2010 5-year est.); Median year structure built: before 1940 (2006-2010 5-year est.).
Safety: Violent crime rate: 0.0 per 10,000 population; Property crime rate: 137.4 per 10,000 population (2011).
Transportation: Commute to work: 96.5% car, 0.0% public transportation, 1.4% walk, 2.2% work from home (2006-2010 5-year est.); Travel time to work: 23.2% less than 15 minutes, 36.5% 15 to 30 minutes, 22.1% 30 to 45 minutes, 2.8% 45 to 60 minutes, 15.5% 60 minutes or more (2006-2010 5-year est.)

REINERTON (CDP). Covers a land area of 0.464 square miles and a water area of 0 square miles. Located at 40.59° N. Lat; 76.54° W. Long. Elevation is 833 feet.
Population: n/a (1990); n/a (2000); 424 (2010); Density: 913.0 persons per square mile (2010); Race: 95.8% White, 1.9% Black, 1.2% Asian, 0.9% American Indian/Alaska Native, 0.0% Native Hawaiian/Other Pacific Islander, 0.2% Other, 0.5% Hispanic of any race (2010); Average household size: 2.36 (2010); Median age: 43.8 (2010); Males per 100 females: 98.1 (2010); Marriage status: 12.6% never married, 73.5% now married, 8.3% widowed, 5.7% divorced (2006-2010 5-year est.); Foreign born: 2.6% (2006-2010 5-year est.); Ancestry (includes multiple ancestries): 60.6% German, 11.9% Dutch, 10.3% Polish, 6.7% Welsh, 6.1% Ukrainian (2006-2010 5-year est.).

Economy: Employment by occupation: 5.1% management, 10.5% professional, 13.2% services, 8.6% sales, 6.6% farming, 12.1% construction, 9.7% production (2006-2010 5-year est.).
Income: Per capita income: $26,644 (2006-2010 5-year est.); Median household income: $53,750 (2006-2010 5-year est.); Average household income: $63,990 (2006-2010 5-year est.); Percent of households with income of $100,000 or more: 17.0% (2006-2010 5-year est.); Poverty rate: 17.2% (2006-2010 5-year est.).
Education: Percent of population age 25 and over with: High school diploma (including GED) or higher: 92.0% (2006-2010 5-year est.); Bachelor's degree or higher: 21.9% (2006-2010 5-year est.); Master's degree or higher: 6.7% (2006-2010 5-year est.).
Housing: Homeownership rate: 83.3% (2010); Median home value: $90,800 (2006-2010 5-year est.); Median contract rent: $446 per month (2006-2010 5-year est.); Median year structure built: before 1940 (2006-2010 5-year est.).
Transportation: Commute to work: 91.1% car, 4.7% public transportation, 0.0% walk, 4.3% work from home (2006-2010 5-year est.); Travel time to work: 17.1% less than 15 minutes, 25.2% 15 to 30 minutes, 16.3% 30 to 45 minutes, 24.8% 45 to 60 minutes, 16.7% 60 minutes or more (2006-2010 5-year est.)

RENNINGERS (CDP). Covers a land area of 1.166 square miles and a water area of 0 square miles. Located at 40.65° N. Lat; 76.15° W. Long. Elevation is 768 feet.
Population: 446 (1990); 380 (2000); 574 (2010); Density: 492.4 persons per square mile (2010); Race: 91.3% White, 0.9% Black, 4.7% Asian, 0.0% American Indian/Alaska Native, 0.0% Native Hawaiian/Other Pacific Islander, 3.1% Other, 2.6% Hispanic of any race (2010); Average household size: 2.65 (2010); Median age: 39.1 (2010); Males per 100 females: 97.3 (2010); Marriage status: 5.4% never married, 75.6% now married, 6.3% widowed, 12.7% divorced (2006-2010 5-year est.); Foreign born: 14.7% (2006-2010 5-year est.); Ancestry (includes multiple ancestries): 24.2% Irish, 18.6% German, 15.0% Polish, 12.7% American, 7.3% English (2006-2010 5-year est.).
Economy: Employment by occupation: 0.0% management, 0.0% professional, 25.3% services, 15.8% sales, 0.0% farming, 4.7% construction, 4.7% production (2006-2010 5-year est.).
Income: Per capita income: $18,504 (2006-2010 5-year est.); Median household income: $53,152 (2006-2010 5-year est.); Average household income: $53,356 (2006-2010 5-year est.); Percent of households with income of $100,000 or more: 4.0% (2006-2010 5-year est.); Poverty rate: 0.0% (2006-2010 5-year est.).
Education: Percent of population age 25 and over with: High school diploma (including GED) or higher: 78.2% (2006-2010 5-year est.); Bachelor's degree or higher: 13.2% (2006-2010 5-year est.); Master's degree or higher: 3.0% (2006-2010 5-year est.).
Housing: Homeownership rate: 86.2% (2010); Median home value: $192,700 (2006-2010 5-year est.); Median contract rent: n/a per month (2006-2010 5-year est.); Median year structure built: 1991 (2006-2010 5-year est.).
Transportation: Commute to work: 94.7% car, 0.0% public transportation, 0.0% walk, 0.0% work from home (2006-2010 5-year est.); Travel time to work: 20.5% less than 15 minutes, 38.9% 15 to 30 minutes, 4.2% 30 to 45 minutes, 0.0% 45 to 60 minutes, 36.3% 60 minutes or more (2006-2010 5-year est.)

RINGTOWN (borough). Covers a land area of 0.439 square miles and a water area of 0 square miles. Located at 40.86° N. Lat; 76.24° W. Long. Elevation is 1,099 feet.
Population: 853 (1990); 826 (2000); 818 (2010); Density: 1,862.6 persons per square mile (2010); Race: 98.8% White, 0.2% Black, 0.1% Asian, 0.0% American Indian/Alaska Native, 0.0% Native Hawaiian/Other Pacific Islander, 0.9% Other, 0.9% Hispanic of any race (2010); Average household size: 2.36 (2010); Median age: 44.8 (2010); Males per 100 females: 92.9 (2010); Marriage status: 24.4% never married, 55.5% now married, 10.0% widowed, 10.2% divorced (2006-2010 5-year est.); Foreign born: 1.4% (2006-2010 5-year est.); Ancestry (includes multiple ancestries): 36.5% German, 20.8% Polish, 16.8% Irish, 10.1% Dutch, 7.6% Lithuanian (2006-2010 5-year est.).
Economy: Single-family building permits issued: 0 (2011); Multi-family building permits issued: 0 (2011); Employment by occupation: 5.0% management, 2.4% professional, 5.2% services, 18.6% sales, 2.6% farming, 9.7% construction, 13.9% production (2006-2010 5-year est.).

Income: Per capita income: $26,912 (2006-2010 5-year est.); Median household income: $52,045 (2006-2010 5-year est.); Average household income: $57,416 (2006-2010 5-year est.); Percent of households with income of $100,000 or more: 8.1% (2006-2010 5-year est.); Poverty rate: 6.4% (2006-2010 5-year est.).
Education: Percent of population age 25 and over with: High school diploma (including GED) or higher: 89.5% (2006-2010 5-year est.); Bachelor's degree or higher: 13.4% (2006-2010 5-year est.); Master's degree or higher: 3.9% (2006-2010 5-year est.).
Housing: Homeownership rate: 81.8% (2010); Median home value: $92,400 (2006-2010 5-year est.); Median contract rent: $427 per month (2006-2010 5-year est.); Median year structure built: before 1940 (2006-2010 5-year est.).
Safety: Violent crime rate: 0.0 per 10,000 population; Property crime rate: 36.5 per 10,000 population (2011).
Transportation: Commute to work: 95.0% car, 0.0% public transportation, 2.9% walk, 1.1% work from home (2006-2010 5-year est.); Travel time to work: 23.9% less than 15 minutes, 38.3% 15 to 30 minutes, 23.1% 30 to 45 minutes, 7.0% 45 to 60 minutes, 7.8% 60 minutes or more (2006-2010 5-year est.)

RUSH (township). Covers a land area of 23.182 square miles and a water area of 1.028 square miles. Located at 40.85° N. Lat; 75.96° W. Long.
Population: 3,517 (1990); 3,957 (2000); 3,412 (2010); Density: 147.2 persons per square mile (2010); Race: 98.6% White, 0.1% Black, 0.4% Asian, 0.0% American Indian/Alaska Native, 0.0% Native Hawaiian/Other Pacific Islander, 0.9% Other, 1.2% Hispanic of any race (2010); Average household size: 2.36 (2010); Median age: 50.4 (2010); Males per 100 females: 94.5 (2010); Marriage status: 22.6% never married, 60.3% now married, 12.1% widowed, 5.0% divorced (2006-2010 5-year est.); Foreign born: 1.4% (2006-2010 5-year est.); Ancestry (includes multiple ancestries): 29.6% German, 18.4% Irish, 13.9% Slovak, 12.9% Polish, 8.1% Italian (2006-2010 5-year est.).
Economy: Single-family building permits issued: 0 (2011); Multi-family building permits issued: 0 (2011); Employment by occupation: 11.9% management, 6.3% professional, 11.0% services, 9.1% sales, 2.2% farming, 8.2% construction, 8.3% production (2006-2010 5-year est.).
Income: Per capita income: $27,302 (2006-2010 5-year est.); Median household income: $49,144 (2006-2010 5-year est.); Average household income: $62,172 (2006-2010 5-year est.); Percent of households with income of $100,000 or more: 22.2% (2006-2010 5-year est.); Poverty rate: 8.8% (2006-2010 5-year est.).
Taxes: Total city taxes per capita: $196 (2009); City property taxes per capita: $76 (2009).
Education: Percent of population age 25 and over with: High school diploma (including GED) or higher: 85.5% (2006-2010 5-year est.); Bachelor's degree or higher: 27.8% (2006-2010 5-year est.); Master's degree or higher: 9.5% (2006-2010 5-year est.).
Housing: Homeownership rate: 90.0% (2010); Median home value: $144,200 (2006-2010 5-year est.); Median contract rent: $247 per month (2006-2010 5-year est.); Median year structure built: 1967 (2006-2010 5-year est.).
Transportation: Commute to work: 91.0% car, 0.0% public transportation, 6.0% walk, 2.9% work from home (2006-2010 5-year est.); Travel time to work: 29.7% less than 15 minutes, 26.9% 15 to 30 minutes, 17.9% 30 to 45 minutes, 17.9% 45 to 60 minutes, 7.8% 60 minutes or more (2006-2010 5-year est.)
Additional Information Contacts
Schuylkill Chamber of Commerce . . . . (570) 622-1942
    http://www.schuylkillchamber.com

RYAN (township). Covers a land area of 17.704 square miles and a water area of 0.265 square miles. Located at 40.79° N. Lat; 76.11° W. Long.
Population: 1,340 (1990); 1,451 (2000); 2,459 (2010); Density: 138.9 persons per square mile (2010); Race: 70.8% White, 22.7% Black, 0.2% Asian, 0.0% American Indian/Alaska Native, 0.0% Native Hawaiian/Other Pacific Islander, 6.3% Other, 6.8% Hispanic of any race (2010); Average household size: 2.40 (2010); Median age: 40.7 (2010); Males per 100 females: 276.0 (2010); Marriage status: 34.7% never married, 49.0% now married, 6.1% widowed, 10.2% divorced (2006-2010 5-year est.); Foreign born: 0.9% (2006-2010 5-year est.); Ancestry (includes multiple ancestries): 15.1% German, 15.0% Irish, 10.8% Polish, 6.2% Italian, 5.9% Lithuanian (2006-2010 5-year est.).

Economy: Single-family building permits issued: 4 (2011); Multi-family building permits issued: 0 (2011); Employment by occupation: 10.3% management, 1.7% professional, 9.5% services, 12.3% sales, 2.5% farming, 16.0% construction, 12.7% production (2006-2010 5-year est.).
Income: Per capita income: $17,724 (2006-2010 5-year est.); Median household income: $50,903 (2006-2010 5-year est.); Average household income: $63,995 (2006-2010 5-year est.); Percent of households with income of $100,000 or more: 18.6% (2006-2010 5-year est.); Poverty rate: 8.5% (2006-2010 5-year est.).
Education: Percent of population age 25 and over with: High school diploma (including GED) or higher: 78.1% (2006-2010 5-year est.); Bachelor's degree or higher: 11.0% (2006-2010 5-year est.); Master's degree or higher: 5.3% (2006-2010 5-year est.).
Housing: Homeownership rate: 91.6% (2010); Median home value: $123,400 (2006-2010 5-year est.); Median contract rent: $652 per month (2006-2010 5-year est.); Median year structure built: 1958 (2006-2010 5-year est.).
Safety: Violent crime rate: 0.0 per 10,000 population; Property crime rate: 12.2 per 10,000 population (2011).
Transportation: Commute to work: 96.3% car, 0.0% public transportation, 0.5% walk, 2.5% work from home (2006-2010 5-year est.); Travel time to work: 21.4% less than 15 minutes, 37.8% 15 to 30 minutes, 20.4% 30 to 45 minutes, 9.5% 45 to 60 minutes, 10.8% 60 minutes or more (2006-2010 5-year est.).
Additional Information Contacts
Schuylkill Chamber of Commerce . . . . (570) 622-1942
http://www.schuylkillchamber.com

SACRAMENTO (unincorporated postal area)
Zip Code: 17968
Covers a land area of 3.909 square miles and a water area of 0 square miles. Located at 40.63° N. Lat; 76.61° W. Long. Elevation is 696 feet.
Population: 329 (2010); Density: 84.2 persons per square mile (2010); Race: 99.1% White, 0.3% Black, 0.0% Asian, 0.3% American Indian/Alaska Native, 0.0% Native Hawaiian/Other Pacific Islander, 0.3% Other, 0.3% Hispanic of any race (2010); Average household size: 2.59 (2010); Median age: 42.5 (2010); Males per 100 females: 97.0 (2010); Homeownership rate: 79.5% (2010)

SAINT CLAIR (borough). Covers a land area of 1.233 square miles and a water area of 0 square miles. Located at 40.72° N. Lat; 76.19° W. Long. Elevation is 738 feet.
Population: 3,524 (1990); 3,254 (2000); 3,004 (2010); Density: 2,436.1 persons per square mile (2010); Race: 96.7% White, 1.0% Black, 0.5% Asian, 0.1% American Indian/Alaska Native, 0.0% Native Hawaiian/Other Pacific Islander, 1.7% Other, 1.6% Hispanic of any race (2010); Average household size: 2.17 (2010); Median age: 44.2 (2010); Males per 100 females: 92.8 (2010); Marriage status: 32.9% never married, 43.1% now married, 14.0% widowed, 10.0% divorced (2006-2010 5-year est.); Foreign born: 3.7% (2006-2010 5-year est.); Ancestry (includes multiple ancestries): 22.6% German, 21.6% Irish, 11.5% Polish, 9.1% Dutch, 7.6% Slovak (2006-2010 5-year est.).
Economy: Single-family building permits issued: 3 (2011); Multi-family building permits issued: 0 (2011); Employment by occupation: 1.6% management, 1.7% professional, 14.9% services, 15.8% sales, 2.9% farming, 14.7% construction, 9.7% production (2006-2010 5-year est.).
Income: Per capita income: $18,507 (2006-2010 5-year est.); Median household income: $32,759 (2006-2010 5-year est.); Average household income: $38,368 (2006-2010 5-year est.); Percent of households with income of $100,000 or more: 2.1% (2006-2010 5-year est.); Poverty rate: 16.7% (2006-2010 5-year est.).
Education: Percent of population age 25 and over with: High school diploma (including GED) or higher: 81.5% (2006-2010 5-year est.); Bachelor's degree or higher: 8.5% (2006-2010 5-year est.); Master's degree or higher: 0.6% (2006-2010 5-year est.).
School District(s)
Saint Clair Area SD (KG-08)
2010-11 Enrollment: 566 . . . . (570) 429-2716
Housing: Homeownership rate: 70.5% (2010); Median home value: $58,800 (2006-2010 5-year est.); Median contract rent: $446 per month (2006-2010 5-year est.); Median year structure built: before 1940 (2006-2010 5-year est.).
Transportation: Commute to work: 91.9% car, 0.0% public transportation, 7.3% walk, 0.8% work from home (2006-2010 5-year est.); Travel time to work: 38.4% less than 15 minutes, 40.6% 15 to 30 minutes, 11.1% 30 to

45 minutes, 3.5% 45 to 60 minutes, 6.5% 60 minutes or more (2006-2010 5-year est.)
Additional Information Contacts
Schuylkill Chamber of Commerce . . . . (570) 622-1942
http://www.schuylkillchamber.com

SCHUYLKILL (township). Covers a land area of 9.656 square miles and a water area of <.001 square miles. Located at 40.79° N. Lat; 76.01° W. Long.
History: Penn. State University-Schuylkill Campus (2-year) here. Settled 1748, laid out 1829, incorporated 1840.
Population: 1,230 (1990); 1,123 (2000); 1,129 (2010); Density: 116.9 persons per square mile (2010); Race: 98.6% White, 0.1% Black, 0.2% Asian, 0.2% American Indian/Alaska Native, 0.1% Native Hawaiian/Other Pacific Islander, 0.8% Other, 1.2% Hispanic of any race (2010); Average household size: 2.21 (2010); Median age: 49.2 (2010); Males per 100 females: 99.1 (2010); Marriage status: 18.5% never married, 56.7% now married, 15.8% widowed, 9.0% divorced (2006-2010 5-year est.); Foreign born: 0.6% (2006-2010 5-year est.); Ancestry (includes multiple ancestries): 27.2% German, 23.0% Irish, 15.0% Slovak, 10.5% Lithuanian, 10.0% Polish (2006-2010 5-year est.).
Economy: Employment by occupation: 0.8% management, 0.8% professional, 9.7% services, 19.1% sales, 2.7% farming, 12.4% construction, 9.7% production (2006-2010 5-year est.).
Income: Per capita income: $18,773 (2006-2010 5-year est.); Median household income: $32,875 (2006-2010 5-year est.); Average household income: $40,008 (2006-2010 5-year est.); Percent of households with income of $100,000 or more: 5.6% (2006-2010 5-year est.); Poverty rate: 11.7% (2006-2010 5-year est.).
Education: Percent of population age 25 and over with: High school diploma (including GED) or higher: 78.6% (2006-2010 5-year est.); Bachelor's degree or higher: 9.9% (2006-2010 5-year est.); Master's degree or higher: 4.7% (2006-2010 5-year est.).
Housing: Homeownership rate: 87.1% (2010); Median home value: $76,100 (2006-2010 5-year est.); Median contract rent: $503 per month (2006-2010 5-year est.); Median year structure built: before 1940 (2006-2010 5-year est.).
Transportation: Commute to work: 96.4% car, 0.0% public transportation, 2.5% walk, 1.1% work from home (2006-2010 5-year est.); Travel time to work: 15.8% less than 15 minutes, 46.6% 15 to 30 minutes, 16.9% 30 to 45 minutes, 7.3% 45 to 60 minutes, 13.3% 60 minutes or more (2006-2010 5-year est.)
Additional Information Contacts
Schuylkill Chamber of Commerce . . . . (570) 622-1942
http://www.schuylkillchamber.com

SCHUYLKILL HAVEN (borough). Covers a land area of 1.398 square miles and a water area of 0.006 square miles. Located at 40.63° N. Lat; 76.17° W. Long. Elevation is 554 feet.
Population: 5,610 (1990); 5,548 (2000); 5,437 (2010); Density: 3,888.9 persons per square mile (2010); Race: 94.5% White, 2.5% Black, 0.9% Asian, 0.3% American Indian/Alaska Native, 0.0% Native Hawaiian/Other Pacific Islander, 1.8% Other, 2.1% Hispanic of any race (2010); Average household size: 2.33 (2010); Median age: 40.2 (2010); Males per 100 females: 89.8 (2010); Marriage status: 26.9% never married, 49.9% now married, 9.4% widowed, 13.8% divorced (2006-2010 5-year est.); Foreign born: 1.5% (2006-2010 5-year est.); Ancestry (includes multiple ancestries): 48.7% German, 14.7% Irish, 13.3% Italian, 8.5% Dutch, 6.4% Pennsylvania German (2006-2010 5-year est.).
Economy: Single-family building permits issued: 0 (2011); Multi-family building permits issued: 0 (2011); Employment by occupation: 6.9% management, 0.8% professional, 9.7% services, 17.0% sales, 4.9% farming, 9.4% construction, 8.3% production (2006-2010 5-year est.).
Income: Per capita income: $23,885 (2006-2010 5-year est.); Median household income: $44,174 (2006-2010 5-year est.); Average household income: $55,389 (2006-2010 5-year est.); Percent of households with income of $100,000 or more: 11.3% (2006-2010 5-year est.); Poverty rate: 12.2% (2006-2010 5-year est.).
Taxes: Total city taxes per capita: $195 (2009); City property taxes per capita: $63 (2009).
Education: Percent of population age 25 and over with: High school diploma (including GED) or higher: 83.6% (2006-2010 5-year est.); Bachelor's degree or higher: 11.5% (2006-2010 5-year est.); Master's degree or higher: 4.7% (2006-2010 5-year est.).

School District(s)

Blue Mountain SD (KG-12)

 2010-11 Enrollment: 2,877 . . . . (570) 366-0515

Schuylkill Haven Area SD (KG-12)

 2010-11 Enrollment: 1,343 . . . . (570) 385-6705

Four-year College(s)

Pennsylvania State University-Penn State Schuylkill (Public)

 Fall 2010 Enrollment: 1,011 . . . . (570) 385-6000

 2011-12 Tuition: In-state $12,994; Out-of-state $19,434

Housing: Homeownership rate: 65.5% (2010); Median home value: $79,600 (2006-2010 5-year est.); Median contract rent: $458 per month (2006-2010 5-year est.); Median year structure built: before 1940 (2006-2010 5-year est.).

Newspapers: The Call (Local news; Circulation 4,047); Press Herald (Community news; Circulation 4,000); West Schuylkill Herald (Community news; Circulation 2,000)

Transportation: Commute to work: 90.5% car, 0.4% public transportation, 7.4% walk, 1.7% work from home (2006-2010 5-year est.); Travel time to work: 35.6% less than 15 minutes, 30.8% 15 to 30 minutes, 17.6% 30 to 45 minutes, 11.1% 45 to 60 minutes, 5.0% 60 minutes or more (2006-2010 5-year est.)

Additional Information Contacts

Borough of Schuylkill Haven . . . . (570) 385-2841

 http://www.schuylkillhaven.org

Schuylkill Chamber of Commerce . . . . (570) 622-1942

 http://www.schuylkillchamber.com

SELTZER (CDP). Covers a land area of 0.070 square miles and a water area of 0 square miles. Located at 40.70° N. Lat; 76.24° W. Long. Elevation is 896 feet.

Population: 285 (1990); 307 (2000); 350 (2010); Density: 5,000.0 persons per square mile (2010); Race: 98.6% White, 0.0% Black, 0.0% Asian, 0.0% American Indian/Alaska Native, 0.0% Native Hawaiian/Other Pacific Islander, 1.4% Other, 2.3% Hispanic of any race (2010); Average household size: 2.36 (2010); Median age: 47.8 (2010); Males per 100 females: 94.4 (2010); Marriage status: 20.7% never married, 55.6% now married, 14.6% widowed, 9.2% divorced (2006-2010 5-year est.); Foreign born: 0.0% (2006-2010 5-year est.); Ancestry (includes multiple ancestries): 32.1% Lithuanian, 24.3% Ukrainian, 19.6% Irish, 17.9% English, 11.8% German (2006-2010 5-year est.).

Economy: Employment by occupation: 4.7% management, 0.0% professional, 4.7% services, 5.4% sales, 5.4% farming, 4.7% construction, 14.0% production (2006-2010 5-year est.).

Income: Per capita income: $17,199 (2006-2010 5-year est.); Median household income: $48,681 (2006-2010 5-year est.); Average household income: $39,726 (2006-2010 5-year est.); Percent of households with income of $100,000 or more: n/a (2006-2010 5-year est.); Poverty rate: 14.9% (2006-2010 5-year est.).

Education: Percent of population age 25 and over with: High school diploma (including GED) or higher: 72.9% (2006-2010 5-year est.); Bachelor's degree or higher: 11.6% (2006-2010 5-year est.); Master's degree or higher: 11.6% (2006-2010 5-year est.).

Housing: Homeownership rate: 84.4% (2010); Median home value: $73,900 (2006-2010 5-year est.); Median contract rent: $466 per month (2006-2010 5-year est.); Median year structure built: before 1940 (2006-2010 5-year est.).

Transportation: Commute to work: 100.0% car, 0.0% public transportation, 0.0% walk, 0.0% work from home (2006-2010 5-year est.); Travel time to work: 50.4% less than 15 minutes, 15.4% 15 to 30 minutes, 0.0% 30 to 45 minutes, 14.6% 45 to 60 minutes, 19.5% 60 minutes or more (2006-2010 5-year est.)

SHENANDOAH (borough). Covers a land area of 1.511 square miles and a water area of 0.067 square miles. Located at 40.82° N. Lat; 76.20° W. Long. Elevation is 1,299 feet.

History: Settled 1835, laid out 1862, incorporated 1866.

Population: 6,221 (1990); 5,624 (2000); 5,071 (2010); Density: 3,356.5 persons per square mile (2010); Race: 86.3% White, 1.7% Black, 0.3% Asian, 0.4% American Indian/Alaska Native, 0.0% Native Hawaiian/Other Pacific Islander, 11.3% Other, 16.7% Hispanic of any race (2010); Average household size: 2.23 (2010); Median age: 41.3 (2010); Males per 100 females: 90.4 (2010); Marriage status: 36.2% never married, 38.5% now married, 12.6% widowed, 12.8% divorced (2006-2010 5-year est.); Foreign born: 8.8% (2006-2010 5-year est.); Ancestry (includes multiple

ancestries): 24.8% Polish, 20.2% Irish, 15.5% German, 10.6% Lithuanian, 9.8% Dutch (2006-2010 5-year est.).

Economy: Single-family building permits issued: 0 (2011); Multi-family building permits issued: 0 (2011); Employment by occupation: 9.0% management, 1.7% professional, 11.9% services, 13.2% sales, 4.7% farming, 16.1% construction, 18.1% production (2006-2010 5-year est.).

Income: Per capita income: $15,003 (2006-2010 5-year est.); Median household income: $27,659 (2006-2010 5-year est.); Average household income: $34,840 (2006-2010 5-year est.); Percent of households with income of $100,000 or more: 3.6% (2006-2010 5-year est.); Poverty rate: 28.9% (2006-2010 5-year est.).

Taxes: Total city taxes per capita: $185 (2009); City property taxes per capita: $104 (2009).

Education: Percent of population age 25 and over with: High school diploma (including GED) or higher: 76.3% (2006-2010 5-year est.); Bachelor's degree or higher: 6.5% (2006-2010 5-year est.); Master's degree or higher: 2.0% (2006-2010 5-year est.).

School District(s)

Shenandoah Valley SD (PK-12)

 2010-11 Enrollment: 1,107 . . . . (570) 462-1936

Housing: Homeownership rate: 60.8% (2010); Median home value: $32,300 (2006-2010 5-year est.); Median contract rent: $349 per month (2006-2010 5-year est.); Median year structure built: before 1940 (2006-2010 5-year est.).

Safety: Violent crime rate: 47.2 per 10,000 population; Property crime rate: 296.8 per 10,000 population (2011).

Transportation: Commute to work: 81.7% car, 1.5% public transportation, 11.5% walk, 5.3% work from home (2006-2010 5-year est.); Travel time to work: 42.3% less than 15 minutes, 27.4% 15 to 30 minutes, 22.2% 30 to 45 minutes, 3.2% 45 to 60 minutes, 4.9% 60 minutes or more (2006-2010 5-year est.)

Additional Information Contacts

Borough of Shenandoah . . . . (570) 462-1904

Schuylkill Chamber of Commerce . . . . (570) 622-1942

 http://www.schuylkillchamber.com

SHENANDOAH HEIGHTS (CDP). Covers a land area of 0.807 square miles and a water area of 0.022 square miles. Located at 40.83° N. Lat; 76.20° W. Long. Elevation is 1,654 feet.

Population: 1,386 (1990); 1,298 (2000); 1,233 (2010); Density: 1,528.6 persons per square mile (2010); Race: 96.8% White, 1.0% Black, 0.1% Asian, 0.0% American Indian/Alaska Native, 0.0% Native Hawaiian/Other Pacific Islander, 2.1% Other, 4.1% Hispanic of any race (2010); Average household size: 2.36 (2010); Median age: 45.4 (2010); Males per 100 females: 101.1 (2010); Marriage status: 28.6% never married, 59.0% now married, 7.5% widowed, 5.0% divorced (2006-2010 5-year est.); Foreign born: 0.0% (2006-2010 5-year est.); Ancestry (includes multiple ancestries): 38.9% Polish, 25.1% Irish, 16.7% Lithuanian, 16.5% Italian, 7.3% German (2006-2010 5-year est.).

Economy: Employment by occupation: 3.0% management, 0.0% professional, 0.0% services, 22.8% sales, 1.4% farming, 16.7% construction, 12.0% production (2006-2010 5-year est.).

Income: Per capita income: $24,412 (2006-2010 5-year est.); Median household income: $43,088 (2006-2010 5-year est.); Average household income: $61,096 (2006-2010 5-year est.); Percent of households with income of $100,000 or more: 13.7% (2006-2010 5-year est.); Poverty rate: 7.2% (2006-2010 5-year est.).

Education: Percent of population age 25 and over with: High school diploma (including GED) or higher: 96.4% (2006-2010 5-year est.); Bachelor's degree or higher: 16.2% (2006-2010 5-year est.); Master's degree or higher: 7.2% (2006-2010 5-year est.).

Housing: Homeownership rate: 88.9% (2010); Median home value: $80,300 (2006-2010 5-year est.); Median contract rent: n/a per month (2006-2010 5-year est.); Median year structure built: 1943 (2006-2010 5-year est.).

Transportation: Commute to work: 98.3% car, 0.0% public transportation, 0.0% walk, 1.7% work from home (2006-2010 5-year est.); Travel time to work: 18.4% less than 15 minutes, 50.7% 15 to 30 minutes, 16.5% 30 to 45 minutes, 9.0% 45 to 60 minutes, 5.4% 60 minutes or more (2006-2010 5-year est.)

Additional Information Contacts

Schuylkill Chamber of Commerce . . . . (570) 622-1942

 http://www.schuylkillchamber.com

SHEPPTON (CDP). Covers a land area of 0.055 square miles and a water area of 0 square miles. Located at 40.90° N. Lat; 76.12° W. Long. Elevation is 1,640 feet.
Population: 231 (1990); 239 (2000); 239 (2010); Density: 4,323.7 persons per square mile (2010); Race: 98.3% White, 0.0% Black, 0.8% Asian, 0.0% American Indian/Alaska Native, 0.0% Native Hawaiian/Other Pacific Islander, 0.9% Other, 0.0% Hispanic of any race (2010); Average household size: 2.51 (2010); Median age: 42.2 (2010); Males per 100 females: 107.8 (2010); Marriage status: 32.3% never married, 34.8% now married, 1.8% widowed, 31.1% divorced (2006-2010 5-year est.); Foreign born: 4.5% (2006-2010 5-year est.); Ancestry (includes multiple ancestries): 28.4% German, 27.0% Italian, 14.4% Scottish, 8.1% Lithuanian, 7.7% Welsh (2006-2010 5-year est.).
Economy: Employment by occupation: 11.9% management, 0.0% professional, 13.6% services, 26.3% sales, 5.1% farming, 22.0% construction, 11.9% production (2006-2010 5-year est.).
Income: Per capita income: $22,011 (2006-2010 5-year est.); Median household income: $57,500 (2006-2010 5-year est.); Average household income: $53,948 (2006-2010 5-year est.); Percent of households with income of $100,000 or more: n/a (2006-2010 5-year est.); Poverty rate: 5.1% (2006-2010 5-year est.).
Education: Percent of population age 25 and over with: High school diploma (including GED) or higher: 97.9% (2006-2010 5-year est.); Bachelor's degree or higher: 4.9% (2006-2010 5-year est.); Master's degree or higher: 2.8% (2006-2010 5-year est.).
Housing: Homeownership rate: 72.3% (2010); Median home value: $67,800 (2006-2010 5-year est.); Median contract rent: $488 per month (2006-2010 5-year est.); Median year structure built: before 1940 (2006-2010 5-year est.).
Transportation: Commute to work: 80.5% car, 0.0% public transportation, 16.9% walk, 2.5% work from home (2006-2010 5-year est.); Travel time to work: 55.7% less than 15 minutes, 18.3% 15 to 30 minutes, 2.6% 30 to 45 minutes, 18.3% 45 to 60 minutes, 5.2% 60 minutes or more (2006-2010 5-year est.)

SOUTH MANHEIM (township). Covers a land area of 20.776 square miles and a water area of 0.393 square miles. Located at 40.59° N. Lat; 76.15° W. Long.
Population: 1,570 (1990); 2,191 (2000); 2,507 (2010); Density: 120.7 persons per square mile (2010); Race: 98.0% White, 0.7% Black, 0.4% Asian, 0.0% American Indian/Alaska Native, 0.0% Native Hawaiian/Other Pacific Islander, 0.9% Other, 1.1% Hispanic of any race (2010); Average household size: 2.60 (2010); Median age: 43.3 (2010); Males per 100 females: 99.6 (2010); Marriage status: 16.7% never married, 69.5% now married, 4.3% widowed, 9.5% divorced (2006-2010 5-year est.); Foreign born: 1.4% (2006-2010 5-year est.); Ancestry (includes multiple ancestries): 48.2% German, 16.1% Irish, 12.3% Polish, 7.2% Dutch, 7.0% American (2006-2010 5-year est.).
Economy: Single-family building permits issued: 5 (2011); Multi-family building permits issued: 0 (2011); Employment by occupation: 16.4% management, 3.6% professional, 7.2% services, 13.9% sales, 3.7% farming, 7.5% construction, 4.8% production (2006-2010 5-year est.).
Income: Per capita income: $27,522 (2006-2010 5-year est.); Median household income: $61,888 (2006-2010 5-year est.); Average household income: $74,915 (2006-2010 5-year est.); Percent of households with income of $100,000 or more: 19.6% (2006-2010 5-year est.); Poverty rate: 3.7% (2006-2010 5-year est.).
Education: Percent of population age 25 and over with: High school diploma (including GED) or higher: 93.6% (2006-2010 5-year est.); Bachelor's degree or higher: 25.1% (2006-2010 5-year est.); Master's degree or higher: 10.6% (2006-2010 5-year est.).
Housing: Homeownership rate: 94.6% (2010); Median home value: $218,300 (2006-2010 5-year est.); Median contract rent: $831 per month (2006-2010 5-year est.); Median year structure built: 1990 (2006-2010 5-year est.).
Transportation: Commute to work: 93.4% car, 0.0% public transportation, 2.4% walk, 4.2% work from home (2006-2010 5-year est.); Travel time to work: 17.1% less than 15 minutes, 29.5% 15 to 30 minutes, 21.7% 30 to 45 minutes, 15.0% 45 to 60 minutes, 16.8% 60 minutes or more (2006-2010 5-year est.)
Additional Information Contacts
Schuylkill Chamber of Commerce . . . . (570) 622-1942
  http://www.schuylkillchamber.com

SPRING GLEN (unincorporated postal area)
Zip Code: 17978
  Covers a land area of 2.775 square miles and a water area of 0 square miles. Located at 40.62° N. Lat; 76.61° W. Long. Elevation is 623 feet. Population: 224 (2010); Density: 80.7 persons per square mile (2010); Race: 97.8% White, 0.0% Black, 0.4% Asian, 0.0% American Indian/Alaska Native, 0.0% Native Hawaiian/Other Pacific Islander, 1.8% Other, 0.4% Hispanic of any race (2010); Average household size: 2.24 (2010); Median age: 45.3 (2010); Males per 100 females: 93.1 (2010); Homeownership rate: 71.0% (2010)

SUMMIT STATION (CDP). Covers a land area of 1.089 square miles and a water area of 0 square miles. Located at 40.56° N. Lat; 76.20° W. Long. Elevation is 728 feet.
Population: 168 (1990); 208 (2000); 174 (2010); Density: 159.8 persons per square mile (2010); Race: 98.9% White, 0.0% Black, 0.6% Asian, 0.0% American Indian/Alaska Native, 0.0% Native Hawaiian/Other Pacific Islander, 0.5% Other, 0.0% Hispanic of any race (2010); Average household size: 2.18 (2010); Median age: 48.8 (2010); Males per 100 females: 87.1 (2010); Marriage status: 22.6% never married, 69.4% now married, 8.1% widowed, 0.0% divorced (2006-2010 5-year est.); Foreign born: 0.0% (2006-2010 5-year est.); Ancestry (includes multiple ancestries): 77.4% German, 46.8% Norwegian, 45.2% Polish, 12.1% Dutch, 8.1% French (2006-2010 5-year est.).
Economy: Employment by occupation: 0.0% management, 50.0% professional, 0.0% services, 23.2% sales, 0.0% farming, 0.0% construction, 0.0% production (2006-2010 5-year est.).
Income: Per capita income: $24,315 (2006-2010 5-year est.); Median household income: $62,634 (2006-2010 5-year est.); Average household income: $57,083 (2006-2010 5-year est.); Percent of households with income of $100,000 or more: n/a (2006-2010 5-year est.); Poverty rate: 0.0% (2006-2010 5-year est.).
Education: Percent of population age 25 and over with: High school diploma (including GED) or higher: 100.0% (2006-2010 5-year est.); Bachelor's degree or higher: 15.6% (2006-2010 5-year est.); Master's degree or higher: 0.0% (2006-2010 5-year est.).
Housing: Homeownership rate: 90.1% (2010); Median home value: n/a (2006-2010 5-year est.); Median contract rent: n/a per month (2006-2010 5-year est.); Median year structure built: before 1940 (2006-2010 5-year est.).
Transportation: Commute to work: 50.0% car, 0.0% public transportation, 0.0% walk, 50.0% work from home (2006-2010 5-year est.); Travel time to work: 0.0% less than 15 minutes, 46.4% 15 to 30 minutes, 53.6% 30 to 45 minutes, 0.0% 45 to 60 minutes, 0.0% 60 minutes or more (2006-2010 5-year est.)

TAMAQUA (borough). Covers a land area of 9.562 square miles and a water area of 0.156 square miles. Located at 40.80° N. Lat; 75.94° W. Long. Elevation is 810 feet.
History: Settled 1799, laid out 1829, incorporated 1832.
Population: 7,943 (1990); 7,174 (2000); 7,107 (2010); Density: 743.2 persons per square mile (2010); Race: 96.1% White, 0.7% Black, 0.3% Asian, 0.2% American Indian/Alaska Native, 0.0% Native Hawaiian/Other Pacific Islander, 2.7% Other, 3.5% Hispanic of any race (2010); Average household size: 2.34 (2010); Median age: 40.4 (2010); Males per 100 females: 95.2 (2010); Marriage status: 32.4% never married, 48.8% now married, 10.3% widowed, 8.4% divorced (2006-2010 5-year est.); Foreign born: 3.6% (2006-2010 5-year est.); Ancestry (includes multiple ancestries): 33.4% German, 22.1% Irish, 9.3% Polish, 8.3% English, 7.5% Italian (2006-2010 5-year est.).
Economy: Single-family building permits issued: 0 (2011); Multi-family building permits issued: 0 (2011); Employment by occupation: 3.9% management, 1.3% professional, 14.4% services, 17.0% sales, 4.8% farming, 9.1% construction, 4.8% production (2006-2010 5-year est.).
Income: Per capita income: $16,303 (2006-2010 5-year est.); Median household income: $28,567 (2006-2010 5-year est.); Average household income: $37,442 (2006-2010 5-year est.); Percent of households with income of $100,000 or more: 4.6% (2006-2010 5-year est.); Poverty rate: 24.2% (2006-2010 5-year est.).
Education: Percent of population age 25 and over with: High school diploma (including GED) or higher: 85.3% (2006-2010 5-year est.); Bachelor's degree or higher: 11.9% (2006-2010 5-year est.); Master's degree or higher: 5.4% (2006-2010 5-year est.).

Tamaqua Area SD (KG-12)

   2010-11 Enrollment: 2,098 . . . . (570) 668-2570

Housing: Homeownership rate: 62.4% (2010); Median home value: $65,000 (2006-2010 5-year est.); Median contract rent: $426 per month (2006-2010 5-year est.); Median year structure built: before 1940 (2006-2010 5-year est.).

Safety: Violent crime rate: 23.8 per 10,000 population; Property crime rate: 307.2 per 10,000 population (2011).

Transportation: Commute to work: 92.2% car, 0.0% public transportation, 3.9% walk, 3.9% work from home (2006-2010 5-year est.); Travel time to work: 37.7% less than 15 minutes, 24.1% 15 to 30 minutes, 23.7% 30 to 45 minutes, 7.6% 45 to 60 minutes, 6.8% 60 minutes or more (2006-2010 5-year est.)

Additional Information Contacts

Borough of Tamaqua . . . . (570) 668-6100

   http://www.tamaqua.net

Tamaqua Area Chamber of Commerce . . . . (570) 668-1880

   http://www.tamaqua.net

TOWER CITY (borough). Covers a land area of 0.315 square miles and a water area of 0 square miles. Located at 40.59° N. Lat; 76.55° W. Long. Elevation is 794 feet.

History: Laid out 1868; incorporated 1892.

Population: 1,514 (1990); 1,396 (2000); 1,346 (2010); Density: 4,279.3 persons per square mile (2010); Race: 98.1% White, 0.3% Black, 0.1% Asian, 0.4% American Indian/Alaska Native, 0.0% Native Hawaiian/Other Pacific Islander, 1.1% Other, 1.3% Hispanic of any race (2010); Average household size: 2.38 (2010); Median age: 40.0 (2010); Males per 100 females: 100.0 (2010); Marriage status: 28.7% never married, 55.5% now married, 6.8% widowed, 9.0% divorced (2006-2010 5-year est.); Foreign born: 0.2% (2006-2010 5-year est.); Ancestry (includes multiple ancestries): 50.7% German, 15.3% Dutch, 8.5% American, 7.9% Irish, 5.5% Polish (2006-2010 5-year est.).

Economy: Employment by occupation: 7.1% management, 1.9% professional, 7.5% services, 14.9% sales, 4.1% farming, 10.9% construction, 13.3% production (2006-2010 5-year est.).

Income: Per capita income: $20,877 (2006-2010 5-year est.); Median household income: $50,132 (2006-2010 5-year est.); Average household income: $52,598 (2006-2010 5-year est.); Percent of households with income of $100,000 or more: 8.4% (2006-2010 5-year est.); Poverty rate: 11.6% (2006-2010 5-year est.).

Education: Percent of population age 25 and over with: High school diploma (including GED) or higher: 83.6% (2006-2010 5-year est.); Bachelor's degree or higher: 8.8% (2006-2010 5-year est.); Master's degree or higher: 4.3% (2006-2010 5-year est.).

School District(s)

Williams Valley SD (KG-12)

   2010-11 Enrollment: 1,028 . . . . (717) 647-2167

Housing: Homeownership rate: 67.8% (2010); Median home value: $82,600 (2006-2010 5-year est.); Median contract rent: $413 per month (2006-2010 5-year est.); Median year structure built: before 1940 (2006-2010 5-year est.).

Transportation: Commute to work: 95.3% car, 0.0% public transportation, 3.6% walk, 1.2% work from home (2006-2010 5-year est.); Travel time to work: 25.6% less than 15 minutes, 29.5% 15 to 30 minutes, 19.0% 30 to 45 minutes, 14.8% 45 to 60 minutes, 11.1% 60 minutes or more (2006-2010 5-year est.).

Additional Information Contacts

Brush Valley Regional Chamber of Commerce. . . . . (570) 648-4675

   http://www.brushvalleychamber.com

TREMONT (borough). Covers a land area of 0.726 square miles and a water area of 0 square miles. Located at 40.63° N. Lat; 76.39° W. Long. Elevation is 751 feet.

Population: 1,814 (1990); 1,784 (2000); 1,752 (2010); Density: 2,414.3 persons per square mile (2010); Race: 98.3% White, 0.6% Black, 0.1% Asian, 0.1% American Indian/Alaska Native, 0.0% Native Hawaiian/Other Pacific Islander, 0.9% Other, 0.5% Hispanic of any race (2010); Average household size: 2.42 (2010); Median age: 42.6 (2010); Males per 100 females: 98.6 (2010); Marriage status: 27.6% never married, 46.4% now married, 11.6% widowed, 14.3% divorced (2006-2010 5-year est.); Foreign born: 0.0% (2006-2010 5-year est.); Ancestry (includes multiple ancestries): 41.2% German, 17.5% Irish, 9.9% American, 8.3% Pennsylvania German, 7.3% Dutch (2006-2010 5-year est.).

Economy: Employment by occupation: 6.5% management, 1.0% professional, 7.8% services, 20.3% sales, 5.5% farming, 12.7% construction, 11.7% production (2006-2010 5-year est.).

Income: Per capita income: $19,069 (2006-2010 5-year est.); Median household income: $36,458 (2006-2010 5-year est.); Average household income: $44,457 (2006-2010 5-year est.); Percent of households with income of $100,000 or more: 5.8% (2006-2010 5-year est.); Poverty rate: 13.8% (2006-2010 5-year est.).

Education: Percent of population age 25 and over with: High school diploma (including GED) or higher: 77.9% (2006-2010 5-year est.); Bachelor's degree or higher: 6.0% (2006-2010 5-year est.); Master's degree or higher: 1.0% (2006-2010 5-year est.).

Housing: Homeownership rate: 72.0% (2010); Median home value: $72,400 (2006-2010 5-year est.); Median contract rent: $386 per month (2006-2010 5-year est.); Median year structure built: before 1940 (2006-2010 5-year est.).

Transportation: Commute to work: 87.8% car, 0.0% public transportation, 5.9% walk, 4.6% work from home (2006-2010 5-year est.); Travel time to work: 31.9% less than 15 minutes, 32.5% 15 to 30 minutes, 19.1% 30 to 45 minutes, 9.1% 45 to 60 minutes, 7.4% 60 minutes or more (2006-2010 5-year est.)

Additional Information Contacts

Schuylkill Chamber of Commerce . . . . (570) 622-1942

   http://www.schuylkillchamber.com

TREMONT (township). Covers a land area of 24.183 square miles and a water area of 0 square miles. Located at 40.59° N. Lat; 76.44° W. Long. Elevation is 751 feet.

History: Laid out 1844, incorporated 1866.

Population: 297 (1990); 250 (2000); 280 (2010); Density: 11.6 persons per square mile (2010); Race: 99.3% White, 0.0% Black, 0.4% Asian, 0.0% American Indian/Alaska Native, 0.0% Native Hawaiian/Other Pacific Islander, 0.3% Other, 1.1% Hispanic of any race (2010); Average household size: 2.29 (2010); Median age: 42.4 (2010); Males per 100 females: 110.5 (2010); Marriage status: 15.6% never married, 65.9% now married, 8.4% widowed, 10.1% divorced (2006-2010 5-year est.); Foreign born: 0.0% (2006-2010 5-year est.); Ancestry (includes multiple ancestries): 40.0% German, 20.0% Irish, 13.0% American, 9.5% Pennsylvania German, 7.0% Dutch (2006-2010 5-year est.).

Economy: Employment by occupation: 15.0% management, 1.9% professional, 0.9% services, 19.6% sales, 0.0% farming, 10.3% construction, 16.8% production (2006-2010 5-year est.).

Income: Per capita income: $24,239 (2006-2010 5-year est.); Median household income: $45,000 (2006-2010 5-year est.); Average household income: $52,064 (2006-2010 5-year est.); Percent of households with income of $100,000 or more: 14.9% (2006-2010 5-year est.); Poverty rate: 15.0% (2006-2010 5-year est.).

Education: Percent of population age 25 and over with: High school diploma (including GED) or higher: 77.8% (2006-2010 5-year est.); Bachelor's degree or higher: 10.2% (2006-2010 5-year est.); Master's degree or higher: 1.2% (2006-2010 5-year est.).

Housing: Homeownership rate: 82.7% (2010); Median home value: $95,000 (2006-2010 5-year est.); Median contract rent: $367 per month (2006-2010 5-year est.); Median year structure built: 1944 (2006-2010 5-year est.).

Transportation: Commute to work: 96.3% car, 0.0% public transportation, 1.9% walk, 1.9% work from home (2006-2010 5-year est.); Travel time to work: 30.2% less than 15 minutes, 31.1% 15 to 30 minutes, 16.0% 30 to 45 minutes, 7.5% 45 to 60 minutes, 15.1% 60 minutes or more (2006-2010 5-year est.)

TUSCARORA (CDP). Covers a land area of 3.499 square miles and a water area of <.001 square miles. Located at 40.76° N. Lat; 76.06° W. Long. Elevation is 1,014 feet.

Population: 1,078 (1990); 939 (2000); 980 (2010); Density: 280.1 persons per square mile (2010); Race: 99.1% White, 0.1% Black, 0.2% Asian, 0.2% American Indian/Alaska Native, 0.1% Native Hawaiian/Other Pacific Islander, 0.3% Other, 1.2% Hispanic of any race (2010); Average household size: 2.22 (2010); Median age: 49.5 (2010); Males per 100 females: 99.2 (2010); Marriage status: 18.6% never married, 56.9% now married, 15.5% widowed, 9.0% divorced (2006-2010 5-year est.); Foreign born: 0.7% (2006-2010 5-year est.); Ancestry (includes multiple ancestries): 24.8% Irish, 24.5% German, 15.9% Slovak, 11.3% Lithuanian, 10.9% Polish (2006-2010 5-year est.).

Economy: Employment by occupation: 0.9% management, 0.9% professional, 9.4% services, 17.8% sales, 3.1% farming, 11.6% construction, 10.3% production (2006-2010 5-year est.).
Income: Per capita income: $18,643 (2006-2010 5-year est.); Median household income: $33,375 (2006-2010 5-year est.); Average household income: $40,054 (2006-2010 5-year est.); Percent of households with income of $100,000 or more: 4.7% (2006-2010 5-year est.); Poverty rate: 12.1% (2006-2010 5-year est.).
Education: Percent of population age 25 and over with: High school diploma (including GED) or higher: 80.3% (2006-2010 5-year est.); Bachelor's degree or higher: 10.5% (2006-2010 5-year est.); Master's degree or higher: 5.1% (2006-2010 5-year est.).
Housing: Homeownership rate: 86.9% (2010); Median home value: $72,300 (2006-2010 5-year est.); Median contract rent: $496 per month (2006-2010 5-year est.); Median year structure built: before 1940 (2006-2010 5-year est.).
Transportation: Commute to work: 95.8% car, 0.0% public transportation, 2.9% walk, 1.3% work from home (2006-2010 5-year est.); Travel time to work: 14.5% less than 15 minutes, 45.9% 15 to 30 minutes, 16.5% 30 to 45 minutes, 8.6% 45 to 60 minutes, 14.5% 60 minutes or more (2006-2010 5-year est.)

UNION (township). Covers a land area of 21.545 square miles and a water area of 0.160 square miles. Located at 40.85° N. Lat; 76.25° W. Long.
Population: 1,458 (1990); 1,308 (2000); 1,273 (2010); Density: 59.1 persons per square mile (2010); Race: 98.8% White, 0.6% Black, 0.0% Asian, 0.0% American Indian/Alaska Native, 0.0% Native Hawaiian/Other Pacific Islander, 0.6% Other, 0.4% Hispanic of any race (2010); Average household size: 2.39 (2010); Median age: 47.1 (2010); Males per 100 females: 106.3 (2010); Marriage status: 25.5% never married, 61.9% now married, 6.7% widowed, 5.9% divorced (2006-2010 5-year est.); Foreign born: 1.5% (2006-2010 5-year est.); Ancestry (includes multiple ancestries): 28.5% German, 21.7% Polish, 19.8% Irish, 13.5% Italian, 11.4% Lithuanian (2006-2010 5-year est.).
Economy: Employment by occupation: 10.9% management, 1.6% professional, 8.4% services, 11.7% sales, 4.4% farming, 13.6% construction, 8.3% production (2006-2010 5-year est.).
Income: Per capita income: $25,780 (2006-2010 5-year est.); Median household income: $47,727 (2006-2010 5-year est.); Average household income: $62,655 (2006-2010 5-year est.); Percent of households with income of $100,000 or more: 19.2% (2006-2010 5-year est.); Poverty rate: 7.8% (2006-2010 5-year est.).
Education: Percent of population age 25 and over with: High school diploma (including GED) or higher: 89.9% (2006-2010 5-year est.); Bachelor's degree or higher: 17.4% (2006-2010 5-year est.); Master's degree or higher: 5.1% (2006-2010 5-year est.).
Housing: Homeownership rate: 91.3% (2010); Median home value: $143,100 (2006-2010 5-year est.); Median contract rent: $385 per month (2006-2010 5-year est.); Median year structure built: 1974 (2006-2010 5-year est.).
Safety: Violent crime rate: 0.0 per 10,000 population; Property crime rate: 0.0 per 10,000 population (2011).
Transportation: Commute to work: 92.0% car, 0.0% public transportation, 0.6% walk, 6.6% work from home (2006-2010 5-year est.); Travel time to work: 25.3% less than 15 minutes, 42.0% 15 to 30 minutes, 18.3% 30 to 45 minutes, 6.7% 45 to 60 minutes, 7.7% 60 minutes or more (2006-2010 5-year est.)
Additional Information Contacts
Schuylkill Chamber of Commerce . . . . (570) 622-1942
http://www.schuylkillchamber.com

UPPER MAHANTONGO (township). Covers a land area of 14.849 square miles and a water area of 0 square miles. Located at 40.67° N. Lat; 76.62° W. Long.
Population: 696 (1990); 652 (2000); 655 (2010); Density: 44.1 persons per square mile (2010); Race: 99.1% White, 0.0% Black, 0.2% Asian, 0.0% American Indian/Alaska Native, 0.0% Native Hawaiian/Other Pacific Islander, 0.7% Other, 0.0% Hispanic of any race (2010); Average household size: 2.47 (2010); Median age: 43.2 (2010); Males per 100 females: 108.6 (2010); Marriage status: 25.9% never married, 63.1% now married, 6.2% widowed, 4.7% divorced (2006-2010 5-year est.); Foreign born: 0.0% (2006-2010 5-year est.); Ancestry (includes multiple ancestries): 54.4% German, 16.1% Pennsylvania German, 11.5% Dutch, 6.4% Italian, 6.1% Irish (2006-2010 5-year est.).

Economy: Employment by occupation: 13.3% management, 2.2% professional, 1.9% services, 16.1% sales, 9.2% farming, 21.2% construction, 13.9% production (2006-2010 5-year est.).
Income: Per capita income: $21,800 (2006-2010 5-year est.); Median household income: $54,432 (2006-2010 5-year est.); Average household income: $57,155 (2006-2010 5-year est.); Percent of households with income of $100,000 or more: 12.7% (2006-2010 5-year est.); Poverty rate: 5.1% (2006-2010 5-year est.).
Education: Percent of population age 25 and over with: High school diploma (including GED) or higher: 84.9% (2006-2010 5-year est.); Bachelor's degree or higher: 9.0% (2006-2010 5-year est.); Master's degree or higher: 3.4% (2006-2010 5-year est.).
Housing: Homeownership rate: 81.1% (2010); Median home value: $139,300 (2006-2010 5-year est.); Median contract rent: $435 per month (2006-2010 5-year est.); Median year structure built: 1957 (2006-2010 5-year est.).
Transportation: Commute to work: 87.1% car, 0.0% public transportation, 6.6% walk, 5.0% work from home (2006-2010 5-year est.); Travel time to work: 29.9% less than 15 minutes, 28.8% 15 to 30 minutes, 13.5% 30 to 45 minutes, 16.3% 45 to 60 minutes, 11.5% 60 minutes or more (2006-2010 5-year est.)

VALLEY VIEW (CDP). Covers a land area of 3.745 square miles and a water area of 0 square miles. Located at 40.65° N. Lat; 76.54° W. Long. Elevation is 807 feet.
Population: 1,789 (1990); 1,677 (2000); 1,683 (2010); Density: 449.4 persons per square mile (2010); Race: 98.5% White, 0.2% Black, 0.2% Asian, 0.1% American Indian/Alaska Native, 0.0% Native Hawaiian/Other Pacific Islander, 1.0% Other, 0.7% Hispanic of any race (2010); Average household size: 2.28 (2010); Median age: 46.6 (2010); Males per 100 females: 95.2 (2010); Marriage status: 21.8% never married, 65.4% now married, 7.7% widowed, 5.2% divorced (2006-2010 5-year est.); Foreign born: 0.0% (2006-2010 5-year est.); Ancestry (includes multiple ancestries): 54.6% German, 11.2% Irish, 9.9% American, 7.7% Dutch, 6.3% Italian (2006-2010 5-year est.).
Economy: Employment by occupation: 5.2% management, 1.3% professional, 11.1% services, 17.5% sales, 0.0% farming, 11.2% construction, 10.4% production (2006-2010 5-year est.).
Income: Per capita income: $25,213 (2006-2010 5-year est.); Median household income: $54,803 (2006-2010 5-year est.); Average household income: $62,653 (2006-2010 5-year est.); Percent of households with income of $100,000 or more: 16.7% (2006-2010 5-year est.); Poverty rate: 2.4% (2006-2010 5-year est.).
Education: Percent of population age 25 and over with: High school diploma (including GED) or higher: 79.6% (2006-2010 5-year est.); Bachelor's degree or higher: 13.9% (2006-2010 5-year est.); Master's degree or higher: 7.0% (2006-2010 5-year est.).
School District(s)
Tri-Valley SD (KG-12)
    2010-11 Enrollment: 871 . . . . (570) 682-9013
Housing: Homeownership rate: 75.7% (2010); Median home value: $122,100 (2006-2010 5-year est.); Median contract rent: $550 per month (2006-2010 5-year est.); Median year structure built: 1946 (2006-2010 5-year est.).
Newspapers: Citizen-Standard (Local news; Circulation 4,550)
Transportation: Commute to work: 86.5% car, 0.0% public transportation, 4.8% walk, 6.2% work from home (2006-2010 5-year est.); Travel time to work: 28.6% less than 15 minutes, 21.0% 15 to 30 minutes, 22.9% 30 to 45 minutes, 5.1% 45 to 60 minutes, 22.4% 60 minutes or more (2006-2010 5-year est.)
Additional Information Contacts
Schuylkill Chamber of Commerce . . . . (570) 622-1942
http://www.schuylkillchamber.com

WALKER (township). Covers a land area of 22.810 square miles and a water area of 0.043 square miles. Located at 40.73° N. Lat; 76.00° W. Long.
Population: 949 (1990); 936 (2000); 1,054 (2010); Density: 46.2 persons per square mile (2010); Race: 98.2% White, 0.5% Black, 0.1% Asian, 0.0% American Indian/Alaska Native, 0.0% Native Hawaiian/Other Pacific Islander, 1.2% Other, 1.3% Hispanic of any race (2010); Average household size: 2.70 (2010); Median age: 44.6 (2010); Males per 100 females: 97.7 (2010); Marriage status: 21.9% never married, 66.6% now married, 6.8% widowed, 4.7% divorced (2006-2010 5-year est.); Foreign born: 2.4% (2006-2010 5-year est.); Ancestry (includes multiple

ancestries): 45.6% German, 18.8% Irish, 9.7% Italian, 6.7% American, 6.5% Swiss (2006-2010 5-year est.).

Economy: Single-family building permits issued: 0 (2011); Multi-family building permits issued: 0 (2011); Employment by occupation: 9.7% management, 3.0% professional, 12.7% services, 13.6% sales, 2.5% farming, 10.7% construction, 6.2% production (2006-2010 5-year est.).

Income: Per capita income: $23,890 (2006-2010 5-year est.); Median household income: $54,706 (2006-2010 5-year est.); Average household income: $59,602 (2006-2010 5-year est.); Percent of households with income of $100,000 or more: 8.9% (2006-2010 5-year est.); Poverty rate: 5.0% (2006-2010 5-year est.).

Education: Percent of population age 25 and over with: High school diploma (including GED) or higher: 85.1% (2006-2010 5-year est.); Bachelor's degree or higher: 15.6% (2006-2010 5-year est.); Master's degree or higher: 5.8% (2006-2010 5-year est.).

Housing: Homeownership rate: 85.0% (2010); Median home value: $166,300 (2006-2010 5-year est.); Median contract rent: $529 per month (2006-2010 5-year est.); Median year structure built: 1962 (2006-2010 5-year est.).

Transportation: Commute to work: 95.5% car, 0.0% public transportation, 2.3% walk, 1.6% work from home (2006-2010 5-year est.); Travel time to work: 23.4% less than 15 minutes, 40.7% 15 to 30 minutes, 19.2% 30 to 45 minutes, 7.7% 45 to 60 minutes, 9.0% 60 minutes or more (2006-2010 5-year est.)

WASHINGTON (township). Covers a land area of 31.016 square miles and a water area of 0.062 square miles. Located at 40.56° N. Lat; 76.30° W. Long.

Population: 2,423 (1990); 2,750 (2000); 3,033 (2010); Density: 97.8 persons per square mile (2010); Race: 98.3% White, 0.4% Black, 0.2% Asian, 0.0% American Indian/Alaska Native, 0.1% Native Hawaiian/Other Pacific Islander, 1.0% Other, 0.5% Hispanic of any race (2010); Average household size: 2.68 (2010); Median age: 41.5 (2010); Males per 100 females: 107.2 (2010); Marriage status: 23.0% never married, 63.1% now married, 5.7% widowed, 8.2% divorced (2006-2010 5-year est.); Foreign born: 0.2% (2006-2010 5-year est.); Ancestry (includes multiple ancestries): 54.6% German, 11.4% Irish, 6.5% Pennsylvania German, 6.3% American, 5.3% Dutch (2006-2010 5-year est.).

Economy: Employment by occupation: 9.9% management, 1.2% professional, 6.7% services, 17.7% sales, 3.9% farming, 14.5% construction, 7.1% production (2006-2010 5-year est.).

Income: Per capita income: $24,499 (2006-2010 5-year est.); Median household income: $61,806 (2006-2010 5-year est.); Average household income: $65,545 (2006-2010 5-year est.); Percent of households with income of $100,000 or more: 18.7% (2006-2010 5-year est.); Poverty rate: 6.1% (2006-2010 5-year est.).

Education: Percent of population age 25 and over with: High school diploma (including GED) or higher: 82.9% (2006-2010 5-year est.); Bachelor's degree or higher: 12.5% (2006-2010 5-year est.); Master's degree or higher: 2.0% (2006-2010 5-year est.).

Housing: Homeownership rate: 88.8% (2010); Median home value: $159,500 (2006-2010 5-year est.); Median contract rent: $472 per month (2006-2010 5-year est.); Median year structure built: 1975 (2006-2010 5-year est.).

Transportation: Commute to work: 89.0% car, 0.1% public transportation, 3.8% walk, 5.0% work from home (2006-2010 5-year est.); Travel time to work: 20.8% less than 15 minutes, 30.9% 15 to 30 minutes, 19.3% 30 to 45 minutes, 17.1% 45 to 60 minutes, 11.8% 60 minutes or more (2006-2010 5-year est.)

Additional Information Contacts

Schuylkill Chamber of Commerce . . . . (570) 622-1942
http://www.schuylkillchamber.com

WAYNE (township). Covers a land area of 35.153 square miles and a water area of 0.056 square miles. Located at 40.58° N. Lat; 76.23° W. Long.

Population: 3,929 (1990); 4,721 (2000); 5,113 (2010); Density: 145.5 persons per square mile (2010); Race: 97.8% White, 0.3% Black, 0.7% Asian, 0.1% American Indian/Alaska Native, 0.0% Native Hawaiian/Other Pacific Islander, 1.1% Other, 1.3% Hispanic of any race (2010); Average household size: 2.47 (2010); Median age: 44.7 (2010); Males per 100 females: 102.8 (2010); Marriage status: 20.8% never married, 65.7% now married, 6.3% widowed, 7.2% divorced (2006-2010 5-year est.); Foreign born: 0.4% (2006-2010 5-year est.); Ancestry (includes multiple

ancestries): 46.4% German, 17.0% Polish, 15.5% Irish, 9.4% English, 9.2% Dutch (2006-2010 5-year est.).

Economy: Single-family building permits issued: 7 (2011); Multi-family building permits issued: 0 (2011); Employment by occupation: 14.8% management, 3.1% professional, 9.4% services, 17.5% sales, 2.5% farming, 7.6% construction, 6.1% production (2006-2010 5-year est.).

Income: Per capita income: $26,103 (2006-2010 5-year est.); Median household income: $56,396 (2006-2010 5-year est.); Average household income: $68,919 (2006-2010 5-year est.); Percent of households with income of $100,000 or more: 16.3% (2006-2010 5-year est.); Poverty rate: 5.7% (2006-2010 5-year est.).

Education: Percent of population age 25 and over with: High school diploma (including GED) or higher: 85.2% (2006-2010 5-year est.); Bachelor's degree or higher: 18.9% (2006-2010 5-year est.); Master's degree or higher: 6.1% (2006-2010 5-year est.).

Housing: Homeownership rate: 88.3% (2010); Median home value: $160,300 (2006-2010 5-year est.); Median contract rent: $553 per month (2006-2010 5-year est.); Median year structure built: 1986 (2006-2010 5-year est.).

Transportation: Commute to work: 91.2% car, 0.0% public transportation, 0.8% walk, 7.6% work from home (2006-2010 5-year est.); Travel time to work: 19.4% less than 15 minutes, 44.8% 15 to 30 minutes, 16.7% 30 to 45 minutes, 9.2% 45 to 60 minutes, 10.0% 60 minutes or more (2006-2010 5-year est.)

Additional Information Contacts

Schuylkill Chamber of Commerce . . . . (570) 622-1942
http://www.schuylkillchamber.com

WEST BRUNSWICK (township). Covers a land area of 30.437 square miles and a water area of 0.152 square miles. Located at 40.63° N. Lat; 76.06° W. Long.

Population: 3,206 (1990); 3,428 (2000); 3,327 (2010); Density: 109.3 persons per square mile (2010); Race: 97.2% White, 0.4% Black, 1.3% Asian, 0.0% American Indian/Alaska Native, 0.1% Native Hawaiian/Other Pacific Islander, 1.0% Other, 0.7% Hispanic of any race (2010); Average household size: 2.34 (2010); Median age: 48.1 (2010); Males per 100 females: 94.0 (2010); Marriage status: 17.1% never married, 67.8% now married, 5.7% widowed, 9.4% divorced (2006-2010 5-year est.); Foreign born: 2.3% (2006-2010 5-year est.); Ancestry (includes multiple ancestries): 45.1% German, 24.8% Irish, 12.0% Polish, 11.8% Italian, 8.4% English (2006-2010 5-year est.).

Economy: Single-family building permits issued: 8 (2011); Multi-family building permits issued: 0 (2011); Employment by occupation: 9.4% management, 3.4% professional, 11.0% services, 6.2% sales, 2.7% farming, 9.0% construction, 16.7% production (2006-2010 5-year est.).

Income: Per capita income: $31,656 (2006-2010 5-year est.); Median household income: $60,154 (2006-2010 5-year est.); Average household income: $74,625 (2006-2010 5-year est.); Percent of households with income of $100,000 or more: 22.2% (2006-2010 5-year est.); Poverty rate: 4.3% (2006-2010 5-year est.).

Education: Percent of population age 25 and over with: High school diploma (including GED) or higher: 80.3% (2006-2010 5-year est.); Bachelor's degree or higher: 24.6% (2006-2010 5-year est.); Master's degree or higher: 13.4% (2006-2010 5-year est.).

Housing: Homeownership rate: 81.0% (2010); Median home value: $156,000 (2006-2010 5-year est.); Median contract rent: $650 per month (2006-2010 5-year est.); Median year structure built: 1982 (2006-2010 5-year est.).

Transportation: Commute to work: 91.7% car, 3.0% public transportation, 0.0% walk, 3.3% work from home (2006-2010 5-year est.); Travel time to work: 30.1% less than 15 minutes, 19.9% 15 to 30 minutes, 30.4% 30 to 45 minutes, 8.7% 45 to 60 minutes, 10.9% 60 minutes or more (2006-2010 5-year est.)

Additional Information Contacts

Schuylkill Chamber of Commerce . . . . (570) 622-1942
http://www.schuylkillchamber.com

WEST MAHANOY (township). Covers a land area of 10.347 square miles and a water area of 0.077 square miles. Located at 40.80° N. Lat; 76.23° W. Long.

Population: 4,539 (1990); 6,166 (2000); 2,872 (2010); Density: 277.6 persons per square mile (2010); Race: 97.1% White, 0.5% Black, 0.2% Asian, 0.0% American Indian/Alaska Native, 0.0% Native Hawaiian/Other Pacific Islander, 2.2% Other, 3.1% Hispanic of any race (2010); Average household size: 2.28 (2010); Median age: 47.8 (2010); Males per 100

females: 102.4 (2010); Marriage status: 26.8% never married, 56.1% now married, 10.2% widowed, 6.9% divorced (2006-2010 5-year est.); Foreign born: 0.0% (2006-2010 5-year est.); Ancestry (includes multiple ancestries): 28.0% Polish, 22.7% Irish, 21.9% Lithuanian, 16.8% Italian, 14.4% German (2006-2010 5-year est.).

Economy: Single-family building permits issued: 1 (2011); Multi-family building permits issued: 0 (2011); Employment by occupation: 7.7% management, 0.0% professional, 3.8% services, 19.3% sales, 4.3% farming, 12.3% construction, 6.6% production (2006-2010 5-year est.).

Income: Per capita income: $24,638 (2006-2010 5-year est.); Median household income: $45,068 (2006-2010 5-year est.); Average household income: $57,362 (2006-2010 5-year est.); Percent of households with income of $100,000 or more: 11.7% (2006-2010 5-year est.); Poverty rate: 9.1% (2006-2010 5-year est.).

Education: Percent of population age 25 and over with: High school diploma (including GED) or higher: 84.1% (2006-2010 5-year est.); Bachelor's degree or higher: 13.2% (2006-2010 5-year est.); Master's degree or higher: 5.8% (2006-2010 5-year est.).

Housing: Homeownership rate: 89.2% (2010); Median home value: $77,500 (2006-2010 5-year est.); Median contract rent: $248 per month (2006-2010 5-year est.); Median year structure built: before 1940 (2006-2010 5-year est.).

Safety: Violent crime rate: 0.0 per 10,000 population; Property crime rate: 41.7 per 10,000 population (2011).

Transportation: Commute to work: 95.7% car, 0.0% public transportation, 1.0% walk, 1.9% work from home (2006-2010 5-year est.); Travel time to work: 24.0% less than 15 minutes, 50.2% 15 to 30 minutes, 12.7% 30 to 45 minutes, 6.1% 45 to 60 minutes, 6.9% 60 minutes or more (2006-2010 5-year est.)

Additional Information Contacts
Schuylkill Chamber of Commerce . . . . (570) 622-1942
   http://www.schuylkillchamber.com
West Mahanoy Township . . . . (570) 462-2958

WEST PENN (township). Covers a land area of 57.778 square miles and a water area of 0.221 square miles. Located at 40.74° N. Lat; 75.87° W. Long. Elevation is 682 feet.

Population: 3,693 (1990); 3,852 (2000); 4,442 (2010); Density: 76.9 persons per square mile (2010); Race: 98.8% White, 0.2% Black, 0.3% Asian, 0.0% American Indian/Alaska Native, 0.0% Native Hawaiian/Other Pacific Islander, 0.7% Other, 0.9% Hispanic of any race (2010); Average household size: 2.45 (2010); Median age: 47.0 (2010); Males per 100 females: 101.4 (2010); Marriage status: 21.4% never married, 56.2% now married, 9.9% widowed, 12.4% divorced (2006-2010 5-year est.); Foreign born: 1.3% (2006-2010 5-year est.); Ancestry (includes multiple ancestries): 36.3% German, 14.2% Pennsylvania German, 10.6% Irish, 8.2% Dutch, 7.6% English (2006-2010 5-year est.).

Economy: Single-family building permits issued: 4 (2011); Multi-family building permits issued: 0 (2011); Employment by occupation: 9.1% management, 2.5% professional, 9.0% services, 13.2% sales, 6.9% farming, 12.0% construction, 15.0% production (2006-2010 5-year est.).

Income: Per capita income: $25,436 (2006-2010 5-year est.); Median household income: $46,927 (2006-2010 5-year est.); Average household income: $56,660 (2006-2010 5-year est.); Percent of households with income of $100,000 or more: 14.0% (2006-2010 5-year est.); Poverty rate: 7.1% (2006-2010 5-year est.).

Education: Percent of population age 25 and over with: High school diploma (including GED) or higher: 86.2% (2006-2010 5-year est.); Bachelor's degree or higher: 16.7% (2006-2010 5-year est.); Master's degree or higher: 4.9% (2006-2010 5-year est.).

Housing: Homeownership rate: 86.7% (2010); Median home value: $157,300 (2006-2010 5-year est.); Median contract rent: $490 per month (2006-2010 5-year est.); Median year structure built: 1979 (2006-2010 5-year est.).

Transportation: Commute to work: 92.9% car, 0.0% public transportation, 1.7% walk, 5.4% work from home (2006-2010 5-year est.); Travel time to work: 24.8% less than 15 minutes, 28.3% 15 to 30 minutes, 32.5% 30 to 45 minutes, 8.7% 45 to 60 minutes, 5.7% 60 minutes or more (2006-2010 5-year est.)

Additional Information Contacts
Tamaqua Area Chamber of Commerce . . . . (570) 668-1880
   http://www.tamaqua.net

ZION GROVE (unincorporated postal area)
Zip Code: 17985

Covers a land area of 26.243 square miles and a water area of 0.133 square miles. Located at 40.91° N. Lat; 76.21° W. Long. Elevation is 827 feet. Population: 1,226 (2010); Density: 46.7 persons per square mile (2010); Race: 97.9% White, 0.4% Black, 0.5% Asian, 0.1% American Indian/Alaska Native, 0.0% Native Hawaiian/Other Pacific Islander, 1.1% Other, 1.5% Hispanic of any race (2010); Average household size: 2.46 (2010); Median age: 45.5 (2010); Males per 100 females: 108.1 (2010); Homeownership rate: 88.8% (2010)

Snyder County

Located in central Pennsylvania; bounded on the east by the Susquehanna River; drained by Penn Creek; crossed by the Jacks Mountains. Covers a land area of 328.705 square miles, a water area of 2.816 square miles, and is located in the Eastern Time Zone at 40.76° N. Lat., 77.07° W. Long. The county was founded in 1855. County seat is Middleburg.

Snyder County is part of the Selinsgrove, PA Micropolitan Statistical Area. The entire metro area includes: Snyder County, PA

Weather Station: Selinsgrove 2 S   Elevation: 419 feet

	Jan	Feb	Mar	Apr	May	Jun	Jul	Aug	Sep	Oct	Nov	Dec
High	35	39	48	61	71	80	84	82	75	63	51	40
Low	19	20	27	37	47	57	61	60	52	40	32	24
Precip	2.8	2.4	3.2	3.8	3.7	4.6	3.7	3.8	4.0	3.5	3.5	3.0
Snow	10.0	6.4	5.5	0.8	tr	0.0	0.0	0.0	0.0	0.1	1.2	4.2

High and Low temperatures in degrees Fahrenheit; Precipitation and Snow in inches

Population: 36,680 (1990); 37,546 (2000); 39,702 (2010); Race: 96.9% White, 1.1% Black, 0.5% Asian, 0.1% American Indian/Alaska Native, 0.0% Native Hawaiian/Other Pacific Islander, 1.4% Other, 1.7% Hispanic of any race (2010); Density: 120.8 persons per square mile (2010); Average household size: 2.53 (2010); Median age: 39.2 (2010); Males per 100 females: 97.5 (2010).

Religion: Six largest groups: 13.2% Methodist/Pietist, 12.4% Lutheran, 4.8% Catholicism, 4.0% Non-Denominational, 2.7% Presbyterian-Reformed, 2.3% Holiness (2010)

Economy: Unemployment rate: 8.1% (August 2012); Total civilian labor force: 19,225 (August 2012); Leading industries: 24.9% manufacturing; 22.4% retail trade; 13.3% accommodation & food services (2010); Farms: 998 totaling 100,179 acres (2007); Companies that employ 500 or more persons: 2 (2010); Companies that employ 100 to 499 persons: 16 (2010); Companies that employ less than 100 persons: 823 (2010); Black-owned businesses: n/a (2007); Hispanic-owned businesses: n/a (2007); Asian-owned businesses: 36 (2007); Women-owned businesses: 733 (2007); Retail sales per capita: $14,659 (2010). Single-family building permits issued: 57 (2011); Multi-family building permits issued: 4 (2011).

Income: Per capita income: $21,072 (2006-2010 5-year est.); Median household income: $44,713 (2006-2010 5-year est.); Average household income: $56,421 (2006-2010 5-year est.); Percent of households with income of $100,000 or more: 12.5% (2006-2010 5-year est.); Poverty rate: 11.7% (2006-2010 5-year est.); Bankruptcy rate: 2.00% (2011).

Education: Percent of population age 25 and over with: High school diploma (including GED) or higher: 81.6% (2006-2010 5-year est.); Bachelor's degree or higher: 15.3% (2006-2010 5-year est.); Master's degree or higher: 5.3% (2006-2010 5-year est.).

Housing: Homeownership rate: 74.2% (2010); Median home value: $122,900 (2006-2010 5-year est.); Median contract rent: $444 per month (2006-2010 5-year est.); Median year structure built: 1971 (2006-2010 5-year est.)

Health: Birth rate: 107.5 per 10,000 population (2011); Death rate: 86.1 per 10,000 population (2011); Age-adjusted cancer mortality rate: 190.7 deaths per 100,000 population (2009); Number of physicians: 10.6 per 10,000 population (2010); Hospital beds: 0.0 per 10,000 population (2008); Hospital admissions: 0.0 per 10,000 population (2008).

Elections: 2012 Presidential election results: 31.2% Obama, 67.2% Romney

National and State Parks: Snyder-Middleswarth State Park

Additional Information Contacts
Snyder County Government . . . . (570) 837-4208
   http://www.snydercounty.org

Snyder County Communities

ADAMS (township). Covers a land area of 20.176 square miles and a water area of 0.416 square miles. Located at 40.81° N. Lat; 77.18° W. Long.
Population: 833 (1990); 852 (2000); 907 (2010); Density: 45.0 persons per square mile (2010); Race: 98.2% White, 0.3% Black, 0.1% Asian, 0.0% American Indian/Alaska Native, 0.0% Native Hawaiian/Other Pacific Islander, 1.4% Other, 0.7% Hispanic of any race (2010); Average household size: 2.74 (2010); Median age: 40.8 (2010); Males per 100 females: 107.1 (2010); Marriage status: 28.5% never married, 57.0% now married, 6.3% widowed, 8.2% divorced (2006-2010 5-year est.); Foreign born: 0.6% (2006-2010 5-year est.); Ancestry (includes multiple ancestries): 49.6% German, 16.8% English, 10.4% American, 7.8% Dutch, 2.4% Irish (2006-2010 5-year est.).
Economy: Single-family building permits issued: 1 (2011); Multi-family building permits issued: 0 (2011); Employment by occupation: 7.5% management, 2.7% professional, 16.2% services, 10.3% sales, 1.1% farming, 20.5% construction, 13.7% production (2006-2010 5-year est.).
Income: Per capita income: $16,349 (2006-2010 5-year est.); Median household income: $45,486 (2006-2010 5-year est.); Average household income: $47,337 (2006-2010 5-year est.); Percent of households with income of $100,000 or more: 3.1% (2006-2010 5-year est.); Poverty rate: 22.5% (2006-2010 5-year est.).
Education: Percent of population age 25 and over with: High school diploma (including GED) or higher: 79.4% (2006-2010 5-year est.); Bachelor's degree or higher: 4.2% (2006-2010 5-year est.); Master's degree or higher: 1.5% (2006-2010 5-year est.).
Housing: Homeownership rate: 82.2% (2010); Median home value: $112,200 (2006-2010 5-year est.); Median contract rent: $471 per month (2006-2010 5-year est.); Median year structure built: 1966 (2006-2010 5-year est.).
Transportation: Commute to work: 91.9% car, 0.0% public transportation, 0.7% walk, 3.8% work from home (2006-2010 5-year est.); Travel time to work: 17.2% less than 15 minutes, 39.4% 15 to 30 minutes, 28.8% 30 to 45 minutes, 6.2% 45 to 60 minutes, 8.4% 60 minutes or more (2006-2010 5-year est.)

BEAVER (township). Covers a land area of 18.383 square miles and a water area of 0.157 square miles. Located at 40.75° N. Lat; 77.15° W. Long.
Population: 516 (1990); 527 (2000); 525 (2010); Density: 28.6 persons per square mile (2010); Race: 99.0% White, 0.4% Black, 0.0% Asian, 0.0% American Indian/Alaska Native, 0.0% Native Hawaiian/Other Pacific Islander, 0.6% Other, 0.2% Hispanic of any race (2010); Average household size: 2.63 (2010); Median age: 45.1 (2010); Males per 100 females: 98.9 (2010); Marriage status: 21.6% never married, 70.8% now married, 3.0% widowed, 4.6% divorced (2006-2010 5-year est.); Foreign born: 0.0% (2006-2010 5-year est.); Ancestry (includes multiple ancestries): 52.1% German, 8.2% Dutch, 6.0% Italian, 5.2% American, 4.8% Polish (2006-2010 5-year est.).
Economy: Single-family building permits issued: 2 (2011); Multi-family building permits issued: 0 (2011); Employment by occupation: 11.4% management, 1.3% professional, 10.5% services, 18.3% sales, 6.6% farming, 13.5% construction, 11.8% production (2006-2010 5-year est.).
Income: Per capita income: $21,944 (2006-2010 5-year est.); Median household income: $42,708 (2006-2010 5-year est.); Average household income: $55,422 (2006-2010 5-year est.); Percent of households with income of $100,000 or more: 12.5% (2006-2010 5-year est.); Poverty rate: 7.4% (2006-2010 5-year est.).
Education: Percent of population age 25 and over with: High school diploma (including GED) or higher: 80.4% (2006-2010 5-year est.); Bachelor's degree or higher: 13.4% (2006-2010 5-year est.); Master's degree or higher: 4.8% (2006-2010 5-year est.).
Housing: Homeownership rate: 81.0% (2010); Median home value: $133,900 (2006-2010 5-year est.); Median contract rent: $435 per month (2006-2010 5-year est.); Median year structure built: 1968 (2006-2010 5-year est.).
Transportation: Commute to work: 91.3% car, 0.0% public transportation, 4.4% walk, 4.4% work from home (2006-2010 5-year est.); Travel time to work: 41.6% less than 15 minutes, 27.4% 15 to 30 minutes, 14.6% 30 to 45 minutes, 9.1% 45 to 60 minutes, 7.3% 60 minutes or more (2006-2010 5-year est.)

BEAVER SPRINGS (CDP). Covers a land area of 1.355 square miles and a water area of 0.005 square miles. Located at 40.74° N. Lat; 77.22° W. Long. Elevation is 594 feet.
Population: 645 (1990); 634 (2000); 674 (2010); Density: 497.5 persons per square mile (2010); Race: 98.8% White, 0.1% Black, 0.1% Asian, 0.0% American Indian/Alaska Native, 0.0% Native Hawaiian/Other Pacific Islander, 1.0% Other, 0.1% Hispanic of any race (2010); Average household size: 2.36 (2010); Median age: 42.1 (2010); Males per 100 females: 93.1 (2010); Marriage status: 19.5% never married, 68.5% now married, 7.5% widowed, 4.5% divorced (2006-2010 5-year est.); Foreign born: 0.9% (2006-2010 5-year est.); Ancestry (includes multiple ancestries): 50.4% German, 16.2% Irish, 8.2% English, 8.1% American, 6.2% Italian (2006-2010 5-year est.).
Economy: Employment by occupation: 5.7% management, 1.7% professional, 9.3% services, 18.0% sales, 2.3% farming, 19.7% construction, 18.7% production (2006-2010 5-year est.).
Income: Per capita income: $17,008 (2006-2010 5-year est.); Median household income: $45,208 (2006-2010 5-year est.); Average household income: $45,412 (2006-2010 5-year est.); Percent of households with income of $100,000 or more: 3.1% (2006-2010 5-year est.); Poverty rate: 7.6% (2006-2010 5-year est.).
Education: Percent of population age 25 and over with: High school diploma (including GED) or higher: 81.8% (2006-2010 5-year est.); Bachelor's degree or higher: 8.1% (2006-2010 5-year est.); Master's degree or higher: 4.4% (2006-2010 5-year est.).
School District(s)
Midd-West SD (KG-12)
   2010-11 Enrollment: 2,202 . . . . (570) 837-0046
Housing: Homeownership rate: 67.0% (2010); Median home value: $98,300 (2006-2010 5-year est.); Median contract rent: $415 per month (2006-2010 5-year est.); Median year structure built: before 1940 (2006-2010 5-year est.).
Transportation: Commute to work: 96.0% car, 0.0% public transportation, 4.0% walk, 0.0% work from home (2006-2010 5-year est.); Travel time to work: 27.9% less than 15 minutes, 27.2% 15 to 30 minutes, 27.2% 30 to 45 minutes, 7.7% 45 to 60 minutes, 9.9% 60 minutes or more (2006-2010 5-year est.)

BEAVERTOWN (borough). Covers a land area of 0.767 square miles and a water area of <.001 square miles. Located at 40.75° N. Lat; 77.17° W. Long. Elevation is 643 feet.
Population: 877 (1990); 870 (2000); 965 (2010); Density: 1,258.4 persons per square mile (2010); Race: 98.3% White, 0.2% Black, 0.2% Asian, 0.0% American Indian/Alaska Native, 0.0% Native Hawaiian/Other Pacific Islander, 1.3% Other, 0.6% Hispanic of any race (2010); Average household size: 2.49 (2010); Median age: 36.9 (2010); Males per 100 females: 95.3 (2010); Marriage status: 22.6% never married, 65.9% now married, 6.1% widowed, 5.3% divorced (2006-2010 5-year est.); Foreign born: 5.5% (2006-2010 5-year est.); Ancestry (includes multiple ancestries): 51.3% German, 15.0% Italian, 6.1% Irish, 4.5% English, 3.2% American (2006-2010 5-year est.).
Economy: Single-family building permits issued: 2 (2011); Multi-family building permits issued: 0 (2011); Employment by occupation: 11.7% management, 1.8% professional, 13.2% services, 14.5% sales, 4.0% farming, 13.2% construction, 17.7% production (2006-2010 5-year est.).
Income: Per capita income: $16,393 (2006-2010 5-year est.); Median household income: $44,286 (2006-2010 5-year est.); Average household income: $47,017 (2006-2010 5-year est.); Percent of households with income of $100,000 or more: 4.5% (2006-2010 5-year est.); Poverty rate: 20.5% (2006-2010 5-year est.).
Education: Percent of population age 25 and over with: High school diploma (including GED) or higher: 88.1% (2006-2010 5-year est.); Bachelor's degree or higher: 6.9% (2006-2010 5-year est.); Master's degree or higher: 2.5% (2006-2010 5-year est.).
Housing: Homeownership rate: 71.9% (2010); Median home value: $107,700 (2006-2010 5-year est.); Median contract rent: $453 per month (2006-2010 5-year est.); Median year structure built: 1952 (2006-2010 5-year est.).
Transportation: Commute to work: 92.1% car, 0.0% public transportation, 0.7% walk, 4.7% work from home (2006-2010 5-year est.); Travel time to work: 41.5% less than 15 minutes, 36.2% 15 to 30 minutes, 14.3% 30 to 45 minutes, 2.2% 45 to 60 minutes, 5.7% 60 minutes or more (2006-2010 5-year est.)

CENTER (township). Covers a land area of 20.979 square miles and a water area of 0.142 square miles. Located at 40.84° N. Lat; 77.07° W. Long.

Population: 1,986 (1990); 2,162 (2000); 2,458 (2010); Density: 117.2 persons per square mile (2010); Race: 98.5% White, 0.7% Black, 0.0% Asian, 0.0% American Indian/Alaska Native, 0.0% Native Hawaiian/Other Pacific Islander, 0.8% Other, 1.3% Hispanic of any race (2010); Average household size: 2.87 (2010); Median age: 34.6 (2010); Males per 100 females: 99.2 (2010); Marriage status: 23.1% never married, 60.4% now married, 6.8% widowed, 9.6% divorced (2006-2010 5-year est.); Foreign born: 1.0% (2006-2010 5-year est.); Ancestry (includes multiple ancestries): 48.5% German, 10.3% English, 10.1% Irish, 8.6% American, 6.7% Dutch (2006-2010 5-year est.).

Economy: Single-family building permits issued: 1 (2011); Multi-family building permits issued: 0 (2011); Employment by occupation: 6.3% management, 0.7% professional, 12.6% services, 11.1% sales, 6.5% farming, 15.3% construction, 9.2% production (2006-2010 5-year est.).

Income: Per capita income: $18,903 (2006-2010 5-year est.); Median household income: $39,879 (2006-2010 5-year est.); Average household income: $53,634 (2006-2010 5-year est.); Percent of households with income of $100,000 or more: 11.2% (2006-2010 5-year est.); Poverty rate: 16.2% (2006-2010 5-year est.).

Education: Percent of population age 25 and over with: High school diploma (including GED) or higher: 72.0% (2006-2010 5-year est.); Bachelor's degree or higher: 9.7% (2006-2010 5-year est.); Master's degree or higher: 2.9% (2006-2010 5-year est.).

Housing: Homeownership rate: 77.3% (2010); Median home value: $119,700 (2006-2010 5-year est.); Median contract rent: $425 per month (2006-2010 5-year est.); Median year structure built: 1979 (2006-2010 5-year est.).

Transportation: Commute to work: 91.1% car, 0.0% public transportation, 2.9% walk, 3.3% work from home (2006-2010 5-year est.); Travel time to work: 27.2% less than 15 minutes, 39.6% 15 to 30 minutes, 23.5% 30 to 45 minutes, 5.0% 45 to 60 minutes, 4.6% 60 minutes or more (2006-2010 5-year est.)

Additional Information Contacts
Central PA Chamber of Commerce . . . . (570) 742-7341
    http://www.centralpachamber.com/index.php

CHAPMAN (township). Covers a land area of 13.535 square miles and a water area of 0.049 square miles. Located at 40.68° N. Lat; 76.94° W. Long. Elevation is 436 feet.

Population: 1,442 (1990); 1,426 (2000); 1,554 (2010); Density: 114.8 persons per square mile (2010); Race: 98.5% White, 1.0% Black, 0.1% Asian, 0.0% American Indian/Alaska Native, 0.0% Native Hawaiian/Other Pacific Islander, 0.4% Other, 0.8% Hispanic of any race (2010); Average household size: 3.48 (2010); Median age: 29.0 (2010); Males per 100 females: 96.2 (2010); Marriage status: 36.1% never married, 51.0% now married, 7.1% widowed, 5.9% divorced (2006-2010 5-year est.); Foreign born: 0.9% (2006-2010 5-year est.); Ancestry (includes multiple ancestries): 47.5% German, 15.6% American, 13.4% Swiss, 5.8% Pennsylvania German, 5.2% French Canadian (2006-2010 5-year est.).

Economy: Single-family building permits issued: 2 (2011); Multi-family building permits issued: 0 (2011); Employment by occupation: 9.4% management, 0.6% professional, 12.4% services, 13.1% sales, 2.8% farming, 5.0% construction, 15.1% production (2006-2010 5-year est.).

Income: Per capita income: $14,799 (2006-2010 5-year est.); Median household income: $53,125 (2006-2010 5-year est.); Average household income: $57,164 (2006-2010 5-year est.); Percent of households with income of $100,000 or more: 12.1% (2006-2010 5-year est.); Poverty rate: 10.7% (2006-2010 5-year est.).

Education: Percent of population age 25 and over with: High school diploma (including GED) or higher: 56.9% (2006-2010 5-year est.); Bachelor's degree or higher: 4.5% (2006-2010 5-year est.); Master's degree or higher: 0.4% (2006-2010 5-year est.).

Housing: Homeownership rate: 83.7% (2010); Median home value: $147,800 (2006-2010 5-year est.); Median contract rent: $343 per month (2006-2010 5-year est.); Median year structure built: 1969 (2006-2010 5-year est.).

Transportation: Commute to work: 70.5% car, 0.9% public transportation, 9.8% walk, 9.2% work from home (2006-2010 5-year est.); Travel time to work: 33.6% less than 15 minutes, 26.1% 15 to 30 minutes, 11.4% 30 to 45 minutes, 18.6% 45 to 60 minutes, 10.3% 60 minutes or more (2006-2010 5-year est.)

Additional Information Contacts
Greater Lehigh Valley Chamber of Commerce . . . . (610) 841-5800
    http://www.lehighvalleychamber.org

FRANKLIN (township). Covers a land area of 27.878 square miles and a water area of 0.193 square miles. Located at 40.78° N. Lat; 77.07° W. Long.

Population: 2,158 (1990); 2,094 (2000); 2,259 (2010); Density: 81.0 persons per square mile (2010); Race: 98.8% White, 0.4% Black, 0.1% Asian, 0.0% American Indian/Alaska Native, 0.0% Native Hawaiian/Other Pacific Islander, 0.7% Other, 0.7% Hispanic of any race (2010); Average household size: 2.46 (2010); Median age: 43.6 (2010); Males per 100 females: 99.0 (2010); Marriage status: 19.6% never married, 63.1% now married, 8.3% widowed, 9.0% divorced (2006-2010 5-year est.); Foreign born: 0.2% (2006-2010 5-year est.); Ancestry (includes multiple ancestries): 57.5% German, 12.0% American, 7.7% Pennsylvania German, 5.5% Dutch, 5.3% Irish (2006-2010 5-year est.).

Economy: Single-family building permits issued: 3 (2011); Multi-family building permits issued: 0 (2011); Employment by occupation: 3.2% management, 2.1% professional, 8.1% services, 10.1% sales, 3.5% farming, 15.2% construction, 19.6% production (2006-2010 5-year est.).

Income: Per capita income: $19,445 (2006-2010 5-year est.); Median household income: $39,028 (2006-2010 5-year est.); Average household income: $45,119 (2006-2010 5-year est.); Percent of households with income of $100,000 or more: 4.8% (2006-2010 5-year est.); Poverty rate: 9.7% (2006-2010 5-year est.).

Education: Percent of population age 25 and over with: High school diploma (including GED) or higher: 77.7% (2006-2010 5-year est.); Bachelor's degree or higher: 14.3% (2006-2010 5-year est.); Master's degree or higher: 1.6% (2006-2010 5-year est.).

Housing: Homeownership rate: 82.0% (2010); Median home value: $109,300 (2006-2010 5-year est.); Median contract rent: $393 per month (2006-2010 5-year est.); Median year structure built: 1968 (2006-2010 5-year est.).

Transportation: Commute to work: 92.8% car, 0.0% public transportation, 1.4% walk, 4.0% work from home (2006-2010 5-year est.); Travel time to work: 36.5% less than 15 minutes, 43.8% 15 to 30 minutes, 10.4% 30 to 45 minutes, 3.8% 45 to 60 minutes, 5.5% 60 minutes or more (2006-2010 5-year est.)

Additional Information Contacts
Greater Susquehanna Valley Chamber of Commerce . . . . (570) 743-4100
    http://www.gsvcc.org

FREEBURG (borough). Covers a land area of 0.319 square miles and a water area of 0 square miles. Located at 40.76° N. Lat; 76.94° W. Long. Elevation is 531 feet.

Population: 640 (1990); 584 (2000); 575 (2010); Density: 1,803.2 persons per square mile (2010); Race: 98.8% White, 0.2% Black, 0.2% Asian, 0.0% American Indian/Alaska Native, 0.0% Native Hawaiian/Other Pacific Islander, 0.8% Other, 0.2% Hispanic of any race (2010); Average household size: 2.24 (2010); Median age: 43.5 (2010); Males per 100 females: 90.4 (2010); Marriage status: 15.6% never married, 67.2% now married, 10.8% widowed, 6.5% divorced (2006-2010 5-year est.); Foreign born: 0.8% (2006-2010 5-year est.); Ancestry (includes multiple ancestries): 61.2% German, 10.5% Irish, 9.7% English, 6.9% Polish, 5.3% Dutch (2006-2010 5-year est.).

Economy: Single-family building permits issued: 0 (2011); Multi-family building permits issued: 0 (2011); Employment by occupation: 3.5% management, 5.9% professional, 12.9% services, 12.9% sales, 2.3% farming, 7.8% construction, 9.0% production (2006-2010 5-year est.).

Income: Per capita income: $20,100 (2006-2010 5-year est.); Median household income: $39,531 (2006-2010 5-year est.); Average household income: $45,311 (2006-2010 5-year est.); Percent of households with income of $100,000 or more: 7.9% (2006-2010 5-year est.); Poverty rate: 4.7% (2006-2010 5-year est.).

Education: Percent of population age 25 and over with: High school diploma (including GED) or higher: 78.7% (2006-2010 5-year est.); Bachelor's degree or higher: 11.2% (2006-2010 5-year est.); Master's degree or higher: 5.2% (2006-2010 5-year est.).

Housing: Homeownership rate: 76.6% (2010); Median home value: $101,400 (2006-2010 5-year est.); Median contract rent: $445 per month (2006-2010 5-year est.); Median year structure built: before 1940 (2006-2010 5-year est.).

Transportation: Commute to work: 89.6% car, 5.4% public transportation, 0.0% walk, 5.0% work from home (2006-2010 5-year est.); Travel time to

work: 23.2% less than 15 minutes, 35.5% 15 to 30 minutes, 13.6% 30 to 45 minutes, 11.4% 45 to 60 minutes, 16.2% 60 minutes or more (2006-2010 5-year est.)

HUMMELS WHARF (CDP). Covers a land area of 0.788 square miles and a water area of 0.009 square miles. Located at 40.83° N. Lat; 76.84° W. Long. Elevation is 456 feet.

Population: 642 (1990); 641 (2000); 1,353 (2010); Density: 1,716.7 persons per square mile (2010); Race: 96.1% White, 1.3% Black, 1.1% Asian, 0.1% American Indian/Alaska Native, 0.1% Native Hawaiian/Other Pacific Islander, 1.3% Other, 2.7% Hispanic of any race (2010); Average household size: 2.24 (2010); Median age: 44.2 (2010); Males per 100 females: 93.6 (2010); Marriage status: 16.6% never married, 68.7% now married, 8.7% widowed, 5.9% divorced (2006-2010 5-year est.); Foreign born: 4.1% (2006-2010 5-year est.); Ancestry (includes multiple ancestries): 56.1% German, 13.4% Irish, 8.3% English, 5.7% Italian, 5.0% Czech (2006-2010 5-year est.).

Economy: Employment by occupation: 7.7% management, 2.5% professional, 9.6% services, 28.3% sales, 1.1% farming, 12.4% construction, 5.6% production (2006-2010 5-year est.).

Income: Per capita income: $32,705 (2006-2010 5-year est.); Median household income: $52,143 (2006-2010 5-year est.); Average household income: $77,586 (2006-2010 5-year est.); Percent of households with income of $100,000 or more: 33.2% (2006-2010 5-year est.); Poverty rate: 3.5% (2006-2010 5-year est.).

Education: Percent of population age 25 and over with: High school diploma (including GED) or higher: 91.8% (2006-2010 5-year est.); Bachelor's degree or higher: 24.3% (2006-2010 5-year est.); Master's degree or higher: 6.0% (2006-2010 5-year est.).

Housing: Homeownership rate: 78.1% (2010); Median home value: $121,600 (2006-2010 5-year est.); Median contract rent: $492 per month (2006-2010 5-year est.); Median year structure built: 1974 (2006-2010 5-year est.).

Transportation: Commute to work: 94.3% car, 0.0% public transportation, 0.0% walk, 5.7% work from home (2006-2010 5-year est.); Travel time to work: 42.3% less than 15 minutes, 36.3% 15 to 30 minutes, 5.9% 30 to 45 minutes, 8.6% 45 to 60 minutes, 6.9% 60 minutes or more (2006-2010 5-year est.)

JACKSON (township). Covers a land area of 14.536 square miles and a water area of 0.300 square miles. Located at 40.86° N. Lat; 76.96° W. Long.

Population: 1,383 (1990); 1,276 (2000); 1,382 (2010); Density: 95.1 persons per square mile (2010); Race: 98.2% White, 0.6% Black, 0.3% Asian, 0.1% American Indian/Alaska Native, 0.0% Native Hawaiian/Other Pacific Islander, 0.8% Other, 0.9% Hispanic of any race (2010); Average household size: 2.67 (2010); Median age: 40.7 (2010); Males per 100 females: 100.0 (2010); Marriage status: 20.7% never married, 65.6% now married, 5.3% widowed, 8.4% divorced (2006-2010 5-year est.); Foreign born: 0.5% (2006-2010 5-year est.); Ancestry (includes multiple ancestries): 65.2% German, 8.4% American, 6.5% Irish, 6.3% Polish, 5.6% Italian (2006-2010 5-year est.).

Economy: Single-family building permits issued: 5 (2011); Multi-family building permits issued: 0 (2011); Employment by occupation: 1.2% management, 1.8% professional, 10.0% services, 26.3% sales, 3.9% farming, 17.6% construction, 9.6% production (2006-2010 5-year est.).

Income: Per capita income: $22,794 (2006-2010 5-year est.); Median household income: $42,955 (2006-2010 5-year est.); Average household income: $61,738 (2006-2010 5-year est.); Percent of households with income of $100,000 or more: 14.5% (2006-2010 5-year est.); Poverty rate: 8.4% (2006-2010 5-year est.).

Education: Percent of population age 25 and over with: High school diploma (including GED) or higher: 87.3% (2006-2010 5-year est.); Bachelor's degree or higher: 11.8% (2006-2010 5-year est.); Master's degree or higher: 3.0% (2006-2010 5-year est.).

Housing: Homeownership rate: 79.9% (2010); Median home value: $122,700 (2006-2010 5-year est.); Median contract rent: $440 per month (2006-2010 5-year est.); Median year structure built: 1966 (2006-2010 5-year est.).

Transportation: Commute to work: 96.9% car, 0.0% public transportation, 0.0% walk, 3.1% work from home (2006-2010 5-year est.); Travel time to work: 29.2% less than 15 minutes, 41.7% 15 to 30 minutes, 10.9% 30 to 45 minutes, 11.3% 45 to 60 minutes, 6.9% 60 minutes or more (2006-2010 5-year est.)

Additional Information Contacts
Greater Susquehanna Valley Chamber of Commerce . . . . (570) 743-4100
http://www.gsvcc.org

KRATZERVILLE (CDP). Covers a land area of 0.953 square miles and a water area of 0.021 square miles. Located at 40.86° N. Lat; 76.90° W. Long. Elevation is 673 feet.

Population: 424 (1990); 391 (2000); 383 (2010); Density: 401.8 persons per square mile (2010); Race: 98.7% White, 0.3% Black, 0.0% Asian, 0.0% American Indian/Alaska Native, 0.0% Native Hawaiian/Other Pacific Islander, 1.0% Other, 0.3% Hispanic of any race (2010); Average household size: 2.29 (2010); Median age: 47.8 (2010); Males per 100 females: 89.6 (2010); Marriage status: 27.1% never married, 55.6% now married, 6.8% widowed, 10.5% divorced (2006-2010 5-year est.); Foreign born: 1.1% (2006-2010 5-year est.); Ancestry (includes multiple ancestries): 70.5% German, 6.9% Irish, 6.8% American, 6.6% English, 4.1% Pennsylvania German (2006-2010 5-year est.).

Economy: Employment by occupation: 1.2% management, 3.2% professional, 8.8% services, 28.9% sales, 6.1% farming, 12.0% construction, 6.4% production (2006-2010 5-year est.).

Income: Per capita income: $25,251 (2006-2010 5-year est.); Median household income: $43,636 (2006-2010 5-year est.); Average household income: $72,480 (2006-2010 5-year est.); Percent of households with income of $100,000 or more: 20.6% (2006-2010 5-year est.); Poverty rate: 10.2% (2006-2010 5-year est.).

Education: Percent of population age 25 and over with: High school diploma (including GED) or higher: 86.1% (2006-2010 5-year est.); Bachelor's degree or higher: 8.4% (2006-2010 5-year est.); Master's degree or higher: 1.4% (2006-2010 5-year est.).

Housing: Homeownership rate: 81.4% (2010); Median home value: $121,400 (2006-2010 5-year est.); Median contract rent: $385 per month (2006-2010 5-year est.); Median year structure built: 1953 (2006-2010 5-year est.).

Transportation: Commute to work: 98.9% car, 0.0% public transportation, 0.0% walk, 1.1% work from home (2006-2010 5-year est.); Travel time to work: 31.0% less than 15 minutes, 46.1% 15 to 30 minutes, 8.4% 30 to 45 minutes, 11.1% 45 to 60 minutes, 3.5% 60 minutes or more (2006-2010 5-year est.)

KREAMER (CDP). Covers a land area of 1.240 square miles and a water area of 0.004 square miles. Located at 40.80° N. Lat; 76.97° W. Long. Elevation is 482 feet.

Population: 702 (1990); 773 (2000); 822 (2010); Density: 662.8 persons per square mile (2010); Race: 98.3% White, 0.7% Black, 0.0% Asian, 0.2% American Indian/Alaska Native, 0.1% Native Hawaiian/Other Pacific Islander, 0.7% Other, 0.0% Hispanic of any race (2010); Average household size: 2.45 (2010); Median age: 42.7 (2010); Males per 100 females: 97.1 (2010); Marriage status: 21.6% never married, 58.8% now married, 6.4% widowed, 13.2% divorced (2006-2010 5-year est.); Foreign born: 2.0% (2006-2010 5-year est.); Ancestry (includes multiple ancestries): 59.4% German, 11.7% Polish, 8.8% Irish, 8.3% American, 3.3% English (2006-2010 5-year est.).

Economy: Employment by occupation: 4.8% management, 1.9% professional, 10.9% services, 21.0% sales, 4.6% farming, 16.1% construction, 5.9% production (2006-2010 5-year est.).

Income: Per capita income: $22,351 (2006-2010 5-year est.); Median household income: $46,250 (2006-2010 5-year est.); Average household income: $53,822 (2006-2010 5-year est.); Percent of households with income of $100,000 or more: 6.9% (2006-2010 5-year est.); Poverty rate: 7.4% (2006-2010 5-year est.).

Education: Percent of population age 25 and over with: High school diploma (including GED) or higher: 90.6% (2006-2010 5-year est.); Bachelor's degree or higher: 17.6% (2006-2010 5-year est.); Master's degree or higher: 5.6% (2006-2010 5-year est.).

Housing: Homeownership rate: 83.7% (2010); Median home value: $126,100 (2006-2010 5-year est.); Median contract rent: $435 per month (2006-2010 5-year est.); Median year structure built: 1975 (2006-2010 5-year est.).

Transportation: Commute to work: 91.2% car, 0.0% public transportation, 4.6% walk, 1.6% work from home (2006-2010 5-year est.); Travel time to work: 46.7% less than 15 minutes, 25.1% 15 to 30 minutes, 17.6% 30 to 45 minutes, 2.4% 45 to 60 minutes, 8.2% 60 minutes or more (2006-2010 5-year est.)

MCCLURE (borough). Covers a land area of 3.754 square miles and a water area of 0.006 square miles. Located at 40.71° N. Lat; 77.31° W. Long. Elevation is 686 feet.

Population: 1,070 (1990); 975 (2000); 941 (2010); Density: 250.7 persons per square mile (2010); Race: 98.3% White, 0.0% Black, 0.2% Asian, 0.0% American Indian/Alaska Native, 0.0% Native Hawaiian/Other Pacific Islander, 1.5% Other, 1.0% Hispanic of any race (2010); Average household size: 2.46 (2010); Median age: 40.0 (2010); Males per 100 females: 94.8 (2010); Marriage status: 29.8% never married, 52.5% now married, 6.9% widowed, 10.8% divorced (2006-2010 5-year est.); Foreign born: 0.2% (2006-2010 5-year est.); Ancestry (includes multiple ancestries): 44.7% German, 9.3% Irish, 9.3% Pennsylvania German, 6.7% Italian, 6.5% American (2006-2010 5-year est.).

Economy: Single-family building permits issued: 1 (2011); Multi-family building permits issued: 0 (2011); Employment by occupation: 2.9% management, 0.0% professional, 14.1% services, 11.7% sales, 1.6% farming, 12.0% construction, 16.4% production (2006-2010 5-year est.).

Income: Per capita income: $17,847 (2006-2010 5-year est.); Median household income: $39,250 (2006-2010 5-year est.); Average household income: $45,701 (2006-2010 5-year est.); Percent of households with income of $100,000 or more: 5.1% (2006-2010 5-year est.); Poverty rate: 16.4% (2006-2010 5-year est.).

Education: Percent of population age 25 and over with: High school diploma (including GED) or higher: 88.1% (2006-2010 5-year est.); Bachelor's degree or higher: 8.7% (2006-2010 5-year est.); Master's degree or higher: 5.5% (2006-2010 5-year est.).

School District(s)

Midd-West SD (KG-12)

   2010-11 Enrollment: 2,202 . . . . (570) 837-0046

Housing: Homeownership rate: 67.3% (2010); Median home value: $84,800 (2006-2010 5-year est.); Median contract rent: $445 per month (2006-2010 5-year est.); Median year structure built: before 1940 (2006-2010 5-year est.).

Transportation: Commute to work: 88.0% car, 0.0% public transportation, 8.4% walk, 3.5% work from home (2006-2010 5-year est.); Travel time to work: 33.2% less than 15 minutes, 31.0% 15 to 30 minutes, 28.2% 30 to 45 minutes, 5.9% 45 to 60 minutes, 1.7% 60 minutes or more (2006-2010 5-year est.)

MIDDLEBURG (borough). County seat. Covers a land area of 0.883 square miles and a water area of 0.036 square miles. Located at 40.79° N. Lat; 77.04° W. Long. Elevation is 486 feet.

History: Settled c.1760, laid out 1800, incorporated 1856.

Population: 1,422 (1990); 1,382 (2000); 1,309 (2010); Density: 1,482.6 persons per square mile (2010); Race: 96.9% White, 1.2% Black, 0.1% Asian, 0.4% American Indian/Alaska Native, 0.0% Native Hawaiian/Other Pacific Islander, 1.4% Other, 0.8% Hispanic of any race (2010); Average household size: 2.28 (2010); Median age: 39.1 (2010); Males per 100 females: 90.8 (2010); Marriage status: 24.9% never married, 55.0% now married, 8.1% widowed, 12.0% divorced (2006-2010 5-year est.); Foreign born: 0.9% (2006-2010 5-year est.); Ancestry (includes multiple ancestries): 54.9% German, 9.0% Irish, 8.0% American, 5.0% Italian, 4.8% English (2006-2010 5-year est.).

Economy: Single-family building permits issued: 0 (2011); Multi-family building permits issued: 0 (2011); Employment by occupation: 6.4% management, 0.9% professional, 15.2% services, 17.6% sales, 3.5% farming, 10.1% construction, 7.9% production (2006-2010 5-year est.).

Income: Per capita income: $18,261 (2006-2010 5-year est.); Median household income: $36,688 (2006-2010 5-year est.); Average household income: $42,168 (2006-2010 5-year est.); Percent of households with income of $100,000 or more: 4.2% (2006-2010 5-year est.); Poverty rate: 14.2% (2006-2010 5-year est.).

Education: Percent of population age 25 and over with: High school diploma (including GED) or higher: 78.2% (2006-2010 5-year est.); Bachelor's degree or higher: 10.8% (2006-2010 5-year est.); Master's degree or higher: 4.5% (2006-2010 5-year est.).

School District(s)

Midd-West SD (KG-12)

   2010-11 Enrollment: 2,202 . . . . (570) 837-0046

Housing: Homeownership rate: 57.2% (2010); Median home value: $100,000 (2006-2010 5-year est.); Median contract rent: $330 per month (2006-2010 5-year est.); Median year structure built: 1958 (2006-2010 5-year est.).

Safety: Violent crime rate: 0.0 per 10,000 population; Property crime rate: 677.8 per 10,000 population (2011).

Newspapers: The Shopper (Community news; Circulation 18,000); Union County Times (Community news; Circulation 16,000)

Transportation: Commute to work: 91.9% car, 0.0% public transportation, 4.9% walk, 2.4% work from home (2006-2010 5-year est.); Travel time to work: 44.2% less than 15 minutes, 29.2% 15 to 30 minutes, 11.0% 30 to 45 minutes, 4.3% 45 to 60 minutes, 11.2% 60 minutes or more (2006-2010 5-year est.)

Additional Information Contacts

Central PA Chamber of Commerce. . . . . (570) 742-7341

   http://www.centralpachamber.com/index.php

MIDDLECREEK (township). Covers a land area of 14.382 square miles and a water area of 0.128 square miles. Located at 40.82° N. Lat; 76.97° W. Long.

Population: 1,791 (1990); 1,971 (2000); 2,114 (2010); Density: 147.0 persons per square mile (2010); Race: 97.7% White, 0.8% Black, 0.1% Asian, 0.1% American Indian/Alaska Native, 0.0% Native Hawaiian/Other Pacific Islander, 1.3% Other, 1.0% Hispanic of any race (2010); Average household size: 2.57 (2010); Median age: 42.4 (2010); Males per 100 females: 102.5 (2010); Marriage status: 21.0% never married, 66.4% now married, 3.6% widowed, 8.9% divorced (2006-2010 5-year est.); Foreign born: 1.3% (2006-2010 5-year est.); Ancestry (includes multiple ancestries): 55.0% German, 8.5% American, 7.1% Polish, 5.2% Irish, 3.6% Dutch (2006-2010 5-year est.).

Economy: Single-family building permits issued: 4 (2011); Multi-family building permits issued: 0 (2011); Employment by occupation: 5.7% management, 2.1% professional, 13.1% services, 17.1% sales, 4.5% farming, 15.8% construction, 8.2% production (2006-2010 5-year est.).

Income: Per capita income: $23,331 (2006-2010 5-year est.); Median household income: $50,515 (2006-2010 5-year est.); Average household income: $60,487 (2006-2010 5-year est.); Percent of households with income of $100,000 or more: 11.7% (2006-2010 5-year est.); Poverty rate: 7.6% (2006-2010 5-year est.).

Education: Percent of population age 25 and over with: High school diploma (including GED) or higher: 85.0% (2006-2010 5-year est.); Bachelor's degree or higher: 11.5% (2006-2010 5-year est.); Master's degree or higher: 3.6% (2006-2010 5-year est.).

Housing: Homeownership rate: 85.2% (2010); Median home value: $124,500 (2006-2010 5-year est.); Median contract rent: $448 per month (2006-2010 5-year est.); Median year structure built: 1977 (2006-2010 5-year est.).

Transportation: Commute to work: 90.5% car, 0.0% public transportation, 3.6% walk, 4.3% work from home (2006-2010 5-year est.); Travel time to work: 43.7% less than 15 minutes, 32.5% 15 to 30 minutes, 12.5% 30 to 45 minutes, 4.2% 45 to 60 minutes, 7.1% 60 minutes or more (2006-2010 5-year est.)

Additional Information Contacts

Central PA Chamber of Commerce. . . . . (570) 742-7341

   http://www.centralpachamber.com/index.php

MONROE (township). Covers a land area of 15.553 square miles and a water area of 0.182 square miles. Located at 40.86° N. Lat; 76.86° W. Long.

Population: 3,881 (1990); 4,012 (2000); 3,895 (2010); Density: 250.4 persons per square mile (2010); Race: 96.2% White, 0.9% Black, 1.6% Asian, 0.1% American Indian/Alaska Native, 0.0% Native Hawaiian/Other Pacific Islander, 1.2% Other, 1.4% Hispanic of any race (2010); Average household size: 2.43 (2010); Median age: 45.7 (2010); Males per 100 females: 97.8 (2010); Marriage status: 18.4% never married, 69.0% now married, 7.8% widowed, 4.8% divorced (2006-2010 5-year est.); Foreign born: 3.7% (2006-2010 5-year est.); Ancestry (includes multiple ancestries): 47.1% German, 14.5% Irish, 8.5% English, 6.7% Italian, 5.6% Dutch (2006-2010 5-year est.).

Economy: Single-family building permits issued: 21 (2011); Multi-family building permits issued: 0 (2011); Employment by occupation: 7.7% management, 2.5% professional, 10.5% services, 19.5% sales, 1.7% farming, 12.3% construction, 9.4% production (2006-2010 5-year est.).

Income: Per capita income: $33,925 (2006-2010 5-year est.); Median household income: $58,684 (2006-2010 5-year est.); Average household income: $84,979 (2006-2010 5-year est.); Percent of households with income of $100,000 or more: 28.9% (2006-2010 5-year est.); Poverty rate: 5.8% (2006-2010 5-year est.).

Education: Percent of population age 25 and over with: High school diploma (including GED) or higher: 94.0% (2006-2010 5-year est.);

Bachelor's degree or higher: 26.9% (2006-2010 5-year est.); Master's degree or higher: 9.7% (2006-2010 5-year est.).
Housing: Homeownership rate: 86.0% (2010); Median home value: $136,900 (2006-2010 5-year est.); Median contract rent: $573 per month (2006-2010 5-year est.); Median year structure built: 1974 (2006-2010 5-year est.).
Transportation: Commute to work: 95.1% car, 0.0% public transportation, 0.7% walk, 4.2% work from home (2006-2010 5-year est.); Travel time to work: 39.6% less than 15 minutes, 39.5% 15 to 30 minutes, 7.6% 30 to 45 minutes, 8.4% 45 to 60 minutes, 4.9% 60 minutes or more (2006-2010 5-year est.)
Additional Information Contacts
Central PA Chamber of Commerce. . . . . (570) 742-7341
　http://www.centralpachamber.com/index.php

MOUNT PLEASANT MILLS (CDP). Aka Freemont. Covers a land area of 1.260 square miles and a water area of 0.004 square miles. Located at 40.72° N. Lat; 77.03° W. Long. Elevation is 564 feet.
Population: 326 (1990); 342 (2000); 464 (2010); Density: 368.1 persons per square mile (2010); Race: 98.3% White, 0.4% Black, 0.0% Asian, 0.4% American Indian/Alaska Native, 0.0% Native Hawaiian/Other Pacific Islander, 0.9% Other, 0.0% Hispanic of any race (2010); Average household size: 2.30 (2010); Median age: 36.8 (2010); Males per 100 females: 106.2 (2010); Marriage status: 26.4% never married, 58.6% now married, 8.7% widowed, 6.3% divorced (2006-2010 5-year est.); Foreign born: 0.0% (2006-2010 5-year est.); Ancestry (includes multiple ancestries): 53.1% German, 11.6% Irish, 5.1% Swiss, 4.6% English, 4.6% American (2006-2010 5-year est.).
Economy: Employment by occupation: 0.0% management, 0.0% professional, 9.0% services, 9.5% sales, 5.4% farming, 22.1% construction, 5.9% production (2006-2010 5-year est.).
Income: Per capita income: $15,369 (2006-2010 5-year est.); Median household income: $39,028 (2006-2010 5-year est.); Average household income: $39,716 (2006-2010 5-year est.); Percent of households with income of $100,000 or more: 3.1% (2006-2010 5-year est.); Poverty rate: 12.4% (2006-2010 5-year est.).
Education: Percent of population age 25 and over with: High school diploma (including GED) or higher: 83.5% (2006-2010 5-year est.); Bachelor's degree or higher: 9.4% (2006-2010 5-year est.); Master's degree or higher: 9.4% (2006-2010 5-year est.).

School District(s)
Midd-West SD (KG-12)
　2010-11 Enrollment: 2,202 . . . . (570) 837-0046
Housing: Homeownership rate: 65.8% (2010); Median home value: $156,900 (2006-2010 5-year est.); Median contract rent: $375 per month (2006-2010 5-year est.); Median year structure built: 1959 (2006-2010 5-year est.).
Transportation: Commute to work: 98.1% car, 0.0% public transportation, 1.9% walk, 0.0% work from home (2006-2010 5-year est.); Travel time to work: 9.3% less than 15 minutes, 49.3% 15 to 30 minutes, 14.4% 30 to 45 minutes, 14.9% 45 to 60 minutes, 12.1% 60 minutes or more (2006-2010 5-year est.)

PAXTONVILLE (CDP). Covers a land area of 0.873 square miles and a water area of 0.002 square miles. Located at 40.77° N. Lat; 77.08° W. Long. Elevation is 535 feet.
Population: 229 (1990); 221 (2000); 265 (2010); Density: 303.7 persons per square mile (2010); Race: 99.6% White, 0.0% Black, 0.0% Asian, 0.0% American Indian/Alaska Native, 0.0% Native Hawaiian/Other Pacific Islander, 0.4% Other, 0.4% Hispanic of any race (2010); Average household size: 2.39 (2010); Median age: 44.4 (2010); Males per 100 females: 87.9 (2010); Marriage status: 17.0% never married, 46.2% now married, 26.4% widowed, 10.4% divorced (2006-2010 5-year est.); Foreign born: 0.0% (2006-2010 5-year est.); Ancestry (includes multiple ancestries): 63.3% German, 24.6% Dutch, 24.6% Irish, 6.8% American, 5.3% Pennsylvania German (2006-2010 5-year est.).
Economy: Employment by occupation: 0.0% management, 0.0% professional, 0.0% services, 20.2% sales, 28.8% farming, 16.3% construction, 18.3% production (2006-2010 5-year est.).
Income: Per capita income: $21,812 (2006-2010 5-year est.); Median household income: $38,594 (2006-2010 5-year est.); Average household income: $42,650 (2006-2010 5-year est.); Percent of households with income of $100,000 or more: n/a (2006-2010 5-year est.); Poverty rate: 0.0% (2006-2010 5-year est.).

Education: Percent of population age 25 and over with: High school diploma (including GED) or higher: 88.6% (2006-2010 5-year est.); Bachelor's degree or higher: 17.7% (2006-2010 5-year est.); Master's degree or higher: 0.0% (2006-2010 5-year est.).
Housing: Homeownership rate: 88.2% (2010); Median home value: $120,600 (2006-2010 5-year est.); Median contract rent: $547 per month (2006-2010 5-year est.); Median year structure built: before 1940 (2006-2010 5-year est.).
Transportation: Commute to work: 100.0% car, 0.0% public transportation, 0.0% walk, 0.0% work from home (2006-2010 5-year est.); Travel time to work: 18.3% less than 15 minutes, 58.7% 15 to 30 minutes, 23.1% 30 to 45 minutes, 0.0% 45 to 60 minutes, 0.0% 60 minutes or more (2006-2010 5-year est.)

PENN (township). Covers a land area of 17.579 square miles and a water area of 0.247 square miles. Located at 40.81° N. Lat; 76.90° W. Long.
Population: 3,208 (1990); 3,781 (2000); 4,324 (2010); Density: 246.0 persons per square mile (2010); Race: 96.1% White, 1.6% Black, 0.7% Asian, 0.2% American Indian/Alaska Native, 0.0% Native Hawaiian/Other Pacific Islander, 1.4% Other, 1.8% Hispanic of any race (2010); Average household size: 2.46 (2010); Median age: 43.0 (2010); Males per 100 females: 97.3 (2010); Marriage status: 34.2% never married, 54.2% now married, 3.2% widowed, 8.3% divorced (2006-2010 5-year est.); Foreign born: 0.4% (2006-2010 5-year est.); Ancestry (includes multiple ancestries): 46.0% German, 7.5% Irish, 6.6% American, 6.0% English, 3.3% Italian (2006-2010 5-year est.).
Economy: Single-family building permits issued: 5 (2011); Multi-family building permits issued: 0 (2011); Employment by occupation: 7.4% management, 4.2% professional, 10.4% services, 13.4% sales, 4.5% farming, 7.5% construction, 6.2% production (2006-2010 5-year est.).
Income: Per capita income: $25,553 (2006-2010 5-year est.); Median household income: $57,734 (2006-2010 5-year est.); Average household income: $68,575 (2006-2010 5-year est.); Percent of households with income of $100,000 or more: 23.5% (2006-2010 5-year est.); Poverty rate: 15.3% (2006-2010 5-year est.).
Education: Percent of population age 25 and over with: High school diploma (including GED) or higher: 76.1% (2006-2010 5-year est.); Bachelor's degree or higher: 24.0% (2006-2010 5-year est.); Master's degree or higher: 11.2% (2006-2010 5-year est.).
Housing: Homeownership rate: 77.8% (2010); Median home value: $155,300 (2006-2010 5-year est.); Median contract rent: $420 per month (2006-2010 5-year est.); Median year structure built: 1988 (2006-2010 5-year est.).
Transportation: Commute to work: 85.2% car, 0.0% public transportation, 1.5% walk, 13.3% work from home (2006-2010 5-year est.); Travel time to work: 53.0% less than 15 minutes, 26.2% 15 to 30 minutes, 10.2% 30 to 45 minutes, 6.0% 45 to 60 minutes, 4.5% 60 minutes or more (2006-2010 5-year est.)
Additional Information Contacts
Central PA Chamber of Commerce. . . . . (570) 742-7341
　http://www.centralpachamber.com/index.php

PENNS CREEK (CDP). Covers a land area of 0.734 square miles and a water area of 0.019 square miles. Located at 40.86° N. Lat; 77.06° W. Long. Elevation is 561 feet.
Population: 614 (1990); 668 (2000); 715 (2010); Density: 974.6 persons per square mile (2010); Race: 97.5% White, 1.3% Black, 0.0% Asian, 0.1% American Indian/Alaska Native, 0.1% Native Hawaiian/Other Pacific Islander, 1.0% Other, 2.2% Hispanic of any race (2010); Average household size: 2.79 (2010); Median age: 28.7 (2010); Males per 100 females: 93.8 (2010); Marriage status: 31.2% never married, 50.7% now married, 7.7% widowed, 10.4% divorced (2006-2010 5-year est.); Foreign born: 1.2% (2006-2010 5-year est.); Ancestry (includes multiple ancestries): 32.8% German, 16.2% Irish, 7.6% American, 6.1% Dutch, 5.5% Romanian (2006-2010 5-year est.).
Economy: Employment by occupation: 0.9% management, 1.4% professional, 21.6% services, 4.1% sales, 3.6% farming, 12.2% construction, 6.8% production (2006-2010 5-year est.).
Income: Per capita income: $15,910 (2006-2010 5-year est.); Median household income: $35,139 (2006-2010 5-year est.); Average household income: $41,273 (2006-2010 5-year est.); Percent of households with income of $100,000 or more: 7.3% (2006-2010 5-year est.); Poverty rate: 17.4% (2006-2010 5-year est.).

Education: Percent of population age 25 and over with: High school diploma (including GED) or higher: 71.1% (2006-2010 5-year est.); Bachelor's degree or higher: 9.4% (2006-2010 5-year est.); Master's degree or higher: 3.7% (2006-2010 5-year est.).

Housing: Homeownership rate: 65.6% (2010); Median home value: $95,500 (2006-2010 5-year est.); Median contract rent: $419 per month (2006-2010 5-year est.); Median year structure built: 1954 (2006-2010 5-year est.).

Transportation: Commute to work: 91.9% car, 0.0% public transportation, 8.1% walk, 0.0% work from home (2006-2010 5-year est.); Travel time to work: 44.3% less than 15 minutes, 32.9% 15 to 30 minutes, 18.6% 30 to 45 minutes, 3.3% 45 to 60 minutes, 1.0% 60 minutes or more (2006-2010 5-year est.)

PERRY (township). Covers a land area of 26.303 square miles and a water area of 0.104 square miles. Located at 40.70° N. Lat; 77.02° W. Long.

Population: 1,873 (1990); 1,973 (2000); 2,183 (2010); Density: 83.0 persons per square mile (2010); Race: 98.9% White, 0.4% Black, 0.0% Asian, 0.1% American Indian/Alaska Native, 0.0% Native Hawaiian/Other Pacific Islander, 0.6% Other, 0.3% Hispanic of any race (2010); Average household size: 2.77 (2010); Median age: 36.9 (2010); Males per 100 females: 105.7 (2010); Marriage status: 22.3% never married, 62.7% now married, 8.4% widowed, 6.6% divorced (2006-2010 5-year est.); Foreign born: 0.8% (2006-2010 5-year est.); Ancestry (includes multiple ancestries): 48.7% German, 13.9% American, 6.7% Irish, 3.1% Swiss, 3.1% Dutch (2006-2010 5-year est.).

Economy: Single-family building permits issued: 3 (2011); Multi-family building permits issued: 4 (2011); Employment by occupation: 3.8% management, 1.7% professional, 14.0% services, 15.2% sales, 2.9% farming, 17.7% construction, 8.1% production (2006-2010 5-year est.).

Income: Per capita income: $16,925 (2006-2010 5-year est.); Median household income: $42,333 (2006-2010 5-year est.); Average household income: $44,647 (2006-2010 5-year est.); Percent of households with income of $100,000 or more: 5.0% (2006-2010 5-year est.); Poverty rate: 11.7% (2006-2010 5-year est.).

Education: Percent of population age 25 and over with: High school diploma (including GED) or higher: 78.1% (2006-2010 5-year est.); Bachelor's degree or higher: 7.2% (2006-2010 5-year est.); Master's degree or higher: 3.7% (2006-2010 5-year est.).

Housing: Homeownership rate: 77.6% (2010); Median home value: $140,300 (2006-2010 5-year est.); Median contract rent: $416 per month (2006-2010 5-year est.); Median year structure built: 1973 (2006-2010 5-year est.).

Transportation: Commute to work: 93.2% car, 0.0% public transportation, 2.3% walk, 3.2% work from home (2006-2010 5-year est.); Travel time to work: 24.7% less than 15 minutes, 38.2% 15 to 30 minutes, 15.8% 30 to 45 minutes, 9.1% 45 to 60 minutes, 12.2% 60 minutes or more (2006-2010 5-year est.)

Additional Information Contacts
Greater Susquehanna Valley Chamber of Commerce . . . . (570) 743-4100
   http://www.gsvcc.org

PORT TREVORTON (CDP). Covers a land area of 3.190 square miles and a water area of 0.006 square miles. Located at 40.69° N. Lat; 76.90° W. Long. Elevation is 469 feet.

Population: 446 (1990); 451 (2000); 769 (2010); Density: 241.0 persons per square mile (2010); Race: 98.7% White, 0.1% Black, 0.4% Asian, 0.0% American Indian/Alaska Native, 0.0% Native Hawaiian/Other Pacific Islander, 0.8% Other, 1.0% Hispanic of any race (2010); Average household size: 2.88 (2010); Median age: 35.9 (2010); Males per 100 females: 106.2 (2010); Marriage status: 36.4% never married, 54.2% now married, 3.8% widowed, 5.7% divorced (2006-2010 5-year est.); Foreign born: 1.3% (2006-2010 5-year est.); Ancestry (includes multiple ancestries): 38.6% German, 8.0% English, 5.2% Dutch, 5.0% American, 3.7% Italian (2006-2010 5-year est.).

Economy: Employment by occupation: 2.9% management, 0.0% professional, 8.9% services, 19.4% sales, 7.1% farming, 12.0% construction, 15.1% production (2006-2010 5-year est.).

Income: Per capita income: $17,760 (2006-2010 5-year est.); Median household income: $39,886 (2006-2010 5-year est.); Average household income: $53,469 (2006-2010 5-year est.); Percent of households with income of $100,000 or more: 10.1% (2006-2010 5-year est.); Poverty rate: 12.2% (2006-2010 5-year est.).

Education: Percent of population age 25 and over with: High school diploma (including GED) or higher: 70.9% (2006-2010 5-year est.); Bachelor's degree or higher: 9.6% (2006-2010 5-year est.); Master's degree or higher: 2.6% (2006-2010 5-year est.).

Housing: Homeownership rate: 74.5% (2010); Median home value: $97,100 (2006-2010 5-year est.); Median contract rent: $505 per month (2006-2010 5-year est.); Median year structure built: 1948 (2006-2010 5-year est.).

Transportation: Commute to work: 80.1% car, 0.0% public transportation, 4.6% walk, 8.4% work from home (2006-2010 5-year est.); Travel time to work: 16.4% less than 15 minutes, 41.5% 15 to 30 minutes, 25.5% 30 to 45 minutes, 12.9% 45 to 60 minutes, 3.8% 60 minutes or more (2006-2010 5-year est.)

SELINSGROVE (borough). Covers a land area of 1.831 square miles and a water area of 0.069 square miles. Located at 40.80° N. Lat; 76.87° W. Long. Elevation is 440 feet.

History: Selinsgrove was laid out in 1790 by Anthony Selin, a Swiss soldier of fortune who accompanied Lafayette to America.

Population: 5,384 (1990); 5,383 (2000); 5,654 (2010); Density: 3,087.4 persons per square mile (2010); Race: 91.7% White, 3.4% Black, 1.2% Asian, 0.2% American Indian/Alaska Native, 0.0% Native Hawaiian/Other Pacific Islander, 3.5% Other, 6.0% Hispanic of any race (2010); Average household size: 2.15 (2010); Median age: 22.9 (2010); Males per 100 females: 86.5 (2010); Marriage status: 55.8% never married, 28.5% now married, 7.8% widowed, 7.9% divorced (2006-2010 5-year est.); Foreign born: 2.6% (2006-2010 5-year est.); Ancestry (includes multiple ancestries): 37.9% German, 14.9% Irish, 12.0% Italian, 9.8% English, 4.3% Polish (2006-2010 5-year est.).

Economy: Single-family building permits issued: 0 (2011); Multi-family building permits issued: 0 (2011); Employment by occupation: 5.4% management, 1.6% professional, 19.6% services, 20.1% sales, 3.7% farming, 7.6% construction, 5.7% production (2006-2010 5-year est.).

Income: Per capita income: $16,087 (2006-2010 5-year est.); Median household income: $32,957 (2006-2010 5-year est.); Average household income: $45,322 (2006-2010 5-year est.); Percent of households with income of $100,000 or more: 7.1% (2006-2010 5-year est.); Poverty rate: 16.5% (2006-2010 5-year est.).

Taxes: Total city taxes per capita: $171 (2009); City property taxes per capita: $85 (2009).

Education: Percent of population age 25 and over with: High school diploma (including GED) or higher: 89.0% (2006-2010 5-year est.); Bachelor's degree or higher: 24.3% (2006-2010 5-year est.); Master's degree or higher: 6.8% (2006-2010 5-year est.).

School District(s)
Selinsgrove Area SD (KG-12)
   2010-11 Enrollment: 2,717 . . . . (570) 374-1144

Four-year College(s)
Susquehanna University (Private, Not-for-profit, Evangelical Lutheran Church)
   Fall 2010 Enrollment: 2,582 . . . . (570) 374-0101
   2011-12 Tuition: In-state $35,860; Out-of-state $35,860

Housing: Homeownership rate: 43.8% (2010); Median home value: $120,900 (2006-2010 5-year est.); Median contract rent: $471 per month (2006-2010 5-year est.); Median year structure built: 1958 (2006-2010 5-year est.).

Safety: Violent crime rate: 116.4 per 10,000 population; Property crime rate: 439.0 per 10,000 population (2011).

Transportation: Commute to work: 73.0% car, 0.0% public transportation, 10.4% walk, 14.1% work from home (2006-2010 5-year est.); Travel time to work: 61.0% less than 15 minutes, 23.0% 15 to 30 minutes, 6.1% 30 to 45 minutes, 6.0% 45 to 60 minutes, 3.9% 60 minutes or more (2006-2010 5-year est.)

Airports: Penn Valley (general aviation)

Additional Information Contacts
Borough of Selinsgrove . . . . (570) 374-2311
Central PA Chamber of Commerce . . . . (570) 742-7341
   http://www.centralpachamber.com/index.php

SHAMOKIN DAM (borough). Covers a land area of 1.845 square miles and a water area of 0.038 square miles. Located at 40.86° N. Lat; 76.83° W. Long. Elevation is 482 feet.

Population: 1,690 (1990); 1,502 (2000); 1,686 (2010); Density: 914.0 persons per square mile (2010); Race: 96.1% White, 0.5% Black, 1.4% Asian, 0.6% American Indian/Alaska Native, 0.0% Native Hawaiian/Other

Pacific Islander, 1.4% Other, 1.4% Hispanic of any race (2010); Average household size: 2.10 (2010); Median age: 49.6 (2010); Males per 100 females: 86.3 (2010); Marriage status: 20.0% never married, 60.1% now married, 10.2% widowed, 9.7% divorced (2006-2010 5-year est.); Foreign born: 1.1% (2006-2010 5-year est.); Ancestry (includes multiple ancestries): 50.3% German, 12.2% Irish, 8.2% English, 8.1% Pennsylvania German, 7.4% Italian (2006-2010 5-year est.).

Economy: Single-family building permits issued: 0 (2011); Multi-family building permits issued: 0 (2011); Employment by occupation: 6.6% management, 0.0% professional, 13.3% services, 12.9% sales, 2.5% farming, 10.9% construction, 6.2% production (2006-2010 5-year est.).

Income: Per capita income: $20,832 (2006-2010 5-year est.); Median household income: $42,988 (2006-2010 5-year est.); Average household income: $48,430 (2006-2010 5-year est.); Percent of households with income of $100,000 or more: 6.5% (2006-2010 5-year est.); Poverty rate: 6.3% (2006-2010 5-year est.).

Education: Percent of population age 25 and over with: High school diploma (including GED) or higher: 85.6% (2006-2010 5-year est.); Bachelor's degree or higher: 19.1% (2006-2010 5-year est.); Master's degree or higher: 4.8% (2006-2010 5-year est.).

Vocational/Technical School(s)
Empire Beauty School-Shamokin Dam (Private, For-profit)
    Fall 2010 Enrollment: 132 . . . . (800) 223-3271
    2011-12 Tuition: $14,490

Housing: Homeownership rate: 63.9% (2010); Median home value: $127,000 (2006-2010 5-year est.); Median contract rent: $464 per month (2006-2010 5-year est.); Median year structure built: 1967 (2006-2010 5-year est.).

Transportation: Commute to work: 95.1% car, 0.0% public transportation, 0.5% walk, 1.9% work from home (2006-2010 5-year est.); Travel time to work: 40.0% less than 15 minutes, 45.8% 15 to 30 minutes, 7.6% 30 to 45 minutes, 3.0% 45 to 60 minutes, 3.7% 60 minutes or more (2006-2010 5-year est.)

Additional Information Contacts
Greater Susquehanna Valley Chamber of Commerce . . . . (570) 743-4100
    http://www.gsvcc.org

SPRING (township). Covers a land area of 37.065 square miles and a water area of 0.343 square miles. Located at 40.77° N. Lat; 77.24° W. Long.

Population: 1,575 (1990); 1,563 (2000); 1,616 (2010); Density: 43.6 persons per square mile (2010); Race: 98.6% White, 0.2% Black, 0.1% Asian, 0.0% American Indian/Alaska Native, 0.0% Native Hawaiian/Other Pacific Islander, 1.1% Other, 0.2% Hispanic of any race (2010); Average household size: 2.63 (2010); Median age: 40.9 (2010); Males per 100 females: 99.8 (2010); Marriage status: 22.8% never married, 65.3% now married, 6.8% widowed, 5.1% divorced (2006-2010 5-year est.); Foreign born: 0.4% (2006-2010 5-year est.); Ancestry (includes multiple ancestries): 49.9% German, 15.7% Irish, 15.4% American, 7.5% English, 4.5% Swiss (2006-2010 5-year est.).

Economy: Single-family building permits issued: 1 (2011); Multi-family building permits issued: 0 (2011); Employment by occupation: 11.3% management, 1.0% professional, 12.7% services, 13.0% sales, 3.8% farming, 21.4% construction, 12.2% production (2006-2010 5-year est.).

Income: Per capita income: $19,383 (2006-2010 5-year est.); Median household income: $47,143 (2006-2010 5-year est.); Average household income: $53,605 (2006-2010 5-year est.); Percent of households with income of $100,000 or more: 8.5% (2006-2010 5-year est.); Poverty rate: 10.7% (2006-2010 5-year est.).

Education: Percent of population age 25 and over with: High school diploma (including GED) or higher: 80.9% (2006-2010 5-year est.); Bachelor's degree or higher: 7.5% (2006-2010 5-year est.); Master's degree or higher: 3.2% (2006-2010 5-year est.).

Housing: Homeownership rate: 76.1% (2010); Median home value: $100,000 (2006-2010 5-year est.); Median contract rent: $420 per month (2006-2010 5-year est.); Median year structure built: 1956 (2006-2010 5-year est.).

Safety: Violent crime rate: 6.2 per 10,000 population; Property crime rate: 37.0 per 10,000 population (2011).

Transportation: Commute to work: 90.1% car, 0.0% public transportation, 4.2% walk, 3.9% work from home (2006-2010 5-year est.); Travel time to work: 29.4% less than 15 minutes, 19.8% 15 to 30 minutes, 29.8% 30 to 45 minutes, 10.6% 45 to 60 minutes, 10.4% 60 minutes or more (2006-2010 5-year est.)

Additional Information Contacts
Juniata River Valley Chamber of Commerce . . . . (717) 248-6713
    http://www.juniatarivervalley.org

TROXELVILLE (CDP). Covers a land area of 0.994 square miles and a water area of <.001 square miles. Located at 40.81° N. Lat; 77.20° W. Long. Elevation is 656 feet.

Population: 188 (1990); 192 (2000); 221 (2010); Density: 222.2 persons per square mile (2010); Race: 98.2% White, 0.5% Black, 0.0% Asian, 0.0% American Indian/Alaska Native, 0.0% Native Hawaiian/Other Pacific Islander, 1.3% Other, 0.0% Hispanic of any race (2010); Average household size: 2.99 (2010); Median age: 39.5 (2010); Males per 100 females: 84.2 (2010); Marriage status: 0.0% never married, 70.5% now married, 8.1% widowed, 21.5% divorced (2006-2010 5-year est.); Foreign born: 1.0% (2006-2010 5-year est.); Ancestry (includes multiple ancestries): 70.9% German, 9.0% French, 8.0% Irish, 5.5% Polish, 5.5% Dutch (2006-2010 5-year est.).

Economy: Employment by occupation: 14.2% management, 10.6% professional, 3.5% services, 10.6% sales, 4.4% farming, 12.4% construction, 6.2% production (2006-2010 5-year est.).

Income: Per capita income: $19,460 (2006-2010 5-year est.); Median household income: $52,500 (2006-2010 5-year est.); Average household income: $49,215 (2006-2010 5-year est.); Percent of households with income of $100,000 or more: n/a (2006-2010 5-year est.); Poverty rate: 3.0% (2006-2010 5-year est.).

Education: Percent of population age 25 and over with: High school diploma (including GED) or higher: 83.9% (2006-2010 5-year est.); Bachelor's degree or higher: 5.4% (2006-2010 5-year est.); Master's degree or higher: 2.7% (2006-2010 5-year est.).

Housing: Homeownership rate: 91.9% (2010); Median home value: $84,200 (2006-2010 5-year est.); Median contract rent: n/a per month (2006-2010 5-year est.); Median year structure built: before 1940 (2006-2010 5-year est.).

Transportation: Commute to work: 97.3% car, 0.0% public transportation, 0.0% walk, 0.0% work from home (2006-2010 5-year est.); Travel time to work: 26.5% less than 15 minutes, 30.1% 15 to 30 minutes, 30.1% 30 to 45 minutes, 0.0% 45 to 60 minutes, 13.3% 60 minutes or more (2006-2010 5-year est.)

UNION (township). Covers a land area of 14.443 square miles and a water area of 0.114 square miles. Located at 40.72° N. Lat; 76.89° W. Long.

Population: 1,466 (1990); 1,519 (2000); 1,520 (2010); Density: 105.2 persons per square mile (2010); Race: 99.1% White, 0.2% Black, 0.3% Asian, 0.0% American Indian/Alaska Native, 0.0% Native Hawaiian/Other Pacific Islander, 0.4% Other, 0.3% Hispanic of any race (2010); Average household size: 2.93 (2010); Median age: 37.6 (2010); Males per 100 females: 109.4 (2010); Marriage status: 23.1% never married, 67.5% now married, 3.3% widowed, 6.1% divorced (2006-2010 5-year est.); Foreign born: 1.1% (2006-2010 5-year est.); Ancestry (includes multiple ancestries): 42.7% German, 9.6% American, 7.0% English, 3.9% Dutch, 3.9% Scotch-Irish (2006-2010 5-year est.).

Economy: Single-family building permits issued: 3 (2011); Multi-family building permits issued: 0 (2011); Employment by occupation: 3.4% management, 2.2% professional, 9.8% services, 16.6% sales, 6.5% farming, 16.1% construction, 11.7% production (2006-2010 5-year est.).

Income: Per capita income: $22,319 (2006-2010 5-year est.); Median household income: $46,771 (2006-2010 5-year est.); Average household income: $62,372 (2006-2010 5-year est.); Percent of households with income of $100,000 or more: 16.3% (2006-2010 5-year est.); Poverty rate: 3.7% (2006-2010 5-year est.).

Education: Percent of population age 25 and over with: High school diploma (including GED) or higher: 80.0% (2006-2010 5-year est.); Bachelor's degree or higher: 12.4% (2006-2010 5-year est.); Master's degree or higher: 3.1% (2006-2010 5-year est.).

Housing: Homeownership rate: 81.3% (2010); Median home value: $126,500 (2006-2010 5-year est.); Median contract rent: $410 per month (2006-2010 5-year est.); Median year structure built: 1950 (2006-2010 5-year est.).

Transportation: Commute to work: 88.3% car, 0.0% public transportation, 2.6% walk, 5.2% work from home (2006-2010 5-year est.); Travel time to work: 22.3% less than 15 minutes, 39.2% 15 to 30 minutes, 22.6% 30 to 45 minutes, 11.1% 45 to 60 minutes, 4.8% 60 minutes or more (2006-2010 5-year est.)

Additional Information Contacts
Greater Susquehanna Valley Chamber of Commerce .... (570) 743-4100
  http://www.gsvcc.org

WASHINGTON (township). Covers a land area of 24.029 square
miles and a water area of 0.168 square miles. Located at 40.76° N. Lat;
76.96° W. Long.
Population: 1,420 (1990); 1,532 (2000); 1,654 (2010); Density: 68.8
persons per square mile (2010); Race: 99.2% White, 0.4% Black, 0.1%
Asian, 0.0% American Indian/Alaska Native, 0.0% Native Hawaiian/Other
Pacific Islander, 0.3% Other, 0.5% Hispanic of any race (2010); Average
household size: 2.83 (2010); Median age: 39.9 (2010); Males per 100
females: 108.3 (2010); Marriage status: 28.1% never married, 61.6% now
married, 5.2% widowed, 5.2% divorced (2006-2010 5-year est.); Foreign
born: 1.2% (2006-2010 5-year est.); Ancestry (includes multiple
ancestries): 58.6% German, 9.8% American, 5.8% Irish, 5.5% English,
5.1% Italian (2006-2010 5-year est.).
Economy: Single-family building permits issued: 2 (2011); Multi-family
building permits issued: 0 (2011); Employment by occupation: 5.5%
management, 0.8% professional, 12.5% services, 16.6% sales, 4.1%
farming, 10.1% construction, 7.8% production (2006-2010 5-year est.).
Income: Per capita income: $22,481 (2006-2010 5-year est.); Median
household income: $49,286 (2006-2010 5-year est.); Average household
income: $61,137 (2006-2010 5-year est.); Percent of households with
income of $100,000 or more: 13.3% (2006-2010 5-year est.); Poverty rate:
4.8% (2006-2010 5-year est.).
Education: Percent of population age 25 and over with: High school
diploma (including GED) or higher: 80.0% (2006-2010 5-year est.);
Bachelor's degree or higher: 12.7% (2006-2010 5-year est.); Master's
degree or higher: 5.5% (2006-2010 5-year est.).
Housing: Homeownership rate: 87.7% (2010); Median home value:
$139,800 (2006-2010 5-year est.); Median contract rent: $383 per month
(2006-2010 5-year est.); Median year structure built: 1976 (2006-2010
5-year est.).
Transportation: Commute to work: 91.3% car, 0.5% public transportation,
1.3% walk, 6.5% work from home (2006-2010 5-year est.); Travel time to
work: 30.1% less than 15 minutes, 42.8% 15 to 30 minutes, 15.8% 30 to
45 minutes, 5.9% 45 to 60 minutes, 5.4% 60 minutes or more (2006-2010
5-year est.)
Additional Information Contacts
Greater Susquehanna Valley Chamber of Commerce .... (570) 743-4100
  http://www.gsvcc.org

WEST BEAVER (township). Covers a land area of 27.480 square
miles and a water area of 0.076 square miles. Located at 40.75° N. Lat;
77.31° W. Long.
Population: 1,096 (1990); 1,124 (2000); 1,110 (2010); Density: 40.4
persons per square mile (2010); Race: 98.1% White, 0.2% Black, 0.0%
Asian, 0.1% American Indian/Alaska Native, 0.0% Native Hawaiian/Other
Pacific Islander, 1.6% Other, 0.7% Hispanic of any race (2010); Average
household size: 2.78 (2010); Median age: 39.1 (2010); Males per 100
females: 109.8 (2010); Marriage status: 21.7% never married, 64.4% now
married, 6.3% widowed, 7.6% divorced (2006-2010 5-year est.); Foreign
born: 0.8% (2006-2010 5-year est.); Ancestry (includes multiple
ancestries): 50.5% German, 12.1% Dutch, 11.0% Irish, 4.7% Swiss, 4.0%
English (2006-2010 5-year est.).
Economy: Single-family building permits issued: 1 (2011); Multi-family
building permits issued: 0 (2011); Employment by occupation: 10.2%
management, 0.6% professional, 10.0% services, 7.1% sales, 1.5%
farming, 24.7% construction, 21.0% production (2006-2010 5-year est.).
Income: Per capita income: $16,205 (2006-2010 5-year est.); Median
household income: $41,346 (2006-2010 5-year est.); Average household
income: $48,376 (2006-2010 5-year est.); Percent of households with
income of $100,000 or more: 8.5% (2006-2010 5-year est.); Poverty rate:
23.1% (2006-2010 5-year est.).
Education: Percent of population age 25 and over with: High school
diploma (including GED) or higher: 67.7% (2006-2010 5-year est.);
Bachelor's degree or higher: 6.0% (2006-2010 5-year est.); Master's
degree or higher: 1.7% (2006-2010 5-year est.).
Housing: Homeownership rate: 81.8% (2010); Median home value:
$118,500 (2006-2010 5-year est.); Median contract rent: $421 per month
(2006-2010 5-year est.); Median year structure built: 1973 (2006-2010
5-year est.).
Transportation: Commute to work: 91.0% car, 2.7% public transportation,
1.9% walk, 4.4% work from home (2006-2010 5-year est.); Travel time to

work: 16.4% less than 15 minutes, 37.7% 15 to 30 minutes, 26.5% 30 to
45 minutes, 9.4% 45 to 60 minutes, 10.0% 60 minutes or more (2006-2010
5-year est.)

WEST PERRY (township). Covers a land area of 26.984 square miles
and a water area of 0.047 square miles. Located at 40.71° N. Lat; 77.14°
W. Long.
Population: 969 (1990); 1,038 (2000); 1,071 (2010); Density: 39.7
persons per square mile (2010); Race: 98.1% White, 0.7% Black, 0.1%
Asian, 0.5% American Indian/Alaska Native, 0.1% Native Hawaiian/Other
Pacific Islander, 0.5% Other, 0.6% Hispanic of any race (2010); Average
household size: 2.72 (2010); Median age: 42.0 (2010); Males per 100
females: 104.0 (2010); Marriage status: 23.6% never married, 66.1% now
married, 4.9% widowed, 5.5% divorced (2006-2010 5-year est.); Foreign
born: 0.3% (2006-2010 5-year est.); Ancestry (includes multiple
ancestries): 58.6% German, 14.3% American, 10.0% Irish, 6.1% Swiss,
3.3% Dutch (2006-2010 5-year est.).
Economy: Single-family building permits issued: 0 (2011); Multi-family
building permits issued: 0 (2011); Employment by occupation: 5.6%
management, 2.7% professional, 16.1% services, 14.9% sales, 3.5%
farming, 19.3% construction, 7.9% production (2006-2010 5-year est.).
Income: Per capita income: $22,347 (2006-2010 5-year est.); Median
household income: $44,625 (2006-2010 5-year est.); Average household
income: $58,885 (2006-2010 5-year est.); Percent of households with
income of $100,000 or more: 19.7% (2006-2010 5-year est.); Poverty rate:
7.2% (2006-2010 5-year est.).
Education: Percent of population age 25 and over with: High school
diploma (including GED) or higher: 86.8% (2006-2010 5-year est.);
Bachelor's degree or higher: 6.8% (2006-2010 5-year est.); Master's
degree or higher: 3.1% (2006-2010 5-year est.).
Housing: Homeownership rate: 82.3% (2010); Median home value:
$135,500 (2006-2010 5-year est.); Median contract rent: $423 per month
(2006-2010 5-year est.); Median year structure built: 1966 (2006-2010
5-year est.).
Transportation: Commute to work: 93.0% car, 0.0% public transportation,
2.4% walk, 3.1% work from home (2006-2010 5-year est.); Travel time to
work: 26.1% less than 15 minutes, 33.7% 15 to 30 minutes, 17.8% 30 to
45 minutes, 13.3% 45 to 60 minutes, 9.2% 60 minutes or more (2006-2010
5-year est.)
Additional Information Contacts
Perry County Chamber of Commerce .... (717) 582-4523
  http://www.perrycountychamber.org

Somerset County

Located in southwestern Pennsylvania; mountainous area, bounded on the
south by Maryland, and on the southwest by the Youghiogheny River, with
the Allegheny Mountains in the east and Laurel Hill on the west; includes
Mt. Davis, the highest point in t he state (3.213 ft). Covers a land area of
1,074.374 square miles, a water area of 6.558 square miles, and is located
in the Eastern Time Zone at 39.98° N. Lat., 79.03° W. Long. The county
was founded in 1795. County seat is Somerset.

Somerset County is part of the Somerset, PA Micropolitan Statistical Area.
The entire metro area includes: Somerset County, PA

Weather Station: Confluence 1 SW Dam								Elevation: 1,490 feet			
	Jan	Feb	Mar	Apr	May	Jun	Jul	Aug	Sep	Oct	Nov	Dec
High	37	41	50	63	72	80	84	83	76	65	53	41
Low	17	18	25	35	44	53	57	56	49	37	29	21
Precip	3.5	3.0	3.9	4.0	4.8	4.1	4.6	3.6	3.8	3.0	3.7	3.5
Snow	18.1	12.0	8.9	1.4	tr	0.0	0.0	0.0	0.0	0.2	3.9	11.5

High and Low temperatures in degrees Fahrenheit; Precipitation and Snow in inches

Population: 78,218 (1990); 80,023 (2000); 77,742 (2010); Race: 96.0%
White, 2.4% Black, 0.3% Asian, 0.1% American Indian/Alaska Native,
0.0% Native Hawaiian/Other Pacific Islander, 1.2% Other, 1.1% Hispanic
of any race (2010); Density: 72.4 persons per square mile (2010); Average
household size: 2.35 (2010); Median age: 44.3 (2010); Males per 100
females: 106.1 (2010).
Religion: Six largest groups: 13.9% Lutheran, 13.2% Catholicism, 9.8%
European Free-Church, 9.1% Methodist/Pietist, 5.0%
Presbyterian-Reformed, 2.2% Holiness (2010)
Economy: Unemployment rate: 8.7% (August 2012); Total civilian labor
force: 39,069 (August 2012); Leading industries: 17.1% health care and
social assistance; 15.2% manufacturing; 13.7% retail trade (2010); Farms:

1,156 totaling 206,651 acres (2007); Companies that employ 500 or more persons: 2 (2010); Companies that employ 100 to 499 persons: 32 (2010); Companies that employ less than 100 persons: 1,707 (2010); Black-owned businesses: n/a (2007); Hispanic-owned businesses: n/a (2007); Asian-owned businesses: n/a (2007); Women-owned businesses: 1,671 (2007); Retail sales per capita: $10,508 (2010). Single-family building permits issued: 46 (2011); Multi-family building permits issued: 0 (2011).
Income: Per capita income: $19,903 (2006-2010 5-year est.); Median household income: $39,194 (2006-2010 5-year est.); Average household income: $49,162 (2006-2010 5-year est.); Percent of households with income of $100,000 or more: 8.3% (2006-2010 5-year est.); Poverty rate: 12.9% (2006-2010 5-year est.); Bankruptcy rate: 2.27% (2011).
Education: Percent of population age 25 and over with: High school diploma (including GED) or higher: 82.9% (2006-2010 5-year est.); Bachelor's degree or higher: 14.3% (2006-2010 5-year est.); Master's degree or higher: 5.2% (2006-2010 5-year est.).
Housing: Homeownership rate: 76.8% (2010); Median home value: $92,200 (2006-2010 5-year est.); Median contract rent: $376 per month (2006-2010 5-year est.); Median year structure built: 1962 (2006-2010 5-year est.)
Health: Birth rate: 87.5 per 10,000 population (2011); Death rate: 120.8 per 10,000 population (2011); Age-adjusted cancer mortality rate: 155.3 deaths per 100,000 population (2009); Number of physicians: 11.2 per 10,000 population (2010); Hospital beds: 26.8 per 10,000 population (2008); Hospital admissions: 1,001.8 per 10,000 population (2008).
Environment: Air Quality Index: 92.9% good, 7.1% moderate, 0.0% unhealthy for sensitive individuals, 0.0% unhealthy (percent of days in 2011)
Elections: 2012 Presidential election results: 27.8% Obama, 70.7% Romney
National and State Parks: Babcock State Forest; Forbes State Forest; Gallitzin State Forest; Kooser State Park; Laurel Hill State Park; Laurel Summit State Park
Additional Information Contacts
Somerset County Government . . . . (814) 445-1400
http://www.co.somerset.pa.us
Somerset County Chamber of Commerce . . . . (814) 445-6431
http://www.somersetcountychamber.com

Somerset County Communities

ACOSTA (unincorporated postal area)
Zip Code: 15520
Covers a land area of 0.677 square miles and a water area of 0 square miles. Located at 40.10° N. Lat; 79.06° W. Long. Elevation is 1,857 feet.
Population: 293 (2010); Density: 432.6 persons per square mile (2010); Race: 96.9% White, 0.3% Black, 1.0% Asian, 0.3% American Indian/Alaska Native, 0.0% Native Hawaiian/Other Pacific Islander, 1.5% Other, 1.0% Hispanic of any race (2010); Average household size: 2.71 (2010); Median age: 40.3 (2010); Males per 100 females: 102.1 (2010); Homeownership rate: 87.1% (2010)

ADDISON (borough). Covers a land area of 0.544 square miles and a water area of 0 square miles. Located at 39.75° N. Lat; 79.33° W. Long. Elevation is 2,047 feet.
Population: 224 (1990); 214 (2000); 207 (2010); Density: 380.8 persons per square mile (2010); Race: 98.1% White, 0.5% Black, 0.0% Asian, 1.0% American Indian/Alaska Native, 0.0% Native Hawaiian/Other Pacific Islander, 0.4% Other, 0.0% Hispanic of any race (2010); Average household size: 2.46 (2010); Median age: 45.5 (2010); Males per 100 females: 113.4 (2010); Marriage status: 6.3% never married, 72.0% now married, 21.7% widowed, 0.0% divorced (2006-2010 5-year est.); Foreign born: 0.0% (2006-2010 5-year est.); Ancestry (includes multiple ancestries): 50.9% German, 18.0% English, 15.6% Irish, 7.8% Dutch, 5.4% Italian (2006-2010 5-year est.).
Economy: Single-family building permits issued: 0 (2011); Multi-family building permits issued: 0 (2011); Employment by occupation: 11.1% management, 3.2% professional, 3.2% services, 12.7% sales, 0.0% farming, 17.5% construction, 15.9% production (2006-2010 5-year est.).
Income: Per capita income: $23,832 (2006-2010 5-year est.); Median household income: $41,250 (2006-2010 5-year est.); Average household income: $51,212 (2006-2010 5-year est.); Percent of households with income of $100,000 or more: 9.6% (2006-2010 5-year est.); Poverty rate: 10.2% (2006-2010 5-year est.).

Education: Percent of population age 25 and over with: High school diploma (including GED) or higher: 86.6% (2006-2010 5-year est.); Bachelor's degree or higher: 19.4% (2006-2010 5-year est.); Master's degree or higher: 8.2% (2006-2010 5-year est.).
Housing: Homeownership rate: 84.5% (2010); Median home value: $119,600 (2006-2010 5-year est.); Median contract rent: n/a per month (2006-2010 5-year est.); Median year structure built: before 1940 (2006-2010 5-year est.).
Transportation: Commute to work: 95.1% car, 1.6% public transportation, 0.0% walk, 3.3% work from home (2006-2010 5-year est.); Travel time to work: 33.9% less than 15 minutes, 40.7% 15 to 30 minutes, 8.5% 30 to 45 minutes, 8.5% 45 to 60 minutes, 8.5% 60 minutes or more (2006-2010 5-year est.)

ADDISON (township). Covers a land area of 61.396 square miles and a water area of 1.804 square miles. Located at 39.78° N. Lat; 79.29° W. Long. Elevation is 2,047 feet.
Population: 934 (1990); 1,019 (2000); 974 (2010); Density: 15.9 persons per square mile (2010); Race: 98.3% White, 0.3% Black, 0.1% Asian, 0.1% American Indian/Alaska Native, 0.0% Native Hawaiian/Other Pacific Islander, 1.2% Other, 0.6% Hispanic of any race (2010); Average household size: 2.34 (2010); Median age: 46.1 (2010); Males per 100 females: 112.7 (2010); Marriage status: 20.4% never married, 60.5% now married, 12.7% widowed, 6.4% divorced (2006-2010 5-year est.); Foreign born: 0.0% (2006-2010 5-year est.); Ancestry (includes multiple ancestries): 43.5% German, 11.1% Irish, 8.0% Italian, 7.4% English, 7.4% American (2006-2010 5-year est.).
Economy: Single-family building permits issued: 0 (2011); Multi-family building permits issued: 0 (2011); Employment by occupation: 9.2% management, 0.6% professional, 9.5% services, 13.0% sales, 4.1% farming, 19.6% construction, 4.4% production (2006-2010 5-year est.).
Income: Per capita income: $19,100 (2006-2010 5-year est.); Median household income: $35,893 (2006-2010 5-year est.); Average household income: $45,340 (2006-2010 5-year est.); Percent of households with income of $100,000 or more: 9.4% (2006-2010 5-year est.); Poverty rate: 19.4% (2006-2010 5-year est.).
Education: Percent of population age 25 and over with: High school diploma (including GED) or higher: 74.7% (2006-2010 5-year est.); Bachelor's degree or higher: 12.7% (2006-2010 5-year est.); Master's degree or higher: 4.0% (2006-2010 5-year est.).
Housing: Homeownership rate: 83.0% (2010); Median home value: $85,000 (2006-2010 5-year est.); Median contract rent: $308 per month (2006-2010 5-year est.); Median year structure built: 1972 (2006-2010 5-year est.).
Transportation: Commute to work: 91.0% car, 0.0% public transportation, 3.3% walk, 5.7% work from home (2006-2010 5-year est.); Travel time to work: 17.0% less than 15 minutes, 30.9% 15 to 30 minutes, 25.2% 30 to 45 minutes, 12.1% 45 to 60 minutes, 14.9% 60 minutes or more (2006-2010 5-year est.)

ALLEGHENY (township). Covers a land area of 51.080 square miles and a water area of 0.006 square miles. Located at 39.94° N. Lat; 78.81° W. Long.
Population: 693 (1990); 654 (2000); 692 (2010); Density: 13.5 persons per square mile (2010); Race: 99.4% White, 0.1% Black, 0.0% Asian, 0.0% American Indian/Alaska Native, 0.0% Native Hawaiian/Other Pacific Islander, 0.5% Other, 0.6% Hispanic of any race (2010); Average household size: 2.38 (2010); Median age: 47.4 (2010); Males per 100 females: 114.2 (2010); Marriage status: 25.2% never married, 57.8% now married, 7.8% widowed, 9.3% divorced (2006-2010 5-year est.); Foreign born: 0.5% (2006-2010 5-year est.); Ancestry (includes multiple ancestries): 58.5% German, 12.7% Italian, 10.4% American, 8.9% Irish, 8.5% English (2006-2010 5-year est.).
Economy: Single-family building permits issued: 0 (2011); Multi-family building permits issued: 0 (2011); Employment by occupation: 9.9% management, 2.3% professional, 6.5% services, 8.4% sales, 2.3% farming, 16.0% construction, 12.2% production (2006-2010 5-year est.).
Income: Per capita income: $25,130 (2006-2010 5-year est.); Median household income: $43,839 (2006-2010 5-year est.); Average household income: $58,480 (2006-2010 5-year est.); Percent of households with income of $100,000 or more: 10.3% (2006-2010 5-year est.); Poverty rate: 11.2% (2006-2010 5-year est.).
Education: Percent of population age 25 and over with: High school diploma (including GED) or higher: 84.3% (2006-2010 5-year est.);

Bachelor's degree or higher: 17.9% (2006-2010 5-year est.); Master's degree or higher: 9.8% (2006-2010 5-year est.).
Housing: Homeownership rate: 82.5% (2010); Median home value: $105,900 (2006-2010 5-year est.); Median contract rent: $404 per month (2006-2010 5-year est.); Median year structure built: 1971 (2006-2010 5-year est.).
Transportation: Commute to work: 84.0% car, 0.0% public transportation, 6.4% walk, 9.6% work from home (2006-2010 5-year est.); Travel time to work: 13.7% less than 15 minutes, 57.1% 15 to 30 minutes, 17.7% 30 to 45 minutes, 8.8% 45 to 60 minutes, 2.7% 60 minutes or more (2006-2010 5-year est.)

BENSON (borough). Aka Holsopple. Covers a land area of 0.354 square miles and a water area of 0 square miles. Located at 40.20° N. Lat; 78.93° W. Long. Elevation is 1,529 feet.
Population: 277 (1990); 194 (2000); 191 (2010); Density: 540.1 persons per square mile (2010); Race: 99.0% White, 0.0% Black, 0.0% Asian, 0.5% American Indian/Alaska Native, 0.0% Native Hawaiian/Other Pacific Islander, 0.5% Other, 1.0% Hispanic of any race (2010); Average household size: 2.45 (2010); Median age: 40.3 (2010); Males per 100 females: 119.5 (2010); Marriage status: 17.5% never married, 57.7% now married, 6.6% widowed, 18.2% divorced (2006-2010 5-year est.); Foreign born: 2.8% (2006-2010 5-year est.); Ancestry (includes multiple ancestries): 51.7% German, 23.3% English, 16.5% Irish, 11.9% Italian, 10.8% Portuguese (2006-2010 5-year est.).
Economy: Single-family building permits issued: 0 (2011); Multi-family building permits issued: 0 (2011); Employment by occupation: 5.5% management, 9.6% professional, 0.0% services, 15.1% sales, 0.0% farming, 15.1% construction, 19.2% production (2006-2010 5-year est.).
Income: Per capita income: $16,436 (2006-2010 5-year est.); Median household income: $41,875 (2006-2010 5-year est.); Average household income: $42,705 (2006-2010 5-year est.); Percent of households with income of $100,000 or more: n/a (2006-2010 5-year est.); Poverty rate: 9.7% (2006-2010 5-year est.).
Education: Percent of population age 25 and over with: High school diploma (including GED) or higher: 95.8% (2006-2010 5-year est.); Bachelor's degree or higher: 18.6% (2006-2010 5-year est.); Master's degree or higher: 5.1% (2006-2010 5-year est.).
Housing: Homeownership rate: 78.2% (2010); Median home value: $75,000 (2006-2010 5-year est.); Median contract rent: n/a per month (2006-2010 5-year est.); Median year structure built: before 1940 (2006-2010 5-year est.).
Transportation: Commute to work: 94.5% car, 0.0% public transportation, 0.0% walk, 0.0% work from home (2006-2010 5-year est.); Travel time to work: 12.3% less than 15 minutes, 68.5% 15 to 30 minutes, 2.7% 30 to 45 minutes, 4.1% 45 to 60 minutes, 12.3% 60 minutes or more (2006-2010 5-year est.)

BERLIN (borough). Covers a land area of 0.916 square miles and a water area of 0 square miles. Located at 39.92° N. Lat; 78.95° W. Long. Elevation is 2,329 feet.
History: Settled c.1769 by Germans, laid out 1784, incorporated 1833.
Population: 2,064 (1990); 2,192 (2000); 2,104 (2010); Density: 2,297.9 persons per square mile (2010); Race: 98.3% White, 0.2% Black, 0.4% Asian, 0.1% American Indian/Alaska Native, 0.1% Native Hawaiian/Other Pacific Islander, 0.9% Other, 0.2% Hispanic of any race (2010); Average household size: 2.23 (2010); Median age: 45.1 (2010); Males per 100 females: 83.1 (2010); Marriage status: 24.2% never married, 47.8% now married, 16.8% widowed, 11.2% divorced (2006-2010 5-year est.); Foreign born: 0.3% (2006-2010 5-year est.); Ancestry (includes multiple ancestries): 46.1% German, 9.7% Irish, 6.0% American, 5.8% English, 5.3% Italian (2006-2010 5-year est.).
Economy: Single-family building permits issued: 1 (2011); Multi-family building permits issued: 0 (2011); Employment by occupation: 5.8% management, 1.3% professional, 15.5% services, 14.1% sales, 6.4% farming, 14.2% construction, 11.5% production (2006-2010 5-year est.).
Income: Per capita income: $19,347 (2006-2010 5-year est.); Median household income: $31,051 (2006-2010 5-year est.); Average household income: $42,834 (2006-2010 5-year est.); Percent of households with income of $100,000 or more: 8.3% (2006-2010 5-year est.); Poverty rate: 16.1% (2006-2010 5-year est.).
Education: Percent of population age 25 and over with: High school diploma (including GED) or higher: 80.9% (2006-2010 5-year est.); Bachelor's degree or higher: 11.4% (2006-2010 5-year est.); Master's degree or higher: 4.0% (2006-2010 5-year est.).

Berlin Brothersvalley SD (PK-12)
  2010-11 Enrollment: 889 . . . . (814) 267-4621
Housing: Homeownership rate: 64.4% (2010); Median home value: $89,000 (2006-2010 5-year est.); Median contract rent: $364 per month (2006-2010 5-year est.); Median year structure built: 1951 (2006-2010 5-year est.).
Safety: Violent crime rate: 0.0 per 10,000 population; Property crime rate: 0.0 per 10,000 population (2011).
Transportation: Commute to work: 97.0% car, 0.0% public transportation, 2.3% walk, 0.7% work from home (2006-2010 5-year est.); Travel time to work: 35.1% less than 15 minutes, 49.6% 15 to 30 minutes, 9.7% 30 to 45 minutes, 2.4% 45 to 60 minutes, 3.1% 60 minutes or more (2006-2010 5-year est.)
Additional Information Contacts
Somerset County Chamber of Commerce . . . . (814) 445-6431
  http://www.somersetcountychamber.com

BLACK (township). Covers a land area of 42.725 square miles and a water area of 0.014 square miles. Located at 39.89° N. Lat; 79.14° W. Long.
Population: 942 (1990); 980 (2000); 926 (2010); Density: 21.7 persons per square mile (2010); Race: 99.5% White, 0.0% Black, 0.2% Asian, 0.0% American Indian/Alaska Native, 0.0% Native Hawaiian/Other Pacific Islander, 0.3% Other, 0.0% Hispanic of any race (2010); Average household size: 2.52 (2010); Median age: 42.2 (2010); Males per 100 females: 107.2 (2010); Marriage status: 28.8% never married, 49.8% now married, 12.7% widowed, 8.7% divorced (2006-2010 5-year est.); Foreign born: 0.3% (2006-2010 5-year est.); Ancestry (includes multiple ancestries): 48.6% German, 13.7% Irish, 10.1% English, 8.9% Italian, 8.8% Scottish (2006-2010 5-year est.).
Economy: Single-family building permits issued: 0 (2011); Multi-family building permits issued: 0 (2011); Employment by occupation: 8.3% management, 0.0% professional, 13.0% services, 9.3% sales, 3.5% farming, 12.5% construction, 10.8% production (2006-2010 5-year est.).
Income: Per capita income: $18,336 (2006-2010 5-year est.); Median household income: $40,104 (2006-2010 5-year est.); Average household income: $45,176 (2006-2010 5-year est.); Percent of households with income of $100,000 or more: 7.5% (2006-2010 5-year est.); Poverty rate: 11.8% (2006-2010 5-year est.).
Education: Percent of population age 25 and over with: High school diploma (including GED) or higher: 76.5% (2006-2010 5-year est.); Bachelor's degree or higher: 9.4% (2006-2010 5-year est.); Master's degree or higher: 3.4% (2006-2010 5-year est.).
Housing: Homeownership rate: 90.7% (2010); Median home value: $75,000 (2006-2010 5-year est.); Median contract rent: $396 per month (2006-2010 5-year est.); Median year structure built: 1962 (2006-2010 5-year est.).
Transportation: Commute to work: 94.9% car, 0.0% public transportation, 0.8% walk, 4.4% work from home (2006-2010 5-year est.); Travel time to work: 15.5% less than 15 minutes, 47.7% 15 to 30 minutes, 20.6% 30 to 45 minutes, 3.5% 45 to 60 minutes, 12.6% 60 minutes or more (2006-2010 5-year est.)

BOSWELL (borough). Covers a land area of 0.739 square miles and a water area of 0 square miles. Located at 40.16° N. Lat; 79.03° W. Long. Elevation is 1,857 feet.
History: Incorporated 1904.
Population: 1,485 (1990); 1,364 (2000); 1,277 (2010); Density: 1,727.4 persons per square mile (2010); Race: 97.7% White, 0.6% Black, 0.5% Asian, 0.0% American Indian/Alaska Native, 0.0% Native Hawaiian/Other Pacific Islander, 1.2% Other, 0.4% Hispanic of any race (2010); Average household size: 2.21 (2010); Median age: 41.9 (2010); Males per 100 females: 90.9 (2010); Marriage status: 26.5% never married, 56.9% now married, 7.2% widowed, 9.4% divorced (2006-2010 5-year est.); Foreign born: 0.3% (2006-2010 5-year est.); Ancestry (includes multiple ancestries): 33.2% German, 21.9% Italian, 16.7% Polish, 14.3% Irish, 6.7% English (2006-2010 5-year est.).
Economy: Single-family building permits issued: 2 (2011); Multi-family building permits issued: 0 (2011); Employment by occupation: 4.7% management, 2.4% professional, 22.9% services, 16.9% sales, 1.9% farming, 6.4% construction, 5.2% production (2006-2010 5-year est.).
Income: Per capita income: $17,948 (2006-2010 5-year est.); Median household income: $29,958 (2006-2010 5-year est.); Average household income: $41,153 (2006-2010 5-year est.); Percent of households with

income of $100,000 or more: 6.2% (2006-2010 5-year est.); Poverty rate: 23.7% (2006-2010 5-year est.).

Education: Percent of population age 25 and over with: High school diploma (including GED) or higher: 86.5% (2006-2010 5-year est.); Bachelor's degree or higher: 8.9% (2006-2010 5-year est.); Master's degree or higher: 5.0% (2006-2010 5-year est.).

School District(s)

North Star SD (PK-12)

    2010-11 Enrollment: 1,192 . . . . (814) 629-5631

Housing: Homeownership rate: 56.8% (2010); Median home value: $66,900 (2006-2010 5-year est.); Median contract rent: $272 per month (2006-2010 5-year est.); Median year structure built: 1944 (2006-2010 5-year est.).

Transportation: Commute to work: 95.8% car, 0.0% public transportation, 3.0% walk, 1.2% work from home (2006-2010 5-year est.); Travel time to work: 20.3% less than 15 minutes, 57.2% 15 to 30 minutes, 18.1% 30 to 45 minutes, 1.9% 45 to 60 minutes, 2.5% 60 minutes or more (2006-2010 5-year est.).

Additional Information Contacts

Greater Johnstown Cambria County Chamber of Commerce . . . . (814) 536-5107

    http://www.johnstownchamber.com

BOYNTON (unincorporated postal area)

Zip Code: 15532

Covers a land area of 0.675 square miles and a water area of 0 square miles. Located at 39.76° N. Lat; 79.06° W. Long. Elevation is 1,988 feet. Population: 142 (2010); Density: 210.3 persons per square mile (2010); Race: 100.0% White, 0.0% Black, 0.0% Asian, 0.0% American Indian/Alaska Native, 0.0% Native Hawaiian/Other Pacific Islander, 0.0% Other, 0.0% Hispanic of any race (2010); Average household size: 2.37 (2010); Median age: 45.8 (2010); Males per 100 females: 97.2 (2010); Homeownership rate: 78.4% (2010)

BROTHERSVALLEY (township). Covers a land area of 62.609 square miles and a water area of 0.020 square miles. Located at 39.91° N. Lat; 78.98° W. Long.

Population: 2,395 (1990); 4,184 (2000); 2,398 (2010); Density: 38.3 persons per square mile (2010); Race: 99.0% White, 0.1% Black, 0.4% Asian, 0.0% American Indian/Alaska Native, 0.0% Native Hawaiian/Other Pacific Islander, 0.5% Other, 0.7% Hispanic of any race (2010); Average household size: 2.59 (2010); Median age: 42.4 (2010); Males per 100 females: 103.7 (2010); Marriage status: 20.7% never married, 63.9% now married, 6.8% widowed, 8.6% divorced (2006-2010 5-year est.); Foreign born: 0.4% (2006-2010 5-year est.); Ancestry (includes multiple ancestries): 50.9% German, 14.7% American, 8.7% English, 6.6% Irish, 3.7% Italian (2006-2010 5-year est.).

Economy: Single-family building permits issued: 3 (2011); Multi-family building permits issued: 0 (2011); Employment by occupation: 8.7% management, 3.0% professional, 9.2% services, 16.5% sales, 4.4% farming, 18.3% construction, 8.6% production (2006-2010 5-year est.).

Income: Per capita income: $20,860 (2006-2010 5-year est.); Median household income: $47,649 (2006-2010 5-year est.); Average household income: $54,937 (2006-2010 5-year est.); Percent of households with income of $100,000 or more: 6.7% (2006-2010 5-year est.); Poverty rate: 6.5% (2006-2010 5-year est.).

Education: Percent of population age 25 and over with: High school diploma (including GED) or higher: 87.5% (2006-2010 5-year est.); Bachelor's degree or higher: 10.2% (2006-2010 5-year est.); Master's degree or higher: 2.6% (2006-2010 5-year est.).

Housing: Homeownership rate: 87.7% (2010); Median home value: $103,300 (2006-2010 5-year est.); Median contract rent: $419 per month (2006-2010 5-year est.); Median year structure built: 1962 (2006-2010 5-year est.).

Transportation: Commute to work: 87.4% car, 0.0% public transportation, 4.7% walk, 6.4% work from home (2006-2010 5-year est.); Travel time to work: 34.6% less than 15 minutes, 40.7% 15 to 30 minutes, 15.9% 30 to 45 minutes, 6.7% 45 to 60 minutes, 2.1% 60 minutes or more (2006-2010 5-year est.).

Additional Information Contacts

Somerset County Chamber of Commerce . . . . (814) 445-6431

    http://www.somersetcountychamber.com

CAIRNBROOK (CDP). Covers a land area of 0.844 square miles and a water area of 0 square miles. Located at 40.12° N. Lat; 78.82° W. Long. Elevation is 2,224 feet.

Population: n/a (1990); n/a (2000); 520 (2010); Density: 615.9 persons per square mile (2010); Race: 99.8% White, 0.0% Black, 0.0% Asian, 0.0% American Indian/Alaska Native, 0.0% Native Hawaiian/Other Pacific Islander, 0.2% Other, 0.2% Hispanic of any race (2010); Average household size: 2.23 (2010); Median age: 43.0 (2010); Males per 100 females: 88.4 (2010); Marriage status: 11.8% never married, 51.3% now married, 17.2% widowed, 19.7% divorced (2006-2010 5-year est.); Foreign born: 0.0% (2006-2010 5-year est.); Ancestry (includes multiple ancestries): 31.2% Polish, 23.5% Ukrainian, 14.4% German, 12.8% Russian, 11.7% Hungarian (2006-2010 5-year est.).

Economy: Employment by occupation: 20.8% management, 0.0% professional, 8.3% services, 9.7% sales, 0.0% farming, 2.1% construction, 4.2% production (2006-2010 5-year est.).

Income: Per capita income: $15,581 (2006-2010 5-year est.); Median household income: $14,333 (2006-2010 5-year est.); Average household income: $29,942 (2006-2010 5-year est.); Percent of households with income of $100,000 or more: 1.3% (2006-2010 5-year est.); Poverty rate: 27.4% (2006-2010 5-year est.).

Education: Percent of population age 25 and over with: High school diploma (including GED) or higher: 80.7% (2006-2010 5-year est.); Bachelor's degree or higher: 2.1% (2006-2010 5-year est.); Master's degree or higher: 0.0% (2006-2010 5-year est.).

School District(s)

Shade-Central City SD (KG-12)

    2010-11 Enrollment: 551 . . . . (814) 754-4648

Housing: Homeownership rate: 86.3% (2010); Median home value: $56,000 (2006-2010 5-year est.); Median contract rent: $355 per month (2006-2010 5-year est.); Median year structure built: before 1940 (2006-2010 5-year est.).

Transportation: Commute to work: 91.0% car, 0.0% public transportation, 9.0% walk, 0.0% work from home (2006-2010 5-year est.); Travel time to work: 31.9% less than 15 minutes, 26.4% 15 to 30 minutes, 38.2% 30 to 45 minutes, 3.5% 45 to 60 minutes, 0.0% 60 minutes or more (2006-2010 5-year est.)

CALLIMONT (borough). Covers a land area of 4.356 square miles and a water area of 0 square miles. Located at 39.80° N. Lat; 78.92° W. Long. Elevation is 2,234 feet.

Population: 55 (1990); 51 (2000); 41 (2010); Density: 9.4 persons per square mile (2010); Race: 97.6% White, 0.0% Black, 0.0% Asian, 0.0% American Indian/Alaska Native, 0.0% Native Hawaiian/Other Pacific Islander, 2.4% Other, 0.0% Hispanic of any race (2010); Average household size: 2.28 (2010); Median age: 55.4 (2010); Males per 100 females: 141.2 (2010); Marriage status: 17.1% never married, 75.6% now married, 0.0% widowed, 7.3% divorced (2006-2010 5-year est.); Foreign born: 0.0% (2006-2010 5-year est.); Ancestry (includes multiple ancestries): 58.5% German, 17.1% French, 12.2% Lithuanian, 9.8% English, 4.9% Czech (2006-2010 5-year est.).

Economy: Single-family building permits issued: 0 (2011); Multi-family building permits issued: 0 (2011); Employment by occupation: 10.0% management, 10.0% professional, 0.0% services, 10.0% sales, 0.0% farming, 60.0% construction, 35.0% production (2006-2010 5-year est.).

Income: Per capita income: $31,588 (2006-2010 5-year est.); Median household income: $70,313 (2006-2010 5-year est.); Average household income: $68,084 (2006-2010 5-year est.); Percent of households with income of $100,000 or more: 10.5% (2006-2010 5-year est.); Poverty rate: 0.0% (2006-2010 5-year est.).

Education: Percent of population age 25 and over with: High school diploma (including GED) or higher: 100.0% (2006-2010 5-year est.); Bachelor's degree or higher: 35.1% (2006-2010 5-year est.); Master's degree or higher: 29.7% (2006-2010 5-year est.).

Housing: Homeownership rate: 100.0% (2010); Median home value: $164,600 (2006-2010 5-year est.); Median contract rent: n/a per month (2006-2010 5-year est.); Median year structure built: 1975 (2006-2010 5-year est.).

Transportation: Commute to work: 100.0% car, 0.0% public transportation, 0.0% walk, 0.0% work from home (2006-2010 5-year est.); Travel time to work: 15.0% less than 15 minutes, 20.0% 15 to 30 minutes, 30.0% 30 to 45 minutes, 25.0% 45 to 60 minutes, 10.0% 60 minutes or more (2006-2010 5-year est.)

CASSELMAN (borough). Covers a land area of 0.201 square miles and a water area of <.001 square miles. Located at 39.89° N. Lat; 79.21° W. Long. Elevation is 1,798 feet.

Population: 89 (1990); 99 (2000); 94 (2010); Density: 467.5 persons per square mile (2010); Race: 100.0% White, 0.0% Black, 0.0% Asian, 0.0% American Indian/Alaska Native, 0.0% Native Hawaiian/Other Pacific Islander, 0.0% Other, 0.0% Hispanic of any race (2010); Average household size: 2.69 (2010); Median age: 34.0 (2010); Males per 100 females: 104.3 (2010); Marriage status: 25.6% never married, 51.2% now married, 9.8% widowed, 13.4% divorced (2006-2010 5-year est.); Foreign born: 2.0% (2006-2010 5-year est.); Ancestry (includes multiple ancestries): 41.4% German, 9.1% Pennsylvania German, 8.1% American, 7.1% Irish, 2.0% Italian (2006-2010 5-year est.).

Economy: Single-family building permits issued: 0 (2011); Multi-family building permits issued: 0 (2011); Employment by occupation: 0.0% management, 0.0% professional, 8.3% services, 33.3% sales, 0.0% farming, 25.0% construction, 13.9% production (2006-2010 5-year est.).

Income: Per capita income: $14,163 (2006-2010 5-year est.); Median household income: $35,833 (2006-2010 5-year est.); Average household income: $36,258 (2006-2010 5-year est.); Percent of households with income of $100,000 or more: n/a (2006-2010 5-year est.); Poverty rate: 5.1% (2006-2010 5-year est.).

Education: Percent of population age 25 and over with: High school diploma (including GED) or higher: 78.5% (2006-2010 5-year est.); Bachelor's degree or higher: 0.0% (2006-2010 5-year est.); Master's degree or higher: 0.0% (2006-2010 5-year est.).

Housing: Homeownership rate: 88.6% (2010); Median home value: $63,600 (2006-2010 5-year est.); Median contract rent: n/a per month (2006-2010 5-year est.); Median year structure built: before 1940 (2006-2010 5-year est.).

Transportation: Commute to work: 100.0% car, 0.0% public transportation, 0.0% walk, 0.0% work from home (2006-2010 5-year est.); Travel time to work: 8.3% less than 15 minutes, 30.6% 15 to 30 minutes, 19.4% 30 to 45 minutes, 25.0% 45 to 60 minutes, 16.7% 60 minutes or more (2006-2010 5-year est.)

CENTRAL CITY (borough). Covers a land area of 0.540 square miles and a water area of 0 square miles. Located at 40.11° N. Lat; 78.80° W. Long. Elevation is 2,198 feet.

History: Incorporated 1918.

Population: 1,246 (1990); 1,258 (2000); 1,124 (2010); Density: 2,083.1 persons per square mile (2010); Race: 99.7% White, 0.0% Black, 0.0% Asian, 0.1% American Indian/Alaska Native, 0.0% Native Hawaiian/Other Pacific Islander, 0.2% Other, 0.1% Hispanic of any race (2010); Average household size: 2.30 (2010); Median age: 44.9 (2010); Males per 100 females: 91.5 (2010); Marriage status: 28.0% never married, 54.2% now married, 10.0% widowed, 7.8% divorced (2006-2010 5-year est.); Foreign born: 0.0% (2006-2010 5-year est.); Ancestry (includes multiple ancestries): 28.4% German, 19.4% Polish, 13.9% Irish, 11.3% Italian, 9.5% Slovak (2006-2010 5-year est.).

Economy: Single-family building permits issued: 0 (2011); Multi-family building permits issued: 0 (2011); Employment by occupation: 4.9% management, 1.0% professional, 14.8% services, 19.1% sales, 2.2% farming, 9.9% construction, 3.7% production (2006-2010 5-year est.).

Income: Per capita income: $15,331 (2006-2010 5-year est.); Median household income: $28,077 (2006-2010 5-year est.); Average household income: $38,314 (2006-2010 5-year est.); Percent of households with income of $100,000 or more: 4.8% (2006-2010 5-year est.); Poverty rate: 20.3% (2006-2010 5-year est.).

Education: Percent of population age 25 and over with: High school diploma (including GED) or higher: 85.1% (2006-2010 5-year est.); Bachelor's degree or higher: 11.0% (2006-2010 5-year est.); Master's degree or higher: 3.6% (2006-2010 5-year est.).

Housing: Homeownership rate: 79.9% (2010); Median home value: $62,500 (2006-2010 5-year est.); Median contract rent: $286 per month (2006-2010 5-year est.); Median year structure built: 1943 (2006-2010 5-year est.).

Transportation: Commute to work: 91.6% car, 0.0% public transportation, 3.8% walk, 1.2% work from home (2006-2010 5-year est.); Travel time to work: 22.8% less than 15 minutes, 29.8% 15 to 30 minutes, 29.8% 30 to 45 minutes, 12.7% 45 to 60 minutes, 4.8% 60 minutes or more (2006-2010 5-year est.)

Additional Information Contacts

Greater Johnstown Cambria County Chamber of Commerce . . . . (814) 536-5107
  http://www.johnstownchamber.com

CONEMAUGH (township). Covers a land area of 41.273 square miles and a water area of 0.574 square miles. Located at 40.24° N. Lat; 78.97° W. Long.

Population: 7,737 (1990); 7,452 (2000); 7,279 (2010); Density: 176.4 persons per square mile (2010); Race: 99.0% White, 0.1% Black, 0.2% Asian, 0.0% American Indian/Alaska Native, 0.0% Native Hawaiian/Other Pacific Islander, 0.7% Other, 0.6% Hispanic of any race (2010); Average household size: 2.33 (2010); Median age: 48.6 (2010); Males per 100 females: 95.0 (2010); Marriage status: 19.4% never married, 63.9% now married, 10.9% widowed, 5.9% divorced (2006-2010 5-year est.); Foreign born: 1.3% (2006-2010 5-year est.); Ancestry (includes multiple ancestries): 39.7% German, 13.6% Irish, 9.4% English, 9.3% Italian, 7.9% Polish (2006-2010 5-year est.).

Economy: Single-family building permits issued: 4 (2011); Multi-family building permits issued: 0 (2011); Employment by occupation: 9.0% management, 1.6% professional, 10.0% services, 16.2% sales, 3.0% farming, 9.0% construction, 8.0% production (2006-2010 5-year est.).

Income: Per capita income: $23,538 (2006-2010 5-year est.); Median household income: $50,063 (2006-2010 5-year est.); Average household income: $54,541 (2006-2010 5-year est.); Percent of households with income of $100,000 or more: 10.3% (2006-2010 5-year est.); Poverty rate: 9.1% (2006-2010 5-year est.).

Education: Percent of population age 25 and over with: High school diploma (including GED) or higher: 85.2% (2006-2010 5-year est.); Bachelor's degree or higher: 20.1% (2006-2010 5-year est.); Master's degree or higher: 6.7% (2006-2010 5-year est.).

Housing: Homeownership rate: 81.9% (2010); Median home value: $93,500 (2006-2010 5-year est.); Median contract rent: $436 per month (2006-2010 5-year est.); Median year structure built: 1953 (2006-2010 5-year est.).

Safety: Violent crime rate: 12.3 per 10,000 population; Property crime rate: 56.1 per 10,000 population (2011).

Transportation: Commute to work: 95.4% car, 0.0% public transportation, 1.3% walk, 2.4% work from home (2006-2010 5-year est.); Travel time to work: 28.8% less than 15 minutes, 48.1% 15 to 30 minutes, 15.7% 30 to 45 minutes, 1.4% 45 to 60 minutes, 6.0% 60 minutes or more (2006-2010 5-year est.)

Additional Information Contacts

Conemaugh Township . . . . (814) 288-1400
  http://www.contwpsupers.us
Greater Johnstown Cambria County Chamber of Commerce . . . . (814) 536-5107
  http://www.johnstownchamber.com

CONFLUENCE (borough). Covers a land area of 1.600 square miles and a water area of 0.080 square miles. Located at 39.81° N. Lat; 79.35° W. Long. Elevation is 1,335 feet.

History: Incorporated 1873.

Population: 873 (1990); 834 (2000); 780 (2010); Density: 487.4 persons per square mile (2010); Race: 96.3% White, 0.3% Black, 0.3% Asian, 0.0% American Indian/Alaska Native, 0.0% Native Hawaiian/Other Pacific Islander, 3.1% Other, 1.7% Hispanic of any race (2010); Average household size: 2.14 (2010); Median age: 45.0 (2010); Males per 100 females: 87.5 (2010); Marriage status: 26.0% never married, 51.7% now married, 11.0% widowed, 11.3% divorced (2006-2010 5-year est.); Foreign born: 1.1% (2006-2010 5-year est.); Ancestry (includes multiple ancestries): 37.1% German, 14.2% American, 9.2% Irish, 8.9% English, 4.7% Dutch (2006-2010 5-year est.).

Economy: Single-family building permits issued: 0 (2011); Multi-family building permits issued: 0 (2011); Employment by occupation: 5.0% management, 0.0% professional, 20.6% services, 18.1% sales, 5.3% farming, 9.6% construction, 12.1% production (2006-2010 5-year est.).

Income: Per capita income: $18,283 (2006-2010 5-year est.); Median household income: $34,479 (2006-2010 5-year est.); Average household income: $38,958 (2006-2010 5-year est.); Percent of households with income of $100,000 or more: 5.0% (2006-2010 5-year est.); Poverty rate: 16.2% (2006-2010 5-year est.).

Education: Percent of population age 25 and over with: High school diploma (including GED) or higher: 79.0% (2006-2010 5-year est.);

Bachelor's degree or higher: 14.7% (2006-2010 5-year est.); Master's degree or higher: 3.3% (2006-2010 5-year est.).

School District(s)

Turkeyfoot Valley Area SD (PK-12)

   2010-11 Enrollment: 410 . . . . (814) 395-3621

Housing: Homeownership rate: 59.6% (2010); Median home value: $87,200 (2006-2010 5-year est.); Median contract rent: $235 per month (2006-2010 5-year est.); Median year structure built: 1955 (2006-2010 5-year est.).

Transportation: Commute to work: 82.1% car, 3.4% public transportation, 8.8% walk, 2.7% work from home (2006-2010 5-year est.); Travel time to work: 42.0% less than 15 minutes, 16.5% 15 to 30 minutes, 22.4% 30 to 45 minutes, 5.9% 45 to 60 minutes, 13.3% 60 minutes or more (2006-2010 5-year est.)

DAVIDSVILLE (CDP). Covers a land area of 2.307 square miles and a water area of 0 square miles. Located at 40.23° N. Lat; 78.94° W. Long. Elevation is 1,736 feet.

Population: 1,142 (1990); 1,119 (2000); 1,130 (2010); Density: 489.8 persons per square mile (2010); Race: 99.6% White, 0.0% Black, 0.3% Asian, 0.0% American Indian/Alaska Native, 0.0% Native Hawaiian/Other Pacific Islander, 0.1% Other, 0.4% Hispanic of any race (2010); Average household size: 2.37 (2010); Median age: 51.0 (2010); Males per 100 females: 96.9 (2010); Marriage status: 16.7% never married, 69.6% now married, 7.4% widowed, 6.3% divorced (2006-2010 5-year est.); Foreign born: 1.2% (2006-2010 5-year est.); Ancestry (includes multiple ancestries): 38.4% German, 18.2% Italian, 16.7% Polish, 12.1% English, 7.6% Irish (2006-2010 5-year est.).

Economy: Employment by occupation: 14.9% management, 0.4% professional, 0.0% services, 20.2% sales, 2.6% farming, 3.3% construction, 5.7% production (2006-2010 5-year est.).

Income: Per capita income: $26,453 (2006-2010 5-year est.); Median household income: $67,262 (2006-2010 5-year est.); Average household income: $68,763 (2006-2010 5-year est.); Percent of households with income of $100,000 or more: 12.5% (2006-2010 5-year est.); Poverty rate: 0.0% (2006-2010 5-year est.).

Education: Percent of population age 25 and over with: High school diploma (including GED) or higher: 93.9% (2006-2010 5-year est.); Bachelor's degree or higher: 43.8% (2006-2010 5-year est.); Master's degree or higher: 14.6% (2006-2010 5-year est.).

School District(s)

Conemaugh Township Area SD (KG-12)

   2010-11 Enrollment: 1,022 . . . . (814) 479-7575

Housing: Homeownership rate: 86.1% (2010); Median home value: $139,700 (2006-2010 5-year est.); Median contract rent: $553 per month (2006-2010 5-year est.); Median year structure built: 1975 (2006-2010 5-year est.).

Transportation: Commute to work: 98.8% car, 0.0% public transportation, 1.2% walk, 0.0% work from home (2006-2010 5-year est.); Travel time to work: 29.7% less than 15 minutes, 47.7% 15 to 30 minutes, 18.1% 30 to 45 minutes, 0.0% 45 to 60 minutes, 4.5% 60 minutes or more (2006-2010 5-year est.).

Additional Information Contacts

Greater Johnstown Cambria County Chamber of Commerce . . . . (814) 536-5107

   http://www.johnstownchamber.com

EDIE (CDP). Covers a land area of 0.565 square miles and a water area of 0 square miles. Located at 40.09° N. Lat; 79.13° W. Long. Elevation is 1,998 feet.

Population: n/a (1990); n/a (2000); 83 (2010); Density: 146.9 persons per square mile (2010); Race: 100.0% White, 0.0% Black, 0.0% Asian, 0.0% American Indian/Alaska Native, 0.0% Native Hawaiian/Other Pacific Islander, 0.0% Other, 0.0% Hispanic of any race (2010); Average household size: 2.24 (2010); Median age: 53.2 (2010); Males per 100 females: 84.4 (2010); Marriage status: 24.7% never married, 60.0% now married, 10.6% widowed, 4.7% divorced (2006-2010 5-year est.); Foreign born: 0.0% (2006-2010 5-year est.); Ancestry (includes multiple ancestries): 57.3% German, 24.7% Irish, 6.7% English, 4.5% Polish, 4.5% American (2006-2010 5-year est.).

Economy: Employment by occupation: 0.0% management, 0.0% professional, 13.8% services, 0.0% sales, 0.0% farming, 0.0% construction, 0.0% production (2006-2010 5-year est.).

Income: Per capita income: $19,627 (2006-2010 5-year est.); Median household income: $24,643 (2006-2010 5-year est.); Average household

income: $43,995 (2006-2010 5-year est.); Percent of households with income of $100,000 or more: 10.0% (2006-2010 5-year est.); Poverty rate: 46.1% (2006-2010 5-year est.).

Education: Percent of population age 25 and over with: High school diploma (including GED) or higher: 70.4% (2006-2010 5-year est.); Bachelor's degree or higher: 19.8% (2006-2010 5-year est.); Master's degree or higher: 3.7% (2006-2010 5-year est.).

Housing: Homeownership rate: 97.3% (2010); Median home value: $118,800 (2006-2010 5-year est.); Median contract rent: n/a per month (2006-2010 5-year est.); Median year structure built: 1971 (2006-2010 5-year est.).

Transportation: Commute to work: 100.0% car, 0.0% public transportation, 0.0% walk, 0.0% work from home (2006-2010 5-year est.); Travel time to work: 26.9% less than 15 minutes, 42.3% 15 to 30 minutes, 30.8% 30 to 45 minutes, 0.0% 45 to 60 minutes, 0.0% 60 minutes or more (2006-2010 5-year est.)

ELK LICK (township). Covers a land area of 57.071 square miles and a water area of 0.580 square miles. Located at 39.77° N. Lat; 79.13° W. Long.

Population: 2,246 (1990); 2,293 (2000); 2,241 (2010); Density: 39.3 persons per square mile (2010); Race: 99.3% White, 0.1% Black, 0.0% Asian, 0.0% American Indian/Alaska Native, 0.0% Native Hawaiian/Other Pacific Islander, 0.6% Other, 0.7% Hispanic of any race (2010); Average household size: 2.90 (2010); Median age: 37.8 (2010); Males per 100 females: 98.1 (2010); Marriage status: 27.7% never married, 56.1% now married, 9.2% widowed, 7.0% divorced (2006-2010 5-year est.); Foreign born: 0.8% (2006-2010 5-year est.); Ancestry (includes multiple ancestries): 53.3% German, 13.4% Swiss, 11.6% American, 7.9% English, 5.9% Irish (2006-2010 5-year est.).

Economy: Single-family building permits issued: 2 (2011); Multi-family building permits issued: 0 (2011); Employment by occupation: 11.7% management, 0.6% professional, 9.6% services, 15.7% sales, 3.1% farming, 20.0% construction, 11.9% production (2006-2010 5-year est.).

Income: Per capita income: $16,810 (2006-2010 5-year est.); Median household income: $39,405 (2006-2010 5-year est.); Average household income: $46,991 (2006-2010 5-year est.); Percent of households with income of $100,000 or more: 7.1% (2006-2010 5-year est.); Poverty rate: 21.4% (2006-2010 5-year est.).

Education: Percent of population age 25 and over with: High school diploma (including GED) or higher: 69.3% (2006-2010 5-year est.); Bachelor's degree or higher: 8.5% (2006-2010 5-year est.); Master's degree or higher: 2.0% (2006-2010 5-year est.).

Housing: Homeownership rate: 78.7% (2010); Median home value: $104,300 (2006-2010 5-year est.); Median contract rent: $297 per month (2006-2010 5-year est.); Median year structure built: 1954 (2006-2010 5-year est.).

Transportation: Commute to work: 76.5% car, 0.0% public transportation, 6.9% walk, 14.9% work from home (2006-2010 5-year est.); Travel time to work: 36.2% less than 15 minutes, 34.9% 15 to 30 minutes, 20.4% 30 to 45 minutes, 3.9% 45 to 60 minutes, 4.7% 60 minutes or more (2006-2010 5-year est.).

Additional Information Contacts

Somerset County Chamber of Commerce . . . . (814) 445-6431

   http://www.somersetcountychamber.com

FAIRHOPE (township). Covers a land area of 14.598 square miles and a water area of <.001 square miles. Located at 39.85° N. Lat; 78.77° W. Long. Elevation is 1,352 feet.

Population: 137 (1990); 137 (2000); 134 (2010); Density: 9.2 persons per square mile (2010); Race: 100.0% White, 0.0% Black, 0.0% Asian, 0.0% American Indian/Alaska Native, 0.0% Native Hawaiian/Other Pacific Islander, 0.0% Other, 0.0% Hispanic of any race (2010); Average household size: 2.16 (2010); Median age: 50.0 (2010); Males per 100 females: 112.7 (2010); Marriage status: 11.2% never married, 67.4% now married, 14.6% widowed, 6.7% divorced (2006-2010 5-year est.); Foreign born: 0.0% (2006-2010 5-year est.); Ancestry (includes multiple ancestries): 57.6% German, 12.1% English, 10.1% Dutch, 5.1% American, 4.0% Italian (2006-2010 5-year est.).

Economy: Single-family building permits issued: 0 (2011); Multi-family building permits issued: 0 (2011); Employment by occupation: 5.6% management, 0.0% professional, 5.6% services, 11.1% sales, 0.0% farming, 25.0% construction, 0.0% production (2006-2010 5-year est.).

Income: Per capita income: $14,936 (2006-2010 5-year est.); Median household income: $21,250 (2006-2010 5-year est.); Average household

income: $27,110 (2006-2010 5-year est.); Percent of households with income of $100,000 or more: n/a (2006-2010 5-year est.); Poverty rate: 18.2% (2006-2010 5-year est.).

Education: Percent of population age 25 and over with: High school diploma (including GED) or higher: 74.2% (2006-2010 5-year est.); Bachelor's degree or higher: 10.1% (2006-2010 5-year est.); Master's degree or higher: 2.2% (2006-2010 5-year est.).

Housing: Homeownership rate: 85.5% (2010); Median home value: $84,500 (2006-2010 5-year est.); Median contract rent: $417 per month (2006-2010 5-year est.); Median year structure built: 1953 (2006-2010 5-year est.).

Transportation: Commute to work: 100.0% car, 0.0% public transportation, 0.0% walk, 0.0% work from home (2006-2010 5-year est.); Travel time to work: 0.0% less than 15 minutes, 13.9% 15 to 30 minutes, 30.6% 30 to 45 minutes, 55.6% 45 to 60 minutes, 0.0% 60 minutes or more (2006-2010 5-year est.)

FORT HILL (unincorporated postal area)

Zip Code: 15540

Covers a land area of 36.004 square miles and a water area of 0.586 square miles. Located at 39.79° N. Lat; 79.23° W. Long. Population: 290 (2010); Density: 8.1 persons per square mile (2010); Race: 99.3% White, 0.0% Black, 0.0% Asian, 0.3% American Indian/Alaska Native, 0.0% Native Hawaiian/Other Pacific Islander, 0.4% Other, 0.3% Hispanic of any race (2010); Average household size: 2.48 (2010); Median age: 45.5 (2010); Males per 100 females: 111.7 (2010); Homeownership rate: 85.5% (2010)

FRIEDENS (CDP). Covers a land area of 3.138 square miles and a water area of 0 square miles. Located at 40.04° N. Lat; 79.00° W. Long. Elevation is 2,113 feet.

Population: 1,576 (1990); 1,673 (2000); 1,523 (2010); Density: 485.3 persons per square mile (2010); Race: 99.6% White, 0.0% Black, 0.1% Asian, 0.1% American Indian/Alaska Native, 0.0% Native Hawaiian/Other Pacific Islander, 0.2% Other, 0.1% Hispanic of any race (2010); Average household size: 2.52 (2010); Median age: 40.6 (2010); Males per 100 females: 99.1 (2010); Marriage status: 20.9% never married, 62.2% now married, 7.9% widowed, 8.9% divorced (2006-2010 5-year est.); Foreign born: 0.9% (2006-2010 5-year est.); Ancestry (includes multiple ancestries): 52.5% German, 7.8% English, 6.4% Italian, 4.9% Polish, 4.8% Slovak (2006-2010 5-year est.).

Economy: Employment by occupation: 8.3% management, 1.5% professional, 7.3% services, 16.6% sales, 0.0% farming, 16.6% construction, 11.7% production (2006-2010 5-year est.).

Income: Per capita income: $21,866 (2006-2010 5-year est.); Median household income: $43,125 (2006-2010 5-year est.); Average household income: $52,189 (2006-2010 5-year est.); Percent of households with income of $100,000 or more: 15.4% (2006-2010 5-year est.); Poverty rate: 8.2% (2006-2010 5-year est.).

Education: Percent of population age 25 and over with: High school diploma (including GED) or higher: 93.2% (2006-2010 5-year est.); Bachelor's degree or higher: 15.5% (2006-2010 5-year est.); Master's degree or higher: 9.0% (2006-2010 5-year est.).

School District(s)

Somerset Area SD (KG-12)

2010-11 Enrollment: 2,392 .... (814) 445-9714

Housing: Homeownership rate: 85.7% (2010); Median home value: $117,900 (2006-2010 5-year est.); Median contract rent: $393 per month (2006-2010 5-year est.); Median year structure built: 1980 (2006-2010 5-year est.).

Transportation: Commute to work: 96.7% car, 0.0% public transportation, 0.0% walk, 3.3% work from home (2006-2010 5-year est.); Travel time to work: 42.3% less than 15 minutes, 36.3% 15 to 30 minutes, 4.7% 30 to 45 minutes, 4.7% 45 to 60 minutes, 12.0% 60 minutes or more (2006-2010 5-year est.)

Additional Information Contacts

Somerset County Chamber of Commerce .... (814) 445-6431
http://www.somersetcountychamber.com

GARRETT (borough). Covers a land area of 0.506 square miles and a water area of 0 square miles. Located at 39.86° N. Lat; 79.06° W. Long. Elevation is 1,923 feet.

Population: 520 (1990); 449 (2000); 456 (2010); Density: 901.8 persons per square mile (2010); Race: 99.8% White, 0.0% Black, 0.0% Asian, 0.0% American Indian/Alaska Native, 0.0% Native Hawaiian/Other Pacific

Islander, 0.2% Other, 0.4% Hispanic of any race (2010); Average household size: 2.58 (2010); Median age: 40.8 (2010); Males per 100 females: 95.7 (2010); Marriage status: 13.5% never married, 64.2% now married, 12.0% widowed, 10.2% divorced (2006-2010 5-year est.); Foreign born: 0.0% (2006-2010 5-year est.); Ancestry (includes multiple ancestries): 44.9% German, 14.3% American, 10.2% English, 7.9% Irish, 5.2% Dutch (2006-2010 5-year est.).

Economy: Single-family building permits issued: 0 (2011); Multi-family building permits issued: 0 (2011); Employment by occupation: 7.0% management, 0.7% professional, 13.4% services, 14.8% sales, 6.3% farming, 10.6% construction, 4.2% production (2006-2010 5-year est.).

Income: Per capita income: $16,478 (2006-2010 5-year est.); Median household income: $36,000 (2006-2010 5-year est.); Average household income: $42,894 (2006-2010 5-year est.); Percent of households with income of $100,000 or more: 3.9% (2006-2010 5-year est.); Poverty rate: 9.6% (2006-2010 5-year est.).

Education: Percent of population age 25 and over with: High school diploma (including GED) or higher: 77.6% (2006-2010 5-year est.); Bachelor's degree or higher: 3.8% (2006-2010 5-year est.); Master's degree or higher: 2.5% (2006-2010 5-year est.).

Housing: Homeownership rate: 86.5% (2010); Median home value: $66,400 (2006-2010 5-year est.); Median contract rent: $342 per month (2006-2010 5-year est.); Median year structure built: 1945 (2006-2010 5-year est.).

Safety: Violent crime rate: 0.0 per 10,000 population; Property crime rate: 0.0 per 10,000 population (2011).

Transportation: Commute to work: 96.4% car, 0.0% public transportation, 0.0% walk, 2.2% work from home (2006-2010 5-year est.); Travel time to work: 18.4% less than 15 minutes, 52.9% 15 to 30 minutes, 19.1% 30 to 45 minutes, 5.9% 45 to 60 minutes, 3.7% 60 minutes or more (2006-2010 5-year est.)

GREENVILLE (township). Covers a land area of 25.062 square miles and a water area of 0.009 square miles. Located at 39.75° N. Lat; 78.97° W. Long.

Population: 664 (1990); 718 (2000); 668 (2010); Density: 26.7 persons per square mile (2010); Race: 99.9% White, 0.0% Black, 0.0% Asian, 0.0% American Indian/Alaska Native, 0.0% Native Hawaiian/Other Pacific Islander, 0.1% Other, 0.6% Hispanic of any race (2010); Average household size: 2.83 (2010); Median age: 37.3 (2010); Males per 100 females: 98.8 (2010); Marriage status: 19.1% never married, 63.1% now married, 7.8% widowed, 9.9% divorced (2006-2010 5-year est.); Foreign born: 0.5% (2006-2010 5-year est.); Ancestry (includes multiple ancestries): 55.9% German, 9.3% English, 8.5% American, 6.8% Irish, 3.7% Italian (2006-2010 5-year est.).

Economy: Single-family building permits issued: 4 (2011); Multi-family building permits issued: 0 (2011); Employment by occupation: 9.0% management, 2.4% professional, 11.3% services, 15.2% sales, 5.7% farming, 14.6% construction, 6.9% production (2006-2010 5-year est.).

Income: Per capita income: $20,587 (2006-2010 5-year est.); Median household income: $37,750 (2006-2010 5-year est.); Average household income: $54,199 (2006-2010 5-year est.); Percent of households with income of $100,000 or more: 12.6% (2006-2010 5-year est.); Poverty rate: 15.0% (2006-2010 5-year est.).

Education: Percent of population age 25 and over with: High school diploma (including GED) or higher: 73.2% (2006-2010 5-year est.); Bachelor's degree or higher: 16.7% (2006-2010 5-year est.); Master's degree or higher: 9.3% (2006-2010 5-year est.).

Housing: Homeownership rate: 81.8% (2010); Median home value: $120,500 (2006-2010 5-year est.); Median contract rent: $219 per month (2006-2010 5-year est.); Median year structure built: 1971 (2006-2010 5-year est.).

Transportation: Commute to work: 90.1% car, 0.0% public transportation, 0.0% walk, 9.0% work from home (2006-2010 5-year est.); Travel time to work: 17.0% less than 15 minutes, 39.7% 15 to 30 minutes, 32.1% 30 to 45 minutes, 7.2% 45 to 60 minutes, 3.9% 60 minutes or more (2006-2010 5-year est.)

HIDDEN VALLEY (unincorporated postal area)

Zip Code: 15502

Covers a land area of 5.984 square miles and a water area of 0.009 square miles. Located at 40.04° N. Lat; 79.24° W. Long. Population: 191 (2010); Density: 31.9 persons per square mile (2010); Race: 97.4% White, 1.0% Black, 0.5% Asian, 0.0% American Indian/Alaska Native, 0.0% Native Hawaiian/Other Pacific Islander, 1.1% Other, 0.0%

Hispanic of any race (2010); Average household size: 1.99 (2010); Median age: 57.6 (2010); Males per 100 females: 114.6 (2010); Homeownership rate: 89.6% (2010)

HOLLSOPPLE (unincorporated postal area)
Zip Code: 15935

Covers a land area of 24.109 square miles and a water area of 1.385 square miles. Located at 40.20° N. Lat; 78.96° W. Long. Population: 2,620 (2010); Density: 108.7 persons per square mile (2010); Race: 99.1% White, 0.1% Black, 0.1% Asian, 0.1% American Indian/Alaska Native, 0.1% Native Hawaiian/Other Pacific Islander, 0.5% Other, 0.8% Hispanic of any race (2010); Average household size: 2.41 (2010); Median age: 46.3 (2010); Males per 100 females: 100.9 (2010); Homeownership rate: 85.1% (2010)

HOOVERSVILLE (borough). Covers a land area of 0.611 square miles and a water area of 0 square miles. Located at 40.15° N. Lat; 78.91° W. Long. Elevation is 1,713 feet.
History: Incorporated 1896.
Population: 731 (1990); 779 (2000); 645 (2010); Density: 1,056.4 persons per square mile (2010); Race: 99.5% White, 0.2% Black, 0.0% Asian, 0.0% American Indian/Alaska Native, 0.0% Native Hawaiian/Other Pacific Islander, 0.3% Other, 0.3% Hispanic of any race (2010); Average household size: 2.26 (2010); Median age: 44.0 (2010); Males per 100 females: 102.2 (2010); Marriage status: 27.5% never married, 43.6% now married, 9.3% widowed, 19.7% divorced (2006-2010 5-year est.); Foreign born: 0.0% (2006-2010 5-year est.); Ancestry (includes multiple ancestries): 47.1% German, 17.7% Irish, 9.4% Dutch, 7.4% Polish, 6.9% Italian (2006-2010 5-year est.).
Economy: Single-family building permits issued: 0 (2011); Multi-family building permits issued: 0 (2011); Employment by occupation: 1.8% management, 1.1% professional, 22.1% services, 19.3% sales, 0.0% farming, 11.6% construction, 9.5% production (2006-2010 5-year est.).
Income: Per capita income: $16,074 (2006-2010 5-year est.); Median household income: $25,833 (2006-2010 5-year est.); Average household income: $34,605 (2006-2010 5-year est.); Percent of households with income of $100,000 or more: 1.4% (2006-2010 5-year est.); Poverty rate: 12.8% (2006-2010 5-year est.).
Education: Percent of population age 25 and over with: High school diploma (including GED) or higher: 77.5% (2006-2010 5-year est.); Bachelor's degree or higher: 9.1% (2006-2010 5-year est.); Master's degree or higher: 1.5% (2006-2010 5-year est.).
Housing: Homeownership rate: 74.0% (2010); Median home value: $63,100 (2006-2010 5-year est.); Median contract rent: $294 per month (2006-2010 5-year est.); Median year structure built: before 1940 (2006-2010 5-year est.).
Safety: Violent crime rate: 30.9 per 10,000 population; Property crime rate: 170.0 per 10,000 population (2011).
Transportation: Commute to work: 83.2% car, 0.0% public transportation, 8.4% walk, 7.7% work from home (2006-2010 5-year est.); Travel time to work: 25.5% less than 15 minutes, 43.3% 15 to 30 minutes, 23.6% 30 to 45 minutes, 5.7% 45 to 60 minutes, 1.9% 60 minutes or more (2006-2010 5-year est.)

INDIAN LAKE (borough). Covers a land area of 3.563 square miles and a water area of 0.786 square miles. Located at 40.04° N. Lat; 78.87° W. Long. Elevation is 2,352 feet.
Population: 388 (1990); 450 (2000); 394 (2010); Density: 110.6 persons per square mile (2010); Race: 98.2% White, 0.8% Black, 0.3% Asian, 0.0% American Indian/Alaska Native, 0.0% Native Hawaiian/Other Pacific Islander, 0.7% Other, 1.0% Hispanic of any race (2010); Average household size: 1.96 (2010); Median age: 56.5 (2010); Males per 100 females: 121.3 (2010); Marriage status: 20.6% never married, 62.5% now married, 2.9% widowed, 14.0% divorced (2006-2010 5-year est.); Foreign born: 2.5% (2006-2010 5-year est.); Ancestry (includes multiple ancestries): 34.3% German, 13.4% American, 9.6% English, 9.3% Irish, 7.8% Polish (2006-2010 5-year est.).
Economy: Single-family building permits issued: 1 (2011); Multi-family building permits issued: 0 (2011); Employment by occupation: 19.0% management, 4.3% professional, 9.5% services, 7.6% sales, 10.0% farming, 2.8% construction, 0.0% production (2006-2010 5-year est.).
Income: Per capita income: $61,929 (2006-2010 5-year est.); Median household income: $77,143 (2006-2010 5-year est.); Average household income: $128,111 (2006-2010 5-year est.); Percent of households with

income of $100,000 or more: 36.7% (2006-2010 5-year est.); Poverty rate: 7.3% (2006-2010 5-year est.).
Education: Percent of population age 25 and over with: High school diploma (including GED) or higher: 96.2% (2006-2010 5-year est.); Bachelor's degree or higher: 40.6% (2006-2010 5-year est.); Master's degree or higher: 20.2% (2006-2010 5-year est.).
Housing: Homeownership rate: 93.0% (2010); Median home value: $305,400 (2006-2010 5-year est.); Median contract rent: n/a per month (2006-2010 5-year est.); Median year structure built: 1973 (2006-2010 5-year est.).
Transportation: Commute to work: 96.0% car, 0.0% public transportation, 1.5% walk, 2.5% work from home (2006-2010 5-year est.); Travel time to work: 15.7% less than 15 minutes, 30.5% 15 to 30 minutes, 34.0% 30 to 45 minutes, 7.1% 45 to 60 minutes, 12.7% 60 minutes or more (2006-2010 5-year est.)
Additional Information Contacts
Borough of Indian Lake . . . . (814) 754-8161
   http://www.indian-lake.pa.us

JEFFERSON (township). Covers a land area of 41.214 square miles and a water area of 0.153 square miles. Located at 40.07° N. Lat; 79.23° W. Long.
Population: 1,462 (1990); 1,375 (2000); 1,423 (2010); Density: 34.5 persons per square mile (2010); Race: 97.3% White, 0.6% Black, 0.8% Asian, 0.0% American Indian/Alaska Native, 0.1% Native Hawaiian/Other Pacific Islander, 1.2% Other, 0.4% Hispanic of any race (2010); Average household size: 2.36 (2010); Median age: 47.1 (2010); Males per 100 females: 109.3 (2010); Marriage status: 22.9% never married, 67.9% now married, 4.1% widowed, 5.1% divorced (2006-2010 5-year est.); Foreign born: 0.3% (2006-2010 5-year est.); Ancestry (includes multiple ancestries): 51.8% German, 10.9% Irish, 10.7% American, 7.8% Italian, 6.4% English (2006-2010 5-year est.).
Economy: Single-family building permits issued: 4 (2011); Multi-family building permits issued: 0 (2011); Employment by occupation: 13.0% management, 2.8% professional, 8.3% services, 17.7% sales, 3.5% farming, 13.3% construction, 7.5% production (2006-2010 5-year est.).
Income: Per capita income: $26,902 (2006-2010 5-year est.); Median household income: $49,327 (2006-2010 5-year est.); Average household income: $64,052 (2006-2010 5-year est.); Percent of households with income of $100,000 or more: 11.6% (2006-2010 5-year est.); Poverty rate: 8.0% (2006-2010 5-year est.).
Education: Percent of population age 25 and over with: High school diploma (including GED) or higher: 90.1% (2006-2010 5-year est.); Bachelor's degree or higher: 24.1% (2006-2010 5-year est.); Master's degree or higher: 10.7% (2006-2010 5-year est.).
Housing: Homeownership rate: 84.0% (2010); Median home value: $133,900 (2006-2010 5-year est.); Median contract rent: $406 per month (2006-2010 5-year est.); Median year structure built: 1983 (2006-2010 5-year est.).
Transportation: Commute to work: 88.1% car, 0.0% public transportation, 2.2% walk, 9.7% work from home (2006-2010 5-year est.); Travel time to work: 21.5% less than 15 minutes, 47.4% 15 to 30 minutes, 13.7% 30 to 45 minutes, 4.2% 45 to 60 minutes, 13.3% 60 minutes or more (2006-2010 5-year est.)
Additional Information Contacts
Somerset County Chamber of Commerce . . . . (814) 445-6431
   http://www.somersetcountychamber.com

JENNER (township). Covers a land area of 64.620 square miles and a water area of 0.497 square miles. Located at 40.18° N. Lat; 79.06° W. Long.
Population: 4,147 (1990); 4,054 (2000); 4,122 (2010); Density: 63.8 persons per square mile (2010); Race: 98.4% White, 0.2% Black, 0.2% Asian, 0.2% American Indian/Alaska Native, 0.0% Native Hawaiian/Other Pacific Islander, 1.0% Other, 0.6% Hispanic of any race (2010); Average household size: 2.48 (2010); Median age: 44.4 (2010); Males per 100 females: 102.4 (2010); Marriage status: 23.1% never married, 57.5% now married, 5.1% widowed, 14.2% divorced (2006-2010 5-year est.); Foreign born: 1.4% (2006-2010 5-year est.); Ancestry (includes multiple ancestries): 42.2% German, 15.7% Irish, 15.6% English, 7.7% Polish, 7.0% Pennsylvania German (2006-2010 5-year est.).
Economy: Single-family building permits issued: 2 (2011); Multi-family building permits issued: 0 (2011); Employment by occupation: 3.5% management, 1.7% professional, 11.9% services, 15.9% sales, 1.8% farming, 15.9% construction, 10.5% production (2006-2010 5-year est.).

Income: Per capita income: $19,881 (2006-2010 5-year est.); Median household income: $48,036 (2006-2010 5-year est.); Average household income: $51,485 (2006-2010 5-year est.); Percent of households with income of $100,000 or more: 7.0% (2006-2010 5-year est.); Poverty rate: 8.7% (2006-2010 5-year est.).

Education: Percent of population age 25 and over with: High school diploma (including GED) or higher: 81.8% (2006-2010 5-year est.); Bachelor's degree or higher: 8.3% (2006-2010 5-year est.); Master's degree or higher: 4.2% (2006-2010 5-year est.).

Housing: Homeownership rate: 83.2% (2010); Median home value: $87,100 (2006-2010 5-year est.); Median contract rent: $313 per month (2006-2010 5-year est.); Median year structure built: 1959 (2006-2010 5-year est.).

Transportation: Commute to work: 89.7% car, 0.0% public transportation, 2.1% walk, 8.2% work from home (2006-2010 5-year est.); Travel time to work: 30.0% less than 15 minutes, 45.1% 15 to 30 minutes, 15.5% 30 to 45 minutes, 2.3% 45 to 60 minutes, 7.0% 60 minutes or more (2006-2010 5-year est.)

Additional Information Contacts

Greater Johnstown Cambria County Chamber of Commerce . . . . (814) 536-5107

http://www.johnstownchamber.com

JENNERS (unincorporated postal area)

Zip Code: 15546

Covers a land area of 0.771 square miles and a water area of 0 square miles. Located at 40.13° N. Lat; 79.04° W. Long. Elevation is 1,837 feet. Population: 386 (2010); Density: 500.3 persons per square mile (2010); Race: 98.4% White, 0.8% Black, 0.3% Asian, 0.0% American Indian/Alaska Native, 0.0% Native Hawaiian/Other Pacific Islander, 0.5% Other, 0.3% Hispanic of any race (2010); Average household size: 2.52 (2010); Median age: 39.7 (2010); Males per 100 females: 104.2 (2010); Homeownership rate: 85.7% (2010)

JENNERSTOWN (borough). Covers a land area of 1.923 square miles and a water area of 0.067 square miles. Located at 40.16° N. Lat; 79.06° W. Long. Elevation is 1,942 feet.

Population: 635 (1990); 714 (2000); 695 (2010); Density: 361.5 persons per square mile (2010); Race: 98.7% White, 0.1% Black, 0.0% Asian, 0.0% American Indian/Alaska Native, 0.0% Native Hawaiian/Other Pacific Islander, 1.2% Other, 0.4% Hispanic of any race (2010); Average household size: 2.34 (2010); Median age: 44.4 (2010); Males per 100 females: 100.9 (2010); Marriage status: 26.0% never married, 58.8% now married, 9.2% widowed, 6.0% divorced (2006-2010 5-year est.); Foreign born: 2.0% (2006-2010 5-year est.); Ancestry (includes multiple ancestries): 54.5% German, 17.4% Polish, 15.6% English, 12.7% Irish, 5.3% Scotch-Irish (2006-2010 5-year est.).

Economy: Single-family building permits issued: 0 (2011); Multi-family building permits issued: 0 (2011); Employment by occupation: 6.0% management, 5.6% professional, 6.7% services, 18.7% sales, 0.0% farming, 13.5% construction, 6.0% production (2006-2010 5-year est.).

Income: Per capita income: $34,212 (2006-2010 5-year est.); Median household income: $49,630 (2006-2010 5-year est.); Average household income: $74,068 (2006-2010 5-year est.); Percent of households with income of $100,000 or more: 14.4% (2006-2010 5-year est.); Poverty rate: 1.6% (2006-2010 5-year est.).

Education: Percent of population age 25 and over with: High school diploma (including GED) or higher: 98.7% (2006-2010 5-year est.); Bachelor's degree or higher: 25.1% (2006-2010 5-year est.); Master's degree or higher: 11.5% (2006-2010 5-year est.).

Housing: Homeownership rate: 88.4% (2010); Median home value: $129,800 (2006-2010 5-year est.); Median contract rent: $397 per month (2006-2010 5-year est.); Median year structure built: 1959 (2006-2010 5-year est.).

Safety: Violent crime rate: 28.7 per 10,000 population; Property crime rate: 28.7 per 10,000 population (2011).

Transportation: Commute to work: 80.5% car, 0.0% public transportation, 9.4% walk, 4.5% work from home (2006-2010 5-year est.); Travel time to work: 31.4% less than 15 minutes, 34.1% 15 to 30 minutes, 21.2% 30 to 45 minutes, 7.5% 45 to 60 minutes, 5.9% 60 minutes or more (2006-2010 5-year est.)

JEROME (CDP). Covers a land area of 2.603 square miles and a water area of 0 square miles. Located at 40.21° N. Lat; 78.98° W. Long. Elevation is 1,788 feet.

Population: 1,057 (1990); 1,068 (2000); 1,017 (2010); Density: 390.7 persons per square mile (2010); Race: 98.0% White, 0.0% Black, 0.3% Asian, 0.0% American Indian/Alaska Native, 0.0% Native Hawaiian/Other Pacific Islander, 1.7% Other, 0.8% Hispanic of any race (2010); Average household size: 2.33 (2010); Median age: 47.7 (2010); Males per 100 females: 90.1 (2010); Marriage status: 22.8% never married, 56.4% now married, 17.9% widowed, 3.0% divorced (2006-2010 5-year est.); Foreign born: 0.0% (2006-2010 5-year est.); Ancestry (includes multiple ancestries): 29.6% German, 26.2% Irish, 5.8% Polish, 5.0% English, 4.8% Italian (2006-2010 5-year est.).

Economy: Employment by occupation: 24.3% management, 0.0% professional, 0.0% services, 0.0% sales, 0.0% farming, 0.0% construction, 0.0% production (2006-2010 5-year est.).

Income: Per capita income: $22,244 (2006-2010 5-year est.); Median household income: $40,469 (2006-2010 5-year est.); Average household income: $47,100 (2006-2010 5-year est.); Percent of households with income of $100,000 or more: 5.1% (2006-2010 5-year est.); Poverty rate: 2.0% (2006-2010 5-year est.).

Education: Percent of population age 25 and over with: High school diploma (including GED) or higher: 64.1% (2006-2010 5-year est.); Bachelor's degree or higher: 12.8% (2006-2010 5-year est.); Master's degree or higher: 4.1% (2006-2010 5-year est.).

School District(s)

Conemaugh Township Area SD (KG-12)

2010-11 Enrollment: 1,022 . . . . (814) 479-7575

Housing: Homeownership rate: 83.8% (2010); Median home value: $51,700 (2006-2010 5-year est.); Median contract rent: $536 per month (2006-2010 5-year est.); Median year structure built: before 1940 (2006-2010 5-year est.).

Transportation: Commute to work: 91.5% car, 0.0% public transportation, 8.5% walk, 0.0% work from home (2006-2010 5-year est.); Travel time to work: 8.5% less than 15 minutes, 75.7% 15 to 30 minutes, 7.9% 30 to 45 minutes, 7.9% 45 to 60 minutes, 0.0% 60 minutes or more (2006-2010 5-year est.)

LARIMER (township). Covers a land area of 16.838 square miles and a water area of 0 square miles. Located at 39.79° N. Lat; 78.93° W. Long.

Population: 547 (1990); 590 (2000); 595 (2010); Density: 35.3 persons per square mile (2010); Race: 99.0% White, 0.0% Black, 0.0% Asian, 0.3% American Indian/Alaska Native, 0.0% Native Hawaiian/Other Pacific Islander, 0.7% Other, 0.3% Hispanic of any race (2010); Average household size: 2.52 (2010); Median age: 46.9 (2010); Males per 100 females: 107.3 (2010); Marriage status: 19.3% never married, 67.7% now married, 10.1% widowed, 2.9% divorced (2006-2010 5-year est.); Foreign born: 0.0% (2006-2010 5-year est.); Ancestry (includes multiple ancestries): 51.4% German, 10.5% Irish, 10.1% English, 7.3% American, 3.5% Welsh (2006-2010 5-year est.).

Economy: Single-family building permits issued: 1 (2011); Multi-family building permits issued: 0 (2011); Employment by occupation: 0.0% management, 3.1% professional, 17.2% services, 9.2% sales, 1.1% farming, 22.5% construction, 10.7% production (2006-2010 5-year est.).

Income: Per capita income: $16,446 (2006-2010 5-year est.); Median household income: $35,694 (2006-2010 5-year est.); Average household income: $39,703 (2006-2010 5-year est.); Percent of households with income of $100,000 or more: 3.3% (2006-2010 5-year est.); Poverty rate: 15.0% (2006-2010 5-year est.).

Education: Percent of population age 25 and over with: High school diploma (including GED) or higher: 79.5% (2006-2010 5-year est.); Bachelor's degree or higher: 8.0% (2006-2010 5-year est.); Master's degree or higher: 3.6% (2006-2010 5-year est.).

Housing: Homeownership rate: 88.1% (2010); Median home value: $90,800 (2006-2010 5-year est.); Median contract rent: $344 per month (2006-2010 5-year est.); Median year structure built: 1978 (2006-2010 5-year est.).

Transportation: Commute to work: 95.5% car, 0.0% public transportation, 0.0% walk, 4.5% work from home (2006-2010 5-year est.); Travel time to work: 21.6% less than 15 minutes, 52.6% 15 to 30 minutes, 19.0% 30 to 45 minutes, 1.3% 45 to 60 minutes, 5.6% 60 minutes or more (2006-2010 5-year est.)

LINCOLN (township). Covers a land area of 25.735 square miles and a water area of 0 square miles. Located at 40.10° N. Lat; 79.11° W. Long.

Population: 1,655 (1990); 1,669 (2000); 1,519 (2010); Density: 59.0 persons per square mile (2010); Race: 98.9% White, 0.1% Black, 0.5% Asian, 0.0% American Indian/Alaska Native, 0.0% Native Hawaiian/Other Pacific Islander, 0.5% Other, 0.4% Hispanic of any race (2010); Average household size: 2.43 (2010); Median age: 45.6 (2010); Males per 100 females: 105.8 (2010); Marriage status: 22.4% never married, 61.2% now married, 5.3% widowed, 11.2% divorced (2006-2010 5-year est.); Foreign born: 0.5% (2006-2010 5-year est.); Ancestry (includes multiple ancestries): 56.2% German, 14.7% Irish, 7.5% Italian, 6.6% English, 5.5% Dutch (2006-2010 5-year est.).

Economy: Single-family building permits issued: 0 (2011); Multi-family building permits issued: 0 (2011); Employment by occupation: 9.5% management, 4.1% professional, 12.4% services, 12.8% sales, 5.3% farming, 15.2% construction, 10.3% production (2006-2010 5-year est.).

Income: Per capita income: $21,008 (2006-2010 5-year est.); Median household income: $42,188 (2006-2010 5-year est.); Average household income: $52,967 (2006-2010 5-year est.); Percent of households with income of $100,000 or more: 9.9% (2006-2010 5-year est.); Poverty rate: 11.6% (2006-2010 5-year est.).

Education: Percent of population age 25 and over with: High school diploma (including GED) or higher: 88.2% (2006-2010 5-year est.); Bachelor's degree or higher: 14.4% (2006-2010 5-year est.); Master's degree or higher: 4.3% (2006-2010 5-year est.).

Housing: Homeownership rate: 87.5% (2010); Median home value: $111,000 (2006-2010 5-year est.); Median contract rent: $383 per month (2006-2010 5-year est.); Median year structure built: 1972 (2006-2010 5-year est.).

Transportation: Commute to work: 92.9% car, 0.4% public transportation, 2.4% walk, 3.9% work from home (2006-2010 5-year est.); Travel time to work: 31.3% less than 15 minutes, 45.2% 15 to 30 minutes, 14.0% 30 to 45 minutes, 5.8% 45 to 60 minutes, 3.8% 60 minutes or more (2006-2010 5-year est.)

Additional Information Contacts

Somerset County Chamber of Commerce . . . . (814) 445-6431
  http://www.somersetcountychamber.com

LOWER TURKEYFOOT (township). Covers a land area of 35.967 square miles and a water area of 0.290 square miles. Located at 39.87° N. Lat; 79.36° W. Long.

Population: 670 (1990); 672 (2000); 603 (2010); Density: 16.8 persons per square mile (2010); Race: 98.8% White, 0.3% Black, 0.0% Asian, 0.3% American Indian/Alaska Native, 0.0% Native Hawaiian/Other Pacific Islander, 0.6% Other, 0.5% Hispanic of any race (2010); Average household size: 2.29 (2010); Median age: 45.8 (2010); Males per 100 females: 105.1 (2010); Marriage status: 24.5% never married, 58.0% now married, 15.9% widowed, 1.6% divorced (2006-2010 5-year est.); Foreign born: 0.0% (2006-2010 5-year est.); Ancestry (includes multiple ancestries): 45.6% German, 20.1% Irish, 7.4% American, 6.6% Dutch, 4.6% English (2006-2010 5-year est.).

Economy: Single-family building permits issued: 0 (2011); Multi-family building permits issued: 0 (2011); Employment by occupation: 4.8% management, 0.0% professional, 14.8% services, 23.3% sales, 0.0% farming, 22.2% construction, 3.2% production (2006-2010 5-year est.).

Income: Per capita income: $16,243 (2006-2010 5-year est.); Median household income: $36,833 (2006-2010 5-year est.); Average household income: $42,594 (2006-2010 5-year est.); Percent of households with income of $100,000 or more: 6.8% (2006-2010 5-year est.); Poverty rate: 12.8% (2006-2010 5-year est.).

Education: Percent of population age 25 and over with: High school diploma (including GED) or higher: 75.5% (2006-2010 5-year est.); Bachelor's degree or higher: 7.5% (2006-2010 5-year est.); Master's degree or higher: 0.5% (2006-2010 5-year est.).

Housing: Homeownership rate: 84.3% (2010); Median home value: $71,900 (2006-2010 5-year est.); Median contract rent: $375 per month (2006-2010 5-year est.); Median year structure built: 1967 (2006-2010 5-year est.).

Transportation: Commute to work: 92.9% car, 0.0% public transportation, 1.6% walk, 5.5% work from home (2006-2010 5-year est.); Travel time to work: 16.8% less than 15 minutes, 30.6% 15 to 30 minutes, 17.9% 30 to 45 minutes, 9.2% 45 to 60 minutes, 25.4% 60 minutes or more (2006-2010 5-year est.)

MARKLETON (unincorporated postal area)
Zip Code: 15551

Covers a land area of 35.923 square miles and a water area of 0.006 square miles. Located at 39.86° N. Lat; 79.28° W. Long. Population: 860 (2010); Density: 23.9 persons per square mile (2010); Race: 99.7% White, 0.1% Black, 0.0% Asian, 0.0% American Indian/Alaska Native, 0.0% Native Hawaiian/Other Pacific Islander, 0.2% Other, 0.5% Hispanic of any race (2010); Average household size: 2.43 (2010); Median age: 46.5 (2010); Males per 100 females: 108.2 (2010); Homeownership rate: 89.6% (2010)

MEYERSDALE (borough). Covers a land area of 0.817 square miles and a water area of 0 square miles. Located at 39.81° N. Lat; 79.03° W. Long. Elevation is 1,985 feet.

History: Laid out 1844, incorporated 1871.

Population: 2,518 (1990); 2,473 (2000); 2,184 (2010); Density: 2,672.9 persons per square mile (2010); Race: 98.8% White, 0.1% Black, 0.2% Asian, 0.1% American Indian/Alaska Native, 0.1% Native Hawaiian/Other Pacific Islander, 0.7% Other, 0.3% Hispanic of any race (2010); Average household size: 2.29 (2010); Median age: 42.8 (2010); Males per 100 females: 89.9 (2010); Marriage status: 24.3% never married, 54.2% now married, 14.4% widowed, 7.1% divorced (2006-2010 5-year est.); Foreign born: 1.6% (2006-2010 5-year est.); Ancestry (includes multiple ancestries): 40.9% German, 19.0% Irish, 7.2% English, 6.4% Italian, 6.3% American (2006-2010 5-year est.).

Economy: Single-family building permits issued: 0 (2011); Multi-family building permits issued: 0 (2011); Employment by occupation: 8.4% management, 1.2% professional, 14.2% services, 15.4% sales, 2.2% farming, 9.4% construction, 6.3% production (2006-2010 5-year est.).

Income: Per capita income: $17,490 (2006-2010 5-year est.); Median household income: $29,923 (2006-2010 5-year est.); Average household income: $39,426 (2006-2010 5-year est.); Percent of households with income of $100,000 or more: 4.6% (2006-2010 5-year est.); Poverty rate: 17.2% (2006-2010 5-year est.).

Taxes: Total city taxes per capita: $186 (2009); City property taxes per capita: $110 (2009).

Education: Percent of population age 25 and over with: High school diploma (including GED) or higher: 80.8% (2006-2010 5-year est.); Bachelor's degree or higher: 11.6% (2006-2010 5-year est.); Master's degree or higher: 2.9% (2006-2010 5-year est.).

School District(s)

Meyersdale Area SD (KG-12)
  2010-11 Enrollment: 914 . . . . (814) 634-5123

Housing: Homeownership rate: 68.3% (2010); Median home value: $73,000 (2006-2010 5-year est.); Median contract rent: $315 per month (2006-2010 5-year est.); Median year structure built: before 1940 (2006-2010 5-year est.).

Hospitals: Meyersdale Medical Center (20 beds)

Safety: Violent crime rate: 9.1 per 10,000 population; Property crime rate: 118.7 per 10,000 population (2011).

Newspapers: New Republic (Community news; Circulation 5,000)

Transportation: Commute to work: 92.7% car, 0.0% public transportation, 4.2% walk, 3.1% work from home (2006-2010 5-year est.); Travel time to work: 40.8% less than 15 minutes, 25.9% 15 to 30 minutes, 20.5% 30 to 45 minutes, 7.2% 45 to 60 minutes, 5.6% 60 minutes or more (2006-2010 5-year est.)

Additional Information Contacts

Somerset County Chamber of Commerce . . . . (814) 445-6431
  http://www.somersetcountychamber.com

MIDDLECREEK (township). Covers a land area of 33.271 square miles and a water area of 0.085 square miles. Located at 39.97° N. Lat; 79.27° W. Long.

Population: 764 (1990); 797 (2000); 875 (2010); Density: 26.3 persons per square mile (2010); Race: 99.1% White, 0.0% Black, 0.0% Asian, 0.1% American Indian/Alaska Native, 0.0% Native Hawaiian/Other Pacific Islander, 0.8% Other, 0.5% Hispanic of any race (2010); Average household size: 2.35 (2010); Median age: 47.6 (2010); Males per 100 females: 107.8 (2010); Marriage status: 15.8% never married, 70.0% now married, 8.0% widowed, 6.3% divorced (2006-2010 5-year est.); Foreign born: 2.4% (2006-2010 5-year est.); Ancestry (includes multiple ancestries): 38.9% German, 27.3% Irish, 10.6% English, 7.9% American, 5.4% Italian (2006-2010 5-year est.).

Economy: Single-family building permits issued: 3 (2011); Multi-family building permits issued: 0 (2011); Employment by occupation: 7.5%

management, 0.0% professional, 11.4% services, 18.4% sales, 2.7% farming, 24.7% construction, 2.4% production (2006-2010 5-year est.).
Income: Per capita income: $20,126 (2006-2010 5-year est.); Median household income: $48,142 (2006-2010 5-year est.); Average household income: $55,143 (2006-2010 5-year est.); Percent of households with income of $100,000 or more: 12.3% (2006-2010 5-year est.); Poverty rate: 7.4% (2006-2010 5-year est.).
Education: Percent of population age 25 and over with: High school diploma (including GED) or higher: 85.8% (2006-2010 5-year est.); Bachelor's degree or higher: 14.0% (2006-2010 5-year est.); Master's degree or higher: 9.5% (2006-2010 5-year est.).
Housing: Homeownership rate: 80.2% (2010); Median home value: $119,400 (2006-2010 5-year est.); Median contract rent: $350 per month (2006-2010 5-year est.); Median year structure built: 1984 (2006-2010 5-year est.).
Transportation: Commute to work: 93.4% car, 0.7% public transportation, 2.9% walk, 2.9% work from home (2006-2010 5-year est.); Travel time to work: 14.1% less than 15 minutes, 55.3% 15 to 30 minutes, 10.9% 30 to 45 minutes, 10.4% 45 to 60 minutes, 9.3% 60 minutes or more (2006-2010 5-year est.)

MILFORD (township). Covers a land area of 29.748 square miles and a water area of 0.005 square miles. Located at 39.96° N. Lat; 79.17° W. Long. Elevation is 1,949 feet.
Population: 1,546 (1990); 1,561 (2000); 1,553 (2010); Density: 52.2 persons per square mile (2010); Race: 98.8% White, 0.1% Black, 0.2% Asian, 0.1% American Indian/Alaska Native, 0.1% Native Hawaiian/Other Pacific Islander, 0.7% Other, 0.7% Hispanic of any race (2010); Average household size: 2.43 (2010); Median age: 45.8 (2010); Males per 100 females: 100.1 (2010); Marriage status: 20.1% never married, 65.7% now married, 7.6% widowed, 6.6% divorced (2006-2010 5-year est.); Foreign born: 1.3% (2006-2010 5-year est.); Ancestry (includes multiple ancestries): 51.4% German, 11.9% Irish, 8.7% English, 8.3% Italian, 4.8% American (2006-2010 5-year est.).
Economy: Single-family building permits issued: 2 (2011); Multi-family building permits issued: 0 (2011); Employment by occupation: 14.1% management, 0.8% professional, 11.5% services, 16.8% sales, 2.6% farming, 14.4% construction, 5.6% production (2006-2010 5-year est.).
Income: Per capita income: $23,842 (2006-2010 5-year est.); Median household income: $47,614 (2006-2010 5-year est.); Average household income: $57,283 (2006-2010 5-year est.); Percent of households with income of $100,000 or more: 10.6% (2006-2010 5-year est.); Poverty rate: 6.0% (2006-2010 5-year est.).
Education: Percent of population age 25 and over with: High school diploma (including GED) or higher: 90.8% (2006-2010 5-year est.); Bachelor's degree or higher: 16.4% (2006-2010 5-year est.); Master's degree or higher: 6.3% (2006-2010 5-year est.).
Housing: Homeownership rate: 88.4% (2010); Median home value: $104,900 (2006-2010 5-year est.); Median contract rent: $366 per month (2006-2010 5-year est.); Median year structure built: 1968 (2006-2010 5-year est.).
Transportation: Commute to work: 88.3% car, 0.0% public transportation, 3.2% walk, 7.0% work from home (2006-2010 5-year est.); Travel time to work: 30.1% less than 15 minutes, 49.1% 15 to 30 minutes, 8.2% 30 to 45 minutes, 7.8% 45 to 60 minutes, 4.8% 60 minutes or more (2006-2010 5-year est.)
Additional Information Contacts
Somerset County Chamber of Commerce . . . . (814) 445-6431
  http://www.somersetcountychamber.com

NEW BALTIMORE (borough). Covers a land area of 0.347 square miles and a water area of 0 square miles. Located at 39.98° N. Lat; 78.77° W. Long. Elevation is 1,424 feet.
Population: 164 (1990); 168 (2000); 180 (2010); Density: 519.2 persons per square mile (2010); Race: 100.0% White, 0.0% Black, 0.0% Asian, 0.0% American Indian/Alaska Native, 0.0% Native Hawaiian/Other Pacific Islander, 0.0% Other, 0.0% Hispanic of any race (2010); Average household size: 2.67 (2010); Median age: 44.7 (2010); Males per 100 females: 104.5 (2010); Marriage status: 42.7% never married, 50.0% now married, 2.8% widowed, 4.5% divorced (2006-2010 5-year est.); Foreign born: 1.9% (2006-2010 5-year est.); Ancestry (includes multiple ancestries): 65.9% German, 19.2% Italian, 12.0% Irish, 10.6% Dutch, 6.3% American (2006-2010 5-year est.).
Economy: Single-family building permits issued: 0 (2011); Multi-family building permits issued: 0 (2011); Employment by occupation: 5.6%

management, 10.2% professional, 10.2% services, 10.2% sales, 1.9% farming, 14.8% construction, 1.9% production (2006-2010 5-year est.).
Income: Per capita income: $22,908 (2006-2010 5-year est.); Median household income: $34,000 (2006-2010 5-year est.); Average household income: $60,231 (2006-2010 5-year est.); Percent of households with income of $100,000 or more: 24.4% (2006-2010 5-year est.); Poverty rate: 9.7% (2006-2010 5-year est.).
Education: Percent of population age 25 and over with: High school diploma (including GED) or higher: 84.4% (2006-2010 5-year est.); Bachelor's degree or higher: 11.7% (2006-2010 5-year est.); Master's degree or higher: 9.7% (2006-2010 5-year est.).
Housing: Homeownership rate: 83.6% (2010); Median home value: $86,800 (2006-2010 5-year est.); Median contract rent: $417 per month (2006-2010 5-year est.); Median year structure built: before 1940 (2006-2010 5-year est.).
Transportation: Commute to work: 85.2% car, 0.0% public transportation, 3.7% walk, 11.1% work from home (2006-2010 5-year est.); Travel time to work: 18.8% less than 15 minutes, 27.1% 15 to 30 minutes, 38.5% 30 to 45 minutes, 6.3% 45 to 60 minutes, 9.4% 60 minutes or more (2006-2010 5-year est.)

NEW CENTERVILLE (borough). Aka Glade. Covers a land area of 0.142 square miles and a water area of 0 square miles. Located at 39.94° N. Lat; 79.19° W. Long. Elevation is 2,149 feet.
Population: 211 (1990); 193 (2000); 133 (2010); Density: 935.4 persons per square mile (2010); Race: 99.2% White, 0.0% Black, 0.8% Asian, 0.0% American Indian/Alaska Native, 0.0% Native Hawaiian/Other Pacific Islander, 0.0% Other, 0.0% Hispanic of any race (2010); Average household size: 2.29 (2010); Median age: 49.3 (2010); Males per 100 females: 107.8 (2010); Marriage status: 27.6% never married, 57.5% now married, 8.2% widowed, 6.7% divorced (2006-2010 5-year est.); Foreign born: 0.0% (2006-2010 5-year est.); Ancestry (includes multiple ancestries): 58.4% German, 18.2% Irish, 12.3% English, 10.4% Italian, 7.8% Russian (2006-2010 5-year est.).
Economy: Single-family building permits issued: 0 (2011); Multi-family building permits issued: 0 (2011); Employment by occupation: 3.5% management, 12.3% professional, 3.5% services, 21.1% sales, 7.0% farming, 12.3% construction, 0.0% production (2006-2010 5-year est.).
Income: Per capita income: $22,369 (2006-2010 5-year est.); Median household income: $53,750 (2006-2010 5-year est.); Average household income: $58,182 (2006-2010 5-year est.); Percent of households with income of $100,000 or more: 19.3% (2006-2010 5-year est.); Poverty rate: 12.3% (2006-2010 5-year est.).
Education: Percent of population age 25 and over with: High school diploma (including GED) or higher: 84.7% (2006-2010 5-year est.); Bachelor's degree or higher: 15.3% (2006-2010 5-year est.); Master's degree or higher: 7.2% (2006-2010 5-year est.).
Housing: Homeownership rate: 87.9% (2010); Median home value: $97,700 (2006-2010 5-year est.); Median contract rent: $379 per month (2006-2010 5-year est.); Median year structure built: 1950 (2006-2010 5-year est.).
Transportation: Commute to work: 88.7% car, 0.0% public transportation, 3.8% walk, 7.5% work from home (2006-2010 5-year est.); Travel time to work: 32.7% less than 15 minutes, 42.9% 15 to 30 minutes, 6.1% 30 to 45 minutes, 0.0% 45 to 60 minutes, 18.4% 60 minutes or more (2006-2010 5-year est.)

NORTHAMPTON (township). Covers a land area of 35.872 square miles and a water area of 0 square miles. Located at 39.84° N. Lat; 78.88° W. Long.
Population: 356 (1990); 366 (2000); 343 (2010); Density: 9.6 persons per square mile (2010); Race: 99.4% White, 0.3% Black, 0.0% Asian, 0.0% American Indian/Alaska Native, 0.0% Native Hawaiian/Other Pacific Islander, 0.3% Other, 0.0% Hispanic of any race (2010); Average household size: 2.49 (2010); Median age: 47.4 (2010); Males per 100 females: 104.2 (2010); Marriage status: 24.1% never married, 63.7% now married, 4.6% widowed, 7.6% divorced (2006-2010 5-year est.); Foreign born: 0.0% (2006-2010 5-year est.); Ancestry (includes multiple ancestries): 69.7% German, 20.4% Irish, 9.9% American, 6.4% Scottish, 5.9% English (2006-2010 5-year est.).
Economy: Single-family building permits issued: 0 (2011); Multi-family building permits issued: 0 (2011); Employment by occupation: 1.2% management, 3.7% professional, 8.1% services, 17.4% sales, 5.6% farming, 18.6% construction, 11.2% production (2006-2010 5-year est.).

Income: Per capita income: $17,687 (2006-2010 5-year est.); Median household income: $44,750 (2006-2010 5-year est.); Average household income: $49,623 (2006-2010 5-year est.); Percent of households with income of $100,000 or more: 4.6% (2006-2010 5-year est.); Poverty rate: 6.2% (2006-2010 5-year est.).

Education: Percent of population age 25 and over with: High school diploma (including GED) or higher: 89.0% (2006-2010 5-year est.); Bachelor's degree or higher: 11.8% (2006-2010 5-year est.); Master's degree or higher: 4.7% (2006-2010 5-year est.).

Housing: Homeownership rate: 85.6% (2010); Median home value: $89,700 (2006-2010 5-year est.); Median contract rent: $413 per month (2006-2010 5-year est.); Median year structure built: 1965 (2006-2010 5-year est.).

Transportation: Commute to work: 94.7% car, 0.0% public transportation, 3.3% walk, 2.0% work from home (2006-2010 5-year est.); Travel time to work: 14.1% less than 15 minutes, 40.9% 15 to 30 minutes, 21.5% 30 to 45 minutes, 12.8% 45 to 60 minutes, 10.7% 60 minutes or more (2006-2010 5-year est.)

OGLE (township). Covers a land area of 34.568 square miles and a water area of 0.014 square miles. Located at 40.19° N. Lat; 78.75° W. Long.

Population: 597 (1990); 588 (2000); 501 (2010); Density: 14.5 persons per square mile (2010); Race: 97.0% White, 0.2% Black, 0.2% Asian, 0.2% American Indian/Alaska Native, 0.0% Native Hawaiian/Other Pacific Islander, 2.4% Other, 0.2% Hispanic of any race (2010); Average household size: 2.48 (2010); Median age: 46.4 (2010); Males per 100 females: 104.5 (2010); Marriage status: 23.2% never married, 58.6% now married, 2.5% widowed, 15.8% divorced (2006-2010 5-year est.); Foreign born: 0.0% (2006-2010 5-year est.); Ancestry (includes multiple ancestries): 39.9% German, 15.2% Irish, 12.0% Slovak, 10.4% Italian, 10.4% Polish (2006-2010 5-year est.).

Economy: Single-family building permits issued: 0 (2011); Multi-family building permits issued: 0 (2011); Employment by occupation: 7.6% management, 3.5% professional, 10.7% services, 15.8% sales, 2.8% farming, 19.2% construction, 5.0% production (2006-2010 5-year est.).

Income: Per capita income: $22,682 (2006-2010 5-year est.); Median household income: $49,583 (2006-2010 5-year est.); Average household income: $56,965 (2006-2010 5-year est.); Percent of households with income of $100,000 or more: 15.4% (2006-2010 5-year est.); Poverty rate: 17.9% (2006-2010 5-year est.).

Education: Percent of population age 25 and over with: High school diploma (including GED) or higher: 88.5% (2006-2010 5-year est.); Bachelor's degree or higher: 14.0% (2006-2010 5-year est.); Master's degree or higher: 7.7% (2006-2010 5-year est.).

Housing: Homeownership rate: 87.7% (2010); Median home value: $122,100 (2006-2010 5-year est.); Median contract rent: $563 per month (2006-2010 5-year est.); Median year structure built: 1974 (2006-2010 5-year est.).

Transportation: Commute to work: 93.5% car, 0.0% public transportation, 1.9% walk, 4.5% work from home (2006-2010 5-year est.); Travel time to work: 18.9% less than 15 minutes, 43.9% 15 to 30 minutes, 22.6% 30 to 45 minutes, 6.4% 45 to 60 minutes, 8.1% 60 minutes or more (2006-2010 5-year est.)

PAINT (borough). Covers a land area of 0.350 square miles and a water area of 0 square miles. Located at 40.24° N. Lat; 78.85° W. Long. Elevation is 1,660 feet.

Population: 1,129 (1990); 1,103 (2000); 1,023 (2010); Density: 2,920.7 persons per square mile (2010); Race: 99.4% White, 0.0% Black, 0.1% Asian, 0.0% American Indian/Alaska Native, 0.0% Native Hawaiian/Other Pacific Islander, 0.5% Other, 0.0% Hispanic of any race (2010); Average household size: 2.06 (2010); Median age: 56.2 (2010); Males per 100 females: 71.9 (2010); Marriage status: 21.1% never married, 54.9% now married, 17.1% widowed, 7.0% divorced (2006-2010 5-year est.); Foreign born: 1.3% (2006-2010 5-year est.); Ancestry (includes multiple ancestries): 26.5% German, 13.7% Slovak, 12.7% Polish, 11.9% Hungarian, 9.3% Irish (2006-2010 5-year est.).

Economy: Single-family building permits issued: 0 (2011); Multi-family building permits issued: 0 (2011); Employment by occupation: 7.2% management, 2.7% professional, 10.7% services, 11.0% sales, 3.7% farming, 16.0% construction, 12.3% production (2006-2010 5-year est.).

Income: Per capita income: $18,554 (2006-2010 5-year est.); Median household income: $33,864 (2006-2010 5-year est.); Average household income: $38,466 (2006-2010 5-year est.); Percent of households with

income of $100,000 or more: 1.8% (2006-2010 5-year est.); Poverty rate: 17.4% (2006-2010 5-year est.).

Education: Percent of population age 25 and over with: High school diploma (including GED) or higher: 81.9% (2006-2010 5-year est.); Bachelor's degree or higher: 8.8% (2006-2010 5-year est.); Master's degree or higher: 4.6% (2006-2010 5-year est.).

Housing: Homeownership rate: 61.9% (2010); Median home value: $74,500 (2006-2010 5-year est.); Median contract rent: $419 per month (2006-2010 5-year est.); Median year structure built: 1942 (2006-2010 5-year est.).

Transportation: Commute to work: 94.1% car, 0.0% public transportation, 1.9% walk, 4.1% work from home (2006-2010 5-year est.); Travel time to work: 49.6% less than 15 minutes, 34.1% 15 to 30 minutes, 8.7% 30 to 45 minutes, 5.4% 45 to 60 minutes, 2.3% 60 minutes or more (2006-2010 5-year est.).

Additional Information Contacts
Somerset County Chamber of Commerce . . . . (814) 445-6431
   http://www.somersetcountychamber.com

PAINT (township). Covers a land area of 32.243 square miles and a water area of 0.136 square miles. Located at 40.21° N. Lat; 78.85° W. Long. Elevation is 1,660 feet.

Population: 3,543 (1990); 3,300 (2000); 3,149 (2010); Density: 97.7 persons per square mile (2010); Race: 99.3% White, 0.0% Black, 0.3% Asian, 0.2% American Indian/Alaska Native, 0.0% Native Hawaiian/Other Pacific Islander, 0.2% Other, 0.6% Hispanic of any race (2010); Average household size: 2.32 (2010); Median age: 49.1 (2010); Males per 100 females: 101.0 (2010); Marriage status: 18.6% never married, 61.2% now married, 11.2% widowed, 9.0% divorced (2006-2010 5-year est.); Foreign born: 0.5% (2006-2010 5-year est.); Ancestry (includes multiple ancestries): 29.8% German, 13.1% Polish, 12.6% Italian, 11.2% English, 9.4% Irish (2006-2010 5-year est.).

Economy: Single-family building permits issued: 11 (2011); Multi-family building permits issued: 0 (2011); Employment by occupation: 7.7% management, 3.9% professional, 8.9% services, 21.1% sales, 7.0% farming, 9.1% construction, 7.5% production (2006-2010 5-year est.).

Income: Per capita income: $21,871 (2006-2010 5-year est.); Median household income: $39,048 (2006-2010 5-year est.); Average household income: $49,244 (2006-2010 5-year est.); Percent of households with income of $100,000 or more: 9.4% (2006-2010 5-year est.); Poverty rate: 5.7% (2006-2010 5-year est.).

Education: Percent of population age 25 and over with: High school diploma (including GED) or higher: 83.3% (2006-2010 5-year est.); Bachelor's degree or higher: 15.0% (2006-2010 5-year est.); Master's degree or higher: 6.0% (2006-2010 5-year est.).

Housing: Homeownership rate: 86.7% (2010); Median home value: $97,300 (2006-2010 5-year est.); Median contract rent: $345 per month (2006-2010 5-year est.); Median year structure built: 1966 (2006-2010 5-year est.).

Safety: Violent crime rate: 117.1 per 10,000 population; Property crime rate: 275.4 per 10,000 population (2011).

Transportation: Commute to work: 90.7% car, 0.0% public transportation, 1.9% walk, 6.6% work from home (2006-2010 5-year est.); Travel time to work: 30.2% less than 15 minutes, 58.9% 15 to 30 minutes, 6.3% 30 to 45 minutes, 3.5% 45 to 60 minutes, 1.1% 60 minutes or more (2006-2010 5-year est.)

Additional Information Contacts
Somerset County Chamber of Commerce . . . . (814) 445-6431
   http://www.somersetcountychamber.com

QUECREEK (unincorporated postal area)
Zip Code: 15555

   Covers a land area of 0.075 square miles and a water area of 0 square miles. Located at 40.09° N. Lat; 79.08° W. Long. Elevation is 1,936 feet. Population: 112 (2010); Density: 1,492.1 persons per square mile (2010); Race: 99.1% White, 0.0% Black, 0.0% Asian, 0.0% American Indian/Alaska Native, 0.0% Native Hawaiian/Other Pacific Islander, 0.9% Other, 0.0% Hispanic of any race (2010); Average household size: 2.55 (2010); Median age: 37.5 (2010); Males per 100 females: 111.3 (2010); Homeownership rate: 81.8% (2010)

QUEMAHONING (township). Covers a land area of 35.097 square miles and a water area of 0.652 square miles. Located at 40.12° N. Lat; 78.96° W. Long.

Population: 2,323 (1990); 2,180 (2000); 2,025 (2010); Density: 57.7 persons per square mile (2010); Race: 98.8% White, 0.1% Black, 0.2% Asian, 0.3% American Indian/Alaska Native, 0.0% Native Hawaiian/Other Pacific Islander, 0.6% Other, 0.2% Hispanic of any race (2010); Average household size: 2.56 (2010); Median age: 43.5 (2010); Males per 100 females: 104.5 (2010); Marriage status: 25.5% never married, 57.2% now married, 6.0% widowed, 11.2% divorced (2006-2010 5-year est.); Foreign born: 0.2% (2006-2010 5-year est.); Ancestry (includes multiple ancestries): 42.6% German, 13.3% American, 12.4% Irish, 7.8% English, 7.0% Italian (2006-2010 5-year est.).

Economy: Single-family building permits issued: 0 (2011); Multi-family building permits issued: 0 (2011); Employment by occupation: 6.8% management, 1.9% professional, 13.1% services, 13.7% sales, 2.9% farming, 10.1% construction, 7.7% production (2006-2010 5-year est.).

Income: Per capita income: $19,559 (2006-2010 5-year est.); Median household income: $41,361 (2006-2010 5-year est.); Average household income: $47,606 (2006-2010 5-year est.); Percent of households with income of $100,000 or more: 5.4% (2006-2010 5-year est.); Poverty rate: 13.8% (2006-2010 5-year est.).

Education: Percent of population age 25 and over with: High school diploma (including GED) or higher: 82.4% (2006-2010 5-year est.); Bachelor's degree or higher: 10.7% (2006-2010 5-year est.); Master's degree or higher: 2.5% (2006-2010 5-year est.).

Housing: Homeownership rate: 86.7% (2010); Median home value: $84,200 (2006-2010 5-year est.); Median contract rent: $317 per month (2006-2010 5-year est.); Median year structure built: 1966 (2006-2010 5-year est.).

Transportation: Commute to work: 89.0% car, 0.8% public transportation, 5.8% walk, 3.1% work from home (2006-2010 5-year est.); Travel time to work: 24.6% less than 15 minutes, 46.6% 15 to 30 minutes, 18.5% 30 to 45 minutes, 1.7% 45 to 60 minutes, 8.6% 60 minutes or more (2006-2010 5-year est.)

Additional Information Contacts

Somerset County Chamber of Commerce . . . . (814) 445-6431
    http://www.somersetcountychamber.com

ROCKWOOD (borough). Covers a land area of 0.334 square miles and a water area of 0 square miles. Located at 39.92° N. Lat; 79.16° W. Long. Elevation is 1,841 feet.

History: Laid out 1857, incorporated 1885.

Population: 1,012 (1990); 954 (2000); 890 (2010); Density: 2,664.1 persons per square mile (2010); Race: 98.7% White, 0.1% Black, 0.0% Asian, 0.4% American Indian/Alaska Native, 0.0% Native Hawaiian/Other Pacific Islander, 0.8% Other, 0.9% Hispanic of any race (2010); Average household size: 2.34 (2010); Median age: 38.1 (2010); Males per 100 females: 89.4 (2010); Marriage status: 24.5% never married, 54.5% now married, 9.6% widowed, 11.5% divorced (2006-2010 5-year est.); Foreign born: 1.2% (2006-2010 5-year est.); Ancestry (includes multiple ancestries): 40.9% German, 10.7% Irish, 5.6% American, 5.5% English, 5.1% Czech (2006-2010 5-year est.).

Economy: Single-family building permits issued: 0 (2011); Multi-family building permits issued: 0 (2011); Employment by occupation: 6.6% management, 2.7% professional, 15.5% services, 11.3% sales, 4.2% farming, 11.6% construction, 9.3% production (2006-2010 5-year est.).

Income: Per capita income: $18,949 (2006-2010 5-year est.); Median household income: $35,917 (2006-2010 5-year est.); Average household income: $43,369 (2006-2010 5-year est.); Percent of households with income of $100,000 or more: 4.6% (2006-2010 5-year est.); Poverty rate: 12.2% (2006-2010 5-year est.).

Education: Percent of population age 25 and over with: High school diploma (including GED) or higher: 84.1% (2006-2010 5-year est.); Bachelor's degree or higher: 8.8% (2006-2010 5-year est.); Master's degree or higher: 3.7% (2006-2010 5-year est.).

School District(s)

Rockwood Area SD (KG-12)
    2010-11 Enrollment: 798 . . . . (814) 926-4913

Housing: Homeownership rate: 62.4% (2010); Median home value: $72,500 (2006-2010 5-year est.); Median contract rent: $336 per month (2006-2010 5-year est.); Median year structure built: before 1940 (2006-2010 5-year est.).

Transportation: Commute to work: 93.3% car, 0.0% public transportation, 3.7% walk, 1.8% work from home (2006-2010 5-year est.); Travel time to

work: 32.6% less than 15 minutes, 38.5% 15 to 30 minutes, 14.6% 30 to 45 minutes, 3.4% 45 to 60 minutes, 10.9% 60 minutes or more (2006-2010 5-year est.)

SALISBURY (borough). Covers a land area of 0.384 square miles and a water area of 0 square miles. Located at 39.75° N. Lat; 79.08° W. Long. Elevation is 2,146 feet.

Population: 783 (1990); 878 (2000); 727 (2010); Density: 1,890.9 persons per square mile (2010); Race: 99.3% White, 0.0% Black, 0.0% Asian, 0.3% American Indian/Alaska Native, 0.0% Native Hawaiian/Other Pacific Islander, 0.4% Other, 0.1% Hispanic of any race (2010); Average household size: 2.20 (2010); Median age: 46.7 (2010); Males per 100 females: 91.3 (2010); Marriage status: 20.3% never married, 59.5% now married, 12.2% widowed, 8.1% divorced (2006-2010 5-year est.); Foreign born: 0.0% (2006-2010 5-year est.); Ancestry (includes multiple ancestries): 57.8% German, 17.8% Irish, 8.8% American, 6.6% Italian, 6.2% English (2006-2010 5-year est.).

Economy: Single-family building permits issued: 1 (2011); Multi-family building permits issued: 0 (2011); Employment by occupation: 4.2% management, 5.6% professional, 9.5% services, 19.0% sales, 2.5% farming, 8.8% construction, 6.3% production (2006-2010 5-year est.).

Income: Per capita income: $21,282 (2006-2010 5-year est.); Median household income: $32,946 (2006-2010 5-year est.); Average household income: $46,568 (2006-2010 5-year est.); Percent of households with income of $100,000 or more: 6.8% (2006-2010 5-year est.); Poverty rate: 8.1% (2006-2010 5-year est.).

Education: Percent of population age 25 and over with: High school diploma (including GED) or higher: 77.9% (2006-2010 5-year est.); Bachelor's degree or higher: 11.8% (2006-2010 5-year est.); Master's degree or higher: 0.8% (2006-2010 5-year est.).

School District(s)

Salisbury-Elk Lick SD (KG-12)
    2010-11 Enrollment: 267 . . . . (814) 662-2733

Housing: Homeownership rate: 70.3% (2010); Median home value: $87,900 (2006-2010 5-year est.); Median contract rent: $283 per month (2006-2010 5-year est.); Median year structure built: 1945 (2006-2010 5-year est.).

Transportation: Commute to work: 88.1% car, 0.0% public transportation, 9.7% walk, 1.1% work from home (2006-2010 5-year est.); Travel time to work: 40.2% less than 15 minutes, 24.4% 15 to 30 minutes, 21.1% 30 to 45 minutes, 5.6% 45 to 60 minutes, 8.6% 60 minutes or more (2006-2010 5-year est.)

SEANOR (unincorporated postal area)

Zip Code: 15953

Covers a land area of 0.828 square miles and a water area of <.001 square miles. Located at 40.20° N. Lat; 78.88° W. Long. Elevation is 1,496 feet. Population: 83 (2010); Density: 100.2 persons per square mile (2010); Race: 100.0% White, 0.0% Black, 0.0% Asian, 0.0% American Indian/Alaska Native, 0.0% Native Hawaiian/Other Pacific Islander, 0.0% Other, 6.0% Hispanic of any race (2010); Average household size: 2.68 (2010); Median age: 43.8 (2010); Males per 100 females: 130.6 (2010); Homeownership rate: 93.6% (2010)

SEVEN SPRINGS (borough). Covers a land area of 0.972 square miles and a water area of 0 square miles. Located at 40.02° N. Lat; 79.29° W. Long. Elevation is 2,520 feet.

Population: 22 (1990); 126 (2000); 11 (2010); Density: 11.3 persons per square mile (2010); Race: 100.0% White, 0.0% Black, 0.0% Asian, 0.0% American Indian/Alaska Native, 0.0% Native Hawaiian/Other Pacific Islander, 0.0% Other, 0.0% Hispanic of any race (2010); Average household size: 1.22 (2010); Median age: 71.3 (2010); Males per 100 females: 83.3 (2010); Marriage status: 7.5% never married, 82.5% now married, 0.0% widowed, 10.0% divorced (2006-2010 5-year est.); Foreign born: 0.0% (2006-2010 5-year est.); Ancestry (includes multiple ancestries): 37.5% English, 35.0% German, 20.0% Polish, 15.0% Italian, 15.0% Irish (2006-2010 5-year est.).

Economy: Employment by occupation: 0.0% management, 0.0% professional, 31.6% services, 10.5% sales, 0.0% farming, 0.0% construction, 0.0% production (2006-2010 5-year est.).

Income: Per capita income: $92,638 (2006-2010 5-year est.); Median household income: $98,125 (2006-2010 5-year est.); Average household income: $163,513 (2006-2010 5-year est.); Percent of households with income of $100,000 or more: 43.5% (2006-2010 5-year est.); Poverty rate: 0.0% (2006-2010 5-year est.).

Education: Percent of population age 25 and over with: High school diploma (including GED) or higher: 100.0% (2006-2010 5-year est.); Bachelor's degree or higher: 56.4% (2006-2010 5-year est.); Master's degree or higher: 43.6% (2006-2010 5-year est.).
Housing: Homeownership rate: 66.6% (2010); Median home value: $312,500 (2006-2010 5-year est.); Median contract rent: n/a per month (2006-2010 5-year est.); Median year structure built: 1985 (2006-2010 5-year est.).
Transportation: Commute to work: 100.0% car, 0.0% public transportation, 0.0% walk, 0.0% work from home (2006-2010 5-year est.); Travel time to work: 26.3% less than 15 minutes, 63.2% 15 to 30 minutes, 0.0% 30 to 45 minutes, 0.0% 45 to 60 minutes, 10.5% 60 minutes or more (2006-2010 5-year est.)

SHADE (township). Covers a land area of 68.726 square miles and a water area of 0.035 square miles. Located at 40.11° N. Lat; 78.83° W. Long.
Population: 3,155 (1990); 2,886 (2000); 2,774 (2010); Density: 40.4 persons per square mile (2010); Race: 98.9% White, 0.1% Black, 0.1% Asian, 0.0% American Indian/Alaska Native, 0.0% Native Hawaiian/Other Pacific Islander, 0.9% Other, 0.4% Hispanic of any race (2010); Average household size: 2.36 (2010); Median age: 45.4 (2010); Males per 100 females: 99.3 (2010); Marriage status: 20.5% never married, 59.0% now married, 11.5% widowed, 9.0% divorced (2006-2010 5-year est.); Foreign born: 0.0% (2006-2010 5-year est.); Ancestry (includes multiple ancestries): 37.9% German, 15.2% Polish, 8.9% English, 6.8% Italian, 6.4% Irish (2006-2010 5-year est.).
Economy: Single-family building permits issued: 0 (2011); Multi-family building permits issued: 0 (2011); Employment by occupation: 7.5% management, 1.0% professional, 10.1% services, 18.0% sales, 4.1% farming, 12.0% construction, 6.6% production (2006-2010 5-year est.).
Income: Per capita income: $18,001 (2006-2010 5-year est.); Median household income: $35,769 (2006-2010 5-year est.); Average household income: $41,875 (2006-2010 5-year est.); Percent of households with income of $100,000 or more: 7.2% (2006-2010 5-year est.); Poverty rate: 11.0% (2006-2010 5-year est.).
Taxes: Total city taxes per capita: $73 (2009); City property taxes per capita: $7 (2009).
Education: Percent of population age 25 and over with: High school diploma (including GED) or higher: 82.1% (2006-2010 5-year est.); Bachelor's degree or higher: 11.0% (2006-2010 5-year est.); Master's degree or higher: 3.1% (2006-2010 5-year est.).
Housing: Homeownership rate: 86.5% (2010); Median home value: $70,900 (2006-2010 5-year est.); Median contract rent: $313 per month (2006-2010 5-year est.); Median year structure built: 1946 (2006-2010 5-year est.).
Transportation: Commute to work: 95.8% car, 0.0% public transportation, 1.1% walk, 0.4% work from home (2006-2010 5-year est.); Travel time to work: 20.1% less than 15 minutes, 41.3% 15 to 30 minutes, 23.7% 30 to 45 minutes, 8.3% 45 to 60 minutes, 6.5% 60 minutes or more (2006-2010 5-year est.)
Additional Information Contacts
Greater Johnstown Cambria County Chamber of Commerce . . . . (814) 536-5107
    http://www.johnstownchamber.com

SHANKSVILLE (borough). Covers a land area of 0.197 square miles and a water area of 0 square miles. Located at 40.02° N. Lat; 78.91° W. Long. Elevation is 2,231 feet.
Population: 235 (1990); 245 (2000); 237 (2010); Density: 1,201.5 persons per square mile (2010); Race: 95.4% White, 0.4% Black, 0.4% Asian, 0.4% American Indian/Alaska Native, 0.0% Native Hawaiian/Other Pacific Islander, 3.4% Other, 0.4% Hispanic of any race (2010); Average household size: 2.69 (2010); Median age: 38.1 (2010); Males per 100 females: 111.6 (2010); Marriage status: 22.5% never married, 74.0% now married, 1.2% widowed, 2.4% divorced (2006-2010 5-year est.); Foreign born: 0.0% (2006-2010 5-year est.); Ancestry (includes multiple ancestries): 65.8% German, 16.3% English, 11.2% Irish, 10.7% Welsh, 8.2% Italian (2006-2010 5-year est.).
Economy: Single-family building permits issued: 0 (2011); Multi-family building permits issued: 0 (2011); Employment by occupation: 0.0% management, 0.0% professional, 25.3% services, 12.0% sales, 13.3% farming, 20.5% construction, 19.3% production (2006-2010 5-year est.).
Income: Per capita income: $19,720 (2006-2010 5-year est.); Median household income: $47,292 (2006-2010 5-year est.); Average household

income: $51,811 (2006-2010 5-year est.); Percent of households with income of $100,000 or more: n/a (2006-2010 5-year est.); Poverty rate: 2.0% (2006-2010 5-year est.).
Education: Percent of population age 25 and over with: High school diploma (including GED) or higher: 98.6% (2006-2010 5-year est.); Bachelor's degree or higher: 12.9% (2006-2010 5-year est.); Master's degree or higher: 10.0% (2006-2010 5-year est.).

School District(s)
Shanksville-Stonycreek SD (PK-12)
    2010-11 Enrollment: 414 . . . . (814) 267-4649
Housing: Homeownership rate: 81.9% (2010); Median home value: $76,400 (2006-2010 5-year est.); Median contract rent: $330 per month (2006-2010 5-year est.); Median year structure built: before 1940 (2006-2010 5-year est.).
Transportation: Commute to work: 92.8% car, 0.0% public transportation, 3.6% walk, 3.6% work from home (2006-2010 5-year est.); Travel time to work: 31.3% less than 15 minutes, 52.5% 15 to 30 minutes, 8.8% 30 to 45 minutes, 7.5% 45 to 60 minutes, 0.0% 60 minutes or more (2006-2010 5-year est.)

SIPESVILLE (unincorporated postal area)
Zip Code: 15561
    Covers a land area of 0.572 square miles and a water area of 0 square miles. Located at 40.09° N. Lat; 79.08° W. Long. Elevation is 2,083 feet.
Population: 168 (2010); Density: 293.6 persons per square mile (2010); Race: 97.6% White, 0.0% Black, 0.6% Asian, 0.0% American Indian/Alaska Native, 0.0% Native Hawaiian/Other Pacific Islander, 1.8% Other, 1.8% Hispanic of any race (2010); Average household size: 2.27 (2010); Median age: 48.6 (2010); Males per 100 females: 110.0 (2010); Homeownership rate: 89.2% (2010)

SOMERSET (borough). County seat. Covers a land area of 2.729 square miles and a water area of 0 square miles. Located at 40.01° N. Lat; 79.08° W. Long. Elevation is 2,195 feet.
History: Somerset was originally called Brunerstown, after Ulrich Bruner, who arrived in 1787.
Population: 6,512 (1990); 6,762 (2000); 6,277 (2010); Density: 2,300.5 persons per square mile (2010); Race: 96.8% White, 0.9% Black, 0.9% Asian, 0.2% American Indian/Alaska Native, 0.0% Native Hawaiian/Other Pacific Islander, 1.3% Other, 1.1% Hispanic of any race (2010); Average household size: 2.06 (2010); Median age: 42.3 (2010); Males per 100 females: 83.4 (2010); Marriage status: 31.5% never married, 43.7% now married, 12.5% widowed, 12.3% divorced (2006-2010 5-year est.); Foreign born: 1.5% (2006-2010 5-year est.); Ancestry (includes multiple ancestries): 48.8% German, 19.1% Irish, 10.8% English, 9.9% Italian, 5.4% Polish (2006-2010 5-year est.).
Economy: Single-family building permits issued: 0 (2011); Multi-family building permits issued: 0 (2011); Employment by occupation: 12.8% management, 0.9% professional, 11.3% services, 17.7% sales, 4.1% farming, 3.4% construction, 4.2% production (2006-2010 5-year est.).
Income: Per capita income: $18,541 (2006-2010 5-year est.); Median household income: $30,891 (2006-2010 5-year est.); Average household income: $41,887 (2006-2010 5-year est.); Percent of households with income of $100,000 or more: 6.5% (2006-2010 5-year est.); Poverty rate: 22.2% (2006-2010 5-year est.).
Education: Percent of population age 25 and over with: High school diploma (including GED) or higher: 83.9% (2006-2010 5-year est.); Bachelor's degree or higher: 22.0% (2006-2010 5-year est.); Master's degree or higher: 8.9% (2006-2010 5-year est.).

School District(s)
Somerset Area SD (KG-12)
    2010-11 Enrollment: 2,392 . . . . (814) 445-9714
Somerset County Technology Center (10-12)
    2010-11 Enrollment: n/a . . . . (814) 443-3651
Two-year College(s)
Somerset County Technology Center (Public)
    Fall 2010 Enrollment: 67 . . . . (814) 443-3651
Housing: Homeownership rate: 47.8% (2010); Median home value: $106,100 (2006-2010 5-year est.); Median contract rent: $394 per month (2006-2010 5-year est.); Median year structure built: 1957 (2006-2010 5-year est.).
Hospitals: Somerset Hospital (167 beds)
Safety: Violent crime rate: 39.7 per 10,000 population; Property crime rate: 284.3 per 10,000 population (2011).

Newspapers: Daily American (Local news; Circulation 13,938); Somerset County Shopper (Community news; Circulation 35,000)

Transportation: Commute to work: 86.4% car, 0.3% public transportation, 8.8% walk, 3.6% work from home (2006-2010 5-year est.); Travel time to work: 67.4% less than 15 minutes, 19.8% 15 to 30 minutes, 6.4% 30 to 45 minutes, 3.6% 45 to 60 minutes, 2.8% 60 minutes or more (2006-2010 5-year est.)

Airports: Somerset County (general aviation)

Additional Information Contacts

Borough of Somerset . . . . (814) 443-2661
   http://www.somersetborough.com

Somerset County Chamber of Commerce . . . . (814) 445-6431
   http://www.somersetcountychamber.com

SOMERSET (township). Covers a land area of 64.166 square miles and a water area of 0.424 square miles. Located at 40.02° N. Lat; 79.06° W. Long. Elevation is 2,195 feet.

History: Somerset Historic Center. Settled 1771, laid out 1787, Incorporated 1804.

Population: 8,674 (1990); 9,319 (2000); 12,122 (2010); Density: 188.9 persons per square mile (2010); Race: 81.5% White, 14.1% Black, 0.6% Asian, 0.1% American Indian/Alaska Native, 0.0% Native Hawaiian/Other Pacific Islander, 3.7% Other, 3.7% Hispanic of any race (2010); Average household size: 2.38 (2010); Median age: 41.6 (2010); Males per 100 females: 178.2 (2010); Marriage status: 28.7% never married, 53.9% now married, 5.9% widowed, 11.5% divorced (2006-2010 5-year est.); Foreign born: 0.7% (2006-2010 5-year est.); Ancestry (includes multiple ancestries): 36.7% German, 8.6% Irish, 6.3% American, 6.1% English, 4.3% Italian (2006-2010 5-year est.).

Economy: Single-family building permits issued: 6 (2011); Multi-family building permits issued: 0 (2011); Employment by occupation: 11.4% management, 2.0% professional, 8.1% services, 15.1% sales, 2.7% farming, 13.1% construction, 10.2% production (2006-2010 5-year est.).

Income: Per capita income: $18,220 (2006-2010 5-year est.); Median household income: $39,955 (2006-2010 5-year est.); Average household income: $54,660 (2006-2010 5-year est.); Percent of households with income of $100,000 or more: 12.6% (2006-2010 5-year est.); Poverty rate: 10.6% (2006-2010 5-year est.).

Education: Percent of population age 25 and over with: High school diploma (including GED) or higher: 83.5% (2006-2010 5-year est.); Bachelor's degree or higher: 14.5% (2006-2010 5-year est.); Master's degree or higher: 5.2% (2006-2010 5-year est.).

Two-year College(s)

Somerset County Technology Center (Public)
   Fall 2010 Enrollment: 67 . . . . (814) 443-3651

Housing: Homeownership rate: 81.4% (2010); Median home value: $112,800 (2006-2010 5-year est.); Median contract rent: $420 per month (2006-2010 5-year est.); Median year structure built: 1973 (2006-2010 5-year est.).

Hospitals: Somerset Hospital (167 beds)

Newspapers: Daily American (Local news; Circulation 13,938); Somerset County Shopper (Community news; Circulation 35,000)

Transportation: Commute to work: 91.9% car, 1.0% public transportation, 3.1% walk, 3.0% work from home (2006-2010 5-year est.); Travel time to work: 50.1% less than 15 minutes, 33.7% 15 to 30 minutes, 7.6% 30 to 45 minutes, 3.9% 45 to 60 minutes, 4.8% 60 minutes or more (2006-2010 5-year est.)

Airports: Somerset County (general aviation)

Additional Information Contacts

Somerset County Chamber of Commerce . . . . (814) 445-6431
   http://www.somersetcountychamber.com

Somerset Township. . . . . (814) 445-4675
   http://www.somersettownshippa.com

SOUTHAMPTON (township). Covers a land area of 29.269 square miles and a water area of 0 square miles. Located at 39.77° N. Lat; 78.83° W. Long.

Population: 553 (1990); 655 (2000); 630 (2010); Density: 21.5 persons per square mile (2010); Race: 99.4% White, 0.0% Black, 0.0% Asian, 0.0% American Indian/Alaska Native, 0.0% Native Hawaiian/Other Pacific Islander, 0.6% Other, 0.3% Hispanic of any race (2010); Average household size: 2.44 (2010); Median age: 44.1 (2010); Males per 100 females: 105.9 (2010); Marriage status: 24.3% never married, 58.3% now married, 4.8% widowed, 12.6% divorced (2006-2010 5-year est.); Foreign born: 0.4% (2006-2010 5-year est.); Ancestry (includes multiple

ancestries): 44.3% German, 14.6% American, 9.6% Irish, 6.5% Polish, 6.0% Scottish (2006-2010 5-year est.).

Economy: Single-family building permits issued: 1 (2011); Multi-family building permits issued: 0 (2011); Employment by occupation: 3.6% management, 0.0% professional, 14.9% services, 12.7% sales, 1.1% farming, 19.9% construction, 5.1% production (2006-2010 5-year est.).

Income: Per capita income: $19,200 (2006-2010 5-year est.); Median household income: $43,958 (2006-2010 5-year est.); Average household income: $49,223 (2006-2010 5-year est.); Percent of households with income of $100,000 or more: 8.2% (2006-2010 5-year est.); Poverty rate: 9.3% (2006-2010 5-year est.).

Education: Percent of population age 25 and over with: High school diploma (including GED) or higher: 80.3% (2006-2010 5-year est.); Bachelor's degree or higher: 6.2% (2006-2010 5-year est.); Master's degree or higher: 4.3% (2006-2010 5-year est.).

Housing: Homeownership rate: 88.8% (2010); Median home value: $109,800 (2006-2010 5-year est.); Median contract rent: $311 per month (2006-2010 5-year est.); Median year structure built: 1970 (2006-2010 5-year est.).

Transportation: Commute to work: 94.3% car, 0.0% public transportation, 0.0% walk, 4.3% work from home (2006-2010 5-year est.); Travel time to work: 7.9% less than 15 minutes, 28.1% 15 to 30 minutes, 39.0% 30 to 45 minutes, 8.6% 45 to 60 minutes, 16.5% 60 minutes or more (2006-2010 5-year est.)

SPRINGS (unincorporated postal area)

Zip Code: 15562

Covers a land area of 1.622 square miles and a water area of 0.006 square miles. Located at 39.73° N. Lat; 79.13° W. Long. Elevation is 2,480 feet. Population: 201 (2010); Density: 123.8 persons per square mile (2010); Race: 100.0% White, 0.0% Black, 0.0% Asian, 0.0% American Indian/Alaska Native, 0.0% Native Hawaiian/Other Pacific Islander, 0.0% Other, 0.0% Hispanic of any race (2010); Average household size: 3.05 (2010); Median age: 38.1 (2010); Males per 100 females: 89.6 (2010); Homeownership rate: 89.4% (2010)

STONYCREEK (township). Covers a land area of 61.363 square miles and a water area of 0.268 square miles. Located at 40.01° N. Lat; 78.88° W. Long.

Population: 2,083 (1990); 2,221 (2000); 2,237 (2010); Density: 36.5 persons per square mile (2010); Race: 99.4% White, 0.0% Black, 0.1% Asian, 0.0% American Indian/Alaska Native, 0.0% Native Hawaiian/Other Pacific Islander, 0.5% Other, 0.2% Hispanic of any race (2010); Average household size: 2.62 (2010); Median age: 42.6 (2010); Males per 100 females: 105.4 (2010); Marriage status: 21.6% never married, 65.7% now married, 5.2% widowed, 7.5% divorced (2006-2010 5-year est.); Foreign born: 0.9% (2006-2010 5-year est.); Ancestry (includes multiple ancestries): 42.3% German, 9.2% American, 8.5% English, 7.6% Italian, 4.9% Dutch (2006-2010 5-year est.).

Economy: Single-family building permits issued: 1 (2011); Multi-family building permits issued: 0 (2011); Employment by occupation: 6.8% management, 5.3% professional, 8.0% services, 16.0% sales, 2.2% farming, 22.5% construction, 10.0% production (2006-2010 5-year est.).

Income: Per capita income: $19,786 (2006-2010 5-year est.); Median household income: $44,118 (2006-2010 5-year est.); Average household income: $54,304 (2006-2010 5-year est.); Percent of households with income of $100,000 or more: 6.2% (2006-2010 5-year est.); Poverty rate: 7.8% (2006-2010 5-year est.).

Education: Percent of population age 25 and over with: High school diploma (including GED) or higher: 84.8% (2006-2010 5-year est.); Bachelor's degree or higher: 9.1% (2006-2010 5-year est.); Master's degree or higher: 2.1% (2006-2010 5-year est.).

Housing: Homeownership rate: 88.9% (2010); Median home value: $118,800 (2006-2010 5-year est.); Median contract rent: $444 per month (2006-2010 5-year est.); Median year structure built: 1968 (2006-2010 5-year est.).

Transportation: Commute to work: 82.8% car, 0.0% public transportation, 9.9% walk, 5.8% work from home (2006-2010 5-year est.); Travel time to work: 31.6% less than 15 minutes, 41.4% 15 to 30 minutes, 19.6% 30 to 45 minutes, 4.5% 45 to 60 minutes, 2.9% 60 minutes or more (2006-2010 5-year est.)

Additional Information Contacts

Somerset County Chamber of Commerce . . . . (814) 445-6431
   http://www.somersetcountychamber.com

STOYSTOWN (borough). Covers a land area of 0.190 square miles and a water area of 0 square miles. Located at 40.10° N. Lat; 78.95° W. Long. Elevation is 1,834 feet.

Population: 389 (1990); 428 (2000); 355 (2010); Density: 1,866.8 persons per square mile (2010); Race: 99.7% White, 0.0% Black, 0.0% Asian, 0.0% American Indian/Alaska Native, 0.0% Native Hawaiian/Other Pacific Islander, 0.3% Other, 0.0% Hispanic of any race (2010); Average household size: 2.11 (2010); Median age: 50.2 (2010); Males per 100 females: 82.1 (2010); Marriage status: 20.2% never married, 50.9% now married, 20.2% widowed, 8.7% divorced (2006-2010 5-year est.); Foreign born: 0.0% (2006-2010 5-year est.); Ancestry (includes multiple ancestries): 51.9% German, 13.4% Polish, 10.9% Irish, 7.1% Italian, 7.1% English (2006-2010 5-year est.).

Economy: Single-family building permits issued: 0 (2011); Multi-family building permits issued: 0 (2011); Employment by occupation: 19.0% management, 2.0% professional, 9.5% services, 18.4% sales, 3.4% farming, 12.2% construction, 4.1% production (2006-2010 5-year est.).

Income: Per capita income: $22,975 (2006-2010 5-year est.); Median household income: $42,727 (2006-2010 5-year est.); Average household income: $46,560 (2006-2010 5-year est.); Percent of households with income of $100,000 or more: 13.5% (2006-2010 5-year est.); Poverty rate: 6.9% (2006-2010 5-year est.).

Education: Percent of population age 25 and over with: High school diploma (including GED) or higher: 90.9% (2006-2010 5-year est.); Bachelor's degree or higher: 14.9% (2006-2010 5-year est.); Master's degree or higher: 7.5% (2006-2010 5-year est.).

School District(s)
North Star SD (PK-12)
   2010-11 Enrollment: 1,192 . . . . (814) 629-5631
Housing: Homeownership rate: 63.7% (2010); Median home value: $76,800 (2006-2010 5-year est.); Median contract rent: $289 per month (2006-2010 5-year est.); Median year structure built: before 1940 (2006-2010 5-year est.).

Transportation: Commute to work: 100.0% car, 0.0% public transportation, 0.0% walk, 0.0% work from home (2006-2010 5-year est.); Travel time to work: 22.3% less than 15 minutes, 56.1% 15 to 30 minutes, 18.0% 30 to 45 minutes, 2.9% 45 to 60 minutes, 0.7% 60 minutes or more (2006-2010 5-year est.)

SUMMIT (township). Covers a land area of 45.226 square miles and a water area of 0.033 square miles. Located at 39.83° N. Lat; 79.06° W. Long.

Population: 2,495 (1990); 2,368 (2000); 2,271 (2010); Density: 50.2 persons per square mile (2010); Race: 98.7% White, 0.4% Black, 0.1% Asian, 0.1% American Indian/Alaska Native, 0.0% Native Hawaiian/Other Pacific Islander, 0.7% Other, 0.5% Hispanic of any race (2010); Average household size: 2.60 (2010); Median age: 43.9 (2010); Males per 100 females: 95.9 (2010); Marriage status: 30.6% never married, 59.1% now married, 4.1% widowed, 6.2% divorced (2006-2010 5-year est.); Foreign born: 0.9% (2006-2010 5-year est.); Ancestry (includes multiple ancestries): 48.1% German, 10.1% Irish, 8.0% American, 6.0% Italian, 4.2% English (2006-2010 5-year est.).

Economy: Single-family building permits issued: 2 (2011); Multi-family building permits issued: 0 (2011); Employment by occupation: 8.3% management, 0.0% professional, 14.8% services, 17.3% sales, 2.7% farming, 13.2% construction, 9.4% production (2006-2010 5-year est.).

Income: Per capita income: $21,252 (2006-2010 5-year est.); Median household income: $45,588 (2006-2010 5-year est.); Average household income: $58,598 (2006-2010 5-year est.); Percent of households with income of $100,000 or more: 14.6% (2006-2010 5-year est.); Poverty rate: 10.9% (2006-2010 5-year est.).

Education: Percent of population age 25 and over with: High school diploma (including GED) or higher: 75.4% (2006-2010 5-year est.); Bachelor's degree or higher: 11.6% (2006-2010 5-year est.); Master's degree or higher: 6.0% (2006-2010 5-year est.).

Housing: Homeownership rate: 83.4% (2010); Median home value: $110,600 (2006-2010 5-year est.); Median contract rent: $297 per month (2006-2010 5-year est.); Median year structure built: 1957 (2006-2010 5-year est.).

Safety: Violent crime rate: 0.0 per 10,000 population; Property crime rate: 30.7 per 10,000 population (2011).

Transportation: Commute to work: 84.5% car, 0.0% public transportation, 4.4% walk, 8.8% work from home (2006-2010 5-year est.); Travel time to work: 34.6% less than 15 minutes, 26.0% 15 to 30 minutes, 23.4% 30 to

45 minutes, 10.9% 45 to 60 minutes, 5.1% 60 minutes or more (2006-2010 5-year est.)

Additional Information Contacts
Somerset County Chamber of Commerce . . . . (814) 445-6431
   http://www.somersetcountychamber.com

UPPER TURKEYFOOT (township). Covers a land area of 38.635 square miles and a water area of 0.024 square miles. Located at 39.89° N. Lat; 79.29° W. Long.

Population: 1,132 (1990); 1,232 (2000); 1,119 (2010); Density: 29.0 persons per square mile (2010); Race: 99.5% White, 0.2% Black, 0.0% Asian, 0.2% American Indian/Alaska Native, 0.0% Native Hawaiian/Other Pacific Islander, 0.1% Other, 0.4% Hispanic of any race (2010); Average household size: 2.46 (2010); Median age: 46.3 (2010); Males per 100 females: 108.0 (2010); Marriage status: 23.3% never married, 65.8% now married, 5.2% widowed, 5.8% divorced (2006-2010 5-year est.); Foreign born: 0.0% (2006-2010 5-year est.); Ancestry (includes multiple ancestries): 46.7% German, 16.2% American, 11.2% English, 7.0% Irish, 3.5% Pennsylvania German (2006-2010 5-year est.).

Economy: Single-family building permits issued: 0 (2011); Multi-family building permits issued: 0 (2011); Employment by occupation: 11.8% management, 1.4% professional, 8.8% services, 11.3% sales, 1.4% farming, 20.8% construction, 6.1% production (2006-2010 5-year est.).

Income: Per capita income: $20,260 (2006-2010 5-year est.); Median household income: $43,750 (2006-2010 5-year est.); Average household income: $48,150 (2006-2010 5-year est.); Percent of households with income of $100,000 or more: 7.4% (2006-2010 5-year est.); Poverty rate: 5.7% (2006-2010 5-year est.).

Education: Percent of population age 25 and over with: High school diploma (including GED) or higher: 82.5% (2006-2010 5-year est.); Bachelor's degree or higher: 13.1% (2006-2010 5-year est.); Master's degree or higher: 3.1% (2006-2010 5-year est.).

Housing: Homeownership rate: 89.9% (2010); Median home value: $97,700 (2006-2010 5-year est.); Median contract rent: $395 per month (2006-2010 5-year est.); Median year structure built: 1964 (2006-2010 5-year est.).

Transportation: Commute to work: 86.7% car, 0.0% public transportation, 4.0% walk, 9.4% work from home (2006-2010 5-year est.); Travel time to work: 10.7% less than 15 minutes, 43.8% 15 to 30 minutes, 17.6% 30 to 45 minutes, 13.6% 45 to 60 minutes, 14.3% 60 minutes or more (2006-2010 5-year est.)

Additional Information Contacts
Somerset County Chamber of Commerce . . . . (814) 445-6431
   http://www.somersetcountychamber.com

URSINA (borough). Covers a land area of 0.900 square miles and a water area of 0 square miles. Located at 39.82° N. Lat; 79.33° W. Long. Elevation is 1,352 feet.

Population: 327 (1990); 254 (2000); 225 (2010); Density: 250.1 persons per square mile (2010); Race: 99.6% White, 0.0% Black, 0.4% Asian, 0.0% American Indian/Alaska Native, 0.0% Native Hawaiian/Other Pacific Islander, 0.0% Other, 0.4% Hispanic of any race (2010); Average household size: 2.23 (2010); Median age: 48.8 (2010); Males per 100 females: 99.1 (2010); Marriage status: 20.3% never married, 62.3% now married, 3.4% widowed, 14.0% divorced (2006-2010 5-year est.); Foreign born: 0.0% (2006-2010 5-year est.); Ancestry (includes multiple ancestries): 23.3% German, 19.4% Pennsylvania German, 14.7% Irish, 8.3% English, 7.8% Dutch (2006-2010 5-year est.).

Economy: Single-family building permits issued: 0 (2011); Multi-family building permits issued: 0 (2011); Employment by occupation: 3.1% management, 2.0% professional, 26.5% services, 8.2% sales, 5.1% farming, 18.4% construction, 7.1% production (2006-2010 5-year est.).

Income: Per capita income: $10,450 (2006-2010 5-year est.); Median household income: $32,917 (2006-2010 5-year est.); Average household income: $39,365 (2006-2010 5-year est.); Percent of households with income of $100,000 or more: 5.0% (2006-2010 5-year est.); Poverty rate: 50.4% (2006-2010 5-year est.).

Education: Percent of population age 25 and over with: High school diploma (including GED) or higher: 63.2% (2006-2010 5-year est.); Bachelor's degree or higher: 7.7% (2006-2010 5-year est.); Master's degree or higher: 1.9% (2006-2010 5-year est.).

Housing: Homeownership rate: 85.2% (2010); Median home value: $66,300 (2006-2010 5-year est.); Median contract rent: $356 per month (2006-2010 5-year est.); Median year structure built: 1952 (2006-2010 5-year est.).

Transportation: Commute to work: 89.3% car, 0.0% public transportation, 2.4% walk, 8.3% work from home (2006-2010 5-year est.); Travel time to work: 31.2% less than 15 minutes, 31.2% 15 to 30 minutes, 24.7% 30 to 45 minutes, 10.4% 45 to 60 minutes, 2.6% 60 minutes or more (2006-2010 5-year est.).

WELLERSBURG (borough). Covers a land area of 0.810 square miles and a water area of 0 square miles. Located at 39.73° N. Lat; 78.85° W. Long. Elevation is 1,371 feet.

Population: 213 (1990); 176 (2000); 181 (2010); Density: 223.4 persons per square mile (2010); Race: 98.3% White, 0.6% Black, 0.6% Asian, 0.0% American Indian/Alaska Native, 0.0% Native Hawaiian/Other Pacific Islander, 0.5% Other, 0.6% Hispanic of any race (2010); Average household size: 2.23 (2010); Median age: 47.9 (2010); Males per 100 females: 94.6 (2010); Marriage status: 20.9% never married, 54.9% now married, 13.7% widowed, 10.4% divorced (2006-2010 5-year est.); Foreign born: 0.0% (2006-2010 5-year est.); Ancestry (includes multiple ancestries): 50.2% German, 18.4% Irish, 10.1% English, 6.9% American, 6.0% European (2006-2010 5-year est.).

Economy: Employment by occupation: 0.0% management, 2.7% professional, 7.2% services, 31.5% sales, 1.8% farming, 14.4% construction, 2.7% production (2006-2010 5-year est.).

Income: Per capita income: $19,858 (2006-2010 5-year est.); Median household income: $46,250 (2006-2010 5-year est.); Average household income: $47,682 (2006-2010 5-year est.); Percent of households with income of $100,000 or more: 13.8% (2006-2010 5-year est.); Poverty rate: 5.1% (2006-2010 5-year est.).

Education: Percent of population age 25 and over with: High school diploma (including GED) or higher: 82.0% (2006-2010 5-year est.); Bachelor's degree or higher: 13.7% (2006-2010 5-year est.); Master's degree or higher: 1.2% (2006-2010 5-year est.).

Housing: Homeownership rate: 90.1% (2010); Median home value: $86,000 (2006-2010 5-year est.); Median contract rent: $250 per month (2006-2010 5-year est.); Median year structure built: 1942 (2006-2010 5-year est.).

Transportation: Commute to work: 98.1% car, 0.0% public transportation, 1.9% walk, 0.0% work from home (2006-2010 5-year est.); Travel time to work: 11.4% less than 15 minutes, 51.4% 15 to 30 minutes, 13.3% 30 to 45 minutes, 5.7% 45 to 60 minutes, 18.1% 60 minutes or more (2006-2010 5-year est.).

WINDBER (borough). Covers a land area of 1.976 square miles and a water area of 0 square miles. Located at 40.24° N. Lat; 78.82° W. Long. Elevation is 1,765 feet.

History: Laid out 1897, incorporated 1900.

Population: 4,666 (1990); 4,395 (2000); 4,138 (2010); Density: 2,094.6 persons per square mile (2010); Race: 98.6% White, 0.3% Black, 0.1% Asian, 0.2% American Indian/Alaska Native, 0.0% Native Hawaiian/Other Pacific Islander, 0.8% Other, 1.4% Hispanic of any race (2010); Average household size: 2.18 (2010); Median age: 42.4 (2010); Males per 100 females: 90.7 (2010); Marriage status: 36.3% never married, 44.6% now married, 10.7% widowed, 8.4% divorced (2006-2010 5-year est.); Foreign born: 0.3% (2006-2010 5-year est.); Ancestry (includes multiple ancestries): 30.4% German, 16.1% Italian, 15.5% Irish, 11.4% Polish, 10.5% Slovak (2006-2010 5-year est.).

Economy: Single-family building permits issued: 0 (2011); Multi-family building permits issued: 0 (2011); Employment by occupation: 7.9% management, 1.9% professional, 9.2% services, 18.8% sales, 5.0% farming, 12.2% construction, 6.6% production (2006-2010 5-year est.).

Income: Per capita income: $16,822 (2006-2010 5-year est.); Median household income: $26,842 (2006-2010 5-year est.); Average household income: $37,422 (2006-2010 5-year est.); Percent of households with income of $100,000 or more: 1.9% (2006-2010 5-year est.); Poverty rate: 21.0% (2006-2010 5-year est.).

Education: Percent of population age 25 and over with: High school diploma (including GED) or higher: 80.6% (2006-2010 5-year est.); Bachelor's degree or higher: 16.8% (2006-2010 5-year est.); Master's degree or higher: 3.9% (2006-2010 5-year est.).

School District(s)

Windber Area SD (PK-12)
    2010-11 Enrollment: 1,302 . . . . (814) 467-5551

Housing: Homeownership rate: 63.6% (2010); Median home value: $72,000 (2006-2010 5-year est.); Median contract rent: $363 per month (2006-2010 5-year est.); Median year structure built: before 1940 (2006-2010 5-year est.).

Hospitals: Windber Medical Center (82 beds)

Transportation: Commute to work: 96.9% car, 0.0% public transportation, 1.1% walk, 2.0% work from home (2006-2010 5-year est.); Travel time to work: 33.8% less than 15 minutes, 50.1% 15 to 30 minutes, 5.2% 30 to 45 minutes, 5.8% 45 to 60 minutes, 5.1% 60 minutes or more (2006-2010 5-year est.).

Additional Information Contacts

Greater Johnstown Cambria County Chamber of Commerce . . . . (814) 536-5107
    http://www.johnstownchamber.com

Sullivan County

Located in northeastern Pennsylvania; mountainous area, drained by Loyalsock and Muncy Creeks; includes many lakes. Covers a land area of 449.940 square miles, a water area of 2.555 square miles, and is located in the Eastern Time Zone at 41.44° N. Lat., 76.51° W. Long. The county was founded in 1847. County seat is Laporte.

Population: 6,104 (1990); 6,556 (2000); 6,428 (2010); Race: 95.9% White, 2.6% Black, 0.3% Asian, 0.4% American Indian/Alaska Native, 0.0% Native Hawaiian/Other Pacific Islander, 0.8% Other, 1.4% Hispanic of any race (2010); Density: 14.3 persons per square mile (2010); Average household size: 2.16 (2010); Median age: 49.9 (2010); Males per 100 females: 106.0 (2010).

Religion: Six largest groups: 15.6% Catholicism, 4.8% Methodist/Pietist, 4.3% Lutheran, 2.1% Pentecostal, 1.7% Holiness, 0.6% Eastern Liturgical (Orthodox) (2010)

Economy: Unemployment rate: 7.2% (August 2012); Total civilian labor force: 3,519 (August 2012); Leading industries: 36.3% health care and social assistance; 23.7% retail trade; 7.7% accommodation & food services (2010); Farms: 165 totaling 27,821 acres (2007); Companies that employ 500 or more persons: 0 (2010); Companies that employ 100 to 499 persons: 2 (2010); Companies that employ less than 100 persons: 161 (2010); Black-owned businesses: n/a (2007); Hispanic-owned businesses: n/a (2007); Asian-owned businesses: n/a (2007); Women-owned businesses: 101 (2007); Retail sales per capita: $6,466 (2010). Single-family building permits issued: 10 (2011); Multi-family building permits issued: 0 (2011).

Income: Per capita income: $19,718 (2006-2010 5-year est.); Median household income: $36,250 (2006-2010 5-year est.); Average household income: $46,502 (2006-2010 5-year est.); Percent of households with income of $100,000 or more: 7.5% (2006-2010 5-year est.); Poverty rate: 15.5% (2006-2010 5-year est.); Bankruptcy rate: 0.92% (2011).

Education: Percent of population age 25 and over with: High school diploma (including GED) or higher: 86.1% (2006-2010 5-year est.); Bachelor's degree or higher: 11.4% (2006-2010 5-year est.); Master's degree or higher: 4.2% (2006-2010 5-year est.).

Housing: Homeownership rate: 80.0% (2010); Median home value: $120,600 (2006-2010 5-year est.); Median contract rent: $339 per month (2006-2010 5-year est.); Median year structure built: 1967 (2006-2010 5-year est.).

Health: Birth rate: 88.0 per 10,000 population (2011); Death rate: 159.0 per 10,000 population (2011); Age-adjusted cancer mortality rate: 211.9 deaths per 100,000 population (2009); Number of physicians: 0.0 per 10,000 population (2010); Hospital beds: 0.0 per 10,000 population (2008); Hospital admissions: 0.0 per 10,000 population (2008).

Elections: 2012 Presidential election results: 35.1% Obama, 63.3% Romney

National and State Parks: Worlds End State Park; Wyoming State Forest

Additional Information Contacts

Sullivan County Government. . . . . (570) 946-5201
    http://www.sullivancounty-pa.us
Sullivan County Chamber of Commerce . . . . (570) 482-4088
    http://www.sullivanpachamber.com/location.html

Sullivan County Communities

CHERRY (township). Covers a land area of 57.933 square miles and a water area of 0.223 square miles. Located at 41.50° N. Lat; 76.40° W. Long.

Population: 1,481 (1990); 1,718 (2000); 1,705 (2010); Density: 29.4 persons per square mile (2010); Race: 98.3% White, 0.2% Black, 0.2% Asian, 0.4% American Indian/Alaska Native, 0.0% Native Hawaiian/Other Pacific Islander, 0.9% Other, 1.5% Hispanic of any race (2010); Average household size: 2.31 (2010); Median age: 48.4 (2010); Males per 100

females: 103.9 (2010); Marriage status: 26.1% never married, 58.7% now married, 9.1% widowed, 6.1% divorced (2006-2010 5-year est.); Foreign born: 0.7% (2006-2010 5-year est.); Ancestry (includes multiple ancestries): 32.2% German, 26.2% Irish, 11.0% Italian, 10.7% Polish, 9.4% English (2006-2010 5-year est.).

Economy: Single-family building permits issued: 2 (2011); Multi-family building permits issued: 0 (2011); Employment by occupation: 6.5% management, 3.1% professional, 8.1% services, 15.4% sales, 2.7% farming, 18.7% construction, 12.7% production (2006-2010 5-year est.).

Income: Per capita income: $19,573 (2006-2010 5-year est.); Median household income: $40,143 (2006-2010 5-year est.); Average household income: $47,947 (2006-2010 5-year est.); Percent of households with income of $100,000 or more: 6.9% (2006-2010 5-year est.); Poverty rate: 15.6% (2006-2010 5-year est.).

Education: Percent of population age 25 and over with: High school diploma (including GED) or higher: 88.8% (2006-2010 5-year est.); Bachelor's degree or higher: 8.2% (2006-2010 5-year est.); Master's degree or higher: 2.8% (2006-2010 5-year est.).

Housing: Homeownership rate: 86.0% (2010); Median home value: $120,300 (2006-2010 5-year est.); Median contract rent: $442 per month (2006-2010 5-year est.); Median year structure built: 1963 (2006-2010 5-year est.).

Transportation: Commute to work: 94.2% car, 1.7% public transportation, 3.2% walk, 0.5% work from home (2006-2010 5-year est.); Travel time to work: 33.0% less than 15 minutes, 18.3% 15 to 30 minutes, 35.3% 30 to 45 minutes, 7.5% 45 to 60 minutes, 5.9% 60 minutes or more (2006-2010 5-year est.)

Additional Information Contacts

Sullivan County Chamber of Commerce . . . . (570) 482-4088
http://www.sullivanpachamber.com/location.html

COLLEY (township). Covers a land area of 58.257 square miles and a water area of 0.958 square miles. Located at 41.46° N. Lat; 76.30° W. Long. Elevation is 1,506 feet.

Population: 600 (1990); 647 (2000); 694 (2010); Density: 11.9 persons per square mile (2010); Race: 76.7% White, 21.6% Black, 1.2% Asian, 0.4% American Indian/Alaska Native, 0.0% Native Hawaiian/Other Pacific Islander, 0.1% Other, 5.8% Hispanic of any race (2010); Average household size: 1.94 (2010); Median age: 25.3 (2010); Males per 100 females: 181.0 (2010); Marriage status: 39.4% never married, 40.5% now married, 17.7% widowed, 2.4% divorced (2006-2010 5-year est.); Foreign born: 4.1% (2006-2010 5-year est.); Ancestry (includes multiple ancestries): 22.5% German, 13.0% Italian, 9.1% Polish, 7.6% Irish, 4.5% English (2006-2010 5-year est.).

Economy: Single-family building permits issued: 0 (2011); Multi-family building permits issued: 0 (2011); Employment by occupation: 6.4% management, 0.0% professional, 3.2% services, 19.2% sales, 3.2% farming, 14.4% construction, 10.4% production (2006-2010 5-year est.).

Income: Per capita income: $14,243 (2006-2010 5-year est.); Median household income: $30,096 (2006-2010 5-year est.); Average household income: $38,299 (2006-2010 5-year est.); Percent of households with income of $100,000 or more: 9.0% (2006-2010 5-year est.); Poverty rate: 31.5% (2006-2010 5-year est.).

Education: Percent of population age 25 and over with: High school diploma (including GED) or higher: 85.4% (2006-2010 5-year est.); Bachelor's degree or higher: 11.3% (2006-2010 5-year est.); Master's degree or higher: 7.0% (2006-2010 5-year est.).

Housing: Homeownership rate: 86.5% (2010); Median home value: $96,700 (2006-2010 5-year est.); Median contract rent: $590 per month (2006-2010 5-year est.); Median year structure built: 1956 (2006-2010 5-year est.).

Transportation: Commute to work: 92.8% car, 0.0% public transportation, 0.0% walk, 7.2% work from home (2006-2010 5-year est.); Travel time to work: 18.1% less than 15 minutes, 48.3% 15 to 30 minutes, 16.4% 30 to 45 minutes, 4.3% 45 to 60 minutes, 12.9% 60 minutes or more (2006-2010 5-year est.)

DAVIDSON (township). Covers a land area of 77.863 square miles and a water area of 0.059 square miles. Located at 41.33° N. Lat; 76.44° W. Long.

Population: 597 (1990); 626 (2000); 573 (2010); Density: 7.4 persons per square mile (2010); Race: 98.1% White, 1.0% Black, 0.3% Asian, 0.0% American Indian/Alaska Native, 0.0% Native Hawaiian/Other Pacific Islander, 0.6% Other, 0.5% Hispanic of any race (2010); Average household size: 2.37 (2010); Median age: 48.1 (2010); Males per 100

females: 94.2 (2010); Marriage status: 32.3% never married, 57.8% now married, 4.3% widowed, 5.5% divorced (2006-2010 5-year est.); Foreign born: 0.9% (2006-2010 5-year est.); Ancestry (includes multiple ancestries): 76.3% German, 13.9% Irish, 8.6% Scotch-Irish, 5.4% Dutch, 3.9% English (2006-2010 5-year est.).

Economy: Single-family building permits issued: 0 (2011); Multi-family building permits issued: 0 (2011); Employment by occupation: 8.7% management, 4.0% professional, 17.3% services, 5.3% sales, 0.0% farming, 18.3% construction, 15.7% production (2006-2010 5-year est.).

Income: Per capita income: $19,912 (2006-2010 5-year est.); Median household income: $36,071 (2006-2010 5-year est.); Average household income: $48,955 (2006-2010 5-year est.); Percent of households with income of $100,000 or more: 9.0% (2006-2010 5-year est.); Poverty rate: 4.7% (2006-2010 5-year est.).

Education: Percent of population age 25 and over with: High school diploma (including GED) or higher: 85.4% (2006-2010 5-year est.); Bachelor's degree or higher: 9.6% (2006-2010 5-year est.); Master's degree or higher: 4.5% (2006-2010 5-year est.).

Housing: Homeownership rate: 85.1% (2010); Median home value: $93,100 (2006-2010 5-year est.); Median contract rent: $391 per month (2006-2010 5-year est.); Median year structure built: 1963 (2006-2010 5-year est.).

Transportation: Commute to work: 84.7% car, 0.0% public transportation, 9.7% walk, 5.7% work from home (2006-2010 5-year est.); Travel time to work: 21.2% less than 15 minutes, 29.3% 15 to 30 minutes, 31.1% 30 to 45 minutes, 17.3% 45 to 60 minutes, 1.1% 60 minutes or more (2006-2010 5-year est.)

DUSHORE (borough). Covers a land area of 0.788 square miles and a water area of 0.016 square miles. Located at 41.53° N. Lat; 76.40° W. Long. Elevation is 1,453 feet.

Population: 738 (1990); 663 (2000); 608 (2010); Density: 771.4 persons per square mile (2010); Race: 98.8% White, 0.0% Black, 0.0% Asian, 0.3% American Indian/Alaska Native, 0.0% Native Hawaiian/Other Pacific Islander, 0.9% Other, 0.5% Hispanic of any race (2010); Average household size: 1.78 (2010); Median age: 49.2 (2010); Males per 100 females: 83.1 (2010); Marriage status: 40.8% never married, 33.7% now married, 11.2% widowed, 14.3% divorced (2006-2010 5-year est.); Foreign born: 1.3% (2006-2010 5-year est.); Ancestry (includes multiple ancestries): 35.2% Irish, 28.5% English, 22.3% German, 15.2% Italian, 7.3% Polish (2006-2010 5-year est.).

Economy: Single-family building permits issued: 1 (2011); Multi-family building permits issued: 0 (2011); Employment by occupation: 6.5% management, 0.9% professional, 16.1% services, 24.3% sales, 2.6% farming, 17.0% construction, 13.5% production (2006-2010 5-year est.).

Income: Per capita income: $18,112 (2006-2010 5-year est.); Median household income: $24,479 (2006-2010 5-year est.); Average household income: $34,930 (2006-2010 5-year est.); Percent of households with income of $100,000 or more: 3.5% (2006-2010 5-year est.); Poverty rate: 21.4% (2006-2010 5-year est.).

Education: Percent of population age 25 and over with: High school diploma (including GED) or higher: 81.3% (2006-2010 5-year est.); Bachelor's degree or higher: 12.9% (2006-2010 5-year est.); Master's degree or higher: 5.4% (2006-2010 5-year est.).

Housing: Homeownership rate: 41.0% (2010); Median home value: $88,300 (2006-2010 5-year est.); Median contract rent: $196 per month (2006-2010 5-year est.); Median year structure built: before 1940 (2006-2010 5-year est.).

Newspapers: Sullivan Review (Local news; Circulation 7,147)

Transportation: Commute to work: 99.1% car, 0.0% public transportation, 0.0% walk, 0.9% work from home (2006-2010 5-year est.); Travel time to work: 40.8% less than 15 minutes, 28.1% 15 to 30 minutes, 16.7% 30 to 45 minutes, 7.9% 45 to 60 minutes, 6.6% 60 minutes or more (2006-2010 5-year est.)

EAGLES MERE (borough). Covers a land area of 2.058 square miles and a water area of 0.186 square miles. Located at 41.41° N. Lat; 76.58° W. Long. Elevation is 2,064 feet.

Population: 123 (1990); 153 (2000); 120 (2010); Density: 58.3 persons per square mile (2010); Race: 99.2% White, 0.0% Black, 0.8% Asian, 0.0% American Indian/Alaska Native, 0.0% Native Hawaiian/Other Pacific Islander, 0.0% Other, 0.8% Hispanic of any race (2010); Average household size: 1.94 (2010); Median age: 63.3 (2010); Males per 100 females: 93.5 (2010); Marriage status: 0.0% never married, 82.4% now married, 13.7% widowed, 3.9% divorced (2006-2010 5-year est.); Foreign

born: 3.9% (2006-2010 5-year est.); Ancestry (includes multiple ancestries): 31.4% Irish, 31.4% German, 19.6% Italian, 19.6% French, 13.7% Scottish (2006-2010 5-year est.).

Economy: Single-family building permits issued: 0 (2011); Multi-family building permits issued: 0 (2011); Employment by occupation: 0.0% management, 0.0% professional, 20.0% services, 80.0% sales, 0.0% farming, 0.0% construction, 0.0% production (2006-2010 5-year est.).

Income: Per capita income: $25,033 (2006-2010 5-year est.); Median household income: $30,469 (2006-2010 5-year est.); Average household income: $41,648 (2006-2010 5-year est.); Percent of households with income of $100,000 or more: 10.3% (2006-2010 5-year est.); Poverty rate: 5.9% (2006-2010 5-year est.).

Taxes: Total city taxes per capita: $924 (2009); City property taxes per capita: $662 (2009).

Education: Percent of population age 25 and over with: High school diploma (including GED) or higher: 84.3% (2006-2010 5-year est.); Bachelor's degree or higher: 17.6% (2006-2010 5-year est.); Master's degree or higher: 5.9% (2006-2010 5-year est.).

Housing: Homeownership rate: 95.2% (2010); Median home value: $225,000 (2006-2010 5-year est.); Median contract rent: n/a per month (2006-2010 5-year est.); Median year structure built: 1949 (2006-2010 5-year est.).

Transportation: Commute to work: 100.0% car, 0.0% public transportation, 0.0% walk, 0.0% work from home (2006-2010 5-year est.); Travel time to work: 100.0% less than 15 minutes, 0.0% 15 to 30 minutes, 0.0% 30 to 45 minutes, 0.0% 45 to 60 minutes, 0.0% 60 minutes or more (2006-2010 5-year est.)

Additional Information Contacts

Borough of Eagles Mere . . . . (570) 525-3247
   http://www.eaglesmere.org

ELKLAND (township). Covers a land area of 38.460 square miles and a water area of 0.230 square miles. Located at 41.53° N. Lat; 76.65° W. Long.

Population: 565 (1990); 607 (2000); 577 (2010); Density: 15.0 persons per square mile (2010); Race: 97.6% White, 0.5% Black, 0.3% Asian, 0.3% American Indian/Alaska Native, 0.0% Native Hawaiian/Other Pacific Islander, 1.3% Other, 0.5% Hispanic of any race (2010); Average household size: 2.22 (2010); Median age: 52.5 (2010); Males per 100 females: 111.4 (2010); Marriage status: 24.4% never married, 59.0% now married, 12.7% widowed, 3.9% divorced (2006-2010 5-year est.); Foreign born: 0.0% (2006-2010 5-year est.); Ancestry (includes multiple ancestries): 39.9% German, 25.0% English, 12.9% Irish, 8.6% Swedish, 6.0% Polish (2006-2010 5-year est.).

Economy: Single-family building permits issued: 0 (2011); Multi-family building permits issued: 0 (2011); Employment by occupation: 11.7% management, 2.5% professional, 25.9% services, 10.9% sales, 2.1% farming, 7.9% construction, 0.0% production (2006-2010 5-year est.).

Income: Per capita income: $22,988 (2006-2010 5-year est.); Median household income: $37,125 (2006-2010 5-year est.); Average household income: $56,316 (2006-2010 5-year est.); Percent of households with income of $100,000 or more: 8.5% (2006-2010 5-year est.); Poverty rate: 1.9% (2006-2010 5-year est.).

Education: Percent of population age 25 and over with: High school diploma (including GED) or higher: 95.0% (2006-2010 5-year est.); Bachelor's degree or higher: 13.9% (2006-2010 5-year est.); Master's degree or higher: 3.2% (2006-2010 5-year est.).

Housing: Homeownership rate: 85.1% (2010); Median home value: $169,800 (2006-2010 5-year est.); Median contract rent: $350 per month (2006-2010 5-year est.); Median year structure built: 1967 (2006-2010 5-year est.).

Transportation: Commute to work: 69.4% car, 0.0% public transportation, 11.9% walk, 10.6% work from home (2006-2010 5-year est.); Travel time to work: 43.3% less than 15 minutes, 19.5% 15 to 30 minutes, 10.0% 30 to 45 minutes, 2.9% 45 to 60 minutes, 24.3% 60 minutes or more (2006-2010 5-year est.).

FORKS (township). Covers a land area of 43.411 square miles and a water area of 0.021 square miles. Located at 41.49° N. Lat; 76.55° W. Long.

Population: 355 (1990); 407 (2000); 377 (2010); Density: 8.7 persons per square mile (2010); Race: 97.6% White, 0.0% Black, 0.3% Asian, 0.0% American Indian/Alaska Native, 0.0% Native Hawaiian/Other Pacific Islander, 2.1% Other, 2.1% Hispanic of any race (2010); Average household size: 2.27 (2010); Median age: 53.1 (2010); Males per 100

females: 109.4 (2010); Marriage status: 29.0% never married, 57.9% now married, 8.3% widowed, 4.8% divorced (2006-2010 5-year est.); Foreign born: 0.2% (2006-2010 5-year est.); Ancestry (includes multiple ancestries): 39.8% German, 25.2% Irish, 19.3% English, 8.1% American, 5.5% Dutch (2006-2010 5-year est.).

Economy: Single-family building permits issued: 1 (2011); Multi-family building permits issued: 0 (2011); Employment by occupation: 14.0% management, 0.0% professional, 8.9% services, 12.2% sales, 0.7% farming, 7.7% construction, 5.2% production (2006-2010 5-year est.).

Income: Per capita income: $22,306 (2006-2010 5-year est.); Median household income: $42,054 (2006-2010 5-year est.); Average household income: $48,818 (2006-2010 5-year est.); Percent of households with income of $100,000 or more: 5.1% (2006-2010 5-year est.); Poverty rate: 9.0% (2006-2010 5-year est.).

Education: Percent of population age 25 and over with: High school diploma (including GED) or higher: 92.7% (2006-2010 5-year est.); Bachelor's degree or higher: 9.9% (2006-2010 5-year est.); Master's degree or higher: 5.8% (2006-2010 5-year est.).

Housing: Homeownership rate: 88.6% (2010); Median home value: $166,700 (2006-2010 5-year est.); Median contract rent: $425 per month (2006-2010 5-year est.); Median year structure built: 1969 (2006-2010 5-year est.).

Transportation: Commute to work: 86.0% car, 0.0% public transportation, 0.8% walk, 5.3% work from home (2006-2010 5-year est.); Travel time to work: 28.4% less than 15 minutes, 24.4% 15 to 30 minutes, 16.4% 30 to 45 minutes, 17.2% 45 to 60 minutes, 13.6% 60 minutes or more (2006-2010 5-year est.)

FORKSVILLE (borough). Covers a land area of 1.573 square miles and a water area of 0 square miles. Located at 41.49° N. Lat; 76.60° W. Long. Elevation is 1,017 feet.

Population: 160 (1990); 147 (2000); 145 (2010); Density: 92.2 persons per square mile (2010); Race: 94.5% White, 2.1% Black, 0.0% Asian, 2.8% American Indian/Alaska Native, 0.0% Native Hawaiian/Other Pacific Islander, 0.6% Other, 0.0% Hispanic of any race (2010); Average household size: 2.16 (2010); Median age: 45.5 (2010); Males per 100 females: 76.8 (2010); Marriage status: 21.1% never married, 38.9% now married, 11.6% widowed, 28.4% divorced (2006-2010 5-year est.); Foreign born: 0.0% (2006-2010 5-year est.); Ancestry (includes multiple ancestries): 69.7% German, 22.2% English, 15.2% Irish, 12.1% French, 8.1% Italian (2006-2010 5-year est.).

Economy: Single-family building permits issued: 0 (2011); Multi-family building permits issued: 0 (2011); Employment by occupation: 12.8% management, 0.0% professional, 8.5% services, 25.5% sales, 6.4% farming, 14.9% construction, 6.4% production (2006-2010 5-year est.).

Income: Per capita income: $17,505 (2006-2010 5-year est.); Median household income: $23,393 (2006-2010 5-year est.); Average household income: $30,847 (2006-2010 5-year est.); Percent of households with income of $100,000 or more: 3.4% (2006-2010 5-year est.); Poverty rate: 29.3% (2006-2010 5-year est.).

Education: Percent of population age 25 and over with: High school diploma (including GED) or higher: 90.7% (2006-2010 5-year est.); Bachelor's degree or higher: 7.0% (2006-2010 5-year est.); Master's degree or higher: 4.7% (2006-2010 5-year est.).

Housing: Homeownership rate: 50.8% (2010); Median home value: $96,700 (2006-2010 5-year est.); Median contract rent: $381 per month (2006-2010 5-year est.); Median year structure built: 1957 (2006-2010 5-year est.).

Transportation: Commute to work: 93.6% car, 0.0% public transportation, 6.4% walk, 0.0% work from home (2006-2010 5-year est.); Travel time to work: 8.5% less than 15 minutes, 31.9% 15 to 30 minutes, 17.0% 30 to 45 minutes, 0.0% 45 to 60 minutes, 42.6% 60 minutes or more (2006-2010 5-year est.)

FOX (township). Covers a land area of 38.858 square miles and a water area of 0.091 square miles. Located at 41.54° N. Lat; 76.75° W. Long.

Population: 300 (1990); 332 (2000); 358 (2010); Density: 9.2 persons per square mile (2010); Race: 98.3% White, 0.0% Black, 0.3% Asian, 0.8% American Indian/Alaska Native, 0.0% Native Hawaiian/Other Pacific Islander, 0.6% Other, 0.3% Hispanic of any race (2010); Average household size: 2.12 (2010); Median age: 52.8 (2010); Males per 100 females: 111.8 (2010); Marriage status: 9.0% never married, 80.5% now married, 6.0% widowed, 4.5% divorced (2006-2010 5-year est.); Foreign born: 0.0% (2006-2010 5-year est.); Ancestry (includes multiple

ancestries): 21.8% German, 18.3% English, 13.1% Italian, 11.4% Irish, 7.4% Dutch (2006-2010 5-year est.).
Economy: Single-family building permits issued: 2 (2011); Multi-family building permits issued: 0 (2011); Employment by occupation: 14.0% management, 0.0% professional, 13.1% services, 18.7% sales, 4.7% farming, 13.1% construction, 5.6% production (2006-2010 5-year est.).
Income: Per capita income: $18,528 (2006-2010 5-year est.); Median household income: $31,250 (2006-2010 5-year est.); Average household income: $40,638 (2006-2010 5-year est.); Percent of households with income of $100,000 or more: 2.0% (2006-2010 5-year est.); Poverty rate: 5.2% (2006-2010 5-year est.).
Education: Percent of population age 25 and over with: High school diploma (including GED) or higher: 82.0% (2006-2010 5-year est.); Bachelor's degree or higher: 5.6% (2006-2010 5-year est.); Master's degree or higher: 1.7% (2006-2010 5-year est.).
Housing: Homeownership rate: 85.8% (2010); Median home value: $100,000 (2006-2010 5-year est.); Median contract rent: $200 per month (2006-2010 5-year est.); Median year structure built: 1972 (2006-2010 5-year est.).
Transportation: Commute to work: 93.5% car, 0.0% public transportation, 6.5% walk, 0.0% work from home (2006-2010 5-year est.); Travel time to work: 34.6% less than 15 minutes, 34.6% 15 to 30 minutes, 16.8% 30 to 45 minutes, 7.5% 45 to 60 minutes, 6.5% 60 minutes or more (2006-2010 5-year est.)

HILLSGROVE (township). Covers a land area of 28.510 square miles and a water area of 0.019 square miles. Located at 41.44° N. Lat; 76.68° W. Long. Elevation is 873 feet.
Population: 337 (1990); 265 (2000); 287 (2010); Density: 10.1 persons per square mile (2010); Race: 99.3% White, 0.0% Black, 0.0% Asian, 0.3% American Indian/Alaska Native, 0.3% Native Hawaiian/Other Pacific Islander, 0.4% Other, 0.0% Hispanic of any race (2010); Average household size: 2.18 (2010); Median age: 48.6 (2010); Males per 100 females: 97.9 (2010); Marriage status: 18.3% never married, 58.0% now married, 18.9% widowed, 4.7% divorced (2006-2010 5-year est.); Foreign born: 0.0% (2006-2010 5-year est.); Ancestry (includes multiple ancestries): 40.8% German, 20.9% English, 18.4% Irish, 12.4% Dutch, 8.0% Polish (2006-2010 5-year est.).
Economy: Single-family building permits issued: 2 (2011); Multi-family building permits issued: 0 (2011); Employment by occupation: 8.7% management, 11.6% professional, 5.8% services, 29.0% sales, 4.3% farming, 11.6% construction, 11.6% production (2006-2010 5-year est.).
Income: Per capita income: $18,192 (2006-2010 5-year est.); Median household income: $26,625 (2006-2010 5-year est.); Average household income: $41,959 (2006-2010 5-year est.); Percent of households with income of $100,000 or more: 6.2% (2006-2010 5-year est.); Poverty rate: 26.4% (2006-2010 5-year est.).
Education: Percent of population age 25 and over with: High school diploma (including GED) or higher: 92.3% (2006-2010 5-year est.); Bachelor's degree or higher: 16.9% (2006-2010 5-year est.); Master's degree or higher: 4.2% (2006-2010 5-year est.).
Housing: Homeownership rate: 83.0% (2010); Median home value: $140,600 (2006-2010 5-year est.); Median contract rent: n/a per month (2006-2010 5-year est.); Median year structure built: 1973 (2006-2010 5-year est.).
Transportation: Commute to work: 83.9% car, 0.0% public transportation, 11.3% walk, 4.8% work from home (2006-2010 5-year est.); Travel time to work: 22.0% less than 15 minutes, 0.0% 15 to 30 minutes, 44.1% 30 to 45 minutes, 33.9% 45 to 60 minutes, 0.0% 60 minutes or more (2006-2010 5-year est.)

LAPORTE (borough). County seat. Covers a land area of 1.068 square miles and a water area of 0.164 square miles. Located at 41.42° N. Lat; 76.49° W. Long. Elevation is 1,959 feet.
Population: 328 (1990); 290 (2000); 316 (2010); Density: 296.0 persons per square mile (2010); Race: 98.1% White, 0.6% Black, 0.3% Asian, 0.9% American Indian/Alaska Native, 0.0% Native Hawaiian/Other Pacific Islander, 0.1% Other, 0.9% Hispanic of any race (2010); Average household size: 2.01 (2010); Median age: 61.7 (2010); Males per 100 females: 84.8 (2010); Marriage status: 29.4% never married, 40.4% now married, 22.2% widowed, 7.9% divorced (2006-2010 5-year est.); Foreign born: 0.0% (2006-2010 5-year est.); Ancestry (includes multiple ancestries): 33.7% German, 17.5% Irish, 9.6% English, 3.5% Pennsylvania German, 3.3% Italian (2006-2010 5-year est.).

Economy: Single-family building permits issued: 0 (2011); Multi-family building permits issued: 0 (2011); Employment by occupation: 0.0% management, 0.0% professional, 38.4% services, 3.0% sales, 4.0% farming, 14.1% construction, 8.1% production (2006-2010 5-year est.).
Income: Per capita income: $15,536 (2006-2010 5-year est.); Median household income: $35,833 (2006-2010 5-year est.); Average household income: $40,398 (2006-2010 5-year est.); Percent of households with income of $100,000 or more: 6.6% (2006-2010 5-year est.); Poverty rate: 19.9% (2006-2010 5-year est.).
Education: Percent of population age 25 and over with: High school diploma (including GED) or higher: 65.6% (2006-2010 5-year est.); Bachelor's degree or higher: 15.9% (2006-2010 5-year est.); Master's degree or higher: 3.3% (2006-2010 5-year est.).

School District(s)
Sullivan County SD (KG-12)
    2010-11 Enrollment: 630 . . . . (570) 928-8194
Housing: Homeownership rate: 84.4% (2010); Median home value: $152,000 (2006-2010 5-year est.); Median contract rent: $375 per month (2006-2010 5-year est.); Median year structure built: 1973 (2006-2010 5-year est.).
Transportation: Commute to work: 91.7% car, 0.0% public transportation, 8.3% walk, 0.0% work from home (2006-2010 5-year est.); Travel time to work: 62.5% less than 15 minutes, 18.8% 15 to 30 minutes, 8.3% 30 to 45 minutes, 0.0% 45 to 60 minutes, 10.4% 60 minutes or more (2006-2010 5-year est.)

LAPORTE (township). Covers a land area of 54.002 square miles and a water area of 0.167 square miles. Located at 41.41° N. Lat; 76.45° W. Long. Elevation is 1,959 feet.
Population: 213 (1990); 373 (2000); 349 (2010); Density: 6.5 persons per square mile (2010); Race: 98.0% White, 0.3% Black, 0.6% American Indian/Alaska Native, 0.0% Native Hawaiian/Other Pacific Islander, 1.1% Other, 0.3% Hispanic of any race (2010); Average household size: 2.14 (2010); Median age: 53.4 (2010); Males per 100 females: 102.9 (2010); Marriage status: 28.3% never married, 55.8% now married, 10.2% widowed, 5.7% divorced (2006-2010 5-year est.); Foreign born: 0.0% (2006-2010 5-year est.); Ancestry (includes multiple ancestries): 37.6% German, 18.3% English, 17.2% Irish, 13.4% Pennsylvania German, 12.4% Polish (2006-2010 5-year est.).
Economy: Single-family building permits issued: 1 (2011); Multi-family building permits issued: 0 (2011); Employment by occupation: 0.0% management, 0.0% professional, 7.5% services, 14.2% sales, 0.0% farming, 26.7% construction, 10.0% production (2006-2010 5-year est.).
Income: Per capita income: $26,005 (2006-2010 5-year est.); Median household income: $59,125 (2006-2010 5-year est.); Average household income: $62,192 (2006-2010 5-year est.); Percent of households with income of $100,000 or more: 16.5% (2006-2010 5-year est.); Poverty rate: 1.7% (2006-2010 5-year est.).
Education: Percent of population age 25 and over with: High school diploma (including GED) or higher: 86.9% (2006-2010 5-year est.); Bachelor's degree or higher: 18.2% (2006-2010 5-year est.); Master's degree or higher: 7.6% (2006-2010 5-year est.).
Housing: Homeownership rate: 90.8% (2010); Median home value: $200,000 (2006-2010 5-year est.); Median contract rent: $438 per month (2006-2010 5-year est.); Median year structure built: 1978 (2006-2010 5-year est.).
Transportation: Commute to work: 95.8% car, 0.0% public transportation, 4.2% walk, 0.0% work from home (2006-2010 5-year est.); Travel time to work: 20.8% less than 15 minutes, 31.7% 15 to 30 minutes, 11.7% 30 to 45 minutes, 19.2% 45 to 60 minutes, 16.7% 60 minutes or more (2006-2010 5-year est.)

LOPEZ (unincorporated postal area)
Zip Code: 18628
    Covers a land area of 20.435 square miles and a water area of 0.428 square miles. Located at 41.43° N. Lat; 76.31° W. Long. Population: 192 (2010); Density: 9.4 persons per square mile (2010); Race: 96.4% White, 0.0% Black, 3.1% Asian, 0.5% American Indian/Alaska Native, 0.0% Native Hawaiian/Other Pacific Islander, 0.0% Other, 0.5% Hispanic of any race (2010); Average household size: 1.86 (2010); Median age: 53.0 (2010); Males per 100 females: 97.9 (2010); Homeownership rate: 86.4% (2010)

MILDRED (unincorporated postal area)
Zip Code: 18632

Covers a land area of 5.204 square miles and a water area of 0.012 square miles. Located at 41.45° N. Lat; 76.37° W. Long. Elevation is 1,831 feet. Population: 409 (2010); Density: 78.6 persons per square mile (2010); Race: 99.3% White, 0.2% Black, 0.5% Asian, 0.0% American Indian/Alaska Native, 0.0% Native Hawaiian/Other Pacific Islander, 0.0% Other, 2.7% Hispanic of any race (2010); Average household size: 2.30 (2010); Median age: 42.4 (2010); Males per 100 females: 90.2 (2010); Homeownership rate: 78.1% (2010)

MUNCY VALLEY (unincorporated postal area)

Zip Code: 17758

Covers a land area of 81.873 square miles and a water area of 0.681 square miles. Located at 41.36° N. Lat; 76.53° W. Long. Population: 919 (2010); Density: 11.2 persons per square mile (2010); Race: 98.4% White, 0.8% Black, 0.2% Asian, 0.2% American Indian/Alaska Native, 0.0% Native Hawaiian/Other Pacific Islander, 0.4% Other, 0.7% Hispanic of any race (2010); Average household size: 2.36 (2010); Median age: 46.8 (2010); Males per 100 females: 98.5 (2010); Homeownership rate: 84.6% (2010)

SHREWSBURY (township). Covers a land area of 47.158 square miles and a water area of 0.421 square miles. Located at 41.39° N. Lat; 76.62° W. Long.

Population: 307 (1990); 328 (2000); 319 (2010); Density: 6.8 persons per square mile (2010); Race: 99.1% White, 0.0% Black, 0.3% Asian, 0.0% American Indian/Alaska Native, 0.0% Native Hawaiian/Other Pacific Islander, 0.6% Other, 1.3% Hispanic of any race (2010); Average household size: 2.28 (2010); Median age: 51.7 (2010); Males per 100 females: 103.2 (2010); Marriage status: 36.7% never married, 44.3% now married, 8.9% widowed, 10.1% divorced (2006-2010 5-year est.); Foreign born: 0.9% (2006-2010 5-year est.); Ancestry (includes multiple ancestries): 28.7% German, 14.3% Irish, 9.9% English, 7.9% Pennsylvania German, 5.6% Polish (2006-2010 5-year est.).
Economy: Single-family building permits issued: 1 (2011); Multi-family building permits issued: 0 (2011); Employment by occupation: 10.2% management, 8.3% professional, 8.9% services, 9.6% sales, 0.0% farming, 17.8% construction, 11.5% production (2006-2010 5-year est.).
Income: Per capita income: $24,393 (2006-2010 5-year est.); Median household income: $34,688 (2006-2010 5-year est.); Average household income: $56,315 (2006-2010 5-year est.); Percent of households with income of $100,000 or more: 14.7% (2006-2010 5-year est.); Poverty rate: 33.0% (2006-2010 5-year est.).
Education: Percent of population age 25 and over with: High school diploma (including GED) or higher: 83.6% (2006-2010 5-year est.); Bachelor's degree or higher: 13.4% (2006-2010 5-year est.); Master's degree or higher: 5.0% (2006-2010 5-year est.).
Housing: Homeownership rate: 85.7% (2010); Median home value: $117,500 (2006-2010 5-year est.); Median contract rent: $388 per month (2006-2010 5-year est.); Median year structure built: 1954 (2006-2010 5-year est.).
Transportation: Commute to work: 95.5% car, 0.0% public transportation, 4.5% walk, 0.0% work from home (2006-2010 5-year est.); Travel time to work: 24.2% less than 15 minutes, 3.8% 15 to 30 minutes, 54.1% 30 to 45 minutes, 14.0% 45 to 60 minutes, 3.8% 60 minutes or more (2006-2010 5-year est.)

SHUNK (unincorporated postal area)

Zip Code: 17768

Covers a land area of 29.380 square miles and a water area of 0.091 square miles. Located at 41.55° N. Lat; 76.75° W. Long. Population: 377 (2010); Density: 12.8 persons per square mile (2010); Race: 97.9% White, 0.0% Black, 0.3% Asian, 0.8% American Indian/Alaska Native, 0.0% Native Hawaiian/Other Pacific Islander, 1.0% Other, 0.3% Hispanic of any race (2010); Average household size: 2.14 (2010); Median age: 51.1 (2010); Males per 100 females: 113.0 (2010); Homeownership rate: 85.3% (2010)

Susquehanna County

Located in northeastern Pennsylvania; bounded on the north by New York; drained by the Susquehanna River; includes the Lackawanna River and several lakes. Covers a land area of 823.435 square miles, a water area of 8.708 square miles, and is located in the Eastern Time Zone at 41.82° N. Lat., 75.80° W. Long. The county was founded in 1810. County seat is Montrose.

Weather Station: Montrose									Elevation: 1,419 feet			
	Jan	Feb	Mar	Apr	May	Jun	Jul	Aug	Sep	Oct	Nov	Dec
High	30	34	42	55	66	75	79	78	70	59	46	35
Low	13	14	22	33	43	52	56	55	47	36	28	19
Precip	3.1	2.7	3.4	4.1	4.0	4.5	4.3	3.5	4.0	3.9	3.8	3.3
Snow	21.5	15.5	16.0	5.6	0.1	0.0	0.0	0.0	tr	0.7	7.0	15.5

High and Low temperatures in degrees Fahrenheit; Precipitation and Snow in inches

Population: 40,380 (1990); 42,238 (2000); 43,356 (2010); Race: 98.0% White, 0.4% Black, 0.3% Asian, 0.1% American Indian/Alaska Native, 0.0% Native Hawaiian/Other Pacific Islander, 1.2% Other, 1.3% Hispanic of any race (2010); Density: 52.7 persons per square mile (2010); Average household size: 2.42 (2010); Median age: 45.1 (2010); Males per 100 females: 101.1 (2010).
Religion: Six largest groups: 12.8% Catholicism, 9.7% Methodist/Pietist, 3.5% Non-Denominational, 1.8% Presbyterian-Reformed, 1.0% Baptist, 1.0% Latter-day Saints (2010)
Economy: Unemployment rate: 7.2% (August 2012); Total civilian labor force: 24,371 (August 2012); Leading industries: 20.4% retail trade; 17.1% health care and social assistance; 12.4% accommodation & food services (2010); Farms: 1,008 totaling 158,218 acres (2007); Companies that employ 500 or more persons: 0 (2010); Companies that employ 100 to 499 persons: 6 (2010); Companies that employ less than 100 persons: 895 (2010); Black-owned businesses: n/a (2007); Hispanic-owned businesses: 44 (2007); Asian-owned businesses: n/a (2007); Women-owned businesses: 1,040 (2007); Retail sales per capita: $8,846 (2010). Single-family building permits issued: 56 (2011); Multi-family building permits issued: 0 (2011).
Income: Per capita income: $22,173 (2006-2010 5-year est.); Median household income: $43,457 (2006-2010 5-year est.); Average household income: $54,600 (2006-2010 5-year est.); Percent of households with income of $100,000 or more: 12.1% (2006-2010 5-year est.); Poverty rate: 11.3% (2006-2010 5-year est.); Bankruptcy rate: 1.66% (2011).
Education: Percent of population age 25 and over with: High school diploma (including GED) or higher: 86.8% (2006-2010 5-year est.); Bachelor's degree or higher: 15.4% (2006-2010 5-year est.); Master's degree or higher: 6.0% (2006-2010 5-year est.).
Housing: Homeownership rate: 78.1% (2010); Median home value: $124,400 (2006-2010 5-year est.); Median contract rent: $450 per month (2006-2010 5-year est.); Median year structure built: 1966 (2006-2010 5-year est.)
Health: Birth rate: 93.1 per 10,000 population (2011); Death rate: 96.1 per 10,000 population (2011); Age-adjusted cancer mortality rate: 148.6 deaths per 100,000 population (2009); Number of physicians: 6.9 per 10,000 population (2010); Hospital beds: 25.4 per 10,000 population (2008); Hospital admissions: 630.4 per 10,000 population (2008).
Elections: 2012 Presidential election results: 38.5% Obama, 59.8% Romney
National and State Parks: Salt Springs State Park
Additional Information Contacts
Susquehanna County Government . . . . (570) 278-4600
http://www.susqco.com

Susquehanna County Communities

APOLACON (township). Covers a land area of 22.474 square miles and a water area of 0.261 square miles. Located at 41.96° N. Lat; 76.10° W. Long.

Population: 493 (1990); 507 (2000); 500 (2010); Density: 22.2 persons per square mile (2010); Race: 98.4% White, 0.4% Black, 0.6% Asian, 0.4% American Indian/Alaska Native, 0.0% Native Hawaiian/Other Pacific Islander, 0.2% Other, 1.0% Hispanic of any race (2010); Average household size: 2.45 (2010); Median age: 46.3 (2010); Males per 100 females: 100.0 (2010); Marriage status: 22.3% never married, 64.2% now married, 6.7% widowed, 6.7% divorced (2006-2010 5-year est.); Foreign born: 1.8% (2006-2010 5-year est.); Ancestry (includes multiple ancestries): 25.9% German, 21.5% English, 17.0% Irish, 12.2% Polish, 6.4% Italian (2006-2010 5-year est.).
Economy: Single-family building permits issued: 3 (2011); Multi-family building permits issued: 0 (2011); Employment by occupation: 7.6% management, 2.5% professional, 6.8% services, 16.5% sales, 0.0% farming, 12.7% construction, 9.3% production (2006-2010 5-year est.).
Income: Per capita income: $23,042 (2006-2010 5-year est.); Median household income: $47,500 (2006-2010 5-year est.); Average household income: $53,400 (2006-2010 5-year est.); Percent of households with

income of $100,000 or more: 11.3% (2006-2010 5-year est.); Poverty rate: 10.4% (2006-2010 5-year est.).

Education: Percent of population age 25 and over with: High school diploma (including GED) or higher: 88.7% (2006-2010 5-year est.); Bachelor's degree or higher: 18.5% (2006-2010 5-year est.); Master's degree or higher: 8.4% (2006-2010 5-year est.).

Housing: Homeownership rate: 90.2% (2010); Median home value: $121,400 (2006-2010 5-year est.); Median contract rent: $443 per month (2006-2010 5-year est.); Median year structure built: 1975 (2006-2010 5-year est.).

Transportation: Commute to work: 93.4% car, 0.0% public transportation, 3.9% walk, 1.7% work from home (2006-2010 5-year est.); Travel time to work: 14.7% less than 15 minutes, 28.4% 15 to 30 minutes, 44.9% 30 to 45 minutes, 5.3% 45 to 60 minutes, 6.7% 60 minutes or more (2006-2010 5-year est.).

ARARAT (township). Covers a land area of 18.578 square miles and a water area of 0.645 square miles. Located at 41.81° N. Lat; 75.52° W. Long. Elevation is 2,021 feet.

Population: 426 (1990); 531 (2000); 563 (2010); Density: 30.3 persons per square mile (2010); Race: 98.4% White, 0.4% Black, 0.2% Asian, 0.4% American Indian/Alaska Native, 0.0% Native Hawaiian/Other Pacific Islander, 0.6% Other, 1.8% Hispanic of any race (2010); Average household size: 2.29 (2010); Median age: 46.3 (2010); Males per 100 females: 101.8 (2010); Marriage status: 23.8% never married, 66.5% now married, 5.8% widowed, 3.9% divorced (2006-2010 5-year est.); Foreign born: 0.0% (2006-2010 5-year est.); Ancestry (includes multiple ancestries): 32.2% German, 24.1% English, 22.0% Italian, 9.2% Irish, 7.3% Welsh (2006-2010 5-year est.).

Economy: Single-family building permits issued: 3 (2011); Multi-family building permits issued: 0 (2011); Employment by occupation: 1.7% management, 0.0% professional, 14.9% services, 20.4% sales, 2.2% farming, 21.0% construction, 3.9% production (2006-2010 5-year est.).

Income: Per capita income: $21,389 (2006-2010 5-year est.); Median household income: $52,639 (2006-2010 5-year est.); Average household income: $54,004 (2006-2010 5-year est.); Percent of households with income of $100,000 or more: 9.1% (2006-2010 5-year est.); Poverty rate: 15.1% (2006-2010 5-year est.).

Education: Percent of population age 25 and over with: High school diploma (including GED) or higher: 90.6% (2006-2010 5-year est.); Bachelor's degree or higher: 17.3% (2006-2010 5-year est.); Master's degree or higher: 7.9% (2006-2010 5-year est.).

Housing: Homeownership rate: 86.2% (2010); Median home value: $164,300 (2006-2010 5-year est.); Median contract rent: <$101 per month (2006-2010 5-year est.); Median year structure built: 1980 (2006-2010 5-year est.).

Transportation: Commute to work: 80.2% car, 0.0% public transportation, 2.3% walk, 17.5% work from home (2006-2010 5-year est.); Travel time to work: 11.6% less than 15 minutes, 32.9% 15 to 30 minutes, 21.9% 30 to 45 minutes, 22.6% 45 to 60 minutes, 11.0% 60 minutes or more (2006-2010 5-year est.).

AUBURN (township). Covers a land area of 50.101 square miles and a water area of 0.242 square miles. Located at 41.69° N. Lat; 76.05° W. Long.

Population: 1,639 (1990); 1,816 (2000); 1,939 (2010); Density: 38.7 persons per square mile (2010); Race: 98.4% White, 0.1% Black, 0.3% Asian, 0.1% American Indian/Alaska Native, 0.0% Native Hawaiian/Other Pacific Islander, 1.1% Other, 1.8% Hispanic of any race (2010); Average household size: 2.55 (2010); Median age: 42.3 (2010); Males per 100 females: 106.5 (2010); Marriage status: 24.2% never married, 57.2% now married, 8.7% widowed, 9.9% divorced (2006-2010 5-year est.); Foreign born: 2.1% (2006-2010 5-year est.); Ancestry (includes multiple ancestries): 30.8% German, 19.5% English, 15.0% Irish, 11.7% Italian, 9.2% Polish (2006-2010 5-year est.).

Economy: Employment by occupation: 11.5% management, 1.9% professional, 12.8% services, 13.6% sales, 1.6% farming, 16.2% construction, 11.1% production (2006-2010 5-year est.).

Income: Per capita income: $21,112 (2006-2010 5-year est.); Median household income: $40,302 (2006-2010 5-year est.); Average household income: $51,800 (2006-2010 5-year est.); Percent of households with income of $100,000 or more: 14.7% (2006-2010 5-year est.); Poverty rate: 15.0% (2006-2010 5-year est.).

Education: Percent of population age 25 and over with: High school diploma (including GED) or higher: 83.0% (2006-2010 5-year est.);

Bachelor's degree or higher: 14.7% (2006-2010 5-year est.); Master's degree or higher: 6.2% (2006-2010 5-year est.).

Housing: Homeownership rate: 79.3% (2010); Median home value: $134,400 (2006-2010 5-year est.); Median contract rent: $431 per month (2006-2010 5-year est.); Median year structure built: 1972 (2006-2010 5-year est.).

Transportation: Commute to work: 92.1% car, 0.0% public transportation, 3.1% walk, 3.7% work from home (2006-2010 5-year est.); Travel time to work: 23.2% less than 15 minutes, 44.4% 15 to 30 minutes, 20.2% 30 to 45 minutes, 2.5% 45 to 60 minutes, 9.6% 60 minutes or more (2006-2010 5-year est.)

Additional Information Contacts
Schuylkill Chamber of Commerce . . . . (570) 622-1942
  http://www.schuylkillchamber.com

BRACKNEY (unincorporated postal area)
Zip Code: 18812
  Covers a land area of 31.510 square miles and a water area of 0.604 square miles. Located at 41.97° N. Lat; 75.96° W. Long. Population: 1,644 (2010); Density: 52.2 persons per square mile (2010); Race: 98.7% White, 0.2% Black, 0.2% Asian, 0.1% American Indian/Alaska Native, 0.0% Native Hawaiian/Other Pacific Islander, 0.8% Other, 0.9% Hispanic of any race (2010); Average household size: 2.42 (2010); Median age: 48.3 (2010); Males per 100 females: 109.2 (2010); Homeownership rate: 89.1% (2010)

BRIDGEWATER (township). Covers a land area of 41.049 square miles and a water area of 0.362 square miles. Located at 41.83° N. Lat; 75.85° W. Long.

Population: 2,368 (1990); 2,668 (2000); 2,844 (2010); Density: 69.3 persons per square mile (2010); Race: 98.1% White, 0.4% Black, 0.4% Asian, 0.2% American Indian/Alaska Native, 0.0% Native Hawaiian/Other Pacific Islander, 0.9% Other, 1.0% Hispanic of any race (2010); Average household size: 2.43 (2010); Median age: 45.7 (2010); Males per 100 females: 97.9 (2010); Marriage status: 23.4% never married, 60.9% now married, 8.2% widowed, 7.5% divorced (2006-2010 5-year est.); Foreign born: 0.7% (2006-2010 5-year est.); Ancestry (includes multiple ancestries): 25.0% English, 24.7% German, 20.3% Irish, 9.0% Polish, 6.4% Dutch (2006-2010 5-year est.).

Economy: Single-family building permits issued: 1 (2011); Multi-family building permits issued: 0 (2011); Employment by occupation: 10.6% management, 3.1% professional, 15.6% services, 20.0% sales, 3.7% farming, 14.9% construction, 6.7% production (2006-2010 5-year est.).

Income: Per capita income: $24,898 (2006-2010 5-year est.); Median household income: $44,188 (2006-2010 5-year est.); Average household income: $58,988 (2006-2010 5-year est.); Percent of households with income of $100,000 or more: 19.2% (2006-2010 5-year est.); Poverty rate: 8.3% (2006-2010 5-year est.).

Education: Percent of population age 25 and over with: High school diploma (including GED) or higher: 87.8% (2006-2010 5-year est.); Bachelor's degree or higher: 13.4% (2006-2010 5-year est.); Master's degree or higher: 8.2% (2006-2010 5-year est.).

Housing: Homeownership rate: 82.9% (2010); Median home value: $146,100 (2006-2010 5-year est.); Median contract rent: $413 per month (2006-2010 5-year est.); Median year structure built: 1970 (2006-2010 5-year est.).

Transportation: Commute to work: 89.4% car, 0.0% public transportation, 4.0% walk, 6.1% work from home (2006-2010 5-year est.); Travel time to work: 44.7% less than 15 minutes, 19.6% 15 to 30 minutes, 21.2% 30 to 45 minutes, 12.2% 45 to 60 minutes, 2.3% 60 minutes or more (2006-2010 5-year est.)

Additional Information Contacts
Beaver Area Chamber of Commerce . . . . (724) 773-6504
  http://beaverareachamber.com

BROOKLYN (township). Covers a land area of 24.285 square miles and a water area of 0.196 square miles. Located at 41.76° N. Lat; 75.80° W. Long. Elevation is 1,099 feet.

Population: 873 (1990); 889 (2000); 963 (2010); Density: 39.7 persons per square mile (2010); Race: 97.8% White, 0.4% Black, 0.5% Asian, 0.0% American Indian/Alaska Native, 0.0% Native Hawaiian/Other Pacific Islander, 1.3% Other, 1.8% Hispanic of any race (2010); Average household size: 2.51 (2010); Median age: 45.0 (2010); Males per 100 females: 105.8 (2010); Marriage status: 22.7% never married, 60.8% now married, 10.6% widowed, 5.9% divorced (2006-2010 5-year est.); Foreign

born: 1.6% (2006-2010 5-year est.); Ancestry (includes multiple ancestries): 23.9% German, 21.5% English, 15.7% Polish, 10.3% Italian, 9.0% Irish (2006-2010 5-year est.).

Economy: Single-family building permits issued: 1 (2011); Multi-family building permits issued: 0 (2011); Employment by occupation: 6.8% management, 5.8% professional, 5.8% services, 8.7% sales, 8.4% farming, 24.4% construction, 12.2% production (2006-2010 5-year est.).

Income: Per capita income: $23,275 (2006-2010 5-year est.); Median household income: $39,792 (2006-2010 5-year est.); Average household income: $51,796 (2006-2010 5-year est.); Percent of households with income of $100,000 or more: 12.8% (2006-2010 5-year est.); Poverty rate: 18.3% (2006-2010 5-year est.).

Education: Percent of population age 25 and over with: High school diploma (including GED) or higher: 87.3% (2006-2010 5-year est.); Bachelor's degree or higher: 19.5% (2006-2010 5-year est.); Master's degree or higher: 5.3% (2006-2010 5-year est.).

Housing: Homeownership rate: 85.4% (2010); Median home value: $124,400 (2006-2010 5-year est.); Median contract rent: $444 per month (2006-2010 5-year est.); Median year structure built: 1958 (2006-2010 5-year est.).

Transportation: Commute to work: 88.3% car, 0.0% public transportation, 6.4% walk, 4.2% work from home (2006-2010 5-year est.); Travel time to work: 20.3% less than 15 minutes, 27.3% 15 to 30 minutes, 24.4% 30 to 45 minutes, 15.5% 45 to 60 minutes, 12.5% 60 minutes or more (2006-2010 5-year est.)

CHOCONUT (township). Covers a land area of 20.147 square miles and a water area of 0.123 square miles. Located at 41.95° N. Lat; 76.01° W. Long. Elevation is 1,115 feet.

Population: 799 (1990); 797 (2000); 713 (2010); Density: 35.4 persons per square mile (2010); Race: 98.6% White, 0.4% Black, 0.0% Asian, 0.1% American Indian/Alaska Native, 0.0% Native Hawaiian/Other Pacific Islander, 0.9% Other, 0.7% Hispanic of any race (2010); Average household size: 2.27 (2010); Median age: 49.0 (2010); Males per 100 females: 115.4 (2010); Marriage status: 19.8% never married, 66.4% now married, 9.0% widowed, 4.7% divorced (2006-2010 5-year est.); Foreign born: 1.3% (2006-2010 5-year est.); Ancestry (includes multiple ancestries): 24.3% German, 19.5% Irish, 17.5% English, 9.6% Polish, 7.2% Italian (2006-2010 5-year est.).

Economy: Single-family building permits issued: 1 (2011); Multi-family building permits issued: 0 (2011); Employment by occupation: 12.2% management, 9.5% professional, 6.1% services, 15.9% sales, 2.0% farming, 18.6% construction, 8.3% production (2006-2010 5-year est.).

Income: Per capita income: $29,742 (2006-2010 5-year est.); Median household income: $54,231 (2006-2010 5-year est.); Average household income: $70,083 (2006-2010 5-year est.); Percent of households with income of $100,000 or more: 24.7% (2006-2010 5-year est.); Poverty rate: 2.4% (2006-2010 5-year est.).

Education: Percent of population age 25 and over with: High school diploma (including GED) or higher: 86.9% (2006-2010 5-year est.); Bachelor's degree or higher: 18.5% (2006-2010 5-year est.); Master's degree or higher: 7.1% (2006-2010 5-year est.).

Housing: Homeownership rate: 83.1% (2010); Median home value: $140,900 (2006-2010 5-year est.); Median contract rent: $445 per month (2006-2010 5-year est.); Median year structure built: 1975 (2006-2010 5-year est.).

Transportation: Commute to work: 93.3% car, 0.0% public transportation, 0.0% walk, 5.2% work from home (2006-2010 5-year est.); Travel time to work: 13.2% less than 15 minutes, 55.8% 15 to 30 minutes, 25.2% 30 to 45 minutes, 3.1% 45 to 60 minutes, 2.6% 60 minutes or more (2006-2010 5-year est.)

CLIFFORD (township). Covers a land area of 40.478 square miles and a water area of 0.449 square miles. Located at 41.67° N. Lat; 75.55° W. Long. Elevation is 1,063 feet.

History: Clifford was settled in 1800 by Adam Miller.

Population: 2,147 (1990); 2,381 (2000); 2,408 (2010); Density: 59.5 persons per square mile (2010); Race: 97.6% White, 0.3% Black, 0.2% Asian, 0.1% American Indian/Alaska Native, 0.1% Native Hawaiian/Other Pacific Islander, 1.7% Other, 1.6% Hispanic of any race (2010); Average household size: 2.43 (2010); Median age: 45.2 (2010); Males per 100 females: 103.2 (2010); Marriage status: 20.2% never married, 57.3% now married, 6.5% widowed, 16.0% divorced (2006-2010 5-year est.); Foreign born: 3.5% (2006-2010 5-year est.); Ancestry (includes multiple

ancestries): 27.4% Irish, 25.4% German, 12.8% Italian, 12.3% Polish, 11.9% English (2006-2010 5-year est.).

Economy: Single-family building permits issued: 6 (2011); Multi-family building permits issued: 0 (2011); Employment by occupation: 15.1% management, 0.7% professional, 3.5% services, 13.7% sales, 5.2% farming, 12.5% construction, 8.6% production (2006-2010 5-year est.).

Income: Per capita income: $26,412 (2006-2010 5-year est.); Median household income: $45,030 (2006-2010 5-year est.); Average household income: $61,661 (2006-2010 5-year est.); Percent of households with income of $100,000 or more: 14.8% (2006-2010 5-year est.); Poverty rate: 7.1% (2006-2010 5-year est.).

Education: Percent of population age 25 and over with: High school diploma (including GED) or higher: 91.6% (2006-2010 5-year est.); Bachelor's degree or higher: 25.0% (2006-2010 5-year est.); Master's degree or higher: 9.2% (2006-2010 5-year est.).

Housing: Homeownership rate: 82.8% (2010); Median home value: $168,600 (2006-2010 5-year est.); Median contract rent: $419 per month (2006-2010 5-year est.); Median year structure built: 1974 (2006-2010 5-year est.).

Transportation: Commute to work: 89.6% car, 0.0% public transportation, 2.5% walk, 6.6% work from home (2006-2010 5-year est.); Travel time to work: 24.8% less than 15 minutes, 32.5% 15 to 30 minutes, 22.3% 30 to 45 minutes, 14.3% 45 to 60 minutes, 6.0% 60 minutes or more (2006-2010 5-year est.)

Additional Information Contacts

Greater Scranton Chamber of Commerce . . . . (570) 342-7711
http://www.scrantonchamber.com

DIMOCK (township). Covers a land area of 29.031 square miles and a water area of 0.451 square miles. Located at 41.74° N. Lat; 75.92° W. Long. Elevation is 1,509 feet.

Population: 1,226 (1990); 1,398 (2000); 1,497 (2010); Density: 51.6 persons per square mile (2010); Race: 97.3% White, 0.1% Black, 0.1% Asian, 0.1% American Indian/Alaska Native, 0.1% Native Hawaiian/Other Pacific Islander, 2.3% Other, 2.0% Hispanic of any race (2010); Average household size: 2.63 (2010); Median age: 42.5 (2010); Males per 100 females: 109.7 (2010); Marriage status: 19.7% never married, 61.5% now married, 8.2% widowed, 10.7% divorced (2006-2010 5-year est.); Foreign born: 0.6% (2006-2010 5-year est.); Ancestry (includes multiple ancestries): 25.3% German, 23.3% English, 12.4% Irish, 11.4% Polish, 7.6% Italian (2006-2010 5-year est.).

Economy: Single-family building permits issued: 2 (2011); Multi-family building permits issued: 0 (2011); Employment by occupation: 14.7% management, 2.1% professional, 10.6% services, 13.3% sales, 2.5% farming, 14.4% construction, 6.5% production (2006-2010 5-year est.).

Income: Per capita income: $22,648 (2006-2010 5-year est.); Median household income: $47,159 (2006-2010 5-year est.); Average household income: $59,922 (2006-2010 5-year est.); Percent of households with income of $100,000 or more: 16.4% (2006-2010 5-year est.); Poverty rate: 8.7% (2006-2010 5-year est.).

Education: Percent of population age 25 and over with: High school diploma (including GED) or higher: 87.7% (2006-2010 5-year est.); Bachelor's degree or higher: 19.5% (2006-2010 5-year est.); Master's degree or higher: 8.5% (2006-2010 5-year est.).

Vocational/Technical School(s)

Susquehanna County Career and Technology Center (Public)
Fall 2010 Enrollment: 19 . . . . (570) 278-9229
2011-12 Tuition: $6,000

Housing: Homeownership rate: 80.1% (2010); Median home value: $136,500 (2006-2010 5-year est.); Median contract rent: $498 per month (2006-2010 5-year est.); Median year structure built: 1974 (2006-2010 5-year est.).

Transportation: Commute to work: 85.8% car, 0.0% public transportation, 1.2% walk, 11.4% work from home (2006-2010 5-year est.); Travel time to work: 24.4% less than 15 minutes, 37.5% 15 to 30 minutes, 12.9% 30 to 45 minutes, 14.9% 45 to 60 minutes, 10.3% 60 minutes or more (2006-2010 5-year est.)

Additional Information Contacts

Montrose Area Chamber of Commerce . . . . (570) 278-1174
http://www.montrosearea.com/news.php

FOREST CITY (borough). Covers a land area of 0.915 square miles and a water area of 0.029 square miles. Located at 41.65° N. Lat; 75.47° W. Long. Elevation is 1,575 feet.

History: Laid out 1871.

Population: 1,846 (1990); 1,855 (2000); 1,911 (2010); Density: 2,089.5 persons per square mile (2010); Race: 96.7% White, 0.9% Black, 0.6% Asian, 0.1% American Indian/Alaska Native, 0.1% Native Hawaiian/Other Pacific Islander, 1.6% Other, 1.5% Hispanic of any race (2010); Average household size: 2.23 (2010); Median age: 43.5 (2010); Males per 100 females: 84.1 (2010); Marriage status: 34.0% never married, 42.6% now married, 14.7% widowed, 8.7% divorced (2006-2010 5-year est.); Foreign born: 2.2% (2006-2010 5-year est.); Ancestry (includes multiple ancestries): 24.6% Irish, 24.2% Polish, 13.8% Italian, 12.8% German, 10.5% English (2006-2010 5-year est.).

Economy: Single-family building permits issued: 0 (2011); Multi-family building permits issued: 0 (2011); Employment by occupation: 4.1% management, 1.7% professional, 9.8% services, 18.0% sales, 6.2% farming, 10.7% construction, 13.2% production (2006-2010 5-year est.).

Income: Per capita income: $19,245 (2006-2010 5-year est.); Median household income: $33,618 (2006-2010 5-year est.); Average household income: $43,403 (2006-2010 5-year est.); Percent of households with income of $100,000 or more: 7.5% (2006-2010 5-year est.); Poverty rate: 21.3% (2006-2010 5-year est.).

Education: Percent of population age 25 and over with: High school diploma (including GED) or higher: 83.9% (2006-2010 5-year est.); Bachelor's degree or higher: 7.6% (2006-2010 5-year est.); Master's degree or higher: 2.5% (2006-2010 5-year est.).

School District(s)

Forest City Regional SD (PK-12)

    2010-11 Enrollment: 853 . . . . (570) 785-2400

Housing: Homeownership rate: 60.7% (2010); Median home value: $87,500 (2006-2010 5-year est.); Median contract rent: $432 per month (2006-2010 5-year est.); Median year structure built: before 1940 (2006-2010 5-year est.).

Safety: Violent crime rate: 15.6 per 10,000 population; Property crime rate: 234.7 per 10,000 population (2011).

Newspapers: The Forest City News (Community news; Circulation 3,370)

Transportation: Commute to work: 94.8% car, 0.0% public transportation, 5.2% walk, 0.0% work from home (2006-2010 5-year est.); Travel time to work: 29.1% less than 15 minutes, 35.0% 15 to 30 minutes, 26.2% 30 to 45 minutes, 9.2% 45 to 60 minutes, 0.5% 60 minutes or more (2006-2010 5-year est.).

Additional Information Contacts

Wayne County Chamber of Commerce . . . . (570) 253-1960
  http://www.waynecountycc.com

FOREST LAKE (township). Covers a land area of 29.800 square miles and a water area of 0.129 square miles. Located at 41.88° N. Lat; 75.99° W. Long. Elevation is 1,542 feet.

Population: 1,229 (1990); 1,194 (2000); 1,193 (2010); Density: 40.0 persons per square mile (2010); Race: 98.7% White, 0.0% Black, 0.3% Asian, 0.0% American Indian/Alaska Native, 0.0% Native Hawaiian/Other Pacific Islander, 1.0% Other, 0.8% Hispanic of any race (2010); Average household size: 2.52 (2010); Median age: 45.2 (2010); Males per 100 females: 105.0 (2010); Marriage status: 19.5% never married, 66.6% now married, 4.8% widowed, 9.0% divorced (2006-2010 5-year est.); Foreign born: 0.2% (2006-2010 5-year est.); Ancestry (includes multiple ancestries): 25.0% Irish, 25.0% German, 20.1% English, 12.9% Polish, 10.2% Italian (2006-2010 5-year est.).

Economy: Single-family building permits issued: 1 (2011); Multi-family building permits issued: 0 (2011); Employment by occupation: 9.7% management, 2.9% professional, 8.1% services, 10.5% sales, 1.9% farming, 20.1% construction, 16.0% production (2006-2010 5-year est.).

Income: Per capita income: $22,251 (2006-2010 5-year est.); Median household income: $47,500 (2006-2010 5-year est.); Average household income: $57,256 (2006-2010 5-year est.); Percent of households with income of $100,000 or more: 9.2% (2006-2010 5-year est.); Poverty rate: 6.9% (2006-2010 5-year est.).

Education: Percent of population age 25 and over with: High school diploma (including GED) or higher: 93.1% (2006-2010 5-year est.); Bachelor's degree or higher: 10.3% (2006-2010 5-year est.); Master's degree or higher: 3.7% (2006-2010 5-year est.).

Housing: Homeownership rate: 83.3% (2010); Median home value: $154,900 (2006-2010 5-year est.); Median contract rent: $334 per month (2006-2010 5-year est.); Median year structure built: 1969 (2006-2010 5-year est.).

Transportation: Commute to work: 86.0% car, 0.0% public transportation, 2.1% walk, 9.6% work from home (2006-2010 5-year est.); Travel time to work: 14.2% less than 15 minutes, 35.8% 15 to 30 minutes, 29.9% 30 to

45 minutes, 7.4% 45 to 60 minutes, 12.8% 60 minutes or more (2006-2010 5-year est.)

Additional Information Contacts

Montrose Area Chamber of Commerce . . . . (570) 278-1174
  http://montrosearea.com/news.php

FRANKLIN (township). Covers a land area of 23.690 square miles and a water area of 0.118 square miles. Located at 41.90° N. Lat; 75.83° W. Long.

Population: 913 (1990); 938 (2000); 937 (2010); Density: 39.6 persons per square mile (2010); Race: 99.9% White, 0.1% Black, 0.0% Asian, 0.0% American Indian/Alaska Native, 0.0% Native Hawaiian/Other Pacific Islander, 0.0% Other, 1.7% Hispanic of any race (2010); Average household size: 2.53 (2010); Median age: 47.3 (2010); Males per 100 females: 103.7 (2010); Marriage status: 28.3% never married, 57.7% now married, 5.6% widowed, 8.5% divorced (2006-2010 5-year est.); Foreign born: 0.7% (2006-2010 5-year est.); Ancestry (includes multiple ancestries): 22.9% English, 17.8% German, 17.2% Irish, 9.1% French, 7.0% Italian (2006-2010 5-year est.).

Economy: Single-family building permits issued: 2 (2011); Multi-family building permits issued: 0 (2011); Employment by occupation: 10.5% management, 0.6% professional, 4.1% services, 17.6% sales, 4.3% farming, 14.2% construction, 10.5% production (2006-2010 5-year est.).

Income: Per capita income: $19,069 (2006-2010 5-year est.); Median household income: $45,833 (2006-2010 5-year est.); Average household income: $50,220 (2006-2010 5-year est.); Percent of households with income of $100,000 or more: 4.6% (2006-2010 5-year est.); Poverty rate: 9.0% (2006-2010 5-year est.).

Education: Percent of population age 25 and over with: High school diploma (including GED) or higher: 89.1% (2006-2010 5-year est.); Bachelor's degree or higher: 12.9% (2006-2010 5-year est.); Master's degree or higher: 6.6% (2006-2010 5-year est.).

Housing: Homeownership rate: 87.6% (2010); Median home value: $125,600 (2006-2010 5-year est.); Median contract rent: $540 per month (2006-2010 5-year est.); Median year structure built: 1975 (2006-2010 5-year est.).

Transportation: Commute to work: 88.4% car, 0.0% public transportation, 2.6% walk, 9.0% work from home (2006-2010 5-year est.); Travel time to work: 23.0% less than 15 minutes, 33.8% 15 to 30 minutes, 20.4% 30 to 45 minutes, 13.4% 45 to 60 minutes, 9.4% 60 minutes or more (2006-2010 5-year est.)

FRIENDSVILLE (borough). Covers a land area of 1.495 square miles and a water area of 0 square miles. Located at 41.92° N. Lat; 76.05° W. Long. Elevation is 1,552 feet.

Population: 102 (1990); 91 (2000); 111 (2010); Density: 74.3 persons per square mile (2010); Race: 91.9% White, 6.3% Black, 0.0% Asian, 1.8% American Indian/Alaska Native, 0.0% Native Hawaiian/Other Pacific Islander, 0.0% Other, 0.0% Hispanic of any race (2010); Average household size: 2.52 (2010); Median age: 42.5 (2010); Males per 100 females: 126.5 (2010); Marriage status: 25.8% never married, 66.3% now married, 3.4% widowed, 4.5% divorced (2006-2010 5-year est.); Foreign born: 0.0% (2006-2010 5-year est.); Ancestry (includes multiple ancestries): 28.8% German, 17.6% English, 13.6% Irish, 10.4% Italian, 7.2% French (2006-2010 5-year est.).

Economy: Employment by occupation: 6.5% management, 0.0% professional, 13.0% services, 13.0% sales, 13.0% farming, 17.4% construction, 8.7% production (2006-2010 5-year est.).

Income: Per capita income: $15,996 (2006-2010 5-year est.); Median household income: $35,625 (2006-2010 5-year est.); Average household income: $43,524 (2006-2010 5-year est.); Percent of households with income of $100,000 or more: n/a (2006-2010 5-year est.); Poverty rate: 9.6% (2006-2010 5-year est.).

Education: Percent of population age 25 and over with: High school diploma (including GED) or higher: 76.9% (2006-2010 5-year est.); Bachelor's degree or higher: 10.3% (2006-2010 5-year est.); Master's degree or higher: 2.6% (2006-2010 5-year est.).

School District(s)

Montrose Area SD (KG-12)

    2010-11 Enrollment: 1,614 . . . . (570) 278-3731

Housing: Homeownership rate: 88.6% (2010); Median home value: $178,600 (2006-2010 5-year est.); Median contract rent: $500 per month (2006-2010 5-year est.); Median year structure built: 1988 (2006-2010 5-year est.).

Transportation: Commute to work: 93.5% car, 0.0% public transportation, 0.0% walk, 6.5% work from home (2006-2010 5-year est.); Travel time to work: 14.0% less than 15 minutes, 30.2% 15 to 30 minutes, 55.8% 30 to 45 minutes, 0.0% 45 to 60 minutes, 0.0% 60 minutes or more (2006-2010 5-year est.)

GIBSON (township). Covers a land area of 31.889 square miles and a water area of 0.241 square miles. Located at 41.77° N. Lat; 75.61° W. Long. Elevation is 1,201 feet.

Population: 1,015 (1990); 1,129 (2000); 1,221 (2010); Density: 38.3 persons per square mile (2010); Race: 97.9% White, 0.4% Black, 0.1% Asian, 0.0% American Indian/Alaska Native, 0.0% Native Hawaiian/Other Pacific Islander, 1.6% Other, 2.2% Hispanic of any race (2010); Average household size: 2.54 (2010); Median age: 45.9 (2010); Males per 100 females: 110.9 (2010); Marriage status: 23.0% never married, 55.1% now married, 13.2% widowed, 8.7% divorced (2006-2010 5-year est.); Foreign born: 0.6% (2006-2010 5-year est.); Ancestry (includes multiple ancestries): 26.2% German, 23.3% Irish, 20.7% English, 11.4% Italian, 7.4% Polish (2006-2010 5-year est.).

Economy: Single-family building permits issued: 3 (2011); Multi-family building permits issued: 0 (2011); Employment by occupation: 18.7% management, 2.4% professional, 12.8% services, 14.8% sales, 2.4% farming, 13.5% construction, 3.3% production (2006-2010 5-year est.).

Income: Per capita income: $20,202 (2006-2010 5-year est.); Median household income: $46,154 (2006-2010 5-year est.); Average household income: $53,820 (2006-2010 5-year est.); Percent of households with income of $100,000 or more: 11.3% (2006-2010 5-year est.); Poverty rate: 10.5% (2006-2010 5-year est.).

Education: Percent of population age 25 and over with: High school diploma (including GED) or higher: 78.4% (2006-2010 5-year est.); Bachelor's degree or higher: 12.2% (2006-2010 5-year est.); Master's degree or higher: 5.6% (2006-2010 5-year est.).

Housing: Homeownership rate: 85.9% (2010); Median home value: $156,400 (2006-2010 5-year est.); Median contract rent: $530 per month (2006-2010 5-year est.); Median year structure built: 1971 (2006-2010 5-year est.).

Transportation: Commute to work: 86.3% car, 0.0% public transportation, 5.0% walk, 6.2% work from home (2006-2010 5-year est.); Travel time to work: 18.7% less than 15 minutes, 44.7% 15 to 30 minutes, 23.7% 30 to 45 minutes, 4.5% 45 to 60 minutes, 8.4% 60 minutes or more (2006-2010 5-year est.)

Additional Information Contacts
Greater Scranton Chamber of Commerce . . . . (570) 342-7711
http://www.scrantonchamber.com

GREAT BEND (borough). Covers a land area of 0.292 square miles and a water area of 0.024 square miles. Located at 41.97° N. Lat; 75.75° W. Long. Elevation is 892 feet.

Population: 704 (1990); 700 (2000); 734 (2010); Density: 2,510.9 persons per square mile (2010); Race: 97.7% White, 0.0% Black, 0.4% Asian, 0.0% American Indian/Alaska Native, 0.0% Native Hawaiian/Other Pacific Islander, 1.9% Other, 1.4% Hispanic of any race (2010); Average household size: 2.15 (2010); Median age: 46.1 (2010); Males per 100 females: 93.7 (2010); Marriage status: 26.4% never married, 53.0% now married, 8.3% widowed, 12.4% divorced (2006-2010 5-year est.); Foreign born: 0.0% (2006-2010 5-year est.); Ancestry (includes multiple ancestries): 27.5% German, 21.5% English, 21.0% Polish, 18.8% Irish, 9.8% Italian (2006-2010 5-year est.).

Economy: Single-family building permits issued: 0 (2011); Multi-family building permits issued: 0 (2011); Employment by occupation: 3.6% management, 5.7% professional, 10.5% services, 14.0% sales, 4.8% farming, 8.0% construction, 5.9% production (2006-2010 5-year est.).

Income: Per capita income: $21,634 (2006-2010 5-year est.); Median household income: $41,776 (2006-2010 5-year est.); Average household income: $49,000 (2006-2010 5-year est.); Percent of households with income of $100,000 or more: 9.6% (2006-2010 5-year est.); Poverty rate: 6.3% (2006-2010 5-year est.).

Education: Percent of population age 25 and over with: High school diploma (including GED) or higher: 88.3% (2006-2010 5-year est.); Bachelor's degree or higher: 14.1% (2006-2010 5-year est.); Master's degree or higher: 4.2% (2006-2010 5-year est.).

Housing: Homeownership rate: 51.9% (2010); Median home value: $95,000 (2006-2010 5-year est.); Median contract rent: $294 per month (2006-2010 5-year est.); Median year structure built: 1955 (2006-2010 5-year est.).

Transportation: Commute to work: 93.5% car, 0.0% public transportation, 5.9% walk, 0.6% work from home (2006-2010 5-year est.); Travel time to work: 30.6% less than 15 minutes, 40.1% 15 to 30 minutes, 12.9% 30 to 45 minutes, 12.2% 45 to 60 minutes, 4.2% 60 minutes or more (2006-2010 5-year est.)

GREAT BEND (township). Covers a land area of 36.098 square miles and a water area of 0.748 square miles. Located at 41.94° N. Lat; 75.71° W. Long. Elevation is 892 feet.

Population: 1,844 (1990); 1,890 (2000); 1,949 (2010); Density: 54.0 persons per square mile (2010); Race: 97.7% White, 0.6% Black, 0.2% Asian, 0.0% American Indian/Alaska Native, 0.1% Native Hawaiian/Other Pacific Islander, 1.4% Other, 1.3% Hispanic of any race (2010); Average household size: 2.47 (2010); Median age: 43.2 (2010); Males per 100 females: 93.7 (2010); Marriage status: 19.9% never married, 61.6% now married, 6.0% widowed, 12.4% divorced (2006-2010 5-year est.); Foreign born: 1.3% (2006-2010 5-year est.); Ancestry (includes multiple ancestries): 28.9% German, 26.6% English, 19.8% Irish, 6.8% Italian, 6.6% Polish (2006-2010 5-year est.).

Economy: Single-family building permits issued: 3 (2011); Multi-family building permits issued: 0 (2011); Employment by occupation: 6.2% management, 5.2% professional, 7.9% services, 20.1% sales, 6.9% farming, 9.2% construction, 9.8% production (2006-2010 5-year est.).

Income: Per capita income: $21,151 (2006-2010 5-year est.); Median household income: $37,134 (2006-2010 5-year est.); Average household income: $50,966 (2006-2010 5-year est.); Percent of households with income of $100,000 or more: 11.2% (2006-2010 5-year est.); Poverty rate: 11.2% (2006-2010 5-year est.).

Education: Percent of population age 25 and over with: High school diploma (including GED) or higher: 88.7% (2006-2010 5-year est.); Bachelor's degree or higher: 12.7% (2006-2010 5-year est.); Master's degree or higher: 8.3% (2006-2010 5-year est.).

Housing: Homeownership rate: 71.5% (2010); Median home value: $119,000 (2006-2010 5-year est.); Median contract rent: $551 per month (2006-2010 5-year est.); Median year structure built: 1968 (2006-2010 5-year est.).

Transportation: Commute to work: 93.5% car, 0.0% public transportation, 1.2% walk, 5.3% work from home (2006-2010 5-year est.); Travel time to work: 26.9% less than 15 minutes, 36.1% 15 to 30 minutes, 25.6% 30 to 45 minutes, 3.8% 45 to 60 minutes, 7.7% 60 minutes or more (2006-2010 5-year est.)

Additional Information Contacts
Greater Binghamton Chamber of Commerce . . . . (607) 772-8860
http://www.greaterbinghamtonchamber.com

HALLSTEAD (borough). Covers a land area of 0.418 square miles and a water area of 0.001 square miles. Located at 41.96° N. Lat; 75.75° W. Long. Elevation is 869 feet.

History: Founded 1787, incorporated 1874.

Population: 1,247 (1990); 1,216 (2000); 1,303 (2010); Density: 3,120.1 persons per square mile (2010); Race: 97.5% White, 0.7% Black, 0.0% Asian, 0.4% American Indian/Alaska Native, 0.0% Native Hawaiian/Other Pacific Islander, 1.4% Other, 1.0% Hispanic of any race (2010); Average household size: 2.28 (2010); Median age: 43.8 (2010); Males per 100 females: 96.8 (2010); Marriage status: 28.4% never married, 49.5% now married, 7.8% widowed, 14.2% divorced (2006-2010 5-year est.); Foreign born: 0.7% (2006-2010 5-year est.); Ancestry (includes multiple ancestries): 27.5% German, 22.6% Irish, 17.8% English, 16.2% Italian, 5.9% Welsh (2006-2010 5-year est.).

Economy: Single-family building permits issued: 0 (2011); Multi-family building permits issued: 0 (2011); Employment by occupation: 6.5% management, 4.5% professional, 17.1% services, 23.9% sales, 2.8% farming, 8.1% construction, 2.9% production (2006-2010 5-year est.).

Income: Per capita income: $18,181 (2006-2010 5-year est.); Median household income: $45,649 (2006-2010 5-year est.); Average household income: $48,195 (2006-2010 5-year est.); Percent of households with income of $100,000 or more: 10.5% (2006-2010 5-year est.); Poverty rate: 13.1% (2006-2010 5-year est.).

Education: Percent of population age 25 and over with: High school diploma (including GED) or higher: 88.1% (2006-2010 5-year est.); Bachelor's degree or higher: 10.9% (2006-2010 5-year est.); Master's degree or higher: 1.8% (2006-2010 5-year est.).

Housing: Homeownership rate: 59.9% (2010); Median home value: $97,100 (2006-2010 5-year est.); Median contract rent: $449 per month

(2006-2010 5-year est.); Median year structure built: before 1940 (2006-2010 5-year est.).

Transportation: Commute to work: 94.1% car, 0.0% public transportation, 3.9% walk, 2.0% work from home (2006-2010 5-year est.); Travel time to work: 29.4% less than 15 minutes, 45.9% 15 to 30 minutes, 17.2% 30 to 45 minutes, 0.8% 45 to 60 minutes, 6.8% 60 minutes or more (2006-2010 5-year est.)

Additional Information Contacts

Montrose Area Chamber of Commerce . . . . (570) 278-1174
  http://montrosearea.com/news.php

HARFORD (township). Covers a land area of 32.882 square miles and a water area of 0.385 square miles. Located at 41.77° N. Lat; 75.72° W. Long. Elevation is 1,276 feet.

Population: 1,100 (1990); 1,301 (2000); 1,430 (2010); Density: 43.5 persons per square mile (2010); Race: 98.8% White, 0.0% Black, 0.1% Asian, 0.1% American Indian/Alaska Native, 0.0% Native Hawaiian/Other Pacific Islander, 1.0% Other, 0.4% Hispanic of any race (2010); Average household size: 2.40 (2010); Median age: 46.0 (2010); Males per 100 females: 102.8 (2010); Marriage status: 23.8% never married, 62.2% now married, 6.5% widowed, 7.6% divorced (2006-2010 5-year est.); Foreign born: 1.2% (2006-2010 5-year est.); Ancestry (includes multiple ancestries): 28.5% German, 27.1% English, 21.5% Irish, 10.6% Italian, 9.0% Polish (2006-2010 5-year est.).

Economy: Single-family building permits issued: 3 (2011); Multi-family building permits issued: 0 (2011); Employment by occupation: 7.9% management, 3.5% professional, 13.8% services, 13.7% sales, 4.2% farming, 13.2% construction, 7.3% production (2006-2010 5-year est.).

Income: Per capita income: $26,006 (2006-2010 5-year est.); Median household income: $53,600 (2006-2010 5-year est.); Average household income: $61,776 (2006-2010 5-year est.); Percent of households with income of $100,000 or more: 13.2% (2006-2010 5-year est.); Poverty rate: 4.8% (2006-2010 5-year est.).

Education: Percent of population age 25 and over with: High school diploma (including GED) or higher: 91.3% (2006-2010 5-year est.); Bachelor's degree or higher: 18.1% (2006-2010 5-year est.); Master's degree or higher: 6.4% (2006-2010 5-year est.).

Housing: Homeownership rate: 82.6% (2010); Median home value: $147,700 (2006-2010 5-year est.); Median contract rent: $506 per month (2006-2010 5-year est.); Median year structure built: 1973 (2006-2010 5-year est.).

Transportation: Commute to work: 91.2% car, 0.3% public transportation, 4.4% walk, 4.1% work from home (2006-2010 5-year est.); Travel time to work: 31.9% less than 15 minutes, 21.7% 15 to 30 minutes, 29.5% 30 to 45 minutes, 12.5% 45 to 60 minutes, 4.4% 60 minutes or more (2006-2010 5-year est.)

Additional Information Contacts

Montrose Area Chamber of Commerce . . . . (570) 278-1174
  http://montrosearea.com/news.php

HARMONY (township). Covers a land area of 31.342 square miles and a water area of 0.276 square miles. Located at 41.96° N. Lat; 75.54° W. Long.

Population: 544 (1990); 558 (2000); 528 (2010); Density: 16.8 persons per square mile (2010); Race: 99.1% White, 0.2% Black, 0.2% Asian, 0.2% American Indian/Alaska Native, 0.0% Native Hawaiian/Other Pacific Islander, 0.3% Other, 1.7% Hispanic of any race (2010); Average household size: 2.47 (2010); Median age: 47.6 (2010); Males per 100 females: 115.5 (2010); Marriage status: 14.9% never married, 67.4% now married, 2.8% widowed, 14.9% divorced (2006-2010 5-year est.); Foreign born: 3.3% (2006-2010 5-year est.); Ancestry (includes multiple ancestries): 26.1% German, 23.9% Irish, 10.4% American, 8.1% Italian, 6.6% French (2006-2010 5-year est.).

Economy: Single-family building permits issued: 0 (2011); Multi-family building permits issued: 0 (2011); Employment by occupation: 17.6% management, 3.3% professional, 5.7% services, 8.1% sales, 0.0% farming, 11.0% construction, 6.2% production (2006-2010 5-year est.).

Income: Per capita income: $29,827 (2006-2010 5-year est.); Median household income: $46,944 (2006-2010 5-year est.); Average household income: $74,105 (2006-2010 5-year est.); Percent of households with income of $100,000 or more: 27.9% (2006-2010 5-year est.); Poverty rate: 7.7% (2006-2010 5-year est.).

Education: Percent of population age 25 and over with: High school diploma (including GED) or higher: 77.5% (2006-2010 5-year est.);

Bachelor's degree or higher: 14.1% (2006-2010 5-year est.); Master's degree or higher: 4.2% (2006-2010 5-year est.).

Housing: Homeownership rate: 89.7% (2010); Median home value: $117,800 (2006-2010 5-year est.); Median contract rent: n/a per month (2006-2010 5-year est.); Median year structure built: 1975 (2006-2010 5-year est.).

Transportation: Commute to work: 79.6% car, 0.0% public transportation, 6.0% walk, 11.9% work from home (2006-2010 5-year est.); Travel time to work: 22.6% less than 15 minutes, 30.5% 15 to 30 minutes, 27.1% 30 to 45 minutes, 11.9% 45 to 60 minutes, 7.9% 60 minutes or more (2006-2010 5-year est.)

HERRICK (township). Covers a land area of 24.650 square miles and a water area of 0.215 square miles. Located at 41.74° N. Lat; 75.52° W. Long.

Population: 563 (1990); 599 (2000); 713 (2010); Density: 28.9 persons per square mile (2010); Race: 97.3% White, 0.6% Black, 0.3% Asian, 0.3% American Indian/Alaska Native, 0.0% Native Hawaiian/Other Pacific Islander, 1.5% Other, 1.4% Hispanic of any race (2010); Average household size: 2.31 (2010); Median age: 49.4 (2010); Males per 100 females: 112.2 (2010); Marriage status: 18.2% never married, 69.4% now married, 3.3% widowed, 9.2% divorced (2006-2010 5-year est.); Foreign born: 3.0% (2006-2010 5-year est.); Ancestry (includes multiple ancestries): 29.4% German, 25.4% Irish, 18.8% English, 16.0% Italian, 15.3% Polish (2006-2010 5-year est.).

Economy: Single-family building permits issued: 3 (2011); Multi-family building permits issued: 0 (2011); Employment by occupation: 11.0% management, 3.5% professional, 16.8% services, 10.5% sales, 0.9% farming, 10.0% construction, 0.0% production (2006-2010 5-year est.).

Income: Per capita income: $32,377 (2006-2010 5-year est.); Median household income: $58,125 (2006-2010 5-year est.); Average household income: $78,908 (2006-2010 5-year est.); Percent of households with income of $100,000 or more: 23.4% (2006-2010 5-year est.); Poverty rate: 4.5% (2006-2010 5-year est.).

Education: Percent of population age 25 and over with: High school diploma (including GED) or higher: 92.0% (2006-2010 5-year est.); Bachelor's degree or higher: 29.7% (2006-2010 5-year est.); Master's degree or higher: 14.3% (2006-2010 5-year est.).

Housing: Homeownership rate: 87.9% (2010); Median home value: $249,300 (2006-2010 5-year est.); Median contract rent: $498 per month (2006-2010 5-year est.); Median year structure built: 1977 (2006-2010 5-year est.).

Transportation: Commute to work: 94.2% car, 0.0% public transportation, 0.0% walk, 4.8% work from home (2006-2010 5-year est.); Travel time to work: 24.7% less than 15 minutes, 19.1% 15 to 30 minutes, 32.6% 30 to 45 minutes, 12.2% 45 to 60 minutes, 11.5% 60 minutes or more (2006-2010 5-year est.)

HERRICK CENTER (unincorporated postal area) Zip Code: 18430

Covers a land area of 1.778 square miles and a water area of 0.006 square miles. Located at 41.75° N. Lat; 75.47° W. Long. Population: 33 (2010); Density: 18.6 persons per square mile (2010); Race: 97.0% White, 3.0% Black, 0.0% Asian, 0.0% American Indian/Alaska Native, 0.0% Native Hawaiian/Other Pacific Islander, 0.0% Other, 0.0% Hispanic of any race (2010); Average household size: 2.54 (2010); Median age: 43.3 (2010); Males per 100 females: 153.8 (2010); Homeownership rate: 69.3% (2010)

HOP BOTTOM (borough). Aka Foster. Covers a land area of 0.606 square miles and a water area of 0.003 square miles. Located at 41.70° N. Lat; 75.77° W. Long. Elevation is 869 feet.

Population: 345 (1990); 333 (2000); 337 (2010); Density: 556.5 persons per square mile (2010); Race: 98.5% White, 0.0% Black, 0.0% Asian, 0.0% American Indian/Alaska Native, 0.0% Native Hawaiian/Other Pacific Islander, 1.5% Other, 1.2% Hispanic of any race (2010); Average household size: 2.44 (2010); Median age: 38.9 (2010); Males per 100 females: 100.6 (2010); Marriage status: 22.4% never married, 53.0% now married, 8.2% widowed, 16.4% divorced (2006-2010 5-year est.); Foreign born: 0.0% (2006-2010 5-year est.); Ancestry (includes multiple ancestries): 23.2% German, 20.8% English, 17.8% Irish, 12.6% Italian, 7.1% Welsh (2006-2010 5-year est.).

Economy: Single-family building permits issued: 0 (2011); Multi-family building permits issued: 0 (2011); Employment by occupation: 10.3%

management, 3.8% professional, 8.3% services, 10.9% sales, 1.9% farming, 14.7% construction, 8.3% production (2006-2010 5-year est.).
Income: Per capita income: $19,665 (2006-2010 5-year est.); Median household income: $42,917 (2006-2010 5-year est.); Average household income: $51,322 (2006-2010 5-year est.); Percent of households with income of $100,000 or more: 11.5% (2006-2010 5-year est.); Poverty rate: 20.8% (2006-2010 5-year est.).
Education: Percent of population age 25 and over with: High school diploma (including GED) or higher: 87.1% (2006-2010 5-year est.); Bachelor's degree or higher: 11.4% (2006-2010 5-year est.); Master's degree or higher: 3.9% (2006-2010 5-year est.).
Housing: Homeownership rate: 67.4% (2010); Median home value: $101,400 (2006-2010 5-year est.); Median contract rent: $523 per month (2006-2010 5-year est.); Median year structure built: before 1940 (2006-2010 5-year est.).
Safety: Violent crime rate: 0.0 per 10,000 population; Property crime rate: 0.0 per 10,000 population (2011).
Transportation: Commute to work: 90.3% car, 0.0% public transportation, 7.1% walk, 1.3% work from home (2006-2010 5-year est.); Travel time to work: 24.3% less than 15 minutes, 29.6% 15 to 30 minutes, 28.9% 30 to 45 minutes, 15.8% 45 to 60 minutes, 1.3% 60 minutes or more (2006-2010 5-year est.)

JACKSON (township). Covers a land area of 26.116 square miles and a water area of 0.407 square miles. Located at 41.87° N. Lat; 75.60° W. Long. Elevation is 1,352 feet.
Population: 751 (1990); 788 (2000); 848 (2010); Density: 32.5 persons per square mile (2010); Race: 99.2% White, 0.5% Black, 0.0% Asian, 0.0% American Indian/Alaska Native, 0.0% Native Hawaiian/Other Pacific Islander, 0.3% Other, 1.2% Hispanic of any race (2010); Average household size: 2.24 (2010); Median age: 51.9 (2010); Males per 100 females: 113.1 (2010); Marriage status: 29.2% never married, 55.6% now married, 4.5% widowed, 10.7% divorced (2006-2010 5-year est.); Foreign born: 1.3% (2006-2010 5-year est.); Ancestry (includes multiple ancestries): 25.6% German, 22.3% Irish, 21.6% English, 13.3% Italian, 9.3% Polish (2006-2010 5-year est.).
Economy: Single-family building permits issued: 0 (2011); Multi-family building permits issued: 0 (2011); Employment by occupation: 10.7% management, 1.8% professional, 3.9% services, 7.4% sales, 4.5% farming, 16.7% construction, 10.7% production (2006-2010 5-year est.).
Income: Per capita income: $24,936 (2006-2010 5-year est.); Median household income: $48,438 (2006-2010 5-year est.); Average household income: $57,041 (2006-2010 5-year est.); Percent of households with income of $100,000 or more: 11.7% (2006-2010 5-year est.); Poverty rate: 9.9% (2006-2010 5-year est.).
Education: Percent of population age 25 and over with: High school diploma (including GED) or higher: 90.7% (2006-2010 5-year est.); Bachelor's degree or higher: 20.7% (2006-2010 5-year est.); Master's degree or higher: 5.6% (2006-2010 5-year est.).
Housing: Homeownership rate: 87.8% (2010); Median home value: $118,100 (2006-2010 5-year est.); Median contract rent: $538 per month (2006-2010 5-year est.); Median year structure built: 1978 (2006-2010 5-year est.).
Transportation: Commute to work: 96.1% car, 0.0% public transportation, 0.0% walk, 3.9% work from home (2006-2010 5-year est.); Travel time to work: 25.3% less than 15 minutes, 24.7% 15 to 30 minutes, 17.5% 30 to 45 minutes, 15.9% 45 to 60 minutes, 16.6% 60 minutes or more (2006-2010 5-year est.)

JESSUP (township). Covers a land area of 21.212 square miles and a water area of 0.067 square miles. Located at 41.81° N. Lat; 75.98° W. Long.
Population: 483 (1990); 564 (2000); 536 (2010); Density: 25.3 persons per square mile (2010); Race: 97.0% White, 0.6% Black, 0.0% Asian, 0.4% American Indian/Alaska Native, 0.0% Native Hawaiian/Other Pacific Islander, 2.0% Other, 3.0% Hispanic of any race (2010); Average household size: 2.54 (2010); Median age: 44.3 (2010); Males per 100 females: 97.1 (2010); Marriage status: 21.4% never married, 66.8% now married, 10.3% widowed, 1.5% divorced (2006-2010 5-year est.); Foreign born: 1.5% (2006-2010 5-year est.); Ancestry (includes multiple ancestries): 25.3% English, 22.9% German, 13.8% Irish, 10.3% French, 9.7% Italian (2006-2010 5-year est.).
Economy: Single-family building permits issued: 0 (2011); Multi-family building permits issued: 0 (2011); Employment by occupation: 17.6%

management, 1.8% professional, 9.7% services, 14.5% sales, 3.0% farming, 20.0% construction, 6.1% production (2006-2010 5-year est.).
Income: Per capita income: $20,661 (2006-2010 5-year est.); Median household income: $41,250 (2006-2010 5-year est.); Average household income: $47,226 (2006-2010 5-year est.); Percent of households with income of $100,000 or more: 5.4% (2006-2010 5-year est.); Poverty rate: 18.5% (2006-2010 5-year est.).
Education: Percent of population age 25 and over with: High school diploma (including GED) or higher: 87.1% (2006-2010 5-year est.); Bachelor's degree or higher: 24.5% (2006-2010 5-year est.); Master's degree or higher: 3.6% (2006-2010 5-year est.).
Housing: Homeownership rate: 83.9% (2010); Median home value: $116,700 (2006-2010 5-year est.); Median contract rent: $675 per month (2006-2010 5-year est.); Median year structure built: 1981 (2006-2010 5-year est.).
Transportation: Commute to work: 82.7% car, 0.0% public transportation, 2.5% walk, 14.8% work from home (2006-2010 5-year est.); Travel time to work: 12.3% less than 15 minutes, 38.4% 15 to 30 minutes, 23.2% 30 to 45 minutes, 19.6% 45 to 60 minutes, 6.5% 60 minutes or more (2006-2010 5-year est.)

LANESBORO (borough). Covers a land area of 2.590 square miles and a water area of 0.062 square miles. Located at 41.96° N. Lat; 75.58° W. Long. Elevation is 919 feet.
Population: 659 (1990); 588 (2000); 506 (2010); Density: 195.4 persons per square mile (2010); Race: 96.4% White, 0.4% Black, 0.4% Asian, 0.4% American Indian/Alaska Native, 0.0% Native Hawaiian/Other Pacific Islander, 2.4% Other, 0.0% Hispanic of any race (2010); Average household size: 2.33 (2010); Median age: 42.5 (2010); Males per 100 females: 82.7 (2010); Marriage status: 24.8% never married, 54.0% now married, 12.7% widowed, 8.5% divorced (2006-2010 5-year est.); Foreign born: 3.7% (2006-2010 5-year est.); Ancestry (includes multiple ancestries): 28.4% Irish, 23.4% English, 15.0% German, 12.2% American, 7.8% Polish (2006-2010 5-year est.).
Economy: Employment by occupation: 3.0% management, 2.4% professional, 10.2% services, 16.9% sales, 0.0% farming, 9.0% construction, 11.4% production (2006-2010 5-year est.).
Income: Per capita income: $16,319 (2006-2010 5-year est.); Median household income: $29,083 (2006-2010 5-year est.); Average household income: $33,795 (2006-2010 5-year est.); Percent of households with income of $100,000 or more: 1.6% (2006-2010 5-year est.); Poverty rate: 19.6% (2006-2010 5-year est.).
Education: Percent of population age 25 and over with: High school diploma (including GED) or higher: 81.8% (2006-2010 5-year est.); Bachelor's degree or higher: 8.6% (2006-2010 5-year est.); Master's degree or higher: 4.7% (2006-2010 5-year est.).
Housing: Homeownership rate: 61.3% (2010); Median home value: $91,400 (2006-2010 5-year est.); Median contract rent: $326 per month (2006-2010 5-year est.); Median year structure built: before 1940 (2006-2010 5-year est.).
Transportation: Commute to work: 83.0% car, 5.0% public transportation, 2.5% walk, 9.4% work from home (2006-2010 5-year est.); Travel time to work: 22.2% less than 15 minutes, 38.2% 15 to 30 minutes, 18.8% 30 to 45 minutes, 18.1% 45 to 60 minutes, 2.8% 60 minutes or more (2006-2010 5-year est.)

LATHROP (township). Covers a land area of 20.365 square miles and a water area of 0.175 square miles. Located at 41.68° N. Lat; 75.81° W. Long.
Population: 794 (1990); 835 (2000); 841 (2010); Density: 41.3 persons per square mile (2010); Race: 99.3% White, 0.0% Black, 0.0% Asian, 0.0% American Indian/Alaska Native, 0.0% Native Hawaiian/Other Pacific Islander, 0.7% Other, 0.2% Hispanic of any race (2010); Average household size: 2.44 (2010); Median age: 46.5 (2010); Males per 100 females: 99.8 (2010); Marriage status: 19.6% never married, 60.4% now married, 9.8% widowed, 10.3% divorced (2006-2010 5-year est.); Foreign born: 4.4% (2006-2010 5-year est.); Ancestry (includes multiple ancestries): 28.2% German, 21.4% Polish, 17.4% Italian, 17.2% English, 11.1% Irish (2006-2010 5-year est.).
Economy: Employment by occupation: 6.1% management, 2.4% professional, 4.9% services, 11.6% sales, 3.6% farming, 20.7% construction, 12.5% production (2006-2010 5-year est.).
Income: Per capita income: $21,481 (2006-2010 5-year est.); Median household income: $35,341 (2006-2010 5-year est.); Average household income: $48,654 (2006-2010 5-year est.); Percent of households with

income of $100,000 or more: 14.4% (2006-2010 5-year est.); Poverty rate: 4.7% (2006-2010 5-year est.).

Education: Percent of population age 25 and over with: High school diploma (including GED) or higher: 86.7% (2006-2010 5-year est.); Bachelor's degree or higher: 13.7% (2006-2010 5-year est.); Master's degree or higher: 5.7% (2006-2010 5-year est.).

Housing: Homeownership rate: 80.3% (2010); Median home value: $95,800 (2006-2010 5-year est.); Median contract rent: $458 per month (2006-2010 5-year est.); Median year structure built: 1961 (2006-2010 5-year est.).

Transportation: Commute to work: 82.7% car, 0.0% public transportation, 7.2% walk, 9.2% work from home (2006-2010 5-year est.); Travel time to work: 16.5% less than 15 minutes, 27.7% 15 to 30 minutes, 41.0% 30 to 45 minutes, 11.2% 45 to 60 minutes, 3.6% 60 minutes or more (2006-2010 5-year est.)

LAWTON (unincorporated postal area)

Zip Code: 18828

Covers a land area of 10.026 square miles and a water area of 0.002 square miles. Located at 41.80° N. Lat; 76.09° W. Long. Elevation is 935 feet. Population: 352 (2010); Density: 35.1 persons per square mile (2010); Race: 97.4% White, 0.0% Black, 0.0% Asian, 0.9% American Indian/Alaska Native, 0.3% Native Hawaiian/Other Pacific Islander, 1.4% Other, 4.3% Hispanic of any race (2010); Average household size: 2.44 (2010); Median age: 44.0 (2010); Males per 100 females: 110.8 (2010); Homeownership rate: 67.4% (2010)

LENOX (township).

Covers a land area of 40.625 square miles and a water area of 0.514 square miles. Located at 41.70° N. Lat; 75.70° W. Long. Elevation is 886 feet.

Population: 1,581 (1990); 1,832 (2000); 1,934 (2010); Density: 47.6 persons per square mile (2010); Race: 98.0% White, 0.3% Black, 0.3% Asian, 0.2% American Indian/Alaska Native, 0.1% Native Hawaiian/Other Pacific Islander, 1.1% Other, 1.2% Hispanic of any race (2010); Average household size: 2.49 (2010); Median age: 44.8 (2010); Males per 100 females: 104.9 (2010); Marriage status: 23.2% never married, 59.2% now married, 5.1% widowed, 12.4% divorced (2006-2010 5-year est.); Foreign born: 3.0% (2006-2010 5-year est.); Ancestry (includes multiple ancestries): 27.0% German, 20.7% English, 17.4% Irish, 16.3% Polish, 10.0% Welsh (2006-2010 5-year est.).

Economy: Single-family building permits issued: 5 (2011); Multi-family building permits issued: 0 (2011); Employment by occupation: 5.5% management, 1.5% professional, 14.4% services, 16.5% sales, 3.4% farming, 16.5% construction, 7.8% production (2006-2010 5-year est.).

Income: Per capita income: $23,674 (2006-2010 5-year est.); Median household income: $42,206 (2006-2010 5-year est.); Average household income: $57,314 (2006-2010 5-year est.); Percent of households with income of $100,000 or more: 10.4% (2006-2010 5-year est.); Poverty rate: 8.9% (2006-2010 5-year est.).

Education: Percent of population age 25 and over with: High school diploma (including GED) or higher: 89.4% (2006-2010 5-year est.); Bachelor's degree or higher: 18.1% (2006-2010 5-year est.); Master's degree or higher: 7.7% (2006-2010 5-year est.).

Housing: Homeownership rate: 84.2% (2010); Median home value: $135,900 (2006-2010 5-year est.); Median contract rent: $469 per month (2006-2010 5-year est.); Median year structure built: 1973 (2006-2010 5-year est.).

Transportation: Commute to work: 94.2% car, 0.0% public transportation, 2.5% walk, 3.3% work from home (2006-2010 5-year est.); Travel time to work: 17.0% less than 15 minutes, 34.4% 15 to 30 minutes, 36.5% 30 to 45 minutes, 8.5% 45 to 60 minutes, 3.6% 60 minutes or more (2006-2010 5-year est.)

Additional Information Contacts

Wyoming County Chamber of Commerce. . . . . (570) 836-7755
http://wyccc.com

LENOXVILLE (unincorporated postal area)

Zip Code: 18441

Covers a land area of 2.920 square miles and a water area of 0.029 square miles. Located at 41.65° N. Lat; 75.61° W. Long. Elevation is 1,001 feet. Population: 289 (2010); Density: 99.0 persons per square mile (2010); Race: 97.9% White, 1.0% Black, 0.3% Asian, 0.3% American Indian/Alaska Native, 0.0% Native Hawaiian/Other Pacific Islander, 0.5% Other, 1.0% Hispanic of any race (2010); Average

household size: 2.47 (2010); Median age: 44.5 (2010); Males per 100 females: 107.9 (2010); Homeownership rate: 77.7% (2010)

LIBERTY (township).

Covers a land area of 29.639 square miles and a water area of 0.260 square miles. Located at 41.96° N. Lat; 75.85° W. Long.

Population: 1,353 (1990); 1,266 (2000); 1,292 (2010); Density: 43.6 persons per square mile (2010); Race: 97.8% White, 0.5% Black, 0.2% Asian, 0.0% American Indian/Alaska Native, 0.0% Native Hawaiian/Other Pacific Islander, 1.5% Other, 1.1% Hispanic of any race (2010); Average household size: 2.55 (2010); Median age: 44.5 (2010); Males per 100 females: 108.4 (2010); Marriage status: 24.8% never married, 65.2% now married, 2.7% widowed, 7.2% divorced (2006-2010 5-year est.); Foreign born: 0.3% (2006-2010 5-year est.); Ancestry (includes multiple ancestries): 23.7% German, 21.8% Irish, 19.4% English, 7.6% Italian, 5.4% American (2006-2010 5-year est.).

Economy: Single-family building permits issued: 0 (2011); Multi-family building permits issued: 0 (2011); Employment by occupation: 14.9% management, 3.3% professional, 13.3% services, 16.1% sales, 2.1% farming, 13.7% construction, 8.3% production (2006-2010 5-year est.).

Income: Per capita income: $23,569 (2006-2010 5-year est.); Median household income: $48,750 (2006-2010 5-year est.); Average household income: $63,625 (2006-2010 5-year est.); Percent of households with income of $100,000 or more: 19.9% (2006-2010 5-year est.); Poverty rate: 12.6% (2006-2010 5-year est.).

Education: Percent of population age 25 and over with: High school diploma (including GED) or higher: 87.1% (2006-2010 5-year est.); Bachelor's degree or higher: 15.3% (2006-2010 5-year est.); Master's degree or higher: 5.0% (2006-2010 5-year est.).

Housing: Homeownership rate: 83.2% (2010); Median home value: $105,600 (2006-2010 5-year est.); Median contract rent: $495 per month (2006-2010 5-year est.); Median year structure built: 1967 (2006-2010 5-year est.).

Transportation: Commute to work: 89.5% car, 0.0% public transportation, 1.5% walk, 4.9% work from home (2006-2010 5-year est.); Travel time to work: 19.1% less than 15 minutes, 45.3% 15 to 30 minutes, 26.8% 30 to 45 minutes, 5.2% 45 to 60 minutes, 3.6% 60 minutes or more (2006-2010 5-year est.)

Additional Information Contacts

Montrose Area Chamber of Commerce . . . . (570) 278-1174
http://www.montrosearea.com/news.php

LITTLE MEADOWS (borough).

Covers a land area of 2.424 square miles and a water area of 0 square miles. Located at 41.99° N. Lat; 76.13° W. Long. Elevation is 1,043 feet.

Population: 326 (1990); 290 (2000); 273 (2010); Density: 112.6 persons per square mile (2010); Race: 99.3% White, 0.0% Black, 0.4% Asian, 0.0% American Indian/Alaska Native, 0.0% Native Hawaiian/Other Pacific Islander, 0.3% Other, 1.5% Hispanic of any race (2010); Average household size: 2.29 (2010); Median age: 52.3 (2010); Males per 100 females: 97.8 (2010); Marriage status: 26.5% never married, 55.6% now married, 8.3% widowed, 9.6% divorced (2006-2010 5-year est.); Foreign born: 0.0% (2006-2010 5-year est.); Ancestry (includes multiple ancestries): 32.3% Irish, 23.6% English, 20.0% German, 11.2% Polish, 5.5% French (2006-2010 5-year est.).

Economy: Single-family building permits issued: 0 (2011); Multi-family building permits issued: 0 (2011); Employment by occupation: 5.2% management, 5.7% professional, 11.5% services, 14.4% sales, 10.3% farming, 21.8% construction, 6.9% production (2006-2010 5-year est.).

Income: Per capita income: $26,027 (2006-2010 5-year est.); Median household income: $48,235 (2006-2010 5-year est.); Average household income: $62,944 (2006-2010 5-year est.); Percent of households with income of $100,000 or more: 22.0% (2006-2010 5-year est.); Poverty rate: 14.6% (2006-2010 5-year est.).

Education: Percent of population age 25 and over with: High school diploma (including GED) or higher: 85.5% (2006-2010 5-year est.); Bachelor's degree or higher: 9.5% (2006-2010 5-year est.); Master's degree or higher: 3.5% (2006-2010 5-year est.).

Housing: Homeownership rate: 83.2% (2010); Median home value: $109,800 (2006-2010 5-year est.); Median contract rent: $584 per month (2006-2010 5-year est.); Median year structure built: 1966 (2006-2010 5-year est.).

Transportation: Commute to work: 92.3% car, 0.0% public transportation, 3.6% walk, 2.4% work from home (2006-2010 5-year est.); Travel time to work: 12.2% less than 15 minutes, 47.0% 15 to 30 minutes, 29.9% 30 to

45 minutes, 0.0% 45 to 60 minutes, 11.0% 60 minutes or more (2006-2010 5-year est.)

MIDDLETOWN (township). Covers a land area of 28.904 square miles and a water area of 0.006 square miles. Located at 41.87° N. Lat; 76.07° W. Long.

Population: 339 (1990); 340 (2000); 382 (2010); Density: 13.2 persons per square mile (2010); Race: 98.4% White, 0.0% Black, 0.5% Asian, 0.0% American Indian/Alaska Native, 0.3% Native Hawaiian/Other Pacific Islander, 0.8% Other, 1.6% Hispanic of any race (2010); Average household size: 2.53 (2010); Median age: 43.8 (2010); Males per 100 females: 118.3 (2010); Marriage status: 27.3% never married, 61.4% now married, 4.8% widowed, 6.5% divorced (2006-2010 5-year est.); Foreign born: 0.5% (2006-2010 5-year est.); Ancestry (includes multiple ancestries): 39.6% Irish, 13.1% Welsh, 12.3% English, 11.5% German, 8.8% Dutch (2006-2010 5-year est.).

Economy: Single-family building permits issued: 0 (2011); Multi-family building permits issued: 0 (2011); Employment by occupation: 13.4% management, 0.0% professional, 6.7% services, 8.5% sales, 3.7% farming, 23.2% construction, 12.8% production (2006-2010 5-year est.).

Income: Per capita income: $19,810 (2006-2010 5-year est.); Median household income: $38,393 (2006-2010 5-year est.); Average household income: $50,405 (2006-2010 5-year est.); Percent of households with income of $100,000 or more: 13.8% (2006-2010 5-year est.); Poverty rate: 25.7% (2006-2010 5-year est.).

Education: Percent of population age 25 and over with: High school diploma (including GED) or higher: 90.2% (2006-2010 5-year est.); Bachelor's degree or higher: 11.7% (2006-2010 5-year est.); Master's degree or higher: 1.6% (2006-2010 5-year est.).

Housing: Homeownership rate: 77.5% (2010); Median home value: $131,900 (2006-2010 5-year est.); Median contract rent: $473 per month (2006-2010 5-year est.); Median year structure built: 1977 (2006-2010 5-year est.).

Transportation: Commute to work: 89.0% car, 0.0% public transportation, 5.8% walk, 3.9% work from home (2006-2010 5-year est.); Travel time to work: 29.7% less than 15 minutes, 22.3% 15 to 30 minutes, 33.8% 30 to 45 minutes, 12.2% 45 to 60 minutes, 2.0% 60 minutes or more (2006-2010 5-year est.)

MONTROSE (borough). County seat. Covers a land area of 1.274 square miles and a water area of 0 square miles. Located at 41.83° N. Lat; 75.88° W. Long. Elevation is 1,663 feet.

History: Settled 1799, incorporated 1824.

Population: 1,982 (1990); 1,664 (2000); 1,617 (2010); Density: 1,269.0 persons per square mile (2010); Race: 98.8% White, 0.2% Black, 0.1% Asian, 0.1% American Indian/Alaska Native, 0.1% Native Hawaiian/Other Pacific Islander, 0.7% Other, 1.1% Hispanic of any race (2010); Average household size: 2.14 (2010); Median age: 44.4 (2010); Males per 100 females: 84.2 (2010); Marriage status: 37.5% never married, 44.1% now married, 8.5% widowed, 9.9% divorced (2006-2010 5-year est.); Foreign born: 3.1% (2006-2010 5-year est.); Ancestry (includes multiple ancestries): 24.2% Irish, 22.0% German, 19.9% English, 14.2% Italian, 6.6% Dutch (2006-2010 5-year est.).

Economy: Single-family building permits issued: 0 (2011); Multi-family building permits issued: 0 (2011); Employment by occupation: 7.7% management, 1.8% professional, 7.8% services, 25.6% sales, 1.5% farming, 8.8% construction, 7.3% production (2006-2010 5-year est.).

Income: Per capita income: $19,255 (2006-2010 5-year est.); Median household income: $37,125 (2006-2010 5-year est.); Average household income: $46,581 (2006-2010 5-year est.); Percent of households with income of $100,000 or more: 9.9% (2006-2010 5-year est.); Poverty rate: 15.5% (2006-2010 5-year est.).

Education: Percent of population age 25 and over with: High school diploma (including GED) or higher: 80.4% (2006-2010 5-year est.); Bachelor's degree or higher: 14.7% (2006-2010 5-year est.); Master's degree or higher: 6.5% (2006-2010 5-year est.).

School District(s)

Montrose Area SD (KG-12)
    2010-11 Enrollment: 1,614 . . . . (570) 278-3731

Housing: Homeownership rate: 58.5% (2010); Median home value: $130,700 (2006-2010 5-year est.); Median contract rent: $499 per month (2006-2010 5-year est.); Median year structure built: before 1940 (2006-2010 5-year est.).

Hospitals: Endless Mountain Health Systems (22 beds)

Newspapers: Susquehanna County Independent (Local news; Circulation 6,800)

Transportation: Commute to work: 88.1% car, 1.3% public transportation, 5.8% walk, 4.8% work from home (2006-2010 5-year est.); Travel time to work: 58.2% less than 15 minutes, 16.6% 15 to 30 minutes, 14.5% 30 to 45 minutes, 5.3% 45 to 60 minutes, 5.4% 60 minutes or more (2006-2010 5-year est.)

Additional Information Contacts

Montrose Area Chamber of Commerce . . . . (570) 278-1174
    http://www.montrosearea.com/news.php

NEW MILFORD (borough). Covers a land area of 1.016 square miles and a water area of 0 square miles. Located at 41.88° N. Lat; 75.73° W. Long. Elevation is 1,112 feet.

Population: 889 (1990); 878 (2000); 868 (2010); Density: 854.5 persons per square mile (2010); Race: 97.2% White, 1.0% Black, 0.2% Asian, 0.0% American Indian/Alaska Native, 0.0% Native Hawaiian/Other Pacific Islander, 1.6% Other, 1.5% Hispanic of any race (2010); Average household size: 2.29 (2010); Median age: 40.6 (2010); Males per 100 females: 97.7 (2010); Marriage status: 25.3% never married, 49.6% now married, 7.9% widowed, 17.1% divorced (2006-2010 5-year est.); Foreign born: 0.0% (2006-2010 5-year est.); Ancestry (includes multiple ancestries): 30.4% English, 27.9% German, 23.6% Irish, 13.7% Italian, 6.7% Polish (2006-2010 5-year est.).

Economy: Single-family building permits issued: 0 (2011); Multi-family building permits issued: 0 (2011); Employment by occupation: 12.8% management, 4.8% professional, 11.4% services, 15.7% sales, 5.2% farming, 9.7% construction, 4.3% production (2006-2010 5-year est.).

Income: Per capita income: $20,067 (2006-2010 5-year est.); Median household income: $38,611 (2006-2010 5-year est.); Average household income: $47,764 (2006-2010 5-year est.); Percent of households with income of $100,000 or more: 8.9% (2006-2010 5-year est.); Poverty rate: 11.7% (2006-2010 5-year est.).

Education: Percent of population age 25 and over with: High school diploma (including GED) or higher: 84.5% (2006-2010 5-year est.); Bachelor's degree or higher: 15.7% (2006-2010 5-year est.); Master's degree or higher: 5.2% (2006-2010 5-year est.).

School District(s)

Blue Ridge SD (KG-12)
    2010-11 Enrollment: 1,142 . . . . (570) 465-3141

Housing: Homeownership rate: 65.9% (2010); Median home value: $90,500 (2006-2010 5-year est.); Median contract rent: $486 per month (2006-2010 5-year est.); Median year structure built: before 1940 (2006-2010 5-year est.).

Transportation: Commute to work: 85.9% car, 0.0% public transportation, 7.0% walk, 6.5% work from home (2006-2010 5-year est.); Travel time to work: 39.0% less than 15 minutes, 21.0% 15 to 30 minutes, 20.3% 30 to 45 minutes, 8.2% 45 to 60 minutes, 11.5% 60 minutes or more (2006-2010 5-year est.)

NEW MILFORD (township). Covers a land area of 44.808 square miles and a water area of 0.599 square miles. Located at 41.85° N. Lat; 75.70° W. Long. Elevation is 1,112 feet.

Population: 1,795 (1990); 1,859 (2000); 2,042 (2010); Density: 45.6 persons per square mile (2010); Race: 98.5% White, 0.3% Black, 0.1% Asian, 0.2% American Indian/Alaska Native, 0.0% Native Hawaiian/Other Pacific Islander, 0.9% Other, 1.0% Hispanic of any race (2010); Average household size: 2.45 (2010); Median age: 46.4 (2010); Males per 100 females: 105.0 (2010); Marriage status: 22.3% never married, 63.0% now married, 4.7% widowed, 10.0% divorced (2006-2010 5-year est.); Foreign born: 2.6% (2006-2010 5-year est.); Ancestry (includes multiple ancestries): 35.4% German, 22.6% Irish, 22.2% English, 11.1% Italian, 6.5% Polish (2006-2010 5-year est.).

Economy: Single-family building permits issued: 2 (2011); Multi-family building permits issued: 0 (2011); Employment by occupation: 5.7% management, 0.9% professional, 16.0% services, 14.9% sales, 3.8% farming, 13.9% construction, 12.7% production (2006-2010 5-year est.).

Income: Per capita income: $22,574 (2006-2010 5-year est.); Median household income: $47,462 (2006-2010 5-year est.); Average household income: $60,023 (2006-2010 5-year est.); Percent of households with income of $100,000 or more: 12.9% (2006-2010 5-year est.); Poverty rate: 11.2% (2006-2010 5-year est.).

Education: Percent of population age 25 and over with: High school diploma (including GED) or higher: 91.5% (2006-2010 5-year est.);

Bachelor's degree or higher: 12.7% (2006-2010 5-year est.); Master's degree or higher: 6.4% (2006-2010 5-year est.).

Housing: Homeownership rate: 88.2% (2010); Median home value: $143,200 (2006-2010 5-year est.); Median contract rent: $491 per month (2006-2010 5-year est.); Median year structure built: 1975 (2006-2010 5-year est.).

Transportation: Commute to work: 93.9% car, 2.2% public transportation, 0.0% walk, 3.4% work from home (2006-2010 5-year est.); Travel time to work: 28.2% less than 15 minutes, 35.9% 15 to 30 minutes, 22.3% 30 to 45 minutes, 3.7% 45 to 60 minutes, 9.8% 60 minutes or more (2006-2010 5-year est.)

Additional Information Contacts

Montrose Area Chamber of Commerce . . . . (570) 278-1174
   http://www.montrosearea.com/news.php

OAKLAND (borough). Covers a land area of 0.446 square miles and a water area of 0.058 square miles. Located at 41.95° N. Lat; 75.61° W. Long. Elevation is 938 feet.

Population: 641 (1990); 622 (2000); 616 (2010); Density: 1,380.5 persons per square mile (2010); Race: 98.4% White, 0.5% Black, 0.6% Asian, 0.0% American Indian/Alaska Native, 0.0% Native Hawaiian/Other Pacific Islander, 0.5% Other, 1.3% Hispanic of any race (2010); Average household size: 2.69 (2010); Median age: 38.7 (2010); Males per 100 females: 99.4 (2010); Marriage status: 23.0% never married, 47.8% now married, 15.3% widowed, 13.9% divorced (2006-2010 5-year est.); Foreign born: 0.0% (2006-2010 5-year est.); Ancestry (includes multiple ancestries): 35.0% Irish, 26.0% German, 21.6% English, 9.9% Italian, 7.2% Dutch (2006-2010 5-year est.).

Economy: Employment by occupation: 1.1% management, 0.0% professional, 13.5% services, 16.7% sales, 1.5% farming, 21.8% construction, 4.4% production (2006-2010 5-year est.).

Income: Per capita income: $16,352 (2006-2010 5-year est.); Median household income: $36,750 (2006-2010 5-year est.); Average household income: $41,333 (2006-2010 5-year est.); Percent of households with income of $100,000 or more: 5.4% (2006-2010 5-year est.); Poverty rate: 11.7% (2006-2010 5-year est.).

Education: Percent of population age 25 and over with: High school diploma (including GED) or higher: 86.4% (2006-2010 5-year est.); Bachelor's degree or higher: 8.5% (2006-2010 5-year est.); Master's degree or higher: 4.2% (2006-2010 5-year est.).

Housing: Homeownership rate: 75.9% (2010); Median home value: $82,600 (2006-2010 5-year est.); Median contract rent: $441 per month (2006-2010 5-year est.); Median year structure built: before 1940 (2006-2010 5-year est.).

Transportation: Commute to work: 95.5% car, 0.0% public transportation, 0.0% walk, 4.5% work from home (2006-2010 5-year est.); Travel time to work: 28.4% less than 15 minutes, 23.3% 15 to 30 minutes, 35.2% 30 to 45 minutes, 5.5% 45 to 60 minutes, 7.6% 60 minutes or more (2006-2010 5-year est.)

OAKLAND (township). Covers a land area of 16.446 square miles and a water area of 0.297 square miles. Located at 41.97° N. Lat; 75.63° W. Long. Elevation is 938 feet.

Population: 544 (1990); 550 (2000); 564 (2010); Density: 34.3 persons per square mile (2010); Race: 96.3% White, 0.5% Black, 1.2% Asian, 0.5% American Indian/Alaska Native, 0.2% Native Hawaiian/Other Pacific Islander, 1.3% Other, 1.2% Hispanic of any race (2010); Average household size: 2.43 (2010); Median age: 47.2 (2010); Males per 100 females: 105.8 (2010); Marriage status: 27.3% never married, 60.7% now married, 4.1% widowed, 7.9% divorced (2006-2010 5-year est.); Foreign born: 2.0% (2006-2010 5-year est.); Ancestry (includes multiple ancestries): 31.9% German, 21.0% Irish, 21.0% English, 9.9% Italian, 8.4% Polish (2006-2010 5-year est.).

Economy: Single-family building permits issued: 0 (2011); Multi-family building permits issued: 0 (2011); Employment by occupation: 14.6% management, 2.4% professional, 4.3% services, 20.3% sales, 11.1% farming, 8.9% construction, 8.4% production (2006-2010 5-year est.).

Income: Per capita income: $25,326 (2006-2010 5-year est.); Median household income: $55,865 (2006-2010 5-year est.); Average household income: $64,118 (2006-2010 5-year est.); Percent of households with income of $100,000 or more: 14.4% (2006-2010 5-year est.); Poverty rate: 7.4% (2006-2010 5-year est.).

Education: Percent of population age 25 and over with: High school diploma (including GED) or higher: 86.3% (2006-2010 5-year est.);

Bachelor's degree or higher: 12.5% (2006-2010 5-year est.); Master's degree or higher: 2.8% (2006-2010 5-year est.).

Housing: Homeownership rate: 84.5% (2010); Median home value: $108,600 (2006-2010 5-year est.); Median contract rent: $432 per month (2006-2010 5-year est.); Median year structure built: 1974 (2006-2010 5-year est.).

Transportation: Commute to work: 93.4% car, 0.0% public transportation, 2.2% walk, 4.4% work from home (2006-2010 5-year est.); Travel time to work: 24.9% less than 15 minutes, 39.1% 15 to 30 minutes, 17.1% 30 to 45 minutes, 4.6% 45 to 60 minutes, 14.2% 60 minutes or more (2006-2010 5-year est.)

RUSH (township). Covers a land area of 38.427 square miles and a water area of 0.143 square miles. Located at 41.78° N. Lat; 76.06° W. Long. Elevation is 988 feet.

Population: 1,126 (1990); 1,290 (2000); 1,267 (2010); Density: 33.0 persons per square mile (2010); Race: 97.6% White, 0.3% Black, 0.9% Asian, 0.2% American Indian/Alaska Native, 0.0% Native Hawaiian/Other Pacific Islander, 1.0% Other, 1.8% Hispanic of any race (2010); Average household size: 2.49 (2010); Median age: 45.2 (2010); Males per 100 females: 108.7 (2010); Marriage status: 21.6% never married, 56.0% now married, 7.0% widowed, 15.4% divorced (2006-2010 5-year est.); Foreign born: 2.9% (2006-2010 5-year est.); Ancestry (includes multiple ancestries): 23.3% English, 22.6% German, 16.1% Irish, 7.5% Dutch, 4.7% Welsh (2006-2010 5-year est.).

Economy: Single-family building permits issued: 5 (2011); Multi-family building permits issued: 0 (2011); Employment by occupation: 4.6% management, 2.4% professional, 15.0% services, 11.5% sales, 6.1% farming, 19.1% construction, 15.0% production (2006-2010 5-year est.).

Income: Per capita income: $20,222 (2006-2010 5-year est.); Median household income: $39,531 (2006-2010 5-year est.); Average household income: $51,503 (2006-2010 5-year est.); Percent of households with income of $100,000 or more: 9.3% (2006-2010 5-year est.); Poverty rate: 9.6% (2006-2010 5-year est.).

Education: Percent of population age 25 and over with: High school diploma (including GED) or higher: 82.8% (2006-2010 5-year est.); Bachelor's degree or higher: 9.2% (2006-2010 5-year est.); Master's degree or higher: 2.4% (2006-2010 5-year est.).

Housing: Homeownership rate: 79.5% (2010); Median home value: $135,200 (2006-2010 5-year est.); Median contract rent: $449 per month (2006-2010 5-year est.); Median year structure built: 1973 (2006-2010 5-year est.).

Transportation: Commute to work: 95.7% car, 0.0% public transportation, 0.0% walk, 3.8% work from home (2006-2010 5-year est.); Travel time to work: 15.4% less than 15 minutes, 39.6% 15 to 30 minutes, 27.7% 30 to 45 minutes, 10.2% 45 to 60 minutes, 7.1% 60 minutes or more (2006-2010 5-year est.)

Additional Information Contacts

Montrose Area Chamber of Commerce . . . . (570) 278-1174
   http://www.montrosearea.com/news.php

SILVER LAKE (township). Covers a land area of 32.708 square miles and a water area of 0.599 square miles. Located at 41.95° N. Lat; 75.94° W. Long.

Population: 1,542 (1990); 1,729 (2000); 1,716 (2010); Density: 52.5 persons per square mile (2010); Race: 98.6% White, 0.2% Black, 0.2% Asian, 0.1% American Indian/Alaska Native, 0.0% Native Hawaiian/Other Pacific Islander, 0.9% Other, 0.7% Hispanic of any race (2010); Average household size: 2.42 (2010); Median age: 48.2 (2010); Males per 100 females: 109.8 (2010); Marriage status: 22.6% never married, 64.2% now married, 5.8% widowed, 7.3% divorced (2006-2010 5-year est.); Foreign born: 1.4% (2006-2010 5-year est.); Ancestry (includes multiple ancestries): 30.5% Irish, 24.3% German, 19.4% English, 11.5% Italian, 9.0% French (2006-2010 5-year est.).

Economy: Single-family building permits issued: 4 (2011); Multi-family building permits issued: 0 (2011); Employment by occupation: 21.4% management, 4.1% professional, 13.4% services, 16.8% sales, 2.0% farming, 8.5% construction, 6.9% production (2006-2010 5-year est.).

Income: Per capita income: $23,493 (2006-2010 5-year est.); Median household income: $56,026 (2006-2010 5-year est.); Average household income: $60,187 (2006-2010 5-year est.); Percent of households with income of $100,000 or more: 10.2% (2006-2010 5-year est.); Poverty rate: 6.8% (2006-2010 5-year est.).

Education: Percent of population age 25 and over with: High school diploma (including GED) or higher: 91.2% (2006-2010 5-year est.);

Bachelor's degree or higher: 24.1% (2006-2010 5-year est.); Master's degree or higher: 7.9% (2006-2010 5-year est.).
Housing: Homeownership rate: 88.7% (2010); Median home value: $149,400 (2006-2010 5-year est.); Median contract rent: $455 per month (2006-2010 5-year est.); Median year structure built: 1970 (2006-2010 5-year est.).
Safety: Violent crime rate: 0.0 per 10,000 population; Property crime rate: 58.1 per 10,000 population (2011).
Transportation: Commute to work: 92.0% car, 0.0% public transportation, 1.1% walk, 6.3% work from home (2006-2010 5-year est.); Travel time to work: 7.6% less than 15 minutes, 59.4% 15 to 30 minutes, 24.4% 30 to 45 minutes, 3.9% 45 to 60 minutes, 4.8% 60 minutes or more (2006-2010 5-year est.)
Additional Information Contacts
Montrose Area Chamber of Commerce . . . . (570) 278-1174
  http://montrosearea.com/news.php

SOUTH GIBSON (unincorporated postal area)
Zip Code: 18842
  Covers a land area of 4.118 square miles and a water area of 0.006 square miles. Located at 41.74° N. Lat; 75.62° W. Long. Elevation is 997 feet. Population: 278 (2010); Density: 67.5 persons per square mile (2010); Race: 96.4% White, 0.7% Black, 0.0% Asian, 0.0% American Indian/Alaska Native, 0.0% Native Hawaiian/Other Pacific Islander, 2.9% Other, 0.0% Hispanic of any race (2010); Average household size: 2.53 (2010); Median age: 46.0 (2010); Males per 100 females: 105.9 (2010); Homeownership rate: 90.0% (2010)

SOUTH MONTROSE (unincorporated postal area)
Zip Code: 18843
  Covers a land area of 0.876 square miles and a water area of 0 square miles. Located at 41.79° N. Lat; 75.89° W. Long. Elevation is 1,644 feet. Population: 277 (2010); Density: 316.0 persons per square mile (2010); Race: 98.9% White, 0.0% Black, 0.0% Asian, 0.0% American Indian/Alaska Native, 0.0% Native Hawaiian/Other Pacific Islander, 1.1% Other, 0.0% Hispanic of any race (2010); Average household size: 2.23 (2010); Median age: 40.5 (2010); Males per 100 females: 91.0 (2010); Homeownership rate: 74.2% (2010)

SPRINGVILLE (township). Covers a land area of 30.594 square miles and a water area of 0.232 square miles. Located at 41.68° N. Lat; 75.91° W. Long. Elevation is 1,152 feet.
Population: 1,424 (1990); 1,555 (2000); 1,641 (2010); Density: 53.6 persons per square mile (2010); Race: 99.0% White, 0.2% Black, 0.2% Asian, 0.1% American Indian/Alaska Native, 0.0% Native Hawaiian/Other Pacific Islander, 0.5% Other, 1.0% Hispanic of any race (2010); Average household size: 2.60 (2010); Median age: 43.5 (2010); Males per 100 females: 97.0 (2010); Marriage status: 23.4% never married, 62.4% now married, 6.2% widowed, 8.0% divorced (2006-2010 5-year est.); Foreign born: 1.0% (2006-2010 5-year est.); Ancestry (includes multiple ancestries): 28.9% English, 24.8% German, 15.5% Irish, 7.8% Polish, 5.9% Italian (2006-2010 5-year est.).
Economy: Single-family building permits issued: 2 (2011); Multi-family building permits issued: 0 (2011); Employment by occupation: 11.7% management, 0.9% professional, 7.0% services, 19.8% sales, 3.2% farming, 22.4% construction, 11.7% production (2006-2010 5-year est.).
Income: Per capita income: $21,062 (2006-2010 5-year est.); Median household income: $51,136 (2006-2010 5-year est.); Average household income: $57,048 (2006-2010 5-year est.); Percent of households with income of $100,000 or more: 8.9% (2006-2010 5-year est.); Poverty rate: 12.9% (2006-2010 5-year est.).
Education: Percent of population age 25 and over with: High school diploma (including GED) or higher: 84.0% (2006-2010 5-year est.); Bachelor's degree or higher: 15.8% (2006-2010 5-year est.); Master's degree or higher: 4.2% (2006-2010 5-year est.).
School District(s)
Elk Lake SD (KG-12)
  2010-11 Enrollment: 1,369 . . . . (570) 278-1106
Susquehanna County CTC (10-12)
  2010-11 Enrollment: n/a . . . . (570) 278-9229
Housing: Homeownership rate: 82.1% (2010); Median home value: $142,400 (2006-2010 5-year est.); Median contract rent: $497 per month (2006-2010 5-year est.); Median year structure built: 1971 (2006-2010 5-year est.).

Transportation: Commute to work: 87.7% car, 0.5% public transportation, 1.8% walk, 9.6% work from home (2006-2010 5-year est.); Travel time to work: 16.5% less than 15 minutes, 57.5% 15 to 30 minutes, 10.9% 30 to 45 minutes, 8.0% 45 to 60 minutes, 7.0% 60 minutes or more (2006-2010 5-year est.)
Additional Information Contacts
Montrose Area Chamber of Commerce . . . . (570) 278-1174
  http://montrosearea.com/news.php

SUSQUEHANNA DEPOT (borough). Aka Susquehanna. Covers a land area of 0.765 square miles and a water area of 0.056 square miles. Located at 41.94° N. Lat; 75.61° W. Long.
History: Also called Susquehanna.
Population: 1,760 (1990); 1,690 (2000); 1,643 (2010); Density: 2,148.9 persons per square mile (2010); Race: 97.1% White, 0.4% Black, 1.0% Asian, 0.3% American Indian/Alaska Native, 0.0% Native Hawaiian/Other Pacific Islander, 1.2% Other, 2.0% Hispanic of any race (2010); Average household size: 2.50 (2010); Median age: 38.1 (2010); Males per 100 females: 91.3 (2010); Marriage status: 27.5% never married, 50.7% now married, 9.0% widowed, 12.7% divorced (2006-2010 5-year est.); Foreign born: 0.2% (2006-2010 5-year est.); Ancestry (includes multiple ancestries): 26.9% Irish, 24.4% German, 14.2% Italian, 13.8% English, 8.4% American (2006-2010 5-year est.).
Economy: Single-family building permits issued: 3 (2011); Multi-family building permits issued: 0 (2011); Employment by occupation: 6.5% management, 4.9% professional, 15.0% services, 14.0% sales, 5.4% farming, 14.0% construction, 6.4% production (2006-2010 5-year est.).
Income: Per capita income: $17,637 (2006-2010 5-year est.); Median household income: $35,197 (2006-2010 5-year est.); Average household income: $44,727 (2006-2010 5-year est.); Percent of households with income of $100,000 or more: 6.7% (2006-2010 5-year est.); Poverty rate: 20.8% (2006-2010 5-year est.).
Taxes: Total city taxes per capita: $258 (2009); City property taxes per capita: $232 (2009).
Education: Percent of population age 25 and over with: High school diploma (including GED) or higher: 79.7% (2006-2010 5-year est.); Bachelor's degree or higher: 16.2% (2006-2010 5-year est.); Master's degree or higher: 5.2% (2006-2010 5-year est.).
School District(s)
Susquehanna Community SD (KG-12)
  2010-11 Enrollment: 857 . . . . (570) 853-4921
Housing: Homeownership rate: 60.7% (2010); Median home value: $81,300 (2006-2010 5-year est.); Median contract rent: $444 per month (2006-2010 5-year est.); Median year structure built: before 1940 (2006-2010 5-year est.).
Hospitals: Barnes-Kasson Hospital (106 beds)
Safety: Violent crime rate: 18.2 per 10,000 population; Property crime rate: 97.1 per 10,000 population (2011).
Newspapers: Susquehanna County Transcript (Community news; Circulation 8,200)
Transportation: Commute to work: 89.3% car, 0.0% public transportation, 3.0% walk, 7.4% work from home (2006-2010 5-year est.); Travel time to work: 45.1% less than 15 minutes, 20.2% 15 to 30 minutes, 24.5% 30 to 45 minutes, 0.7% 45 to 60 minutes, 9.4% 60 minutes or more (2006-2010 5-year est.)
Additional Information Contacts
Montrose Area Chamber of Commerce . . . . (570) 278-1174
  http://montrosearea.com/news.php

THOMPSON (borough). Covers a land area of 0.512 square miles and a water area of 0 square miles. Located at 41.86° N. Lat; 75.51° W. Long. Elevation is 1,657 feet.
Population: 291 (1990); 299 (2000); 299 (2010); Density: 583.9 persons per square mile (2010); Race: 98.7% White, 0.3% Black, 0.0% Asian, 0.0% American Indian/Alaska Native, 0.0% Native Hawaiian/Other Pacific Islander, 1.0% Other, 0.7% Hispanic of any race (2010); Average household size: 2.37 (2010); Median age: 42.4 (2010); Males per 100 females: 94.2 (2010); Marriage status: 30.8% never married, 46.5% now married, 4.5% widowed, 18.2% divorced (2006-2010 5-year est.); Foreign born: 2.9% (2006-2010 5-year est.); Ancestry (includes multiple ancestries): 30.9% German, 23.7% Irish, 17.9% English, 16.2% Italian, 13.3% Polish (2006-2010 5-year est.).
Economy: Single-family building permits issued: 0 (2011); Multi-family building permits issued: 0 (2011); Employment by occupation: 13.8%

management, 0.0% professional, 11.2% services, 17.2% sales, 0.0% farming, 18.1% construction, 6.0% production (2006-2010 5-year est.).
Income: Per capita income: $14,883 (2006-2010 5-year est.); Median household income: $31,875 (2006-2010 5-year est.); Average household income: $42,274 (2006-2010 5-year est.); Percent of households with income of $100,000 or more: 8.6% (2006-2010 5-year est.); Poverty rate: 25.1% (2006-2010 5-year est.).
Education: Percent of population age 25 and over with: High school diploma (including GED) or higher: 76.3% (2006-2010 5-year est.); Bachelor's degree or higher: 6.8% (2006-2010 5-year est.); Master's degree or higher: 5.9% (2006-2010 5-year est.).
Housing: Homeownership rate: 74.6% (2010); Median home value: $92,000 (2006-2010 5-year est.); Median contract rent: $419 per month (2006-2010 5-year est.); Median year structure built: before 1940 (2006-2010 5-year est.).
Transportation: Commute to work: 97.3% car, 0.0% public transportation, 0.0% walk, 2.7% work from home (2006-2010 5-year est.); Travel time to work: 15.6% less than 15 minutes, 34.9% 15 to 30 minutes, 13.8% 30 to 45 minutes, 27.5% 45 to 60 minutes, 8.3% 60 minutes or more (2006-2010 5-year est.)

THOMPSON (township). Covers a land area of 21.940 square miles and a water area of 0.271 square miles. Located at 41.87° N. Lat; 75.52° W. Long. Elevation is 1,657 feet.
Population: 374 (1990); 440 (2000); 410 (2010); Density: 18.7 persons per square mile (2010); Race: 98.3% White, 0.2% Black, 0.0% Asian, 0.0% American Indian/Alaska Native, 0.2% Native Hawaiian/Other Pacific Islander, 1.3% Other, 1.7% Hispanic of any race (2010); Average household size: 2.10 (2010); Median age: 51.1 (2010); Males per 100 females: 100.0 (2010); Marriage status: 22.4% never married, 60.2% now married, 5.0% widowed, 12.4% divorced (2006-2010 5-year est.); Foreign born: 0.0% (2006-2010 5-year est.); Ancestry (includes multiple ancestries): 33.9% English, 20.7% German, 20.1% Irish, 13.7% Italian, 8.8% Polish (2006-2010 5-year est.).
Economy: Single-family building permits issued: 3 (2011); Multi-family building permits issued: 0 (2011); Employment by occupation: 6.7% management, 0.0% professional, 9.1% services, 33.5% sales, 1.4% farming, 18.2% construction, 9.6% production (2006-2010 5-year est.).
Income: Per capita income: $26,151 (2006-2010 5-year est.); Median household income: $36,667 (2006-2010 5-year est.); Average household income: $55,861 (2006-2010 5-year est.); Percent of households with income of $100,000 or more: 12.4% (2006-2010 5-year est.); Poverty rate: 8.0% (2006-2010 5-year est.).
Education: Percent of population age 25 and over with: High school diploma (including GED) or higher: 90.2% (2006-2010 5-year est.); Bachelor's degree or higher: 20.3% (2006-2010 5-year est.); Master's degree or higher: 7.3% (2006-2010 5-year est.).
Housing: Homeownership rate: 87.7% (2010); Median home value: $152,200 (2006-2010 5-year est.); Median contract rent: $475 per month (2006-2010 5-year est.); Median year structure built: 1967 (2006-2010 5-year est.).
Transportation: Commute to work: 98.9% car, 0.0% public transportation, 1.1% walk, 0.0% work from home (2006-2010 5-year est.); Travel time to work: 18.5% less than 15 minutes, 22.2% 15 to 30 minutes, 34.9% 30 to 45 minutes, 17.5% 45 to 60 minutes, 6.9% 60 minutes or more (2006-2010 5-year est.)

UNION DALE (borough). Aka Uniondale. Covers a land area of 2.406 square miles and a water area of 0.062 square miles. Located at 41.71° N. Lat; 75.48° W. Long. Elevation is 1,690 feet.
Population: 303 (1990); 368 (2000); 267 (2010); Density: 111.0 persons per square mile (2010); Race: 98.5% White, 1.1% Black, 0.0% Asian, 0.0% American Indian/Alaska Native, 0.0% Native Hawaiian/Other Pacific Islander, 0.4% Other, 1.5% Hispanic of any race (2010); Average household size: 2.05 (2010); Median age: 48.1 (2010); Males per 100 females: 102.3 (2010); Marriage status: 21.8% never married, 55.6% now married, 11.3% widowed, 11.3% divorced (2006-2010 5-year est.); Foreign born: 0.0% (2006-2010 5-year est.); Ancestry (includes multiple ancestries): 23.9% English, 18.8% Italian, 17.9% Polish, 15.8% Irish, 15.5% German (2006-2010 5-year est.).
Economy: Single-family building permits issued: 0 (2011); Multi-family building permits issued: 0 (2011); Employment by occupation: 9.8% management, 5.2% professional, 15.7% services, 12.4% sales, 0.0% farming, 16.3% construction, 10.5% production (2006-2010 5-year est.).

Income: Per capita income: $20,908 (2006-2010 5-year est.); Median household income: $39,375 (2006-2010 5-year est.); Average household income: $45,943 (2006-2010 5-year est.); Percent of households with income of $100,000 or more: 6.6% (2006-2010 5-year est.); Poverty rate: 12.5% (2006-2010 5-year est.).
Education: Percent of population age 25 and over with: High school diploma (including GED) or higher: 78.0% (2006-2010 5-year est.); Bachelor's degree or higher: 13.5% (2006-2010 5-year est.); Master's degree or higher: 3.1% (2006-2010 5-year est.).
Housing: Homeownership rate: 84.6% (2010); Median home value: $110,000 (2006-2010 5-year est.); Median contract rent: $656 per month (2006-2010 5-year est.); Median year structure built: 1971 (2006-2010 5-year est.).
Transportation: Commute to work: 96.4% car, 0.0% public transportation, 0.0% walk, 1.4% work from home (2006-2010 5-year est.); Travel time to work: 34.8% less than 15 minutes, 34.1% 15 to 30 minutes, 18.1% 30 to 45 minutes, 6.5% 45 to 60 minutes, 6.5% 60 minutes or more (2006-2010 5-year est.)

Tioga County

Located in northern Pennsylvania; bounded on the north by New York; drained by the Tioga River. Covers a land area of 1,133.788 square miles, a water area of 3.178 square miles, and is located in the Eastern Time Zone at 41.77° N. Lat., 77.26° W. Long. The county was founded in 1804. County seat is Wellsboro.

Weather Station: Wellsboro 4 SSE   Elevation: 1,859 feet

	Jan	Feb	Mar	Apr	May	Jun	Jul	Aug	Sep	Oct	Nov	Dec
High	30	33	41	55	66	73	77	76	69	58	47	34
Low	14	15	21	33	42	51	56	55	47	37	30	19
Precip	1.9	1.9	2.9	2.9	3.1	4.4	3.8	3.4	3.3	2.8	2.9	2.4
Snow	12.0	12.2	13.8	3.2	0.1	0.0	0.0	0.0	0.0	0.6	4.3	10.6

High and Low temperatures in degrees Fahrenheit; Precipitation and Snow in inches

Population: 41,126 (1990); 41,373 (2000); 41,981 (2010); Race: 97.3% White, 0.8% Black, 0.4% Asian, 0.2% American Indian/Alaska Native, 0.0% Native Hawaiian/Other Pacific Islander, 1.3% Other, 1.0% Hispanic of any race (2010); Density: 37.0 persons per square mile (2010); Average household size: 2.39 (2010); Median age: 42.4 (2010); Males per 100 females: 96.1 (2010).
Religion: Six largest groups: 8.4% Methodist/Pietist, 7.1% Catholicism, 4.3% Non-Denominational, 3.9% Baptist, 1.6% Pentecostal, 1.6% Lutheran (2010)
Economy: Unemployment rate: 7.6% (August 2012); Total civilian labor force: 23,484 (August 2012); Leading industries: 22.9% manufacturing; 19.3% health care and social assistance; 17.8% retail trade (2010); Farms: 1,011 totaling 184,108 acres (2007); Companies that employ 500 or more persons: 0 (2010); Companies that employ 100 to 499 persons: 16 (2010); Companies that employ less than 100 persons: 844 (2010); Black-owned businesses: n/a (2007); Hispanic-owned businesses: n/a (2007); Asian-owned businesses: n/a (2007); Women-owned businesses: 743 (2007); Retail sales per capita: $10,503 (2010). Single-family building permits issued: 78 (2011); Multi-family building permits issued: 2 (2011).
Income: Per capita income: $20,358 (2006-2010 5-year est.); Median household income: $40,338 (2006-2010 5-year est.); Average household income: $49,379 (2006-2010 5-year est.); Percent of households with income of $100,000 or more: 8.8% (2006-2010 5-year est.); Poverty rate: 15.8% (2006-2010 5-year est.); Bankruptcy rate: 1.67% (2011).
Education: Percent of population age 25 and over with: High school diploma (including GED) or higher: 87.1% (2006-2010 5-year est.); Bachelor's degree or higher: 17.7% (2006-2010 5-year est.); Master's degree or higher: 6.7% (2006-2010 5-year est.).
Housing: Homeownership rate: 74.6% (2010); Median home value: $105,700 (2006-2010 5-year est.); Median contract rent: $417 per month (2006-2010 5-year est.); Median year structure built: 1968 (2006-2010 5-year est.)
Health: Birth rate: 99.7 per 10,000 population (2011); Death rate: 104.4 per 10,000 population (2011); Age-adjusted cancer mortality rate: 169.5 deaths per 100,000 population (2009); Number of physicians: 10.2 per 10,000 population (2010); Hospital beds: 20.3 per 10,000 population (2008); Hospital admissions: 630.8 per 10,000 population (2008).
Environment: Air Quality Index: 92.3% good, 7.7% moderate, 0.0% unhealthy for sensitive individuals, 0.0% unhealthy (percent of days in 2011)

Elections: 2012 Presidential election results: 31.7% Obama, 66.5% Romney

National and State Parks: Hills Creek State Park; Leonard Harrison State Park; Tioga State Forest

Additional Information Contacts

Tioga County Government . . . . (570) 723-8191
http://www.tiogacountypa.us

Tioga County Communities

ARNOT (CDP). Covers a land area of 1.026 square miles and a water area of 0.011 square miles. Located at 41.66° N. Lat; 77.12° W. Long. Elevation is 1,690 feet.

Population: n/a (1990); n/a (2000); 332 (2010); Density: 323.5 persons per square mile (2010); Race: 100.0% White, 0.0% Black, 0.0% Asian, 0.0% American Indian/Alaska Native, 0.0% Native Hawaiian/Other Pacific Islander, 0.0% Other, 0.0% Hispanic of any race (2010); Average household size: 2.35 (2010); Median age: 48.4 (2010); Males per 100 females: 97.6 (2010); Marriage status: 25.9% never married, 55.5% now married, 6.1% widowed, 12.6% divorced (2006-2010 5-year est.); Foreign born: 0.9% (2006-2010 5-year est.); Ancestry (includes multiple ancestries): 33.2% German, 17.2% English, 12.3% Polish, 7.1% Scottish, 6.5% Irish (2006-2010 5-year est.).

Economy: Employment by occupation: 0.0% management, 2.1% professional, 9.7% services, 20.8% sales, 1.4% farming, 9.0% construction, 14.6% production (2006-2010 5-year est.).

Income: Per capita income: $18,676 (2006-2010 5-year est.); Median household income: $42,833 (2006-2010 5-year est.); Average household income: $50,035 (2006-2010 5-year est.); Percent of households with income of $100,000 or more: 10.6% (2006-2010 5-year est.); Poverty rate: 7.6% (2006-2010 5-year est.).

Education: Percent of population age 25 and over with: High school diploma (including GED) or higher: 84.0% (2006-2010 5-year est.); Bachelor's degree or higher: 13.1% (2006-2010 5-year est.); Master's degree or higher: 0.0% (2006-2010 5-year est.).

Housing: Homeownership rate: 91.5% (2010); Median home value: $80,000 (2006-2010 5-year est.); Median contract rent: $514 per month (2006-2010 5-year est.); Median year structure built: before 1940 (2006-2010 5-year est.).

Transportation: Commute to work: 88.7% car, 0.0% public transportation, 9.2% walk, 2.1% work from home (2006-2010 5-year est.); Travel time to work: 41.3% less than 15 minutes, 50.0% 15 to 30 minutes, 6.5% 30 to 45 minutes, 0.0% 45 to 60 minutes, 2.2% 60 minutes or more (2006-2010 5-year est.)

BLOSS (township). Covers a land area of 23.434 square miles and a water area of 0.088 square miles. Located at 41.67° N. Lat; 77.14° W. Long.

History: Settled c.1802.

Population: 388 (1990); 354 (2000); 353 (2010); Density: 15.1 persons per square mile (2010); Race: 100.0% White, 0.0% Black, 0.0% Asian, 0.0% American Indian/Alaska Native, 0.0% Native Hawaiian/Other Pacific Islander, 0.0% Other, 0.0% Hispanic of any race (2010); Average household size: 2.35 (2010); Median age: 48.2 (2010); Males per 100 females: 98.3 (2010); Marriage status: 26.0% never married, 57.4% now married, 5.4% widowed, 11.2% divorced (2006-2010 5-year est.); Foreign born: 0.8% (2006-2010 5-year est.); Ancestry (includes multiple ancestries): 37.8% German, 18.6% English, 14.5% Polish, 6.3% Scottish, 5.8% Irish (2006-2010 5-year est.).

Economy: Single-family building permits issued: 0 (2011); Multi-family building permits issued: 0 (2011); Employment by occupation: 5.4% management, 1.8% professional, 9.6% services, 20.5% sales, 3.0% farming, 7.8% construction, 12.7% production (2006-2010 5-year est.).

Income: Per capita income: $19,308 (2006-2010 5-year est.); Median household income: $43,333 (2006-2010 5-year est.); Average household income: $50,990 (2006-2010 5-year est.); Percent of households with income of $100,000 or more: 9.5% (2006-2010 5-year est.); Poverty rate: 6.7% (2006-2010 5-year est.).

Education: Percent of population age 25 and over with: High school diploma (including GED) or higher: 86.0% (2006-2010 5-year est.); Bachelor's degree or higher: 13.1% (2006-2010 5-year est.); Master's degree or higher: 0.0% (2006-2010 5-year est.).

Housing: Homeownership rate: 92.0% (2010); Median home value: $82,800 (2006-2010 5-year est.); Median contract rent: $514 per month

(2006-2010 5-year est.); Median year structure built: 1954 (2006-2010 5-year est.).

Transportation: Commute to work: 90.2% car, 0.0% public transportation, 8.0% walk, 1.8% work from home (2006-2010 5-year est.); Travel time to work: 35.6% less than 15 minutes, 51.2% 15 to 30 minutes, 11.3% 30 to 45 minutes, 0.0% 45 to 60 minutes, 1.9% 60 minutes or more (2006-2010 5-year est.)

BLOSSBURG (borough). Covers a land area of 4.646 square miles and a water area of 0 square miles. Located at 41.68° N. Lat; 77.07° W. Long. Elevation is 1,339 feet.

Population: 1,571 (1990); 1,480 (2000); 1,538 (2010); Density: 331.0 persons per square mile (2010); Race: 98.6% White, 0.1% Black, 0.4% Asian, 0.4% American Indian/Alaska Native, 0.0% Native Hawaiian/Other Pacific Islander, 0.5% Other, 1.3% Hispanic of any race (2010); Average household size: 2.38 (2010); Median age: 40.4 (2010); Males per 100 females: 100.8 (2010); Marriage status: 23.1% never married, 49.9% now married, 11.2% widowed, 15.8% divorced (2006-2010 5-year est.); Foreign born: 1.7% (2006-2010 5-year est.); Ancestry (includes multiple ancestries): 19.1% Polish, 17.5% English, 16.8% German, 12.1% Irish, 8.3% American (2006-2010 5-year est.).

Economy: Single-family building permits issued: 0 (2011); Multi-family building permits issued: 0 (2011); Employment by occupation: 3.4% management, 0.9% professional, 15.2% services, 15.0% sales, 3.3% farming, 14.6% construction, 9.5% production (2006-2010 5-year est.).

Income: Per capita income: $20,295 (2006-2010 5-year est.); Median household income: $34,924 (2006-2010 5-year est.); Average household income: $45,144 (2006-2010 5-year est.); Percent of households with income of $100,000 or more: 6.2% (2006-2010 5-year est.); Poverty rate: 12.4% (2006-2010 5-year est.).

Education: Percent of population age 25 and over with: High school diploma (including GED) or higher: 86.8% (2006-2010 5-year est.); Bachelor's degree or higher: 18.9% (2006-2010 5-year est.); Master's degree or higher: 6.9% (2006-2010 5-year est.).

School District(s)

Southern Tioga SD (KG-12)
2010-11 Enrollment: 1,994 . . . . (570) 638-2183

Housing: Homeownership rate: 67.2% (2010); Median home value: $82,100 (2006-2010 5-year est.); Median contract rent: $344 per month (2006-2010 5-year est.); Median year structure built: 1957 (2006-2010 5-year est.).

Transportation: Commute to work: 91.5% car, 0.0% public transportation, 6.1% walk, 1.3% work from home (2006-2010 5-year est.); Travel time to work: 42.6% less than 15 minutes, 36.7% 15 to 30 minutes, 10.6% 30 to 45 minutes, 5.1% 45 to 60 minutes, 5.0% 60 minutes or more (2006-2010 5-year est.)

Additional Information Contacts

Mansfield Chamber of Commerce, Inc. . . . . (570) 662-3442
http://www.mansfield.org

BROOKFIELD (township). Covers a land area of 31.773 square miles and a water area of 0 square miles. Located at 41.97° N. Lat; 77.55° W. Long. Elevation is 1,913 feet.

Population: 432 (1990); 443 (2000); 421 (2010); Density: 13.3 persons per square mile (2010); Race: 97.1% White, 0.2% Black, 0.0% Asian, 0.0% American Indian/Alaska Native, 0.0% Native Hawaiian/Other Pacific Islander, 2.7% Other, 2.6% Hispanic of any race (2010); Average household size: 2.43 (2010); Median age: 48.3 (2010); Males per 100 females: 109.5 (2010); Marriage status: 16.4% never married, 72.0% now married, 4.6% widowed, 6.9% divorced (2006-2010 5-year est.); Foreign born: 0.0% (2006-2010 5-year est.); Ancestry (includes multiple ancestries): 20.0% English, 17.1% German, 16.1% Irish, 9.9% American, 4.3% Scottish (2006-2010 5-year est.).

Economy: Employment by occupation: 9.6% management, 1.1% professional, 5.3% services, 20.7% sales, 8.0% farming, 16.0% construction, 17.0% production (2006-2010 5-year est.).

Income: Per capita income: $25,144 (2006-2010 5-year est.); Median household income: $41,905 (2006-2010 5-year est.); Average household income: $63,133 (2006-2010 5-year est.); Percent of households with income of $100,000 or more: 10.8% (2006-2010 5-year est.); Poverty rate: 3.8% (2006-2010 5-year est.).

Education: Percent of population age 25 and over with: High school diploma (including GED) or higher: 84.9% (2006-2010 5-year est.); Bachelor's degree or higher: 13.1% (2006-2010 5-year est.); Master's degree or higher: 4.6% (2006-2010 5-year est.).

Housing: Homeownership rate: 82.7% (2010); Median home value: $87,900 (2006-2010 5-year est.); Median contract rent: $381 per month (2006-2010 5-year est.); Median year structure built: 1967 (2006-2010 5-year est.).

Transportation: Commute to work: 88.0% car, 0.0% public transportation, 10.4% walk, 1.6% work from home (2006-2010 5-year est.); Travel time to work: 25.0% less than 15 minutes, 35.0% 15 to 30 minutes, 22.8% 30 to 45 minutes, 6.7% 45 to 60 minutes, 10.6% 60 minutes or more (2006-2010 5-year est.)

CHARLESTON (township). Covers a land area of 52.182 square miles and a water area of 0.341 square miles. Located at 41.74° N. Lat; 77.22° W. Long. Elevation is 1,391 feet.

Population: 2,957 (1990); 3,233 (2000); 3,360 (2010); Density: 64.4 persons per square mile (2010); Race: 98.0% White, 0.4% Black, 0.4% Asian, 0.2% American Indian/Alaska Native, 0.0% Native Hawaiian/Other Pacific Islander, 1.0% Other, 1.3% Hispanic of any race (2010); Average household size: 2.41 (2010); Median age: 45.2 (2010); Males per 100 females: 95.5 (2010); Marriage status: 14.6% never married, 67.6% now married, 12.0% widowed, 5.8% divorced (2006-2010 5-year est.); Foreign born: 0.4% (2006-2010 5-year est.); Ancestry (includes multiple ancestries): 34.7% German, 12.6% Irish, 11.9% English, 9.3% American, 7.8% Italian (2006-2010 5-year est.).

Economy: Single-family building permits issued: 19 (2011); Multi-family building permits issued: 0 (2011); Employment by occupation: 10.7% management, 4.3% professional, 6.9% services, 19.9% sales, 4.7% farming, 8.5% construction, 6.5% production (2006-2010 5-year est.).

Income: Per capita income: $24,528 (2006-2010 5-year est.); Median household income: $52,143 (2006-2010 5-year est.); Average household income: $59,562 (2006-2010 5-year est.); Percent of households with income of $100,000 or more: 12.3% (2006-2010 5-year est.); Poverty rate: 5.3% (2006-2010 5-year est.).

Education: Percent of population age 25 and over with: High school diploma (including GED) or higher: 92.6% (2006-2010 5-year est.); Bachelor's degree or higher: 28.8% (2006-2010 5-year est.); Master's degree or higher: 7.4% (2006-2010 5-year est.).

Housing: Homeownership rate: 81.9% (2010); Median home value: $141,800 (2006-2010 5-year est.); Median contract rent: $538 per month (2006-2010 5-year est.); Median year structure built: 1980 (2006-2010 5-year est.).

Transportation: Commute to work: 96.6% car, 0.9% public transportation, 0.0% walk, 2.5% work from home (2006-2010 5-year est.); Travel time to work: 45.8% less than 15 minutes, 38.6% 15 to 30 minutes, 5.7% 30 to 45 minutes, 4.0% 45 to 60 minutes, 5.9% 60 minutes or more (2006-2010 5-year est.)

Additional Information Contacts
Wellsboro Area Chamber of Commerce . . . . (570) 724-1926
http://www.wellsboropa.com

CHATHAM (township). Covers a land area of 35.163 square miles and a water area of 0.036 square miles. Located at 41.87° N. Lat; 77.42° W. Long.

Population: 607 (1990); 587 (2000); 588 (2010); Density: 16.7 persons per square mile (2010); Race: 97.4% White, 0.5% Black, 0.3% Asian, 0.5% American Indian/Alaska Native, 0.0% Native Hawaiian/Other Pacific Islander, 1.3% Other, 1.7% Hispanic of any race (2010); Average household size: 2.36 (2010); Median age: 49.0 (2010); Males per 100 females: 100.0 (2010); Marriage status: 15.9% never married, 69.5% now married, 6.3% widowed, 8.4% divorced (2006-2010 5-year est.); Foreign born: 0.0% (2006-2010 5-year est.); Ancestry (includes multiple ancestries): 27.0% German, 19.0% English, 13.5% American, 11.1% French, 8.8% Irish (2006-2010 5-year est.).

Economy: Single-family building permits issued: 0 (2011); Multi-family building permits issued: 0 (2011); Employment by occupation: 13.6% management, 1.9% professional, 5.7% services, 12.5% sales, 2.3% farming, 25.3% construction, 9.4% production (2006-2010 5-year est.).

Income: Per capita income: $22,684 (2006-2010 5-year est.); Median household income: $39,375 (2006-2010 5-year est.); Average household income: $58,771 (2006-2010 5-year est.); Percent of households with income of $100,000 or more: 9.3% (2006-2010 5-year est.); Poverty rate: 15.2% (2006-2010 5-year est.).

Education: Percent of population age 25 and over with: High school diploma (including GED) or higher: 83.8% (2006-2010 5-year est.); Bachelor's degree or higher: 12.7% (2006-2010 5-year est.); Master's degree or higher: 4.0% (2006-2010 5-year est.).

Housing: Homeownership rate: 91.2% (2010); Median home value: $114,000 (2006-2010 5-year est.); Median contract rent: $365 per month (2006-2010 5-year est.); Median year structure built: 1979 (2006-2010 5-year est.).

Transportation: Commute to work: 83.8% car, 1.1% public transportation, 1.5% walk, 13.6% work from home (2006-2010 5-year est.); Travel time to work: 12.7% less than 15 minutes, 55.9% 15 to 30 minutes, 22.3% 30 to 45 minutes, 4.8% 45 to 60 minutes, 4.4% 60 minutes or more (2006-2010 5-year est.)

CLYMER (township). Covers a land area of 33.866 square miles and a water area of 0.158 square miles. Located at 41.84° N. Lat; 77.54° W. Long. Elevation is 2,051 feet.

Population: 597 (1990); 597 (2000); 581 (2010); Density: 17.2 persons per square mile (2010); Race: 99.7% White, 0.2% Black, 0.0% Asian, 0.2% American Indian/Alaska Native, 0.0% Native Hawaiian/Other Pacific Islander, 0.0% Other, 0.2% Hispanic of any race (2010); Average household size: 2.40 (2010); Median age: 47.6 (2010); Males per 100 females: 106.0 (2010); Marriage status: 21.3% never married, 63.8% now married, 4.5% widowed, 10.3% divorced (2006-2010 5-year est.); Foreign born: 0.5% (2006-2010 5-year est.); Ancestry (includes multiple ancestries): 23.1% German, 12.9% English, 11.6% American, 11.1% Irish, 4.2% Scottish (2006-2010 5-year est.).

Economy: Single-family building permits issued: 0 (2011); Multi-family building permits issued: 0 (2011); Employment by occupation: 1.9% management, 0.0% professional, 5.1% services, 5.1% sales, 0.0% farming, 28.2% construction, 21.8% production (2006-2010 5-year est.).

Income: Per capita income: $18,280 (2006-2010 5-year est.); Median household income: $36,900 (2006-2010 5-year est.); Average household income: $43,779 (2006-2010 5-year est.); Percent of households with income of $100,000 or more: 14.4% (2006-2010 5-year est.); Poverty rate: 25.4% (2006-2010 5-year est.).

Education: Percent of population age 25 and over with: High school diploma (including GED) or higher: 81.4% (2006-2010 5-year est.); Bachelor's degree or higher: 10.3% (2006-2010 5-year est.); Master's degree or higher: 2.4% (2006-2010 5-year est.).

Housing: Homeownership rate: 78.1% (2010); Median home value: $77,700 (2006-2010 5-year est.); Median contract rent: $420 per month (2006-2010 5-year est.); Median year structure built: 1967 (2006-2010 5-year est.).

Transportation: Commute to work: 96.2% car, 0.0% public transportation, 0.0% walk, 1.9% work from home (2006-2010 5-year est.); Travel time to work: 20.7% less than 15 minutes, 49.0% 15 to 30 minutes, 25.5% 30 to 45 minutes, 1.4% 45 to 60 minutes, 3.4% 60 minutes or more (2006-2010 5-year est.)

COVINGTON (township). Covers a land area of 36.380 square miles and a water area of 0.037 square miles. Located at 41.73° N. Lat; 77.10° W. Long. Elevation is 1,194 feet.

History: Formerly a borough.

Population: 918 (1990); 1,047 (2000); 1,022 (2010); Density: 28.1 persons per square mile (2010); Race: 98.6% White, 0.4% Black, 0.3% Asian, 0.2% American Indian/Alaska Native, 0.0% Native Hawaiian/Other Pacific Islander, 0.5% Other, 0.6% Hispanic of any race (2010); Average household size: 2.57 (2010); Median age: 44.6 (2010); Males per 100 females: 102.4 (2010); Marriage status: 21.4% never married, 66.7% now married, 5.1% widowed, 6.8% divorced (2006-2010 5-year est.); Foreign born: 0.0% (2006-2010 5-year est.); Ancestry (includes multiple ancestries): 26.8% German, 19.1% Irish, 16.5% English, 10.3% Italian, 7.4% Polish (2006-2010 5-year est.).

Economy: Single-family building permits issued: 1 (2011); Multi-family building permits issued: 0 (2011); Employment by occupation: 10.6% management, 2.9% professional, 11.6% services, 15.1% sales, 3.3% farming, 14.5% construction, 11.0% production (2006-2010 5-year est.).

Income: Per capita income: $21,079 (2006-2010 5-year est.); Median household income: $43,333 (2006-2010 5-year est.); Average household income: $54,354 (2006-2010 5-year est.); Percent of households with income of $100,000 or more: 11.7% (2006-2010 5-year est.); Poverty rate: 15.0% (2006-2010 5-year est.).

Education: Percent of population age 25 and over with: High school diploma (including GED) or higher: 87.4% (2006-2010 5-year est.); Bachelor's degree or higher: 13.0% (2006-2010 5-year est.); Master's degree or higher: 5.3% (2006-2010 5-year est.).

Housing: Homeownership rate: 83.4% (2010); Median home value: $121,700 (2006-2010 5-year est.); Median contract rent: $454 per month

(2006-2010 5-year est.); Median year structure built: 1973 (2006-2010 5-year est.).

Transportation: Commute to work: 85.3% car, 0.0% public transportation, 4.2% walk, 8.8% work from home (2006-2010 5-year est.); Travel time to work: 44.7% less than 15 minutes, 35.3% 15 to 30 minutes, 10.6% 30 to 45 minutes, 4.1% 45 to 60 minutes, 5.3% 60 minutes or more (2006-2010 5-year est.)

Additional Information Contacts

Mansfield Chamber of Commerce, Inc.................. (570) 662-3442
   http://www.mansfield.org

DEERFIELD (township). Covers a land area of 29.243 square miles and a water area of 0 square miles. Located at 41.95° N. Lat; 77.42° W. Long.

Population: 647 (1990); 659 (2000); 662 (2010); Density: 22.6 persons per square mile (2010); Race: 97.4% White, 0.5% Black, 0.6% Asian, 0.0% American Indian/Alaska Native, 0.0% Native Hawaiian/Other Pacific Islander, 1.5% Other, 1.1% Hispanic of any race (2010); Average household size: 2.58 (2010); Median age: 45.1 (2010); Males per 100 females: 107.5 (2010); Marriage status: 23.0% never married, 64.3% now married, 4.4% widowed, 8.3% divorced (2006-2010 5-year est.); Foreign born: 0.5% (2006-2010 5-year est.); Ancestry (includes multiple ancestries): 30.8% German, 16.3% English, 8.0% Irish, 7.3% American, 5.6% Polish (2006-2010 5-year est.).

Economy: Single-family building permits issued: 2 (2011); Multi-family building permits issued: 0 (2011); Employment by occupation: 13.1% management, 4.2% professional, 1.7% services, 16.4% sales, 0.8% farming, 16.1% construction, 9.7% production (2006-2010 5-year est.).

Income: Per capita income: $22,856 (2006-2010 5-year est.); Median household income: $44,327 (2006-2010 5-year est.); Average household income: $53,719 (2006-2010 5-year est.); Percent of households with income of $100,000 or more: 13.6% (2006-2010 5-year est.); Poverty rate: 10.0% (2006-2010 5-year est.).

Education: Percent of population age 25 and over with: High school diploma (including GED) or higher: 93.0% (2006-2010 5-year est.); Bachelor's degree or higher: 19.3% (2006-2010 5-year est.); Master's degree or higher: 7.4% (2006-2010 5-year est.).

Housing: Homeownership rate: 81.7% (2010); Median home value: $138,800 (2006-2010 5-year est.); Median contract rent: $338 per month (2006-2010 5-year est.); Median year structure built: 1966 (2006-2010 5-year est.).

Transportation: Commute to work: 85.6% car, 0.0% public transportation, 8.8% walk, 5.6% work from home (2006-2010 5-year est.); Travel time to work: 32.3% less than 15 minutes, 38.2% 15 to 30 minutes, 23.0% 30 to 45 minutes, 5.6% 45 to 60 minutes, 0.9% 60 minutes or more (2006-2010 5-year est.)

DELMAR (township). Covers a land area of 80.728 square miles and a water area of 0.169 square miles. Located at 41.72° N. Lat; 77.36° W. Long.

Population: 3,048 (1990); 2,893 (2000); 2,856 (2010); Density: 35.4 persons per square mile (2010); Race: 97.8% White, 0.6% Black, 0.4% Asian, 0.4% American Indian/Alaska Native, 0.0% Native Hawaiian/Other Pacific Islander, 0.8% Other, 1.0% Hispanic of any race (2010); Average household size: 2.48 (2010); Median age: 47.1 (2010); Males per 100 females: 102.7 (2010); Marriage status: 18.3% never married, 68.6% now married, 4.8% widowed, 8.3% divorced (2006-2010 5-year est.); Foreign born: 0.4% (2006-2010 5-year est.); Ancestry (includes multiple ancestries): 30.9% German, 17.0% English, 11.4% Irish, 7.8% American, 6.6% Italian (2006-2010 5-year est.).

Economy: Single-family building permits issued: 7 (2011); Multi-family building permits issued: 0 (2011); Employment by occupation: 8.7% management, 2.0% professional, 8.7% services, 16.7% sales, 6.2% farming, 15.2% construction, 7.2% production (2006-2010 5-year est.).

Income: Per capita income: $24,031 (2006-2010 5-year est.); Median household income: $55,127 (2006-2010 5-year est.); Average household income: $57,769 (2006-2010 5-year est.); Percent of households with income of $100,000 or more: 7.5% (2006-2010 5-year est.); Poverty rate: 7.6% (2006-2010 5-year est.).

Education: Percent of population age 25 and over with: High school diploma (including GED) or higher: 88.1% (2006-2010 5-year est.); Bachelor's degree or higher: 19.7% (2006-2010 5-year est.); Master's degree or higher: 5.2% (2006-2010 5-year est.).

Housing: Homeownership rate: 84.7% (2010); Median home value: $125,400 (2006-2010 5-year est.); Median contract rent: $523 per month

(2006-2010 5-year est.); Median year structure built: 1970 (2006-2010 5-year est.).

Transportation: Commute to work: 83.0% car, 0.5% public transportation, 4.3% walk, 12.2% work from home (2006-2010 5-year est.); Travel time to work: 55.8% less than 15 minutes, 23.1% 15 to 30 minutes, 14.9% 30 to 45 minutes, 2.3% 45 to 60 minutes, 3.8% 60 minutes or more (2006-2010 5-year est.)

Additional Information Contacts

Mansfield Chamber of Commerce, Inc.................. (570) 662-3442
   http://www.mansfield.org

DUNCAN (township). Covers a land area of 19.822 square miles and a water area of 0 square miles. Located at 41.65° N. Lat; 77.25° W. Long. Elevation is 1,844 feet.

Population: 248 (1990); 213 (2000); 208 (2010); Density: 10.5 persons per square mile (2010); Race: 99.0% White, 0.0% Black, 0.0% Asian, 1.0% American Indian/Alaska Native, 0.0% Native Hawaiian/Other Pacific Islander, 0.0% Other, 1.0% Hispanic of any race (2010); Average household size: 2.14 (2010); Median age: 47.4 (2010); Males per 100 females: 108.0 (2010); Marriage status: 26.6% never married, 45.3% now married, 13.3% widowed, 14.8% divorced (2006-2010 5-year est.); Foreign born: 1.2% (2006-2010 5-year est.); Ancestry (includes multiple ancestries): 17.4% German, 15.1% Polish, 14.5% American, 14.0% Irish, 7.0% English (2006-2010 5-year est.).

Economy: Employment by occupation: 7.7% management, 0.0% professional, 5.1% services, 12.8% sales, 0.0% farming, 11.5% construction, 5.1% production (2006-2010 5-year est.).

Income: Per capita income: $15,962 (2006-2010 5-year est.); Median household income: $36,250 (2006-2010 5-year est.); Average household income: $35,173 (2006-2010 5-year est.); Percent of households with income of $100,000 or more: 1.3% (2006-2010 5-year est.); Poverty rate: 16.9% (2006-2010 5-year est.).

Education: Percent of population age 25 and over with: High school diploma (including GED) or higher: 82.4% (2006-2010 5-year est.); Bachelor's degree or higher: 7.6% (2006-2010 5-year est.); Master's degree or higher: 0.0% (2006-2010 5-year est.).

Housing: Homeownership rate: 82.5% (2010); Median home value: $55,000 (2006-2010 5-year est.); Median contract rent: $413 per month (2006-2010 5-year est.); Median year structure built: before 1940 (2006-2010 5-year est.).

Transportation: Commute to work: 94.9% car, 0.0% public transportation, 2.6% walk, 2.6% work from home (2006-2010 5-year est.); Travel time to work: 28.9% less than 15 minutes, 44.7% 15 to 30 minutes, 3.9% 30 to 45 minutes, 15.8% 45 to 60 minutes, 6.6% 60 minutes or more (2006-2010 5-year est.)

ELK (township). Covers a land area of 73.084 square miles and a water area of 0.109 square miles. Located at 41.63° N. Lat; 77.53° W. Long.

History: Incorporated 1850.

Population: 42 (1990); 51 (2000); 49 (2010); Density: 0.7 persons per square mile (2010); Race: 100.0% White, 0.0% Black, 0.0% Asian, 0.0% American Indian/Alaska Native, 0.0% Native Hawaiian/Other Pacific Islander, 0.0% Other, 0.0% Hispanic of any race (2010); Average household size: 1.88 (2010); Median age: 56.8 (2010); Males per 100 females: 104.2 (2010); Marriage status: 18.2% never married, 69.7% now married, 12.1% widowed, 0.0% divorced (2006-2010 5-year est.); Foreign born: 0.0% (2006-2010 5-year est.); Ancestry (includes multiple ancestries): 30.3% German, 12.1% Scottish, 12.1% Irish, 12.1% American, 9.1% English (2006-2010 5-year est.).

Economy: Single-family building permits issued: 0 (2011); Multi-family building permits issued: 0 (2011); Employment by occupation: 23.5% management, 0.0% professional, 17.6% services, 17.6% sales, 0.0% farming, 23.5% construction, 0.0% production (2006-2010 5-year est.).

Income: Per capita income: $19,912 (2006-2010 5-year est.); Median household income: $38,333 (2006-2010 5-year est.); Average household income: $28,709 (2006-2010 5-year est.); Percent of households with income of $100,000 or more: n/a (2006-2010 5-year est.); Poverty rate: 18.2% (2006-2010 5-year est.).

Education: Percent of population age 25 and over with: High school diploma (including GED) or higher: 84.8% (2006-2010 5-year est.); Bachelor's degree or higher: 0.0% (2006-2010 5-year est.); Master's degree or higher: 0.0% (2006-2010 5-year est.).

Housing: Homeownership rate: 92.4% (2010); Median home value: $144,600 (2006-2010 5-year est.); Median contract rent: $456 per month

(2006-2010 5-year est.); Median year structure built: 1955 (2006-2010 5-year est.).

Transportation: Commute to work: 63.6% car, 0.0% public transportation, 0.0% walk, 36.4% work from home (2006-2010 5-year est.); Travel time to work: 0.0% less than 15 minutes, 71.4% 15 to 30 minutes, 28.6% 30 to 45 minutes, 0.0% 45 to 60 minutes, 0.0% 60 minutes or more (2006-2010 5-year est.)

ELKLAND (borough). Covers a land area of 2.445 square miles and a water area of 0 square miles. Located at 41.99° N. Lat; 77.32° W. Long. Elevation is 1,129 feet.

Population: 1,849 (1990); 1,786 (2000); 1,821 (2010); Density: 744.8 persons per square mile (2010); Race: 98.0% White, 0.3% Black, 0.1% Asian, 0.2% American Indian/Alaska Native, 0.0% Native Hawaiian/Other Pacific Islander, 1.4% Other, 0.9% Hispanic of any race (2010); Average household size: 2.33 (2010); Median age: 40.4 (2010); Males per 100 females: 92.1 (2010); Marriage status: 30.2% never married, 52.9% now married, 5.4% widowed, 11.5% divorced (2006-2010 5-year est.); Foreign born: 1.1% (2006-2010 5-year est.); Ancestry (includes multiple ancestries): 32.2% German, 14.7% English, 13.8% Irish, 9.9% Italian, 5.9% American (2006-2010 5-year est.).

Economy: Single-family building permits issued: 0 (2011); Multi-family building permits issued: 0 (2011); Employment by occupation: 8.3% management, 5.5% professional, 18.0% services, 10.4% sales, 1.5% farming, 5.8% construction, 10.2% production (2006-2010 5-year est.).

Income: Per capita income: $18,635 (2006-2010 5-year est.); Median household income: $36,683 (2006-2010 5-year est.); Average household income: $46,312 (2006-2010 5-year est.); Percent of households with income of $100,000 or more: 7.9% (2006-2010 5-year est.); Poverty rate: 24.0% (2006-2010 5-year est.).

Education: Percent of population age 25 and over with: High school diploma (including GED) or higher: 85.1% (2006-2010 5-year est.); Bachelor's degree or higher: 9.6% (2006-2010 5-year est.); Master's degree or higher: 4.8% (2006-2010 5-year est.).

School District(s)

Northern Tioga SD (KG-12)

    2010-11 Enrollment: 2,139 . . . . (814) 258-5642

Housing: Homeownership rate: 62.8% (2010); Median home value: $67,500 (2006-2010 5-year est.); Median contract rent: $354 per month (2006-2010 5-year est.); Median year structure built: 1949 (2006-2010 5-year est.).

Transportation: Commute to work: 88.0% car, 0.6% public transportation, 5.3% walk, 4.9% work from home (2006-2010 5-year est.); Travel time to work: 31.7% less than 15 minutes, 22.8% 15 to 30 minutes, 31.1% 30 to 45 minutes, 7.8% 45 to 60 minutes, 6.6% 60 minutes or more (2006-2010 5-year est.)

Additional Information Contacts

Elkland Area Chamber of Commerce . . . . (814) 258-5148
    http://www.elklandareacc.webs.com

FARMINGTON (township). Covers a land area of 31.735 square miles and a water area of 0 square miles. Located at 41.93° N. Lat; 77.27° W. Long.

Population: 644 (1990); 636 (2000); 637 (2010); Density: 20.1 persons per square mile (2010); Race: 98.4% White, 0.3% Black, 0.0% Asian, 0.0% American Indian/Alaska Native, 0.0% Native Hawaiian/Other Pacific Islander, 1.3% Other, 0.6% Hispanic of any race (2010); Average household size: 2.39 (2010); Median age: 45.9 (2010); Males per 100 females: 99.1 (2010); Marriage status: 16.7% never married, 61.3% now married, 11.9% widowed, 10.1% divorced (2006-2010 5-year est.); Foreign born: 1.8% (2006-2010 5-year est.); Ancestry (includes multiple ancestries): 25.9% German, 19.3% Irish, 15.5% English, 12.2% American, 7.5% Italian (2006-2010 5-year est.).

Economy: Single-family building permits issued: 0 (2011); Multi-family building permits issued: 0 (2011); Employment by occupation: 7.0% management, 5.0% professional, 16.0% services, 17.5% sales, 1.5% farming, 23.0% construction, 17.5% production (2006-2010 5-year est.).

Income: Per capita income: $22,167 (2006-2010 5-year est.); Median household income: $37,063 (2006-2010 5-year est.); Average household income: $47,258 (2006-2010 5-year est.); Percent of households with income of $100,000 or more: 5.6% (2006-2010 5-year est.); Poverty rate: 8.0% (2006-2010 5-year est.).

Education: Percent of population age 25 and over with: High school diploma (including GED) or higher: 78.3% (2006-2010 5-year est.);

Bachelor's degree or higher: 8.2% (2006-2010 5-year est.); Master's degree or higher: 3.7% (2006-2010 5-year est.).

Housing: Homeownership rate: 85.4% (2010); Median home value: $109,000 (2006-2010 5-year est.); Median contract rent: $381 per month (2006-2010 5-year est.); Median year structure built: 1972 (2006-2010 5-year est.).

Transportation: Commute to work: 91.0% car, 0.0% public transportation, 0.0% walk, 5.5% work from home (2006-2010 5-year est.); Travel time to work: 25.9% less than 15 minutes, 35.4% 15 to 30 minutes, 24.9% 30 to 45 minutes, 11.1% 45 to 60 minutes, 2.6% 60 minutes or more (2006-2010 5-year est.)

GAINES (township). Covers a land area of 48.632 square miles and a water area of 0.013 square miles. Located at 41.76° N. Lat; 77.56° W. Long. Elevation is 1,289 feet.

Population: 601 (1990); 553 (2000); 542 (2010); Density: 11.1 persons per square mile (2010); Race: 98.9% White, 0.0% Black, 0.0% Asian, 0.2% American Indian/Alaska Native, 0.2% Native Hawaiian/Other Pacific Islander, 0.7% Other, 0.6% Hispanic of any race (2010); Average household size: 2.14 (2010); Median age: 54.0 (2010); Males per 100 females: 97.1 (2010); Marriage status: 17.0% never married, 66.7% now married, 4.7% widowed, 11.6% divorced (2006-2010 5-year est.); Foreign born: 1.9% (2006-2010 5-year est.); Ancestry (includes multiple ancestries): 29.3% German, 17.0% English, 16.9% Irish, 10.2% Welsh, 7.8% Italian (2006-2010 5-year est.).

Economy: Single-family building permits issued: 3 (2011); Multi-family building permits issued: 0 (2011); Employment by occupation: 11.0% management, 1.6% professional, 6.5% services, 22.9% sales, 6.1% farming, 6.9% construction, 8.2% production (2006-2010 5-year est.).

Income: Per capita income: $19,770 (2006-2010 5-year est.); Median household income: $34,167 (2006-2010 5-year est.); Average household income: $40,384 (2006-2010 5-year est.); Percent of households with income of $100,000 or more: 4.6% (2006-2010 5-year est.); Poverty rate: 12.4% (2006-2010 5-year est.).

Education: Percent of population age 25 and over with: High school diploma (including GED) or higher: 84.7% (2006-2010 5-year est.); Bachelor's degree or higher: 6.9% (2006-2010 5-year est.); Master's degree or higher: 1.3% (2006-2010 5-year est.).

Housing: Homeownership rate: 80.2% (2010); Median home value: $92,700 (2006-2010 5-year est.); Median contract rent: $368 per month (2006-2010 5-year est.); Median year structure built: 1973 (2006-2010 5-year est.).

Safety: Violent crime rate: 0.0 per 10,000 population; Property crime rate: 477.9 per 10,000 population (2011).

Transportation: Commute to work: 88.6% car, 0.0% public transportation, 9.7% walk, 0.0% work from home (2006-2010 5-year est.); Travel time to work: 41.8% less than 15 minutes, 38.4% 15 to 30 minutes, 15.2% 30 to 45 minutes, 4.6% 45 to 60 minutes, 0.0% 60 minutes or more (2006-2010 5-year est.)

HAMILTON (township). Covers a land area of 11.008 square miles and a water area of 0.011 square miles. Located at 41.67° N. Lat; 77.04° W. Long.

Population: 496 (1990); 462 (2000); 499 (2010); Density: 45.3 persons per square mile (2010); Race: 98.2% White, 0.2% Black, 0.0% Asian, 0.6% American Indian/Alaska Native, 0.0% Native Hawaiian/Other Pacific Islander, 1.0% Other, 0.6% Hispanic of any race (2010); Average household size: 2.51 (2010); Median age: 41.4 (2010); Males per 100 females: 107.9 (2010); Marriage status: 23.8% never married, 60.3% now married, 0.5% widowed, 15.3% divorced (2006-2010 5-year est.); Foreign born: 0.6% (2006-2010 5-year est.); Ancestry (includes multiple ancestries): 34.6% German, 23.4% Polish, 14.6% Swedish, 14.0% American, 11.4% Irish (2006-2010 5-year est.).

Economy: Single-family building permits issued: 0 (2011); Multi-family building permits issued: 0 (2011); Employment by occupation: 6.1% management, 0.0% professional, 9.2% services, 26.8% sales, 0.9% farming, 13.2% construction, 18.9% production (2006-2010 5-year est.).

Income: Per capita income: $16,525 (2006-2010 5-year est.); Median household income: $38,750 (2006-2010 5-year est.); Average household income: $48,284 (2006-2010 5-year est.); Percent of households with income of $100,000 or more: 6.5% (2006-2010 5-year est.); Poverty rate: 13.0% (2006-2010 5-year est.).

Education: Percent of population age 25 and over with: High school diploma (including GED) or higher: 88.2% (2006-2010 5-year est.);

Bachelor's degree or higher: 7.7% (2006-2010 5-year est.); Master's degree or higher: 0.6% (2006-2010 5-year est.).
Housing: Homeownership rate: 74.1% (2010); Median home value: $83,500 (2006-2010 5-year est.); Median contract rent: $392 per month (2006-2010 5-year est.); Median year structure built: before 1940 (2006-2010 5-year est.).
Transportation: Commute to work: 95.1% car, 0.0% public transportation, 2.2% walk, 2.7% work from home (2006-2010 5-year est.); Travel time to work: 42.9% less than 15 minutes, 20.5% 15 to 30 minutes, 21.5% 30 to 45 minutes, 14.2% 45 to 60 minutes, 0.9% 60 minutes or more (2006-2010 5-year est.)

JACKSON (township). Covers a land area of 40.826 square miles and a water area of 0.028 square miles. Located at 41.95° N. Lat; 77.00° W. Long.
Population: 2,072 (1990); 2,054 (2000); 1,887 (2010); Density: 46.2 persons per square mile (2010); Race: 98.5% White, 0.2% Black, 0.3% Asian, 0.1% American Indian/Alaska Native, 0.0% Native Hawaiian/Other Pacific Islander, 0.9% Other, 0.6% Hispanic of any race (2010); Average household size: 2.51 (2010); Median age: 45.2 (2010); Males per 100 females: 101.4 (2010); Marriage status: 16.8% never married, 68.6% now married, 8.4% widowed, 6.2% divorced (2006-2010 5-year est.); Foreign born: 0.7% (2006-2010 5-year est.); Ancestry (includes multiple ancestries): 28.8% English, 21.9% German, 14.9% American, 10.3% Irish, 5.2% Polish (2006-2010 5-year est.).
Economy: Single-family building permits issued: 3 (2011); Multi-family building permits issued: 0 (2011); Employment by occupation: 7.7% management, 3.9% professional, 5.4% services, 24.0% sales, 1.2% farming, 11.8% construction, 9.5% production (2006-2010 5-year est.).
Income: Per capita income: $21,480 (2006-2010 5-year est.); Median household income: $50,536 (2006-2010 5-year est.); Average household income: $51,737 (2006-2010 5-year est.); Percent of households with income of $100,000 or more: 4.4% (2006-2010 5-year est.); Poverty rate: 9.1% (2006-2010 5-year est.).
Education: Percent of population age 25 and over with: High school diploma (including GED) or higher: 84.3% (2006-2010 5-year est.); Bachelor's degree or higher: 12.6% (2006-2010 5-year est.); Master's degree or higher: 7.5% (2006-2010 5-year est.).
Housing: Homeownership rate: 84.2% (2010); Median home value: $103,000 (2006-2010 5-year est.); Median contract rent: $422 per month (2006-2010 5-year est.); Median year structure built: 1966 (2006-2010 5-year est.).
Transportation: Commute to work: 88.7% car, 0.3% public transportation, 3.4% walk, 6.1% work from home (2006-2010 5-year est.); Travel time to work: 16.4% less than 15 minutes, 34.9% 15 to 30 minutes, 34.7% 30 to 45 minutes, 8.8% 45 to 60 minutes, 5.2% 60 minutes or more (2006-2010 5-year est.)
Additional Information Contacts
Mansfield Chamber of Commerce, Inc.. . . . . (570) 662-3442
    http://www.mansfield.org

KNOXVILLE (borough). Covers a land area of 0.457 square miles and a water area of 0 square miles. Located at 41.96° N. Lat; 77.44° W. Long. Elevation is 1,243 feet.
Population: 589 (1990); 617 (2000); 629 (2010); Density: 1,376.8 persons per square mile (2010); Race: 98.7% White, 0.0% Black, 0.2% Asian, 0.0% American Indian/Alaska Native, 0.0% Native Hawaiian/Other Pacific Islander, 1.1% Other, 0.0% Hispanic of any race (2010); Average household size: 2.57 (2010); Median age: 37.1 (2010); Males per 100 females: 104.2 (2010); Marriage status: 18.4% never married, 54.1% now married, 6.4% widowed, 21.0% divorced (2006-2010 5-year est.); Foreign born: 0.6% (2006-2010 5-year est.); Ancestry (includes multiple ancestries): 25.9% German, 18.9% English, 13.0% Irish, 9.9% American, 3.7% Scotch-Irish (2006-2010 5-year est.).
Economy: Single-family building permits issued: 1 (2011); Multi-family building permits issued: 2 (2011); Employment by occupation: 3.3% management, 4.4% professional, 7.7% services, 11.0% sales, 2.9% farming, 12.5% construction, 18.8% production (2006-2010 5-year est.).
Income: Per capita income: $16,551 (2006-2010 5-year est.); Median household income: $24,250 (2006-2010 5-year est.); Average household income: $37,043 (2006-2010 5-year est.); Percent of households with income of $100,000 or more: 3.0% (2006-2010 5-year est.); Poverty rate: 15.1% (2006-2010 5-year est.).
Education: Percent of population age 25 and over with: High school diploma (including GED) or higher: 92.3% (2006-2010 5-year est.);

Bachelor's degree or higher: 16.3% (2006-2010 5-year est.); Master's degree or higher: 3.6% (2006-2010 5-year est.).
Housing: Homeownership rate: 74.2% (2010); Median home value: $50,200 (2006-2010 5-year est.); Median contract rent: $325 per month (2006-2010 5-year est.); Median year structure built: before 1940 (2006-2010 5-year est.).
Transportation: Commute to work: 88.2% car, 0.0% public transportation, 6.3% walk, 4.8% work from home (2006-2010 5-year est.); Travel time to work: 31.7% less than 15 minutes, 12.0% 15 to 30 minutes, 24.7% 30 to 45 minutes, 24.7% 45 to 60 minutes, 6.9% 60 minutes or more (2006-2010 5-year est.)

LAWRENCE (township). Covers a land area of 34.280 square miles and a water area of 0 square miles. Located at 41.97° N. Lat; 77.14° W. Long.
Population: 1,519 (1990); 1,721 (2000); 1,718 (2010); Density: 50.1 persons per square mile (2010); Race: 98.0% White, 0.2% Black, 0.2% Asian, 0.1% American Indian/Alaska Native, 0.0% Native Hawaiian/Other Pacific Islander, 1.5% Other, 0.5% Hispanic of any race (2010); Average household size: 2.47 (2010); Median age: 44.1 (2010); Males per 100 females: 99.3 (2010); Marriage status: 24.3% never married, 61.9% now married, 5.2% widowed, 8.5% divorced (2006-2010 5-year est.); Foreign born: 0.2% (2006-2010 5-year est.); Ancestry (includes multiple ancestries): 27.9% German, 25.0% English, 11.4% Irish, 10.7% Italian, 7.6% Swedish (2006-2010 5-year est.).
Economy: Single-family building permits issued: 0 (2011); Multi-family building permits issued: 0 (2011); Employment by occupation: 17.4% management, 5.6% professional, 11.8% services, 16.5% sales, 1.6% farming, 8.7% construction, 14.4% production (2006-2010 5-year est.).
Income: Per capita income: $18,573 (2006-2010 5-year est.); Median household income: $36,466 (2006-2010 5-year est.); Average household income: $45,870 (2006-2010 5-year est.); Percent of households with income of $100,000 or more: 9.0% (2006-2010 5-year est.); Poverty rate: 11.8% (2006-2010 5-year est.).
Education: Percent of population age 25 and over with: High school diploma (including GED) or higher: 85.3% (2006-2010 5-year est.); Bachelor's degree or higher: 9.7% (2006-2010 5-year est.); Master's degree or higher: 2.9% (2006-2010 5-year est.).
Housing: Homeownership rate: 81.6% (2010); Median home value: $122,000 (2006-2010 5-year est.); Median contract rent: $315 per month (2006-2010 5-year est.); Median year structure built: 1980 (2006-2010 5-year est.).
Safety: Violent crime rate: 11.6 per 10,000 population; Property crime rate: 5.8 per 10,000 population (2011).
Transportation: Commute to work: 95.5% car, 0.0% public transportation, 0.9% walk, 3.6% work from home (2006-2010 5-year est.); Travel time to work: 28.2% less than 15 minutes, 23.0% 15 to 30 minutes, 39.0% 30 to 45 minutes, 5.4% 45 to 60 minutes, 4.5% 60 minutes or more (2006-2010 5-year est.)
Additional Information Contacts
Mansfield Chamber of Commerce, Inc.. . . . . (570) 662-3442
    http://www.mansfield.org

LAWRENCEVILLE (borough). Covers a land area of 0.583 square miles and a water area of 0 square miles. Located at 42.00° N. Lat; 77.13° W. Long. Elevation is 988 feet.
Population: 481 (1990); 627 (2000); 581 (2010); Density: 997.0 persons per square mile (2010); Race: 98.1% White, 0.5% Black, 0.0% Asian, 0.7% American Indian/Alaska Native, 0.0% Native Hawaiian/Other Pacific Islander, 0.7% Other, 1.0% Hispanic of any race (2010); Average household size: 2.27 (2010); Median age: 39.4 (2010); Males per 100 females: 86.8 (2010); Marriage status: 21.0% never married, 66.3% now married, 7.5% widowed, 5.1% divorced (2006-2010 5-year est.); Foreign born: 0.0% (2006-2010 5-year est.); Ancestry (includes multiple ancestries): 25.6% German, 15.0% English, 10.4% Irish, 6.1% Italian, 6.1% Polish (2006-2010 5-year est.).
Economy: Single-family building permits issued: 5 (2011); Multi-family building permits issued: 0 (2011); Employment by occupation: 2.1% management, 3.7% professional, 9.1% services, 16.8% sales, 3.4% farming, 7.3% construction, 11.0% production (2006-2010 5-year est.).
Income: Per capita income: $20,082 (2006-2010 5-year est.); Median household income: $42,361 (2006-2010 5-year est.); Average household income: $49,457 (2006-2010 5-year est.); Percent of households with income of $100,000 or more: 12.2% (2006-2010 5-year est.); Poverty rate: 23.0% (2006-2010 5-year est.).

Education: Percent of population age 25 and over with: High school diploma (including GED) or higher: 88.8% (2006-2010 5-year est.); Bachelor's degree or higher: 16.8% (2006-2010 5-year est.); Master's degree or higher: 1.6% (2006-2010 5-year est.).
Housing: Homeownership rate: 55.1% (2010); Median home value: $98,800 (2006-2010 5-year est.); Median contract rent: $426 per month (2006-2010 5-year est.); Median year structure built: 1976 (2006-2010 5-year est.).
Transportation: Commute to work: 96.6% car, 0.0% public transportation, 2.5% walk, 0.0% work from home (2006-2010 5-year est.); Travel time to work: 24.7% less than 15 minutes, 35.6% 15 to 30 minutes, 27.5% 30 to 45 minutes, 6.3% 45 to 60 minutes, 5.9% 60 minutes or more (2006-2010 5-year est.)

LIBERTY (borough). Covers a land area of 0.576 square miles and a water area of 0 square miles. Located at 41.56° N. Lat; 77.11° W. Long. Elevation is 1,545 feet.
Population: 199 (1990); 230 (2000); 249 (2010); Density: 432.6 persons per square mile (2010); Race: 97.6% White, 1.6% Black, 0.0% Asian, 0.0% American Indian/Alaska Native, 0.0% Native Hawaiian/Other Pacific Islander, 0.8% Other, 0.0% Hispanic of any race (2010); Average household size: 2.93 (2010); Median age: 33.6 (2010); Males per 100 females: 99.2 (2010); Marriage status: 29.0% never married, 52.9% now married, 8.6% widowed, 9.5% divorced (2006-2010 5-year est.); Foreign born: 4.2% (2006-2010 5-year est.); Ancestry (includes multiple ancestries): 35.3% German, 23.8% Irish, 14.3% English, 7.0% French Canadian, 5.9% Italian (2006-2010 5-year est.).
Economy: Single-family building permits issued: 0 (2011); Multi-family building permits issued: 0 (2011); Employment by occupation: 6.8% management, 3.4% professional, 9.3% services, 17.8% sales, 13.6% farming, 8.5% construction, 6.8% production (2006-2010 5-year est.).
Income: Per capita income: $15,847 (2006-2010 5-year est.); Median household income: $41,875 (2006-2010 5-year est.); Average household income: $47,260 (2006-2010 5-year est.); Percent of households with income of $100,000 or more: 10.0% (2006-2010 5-year est.); Poverty rate: 22.7% (2006-2010 5-year est.).
Education: Percent of population age 25 and over with: High school diploma (including GED) or higher: 91.1% (2006-2010 5-year est.); Bachelor's degree or higher: 19.9% (2006-2010 5-year est.); Master's degree or higher: 7.5% (2006-2010 5-year est.).
School District(s)
Southern Tioga SD (KG-12)
   2010-11 Enrollment: 1,994 . . . . (570) 638-2183
Housing: Homeownership rate: 68.2% (2010); Median home value: $88,900 (2006-2010 5-year est.); Median contract rent: $428 per month (2006-2010 5-year est.); Median year structure built: before 1940 (2006-2010 5-year est.).
Transportation: Commute to work: 94.1% car, 0.0% public transportation, 5.9% walk, 0.0% work from home (2006-2010 5-year est.); Travel time to work: 26.3% less than 15 minutes, 32.2% 15 to 30 minutes, 19.5% 30 to 45 minutes, 11.0% 45 to 60 minutes, 11.0% 60 minutes or more (2006-2010 5-year est.)

LIBERTY (township). Covers a land area of 64.636 square miles and a water area of 0.036 square miles. Located at 41.59° N. Lat; 77.12° W. Long. Elevation is 1,545 feet.
Population: 930 (1990); 868 (2000); 1,042 (2010); Density: 16.1 persons per square mile (2010); Race: 97.1% White, 0.0% Black, 0.2% Asian, 0.1% American Indian/Alaska Native, 0.0% Native Hawaiian/Other Pacific Islander, 2.6% Other, 0.6% Hispanic of any race (2010); Average household size: 2.61 (2010); Median age: 41.6 (2010); Males per 100 females: 95.9 (2010); Marriage status: 17.8% never married, 71.0% now married, 7.6% widowed, 3.6% divorced (2006-2010 5-year est.); Foreign born: 0.0% (2006-2010 5-year est.); Ancestry (includes multiple ancestries): 40.4% German, 19.0% English, 14.1% Irish, 7.5% Pennsylvania German, 6.2% American (2006-2010 5-year est.).
Economy: Single-family building permits issued: 0 (2011); Multi-family building permits issued: 0 (2011); Employment by occupation: 13.5% management, 2.9% professional, 7.9% services, 17.1% sales, 4.7% farming, 18.0% construction, 8.3% production (2006-2010 5-year est.).
Income: Per capita income: $18,224 (2006-2010 5-year est.); Median household income: $37,222 (2006-2010 5-year est.); Average household income: $49,640 (2006-2010 5-year est.); Percent of households with income of $100,000 or more: 9.1% (2006-2010 5-year est.); Poverty rate: 14.1% (2006-2010 5-year est.).

Education: Percent of population age 25 and over with: High school diploma (including GED) or higher: 85.4% (2006-2010 5-year est.); Bachelor's degree or higher: 17.4% (2006-2010 5-year est.); Master's degree or higher: 3.6% (2006-2010 5-year est.).
Housing: Homeownership rate: 84.5% (2010); Median home value: $124,400 (2006-2010 5-year est.); Median contract rent: $431 per month (2006-2010 5-year est.); Median year structure built: 1970 (2006-2010 5-year est.).
Transportation: Commute to work: 91.5% car, 0.0% public transportation, 2.5% walk, 6.0% work from home (2006-2010 5-year est.); Travel time to work: 27.9% less than 15 minutes, 27.5% 15 to 30 minutes, 28.4% 30 to 45 minutes, 8.1% 45 to 60 minutes, 8.1% 60 minutes or more (2006-2010 5-year est.)

MAINESBURG (unincorporated postal area)
Zip Code: 16932
   Covers a land area of 21.259 square miles and a water area of 0.038 square miles. Located at 41.77° N. Lat; 76.93° W. Long. Population: 734 (2010); Density: 34.5 persons per square mile (2010); Race: 97.5% White, 0.1% Black, 0.7% Asian, 0.3% American Indian/Alaska Native, 0.0% Native Hawaiian/Other Pacific Islander, 1.4% Other, 1.4% Hispanic of any race (2010); Average household size: 2.75 (2010); Median age: 41.2 (2010); Males per 100 females: 96.8 (2010); Homeownership rate: 82.0% (2010)

MANSFIELD (borough). Covers a land area of 1.914 square miles and a water area of 0.002 square miles. Located at 41.81° N. Lat; 77.08° W. Long. Elevation is 1,161 feet.
History: Mansfield was named for Asa Mann, an early settler.
Population: 3,538 (1990); 3,411 (2000); 3,625 (2010); Density: 1,894.1 persons per square mile (2010); Race: 90.2% White, 5.2% Black, 1.3% Asian, 0.2% American Indian/Alaska Native, 0.1% Native Hawaiian/Other Pacific Islander, 3.0% Other, 3.1% Hispanic of any race (2010); Average household size: 2.15 (2010); Median age: 21.7 (2010); Males per 100 females: 86.6 (2010); Marriage status: 62.3% never married, 28.6% now married, 4.2% widowed, 4.9% divorced (2006-2010 5-year est.); Foreign born: 4.2% (2006-2010 5-year est.); Ancestry (includes multiple ancestries): 25.9% German, 19.2% Irish, 13.9% English, 10.3% Italian, 4.8% American (2006-2010 5-year est.).
Economy: Single-family building permits issued: 4 (2011); Multi-family building permits issued: 0 (2011); Employment by occupation: 7.8% management, 2.9% professional, 8.1% services, 20.1% sales, 4.7% farming, 6.6% construction, 6.8% production (2006-2010 5-year est.).
Income: Per capita income: $16,591 (2006-2010 5-year est.); Median household income: $28,333 (2006-2010 5-year est.); Average household income: $45,812 (2006-2010 5-year est.); Percent of households with income of $100,000 or more: 12.5% (2006-2010 5-year est.); Poverty rate: 31.3% (2006-2010 5-year est.).
Taxes: Total city taxes per capita: $224 (2009); City property taxes per capita: $132 (2009).
Education: Percent of population age 25 and over with: High school diploma (including GED) or higher: 92.0% (2006-2010 5-year est.); Bachelor's degree or higher: 42.5% (2006-2010 5-year est.); Master's degree or higher: 24.9% (2006-2010 5-year est.).
School District(s)
Southern Tioga SD (KG-12)
   2010-11 Enrollment: 1,994 . . . . (570) 638-2183
Four-year College(s)
Mansfield University of Pennsylvania (Public)
   Fall 2010 Enrollment: 3,181 . . . . (570) 662-4000
   2011-12 Tuition: In-state $8,654; Out-of-state $18,192
Housing: Homeownership rate: 43.7% (2010); Median home value: $119,500 (2006-2010 5-year est.); Median contract rent: $528 per month (2006-2010 5-year est.); Median year structure built: 1970 (2006-2010 5-year est.).
Safety: Violent crime rate: 0.0 per 10,000 population; Property crime rate: 11.0 per 10,000 population (2011).
Transportation: Commute to work: 71.2% car, 0.6% public transportation, 22.3% walk, 5.3% work from home (2006-2010 5-year est.); Travel time to work: 64.8% less than 15 minutes, 19.6% 15 to 30 minutes, 5.4% 30 to 45 minutes, 6.0% 45 to 60 minutes, 4.3% 60 minutes or more (2006-2010 5-year est.)
Additional Information Contacts
Mansfield Chamber of Commerce, Inc. . . . . (570) 662-3442
   http://www.mansfield.org

MIDDLEBURY (township). Covers a land area of 49.037 square miles and a water area of 0.314 square miles. Located at 41.86° N. Lat; 77.27° W. Long.

Population: 1,244 (1990); 1,221 (2000); 1,285 (2010); Density: 26.2 persons per square mile (2010); Race: 99.4% White, 0.0% Black, 0.1% Asian, 0.2% American Indian/Alaska Native, 0.0% Native Hawaiian/Other Pacific Islander, 0.3% Other, 0.5% Hispanic of any race (2010); Average household size: 2.47 (2010); Median age: 43.4 (2010); Males per 100 females: 103.3 (2010); Marriage status: 18.6% never married, 68.1% now married, 1.5% widowed, 11.9% divorced (2006-2010 5-year est.); Foreign born: 1.4% (2006-2010 5-year est.); Ancestry (includes multiple ancestries): 24.5% English, 23.9% German, 12.4% Irish, 11.6% American, 7.6% Italian (2006-2010 5-year est.).

Economy: Single-family building permits issued: 3 (2011); Multi-family building permits issued: 0 (2011); Employment by occupation: 7.1% management, 1.3% professional, 15.3% services, 17.9% sales, 2.9% farming, 18.5% construction, 11.3% production (2006-2010 5-year est.).

Income: Per capita income: $20,626 (2006-2010 5-year est.); Median household income: $46,429 (2006-2010 5-year est.); Average household income: $50,754 (2006-2010 5-year est.); Percent of households with income of $100,000 or more: 6.9% (2006-2010 5-year est.); Poverty rate: 9.6% (2006-2010 5-year est.).

Education: Percent of population age 25 and over with: High school diploma (including GED) or higher: 87.8% (2006-2010 5-year est.); Bachelor's degree or higher: 15.2% (2006-2010 5-year est.); Master's degree or higher: 7.1% (2006-2010 5-year est.).

Housing: Homeownership rate: 83.3% (2010); Median home value: $107,700 (2006-2010 5-year est.); Median contract rent: $435 per month (2006-2010 5-year est.); Median year structure built: 1975 (2006-2010 5-year est.).

Transportation: Commute to work: 86.4% car, 0.0% public transportation, 3.9% walk, 8.5% work from home (2006-2010 5-year est.); Travel time to work: 29.1% less than 15 minutes, 50.7% 15 to 30 minutes, 7.6% 30 to 45 minutes, 1.5% 45 to 60 minutes, 11.0% 60 minutes or more (2006-2010 5-year est.)

Additional Information Contacts

Wellsboro Area Chamber of Commerce . . . . (570) 724-1926
   http://www.wellsboropa.com

MIDDLEBURY CENTER (unincorporated postal area)

Zip Code: 16935

Covers a land area of 50.029 square miles and a water area of 0.007 square miles. Located at 41.87° N. Lat; 77.30° W. Long. Population: 1,256 (2010); Density: 25.1 persons per square mile (2010); Race: 99.2% White, 0.1% Black, 0.1% Asian, 0.2% American Indian/Alaska Native, 0.0% Native Hawaiian/Other Pacific Islander, 0.4% Other, 0.6% Hispanic of any race (2010); Average household size: 2.50 (2010); Median age: 44.8 (2010); Males per 100 females: 102.6 (2010); Homeownership rate: 85.5% (2010)

MILLERTON (CDP). Covers a land area of 0.857 square miles and a water area of 0 square miles. Located at 41.99° N. Lat; 76.94° W. Long. Elevation is 1,184 feet.

Population: n/a (1990); n/a (2000); 316 (2010); Density: 368.6 persons per square mile (2010); Race: 97.2% White, 0.6% Black, 0.6% Asian, 0.0% American Indian/Alaska Native, 0.0% Native Hawaiian/Other Pacific Islander, 1.6% Other, 0.0% Hispanic of any race (2010); Average household size: 2.39 (2010); Median age: 47.0 (2010); Males per 100 females: 107.9 (2010); Marriage status: 13.4% never married, 72.0% now married, 6.3% widowed, 8.3% divorced (2006-2010 5-year est.); Foreign born: 0.0% (2006-2010 5-year est.); Ancestry (includes multiple ancestries): 32.1% English, 25.3% German, 15.3% Swiss, 15.3% Irish, 12.7% American (2006-2010 5-year est.).

Economy: Employment by occupation: 3.8% management, 3.8% professional, 5.7% services, 20.9% sales, 0.0% farming, 20.9% construction, 9.5% production (2006-2010 5-year est.).

Income: Per capita income: $18,716 (2006-2010 5-year est.); Median household income: $39,375 (2006-2010 5-year est.); Average household income: $42,597 (2006-2010 5-year est.); Percent of households with income of $100,000 or more: 3.0% (2006-2010 5-year est.); Poverty rate: 10.2% (2006-2010 5-year est.).

Education: Percent of population age 25 and over with: High school diploma (including GED) or higher: 81.9% (2006-2010 5-year est.); Bachelor's degree or higher: 16.4% (2006-2010 5-year est.); Master's degree or higher: 3.0% (2006-2010 5-year est.).

Housing: Homeownership rate: 75.0% (2010); Median home value: $92,100 (2006-2010 5-year est.); Median contract rent: $466 per month (2006-2010 5-year est.); Median year structure built: 1950 (2006-2010 5-year est.).

Transportation: Commute to work: 85.1% car, 0.0% public transportation, 9.1% walk, 5.8% work from home (2006-2010 5-year est.); Travel time to work: 16.6% less than 15 minutes, 45.5% 15 to 30 minutes, 35.2% 30 to 45 minutes, 0.0% 45 to 60 minutes, 2.8% 60 minutes or more (2006-2010 5-year est.)

MORRIS (township). Covers a land area of 73.992 square miles and a water area of 0.023 square miles. Located at 41.60° N. Lat; 77.33° W. Long. Elevation is 1,040 feet.

Population: 675 (1990); 646 (2000); 606 (2010); Density: 8.2 persons per square mile (2010); Race: 99.3% White, 0.0% Black, 0.3% Asian, 0.0% American Indian/Alaska Native, 0.0% Native Hawaiian/Other Pacific Islander, 0.4% Other, 2.0% Hispanic of any race (2010); Average household size: 2.33 (2010); Median age: 47.6 (2010); Males per 100 females: 108.2 (2010); Marriage status: 12.8% never married, 71.1% now married, 8.0% widowed, 8.2% divorced (2006-2010 5-year est.); Foreign born: 0.0% (2006-2010 5-year est.); Ancestry (includes multiple ancestries): 37.3% German, 25.8% English, 9.0% Irish, 7.6% Swedish, 5.4% Scotch-Irish (2006-2010 5-year est.).

Economy: Single-family building permits issued: 0 (2011); Multi-family building permits issued: 0 (2011); Employment by occupation: 15.3% management, 0.0% professional, 8.0% services, 18.2% sales, 4.4% farming, 8.0% construction, 6.9% production (2006-2010 5-year est.).

Income: Per capita income: $24,318 (2006-2010 5-year est.); Median household income: $36,635 (2006-2010 5-year est.); Average household income: $52,197 (2006-2010 5-year est.); Percent of households with income of $100,000 or more: 8.9% (2006-2010 5-year est.); Poverty rate: 4.6% (2006-2010 5-year est.).

Education: Percent of population age 25 and over with: High school diploma (including GED) or higher: 90.7% (2006-2010 5-year est.); Bachelor's degree or higher: 13.8% (2006-2010 5-year est.); Master's degree or higher: 5.0% (2006-2010 5-year est.).

Housing: Homeownership rate: 85.9% (2010); Median home value: $91,000 (2006-2010 5-year est.); Median contract rent: $317 per month (2006-2010 5-year est.); Median year structure built: 1968 (2006-2010 5-year est.).

Transportation: Commute to work: 78.6% car, 0.0% public transportation, 5.9% walk, 13.7% work from home (2006-2010 5-year est.); Travel time to work: 21.4% less than 15 minutes, 41.9% 15 to 30 minutes, 31.6% 30 to 45 minutes, 1.3% 45 to 60 minutes, 3.8% 60 minutes or more (2006-2010 5-year est.)

MORRIS RUN (unincorporated postal area)

Zip Code: 16939

Covers a land area of 2.691 square miles and a water area of 0.007 square miles. Located at 41.66° N. Lat; 77.02° W. Long. Elevation is 1,693 feet. Population: 295 (2010); Density: 109.6 persons per square mile (2010); Race: 99.0% White, 0.3% Black, 0.0% Asian, 0.0% American Indian/Alaska Native, 0.0% Native Hawaiian/Other Pacific Islander, 0.7% Other, 0.7% Hispanic of any race (2010); Average household size: 2.40 (2010); Median age: 38.4 (2010); Males per 100 females: 100.7 (2010); Homeownership rate: 72.7% (2010)

NELSON (township). Covers a land area of 11.547 square miles and a water area of 0.010 square miles. Located at 41.97° N. Lat; 77.28° W. Long. Elevation is 1,089 feet.

Population: 564 (1990); 587 (2000); 571 (2010); Density: 49.5 persons per square mile (2010); Race: 97.7% White, 1.2% Black, 0.2% Asian, 0.4% American Indian/Alaska Native, 0.0% Native Hawaiian/Other Pacific Islander, 0.5% Other, 0.5% Hispanic of any race (2010); Average household size: 2.41 (2010); Median age: 46.3 (2010); Males per 100 females: 94.9 (2010); Marriage status: 13.8% never married, 68.2% now married, 7.6% widowed, 10.4% divorced (2006-2010 5-year est.); Foreign born: 0.5% (2006-2010 5-year est.); Ancestry (includes multiple ancestries): 35.8% English, 24.0% German, 16.5% Irish, 6.1% American, 4.2% Welsh (2006-2010 5-year est.).

Economy: Single-family building permits issued: 1 (2011); Multi-family building permits issued: 0 (2011); Employment by occupation: 19.7% management, 5.9% professional, 7.1% services, 24.4% sales, 5.5% farming, 9.2% construction, 7.1% production (2006-2010 5-year est.).

Income: Per capita income: $17,592 (2006-2010 5-year est.); Median household income: $31,667 (2006-2010 5-year est.); Average household income: $43,679 (2006-2010 5-year est.); Percent of households with income of $100,000 or more: 5.6% (2006-2010 5-year est.); Poverty rate: 15.5% (2006-2010 5-year est.).

Education: Percent of population age 25 and over with: High school diploma (including GED) or higher: 82.8% (2006-2010 5-year est.); Bachelor's degree or higher: 18.6% (2006-2010 5-year est.); Master's degree or higher: 4.2% (2006-2010 5-year est.).

Housing: Homeownership rate: 79.8% (2010); Median home value: $87,100 (2006-2010 5-year est.); Median contract rent: $172 per month (2006-2010 5-year est.); Median year structure built: 1970 (2006-2010 5-year est.).

Transportation: Commute to work: 95.7% car, 0.0% public transportation, 0.0% walk, 0.0% work from home (2006-2010 5-year est.); Travel time to work: 38.7% less than 15 minutes, 18.3% 15 to 30 minutes, 32.3% 30 to 45 minutes, 8.9% 45 to 60 minutes, 1.7% 60 minutes or more (2006-2010 5-year est.)

OSCEOLA (township). Covers a land area of 13.582 square miles and a water area of 0 square miles. Located at 41.98° N. Lat; 77.37° W. Long. Elevation is 1,158 feet.

Population: 783 (1990); 700 (2000); 659 (2010); Density: 48.5 persons per square mile (2010); Race: 98.5% White, 0.3% Black, 0.0% Asian, 0.0% American Indian/Alaska Native, 0.0% Native Hawaiian/Other Pacific Islander, 1.2% Other, 0.2% Hispanic of any race (2010); Average household size: 2.57 (2010); Median age: 43.7 (2010); Males per 100 females: 102.1 (2010); Marriage status: 16.3% never married, 63.5% now married, 4.4% widowed, 15.8% divorced (2006-2010 5-year est.); Foreign born: 0.0% (2006-2010 5-year est.); Ancestry (includes multiple ancestries): 24.9% German, 24.4% English, 14.8% American, 13.8% Irish, 5.6% Italian (2006-2010 5-year est.).

Economy: Single-family building permits issued: 0 (2011); Multi-family building permits issued: 0 (2011); Employment by occupation: 2.7% management, 4.4% professional, 4.9% services, 8.7% sales, 2.2% farming, 6.6% construction, 27.9% production (2006-2010 5-year est.).

Income: Per capita income: $19,161 (2006-2010 5-year est.); Median household income: $40,352 (2006-2010 5-year est.); Average household income: $39,765 (2006-2010 5-year est.); Percent of households with income of $100,000 or more: 4.3% (2006-2010 5-year est.); Poverty rate: 29.6% (2006-2010 5-year est.).

Education: Percent of population age 25 and over with: High school diploma (including GED) or higher: 80.0% (2006-2010 5-year est.); Bachelor's degree or higher: 17.4% (2006-2010 5-year est.); Master's degree or higher: 6.8% (2006-2010 5-year est.).

Housing: Homeownership rate: 79.6% (2010); Median home value: $92,800 (2006-2010 5-year est.); Median contract rent: $405 per month (2006-2010 5-year est.); Median year structure built: before 1940 (2006-2010 5-year est.).

Safety: Violent crime rate: 0.0 per 10,000 population; Property crime rate: 0.0 per 10,000 population (2011).

Transportation: Commute to work: 91.1% car, 3.4% public transportation, 0.0% walk, 5.6% work from home (2006-2010 5-year est.); Travel time to work: 26.0% less than 15 minutes, 20.1% 15 to 30 minutes, 35.5% 30 to 45 minutes, 14.2% 45 to 60 minutes, 4.1% 60 minutes or more (2006-2010 5-year est.)

PUTNAM (township). Covers a land area of 0.625 square miles and a water area of 0 square miles. Located at 41.74° N. Lat; 77.08° W. Long.

Population: 444 (1990); 428 (2000); 425 (2010); Density: 680.4 persons per square mile (2010); Race: 99.8% White, 0.0% Black, 0.0% Asian, 0.0% American Indian/Alaska Native, 0.0% Native Hawaiian/Other Pacific Islander, 0.2% Other, 0.9% Hispanic of any race (2010); Average household size: 2.46 (2010); Median age: 38.3 (2010); Males per 100 females: 101.4 (2010); Marriage status: 43.3% never married, 41.5% now married, 1.5% widowed, 13.8% divorced (2006-2010 5-year est.); Foreign born: 0.0% (2006-2010 5-year est.); Ancestry (includes multiple ancestries): 22.5% German, 18.7% English, 18.5% American, 11.2% Polish, 10.3% Irish (2006-2010 5-year est.).

Economy: Single-family building permits issued: 0 (2011); Multi-family building permits issued: 0 (2011); Employment by occupation: 9.7% management, 7.4% professional, 15.6% services, 11.3% sales, 1.6% farming, 8.9% construction, 10.1% production (2006-2010 5-year est.).

Income: Per capita income: $15,515 (2006-2010 5-year est.); Median household income: $39,688 (2006-2010 5-year est.); Average household

income: $42,845 (2006-2010 5-year est.); Percent of households with income of $100,000 or more: 1.5% (2006-2010 5-year est.); Poverty rate: 20.2% (2006-2010 5-year est.).

Education: Percent of population age 25 and over with: High school diploma (including GED) or higher: 92.3% (2006-2010 5-year est.); Bachelor's degree or higher: 7.7% (2006-2010 5-year est.); Master's degree or higher: 2.3% (2006-2010 5-year est.).

Housing: Homeownership rate: 61.9% (2010); Median home value: $97,700 (2006-2010 5-year est.); Median contract rent: $496 per month (2006-2010 5-year est.); Median year structure built: 1943 (2006-2010 5-year est.).

Transportation: Commute to work: 94.0% car, 0.0% public transportation, 2.0% walk, 1.2% work from home (2006-2010 5-year est.); Travel time to work: 58.1% less than 15 minutes, 13.4% 15 to 30 minutes, 19.5% 30 to 45 minutes, 4.5% 45 to 60 minutes, 4.5% 60 minutes or more (2006-2010 5-year est.)

RICHMOND (township). Covers a land area of 50.658 square miles and a water area of 0.073 square miles. Located at 41.81° N. Lat; 77.10° W. Long.

Population: 2,305 (1990); 2,475 (2000); 2,396 (2010); Density: 47.3 persons per square mile (2010); Race: 97.2% White, 0.8% Black, 0.7% Asian, 0.3% American Indian/Alaska Native, 0.0% Native Hawaiian/Other Pacific Islander, 1.0% Other, 0.9% Hispanic of any race (2010); Average household size: 2.38 (2010); Median age: 44.1 (2010); Males per 100 females: 87.0 (2010); Marriage status: 26.1% never married, 60.3% now married, 5.7% widowed, 7.9% divorced (2006-2010 5-year est.); Foreign born: 1.1% (2006-2010 5-year est.); Ancestry (includes multiple ancestries): 34.9% German, 21.4% English, 14.6% Irish, 7.8% American, 7.5% Polish (2006-2010 5-year est.).

Economy: Single-family building permits issued: 10 (2011); Multi-family building permits issued: 0 (2011); Employment by occupation: 8.2% management, 2.1% professional, 14.7% services, 12.8% sales, 2.2% farming, 10.8% construction, 7.8% production (2006-2010 5-year est.).

Income: Per capita income: $20,594 (2006-2010 5-year est.); Median household income: $40,507 (2006-2010 5-year est.); Average household income: $51,350 (2006-2010 5-year est.); Percent of households with income of $100,000 or more: 9.8% (2006-2010 5-year est.); Poverty rate: 20.2% (2006-2010 5-year est.).

Education: Percent of population age 25 and over with: High school diploma (including GED) or higher: 90.9% (2006-2010 5-year est.); Bachelor's degree or higher: 20.9% (2006-2010 5-year est.); Master's degree or higher: 10.3% (2006-2010 5-year est.).

Housing: Homeownership rate: 79.0% (2010); Median home value: $125,200 (2006-2010 5-year est.); Median contract rent: $430 per month (2006-2010 5-year est.); Median year structure built: 1977 (2006-2010 5-year est.).

Transportation: Commute to work: 89.2% car, 0.6% public transportation, 2.8% walk, 7.4% work from home (2006-2010 5-year est.); Travel time to work: 45.2% less than 15 minutes, 34.6% 15 to 30 minutes, 9.2% 30 to 45 minutes, 3.8% 45 to 60 minutes, 7.1% 60 minutes or more (2006-2010 5-year est.)

Additional Information Contacts
Mansfield Chamber of Commerce, Inc. . . . . (570) 662-3442
http://www.mansfield.org

ROARING BRANCH (unincorporated postal area)
Zip Code: 17765

Covers a land area of 82.635 square miles and a water area of 0.427 square miles. Located at 41.56° N. Lat; 76.97° W. Long. Population: 1,162 (2010); Density: 14.1 persons per square mile (2010); Race: 98.5% White, 0.0% Black, 0.4% Asian, 0.0% American Indian/Alaska Native, 0.1% Native Hawaiian/Other Pacific Islander, 1.0% Other, 0.6% Hispanic of any race (2010); Average household size: 2.57 (2010); Median age: 42.7 (2010); Males per 100 females: 103.5 (2010); Homeownership rate: 83.0% (2010)

ROSEVILLE (borough). Aka Rutland. Covers a land area of 0.455 square miles and a water area of 0 square miles. Located at 41.86° N. Lat; 76.96° W. Long. Elevation is 1,355 feet.

Population: 230 (1990); 207 (2000); 189 (2010); Density: 415.2 persons per square mile (2010); Race: 95.2% White, 0.0% Black, 1.1% Asian, 1.1% American Indian/Alaska Native, 0.0% Native Hawaiian/Other Pacific Islander, 2.6% Other, 0.5% Hispanic of any race (2010); Average household size: 2.52 (2010); Median age: 41.8 (2010); Males per 100

females: 92.9 (2010); Marriage status: 17.6% never married, 64.8% now married, 8.8% widowed, 8.8% divorced (2006-2010 5-year est.); Foreign born: 5.8% (2006-2010 5-year est.); Ancestry (includes multiple ancestries): 24.5% English, 23.2% German, 18.1% Irish, 16.8% Slovak, 7.7% Swedish (2006-2010 5-year est.).

Economy: Employment by occupation: 12.3% management, 0.0% professional, 6.2% services, 12.3% sales, 7.7% farming, 6.2% construction, 21.5% production (2006-2010 5-year est.).

Income: Per capita income: $19,432 (2006-2010 5-year est.); Median household income: $33,750 (2006-2010 5-year est.); Average household income: $46,223 (2006-2010 5-year est.); Percent of households with income of $100,000 or more: 10.9% (2006-2010 5-year est.); Poverty rate: 6.5% (2006-2010 5-year est.).

Education: Percent of population age 25 and over with: High school diploma (including GED) or higher: 90.0% (2006-2010 5-year est.); Bachelor's degree or higher: 27.3% (2006-2010 5-year est.); Master's degree or higher: 7.3% (2006-2010 5-year est.).

Housing: Homeownership rate: 74.6% (2010); Median home value: $112,500 (2006-2010 5-year est.); Median contract rent: $200 per month (2006-2010 5-year est.); Median year structure built: before 1940 (2006-2010 5-year est.).

Transportation: Commute to work: 93.7% car, 0.0% public transportation, 3.2% walk, 3.2% work from home (2006-2010 5-year est.); Travel time to work: 11.5% less than 15 minutes, 34.4% 15 to 30 minutes, 16.4% 30 to 45 minutes, 18.0% 45 to 60 minutes, 19.7% 60 minutes or more (2006-2010 5-year est.)

RUTLAND (township). Aka Roseville. Covers a land area of 35.405 square miles and a water area of 0.017 square miles. Located at 41.87° N. Lat; 76.98° W. Long.

Population: 646 (1990); 736 (2000); 805 (2010); Density: 22.7 persons per square mile (2010); Race: 98.6% White, 0.4% Black, 0.1% Asian, 0.2% American Indian/Alaska Native, 0.0% Native Hawaiian/Other Pacific Islander, 0.7% Other, 0.5% Hispanic of any race (2010); Average household size: 2.59 (2010); Median age: 43.0 (2010); Males per 100 females: 118.2 (2010); Marriage status: 23.5% never married, 69.6% now married, 2.4% widowed, 4.5% divorced (2006-2010 5-year est.); Foreign born: 2.3% (2006-2010 5-year est.); Ancestry (includes multiple ancestries): 33.1% Irish, 23.7% German, 14.7% American, 13.0% English, 5.0% Scottish (2006-2010 5-year est.).

Economy: Single-family building permits issued: 2 (2011); Multi-family building permits issued: 0 (2011); Employment by occupation: 19.2% management, 2.6% professional, 22.6% services, 5.6% sales, 1.3% farming, 7.7% construction, 6.0% production (2006-2010 5-year est.).

Income: Per capita income: $14,763 (2006-2010 5-year est.); Median household income: $34,318 (2006-2010 5-year est.); Average household income: $40,792 (2006-2010 5-year est.); Percent of households with income of $100,000 or more: 2.6% (2006-2010 5-year est.); Poverty rate: 26.9% (2006-2010 5-year est.).

Education: Percent of population age 25 and over with: High school diploma (including GED) or higher: 83.5% (2006-2010 5-year est.); Bachelor's degree or higher: 17.0% (2006-2010 5-year est.); Master's degree or higher: 3.1% (2006-2010 5-year est.).

Housing: Homeownership rate: 82.6% (2010); Median home value: $145,700 (2006-2010 5-year est.); Median contract rent: $428 per month (2006-2010 5-year est.); Median year structure built: 1974 (2006-2010 5-year est.).

Transportation: Commute to work: 84.6% car, 0.0% public transportation, 3.2% walk, 10.4% work from home (2006-2010 5-year est.); Travel time to work: 16.2% less than 15 minutes, 23.7% 15 to 30 minutes, 46.5% 30 to 45 minutes, 3.5% 45 to 60 minutes, 10.1% 60 minutes or more (2006-2010 5-year est.)

SABINSVILLE (unincorporated postal area)
Zip Code: 16943
Covers a land area of 37.703 square miles and a water area of 0.016 square miles. Located at 41.83° N. Lat; 77.61° W. Long. Population: 549 (2010); Density: 14.6 persons per square mile (2010); Race: 99.6% White, 0.4% Black, 0.0% Asian, 0.0% American Indian/Alaska Native, 0.0% Native Hawaiian/Other Pacific Islander, 0.0% Other, 0.2% Hispanic of any race (2010); Average household size: 2.34 (2010); Median age: 50.1 (2010); Males per 100 females: 104.1 (2010); Homeownership rate: 79.5% (2010)

SHIPPEN (township). Covers a land area of 48.773 square miles and a water area of 0.032 square miles. Located at 41.76° N. Lat; 77.45° W. Long.

Population: 508 (1990); 472 (2000); 527 (2010); Density: 10.8 persons per square mile (2010); Race: 97.9% White, 0.6% Black, 0.4% Asian, 0.0% American Indian/Alaska Native, 0.0% Native Hawaiian/Other Pacific Islander, 1.1% Other, 1.5% Hispanic of any race (2010); Average household size: 2.60 (2010); Median age: 44.0 (2010); Males per 100 females: 94.5 (2010); Marriage status: 17.7% never married, 62.5% now married, 12.2% widowed, 7.6% divorced (2006-2010 5-year est.); Foreign born: 5.2% (2006-2010 5-year est.); Ancestry (includes multiple ancestries): 27.6% German, 18.9% Irish, 11.4% English, 9.5% American, 5.0% French (2006-2010 5-year est.).

Economy: Single-family building permits issued: 2 (2011); Multi-family building permits issued: 0 (2011); Employment by occupation: 4.3% management, 3.0% professional, 11.7% services, 17.8% sales, 3.0% farming, 22.6% construction, 13.5% production (2006-2010 5-year est.).

Income: Per capita income: $24,971 (2006-2010 5-year est.); Median household income: $42,500 (2006-2010 5-year est.); Average household income: $57,637 (2006-2010 5-year est.); Percent of households with income of $100,000 or more: 16.5% (2006-2010 5-year est.); Poverty rate: 8.7% (2006-2010 5-year est.).

Education: Percent of population age 25 and over with: High school diploma (including GED) or higher: 84.7% (2006-2010 5-year est.); Bachelor's degree or higher: 15.8% (2006-2010 5-year est.); Master's degree or higher: 3.3% (2006-2010 5-year est.).

Housing: Homeownership rate: 81.3% (2010); Median home value: $125,000 (2006-2010 5-year est.); Median contract rent: $554 per month (2006-2010 5-year est.); Median year structure built: 1965 (2006-2010 5-year est.).

Transportation: Commute to work: 86.2% car, 0.0% public transportation, 6.2% walk, 5.3% work from home (2006-2010 5-year est.); Travel time to work: 35.7% less than 15 minutes, 40.4% 15 to 30 minutes, 16.0% 30 to 45 minutes, 6.1% 45 to 60 minutes, 1.9% 60 minutes or more (2006-2010 5-year est.)

SULLIVAN (township). Covers a land area of 42.302 square miles and a water area of 0.105 square miles. Located at 41.79° N. Lat; 76.97° W. Long.

Population: 1,140 (1990); 1,322 (2000); 1,453 (2010); Density: 34.3 persons per square mile (2010); Race: 97.9% White, 0.1% Black, 0.5% Asian, 0.2% American Indian/Alaska Native, 0.0% Native Hawaiian/Other Pacific Islander, 1.3% Other, 0.9% Hispanic of any race (2010); Average household size: 2.64 (2010); Median age: 42.7 (2010); Males per 100 females: 95.6 (2010); Marriage status: 20.1% never married, 67.9% now married, 4.8% widowed, 7.2% divorced (2006-2010 5-year est.); Foreign born: 1.2% (2006-2010 5-year est.); Ancestry (includes multiple ancestries): 27.6% German, 17.7% Irish, 16.8% English, 8.2% American, 5.2% Polish (2006-2010 5-year est.).

Economy: Single-family building permits issued: 3 (2011); Multi-family building permits issued: 0 (2011); Employment by occupation: 12.2% management, 2.3% professional, 10.3% services, 14.1% sales, 3.4% farming, 13.7% construction, 11.9% production (2006-2010 5-year est.).

Income: Per capita income: $19,075 (2006-2010 5-year est.); Median household income: $40,461 (2006-2010 5-year est.); Average household income: $50,369 (2006-2010 5-year est.); Percent of households with income of $100,000 or more: 9.1% (2006-2010 5-year est.); Poverty rate: 20.5% (2006-2010 5-year est.).

Education: Percent of population age 25 and over with: High school diploma (including GED) or higher: 89.8% (2006-2010 5-year est.); Bachelor's degree or higher: 12.1% (2006-2010 5-year est.); Master's degree or higher: 4.6% (2006-2010 5-year est.).

Housing: Homeownership rate: 85.8% (2010); Median home value: $128,500 (2006-2010 5-year est.); Median contract rent: $406 per month (2006-2010 5-year est.); Median year structure built: 1976 (2006-2010 5-year est.).

Transportation: Commute to work: 90.0% car, 0.0% public transportation, 3.3% walk, 5.1% work from home (2006-2010 5-year est.); Travel time to work: 17.6% less than 15 minutes, 43.4% 15 to 30 minutes, 22.3% 30 to 45 minutes, 6.5% 45 to 60 minutes, 10.2% 60 minutes or more (2006-2010 5-year est.)

Additional Information Contacts
Mansfield Chamber of Commerce, Inc. . . . . (570) 662-3442
http://www.mansfield.org

TIOGA (borough). Aka Brooklyn. Covers a land area of 0.452 square miles and a water area of 0.023 square miles. Located at 41.90° N. Lat; 77.13° W. Long. Elevation is 1,030 feet.
Population: 638 (1990); 622 (2000); 666 (2010); Density: 1,472.0 persons per square mile (2010); Race: 98.2% White, 0.6% Black, 0.0% Asian, 0.2% American Indian/Alaska Native, 0.0% Native Hawaiian/Other Pacific Islander, 1.0% Other, 0.2% Hispanic of any race (2010); Average household size: 2.41 (2010); Median age: 38.0 (2010); Males per 100 females: 99.4 (2010); Marriage status: 32.7% never married, 42.4% now married, 4.5% widowed, 20.4% divorced (2006-2010 5-year est.); Foreign born: 0.7% (2006-2010 5-year est.); Ancestry (includes multiple ancestries): 26.0% German, 16.4% Irish, 13.5% English, 7.9% American, 3.8% Dutch (2006-2010 5-year est.).
Economy: Single-family building permits issued: 1 (2011); Multi-family building permits issued: 0 (2011); Employment by occupation: 3.9% management, 0.7% professional, 13.6% services, 21.9% sales, 3.6% farming, 10.8% construction, 9.3% production (2006-2010 5-year est.).
Income: Per capita income: $18,760 (2006-2010 5-year est.); Median household income: $37,083 (2006-2010 5-year est.); Average household income: $46,382 (2006-2010 5-year est.); Percent of households with income of $100,000 or more: 8.3% (2006-2010 5-year est.); Poverty rate: 15.6% (2006-2010 5-year est.).
Education: Percent of population age 25 and over with: High school diploma (including GED) or higher: 77.3% (2006-2010 5-year est.); Bachelor's degree or higher: 14.3% (2006-2010 5-year est.); Master's degree or higher: 2.7% (2006-2010 5-year est.).

School District(s)
Northern Tioga SD (KG-12)
   2010-11 Enrollment: 2,139 . . . . (814) 258-5642
Housing: Homeownership rate: 71.6% (2010); Median home value: $70,000 (2006-2010 5-year est.); Median contract rent: $439 per month (2006-2010 5-year est.); Median year structure built: before 1940 (2006-2010 5-year est.).
Safety: Violent crime rate: 15.0 per 10,000 population; Property crime rate: 44.9 per 10,000 population (2011).
Transportation: Commute to work: 90.0% car, 0.0% public transportation, 7.4% walk, 2.6% work from home (2006-2010 5-year est.); Travel time to work: 20.6% less than 15 minutes, 31.7% 15 to 30 minutes, 24.4% 30 to 45 minutes, 15.3% 45 to 60 minutes, 8.0% 60 minutes or more (2006-2010 5-year est.)

TIOGA (township). Aka Brooklyn. Covers a land area of 38.930 square miles and a water area of 1.509 square miles. Located at 41.89° N. Lat; 77.09° W. Long. Elevation is 1,030 feet.
Population: 1,019 (1990); 995 (2000); 991 (2010); Density: 25.5 persons per square mile (2010); Race: 97.2% White, 0.5% Black, 0.3% Asian, 0.0% American Indian/Alaska Native, 0.0% Native Hawaiian/Other Pacific Islander, 2.0% Other, 1.1% Hispanic of any race (2010); Average household size: 2.43 (2010); Median age: 44.3 (2010); Males per 100 females: 106.0 (2010); Marriage status: 13.3% never married, 71.9% now married, 6.6% widowed, 8.1% divorced (2006-2010 5-year est.); Foreign born: 0.9% (2006-2010 5-year est.); Ancestry (includes multiple ancestries): 20.5% American, 16.3% German, 10.6% English, 7.9% Italian, 6.8% Polish (2006-2010 5-year est.).
Economy: Single-family building permits issued: 0 (2011); Multi-family building permits issued: 0 (2011); Employment by occupation: 6.7% management, 3.7% professional, 13.6% services, 17.7% sales, 4.4% farming, 12.9% construction, 9.0% production (2006-2010 5-year est.).
Income: Per capita income: $21,644 (2006-2010 5-year est.); Median household income: $56,167 (2006-2010 5-year est.); Average household income: $54,798 (2006-2010 5-year est.); Percent of households with income of $100,000 or more: 11.2% (2006-2010 5-year est.); Poverty rate: 8.1% (2006-2010 5-year est.).
Education: Percent of population age 25 and over with: High school diploma (including GED) or higher: 85.1% (2006-2010 5-year est.); Bachelor's degree or higher: 12.9% (2006-2010 5-year est.); Master's degree or higher: 5.6% (2006-2010 5-year est.).
Housing: Homeownership rate: 76.9% (2010); Median home value: $104,800 (2006-2010 5-year est.); Median contract rent: $354 per month (2006-2010 5-year est.); Median year structure built: 1975 (2006-2010 5-year est.).
Transportation: Commute to work: 92.1% car, 1.0% public transportation, 3.8% walk, 3.1% work from home (2006-2010 5-year est.); Travel time to work: 20.9% less than 15 minutes, 31.2% 15 to 30 minutes, 33.2% 30 to

45 minutes, 10.6% 45 to 60 minutes, 4.2% 60 minutes or more (2006-2010 5-year est.)
Additional Information Contacts
Wellsboro Area Chamber of Commerce . . . . (570) 724-1926
   http://www.wellsboropa.com

UNION (township). Covers a land area of 47.017 square miles and a water area of 0.013 square miles. Located at 41.61° N. Lat; 76.96° W. Long.
Population: 931 (1990); 945 (2000); 1,000 (2010); Density: 21.3 persons per square mile (2010); Race: 98.9% White, 0.0% Black, 0.4% Asian, 0.0% American Indian/Alaska Native, 0.1% Native Hawaiian/Other Pacific Islander, 0.6% Other, 0.5% Hispanic of any race (2010); Average household size: 2.56 (2010); Median age: 42.7 (2010); Males per 100 females: 99.6 (2010); Marriage status: 21.6% never married, 59.4% now married, 6.6% widowed, 12.4% divorced (2006-2010 5-year est.); Foreign born: 1.9% (2006-2010 5-year est.); Ancestry (includes multiple ancestries): 34.4% German, 17.1% English, 13.7% Irish, 11.4% Polish, 6.0% Dutch (2006-2010 5-year est.).
Economy: Single-family building permits issued: 0 (2011); Multi-family building permits issued: 0 (2011); Employment by occupation: 13.3% management, 0.9% professional, 15.0% services, 11.7% sales, 0.9% farming, 19.3% construction, 10.9% production (2006-2010 5-year est.).
Income: Per capita income: $18,348 (2006-2010 5-year est.); Median household income: $40,568 (2006-2010 5-year est.); Average household income: $45,614 (2006-2010 5-year est.); Percent of households with income of $100,000 or more: 6.4% (2006-2010 5-year est.); Poverty rate: 21.9% (2006-2010 5-year est.).
Education: Percent of population age 25 and over with: High school diploma (including GED) or higher: 87.0% (2006-2010 5-year est.); Bachelor's degree or higher: 7.7% (2006-2010 5-year est.); Master's degree or higher: 1.9% (2006-2010 5-year est.).
Housing: Homeownership rate: 84.2% (2010); Median home value: $95,800 (2006-2010 5-year est.); Median contract rent: $392 per month (2006-2010 5-year est.); Median year structure built: 1968 (2006-2010 5-year est.).
Transportation: Commute to work: 88.4% car, 0.0% public transportation, 4.0% walk, 7.0% work from home (2006-2010 5-year est.); Travel time to work: 37.6% less than 15 minutes, 27.4% 15 to 30 minutes, 16.6% 30 to 45 minutes, 11.9% 45 to 60 minutes, 6.5% 60 minutes or more (2006-2010 5-year est.)
Additional Information Contacts
Wellsboro Area Chamber of Commerce . . . . (570) 724-1926
   http://www.wellsboropa.com/pages/community/links.php

WARD (township). Covers a land area of 34.383 square miles and a water area of 0.003 square miles. Located at 41.71° N. Lat; 76.94° W. Long.
Population: 55 (1990); 128 (2000); 166 (2010); Density: 4.8 persons per square mile (2010); Race: 95.8% White, 0.0% Black, 0.0% Asian, 0.0% American Indian/Alaska Native, 0.0% Native Hawaiian/Other Pacific Islander, 4.2% Other, 0.0% Hispanic of any race (2010); Average household size: 2.02 (2010); Median age: 52.3 (2010); Males per 100 females: 130.6 (2010); Marriage status: 16.0% never married, 52.0% now married, 10.4% widowed, 21.6% divorced (2006-2010 5-year est.); Foreign born: 0.0% (2006-2010 5-year est.); Ancestry (includes multiple ancestries): 26.1% Irish, 18.8% English, 15.9% German, 13.0% American, 12.3% Dutch (2006-2010 5-year est.).
Economy: Single-family building permits issued: 10 (2011); Multi-family building permits issued: 0 (2011); Employment by occupation: 11.3% management, 0.0% professional, 7.0% services, 0.0% sales, 0.0% farming, 11.3% construction, 23.9% production (2006-2010 5-year est.).
Income: Per capita income: $20,034 (2006-2010 5-year est.); Median household income: $30,625 (2006-2010 5-year est.); Average household income: $39,415 (2006-2010 5-year est.); Percent of households with income of $100,000 or more: 7.0% (2006-2010 5-year est.); Poverty rate: 8.7% (2006-2010 5-year est.).
Education: Percent of population age 25 and over with: High school diploma (including GED) or higher: 89.9% (2006-2010 5-year est.); Bachelor's degree or higher: 9.2% (2006-2010 5-year est.); Master's degree or higher: 5.5% (2006-2010 5-year est.).
Housing: Homeownership rate: 96.3% (2010); Median home value: $89,400 (2006-2010 5-year est.); Median contract rent: n/a per month (2006-2010 5-year est.); Median year structure built: 1980 (2006-2010 5-year est.).

Transportation: Commute to work: 92.2% car, 0.0% public transportation, 0.0% walk, 0.0% work from home (2006-2010 5-year est.); Travel time to work: 7.8% less than 15 minutes, 51.6% 15 to 30 minutes, 10.9% 30 to 45 minutes, 20.3% 45 to 60 minutes, 9.4% 60 minutes or more (2006-2010 5-year est.)

WELLSBORO (borough). County seat. Covers a land area of 4.885 square miles and a water area of 0.028 square miles. Located at 41.75° N. Lat; 77.30° W. Long. Elevation is 1,299 feet.

History: Settled c.1800, laid out 1806, incorporated 1830.

Population: 3,430 (1990); 3,328 (2000); 3,263 (2010); Density: 667.9 persons per square mile (2010); Race: 96.1% White, 0.6% Black, 1.3% Asian, 0.3% American Indian/Alaska Native, 0.0% Native Hawaiian/Other Pacific Islander, 1.7% Other, 1.1% Hispanic of any race (2010); Average household size: 2.08 (2010); Median age: 47.5 (2010); Males per 100 females: 79.8 (2010); Marriage status: 27.0% never married, 45.7% now married, 17.5% widowed, 9.8% divorced (2006-2010 5-year est.); Foreign born: 3.0% (2006-2010 5-year est.); Ancestry (includes multiple ancestries): 31.6% German, 18.7% English, 12.4% Irish, 8.7% American, 5.9% Italian (2006-2010 5-year est.).

Economy: Single-family building permits issued: 0 (2011); Multi-family building permits issued: 0 (2011); Employment by occupation: 12.2% management, 4.5% professional, 11.5% services, 18.1% sales, 4.4% farming, 5.1% construction, 3.7% production (2006-2010 5-year est.).

Income: Per capita income: $24,042 (2006-2010 5-year est.); Median household income: $32,857 (2006-2010 5-year est.); Average household income: $49,949 (2006-2010 5-year est.); Percent of households with income of $100,000 or more: 10.8% (2006-2010 5-year est.); Poverty rate: 18.7% (2006-2010 5-year est.).

Education: Percent of population age 25 and over with: High school diploma (including GED) or higher: 85.9% (2006-2010 5-year est.); Bachelor's degree or higher: 23.6% (2006-2010 5-year est.); Master's degree or higher: 12.0% (2006-2010 5-year est.).

School District(s)

Wellsboro Area SD (KG-12)

   2010-11 Enrollment: 1,538 . . . . (570) 724-4424

Housing: Homeownership rate: 57.1% (2010); Median home value: $121,100 (2006-2010 5-year est.); Median contract rent: $428 per month (2006-2010 5-year est.); Median year structure built: before 1940 (2006-2010 5-year est.).

Hospitals: Soldiers and Sailors Memorial Hospital (103 beds)

Safety: Violent crime rate: 3.1 per 10,000 population; Property crime rate: 122.2 per 10,000 population (2011).

Newspapers: Gazette (Community news; Circulation 7,200); Wellsboro Gazette (Community news)

Transportation: Commute to work: 78.9% car, 1.0% public transportation, 13.1% walk, 6.3% work from home (2006-2010 5-year est.); Travel time to work: 67.2% less than 15 minutes, 18.8% 15 to 30 minutes, 6.3% 30 to 45 minutes, 3.1% 45 to 60 minutes, 4.6% 60 minutes or more (2006-2010 5-year est.)

Additional Information Contacts

Wellsboro Area Chamber of Commerce . . . . (570) 724-1926

   http://www.wellsboropa.com

WESTFIELD (borough). Covers a land area of 0.968 square miles and a water area of 0 square miles. Located at 41.92° N. Lat; 77.54° W. Long. Elevation is 1,365 feet.

Population: 1,119 (1990); 1,190 (2000); 1,064 (2010); Density: 1,099.7 persons per square mile (2010); Race: 97.8% White, 1.0% Black, 0.1% Asian, 0.4% American Indian/Alaska Native, 0.0% Native Hawaiian/Other Pacific Islander, 0.7% Other, 0.8% Hispanic of any race (2010); Average household size: 2.32 (2010); Median age: 42.2 (2010); Males per 100 females: 88.7 (2010); Marriage status: 24.3% never married, 52.6% now married, 9.5% widowed, 13.6% divorced (2006-2010 5-year est.); Foreign born: 0.2% (2006-2010 5-year est.); Ancestry (includes multiple ancestries): 23.1% German, 14.9% English, 10.5% American, 8.9% Irish, 5.8% Italian (2006-2010 5-year est.).

Economy: Single-family building permits issued: 1 (2011); Multi-family building permits issued: 0 (2011); Employment by occupation: 2.4% management, 2.2% professional, 15.6% services, 7.7% sales, 5.9% farming, 4.3% construction, 14.8% production (2006-2010 5-year est.).

Income: Per capita income: $16,699 (2006-2010 5-year est.); Median household income: $32,171 (2006-2010 5-year est.); Average household income: $39,318 (2006-2010 5-year est.); Percent of households with

income of $100,000 or more: 5.0% (2006-2010 5-year est.); Poverty rate: 26.6% (2006-2010 5-year est.).

Education: Percent of population age 25 and over with: High school diploma (including GED) or higher: 81.6% (2006-2010 5-year est.); Bachelor's degree or higher: 12.2% (2006-2010 5-year est.); Master's degree or higher: 4.5% (2006-2010 5-year est.).

School District(s)

Northern Tioga SD (KG-12)

   2010-11 Enrollment: 2,139 . . . . (814) 258-5642

Housing: Homeownership rate: 55.0% (2010); Median home value: $66,900 (2006-2010 5-year est.); Median contract rent: $322 per month (2006-2010 5-year est.); Median year structure built: 1941 (2006-2010 5-year est.).

Newspapers: Dollar Saver (Community news; Circulation 17,000); Free Press Courier (Local news; Circulation 4,000)

Transportation: Commute to work: 85.7% car, 0.0% public transportation, 10.1% walk, 1.7% work from home (2006-2010 5-year est.); Travel time to work: 47.7% less than 15 minutes, 18.5% 15 to 30 minutes, 7.6% 30 to 45 minutes, 20.0% 45 to 60 minutes, 6.3% 60 minutes or more (2006-2010 5-year est.)

Additional Information Contacts

Wellsboro Area Chamber of Commerce . . . . (570) 724-1926

   http://www.wellsboropa.com

WESTFIELD (township). Covers a land area of 23.364 square miles and a water area of 0 square miles. Located at 41.91° N. Lat; 77.53° W. Long. Elevation is 1,365 feet.

History: Incorporated 1867.

Population: 1,022 (1990); 849 (2000); 1,047 (2010); Density: 44.8 persons per square mile (2010); Race: 99.3% White, 0.1% Black, 0.2% Asian, 0.1% American Indian/Alaska Native, 0.0% Native Hawaiian/Other Pacific Islander, 0.3% Other, 0.4% Hispanic of any race (2010); Average household size: 2.42 (2010); Median age: 46.4 (2010); Males per 100 females: 98.3 (2010); Marriage status: 15.9% never married, 65.9% now married, 10.8% widowed, 7.3% divorced (2006-2010 5-year est.); Foreign born: 0.8% (2006-2010 5-year est.); Ancestry (includes multiple ancestries): 27.3% German, 19.5% English, 12.7% Irish, 8.6% American, 7.6% Italian (2006-2010 5-year est.).

Economy: Single-family building permits issued: 0 (2011); Multi-family building permits issued: 0 (2011); Employment by occupation: 6.9% management, 3.9% professional, 16.8% services, 9.6% sales, 0.0% farming, 14.9% construction, 24.5% production (2006-2010 5-year est.).

Income: Per capita income: $17,257 (2006-2010 5-year est.); Median household income: $33,889 (2006-2010 5-year est.); Average household income: $40,386 (2006-2010 5-year est.); Percent of households with income of $100,000 or more: 5.2% (2006-2010 5-year est.); Poverty rate: 10.2% (2006-2010 5-year est.).

Education: Percent of population age 25 and over with: High school diploma (including GED) or higher: 78.5% (2006-2010 5-year est.); Bachelor's degree or higher: 9.5% (2006-2010 5-year est.); Master's degree or higher: 3.3% (2006-2010 5-year est.).

Housing: Homeownership rate: 79.3% (2010); Median home value: $77,900 (2006-2010 5-year est.); Median contract rent: $280 per month (2006-2010 5-year est.); Median year structure built: 1950 (2006-2010 5-year est.).

Newspapers: Dollar Saver (Community news; Circulation 17,000); Free Press Courier (Local news; Circulation 4,000)

Transportation: Commute to work: 93.8% car, 0.0% public transportation, 0.8% walk, 4.2% work from home (2006-2010 5-year est.); Travel time to work: 36.6% less than 15 minutes, 20.1% 15 to 30 minutes, 17.7% 30 to 45 minutes, 17.1% 45 to 60 minutes, 8.6% 60 minutes or more (2006-2010 5-year est.)

Union County

Located in central Pennsylvania; bounded on the east by the West Branch of the Susquehanna River. Covers a land area of 315.982 square miles, a water area of 1.795 square miles, and is located in the Eastern Time Zone at 40.96° N. Lat., 77.06° W. Long. The county was founded in 1813. County seat is Lewisburg.

Union County is part of the Lewisburg, PA Micropolitan Statistical Area. The entire metro area includes: Union County, PA

Weather Station: Laurelton Center   Elevation: 799 feet

	Jan	Feb	Mar	Apr	May	Jun	Jul	Aug	Sep	Oct	Nov	Dec
High	37	42	51	65	76	83	86	85	76	65	53	40
Low	18	21	27	37	47	55	60	59	52	40	32	23
Precip	2.8	2.5	3.4	3.9	4.0	4.4	4.1	4.0	4.5	3.4	3.9	2.7
Snow	9.4	na	4.2	0.9	0.0	0.0	0.0	0.0	0.0	0.1	0.8	na

High and Low temperatures in degrees Fahrenheit; Precipitation and Snow in inches

Population: 36,176 (1990); 41,624 (2000); 44,947 (2010); Race: 87.7% White, 7.4% Black, 1.2% Asian, 0.4% American Indian/Alaska Native, 0.1% Native Hawaiian/Other Pacific Islander, 3.2% Other, 5.2% Hispanic of any race (2010); Density: 142.2 persons per square mile (2010); Average household size: 2.43 (2010); Median age: 38.5 (2010); Males per 100 females: 122.1 (2010).
Religion: Six largest groups: 7.5% Lutheran, 6.0% Presbyterian-Reformed, 5.8% Methodist/Pietist, 4.4% Catholicism, 3.0% Non-Denominational, 2.4% European Free-Church (2010)
Economy: Unemployment rate: 7.9% (August 2012); Total civilian labor force: 17,721 (August 2012); Leading industries: 24.1% health care and social assistance; 13.2% accommodation & food services; 11.2% retail trade (2010); Farms: 575 totaling 63,795 acres (2007); Companies that employ 500 or more persons: 2 (2010); Companies that employ 100 to 499 persons: 19 (2010); Companies that employ less than 100 persons: 890 (2010); Black-owned businesses: n/a (2007); Hispanic-owned businesses: n/a (2007); Asian-owned businesses: n/a (2007); Women-owned businesses: 809 (2007); Retail sales per capita: $8,700 (2010). Single-family building permits issued: 37 (2011); Multi-family building permits issued: 0 (2011).
Income: Per capita income: $21,612 (2006-2010 5-year est.); Median household income: $45,474 (2006-2010 5-year est.); Average household income: $60,805 (2006-2010 5-year est.); Percent of households with income of $100,000 or more: 14.9% (2006-2010 5-year est.); Poverty rate: 12.6% (2006-2010 5-year est.); Bankruptcy rate: 1.53% (2011).
Taxes: Total county taxes per capita: $213 (2009); County property taxes per capita: $213 (2009).
Education: Percent of population age 25 and over with: High school diploma (including GED) or higher: 83.1% (2006-2010 5-year est.); Bachelor's degree or higher: 22.2% (2006-2010 5-year est.); Master's degree or higher: 9.2% (2006-2010 5-year est.).
Housing: Homeownership rate: 71.1% (2010); Median home value: $143,200 (2006-2010 5-year est.); Median contract rent: $501 per month (2006-2010 5-year est.); Median year structure built: 1971 (2006-2010 5-year est.)
Health: Birth rate: 82.3 per 10,000 population (2011); Death rate: 85.2 per 10,000 population (2011); Age-adjusted cancer mortality rate: 152.0 deaths per 100,000 population (2009); Number of physicians: 32.9 per 10,000 population (2010); Hospital beds: 32.1 per 10,000 population (2008); Hospital admissions: 1,575.4 per 10,000 population (2008).
Elections: 2012 Presidential election results: 37.5% Obama, 60.9% Romney
National and State Parks: Raymond B Winter State Park; Sand Bridge State Park; Shikellamy State Park
Additional Information Contacts
Union County Government . . . . (570) 524-8686
  http://unioncountypa.org

Union County Communities

ALLENWOOD (CDP). Covers a land area of 0.588 square miles and a water area of 0 square miles. Located at 41.11° N. Lat; 76.90° W. Long. Elevation is 482 feet.
Population: n/a (1990); n/a (2000); 321 (2010); Density: 546.3 persons per square mile (2010); Race: 95.0% White, 4.4% Black, 0.3% Asian, 0.0% American Indian/Alaska Native, 0.0% Native Hawaiian/Other Pacific Islander, 0.3% Other, 1.2% Hispanic of any race (2010); Average household size: 2.34 (2010); Median age: 44.7 (2010); Males per 100 females: 94.5 (2010); Marriage status: 20.3% never married, 57.6% now married, 5.6% widowed, 16.5% divorced (2006-2010 5-year est.); Foreign born: 7.5% (2006-2010 5-year est.); Ancestry (includes multiple ancestries): 49.3% German, 21.6% Irish, 10.7% English, 10.5% American, 8.6% Italian (2006-2010 5-year est.).
Economy: Employment by occupation: 6.9% management, 1.8% professional, 14.2% services, 16.4% sales, 8.4% farming, 12.8% construction, 9.1% production (2006-2010 5-year est.).

Income: Per capita income: $20,821 (2006-2010 5-year est.); Median household income: $45,750 (2006-2010 5-year est.); Average household income: $50,166 (2006-2010 5-year est.); Percent of households with income of $100,000 or more: 7.9% (2006-2010 5-year est.); Poverty rate: 5.7% (2006-2010 5-year est.).
Education: Percent of population age 25 and over with: High school diploma (including GED) or higher: 83.6% (2006-2010 5-year est.); Bachelor's degree or higher: 11.4% (2006-2010 5-year est.); Master's degree or higher: 3.7% (2006-2010 5-year est.).
School District(s)
Montgomery Area SD (KG-12)
  2010-11 Enrollment: 915 . . . . (570) 547-1608
Housing: Homeownership rate: 81.8% (2010); Median home value: $96,300 (2006-2010 5-year est.); Median contract rent: $521 per month (2006-2010 5-year est.); Median year structure built: 1975 (2006-2010 5-year est.).
Transportation: Commute to work: 89.9% car, 0.0% public transportation, 3.2% walk, 2.8% work from home (2006-2010 5-year est.); Travel time to work: 23.8% less than 15 minutes, 48.3% 15 to 30 minutes, 23.8% 30 to 45 minutes, 1.3% 45 to 60 minutes, 2.9% 60 minutes or more (2006-2010 5-year est.)

BUFFALO (township). Covers a land area of 30.132 square miles and a water area of 0.199 square miles. Located at 40.97° N. Lat; 76.98° W. Long.
Population: 2,877 (1990); 3,207 (2000); 3,538 (2010); Density: 117.4 persons per square mile (2010); Race: 97.1% White, 0.9% Black, 0.1% Asian, 0.1% American Indian/Alaska Native, 0.0% Native Hawaiian/Other Pacific Islander, 1.8% Other, 2.0% Hispanic of any race (2010); Average household size: 2.73 (2010); Median age: 38.2 (2010); Males per 100 females: 100.7 (2010); Marriage status: 20.0% never married, 68.7% now married, 6.7% widowed, 4.6% divorced (2006-2010 5-year est.); Foreign born: 0.1% (2006-2010 5-year est.); Ancestry (includes multiple ancestries): 42.1% German, 14.1% Swiss, 10.5% Irish, 9.3% English, 5.7% Italian (2006-2010 5-year est.).
Economy: Single-family building permits issued: 3 (2011); Multi-family building permits issued: 0 (2011); Employment by occupation: 13.0% management, 2.8% professional, 8.7% services, 19.5% sales, 1.0% farming, 13.6% construction, 7.4% production (2006-2010 5-year est.).
Income: Per capita income: $22,255 (2006-2010 5-year est.); Median household income: $45,451 (2006-2010 5-year est.); Average household income: $60,919 (2006-2010 5-year est.); Percent of households with income of $100,000 or more: 15.2% (2006-2010 5-year est.); Poverty rate: 23.6% (2006-2010 5-year est.).
Education: Percent of population age 25 and over with: High school diploma (including GED) or higher: 82.2% (2006-2010 5-year est.); Bachelor's degree or higher: 17.2% (2006-2010 5-year est.); Master's degree or higher: 6.4% (2006-2010 5-year est.).
Housing: Homeownership rate: 72.3% (2010); Median home value: $126,800 (2006-2010 5-year est.); Median contract rent: $618 per month (2006-2010 5-year est.); Median year structure built: 1972 (2006-2010 5-year est.).
Transportation: Commute to work: 82.9% car, 0.0% public transportation, 2.2% walk, 10.9% work from home (2006-2010 5-year est.); Travel time to work: 35.3% less than 15 minutes, 40.0% 15 to 30 minutes, 13.2% 30 to 45 minutes, 7.0% 45 to 60 minutes, 4.5% 60 minutes or more (2006-2010 5-year est.)
Additional Information Contacts
Central PA Chamber of Commerce. . . . . (570) 742-7341
  http://www.centralpachamber.com/index.php

EAST BUFFALO (township). Covers a land area of 15.151 square miles and a water area of 0.010 square miles. Located at 40.93° N. Lat; 76.91° W. Long.
History: The history of East Buffalo Township began March 21, 1772, when the legislature of Pennsylvania erected Northumberland County; at the January 1792 Quarter Sessions Court of Northumberland County, what was left of Buffalo Township, was divided into West Buffalo and East Buffalo Townships.
Population: 5,245 (1990); 5,730 (2000); 6,414 (2010); Density: 423.3 persons per square mile (2010); Race: 92.4% White, 2.0% Black, 2.6% Asian, 0.3% American Indian/Alaska Native, 0.0% Native Hawaiian/Other Pacific Islander, 2.7% Other, 2.5% Hispanic of any race (2010); Average household size: 2.51 (2010); Median age: 38.4 (2010); Males per 100 females: 96.7 (2010); Marriage status: 31.4% never married, 55.9% now

married, 5.7% widowed, 7.0% divorced (2006-2010 5-year est.); Foreign born: 4.8% (2006-2010 5-year est.); Ancestry (includes multiple ancestries): 37.2% German, 17.5% Irish, 14.3% English, 10.9% Italian, 7.0% Polish (2006-2010 5-year est.).

Economy: Single-family building permits issued: 5 (2011); Multi-family building permits issued: 0 (2011); Employment by occupation: 20.4% management, 8.3% professional, 6.2% services, 10.5% sales, 1.3% farming, 3.0% construction, 2.2% production (2006-2010 5-year est.).

Income: Per capita income: $35,902 (2006-2010 5-year est.); Median household income: $73,399 (2006-2010 5-year est.); Average household income: $102,088 (2006-2010 5-year est.); Percent of households with income of $100,000 or more: 37.2% (2006-2010 5-year est.); Poverty rate: 5.8% (2006-2010 5-year est.).

Education: Percent of population age 25 and over with: High school diploma (including GED) or higher: 95.5% (2006-2010 5-year est.); Bachelor's degree or higher: 58.3% (2006-2010 5-year est.); Master's degree or higher: 30.4% (2006-2010 5-year est.).

Housing: Homeownership rate: 85.2% (2010); Median home value: $218,200 (2006-2010 5-year est.); Median contract rent: $532 per month (2006-2010 5-year est.); Median year structure built: 1971 (2006-2010 5-year est.).

Safety: Violent crime rate: 4.7 per 10,000 population; Property crime rate: 54.4 per 10,000 population (2011).

Transportation: Commute to work: 82.9% car, 0.0% public transportation, 8.7% walk, 7.0% work from home (2006-2010 5-year est.); Travel time to work: 56.4% less than 15 minutes, 23.8% 15 to 30 minutes, 13.0% 30 to 45 minutes, 0.6% 45 to 60 minutes, 6.2% 60 minutes or more (2006-2010 5-year est.)

Additional Information Contacts

Central PA Chamber of Commerce . . . . (570) 742-7341
   http://www.centralpachamber.com/index.php
East Buffalo Township . . . . (570) 523-6320
   http://www.ebtwp.org

GREGG (township). Covers a land area of 14.889 square miles and a water area of 0.228 square miles. Located at 41.11° N. Lat; 76.94° W. Long.

Population: 1,114 (1990); 4,687 (2000); 4,984 (2010); Density: 334.7 persons per square mile (2010); Race: 47.7% White, 38.4% Black, 1.6% Asian, 1.4% American Indian/Alaska Native, 0.1% Native Hawaiian/Other Pacific Islander, 10.8% Other, 22.3% Hispanic of any race (2010); Average household size: 2.47 (2010); Median age: 38.4 (2010); Males per 100 females: 793.2 (2010); Marriage status: 45.8% never married, 41.2% now married, 2.4% widowed, 10.6% divorced (2006-2010 5-year est.); Foreign born: 20.2% (2006-2010 5-year est.); Ancestry (includes multiple ancestries): 12.6% German, 5.9% Irish, 3.9% Italian, 3.5% American, 3.4% English (2006-2010 5-year est.).

Economy: Employment by occupation: 11.1% management, 0.8% professional, 14.8% services, 13.9% sales, 5.1% farming, 16.1% construction, 16.0% production (2006-2010 5-year est.).

Income: Per capita income: $10,432 (2006-2010 5-year est.); Median household income: $38,971 (2006-2010 5-year est.); Average household income: $48,442 (2006-2010 5-year est.); Percent of households with income of $100,000 or more: 7.0% (2006-2010 5-year est.); Poverty rate: 26.5% (2006-2010 5-year est.).

Education: Percent of population age 25 and over with: High school diploma (including GED) or higher: 68.8% (2006-2010 5-year est.); Bachelor's degree or higher: 5.9% (2006-2010 5-year est.); Master's degree or higher: 1.5% (2006-2010 5-year est.).

Housing: Homeownership rate: 75.3% (2010); Median home value: $110,500 (2006-2010 5-year est.); Median contract rent: $461 per month (2006-2010 5-year est.); Median year structure built: 1973 (2006-2010 5-year est.).

Transportation: Commute to work: 94.2% car, 0.0% public transportation, 2.7% walk, 1.3% work from home (2006-2010 5-year est.); Travel time to work: 24.2% less than 15 minutes, 46.7% 15 to 30 minutes, 22.1% 30 to 45 minutes, 5.0% 45 to 60 minutes, 2.0% 60 minutes or more (2006-2010 5-year est.)

Additional Information Contacts

Williamsport/Lycoming Chamber of Commerce . . . . (570) 326-1971
   http://www.williamsport.org

HARTLETON (borough). Covers a land area of 0.908 square miles and a water area of 0 square miles. Located at 40.90° N. Lat; 77.16° W. Long. Elevation is 653 feet.

Population: 246 (1990); 260 (2000); 283 (2010); Density: 311.6 persons per square mile (2010); Race: 98.6% White, 0.0% Black, 0.0% Asian, 0.0% American Indian/Alaska Native, 0.0% Native Hawaiian/Other Pacific Islander, 1.4% Other, 0.0% Hispanic of any race (2010); Average household size: 2.83 (2010); Median age: 41.3 (2010); Males per 100 females: 99.3 (2010); Marriage status: 19.9% never married, 63.4% now married, 8.1% widowed, 8.6% divorced (2006-2010 5-year est.); Foreign born: 0.0% (2006-2010 5-year est.); Ancestry (includes multiple ancestries): 51.7% German, 9.8% American, 6.8% English, 4.5% Irish, 3.0% French (2006-2010 5-year est.).

Economy: Employment by occupation: 17.5% management, 0.0% professional, 12.3% services, 6.1% sales, 0.9% farming, 27.2% construction, 10.5% production (2006-2010 5-year est.).

Income: Per capita income: $17,950 (2006-2010 5-year est.); Median household income: $47,857 (2006-2010 5-year est.); Average household income: $52,572 (2006-2010 5-year est.); Percent of households with income of $100,000 or more: 8.9% (2006-2010 5-year est.); Poverty rate: 9.1% (2006-2010 5-year est.).

Education: Percent of population age 25 and over with: High school diploma (including GED) or higher: 66.5% (2006-2010 5-year est.); Bachelor's degree or higher: 8.7% (2006-2010 5-year est.); Master's degree or higher: 1.9% (2006-2010 5-year est.).

Housing: Homeownership rate: 87.0% (2010); Median home value: $100,000 (2006-2010 5-year est.); Median contract rent: $575 per month (2006-2010 5-year est.); Median year structure built: before 1940 (2006-2010 5-year est.).

Safety: Violent crime rate: 0.0 per 10,000 population; Property crime rate: 35.2 per 10,000 population (2011).

Transportation: Commute to work: 71.9% car, 0.0% public transportation, 13.2% walk, 9.6% work from home (2006-2010 5-year est.); Travel time to work: 41.7% less than 15 minutes, 24.3% 15 to 30 minutes, 23.3% 30 to 45 minutes, 1.9% 45 to 60 minutes, 8.7% 60 minutes or more (2006-2010 5-year est.)

HARTLEY (township). Covers a land area of 79.602 square miles and a water area of 0.549 square miles. Located at 40.89° N. Lat; 77.27° W. Long.

Population: 1,896 (1990); 1,714 (2000); 1,820 (2010); Density: 22.9 persons per square mile (2010); Race: 99.0% White, 0.2% Black, 0.2% Asian, 0.2% American Indian/Alaska Native, 0.0% Native Hawaiian/Other Pacific Islander, 0.4% Other, 1.1% Hispanic of any race (2010); Average household size: 2.60 (2010); Median age: 41.5 (2010); Males per 100 females: 98.9 (2010); Marriage status: 16.3% never married, 70.3% now married, 5.3% widowed, 8.0% divorced (2006-2010 5-year est.); Foreign born: 0.3% (2006-2010 5-year est.); Ancestry (includes multiple ancestries): 49.4% German, 11.2% Irish, 10.1% Polish, 7.0% American, 6.3% English (2006-2010 5-year est.).

Economy: Single-family building permits issued: 6 (2011); Multi-family building permits issued: 0 (2011); Employment by occupation: 5.7% management, 1.4% professional, 12.0% services, 14.3% sales, 1.3% farming, 26.6% construction, 13.7% production (2006-2010 5-year est.).

Income: Per capita income: $18,341 (2006-2010 5-year est.); Median household income: $42,406 (2006-2010 5-year est.); Average household income: $49,717 (2006-2010 5-year est.); Percent of households with income of $100,000 or more: 5.6% (2006-2010 5-year est.); Poverty rate: 13.0% (2006-2010 5-year est.).

Education: Percent of population age 25 and over with: High school diploma (including GED) or higher: 81.0% (2006-2010 5-year est.); Bachelor's degree or higher: 10.8% (2006-2010 5-year est.); Master's degree or higher: 2.3% (2006-2010 5-year est.).

Housing: Homeownership rate: 81.2% (2010); Median home value: $114,400 (2006-2010 5-year est.); Median contract rent: $454 per month (2006-2010 5-year est.); Median year structure built: 1963 (2006-2010 5-year est.).

Transportation: Commute to work: 88.7% car, 0.0% public transportation, 0.7% walk, 9.9% work from home (2006-2010 5-year est.); Travel time to work: 23.8% less than 15 minutes, 23.4% 15 to 30 minutes, 20.6% 30 to 45 minutes, 19.6% 45 to 60 minutes, 12.6% 60 minutes or more (2006-2010 5-year est.)

Additional Information Contacts

Greater Susquehanna Valley Chamber of Commerce . . . . (570) 743-4100
   http://www.gsvcc.org

KELLY (township). Covers a land area of 17.168 square miles and a water area of 0.032 square miles. Located at 41.00° N. Lat; 76.92° W. Long.

Population: 4,561 (1990); 4,502 (2000); 5,491 (2010); Density: 319.8 persons per square mile (2010); Race: 74.8% White, 16.8% Black, 0.9% Asian, 0.7% American Indian/Alaska Native, 0.1% Native Hawaiian/Other Pacific Islander, 6.7% Other, 11.4% Hispanic of any race (2010); Average household size: 2.23 (2010); Median age: 40.2 (2010); Males per 100 females: 165.7 (2010); Marriage status: 30.2% never married, 48.4% now married, 10.2% widowed, 11.2% divorced (2006-2010 5-year est.); Foreign born: 6.2% (2006-2010 5-year est.); Ancestry (includes multiple ancestries): 26.0% German, 11.7% Irish, 8.5% English, 7.0% Italian, 5.6% American (2006-2010 5-year est.).

Economy: Single-family building permits issued: 3 (2011); Multi-family building permits issued: 0 (2011); Employment by occupation: 10.3% management, 1.3% professional, 14.1% services, 15.9% sales, 0.0% farming, 10.8% construction, 3.6% production (2006-2010 5-year est.).

Income: Per capita income: $18,125 (2006-2010 5-year est.); Median household income: $30,146 (2006-2010 5-year est.); Average household income: $45,100 (2006-2010 5-year est.); Percent of households with income of $100,000 or more: 8.1% (2006-2010 5-year est.); Poverty rate: 16.2% (2006-2010 5-year est.).

Education: Percent of population age 25 and over with: High school diploma (including GED) or higher: 84.7% (2006-2010 5-year est.); Bachelor's degree or higher: 18.0% (2006-2010 5-year est.); Master's degree or higher: 8.1% (2006-2010 5-year est.).

Housing: Homeownership rate: 57.7% (2010); Median home value: $168,100 (2006-2010 5-year est.); Median contract rent: $462 per month (2006-2010 5-year est.); Median year structure built: 1981 (2006-2010 5-year est.).

Transportation: Commute to work: 88.3% car, 0.6% public transportation, 3.7% walk, 7.4% work from home (2006-2010 5-year est.); Travel time to work: 71.3% less than 15 minutes, 18.5% 15 to 30 minutes, 8.9% 30 to 45 minutes, 1.2% 45 to 60 minutes, 0.0% 60 minutes or more (2006-2010 5-year est.)

Additional Information Contacts

Central PA Chamber of Commerce . . . . (570) 742-7341
  http://www.centralpachamber.com/index.php

LAURELTON (CDP). Covers a land area of 0.570 square miles and a water area of 0.001 square miles. Located at 40.88° N. Lat; 77.20° W. Long. Elevation is 653 feet.

Population: n/a (1990); n/a (2000); 221 (2010); Density: 387.4 persons per square mile (2010); Race: 99.1% White, 0.0% Black, 0.9% Asian, 0.0% American Indian/Alaska Native, 0.0% Native Hawaiian/Other Pacific Islander, 0.0% Other, 0.0% Hispanic of any race (2010); Average household size: 2.51 (2010); Median age: 38.2 (2010); Males per 100 females: 84.2 (2010); Marriage status: 31.2% never married, 61.1% now married, 1.9% widowed, 5.7% divorced (2006-2010 5-year est.); Foreign born: 0.0% (2006-2010 5-year est.); Ancestry (includes multiple ancestries): 50.0% German, 12.4% Dutch, 9.2% Italian, 8.3% Irish, 6.4% Scottish (2006-2010 5-year est.).

Economy: Employment by occupation: 4.2% management, 0.0% professional, 12.5% services, 2.5% sales, 0.0% farming, 15.0% construction, 9.2% production (2006-2010 5-year est.).

Income: Per capita income: $22,205 (2006-2010 5-year est.); Median household income: $48,438 (2006-2010 5-year est.); Average household income: $53,374 (2006-2010 5-year est.); Percent of households with income of $100,000 or more: 3.3% (2006-2010 5-year est.); Poverty rate: 11.6% (2006-2010 5-year est.).

Education: Percent of population age 25 and over with: High school diploma (including GED) or higher: 90.8% (2006-2010 5-year est.); Bachelor's degree or higher: 3.9% (2006-2010 5-year est.); Master's degree or higher: 0.0% (2006-2010 5-year est.).

School District(s)

Mifflinburg Area SD (KG-12)
  2010-11 Enrollment: 2,150 . . . . (570) 966-8200

Housing: Homeownership rate: 77.3% (2010); Median home value: $87,600 (2006-2010 5-year est.); Median contract rent: $525 per month (2006-2010 5-year est.); Median year structure built: before 1940 (2006-2010 5-year est.).

Transportation: Commute to work: 87.2% car, 0.0% public transportation, 0.0% walk, 12.8% work from home (2006-2010 5-year est.); Travel time to work: 24.2% less than 15 minutes, 31.6% 15 to 30 minutes, 32.6% 30 to

45 minutes, 0.0% 45 to 60 minutes, 11.6% 60 minutes or more (2006-2010 5-year est.)

LEWIS (township). Covers a land area of 38.721 square miles and a water area of 0.185 square miles. Located at 40.95° N. Lat; 77.12° W. Long.

Population: 1,222 (1990); 1,405 (2000); 1,480 (2010); Density: 38.2 persons per square mile (2010); Race: 97.2% White, 1.7% Black, 0.1% Asian, 0.1% American Indian/Alaska Native, 0.0% Native Hawaiian/Other Pacific Islander, 0.9% Other, 0.3% Hispanic of any race (2010); Average household size: 2.79 (2010); Median age: 36.4 (2010); Males per 100 females: 104.1 (2010); Marriage status: 16.7% never married, 71.8% now married, 3.4% widowed, 8.1% divorced (2006-2010 5-year est.); Foreign born: 0.2% (2006-2010 5-year est.); Ancestry (includes multiple ancestries): 48.5% German, 14.6% American, 6.2% Dutch, 4.4% English, 4.3% Irish (2006-2010 5-year est.).

Economy: Single-family building permits issued: 3 (2011); Multi-family building permits issued: 0 (2011); Employment by occupation: 12.5% management, 3.9% professional, 8.5% services, 16.4% sales, 4.1% farming, 16.9% construction, 6.9% production (2006-2010 5-year est.).

Income: Per capita income: $21,882 (2006-2010 5-year est.); Median household income: $40,417 (2006-2010 5-year est.); Average household income: $53,872 (2006-2010 5-year est.); Percent of households with income of $100,000 or more: 7.9% (2006-2010 5-year est.); Poverty rate: 12.8% (2006-2010 5-year est.).

Education: Percent of population age 25 and over with: High school diploma (including GED) or higher: 70.9% (2006-2010 5-year est.); Bachelor's degree or higher: 10.6% (2006-2010 5-year est.); Master's degree or higher: 1.1% (2006-2010 5-year est.).

Housing: Homeownership rate: 77.5% (2010); Median home value: $121,600 (2006-2010 5-year est.); Median contract rent: $448 per month (2006-2010 5-year est.); Median year structure built: 1969 (2006-2010 5-year est.).

Transportation: Commute to work: 79.4% car, 0.0% public transportation, 2.5% walk, 14.1% work from home (2006-2010 5-year est.); Travel time to work: 20.1% less than 15 minutes, 44.6% 15 to 30 minutes, 15.8% 30 to 45 minutes, 11.5% 45 to 60 minutes, 8.0% 60 minutes or more (2006-2010 5-year est.)

Additional Information Contacts

Williamsport/Lycoming Chamber of Commerce . . . . (570) 326-1971
  http://www.williamsport.org

LEWISBURG (borough). County seat. Covers a land area of 0.973 square miles and a water area of 0 square miles. Located at 40.96° N. Lat; 76.89° W. Long. Elevation is 472 feet.

History: Lewisburg was laid out in 1785 and named for Ludwig (Lewis) Doerr, early settler. Bucknell University was founded here in 1846.

Population: 5,785 (1990); 5,620 (2000); 5,792 (2010); Density: 5,951.5 persons per square mile (2010); Race: 90.0% White, 3.2% Black, 3.2% Asian, 0.2% American Indian/Alaska Native, 0.0% Native Hawaiian/Other Pacific Islander, 3.4% Other, 4.0% Hispanic of any race (2010); Average household size: 1.90 (2010); Median age: 22.8 (2010); Males per 100 females: 86.1 (2010); Marriage status: 62.9% never married, 21.4% now married, 6.8% widowed, 8.9% divorced (2006-2010 5-year est.); Foreign born: 3.7% (2006-2010 5-year est.); Ancestry (includes multiple ancestries): 33.4% German, 15.7% Irish, 14.0% Italian, 12.5% English, 4.8% Polish (2006-2010 5-year est.).

Economy: Employment by occupation: 11.0% management, 4.8% professional, 16.1% services, 16.8% sales, 5.2% farming, 2.9% construction, 2.8% production (2006-2010 5-year est.).

Income: Per capita income: $17,384 (2006-2010 5-year est.); Median household income: $32,934 (2006-2010 5-year est.); Average household income: $53,564 (2006-2010 5-year est.); Percent of households with income of $100,000 or more: 17.1% (2006-2010 5-year est.); Poverty rate: 20.9% (2006-2010 5-year est.).

Education: Percent of population age 25 and over with: High school diploma (including GED) or higher: 87.2% (2006-2010 5-year est.); Bachelor's degree or higher: 38.4% (2006-2010 5-year est.); Master's degree or higher: 16.6% (2006-2010 5-year est.).

School District(s)

Lewisburg Area SD (KG-12)
  2010-11 Enrollment: 1,911 . . . . (570) 523-3220
Mifflinburg Area SD (KG-12)
  2010-11 Enrollment: 2,150 . . . . (570) 966-8200

Four-year College(s)

Bucknell University (Private, Not-for-profit)

Fall 2010 Enrollment: 4,047 . . . . (570) 577-2000

2011-12 Tuition: In-state $43,866; Out-of-state $43,866

Housing: Homeownership rate: 35.8% (2010); Median home value: $157,500 (2006-2010 5-year est.); Median contract rent: $540 per month (2006-2010 5-year est.); Median year structure built: 1945 (2006-2010 5-year est.).

Hospitals: Evangelical Community Hospital (134 beds)

Safety: Violent crime rate: 22.4 per 10,000 population; Property crime rate: 156.6 per 10,000 population (2011).

Transportation: Commute to work: 46.3% car, 0.0% public transportation, 33.4% walk, 17.9% work from home (2006-2010 5-year est.); Travel time to work: 67.6% less than 15 minutes, 21.0% 15 to 30 minutes, 7.5% 30 to 45 minutes, 2.0% 45 to 60 minutes, 1.9% 60 minutes or more (2006-2010 5-year est.).

Additional Information Contacts

Borough of Lewisburg . . . . (570) 523-3614

http://www.lewisburgborough.org

Central PA Chamber of Commerce. . . . . (570) 742-7341

http://www.centralpachamber.com/index.php

LIMESTONE (township). Covers a land area of 20.540 square miles and a water area of 0.179 square miles. Located at 40.90° N. Lat; 77.02° W. Long.

Population: 1,364 (1990); 1,572 (2000); 1,723 (2010); Density: 83.9 persons per square mile (2010); Race: 98.0% White, 0.6% Black, 0.4% Asian, 0.2% American Indian/Alaska Native, 0.0% Native Hawaiian/Other Pacific Islander, 0.8% Other, 0.8% Hispanic of any race (2010); Average household size: 2.94 (2010); Median age: 36.7 (2010); Males per 100 females: 100.3 (2010); Marriage status: 18.1% never married, 73.6% now married, 4.9% widowed, 3.4% divorced (2006-2010 5-year est.); Foreign born: 0.1% (2006-2010 5-year est.); Ancestry (includes multiple ancestries): 45.0% German, 14.1% American, 9.0% Swiss, 5.8% Polish, 4.7% Irish (2006-2010 5-year est.).

Economy: Single-family building permits issued: 7 (2011); Multi-family building permits issued: 0 (2011); Employment by occupation: 11.5% management, 2.5% professional, 9.5% services, 11.1% sales, 1.6% farming, 24.4% construction, 11.2% production (2006-2010 5-year est.).

Income: Per capita income: $22,781 (2006-2010 5-year est.); Median household income: $48,625 (2006-2010 5-year est.); Average household income: $63,603 (2006-2010 5-year est.); Percent of households with income of $100,000 or more: 16.3% (2006-2010 5-year est.); Poverty rate: 8.4% (2006-2010 5-year est.).

Education: Percent of population age 25 and over with: High school diploma (including GED) or higher: 78.4% (2006-2010 5-year est.); Bachelor's degree or higher: 18.7% (2006-2010 5-year est.); Master's degree or higher: 9.3% (2006-2010 5-year est.).

Housing: Homeownership rate: 88.6% (2010); Median home value: $152,900 (2006-2010 5-year est.); Median contract rent: $446 per month (2006-2010 5-year est.); Median year structure built: 1972 (2006-2010 5-year est.).

Transportation: Commute to work: 76.5% car, 0.3% public transportation, 5.9% walk, 8.3% work from home (2006-2010 5-year est.); Travel time to work: 35.5% less than 15 minutes, 43.8% 15 to 30 minutes, 8.9% 30 to 45 minutes, 5.3% 45 to 60 minutes, 6.5% 60 minutes or more (2006-2010 5-year est.)

Additional Information Contacts

Central PA Chamber of Commerce. . . . . (570) 742-7341

http://www.centralpachamber.com/index.php

LINNTOWN (CDP). Covers a land area of 0.709 square miles and a water area of 0 square miles. Located at 40.96° N. Lat; 76.90° W. Long. Elevation is 469 feet.

Population: 1,640 (1990); 1,542 (2000); 1,489 (2010); Density: 2,098.7 persons per square mile (2010); Race: 94.6% White, 1.5% Black, 1.7% Asian, 0.3% American Indian/Alaska Native, 0.1% Native Hawaiian/Other Pacific Islander, 1.8% Other, 1.8% Hispanic of any race (2010); Average household size: 2.21 (2010); Median age: 46.6 (2010); Males per 100 females: 85.2 (2010); Marriage status: 22.3% never married, 61.3% now married, 5.2% widowed, 11.2% divorced (2006-2010 5-year est.); Foreign born: 6.0% (2006-2010 5-year est.); Ancestry (includes multiple ancestries): 41.8% German, 14.9% English, 10.9% Irish, 6.9% Welsh, 6.2% American (2006-2010 5-year est.).

Economy: Employment by occupation: 10.1% management, 5.3% professional, 6.2% services, 17.3% sales, 2.4% farming, 1.4% construction, 2.8% production (2006-2010 5-year est.).

Income: Per capita income: $29,736 (2006-2010 5-year est.); Median household income: $53,011 (2006-2010 5-year est.); Average household income: $62,448 (2006-2010 5-year est.); Percent of households with income of $100,000 or more: 14.0% (2006-2010 5-year est.); Poverty rate: 11.0% (2006-2010 5-year est.).

Education: Percent of population age 25 and over with: High school diploma (including GED) or higher: 97.0% (2006-2010 5-year est.); Bachelor's degree or higher: 57.9% (2006-2010 5-year est.); Master's degree or higher: 31.5% (2006-2010 5-year est.).

Housing: Homeownership rate: 79.3% (2010); Median home value: $161,500 (2006-2010 5-year est.); Median contract rent: $530 per month (2006-2010 5-year est.); Median year structure built: 1958 (2006-2010 5-year est.).

Transportation: Commute to work: 92.4% car, 0.0% public transportation, 6.2% walk, 1.4% work from home (2006-2010 5-year est.); Travel time to work: 54.4% less than 15 minutes, 28.2% 15 to 30 minutes, 9.9% 30 to 45 minutes, 0.0% 45 to 60 minutes, 7.5% 60 minutes or more (2006-2010 5-year est.)

Additional Information Contacts

Central PA Chamber of Commerce. . . . . (570) 742-7341

http://www.centralpachamber.com/index.php

MIFFLINBURG (borough). Covers a land area of 1.804 square miles and a water area of <.001 square miles. Located at 40.92° N. Lat; 77.05° W. Long. Elevation is 584 feet.

History: Laid out 1792; incorporated 1827.

Population: 3,464 (1990); 3,594 (2000); 3,540 (2010); Density: 1,962.3 persons per square mile (2010); Race: 98.3% White, 0.6% Black, 0.3% Asian, 0.0% American Indian/Alaska Native, 0.1% Native Hawaiian/Other Pacific Islander, 0.7% Other, 0.9% Hispanic of any race (2010); Average household size: 2.28 (2010); Median age: 41.4 (2010); Males per 100 females: 92.2 (2010); Marriage status: 21.3% never married, 63.7% now married, 5.5% widowed, 9.5% divorced (2006-2010 5-year est.); Foreign born: 0.9% (2006-2010 5-year est.); Ancestry (includes multiple ancestries): 56.0% German, 9.1% Irish, 8.8% Italian, 8.2% English, 8.0% American (2006-2010 5-year est.).

Economy: Employment by occupation: 6.5% management, 2.2% professional, 9.8% services, 10.8% sales, 3.5% farming, 6.1% construction, 8.7% production (2006-2010 5-year est.).

Income: Per capita income: $21,956 (2006-2010 5-year est.); Median household income: $42,692 (2006-2010 5-year est.); Average household income: $50,306 (2006-2010 5-year est.); Percent of households with income of $100,000 or more: 8.0% (2006-2010 5-year est.); Poverty rate: 5.3% (2006-2010 5-year est.).

Education: Percent of population age 25 and over with: High school diploma (including GED) or higher: 90.2% (2006-2010 5-year est.); Bachelor's degree or higher: 24.3% (2006-2010 5-year est.); Master's degree or higher: 8.7% (2006-2010 5-year est.).

School District(s)

Mifflinburg Area SD (KG-12)

2010-11 Enrollment: 2,150 . . . . (570) 966-8200

Housing: Homeownership rate: 65.6% (2010); Median home value: $119,000 (2006-2010 5-year est.); Median contract rent: $435 per month (2006-2010 5-year est.); Median year structure built: 1963 (2006-2010 5-year est.).

Safety: Violent crime rate: 5.6 per 10,000 population; Property crime rate: 228.1 per 10,000 population (2011).

Newspapers: Mifflinburg Telegraph (Community news; Circulation 900)

Transportation: Commute to work: 88.8% car, 0.0% public transportation, 5.4% walk, 5.9% work from home (2006-2010 5-year est.); Travel time to work: 39.6% less than 15 minutes, 34.9% 15 to 30 minutes, 16.1% 30 to 45 minutes, 4.1% 45 to 60 minutes, 5.3% 60 minutes or more (2006-2010 5-year est.)

Additional Information Contacts

Central PA Chamber of Commerce. . . . . (570) 742-7341

http://www.centralpachamber.com/index.php

MILLMONT (unincorporated postal area)

Zip Code: 17845

Covers a land area of 65.486 square miles and a water area of 0.486 square miles. Located at 40.88° N. Lat; 77.21° W. Long. Population: 2,245 (2010); Density: 34.3 persons per square mile (2010); Race:

97.8% White, 1.2% Black, 0.0% Asian, 0.2% American Indian/Alaska Native, 0.0% Native Hawaiian/Other Pacific Islander, 0.8% Other, 0.9% Hispanic of any race (2010); Average household size: 2.67 (2010); Median age: 40.3 (2010); Males per 100 females: 97.8 (2010); Homeownership rate: 79.9% (2010)

NEW BERLIN (borough). Covers a land area of 0.388 square miles and a water area of 0.010 square miles. Located at 40.88° N. Lat; 76.98° W. Long. Elevation is 545 feet.

Population: 890 (1990); 838 (2000); 873 (2010); Density: 2,250.9 persons per square mile (2010); Race: 99.1% White, 0.2% Black, 0.2% Asian, 0.1% American Indian/Alaska Native, 0.0% Native Hawaiian/Other Pacific Islander, 0.4% Other, 0.2% Hispanic of any race (2010); Average household size: 2.50 (2010); Median age: 41.3 (2010); Males per 100 females: 94.0 (2010); Marriage status: 25.7% never married, 60.1% now married, 2.0% widowed, 12.3% divorced (2006-2010 5-year est.); Foreign born: 0.7% (2006-2010 5-year est.); Ancestry (includes multiple ancestries): 57.2% German, 9.6% Irish, 9.2% English, 7.3% American, 6.5% Dutch (2006-2010 5-year est.).

Economy: Single-family building permits issued: 0 (2011); Multi-family building permits issued: 0 (2011); Employment by occupation: 2.1% management, 2.9% professional, 11.8% services, 13.6% sales, 1.6% farming, 12.6% construction, 7.6% production (2006-2010 5-year est.).

Income: Per capita income: $22,410 (2006-2010 5-year est.); Median household income: $47,656 (2006-2010 5-year est.); Average household income: $55,338 (2006-2010 5-year est.); Percent of households with income of $100,000 or more: 10.0% (2006-2010 5-year est.); Poverty rate: 6.4% (2006-2010 5-year est.).

Education: Percent of population age 25 and over with: High school diploma (including GED) or higher: 89.1% (2006-2010 5-year est.); Bachelor's degree or higher: 14.6% (2006-2010 5-year est.); Master's degree or higher: 5.4% (2006-2010 5-year est.).

School District(s)

Mifflinburg Area SD (KG-12)

2010-11 Enrollment: 2,150 . . . . (570) 966-8200

Sun Area Technical Institute (09-12)

2010-11 Enrollment: n/a . . . . (570) 966-1034

Housing: Homeownership rate: 78.5% (2010); Median home value: $102,100 (2006-2010 5-year est.); Median contract rent: $436 per month (2006-2010 5-year est.); Median year structure built: 1951 (2006-2010 5-year est.).

Transportation: Commute to work: 83.2% car, 0.0% public transportation, 6.8% walk, 5.6% work from home (2006-2010 5-year est.); Travel time to work: 29.1% less than 15 minutes, 45.4% 15 to 30 minutes, 11.5% 30 to 45 minutes, 9.8% 45 to 60 minutes, 4.2% 60 minutes or more (2006-2010 5-year est.).

NEW COLUMBIA (CDP). Covers a land area of 1.940 square miles and a water area of 0.002 square miles. Located at 41.04° N. Lat; 76.88° W. Long. Elevation is 469 feet.

Population: n/a (1990); n/a (2000); 1,013 (2010); Density: 522.1 persons per square mile (2010); Race: 96.5% White, 0.9% Black, 0.1% Asian, 0.1% American Indian/Alaska Native, 0.2% Native Hawaiian/Other Pacific Islander, 2.2% Other, 1.8% Hispanic of any race (2010); Average household size: 2.32 (2010); Median age: 42.0 (2010); Males per 100 females: 86.2 (2010); Marriage status: 21.5% never married, 60.7% now married, 3.0% widowed, 14.8% divorced (2006-2010 5-year est.); Foreign born: 0.0% (2006-2010 5-year est.); Ancestry (includes multiple ancestries): 53.5% German, 9.0% American, 6.9% Irish, 5.6% Dutch, 5.6% Czech (2006-2010 5-year est.).

Economy: Employment by occupation: 4.3% management, 0.0% professional, 4.7% services, 26.7% sales, 4.6% farming, 14.1% construction, 14.1% production (2006-2010 5-year est.).

Income: Per capita income: $27,935 (2006-2010 5-year est.); Median household income: $55,350 (2006-2010 5-year est.); Average household income: $68,187 (2006-2010 5-year est.); Percent of households with income of $100,000 or more: 22.5% (2006-2010 5-year est.); Poverty rate: 6.2% (2006-2010 5-year est.).

Education: Percent of population age 25 and over with: High school diploma (including GED) or higher: 93.6% (2006-2010 5-year est.); Bachelor's degree or higher: 20.5% (2006-2010 5-year est.); Master's degree or higher: 0.0% (2006-2010 5-year est.).

School District(s)

Milton Area SD (KG-12)

2010-11 Enrollment: 2,283 . . . . (570) 742-7614

Housing: Homeownership rate: 69.4% (2010); Median home value: $128,800 (2006-2010 5-year est.); Median contract rent: $556 per month (2006-2010 5-year est.); Median year structure built: 1992 (2006-2010 5-year est.).

Transportation: Commute to work: 96.1% car, 0.0% public transportation, 0.0% walk, 1.8% work from home (2006-2010 5-year est.); Travel time to work: 44.9% less than 15 minutes, 42.7% 15 to 30 minutes, 7.9% 30 to 45 minutes, 0.0% 45 to 60 minutes, 4.6% 60 minutes or more (2006-2010 5-year est.)

SWENGEL (unincorporated postal area)

Zip Code: 17880

Covers a land area of 0.124 square miles and a water area of 0 square miles. Located at 40.89° N. Lat; 77.12° W. Long. Elevation is 614 feet. Population: 72 (2010); Density: 579.7 persons per square mile (2010); Race: 100.0% White, 0.0% Black, 0.0% Asian, 0.0% American Indian/Alaska Native, 0.0% Native Hawaiian/Other Pacific Islander, 0.0% Other, 0.0% Hispanic of any race (2010); Average household size: 2.77 (2010); Median age: 27.3 (2010); Males per 100 females: 105.7 (2010); Homeownership rate: 46.2% (2010)

UNION (township). Covers a land area of 11.277 square miles and a water area of 0.054 square miles. Located at 40.90° N. Lat; 76.89° W. Long.

Population: 1,300 (1990); 1,427 (2000); 1,589 (2010); Density: 140.9 persons per square mile (2010); Race: 97.8% White, 0.4% Black, 0.6% Asian, 0.1% American Indian/Alaska Native, 0.0% Native Hawaiian/Other Pacific Islander, 1.1% Other, 0.6% Hispanic of any race (2010); Average household size: 2.48 (2010); Median age: 47.3 (2010); Males per 100 females: 103.7 (2010); Marriage status: 19.0% never married, 67.2% now married, 5.7% widowed, 8.2% divorced (2006-2010 5-year est.); Foreign born: 1.4% (2006-2010 5-year est.); Ancestry (includes multiple ancestries): 49.1% German, 14.2% American, 13.8% English, 9.2% Irish, 6.0% Polish (2006-2010 5-year est.).

Economy: Single-family building permits issued: 1 (2011); Multi-family building permits issued: 0 (2011); Employment by occupation: 14.6% management, 3.5% professional, 18.6% services, 12.1% sales, 2.4% farming, 8.7% construction, 6.4% production (2006-2010 5-year est.).

Income: Per capita income: $30,815 (2006-2010 5-year est.); Median household income: $57,955 (2006-2010 5-year est.); Average household income: $72,268 (2006-2010 5-year est.); Percent of households with income of $100,000 or more: 19.0% (2006-2010 5-year est.); Poverty rate: 4.7% (2006-2010 5-year est.).

Education: Percent of population age 25 and over with: High school diploma (including GED) or higher: 88.7% (2006-2010 5-year est.); Bachelor's degree or higher: 21.8% (2006-2010 5-year est.); Master's degree or higher: 9.5% (2006-2010 5-year est.).

Housing: Homeownership rate: 87.0% (2010); Median home value: $158,900 (2006-2010 5-year est.); Median contract rent: $445 per month (2006-2010 5-year est.); Median year structure built: 1973 (2006-2010 5-year est.).

Transportation: Commute to work: 94.1% car, 0.0% public transportation, 1.1% walk, 2.7% work from home (2006-2010 5-year est.); Travel time to work: 28.0% less than 15 minutes, 52.5% 15 to 30 minutes, 13.2% 30 to 45 minutes, 4.1% 45 to 60 minutes, 2.2% 60 minutes or more (2006-2010 5-year est.)

Additional Information Contacts

Greater Susquehanna Valley Chamber of Commerce . . . . (570) 743-4100

http://www.gsvcc.org

VICKSBURG (CDP). Covers a land area of 0.472 square miles and a water area of 0 square miles. Located at 40.94° N. Lat; 76.99° W. Long. Elevation is 531 feet.

Population: n/a (1990); n/a (2000); 261 (2010); Density: 552.9 persons per square mile (2010); Race: 99.6% White, 0.4% Black, 0.0% Asian, 0.0% American Indian/Alaska Native, 0.0% Native Hawaiian/Other Pacific Islander, 0.0% Other, 0.0% Hispanic of any race (2010); Average household size: 2.93 (2010); Median age: 39.1 (2010); Males per 100 females: 99.2 (2010); Marriage status: 31.3% never married, 60.7% now married, 0.0% widowed, 7.9% divorced (2006-2010 5-year est.); Foreign born: 0.0% (2006-2010 5-year est.); Ancestry (includes multiple ancestries): 50.9% German, 21.2% Austrian, 16.4% Welsh, 13.3% American, 11.9% Irish (2006-2010 5-year est.).

Economy: Employment by occupation: 0.0% management, 0.0% professional, 0.0% services, 21.3% sales, 0.0% farming, 20.4% construction, 29.6% production (2006-2010 5-year est.).

Income: Per capita income: $24,562 (2006-2010 5-year est.); Median household income: $44,464 (2006-2010 5-year est.); Average household income: $60,811 (2006-2010 5-year est.); Percent of households with income of $100,000 or more: 25.0% (2006-2010 5-year est.); Poverty rate: 0.0% (2006-2010 5-year est.).

Education: Percent of population age 25 and over with: High school diploma (including GED) or higher: 93.4% (2006-2010 5-year est.); Bachelor's degree or higher: 6.6% (2006-2010 5-year est.); Master's degree or higher: 0.0% (2006-2010 5-year est.).

Housing: Homeownership rate: 86.5% (2010); Median home value: $135,700 (2006-2010 5-year est.); Median contract rent: n/a per month (2006-2010 5-year est.); Median year structure built: 1973 (2006-2010 5-year est.).

Transportation: Commute to work: 85.4% car, 0.0% public transportation, 0.0% walk, 14.6% work from home (2006-2010 5-year est.); Travel time to work: 37.8% less than 15 minutes, 42.7% 15 to 30 minutes, 19.5% 30 to 45 minutes, 0.0% 45 to 60 minutes, 0.0% 60 minutes or more (2006-2010 5-year est.)

WEIKERT (unincorporated postal area)

Zip Code: 17885

Covers a land area of 10.826 square miles and a water area of 0.155 square miles. Located at 40.86° N. Lat; 77.31° W. Long. Elevation is 738 feet. Population: 141 (2010); Density: 13.0 persons per square mile (2010); Race: 99.3% White, 0.0% Black, 0.0% Asian, 0.0% American Indian/Alaska Native, 0.0% Native Hawaiian/Other Pacific Islander, 0.0% Other, 1.4% Hispanic of any race (2010); Average household size: 2.47 (2010); Median age: 45.7 (2010); Males per 100 females: 123.8 (2010); Homeownership rate: 78.9% (2010)

WEST BUFFALO (township). Covers a land area of 38.257 square miles and a water area of 0.085 square miles. Located at 41.01° N. Lat; 77.06° W. Long.

Population: 2,254 (1990); 2,795 (2000); 2,983 (2010); Density: 78.0 persons per square mile (2010); Race: 98.3% White, 0.6% Black, 0.1% Asian, 0.1% American Indian/Alaska Native, 0.0% Native Hawaiian/Other Pacific Islander, 0.9% Other, 0.8% Hispanic of any race (2010); Average household size: 2.67 (2010); Median age: 40.4 (2010); Males per 100 females: 99.5 (2010); Marriage status: 23.9% never married, 59.4% now married, 4.9% widowed, 11.8% divorced (2006-2010 5-year est.); Foreign born: 0.2% (2006-2010 5-year est.); Ancestry (includes multiple ancestries): 52.6% German, 8.9% American, 7.4% Pennsylvania German, 6.4% Irish, 6.1% English (2006-2010 5-year est.).

Economy: Single-family building permits issued: 1 (2011); Multi-family building permits issued: 0 (2011); Employment by occupation: 13.4% management, 2.3% professional, 10.7% services, 18.8% sales, 7.5% farming, 14.1% construction, 5.9% production (2006-2010 5-year est.).

Income: Per capita income: $21,791 (2006-2010 5-year est.); Median household income: $49,375 (2006-2010 5-year est.); Average household income: $55,416 (2006-2010 5-year est.); Percent of households with income of $100,000 or more: 9.6% (2006-2010 5-year est.); Poverty rate: 7.1% (2006-2010 5-year est.).

Education: Percent of population age 25 and over with: High school diploma (including GED) or higher: 74.1% (2006-2010 5-year est.); Bachelor's degree or higher: 13.7% (2006-2010 5-year est.); Master's degree or higher: 5.0% (2006-2010 5-year est.).

Housing: Homeownership rate: 81.5% (2010); Median home value: $150,400 (2006-2010 5-year est.); Median contract rent: $652 per month (2006-2010 5-year est.); Median year structure built: 1982 (2006-2010 5-year est.).

Transportation: Commute to work: 88.4% car, 0.0% public transportation, 1.1% walk, 5.0% work from home (2006-2010 5-year est.); Travel time to work: 28.8% less than 15 minutes, 46.4% 15 to 30 minutes, 12.5% 30 to 45 minutes, 6.0% 45 to 60 minutes, 6.3% 60 minutes or more (2006-2010 5-year est.)

Additional Information Contacts

Central PA Chamber of Commerce. . . . . (570) 742-7341
http://www.centralpachamber.com/index.php

WEST MILTON (CDP). Covers a land area of 0.830 square miles and a water area of 0 square miles. Located at 41.02° N. Lat; 76.88° W. Long. Elevation is 509 feet.

Population: n/a (1990); n/a (2000); 900 (2010); Density: 1,084.3 persons per square mile (2010); Race: 91.4% White, 4.9% Black, 0.1% Asian, 0.0% American Indian/Alaska Native, 0.0% Native Hawaiian/Other Pacific Islander, 3.6% Other, 3.4% Hispanic of any race (2010); Average household size: 2.35 (2010); Median age: 37.7 (2010); Males per 100 females: 96.1 (2010); Marriage status: 28.9% never married, 36.5% now married, 14.4% widowed, 20.2% divorced (2006-2010 5-year est.); Foreign born: 0.0% (2006-2010 5-year est.); Ancestry (includes multiple ancestries): 23.5% American, 21.6% Pennsylvania German, 19.8% German, 9.3% Russian, 8.0% Irish (2006-2010 5-year est.).

Economy: Employment by occupation: 8.6% management, 0.0% professional, 27.3% services, 23.3% sales, 0.0% farming, 3.1% construction, 3.1% production (2006-2010 5-year est.).

Income: Per capita income: $23,701 (2006-2010 5-year est.); Median household income: $23,854 (2006-2010 5-year est.); Average household income: $42,392 (2006-2010 5-year est.); Percent of households with income of $100,000 or more: 10.1% (2006-2010 5-year est.); Poverty rate: 11.3% (2006-2010 5-year est.).

Education: Percent of population age 25 and over with: High school diploma (including GED) or higher: 93.0% (2006-2010 5-year est.); Bachelor's degree or higher: 12.7% (2006-2010 5-year est.); Master's degree or higher: 6.8% (2006-2010 5-year est.).

Housing: Homeownership rate: 60.6% (2010); Median home value: $93,900 (2006-2010 5-year est.); Median contract rent: $293 per month (2006-2010 5-year est.); Median year structure built: 1953 (2006-2010 5-year est.).

Transportation: Commute to work: 95.6% car, 0.0% public transportation, 4.4% walk, 0.0% work from home (2006-2010 5-year est.); Travel time to work: 74.4% less than 15 minutes, 19.8% 15 to 30 minutes, 5.8% 30 to 45 minutes, 0.0% 45 to 60 minutes, 0.0% 60 minutes or more (2006-2010 5-year est.)

WHITE DEER (township). Covers a land area of 46.171 square miles and a water area of 0.262 square miles. Located at 41.05° N. Lat; 76.95° W. Long. Elevation is 466 feet.

Population: 3,958 (1990); 4,273 (2000); 4,437 (2010); Density: 96.1 persons per square mile (2010); Race: 97.1% White, 1.1% Black, 0.1% Asian, 0.1% American Indian/Alaska Native, 0.1% Native Hawaiian/Other Pacific Islander, 1.5% Other, 1.0% Hispanic of any race (2010); Average household size: 2.45 (2010); Median age: 43.6 (2010); Males per 100 females: 95.8 (2010); Marriage status: 18.4% never married, 66.3% now married, 5.7% widowed, 9.6% divorced (2006-2010 5-year est.); Foreign born: 1.5% (2006-2010 5-year est.); Ancestry (includes multiple ancestries): 43.5% German, 8.9% American, 8.6% Irish, 8.0% English, 7.7% Dutch (2006-2010 5-year est.).

Economy: Single-family building permits issued: 8 (2011); Multi-family building permits issued: 0 (2011); Employment by occupation: 4.0% management, 1.4% professional, 10.0% services, 22.0% sales, 3.3% farming, 13.8% construction, 12.7% production (2006-2010 5-year est.).

Income: Per capita income: $20,698 (2006-2010 5-year est.); Median household income: $46,231 (2006-2010 5-year est.); Average household income: $52,317 (2006-2010 5-year est.); Percent of households with income of $100,000 or more: 8.9% (2006-2010 5-year est.); Poverty rate: 13.2% (2006-2010 5-year est.).

Education: Percent of population age 25 and over with: High school diploma (including GED) or higher: 87.7% (2006-2010 5-year est.); Bachelor's degree or higher: 12.5% (2006-2010 5-year est.); Master's degree or higher: 0.9% (2006-2010 5-year est.).

Housing: Homeownership rate: 82.3% (2010); Median home value: $119,500 (2006-2010 5-year est.); Median contract rent: $381 per month (2006-2010 5-year est.); Median year structure built: 1978 (2006-2010 5-year est.).

Transportation: Commute to work: 96.2% car, 0.0% public transportation, 1.8% walk, 0.9% work from home (2006-2010 5-year est.); Travel time to work: 39.4% less than 15 minutes, 46.2% 15 to 30 minutes, 10.9% 30 to 45 minutes, 1.3% 45 to 60 minutes, 2.2% 60 minutes or more (2006-2010 5-year est.)

Additional Information Contacts

Central PA Chamber of Commerce. . . . . (570) 742-7341
http://www.centralpachamber.com/index.php

WINFIELD (CDP). Covers a land area of 2.881 square miles and a water area of 0.048 square miles. Located at 40.89° N. Lat; 76.86° W. Long. Elevation is 446 feet.

Population: n/a (1990); n/a (2000); 900 (2010); Density: 312.4 persons per square mile (2010); Race: 97.8% White, 0.3% Black, 0.8% Asian, 0.1% American Indian/Alaska Native, 0.0% Native Hawaiian/Other Pacific Islander, 1.0% Other, 1.0% Hispanic of any race (2010); Average household size: 2.45 (2010); Median age: 46.7 (2010); Males per 100 females: 104.1 (2010); Marriage status: 13.4% never married, 68.3% now married, 7.8% widowed, 10.6% divorced (2006-2010 5-year est.); Foreign born: 0.6% (2006-2010 5-year est.); Ancestry (includes multiple ancestries): 53.9% German, 13.8% English, 13.1% American, 8.6% Irish, 6.3% Italian (2006-2010 5-year est.).

Economy: Employment by occupation: 8.6% management, 6.0% professional, 23.0% services, 9.9% sales, 1.1% farming, 11.4% construction, 7.1% production (2006-2010 5-year est.).

Income: Per capita income: $31,247 (2006-2010 5-year est.); Median household income: $58,750 (2006-2010 5-year est.); Average household income: $70,347 (2006-2010 5-year est.); Percent of households with income of $100,000 or more: 18.8% (2006-2010 5-year est.); Poverty rate: 3.0% (2006-2010 5-year est.).

Education: Percent of population age 25 and over with: High school diploma (including GED) or higher: 86.7% (2006-2010 5-year est.); Bachelor's degree or higher: 21.8% (2006-2010 5-year est.); Master's degree or higher: 7.6% (2006-2010 5-year est.).

Housing: Homeownership rate: 86.3% (2010); Median home value: $155,300 (2006-2010 5-year est.); Median contract rent: $447 per month (2006-2010 5-year est.); Median year structure built: 1971 (2006-2010 5-year est.).

Transportation: Commute to work: 93.0% car, 0.0% public transportation, 1.1% walk, 1.8% work from home (2006-2010 5-year est.); Travel time to work: 26.2% less than 15 minutes, 49.5% 15 to 30 minutes, 15.5% 30 to 45 minutes, 6.5% 45 to 60 minutes, 2.3% 60 minutes or more (2006-2010 5-year est.).

Venango County

Located in northwestern Pennsylvania; drained by the Allegheny River. Covers a land area of 674.284 square miles, a water area of 8.552 square miles, and is located in the Eastern Time Zone at 41.40° N. Lat., 79.75° W. Long. The county was founded in 1800. County seat is Franklin.

Venango County is part of the Oil City, PA Micropolitan Statistical Area. The entire metro area includes: Venango County, PA

Weather Station: Franklin											Elevation: 990 feet
	Jan	Feb	Mar	Apr	May	Jun	Jul	Aug	Sep	Oct	Nov	Dec
High	35	37	46	60	71	79	83	82	74	62	50	38
Low	18	19	25	35	44	54	58	57	51	40	32	23
Precip	2.8	2.5	3.3	3.8	4.1	4.7	5.4	4.3	4.0	3.4	3.6	3.3
Snow	16.7	11.4	10.1	1.5	0.0	0.0	0.0	0.0	0.0	tr	2.4	12.4

High and Low temperatures in degrees Fahrenheit; Precipitation and Snow in inches

Population: 59,381 (1990); 57,565 (2000); 54,984 (2010); Race: 97.1% White, 1.0% Black, 0.4% Asian, 0.2% American Indian/Alaska Native, 0.0% Native Hawaiian/Other Pacific Islander, 1.3% Other, 0.9% Hispanic of any race (2010); Density: 81.5 persons per square mile (2010); Average household size: 2.37 (2010); Median age: 44.3 (2010); Males per 100 females: 95.9 (2010).

Religion: Six largest groups: 19.5% Methodist/Pietist, 16.5% Catholicism, 4.3% Non-Denominational, 3.9% Presbyterian-Reformed, 3.3% Holiness, 1.9% Lutheran (2010)

Economy: Unemployment rate: 8.2% (August 2012); Total civilian labor force: 26,929 (August 2012); Leading industries: 23.0% manufacturing; 22.6% health care and social assistance; 15.1% retail trade (2010); Farms: 487 totaling 64,796 acres (2007); Companies that employ 500 or more persons: 2 (2010); Companies that employ 100 to 499 persons: 24 (2010); Companies that employ less than 100 persons: 1,159 (2010); Black-owned businesses: n/a (2007); Hispanic-owned businesses: n/a (2007); Asian-owned businesses: n/a (2007); Women-owned businesses: 677 (2007); Retail sales per capita: $11,078 (2010). Single-family building permits issued: 33 (2011); Multi-family building permits issued: 0 (2011).

Income: Per capita income: $20,522 (2006-2010 5-year est.); Median household income: $39,812 (2006-2010 5-year est.); Average household income: $49,130 (2006-2010 5-year est.); Percent of households with

income of $100,000 or more: 7.9% (2006-2010 5-year est.); Poverty rate: 15.7% (2006-2010 5-year est.); Bankruptcy rate: 2.50% (2011).

Education: Percent of population age 25 and over with: High school diploma (including GED) or higher: 87.3% (2006-2010 5-year est.); Bachelor's degree or higher: 14.1% (2006-2010 5-year est.); Master's degree or higher: 4.9% (2006-2010 5-year est.).

Housing: Homeownership rate: 74.6% (2010); Median home value: $76,500 (2006-2010 5-year est.); Median contract rent: $383 per month (2006-2010 5-year est.); Median year structure built: 1953 (2006-2010 5-year est.).

Health: Birth rate: 102.8 per 10,000 population (2011); Death rate: 118.9 per 10,000 population (2011); Age-adjusted cancer mortality rate: 227.8 deaths per 100,000 population (2009); Number of physicians: 17.1 per 10,000 population (2010); Hospital beds: 34.5 per 10,000 population (2008); Hospital admissions: 1,523.7 per 10,000 population (2008).

Elections: 2012 Presidential election results: 35.8% Obama, 62.3% Romney

National and State Parks: Drake Well State Park; Oil Creek State Park

Additional Information Contacts

Venango County Government . . . . (814) 432-9512
http://www.co.venango.pa.us

Venango County Communities

ALLEGHENY (township). Covers a land area of 24.972 square miles and a water area of 0 square miles. Located at 41.57° N. Lat; 79.54° W. Long.

Population: 281 (1990); 281 (2000); 276 (2010); Density: 11.1 persons per square mile (2010); Race: 98.9% White, 0.0% Black, 0.4% Asian, 0.0% American Indian/Alaska Native, 0.0% Native Hawaiian/Other Pacific Islander, 0.7% Other, 0.7% Hispanic of any race (2010); Average household size: 2.34 (2010); Median age: 50.1 (2010); Males per 100 females: 94.4 (2010); Marriage status: 22.4% never married, 56.8% now married, 9.2% widowed, 11.6% divorced (2006-2010 5-year est.); Foreign born: 3.5% (2006-2010 5-year est.); Ancestry (includes multiple ancestries): 46.5% German, 20.3% Irish, 19.1% English, 9.9% Polish, 7.2% Italian (2006-2010 5-year est.).

Economy: Single-family building permits issued: 0 (2011); Multi-family building permits issued: 0 (2011); Employment by occupation: 5.8% management, 0.0% professional, 10.9% services, 25.5% sales, 5.8% farming, 9.5% construction, 0.7% production (2006-2010 5-year est.).

Income: Per capita income: $18,592 (2006-2010 5-year est.); Median household income: $43,000 (2006-2010 5-year est.); Average household income: $54,686 (2006-2010 5-year est.); Percent of households with income of $100,000 or more: 7.2% (2006-2010 5-year est.); Poverty rate: 29.7% (2006-2010 5-year est.).

Education: Percent of population age 25 and over with: High school diploma (including GED) or higher: 76.1% (2006-2010 5-year est.); Bachelor's degree or higher: 11.2% (2006-2010 5-year est.); Master's degree or higher: 6.4% (2006-2010 5-year est.).

Housing: Homeownership rate: 91.5% (2010); Median home value: $71,700 (2006-2010 5-year est.); Median contract rent: $357 per month (2006-2010 5-year est.); Median year structure built: 1974 (2006-2010 5-year est.).

Transportation: Commute to work: 94.3% car, 0.0% public transportation, 1.6% walk, 4.1% work from home (2006-2010 5-year est.); Travel time to work: 41.0% less than 15 minutes, 35.9% 15 to 30 minutes, 5.1% 30 to 45 minutes, 8.5% 45 to 60 minutes, 9.4% 60 minutes or more (2006-2010 5-year est.).

BARKEYVILLE (borough). Covers a land area of 3.088 square miles and a water area of 0 square miles. Located at 41.20° N. Lat; 79.98° W. Long. Elevation is 1,483 feet.

Population: 274 (1990); 237 (2000); 207 (2010); Density: 67.0 persons per square mile (2010); Race: 96.6% White, 0.0% Black, 0.5% Asian, 0.0% American Indian/Alaska Native, 0.0% Native Hawaiian/Other Pacific Islander, 2.9% Other, 5.3% Hispanic of any race (2010); Average household size: 2.56 (2010); Median age: 37.8 (2010); Males per 100 females: 78.4 (2010); Marriage status: 26.6% never married, 54.1% now married, 11.8% widowed, 7.4% divorced (2006-2010 5-year est.); Foreign born: 0.0% (2006-2010 5-year est.); Ancestry (includes multiple ancestries): 40.6% German, 31.2% Irish, 8.7% English, 6.7% Scottish, 4.4% Welsh (2006-2010 5-year est.).

Economy: Single-family building permits issued: 1 (2011); Multi-family building permits issued: 0 (2011); Employment by occupation: 8.5%

management, 2.3% professional, 23.3% services, 9.3% sales, 1.6% farming, 14.0% construction, 7.8% production (2006-2010 5-year est.).
Income: Per capita income: $32,787 (2006-2010 5-year est.); Median household income: $41,250 (2006-2010 5-year est.); Average household income: $90,619 (2006-2010 5-year est.); Percent of households with income of $100,000 or more: 10.3% (2006-2010 5-year est.); Poverty rate: 9.4% (2006-2010 5-year est.).
Education: Percent of population age 25 and over with: High school diploma (including GED) or higher: 89.9% (2006-2010 5-year est.); Bachelor's degree or higher: 10.1% (2006-2010 5-year est.); Master's degree or higher: 2.7% (2006-2010 5-year est.).
Housing: Homeownership rate: 72.8% (2010); Median home value: $88,800 (2006-2010 5-year est.); Median contract rent: $556 per month (2006-2010 5-year est.); Median year structure built: 1971 (2006-2010 5-year est.).
Transportation: Commute to work: 95.9% car, 0.0% public transportation, 0.0% walk, 4.1% work from home (2006-2010 5-year est.); Travel time to work: 26.3% less than 15 minutes, 57.6% 15 to 30 minutes, 14.4% 30 to 45 minutes, 0.0% 45 to 60 minutes, 1.7% 60 minutes or more (2006-2010 5-year est.).

CANAL (township). Covers a land area of 24.312 square miles and a water area of 0.121 square miles. Located at 41.48° N. Lat; 79.94° W. Long.
Population: 1,067 (1990); 1,008 (2000); 1,023 (2010); Density: 42.1 persons per square mile (2010); Race: 98.6% White, 0.4% Black, 0.1% Asian, 0.2% American Indian/Alaska Native, 0.0% Native Hawaiian/Other Pacific Islander, 0.7% Other, 0.1% Hispanic of any race (2010); Average household size: 2.51 (2010); Median age: 45.3 (2010); Males per 100 females: 97.5 (2010); Marriage status: 26.0% never married, 59.7% now married, 4.7% widowed, 9.6% divorced (2006-2010 5-year est.); Foreign born: 0.0% (2006-2010 5-year est.); Ancestry (includes multiple ancestries): 30.8% German, 19.0% Irish, 12.0% American, 9.0% English, 7.6% Dutch (2006-2010 5-year est.).
Economy: Single-family building permits issued: 1 (2011); Multi-family building permits issued: 0 (2011); Employment by occupation: 9.0% management, 0.0% professional, 11.9% services, 16.7% sales, 2.0% farming, 16.0% construction, 5.2% production (2006-2010 5-year est.).
Income: Per capita income: $20,749 (2006-2010 5-year est.); Median household income: $44,091 (2006-2010 5-year est.); Average household income: $52,913 (2006-2010 5-year est.); Percent of households with income of $100,000 or more: 9.2% (2006-2010 5-year est.); Poverty rate: 3.6% (2006-2010 5-year est.).
Education: Percent of population age 25 and over with: High school diploma (including GED) or higher: 89.1% (2006-2010 5-year est.); Bachelor's degree or higher: 7.8% (2006-2010 5-year est.); Master's degree or higher: 2.7% (2006-2010 5-year est.).
Housing: Homeownership rate: 88.5% (2010); Median home value: $88,200 (2006-2010 5-year est.); Median contract rent: $325 per month (2006-2010 5-year est.); Median year structure built: 1973 (2006-2010 5-year est.).
Transportation: Commute to work: 96.7% car, 0.5% public transportation, 1.2% walk, 1.6% work from home (2006-2010 5-year est.); Travel time to work: 12.9% less than 15 minutes, 46.7% 15 to 30 minutes, 20.7% 30 to 45 minutes, 13.1% 45 to 60 minutes, 6.7% 60 minutes or more (2006-2010 5-year est.).

CHERRYTREE (township). Covers a land area of 36.698 square miles and a water area of 0 square miles. Located at 41.57° N. Lat; 79.71° W. Long. Elevation is 1,299 feet.
Population: 1,601 (1990); 1,543 (2000); 1,540 (2010); Density: 42.0 persons per square mile (2010); Race: 98.9% White, 0.2% Black, 0.3% Asian, 0.1% American Indian/Alaska Native, 0.1% Native Hawaiian/Other Pacific Islander, 0.4% Other, 0.3% Hispanic of any race (2010); Average household size: 2.46 (2010); Median age: 46.9 (2010); Males per 100 females: 104.2 (2010); Marriage status: 16.6% never married, 63.4% now married, 8.3% widowed, 11.7% divorced (2006-2010 5-year est.); Foreign born: 0.7% (2006-2010 5-year est.); Ancestry (includes multiple ancestries): 26.3% German, 15.7% Irish, 15.0% English, 13.0% American, 5.0% Polish (2006-2010 5-year est.).
Economy: Single-family building permits issued: 0 (2011); Multi-family building permits issued: 0 (2011); Employment by occupation: 8.8% management, 3.8% professional, 11.8% services, 14.7% sales, 2.7% farming, 9.3% construction, 8.9% production (2006-2010 5-year est.).

Income: Per capita income: $20,613 (2006-2010 5-year est.); Median household income: $42,361 (2006-2010 5-year est.); Average household income: $51,180 (2006-2010 5-year est.); Percent of households with income of $100,000 or more: 7.5% (2006-2010 5-year est.); Poverty rate: 9.6% (2006-2010 5-year est.).
Education: Percent of population age 25 and over with: High school diploma (including GED) or higher: 86.8% (2006-2010 5-year est.); Bachelor's degree or higher: 13.7% (2006-2010 5-year est.); Master's degree or higher: 4.0% (2006-2010 5-year est.).
Housing: Homeownership rate: 83.9% (2010); Median home value: $88,200 (2006-2010 5-year est.); Median contract rent: $388 per month (2006-2010 5-year est.); Median year structure built: 1971 (2006-2010 5-year est.).
Transportation: Commute to work: 96.9% car, 0.0% public transportation, 1.3% walk, 1.8% work from home (2006-2010 5-year est.); Travel time to work: 35.7% less than 15 minutes, 32.2% 15 to 30 minutes, 11.4% 30 to 45 minutes, 8.4% 45 to 60 minutes, 12.2% 60 minutes or more (2006-2010 5-year est.)
Additional Information Contacts
Titusville Area Chamber of Commerce . . . . (814) 827-2941
http://titusvillechamber.com

CLINTON (township). Covers a land area of 28.445 square miles and a water area of 0.274 square miles. Located at 41.22° N. Lat; 79.87° W. Long.
Population: 733 (1990); 758 (2000); 854 (2010); Density: 30.0 persons per square mile (2010); Race: 99.3% White, 0.4% Black, 0.1% Asian, 0.0% American Indian/Alaska Native, 0.0% Native Hawaiian/Other Pacific Islander, 0.2% Other, 0.5% Hispanic of any race (2010); Average household size: 2.67 (2010); Median age: 38.4 (2010); Males per 100 females: 99.1 (2010); Marriage status: 17.8% never married, 64.2% now married, 6.7% widowed, 11.3% divorced (2006-2010 5-year est.); Foreign born: 0.7% (2006-2010 5-year est.); Ancestry (includes multiple ancestries): 46.2% German, 22.0% Irish, 21.7% English, 15.6% Scotch-Irish, 6.9% Dutch (2006-2010 5-year est.).
Economy: Single-family building permits issued: 0 (2011); Multi-family building permits issued: 0 (2011); Employment by occupation: 1.5% management, 0.0% professional, 10.9% services, 14.5% sales, 5.5% farming, 21.5% construction, 5.5% production (2006-2010 5-year est.).
Income: Per capita income: $19,243 (2006-2010 5-year est.); Median household income: $47,411 (2006-2010 5-year est.); Average household income: $52,253 (2006-2010 5-year est.); Percent of households with income of $100,000 or more: 6.4% (2006-2010 5-year est.); Poverty rate: 4.1% (2006-2010 5-year est.).
Education: Percent of population age 25 and over with: High school diploma (including GED) or higher: 81.3% (2006-2010 5-year est.); Bachelor's degree or higher: 8.7% (2006-2010 5-year est.); Master's degree or higher: 4.2% (2006-2010 5-year est.).
Housing: Homeownership rate: 85.3% (2010); Median home value: $80,000 (2006-2010 5-year est.); Median contract rent: $347 per month (2006-2010 5-year est.); Median year structure built: 1971 (2006-2010 5-year est.).
Transportation: Commute to work: 89.4% car, 0.0% public transportation, 2.6% walk, 4.2% work from home (2006-2010 5-year est.); Travel time to work: 20.5% less than 15 minutes, 45.3% 15 to 30 minutes, 20.9% 30 to 45 minutes, 6.3% 45 to 60 minutes, 7.1% 60 minutes or more (2006-2010 5-year est.)

CLINTONVILLE (borough). Covers a land area of 1.091 square miles and a water area of 0.003 square miles. Located at 41.20° N. Lat; 79.87° W. Long. Elevation is 1,424 feet.
Population: 520 (1990); 528 (2000); 508 (2010); Density: 465.6 persons per square mile (2010); Race: 97.8% White, 0.0% Black, 1.2% Asian, 0.4% American Indian/Alaska Native, 0.0% Native Hawaiian/Other Pacific Islander, 0.6% Other, 1.0% Hispanic of any race (2010); Average household size: 2.30 (2010); Median age: 37.3 (2010); Males per 100 females: 104.0 (2010); Marriage status: 24.4% never married, 51.0% now married, 3.7% widowed, 20.9% divorced (2006-2010 5-year est.); Foreign born: 0.0% (2006-2010 5-year est.); Ancestry (includes multiple ancestries): 40.6% German, 16.3% Irish, 7.5% Italian, 7.5% English, 7.1% Polish (2006-2010 5-year est.).
Economy: Single-family building permits issued: 0 (2011); Multi-family building permits issued: 0 (2011); Employment by occupation: 4.6% management, 1.7% professional, 23.8% services, 12.5% sales, 2.5% farming, 5.4% construction, 7.5% production (2006-2010 5-year est.).

Income: Per capita income: $18,473 (2006-2010 5-year est.); Median household income: $31,875 (2006-2010 5-year est.); Average household income: $39,299 (2006-2010 5-year est.); Percent of households with income of $100,000 or more: 0.9% (2006-2010 5-year est.); Poverty rate: 16.1% (2006-2010 5-year est.).

Education: Percent of population age 25 and over with: High school diploma (including GED) or higher: 85.6% (2006-2010 5-year est.); Bachelor's degree or higher: 12.7% (2006-2010 5-year est.); Master's degree or higher: 5.8% (2006-2010 5-year est.).

Housing: Homeownership rate: 63.4% (2010); Median home value: $60,400 (2006-2010 5-year est.); Median contract rent: $377 per month (2006-2010 5-year est.); Median year structure built: 1963 (2006-2010 5-year est.).

Transportation: Commute to work: 87.8% car, 0.0% public transportation, 10.8% walk, 0.0% work from home (2006-2010 5-year est.); Travel time to work: 38.3% less than 15 minutes, 32.9% 15 to 30 minutes, 24.3% 30 to 45 minutes, 0.0% 45 to 60 minutes, 4.5% 60 minutes or more (2006-2010 5-year est.)

COOPERSTOWN (borough).
Covers a land area of 0.554 square miles and a water area of 0 square miles. Located at 41.50° N. Lat; 79.87° W. Long. Elevation is 1,119 feet.

Population: 529 (1990); 460 (2000); 460 (2010); Density: 830.9 persons per square mile (2010); Race: 98.9% White, 0.4% Black, 0.4% Asian, 0.2% American Indian/Alaska Native, 0.0% Native Hawaiian/Other Pacific Islander, 0.1% Other, 0.4% Hispanic of any race (2010); Average household size: 2.49 (2010); Median age: 43.2 (2010); Males per 100 females: 104.4 (2010); Marriage status: 22.6% never married, 63.1% now married, 8.1% widowed, 6.2% divorced (2006-2010 5-year est.); Foreign born: 0.0% (2006-2010 5-year est.); Ancestry (includes multiple ancestries): 40.0% German, 14.2% English, 9.4% American, 7.9% Irish, 7.1% Dutch (2006-2010 5-year est.).

Economy: Single-family building permits issued: 0 (2011); Multi-family building permits issued: 0 (2011); Employment by occupation: 6.3% management, 0.0% professional, 13.2% services, 18.4% sales, 7.0% farming, 12.9% construction, 11.4% production (2006-2010 5-year est.).

Income: Per capita income: $20,030 (2006-2010 5-year est.); Median household income: $49,750 (2006-2010 5-year est.); Average household income: $52,348 (2006-2010 5-year est.); Percent of households with income of $100,000 or more: 2.6% (2006-2010 5-year est.); Poverty rate: 11.1% (2006-2010 5-year est.).

Education: Percent of population age 25 and over with: High school diploma (including GED) or higher: 91.4% (2006-2010 5-year est.); Bachelor's degree or higher: 14.8% (2006-2010 5-year est.); Master's degree or higher: 3.2% (2006-2010 5-year est.).

School District(s)
Oil City Area SD (KG-12)
    2010-11 Enrollment: 2,148 . . . . (814) 676-1867

Housing: Homeownership rate: 89.8% (2010); Median home value: $74,000 (2006-2010 5-year est.); Median contract rent: $229 per month (2006-2010 5-year est.); Median year structure built: 1963 (2006-2010 5-year est.).

Transportation: Commute to work: 96.9% car, 0.0% public transportation, 2.3% walk, 0.0% work from home (2006-2010 5-year est.); Travel time to work: 12.0% less than 15 minutes, 49.4% 15 to 30 minutes, 29.7% 30 to 45 minutes, 3.1% 45 to 60 minutes, 5.8% 60 minutes or more (2006-2010 5-year est.)

CORNPLANTER (township).
Covers a land area of 37.444 square miles and a water area of 0.543 square miles. Located at 41.50° N. Lat; 79.66° W. Long.

Population: 2,968 (1990); 2,687 (2000); 2,418 (2010); Density: 64.6 persons per square mile (2010); Race: 98.6% White, 0.7% Black, 0.3% Asian, 0.0% American Indian/Alaska Native, 0.0% Native Hawaiian/Other Pacific Islander, 0.4% Other, 0.5% Hispanic of any race (2010); Average household size: 2.36 (2010); Median age: 49.5 (2010); Males per 100 females: 96.3 (2010); Marriage status: 19.5% never married, 54.3% now married, 14.1% widowed, 12.1% divorced (2006-2010 5-year est.); Foreign born: 0.4% (2006-2010 5-year est.); Ancestry (includes multiple ancestries): 43.7% German, 24.1% Irish, 9.1% English, 7.9% Polish, 7.8% American (2006-2010 5-year est.).

Economy: Single-family building permits issued: 0 (2011); Multi-family building permits issued: 0 (2011); Employment by occupation: 6.1% management, 1.8% professional, 10.6% services, 21.3% sales, 4.3% farming, 6.1% construction, 2.1% production (2006-2010 5-year est.).

Income: Per capita income: $24,539 (2006-2010 5-year est.); Median household income: $41,809 (2006-2010 5-year est.); Average household income: $56,878 (2006-2010 5-year est.); Percent of households with income of $100,000 or more: 12.3% (2006-2010 5-year est.); Poverty rate: 15.7% (2006-2010 5-year est.).

Education: Percent of population age 25 and over with: High school diploma (including GED) or higher: 86.8% (2006-2010 5-year est.); Bachelor's degree or higher: 18.1% (2006-2010 5-year est.); Master's degree or higher: 4.8% (2006-2010 5-year est.).

Housing: Homeownership rate: 87.6% (2010); Median home value: $84,200 (2006-2010 5-year est.); Median contract rent: $307 per month (2006-2010 5-year est.); Median year structure built: 1959 (2006-2010 5-year est.).

Transportation: Commute to work: 95.4% car, 0.0% public transportation, 0.6% walk, 4.0% work from home (2006-2010 5-year est.); Travel time to work: 30.5% less than 15 minutes, 50.3% 15 to 30 minutes, 8.2% 30 to 45 minutes, 3.3% 45 to 60 minutes, 7.8% 60 minutes or more (2006-2010 5-year est.)

Additional Information Contacts
Wellsboro Area Chamber of Commerce . . . . (570) 724-1926
    http://www.wellsboropa.com

CRANBERRY (township).
Covers a land area of 69.801 square miles and a water area of 0.223 square miles. Located at 41.37° N. Lat; 79.69° W. Long. Elevation is 1,417 feet.

Population: 7,256 (1990); 7,014 (2000); 6,685 (2010); Density: 95.8 persons per square mile (2010); Race: 98.1% White, 0.3% Black, 0.4% Asian, 0.1% American Indian/Alaska Native, 0.1% Native Hawaiian/Other Pacific Islander, 1.0% Other, 0.6% Hispanic of any race (2010); Average household size: 2.33 (2010); Median age: 46.0 (2010); Males per 100 females: 92.8 (2010); Marriage status: 19.7% never married, 60.8% now married, 9.8% widowed, 9.7% divorced (2006-2010 5-year est.); Foreign born: 0.6% (2006-2010 5-year est.); Ancestry (includes multiple ancestries): 48.2% German, 14.3% English, 13.5% Irish, 6.2% American, 6.1% Italian (2006-2010 5-year est.).

Economy: Single-family building permits issued: 8 (2011); Multi-family building permits issued: 0 (2011); Employment by occupation: 6.8% management, 2.8% professional, 11.4% services, 21.2% sales, 2.9% farming, 10.9% construction, 4.4% production (2006-2010 5-year est.).

Income: Per capita income: $21,744 (2006-2010 5-year est.); Median household income: $46,662 (2006-2010 5-year est.); Average household income: $50,020 (2006-2010 5-year est.); Percent of households with income of $100,000 or more: 8.4% (2006-2010 5-year est.); Poverty rate: 18.0% (2006-2010 5-year est.).

Education: Percent of population age 25 and over with: High school diploma (including GED) or higher: 90.7% (2006-2010 5-year est.); Bachelor's degree or higher: 15.2% (2006-2010 5-year est.); Master's degree or higher: 4.9% (2006-2010 5-year est.).

Housing: Homeownership rate: 77.8% (2010); Median home value: $86,500 (2006-2010 5-year est.); Median contract rent: $416 per month (2006-2010 5-year est.); Median year structure built: 1959 (2006-2010 5-year est.).

Transportation: Commute to work: 91.3% car, 0.3% public transportation, 2.6% walk, 5.0% work from home (2006-2010 5-year est.); Travel time to work: 54.4% less than 15 minutes, 31.8% 15 to 30 minutes, 9.8% 30 to 45 minutes, 3.7% 45 to 60 minutes, 0.2% 60 minutes or more (2006-2010 5-year est.)

Additional Information Contacts
Cranberry Township . . . . (724) 776-4806
    http://www.twp.cranberry.pa.us
Venango Area Chamber of Commerce . . . . (814) 676-8521
    http://www.venangochamber.org

EMLENTON (borough).
Covers a land area of 0.582 square miles and a water area of 0.005 square miles. Located at 41.18° N. Lat; 79.71° W. Long. Elevation is 912 feet.

Population: 834 (1990); 784 (2000); 625 (2010); Density: 1,074.3 persons per square mile (2010); Race: 99.0% White, 0.2% Black, 0.6% Asian, 0.0% American Indian/Alaska Native, 0.0% Native Hawaiian/Other Pacific Islander, 0.2% Other, 0.6% Hispanic of any race (2010); Average household size: 2.19 (2010); Median age: 43.3 (2010); Males per 100 females: 89.4 (2010); Marriage status: 30.1% never married, 51.5% now married, 6.4% widowed, 12.0% divorced (2006-2010 5-year est.); Foreign born: 0.5% (2006-2010 5-year est.); Ancestry (includes multiple

ancestries): 40.0% German, 23.0% Irish, 12.9% English, 6.0% Croatian, 5.6% Scotch-Irish (2006-2010 5-year est.).

Economy: Single-family building permits issued: 0 (2011); Multi-family building permits issued: 0 (2011); Employment by occupation: 7.4% management, 0.0% professional, 14.0% services, 12.5% sales, 3.1% farming, 10.5% construction, 5.8% production (2006-2010 5-year est.).

Income: Per capita income: $19,740 (2006-2010 5-year est.); Median household income: $41,146 (2006-2010 5-year est.); Average household income: $48,769 (2006-2010 5-year est.); Percent of households with income of $100,000 or more: 8.5% (2006-2010 5-year est.); Poverty rate: 13.9% (2006-2010 5-year est.).

Education: Percent of population age 25 and over with: High school diploma (including GED) or higher: 86.8% (2006-2010 5-year est.); Bachelor's degree or higher: 16.9% (2006-2010 5-year est.); Master's degree or higher: 8.2% (2006-2010 5-year est.).

Housing: Homeownership rate: 58.6% (2010); Median home value: $85,900 (2006-2010 5-year est.); Median contract rent: $380 per month (2006-2010 5-year est.); Median year structure built: before 1940 (2006-2010 5-year est.).

Safety: Violent crime rate: 15.9 per 10,000 population; Property crime rate: 0.0 per 10,000 population (2011).

Newspapers: Progress News (Community news; Circulation 15,000)

Transportation: Commute to work: 87.2% car, 0.0% public transportation, 3.5% walk, 9.3% work from home (2006-2010 5-year est.); Travel time to work: 46.8% less than 15 minutes, 14.2% 15 to 30 minutes, 15.5% 30 to 45 minutes, 12.0% 45 to 60 minutes, 11.6% 60 minutes or more (2006-2010 5-year est.)

FRANKLIN (city). County seat. Covers a land area of 4.677 square miles and a water area of 0.127 square miles. Located at 41.38° N. Lat; 79.83° W. Long. Elevation is 1,010 feet.

History: Site of Indian village and of early French, British, and American forts. Oil discovered 1860. Laid out 1795, incorporated as borough 1828, as city 1868.

Population: 7,293 (1990); 7,212 (2000); 6,545 (2010); Density: 1,399.4 persons per square mile (2010); Race: 93.4% White, 2.7% Black, 0.7% Asian, 0.3% American Indian/Alaska Native, 0.0% Native Hawaiian/Other Pacific Islander, 2.9% Other, 1.3% Hispanic of any race (2010); Average household size: 2.19 (2010); Median age: 42.4 (2010); Males per 100 females: 86.0 (2010); Marriage status: 25.7% never married, 47.6% now married, 10.9% widowed, 15.7% divorced (2006-2010 5-year est.); Foreign born: 1.3% (2006-2010 5-year est.); Ancestry (includes multiple ancestries): 27.2% German, 16.4% Irish, 12.7% Italian, 11.7% English, 4.9% Polish (2006-2010 5-year est.).

Economy: Single-family building permits issued: 3 (2011); Multi-family building permits issued: 0 (2011); Employment by occupation: 8.5% management, 0.8% professional, 13.5% services, 15.0% sales, 3.5% farming, 6.1% construction, 6.1% production (2006-2010 5-year est.).

Income: Per capita income: $23,150 (2006-2010 5-year est.); Median household income: $34,732 (2006-2010 5-year est.); Average household income: $47,879 (2006-2010 5-year est.); Percent of households with income of $100,000 or more: 5.4% (2006-2010 5-year est.); Poverty rate: 16.3% (2006-2010 5-year est.).

Education: Percent of population age 25 and over with: High school diploma (including GED) or higher: 90.9% (2006-2010 5-year est.); Bachelor's degree or higher: 20.7% (2006-2010 5-year est.); Master's degree or higher: 7.4% (2006-2010 5-year est.).

School District(s)

Franklin Area SD (KG-12)

    2010-11 Enrollment: 2,068 . . . . (814) 432-8917

Valley Grove SD (KG-12)

    2010-11 Enrollment: 990 . . . . (814) 432-4919

Housing: Homeownership rate: 54.3% (2010); Median home value: $61,300 (2006-2010 5-year est.); Median contract rent: $408 per month (2006-2010 5-year est.); Median year structure built: before 1940 (2006-2010 5-year est.).

Hospitals: Northwest Medical Center (96 beds)

Safety: Violent crime rate: 19.8 per 10,000 population; Property crime rate: 257.4 per 10,000 population (2011).

Transportation: Commute to work: 86.6% car, 1.8% public transportation, 6.8% walk, 3.5% work from home (2006-2010 5-year est.); Travel time to work: 52.9% less than 15 minutes, 28.2% 15 to 30 minutes, 11.7% 30 to 45 minutes, 4.1% 45 to 60 minutes, 3.2% 60 minutes or more (2006-2010 5-year est.)

Airports: Venango Regional (general aviation)

Additional Information Contacts

City of Franklin . . . . (814) 437-1670

    http://www.franklinpa.gov

Franklin Area Chamber of Commerce. . . . . (814) 432-5823

    http://www.franklinareachamber.org

FRENCHCREEK (township). Covers a land area of 29.134 square miles and a water area of 0.208 square miles. Located at 41.40° N. Lat; 79.94° W. Long.

Population: 1,765 (1990); 1,605 (2000); 1,542 (2010); Density: 52.9 persons per square mile (2010); Race: 97.6% White, 0.3% Black, 0.3% Asian, 0.3% American Indian/Alaska Native, 0.0% Native Hawaiian/Other Pacific Islander, 1.5% Other, 0.9% Hispanic of any race (2010); Average household size: 2.31 (2010); Median age: 48.7 (2010); Males per 100 females: 98.5 (2010); Marriage status: 23.2% never married, 63.0% now married, 4.4% widowed, 9.4% divorced (2006-2010 5-year est.); Foreign born: 0.0% (2006-2010 5-year est.); Ancestry (includes multiple ancestries): 37.7% German, 11.5% English, 11.4% Irish, 6.8% Scotch-Irish, 4.8% American (2006-2010 5-year est.).

Economy: Single-family building permits issued: 1 (2011); Multi-family building permits issued: 0 (2011); Employment by occupation: 10.1% management, 2.4% professional, 13.8% services, 15.9% sales, 1.4% farming, 9.9% construction, 5.7% production (2006-2010 5-year est.).

Income: Per capita income: $24,138 (2006-2010 5-year est.); Median household income: $47,050 (2006-2010 5-year est.); Average household income: $57,848 (2006-2010 5-year est.); Percent of households with income of $100,000 or more: 10.4% (2006-2010 5-year est.); Poverty rate: 10.2% (2006-2010 5-year est.).

Education: Percent of population age 25 and over with: High school diploma (including GED) or higher: 92.3% (2006-2010 5-year est.); Bachelor's degree or higher: 13.2% (2006-2010 5-year est.); Master's degree or higher: 6.8% (2006-2010 5-year est.).

Housing: Homeownership rate: 83.5% (2010); Median home value: $93,600 (2006-2010 5-year est.); Median contract rent: $376 per month (2006-2010 5-year est.); Median year structure built: 1970 (2006-2010 5-year est.).

Transportation: Commute to work: 93.9% car, 0.0% public transportation, 1.3% walk, 4.8% work from home (2006-2010 5-year est.); Travel time to work: 44.1% less than 15 minutes, 33.4% 15 to 30 minutes, 15.3% 30 to 45 minutes, 2.3% 45 to 60 minutes, 4.9% 60 minutes or more (2006-2010 5-year est.)

Additional Information Contacts

Franklin Area Chamber of Commerce. . . . . (814) 432-5823

    http://www.franklinareachamber.org

HANNASVILLE (CDP). Covers a land area of 1.515 square miles and a water area of 0 square miles. Located at 41.47° N. Lat; 79.93° W. Long. Elevation is 1,263 feet.

Population: n/a (1990); n/a (2000); 176 (2010); Density: 116.2 persons per square mile (2010); Race: 95.5% White, 2.3% Black, 0.0% Asian, 1.1% American Indian/Alaska Native, 0.0% Native Hawaiian/Other Pacific Islander, 1.1% Other, 0.6% Hispanic of any race (2010); Average household size: 2.59 (2010); Median age: 40.3 (2010); Males per 100 females: 97.8 (2010); Marriage status: 21.7% never married, 56.1% now married, 8.3% widowed, 14.0% divorced (2006-2010 5-year est.); Foreign born: 0.0% (2006-2010 5-year est.); Ancestry (includes multiple ancestries): 46.0% German, 23.3% Irish, 14.8% English, 13.8% American, 10.6% Dutch (2006-2010 5-year est.).

Economy: Employment by occupation: 12.0% management, 0.0% professional, 8.4% services, 10.8% sales, 0.0% farming, 16.9% construction, 8.4% production (2006-2010 5-year est.).

Income: Per capita income: $20,402 (2006-2010 5-year est.); Median household income: $40,833 (2006-2010 5-year est.); Average household income: $47,920 (2006-2010 5-year est.); Percent of households with income of $100,000 or more: 5.0% (2006-2010 5-year est.); Poverty rate: 3.2% (2006-2010 5-year est.).

Education: Percent of population age 25 and over with: High school diploma (including GED) or higher: 94.7% (2006-2010 5-year est.); Bachelor's degree or higher: 12.8% (2006-2010 5-year est.); Master's degree or higher: 4.5% (2006-2010 5-year est.).

Housing: Homeownership rate: 88.2% (2010); Median home value: $86,700 (2006-2010 5-year est.); Median contract rent: $425 per month (2006-2010 5-year est.); Median year structure built: 1980 (2006-2010 5-year est.).

Transportation: Commute to work: 94.0% car, 0.0% public transportation, 2.4% walk, 3.6% work from home (2006-2010 5-year est.); Travel time to work: 5.0% less than 15 minutes, 72.5% 15 to 30 minutes, 12.5% 30 to 45 minutes, 6.3% 45 to 60 minutes, 3.8% 60 minutes or more (2006-2010 5-year est.)

HASSON HEIGHTS (CDP). Covers a land area of 1.526 square miles and a water area of 0 square miles. Located at 41.45° N. Lat; 79.68° W. Long. Elevation is 1,486 feet.

Population: 1,605 (1990); 1,495 (2000); 1,351 (2010); Density: 885.3 persons per square mile (2010); Race: 98.1% White, 1.0% Black, 0.5% Asian, 0.0% American Indian/Alaska Native, 0.0% Native Hawaiian/Other Pacific Islander, 0.4% Other, 0.7% Hispanic of any race (2010); Average household size: 2.34 (2010); Median age: 48.4 (2010); Males per 100 females: 93.8 (2010); Marriage status: 22.0% never married, 59.5% now married, 8.1% widowed, 10.4% divorced (2006-2010 5-year est.); Foreign born: 0.0% (2006-2010 5-year est.); Ancestry (includes multiple ancestries): 44.5% German, 30.5% Irish, 9.6% Polish, 9.1% English, 5.3% Scotch-Irish (2006-2010 5-year est.).

Economy: Employment by occupation: 8.0% management, 2.0% professional, 9.8% services, 23.4% sales, 2.8% farming, 4.3% construction, 1.1% production (2006-2010 5-year est.).

Income: Per capita income: $28,046 (2006-2010 5-year est.); Median household income: $46,023 (2006-2010 5-year est.); Average household income: $63,008 (2006-2010 5-year est.); Percent of households with income of $100,000 or more: 18.4% (2006-2010 5-year est.); Poverty rate: 13.2% (2006-2010 5-year est.).

Education: Percent of population age 25 and over with: High school diploma (including GED) or higher: 93.7% (2006-2010 5-year est.); Bachelor's degree or higher: 26.7% (2006-2010 5-year est.); Master's degree or higher: 8.6% (2006-2010 5-year est.).

Housing: Homeownership rate: 87.3% (2010); Median home value: $90,000 (2006-2010 5-year est.); Median contract rent: $229 per month (2006-2010 5-year est.); Median year structure built: 1958 (2006-2010 5-year est.).

Transportation: Commute to work: 96.4% car, 0.0% public transportation, 0.0% walk, 3.6% work from home (2006-2010 5-year est.); Travel time to work: 28.9% less than 15 minutes, 48.9% 15 to 30 minutes, 8.4% 30 to 45 minutes, 4.7% 45 to 60 minutes, 9.2% 60 minutes or more (2006-2010 5-year est.)

Additional Information Contacts
Venango Area Chamber of Commerce . . . . (814) 676-8521
  http://www.venangochamber.org

IRWIN (township). Covers a land area of 30.536 square miles and a water area of 0 square miles. Located at 41.23° N. Lat; 79.95° W. Long.

Population: 1,182 (1990); 1,309 (2000); 1,391 (2010); Density: 45.6 persons per square mile (2010); Race: 98.6% White, 0.6% Black, 0.1% Asian, 0.1% American Indian/Alaska Native, 0.0% Native Hawaiian/Other Pacific Islander, 0.6% Other, 0.3% Hispanic of any race (2010); Average household size: 2.61 (2010); Median age: 41.7 (2010); Males per 100 females: 99.0 (2010); Marriage status: 20.4% never married, 64.9% now married, 7.6% widowed, 7.2% divorced (2006-2010 5-year est.); Foreign born: 0.8% (2006-2010 5-year est.); Ancestry (includes multiple ancestries): 40.7% German, 23.0% Irish, 12.8% English, 9.2% Italian, 6.1% Scottish (2006-2010 5-year est.).

Economy: Single-family building permits issued: 0 (2011); Multi-family building permits issued: 0 (2011); Employment by occupation: 5.8% management, 2.1% professional, 15.5% services, 15.1% sales, 3.0% farming, 18.0% construction, 10.7% production (2006-2010 5-year est.).

Income: Per capita income: $22,357 (2006-2010 5-year est.); Median household income: $50,083 (2006-2010 5-year est.); Average household income: $56,943 (2006-2010 5-year est.); Percent of households with income of $100,000 or more: 12.3% (2006-2010 5-year est.); Poverty rate: 7.3% (2006-2010 5-year est.).

Education: Percent of population age 25 and over with: High school diploma (including GED) or higher: 83.5% (2006-2010 5-year est.); Bachelor's degree or higher: 7.8% (2006-2010 5-year est.); Master's degree or higher: 2.3% (2006-2010 5-year est.).

Housing: Homeownership rate: 84.2% (2010); Median home value: $104,000 (2006-2010 5-year est.); Median contract rent: $362 per month (2006-2010 5-year est.); Median year structure built: 1978 (2006-2010 5-year est.).

Transportation: Commute to work: 93.5% car, 0.7% public transportation, 0.9% walk, 4.1% work from home (2006-2010 5-year est.); Travel time to

work: 22.6% less than 15 minutes, 39.2% 15 to 30 minutes, 18.0% 30 to 45 minutes, 8.6% 45 to 60 minutes, 11.7% 60 minutes or more (2006-2010 5-year est.)

Additional Information Contacts
Venango Area Chamber of Commerce . . . . (814) 676-8521
  http://www.venangochamber.org

JACKSON (township). Covers a land area of 24.694 square miles and a water area of 0 square miles. Located at 41.51° N. Lat; 79.88° W. Long.

Population: 1,066 (1990); 1,168 (2000); 1,147 (2010); Density: 46.4 persons per square mile (2010); Race: 98.0% White, 0.1% Black, 0.0% Asian, 0.2% American Indian/Alaska Native, 0.0% Native Hawaiian/Other Pacific Islander, 1.7% Other, 0.5% Hispanic of any race (2010); Average household size: 2.55 (2010); Median age: 41.9 (2010); Males per 100 females: 96.7 (2010); Marriage status: 21.0% never married, 66.3% now married, 4.3% widowed, 8.4% divorced (2006-2010 5-year est.); Foreign born: 1.3% (2006-2010 5-year est.); Ancestry (includes multiple ancestries): 38.4% German, 15.8% Irish, 8.5% English, 7.9% Italian, 5.1% Scotch-Irish (2006-2010 5-year est.).

Economy: Single-family building permits issued: 5 (2011); Multi-family building permits issued: 0 (2011); Employment by occupation: 14.1% management, 1.7% professional, 5.4% services, 11.1% sales, 4.3% farming, 16.5% construction, 7.8% production (2006-2010 5-year est.).

Income: Per capita income: $23,986 (2006-2010 5-year est.); Median household income: $47,500 (2006-2010 5-year est.); Average household income: $60,007 (2006-2010 5-year est.); Percent of households with income of $100,000 or more: 15.2% (2006-2010 5-year est.); Poverty rate: 16.0% (2006-2010 5-year est.).

Education: Percent of population age 25 and over with: High school diploma (including GED) or higher: 89.5% (2006-2010 5-year est.); Bachelor's degree or higher: 11.8% (2006-2010 5-year est.); Master's degree or higher: 4.7% (2006-2010 5-year est.).

Housing: Homeownership rate: 79.5% (2010); Median home value: $91,000 (2006-2010 5-year est.); Median contract rent: $323 per month (2006-2010 5-year est.); Median year structure built: 1974 (2006-2010 5-year est.).

Transportation: Commute to work: 91.9% car, 0.7% public transportation, 2.7% walk, 4.1% work from home (2006-2010 5-year est.); Travel time to work: 17.6% less than 15 minutes, 44.4% 15 to 30 minutes, 21.8% 30 to 45 minutes, 9.2% 45 to 60 minutes, 7.0% 60 minutes or more (2006-2010 5-year est.)

Additional Information Contacts
Venango Area Chamber of Commerce . . . . (814) 676-8521
  http://www.venangochamber.org

KENNERDELL (CDP). Covers a land area of 2.249 square miles and a water area of 0 square miles. Located at 41.28° N. Lat; 79.82° W. Long. Elevation is 1,017 feet.

Population: n/a (1990); n/a (2000); 247 (2010); Density: 109.8 persons per square mile (2010); Race: 98.0% White, 0.0% Black, 0.8% Asian, 0.0% American Indian/Alaska Native, 0.0% Native Hawaiian/Other Pacific Islander, 1.2% Other, 0.0% Hispanic of any race (2010); Average household size: 2.11 (2010); Median age: 54.2 (2010); Males per 100 females: 107.6 (2010); Marriage status: 24.4% never married, 67.1% now married, 8.5% widowed, 0.0% divorced (2006-2010 5-year est.); Foreign born: 0.0% (2006-2010 5-year est.); Ancestry (includes multiple ancestries): 52.1% German, 34.6% Irish, 6.9% Scottish, 6.4% French Canadian, 4.3% Scotch-Irish (2006-2010 5-year est.).

Economy: Employment by occupation: 0.0% management, 0.0% professional, 15.5% services, 19.6% sales, 5.2% farming, 10.3% construction, 6.2% production (2006-2010 5-year est.).

Income: Per capita income: $22,309 (2006-2010 5-year est.); Median household income: $44,750 (2006-2010 5-year est.); Average household income: $53,258 (2006-2010 5-year est.); Percent of households with income of $100,000 or more: 5.2% (2006-2010 5-year est.); Poverty rate: 3.7% (2006-2010 5-year est.).

Education: Percent of population age 25 and over with: High school diploma (including GED) or higher: 94.1% (2006-2010 5-year est.); Bachelor's degree or higher: 25.2% (2006-2010 5-year est.); Master's degree or higher: 6.7% (2006-2010 5-year est.).

School District(s)
Cranberry Area SD (KG-12)
  2010-11 Enrollment: 1,183 . . . . (814) 676-5628

Housing: Homeownership rate: 88.9% (2010); Median home value: $73,300 (2006-2010 5-year est.); Median contract rent: $525 per month

(2006-2010 5-year est.); Median year structure built: 1966 (2006-2010 5-year est.).

Transportation: Commute to work: 84.8% car, 0.0% public transportation, 5.4% walk, 9.8% work from home (2006-2010 5-year est.); Travel time to work: 24.1% less than 15 minutes, 63.9% 15 to 30 minutes, 2.4% 30 to 45 minutes, 4.8% 45 to 60 minutes, 4.8% 60 minutes or more (2006-2010 5-year est.)

MINERAL (township). Covers a land area of 22.273 square miles and a water area of 0 square miles. Located at 41.32° N. Lat; 79.97° W. Long.

Population: 514 (1990); 533 (2000); 538 (2010); Density: 24.2 persons per square mile (2010); Race: 98.0% White, 0.4% Black, 0.6% Asian, 0.0% American Indian/Alaska Native, 0.0% Native Hawaiian/Other Pacific Islander, 1.0% Other, 0.4% Hispanic of any race (2010); Average household size: 2.39 (2010); Median age: 48.3 (2010); Males per 100 females: 115.2 (2010); Marriage status: 18.1% never married, 61.0% now married, 7.2% widowed, 13.7% divorced (2006-2010 5-year est.); Foreign born: 1.2% (2006-2010 5-year est.); Ancestry (includes multiple ancestries): 43.5% German, 19.9% Irish, 9.3% Scotch-Irish, 7.5% French, 7.5% Dutch (2006-2010 5-year est.).

Economy: Single-family building permits issued: 2 (2011); Multi-family building permits issued: 0 (2011); Employment by occupation: 8.9% management, 2.6% professional, 15.6% services, 12.5% sales, 0.0% farming, 8.9% construction, 1.6% production (2006-2010 5-year est.).

Income: Per capita income: $22,808 (2006-2010 5-year est.); Median household income: $46,667 (2006-2010 5-year est.); Average household income: $52,462 (2006-2010 5-year est.); Percent of households with income of $100,000 or more: 9.6% (2006-2010 5-year est.); Poverty rate: 4.0% (2006-2010 5-year est.).

Education: Percent of population age 25 and over with: High school diploma (including GED) or higher: 80.7% (2006-2010 5-year est.); Bachelor's degree or higher: 8.0% (2006-2010 5-year est.); Master's degree or higher: 0.8% (2006-2010 5-year est.).

Housing: Homeownership rate: 87.6% (2010); Median home value: $84,800 (2006-2010 5-year est.); Median contract rent: $608 per month (2006-2010 5-year est.); Median year structure built: 1978 (2006-2010 5-year est.).

Transportation: Commute to work: 93.9% car, 0.0% public transportation, 0.0% walk, 6.1% work from home (2006-2010 5-year est.); Travel time to work: 10.7% less than 15 minutes, 43.2% 15 to 30 minutes, 29.6% 30 to 45 minutes, 8.3% 45 to 60 minutes, 8.3% 60 minutes or more (2006-2010 5-year est.)

OAKLAND (township). Covers a land area of 28.804 square miles and a water area of 0.179 square miles. Located at 41.50° N. Lat; 79.77° W. Long.

Population: 1,527 (1990); 1,565 (2000); 1,504 (2010); Density: 52.2 persons per square mile (2010); Race: 98.9% White, 0.1% Black, 0.2% Asian, 0.1% American Indian/Alaska Native, 0.1% Native Hawaiian/Other Pacific Islander, 0.6% Other, 0.5% Hispanic of any race (2010); Average household size: 2.54 (2010); Median age: 45.7 (2010); Males per 100 females: 98.9 (2010); Marriage status: 19.6% never married, 63.5% now married, 8.2% widowed, 8.7% divorced (2006-2010 5-year est.); Foreign born: 0.2% (2006-2010 5-year est.); Ancestry (includes multiple ancestries): 44.8% German, 18.5% Irish, 11.9% American, 6.9% English, 4.5% Italian (2006-2010 5-year est.).

Economy: Single-family building permits issued: 1 (2011); Multi-family building permits issued: 0 (2011); Employment by occupation: 10.2% management, 3.3% professional, 5.5% services, 21.1% sales, 3.9% farming, 13.0% construction, 8.5% production (2006-2010 5-year est.).

Income: Per capita income: $22,898 (2006-2010 5-year est.); Median household income: $53,026 (2006-2010 5-year est.); Average household income: $58,098 (2006-2010 5-year est.); Percent of households with income of $100,000 or more: 12.9% (2006-2010 5-year est.); Poverty rate: 6.5% (2006-2010 5-year est.).

Education: Percent of population age 25 and over with: High school diploma (including GED) or higher: 93.8% (2006-2010 5-year est.); Bachelor's degree or higher: 16.2% (2006-2010 5-year est.); Master's degree or higher: 5.1% (2006-2010 5-year est.).

Housing: Homeownership rate: 89.2% (2010); Median home value: $97,200 (2006-2010 5-year est.); Median contract rent: $470 per month (2006-2010 5-year est.); Median year structure built: 1972 (2006-2010 5-year est.).

Transportation: Commute to work: 94.7% car, 0.0% public transportation, 2.3% walk, 3.0% work from home (2006-2010 5-year est.); Travel time to

work: 26.8% less than 15 minutes, 58.1% 15 to 30 minutes, 10.0% 30 to 45 minutes, 2.0% 45 to 60 minutes, 3.0% 60 minutes or more (2006-2010 5-year est.)

Additional Information Contacts
Venango Area Chamber of Commerce . . . . (814) 676-8521
　http://www.venangochamber.org

OIL CITY (city). Covers a land area of 4.493 square miles and a water area of 0.345 square miles. Located at 41.43° N. Lat; 79.71° W. Long. Elevation is 1,024 feet.

History: Oil City emerged in 1860 as an important oil center.

Population: 11,949 (1990); 11,504 (2000); 10,557 (2010); Density: 2,349.9 persons per square mile (2010); Race: 96.2% White, 1.5% Black, 0.3% Asian, 0.2% American Indian/Alaska Native, 0.0% Native Hawaiian/Other Pacific Islander, 1.8% Other, 1.2% Hispanic of any race (2010); Average household size: 2.34 (2010); Median age: 39.9 (2010); Males per 100 females: 90.1 (2010); Marriage status: 28.6% never married, 46.0% now married, 10.7% widowed, 14.7% divorced (2006-2010 5-year est.); Foreign born: 1.0% (2006-2010 5-year est.); Ancestry (includes multiple ancestries): 35.6% German, 20.9% Irish, 9.9% English, 7.6% Polish, 7.4% Italian (2006-2010 5-year est.).

Economy: Single-family building permits issued: 0 (2011); Multi-family building permits issued: 0 (2011); Employment by occupation: 6.6% management, 1.4% professional, 14.2% services, 18.2% sales, 3.5% farming, 8.1% construction, 6.4% production (2006-2010 5-year est.).

Income: Per capita income: $15,904 (2006-2010 5-year est.); Median household income: $30,000 (2006-2010 5-year est.); Average household income: $38,502 (2006-2010 5-year est.); Percent of households with income of $100,000 or more: 4.5% (2006-2010 5-year est.); Poverty rate: 28.1% (2006-2010 5-year est.).

Education: Percent of population age 25 and over with: High school diploma (including GED) or higher: 83.8% (2006-2010 5-year est.); Bachelor's degree or higher: 13.3% (2006-2010 5-year est.); Master's degree or higher: 5.0% (2006-2010 5-year est.).

School District(s)
Oil City Area SD (KG-12)
　2010-11 Enrollment: 2,148 . . . . (814) 676-1867
Venango Technology Center (10-12)
　2010-11 Enrollment: n/a . . . . (814) 677-3097

Two-year College(s)
Du Bois Business College-Oil City (Private, For-profit)
　Fall 2010 Enrollment: 43 . . . . (814) 371-6920
　2011-12 Tuition: In-state $10,305; Out-of-state $10,305

Vocational/Technical School(s)
Venango County Area Vocational Technical School (Public)
　Fall 2010 Enrollment: 85 . . . . (814) 677-3097
　2011-12 Tuition: $10,405

Housing: Homeownership rate: 60.1% (2010); Median home value: $48,000 (2006-2010 5-year est.); Median contract rent: $350 per month (2006-2010 5-year est.); Median year structure built: before 1940 (2006-2010 5-year est.).

Safety: Violent crime rate: 20.8 per 10,000 population; Property crime rate: 109.5 per 10,000 population (2011).

Newspapers: The News Herald (Local news; Circulation 8,900); Oil City Derrick (Community news; Circulation 28,000)

Transportation: Commute to work: 91.8% car, 0.5% public transportation, 4.1% walk, 2.5% work from home (2006-2010 5-year est.); Travel time to work: 42.5% less than 15 minutes, 39.9% 15 to 30 minutes, 9.4% 30 to 45 minutes, 3.9% 45 to 60 minutes, 4.4% 60 minutes or more (2006-2010 5-year est.)

Additional Information Contacts
City of Oil City . . . . (814) 678-3012
　http://www.oilcity.org
Venango Area Chamber of Commerce . . . . (814) 676-8521
　http://www.venangochamber.org

OIL CREEK (township). Covers a land area of 23.026 square miles and a water area of 0 square miles. Located at 41.58° N. Lat; 79.61° W. Long.

Population: 915 (1990); 840 (2000); 854 (2010); Density: 37.1 persons per square mile (2010); Race: 99.3% White, 0.0% Black, 0.1% Asian, 0.0% American Indian/Alaska Native, 0.0% Native Hawaiian/Other Pacific Islander, 0.6% Other, 0.4% Hispanic of any race (2010); Average household size: 2.49 (2010); Median age: 48.1 (2010); Males per 100 females: 104.8 (2010); Marriage status: 18.3% never married, 63.1% now

married, 7.8% widowed, 10.8% divorced (2006-2010 5-year est.); Foreign born: 0.0% (2006-2010 5-year est.); Ancestry (includes multiple ancestries): 40.8% German, 17.2% English, 15.0% Irish, 7.3% Polish, 5.9% American (2006-2010 5-year est.).

Economy: Single-family building permits issued: 0 (2011); Multi-family building permits issued: 0 (2011); Employment by occupation: 8.9% management, 3.7% professional, 8.6% services, 15.6% sales, 3.1% farming, 8.6% construction, 7.4% production (2006-2010 5-year est.).

Income: Per capita income: $20,133 (2006-2010 5-year est.); Median household income: $41,618 (2006-2010 5-year est.); Average household income: $51,309 (2006-2010 5-year est.); Percent of households with income of $100,000 or more: 13.9% (2006-2010 5-year est.); Poverty rate: 9.5% (2006-2010 5-year est.).

Education: Percent of population age 25 and over with: High school diploma (including GED) or higher: 87.5% (2006-2010 5-year est.); Bachelor's degree or higher: 9.3% (2006-2010 5-year est.); Master's degree or higher: 3.9% (2006-2010 5-year est.).

Housing: Homeownership rate: 92.2% (2010); Median home value: $79,700 (2006-2010 5-year est.); Median contract rent: n/a per month (2006-2010 5-year est.); Median year structure built: 1976 (2006-2010 5-year est.).

Transportation: Commute to work: 98.1% car, 0.0% public transportation, 1.9% walk, 0.0% work from home (2006-2010 5-year est.); Travel time to work: 37.0% less than 15 minutes, 37.0% 15 to 30 minutes, 6.5% 30 to 45 minutes, 17.6% 45 to 60 minutes, 1.9% 60 minutes or more (2006-2010 5-year est.)

PINEGROVE (township). Covers a land area of 37.019 square miles and a water area of 0 square miles. Located at 41.37° N. Lat; 79.54° W. Long.

Population: 1,395 (1990); 1,338 (2000); 1,354 (2010); Density: 36.6 persons per square mile (2010); Race: 98.2% White, 0.1% Black, 0.4% Asian, 0.3% American Indian/Alaska Native, 0.0% Native Hawaiian/Other Pacific Islander, 1.0% Other, 0.1% Hispanic of any race (2010); Average household size: 2.61 (2010); Median age: 43.3 (2010); Males per 100 females: 98.5 (2010); Marriage status: 17.0% never married, 64.5% now married, 7.1% widowed, 11.4% divorced (2006-2010 5-year est.); Foreign born: 0.0% (2006-2010 5-year est.); Ancestry (includes multiple ancestries): 44.4% German, 14.8% Irish, 11.2% English, 8.2% Italian, 7.4% American (2006-2010 5-year est.).

Economy: Single-family building permits issued: 1 (2011); Multi-family building permits issued: 0 (2011); Employment by occupation: 4.6% management, 1.9% professional, 14.5% services, 15.9% sales, 2.6% farming, 11.3% construction, 5.5% production (2006-2010 5-year est.).

Income: Per capita income: $19,502 (2006-2010 5-year est.); Median household income: $46,250 (2006-2010 5-year est.); Average household income: $50,207 (2006-2010 5-year est.); Percent of households with income of $100,000 or more: 8.0% (2006-2010 5-year est.); Poverty rate: 11.4% (2006-2010 5-year est.).

Education: Percent of population age 25 and over with: High school diploma (including GED) or higher: 87.9% (2006-2010 5-year est.); Bachelor's degree or higher: 15.8% (2006-2010 5-year est.); Master's degree or higher: 4.9% (2006-2010 5-year est.).

Housing: Homeownership rate: 84.0% (2010); Median home value: $89,300 (2006-2010 5-year est.); Median contract rent: $332 per month (2006-2010 5-year est.); Median year structure built: 1962 (2006-2010 5-year est.).

Transportation: Commute to work: 94.9% car, 0.0% public transportation, 0.5% walk, 4.2% work from home (2006-2010 5-year est.); Travel time to work: 13.1% less than 15 minutes, 52.2% 15 to 30 minutes, 20.6% 30 to 45 minutes, 6.1% 45 to 60 minutes, 8.0% 60 minutes or more (2006-2010 5-year est.)

Additional Information Contacts

Venango Area Chamber of Commerce . . . . (814) 676-8521
   http://www.venangochamber.org

PLEASANTVILLE (borough). Covers a land area of 0.950 square miles and a water area of 0 square miles. Located at 41.59° N. Lat; 79.58° W. Long. Elevation is 1,650 feet.

History: Pithole City Historic Site to South.

Population: 991 (1990); 850 (2000); 892 (2010); Density: 938.7 persons per square mile (2010); Race: 98.0% White, 0.2% Black, 1.1% Asian, 0.0% American Indian/Alaska Native, 0.0% Native Hawaiian/Other Pacific Islander, 0.7% Other, 0.3% Hispanic of any race (2010); Average household size: 2.54 (2010); Median age: 39.2 (2010); Males per 100

females: 96.5 (2010); Marriage status: 28.6% never married, 56.5% now married, 6.3% widowed, 8.6% divorced (2006-2010 5-year est.); Foreign born: 0.4% (2006-2010 5-year est.); Ancestry (includes multiple ancestries): 43.0% German, 27.3% Irish, 11.5% English, 6.1% American, 5.2% Swedish (2006-2010 5-year est.).

Economy: Single-family building permits issued: 0 (2011); Multi-family building permits issued: 0 (2011); Employment by occupation: 7.6% management, 3.3% professional, 24.1% services, 9.8% sales, 2.6% farming, 11.9% construction, 7.8% production (2006-2010 5-year est.).

Income: Per capita income: $20,606 (2006-2010 5-year est.); Median household income: $44,107 (2006-2010 5-year est.); Average household income: $50,864 (2006-2010 5-year est.); Percent of households with income of $100,000 or more: 9.5% (2006-2010 5-year est.); Poverty rate: 9.9% (2006-2010 5-year est.).

Education: Percent of population age 25 and over with: High school diploma (including GED) or higher: 90.4% (2006-2010 5-year est.); Bachelor's degree or higher: 9.0% (2006-2010 5-year est.); Master's degree or higher: 1.5% (2006-2010 5-year est.).

School District(s)

Titusville Area SD (KG-12)
   2010-11 Enrollment: 2,077 . . . . (814) 827-2715

Housing: Homeownership rate: 81.2% (2010); Median home value: $72,600 (2006-2010 5-year est.); Median contract rent: $366 per month (2006-2010 5-year est.); Median year structure built: before 1940 (2006-2010 5-year est.).

Transportation: Commute to work: 87.7% car, 0.0% public transportation, 9.4% walk, 0.7% work from home (2006-2010 5-year est.); Travel time to work: 47.0% less than 15 minutes, 23.7% 15 to 30 minutes, 8.4% 30 to 45 minutes, 12.9% 45 to 60 minutes, 8.1% 60 minutes or more (2006-2010 5-year est.)

PLUM (township). Aka Chapmanville. Covers a land area of 26.597 square miles and a water area of 0 square miles. Located at 41.58° N. Lat; 79.82° W. Long.

Population: 1,031 (1990); 1,060 (2000); 1,056 (2010); Density: 39.7 persons per square mile (2010); Race: 99.4% White, 0.0% Black, 0.1% Asian, 0.0% American Indian/Alaska Native, 0.0% Native Hawaiian/Other Pacific Islander, 0.5% Other, 0.1% Hispanic of any race (2010); Average household size: 2.63 (2010); Median age: 45.5 (2010); Males per 100 females: 105.8 (2010); Marriage status: 23.4% never married, 67.4% now married, 4.2% widowed, 5.0% divorced (2006-2010 5-year est.); Foreign born: 0.0% (2006-2010 5-year est.); Ancestry (includes multiple ancestries): 40.8% German, 16.4% Irish, 9.6% Italian, 9.3% Scotch-Irish, 7.4% English (2006-2010 5-year est.).

Economy: Single-family building permits issued: 1 (2011); Multi-family building permits issued: 0 (2011); Employment by occupation: 9.2% management, 2.0% professional, 9.7% services, 16.3% sales, 4.0% farming, 7.3% construction, 10.1% production (2006-2010 5-year est.).

Income: Per capita income: $18,022 (2006-2010 5-year est.); Median household income: $41,667 (2006-2010 5-year est.); Average household income: $49,678 (2006-2010 5-year est.); Percent of households with income of $100,000 or more: 6.3% (2006-2010 5-year est.); Poverty rate: 10.3% (2006-2010 5-year est.).

Education: Percent of population age 25 and over with: High school diploma (including GED) or higher: 88.2% (2006-2010 5-year est.); Bachelor's degree or higher: 11.5% (2006-2010 5-year est.); Master's degree or higher: 3.4% (2006-2010 5-year est.).

Housing: Homeownership rate: 89.7% (2010); Median home value: $96,500 (2006-2010 5-year est.); Median contract rent: $321 per month (2006-2010 5-year est.); Median year structure built: 1971 (2006-2010 5-year est.).

Transportation: Commute to work: 97.0% car, 0.0% public transportation, 0.0% walk, 3.0% work from home (2006-2010 5-year est.); Travel time to work: 10.3% less than 15 minutes, 48.2% 15 to 30 minutes, 23.4% 30 to 45 minutes, 8.7% 45 to 60 minutes, 9.5% 60 minutes or more (2006-2010 5-year est.)

Additional Information Contacts

Franklin Area Chamber of Commerce . . . . (814) 432-5823
   http://www.franklinareachamber.org

POLK (borough). Covers a land area of 2.028 square miles and a water area of 0.013 square miles. Located at 41.37° N. Lat; 79.93° W. Long. Elevation is 1,056 feet.

History: Settled c.1798, laid out 1839, incorporated 1886.

Population: 1,267 (1990); 1,031 (2000); 816 (2010); Density: 402.4 persons per square mile (2010); Race: 97.3% White, 2.0% Black, 0.1% Asian, 0.1% American Indian/Alaska Native, 0.0% Native Hawaiian/Other Pacific Islander, 0.5% Other, 0.2% Hispanic of any race (2010); Average household size: 2.48 (2010); Median age: 48.7 (2010); Males per 100 females: 96.6 (2010); Marriage status: 61.5% never married, 28.5% now married, 3.4% widowed, 6.6% divorced (2006-2010 5-year est.); Foreign born: 1.4% (2006-2010 5-year est.); Ancestry (includes multiple ancestries): 22.2% German, 6.8% English, 5.5% Polish, 5.1% Irish, 5.0% Scotch-Irish (2006-2010 5-year est.).

Economy: Single-family building permits issued: 0 (2011); Multi-family building permits issued: 0 (2011); Employment by occupation: 4.5% management, 3.4% professional, 8.4% services, 11.3% sales, 5.3% farming, 13.3% construction, 14.5% production (2006-2010 5-year est.).

Income: Per capita income: $17,569 (2006-2010 5-year est.); Median household income: $55,833 (2006-2010 5-year est.); Average household income: $59,015 (2006-2010 5-year est.); Percent of households with income of $100,000 or more: 16.3% (2006-2010 5-year est.); Poverty rate: 30.8% (2006-2010 5-year est.).

Education: Percent of population age 25 and over with: High school diploma (including GED) or higher: 62.7% (2006-2010 5-year est.); Bachelor's degree or higher: 6.6% (2006-2010 5-year est.); Master's degree or higher: 3.4% (2006-2010 5-year est.).

School District(s)

Franklin Area SD (KG-12)

    2010-11 Enrollment: 2,068 . . . . (814) 432-8917

Housing: Homeownership rate: 71.4% (2010); Median home value: $69,500 (2006-2010 5-year est.); Median contract rent: $413 per month (2006-2010 5-year est.); Median year structure built: before 1940 (2006-2010 5-year est.).

Safety: Violent crime rate: 0.0 per 10,000 population; Property crime rate: 12.2 per 10,000 population (2011).

Transportation: Commute to work: 51.4% car, 5.6% public transportation, 41.6% walk, 1.3% work from home (2006-2010 5-year est.); Travel time to work: 54.4% less than 15 minutes, 25.1% 15 to 30 minutes, 15.3% 30 to 45 minutes, 1.6% 45 to 60 minutes, 3.6% 60 minutes or more (2006-2010 5-year est.)

Additional Information Contacts

Franklin Area Chamber of Commerce. . . . . (814) 432-5823
    http://www.franklinareachamber.org

PRESIDENT (township). Covers a land area of 37.790 square miles and a water area of 1.122 square miles. Located at 41.46° N. Lat; 79.57° W. Long. Elevation is 1,037 feet.

Population: 501 (1990); 543 (2000); 540 (2010); Density: 14.3 persons per square mile (2010); Race: 98.7% White, 0.2% Black, 0.0% Asian, 0.4% American Indian/Alaska Native, 0.0% Native Hawaiian/Other Pacific Islander, 0.7% Other, 0.4% Hispanic of any race (2010); Average household size: 2.05 (2010); Median age: 53.2 (2010); Males per 100 females: 107.7 (2010); Marriage status: 23.6% never married, 63.2% now married, 5.8% widowed, 7.4% divorced (2006-2010 5-year est.); Foreign born: 0.0% (2006-2010 5-year est.); Ancestry (includes multiple ancestries): 50.3% German, 33.5% Irish, 18.5% English, 6.7% Scotch-Irish, 6.7% Dutch (2006-2010 5-year est.).

Economy: Single-family building permits issued: 2 (2011); Multi-family building permits issued: 0 (2011); Employment by occupation: 4.0% management, 4.8% professional, 6.9% services, 19.4% sales, 0.0% farming, 14.9% construction, 6.0% production (2006-2010 5-year est.).

Income: Per capita income: $22,505 (2006-2010 5-year est.); Median household income: $41,827 (2006-2010 5-year est.); Average household income: $47,932 (2006-2010 5-year est.); Percent of households with income of $100,000 or more: 8.3% (2006-2010 5-year est.); Poverty rate: 3.7% (2006-2010 5-year est.).

Education: Percent of population age 25 and over with: High school diploma (including GED) or higher: 90.5% (2006-2010 5-year est.); Bachelor's degree or higher: 23.5% (2006-2010 5-year est.); Master's degree or higher: 7.6% (2006-2010 5-year est.).

Housing: Homeownership rate: 91.6% (2010); Median home value: $89,200 (2006-2010 5-year est.); Median contract rent: $278 per month (2006-2010 5-year est.); Median year structure built: 1961 (2006-2010 5-year est.).

Transportation: Commute to work: 98.8% car, 0.0% public transportation, 1.2% walk, 0.0% work from home (2006-2010 5-year est.); Travel time to work: 6.0% less than 15 minutes, 44.4% 15 to 30 minutes, 23.4% 30 to 45

minutes, 9.5% 45 to 60 minutes, 16.7% 60 minutes or more (2006-2010 5-year est.)

RENO (unincorporated postal area)

Zip Code: 16343

    Covers a land area of 4.753 square miles and a water area of 0.719 square miles. Located at 41.42° N. Lat; 79.75° W. Long. Elevation is 1,017 feet. Population: 449 (2010); Density: 94.4 persons per square mile (2010); Race: 98.0% White, 1.3% Black, 0.0% Asian, 0.2% American Indian/Alaska Native, 0.0% Native Hawaiian/Other Pacific Islander, 0.5% Other, 0.0% Hispanic of any race (2010); Average household size: 2.30 (2010); Median age: 43.7 (2010); Males per 100 females: 99.6 (2010); Homeownership rate: 81.5% (2010)

RICHLAND (township). Covers a land area of 22.223 square miles and a water area of 0.192 square miles. Located at 41.24° N. Lat; 79.68° W. Long.

Population: 775 (1990); 744 (2000); 777 (2010); Density: 35.0 persons per square mile (2010); Race: 97.4% White, 0.6% Black, 0.0% Asian, 0.6% American Indian/Alaska Native, 0.0% Native Hawaiian/Other Pacific Islander, 1.4% Other, 0.4% Hispanic of any race (2010); Average household size: 2.43 (2010); Median age: 45.8 (2010); Males per 100 females: 100.8 (2010); Marriage status: 31.3% never married, 51.6% now married, 8.2% widowed, 8.9% divorced (2006-2010 5-year est.); Foreign born: 0.0% (2006-2010 5-year est.); Ancestry (includes multiple ancestries): 46.1% German, 14.2% English, 11.8% Irish, 9.2% Scotch-Irish, 5.5% Dutch (2006-2010 5-year est.).

Economy: Single-family building permits issued: 0 (2011); Multi-family building permits issued: 0 (2011); Employment by occupation: 11.4% management, 3.5% professional, 10.3% services, 20.5% sales, 0.0% farming, 15.5% construction, 1.5% production (2006-2010 5-year est.).

Income: Per capita income: $20,093 (2006-2010 5-year est.); Median household income: $42,039 (2006-2010 5-year est.); Average household income: $49,930 (2006-2010 5-year est.); Percent of households with income of $100,000 or more: 8.2% (2006-2010 5-year est.); Poverty rate: 8.1% (2006-2010 5-year est.).

Education: Percent of population age 25 and over with: High school diploma (including GED) or higher: 85.6% (2006-2010 5-year est.); Bachelor's degree or higher: 18.7% (2006-2010 5-year est.); Master's degree or higher: 2.6% (2006-2010 5-year est.).

Housing: Homeownership rate: 81.9% (2010); Median home value: $92,000 (2006-2010 5-year est.); Median contract rent: $196 per month (2006-2010 5-year est.); Median year structure built: 1955 (2006-2010 5-year est.).

Transportation: Commute to work: 91.8% car, 0.0% public transportation, 5.3% walk, 2.9% work from home (2006-2010 5-year est.); Travel time to work: 32.3% less than 15 minutes, 29.6% 15 to 30 minutes, 29.0% 30 to 45 minutes, 5.1% 45 to 60 minutes, 3.9% 60 minutes or more (2006-2010 5-year est.)

ROCKLAND (township). Covers a land area of 49.585 square miles and a water area of 0 square miles. Located at 41.28° N. Lat; 79.75° W. Long. Elevation is 1,430 feet.

Population: 1,320 (1990); 1,346 (2000); 1,456 (2010); Density: 29.4 persons per square mile (2010); Race: 98.3% White, 0.0% Black, 0.1% Asian, 0.1% American Indian/Alaska Native, 0.0% Native Hawaiian/Other Pacific Islander, 1.5% Other, 0.5% Hispanic of any race (2010); Average household size: 2.37 (2010); Median age: 48.6 (2010); Males per 100 females: 113.8 (2010); Marriage status: 22.3% never married, 59.6% now married, 9.3% widowed, 8.8% divorced (2006-2010 5-year est.); Foreign born: 0.1% (2006-2010 5-year est.); Ancestry (includes multiple ancestries): 50.2% German, 20.4% Irish, 10.4% English, 6.0% Scottish, 5.7% Dutch (2006-2010 5-year est.).

Economy: Single-family building permits issued: 1 (2011); Multi-family building permits issued: 0 (2011); Employment by occupation: 2.8% management, 0.8% professional, 11.3% services, 16.9% sales, 3.3% farming, 14.4% construction, 8.4% production (2006-2010 5-year est.).

Income: Per capita income: $22,259 (2006-2010 5-year est.); Median household income: $42,237 (2006-2010 5-year est.); Average household income: $52,470 (2006-2010 5-year est.); Percent of households with income of $100,000 or more: 8.2% (2006-2010 5-year est.); Poverty rate: 9.3% (2006-2010 5-year est.).

Education: Percent of population age 25 and over with: High school diploma (including GED) or higher: 89.1% (2006-2010 5-year est.);

Bachelor's degree or higher: 13.7% (2006-2010 5-year est.); Master's degree or higher: 3.4% (2006-2010 5-year est.).

Housing: Homeownership rate: 87.9% (2010); Median home value: $79,700 (2006-2010 5-year est.); Median contract rent: $475 per month (2006-2010 5-year est.); Median year structure built: 1967 (2006-2010 5-year est.).

Transportation: Commute to work: 92.5% car, 1.5% public transportation, 1.7% walk, 3.7% work from home (2006-2010 5-year est.); Travel time to work: 21.1% less than 15 minutes, 52.4% 15 to 30 minutes, 20.0% 30 to 45 minutes, 3.4% 45 to 60 minutes, 3.2% 60 minutes or more (2006-2010 5-year est.)

Additional Information Contacts

Franklin Area Chamber of Commerce. . . . . (814) 432-5823
http://www.franklinareachamber.org

ROUSEVILLE (borough). Covers a land area of 0.893 square miles and a water area of 0.012 square miles. Located at 41.47° N. Lat; 79.68° W. Long. Elevation is 1,037 feet.

Population: 583 (1990); 472 (2000); 523 (2010); Density: 585.4 persons per square mile (2010); Race: 99.6% White, 0.0% Black, 0.0% Asian, 0.0% American Indian/Alaska Native, 0.0% Native Hawaiian/Other Pacific Islander, 0.4% Other, 0.6% Hispanic of any race (2010); Average household size: 2.58 (2010); Median age: 39.6 (2010); Males per 100 females: 101.2 (2010); Marriage status: 20.7% never married, 56.4% now married, 8.8% widowed, 14.1% divorced (2006-2010 5-year est.); Foreign born: 1.4% (2006-2010 5-year est.); Ancestry (includes multiple ancestries): 47.7% German, 22.2% Irish, 15.3% English, 10.1% Polish, 6.2% Dutch (2006-2010 5-year est.).

Economy: Single-family building permits issued: 0 (2011); Multi-family building permits issued: 0 (2011); Employment by occupation: 6.7% management, 4.0% professional, 13.3% services, 21.3% sales, 2.2% farming, 6.7% construction, 11.1% production (2006-2010 5-year est.).

Income: Per capita income: $14,810 (2006-2010 5-year est.); Median household income: $30,789 (2006-2010 5-year est.); Average household income: $38,603 (2006-2010 5-year est.); Percent of households with income of $100,000 or more: 2.8% (2006-2010 5-year est.); Poverty rate: 7.1% (2006-2010 5-year est.).

Education: Percent of population age 25 and over with: High school diploma (including GED) or higher: 89.6% (2006-2010 5-year est.); Bachelor's degree or higher: 5.1% (2006-2010 5-year est.); Master's degree or higher: 0.0% (2006-2010 5-year est.).

Housing: Homeownership rate: 79.8% (2010); Median home value: $43,700 (2006-2010 5-year est.); Median contract rent: $405 per month (2006-2010 5-year est.); Median year structure built: before 1940 (2006-2010 5-year est.).

Transportation: Commute to work: 95.5% car, 0.0% public transportation, 2.7% walk, 0.9% work from home (2006-2010 5-year est.); Travel time to work: 27.1% less than 15 minutes, 58.8% 15 to 30 minutes, 8.1% 30 to 45 minutes, 4.5% 45 to 60 minutes, 1.4% 60 minutes or more (2006-2010 5-year est.)

SANDYCREEK (township). Covers a land area of 17.765 square miles and a water area of 1.328 square miles. Located at 41.35° N. Lat; 79.83° W. Long.

Population: 2,495 (1990); 2,406 (2000); 2,260 (2010); Density: 127.2 persons per square mile (2010); Race: 92.8% White, 5.0% Black, 0.5% Asian, 0.0% American Indian/Alaska Native, 0.0% Native Hawaiian/Other Pacific Islander, 1.7% Other, 2.3% Hispanic of any race (2010); Average household size: 2.39 (2010); Median age: 45.3 (2010); Males per 100 females: 112.8 (2010); Marriage status: 23.9% never married, 61.4% now married, 5.6% widowed, 9.0% divorced (2006-2010 5-year est.); Foreign born: 1.2% (2006-2010 5-year est.); Ancestry (includes multiple ancestries): 38.1% German, 17.6% Irish, 14.1% English, 7.5% Italian, 5.1% American (2006-2010 5-year est.).

Economy: Single-family building permits issued: 4 (2011); Multi-family building permits issued: 0 (2011); Employment by occupation: 8.7% management, 1.6% professional, 10.0% services, 16.7% sales, 2.4% farming, 7.3% construction, 9.1% production (2006-2010 5-year est.).

Income: Per capita income: $25,753 (2006-2010 5-year est.); Median household income: $50,889 (2006-2010 5-year est.); Average household income: $61,935 (2006-2010 5-year est.); Percent of households with income of $100,000 or more: 16.2% (2006-2010 5-year est.); Poverty rate: 8.8% (2006-2010 5-year est.).

Education: Percent of population age 25 and over with: High school diploma (including GED) or higher: 86.4% (2006-2010 5-year est.);

Bachelor's degree or higher: 19.1% (2006-2010 5-year est.); Master's degree or higher: 9.9% (2006-2010 5-year est.).

Housing: Homeownership rate: 87.1% (2010); Median home value: $98,100 (2006-2010 5-year est.); Median contract rent: $488 per month (2006-2010 5-year est.); Median year structure built: 1963 (2006-2010 5-year est.).

Transportation: Commute to work: 94.0% car, 0.0% public transportation, 2.7% walk, 2.1% work from home (2006-2010 5-year est.); Travel time to work: 47.4% less than 15 minutes, 28.0% 15 to 30 minutes, 8.4% 30 to 45 minutes, 7.3% 45 to 60 minutes, 8.8% 60 minutes or more (2006-2010 5-year est.)

Additional Information Contacts

Franklin Area Chamber of Commerce. . . . . (814) 432-5823
http://www.franklinareachamber.org

SCRUBGRASS (township). Covers a land area of 25.872 square miles and a water area of 1.937 square miles. Located at 41.22° N. Lat; 79.77° W. Long.

Population: 673 (1990); 799 (2000); 751 (2010); Density: 29.0 persons per square mile (2010); Race: 95.9% White, 0.7% Black, 0.9% Asian, 0.1% American Indian/Alaska Native, 0.0% Native Hawaiian/Other Pacific Islander, 2.4% Other, 1.2% Hispanic of any race (2010); Average household size: 2.42 (2010); Median age: 45.0 (2010); Males per 100 females: 113.4 (2010); Marriage status: 13.7% never married, 72.9% now married, 4.4% widowed, 9.0% divorced (2006-2010 5-year est.); Foreign born: 0.1% (2006-2010 5-year est.); Ancestry (includes multiple ancestries): 58.0% German, 17.9% Irish, 12.8% English, 8.2% Italian, 7.9% Scottish (2006-2010 5-year est.).

Economy: Single-family building permits issued: 0 (2011); Multi-family building permits issued: 0 (2011); Employment by occupation: 10.1% management, 0.0% professional, 18.1% services, 17.6% sales, 0.0% farming, 14.6% construction, 8.0% production (2006-2010 5-year est.).

Income: Per capita income: $18,814 (2006-2010 5-year est.); Median household income: $47,969 (2006-2010 5-year est.); Average household income: $50,507 (2006-2010 5-year est.); Percent of households with income of $100,000 or more: 4.9% (2006-2010 5-year est.); Poverty rate: 14.4% (2006-2010 5-year est.).

Education: Percent of population age 25 and over with: High school diploma (including GED) or higher: 90.6% (2006-2010 5-year est.); Bachelor's degree or higher: 6.6% (2006-2010 5-year est.); Master's degree or higher: 2.4% (2006-2010 5-year est.).

Housing: Homeownership rate: 83.9% (2010); Median home value: $108,500 (2006-2010 5-year est.); Median contract rent: $279 per month (2006-2010 5-year est.); Median year structure built: 1961 (2006-2010 5-year est.).

Transportation: Commute to work: 98.2% car, 1.3% public transportation, 0.0% walk, 0.5% work from home (2006-2010 5-year est.); Travel time to work: 27.2% less than 15 minutes, 39.3% 15 to 30 minutes, 16.5% 30 to 45 minutes, 12.4% 45 to 60 minutes, 4.6% 60 minutes or more (2006-2010 5-year est.)

SENECA (CDP). Covers a land area of 2.248 square miles and a water area of 0 square miles. Located at 41.38° N. Lat; 79.71° W. Long. Elevation is 1,453 feet.

Population: 1,014 (1990); 966 (2000); 1,065 (2010); Density: 473.8 persons per square mile (2010); Race: 97.1% White, 0.5% Black, 1.0% Asian, 0.3% American Indian/Alaska Native, 0.4% Native Hawaiian/Other Pacific Islander, 0.7% Other, 0.2% Hispanic of any race (2010); Average household size: 2.24 (2010); Median age: 49.1 (2010); Males per 100 females: 83.9 (2010); Marriage status: 16.2% never married, 70.1% now married, 5.1% widowed, 8.6% divorced (2006-2010 5-year est.); Foreign born: 1.0% (2006-2010 5-year est.); Ancestry (includes multiple ancestries): 52.5% German, 12.9% English, 11.9% Irish, 8.2% Dutch, 7.3% American (2006-2010 5-year est.).

Economy: Employment by occupation: 8.5% management, 3.5% professional, 11.0% services, 20.4% sales, 3.9% farming, 5.6% construction, 1.9% production (2006-2010 5-year est.).

Income: Per capita income: $25,505 (2006-2010 5-year est.); Median household income: $53,125 (2006-2010 5-year est.); Average household income: $52,889 (2006-2010 5-year est.); Percent of households with income of $100,000 or more: 12.3% (2006-2010 5-year est.); Poverty rate: 8.8% (2006-2010 5-year est.).

Education: Percent of population age 25 and over with: High school diploma (including GED) or higher: 97.5% (2006-2010 5-year est.);

Bachelor's degree or higher: 15.0% (2006-2010 5-year est.); Master's degree or higher: 3.4% (2006-2010 5-year est.).

School District(s)

Cranberry Area SD (KG-12)

2010-11 Enrollment: 1,183 . . . . (814) 676-5628

Housing: Homeownership rate: 77.3% (2010); Median home value: $92,400 (2006-2010 5-year est.); Median contract rent: $243 per month (2006-2010 5-year est.); Median year structure built: 1962 (2006-2010 5-year est.).

Hospitals: UPMS Northwest (189 beds)

Transportation: Commute to work: 90.4% car, 0.0% public transportation, 0.0% walk, 7.1% work from home (2006-2010 5-year est.); Travel time to work: 58.7% less than 15 minutes, 23.9% 15 to 30 minutes, 15.4% 30 to 45 minutes, 2.1% 45 to 60 minutes, 0.0% 60 minutes or more (2006-2010 5-year est.)

Additional Information Contacts

Venango Area Chamber of Commerce . . . . (814) 676-8521

http://www.venangochamber.org

SUGARCREEK (borough). Covers a land area of 37.513 square miles and a water area of 1.137 square miles. Located at 41.43° N. Lat; 79.82° W. Long. Elevation is 1,037 feet.

History: Formerly a township.

Population: 5,479 (1990); 5,331 (2000); 5,294 (2010); Density: 141.1 persons per square mile (2010); Race: 98.1% White, 0.5% Black, 0.2% Asian, 0.1% American Indian/Alaska Native, 0.0% Native Hawaiian/Other Pacific Islander, 1.1% Other, 1.0% Hispanic of any race (2010); Average household size: 2.38 (2010); Median age: 45.5 (2010); Males per 100 females: 95.6 (2010); Marriage status: 18.2% never married, 63.0% now married, 7.5% widowed, 11.3% divorced (2006-2010 5-year est.); Foreign born: 0.7% (2006-2010 5-year est.); Ancestry (includes multiple ancestries): 29.3% German, 17.0% Irish, 9.0% American, 8.2% Italian, 6.8% Polish (2006-2010 5-year est.).

Economy: Single-family building permits issued: 2 (2011); Multi-family building permits issued: 0 (2011); Employment by occupation: 11.5% management, 0.6% professional, 12.6% services, 15.6% sales, 3.3% farming, 8.0% construction, 8.7% production (2006-2010 5-year est.).

Income: Per capita income: $19,158 (2006-2010 5-year est.); Median household income: $35,042 (2006-2010 5-year est.); Average household income: $46,502 (2006-2010 5-year est.); Percent of households with income of $100,000 or more: 8.0% (2006-2010 5-year est.); Poverty rate: 10.2% (2006-2010 5-year est.).

Taxes: Total city taxes per capita: $227 (2009); City property taxes per capita: $128 (2009).

Education: Percent of population age 25 and over with: High school diploma (including GED) or higher: 89.0% (2006-2010 5-year est.); Bachelor's degree or higher: 9.1% (2006-2010 5-year est.); Master's degree or higher: 2.4% (2006-2010 5-year est.).

Housing: Homeownership rate: 79.8% (2010); Median home value: $71,600 (2006-2010 5-year est.); Median contract rent: $424 per month (2006-2010 5-year est.); Median year structure built: 1941 (2006-2010 5-year est.).

Safety: Violent crime rate: 3.8 per 10,000 population; Property crime rate: 94.1 per 10,000 population (2011).

Transportation: Commute to work: 94.7% car, 0.0% public transportation, 1.3% walk, 2.0% work from home (2006-2010 5-year est.); Travel time to work: 37.1% less than 15 minutes, 43.3% 15 to 30 minutes, 13.4% 30 to 45 minutes, 2.6% 45 to 60 minutes, 3.5% 60 minutes or more (2006-2010 5-year est.)

Additional Information Contacts

Borough of Sugarcreek . . . . (814) 432-9512

Venango Area Chamber of Commerce . . . . (814) 676-8521

http://www.venangochamber.org

UTICA (borough). Covers a land area of 1.399 square miles and a water area of 0.060 square miles. Located at 41.44° N. Lat; 79.97° W. Long. Elevation is 1,050 feet.

Population: 242 (1990); 211 (2000); 189 (2010); Density: 135.1 persons per square mile (2010); Race: 99.5% White, 0.0% Black, 0.0% Asian, 0.5% American Indian/Alaska Native, 0.0% Native Hawaiian/Other Pacific Islander, 0.0% Other, 1.1% Hispanic of any race (2010); Average household size: 2.49 (2010); Median age: 44.5 (2010); Males per 100 females: 92.9 (2010); Marriage status: 26.7% never married, 61.1% now married, 5.3% widowed, 6.9% divorced (2006-2010 5-year est.); Foreign born: 3.8% (2006-2010 5-year est.); Ancestry (includes multiple

ancestries): 27.0% German, 17.0% Irish, 12.6% English, 11.3% Egyptian, 10.7% Dutch (2006-2010 5-year est.).

Economy: Single-family building permits issued: 0 (2011); Multi-family building permits issued: 0 (2011); Employment by occupation: 16.7% management, 0.0% professional, 18.5% services, 0.0% sales, 0.0% farming, 20.4% construction, 7.4% production (2006-2010 5-year est.).

Income: Per capita income: $19,654 (2006-2010 5-year est.); Median household income: $36,667 (2006-2010 5-year est.); Average household income: $50,645 (2006-2010 5-year est.); Percent of households with income of $100,000 or more: 11.3% (2006-2010 5-year est.); Poverty rate: 12.6% (2006-2010 5-year est.).

Education: Percent of population age 25 and over with: High school diploma (including GED) or higher: 91.5% (2006-2010 5-year est.); Bachelor's degree or higher: 9.4% (2006-2010 5-year est.); Master's degree or higher: 4.3% (2006-2010 5-year est.).

School District(s)

Franklin Area SD (KG-12)

2010-11 Enrollment: 2,068 . . . . (814) 432-8917

Housing: Homeownership rate: 84.2% (2010); Median home value: $62,700 (2006-2010 5-year est.); Median contract rent: n/a per month (2006-2010 5-year est.); Median year structure built: before 1940 (2006-2010 5-year est.).

Transportation: Commute to work: 94.4% car, 0.0% public transportation, 5.6% walk, 0.0% work from home (2006-2010 5-year est.); Travel time to work: 29.6% less than 15 minutes, 29.6% 15 to 30 minutes, 40.7% 30 to 45 minutes, 0.0% 45 to 60 minutes, 0.0% 60 minutes or more (2006-2010 5-year est.)

VENUS (unincorporated postal area)

Zip Code: 16364

Covers a land area of 33.407 square miles and a water area of 0.010 square miles. Located at 41.35° N. Lat; 79.52° W. Long. Elevation is 1,598 feet. Population: 1,347 (2010); Density: 40.3 persons per square mile (2010); Race: 98.4% White, 0.1% Black, 0.1% Asian, 0.6% American Indian/Alaska Native, 0.0% Native Hawaiian/Other Pacific Islander, 0.8% Other, 0.4% Hispanic of any race (2010); Average household size: 2.68 (2010); Median age: 41.0 (2010); Males per 100 females: 99.0 (2010); Homeownership rate: 83.0% (2010)

VICTORY (township). Covers a land area of 20.125 square miles and a water area of 0.726 square miles. Located at 41.32° N. Lat; 79.89° W. Long.

Population: 365 (1990); 408 (2000); 410 (2010); Density: 20.4 persons per square mile (2010); Race: 99.3% White, 0.0% Black, 0.0% Asian, 0.0% American Indian/Alaska Native, 0.0% Native Hawaiian/Other Pacific Islander, 0.7% Other, 0.5% Hispanic of any race (2010); Average household size: 2.33 (2010); Median age: 49.6 (2010); Males per 100 females: 114.7 (2010); Marriage status: 26.8% never married, 63.6% now married, 5.6% widowed, 4.0% divorced (2006-2010 5-year est.); Foreign born: 0.0% (2006-2010 5-year est.); Ancestry (includes multiple ancestries): 53.3% German, 19.4% Irish, 13.4% English, 10.4% Hungarian, 5.7% Norwegian (2006-2010 5-year est.).

Economy: Single-family building permits issued: 0 (2011); Multi-family building permits issued: 0 (2011); Employment by occupation: 11.8% management, 0.0% professional, 7.6% services, 14.2% sales, 0.0% farming, 8.1% construction, 5.7% production (2006-2010 5-year est.).

Income: Per capita income: $24,050 (2006-2010 5-year est.); Median household income: $49,286 (2006-2010 5-year est.); Average household income: $59,907 (2006-2010 5-year est.); Percent of households with income of $100,000 or more: 11.7% (2006-2010 5-year est.); Poverty rate: 7.3% (2006-2010 5-year est.).

Education: Percent of population age 25 and over with: High school diploma (including GED) or higher: 77.2% (2006-2010 5-year est.); Bachelor's degree or higher: 20.5% (2006-2010 5-year est.); Master's degree or higher: 2.6% (2006-2010 5-year est.).

Housing: Homeownership rate: 88.6% (2010); Median home value: $105,800 (2006-2010 5-year est.); Median contract rent: $388 per month (2006-2010 5-year est.); Median year structure built: 1976 (2006-2010 5-year est.).

Transportation: Commute to work: 90.5% car, 1.4% public transportation, 1.9% walk, 4.7% work from home (2006-2010 5-year est.); Travel time to work: 15.4% less than 15 minutes, 47.3% 15 to 30 minutes, 19.4% 30 to 45 minutes, 2.0% 45 to 60 minutes, 15.9% 60 minutes or more (2006-2010 5-year est.)

WOODLAND HEIGHTS (CDP). Covers a land area of 1.631 square miles and a water area of 0.051 square miles. Located at 41.41° N. Lat; 79.70° W. Long. Elevation is 1,411 feet.

Population: 1,471 (1990); 1,402 (2000); 1,261 (2010); Density: 773.3 persons per square mile (2010); Race: 97.2% White, 0.3% Black, 0.1% Asian, 0.0% American Indian/Alaska Native, 0.0% Native Hawaiian/Other Pacific Islander, 2.4% Other, 1.3% Hispanic of any race (2010); Average household size: 2.29 (2010); Median age: 41.8 (2010); Males per 100 females: 89.6 (2010); Marriage status: 28.8% never married, 52.7% now married, 5.2% widowed, 13.3% divorced (2006-2010 5-year est.); Foreign born: 0.0% (2006-2010 5-year est.); Ancestry (includes multiple ancestries): 42.8% German, 25.5% Irish, 14.4% American, 5.7% Dutch, 4.9% Italian (2006-2010 5-year est.).

Economy: Employment by occupation: 2.9% management, 1.2% professional, 20.6% services, 22.7% sales, 4.2% farming, 7.1% construction, 3.1% production (2006-2010 5-year est.).

Income: Per capita income: $18,643 (2006-2010 5-year est.); Median household income: $32,344 (2006-2010 5-year est.); Average household income: $43,016 (2006-2010 5-year est.); Percent of households with income of $100,000 or more: 6.3% (2006-2010 5-year est.); Poverty rate: 27.6% (2006-2010 5-year est.).

Education: Percent of population age 25 and over with: High school diploma (including GED) or higher: 88.9% (2006-2010 5-year est.); Bachelor's degree or higher: 13.5% (2006-2010 5-year est.); Master's degree or higher: 1.6% (2006-2010 5-year est.).

Housing: Homeownership rate: 68.6% (2010); Median home value: $65,000 (2006-2010 5-year est.); Median contract rent: $333 per month (2006-2010 5-year est.); Median year structure built: 1953 (2006-2010 5-year est.).

Transportation: Commute to work: 96.5% car, 1.6% public transportation, 0.0% walk, 1.9% work from home (2006-2010 5-year est.); Travel time to work: 57.3% less than 15 minutes, 24.6% 15 to 30 minutes, 12.9% 30 to 45 minutes, 5.2% 45 to 60 minutes, 0.0% 60 minutes or more (2006-2010 5-year est.).

Additional Information Contacts
Venango Area Chamber of Commerce . . . . (814) 676-8521
    http://www.venangochamber.org

Warren County

Located in northwestern Pennsylvania; bounded on the north by New York; plateau area, drained by the Allegheny River. Covers a land area of 884.135 square miles, a water area of 14.428 square miles, and is located in the Eastern Time Zone at 41.84° N. Lat., 79.31° W. Long. The county was founded in 1800. County seat is Warren.

Warren County is part of the Warren, PA Micropolitan Statistical Area. The entire metro area includes: Warren County, PA

Weather Station: Warren   Elevation: 1,209 feet

	Jan	Feb	Mar	Apr	May	Jun	Jul	Aug	Sep	Oct	Nov	Dec
High	33	36	45	58	69	78	82	80	73	61	48	37
Low	17	18	24	35	44	54	58	57	51	40	32	23
Precip	3.2	2.5	3.3	4.0	4.3	5.0	4.8	4.4	4.1	3.6	4.0	3.7
Snow	16.6	11.0	9.5	1.8	tr	0.0	0.0	0.0	0.0	0.1	6.5	15.1

High and Low temperatures in degrees Fahrenheit; Precipitation and Snow in inches

Population: 45,083 (1990); 43,863 (2000); 41,815 (2010); Race: 98.1% White, 0.4% Black, 0.4% Asian, 0.2% American Indian/Alaska Native, 0.0% Native Hawaiian/Other Pacific Islander, 0.9% Other, 0.7% Hispanic of any race (2010); Density: 47.3 persons per square mile (2010); Average household size: 2.31 (2010); Median age: 45.1 (2010); Males per 100 females: 99.2 (2010).

Religion: Six largest groups: 17.5% Catholicism, 13.1% Methodist/Pietist, 3.9% Lutheran, 3.4% Holiness, 3.3% Presbyterian-Reformed, 2.0% Non-Denominational (2010)

Economy: Unemployment rate: 7.3% (August 2012); Total civilian labor force: 21,511 (August 2012); Leading industries: 22.0% health care and social assistance; 19.6% manufacturing; 17.9% retail trade (2010); Farms: 831 totaling 99,582 acres (2007); Companies that employ 500 or more persons: 5 (2010); Companies that employ 100 to 499 persons: 14 (2010); Companies that employ less than 100 persons: 869 (2010); Black-owned businesses: n/a (2007); Hispanic-owned businesses: n/a (2007); Asian-owned businesses: n/a (2007); Women-owned businesses: 650 (2007); Retail sales per capita: $18,369 (2010). Single-family building permits issued: 26 (2011); Multi-family building permits issued: 0 (2011).

Income: Per capita income: $22,170 (2006-2010 5-year est.); Median household income: $41,286 (2006-2010 5-year est.); Average household income: $52,371 (2006-2010 5-year est.); Percent of households with income of $100,000 or more: 9.4% (2006-2010 5-year est.); Poverty rate: 12.2% (2006-2010 5-year est.); Bankruptcy rate: 2.63% (2011).

Taxes: Total county taxes per capita: $211 (2009); County property taxes per capita: $207 (2009).

Education: Percent of population age 25 and over with: High school diploma (including GED) or higher: 88.9% (2006-2010 5-year est.); Bachelor's degree or higher: 16.9% (2006-2010 5-year est.); Master's degree or higher: 5.5% (2006-2010 5-year est.).

Housing: Homeownership rate: 76.7% (2010); Median home value: $83,900 (2006-2010 5-year est.); Median contract rent: $387 per month (2006-2010 5-year est.); Median year structure built: 1957 (2006-2010 5-year est.)

Health: Birth rate: 91.9 per 10,000 population (2011); Death rate: 120.9 per 10,000 population (2011); Age-adjusted cancer mortality rate: 207.4 deaths per 100,000 population (2009); Number of physicians: 16.3 per 10,000 population (2010); Hospital beds: 87.1 per 10,000 population (2008); Hospital admissions: 1,081.5 per 10,000 population (2008).

Environment: Air Quality Index: 87.4% good, 10.3% moderate, 2.3% unhealthy for sensitive individuals, 0.0% unhealthy (percent of days in 2011)

Elections: 2012 Presidential election results: 40.4% Obama, 57.9% Romney

National and State Parks: Allegheny National Forest; Chapman State Park

Additional Information Contacts
Warren County Government . . . . (814) 728-3406
    http://www.warren-county.net
Warren County Chamber of Business and Industry . . . . . . (814) 723-3050
    http://wccbi.org
Warren County Chamber of Business and Industry . . . . . . (814) 723-3050
    http://www.wccbi.org

Warren County Communities

BEAR LAKE (borough). Covers a land area of 0.695 square miles and a water area of 0 square miles. Located at 41.99° N. Lat; 79.50° W. Long. Elevation is 1,555 feet.

Population: 193 (1990); 193 (2000); 164 (2010); Density: 236.0 persons per square mile (2010); Race: 90.9% White, 0.0% Black, 0.0% Asian, 0.0% American Indian/Alaska Native, 0.0% Native Hawaiian/Other Pacific Islander, 9.1% Other, 7.9% Hispanic of any race (2010); Average household size: 2.60 (2010); Median age: 43.7 (2010); Males per 100 females: 105.0 (2010); Marriage status: 13.5% never married, 67.1% now married, 13.5% widowed, 5.8% divorced (2006-2010 5-year est.); Foreign born: 1.4% (2006-2010 5-year est.); Ancestry (includes multiple ancestries): 51.2% German, 24.6% Irish, 19.8% English, 13.0% Dutch, 3.4% Pennsylvania German (2006-2010 5-year est.).

Economy: Employment by occupation: 3.9% management, 0.0% professional, 9.1% services, 23.4% sales, 0.0% farming, 19.5% construction, 15.6% production (2006-2010 5-year est.).

Income: Per capita income: $14,454 (2006-2010 5-year est.); Median household income: $35,455 (2006-2010 5-year est.); Average household income: $38,794 (2006-2010 5-year est.); Percent of households with income of $100,000 or more: n/a (2006-2010 5-year est.); Poverty rate: 11.1% (2006-2010 5-year est.).

Education: Percent of population age 25 and over with: High school diploma (including GED) or higher: 70.1% (2006-2010 5-year est.); Bachelor's degree or higher: 4.4% (2006-2010 5-year est.); Master's degree or higher: 0.0% (2006-2010 5-year est.).

Housing: Homeownership rate: 90.5% (2010); Median home value: $63,300 (2006-2010 5-year est.); Median contract rent: $344 per month (2006-2010 5-year est.); Median year structure built: before 1940 (2006-2010 5-year est.).

Transportation: Commute to work: 89.2% car, 0.0% public transportation, 0.0% walk, 10.8% work from home (2006-2010 5-year est.); Travel time to work: 13.6% less than 15 minutes, 72.7% 15 to 30 minutes, 9.1% 30 to 45 minutes, 4.5% 45 to 60 minutes, 0.0% 60 minutes or more (2006-2010 5-year est.)

BROKENSTRAW (township). Covers a land area of 38.046 square miles and a water area of 0.180 square miles. Located at 41.84° N. Lat; 79.31° W. Long.
Population: 1,962 (1990); 2,068 (2000); 1,884 (2010); Density: 49.5 persons per square mile (2010); Race: 98.7% White, 0.0% Black, 0.2% Asian, 0.4% American Indian/Alaska Native, 0.0% Native Hawaiian/Other Pacific Islander, 0.7% Other, 0.4% Hispanic of any race (2010); Average household size: 2.20 (2010); Median age: 51.2 (2010); Males per 100 females: 92.6 (2010); Marriage status: 23.9% never married, 54.9% now married, 13.5% widowed, 7.7% divorced (2006-2010 5-year est.); Foreign born: 2.6% (2006-2010 5-year est.); Ancestry (includes multiple ancestries): 32.1% German, 20.3% Irish, 17.1% English, 8.6% Polish, 7.4% Swedish (2006-2010 5-year est.).
Economy: Single-family building permits issued: 0 (2011); Multi-family building permits issued: 0 (2011); Employment by occupation: 4.3% management, 2.2% professional, 11.0% services, 13.7% sales, 2.1% farming, 13.3% construction, 14.6% production (2006-2010 5-year est.).
Income: Per capita income: $17,453 (2006-2010 5-year est.); Median household income: $35,667 (2006-2010 5-year est.); Average household income: $44,360 (2006-2010 5-year est.); Percent of households with income of $100,000 or more: 4.6% (2006-2010 5-year est.); Poverty rate: 18.2% (2006-2010 5-year est.).
Education: Percent of population age 25 and over with: High school diploma (including GED) or higher: 90.6% (2006-2010 5-year est.); Bachelor's degree or higher: 15.6% (2006-2010 5-year est.); Master's degree or higher: 5.9% (2006-2010 5-year est.).
Housing: Homeownership rate: 74.8% (2010); Median home value: $93,400 (2006-2010 5-year est.); Median contract rent: $319 per month (2006-2010 5-year est.); Median year structure built: 1967 (2006-2010 5-year est.).
Transportation: Commute to work: 95.0% car, 0.0% public transportation, 4.4% walk, 0.6% work from home (2006-2010 5-year est.); Travel time to work: 34.5% less than 15 minutes, 38.9% 15 to 30 minutes, 18.7% 30 to 45 minutes, 4.2% 45 to 60 minutes, 3.8% 60 minutes or more (2006-2010 5-year est.)
Additional Information Contacts
Warren County Chamber of Business and Industry . . . . . . (814) 723-3050
    http://www.wccbi.org

CHANDLERS VALLEY (unincorporated postal area)
Zip Code: 16312
    Covers a land area of 0.027 square miles and a water area of 0 square miles. Located at 41.93° N. Lat; 79.30° W. Long. Elevation is 1,509 feet. Population: 25 (2010); Density: 895.6 persons per square mile (2010); Race: 100.0% White, 0.0% Black, 0.0% Asian, 0.0% American Indian/Alaska Native, 0.0% Native Hawaiian/Other Pacific Islander, 0.0% Other, 0.0% Hispanic of any race (2010); Average household size: 2.27 (2010); Median age: 38.8 (2010); Males per 100 females: 92.3 (2010); Homeownership rate: 81.9% (2010)

CHERRY GROVE (township). Covers a land area of 46.271 square miles and a water area of 0 square miles. Located at 41.68° N. Lat; 79.15° W. Long. Elevation is 1,946 feet.
Population: 155 (1990); 228 (2000); 216 (2010); Density: 4.7 persons per square mile (2010); Race: 97.7% White, 1.9% Black, 0.0% Asian, 0.0% American Indian/Alaska Native, 0.0% Native Hawaiian/Other Pacific Islander, 0.4% Other, 2.3% Hispanic of any race (2010); Average household size: 2.25 (2010); Median age: 50.5 (2010); Males per 100 females: 113.9 (2010); Marriage status: 20.7% never married, 61.5% now married, 6.7% widowed, 11.1% divorced (2006-2010 5-year est.); Foreign born: 0.0% (2006-2010 5-year est.); Ancestry (includes multiple ancestries): 36.8% Swedish, 32.2% German, 30.6% English, 8.7% American, 5.0% Scotch-Irish (2006-2010 5-year est.).
Economy: Employment by occupation: 0.0% management, 0.0% professional, 26.5% services, 17.1% sales, 0.0% farming, 6.8% construction, 1.7% production (2006-2010 5-year est.).
Income: Per capita income: $16,471 (2006-2010 5-year est.); Median household income: $33,906 (2006-2010 5-year est.); Average household income: $39,432 (2006-2010 5-year est.); Percent of households with income of $100,000 or more: 3.8% (2006-2010 5-year est.); Poverty rate: 6.2% (2006-2010 5-year est.).
Education: Percent of population age 25 and over with: High school diploma (including GED) or higher: 92.7% (2006-2010 5-year est.); Bachelor's degree or higher: 14.5% (2006-2010 5-year est.); Master's degree or higher: 0.0% (2006-2010 5-year est.).

Housing: Homeownership rate: 93.8% (2010); Median home value: $99,700 (2006-2010 5-year est.); Median contract rent: n/a per month (2006-2010 5-year est.); Median year structure built: 1963 (2006-2010 5-year est.).
Transportation: Commute to work: 93.2% car, 0.0% public transportation, 0.0% walk, 6.8% work from home (2006-2010 5-year est.); Travel time to work: 24.8% less than 15 minutes, 38.5% 15 to 30 minutes, 33.0% 30 to 45 minutes, 3.7% 45 to 60 minutes, 0.0% 60 minutes or more (2006-2010 5-year est.)

CLARENDON (borough). Covers a land area of 0.337 square miles and a water area of 0 square miles. Located at 41.78° N. Lat; 79.09° W. Long. Elevation is 1,401 feet.
Population: 650 (1990); 564 (2000); 450 (2010); Density: 1,336.1 persons per square mile (2010); Race: 98.9% White, 0.7% Black, 0.0% Asian, 0.2% American Indian/Alaska Native, 0.0% Native Hawaiian/Other Pacific Islander, 0.2% Other, 0.7% Hispanic of any race (2010); Average household size: 2.34 (2010); Median age: 39.4 (2010); Males per 100 females: 106.4 (2010); Marriage status: 24.3% never married, 51.2% now married, 8.6% widowed, 15.9% divorced (2006-2010 5-year est.); Foreign born: 2.1% (2006-2010 5-year est.); Ancestry (includes multiple ancestries): 28.8% German, 15.5% Swedish, 10.8% Italian, 9.7% Irish, 9.7% English (2006-2010 5-year est.).
Economy: Employment by occupation: 4.6% management, 6.7% professional, 21.7% services, 12.9% sales, 0.0% farming, 4.2% construction, 2.9% production (2006-2010 5-year est.).
Income: Per capita income: $21,308 (2006-2010 5-year est.); Median household income: $42,670 (2006-2010 5-year est.); Average household income: $46,059 (2006-2010 5-year est.); Percent of households with income of $100,000 or more: 6.6% (2006-2010 5-year est.); Poverty rate: 9.9% (2006-2010 5-year est.).
Education: Percent of population age 25 and over with: High school diploma (including GED) or higher: 87.3% (2006-2010 5-year est.); Bachelor's degree or higher: 4.3% (2006-2010 5-year est.); Master's degree or higher: 1.3% (2006-2010 5-year est.).
School District(s)
Warren County SD (KG-12)
    2010-11 Enrollment: 4,928 . . . . (814) 723-6900
Housing: Homeownership rate: 75.6% (2010); Median home value: $51,100 (2006-2010 5-year est.); Median contract rent: $507 per month (2006-2010 5-year est.); Median year structure built: before 1940 (2006-2010 5-year est.).
Transportation: Commute to work: 83.3% car, 4.6% public transportation, 10.0% walk, 0.0% work from home (2006-2010 5-year est.); Travel time to work: 32.5% less than 15 minutes, 48.3% 15 to 30 minutes, 4.2% 30 to 45 minutes, 3.8% 45 to 60 minutes, 11.3% 60 minutes or more (2006-2010 5-year est.)

COLUMBUS (CDP). Covers a land area of 2.284 square miles and a water area of 0 square miles. Located at 41.95° N. Lat; 79.58° W. Long. Elevation is 1,401 feet.
Population: n/a (1990); n/a (2000); 824 (2010); Density: 360.8 persons per square mile (2010); Race: 98.8% White, 0.0% Black, 0.2% Asian, 0.0% American Indian/Alaska Native, 0.0% Native Hawaiian/Other Pacific Islander, 1.0% Other, 0.2% Hispanic of any race (2010); Average household size: 2.56 (2010); Median age: 44.4 (2010); Males per 100 females: 97.6 (2010); Marriage status: 25.4% never married, 55.7% now married, 7.8% widowed, 11.1% divorced (2006-2010 5-year est.); Foreign born: 1.1% (2006-2010 5-year est.); Ancestry (includes multiple ancestries): 27.0% German, 15.7% English, 11.2% Polish, 8.3% Irish, 7.9% Italian (2006-2010 5-year est.).
Economy: Employment by occupation: 9.4% management, 2.8% professional, 9.7% services, 14.4% sales, 0.8% farming, 13.5% construction, 11.6% production (2006-2010 5-year est.).
Income: Per capita income: $18,674 (2006-2010 5-year est.); Median household income: $48,875 (2006-2010 5-year est.); Average household income: $53,577 (2006-2010 5-year est.); Percent of households with income of $100,000 or more: 6.9% (2006-2010 5-year est.); Poverty rate: 9.0% (2006-2010 5-year est.).
Education: Percent of population age 25 and over with: High school diploma (including GED) or higher: 92.0% (2006-2010 5-year est.); Bachelor's degree or higher: 15.3% (2006-2010 5-year est.); Master's degree or higher: 3.2% (2006-2010 5-year est.).
Housing: Homeownership rate: 85.4% (2010); Median home value: $78,700 (2006-2010 5-year est.); Median contract rent: $410 per month

(2006-2010 5-year est.); Median year structure built: 1954 (2006-2010 5-year est.).

Transportation: Commute to work: 96.2% car, 0.0% public transportation, 1.8% walk, 2.0% work from home (2006-2010 5-year est.); Travel time to work: 44.5% less than 15 minutes, 23.6% 15 to 30 minutes, 4.5% 30 to 45 minutes, 17.9% 45 to 60 minutes, 9.6% 60 minutes or more (2006-2010 5-year est.)

COLUMBUS (township).

COLUMBUS (township). Covers a land area of 40.665 square miles and a water area of 0.003 square miles. Located at 41.94° N. Lat; 79.56° W. Long. Elevation is 1,401 feet.

Population: 1,801 (1990); 1,741 (2000); 2,034 (2010); Density: 50.0 persons per square mile (2010); Race: 98.4% White, 0.1% Black, 0.3% Asian, 0.0% American Indian/Alaska Native, 0.2% Native Hawaiian/Other Pacific Islander, 1.0% Other, 0.6% Hispanic of any race (2010); Average household size: 2.59 (2010); Median age: 43.6 (2010); Males per 100 females: 100.4 (2010); Marriage status: 27.0% never married, 58.2% now married, 4.9% widowed, 9.9% divorced (2006-2010 5-year est.); Foreign born: 0.9% (2006-2010 5-year est.); Ancestry (includes multiple ancestries): 29.7% German, 17.7% Irish, 15.3% English, 12.2% Polish, 8.5% Dutch (2006-2010 5-year est.).

Economy: Employment by occupation: 8.3% management, 1.1% professional, 13.8% services, 14.9% sales, 1.5% farming, 16.5% construction, 16.3% production (2006-2010 5-year est.).

Income: Per capita income: $20,304 (2006-2010 5-year est.); Median household income: $49,971 (2006-2010 5-year est.); Average household income: $56,615 (2006-2010 5-year est.); Percent of households with income of $100,000 or more: 10.0% (2006-2010 5-year est.); Poverty rate: 11.5% (2006-2010 5-year est.).

Education: Percent of population age 25 and over with: High school diploma (including GED) or higher: 88.8% (2006-2010 5-year est.); Bachelor's degree or higher: 12.3% (2006-2010 5-year est.); Master's degree or higher: 2.3% (2006-2010 5-year est.).

Housing: Homeownership rate: 85.2% (2010); Median home value: $90,200 (2006-2010 5-year est.); Median contract rent: $334 per month (2006-2010 5-year est.); Median year structure built: 1959 (2006-2010 5-year est.).

Transportation: Commute to work: 93.0% car, 0.0% public transportation, 1.1% walk, 5.9% work from home (2006-2010 5-year est.); Travel time to work: 50.3% less than 15 minutes, 18.4% 15 to 30 minutes, 8.6% 30 to 45 minutes, 11.9% 45 to 60 minutes, 10.8% 60 minutes or more (2006-2010 5-year est.)

Additional Information Contacts

Corry Area Chamber of Commerce. . . . . (814) 665-9925
   http://www.corrychamber.com

CONEWANGO (township).

CONEWANGO (township). Covers a land area of 29.956 square miles and a water area of 0.459 square miles. Located at 41.89° N. Lat; 79.22° W. Long.

Population: 4,475 (1990); 3,915 (2000); 3,594 (2010); Density: 120.0 persons per square mile (2010); Race: 96.9% White, 1.1% Black, 0.5% Asian, 0.2% American Indian/Alaska Native, 0.0% Native Hawaiian/Other Pacific Islander, 1.3% Other, 0.6% Hispanic of any race (2010); Average household size: 2.27 (2010); Median age: 46.4 (2010); Males per 100 females: 103.4 (2010); Marriage status: 25.6% never married, 56.5% now married, 6.7% widowed, 11.1% divorced (2006-2010 5-year est.); Foreign born: 1.7% (2006-2010 5-year est.); Ancestry (includes multiple ancestries): 31.4% German, 15.2% Irish, 14.8% Swedish, 13.7% English, 11.0% Italian (2006-2010 5-year est.).

Economy: Employment by occupation: 8.8% management, 4.4% professional, 11.9% services, 11.4% sales, 4.0% farming, 9.6% construction, 9.4% production (2006-2010 5-year est.).

Income: Per capita income: $24,902 (2006-2010 5-year est.); Median household income: $43,625 (2006-2010 5-year est.); Average household income: $56,171 (2006-2010 5-year est.); Percent of households with income of $100,000 or more: 14.3% (2006-2010 5-year est.); Poverty rate: 5.8% (2006-2010 5-year est.).

Education: Percent of population age 25 and over with: High school diploma (including GED) or higher: 87.0% (2006-2010 5-year est.); Bachelor's degree or higher: 16.8% (2006-2010 5-year est.); Master's degree or higher: 6.0% (2006-2010 5-year est.).

Housing: Homeownership rate: 81.6% (2010); Median home value: $78,700 (2006-2010 5-year est.); Median contract rent: $412 per month (2006-2010 5-year est.); Median year structure built: 1960 (2006-2010 5-year est.).

Safety: Violent crime rate: 19.4 per 10,000 population; Property crime rate: 491.0 per 10,000 population (2011).

Transportation: Commute to work: 91.6% car, 0.0% public transportation, 3.6% walk, 4.8% work from home (2006-2010 5-year est.); Travel time to work: 51.2% less than 15 minutes, 38.6% 15 to 30 minutes, 6.6% 30 to 45 minutes, 0.7% 45 to 60 minutes, 2.9% 60 minutes or more (2006-2010 5-year est.)

Additional Information Contacts

Warren County Chamber of Business and Industry . . . . . . (814) 723-3050
   http://www.wccbi.org

DEERFIELD (township).

DEERFIELD (township). Covers a land area of 43.224 square miles and a water area of 0.559 square miles. Located at 41.74° N. Lat; 79.37° W. Long.

Population: 274 (1990); 333 (2000); 339 (2010); Density: 7.8 persons per square mile (2010); Race: 99.7% White, 0.0% Black, 0.3% Asian, 0.0% American Indian/Alaska Native, 0.0% Native Hawaiian/Other Pacific Islander, 0.0% Other, 0.0% Hispanic of any race (2010); Average household size: 2.05 (2010); Median age: 53.6 (2010); Males per 100 females: 117.3 (2010); Marriage status: 20.4% never married, 66.9% now married, 6.6% widowed, 6.1% divorced (2006-2010 5-year est.); Foreign born: 0.0% (2006-2010 5-year est.); Ancestry (includes multiple ancestries): 25.1% German, 19.4% English, 12.6% Swedish, 12.0% American, 12.0% Irish (2006-2010 5-year est.).

Economy: Employment by occupation: 10.6% management, 0.0% professional, 9.1% services, 25.8% sales, 3.0% farming, 12.1% construction, 3.0% production (2006-2010 5-year est.).

Income: Per capita income: $19,884 (2006-2010 5-year est.); Median household income: $32,857 (2006-2010 5-year est.); Average household income: $37,588 (2006-2010 5-year est.); Percent of households with income of $100,000 or more: 3.8% (2006-2010 5-year est.); Poverty rate: 2.1% (2006-2010 5-year est.).

Education: Percent of population age 25 and over with: High school diploma (including GED) or higher: 75.9% (2006-2010 5-year est.); Bachelor's degree or higher: 10.3% (2006-2010 5-year est.); Master's degree or higher: 3.4% (2006-2010 5-year est.).

Housing: Homeownership rate: 90.9% (2010); Median home value: $75,500 (2006-2010 5-year est.); Median contract rent: n/a per month (2006-2010 5-year est.); Median year structure built: 1963 (2006-2010 5-year est.).

Transportation: Commute to work: 87.5% car, 0.0% public transportation, 0.0% walk, 12.5% work from home (2006-2010 5-year est.); Travel time to work: 14.3% less than 15 minutes, 32.1% 15 to 30 minutes, 50.0% 30 to 45 minutes, 3.6% 45 to 60 minutes, 0.0% 60 minutes or more (2006-2010 5-year est.)

ELDRED (township).

ELDRED (township). Covers a land area of 36.215 square miles and a water area of 0 square miles. Located at 41.75° N. Lat; 79.55° W. Long.

Population: 669 (1990); 709 (2000); 650 (2010); Density: 17.9 persons per square mile (2010); Race: 99.7% White, 0.0% Black, 0.0% Asian, 0.0% American Indian/Alaska Native, 0.0% Native Hawaiian/Other Pacific Islander, 0.3% Other, 0.0% Hispanic of any race (2010); Average household size: 2.47 (2010); Median age: 44.6 (2010); Males per 100 females: 119.6 (2010); Marriage status: 17.7% never married, 70.6% now married, 7.0% widowed, 4.6% divorced (2006-2010 5-year est.); Foreign born: 0.0% (2006-2010 5-year est.); Ancestry (includes multiple ancestries): 28.4% English, 27.2% German, 7.3% Irish, 5.9% Swedish, 4.2% Polish (2006-2010 5-year est.).

Economy: Employment by occupation: 8.1% management, 0.0% professional, 10.3% services, 14.4% sales, 4.1% farming, 14.4% construction, 16.6% production (2006-2010 5-year est.).

Income: Per capita income: $15,982 (2006-2010 5-year est.); Median household income: $45,326 (2006-2010 5-year est.); Average household income: $47,229 (2006-2010 5-year est.); Percent of households with income of $100,000 or more: 3.9% (2006-2010 5-year est.); Poverty rate: 17.5% (2006-2010 5-year est.).

Education: Percent of population age 25 and over with: High school diploma (including GED) or higher: 87.4% (2006-2010 5-year est.); Bachelor's degree or higher: 11.5% (2006-2010 5-year est.); Master's degree or higher: 1.8% (2006-2010 5-year est.).

Housing: Homeownership rate: 90.5% (2010); Median home value: $103,300 (2006-2010 5-year est.); Median contract rent: $515 per month (2006-2010 5-year est.); Median year structure built: 1974 (2006-2010 5-year est.).

Transportation: Commute to work: 94.3% car, 0.0% public transportation, 5.7% walk, 0.0% work from home (2006-2010 5-year est.); Travel time to work: 16.7% less than 15 minutes, 37.1% 15 to 30 minutes, 16.7% 30 to 45 minutes, 10.2% 45 to 60 minutes, 19.3% 60 minutes or more (2006-2010 5-year est.)

ELK (township). Covers a land area of 41.024 square miles and a water area of 2.707 square miles. Located at 41.96° N. Lat; 78.97° W. Long.
Population: 541 (1990); 551 (2000); 520 (2010); Density: 12.7 persons per square mile (2010); Race: 98.8% White, 0.0% Black, 0.2% Asian, 0.6% American Indian/Alaska Native, 0.0% Native Hawaiian/Other Pacific Islander, 0.4% Other, 0.0% Hispanic of any race (2010); Average household size: 2.27 (2010); Median age: 50.3 (2010); Males per 100 females: 108.8 (2010); Marriage status: 18.5% never married, 62.7% now married, 10.9% widowed, 7.8% divorced (2006-2010 5-year est.); Foreign born: 2.0% (2006-2010 5-year est.); Ancestry (includes multiple ancestries): 33.7% German, 23.4% Swedish, 15.8% Irish, 13.3% English, 9.1% American (2006-2010 5-year est.).
Economy: Employment by occupation: 8.6% management, 2.2% professional, 10.8% services, 12.3% sales, 0.0% farming, 18.5% construction, 15.7% production (2006-2010 5-year est.).
Income: Per capita income: $28,322 (2006-2010 5-year est.); Median household income: $54,219 (2006-2010 5-year est.); Average household income: $62,978 (2006-2010 5-year est.); Percent of households with income of $100,000 or more: 11.6% (2006-2010 5-year est.); Poverty rate: 5.1% (2006-2010 5-year est.).
Education: Percent of population age 25 and over with: High school diploma (including GED) or higher: 91.0% (2006-2010 5-year est.); Bachelor's degree or higher: 19.2% (2006-2010 5-year est.); Master's degree or higher: 1.9% (2006-2010 5-year est.).
Housing: Homeownership rate: 93.8% (2010); Median home value: $111,100 (2006-2010 5-year est.); Median contract rent: $550 per month (2006-2010 5-year est.); Median year structure built: 1973 (2006-2010 5-year est.).
Transportation: Commute to work: 99.1% car, 0.9% public transportation, 0.0% walk, 0.0% work from home (2006-2010 5-year est.); Travel time to work: 14.8% less than 15 minutes, 54.3% 15 to 30 minutes, 25.3% 30 to 45 minutes, 0.0% 45 to 60 minutes, 5.6% 60 minutes or more (2006-2010 5-year est.)

FARMINGTON (township). Covers a land area of 34.192 square miles and a water area of 0.025 square miles. Located at 41.95° N. Lat; 79.23° W. Long.
Population: 1,292 (1990); 1,353 (2000); 1,259 (2010); Density: 36.8 persons per square mile (2010); Race: 98.6% White, 0.3% Black, 0.2% Asian, 0.1% American Indian/Alaska Native, 0.0% Native Hawaiian/Other Pacific Islander, 0.8% Other, 1.0% Hispanic of any race (2010); Average household size: 2.60 (2010); Median age: 43.2 (2010); Males per 100 females: 108.1 (2010); Marriage status: 16.7% never married, 70.1% now married, 7.4% widowed, 5.7% divorced (2006-2010 5-year est.); Foreign born: 0.8% (2006-2010 5-year est.); Ancestry (includes multiple ancestries): 30.9% German, 21.7% Swedish, 16.8% English, 11.0% Irish, 9.6% Italian (2006-2010 5-year est.).
Economy: Employment by occupation: 10.1% management, 4.4% professional, 11.1% services, 19.6% sales, 2.6% farming, 20.9% construction, 9.3% production (2006-2010 5-year est.).
Income: Per capita income: $19,623 (2006-2010 5-year est.); Median household income: $42,917 (2006-2010 5-year est.); Average household income: $53,740 (2006-2010 5-year est.); Percent of households with income of $100,000 or more: 9.8% (2006-2010 5-year est.); Poverty rate: 15.7% (2006-2010 5-year est.).
Education: Percent of population age 25 and over with: High school diploma (including GED) or higher: 88.7% (2006-2010 5-year est.); Bachelor's degree or higher: 13.8% (2006-2010 5-year est.); Master's degree or higher: 4.8% (2006-2010 5-year est.).
Housing: Homeownership rate: 89.1% (2010); Median home value: $87,800 (2006-2010 5-year est.); Median contract rent: $419 per month (2006-2010 5-year est.); Median year structure built: 1973 (2006-2010 5-year est.).
Transportation: Commute to work: 93.0% car, 0.0% public transportation, 5.1% walk, 1.3% work from home (2006-2010 5-year est.); Travel time to work: 20.6% less than 15 minutes, 58.3% 15 to 30 minutes, 15.2% 30 to 45 minutes, 3.9% 45 to 60 minutes, 2.0% 60 minutes or more (2006-2010 5-year est.)

Additional Information Contacts
Warren County Chamber of Business and Industry . . . . . . (814) 723-3050
  http://www.wccbi.org

FREEHOLD (township). Covers a land area of 35.741 square miles and a water area of 0.043 square miles. Located at 41.96° N. Lat; 79.45° W. Long.
Population: 1,318 (1990); 1,402 (2000); 1,510 (2010); Density: 42.2 persons per square mile (2010); Race: 98.9% White, 0.2% Black, 0.1% Asian, 0.3% American Indian/Alaska Native, 0.0% Native Hawaiian/Other Pacific Islander, 0.5% Other, 0.3% Hispanic of any race (2010); Average household size: 2.89 (2010); Median age: 38.2 (2010); Males per 100 females: 100.3 (2010); Marriage status: 26.8% never married, 60.4% now married, 5.6% widowed, 7.2% divorced (2006-2010 5-year est.); Foreign born: 0.2% (2006-2010 5-year est.); Ancestry (includes multiple ancestries): 41.9% German, 14.9% English, 14.2% Irish, 9.3% Swedish, 6.3% Italian (2006-2010 5-year est.).
Economy: Single-family building permits issued: 4 (2011); Multi-family building permits issued: 0 (2011); Employment by occupation: 9.8% management, 0.7% professional, 10.0% services, 13.4% sales, 1.8% farming, 15.9% construction, 15.5% production (2006-2010 5-year est.).
Income: Per capita income: $14,488 (2006-2010 5-year est.); Median household income: $34,612 (2006-2010 5-year est.); Average household income: $42,263 (2006-2010 5-year est.); Percent of households with income of $100,000 or more: 3.6% (2006-2010 5-year est.); Poverty rate: 19.4% (2006-2010 5-year est.).
Education: Percent of population age 25 and over with: High school diploma (including GED) or higher: 75.8% (2006-2010 5-year est.); Bachelor's degree or higher: 6.6% (2006-2010 5-year est.); Master's degree or higher: 1.6% (2006-2010 5-year est.).
Housing: Homeownership rate: 86.0% (2010); Median home value: $88,100 (2006-2010 5-year est.); Median contract rent: $421 per month (2006-2010 5-year est.); Median year structure built: 1968 (2006-2010 5-year est.).
Transportation: Commute to work: 85.9% car, 1.0% public transportation, 3.4% walk, 8.3% work from home (2006-2010 5-year est.); Travel time to work: 21.8% less than 15 minutes, 33.2% 15 to 30 minutes, 30.0% 30 to 45 minutes, 9.0% 45 to 60 minutes, 6.1% 60 minutes or more (2006-2010 5-year est.)
Additional Information Contacts
Corry Area Chamber of Commerce. . . . . (814) 665-9925
  http://www.corrychamber.com

GARLAND (unincorporated postal area)
Zip Code: 16416
  Covers a land area of 3.910 square miles and a water area of 0 square miles. Located at 41.82° N. Lat; 79.47° W. Long. Population: 203 (2010); Density: 51.9 persons per square mile (2010); Race: 99.0% White, 0.0% Black, 1.0% Asian, 0.0% American Indian/Alaska Native, 0.0% Native Hawaiian/Other Pacific Islander, 0.0% Other, 0.0% Hispanic of any race (2010); Average household size: 2.45 (2010); Median age: 36.5 (2010); Males per 100 females: 99.0 (2010); Homeownership rate: 73.5% (2010)

GLADE (township). Covers a land area of 36.018 square miles and a water area of 0.817 square miles. Located at 41.87° N. Lat; 79.06° W. Long. Elevation is 1,198 feet.
Population: 2,372 (1990); 2,319 (2000); 2,308 (2010); Density: 64.1 persons per square mile (2010); Race: 98.5% White, 0.3% Black, 0.6% Asian, 0.3% American Indian/Alaska Native, 0.0% Native Hawaiian/Other Pacific Islander, 0.3% Other, 0.7% Hispanic of any race (2010); Average household size: 2.23 (2010); Median age: 48.8 (2010); Males per 100 females: 94.4 (2010); Marriage status: 20.2% never married, 64.1% now married, 8.6% widowed, 7.2% divorced (2006-2010 5-year est.); Foreign born: 2.2% (2006-2010 5-year est.); Ancestry (includes multiple ancestries): 33.6% German, 21.7% English, 21.3% Swedish, 13.9% Irish, 11.4% Italian (2006-2010 5-year est.).
Economy: Employment by occupation: 7.0% management, 1.8% professional, 6.0% services, 21.2% sales, 6.2% farming, 8.4% construction, 9.2% production (2006-2010 5-year est.).
Income: Per capita income: $28,213 (2006-2010 5-year est.); Median household income: $48,207 (2006-2010 5-year est.); Average household income: $65,903 (2006-2010 5-year est.); Percent of households with income of $100,000 or more: 15.0% (2006-2010 5-year est.); Poverty rate: 5.0% (2006-2010 5-year est.).

Education: Percent of population age 25 and over with: High school diploma (including GED) or higher: 89.5% (2006-2010 5-year est.); Bachelor's degree or higher: 20.7% (2006-2010 5-year est.); Master's degree or higher: 6.9% (2006-2010 5-year est.).

Housing: Homeownership rate: 79.1% (2010); Median home value: $107,500 (2006-2010 5-year est.); Median contract rent: $424 per month (2006-2010 5-year est.); Median year structure built: 1965 (2006-2010 5-year est.).

Transportation: Commute to work: 95.7% car, 0.3% public transportation, 2.2% walk, 1.8% work from home (2006-2010 5-year est.); Travel time to work: 46.1% less than 15 minutes, 35.9% 15 to 30 minutes, 12.2% 30 to 45 minutes, 2.0% 45 to 60 minutes, 3.8% 60 minutes or more (2006-2010 5-year est.)

Additional Information Contacts

Warren County Chamber of Business and Industry . . . . . . (814) 723-3050
http://www.wccbi.org

GRAND VALLEY (unincorporated postal area)

Zip Code: 16420

Covers a land area of 48.636 square miles and a water area of 0 square miles. Located at 41.69° N. Lat; 79.54° W. Long. Elevation is 1,411 feet. Population: 650 (2010); Density: 13.4 persons per square mile (2010); Race: 99.5% White, 0.0% Black, 0.0% Asian, 0.0% American Indian/Alaska Native, 0.0% Native Hawaiian/Other Pacific Islander, 0.5% Other, 1.5% Hispanic of any race (2010); Average household size: 2.49 (2010); Median age: 43.6 (2010); Males per 100 females: 107.7 (2010); Homeownership rate: 88.5% (2010)

IRVINE (unincorporated postal area)

Zip Code: 16329

Covers a land area of 8.217 square miles and a water area of 0.715 square miles. Located at 41.79° N. Lat; 79.25° W. Long. Elevation is 1,168 feet. Population: 528 (2010); Density: 64.3 persons per square mile (2010); Race: 97.9% White, 0.0% Black, 0.6% Asian, 0.4% American Indian/Alaska Native, 0.0% Native Hawaiian/Other Pacific Islander, 1.1% Other, 0.0% Hispanic of any race (2010); Average household size: 2.31 (2010); Median age: 48.1 (2010); Males per 100 females: 109.5 (2010); Homeownership rate: 88.7% (2010)

LIMESTONE (township). Covers a land area of 31.425 square miles and a water area of 0.483 square miles. Located at 41.67° N. Lat; 79.33° W. Long.

Population: 359 (1990); 418 (2000); 403 (2010); Density: 12.8 persons per square mile (2010); Race: 99.3% White, 0.0% Black, 0.0% Asian, 0.0% American Indian/Alaska Native, 0.5% Native Hawaiian/Other Pacific Islander, 0.2% Other, 0.0% Hispanic of any race (2010); Average household size: 2.00 (2010); Median age: 51.3 (2010); Males per 100 females: 108.8 (2010); Marriage status: 15.0% never married, 57.1% now married, 17.6% widowed, 10.3% divorced (2006-2010 5-year est.); Foreign born: 0.0% (2006-2010 5-year est.); Ancestry (includes multiple ancestries): 37.0% German, 11.3% Irish, 9.4% Hungarian, 9.1% English, 5.7% Pennsylvania German (2006-2010 5-year est.).

Economy: Single-family building permits issued: 0 (2011); Multi-family building permits issued: 0 (2011); Employment by occupation: 2.3% management, 0.0% professional, 16.3% services, 31.4% sales, 0.0% farming, 14.0% construction, 3.5% production (2006-2010 5-year est.).

Income: Per capita income: $21,675 (2006-2010 5-year est.); Median household income: $32,614 (2006-2010 5-year est.); Average household income: $40,581 (2006-2010 5-year est.); Percent of households with income of $100,000 or more: 5.0% (2006-2010 5-year est.); Poverty rate: 20.8% (2006-2010 5-year est.).

Education: Percent of population age 25 and over with: High school diploma (including GED) or higher: 95.0% (2006-2010 5-year est.); Bachelor's degree or higher: 9.9% (2006-2010 5-year est.); Master's degree or higher: 3.2% (2006-2010 5-year est.).

Housing: Homeownership rate: 83.0% (2010); Median home value: $80,300 (2006-2010 5-year est.); Median contract rent: $538 per month (2006-2010 5-year est.); Median year structure built: 1964 (2006-2010 5-year est.).

Transportation: Commute to work: 91.7% car, 0.0% public transportation, 0.0% walk, 8.3% work from home (2006-2010 5-year est.); Travel time to work: 7.8% less than 15 minutes, 40.3% 15 to 30 minutes, 32.5% 30 to 45 minutes, 13.0% 45 to 60 minutes, 6.5% 60 minutes or more (2006-2010 5-year est.)

MEAD (township). Covers a land area of 78.587 square miles and a water area of 7.051 square miles. Located at 41.81° N. Lat; 79.02° W. Long.

Population: 1,579 (1990); 1,555 (2000); 1,386 (2010); Density: 17.6 persons per square mile (2010); Race: 98.3% White, 0.1% Black, 0.6% Asian, 0.0% American Indian/Alaska Native, 0.1% Native Hawaiian/Other Pacific Islander, 0.9% Other, 0.4% Hispanic of any race (2010); Average household size: 2.20 (2010); Median age: 49.6 (2010); Males per 100 females: 112.3 (2010); Marriage status: 24.3% never married, 62.9% now married, 6.3% widowed, 6.6% divorced (2006-2010 5-year est.); Foreign born: 2.3% (2006-2010 5-year est.); Ancestry (includes multiple ancestries): 25.7% German, 18.5% Irish, 11.6% English, 11.0% Italian, 9.2% Swedish (2006-2010 5-year est.).

Economy: Employment by occupation: 4.6% management, 0.5% professional, 19.0% services, 17.3% sales, 4.8% farming, 8.2% construction, 10.7% production (2006-2010 5-year est.).

Income: Per capita income: $21,061 (2006-2010 5-year est.); Median household income: $41,972 (2006-2010 5-year est.); Average household income: $50,323 (2006-2010 5-year est.); Percent of households with income of $100,000 or more: 4.4% (2006-2010 5-year est.); Poverty rate: 12.3% (2006-2010 5-year est.).

Education: Percent of population age 25 and over with: High school diploma (including GED) or higher: 86.7% (2006-2010 5-year est.); Bachelor's degree or higher: 9.2% (2006-2010 5-year est.); Master's degree or higher: 3.6% (2006-2010 5-year est.).

Housing: Homeownership rate: 87.4% (2010); Median home value: $76,300 (2006-2010 5-year est.); Median contract rent: $405 per month (2006-2010 5-year est.); Median year structure built: 1960 (2006-2010 5-year est.).

Transportation: Commute to work: 97.4% car, 0.0% public transportation, 0.0% walk, 2.0% work from home (2006-2010 5-year est.); Travel time to work: 31.7% less than 15 minutes, 41.6% 15 to 30 minutes, 19.9% 30 to 45 minutes, 3.1% 45 to 60 minutes, 3.7% 60 minutes or more (2006-2010 5-year est.)

Additional Information Contacts

Warren County Chamber of Business and Industry . . . . . . (814) 723-3050
http://www.wccbi.org

NORTH WARREN (CDP). Covers a land area of 8.200 square miles and a water area of 0.039 square miles. Located at 41.88° N. Lat; 79.17° W. Long. Elevation is 1,214 feet.

Population: n/a (1990); n/a (2000); 1,934 (2010); Density: 235.9 persons per square mile (2010); Race: 96.1% White, 1.5% Black, 0.8% Asian, 0.3% American Indian/Alaska Native, 0.1% Native Hawaiian/Other Pacific Islander, 1.2% Other, 0.7% Hispanic of any race (2010); Average household size: 2.23 (2010); Median age: 47.2 (2010); Males per 100 females: 107.7 (2010); Marriage status: 27.6% never married, 53.0% now married, 6.8% widowed, 12.6% divorced (2006-2010 5-year est.); Foreign born: 2.3% (2006-2010 5-year est.); Ancestry (includes multiple ancestries): 25.0% German, 14.4% Italian, 14.0% English, 13.6% Swedish, 12.4% Irish (2006-2010 5-year est.).

Economy: Employment by occupation: 7.1% management, 3.6% professional, 11.1% services, 8.8% sales, 4.4% farming, 5.7% construction, 6.2% production (2006-2010 5-year est.).

Income: Per capita income: $23,859 (2006-2010 5-year est.); Median household income: $40,000 (2006-2010 5-year est.); Average household income: $55,942 (2006-2010 5-year est.); Percent of households with income of $100,000 or more: 15.8% (2006-2010 5-year est.); Poverty rate: 7.5% (2006-2010 5-year est.).

Education: Percent of population age 25 and over with: High school diploma (including GED) or higher: 87.7% (2006-2010 5-year est.); Bachelor's degree or higher: 20.3% (2006-2010 5-year est.); Master's degree or higher: 6.4% (2006-2010 5-year est.).

Housing: Homeownership rate: 82.6% (2010); Median home value: $79,500 (2006-2010 5-year est.); Median contract rent: $422 per month (2006-2010 5-year est.); Median year structure built: 1955 (2006-2010 5-year est.).

Transportation: Commute to work: 88.6% car, 0.0% public transportation, 5.3% walk, 6.2% work from home (2006-2010 5-year est.); Travel time to work: 66.1% less than 15 minutes, 28.5% 15 to 30 minutes, 4.2% 30 to 45 minutes, 0.0% 45 to 60 minutes, 1.1% 60 minutes or more (2006-2010 5-year est.)

PINE GROVE (township). Covers a land area of 39.650 square miles and a water area of 0.247 square miles. Located at 41.95° N. Lat; 79.10° W. Long.

Population: 2,772 (1990); 2,712 (2000); 2,695 (2010); Density: 68.0 persons per square mile (2010); Race: 97.9% White, 0.4% Black, 0.5% Asian, 0.2% American Indian/Alaska Native, 0.0% Native Hawaiian/Other Pacific Islander, 1.0% Other, 0.8% Hispanic of any race (2010); Average household size: 2.38 (2010); Median age: 47.8 (2010); Males per 100 females: 97.6 (2010); Marriage status: 14.0% never married, 73.9% now married, 5.6% widowed, 6.4% divorced (2006-2010 5-year est.); Foreign born: 0.3% (2006-2010 5-year est.); Ancestry (includes multiple ancestries): 23.4% German, 17.6% Swedish, 13.9% English, 10.2% Irish, 7.6% American (2006-2010 5-year est.).

Economy: Employment by occupation: 10.6% management, 2.7% professional, 5.7% services, 15.6% sales, 4.8% farming, 7.7% construction, 3.6% production (2006-2010 5-year est.).

Income: Per capita income: $29,840 (2006-2010 5-year est.); Median household income: $56,198 (2006-2010 5-year est.); Average household income: $73,447 (2006-2010 5-year est.); Percent of households with income of $100,000 or more: 18.7% (2006-2010 5-year est.); Poverty rate: 10.6% (2006-2010 5-year est.).

Education: Percent of population age 25 and over with: High school diploma (including GED) or higher: 94.4% (2006-2010 5-year est.); Bachelor's degree or higher: 25.3% (2006-2010 5-year est.); Master's degree or higher: 9.6% (2006-2010 5-year est.).

Housing: Homeownership rate: 87.8% (2010); Median home value: $124,300 (2006-2010 5-year est.); Median contract rent: $377 per month (2006-2010 5-year est.); Median year structure built: 1966 (2006-2010 5-year est.).

Transportation: Commute to work: 90.9% car, 0.0% public transportation, 1.1% walk, 6.7% work from home (2006-2010 5-year est.); Travel time to work: 31.7% less than 15 minutes, 49.1% 15 to 30 minutes, 11.9% 30 to 45 minutes, 4.8% 45 to 60 minutes, 2.6% 60 minutes or more (2006-2010 5-year est.)

Additional Information Contacts
Warren County Chamber of Business and Industry . . . . . . (814) 723-3050
  http://www.wccbi.org

PITTSFIELD (township). Covers a land area of 55.646 square miles and a water area of 0 square miles. Located at 41.83° N. Lat; 79.43° W. Long. Elevation is 1,247 feet.

Population: 1,543 (1990); 1,519 (2000); 1,405 (2010); Density: 25.2 persons per square mile (2010); Race: 98.6% White, 0.1% Black, 0.2% Asian, 0.0% American Indian/Alaska Native, 0.0% Native Hawaiian/Other Pacific Islander, 1.1% Other, 1.1% Hispanic of any race (2010); Average household size: 2.46 (2010); Median age: 44.6 (2010); Males per 100 females: 106.0 (2010); Marriage status: 24.8% never married, 63.0% now married, 3.5% widowed, 8.7% divorced (2006-2010 5-year est.); Foreign born: 1.0% (2006-2010 5-year est.); Ancestry (includes multiple ancestries): 31.4% German, 16.9% Swedish, 15.4% Irish, 15.3% English, 8.2% Polish (2006-2010 5-year est.).

Economy: Single-family building permits issued: 1 (2011); Multi-family building permits issued: 0 (2011); Employment by occupation: 5.6% management, 1.6% professional, 12.6% services, 12.9% sales, 2.6% farming, 12.9% construction, 8.8% production (2006-2010 5-year est.).

Income: Per capita income: $21,757 (2006-2010 5-year est.); Median household income: $46,667 (2006-2010 5-year est.); Average household income: $53,652 (2006-2010 5-year est.); Percent of households with income of $100,000 or more: 11.1% (2006-2010 5-year est.); Poverty rate: 8.4% (2006-2010 5-year est.).

Education: Percent of population age 25 and over with: High school diploma (including GED) or higher: 90.9% (2006-2010 5-year est.); Bachelor's degree or higher: 9.2% (2006-2010 5-year est.); Master's degree or higher: 1.9% (2006-2010 5-year est.).

Housing: Homeownership rate: 86.4% (2010); Median home value: $89,200 (2006-2010 5-year est.); Median contract rent: $315 per month (2006-2010 5-year est.); Median year structure built: 1965 (2006-2010 5-year est.).

Transportation: Commute to work: 93.7% car, 0.3% public transportation, 1.9% walk, 4.0% work from home (2006-2010 5-year est.); Travel time to work: 19.1% less than 15 minutes, 47.6% 15 to 30 minutes, 18.1% 30 to 45 minutes, 5.2% 45 to 60 minutes, 10.1% 60 minutes or more (2006-2010 5-year est.)

Additional Information Contacts
Warren County Chamber of Business and Industry . . . . . . (814) 723-3050
  http://www.wccbi.org

PLEASANT (township). Covers a land area of 33.689 square miles and a water area of 0.848 square miles. Located at 41.79° N. Lat; 79.19° W. Long.

Population: 2,663 (1990); 2,528 (2000); 2,444 (2010); Density: 72.5 persons per square mile (2010); Race: 99.1% White, 0.1% Black, 0.2% Asian, 0.1% American Indian/Alaska Native, 0.0% Native Hawaiian/Other Pacific Islander, 0.5% Other, 0.5% Hispanic of any race (2010); Average household size: 2.23 (2010); Median age: 52.3 (2010); Males per 100 females: 91.4 (2010); Marriage status: 18.1% never married, 63.0% now married, 9.0% widowed, 9.8% divorced (2006-2010 5-year est.); Foreign born: 2.0% (2006-2010 5-year est.); Ancestry (includes multiple ancestries): 34.9% German, 17.2% English, 14.2% Irish, 13.1% Swedish, 11.9% Italian (2006-2010 5-year est.).

Economy: Employment by occupation: 7.7% management, 3.0% professional, 12.8% services, 19.0% sales, 3.2% farming, 4.3% construction, 7.5% production (2006-2010 5-year est.).

Income: Per capita income: $24,520 (2006-2010 5-year est.); Median household income: $49,135 (2006-2010 5-year est.); Average household income: $56,164 (2006-2010 5-year est.); Percent of households with income of $100,000 or more: 11.9% (2006-2010 5-year est.); Poverty rate: 7.4% (2006-2010 5-year est.).

Education: Percent of population age 25 and over with: High school diploma (including GED) or higher: 92.4% (2006-2010 5-year est.); Bachelor's degree or higher: 20.7% (2006-2010 5-year est.); Master's degree or higher: 7.2% (2006-2010 5-year est.).

Housing: Homeownership rate: 85.0% (2010); Median home value: $98,700 (2006-2010 5-year est.); Median contract rent: $467 per month (2006-2010 5-year est.); Median year structure built: 1964 (2006-2010 5-year est.).

Transportation: Commute to work: 95.7% car, 0.8% public transportation, 2.0% walk, 1.5% work from home (2006-2010 5-year est.); Travel time to work: 50.8% less than 15 minutes, 30.3% 15 to 30 minutes, 10.7% 30 to 45 minutes, 1.2% 45 to 60 minutes, 7.0% 60 minutes or more (2006-2010 5-year est.)

Additional Information Contacts
Warren County Chamber of Business and Industry . . . . . . (814) 723-3050
  http://www.wccbi.org

RUSSELL (CDP). Covers a land area of 3.523 square miles and a water area of 0.142 square miles. Located at 41.94° N. Lat; 79.14° W. Long. Elevation is 1,257 feet.

Population: n/a (1990); n/a (2000); 1,408 (2010); Density: 399.6 persons per square mile (2010); Race: 97.2% White, 0.4% Black, 0.9% Asian, 0.4% American Indian/Alaska Native, 0.0% Native Hawaiian/Other Pacific Islander, 1.1% Other, 0.8% Hispanic of any race (2010); Average household size: 2.43 (2010); Median age: 46.5 (2010); Males per 100 females: 92.9 (2010); Marriage status: 15.5% never married, 71.8% now married, 6.2% widowed, 6.4% divorced (2006-2010 5-year est.); Foreign born: 0.7% (2006-2010 5-year est.); Ancestry (includes multiple ancestries): 22.2% German, 15.7% Swedish, 13.7% English, 13.0% Irish, 10.3% Italian (2006-2010 5-year est.).

Economy: Employment by occupation: 12.9% management, 4.4% professional, 8.7% services, 12.6% sales, 6.9% farming, 4.1% construction, 5.1% production (2006-2010 5-year est.).

Income: Per capita income: $32,057 (2006-2010 5-year est.); Median household income: $52,552 (2006-2010 5-year est.); Average household income: $79,896 (2006-2010 5-year est.); Percent of households with income of $100,000 or more: 19.5% (2006-2010 5-year est.); Poverty rate: 19.7% (2006-2010 5-year est.).

Education: Percent of population age 25 and over with: High school diploma (including GED) or higher: 94.0% (2006-2010 5-year est.); Bachelor's degree or higher: 30.8% (2006-2010 5-year est.); Master's degree or higher: 11.8% (2006-2010 5-year est.).

School District(s)
Warren County SD (KG-12)
    2010-11 Enrollment: 4,928 . . . . (814) 723-6900
Housing: Homeownership rate: 85.4% (2010); Median home value: $163,900 (2006-2010 5-year est.); Median contract rent: $425 per month (2006-2010 5-year est.); Median year structure built: 1965 (2006-2010 5-year est.).

Transportation: Commute to work: 91.1% car, 0.0% public transportation, 0.0% walk, 7.1% work from home (2006-2010 5-year est.); Travel time to work: 24.6% less than 15 minutes, 52.0% 15 to 30 minutes, 8.4% 30 to 45 minutes, 9.8% 45 to 60 minutes, 5.3% 60 minutes or more (2006-2010 5-year est.)

SHEFFIELD (CDP). Covers a land area of 1.775 square miles and a water area of 0 square miles. Located at 41.70° N. Lat; 79.03° W. Long. Elevation is 1,342 feet.

Population: 1,294 (1990); 1,268 (2000); 1,132 (2010); Density: 637.8 persons per square mile (2010); Race: 99.3% White, 0.1% Black, 0.2% Asian, 0.0% American Indian/Alaska Native, 0.0% Native Hawaiian/Other Pacific Islander, 0.4% Other, 0.2% Hispanic of any race (2010); Average household size: 2.35 (2010); Median age: 43.2 (2010); Males per 100 females: 100.7 (2010); Marriage status: 21.7% never married, 59.3% now married, 13.7% widowed, 5.2% divorced (2006-2010 5-year est.); Foreign born: 3.1% (2006-2010 5-year est.); Ancestry (includes multiple ancestries): 26.9% English, 25.0% German, 8.8% Swedish, 8.1% Irish, 8.0% Polish (2006-2010 5-year est.).

Economy: Employment by occupation: 3.3% management, 0.0% professional, 12.6% services, 19.7% sales, 0.0% farming, 18.4% construction, 14.0% production (2006-2010 5-year est.).

Income: Per capita income: $24,395 (2006-2010 5-year est.); Median household income: $41,429 (2006-2010 5-year est.); Average household income: $54,435 (2006-2010 5-year est.); Percent of households with income of $100,000 or more: 4.4% (2006-2010 5-year est.); Poverty rate: 20.5% (2006-2010 5-year est.).

Education: Percent of population age 25 and over with: High school diploma (including GED) or higher: 85.5% (2006-2010 5-year est.); Bachelor's degree or higher: 14.4% (2006-2010 5-year est.); Master's degree or higher: 4.2% (2006-2010 5-year est.).

School District(s)
Warren County SD (KG-12)
  2010-11 Enrollment: 4,928 . . . . (814) 723-6900

Housing: Homeownership rate: 73.6% (2010); Median home value: $64,000 (2006-2010 5-year est.); Median contract rent: $375 per month (2006-2010 5-year est.); Median year structure built: before 1940 (2006-2010 5-year est.).

Newspapers: Valley Voice (Community news; Circulation 3,000)

Transportation: Commute to work: 77.8% car, 5.3% public transportation, 6.2% walk, 10.8% work from home (2006-2010 5-year est.); Travel time to work: 38.5% less than 15 minutes, 31.5% 15 to 30 minutes, 21.0% 30 to 45 minutes, 0.0% 45 to 60 minutes, 9.0% 60 minutes or more (2006-2010 5-year est.)

Additional Information Contacts
Kane Chamber of Commerce . . . . (814) 837-6565
  http://www.kanepa.com

SHEFFIELD (township). Covers a land area of 59.165 square miles and a water area of 0.005 square miles. Located at 41.69° N. Lat; 79.02° W. Long. Elevation is 1,342 feet.

History: Founded 1864.

Population: 2,382 (1990); 2,346 (2000); 2,121 (2010); Density: 35.8 persons per square mile (2010); Race: 98.8% White, 0.2% Black, 0.1% Asian, 0.2% American Indian/Alaska Native, 0.0% Native Hawaiian/Other Pacific Islander, 0.7% Other, 0.5% Hispanic of any race (2010); Average household size: 2.32 (2010); Median age: 46.0 (2010); Males per 100 females: 99.2 (2010); Marriage status: 21.0% never married, 63.6% now married, 9.3% widowed, 6.2% divorced (2006-2010 5-year est.); Foreign born: 1.6% (2006-2010 5-year est.); Ancestry (includes multiple ancestries): 24.8% English, 23.2% German, 10.0% Irish, 8.6% Swedish, 8.4% Polish (2006-2010 5-year est.).

Economy: Single-family building permits issued: 1 (2011); Multi-family building permits issued: 0 (2011); Employment by occupation: 10.2% management, 2.1% professional, 15.5% services, 12.6% sales, 0.0% farming, 15.7% construction, 10.2% production (2006-2010 5-year est.).

Income: Per capita income: $26,948 (2006-2010 5-year est.); Median household income: $45,587 (2006-2010 5-year est.); Average household income: $60,502 (2006-2010 5-year est.); Percent of households with income of $100,000 or more: 6.5% (2006-2010 5-year est.); Poverty rate: 16.7% (2006-2010 5-year est.).

Education: Percent of population age 25 and over with: High school diploma (including GED) or higher: 84.3% (2006-2010 5-year est.); Bachelor's degree or higher: 11.4% (2006-2010 5-year est.); Master's degree or higher: 3.2% (2006-2010 5-year est.).

Housing: Homeownership rate: 80.6% (2010); Median home value: $72,500 (2006-2010 5-year est.); Median contract rent: $372 per month (2006-2010 5-year est.); Median year structure built: 1944 (2006-2010 5-year est.).

Newspapers: Valley Voice (Community news; Circulation 3,000)

Transportation: Commute to work: 85.3% car, 2.4% public transportation, 2.9% walk, 9.4% work from home (2006-2010 5-year est.); Travel time to work: 35.4% less than 15 minutes, 34.9% 15 to 30 minutes, 22.3% 30 to 45 minutes, 2.3% 45 to 60 minutes, 5.0% 60 minutes or more (2006-2010 5-year est.)

Additional Information Contacts
Kane Chamber of Commerce . . . . (814) 837-6565
  http://www.kanepa.com

SOUTHWEST (township). Covers a land area of 34.039 square miles and a water area of 0 square miles. Located at 41.66° N. Lat; 79.55° W. Long.

Population: 610 (1990); 561 (2000); 527 (2010); Density: 15.5 persons per square mile (2010); Race: 99.2% White, 0.0% Black, 0.0% Asian, 0.0% American Indian/Alaska Native, 0.0% Native Hawaiian/Other Pacific Islander, 0.8% Other, 2.8% Hispanic of any race (2010); Average household size: 2.60 (2010); Median age: 41.4 (2010); Males per 100 females: 96.6 (2010); Marriage status: 19.1% never married, 60.9% now married, 10.0% widowed, 10.0% divorced (2006-2010 5-year est.); Foreign born: 0.0% (2006-2010 5-year est.); Ancestry (includes multiple ancestries): 19.6% German, 15.3% English, 15.3% Irish, 9.7% American, 8.4% Italian (2006-2010 5-year est.).

Economy: Employment by occupation: 3.0% management, 5.5% professional, 19.4% services, 8.5% sales, 7.3% farming, 21.2% construction, 7.3% production (2006-2010 5-year est.).

Income: Per capita income: $18,079 (2006-2010 5-year est.); Median household income: $31,750 (2006-2010 5-year est.); Average household income: $42,617 (2006-2010 5-year est.); Percent of households with income of $100,000 or more: 7.7% (2006-2010 5-year est.); Poverty rate: 17.7% (2006-2010 5-year est.).

Education: Percent of population age 25 and over with: High school diploma (including GED) or higher: 75.1% (2006-2010 5-year est.); Bachelor's degree or higher: 10.0% (2006-2010 5-year est.); Master's degree or higher: 4.9% (2006-2010 5-year est.).

Housing: Homeownership rate: 87.2% (2010); Median home value: $78,500 (2006-2010 5-year est.); Median contract rent: $319 per month (2006-2010 5-year est.); Median year structure built: 1968 (2006-2010 5-year est.).

Transportation: Commute to work: 98.2% car, 0.0% public transportation, 0.0% walk, 1.8% work from home (2006-2010 5-year est.); Travel time to work: 19.3% less than 15 minutes, 35.4% 15 to 30 minutes, 14.9% 30 to 45 minutes, 18.6% 45 to 60 minutes, 11.8% 60 minutes or more (2006-2010 5-year est.)

SPRING CREEK (township). Covers a land area of 48.688 square miles and a water area of 0.076 square miles. Located at 41.85° N. Lat; 79.54° W. Long. Elevation is 1,404 feet.

Population: 843 (1990); 872 (2000); 852 (2010); Density: 17.5 persons per square mile (2010); Race: 99.1% White, 0.5% Black, 0.0% Asian, 0.0% American Indian/Alaska Native, 0.0% Native Hawaiian/Other Pacific Islander, 0.4% Other, 0.2% Hispanic of any race (2010); Average household size: 2.50 (2010); Median age: 43.3 (2010); Males per 100 females: 114.6 (2010); Marriage status: 37.9% never married, 52.7% now married, 1.9% widowed, 7.6% divorced (2006-2010 5-year est.); Foreign born: 1.4% (2006-2010 5-year est.); Ancestry (includes multiple ancestries): 28.7% German, 23.9% English, 11.7% Irish, 7.5% Polish, 4.6% Danish (2006-2010 5-year est.).

Economy: Single-family building permits issued: 0 (2011); Multi-family building permits issued: 0 (2011); Employment by occupation: 12.6% management, 2.1% professional, 11.8% services, 14.5% sales, 1.9% farming, 10.9% construction, 6.4% production (2006-2010 5-year est.).

Income: Per capita income: $19,429 (2006-2010 5-year est.); Median household income: $50,000 (2006-2010 5-year est.); Average household income: $54,351 (2006-2010 5-year est.); Percent of households with income of $100,000 or more: 8.7% (2006-2010 5-year est.); Poverty rate: 15.9% (2006-2010 5-year est.).

Education: Percent of population age 25 and over with: High school diploma (including GED) or higher: 91.0% (2006-2010 5-year est.); Bachelor's degree or higher: 11.3% (2006-2010 5-year est.); Master's degree or higher: 5.1% (2006-2010 5-year est.).

Housing: Homeownership rate: 84.5% (2010); Median home value: $88,500 (2006-2010 5-year est.); Median contract rent: $351 per month (2006-2010 5-year est.); Median year structure built: 1976 (2006-2010 5-year est.).

Transportation: Commute to work: 80.9% car, 0.0% public transportation, 16.0% walk, 3.1% work from home (2006-2010 5-year est.); Travel time to work: 37.1% less than 15 minutes, 38.7% 15 to 30 minutes, 12.0% 30 to 45 minutes, 4.3% 45 to 60 minutes, 7.9% 60 minutes or more (2006-2010 5-year est.).

STARBRICK (CDP).
Covers a land area of 1.184 square miles and a water area of 0.116 square miles. Located at 41.84° N. Lat; 79.21° W. Long. Elevation is 1,194 feet.

Population: n/a (1990); n/a (2000); 522 (2010); Density: 440.7 persons per square mile (2010); Race: 96.7% White, 0.4% Black, 0.0% Asian, 0.0% American Indian/Alaska Native, 0.0% Native Hawaiian/Other Pacific Islander, 2.9% Other, 0.4% Hispanic of any race (2010); Average household size: 2.06 (2010); Median age: 44.8 (2010); Males per 100 females: 92.6 (2010); Marriage status: 30.5% never married, 45.3% now married, 8.7% widowed, 15.5% divorced (2006-2010 5-year est.); Foreign born: 1.6% (2006-2010 5-year est.); Ancestry (includes multiple ancestries): 28.9% German, 13.2% Irish, 12.9% American, 9.7% English, 7.9% Russian (2006-2010 5-year est.).

Economy: Employment by occupation: 20.2% management, 0.0% professional, 0.0% services, 5.2% sales, 0.0% farming, 8.1% construction, 31.2% production (2006-2010 5-year est.).

Income: Per capita income: $23,814 (2006-2010 5-year est.); Median household income: $37,917 (2006-2010 5-year est.); Average household income: $46,788 (2006-2010 5-year est.); Percent of households with income of $100,000 or more: 18.4% (2006-2010 5-year est.); Poverty rate: 6.8% (2006-2010 5-year est.).

Education: Percent of population age 25 and over with: High school diploma (including GED) or higher: 76.7% (2006-2010 5-year est.); Bachelor's degree or higher: 15.2% (2006-2010 5-year est.); Master's degree or higher: 5.5% (2006-2010 5-year est.).

Housing: Homeownership rate: 79.8% (2010); Median home value: $32,800 (2006-2010 5-year est.); Median contract rent: n/a per month (2006-2010 5-year est.); Median year structure built: 1971 (2006-2010 5-year est.).

Transportation: Commute to work: 100.0% car, 0.0% public transportation, 0.0% walk, 0.0% work from home (2006-2010 5-year est.); Travel time to work: 53.8% less than 15 minutes, 23.4% 15 to 30 minutes, 14.6% 30 to 45 minutes, 0.0% 45 to 60 minutes, 8.2% 60 minutes or more (2006-2010 5-year est.)

SUGAR GROVE (borough).
Aka Sugargrove. Covers a land area of 1.121 square miles and a water area of 0 square miles. Located at 41.98° N. Lat; 79.34° W. Long. Elevation is 1,398 feet.

Population: 604 (1990); 613 (2000); 614 (2010); Density: 547.8 persons per square mile (2010); Race: 96.6% White, 0.8% Black, 0.5% Asian, 0.2% American Indian/Alaska Native, 0.2% Native Hawaiian/Other Pacific Islander, 1.7% Other, 0.0% Hispanic of any race (2010); Average household size: 2.70 (2010); Median age: 37.8 (2010); Males per 100 females: 98.1 (2010); Marriage status: 32.1% never married, 57.1% now married, 4.7% widowed, 6.1% divorced (2006-2010 5-year est.); Foreign born: 0.2% (2006-2010 5-year est.); Ancestry (includes multiple ancestries): 29.9% German, 16.6% Irish, 14.9% Swedish, 11.8% English, 9.2% Italian (2006-2010 5-year est.).

Economy: Employment by occupation: 17.5% management, 1.7% professional, 22.7% services, 15.3% sales, 0.0% farming, 4.7% construction, 10.4% production (2006-2010 5-year est.).

Income: Per capita income: $20,906 (2006-2010 5-year est.); Median household income: $50,526 (2006-2010 5-year est.); Average household income: $59,870 (2006-2010 5-year est.); Percent of households with income of $100,000 or more: 15.7% (2006-2010 5-year est.); Poverty rate: 9.1% (2006-2010 5-year est.).

Education: Percent of population age 25 and over with: High school diploma (including GED) or higher: 87.4% (2006-2010 5-year est.); Bachelor's degree or higher: 12.8% (2006-2010 5-year est.); Master's degree or higher: 5.2% (2006-2010 5-year est.).

School District(s)
Warren County SD (KG-12)

    2010-11 Enrollment: 4,928 .... (814) 723-6900

Housing: Homeownership rate: 78.0% (2010); Median home value: $90,100 (2006-2010 5-year est.); Median contract rent: $395 per month

(2006-2010 5-year est.); Median year structure built: before 1940 (2006-2010 5-year est.).

Transportation: Commute to work: 92.8% car, 0.0% public transportation, 1.0% walk, 6.2% work from home (2006-2010 5-year est.); Travel time to work: 27.3% less than 15 minutes, 53.0% 15 to 30 minutes, 14.2% 30 to 45 minutes, 0.0% 45 to 60 minutes, 5.5% 60 minutes or more (2006-2010 5-year est.)

SUGAR GROVE (township).
Aka Sugargrove. Covers a land area of 35.370 square miles and a water area of 0.034 square miles. Located at 41.95° N. Lat; 79.34° W. Long. Elevation is 1,398 feet.

Population: 1,745 (1990); 1,870 (2000); 1,723 (2010); Density: 48.7 persons per square mile (2010); Race: 98.0% White, 0.0% Black, 0.8% Asian, 0.2% American Indian/Alaska Native, 0.0% Native Hawaiian/Other Pacific Islander, 1.0% Other, 0.5% Hispanic of any race (2010); Average household size: 2.63 (2010); Median age: 40.0 (2010); Males per 100 females: 112.2 (2010); Marriage status: 23.9% never married, 60.8% now married, 6.6% widowed, 8.7% divorced (2006-2010 5-year est.); Foreign born: 1.0% (2006-2010 5-year est.); Ancestry (includes multiple ancestries): 40.3% German, 15.8% Swedish, 10.6% English, 10.2% Italian, 9.3% Polish (2006-2010 5-year est.).

Economy: Single-family building permits issued: 3 (2011); Multi-family building permits issued: 0 (2011); Employment by occupation: 8.3% management, 1.1% professional, 11.3% services, 12.7% sales, 6.1% farming, 11.7% construction, 8.1% production (2006-2010 5-year est.).

Income: Per capita income: $19,807 (2006-2010 5-year est.); Median household income: $42,083 (2006-2010 5-year est.); Average household income: $52,606 (2006-2010 5-year est.); Percent of households with income of $100,000 or more: 9.5% (2006-2010 5-year est.); Poverty rate: 15.5% (2006-2010 5-year est.).

Education: Percent of population age 25 and over with: High school diploma (including GED) or higher: 83.2% (2006-2010 5-year est.); Bachelor's degree or higher: 9.7% (2006-2010 5-year est.); Master's degree or higher: 3.9% (2006-2010 5-year est.).

Housing: Homeownership rate: 85.5% (2010); Median home value: $90,800 (2006-2010 5-year est.); Median contract rent: $336 per month (2006-2010 5-year est.); Median year structure built: 1971 (2006-2010 5-year est.).

Transportation: Commute to work: 88.7% car, 0.0% public transportation, 4.1% walk, 6.6% work from home (2006-2010 5-year est.); Travel time to work: 33.2% less than 15 minutes, 46.7% 15 to 30 minutes, 14.6% 30 to 45 minutes, 4.5% 45 to 60 minutes, 1.0% 60 minutes or more (2006-2010 5-year est.)

Additional Information Contacts

Warren County Chamber of Business and Industry .... (814) 723-3050
  http://www.wccbi.org

TIDIOUTE (borough).
Covers a land area of 1.073 square miles and a water area of 0.132 square miles. Located at 41.69° N. Lat; 79.39° W. Long. Elevation is 1,125 feet.

Population: 827 (1990); 792 (2000); 688 (2010); Density: 641.2 persons per square mile (2010); Race: 99.3% White, 0.0% Black, 0.0% Asian, 0.1% American Indian/Alaska Native, 0.0% Native Hawaiian/Other Pacific Islander, 0.6% Other, 0.9% Hispanic of any race (2010); Average household size: 2.19 (2010); Median age: 47.1 (2010); Males per 100 females: 91.1 (2010); Marriage status: 20.6% never married, 57.2% now married, 14.0% widowed, 8.1% divorced (2006-2010 5-year est.); Foreign born: 1.0% (2006-2010 5-year est.); Ancestry (includes multiple ancestries): 31.7% German, 23.6% Irish, 12.9% English, 10.3% Swedish, 8.4% Polish (2006-2010 5-year est.).

Economy: Employment by occupation: 2.8% management, 1.3% professional, 13.5% services, 15.7% sales, 7.2% farming, 12.5% construction, 11.6% production (2006-2010 5-year est.).

Income: Per capita income: $18,883 (2006-2010 5-year est.); Median household income: $34,792 (2006-2010 5-year est.); Average household income: $42,339 (2006-2010 5-year est.); Percent of households with income of $100,000 or more: 6.1% (2006-2010 5-year est.); Poverty rate: 8.7% (2006-2010 5-year est.).

Education: Percent of population age 25 and over with: High school diploma (including GED) or higher: 87.3% (2006-2010 5-year est.); Bachelor's degree or higher: 8.3% (2006-2010 5-year est.); Master's degree or higher: 4.6% (2006-2010 5-year est.).

School District(s)
Tidioute Community CS (KG-12)

    2010-11 Enrollment: 279........................ (814) 484-3550

Housing: Homeownership rate: 69.7% (2010); Median home value: $67,600 (2006-2010 5-year est.); Median contract rent: $375 per month (2006-2010 5-year est.); Median year structure built: before 1940 (2006-2010 5-year est.).

Safety: Violent crime rate: 14.5 per 10,000 population; Property crime rate: 101.4 per 10,000 population (2011).

Transportation: Commute to work: 83.9% car, 0.0% public transportation, 5.1% walk, 6.5% work from home (2006-2010 5-year est.); Travel time to work: 37.4% less than 15 minutes, 27.1% 15 to 30 minutes, 19.8% 30 to 45 minutes, 11.4% 45 to 60 minutes, 4.4% 60 minutes or more (2006-2010 5-year est.)

TIONA (unincorporated postal area)

Zip Code: 16352

Covers a land area of 12.806 square miles and a water area of 0 square miles. Located at 41.76° N. Lat; 79.03° W. Long. Population: 245 (2010); Density: 19.1 persons per square mile (2010); Race: 99.2% White, 0.0% Black, 0.0% Asian, 0.0% American Indian/Alaska Native, 0.0% Native Hawaiian/Other Pacific Islander, 0.8% Other, 1.2% Hispanic of any race (2010); Average household size: 2.23 (2010); Median age: 47.5 (2010); Males per 100 females: 116.8 (2010); Homeownership rate: 90.0% (2010)

TRIUMPH (township).

Covers a land area of 28.232 square miles and a water area of 0.232 square miles. Located at 41.68° N. Lat; 79.45° W. Long. Elevation is 1,686 feet.

Population: 281 (1990); 286 (2000); 316 (2010); Density: 11.2 persons per square mile (2010); Race: 95.9% White, 0.6% Black, 0.3% Asian, 0.0% American Indian/Alaska Native, 0.0% Native Hawaiian/Other Pacific Islander, 3.2% Other, 1.3% Hispanic of any race (2010); Average household size: 2.24 (2010); Median age: 51.2 (2010); Males per 100 females: 119.4 (2010); Marriage status: 22.0% never married, 62.5% now married, 4.3% widowed, 11.2% divorced (2006-2010 5-year est.); Foreign born: 2.7% (2006-2010 5-year est.); Ancestry (includes multiple ancestries): 36.1% German, 18.6% Irish, 14.2% Italian, 12.2% English, 7.8% American (2006-2010 5-year est.).

Economy: Single-family building permits issued: 0 (2011); Multi-family building permits issued: 0 (2011); Employment by occupation: 10.8% management, 0.0% professional, 11.7% services, 17.1% sales, 1.8% farming, 16.2% construction, 18.0% production (2006-2010 5-year est.).

Income: Per capita income: $17,330 (2006-2010 5-year est.); Median household income: $26,667 (2006-2010 5-year est.); Average household income: $37,335 (2006-2010 5-year est.); Percent of households with income of $100,000 or more: 6.6% (2006-2010 5-year est.); Poverty rate: 15.9% (2006-2010 5-year est.).

Education: Percent of population age 25 and over with: High school diploma (including GED) or higher: 86.1% (2006-2010 5-year est.); Bachelor's degree or higher: 0.8% (2006-2010 5-year est.); Master's degree or higher: 0.0% (2006-2010 5-year est.).

Housing: Homeownership rate: 90.1% (2010); Median home value: $71,900 (2006-2010 5-year est.); Median contract rent: $510 per month (2006-2010 5-year est.); Median year structure built: 1964 (2006-2010 5-year est.).

Transportation: Commute to work: 86.1% car, 0.0% public transportation, 0.0% walk, 13.9% work from home (2006-2010 5-year est.); Travel time to work: 22.6% less than 15 minutes, 19.4% 15 to 30 minutes, 29.0% 30 to 45 minutes, 20.4% 45 to 60 minutes, 8.6% 60 minutes or more (2006-2010 5-year est.)

WARREN (city).

County seat. Covers a land area of 2.913 square miles and a water area of 0.175 square miles. Located at 41.84° N. Lat; 79.14° W. Long. Elevation is 1,201 feet.

History: Warren was laid out about 1795. Lots were sold at auction in distant communities to speculative bidders, few of whom settled on or paid for their lots. The town grew slowly until lumbering began. In 1860 there was an oil boom.

Population: 11,122 (1990); 10,259 (2000); 9,710 (2010); Density: 3,333.3 persons per square mile (2010); Race: 97.5% White, 0.5% Black, 0.6% Asian, 0.3% American Indian/Alaska Native, 0.0% Native Hawaiian/Other Pacific Islander, 1.1% Other, 0.9% Hispanic of any race (2010); Average household size: 2.13 (2010); Median age: 41.2 (2010); Males per 100 females: 94.2 (2010); Marriage status: 26.3% never married, 49.1% now married, 8.5% widowed, 16.1% divorced (2006-2010 5-year est.); Foreign born: 1.0% (2006-2010 5-year est.); Ancestry (includes multiple

ancestries): 30.0% German, 15.3% Irish, 15.2% English, 12.9% Italian, 12.9% Swedish (2006-2010 5-year est.).

Economy: Single-family building permits issued: 0 (2011); Multi-family building permits issued: 0 (2011); Employment by occupation: 10.5% management, 3.9% professional, 8.2% services, 16.7% sales, 5.0% farming, 8.5% construction, 8.2% production (2006-2010 5-year est.).

Income: Per capita income: $20,617 (2006-2010 5-year est.); Median household income: $34,992 (2006-2010 5-year est.); Average household income: $45,085 (2006-2010 5-year est.); Percent of households with income of $100,000 or more: 6.5% (2006-2010 5-year est.); Poverty rate: 14.0% (2006-2010 5-year est.).

Taxes: Total city taxes per capita: $573 (2009); City property taxes per capita: $190 (2009).

Education: Percent of population age 25 and over with: High school diploma (including GED) or higher: 90.9% (2006-2010 5-year est.); Bachelor's degree or higher: 24.1% (2006-2010 5-year est.); Master's degree or higher: 7.5% (2006-2010 5-year est.).

School District(s)

Warren County Avts (10-12)
    2010-11 Enrollment: n/a . . . . (814) 726-1260
Warren County SD (KG-12)
    2010-11 Enrollment: 4,928 . . . . (814) 723-6900

Housing: Homeownership rate: 57.5% (2010); Median home value: $70,600 (2006-2010 5-year est.); Median contract rent: $381 per month (2006-2010 5-year est.); Median year structure built: before 1940 (2006-2010 5-year est.).

Hospitals: Warren Dental Arts Hospital (6 beds); Warren General Hospital (89 beds); Warren State Hospital (230 beds)

Safety: Violent crime rate: 42.1 per 10,000 population; Property crime rate: 266.9 per 10,000 population (2011).

Newspapers: Times Observer (Community news; Circulation 10,622)

Transportation: Commute to work: 84.8% car, 0.6% public transportation, 10.9% walk, 3.0% work from home (2006-2010 5-year est.); Travel time to work: 64.9% less than 15 minutes, 21.7% 15 to 30 minutes, 7.0% 30 to 45 minutes, 2.3% 45 to 60 minutes, 4.1% 60 minutes or more (2006-2010 5-year est.)

Additional Information Contacts

City of Warren . . . . (814) 723-6300
    http://www.cityofwarrenpa.org
Warren County Chamber of Business and Industry . . . . . . (814) 723-3050
    http://wccbi.org

WATSON (township).

Covers a land area of 50.821 square miles and a water area of 0.351 square miles. Located at 41.69° N. Lat; 79.27° W. Long.

Population: 276 (1990); 322 (2000); 274 (2010); Density: 5.4 persons per square mile (2010); Race: 99.3% White, 0.4% Black, 0.0% Asian, 0.0% American Indian/Alaska Native, 0.0% Native Hawaiian/Other Pacific Islander, 0.3% Other, 0.4% Hispanic of any race (2010); Average household size: 2.16 (2010); Median age: 49.0 (2010); Males per 100 females: 122.8 (2010); Marriage status: 22.6% never married, 62.9% now married, 6.3% widowed, 8.1% divorced (2006-2010 5-year est.); Foreign born: 0.0% (2006-2010 5-year est.); Ancestry (includes multiple ancestries): 31.0% German, 27.8% English, 11.3% Dutch, 10.9% Italian, 10.1% Swedish (2006-2010 5-year est.).

Economy: Employment by occupation: 3.1% management, 3.9% professional, 8.7% services, 14.2% sales, 3.1% farming, 7.9% construction, 15.7% production (2006-2010 5-year est.).

Income: Per capita income: $25,452 (2006-2010 5-year est.); Median household income: $58,750 (2006-2010 5-year est.); Average household income: $60,498 (2006-2010 5-year est.); Percent of households with income of $100,000 or more: 6.7% (2006-2010 5-year est.); Poverty rate: 11.3% (2006-2010 5-year est.).

Education: Percent of population age 25 and over with: High school diploma (including GED) or higher: 92.9% (2006-2010 5-year est.); Bachelor's degree or higher: 16.5% (2006-2010 5-year est.); Master's degree or higher: 2.7% (2006-2010 5-year est.).

Housing: Homeownership rate: 92.9% (2010); Median home value: $92,000 (2006-2010 5-year est.); Median contract rent: n/a per month (2006-2010 5-year est.); Median year structure built: 1960 (2006-2010 5-year est.).

Transportation: Commute to work: 93.7% car, 0.0% public transportation, 0.0% walk, 6.3% work from home (2006-2010 5-year est.); Travel time to work: 9.2% less than 15 minutes, 52.1% 15 to 30 minutes, 32.8% 30 to 45

minutes, 2.5% 45 to 60 minutes, 3.4% 60 minutes or more (2006-2010 5-year est.)

YOUNGSVILLE (borough). Covers a land area of 1.330 square miles and a water area of 0 square miles. Located at 41.85° N. Lat; 79.32° W. Long. Elevation is 1,201 feet.

History: Settled 1795.

Population: 1,775 (1990); 1,834 (2000); 1,729 (2010); Density: 1,299.6 persons per square mile (2010); Race: 98.2% White, 0.5% Black, 0.2% Asian, 0.1% American Indian/Alaska Native, 0.0% Native Hawaiian/Other Pacific Islander, 1.0% Other, 1.0% Hispanic of any race (2010); Average household size: 2.32 (2010); Median age: 41.9 (2010); Males per 100 females: 85.1 (2010); Marriage status: 17.4% never married, 60.5% now married, 11.2% widowed, 10.9% divorced (2006-2010 5-year est.); Foreign born: 0.7% (2006-2010 5-year est.); Ancestry (includes multiple ancestries): 31.5% German, 16.6% English, 14.0% Swedish, 13.4% Irish, 8.3% Polish (2006-2010 5-year est.).

Economy: Single-family building permits issued: 1 (2011); Multi-family building permits issued: 0 (2011); Employment by occupation: 7.3% management, 1.5% professional, 13.5% services, 13.6% sales, 1.7% farming, 8.8% construction, 7.4% production (2006-2010 5-year est.).

Income: Per capita income: $21,080 (2006-2010 5-year est.); Median household income: $36,699 (2006-2010 5-year est.); Average household income: $45,649 (2006-2010 5-year est.); Percent of households with income of $100,000 or more: 9.0% (2006-2010 5-year est.); Poverty rate: 15.2% (2006-2010 5-year est.).

Education: Percent of population age 25 and over with: High school diploma (including GED) or higher: 90.7% (2006-2010 5-year est.); Bachelor's degree or higher: 15.9% (2006-2010 5-year est.); Master's degree or higher: 4.9% (2006-2010 5-year est.).

School District(s)

Warren County SD (KG-12)

   2010-11 Enrollment: 4,928 . . . . (814) 723-6900

Housing: Homeownership rate: 70.8% (2010); Median home value: $79,600 (2006-2010 5-year est.); Median contract rent: $350 per month (2006-2010 5-year est.); Median year structure built: 1946 (2006-2010 5-year est.).

Transportation: Commute to work: 90.8% car, 0.4% public transportation, 3.8% walk, 4.5% work from home (2006-2010 5-year est.); Travel time to work: 42.1% less than 15 minutes, 37.7% 15 to 30 minutes, 12.0% 30 to 45 minutes, 3.4% 45 to 60 minutes, 4.9% 60 minutes or more (2006-2010 5-year est.)

Additional Information Contacts

Warren County Chamber of Business and Industry . . . . . . (814) 723-3050
   http://wccbi.org

Washington County

Located in southwestern Pennsylvania; bounded on the west by West Virginia, and on the east by the Monongahela River. Covers a land area of 856.989 square miles, a water area of 3.918 square miles, and is located in the Eastern Time Zone at 40.20° N. Lat., 80.25° W. Long. The county was founded in 1781. County seat is Washington.

Washington County is part of the Pittsburgh, PA Metropolitan Statistical Area. The entire metro area includes: Allegheny County, PA; Armstrong County, PA; Beaver County, PA; Butler County, PA; Fayette County, PA; Washington County, PA; Westmoreland County, PA

Weather Station: Donora 1 SW   Elevation: 762 feet

	Jan	Feb	Mar	Apr	May	Jun	Jul	Aug	Sep	Oct	Nov	Dec
High	40	43	52	65	74	82	85	84	78	67	55	43
Low	22	24	30	40	49	58	63	62	55	43	35	26
Precip	2.5	2.2	3.2	3.2	4.1	3.9	3.9	3.5	2.9	2.5	3.1	2.7
Snow	6.1	3.1	3.4	0.2	0.0	0.0	0.0	0.0	0.0	tr	0.6	3.6

High and Low temperatures in degrees Fahrenheit; Precipitation and Snow in inches

Weather Station: Washington 3 NE   Elevation: 1,299 feet

	Jan	Feb	Mar	Apr	May	Jun	Jul	Aug	Sep	Oct	Nov	Dec
High	36	39	49	61	70	78	82	81	74	62	51	40
Low	20	22	28	39	48	57	61	59	52	41	34	24
Precip	3.0	2.3	3.3	3.0	4.3	3.9	3.9	3.2	3.4	2.4	3.5	3.0
Snow	8.5	5.4	4.8	0.9	tr	0.0	0.0	0.0	0.0	tr	1.4	5.1

High and Low temperatures in degrees Fahrenheit; Precipitation and Snow in inches

Population: 204,584 (1990); 202,897 (2000); 207,820 (2010); Race: 94.1% White, 3.3% Black, 0.6% Asian, 0.1% American Indian/Alaska Native, 0.0% Native Hawaiian/Other Pacific Islander, 1.9% Other, 1.1% Hispanic of any race (2010); Density: 242.5 persons per square mile (2010); Average household size: 2.37 (2010); Median age: 43.6 (2010); Males per 100 females: 94.6 (2010).

Religion: Six largest groups: 25.9% Catholicism, 5.6% Methodist/Pietist, 5.6% Presbyterian-Reformed, 4.1% Non-Denominational, 3.6% Baptist, 1.2% Holiness (2010)

Economy: Unemployment rate: 7.2% (August 2012); Total civilian labor force: 109,943 (August 2012); Leading industries: 16.8% construction; 16.3% health care and social assistance; 11.9% manufacturing (2010); Farms: 2,023 totaling 211,053 acres (2007); Companies that employ 500 or more persons: 9 (2010); Companies that employ 100 to 499 persons: 109 (2010); Companies that employ less than 100 persons: 4,910 (2010); Black-owned businesses: n/a (2007); Hispanic-owned businesses: 138 (2007); Asian-owned businesses: 84 (2007); Women-owned businesses: 3,852 (2007); Retail sales per capita: $10,803 (2010). Single-family building permits issued: 359 (2011); Multi-family building permits issued: 32 (2011).

Income: Per capita income: $26,045 (2006-2010 5-year est.); Median household income: $49,687 (2006-2010 5-year est.); Average household income: $63,193 (2006-2010 5-year est.); Percent of households with income of $100,000 or more: 17.1% (2006-2010 5-year est.); Poverty rate: 10.4% (2006-2010 5-year est.); Bankruptcy rate: 2.94% (2011).

Taxes: Total county taxes per capita: $157 (2009); County property taxes per capita: $152 (2009).

Education: Percent of population age 25 and over with: High school diploma (including GED) or higher: 89.0% (2006-2010 5-year est.); Bachelor's degree or higher: 24.2% (2006-2010 5-year est.); Master's degree or higher: 8.2% (2006-2010 5-year est.).

Housing: Homeownership rate: 75.9% (2010); Median home value: $130,300 (2006-2010 5-year est.); Median contract rent: $437 per month (2006-2010 5-year est.); Median year structure built: 1959 (2006-2010 5-year est.)

Health: Birth rate: 97.2 per 10,000 population (2011); Death rate: 118.0 per 10,000 population (2011); Age-adjusted cancer mortality rate: 199.2 deaths per 100,000 population (2009); Number of physicians: 19.6 per 10,000 population (2010); Hospital beds: 28.7 per 10,000 population (2008); Hospital admissions: 1,439.1 per 10,000 population (2008).

Environment: Air Quality Index: 67.1% good, 32.6% moderate, 0.3% unhealthy for sensitive individuals, 0.0% unhealthy (percent of days in 2011)

Elections: 2012 Presidential election results: 42.7% Obama, 56.0% Romney

National and State Parks: Hillman State Park

Additional Information Contacts

Washington County Government . . . . (724) 228-6700
   http://www.co.washington.pa.us
Washington County Chamber of Commerce. . . . . (724) 225-3010
   http://www.washcochamber.com

Washington County Communities

AARONSBURG (CDP). Covers a land area of 0.552 square miles and a water area of 0 square miles. Located at 40.01° N. Lat; 80.00° W. Long.

Population: n/a (1990); n/a (2000); 259 (2010); Density: 469.4 persons per square mile (2010); Race: 90.7% White, 1.5% Black, 0.0% Asian, 1.2% American Indian/Alaska Native, 0.0% Native Hawaiian/Other Pacific Islander, 6.6% Other, 1.5% Hispanic of any race (2010); Average household size: 2.62 (2010); Median age: 36.6 (2010); Males per 100 females: 89.1 (2010); Marriage status: 28.0% never married, 39.0% now married, 8.9% widowed, 24.2% divorced (2006-2010 5-year est.); Foreign born: 0.0% (2006-2010 5-year est.); Ancestry (includes multiple ancestries): 33.2% Polish, 26.4% Irish, 20.9% German, 17.3% Dutch, 6.9% Slovak (2006-2010 5-year est.).

Economy: Employment by occupation: 19.6% management, 6.5% professional, 29.9% services, 14.0% sales, 8.4% farming, 11.2% construction, 5.6% production (2006-2010 5-year est.).

Income: Per capita income: $20,718 (2006-2010 5-year est.); Median household income: $65,875 (2006-2010 5-year est.); Average household income: $54,292 (2006-2010 5-year est.); Percent of households with income of $100,000 or more: 19.8% (2006-2010 5-year est.); Poverty rate: 23.8% (2006-2010 5-year est.).

Education: Percent of population age 25 and over with: High school diploma (including GED) or higher: 77.3% (2006-2010 5-year est.); Bachelor's degree or higher: 17.6% (2006-2010 5-year est.); Master's degree or higher: 2.8% (2006-2010 5-year est.).

Housing: Homeownership rate: 68.7% (2010); Median home value: $99,300 (2006-2010 5-year est.); Median contract rent: $169 per month (2006-2010 5-year est.); Median year structure built: before 1940 (2006-2010 5-year est.).

Transportation: Commute to work: 100.0% car, 0.0% public transportation, 0.0% walk, 0.0% work from home (2006-2010 5-year est.); Travel time to work: 29.7% less than 15 minutes, 36.6% 15 to 30 minutes, 14.9% 30 to 45 minutes, 12.9% 45 to 60 minutes, 5.9% 60 minutes or more (2006-2010 5-year est.)

ALLENPORT (borough). Covers a land area of 2.117 square miles and a water area of 0.091 square miles. Located at 40.09° N. Lat; 79.86° W. Long. Elevation is 791 feet.

Population: 516 (1990); 549 (2000); 537 (2010); Density: 253.6 persons per square mile (2010); Race: 99.1% White, 0.6% Black, 0.0% Asian, 0.0% American Indian/Alaska Native, 0.0% Native Hawaiian/Other Pacific Islander, 0.3% Other, 0.2% Hispanic of any race (2010); Average household size: 2.25 (2010); Median age: 47.7 (2010); Males per 100 females: 93.9 (2010); Marriage status: 22.2% never married, 57.4% now married, 9.7% widowed, 10.6% divorced (2006-2010 5-year est.); Foreign born: 0.7% (2006-2010 5-year est.); Ancestry (includes multiple ancestries): 29.1% English, 19.3% Irish, 16.3% German, 12.4% Italian, 9.4% Slovak (2006-2010 5-year est.).

Economy: Single-family building permits issued: 1 (2011); Multi-family building permits issued: 0 (2011); Employment by occupation: 5.6% management, 0.0% professional, 14.9% services, 21.7% sales, 1.9% farming, 9.3% construction, 5.6% production (2006-2010 5-year est.).

Income: Per capita income: $20,030 (2006-2010 5-year est.); Median household income: $43,250 (2006-2010 5-year est.); Average household income: $53,119 (2006-2010 5-year est.); Percent of households with income of $100,000 or more: 16.4% (2006-2010 5-year est.); Poverty rate: 15.0% (2006-2010 5-year est.).

Education: Percent of population age 25 and over with: High school diploma (including GED) or higher: 90.1% (2006-2010 5-year est.); Bachelor's degree or higher: 27.0% (2006-2010 5-year est.); Master's degree or higher: 12.6% (2006-2010 5-year est.).

Housing: Homeownership rate: 80.3% (2010); Median home value: $92,500 (2006-2010 5-year est.); Median contract rent: $245 per month (2006-2010 5-year est.); Median year structure built: 1943 (2006-2010 5-year est.).

Transportation: Commute to work: 100.0% car, 0.0% public transportation, 0.0% walk, 0.0% work from home (2006-2010 5-year est.); Travel time to work: 21.1% less than 15 minutes, 39.1% 15 to 30 minutes, 26.7% 30 to 45 minutes, 5.0% 45 to 60 minutes, 8.1% 60 minutes or more (2006-2010 5-year est.)

AMWELL (township). Covers a land area of 44.784 square miles and a water area of 0 square miles. Located at 40.08° N. Lat; 80.19° W. Long.

Population: 4,176 (1990); 3,960 (2000); 3,751 (2010); Density: 83.8 persons per square mile (2010); Race: 98.0% White, 0.5% Black, 0.2% Asian, 0.2% American Indian/Alaska Native, 0.0% Native Hawaiian/Other Pacific Islander, 1.1% Other, 0.6% Hispanic of any race (2010); Average household size: 2.52 (2010); Median age: 44.9 (2010); Males per 100 females: 97.9 (2010); Marriage status: 26.3% never married, 58.4% now married, 7.7% widowed, 7.6% divorced (2006-2010 5-year est.); Foreign born: 0.5% (2006-2010 5-year est.); Ancestry (includes multiple ancestries): 38.6% German, 25.8% Irish, 15.7% English, 13.5% Scotch-Irish, 11.6% Polish (2006-2010 5-year est.).

Economy: Single-family building permits issued: 2 (2011); Multi-family building permits issued: 0 (2011); Employment by occupation: 12.5% management, 1.0% professional, 7.3% services, 14.9% sales, 2.8% farming, 17.7% construction, 10.5% production (2006-2010 5-year est.).

Income: Per capita income: $28,207 (2006-2010 5-year est.); Median household income: $57,185 (2006-2010 5-year est.); Average household income: $69,690 (2006-2010 5-year est.); Percent of households with income of $100,000 or more: 16.4% (2006-2010 5-year est.); Poverty rate: 6.4% (2006-2010 5-year est.).

Education: Percent of population age 25 and over with: High school diploma (including GED) or higher: 89.5% (2006-2010 5-year est.); Bachelor's degree or higher: 21.5% (2006-2010 5-year est.); Master's degree or higher: 6.0% (2006-2010 5-year est.).

Housing: Homeownership rate: 84.8% (2010); Median home value: $128,800 (2006-2010 5-year est.); Median contract rent: $575 per month (2006-2010 5-year est.); Median year structure built: 1971 (2006-2010 5-year est.).

Transportation: Commute to work: 95.6% car, 0.0% public transportation, 0.0% walk, 3.8% work from home (2006-2010 5-year est.); Travel time to work: 13.8% less than 15 minutes, 54.7% 15 to 30 minutes, 17.0% 30 to 45 minutes, 5.8% 45 to 60 minutes, 8.8% 60 minutes or more (2006-2010 5-year est.)

Additional Information Contacts
Washington County Chamber of Commerce. . . . . (724) 225-3010
 http://www.washcochamber.com

ATLASBURG (CDP). Covers a land area of 0.674 square miles and a water area of 0 square miles. Located at 40.34° N. Lat; 80.38° W. Long. Elevation is 1,083 feet.

Population: n/a (1990); n/a (2000); 401 (2010); Density: 594.5 persons per square mile (2010); Race: 99.5% White, 0.0% Black, 0.0% Asian, 0.0% American Indian/Alaska Native, 0.0% Native Hawaiian/Other Pacific Islander, 0.5% Other, 0.5% Hispanic of any race (2010); Average household size: 2.46 (2010); Median age: 43.3 (2010); Males per 100 females: 99.5 (2010); Marriage status: 28.2% never married, 54.1% now married, 11.5% widowed, 6.2% divorced (2006-2010 5-year est.); Foreign born: 0.0% (2006-2010 5-year est.); Ancestry (includes multiple ancestries): 62.9% Italian, 40.2% Irish, 16.6% German, 15.7% Slovak, 10.5% Czech (2006-2010 5-year est.).

Economy: Employment by occupation: 0.0% management, 0.0% professional, 9.7% services, 21.2% sales, 11.5% farming, 0.0% construction, 0.0% production (2006-2010 5-year est.).

Income: Per capita income: $29,915 (2006-2010 5-year est.); Median household income: $24,896 (2006-2010 5-year est.); Average household income: $63,919 (2006-2010 5-year est.); Percent of households with income of $100,000 or more: 36.2% (2006-2010 5-year est.); Poverty rate: 0.0% (2006-2010 5-year est.).

Education: Percent of population age 25 and over with: High school diploma (including GED) or higher: 83.2% (2006-2010 5-year est.); Bachelor's degree or higher: 18.4% (2006-2010 5-year est.); Master's degree or higher: 7.0% (2006-2010 5-year est.).

Housing: Homeownership rate: 77.9% (2010); Median home value: $118,100 (2006-2010 5-year est.); Median contract rent: n/a per month (2006-2010 5-year est.); Median year structure built: 1952 (2006-2010 5-year est.).

Transportation: Commute to work: 100.0% car, 0.0% public transportation, 0.0% walk, 0.0% work from home (2006-2010 5-year est.); Travel time to work: 0.0% less than 15 minutes, 33.3% 15 to 30 minutes, 52.9% 30 to 45 minutes, 0.0% 45 to 60 minutes, 13.7% 60 minutes or more (2006-2010 5-year est.)

AVELLA (CDP). Covers a land area of 0.901 square miles and a water area of 0 square miles. Located at 40.27° N. Lat; 80.47° W. Long. Elevation is 915 feet.

Population: n/a (1990); n/a (2000); 804 (2010); Density: 892.1 persons per square mile (2010); Race: 96.4% White, 1.9% Black, 0.1% Asian, 0.2% American Indian/Alaska Native, 0.0% Native Hawaiian/Other Pacific Islander, 1.4% Other, 1.0% Hispanic of any race (2010); Average household size: 2.54 (2010); Median age: 39.4 (2010); Males per 100 females: 95.1 (2010); Marriage status: 27.6% never married, 59.4% now married, 7.0% widowed, 6.0% divorced (2006-2010 5-year est.); Foreign born: 0.4% (2006-2010 5-year est.); Ancestry (includes multiple ancestries): 24.4% Italian, 23.6% Irish, 21.9% German, 12.0% Polish, 8.8% English (2006-2010 5-year est.).

Economy: Employment by occupation: 6.1% management, 2.1% professional, 8.9% services, 15.4% sales, 3.6% farming, 16.4% construction, 5.4% production (2006-2010 5-year est.).

Income: Per capita income: $19,038 (2006-2010 5-year est.); Median household income: $41,250 (2006-2010 5-year est.); Average household income: $52,597 (2006-2010 5-year est.); Percent of households with income of $100,000 or more: 11.4% (2006-2010 5-year est.); Poverty rate: 7.3% (2006-2010 5-year est.).

Education: Percent of population age 25 and over with: High school diploma (including GED) or higher: 81.6% (2006-2010 5-year est.); Bachelor's degree or higher: 9.5% (2006-2010 5-year est.); Master's degree or higher: 2.7% (2006-2010 5-year est.).

Avella Area SD (KG-12)
2010-11 Enrollment: 633 . . . . (724) 356-2218
Housing: Homeownership rate: 75.8% (2010); Median home value: $82,800 (2006-2010 5-year est.); Median contract rent: $496 per month (2006-2010 5-year est.); Median year structure built: 1943 (2006-2010 5-year est.).
Transportation: Commute to work: 97.5% car, 0.0% public transportation, 1.4% walk, 1.1% work from home (2006-2010 5-year est.); Travel time to work: 13.8% less than 15 minutes, 23.3% 15 to 30 minutes, 32.0% 30 to 45 minutes, 16.7% 45 to 60 minutes, 14.2% 60 minutes or more (2006-2010 5-year est.)

BAIDLAND (CDP). Covers a land area of 1.953 square miles and a water area of 0 square miles. Located at 40.19° N. Lat; 79.95° W. Long. Elevation is 994 feet.
Population: 1,620 (1990); 1,576 (2000); 1,563 (2010); Density: 800.3 persons per square mile (2010); Race: 98.8% White, 0.4% Black, 0.1% Asian, 0.1% American Indian/Alaska Native, 0.0% Native Hawaiian/Other Pacific Islander, 0.6% Other, 1.6% Hispanic of any race (2010); Average household size: 2.42 (2010); Median age: 48.6 (2010); Males per 100 females: 95.1 (2010); Marriage status: 29.3% never married, 57.0% now married, 8.1% widowed, 5.6% divorced (2006-2010 5-year est.); Foreign born: 0.5% (2006-2010 5-year est.); Ancestry (includes multiple ancestries): 47.3% Italian, 22.3% German, 13.6% Polish, 13.4% English, 13.1% Irish (2006-2010 5-year est.).
Economy: Employment by occupation: 21.0% management, 4.6% professional, 2.8% services, 13.1% sales, 5.2% farming, 10.2% construction, 3.5% production (2006-2010 5-year est.).
Income: Per capita income: $26,889 (2006-2010 5-year est.); Median household income: $71,023 (2006-2010 5-year est.); Average household income: $87,360 (2006-2010 5-year est.); Percent of households with income of $100,000 or more: 30.6% (2006-2010 5-year est.); Poverty rate: 2.2% (2006-2010 5-year est.).
Education: Percent of population age 25 and over with: High school diploma (including GED) or higher: 86.1% (2006-2010 5-year est.); Bachelor's degree or higher: 23.0% (2006-2010 5-year est.); Master's degree or higher: 5.1% (2006-2010 5-year est.).
Housing: Homeownership rate: 89.6% (2010); Median home value: $149,500 (2006-2010 5-year est.); Median contract rent: n/a per month (2006-2010 5-year est.); Median year structure built: 1965 (2006-2010 5-year est.).
Transportation: Commute to work: 91.5% car, 4.4% public transportation, 0.0% walk, 4.1% work from home (2006-2010 5-year est.); Travel time to work: 26.1% less than 15 minutes, 33.0% 15 to 30 minutes, 16.7% 30 to 45 minutes, 10.9% 45 to 60 minutes, 13.2% 60 minutes or more (2006-2010 5-year est.)
Additional Information Contacts
Greater Philadelphia Chamber of Commerce . . . . (215) 545-1234
http://www.greaterphilachamber.com

BEALLSVILLE (borough). Covers a land area of 2.428 square miles and a water area of 0 square miles. Located at 40.06° N. Lat; 80.03° W. Long. Elevation is 1,138 feet.
Population: 530 (1990); 511 (2000); 466 (2010); Density: 192.0 persons per square mile (2010); Race: 98.1% White, 0.4% Black, 0.6% Asian, 0.2% American Indian/Alaska Native, 0.0% Native Hawaiian/Other Pacific Islander, 0.7% Other, 0.6% Hispanic of any race (2010); Average household size: 2.47 (2010); Median age: 46.6 (2010); Males per 100 females: 97.5 (2010); Marriage status: 29.3% never married, 58.7% now married, 6.5% widowed, 5.4% divorced (2006-2010 5-year est.); Foreign born: 0.9% (2006-2010 5-year est.); Ancestry (includes multiple ancestries): 22.4% English, 18.8% German, 17.8% Polish, 14.0% Irish, 10.3% Hungarian (2006-2010 5-year est.).
Economy: Single-family building permits issued: 0 (2011); Multi-family building permits issued: 0 (2011); Employment by occupation: 7.2% management, 5.8% professional, 15.7% services, 17.5% sales, 0.0% farming, 10.8% construction, 1.3% production (2006-2010 5-year est.).
Income: Per capita income: $21,869 (2006-2010 5-year est.); Median household income: $37,273 (2006-2010 5-year est.); Average household income: $51,461 (2006-2010 5-year est.); Percent of households with income of $100,000 or more: 9.1% (2006-2010 5-year est.); Poverty rate: 13.7% (2006-2010 5-year est.).
Education: Percent of population age 25 and over with: High school diploma (including GED) or higher: 97.3% (2006-2010 5-year est.);

Bachelor's degree or higher: 18.2% (2006-2010 5-year est.); Master's degree or higher: 5.1% (2006-2010 5-year est.).
Housing: Homeownership rate: 87.8% (2010); Median home value: $128,500 (2006-2010 5-year est.); Median contract rent: n/a per month (2006-2010 5-year est.); Median year structure built: 1943 (2006-2010 5-year est.).
Transportation: Commute to work: 88.9% car, 0.0% public transportation, 1.4% walk, 9.7% work from home (2006-2010 5-year est.); Travel time to work: 22.4% less than 15 minutes, 28.6% 15 to 30 minutes, 15.3% 30 to 45 minutes, 12.8% 45 to 60 minutes, 20.9% 60 minutes or more (2006-2010 5-year est.)

BENTLEYVILLE (borough). Covers a land area of 3.695 square miles and a water area of 0 square miles. Located at 40.12° N. Lat; 80.00° W. Long. Elevation is 955 feet.
History: Laid out 1816, incorporated 1868.
Population: 2,673 (1990); 2,502 (2000); 2,581 (2010); Density: 698.5 persons per square mile (2010); Race: 95.4% White, 2.7% Black, 0.2% Asian, 0.0% American Indian/Alaska Native, 0.0% Native Hawaiian/Other Pacific Islander, 1.7% Other, 0.7% Hispanic of any race (2010); Average household size: 2.26 (2010); Median age: 40.8 (2010); Males per 100 females: 91.9 (2010); Marriage status: 32.9% never married, 47.6% now married, 9.7% widowed, 9.8% divorced (2006-2010 5-year est.); Foreign born: 1.0% (2006-2010 5-year est.); Ancestry (includes multiple ancestries): 21.6% German, 17.3% Irish, 16.0% Italian, 12.7% Slovak, 10.0% Polish (2006-2010 5-year est.).
Economy: Single-family building permits issued: 0 (2011); Multi-family building permits issued: 0 (2011); Employment by occupation: 8.7% management, 6.1% professional, 13.3% services, 12.1% sales, 4.0% farming, 8.2% construction, 5.8% production (2006-2010 5-year est.).
Income: Per capita income: $17,965 (2006-2010 5-year est.); Median household income: $29,868 (2006-2010 5-year est.); Average household income: $41,150 (2006-2010 5-year est.); Percent of households with income of $100,000 or more: 11.1% (2006-2010 5-year est.); Poverty rate: 28.5% (2006-2010 5-year est.).
Education: Percent of population age 25 and over with: High school diploma (including GED) or higher: 84.6% (2006-2010 5-year est.); Bachelor's degree or higher: 18.1% (2006-2010 5-year est.); Master's degree or higher: 6.5% (2006-2010 5-year est.).
Bentworth SD (KG-12)
2010-11 Enrollment: 1,221 . . . . (724) 239-2861
Housing: Homeownership rate: 61.0% (2010); Median home value: $92,000 (2006-2010 5-year est.); Median contract rent: $269 per month (2006-2010 5-year est.); Median year structure built: 1956 (2006-2010 5-year est.).
Transportation: Commute to work: 93.1% car, 1.5% public transportation, 2.0% walk, 2.8% work from home (2006-2010 5-year est.); Travel time to work: 22.6% less than 15 minutes, 33.0% 15 to 30 minutes, 28.2% 30 to 45 minutes, 9.2% 45 to 60 minutes, 7.0% 60 minutes or more (2006-2010 5-year est.)
Additional Information Contacts
Borough of Bentleyville . . . . (724) 239-2112
http://www.bentleyville.org
Washington County Chamber of Commerce . . . . (724) 225-3010
http://www.washcochamber.com

BLAINE (township). Covers a land area of 11.883 square miles and a water area of 0 square miles. Located at 40.18° N. Lat; 80.40° W. Long.
Population: 682 (1990); 597 (2000); 690 (2010); Density: 58.1 persons per square mile (2010); Race: 98.3% White, 0.1% Black, 0.6% Asian, 0.0% American Indian/Alaska Native, 0.0% Native Hawaiian/Other Pacific Islander, 1.0% Other, 0.1% Hispanic of any race (2010); Average household size: 2.78 (2010); Median age: 39.9 (2010); Males per 100 females: 95.5 (2010); Marriage status: 19.9% never married, 72.1% now married, 4.5% widowed, 3.5% divorced (2006-2010 5-year est.); Foreign born: 0.0% (2006-2010 5-year est.); Ancestry (includes multiple ancestries): 22.0% German, 16.7% Irish, 9.1% American, 8.7% Italian, 7.5% Scotch-Irish (2006-2010 5-year est.).
Economy: Single-family building permits issued: 0 (2011); Multi-family building permits issued: 0 (2011); Employment by occupation: 4.7% management, 4.7% professional, 12.6% services, 23.7% sales, 2.5% farming, 18.0% construction, 11.9% production (2006-2010 5-year est.).
Income: Per capita income: $24,927 (2006-2010 5-year est.); Median household income: $57,500 (2006-2010 5-year est.); Average household

income: $64,545 (2006-2010 5-year est.); Percent of households with income of $100,000 or more: 16.0% (2006-2010 5-year est.); Poverty rate: 6.3% (2006-2010 5-year est.).

Education: Percent of population age 25 and over with: High school diploma (including GED) or higher: 86.8% (2006-2010 5-year est.); Bachelor's degree or higher: 17.6% (2006-2010 5-year est.); Master's degree or higher: 5.0% (2006-2010 5-year est.).

Housing: Homeownership rate: 85.0% (2010); Median home value: $141,100 (2006-2010 5-year est.); Median contract rent: $258 per month (2006-2010 5-year est.); Median year structure built: 1980 (2006-2010 5-year est.).

Transportation: Commute to work: 93.3% car, 0.0% public transportation, 0.0% walk, 5.2% work from home (2006-2010 5-year est.); Travel time to work: 18.4% less than 15 minutes, 41.0% 15 to 30 minutes, 18.0% 30 to 45 minutes, 16.8% 45 to 60 minutes, 5.9% 60 minutes or more (2006-2010 5-year est.)

BUFFALO (township). Covers a land area of 20.362 square miles and a water area of 0.007 square miles. Located at 40.15° N. Lat; 80.35° W. Long. Elevation is 1,283 feet.

Population: 2,148 (1990); 2,100 (2000); 2,069 (2010); Density: 101.6 persons per square mile (2010); Race: 98.5% White, 0.4% Black, 0.1% Asian, 0.2% American Indian/Alaska Native, 0.0% Native Hawaiian/Other Pacific Islander, 0.8% Other, 0.8% Hispanic of any race (2010); Average household size: 2.48 (2010); Median age: 48.0 (2010); Males per 100 females: 102.4 (2010); Marriage status: 19.2% never married, 71.3% now married, 2.5% widowed, 6.9% divorced (2006-2010 5-year est.); Foreign born: 0.8% (2006-2010 5-year est.); Ancestry (includes multiple ancestries): 22.9% German, 19.3% Irish, 17.4% Scotch-Irish, 16.8% Italian, 10.7% English (2006-2010 5-year est.).

Economy: Single-family building permits issued: 2 (2011); Multi-family building permits issued: 0 (2011); Employment by occupation: 9.1% management, 6.9% professional, 9.9% services, 17.2% sales, 5.2% farming, 10.0% construction, 9.3% production (2006-2010 5-year est.).

Income: Per capita income: $24,445 (2006-2010 5-year est.); Median household income: $57,539 (2006-2010 5-year est.); Average household income: $61,107 (2006-2010 5-year est.); Percent of households with income of $100,000 or more: 12.9% (2006-2010 5-year est.); Poverty rate: 5.0% (2006-2010 5-year est.).

Education: Percent of population age 25 and over with: High school diploma (including GED) or higher: 87.6% (2006-2010 5-year est.); Bachelor's degree or higher: 18.8% (2006-2010 5-year est.); Master's degree or higher: 5.2% (2006-2010 5-year est.).

Housing: Homeownership rate: 87.0% (2010); Median home value: $158,200 (2006-2010 5-year est.); Median contract rent: $420 per month (2006-2010 5-year est.); Median year structure built: 1973 (2006-2010 5-year est.).

Transportation: Commute to work: 96.0% car, 0.0% public transportation, 1.3% walk, 2.7% work from home (2006-2010 5-year est.); Travel time to work: 29.6% less than 15 minutes, 37.8% 15 to 30 minutes, 18.2% 30 to 45 minutes, 6.4% 45 to 60 minutes, 7.9% 60 minutes or more (2006-2010 5-year est.)

Additional Information Contacts
Washington County Chamber of Commerce . . . . (724) 225-3010
http://www.washcochamber.com

BULGER (CDP). Covers a land area of 1.438 square miles and a water area of 0 square miles. Located at 40.38° N. Lat; 80.32° W. Long. Elevation is 1,198 feet.

Population: n/a (1990); n/a (2000); 407 (2010); Density: 283.1 persons per square mile (2010); Race: 95.8% White, 0.5% Black, 0.7% Asian, 0.0% American Indian/Alaska Native, 0.0% Native Hawaiian/Other Pacific Islander, 3.0% Other, 0.7% Hispanic of any race (2010); Average household size: 2.31 (2010); Median age: 44.7 (2010); Males per 100 females: 97.6 (2010); Marriage status: 30.0% never married, 52.4% now married, 16.9% widowed, 0.7% divorced (2006-2010 5-year est.); Foreign born: 0.0% (2006-2010 5-year est.); Ancestry (includes multiple ancestries): 32.6% Italian, 27.1% German, 19.9% Polish, 11.9% Belgian, 9.0% Croatian (2006-2010 5-year est.).

Economy: Employment by occupation: 14.9% management, 0.0% professional, 23.8% services, 13.4% sales, 0.0% farming, 6.1% construction, 0.0% production (2006-2010 5-year est.).

Income: Per capita income: $21,708 (2006-2010 5-year est.); Median household income: $32,177 (2006-2010 5-year est.); Average household income: $48,198 (2006-2010 5-year est.); Percent of households with

income of $100,000 or more: 20.2% (2006-2010 5-year est.); Poverty rate: 20.1% (2006-2010 5-year est.).

Education: Percent of population age 25 and over with: High school diploma (including GED) or higher: 86.9% (2006-2010 5-year est.); Bachelor's degree or higher: 20.1% (2006-2010 5-year est.); Master's degree or higher: 3.9% (2006-2010 5-year est.).

Housing: Homeownership rate: 76.1% (2010); Median home value: $111,900 (2006-2010 5-year est.); Median contract rent: $566 per month (2006-2010 5-year est.); Median year structure built: 1946 (2006-2010 5-year est.).

Transportation: Commute to work: 88.6% car, 11.4% public transportation, 0.0% walk, 0.0% work from home (2006-2010 5-year est.); Travel time to work: 11.8% less than 15 minutes, 72.0% 15 to 30 minutes, 16.3% 30 to 45 minutes, 0.0% 45 to 60 minutes, 0.0% 60 minutes or more (2006-2010 5-year est.)

BURGETTSTOWN (borough). Aka Dinsmore. Covers a land area of 0.622 square miles and a water area of 0 square miles. Located at 40.38° N. Lat; 80.39° W. Long. Elevation is 991 feet.

History: Laid out 1795, incorporated 1881.

Population: 1,634 (1990); 1,576 (2000); 1,388 (2010); Density: 2,232.8 persons per square mile (2010); Race: 96.0% White, 1.7% Black, 0.4% Asian, 0.1% American Indian/Alaska Native, 0.0% Native Hawaiian/Other Pacific Islander, 1.8% Other, 1.4% Hispanic of any race (2010); Average household size: 2.30 (2010); Median age: 40.9 (2010); Males per 100 females: 96.6 (2010); Marriage status: 25.8% never married, 49.2% now married, 9.2% widowed, 15.7% divorced (2006-2010 5-year est.); Foreign born: 1.4% (2006-2010 5-year est.); Ancestry (includes multiple ancestries): 26.5% Irish, 26.2% German, 21.6% Italian, 13.4% English, 11.7% Polish (2006-2010 5-year est.).

Economy: Single-family building permits issued: 0 (2011); Multi-family building permits issued: 0 (2011); Employment by occupation: 10.8% management, 1.7% professional, 9.8% services, 18.1% sales, 7.7% farming, 12.0% construction, 4.2% production (2006-2010 5-year est.).

Income: Per capita income: $25,546 (2006-2010 5-year est.); Median household income: $50,125 (2006-2010 5-year est.); Average household income: $61,813 (2006-2010 5-year est.); Percent of households with income of $100,000 or more: 10.6% (2006-2010 5-year est.); Poverty rate: 11.4% (2006-2010 5-year est.).

Education: Percent of population age 25 and over with: High school diploma (including GED) or higher: 89.7% (2006-2010 5-year est.); Bachelor's degree or higher: 16.1% (2006-2010 5-year est.); Master's degree or higher: 5.8% (2006-2010 5-year est.).

School District(s)
Burgettstown Area SD (KG-12)
    2010-11 Enrollment: 1,370 . . . . (724) 947-8136

Housing: Homeownership rate: 68.3% (2010); Median home value: $99,600 (2006-2010 5-year est.); Median contract rent: $440 per month (2006-2010 5-year est.); Median year structure built: before 1940 (2006-2010 5-year est.).

Transportation: Commute to work: 94.9% car, 0.3% public transportation, 3.2% walk, 1.6% work from home (2006-2010 5-year est.); Travel time to work: 20.8% less than 15 minutes, 22.7% 15 to 30 minutes, 30.8% 30 to 45 minutes, 14.6% 45 to 60 minutes, 11.1% 60 minutes or more (2006-2010 5-year est.)

Additional Information Contacts
Pittsburgh Airport Area Chamber of Commerce . . . . (412) 264-6270
http://www.paacc.com

CALIFORNIA (borough). Covers a land area of 11.011 square miles and a water area of 0.220 square miles. Located at 40.07° N. Lat; 79.91° W. Long. Elevation is 787 feet.

History: Seat of California University of Pennsylvania. Laid out c. 1850, incorporated c. 1863.

Population: 5,748 (1990); 5,274 (2000); 6,795 (2010); Density: 617.1 persons per square mile (2010); Race: 91.0% White, 6.6% Black, 0.5% Asian, 0.2% American Indian/Alaska Native, 0.0% Native Hawaiian/Other Pacific Islander, 1.7% Other, 1.5% Hispanic of any race (2010); Average household size: 2.24 (2010); Median age: 21.5 (2010); Males per 100 females: 93.7 (2010); Marriage status: 56.6% never married, 32.4% now married, 6.0% widowed, 5.0% divorced (2006-2010 5-year est.); Foreign born: 2.5% (2006-2010 5-year est.); Ancestry (includes multiple ancestries): 24.0% Italian, 21.5% German, 11.5% Irish, 11.1% English, 10.4% Polish (2006-2010 5-year est.).

Economy: Single-family building permits issued: 1 (2011); Multi-family building permits issued: 0 (2011); Employment by occupation: 6.7% management, 1.5% professional, 18.0% services, 18.3% sales, 5.8% farming, 7.7% construction, 5.2% production (2006-2010 5-year est.).
Income: Per capita income: $17,379 (2006-2010 5-year est.); Median household income: $34,724 (2006-2010 5-year est.); Average household income: $44,199 (2006-2010 5-year est.); Percent of households with income of $100,000 or more: 9.2% (2006-2010 5-year est.); Poverty rate: 30.6% (2006-2010 5-year est.).
Education: Percent of population age 25 and over with: High school diploma (including GED) or higher: 88.8% (2006-2010 5-year est.); Bachelor's degree or higher: 39.2% (2006-2010 5-year est.); Master's degree or higher: 16.1% (2006-2010 5-year est.).

Four-year College(s)
California University of Pennsylvania (Public)
　Fall 2010 Enrollment: 9,007 . . . . (724) 938-4400
　2011-12 Tuition: In-state $8,912; Out-of-state $13,786
Housing: Homeownership rate: 42.2% (2010); Median home value: $111,600 (2006-2010 5-year est.); Median contract rent: $394 per month (2006-2010 5-year est.); Median year structure built: 1955 (2006-2010 5-year est.).
Safety: Violent crime rate: 29.3 per 10,000 population; Property crime rate: 171.6 per 10,000 population (2011).
Transportation: Commute to work: 82.7% car, 0.7% public transportation, 14.9% walk, 1.7% work from home (2006-2010 5-year est.); Travel time to work: 50.0% less than 15 minutes, 20.1% 15 to 30 minutes, 20.2% 30 to 45 minutes, 7.5% 45 to 60 minutes, 2.1% 60 minutes or more (2006-2010 5-year est.)

Additional Information Contacts
Borough of California . . . . (724) 938-8878
　http://www.californiapa.net
Mon Valley Regional Chamber of Commerce . . . . (724) 483-3507
　http://www.mvrchamber.org/directory-alpha/c-d.html

CANONSBURG (borough). Covers a land area of 2.310 square miles and a water area of 0 square miles. Located at 40.26° N. Lat; 80.19° W. Long. Elevation is 1,096 feet.
History: Its steel and coal industries have declined. A gram of radium produced here was presented to Marie Curie in 1921 when she visited the town. The Log Cabin School (established 1777; the first school west of the Allegheny Mts.) is preserved. The Black Horse Tavern was a famous gathering place for leaders of the Whiskey Rebellion (1794). Roberts House (1804) is an example of Western Pennsylvania manor architecture. Incorporated 1802.
Population: 9,200 (1990); 8,607 (2000); 8,992 (2010); Density: 3,892.6 persons per square mile (2010); Race: 87.4% White, 7.6% Black, 1.0% Asian, 0.1% American Indian/Alaska Native, 0.0% Native Hawaiian/Other Pacific Islander, 3.9% Other, 1.8% Hispanic of any race (2010); Average household size: 2.18 (2010); Median age: 39.6 (2010); Males per 100 females: 91.2 (2010); Marriage status: 28.9% never married, 49.8% now married, 9.3% widowed, 12.0% divorced (2006-2010 5-year est.); Foreign born: 3.0% (2006-2010 5-year est.); Ancestry (includes multiple ancestries): 25.7% German, 20.1% Italian, 15.3% Irish, 14.3% Polish, 8.9% English (2006-2010 5-year est.).
Economy: Single-family building permits issued: 11 (2011); Multi-family building permits issued: 0 (2011); Employment by occupation: 8.2% management, 4.1% professional, 11.9% services, 18.8% sales, 5.4% farming, 6.8% construction, 5.3% production (2006-2010 5-year est.).
Income: Per capita income: $22,286 (2006-2010 5-year est.); Median household income: $47,228 (2006-2010 5-year est.); Average household income: $49,841 (2006-2010 5-year est.); Percent of households with income of $100,000 or more: 6.9% (2006-2010 5-year est.); Poverty rate: 8.5% (2006-2010 5-year est.).
Education: Percent of population age 25 and over with: High school diploma (including GED) or higher: 88.4% (2006-2010 5-year est.); Bachelor's degree or higher: 23.3% (2006-2010 5-year est.); Master's degree or higher: 7.0% (2006-2010 5-year est.).

School District(s)
Canon-Mcmillan SD (KG-12)
　2010-11 Enrollment: 4,954 . . . . (724) 746-2940
Western Area CTC (10-12)
　2010-11 Enrollment: n/a . . . . (724) 746-2890

Vocational/Technical School(s)
Western Area Career and Technology Center (Public)
　Fall 2010 Enrollment: 143 . . . . (724) 746-2890
　2011-12 Tuition: $9,224
Housing: Homeownership rate: 56.6% (2010); Median home value: $115,200 (2006-2010 5-year est.); Median contract rent: $490 per month (2006-2010 5-year est.); Median year structure built: 1953 (2006-2010 5-year est.).
Hospitals: Canonsburg General Hospital (120 beds)
Transportation: Commute to work: 94.3% car, 0.7% public transportation, 2.0% walk, 1.6% work from home (2006-2010 5-year est.); Travel time to work: 34.9% less than 15 minutes, 38.1% 15 to 30 minutes, 13.0% 30 to 45 minutes, 7.0% 45 to 60 minutes, 7.0% 60 minutes or more (2006-2010 5-year est.)

Additional Information Contacts
Borough of Canonsburg . . . . (724) 745-1800
　http://www.canonsburgboro.com
Greater Canonsburg Chamber of Commerce . . . . (724) 745-1812
　http://www.canonchamber.com

CANTON (township). Covers a land area of 14.867 square miles and a water area of 0 square miles. Located at 40.20° N. Lat; 80.30° W. Long.
Population: 9,256 (1990); 8,826 (2000); 8,375 (2010); Density: 563.3 persons per square mile (2010); Race: 95.2% White, 3.0% Black, 0.1% Asian, 0.1% American Indian/Alaska Native, 0.0% Native Hawaiian/Other Pacific Islander, 1.6% Other, 1.1% Hispanic of any race (2010); Average household size: 2.36 (2010); Median age: 44.8 (2010); Males per 100 females: 92.2 (2010); Marriage status: 24.8% never married, 56.2% now married, 5.6% widowed, 13.4% divorced (2006-2010 5-year est.); Foreign born: 0.4% (2006-2010 5-year est.); Ancestry (includes multiple ancestries): 28.7% German, 22.8% Irish, 15.6% Italian, 13.1% Polish, 12.0% English (2006-2010 5-year est.).
Economy: Single-family building permits issued: 7 (2011); Multi-family building permits issued: 0 (2011); Employment by occupation: 10.3% management, 3.0% professional, 8.8% services, 23.8% sales, 2.3% farming, 12.5% construction, 9.6% production (2006-2010 5-year est.).
Income: Per capita income: $23,351 (2006-2010 5-year est.); Median household income: $51,125 (2006-2010 5-year est.); Average household income: $56,157 (2006-2010 5-year est.); Percent of households with income of $100,000 or more: 11.0% (2006-2010 5-year est.); Poverty rate: 12.0% (2006-2010 5-year est.).
Education: Percent of population age 25 and over with: High school diploma (including GED) or higher: 85.2% (2006-2010 5-year est.); Bachelor's degree or higher: 10.9% (2006-2010 5-year est.); Master's degree or higher: 2.6% (2006-2010 5-year est.).
Housing: Homeownership rate: 81.3% (2010); Median home value: $88,700 (2006-2010 5-year est.); Median contract rent: $343 per month (2006-2010 5-year est.); Median year structure built: 1965 (2006-2010 5-year est.).
Transportation: Commute to work: 95.8% car, 0.0% public transportation, 2.0% walk, 0.8% work from home (2006-2010 5-year est.); Travel time to work: 46.3% less than 15 minutes, 35.0% 15 to 30 minutes, 9.0% 30 to 45 minutes, 4.7% 45 to 60 minutes, 4.9% 60 minutes or more (2006-2010 5-year est.)

Additional Information Contacts
Canton Township . . . . (724) 225-8990
　http://www.yourcanton.com
Washington County Chamber of Commerce . . . . (724) 225-3010
　http://www.washcochamber.com

CARROLL (township). Covers a land area of 13.480 square miles and a water area of 0.298 square miles. Located at 40.17° N. Lat; 79.93° W. Long.
Population: 6,210 (1990); 5,677 (2000); 5,640 (2010); Density: 418.4 persons per square mile (2010); Race: 97.7% White, 1.1% Black, 0.2% Asian, 0.0% American Indian/Alaska Native, 0.0% Native Hawaiian/Other Pacific Islander, 1.0% Other, 1.2% Hispanic of any race (2010); Average household size: 2.32 (2010); Median age: 50.3 (2010); Males per 100 females: 92.5 (2010); Marriage status: 24.4% never married, 59.7% now married, 9.2% widowed, 6.7% divorced (2006-2010 5-year est.); Foreign born: 1.0% (2006-2010 5-year est.); Ancestry (includes multiple ancestries): 34.7% Italian, 24.4% German, 12.6% Polish, 12.2% English, 10.4% Irish (2006-2010 5-year est.).
Economy: Single-family building permits issued: 5 (2011); Multi-family building permits issued: 0 (2011); Employment by occupation: 13.0%

management, 2.6% professional, 7.6% services, 15.8% sales, 1.9% farming, 10.8% construction, 6.7% production (2006-2010 5-year est.).
Income: Per capita income: $28,429 (2006-2010 5-year est.); Median household income: $51,442 (2006-2010 5-year est.); Average household income: $69,341 (2006-2010 5-year est.); Percent of households with income of $100,000 or more: 21.4% (2006-2010 5-year est.); Poverty rate: 6.1% (2006-2010 5-year est.).
Education: Percent of population age 25 and over with: High school diploma (including GED) or higher: 89.3% (2006-2010 5-year est.); Bachelor's degree or higher: 22.7% (2006-2010 5-year est.); Master's degree or higher: 6.3% (2006-2010 5-year est.).
Housing: Homeownership rate: 86.8% (2010); Median home value: $118,400 (2006-2010 5-year est.); Median contract rent: $419 per month (2006-2010 5-year est.); Median year structure built: 1959 (2006-2010 5-year est.).
Safety: Violent crime rate: 37.1 per 10,000 population; Property crime rate: 102.5 per 10,000 population (2011).
Transportation: Commute to work: 93.3% car, 2.1% public transportation, 0.0% walk, 4.6% work from home (2006-2010 5-year est.); Travel time to work: 29.2% less than 15 minutes, 35.0% 15 to 30 minutes, 15.3% 30 to 45 minutes, 9.8% 45 to 60 minutes, 10.8% 60 minutes or more (2006-2010 5-year est.)
Additional Information Contacts
Mon Valley Regional Chamber of Commerce . . . . (724) 483-3507
 http://www.mvrchamber.org/directory-alpha/c-d.html

CECIL (township). Covers a land area of 26.296 square miles and a water area of 0.081 square miles. Located at 40.31° N. Lat; 80.19° W. Long. Elevation is 1,198 feet.
Population: 8,948 (1990); 9,756 (2000); 11,271 (2010); Density: 428.6 persons per square mile (2010); Race: 96.2% White, 1.7% Black, 0.7% Asian, 0.1% American Indian/Alaska Native, 0.0% Native Hawaiian/Other Pacific Islander, 1.3% Other, 0.7% Hispanic of any race (2010); Average household size: 2.49 (2010); Median age: 42.9 (2010); Males per 100 females: 96.2 (2010); Marriage status: 20.8% never married, 64.8% now married, 6.3% widowed, 8.2% divorced (2006-2010 5-year est.); Foreign born: 1.1% (2006-2010 5-year est.); Ancestry (includes multiple ancestries): 30.8% German, 24.1% Italian, 20.7% Irish, 16.9% Polish, 9.1% English (2006-2010 5-year est.).
Economy: Single-family building permits issued: 57 (2011); Multi-family building permits issued: 4 (2011); Employment by occupation: 14.0% management, 5.4% professional, 6.3% services, 19.2% sales, 3.2% farming, 11.0% construction, 6.9% production (2006-2010 5-year est.).
Income: Per capita income: $31,481 (2006-2010 5-year est.); Median household income: $62,966 (2006-2010 5-year est.); Average household income: $80,385 (2006-2010 5-year est.); Percent of households with income of $100,000 or more: 25.0% (2006-2010 5-year est.); Poverty rate: 5.0% (2006-2010 5-year est.).
Taxes: Total city taxes per capita: $420 (2009); City property taxes per capita: $208 (2009).
Education: Percent of population age 25 and over with: High school diploma (including GED) or higher: 92.8% (2006-2010 5-year est.); Bachelor's degree or higher: 33.1% (2006-2010 5-year est.); Master's degree or higher: 8.5% (2006-2010 5-year est.).
School District(s)
Canon-Mcmillan SD (KG-12)
 2010-11 Enrollment: 4,954 . . . . (724) 746-2940
Housing: Homeownership rate: 86.4% (2010); Median home value: $166,900 (2006-2010 5-year est.); Median contract rent: $493 per month (2006-2010 5-year est.); Median year structure built: 1980 (2006-2010 5-year est.).
Safety: Violent crime rate: 1.8 per 10,000 population; Property crime rate: 7.1 per 10,000 population (2011).
Transportation: Commute to work: 93.6% car, 1.2% public transportation, 0.6% walk, 3.5% work from home (2006-2010 5-year est.); Travel time to work: 24.5% less than 15 minutes, 38.0% 15 to 30 minutes, 20.7% 30 to 45 minutes, 9.1% 45 to 60 minutes, 7.8% 60 minutes or more (2006-2010 5-year est.)
Additional Information Contacts
Cecil Township . . . . (724) 745-2227
 http://www.ceciltownship-pa.gov
Greater Canonsburg Chamber of Commerce . . . . (724) 745-1812
 http://www.canonchamber.com

CECIL-BISHOP (CDP). Covers a land area of 2.541 square miles and a water area of 0 square miles. Located at 40.32° N. Lat; 80.19° W. Long.
Population: 2,701 (1990); 2,585 (2000); 2,476 (2010); Density: 974.3 persons per square mile (2010); Race: 97.6% White, 1.0% Black, 0.3% Asian, 0.0% American Indian/Alaska Native, 0.0% Native Hawaiian/Other Pacific Islander, 1.1% Other, 0.7% Hispanic of any race (2010); Average household size: 2.53 (2010); Median age: 44.4 (2010); Males per 100 females: 100.2 (2010); Marriage status: 18.4% never married, 68.7% now married, 6.2% widowed, 6.7% divorced (2006-2010 5-year est.); Foreign born: 0.9% (2006-2010 5-year est.); Ancestry (includes multiple ancestries): 32.1% German, 27.8% Italian, 20.8% Irish, 16.8% Polish, 10.3% English (2006-2010 5-year est.).
Economy: Employment by occupation: 8.5% management, 5.9% professional, 10.9% services, 27.2% sales, 4.8% farming, 13.4% construction, 3.5% production (2006-2010 5-year est.).
Income: Per capita income: $31,815 (2006-2010 5-year est.); Median household income: $58,696 (2006-2010 5-year est.); Average household income: $77,823 (2006-2010 5-year est.); Percent of households with income of $100,000 or more: 16.5% (2006-2010 5-year est.); Poverty rate: 4.2% (2006-2010 5-year est.).
Education: Percent of population age 25 and over with: High school diploma (including GED) or higher: 89.9% (2006-2010 5-year est.); Bachelor's degree or higher: 28.4% (2006-2010 5-year est.); Master's degree or higher: 2.1% (2006-2010 5-year est.).
Housing: Homeownership rate: 84.4% (2010); Median home value: $163,900 (2006-2010 5-year est.); Median contract rent: $563 per month (2006-2010 5-year est.); Median year structure built: 1976 (2006-2010 5-year est.).
Transportation: Commute to work: 90.8% car, 1.6% public transportation, 2.6% walk, 3.4% work from home (2006-2010 5-year est.); Travel time to work: 26.8% less than 15 minutes, 42.3% 15 to 30 minutes, 14.5% 30 to 45 minutes, 7.6% 45 to 60 minutes, 8.8% 60 minutes or more (2006-2010 5-year est.)
Additional Information Contacts
Greater Canonsburg Chamber of Commerce . . . . (724) 745-1812
 http://www.canonchamber.com

CENTERVILLE (borough). Covers a land area of 13.227 square miles and a water area of 0.385 square miles. Located at 40.03° N. Lat; 79.96° W. Long. Elevation is 1,178 feet.
History: Settled 1766, laid out 1821, incorporated 1895.
Population: 3,842 (1990); 3,390 (2000); 3,263 (2010); Density: 246.7 persons per square mile (2010); Race: 96.5% White, 1.2% Black, 0.2% Asian, 0.2% American Indian/Alaska Native, 0.0% Native Hawaiian/Other Pacific Islander, 1.9% Other, 1.1% Hispanic of any race (2010); Average household size: 2.42 (2010); Median age: 45.7 (2010); Males per 100 females: 92.5 (2010); Marriage status: 22.6% never married, 58.6% now married, 9.7% widowed, 9.1% divorced (2006-2010 5-year est.); Foreign born: 0.6% (2006-2010 5-year est.); Ancestry (includes multiple ancestries): 15.9% Hungarian, 14.7% German, 13.1% Polish, 12.8% Italian, 12.3% Irish (2006-2010 5-year est.).
Economy: Single-family building permits issued: 0 (2011); Multi-family building permits issued: 0 (2011); Employment by occupation: 8.6% management, 3.9% professional, 9.1% services, 16.9% sales, 5.2% farming, 17.6% construction, 5.9% production (2006-2010 5-year est.).
Income: Per capita income: $24,024 (2006-2010 5-year est.); Median household income: $47,200 (2006-2010 5-year est.); Average household income: $57,526 (2006-2010 5-year est.); Percent of households with income of $100,000 or more: 15.9% (2006-2010 5-year est.); Poverty rate: 5.9% (2006-2010 5-year est.).
Education: Percent of population age 25 and over with: High school diploma (including GED) or higher: 88.5% (2006-2010 5-year est.); Bachelor's degree or higher: 18.6% (2006-2010 5-year est.); Master's degree or higher: 6.7% (2006-2010 5-year est.).
Housing: Homeownership rate: 85.3% (2010); Median home value: $89,700 (2006-2010 5-year est.); Median contract rent: $448 per month (2006-2010 5-year est.); Median year structure built: 1944 (2006-2010 5-year est.).
Safety: Violent crime rate: 3.1 per 10,000 population; Property crime rate: 51.9 per 10,000 population (2011).
Transportation: Commute to work: 95.8% car, 0.0% public transportation, 1.9% walk, 2.3% work from home (2006-2010 5-year est.); Travel time to work: 18.5% less than 15 minutes, 28.9% 15 to 30 minutes, 27.5% 30 to

45 minutes, 7.8% 45 to 60 minutes, 17.2% 60 minutes or more (2006-2010 5-year est.)

Additional Information Contacts
Mon Valley Regional Chamber of Commerce . . . . (724) 483-3507
http://www.mvrchamber.org/directory-alpha/c-d.html

CHARLEROI (borough). Covers a land area of 0.762 square miles and a water area of 0.100 square miles. Located at 40.14° N. Lat; 79.90° W. Long. Elevation is 778 feet.
History: Laid out 1890, incorporated 1892.
Population: 5,014 (1990); 4,871 (2000); 4,120 (2010); Density: 5,405.9 persons per square mile (2010); Race: 90.0% White, 5.7% Black, 1.0% Asian, 0.1% American Indian/Alaska Native, 0.0% Native Hawaiian/Other Pacific Islander, 3.2% Other, 1.9% Hispanic of any race (2010); Average household size: 2.10 (2010); Median age: 42.0 (2010); Males per 100 females: 87.4 (2010); Marriage status: 35.8% never married, 43.2% now married, 10.5% widowed, 10.6% divorced (2006-2010 5-year est.); Foreign born: 0.9% (2006-2010 5-year est.); Ancestry (includes multiple ancestries): 22.9% German, 20.6% Italian, 14.2% Irish, 13.7% English, 8.3% Polish (2006-2010 5-year est.).
Economy: Single-family building permits issued: 0 (2011); Multi-family building permits issued: 0 (2011); Employment by occupation: 5.7% management, 0.0% professional, 15.9% services, 26.6% sales, 3.2% farming, 8.4% construction, 9.2% production (2006-2010 5-year est.).
Income: Per capita income: $17,291 (2006-2010 5-year est.); Median household income: $24,066 (2006-2010 5-year est.); Average household income: $35,158 (2006-2010 5-year est.); Percent of households with income of $100,000 or more: 3.9% (2006-2010 5-year est.); Poverty rate: 22.9% (2006-2010 5-year est.).
Education: Percent of population age 25 and over with: High school diploma (including GED) or higher: 87.6% (2006-2010 5-year est.); Bachelor's degree or higher: 12.1% (2006-2010 5-year est.); Master's degree or higher: 2.6% (2006-2010 5-year est.).

School District(s)
Charleroi SD (KG-12)
2010-11 Enrollment: 1,671 . . . . (724) 483-3509
Mon Valley CTC (10-12)
2010-11 Enrollment: n/a . . . . (724) 489-9581
Housing: Homeownership rate: 50.7% (2010); Median home value: $47,200 (2006-2010 5-year est.); Median contract rent: $348 per month (2006-2010 5-year est.); Median year structure built: before 1940 (2006-2010 5-year est.).
Safety: Violent crime rate: 58.6 per 10,000 population; Property crime rate: 442.3 per 10,000 population (2011).
Transportation: Commute to work: 80.3% car, 0.6% public transportation, 15.5% walk, 1.1% work from home (2006-2010 5-year est.); Travel time to work: 46.9% less than 15 minutes, 26.6% 15 to 30 minutes, 14.3% 30 to 45 minutes, 7.9% 45 to 60 minutes, 4.3% 60 minutes or more (2006-2010 5-year est.)

Additional Information Contacts
Borough of Charleroi . . . . (724) 483-6961
http://www.charleroiboro.org
Mon Valley Regional Chamber of Commerce . . . . (724) 483-3507
http://www.mvrchamber.org/directory-alpha/c-d.html

CHARTIERS (township). Covers a land area of 24.614 square miles and a water area of 0 square miles. Located at 40.25° N. Lat; 80.25° W. Long.
Population: 7,603 (1990); 7,154 (2000); 7,818 (2010); Density: 317.6 persons per square mile (2010); Race: 95.0% White, 2.8% Black, 0.2% Asian, 0.1% American Indian/Alaska Native, 0.0% Native Hawaiian/Other Pacific Islander, 1.9% Other, 1.3% Hispanic of any race (2010); Average household size: 2.35 (2010); Median age: 47.5 (2010); Males per 100 females: 92.6 (2010); Marriage status: 21.3% never married, 55.4% now married, 11.9% widowed, 11.4% divorced (2006-2010 5-year est.); Foreign born: 2.0% (2006-2010 5-year est.); Ancestry (includes multiple ancestries): 25.2% German, 20.7% Italian, 16.2% Polish, 14.7% Irish, 11.3% English (2006-2010 5-year est.).
Economy: Single-family building permits issued: 20 (2011); Multi-family building permits issued: 4 (2011); Employment by occupation: 11.2% management, 4.9% professional, 14.0% services, 20.1% sales, 3.3% farming, 8.6% construction, 4.7% production (2006-2010 5-year est.).
Income: Per capita income: $28,213 (2006-2010 5-year est.); Median household income: $53,977 (2006-2010 5-year est.); Average household income: $67,509 (2006-2010 5-year est.); Percent of households with income of $100,000 or more: 19.7% (2006-2010 5-year est.); Poverty rate: 5.5% (2006-2010 5-year est.).
Education: Percent of population age 25 and over with: High school diploma (including GED) or higher: 88.7% (2006-2010 5-year est.); Bachelor's degree or higher: 21.4% (2006-2010 5-year est.); Master's degree or higher: 5.9% (2006-2010 5-year est.).
Housing: Homeownership rate: 84.2% (2010); Median home value: $134,800 (2006-2010 5-year est.); Median contract rent: $568 per month (2006-2010 5-year est.); Median year structure built: 1965 (2006-2010 5-year est.).
Safety: Violent crime rate: 2.6 per 10,000 population; Property crime rate: 84.2 per 10,000 population (2011).
Transportation: Commute to work: 93.4% car, 0.5% public transportation, 2.3% walk, 3.2% work from home (2006-2010 5-year est.); Travel time to work: 35.9% less than 15 minutes, 39.1% 15 to 30 minutes, 12.7% 30 to 45 minutes, 8.6% 45 to 60 minutes, 3.8% 60 minutes or more (2006-2010 5-year est.)

Additional Information Contacts
Chartiers Township . . . . (724) 745-3415
http://www.chartierstwp.com
Washington County Chamber of Commerce . . . . (724) 225-3010
http://www.washcochamber.com

CLAYSVILLE (borough). Covers a land area of 0.309 square miles and a water area of 0.006 square miles. Located at 40.12° N. Lat; 80.41° W. Long. Elevation is 1,152 feet.
Population: 962 (1990); 724 (2000); 829 (2010); Density: 2,679.2 persons per square mile (2010); Race: 97.1% White, 0.5% Black, 0.4% Asian, 0.4% American Indian/Alaska Native, 0.0% Native Hawaiian/Other Pacific Islander, 1.6% Other, 0.6% Hispanic of any race (2010); Average household size: 2.36 (2010); Median age: 44.8 (2010); Males per 100 females: 103.7 (2010); Marriage status: 21.7% never married, 48.5% now married, 12.5% widowed, 17.3% divorced (2006-2010 5-year est.); Foreign born: 1.6% (2006-2010 5-year est.); Ancestry (includes multiple ancestries): 47.4% German, 20.7% English, 14.4% Italian, 11.5% Irish, 9.5% Polish (2006-2010 5-year est.).
Economy: Single-family building permits issued: 0 (2011); Multi-family building permits issued: 0 (2011); Employment by occupation: 8.0% management, 2.0% professional, 11.6% services, 9.6% sales, 3.6% farming, 18.4% construction, 4.4% production (2006-2010 5-year est.).
Income: Per capita income: $20,854 (2006-2010 5-year est.); Median household income: $56,071 (2006-2010 5-year est.); Average household income: $60,108 (2006-2010 5-year est.); Percent of households with income of $100,000 or more: 7.1% (2006-2010 5-year est.); Poverty rate: 1.6% (2006-2010 5-year est.).
Education: Percent of population age 25 and over with: High school diploma (including GED) or higher: 79.2% (2006-2010 5-year est.); Bachelor's degree or higher: 7.6% (2006-2010 5-year est.); Master's degree or higher: 2.9% (2006-2010 5-year est.).

School District(s)
Mcguffey SD (KG-12)
2010-11 Enrollment: 1,999 . . . . (724) 948-3731
Housing: Homeownership rate: 65.7% (2010); Median home value: $89,500 (2006-2010 5-year est.); Median contract rent: $538 per month (2006-2010 5-year est.); Median year structure built: before 1940 (2006-2010 5-year est.).
Safety: Violent crime rate: 0.0 per 10,000 population; Property crime rate: 72.1 per 10,000 population (2011).
Newspapers: The Weekly Recorder (Local news; Circulation 3,500)
Transportation: Commute to work: 96.8% car, 0.0% public transportation, 0.0% walk, 1.6% work from home (2006-2010 5-year est.); Travel time to work: 14.2% less than 15 minutes, 47.2% 15 to 30 minutes, 28.5% 30 to 45 minutes, 2.0% 45 to 60 minutes, 8.1% 60 minutes or more (2006-2010 5-year est.)

COAL CENTER (borough). Covers a land area of 0.114 square miles and a water area of 0.024 square miles. Located at 40.07° N. Lat; 79.90° W. Long. Elevation is 820 feet.
Population: 184 (1990); 134 (2000); 139 (2010); Density: 1,220.7 persons per square mile (2010); Race: 92.8% White, 2.9% Black, 0.7% Asian, 0.0% American Indian/Alaska Native, 0.0% Native Hawaiian/Other Pacific Islander, 3.6% Other, 0.0% Hispanic of any race (2010); Average household size: 2.14 (2010); Median age: 25.1 (2010); Males per 100 females: 117.2 (2010); Marriage status: 54.6% never married, 39.9% now married, 4.1% widowed, 1.4% divorced (2006-2010 5-year est.); Foreign

born: 0.0% (2006-2010 5-year est.); Ancestry (includes multiple ancestries): 16.8% Irish, 15.4% Dutch, 14.7% Russian, 13.3% Hungarian, 10.0% Italian (2006-2010 5-year est.).

Economy: Single-family building permits issued: 0 (2011); Multi-family building permits issued: 0 (2011); Employment by occupation: 3.2% management, 0.0% professional, 4.8% services, 21.8% sales, 15.3% farming, 5.6% construction, 2.4% production (2006-2010 5-year est.).

Income: Per capita income: $18,866 (2006-2010 5-year est.); Median household income: $31,645 (2006-2010 5-year est.); Average household income: $53,927 (2006-2010 5-year est.); Percent of households with income of $100,000 or more: 12.9% (2006-2010 5-year est.); Poverty rate: 42.3% (2006-2010 5-year est.).

Education: Percent of population age 25 and over with: High school diploma (including GED) or higher: 71.8% (2006-2010 5-year est.); Bachelor's degree or higher: 25.0% (2006-2010 5-year est.); Master's degree or higher: 18.5% (2006-2010 5-year est.).

School District(s)

California Area SD (KG-12)

   2010-11 Enrollment: 934 . . . . (724) 785-5800

Housing: Homeownership rate: 44.7% (2010); Median home value: $78,000 (2006-2010 5-year est.); Median contract rent: $813 per month (2006-2010 5-year est.); Median year structure built: 1949 (2006-2010 5-year est.).

Transportation: Commute to work: 96.8% car, 0.0% public transportation, 3.2% walk, 0.0% work from home (2006-2010 5-year est.); Travel time to work: 40.3% less than 15 minutes, 26.6% 15 to 30 minutes, 10.5% 30 to 45 minutes, 6.5% 45 to 60 minutes, 16.1% 60 minutes or more (2006-2010 5-year est.)

COKEBURG (borough). Covers a land area of 0.352 square miles and a water area of 0 square miles. Located at 40.10° N. Lat; 80.07° W. Long. Elevation is 1,142 feet.

History: Incorporated 1906.

Population: 750 (1990); 705 (2000); 630 (2010); Density: 1,791.9 persons per square mile (2010); Race: 97.0% White, 1.0% Black, 0.5% Asian, 0.0% American Indian/Alaska Native, 0.0% Native Hawaiian/Other Pacific Islander, 1.5% Other, 0.3% Hispanic of any race (2010); Average household size: 2.21 (2010); Median age: 41.8 (2010); Males per 100 females: 79.0 (2010); Marriage status: 26.8% never married, 50.6% now married, 8.5% widowed, 14.2% divorced (2006-2010 5-year est.); Foreign born: 0.8% (2006-2010 5-year est.); Ancestry (includes multiple ancestries): 25.9% Italian, 18.8% Irish, 18.3% German, 14.0% Polish, 8.5% American (2006-2010 5-year est.).

Economy: Single-family building permits issued: 2 (2011); Multi-family building permits issued: 0 (2011); Employment by occupation: 4.4% management, 3.7% professional, 22.1% services, 19.7% sales, 4.1% farming, 15.0% construction, 1.4% production (2006-2010 5-year est.).

Income: Per capita income: $20,351 (2006-2010 5-year est.); Median household income: $48,077 (2006-2010 5-year est.); Average household income: $47,020 (2006-2010 5-year est.); Percent of households with income of $100,000 or more: 1.0% (2006-2010 5-year est.); Poverty rate: 7.9% (2006-2010 5-year est.).

Education: Percent of population age 25 and over with: High school diploma (including GED) or higher: 80.2% (2006-2010 5-year est.); Bachelor's degree or higher: 8.4% (2006-2010 5-year est.); Master's degree or higher: 3.0% (2006-2010 5-year est.).

Housing: Homeownership rate: 68.1% (2010); Median home value: $73,100 (2006-2010 5-year est.); Median contract rent: $515 per month (2006-2010 5-year est.); Median year structure built: before 1940 (2006-2010 5-year est.).

Transportation: Commute to work: 98.9% car, 0.0% public transportation, 0.0% walk, 1.1% work from home (2006-2010 5-year est.); Travel time to work: 16.4% less than 15 minutes, 38.1% 15 to 30 minutes, 31.7% 30 to 45 minutes, 9.3% 45 to 60 minutes, 4.6% 60 minutes or more (2006-2010 5-year est.)

CROSS CREEK (CDP). Covers a land area of 0.363 square miles and a water area of 0 square miles. Located at 40.33° N. Lat; 80.41° W. Long. Elevation is 1,342 feet.

Population: n/a (1990); n/a (2000); 137 (2010); Density: 377.3 persons per square mile (2010); Race: 97.8% White, 2.2% Black, 0.0% Asian, 0.0% American Indian/Alaska Native, 0.0% Native Hawaiian/Other Pacific Islander, 0.0% Other, 5.1% Hispanic of any race (2010); Average household size: 2.49 (2010); Median age: 45.8 (2010); Males per 100 females: 95.7 (2010); Marriage status: 19.8% never married, 62.1% now

married, 5.2% widowed, 12.9% divorced (2006-2010 5-year est.); Foreign born: 0.0% (2006-2010 5-year est.); Ancestry (includes multiple ancestries): 38.4% German, 23.2% Irish, 21.7% French, 19.6% Scotch-Irish, 18.1% English (2006-2010 5-year est.).

Economy: Employment by occupation: 0.0% management, 4.6% professional, 4.6% services, 15.4% sales, 18.5% farming, 23.1% construction, 0.0% production (2006-2010 5-year est.).

Income: Per capita income: $23,971 (2006-2010 5-year est.); Median household income: $43,611 (2006-2010 5-year est.); Average household income: $57,122 (2006-2010 5-year est.); Percent of households with income of $100,000 or more: 15.5% (2006-2010 5-year est.); Poverty rate: 23.2% (2006-2010 5-year est.).

Education: Percent of population age 25 and over with: High school diploma (including GED) or higher: 81.8% (2006-2010 5-year est.); Bachelor's degree or higher: 3.0% (2006-2010 5-year est.); Master's degree or higher: 3.0% (2006-2010 5-year est.).

Housing: Homeownership rate: 94.6% (2010); Median home value: $98,300 (2006-2010 5-year est.); Median contract rent: <$101 per month (2006-2010 5-year est.); Median year structure built: before 1940 (2006-2010 5-year est.).

Transportation: Commute to work: 100.0% car, 0.0% public transportation, 0.0% walk, 0.0% work from home (2006-2010 5-year est.); Travel time to work: 11.3% less than 15 minutes, 14.5% 15 to 30 minutes, 50.0% 30 to 45 minutes, 19.4% 45 to 60 minutes, 4.8% 60 minutes or more (2006-2010 5-year est.)

CROSS CREEK (township). Covers a land area of 27.592 square miles and a water area of 0 square miles. Located at 40.30° N. Lat; 80.41° W. Long. Elevation is 1,342 feet.

Population: 1,581 (1990); 1,685 (2000); 1,556 (2010); Density: 56.4 persons per square mile (2010); Race: 98.2% White, 0.2% Black, 0.0% Asian, 0.1% American Indian/Alaska Native, 0.0% Native Hawaiian/Other Pacific Islander, 1.5% Other, 0.8% Hispanic of any race (2010); Average household size: 2.49 (2010); Median age: 46.5 (2010); Males per 100 females: 99.2 (2010); Marriage status: 25.4% never married, 61.0% now married, 8.2% widowed, 5.3% divorced (2006-2010 5-year est.); Foreign born: 1.0% (2006-2010 5-year est.); Ancestry (includes multiple ancestries): 22.5% German, 19.5% Italian, 18.6% Irish, 13.0% English, 11.5% Polish (2006-2010 5-year est.).

Economy: Single-family building permits issued: 0 (2011); Multi-family building permits issued: 0 (2011); Employment by occupation: 9.0% management, 1.3% professional, 9.5% services, 13.8% sales, 5.6% farming, 21.3% construction, 12.4% production (2006-2010 5-year est.).

Income: Per capita income: $23,464 (2006-2010 5-year est.); Median household income: $51,078 (2006-2010 5-year est.); Average household income: $61,297 (2006-2010 5-year est.); Percent of households with income of $100,000 or more: 17.1% (2006-2010 5-year est.); Poverty rate: 7.7% (2006-2010 5-year est.).

Education: Percent of population age 25 and over with: High school diploma (including GED) or higher: 86.9% (2006-2010 5-year est.); Bachelor's degree or higher: 12.0% (2006-2010 5-year est.); Master's degree or higher: 5.3% (2006-2010 5-year est.).

Housing: Homeownership rate: 83.4% (2010); Median home value: $133,300 (2006-2010 5-year est.); Median contract rent: $467 per month (2006-2010 5-year est.); Median year structure built: 1967 (2006-2010 5-year est.).

Transportation: Commute to work: 92.0% car, 0.5% public transportation, 2.9% walk, 4.1% work from home (2006-2010 5-year est.); Travel time to work: 15.5% less than 15 minutes, 16.2% 15 to 30 minutes, 43.0% 30 to 45 minutes, 11.3% 45 to 60 minutes, 13.9% 60 minutes or more (2006-2010 5-year est.)

Additional Information Contacts

Washington County Chamber of Commerce . . . . (724) 225-3010
   http://www.washcochamber.com

DEEMSTON (borough). Covers a land area of 9.589 square miles and a water area of 0 square miles. Located at 40.03° N. Lat; 80.03° W. Long. Elevation is 1,145 feet.

Population: 770 (1990); 809 (2000); 722 (2010); Density: 75.3 persons per square mile (2010); Race: 98.3% White, 0.3% Black, 0.3% Asian, 0.4% American Indian/Alaska Native, 0.0% Native Hawaiian/Other Pacific Islander, 0.7% Other, 0.8% Hispanic of any race (2010); Average household size: 2.37 (2010); Median age: 47.1 (2010); Males per 100 females: 100.0 (2010); Marriage status: 19.5% never married, 66.3% now married, 5.5% widowed, 8.7% divorced (2006-2010 5-year est.); Foreign

born: 0.0% (2006-2010 5-year est.); Ancestry (includes multiple ancestries): 34.2% German, 17.8% Irish, 15.5% English, 13.6% Italian, 8.4% Russian (2006-2010 5-year est.).

Economy: Single-family building permits issued: 1 (2011); Multi-family building permits issued: 0 (2011); Employment by occupation: 9.7% management, 1.7% professional, 13.0% services, 13.4% sales, 1.1% farming, 17.7% construction, 9.7% production (2006-2010 5-year est.).

Income: Per capita income: $26,016 (2006-2010 5-year est.); Median household income: $60,694 (2006-2010 5-year est.); Average household income: $62,040 (2006-2010 5-year est.); Percent of households with income of $100,000 or more: 11.8% (2006-2010 5-year est.); Poverty rate: 6.3% (2006-2010 5-year est.).

Education: Percent of population age 25 and over with: High school diploma (including GED) or higher: 91.7% (2006-2010 5-year est.); Bachelor's degree or higher: 26.2% (2006-2010 5-year est.); Master's degree or higher: 8.4% (2006-2010 5-year est.).

Housing: Homeownership rate: 92.4% (2010); Median home value: $147,000 (2006-2010 5-year est.); Median contract rent: $446 per month (2006-2010 5-year est.); Median year structure built: 1956 (2006-2010 5-year est.).

Transportation: Commute to work: 95.2% car, 1.2% public transportation, 0.8% walk, 1.2% work from home (2006-2010 5-year est.); Travel time to work: 16.9% less than 15 minutes, 22.2% 15 to 30 minutes, 35.3% 30 to 45 minutes, 12.1% 45 to 60 minutes, 13.5% 60 minutes or more (2006-2010 5-year est.)

DENBO (unincorporated postal area)

Zip Code: 15429

Covers a land area of 0.310 square miles and a water area of 0.163 square miles. Located at 40.00° N. Lat; 79.93° W. Long. Elevation is 791 feet. Population: 126 (2010); Density: 406.4 persons per square mile (2010); Race: 92.1% White, 1.6% Black, 0.0% Asian, 0.0% American Indian/Alaska Native, 0.0% Native Hawaiian/Other Pacific Islander, 6.3% Other, 0.0% Hispanic of any race (2010); Average household size: 2.52 (2010); Median age: 38.0 (2010); Males per 100 females: 88.1 (2010); Homeownership rate: 62.0% (2010)

DONEGAL (township). Covers a land area of 41.484 square miles and a water area of 0.173 square miles. Located at 40.14° N. Lat; 80.46° W. Long.

Population: 2,410 (1990); 2,428 (2000); 2,465 (2010); Density: 59.4 persons per square mile (2010); Race: 98.8% White, 0.3% Black, 0.1% Asian, 0.0% American Indian/Alaska Native, 0.0% Native Hawaiian/Other Pacific Islander, 0.8% Other, 0.5% Hispanic of any race (2010); Average household size: 2.50 (2010); Median age: 44.2 (2010); Males per 100 females: 98.3 (2010); Marriage status: 24.7% never married, 56.2% now married, 9.7% widowed, 9.4% divorced (2006-2010 5-year est.); Foreign born: 0.3% (2006-2010 5-year est.); Ancestry (includes multiple ancestries): 29.3% German, 21.2% Scotch-Irish, 13.4% Irish, 12.7% Italian, 11.9% English (2006-2010 5-year est.).

Economy: Single-family building permits issued: 4 (2011); Multi-family building permits issued: 0 (2011); Employment by occupation: 4.5% management, 4.4% professional, 12.2% services, 19.4% sales, 2.2% farming, 13.0% construction, 6.4% production (2006-2010 5-year est.).

Income: Per capita income: $19,588 (2006-2010 5-year est.); Median household income: $40,505 (2006-2010 5-year est.); Average household income: $50,291 (2006-2010 5-year est.); Percent of households with income of $100,000 or more: 11.8% (2006-2010 5-year est.); Poverty rate: 9.0% (2006-2010 5-year est.).

Education: Percent of population age 25 and over with: High school diploma (including GED) or higher: 89.1% (2006-2010 5-year est.); Bachelor's degree or higher: 6.8% (2006-2010 5-year est.); Master's degree or higher: 2.3% (2006-2010 5-year est.).

Housing: Homeownership rate: 84.5% (2010); Median home value: $98,700 (2006-2010 5-year est.); Median contract rent: $530 per month (2006-2010 5-year est.); Median year structure built: 1970 (2006-2010 5-year est.).

Safety: Violent crime rate: 0.0 per 10,000 population; Property crime rate: 40.4 per 10,000 population (2011).

Transportation: Commute to work: 96.8% car, 0.0% public transportation, 0.8% walk, 0.3% work from home (2006-2010 5-year est.); Travel time to work: 14.4% less than 15 minutes, 46.3% 15 to 30 minutes, 21.1% 30 to 45 minutes, 9.9% 45 to 60 minutes, 8.4% 60 minutes or more (2006-2010 5-year est.)

Additional Information Contacts

Washington County Chamber of Commerce . . . . (724) 225-3010
  http://www.washcochamber.com

DONORA (borough). Covers a land area of 1.899 square miles and a water area of 0.149 square miles. Located at 40.18° N. Lat; 79.86° W. Long. Elevation is 827 feet.

History: Incorporated 1901.

Population: 5,928 (1990); 5,653 (2000); 4,781 (2010); Density: 2,517.0 persons per square mile (2010); Race: 79.7% White, 15.1% Black, 0.4% Asian, 0.1% American Indian/Alaska Native, 0.0% Native Hawaiian/Other Pacific Islander, 4.7% Other, 3.1% Hispanic of any race (2010); Average household size: 2.23 (2010); Median age: 43.2 (2010); Males per 100 females: 83.2 (2010); Marriage status: 32.8% never married, 42.1% now married, 11.4% widowed, 13.7% divorced (2006-2010 5-year est.); Foreign born: 2.6% (2006-2010 5-year est.); Ancestry (includes multiple ancestries): 15.0% German, 14.3% Italian, 12.3% Slovak, 12.2% Irish, 9.7% Polish (2006-2010 5-year est.).

Economy: Single-family building permits issued: 0 (2011); Multi-family building permits issued: 0 (2011); Employment by occupation: 4.4% management, 1.9% professional, 15.4% services, 17.4% sales, 5.8% farming, 8.1% construction, 4.6% production (2006-2010 5-year est.).

Income: Per capita income: $18,050 (2006-2010 5-year est.); Median household income: $27,708 (2006-2010 5-year est.); Average household income: $38,460 (2006-2010 5-year est.); Percent of households with income of $100,000 or more: 5.5% (2006-2010 5-year est.); Poverty rate: 18.5% (2006-2010 5-year est.).

Education: Percent of population age 25 and over with: High school diploma (including GED) or higher: 84.1% (2006-2010 5-year est.); Bachelor's degree or higher: 14.7% (2006-2010 5-year est.); Master's degree or higher: 3.5% (2006-2010 5-year est.).

School District(s)

Ringgold SD (KG-12)
  2010-11 Enrollment: 3,057 . . . . (724) 258-9329

Housing: Homeownership rate: 61.5% (2010); Median home value: $50,000 (2006-2010 5-year est.); Median contract rent: $387 per month (2006-2010 5-year est.); Median year structure built: before 1940 (2006-2010 5-year est.).

Transportation: Commute to work: 89.1% car, 1.5% public transportation, 4.6% walk, 0.7% work from home (2006-2010 5-year est.); Travel time to work: 41.3% less than 15 minutes, 17.5% 15 to 30 minutes, 28.5% 30 to 45 minutes, 2.9% 45 to 60 minutes, 9.7% 60 minutes or more (2006-2010 5-year est.)

Additional Information Contacts

Borough of Donora . . . . (724) 379-6600
Washington County Chamber of Commerce . . . . (724) 225-3010
  http://www.washcochamber.com

DUNLEVY (borough). Covers a land area of 0.519 square miles and a water area of 0.059 square miles. Located at 40.11° N. Lat; 79.86° W. Long. Elevation is 781 feet.

Population: 417 (1990); 397 (2000); 381 (2010); Density: 734.1 persons per square mile (2010); Race: 97.6% White, 1.3% Black, 0.0% Asian, 0.0% American Indian/Alaska Native, 0.0% Native Hawaiian/Other Pacific Islander, 1.1% Other, 0.0% Hispanic of any race (2010); Average household size: 2.13 (2010); Median age: 48.4 (2010); Males per 100 females: 91.5 (2010); Marriage status: 32.6% never married, 47.0% now married, 10.8% widowed, 9.7% divorced (2006-2010 5-year est.); Foreign born: 0.0% (2006-2010 5-year est.); Ancestry (includes multiple ancestries): 31.4% Italian, 17.5% English, 16.8% Irish, 12.9% German, 9.6% Polish (2006-2010 5-year est.).

Economy: Single-family building permits issued: 1 (2011); Multi-family building permits issued: 0 (2011); Employment by occupation: 7.3% management, 1.5% professional, 18.2% services, 8.8% sales, 2.2% farming, 13.1% construction, 9.5% production (2006-2010 5-year est.).

Income: Per capita income: $22,055 (2006-2010 5-year est.); Median household income: $41,667 (2006-2010 5-year est.); Average household income: $45,303 (2006-2010 5-year est.); Percent of households with income of $100,000 or more: 4.2% (2006-2010 5-year est.); Poverty rate: 7.9% (2006-2010 5-year est.).

Education: Percent of population age 25 and over with: High school diploma (including GED) or higher: 89.8% (2006-2010 5-year est.); Bachelor's degree or higher: 12.7% (2006-2010 5-year est.); Master's degree or higher: 1.6% (2006-2010 5-year est.).

Housing: Homeownership rate: 78.8% (2010); Median home value: $73,300 (2006-2010 5-year est.); Median contract rent: $294 per month (2006-2010 5-year est.); Median year structure built: 1956 (2006-2010 5-year est.).

Transportation: Commute to work: 92.5% car, 0.0% public transportation, 3.8% walk, 2.3% work from home (2006-2010 5-year est.); Travel time to work: 45.4% less than 15 minutes, 23.8% 15 to 30 minutes, 19.2% 30 to 45 minutes, 8.5% 45 to 60 minutes, 3.1% 60 minutes or more (2006-2010 5-year est.)

EAST BETHLEHEM (township). Covers a land area of 5.065 square miles and a water area of 0.255 square miles. Located at 40.00° N. Lat; 80.02° W. Long.

Population: 2,799 (1990); 2,524 (2000); 2,354 (2010); Density: 464.7 persons per square mile (2010); Race: 95.1% White, 2.3% Black, 0.0% Asian, 0.3% American Indian/Alaska Native, 0.0% Native Hawaiian/Other Pacific Islander, 2.3% Other, 0.6% Hispanic of any race (2010); Average household size: 2.52 (2010); Median age: 39.5 (2010); Males per 100 females: 91.5 (2010); Marriage status: 24.6% never married, 57.4% now married, 6.8% widowed, 11.3% divorced (2006-2010 5-year est.); Foreign born: 2.3% (2006-2010 5-year est.); Ancestry (includes multiple ancestries): 21.8% Irish, 18.5% German, 13.9% Polish, 12.3% Italian, 8.9% English (2006-2010 5-year est.).

Economy: Single-family building permits issued: 0 (2011); Multi-family building permits issued: 0 (2011); Employment by occupation: 4.6% management, 2.9% professional, 15.2% services, 15.0% sales, 1.8% farming, 8.5% construction, 3.2% production (2006-2010 5-year est.).

Income: Per capita income: $22,248 (2006-2010 5-year est.); Median household income: $50,560 (2006-2010 5-year est.); Average household income: $53,940 (2006-2010 5-year est.); Percent of households with income of $100,000 or more: 18.0% (2006-2010 5-year est.); Poverty rate: 16.5% (2006-2010 5-year est.).

Education: Percent of population age 25 and over with: High school diploma (including GED) or higher: 84.4% (2006-2010 5-year est.); Bachelor's degree or higher: 12.3% (2006-2010 5-year est.); Master's degree or higher: 3.6% (2006-2010 5-year est.).

Housing: Homeownership rate: 78.9% (2010); Median home value: $87,500 (2006-2010 5-year est.); Median contract rent: $258 per month (2006-2010 5-year est.); Median year structure built: before 1940 (2006-2010 5-year est.).

Safety: Violent crime rate: 12.7 per 10,000 population; Property crime rate: 165.1 per 10,000 population (2011).

Transportation: Commute to work: 97.2% car, 1.1% public transportation, 1.2% walk, 0.6% work from home (2006-2010 5-year est.); Travel time to work: 21.5% less than 15 minutes, 24.1% 15 to 30 minutes, 31.0% 30 to 45 minutes, 16.2% 45 to 60 minutes, 7.1% 60 minutes or more (2006-2010 5-year est.)

Additional Information Contacts

Waynesburg Area Chamber of Commerce . . . . (724) 627-5926
http://www.waynesburgchamber.com

EAST FINLEY (township). Covers a land area of 35.114 square miles and a water area of 0 square miles. Located at 40.05° N. Lat; 80.39° W. Long. Elevation is 1,106 feet.

Population: 1,479 (1990); 1,489 (2000); 1,392 (2010); Density: 39.6 persons per square mile (2010); Race: 98.6% White, 0.1% Black, 0.0% Asian, 0.0% American Indian/Alaska Native, 0.0% Native Hawaiian/Other Pacific Islander, 1.3% Other, 0.9% Hispanic of any race (2010); Average household size: 2.68 (2010); Median age: 40.4 (2010); Males per 100 females: 103.8 (2010); Marriage status: 24.0% never married, 59.4% now married, 8.3% widowed, 8.2% divorced (2006-2010 5-year est.); Foreign born: 0.3% (2006-2010 5-year est.); Ancestry (includes multiple ancestries): 24.5% German, 20.1% Irish, 12.5% Scotch-Irish, 9.5% American, 9.2% Polish (2006-2010 5-year est.).

Economy: Single-family building permits issued: 3 (2011); Multi-family building permits issued: 0 (2011); Employment by occupation: 10.0% management, 2.6% professional, 10.2% services, 15.2% sales, 3.1% farming, 18.0% construction, 8.7% production (2006-2010 5-year est.).

Income: Per capita income: $19,445 (2006-2010 5-year est.); Median household income: $47,750 (2006-2010 5-year est.); Average household income: $53,598 (2006-2010 5-year est.); Percent of households with income of $100,000 or more: 9.1% (2006-2010 5-year est.); Poverty rate: 9.4% (2006-2010 5-year est.).

Education: Percent of population age 25 and over with: High school diploma (including GED) or higher: 84.4% (2006-2010 5-year est.);

Bachelor's degree or higher: 10.3% (2006-2010 5-year est.); Master's degree or higher: 4.6% (2006-2010 5-year est.).

Housing: Homeownership rate: 73.7% (2010); Median home value: $149,800 (2006-2010 5-year est.); Median contract rent: $429 per month (2006-2010 5-year est.); Median year structure built: 1977 (2006-2010 5-year est.).

Transportation: Commute to work: 95.6% car, 0.0% public transportation, 1.9% walk, 2.4% work from home (2006-2010 5-year est.); Travel time to work: 13.1% less than 15 minutes, 35.7% 15 to 30 minutes, 28.9% 30 to 45 minutes, 11.1% 45 to 60 minutes, 11.2% 60 minutes or more (2006-2010 5-year est.)

Additional Information Contacts

Washington County Chamber of Commerce . . . . (724) 225-3010
http://www.washcochamber.com

EAST WASHINGTON (borough). Covers a land area of 0.449 square miles and a water area of 0 square miles. Located at 40.17° N. Lat; 80.23° W. Long. Elevation is 1,142 feet.

History: Incorporated 1892.

Population: 2,156 (1990); 1,930 (2000); 2,234 (2010); Density: 4,977.0 persons per square mile (2010); Race: 90.3% White, 5.3% Black, 1.0% Asian, 0.1% American Indian/Alaska Native, 0.0% Native Hawaiian/Other Pacific Islander, 3.3% Other, 2.0% Hispanic of any race (2010); Average household size: 2.08 (2010); Median age: 32.3 (2010); Males per 100 females: 78.3 (2010); Marriage status: 50.6% never married, 40.9% now married, 3.7% widowed, 4.8% divorced (2006-2010 5-year est.); Foreign born: 0.8% (2006-2010 5-year est.); Ancestry (includes multiple ancestries): 31.9% German, 26.4% Italian, 22.7% Irish, 12.9% English, 7.0% Scotch-Irish (2006-2010 5-year est.).

Economy: Single-family building permits issued: 0 (2011); Multi-family building permits issued: 0 (2011); Employment by occupation: 14.1% management, 1.8% professional, 7.2% services, 17.7% sales, 7.6% farming, 3.8% construction, 3.0% production (2006-2010 5-year est.).

Income: Per capita income: $30,766 (2006-2010 5-year est.); Median household income: $70,495 (2006-2010 5-year est.); Average household income: $87,398 (2006-2010 5-year est.); Percent of households with income of $100,000 or more: 28.7% (2006-2010 5-year est.); Poverty rate: 13.0% (2006-2010 5-year est.).

Education: Percent of population age 25 and over with: High school diploma (including GED) or higher: 95.0% (2006-2010 5-year est.); Bachelor's degree or higher: 58.5% (2006-2010 5-year est.); Master's degree or higher: 26.3% (2006-2010 5-year est.).

Housing: Homeownership rate: 51.6% (2010); Median home value: $196,300 (2006-2010 5-year est.); Median contract rent: $514 per month (2006-2010 5-year est.); Median year structure built: before 1940 (2006-2010 5-year est.).

Safety: Violent crime rate: 35.7 per 10,000 population; Property crime rate: 196.3 per 10,000 population (2011).

Transportation: Commute to work: 70.6% car, 0.0% public transportation, 23.4% walk, 4.9% work from home (2006-2010 5-year est.); Travel time to work: 63.9% less than 15 minutes, 19.7% 15 to 30 minutes, 5.6% 30 to 45 minutes, 6.3% 45 to 60 minutes, 4.5% 60 minutes or more (2006-2010 5-year est.)

Additional Information Contacts

Washington County Chamber of Commerce . . . . (724) 225-3010
http://www.washcochamber.com

EIGHTY FOUR (CDP). Covers a land area of 6.601 square miles and a water area of 0 square miles. Located at 40.18° N. Lat; 80.13° W. Long. Elevation is 1,033 feet.

Population: n/a (1990); n/a (2000); 657 (2010); Density: 99.5 persons per square mile (2010); Race: 98.9% White, 0.6% Black, 0.2% Asian, 0.0% American Indian/Alaska Native, 0.0% Native Hawaiian/Other Pacific Islander, 0.3% Other, 0.3% Hispanic of any race (2010); Average household size: 2.38 (2010); Median age: 47.8 (2010); Males per 100 females: 109.9 (2010); Marriage status: 22.3% never married, 67.0% now married, 5.8% widowed, 4.9% divorced (2006-2010 5-year est.); Foreign born: 1.1% (2006-2010 5-year est.); Ancestry (includes multiple ancestries): 35.7% Irish, 35.1% German, 16.9% English, 14.9% Italian, 8.2% Slovak (2006-2010 5-year est.).

Economy: Employment by occupation: 1.9% management, 0.0% professional, 18.0% services, 12.4% sales, 4.0% farming, 5.3% construction, 0.0% production (2006-2010 5-year est.).

Income: Per capita income: $24,239 (2006-2010 5-year est.); Median household income: $50,926 (2006-2010 5-year est.); Average household

income: $62,010 (2006-2010 5-year est.); Percent of households with income of $100,000 or more: 13.5% (2006-2010 5-year est.); Poverty rate: 0.0% (2006-2010 5-year est.).

Education: Percent of population age 25 and over with: High school diploma (including GED) or higher: 90.0% (2006-2010 5-year est.); Bachelor's degree or higher: 13.4% (2006-2010 5-year est.); Master's degree or higher: 4.4% (2006-2010 5-year est.).

School District(s)

Canon-Mcmillan SD (KG-12)

   2010-11 Enrollment: 4,954 . . . . (724) 746-2940

Housing: Homeownership rate: 82.2% (2010); Median home value: $165,100 (2006-2010 5-year est.); Median contract rent: $654 per month (2006-2010 5-year est.); Median year structure built: 1971 (2006-2010 5-year est.).

Transportation: Commute to work: 93.5% car, 0.0% public transportation, 0.0% walk, 6.5% work from home (2006-2010 5-year est.); Travel time to work: 22.6% less than 15 minutes, 35.2% 15 to 30 minutes, 23.6% 30 to 45 minutes, 15.9% 45 to 60 minutes, 2.7% 60 minutes or more (2006-2010 5-year est.)

ELCO (borough). Aka Wood Run. Covers a land area of 0.276 square miles and a water area of 0.079 square miles. Located at 40.08° N. Lat; 79.88° W. Long. Elevation is 764 feet.

Population: 341 (1990); 362 (2000); 323 (2010); Density: 1,171.0 persons per square mile (2010); Race: 98.1% White, 0.6% Black, 0.3% Asian, 0.0% American Indian/Alaska Native, 0.0% Native Hawaiian/Other Pacific Islander, 1.0% Other, 0.0% Hispanic of any race (2010); Average household size: 2.25 (2010); Median age: 49.3 (2010); Males per 100 females: 81.5 (2010); Marriage status: 21.3% never married, 53.2% now married, 11.1% widowed, 14.5% divorced (2006-2010 5-year est.); Foreign born: 0.0% (2006-2010 5-year est.); Ancestry (includes multiple ancestries): 30.2% German, 21.4% English, 16.7% Italian, 9.3% Slovak, 7.5% Scotch-Irish (2006-2010 5-year est.).

Economy: Single-family building permits issued: 0 (2011); Multi-family building permits issued: 0 (2011); Employment by occupation: 16.2% management, 7.7% professional, 12.8% services, 10.3% sales, 5.1% farming, 10.3% construction, 0.0% production (2006-2010 5-year est.).

Income: Per capita income: $19,879 (2006-2010 5-year est.); Median household income: $31,000 (2006-2010 5-year est.); Average household income: $41,807 (2006-2010 5-year est.); Percent of households with income of $100,000 or more: 6.4% (2006-2010 5-year est.); Poverty rate: 12.1% (2006-2010 5-year est.).

Education: Percent of population age 25 and over with: High school diploma (including GED) or higher: 87.4% (2006-2010 5-year est.); Bachelor's degree or higher: 14.4% (2006-2010 5-year est.); Master's degree or higher: 7.2% (2006-2010 5-year est.).

Housing: Homeownership rate: 75.1% (2010); Median home value: $67,100 (2006-2010 5-year est.); Median contract rent: $468 per month (2006-2010 5-year est.); Median year structure built: before 1940 (2006-2010 5-year est.).

Transportation: Commute to work: 99.1% car, 0.0% public transportation, 0.0% walk, 0.9% work from home (2006-2010 5-year est.); Travel time to work: 28.4% less than 15 minutes, 19.8% 15 to 30 minutes, 14.7% 30 to 45 minutes, 4.3% 45 to 60 minutes, 32.8% 60 minutes or more (2006-2010 5-year est.)

ELLSWORTH (borough). Covers a land area of 0.739 square miles and a water area of 0.017 square miles. Located at 40.11° N. Lat; 80.02° W. Long. Elevation is 997 feet.

History: Incorporated 1900.

Population: 1,048 (1990); 1,083 (2000); 1,027 (2010); Density: 1,389.5 persons per square mile (2010); Race: 95.9% White, 2.4% Black, 0.0% Asian, 0.1% American Indian/Alaska Native, 0.0% Native Hawaiian/Other Pacific Islander, 1.6% Other, 0.8% Hispanic of any race (2010); Average household size: 2.34 (2010); Median age: 40.7 (2010); Males per 100 females: 98.6 (2010); Marriage status: 30.1% never married, 57.1% now married, 6.3% widowed, 6.4% divorced (2006-2010 5-year est.); Foreign born: 0.0% (2006-2010 5-year est.); Ancestry (includes multiple ancestries): 30.0% German, 27.6% Italian, 16.8% Irish, 11.8% Polish, 8.9% Russian (2006-2010 5-year est.).

Economy: Single-family building permits issued: 0 (2011); Multi-family building permits issued: 0 (2011); Employment by occupation: 13.3% management, 3.3% professional, 14.3% services, 16.4% sales, 0.0% farming, 14.5% construction, 12.2% production (2006-2010 5-year est.).

Income: Per capita income: $18,232 (2006-2010 5-year est.); Median household income: $32,386 (2006-2010 5-year est.); Average household income: $42,367 (2006-2010 5-year est.); Percent of households with income of $100,000 or more: 5.2% (2006-2010 5-year est.); Poverty rate: 12.8% (2006-2010 5-year est.).

Education: Percent of population age 25 and over with: High school diploma (including GED) or higher: 87.8% (2006-2010 5-year est.); Bachelor's degree or higher: 23.3% (2006-2010 5-year est.); Master's degree or higher: 8.1% (2006-2010 5-year est.).

Housing: Homeownership rate: 68.4% (2010); Median home value: $77,100 (2006-2010 5-year est.); Median contract rent: $396 per month (2006-2010 5-year est.); Median year structure built: before 1940 (2006-2010 5-year est.).

Transportation: Commute to work: 94.9% car, 0.0% public transportation, 0.0% walk, 2.4% work from home (2006-2010 5-year est.); Travel time to work: 36.1% less than 15 minutes, 28.2% 15 to 30 minutes, 18.1% 30 to 45 minutes, 11.1% 45 to 60 minutes, 6.4% 60 minutes or more (2006-2010 5-year est.)

ELRAMA (CDP). Covers a land area of 0.149 square miles and a water area of 0 square miles. Located at 40.25° N. Lat; 79.92° W. Long. Elevation is 837 feet.

Population: n/a (1990); n/a (2000); 307 (2010); Density: 2,065.8 persons per square mile (2010); Race: 99.3% White, 0.0% Black, 0.0% Asian, 0.7% American Indian/Alaska Native, 0.0% Native Hawaiian/Other Pacific Islander, 0.0% Other, 0.0% Hispanic of any race (2010); Average household size: 2.29 (2010); Median age: 44.9 (2010); Males per 100 females: 96.8 (2010); Marriage status: 33.1% never married, 52.8% now married, 0.0% widowed, 14.2% divorced (2006-2010 5-year est.); Foreign born: 0.0% (2006-2010 5-year est.); Ancestry (includes multiple ancestries): 37.9% Italian, 25.6% German, 17.1% Irish, 16.7% Slovak, 10.6% American (2006-2010 5-year est.).

Economy: Employment by occupation: 0.0% management, 0.0% professional, 20.7% services, 17.9% sales, 0.0% farming, 25.7% construction, 8.6% production (2006-2010 5-year est.).

Income: Per capita income: $16,605 (2006-2010 5-year est.); Median household income: $50,130 (2006-2010 5-year est.); Average household income: $42,537 (2006-2010 5-year est.); Percent of households with income of $100,000 or more: n/a (2006-2010 5-year est.); Poverty rate: 4.4% (2006-2010 5-year est.).

Education: Percent of population age 25 and over with: High school diploma (including GED) or higher: 73.7% (2006-2010 5-year est.); Bachelor's degree or higher: 0.0% (2006-2010 5-year est.); Master's degree or higher: 0.0% (2006-2010 5-year est.).

Housing: Homeownership rate: 81.3% (2010); Median home value: $104,300 (2006-2010 5-year est.); Median contract rent: n/a per month (2006-2010 5-year est.); Median year structure built: 1956 (2006-2010 5-year est.).

Transportation: Commute to work: 100.0% car, 0.0% public transportation, 0.0% walk, 0.0% work from home (2006-2010 5-year est.); Travel time to work: 18.6% less than 15 minutes, 62.1% 15 to 30 minutes, 19.3% 30 to 45 minutes, 0.0% 45 to 60 minutes, 0.0% 60 minutes or more (2006-2010 5-year est.)

FALLOWFIELD (township). Covers a land area of 21.272 square miles and a water area of 0.047 square miles. Located at 40.14° N. Lat; 79.97° W. Long.

Population: 4,972 (1990); 4,461 (2000); 4,321 (2010); Density: 203.1 persons per square mile (2010); Race: 97.1% White, 1.6% Black, 0.1% Asian, 0.0% American Indian/Alaska Native, 0.0% Native Hawaiian/Other Pacific Islander, 1.2% Other, 0.8% Hispanic of any race (2010); Average household size: 2.40 (2010); Median age: 47.4 (2010); Males per 100 females: 98.1 (2010); Marriage status: 24.2% never married, 60.0% now married, 9.3% widowed, 6.5% divorced (2006-2010 5-year est.); Foreign born: 0.5% (2006-2010 5-year est.); Ancestry (includes multiple ancestries): 26.8% German, 21.8% Irish, 21.6% Italian, 14.5% English, 10.4% Polish (2006-2010 5-year est.).

Economy: Single-family building permits issued: 3 (2011); Multi-family building permits issued: 0 (2011); Employment by occupation: 7.0% management, 6.4% professional, 8.0% services, 14.2% sales, 6.2% farming, 11.7% construction, 10.6% production (2006-2010 5-year est.).

Income: Per capita income: $24,436 (2006-2010 5-year est.); Median household income: $46,056 (2006-2010 5-year est.); Average household income: $57,583 (2006-2010 5-year est.); Percent of households with

income of $100,000 or more: 15.4% (2006-2010 5-year est.); Poverty rate: 7.8% (2006-2010 5-year est.).

Education: Percent of population age 25 and over with: High school diploma (including GED) or higher: 90.6% (2006-2010 5-year est.); Bachelor's degree or higher: 17.2% (2006-2010 5-year est.); Master's degree or higher: 4.6% (2006-2010 5-year est.).

Housing: Homeownership rate: 89.4% (2010); Median home value: $98,600 (2006-2010 5-year est.); Median contract rent: $346 per month (2006-2010 5-year est.); Median year structure built: 1955 (2006-2010 5-year est.).

Transportation: Commute to work: 97.3% car, 0.5% public transportation, 0.6% walk, 1.0% work from home (2006-2010 5-year est.); Travel time to work: 30.1% less than 15 minutes, 36.5% 15 to 30 minutes, 15.9% 30 to 45 minutes, 8.1% 45 to 60 minutes, 9.4% 60 minutes or more (2006-2010 5-year est.)

Additional Information Contacts

Mon Valley Regional Chamber of Commerce . . . . (724) 483-3507
http://www.mvrchamber.org

FINLEYVILLE (borough). Covers a land area of 0.167 square miles and a water area of 0 square miles. Located at 40.25° N. Lat; 80.00° W. Long. Elevation is 955 feet.

Population: 446 (1990); 459 (2000); 461 (2010); Density: 2,756.1 persons per square mile (2010); Race: 93.3% White, 4.1% Black, 0.7% Asian, 0.0% American Indian/Alaska Native, 0.0% Native Hawaiian/Other Pacific Islander, 1.9% Other, 2.0% Hispanic of any race (2010); Average household size: 1.87 (2010); Median age: 40.8 (2010); Males per 100 females: 103.1 (2010); Marriage status: 29.1% never married, 36.9% now married, 11.0% widowed, 23.1% divorced (2006-2010 5-year est.); Foreign born: 7.3% (2006-2010 5-year est.); Ancestry (includes multiple ancestries): 41.2% German, 20.4% Italian, 15.1% Irish, 12.8% English, 9.5% Scotch-Irish (2006-2010 5-year est.).

Economy: Single-family building permits issued: 0 (2011); Multi-family building permits issued: 0 (2011); Employment by occupation: 3.9% management, 2.6% professional, 10.5% services, 15.8% sales, 2.6% farming, 12.7% construction, 18.0% production (2006-2010 5-year est.).

Income: Per capita income: $21,291 (2006-2010 5-year est.); Median household income: $30,469 (2006-2010 5-year est.); Average household income: $36,514 (2006-2010 5-year est.); Percent of households with income of $100,000 or more: 3.0% (2006-2010 5-year est.); Poverty rate: 20.6% (2006-2010 5-year est.).

Education: Percent of population age 25 and over with: High school diploma (including GED) or higher: 97.1% (2006-2010 5-year est.); Bachelor's degree or higher: 23.7% (2006-2010 5-year est.); Master's degree or higher: 4.5% (2006-2010 5-year est.).

School District(s)

Ringgold SD (KG-12)
    2010-11 Enrollment: 3,057 . . . . (724) 258-9329

Housing: Homeownership rate: 47.4% (2010); Median home value: $104,800 (2006-2010 5-year est.); Median contract rent: $476 per month (2006-2010 5-year est.); Median year structure built: 1940 (2006-2010 5-year est.).

Transportation: Commute to work: 74.6% car, 8.3% public transportation, 14.5% walk, 2.6% work from home (2006-2010 5-year est.); Travel time to work: 29.7% less than 15 minutes, 35.6% 15 to 30 minutes, 9.0% 30 to 45 minutes, 12.6% 45 to 60 minutes, 13.1% 60 minutes or more (2006-2010 5-year est.)

FREDERICKTOWN (CDP). Covers a land area of 0.970 square miles and a water area of 0 square miles. Located at 40.00° N. Lat; 80.01° W. Long. Elevation is 791 feet.

Population: n/a (1990); n/a (2000); 403 (2010); Density: 415.3 persons per square mile (2010); Race: 92.8% White, 5.2% Black, 0.0% Asian, 0.2% American Indian/Alaska Native, 0.0% Native Hawaiian/Other Pacific Islander, 1.8% Other, 1.2% Hispanic of any race (2010); Average household size: 2.44 (2010); Median age: 40.4 (2010); Males per 100 females: 95.6 (2010); Marriage status: 37.3% never married, 42.7% now married, 9.7% widowed, 10.3% divorced (2006-2010 5-year est.); Foreign born: 2.5% (2006-2010 5-year est.); Ancestry (includes multiple ancestries): 24.7% Irish, 15.9% German, 13.6% English, 12.4% Dutch, 11.1% Italian (2006-2010 5-year est.).

Economy: Employment by occupation: 0.0% management, 0.0% professional, 6.9% services, 5.2% sales, 0.0% farming, 10.4% construction, 0.0% production (2006-2010 5-year est.).

Income: Per capita income: $17,098 (2006-2010 5-year est.); Median household income: $34,318 (2006-2010 5-year est.); Average household income: $46,999 (2006-2010 5-year est.); Percent of households with income of $100,000 or more: 15.2% (2006-2010 5-year est.); Poverty rate: 19.9% (2006-2010 5-year est.).

Education: Percent of population age 25 and over with: High school diploma (including GED) or higher: 95.4% (2006-2010 5-year est.); Bachelor's degree or higher: 17.6% (2006-2010 5-year est.); Master's degree or higher: 9.9% (2006-2010 5-year est.).

School District(s)

Bethlehem-Center SD (PK-12)
    2010-11 Enrollment: 1,343 . . . . (724) 267-4910

Housing: Homeownership rate: 74.6% (2010); Median home value: $93,200 (2006-2010 5-year est.); Median contract rent: <$101 per month (2006-2010 5-year est.); Median year structure built: before 1940 (2006-2010 5-year est.).

Transportation: Commute to work: 91.6% car, 5.4% public transportation, 0.0% walk, 3.0% work from home (2006-2010 5-year est.); Travel time to work: 21.7% less than 15 minutes, 23.6% 15 to 30 minutes, 39.8% 30 to 45 minutes, 11.8% 45 to 60 minutes, 3.1% 60 minutes or more (2006-2010 5-year est.)

GASTONVILLE (CDP). Covers a land area of 2.724 square miles and a water area of 0 square miles. Located at 40.27° N. Lat; 80.01° W. Long. Elevation is 978 feet.

Population: 3,090 (1990); 3,002 (2000); 2,818 (2010); Density: 1,034.3 persons per square mile (2010); Race: 97.9% White, 0.6% Black, 0.4% Asian, 0.1% American Indian/Alaska Native, 0.0% Native Hawaiian/Other Pacific Islander, 1.0% Other, 0.9% Hispanic of any race (2010); Average household size: 2.20 (2010); Median age: 49.2 (2010); Males per 100 females: 92.4 (2010); Marriage status: 25.7% never married, 55.2% now married, 8.5% widowed, 10.6% divorced (2006-2010 5-year est.); Foreign born: 0.3% (2006-2010 5-year est.); Ancestry (includes multiple ancestries): 38.0% German, 28.6% Irish, 18.8% Italian, 15.1% English, 9.9% Polish (2006-2010 5-year est.).

Economy: Employment by occupation: 4.1% management, 2.4% professional, 10.6% services, 21.2% sales, 4.5% farming, 15.3% construction, 5.9% production (2006-2010 5-year est.).

Income: Per capita income: $23,567 (2006-2010 5-year est.); Median household income: $47,061 (2006-2010 5-year est.); Average household income: $55,127 (2006-2010 5-year est.); Percent of households with income of $100,000 or more: 17.5% (2006-2010 5-year est.); Poverty rate: 9.4% (2006-2010 5-year est.).

Education: Percent of population age 25 and over with: High school diploma (including GED) or higher: 94.3% (2006-2010 5-year est.); Bachelor's degree or higher: 17.6% (2006-2010 5-year est.); Master's degree or higher: 5.2% (2006-2010 5-year est.).

Housing: Homeownership rate: 88.1% (2010); Median home value: $124,400 (2006-2010 5-year est.); Median contract rent: $537 per month (2006-2010 5-year est.); Median year structure built: 1968 (2006-2010 5-year est.).

Transportation: Commute to work: 87.3% car, 6.3% public transportation, 0.0% walk, 4.7% work from home (2006-2010 5-year est.); Travel time to work: 15.5% less than 15 minutes, 33.6% 15 to 30 minutes, 26.5% 30 to 45 minutes, 7.8% 45 to 60 minutes, 16.6% 60 minutes or more (2006-2010 5-year est.)

Additional Information Contacts

South West Communities Chamber of Commerce . . . . (412) 221-4100
http://www.swccoc.org

GREEN HILLS (borough). Covers a land area of 0.923 square miles and a water area of 0.015 square miles. Located at 40.12° N. Lat; 80.31° W. Long. Elevation is 1,230 feet.

Population: 21 (1990); 18 (2000); 29 (2010); Density: 31.4 persons per square mile (2010); Race: 100.0% White, 0.0% Black, 0.0% Asian, 0.0% American Indian/Alaska Native, 0.0% Native Hawaiian/Other Pacific Islander, 0.0% Other, 0.0% Hispanic of any race (2010); Average household size: 3.22 (2010); Median age: 35.5 (2010); Males per 100 females: 107.1 (2010); Marriage status: 14.3% never married, 85.7% now married, 0.0% widowed, 0.0% divorced (2006-2010 5-year est.); Foreign born: 0.0% (2006-2010 5-year est.); Ancestry (includes multiple ancestries): 42.9% Irish, 42.9% English, 28.6% German, 14.3% Welsh, 14.3% Scotch-Irish (2006-2010 5-year est.).

Economy: Employment by occupation: 50.0% management, 0.0% professional, 0.0% services, 0.0% sales, 0.0% farming, 0.0% construction, 0.0% production (2006-2010 5-year est.).
Income: Per capita income: $63,679 (2006-2010 5-year est.); Median household income: $91,250 (2006-2010 5-year est.); Average household income: $148,583 (2006-2010 5-year est.); Percent of households with income of $100,000 or more: 33.3% (2006-2010 5-year est.); Poverty rate: 0.0% (2006-2010 5-year est.).
Education: Percent of population age 25 and over with: High school diploma (including GED) or higher: 100.0% (2006-2010 5-year est.); Bachelor's degree or higher: 33.3% (2006-2010 5-year est.); Master's degree or higher: 16.7% (2006-2010 5-year est.).
Housing: Homeownership rate: 100.0% (2010); Median home value: $225,000 (2006-2010 5-year est.); Median contract rent: n/a per month (2006-2010 5-year est.); Median year structure built: 1965 (2006-2010 5-year est.).
Transportation: Commute to work: 75.0% car, 0.0% public transportation, 0.0% walk, 0.0% work from home (2006-2010 5-year est.); Travel time to work: 25.0% less than 15 minutes, 50.0% 15 to 30 minutes, 0.0% 30 to 45 minutes, 0.0% 45 to 60 minutes, 25.0% 60 minutes or more (2006-2010 5-year est.)

HANOVER (township). Covers a land area of 47.596 square miles and a water area of 0.027 square miles. Located at 40.43° N. Lat; 80.46° W. Long.
Population: 2,883 (1990); 2,795 (2000); 2,673 (2010); Density: 56.2 persons per square mile (2010); Race: 98.1% White, 0.2% Black, 0.4% Asian, 0.0% American Indian/Alaska Native, 0.1% Native Hawaiian/Other Pacific Islander, 1.2% Other, 0.4% Hispanic of any race (2010); Average household size: 2.51 (2010); Median age: 45.9 (2010); Males per 100 females: 103.1 (2010); Marriage status: 26.5% never married, 61.3% now married, 3.8% widowed, 8.5% divorced (2006-2010 5-year est.); Foreign born: 0.6% (2006-2010 5-year est.); Ancestry (includes multiple ancestries): 37.7% German, 27.8% Irish, 12.8% Polish, 10.4% English, 9.1% American (2006-2010 5-year est.).
Economy: Single-family building permits issued: 1 (2011); Multi-family building permits issued: 0 (2011); Employment by occupation: 7.8% management, 7.3% professional, 9.5% services, 20.9% sales, 3.8% farming, 16.5% construction, 8.8% production (2006-2010 5-year est.).
Income: Per capita income: $23,221 (2006-2010 5-year est.); Median household income: $50,500 (2006-2010 5-year est.); Average household income: $58,966 (2006-2010 5-year est.); Percent of households with income of $100,000 or more: 12.8% (2006-2010 5-year est.); Poverty rate: 11.7% (2006-2010 5-year est.).
Education: Percent of population age 25 and over with: High school diploma (including GED) or higher: 88.6% (2006-2010 5-year est.); Bachelor's degree or higher: 13.1% (2006-2010 5-year est.); Master's degree or higher: 4.1% (2006-2010 5-year est.).
Housing: Homeownership rate: 84.4% (2010); Median home value: $125,000 (2006-2010 5-year est.); Median contract rent: $449 per month (2006-2010 5-year est.); Median year structure built: 1977 (2006-2010 5-year est.).
Transportation: Commute to work: 94.9% car, 0.0% public transportation, 0.6% walk, 3.6% work from home (2006-2010 5-year est.); Travel time to work: 7.2% less than 15 minutes, 36.3% 15 to 30 minutes, 31.3% 30 to 45 minutes, 15.6% 45 to 60 minutes, 9.7% 60 minutes or more (2006-2010 5-year est.)
Additional Information Contacts
Washington County Chamber of Commerce . . . . (724) 225-3010
http://www.washcochamber.com

HENDERSONVILLE (CDP). Covers a land area of 0.398 square miles and a water area of 0 square miles. Located at 40.30° N. Lat; 80.16° W. Long. Elevation is 991 feet.
Population: n/a (1990); n/a (2000); 325 (2010); Density: 815.7 persons per square mile (2010); Race: 90.8% White, 6.5% Black, 0.0% Asian, 0.0% American Indian/Alaska Native, 0.0% Native Hawaiian/Other Pacific Islander, 2.7% Other, 0.0% Hispanic of any race (2010); Average household size: 2.32 (2010); Median age: 43.1 (2010); Males per 100 females: 103.1 (2010); Marriage status: 25.4% never married, 59.9% now married, 7.0% widowed, 7.7% divorced (2006-2010 5-year est.); Foreign born: 0.0% (2006-2010 5-year est.); Ancestry (includes multiple ancestries): 41.8% Russian, 36.7% Croatian, 36.7% Italian, 9.2% Swedish, 5.6% German (2006-2010 5-year est.).

Economy: Employment by occupation: 24.0% management, 14.7% professional, 13.3% services, 0.0% sales, 0.0% farming, 0.0% construction, 0.0% production (2006-2010 5-year est.).
Income: Per capita income: $18,814 (2006-2010 5-year est.); Median household income: $45,125 (2006-2010 5-year est.); Average household income: $46,032 (2006-2010 5-year est.); Percent of households with income of $100,000 or more: n/a (2006-2010 5-year est.); Poverty rate: 0.0% (2006-2010 5-year est.).
Education: Percent of population age 25 and over with: High school diploma (including GED) or higher: 100.0% (2006-2010 5-year est.); Bachelor's degree or higher: 12.7% (2006-2010 5-year est.); Master's degree or higher: 0.0% (2006-2010 5-year est.).
Housing: Homeownership rate: 75.7% (2010); Median home value: $68,200 (2006-2010 5-year est.); Median contract rent: n/a per month (2006-2010 5-year est.); Median year structure built: before 1940 (2006-2010 5-year est.).
Transportation: Commute to work: 100.0% car, 0.0% public transportation, 0.0% walk, 0.0% work from home (2006-2010 5-year est.); Travel time to work: 76.0% less than 15 minutes, 24.0% 15 to 30 minutes, 0.0% 30 to 45 minutes, 0.0% 45 to 60 minutes, 0.0% 60 minutes or more (2006-2010 5-year est.)

HICKORY (CDP). Covers a land area of 2.845 square miles and a water area of 0 square miles. Located at 40.30° N. Lat; 80.31° W. Long. Elevation is 1,299 feet.
Population: n/a (1990); n/a (2000); 740 (2010); Density: 260.2 persons per square mile (2010); Race: 98.5% White, 0.0% Black, 0.1% Asian, 0.0% American Indian/Alaska Native, 0.0% Native Hawaiian/Other Pacific Islander, 1.4% Other, 0.1% Hispanic of any race (2010); Average household size: 2.44 (2010); Median age: 45.5 (2010); Males per 100 females: 102.7 (2010); Marriage status: 12.5% never married, 73.4% now married, 4.2% widowed, 9.9% divorced (2006-2010 5-year est.); Foreign born: 0.0% (2006-2010 5-year est.); Ancestry (includes multiple ancestries): 28.4% German, 27.0% Italian, 16.3% Irish, 15.8% Scotch-Irish, 11.0% English (2006-2010 5-year est.).
Economy: Employment by occupation: 6.8% management, 4.2% professional, 16.0% services, 12.7% sales, 5.7% farming, 4.6% construction, 2.2% production (2006-2010 5-year est.).
Income: Per capita income: $30,556 (2006-2010 5-year est.); Median household income: $79,333 (2006-2010 5-year est.); Average household income: $81,174 (2006-2010 5-year est.); Percent of households with income of $100,000 or more: 25.3% (2006-2010 5-year est.); Poverty rate: 6.8% (2006-2010 5-year est.).
Education: Percent of population age 25 and over with: High school diploma (including GED) or higher: 92.0% (2006-2010 5-year est.); Bachelor's degree or higher: 20.9% (2006-2010 5-year est.); Master's degree or higher: 10.8% (2006-2010 5-year est.).
Housing: Homeownership rate: 84.8% (2010); Median home value: $161,500 (2006-2010 5-year est.); Median contract rent: $500 per month (2006-2010 5-year est.); Median year structure built: 1950 (2006-2010 5-year est.).
Transportation: Commute to work: 93.0% car, 0.0% public transportation, 4.2% walk, 2.9% work from home (2006-2010 5-year est.); Travel time to work: 19.0% less than 15 minutes, 47.4% 15 to 30 minutes, 17.6% 30 to 45 minutes, 9.3% 45 to 60 minutes, 6.8% 60 minutes or more (2006-2010 5-year est.)

HOPEWELL (township). Covers a land area of 20.552 square miles and a water area of 0 square miles. Located at 40.23° N. Lat; 80.39° W. Long.
Population: 942 (1990); 992 (2000); 957 (2010); Density: 46.6 persons per square mile (2010); Race: 95.9% White, 1.0% Black, 0.0% Asian, 0.6% American Indian/Alaska Native, 0.0% Native Hawaiian/Other Pacific Islander, 2.5% Other, 1.5% Hispanic of any race (2010); Average household size: 2.61 (2010); Median age: 46.1 (2010); Males per 100 females: 102.8 (2010); Marriage status: 20.8% never married, 68.4% now married, 4.4% widowed, 6.4% divorced (2006-2010 5-year est.); Foreign born: 0.4% (2006-2010 5-year est.); Ancestry (includes multiple ancestries): 28.6% German, 24.1% Irish, 14.4% Italian, 14.0% English, 12.5% Scotch-Irish (2006-2010 5-year est.).
Economy: Single-family building permits issued: 0 (2011); Multi-family building permits issued: 0 (2011); Employment by occupation: 15.1% management, 2.1% professional, 9.9% services, 11.8% sales, 4.6% farming, 18.0% construction, 8.6% production (2006-2010 5-year est.).

Income: Per capita income: $27,738 (2006-2010 5-year est.); Median household income: $62,375 (2006-2010 5-year est.); Average household income: $76,788 (2006-2010 5-year est.); Percent of households with income of $100,000 or more: 23.5% (2006-2010 5-year est.); Poverty rate: 4.4% (2006-2010 5-year est.).

Education: Percent of population age 25 and over with: High school diploma (including GED) or higher: 91.3% (2006-2010 5-year est.); Bachelor's degree or higher: 15.9% (2006-2010 5-year est.); Master's degree or higher: 7.0% (2006-2010 5-year est.).

Housing: Homeownership rate: 87.7% (2010); Median home value: $177,500 (2006-2010 5-year est.); Median contract rent: $408 per month (2006-2010 5-year est.); Median year structure built: 1966 (2006-2010 5-year est.).

Transportation: Commute to work: 83.3% car, 0.7% public transportation, 2.9% walk, 9.3% work from home (2006-2010 5-year est.); Travel time to work: 14.4% less than 15 minutes, 46.1% 15 to 30 minutes, 17.5% 30 to 45 minutes, 13.1% 45 to 60 minutes, 8.9% 60 minutes or more (2006-2010 5-year est.)

Additional Information Contacts
Washington County Chamber of Commerce. . . . . (724) 225-3010
  http://www.washcochamber.com

HOUSTON (borough). Covers a land area of 0.411 square miles and a water area of 0 square miles. Located at 40.25° N. Lat; 80.21° W. Long. Elevation is 991 feet.

History: Laid out 1871, incorporated 1901.

Population: 1,445 (1990); 1,314 (2000); 1,296 (2010); Density: 3,154.2 persons per square mile (2010); Race: 91.7% White, 3.4% Black, 0.4% Asian, 0.2% American Indian/Alaska Native, 0.0% Native Hawaiian/Other Pacific Islander, 4.3% Other, 1.2% Hispanic of any race (2010); Average household size: 2.13 (2010); Median age: 43.3 (2010); Males per 100 females: 94.3 (2010); Marriage status: 32.9% never married, 43.9% now married, 8.1% widowed, 15.1% divorced (2006-2010 5-year est.); Foreign born: 0.5% (2006-2010 5-year est.); Ancestry (includes multiple ancestries): 24.0% German, 23.9% Italian, 16.2% Irish, 11.3% English, 9.9% Scotch-Irish (2006-2010 5-year est.).

Economy: Single-family building permits issued: 2 (2011); Multi-family building permits issued: 0 (2011); Employment by occupation: 5.2% management, 4.3% professional, 9.1% services, 23.2% sales, 4.6% farming, 11.9% construction, 5.4% production (2006-2010 5-year est.).

Income: Per capita income: $22,365 (2006-2010 5-year est.); Median household income: $37,969 (2006-2010 5-year est.); Average household income: $46,707 (2006-2010 5-year est.); Percent of households with income of $100,000 or more: 8.7% (2006-2010 5-year est.); Poverty rate: 14.7% (2006-2010 5-year est.).

Education: Percent of population age 25 and over with: High school diploma (including GED) or higher: 84.5% (2006-2010 5-year est.); Bachelor's degree or higher: 9.9% (2006-2010 5-year est.); Master's degree or higher: 1.4% (2006-2010 5-year est.).

School District(s)
Chartiers-Houston SD (KG-12)
  2010-11 Enrollment: 1,117 . . . . (724) 746-1400

Housing: Homeownership rate: 56.5% (2010); Median home value: $109,200 (2006-2010 5-year est.); Median contract rent: $440 per month (2006-2010 5-year est.); Median year structure built: 1941 (2006-2010 5-year est.).

Safety: Violent crime rate: 0.0 per 10,000 population; Property crime rate: 7.7 per 10,000 population (2011).

Transportation: Commute to work: 98.1% car, 0.0% public transportation, 0.4% walk, 1.0% work from home (2006-2010 5-year est.); Travel time to work: 35.9% less than 15 minutes, 43.3% 15 to 30 minutes, 12.6% 30 to 45 minutes, 3.9% 45 to 60 minutes, 4.4% 60 minutes or more (2006-2010 5-year est.)

Additional Information Contacts
Washington County Chamber of Commerce. . . . . (724) 225-3010
  http://www.washcochamber.com

INDEPENDENCE (township). Covers a land area of 25.752 square miles and a water area of 0.014 square miles. Located at 40.24° N. Lat; 80.48° W. Long.

Population: 1,868 (1990); 1,676 (2000); 1,557 (2010); Density: 60.5 persons per square mile (2010); Race: 97.6% White, 1.1% Black, 0.1% Asian, 0.1% American Indian/Alaska Native, 0.1% Native Hawaiian/Other Pacific Islander, 1.0% Other, 1.2% Hispanic of any race (2010); Average household size: 2.49 (2010); Median age: 44.6 (2010); Males per 100

females: 103.8 (2010); Marriage status: 23.6% never married, 60.7% now married, 8.5% widowed, 7.2% divorced (2006-2010 5-year est.); Foreign born: 0.2% (2006-2010 5-year est.); Ancestry (includes multiple ancestries): 25.6% German, 24.3% Irish, 18.7% Italian, 10.5% Polish, 10.3% English (2006-2010 5-year est.).

Economy: Single-family building permits issued: 0 (2011); Multi-family building permits issued: 0 (2011); Employment by occupation: 9.3% management, 4.2% professional, 10.4% services, 16.6% sales, 4.5% farming, 17.0% construction, 4.5% production (2006-2010 5-year est.).

Income: Per capita income: $20,444 (2006-2010 5-year est.); Median household income: $46,979 (2006-2010 5-year est.); Average household income: $55,015 (2006-2010 5-year est.); Percent of households with income of $100,000 or more: 13.2% (2006-2010 5-year est.); Poverty rate: 10.3% (2006-2010 5-year est.).

Education: Percent of population age 25 and over with: High school diploma (including GED) or higher: 83.8% (2006-2010 5-year est.); Bachelor's degree or higher: 16.3% (2006-2010 5-year est.); Master's degree or higher: 3.5% (2006-2010 5-year est.).

Housing: Homeownership rate: 86.7% (2010); Median home value: $105,400 (2006-2010 5-year est.); Median contract rent: $479 per month (2006-2010 5-year est.); Median year structure built: 1958 (2006-2010 5-year est.).

Transportation: Commute to work: 92.3% car, 0.0% public transportation, 1.8% walk, 5.9% work from home (2006-2010 5-year est.); Travel time to work: 14.4% less than 15 minutes, 23.2% 15 to 30 minutes, 35.3% 30 to 45 minutes, 16.1% 45 to 60 minutes, 11.0% 60 minutes or more (2006-2010 5-year est.)

Additional Information Contacts
Washington County Chamber of Commerce. . . . . (724) 225-3010
  http://www.washcochamber.com

JEFFERSON (township). Covers a land area of 22.626 square miles and a water area of 0.015 square miles. Located at 40.33° N. Lat; 80.48° W. Long. Elevation is 965 feet.

Population: 1,358 (1990); 1,218 (2000); 1,162 (2010); Density: 51.4 persons per square mile (2010); Race: 98.9% White, 0.2% Black, 0.2% Asian, 0.0% American Indian/Alaska Native, 0.0% Native Hawaiian/Other Pacific Islander, 0.7% Other, 1.2% Hispanic of any race (2010); Average household size: 2.52 (2010); Median age: 46.1 (2010); Males per 100 females: 96.0 (2010); Marriage status: 18.8% never married, 65.1% now married, 9.5% widowed, 6.6% divorced (2006-2010 5-year est.); Foreign born: 0.5% (2006-2010 5-year est.); Ancestry (includes multiple ancestries): 34.7% German, 19.9% Irish, 16.8% Polish, 15.7% Italian, 11.6% English (2006-2010 5-year est.).

Economy: Single-family building permits issued: 0 (2011); Multi-family building permits issued: 0 (2011); Employment by occupation: 8.5% management, 5.3% professional, 12.2% services, 15.4% sales, 3.5% farming, 17.3% construction, 11.2% production (2006-2010 5-year est.).

Income: Per capita income: $24,268 (2006-2010 5-year est.); Median household income: $61,544 (2006-2010 5-year est.); Average household income: $67,250 (2006-2010 5-year est.); Percent of households with income of $100,000 or more: 19.8% (2006-2010 5-year est.); Poverty rate: 9.7% (2006-2010 5-year est.).

Education: Percent of population age 25 and over with: High school diploma (including GED) or higher: 87.2% (2006-2010 5-year est.); Bachelor's degree or higher: 16.7% (2006-2010 5-year est.); Master's degree or higher: 5.6% (2006-2010 5-year est.).

Housing: Homeownership rate: 92.0% (2010); Median home value: $142,700 (2006-2010 5-year est.); Median contract rent: $246 per month (2006-2010 5-year est.); Median year structure built: 1966 (2006-2010 5-year est.).

Transportation: Commute to work: 97.2% car, 0.0% public transportation, 0.0% walk, 2.8% work from home (2006-2010 5-year est.); Travel time to work: 12.4% less than 15 minutes, 21.0% 15 to 30 minutes, 40.6% 30 to 45 minutes, 15.7% 45 to 60 minutes, 10.3% 60 minutes or more (2006-2010 5-year est.)

Additional Information Contacts
Washington County Chamber of Commerce. . . . . (724) 225-3010
  http://www.washcochamber.com

JOFFRE (CDP). Covers a land area of 0.897 square miles and a water area of 0 square miles. Located at 40.38° N. Lat; 80.35° W. Long. Elevation is 1,004 feet.

Population: n/a (1990); n/a (2000); 536 (2010); Density: 597.8 persons per square mile (2010); Race: 96.5% White, 0.2% Black, 0.9% Asian,

0.0% American Indian/Alaska Native, 0.0% Native Hawaiian/Other Pacific Islander, 2.4% Other, 0.4% Hispanic of any race (2010); Average household size: 2.29 (2010); Median age: 43.6 (2010); Males per 100 females: 102.3 (2010); Marriage status: 29.6% never married, 44.0% now married, 11.4% widowed, 15.0% divorced (2006-2010 5-year est.); Foreign born: 0.0% (2006-2010 5-year est.); Ancestry (includes multiple ancestries): 26.6% German, 12.6% English, 10.5% American, 9.5% Irish, 8.6% Italian (2006-2010 5-year est.).

Economy: Employment by occupation: 0.0% management, 0.0% professional, 14.0% services, 20.1% sales, 0.0% farming, 26.6% construction, 19.6% production (2006-2010 5-year est.).

Income: Per capita income: $18,287 (2006-2010 5-year est.); Median household income: $41,574 (2006-2010 5-year est.); Average household income: $42,888 (2006-2010 5-year est.); Percent of households with income of $100,000 or more: 5.2% (2006-2010 5-year est.); Poverty rate: 14.5% (2006-2010 5-year est.).

Education: Percent of population age 25 and over with: High school diploma (including GED) or higher: 72.7% (2006-2010 5-year est.); Bachelor's degree or higher: 3.6% (2006-2010 5-year est.); Master's degree or higher: 0.0% (2006-2010 5-year est.).

Housing: Homeownership rate: 83.7% (2010); Median home value: $97,000 (2006-2010 5-year est.); Median contract rent: $337 per month (2006-2010 5-year est.); Median year structure built: 1974 (2006-2010 5-year est.).

Transportation: Commute to work: 92.1% car, 0.0% public transportation, 0.0% walk, 7.9% work from home (2006-2010 5-year est.); Travel time to work: 1.5% less than 15 minutes, 21.3% 15 to 30 minutes, 66.0% 30 to 45 minutes, 9.6% 45 to 60 minutes, 1.5% 60 minutes or more (2006-2010 5-year est.)

LANGELOTH (CDP). Covers a land area of 1.041 square miles and a water area of 0 square miles. Located at 40.36° N. Lat; 80.41° W. Long. Elevation is 1,220 feet.

Population: n/a (1990); n/a (2000); 717 (2010); Density: 688.8 persons per square mile (2010); Race: 98.3% White, 0.6% Black, 0.3% Asian, 0.0% American Indian/Alaska Native, 0.0% Native Hawaiian/Other Pacific Islander, 0.8% Other, 4.5% Hispanic of any race (2010); Average household size: 2.36 (2010); Median age: 43.1 (2010); Males per 100 females: 91.7 (2010); Marriage status: 33.6% never married, 46.9% now married, 12.0% widowed, 7.5% divorced (2006-2010 5-year est.); Foreign born: 0.0% (2006-2010 5-year est.); Ancestry (includes multiple ancestries): 27.6% Irish, 16.9% German, 16.0% English, 13.9% Polish, 7.5% Greek (2006-2010 5-year est.).

Economy: Employment by occupation: 0.0% management, 9.7% professional, 24.6% services, 4.0% sales, 0.0% farming, 23.0% construction, 0.0% production (2006-2010 5-year est.).

Income: Per capita income: $24,483 (2006-2010 5-year est.); Median household income: $48,065 (2006-2010 5-year est.); Average household income: $44,424 (2006-2010 5-year est.); Percent of households with income of $100,000 or more: 4.2% (2006-2010 5-year est.); Poverty rate: 11.9% (2006-2010 5-year est.).

Education: Percent of population age 25 and over with: High school diploma (including GED) or higher: 80.6% (2006-2010 5-year est.); Bachelor's degree or higher: 14.6% (2006-2010 5-year est.); Master's degree or higher: 11.7% (2006-2010 5-year est.).

Housing: Homeownership rate: 70.7% (2010); Median home value: $73,500 (2006-2010 5-year est.); Median contract rent: $351 per month (2006-2010 5-year est.); Median year structure built: before 1940 (2006-2010 5-year est.).

Transportation: Commute to work: 86.6% car, 0.0% public transportation, 10.1% walk, 3.2% work from home (2006-2010 5-year est.); Travel time to work: 10.5% less than 15 minutes, 55.2% 15 to 30 minutes, 27.1% 30 to 45 minutes, 1.4% 45 to 60 minutes, 5.7% 60 minutes or more (2006-2010 5-year est.)

LAWRENCE (CDP). Covers a land area of 0.243 square miles and a water area of 0.010 square miles. Located at 40.30° N. Lat; 80.12° W. Long. Elevation is 1,020 feet.

Population: n/a (1990); n/a (2000); 540 (2010); Density: 2,218.6 persons per square mile (2010); Race: 89.6% White, 6.1% Black, 0.9% Asian, 0.6% American Indian/Alaska Native, 0.2% Native Hawaiian/Other Pacific Islander, 2.6% Other, 0.4% Hispanic of any race (2010); Average household size: 2.18 (2010); Median age: 45.2 (2010); Males per 100 females: 90.1 (2010); Marriage status: 19.7% never married, 51.3% now married, 11.1% widowed, 17.9% divorced (2006-2010 5-year est.); Foreign

born: 0.0% (2006-2010 5-year est.); Ancestry (includes multiple ancestries): 31.0% German, 27.5% Irish, 22.9% Polish, 16.7% English, 15.8% Slovak (2006-2010 5-year est.).

Economy: Employment by occupation: 0.0% management, 0.0% professional, 0.0% services, 14.6% sales, 0.0% farming, 13.6% construction, 9.1% production (2006-2010 5-year est.).

Income: Per capita income: $20,957 (2006-2010 5-year est.); Median household income: $42,153 (2006-2010 5-year est.); Average household income: $61,301 (2006-2010 5-year est.); Percent of households with income of $100,000 or more: 12.8% (2006-2010 5-year est.); Poverty rate: 6.7% (2006-2010 5-year est.).

Education: Percent of population age 25 and over with: High school diploma (including GED) or higher: 96.2% (2006-2010 5-year est.); Bachelor's degree or higher: 19.6% (2006-2010 5-year est.); Master's degree or higher: 0.0% (2006-2010 5-year est.).

Housing: Homeownership rate: 62.9% (2010); Median home value: $109,500 (2006-2010 5-year est.); Median contract rent: $493 per month (2006-2010 5-year est.); Median year structure built: before 1940 (2006-2010 5-year est.).

Transportation: Commute to work: 100.0% car, 0.0% public transportation, 0.0% walk, 0.0% work from home (2006-2010 5-year est.); Travel time to work: 17.1% less than 15 minutes, 57.0% 15 to 30 minutes, 11.4% 30 to 45 minutes, 14.6% 45 to 60 minutes, 0.0% 60 minutes or more (2006-2010 5-year est.)

LONG BRANCH (borough). Covers a land area of 3.191 square miles and a water area of 0 square miles. Located at 40.10° N. Lat; 79.88° W. Long. Elevation is 1,093 feet.

Population: 593 (1990); 539 (2000); 447 (2010); Density: 140.1 persons per square mile (2010); Race: 98.9% White, 0.7% Black, 0.0% Asian, 0.4% American Indian/Alaska Native, 0.0% Native Hawaiian/Other Pacific Islander, 0.0% Other, 0.0% Hispanic of any race (2010); Average household size: 2.40 (2010); Median age: 48.2 (2010); Males per 100 females: 95.2 (2010); Marriage status: 25.1% never married, 66.5% now married, 1.8% widowed, 6.6% divorced (2006-2010 5-year est.); Foreign born: 0.5% (2006-2010 5-year est.); Ancestry (includes multiple ancestries): 27.3% German, 22.7% Italian, 18.0% English, 16.8% Irish, 9.0% Polish (2006-2010 5-year est.).

Economy: Single-family building permits issued: 0 (2011); Multi-family building permits issued: 0 (2011); Employment by occupation: 14.2% management, 3.0% professional, 2.2% services, 21.6% sales, 1.9% farming, 11.2% construction, 3.4% production (2006-2010 5-year est.).

Income: Per capita income: $20,189 (2006-2010 5-year est.); Median household income: $43,750 (2006-2010 5-year est.); Average household income: $52,677 (2006-2010 5-year est.); Percent of households with income of $100,000 or more: 10.5% (2006-2010 5-year est.); Poverty rate: 11.6% (2006-2010 5-year est.).

Education: Percent of population age 25 and over with: High school diploma (including GED) or higher: 90.8% (2006-2010 5-year est.); Bachelor's degree or higher: 19.3% (2006-2010 5-year est.); Master's degree or higher: 8.4% (2006-2010 5-year est.).

Housing: Homeownership rate: 93.5% (2010); Median home value: $112,200 (2006-2010 5-year est.); Median contract rent: $625 per month (2006-2010 5-year est.); Median year structure built: 1959 (2006-2010 5-year est.).

Transportation: Commute to work: 99.2% car, 0.0% public transportation, 0.0% walk, 0.8% work from home (2006-2010 5-year est.); Travel time to work: 28.8% less than 15 minutes, 42.0% 15 to 30 minutes, 10.7% 30 to 45 minutes, 5.8% 45 to 60 minutes, 12.8% 60 minutes or more (2006-2010 5-year est.)

MARIANNA (borough). Covers a land area of 1.956 square miles and a water area of 0 square miles. Located at 40.01° N. Lat; 80.11° W. Long. Elevation is 1,050 feet.

History: Incorporated 1901.

Population: 616 (1990); 626 (2000); 494 (2010); Density: 252.5 persons per square mile (2010); Race: 91.9% White, 3.6% Black, 0.0% Asian, 1.0% American Indian/Alaska Native, 0.0% Native Hawaiian/Other Pacific Islander, 3.5% Other, 0.4% Hispanic of any race (2010); Average household size: 2.47 (2010); Median age: 35.7 (2010); Males per 100 females: 96.0 (2010); Marriage status: 28.5% never married, 53.9% now married, 10.9% widowed, 6.7% divorced (2006-2010 5-year est.); Foreign born: 0.0% (2006-2010 5-year est.); Ancestry (includes multiple ancestries): 24.6% Irish, 14.7% Polish, 14.5% German, 13.2% Italian, 10.3% Welsh (2006-2010 5-year est.).

Economy: Single-family building permits issued: 0 (2011); Multi-family building permits issued: 0 (2011); Employment by occupation: 0.0% management, 3.4% professional, 5.6% services, 23.6% sales, 6.7% farming, 11.2% construction, 5.1% production (2006-2010 5-year est.).
Income: Per capita income: $19,532 (2006-2010 5-year est.); Median household income: $45,000 (2006-2010 5-year est.); Average household income: $49,858 (2006-2010 5-year est.); Percent of households with income of $100,000 or more: 5.1% (2006-2010 5-year est.); Poverty rate: 12.4% (2006-2010 5-year est.).
Education: Percent of population age 25 and over with: High school diploma (including GED) or higher: 80.0% (2006-2010 5-year est.); Bachelor's degree or higher: 11.3% (2006-2010 5-year est.); Master's degree or higher: 2.5% (2006-2010 5-year est.).
Housing: Homeownership rate: 76.5% (2010); Median home value: $43,500 (2006-2010 5-year est.); Median contract rent: $425 per month (2006-2010 5-year est.); Median year structure built: before 1940 (2006-2010 5-year est.).
Transportation: Commute to work: 98.3% car, 0.0% public transportation, 1.7% walk, 0.0% work from home (2006-2010 5-year est.); Travel time to work: 1.7% less than 15 minutes, 26.7% 15 to 30 minutes, 46.0% 30 to 45 minutes, 18.8% 45 to 60 minutes, 6.8% 60 minutes or more (2006-2010 5-year est.)

MCDONALD (borough). Covers a land area of 0.522 square miles and a water area of 0 square miles. Located at 40.37° N. Lat; 80.23° W. Long. Elevation is 994 feet.
Population: 2,252 (1990); 2,281 (2000); 2,149 (2010); Density: 4,116.9 persons per square mile (2010); Race: 94.9% White, 3.1% Black, 0.5% Asian, 0.2% American Indian/Alaska Native, 0.2% Native Hawaiian/Other Pacific Islander, 1.1% Other, 1.1% Hispanic of any race (2010); Average household size: 2.21 (2010); Median age: 42.8 (2010); Males per 100 females: 93.1 (2010); Marriage status: 33.9% never married, 39.0% now married, 14.2% widowed, 12.9% divorced (2006-2010 5-year est.); Foreign born: 0.0% (2006-2010 5-year est.); Ancestry (includes multiple ancestries): 39.9% German, 23.6% Irish, 15.7% English, 11.3% Italian, 8.0% Polish (2006-2010 5-year est.).
Economy: Single-family building permits issued: 0 (2011); Multi-family building permits issued: 0 (2011); Employment by occupation: 3.4% management, 3.4% professional, 10.9% services, 19.9% sales, 4.0% farming, 18.4% construction, 11.0% production (2006-2010 5-year est.).
Income: Per capita income: $20,608 (2006-2010 5-year est.); Median household income: $40,948 (2006-2010 5-year est.); Average household income: $45,895 (2006-2010 5-year est.); Percent of households with income of $100,000 or more: 5.4% (2006-2010 5-year est.); Poverty rate: 10.3% (2006-2010 5-year est.).
Education: Percent of population age 25 and over with: High school diploma (including GED) or higher: 81.1% (2006-2010 5-year est.); Bachelor's degree or higher: 9.5% (2006-2010 5-year est.); Master's degree or higher: 3.2% (2006-2010 5-year est.).

School District(s)
Canon-Mcmillan SD (KG-12)
    2010-11 Enrollment: 4,954 . . . . (724) 746-2940
Fort Cherry SD (KG-12)
    2010-11 Enrollment: 1,112 . . . . (724) 796-1551
South Fayette Township SD (KG-12)
    2010-11 Enrollment: 2,486 . . . . (412) 221-4542
Housing: Homeownership rate: 56.8% (2010); Median home value: $97,900 (2006-2010 5-year est.); Median contract rent: $391 per month (2006-2010 5-year est.); Median year structure built: before 1940 (2006-2010 5-year est.).
Safety: Violent crime rate: 23.2 per 10,000 population; Property crime rate: 236.5 per 10,000 population (2011).
Transportation: Commute to work: 89.3% car, 1.7% public transportation, 6.5% walk, 2.5% work from home (2006-2010 5-year est.); Travel time to work: 16.8% less than 15 minutes, 43.6% 15 to 30 minutes, 26.1% 30 to 45 minutes, 6.7% 45 to 60 minutes, 6.7% 60 minutes or more (2006-2010 5-year est.)
Additional Information Contacts
South West Communities Chamber of Commerce . . . . (412) 221-4100
    http://www.swccoc.org

MCGOVERN (CDP). Covers a land area of 1.834 square miles and a water area of 0 square miles. Located at 40.24° N. Lat; 80.23° W. Long. Elevation is 991 feet.
Population: 2,517 (1990); 2,538 (2000); 2,742 (2010); Density: 1,495.4 persons per square mile (2010); Race: 97.4% White, 1.4% Black, 0.1% Asian, 0.1% American Indian/Alaska Native, 0.0% Native Hawaiian/Other Pacific Islander, 1.0% Other, 0.9% Hispanic of any race (2010); Average household size: 2.32 (2010); Median age: 46.7 (2010); Males per 100 females: 92.6 (2010); Marriage status: 20.9% never married, 60.4% now married, 9.3% widowed, 9.3% divorced (2006-2010 5-year est.); Foreign born: 0.6% (2006-2010 5-year est.); Ancestry (includes multiple ancestries): 22.1% German, 21.3% Italian, 19.1% Polish, 12.1% Irish, 11.0% English (2006-2010 5-year est.).
Economy: Employment by occupation: 13.6% management, 6.0% professional, 17.0% services, 21.9% sales, 2.4% farming, 4.8% construction, 2.0% production (2006-2010 5-year est.).
Income: Per capita income: $29,607 (2006-2010 5-year est.); Median household income: $56,802 (2006-2010 5-year est.); Average household income: $72,960 (2006-2010 5-year est.); Percent of households with income of $100,000 or more: 23.0% (2006-2010 5-year est.); Poverty rate: 1.7% (2006-2010 5-year est.).
Education: Percent of population age 25 and over with: High school diploma (including GED) or higher: 95.9% (2006-2010 5-year est.); Bachelor's degree or higher: 27.6% (2006-2010 5-year est.); Master's degree or higher: 6.7% (2006-2010 5-year est.).
Housing: Homeownership rate: 85.9% (2010); Median home value: $147,400 (2006-2010 5-year est.); Median contract rent: $655 per month (2006-2010 5-year est.); Median year structure built: 1966 (2006-2010 5-year est.).
Transportation: Commute to work: 94.0% car, 0.6% public transportation, 2.2% walk, 1.7% work from home (2006-2010 5-year est.); Travel time to work: 42.1% less than 15 minutes, 37.1% 15 to 30 minutes, 9.3% 30 to 45 minutes, 7.4% 45 to 60 minutes, 4.1% 60 minutes or more (2006-2010 5-year est.)
Additional Information Contacts
Washington County Chamber of Commerce . . . . (724) 225-3010
    http://www.washcochamber.com

MCMURRAY (CDP). Covers a land area of 3.068 square miles and a water area of 0 square miles. Located at 40.28° N. Lat; 80.09° W. Long. Elevation is 994 feet.
History: McMurray is situated near the central point of the Whiskey Rebellion of 1794. The area is in a rich coal district, and most of the work force once worked in local steel mills or coal mines.
Population: 4,082 (1990); 4,726 (2000); 4,647 (2010); Density: 1,514.9 persons per square mile (2010); Race: 97.7% White, 0.7% Black, 0.8% Asian, 0.0% American Indian/Alaska Native, 0.0% Native Hawaiian/Other Pacific Islander, 0.8% Other, 1.5% Hispanic of any race (2010); Average household size: 2.82 (2010); Median age: 45.2 (2010); Males per 100 females: 98.1 (2010); Marriage status: 23.5% never married, 69.4% now married, 4.4% widowed, 2.7% divorced (2006-2010 5-year est.); Foreign born: 1.9% (2006-2010 5-year est.); Ancestry (includes multiple ancestries): 33.2% German, 21.6% Irish, 17.2% Italian, 15.1% English, 13.0% Polish (2006-2010 5-year est.).
Economy: Employment by occupation: 16.1% management, 4.7% professional, 6.2% services, 14.7% sales, 4.7% farming, 5.5% construction, 2.0% production (2006-2010 5-year est.).
Income: Per capita income: $38,998 (2006-2010 5-year est.); Median household income: $92,375 (2006-2010 5-year est.); Average household income: $118,337 (2006-2010 5-year est.); Percent of households with income of $100,000 or more: 45.8% (2006-2010 5-year est.); Poverty rate: 1.4% (2006-2010 5-year est.).
Education: Percent of population age 25 and over with: High school diploma (including GED) or higher: 97.2% (2006-2010 5-year est.); Bachelor's degree or higher: 58.8% (2006-2010 5-year est.); Master's degree or higher: 23.5% (2006-2010 5-year est.).

School District(s)
Peters Township SD (KG-12)
    2010-11 Enrollment: 4,506 . . . . (724) 941-6251
Housing: Homeownership rate: 96.3% (2010); Median home value: $285,000 (2006-2010 5-year est.); Median contract rent: $1,136 per month (2006-2010 5-year est.); Median year structure built: 1974 (2006-2010 5-year est.).
Newspapers: The Almanac (Local news; Circulation 59,896)

Transportation: Commute to work: 80.9% car, 6.2% public transportation, 3.1% walk, 9.3% work from home (2006-2010 5-year est.); Travel time to work: 32.0% less than 15 minutes, 22.7% 15 to 30 minutes, 25.9% 30 to 45 minutes, 12.9% 45 to 60 minutes, 6.4% 60 minutes or more (2006-2010 5-year est.)

Additional Information Contacts

Peters Township Chamber of Commerce . . . . (724) 941-6345
    http://www.peterstownshipchamber.com

MEADOWLANDS (CDP). Covers a land area of 0.893 square miles and a water area of 0 square miles. Located at 40.22° N. Lat; 80.23° W. Long. Elevation is 978 feet.

Population: n/a (1990); n/a (2000); 822 (2010); Density: 921.0 persons per square mile (2010); Race: 96.5% White, 1.7% Black, 0.0% Asian, 0.2% American Indian/Alaska Native, 0.0% Native Hawaiian/Other Pacific Islander, 1.6% Other, 1.1% Hispanic of any race (2010); Average household size: 2.27 (2010); Median age: 42.8 (2010); Males per 100 females: 94.3 (2010); Marriage status: 0.0% never married, 34.5% now married, 23.0% widowed, 42.6% divorced (2006-2010 5-year est.); Foreign born: 0.0% (2006-2010 5-year est.); Ancestry (includes multiple ancestries): 58.3% German, 51.4% Italian, 23.5% Polish, 13.3% Slovak, 2.5% Irish (2006-2010 5-year est.).

Economy: Employment by occupation: 36.8% management, 0.0% professional, 0.0% services, 0.0% sales, 20.6% farming, 0.0% construction, 0.0% production (2006-2010 5-year est.).

Income: Per capita income: $16,706 (2006-2010 5-year est.); Median household income: $23,631 (2006-2010 5-year est.); Average household income: $37,492 (2006-2010 5-year est.); Percent of households with income of $100,000 or more: 13.5% (2006-2010 5-year est.); Poverty rate: 0.0% (2006-2010 5-year est.).

Education: Percent of population age 25 and over with: High school diploma (including GED) or higher: 100.0% (2006-2010 5-year est.); Bachelor's degree or higher: 54.0% (2006-2010 5-year est.); Master's degree or higher: 19.1% (2006-2010 5-year est.).

Housing: Homeownership rate: 71.0% (2010); Median home value: $78,900 (2006-2010 5-year est.); Median contract rent: n/a per month (2006-2010 5-year est.); Median year structure built: before 1940 (2006-2010 5-year est.).

Transportation: Commute to work: 72.1% car, 0.0% public transportation, 27.9% walk, 0.0% work from home (2006-2010 5-year est.); Travel time to work: 64.7% less than 15 minutes, 14.7% 15 to 30 minutes, 0.0% 30 to 45 minutes, 20.6% 45 to 60 minutes, 0.0% 60 minutes or more (2006-2010 5-year est.)

MIDWAY (borough). Covers a land area of 0.440 square miles and a water area of 0 square miles. Located at 40.37° N. Lat; 80.29° W. Long. Elevation is 1,106 feet.

Population: 1,043 (1990); 982 (2000); 913 (2010); Density: 2,075.1 persons per square mile (2010); Race: 98.5% White, 0.7% Black, 0.1% Asian, 0.1% American Indian/Alaska Native, 0.1% Native Hawaiian/Other Pacific Islander, 0.5% Other, 0.5% Hispanic of any race (2010); Average household size: 2.47 (2010); Median age: 41.7 (2010); Males per 100 females: 94.3 (2010); Marriage status: 18.8% never married, 68.7% now married, 6.0% widowed, 6.6% divorced (2006-2010 5-year est.); Foreign born: 0.6% (2006-2010 5-year est.); Ancestry (includes multiple ancestries): 36.4% German, 25.6% Irish, 15.9% Italian, 14.1% French, 12.1% English (2006-2010 5-year est.).

Economy: Single-family building permits issued: 0 (2011); Multi-family building permits issued: 0 (2011); Employment by occupation: 6.5% management, 5.2% professional, 12.2% services, 18.1% sales, 5.2% farming, 11.9% construction, 11.4% production (2006-2010 5-year est.).

Income: Per capita income: $20,085 (2006-2010 5-year est.); Median household income: $46,917 (2006-2010 5-year est.); Average household income: $50,853 (2006-2010 5-year est.); Percent of households with income of $100,000 or more: 6.8% (2006-2010 5-year est.); Poverty rate: 11.0% (2006-2010 5-year est.).

Education: Percent of population age 25 and over with: High school diploma (including GED) or higher: 88.6% (2006-2010 5-year est.); Bachelor's degree or higher: 10.9% (2006-2010 5-year est.); Master's degree or higher: 4.1% (2006-2010 5-year est.).

Housing: Homeownership rate: 75.9% (2010); Median home value: $97,400 (2006-2010 5-year est.); Median contract rent: $461 per month (2006-2010 5-year est.); Median year structure built: before 1940 (2006-2010 5-year est.).

Transportation: Commute to work: 96.1% car, 0.8% public transportation, 3.1% walk, 0.0% work from home (2006-2010 5-year est.); Travel time to work: 20.1% less than 15 minutes, 32.4% 15 to 30 minutes, 31.1% 30 to 45 minutes, 9.1% 45 to 60 minutes, 7.3% 60 minutes or more (2006-2010 5-year est.)

MILLSBORO (CDP). Covers a land area of 0.788 square miles and a water area of 0 square miles. Located at 39.99° N. Lat; 80.00° W. Long. Elevation is 771 feet.

Population: n/a (1990); n/a (2000); 666 (2010); Density: 844.7 persons per square mile (2010); Race: 97.4% White, 0.6% Black, 0.0% Asian, 0.0% American Indian/Alaska Native, 0.0% Native Hawaiian/Other Pacific Islander, 2.0% Other, 0.2% Hispanic of any race (2010); Average household size: 2.58 (2010); Median age: 37.6 (2010); Males per 100 females: 84.5 (2010); Marriage status: 26.0% never married, 56.8% now married, 6.9% widowed, 10.2% divorced (2006-2010 5-year est.); Foreign born: 0.0% (2006-2010 5-year est.); Ancestry (includes multiple ancestries): 16.1% Irish, 16.1% Italian, 15.7% Polish, 12.3% German, 8.6% Croatian (2006-2010 5-year est.).

Economy: Employment by occupation: 0.0% management, 0.0% professional, 2.0% services, 31.5% sales, 0.0% farming, 2.0% construction, 0.0% production (2006-2010 5-year est.).

Income: Per capita income: $26,283 (2006-2010 5-year est.); Median household income: $53,150 (2006-2010 5-year est.); Average household income: $57,592 (2006-2010 5-year est.); Percent of households with income of $100,000 or more: 28.7% (2006-2010 5-year est.); Poverty rate: 13.3% (2006-2010 5-year est.).

Education: Percent of population age 25 and over with: High school diploma (including GED) or higher: 90.6% (2006-2010 5-year est.); Bachelor's degree or higher: 3.3% (2006-2010 5-year est.); Master's degree or higher: 0.0% (2006-2010 5-year est.).

Housing: Homeownership rate: 82.2% (2010); Median home value: $96,100 (2006-2010 5-year est.); Median contract rent: $340 per month (2006-2010 5-year est.); Median year structure built: 1941 (2006-2010 5-year est.).

Transportation: Commute to work: 96.1% car, 0.0% public transportation, 3.9% walk, 0.0% work from home (2006-2010 5-year est.); Travel time to work: 28.7% less than 15 minutes, 17.3% 15 to 30 minutes, 29.9% 30 to 45 minutes, 7.9% 45 to 60 minutes, 16.1% 60 minutes or more (2006-2010 5-year est.)

MONONGAHELA (city). Covers a land area of 1.913 square miles and a water area of 0.220 square miles. Located at 40.19° N. Lat; 79.92° W. Long. Elevation is 758 feet.

History: A center of Whisky Rebellion, 1794. Settled 1770, incorporated as borough 1833, as city 1873.

Population: 4,929 (1990); 4,761 (2000); 4,300 (2010); Density: 2,247.8 persons per square mile (2010); Race: 94.6% White, 2.6% Black, 0.5% Asian, 0.3% American Indian/Alaska Native, 0.0% Native Hawaiian/Other Pacific Islander, 2.0% Other, 1.1% Hispanic of any race (2010); Average household size: 2.19 (2010); Median age: 43.6 (2010); Males per 100 females: 89.3 (2010); Marriage status: 31.7% never married, 43.9% now married, 14.1% widowed, 10.3% divorced (2006-2010 5-year est.); Foreign born: 0.3% (2006-2010 5-year est.); Ancestry (includes multiple ancestries): 24.0% Italian, 23.9% Irish, 20.1% German, 15.8% English, 7.0% Polish (2006-2010 5-year est.).

Economy: Single-family building permits issued: 0 (2011); Multi-family building permits issued: 0 (2011); Employment by occupation: 5.2% management, 2.1% professional, 15.1% services, 21.2% sales, 4.7% farming, 9.3% construction, 6.6% production (2006-2010 5-year est.).

Income: Per capita income: $21,359 (2006-2010 5-year est.); Median household income: $37,074 (2006-2010 5-year est.); Average household income: $46,806 (2006-2010 5-year est.); Percent of households with income of $100,000 or more: 7.4% (2006-2010 5-year est.); Poverty rate: 16.6% (2006-2010 5-year est.).

Education: Percent of population age 25 and over with: High school diploma (including GED) or higher: 87.3% (2006-2010 5-year est.); Bachelor's degree or higher: 15.3% (2006-2010 5-year est.); Master's degree or higher: 4.4% (2006-2010 5-year est.).

School District(s)

Elizabeth Forward SD (KG-12)
    2010-11 Enrollment: 2,491 . . . . (412) 896-2300
Ringgold SD (KG-12)
    2010-11 Enrollment: 3,057 . . . . (724) 258-9329

Housing: Homeownership rate: 61.6% (2010); Median home value: $79,800 (2006-2010 5-year est.); Median contract rent: $395 per month (2006-2010 5-year est.); Median year structure built: 1941 (2006-2010 5-year est.).

Hospitals: Monongahela Valley Hospital (226 beds)

Safety: Violent crime rate: 39.4 per 10,000 population; Property crime rate: 343.1 per 10,000 population (2011).

Transportation: Commute to work: 87.1% car, 3.6% public transportation, 3.9% walk, 2.7% work from home (2006-2010 5-year est.); Travel time to work: 34.0% less than 15 minutes, 20.4% 15 to 30 minutes, 22.8% 30 to 45 minutes, 12.3% 45 to 60 minutes, 10.4% 60 minutes or more (2006-2010 5-year est.)

Additional Information Contacts

City of Monongahela . . . . (724) 258-5500
  http://cityofmonongahela-pa.gov
Mon Valley Regional Chamber of Commerce . . . . (724) 483-3507
  http://www.mvrchamber.org

MORRIS (township). Covers a land area of 28.418 square miles and a water area of 0.011 square miles. Located at 40.04° N. Lat; 80.30° W. Long.

Population: 1,145 (1990); 1,272 (2000); 1,105 (2010); Density: 38.9 persons per square mile (2010); Race: 97.0% White, 1.3% Black, 0.1% Asian, 0.7% American Indian/Alaska Native, 0.0% Native Hawaiian/Other Pacific Islander, 0.9% Other, 1.7% Hispanic of any race (2010); Average household size: 2.60 (2010); Median age: 43.4 (2010); Males per 100 females: 115.8 (2010); Marriage status: 23.2% never married, 58.9% now married, 4.9% widowed, 13.0% divorced (2006-2010 5-year est.); Foreign born: 0.6% (2006-2010 5-year est.); Ancestry (includes multiple ancestries): 38.1% German, 21.9% Irish, 17.4% English, 15.1% Scotch-Irish, 12.1% Italian (2006-2010 5-year est.).

Economy: Single-family building permits issued: 0 (2011); Multi-family building permits issued: 0 (2011); Employment by occupation: 10.4% management, 5.3% professional, 10.5% services, 13.5% sales, 1.8% farming, 14.9% construction, 8.6% production (2006-2010 5-year est.).

Income: Per capita income: $21,705 (2006-2010 5-year est.); Median household income: $49,375 (2006-2010 5-year est.); Average household income: $60,272 (2006-2010 5-year est.); Percent of households with income of $100,000 or more: 9.7% (2006-2010 5-year est.); Poverty rate: 12.8% (2006-2010 5-year est.).

Education: Percent of population age 25 and over with: High school diploma (including GED) or higher: 86.4% (2006-2010 5-year est.); Bachelor's degree or higher: 14.8% (2006-2010 5-year est.); Master's degree or higher: 3.8% (2006-2010 5-year est.).

Housing: Homeownership rate: 77.7% (2010); Median home value: $147,900 (2006-2010 5-year est.); Median contract rent: $467 per month (2006-2010 5-year est.); Median year structure built: 1973 (2006-2010 5-year est.).

Transportation: Commute to work: 94.8% car, 0.7% public transportation, 2.9% walk, 1.6% work from home (2006-2010 5-year est.); Travel time to work: 11.6% less than 15 minutes, 36.0% 15 to 30 minutes, 29.3% 30 to 45 minutes, 11.8% 45 to 60 minutes, 11.3% 60 minutes or more (2006-2010 5-year est.)

Additional Information Contacts

Washington County Chamber of Commerce . . . . (724) 225-3010
  http://www.washcochamber.com

MOUNT PLEASANT (township). Covers a land area of 35.591 square miles and a water area of 0.082 square miles. Located at 40.30° N. Lat; 80.31° W. Long. Elevation is 1,345 feet.

Population: 3,555 (1990); 3,422 (2000); 3,515 (2010); Density: 98.8 persons per square mile (2010); Race: 97.0% White, 2.0% Black, 0.2% Asian, 0.0% American Indian/Alaska Native, 0.0% Native Hawaiian/Other Pacific Islander, 0.8% Other, 0.6% Hispanic of any race (2010); Average household size: 2.51 (2010); Median age: 46.4 (2010); Males per 100 females: 105.0 (2010); Marriage status: 19.6% never married, 61.0% now married, 9.9% widowed, 9.6% divorced (2006-2010 5-year est.); Foreign born: 0.9% (2006-2010 5-year est.); Ancestry (includes multiple ancestries): 33.5% German, 20.6% Italian, 16.7% Irish, 14.4% English, 10.9% French (2006-2010 5-year est.).

Economy: Single-family building permits issued: 1 (2011); Multi-family building permits issued: 0 (2011); Employment by occupation: 10.6% management, 5.1% professional, 14.5% services, 14.1% sales, 2.0% farming, 13.3% construction, 7.7% production (2006-2010 5-year est.).

Income: Per capita income: $29,769 (2006-2010 5-year est.); Median household income: $63,854 (2006-2010 5-year est.); Average household income: $76,471 (2006-2010 5-year est.); Percent of households with income of $100,000 or more: 20.1% (2006-2010 5-year est.); Poverty rate: 3.0% (2006-2010 5-year est.).

Education: Percent of population age 25 and over with: High school diploma (including GED) or higher: 89.0% (2006-2010 5-year est.); Bachelor's degree or higher: 21.6% (2006-2010 5-year est.); Master's degree or higher: 5.2% (2006-2010 5-year est.).

Housing: Homeownership rate: 86.4% (2010); Median home value: $154,600 (2006-2010 5-year est.); Median contract rent: $479 per month (2006-2010 5-year est.); Median year structure built: 1971 (2006-2010 5-year est.).

Safety: Violent crime rate: 11.3 per 10,000 population; Property crime rate: 79.4 per 10,000 population (2011).

Transportation: Commute to work: 89.5% car, 0.6% public transportation, 4.2% walk, 4.2% work from home (2006-2010 5-year est.); Travel time to work: 15.3% less than 15 minutes, 43.5% 15 to 30 minutes, 19.3% 30 to 45 minutes, 12.2% 45 to 60 minutes, 9.7% 60 minutes or more (2006-2010 5-year est.)

Additional Information Contacts

Greater Canonsburg Chamber of Commerce . . . . (724) 745-1812
  http://www.canonchamber.com

MUSE (CDP). Covers a land area of 1.552 square miles and a water area of 0 square miles. Located at 40.29° N. Lat; 80.21° W. Long. Elevation is 1,053 feet.

Population: n/a (1990); n/a (2000); 2,504 (2010); Density: 1,612.9 persons per square mile (2010); Race: 96.5% White, 1.4% Black, 1.0% Asian, 0.2% American Indian/Alaska Native, 0.0% Native Hawaiian/Other Pacific Islander, 0.9% Other, 0.6% Hispanic of any race (2010); Average household size: 2.93 (2010); Median age: 37.4 (2010); Males per 100 females: 98.4 (2010); Marriage status: 19.7% never married, 66.8% now married, 4.5% widowed, 9.0% divorced (2006-2010 5-year est.); Foreign born: 2.8% (2006-2010 5-year est.); Ancestry (includes multiple ancestries): 32.0% German, 26.4% Irish, 22.9% Polish, 20.0% Italian, 4.4% English (2006-2010 5-year est.).

Economy: Employment by occupation: 12.6% management, 2.6% professional, 2.4% services, 24.0% sales, 3.9% farming, 7.0% construction, 9.2% production (2006-2010 5-year est.).

Income: Per capita income: $25,179 (2006-2010 5-year est.); Median household income: $66,960 (2006-2010 5-year est.); Average household income: $78,175 (2006-2010 5-year est.); Percent of households with income of $100,000 or more: 30.5% (2006-2010 5-year est.); Poverty rate: 9.8% (2006-2010 5-year est.).

Education: Percent of population age 25 and over with: High school diploma (including GED) or higher: 91.2% (2006-2010 5-year est.); Bachelor's degree or higher: 37.0% (2006-2010 5-year est.); Master's degree or higher: 11.9% (2006-2010 5-year est.).

School District(s)

Canon-Mcmillan SD (KG-12)
  2010-11 Enrollment: 4,954 . . . . (724) 746-2940

Housing: Homeownership rate: 86.4% (2010); Median home value: $210,800 (2006-2010 5-year est.); Median contract rent: $471 per month (2006-2010 5-year est.); Median year structure built: 1993 (2006-2010 5-year est.).

Transportation: Commute to work: 92.5% car, 0.8% public transportation, 0.0% walk, 6.0% work from home (2006-2010 5-year est.); Travel time to work: 25.7% less than 15 minutes, 37.0% 15 to 30 minutes, 23.9% 30 to 45 minutes, 8.5% 45 to 60 minutes, 4.9% 60 minutes or more (2006-2010 5-year est.)

NEW EAGLE (borough). Covers a land area of 1.016 square miles and a water area of 0.107 square miles. Located at 40.21° N. Lat; 79.95° W. Long. Elevation is 787 feet.

History: Incorporated 1912.

Population: 2,171 (1990); 2,262 (2000); 2,184 (2010); Density: 2,149.2 persons per square mile (2010); Race: 97.3% White, 0.8% Black, 0.6% Asian, 0.1% American Indian/Alaska Native, 0.0% Native Hawaiian/Other Pacific Islander, 1.2% Other, 0.5% Hispanic of any race (2010); Average household size: 2.22 (2010); Median age: 44.2 (2010); Males per 100 females: 91.9 (2010); Marriage status: 24.4% never married, 47.2% now married, 14.6% widowed, 13.8% divorced (2006-2010 5-year est.); Foreign born: 2.9% (2006-2010 5-year est.); Ancestry (includes multiple

ancestries): 23.9% Italian, 22.4% German, 18.4% Irish, 17.7% English, 6.9% Polish (2006-2010 5-year est.).

Economy: Single-family building permits issued: 0 (2011); Multi-family building permits issued: 0 (2011); Employment by occupation: 4.5% management, 4.1% professional, 14.4% services, 16.1% sales, 5.4% farming, 10.2% construction, 6.9% production (2006-2010 5-year est.).

Income: Per capita income: $18,810 (2006-2010 5-year est.); Median household income: $34,831 (2006-2010 5-year est.); Average household income: $43,678 (2006-2010 5-year est.); Percent of households with income of $100,000 or more: 6.4% (2006-2010 5-year est.); Poverty rate: 15.7% (2006-2010 5-year est.).

Education: Percent of population age 25 and over with: High school diploma (including GED) or higher: 88.1% (2006-2010 5-year est.); Bachelor's degree or higher: 15.4% (2006-2010 5-year est.); Master's degree or higher: 3.0% (2006-2010 5-year est.).

Housing: Homeownership rate: 74.1% (2010); Median home value: $72,700 (2006-2010 5-year est.); Median contract rent: $442 per month (2006-2010 5-year est.); Median year structure built: 1964 (2006-2010 5-year est.).

Transportation: Commute to work: 90.0% car, 4.1% public transportation, 3.6% walk, 1.1% work from home (2006-2010 5-year est.); Travel time to work: 23.5% less than 15 minutes, 33.0% 15 to 30 minutes, 23.3% 30 to 45 minutes, 9.0% 45 to 60 minutes, 11.2% 60 minutes or more (2006-2010 5-year est.)

Additional Information Contacts

Mon Valley Regional Chamber of Commerce . . . . (724) 483-3507
  http://www.mvrchamber.org

NORTH BETHLEHEM (township). Covers a land area of 22.083 square miles and a water area of 0 square miles. Located at 40.10° N. Lat; 80.10° W. Long.

Population: 1,938 (1990); 1,746 (2000); 1,631 (2010); Density: 73.9 persons per square mile (2010); Race: 98.5% White, 0.2% Black, 0.2% Asian, 0.1% American Indian/Alaska Native, 0.0% Native Hawaiian/Other Pacific Islander, 1.0% Other, 0.6% Hispanic of any race (2010); Average household size: 2.45 (2010); Median age: 44.5 (2010); Males per 100 females: 99.4 (2010); Marriage status: 23.0% never married, 61.5% now married, 7.4% widowed, 8.0% divorced (2006-2010 5-year est.); Foreign born: 0.9% (2006-2010 5-year est.); Ancestry (includes multiple ancestries): 28.9% German, 18.0% Irish, 16.6% Italian, 15.5% English, 11.0% Polish (2006-2010 5-year est.).

Economy: Single-family building permits issued: 2 (2011); Multi-family building permits issued: 0 (2011); Employment by occupation: 14.0% management, 3.5% professional, 6.5% services, 15.0% sales, 2.4% farming, 17.0% construction, 7.4% production (2006-2010 5-year est.).

Income: Per capita income: $32,542 (2006-2010 5-year est.); Median household income: $59,167 (2006-2010 5-year est.); Average household income: $81,874 (2006-2010 5-year est.); Percent of households with income of $100,000 or more: 20.4% (2006-2010 5-year est.); Poverty rate: 5.6% (2006-2010 5-year est.).

Education: Percent of population age 25 and over with: High school diploma (including GED) or higher: 89.5% (2006-2010 5-year est.); Bachelor's degree or higher: 26.5% (2006-2010 5-year est.); Master's degree or higher: 7.3% (2006-2010 5-year est.).

Housing: Homeownership rate: 82.8% (2010); Median home value: $151,800 (2006-2010 5-year est.); Median contract rent: $494 per month (2006-2010 5-year est.); Median year structure built: 1957 (2006-2010 5-year est.).

Transportation: Commute to work: 93.7% car, 0.0% public transportation, 1.3% walk, 4.1% work from home (2006-2010 5-year est.); Travel time to work: 18.3% less than 15 minutes, 40.2% 15 to 30 minutes, 19.5% 30 to 45 minutes, 7.2% 45 to 60 minutes, 14.7% 60 minutes or more (2006-2010 5-year est.)

Additional Information Contacts

Washington County Chamber of Commerce . . . . (724) 225-3010
  http://www.washcochamber.com

NORTH CHARLEROI (borough). Aka West Monesson. Covers a land area of 0.257 square miles and a water area of 0.037 square miles. Located at 40.15° N. Lat; 79.91° W. Long. Elevation is 810 feet.

History: Incorporated 1894.

Population: 1,562 (1990); 1,409 (2000); 1,313 (2010); Density: 5,108.6 persons per square mile (2010); Race: 96.3% White, 1.8% Black, 0.2% Asian, 0.1% American Indian/Alaska Native, 0.0% Native Hawaiian/Other Pacific Islander, 1.6% Other, 1.2% Hispanic of any race (2010); Average

household size: 2.10 (2010); Median age: 46.7 (2010); Males per 100 females: 81.4 (2010); Marriage status: 28.5% never married, 48.1% now married, 16.2% widowed, 7.2% divorced (2006-2010 5-year est.); Foreign born: 0.4% (2006-2010 5-year est.); Ancestry (includes multiple ancestries): 26.0% Italian, 24.3% German, 17.4% English, 13.5% Irish, 12.3% Polish (2006-2010 5-year est.).

Economy: Single-family building permits issued: 0 (2011); Multi-family building permits issued: 0 (2011); Employment by occupation: 9.5% management, 2.7% professional, 14.9% services, 21.6% sales, 3.6% farming, 7.3% construction, 5.9% production (2006-2010 5-year est.).

Income: Per capita income: $20,257 (2006-2010 5-year est.); Median household income: $33,750 (2006-2010 5-year est.); Average household income: $41,292 (2006-2010 5-year est.); Percent of households with income of $100,000 or more: 7.8% (2006-2010 5-year est.); Poverty rate: 9.8% (2006-2010 5-year est.).

Education: Percent of population age 25 and over with: High school diploma (including GED) or higher: 86.0% (2006-2010 5-year est.); Bachelor's degree or higher: 18.2% (2006-2010 5-year est.); Master's degree or higher: 5.7% (2006-2010 5-year est.).

Housing: Homeownership rate: 60.2% (2010); Median home value: $62,200 (2006-2010 5-year est.); Median contract rent: $308 per month (2006-2010 5-year est.); Median year structure built: before 1940 (2006-2010 5-year est.).

Safety: Violent crime rate: 7.6 per 10,000 population; Property crime rate: 45.6 per 10,000 population (2011).

Transportation: Commute to work: 93.4% car, 3.9% public transportation, 0.8% walk, 1.9% work from home (2006-2010 5-year est.); Travel time to work: 39.5% less than 15 minutes, 25.8% 15 to 30 minutes, 16.5% 30 to 45 minutes, 9.9% 45 to 60 minutes, 8.3% 60 minutes or more (2006-2010 5-year est.)

Additional Information Contacts

Mon Valley Regional Chamber of Commerce . . . . (724) 483-3507
  http://www.mvrchamber.org

NORTH FRANKLIN (township). Covers a land area of 7.295 square miles and a water area of 0.164 square miles. Located at 40.15° N. Lat; 80.25° W. Long.

Population: 4,997 (1990); 4,818 (2000); 4,583 (2010); Density: 628.2 persons per square mile (2010); Race: 96.3% White, 2.1% Black, 0.3% Asian, 0.1% American Indian/Alaska Native, 0.0% Native Hawaiian/Other Pacific Islander, 1.2% Other, 0.9% Hispanic of any race (2010); Average household size: 2.29 (2010); Median age: 48.1 (2010); Males per 100 females: 87.2 (2010); Marriage status: 21.5% never married, 57.2% now married, 15.6% widowed, 5.7% divorced (2006-2010 5-year est.); Foreign born: 1.3% (2006-2010 5-year est.); Ancestry (includes multiple ancestries): 32.7% German, 16.0% English, 15.5% Irish, 15.3% Italian, 8.9% Polish (2006-2010 5-year est.).

Economy: Single-family building permits issued: 6 (2011); Multi-family building permits issued: 0 (2011); Employment by occupation: 9.8% management, 3.2% professional, 10.6% services, 19.0% sales, 3.9% farming, 2.7% construction, 3.2% production (2006-2010 5-year est.).

Income: Per capita income: $25,242 (2006-2010 5-year est.); Median household income: $51,441 (2006-2010 5-year est.); Average household income: $64,741 (2006-2010 5-year est.); Percent of households with income of $100,000 or more: 18.7% (2006-2010 5-year est.); Poverty rate: 10.5% (2006-2010 5-year est.).

Education: Percent of population age 25 and over with: High school diploma (including GED) or higher: 88.6% (2006-2010 5-year est.); Bachelor's degree or higher: 23.6% (2006-2010 5-year est.); Master's degree or higher: 9.4% (2006-2010 5-year est.).

Housing: Homeownership rate: 75.1% (2010); Median home value: $156,000 (2006-2010 5-year est.); Median contract rent: $473 per month (2006-2010 5-year est.); Median year structure built: 1960 (2006-2010 5-year est.).

Safety: Violent crime rate: 30.4 per 10,000 population; Property crime rate: 267.5 per 10,000 population (2011).

Transportation: Commute to work: 93.8% car, 0.0% public transportation, 1.7% walk, 3.5% work from home (2006-2010 5-year est.); Travel time to work: 44.7% less than 15 minutes, 29.8% 15 to 30 minutes, 16.5% 30 to 45 minutes, 6.5% 45 to 60 minutes, 2.5% 60 minutes or more (2006-2010 5-year est.)

Additional Information Contacts

North Franklin Township . . . . (724) 228-2150
  http://www.northfranklintownship.com

Washington County Chamber of Commerce . . . . (724) 225-3010
  http://www.washcochamber.com

NORTH STRABANE (township). Covers a land area of 27.264
square miles and a water area of 0.135 square miles. Located at 40.23° N.
Lat; 80.15° W. Long.
Population: 8,146 (1990); 10,057 (2000); 13,408 (2010); Density: 491.8
persons per square mile (2010); Race: 96.0% White, 1.6% Black, 1.2%
Asian, 0.1% American Indian/Alaska Native, 0.0% Native Hawaiian/Other
Pacific Islander, 1.1% Other, 1.1% Hispanic of any race (2010); Average
household size: 2.43 (2010); Median age: 42.8 (2010); Males per 100
females: 93.1 (2010); Marriage status: 21.3% never married, 61.2% now
married, 8.2% widowed, 9.3% divorced (2006-2010 5-year est.); Foreign
born: 1.6% (2006-2010 5-year est.); Ancestry (includes multiple
ancestries): 25.7% German, 20.7% Irish, 20.0% Italian, 12.2% Polish,
11.5% English (2006-2010 5-year est.).
Economy: Single-family building permits issued: 43 (2011); Multi-family
building permits issued: 17 (2011); Employment by occupation: 15.5%
management, 4.9% professional, 9.9% services, 19.9% sales, 1.8%
farming, 5.4% construction, 3.4% production (2006-2010 5-year est.).
Income: Per capita income: $31,251 (2006-2010 5-year est.); Median
household income: $65,602 (2006-2010 5-year est.); Average household
income: $77,646 (2006-2010 5-year est.); Percent of households with
income of $100,000 or more: 25.0% (2006-2010 5-year est.); Poverty rate:
3.5% (2006-2010 5-year est.).
Education: Percent of population age 25 and over with: High school
diploma (including GED) or higher: 92.4% (2006-2010 5-year est.);
Bachelor's degree or higher: 36.1% (2006-2010 5-year est.); Master's
degree or higher: 12.3% (2006-2010 5-year est.).
Housing: Homeownership rate: 88.3% (2010); Median home value:
$183,600 (2006-2010 5-year est.); Median contract rent: $529 per month
(2006-2010 5-year est.); Median year structure built: 1978 (2006-2010
5-year est.).
Safety: Violent crime rate: 6.7 per 10,000 population; Property crime rate:
113.0 per 10,000 population (2011).
Transportation: Commute to work: 92.5% car, 2.5% public transportation,
0.3% walk, 4.0% work from home (2006-2010 5-year est.); Travel time to
work: 24.5% less than 15 minutes, 36.6% 15 to 30 minutes, 24.6% 30 to
45 minutes, 7.8% 45 to 60 minutes, 6.6% 60 minutes or more (2006-2010
5-year est.).
Additional Information Contacts
Greater Canonsburg Chamber of Commerce . . . . (724) 745-1812
  http://www.canonchamber.com
North Strabane Township . . . . (724) 745-7220
  http://www.northstrabanetwp.com

NOTTINGHAM (township). Covers a land area of 20.289 square
miles and a water area of 0 square miles. Located at 40.21° N. Lat; 80.05°
W. Long.
Population: 2,239 (1990); 2,522 (2000); 3,036 (2010); Density: 149.6
persons per square mile (2010); Race: 98.5% White, 0.4% Black, 0.3%
Asian, 0.1% American Indian/Alaska Native, 0.0% Native Hawaiian/Other
Pacific Islander, 0.7% Other, 1.0% Hispanic of any race (2010); Average
household size: 2.44 (2010); Median age: 48.8 (2010); Males per 100
females: 102.4 (2010); Marriage status: 20.8% never married, 64.3% now
married, 5.7% widowed, 9.2% divorced (2006-2010 5-year est.); Foreign
born: 1.6% (2006-2010 5-year est.); Ancestry (includes multiple
ancestries): 39.4% German, 24.2% Irish, 12.4% Polish, 12.3% English,
9.1% Italian (2006-2010 5-year est.).
Economy: Single-family building permits issued: 5 (2011); Multi-family
building permits issued: 0 (2011); Employment by occupation: 10.2%
management, 4.0% professional, 10.6% services, 13.7% sales, 4.0%
farming, 18.3% construction, 8.8% production (2006-2010 5-year est.).
Income: Per capita income: $30,178 (2006-2010 5-year est.); Median
household income: $59,099 (2006-2010 5-year est.); Average household
income: $71,150 (2006-2010 5-year est.); Percent of households with
income of $100,000 or more: 25.6% (2006-2010 5-year est.); Poverty rate:
8.4% (2006-2010 5-year est.).
Education: Percent of population age 25 and over with: High school
diploma (including GED) or higher: 94.3% (2006-2010 5-year est.);
Bachelor's degree or higher: 27.0% (2006-2010 5-year est.); Master's
degree or higher: 7.3% (2006-2010 5-year est.).
Housing: Homeownership rate: 94.4% (2010); Median home value:
$207,900 (2006-2010 5-year est.); Median contract rent: $521 per month

(2006-2010 5-year est.); Median year structure built: 1978 (2006-2010
5-year est.).
Transportation: Commute to work: 91.4% car, 2.4% public transportation,
1.1% walk, 4.5% work from home (2006-2010 5-year est.); Travel time to
work: 18.5% less than 15 minutes, 35.0% 15 to 30 minutes, 19.8% 30 to
45 minutes, 12.0% 45 to 60 minutes, 14.6% 60 minutes or more
(2006-2010 5-year est.)
Additional Information Contacts
Oxford Area Chamber of Commerce . . . . (610) 932-0740
  http://www.oxfordpa.org

PARIS (CDP). Covers a land area of 2.111 square miles and a water
area of 0 square miles. Located at 40.41° N. Lat; 80.51° W. Long.
Elevation is 1,227 feet.
Population: n/a (1990); n/a (2000); 732 (2010); Density: 346.8 persons
per square mile (2010); Race: 98.2% White, 0.7% Black, 0.4% Asian,
0.0% American Indian/Alaska Native, 0.0% Native Hawaiian/Other Pacific
Islander, 0.7% Other, 0.4% Hispanic of any race (2010); Average
household size: 2.48 (2010); Median age: 46.8 (2010); Males per 100
females: 106.2 (2010); Marriage status: 27.1% never married, 63.2% now
married, 6.0% widowed, 3.7% divorced (2006-2010 5-year est.); Foreign
born: 0.0% (2006-2010 5-year est.); Ancestry (includes multiple
ancestries): 37.8% Irish, 33.6% German, 15.5% American, 10.2% English,
7.0% Polish (2006-2010 5-year est.).
Economy: Employment by occupation: 7.8% management, 8.8%
professional, 6.4% services, 19.9% sales, 4.1% farming, 22.6%
construction, 14.2% production (2006-2010 5-year est.).
Income: Per capita income: $21,022 (2006-2010 5-year est.); Median
household income: $42,188 (2006-2010 5-year est.); Average household
income: $55,587 (2006-2010 5-year est.); Percent of households with
income of $100,000 or more: 9.4% (2006-2010 5-year est.); Poverty rate:
9.1% (2006-2010 5-year est.).
Education: Percent of population age 25 and over with: High school
diploma (including GED) or higher: 91.9% (2006-2010 5-year est.);
Bachelor's degree or higher: 6.9% (2006-2010 5-year est.); Master's
degree or higher: 2.3% (2006-2010 5-year est.).
Housing: Homeownership rate: 87.5% (2010); Median home value:
$101,500 (2006-2010 5-year est.); Median contract rent: $435 per month
(2006-2010 5-year est.); Median year structure built: 1963 (2006-2010
5-year est.).
Transportation: Commute to work: 95.9% car, 0.0% public transportation,
0.0% walk, 2.4% work from home (2006-2010 5-year est.); Travel time to
work: 6.3% less than 15 minutes, 34.9% 15 to 30 minutes, 30.3% 30 to 45
minutes, 16.2% 45 to 60 minutes, 12.3% 60 minutes or more (2006-2010
5-year est.)

PETERS (township). Covers a land area of 19.551 square miles and a
water area of 0.175 square miles. Located at 40.27° N. Lat; 80.08° W.
Long.
History: Peters Township was incorporated in 1781 as one of the 13
original Townships of Washington County when it became part of
Pennsylvania. Prior to 1781, the Peters Township area was part of
Virginia.
Population: 14,542 (1990); 17,566 (2000); 21,213 (2010); Density:
1,085.0 persons per square mile (2010); Race: 96.2% White, 0.5% Black,
2.0% Asian, 0.1% American Indian/Alaska Native, 0.0% Native
Hawaiian/Other Pacific Islander, 1.2% Other, 1.5% Hispanic of any race
(2010); Average household size: 2.88 (2010); Median age: 43.0 (2010);
Males per 100 females: 96.8 (2010); Marriage status: 19.4% never
married, 69.6% now married, 5.7% widowed, 5.3% divorced (2006-2010
5-year est.); Foreign born: 3.4% (2006-2010 5-year est.); Ancestry
(includes multiple ancestries): 30.2% German, 21.8% Irish, 21.0% Italian,
13.9% English, 12.1% Polish (2006-2010 5-year est.).
Economy: Single-family building permits issued: 85 (2011); Multi-family
building permits issued: 0 (2011); Employment by occupation: 20.0%
management, 5.4% professional, 6.6% services, 15.2% sales, 3.1%
farming, 5.4% construction, 2.5% production (2006-2010 5-year est.).
Income: Per capita income: $40,461 (2006-2010 5-year est.); Median
household income: $100,109 (2006-2010 5-year est.); Average household
income: $121,750 (2006-2010 5-year est.); Percent of households with
income of $100,000 or more: 50.0% (2006-2010 5-year est.); Poverty rate:
3.8% (2006-2010 5-year est.).
Education: Percent of population age 25 and over with: High school
diploma (including GED) or higher: 94.6% (2006-2010 5-year est.);

Bachelor's degree or higher: 54.0% (2006-2010 5-year est.); Master's degree or higher: 23.4% (2006-2010 5-year est.).

Housing: Homeownership rate: 94.2% (2010); Median home value: $286,600 (2006-2010 5-year est.); Median contract rent: $680 per month (2006-2010 5-year est.); Median year structure built: 1979 (2006-2010 5-year est.).

Safety: Violent crime rate: 3.8 per 10,000 population; Property crime rate: 67.7 per 10,000 population (2011).

Transportation: Commute to work: 85.6% car, 3.9% public transportation, 1.7% walk, 7.6% work from home (2006-2010 5-year est.); Travel time to work: 23.7% less than 15 minutes, 32.1% 15 to 30 minutes, 24.5% 30 to 45 minutes, 12.0% 45 to 60 minutes, 7.7% 60 minutes or more (2006-2010 5-year est.)

Additional Information Contacts
Peters Township . . . . (724) 941-4180
    http://www.peterstownship.com
Washington County Chamber of Commerce. . . . . (724) 225-3010
    http://www.washcochamber.com

PROSPERITY (unincorporated postal area)
Zip Code: 15329

Covers a land area of 40.546 square miles and a water area of 0.028 square miles. Located at 40.02° N. Lat; 80.27° W. Long. Elevation is 1,037 feet. Population: 1,709 (2010); Density: 42.1 persons per square mile (2010); Race: 97.2% White, 1.1% Black, 0.2% Asian, 0.0% American Indian/Alaska Native, 0.0% Native Hawaiian/Other Pacific Islander, 1.5% Other, 1.1% Hispanic of any race (2010); Average household size: 2.59 (2010); Median age: 43.9 (2010); Males per 100 females: 106.7 (2010); Homeownership rate: 77.9% (2010)

RICHEYVILLE (unincorporated postal area)
Zip Code: 15358

Covers a land area of 0.845 square miles and a water area of 0 square miles. Located at 40.05° N. Lat; 80.00° W. Long. Elevation is 1,194 feet. Population: 923 (2010); Density: 1,091.7 persons per square mile (2010); Race: 96.5% White, 1.0% Black, 0.0% Asian, 0.2% American Indian/Alaska Native, 0.1% Native Hawaiian/Other Pacific Islander, 2.2% Other, 1.5% Hispanic of any race (2010); Average household size: 2.40 (2010); Median age: 42.5 (2010); Males per 100 females: 91.5 (2010); Homeownership rate: 78.4% (2010)

ROBINSON (township). Covers a land area of 21.124 square miles and a water area of 0.057 square miles. Located at 40.41° N. Lat; 80.30° W. Long. Elevation is 1,178 feet.

Population: 2,160 (1990); 2,193 (2000); 1,931 (2010); Density: 91.4 persons per square mile (2010); Race: 97.2% White, 1.2% Black, 0.3% Asian, 0.1% American Indian/Alaska Native, 0.1% Native Hawaiian/Other Pacific Islander, 1.1% Other, 0.3% Hispanic of any race (2010); Average household size: 2.41 (2010); Median age: 44.6 (2010); Males per 100 females: 106.3 (2010); Marriage status: 28.9% never married, 56.0% now married, 9.3% widowed, 5.8% divorced (2006-2010 5-year est.); Foreign born: 0.9% (2006-2010 5-year est.); Ancestry (includes multiple ancestries): 34.7% German, 22.8% Irish, 22.4% Italian, 13.5% Polish, 11.0% English (2006-2010 5-year est.).

Economy: Single-family building permits issued: 2 (2011); Multi-family building permits issued: 0 (2011); Employment by occupation: 6.9% management, 4.9% professional, 8.7% services, 16.5% sales, 10.1% farming, 15.9% construction, 10.1% production (2006-2010 5-year est.).

Income: Per capita income: $23,409 (2006-2010 5-year est.); Median household income: $46,917 (2006-2010 5-year est.); Average household income: $54,768 (2006-2010 5-year est.); Percent of households with income of $100,000 or more: 9.6% (2006-2010 5-year est.); Poverty rate: 14.0% (2006-2010 5-year est.).

Education: Percent of population age 25 and over with: High school diploma (including GED) or higher: 86.7% (2006-2010 5-year est.); Bachelor's degree or higher: 12.8% (2006-2010 5-year est.); Master's degree or higher: 3.7% (2006-2010 5-year est.).

Housing: Homeownership rate: 84.1% (2010); Median home value: $125,100 (2006-2010 5-year est.); Median contract rent: $480 per month (2006-2010 5-year est.); Median year structure built: 1964 (2006-2010 5-year est.).

Safety: Violent crime rate: 20.7 per 10,000 population; Property crime rate: 180.7 per 10,000 population (2011).

Transportation: Commute to work: 93.9% car, 1.0% public transportation, 1.8% walk, 2.6% work from home (2006-2010 5-year est.); Travel time to

work: 20.8% less than 15 minutes, 44.4% 15 to 30 minutes, 21.3% 30 to 45 minutes, 7.8% 45 to 60 minutes, 5.7% 60 minutes or more (2006-2010 5-year est.)

Additional Information Contacts
Pittsburgh Airport Area Chamber of Commerce . . . . (412) 264-6270
    http://www.paacc.com

ROSCOE (borough). Covers a land area of 0.179 square miles and a water area of 0.065 square miles. Located at 40.08° N. Lat; 79.86° W. Long. Elevation is 774 feet.

History: Incorporated 1892.

Population: 872 (1990); 848 (2000); 812 (2010); Density: 4,524.7 persons per square mile (2010); Race: 96.6% White, 1.0% Black, 0.0% Asian, 0.2% American Indian/Alaska Native, 0.0% Native Hawaiian/Other Pacific Islander, 2.2% Other, 0.6% Hispanic of any race (2010); Average household size: 2.26 (2010); Median age: 47.0 (2010); Males per 100 females: 83.3 (2010); Marriage status: 22.6% never married, 54.5% now married, 14.6% widowed, 8.2% divorced (2006-2010 5-year est.); Foreign born: 1.7% (2006-2010 5-year est.); Ancestry (includes multiple ancestries): 24.4% German, 23.2% English, 14.6% Italian, 12.4% Polish, 9.9% Russian (2006-2010 5-year est.).

Economy: Single-family building permits issued: 0 (2011); Multi-family building permits issued: 0 (2011); Employment by occupation: 4.8% management, 4.8% professional, 11.4% services, 17.4% sales, 0.9% farming, 12.6% construction, 9.9% production (2006-2010 5-year est.).

Income: Per capita income: $22,695 (2006-2010 5-year est.); Median household income: $38,625 (2006-2010 5-year est.); Average household income: $48,377 (2006-2010 5-year est.); Percent of households with income of $100,000 or more: 12.3% (2006-2010 5-year est.); Poverty rate: 5.2% (2006-2010 5-year est.).

Education: Percent of population age 25 and over with: High school diploma (including GED) or higher: 92.1% (2006-2010 5-year est.); Bachelor's degree or higher: 18.3% (2006-2010 5-year est.); Master's degree or higher: 4.5% (2006-2010 5-year est.).

Housing: Homeownership rate: 73.1% (2010); Median home value: $82,200 (2006-2010 5-year est.); Median contract rent: $367 per month (2006-2010 5-year est.); Median year structure built: 1945 (2006-2010 5-year est.).

Transportation: Commute to work: 94.6% car, 0.0% public transportation, 2.2% walk, 0.9% work from home (2006-2010 5-year est.); Travel time to work: 29.0% less than 15 minutes, 36.3% 15 to 30 minutes, 16.9% 30 to 45 minutes, 11.1% 45 to 60 minutes, 6.7% 60 minutes or more (2006-2010 5-year est.)

SCENERY HILL (unincorporated postal area)
Zip Code: 15360

Covers a land area of 25.596 square miles and a water area of 0 square miles. Located at 40.08° N. Lat; 80.08° W. Long. Elevation is 1,388 feet. Population: 1,731 (2010); Density: 67.6 persons per square mile (2010); Race: 98.2% White, 0.2% Black, 0.2% Asian, 0.2% American Indian/Alaska Native, 0.0% Native Hawaiian/Other Pacific Islander, 1.2% Other, 0.6% Hispanic of any race (2010); Average household size: 2.52 (2010); Median age: 45.2 (2010); Males per 100 females: 103.4 (2010); Homeownership rate: 86.9% (2010)

SLOVAN (CDP). Covers a land area of 0.587 square miles and a water area of 0 square miles. Located at 40.36° N. Lat; 80.39° W. Long. Elevation is 1,040 feet.

Population: n/a (1990); n/a (2000); 555 (2010); Density: 945.1 persons per square mile (2010); Race: 97.5% White, 0.5% Black, 0.2% Asian, 0.2% American Indian/Alaska Native, 0.0% Native Hawaiian/Other Pacific Islander, 1.6% Other, 1.3% Hispanic of any race (2010); Average household size: 2.17 (2010); Median age: 44.9 (2010); Males per 100 females: 87.5 (2010); Marriage status: 12.7% never married, 71.2% now married, 13.4% widowed, 2.7% divorced (2006-2010 5-year est.); Foreign born: 0.0% (2006-2010 5-year est.); Ancestry (includes multiple ancestries): 52.6% German, 37.7% English, 13.6% Polish, 11.4% Irish, 10.7% Serbian (2006-2010 5-year est.).

Economy: Employment by occupation: 0.0% management, 30.6% professional, 9.9% services, 39.7% sales, 0.0% farming, 7.3% construction, 0.0% production (2006-2010 5-year est.).

Income: Per capita income: $26,097 (2006-2010 5-year est.); Median household income: $33,900 (2006-2010 5-year est.); Average household income: $40,032 (2006-2010 5-year est.); Percent of households with

income of $100,000 or more: n/a (2006-2010 5-year est.); Poverty rate: 2.2% (2006-2010 5-year est.).

Education: Percent of population age 25 and over with: High school diploma (including GED) or higher: 77.7% (2006-2010 5-year est.); Bachelor's degree or higher: 7.2% (2006-2010 5-year est.); Master's degree or higher: 3.0% (2006-2010 5-year est.).

Housing: Homeownership rate: 67.1% (2010); Median home value: $101,000 (2006-2010 5-year est.); Median contract rent: n/a per month (2006-2010 5-year est.); Median year structure built: before 1940 (2006-2010 5-year est.).

Transportation: Commute to work: 100.0% car, 0.0% public transportation, 0.0% walk, 0.0% work from home (2006-2010 5-year est.); Travel time to work: 47.8% less than 15 minutes, 5.2% 15 to 30 minutes, 16.4% 30 to 45 minutes, 30.6% 45 to 60 minutes, 0.0% 60 minutes or more (2006-2010 5-year est.)

SMITH (township). Covers a land area of 34.439 square miles and a water area of 0.017 square miles. Located at 40.37° N. Lat; 80.38° W. Long.

Population: 4,844 (1990); 4,567 (2000); 4,476 (2010); Density: 130.0 persons per square mile (2010); Race: 96.8% White, 1.1% Black, 0.3% Asian, 0.0% American Indian/Alaska Native, 0.0% Native Hawaiian/Other Pacific Islander, 1.8% Other, 1.2% Hispanic of any race (2010); Average household size: 2.37 (2010); Median age: 44.9 (2010); Males per 100 females: 96.7 (2010); Marriage status: 26.9% never married, 55.9% now married, 10.3% widowed, 6.9% divorced (2006-2010 5-year est.); Foreign born: 0.9% (2006-2010 5-year est.); Ancestry (includes multiple ancestries): 27.5% German, 24.1% Italian, 19.3% Irish, 10.8% Polish, 8.1% English (2006-2010 5-year est.).

Economy: Single-family building permits issued: 3 (2011); Multi-family building permits issued: 0 (2011); Employment by occupation: 4.7% management, 4.3% professional, 20.4% services, 19.1% sales, 1.0% farming, 12.2% construction, 5.7% production (2006-2010 5-year est.).

Income: Per capita income: $22,309 (2006-2010 5-year est.); Median household income: $44,028 (2006-2010 5-year est.); Average household income: $49,315 (2006-2010 5-year est.); Percent of households with income of $100,000 or more: 11.1% (2006-2010 5-year est.); Poverty rate: 11.0% (2006-2010 5-year est.).

Education: Percent of population age 25 and over with: High school diploma (including GED) or higher: 84.4% (2006-2010 5-year est.); Bachelor's degree or higher: 14.6% (2006-2010 5-year est.); Master's degree or higher: 5.6% (2006-2010 5-year est.).

Housing: Homeownership rate: 79.5% (2010); Median home value: $97,200 (2006-2010 5-year est.); Median contract rent: $373 per month (2006-2010 5-year est.); Median year structure built: 1953 (2006-2010 5-year est.).

Safety: Violent crime rate: 0.0 per 10,000 population; Property crime rate: 0.0 per 10,000 population (2011).

Transportation: Commute to work: 93.8% car, 2.3% public transportation, 1.1% walk, 2.9% work from home (2006-2010 5-year est.); Travel time to work: 20.5% less than 15 minutes, 32.1% 15 to 30 minutes, 32.5% 30 to 45 minutes, 6.8% 45 to 60 minutes, 8.1% 60 minutes or more (2006-2010 5-year est.)

Additional Information Contacts

Smith Township . . . . (724) 947-9456
  http://www.smithtownship.org
Washington County Chamber of Commerce . . . . (724) 225-3010
  http://www.washcochamber.com

SOMERSET (township). Covers a land area of 32.146 square miles and a water area of 0.040 square miles. Located at 40.15° N. Lat; 80.06° W. Long.

Population: 2,947 (1990); 2,701 (2000); 2,684 (2010); Density: 83.5 persons per square mile (2010); Race: 98.8% White, 0.6% Black, 0.1% Asian, 0.0% American Indian/Alaska Native, 0.0% Native Hawaiian/Other Pacific Islander, 0.5% Other, 0.6% Hispanic of any race (2010); Average household size: 2.47 (2010); Median age: 47.2 (2010); Males per 100 females: 106.1 (2010); Marriage status: 26.8% never married, 56.7% now married, 7.9% widowed, 8.6% divorced (2006-2010 5-year est.); Foreign born: 0.6% (2006-2010 5-year est.); Ancestry (includes multiple ancestries): 30.4% German, 22.0% Irish, 17.3% Italian, 13.7% English, 10.4% Polish (2006-2010 5-year est.).

Economy: Single-family building permits issued: 0 (2011); Multi-family building permits issued: 0 (2011); Employment by occupation: 8.0%

management, 6.0% professional, 7.8% services, 16.9% sales, 4.1% farming, 14.9% construction, 5.8% production (2006-2010 5-year est.).

Income: Per capita income: $26,631 (2006-2010 5-year est.); Median household income: $52,449 (2006-2010 5-year est.); Average household income: $66,269 (2006-2010 5-year est.); Percent of households with income of $100,000 or more: 23.0% (2006-2010 5-year est.); Poverty rate: 7.8% (2006-2010 5-year est.).

Education: Percent of population age 25 and over with: High school diploma (including GED) or higher: 87.2% (2006-2010 5-year est.); Bachelor's degree or higher: 17.7% (2006-2010 5-year est.); Master's degree or higher: 5.2% (2006-2010 5-year est.).

Housing: Homeownership rate: 85.8% (2010); Median home value: $161,400 (2006-2010 5-year est.); Median contract rent: $462 per month (2006-2010 5-year est.); Median year structure built: 1971 (2006-2010 5-year est.).

Transportation: Commute to work: 91.4% car, 0.0% public transportation, 4.0% walk, 4.6% work from home (2006-2010 5-year est.); Travel time to work: 18.6% less than 15 minutes, 38.6% 15 to 30 minutes, 26.8% 30 to 45 minutes, 6.7% 45 to 60 minutes, 9.2% 60 minutes or more (2006-2010 5-year est.)

Additional Information Contacts

Washington County Chamber of Commerce . . . . (724) 225-3010
  http://www.washcochamber.com

SOUTH FRANKLIN (township). Covers a land area of 20.578 square miles and a water area of 0.092 square miles. Located at 40.09° N. Lat; 80.29° W. Long.

Population: 3,665 (1990); 3,796 (2000); 3,310 (2010); Density: 160.9 persons per square mile (2010); Race: 98.0% White, 0.5% Black, 0.2% Asian, 0.0% American Indian/Alaska Native, 0.0% Native Hawaiian/Other Pacific Islander, 1.3% Other, 0.7% Hispanic of any race (2010); Average household size: 2.56 (2010); Median age: 44.3 (2010); Males per 100 females: 99.6 (2010); Marriage status: 25.4% never married, 61.6% now married, 4.2% widowed, 8.8% divorced (2006-2010 5-year est.); Foreign born: 0.9% (2006-2010 5-year est.); Ancestry (includes multiple ancestries): 31.5% Irish, 29.4% German, 19.1% Italian, 17.6% English, 9.1% Scotch-Irish (2006-2010 5-year est.).

Economy: Single-family building permits issued: 2 (2011); Multi-family building permits issued: 0 (2011); Employment by occupation: 12.9% management, 4.1% professional, 13.2% services, 20.4% sales, 4.4% farming, 10.8% construction, 3.6% production (2006-2010 5-year est.).

Income: Per capita income: $27,233 (2006-2010 5-year est.); Median household income: $58,504 (2006-2010 5-year est.); Average household income: $69,543 (2006-2010 5-year est.); Percent of households with income of $100,000 or more: 20.6% (2006-2010 5-year est.); Poverty rate: 3.8% (2006-2010 5-year est.).

Education: Percent of population age 25 and over with: High school diploma (including GED) or higher: 93.0% (2006-2010 5-year est.); Bachelor's degree or higher: 27.0% (2006-2010 5-year est.); Master's degree or higher: 6.5% (2006-2010 5-year est.).

Housing: Homeownership rate: 85.2% (2010); Median home value: $157,500 (2006-2010 5-year est.); Median contract rent: $402 per month (2006-2010 5-year est.); Median year structure built: 1977 (2006-2010 5-year est.).

Transportation: Commute to work: 93.7% car, 0.0% public transportation, 0.0% walk, 3.8% work from home (2006-2010 5-year est.); Travel time to work: 18.7% less than 15 minutes, 47.8% 15 to 30 minutes, 20.5% 30 to 45 minutes, 8.9% 45 to 60 minutes, 4.1% 60 minutes or more (2006-2010 5-year est.)

Additional Information Contacts

Washington County Chamber of Commerce . . . . (724) 225-3010
  http://www.washcochamber.com

SOUTH STRABANE (township). Covers a land area of 23.002 square miles and a water area of 0.005 square miles. Located at 40.17° N. Lat; 80.19° W. Long. Elevation is 1,188 feet.

Population: 7,676 (1990); 7,987 (2000); 9,346 (2010); Density: 406.3 persons per square mile (2010); Race: 95.7% White, 1.8% Black, 1.0% Asian, 0.1% American Indian/Alaska Native, 0.0% Native Hawaiian/Other Pacific Islander, 1.4% Other, 0.8% Hispanic of any race (2010); Average household size: 2.17 (2010); Median age: 48.6 (2010); Males per 100 females: 85.8 (2010); Marriage status: 22.1% never married, 57.4% now married, 13.6% widowed, 6.9% divorced (2006-2010 5-year est.); Foreign born: 2.5% (2006-2010 5-year est.); Ancestry (includes multiple

ancestries): 24.4% German, 20.2% Italian, 17.9% Irish, 16.3% English, 10.4% Polish (2006-2010 5-year est.).

Economy: Single-family building permits issued: 52 (2011); Multi-family building permits issued: 7 (2011); Employment by occupation: 19.5% management, 3.2% professional, 8.5% services, 16.9% sales, 2.2% farming, 5.4% construction, 3.6% production (2006-2010 5-year est.).

Income: Per capita income: $28,561 (2006-2010 5-year est.); Median household income: $52,791 (2006-2010 5-year est.); Average household income: $63,299 (2006-2010 5-year est.); Percent of households with income of $100,000 or more: 16.6% (2006-2010 5-year est.); Poverty rate: 6.4% (2006-2010 5-year est.).

Education: Percent of population age 25 and over with: High school diploma (including GED) or higher: 90.9% (2006-2010 5-year est.); Bachelor's degree or higher: 31.5% (2006-2010 5-year est.); Master's degree or higher: 11.5% (2006-2010 5-year est.).

Housing: Homeownership rate: 68.5% (2010); Median home value: $171,900 (2006-2010 5-year est.); Median contract rent: $672 per month (2006-2010 5-year est.); Median year structure built: 1974 (2006-2010 5-year est.).

Safety: Violent crime rate: 20.3 per 10,000 population; Property crime rate: 503.4 per 10,000 population (2011).

Transportation: Commute to work: 93.3% car, 1.0% public transportation, 1.1% walk, 2.9% work from home (2006-2010 5-year est.); Travel time to work: 39.6% less than 15 minutes, 22.2% 15 to 30 minutes, 19.8% 30 to 45 minutes, 9.3% 45 to 60 minutes, 9.1% 60 minutes or more (2006-2010 5-year est.)

Additional Information Contacts

South Strabane Township . . . . (724) 225-9055
  http://www.southstrabane.com
Washington County Chamber of Commerce. . . . . (724) 225-3010
  http://www.washcochamber.com

SOUTHVIEW (CDP). Covers a land area of 0.897 square miles and a water area of 0 square miles. Located at 40.33° N. Lat; 80.26° W. Long. Elevation is 1,109 feet.

Population: n/a (1990); n/a (2000); 276 (2010); Density: 307.8 persons per square mile (2010); Race: 99.3% White, 0.7% Black, 0.0% Asian, 0.0% American Indian/Alaska Native, 0.0% Native Hawaiian/Other Pacific Islander, 0.0% Other, 0.0% Hispanic of any race (2010); Average household size: 2.56 (2010); Median age: 45.7 (2010); Males per 100 females: 95.7 (2010); Marriage status: 18.6% never married, 48.6% now married, 25.7% widowed, 7.1% divorced (2006-2010 5-year est.); Foreign born: 0.0% (2006-2010 5-year est.); Ancestry (includes multiple ancestries): 28.7% German, 24.0% Irish, 16.0% African, 15.3% Scotch-Irish, 12.7% Italian (2006-2010 5-year est.).

Economy: Employment by occupation: 11.1% management, 0.0% professional, 0.0% services, 0.0% sales, 12.3% farming, 0.0% construction, 0.0% production (2006-2010 5-year est.).

Income: Per capita income: $21,665 (2006-2010 5-year est.); Median household income: $34,559 (2006-2010 5-year est.); Average household income: $46,846 (2006-2010 5-year est.); Percent of households with income of $100,000 or more: n/a (2006-2010 5-year est.); Poverty rate: 0.0% (2006-2010 5-year est.).

Education: Percent of population age 25 and over with: High school diploma (including GED) or higher: 51.2% (2006-2010 5-year est.); Bachelor's degree or higher: 7.3% (2006-2010 5-year est.); Master's degree or higher: 0.0% (2006-2010 5-year est.).

Housing: Homeownership rate: 89.9% (2010); Median home value: $95,000 (2006-2010 5-year est.); Median contract rent: $488 per month (2006-2010 5-year est.); Median year structure built: before 1940 (2006-2010 5-year est.).

Transportation: Commute to work: 85.9% car, 0.0% public transportation, 0.0% walk, 14.1% work from home (2006-2010 5-year est.); Travel time to work: 0.0% less than 15 minutes, 43.6% 15 to 30 minutes, 38.2% 30 to 45 minutes, 18.2% 45 to 60 minutes, 0.0% 60 minutes or more (2006-2010 5-year est.)

SPEERS (borough). Aka West Belle Vernon. Covers a land area of 0.969 square miles and a water area of 0.122 square miles. Located at 40.12° N. Lat; 79.88° W. Long. Elevation is 787 feet.

Population: 1,284 (1990); 1,241 (2000); 1,154 (2010); Density: 1,191.4 persons per square mile (2010); Race: 95.8% White, 1.9% Black, 0.6% Asian, 0.2% American Indian/Alaska Native, 0.1% Native Hawaiian/Other Pacific Islander, 1.4% Other, 0.5% Hispanic of any race (2010); Average household size: 2.14 (2010); Median age: 50.3 (2010); Males per 100

females: 93.0 (2010); Marriage status: 24.0% never married, 53.8% now married, 11.0% widowed, 11.2% divorced (2006-2010 5-year est.); Foreign born: 2.1% (2006-2010 5-year est.); Ancestry (includes multiple ancestries): 23.2% Italian, 22.1% German, 12.3% Polish, 12.2% English, 9.3% Irish (2006-2010 5-year est.).

Economy: Single-family building permits issued: 0 (2011); Multi-family building permits issued: 0 (2011); Employment by occupation: 10.6% management, 3.0% professional, 10.2% services, 11.0% sales, 2.1% farming, 5.7% construction, 4.9% production (2006-2010 5-year est.).

Income: Per capita income: $26,352 (2006-2010 5-year est.); Median household income: $42,303 (2006-2010 5-year est.); Average household income: $55,918 (2006-2010 5-year est.); Percent of households with income of $100,000 or more: 12.3% (2006-2010 5-year est.); Poverty rate: 9.9% (2006-2010 5-year est.).

Education: Percent of population age 25 and over with: High school diploma (including GED) or higher: 92.5% (2006-2010 5-year est.); Bachelor's degree or higher: 25.3% (2006-2010 5-year est.); Master's degree or higher: 8.5% (2006-2010 5-year est.).

Housing: Homeownership rate: 86.3% (2010); Median home value: $103,500 (2006-2010 5-year est.); Median contract rent: $475 per month (2006-2010 5-year est.); Median year structure built: 1954 (2006-2010 5-year est.).

Transportation: Commute to work: 96.2% car, 2.1% public transportation, 0.6% walk, 0.8% work from home (2006-2010 5-year est.); Travel time to work: 33.1% less than 15 minutes, 31.6% 15 to 30 minutes, 17.0% 30 to 45 minutes, 9.6% 45 to 60 minutes, 8.7% 60 minutes or more (2006-2010 5-year est.)

Additional Information Contacts

Mon Valley Regional Chamber of Commerce . . . . (724) 483-3507
  http://www.mvrchamber.org

STOCKDALE (borough). Covers a land area of 0.271 square miles and a water area of 0.037 square miles. Located at 40.08° N. Lat; 79.85° W. Long. Elevation is 768 feet.

Population: 630 (1990); 555 (2000); 502 (2010); Density: 1,852.1 persons per square mile (2010); Race: 98.0% White, 0.0% Black, 0.0% Asian, 0.0% American Indian/Alaska Native, 0.0% Native Hawaiian/Other Pacific Islander, 2.0% Other, 0.8% Hispanic of any race (2010); Average household size: 2.20 (2010); Median age: 42.9 (2010); Males per 100 females: 97.6 (2010); Marriage status: 29.8% never married, 50.5% now married, 12.9% widowed, 6.8% divorced (2006-2010 5-year est.); Foreign born: 0.0% (2006-2010 5-year est.); Ancestry (includes multiple ancestries): 30.9% Italian, 21.4% Slovak, 18.4% English, 15.4% Irish, 15.0% German (2006-2010 5-year est.).

Economy: Single-family building permits issued: 4 (2011); Multi-family building permits issued: 0 (2011); Employment by occupation: 19.0% management, 1.2% professional, 9.9% services, 7.5% sales, 2.0% farming, 16.2% construction, 9.5% production (2006-2010 5-year est.).

Income: Per capita income: $25,222 (2006-2010 5-year est.); Median household income: $38,542 (2006-2010 5-year est.); Average household income: $48,872 (2006-2010 5-year est.); Percent of households with income of $100,000 or more: 8.4% (2006-2010 5-year est.); Poverty rate: 5.5% (2006-2010 5-year est.).

Education: Percent of population age 25 and over with: High school diploma (including GED) or higher: 84.0% (2006-2010 5-year est.); Bachelor's degree or higher: 10.4% (2006-2010 5-year est.); Master's degree or higher: 2.8% (2006-2010 5-year est.).

Housing: Homeownership rate: 70.2% (2010); Median home value: $103,800 (2006-2010 5-year est.); Median contract rent: $407 per month (2006-2010 5-year est.); Median year structure built: 1941 (2006-2010 5-year est.).

Transportation: Commute to work: 92.8% car, 0.0% public transportation, 6.0% walk, 0.0% work from home (2006-2010 5-year est.); Travel time to work: 34.0% less than 15 minutes, 36.8% 15 to 30 minutes, 10.8% 30 to 45 minutes, 6.8% 45 to 60 minutes, 11.6% 60 minutes or more (2006-2010 5-year est.)

STRABANE (unincorporated postal area)

Zip Code: 15363

Covers a land area of 0.230 square miles and a water area of 0 square miles. Located at 40.25° N. Lat; 80.19° W. Long. Elevation is 1,073 feet. Population: 760 (2010); Density: 3,292.0 persons per square mile (2010); Race: 97.1% White, 0.7% Black, 0.4% Asian, 0.1% American Indian/Alaska Native, 0.0% Native Hawaiian/Other Pacific Islander, 1.7% Other, 1.2% Hispanic of any race (2010); Average household size:

2.35 (2010); Median age: 42.0 (2010); Males per 100 females: 95.4 (2010); Homeownership rate: 73.0% (2010)

TAYLORSTOWN (CDP). Covers a land area of 1.018 square miles and a water area of 0 square miles. Located at 40.16° N. Lat; 80.39° W. Long. Elevation is 1,027 feet.

Population: n/a (1990); n/a (2000); 217 (2010); Density: 213.3 persons per square mile (2010); Race: 97.2% White, 0.0% Black, 0.9% Asian, 0.0% American Indian/Alaska Native, 0.0% Native Hawaiian/Other Pacific Islander, 1.9% Other, 0.5% Hispanic of any race (2010); Average household size: 2.65 (2010); Median age: 41.1 (2010); Males per 100 females: 87.1 (2010); Marriage status: 22.6% never married, 63.4% now married, 9.7% widowed, 4.3% divorced (2006-2010 5-year est.); Foreign born: 0.0% (2006-2010 5-year est.); Ancestry (includes multiple ancestries): 14.4% American, 14.4% Irish, 14.4% German, 13.4% Scotch-Irish, 11.3% Polish (2006-2010 5-year est.).
Economy: Employment by occupation: 0.0% management, 0.0% professional, 17.8% services, 15.6% sales, 0.0% farming, 15.6% construction, 0.0% production (2006-2010 5-year est.).
Income: Per capita income: $20,255 (2006-2010 5-year est.); Median household income: $44,250 (2006-2010 5-year est.); Average household income: $48,450 (2006-2010 5-year est.); Percent of households with income of $100,000 or more: 10.0% (2006-2010 5-year est.); Poverty rate: 0.0% (2006-2010 5-year est.).
Education: Percent of population age 25 and over with: High school diploma (including GED) or higher: 86.1% (2006-2010 5-year est.); Bachelor's degree or higher: 12.7% (2006-2010 5-year est.); Master's degree or higher: 3.8% (2006-2010 5-year est.).
Housing: Homeownership rate: 80.5% (2010); Median home value: $113,800 (2006-2010 5-year est.); Median contract rent: n/a per month (2006-2010 5-year est.); Median year structure built: before 1940 (2006-2010 5-year est.).
Transportation: Commute to work: 100.0% car, 0.0% public transportation, 0.0% walk, 0.0% work from home (2006-2010 5-year est.); Travel time to work: 28.9% less than 15 minutes, 35.6% 15 to 30 minutes, 15.6% 30 to 45 minutes, 8.9% 45 to 60 minutes, 11.1% 60 minutes or more (2006-2010 5-year est.)

THOMPSONVILLE (CDP). Covers a land area of 2.069 square miles and a water area of 0.025 square miles. Located at 40.28° N. Lat; 80.12° W. Long. Elevation is 938 feet.

History: The area known today as Thompsonville is adjacent to the site where the first shots were fired in The Whiskey Rebellion. The Wiskey Rebellion was a popular uprising that had its beginnings in 1791 in nearby South Park Township.
Population: 3,560 (1990); 3,592 (2000); 3,520 (2010); Density: 1,701.3 persons per square mile (2010); Race: 97.2% White, 0.7% Black, 1.0% Asian, 0.2% American Indian/Alaska Native, 0.0% Native Hawaiian/Other Pacific Islander, 0.9% Other, 1.4% Hispanic of any race (2010); Average household size: 2.59 (2010); Median age: 49.3 (2010); Males per 100 females: 89.7 (2010); Marriage status: 17.0% never married, 57.9% now married, 15.8% widowed, 9.3% divorced (2006-2010 5-year est.); Foreign born: 3.0% (2006-2010 5-year est.); Ancestry (includes multiple ancestries): 27.6% German, 21.0% Italian, 19.3% Irish, 14.2% English, 10.8% Polish (2006-2010 5-year est.).
Economy: Employment by occupation: 19.3% management, 6.2% professional, 9.5% services, 16.1% sales, 4.4% farming, 4.3% construction, 1.1% production (2006-2010 5-year est.).
Income: Per capita income: $35,916 (2006-2010 5-year est.); Median household income: $91,979 (2006-2010 5-year est.); Average household income: $108,021 (2006-2010 5-year est.); Percent of households with income of $100,000 or more: 45.1% (2006-2010 5-year est.); Poverty rate: 2.7% (2006-2010 5-year est.).
Education: Percent of population age 25 and over with: High school diploma (including GED) or higher: 84.1% (2006-2010 5-year est.); Bachelor's degree or higher: 40.9% (2006-2010 5-year est.); Master's degree or higher: 18.6% (2006-2010 5-year est.).
Housing: Homeownership rate: 93.2% (2010); Median home value: $245,700 (2006-2010 5-year est.); Median contract rent: $658 per month (2006-2010 5-year est.); Median year structure built: 1970 (2006-2010 5-year est.).
Transportation: Commute to work: 86.7% car, 4.0% public transportation, 0.9% walk, 8.4% work from home (2006-2010 5-year est.); Travel time to work: 26.4% less than 15 minutes, 33.5% 15 to 30 minutes, 24.3% 30 to

45 minutes, 10.5% 45 to 60 minutes, 5.4% 60 minutes or more (2006-2010 5-year est.)
Additional Information Contacts
Washington County Chamber of Commerce............ (724) 225-3010
  http://www.washcochamber.com

TWILIGHT (borough). Covers a land area of 1.610 square miles and a water area of 0 square miles. Located at 40.12° N. Lat; 79.89° W. Long. Elevation is 896 feet.

Population: 252 (1990); 241 (2000); 233 (2010); Density: 144.7 persons per square mile (2010); Race: 98.7% White, 1.3% Black, 0.0% Asian, 0.0% American Indian/Alaska Native, 0.0% Native Hawaiian/Other Pacific Islander, 0.0% Other, 0.0% Hispanic of any race (2010); Average household size: 2.51 (2010); Median age: 43.8 (2010); Males per 100 females: 99.1 (2010); Marriage status: 21.5% never married, 68.3% now married, 4.3% widowed, 5.9% divorced (2006-2010 5-year est.); Foreign born: 0.8% (2006-2010 5-year est.); Ancestry (includes multiple ancestries): 16.1% Italian, 14.6% German, 13.0% Irish, 11.4% Polish, 9.1% English (2006-2010 5-year est.).
Economy: Single-family building permits issued: 0 (2011); Multi-family building permits issued: 0 (2011); Employment by occupation: 1.7% management, 7.0% professional, 17.4% services, 8.7% sales, 4.3% farming, 14.8% construction, 24.3% production (2006-2010 5-year est.).
Income: Per capita income: $19,645 (2006-2010 5-year est.); Median household income: $52,917 (2006-2010 5-year est.); Average household income: $58,880 (2006-2010 5-year est.); Percent of households with income of $100,000 or more: 8.9% (2006-2010 5-year est.); Poverty rate: 15.7% (2006-2010 5-year est.).
Education: Percent of population age 25 and over with: High school diploma (including GED) or higher: 86.9% (2006-2010 5-year est.); Bachelor's degree or higher: 20.2% (2006-2010 5-year est.); Master's degree or higher: 8.3% (2006-2010 5-year est.).
Housing: Homeownership rate: 89.2% (2010); Median home value: $105,000 (2006-2010 5-year est.); Median contract rent: $282 per month (2006-2010 5-year est.); Median year structure built: 1955 (2006-2010 5-year est.).
Transportation: Commute to work: 95.6% car, 0.0% public transportation, 4.4% walk, 0.0% work from home (2006-2010 5-year est.); Travel time to work: 42.5% less than 15 minutes, 22.1% 15 to 30 minutes, 18.6% 30 to 45 minutes, 4.4% 45 to 60 minutes, 12.4% 60 minutes or more (2006-2010 5-year est.)

UNION (township). Covers a land area of 15.380 square miles and a water area of 0.369 square miles. Located at 40.24° N. Lat; 79.98° W. Long.

Population: 6,322 (1990); 5,599 (2000); 5,700 (2010); Density: 370.6 persons per square mile (2010); Race: 98.0% White, 0.7% Black, 0.3% Asian, 0.2% American Indian/Alaska Native, 0.0% Native Hawaiian/Other Pacific Islander, 0.8% Other, 0.7% Hispanic of any race (2010); Average household size: 2.26 (2010); Median age: 47.8 (2010); Males per 100 females: 95.7 (2010); Marriage status: 24.0% never married, 57.3% now married, 8.7% widowed, 9.9% divorced (2006-2010 5-year est.); Foreign born: 0.2% (2006-2010 5-year est.); Ancestry (includes multiple ancestries): 34.4% German, 24.4% Irish, 18.4% Italian, 13.1% English, 13.0% Polish (2006-2010 5-year est.).
Economy: Single-family building permits issued: 25 (2011); Multi-family building permits issued: 0 (2011); Employment by occupation: 5.2% management, 3.7% professional, 14.9% services, 14.4% sales, 4.9% farming, 16.8% construction, 8.5% production (2006-2010 5-year est.).
Income: Per capita income: $24,641 (2006-2010 5-year est.); Median household income: $52,152 (2006-2010 5-year est.); Average household income: $60,693 (2006-2010 5-year est.); Percent of households with income of $100,000 or more: 17.9% (2006-2010 5-year est.); Poverty rate: 8.9% (2006-2010 5-year est.).
Education: Percent of population age 25 and over with: High school diploma (including GED) or higher: 90.8% (2006-2010 5-year est.); Bachelor's degree or higher: 15.0% (2006-2010 5-year est.); Master's degree or higher: 5.4% (2006-2010 5-year est.).
Housing: Homeownership rate: 87.7% (2010); Median home value: $131,500 (2006-2010 5-year est.); Median contract rent: $520 per month (2006-2010 5-year est.); Median year structure built: 1968 (2006-2010 5-year est.).
Transportation: Commute to work: 91.7% car, 4.8% public transportation, 0.3% walk, 2.3% work from home (2006-2010 5-year est.); Travel time to work: 16.7% less than 15 minutes, 33.6% 15 to 30 minutes, 21.4% 30 to

45 minutes, 11.1% 45 to 60 minutes, 17.2% 60 minutes or more (2006-2010 5-year est.)

Additional Information Contacts

Union Township. . . . . (724) 348-4229
    http://www.uniontwp.com

Washington County Chamber of Commerce. . . . . (724) 225-3010
    http://www.washcochamber.com

VAN VOORHIS (CDP).
Covers a land area of 0.380 square miles and a water area of 0 square miles. Located at 40.16° N. Lat; 79.97° W. Long. Elevation is 942 feet.

Population: n/a (1990); n/a (2000); 166 (2010); Density: 437.2 persons per square mile (2010); Race: 98.2% White, 0.0% Black, 0.6% Asian, 0.0% American Indian/Alaska Native, 0.0% Native Hawaiian/Other Pacific Islander, 1.2% Other, 0.0% Hispanic of any race (2010); Average household size: 2.24 (2010); Median age: 51.0 (2010); Males per 100 females: 110.1 (2010); Marriage status: 14.9% never married, 85.1% now married, 0.0% widowed, 0.0% divorced (2006-2010 5-year est.); Foreign born: 0.0% (2006-2010 5-year est.); Ancestry (includes multiple ancestries): 74.3% Irish, 71.4% German, 15.2% Hungarian, 5.2% Italian, 2.6% English (2006-2010 5-year est.).

Economy: Employment by occupation: 0.0% management, 35.6% professional, 0.0% services, 27.1% sales, 0.0% farming, 28.0% construction, 28.0% production (2006-2010 5-year est.).

Income: Per capita income: $22,092 (2006-2010 5-year est.); Median household income: $93,750 (2006-2010 5-year est.); Average household income: $80,115 (2006-2010 5-year est.); Percent of households with income of $100,000 or more: 50.0% (2006-2010 5-year est.); Poverty rate: 5.2% (2006-2010 5-year est.).

Education: Percent of population age 25 and over with: High school diploma (including GED) or higher: 95.7% (2006-2010 5-year est.); Bachelor's degree or higher: 8.9% (2006-2010 5-year est.); Master's degree or higher: 4.7% (2006-2010 5-year est.).

Housing: Homeownership rate: 89.1% (2010); Median home value: $35,200 (2006-2010 5-year est.); Median contract rent: n/a per month (2006-2010 5-year est.); Median year structure built: before 1940 (2006-2010 5-year est.).

Transportation: Commute to work: 100.0% car, 0.0% public transportation, 0.0% walk, 0.0% work from home (2006-2010 5-year est.); Travel time to work: 36.4% less than 15 minutes, 35.6% 15 to 30 minutes, 0.0% 30 to 45 minutes, 0.0% 45 to 60 minutes, 28.0% 60 minutes or more (2006-2010 5-year est.).

VENETIA (unincorporated postal area)
Zip Code: 15367

Covers a land area of 9.214 square miles and a water area of 0.023 square miles. Located at 40.26° N. Lat; 80.05° W. Long. Population: 8,731 (2010); Density: 947.6 persons per square mile (2010); Race: 96.0% White, 0.3% Black, 2.5% Asian, 0.1% American Indian/Alaska Native, 0.0% Native Hawaiian/Other Pacific Islander, 1.1% Other, 1.6% Hispanic of any race (2010); Average household size: 3.05 (2010); Median age: 39.6 (2010); Males per 100 females: 96.6 (2010); Homeownership rate: 92.8% (2010)

VESTABURG (unincorporated postal area)
Zip Code: 15368

Covers a land area of 0.190 square miles and a water area of 0.068 square miles. Located at 40.01° N. Lat; 79.98° W. Long. Elevation is 951 feet. Population: 473 (2010); Density: 2,482.8 persons per square mile (2010); Race: 96.6% White, 0.4% Black, 0.0% Asian, 0.2% American Indian/Alaska Native, 0.0% Native Hawaiian/Other Pacific Islander, 2.8% Other, 0.4% Hispanic of any race (2010); Average household size: 2.46 (2010); Median age: 38.6 (2010); Males per 100 females: 98.7 (2010); Homeownership rate: 73.5% (2010)

WASHINGTON (city).
County seat. Covers a land area of 2.948 square miles and a water area of 0 square miles. Located at 40.17° N. Lat; 80.25° W. Long. Elevation is 1,168 feet.

History: Named for George Washington, first President of the U.S. The site of Washington was once a Delaware village known as Catfish's Camp, the headquarters of Chief Tingoocqua. A town laid out in 1781 shortly became the county seat of newly created Washington County. Incorporated as a borough in 1810, Washington was chartered as a city in 1924.

Population: 15,834 (1990); 15,268 (2000); 13,663 (2010); Density: 4,635.4 persons per square mile (2010); Race: 77.7% White, 15.9% Black, 0.7% Asian, 0.2% American Indian/Alaska Native, 0.1% Native Hawaiian/Other Pacific Islander, 5.4% Other, 1.8% Hispanic of any race (2010); Average household size: 2.11 (2010); Median age: 38.2 (2010); Males per 100 females: 97.4 (2010); Marriage status: 40.8% never married, 35.5% now married, 9.0% widowed, 14.7% divorced (2006-2010 5-year est.); Foreign born: 0.7% (2006-2010 5-year est.); Ancestry (includes multiple ancestries): 18.2% German, 16.1% Irish, 14.6% Italian, 8.1% English, 7.1% Scotch-Irish (2006-2010 5-year est.).

Economy: Single-family building permits issued: 4 (2011); Multi-family building permits issued: 0 (2011); Employment by occupation: 7.4% management, 0.9% professional, 14.2% services, 16.3% sales, 5.6% farming, 7.9% construction, 4.4% production (2006-2010 5-year est.).

Income: Per capita income: $18,829 (2006-2010 5-year est.); Median household income: $31,775 (2006-2010 5-year est.); Average household income: $40,898 (2006-2010 5-year est.); Percent of households with income of $100,000 or more: 5.5% (2006-2010 5-year est.); Poverty rate: 24.1% (2006-2010 5-year est.).

Taxes: Total city taxes per capita: $441 (2009); City property taxes per capita: $288 (2009).

Education: Percent of population age 25 and over with: High school diploma (including GED) or higher: 82.8% (2006-2010 5-year est.); Bachelor's degree or higher: 13.1% (2006-2010 5-year est.); Master's degree or higher: 3.3% (2006-2010 5-year est.).

School District(s)

Mcguffey SD (KG-12)
    2010-11 Enrollment: 1,999 . . . . (724) 948-3731
Trinity Area SD (KG-12)
    2010-11 Enrollment: 3,387 . . . . (724) 223-2000
Washington SD (KG-12)
    2010-11 Enrollment: 1,588 . . . . (724) 223-5010

Four-year College(s)

Washington & Jefferson College (Private, Not-for-profit)
    Fall 2010 Enrollment: 1,445 . . . . (724) 503-1001
    2011-12 Tuition: In-state $36,420; Out-of-state $36,420

Two-year College(s)

Penn Commercial Business/Technical School (Private, For-profit)
    Fall 2010 Enrollment: 529 . . . . (724) 222-5330
    2011-12 Tuition: In-state $20,600; Out-of-state $20,600
Washington Hospital School of Nursing (Private, Not-for-profit)
    Fall 2010 Enrollment: 136 . . . . (724) 223-3167
    2011-12 Tuition: In-state $12,429; Out-of-state $12,429
Washington Hospital School of Radiography (Private, Not-for-profit)
    Fall 2010 Enrollment: 38 . . . . (724) 223-3326

Housing: Homeownership rate: 44.3% (2010); Median home value: $92,300 (2006-2010 5-year est.); Median contract rent: $431 per month (2006-2010 5-year est.); Median year structure built: 1942 (2006-2010 5-year est.).

Hospitals: Presbyterian Medical Center (159 beds); Washington Hospital (239 beds)

Safety: Violent crime rate: 66.4 per 10,000 population; Property crime rate: 434.8 per 10,000 population (2011).

Newspapers: Observer-Reporter (Local news; Circulation 34,875)

Transportation: Commute to work: 82.9% car, 1.8% public transportation, 11.3% walk, 2.1% work from home (2006-2010 5-year est.); Travel time to work: 56.3% less than 15 minutes, 22.3% 15 to 30 minutes, 10.7% 30 to 45 minutes, 4.6% 45 to 60 minutes, 6.1% 60 minutes or more (2006-2010 5-year est.)

Airports: Washington County (general aviation)

Additional Information Contacts

City of Washington . . . . (724) 223-4200
    http://www.washingtonpa.us

Washington County Chamber of Commerce. . . . . (724) 225-3010
    http://www.washcochamber.com

WEST ALEXANDER (CDP).
Covers a land area of 1.223 square miles and a water area of 0 square miles. Located at 40.11° N. Lat; 80.51° W. Long. Elevation is 1,332 feet.

History: Several covered bridges in area, especially to South.

Population: 238 (1990); 320 (2000); 604 (2010); Density: 494.0 persons per square mile (2010); Race: 99.2% White, 0.5% Black, 0.0% Asian, 0.0% American Indian/Alaska Native, 0.0% Native Hawaiian/Other Pacific Islander, 0.3% Other, 0.7% Hispanic of any race (2010); Average household size: 2.59 (2010); Median age: 39.3 (2010); Males per 100

females: 89.9 (2010); Marriage status: 23.6% never married, 57.1% now married, 8.7% widowed, 10.6% divorced (2006-2010 5-year est.); Foreign born: 0.0% (2006-2010 5-year est.); Ancestry (includes multiple ancestries): 41.9% German, 30.0% Scotch-Irish, 13.8% English, 11.9% Irish, 9.4% American (2006-2010 5-year est.).

Economy: Employment by occupation: 3.4% management, 0.0% professional, 12.7% services, 24.6% sales, 3.6% farming, 18.9% construction, 7.3% production (2006-2010 5-year est.).

Income: Per capita income: $14,874 (2006-2010 5-year est.); Median household income: $33,036 (2006-2010 5-year est.); Average household income: $41,808 (2006-2010 5-year est.); Percent of households with income of $100,000 or more: 6.5% (2006-2010 5-year est.); Poverty rate: 16.6% (2006-2010 5-year est.).

Education: Percent of population age 25 and over with: High school diploma (including GED) or higher: 88.5% (2006-2010 5-year est.); Bachelor's degree or higher: 10.9% (2006-2010 5-year est.); Master's degree or higher: 5.3% (2006-2010 5-year est.).

Housing: Homeownership rate: 77.5% (2010); Median home value: $90,700 (2006-2010 5-year est.); Median contract rent: $617 per month (2006-2010 5-year est.); Median year structure built: before 1940 (2006-2010 5-year est.).

Transportation: Commute to work: 96.3% car, 0.0% public transportation, 2.7% walk, 1.1% work from home (2006-2010 5-year est.); Travel time to work: 21.3% less than 15 minutes, 55.3% 15 to 30 minutes, 11.1% 30 to 45 minutes, 7.3% 45 to 60 minutes, 5.1% 60 minutes or more (2006-2010 5-year est.)

WEST BETHLEHEM (township). Covers a land area of 22.420 square miles and a water area of 0 square miles. Located at 40.04° N. Lat; 80.11° W. Long.

Population: 1,509 (1990); 1,432 (2000); 1,460 (2010); Density: 65.1 persons per square mile (2010); Race: 98.2% White, 0.4% Black, 0.2% Asian, 0.2% American Indian/Alaska Native, 0.0% Native Hawaiian/Other Pacific Islander, 1.0% Other, 0.2% Hispanic of any race (2010); Average household size: 2.43 (2010); Median age: 45.3 (2010); Males per 100 females: 107.4 (2010); Marriage status: 22.1% never married, 58.6% now married, 9.9% widowed, 9.4% divorced (2006-2010 5-year est.); Foreign born: 1.7% (2006-2010 5-year est.); Ancestry (includes multiple ancestries): 27.3% German, 17.9% Italian, 17.4% Irish, 16.0% English, 7.4% Polish (2006-2010 5-year est.).

Economy: Single-family building permits issued: 1 (2011); Multi-family building permits issued: 0 (2011); Employment by occupation: 5.8% management, 2.9% professional, 15.4% services, 12.6% sales, 3.6% farming, 15.3% construction, 9.8% production (2006-2010 5-year est.).

Income: Per capita income: $23,806 (2006-2010 5-year est.); Median household income: $45,833 (2006-2010 5-year est.); Average household income: $56,516 (2006-2010 5-year est.); Percent of households with income of $100,000 or more: 11.1% (2006-2010 5-year est.); Poverty rate: 7.7% (2006-2010 5-year est.).

Education: Percent of population age 25 and over with: High school diploma (including GED) or higher: 90.2% (2006-2010 5-year est.); Bachelor's degree or higher: 16.3% (2006-2010 5-year est.); Master's degree or higher: 5.4% (2006-2010 5-year est.).

Housing: Homeownership rate: 83.6% (2010); Median home value: $105,800 (2006-2010 5-year est.); Median contract rent: $334 per month (2006-2010 5-year est.); Median year structure built: 1941 (2006-2010 5-year est.).

Transportation: Commute to work: 94.2% car, 0.0% public transportation, 1.3% walk, 4.6% work from home (2006-2010 5-year est.); Travel time to work: 14.1% less than 15 minutes, 34.0% 15 to 30 minutes, 27.7% 30 to 45 minutes, 7.4% 45 to 60 minutes, 16.8% 60 minutes or more (2006-2010 5-year est.)

Additional Information Contacts
Waynesburg Area Chamber of Commerce . . . . (724) 627-5926
   http://www.waynesburgchamber.com

WEST BROWNSVILLE (borough). Covers a land area of 1.299 square miles and a water area of 0.124 square miles. Located at 40.03° N. Lat; 79.89° W. Long. Elevation is 768 feet.

History: James G. Blaine born here, 1830. Laid out 1831, incorporated c.1852.

Population: 1,170 (1990); 1,075 (2000); 992 (2010); Density: 763.7 persons per square mile (2010); Race: 96.2% White, 1.4% Black, 0.2% Asian, 0.7% American Indian/Alaska Native, 0.0% Native Hawaiian/Other Pacific Islander, 1.5% Other, 1.2% Hispanic of any race (2010); Average

household size: 2.31 (2010); Median age: 45.2 (2010); Males per 100 females: 91.1 (2010); Marriage status: 21.9% never married, 53.5% now married, 11.4% widowed, 13.3% divorced (2006-2010 5-year est.); Foreign born: 0.3% (2006-2010 5-year est.); Ancestry (includes multiple ancestries): 29.1% German, 21.6% Irish, 17.8% English, 13.3% Italian, 9.5% Hungarian (2006-2010 5-year est.).

Economy: Single-family building permits issued: 0 (2011); Multi-family building permits issued: 0 (2011); Employment by occupation: 5.5% management, 3.6% professional, 13.8% services, 18.6% sales, 2.4% farming, 6.2% construction, 5.7% production (2006-2010 5-year est.).

Income: Per capita income: $22,525 (2006-2010 5-year est.); Median household income: $38,750 (2006-2010 5-year est.); Average household income: $48,795 (2006-2010 5-year est.); Percent of households with income of $100,000 or more: 9.7% (2006-2010 5-year est.); Poverty rate: 11.4% (2006-2010 5-year est.).

Education: Percent of population age 25 and over with: High school diploma (including GED) or higher: 89.5% (2006-2010 5-year est.); Bachelor's degree or higher: 18.2% (2006-2010 5-year est.); Master's degree or higher: 5.9% (2006-2010 5-year est.).

Housing: Homeownership rate: 76.1% (2010); Median home value: $65,200 (2006-2010 5-year est.); Median contract rent: $422 per month (2006-2010 5-year est.); Median year structure built: before 1940 (2006-2010 5-year est.).

Transportation: Commute to work: 96.8% car, 0.0% public transportation, 0.2% walk, 1.5% work from home (2006-2010 5-year est.); Travel time to work: 28.3% less than 15 minutes, 25.4% 15 to 30 minutes, 29.8% 30 to 45 minutes, 8.6% 45 to 60 minutes, 7.9% 60 minutes or more (2006-2010 5-year est.)

Additional Information Contacts
Mon Valley Regional Chamber of Commerce . . . . (724) 483-3507
   http://www.mvrchamber.org

WEST FINLEY (township). Aka Burnsville. Covers a land area of 39.120 square miles and a water area of 0 square miles. Located at 40.02° N. Lat; 80.47° W. Long. Elevation is 1,404 feet.

Population: 972 (1990); 951 (2000); 878 (2010); Density: 22.4 persons per square mile (2010); Race: 98.7% White, 0.1% Black, 0.5% Asian, 0.0% American Indian/Alaska Native, 0.0% Native Hawaiian/Other Pacific Islander, 0.7% Other, 0.3% Hispanic of any race (2010); Average household size: 2.59 (2010); Median age: 42.4 (2010); Males per 100 females: 111.6 (2010); Marriage status: 20.0% never married, 65.6% now married, 7.9% widowed, 6.5% divorced (2006-2010 5-year est.); Foreign born: 0.6% (2006-2010 5-year est.); Ancestry (includes multiple ancestries): 35.3% German, 20.7% Irish, 11.0% English, 9.8% Scotch-Irish, 8.7% Italian (2006-2010 5-year est.).

Economy: Single-family building permits issued: 0 (2011); Multi-family building permits issued: 0 (2011); Employment by occupation: 8.5% management, 2.9% professional, 9.3% services, 24.9% sales, 1.6% farming, 11.9% construction, 5.3% production (2006-2010 5-year est.).

Income: Per capita income: $22,917 (2006-2010 5-year est.); Median household income: $45,521 (2006-2010 5-year est.); Average household income: $55,503 (2006-2010 5-year est.); Percent of households with income of $100,000 or more: 10.1% (2006-2010 5-year est.); Poverty rate: 7.7% (2006-2010 5-year est.).

Education: Percent of population age 25 and over with: High school diploma (including GED) or higher: 86.2% (2006-2010 5-year est.); Bachelor's degree or higher: 13.5% (2006-2010 5-year est.); Master's degree or higher: 4.6% (2006-2010 5-year est.).

Housing: Homeownership rate: 88.0% (2010); Median home value: $151,200 (2006-2010 5-year est.); Median contract rent: $388 per month (2006-2010 5-year est.); Median year structure built: 1971 (2006-2010 5-year est.).

Transportation: Commute to work: 93.8% car, 0.0% public transportation, 0.0% walk, 4.6% work from home (2006-2010 5-year est.); Travel time to work: 11.3% less than 15 minutes, 23.7% 15 to 30 minutes, 32.5% 30 to 45 minutes, 21.8% 45 to 60 minutes, 10.7% 60 minutes or more (2006-2010 5-year est.)

WEST MIDDLETOWN (borough). Covers a land area of 0.406 square miles and a water area of 0 square miles. Located at 40.24° N. Lat; 80.43° W. Long. Elevation is 1,325 feet.

Population: 166 (1990); 144 (2000); 139 (2010); Density: 342.4 persons per square mile (2010); Race: 91.4% White, 6.5% Black, 0.7% Asian, 0.0% American Indian/Alaska Native, 0.0% Native Hawaiian/Other Pacific Islander, 1.4% Other, 0.0% Hispanic of any race (2010); Average

household size: 2.32 (2010); Median age: 47.9 (2010); Males per 100 females: 117.2 (2010); Marriage status: 11.5% never married, 55.2% now married, 12.6% widowed, 20.7% divorced (2006-2010 5-year est.); Foreign born: 0.0% (2006-2010 5-year est.); Ancestry (includes multiple ancestries): 20.2% German, 17.7% English, 8.9% Irish, 8.1% Scotch-Irish, 4.8% American (2006-2010 5-year est.).

Economy: Single-family building permits issued: 0 (2011); Multi-family building permits issued: 0 (2011); Employment by occupation: 15.2% management, 4.3% professional, 17.4% services, 4.3% sales, 15.0% farming, 17.4% construction, 10.9% production (2006-2010 5-year est.).

Income: Per capita income: $18,935 (2006-2010 5-year est.); Median household income: $46,429 (2006-2010 5-year est.); Average household income: $47,077 (2006-2010 5-year est.); Percent of households with income of $100,000 or more: n/a (2006-2010 5-year est.); Poverty rate: 35.5% (2006-2010 5-year est.).

Education: Percent of population age 25 and over with: High school diploma (including GED) or higher: 82.4% (2006-2010 5-year est.); Bachelor's degree or higher: 24.7% (2006-2010 5-year est.); Master's degree or higher: 8.2% (2006-2010 5-year est.).

Housing: Homeownership rate: 88.3% (2010); Median home value: $78,600 (2006-2010 5-year est.); Median contract rent: $531 per month (2006-2010 5-year est.); Median year structure built: before 1940 (2006-2010 5-year est.).

Transportation: Commute to work: 100.0% car, 0.0% public transportation, 0.0% walk, 0.0% work from home (2006-2010 5-year est.); Travel time to work: 4.3% less than 15 minutes, 54.3% 15 to 30 minutes, 4.3% 30 to 45 minutes, 17.4% 45 to 60 minutes, 19.6% 60 minutes or more (2006-2010 5-year est.)

WEST PIKE RUN (township).
Covers a land area of 16.251 square miles and a water area of 0 square miles. Located at 40.08° N. Lat; 79.98° W. Long.

Population: 1,818 (1990); 1,925 (2000); 1,587 (2010); Density: 97.7 persons per square mile (2010); Race: 94.3% White, 3.7% Black, 0.1% Asian, 0.4% American Indian/Alaska Native, 0.0% Native Hawaiian/Other Pacific Islander, 1.5% Other, 0.6% Hispanic of any race (2010); Average household size: 2.33 (2010); Median age: 48.7 (2010); Males per 100 females: 101.1 (2010); Marriage status: 27.7% never married, 55.4% now married, 7.6% widowed, 9.4% divorced (2006-2010 5-year est.); Foreign born: 0.4% (2006-2010 5-year est.); Ancestry (includes multiple ancestries): 20.1% German, 16.0% English, 13.7% Irish, 9.9% Polish, 8.2% Italian (2006-2010 5-year est.).

Economy: Single-family building permits issued: 1 (2011); Multi-family building permits issued: 0 (2011); Employment by occupation: 8.5% management, 1.6% professional, 13.5% services, 12.8% sales, 1.9% farming, 18.4% construction, 5.1% production (2006-2010 5-year est.).

Income: Per capita income: $26,393 (2006-2010 5-year est.); Median household income: $49,708 (2006-2010 5-year est.); Average household income: $60,683 (2006-2010 5-year est.); Percent of households with income of $100,000 or more: 20.0% (2006-2010 5-year est.); Poverty rate: 8.8% (2006-2010 5-year est.).

Education: Percent of population age 25 and over with: High school diploma (including GED) or higher: 88.6% (2006-2010 5-year est.); Bachelor's degree or higher: 19.6% (2006-2010 5-year est.); Master's degree or higher: 6.6% (2006-2010 5-year est.).

Housing: Homeownership rate: 88.5% (2010); Median home value: $113,800 (2006-2010 5-year est.); Median contract rent: $420 per month (2006-2010 5-year est.); Median year structure built: 1956 (2006-2010 5-year est.).

Safety: Violent crime rate: 0.0 per 10,000 population; Property crime rate: 81.7 per 10,000 population (2011).

Transportation: Commute to work: 93.4% car, 0.0% public transportation, 2.0% walk, 4.6% work from home (2006-2010 5-year est.); Travel time to work: 21.3% less than 15 minutes, 37.0% 15 to 30 minutes, 31.4% 30 to 45 minutes, 6.8% 45 to 60 minutes, 3.5% 60 minutes or more (2006-2010 5-year est.)

Additional Information Contacts
Mon Valley Regional Chamber of Commerce . . . . (724) 483-3507
  http://www.mvrchamber.org

WESTLAND (CDP).
Covers a land area of 0.182 square miles and a water area of 0 square miles. Located at 40.28° N. Lat; 80.27° W. Long. Elevation is 1,047 feet.

Population: n/a (1990); n/a (2000); 167 (2010); Density: 916.4 persons per square mile (2010); Race: 67.1% White, 31.7% Black, 0.6% Asian,

0.0% American Indian/Alaska Native, 0.0% Native Hawaiian/Other Pacific Islander, 0.6% Other, 0.0% Hispanic of any race (2010); Average household size: 2.49 (2010); Median age: 41.8 (2010); Males per 100 females: 101.2 (2010); Marriage status: 47.5% never married, 0.0% now married, 37.6% widowed, 14.9% divorced (2006-2010 5-year est.); Foreign born: 0.0% (2006-2010 5-year est.); Ancestry (includes multiple ancestries): 70.3% Italian (2006-2010 5-year est.).

Economy: Employment by occupation: 0.0% management, 0.0% professional, 100.0% services, 0.0% sales, 0.0% farming, 0.0% construction, 0.0% production (2006-2010 5-year est.).

Income: Per capita income: $16,888 (2006-2010 5-year est.); Median household income: $29,318 (2006-2010 5-year est.); Average household income: n/a (2006-2010 5-year est.); Percent of households with income of $100,000 or more: n/a (2006-2010 5-year est.); Poverty rate: 0.0% (2006-2010 5-year est.).

Education: Percent of population age 25 and over with: High school diploma (including GED) or higher: 62.4% (2006-2010 5-year est.); Bachelor's degree or higher: 0.0% (2006-2010 5-year est.); Master's degree or higher: 0.0% (2006-2010 5-year est.).

Housing: Homeownership rate: 61.2% (2010); Median home value: $28,600 (2006-2010 5-year est.); Median contract rent: n/a per month (2006-2010 5-year est.); Median year structure built: before 1940 (2006-2010 5-year est.).

Transportation: Commute to work: 100.0% car, 0.0% public transportation, 0.0% walk, 0.0% work from home (2006-2010 5-year est.); Travel time to work: 0.0% less than 15 minutes, 100.0% 15 to 30 minutes, 0.0% 30 to 45 minutes, 0.0% 45 to 60 minutes, 0.0% 60 minutes or more (2006-2010 5-year est.)

WICKERHAM MANOR-FISHER (CDP).
Covers a land area of 2.151 square miles and a water area of 0 square miles. Located at 40.18° N. Lat; 79.91° W. Long.

Population: 1,931 (1990); 1,783 (2000); 1,728 (2010); Density: 803.5 persons per square mile (2010); Race: 97.6% White, 0.8% Black, 0.4% Asian, 0.0% American Indian/Alaska Native, 0.0% Native Hawaiian/Other Pacific Islander, 1.2% Other, 0.7% Hispanic of any race (2010); Average household size: 2.28 (2010); Median age: 53.6 (2010); Males per 100 females: 83.8 (2010); Marriage status: 14.7% never married, 73.5% now married, 6.8% widowed, 5.0% divorced (2006-2010 5-year est.); Foreign born: 2.2% (2006-2010 5-year est.); Ancestry (includes multiple ancestries): 28.6% Italian, 28.5% German, 15.3% English, 13.3% Polish, 7.6% Irish (2006-2010 5-year est.).

Economy: Employment by occupation: 13.6% management, 0.0% professional, 5.5% services, 18.1% sales, 0.0% farming, 0.7% construction, 6.0% production (2006-2010 5-year est.).

Income: Per capita income: $32,639 (2006-2010 5-year est.); Median household income: $42,969 (2006-2010 5-year est.); Average household income: $71,659 (2006-2010 5-year est.); Percent of households with income of $100,000 or more: 22.6% (2006-2010 5-year est.); Poverty rate: 9.7% (2006-2010 5-year est.).

Education: Percent of population age 25 and over with: High school diploma (including GED) or higher: 93.8% (2006-2010 5-year est.); Bachelor's degree or higher: 31.1% (2006-2010 5-year est.); Master's degree or higher: 11.8% (2006-2010 5-year est.).

Housing: Homeownership rate: 89.1% (2010); Median home value: $137,700 (2006-2010 5-year est.); Median contract rent: $926 per month (2006-2010 5-year est.); Median year structure built: 1953 (2006-2010 5-year est.).

Transportation: Commute to work: 95.2% car, 0.0% public transportation, 0.0% walk, 4.8% work from home (2006-2010 5-year est.); Travel time to work: 40.3% less than 15 minutes, 37.2% 15 to 30 minutes, 13.7% 30 to 45 minutes, 7.6% 45 to 60 minutes, 1.3% 60 minutes or more (2006-2010 5-year est.)

Additional Information Contacts
Monessen Chamber of Commerce . . . . (724) 684-3200
  http://www.monessenchamberofcommerce.com

WOLFDALE (CDP).
Covers a land area of 2.403 square miles and a water area of 0 square miles. Located at 40.20° N. Lat; 80.30° W. Long. Elevation is 1,053 feet.

Population: 2,933 (1990); 2,873 (2000); 2,888 (2010); Density: 1,201.6 persons per square mile (2010); Race: 97.5% White, 1.3% Black, 0.2% Asian, 0.0% American Indian/Alaska Native, 0.0% Native Hawaiian/Other Pacific Islander, 1.0% Other, 0.9% Hispanic of any race (2010); Average household size: 2.28 (2010); Median age: 47.3 (2010); Males per 100

females: 87.8 (2010); Marriage status: 20.5% never married, 59.2% now married, 4.5% widowed, 15.7% divorced (2006-2010 5-year est.); Foreign born: 0.3% (2006-2010 5-year est.); Ancestry (includes multiple ancestries): 35.2% German, 22.8% Irish, 15.9% Italian, 15.6% Polish, 12.8% English (2006-2010 5-year est.).

Economy: Employment by occupation: 14.9% management, 5.5% professional, 13.7% services, 20.5% sales, 1.7% farming, 6.8% construction, 6.0% production (2006-2010 5-year est.).

Income: Per capita income: $23,964 (2006-2010 5-year est.); Median household income: $47,115 (2006-2010 5-year est.); Average household income: $55,121 (2006-2010 5-year est.); Percent of households with income of $100,000 or more: 13.1% (2006-2010 5-year est.); Poverty rate: 10.7% (2006-2010 5-year est.).

Education: Percent of population age 25 and over with: High school diploma (including GED) or higher: 85.6% (2006-2010 5-year est.); Bachelor's degree or higher: 14.4% (2006-2010 5-year est.); Master's degree or higher: 4.1% (2006-2010 5-year est.).

Housing: Homeownership rate: 88.7% (2010); Median home value: $86,200 (2006-2010 5-year est.); Median contract rent: $253 per month (2006-2010 5-year est.); Median year structure built: 1972 (2006-2010 5-year est.).

Transportation: Commute to work: 93.7% car, 0.0% public transportation, 1.2% walk, 1.3% work from home (2006-2010 5-year est.); Travel time to work: 42.8% less than 15 minutes, 34.1% 15 to 30 minutes, 13.3% 30 to 45 minutes, 6.9% 45 to 60 minutes, 2.8% 60 minutes or more (2006-2010 5-year est.)

Additional Information Contacts
Washington County Chamber of Commerce . . . . (724) 225-3010
    http://www.washcochamber.com

WYLANDVILLE (CDP). Covers a land area of 1.467 square miles and a water area of 0 square miles. Located at 40.21° N. Lat; 80.13° W. Long. Elevation is 1,010 feet.

Population: n/a (1990); n/a (2000); 391 (2010); Density: 266.6 persons per square mile (2010); Race: 95.1% White, 3.6% Black, 0.0% Asian, 0.0% American Indian/Alaska Native, 0.0% Native Hawaiian/Other Pacific Islander, 1.3% Other, 1.0% Hispanic of any race (2010); Average household size: 2.33 (2010); Median age: 46.1 (2010); Males per 100 females: 111.4 (2010); Marriage status: 30.9% never married, 64.1% now married, 3.6% widowed, 1.5% divorced (2006-2010 5-year est.); Foreign born: 0.0% (2006-2010 5-year est.); Ancestry (includes multiple ancestries): 21.8% Italian, 18.1% Irish, 10.6% German, 8.6% Polish, 5.5% Scotch-Irish (2006-2010 5-year est.).

Economy: Employment by occupation: 3.7% management, 3.7% professional, 8.2% services, 30.1% sales, 8.2% farming, 14.6% construction, 5.5% production (2006-2010 5-year est.).

Income: Per capita income: $34,563 (2006-2010 5-year est.); Median household income: $59,375 (2006-2010 5-year est.); Average household income: $73,921 (2006-2010 5-year est.); Percent of households with income of $100,000 or more: 4.9% (2006-2010 5-year est.); Poverty rate: 0.0% (2006-2010 5-year est.).

Education: Percent of population age 25 and over with: High school diploma (including GED) or higher: 74.5% (2006-2010 5-year est.); Bachelor's degree or higher: 15.0% (2006-2010 5-year est.); Master's degree or higher: 2.8% (2006-2010 5-year est.).

Housing: Homeownership rate: 86.9% (2010); Median home value: $283,300 (2006-2010 5-year est.); Median contract rent: n/a per month (2006-2010 5-year est.); Median year structure built: 1973 (2006-2010 5-year est.).

Transportation: Commute to work: 96.3% car, 0.0% public transportation, 0.0% walk, 3.7% work from home (2006-2010 5-year est.); Travel time to work: 15.6% less than 15 minutes, 51.7% 15 to 30 minutes, 28.9% 30 to 45 minutes, 3.8% 45 to 60 minutes, 0.0% 60 minutes or more (2006-2010 5-year est.)

Wayne County

Located in northeastern Pennsylvania; bounded on the north by New York, and on the east by the Delaware River and the New York border; drained by the Lackawaxen River; includes Lake Wallenpaupack. Covers a land area of 725.604 square miles, a water area of 25.011 square miles, and is located in the Eastern Time Zone at 41.65° N. Lat., 75.29° W. Long. The county was founded in 1798. County seat is Honesdale.

Weather Station: Pleasant Mount 1 W   Elevation: 1,798 feet

	Jan	Feb	Mar	Apr	May	Jun	Jul	Aug	Sep	Oct	Nov	Dec
High	29	32	40	53	64	72	77	75	68	57	45	33
Low	11	13	20	32	42	51	56	54	47	36	28	17
Precip	3.2	2.7	3.4	4.2	4.7	5.0	4.6	4.1	4.8	4.5	4.1	3.6
Snow	18.9	13.6	11.7	3.3	tr	0.0	0.0	0.0	0.0	0.4	4.5	13.4

High and Low temperatures in degrees Fahrenheit; Precipitation and Snow in inches

Population: 39,944 (1990); 47,722 (2000); 52,822 (2010); Race: 94.2% White, 3.1% Black, 0.5% Asian, 0.2% American Indian/Alaska Native, 0.0% Native Hawaiian/Other Pacific Islander, 2.0% Other, 3.4% Hispanic of any race (2010); Density: 72.8 persons per square mile (2010); Average household size: 2.38 (2010); Median age: 45.9 (2010); Males per 100 females: 110.3 (2010).

Religion: Six largest groups: 30.3% Catholicism, 8.8% Methodist/Pietist, 3.2% Lutheran, 1.9% Hindu, 1.7% Non-Denominational, 1.2% Presbyterian-Reformed (2010)

Economy: Unemployment rate: 6.6% (August 2012); Total civilian labor force: 28,329 (August 2012); Leading industries: 21.8% retail trade; 20.8% health care and social assistance; 12.0% accommodation & food services (2010); Farms: 603 totaling 92,939 acres (2007); Companies that employ 500 or more persons: 1 (2010); Companies that employ 100 to 499 persons: 17 (2010); Companies that employ less than 100 persons: 1,339 (2010); Black-owned businesses: n/a (2007); Hispanic-owned businesses: n/a (2007); Asian-owned businesses: n/a (2007); Women-owned businesses: 1,556 (2007); Retail sales per capita: $14,049 (2010). Single-family building permits issued: 98 (2011); Multi-family building permits issued: 0 (2011).

Income: Per capita income: $22,525 (2006-2010 5-year est.); Median household income: $45,930 (2006-2010 5-year est.); Average household income: $56,816 (2006-2010 5-year est.); Percent of households with income of $100,000 or more: 12.6% (2006-2010 5-year est.); Poverty rate: 10.9% (2006-2010 5-year est.); Bankruptcy rate: 2.84% (2011).

Education: Percent of population age 25 and over with: High school diploma (including GED) or higher: 86.7% (2006-2010 5-year est.); Bachelor's degree or higher: 17.9% (2006-2010 5-year est.); Master's degree or higher: 7.3% (2006-2010 5-year est.).

Housing: Homeownership rate: 80.8% (2010); Median home value: $173,600 (2006-2010 5-year est.); Median contract rent: $545 per month (2006-2010 5-year est.); Median year structure built: 1976 (2006-2010 5-year est.)

Health: Birth rate: 78.3 per 10,000 population (2011); Death rate: 107.2 per 10,000 population (2011); Age-adjusted cancer mortality rate: 186.2 deaths per 100,000 population (2009); Number of physicians: 10.6 per 10,000 population (2010); Hospital beds: 20.3 per 10,000 population (2008); Hospital admissions: 954.0 per 10,000 population (2008).

Elections: 2012 Presidential election results: 38.5% Obama, 60.1% Romney

National and State Parks: Prompton State Park; Tobyhanna State Park

Additional Information Contacts
Wayne County Government . . . . (570) 253-5970
    http://www.co.wayne.pa.us
Wayne County Chamber of Commerce . . . . (570) 253-1960
    http://www.waynecountycc.com

Wayne County Communities

BEACH LAKE (unincorporated postal area)
Zip Code: 18405
    Covers a land area of 36.891 square miles and a water area of 1.511 square miles. Located at 41.59° N. Lat; 75.10° W. Long. Elevation is 1,312 feet. Population: 2,561 (2010); Density: 69.4 persons per square mile (2010); Race: 98.2% White, 0.2% Black, 0.2% Asian, 0.1% American Indian/Alaska Native, 0.0% Native Hawaiian/Other Pacific Islander, 1.3% Other, 3.1% Hispanic of any race (2010); Average household size: 2.48 (2010); Median age: 43.6 (2010); Males per 100 females: 99.5 (2010); Homeownership rate: 81.1% (2010)

BERLIN (township). Covers a land area of 38.450 square miles and a water area of 1.108 square miles. Located at 41.58° N. Lat; 75.16° W. Long.

Population: 1,622 (1990); 2,188 (2000); 2,578 (2010); Density: 67.0 persons per square mile (2010); Race: 97.5% White, 0.6% Black, 0.7% Asian, 0.1% American Indian/Alaska Native, 0.0% Native Hawaiian/Other Pacific Islander, 1.1% Other, 2.4% Hispanic of any race (2010); Average household size: 2.55 (2010); Median age: 42.8 (2010); Males per 100

females: 103.5 (2010); Marriage status: 22.2% never married, 65.2% now married, 4.9% widowed, 7.7% divorced (2006-2010 5-year est.); Foreign born: 4.0% (2006-2010 5-year est.); Ancestry (includes multiple ancestries): 43.4% German, 25.4% Irish, 16.9% Italian, 15.4% English, 11.1% Polish (2006-2010 5-year est.).

Economy: Single-family building permits issued: 4 (2011); Multi-family building permits issued: 0 (2011); Employment by occupation: 15.7% management, 0.5% professional, 13.9% services, 16.9% sales, 0.9% farming, 14.4% construction, 8.5% production (2006-2010 5-year est.).

Income: Per capita income: $27,739 (2006-2010 5-year est.); Median household income: $54,844 (2006-2010 5-year est.); Average household income: $71,449 (2006-2010 5-year est.); Percent of households with income of $100,000 or more: 20.9% (2006-2010 5-year est.); Poverty rate: 10.4% (2006-2010 5-year est.).

Education: Percent of population age 25 and over with: High school diploma (including GED) or higher: 90.8% (2006-2010 5-year est.); Bachelor's degree or higher: 17.0% (2006-2010 5-year est.); Master's degree or higher: 7.3% (2006-2010 5-year est.).

Housing: Homeownership rate: 79.6% (2010); Median home value: $208,400 (2006-2010 5-year est.); Median contract rent: $557 per month (2006-2010 5-year est.); Median year structure built: 1979 (2006-2010 5-year est.).

Transportation: Commute to work: 93.0% car, 0.0% public transportation, 2.4% walk, 4.2% work from home (2006-2010 5-year est.); Travel time to work: 35.9% less than 15 minutes, 39.2% 15 to 30 minutes, 3.9% 30 to 45 minutes, 12.0% 45 to 60 minutes, 9.0% 60 minutes or more (2006-2010 5-year est.)

Additional Information Contacts
Wayne County Chamber of Commerce . . . . (570) 253-1960
    http://www.waynecountycc.com

BETHANY (borough). Covers a land area of 0.498 square miles and a water area of 0.003 square miles. Located at 41.61° N. Lat; 75.29° W. Long. Elevation is 1,385 feet.

Population: 245 (1990); 292 (2000); 246 (2010); Density: 494.4 persons per square mile (2010); Race: 98.0% White, 1.6% Black, 0.0% Asian, 0.4% American Indian/Alaska Native, 0.0% Native Hawaiian/Other Pacific Islander, 0.0% Other, 1.6% Hispanic of any race (2010); Average household size: 2.28 (2010); Median age: 48.0 (2010); Males per 100 females: 90.7 (2010); Marriage status: 26.7% never married, 61.4% now married, 8.2% widowed, 3.7% divorced (2006-2010 5-year est.); Foreign born: 3.0% (2006-2010 5-year est.); Ancestry (includes multiple ancestries): 23.0% German, 12.6% Irish, 12.6% American, 11.6% English, 11.6% Italian (2006-2010 5-year est.).

Economy: Single-family building permits issued: 0 (2011); Multi-family building permits issued: 0 (2011); Employment by occupation: 8.7% management, 2.4% professional, 7.1% services, 18.3% sales, 0.8% farming, 17.9% construction, 7.1% production (2006-2010 5-year est.).

Income: Per capita income: $30,721 (2006-2010 5-year est.); Median household income: $70,938 (2006-2010 5-year est.); Average household income: $67,363 (2006-2010 5-year est.); Percent of households with income of $100,000 or more: 16.9% (2006-2010 5-year est.); Poverty rate: 1.8% (2006-2010 5-year est.).

Education: Percent of population age 25 and over with: High school diploma (including GED) or higher: 91.6% (2006-2010 5-year est.); Bachelor's degree or higher: 30.0% (2006-2010 5-year est.); Master's degree or higher: 14.2% (2006-2010 5-year est.).

Housing: Homeownership rate: 82.4% (2010); Median home value: $193,800 (2006-2010 5-year est.); Median contract rent: $558 per month (2006-2010 5-year est.); Median year structure built: 1960 (2006-2010 5-year est.).

Transportation: Commute to work: 92.9% car, 0.0% public transportation, 1.2% walk, 6.0% work from home (2006-2010 5-year est.); Travel time to work: 38.0% less than 15 minutes, 41.8% 15 to 30 minutes, 5.1% 30 to 45 minutes, 11.4% 45 to 60 minutes, 3.8% 60 minutes or more (2006-2010 5-year est.)

BUCKINGHAM (township). Covers a land area of 44.168 square miles and a water area of 1.203 square miles. Located at 41.88° N. Lat; 75.29° W. Long.

Population: 648 (1990); 656 (2000); 520 (2010); Density: 11.8 persons per square mile (2010); Race: 97.7% White, 0.2% Black, 0.6% Asian, 0.0% American Indian/Alaska Native, 0.0% Native Hawaiian/Other Pacific Islander, 1.5% Other, 2.5% Hispanic of any race (2010); Average household size: 2.00 (2010); Median age: 53.3 (2010); Males per 100

females: 95.5 (2010); Marriage status: 23.0% never married, 56.5% now married, 10.1% widowed, 10.4% divorced (2006-2010 5-year est.); Foreign born: 5.9% (2006-2010 5-year est.); Ancestry (includes multiple ancestries): 33.0% German, 24.0% Irish, 19.1% Polish, 12.6% English, 11.2% French (2006-2010 5-year est.).

Economy: Single-family building permits issued: 1 (2011); Multi-family building permits issued: 0 (2011); Employment by occupation: 8.0% management, 2.2% professional, 3.1% services, 11.2% sales, 4.9% farming, 10.3% construction, 8.0% production (2006-2010 5-year est.).

Income: Per capita income: $26,796 (2006-2010 5-year est.); Median household income: $40,268 (2006-2010 5-year est.); Average household income: $58,762 (2006-2010 5-year est.); Percent of households with income of $100,000 or more: 7.2% (2006-2010 5-year est.); Poverty rate: 11.4% (2006-2010 5-year est.).

Education: Percent of population age 25 and over with: High school diploma (including GED) or higher: 89.6% (2006-2010 5-year est.); Bachelor's degree or higher: 10.2% (2006-2010 5-year est.); Master's degree or higher: 5.2% (2006-2010 5-year est.).

Housing: Homeownership rate: 83.4% (2010); Median home value: $150,400 (2006-2010 5-year est.); Median contract rent: n/a per month (2006-2010 5-year est.); Median year structure built: 1964 (2006-2010 5-year est.).

Transportation: Commute to work: 87.8% car, 0.0% public transportation, 0.0% walk, 12.2% work from home (2006-2010 5-year est.); Travel time to work: 29.2% less than 15 minutes, 10.8% 15 to 30 minutes, 35.9% 30 to 45 minutes, 5.1% 45 to 60 minutes, 19.0% 60 minutes or more (2006-2010 5-year est.)

CANAAN (township). Covers a land area of 18.257 square miles and a water area of 0.937 square miles. Located at 41.57° N. Lat; 75.39° W. Long.

Population: 1,296 (1990); 1,916 (2000); 3,963 (2010); Density: 217.1 persons per square mile (2010); Race: 60.3% White, 29.4% Black, 0.6% Asian, 1.1% American Indian/Alaska Native, 0.0% Native Hawaiian/Other Pacific Islander, 8.6% Other, 13.6% Hispanic of any race (2010); Average household size: 2.49 (2010); Median age: 40.1 (2010); Males per 100 females: 748.6 (2010); Marriage status: 31.4% never married, 47.4% now married, 2.5% widowed, 18.7% divorced (2006-2010 5-year est.); Foreign born: 4.9% (2006-2010 5-year est.); Ancestry (includes multiple ancestries): 8.7% American, 8.6% German, 5.6% Irish, 3.6% English, 3.5% Italian (2006-2010 5-year est.).

Economy: Single-family building permits issued: 0 (2011); Multi-family building permits issued: 0 (2011); Employment by occupation: 11.2% management, 1.3% professional, 10.3% services, 21.1% sales, 6.3% farming, 15.7% construction, 11.5% production (2006-2010 5-year est.).

Income: Per capita income: $13,640 (2006-2010 5-year est.); Median household income: $46,667 (2006-2010 5-year est.); Average household income: $52,203 (2006-2010 5-year est.); Percent of households with income of $100,000 or more: 9.4% (2006-2010 5-year est.); Poverty rate: 12.4% (2006-2010 5-year est.).

Education: Percent of population age 25 and over with: High school diploma (including GED) or higher: 78.1% (2006-2010 5-year est.); Bachelor's degree or higher: 10.9% (2006-2010 5-year est.); Master's degree or higher: 6.1% (2006-2010 5-year est.).

Housing: Homeownership rate: 80.2% (2010); Median home value: $180,100 (2006-2010 5-year est.); Median contract rent: $375 per month (2006-2010 5-year est.); Median year structure built: 1965 (2006-2010 5-year est.).

Transportation: Commute to work: 84.5% car, 0.0% public transportation, 1.1% walk, 13.7% work from home (2006-2010 5-year est.); Travel time to work: 45.6% less than 15 minutes, 34.1% 15 to 30 minutes, 6.3% 30 to 45 minutes, 6.0% 45 to 60 minutes, 8.1% 60 minutes or more (2006-2010 5-year est.)

Additional Information Contacts
Wayne County Chamber of Commerce . . . . (570) 253-1960
    http://www.waynecountycc.com

CHERRY RIDGE (township). Covers a land area of 21.423 square miles and a water area of 0.835 square miles. Located at 41.53° N. Lat; 75.29° W. Long. Elevation is 1,227 feet.

Population: 1,617 (1990); 1,817 (2000); 1,895 (2010); Density: 88.5 persons per square mile (2010); Race: 98.6% White, 0.1% Black, 0.1% Asian, 0.1% American Indian/Alaska Native, 0.0% Native Hawaiian/Other Pacific Islander, 1.1% Other, 2.0% Hispanic of any race (2010); Average household size: 2.45 (2010); Median age: 44.7 (2010); Males per 100

females: 102.2 (2010); Marriage status: 25.6% never married, 57.9% now married, 7.0% widowed, 9.5% divorced (2006-2010 5-year est.); Foreign born: 1.0% (2006-2010 5-year est.); Ancestry (includes multiple ancestries): 45.4% German, 28.0% Irish, 12.5% Italian, 12.1% English, 8.6% Polish (2006-2010 5-year est.).

Economy: Single-family building permits issued: 2 (2011); Multi-family building permits issued: 0 (2011); Employment by occupation: 8.0% management, 1.3% professional, 11.8% services, 16.5% sales, 2.0% farming, 11.7% construction, 11.1% production (2006-2010 5-year est.).

Income: Per capita income: $24,824 (2006-2010 5-year est.); Median household income: $49,375 (2006-2010 5-year est.); Average household income: $59,689 (2006-2010 5-year est.); Percent of households with income of $100,000 or more: 11.9% (2006-2010 5-year est.); Poverty rate: 6.0% (2006-2010 5-year est.).

Education: Percent of population age 25 and over with: High school diploma (including GED) or higher: 86.2% (2006-2010 5-year est.); Bachelor's degree or higher: 17.2% (2006-2010 5-year est.); Master's degree or higher: 9.5% (2006-2010 5-year est.).

Housing: Homeownership rate: 81.0% (2010); Median home value: $180,500 (2006-2010 5-year est.); Median contract rent: $656 per month (2006-2010 5-year est.); Median year structure built: 1979 (2006-2010 5-year est.).

Transportation: Commute to work: 93.0% car, 1.0% public transportation, 2.9% walk, 3.1% work from home (2006-2010 5-year est.); Travel time to work: 53.6% less than 15 minutes, 25.9% 15 to 30 minutes, 13.7% 30 to 45 minutes, 1.7% 45 to 60 minutes, 5.1% 60 minutes or more (2006-2010 5-year est.)

Additional Information Contacts
Wayne County Chamber of Commerce . . . . (570) 253-1960
   http://www.waynecountycc.com

CLINTON (township).
Covers a land area of 38.243 square miles and a water area of 1.324 square miles. Located at 41.65° N. Lat; 75.41° W. Long.

Population: 1,503 (1990); 1,926 (2000); 2,053 (2010); Density: 53.7 persons per square mile (2010); Race: 98.5% White, 0.2% Black, 0.2% Asian, 0.0% American Indian/Alaska Native, 0.0% Native Hawaiian/Other Pacific Islander, 1.1% Other, 0.9% Hispanic of any race (2010); Average household size: 2.41 (2010); Median age: 44.9 (2010); Males per 100 females: 106.5 (2010); Marriage status: 22.0% never married, 58.7% now married, 8.0% widowed, 11.2% divorced (2006-2010 5-year est.); Foreign born: 1.5% (2006-2010 5-year est.); Ancestry (includes multiple ancestries): 30.1% German, 17.1% Irish, 16.6% Polish, 14.0% Italian, 11.6% American (2006-2010 5-year est.).

Economy: Single-family building permits issued: 8 (2011); Multi-family building permits issued: 0 (2011); Employment by occupation: 6.9% management, 9.2% professional, 9.9% services, 19.3% sales, 4.2% farming, 11.1% construction, 6.7% production (2006-2010 5-year est.).

Income: Per capita income: $25,281 (2006-2010 5-year est.); Median household income: $48,125 (2006-2010 5-year est.); Average household income: $64,246 (2006-2010 5-year est.); Percent of households with income of $100,000 or more: 13.5% (2006-2010 5-year est.); Poverty rate: 8.6% (2006-2010 5-year est.).

Education: Percent of population age 25 and over with: High school diploma (including GED) or higher: 83.9% (2006-2010 5-year est.); Bachelor's degree or higher: 14.0% (2006-2010 5-year est.); Master's degree or higher: 6.6% (2006-2010 5-year est.).

Housing: Homeownership rate: 88.0% (2010); Median home value: $171,800 (2006-2010 5-year est.); Median contract rent: $422 per month (2006-2010 5-year est.); Median year structure built: 1963 (2006-2010 5-year est.).

Transportation: Commute to work: 95.0% car, 1.1% public transportation, 0.0% walk, 3.9% work from home (2006-2010 5-year est.); Travel time to work: 28.6% less than 15 minutes, 34.0% 15 to 30 minutes, 18.8% 30 to 45 minutes, 10.1% 45 to 60 minutes, 8.5% 60 minutes or more (2006-2010 5-year est.)

Additional Information Contacts
Wayne County Chamber of Commerce . . . . (570) 253-1960
   http://www.waynecountycc.com

DAMASCUS (township).
Covers a land area of 78.685 square miles and a water area of 1.592 square miles. Located at 41.70° N. Lat; 75.13° W. Long. Elevation is 722 feet.

Population: 3,192 (1990); 3,662 (2000); 3,659 (2010); Density: 46.5 persons per square mile (2010); Race: 97.7% White, 0.5% Black, 0.4%

Asian, 0.1% American Indian/Alaska Native, 0.0% Native Hawaiian/Other Pacific Islander, 1.3% Other, 2.2% Hispanic of any race (2010); Average household size: 2.30 (2010); Median age: 48.0 (2010); Males per 100 females: 101.5 (2010); Marriage status: 20.1% never married, 66.8% now married, 9.2% widowed, 3.9% divorced (2006-2010 5-year est.); Foreign born: 4.4% (2006-2010 5-year est.); Ancestry (includes multiple ancestries): 44.2% German, 24.7% Irish, 18.1% English, 10.5% Italian, 7.8% Polish (2006-2010 5-year est.).

Economy: Single-family building permits issued: 14 (2011); Multi-family building permits issued: 0 (2011); Employment by occupation: 7.0% management, 0.8% professional, 12.9% services, 14.7% sales, 1.6% farming, 19.8% construction, 6.2% production (2006-2010 5-year est.).

Income: Per capita income: $24,463 (2006-2010 5-year est.); Median household income: $47,772 (2006-2010 5-year est.); Average household income: $60,531 (2006-2010 5-year est.); Percent of households with income of $100,000 or more: 12.8% (2006-2010 5-year est.); Poverty rate: 7.4% (2006-2010 5-year est.).

Education: Percent of population age 25 and over with: High school diploma (including GED) or higher: 84.0% (2006-2010 5-year est.); Bachelor's degree or higher: 14.9% (2006-2010 5-year est.); Master's degree or higher: 6.0% (2006-2010 5-year est.).

School District(s)
Wayne Highlands SD (PK-12)
   2010-11 Enrollment: 2,983 . . . . (570) 253-4661
Housing: Homeownership rate: 87.4% (2010); Median home value: $182,300 (2006-2010 5-year est.); Median contract rent: $604 per month (2006-2010 5-year est.); Median year structure built: 1973 (2006-2010 5-year est.).

Transportation: Commute to work: 90.7% car, 0.5% public transportation, 3.3% walk, 5.4% work from home (2006-2010 5-year est.); Travel time to work: 19.3% less than 15 minutes, 41.1% 15 to 30 minutes, 10.7% 30 to 45 minutes, 12.1% 45 to 60 minutes, 16.8% 60 minutes or more (2006-2010 5-year est.)

Additional Information Contacts
Damascus Township . . . . (570) 224-4410
   http://damascustwp.org
Wayne County Chamber of Commerce . . . . (570) 253-1960
   http://www.waynecountycc.com

DREHER (township).
Covers a land area of 14.850 square miles and a water area of 0.255 square miles. Located at 41.30° N. Lat; 75.36° W. Long.

Population: 984 (1990); 1,280 (2000); 1,412 (2010); Density: 95.1 persons per square mile (2010); Race: 95.6% White, 2.1% Black, 0.4% Asian, 0.3% American Indian/Alaska Native, 0.1% Native Hawaiian/Other Pacific Islander, 1.5% Other, 4.9% Hispanic of any race (2010); Average household size: 2.44 (2010); Median age: 45.6 (2010); Males per 100 females: 102.9 (2010); Marriage status: 26.6% never married, 51.5% now married, 10.6% widowed, 11.4% divorced (2006-2010 5-year est.); Foreign born: 5.5% (2006-2010 5-year est.); Ancestry (includes multiple ancestries): 42.3% German, 28.7% Irish, 11.1% Polish, 8.3% English, 7.3% French (2006-2010 5-year est.).

Economy: Single-family building permits issued: 3 (2011); Multi-family building permits issued: 0 (2011); Employment by occupation: 8.0% management, 4.1% professional, 9.6% services, 15.3% sales, 3.7% farming, 12.0% construction, 9.0% production (2006-2010 5-year est.).

Income: Per capita income: $21,666 (2006-2010 5-year est.); Median household income: $40,278 (2006-2010 5-year est.); Average household income: $52,580 (2006-2010 5-year est.); Percent of households with income of $100,000 or more: 12.8% (2006-2010 5-year est.); Poverty rate: 13.3% (2006-2010 5-year est.).

Education: Percent of population age 25 and over with: High school diploma (including GED) or higher: 91.9% (2006-2010 5-year est.); Bachelor's degree or higher: 24.9% (2006-2010 5-year est.); Master's degree or higher: 11.2% (2006-2010 5-year est.).

Housing: Homeownership rate: 81.4% (2010); Median home value: $181,000 (2006-2010 5-year est.); Median contract rent: $494 per month (2006-2010 5-year est.); Median year structure built: 1970 (2006-2010 5-year est.).

Transportation: Commute to work: 83.3% car, 0.0% public transportation, 9.4% walk, 7.3% work from home (2006-2010 5-year est.); Travel time to work: 32.3% less than 15 minutes, 26.5% 15 to 30 minutes, 21.7% 30 to 45 minutes, 10.4% 45 to 60 minutes, 9.2% 60 minutes or more (2006-2010 5-year est.)

Additional Information Contacts
Greater Scranton Chamber of Commerce . . . . (570) 342-7711
http://www.scrantonchamber.com

DYBERRY (township). Covers a land area of 22.169 square miles and a water area of 0.727 square miles. Located at 41.65° N. Lat; 75.29° W. Long. Elevation is 1,030 feet.
Population: 1,003 (1990); 1,353 (2000); 1,401 (2010); Density: 63.2 persons per square mile (2010); Race: 97.1% White, 0.5% Black, 0.7% Asian, 0.0% American Indian/Alaska Native, 0.0% Native Hawaiian/Other Pacific Islander, 1.7% Other, 1.5% Hispanic of any race (2010); Average household size: 2.38 (2010); Median age: 46.7 (2010); Males per 100 females: 95.1 (2010); Marriage status: 31.9% never married, 47.4% now married, 8.1% widowed, 12.7% divorced (2006-2010 5-year est.); Foreign born: 4.5% (2006-2010 5-year est.); Ancestry (includes multiple ancestries): 37.3% German, 30.2% Irish, 17.4% English, 10.0% Polish, 9.3% Italian (2006-2010 5-year est.).
Economy: Single-family building permits issued: 0 (2011); Multi-family building permits issued: 0 (2011); Employment by occupation: 8.5% management, 2.2% professional, 12.3% services, 19.1% sales, 1.1% farming, 12.5% construction, 10.2% production (2006-2010 5-year est.).
Income: Per capita income: $21,428 (2006-2010 5-year est.); Median household income: $47,463 (2006-2010 5-year est.); Average household income: $60,739 (2006-2010 5-year est.); Percent of households with income of $100,000 or more: 17.2% (2006-2010 5-year est.); Poverty rate: 23.4% (2006-2010 5-year est.).
Education: Percent of population age 25 and over with: High school diploma (including GED) or higher: 91.8% (2006-2010 5-year est.); Bachelor's degree or higher: 35.5% (2006-2010 5-year est.); Master's degree or higher: 9.5% (2006-2010 5-year est.).
Housing: Homeownership rate: 84.6% (2010); Median home value: $203,700 (2006-2010 5-year est.); Median contract rent: $575 per month (2006-2010 5-year est.); Median year structure built: 1977 (2006-2010 5-year est.).
Transportation: Commute to work: 78.7% car, 0.3% public transportation, 11.6% walk, 7.9% work from home (2006-2010 5-year est.); Travel time to work: 49.3% less than 15 minutes, 28.1% 15 to 30 minutes, 8.3% 30 to 45 minutes, 7.9% 45 to 60 minutes, 6.4% 60 minutes or more (2006-2010 5-year est.).
Additional Information Contacts
Wayne County Chamber of Commerce . . . . (570) 253-1960
http://www.waynecountycc.com

EQUINUNK (unincorporated postal area)
Zip Code: 18417
Covers a land area of 58.482 square miles and a water area of 1.487 square miles. Located at 41.80° N. Lat; 75.20° W. Long. Population: 1,121 (2010); Density: 19.2 persons per square mile (2010); Race: 97.5% White, 0.4% Black, 0.3% Asian, 0.1% American Indian/Alaska Native, 0.0% Native Hawaiian/Other Pacific Islander, 1.7% Other, 0.9% Hispanic of any race (2010); Average household size: 2.28 (2010); Median age: 49.0 (2010); Males per 100 females: 107.6 (2010); Homeownership rate: 82.3% (2010)

GOULDSBORO (CDP). Covers a land area of 2.596 square miles and a water area of 0.408 square miles. Located at 41.25° N. Lat; 75.44° W. Long. Elevation is 1,906 feet.
Population: n/a (1990); n/a (2000); 890 (2010); Density: 342.9 persons per square mile (2010); Race: 94.9% White, 1.0% Black, 1.3% Asian, 0.1% American Indian/Alaska Native, 0.1% Native Hawaiian/Other Pacific Islander, 2.6% Other, 4.0% Hispanic of any race (2010); Average household size: 2.52 (2010); Median age: 45.4 (2010); Males per 100 females: 98.7 (2010); Marriage status: 15.3% never married, 74.1% now married, 5.2% widowed, 5.5% divorced (2006-2010 5-year est.); Foreign born: 2.2% (2006-2010 5-year est.); Ancestry (includes multiple ancestries): 40.4% German, 38.5% Irish, 18.4% Italian, 16.7% English, 10.1% Polish (2006-2010 5-year est.).
Economy: Employment by occupation: 10.1% management, 4.9% professional, 8.8% services, 14.1% sales, 4.2% farming, 8.8% construction, 3.3% production (2006-2010 5-year est.).
Income: Per capita income: $21,669 (2006-2010 5-year est.); Median household income: $48,889 (2006-2010 5-year est.); Average household income: $60,907 (2006-2010 5-year est.); Percent of households with income of $100,000 or more: 16.3% (2006-2010 5-year est.); Poverty rate: 2.8% (2006-2010 5-year est.).

Education: Percent of population age 25 and over with: High school diploma (including GED) or higher: 82.3% (2006-2010 5-year est.); Bachelor's degree or higher: 17.7% (2006-2010 5-year est.); Master's degree or higher: 5.2% (2006-2010 5-year est.).
Housing: Homeownership rate: 79.8% (2010); Median home value: $196,400 (2006-2010 5-year est.); Median contract rent: $546 per month (2006-2010 5-year est.); Median year structure built: 1965 (2006-2010 5-year est.).
Transportation: Commute to work: 97.7% car, 0.0% public transportation, 0.0% walk, 2.3% work from home (2006-2010 5-year est.); Travel time to work: 31.4% less than 15 minutes, 26.8% 15 to 30 minutes, 21.1% 30 to 45 minutes, 12.4% 45 to 60 minutes, 8.4% 60 minutes or more (2006-2010 5-year est.)

HAWLEY (borough). Covers a land area of 0.581 square miles and a water area of 0.036 square miles. Located at 41.48° N. Lat; 75.18° W. Long. Elevation is 906 feet.
History: Settled 1803, incorporated 1884.
Population: 1,244 (1990); 1,303 (2000); 1,211 (2010); Density: 2,085.4 persons per square mile (2010); Race: 96.4% White, 0.5% Black, 0.1% Asian, 0.0% American Indian/Alaska Native, 0.0% Native Hawaiian/Other Pacific Islander, 3.0% Other, 5.0% Hispanic of any race (2010); Average household size: 2.21 (2010); Median age: 44.4 (2010); Males per 100 females: 91.6 (2010); Marriage status: 33.0% never married, 38.9% now married, 12.1% widowed, 16.0% divorced (2006-2010 5-year est.); Foreign born: 1.5% (2006-2010 5-year est.); Ancestry (includes multiple ancestries): 34.6% German, 27.8% Irish, 17.3% Italian, 14.3% English, 6.8% Polish (2006-2010 5-year est.).
Economy: Employment by occupation: 9.5% management, 3.7% professional, 12.5% services, 13.4% sales, 3.0% farming, 10.4% construction, 4.5% production (2006-2010 5-year est.).
Income: Per capita income: $20,669 (2006-2010 5-year est.); Median household income: $36,700 (2006-2010 5-year est.); Average household income: $47,176 (2006-2010 5-year est.); Percent of households with income of $100,000 or more: 9.7% (2006-2010 5-year est.); Poverty rate: 21.8% (2006-2010 5-year est.).
Education: Percent of population age 25 and over with: High school diploma (including GED) or higher: 87.7% (2006-2010 5-year est.); Bachelor's degree or higher: 18.7% (2006-2010 5-year est.); Master's degree or higher: 6.5% (2006-2010 5-year est.).
School District(s)
Wallenpaupack Area SD (KG-12)
2010-11 Enrollment: 3,586 . . . . (570) 226-4557
Housing: Homeownership rate: 53.0% (2010); Median home value: $153,100 (2006-2010 5-year est.); Median contract rent: $530 per month (2006-2010 5-year est.); Median year structure built: before 1940 (2006-2010 5-year est.).
Safety: Violent crime rate: 0.0 per 10,000 population; Property crime rate: 65.8 per 10,000 population (2011).
Newspapers: The News Eagle (Local news; Circulation 7,500)
Transportation: Commute to work: 80.0% car, 1.1% public transportation, 13.8% walk, 5.1% work from home (2006-2010 5-year est.); Travel time to work: 44.2% less than 15 minutes, 33.3% 15 to 30 minutes, 9.6% 30 to 45 minutes, 3.4% 45 to 60 minutes, 9.6% 60 minutes or more (2006-2010 5-year est.)
Additional Information Contacts
Pocono Lake Region Chamber of Commerce. . . . . (570) 226-3191
http://www.lakeregioncc.com

HONESDALE (borough). County seat. Covers a land area of 3.881 square miles and a water area of 0.141 square miles. Located at 41.58° N. Lat; 75.25° W. Long. Elevation is 974 feet.
History: After 1808, Honesdale became one of the foremost coal storage and shipping points. In 1826, Philip Hone, mayor of New York City, came to the settlement to push construction of a canal that would divert the flow of coal to his city.
Population: 5,256 (1990); 4,874 (2000); 4,480 (2010); Density: 1,154.2 persons per square mile (2010); Race: 96.8% White, 0.9% Black, 0.4% Asian, 0.1% American Indian/Alaska Native, 0.0% Native Hawaiian/Other Pacific Islander, 1.8% Other, 2.8% Hispanic of any race (2010); Average household size: 2.15 (2010); Median age: 42.1 (2010); Males per 100 females: 85.5 (2010); Marriage status: 32.4% never married, 43.9% now married, 10.5% widowed, 13.1% divorced (2006-2010 5-year est.); Foreign born: 3.7% (2006-2010 5-year est.); Ancestry (includes multiple

ancestries): 31.9% German, 22.7% Irish, 21.8% English, 12.2% Polish, 10.0% Italian (2006-2010 5-year est.).

Economy: Single-family building permits issued: 1 (2011); Multi-family building permits issued: 0 (2011); Employment by occupation: 8.5% management, 3.6% professional, 10.0% services, 23.1% sales, 1.4% farming, 11.2% construction, 7.7% production (2006-2010 5-year est.).

Income: Per capita income: $20,122 (2006-2010 5-year est.); Median household income: $32,644 (2006-2010 5-year est.); Average household income: $41,452 (2006-2010 5-year est.); Percent of households with income of $100,000 or more: 4.9% (2006-2010 5-year est.); Poverty rate: 19.6% (2006-2010 5-year est.).

Education: Percent of population age 25 and over with: High school diploma (including GED) or higher: 83.9% (2006-2010 5-year est.); Bachelor's degree or higher: 15.8% (2006-2010 5-year est.); Master's degree or higher: 4.5% (2006-2010 5-year est.).

School District(s)

Wayne Highlands SD (PK-12)

   2010-11 Enrollment: 2,983 . . . . (570) 253-4661

Housing: Homeownership rate: 54.5% (2010); Median home value: $126,300 (2006-2010 5-year est.); Median contract rent: $507 per month (2006-2010 5-year est.); Median year structure built: before 1940 (2006-2010 5-year est.).

Hospitals: Wayne Memorial Hospital (95 beds)

Safety: Violent crime rate: 8.9 per 10,000 population; Property crime rate: 318.2 per 10,000 population (2011).

Newspapers: The Wayne Independent (Local news; Circulation 9,000); The Weekly Almanac (Local news; Circulation 5,000)

Transportation: Commute to work: 79.8% car, 1.9% public transportation, 10.3% walk, 4.3% work from home (2006-2010 5-year est.); Travel time to work: 58.1% less than 15 minutes, 31.0% 15 to 30 minutes, 2.8% 30 to 45 minutes, 2.0% 45 to 60 minutes, 6.1% 60 minutes or more (2006-2010 5-year est.)

Airports: Cherry Ridge (general aviation)

Additional Information Contacts

Wayne County Chamber of Commerce . . . . (570) 253-1960

   http://www.waynecountycc.com

LAKE (township). Covers a land area of 27.796 square miles and a water area of 2.045 square miles. Located at 41.46° N. Lat; 75.37° W. Long.

Population: 3,140 (1990); 4,361 (2000); 5,269 (2010); Density: 189.6 persons per square mile (2010); Race: 96.0% White, 1.6% Black, 0.4% Asian, 0.2% American Indian/Alaska Native, 0.0% Native Hawaiian/Other Pacific Islander, 1.8% Other, 2.9% Hispanic of any race (2010); Average household size: 2.39 (2010); Median age: 49.0 (2010); Males per 100 females: 95.7 (2010); Marriage status: 23.6% never married, 59.2% now married, 6.8% widowed, 10.4% divorced (2006-2010 5-year est.); Foreign born: 3.4% (2006-2010 5-year est.); Ancestry (includes multiple ancestries): 28.9% Irish, 25.7% German, 17.0% Italian, 13.3% English, 13.1% Polish (2006-2010 5-year est.).

Economy: Single-family building permits issued: 9 (2011); Multi-family building permits issued: 0 (2011); Employment by occupation: 7.9% management, 2.6% professional, 11.1% services, 15.8% sales, 2.3% farming, 13.9% construction, 10.7% production (2006-2010 5-year est.).

Income: Per capita income: $24,483 (2006-2010 5-year est.); Median household income: $49,625 (2006-2010 5-year est.); Average household income: $63,471 (2006-2010 5-year est.); Percent of households with income of $100,000 or more: 15.5% (2006-2010 5-year est.); Poverty rate: 7.2% (2006-2010 5-year est.).

Education: Percent of population age 25 and over with: High school diploma (including GED) or higher: 88.4% (2006-2010 5-year est.); Bachelor's degree or higher: 18.1% (2006-2010 5-year est.); Master's degree or higher: 5.6% (2006-2010 5-year est.).

Housing: Homeownership rate: 87.4% (2010); Median home value: $183,600 (2006-2010 5-year est.); Median contract rent: $598 per month (2006-2010 5-year est.); Median year structure built: 1983 (2006-2010 5-year est.).

Transportation: Commute to work: 88.3% car, 0.2% public transportation, 0.6% walk, 9.9% work from home (2006-2010 5-year est.); Travel time to work: 22.2% less than 15 minutes, 37.3% 15 to 30 minutes, 30.1% 30 to 45 minutes, 6.1% 45 to 60 minutes, 4.4% 60 minutes or more (2006-2010 5-year est.)

Additional Information Contacts

Wayne County Chamber of Commerce . . . . (570) 253-1960

   http://www.waynecountycc.com

LAKE ARIEL (unincorporated postal area)

Zip Code: 18436

   Covers a land area of 90.856 square miles and a water area of 3.573 square miles. Located at 41.44° N. Lat; 75.39° W. Long. Population: 13,853 (2010); Density: 152.5 persons per square mile (2010); Race: 96.6% White, 1.3% Black, 0.4% Asian, 0.2% American Indian/Alaska Native, 0.0% Native Hawaiian/Other Pacific Islander, 1.5% Other, 2.7% Hispanic of any race (2010); Average household size: 2.44 (2010); Median age: 47.9 (2010); Males per 100 females: 99.6 (2010); Homeownership rate: 87.3% (2010)

LAKE COMO (unincorporated postal area)

Zip Code: 18437

   Covers a land area of 11.832 square miles and a water area of 0.332 square miles. Located at 41.87° N. Lat; 75.31° W. Long. Population: 211 (2010); Density: 17.8 persons per square mile (2010); Race: 96.7% White, 0.0% Black, 0.5% Asian, 0.0% American Indian/Alaska Native, 0.0% Native Hawaiian/Other Pacific Islander, 2.8% Other, 3.8% Hispanic of any race (2010); Average household size: 2.32 (2010); Median age: 48.9 (2010); Males per 100 females: 88.4 (2010); Homeownership rate: 73.7% (2010)

LAKEVILLE (unincorporated postal area)

Zip Code: 18438

   Covers a land area of 7.352 square miles and a water area of 0.417 square miles. Located at 41.43° N. Lat; 75.25° W. Long. Elevation is 1,257 feet. Population: 1,172 (2010); Density: 159.4 persons per square mile (2010); Race: 98.0% White, 0.2% Black, 0.8% Asian, 0.0% American Indian/Alaska Native, 0.0% Native Hawaiian/Other Pacific Islander, 1.0% Other, 3.3% Hispanic of any race (2010); Average household size: 2.26 (2010); Median age: 54.3 (2010); Males per 100 females: 93.7 (2010); Homeownership rate: 90.4% (2010)

LAKEWOOD (unincorporated postal area)

Zip Code: 18439

   Covers a land area of 30.520 square miles and a water area of 1.236 square miles. Located at 41.82° N. Lat; 75.34° W. Long. Population: 500 (2010); Density: 16.4 persons per square mile (2010); Race: 99.2% White, 0.0% Black, 0.6% Asian, 0.0% American Indian/Alaska Native, 0.0% Native Hawaiian/Other Pacific Islander, 0.2% Other, 0.8% Hispanic of any race (2010); Average household size: 2.22 (2010); Median age: 49.1 (2010); Males per 100 females: 100.8 (2010); Homeownership rate: 84.9% (2010)

LEBANON (township). Covers a land area of 37.234 square miles and a water area of 0.918 square miles. Located at 41.70° N. Lat; 75.27° W. Long.

Population: 464 (1990); 645 (2000); 684 (2010); Density: 18.4 persons per square mile (2010); Race: 97.1% White, 1.6% Black, 0.4% Asian, 0.0% American Indian/Alaska Native, 0.0% Native Hawaiian/Other Pacific Islander, 0.9% Other, 1.6% Hispanic of any race (2010); Average household size: 2.45 (2010); Median age: 46.9 (2010); Males per 100 females: 98.3 (2010); Marriage status: 21.9% never married, 64.5% now married, 8.3% widowed, 5.3% divorced (2006-2010 5-year est.); Foreign born: 1.9% (2006-2010 5-year est.); Ancestry (includes multiple ancestries): 39.8% German, 18.1% English, 15.0% Irish, 11.8% Italian, 5.5% Polish (2006-2010 5-year est.).

Economy: Single-family building permits issued: 3 (2011); Multi-family building permits issued: 0 (2011); Employment by occupation: 14.5% management, 0.0% professional, 3.8% services, 29.6% sales, 3.5% farming, 18.9% construction, 4.7% production (2006-2010 5-year est.).

Income: Per capita income: $29,011 (2006-2010 5-year est.); Median household income: $42,000 (2006-2010 5-year est.); Average household income: $59,929 (2006-2010 5-year est.); Percent of households with income of $100,000 or more: 16.0% (2006-2010 5-year est.); Poverty rate: 10.1% (2006-2010 5-year est.).

Education: Percent of population age 25 and over with: High school diploma (including GED) or higher: 84.9% (2006-2010 5-year est.); Bachelor's degree or higher: 15.9% (2006-2010 5-year est.); Master's degree or higher: 6.2% (2006-2010 5-year est.).

Housing: Homeownership rate: 87.8% (2010); Median home value: $169,400 (2006-2010 5-year est.); Median contract rent: $668 per month (2006-2010 5-year est.); Median year structure built: 1977 (2006-2010 5-year est.).

Transportation: Commute to work: 93.6% car, 0.0% public transportation, 1.0% walk, 5.4% work from home (2006-2010 5-year est.); Travel time to work: 8.4% less than 15 minutes, 42.9% 15 to 30 minutes, 14.2% 30 to 45 minutes, 22.0% 45 to 60 minutes, 12.5% 60 minutes or more (2006-2010 5-year est.)

LEHIGH (township). Covers a land area of 12.014 square miles and a water area of 0.602 square miles. Located at 41.25° N. Lat; 75.40° W. Long.

Population: 1,287 (1990); 1,639 (2000); 1,881 (2010); Density: 156.6 persons per square mile (2010); Race: 94.3% White, 2.2% Black, 1.0% Asian, 0.1% American Indian/Alaska Native, 0.1% Native Hawaiian/Other Pacific Islander, 2.3% Other, 4.0% Hispanic of any race (2010); Average household size: 2.43 (2010); Median age: 47.2 (2010); Males per 100 females: 101.8 (2010); Marriage status: 24.6% never married, 58.8% now married, 6.5% widowed, 10.1% divorced (2006-2010 5-year est.); Foreign born: 3.4% (2006-2010 5-year est.); Ancestry (includes multiple ancestries): 34.2% German, 25.2% Irish, 16.0% Italian, 9.1% Polish, 8.6% English (2006-2010 5-year est.).

Economy: Single-family building permits issued: 3 (2011); Multi-family building permits issued: 0 (2011); Employment by occupation: 10.3% management, 4.2% professional, 8.3% services, 15.9% sales, 5.0% farming, 8.3% construction, 7.8% production (2006-2010 5-year est.).

Income: Per capita income: $25,300 (2006-2010 5-year est.); Median household income: $43,618 (2006-2010 5-year est.); Average household income: $65,956 (2006-2010 5-year est.); Percent of households with income of $100,000 or more: 21.6% (2006-2010 5-year est.); Poverty rate: 14.5% (2006-2010 5-year est.).

Education: Percent of population age 25 and over with: High school diploma (including GED) or higher: 87.1% (2006-2010 5-year est.); Bachelor's degree or higher: 18.2% (2006-2010 5-year est.); Master's degree or higher: 7.1% (2006-2010 5-year est.).

Housing: Homeownership rate: 86.2% (2010); Median home value: $136,700 (2006-2010 5-year est.); Median contract rent: $566 per month (2006-2010 5-year est.); Median year structure built: 1982 (2006-2010 5-year est.).

Transportation: Commute to work: 92.4% car, 2.5% public transportation, 2.4% walk, 2.3% work from home (2006-2010 5-year est.); Travel time to work: 30.3% less than 15 minutes, 30.9% 15 to 30 minutes, 20.1% 30 to 45 minutes, 9.0% 45 to 60 minutes, 9.7% 60 minutes or more (2006-2010 5-year est.)

Additional Information Contacts
Greater Scranton Chamber of Commerce . . . . (570) 342-7711
http://www.scrantonchamber.com

MANCHESTER (township). Covers a land area of 44.124 square miles and a water area of 0.891 square miles. Located at 41.82° N. Lat; 75.17° W. Long.

Population: 624 (1990); 888 (2000); 836 (2010); Density: 18.9 persons per square mile (2010); Race: 98.0% White, 0.6% Black, 0.1% Asian, 0.0% American Indian/Alaska Native, 0.0% Native Hawaiian/Other Pacific Islander, 1.3% Other, 1.0% Hispanic of any race (2010); Average household size: 2.33 (2010); Median age: 48.0 (2010); Males per 100 females: 110.1 (2010); Marriage status: 19.0% never married, 47.2% now married, 12.5% widowed, 21.3% divorced (2006-2010 5-year est.); Foreign born: 4.2% (2006-2010 5-year est.); Ancestry (includes multiple ancestries): 31.0% German, 27.9% Irish, 14.4% English, 12.5% Italian, 7.8% Polish (2006-2010 5-year est.).

Economy: Single-family building permits issued: 2 (2011); Multi-family building permits issued: 0 (2011); Employment by occupation: 11.3% management, 1.9% professional, 10.8% services, 17.5% sales, 4.6% farming, 13.5% construction, 11.6% production (2006-2010 5-year est.).

Income: Per capita income: $22,126 (2006-2010 5-year est.); Median household income: $35,873 (2006-2010 5-year est.); Average household income: $44,806 (2006-2010 5-year est.); Percent of households with income of $100,000 or more: 7.4% (2006-2010 5-year est.); Poverty rate: 18.6% (2006-2010 5-year est.).

Education: Percent of population age 25 and over with: High school diploma (including GED) or higher: 83.6% (2006-2010 5-year est.); Bachelor's degree or higher: 11.6% (2006-2010 5-year est.); Master's degree or higher: 6.4% (2006-2010 5-year est.).

Housing: Homeownership rate: 81.9% (2010); Median home value: $197,300 (2006-2010 5-year est.); Median contract rent: $343 per month (2006-2010 5-year est.); Median year structure built: 1977 (2006-2010 5-year est.).

Transportation: Commute to work: 82.8% car, 0.0% public transportation, 10.5% walk, 6.6% work from home (2006-2010 5-year est.); Travel time to work: 26.7% less than 15 minutes, 18.1% 15 to 30 minutes, 37.4% 30 to 45 minutes, 8.6% 45 to 60 minutes, 9.2% 60 minutes or more (2006-2010 5-year est.)

Additional Information Contacts
Wayne County Chamber of Commerce . . . . (570) 253-1960
http://www.waynecountycc.com

MILANVILLE (unincorporated postal area)
Zip Code: 18443

Covers a land area of 13.726 square miles and a water area of 0.191 square miles. Located at 41.66° N. Lat; 75.10° W. Long. Elevation is 751 feet. Population: 458 (2010); Density: 33.4 persons per square mile (2010); Race: 96.3% White, 0.9% Black, 0.2% Asian, 0.0% American Indian/Alaska Native, 0.0% Native Hawaiian/Other Pacific Islander, 2.6% Other, 2.8% Hispanic of any race (2010); Average household size: 2.29 (2010); Median age: 49.3 (2010); Males per 100 females: 112.0 (2010); Homeownership rate: 85.5% (2010)

MOUNT PLEASANT (township). Covers a land area of 56.456 square miles and a water area of 1.116 square miles. Located at 41.74° N. Lat; 75.40° W. Long.

Population: 1,338 (1990); 1,345 (2000); 1,357 (2010); Density: 24.0 persons per square mile (2010); Race: 97.1% White, 0.7% Black, 0.9% Asian, 0.2% American Indian/Alaska Native, 0.0% Native Hawaiian/Other Pacific Islander, 1.1% Other, 2.8% Hispanic of any race (2010); Average household size: 2.40 (2010); Median age: 48.6 (2010); Males per 100 females: 100.1 (2010); Marriage status: 19.7% never married, 62.4% now married, 8.5% widowed, 9.4% divorced (2006-2010 5-year est.); Foreign born: 2.5% (2006-2010 5-year est.); Ancestry (includes multiple ancestries): 31.2% Irish, 23.1% English, 21.6% German, 14.7% Polish, 7.3% Italian (2006-2010 5-year est.).

Economy: Single-family building permits issued: 3 (2011); Multi-family building permits issued: 0 (2011); Employment by occupation: 13.3% management, 0.0% professional, 12.2% services, 23.3% sales, 2.6% farming, 6.6% construction, 4.4% production (2006-2010 5-year est.).

Income: Per capita income: $25,987 (2006-2010 5-year est.); Median household income: $53,424 (2006-2010 5-year est.); Average household income: $58,462 (2006-2010 5-year est.); Percent of households with income of $100,000 or more: 13.5% (2006-2010 5-year est.); Poverty rate: 1.8% (2006-2010 5-year est.).

Education: Percent of population age 25 and over with: High school diploma (including GED) or higher: 94.6% (2006-2010 5-year est.); Bachelor's degree or higher: 18.7% (2006-2010 5-year est.); Master's degree or higher: 8.1% (2006-2010 5-year est.).

Housing: Homeownership rate: 86.9% (2010); Median home value: $193,100 (2006-2010 5-year est.); Median contract rent: $445 per month (2006-2010 5-year est.); Median year structure built: 1977 (2006-2010 5-year est.).

Transportation: Commute to work: 90.3% car, 0.5% public transportation, 1.2% walk, 7.9% work from home (2006-2010 5-year est.); Travel time to work: 12.9% less than 15 minutes, 42.4% 15 to 30 minutes, 32.1% 30 to 45 minutes, 6.8% 45 to 60 minutes, 5.8% 60 minutes or more (2006-2010 5-year est.)

Additional Information Contacts
Wayne County Chamber of Commerce . . . . (570) 253-1960
http://www.waynecountycc.com

NEWFOUNDLAND (unincorporated postal area)
Zip Code: 18445

Covers a land area of 36.439 square miles and a water area of 0.580 square miles. Located at 41.29° N. Lat; 75.35° W. Long. Population: 2,329 (2010); Density: 63.9 persons per square mile (2010); Race: 94.8% White, 2.4% Black, 0.6% Asian, 0.3% American Indian/Alaska Native, 0.1% Native Hawaiian/Other Pacific Islander, 1.8% Other, 4.3% Hispanic of any race (2010); Average household size: 2.37 (2010); Median age: 47.0 (2010); Males per 100 females: 103.4 (2010); Homeownership rate: 85.4% (2010)

OREGON (township). Covers a land area of 17.701 square miles and a water area of 0.272 square miles. Located at 41.66° N. Lat; 75.20° W. Long.

Population: 621 (1990); 745 (2000); 781 (2010); Density: 44.1 persons per square mile (2010); Race: 99.2% White, 0.1% Black, 0.3% Asian,

0.1% American Indian/Alaska Native, 0.0% Native Hawaiian/Other Pacific Islander, 0.3% Other, 0.6% Hispanic of any race (2010); Average household size: 2.49 (2010); Median age: 46.6 (2010); Males per 100 females: 104.5 (2010); Marriage status: 25.5% never married, 62.2% now married, 4.4% widowed, 7.8% divorced (2006-2010 5-year est.); Foreign born: 5.0% (2006-2010 5-year est.); Ancestry (includes multiple ancestries): 36.7% German, 20.8% Irish, 12.1% English, 11.1% Italian, 7.7% Polish (2006-2010 5-year est.).

Economy: Single-family building permits issued: 2 (2011); Multi-family building permits issued: 0 (2011); Employment by occupation: 7.9% management, 3.8% professional, 5.3% services, 21.9% sales, 1.8% farming, 19.6% construction, 4.4% production (2006-2010 5-year est.).

Income: Per capita income: $20,458 (2006-2010 5-year est.); Median household income: $48,750 (2006-2010 5-year est.); Average household income: $54,357 (2006-2010 5-year est.); Percent of households with income of $100,000 or more: 12.2% (2006-2010 5-year est.); Poverty rate: 8.4% (2006-2010 5-year est.).

Education: Percent of population age 25 and over with: High school diploma (including GED) or higher: 81.0% (2006-2010 5-year est.); Bachelor's degree or higher: 15.5% (2006-2010 5-year est.); Master's degree or higher: 7.0% (2006-2010 5-year est.).

Housing: Homeownership rate: 85.4% (2010); Median home value: $237,500 (2006-2010 5-year est.); Median contract rent: $338 per month (2006-2010 5-year est.); Median year structure built: 1978 (2006-2010 5-year est.).

Transportation: Commute to work: 87.3% car, 1.5% public transportation, 4.5% walk, 6.6% work from home (2006-2010 5-year est.); Travel time to work: 23.9% less than 15 minutes, 46.6% 15 to 30 minutes, 7.4% 30 to 45 minutes, 11.0% 45 to 60 minutes, 11.0% 60 minutes or more (2006-2010 5-year est.)

PALMYRA (township). Covers a land area of 15.898 square miles and a water area of 0.443 square miles. Located at 41.51° N. Lat; 75.19° W. Long.

Population: 977 (1990); 1,127 (2000); 1,339 (2010); Density: 84.2 persons per square mile (2010); Race: 96.5% White, 1.6% Black, 0.4% Asian, 0.1% American Indian/Alaska Native, 0.0% Native Hawaiian/Other Pacific Islander, 1.4% Other, 2.8% Hispanic of any race (2010); Average household size: 2.43 (2010); Median age: 47.5 (2010); Males per 100 females: 94.1 (2010); Marriage status: 21.4% never married, 59.4% now married, 6.8% widowed, 12.5% divorced (2006-2010 5-year est.); Foreign born: 3.8% (2006-2010 5-year est.); Ancestry (includes multiple ancestries): 45.3% German, 34.1% Irish, 13.6% Italian, 10.9% English, 8.6% Polish (2006-2010 5-year est.).

Economy: Single-family building permits issued: 1 (2011); Multi-family building permits issued: 0 (2011); Employment by occupation: 6.8% management, 0.2% professional, 14.2% services, 16.1% sales, 1.0% farming, 16.7% construction, 8.8% production (2006-2010 5-year est.).

Income: Per capita income: $21,858 (2006-2010 5-year est.); Median household income: $44,191 (2006-2010 5-year est.); Average household income: $53,138 (2006-2010 5-year est.); Percent of households with income of $100,000 or more: 11.5% (2006-2010 5-year est.); Poverty rate: 12.8% (2006-2010 5-year est.).

Education: Percent of population age 25 and over with: High school diploma (including GED) or higher: 86.6% (2006-2010 5-year est.); Bachelor's degree or higher: 17.1% (2006-2010 5-year est.); Master's degree or higher: 10.2% (2006-2010 5-year est.).

Housing: Homeownership rate: 87.6% (2010); Median home value: $195,900 (2006-2010 5-year est.); Median contract rent: $573 per month (2006-2010 5-year est.); Median year structure built: 1978 (2006-2010 5-year est.).

Transportation: Commute to work: 93.6% car, 2.2% public transportation, 2.0% walk, 2.2% work from home (2006-2010 5-year est.); Travel time to work: 38.7% less than 15 minutes, 28.6% 15 to 30 minutes, 9.1% 30 to 45 minutes, 8.8% 45 to 60 minutes, 14.8% 60 minutes or more (2006-2010 5-year est.)

Additional Information Contacts
Wayne County Chamber of Commerce . . . . (570) 253-1960
  http://www.waynecountycc.com

PAUPACK (township). Covers a land area of 28.010 square miles and a water area of 5.135 square miles. Located at 41.44° N. Lat; 75.26° W. Long.

Population: 1,673 (1990); 2,959 (2000); 3,828 (2010); Density: 136.7 persons per square mile (2010); Race: 97.3% White, 1.1% Black, 0.4%

Asian, 0.1% American Indian/Alaska Native, 0.0% Native Hawaiian/Other Pacific Islander, 1.1% Other, 3.4% Hispanic of any race (2010); Average household size: 2.33 (2010); Median age: 51.1 (2010); Males per 100 females: 96.6 (2010); Marriage status: 17.7% never married, 62.3% now married, 5.9% widowed, 14.1% divorced (2006-2010 5-year est.); Foreign born: 4.4% (2006-2010 5-year est.); Ancestry (includes multiple ancestries): 37.2% German, 23.5% Irish, 20.7% Italian, 8.6% English, 6.6% Polish (2006-2010 5-year est.).

Economy: Single-family building permits issued: 13 (2011); Multi-family building permits issued: 0 (2011); Employment by occupation: 11.5% management, 1.0% professional, 10.7% services, 17.3% sales, 1.3% farming, 10.9% construction, 6.0% production (2006-2010 5-year est.).

Income: Per capita income: $27,280 (2006-2010 5-year est.); Median household income: $46,282 (2006-2010 5-year est.); Average household income: $64,422 (2006-2010 5-year est.); Percent of households with income of $100,000 or more: 18.4% (2006-2010 5-year est.); Poverty rate: 6.4% (2006-2010 5-year est.).

Education: Percent of population age 25 and over with: High school diploma (including GED) or higher: 92.4% (2006-2010 5-year est.); Bachelor's degree or higher: 22.0% (2006-2010 5-year est.); Master's degree or higher: 8.2% (2006-2010 5-year est.).

Housing: Homeownership rate: 90.8% (2010); Median home value: $200,800 (2006-2010 5-year est.); Median contract rent: $794 per month (2006-2010 5-year est.); Median year structure built: 1980 (2006-2010 5-year est.).

Transportation: Commute to work: 88.5% car, 0.8% public transportation, 2.9% walk, 7.7% work from home (2006-2010 5-year est.); Travel time to work: 23.6% less than 15 minutes, 28.5% 15 to 30 minutes, 15.3% 30 to 45 minutes, 8.6% 45 to 60 minutes, 24.1% 60 minutes or more (2006-2010 5-year est.)

Additional Information Contacts
Pocono Lake Region Chamber of Commerce . . . . (570) 226-3191
  http://www.lakeregioncc.com

PLEASANT MOUNT (unincorporated postal area)
Zip Code: 18453

Covers a land area of 50.550 square miles and a water area of 1.295 square miles. Located at 41.75° N. Lat; 75.37° W. Long. Population: 1,104 (2010); Density: 21.8 persons per square mile (2010); Race: 96.4% White, 0.8% Black, 1.1% Asian, 0.3% American Indian/Alaska Native, 0.0% Native Hawaiian/Other Pacific Islander, 1.4% Other, 2.9% Hispanic of any race (2010); Average household size: 2.36 (2010); Median age: 49.7 (2010); Males per 100 females: 103.7 (2010); Homeownership rate: 89.9% (2010)

POCONO SPRINGS (CDP). Covers a land area of 3.804 square miles and a water area of 0.176 square miles. Located at 41.28° N. Lat; 75.40° W. Long. Elevation is 2,067 feet.

Population: n/a (1990); n/a (2000); 926 (2010); Density: 243.4 persons per square mile (2010); Race: 92.1% White, 3.5% Black, 1.1% Asian, 0.0% American Indian/Alaska Native, 0.1% Native Hawaiian/Other Pacific Islander, 3.2% Other, 5.1% Hispanic of any race (2010); Average household size: 2.42 (2010); Median age: 46.6 (2010); Males per 100 females: 103.5 (2010); Marriage status: 15.1% never married, 59.2% now married, 7.8% widowed, 17.9% divorced (2006-2010 5-year est.); Foreign born: 6.3% (2006-2010 5-year est.); Ancestry (includes multiple ancestries): 34.5% German, 18.2% Irish, 9.7% Italian, 8.6% Polish, 8.0% Romanian (2006-2010 5-year est.).

Economy: Employment by occupation: 11.0% management, 3.7% professional, 13.2% services, 20.8% sales, 6.5% farming, 7.6% construction, 7.3% production (2006-2010 5-year est.).

Income: Per capita income: $28,755 (2006-2010 5-year est.); Median household income: $49,167 (2006-2010 5-year est.); Average household income: $67,225 (2006-2010 5-year est.); Percent of households with income of $100,000 or more: 19.7% (2006-2010 5-year est.); Poverty rate: 13.3% (2006-2010 5-year est.).

Education: Percent of population age 25 and over with: High school diploma (including GED) or higher: 92.4% (2006-2010 5-year est.); Bachelor's degree or higher: 15.3% (2006-2010 5-year est.); Master's degree or higher: 9.4% (2006-2010 5-year est.).

Housing: Homeownership rate: 94.3% (2010); Median home value: $125,700 (2006-2010 5-year est.); Median contract rent: $388 per month (2006-2010 5-year est.); Median year structure built: 1981 (2006-2010 5-year est.).

Transportation: Commute to work: 92.4% car, 2.2% public transportation, 2.2% walk, 3.3% work from home (2006-2010 5-year est.); Travel time to work: 18.9% less than 15 minutes, 38.6% 15 to 30 minutes, 19.2% 30 to 45 minutes, 11.0% 45 to 60 minutes, 12.4% 60 minutes or more (2006-2010 5-year est.)

POYNTELLE (unincorporated postal area)

Zip Code: 18454

Covers a land area of 2.705 square miles and a water area of 0.382 square miles. Located at 41.82° N. Lat; 75.42° W. Long. Elevation is 2,073 feet. Population: 64 (2010); Density: 23.7 persons per square mile (2010); Race: 100.0% White, 0.0% Black, 0.0% Asian, 0.0% American Indian/Alaska Native, 0.0% Native Hawaiian/Other Pacific Islander, 0.0% Other, 0.0% Hispanic of any race (2010); Average household size: 1.94 (2010); Median age: 56.5 (2010); Males per 100 females: 120.7 (2010); Homeownership rate: 97.0% (2010)

PRESTON (township). Covers a land area of 49.416 square miles and a water area of 2.126 square miles. Located at 41.85° N. Lat; 75.40° W. Long.

Population: 951 (1990); 1,107 (2000); 1,014 (2010); Density: 20.5 persons per square mile (2010); Race: 98.6% White, 0.0% Black, 0.4% Asian, 0.1% American Indian/Alaska Native, 0.0% Native Hawaiian/Other Pacific Islander, 0.9% Other, 0.5% Hispanic of any race (2010); Average household size: 2.31 (2010); Median age: 48.0 (2010); Males per 100 females: 98.0 (2010); Marriage status: 18.3% never married, 66.7% now married, 6.3% widowed, 8.7% divorced (2006-2010 5-year est.); Foreign born: 4.3% (2006-2010 5-year est.); Ancestry (includes multiple ancestries): 35.8% German, 21.4% English, 20.7% Irish, 12.0% Polish, 5.1% Russian (2006-2010 5-year est.).
Economy: Single-family building permits issued: 10 (2011); Multi-family building permits issued: 0 (2011); Employment by occupation: 14.7% management, 0.9% professional, 11.6% services, 13.5% sales, 3.8% farming, 17.3% construction, 5.2% production (2006-2010 5-year est.).
Income: Per capita income: $20,431 (2006-2010 5-year est.); Median household income: $46,094 (2006-2010 5-year est.); Average household income: $55,172 (2006-2010 5-year est.); Percent of households with income of $100,000 or more: 10.5% (2006-2010 5-year est.); Poverty rate: 15.7% (2006-2010 5-year est.).
Education: Percent of population age 25 and over with: High school diploma (including GED) or higher: 85.7% (2006-2010 5-year est.); Bachelor's degree or higher: 18.6% (2006-2010 5-year est.); Master's degree or higher: 7.9% (2006-2010 5-year est.).
Housing: Homeownership rate: 86.3% (2010); Median home value: $169,900 (2006-2010 5-year est.); Median contract rent: $438 per month (2006-2010 5-year est.); Median year structure built: 1962 (2006-2010 5-year est.).
Transportation: Commute to work: 91.6% car, 0.0% public transportation, 4.6% walk, 3.8% work from home (2006-2010 5-year est.); Travel time to work: 37.0% less than 15 minutes, 20.5% 15 to 30 minutes, 29.0% 30 to 45 minutes, 7.2% 45 to 60 minutes, 6.4% 60 minutes or more (2006-2010 5-year est.)

Additional Information Contacts
Wayne County Chamber of Commerce . . . . (570) 253-1960
  http://www.waynecountycc.com

PRESTON PARK (unincorporated postal area)

Zip Code: 18455

Covers a land area of 4.461 square miles and a water area of 0.228 square miles. Located at 41.89° N. Lat; 75.35° W. Long. Elevation is 1,450 feet. Population: 105 (2010); Density: 23.5 persons per square mile (2010); Race: 99.0% White, 0.0% Black, 0.0% Asian, 0.0% American Indian/Alaska Native, 0.0% Native Hawaiian/Other Pacific Islander, 1.0% Other, 1.0% Hispanic of any race (2010); Average household size: 2.69 (2010); Median age: 38.4 (2010); Males per 100 females: 87.5 (2010); Homeownership rate: 76.9% (2010)

PROMPTON (borough). Covers a land area of 1.548 square miles and a water area of 0.141 square miles. Located at 41.59° N. Lat; 75.33° W. Long. Elevation is 1,099 feet.

Population: 259 (1990); 243 (2000); 250 (2010); Density: 161.5 persons per square mile (2010); Race: 96.8% White, 0.0% Black, 0.0% Asian, 0.0% American Indian/Alaska Native, 0.0% Native Hawaiian/Other Pacific Islander, 3.2% Other, 3.2% Hispanic of any race (2010); Average household size: 2.40 (2010); Median age: 39.7 (2010); Males per 100

females: 85.2 (2010); Marriage status: 24.9% never married, 50.3% now married, 17.3% widowed, 7.5% divorced (2006-2010 5-year est.); Foreign born: 0.0% (2006-2010 5-year est.); Ancestry (includes multiple ancestries): 28.1% German, 20.1% American, 18.6% English, 15.6% Irish, 11.1% Pennsylvania German (2006-2010 5-year est.).
Economy: Single-family building permits issued: 0 (2011); Multi-family building permits issued: 0 (2011); Employment by occupation: 9.5% management, 6.0% professional, 7.8% services, 26.7% sales, 5.2% farming, 6.0% construction, 13.8% production (2006-2010 5-year est.).
Income: Per capita income: $23,902 (2006-2010 5-year est.); Median household income: $47,045 (2006-2010 5-year est.); Average household income: $54,476 (2006-2010 5-year est.); Percent of households with income of $100,000 or more: 4.7% (2006-2010 5-year est.); Poverty rate: 3.5% (2006-2010 5-year est.).
Education: Percent of population age 25 and over with: High school diploma (including GED) or higher: 90.4% (2006-2010 5-year est.); Bachelor's degree or higher: 18.5% (2006-2010 5-year est.); Master's degree or higher: 3.4% (2006-2010 5-year est.).
Housing: Homeownership rate: 71.2% (2010); Median home value: $154,800 (2006-2010 5-year est.); Median contract rent: $485 per month (2006-2010 5-year est.); Median year structure built: 1960 (2006-2010 5-year est.).
Transportation: Commute to work: 79.3% car, 0.0% public transportation, 10.3% walk, 10.3% work from home (2006-2010 5-year est.); Travel time to work: 43.3% less than 15 minutes, 29.8% 15 to 30 minutes, 7.7% 30 to 45 minutes, 12.5% 45 to 60 minutes, 6.7% 60 minutes or more (2006-2010 5-year est.)

SALEM (township). Covers a land area of 30.557 square miles and a water area of 0.880 square miles. Located at 41.40° N. Lat; 75.37° W. Long.

Population: 3,142 (1990); 3,664 (2000); 4,271 (2010); Density: 139.8 persons per square mile (2010); Race: 96.9% White, 1.1% Black, 0.5% Asian, 0.0% American Indian/Alaska Native, 0.0% Native Hawaiian/Other Pacific Islander, 1.5% Other, 3.3% Hispanic of any race (2010); Average household size: 2.40 (2010); Median age: 47.9 (2010); Males per 100 females: 103.6 (2010); Marriage status: 18.2% never married, 61.5% now married, 8.6% widowed, 11.7% divorced (2006-2010 5-year est.); Foreign born: 2.8% (2006-2010 5-year est.); Ancestry (includes multiple ancestries): 29.1% Irish, 24.7% German, 15.2% Italian, 14.7% Polish, 11.9% English (2006-2010 5-year est.).
Economy: Single-family building permits issued: 6 (2011); Multi-family building permits issued: 0 (2011); Employment by occupation: 8.9% management, 1.2% professional, 17.5% services, 14.6% sales, 3.3% farming, 13.2% construction, 12.7% production (2006-2010 5-year est.).
Income: Per capita income: $20,721 (2006-2010 5-year est.); Median household income: $48,551 (2006-2010 5-year est.); Average household income: $51,017 (2006-2010 5-year est.); Percent of households with income of $100,000 or more: 7.3% (2006-2010 5-year est.); Poverty rate: 8.9% (2006-2010 5-year est.).
Education: Percent of population age 25 and over with: High school diploma (including GED) or higher: 87.3% (2006-2010 5-year est.); Bachelor's degree or higher: 20.6% (2006-2010 5-year est.); Master's degree or higher: 9.7% (2006-2010 5-year est.).
Housing: Homeownership rate: 83.6% (2010); Median home value: $167,900 (2006-2010 5-year est.); Median contract rent: $558 per month (2006-2010 5-year est.); Median year structure built: 1983 (2006-2010 5-year est.).
Transportation: Commute to work: 88.6% car, 1.1% public transportation, 2.6% walk, 7.7% work from home (2006-2010 5-year est.); Travel time to work: 28.7% less than 15 minutes, 33.9% 15 to 30 minutes, 24.5% 30 to 45 minutes, 2.9% 45 to 60 minutes, 10.0% 60 minutes or more (2006-2010 5-year est.)

Additional Information Contacts
Greater Scranton Chamber of Commerce . . . . (570) 342-7711
  http://www.scrantonchamber.com

SCOTT (township). Covers a land area of 43.543 square miles and a water area of 0.777 square miles. Located at 41.95° N. Lat; 75.40° W. Long.

Population: 553 (1990); 669 (2000); 593 (2010); Density: 13.6 persons per square mile (2010); Race: 98.5% White, 0.2% Black, 0.5% Asian, 0.3% American Indian/Alaska Native, 0.0% Native Hawaiian/Other Pacific Islander, 0.5% Other, 1.0% Hispanic of any race (2010); Average household size: 2.51 (2010); Median age: 46.3 (2010); Males per 100

females: 103.1 (2010); Marriage status: 19.2% never married, 65.7% now married, 5.2% widowed, 9.9% divorced (2006-2010 5-year est.); Foreign born: 0.5% (2006-2010 5-year est.); Ancestry (includes multiple ancestries): 42.0% German, 22.8% English, 12.9% Irish, 7.9% Italian, 7.0% Dutch (2006-2010 5-year est.).

Economy: Single-family building permits issued: 3 (2011); Multi-family building permits issued: 0 (2011); Employment by occupation: 8.9% management, 0.0% professional, 11.5% services, 12.5% sales, 2.6% farming, 22.9% construction, 4.2% production (2006-2010 5-year est.).

Income: Per capita income: $20,336 (2006-2010 5-year est.); Median household income: $27,206 (2006-2010 5-year est.); Average household income: $42,670 (2006-2010 5-year est.); Percent of households with income of $100,000 or more: 12.1% (2006-2010 5-year est.); Poverty rate: 6.3% (2006-2010 5-year est.).

Education: Percent of population age 25 and over with: High school diploma (including GED) or higher: 83.0% (2006-2010 5-year est.); Bachelor's degree or higher: 7.1% (2006-2010 5-year est.); Master's degree or higher: 4.3% (2006-2010 5-year est.).

Housing: Homeownership rate: 85.1% (2010); Median home value: $102,100 (2006-2010 5-year est.); Median contract rent: $344 per month (2006-2010 5-year est.); Median year structure built: 1972 (2006-2010 5-year est.).

Transportation: Commute to work: 86.5% car, 0.0% public transportation, 7.3% walk, 6.3% work from home (2006-2010 5-year est.); Travel time to work: 23.9% less than 15 minutes, 27.8% 15 to 30 minutes, 7.8% 30 to 45 minutes, 22.8% 45 to 60 minutes, 17.8% 60 minutes or more (2006-2010 5-year est.)

SOUTH CANAAN (township). Covers a land area of 27.464 square miles and a water area of 0.771 square miles. Located at 41.51° N. Lat; 75.40° W. Long. Elevation is 1,424 feet.

Population: 1,227 (1990); 1,666 (2000); 1,768 (2010); Density: 64.4 persons per square mile (2010); Race: 96.9% White, 0.5% Black, 1.1% Asian, 0.2% American Indian/Alaska Native, 0.0% Native Hawaiian/Other Pacific Islander, 1.3% Other, 1.3% Hispanic of any race (2010); Average household size: 2.68 (2010); Median age: 42.3 (2010); Males per 100 females: 107.0 (2010); Marriage status: 36.9% never married, 49.9% now married, 7.6% widowed, 5.6% divorced (2006-2010 5-year est.); Foreign born: 4.3% (2006-2010 5-year est.); Ancestry (includes multiple ancestries): 42.1% German, 22.2% Irish, 16.3% English, 15.2% Polish, 10.3% Italian (2006-2010 5-year est.).

Economy: Single-family building permits issued: 4 (2011); Multi-family building permits issued: 0 (2011); Employment by occupation: 7.3% management, 3.9% professional, 10.2% services, 17.5% sales, 1.3% farming, 20.5% construction, 11.3% production (2006-2010 5-year est.).

Income: Per capita income: $18,747 (2006-2010 5-year est.); Median household income: $47,604 (2006-2010 5-year est.); Average household income: $57,974 (2006-2010 5-year est.); Percent of households with income of $100,000 or more: 14.5% (2006-2010 5-year est.); Poverty rate: 8.8% (2006-2010 5-year est.).

Education: Percent of population age 25 and over with: High school diploma (including GED) or higher: 92.6% (2006-2010 5-year est.); Bachelor's degree or higher: 34.7% (2006-2010 5-year est.); Master's degree or higher: 16.8% (2006-2010 5-year est.).

Housing: Homeownership rate: 84.4% (2010); Median home value: $187,000 (2006-2010 5-year est.); Median contract rent: $587 per month (2006-2010 5-year est.); Median year structure built: 1970 (2006-2010 5-year est.).

Transportation: Commute to work: 89.4% car, 0.0% public transportation, 6.4% walk, 4.2% work from home (2006-2010 5-year est.); Travel time to work: 19.9% less than 15 minutes, 34.7% 15 to 30 minutes, 26.7% 30 to 45 minutes, 6.4% 45 to 60 minutes, 12.3% 60 minutes or more (2006-2010 5-year est.)

Additional Information Contacts

Greater Scranton Chamber of Commerce . . . . (570) 342-7711
http://www.scrantonchamber.com

SOUTH STERLING (unincorporated postal area)
Zip Code: 18460

Covers a land area of 3.309 square miles and a water area of 0.057 square miles. Located at 41.24° N. Lat; 75.31° W. Long. Population: 184 (2010); Density: 55.6 persons per square mile (2010); Race: 98.4% White, 0.0% Black, 1.1% Asian, 0.0% American Indian/Alaska Native, 0.0% Native Hawaiian/Other Pacific Islander, 0.5% Other, 2.7% Hispanic of any race (2010); Average household size: 2.36 (2010);

Median age: 48.5 (2010); Males per 100 females: 102.2 (2010); Homeownership rate: 87.2% (2010)

STARLIGHT (unincorporated postal area)
Zip Code: 18461

Covers a land area of 21.427 square miles and a water area of 0.643 square miles. Located at 41.92° N. Lat; 75.32° W. Long. Elevation is 1,355 feet. Population: 404 (2010); Density: 18.9 persons per square mile (2010); Race: 98.3% White, 0.2% Black, 0.5% Asian, 0.0% American Indian/Alaska Native, 0.0% Native Hawaiian/Other Pacific Islander, 1.0% Other, 0.7% Hispanic of any race (2010); Average household size: 2.18 (2010); Median age: 49.5 (2010); Males per 100 females: 113.8 (2010); Homeownership rate: 82.1% (2010)

STARRUCCA (borough). Covers a land area of 8.915 square miles and a water area of 0.070 square miles. Located at 41.89° N. Lat; 75.45° W. Long. Elevation is 1,312 feet.

History: Also spelled Starucca.

Population: 262 (1990); 216 (2000); 173 (2010); Density: 19.4 persons per square mile (2010); Race: 96.0% White, 1.7% Black, 0.6% Asian, 0.0% American Indian/Alaska Native, 0.0% Native Hawaiian/Other Pacific Islander, 1.7% Other, 4.0% Hispanic of any race (2010); Average household size: 2.31 (2010); Median age: 49.3 (2010); Males per 100 females: 127.6 (2010); Marriage status: 18.2% never married, 58.8% now married, 14.2% widowed, 8.8% divorced (2006-2010 5-year est.); Foreign born: 1.0% (2006-2010 5-year est.); Ancestry (includes multiple ancestries): 49.5% German, 26.2% Dutch, 17.8% Irish, 14.9% English, 9.4% Italian (2006-2010 5-year est.).

Economy: Single-family building permits issued: 0 (2011); Multi-family building permits issued: 0 (2011); Employment by occupation: 10.6% management, 0.0% professional, 6.4% services, 18.1% sales, 4.3% farming, 24.5% construction, 7.4% production (2006-2010 5-year est.).

Income: Per capita income: $25,570 (2006-2010 5-year est.); Median household income: $54,375 (2006-2010 5-year est.); Average household income: $65,557 (2006-2010 5-year est.); Percent of households with income of $100,000 or more: 21.5% (2006-2010 5-year est.); Poverty rate: 1.0% (2006-2010 5-year est.).

Education: Percent of population age 25 and over with: High school diploma (including GED) or higher: 91.9% (2006-2010 5-year est.); Bachelor's degree or higher: 22.1% (2006-2010 5-year est.); Master's degree or higher: 10.3% (2006-2010 5-year est.).

Housing: Homeownership rate: 82.7% (2010); Median home value: $117,200 (2006-2010 5-year est.); Median contract rent: n/a per month (2006-2010 5-year est.); Median year structure built: 1945 (2006-2010 5-year est.).

Transportation: Commute to work: 95.6% car, 0.0% public transportation, 0.0% walk, 2.2% work from home (2006-2010 5-year est.); Travel time to work: 13.6% less than 15 minutes, 15.9% 15 to 30 minutes, 14.8% 30 to 45 minutes, 29.5% 45 to 60 minutes, 26.1% 60 minutes or more (2006-2010 5-year est.)

STERLING (township). Covers a land area of 26.997 square miles and a water area of 0.232 square miles. Located at 41.33° N. Lat; 75.41° W. Long. Elevation is 1,614 feet.

Population: 903 (1990); 1,251 (2000); 1,450 (2010); Density: 53.7 persons per square mile (2010); Race: 95.9% White, 2.2% Black, 0.3% Asian, 0.1% American Indian/Alaska Native, 0.0% Native Hawaiian/Other Pacific Islander, 1.5% Other, 2.7% Hispanic of any race (2010); Average household size: 2.54 (2010); Median age: 45.4 (2010); Males per 100 females: 104.2 (2010); Marriage status: 16.1% never married, 63.8% now married, 8.4% widowed, 11.7% divorced (2006-2010 5-year est.); Foreign born: 1.8% (2006-2010 5-year est.); Ancestry (includes multiple ancestries): 34.8% German, 31.4% Irish, 13.1% English, 11.8% Polish, 11.5% Italian (2006-2010 5-year est.).

Economy: Single-family building permits issued: 3 (2011); Multi-family building permits issued: 0 (2011); Employment by occupation: 5.8% management, 1.2% professional, 8.5% services, 16.6% sales, 9.1% farming, 10.8% construction, 7.7% production (2006-2010 5-year est.).

Income: Per capita income: $25,700 (2006-2010 5-year est.); Median household income: $50,489 (2006-2010 5-year est.); Average household income: $62,838 (2006-2010 5-year est.); Percent of households with income of $100,000 or more: 10.3% (2006-2010 5-year est.); Poverty rate: 11.6% (2006-2010 5-year est.).

Education: Percent of population age 25 and over with: High school diploma (including GED) or higher: 87.1% (2006-2010 5-year est.);

Bachelor's degree or higher: 12.3% (2006-2010 5-year est.); Master's degree or higher: 3.5% (2006-2010 5-year est.).

Housing: Homeownership rate: 88.1% (2010); Median home value: $147,800 (2006-2010 5-year est.); Median contract rent: $438 per month (2006-2010 5-year est.); Median year structure built: 1981 (2006-2010 5-year est.).

Transportation: Commute to work: 91.1% car, 0.0% public transportation, 1.8% walk, 7.1% work from home (2006-2010 5-year est.); Travel time to work: 19.9% less than 15 minutes, 31.4% 15 to 30 minutes, 31.8% 30 to 45 minutes, 7.9% 45 to 60 minutes, 9.0% 60 minutes or more (2006-2010 5-year est.)

Additional Information Contacts

Greater Scranton Chamber of Commerce . . . . (570) 342-7711
    http://www.scrantonchamber.com

TEXAS (township). Covers a land area of 14.036 square miles and a water area of 0.363 square miles. Located at 41.55° N. Lat; 75.26° W. Long.

Population: 2,585 (1990); 2,501 (2000); 2,569 (2010); Density: 183.0 persons per square mile (2010); Race: 96.1% White, 1.3% Black, 0.7% Asian, 0.4% American Indian/Alaska Native, 0.0% Native Hawaiian/Other Pacific Islander, 1.5% Other, 2.5% Hispanic of any race (2010); Average household size: 2.41 (2010); Median age: 45.1 (2010); Males per 100 females: 97.0 (2010); Marriage status: 35.9% never married, 51.4% now married, 7.5% widowed, 5.2% divorced (2006-2010 5-year est.); Foreign born: 1.2% (2006-2010 5-year est.); Ancestry (includes multiple ancestries): 35.5% German, 29.5% Irish, 15.8% American, 13.9% Italian, 10.7% English (2006-2010 5-year est.).

Economy: Single-family building permits issued: 3 (2011); Multi-family building permits issued: 0 (2011); Employment by occupation: 9.2% management, 1.9% professional, 10.2% services, 26.1% sales, 3.6% farming, 10.9% construction, 12.4% production (2006-2010 5-year est.).

Income: Per capita income: $18,596 (2006-2010 5-year est.); Median household income: $36,518 (2006-2010 5-year est.); Average household income: $49,999 (2006-2010 5-year est.); Percent of households with income of $100,000 or more: 8.2% (2006-2010 5-year est.); Poverty rate: 15.0% (2006-2010 5-year est.).

Education: Percent of population age 25 and over with: High school diploma (including GED) or higher: 84.6% (2006-2010 5-year est.); Bachelor's degree or higher: 10.3% (2006-2010 5-year est.); Master's degree or higher: 3.9% (2006-2010 5-year est.).

Housing: Homeownership rate: 80.1% (2010); Median home value: $168,500 (2006-2010 5-year est.); Median contract rent: $738 per month (2006-2010 5-year est.); Median year structure built: 1971 (2006-2010 5-year est.).

Transportation: Commute to work: 91.8% car, 0.0% public transportation, 2.2% walk, 5.1% work from home (2006-2010 5-year est.); Travel time to work: 58.6% less than 15 minutes, 25.0% 15 to 30 minutes, 9.6% 30 to 45 minutes, 4.2% 45 to 60 minutes, 2.6% 60 minutes or more (2006-2010 5-year est.)

Additional Information Contacts

Greater Scranton Chamber of Commerce . . . . (570) 342-7711
    http://www.scrantonchamber.com

THE HIDEOUT (CDP). Covers a land area of 6.110 square miles and a water area of 0.582 square miles. Located at 41.44° N. Lat; 75.35° W. Long.

Population: n/a (1990); n/a (2000); 3,013 (2010); Density: 493.2 persons per square mile (2010); Race: 94.5% White, 2.8% Black, 0.3% Asian, 0.2% American Indian/Alaska Native, 0.0% Native Hawaiian/Other Pacific Islander, 2.2% Other, 5.2% Hispanic of any race (2010); Average household size: 2.27 (2010); Median age: 54.7 (2010); Males per 100 females: 93.8 (2010); Marriage status: 15.7% never married, 70.5% now married, 8.5% widowed, 5.3% divorced (2006-2010 5-year est.); Foreign born: 5.0% (2006-2010 5-year est.); Ancestry (includes multiple ancestries): 37.1% Irish, 25.3% Italian, 18.0% German, 12.6% Polish, 10.4% American (2006-2010 5-year est.).

Economy: Employment by occupation: 12.2% management, 3.4% professional, 14.0% services, 17.9% sales, 0.0% farming, 9.2% construction, 6.7% production (2006-2010 5-year est.).

Income: Per capita income: $22,299 (2006-2010 5-year est.); Median household income: $47,368 (2006-2010 5-year est.); Average household income: $55,576 (2006-2010 5-year est.); Percent of households with income of $100,000 or more: 13.6% (2006-2010 5-year est.); Poverty rate: 3.5% (2006-2010 5-year est.).

Education: Percent of population age 25 and over with: High school diploma (including GED) or higher: 94.0% (2006-2010 5-year est.); Bachelor's degree or higher: 20.7% (2006-2010 5-year est.); Master's degree or higher: 4.4% (2006-2010 5-year est.).

Housing: Homeownership rate: 90.7% (2010); Median home value: $193,700 (2006-2010 5-year est.); Median contract rent: $734 per month (2006-2010 5-year est.); Median year structure built: 1985 (2006-2010 5-year est.).

Transportation: Commute to work: 91.0% car, 0.5% public transportation, 1.9% walk, 6.6% work from home (2006-2010 5-year est.); Travel time to work: 19.1% less than 15 minutes, 27.2% 15 to 30 minutes, 35.2% 30 to 45 minutes, 1.7% 45 to 60 minutes, 16.8% 60 minutes or more (2006-2010 5-year est.)

TYLER HILL (unincorporated postal area)

Zip Code: 18469

Covers a land area of 9.265 square miles and a water area of 0.198 square miles. Located at 41.70° N. Lat; 75.13° W. Long. Elevation is 1,230 feet. Population: 357 (2010); Density: 38.5 persons per square mile (2010); Race: 97.5% White, 2.0% Black, 0.3% Asian, 0.3% American Indian/Alaska Native, 0.0% Native Hawaiian/Other Pacific Islander, 0.0% Other, 2.0% Hispanic of any race (2010); Average household size: 2.35 (2010); Median age: 46.2 (2010); Males per 100 females: 95.1 (2010); Homeownership rate: 76.3% (2010)

WALLENPAUPACK LAKE ESTATES (CDP). Covers a land area of 1.728 square miles and a water area of 0.385 square miles. Located at 41.40° N. Lat; 75.27° W. Long.

Population: n/a (1990); n/a (2000); 1,279 (2010); Density: 740.2 persons per square mile (2010); Race: 96.0% White, 2.3% Black, 0.3% Asian, 0.2% American Indian/Alaska Native, 0.0% Native Hawaiian/Other Pacific Islander, 1.2% Other, 3.6% Hispanic of any race (2010); Average household size: 2.38 (2010); Median age: 51.5 (2010); Males per 100 females: 97.7 (2010); Marriage status: 18.5% never married, 54.2% now married, 6.5% widowed, 20.8% divorced (2006-2010 5-year est.); Foreign born: 4.6% (2006-2010 5-year est.); Ancestry (includes multiple ancestries): 33.0% German, 26.3% Italian, 21.1% Irish, 7.1% Polish, 5.3% French (2006-2010 5-year est.).

Economy: Employment by occupation: 7.6% management, 0.0% professional, 2.3% services, 33.1% sales, 0.0% farming, 6.0% construction, 5.2% production (2006-2010 5-year est.).

Income: Per capita income: $23,067 (2006-2010 5-year est.); Median household income: $39,583 (2006-2010 5-year est.); Average household income: $55,003 (2006-2010 5-year est.); Percent of households with income of $100,000 or more: 15.6% (2006-2010 5-year est.); Poverty rate: 5.9% (2006-2010 5-year est.).

Education: Percent of population age 25 and over with: High school diploma (including GED) or higher: 91.7% (2006-2010 5-year est.); Bachelor's degree or higher: 6.9% (2006-2010 5-year est.); Master's degree or higher: 2.9% (2006-2010 5-year est.).

Housing: Homeownership rate: 91.8% (2010); Median home value: $188,600 (2006-2010 5-year est.); Median contract rent: $675 per month (2006-2010 5-year est.); Median year structure built: 1984 (2006-2010 5-year est.).

Transportation: Commute to work: 78.8% car, 0.0% public transportation, 7.9% walk, 13.2% work from home (2006-2010 5-year est.); Travel time to work: 8.7% less than 15 minutes, 36.2% 15 to 30 minutes, 22.1% 30 to 45 minutes, 5.9% 45 to 60 minutes, 27.2% 60 minutes or more (2006-2010 5-year est.)

WAYMART (borough). Covers a land area of 2.691 square miles and a water area of 0.068 square miles. Located at 41.59° N. Lat; 75.40° W. Long. Elevation is 1,398 feet.

History: Incorporated 1851.

Population: 1,328 (1990); 1,429 (2000); 1,341 (2010); Density: 498.3 persons per square mile (2010); Race: 97.2% White, 0.3% Black, 0.1% Asian, 0.3% American Indian/Alaska Native, 0.0% Native Hawaiian/Other Pacific Islander, 2.1% Other, 2.2% Hispanic of any race (2010); Average household size: 2.40 (2010); Median age: 43.8 (2010); Males per 100 females: 82.2 (2010); Marriage status: 25.3% never married, 50.9% now married, 17.0% widowed, 6.9% divorced (2006-2010 5-year est.); Foreign born: 2.6% (2006-2010 5-year est.); Ancestry (includes multiple ancestries): 28.7% German, 20.2% Irish, 19.9% Polish, 15.5% English, 9.0% American (2006-2010 5-year est.).

Economy: Single-family building permits issued: 0 (2011); Multi-family building permits issued: 0 (2011); Employment by occupation: 7.7% management, 1.3% professional, 13.1% services, 14.7% sales, 1.7% farming, 13.1% construction, 6.3% production (2006-2010 5-year est.).
Income: Per capita income: $20,042 (2006-2010 5-year est.); Median household income: $43,819 (2006-2010 5-year est.); Average household income: $54,251 (2006-2010 5-year est.); Percent of households with income of $100,000 or more: 14.0% (2006-2010 5-year est.); Poverty rate: 5.1% (2006-2010 5-year est.).
Education: Percent of population age 25 and over with: High school diploma (including GED) or higher: 82.6% (2006-2010 5-year est.); Bachelor's degree or higher: 14.4% (2006-2010 5-year est.); Master's degree or higher: 5.4% (2006-2010 5-year est.).

School District(s)

Western Wayne SD (PK-12)
  2010-11 Enrollment: 2,251 . . . . (570) 937-4270
Housing: Homeownership rate: 64.7% (2010); Median home value: $150,600 (2006-2010 5-year est.); Median contract rent: $513 per month (2006-2010 5-year est.); Median year structure built: 1953 (2006-2010 5-year est.).
Safety: Violent crime rate: 0.0 per 10,000 population; Property crime rate: 74.3 per 10,000 population (2011).
Transportation: Commute to work: 96.1% car, 0.0% public transportation, 0.6% walk, 3.4% work from home (2006-2010 5-year est.); Travel time to work: 37.5% less than 15 minutes, 36.4% 15 to 30 minutes, 16.1% 30 to 45 minutes, 6.0% 45 to 60 minutes, 3.9% 60 minutes or more (2006-2010 5-year est.)

Additional Information Contacts

Greater Scranton Chamber of Commerce . . . . (570) 342-7711
  http://www.scrantonchamber.com

WHITE MILLS (CDP). Covers a land area of 1.483 square miles and a water area of 0.034 square miles. Located at 41.54° N. Lat; 75.20° W. Long. Elevation is 938 feet.
Population: n/a (1990); n/a (2000); 659 (2010); Density: 444.5 persons per square mile (2010); Race: 96.7% White, 1.1% Black, 0.2% Asian, 1.1% American Indian/Alaska Native, 0.0% Native Hawaiian/Other Pacific Islander, 0.9% Other, 3.0% Hispanic of any race (2010); Average household size: 2.35 (2010); Median age: 45.2 (2010); Males per 100 females: 97.9 (2010); Marriage status: 22.0% never married, 60.0% now married, 13.0% widowed, 4.9% divorced (2006-2010 5-year est.); Foreign born: 3.7% (2006-2010 5-year est.); Ancestry (includes multiple ancestries): 46.9% German, 30.8% Irish, 18.4% Italian, 11.2% Polish, 8.3% American (2006-2010 5-year est.).
Economy: Employment by occupation: 19.0% management, 3.7% professional, 9.5% services, 14.7% sales, 0.0% farming, 1.8% construction, 13.9% production (2006-2010 5-year est.).
Income: Per capita income: $16,967 (2006-2010 5-year est.); Median household income: $31,389 (2006-2010 5-year est.); Average household income: $36,255 (2006-2010 5-year est.); Percent of households with income of $100,000 or more: n/a (2006-2010 5-year est.); Poverty rate: 21.0% (2006-2010 5-year est.).
Education: Percent of population age 25 and over with: High school diploma (including GED) or higher: 76.0% (2006-2010 5-year est.); Bachelor's degree or higher: 3.7% (2006-2010 5-year est.); Master's degree or higher: 1.7% (2006-2010 5-year est.).
Housing: Homeownership rate: 84.3% (2010); Median home value: $119,400 (2006-2010 5-year est.); Median contract rent: $813 per month (2006-2010 5-year est.); Median year structure built: 1953 (2006-2010 5-year est.).
Transportation: Commute to work: 96.3% car, 0.0% public transportation, 0.0% walk, 3.7% work from home (2006-2010 5-year est.); Travel time to work: 73.8% less than 15 minutes, 15.2% 15 to 30 minutes, 6.8% 30 to 45 minutes, 4.2% 45 to 60 minutes, 0.0% 60 minutes or more (2006-2010 5-year est.)

Westmoreland County

Located in southwestern Pennsylvania; bounded on the north by the Kiskiminetas and Conemaugh Rivers, on the southwest by the Monongahela River, and on the northwest by the Allegheny River; drained by the Youghiogheny River. Covers a land area of 1,027.554 square miles, a water area of 8.520 square miles, and is located in the Eastern Time Zone at 40.31° N. Lat., 79.47° W. Long. The county was founded in 1773. County seat is Greensburg.

Westmoreland County is part of the Pittsburgh, PA Metropolitan Statistical Area. The entire metro area includes: Allegheny County, PA; Armstrong County, PA; Beaver County, PA; Butler County, PA; Fayette County, PA; Washington County, PA; Westmoreland County, PA

Weather Station: Derry 4 SW   Elevation: 1,060 feet

	Jan	Feb	Mar	Apr	May	Jun	Jul	Aug	Sep	Oct	Nov	Dec
High	37	40	49	62	71	80	83	82	75	64	52	41
Low	20	21	27	37	46	56	60	59	52	41	33	24
Precip	3.6	3.1	4.1	4.3	4.8	4.8	5.0	4.3	4.4	3.1	4.4	3.6
Snow	14.4	9.7	7.9	1.2	tr	0.0	0.0	0.0	0.0	0.2	2.1	9.3

High and Low temperatures in degrees Fahrenheit; Precipitation and Snow in inches

Weather Station: Salina 3 W   Elevation: 1,108 feet

	Jan	Feb	Mar	Apr	May	Jun	Jul	Aug	Sep	Oct	Nov	Dec
High	37	40	49	62	71	80	83	82	76	64	52	41
Low	17	19	25	35	44	53	58	56	49	38	31	22
Precip	2.9	2.4	3.3	3.5	4.2	4.3	4.7	4.0	3.5	2.6	3.7	3.1
Snow	9.8	6.6	4.6	0.6	0.0	0.0	0.0	0.0	0.0	tr	1.4	5.2

High and Low temperatures in degrees Fahrenheit; Precipitation and Snow in inches

Population: 370,321 (1990); 369,993 (2000); 365,169 (2010); Race: 95.3% White, 2.3% Black, 0.7% Asian, 0.1% American Indian/Alaska Native, 0.0% Native Hawaiian/Other Pacific Islander, 1.6% Other, 0.9% Hispanic of any race (2010); Density: 355.4 persons per square mile (2010); Average household size: 2.32 (2010); Median age: 45.1 (2010); Males per 100 females: 94.8 (2010).
Religion: Six largest groups: 33.3% Catholicism, 8.0% Methodist/Pietist, 5.8% Lutheran, 5.2% Presbyterian-Reformed, 2.5% Non-Denominational, 1.6% Baptist (2010)
Economy: Unemployment rate: 7.8% (August 2012); Total civilian labor force: 196,824 (August 2012); Leading industries: 16.9% health care and social assistance; 15.3% retail trade; 14.9% manufacturing (2010); Farms: 1,415 totaling 167,489 acres (2007); Companies that employ 500 or more persons: 18 (2010); Companies that employ 100 to 499 persons: 153 (2010); Companies that employ less than 100 persons: 8,579 (2010); Black-owned businesses: 347 (2007); Hispanic-owned businesses: 95 (2007); Asian-owned businesses: 372 (2007); Women-owned businesses: 7,489 (2007); Retail sales per capita: $14,548 (2010). Single-family building permits issued: 301 (2011); Multi-family building permits issued: 36 (2011).
Income: Per capita income: $25,845 (2006-2010 5-year est.); Median household income: $47,689 (2006-2010 5-year est.); Average household income: $60,999 (2006-2010 5-year est.); Percent of households with income of $100,000 or more: 16.0% (2006-2010 5-year est.); Poverty rate: 9.8% (2006-2010 5-year est.); Bankruptcy rate: 3.46% (2011).
Taxes: Total county taxes per capita: $221 (2009); County property taxes per capita: $217 (2009).
Education: Percent of population age 25 and over with: High school diploma (including GED) or higher: 91.4% (2006-2010 5-year est.); Bachelor's degree or higher: 24.0% (2006-2010 5-year est.); Master's degree or higher: 8.0% (2006-2010 5-year est.).
Housing: Homeownership rate: 76.7% (2010); Median home value: $126,800 (2006-2010 5-year est.); Median contract rent: $442 per month (2006-2010 5-year est.); Median year structure built: 1960 (2006-2010 5-year est.)
Health: Birth rate: 88.9 per 10,000 population (2011); Death rate: 119.1 per 10,000 population (2011); Age-adjusted cancer mortality rate: 185.3 deaths per 100,000 population (2009); Number of physicians: 18.8 per 10,000 population (2010); Hospital beds: 28.3 per 10,000 population (2008); Hospital admissions: 1,099.4 per 10,000 population (2008).
Environment: Air Quality Index: 65.2% good, 34.2% moderate, 0.5% unhealthy for sensitive individuals, 0.0% unhealthy (percent of days in 2011)
Elections: 2012 Presidential election results: 37.6% Obama, 61.3% Romney
National and State Parks: Bushy Run Battlefield State Park; Forbes State Forest; Keystone State Park; Laurel Mountain State Park; Linn Run State Park; Loyalhanna Lake National Recreation Area; State Forest Lands

Additional Information Contacts

Westmoreland County Government . . . . (724) 830-3106
  http://www.co.westmoreland.pa.us

Westmoreland County Communities

ACME (unincorporated postal area)
Zip Code: 15610
  Covers a land area of 38.568 square miles and a water area of 0.061 square miles. Located at 40.14° N. Lat; 79.41° W. Long. Elevation is 1,916 feet. Population: 3,738 (2010); Density: 96.9 persons per square mile (2010); Race: 99.3% White, 0.1% Black, 0.2% Asian, 0.1% American Indian/Alaska Native, 0.0% Native Hawaiian/Other Pacific Islander, 0.3% Other, 0.5% Hispanic of any race (2010); Average household size: 2.46 (2010); Median age: 45.1 (2010); Males per 100 females: 101.4 (2010); Homeownership rate: 90.9% (2010)

ADAMSBURG (borough). Covers a land area of 0.280 square miles and a water area of 0 square miles. Located at 40.31° N. Lat; 79.65° W. Long. Elevation is 1,175 feet.
Population: 257 (1990); 221 (2000); 172 (2010); Density: 614.8 persons per square mile (2010); Race: 97.7% White, 1.2% Black, 1.2% Asian, 0.0% American Indian/Alaska Native, 0.0% Native Hawaiian/Other Pacific Islander, 0.0% Other, 0.6% Hispanic of any race (2010); Average household size: 2.29 (2010); Median age: 44.0 (2010); Males per 100 females: 100.0 (2010); Marriage status: 21.7% never married, 65.5% now married, 7.5% widowed, 5.3% divorced (2006-2010 5-year est.); Foreign born: 0.0% (2006-2010 5-year est.); Ancestry (includes multiple ancestries): 35.7% German, 11.6% English, 11.6% Irish, 11.2% Italian, 6.2% Russian (2006-2010 5-year est.).
Economy: Single-family building permits issued: 0 (2011); Multi-family building permits issued: 0 (2011); Employment by occupation: 0.0% management, 0.0% professional, 4.4% services, 36.5% sales, 3.8% farming, 15.1% construction, 13.2% production (2006-2010 5-year est.).
Income: Per capita income: $32,789 (2006-2010 5-year est.); Median household income: $59,531 (2006-2010 5-year est.); Average household income: $66,175 (2006-2010 5-year est.); Percent of households with income of $100,000 or more: 33.3% (2006-2010 5-year est.); Poverty rate: 0.8% (2006-2010 5-year est.).
Education: Percent of population age 25 and over with: High school diploma (including GED) or higher: 99.0% (2006-2010 5-year est.); Bachelor's degree or higher: 9.5% (2006-2010 5-year est.); Master's degree or higher: 2.9% (2006-2010 5-year est.).
Housing: Homeownership rate: 62.6% (2010); Median home value: $152,200 (2006-2010 5-year est.); Median contract rent: $494 per month (2006-2010 5-year est.); Median year structure built: 1953 (2006-2010 5-year est.).
Transportation: Commute to work: 74.8% car, 0.0% public transportation, 25.2% walk, 0.0% work from home (2006-2010 5-year est.); Travel time to work: 61.0% less than 15 minutes, 16.4% 15 to 30 minutes, 6.9% 30 to 45 minutes, 7.5% 45 to 60 minutes, 8.2% 60 minutes or more (2006-2010 5-year est.)

ALLEGHENY (township). Covers a land area of 31.089 square miles and a water area of 0.804 square miles. Located at 40.61° N. Lat; 79.64° W. Long.
Population: 8,049 (1990); 8,002 (2000); 8,164 (2010); Density: 262.6 persons per square mile (2010); Race: 97.7% White, 0.9% Black, 0.1% Asian, 0.1% American Indian/Alaska Native, 0.0% Native Hawaiian/Other Pacific Islander, 1.2% Other, 0.4% Hispanic of any race (2010); Average household size: 2.46 (2010); Median age: 46.1 (2010); Males per 100 females: 98.7 (2010); Marriage status: 24.6% never married, 56.4% now married, 9.7% widowed, 9.3% divorced (2006-2010 5-year est.); Foreign born: 1.4% (2006-2010 5-year est.); Ancestry (includes multiple ancestries): 35.5% German, 24.3% Italian, 12.8% Irish, 12.0% Polish, 10.7% English (2006-2010 5-year est.).
Economy: Single-family building permits issued: 10 (2011); Multi-family building permits issued: 17 (2011); Employment by occupation: 11.6% management, 7.7% professional, 7.3% services, 13.6% sales, 5.2% farming, 11.7% construction, 11.9% production (2006-2010 5-year est.).
Income: Per capita income: $28,228 (2006-2010 5-year est.); Median household income: $56,486 (2006-2010 5-year est.); Average household income: $71,236 (2006-2010 5-year est.); Percent of households with income of $100,000 or more: 21.9% (2006-2010 5-year est.); Poverty rate: 8.7% (2006-2010 5-year est.).
Education: Percent of population age 25 and over with: High school diploma (including GED) or higher: 89.5% (2006-2010 5-year est.);
Bachelor's degree or higher: 25.8% (2006-2010 5-year est.); Master's degree or higher: 9.2% (2006-2010 5-year est.).
Housing: Homeownership rate: 86.1% (2010); Median home value: $142,900 (2006-2010 5-year est.); Median contract rent: $263 per month (2006-2010 5-year est.); Median year structure built: 1971 (2006-2010 5-year est.).
Safety: Violent crime rate: 4.9 per 10,000 population; Property crime rate: 130.6 per 10,000 population (2011).
Transportation: Commute to work: 96.4% car, 1.1% public transportation, 1.0% walk, 1.3% work from home (2006-2010 5-year est.); Travel time to work: 22.8% less than 15 minutes, 29.9% 15 to 30 minutes, 20.1% 30 to 45 minutes, 12.3% 45 to 60 minutes, 14.9% 60 minutes or more (2006-2010 5-year est.)
Additional Information Contacts
Allegheny Township . . . . (724) 842-4641
  http://alleghenytownship.net
Northside Northshore Chamber of Commerce . . . . (412) 231-6500
  http://www.northsidechamberofcommerce.com

ALVERTON (unincorporated postal area)
Zip Code: 15612
  Covers a land area of 2.507 square miles and a water area of 0 square miles. Located at 40.13° N. Lat; 79.59° W. Long. Elevation is 1,099 feet. Population: 474 (2010); Density: 189.0 persons per square mile (2010); Race: 98.7% White, 0.0% Black, 0.0% Asian, 0.6% American Indian/Alaska Native, 0.0% Native Hawaiian/Other Pacific Islander, 0.7% Other, 0.8% Hispanic of any race (2010); Average household size: 2.47 (2010); Median age: 45.7 (2010); Males per 100 females: 95.1 (2010); Homeownership rate: 91.1% (2010)

ARDARA (unincorporated postal area)
Zip Code: 15615
  Covers a land area of 0.983 square miles and a water area of 0 square miles. Located at 40.36° N. Lat; 79.73° W. Long. Elevation is 978 feet. Population: 387 (2010); Density: 393.4 persons per square mile (2010); Race: 98.7% White, 1.0% Black, 0.0% Asian, 0.0% American Indian/Alaska Native, 0.0% Native Hawaiian/Other Pacific Islander, 0.3% Other, 0.5% Hispanic of any race (2010); Average household size: 2.65 (2010); Median age: 44.3 (2010); Males per 100 females: 96.4 (2010); Homeownership rate: 87.7% (2010)

ARMBRUST (unincorporated postal area)
Zip Code: 15616
  Covers a land area of 0.053 square miles and a water area of 0.006 square miles. Located at 40.22° N. Lat; 79.55° W. Long. Elevation is 965 feet. Population: 23 (2010); Density: 430.4 persons per square mile (2010); Race: 87.0% White, 0.0% Black, 0.0% Asian, 0.0% American Indian/Alaska Native, 0.0% Native Hawaiian/Other Pacific Islander, 13.0% Other, 4.3% Hispanic of any race (2010); Average household size: 1.92 (2010); Median age: 44.3 (2010); Males per 100 females: 64.3 (2010); Homeownership rate: 75.0% (2010)

ARNOLD (city). Covers a land area of 0.732 square miles and a water area of 0.090 square miles. Located at 40.58° N. Lat; 79.77° W. Long. Elevation is 791 feet.
History: Incorporated 1895.
Population: 6,113 (1990); 5,667 (2000); 5,157 (2010); Density: 7,044.7 persons per square mile (2010); Race: 74.0% White, 20.0% Black, 0.2% Asian, 0.2% American Indian/Alaska Native, 0.0% Native Hawaiian/Other Pacific Islander, 5.6% Other, 2.3% Hispanic of any race (2010); Average household size: 2.21 (2010); Median age: 39.6 (2010); Males per 100 females: 91.7 (2010); Marriage status: 41.1% never married, 36.4% now married, 9.3% widowed, 13.1% divorced (2006-2010 5-year est.); Foreign born: 1.4% (2006-2010 5-year est.); Ancestry (includes multiple ancestries): 23.1% German, 20.6% Italian, 19.0% Irish, 9.7% Polish, 7.0% English (2006-2010 5-year est.).
Economy: Single-family building permits issued: 0 (2011); Multi-family building permits issued: 0 (2011); Employment by occupation: 7.0% management, 3.1% professional, 18.9% services, 18.4% sales, 3.3% farming, 4.6% construction, 11.1% production (2006-2010 5-year est.).
Income: Per capita income: $16,422 (2006-2010 5-year est.); Median household income: $24,444 (2006-2010 5-year est.); Average household income: $36,215 (2006-2010 5-year est.); Percent of households with income of $100,000 or more: 4.4% (2006-2010 5-year est.); Poverty rate: 25.0% (2006-2010 5-year est.).

Education: Percent of population age 25 and over with: High school diploma (including GED) or higher: 91.9% (2006-2010 5-year est.); Bachelor's degree or higher: 11.2% (2006-2010 5-year est.); Master's degree or higher: 4.3% (2006-2010 5-year est.).

School District(s)

New Kensington-Arnold SD (PK-12)

   2010-11 Enrollment: 2,138 . . . . (724) 335-8581

Housing: Homeownership rate: 52.0% (2010); Median home value: $65,000 (2006-2010 5-year est.); Median contract rent: $424 per month (2006-2010 5-year est.); Median year structure built: 1944 (2006-2010 5-year est.).

Safety: Violent crime rate: 23.2 per 10,000 population; Property crime rate: 162.4 per 10,000 population (2011).

Transportation: Commute to work: 85.2% car, 4.9% public transportation, 6.7% walk, 1.2% work from home (2006-2010 5-year est.); Travel time to work: 34.6% less than 15 minutes, 31.2% 15 to 30 minutes, 21.4% 30 to 45 minutes, 6.4% 45 to 60 minutes, 6.4% 60 minutes or more (2006-2010 5-year est.)

Additional Information Contacts

City of Arnold. . . . . (724) 337-4441
   http://www.arnoldpa.org
New Kensington Area Chamber of Commerce . . . . (724) 339-6616
   http://www.nkchamber.org

ARONA (borough). Covers a land area of 0.522 square miles and a water area of 0.003 square miles. Located at 40.27° N. Lat; 79.66° W. Long. Elevation is 961 feet.

Population: 397 (1990); 407 (2000); 370 (2010); Density: 708.3 persons per square mile (2010); Race: 100.0% White, 0.0% Black, 0.0% Asian, 0.0% American Indian/Alaska Native, 0.0% Native Hawaiian/Other Pacific Islander, 0.0% Other, 0.0% Hispanic of any race (2010); Average household size: 2.42 (2010); Median age: 42.4 (2010); Males per 100 females: 97.9 (2010); Marriage status: 26.7% never married, 58.9% now married, 4.3% widowed, 10.1% divorced (2006-2010 5-year est.); Foreign born: 0.7% (2006-2010 5-year est.); Ancestry (includes multiple ancestries): 45.0% German, 15.4% English, 15.1% Italian, 14.5% Irish, 7.6% Scottish (2006-2010 5-year est.).

Economy: Single-family building permits issued: 0 (2011); Multi-family building permits issued: 0 (2011); Employment by occupation: 7.8% management, 1.4% professional, 8.7% services, 22.9% sales, 3.7% farming, 6.4% construction, 4.6% production (2006-2010 5-year est.).

Income: Per capita income: $21,704 (2006-2010 5-year est.); Median household income: $40,417 (2006-2010 5-year est.); Average household income: $51,331 (2006-2010 5-year est.); Percent of households with income of $100,000 or more: 10.4% (2006-2010 5-year est.); Poverty rate: 4.5% (2006-2010 5-year est.).

Education: Percent of population age 25 and over with: High school diploma (including GED) or higher: 89.9% (2006-2010 5-year est.); Bachelor's degree or higher: 8.5% (2006-2010 5-year est.); Master's degree or higher: 2.5% (2006-2010 5-year est.).

Housing: Homeownership rate: 85.6% (2010); Median home value: $98,100 (2006-2010 5-year est.); Median contract rent: $500 per month (2006-2010 5-year est.); Median year structure built: before 1940 (2006-2010 5-year est.).

Transportation: Commute to work: 85.8% car, 0.0% public transportation, 0.0% walk, 9.4% work from home (2006-2010 5-year est.); Travel time to work: 26.6% less than 15 minutes, 49.0% 15 to 30 minutes, 14.1% 30 to 45 minutes, 4.7% 45 to 60 minutes, 5.7% 60 minutes or more (2006-2010 5-year est.)

AVONMORE (borough). Covers a land area of 1.471 square miles and a water area of 0.085 square miles. Located at 40.53° N. Lat; 79.47° W. Long. Elevation is 932 feet.

History: Incorporated 1893.

Population: 1,089 (1990); 820 (2000); 1,011 (2010); Density: 687.5 persons per square mile (2010); Race: 97.4% White, 1.4% Black, 0.1% Asian, 0.0% American Indian/Alaska Native, 0.0% Native Hawaiian/Other Pacific Islander, 1.1% Other, 0.5% Hispanic of any race (2010); Average household size: 2.26 (2010); Median age: 45.0 (2010); Males per 100 females: 91.5 (2010); Marriage status: 20.9% never married, 60.5% now married, 12.4% widowed, 6.2% divorced (2006-2010 5-year est.); Foreign born: 1.9% (2006-2010 5-year est.); Ancestry (includes multiple ancestries): 36.5% German, 29.6% Italian, 20.8% Irish, 19.6% Polish, 10.0% English (2006-2010 5-year est.).

Economy: Single-family building permits issued: 0 (2011); Multi-family building permits issued: 0 (2011); Employment by occupation: 5.2% management, 4.6% professional, 21.8% services, 10.1% sales, 2.2% farming, 11.7% construction, 10.9% production (2006-2010 5-year est.).

Income: Per capita income: $21,917 (2006-2010 5-year est.); Median household income: $36,167 (2006-2010 5-year est.); Average household income: $50,841 (2006-2010 5-year est.); Percent of households with income of $100,000 or more: 11.8% (2006-2010 5-year est.); Poverty rate: 22.3% (2006-2010 5-year est.).

Education: Percent of population age 25 and over with: High school diploma (including GED) or higher: 87.5% (2006-2010 5-year est.); Bachelor's degree or higher: 8.0% (2006-2010 5-year est.); Master's degree or higher: 0.4% (2006-2010 5-year est.).

Housing: Homeownership rate: 74.8% (2010); Median home value: $86,300 (2006-2010 5-year est.); Median contract rent: $366 per month (2006-2010 5-year est.); Median year structure built: 1953 (2006-2010 5-year est.).

Safety: Violent crime rate: 0.0 per 10,000 population; Property crime rate: 0.0 per 10,000 population (2011).

Transportation: Commute to work: 92.6% car, 0.0% public transportation, 6.3% walk, 1.1% work from home (2006-2010 5-year est.); Travel time to work: 24.4% less than 15 minutes, 26.9% 15 to 30 minutes, 25.3% 30 to 45 minutes, 15.0% 45 to 60 minutes, 8.3% 60 minutes or more (2006-2010 5-year est.)

BELL (township). Covers a land area of 21.489 square miles and a water area of 0.651 square miles. Located at 40.51° N. Lat; 79.51° W. Long.

History: Incorporated 1876.

Population: 2,363 (1990); 2,458 (2000); 2,348 (2010); Density: 109.3 persons per square mile (2010); Race: 97.7% White, 1.1% Black, 0.1% Asian, 0.3% American Indian/Alaska Native, 0.0% Native Hawaiian/Other Pacific Islander, 0.8% Other, 0.6% Hispanic of any race (2010); Average household size: 2.44 (2010); Median age: 46.3 (2010); Males per 100 females: 98.8 (2010); Marriage status: 19.4% never married, 69.6% now married, 6.7% widowed, 4.2% divorced (2006-2010 5-year est.); Foreign born: 1.9% (2006-2010 5-year est.); Ancestry (includes multiple ancestries): 42.6% German, 18.4% Italian, 17.8% Irish, 9.4% Polish, 7.6% English (2006-2010 5-year est.).

Economy: Single-family building permits issued: 4 (2011); Multi-family building permits issued: 0 (2011); Employment by occupation: 9.1% management, 1.0% professional, 6.1% services, 16.1% sales, 5.1% farming, 15.7% construction, 7.7% production (2006-2010 5-year est.).

Income: Per capita income: $23,968 (2006-2010 5-year est.); Median household income: $50,096 (2006-2010 5-year est.); Average household income: $59,946 (2006-2010 5-year est.); Percent of households with income of $100,000 or more: 13.7% (2006-2010 5-year est.); Poverty rate: 6.0% (2006-2010 5-year est.).

Education: Percent of population age 25 and over with: High school diploma (including GED) or higher: 90.3% (2006-2010 5-year est.); Bachelor's degree or higher: 13.8% (2006-2010 5-year est.); Master's degree or higher: 5.2% (2006-2010 5-year est.).

Housing: Homeownership rate: 89.3% (2010); Median home value: $134,100 (2006-2010 5-year est.); Median contract rent: $348 per month (2006-2010 5-year est.); Median year structure built: 1968 (2006-2010 5-year est.).

Transportation: Commute to work: 87.9% car, 0.9% public transportation, 9.4% walk, 1.8% work from home (2006-2010 5-year est.); Travel time to work: 26.3% less than 15 minutes, 33.4% 15 to 30 minutes, 19.4% 30 to 45 minutes, 14.0% 45 to 60 minutes, 6.9% 60 minutes or more (2006-2010 5-year est.)

Additional Information Contacts

Westmoreland Chamber of Commerce . . . . (724) 834-2900
   http://www.westmorelandchamber.com

BOLIVAR (borough). Covers a land area of 0.171 square miles and a water area of 0.008 square miles. Located at 40.40° N. Lat; 79.15° W. Long. Elevation is 1,033 feet.

Population: 544 (1990); 501 (2000); 465 (2010); Density: 2,727.0 persons per square mile (2010); Race: 98.9% White, 0.0% Black, 0.4% Asian, 0.4% American Indian/Alaska Native, 0.2% Native Hawaiian/Other Pacific Islander, 0.1% Other, 0.9% Hispanic of any race (2010); Average household size: 2.42 (2010); Median age: 43.7 (2010); Males per 100 females: 99.6 (2010); Marriage status: 20.1% never married, 67.9% now married, 8.0% widowed, 4.1% divorced (2006-2010 5-year est.); Foreign

born: 0.4% (2006-2010 5-year est.); Ancestry (includes multiple ancestries): 31.8% German, 21.9% Irish, 12.6% Italian, 8.2% English, 7.8% Polish (2006-2010 5-year est.).

Economy: Single-family building permits issued: 0 (2011); Multi-family building permits issued: 0 (2011); Employment by occupation: 3.4% management, 1.1% professional, 17.7% services, 14.3% sales, 0.0% farming, 18.3% construction, 9.1% production (2006-2010 5-year est.).

Income: Per capita income: $16,677 (2006-2010 5-year est.); Median household income: $29,500 (2006-2010 5-year est.); Average household income: $42,014 (2006-2010 5-year est.); Percent of households with income of $100,000 or more: 6.0% (2006-2010 5-year est.); Poverty rate: 15.2% (2006-2010 5-year est.).

Education: Percent of population age 25 and over with: High school diploma (including GED) or higher: 93.8% (2006-2010 5-year est.); Bachelor's degree or higher: 10.3% (2006-2010 5-year est.); Master's degree or higher: 2.8% (2006-2010 5-year est.).

Housing: Homeownership rate: 85.8% (2010); Median home value: $73,000 (2006-2010 5-year est.); Median contract rent: $395 per month (2006-2010 5-year est.); Median year structure built: before 1940 (2006-2010 5-year est.).

Safety: Violent crime rate: 21.5 per 10,000 population; Property crime rate: 0.0 per 10,000 population (2011).

Transportation: Commute to work: 93.1% car, 1.1% public transportation, 1.7% walk, 4.0% work from home (2006-2010 5-year est.); Travel time to work: 9.5% less than 15 minutes, 25.0% 15 to 30 minutes, 38.7% 30 to 45 minutes, 21.4% 45 to 60 minutes, 5.4% 60 minutes or more (2006-2010 5-year est.)

BRADENVILLE (CDP). Covers a land area of 0.409 square miles and a water area of 0 square miles. Located at 40.32° N. Lat; 79.34° W. Long. Elevation is 1,102 feet.

Population: n/a (1990); n/a (2000); 545 (2010); Density: 1,332.0 persons per square mile (2010); Race: 99.1% White, 0.7% Black, 0.2% Asian, 0.0% American Indian/Alaska Native, 0.0% Native Hawaiian/Other Pacific Islander, 0.0% Other, 0.7% Hispanic of any race (2010); Average household size: 2.30 (2010); Median age: 42.7 (2010); Males per 100 females: 96.8 (2010); Marriage status: 17.1% never married, 73.2% now married, 6.7% widowed, 3.0% divorced (2006-2010 5-year est.); Foreign born: 0.0% (2006-2010 5-year est.); Ancestry (includes multiple ancestries): 43.7% German, 41.4% Italian, 19.3% Irish, 9.9% Dutch, 9.3% Polish (2006-2010 5-year est.).

Economy: Employment by occupation: 0.0% management, 9.7% professional, 8.2% services, 0.0% sales, 0.0% farming, 10.3% construction, 10.3% production (2006-2010 5-year est.).

Income: Per capita income: $15,391 (2006-2010 5-year est.); Median household income: $43,594 (2006-2010 5-year est.); Average household income: $44,382 (2006-2010 5-year est.); Percent of households with income of $100,000 or more: 11.0% (2006-2010 5-year est.); Poverty rate: 9.9% (2006-2010 5-year est.).

Education: Percent of population age 25 and over with: High school diploma (including GED) or higher: 92.9% (2006-2010 5-year est.); Bachelor's degree or higher: 11.2% (2006-2010 5-year est.); Master's degree or higher: 0.0% (2006-2010 5-year est.).

Housing: Homeownership rate: 73.8% (2010); Median home value: $86,800 (2006-2010 5-year est.); Median contract rent: $554 per month (2006-2010 5-year est.); Median year structure built: 1946 (2006-2010 5-year est.).

Transportation: Commute to work: 100.0% car, 0.0% public transportation, 0.0% walk, 0.0% work from home (2006-2010 5-year est.); Travel time to work: 55.9% less than 15 minutes, 23.6% 15 to 30 minutes, 10.3% 30 to 45 minutes, 0.0% 45 to 60 minutes, 10.3% 60 minutes or more (2006-2010 5-year est.)

CALUMET (CDP). Covers a land area of 2.181 square miles and a water area of 0 square miles. Located at 40.22° N. Lat; 79.49° W. Long. Elevation is 1,001 feet.

Population: n/a (1990); n/a (2000); 1,241 (2010); Density: 569.0 persons per square mile (2010); Race: 99.3% White, 0.1% Black, 0.0% Asian, 0.2% American Indian/Alaska Native, 0.0% Native Hawaiian/Other Pacific Islander, 0.4% Other, 0.3% Hispanic of any race (2010); Average household size: 2.45 (2010); Median age: 45.2 (2010); Males per 100 females: 94.8 (2010); Marriage status: 32.7% never married, 60.4% now married, 3.0% widowed, 4.0% divorced (2006-2010 5-year est.); Foreign born: 0.0% (2006-2010 5-year est.); Ancestry (includes multiple

ancestries): 23.4% German, 16.4% Italian, 16.2% Polish, 15.2% Slovak, 10.8% English (2006-2010 5-year est.).

Economy: Employment by occupation: 4.1% management, 4.3% professional, 20.5% services, 22.0% sales, 5.8% farming, 14.3% construction, 9.8% production (2006-2010 5-year est.).

Income: Per capita income: $21,939 (2006-2010 5-year est.); Median household income: $49,375 (2006-2010 5-year est.); Average household income: $51,562 (2006-2010 5-year est.); Percent of households with income of $100,000 or more: 13.4% (2006-2010 5-year est.); Poverty rate: 6.8% (2006-2010 5-year est.).

Education: Percent of population age 25 and over with: High school diploma (including GED) or higher: 92.1% (2006-2010 5-year est.); Bachelor's degree or higher: 14.8% (2006-2010 5-year est.); Master's degree or higher: 3.6% (2006-2010 5-year est.).

Housing: Homeownership rate: 86.0% (2010); Median home value: $104,100 (2006-2010 5-year est.); Median contract rent: n/a per month (2006-2010 5-year est.); Median year structure built: before 1940 (2006-2010 5-year est.).

Transportation: Commute to work: 98.5% car, 0.0% public transportation, 0.0% walk, 1.5% work from home (2006-2010 5-year est.); Travel time to work: 10.1% less than 15 minutes, 70.4% 15 to 30 minutes, 5.4% 30 to 45 minutes, 6.1% 45 to 60 minutes, 8.0% 60 minutes or more (2006-2010 5-year est.)

CHAMPION (unincorporated postal area)
Zip Code: 15622

Covers a land area of 32.393 square miles and a water area of 0.005 square miles. Located at 40.04° N. Lat; 79.32° W. Long. Population: 1,387 (2010); Density: 42.8 persons per square mile (2010); Race: 99.4% White, 0.0% Black, 0.1% Asian, 0.0% American Indian/Alaska Native, 0.0% Native Hawaiian/Other Pacific Islander, 0.5% Other, 0.7% Hispanic of any race (2010); Average household size: 2.23 (2010); Median age: 47.4 (2010); Males per 100 females: 109.2 (2010); Homeownership rate: 79.7% (2010)

CLARIDGE (unincorporated postal area)
Zip Code: 15623

Covers a land area of 1.740 square miles and a water area of 0 square miles. Located at 40.36° N. Lat; 79.62° W. Long. Elevation is 1,053 feet. Population: 762 (2010); Density: 437.9 persons per square mile (2010); Race: 97.2% White, 1.3% Black, 0.3% Asian, 0.0% American Indian/Alaska Native, 0.0% Native Hawaiian/Other Pacific Islander, 1.2% Other, 0.9% Hispanic of any race (2010); Average household size: 2.47 (2010); Median age: 42.1 (2010); Males per 100 females: 100.0 (2010); Homeownership rate: 85.1% (2010)

COLLINSBURG (CDP). Covers a land area of 1.735 square miles and a water area of 0.023 square miles. Located at 40.22° N. Lat; 79.78° W. Long. Elevation is 784 feet.

Population: n/a (1990); n/a (2000); 1,125 (2010); Density: 648.3 persons per square mile (2010); Race: 97.7% White, 1.1% Black, 0.2% Asian, 0.0% American Indian/Alaska Native, 0.0% Native Hawaiian/Other Pacific Islander, 1.0% Other, 0.5% Hispanic of any race (2010); Average household size: 2.31 (2010); Median age: 46.9 (2010); Males per 100 females: 103.8 (2010); Marriage status: 19.0% never married, 58.8% now married, 8.7% widowed, 13.5% divorced (2006-2010 5-year est.); Foreign born: 0.0% (2006-2010 5-year est.); Ancestry (includes multiple ancestries): 33.9% German, 28.9% Italian, 10.4% English, 6.5% Slovak, 6.5% Scottish (2006-2010 5-year est.).

Economy: Employment by occupation: 2.2% management, 2.4% professional, 15.1% services, 17.3% sales, 2.2% farming, 11.1% construction, 7.5% production (2006-2010 5-year est.).

Income: Per capita income: $23,310 (2006-2010 5-year est.); Median household income: $43,269 (2006-2010 5-year est.); Average household income: $50,799 (2006-2010 5-year est.); Percent of households with income of $100,000 or more: 8.8% (2006-2010 5-year est.); Poverty rate: 5.3% (2006-2010 5-year est.).

Education: Percent of population age 25 and over with: High school diploma (including GED) or higher: 95.3% (2006-2010 5-year est.); Bachelor's degree or higher: 14.0% (2006-2010 5-year est.); Master's degree or higher: 3.6% (2006-2010 5-year est.).

Housing: Homeownership rate: 92.0% (2010); Median home value: $45,000 (2006-2010 5-year est.); Median contract rent: $437 per month (2006-2010 5-year est.); Median year structure built: 1980 (2006-2010 5-year est.).

Transportation: Commute to work: 83.5% car, 7.1% public transportation, 2.2% walk, 7.3% work from home (2006-2010 5-year est.); Travel time to work: 14.5% less than 15 minutes, 29.2% 15 to 30 minutes, 27.1% 30 to 45 minutes, 20.0% 45 to 60 minutes, 9.2% 60 minutes or more (2006-2010 5-year est.)

COOK (township). Covers a land area of 46.760 square miles and a water area of 0.018 square miles. Located at 40.17° N. Lat; 79.29° W. Long.

Population: 2,320 (1990); 2,403 (2000); 2,250 (2010); Density: 48.1 persons per square mile (2010); Race: 99.4% White, 0.0% Black, 0.1% Asian, 0.2% American Indian/Alaska Native, 0.0% Native Hawaiian/Other Pacific Islander, 0.3% Other, 0.6% Hispanic of any race (2010); Average household size: 2.41 (2010); Median age: 47.5 (2010); Males per 100 females: 97.5 (2010); Marriage status: 12.4% never married, 73.6% now married, 7.2% widowed, 6.8% divorced (2006-2010 5-year est.); Foreign born: 3.0% (2006-2010 5-year est.); Ancestry (includes multiple ancestries): 38.4% German, 13.7% Irish, 10.7% Italian, 9.6% Polish, 7.8% English (2006-2010 5-year est.).

Economy: Employment by occupation: 13.1% management, 0.4% professional, 11.9% services, 11.9% sales, 0.0% farming, 17.9% construction, 6.5% production (2006-2010 5-year est.).

Income: Per capita income: $29,740 (2006-2010 5-year est.); Median household income: $50,762 (2006-2010 5-year est.); Average household income: $68,744 (2006-2010 5-year est.); Percent of households with income of $100,000 or more: 20.2% (2006-2010 5-year est.); Poverty rate: 6.7% (2006-2010 5-year est.).

Education: Percent of population age 25 and over with: High school diploma (including GED) or higher: 87.5% (2006-2010 5-year est.); Bachelor's degree or higher: 20.4% (2006-2010 5-year est.); Master's degree or higher: 6.6% (2006-2010 5-year est.).

Housing: Homeownership rate: 90.1% (2010); Median home value: $141,900 (2006-2010 5-year est.); Median contract rent: $425 per month (2006-2010 5-year est.); Median year structure built: 1962 (2006-2010 5-year est.).

Transportation: Commute to work: 86.5% car, 1.7% public transportation, 3.1% walk, 8.3% work from home (2006-2010 5-year est.); Travel time to work: 23.0% less than 15 minutes, 35.8% 15 to 30 minutes, 20.8% 30 to 45 minutes, 6.8% 45 to 60 minutes, 13.7% 60 minutes or more (2006-2010 5-year est.)

Additional Information Contacts
Wellsboro Area Chamber of Commerce . . . . (570) 724-1926
http://www.wellsboropa.com

CRABTREE (CDP). Covers a land area of 0.094 square miles and a water area of 0 square miles. Located at 40.36° N. Lat; 79.47° W. Long. Elevation is 1,014 feet.

Population: 353 (1990); 320 (2000); 277 (2010); Density: 2,953.1 persons per square mile (2010); Race: 98.2% White, 0.4% Black, 0.4% Asian, 0.4% American Indian/Alaska Native, 0.0% Native Hawaiian/Other Pacific Islander, 0.6% Other, 0.4% Hispanic of any race (2010); Average household size: 2.11 (2010); Median age: 45.7 (2010); Males per 100 females: 88.4 (2010); Marriage status: 12.1% never married, 61.4% now married, 22.9% widowed, 3.6% divorced (2006-2010 5-year est.); Foreign born: 9.4% (2006-2010 5-year est.); Ancestry (includes multiple ancestries): 41.2% Italian, 31.2% German, 21.6% Slovak, 20.3% Polish, 14.2% English (2006-2010 5-year est.).

Economy: Employment by occupation: 25.7% management, 0.0% professional, 4.9% services, 7.3% sales, 0.0% farming, 23.3% construction, 0.0% production (2006-2010 5-year est.).

Income: Per capita income: $18,987 (2006-2010 5-year est.); Median household income: $35,750 (2006-2010 5-year est.); Average household income: $41,307 (2006-2010 5-year est.); Percent of households with income of $100,000 or more: n/a (2006-2010 5-year est.); Poverty rate: 2.8% (2006-2010 5-year est.).

Education: Percent of population age 25 and over with: High school diploma (including GED) or higher: 54.5% (2006-2010 5-year est.); Bachelor's degree or higher: 10.3% (2006-2010 5-year est.); Master's degree or higher: 5.9% (2006-2010 5-year est.).

Housing: Homeownership rate: 61.8% (2010); Median home value: $67,800 (2006-2010 5-year est.); Median contract rent: n/a per month (2006-2010 5-year est.); Median year structure built: before 1940 (2006-2010 5-year est.).

Transportation: Commute to work: 95.1% car, 0.0% public transportation, 4.9% walk, 0.0% work from home (2006-2010 5-year est.); Travel time to

work: 4.9% less than 15 minutes, 28.6% 15 to 30 minutes, 28.6% 30 to 45 minutes, 32.5% 45 to 60 minutes, 5.3% 60 minutes or more (2006-2010 5-year est.)

DARRAGH (unincorporated postal area)
Zip Code: 15625
Covers a land area of 0.586 square miles and a water area of 0 square miles. Located at 40.26° N. Lat; 79.67° W. Long. Elevation is 971 feet. Population: 144 (2010); Density: 245.5 persons per square mile (2010); Race: 99.3% White, 0.0% Black, 0.0% Asian, 0.7% American Indian/Alaska Native, 0.0% Native Hawaiian/Other Pacific Islander, 0.0% Other, 0.0% Hispanic of any race (2010); Average household size: 2.53 (2010); Median age: 43.7 (2010); Males per 100 females: 100.0 (2010); Homeownership rate: 87.7% (2010)

DELMONT (borough). Aka New Salem. Covers a land area of 1.056 square miles and a water area of 0 square miles. Located at 40.41° N. Lat; 79.57° W. Long. Elevation is 1,260 feet.

Population: 2,041 (1990); 2,497 (2000); 2,686 (2010); Density: 2,543.4 persons per square mile (2010); Race: 95.8% White, 0.9% Black, 1.5% Asian, 0.2% American Indian/Alaska Native, 0.0% Native Hawaiian/Other Pacific Islander, 1.6% Other, 1.7% Hispanic of any race (2010); Average household size: 2.26 (2010); Median age: 42.6 (2010); Males per 100 females: 95.2 (2010); Marriage status: 26.9% never married, 58.9% now married, 4.8% widowed, 9.3% divorced (2006-2010 5-year est.); Foreign born: 2.0% (2006-2010 5-year est.); Ancestry (includes multiple ancestries): 35.4% German, 25.5% Italian, 22.5% Irish, 13.2% Polish, 7.1% English (2006-2010 5-year est.).

Economy: Single-family building permits issued: 1 (2011); Multi-family building permits issued: 0 (2011); Employment by occupation: 12.8% management, 7.6% professional, 5.0% services, 12.9% sales, 3.0% farming, 8.5% construction, 6.8% production (2006-2010 5-year est.).

Income: Per capita income: $26,273 (2006-2010 5-year est.); Median household income: $48,462 (2006-2010 5-year est.); Average household income: $58,907 (2006-2010 5-year est.); Percent of households with income of $100,000 or more: 20.0% (2006-2010 5-year est.); Poverty rate: 11.9% (2006-2010 5-year est.).

Education: Percent of population age 25 and over with: High school diploma (including GED) or higher: 96.3% (2006-2010 5-year est.); Bachelor's degree or higher: 32.1% (2006-2010 5-year est.); Master's degree or higher: 10.9% (2006-2010 5-year est.).

Housing: Homeownership rate: 68.6% (2010); Median home value: $149,100 (2006-2010 5-year est.); Median contract rent: $390 per month (2006-2010 5-year est.); Median year structure built: 1972 (2006-2010 5-year est.).

Safety: Violent crime rate: 33.4 per 10,000 population; Property crime rate: 103.9 per 10,000 population (2011).

Transportation: Commute to work: 91.5% car, 0.5% public transportation, 1.6% walk, 3.1% work from home (2006-2010 5-year est.); Travel time to work: 21.3% less than 15 minutes, 35.1% 15 to 30 minutes, 20.9% 30 to 45 minutes, 12.4% 45 to 60 minutes, 10.2% 60 minutes or more (2006-2010 5-year est.)

Additional Information Contacts
Westmoreland Chamber of Commerce . . . . (724) 834-2900
http://www.westmorelandchamber.com

DERRY (borough). Covers a land area of 0.772 square miles and a water area of 0.024 square miles. Located at 40.33° N. Lat; 79.30° W. Long. Elevation is 1,178 feet.

Population: 2,950 (1990); 2,991 (2000); 2,688 (2010); Density: 3,482.3 persons per square mile (2010); Race: 98.2% White, 0.6% Black, 0.3% Asian, 0.1% American Indian/Alaska Native, 0.0% Native Hawaiian/Other Pacific Islander, 0.8% Other, 0.8% Hispanic of any race (2010); Average household size: 2.37 (2010); Median age: 40.7 (2010); Males per 100 females: 94.2 (2010); Marriage status: 16.5% never married, 57.1% now married, 16.7% widowed, 9.7% divorced (2006-2010 5-year est.); Foreign born: 0.0% (2006-2010 5-year est.); Ancestry (includes multiple ancestries): 31.5% German, 26.6% Irish, 19.3% Italian, 10.6% English, 6.1% French (2006-2010 5-year est.).

Economy: Single-family building permits issued: 0 (2011); Multi-family building permits issued: 0 (2011); Employment by occupation: 8.7% management, 0.9% professional, 15.9% services, 16.5% sales, 1.9% farming, 5.8% construction, 6.3% production (2006-2010 5-year est.).

Income: Per capita income: $19,737 (2006-2010 5-year est.); Median household income: $32,350 (2006-2010 5-year est.); Average household

income: $43,751 (2006-2010 5-year est.); Percent of households with income of $100,000 or more: 4.8% (2006-2010 5-year est.); Poverty rate: 19.3% (2006-2010 5-year est.).

Education: Percent of population age 25 and over with: High school diploma (including GED) or higher: 91.0% (2006-2010 5-year est.); Bachelor's degree or higher: 16.9% (2006-2010 5-year est.); Master's degree or higher: 4.8% (2006-2010 5-year est.).

School District(s)

Derry Area SD (KG-12)

    2010-11 Enrollment: 2,245 . . . . (724) 694-1401

Housing: Homeownership rate: 68.8% (2010); Median home value: $93,900 (2006-2010 5-year est.); Median contract rent: $405 per month (2006-2010 5-year est.); Median year structure built: 1941 (2006-2010 5-year est.).

Safety: Violent crime rate: 26.0 per 10,000 population; Property crime rate: 18.5 per 10,000 population (2011).

Transportation: Commute to work: 93.1% car, 0.0% public transportation, 5.1% walk, 1.1% work from home (2006-2010 5-year est.); Travel time to work: 35.8% less than 15 minutes, 38.5% 15 to 30 minutes, 17.2% 30 to 45 minutes, 4.1% 45 to 60 minutes, 4.4% 60 minutes or more (2006-2010 5-year est.)

Additional Information Contacts

Latrobe Area Chamber of Commerce . . . . (724) 537-2671
    http://www.latrobearea.com

DERRY (township). Covers a land area of 95.091 square miles and a water area of 1.191 square miles. Located at 40.37° N. Lat; 79.31° W. Long. Elevation is 1,178 feet.

History: Incorporated 1881.

Population: 15,446 (1990); 14,726 (2000); 14,502 (2010); Density: 152.5 persons per square mile (2010); Race: 97.6% White, 1.3% Black, 0.2% Asian, 0.1% American Indian/Alaska Native, 0.0% Native Hawaiian/Other Pacific Islander, 0.8% Other, 0.6% Hispanic of any race (2010); Average household size: 2.30 (2010); Median age: 46.2 (2010); Males per 100 females: 98.8 (2010); Marriage status: 23.1% never married, 55.7% now married, 11.4% widowed, 9.9% divorced (2006-2010 5-year est.); Foreign born: 1.1% (2006-2010 5-year est.); Ancestry (includes multiple ancestries): 33.4% German, 18.1% Italian, 17.4% Irish, 8.7% Polish, 8.0% Slovak (2006-2010 5-year est.).

Economy: Single-family building permits issued: 8 (2011); Multi-family building permits issued: 0 (2011); Employment by occupation: 8.2% management, 3.7% professional, 14.4% services, 13.7% sales, 2.6% farming, 12.1% construction, 8.1% production (2006-2010 5-year est.).

Income: Per capita income: $21,784 (2006-2010 5-year est.); Median household income: $42,904 (2006-2010 5-year est.); Average household income: $52,361 (2006-2010 5-year est.); Percent of households with income of $100,000 or more: 10.9% (2006-2010 5-year est.); Poverty rate: 12.3% (2006-2010 5-year est.).

Education: Percent of population age 25 and over with: High school diploma (including GED) or higher: 86.0% (2006-2010 5-year est.); Bachelor's degree or higher: 12.1% (2006-2010 5-year est.); Master's degree or higher: 2.9% (2006-2010 5-year est.).

Housing: Homeownership rate: 79.9% (2010); Median home value: $103,900 (2006-2010 5-year est.); Median contract rent: $448 per month (2006-2010 5-year est.); Median year structure built: 1968 (2006-2010 5-year est.).

Transportation: Commute to work: 94.9% car, 0.0% public transportation, 1.2% walk, 3.1% work from home (2006-2010 5-year est.); Travel time to work: 37.9% less than 15 minutes, 34.0% 15 to 30 minutes, 14.7% 30 to 45 minutes, 5.8% 45 to 60 minutes, 7.6% 60 minutes or more (2006-2010 5-year est.)

Additional Information Contacts

Derry Township . . . . (717) 533-2057
    http://www.derrytownship.org
Latrobe Area Chamber of Commerce . . . . (724) 537-2671
    http://www.latrobearea.com

DONEGAL (borough). Covers a land area of 0.227 square miles and a water area of 0 square miles. Located at 40.11° N. Lat; 79.38° W. Long. Elevation is 1,814 feet.

Population: 152 (1990); 165 (2000); 120 (2010); Density: 527.6 persons per square mile (2010); Race: 99.2% White, 0.0% Black, 0.8% Asian, 0.0% American Indian/Alaska Native, 0.0% Native Hawaiian/Other Pacific Islander, 0.0% Other, 0.0% Hispanic of any race (2010); Average household size: 1.97 (2010); Median age: 49.3 (2010); Males per 100

females: 79.1 (2010); Marriage status: 22.3% never married, 56.2% now married, 6.9% widowed, 14.6% divorced (2006-2010 5-year est.); Foreign born: 0.0% (2006-2010 5-year est.); Ancestry (includes multiple ancestries): 42.5% German, 14.4% Irish, 13.7% English, 7.5% Polish, 6.8% Slovak (2006-2010 5-year est.).

Economy: Single-family building permits issued: 0 (2011); Multi-family building permits issued: 0 (2011); Employment by occupation: 15.5% management, 2.1% professional, 19.6% services, 16.5% sales, 0.0% farming, 18.6% construction, 11.3% production (2006-2010 5-year est.).

Income: Per capita income: $30,053 (2006-2010 5-year est.); Median household income: $58,472 (2006-2010 5-year est.); Average household income: $64,155 (2006-2010 5-year est.); Percent of households with income of $100,000 or more: 27.5% (2006-2010 5-year est.); Poverty rate: 14.4% (2006-2010 5-year est.).

Education: Percent of population age 25 and over with: High school diploma (including GED) or higher: 88.4% (2006-2010 5-year est.); Bachelor's degree or higher: 16.5% (2006-2010 5-year est.); Master's degree or higher: 6.6% (2006-2010 5-year est.).

Housing: Homeownership rate: 72.2% (2010); Median home value: $140,000 (2006-2010 5-year est.); Median contract rent: $388 per month (2006-2010 5-year est.); Median year structure built: 1956 (2006-2010 5-year est.).

Transportation: Commute to work: 71.1% car, 0.0% public transportation, 1.0% walk, 27.8% work from home (2006-2010 5-year est.); Travel time to work: 27.1% less than 15 minutes, 45.7% 15 to 30 minutes, 22.9% 30 to 45 minutes, 0.0% 45 to 60 minutes, 4.3% 60 minutes or more (2006-2010 5-year est.)

DONEGAL (township). Covers a land area of 49.130 square miles and a water area of 0.127 square miles. Located at 40.10° N. Lat; 79.33° W. Long. Elevation is 1,814 feet.

Population: 2,206 (1990); 2,442 (2000); 2,403 (2010); Density: 48.9 persons per square mile (2010); Race: 99.0% White, 0.1% Black, 0.2% Asian, 0.0% American Indian/Alaska Native, 0.1% Native Hawaiian/Other Pacific Islander, 0.6% Other, 1.0% Hispanic of any race (2010); Average household size: 2.37 (2010); Median age: 46.0 (2010); Males per 100 females: 97.8 (2010); Marriage status: 22.9% never married, 64.0% now married, 8.7% widowed, 4.4% divorced (2006-2010 5-year est.); Foreign born: 0.0% (2006-2010 5-year est.); Ancestry (includes multiple ancestries): 49.8% German, 18.0% Irish, 11.9% English, 10.9% Italian, 7.1% Polish (2006-2010 5-year est.).

Economy: Single-family building permits issued: 2 (2011); Multi-family building permits issued: 0 (2011); Employment by occupation: 8.2% management, 3.5% professional, 12.2% services, 12.6% sales, 6.4% farming, 16.3% construction, 10.2% production (2006-2010 5-year est.).

Income: Per capita income: $20,592 (2006-2010 5-year est.); Median household income: $42,601 (2006-2010 5-year est.); Average household income: $51,514 (2006-2010 5-year est.); Percent of households with income of $100,000 or more: 11.7% (2006-2010 5-year est.); Poverty rate: 12.4% (2006-2010 5-year est.).

Education: Percent of population age 25 and over with: High school diploma (including GED) or higher: 88.9% (2006-2010 5-year est.); Bachelor's degree or higher: 16.2% (2006-2010 5-year est.); Master's degree or higher: 6.5% (2006-2010 5-year est.).

Housing: Homeownership rate: 85.5% (2010); Median home value: $130,900 (2006-2010 5-year est.); Median contract rent: $382 per month (2006-2010 5-year est.); Median year structure built: 1978 (2006-2010 5-year est.).

Transportation: Commute to work: 96.2% car, 0.0% public transportation, 0.0% walk, 3.8% work from home (2006-2010 5-year est.); Travel time to work: 29.5% less than 15 minutes, 24.9% 15 to 30 minutes, 25.6% 30 to 45 minutes, 8.9% 45 to 60 minutes, 11.2% 60 minutes or more (2006-2010 5-year est.)

Additional Information Contacts

Mountain Laurel Chamber of Commerce . . . . (724) 593-8900
    http://mountainlaurelchamber.com/index.php

EAST HUNTINGDON (township). Covers a land area of 32.955 square miles and a water area of 0.007 square miles. Located at 40.14° N. Lat; 79.60° W. Long.

Population: 7,626 (1990); 7,781 (2000); 7,963 (2010); Density: 241.6 persons per square mile (2010); Race: 97.4% White, 0.7% Black, 0.5% Asian, 0.1% American Indian/Alaska Native, 0.0% Native Hawaiian/Other Pacific Islander, 1.3% Other, 0.8% Hispanic of any race (2010); Average household size: 2.35 (2010); Median age: 45.0 (2010); Males per 100

females: 91.3 (2010); Marriage status: 22.7% never married, 58.0% now married, 9.2% widowed, 10.1% divorced (2006-2010 5-year est.); Foreign born: 1.1% (2006-2010 5-year est.); Ancestry (includes multiple ancestries): 35.5% German, 18.2% Irish, 13.7% Italian, 12.0% English, 11.0% Polish (2006-2010 5-year est.).

Economy: Single-family building permits issued: 4 (2011); Multi-family building permits issued: 10 (2011); Employment by occupation: 8.5% management, 2.4% professional, 9.8% services, 16.8% sales, 3.7% farming, 12.6% construction, 8.4% production (2006-2010 5-year est.).

Income: Per capita income: $20,408 (2006-2010 5-year est.); Median household income: $34,659 (2006-2010 5-year est.); Average household income: $44,264 (2006-2010 5-year est.); Percent of households with income of $100,000 or more: 4.8% (2006-2010 5-year est.); Poverty rate: 17.4% (2006-2010 5-year est.).

Education: Percent of population age 25 and over with: High school diploma (including GED) or higher: 87.3% (2006-2010 5-year est.); Bachelor's degree or higher: 10.7% (2006-2010 5-year est.); Master's degree or higher: 2.6% (2006-2010 5-year est.).

Housing: Homeownership rate: 78.9% (2010); Median home value: $101,300 (2006-2010 5-year est.); Median contract rent: $349 per month (2006-2010 5-year est.); Median year structure built: 1972 (2006-2010 5-year est.).

Transportation: Commute to work: 94.2% car, 0.0% public transportation, 1.0% walk, 4.1% work from home (2006-2010 5-year est.); Travel time to work: 30.1% less than 15 minutes, 36.9% 15 to 30 minutes, 15.4% 30 to 45 minutes, 6.9% 45 to 60 minutes, 10.7% 60 minutes or more (2006-2010 5-year est.)

Additional Information Contacts

East Huntingdon Township . . . . (724) 887-6141
Laurel Highlands Chamber of Commerce . . . . (724) 547-7521
  http://www.laurelhighlandschamber.com

EAST VANDERGRIFT (borough). Covers a land area of 0.126 square miles and a water area of 0.019 square miles. Located at 40.60° N. Lat; 79.56° W. Long. Elevation is 801 feet.

Population: 787 (1990); 742 (2000); 674 (2010); Density: 5,342.7 persons per square mile (2010); Race: 95.3% White, 1.9% Black, 0.6% Asian, 0.1% American Indian/Alaska Native, 0.0% Native Hawaiian/Other Pacific Islander, 2.1% Other, 1.0% Hispanic of any race (2010); Average household size: 2.16 (2010); Median age: 44.0 (2010); Males per 100 females: 91.5 (2010); Marriage status: 24.8% never married, 58.3% now married, 10.9% widowed, 6.0% divorced (2006-2010 5-year est.); Foreign born: 0.3% (2006-2010 5-year est.); Ancestry (includes multiple ancestries): 32.2% German, 18.8% Polish, 18.6% Irish, 13.0% Italian, 7.4% Slovak (2006-2010 5-year est.).

Economy: Single-family building permits issued: 0 (2011); Multi-family building permits issued: 0 (2011); Employment by occupation: 6.8% management, 2.7% professional, 11.4% services, 19.8% sales, 1.5% farming, 12.9% construction, 17.9% production (2006-2010 5-year est.).

Income: Per capita income: $17,120 (2006-2010 5-year est.); Median household income: $33,542 (2006-2010 5-year est.); Average household income: $40,252 (2006-2010 5-year est.); Percent of households with income of $100,000 or more: 2.2% (2006-2010 5-year est.); Poverty rate: 13.8% (2006-2010 5-year est.).

Education: Percent of population age 25 and over with: High school diploma (including GED) or higher: 89.7% (2006-2010 5-year est.); Bachelor's degree or higher: 10.5% (2006-2010 5-year est.); Master's degree or higher: 2.7% (2006-2010 5-year est.).

Housing: Homeownership rate: 73.4% (2010); Median home value: $59,200 (2006-2010 5-year est.); Median contract rent: $460 per month (2006-2010 5-year est.); Median year structure built: before 1940 (2006-2010 5-year est.).

Transportation: Commute to work: 93.2% car, 0.0% public transportation, 1.5% walk, 0.0% work from home (2006-2010 5-year est.); Travel time to work: 38.4% less than 15 minutes, 22.4% 15 to 30 minutes, 25.1% 30 to 45 minutes, 8.0% 45 to 60 minutes, 6.1% 60 minutes or more (2006-2010 5-year est.)

EXPORT (borough). Covers a land area of 0.403 square miles and a water area of 0 square miles. Located at 40.42° N. Lat; 79.62° W. Long. Elevation is 997 feet.

History: Incorporated 1911.

Population: 853 (1990); 895 (2000); 917 (2010); Density: 2,273.2 persons per square mile (2010); Race: 98.3% White, 0.7% Black, 0.5% Asian, 0.0% American Indian/Alaska Native, 0.0% Native Hawaiian/Other Pacific

Islander, 0.5% Other, 0.0% Hispanic of any race (2010); Average household size: 2.07 (2010); Median age: 39.4 (2010); Males per 100 females: 107.0 (2010); Marriage status: 37.2% never married, 45.0% now married, 7.8% widowed, 10.0% divorced (2006-2010 5-year est.); Foreign born: 2.0% (2006-2010 5-year est.); Ancestry (includes multiple ancestries): 32.3% German, 26.6% Italian, 14.5% Irish, 9.7% Polish, 7.3% English (2006-2010 5-year est.).

Economy: Single-family building permits issued: 0 (2011); Multi-family building permits issued: 0 (2011); Employment by occupation: 5.2% management, 0.0% professional, 18.1% services, 24.9% sales, 1.2% farming, 13.4% construction, 11.5% production (2006-2010 5-year est.).

Income: Per capita income: $17,343 (2006-2010 5-year est.); Median household income: $25,694 (2006-2010 5-year est.); Average household income: $35,781 (2006-2010 5-year est.); Percent of households with income of $100,000 or more: 1.6% (2006-2010 5-year est.); Poverty rate: 19.9% (2006-2010 5-year est.).

Education: Percent of population age 25 and over with: High school diploma (including GED) or higher: 86.4% (2006-2010 5-year est.); Bachelor's degree or higher: 9.0% (2006-2010 5-year est.); Master's degree or higher: 2.3% (2006-2010 5-year est.).

School District(s)

Kiski Area SD (KG-12)
  2010-11 Enrollment: 3,967 . . . . (724) 845-2022

Housing: Homeownership rate: 50.4% (2010); Median home value: $91,300 (2006-2010 5-year est.); Median contract rent: $477 per month (2006-2010 5-year est.); Median year structure built: before 1940 (2006-2010 5-year est.).

Transportation: Commute to work: 91.0% car, 1.2% public transportation, 5.8% walk, 1.9% work from home (2006-2010 5-year est.); Travel time to work: 62.3% less than 15 minutes, 19.4% 15 to 30 minutes, 9.2% 30 to 45 minutes, 4.5% 45 to 60 minutes, 4.7% 60 minutes or more (2006-2010 5-year est.)

FAIRFIELD (township). Covers a land area of 61.375 square miles and a water area of 0.217 square miles. Located at 40.33° N. Lat; 79.14° W. Long.

Population: 2,276 (1990); 2,536 (2000); 2,424 (2010); Density: 39.5 persons per square mile (2010); Race: 98.1% White, 0.7% Black, 0.1% Asian, 0.1% American Indian/Alaska Native, 0.3% Native Hawaiian/Other Pacific Islander, 0.7% Other, 1.2% Hispanic of any race (2010); Average household size: 2.46 (2010); Median age: 44.6 (2010); Males per 100 females: 103.2 (2010); Marriage status: 22.2% never married, 58.2% now married, 8.1% widowed, 11.6% divorced (2006-2010 5-year est.); Foreign born: 0.6% (2006-2010 5-year est.); Ancestry (includes multiple ancestries): 42.5% German, 17.8% Irish, 10.8% American, 9.9% Polish, 8.2% English (2006-2010 5-year est.).

Economy: Employment by occupation: 12.8% management, 1.3% professional, 8.6% services, 16.0% sales, 4.4% farming, 14.9% construction, 7.1% production (2006-2010 5-year est.).

Income: Per capita income: $20,075 (2006-2010 5-year est.); Median household income: $43,919 (2006-2010 5-year est.); Average household income: $51,891 (2006-2010 5-year est.); Percent of households with income of $100,000 or more: 9.6% (2006-2010 5-year est.); Poverty rate: 8.2% (2006-2010 5-year est.).

Education: Percent of population age 25 and over with: High school diploma (including GED) or higher: 86.4% (2006-2010 5-year est.); Bachelor's degree or higher: 11.1% (2006-2010 5-year est.); Master's degree or higher: 3.4% (2006-2010 5-year est.).

Housing: Homeownership rate: 88.3% (2010); Median home value: $109,600 (2006-2010 5-year est.); Median contract rent: $354 per month (2006-2010 5-year est.); Median year structure built: 1971 (2006-2010 5-year est.).

Transportation: Commute to work: 94.8% car, 0.0% public transportation, 1.4% walk, 3.8% work from home (2006-2010 5-year est.); Travel time to work: 22.4% less than 15 minutes, 25.6% 15 to 30 minutes, 30.1% 30 to 45 minutes, 12.4% 45 to 60 minutes, 9.4% 60 minutes or more (2006-2010 5-year est.)

Additional Information Contacts

Westmoreland Chamber of Commerce . . . . (724) 834-2900
  http://www.westmorelandchamber.com

FELLSBURG (CDP).

Covers a land area of 1.238 square miles and a water area of 0 square miles. Located at 40.18° N. Lat; 79.83° W. Long. Elevation is 1,102 feet.

Population: n/a (1990); n/a (2000); 1,180 (2010); Density: 953.3 persons per square mile (2010); Race: 97.5% White, 0.7% Black, 0.3% Asian, 0.0% American Indian/Alaska Native, 0.0% Native Hawaiian/Other Pacific Islander, 1.5% Other, 1.7% Hispanic of any race (2010); Average household size: 2.63 (2010); Median age: 44.8 (2010); Males per 100 females: 98.0 (2010); Marriage status: 16.8% never married, 71.1% now married, 5.8% widowed, 6.4% divorced (2006-2010 5-year est.); Foreign born: 1.5% (2006-2010 5-year est.); Ancestry (includes multiple ancestries): 23.3% German, 14.3% Italian, 13.5% English, 10.8% Polish, 7.1% Irish (2006-2010 5-year est.).

Economy: Employment by occupation: 8.3% management, 0.0% professional, 9.3% services, 12.8% sales, 10.0% farming, 14.6% construction, 8.3% production (2006-2010 5-year est.).

Income: Per capita income: $22,760 (2006-2010 5-year est.); Median household income: $45,625 (2006-2010 5-year est.); Average household income: $57,764 (2006-2010 5-year est.); Percent of households with income of $100,000 or more: 14.8% (2006-2010 5-year est.); Poverty rate: 1.7% (2006-2010 5-year est.).

Education: Percent of population age 25 and over with: High school diploma (including GED) or higher: 90.7% (2006-2010 5-year est.); Bachelor's degree or higher: 18.7% (2006-2010 5-year est.); Master's degree or higher: 1.6% (2006-2010 5-year est.).

Housing: Homeownership rate: 93.3% (2010); Median home value: $99,300 (2006-2010 5-year est.); Median contract rent: n/a per month (2006-2010 5-year est.); Median year structure built: 1954 (2006-2010 5-year est.).

Transportation: Commute to work: 91.4% car, 0.0% public transportation, 2.6% walk, 5.9% work from home (2006-2010 5-year est.); Travel time to work: 29.4% less than 15 minutes, 26.8% 15 to 30 minutes, 21.7% 30 to 45 minutes, 4.2% 45 to 60 minutes, 17.9% 60 minutes or more (2006-2010 5-year est.)

FORBES ROAD (unincorporated postal area)

Zip Code: 15633

Covers a land area of 0.630 square miles and a water area of 0 square miles. Located at 40.35° N. Lat; 79.52° W. Long. Elevation is 1,093 feet. Population: 293 (2010); Density: 464.9 persons per square mile (2010); Race: 98.0% White, 1.0% Black, 0.0% Asian, 0.0% American Indian/Alaska Native, 0.3% Native Hawaiian/Other Pacific Islander, 0.7% Other, 1.0% Hispanic of any race (2010); Average household size: 2.38 (2010); Median age: 45.5 (2010); Males per 100 females: 96.6 (2010); Homeownership rate: 69.1% (2010)

GRAPEVILLE (CDP).

Covers a land area of 0.127 square miles and a water area of 0 square miles. Located at 40.33° N. Lat; 79.61° W. Long. Elevation is 1,125 feet.

Population: 745 (1990); 676 (2000); 538 (2010); Density: 4,252.6 persons per square mile (2010); Race: 98.5% White, 0.2% Black, 0.6% Asian, 0.2% American Indian/Alaska Native, 0.0% Native Hawaiian/Other Pacific Islander, 0.5% Other, 1.1% Hispanic of any race (2010); Average household size: 2.23 (2010); Median age: 41.8 (2010); Males per 100 females: 89.4 (2010); Marriage status: 26.2% never married, 58.2% now married, 3.4% widowed, 12.3% divorced (2006-2010 5-year est.); Foreign born: 0.0% (2006-2010 5-year est.); Ancestry (includes multiple ancestries): 57.6% German, 34.7% Polish, 26.1% Italian, 9.4% Irish, 8.2% American (2006-2010 5-year est.).

Economy: Employment by occupation: 27.1% management, 0.0% professional, 18.2% services, 17.7% sales, 0.0% farming, 10.5% construction, 0.0% production (2006-2010 5-year est.).

Income: Per capita income: $17,223 (2006-2010 5-year est.); Median household income: $33,523 (2006-2010 5-year est.); Average household income: $39,855 (2006-2010 5-year est.); Percent of households with income of $100,000 or more: n/a (2006-2010 5-year est.); Poverty rate: 5.9% (2006-2010 5-year est.).

Education: Percent of population age 25 and over with: High school diploma (including GED) or higher: 81.1% (2006-2010 5-year est.); Bachelor's degree or higher: 11.0% (2006-2010 5-year est.); Master's degree or higher: 4.3% (2006-2010 5-year est.).

Housing: Homeownership rate: 75.5% (2010); Median home value: $87,500 (2006-2010 5-year est.); Median contract rent: $615 per month (2006-2010 5-year est.); Median year structure built: 1958 (2006-2010 5-year est.).

Transportation: Commute to work: 93.4% car, 6.6% public transportation, 0.0% walk, 0.0% work from home (2006-2010 5-year est.); Travel time to work: 51.9% less than 15 minutes, 29.8% 15 to 30 minutes, 0.0% 30 to 45 minutes, 5.5% 45 to 60 minutes, 12.7% 60 minutes or more (2006-2010 5-year est.)

GREENSBURG (city).

County seat. Covers a land area of 4.055 square miles and a water area of 0 square miles. Located at 40.31° N. Lat; 79.54° W. Long. Elevation is 1,027 feet.

History: Greensburg is named for Nathanael Greene (1742-1786), Revolutionary War general. Its early residents were landed country squires. The advent of the railroad and the opening of coal mines transformed it into an industrial center.

Population: 16,318 (1990); 15,889 (2000); 14,892 (2010); Density: 3,672.4 persons per square mile (2010); Race: 91.3% White, 4.8% Black, 0.8% Asian, 0.2% American Indian/Alaska Native, 0.0% Native Hawaiian/Other Pacific Islander, 2.9% Other, 1.5% Hispanic of any race (2010); Average household size: 2.04 (2010); Median age: 40.2 (2010); Males per 100 females: 84.5 (2010); Marriage status: 34.2% never married, 43.4% now married, 10.4% widowed, 11.9% divorced (2006-2010 5-year est.); Foreign born: 2.3% (2006-2010 5-year est.); Ancestry (includes multiple ancestries): 34.5% German, 21.9% Irish, 20.3% Italian, 8.8% English, 6.8% Polish (2006-2010 5-year est.).

Economy: Single-family building permits issued: 1 (2011); Multi-family building permits issued: 2 (2011); Employment by occupation: 8.9% management, 4.0% professional, 12.4% services, 15.6% sales, 4.9% farming, 8.0% construction, 3.0% production (2006-2010 5-year est.).

Income: Per capita income: $25,051 (2006-2010 5-year est.); Median household income: $39,529 (2006-2010 5-year est.); Average household income: $50,643 (2006-2010 5-year est.); Percent of households with income of $100,000 or more: 12.1% (2006-2010 5-year est.); Poverty rate: 13.5% (2006-2010 5-year est.).

Education: Percent of population age 25 and over with: High school diploma (including GED) or higher: 94.8% (2006-2010 5-year est.); Bachelor's degree or higher: 33.4% (2006-2010 5-year est.); Master's degree or higher: 10.6% (2006-2010 5-year est.).

School District(s)

Greater Latrobe SD (KG-12)
  2010-11 Enrollment: 4,173 . . . . (724) 539-4200
Greensburg Salem SD (KG-12)
  2010-11 Enrollment: 2,879 . . . . (724) 832-2901
Hempfield Area SD (KG-12)
  2010-11 Enrollment: 6,236 . . . . (724) 834-2590

Four-year College(s)

Seton Hill University (Private, Not-for-profit, Roman Catholic)
  Fall 2010 Enrollment: 2,197 . . . . (724) 834-2200
  2011-12 Tuition: In-state $28,354; Out-of-state $28,354
University of Pittsburgh-Greensburg (Public)
  Fall 2010 Enrollment: 1,713 . . . . (724) 837-7040
  2011-12 Tuition: In-state $12,626; Out-of-state $22,818

Two-year College(s)

Triangle Tech Inc-Greensburg (Private, For-profit)
  Fall 2010 Enrollment: 429 . . . . (724) 832-1050
  2011-12 Tuition: In-state $15,594; Out-of-state $15,594

Vocational/Technical School(s)

Education and Technology Institute (Private, Not-for-profit)
  Fall 2010 Enrollment: 25 . . . . (724) 836-2395
  2011-12 Tuition: $5,125

Housing: Homeownership rate: 52.0% (2010); Median home value: $113,500 (2006-2010 5-year est.); Median contract rent: $451 per month (2006-2010 5-year est.); Median year structure built: 1953 (2006-2010 5-year est.).

Hospitals: Westmoreland Regional Hospital (302 beds)

Safety: Violent crime rate: 24.1 per 10,000 population; Property crime rate: 257.7 per 10,000 population (2011).

Newspapers: The Catholic Accent (Regional news; Circulation 50,000); Tribune-Review (Local news; Circulation 185,331)

Transportation: Commute to work: 86.2% car, 0.5% public transportation, 9.0% walk, 3.7% work from home (2006-2010 5-year est.); Travel time to work: 45.7% less than 15 minutes, 25.8% 15 to 30 minutes, 14.9% 30 to 45 minutes, 5.9% 45 to 60 minutes, 7.7% 60 minutes or more (2006-2010 5-year est.); Amtrak: train service available.

Additional Information Contacts

City of Greensburg . . . . (724) 838-4324
  http://www.city.greensburg.pa.us

Westmoreland Chamber of Commerce . . . . (724) 834-2900
http://www.westmorelandchamber.com

HANNASTOWN (unincorporated postal area)
Zip Code: 15635

Covers a land area of 0.301 square miles and a water area of 0.005 square miles. Located at 40.34° N. Lat; 79.50° W. Long. Population: 220 (2010); Density: 728.6 persons per square mile (2010); Race: 95.9% White, 0.9% Black, 2.7% Asian, 0.0% American Indian/Alaska Native, 0.0% Native Hawaiian/Other Pacific Islander, 0.5% Other, 0.9% Hispanic of any race (2010); Average household size: 2.34 (2010); Median age: 44.3 (2010); Males per 100 females: 111.5 (2010); Homeownership rate: 65.9% (2010)

HARRISON CITY (CDP). Covers a land area of 0.049 square miles and a water area of 0 square miles. Located at 40.35° N. Lat; 79.65° W. Long. Elevation is 978 feet.
History: Bushy Run Battlefield Historical Site to East.
Population: 199 (1990); 155 (2000); 134 (2010); Density: 2,740.5 persons per square mile (2010); Race: 99.3% White, 0.7% Black, 0.0% Asian, 0.0% American Indian/Alaska Native, 0.0% Native Hawaiian/Other Pacific Islander, 0.0% Other, 0.0% Hispanic of any race (2010); Average household size: 1.97 (2010); Median age: 47.3 (2010); Males per 100 females: 71.8 (2010); Marriage status: 54.0% never married, 18.6% now married, 0.0% widowed, 27.4% divorced (2006-2010 5-year est.); Foreign born: 0.0% (2006-2010 5-year est.); Ancestry (includes multiple ancestries): 40.7% Irish, 40.7% German, 14.2% Croatian, 13.3% Czechoslovakian, 13.3% Czech (2006-2010 5-year est.).
Economy: Employment by occupation: n/a management, n/a professional, n/a services, n/a sales, n/a farming, n/a construction, n/a production (2006-2010 5-year est.).
Income: Per capita income: $7,847 (2006-2010 5-year est.); Median household income: $22,667 (2006-2010 5-year est.); Average household income: $17,704 (2006-2010 5-year est.); Percent of households with income of $100,000 or more: n/a (2006-2010 5-year est.); Poverty rate: 67.3% (2006-2010 5-year est.).
Education: Percent of population age 25 and over with: High school diploma (including GED) or higher: 100.0% (2006-2010 5-year est.); Bachelor's degree or higher: 28.0% (2006-2010 5-year est.); Master's degree or higher: 13.3% (2006-2010 5-year est.).

School District(s)
Penn-Trafford SD (KG-12)
　2010-11 Enrollment: 4,239 . . . . (724) 744-4496
Housing: Homeownership rate: 63.2% (2010); Median home value: n/a (2006-2010 5-year est.); Median contract rent: <$101 per month (2006-2010 5-year est.); Median year structure built: 1954 (2006-2010 5-year est.).
Transportation: Commute to work: n/a car, n/a public transportation, n/a walk, n/a work from home (2006-2010 5-year est.); Travel time to work: n/a less than 15 minutes, n/a 15 to 30 minutes, n/a 30 to 45 minutes, n/a 45 to 60 minutes, n/a 60 minutes or more (2006-2010 5-year est.)

HEMPFIELD (township). Covers a land area of 76.727 square miles and a water area of 0.143 square miles. Located at 40.28° N. Lat; 79.58° W. Long.
Population: 42,694 (1990); 40,721 (2000); 43,241 (2010); Density: 563.6 persons per square mile (2010); Race: 95.5% White, 2.4% Black, 0.9% Asian, 0.1% American Indian/Alaska Native, 0.0% Native Hawaiian/Other Pacific Islander, 1.1% Other, 0.9% Hispanic of any race (2010); Average household size: 2.30 (2010); Median age: 46.2 (2010); Males per 100 females: 98.8 (2010); Marriage status: 25.1% never married, 57.8% now married, 8.0% widowed, 9.1% divorced (2006-2010 5-year est.); Foreign born: 1.6% (2006-2010 5-year est.); Ancestry (includes multiple ancestries): 37.5% German, 21.1% Italian, 16.6% Irish, 11.0% English, 10.7% Polish (2006-2010 5-year est.).
Economy: Unemployment rate: 7.0% (August 2012); Total civilian labor force: 23,752 (August 2012); Single-family building permits issued: 47 (2011); Multi-family building permits issued: 0 (2011); Employment by occupation: 11.8% management, 4.7% professional, 9.6% services, 17.2% sales, 3.9% farming, 7.5% construction, 6.0% production (2006-2010 5-year est.).
Income: Per capita income: $29,213 (2006-2010 5-year est.); Median household income: $55,416 (2006-2010 5-year est.); Average household income: $72,079 (2006-2010 5-year est.); Percent of households with

income of $100,000 or more: 21.4% (2006-2010 5-year est.); Poverty rate: 5.8% (2006-2010 5-year est.).
Education: Percent of population age 25 and over with: High school diploma (including GED) or higher: 92.8% (2006-2010 5-year est.); Bachelor's degree or higher: 28.5% (2006-2010 5-year est.); Master's degree or higher: 10.0% (2006-2010 5-year est.).
Housing: Homeownership rate: 81.4% (2010); Median home value: $148,200 (2006-2010 5-year est.); Median contract rent: $481 per month (2006-2010 5-year est.); Median year structure built: 1971 (2006-2010 5-year est.).
Transportation: Commute to work: 94.7% car, 0.7% public transportation, 1.4% walk, 3.0% work from home (2006-2010 5-year est.); Travel time to work: 36.9% less than 15 minutes, 34.7% 15 to 30 minutes, 12.0% 30 to 45 minutes, 7.5% 45 to 60 minutes, 8.9% 60 minutes or more (2006-2010 5-year est.)
Additional Information Contacts
Hempfield Township . . . . (717) 898-3100
http://www.easthempfield.org
Westmoreland Chamber of Commerce . . . . (724) 834-2900
http://www.westmorelandchamber.com

HERMINIE (CDP). Covers a land area of 0.243 square miles and a water area of 0 square miles. Located at 40.26° N. Lat; 79.71° W. Long. Elevation is 978 feet.
Population: 912 (1990); 856 (2000); 789 (2010); Density: 3,248.7 persons per square mile (2010); Race: 98.6% White, 0.6% Black, 0.3% Asian, 0.0% American Indian/Alaska Native, 0.0% Native Hawaiian/Other Pacific Islander, 0.5% Other, 1.6% Hispanic of any race (2010); Average household size: 2.39 (2010); Median age: 36.9 (2010); Males per 100 females: 91.0 (2010); Marriage status: 27.6% never married, 41.1% now married, 1.2% widowed, 30.1% divorced (2006-2010 5-year est.); Foreign born: 0.0% (2006-2010 5-year est.); Ancestry (includes multiple ancestries): 27.9% German, 21.2% Italian, 19.0% Irish, 12.6% Polish, 12.4% English (2006-2010 5-year est.).
Economy: Employment by occupation: 3.5% management, 4.9% professional, 14.5% services, 14.7% sales, 8.7% farming, 14.5% construction, 13.0% production (2006-2010 5-year est.).
Income: Per capita income: $23,276 (2006-2010 5-year est.); Median household income: $27,375 (2006-2010 5-year est.); Average household income: $48,531 (2006-2010 5-year est.); Percent of households with income of $100,000 or more: 15.1% (2006-2010 5-year est.); Poverty rate: 12.0% (2006-2010 5-year est.).
Education: Percent of population age 25 and over with: High school diploma (including GED) or higher: 91.5% (2006-2010 5-year est.); Bachelor's degree or higher: 16.8% (2006-2010 5-year est.); Master's degree or higher: 0.0% (2006-2010 5-year est.).

School District(s)
Yough SD (KG-12)
　2010-11 Enrollment: 2,323 . . . . (724) 446-7272
Housing: Homeownership rate: 51.8% (2010); Median home value: $82,800 (2006-2010 5-year est.); Median contract rent: $458 per month (2006-2010 5-year est.); Median year structure built: before 1940 (2006-2010 5-year est.).
Transportation: Commute to work: 94.2% car, 0.0% public transportation, 2.9% walk, 0.0% work from home (2006-2010 5-year est.); Travel time to work: 31.8% less than 15 minutes, 36.1% 15 to 30 minutes, 13.6% 30 to 45 minutes, 1.7% 45 to 60 minutes, 16.8% 60 minutes or more (2006-2010 5-year est.)

HOSTETTER (CDP). Covers a land area of 0.726 square miles and a water area of 0 square miles. Located at 40.26° N. Lat; 79.40° W. Long. Elevation is 1,165 feet.
Population: n/a (1990); n/a (2000); 740 (2010); Density: 1,019.0 persons per square mile (2010); Race: 97.2% White, 0.4% Black, 1.4% Asian, 0.0% American Indian/Alaska Native, 0.0% Native Hawaiian/Other Pacific Islander, 1.0% Other, 0.5% Hispanic of any race (2010); Average household size: 2.41 (2010); Median age: 42.4 (2010); Males per 100 females: 97.9 (2010); Marriage status: 22.7% never married, 56.3% now married, 9.3% widowed, 11.6% divorced (2006-2010 5-year est.); Foreign born: 0.0% (2006-2010 5-year est.); Ancestry (includes multiple ancestries): 30.6% German, 25.8% Italian, 22.5% Irish, 19.1% Hungarian, 17.6% Slovak (2006-2010 5-year est.).
Economy: Employment by occupation: 4.6% management, 12.4% professional, 18.7% services, 15.9% sales, 3.9% farming, 16.3% construction, 11.7% production (2006-2010 5-year est.).

Income: Per capita income: $22,099 (2006-2010 5-year est.); Median household income: $39,205 (2006-2010 5-year est.); Average household income: $49,116 (2006-2010 5-year est.); Percent of households with income of $100,000 or more: 7.7% (2006-2010 5-year est.); Poverty rate: 15.7% (2006-2010 5-year est.).

Education: Percent of population age 25 and over with: High school diploma (including GED) or higher: 86.2% (2006-2010 5-year est.); Bachelor's degree or higher: 8.2% (2006-2010 5-year est.); Master's degree or higher: 0.0% (2006-2010 5-year est.).

Housing: Homeownership rate: 77.6% (2010); Median home value: $103,700 (2006-2010 5-year est.); Median contract rent: $605 per month (2006-2010 5-year est.); Median year structure built: before 1940 (2006-2010 5-year est.).

Transportation: Commute to work: 95.1% car, 0.0% public transportation, 0.0% walk, 4.9% work from home (2006-2010 5-year est.); Travel time to work: 61.0% less than 15 minutes, 13.4% 15 to 30 minutes, 3.3% 30 to 45 minutes, 4.8% 45 to 60 minutes, 17.5% 60 minutes or more (2006-2010 5-year est.)

HUNKER (borough). Covers a land area of 0.253 square miles and a water area of 0 square miles. Located at 40.20° N. Lat; 79.62° W. Long. Elevation is 935 feet.

Population: 328 (1990); 329 (2000); 291 (2010); Density: 1,149.8 persons per square mile (2010); Race: 96.6% White, 0.0% Black, 0.7% Asian, 0.0% American Indian/Alaska Native, 0.0% Native Hawaiian/Other Pacific Islander, 2.7% Other, 1.0% Hispanic of any race (2010); Average household size: 2.20 (2010); Median age: 49.9 (2010); Males per 100 females: 95.3 (2010); Marriage status: 19.2% never married, 63.6% now married, 7.3% widowed, 10.0% divorced (2006-2010 5-year est.); Foreign born: 2.5% (2006-2010 5-year est.); Ancestry (includes multiple ancestries): 43.2% German, 14.2% Slovak, 10.4% Irish, 9.8% English, 8.8% French (2006-2010 5-year est.).

Economy: Single-family building permits issued: 0 (2011); Multi-family building permits issued: 0 (2011); Employment by occupation: 2.2% management, 1.7% professional, 20.6% services, 17.2% sales, 1.1% farming, 13.9% construction, 12.2% production (2006-2010 5-year est.).

Income: Per capita income: $19,659 (2006-2010 5-year est.); Median household income: $48,542 (2006-2010 5-year est.); Average household income: $48,154 (2006-2010 5-year est.); Percent of households with income of $100,000 or more: n/a (2006-2010 5-year est.); Poverty rate: 0.0% (2006-2010 5-year est.).

Education: Percent of population age 25 and over with: High school diploma (including GED) or higher: 94.8% (2006-2010 5-year est.); Bachelor's degree or higher: 15.6% (2006-2010 5-year est.); Master's degree or higher: 6.1% (2006-2010 5-year est.).

Housing: Homeownership rate: 94.7% (2010); Median home value: $99,300 (2006-2010 5-year est.); Median contract rent: n/a per month (2006-2010 5-year est.); Median year structure built: before 1940 (2006-2010 5-year est.).

Transportation: Commute to work: 96.5% car, 0.0% public transportation, 1.7% walk, 1.7% work from home (2006-2010 5-year est.); Travel time to work: 44.4% less than 15 minutes, 39.6% 15 to 30 minutes, 5.3% 30 to 45 minutes, 7.1% 45 to 60 minutes, 3.6% 60 minutes or more (2006-2010 5-year est.)

HUTCHINSON (unincorporated postal area)

Zip Code: 15640

Covers a land area of 0.722 square miles and a water area of 0 square miles. Located at 40.22° N. Lat; 79.72° W. Long. Elevation is 1,024 feet. Population: 378 (2010); Density: 523.2 persons per square mile (2010); Race: 100.0% White, 0.0% Black, 0.0% Asian, 0.0% American Indian/Alaska Native, 0.0% Native Hawaiian/Other Pacific Islander, 0.0% Other, 0.0% Hispanic of any race (2010); Average household size: 2.49 (2010); Median age: 40.4 (2010); Males per 100 females: 97.9 (2010); Homeownership rate: 87.5% (2010)

HYDE PARK (borough). Covers a land area of 0.240 square miles and a water area of 0.055 square miles. Located at 40.63° N. Lat; 79.59° W. Long. Elevation is 804 feet.

Population: 542 (1990); 513 (2000); 500 (2010); Density: 2,079.7 persons per square mile (2010); Race: 99.0% White, 0.2% Black, 0.0% Asian, 0.0% American Indian/Alaska Native, 0.0% Native Hawaiian/Other Pacific Islander, 0.8% Other, 0.6% Hispanic of any race (2010); Average household size: 2.28 (2010); Median age: 44.9 (2010); Males per 100 females: 86.6 (2010); Marriage status: 30.3% never married, 49.1% now

married, 7.3% widowed, 13.3% divorced (2006-2010 5-year est.); Foreign born: 0.0% (2006-2010 5-year est.); Ancestry (includes multiple ancestries): 53.1% German, 20.6% Italian, 17.1% Polish, 15.3% Irish, 10.7% English (2006-2010 5-year est.).

Economy: Single-family building permits issued: 0 (2011); Multi-family building permits issued: 0 (2011); Employment by occupation: 12.8% management, 1.0% professional, 10.6% services, 17.3% sales, 2.2% farming, 8.7% construction, 9.3% production (2006-2010 5-year est.).

Income: Per capita income: $24,056 (2006-2010 5-year est.); Median household income: $40,357 (2006-2010 5-year est.); Average household income: $54,936 (2006-2010 5-year est.); Percent of households with income of $100,000 or more: 10.3% (2006-2010 5-year est.); Poverty rate: 7.9% (2006-2010 5-year est.).

Education: Percent of population age 25 and over with: High school diploma (including GED) or higher: 85.6% (2006-2010 5-year est.); Bachelor's degree or higher: 8.7% (2006-2010 5-year est.); Master's degree or higher: 2.4% (2006-2010 5-year est.).

Housing: Homeownership rate: 72.6% (2010); Median home value: $83,100 (2006-2010 5-year est.); Median contract rent: $445 per month (2006-2010 5-year est.); Median year structure built: before 1940 (2006-2010 5-year est.).

Transportation: Commute to work: 99.0% car, 0.0% public transportation, 0.0% walk, 1.0% work from home (2006-2010 5-year est.); Travel time to work: 35.6% less than 15 minutes, 30.7% 15 to 30 minutes, 14.2% 30 to 45 minutes, 12.9% 45 to 60 minutes, 6.5% 60 minutes or more (2006-2010 5-year est.)

IRWIN (borough). Aka Lash. Covers a land area of 0.837 square miles and a water area of 0 square miles. Located at 40.33° N. Lat; 79.70° W. Long. Elevation is 1,001 feet.

History: Laid out 1853, incorporated 1864.

Population: 4,410 (1990); 4,366 (2000); 3,973 (2010); Density: 4,746.2 persons per square mile (2010); Race: 96.5% White, 1.2% Black, 0.9% Asian, 0.0% American Indian/Alaska Native, 0.1% Native Hawaiian/Other Pacific Islander, 1.3% Other, 1.0% Hispanic of any race (2010); Average household size: 1.96 (2010); Median age: 40.2 (2010); Males per 100 females: 87.0 (2010); Marriage status: 27.8% never married, 50.3% now married, 9.3% widowed, 12.6% divorced (2006-2010 5-year est.); Foreign born: 2.2% (2006-2010 5-year est.); Ancestry (includes multiple ancestries): 30.4% German, 28.6% Irish, 20.3% Italian, 14.2% Polish, 12.6% English (2006-2010 5-year est.).

Economy: Single-family building permits issued: 0 (2011); Multi-family building permits issued: 0 (2011); Employment by occupation: 5.4% management, 4.3% professional, 8.8% services, 22.7% sales, 5.2% farming, 5.6% construction, 4.5% production (2006-2010 5-year est.).

Income: Per capita income: $26,286 (2006-2010 5-year est.); Median household income: $40,431 (2006-2010 5-year est.); Average household income: $50,318 (2006-2010 5-year est.); Percent of households with income of $100,000 or more: 8.3% (2006-2010 5-year est.); Poverty rate: 3.5% (2006-2010 5-year est.).

Education: Percent of population age 25 and over with: High school diploma (including GED) or higher: 93.3% (2006-2010 5-year est.); Bachelor's degree or higher: 21.8% (2006-2010 5-year est.); Master's degree or higher: 5.0% (2006-2010 5-year est.).

School District(s)

Hempfield Area SD (KG-12)

   2010-11 Enrollment: 6,236 . . . . (724) 834-2590

Penn-Trafford SD (KG-12)

   2010-11 Enrollment: 4,239 . . . . (724) 744-4496

Housing: Homeownership rate: 41.2% (2010); Median home value: $125,800 (2006-2010 5-year est.); Median contract rent: $477 per month (2006-2010 5-year est.); Median year structure built: 1956 (2006-2010 5-year est.).

Transportation: Commute to work: 93.4% car, 0.5% public transportation, 4.8% walk, 0.4% work from home (2006-2010 5-year est.); Travel time to work: 32.9% less than 15 minutes, 33.9% 15 to 30 minutes, 19.6% 30 to 45 minutes, 8.1% 45 to 60 minutes, 5.4% 60 minutes or more (2006-2010 5-year est.)

Additional Information Contacts

Westmoreland Chamber of Commerce . . . . (724) 834-2900
   http://www.westmorelandchamber.com

JACOBS CREEK (unincorporated postal area)

Zip Code: 15448

Covers a land area of 0.957 square miles and a water area of 0.057 square miles. Located at 40.13° N. Lat; 79.73° W. Long. Elevation is 791 feet. Population: 192 (2010); Density: 200.5 persons per square mile (2010); Race: 93.2% White, 0.5% Black, 0.0% Asian, 0.0% American Indian/Alaska Native, 0.0% Native Hawaiian/Other Pacific Islander, 6.3% Other, 0.0% Hispanic of any race (2010); Average household size: 2.74 (2010); Median age: 37.7 (2010); Males per 100 females: 108.7 (2010); Homeownership rate: 82.9% (2010)

JEANNETTE (city). Covers a land area of 2.388 square miles and a water area of 0 square miles. Located at 40.33° N. Lat; 79.61° W. Long. Elevation is 1,027 feet.

History: Named for Jeannette McKee, wife of a settler who helped to found a glass works in the area. Glassworks date from 1889. Bushy Run Battleground historic site to North. Laid out 1888. Incorporated as a city 1937.

Population: 11,221 (1990); 10,654 (2000); 9,654 (2010); Density: 4,042.2 persons per square mile (2010); Race: 88.5% White, 6.9% Black, 0.2% Asian, 0.2% American Indian/Alaska Native, 0.0% Native Hawaiian/Other Pacific Islander, 4.2% Other, 0.9% Hispanic of any race (2010); Average household size: 2.22 (2010); Median age: 42.3 (2010); Males per 100 females: 90.6 (2010); Marriage status: 29.7% never married, 47.8% now married, 11.9% widowed, 10.7% divorced (2006-2010 5-year est.); Foreign born: 1.7% (2006-2010 5-year est.); Ancestry (includes multiple ancestries): 28.0% German, 23.0% Italian, 14.2% Irish, 10.4% Polish, 9.6% English (2006-2010 5-year est.).

Economy: Single-family building permits issued: 0 (2011); Multi-family building permits issued: 0 (2011); Employment by occupation: 8.9% management, 2.0% professional, 13.1% services, 14.9% sales, 3.9% farming, 6.6% construction, 6.0% production (2006-2010 5-year est.).

Income: Per capita income: $19,633 (2006-2010 5-year est.); Median household income: $33,083 (2006-2010 5-year est.); Average household income: $41,450 (2006-2010 5-year est.); Percent of households with income of $100,000 or more: 6.4% (2006-2010 5-year est.); Poverty rate: 18.2% (2006-2010 5-year est.).

Education: Percent of population age 25 and over with: High school diploma (including GED) or higher: 89.0% (2006-2010 5-year est.); Bachelor's degree or higher: 17.1% (2006-2010 5-year est.); Master's degree or higher: 3.0% (2006-2010 5-year est.).

School District(s)

Jeannette City SD (KG-12)

    2010-11 Enrollment: 1,178 . . . . (724) 523-5497

Penn-Trafford SD (KG-12)

    2010-11 Enrollment: 4,239 . . . . (724) 744-4496

Housing: Homeownership rate: 63.9% (2010); Median home value: $81,200 (2006-2010 5-year est.); Median contract rent: $418 per month (2006-2010 5-year est.); Median year structure built: 1946 (2006-2010 5-year est.).

Hospitals: Mercy Jeannette Hospital (149 beds)

Safety: Violent crime rate: 9.3 per 10,000 population; Property crime rate: 70.2 per 10,000 population (2011).

Transportation: Commute to work: 94.6% car, 0.7% public transportation, 2.2% walk, 1.9% work from home (2006-2010 5-year est.); Travel time to work: 39.3% less than 15 minutes, 37.3% 15 to 30 minutes, 11.8% 30 to 45 minutes, 3.7% 45 to 60 minutes, 7.9% 60 minutes or more (2006-2010 5-year est.)

Additional Information Contacts

City of Jeannette . . . . (724) 527-4000

Westmoreland Chamber of Commerce . . . . (724) 834-2900

    http://www.westmorelandchamber.com

JONES MILLS (unincorporated postal area)

Zip Code: 15646

    Covers a land area of 1.427 square miles and a water area of 0 square miles. Located at 40.08° N. Lat; 79.32° W. Long. Elevation is 1,558 feet. Population: 233 (2010); Density: 163.2 persons per square mile (2010); Race: 97.0% White, 0.0% Black, 0.9% Asian, 0.0% American Indian/Alaska Native, 0.0% Native Hawaiian/Other Pacific Islander, 2.1% Other, 4.3% Hispanic of any race (2010); Average household size: 2.45 (2010); Median age: 44.5 (2010); Males per 100 females: 92.6 (2010); Homeownership rate: 82.6% (2010)

LATROBE (city). Aka Klondike. Covers a land area of 2.316 square miles and a water area of 0 square miles. Located at 40.31° N. Lat; 79.38° W. Long. Elevation is 997 feet.

History: St. Vincent College to Southwest. Incorporated 1854.

Population: 9,265 (1990); 8,994 (2000); 8,338 (2010); Density: 3,600.9 persons per square mile (2010); Race: 97.5% White, 0.8% Black, 0.6% Asian, 0.1% American Indian/Alaska Native, 0.0% Native Hawaiian/Other Pacific Islander, 1.0% Other, 0.7% Hispanic of any race (2010); Average household size: 2.20 (2010); Median age: 43.6 (2010); Males per 100 females: 90.6 (2010); Marriage status: 30.2% never married, 44.8% now married, 11.3% widowed, 13.6% divorced (2006-2010 5-year est.); Foreign born: 1.9% (2006-2010 5-year est.); Ancestry (includes multiple ancestries): 30.0% German, 22.4% Italian, 18.1% Irish, 11.4% Polish, 9.4% English (2006-2010 5-year est.).

Economy: Single-family building permits issued: 2 (2011); Multi-family building permits issued: 0 (2011); Employment by occupation: 6.6% management, 1.8% professional, 15.1% services, 18.1% sales, 2.5% farming, 7.3% construction, 6.5% production (2006-2010 5-year est.).

Income: Per capita income: $20,229 (2006-2010 5-year est.); Median household income: $34,819 (2006-2010 5-year est.); Average household income: $44,587 (2006-2010 5-year est.); Percent of households with income of $100,000 or more: 6.9% (2006-2010 5-year est.); Poverty rate: 15.0% (2006-2010 5-year est.).

Education: Percent of population age 25 and over with: High school diploma (including GED) or higher: 89.4% (2006-2010 5-year est.); Bachelor's degree or higher: 18.6% (2006-2010 5-year est.); Master's degree or higher: 4.8% (2006-2010 5-year est.).

School District(s)

Derry Area SD (KG-12)

    2010-11 Enrollment: 2,245 . . . . (724) 694-1401

Dr Robert Ketterer CS (03-12)

    2010-11 Enrollment: 216 . . . . (724) 537-9110

Eastern Westmoreland CTC (09-12)

    2010-11 Enrollment: n/a . . . . (724) 539-9788

Greater Latrobe SD (KG-12)

    2010-11 Enrollment: 4,173 . . . . (724) 539-4200

Four-year College(s)

Saint Vincent College (Private, Not-for-profit, Roman Catholic)

    Fall 2010 Enrollment: 1,968 . . . . (724) 539-9761

    2011-12 Tuition: In-state $28,804; Out-of-state $28,804

Saint Vincent Seminary (Private, Not-for-profit, Roman Catholic)

    Fall 2010 Enrollment: 83 . . . . (724) 805-2592

Housing: Homeownership rate: 61.6% (2010); Median home value: $97,500 (2006-2010 5-year est.); Median contract rent: $428 per month (2006-2010 5-year est.); Median year structure built: 1947 (2006-2010 5-year est.).

Hospitals: Latrobe Area Hospital (221 beds)

Safety: Violent crime rate: 38.3 per 10,000 population; Property crime rate: 252.2 per 10,000 population (2011).

Newspapers: Latrobe Bulletin (Local news; Circulation 8,000)

Transportation: Commute to work: 90.3% car, 0.7% public transportation, 6.0% walk, 2.1% work from home (2006-2010 5-year est.); Travel time to work: 48.4% less than 15 minutes, 29.6% 15 to 30 minutes, 9.3% 30 to 45 minutes, 6.4% 45 to 60 minutes, 6.4% 60 minutes or more (2006-2010 5-year est.); Amtrak: train service available.

Airports: Arnold Palmer Regional (primary service)

Additional Information Contacts

City of Latrobe . . . . (724) 539-8548

    http://www.cityoflatrobe.com

Latrobe Area Chamber of Commerce . . . . (724) 537-2671

    http://www.latrobearea.com

LAUGHLINTOWN (unincorporated postal area)

Zip Code: 15655

    Covers a land area of 12.886 square miles and a water area of 0.008 square miles. Located at 40.19° N. Lat; 79.16° W. Long. Elevation is 1,286 feet. Population: 423 (2010); Density: 32.8 persons per square mile (2010); Race: 99.5% White, 0.2% Black, 0.0% Asian, 0.0% American Indian/Alaska Native, 0.0% Native Hawaiian/Other Pacific Islander, 0.3% Other, 2.4% Hispanic of any race (2010); Average household size: 2.31 (2010); Median age: 46.9 (2010); Males per 100 females: 99.5 (2010); Homeownership rate: 73.2% (2010)

LAUREL MOUNTAIN (borough). Aka Laurel Mount Boro. Covers a land area of 0.129 square miles and a water area of 0 square miles. Located at 40.21° N. Lat; 79.19° W. Long. Elevation is 1,421 feet.
Population: 195 (1990); 185 (2000); 167 (2010); Density: 1,293.9 persons per square mile (2010); Race: 99.4% White, 0.0% Black, 0.6% Asian, 0.0% American Indian/Alaska Native, 0.0% Native Hawaiian/Other Pacific Islander, 0.0% Other, 0.6% Hispanic of any race (2010); Average household size: 2.14 (2010); Median age: 51.3 (2010); Males per 100 females: 96.5 (2010); Marriage status: 15.8% never married, 66.7% now married, 0.0% widowed, 17.5% divorced (2006-2010 5-year est.); Foreign born: 6.4% (2006-2010 5-year est.); Ancestry (includes multiple ancestries): 26.5% Italian, 22.6% German, 20.5% Swiss, 20.1% Irish, 13.7% English (2006-2010 5-year est.).
Economy: Single-family building permits issued: 0 (2011); Multi-family building permits issued: 0 (2011); Employment by occupation: 29.7% management, 0.0% professional, 4.4% services, 5.5% sales, 6.6% farming, 5.5% construction, 2.2% production (2006-2010 5-year est.).
Income: Per capita income: $32,490 (2006-2010 5-year est.); Median household income: $55,357 (2006-2010 5-year est.); Average household income: $72,262 (2006-2010 5-year est.); Percent of households with income of $100,000 or more: 9.6% (2006-2010 5-year est.); Poverty rate: 2.6% (2006-2010 5-year est.).
Education: Percent of population age 25 and over with: High school diploma (including GED) or higher: 98.3% (2006-2010 5-year est.); Bachelor's degree or higher: 43.6% (2006-2010 5-year est.); Master's degree or higher: 15.1% (2006-2010 5-year est.).
Housing: Homeownership rate: 80.8% (2010); Median home value: $138,500 (2006-2010 5-year est.); Median contract rent: $604 per month (2006-2010 5-year est.); Median year structure built: 1946 (2006-2010 5-year est.).
Transportation: Commute to work: 91.2% car, 0.0% public transportation, 0.0% walk, 8.8% work from home (2006-2010 5-year est.); Travel time to work: 26.5% less than 15 minutes, 21.7% 15 to 30 minutes, 27.7% 30 to 45 minutes, 14.5% 45 to 60 minutes, 9.6% 60 minutes or more (2006-2010 5-year est.)

LAWSON HEIGHTS (CDP). Covers a land area of 1.530 square miles and a water area of 0 square miles. Located at 40.29° N. Lat; 79.39° W. Long. Elevation is 1,181 feet.
History: St. Vincent College to West.
Population: 2,509 (1990); 2,339 (2000); 2,194 (2010); Density: 1,434.4 persons per square mile (2010); Race: 98.1% White, 0.2% Black, 1.0% Asian, 0.0% American Indian/Alaska Native, 0.0% Native Hawaiian/Other Pacific Islander, 0.7% Other, 0.5% Hispanic of any race (2010); Average household size: 2.24 (2010); Median age: 48.2 (2010); Males per 100 females: 89.6 (2010); Marriage status: 20.7% never married, 59.9% now married, 13.5% widowed, 5.8% divorced (2006-2010 5-year est.); Foreign born: 1.1% (2006-2010 5-year est.); Ancestry (includes multiple ancestries): 28.4% German, 22.0% Irish, 16.3% Italian, 10.7% Polish, 10.3% Slovak (2006-2010 5-year est.).
Economy: Employment by occupation: 6.3% management, 3.5% professional, 7.5% services, 15.1% sales, 2.2% farming, 7.8% construction, 3.2% production (2006-2010 5-year est.).
Income: Per capita income: $22,914 (2006-2010 5-year est.); Median household income: $41,563 (2006-2010 5-year est.); Average household income: $52,953 (2006-2010 5-year est.); Percent of households with income of $100,000 or more: 6.9% (2006-2010 5-year est.); Poverty rate: 4.1% (2006-2010 5-year est.).
Education: Percent of population age 25 and over with: High school diploma (including GED) or higher: 89.8% (2006-2010 5-year est.); Bachelor's degree or higher: 22.4% (2006-2010 5-year est.); Master's degree or higher: 8.6% (2006-2010 5-year est.).
Housing: Homeownership rate: 76.4% (2010); Median home value: $148,200 (2006-2010 5-year est.); Median contract rent: $471 per month (2006-2010 5-year est.); Median year structure built: 1958 (2006-2010 5-year est.).
Transportation: Commute to work: 95.6% car, 0.0% public transportation, 1.1% walk, 3.3% work from home (2006-2010 5-year est.); Travel time to work: 53.1% less than 15 minutes, 29.7% 15 to 30 minutes, 12.5% 30 to 45 minutes, 4.8% 45 to 60 minutes, 0.0% 60 minutes or more (2006-2010 5-year est.)
Additional Information Contacts
Westmoreland Chamber of Commerce . . . . (724) 834-2900
   http://www.westmorelandchamber.com

LEVEL GREEN (CDP). Covers a land area of 3.801 square miles and a water area of 0 square miles. Located at 40.39° N. Lat; 79.72° W. Long. Elevation is 1,043 feet.
Population: n/a (1990); n/a (2000); 4,020 (2010); Density: 1,057.7 persons per square mile (2010); Race: 98.7% White, 0.2% Black, 0.6% Asian, 0.0% American Indian/Alaska Native, 0.0% Native Hawaiian/Other Pacific Islander, 0.5% Other, 0.6% Hispanic of any race (2010); Average household size: 2.60 (2010); Median age: 46.4 (2010); Males per 100 females: 98.9 (2010); Marriage status: 21.2% never married, 65.0% now married, 6.8% widowed, 7.0% divorced (2006-2010 5-year est.); Foreign born: 0.9% (2006-2010 5-year est.); Ancestry (includes multiple ancestries): 37.4% German, 26.1% Italian, 14.9% Irish, 9.1% Slovak, 7.9% English (2006-2010 5-year est.).
Economy: Employment by occupation: 13.5% management, 6.5% professional, 6.3% services, 20.8% sales, 2.8% farming, 14.2% construction, 7.3% production (2006-2010 5-year est.).
Income: Per capita income: $33,727 (2006-2010 5-year est.); Median household income: $66,941 (2006-2010 5-year est.); Average household income: $85,101 (2006-2010 5-year est.); Percent of households with income of $100,000 or more: 33.3% (2006-2010 5-year est.); Poverty rate: 6.7% (2006-2010 5-year est.).
Education: Percent of population age 25 and over with: High school diploma (including GED) or higher: 97.8% (2006-2010 5-year est.); Bachelor's degree or higher: 32.2% (2006-2010 5-year est.); Master's degree or higher: 13.3% (2006-2010 5-year est.).
Housing: Homeownership rate: 93.4% (2010); Median home value: $163,300 (2006-2010 5-year est.); Median contract rent: $443 per month (2006-2010 5-year est.); Median year structure built: 1959 (2006-2010 5-year est.).
Transportation: Commute to work: 95.7% car, 2.5% public transportation, 0.0% walk, 1.8% work from home (2006-2010 5-year est.); Travel time to work: 24.0% less than 15 minutes, 35.4% 15 to 30 minutes, 22.0% 30 to 45 minutes, 6.3% 45 to 60 minutes, 12.4% 60 minutes or more (2006-2010 5-year est.)

LIGONIER (borough). Covers a land area of 0.504 square miles and a water area of 0 square miles. Located at 40.24° N. Lat; 79.24° W. Long. Elevation is 1,198 feet.
Population: 1,638 (1990); 1,695 (2000); 1,573 (2010); Density: 3,120.9 persons per square mile (2010); Race: 98.9% White, 0.0% Black, 0.2% Asian, 0.0% American Indian/Alaska Native, 0.0% Native Hawaiian/Other Pacific Islander, 0.9% Other, 0.9% Hispanic of any race (2010); Average household size: 1.90 (2010); Median age: 52.9 (2010); Males per 100 females: 81.0 (2010); Marriage status: 19.5% never married, 57.3% now married, 10.0% widowed, 13.2% divorced (2006-2010 5-year est.); Foreign born: 2.0% (2006-2010 5-year est.); Ancestry (includes multiple ancestries): 34.1% German, 18.6% Irish, 13.8% English, 10.3% Italian, 7.2% Polish (2006-2010 5-year est.).
Economy: Single-family building permits issued: 0 (2011); Multi-family building permits issued: 0 (2011); Employment by occupation: 10.5% management, 1.3% professional, 14.8% services, 14.4% sales, 2.6% farming, 4.6% construction, 2.4% production (2006-2010 5-year est.).
Income: Per capita income: $25,363 (2006-2010 5-year est.); Median household income: $45,947 (2006-2010 5-year est.); Average household income: $50,648 (2006-2010 5-year est.); Percent of households with income of $100,000 or more: 8.4% (2006-2010 5-year est.); Poverty rate: 4.3% (2006-2010 5-year est.).
Taxes: Total city taxes per capita: $286 (2009); City property taxes per capita: $182 (2009).
Education: Percent of population age 25 and over with: High school diploma (including GED) or higher: 87.7% (2006-2010 5-year est.); Bachelor's degree or higher: 32.0% (2006-2010 5-year est.); Master's degree or higher: 13.8% (2006-2010 5-year est.).
School District(s)
Ligonier Valley SD (PK-12)
   2010-11 Enrollment: 1,697 . . . . (724) 238-5696
Housing: Homeownership rate: 57.4% (2010); Median home value: $148,200 (2006-2010 5-year est.); Median contract rent: $469 per month (2006-2010 5-year est.); Median year structure built: 1942 (2006-2010 5-year est.).
Safety: Violent crime rate: 12.7 per 10,000 population; Property crime rate: 114.1 per 10,000 population (2011).
Newspapers: The Ligonier Echo (Community news; Circulation 4,692)
Transportation: Commute to work: 74.6% car, 0.0% public transportation, 16.2% walk, 9.2% work from home (2006-2010 5-year est.); Travel time to

work: 43.8% less than 15 minutes, 21.5% 15 to 30 minutes, 18.3% 30 to 45 minutes, 7.4% 45 to 60 minutes, 9.0% 60 minutes or more (2006-2010 5-year est.)

Additional Information Contacts
Ligonier Valley Chamber of Commerce . . . . (724) 238-4200
  http://visitligonier.com

LIGONIER (township).
Covers a land area of 92.421 square miles and a water area of 0.299 square miles. Located at 40.23° N. Lat; 79.22° W. Long. Elevation is 1,198 feet.
History: Fort Ligonier built c.1758. Laid out 1817; incorporated 1834.
Population: 6,979 (1990); 6,973 (2000); 6,603 (2010); Density: 71.4 persons per square mile (2010); Race: 99.3% White, 0.2% Black, 0.2% Asian, 0.1% American Indian/Alaska Native, 0.0% Native Hawaiian/Other Pacific Islander, 0.2% Other, 0.6% Hispanic of any race (2010); Average household size: 2.27 (2010); Median age: 50.0 (2010); Males per 100 females: 100.2 (2010); Marriage status: 18.4% never married, 61.7% now married, 11.4% widowed, 8.4% divorced (2006-2010 5-year est.); Foreign born: 1.4% (2006-2010 5-year est.); Ancestry (includes multiple ancestries): 38.6% German, 18.2% Irish, 13.2% English, 11.2% Italian, 8.4% Polish (2006-2010 5-year est.).
Economy: Single-family building permits issued: 2 (2011); Multi-family building permits issued: 0 (2011); Employment by occupation: 9.9% management, 5.1% professional, 10.7% services, 19.4% sales, 1.8% farming, 11.8% construction, 5.5% production (2006-2010 5-year est.).
Income: Per capita income: $27,341 (2006-2010 5-year est.); Median household income: $50,044 (2006-2010 5-year est.); Average household income: $63,615 (2006-2010 5-year est.); Percent of households with income of $100,000 or more: 12.8% (2006-2010 5-year est.); Poverty rate: 6.1% (2006-2010 5-year est.).
Education: Percent of population age 25 and over with: High school diploma (including GED) or higher: 90.9% (2006-2010 5-year est.); Bachelor's degree or higher: 23.5% (2006-2010 5-year est.); Master's degree or higher: 9.3% (2006-2010 5-year est.).
Housing: Homeownership rate: 82.4% (2010); Median home value: $156,800 (2006-2010 5-year est.); Median contract rent: $436 per month (2006-2010 5-year est.); Median year structure built: 1961 (2006-2010 5-year est.).
Safety: Violent crime rate: 25.7 per 10,000 population; Property crime rate: 54.3 per 10,000 population (2011).
Newspapers: The Ligonier Echo (Community news; Circulation 4,692)
Transportation: Commute to work: 91.9% car, 0.0% public transportation, 1.8% walk, 5.3% work from home (2006-2010 5-year est.); Travel time to work: 32.6% less than 15 minutes, 32.0% 15 to 30 minutes, 19.8% 30 to 45 minutes, 5.2% 45 to 60 minutes, 10.4% 60 minutes or more (2006-2010 5-year est.)
Additional Information Contacts
Ligonier Township . . . . (724) 238-2725
  http://www.ligoniertwp.com
Ligonier Valley Chamber of Commerce . . . . (724) 238-4200
  http://visitligonier.com

LOWBER (unincorporated postal area)
Zip Code: 15660
  Covers a land area of 0.521 square miles and a water area of 0 square miles. Located at 40.24° N. Lat; 79.77° W. Long. Elevation is 781 feet. Population: 323 (2010); Density: 618.8 persons per square mile (2010); Race: 99.7% White, 0.0% Black, 0.0% Asian, 0.0% American Indian/Alaska Native, 0.0% Native Hawaiian/Other Pacific Islander, 0.3% Other, 0.0% Hispanic of any race (2010); Average household size: 2.38 (2010); Median age: 46.9 (2010); Males per 100 females: 87.8 (2010); Homeownership rate: 86.7% (2010)

LOWER BURRELL (city).
Covers a land area of 11.264 square miles and a water area of 0.256 square miles. Located at 40.58° N. Lat; 79.71° W. Long. Elevation is 751 feet.
History: City's steel-based economy declined in the 1970s and 1980s. Incorporated 1959.
Population: 12,251 (1990); 12,608 (2000); 11,761 (2010); Density: 1,044.1 persons per square mile (2010); Race: 97.3% White, 1.1% Black, 0.4% Asian, 0.1% American Indian/Alaska Native, 0.0% Native Hawaiian/Other Pacific Islander, 1.1% Other, 0.5% Hispanic of any race (2010); Average household size: 2.29 (2010); Median age: 47.1 (2010); Males per 100 females: 91.8 (2010); Marriage status: 25.2% never married, 56.9% now married, 9.0% widowed, 8.9% divorced (2006-2010

5-year est.); Foreign born: 2.0% (2006-2010 5-year est.); Ancestry (includes multiple ancestries): 31.7% German, 23.0% Italian, 18.9% Polish, 17.7% Irish, 10.5% English (2006-2010 5-year est.).
Economy: Single-family building permits issued: 0 (2011); Multi-family building permits issued: 0 (2011); Employment by occupation: 9.5% management, 6.6% professional, 10.5% services, 22.8% sales, 3.1% farming, 8.5% construction, 5.5% production (2006-2010 5-year est.).
Income: Per capita income: $24,059 (2006-2010 5-year est.); Median household income: $47,073 (2006-2010 5-year est.); Average household income: $56,227 (2006-2010 5-year est.); Percent of households with income of $100,000 or more: 10.8% (2006-2010 5-year est.); Poverty rate: 13.6% (2006-2010 5-year est.).
Education: Percent of population age 25 and over with: High school diploma (including GED) or higher: 91.7% (2006-2010 5-year est.); Bachelor's degree or higher: 21.3% (2006-2010 5-year est.); Master's degree or higher: 6.7% (2006-2010 5-year est.).

School District(s)
Burrell SD (KG-12)
  2010-11 Enrollment: 1,893 . . . . (724) 334-1406

Two-year College(s)
Newport Business Institute-Lower Burrell (Private, For-profit)
  Fall 2010 Enrollment: 133 . . . . (724) 339-0455
  2011-12 Tuition: In-state $11,775; Out-of-state $11,775
Oakbridge Academy of Arts (Private, For-profit)
  Fall 2010 Enrollment: 34 . . . . (724) 335-5336
  2011-12 Tuition: In-state $11,475; Out-of-state $11,475
Housing: Homeownership rate: 79.3% (2010); Median home value: $124,900 (2006-2010 5-year est.); Median contract rent: $538 per month (2006-2010 5-year est.); Median year structure built: 1961 (2006-2010 5-year est.).
Safety: Violent crime rate: 5.1 per 10,000 population; Property crime rate: 150.0 per 10,000 population (2011).
Transportation: Commute to work: 93.9% car, 2.1% public transportation, 1.1% walk, 2.3% work from home (2006-2010 5-year est.); Travel time to work: 27.3% less than 15 minutes, 35.9% 15 to 30 minutes, 15.3% 30 to 45 minutes, 9.9% 45 to 60 minutes, 11.6% 60 minutes or more (2006-2010 5-year est.)
Additional Information Contacts
City of Lower Burrell . . . . (724) 335-9875
  http://www.cityoflowerburrell.com
Strongland Chamber of Commerce. . . . . (724) 845-5426
  http://www.strongland.org

LOYALHANNA (CDP).
Covers a land area of 2.355 square miles and a water area of 0 square miles. Located at 40.31° N. Lat; 79.36° W. Long. Elevation is 994 feet.
Population: n/a (1990); n/a (2000); 3,428 (2010); Density: 1,455.8 persons per square mile (2010); Race: 98.5% White, 0.6% Black, 0.1% Asian, 0.1% American Indian/Alaska Native, 0.0% Native Hawaiian/Other Pacific Islander, 0.7% Other, 0.3% Hispanic of any race (2010); Average household size: 2.11 (2010); Median age: 49.5 (2010); Males per 100 females: 90.6 (2010); Marriage status: 22.5% never married, 60.3% now married, 9.9% widowed, 7.3% divorced (2006-2010 5-year est.); Foreign born: 0.6% (2006-2010 5-year est.); Ancestry (includes multiple ancestries): 36.8% German, 20.4% Italian, 17.1% Irish, 15.7% Slovak, 8.3% Polish (2006-2010 5-year est.).
Economy: Employment by occupation: 8.3% management, 3.7% professional, 14.5% services, 15.2% sales, 3.7% farming, 7.6% construction, 4.8% production (2006-2010 5-year est.).
Income: Per capita income: $23,636 (2006-2010 5-year est.); Median household income: $42,455 (2006-2010 5-year est.); Average household income: $49,636 (2006-2010 5-year est.); Percent of households with income of $100,000 or more: 9.2% (2006-2010 5-year est.); Poverty rate: 7.6% (2006-2010 5-year est.).
Education: Percent of population age 25 and over with: High school diploma (including GED) or higher: 91.6% (2006-2010 5-year est.); Bachelor's degree or higher: 15.6% (2006-2010 5-year est.); Master's degree or higher: 4.6% (2006-2010 5-year est.).
Housing: Homeownership rate: 78.0% (2010); Median home value: $99,000 (2006-2010 5-year est.); Median contract rent: $502 per month (2006-2010 5-year est.); Median year structure built: 1960 (2006-2010 5-year est.).
Transportation: Commute to work: 95.5% car, 0.0% public transportation, 0.0% walk, 3.8% work from home (2006-2010 5-year est.); Travel time to work: 53.8% less than 15 minutes, 17.7% 15 to 30 minutes, 14.6% 30 to

45 minutes, 4.6% 45 to 60 minutes, 9.3% 60 minutes or more (2006-2010 5-year est.)

LOYALHANNA (township). Covers a land area of 21.566 square miles and a water area of 0.773 square miles. Located at 40.46° N. Lat; 79.44° W. Long. Elevation is 994 feet.

Population: 2,171 (1990); 2,301 (2000); 2,382 (2010); Density: 110.5 persons per square mile (2010); Race: 96.1% White, 1.4% Black, 0.8% Asian, 0.0% American Indian/Alaska Native, 0.0% Native Hawaiian/Other Pacific Islander, 1.7% Other, 1.0% Hispanic of any race (2010); Average household size: 2.48 (2010); Median age: 41.5 (2010); Males per 100 females: 122.2 (2010); Marriage status: 27.5% never married, 60.2% now married, 6.1% widowed, 6.3% divorced (2006-2010 5-year est.); Foreign born: 0.3% (2006-2010 5-year est.); Ancestry (includes multiple ancestries): 37.6% German, 22.1% Italian, 20.3% Irish, 16.2% English, 8.3% Polish (2006-2010 5-year est.).

Economy: Single-family building permits issued: 1 (2011); Multi-family building permits issued: 0 (2011); Employment by occupation: 14.2% management, 7.8% professional, 9.3% services, 12.7% sales, 5.6% farming, 14.5% construction, 9.4% production (2006-2010 5-year est.).

Income: Per capita income: $22,001 (2006-2010 5-year est.); Median household income: $45,313 (2006-2010 5-year est.); Average household income: $54,424 (2006-2010 5-year est.); Percent of households with income of $100,000 or more: 16.1% (2006-2010 5-year est.); Poverty rate: 12.3% (2006-2010 5-year est.).

Education: Percent of population age 25 and over with: High school diploma (including GED) or higher: 90.6% (2006-2010 5-year est.); Bachelor's degree or higher: 16.4% (2006-2010 5-year est.); Master's degree or higher: 1.5% (2006-2010 5-year est.).

Housing: Homeownership rate: 82.0% (2010); Median home value: $105,400 (2006-2010 5-year est.); Median contract rent: $503 per month (2006-2010 5-year est.); Median year structure built: 1960 (2006-2010 5-year est.).

Transportation: Commute to work: 95.9% car, 0.0% public transportation, 0.8% walk, 3.3% work from home (2006-2010 5-year est.); Travel time to work: 12.5% less than 15 minutes, 36.3% 15 to 30 minutes, 29.2% 30 to 45 minutes, 10.2% 45 to 60 minutes, 11.8% 60 minutes or more (2006-2010 5-year est.)

Additional Information Contacts

Latrobe Area Chamber of Commerce . . . . (724) 537-2671
http://www.latrobearea.com

LUXOR (unincorporated postal area)

Zip Code: 15662

Covers a land area of 0.164 square miles and a water area of 0 square miles. Located at 40.33° N. Lat; 79.47° W. Long. Elevation is 1,106 feet. Population: 271 (2010); Density: 1,651.6 persons per square mile (2010); Race: 97.0% White, 1.1% Black, 1.5% Asian, 0.0% American Indian/Alaska Native, 0.0% Native Hawaiian/Other Pacific Islander, 0.4% Other, 0.4% Hispanic of any race (2010); Average household size: 2.24 (2010); Median age: 39.5 (2010); Males per 100 females: 102.2 (2010); Homeownership rate: 67.0% (2010)

LYNNWOOD-PRICEDALE (CDP). Covers a land area of 1.240 square miles and a water area of 0.037 square miles. Located at 40.13° N. Lat; 79.85° W. Long.

Population: 2,664 (1990); 2,168 (2000); 2,031 (2010); Density: 1,638.0 persons per square mile (2010); Race: 96.3% White, 2.0% Black, 0.6% Asian, 0.0% American Indian/Alaska Native, 0.0% Native Hawaiian/Other Pacific Islander, 1.1% Other, 0.5% Hispanic of any race (2010); Average household size: 2.14 (2010); Median age: 48.4 (2010); Males per 100 females: 89.6 (2010); Marriage status: 28.1% never married, 52.9% now married, 6.6% widowed, 12.4% divorced (2006-2010 5-year est.); Foreign born: 8.4% (2006-2010 5-year est.); Ancestry (includes multiple ancestries): 15.1% German, 14.5% Italian, 11.9% Polish, 11.8% English, 9.0% Slovak (2006-2010 5-year est.).

Economy: Employment by occupation: 5.3% management, 1.2% professional, 10.5% services, 21.6% sales, 2.5% farming, 7.3% construction, 6.4% production (2006-2010 5-year est.).

Income: Per capita income: $19,350 (2006-2010 5-year est.); Median household income: $37,555 (2006-2010 5-year est.); Average household income: $44,810 (2006-2010 5-year est.); Percent of households with income of $100,000 or more: 2.9% (2006-2010 5-year est.); Poverty rate: 10.8% (2006-2010 5-year est.).

Education: Percent of population age 25 and over with: High school diploma (including GED) or higher: 86.9% (2006-2010 5-year est.); Bachelor's degree or higher: 16.7% (2006-2010 5-year est.); Master's degree or higher: 4.2% (2006-2010 5-year est.).

Housing: Homeownership rate: 76.5% (2010); Median home value: $90,900 (2006-2010 5-year est.); Median contract rent: $504 per month (2006-2010 5-year est.); Median year structure built: 1952 (2006-2010 5-year est.).

Transportation: Commute to work: 99.3% car, 0.0% public transportation, 0.0% walk, 0.7% work from home (2006-2010 5-year est.); Travel time to work: 42.7% less than 15 minutes, 25.3% 15 to 30 minutes, 16.0% 30 to 45 minutes, 4.3% 45 to 60 minutes, 11.8% 60 minutes or more (2006-2010 5-year est.)

Additional Information Contacts

Monessen Chamber of Commerce . . . . (724) 684-3200
http://www.monessenchamberofcommerce.com

MADISON (borough). Covers a land area of 0.436 square miles and a water area of 0 square miles. Located at 40.25° N. Lat; 79.67° W. Long. Elevation is 1,132 feet.

Population: 539 (1990); 510 (2000); 397 (2010); Density: 909.6 persons per square mile (2010); Race: 99.5% White, 0.3% Black, 0.0% Asian, 0.0% American Indian/Alaska Native, 0.0% Native Hawaiian/Other Pacific Islander, 0.2% Other, 0.5% Hispanic of any race (2010); Average household size: 2.18 (2010); Median age: 52.1 (2010); Males per 100 females: 86.4 (2010); Marriage status: 26.7% never married, 58.0% now married, 11.5% widowed, 3.7% divorced (2006-2010 5-year est.); Foreign born: 0.8% (2006-2010 5-year est.); Ancestry (includes multiple ancestries): 38.9% German, 18.5% Irish, 18.2% Italian, 13.7% English, 12.6% Pennsylvania German (2006-2010 5-year est.).

Economy: Single-family building permits issued: 0 (2011); Multi-family building permits issued: 0 (2011); Employment by occupation: 0.0% management, 9.1% professional, 11.6% services, 13.1% sales, 12.6% farming, 7.6% construction, 6.1% production (2006-2010 5-year est.).

Income: Per capita income: $25,173 (2006-2010 5-year est.); Median household income: $39,432 (2006-2010 5-year est.); Average household income: $49,359 (2006-2010 5-year est.); Percent of households with income of $100,000 or more: 4.8% (2006-2010 5-year est.); Poverty rate: 8.8% (2006-2010 5-year est.).

Education: Percent of population age 25 and over with: High school diploma (including GED) or higher: 93.7% (2006-2010 5-year est.); Bachelor's degree or higher: 19.4% (2006-2010 5-year est.); Master's degree or higher: 4.2% (2006-2010 5-year est.).

Housing: Homeownership rate: 79.7% (2010); Median home value: $95,300 (2006-2010 5-year est.); Median contract rent: $392 per month (2006-2010 5-year est.); Median year structure built: before 1940 (2006-2010 5-year est.).

Transportation: Commute to work: 98.5% car, 0.0% public transportation, 0.0% walk, 1.5% work from home (2006-2010 5-year est.); Travel time to work: 36.9% less than 15 minutes, 42.1% 15 to 30 minutes, 13.8% 30 to 45 minutes, 7.2% 45 to 60 minutes, 0.0% 60 minutes or more (2006-2010 5-year est.)

MAMMOTH (CDP). Covers a land area of 2.022 square miles and a water area of 0 square miles. Located at 40.20° N. Lat; 79.46° W. Long. Elevation is 1,106 feet.

Population: n/a (1990); n/a (2000); 525 (2010); Density: 259.7 persons per square mile (2010); Race: 99.2% White, 0.0% Black, 0.0% Asian, 0.0% American Indian/Alaska Native, 0.2% Native Hawaiian/Other Pacific Islander, 0.6% Other, 0.0% Hispanic of any race (2010); Average household size: 2.39 (2010); Median age: 47.4 (2010); Males per 100 females: 88.8 (2010); Marriage status: 38.2% never married, 53.4% now married, 6.7% widowed, 1.7% divorced (2006-2010 5-year est.); Foreign born: 0.0% (2006-2010 5-year est.); Ancestry (includes multiple ancestries): 40.6% Slovak, 37.6% Irish, 16.5% German, 14.4% Italian, 8.0% English (2006-2010 5-year est.).

Economy: Employment by occupation: 15.2% management, 0.0% professional, 2.2% services, 16.0% sales, 0.0% farming, 6.6% construction, 7.7% production (2006-2010 5-year est.).

Income: Per capita income: $26,463 (2006-2010 5-year est.); Median household income: $63,875 (2006-2010 5-year est.); Average household income: $63,826 (2006-2010 5-year est.); Percent of households with income of $100,000 or more: 8.5% (2006-2010 5-year est.); Poverty rate: 1.7% (2006-2010 5-year est.).

Education: Percent of population age 25 and over with: High school diploma (including GED) or higher: 96.3% (2006-2010 5-year est.); Bachelor's degree or higher: 19.5% (2006-2010 5-year est.); Master's degree or higher: 8.5% (2006-2010 5-year est.).
Housing: Homeownership rate: 84.1% (2010); Median home value: $148,600 (2006-2010 5-year est.); Median contract rent: n/a per month (2006-2010 5-year est.); Median year structure built: 1956 (2006-2010 5-year est.).
Transportation: Commute to work: 93.1% car, 0.0% public transportation, 0.0% walk, 6.9% work from home (2006-2010 5-year est.); Travel time to work: 17.8% less than 15 minutes, 62.0% 15 to 30 minutes, 5.0% 30 to 45 minutes, 15.1% 45 to 60 minutes, 0.0% 60 minutes or more (2006-2010 5-year est.)

MANOR (borough). Covers a land area of 1.913 square miles and a water area of 0 square miles. Located at 40.35° N. Lat; 79.67° W. Long. Elevation is 951 feet.
History: Laid out 1873, incorporated 1890.
Population: 2,627 (1990); 2,796 (2000); 3,239 (2010); Density: 1,693.5 persons per square mile (2010); Race: 98.2% White, 0.3% Black, 0.8% Asian, 0.0% American Indian/Alaska Native, 0.0% Native Hawaiian/Other Pacific Islander, 0.7% Other, 0.7% Hispanic of any race (2010); Average household size: 2.61 (2010); Median age: 40.5 (2010); Males per 100 females: 93.4 (2010); Marriage status: 18.3% never married, 68.4% now married, 4.8% widowed, 8.4% divorced (2006-2010 5-year est.); Foreign born: 0.6% (2006-2010 5-year est.); Ancestry (includes multiple ancestries): 38.7% German, 21.2% Irish, 17.2% Italian, 14.5% Polish, 10.8% English (2006-2010 5-year est.).
Economy: Single-family building permits issued: 14 (2011); Multi-family building permits issued: 0 (2011); Employment by occupation: 12.5% management, 6.1% professional, 10.1% services, 20.0% sales, 0.5% farming, 7.5% construction, 5.0% production (2006-2010 5-year est.).
Income: Per capita income: $26,561 (2006-2010 5-year est.); Median household income: $64,792 (2006-2010 5-year est.); Average household income: $72,466 (2006-2010 5-year est.); Percent of households with income of $100,000 or more: 22.5% (2006-2010 5-year est.); Poverty rate: 4.1% (2006-2010 5-year est.).
Education: Percent of population age 25 and over with: High school diploma (including GED) or higher: 96.5% (2006-2010 5-year est.); Bachelor's degree or higher: 33.6% (2006-2010 5-year est.); Master's degree or higher: 12.0% (2006-2010 5-year est.).
Housing: Homeownership rate: 85.8% (2010); Median home value: $145,300 (2006-2010 5-year est.); Median contract rent: $624 per month (2006-2010 5-year est.); Median year structure built: 1974 (2006-2010 5-year est.).
Safety: Violent crime rate: 9.2 per 10,000 population; Property crime rate: 40.0 per 10,000 population (2011).
Transportation: Commute to work: 93.4% car, 2.0% public transportation, 1.2% walk, 2.5% work from home (2006-2010 5-year est.); Travel time to work: 18.0% less than 15 minutes, 35.8% 15 to 30 minutes, 23.4% 30 to 45 minutes, 8.5% 45 to 60 minutes, 14.3% 60 minutes or more (2006-2010 5-year est.)
Additional Information Contacts
Westmoreland Chamber of Commerce . . . . (724) 834-2900
  http://www.westmorelandchamber.com

MILLWOOD (CDP). Covers a land area of 0.620 square miles and a water area of 0 square miles. Located at 40.35° N. Lat; 79.29° W. Long. Elevation is 1,191 feet.
Population: n/a (1990); n/a (2000); 566 (2010); Density: 913.2 persons per square mile (2010); Race: 98.1% White, 1.1% Black, 0.4% Asian, 0.0% American Indian/Alaska Native, 0.0% Native Hawaiian/Other Pacific Islander, 0.4% Other, 1.2% Hispanic of any race (2010); Average household size: 2.31 (2010); Median age: 44.4 (2010); Males per 100 females: 102.9 (2010); Marriage status: 31.9% never married, 41.1% now married, 13.2% widowed, 13.8% divorced (2006-2010 5-year est.); Foreign born: 0.0% (2006-2010 5-year est.); Ancestry (includes multiple ancestries): 39.0% German, 36.4% Italian, 15.5% Irish, 10.5% American, 7.3% Hungarian (2006-2010 5-year est.).
Economy: Employment by occupation: 0.0% management, 0.0% professional, 22.2% services, 17.2% sales, 9.1% farming, 9.1% construction, 0.0% production (2006-2010 5-year est.).
Income: Per capita income: $16,580 (2006-2010 5-year est.); Median household income: $17,955 (2006-2010 5-year est.); Average household income: $32,309 (2006-2010 5-year est.); Percent of households with

income of $100,000 or more: 6.7% (2006-2010 5-year est.); Poverty rate: 28.0% (2006-2010 5-year est.).
Education: Percent of population age 25 and over with: High school diploma (including GED) or higher: 96.1% (2006-2010 5-year est.); Bachelor's degree or higher: 7.2% (2006-2010 5-year est.); Master's degree or higher: 2.6% (2006-2010 5-year est.).
Housing: Homeownership rate: 82.8% (2010); Median home value: $60,800 (2006-2010 5-year est.); Median contract rent: $425 per month (2006-2010 5-year est.); Median year structure built: 1973 (2006-2010 5-year est.).
Transportation: Commute to work: 100.0% car, 0.0% public transportation, 0.0% walk, 0.0% work from home (2006-2010 5-year est.); Travel time to work: 25.0% less than 15 minutes, 44.3% 15 to 30 minutes, 8.0% 30 to 45 minutes, 0.0% 45 to 60 minutes, 22.7% 60 minutes or more (2006-2010 5-year est.)

MONESSEN (city). Covers a land area of 2.887 square miles and a water area of 0.137 square miles. Located at 40.15° N. Lat; 79.88° W. Long. Elevation is 1,129 feet.
History: Monessen's steel mill was closed as a result of the industry's decline. Founded 1898, incorporated 1921.
Population: 9,901 (1990); 8,669 (2000); 7,720 (2010); Density: 2,674.0 persons per square mile (2010); Race: 80.6% White, 14.9% Black, 0.3% Asian, 0.1% American Indian/Alaska Native, 0.0% Native Hawaiian/Other Pacific Islander, 4.1% Other, 1.8% Hispanic of any race (2010); Average household size: 2.17 (2010); Median age: 46.0 (2010); Males per 100 females: 86.2 (2010); Marriage status: 30.3% never married, 43.3% now married, 13.3% widowed, 13.1% divorced (2006-2010 5-year est.); Foreign born: 2.9% (2006-2010 5-year est.); Ancestry (includes multiple ancestries): 26.9% Italian, 12.4% German, 8.4% Irish, 7.9% Slovak, 7.1% English (2006-2010 5-year est.).
Economy: Single-family building permits issued: 0 (2011); Multi-family building permits issued: 0 (2011); Employment by occupation: 6.4% management, 4.8% professional, 13.7% services, 18.4% sales, 5.9% farming, 4.8% construction, 9.6% production (2006-2010 5-year est.).
Income: Per capita income: $19,816 (2006-2010 5-year est.); Median household income: $28,270 (2006-2010 5-year est.); Average household income: $41,257 (2006-2010 5-year est.); Percent of households with income of $100,000 or more: 5.8% (2006-2010 5-year est.); Poverty rate: 17.6% (2006-2010 5-year est.).
Education: Percent of population age 25 and over with: High school diploma (including GED) or higher: 86.2% (2006-2010 5-year est.); Bachelor's degree or higher: 15.0% (2006-2010 5-year est.); Master's degree or higher: 4.1% (2006-2010 5-year est.).

School District(s)
Monessen City SD (KG-12)
  2010-11 Enrollment: 913 . . . . (724) 684-3600
Two-year College(s)
Douglas Education Center (Private, For-profit)
  Fall 2010 Enrollment: 579 . . . . (724) 684-3684
  2011-12 Tuition: In-state $19,114; Out-of-state $19,114
Housing: Homeownership rate: 71.0% (2010); Median home value: $74,500 (2006-2010 5-year est.); Median contract rent: $392 per month (2006-2010 5-year est.); Median year structure built: 1951 (2006-2010 5-year est.).
Safety: Violent crime rate: 83.9 per 10,000 population; Property crime rate: 346.0 per 10,000 population (2011).
Newspapers: Valley Independent (Regional news)
Transportation: Commute to work: 94.9% car, 0.4% public transportation, 1.8% walk, 2.0% work from home (2006-2010 5-year est.); Travel time to work: 41.3% less than 15 minutes, 24.4% 15 to 30 minutes, 17.9% 30 to 45 minutes, 10.5% 45 to 60 minutes, 5.9% 60 minutes or more (2006-2010 5-year est.)
Additional Information Contacts
City of Monessen . . . . (724) 684-9715
Monessen Chamber of Commerce . . . . (724) 684-3200
  http://www.monessenchamberofcommerce.com

MOUNT PLEASANT (borough). Aka Moline. Covers a land area of 1.001 square miles and a water area of 0 square miles. Located at 40.15° N. Lat; 79.54° W. Long. Elevation is 1,161 feet.
Population: 4,706 (1990); 4,728 (2000); 4,454 (2010); Density: 4,449.0 persons per square mile (2010); Race: 97.1% White, 1.7% Black, 0.1% Asian, 0.1% American Indian/Alaska Native, 0.0% Native Hawaiian/Other Pacific Islander, 1.0% Other, 0.7% Hispanic of any race (2010); Average

household size: 2.11 (2010); Median age: 46.3 (2010); Males per 100 females: 87.9 (2010); Marriage status: 24.0% never married, 51.4% now married, 9.6% widowed, 15.1% divorced (2006-2010 5-year est.); Foreign born: 0.6% (2006-2010 5-year est.); Ancestry (includes multiple ancestries): 25.5% German, 18.0% Italian, 17.3% Polish, 12.1% Irish, 11.5% English (2006-2010 5-year est.).

Economy: Single-family building permits issued: 0 (2011); Multi-family building permits issued: 0 (2011); Employment by occupation: 1.8% management, 6.4% professional, 16.1% services, 17.9% sales, 3.2% farming, 9.9% construction, 4.7% production (2006-2010 5-year est.).

Income: Per capita income: $21,482 (2006-2010 5-year est.); Median household income: $34,432 (2006-2010 5-year est.); Average household income: $45,544 (2006-2010 5-year est.); Percent of households with income of $100,000 or more: 8.0% (2006-2010 5-year est.); Poverty rate: 16.7% (2006-2010 5-year est.).

Education: Percent of population age 25 and over with: High school diploma (including GED) or higher: 86.1% (2006-2010 5-year est.); Bachelor's degree or higher: 18.6% (2006-2010 5-year est.); Master's degree or higher: 5.8% (2006-2010 5-year est.).

School District(s)

Mount Pleasant Area SD (KG-12)

   2010-11 Enrollment: 2,166 . . . . (724) 547-4100

Housing: Homeownership rate: 61.7% (2010); Median home value: $107,600 (2006-2010 5-year est.); Median contract rent: $392 per month (2006-2010 5-year est.); Median year structure built: 1945 (2006-2010 5-year est.).

Hospitals: Frick Hospital (102 beds)

Safety: Violent crime rate: 4.5 per 10,000 population; Property crime rate: 158.9 per 10,000 population (2011).

Newspapers: Mount Pleasant Journal (Community news; Circulation 5,893)

Transportation: Commute to work: 95.2% car, 0.0% public transportation, 3.5% walk, 0.9% work from home (2006-2010 5-year est.); Travel time to work: 35.8% less than 15 minutes, 24.2% 15 to 30 minutes, 16.8% 30 to 45 minutes, 9.6% 45 to 60 minutes, 13.7% 60 minutes or more (2006-2010 5-year est.)

Additional Information Contacts

Westmoreland Chamber of Commerce . . . . (724) 834-2900

   http://www.westmorelandchamber.com

MOUNT PLEASANT (township). Aka Moline. Covers a land area of 55.944 square miles and a water area of 0.145 square miles. Located at 40.18° N. Lat; 79.47° W. Long.

History: Laid out c.1897, incorporated 1828.

Population: 11,544 (1990); 11,153 (2000); 10,911 (2010); Density: 195.0 persons per square mile (2010); Race: 98.5% White, 0.3% Black, 0.2% Asian, 0.1% American Indian/Alaska Native, 0.0% Native Hawaiian/Other Pacific Islander, 0.9% Other, 0.5% Hispanic of any race (2010); Average household size: 2.39 (2010); Median age: 45.8 (2010); Males per 100 females: 95.5 (2010); Marriage status: 25.4% never married, 56.5% now married, 8.0% widowed, 10.1% divorced (2006-2010 5-year est.); Foreign born: 0.5% (2006-2010 5-year est.); Ancestry (includes multiple ancestries): 32.6% German, 16.3% Polish, 16.0% Irish, 12.7% Italian, 11.5% Slovak (2006-2010 5-year est.).

Economy: Single-family building permits issued: 0 (2011); Multi-family building permits issued: 0 (2011); Employment by occupation: 8.1% management, 2.9% professional, 13.1% services, 15.1% sales, 4.3% farming, 12.3% construction, 6.6% production (2006-2010 5-year est.).

Income: Per capita income: $23,282 (2006-2010 5-year est.); Median household income: $49,777 (2006-2010 5-year est.); Average household income: $56,649 (2006-2010 5-year est.); Percent of households with income of $100,000 or more: 12.8% (2006-2010 5-year est.); Poverty rate: 9.1% (2006-2010 5-year est.).

Education: Percent of population age 25 and over with: High school diploma (including GED) or higher: 89.9% (2006-2010 5-year est.); Bachelor's degree or higher: 13.4% (2006-2010 5-year est.); Master's degree or higher: 4.8% (2006-2010 5-year est.).

Housing: Homeownership rate: 82.5% (2010); Median home value: $119,800 (2006-2010 5-year est.); Median contract rent: $430 per month (2006-2010 5-year est.); Median year structure built: 1957 (2006-2010 5-year est.).

Hospitals: Frick Hospital (102 beds)

Newspapers: Mount Pleasant Journal (Community news; Circulation 5,893)

Transportation: Commute to work: 95.4% car, 0.0% public transportation, 0.7% walk, 3.3% work from home (2006-2010 5-year est.); Travel time to work: 23.4% less than 15 minutes, 46.5% 15 to 30 minutes, 17.1% 30 to 45 minutes, 6.5% 45 to 60 minutes, 6.4% 60 minutes or more (2006-2010 5-year est.)

Additional Information Contacts

Mount Pleasant Township . . . . (724) 356-7974

   http://www.mpt-pa.com

Westmoreland Chamber of Commerce . . . . (724) 834-2900

   http://www.westmorelandchamber.com

MURRYSVILLE (municipality). Covers a land area of 36.837 square miles and a water area of 0.007 square miles. Located at 40.44° N. Lat; 79.65° W. Long. Elevation is 899 feet.

History: Originally settled in 1788 as Franklin Township, Since 1933, Murrysville has had a "tree sign" spelling out the word "Murrysville". The trees were landscaped to grow and form the letters by local Boy Scouts. The sign is situated on a large hill as one enters the borough from the Murrysville/Monroeville border, near U.S. Route 22.

Population: 17,368 (1990); 18,872 (2000); 20,079 (2010); Density: 545.1 persons per square mile (2010); Race: 93.7% White, 0.8% Black, 4.4% Asian, 0.1% American Indian/Alaska Native, 0.0% Native Hawaiian/Other Pacific Islander, 1.0% Other, 1.0% Hispanic of any race (2010); Average household size: 2.51 (2010); Median age: 47.4 (2010); Males per 100 females: 96.5 (2010); Marriage status: 21.2% never married, 66.7% now married, 5.5% widowed, 6.6% divorced (2006-2010 5-year est.); Foreign born: 5.6% (2006-2010 5-year est.); Ancestry (includes multiple ancestries): 34.8% German, 22.0% Italian, 18.5% Irish, 14.7% English, 7.9% Polish (2006-2010 5-year est.).

Economy: Single-family building permits issued: 56 (2011); Multi-family building permits issued: 0 (2011); Employment by occupation: 18.3% management, 7.6% professional, 4.9% services, 14.8% sales, 1.7% farming, 6.0% construction, 4.4% production (2006-2010 5-year est.).

Income: Per capita income: $41,817 (2006-2010 5-year est.); Median household income: $81,883 (2006-2010 5-year est.); Average household income: $104,408 (2006-2010 5-year est.); Percent of households with income of $100,000 or more: 38.1% (2006-2010 5-year est.); Poverty rate: 2.4% (2006-2010 5-year est.).

Education: Percent of population age 25 and over with: High school diploma (including GED) or higher: 96.3% (2006-2010 5-year est.); Bachelor's degree or higher: 49.0% (2006-2010 5-year est.); Master's degree or higher: 19.4% (2006-2010 5-year est.).

School District(s)

Franklin Regional SD (KG-12)

   2010-11 Enrollment: 3,749 . . . . (724) 327-5456

Housing: Homeownership rate: 89.0% (2010); Median home value: $207,700 (2006-2010 5-year est.); Median contract rent: $609 per month (2006-2010 5-year est.); Median year structure built: 1973 (2006-2010 5-year est.).

Safety: Violent crime rate: 3.0 per 10,000 population; Property crime rate: 46.7 per 10,000 population (2011).

Newspapers: The Delmont-Salem News (Community news; Circulation 628); The Marketplace (Community news; Circulation 14,000); The Penn-Franklin News (Local news; Circulation 6,178); The Penn-Trafford News (Local news; Circulation 1,450)

Transportation: Commute to work: 91.3% car, 1.7% public transportation, 0.5% walk, 6.1% work from home (2006-2010 5-year est.); Travel time to work: 24.4% less than 15 minutes, 28.7% 15 to 30 minutes, 22.7% 30 to 45 minutes, 14.7% 45 to 60 minutes, 9.6% 60 minutes or more (2006-2010 5-year est.)

Additional Information Contacts

Municipality of Murrysville . . . . (724) 327-2100

   http://www.murrysville.com

Norwin Chamber of Commerce . . . . (724) 863-0888

   http://www.norwinchamber.com/index.php

NEW ALEXANDRIA (borough). Covers a land area of 0.847 square miles and a water area of 0 square miles. Located at 40.39° N. Lat; 79.42° W. Long. Elevation is 1,024 feet.

Population: 571 (1990); 595 (2000); 560 (2010); Density: 661.1 persons per square mile (2010); Race: 96.1% White, 0.9% Black, 1.6% Asian, 0.0% American Indian/Alaska Native, 0.0% Native Hawaiian/Other Pacific Islander, 1.4% Other, 0.0% Hispanic of any race (2010); Average household size: 2.25 (2010); Median age: 49.5 (2010); Males per 100 females: 100.0 (2010); Marriage status: 22.8% never married, 68.1% now

married, 6.2% widowed, 2.9% divorced (2006-2010 5-year est.); Foreign born: 0.0% (2006-2010 5-year est.); Ancestry (includes multiple ancestries): 42.6% German, 18.2% Irish, 12.3% English, 9.8% Polish, 9.8% Slovak (2006-2010 5-year est.).

Economy: Single-family building permits issued: 1 (2011); Multi-family building permits issued: 0 (2011); Employment by occupation: 6.8% management, 3.4% professional, 14.7% services, 13.2% sales, 3.0% farming, 10.2% construction, 10.2% production (2006-2010 5-year est.).

Income: Per capita income: $23,724 (2006-2010 5-year est.); Median household income: $46,875 (2006-2010 5-year est.); Average household income: $53,377 (2006-2010 5-year est.); Percent of households with income of $100,000 or more: 12.4% (2006-2010 5-year est.); Poverty rate: 1.7% (2006-2010 5-year est.).

Education: Percent of population age 25 and over with: High school diploma (including GED) or higher: 90.7% (2006-2010 5-year est.); Bachelor's degree or higher: 19.2% (2006-2010 5-year est.); Master's degree or higher: 8.6% (2006-2010 5-year est.).

School District(s)

Greensburg Salem SD (KG-12)

   2010-11 Enrollment: 2,879 . . . . (724) 832-2901

Housing: Homeownership rate: 79.1% (2010); Median home value: $123,300 (2006-2010 5-year est.); Median contract rent: $515 per month (2006-2010 5-year est.); Median year structure built: 1951 (2006-2010 5-year est.).

Transportation: Commute to work: 89.8% car, 0.0% public transportation, 5.7% walk, 4.5% work from home (2006-2010 5-year est.); Travel time to work: 26.9% less than 15 minutes, 39.1% 15 to 30 minutes, 20.2% 30 to 45 minutes, 3.6% 45 to 60 minutes, 10.3% 60 minutes or more (2006-2010 5-year est.)

NEW DERRY (unincorporated postal area)

Zip Code: 15671

Covers a land area of 3.192 square miles and a water area of 0 square miles. Located at 40.35° N. Lat; 79.32° W. Long. Elevation is 1,280 feet. Population: 865 (2010); Density: 270.9 persons per square mile (2010); Race: 98.8% White, 0.2% Black, 0.0% Asian, 0.0% American Indian/Alaska Native, 0.0% Native Hawaiian/Other Pacific Islander, 1.0% Other, 0.5% Hispanic of any race (2010); Average household size: 2.46 (2010); Median age: 44.1 (2010); Males per 100 females: 103.1 (2010); Homeownership rate: 85.7% (2010)

NEW FLORENCE (borough). Covers a land area of 0.328 square miles and a water area of 0 square miles. Located at 40.38° N. Lat; 79.08° W. Long. Elevation is 1,079 feet.

Population: 854 (1990); 784 (2000); 689 (2010); Density: 2,102.8 persons per square mile (2010); Race: 98.1% White, 0.4% Black, 0.0% Asian, 0.1% American Indian/Alaska Native, 0.0% Native Hawaiian/Other Pacific Islander, 1.4% Other, 1.5% Hispanic of any race (2010); Average household size: 2.28 (2010); Median age: 45.5 (2010); Males per 100 females: 94.1 (2010); Marriage status: 22.4% never married, 55.2% now married, 14.2% widowed, 8.2% divorced (2006-2010 5-year est.); Foreign born: 0.0% (2006-2010 5-year est.); Ancestry (includes multiple ancestries): 49.5% German, 36.3% Irish, 7.0% English, 5.3% American, 4.8% Italian (2006-2010 5-year est.).

Economy: Single-family building permits issued: 0 (2011); Multi-family building permits issued: 0 (2011); Employment by occupation: 6.6% management, 3.3% professional, 5.0% services, 10.3% sales, 2.9% farming, 16.1% construction, 5.8% production (2006-2010 5-year est.).

Income: Per capita income: $21,165 (2006-2010 5-year est.); Median household income: $32,500 (2006-2010 5-year est.); Average household income: $46,837 (2006-2010 5-year est.); Percent of households with income of $100,000 or more: 11.9% (2006-2010 5-year est.); Poverty rate: 8.3% (2006-2010 5-year est.).

Education: Percent of population age 25 and over with: High school diploma (including GED) or higher: 86.6% (2006-2010 5-year est.); Bachelor's degree or higher: 15.0% (2006-2010 5-year est.); Master's degree or higher: 4.5% (2006-2010 5-year est.).

School District(s)

Ligonier Valley SD (PK-12)

   2010-11 Enrollment: 1,697 . . . . (724) 238-5696

Housing: Homeownership rate: 69.5% (2010); Median home value: $94,000 (2006-2010 5-year est.); Median contract rent: $416 per month (2006-2010 5-year est.); Median year structure built: 1947 (2006-2010 5-year est.).

Transportation: Commute to work: 96.1% car, 0.0% public transportation, 0.0% walk, 3.9% work from home (2006-2010 5-year est.); Travel time to work: 27.0% less than 15 minutes, 28.8% 15 to 30 minutes, 29.3% 30 to 45 minutes, 2.7% 45 to 60 minutes, 12.2% 60 minutes or more (2006-2010 5-year est.)

NEW KENSINGTON (city). Covers a land area of 3.949 square miles and a water area of 0.258 square miles. Located at 40.57° N. Lat; 79.75° W. Long. Elevation is 784 feet.

History: Named for the London district of Kensington. Pennsylvania State University New Kensington campus. Laid out 1891 on the site of Fort Crawford (1778). Incorporated as a city 1933.

Population: 15,894 (1990); 14,701 (2000); 13,116 (2010); Density: 3,321.2 persons per square mile (2010); Race: 84.1% White, 10.6% Black, 0.5% Asian, 0.2% American Indian/Alaska Native, 0.0% Native Hawaiian/Other Pacific Islander, 4.6% Other, 1.5% Hispanic of any race (2010); Average household size: 2.19 (2010); Median age: 45.3 (2010); Males per 100 females: 88.3 (2010); Marriage status: 29.9% never married, 48.6% now married, 10.4% widowed, 11.1% divorced (2006-2010 5-year est.); Foreign born: 1.5% (2006-2010 5-year est.); Ancestry (includes multiple ancestries): 28.2% German, 18.6% Irish, 18.2% Italian, 16.2% Polish, 7.3% English (2006-2010 5-year est.).

Economy: Single-family building permits issued: 0 (2011); Multi-family building permits issued: 0 (2011); Employment by occupation: 10.0% management, 3.9% professional, 11.5% services, 16.6% sales, 5.9% farming, 7.3% construction, 7.7% production (2006-2010 5-year est.).

Income: Per capita income: $22,948 (2006-2010 5-year est.); Median household income: $36,652 (2006-2010 5-year est.); Average household income: $49,680 (2006-2010 5-year est.); Percent of households with income of $100,000 or more: 8.7% (2006-2010 5-year est.); Poverty rate: 18.4% (2006-2010 5-year est.).

Education: Percent of population age 25 and over with: High school diploma (including GED) or higher: 88.5% (2006-2010 5-year est.); Bachelor's degree or higher: 16.7% (2006-2010 5-year est.); Master's degree or higher: 5.8% (2006-2010 5-year est.).

School District(s)

New Kensington-Arnold SD (PK-12)

   2010-11 Enrollment: 2,138 . . . . (724) 335-8581

Northern Westmoreland CTC (10-12)

   2010-11 Enrollment: n/a . . . . (724) 335-9389

Two-year College(s)

Career Training Academy-New Kensington (Private, For-profit)

   Fall 2010 Enrollment: 75 . . . . (724) 337-1000

Citizens School of Nursing (Private, Not-for-profit)

   Fall 2010 Enrollment: 177 . . . . (724) 337-5090

Housing: Homeownership rate: 61.1% (2010); Median home value: $90,200 (2006-2010 5-year est.); Median contract rent: $398 per month (2006-2010 5-year est.); Median year structure built: 1949 (2006-2010 5-year est.).

Safety: Violent crime rate: 33.4 per 10,000 population; Property crime rate: 351.9 per 10,000 population (2011).

Transportation: Commute to work: 92.6% car, 1.2% public transportation, 4.1% walk, 1.6% work from home (2006-2010 5-year est.); Travel time to work: 32.7% less than 15 minutes, 32.2% 15 to 30 minutes, 16.8% 30 to 45 minutes, 11.0% 45 to 60 minutes, 7.3% 60 minutes or more (2006-2010 5-year est.)

Additional Information Contacts

City of New Kensington . . . . (724) 337-4525

   http://www.newkensington.org

New Kensington Area Chamber of Commerce . . . . (724) 339-6616

   http://www.nkchamber.org

NEW STANTON (borough). Covers a land area of 4.006 square miles and a water area of 0.024 square miles. Located at 40.22° N. Lat; 79.61° W. Long. Elevation is 974 feet.

Population: 2,081 (1990); 1,906 (2000); 2,173 (2010); Density: 542.4 persons per square mile (2010); Race: 95.8% White, 2.0% Black, 0.9% Asian, 0.0% American Indian/Alaska Native, 0.0% Native Hawaiian/Other Pacific Islander, 1.3% Other, 1.8% Hispanic of any race (2010); Average household size: 2.24 (2010); Median age: 41.0 (2010); Males per 100 females: 101.2 (2010); Marriage status: 24.4% never married, 57.7% now married, 5.6% widowed, 12.4% divorced (2006-2010 5-year est.); Foreign born: 1.8% (2006-2010 5-year est.); Ancestry (includes multiple ancestries): 32.8% German, 21.6% Italian, 14.1% Irish, 13.3% Polish, 10.9% English (2006-2010 5-year est.).

Economy: Single-family building permits issued: 1 (2011); Multi-family building permits issued: 0 (2011); Employment by occupation: 12.8% management, 7.2% professional, 10.8% services, 21.7% sales, 4.3% farming, 7.8% construction, 6.2% production (2006-2010 5-year est.).

Income: Per capita income: $23,138 (2006-2010 5-year est.); Median household income: $39,263 (2006-2010 5-year est.); Average household income: $49,187 (2006-2010 5-year est.); Percent of households with income of $100,000 or more: 12.9% (2006-2010 5-year est.); Poverty rate: 19.7% (2006-2010 5-year est.).

Education: Percent of population age 25 and over with: High school diploma (including GED) or higher: 92.7% (2006-2010 5-year est.); Bachelor's degree or higher: 24.4% (2006-2010 5-year est.); Master's degree or higher: 6.9% (2006-2010 5-year est.).

School District(s)

Central Westmoreland CTC (09-12)

　　2010-11 Enrollment: n/a . . . . (724) 925-3532

Hempfield Area SD (KG-12)

　　2010-11 Enrollment: 6,236 . . . . (724) 834-2590

Housing: Homeownership rate: 55.8% (2010); Median home value: $161,200 (2006-2010 5-year est.); Median contract rent: $490 per month (2006-2010 5-year est.); Median year structure built: 1975 (2006-2010 5-year est.).

Transportation: Commute to work: 95.4% car, 0.0% public transportation, 2.1% walk, 2.5% work from home (2006-2010 5-year est.); Travel time to work: 21.2% less than 15 minutes, 48.3% 15 to 30 minutes, 12.9% 30 to 45 minutes, 7.6% 45 to 60 minutes, 10.0% 60 minutes or more (2006-2010 5-year est.)

Additional Information Contacts

Greater Connellsville Chamber of Commerce. . . . . (724) 628-5500
　　http://www.greaterconnellsville.org

NORTH BELLE VERNON (borough). Covers a land area of 0.423 square miles and a water area of 0 square miles. Located at 40.13° N. Lat; 79.86° W. Long. Elevation is 922 feet.

Population: 2,112 (1990); 2,107 (2000); 1,971 (2010); Density: 4,659.7 persons per square mile (2010); Race: 94.7% White, 2.6% Black, 0.8% Asian, 0.1% American Indian/Alaska Native, 0.0% Native Hawaiian/Other Pacific Islander, 1.8% Other, 1.4% Hispanic of any race (2010); Average household size: 2.26 (2010); Median age: 43.2 (2010); Males per 100 females: 81.5 (2010); Marriage status: 28.1% never married, 49.5% now married, 11.8% widowed, 10.6% divorced (2006-2010 5-year est.); Foreign born: 1.6% (2006-2010 5-year est.); Ancestry (includes multiple ancestries): 30.7% Italian, 18.6% German, 16.2% Polish, 15.0% Irish, 11.0% English (2006-2010 5-year est.).

Economy: Single-family building permits issued: 0 (2011); Multi-family building permits issued: 0 (2011); Employment by occupation: 6.2% management, 3.7% professional, 13.4% services, 17.5% sales, 4.4% farming, 6.1% construction, 7.5% production (2006-2010 5-year est.).

Income: Per capita income: $19,824 (2006-2010 5-year est.); Median household income: $37,778 (2006-2010 5-year est.); Average household income: $48,311 (2006-2010 5-year est.); Percent of households with income of $100,000 or more: 10.8% (2006-2010 5-year est.); Poverty rate: 21.7% (2006-2010 5-year est.).

Taxes: Total city taxes per capita: $243 (2009); City property taxes per capita: $141 (2009).

Education: Percent of population age 25 and over with: High school diploma (including GED) or higher: 93.3% (2006-2010 5-year est.); Bachelor's degree or higher: 18.8% (2006-2010 5-year est.); Master's degree or higher: 6.9% (2006-2010 5-year est.).

Housing: Homeownership rate: 64.4% (2010); Median home value: $84,400 (2006-2010 5-year est.); Median contract rent: $386 per month (2006-2010 5-year est.); Median year structure built: 1944 (2006-2010 5-year est.).

Safety: Violent crime rate: 80.9 per 10,000 population; Property crime rate: 551.3 per 10,000 population (2011).

Transportation: Commute to work: 92.6% car, 0.6% public transportation, 4.7% walk, 2.1% work from home (2006-2010 5-year est.); Travel time to work: 37.3% less than 15 minutes, 23.4% 15 to 30 minutes, 22.1% 30 to 45 minutes, 5.2% 45 to 60 minutes, 12.0% 60 minutes or more (2006-2010 5-year est.)

Additional Information Contacts

Greater Rostraver Chamber of Commerce . . . . (724) 929-3329
　　http://www.greaterrostraverchamber.org

NORTH HUNTINGDON (township). Covers a land area of 27.257 square miles and a water area of 0.059 square miles. Located at 40.33° N. Lat; 79.73° W. Long.

Population: 28,325 (1990); 29,123 (2000); 30,609 (2010); Density: 1,123.0 persons per square mile (2010); Race: 97.8% White, 0.7% Black, 0.6% Asian, 0.1% American Indian/Alaska Native, 0.0% Native Hawaiian/Other Pacific Islander, 0.8% Other, 0.6% Hispanic of any race (2010); Average household size: 2.47 (2010); Median age: 44.9 (2010); Males per 100 females: 94.8 (2010); Marriage status: 21.1% never married, 65.7% now married, 7.5% widowed, 5.8% divorced (2006-2010 5-year est.); Foreign born: 1.3% (2006-2010 5-year est.); Ancestry (includes multiple ancestries): 33.7% German, 21.8% Irish, 17.6% Italian, 11.2% English, 10.9% Polish (2006-2010 5-year est.).

Economy: Unemployment rate: 6.8% (August 2012); Total civilian labor force: 17,390 (August 2012); Single-family building permits issued: 52 (2011); Multi-family building permits issued: 4 (2011); Employment by occupation: 11.8% management, 6.6% professional, 8.8% services, 16.7% sales, 3.5% farming, 9.0% construction, 6.8% production (2006-2010 5-year est.).

Income: Per capita income: $28,035 (2006-2010 5-year est.); Median household income: $64,282 (2006-2010 5-year est.); Average household income: $71,358 (2006-2010 5-year est.); Percent of households with income of $100,000 or more: 22.6% (2006-2010 5-year est.); Poverty rate: 4.2% (2006-2010 5-year est.).

Education: Percent of population age 25 and over with: High school diploma (including GED) or higher: 94.6% (2006-2010 5-year est.); Bachelor's degree or higher: 27.1% (2006-2010 5-year est.); Master's degree or higher: 9.7% (2006-2010 5-year est.).

School District(s)

Norwin SD (KG-12)

　　2010-11 Enrollment: 5,197 . . . . (724) 861-3000

Housing: Homeownership rate: 87.1% (2010); Median home value: $147,500 (2006-2010 5-year est.); Median contract rent: $510 per month (2006-2010 5-year est.); Median year structure built: 1966 (2006-2010 5-year est.).

Safety: Violent crime rate: 4.2 per 10,000 population; Property crime rate: 109.4 per 10,000 population (2011).

Transportation: Commute to work: 93.4% car, 2.4% public transportation, 0.4% walk, 3.3% work from home (2006-2010 5-year est.); Travel time to work: 25.4% less than 15 minutes, 32.4% 15 to 30 minutes, 20.4% 30 to 45 minutes, 11.4% 45 to 60 minutes, 10.4% 60 minutes or more (2006-2010 5-year est.)

Additional Information Contacts

North Huntingdon Township . . . . (724) 863-3806
　　http://www.township.north-huntingdon.pa.us
Norwin Chamber of Commerce . . . . (724) 863-0888
　　http://www.norwinchamber.com/index.php

NORTH IRWIN (borough). Covers a land area of 0.202 square miles and a water area of 0 square miles. Located at 40.34° N. Lat; 79.71° W. Long. Elevation is 958 feet.

History: Incorporated 1894.

Population: 956 (1990); 879 (2000); 846 (2010); Density: 4,183.2 persons per square mile (2010); Race: 98.8% White, 0.4% Black, 0.2% Asian, 0.0% American Indian/Alaska Native, 0.1% Native Hawaiian/Other Pacific Islander, 0.5% Other, 1.2% Hispanic of any race (2010); Average household size: 2.29 (2010); Median age: 38.7 (2010); Males per 100 females: 93.6 (2010); Marriage status: 23.3% never married, 57.3% now married, 10.2% widowed, 9.2% divorced (2006-2010 5-year est.); Foreign born: 1.5% (2006-2010 5-year est.); Ancestry (includes multiple ancestries): 30.2% German, 26.6% Italian, 25.1% Irish, 10.4% English, 9.2% Polish (2006-2010 5-year est.).

Economy: Single-family building permits issued: 0 (2011); Multi-family building permits issued: 0 (2011); Employment by occupation: 5.9% management, 4.4% professional, 11.5% services, 21.4% sales, 6.1% farming, 10.3% construction, 5.2% production (2006-2010 5-year est.).

Income: Per capita income: $22,519 (2006-2010 5-year est.); Median household income: $45,568 (2006-2010 5-year est.); Average household income: $48,545 (2006-2010 5-year est.); Percent of households with income of $100,000 or more: 6.6% (2006-2010 5-year est.); Poverty rate: 7.5% (2006-2010 5-year est.).

Education: Percent of population age 25 and over with: High school diploma (including GED) or higher: 94.7% (2006-2010 5-year est.); Bachelor's degree or higher: 10.3% (2006-2010 5-year est.); Master's degree or higher: 2.7% (2006-2010 5-year est.).

Housing: Homeownership rate: 63.2% (2010); Median home value: $92,100 (2006-2010 5-year est.); Median contract rent: $441 per month (2006-2010 5-year est.); Median year structure built: 1944 (2006-2010 5-year est.).

Transportation: Commute to work: 96.7% car, 0.0% public transportation, 2.0% walk, 1.3% work from home (2006-2010 5-year est.); Travel time to work: 27.2% less than 15 minutes, 38.1% 15 to 30 minutes, 16.8% 30 to 45 minutes, 6.6% 45 to 60 minutes, 11.4% 60 minutes or more (2006-2010 5-year est.)

NORVELT (CDP). Covers a land area of 1.792 square miles and a water area of 0 square miles. Located at 40.20° N. Lat; 79.50° W. Long. Elevation is 1,010 feet.

Population: n/a (1990); n/a (2000); 948 (2010); Density: 529.0 persons per square mile (2010); Race: 99.2% White, 0.0% Black, 0.1% Asian, 0.0% American Indian/Alaska Native, 0.0% Native Hawaiian/Other Pacific Islander, 0.7% Other, 0.2% Hispanic of any race (2010); Average household size: 2.35 (2010); Median age: 50.2 (2010); Males per 100 females: 95.5 (2010); Marriage status: 18.9% never married, 69.2% now married, 4.2% widowed, 7.7% divorced (2006-2010 5-year est.); Foreign born: 0.0% (2006-2010 5-year est.); Ancestry (includes multiple ancestries): 49.6% German, 29.2% Slovak, 19.7% Irish, 12.8% English, 11.8% Polish (2006-2010 5-year est.).

Economy: Employment by occupation: 2.5% management, 0.0% professional, 7.5% services, 8.8% sales, 10.3% farming, 10.8% construction, 7.2% production (2006-2010 5-year est.).

Income: Per capita income: $28,269 (2006-2010 5-year est.); Median household income: $56,750 (2006-2010 5-year est.); Average household income: $64,082 (2006-2010 5-year est.); Percent of households with income of $100,000 or more: 16.5% (2006-2010 5-year est.); Poverty rate: 0.0% (2006-2010 5-year est.).

Education: Percent of population age 25 and over with: High school diploma (including GED) or higher: 92.0% (2006-2010 5-year est.); Bachelor's degree or higher: 7.3% (2006-2010 5-year est.); Master's degree or higher: 4.5% (2006-2010 5-year est.).

Housing: Homeownership rate: 92.6% (2010); Median home value: $124,600 (2006-2010 5-year est.); Median contract rent: n/a per month (2006-2010 5-year est.); Median year structure built: 1948 (2006-2010 5-year est.).

Transportation: Commute to work: 100.0% car, 0.0% public transportation, 0.0% walk, 0.0% work from home (2006-2010 5-year est.); Travel time to work: 34.6% less than 15 minutes, 56.7% 15 to 30 minutes, 4.8% 30 to 45 minutes, 0.0% 45 to 60 minutes, 4.0% 60 minutes or more (2006-2010 5-year est.)

OKLAHOMA (borough). Covers a land area of 0.607 square miles and a water area of 0.034 square miles. Located at 40.58° N. Lat; 79.58° W. Long. Elevation is 955 feet.

Population: 977 (1990); 915 (2000); 809 (2010); Density: 1,333.1 persons per square mile (2010); Race: 98.3% White, 0.7% Black, 0.2% Asian, 0.0% American Indian/Alaska Native, 0.0% Native Hawaiian/Other Pacific Islander, 0.8% Other, 0.6% Hispanic of any race (2010); Average household size: 2.26 (2010); Median age: 47.9 (2010); Males per 100 females: 94.0 (2010); Marriage status: 23.3% never married, 55.1% married, 10.6% widowed, 10.9% divorced (2006-2010 5-year est.); Foreign born: 0.4% (2006-2010 5-year est.); Ancestry (includes multiple ancestries): 43.3% German, 26.0% Italian, 19.8% Irish, 13.4% Slovak, 7.5% Polish (2006-2010 5-year est.).

Economy: Single-family building permits issued: 0 (2011); Multi-family building permits issued: 0 (2011); Employment by occupation: 5.6% management, 6.4% professional, 9.7% services, 19.9% sales, 3.1% farming, 12.3% construction, 8.2% production (2006-2010 5-year est.).

Income: Per capita income: $23,910 (2006-2010 5-year est.); Median household income: $47,935 (2006-2010 5-year est.); Average household income: $56,949 (2006-2010 5-year est.); Percent of households with income of $100,000 or more: 13.7% (2006-2010 5-year est.); Poverty rate: 10.6% (2006-2010 5-year est.).

Education: Percent of population age 25 and over with: High school diploma (including GED) or higher: 85.5% (2006-2010 5-year est.); Bachelor's degree or higher: 13.3% (2006-2010 5-year est.); Master's degree or higher: 4.6% (2006-2010 5-year est.).

Housing: Homeownership rate: 77.9% (2010); Median home value: $90,700 (2006-2010 5-year est.); Median contract rent: $439 per month (2006-2010 5-year est.); Median year structure built: 1952 (2006-2010 5-year est.).

Transportation: Commute to work: 90.5% car, 0.8% public transportation, 4.8% walk, 1.6% work from home (2006-2010 5-year est.); Travel time to work: 22.8% less than 15 minutes, 26.3% 15 to 30 minutes, 28.0% 30 to 45 minutes, 11.8% 45 to 60 minutes, 11.0% 60 minutes or more (2006-2010 5-year est.)

Additional Information Contacts
Strongland Chamber of Commerce. . . . . (724) 845-5426
   http://www.strongland.org

PENN (borough). Covers a land area of 0.157 square miles and a water area of 0 square miles. Located at 40.33° N. Lat; 79.64° W. Long. Elevation is 984 feet.

Population: 511 (1990); 460 (2000); 475 (2010); Density: 3,030.5 persons per square mile (2010); Race: 95.8% White, 2.3% Black, 0.0% Asian, 0.0% American Indian/Alaska Native, 0.0% Native Hawaiian/Other Pacific Islander, 1.9% Other, 1.1% Hispanic of any race (2010); Average household size: 2.54 (2010); Median age: 39.2 (2010); Males per 100 females: 90.8 (2010); Marriage status: 26.2% never married, 65.4% now married, 3.6% widowed, 4.8% divorced (2006-2010 5-year est.); Foreign born: 0.0% (2006-2010 5-year est.); Ancestry (includes multiple ancestries): 32.7% German, 27.5% Irish, 14.6% Italian, 6.4% American, 4.7% Polish (2006-2010 5-year est.).

Economy: Single-family building permits issued: 0 (2011); Multi-family building permits issued: 0 (2011); Employment by occupation: 0.8% management, 6.2% professional, 20.3% services, 15.8% sales, 5.4% farming, 6.2% construction, 4.6% production (2006-2010 5-year est.).

Income: Per capita income: $20,042 (2006-2010 5-year est.); Median household income: $53,036 (2006-2010 5-year est.); Average household income: $56,032 (2006-2010 5-year est.); Percent of households with income of $100,000 or more: 9.4% (2006-2010 5-year est.); Poverty rate: 7.4% (2006-2010 5-year est.).

Education: Percent of population age 25 and over with: High school diploma (including GED) or higher: 92.2% (2006-2010 5-year est.); Bachelor's degree or higher: 14.9% (2006-2010 5-year est.); Master's degree or higher: 3.4% (2006-2010 5-year est.).

Housing: Homeownership rate: 71.6% (2010); Median home value: $89,200 (2006-2010 5-year est.); Median contract rent: $406 per month (2006-2010 5-year est.); Median year structure built: before 1940 (2006-2010 5-year est.).

Transportation: Commute to work: 93.3% car, 2.1% public transportation, 0.4% walk, 4.2% work from home (2006-2010 5-year est.); Travel time to work: 22.7% less than 15 minutes, 35.4% 15 to 30 minutes, 18.3% 30 to 45 minutes, 7.0% 45 to 60 minutes, 16.6% 60 minutes or more (2006-2010 5-year est.)

PENN (township). Covers a land area of 30.764 square miles and a water area of 0 square miles. Located at 40.37° N. Lat; 79.65° W. Long. Elevation is 984 feet.

History: Bushy Run Battlefield historic site to North. Laid out 1859, incorporated 1865.

Population: 16,059 (1990); 19,591 (2000); 20,005 (2010); Density: 650.3 persons per square mile (2010); Race: 98.2% White, 0.5% Black, 0.5% Asian, 0.1% American Indian/Alaska Native, 0.0% Native Hawaiian/Other Pacific Islander, 0.7% Other, 0.7% Hispanic of any race (2010); Average household size: 2.63 (2010); Median age: 44.9 (2010); Males per 100 females: 96.8 (2010); Marriage status: 22.6% never married, 64.1% now married, 6.3% widowed, 6.9% divorced (2006-2010 5-year est.); Foreign born: 1.7% (2006-2010 5-year est.); Ancestry (includes multiple ancestries): 34.7% German, 22.8% Italian, 19.7% Irish, 12.9% English, 8.9% Polish (2006-2010 5-year est.).

Economy: Single-family building permits issued: 13 (2011); Multi-family building permits issued: 0 (2011); Employment by occupation: 15.8% management, 8.3% professional, 8.5% services, 14.5% sales, 3.5% farming, 8.9% construction, 5.9% production (2006-2010 5-year est.).

Income: Per capita income: $30,345 (2006-2010 5-year est.); Median household income: $67,720 (2006-2010 5-year est.); Average household income: $80,107 (2006-2010 5-year est.); Percent of households with income of $100,000 or more: 31.0% (2006-2010 5-year est.); Poverty rate: 6.0% (2006-2010 5-year est.).

Taxes: Total city taxes per capita: $323 (2009); City property taxes per capita: $160 (2009).

Education: Percent of population age 25 and over with: High school diploma (including GED) or higher: 94.3% (2006-2010 5-year est.); Bachelor's degree or higher: 36.0% (2006-2010 5-year est.); Master's degree or higher: 12.4% (2006-2010 5-year est.).

Housing: Homeownership rate: 90.7% (2010); Median home value: $172,900 (2006-2010 5-year est.); Median contract rent: $439 per month (2006-2010 5-year est.); Median year structure built: 1975 (2006-2010 5-year est.).

Safety: Violent crime rate: 7.0 per 10,000 population; Property crime rate: 60.8 per 10,000 population (2011).

Transportation: Commute to work: 94.9% car, 1.9% public transportation, 0.1% walk, 2.8% work from home (2006-2010 5-year est.); Travel time to work: 21.5% less than 15 minutes, 35.0% 15 to 30 minutes, 19.4% 30 to 45 minutes, 9.6% 45 to 60 minutes, 14.5% 60 minutes or more (2006-2010 5-year est.)

Additional Information Contacts

Penn Township . . . . (724) 744-2171
    http://www.penntwp.org
Westmoreland Chamber of Commerce . . . . (724) 834-2900
    http://www.westmorelandchamber.com

PLEASANT UNITY (unincorporated postal area)

Zip Code: 15676

Covers a land area of 0.929 square miles and a water area of 0 square miles. Located at 40.24° N. Lat; 79.46° W. Long. Elevation is 1,086 feet. Population: 437 (2010); Density: 470.3 persons per square mile (2010); Race: 98.9% White, 0.2% Black, 0.5% Asian, 0.0% American Indian/Alaska Native, 0.2% Native Hawaiian/Other Pacific Islander, 0.2% Other, 0.0% Hispanic of any race (2010); Average household size: 2.37 (2010); Median age: 40.3 (2010); Males per 100 females: 103.3 (2010); Homeownership rate: 72.1% (2010)

PRICEDALE (unincorporated postal area)

Zip Code: 15072

Covers a land area of 0.067 square miles and a water area of 0 square miles. Located at 40.13° N. Lat; 79.85° W. Long. Population: 101 (2010); Density: 1,486.1 persons per square mile (2010); Race: 74.3% White, 22.8% Black, 0.0% Asian, 0.0% American Indian/Alaska Native, 0.0% Native Hawaiian/Other Pacific Islander, 2.9% Other, 2.0% Hispanic of any race (2010); Average household size: 2.15 (2010); Median age: 44.2 (2010); Males per 100 females: 110.4 (2010); Homeownership rate: 80.9% (2010)

RECTOR (unincorporated postal area)

Zip Code: 15677

Covers a land area of 19.646 square miles and a water area of 0 square miles. Located at 40.14° N. Lat; 79.23° W. Long. Population: 389 (2010); Density: 19.8 persons per square mile (2010); Race: 98.5% White, 0.0% Black, 0.0% Asian, 0.8% American Indian/Alaska Native, 0.0% Native Hawaiian/Other Pacific Islander, 0.7% Other, 1.5% Hispanic of any race (2010); Average household size: 2.27 (2010); Median age: 46.1 (2010); Males per 100 females: 100.5 (2010); Homeownership rate: 83.1% (2010)

RILLTON (unincorporated postal area)

Zip Code: 15678

Covers a land area of 0.573 square miles and a water area of 0 square miles. Located at 40.28° N. Lat; 79.72° W. Long. Elevation is 1,096 feet. Population: 476 (2010); Density: 830.1 persons per square mile (2010); Race: 99.2% White, 0.2% Black, 0.2% Asian, 0.0% American Indian/Alaska Native, 0.0% Native Hawaiian/Other Pacific Islander, 0.4% Other, 1.3% Hispanic of any race (2010); Average household size: 2.31 (2010); Median age: 42.6 (2010); Males per 100 females: 88.1 (2010); Homeownership rate: 70.4% (2010)

ROSTRAVER (township). Covers a land area of 32.283 square miles and a water area of 0.668 square miles. Located at 40.17° N. Lat; 79.80° W. Long.

Population: 11,224 (1990); 11,634 (2000); 11,363 (2010); Density: 352.0 persons per square mile (2010); Race: 96.0% White, 1.7% Black, 0.9% Asian, 0.1% American Indian/Alaska Native, 0.0% Native Hawaiian/Other Pacific Islander, 1.3% Other, 1.1% Hispanic of any race (2010); Average household size: 2.44 (2010); Median age: 45.3 (2010); Males per 100 females: 95.8 (2010); Marriage status: 22.7% never married, 64.0% now married, 5.3% widowed, 8.0% divorced (2006-2010 5-year est.); Foreign born: 0.6% (2006-2010 5-year est.); Ancestry (includes multiple ancestries): 21.7% Italian, 21.1% German, 13.7% Irish, 13.6% English, 13.5% Polish (2006-2010 5-year est.).

Economy: Single-family building permits issued: 16 (2011); Multi-family building permits issued: 0 (2011); Employment by occupation: 6.6% management, 4.7% professional, 7.7% services, 18.2% sales, 4.9% farming, 12.2% construction, 10.1% production (2006-2010 5-year est.).

Income: Per capita income: $25,439 (2006-2010 5-year est.); Median household income: $52,195 (2006-2010 5-year est.); Average household income: $63,860 (2006-2010 5-year est.); Percent of households with income of $100,000 or more: 18.7% (2006-2010 5-year est.); Poverty rate: 10.4% (2006-2010 5-year est.).

Education: Percent of population age 25 and over with: High school diploma (including GED) or higher: 93.5% (2006-2010 5-year est.); Bachelor's degree or higher: 24.8% (2006-2010 5-year est.); Master's degree or higher: 8.8% (2006-2010 5-year est.).

Housing: Homeownership rate: 85.1% (2010); Median home value: $135,100 (2006-2010 5-year est.); Median contract rent: $520 per month (2006-2010 5-year est.); Median year structure built: 1964 (2006-2010 5-year est.).

Safety: Violent crime rate: 11.4 per 10,000 population; Property crime rate: 343.9 per 10,000 population (2011).

Transportation: Commute to work: 94.0% car, 1.9% public transportation, 1.2% walk, 2.8% work from home (2006-2010 5-year est.); Travel time to work: 26.1% less than 15 minutes, 30.8% 15 to 30 minutes, 15.6% 30 to 45 minutes, 11.8% 45 to 60 minutes, 15.8% 60 minutes or more (2006-2010 5-year est.)

Additional Information Contacts

Greater Rostraver Chamber of Commerce . . . . (724) 929-3329
    http://www.greaterrostraverchamber.org
Rostraver Township . . . . (724) 929-8877
    http://www.rostraver.us

RUFFS DALE (unincorporated postal area)

Zip Code: 15679

Covers a land area of 23.505 square miles and a water area of 0.047 square miles. Located at 40.17° N. Lat; 79.65° W. Long. Population: 3,343 (2010); Density: 142.2 persons per square mile (2010); Race: 97.8% White, 0.7% Black, 0.1% Asian, 0.2% American Indian/Alaska Native, 0.0% Native Hawaiian/Other Pacific Islander, 1.2% Other, 0.6% Hispanic of any race (2010); Average household size: 2.40 (2010); Median age: 45.2 (2010); Males per 100 females: 102.0 (2010); Homeownership rate: 84.8% (2010)

SAINT CLAIR (township). Covers a land area of 28.138 square miles and a water area of 0.273 square miles. Located at 40.35° N. Lat; 79.03° W. Long.

Population: 1,603 (1990); 1,398 (2000); 1,518 (2010); Density: 53.9 persons per square mile (2010); Race: 98.3% White, 0.3% Black, 0.5% Asian, 0.2% American Indian/Alaska Native, 0.0% Native Hawaiian/Other Pacific Islander, 0.7% Other, 1.0% Hispanic of any race (2010); Average household size: 2.39 (2010); Median age: 44.4 (2010); Males per 100 females: 99.0 (2010); Marriage status: 19.4% never married, 64.1% now married, 8.7% widowed, 7.7% divorced (2006-2010 5-year est.); Foreign born: 0.2% (2006-2010 5-year est.); Ancestry (includes multiple ancestries): 42.0% German, 22.0% Irish, 9.5% Polish, 9.0% English, 7.5% Italian (2006-2010 5-year est.).

Economy: Single-family building permits issued: 0 (2011); Multi-family building permits issued: 0 (2011); Employment by occupation: 4.7% management, 3.8% professional, 13.4% services, 18.0% sales, 1.1% farming, 10.0% construction, 2.7% production (2006-2010 5-year est.).

Income: Per capita income: $18,353 (2006-2010 5-year est.); Median household income: $38,563 (2006-2010 5-year est.); Average household income: $45,518 (2006-2010 5-year est.); Percent of households with income of $100,000 or more: 6.3% (2006-2010 5-year est.); Poverty rate: 22.0% (2006-2010 5-year est.).

Education: Percent of population age 25 and over with: High school diploma (including GED) or higher: 86.7% (2006-2010 5-year est.); Bachelor's degree or higher: 13.0% (2006-2010 5-year est.); Master's degree or higher: 4.3% (2006-2010 5-year est.).

Housing: Homeownership rate: 80.6% (2010); Median home value: $86,800 (2006-2010 5-year est.); Median contract rent: $325 per month (2006-2010 5-year est.); Median year structure built: 1962 (2006-2010 5-year est.).

Transportation: Commute to work: 92.8% car, 0.7% public transportation, 1.3% walk, 5.2% work from home (2006-2010 5-year est.); Travel time to work: 22.0% less than 15 minutes, 34.0% 15 to 30 minutes, 27.0% 30 to

45 minutes, 11.9% 45 to 60 minutes, 5.2% 60 minutes or more (2006-2010 5-year est.)
Additional Information Contacts
Westmoreland Chamber of Commerce . . . . (724) 834-2900
http://www.westmorelandchamber.com

SAINT VINCENT COLLEGE (CDP). Covers a land area of 0.504 square miles and a water area of 0 square miles. Located at 40.29° N. Lat; 79.41° W. Long.
Population: n/a (1990); n/a (2000); 1,357 (2010); Density: 2,694.9 persons per square mile (2010); Race: 90.9% White, 5.4% Black, 1.0% Asian, 0.0% American Indian/Alaska Native, 0.0% Native Hawaiian/Other Pacific Islander, 2.7% Other, 3.0% Hispanic of any race (2010); Average household size: 0.00 (2010); Median age: 20.5 (2010); Males per 100 females: 146.3 (2010); Marriage status: 100.0% never married, 0.0% now married, 0.0% widowed, 0.0% divorced (2006-2010 5-year est.); Foreign born: 1.4% (2006-2010 5-year est.); Ancestry (includes multiple ancestries): 32.7% German, 28.7% Italian, 23.9% Irish, 15.0% Polish, 10.3% English (2006-2010 5-year est.).
Economy: Employment by occupation: 7.5% management, 8.3% professional, 12.8% services, 27.8% sales, 7.3% farming, 2.5% construction, 0.0% production (2006-2010 5-year est.).
Income: Per capita income: $4,913 (2006-2010 5-year est.); Median household income: n/a (2006-2010 5-year est.); Average household income: n/a (2006-2010 5-year est.); Percent of households with income of $100,000 or more: n/a (2006-2010 5-year est.); Poverty rate: 70.1% (2006-2010 5-year est.).
Education: Percent of population age 25 and over with: High school diploma (including GED) or higher: 100.0% (2006-2010 5-year est.); Bachelor's degree or higher: 100.0% (2006-2010 5-year est.); Master's degree or higher: 77.5% (2006-2010 5-year est.).
Housing: Homeownership rate: 0.0% (2010); Median home value: n/a (2006-2010 5-year est.); Median contract rent: n/a per month (2006-2010 5-year est.); Median year structure built: n/a (2006-2010 5-year est.).
Transportation: Commute to work: 18.3% car, 0.0% public transportation, 49.9% walk, 31.8% work from home (2006-2010 5-year est.); Travel time to work: 77.6% less than 15 minutes, 8.6% 15 to 30 minutes, 9.9% 30 to 45 minutes, 1.1% 45 to 60 minutes, 2.7% 60 minutes or more (2006-2010 5-year est.)

SALEM (township). Covers a land area of 47.093 square miles and a water area of 0.329 square miles. Located at 40.42° N. Lat; 79.52° W. Long.
Population: 7,260 (1990); 6,939 (2000); 6,623 (2010); Density: 140.6 persons per square mile (2010); Race: 97.0% White, 1.2% Black, 0.4% Asian, 0.2% American Indian/Alaska Native, 0.0% Native Hawaiian/Other Pacific Islander, 1.2% Other, 0.5% Hispanic of any race (2010); Average household size: 2.21 (2010); Median age: 49.1 (2010); Males per 100 females: 96.8 (2010); Marriage status: 19.8% never married, 59.9% now married, 9.2% widowed, 11.2% divorced (2006-2010 5-year est.); Foreign born: 2.3% (2006-2010 5-year est.); Ancestry (includes multiple ancestries): 32.2% German, 21.7% Italian, 18.5% Irish, 8.2% English, 6.8% Polish (2006-2010 5-year est.).
Economy: Single-family building permits issued: 9 (2011); Multi-family building permits issued: 3 (2011); Employment by occupation: 9.2% management, 5.2% professional, 13.1% services, 14.6% sales, 1.6% farming, 14.1% construction, 6.5% production (2006-2010 5-year est.).
Income: Per capita income: $23,790 (2006-2010 5-year est.); Median household income: $52,604 (2006-2010 5-year est.); Average household income: $55,375 (2006-2010 5-year est.); Percent of households with income of $100,000 or more: 10.3% (2006-2010 5-year est.); Poverty rate: 9.7% (2006-2010 5-year est.).
Education: Percent of population age 25 and over with: High school diploma (including GED) or higher: 86.9% (2006-2010 5-year est.); Bachelor's degree or higher: 20.6% (2006-2010 5-year est.); Master's degree or higher: 3.4% (2006-2010 5-year est.).
Housing: Homeownership rate: 82.5% (2010); Median home value: $117,800 (2006-2010 5-year est.); Median contract rent: $447 per month (2006-2010 5-year est.); Median year structure built: 1972 (2006-2010 5-year est.).
Transportation: Commute to work: 90.0% car, 0.4% public transportation, 2.2% walk, 5.1% work from home (2006-2010 5-year est.); Travel time to work: 22.7% less than 15 minutes, 46.9% 15 to 30 minutes, 17.2% 30 to 45 minutes, 7.8% 45 to 60 minutes, 5.4% 60 minutes or more (2006-2010 5-year est.)

Additional Information Contacts
Salem Township . . . . (724) 668-7500
Westmoreland Chamber of Commerce . . . . (724) 834-2900
http://www.westmorelandchamber.com

SALINA (unincorporated postal area)
Zip Code: 15680
Covers a land area of 0.011 square miles and a water area of 0 square miles. Located at 40.52° N. Lat; 79.49° W. Long. Elevation is 997 feet. Population: 101 (2010); Density: 8,510.3 persons per square mile (2010); Race: 99.0% White, 0.0% Black, 0.0% Asian, 0.0% American Indian/Alaska Native, 0.0% Native Hawaiian/Other Pacific Islander, 1.0% Other, 1.0% Hispanic of any race (2010); Average household size: 2.40 (2010); Median age: 49.8 (2010); Males per 100 females: 106.1 (2010); Homeownership rate: 85.7% (2010)

SCOTTDALE (borough). Aka Meadow Mill. Covers a land area of 1.158 square miles and a water area of 0 square miles. Located at 40.10° N. Lat; 79.59° W. Long. Elevation is 1,040 feet.
History: Laid out 1872, incorporated 1874.
Population: 5,266 (1990); 4,772 (2000); 4,384 (2010); Density: 3,786.6 persons per square mile (2010); Race: 97.7% White, 0.9% Black, 0.1% Asian, 0.1% American Indian/Alaska Native, 0.0% Native Hawaiian/Other Pacific Islander, 1.2% Other, 0.8% Hispanic of any race (2010); Average household size: 2.24 (2010); Median age: 43.8 (2010); Males per 100 females: 91.6 (2010); Marriage status: 26.8% never married, 51.2% now married, 10.4% widowed, 11.6% divorced (2006-2010 5-year est.); Foreign born: 0.0% (2006-2010 5-year est.); Ancestry (includes multiple ancestries): 44.0% German, 14.3% Irish, 13.8% Polish, 12.4% Italian, 9.8% American (2006-2010 5-year est.).
Economy: Single-family building permits issued: 1 (2011); Multi-family building permits issued: 0 (2011); Employment by occupation: 7.0% management, 3.5% professional, 15.1% services, 13.2% sales, 2.8% farming, 9.7% construction, 4.4% production (2006-2010 5-year est.).
Income: Per capita income: $23,094 (2006-2010 5-year est.); Median household income: $37,250 (2006-2010 5-year est.); Average household income: $46,878 (2006-2010 5-year est.); Percent of households with income of $100,000 or more: 10.8% (2006-2010 5-year est.); Poverty rate: 8.7% (2006-2010 5-year est.).
Education: Percent of population age 25 and over with: High school diploma (including GED) or higher: 92.6% (2006-2010 5-year est.); Bachelor's degree or higher: 15.6% (2006-2010 5-year est.); Master's degree or higher: 4.3% (2006-2010 5-year est.).
School District(s)
Southmoreland SD (KG-12)
2010-11 Enrollment: 1,961 . . . . (724) 887-2000
Housing: Homeownership rate: 67.9% (2010); Median home value: $98,000 (2006-2010 5-year est.); Median contract rent: $439 per month (2006-2010 5-year est.); Median year structure built: 1941 (2006-2010 5-year est.).
Safety: Violent crime rate: 40.9 per 10,000 population; Property crime rate: 209.2 per 10,000 population (2011).
Newspapers: Advisor (Community news; Circulation 3,393); The Independent Observer (Community news; Circulation 4,300); Jeannette Spirit (Local news; Circulation 2,100)
Transportation: Commute to work: 96.5% car, 1.2% public transportation, 0.5% walk, 1.8% work from home (2006-2010 5-year est.); Travel time to work: 37.5% less than 15 minutes, 30.3% 15 to 30 minutes, 12.7% 30 to 45 minutes, 9.3% 45 to 60 minutes, 10.2% 60 minutes or more (2006-2010 5-year est.)
Additional Information Contacts
Scottdale Area Chamber of Commerce . . . . (724) 887-3611
http://www.scottdale.com

SEWARD (borough). Covers a land area of 0.202 square miles and a water area of 0 square miles. Located at 40.41° N. Lat; 79.02° W. Long. Elevation is 1,138 feet.
Population: 522 (1990); 484 (2000); 495 (2010); Density: 2,449.4 persons per square mile (2010); Race: 98.8% White, 0.2% Black, 0.0% Asian, 0.0% American Indian/Alaska Native, 0.0% Native Hawaiian/Other Pacific Islander, 1.0% Other, 0.2% Hispanic of any race (2010); Average household size: 2.36 (2010); Median age: 44.1 (2010); Males per 100 females: 95.7 (2010); Marriage status: 14.0% never married, 64.0% now married, 12.7% widowed, 9.4% divorced (2006-2010 5-year est.); Foreign born: 0.7% (2006-2010 5-year est.); Ancestry (includes multiple

ancestries): 43.2% German, 40.1% Irish, 11.6% English, 9.9% Polish, 3.1% Scottish (2006-2010 5-year est.).
Economy: Single-family building permits issued: 0 (2011); Multi-family building permits issued: 0 (2011); Employment by occupation: 0.0% management, 0.0% professional, 5.7% services, 18.7% sales, 0.0% farming, 27.6% construction, 24.4% production (2006-2010 5-year est.).
Income: Per capita income: $14,258 (2006-2010 5-year est.); Median household income: $30,250 (2006-2010 5-year est.); Average household income: $33,990 (2006-2010 5-year est.); Percent of households with income of $100,000 or more: n/a (2006-2010 5-year est.); Poverty rate: 12.1% (2006-2010 5-year est.).
Education: Percent of population age 25 and over with: High school diploma (including GED) or higher: 79.5% (2006-2010 5-year est.); Bachelor's degree or higher: 1.7% (2006-2010 5-year est.); Master's degree or higher: 0.0% (2006-2010 5-year est.).
Housing: Homeownership rate: 75.7% (2010); Median home value: $70,400 (2006-2010 5-year est.); Median contract rent: $326 per month (2006-2010 5-year est.); Median year structure built: 1943 (2006-2010 5-year est.).
Safety: Violent crime rate: 0.0 per 10,000 population; Property crime rate: 40.2 per 10,000 population (2011).
Transportation: Commute to work: 97.6% car, 0.0% public transportation, 2.4% walk, 0.0% work from home (2006-2010 5-year est.); Travel time to work: 25.2% less than 15 minutes, 22.8% 15 to 30 minutes, 31.7% 30 to 45 minutes, 14.6% 45 to 60 minutes, 5.7% 60 minutes or more (2006-2010 5-year est.)

SEWICKLEY (township). Covers a land area of 26.759 square miles and a water area of 0.210 square miles. Located at 40.25° N. Lat; 79.73° W. Long.
Population: 6,642 (1990); 6,230 (2000); 5,996 (2010); Density: 224.1 persons per square mile (2010); Race: 98.5% White, 0.4% Black, 0.3% Asian, 0.0% American Indian/Alaska Native, 0.0% Native Hawaiian/Other Pacific Islander, 0.8% Other, 0.6% Hispanic of any race (2010); Average household size: 2.37 (2010); Median age: 45.0 (2010); Males per 100 females: 98.5 (2010); Marriage status: 22.9% never married, 56.5% now married, 8.4% widowed, 12.2% divorced (2006-2010 5-year est.); Foreign born: 1.1% (2006-2010 5-year est.); Ancestry (includes multiple ancestries): 36.7% German, 19.7% Italian, 19.3% Irish, 15.0% Polish, 13.2% English (2006-2010 5-year est.).
Economy: Single-family building permits issued: 6 (2011); Multi-family building permits issued: 0 (2011); Employment by occupation: 6.3% management, 5.2% professional, 9.5% services, 16.1% sales, 6.0% farming, 12.2% construction, 11.4% production (2006-2010 5-year est.).
Income: Per capita income: $22,788 (2006-2010 5-year est.); Median household income: $45,847 (2006-2010 5-year est.); Average household income: $55,228 (2006-2010 5-year est.); Percent of households with income of $100,000 or more: 13.3% (2006-2010 5-year est.); Poverty rate: 9.2% (2006-2010 5-year est.).
Education: Percent of population age 25 and over with: High school diploma (including GED) or higher: 89.7% (2006-2010 5-year est.); Bachelor's degree or higher: 16.2% (2006-2010 5-year est.); Master's degree or higher: 3.7% (2006-2010 5-year est.).
Housing: Homeownership rate: 81.2% (2010); Median home value: $116,600 (2006-2010 5-year est.); Median contract rent: $434 per month (2006-2010 5-year est.); Median year structure built: 1961 (2006-2010 5-year est.).
Transportation: Commute to work: 95.8% car, 0.3% public transportation, 0.5% walk, 2.7% work from home (2006-2010 5-year est.); Travel time to work: 22.7% less than 15 minutes, 43.2% 15 to 30 minutes, 17.5% 30 to 45 minutes, 8.5% 45 to 60 minutes, 8.2% 60 minutes or more (2006-2010 5-year est.)
Additional Information Contacts
Sewickley Township . . . . (724) 446-7202
Westmoreland Chamber of Commerce . . . . (724) 834-2900
    http://www.westmorelandchamber.com

SLICKVILLE (CDP). Covers a land area of 0.518 square miles and a water area of 0 square miles. Located at 40.46° N. Lat; 79.52° W. Long. Elevation is 1,165 feet.
Population: 332 (1990); 372 (2000); 388 (2010); Density: 749.2 persons per square mile (2010); Race: 96.1% White, 2.3% Black, 0.0% Asian, 0.0% American Indian/Alaska Native, 0.0% Native Hawaiian/Other Pacific Islander, 1.6% Other, 0.8% Hispanic of any race (2010); Average household size: 2.47 (2010); Median age: 41.3 (2010); Males per 100

females: 98.0 (2010); Marriage status: 49.8% never married, 45.1% now married, 5.1% widowed, 0.0% divorced (2006-2010 5-year est.); Foreign born: 8.8% (2006-2010 5-year est.); Ancestry (includes multiple ancestries): 43.3% African, 23.5% British West Indian, 16.2% German, 13.4% Ukrainian, 11.1% Barbadian (2006-2010 5-year est.).
Economy: Employment by occupation: 13.3% management, 0.0% professional, 17.8% services, 37.8% sales, 0.0% farming, 7.8% construction, 7.8% production (2006-2010 5-year est.).
Income: Per capita income: $12,250 (2006-2010 5-year est.); Median household income: $22,820 (2006-2010 5-year est.); Average household income: $30,904 (2006-2010 5-year est.); Percent of households with income of $100,000 or more: 4.5% (2006-2010 5-year est.); Poverty rate: 48.7% (2006-2010 5-year est.).
Education: Percent of population age 25 and over with: High school diploma (including GED) or higher: 76.9% (2006-2010 5-year est.); Bachelor's degree or higher: 12.8% (2006-2010 5-year est.); Master's degree or higher: 0.0% (2006-2010 5-year est.).
Housing: Homeownership rate: 79.0% (2010); Median home value: $48,800 (2006-2010 5-year est.); Median contract rent: n/a per month (2006-2010 5-year est.); Median year structure built: before 1940 (2006-2010 5-year est.).
Transportation: Commute to work: 100.0% car, 0.0% public transportation, 0.0% walk, 0.0% work from home (2006-2010 5-year est.); Travel time to work: 10.0% less than 15 minutes, 55.6% 15 to 30 minutes, 34.4% 30 to 45 minutes, 0.0% 45 to 60 minutes, 0.0% 60 minutes or more (2006-2010 5-year est.)

SMITHTON (borough). Covers a land area of 0.102 square miles and a water area of 0.015 square miles. Located at 40.15° N. Lat; 79.74° W. Long. Elevation is 797 feet.
Population: 376 (1990); 444 (2000); 399 (2010); Density: 3,904.6 persons per square mile (2010); Race: 98.5% White, 0.0% Black, 0.5% Asian, 0.0% American Indian/Alaska Native, 0.0% Native Hawaiian/Other Pacific Islander, 1.0% Other, 1.8% Hispanic of any race (2010); Average household size: 2.40 (2010); Median age: 40.4 (2010); Males per 100 females: 95.6 (2010); Marriage status: 36.4% never married, 46.9% now married, 9.7% widowed, 7.0% divorced (2006-2010 5-year est.); Foreign born: 1.3% (2006-2010 5-year est.); Ancestry (includes multiple ancestries): 36.0% German, 32.4% Italian, 20.7% Irish, 16.5% English, 7.4% Slovak (2006-2010 5-year est.).
Economy: Single-family building permits issued: 0 (2011); Multi-family building permits issued: 0 (2011); Employment by occupation: 4.4% management, 4.0% professional, 17.1% services, 18.5% sales, 4.4% farming, 13.1% construction, 7.0% production (2006-2010 5-year est.).
Income: Per capita income: $21,788 (2006-2010 5-year est.); Median household income: $62,500 (2006-2010 5-year est.); Average household income: $59,246 (2006-2010 5-year est.); Percent of households with income of $100,000 or more: 10.3% (2006-2010 5-year est.); Poverty rate: 4.9% (2006-2010 5-year est.).
Education: Percent of population age 25 and over with: High school diploma (including GED) or higher: 94.2% (2006-2010 5-year est.); Bachelor's degree or higher: 14.3% (2006-2010 5-year est.); Master's degree or higher: 5.0% (2006-2010 5-year est.).
Housing: Homeownership rate: 69.2% (2010); Median home value: $93,300 (2006-2010 5-year est.); Median contract rent: $489 per month (2006-2010 5-year est.); Median year structure built: before 1940 (2006-2010 5-year est.).
Safety: Violent crime rate: 0.0 per 10,000 population; Property crime rate: 50.0 per 10,000 population (2011).
Transportation: Commute to work: 95.0% car, 0.0% public transportation, 5.0% walk, 0.0% work from home (2006-2010 5-year est.); Travel time to work: 24.6% less than 15 minutes, 41.5% 15 to 30 minutes, 14.6% 30 to 45 minutes, 10.0% 45 to 60 minutes, 9.2% 60 minutes or more (2006-2010 5-year est.)

SOUTH GREENSBURG (borough). Covers a land area of 0.707 square miles and a water area of 0 square miles. Located at 40.28° N. Lat; 79.55° W. Long. Elevation is 1,073 feet.
History: Incorporated 1891.
Population: 2,237 (1990); 2,280 (2000); 2,117 (2010); Density: 2,994.7 persons per square mile (2010); Race: 97.3% White, 0.9% Black, 0.5% Asian, 0.2% American Indian/Alaska Native, 0.0% Native Hawaiian/Other Pacific Islander, 1.1% Other, 0.9% Hispanic of any race (2010); Average household size: 2.05 (2010); Median age: 46.0 (2010); Males per 100 females: 90.0 (2010); Marriage status: 31.0% never married, 52.3% now

married, 6.7% widowed, 10.0% divorced (2006-2010 5-year est.); Foreign born: 0.3% (2006-2010 5-year est.); Ancestry (includes multiple ancestries): 30.3% German, 29.4% Italian, 13.9% Irish, 13.5% Polish, 8.6% Slovak (2006-2010 5-year est.).

Economy: Single-family building permits issued: 0 (2011); Multi-family building permits issued: 0 (2011); Employment by occupation: 7.7% management, 2.3% professional, 12.0% services, 19.7% sales, 4.2% farming, 12.3% construction, 3.7% production (2006-2010 5-year est.).

Income: Per capita income: $23,779 (2006-2010 5-year est.); Median household income: $41,141 (2006-2010 5-year est.); Average household income: $49,316 (2006-2010 5-year est.); Percent of households with income of $100,000 or more: 4.9% (2006-2010 5-year est.); Poverty rate: 10.0% (2006-2010 5-year est.).

Education: Percent of population age 25 and over with: High school diploma (including GED) or higher: 93.6% (2006-2010 5-year est.); Bachelor's degree or higher: 19.9% (2006-2010 5-year est.); Master's degree or higher: 5.3% (2006-2010 5-year est.).

Housing: Homeownership rate: 70.8% (2010); Median home value: $87,800 (2006-2010 5-year est.); Median contract rent: $464 per month (2006-2010 5-year est.); Median year structure built: 1950 (2006-2010 5-year est.).

Safety: Violent crime rate: 23.5 per 10,000 population; Property crime rate: 193.0 per 10,000 population (2011).

Transportation: Commute to work: 95.3% car, 0.5% public transportation, 2.3% walk, 1.9% work from home (2006-2010 5-year est.); Travel time to work: 47.8% less than 15 minutes, 30.9% 15 to 30 minutes, 9.7% 30 to 45 minutes, 5.2% 45 to 60 minutes, 6.4% 60 minutes or more (2006-2010 5-year est.)

Additional Information Contacts
Westmoreland Chamber of Commerce . . . . (724) 834-2900
   http://www.westmorelandchamber.com

SOUTH HUNTINGDON (township). Covers a land area of 45.423 square miles and a water area of 0.386 square miles. Located at 40.18° N. Lat; 79.70° W. Long.

Population: 6,364 (1990); 6,175 (2000); 5,796 (2010); Density: 127.6 persons per square mile (2010); Race: 97.9% White, 0.8% Black, 0.1% Asian, 0.1% American Indian/Alaska Native, 0.0% Native Hawaiian/Other Pacific Islander, 1.1% Other, 0.7% Hispanic of any race (2010); Average household size: 2.42 (2010); Median age: 44.7 (2010); Males per 100 females: 101.6 (2010); Marriage status: 24.4% never married, 58.0% now married, 7.4% widowed, 10.3% divorced (2006-2010 5-year est.); Foreign born: 1.0% (2006-2010 5-year est.); Ancestry (includes multiple ancestries): 33.4% German, 18.3% Italian, 16.4% Irish, 13.8% Polish, 10.6% English (2006-2010 5-year est.).

Economy: Single-family building permits issued: 2 (2011); Multi-family building permits issued: 0 (2011); Employment by occupation: 5.0% management, 4.8% professional, 13.4% services, 19.1% sales, 3.2% farming, 16.8% construction, 12.3% production (2006-2010 5-year est.).

Income: Per capita income: $23,525 (2006-2010 5-year est.); Median household income: $46,429 (2006-2010 5-year est.); Average household income: $56,097 (2006-2010 5-year est.); Percent of households with income of $100,000 or more: 15.4% (2006-2010 5-year est.); Poverty rate: 5.8% (2006-2010 5-year est.).

Education: Percent of population age 25 and over with: High school diploma (including GED) or higher: 87.3% (2006-2010 5-year est.); Bachelor's degree or higher: 14.2% (2006-2010 5-year est.); Master's degree or higher: 4.9% (2006-2010 5-year est.).

Housing: Homeownership rate: 82.2% (2010); Median home value: $123,800 (2006-2010 5-year est.); Median contract rent: $442 per month (2006-2010 5-year est.); Median year structure built: 1960 (2006-2010 5-year est.).

Transportation: Commute to work: 96.5% car, 0.0% public transportation, 0.8% walk, 2.7% work from home (2006-2010 5-year est.); Travel time to work: 24.0% less than 15 minutes, 36.5% 15 to 30 minutes, 24.1% 30 to 45 minutes, 9.3% 45 to 60 minutes, 6.1% 60 minutes or more (2006-2010 5-year est.)

Additional Information Contacts
Scottdale Area Chamber of Commerce . . . . (724) 887-3611
   http://www.scottdale.com
South Huntingdon Township . . . . (724) 872-8474

SOUTHWEST GREENSBURG (borough). Covers a land area of 0.392 square miles and a water area of 0 square miles. Located at 40.29° N. Lat; 79.55° W. Long. Elevation is 1,089 feet.

History: Incorporated 1890.

Population: 2,456 (1990); 2,398 (2000); 2,155 (2010); Density: 5,500.5 persons per square mile (2010); Race: 94.2% White, 2.7% Black, 0.3% Asian, 0.0% American Indian/Alaska Native, 0.0% Native Hawaiian/Other Pacific Islander, 2.8% Other, 0.6% Hispanic of any race (2010); Average household size: 2.08 (2010); Median age: 41.7 (2010); Males per 100 females: 91.7 (2010); Marriage status: 31.5% never married, 50.0% now married, 4.9% widowed, 13.7% divorced (2006-2010 5-year est.); Foreign born: 0.4% (2006-2010 5-year est.); Ancestry (includes multiple ancestries): 33.3% German, 20.9% Italian, 17.2% Irish, 10.5% English, 9.5% Polish (2006-2010 5-year est.).

Economy: Single-family building permits issued: 0 (2011); Multi-family building permits issued: 0 (2011); Employment by occupation: 10.3% management, 3.3% professional, 13.0% services, 18.0% sales, 5.8% farming, 3.9% construction, 4.4% production (2006-2010 5-year est.).

Income: Per capita income: $22,107 (2006-2010 5-year est.); Median household income: $35,000 (2006-2010 5-year est.); Average household income: $48,099 (2006-2010 5-year est.); Percent of households with income of $100,000 or more: 10.2% (2006-2010 5-year est.); Poverty rate: 16.9% (2006-2010 5-year est.).

Education: Percent of population age 25 and over with: High school diploma (including GED) or higher: 93.6% (2006-2010 5-year est.); Bachelor's degree or higher: 28.6% (2006-2010 5-year est.); Master's degree or higher: 7.0% (2006-2010 5-year est.).

Housing: Homeownership rate: 56.8% (2010); Median home value: $110,300 (2006-2010 5-year est.); Median contract rent: $472 per month (2006-2010 5-year est.); Median year structure built: before 1940 (2006-2010 5-year est.).

Safety: Violent crime rate: 37.0 per 10,000 population; Property crime rate: 300.6 per 10,000 population (2011).

Transportation: Commute to work: 89.9% car, 1.0% public transportation, 6.8% walk, 1.8% work from home (2006-2010 5-year est.); Travel time to work: 47.0% less than 15 minutes, 27.3% 15 to 30 minutes, 11.8% 30 to 45 minutes, 1.0% 45 to 60 minutes, 12.9% 60 minutes or more (2006-2010 5-year est.)

Additional Information Contacts
Westmoreland Chamber of Commerce . . . . (724) 834-2900
   http://www.westmorelandchamber.com

STAHLSTOWN (unincorporated postal area)
Zip Code: 15687
   Covers a land area of 28.870 square miles and a water area of 0.131 square miles. Located at 40.13° N. Lat; 79.31° W. Long. Population: 1,476 (2010); Density: 51.1 persons per square mile (2010); Race: 99.3% White, 0.1% Black, 0.1% Asian, 0.1% American Indian/Alaska Native, 0.2% Native Hawaiian/Other Pacific Islander, 0.2% Other, 0.9% Hispanic of any race (2010); Average household size: 2.44 (2010); Median age: 44.9 (2010); Males per 100 females: 92.9 (2010); Homeownership rate: 87.8% (2010)

SUTERSVILLE (borough). Aka Suter. Covers a land area of 0.272 square miles and a water area of 0.023 square miles. Located at 40.23° N. Lat; 79.80° W. Long. Elevation is 942 feet.

Population: 755 (1990); 636 (2000); 605 (2010); Density: 2,226.6 persons per square mile (2010); Race: 99.2% White, 0.0% Black, 0.0% Asian, 0.0% American Indian/Alaska Native, 0.0% Native Hawaiian/Other Pacific Islander, 0.8% Other, 0.0% Hispanic of any race (2010); Average household size: 2.54 (2010); Median age: 41.1 (2010); Males per 100 females: 98.4 (2010); Marriage status: 26.5% never married, 52.1% now married, 9.4% widowed, 12.0% divorced (2006-2010 5-year est.); Foreign born: 0.5% (2006-2010 5-year est.); Ancestry (includes multiple ancestries): 27.1% Italian, 24.6% Slovak, 22.4% Irish, 21.5% German, 10.7% English (2006-2010 5-year est.).

Economy: Single-family building permits issued: 0 (2011); Multi-family building permits issued: 0 (2011); Employment by occupation: 0.3% management, 3.5% professional, 12.3% services, 16.1% sales, 0.0% farming, 11.0% construction, 16.1% production (2006-2010 5-year est.).

Income: Per capita income: $20,287 (2006-2010 5-year est.); Median household income: $42,500 (2006-2010 5-year est.); Average household income: $49,266 (2006-2010 5-year est.); Percent of households with income of $100,000 or more: 9.5% (2006-2010 5-year est.); Poverty rate: 15.6% (2006-2010 5-year est.).

Education: Percent of population age 25 and over with: High school diploma (including GED) or higher: 90.6% (2006-2010 5-year est.); Bachelor's degree or higher: 12.0% (2006-2010 5-year est.); Master's degree or higher: 1.8% (2006-2010 5-year est.).
Housing: Homeownership rate: 79.8% (2010); Median home value: $94,300 (2006-2010 5-year est.); Median contract rent: $313 per month (2006-2010 5-year est.); Median year structure built: 1941 (2006-2010 5-year est.).
Safety: Violent crime rate: 0.0 per 10,000 population; Property crime rate: 0.0 per 10,000 population (2011).
Transportation: Commute to work: 92.6% car, 0.0% public transportation, 2.0% walk, 4.0% work from home (2006-2010 5-year est.); Travel time to work: 16.4% less than 15 minutes, 33.4% 15 to 30 minutes, 31.0% 30 to 45 minutes, 13.9% 45 to 60 minutes, 5.2% 60 minutes or more (2006-2010 5-year est.)

TARRS (unincorporated postal area)
Zip Code: 15688
Covers a land area of 1.555 square miles and a water area of 0 square miles. Located at 40.16° N. Lat; 79.58° W. Long. Elevation is 1,158 feet. Population: 641 (2010); Density: 412.0 persons per square mile (2010); Race: 99.4% White, 0.3% Black, 0.2% Asian, 0.0% American Indian/Alaska Native, 0.0% Native Hawaiian/Other Pacific Islander, 0.1% Other, 0.6% Hispanic of any race (2010); Average household size: 2.26 (2010); Median age: 46.8 (2010); Males per 100 females: 92.5 (2010); Homeownership rate: 81.4% (2010)

TORRANCE (unincorporated postal area)
Zip Code: 15779
Covers a land area of 7.909 square miles and a water area of 0.120 square miles. Located at 40.38° N. Lat; 79.21° W. Long. Elevation is 1,181 feet. Population: 414 (2010); Density: 52.3 persons per square mile (2010); Race: 86.5% White, 10.6% Black, 0.5% Asian, 0.2% American Indian/Alaska Native, 0.0% Native Hawaiian/Other Pacific Islander, 2.2% Other, 2.2% Hispanic of any race (2010); Average household size: 2.45 (2010); Median age: 37.6 (2010); Males per 100 females: 183.6 (2010); Homeownership rate: 80.7% (2010)

TRAFFORD (borough). Covers a land area of 1.433 square miles and a water area of 0 square miles. Located at 40.38° N. Lat; 79.76° W. Long. Elevation is 860 feet.
Population: 3,270 (1990); 3,236 (2000); 3,174 (2010); Density: 2,214.9 persons per square mile (2010); Race: 95.9% White, 1.6% Black, 1.1% Asian, 0.0% American Indian/Alaska Native, 0.0% Native Hawaiian/Other Pacific Islander, 1.4% Other, 0.9% Hispanic of any race (2010); Average household size: 2.11 (2010); Median age: 42.9 (2010); Males per 100 females: 87.3 (2010); Marriage status: 29.8% never married, 44.0% now married, 10.1% widowed, 16.0% divorced (2006-2010 5-year est.); Foreign born: 0.0% (2006-2010 5-year est.); Ancestry (includes multiple ancestries): 29.3% German, 28.5% Italian, 19.5% Irish, 10.4% Polish, 7.8% English (2006-2010 5-year est.).
Economy: Single-family building permits issued: 0 (2011); Multi-family building permits issued: 0 (2011); Employment by occupation: 12.8% management, 9.9% professional, 8.6% services, 23.8% sales, 0.9% farming, 8.3% construction, 6.3% production (2006-2010 5-year est.).
Income: Per capita income: $26,117 (2006-2010 5-year est.); Median household income: $41,645 (2006-2010 5-year est.); Average household income: $55,351 (2006-2010 5-year est.); Percent of households with income of $100,000 or more: 15.4% (2006-2010 5-year est.); Poverty rate: 9.2% (2006-2010 5-year est.).
Education: Percent of population age 25 and over with: High school diploma (including GED) or higher: 93.0% (2006-2010 5-year est.); Bachelor's degree or higher: 27.0% (2006-2010 5-year est.); Master's degree or higher: 7.5% (2006-2010 5-year est.).
School District(s)
Penn-Trafford SD (KG-12)
    2010-11 Enrollment: 4,239 . . . . (724) 744-4496
Housing: Homeownership rate: 70.4% (2010); Median home value: $107,600 (2006-2010 5-year est.); Median contract rent: $405 per month (2006-2010 5-year est.); Median year structure built: 1949 (2006-2010 5-year est.).
Safety: Violent crime rate: 40.8 per 10,000 population; Property crime rate: 163.3 per 10,000 population (2011).
Transportation: Commute to work: 87.4% car, 3.3% public transportation, 4.1% walk, 5.1% work from home (2006-2010 5-year est.); Travel time to

work: 23.5% less than 15 minutes, 33.5% 15 to 30 minutes, 20.3% 30 to 45 minutes, 14.1% 45 to 60 minutes, 8.6% 60 minutes or more (2006-2010 5-year est.)
Additional Information Contacts
Norwin Chamber of Commerce . . . . (724) 863-0888
    http://www.norwinchamber.com/index.php

UNITED (unincorporated postal area)
Zip Code: 15689
Covers a land area of 0.101 square miles and a water area of 0 square miles. Located at 40.22° N. Lat; 79.49° W. Long. Elevation is 1,063 feet. Population: 229 (2010); Density: 2,266.6 persons per square mile (2010); Race: 100.0% White, 0.0% Black, 0.0% Asian, 0.0% American Indian/Alaska Native, 0.0% Native Hawaiian/Other Pacific Islander, 0.0% Other, 0.0% Hispanic of any race (2010); Average household size: 2.27 (2010); Median age: 38.7 (2010); Males per 100 females: 99.1 (2010); Homeownership rate: 71.3% (2010)

UNITY (township). Covers a land area of 67.442 square miles and a water area of 0.136 square miles. Located at 40.28° N. Lat; 79.43° W. Long.
Population: 19,973 (1990); 21,137 (2000); 22,607 (2010); Density: 335.2 persons per square mile (2010); Race: 97.2% White, 0.7% Black, 1.0% Asian, 0.1% American Indian/Alaska Native, 0.0% Native Hawaiian/Other Pacific Islander, 1.0% Other, 0.9% Hispanic of any race (2010); Average household size: 2.40 (2010); Median age: 44.1 (2010); Males per 100 females: 98.6 (2010); Marriage status: 29.9% never married, 54.8% now married, 7.8% widowed, 7.5% divorced (2006-2010 5-year est.); Foreign born: 1.7% (2006-2010 5-year est.); Ancestry (includes multiple ancestries): 31.0% German, 23.8% Italian, 17.9% Irish, 11.4% English, 10.8% Polish (2006-2010 5-year est.).
Economy: Single-family building permits issued: 43 (2011); Multi-family building permits issued: 0 (2011); Employment by occupation: 12.7% management, 5.0% professional, 9.9% services, 17.0% sales, 2.3% farming, 6.2% construction, 5.2% production (2006-2010 5-year est.).
Income: Per capita income: $27,972 (2006-2010 5-year est.); Median household income: $56,474 (2006-2010 5-year est.); Average household income: $72,213 (2006-2010 5-year est.); Percent of households with income of $100,000 or more: 21.2% (2006-2010 5-year est.); Poverty rate: 7.5% (2006-2010 5-year est.).
Education: Percent of population age 25 and over with: High school diploma (including GED) or higher: 91.9% (2006-2010 5-year est.); Bachelor's degree or higher: 30.6% (2006-2010 5-year est.); Master's degree or higher: 12.4% (2006-2010 5-year est.).
Housing: Homeownership rate: 80.3% (2010); Median home value: $162,000 (2006-2010 5-year est.); Median contract rent: $503 per month (2006-2010 5-year est.); Median year structure built: 1969 (2006-2010 5-year est.).
Transportation: Commute to work: 90.0% car, 0.8% public transportation, 3.9% walk, 5.3% work from home (2006-2010 5-year est.); Travel time to work: 43.7% less than 15 minutes, 34.9% 15 to 30 minutes, 11.0% 30 to 45 minutes, 4.8% 45 to 60 minutes, 5.6% 60 minutes or more (2006-2010 5-year est.)
Additional Information Contacts
Unity Township . . . . (724) 539-2546
    http://www.unitytownship.org
Westmoreland Chamber of Commerce . . . . (724) 834-2900
    http://www.westmorelandchamber.com

UPPER BURRELL (township). Covers a land area of 15.132 square miles and a water area of 0 square miles. Located at 40.55° N. Lat; 79.67° W. Long.
Population: 2,258 (1990); 2,240 (2000); 2,326 (2010); Density: 153.7 persons per square mile (2010); Race: 96.0% White, 2.3% Black, 0.6% Asian, 0.1% American Indian/Alaska Native, 0.0% Native Hawaiian/Other Pacific Islander, 1.0% Other, 0.9% Hispanic of any race (2010); Average household size: 2.51 (2010); Median age: 44.9 (2010); Males per 100 females: 102.4 (2010); Marriage status: 19.7% never married, 65.3% now married, 7.8% widowed, 7.3% divorced (2006-2010 5-year est.); Foreign born: 0.3% (2006-2010 5-year est.); Ancestry (includes multiple ancestries): 35.1% German, 25.6% Irish, 21.4% English, 17.1% Polish, 13.3% Italian (2006-2010 5-year est.).
Economy: Single-family building permits issued: 2 (2011); Multi-family building permits issued: 0 (2011); Employment by occupation: 15.0%

management, 5.0% professional, 12.7% services, 20.3% sales, 5.0% farming, 12.6% construction, 4.7% production (2006-2010 5-year est.).
Income: Per capita income: $26,354 (2006-2010 5-year est.); Median household income: $57,738 (2006-2010 5-year est.); Average household income: $67,181 (2006-2010 5-year est.); Percent of households with income of $100,000 or more: 18.4% (2006-2010 5-year est.); Poverty rate: 7.9% (2006-2010 5-year est.).
Education: Percent of population age 25 and over with: High school diploma (including GED) or higher: 93.4% (2006-2010 5-year est.); Bachelor's degree or higher: 19.4% (2006-2010 5-year est.); Master's degree or higher: 5.3% (2006-2010 5-year est.).
Four-year College(s)
Pennsylvania State University-Penn State New Kensington (Public)
    Fall 2010 Enrollment: 758 . . . . (724) 334-5466
    2011-12 Tuition: In-state $13,048; Out-of-state $19,488
Housing: Homeownership rate: 84.8% (2010); Median home value: $158,900 (2006-2010 5-year est.); Median contract rent: $423 per month (2006-2010 5-year est.); Median year structure built: 1975 (2006-2010 5-year est.).
Safety: Violent crime rate: 0.0 per 10,000 population; Property crime rate: 171.5 per 10,000 population (2011).
Transportation: Commute to work: 86.8% car, 1.5% public transportation, 2.6% walk, 6.9% work from home (2006-2010 5-year est.); Travel time to work: 19.0% less than 15 minutes, 32.6% 15 to 30 minutes, 27.5% 30 to 45 minutes, 9.5% 45 to 60 minutes, 11.4% 60 minutes or more (2006-2010 5-year est.)
Additional Information Contacts
Westmoreland Chamber of Commerce. . . . . (724) 834-2900
    http://www.westmorelandchamber.com

VANDERGRIFT (borough). Covers a land area of 1.361 square miles and a water area of 0.059 square miles. Located at 40.60° N. Lat; 79.58° W. Long. Elevation is 879 feet.
History: Incorporated 1901.
Population: 5,750 (1990); 5,455 (2000); 5,205 (2010); Density: 3,825.7 persons per square mile (2010); Race: 91.6% White, 4.8% Black, 0.3% Asian, 0.1% American Indian/Alaska Native, 0.0% Native Hawaiian/Other Pacific Islander, 3.2% Other, 0.9% Hispanic of any race (2010); Average household size: 2.31 (2010); Median age: 39.5 (2010); Males per 100 females: 92.8 (2010); Marriage status: 30.9% never married, 49.2% now married, 8.9% widowed, 11.1% divorced (2006-2010 5-year est.); Foreign born: 1.1% (2006-2010 5-year est.); Ancestry (includes multiple ancestries): 40.0% German, 26.4% Italian, 18.4% Irish, 8.4% English, 6.6% Polish (2006-2010 5-year est.).
Economy: Single-family building permits issued: 0 (2011); Multi-family building permits issued: 0 (2011); Employment by occupation: 5.3% management, 1.2% professional, 12.6% services, 16.8% sales, 6.3% farming, 10.6% construction, 8.9% production (2006-2010 5-year est.).
Income: Per capita income: $17,628 (2006-2010 5-year est.); Median household income: $32,669 (2006-2010 5-year est.); Average household income: $39,755 (2006-2010 5-year est.); Percent of households with income of $100,000 or more: 2.5% (2006-2010 5-year est.); Poverty rate: 13.1% (2006-2010 5-year est.).
Education: Percent of population age 25 and over with: High school diploma (including GED) or higher: 87.2% (2006-2010 5-year est.); Bachelor's degree or higher: 13.5% (2006-2010 5-year est.); Master's degree or higher: 3.0% (2006-2010 5-year est.).
School District(s)
Kiski Area SD (KG-12)
    2010-11 Enrollment: 3,967 . . . . (724) 845-2022
Kiski Area SD (KG-12)
    2010-11 Enrollment: 3,967 . . . . (724) 845-2022
Housing: Homeownership rate: 59.4% (2010); Median home value: $72,100 (2006-2010 5-year est.); Median contract rent: $379 per month (2006-2010 5-year est.); Median year structure built: before 1940 (2006-2010 5-year est.).
Safety: Violent crime rate: 55.5 per 10,000 population; Property crime rate: 28.7 per 10,000 population (2011).
Newspapers: Apollo News Record (Community news; Circulation 3,000); Leechburg Advance (Community news; Circulation 2,000); Vandergrift News (Community news; Circulation 2,836)
Transportation: Commute to work: 93.7% car, 0.0% public transportation, 3.2% walk, 1.7% work from home (2006-2010 5-year est.); Travel time to work: 22.7% less than 15 minutes, 29.8% 15 to 30 minutes, 22.2% 30 to

45 minutes, 9.6% 45 to 60 minutes, 15.7% 60 minutes or more (2006-2010 5-year est.)
Additional Information Contacts
Borough of Vandergrift . . . . (724) 567-5377
Strongland Chamber of Commerce. . . . . (724) 845-5426
    http://www.strongland.org

WASHINGTON (township). Covers a land area of 31.952 square miles and a water area of 0.856 square miles. Located at 40.51° N. Lat; 79.60° W. Long.
Population: 7,725 (1990); 7,384 (2000); 7,422 (2010); Density: 232.3 persons per square mile (2010); Race: 98.3% White, 0.7% Black, 0.2% Asian, 0.1% American Indian/Alaska Native, 0.0% Native Hawaiian/Other Pacific Islander, 0.7% Other, 0.5% Hispanic of any race (2010); Average household size: 2.40 (2010); Median age: 49.5 (2010); Males per 100 females: 96.8 (2010); Marriage status: 20.4% never married, 61.7% now married, 10.7% widowed, 7.2% divorced (2006-2010 5-year est.); Foreign born: 0.4% (2006-2010 5-year est.); Ancestry (includes multiple ancestries): 39.8% German, 20.8% Irish, 17.1% Italian, 13.0% English, 9.5% Polish (2006-2010 5-year est.).
Economy: Single-family building permits issued: 3 (2011); Multi-family building permits issued: 0 (2011); Employment by occupation: 10.5% management, 5.3% professional, 9.5% services, 15.5% sales, 3.3% farming, 17.7% construction, 8.5% production (2006-2010 5-year est.).
Income: Per capita income: $26,201 (2006-2010 5-year est.); Median household income: $55,512 (2006-2010 5-year est.); Average household income: $63,895 (2006-2010 5-year est.); Percent of households with income of $100,000 or more: 18.2% (2006-2010 5-year est.); Poverty rate: 5.7% (2006-2010 5-year est.).
Education: Percent of population age 25 and over with: High school diploma (including GED) or higher: 89.3% (2006-2010 5-year est.); Bachelor's degree or higher: 21.3% (2006-2010 5-year est.); Master's degree or higher: 6.4% (2006-2010 5-year est.).
Housing: Homeownership rate: 87.9% (2010); Median home value: $150,700 (2006-2010 5-year est.); Median contract rent: $469 per month (2006-2010 5-year est.); Median year structure built: 1972 (2006-2010 5-year est.).
Safety: Violent crime rate: 16.1 per 10,000 population; Property crime rate: 60.4 per 10,000 population (2011).
Transportation: Commute to work: 94.3% car, 1.3% public transportation, 1.1% walk, 3.0% work from home (2006-2010 5-year est.); Travel time to work: 17.8% less than 15 minutes, 32.3% 15 to 30 minutes, 31.4% 30 to 45 minutes, 9.9% 45 to 60 minutes, 8.6% 60 minutes or more (2006-2010 5-year est.)
Additional Information Contacts
Washington Township. . . . . (724) 727-3515
    http://www.washingtontownship.com
Westmoreland Chamber of Commerce. . . . . (724) 834-2900
    http://www.westmorelandchamber.com

WEBSTER (CDP). Covers a land area of 0.588 square miles and a water area of 0.077 square miles. Located at 40.19° N. Lat; 79.85° W. Long. Elevation is 774 feet.
Population: n/a (1990); n/a (2000); 255 (2010); Density: 433.8 persons per square mile (2010); Race: 96.1% White, 0.0% Black, 2.4% Asian, 0.4% American Indian/Alaska Native, 0.0% Native Hawaiian/Other Pacific Islander, 1.1% Other, 0.8% Hispanic of any race (2010); Average household size: 2.45 (2010); Median age: 44.6 (2010); Males per 100 females: 97.7 (2010); Marriage status: 38.2% never married, 61.8% now married, 0.0% widowed, 0.0% divorced (2006-2010 5-year est.); Foreign born: 0.0% (2006-2010 5-year est.); Ancestry (includes multiple ancestries): 38.4% German, 24.7% Irish, 20.6% Italian, 16.3% Slovak, 15.9% Polish (2006-2010 5-year est.).
Economy: Employment by occupation: 21.4% management, 0.0% professional, 17.9% services, 0.0% sales, 0.0% farming, 40.5% construction, 40.5% production (2006-2010 5-year est.).
Income: Per capita income: $19,757 (2006-2010 5-year est.); Median household income: $72,656 (2006-2010 5-year est.); Average household income: $62,338 (2006-2010 5-year est.); Percent of households with income of $100,000 or more: 17.7% (2006-2010 5-year est.); Poverty rate: 24.7% (2006-2010 5-year est.).
Education: Percent of population age 25 and over with: High school diploma (including GED) or higher: 91.4% (2006-2010 5-year est.); Bachelor's degree or higher: 0.0% (2006-2010 5-year est.); Master's degree or higher: 0.0% (2006-2010 5-year est.).

Housing: Homeownership rate: 74.1% (2010); Median home value: $69,700 (2006-2010 5-year est.); Median contract rent: $725 per month (2006-2010 5-year est.); Median year structure built: before 1940 (2006-2010 5-year est.).
Transportation: Commute to work: 100.0% car, 0.0% public transportation, 0.0% walk, 0.0% work from home (2006-2010 5-year est.); Travel time to work: 60.7% less than 15 minutes, 20.2% 15 to 30 minutes, 0.0% 30 to 45 minutes, 0.0% 45 to 60 minutes, 19.0% 60 minutes or more (2006-2010 5-year est.)

WENDEL (unincorporated postal area)
Zip Code: 15691
Covers a land area of 0.033 square miles and a water area of 0 square miles. Located at 40.29° N. Lat; 79.68° W. Long. Elevation is 1,119 feet.
Population: 70 (2010); Density: 2,104.9 persons per square mile (2010); Race: 95.7% White, 0.0% Black, 0.0% Asian, 2.9% American Indian/Alaska Native, 0.0% Native Hawaiian/Other Pacific Islander, 1.4% Other, 0.0% Hispanic of any race (2010); Average household size: 2.50 (2010); Median age: 50.3 (2010); Males per 100 females: 79.5 (2010); Homeownership rate: 85.8% (2010)

WEST LEECHBURG (borough). Covers a land area of 0.955 square miles and a water area of 0.042 square miles. Located at 40.63° N. Lat; 79.62° W. Long. Elevation is 994 feet.
History: Incorporated 1928.
Population: 1,359 (1990); 1,290 (2000); 1,294 (2010); Density: 1,355.1 persons per square mile (2010); Race: 98.7% White, 0.9% Black, 0.1% Asian, 0.0% American Indian/Alaska Native, 0.0% Native Hawaiian/Other Pacific Islander, 0.3% Other, 1.0% Hispanic of any race (2010); Average household size: 2.31 (2010); Median age: 46.1 (2010); Males per 100 females: 101.6 (2010); Marriage status: 25.3% never married, 56.1% now married, 9.3% widowed, 9.3% divorced (2006-2010 5-year est.); Foreign born: 0.0% (2006-2010 5-year est.); Ancestry (includes multiple ancestries): 34.3% German, 23.6% Italian, 22.1% Polish, 18.5% Irish, 15.4% Slovak (2006-2010 5-year est.).
Economy: Single-family building permits issued: 0 (2011); Multi-family building permits issued: 0 (2011); Employment by occupation: 4.0% management, 1.6% professional, 10.3% services, 19.3% sales, 3.9% farming, 7.9% construction, 5.5% production (2006-2010 5-year est.).
Income: Per capita income: $22,091 (2006-2010 5-year est.); Median household income: $49,423 (2006-2010 5-year est.); Average household income: $54,441 (2006-2010 5-year est.); Percent of households with income of $100,000 or more: 11.0% (2006-2010 5-year est.); Poverty rate: 11.7% (2006-2010 5-year est.).
Education: Percent of population age 25 and over with: High school diploma (including GED) or higher: 91.4% (2006-2010 5-year est.); Bachelor's degree or higher: 16.8% (2006-2010 5-year est.); Master's degree or higher: 4.0% (2006-2010 5-year est.).
Housing: Homeownership rate: 83.1% (2010); Median home value: $109,800 (2006-2010 5-year est.); Median contract rent: $431 per month (2006-2010 5-year est.); Median year structure built: 1963 (2006-2010 5-year est.).
Transportation: Commute to work: 92.4% car, 0.0% public transportation, 0.5% walk, 4.6% work from home (2006-2010 5-year est.); Travel time to work: 27.8% less than 15 minutes, 29.5% 15 to 30 minutes, 17.4% 30 to 45 minutes, 14.3% 45 to 60 minutes, 11.0% 60 minutes or more (2006-2010 5-year est.)
Additional Information Contacts
Strongland Chamber of Commerce. . . . . (724) 845-5426
  http://www.strongland.org

WEST NEWTON (borough). Covers a land area of 1.037 square miles and a water area of 0.085 square miles. Located at 40.21° N. Lat; 79.77° W. Long. Elevation is 778 feet.
History: Site Native American massacre of settlers, 1763. Laid out 1796, incorporated 1842.
Population: 3,152 (1990); 3,083 (2000); 2,633 (2010); Density: 2,539.2 persons per square mile (2010); Race: 96.4% White, 1.7% Black, 0.2% Asian, 0.0% American Indian/Alaska Native, 0.0% Native Hawaiian/Other Pacific Islander, 1.7% Other, 0.9% Hispanic of any race (2010); Average household size: 2.15 (2010); Median age: 46.5 (2010); Males per 100 females: 84.5 (2010); Marriage status: 29.6% never married, 46.6% now married, 11.3% widowed, 12.4% divorced (2006-2010 5-year est.); Foreign born: 1.5% (2006-2010 5-year est.); Ancestry (includes multiple

ancestries): 23.3% Italian, 20.3% German, 18.8% Irish, 12.4% English, 5.7% American (2006-2010 5-year est.).
Economy: Single-family building permits issued: 0 (2011); Multi-family building permits issued: 0 (2011); Employment by occupation: 8.5% management, 5.3% professional, 18.1% services, 6.6% sales, 3.2% farming, 7.9% construction, 3.3% production (2006-2010 5-year est.).
Income: Per capita income: $19,261 (2006-2010 5-year est.); Median household income: $31,711 (2006-2010 5-year est.); Average household income: $41,792 (2006-2010 5-year est.); Percent of households with income of $100,000 or more: 5.3% (2006-2010 5-year est.); Poverty rate: 17.2% (2006-2010 5-year est.).
Education: Percent of population age 25 and over with: High school diploma (including GED) or higher: 82.1% (2006-2010 5-year est.); Bachelor's degree or higher: 12.3% (2006-2010 5-year est.); Master's degree or higher: 3.8% (2006-2010 5-year est.).
School District(s)
Yough SD (KG-12)
    2010-11 Enrollment: 2,323 . . . . (724) 446-7272
Housing: Homeownership rate: 66.9% (2010); Median home value: $88,700 (2006-2010 5-year est.); Median contract rent: $401 per month (2006-2010 5-year est.); Median year structure built: 1943 (2006-2010 5-year est.).
Safety: Violent crime rate: 22.7 per 10,000 population; Property crime rate: 310.5 per 10,000 population (2011).
Newspapers: West Newton Times-Sun (Local news; Circulation 3,300)
Transportation: Commute to work: 92.6% car, 0.0% public transportation, 5.6% walk, 1.0% work from home (2006-2010 5-year est.); Travel time to work: 27.9% less than 15 minutes, 38.6% 15 to 30 minutes, 24.5% 30 to 45 minutes, 5.4% 45 to 60 minutes, 3.6% 60 minutes or more (2006-2010 5-year est.)
Airports: Rostraver (general aviation)
Additional Information Contacts
Norwin Chamber of Commerce. (724) 863-0888
  http://www.norwinchamber.com/index.php

WESTMORELAND CITY (unincorporated postal area)
Zip Code: 15692
Covers a land area of 0.455 square miles and a water area of 0 square miles. Located at 40.33° N. Lat; 79.67° W. Long. Elevation is 994 feet.
Population: 941 (2010); Density: 2,067.4 persons per square mile (2010); Race: 97.6% White, 0.1% Black, 0.2% Asian, 0.3% American Indian/Alaska Native, 0.0% Native Hawaiian/Other Pacific Islander, 1.8% Other, 0.9% Hispanic of any race (2010); Average household size: 2.25 (2010); Median age: 44.4 (2010); Males per 100 females: 98.9 (2010); Homeownership rate: 83.3% (2010)

WHITNEY (unincorporated postal area)
Zip Code: 15693
Covers a land area of 0.069 square miles and a water area of 0 square miles. Located at 40.25° N. Lat; 79.40° W. Long. Elevation is 1,115 feet.
Population: 189 (2010); Density: 2,733.7 persons per square mile (2010); Race: 96.3% White, 1.1% Black, 0.0% Asian, 0.0% American Indian/Alaska Native, 0.0% Native Hawaiian/Other Pacific Islander, 2.6% Other, 0.0% Hispanic of any race (2010); Average household size: 2.55 (2010); Median age: 37.7 (2010); Males per 100 females: 89.0 (2010); Homeownership rate: 71.6% (2010)

WYANO (CDP). Covers a land area of 1.178 square miles and a water area of 0 square miles. Located at 40.20° N. Lat; 79.69° W. Long. Elevation is 984 feet.
Population: n/a (1990); n/a (2000); 484 (2010); Density: 410.8 persons per square mile (2010); Race: 98.1% White, 0.6% Black, 0.0% Asian, 0.2% American Indian/Alaska Native, 0.0% Native Hawaiian/Other Pacific Islander, 1.1% Other, 1.0% Hispanic of any race (2010); Average household size: 2.47 (2010); Median age: 41.4 (2010); Males per 100 females: 96.0 (2010); Marriage status: 21.5% never married, 35.1% now married, 21.2% widowed, 22.2% divorced (2006-2010 5-year est.); Foreign born: 0.0% (2006-2010 5-year est.); Ancestry (includes multiple ancestries): 42.6% German, 29.0% Italian, 21.6% Irish, 16.7% Polish, 14.8% English (2006-2010 5-year est.).
Economy: Employment by occupation: 6.6% management, 0.0% professional, 8.2% services, 29.5% sales, 0.0% farming, 10.7% construction, 0.0% production (2006-2010 5-year est.).
Income: Per capita income: $18,018 (2006-2010 5-year est.); Median household income: $29,792 (2006-2010 5-year est.); Average household

income: $39,511 (2006-2010 5-year est.); Percent of households with income of $100,000 or more: 12.5% (2006-2010 5-year est.); Poverty rate: 3.4% (2006-2010 5-year est.).
Education: Percent of population age 25 and over with: High school diploma (including GED) or higher: 73.9% (2006-2010 5-year est.); Bachelor's degree or higher: 0.0% (2006-2010 5-year est.); Master's degree or higher: 0.0% (2006-2010 5-year est.).
Housing: Homeownership rate: 83.7% (2010); Median home value: $84,800 (2006-2010 5-year est.); Median contract rent: n/a per month (2006-2010 5-year est.); Median year structure built: before 1940 (2006-2010 5-year est.).
Transportation: Commute to work: 100.0% car, 0.0% public transportation, 0.0% walk, 0.0% work from home (2006-2010 5-year est.); Travel time to work: 8.5% less than 15 minutes, 38.3% 15 to 30 minutes, 37.2% 30 to 45 minutes, 8.5% 45 to 60 minutes, 7.4% 60 minutes or more (2006-2010 5-year est.)

YOUNGSTOWN (borough). Covers a land area of 0.111 square miles and a water area of 0 square miles. Located at 40.28° N. Lat; 79.37° W. Long. Elevation is 1,076 feet.
Population: 370 (1990); 400 (2000); 326 (2010); Density: 2,927.9 persons per square mile (2010); Race: 99.4% White, 0.0% Black, 0.0% Asian, 0.0% American Indian/Alaska Native, 0.0% Native Hawaiian/Other Pacific Islander, 0.6% Other, 0.6% Hispanic of any race (2010); Average household size: 2.26 (2010); Median age: 46.2 (2010); Males per 100 females: 85.2 (2010); Marriage status: 23.1% never married, 62.1% now married, 9.3% widowed, 5.5% divorced (2006-2010 5-year est.); Foreign born: 0.9% (2006-2010 5-year est.); Ancestry (includes multiple ancestries): 40.7% German, 18.7% Irish, 10.7% Polish, 9.8% English, 7.9% Slovak (2006-2010 5-year est.).
Economy: Single-family building permits issued: 0 (2011); Multi-family building permits issued: 0 (2011); Employment by occupation: 23.1% management, 2.2% professional, 7.7% services, 24.2% sales, 0.0% farming, 11.0% construction, 0.0% production (2006-2010 5-year est.).
Income: Per capita income: $21,424 (2006-2010 5-year est.); Median household income: $40,000 (2006-2010 5-year est.); Average household income: $45,741 (2006-2010 5-year est.); Percent of households with income of $100,000 or more: 5.0% (2006-2010 5-year est.); Poverty rate: 3.7% (2006-2010 5-year est.).
Education: Percent of population age 25 and over with: High school diploma (including GED) or higher: 80.5% (2006-2010 5-year est.); Bachelor's degree or higher: 4.3% (2006-2010 5-year est.); Master's degree or higher: 1.8% (2006-2010 5-year est.).
Housing: Homeownership rate: 69.4% (2010); Median home value: $93,900 (2006-2010 5-year est.); Median contract rent: $579 per month (2006-2010 5-year est.); Median year structure built: before 1940 (2006-2010 5-year est.).
Transportation: Commute to work: 95.6% car, 0.0% public transportation, 3.3% walk, 1.1% work from home (2006-2010 5-year est.); Travel time to work: 38.9% less than 15 minutes, 25.6% 15 to 30 minutes, 20.0% 30 to 45 minutes, 10.0% 45 to 60 minutes, 5.6% 60 minutes or more (2006-2010 5-year est.)

YOUNGWOOD (borough). Covers a land area of 1.918 square miles and a water area of 0.004 square miles. Located at 40.24° N. Lat; 79.58° W. Long. Elevation is 955 feet.
History: Incorporated 1902.
Population: 3,343 (1990); 4,138 (2000); 3,050 (2010); Density: 1,590.2 persons per square mile (2010); Race: 97.7% White, 0.8% Black, 0.2% Asian, 0.1% American Indian/Alaska Native, 0.0% Native Hawaiian/Other Pacific Islander, 1.2% Other, 0.6% Hispanic of any race (2010); Average household size: 2.09 (2010); Median age: 43.1 (2010); Males per 100 females: 94.8 (2010); Marriage status: 32.0% never married, 51.4% now married, 7.0% widowed, 9.6% divorced (2006-2010 5-year est.); Foreign born: 0.0% (2006-2010 5-year est.); Ancestry (includes multiple ancestries): 37.2% German, 16.5% English, 12.3% Irish, 12.2% Italian, 5.3% Scotch-Irish (2006-2010 5-year est.).
Economy: Single-family building permits issued: 0 (2011); Multi-family building permits issued: 0 (2011); Employment by occupation: 7.4% management, 5.7% professional, 11.2% services, 23.2% sales, 8.8% farming, 9.2% construction, 3.2% production (2006-2010 5-year est.).
Income: Per capita income: $22,993 (2006-2010 5-year est.); Median household income: $39,299 (2006-2010 5-year est.); Average household income: $48,897 (2006-2010 5-year est.); Percent of households with

income of $100,000 or more: 8.8% (2006-2010 5-year est.); Poverty rate: 6.1% (2006-2010 5-year est.).
Education: Percent of population age 25 and over with: High school diploma (including GED) or higher: 94.6% (2006-2010 5-year est.); Bachelor's degree or higher: 16.1% (2006-2010 5-year est.); Master's degree or higher: 2.9% (2006-2010 5-year est.).

Two-year College(s)
Westmoreland County Community College (Public)
Fall 2010 Enrollment: 5,455 . . . . (724) 925-4000
2011-12 Tuition: In-state $5,490; Out-of-state $7,890
Housing: Homeownership rate: 62.6% (2010); Median home value: $99,400 (2006-2010 5-year est.); Median contract rent: $445 per month (2006-2010 5-year est.); Median year structure built: 1949 (2006-2010 5-year est.).
Transportation: Commute to work: 92.3% car, 0.0% public transportation, 3.5% walk, 3.0% work from home (2006-2010 5-year est.); Travel time to work: 30.8% less than 15 minutes, 42.8% 15 to 30 minutes, 13.4% 30 to 45 minutes, 6.2% 45 to 60 minutes, 6.8% 60 minutes or more (2006-2010 5-year est.)
Additional Information Contacts
Borough of Youngwood. . . . . (724) 925-3660
http://www.youngwood.org
Westmoreland Chamber of Commerce . . . . (724) 834-2900
http://www.westmorelandchamber.com

YUKON (CDP). Covers a land area of 0.938 square miles and a water area of 0.015 square miles. Located at 40.21° N. Lat; 79.69° W. Long. Elevation is 942 feet.
Population: n/a (1990); n/a (2000); 677 (2010); Density: 721.6 persons per square mile (2010); Race: 99.7% White, 0.0% Black, 0.0% Asian, 0.0% American Indian/Alaska Native, 0.0% Native Hawaiian/Other Pacific Islander, 0.3% Other, 0.6% Hispanic of any race (2010); Average household size: 2.21 (2010); Median age: 43.0 (2010); Males per 100 females: 98.5 (2010); Marriage status: 24.4% never married, 37.1% now married, 16.4% widowed, 22.0% divorced (2006-2010 5-year est.); Foreign born: 1.1% (2006-2010 5-year est.); Ancestry (includes multiple ancestries): 22.6% German, 20.1% Italian, 15.8% English, 15.2% Polish, 12.0% Irish (2006-2010 5-year est.).
Economy: Employment by occupation: 0.0% management, 0.0% professional, 28.9% services, 0.0% sales, 0.0% farming, 22.5% construction, 7.5% production (2006-2010 5-year est.).
Income: Per capita income: $18,357 (2006-2010 5-year est.); Median household income: $29,018 (2006-2010 5-year est.); Average household income: $33,941 (2006-2010 5-year est.); Percent of households with income of $100,000 or more: n/a (2006-2010 5-year est.); Poverty rate: 10.9% (2006-2010 5-year est.).
Education: Percent of population age 25 and over with: High school diploma (including GED) or higher: 72.1% (2006-2010 5-year est.); Bachelor's degree or higher: 9.4% (2006-2010 5-year est.); Master's degree or higher: 5.3% (2006-2010 5-year est.).
Housing: Homeownership rate: 75.2% (2010); Median home value: $61,900 (2006-2010 5-year est.); Median contract rent: $528 per month (2006-2010 5-year est.); Median year structure built: before 1940 (2006-2010 5-year est.).
Transportation: Commute to work: 100.0% car, 0.0% public transportation, 0.0% walk, 0.0% work from home (2006-2010 5-year est.); Travel time to work: 26.7% less than 15 minutes, 39.6% 15 to 30 minutes, 7.0% 30 to 45 minutes, 18.7% 45 to 60 minutes, 8.0% 60 minutes or more (2006-2010 5-year est.)

Wyoming County

Located in northeastern Pennsylvania; hilly area, drained by the Susquehanna River. Covers a land area of 397.323 square miles, a water area of 7.730 square miles, and is located in the Eastern Time Zone at 41.53° N. Lat., 76.01° W. Long. The county was founded in 1842. County seat is Tunkhannock.

Wyoming County is part of the Scranton—Wilkes-Barre, PA Metropolitan Statistical Area. The entire metro area includes: Lackawanna County, PA; Luzerne County, PA; Wyoming County, PA

Population: 28,076 (1990); 28,080 (2000); 28,276 (2010); Race: 97.4% White, 0.7% Black, 0.3% Asian, 0.2% American Indian/Alaska Native, 0.0% Native Hawaiian/Other Pacific Islander, 1.4% Other, 1.5% Hispanic

of any race (2010); Density: 71.2 persons per square mile (2010); Average household size: 2.46 (2010); Median age: 42.3 (2010); Males per 100 females: 99.9 (2010).

Religion: Six largest groups: 21.2% Catholicism, 11.4% Methodist/Pietist, 3.9% Non-Denominational, 1.2% Pentecostal, 1.1% Baptist, 0.9% Lutheran (2010)

Economy: Unemployment rate: 9.3% (August 2012); Total civilian labor force: 14,698 (August 2012); Leading industries: 14.9% retail trade; 13.2% health care and social assistance; 8.0% administration, support, waste management, remediation services (2010); Farms: 649 totaling 77,957 acres (2007); Companies that employ 500 or more persons: 1 (2010); Companies that employ 100 to 499 persons: 11 (2010); Companies that employ less than 100 persons: 635 (2010); Black-owned businesses: n/a (2007); Hispanic-owned businesses: n/a (2007); Asian-owned businesses: n/a (2007); Women-owned businesses: n/a (2007); Retail sales per capita: $9,735 (2010). Single-family building permits issued: 72 (2011); Multi-family building permits issued: 0 (2011).

Income: Per capita income: $22,899 (2006-2010 5-year est.); Median household income: $47,403 (2006-2010 5-year est.); Average household income: $57,383 (2006-2010 5-year est.); Percent of households with income of $100,000 or more: 13.1% (2006-2010 5-year est.); Poverty rate: 10.9% (2006-2010 5-year est.); Bankruptcy rate: 1.54% (2011).

Education: Percent of population age 25 and over with: High school diploma (including GED) or higher: 89.1% (2006-2010 5-year est.); Bachelor's degree or higher: 16.8% (2006-2010 5-year est.); Master's degree or higher: 5.7% (2006-2010 5-year est.).

Housing: Homeownership rate: 76.7% (2010); Median home value: $140,800 (2006-2010 5-year est.); Median contract rent: $475 per month (2006-2010 5-year est.); Median year structure built: 1970 (2006-2010 5-year est.)

Health: Birth rate: 94.3 per 10,000 population (2011); Death rate: 107.4 per 10,000 population (2011); Age-adjusted cancer mortality rate: 212.0 deaths per 100,000 population (2009); Number of physicians: 7.1 per 10,000 population (2010); Hospital beds: 20.8 per 10,000 population (2008); Hospital admissions: 880.9 per 10,000 population (2008).

Elections: 2012 Presidential election results: 42.9% Obama, 55.2% Romney

Additional Information Contacts

Wyoming County Government . . . . (570) 996-2273
   http://www.wycopa.org
Wyoming County Chamber of Commerce. . . . . (570) 836-7755
   http://www.wyccc.com
Wyoming County Chamber of Commerce. . . . . (570) 836-7755
   http://wyccc.com

Wyoming County Communities

BRAINTRIM (township). Covers a land area of 5.831 square miles and a water area of 0.337 square miles. Located at 41.64° N. Lat; 76.15° W. Long.

Population: 465 (1990); 508 (2000); 502 (2010); Density: 86.1 persons per square mile (2010); Race: 99.0% White, 0.0% Black, 0.2% Asian, 0.0% American Indian/Alaska Native, 0.0% Native Hawaiian/Other Pacific Islander, 0.8% Other, 2.2% Hispanic of any race (2010); Average household size: 2.41 (2010); Median age: 36.4 (2010); Males per 100 females: 94.6 (2010); Marriage status: 36.0% never married, 49.1% now married, 5.2% widowed, 9.7% divorced (2006-2010 5-year est.); Foreign born: 1.5% (2006-2010 5-year est.); Ancestry (includes multiple ancestries): 30.7% German, 28.2% Irish, 14.1% English, 6.1% Italian, 4.3% American (2006-2010 5-year est.).

Economy: Single-family building permits issued: 1 (2011); Multi-family building permits issued: 0 (2011); Employment by occupation: 8.4% management, 0.0% professional, 8.4% services, 12.4% sales, 3.9% farming, 8.4% construction, 10.1% production (2006-2010 5-year est.).

Income: Per capita income: $21,264 (2006-2010 5-year est.); Median household income: $44,750 (2006-2010 5-year est.); Average household income: $50,611 (2006-2010 5-year est.); Percent of households with income of $100,000 or more: 7.4% (2006-2010 5-year est.); Poverty rate: 11.2% (2006-2010 5-year est.).

Education: Percent of population age 25 and over with: High school diploma (including GED) or higher: 88.9% (2006-2010 5-year est.); Bachelor's degree or higher: 9.3% (2006-2010 5-year est.); Master's degree or higher: 1.8% (2006-2010 5-year est.).

Housing: Homeownership rate: 68.8% (2010); Median home value: $97,500 (2006-2010 5-year est.); Median contract rent: $525 per month

(2006-2010 5-year est.); Median year structure built: 1973 (2006-2010 5-year est.).

Transportation: Commute to work: 93.6% car, 0.0% public transportation, 4.1% walk, 0.0% work from home (2006-2010 5-year est.); Travel time to work: 35.5% less than 15 minutes, 45.9% 15 to 30 minutes, 9.3% 30 to 45 minutes, 6.4% 45 to 60 minutes, 2.9% 60 minutes or more (2006-2010 5-year est.)

CLINTON (township). Covers a land area of 12.372 square miles and a water area of 0.019 square miles. Located at 41.57° N. Lat; 75.82° W. Long.

Population: 1,063 (1990); 1,343 (2000); 1,367 (2010); Density: 110.5 persons per square mile (2010); Race: 96.3% White, 0.7% Black, 0.4% Asian, 0.2% American Indian/Alaska Native, 0.0% Native Hawaiian/Other Pacific Islander, 2.4% Other, 1.7% Hispanic of any race (2010); Average household size: 2.56 (2010); Median age: 42.8 (2010); Males per 100 females: 99.9 (2010); Marriage status: 24.4% never married, 62.6% now married, 7.2% widowed, 5.7% divorced (2006-2010 5-year est.); Foreign born: 2.1% (2006-2010 5-year est.); Ancestry (includes multiple ancestries): 33.5% German, 23.7% Irish, 15.4% Italian, 15.4% English, 14.3% Polish (2006-2010 5-year est.).

Economy: Single-family building permits issued: 0 (2011); Multi-family building permits issued: 0 (2011); Employment by occupation: 8.3% management, 1.0% professional, 14.6% services, 20.4% sales, 2.4% farming, 14.9% construction, 10.1% production (2006-2010 5-year est.).

Income: Per capita income: $27,607 (2006-2010 5-year est.); Median household income: $55,781 (2006-2010 5-year est.); Average household income: $70,033 (2006-2010 5-year est.); Percent of households with income of $100,000 or more: 18.3% (2006-2010 5-year est.); Poverty rate: 7.9% (2006-2010 5-year est.).

Education: Percent of population age 25 and over with: High school diploma (including GED) or higher: 92.8% (2006-2010 5-year est.); Bachelor's degree or higher: 16.0% (2006-2010 5-year est.); Master's degree or higher: 6.6% (2006-2010 5-year est.).

Housing: Homeownership rate: 83.3% (2010); Median home value: $165,800 (2006-2010 5-year est.); Median contract rent: $562 per month (2006-2010 5-year est.); Median year structure built: 1980 (2006-2010 5-year est.).

Transportation: Commute to work: 92.6% car, 0.0% public transportation, 0.0% walk, 7.4% work from home (2006-2010 5-year est.); Travel time to work: 22.3% less than 15 minutes, 41.9% 15 to 30 minutes, 28.4% 30 to 45 minutes, 2.4% 45 to 60 minutes, 5.0% 60 minutes or more (2006-2010 5-year est.)

Additional Information Contacts

Greater Scranton Chamber of Commerce . . . . (570) 342-7711
   http://www.scrantonchamber.com

EATON (township). Covers a land area of 35.991 square miles and a water area of 1.138 square miles. Located at 41.49° N. Lat; 75.96° W. Long.

Population: 1,609 (1990); 1,644 (2000); 1,519 (2010); Density: 42.2 persons per square mile (2010); Race: 98.0% White, 0.6% Black, 0.3% Asian, 0.2% American Indian/Alaska Native, 0.0% Native Hawaiian/Other Pacific Islander, 0.9% Other, 0.3% Hispanic of any race (2010); Average household size: 2.40 (2010); Median age: 47.3 (2010); Males per 100 females: 97.8 (2010); Marriage status: 26.4% never married, 55.7% now married, 5.4% widowed, 12.5% divorced (2006-2010 5-year est.); Foreign born: 1.5% (2006-2010 5-year est.); Ancestry (includes multiple ancestries): 25.9% German, 17.5% Irish, 13.0% English, 11.0% Polish, 9.9% American (2006-2010 5-year est.).

Economy: Single-family building permits issued: 9 (2011); Multi-family building permits issued: 0 (2011); Employment by occupation: 5.5% management, 2.5% professional, 12.5% services, 17.6% sales, 6.8% farming, 18.9% construction, 13.4% production (2006-2010 5-year est.).

Income: Per capita income: $24,354 (2006-2010 5-year est.); Median household income: $51,500 (2006-2010 5-year est.); Average household income: $59,544 (2006-2010 5-year est.); Percent of households with income of $100,000 or more: 10.6% (2006-2010 5-year est.); Poverty rate: 10.5% (2006-2010 5-year est.).

Education: Percent of population age 25 and over with: High school diploma (including GED) or higher: 88.6% (2006-2010 5-year est.); Bachelor's degree or higher: 18.0% (2006-2010 5-year est.); Master's degree or higher: 8.2% (2006-2010 5-year est.).

Housing: Homeownership rate: 84.1% (2010); Median home value: $135,600 (2006-2010 5-year est.); Median contract rent: $422 per month

(2006-2010 5-year est.); Median year structure built: 1972 (2006-2010 5-year est.).

Transportation: Commute to work: 92.0% car, 0.0% public transportation, 3.7% walk, 4.2% work from home (2006-2010 5-year est.); Travel time to work: 29.2% less than 15 minutes, 33.9% 15 to 30 minutes, 19.8% 30 to 45 minutes, 8.6% 45 to 60 minutes, 8.6% 60 minutes or more (2006-2010 5-year est.)

Additional Information Contacts

Wyoming County Chamber of Commerce. . . . . (570) 836-7755
http://www.wyccc.com

EXETER (township). Covers a land area of 3.135 square miles and a water area of 0.260 square miles. Located at 41.43° N. Lat; 75.85° W. Long.

Population: 763 (1990); 748 (2000); 690 (2010); Density: 220.1 persons per square mile (2010); Race: 98.7% White, 0.9% Black, 0.0% Asian, 0.0% American Indian/Alaska Native, 0.0% Native Hawaiian/Other Pacific Islander, 0.4% Other, 1.4% Hispanic of any race (2010); Average household size: 2.22 (2010); Median age: 49.4 (2010); Males per 100 females: 98.3 (2010); Marriage status: 18.9% never married, 54.9% now married, 7.8% widowed, 18.4% divorced (2006-2010 5-year est.); Foreign born: 0.0% (2006-2010 5-year est.); Ancestry (includes multiple ancestries): 23.5% Italian, 21.4% Polish, 21.4% German, 12.3% Irish, 11.3% American (2006-2010 5-year est.).

Economy: Single-family building permits issued: 1 (2011); Multi-family building permits issued: 0 (2011); Employment by occupation: 7.1% management, 4.0% professional, 13.9% services, 16.7% sales, 2.5% farming, 16.9% construction, 10.4% production (2006-2010 5-year est.).

Income: Per capita income: $23,003 (2006-2010 5-year est.); Median household income: $44,464 (2006-2010 5-year est.); Average household income: $52,224 (2006-2010 5-year est.); Percent of households with income of $100,000 or more: 9.8% (2006-2010 5-year est.); Poverty rate: 6.8% (2006-2010 5-year est.).

Education: Percent of population age 25 and over with: High school diploma (including GED) or higher: 91.4% (2006-2010 5-year est.); Bachelor's degree or higher: 14.8% (2006-2010 5-year est.); Master's degree or higher: 3.3% (2006-2010 5-year est.).

Housing: Homeownership rate: 83.3% (2010); Median home value: $126,000 (2006-2010 5-year est.); Median contract rent: $358 per month (2006-2010 5-year est.); Median year structure built: 1971 (2006-2010 5-year est.).

Transportation: Commute to work: 94.1% car, 0.0% public transportation, 3.3% walk, 1.5% work from home (2006-2010 5-year est.); Travel time to work: 13.5% less than 15 minutes, 43.0% 15 to 30 minutes, 29.0% 30 to 45 minutes, 11.1% 45 to 60 minutes, 3.4% 60 minutes or more (2006-2010 5-year est.)

FACTORYVILLE (borough). Covers a land area of 0.714 square miles and a water area of 0 square miles. Located at 41.56° N. Lat; 75.78° W. Long. Elevation is 820 feet.

Population: 1,310 (1990); 1,144 (2000); 1,158 (2010); Density: 1,622.2 persons per square mile (2010); Race: 92.5% White, 4.6% Black, 0.7% Asian, 0.1% American Indian/Alaska Native, 0.0% Native Hawaiian/Other Pacific Islander, 2.1% Other, 4.0% Hispanic of any race (2010); Average household size: 2.43 (2010); Median age: 23.6 (2010); Males per 100 females: 99.0 (2010); Marriage status: 50.6% never married, 33.7% now married, 6.1% widowed, 9.6% divorced (2006-2010 5-year est.); Foreign born: 1.8% (2006-2010 5-year est.); Ancestry (includes multiple ancestries): 26.5% Irish, 26.0% German, 19.6% Italian, 15.9% Polish, 9.1% English (2006-2010 5-year est.).

Economy: Single-family building permits issued: 0 (2011); Multi-family building permits issued: 0 (2011); Employment by occupation: 4.4% management, 1.2% professional, 18.3% services, 18.6% sales, 6.7% farming, 6.9% construction, 6.6% production (2006-2010 5-year est.).

Income: Per capita income: $16,926 (2006-2010 5-year est.); Median household income: $43,482 (2006-2010 5-year est.); Average household income: $49,181 (2006-2010 5-year est.); Percent of households with income of $100,000 or more: 8.9% (2006-2010 5-year est.); Poverty rate: 7.6% (2006-2010 5-year est.).

Education: Percent of population age 25 and over with: High school diploma (including GED) or higher: 97.5% (2006-2010 5-year est.); Bachelor's degree or higher: 25.1% (2006-2010 5-year est.); Master's degree or higher: 5.8% (2006-2010 5-year est.).

School District(s)

Lackawanna Trail SD (KG-12)
    2010-11 Enrollment: 1,173 . . . . (570) 945-5184

Housing: Homeownership rate: 66.0% (2010); Median home value: $145,700 (2006-2010 5-year est.); Median contract rent: $470 per month (2006-2010 5-year est.); Median year structure built: before 1940 (2006-2010 5-year est.).

Transportation: Commute to work: 77.3% car, 0.0% public transportation, 17.6% walk, 4.5% work from home (2006-2010 5-year est.); Travel time to work: 41.9% less than 15 minutes, 30.7% 15 to 30 minutes, 13.9% 30 to 45 minutes, 2.5% 45 to 60 minutes, 11.0% 60 minutes or more (2006-2010 5-year est.)

Additional Information Contacts

Wyoming County Chamber of Commerce. . . . . (570) 836-7755
http://wyccc.com

FALLS (township). Covers a land area of 20.591 square miles and a water area of 0.550 square miles. Located at 41.48° N. Lat; 75.84° W. Long. Elevation is 607 feet.

Population: 2,055 (1990); 1,997 (2000); 1,995 (2010); Density: 96.9 persons per square mile (2010); Race: 97.5% White, 1.1% Black, 0.1% Asian, 0.1% American Indian/Alaska Native, 0.1% Native Hawaiian/Other Pacific Islander, 1.1% Other, 1.3% Hispanic of any race (2010); Average household size: 2.52 (2010); Median age: 42.8 (2010); Males per 100 females: 98.7 (2010); Marriage status: 26.9% never married, 59.1% now married, 6.3% widowed, 7.7% divorced (2006-2010 5-year est.); Foreign born: 0.5% (2006-2010 5-year est.); Ancestry (includes multiple ancestries): 28.5% German, 16.6% Italian, 16.1% Irish, 13.3% English, 12.6% Polish (2006-2010 5-year est.).

Economy: Single-family building permits issued: 2 (2011); Multi-family building permits issued: 0 (2011); Employment by occupation: 10.7% management, 3.7% professional, 10.7% services, 14.6% sales, 4.0% farming, 14.0% construction, 8.9% production (2006-2010 5-year est.).

Income: Per capita income: $21,217 (2006-2010 5-year est.); Median household income: $51,019 (2006-2010 5-year est.); Average household income: $55,199 (2006-2010 5-year est.); Percent of households with income of $100,000 or more: 10.7% (2006-2010 5-year est.); Poverty rate: 13.0% (2006-2010 5-year est.).

Education: Percent of population age 25 and over with: High school diploma (including GED) or higher: 91.6% (2006-2010 5-year est.); Bachelor's degree or higher: 19.7% (2006-2010 5-year est.); Master's degree or higher: 6.1% (2006-2010 5-year est.).

Housing: Homeownership rate: 80.4% (2010); Median home value: $143,900 (2006-2010 5-year est.); Median contract rent: $450 per month (2006-2010 5-year est.); Median year structure built: 1972 (2006-2010 5-year est.).

Transportation: Commute to work: 93.1% car, 0.0% public transportation, 2.2% walk, 4.2% work from home (2006-2010 5-year est.); Travel time to work: 13.5% less than 15 minutes, 50.2% 15 to 30 minutes, 27.0% 30 to 45 minutes, 4.9% 45 to 60 minutes, 4.5% 60 minutes or more (2006-2010 5-year est.)

Additional Information Contacts

Wyoming County Chamber of Commerce. . . . . (570) 836-7755
http://wyccc.com

FORKSTON (township). Covers a land area of 70.413 square miles and a water area of 0.166 square miles. Located at 41.46° N. Lat; 76.16° W. Long.

Population: 316 (1990); 386 (2000); 397 (2010); Density: 5.6 persons per square mile (2010); Race: 98.0% White, 0.0% Black, 0.3% Asian, 1.0% American Indian/Alaska Native, 0.0% Native Hawaiian/Other Pacific Islander, 0.7% Other, 0.5% Hispanic of any race (2010); Average household size: 2.34 (2010); Median age: 46.3 (2010); Males per 100 females: 116.9 (2010); Marriage status: 22.8% never married, 60.1% now married, 3.6% widowed, 13.6% divorced (2006-2010 5-year est.); Foreign born: 0.4% (2006-2010 5-year est.); Ancestry (includes multiple ancestries): 27.5% German, 21.9% English, 14.0% Italian, 11.8% Polish, 10.5% Irish (2006-2010 5-year est.).

Economy: Single-family building permits issued: 0 (2011); Multi-family building permits issued: 0 (2011); Employment by occupation: 2.1% management, 3.7% professional, 12.0% services, 7.3% sales, 6.3% farming, 9.9% construction, 13.1% production (2006-2010 5-year est.).

Income: Per capita income: $24,474 (2006-2010 5-year est.); Median household income: $47,266 (2006-2010 5-year est.); Average household income: $61,312 (2006-2010 5-year est.); Percent of households with

income of $100,000 or more: 12.0% (2006-2010 5-year est.); Poverty rate: 13.8% (2006-2010 5-year est.).

Education: Percent of population age 25 and over with: High school diploma (including GED) or higher: 82.8% (2006-2010 5-year est.); Bachelor's degree or higher: 13.0% (2006-2010 5-year est.); Master's degree or higher: 3.9% (2006-2010 5-year est.).

Housing: Homeownership rate: 80.6% (2010); Median home value: $138,600 (2006-2010 5-year est.); Median contract rent: $567 per month (2006-2010 5-year est.); Median year structure built: 1957 (2006-2010 5-year est.).

Transportation: Commute to work: 89.4% car, 0.0% public transportation, 6.7% walk, 0.0% work from home (2006-2010 5-year est.); Travel time to work: 17.9% less than 15 minutes, 44.1% 15 to 30 minutes, 22.3% 30 to 45 minutes, 11.7% 45 to 60 minutes, 3.9% 60 minutes or more (2006-2010 5-year est.)

LACEYVILLE (borough). Covers a land area of 0.193 square miles and a water area of 0 square miles. Located at 41.65° N. Lat; 76.16° W. Long. Elevation is 692 feet.

Population: 436 (1990); 396 (2000); 379 (2010); Density: 1,961.4 persons per square mile (2010); Race: 94.5% White, 0.5% Black, 0.0% Asian, 0.0% American Indian/Alaska Native, 0.0% Native Hawaiian/Other Pacific Islander, 5.0% Other, 7.9% Hispanic of any race (2010); Average household size: 2.37 (2010); Median age: 39.4 (2010); Males per 100 females: 88.6 (2010); Marriage status: 29.8% never married, 51.2% now married, 10.8% widowed, 8.2% divorced (2006-2010 5-year est.); Foreign born: 4.2% (2006-2010 5-year est.); Ancestry (includes multiple ancestries): 28.6% German, 21.5% Irish, 16.1% English, 10.7% Polish, 6.6% French (2006-2010 5-year est.).

Economy: Single-family building permits issued: 0 (2011); Multi-family building permits issued: 0 (2011); Employment by occupation: 2.4% management, 4.0% professional, 16.0% services, 22.8% sales, 4.0% farming, 10.0% construction, 16.4% production (2006-2010 5-year est.).

Income: Per capita income: $18,594 (2006-2010 5-year est.); Median household income: $46,667 (2006-2010 5-year est.); Average household income: $49,324 (2006-2010 5-year est.); Percent of households with income of $100,000 or more: 2.7% (2006-2010 5-year est.); Poverty rate: 15.1% (2006-2010 5-year est.).

Education: Percent of population age 25 and over with: High school diploma (including GED) or higher: 81.2% (2006-2010 5-year est.); Bachelor's degree or higher: 9.6% (2006-2010 5-year est.); Master's degree or higher: 0.0% (2006-2010 5-year est.).

School District(s)

Wyalusing Area SD (KG-12)

    2010-11 Enrollment: 1,435 . . . . (570) 746-1605

Housing: Homeownership rate: 56.9% (2010); Median home value: $93,200 (2006-2010 5-year est.); Median contract rent: $430 per month (2006-2010 5-year est.); Median year structure built: before 1940 (2006-2010 5-year est.).

Transportation: Commute to work: 80.4% car, 0.0% public transportation, 9.8% walk, 9.8% work from home (2006-2010 5-year est.); Travel time to work: 33.0% less than 15 minutes, 39.4% 15 to 30 minutes, 18.6% 30 to 45 minutes, 0.9% 45 to 60 minutes, 8.1% 60 minutes or more (2006-2010 5-year est.)

LAKE WINOLA (CDP). Covers a land area of 1.541 square miles and a water area of 0.289 square miles. Located at 41.51° N. Lat; 75.85° W. Long. Elevation is 1,138 feet.

Population: n/a (1990); n/a (2000); 748 (2010); Density: 485.3 persons per square mile (2010); Race: 97.7% White, 0.7% Black, 0.1% Asian, 0.3% American Indian/Alaska Native, 0.0% Native Hawaiian/Other Pacific Islander, 1.2% Other, 2.3% Hispanic of any race (2010); Average household size: 2.11 (2010); Median age: 49.9 (2010); Males per 100 females: 88.9 (2010); Marriage status: 28.3% never married, 49.8% now married, 9.8% widowed, 12.0% divorced (2006-2010 5-year est.); Foreign born: 0.0% (2006-2010 5-year est.); Ancestry (includes multiple ancestries): 30.2% Irish, 29.7% German, 18.4% Polish, 14.3% English, 8.4% Italian (2006-2010 5-year est.).

Economy: Employment by occupation: 9.4% management, 9.7% professional, 10.9% services, 17.6% sales, 0.0% farming, 12.0% construction, 7.0% production (2006-2010 5-year est.).

Income: Per capita income: $26,471 (2006-2010 5-year est.); Median household income: $47,000 (2006-2010 5-year est.); Average household income: $55,875 (2006-2010 5-year est.); Percent of households with

income of $100,000 or more: 12.3% (2006-2010 5-year est.); Poverty rate: 1.4% (2006-2010 5-year est.).

Education: Percent of population age 25 and over with: High school diploma (including GED) or higher: 97.1% (2006-2010 5-year est.); Bachelor's degree or higher: 17.3% (2006-2010 5-year est.); Master's degree or higher: 7.7% (2006-2010 5-year est.).

Housing: Homeownership rate: 68.4% (2010); Median home value: $188,800 (2006-2010 5-year est.); Median contract rent: $625 per month (2006-2010 5-year est.); Median year structure built: 1953 (2006-2010 5-year est.).

Transportation: Commute to work: 92.3% car, 0.0% public transportation, 5.3% walk, 2.4% work from home (2006-2010 5-year est.); Travel time to work: 31.3% less than 15 minutes, 37.7% 15 to 30 minutes, 18.5% 30 to 45 minutes, 9.1% 45 to 60 minutes, 3.3% 60 minutes or more (2006-2010 5-year est.)

LEMON (township). Aka Aldovin. Covers a land area of 16.058 square miles and a water area of 0.598 square miles. Located at 41.61° N. Lat; 75.91° W. Long. Elevation is 1,099 feet.

Population: 1,257 (1990); 1,189 (2000); 1,243 (2010); Density: 77.4 persons per square mile (2010); Race: 99.2% White, 0.0% Black, 0.2% Asian, 0.0% American Indian/Alaska Native, 0.0% Native Hawaiian/Other Pacific Islander, 0.6% Other, 1.3% Hispanic of any race (2010); Average household size: 2.35 (2010); Median age: 44.3 (2010); Males per 100 females: 111.8 (2010); Marriage status: 27.4% never married, 54.3% now married, 8.6% widowed, 9.7% divorced (2006-2010 5-year est.); Foreign born: 0.2% (2006-2010 5-year est.); Ancestry (includes multiple ancestries): 29.3% German, 16.5% Irish, 14.6% Polish, 14.3% English, 10.9% Italian (2006-2010 5-year est.).

Economy: Single-family building permits issued: 2 (2011); Multi-family building permits issued: 0 (2011); Employment by occupation: 10.7% management, 3.6% professional, 16.2% services, 13.9% sales, 5.3% farming, 9.7% construction, 9.0% production (2006-2010 5-year est.).

Income: Per capita income: $24,561 (2006-2010 5-year est.); Median household income: $47,604 (2006-2010 5-year est.); Average household income: $56,932 (2006-2010 5-year est.); Percent of households with income of $100,000 or more: 11.5% (2006-2010 5-year est.); Poverty rate: 6.4% (2006-2010 5-year est.).

Education: Percent of population age 25 and over with: High school diploma (including GED) or higher: 91.3% (2006-2010 5-year est.); Bachelor's degree or higher: 20.5% (2006-2010 5-year est.); Master's degree or higher: 7.1% (2006-2010 5-year est.).

Housing: Homeownership rate: 76.1% (2010); Median home value: $144,900 (2006-2010 5-year est.); Median contract rent: $539 per month (2006-2010 5-year est.); Median year structure built: 1969 (2006-2010 5-year est.).

Transportation: Commute to work: 91.7% car, 0.0% public transportation, 0.6% walk, 6.3% work from home (2006-2010 5-year est.); Travel time to work: 36.8% less than 15 minutes, 28.5% 15 to 30 minutes, 20.5% 30 to 45 minutes, 7.8% 45 to 60 minutes, 6.3% 60 minutes or more (2006-2010 5-year est.)

Additional Information Contacts

Wyoming County Chamber of Commerce . . . . (570) 836-7755

    http://wyccc.com

MEHOOPANY (township). Covers a land area of 17.180 square miles and a water area of 0.707 square miles. Located at 41.56° N. Lat; 76.08° W. Long. Elevation is 653 feet.

Population: 888 (1990); 993 (2000); 892 (2010); Density: 51.9 persons per square mile (2010); Race: 96.4% White, 1.0% Black, 0.2% Asian, 0.8% American Indian/Alaska Native, 0.0% Native Hawaiian/Other Pacific Islander, 1.6% Other, 2.4% Hispanic of any race (2010); Average household size: 2.66 (2010); Median age: 40.1 (2010); Males per 100 females: 100.0 (2010); Marriage status: 19.0% never married, 61.0% now married, 8.3% widowed, 11.7% divorced (2006-2010 5-year est.); Foreign born: 1.8% (2006-2010 5-year est.); Ancestry (includes multiple ancestries): 33.8% German, 24.3% Irish, 15.4% Italian, 15.0% English, 13.6% Polish (2006-2010 5-year est.).

Economy: Single-family building permits issued: 5 (2011); Multi-family building permits issued: 0 (2011); Employment by occupation: 6.2% management, 1.8% professional, 7.1% services, 26.8% sales, 3.5% farming, 7.4% construction, 7.9% production (2006-2010 5-year est.).

Income: Per capita income: $21,962 (2006-2010 5-year est.); Median household income: $47,778 (2006-2010 5-year est.); Average household income: $54,104 (2006-2010 5-year est.); Percent of households with

income of $100,000 or more: 13.3% (2006-2010 5-year est.); Poverty rate: 15.2% (2006-2010 5-year est.).

Education: Percent of population age 25 and over with: High school diploma (including GED) or higher: 91.0% (2006-2010 5-year est.); Bachelor's degree or higher: 13.0% (2006-2010 5-year est.); Master's degree or higher: 1.2% (2006-2010 5-year est.).

School District(s)

Tunkhannock Area SD (KG-12)

   2010-11 Enrollment: 2,818 . . . . (570) 836-3111

Housing: Homeownership rate: 74.4% (2010); Median home value: $123,000 (2006-2010 5-year est.); Median contract rent: $475 per month (2006-2010 5-year est.); Median year structure built: 1963 (2006-2010 5-year est.).

Transportation: Commute to work: 94.0% car, 0.0% public transportation, 1.8% walk, 0.9% work from home (2006-2010 5-year est.); Travel time to work: 31.3% less than 15 minutes, 37.1% 15 to 30 minutes, 6.7% 30 to 45 minutes, 14.9% 45 to 60 minutes, 10.0% 60 minutes or more (2006-2010 5-year est.)

Additional Information Contacts

Wyoming County Chamber of Commerce. . . . . (570) 836-7755
  http://wyccc.com

MESHOPPEN (borough). Covers a land area of 0.691 square miles and a water area of 0.086 square miles. Located at 41.61° N. Lat; 76.04° W. Long. Elevation is 656 feet.

Population: 439 (1990); 459 (2000); 563 (2010); Density: 815.1 persons per square mile (2010); Race: 89.2% White, 3.7% Black, 0.7% Asian, 0.7% American Indian/Alaska Native, 0.0% Native Hawaiian/Other Pacific Islander, 5.7% Other, 10.1% Hispanic of any race (2010); Average household size: 2.96 (2010); Median age: 29.1 (2010); Males per 100 females: 104.7 (2010); Marriage status: 39.4% never married, 43.4% now married, 4.0% widowed, 13.2% divorced (2006-2010 5-year est.); Foreign born: 4.4% (2006-2010 5-year est.); Ancestry (includes multiple ancestries): 31.0% German, 21.0% Irish, 14.4% English, 8.1% Polish, 7.9% American (2006-2010 5-year est.).

Economy: Single-family building permits issued: 0 (2011); Multi-family building permits issued: 0 (2011); Employment by occupation: 2.3% management, 2.6% professional, 5.6% services, 20.8% sales, 8.9% farming, 14.5% construction, 9.6% production (2006-2010 5-year est.).

Income: Per capita income: $16,588 (2006-2010 5-year est.); Median household income: $40,714 (2006-2010 5-year est.); Average household income: $47,588 (2006-2010 5-year est.); Percent of households with income of $100,000 or more: 8.3% (2006-2010 5-year est.); Poverty rate: 22.7% (2006-2010 5-year est.).

Education: Percent of population age 25 and over with: High school diploma (including GED) or higher: 85.9% (2006-2010 5-year est.); Bachelor's degree or higher: 12.6% (2006-2010 5-year est.); Master's degree or higher: 6.4% (2006-2010 5-year est.).

Housing: Homeownership rate: 48.4% (2010); Median home value: $95,600 (2006-2010 5-year est.); Median contract rent: $476 per month (2006-2010 5-year est.); Median year structure built: before 1940 (2006-2010 5-year est.).

Safety: Violent crime rate: 0.0 per 10,000 population; Property crime rate: 0.0 per 10,000 population (2011).

Transportation: Commute to work: 90.3% car, 0.0% public transportation, 2.3% walk, 2.7% work from home (2006-2010 5-year est.); Travel time to work: 46.2% less than 15 minutes, 33.9% 15 to 30 minutes, 7.2% 30 to 45 minutes, 2.4% 45 to 60 minutes, 10.3% 60 minutes or more (2006-2010 5-year est.)

MESHOPPEN (township). Covers a land area of 15.711 square miles and a water area of 0.394 square miles. Located at 41.63° N. Lat; 76.06° W. Long. Elevation is 656 feet.

Population: 879 (1990); 877 (2000); 1,073 (2010); Density: 68.3 persons per square mile (2010); Race: 97.7% White, 0.5% Black, 0.2% Asian, 0.1% American Indian/Alaska Native, 0.0% Native Hawaiian/Other Pacific Islander, 1.5% Other, 1.4% Hispanic of any race (2010); Average household size: 2.50 (2010); Median age: 37.8 (2010); Males per 100 females: 103.2 (2010); Marriage status: 29.9% never married, 54.4% now married, 5.5% widowed, 10.2% divorced (2006-2010 5-year est.); Foreign born: 1.4% (2006-2010 5-year est.); Ancestry (includes multiple ancestries): 31.3% German, 23.4% Irish, 10.4% American, 8.8% Polish, 8.1% Italian (2006-2010 5-year est.).

Economy: Single-family building permits issued: 0 (2011); Multi-family building permits issued: 0 (2011); Employment by occupation: 2.9%

management, 0.5% professional, 12.6% services, 17.1% sales, 2.6% farming, 17.6% construction, 11.9% production (2006-2010 5-year est.).

Income: Per capita income: $19,146 (2006-2010 5-year est.); Median household income: $41,765 (2006-2010 5-year est.); Average household income: $54,257 (2006-2010 5-year est.); Percent of households with income of $100,000 or more: 11.9% (2006-2010 5-year est.); Poverty rate: 16.6% (2006-2010 5-year est.).

Taxes: Total city taxes per capita: $170 (2009); City property taxes per capita: $67 (2009).

Education: Percent of population age 25 and over with: High school diploma (including GED) or higher: 87.5% (2006-2010 5-year est.); Bachelor's degree or higher: 6.3% (2006-2010 5-year est.); Master's degree or higher: 1.8% (2006-2010 5-year est.).

Housing: Homeownership rate: 71.4% (2010); Median home value: $90,700 (2006-2010 5-year est.); Median contract rent: $420 per month (2006-2010 5-year est.); Median year structure built: 1978 (2006-2010 5-year est.).

Transportation: Commute to work: 93.6% car, 0.0% public transportation, 2.2% walk, 4.2% work from home (2006-2010 5-year est.); Travel time to work: 36.2% less than 15 minutes, 36.7% 15 to 30 minutes, 7.7% 30 to 45 minutes, 8.7% 45 to 60 minutes, 10.8% 60 minutes or more (2006-2010 5-year est.)

MONROE (township). Covers a land area of 21.189 square miles and a water area of 0.085 square miles. Located at 41.43° N. Lat; 75.99° W. Long.

Population: 1,802 (1990); 1,836 (2000); 1,652 (2010); Density: 78.0 persons per square mile (2010); Race: 98.4% White, 0.7% Black, 0.2% Asian, 0.0% American Indian/Alaska Native, 0.0% Native Hawaiian/Other Pacific Islander, 0.7% Other, 1.0% Hispanic of any race (2010); Average household size: 2.45 (2010); Median age: 42.8 (2010); Males per 100 females: 102.5 (2010); Marriage status: 21.4% never married, 60.7% now married, 5.6% widowed, 12.3% divorced (2006-2010 5-year est.); Foreign born: 0.2% (2006-2010 5-year est.); Ancestry (includes multiple ancestries): 28.2% German, 20.1% English, 15.9% Polish, 12.9% Irish, 6.1% Russian (2006-2010 5-year est.).

Economy: Single-family building permits issued: 4 (2011); Multi-family building permits issued: 0 (2011); Employment by occupation: 5.8% management, 3.2% professional, 11.2% services, 18.0% sales, 5.3% farming, 14.9% construction, 15.5% production (2006-2010 5-year est.).

Income: Per capita income: $23,421 (2006-2010 5-year est.); Median household income: $43,625 (2006-2010 5-year est.); Average household income: $56,037 (2006-2010 5-year est.); Percent of households with income of $100,000 or more: 10.7% (2006-2010 5-year est.); Poverty rate: 9.0% (2006-2010 5-year est.).

Education: Percent of population age 25 and over with: High school diploma (including GED) or higher: 88.3% (2006-2010 5-year est.); Bachelor's degree or higher: 14.1% (2006-2010 5-year est.); Master's degree or higher: 5.9% (2006-2010 5-year est.).

Housing: Homeownership rate: 79.1% (2010); Median home value: $129,000 (2006-2010 5-year est.); Median contract rent: $426 per month (2006-2010 5-year est.); Median year structure built: 1976 (2006-2010 5-year est.).

Transportation: Commute to work: 85.1% car, 0.8% public transportation, 1.9% walk, 9.5% work from home (2006-2010 5-year est.); Travel time to work: 22.5% less than 15 minutes, 33.1% 15 to 30 minutes, 31.4% 30 to 45 minutes, 8.7% 45 to 60 minutes, 4.2% 60 minutes or more (2006-2010 5-year est.)

Additional Information Contacts

Wyoming County Chamber of Commerce. . . . . (570) 836-7755
  http://wyccc.com

NICHOLSON (borough). Covers a land area of 1.167 square miles and a water area of 0.014 square miles. Located at 41.63° N. Lat; 75.79° W. Long. Elevation is 735 feet.

Population: 857 (1990); 713 (2000); 767 (2010); Density: 657.1 persons per square mile (2010); Race: 97.0% White, 0.1% Black, 0.0% Asian, 0.1% American Indian/Alaska Native, 0.1% Native Hawaiian/Other Pacific Islander, 2.7% Other, 1.4% Hispanic of any race (2010); Average household size: 2.54 (2010); Median age: 36.9 (2010); Males per 100 females: 90.3 (2010); Marriage status: 34.0% never married, 47.6% now married, 10.1% widowed, 8.3% divorced (2006-2010 5-year est.); Foreign born: 0.7% (2006-2010 5-year est.); Ancestry (includes multiple ancestries): 28.9% German, 15.5% Polish, 15.1% Irish, 9.8% English, 8.3% Italian (2006-2010 5-year est.).

Economy: Single-family building permits issued: 1 (2011); Multi-family building permits issued: 0 (2011); Employment by occupation: 10.5% management, 0.0% professional, 9.6% services, 25.8% sales, 8.8% farming, 8.8% construction, 0.0% production (2006-2010 5-year est.).
Income: Per capita income: $21,449 (2006-2010 5-year est.); Median household income: $38,650 (2006-2010 5-year est.); Average household income: $53,976 (2006-2010 5-year est.); Percent of households with income of $100,000 or more: 17.2% (2006-2010 5-year est.); Poverty rate: 24.8% (2006-2010 5-year est.).
Education: Percent of population age 25 and over with: High school diploma (including GED) or higher: 83.2% (2006-2010 5-year est.); Bachelor's degree or higher: 24.9% (2006-2010 5-year est.); Master's degree or higher: 8.7% (2006-2010 5-year est.).
Housing: Homeownership rate: 63.9% (2010); Median home value: $118,300 (2006-2010 5-year est.); Median contract rent: $434 per month (2006-2010 5-year est.); Median year structure built: before 1940 (2006-2010 5-year est.).
Transportation: Commute to work: 81.7% car, 0.0% public transportation, 8.9% walk, 6.8% work from home (2006-2010 5-year est.); Travel time to work: 39.7% less than 15 minutes, 34.3% 15 to 30 minutes, 16.2% 30 to 45 minutes, 2.2% 45 to 60 minutes, 7.6% 60 minutes or more (2006-2010 5-year est.)

NICHOLSON (township). Covers a land area of 22.842 square miles and a water area of 0.261 square miles. Located at 41.63° N. Lat; 75.82° W. Long. Elevation is 735 feet.

Population: 1,294 (1990); 1,361 (2000); 1,385 (2010); Density: 60.6 persons per square mile (2010); Race: 98.3% White, 0.5% Black, 0.3% Asian, 0.4% American Indian/Alaska Native, 0.0% Native Hawaiian/Other Pacific Islander, 0.5% Other, 0.9% Hispanic of any race (2010); Average household size: 2.42 (2010); Median age: 45.9 (2010); Males per 100 females: 104.6 (2010); Marriage status: 24.9% never married, 54.6% now married, 10.0% widowed, 10.5% divorced (2006-2010 5-year est.); Foreign born: 3.5% (2006-2010 5-year est.); Ancestry (includes multiple ancestries): 30.7% Irish, 26.5% German, 18.0% Italian, 17.5% Polish, 14.7% English (2006-2010 5-year est.).
Economy: Single-family building permits issued: 1 (2011); Multi-family building permits issued: 0 (2011); Employment by occupation: 11.9% management, 1.5% professional, 11.2% services, 14.0% sales, 1.5% farming, 10.3% construction, 8.5% production (2006-2010 5-year est.).
Income: Per capita income: $23,813 (2006-2010 5-year est.); Median household income: $40,481 (2006-2010 5-year est.); Average household income: $57,117 (2006-2010 5-year est.); Percent of households with income of $100,000 or more: 15.7% (2006-2010 5-year est.); Poverty rate: 9.4% (2006-2010 5-year est.).
Education: Percent of population age 25 and over with: High school diploma (including GED) or higher: 90.4% (2006-2010 5-year est.); Bachelor's degree or higher: 10.8% (2006-2010 5-year est.); Master's degree or higher: 2.0% (2006-2010 5-year est.).
Housing: Homeownership rate: 82.6% (2010); Median home value: $147,300 (2006-2010 5-year est.); Median contract rent: $431 per month (2006-2010 5-year est.); Median year structure built: 1974 (2006-2010 5-year est.).
Transportation: Commute to work: 93.3% car, 0.6% public transportation, 1.1% walk, 5.0% work from home (2006-2010 5-year est.); Travel time to work: 23.4% less than 15 minutes, 26.9% 15 to 30 minutes, 38.0% 30 to 45 minutes, 5.8% 45 to 60 minutes, 5.8% 60 minutes or more (2006-2010 5-year est.)
Additional Information Contacts
Wyoming County Chamber of Commerce. . . . . (570) 836-7755
  http://wyccc.com

NORTH BRANCH (township). Covers a land area of 22.371 square miles and a water area of 0.133 square miles. Located at 41.50° N. Lat; 76.19° W. Long.

Population: 168 (1990); 197 (2000); 206 (2010); Density: 9.2 persons per square mile (2010); Race: 96.6% White, 0.0% Black, 1.0% Asian, 0.5% American Indian/Alaska Native, 0.0% Native Hawaiian/Other Pacific Islander, 1.9% Other, 3.9% Hispanic of any race (2010); Average household size: 2.22 (2010); Median age: 49.0 (2010); Males per 100 females: 104.0 (2010); Marriage status: 16.3% never married, 65.0% now married, 11.3% widowed, 7.5% divorced (2006-2010 5-year est.); Foreign born: 0.0% (2006-2010 5-year est.); Ancestry (includes multiple ancestries): 33.1% English, 18.9% German, 17.2% Irish, 8.9% Welsh, 8.9% American (2006-2010 5-year est.).

Economy: Single-family building permits issued: 2 (2011); Multi-family building permits issued: 0 (2011); Employment by occupation: 13.2% management, 2.6% professional, 9.2% services, 13.2% sales, 2.6% farming, 15.8% construction, 6.6% production (2006-2010 5-year est.).
Income: Per capita income: $24,713 (2006-2010 5-year est.); Median household income: $47,083 (2006-2010 5-year est.); Average household income: $49,927 (2006-2010 5-year est.); Percent of households with income of $100,000 or more: 9.7% (2006-2010 5-year est.); Poverty rate: 11.3% (2006-2010 5-year est.).
Education: Percent of population age 25 and over with: High school diploma (including GED) or higher: 83.7% (2006-2010 5-year est.); Bachelor's degree or higher: 10.9% (2006-2010 5-year est.); Master's degree or higher: 4.1% (2006-2010 5-year est.).
Housing: Homeownership rate: 85.0% (2010); Median home value: $189,200 (2006-2010 5-year est.); Median contract rent: n/a per month (2006-2010 5-year est.); Median year structure built: 1969 (2006-2010 5-year est.).
Transportation: Commute to work: 100.0% car, 0.0% public transportation, 0.0% walk, 0.0% work from home (2006-2010 5-year est.); Travel time to work: 20.3% less than 15 minutes, 40.5% 15 to 30 minutes, 27.0% 30 to 45 minutes, 5.4% 45 to 60 minutes, 6.8% 60 minutes or more (2006-2010 5-year est.)

NORTHMORELAND (township). Covers a land area of 19.656 square miles and a water area of 0.175 square miles. Located at 41.44° N. Lat; 75.93° W. Long.

Population: 1,453 (1990); 1,463 (2000); 1,558 (2010); Density: 79.3 persons per square mile (2010); Race: 99.0% White, 0.3% Black, 0.1% Asian, 0.1% American Indian/Alaska Native, 0.0% Native Hawaiian/Other Pacific Islander, 0.5% Other, 0.9% Hispanic of any race (2010); Average household size: 2.65 (2010); Median age: 43.2 (2010); Males per 100 females: 112.8 (2010); Marriage status: 25.0% never married, 57.8% now married, 8.2% widowed, 9.0% divorced (2006-2010 5-year est.); Foreign born: 0.5% (2006-2010 5-year est.); Ancestry (includes multiple ancestries): 30.0% German, 14.7% Polish, 14.6% Irish, 13.0% Italian, 12.3% English (2006-2010 5-year est.).
Economy: Single-family building permits issued: 1 (2011); Multi-family building permits issued: 0 (2011); Employment by occupation: 8.6% management, 0.8% professional, 12.6% services, 20.3% sales, 2.2% farming, 10.0% construction, 7.9% production (2006-2010 5-year est.).
Income: Per capita income: $24,678 (2006-2010 5-year est.); Median household income: $47,500 (2006-2010 5-year est.); Average household income: $65,160 (2006-2010 5-year est.); Percent of households with income of $100,000 or more: 17.3% (2006-2010 5-year est.); Poverty rate: 11.4% (2006-2010 5-year est.).
Education: Percent of population age 25 and over with: High school diploma (including GED) or higher: 89.8% (2006-2010 5-year est.); Bachelor's degree or higher: 17.0% (2006-2010 5-year est.); Master's degree or higher: 3.0% (2006-2010 5-year est.).
Housing: Homeownership rate: 88.9% (2010); Median home value: $164,200 (2006-2010 5-year est.); Median contract rent: $506 per month (2006-2010 5-year est.); Median year structure built: 1975 (2006-2010 5-year est.).
Transportation: Commute to work: 94.5% car, 0.4% public transportation, 3.5% walk, 1.7% work from home (2006-2010 5-year est.); Travel time to work: 13.3% less than 15 minutes, 33.1% 15 to 30 minutes, 37.7% 30 to 45 minutes, 12.3% 45 to 60 minutes, 3.7% 60 minutes or more (2006-2010 5-year est.)
Additional Information Contacts
Wyoming County Chamber of Commerce. . . . . (570) 836-7755
  http://www.wyccc.com

NOXEN (CDP). Covers a land area of 1.982 square miles and a water area of 0.012 square miles. Located at 41.42° N. Lat; 76.07° W. Long. Elevation is 984 feet.

Population: n/a (1990); n/a (2000); 633 (2010); Density: 319.4 persons per square mile (2010); Race: 98.9% White, 0.0% Black, 0.0% Asian, 0.0% American Indian/Alaska Native, 0.0% Native Hawaiian/Other Pacific Islander, 1.1% Other, 0.3% Hispanic of any race (2010); Average household size: 2.43 (2010); Median age: 42.3 (2010); Males per 100 females: 92.4 (2010); Marriage status: 28.7% never married, 51.1% now married, 5.5% widowed, 14.7% divorced (2006-2010 5-year est.); Foreign born: 0.0% (2006-2010 5-year est.); Ancestry (includes multiple ancestries): 28.8% German, 21.8% Irish, 16.7% English, 11.1% Polish, 8.7% Welsh (2006-2010 5-year est.).

Economy: Employment by occupation: 1.3% management, 0.0% professional, 21.9% services, 14.1% sales, 1.0% farming, 23.2% construction, 15.5% production (2006-2010 5-year est.).
Income: Per capita income: $20,582 (2006-2010 5-year est.); Median household income: $47,500 (2006-2010 5-year est.); Average household income: $48,259 (2006-2010 5-year est.); Percent of households with income of $100,000 or more: 9.0% (2006-2010 5-year est.); Poverty rate: 12.4% (2006-2010 5-year est.).
Education: Percent of population age 25 and over with: High school diploma (including GED) or higher: 81.5% (2006-2010 5-year est.); Bachelor's degree or higher: 9.4% (2006-2010 5-year est.); Master's degree or higher: 2.5% (2006-2010 5-year est.).
Housing: Homeownership rate: 75.1% (2010); Median home value: $94,800 (2006-2010 5-year est.); Median contract rent: $406 per month (2006-2010 5-year est.); Median year structure built: before 1940 (2006-2010 5-year est.).
Transportation: Commute to work: 89.4% car, 0.0% public transportation, 0.0% walk, 10.6% work from home (2006-2010 5-year est.); Travel time to work: 9.4% less than 15 minutes, 31.9% 15 to 30 minutes, 39.4% 30 to 45 minutes, 10.6% 45 to 60 minutes, 8.7% 60 minutes or more (2006-2010 5-year est.)

NOXEN (township). Covers a land area of 28.713 square miles and a water area of 0.033 square miles. Located at 41.41° N. Lat; 76.13° W. Long. Elevation is 984 feet.
Population: 944 (1990); 951 (2000); 902 (2010); Density: 31.4 persons per square mile (2010); Race: 98.8% White, 0.0% Black, 0.0% Asian, 0.2% American Indian/Alaska Native, 0.0% Native Hawaiian/Other Pacific Islander, 1.0% Other, 0.3% Hispanic of any race (2010); Average household size: 2.48 (2010); Median age: 41.4 (2010); Males per 100 females: 98.2 (2010); Marriage status: 22.8% never married, 58.4% now married, 5.2% widowed, 13.7% divorced (2006-2010 5-year est.); Foreign born: 0.0% (2006-2010 5-year est.); Ancestry (includes multiple ancestries): 29.3% German, 22.3% Irish, 16.2% English, 10.8% Polish, 8.9% Welsh (2006-2010 5-year est.).
Economy: Single-family building permits issued: 1 (2011); Multi-family building permits issued: 0 (2011); Employment by occupation: 2.7% management, 0.0% professional, 22.3% services, 13.3% sales, 4.6% farming, 23.3% construction, 15.8% production (2006-2010 5-year est.).
Income: Per capita income: $20,386 (2006-2010 5-year est.); Median household income: $46,932 (2006-2010 5-year est.); Average household income: $47,582 (2006-2010 5-year est.); Percent of households with income of $100,000 or more: 7.4% (2006-2010 5-year est.); Poverty rate: 9.2% (2006-2010 5-year est.).
Education: Percent of population age 25 and over with: High school diploma (including GED) or higher: 81.3% (2006-2010 5-year est.); Bachelor's degree or higher: 9.7% (2006-2010 5-year est.); Master's degree or higher: 2.4% (2006-2010 5-year est.).
Housing: Homeownership rate: 78.5% (2010); Median home value: $95,100 (2006-2010 5-year est.); Median contract rent: $400 per month (2006-2010 5-year est.); Median year structure built: 1944 (2006-2010 5-year est.).
Transportation: Commute to work: 86.0% car, 0.0% public transportation, 1.3% walk, 12.8% work from home (2006-2010 5-year est.); Travel time to work: 11.2% less than 15 minutes, 34.2% 15 to 30 minutes, 34.8% 30 to 45 minutes, 10.6% 45 to 60 minutes, 9.2% 60 minutes or more (2006-2010 5-year est.)

OVERFIELD (township). Covers a land area of 9.939 square miles and a water area of 0.322 square miles. Located at 41.53° N. Lat; 75.82° W. Long.
Population: 1,466 (1990); 1,532 (2000); 1,666 (2010); Density: 167.6 persons per square mile (2010); Race: 98.1% White, 0.6% Black, 0.1% Asian, 0.2% American Indian/Alaska Native, 0.0% Native Hawaiian/Other Pacific Islander, 1.0% Other, 1.6% Hispanic of any race (2010); Average household size: 2.37 (2010); Median age: 46.5 (2010); Males per 100 females: 97.2 (2010); Marriage status: 23.4% never married, 57.0% now married, 8.0% widowed, 11.6% divorced (2006-2010 5-year est.); Foreign born: 1.5% (2006-2010 5-year est.); Ancestry (includes multiple ancestries): 26.7% Irish, 25.1% German, 17.3% Polish, 16.7% English, 9.8% Italian (2006-2010 5-year est.).
Economy: Single-family building permits issued: 2 (2011); Multi-family building permits issued: 0 (2011); Employment by occupation: 9.4% management, 5.4% professional, 9.6% services, 14.2% sales, 2.3% farming, 9.4% construction, 5.2% production (2006-2010 5-year est.).

Income: Per capita income: $25,158 (2006-2010 5-year est.); Median household income: $48,889 (2006-2010 5-year est.); Average household income: $57,152 (2006-2010 5-year est.); Percent of households with income of $100,000 or more: 12.4% (2006-2010 5-year est.); Poverty rate: 2.2% (2006-2010 5-year est.).
Education: Percent of population age 25 and over with: High school diploma (including GED) or higher: 89.8% (2006-2010 5-year est.); Bachelor's degree or higher: 18.5% (2006-2010 5-year est.); Master's degree or higher: 5.2% (2006-2010 5-year est.).
Housing: Homeownership rate: 77.0% (2010); Median home value: $167,000 (2006-2010 5-year est.); Median contract rent: $611 per month (2006-2010 5-year est.); Median year structure built: 1960 (2006-2010 5-year est.).
Transportation: Commute to work: 90.1% car, 0.0% public transportation, 4.5% walk, 4.0% work from home (2006-2010 5-year est.); Travel time to work: 25.2% less than 15 minutes, 39.1% 15 to 30 minutes, 23.4% 30 to 45 minutes, 7.8% 45 to 60 minutes, 4.5% 60 minutes or more (2006-2010 5-year est.).
Additional Information Contacts
Greater Scranton Chamber of Commerce . . . . (570) 342-7711
   http://www.scrantonchamber.com

TUNKHANNOCK (borough). County seat. Covers a land area of 0.912 square miles and a water area of 0.051 square miles. Located at 41.54° N. Lat; 75.95° W. Long. Elevation is 636 feet.
History: Attracted by the trading possibilities, Jeremiah Osterhout, a native of Holland, built a cabin in 1775.
Population: 2,251 (1990); 1,911 (2000); 1,836 (2010); Density: 2,013.0 persons per square mile (2010); Race: 95.9% White, 0.9% Black, 1.1% Asian, 0.2% American Indian/Alaska Native, 0.1% Native Hawaiian/Other Pacific Islander, 1.8% Other, 1.3% Hispanic of any race (2010); Average household size: 2.15 (2010); Median age: 43.5 (2010); Males per 100 females: 87.2 (2010); Marriage status: 23.4% never married, 52.6% now married, 11.7% widowed, 12.2% divorced (2006-2010 5-year est.); Foreign born: 0.7% (2006-2010 5-year est.); Ancestry (includes multiple ancestries): 23.3% German, 18.7% English, 13.9% Irish, 13.2% Italian, 9.3% Polish (2006-2010 5-year est.).
Economy: Single-family building permits issued: 0 (2011); Multi-family building permits issued: 0 (2011); Employment by occupation: 13.0% management, 1.6% professional, 13.0% services, 11.9% sales, 3.4% farming, 9.6% construction, 9.7% production (2006-2010 5-year est.).
Income: Per capita income: $23,110 (2006-2010 5-year est.); Median household income: $37,071 (2006-2010 5-year est.); Average household income: $52,534 (2006-2010 5-year est.); Percent of households with income of $100,000 or more: 13.4% (2006-2010 5-year est.); Poverty rate: 6.9% (2006-2010 5-year est.).
Education: Percent of population age 25 and over with: High school diploma (including GED) or higher: 87.8% (2006-2010 5-year est.); Bachelor's degree or higher: 26.0% (2006-2010 5-year est.); Master's degree or higher: 14.0% (2006-2010 5-year est.).
School District(s)
Tunkhannock Area SD (KG-12)
   2010-11 Enrollment: 2,818 . . . . (570) 836-3111
Housing: Homeownership rate: 49.9% (2010); Median home value: $150,200 (2006-2010 5-year est.); Median contract rent: $493 per month (2006-2010 5-year est.); Median year structure built: before 1940 (2006-2010 5-year est.).
Hospitals: Tyler Memorial Hospital (48 beds)
Newspapers: New Age-Examiner (Community news; Circulation 5,500); Wyoming County Press Examiner (Community news; Circulation 16,000)
Transportation: Commute to work: 87.4% car, 0.0% public transportation, 9.8% walk, 1.8% work from home (2006-2010 5-year est.); Travel time to work: 53.6% less than 15 minutes, 27.5% 15 to 30 minutes, 8.3% 30 to 45 minutes, 8.9% 45 to 60 minutes, 1.8% 60 minutes or more (2006-2010 5-year est.)
Additional Information Contacts
Wyoming County Chamber of Commerce . . . . (570) 836-7755
   http://wyccc.com

TUNKHANNOCK (township). Covers a land area of 30.646 square miles and a water area of 0.853 square miles. Located at 41.55° N. Lat; 75.91° W. Long. Elevation is 636 feet.
Population: 4,371 (1990); 4,298 (2000); 4,273 (2010); Density: 139.4 persons per square mile (2010); Race: 98.4% White, 0.3% Black, 0.6% Asian, 0.1% American Indian/Alaska Native, 0.0% Native Hawaiian/Other

Pacific Islander, 0.6% Other, 0.7% Hispanic of any race (2010); Average household size: 2.48 (2010); Median age: 44.4 (2010); Males per 100 females: 99.5 (2010); Marriage status: 24.7% never married, 60.5% now married, 7.4% widowed, 7.5% divorced (2006-2010 5-year est.); Foreign born: 1.6% (2006-2010 5-year est.); Ancestry (includes multiple ancestries): 21.4% Irish, 18.1% German, 15.8% Polish, 15.7% Italian, 14.1% English (2006-2010 5-year est.).

Economy: Single-family building permits issued: 40 (2011); Multi-family building permits issued: 0 (2011); Employment by occupation: 9.8% management, 4.0% professional, 8.1% services, 14.6% sales, 3.1% farming, 13.6% construction, 12.3% production (2006-2010 5-year est.).

Income: Per capita income: $24,874 (2006-2010 5-year est.); Median household income: $55,647 (2006-2010 5-year est.); Average household income: $64,565 (2006-2010 5-year est.); Percent of households with income of $100,000 or more: 18.6% (2006-2010 5-year est.); Poverty rate: 12.1% (2006-2010 5-year est.).

Education: Percent of population age 25 and over with: High school diploma (including GED) or higher: 90.0% (2006-2010 5-year est.); Bachelor's degree or higher: 20.3% (2006-2010 5-year est.); Master's degree or higher: 6.9% (2006-2010 5-year est.).

Housing: Homeownership rate: 82.6% (2010); Median home value: $157,200 (2006-2010 5-year est.); Median contract rent: $486 per month (2006-2010 5-year est.); Median year structure built: 1975 (2006-2010 5-year est.).

Hospitals: Tyler Memorial Hospital (48 beds)

Safety: Violent crime rate: 4.7 per 10,000 population; Property crime rate: 165.6 per 10,000 population (2011).

Newspapers: New Age-Examiner (Community news; Circulation 5,500); Wyoming County Press Examiner (Community news; Circulation 16,000)

Transportation: Commute to work: 94.0% car, 1.2% public transportation, 0.8% walk, 3.4% work from home (2006-2010 5-year est.); Travel time to work: 41.8% less than 15 minutes, 23.6% 15 to 30 minutes, 12.9% 30 to 45 minutes, 16.2% 45 to 60 minutes, 5.6% 60 minutes or more (2006-2010 5-year est.)

Additional Information Contacts

Wyoming County Chamber of Commerce . . . . (570) 836-7755
http://wyccc.com

WASHINGTON (township). Covers a land area of 18.747 square miles and a water area of 0.652 square miles. Located at 41.59° N. Lat; 75.99° W. Long.

Population: 1,212 (1990); 1,306 (2000); 1,412 (2010); Density: 75.3 persons per square mile (2010); Race: 97.1% White, 0.6% Black, 0.1% Asian, 0.6% American Indian/Alaska Native, 0.0% Native Hawaiian/Other Pacific Islander, 1.6% Other, 1.4% Hispanic of any race (2010); Average household size: 2.74 (2010); Median age: 39.1 (2010); Males per 100 females: 98.0 (2010); Marriage status: 27.1% never married, 55.9% now married, 8.0% widowed, 9.0% divorced (2006-2010 5-year est.); Foreign born: 2.5% (2006-2010 5-year est.); Ancestry (includes multiple ancestries): 27.0% Irish, 21.7% German, 14.9% English, 12.9% Polish, 8.5% American (2006-2010 5-year est.).

Economy: Single-family building permits issued: 0 (2011); Multi-family building permits issued: 0 (2011); Employment by occupation: 11.0% management, 4.0% professional, 14.6% services, 19.7% sales, 2.2% farming, 16.4% construction, 14.1% production (2006-2010 5-year est.).

Income: Per capita income: $23,028 (2006-2010 5-year est.); Median household income: $51,447 (2006-2010 5-year est.); Average household income: $59,664 (2006-2010 5-year est.); Percent of households with income of $100,000 or more: 12.6% (2006-2010 5-year est.); Poverty rate: 10.4% (2006-2010 5-year est.).

Education: Percent of population age 25 and over with: High school diploma (including GED) or higher: 90.6% (2006-2010 5-year est.); Bachelor's degree or higher: 13.4% (2006-2010 5-year est.); Master's degree or higher: 3.9% (2006-2010 5-year est.).

Housing: Homeownership rate: 80.1% (2010); Median home value: $142,300 (2006-2010 5-year est.); Median contract rent: $650 per month (2006-2010 5-year est.); Median year structure built: 1976 (2006-2010 5-year est.).

Transportation: Commute to work: 97.9% car, 0.0% public transportation, 0.0% walk, 1.6% work from home (2006-2010 5-year est.); Travel time to work: 46.1% less than 15 minutes, 27.3% 15 to 30 minutes, 9.0% 30 to 45 minutes, 14.3% 45 to 60 minutes, 3.3% 60 minutes or more (2006-2010 5-year est.)

Additional Information Contacts

Wyoming County Chamber of Commerce . . . . (570) 836-7755
http://wyccc.com

WEST FALLS (CDP). Covers a land area of 1.075 square miles and a water area of 0.152 square miles. Located at 41.45° N. Lat; 75.86° W. Long. Elevation is 587 feet.

Population: n/a (1990); n/a (2000); 382 (2010); Density: 355.4 persons per square mile (2010); Race: 98.7% White, 0.8% Black, 0.0% Asian, 0.0% American Indian/Alaska Native, 0.0% Native Hawaiian/Other Pacific Islander, 0.5% Other, 2.6% Hispanic of any race (2010); Average household size: 2.13 (2010); Median age: 52.7 (2010); Males per 100 females: 105.4 (2010); Marriage status: 20.7% never married, 50.6% now married, 9.3% widowed, 19.3% divorced (2006-2010 5-year est.); Foreign born: 0.0% (2006-2010 5-year est.); Ancestry (includes multiple ancestries): 30.3% Italian, 20.3% German, 20.3% Polish, 15.2% American, 12.7% Welsh (2006-2010 5-year est.).

Economy: Employment by occupation: 10.9% management, 4.3% professional, 14.4% services, 16.0% sales, 2.7% farming, 13.2% construction, 7.8% production (2006-2010 5-year est.).

Income: Per capita income: $19,745 (2006-2010 5-year est.); Median household income: $44,167 (2006-2010 5-year est.); Average household income: $47,904 (2006-2010 5-year est.); Percent of households with income of $100,000 or more: 2.9% (2006-2010 5-year est.); Poverty rate: 8.4% (2006-2010 5-year est.).

Education: Percent of population age 25 and over with: High school diploma (including GED) or higher: 87.8% (2006-2010 5-year est.); Bachelor's degree or higher: 15.5% (2006-2010 5-year est.); Master's degree or higher: 1.6% (2006-2010 5-year est.).

Housing: Homeownership rate: 79.9% (2010); Median home value: $115,200 (2006-2010 5-year est.); Median contract rent: $333 per month (2006-2010 5-year est.); Median year structure built: 1958 (2006-2010 5-year est.).

Transportation: Commute to work: 92.5% car, 0.0% public transportation, 5.1% walk, 2.4% work from home (2006-2010 5-year est.); Travel time to work: 19.8% less than 15 minutes, 38.9% 15 to 30 minutes, 25.5% 30 to 45 minutes, 13.4% 45 to 60 minutes, 2.4% 60 minutes or more (2006-2010 5-year est.)

WINDHAM (township). Covers a land area of 22.260 square miles and a water area of 0.897 square miles. Located at 41.61° N. Lat; 76.17° W. Long.

Population: 778 (1990); 828 (2000); 841 (2010); Density: 37.8 persons per square mile (2010); Race: 97.7% White, 0.2% Black, 0.4% Asian, 0.1% American Indian/Alaska Native, 0.0% Native Hawaiian/Other Pacific Islander, 1.6% Other, 1.5% Hispanic of any race (2010); Average household size: 2.53 (2010); Median age: 43.6 (2010); Males per 100 females: 103.6 (2010); Marriage status: 24.5% never married, 59.3% now married, 4.7% widowed, 11.6% divorced (2006-2010 5-year est.); Foreign born: 0.4% (2006-2010 5-year est.); Ancestry (includes multiple ancestries): 24.2% German, 17.3% English, 16.7% Irish, 9.9% Polish, 8.7% American (2006-2010 5-year est.).

Economy: Single-family building permits issued: 0 (2011); Multi-family building permits issued: 0 (2011); Employment by occupation: 8.8% management, 2.6% professional, 7.4% services, 20.9% sales, 1.0% farming, 13.3% construction, 14.3% production (2006-2010 5-year est.).

Income: Per capita income: $18,837 (2006-2010 5-year est.); Median household income: $49,554 (2006-2010 5-year est.); Average household income: $53,317 (2006-2010 5-year est.); Percent of households with income of $100,000 or more: 12.2% (2006-2010 5-year est.); Poverty rate: 13.2% (2006-2010 5-year est.).

Education: Percent of population age 25 and over with: High school diploma (including GED) or higher: 84.8% (2006-2010 5-year est.); Bachelor's degree or higher: 8.8% (2006-2010 5-year est.); Master's degree or higher: 2.6% (2006-2010 5-year est.).

Housing: Homeownership rate: 86.1% (2010); Median home value: $130,400 (2006-2010 5-year est.); Median contract rent: $450 per month (2006-2010 5-year est.); Median year structure built: 1973 (2006-2010 5-year est.).

Transportation: Commute to work: 92.6% car, 0.0% public transportation, 3.8% walk, 2.9% work from home (2006-2010 5-year est.); Travel time to work: 37.8% less than 15 minutes, 39.0% 15 to 30 minutes, 8.9% 30 to 45 minutes, 5.7% 45 to 60 minutes, 8.6% 60 minutes or more (2006-2010 5-year est.)

York County

Located in southern Pennsylvania; bounded on the east by the Susquehanna River, and on the south by Maryland; includes part of South Mountain. Covers a land area of 904.181 square miles, a water area of 6.541 square miles, and is located in the Eastern Time Zone at 39.92° N. Lat., 76.73° W. Long. The county was founded in 1749. County seat is York.

York County is part of the York-Hanover, PA Metropolitan Statistical Area. The entire metro area includes: York County, PA

Weather Station: York 3 SSW Pump Stn   Elevation: 390 feet

	Jan	Feb	Mar	Apr	May	Jun	Jul	Aug	Sep	Oct	Nov	Dec
High	41	45	54	66	76	84	87	86	79	68	56	44
Low	22	24	30	40	49	58	63	62	54	43	34	26
Precip	3.0	2.8	3.8	3.6	4.2	3.7	3.9	3.4	4.1	3.3	3.6	3.2
Snow	8.5	7.7	3.5	0.5	0.0	0.0	0.0	0.0	0.0	0.0	0.7	3.2

High and Low temperatures in degrees Fahrenheit; Precipitation and Snow in inches

Population: 339,574 (1990); 381,751 (2000); 434,972 (2010); Race: 88.5% White, 5.6% Black, 1.2% Asian, 0.2% American Indian/Alaska Native, 0.0% Native Hawaiian/Other Pacific Islander, 4.5% Other, 5.6% Hispanic of any race (2010); Density: 481.1 persons per square mile (2010); Average household size: 2.53 (2010); Median age: 40.1 (2010); Males per 100 females: 97.3 (2010).
Religion: Six largest groups: 8.2% Catholicism, 7.8% Lutheran, 7.2% Methodist/Pietist, 4.9% Presbyterian-Reformed, 4.6% Non-Denominational, 1.4% Holiness (2010)
Economy: Unemployment rate: 8.0% (August 2012); Total civilian labor force: 230,848 (August 2012); Leading industries: 21.6% manufacturing; 14.9% health care and social assistance; 14.0% retail trade (2010); Farms: 2,370 totaling 292,507 acres (2007); Companies that employ 500 or more persons: 20 (2010); Companies that employ 100 to 499 persons: 241 (2010); Companies that employ less than 100 persons: 8,319 (2010); Black-owned businesses: n/a (2007); Hispanic-owned businesses: 528 (2007); Asian-owned businesses: 652 (2007); Women-owned businesses: 9,785 (2007); Retail sales per capita: $10,332 (2010). Single-family building permits issued: 582 (2011); Multi-family building permits issued: 56 (2011).
Income: Per capita income: $27,196 (2006-2010 5-year est.); Median household income: $57,494 (2006-2010 5-year est.); Average household income: $68,971 (2006-2010 5-year est.); Percent of households with income of $100,000 or more: 20.3% (2006-2010 5-year est.); Poverty rate: 9.0% (2006-2010 5-year est.); Bankruptcy rate: 3.32% (2011).
Taxes: Total county taxes per capita: $248 (2009); County property taxes per capita: $244 (2009).
Education: Percent of population age 25 and over with: High school diploma (including GED) or higher: 86.8% (2006-2010 5-year est.); Bachelor's degree or higher: 21.5% (2006-2010 5-year est.); Master's degree or higher: 7.4% (2006-2010 5-year est.).
Housing: Homeownership rate: 75.5% (2010); Median home value: $175,500 (2006-2010 5-year est.); Median contract rent: $604 per month (2006-2010 5-year est.); Median year structure built: 1972 (2006-2010 5-year est.)
Health: Birth rate: 115.4 per 10,000 population (2011); Death rate: 81.5 per 10,000 population (2011); Age-adjusted cancer mortality rate: 180.7 deaths per 100,000 population (2009); Number of physicians: 22.7 per 10,000 population (2010); Hospital beds: 19.7 per 10,000 population (2008); Hospital admissions: 997.9 per 10,000 population (2008).
Environment: Air Quality Index: 61.4% good, 37.0% moderate, 1.4% unhealthy for sensitive individuals, 0.3% unhealthy (percent of days in 2011)
Elections: 2012 Presidential election results: 38.7% Obama, 59.9% Romney
National and State Parks: Codorus State Park; Gifford Pinchot State Park; Samuel S Lewis State Park; State Game Propagation Area
Additional Information Contacts
York County Government . . . . (717) 771-9964
  http://www.york-county.org
York County Chamber of Commerce . . . . (717) 848-4000
  http://www.yorkchamber.com

York County Communities

AIRVILLE (unincorporated postal area)
Zip Code: 17302
  Covers a land area of 38.438 square miles and a water area of 0.136 square miles. Located at 39.81° N. Lat; 76.41° W. Long. Elevation is 679 feet. Population: 3,083 (2010); Density: 80.2 persons per square mile (2010); Race: 96.7% White, 1.1% Black, 0.5% Asian, 0.2% American Indian/Alaska Native, 0.0% Native Hawaiian/Other Pacific Islander, 1.5% Other, 0.8% Hispanic of any race (2010); Average household size: 2.81 (2010); Median age: 39.2 (2010); Males per 100 females: 104.6 (2010); Homeownership rate: 82.9% (2010)

BROGUE (unincorporated postal area)
Zip Code: 17309
  Covers a land area of 24.785 square miles and a water area of 0 square miles. Located at 39.87° N. Lat; 76.45° W. Long. Elevation is 817 feet. Population: 2,086 (2010); Density: 84.2 persons per square mile (2010); Race: 97.7% White, 0.3% Black, 0.2% Asian, 0.0% American Indian/Alaska Native, 0.0% Native Hawaiian/Other Pacific Islander, 1.8% Other, 0.7% Hispanic of any race (2010); Average household size: 2.62 (2010); Median age: 42.7 (2010); Males per 100 females: 108.2 (2010); Homeownership rate: 86.3% (2010)

CARROLL (township). Covers a land area of 15.005 square miles and a water area of <.001 square miles. Located at 40.11° N. Lat; 77.02° W. Long.
Population: 3,265 (1990); 4,715 (2000); 5,939 (2010); Density: 395.8 persons per square mile (2010); Race: 96.2% White, 0.7% Black, 2.0% Asian, 0.2% American Indian/Alaska Native, 0.0% Native Hawaiian/Other Pacific Islander, 0.9% Other, 1.2% Hispanic of any race (2010); Average household size: 2.72 (2010); Median age: 40.9 (2010); Males per 100 females: 98.0 (2010); Marriage status: 17.8% never married, 68.9% now married, 4.1% widowed, 9.1% divorced (2006-2010 5-year est.); Foreign born: 1.6% (2006-2010 5-year est.); Ancestry (includes multiple ancestries): 39.7% German, 12.8% Irish, 7.9% American, 6.9% English, 6.3% Italian (2006-2010 5-year est.).
Economy: Single-family building permits issued: 24 (2011); Multi-family building permits issued: 0 (2011); Employment by occupation: 16.6% management, 6.1% professional, 10.0% services, 13.2% sales, 4.5% farming, 9.0% construction, 4.4% production (2006-2010 5-year est.).
Income: Per capita income: $30,047 (2006-2010 5-year est.); Median household income: $73,859 (2006-2010 5-year est.); Average household income: $86,207 (2006-2010 5-year est.); Percent of households with income of $100,000 or more: 34.4% (2006-2010 5-year est.); Poverty rate: 3.0% (2006-2010 5-year est.).
Education: Percent of population age 25 and over with: High school diploma (including GED) or higher: 94.3% (2006-2010 5-year est.); Bachelor's degree or higher: 36.4% (2006-2010 5-year est.); Master's degree or higher: 9.9% (2006-2010 5-year est.).
Housing: Homeownership rate: 86.4% (2010); Median home value: $245,200 (2006-2010 5-year est.); Median contract rent: $688 per month (2006-2010 5-year est.); Median year structure built: 1983 (2006-2010 5-year est.).
Safety: Violent crime rate: 11.7 per 10,000 population; Property crime rate: 179.6 per 10,000 population (2011).
Transportation: Commute to work: 93.7% car, 0.4% public transportation, 1.2% walk, 4.1% work from home (2006-2010 5-year est.); Travel time to work: 20.6% less than 15 minutes, 43.7% 15 to 30 minutes, 24.5% 30 to 45 minutes, 5.7% 45 to 60 minutes, 5.5% 60 minutes or more (2006-2010 5-year est.)
Additional Information Contacts
Carroll Township . . . . (717) 432-4951
  http://www.carrolltownship.com
West Shore Chamber of Commerce . . . . (717) 761-0702
  http://www.wschamber.org

CHANCEFORD (township). Covers a land area of 48.459 square miles and a water area of 0 square miles. Located at 39.88° N. Lat; 76.48° W. Long.
Population: 5,026 (1990); 5,973 (2000); 6,111 (2010); Density: 126.1 persons per square mile (2010); Race: 97.0% White, 0.9% Black, 0.3% Asian, 0.2% American Indian/Alaska Native, 0.0% Native Hawaiian/Other Pacific Islander, 1.6% Other, 1.0% Hispanic of any race (2010); Average

household size: 2.71 (2010); Median age: 41.3 (2010); Males per 100 females: 105.1 (2010); Marriage status: 22.5% never married, 65.9% now married, 3.7% widowed, 7.9% divorced (2006-2010 5-year est.); Foreign born: 1.2% (2006-2010 5-year est.); Ancestry (includes multiple ancestries): 49.0% German, 11.1% American, 10.1% Irish, 8.9% English, 3.9% Italian (2006-2010 5-year est.).

Economy: Single-family building permits issued: 7 (2011); Multi-family building permits issued: 0 (2011); Employment by occupation: 10.5% management, 1.0% professional, 7.7% services, 14.4% sales, 3.9% farming, 17.2% construction, 17.9% production (2006-2010 5-year est.).

Income: Per capita income: $26,461 (2006-2010 5-year est.); Median household income: $65,500 (2006-2010 5-year est.); Average household income: $70,580 (2006-2010 5-year est.); Percent of households with income of $100,000 or more: 21.5% (2006-2010 5-year est.); Poverty rate: 4.9% (2006-2010 5-year est.).

Education: Percent of population age 25 and over with: High school diploma (including GED) or higher: 87.9% (2006-2010 5-year est.); Bachelor's degree or higher: 10.2% (2006-2010 5-year est.); Master's degree or higher: 3.5% (2006-2010 5-year est.).

Housing: Homeownership rate: 88.3% (2010); Median home value: $181,700 (2006-2010 5-year est.); Median contract rent: $489 per month (2006-2010 5-year est.); Median year structure built: 1979 (2006-2010 5-year est.).

Transportation: Commute to work: 95.2% car, 0.2% public transportation, 0.6% walk, 2.6% work from home (2006-2010 5-year est.); Travel time to work: 14.0% less than 15 minutes, 30.7% 15 to 30 minutes, 34.4% 30 to 45 minutes, 8.7% 45 to 60 minutes, 12.1% 60 minutes or more (2006-2010 5-year est.)

Additional Information Contacts
Chanceford Township . . . . (717) 927-6401
  http://www.chancefordtwp.com
Lancaster Chamber of Commerce & Industry . . . . (717) 397-3531
  http://www.lancasterchamber.com

CODORUS (township). Aka Jefferson. Covers a land area of 33.451 square miles and a water area of 0 square miles. Located at 39.78° N. Lat; 76.79° W. Long.

Population: 3,606 (1990); 3,646 (2000); 3,796 (2010); Density: 113.5 persons per square mile (2010); Race: 96.0% White, 1.3% Black, 0.3% Asian, 0.2% American Indian/Alaska Native, 0.0% Native Hawaiian/Other Pacific Islander, 2.2% Other, 1.7% Hispanic of any race (2010); Average household size: 2.60 (2010); Median age: 45.1 (2010); Males per 100 females: 106.0 (2010); Marriage status: 21.9% never married, 66.7% now married, 3.6% widowed, 7.9% divorced (2006-2010 5-year est.); Foreign born: 0.2% (2006-2010 5-year est.); Ancestry (includes multiple ancestries): 49.6% German, 14.9% Irish, 12.6% American, 10.7% Italian, 9.7% English (2006-2010 5-year est.).

Economy: Single-family building permits issued: 10 (2011); Multi-family building permits issued: 0 (2011); Employment by occupation: 13.6% management, 4.1% professional, 7.8% services, 11.1% sales, 3.7% farming, 17.0% construction, 11.5% production (2006-2010 5-year est.).

Income: Per capita income: $26,142 (2006-2010 5-year est.); Median household income: $57,644 (2006-2010 5-year est.); Average household income: $70,568 (2006-2010 5-year est.); Percent of households with income of $100,000 or more: 20.5% (2006-2010 5-year est.); Poverty rate: 10.8% (2006-2010 5-year est.).

Education: Percent of population age 25 and over with: High school diploma (including GED) or higher: 80.9% (2006-2010 5-year est.); Bachelor's degree or higher: 13.5% (2006-2010 5-year est.); Master's degree or higher: 3.3% (2006-2010 5-year est.).

Housing: Homeownership rate: 85.0% (2010); Median home value: $209,000 (2006-2010 5-year est.); Median contract rent: $621 per month (2006-2010 5-year est.); Median year structure built: 1971 (2006-2010 5-year est.).

Transportation: Commute to work: 90.4% car, 0.0% public transportation, 1.4% walk, 5.1% work from home (2006-2010 5-year est.); Travel time to work: 13.9% less than 15 minutes, 34.4% 15 to 30 minutes, 23.6% 30 to 45 minutes, 12.4% 45 to 60 minutes, 15.7% 60 minutes or more (2006-2010 5-year est.)

Additional Information Contacts
Hanover Area Chamber of Commerce . . . . (717) 637-6130
  http://www.hanoverchamber.com

CONEWAGO (township). Covers a land area of 24.437 square miles and a water area of 0.177 square miles. Located at 40.07° N. Lat; 76.80° W. Long.

Population: 4,926 (1990); 5,278 (2000); 7,510 (2010); Density: 307.3 persons per square mile (2010); Race: 87.4% White, 8.4% Black, 1.0% Asian, 0.2% American Indian/Alaska Native, 0.0% Native Hawaiian/Other Pacific Islander, 3.0% Other, 3.9% Hispanic of any race (2010); Average household size: 2.66 (2010); Median age: 37.9 (2010); Males per 100 females: 99.4 (2010); Marriage status: 27.2% never married, 59.5% now married, 4.2% widowed, 9.1% divorced (2006-2010 5-year est.); Foreign born: 3.1% (2006-2010 5-year est.); Ancestry (includes multiple ancestries): 40.7% German, 12.4% Irish, 8.1% English, 8.0% American, 4.4% Italian (2006-2010 5-year est.).

Economy: Single-family building permits issued: 27 (2011); Multi-family building permits issued: 0 (2011); Employment by occupation: 8.1% management, 4.2% professional, 4.2% services, 18.3% sales, 3.3% farming, 12.1% construction, 16.9% production (2006-2010 5-year est.).

Income: Per capita income: $26,798 (2006-2010 5-year est.); Median household income: $60,380 (2006-2010 5-year est.); Average household income: $68,943 (2006-2010 5-year est.); Percent of households with income of $100,000 or more: 20.0% (2006-2010 5-year est.); Poverty rate: 7.0% (2006-2010 5-year est.).

Education: Percent of population age 25 and over with: High school diploma (including GED) or higher: 87.3% (2006-2010 5-year est.); Bachelor's degree or higher: 17.5% (2006-2010 5-year est.); Master's degree or higher: 5.8% (2006-2010 5-year est.).

Housing: Homeownership rate: 82.5% (2010); Median home value: $189,300 (2006-2010 5-year est.); Median contract rent: $535 per month (2006-2010 5-year est.); Median year structure built: 1985 (2006-2010 5-year est.).

Transportation: Commute to work: 95.6% car, 0.0% public transportation, 1.7% walk, 1.9% work from home (2006-2010 5-year est.); Travel time to work: 19.0% less than 15 minutes, 44.2% 15 to 30 minutes, 21.3% 30 to 45 minutes, 5.5% 45 to 60 minutes, 10.0% 60 minutes or more (2006-2010 5-year est.)

Additional Information Contacts
Conewago Township . . . . (717) 266-2122
  http://www.conewagotwp.com
York County Chamber of Commerce . . . . (717) 848-4000
  http://www.yorkchamber.com

CROSS ROADS (borough). Covers a land area of 1.818 square miles and a water area of 0 square miles. Located at 39.82° N. Lat; 76.57° W. Long. Elevation is 801 feet.

Population: 393 (1990); 518 (2000); 512 (2010); Density: 281.7 persons per square mile (2010); Race: 97.5% White, 1.8% Black, 0.4% Asian, 0.0% American Indian/Alaska Native, 0.0% Native Hawaiian/Other Pacific Islander, 0.3% Other, 0.8% Hispanic of any race (2010); Average household size: 2.65 (2010); Median age: 42.7 (2010); Males per 100 females: 95.4 (2010); Marriage status: 20.3% never married, 65.3% now married, 4.3% widowed, 10.1% divorced (2006-2010 5-year est.); Foreign born: 4.7% (2006-2010 5-year est.); Ancestry (includes multiple ancestries): 40.2% German, 16.9% Irish, 16.8% English, 4.8% American, 3.2% Welsh (2006-2010 5-year est.).

Economy: Single-family building permits issued: 0 (2011); Multi-family building permits issued: 0 (2011); Employment by occupation: 13.2% management, 8.2% professional, 10.1% services, 12.3% sales, 8.2% farming, 10.4% construction, 10.4% production (2006-2010 5-year est.).

Income: Per capita income: $27,194 (2006-2010 5-year est.); Median household income: $76,071 (2006-2010 5-year est.); Average household income: $79,177 (2006-2010 5-year est.); Percent of households with income of $100,000 or more: 26.9% (2006-2010 5-year est.); Poverty rate: 1.9% (2006-2010 5-year est.).

Education: Percent of population age 25 and over with: High school diploma (including GED) or higher: 92.8% (2006-2010 5-year est.); Bachelor's degree or higher: 21.7% (2006-2010 5-year est.); Master's degree or higher: 5.3% (2006-2010 5-year est.).

Housing: Homeownership rate: 87.1% (2010); Median home value: $214,600 (2006-2010 5-year est.); Median contract rent: $778 per month (2006-2010 5-year est.); Median year structure built: 1985 (2006-2010 5-year est.).

Transportation: Commute to work: 99.4% car, 0.0% public transportation, 0.0% walk, 0.0% work from home (2006-2010 5-year est.); Travel time to work: 13.1% less than 15 minutes, 23.9% 15 to 30 minutes, 33.1% 30 to

45 minutes, 9.6% 45 to 60 minutes, 20.4% 60 minutes or more (2006-2010 5-year est.)

DALLASTOWN (borough). Covers a land area of 0.777 square miles and a water area of 0 square miles. Located at 39.90° N. Lat; 76.64° W. Long. Elevation is 886 feet.

History: Incorporated 1867.

Population: 3,994 (1990); 4,087 (2000); 4,049 (2010); Density: 5,208.9 persons per square mile (2010); Race: 94.1% White, 2.6% Black, 0.1% Asian, 0.1% American Indian/Alaska Native, 0.0% Native Hawaiian/Other Pacific Islander, 3.1% Other, 4.0% Hispanic of any race (2010); Average household size: 2.36 (2010); Median age: 37.7 (2010); Males per 100 females: 93.5 (2010); Marriage status: 29.1% never married, 48.0% now married, 8.8% widowed, 14.2% divorced (2006-2010 5-year est.); Foreign born: 3.3% (2006-2010 5-year est.); Ancestry (includes multiple ancestries): 37.9% German, 9.7% American, 6.8% Italian, 6.0% English, 3.7% Pennsylvania German (2006-2010 5-year est.).

Economy: Single-family building permits issued: 0 (2011); Multi-family building permits issued: 0 (2011); Employment by occupation: 9.2% management, 5.0% professional, 8.4% services, 14.5% sales, 1.3% farming, 10.8% construction, 12.1% production (2006-2010 5-year est.).

Income: Per capita income: $24,596 (2006-2010 5-year est.); Median household income: $43,862 (2006-2010 5-year est.); Average household income: $56,834 (2006-2010 5-year est.); Percent of households with income of $100,000 or more: 12.4% (2006-2010 5-year est.); Poverty rate: 6.6% (2006-2010 5-year est.).

Education: Percent of population age 25 and over with: High school diploma (including GED) or higher: 80.6% (2006-2010 5-year est.); Bachelor's degree or higher: 12.7% (2006-2010 5-year est.); Master's degree or higher: 3.6% (2006-2010 5-year est.).

School District(s)

Dallastown Area SD (KG-12)

   2010-11 Enrollment: 6,050 . . . . (717) 244-4021

Housing: Homeownership rate: 55.6% (2010); Median home value: $125,000 (2006-2010 5-year est.); Median contract rent: $607 per month (2006-2010 5-year est.); Median year structure built: 1952 (2006-2010 5-year est.).

Transportation: Commute to work: 91.2% car, 0.0% public transportation, 4.2% walk, 3.7% work from home (2006-2010 5-year est.); Travel time to work: 26.7% less than 15 minutes, 40.0% 15 to 30 minutes, 20.7% 30 to 45 minutes, 9.5% 45 to 60 minutes, 3.0% 60 minutes or more (2006-2010 5-year est.)

Additional Information Contacts

York County Chamber of Commerce . . . . (717) 848-4000

   http://www.yorkchamber.com

DELTA (borough). Covers a land area of 0.262 square miles and a water area of 0 square miles. Located at 39.73° N. Lat; 76.33° W. Long. Elevation is 456 feet.

Population: 761 (1990); 741 (2000); 728 (2010); Density: 2,779.6 persons per square mile (2010); Race: 95.7% White, 1.5% Black, 0.4% Asian, 0.3% American Indian/Alaska Native, 0.0% Native Hawaiian/Other Pacific Islander, 2.1% Other, 1.4% Hispanic of any race (2010); Average household size: 2.63 (2010); Median age: 36.4 (2010); Males per 100 females: 93.6 (2010); Marriage status: 18.8% never married, 64.5% now married, 9.1% widowed, 7.5% divorced (2006-2010 5-year est.); Foreign born: 0.5% (2006-2010 5-year est.); Ancestry (includes multiple ancestries): 26.1% German, 24.2% Irish, 22.1% English, 12.2% American, 5.5% Polish (2006-2010 5-year est.).

Economy: Single-family building permits issued: 0 (2011); Multi-family building permits issued: 0 (2011); Employment by occupation: 6.2% management, 7.2% professional, 3.6% services, 23.6% sales, 6.5% farming, 13.0% construction, 8.0% production (2006-2010 5-year est.).

Income: Per capita income: $21,997 (2006-2010 5-year est.); Median household income: $41,797 (2006-2010 5-year est.); Average household income: $55,913 (2006-2010 5-year est.); Percent of households with income of $100,000 or more: 15.6% (2006-2010 5-year est.); Poverty rate: 5.1% (2006-2010 5-year est.).

Education: Percent of population age 25 and over with: High school diploma (including GED) or higher: 81.5% (2006-2010 5-year est.); Bachelor's degree or higher: 14.0% (2006-2010 5-year est.); Master's degree or higher: 4.0% (2006-2010 5-year est.).

School District(s)

South Eastern SD (PK-12)

   2010-11 Enrollment: 2,954 . . . . (717) 382-4843

Housing: Homeownership rate: 61.3% (2010); Median home value: $157,700 (2006-2010 5-year est.); Median contract rent: $521 per month (2006-2010 5-year est.); Median year structure built: before 1940 (2006-2010 5-year est.).

Newspapers: Star (Community news; Circulation 2,100)

Transportation: Commute to work: 95.0% car, 0.0% public transportation, 1.9% walk, 3.1% work from home (2006-2010 5-year est.); Travel time to work: 13.0% less than 15 minutes, 18.1% 15 to 30 minutes, 33.9% 30 to 45 minutes, 20.9% 45 to 60 minutes, 14.2% 60 minutes or more (2006-2010 5-year est.)

DILLSBURG (borough). Covers a land area of 0.799 square miles and a water area of 0 square miles. Located at 40.11° N. Lat; 77.03° W. Long. Elevation is 568 feet.

History: Appalachian Trail passes to West. Laid out 1880, incorporated 1833.

Population: 1,947 (1990); 2,063 (2000); 2,563 (2010); Density: 3,207.1 persons per square mile (2010); Race: 95.6% White, 0.9% Black, 1.1% Asian, 0.2% American Indian/Alaska Native, 0.0% Native Hawaiian/Other Pacific Islander, 2.2% Other, 1.7% Hispanic of any race (2010); Average household size: 2.38 (2010); Median age: 37.0 (2010); Males per 100 females: 91.0 (2010); Marriage status: 20.3% never married, 62.3% now married, 5.5% widowed, 11.9% divorced (2006-2010 5-year est.); Foreign born: 1.4% (2006-2010 5-year est.); Ancestry (includes multiple ancestries): 52.0% German, 13.0% Irish, 11.0% English, 7.0% American, 5.6% Italian (2006-2010 5-year est.).

Economy: Single-family building permits issued: 3 (2011); Multi-family building permits issued: 0 (2011); Employment by occupation: 9.0% management, 7.5% professional, 10.0% services, 21.5% sales, 6.5% farming, 6.4% construction, 5.9% production (2006-2010 5-year est.).

Income: Per capita income: $25,628 (2006-2010 5-year est.); Median household income: $54,088 (2006-2010 5-year est.); Average household income: $61,022 (2006-2010 5-year est.); Percent of households with income of $100,000 or more: 17.4% (2006-2010 5-year est.); Poverty rate: 2.9% (2006-2010 5-year est.).

Education: Percent of population age 25 and over with: High school diploma (including GED) or higher: 91.7% (2006-2010 5-year est.); Bachelor's degree or higher: 24.0% (2006-2010 5-year est.); Master's degree or higher: 7.4% (2006-2010 5-year est.).

School District(s)

Northern York County SD (KG-12)

   2010-11 Enrollment: 3,178 . . . . (717) 432-8691

Housing: Homeownership rate: 67.1% (2010); Median home value: $157,200 (2006-2010 5-year est.); Median contract rent: $540 per month (2006-2010 5-year est.); Median year structure built: 1971 (2006-2010 5-year est.).

Newspapers: Dillsburg Banner (Community news; Circulation 3,000); The Patriot-News - Dillsburg Bureau (Local news)

Transportation: Commute to work: 95.8% car, 0.0% public transportation, 0.6% walk, 2.1% work from home (2006-2010 5-year est.); Travel time to work: 20.7% less than 15 minutes, 44.8% 15 to 30 minutes, 25.0% 30 to 45 minutes, 7.3% 45 to 60 minutes, 2.3% 60 minutes or more (2006-2010 5-year est.)

Additional Information Contacts

Borough of Dillsburg . . . . (717) 432-9969

   http://www.dillsburg.com

Greater Carlisle Area Chamber of Commerce . . . . (717) 243-4515

   http://carlislechamber.org

DOVER (borough). Covers a land area of 0.543 square miles and a water area of 0 square miles. Located at 40.00° N. Lat; 76.85° W. Long. Elevation is 446 feet.

Population: 1,884 (1990); 1,815 (2000); 2,007 (2010); Density: 3,698.4 persons per square mile (2010); Race: 94.4% White, 2.0% Black, 0.5% Asian, 0.1% American Indian/Alaska Native, 0.0% Native Hawaiian/Other Pacific Islander, 3.0% Other, 2.5% Hispanic of any race (2010); Average household size: 2.46 (2010); Median age: 36.9 (2010); Males per 100 females: 96.4 (2010); Marriage status: 26.1% never married, 57.7% now married, 7.9% widowed, 8.3% divorced (2006-2010 5-year est.); Foreign born: 2.0% (2006-2010 5-year est.); Ancestry (includes multiple ancestries): 53.9% German, 14.1% Irish, 9.3% American, 9.1% English, 4.5% Italian (2006-2010 5-year est.).

Economy: Single-family building permits issued: 0 (2011); Multi-family building permits issued: 0 (2011); Employment by occupation: 6.3%

management, 4.8% professional, 10.3% services, 16.4% sales, 8.1% farming, 10.8% construction, 8.3% production (2006-2010 5-year est.).
Income: Per capita income: $23,650 (2006-2010 5-year est.); Median household income: $51,483 (2006-2010 5-year est.); Average household income: $55,628 (2006-2010 5-year est.); Percent of households with income of $100,000 or more: 12.1% (2006-2010 5-year est.); Poverty rate: 4.6% (2006-2010 5-year est.).
Education: Percent of population age 25 and over with: High school diploma (including GED) or higher: 86.1% (2006-2010 5-year est.); Bachelor's degree or higher: 12.4% (2006-2010 5-year est.); Master's degree or higher: 4.1% (2006-2010 5-year est.).

School District(s)
Dover Area SD (KG-12)
    2010-11 Enrollment: 3,613 . . . . (717) 292-3671
Housing: Homeownership rate: 61.9% (2010); Median home value: $150,400 (2006-2010 5-year est.); Median contract rent: $558 per month (2006-2010 5-year est.); Median year structure built: 1971 (2006-2010 5-year est.).
Transportation: Commute to work: 94.3% car, 1.7% public transportation, 0.0% walk, 2.9% work from home (2006-2010 5-year est.); Travel time to work: 21.7% less than 15 minutes, 43.2% 15 to 30 minutes, 20.6% 30 to 45 minutes, 8.2% 45 to 60 minutes, 6.4% 60 minutes or more (2006-2010 5-year est.).
Additional Information Contacts
York County Chamber of Commerce . . . . (717) 848-4000
    http://www.yorkchamber.com

DOVER (township). Covers a land area of 41.558 square miles and a water area of 0.234 square miles. Located at 40.00° N. Lat; 76.87° W. Long. Elevation is 446 feet.
Population: 15,726 (1990); 18,074 (2000); 21,078 (2010); Density: 507.2 persons per square mile (2010); Race: 93.1% White, 3.3% Black, 0.7% Asian, 0.3% American Indian/Alaska Native, 0.0% Native Hawaiian/Other Pacific Islander, 2.6% Other, 3.2% Hispanic of any race (2010); Average household size: 2.52 (2010); Median age: 40.9 (2010); Males per 100 females: 96.6 (2010); Marriage status: 21.4% never married, 60.9% now married, 6.2% widowed, 11.5% divorced (2006-2010 5-year est.); Foreign born: 1.3% (2006-2010 5-year est.); Ancestry (includes multiple ancestries): 47.8% German, 11.7% Irish, 8.5% American, 7.6% English, 3.7% Italian (2006-2010 5-year est.).
Economy: Single-family building permits issued: 41 (2011); Multi-family building permits issued: 0 (2011); Employment by occupation: 8.1% management, 4.0% professional, 10.1% services, 20.2% sales, 5.6% farming, 11.3% construction, 12.0% production (2006-2010 5-year est.).
Income: Per capita income: $25,202 (2006-2010 5-year est.); Median household income: $52,247 (2006-2010 5-year est.); Average household income: $61,529 (2006-2010 5-year est.); Percent of households with income of $100,000 or more: 15.0% (2006-2010 5-year est.); Poverty rate: 6.1% (2006-2010 5-year est.).
Taxes: Total city taxes per capita: $208 (2009); City property taxes per capita: $52 (2009).
Education: Percent of population age 25 and over with: High school diploma (including GED) or higher: 86.0% (2006-2010 5-year est.); Bachelor's degree or higher: 13.7% (2006-2010 5-year est.); Master's degree or higher: 4.7% (2006-2010 5-year est.).
Housing: Homeownership rate: 83.9% (2010); Median home value: $156,600 (2006-2010 5-year est.); Median contract rent: $640 per month (2006-2010 5-year est.); Median year structure built: 1981 (2006-2010 5-year est.).
Transportation: Commute to work: 94.7% car, 0.2% public transportation, 1.0% walk, 3.4% work from home (2006-2010 5-year est.); Travel time to work: 20.9% less than 15 minutes, 44.3% 15 to 30 minutes, 21.3% 30 to 45 minutes, 6.5% 45 to 60 minutes, 6.9% 60 minutes or more (2006-2010 5-year est.).
Additional Information Contacts
Dover Township . . . . (717) 292-3634
    http://www.dovertownship.org
York County Chamber of Commerce . . . . (717) 848-4000
    http://www.yorkchamber.com

EAST HOPEWELL (township). Covers a land area of 20.560 square miles and a water area of 0 square miles. Located at 39.80° N. Lat; 76.53° W. Long.
Population: 1,858 (1990); 2,209 (2000); 2,416 (2010); Density: 117.5 persons per square mile (2010); Race: 98.1% White, 0.5% Black, 0.5%

Asian, 0.1% American Indian/Alaska Native, 0.0% Native Hawaiian/Other Pacific Islander, 0.8% Other, 1.0% Hispanic of any race (2010); Average household size: 2.81 (2010); Median age: 43.4 (2010); Males per 100 females: 100.7 (2010); Marriage status: 20.2% never married, 70.2% now married, 4.7% widowed, 4.8% divorced (2006-2010 5-year est.); Foreign born: 3.3% (2006-2010 5-year est.); Ancestry (includes multiple ancestries): 47.2% German, 20.7% Irish, 14.4% English, 8.7% American, 8.1% Italian (2006-2010 5-year est.).
Economy: Single-family building permits issued: 1 (2011); Multi-family building permits issued: 0 (2011); Employment by occupation: 10.1% management, 4.4% professional, 8.0% services, 18.7% sales, 4.3% farming, 9.8% construction, 6.1% production (2006-2010 5-year est.).
Income: Per capita income: $31,390 (2006-2010 5-year est.); Median household income: $78,854 (2006-2010 5-year est.); Average household income: $88,941 (2006-2010 5-year est.); Percent of households with income of $100,000 or more: 37.0% (2006-2010 5-year est.); Poverty rate: 5.3% (2006-2010 5-year est.).
Education: Percent of population age 25 and over with: High school diploma (including GED) or higher: 88.4% (2006-2010 5-year est.); Bachelor's degree or higher: 25.1% (2006-2010 5-year est.); Master's degree or higher: 9.0% (2006-2010 5-year est.).
Housing: Homeownership rate: 93.4% (2010); Median home value: $244,100 (2006-2010 5-year est.); Median contract rent: $625 per month (2006-2010 5-year est.); Median year structure built: 1983 (2006-2010 5-year est.).
Transportation: Commute to work: 97.1% car, 0.0% public transportation, 0.5% walk, 1.8% work from home (2006-2010 5-year est.); Travel time to work: 10.9% less than 15 minutes, 22.8% 15 to 30 minutes, 24.7% 30 to 45 minutes, 23.5% 45 to 60 minutes, 18.0% 60 minutes or more (2006-2010 5-year est.)
Additional Information Contacts
York County Chamber of Commerce . . . . (717) 848-4000
    http://www.yorkchamber.com

EAST MANCHESTER (township). Covers a land area of 16.645 square miles and a water area of 0.536 square miles. Located at 40.04° N. Lat; 76.71° W. Long.
Population: 3,775 (1990); 5,078 (2000); 7,264 (2010); Density: 436.4 persons per square mile (2010); Race: 91.6% White, 4.5% Black, 1.2% Asian, 0.2% American Indian/Alaska Native, 0.0% Native Hawaiian/Other Pacific Islander, 2.5% Other, 2.6% Hispanic of any race (2010); Average household size: 2.77 (2010); Median age: 37.6 (2010); Males per 100 females: 99.9 (2010); Marriage status: 20.8% never married, 65.2% now married, 4.5% widowed, 9.5% divorced (2006-2010 5-year est.); Foreign born: 4.0% (2006-2010 5-year est.); Ancestry (includes multiple ancestries): 43.1% German, 10.5% Irish, 8.2% American, 8.0% English, 7.4% Italian (2006-2010 5-year est.).
Economy: Single-family building permits issued: 16 (2011); Multi-family building permits issued: 0 (2011); Employment by occupation: 12.8% management, 3.9% professional, 10.9% services, 14.2% sales, 3.2% farming, 10.2% construction, 11.1% production (2006-2010 5-year est.).
Income: Per capita income: $26,653 (2006-2010 5-year est.); Median household income: $65,625 (2006-2010 5-year est.); Average household income: $73,070 (2006-2010 5-year est.); Percent of households with income of $100,000 or more: 22.4% (2006-2010 5-year est.); Poverty rate: 4.9% (2006-2010 5-year est.).
Education: Percent of population age 25 and over with: High school diploma (including GED) or higher: 85.8% (2006-2010 5-year est.); Bachelor's degree or higher: 18.4% (2006-2010 5-year est.); Master's degree or higher: 7.7% (2006-2010 5-year est.).
Housing: Homeownership rate: 92.2% (2010); Median home value: $188,100 (2006-2010 5-year est.); Median contract rent: $578 per month (2006-2010 5-year est.); Median year structure built: 1991 (2006-2010 5-year est.).
Transportation: Commute to work: 97.9% car, 0.0% public transportation, 0.3% walk, 1.3% work from home (2006-2010 5-year est.); Travel time to work: 30.8% less than 15 minutes, 45.7% 15 to 30 minutes, 13.1% 30 to 45 minutes, 3.6% 45 to 60 minutes, 6.9% 60 minutes or more (2006-2010 5-year est.)
Additional Information Contacts
East Manchester Township . . . . (717) 266-6735
    http://www.emanchestertwp.com
York County Chamber of Commerce . . . . (717) 848-4000
    http://www.yorkchamber.com

EAST PROSPECT

EAST PROSPECT (borough). Covers a land area of 0.319 square miles and a water area of 0 square miles. Located at 39.97° N. Lat; 76.52° W. Long. Elevation is 466 feet.

Population: 611 (1990); 678 (2000); 905 (2010); Density: 2,833.8 persons per square mile (2010); Race: 96.7% White, 1.2% Black, 0.2% Asian, 0.0% American Indian/Alaska Native, 0.0% Native Hawaiian/Other Pacific Islander, 1.9% Other, 2.5% Hispanic of any race (2010); Average household size: 2.85 (2010); Median age: 34.5 (2010); Males per 100 females: 92.6 (2010); Marriage status: 20.8% never married, 63.9% now married, 3.8% widowed, 11.5% divorced (2006-2010 5-year est.); Foreign born: 0.0% (2006-2010 5-year est.); Ancestry (includes multiple ancestries): 51.0% German, 10.7% American, 9.1% Irish, 7.9% English, 6.6% Italian (2006-2010 5-year est.).

Economy: Single-family building permits issued: 1 (2011); Multi-family building permits issued: 0 (2011); Employment by occupation: 13.5% management, 1.3% professional, 9.4% services, 9.4% sales, 0.0% farming, 12.9% construction, 15.1% production (2006-2010 5-year est.).

Income: Per capita income: $21,691 (2006-2010 5-year est.); Median household income: $61,786 (2006-2010 5-year est.); Average household income: $62,429 (2006-2010 5-year est.); Percent of households with income of $100,000 or more: 12.9% (2006-2010 5-year est.); Poverty rate: 7.7% (2006-2010 5-year est.).

Education: Percent of population age 25 and over with: High school diploma (including GED) or higher: 85.5% (2006-2010 5-year est.); Bachelor's degree or higher: 10.4% (2006-2010 5-year est.); Master's degree or higher: 2.0% (2006-2010 5-year est.).

School District(s)

Eastern York SD (KG-12)

   2010-11 Enrollment: 2,583 . . . . (717) 252-1555

Housing: Homeownership rate: 80.8% (2010); Median home value: $153,800 (2006-2010 5-year est.); Median contract rent: $463 per month (2006-2010 5-year est.); Median year structure built: 1964 (2006-2010 5-year est.).

Transportation: Commute to work: 99.0% car, 0.0% public transportation, 0.0% walk, 1.0% work from home (2006-2010 5-year est.); Travel time to work: 9.9% less than 15 minutes, 45.5% 15 to 30 minutes, 22.8% 30 to 45 minutes, 15.4% 45 to 60 minutes, 6.4% 60 minutes or more (2006-2010 5-year est.)

EAST YORK

EAST YORK (CDP). Covers a land area of 2.839 square miles and a water area of 0 square miles. Located at 39.97° N. Lat; 76.68° W. Long. Elevation is 417 feet.

Population: 8,487 (1990); 8,782 (2000); 8,777 (2010); Density: 3,091.5 persons per square mile (2010); Race: 88.7% White, 4.1% Black, 4.2% Asian, 0.2% American Indian/Alaska Native, 0.0% Native Hawaiian/Other Pacific Islander, 2.8% Other, 3.8% Hispanic of any race (2010); Average household size: 2.29 (2010); Median age: 45.0 (2010); Males per 100 females: 88.9 (2010); Marriage status: 21.3% never married, 56.8% now married, 11.8% widowed, 10.1% divorced (2006-2010 5-year est.); Foreign born: 5.6% (2006-2010 5-year est.); Ancestry (includes multiple ancestries): 43.8% German, 14.1% Irish, 11.1% English, 6.7% American, 6.1% Italian (2006-2010 5-year est.).

Economy: Employment by occupation: 17.5% management, 3.1% professional, 9.8% services, 15.9% sales, 3.4% farming, 6.3% construction, 5.3% production (2006-2010 5-year est.).

Income: Per capita income: $30,361 (2006-2010 5-year est.); Median household income: $60,194 (2006-2010 5-year est.); Average household income: $70,849 (2006-2010 5-year est.); Percent of households with income of $100,000 or more: 22.2% (2006-2010 5-year est.); Poverty rate: 5.7% (2006-2010 5-year est.).

Education: Percent of population age 25 and over with: High school diploma (including GED) or higher: 90.0% (2006-2010 5-year est.); Bachelor's degree or higher: 32.7% (2006-2010 5-year est.); Master's degree or higher: 13.4% (2006-2010 5-year est.).

Housing: Homeownership rate: 72.2% (2010); Median home value: $173,700 (2006-2010 5-year est.); Median contract rent: $744 per month (2006-2010 5-year est.); Median year structure built: 1963 (2006-2010 5-year est.).

Transportation: Commute to work: 92.5% car, 2.0% public transportation, 2.5% walk, 3.0% work from home (2006-2010 5-year est.); Travel time to work: 41.4% less than 15 minutes, 31.7% 15 to 30 minutes, 12.3% 30 to 45 minutes, 8.0% 45 to 60 minutes, 6.5% 60 minutes or more (2006-2010 5-year est.)

Additional Information Contacts

York County Chamber of Commerce . . . . (717) 848-4000
  http://www.yorkchamber.com

EMIGSVILLE

EMIGSVILLE (CDP). Covers a land area of 1.193 square miles and a water area of 0.001 square miles. Located at 40.01° N. Lat; 76.73° W. Long. Elevation is 397 feet.

Population: 2,580 (1990); 2,467 (2000); 2,672 (2010); Density: 2,240.2 persons per square mile (2010); Race: 90.8% White, 4.0% Black, 1.1% Asian, 0.3% American Indian/Alaska Native, 0.0% Native Hawaiian/Other Pacific Islander, 3.8% Other, 3.7% Hispanic of any race (2010); Average household size: 2.44 (2010); Median age: 39.7 (2010); Males per 100 females: 88.7 (2010); Marriage status: 28.1% never married, 58.4% now married, 7.2% widowed, 6.3% divorced (2006-2010 5-year est.); Foreign born: 3.7% (2006-2010 5-year est.); Ancestry (includes multiple ancestries): 51.2% German, 7.5% Irish, 6.9% American, 5.2% Italian, 4.3% Scotch-Irish (2006-2010 5-year est.).

Economy: Employment by occupation: 5.8% management, 1.5% professional, 12.0% services, 17.1% sales, 2.7% farming, 11.1% construction, 6.1% production (2006-2010 5-year est.).

Income: Per capita income: $20,754 (2006-2010 5-year est.); Median household income: $46,813 (2006-2010 5-year est.); Average household income: $48,976 (2006-2010 5-year est.); Percent of households with income of $100,000 or more: 6.9% (2006-2010 5-year est.); Poverty rate: 10.7% (2006-2010 5-year est.).

Education: Percent of population age 25 and over with: High school diploma (including GED) or higher: 83.2% (2006-2010 5-year est.); Bachelor's degree or higher: 11.9% (2006-2010 5-year est.); Master's degree or higher: 4.3% (2006-2010 5-year est.).

Housing: Homeownership rate: 74.1% (2010); Median home value: $136,300 (2006-2010 5-year est.); Median contract rent: $770 per month (2006-2010 5-year est.); Median year structure built: 1958 (2006-2010 5-year est.).

Transportation: Commute to work: 93.6% car, 0.0% public transportation, 3.3% walk, 3.1% work from home (2006-2010 5-year est.); Travel time to work: 45.0% less than 15 minutes, 39.0% 15 to 30 minutes, 6.3% 30 to 45 minutes, 5.9% 45 to 60 minutes, 3.7% 60 minutes or more (2006-2010 5-year est.)

Additional Information Contacts

York County Chamber of Commerce . . . . (717) 848-4000
  http://www.yorkchamber.com

ETTERS

ETTERS (unincorporated postal area)

Zip Code: 17319

  Covers a land area of 17.332 square miles and a water area of 0.002 square miles. Located at 40.16° N. Lat; 76.79° W. Long. Population: 10,417 (2010); Density: 601.0 persons per square mile (2010); Race: 95.3% White, 1.3% Black, 0.9% Asian, 0.2% American Indian/Alaska Native, 0.0% Native Hawaiian/Other Pacific Islander, 2.3% Other, 2.6% Hispanic of any race (2010); Average household size: 2.64 (2010); Median age: 38.4 (2010); Males per 100 females: 97.5 (2010); Homeownership rate: 87.7% (2010)

FAIRVIEW

FAIRVIEW (township). Covers a land area of 35.580 square miles and a water area of 0.077 square miles. Located at 40.17° N. Lat; 76.86° W. Long.

Population: 13,258 (1990); 14,321 (2000); 16,668 (2010); Density: 468.5 persons per square mile (2010); Race: 94.5% White, 1.6% Black, 1.4% Asian, 0.2% American Indian/Alaska Native, 0.0% Native Hawaiian/Other Pacific Islander, 2.3% Other, 3.3% Hispanic of any race (2010); Average household size: 2.53 (2010); Median age: 42.5 (2010); Males per 100 females: 100.5 (2010); Marriage status: 19.5% never married, 66.1% now married, 4.8% widowed, 9.6% divorced (2006-2010 5-year est.); Foreign born: 2.5% (2006-2010 5-year est.); Ancestry (includes multiple ancestries): 41.4% German, 13.7% Irish, 10.5% Italian, 9.8% English, 5.0% American (2006-2010 5-year est.).

Economy: Single-family building permits issued: 33 (2011); Multi-family building permits issued: 12 (2011); Employment by occupation: 14.9% management, 5.8% professional, 5.8% services, 20.8% sales, 4.7% farming, 6.5% construction, 5.6% production (2006-2010 5-year est.).

Income: Per capita income: $34,010 (2006-2010 5-year est.); Median household income: $73,914 (2006-2010 5-year est.); Average household income: $86,466 (2006-2010 5-year est.); Percent of households with income of $100,000 or more: 32.4% (2006-2010 5-year est.); Poverty rate: 3.8% (2006-2010 5-year est.).

Education: Percent of population age 25 and over with: High school diploma (including GED) or higher: 94.3% (2006-2010 5-year est.); Bachelor's degree or higher: 34.8% (2006-2010 5-year est.); Master's degree or higher: 11.2% (2006-2010 5-year est.).

Housing: Homeownership rate: 84.4% (2010); Median home value: $192,600 (2006-2010 5-year est.); Median contract rent: $649 per month (2006-2010 5-year est.); Median year structure built: 1978 (2006-2010 5-year est.).

Safety: Violent crime rate: 16.1 per 10,000 population; Property crime rate: 168.1 per 10,000 population (2011).

Transportation: Commute to work: 92.8% car, 0.5% public transportation, 1.9% walk, 3.7% work from home (2006-2010 5-year est.); Travel time to work: 24.4% less than 15 minutes, 51.2% 15 to 30 minutes, 18.2% 30 to 45 minutes, 2.0% 45 to 60 minutes, 4.3% 60 minutes or more (2006-2010 5-year est.)

Additional Information Contacts
Fairview Township. . . . . (717) 901-5210
 http://www.twp.fairview.pa.us
York County Chamber of Commerce . . . . (717) 848-4000
 http://www.yorkchamber.com

FAWN (township). Covers a land area of 27.105 square miles and a water area of 0.006 square miles. Located at 39.76° N. Lat; 76.47° W. Long.

Population: 2,175 (1990); 2,727 (2000); 3,099 (2010); Density: 114.3 persons per square mile (2010); Race: 97.3% White, 0.7% Black, 0.5% Asian, 0.1% American Indian/Alaska Native, 0.0% Native Hawaiian/Other Pacific Islander, 1.4% Other, 0.5% Hispanic of any race (2010); Average household size: 2.82 (2010); Median age: 42.2 (2010); Males per 100 females: 102.7 (2010); Marriage status: 22.1% never married, 61.8% now married, 4.6% widowed, 11.5% divorced (2006-2010 5-year est.); Foreign born: 1.5% (2006-2010 5-year est.); Ancestry (includes multiple ancestries): 38.1% German, 21.8% Irish, 13.1% English, 6.6% American, 6.6% Italian (2006-2010 5-year est.).

Economy: Single-family building permits issued: 1 (2011); Multi-family building permits issued: 0 (2011); Employment by occupation: 10.6% management, 6.0% professional, 10.9% services, 21.4% sales, 3.9% farming, 17.2% construction, 6.6% production (2006-2010 5-year est.).

Income: Per capita income: $28,679 (2006-2010 5-year est.); Median household income: $73,673 (2006-2010 5-year est.); Average household income: $80,916 (2006-2010 5-year est.); Percent of households with income of $100,000 or more: 27.6% (2006-2010 5-year est.); Poverty rate: 5.6% (2006-2010 5-year est.).

Education: Percent of population age 25 and over with: High school diploma (including GED) or higher: 90.1% (2006-2010 5-year est.); Bachelor's degree or higher: 15.4% (2006-2010 5-year est.); Master's degree or higher: 8.6% (2006-2010 5-year est.).

Housing: Homeownership rate: 88.6% (2010); Median home value: $258,900 (2006-2010 5-year est.); Median contract rent: $689 per month (2006-2010 5-year est.); Median year structure built: 1980 (2006-2010 5-year est.).

Transportation: Commute to work: 95.9% car, 0.0% public transportation, 0.7% walk, 3.4% work from home (2006-2010 5-year est.); Travel time to work: 14.1% less than 15 minutes, 17.0% 15 to 30 minutes, 27.8% 30 to 45 minutes, 21.2% 45 to 60 minutes, 19.8% 60 minutes or more (2006-2010 5-year est.)

Additional Information Contacts
York County Chamber of Commerce . . . . (717) 848-4000
 http://www.yorkchamber.com

FAWN GROVE (borough). Covers a land area of 1.645 square miles and a water area of 0 square miles. Located at 39.73° N. Lat; 76.45° W. Long. Elevation is 728 feet.

Population: 489 (1990); 463 (2000); 452 (2010); Density: 274.7 persons per square mile (2010); Race: 99.1% White, 0.0% Black, 0.2% Asian, 0.0% American Indian/Alaska Native, 0.2% Native Hawaiian/Other Pacific Islander, 0.5% Other, 0.4% Hispanic of any race (2010); Average household size: 2.47 (2010); Median age: 40.4 (2010); Males per 100 females: 94.0 (2010); Marriage status: 18.2% never married, 61.4% now married, 7.0% widowed, 13.4% divorced (2006-2010 5-year est.); Foreign born: 0.4% (2006-2010 5-year est.); Ancestry (includes multiple ancestries): 34.0% German, 17.8% Irish, 11.6% English, 10.6% American, 5.4% Welsh (2006-2010 5-year est.).

Economy: Single-family building permits issued: 2 (2011); Multi-family building permits issued: 0 (2011); Employment by occupation: 12.6%

management, 5.8% professional, 8.1% services, 20.4% sales, 2.3% farming, 14.6% construction, 10.7% production (2006-2010 5-year est.).

Income: Per capita income: $28,214 (2006-2010 5-year est.); Median household income: $63,750 (2006-2010 5-year est.); Average household income: $69,772 (2006-2010 5-year est.); Percent of households with income of $100,000 or more: 19.1% (2006-2010 5-year est.); Poverty rate: 10.0% (2006-2010 5-year est.).

Education: Percent of population age 25 and over with: High school diploma (including GED) or higher: 84.0% (2006-2010 5-year est.); Bachelor's degree or higher: 19.9% (2006-2010 5-year est.); Master's degree or higher: 7.6% (2006-2010 5-year est.).

School District(s)

South Eastern SD (PK-12)
 2010-11 Enrollment: 2,954 . . . . (717) 382-4843

Housing: Homeownership rate: 73.8% (2010); Median home value: $192,900 (2006-2010 5-year est.); Median contract rent: $642 per month (2006-2010 5-year est.); Median year structure built: 1962 (2006-2010 5-year est.).

Transportation: Commute to work: 94.4% car, 1.0% public transportation, 2.7% walk, 2.0% work from home (2006-2010 5-year est.); Travel time to work: 21.4% less than 15 minutes, 22.0% 15 to 30 minutes, 25.8% 30 to 45 minutes, 11.2% 45 to 60 minutes, 19.7% 60 minutes or more (2006-2010 5-year est.)

FELTON (borough). Covers a land area of 0.630 square miles and a water area of 0 square miles. Located at 39.86° N. Lat; 76.56° W. Long. Elevation is 545 feet.

Population: 438 (1990); 449 (2000); 506 (2010); Density: 803.4 persons per square mile (2010); Race: 98.8% White, 0.6% Black, 0.0% Asian, 0.0% American Indian/Alaska Native, 0.0% Native Hawaiian/Other Pacific Islander, 0.6% Other, 1.6% Hispanic of any race (2010); Average household size: 2.68 (2010); Median age: 38.8 (2010); Males per 100 females: 100.0 (2010); Marriage status: 22.6% never married, 61.6% now married, 4.7% widowed, 11.1% divorced (2006-2010 5-year est.); Foreign born: 0.7% (2006-2010 5-year est.); Ancestry (includes multiple ancestries): 34.5% German, 22.6% English, 13.4% American, 6.5% Irish, 4.3% Scotch-Irish (2006-2010 5-year est.).

Economy: Single-family building permits issued: 0 (2011); Multi-family building permits issued: 0 (2011); Employment by occupation: 6.8% management, 0.9% professional, 13.7% services, 17.1% sales, 2.6% farming, 19.2% construction, 11.5% production (2006-2010 5-year est.).

Income: Per capita income: $23,073 (2006-2010 5-year est.); Median household income: $49,196 (2006-2010 5-year est.); Average household income: $56,433 (2006-2010 5-year est.); Percent of households with income of $100,000 or more: 10.2% (2006-2010 5-year est.); Poverty rate: 1.7% (2006-2010 5-year est.).

Education: Percent of population age 25 and over with: High school diploma (including GED) or higher: 75.6% (2006-2010 5-year est.); Bachelor's degree or higher: 14.6% (2006-2010 5-year est.); Master's degree or higher: 4.5% (2006-2010 5-year est.).

Housing: Homeownership rate: 84.7% (2010); Median home value: $168,400 (2006-2010 5-year est.); Median contract rent: $663 per month (2006-2010 5-year est.); Median year structure built: 1943 (2006-2010 5-year est.).

Transportation: Commute to work: 97.3% car, 1.8% public transportation, 0.9% walk, 0.0% work from home (2006-2010 5-year est.); Travel time to work: 15.6% less than 15 minutes, 29.5% 15 to 30 minutes, 21.9% 30 to 45 minutes, 11.2% 45 to 60 minutes, 21.9% 60 minutes or more (2006-2010 5-year est.)

FRANKLIN (township). Covers a land area of 19.192 square miles and a water area of 0.044 square miles. Located at 40.07° N. Lat; 77.07° W. Long.

Population: 3,852 (1990); 4,515 (2000); 4,678 (2010); Density: 243.7 persons per square mile (2010); Race: 97.4% White, 0.6% Black, 0.5% Asian, 0.1% American Indian/Alaska Native, 0.0% Native Hawaiian/Other Pacific Islander, 1.4% Other, 1.6% Hispanic of any race (2010); Average household size: 2.47 (2010); Median age: 42.9 (2010); Males per 100 females: 99.0 (2010); Marriage status: 23.8% never married, 64.2% now married, 4.6% widowed, 7.4% divorced (2006-2010 5-year est.); Foreign born: 1.8% (2006-2010 5-year est.); Ancestry (includes multiple ancestries): 47.7% German, 19.8% Irish, 9.0% English, 6.6% Italian, 5.9% Dutch (2006-2010 5-year est.).

Economy: Single-family building permits issued: 7 (2011); Multi-family building permits issued: 0 (2011); Employment by occupation: 10.6%

management, 1.5% professional, 11.6% services, 15.7% sales, 4.3% farming, 17.1% construction, 11.8% production (2006-2010 5-year est.).
Income: Per capita income: $29,036 (2006-2010 5-year est.); Median household income: $64,325 (2006-2010 5-year est.); Average household income: $74,009 (2006-2010 5-year est.); Percent of households with income of $100,000 or more: 22.4% (2006-2010 5-year est.); Poverty rate: 3.8% (2006-2010 5-year est.).
Taxes: Total city taxes per capita: $142 (2009); City property taxes per capita: $15 (2009).
Education: Percent of population age 25 and over with: High school diploma (including GED) or higher: 92.1% (2006-2010 5-year est.); Bachelor's degree or higher: 29.1% (2006-2010 5-year est.); Master's degree or higher: 9.4% (2006-2010 5-year est.).
Housing: Homeownership rate: 81.5% (2010); Median home value: $193,800 (2006-2010 5-year est.); Median contract rent: $582 per month (2006-2010 5-year est.); Median year structure built: 1985 (2006-2010 5-year est.).
Transportation: Commute to work: 92.0% car, 1.1% public transportation, 0.0% walk, 6.9% work from home (2006-2010 5-year est.); Travel time to work: 15.8% less than 15 minutes, 46.3% 15 to 30 minutes, 29.6% 30 to 45 minutes, 7.1% 45 to 60 minutes, 1.2% 60 minutes or more (2006-2010 5-year est.).
Additional Information Contacts
Franklin Township . . . . (717) 432-3773
    http://www.franklintownship.org
York County Chamber of Commerce . . . . (717) 848-4000
    http://www.yorkchamber.com

FRANKLINTOWN (borough). Covers a land area of 0.250 square miles and a water area of 0 square miles. Located at 40.08° N. Lat; 77.03° W. Long. Elevation is 692 feet.
Population: 373 (1990); 532 (2000); 489 (2010); Density: 1,955.3 persons per square mile (2010); Race: 95.1% White, 1.4% Black, 0.4% Asian, 0.0% American Indian/Alaska Native, 0.0% Native Hawaiian/Other Pacific Islander, 3.1% Other, 2.5% Hispanic of any race (2010); Average household size: 2.33 (2010); Median age: 35.2 (2010); Males per 100 females: 98.8 (2010); Marriage status: 26.7% never married, 58.3% now married, 1.5% widowed, 13.5% divorced (2006-2010 5-year est.); Foreign born: 1.7% (2006-2010 5-year est.); Ancestry (includes multiple ancestries): 62.9% German, 10.6% Irish, 9.2% English, 5.0% Scotch-Irish, 4.3% American (2006-2010 5-year est.).
Economy: Single-family building permits issued: 0 (2011); Multi-family building permits issued: 0 (2011); Employment by occupation: 19.3% management, 0.0% professional, 5.9% services, 30.3% sales, 4.7% farming, 6.3% construction, 7.9% production (2006-2010 5-year est.).
Income: Per capita income: $22,314 (2006-2010 5-year est.); Median household income: $43,654 (2006-2010 5-year est.); Average household income: $52,097 (2006-2010 5-year est.); Percent of households with income of $100,000 or more: 8.9% (2006-2010 5-year est.); Poverty rate: 9.7% (2006-2010 5-year est.).
Education: Percent of population age 25 and over with: High school diploma (including GED) or higher: 87.7% (2006-2010 5-year est.); Bachelor's degree or higher: 18.5% (2006-2010 5-year est.); Master's degree or higher: 1.6% (2006-2010 5-year est.).
Housing: Homeownership rate: 61.9% (2010); Median home value: $166,700 (2006-2010 5-year est.); Median contract rent: $543 per month (2006-2010 5-year est.); Median year structure built: 1983 (2006-2010 5-year est.).
Transportation: Commute to work: 100.0% car, 0.0% public transportation, 0.0% walk, 0.0% work from home (2006-2010 5-year est.); Travel time to work: 21.2% less than 15 minutes, 24.9% 15 to 30 minutes, 41.2% 30 to 45 minutes, 12.7% 45 to 60 minutes, 0.0% 60 minutes or more (2006-2010 5-year est.)
Additional Information Contacts
Borough of Franklintown . . . . (717) 432-4047
    http://franklintownborough.com

GLEN ROCK (borough). Covers a land area of 0.801 square miles and a water area of 0 square miles. Located at 39.79° N. Lat; 76.73° W. Long. Elevation is 545 feet.
History: Incorporated 1860.
Population: 1,688 (1990); 1,809 (2000); 2,025 (2010); Density: 2,528.0 persons per square mile (2010); Race: 94.6% White, 2.2% Black, 0.3% Asian, 0.4% American Indian/Alaska Native, 0.0% Native Hawaiian/Other Pacific Islander, 2.5% Other, 2.3% Hispanic of any race (2010); Average

household size: 2.58 (2010); Median age: 35.4 (2010); Males per 100 females: 96.6 (2010); Marriage status: 29.3% never married, 57.1% now married, 3.8% widowed, 9.8% divorced (2006-2010 5-year est.); Foreign born: 0.4% (2006-2010 5-year est.); Ancestry (includes multiple ancestries): 43.6% German, 21.0% Irish, 9.4% Italian, 8.5% American, 7.4% English (2006-2010 5-year est.).
Economy: Single-family building permits issued: 0 (2011); Multi-family building permits issued: 0 (2011); Employment by occupation: 7.3% management, 7.6% professional, 9.9% services, 16.8% sales, 4.7% farming, 10.0% construction, 8.8% production (2006-2010 5-year est.).
Income: Per capita income: $24,859 (2006-2010 5-year est.); Median household income: $59,954 (2006-2010 5-year est.); Average household income: $67,456 (2006-2010 5-year est.); Percent of households with income of $100,000 or more: 19.8% (2006-2010 5-year est.); Poverty rate: 5.3% (2006-2010 5-year est.).
Education: Percent of population age 25 and over with: High school diploma (including GED) or higher: 87.0% (2006-2010 5-year est.); Bachelor's degree or higher: 19.9% (2006-2010 5-year est.); Master's degree or higher: 8.5% (2006-2010 5-year est.).
School District(s)
Southern York County SD (KG-12)
    2010-11 Enrollment: 3,176 . . . . (717) 235-4811
Housing: Homeownership rate: 64.5% (2010); Median home value: $181,400 (2006-2010 5-year est.); Median contract rent: $640 per month (2006-2010 5-year est.); Median year structure built: 1952 (2006-2010 5-year est.).
Transportation: Commute to work: 97.2% car, 0.0% public transportation, 0.6% walk, 2.1% work from home (2006-2010 5-year est.); Travel time to work: 22.5% less than 15 minutes, 24.6% 15 to 30 minutes, 23.7% 30 to 45 minutes, 15.5% 45 to 60 minutes, 13.7% 60 minutes or more (2006-2010 5-year est.)
Additional Information Contacts
York County Chamber of Commerce . . . . (717) 848-4000
    http://www.yorkchamber.com

GLENVILLE (unincorporated postal area)
Zip Code: 17329
    Covers a land area of 16.358 square miles and a water area of 0 square miles. Located at 39.76° N. Lat; 76.85° W. Long. Population: 2,494 (2010); Density: 152.5 persons per square mile (2010); Race: 97.5% White, 0.4% Black, 0.3% Asian, 0.1% American Indian/Alaska Native, 0.0% Native Hawaiian/Other Pacific Islander, 1.7% Other, 0.7% Hispanic of any race (2010); Average household size: 2.71 (2010); Median age: 44.6 (2010); Males per 100 females: 102.1 (2010); Homeownership rate: 92.2% (2010)

GOLDSBORO (borough). Aka Etters. Covers a land area of 0.451 square miles and a water area of 0.003 square miles. Located at 40.15° N. Lat; 76.75° W. Long. Elevation is 305 feet.
Population: 452 (1990); 939 (2000); 952 (2010); Density: 2,111.7 persons per square mile (2010); Race: 96.2% White, 0.8% Black, 0.6% Asian, 0.1% American Indian/Alaska Native, 0.1% Native Hawaiian/Other Pacific Islander, 2.2% Other, 3.4% Hispanic of any race (2010); Average household size: 2.81 (2010); Median age: 36.2 (2010); Males per 100 females: 100.0 (2010); Marriage status: 28.7% never married, 56.8% now married, 2.2% widowed, 12.2% divorced (2006-2010 5-year est.); Foreign born: 0.5% (2006-2010 5-year est.); Ancestry (includes multiple ancestries): 40.7% German, 18.4% Irish, 12.7% Italian, 12.1% Polish, 8.3% English (2006-2010 5-year est.).
Economy: Single-family building permits issued: 0 (2011); Multi-family building permits issued: 0 (2011); Employment by occupation: 12.0% management, 4.1% professional, 9.7% services, 14.3% sales, 4.8% farming, 13.3% construction, 10.1% production (2006-2010 5-year est.).
Income: Per capita income: $26,650 (2006-2010 5-year est.); Median household income: $60,000 (2006-2010 5-year est.); Average household income: $70,585 (2006-2010 5-year est.); Percent of households with income of $100,000 or more: 22.3% (2006-2010 5-year est.); Poverty rate: 3.7% (2006-2010 5-year est.).
Education: Percent of population age 25 and over with: High school diploma (including GED) or higher: 92.0% (2006-2010 5-year est.); Bachelor's degree or higher: 13.1% (2006-2010 5-year est.); Master's degree or higher: 2.0% (2006-2010 5-year est.).
Housing: Homeownership rate: 84.6% (2010); Median home value: $145,000 (2006-2010 5-year est.); Median contract rent: $650 per month

(2006-2010 5-year est.); Median year structure built: 1990 (2006-2010 5-year est.).

Transportation: Commute to work: 94.5% car, 0.0% public transportation, 0.0% walk, 4.9% work from home (2006-2010 5-year est.); Travel time to work: 30.7% less than 15 minutes, 31.1% 15 to 30 minutes, 26.9% 30 to 45 minutes, 5.1% 45 to 60 minutes, 6.2% 60 minutes or more (2006-2010 5-year est.)

Additional Information Contacts

Wayne County Chamber of Commerce . . . . (570) 253-1960
   http://www.waynecountycc.com

GRANTLEY (CDP). Covers a land area of 1.671 square miles and a water area of 0.015 square miles. Located at 39.94° N. Lat; 76.73° W. Long. Elevation is 561 feet.

History: Home of York College. York County Academy was founded in 1787. In 1929, the Academy merged with the York Collegiate Institute, allowing further growth of both schools. It was in 1941 that the school's charter was amended,.

Population: 3,036 (1990); 3,580 (2000); 3,628 (2010); Density: 2,171.8 persons per square mile (2010); Race: 92.8% White, 3.9% Black, 1.2% Asian, 0.2% American Indian/Alaska Native, 0.0% Native Hawaiian/Other Pacific Islander, 1.9% Other, 3.9% Hispanic of any race (2010); Average household size: 2.51 (2010); Median age: 21.2 (2010); Males per 100 females: 94.5 (2010); Marriage status: 50.5% never married, 41.4% now married, 5.1% widowed, 3.0% divorced (2006-2010 5-year est.); Foreign born: 4.0% (2006-2010 5-year est.); Ancestry (includes multiple ancestries): 38.8% German, 21.9% Irish, 13.5% Italian, 7.5% English, 5.3% Polish (2006-2010 5-year est.).

Economy: Employment by occupation: 12.4% management, 8.2% professional, 9.4% services, 22.3% sales, 1.9% farming, 2.5% construction, 1.1% production (2006-2010 5-year est.).

Income: Per capita income: $28,315 (2006-2010 5-year est.); Median household income: $90,380 (2006-2010 5-year est.); Average household income: $124,016 (2006-2010 5-year est.); Percent of households with income of $100,000 or more: 43.5% (2006-2010 5-year est.); Poverty rate: 5.8% (2006-2010 5-year est.).

Education: Percent of population age 25 and over with: High school diploma (including GED) or higher: 94.9% (2006-2010 5-year est.); Bachelor's degree or higher: 60.8% (2006-2010 5-year est.); Master's degree or higher: 25.4% (2006-2010 5-year est.).

Housing: Homeownership rate: 87.4% (2010); Median home value: $273,100 (2006-2010 5-year est.); Median contract rent: $1,042 per month (2006-2010 5-year est.); Median year structure built: 1955 (2006-2010 5-year est.).

Transportation: Commute to work: 81.4% car, 0.9% public transportation, 15.7% walk, 1.3% work from home (2006-2010 5-year est.); Travel time to work: 53.3% less than 15 minutes, 27.5% 15 to 30 minutes, 2.8% 30 to 45 minutes, 9.2% 45 to 60 minutes, 7.3% 60 minutes or more (2006-2010 5-year est.)

Additional Information Contacts

York County Chamber of Commerce . . . . (717) 848-4000
   http://www.yorkchamber.com

HALLAM (borough). Aka Hellam. Covers a land area of 0.635 square miles and a water area of 0 square miles. Located at 40.00° N. Lat; 76.60° W. Long. Elevation is 367 feet.

History: Post office name is Hellam; borough surrounded by Hellam township.

Population: 1,375 (1990); 1,532 (2000); 2,673 (2010); Density: 4,209.1 persons per square mile (2010); Race: 92.5% White, 4.2% Black, 1.1% Asian, 0.1% American Indian/Alaska Native, 0.0% Native Hawaiian/Other Pacific Islander, 2.1% Other, 2.3% Hispanic of any race (2010); Average household size: 2.22 (2010); Median age: 34.7 (2010); Males per 100 females: 94.0 (2010); Marriage status: 24.5% never married, 54.5% now married, 5.2% widowed, 15.8% divorced (2006-2010 5-year est.); Foreign born: 3.6% (2006-2010 5-year est.); Ancestry (includes multiple ancestries): 54.7% German, 15.4% Irish, 11.2% English, 8.2% American, 6.7% Italian (2006-2010 5-year est.).

Economy: Single-family building permits issued: 0 (2011); Multi-family building permits issued: 0 (2011); Employment by occupation: 10.0% management, 5.0% professional, 10.0% services, 19.9% sales, 5.6% farming, 7.3% construction, 14.3% production (2006-2010 5-year est.).

Income: Per capita income: $28,280 (2006-2010 5-year est.); Median household income: $51,578 (2006-2010 5-year est.); Average household income: $58,024 (2006-2010 5-year est.); Percent of households with

income of $100,000 or more: 10.3% (2006-2010 5-year est.); Poverty rate: 4.4% (2006-2010 5-year est.).

Education: Percent of population age 25 and over with: High school diploma (including GED) or higher: 91.8% (2006-2010 5-year est.); Bachelor's degree or higher: 25.6% (2006-2010 5-year est.); Master's degree or higher: 5.3% (2006-2010 5-year est.).

Housing: Homeownership rate: 54.1% (2010); Median home value: $140,300 (2006-2010 5-year est.); Median contract rent: $767 per month (2006-2010 5-year est.); Median year structure built: 1994 (2006-2010 5-year est.).

Transportation: Commute to work: 97.0% car, 0.4% public transportation, 0.4% walk, 2.2% work from home (2006-2010 5-year est.); Travel time to work: 26.5% less than 15 minutes, 43.4% 15 to 30 minutes, 16.6% 30 to 45 minutes, 7.9% 45 to 60 minutes, 5.6% 60 minutes or more (2006-2010 5-year est.)

Additional Information Contacts

York County Chamber of Commerce . . . . (717) 848-4000
   http://www.yorkchamber.com

HANOVER (borough). Covers a land area of 3.713 square miles and a water area of 0 square miles. Located at 39.81° N. Lat; 76.98° W. Long. Elevation is 600 feet.

History: Standardbred horses raised here (many famous trotters have Hanover in their names). A cavalry action preceding the battle of Gettysburg was fought here in June 1863. Incorporated 1815.

Population: 14,399 (1990); 14,535 (2000); 15,289 (2010); Density: 4,117.6 persons per square mile (2010); Race: 91.9% White, 1.2% Black, 1.0% Asian, 0.2% American Indian/Alaska Native, 0.0% Native Hawaiian/Other Pacific Islander, 5.7% Other, 7.3% Hispanic of any race (2010); Average household size: 2.22 (2010); Median age: 40.7 (2010); Males per 100 females: 92.0 (2010); Marriage status: 24.8% never married, 53.1% now married, 8.6% widowed, 13.5% divorced (2006-2010 5-year est.); Foreign born: 4.5% (2006-2010 5-year est.); Ancestry (includes multiple ancestries): 43.6% German, 14.5% Irish, 10.5% American, 8.6% English, 4.1% Italian (2006-2010 5-year est.).

Economy: Single-family building permits issued: 16 (2011); Multi-family building permits issued: 6 (2011); Employment by occupation: 6.8% management, 2.0% professional, 11.3% services, 18.0% sales, 3.3% farming, 8.2% construction, 9.5% production (2006-2010 5-year est.).

Income: Per capita income: $25,257 (2006-2010 5-year est.); Median household income: $44,900 (2006-2010 5-year est.); Average household income: $56,907 (2006-2010 5-year est.); Percent of households with income of $100,000 or more: 10.8% (2006-2010 5-year est.); Poverty rate: 10.6% (2006-2010 5-year est.).

Taxes: Total city taxes per capita: $407 (2009); City property taxes per capita: $255 (2009).

Education: Percent of population age 25 and over with: High school diploma (including GED) or higher: 83.2% (2006-2010 5-year est.); Bachelor's degree or higher: 17.5% (2006-2010 5-year est.); Master's degree or higher: 6.1% (2006-2010 5-year est.).

School District(s)

Conewago Valley SD (KG-12)
   2010-11 Enrollment: 3,941 . . . . (717) 624-2157
Hanover Public SD (KG-12)
   2010-11 Enrollment: 1,627 . . . . (717) 637-9000
South Western SD (KG-12)
   2010-11 Enrollment: 4,097 . . . . (717) 632-2500

Vocational/Technical School(s)

Empire Beauty School-Hanover (Private, For-profit)
   Fall 2010 Enrollment: 207 . . . . (800) 223-3271
   2011-12 Tuition: $14,490
Hanover Public School District Practical Nursing Program (Public)
   Fall 2010 Enrollment: 66 . . . . (717) 637-2111
   2011-12 Tuition: $8,330

Housing: Homeownership rate: 54.4% (2010); Median home value: $165,900 (2006-2010 5-year est.); Median contract rent: $591 per month (2006-2010 5-year est.); Median year structure built: 1952 (2006-2010 5-year est.).

Hospitals: Hanover Hospital (117 beds)

Safety: Violent crime rate: 17.0 per 10,000 population; Property crime rate: 440.1 per 10,000 population (2011).

Newspapers: The Evening Sun (Local news)

Transportation: Commute to work: 88.6% car, 0.2% public transportation, 5.1% walk, 3.7% work from home (2006-2010 5-year est.); Travel time to work: 54.6% less than 15 minutes, 19.1% 15 to 30 minutes, 11.4% 30 to

45 minutes, 6.0% 45 to 60 minutes, 8.8% 60 minutes or more (2006-2010 5-year est.)
Additional Information Contacts
Borough of Hanover . . . . (717) 637-3877
　http://www.borough.hanover.pa.us
Hanover Area Chamber of Commerce . . . . (717) 637-6130
　http://hanoverchamber.com

HEIDELBERG (township). Covers a land area of 14.016 square miles and a water area of 0.538 square miles. Located at 39.83° N. Lat; 76.92° W. Long.
Population: 2,622 (1990); 2,970 (2000); 3,078 (2010); Density: 219.6 persons per square mile (2010); Race: 98.1% White, 0.7% Black, 0.2% Asian, 0.3% American Indian/Alaska Native, 0.0% Native Hawaiian/Other Pacific Islander, 0.7% Other, 0.9% Hispanic of any race (2010); Average household size: 2.68 (2010); Median age: 45.7 (2010); Males per 100 females: 98.7 (2010); Marriage status: 21.8% never married, 66.0% now married, 3.4% widowed, 8.8% divorced (2006-2010 5-year est.); Foreign born: 3.4% (2006-2010 5-year est.); Ancestry (includes multiple ancestries): 49.4% German, 11.9% American, 8.1% Irish, 7.8% English, 4.7% Italian (2006-2010 5-year est.).
Economy: Single-family building permits issued: 0 (2011); Multi-family building permits issued: 0 (2011); Employment by occupation: 11.8% management, 3.4% professional, 11.2% services, 11.1% sales, 2.0% farming, 18.5% construction, 12.5% production (2006-2010 5-year est.).
Income: Per capita income: $29,448 (2006-2010 5-year est.); Median household income: $64,688 (2006-2010 5-year est.); Average household income: $82,029 (2006-2010 5-year est.); Percent of households with income of $100,000 or more: 23.7% (2006-2010 5-year est.); Poverty rate: 6.5% (2006-2010 5-year est.).
Education: Percent of population age 25 and over with: High school diploma (including GED) or higher: 84.1% (2006-2010 5-year est.); Bachelor's degree or higher: 21.9% (2006-2010 5-year est.); Master's degree or higher: 6.2% (2006-2010 5-year est.).
Housing: Homeownership rate: 89.0% (2010); Median home value: $218,800 (2006-2010 5-year est.); Median contract rent: $618 per month (2006-2010 5-year est.); Median year structure built: 1978 (2006-2010 5-year est.).
Transportation: Commute to work: 93.9% car, 0.0% public transportation, 2.4% walk, 3.4% work from home (2006-2010 5-year est.); Travel time to work: 25.1% less than 15 minutes, 41.2% 15 to 30 minutes, 14.3% 30 to 45 minutes, 6.6% 45 to 60 minutes, 12.8% 60 minutes or more (2006-2010 5-year est.)
Additional Information Contacts
York County Chamber of Commerce . . . . (717) 848-4000
　http://www.yorkchamber.com

HELLAM (township). Aka Hallam. Covers a land area of 28.227 square miles and a water area of 0.026 square miles. Located at 40.02° N. Lat; 76.60° W. Long.
Population: 5,301 (1990); 5,930 (2000); 6,043 (2010); Density: 214.1 persons per square mile (2010); Race: 96.4% White, 1.1% Black, 0.4% Asian, 0.1% American Indian/Alaska Native, 0.0% Native Hawaiian/Other Pacific Islander, 2.0% Other, 1.8% Hispanic of any race (2010); Average household size: 2.47 (2010); Median age: 45.4 (2010); Males per 100 females: 100.3 (2010); Marriage status: 25.7% never married, 60.8% now married, 3.9% widowed, 9.7% divorced (2006-2010 5-year est.); Foreign born: 3.1% (2006-2010 5-year est.); Ancestry (includes multiple ancestries): 49.1% German, 12.7% Irish, 7.8% American, 6.1% English, 4.9% Italian (2006-2010 5-year est.).
Economy: Single-family building permits issued: 5 (2011); Multi-family building permits issued: 0 (2011); Employment by occupation: 14.9% management, 4.7% professional, 7.8% services, 13.7% sales, 1.3% farming, 9.9% construction, 9.3% production (2006-2010 5-year est.).
Income: Per capita income: $32,795 (2006-2010 5-year est.); Median household income: $66,386 (2006-2010 5-year est.); Average household income: $82,299 (2006-2010 5-year est.); Percent of households with income of $100,000 or more: 23.3% (2006-2010 5-year est.); Poverty rate: 4.4% (2006-2010 5-year est.).
Education: Percent of population age 25 and over with: High school diploma (including GED) or higher: 89.0% (2006-2010 5-year est.); Bachelor's degree or higher: 21.6% (2006-2010 5-year est.); Master's degree or higher: 5.6% (2006-2010 5-year est.).

School District(s)
Eastern York SD (KG-12)
　2010-11 Enrollment: 2,583 . . . . (717) 252-1555
Housing: Homeownership rate: 80.8% (2010); Median home value: $174,300 (2006-2010 5-year est.); Median contract rent: $828 per month (2006-2010 5-year est.); Median year structure built: 1974 (2006-2010 5-year est.).
Safety: Violent crime rate: 30.9 per 10,000 population; Property crime rate: 114.4 per 10,000 population (2011).
Transportation: Commute to work: 90.4% car, 0.0% public transportation, 0.0% walk, 8.2% work from home (2006-2010 5-year est.); Travel time to work: 22.0% less than 15 minutes, 54.2% 15 to 30 minutes, 15.3% 30 to 45 minutes, 4.4% 45 to 60 minutes, 4.1% 60 minutes or more (2006-2010 5-year est.)
Additional Information Contacts
Hellam Township. . . . . (717) 434-1300
　http://www.hellamtownship.com
York County Chamber of Commerce . . . . (717) 848-4000
　http://www.yorkchamber.com

HOPEWELL (township). Covers a land area of 26.779 square miles and a water area of 0 square miles. Located at 39.74° N. Lat; 76.56° W. Long.
Population: 3,153 (1990); 5,062 (2000); 5,435 (2010); Density: 203.0 persons per square mile (2010); Race: 96.0% White, 1.7% Black, 0.6% Asian, 0.1% American Indian/Alaska Native, 0.1% Native Hawaiian/Other Pacific Islander, 1.5% Other, 0.9% Hispanic of any race (2010); Average household size: 2.75 (2010); Median age: 43.4 (2010); Males per 100 females: 101.5 (2010); Marriage status: 20.0% never married, 68.9% now married, 5.0% widowed, 6.1% divorced (2006-2010 5-year est.); Foreign born: 2.6% (2006-2010 5-year est.); Ancestry (includes multiple ancestries): 46.9% German, 24.3% Irish, 19.1% English, 9.6% Italian, 8.8% Polish (2006-2010 5-year est.).
Economy: Single-family building permits issued: 2 (2011); Multi-family building permits issued: 0 (2011); Employment by occupation: 10.7% management, 13.3% professional, 8.0% services, 18.8% sales, 2.4% farming, 8.7% construction, 4.6% production (2006-2010 5-year est.).
Income: Per capita income: $35,609 (2006-2010 5-year est.); Median household income: $85,951 (2006-2010 5-year est.); Average household income: $99,414 (2006-2010 5-year est.); Percent of households with income of $100,000 or more: 39.0% (2006-2010 5-year est.); Poverty rate: 1.3% (2006-2010 5-year est.).
Education: Percent of population age 25 and over with: High school diploma (including GED) or higher: 87.9% (2006-2010 5-year est.); Bachelor's degree or higher: 27.6% (2006-2010 5-year est.); Master's degree or higher: 8.8% (2006-2010 5-year est.).
Housing: Homeownership rate: 90.4% (2010); Median home value: $248,800 (2006-2010 5-year est.); Median contract rent: $725 per month (2006-2010 5-year est.); Median year structure built: 1991 (2006-2010 5-year est.).
Transportation: Commute to work: 97.6% car, 0.0% public transportation, 0.4% walk, 1.6% work from home (2006-2010 5-year est.); Travel time to work: 16.9% less than 15 minutes, 16.1% 15 to 30 minutes, 20.9% 30 to 45 minutes, 20.7% 45 to 60 minutes, 25.5% 60 minutes or more (2006-2010 5-year est.)
Additional Information Contacts
Hopewell Township . . . . (717) 993-2027
　http://www.hopewelltownship.com
York County Chamber of Commerce . . . . (717) 848-4000
　http://www.yorkchamber.com

JACKSON (township). Covers a land area of 22.578 square miles and a water area of 0.233 square miles. Located at 39.91° N. Lat; 76.88° W. Long.
Population: 6,269 (1990); 6,095 (2000); 7,494 (2010); Density: 331.9 persons per square mile (2010); Race: 93.4% White, 3.4% Black, 0.8% Asian, 0.1% American Indian/Alaska Native, 0.0% Native Hawaiian/Other Pacific Islander, 2.3% Other, 2.7% Hispanic of any race (2010); Average household size: 2.67 (2010); Median age: 40.4 (2010); Males per 100 females: 102.2 (2010); Marriage status: 21.0% never married, 62.7% now married, 5.2% widowed, 11.1% divorced (2006-2010 5-year est.); Foreign born: 2.2% (2006-2010 5-year est.); Ancestry (includes multiple ancestries): 48.6% German, 11.7% American, 9.8% Irish, 6.7% English, 4.7% Italian (2006-2010 5-year est.).

Economy: Single-family building permits issued: 13 (2011); Multi-family building permits issued: 0 (2011); Employment by occupation: 11.4% management, 4.1% professional, 9.5% services, 18.4% sales, 2.0% farming, 12.4% construction, 11.6% production (2006-2010 5-year est.).
Income: Per capita income: $26,331 (2006-2010 5-year est.); Median household income: $65,367 (2006-2010 5-year est.); Average household income: $70,651 (2006-2010 5-year est.); Percent of households with income of $100,000 or more: 19.1% (2006-2010 5-year est.); Poverty rate: 3.3% (2006-2010 5-year est.).
Education: Percent of population age 25 and over with: High school diploma (including GED) or higher: 85.6% (2006-2010 5-year est.); Bachelor's degree or higher: 16.6% (2006-2010 5-year est.); Master's degree or higher: 6.6% (2006-2010 5-year est.).
Housing: Homeownership rate: 91.2% (2010); Median home value: $176,400 (2006-2010 5-year est.); Median contract rent: $540 per month (2006-2010 5-year est.); Median year structure built: 1979 (2006-2010 5-year est.).
Transportation: Commute to work: 92.8% car, 0.7% public transportation, 0.9% walk, 4.1% work from home (2006-2010 5-year est.); Travel time to work: 28.0% less than 15 minutes, 40.5% 15 to 30 minutes, 16.4% 30 to 45 minutes, 4.7% 45 to 60 minutes, 10.5% 60 minutes or more (2006-2010 5-year est.)
Additional Information Contacts
Jackson Township . . . . (717) 225-5661
York County Chamber of Commerce . . . . (717) 848-4000
http://www.yorkchamber.com

JACOBUS (borough). Covers a land area of 0.940 square miles and a water area of 0 square miles. Located at 39.88° N. Lat; 76.71° W. Long. Elevation is 659 feet.
Population: 1,370 (1990); 1,203 (2000); 1,841 (2010); Density: 1,958.1 persons per square mile (2010); Race: 91.3% White, 5.1% Black, 1.4% Asian, 0.1% American Indian/Alaska Native, 0.0% Native Hawaiian/Other Pacific Islander, 2.1% Other, 3.5% Hispanic of any race (2010); Average household size: 2.77 (2010); Median age: 37.9 (2010); Males per 100 females: 98.8 (2010); Marriage status: 16.8% never married, 73.0% now married, 4.5% widowed, 5.7% divorced (2006-2010 5-year est.); Foreign born: 2.7% (2006-2010 5-year est.); Ancestry (includes multiple ancestries): 38.3% German, 14.9% American, 8.9% English, 8.7% Irish, 4.5% Italian (2006-2010 5-year est.).
Economy: Single-family building permits issued: 0 (2011); Multi-family building permits issued: 0 (2011); Employment by occupation: 14.1% management, 5.5% professional, 4.6% services, 14.8% sales, 4.2% farming, 6.5% construction, 9.9% production (2006-2010 5-year est.).
Income: Per capita income: $30,290 (2006-2010 5-year est.); Median household income: $72,054 (2006-2010 5-year est.); Average household income: $80,229 (2006-2010 5-year est.); Percent of households with income of $100,000 or more: 33.9% (2006-2010 5-year est.); Poverty rate: 1.1% (2006-2010 5-year est.).
Education: Percent of population age 25 and over with: High school diploma (including GED) or higher: 85.1% (2006-2010 5-year est.); Bachelor's degree or higher: 28.9% (2006-2010 5-year est.); Master's degree or higher: 5.9% (2006-2010 5-year est.).
Housing: Homeownership rate: 88.2% (2010); Median home value: $182,500 (2006-2010 5-year est.); Median contract rent: $686 per month (2006-2010 5-year est.); Median year structure built: 1966 (2006-2010 5-year est.).
Transportation: Commute to work: 94.6% car, 0.2% public transportation, 1.1% walk, 3.4% work from home (2006-2010 5-year est.); Travel time to work: 20.7% less than 15 minutes, 32.9% 15 to 30 minutes, 13.0% 30 to 45 minutes, 19.1% 45 to 60 minutes, 14.3% 60 minutes or more (2006-2010 5-year est.)
Additional Information Contacts
York County Chamber of Commerce . . . . (717) 848-4000
http://www.yorkchamber.com

JEFFERSON (borough). Aka Codorus. Covers a land area of 0.606 square miles and a water area of <.001 square miles. Located at 39.82° N. Lat; 76.84° W. Long. Elevation is 653 feet.
Population: 675 (1990); 631 (2000); 733 (2010); Density: 1,208.9 persons per square mile (2010); Race: 98.2% White, 0.8% Black, 0.0% Asian, 0.1% American Indian/Alaska Native, 0.0% Native Hawaiian/Other Pacific Islander, 0.9% Other, 0.4% Hispanic of any race (2010); Average household size: 2.55 (2010); Median age: 40.9 (2010); Males per 100 females: 104.7 (2010); Marriage status: 19.4% never married, 57.8% now

married, 9.3% widowed, 13.5% divorced (2006-2010 5-year est.); Foreign born: 1.0% (2006-2010 5-year est.); Ancestry (includes multiple ancestries): 51.0% German, 19.1% Irish, 10.9% American, 8.7% Pennsylvania German, 4.1% Italian (2006-2010 5-year est.).
Economy: Single-family building permits issued: 1 (2011); Multi-family building permits issued: 0 (2011); Employment by occupation: 3.1% management, 4.7% professional, 11.2% services, 14.0% sales, 4.0% farming, 15.8% construction, 18.3% production (2006-2010 5-year est.).
Income: Per capita income: $22,082 (2006-2010 5-year est.); Median household income: $53,750 (2006-2010 5-year est.); Average household income: $56,309 (2006-2010 5-year est.); Percent of households with income of $100,000 or more: 10.0% (2006-2010 5-year est.); Poverty rate: 16.5% (2006-2010 5-year est.).
Education: Percent of population age 25 and over with: High school diploma (including GED) or higher: 79.1% (2006-2010 5-year est.); Bachelor's degree or higher: 10.8% (2006-2010 5-year est.); Master's degree or higher: 3.3% (2006-2010 5-year est.).
Housing: Homeownership rate: 82.6% (2010); Median home value: $159,500 (2006-2010 5-year est.); Median contract rent: $475 per month (2006-2010 5-year est.); Median year structure built: 1947 (2006-2010 5-year est.).
Transportation: Commute to work: 97.8% car, 0.0% public transportation, 0.0% walk, 1.2% work from home (2006-2010 5-year est.); Travel time to work: 13.8% less than 15 minutes, 30.8% 15 to 30 minutes, 32.4% 30 to 45 minutes, 4.7% 45 to 60 minutes, 18.2% 60 minutes or more (2006-2010 5-year est.)

LEWISBERRY (borough). Covers a land area of 0.139 square miles and a water area of 0 square miles. Located at 40.14° N. Lat; 76.86° W. Long. Elevation is 436 feet.
Population: 309 (1990); 385 (2000); 362 (2010); Density: 2,607.4 persons per square mile (2010); Race: 95.9% White, 0.3% Black, 0.6% Asian, 0.3% American Indian/Alaska Native, 0.0% Native Hawaiian/Other Pacific Islander, 2.9% Other, 3.0% Hispanic of any race (2010); Average household size: 2.45 (2010); Median age: 38.8 (2010); Males per 100 females: 91.5 (2010); Marriage status: 23.1% never married, 64.2% now married, 4.6% widowed, 8.1% divorced (2006-2010 5-year est.); Foreign born: 0.0% (2006-2010 5-year est.); Ancestry (includes multiple ancestries): 51.1% German, 14.6% Irish, 11.9% Italian, 9.6% English, 5.9% American (2006-2010 5-year est.).
Economy: Single-family building permits issued: 0 (2011); Multi-family building permits issued: 0 (2011); Employment by occupation: 3.6% management, 2.4% professional, 5.6% services, 24.0% sales, 8.4% farming, 12.8% construction, 7.6% production (2006-2010 5-year est.).
Income: Per capita income: $27,249 (2006-2010 5-year est.); Median household income: $69,375 (2006-2010 5-year est.); Average household income: $65,513 (2006-2010 5-year est.); Percent of households with income of $100,000 or more: 11.4% (2006-2010 5-year est.); Poverty rate: 4.4% (2006-2010 5-year est.).
Education: Percent of population age 25 and over with: High school diploma (including GED) or higher: 83.6% (2006-2010 5-year est.); Bachelor's degree or higher: 19.3% (2006-2010 5-year est.); Master's degree or higher: 3.9% (2006-2010 5-year est.).
School District(s)
West Shore SD (KG-12)
    2010-11 Enrollment: 7,943 . . . . (717) 938-9577
Housing: Homeownership rate: 66.9% (2010); Median home value: $156,500 (2006-2010 5-year est.); Median contract rent: $628 per month (2006-2010 5-year est.); Median year structure built: 1965 (2006-2010 5-year est.).
Transportation: Commute to work: 97.5% car, 0.0% public transportation, 0.0% walk, 1.7% work from home (2006-2010 5-year est.); Travel time to work: 9.7% less than 15 minutes, 44.3% 15 to 30 minutes, 38.8% 30 to 45 minutes, 5.5% 45 to 60 minutes, 1.7% 60 minutes or more (2006-2010 5-year est.)

LOGANVILLE (borough). Covers a land area of 0.993 square miles and a water area of 0 square miles. Located at 39.86° N. Lat; 76.71° W. Long. Elevation is 784 feet.
Population: 954 (1990); 908 (2000); 1,240 (2010); Density: 1,248.7 persons per square mile (2010); Race: 96.3% White, 1.4% Black, 1.2% Asian, 0.0% American Indian/Alaska Native, 0.0% Native Hawaiian/Other Pacific Islander, 1.1% Other, 0.8% Hispanic of any race (2010); Average household size: 2.58 (2010); Median age: 39.5 (2010); Males per 100 females: 97.5 (2010); Marriage status: 17.3% never married, 67.8% now

married, 3.9% widowed, 11.0% divorced (2006-2010 5-year est.); Foreign born: 0.7% (2006-2010 5-year est.); Ancestry (includes multiple ancestries): 50.0% German, 11.4% Irish, 10.9% American, 7.8% English, 5.7% Polish (2006-2010 5-year est.).

Economy: Single-family building permits issued: 0 (2011); Multi-family building permits issued: 0 (2011); Employment by occupation: 5.1% management, 2.6% professional, 10.7% services, 19.9% sales, 2.9% farming, 13.9% construction, 11.0% production (2006-2010 5-year est.).

Income: Per capita income: $25,286 (2006-2010 5-year est.); Median household income: $60,042 (2006-2010 5-year est.); Average household income: $62,278 (2006-2010 5-year est.); Percent of households with income of $100,000 or more: 11.7% (2006-2010 5-year est.); Poverty rate: 8.3% (2006-2010 5-year est.).

Education: Percent of population age 25 and over with: High school diploma (including GED) or higher: 88.9% (2006-2010 5-year est.); Bachelor's degree or higher: 13.0% (2006-2010 5-year est.); Master's degree or higher: 4.7% (2006-2010 5-year est.).

Housing: Homeownership rate: 83.2% (2010); Median home value: $184,600 (2006-2010 5-year est.); Median contract rent: $561 per month (2006-2010 5-year est.); Median year structure built: 1965 (2006-2010 5-year est.).

Transportation: Commute to work: 94.7% car, 1.0% public transportation, 1.0% walk, 2.8% work from home (2006-2010 5-year est.); Travel time to work: 13.6% less than 15 minutes, 40.7% 15 to 30 minutes, 17.8% 30 to 45 minutes, 5.0% 45 to 60 minutes, 23.0% 60 minutes or more (2006-2010 5-year est.)

Additional Information Contacts
York County Chamber of Commerce . . . . (717) 848-4000
  http://www.yorkchamber.com

LOWER CHANCEFORD (township). Covers a land area of 41.506 square miles and a water area of 0.193 square miles. Located at 39.81° N. Lat; 76.38° W. Long.

Population: 2,454 (1990); 2,899 (2000); 3,028 (2010); Density: 73.0 persons per square mile (2010); Race: 97.5% White, 0.5% Black, 0.3% Asian, 0.2% American Indian/Alaska Native, 0.0% Native Hawaiian/Other Pacific Islander, 1.5% Other, 0.9% Hispanic of any race (2010); Average household size: 2.87 (2010); Median age: 38.2 (2010); Males per 100 females: 103.9 (2010); Marriage status: 19.5% never married, 68.7% now married, 5.3% widowed, 6.4% divorced (2006-2010 5-year est.); Foreign born: 2.0% (2006-2010 5-year est.); Ancestry (includes multiple ancestries): 37.6% German, 21.9% Irish, 13.9% English, 8.2% French, 5.5% American (2006-2010 5-year est.).

Economy: Single-family building permits issued: 7 (2011); Multi-family building permits issued: 0 (2011); Employment by occupation: 10.8% management, 3.9% professional, 11.8% services, 13.8% sales, 3.1% farming, 21.9% construction, 11.8% production (2006-2010 5-year est.).

Income: Per capita income: $22,759 (2006-2010 5-year est.); Median household income: $55,729 (2006-2010 5-year est.); Average household income: $68,029 (2006-2010 5-year est.); Percent of households with income of $100,000 or more: 20.7% (2006-2010 5-year est.); Poverty rate: 15.4% (2006-2010 5-year est.).

Education: Percent of population age 25 and over with: High school diploma (including GED) or higher: 79.7% (2006-2010 5-year est.); Bachelor's degree or higher: 8.7% (2006-2010 5-year est.); Master's degree or higher: 3.8% (2006-2010 5-year est.).

Housing: Homeownership rate: 80.2% (2010); Median home value: $220,800 (2006-2010 5-year est.); Median contract rent: $642 per month (2006-2010 5-year est.); Median year structure built: 1972 (2006-2010 5-year est.).

Transportation: Commute to work: 86.4% car, 0.7% public transportation, 4.2% walk, 8.3% work from home (2006-2010 5-year est.); Travel time to work: 16.0% less than 15 minutes, 18.5% 15 to 30 minutes, 29.1% 30 to 45 minutes, 18.8% 45 to 60 minutes, 17.6% 60 minutes or more (2006-2010 5-year est.)

Additional Information Contacts
Lancaster Chamber of Commerce & Industry . . . . (717) 397-3531
  http://www.lancasterchamber.com

LOWER WINDSOR (township). Covers a land area of 25.015 square miles and a water area of 0 square miles. Located at 39.96° N. Lat; 76.54° W. Long.

Population: 6,974 (1990); 7,405 (2000); 7,382 (2010); Density: 295.1 persons per square mile (2010); Race: 97.2% White, 0.6% Black, 0.2% Asian, 0.2% American Indian/Alaska Native, 0.0% Native Hawaiian/Other

Pacific Islander, 1.8% Other, 1.7% Hispanic of any race (2010); Average household size: 2.58 (2010); Median age: 42.9 (2010); Males per 100 females: 101.4 (2010); Marriage status: 21.5% never married, 60.5% now married, 5.5% widowed, 12.4% divorced (2006-2010 5-year est.); Foreign born: 1.2% (2006-2010 5-year est.); Ancestry (includes multiple ancestries): 40.4% German, 11.9% Irish, 10.0% American, 7.1% English, 4.2% Italian (2006-2010 5-year est.).

Economy: Single-family building permits issued: 10 (2011); Multi-family building permits issued: 0 (2011); Employment by occupation: 7.4% management, 3.4% professional, 8.4% services, 17.5% sales, 3.3% farming, 13.7% construction, 10.8% production (2006-2010 5-year est.).

Income: Per capita income: $28,216 (2006-2010 5-year est.); Median household income: $54,444 (2006-2010 5-year est.); Average household income: $70,287 (2006-2010 5-year est.); Percent of households with income of $100,000 or more: 15.6% (2006-2010 5-year est.); Poverty rate: 9.9% (2006-2010 5-year est.).

Education: Percent of population age 25 and over with: High school diploma (including GED) or higher: 79.4% (2006-2010 5-year est.); Bachelor's degree or higher: 10.6% (2006-2010 5-year est.); Master's degree or higher: 3.5% (2006-2010 5-year est.).

Housing: Homeownership rate: 86.4% (2010); Median home value: $151,700 (2006-2010 5-year est.); Median contract rent: $644 per month (2006-2010 5-year est.); Median year structure built: 1977 (2006-2010 5-year est.).

Safety: Violent crime rate: 21.6 per 10,000 population; Property crime rate: 83.7 per 10,000 population (2011).

Transportation: Commute to work: 93.7% car, 0.0% public transportation, 2.8% walk, 1.2% work from home (2006-2010 5-year est.); Travel time to work: 18.9% less than 15 minutes, 38.9% 15 to 30 minutes, 32.1% 30 to 45 minutes, 5.3% 45 to 60 minutes, 4.7% 60 minutes or more (2006-2010 5-year est.)

Additional Information Contacts
Lower Windsor Township . . . . (717) 244-6813
  http://www.lowerwindsor.com
York County Chamber of Commerce . . . . (717) 848-4000
  http://www.yorkchamber.com

MANCHESTER (borough). Covers a land area of 0.785 square miles and a water area of 0 square miles. Located at 40.06° N. Lat; 76.72° W. Long. Elevation is 502 feet.

Population: 1,840 (1990); 2,350 (2000); 2,763 (2010); Density: 3,518.0 persons per square mile (2010); Race: 92.4% White, 3.2% Black, 1.0% Asian, 0.0% American Indian/Alaska Native, 0.1% Native Hawaiian/Other Pacific Islander, 3.3% Other, 3.9% Hispanic of any race (2010); Average household size: 2.35 (2010); Median age: 37.9 (2010); Males per 100 females: 94.3 (2010); Marriage status: 24.2% never married, 61.2% now married, 5.7% widowed, 8.9% divorced (2006-2010 5-year est.); Foreign born: 3.0% (2006-2010 5-year est.); Ancestry (includes multiple ancestries): 50.8% German, 15.4% Irish, 8.7% American, 8.1% English, 5.5% Italian (2006-2010 5-year est.).

Economy: Single-family building permits issued: 0 (2011); Multi-family building permits issued: 0 (2011); Employment by occupation: 8.8% management, 2.6% professional, 7.3% services, 19.9% sales, 4.3% farming, 8.5% construction, 14.8% production (2006-2010 5-year est.).

Income: Per capita income: $22,230 (2006-2010 5-year est.); Median household income: $53,051 (2006-2010 5-year est.); Average household income: $55,814 (2006-2010 5-year est.); Percent of households with income of $100,000 or more: 11.7% (2006-2010 5-year est.); Poverty rate: 7.1% (2006-2010 5-year est.).

Education: Percent of population age 25 and over with: High school diploma (including GED) or higher: 83.9% (2006-2010 5-year est.); Bachelor's degree or higher: 12.8% (2006-2010 5-year est.); Master's degree or higher: 3.8% (2006-2010 5-year est.).

School District(s)
Northeastern York SD (KG-12)
  2010-11 Enrollment: 3,766 . . . . (717) 266-3667

Housing: Homeownership rate: 57.7% (2010); Median home value: $147,500 (2006-2010 5-year est.); Median contract rent: $635 per month (2006-2010 5-year est.); Median year structure built: 1968 (2006-2010 5-year est.).

Transportation: Commute to work: 98.1% car, 0.0% public transportation, 0.5% walk, 0.5% work from home (2006-2010 5-year est.); Travel time to work: 33.4% less than 15 minutes, 39.0% 15 to 30 minutes, 18.3% 30 to 45 minutes, 2.2% 45 to 60 minutes, 7.1% 60 minutes or more (2006-2010 5-year est.)

Additional Information Contacts
York County Chamber of Commerce . . . . (717) 848-4000
http://www.yorkchamber.com

MANCHESTER (township). Covers a land area of 15.884 square miles and a water area of 0.017 square miles. Located at 40.02° N. Lat; 76.76° W. Long. Elevation is 502 feet.

History: Laid out c.1815, incorporated c.1869.

Population: 7,509 (1990); 12,700 (2000); 18,161 (2010); Density: 1,143.4 persons per square mile (2010); Race: 87.1% White, 5.9% Black, 3.5% Asian, 0.2% American Indian/Alaska Native, 0.1% Native Hawaiian/Other Pacific Islander, 3.2% Other, 3.6% Hispanic of any race (2010); Average household size: 2.64 (2010); Median age: 39.9 (2010); Males per 100 females: 92.1 (2010); Marriage status: 21.8% never married, 63.9% now married, 7.5% widowed, 6.8% divorced (2006-2010 5-year est.); Foreign born: 5.6% (2006-2010 5-year est.); Ancestry (includes multiple ancestries): 44.3% German, 13.1% Irish, 9.5% English, 6.6% Italian, 6.5% American (2006-2010 5-year est.).

Economy: Single-family building permits issued: 32 (2011); Multi-family building permits issued: 0 (2011); Employment by occupation: 17.4% management, 6.0% professional, 7.8% services, 16.2% sales, 2.5% farming, 6.2% construction, 4.9% production (2006-2010 5-year est.).

Income: Per capita income: $31,554 (2006-2010 5-year est.); Median household income: $73,910 (2006-2010 5-year est.); Average household income: $83,293 (2006-2010 5-year est.); Percent of households with income of $100,000 or more: 32.2% (2006-2010 5-year est.); Poverty rate: 4.0% (2006-2010 5-year est.).

Education: Percent of population age 25 and over with: High school diploma (including GED) or higher: 91.5% (2006-2010 5-year est.); Bachelor's degree or higher: 37.0% (2006-2010 5-year est.); Master's degree or higher: 13.7% (2006-2010 5-year est.).

Housing: Homeownership rate: 88.3% (2010); Median home value: $201,500 (2006-2010 5-year est.); Median contract rent: $692 per month (2006-2010 5-year est.); Median year structure built: 1994 (2006-2010 5-year est.).

Transportation: Commute to work: 94.2% car, 0.4% public transportation, 0.6% walk, 4.3% work from home (2006-2010 5-year est.); Travel time to work: 32.1% less than 15 minutes, 39.8% 15 to 30 minutes, 11.4% 30 to 45 minutes, 6.9% 45 to 60 minutes, 9.7% 60 minutes or more (2006-2010 5-year est.)

Additional Information Contacts
Manchester Township . . . . (717) 764-4646
http://www.mantwp.com
York County Chamber of Commerce . . . . (717) 848-4000
http://www.yorkchamber.com

MANHEIM (township). Covers a land area of 21.544 square miles and a water area of 0.960 square miles. Located at 39.76° N. Lat; 76.87° W. Long.

Population: 2,739 (1990); 3,119 (2000); 3,380 (2010); Density: 156.9 persons per square mile (2010); Race: 97.8% White, 0.4% Black, 0.3% Asian, 0.1% American Indian/Alaska Native, 0.0% Native Hawaiian/Other Pacific Islander, 1.4% Other, 0.8% Hispanic of any race (2010); Average household size: 2.72 (2010); Median age: 45.1 (2010); Males per 100 females: 101.8 (2010); Marriage status: 21.6% never married, 70.9% now married, 5.4% widowed, 2.1% divorced (2006-2010 5-year est.); Foreign born: 0.6% (2006-2010 5-year est.); Ancestry (includes multiple ancestries): 48.2% German, 16.8% Irish, 12.2% English, 9.9% American, 7.0% Italian (2006-2010 5-year est.).

Economy: Single-family building permits issued: 5 (2011); Multi-family building permits issued: 0 (2011); Employment by occupation: 11.5% management, 4.6% professional, 5.2% services, 16.6% sales, 5.1% farming, 18.7% construction, 9.0% production (2006-2010 5-year est.).

Income: Per capita income: $30,830 (2006-2010 5-year est.); Median household income: $77,454 (2006-2010 5-year est.); Average household income: $83,970 (2006-2010 5-year est.); Percent of households with income of $100,000 or more: 30.8% (2006-2010 5-year est.); Poverty rate: 3.5% (2006-2010 5-year est.).

Education: Percent of population age 25 and over with: High school diploma (including GED) or higher: 86.6% (2006-2010 5-year est.); Bachelor's degree or higher: 16.7% (2006-2010 5-year est.); Master's degree or higher: 5.9% (2006-2010 5-year est.).

Housing: Homeownership rate: 92.2% (2010); Median home value: $277,000 (2006-2010 5-year est.); Median contract rent: $733 per month

(2006-2010 5-year est.); Median year structure built: 1982 (2006-2010 5-year est.).

Transportation: Commute to work: 94.4% car, 0.0% public transportation, 1.4% walk, 3.8% work from home (2006-2010 5-year est.); Travel time to work: 9.5% less than 15 minutes, 30.5% 15 to 30 minutes, 21.9% 30 to 45 minutes, 19.4% 45 to 60 minutes, 18.7% 60 minutes or more (2006-2010 5-year est.).

Additional Information Contacts
York County Chamber of Commerce . . . . (717) 848-4000
http://www.yorkchamber.com

MONAGHAN (township). Covers a land area of 12.864 square miles and a water area of 0.005 square miles. Located at 40.14° N. Lat; 76.95° W. Long.

Population: 2,009 (1990); 2,132 (2000); 2,630 (2010); Density: 204.5 persons per square mile (2010); Race: 97.8% White, 0.9% Black, 0.4% Asian, 0.0% American Indian/Alaska Native, 0.0% Native Hawaiian/Other Pacific Islander, 0.9% Other, 0.7% Hispanic of any race (2010); Average household size: 2.61 (2010); Median age: 45.3 (2010); Males per 100 females: 106.9 (2010); Marriage status: 21.2% never married, 68.0% now married, 3.7% widowed, 7.2% divorced (2006-2010 5-year est.); Foreign born: 2.6% (2006-2010 5-year est.); Ancestry (includes multiple ancestries): 44.8% German, 13.3% Irish, 9.6% English, 7.7% American, 3.4% Scotch-Irish (2006-2010 5-year est.).

Economy: Single-family building permits issued: 3 (2011); Multi-family building permits issued: 0 (2011); Employment by occupation: 15.2% management, 2.4% professional, 3.9% services, 20.1% sales, 3.8% farming, 11.8% construction, 6.4% production (2006-2010 5-year est.).

Income: Per capita income: $33,460 (2006-2010 5-year est.); Median household income: $71,591 (2006-2010 5-year est.); Average household income: $89,758 (2006-2010 5-year est.); Percent of households with income of $100,000 or more: 31.8% (2006-2010 5-year est.); Poverty rate: 3.2% (2006-2010 5-year est.).

Education: Percent of population age 25 and over with: High school diploma (including GED) or higher: 94.4% (2006-2010 5-year est.); Bachelor's degree or higher: 33.4% (2006-2010 5-year est.); Master's degree or higher: 13.5% (2006-2010 5-year est.).

Housing: Homeownership rate: 87.5% (2010); Median home value: $212,400 (2006-2010 5-year est.); Median contract rent: $610 per month (2006-2010 5-year est.); Median year structure built: 1979 (2006-2010 5-year est.).

Transportation: Commute to work: 91.8% car, 0.0% public transportation, 2.5% walk, 5.7% work from home (2006-2010 5-year est.); Travel time to work: 27.2% less than 15 minutes, 36.0% 15 to 30 minutes, 29.8% 30 to 45 minutes, 3.8% 45 to 60 minutes, 3.3% 60 minutes or more (2006-2010 5-year est.).

Additional Information Contacts
Mechanicsburg Chamber of Commerce . . . . (717) 796-0811
http://mechanicsburgchamber.org

MOUNT WOLF (borough). Covers a land area of 0.524 square miles and a water area of 0 square miles. Located at 40.06° N. Lat; 76.71° W. Long. Elevation is 427 feet.

Population: 1,365 (1990); 1,373 (2000); 1,393 (2010); Density: 2,656.7 persons per square mile (2010); Race: 95.0% White, 1.0% Black, 0.6% Asian, 0.1% American Indian/Alaska Native, 0.0% Native Hawaiian/Other Pacific Islander, 3.3% Other, 3.2% Hispanic of any race (2010); Average household size: 2.47 (2010); Median age: 41.1 (2010); Males per 100 females: 95.6 (2010); Marriage status: 25.0% never married, 56.8% now married, 8.9% widowed, 9.3% divorced (2006-2010 5-year est.); Foreign born: 0.6% (2006-2010 5-year est.); Ancestry (includes multiple ancestries): 60.8% German, 13.9% Irish, 9.3% Italian, 7.5% English, 6.8% Welsh (2006-2010 5-year est.).

Economy: Single-family building permits issued: 0 (2011); Multi-family building permits issued: 0 (2011); Employment by occupation: 4.0% management, 3.3% professional, 10.6% services, 19.9% sales, 13.0% farming, 5.3% construction, 9.3% production (2006-2010 5-year est.).

Income: Per capita income: $26,825 (2006-2010 5-year est.); Median household income: $47,009 (2006-2010 5-year est.); Average household income: $61,247 (2006-2010 5-year est.); Percent of households with income of $100,000 or more: 15.2% (2006-2010 5-year est.); Poverty rate: 6.2% (2006-2010 5-year est.).

Education: Percent of population age 25 and over with: High school diploma (including GED) or higher: 85.3% (2006-2010 5-year est.);

Bachelor's degree or higher: 23.1% (2006-2010 5-year est.); Master's degree or higher: 6.4% (2006-2010 5-year est.).

School District(s)

Northeastern York SD (KG-12)

2010-11 Enrollment: 3,766 . . . . (717) 266-3667

Housing: Homeownership rate: 70.8% (2010); Median home value: $131,400 (2006-2010 5-year est.); Median contract rent: $721 per month (2006-2010 5-year est.); Median year structure built: 1947 (2006-2010 5-year est.).

Transportation: Commute to work: 95.5% car, 0.4% public transportation, 3.7% walk, 0.4% work from home (2006-2010 5-year est.); Travel time to work: 39.7% less than 15 minutes, 31.1% 15 to 30 minutes, 22.4% 30 to 45 minutes, 5.6% 45 to 60 minutes, 1.2% 60 minutes or more (2006-2010 5-year est.)

Additional Information Contacts

York County Chamber of Commerce . . . . (717) 848-4000
http://www.yorkchamber.com

NEW FREEDOM (borough). Covers a land area of 2.081 square miles and a water area of 0 square miles. Located at 39.74° N. Lat; 76.70° W. Long. Elevation is 820 feet.

History: Incorporated 1879.

Population: 2,920 (1990); 3,512 (2000); 4,464 (2010); Density: 2,145.6 persons per square mile (2010); Race: 94.2% White, 2.3% Black, 1.4% Asian, 0.3% American Indian/Alaska Native, 0.0% Native Hawaiian/Other Pacific Islander, 1.8% Other, 2.2% Hispanic of any race (2010); Average household size: 2.70 (2010); Median age: 40.8 (2010); Males per 100 females: 91.1 (2010); Marriage status: 19.2% never married, 66.0% now married, 7.8% widowed, 6.9% divorced (2006-2010 5-year est.); Foreign born: 3.0% (2006-2010 5-year est.); Ancestry (includes multiple ancestries): 33.2% German, 22.2% Irish, 14.3% English, 12.1% American, 12.0% Italian (2006-2010 5-year est.).

Economy: Single-family building permits issued: 13 (2011); Multi-family building permits issued: 0 (2011); Employment by occupation: 21.4% management, 9.9% professional, 9.6% services, 11.9% sales, 4.2% farming, 5.5% construction, 5.0% production (2006-2010 5-year est.).

Income: Per capita income: $32,450 (2006-2010 5-year est.); Median household income: $73,309 (2006-2010 5-year est.); Average household income: $84,697 (2006-2010 5-year est.); Percent of households with income of $100,000 or more: 32.7% (2006-2010 5-year est.); Poverty rate: 3.3% (2006-2010 5-year est.).

Education: Percent of population age 25 and over with: High school diploma (including GED) or higher: 91.9% (2006-2010 5-year est.); Bachelor's degree or higher: 39.5% (2006-2010 5-year est.); Master's degree or higher: 11.8% (2006-2010 5-year est.).

Housing: Homeownership rate: 87.7% (2010); Median home value: $272,400 (2006-2010 5-year est.); Median contract rent: $651 per month (2006-2010 5-year est.); Median year structure built: 1985 (2006-2010 5-year est.).

Transportation: Commute to work: 90.2% car, 0.0% public transportation, 3.4% walk, 6.2% work from home (2006-2010 5-year est.); Travel time to work: 28.7% less than 15 minutes, 11.6% 15 to 30 minutes, 33.3% 30 to 45 minutes, 11.8% 45 to 60 minutes, 14.6% 60 minutes or more (2006-2010 5-year est.)

Additional Information Contacts

Borough of New Freedom . . . . (717) 235-2337
http://www.newfreedomboro.org
York County Chamber of Commerce . . . . (717) 848-4000
http://www.yorkchamber.com

NEW MARKET (CDP). Covers a land area of 0.184 square miles and a water area of 0 square miles. Located at 40.22° N. Lat; 76.86° W. Long. Elevation is 308 feet.

Population: n/a (1990); n/a (2000); 816 (2010); Density: 4,432.0 persons per square mile (2010); Race: 84.9% White, 5.9% Black, 2.1% Asian, 0.4% American Indian/Alaska Native, 0.0% Native Hawaiian/Other Pacific Islander, 6.7% Other, 11.5% Hispanic of any race (2010); Average household size: 1.96 (2010); Median age: 38.8 (2010); Males per 100 females: 84.2 (2010); Marriage status: 27.3% never married, 40.3% now married, 10.2% widowed, 22.2% divorced (2006-2010 5-year est.); Foreign born: 0.0% (2006-2010 5-year est.); Ancestry (includes multiple ancestries): 25.7% German, 12.4% English, 8.1% American, 5.5% Slovak, 5.5% Hungarian (2006-2010 5-year est.).

Economy: Employment by occupation: 0.0% management, 0.0% professional, 13.4% services, 29.8% sales, 10.0% farming, 8.6% construction, 8.1% production (2006-2010 5-year est.).

Income: Per capita income: $16,872 (2006-2010 5-year est.); Median household income: $23,417 (2006-2010 5-year est.); Average household income: $34,070 (2006-2010 5-year est.); Percent of households with income of $100,000 or more: 2.8% (2006-2010 5-year est.); Poverty rate: 23.5% (2006-2010 5-year est.).

Education: Percent of population age 25 and over with: High school diploma (including GED) or higher: 79.5% (2006-2010 5-year est.); Bachelor's degree or higher: 8.9% (2006-2010 5-year est.); Master's degree or higher: 3.8% (2006-2010 5-year est.).

Housing: Homeownership rate: 31.4% (2010); Median home value: $62,500 (2006-2010 5-year est.); Median contract rent: $630 per month (2006-2010 5-year est.); Median year structure built: 1968 (2006-2010 5-year est.).

Transportation: Commute to work: 81.6% car, 0.0% public transportation, 14.0% walk, 0.0% work from home (2006-2010 5-year est.); Travel time to work: 51.5% less than 15 minutes, 37.2% 15 to 30 minutes, 6.9% 30 to 45 minutes, 0.0% 45 to 60 minutes, 4.3% 60 minutes or more (2006-2010 5-year est.)

NEW PARK (unincorporated postal area)

Zip Code: 17352

Covers a land area of 13.786 square miles and a water area of 0 square miles. Located at 39.76° N. Lat; 76.49° W. Long. Population: 1,292 (2010); Density: 93.7 persons per square mile (2010); Race: 98.0% White, 0.5% Black, 0.4% Asian, 0.1% American Indian/Alaska Native, 0.0% Native Hawaiian/Other Pacific Islander, 1.0% Other, 0.7% Hispanic of any race (2010); Average household size: 2.78 (2010); Median age: 41.4 (2010); Males per 100 females: 102.2 (2010); Homeownership rate: 85.9% (2010)

NEW SALEM (borough). Aka York New Salem. Covers a land area of 0.473 square miles and a water area of 0 square miles. Located at 39.90° N. Lat; 76.79° W. Long. Elevation is 607 feet.

Population: 669 (1990); 648 (2000); 724 (2010); Density: 1,531.6 persons per square mile (2010); Race: 96.1% White, 2.5% Black, 0.1% Asian, 0.0% American Indian/Alaska Native, 0.0% Native Hawaiian/Other Pacific Islander, 1.3% Other, 1.7% Hispanic of any race (2010); Average household size: 2.50 (2010); Median age: 45.3 (2010); Males per 100 females: 108.0 (2010); Marriage status: 23.9% never married, 54.8% now married, 8.6% widowed, 12.8% divorced (2006-2010 5-year est.); Foreign born: 0.0% (2006-2010 5-year est.); Ancestry (includes multiple ancestries): 59.9% German, 15.6% Irish, 7.1% American, 5.6% Italian, 5.3% English (2006-2010 5-year est.).

Economy: Single-family building permits issued: 0 (2011); Multi-family building permits issued: 0 (2011); Employment by occupation: 8.9% management, 6.9% professional, 6.0% services, 18.6% sales, 2.6% farming, 14.0% construction, 8.0% production (2006-2010 5-year est.).

Income: Per capita income: $35,118 (2006-2010 5-year est.); Median household income: $61,389 (2006-2010 5-year est.); Average household income: $74,405 (2006-2010 5-year est.); Percent of households with income of $100,000 or more: 29.9% (2006-2010 5-year est.); Poverty rate: 4.6% (2006-2010 5-year est.).

Education: Percent of population age 25 and over with: High school diploma (including GED) or higher: 84.7% (2006-2010 5-year est.); Bachelor's degree or higher: 25.9% (2006-2010 5-year est.); Master's degree or higher: 11.2% (2006-2010 5-year est.).

Housing: Homeownership rate: 88.2% (2010); Median home value: $189,300 (2006-2010 5-year est.); Median contract rent: $610 per month (2006-2010 5-year est.); Median year structure built: 1971 (2006-2010 5-year est.).

Transportation: Commute to work: 94.4% car, 0.0% public transportation, 0.9% walk, 4.7% work from home (2006-2010 5-year est.); Travel time to work: 26.0% less than 15 minutes, 36.8% 15 to 30 minutes, 20.1% 30 to 45 minutes, 4.0% 45 to 60 minutes, 13.0% 60 minutes or more (2006-2010 5-year est.)

NEWBERRY (township). Covers a land area of 30.413 square miles and a water area of 0.314 square miles. Located at 40.13° N. Lat; 76.79° W. Long.

Population: 12,014 (1990); 14,332 (2000); 15,285 (2010); Density: 502.6 persons per square mile (2010); Race: 96.1% White, 1.0% Black, 0.6% Asian, 0.2% American Indian/Alaska Native, 0.0% Native Hawaiian/Other

Pacific Islander, 2.1% Other, 2.2% Hispanic of any race (2010); Average household size: 2.63 (2010); Median age: 38.9 (2010); Males per 100 females: 98.7 (2010); Marriage status: 21.0% never married, 62.0% now married, 4.3% widowed, 12.7% divorced (2006-2010 5-year est.); Foreign born: 1.0% (2006-2010 5-year est.); Ancestry (includes multiple ancestries): 49.0% German, 13.8% Irish, 8.0% American, 6.8% Italian, 6.7% English (2006-2010 5-year est.).

Economy: Single-family building permits issued: 30 (2011); Multi-family building permits issued: 0 (2011); Employment by occupation: 9.6% management, 5.7% professional, 8.5% services, 18.6% sales, 6.3% farming, 11.5% construction, 8.7% production (2006-2010 5-year est.).

Income: Per capita income: $25,784 (2006-2010 5-year est.); Median household income: $58,639 (2006-2010 5-year est.); Average household income: $66,282 (2006-2010 5-year est.); Percent of households with income of $100,000 or more: 18.3% (2006-2010 5-year est.); Poverty rate: 6.5% (2006-2010 5-year est.).

Taxes: Total city taxes per capita: $226 (2009); City property taxes per capita: $88 (2009).

Education: Percent of population age 25 and over with: High school diploma (including GED) or higher: 86.7% (2006-2010 5-year est.); Bachelor's degree or higher: 15.3% (2006-2010 5-year est.); Master's degree or higher: 3.9% (2006-2010 5-year est.).

Housing: Homeownership rate: 87.8% (2010); Median home value: $138,800 (2006-2010 5-year est.); Median contract rent: $577 per month (2006-2010 5-year est.); Median year structure built: 1982 (2006-2010 5-year est.).

Safety: Violent crime rate: 11.1 per 10,000 population; Property crime rate: 222.4 per 10,000 population (2011).

Transportation: Commute to work: 97.7% car, 0.3% public transportation, 0.0% walk, 1.8% work from home (2006-2010 5-year est.); Travel time to work: 15.6% less than 15 minutes, 42.2% 15 to 30 minutes, 31.4% 30 to 45 minutes, 5.3% 45 to 60 minutes, 5.6% 60 minutes or more (2006-2010 5-year est.)

Additional Information Contacts
Newberry Township. . . . . (717) 938-6992
 http://www.newberrytwp.com
York County Chamber of Commerce . . . . (717) 848-4000
 http://www.yorkchamber.com

NORTH CODORUS (township). Covers a land area of 32.216 square miles and a water area of 0.075 square miles. Located at 39.87° N. Lat; 76.82° W. Long.

Population: 7,565 (1990); 7,915 (2000); 8,905 (2010); Density: 276.4 persons per square mile (2010); Race: 94.8% White, 2.8% Black, 0.5% Asian, 0.1% American Indian/Alaska Native, 0.0% Native Hawaiian/Other Pacific Islander, 1.8% Other, 1.7% Hispanic of any race (2010); Average household size: 2.59 (2010); Median age: 42.2 (2010); Males per 100 females: 102.1 (2010); Marriage status: 25.2% never married, 63.6% now married, 5.5% widowed, 5.7% divorced (2006-2010 5-year est.); Foreign born: 2.2% (2006-2010 5-year est.); Ancestry (includes multiple ancestries): 56.5% German, 10.8% American, 10.0% English, 8.6% Irish, 4.5% Italian (2006-2010 5-year est.).

Economy: Single-family building permits issued: 7 (2011); Multi-family building permits issued: 0 (2011); Employment by occupation: 10.7% management, 5.1% professional, 9.6% services, 14.8% sales, 2.3% farming, 11.5% construction, 8.5% production (2006-2010 5-year est.).

Income: Per capita income: $26,391 (2006-2010 5-year est.); Median household income: $60,239 (2006-2010 5-year est.); Average household income: $70,873 (2006-2010 5-year est.); Percent of households with income of $100,000 or more: 19.7% (2006-2010 5-year est.); Poverty rate: 6.5% (2006-2010 5-year est.).

Education: Percent of population age 25 and over with: High school diploma (including GED) or higher: 85.5% (2006-2010 5-year est.); Bachelor's degree or higher: 16.8% (2006-2010 5-year est.); Master's degree or higher: 3.5% (2006-2010 5-year est.).

Housing: Homeownership rate: 84.6% (2010); Median home value: $179,700 (2006-2010 5-year est.); Median contract rent: $704 per month (2006-2010 5-year est.); Median year structure built: 1976 (2006-2010 5-year est.).

Transportation: Commute to work: 92.6% car, 0.2% public transportation, 4.4% walk, 2.2% work from home (2006-2010 5-year est.); Travel time to work: 21.9% less than 15 minutes, 45.3% 15 to 30 minutes, 15.9% 30 to 45 minutes, 4.9% 45 to 60 minutes, 12.0% 60 minutes or more (2006-2010 5-year est.).

Additional Information Contacts
North Codorus Township. . . . . (717) 225-4812
 http://www.northcodorustwp.com
York County Chamber of Commerce . . . . (717) 848-4000
 http://www.yorkchamber.com

NORTH HOPEWELL (township). Covers a land area of 18.699 square miles and a water area of 0 square miles. Located at 39.83° N. Lat; 76.60° W. Long.

Population: 2,205 (1990); 2,507 (2000); 2,791 (2010); Density: 149.3 persons per square mile (2010); Race: 97.5% White, 0.5% Black, 0.4% Asian, 0.0% American Indian/Alaska Native, 0.1% Native Hawaiian/Other Pacific Islander, 1.5% Other, 0.8% Hispanic of any race (2010); Average household size: 2.59 (2010); Median age: 44.3 (2010); Males per 100 females: 107.8 (2010); Marriage status: 18.3% never married, 66.9% now married, 7.0% widowed, 7.8% divorced (2006-2010 5-year est.); Foreign born: 1.1% (2006-2010 5-year est.); Ancestry (includes multiple ancestries): 40.1% German, 15.8% American, 13.3% Irish, 10.8% English, 5.9% Italian (2006-2010 5-year est.).

Economy: Single-family building permits issued: 5 (2011); Multi-family building permits issued: 0 (2011); Employment by occupation: 4.2% management, 5.6% professional, 9.5% services, 15.1% sales, 3.0% farming, 18.8% construction, 10.6% production (2006-2010 5-year est.).

Income: Per capita income: $25,653 (2006-2010 5-year est.); Median household income: $58,804 (2006-2010 5-year est.); Average household income: $69,253 (2006-2010 5-year est.); Percent of households with income of $100,000 or more: 20.5% (2006-2010 5-year est.); Poverty rate: 7.5% (2006-2010 5-year est.).

Education: Percent of population age 25 and over with: High school diploma (including GED) or higher: 79.8% (2006-2010 5-year est.); Bachelor's degree or higher: 16.2% (2006-2010 5-year est.); Master's degree or higher: 5.2% (2006-2010 5-year est.).

Housing: Homeownership rate: 89.2% (2010); Median home value: $206,300 (2006-2010 5-year est.); Median contract rent: $617 per month (2006-2010 5-year est.); Median year structure built: 1986 (2006-2010 5-year est.).

Transportation: Commute to work: 95.8% car, 0.0% public transportation, 1.1% walk, 3.2% work from home (2006-2010 5-year est.); Travel time to work: 15.9% less than 15 minutes, 22.6% 15 to 30 minutes, 36.2% 30 to 45 minutes, 15.2% 45 to 60 minutes, 10.2% 60 minutes or more (2006-2010 5-year est.)

Additional Information Contacts
York County Chamber of Commerce . . . . (717) 848-4000
 http://www.yorkchamber.com

NORTH YORK (borough). Covers a land area of 0.303 square miles and a water area of 0.009 square miles. Located at 39.98° N. Lat; 76.73° W. Long. Elevation is 404 feet.

Population: 1,689 (1990); 1,689 (2000); 1,914 (2010); Density: 6,321.2 persons per square mile (2010); Race: 81.1% White, 8.4% Black, 1.4% Asian, 0.5% American Indian/Alaska Native, 0.0% Native Hawaiian/Other Pacific Islander, 8.6% Other, 9.9% Hispanic of any race (2010); Average household size: 2.48 (2010); Median age: 33.7 (2010); Males per 100 females: 95.1 (2010); Marriage status: 37.7% never married, 41.2% now married, 5.1% widowed, 16.0% divorced (2006-2010 5-year est.); Foreign born: 4.4% (2006-2010 5-year est.); Ancestry (includes multiple ancestries): 42.6% German, 11.4% Irish, 8.7% English, 4.7% American, 4.1% Scotch-Irish (2006-2010 5-year est.).

Economy: Single-family building permits issued: 6 (2011); Multi-family building permits issued: 0 (2011); Employment by occupation: 6.1% management, 1.6% professional, 17.3% services, 14.2% sales, 0.8% farming, 8.0% construction, 9.4% production (2006-2010 5-year est.).

Income: Per capita income: $19,036 (2006-2010 5-year est.); Median household income: $37,465 (2006-2010 5-year est.); Average household income: $47,417 (2006-2010 5-year est.); Percent of households with income of $100,000 or more: 6.9% (2006-2010 5-year est.); Poverty rate: 16.1% (2006-2010 5-year est.).

Education: Percent of population age 25 and over with: High school diploma (including GED) or higher: 81.0% (2006-2010 5-year est.); Bachelor's degree or higher: 8.3% (2006-2010 5-year est.); Master's degree or higher: 2.4% (2006-2010 5-year est.).

Housing: Homeownership rate: 53.0% (2010); Median home value: $93,400 (2006-2010 5-year est.); Median contract rent: $562 per month (2006-2010 5-year est.); Median year structure built: before 1940 (2006-2010 5-year est.).

Transportation: Commute to work: 86.2% car, 6.3% public transportation, 3.1% walk, 1.8% work from home (2006-2010 5-year est.); Travel time to work: 38.6% less than 15 minutes, 43.5% 15 to 30 minutes, 9.8% 30 to 45 minutes, 5.3% 45 to 60 minutes, 2.7% 60 minutes or more (2006-2010 5-year est.)

Additional Information Contacts
York County Chamber of Commerce . . . . (717) 848-4000
http://www.yorkchamber.com

PARADISE (township). Covers a land area of 20.241 square miles and a water area of 0.008 square miles. Located at 39.91° N. Lat; 76.95° W. Long.

Population: 3,205 (1990); 3,600 (2000); 3,766 (2010); Density: 186.1 persons per square mile (2010); Race: 97.5% White, 0.3% Black, 0.4% Asian, 0.1% American Indian/Alaska Native, 0.3% Native Hawaiian/Other Pacific Islander, 1.4% Other, 1.9% Hispanic of any race (2010); Average household size: 2.67 (2010); Median age: 42.2 (2010); Males per 100 females: 103.2 (2010); Marriage status: 23.1% never married, 67.8% now married, 2.1% widowed, 6.9% divorced (2006-2010 5-year est.); Foreign born: 0.5% (2006-2010 5-year est.); Ancestry (includes multiple ancestries): 52.6% German, 9.8% English, 8.6% Irish, 8.6% American, 3.4% Dutch (2006-2010 5-year est.).

Economy: Single-family building permits issued: 12 (2011); Multi-family building permits issued: 0 (2011); Employment by occupation: 6.1% management, 3.1% professional, 9.3% services, 16.3% sales, 6.2% farming, 13.7% construction, 10.8% production (2006-2010 5-year est.).

Income: Per capita income: $25,933 (2006-2010 5-year est.); Median household income: $66,791 (2006-2010 5-year est.); Average household income: $73,635 (2006-2010 5-year est.); Percent of households with income of $100,000 or more: 23.2% (2006-2010 5-year est.); Poverty rate: 4.5% (2006-2010 5-year est.).

Education: Percent of population age 25 and over with: High school diploma (including GED) or higher: 86.6% (2006-2010 5-year est.); Bachelor's degree or higher: 15.5% (2006-2010 5-year est.); Master's degree or higher: 3.7% (2006-2010 5-year est.).

Housing: Homeownership rate: 89.3% (2010); Median home value: $194,200 (2006-2010 5-year est.); Median contract rent: $654 per month (2006-2010 5-year est.); Median year structure built: 1976 (2006-2010 5-year est.).

Transportation: Commute to work: 88.9% car, 0.5% public transportation, 2.2% walk, 7.6% work from home (2006-2010 5-year est.); Travel time to work: 17.3% less than 15 minutes, 45.6% 15 to 30 minutes, 25.2% 30 to 45 minutes, 5.2% 45 to 60 minutes, 6.7% 60 minutes or more (2006-2010 5-year est.)

Additional Information Contacts
York County Chamber of Commerce . . . . (717) 848-4000
http://www.yorkchamber.com

PARKVILLE (CDP). Covers a land area of 2.914 square miles and a water area of 0 square miles. Located at 39.79° N. Lat; 76.97° W. Long. Elevation is 764 feet.

Population: 6,014 (1990); 6,593 (2000); 6,706 (2010); Density: 2,301.2 persons per square mile (2010); Race: 95.5% White, 0.8% Black, 0.8% Asian, 0.2% American Indian/Alaska Native, 0.0% Native Hawaiian/Other Pacific Islander, 2.7% Other, 3.0% Hispanic of any race (2010); Average household size: 2.50 (2010); Median age: 36.6 (2010); Males per 100 females: 95.9 (2010); Marriage status: 28.6% never married, 55.3% now married, 4.2% widowed, 11.9% divorced (2006-2010 5-year est.); Foreign born: 0.9% (2006-2010 5-year est.); Ancestry (includes multiple ancestries): 46.9% German, 12.0% American, 9.7% Irish, 6.5% Italian, 5.3% English (2006-2010 5-year est.).

Economy: Employment by occupation: 2.9% management, 3.3% professional, 11.5% services, 17.7% sales, 2.7% farming, 13.2% construction, 11.5% production (2006-2010 5-year est.).

Income: Per capita income: $22,899 (2006-2010 5-year est.); Median household income: $51,184 (2006-2010 5-year est.); Average household income: $54,913 (2006-2010 5-year est.); Percent of households with income of $100,000 or more: 10.9% (2006-2010 5-year est.); Poverty rate: 8.2% (2006-2010 5-year est.).

Education: Percent of population age 25 and over with: High school diploma (including GED) or higher: 85.8% (2006-2010 5-year est.); Bachelor's degree or higher: 11.9% (2006-2010 5-year est.); Master's degree or higher: 4.7% (2006-2010 5-year est.).

Housing: Homeownership rate: 71.6% (2010); Median home value: $145,500 (2006-2010 5-year est.); Median contract rent: $585 per month

(2006-2010 5-year est.); Median year structure built: 1964 (2006-2010 5-year est.).

Transportation: Commute to work: 97.1% car, 0.8% public transportation, 0.5% walk, 0.8% work from home (2006-2010 5-year est.); Travel time to work: 44.3% less than 15 minutes, 21.1% 15 to 30 minutes, 11.2% 30 to 45 minutes, 10.0% 45 to 60 minutes, 13.4% 60 minutes or more (2006-2010 5-year est.)

Additional Information Contacts
Hanover Area Chamber of Commerce . . . . (717) 637-6130
http://www.hanoverchamber.com

PEACH BOTTOM (township). Covers a land area of 29.215 square miles and a water area of 0.546 square miles. Located at 39.75° N. Lat; 76.33° W. Long.

Population: 3,444 (1990); 4,412 (2000); 4,813 (2010); Density: 164.7 persons per square mile (2010); Race: 96.0% White, 1.5% Black, 0.4% Asian, 0.3% American Indian/Alaska Native, 0.0% Native Hawaiian/Other Pacific Islander, 1.8% Other, 1.3% Hispanic of any race (2010); Average household size: 2.75 (2010); Median age: 39.5 (2010); Males per 100 females: 102.1 (2010); Marriage status: 21.1% never married, 66.9% now married, 5.7% widowed, 6.3% divorced (2006-2010 5-year est.); Foreign born: 3.4% (2006-2010 5-year est.); Ancestry (includes multiple ancestries): 36.1% German, 13.5% Irish, 8.4% American, 6.0% English, 5.7% Italian (2006-2010 5-year est.).

Economy: Single-family building permits issued: 6 (2011); Multi-family building permits issued: 0 (2011); Employment by occupation: 5.3% management, 2.3% professional, 11.0% services, 22.3% sales, 2.4% farming, 23.1% construction, 15.7% production (2006-2010 5-year est.).

Income: Per capita income: $27,025 (2006-2010 5-year est.); Median household income: $59,273 (2006-2010 5-year est.); Average household income: $66,145 (2006-2010 5-year est.); Percent of households with income of $100,000 or more: 17.9% (2006-2010 5-year est.); Poverty rate: 10.6% (2006-2010 5-year est.).

Education: Percent of population age 25 and over with: High school diploma (including GED) or higher: 80.8% (2006-2010 5-year est.); Bachelor's degree or higher: 7.0% (2006-2010 5-year est.); Master's degree or higher: 2.8% (2006-2010 5-year est.).

Housing: Homeownership rate: 86.7% (2010); Median home value: $204,500 (2006-2010 5-year est.); Median contract rent: $561 per month (2006-2010 5-year est.); Median year structure built: 1976 (2006-2010 5-year est.).

Transportation: Commute to work: 98.1% car, 0.0% public transportation, 0.0% walk, 1.9% work from home (2006-2010 5-year est.); Travel time to work: 15.7% less than 15 minutes, 14.3% 15 to 30 minutes, 31.2% 30 to 45 minutes, 20.2% 45 to 60 minutes, 18.6% 60 minutes or more (2006-2010 5-year est.)

Additional Information Contacts
Lancaster Chamber of Commerce & Industry . . . . (717) 397-3531
http://www.lancasterchamber.com

PENN (township). Covers a land area of 12.941 square miles and a water area of 0.163 square miles. Located at 39.80° N. Lat; 76.96° W. Long.

Population: 11,658 (1990); 14,592 (2000); 15,612 (2010); Density: 1,206.4 persons per square mile (2010); Race: 95.5% White, 1.2% Black, 1.1% Asian, 0.1% American Indian/Alaska Native, 0.0% Native Hawaiian/Other Pacific Islander, 2.1% Other, 2.3% Hispanic of any race (2010); Average household size: 2.56 (2010); Median age: 41.3 (2010); Males per 100 females: 95.9 (2010); Marriage status: 21.4% never married, 63.0% now married, 4.7% widowed, 10.8% divorced (2006-2010 5-year est.); Foreign born: 1.5% (2006-2010 5-year est.); Ancestry (includes multiple ancestries): 44.8% German, 13.7% Irish, 11.8% American, 9.6% English, 5.8% Italian (2006-2010 5-year est.).

Economy: Single-family building permits issued: 19 (2011); Multi-family building permits issued: 7 (2011); Employment by occupation: 6.2% management, 3.1% professional, 9.7% services, 19.2% sales, 3.4% farming, 11.6% construction, 10.3% production (2006-2010 5-year est.).

Income: Per capita income: $27,268 (2006-2010 5-year est.); Median household income: $59,205 (2006-2010 5-year est.); Average household income: $69,004 (2006-2010 5-year est.); Percent of households with income of $100,000 or more: 19.3% (2006-2010 5-year est.); Poverty rate: 6.0% (2006-2010 5-year est.).

Education: Percent of population age 25 and over with: High school diploma (including GED) or higher: 89.3% (2006-2010 5-year est.);

Bachelor's degree or higher: 19.1% (2006-2010 5-year est.); Master's degree or higher: 7.5% (2006-2010 5-year est.).

Housing: Homeownership rate: 79.8% (2010); Median home value: $186,100 (2006-2010 5-year est.); Median contract rent: $646 per month (2006-2010 5-year est.); Median year structure built: 1977 (2006-2010 5-year est.).

Safety: Violent crime rate: 15.3 per 10,000 population; Property crime rate: 164.1 per 10,000 population (2011).

Transportation: Commute to work: 96.0% car, 0.5% public transportation, 1.3% walk, 1.6% work from home (2006-2010 5-year est.); Travel time to work: 42.2% less than 15 minutes, 20.8% 15 to 30 minutes, 12.8% 30 to 45 minutes, 10.5% 45 to 60 minutes, 13.6% 60 minutes or more (2006-2010 5-year est.)

Additional Information Contacts
Hanover Area Chamber of Commerce . . . . (717) 637-6130
   http://www.hanoverchamber.com
Penn Township . . . . (717) 632-7366
   http://www.penntwp.com

PENNVILLE (CDP).

Covers a land area of 0.731 square miles and a water area of 0 square miles. Located at 39.79° N. Lat; 76.99° W. Long. Elevation is 558 feet.

Population: 1,559 (1990); 1,964 (2000); 1,947 (2010); Density: 2,663.8 persons per square mile (2010); Race: 96.0% White, 1.4% Black, 0.5% Asian, 0.2% American Indian/Alaska Native, 0.0% Native Hawaiian/Other Pacific Islander, 1.9% Other, 2.0% Hispanic of any race (2010); Average household size: 2.30 (2010); Median age: 43.6 (2010); Males per 100 females: 78.8 (2010); Marriage status: 17.3% never married, 55.5% now married, 5.6% widowed, 21.6% divorced (2006-2010 5-year est.); Foreign born: 2.0% (2006-2010 5-year est.); Ancestry (includes multiple ancestries): 47.8% German, 14.3% Irish, 8.5% American, 7.8% English, 3.4% Italian (2006-2010 5-year est.).

Economy: Employment by occupation: 8.6% management, 0.0% professional, 13.5% services, 19.9% sales, 4.0% farming, 9.1% construction, 9.3% production (2006-2010 5-year est.).

Income: Per capita income: $24,069 (2006-2010 5-year est.); Median household income: $50,592 (2006-2010 5-year est.); Average household income: $60,466 (2006-2010 5-year est.); Percent of households with income of $100,000 or more: 15.7% (2006-2010 5-year est.); Poverty rate: 11.9% (2006-2010 5-year est.).

Education: Percent of population age 25 and over with: High school diploma (including GED) or higher: 85.7% (2006-2010 5-year est.); Bachelor's degree or higher: 18.9% (2006-2010 5-year est.); Master's degree or higher: 6.2% (2006-2010 5-year est.).

Housing: Homeownership rate: 67.7% (2010); Median home value: $152,000 (2006-2010 5-year est.); Median contract rent: $752 per month (2006-2010 5-year est.); Median year structure built: 1972 (2006-2010 5-year est.).

Transportation: Commute to work: 96.3% car, 0.0% public transportation, 3.7% walk, 0.0% work from home (2006-2010 5-year est.); Travel time to work: 41.4% less than 15 minutes, 20.0% 15 to 30 minutes, 12.2% 30 to 45 minutes, 18.4% 45 to 60 minutes, 7.9% 60 minutes or more (2006-2010 5-year est.).

Additional Information Contacts
Hanover Area Chamber of Commerce . . . . (717) 637-6130
   http://www.hanoverchamber.com

QUEENS GATE (CDP).

Covers a land area of 0.584 square miles and a water area of 0 square miles. Located at 39.94° N. Lat; 76.69° W. Long.

Population: n/a (1990); n/a (2000); 1,464 (2010); Density: 2,507.5 persons per square mile (2010); Race: 79.9% White, 7.2% Black, 7.4% Asian, 0.2% American Indian/Alaska Native, 0.1% Native Hawaiian/Other Pacific Islander, 5.2% Other, 7.6% Hispanic of any race (2010); Average household size: 1.82 (2010); Median age: 33.8 (2010); Males per 100 females: 94.7 (2010); Marriage status: 27.6% never married, 43.3% now married, 6.1% widowed, 23.0% divorced (2006-2010 5-year est.); Foreign born: 11.5% (2006-2010 5-year est.); Ancestry (includes multiple ancestries): 37.6% German, 17.9% English, 7.7% Irish, 6.7% Polish, 5.3% American (2006-2010 5-year est.).

Economy: Employment by occupation: 14.7% management, 9.6% professional, 14.8% services, 22.5% sales, 3.3% farming, 8.2% construction, 4.0% production (2006-2010 5-year est.).

Income: Per capita income: $28,246 (2006-2010 5-year est.); Median household income: $59,479 (2006-2010 5-year est.); Average household

income: $60,440 (2006-2010 5-year est.); Percent of households with income of $100,000 or more: 11.9% (2006-2010 5-year est.); Poverty rate: 16.2% (2006-2010 5-year est.).

Education: Percent of population age 25 and over with: High school diploma (including GED) or higher: 85.4% (2006-2010 5-year est.); Bachelor's degree or higher: 22.5% (2006-2010 5-year est.); Master's degree or higher: 7.3% (2006-2010 5-year est.).

Housing: Homeownership rate: 22.1% (2010); Median home value: $144,800 (2006-2010 5-year est.); Median contract rent: $719 per month (2006-2010 5-year est.); Median year structure built: 1970 (2006-2010 5-year est.).

Transportation: Commute to work: 100.0% car, 0.0% public transportation, 0.0% walk, 0.0% work from home (2006-2010 5-year est.); Travel time to work: 33.8% less than 15 minutes, 43.4% 15 to 30 minutes, 9.0% 30 to 45 minutes, 13.7% 45 to 60 minutes, 0.0% 60 minutes or more (2006-2010 5-year est.).

RAILROAD (borough).

Covers a land area of 0.638 square miles and a water area of 0 square miles. Located at 39.76° N. Lat; 76.70° W. Long. Elevation is 745 feet.

Population: 317 (1990); 300 (2000); 278 (2010); Density: 435.5 persons per square mile (2010); Race: 97.8% White, 1.4% Black, 0.0% Asian, 0.0% American Indian/Alaska Native, 0.0% Native Hawaiian/Other Pacific Islander, 0.8% Other, 0.0% Hispanic of any race (2010); Average household size: 2.42 (2010); Median age: 40.0 (2010); Males per 100 females: 110.6 (2010); Marriage status: 24.4% never married, 58.7% now married, 4.5% widowed, 12.4% divorced (2006-2010 5-year est.); Foreign born: 1.2% (2006-2010 5-year est.); Ancestry (includes multiple ancestries): 37.7% German, 27.1% English, 17.4% Irish, 10.1% Italian, 4.9% American (2006-2010 5-year est.).

Economy: Single-family building permits issued: 0 (2011); Multi-family building permits issued: 0 (2011); Employment by occupation: 8.8% management, 6.3% professional, 11.9% services, 10.7% sales, 1.3% farming, 27.0% construction, 4.4% production (2006-2010 5-year est.).

Income: Per capita income: $29,498 (2006-2010 5-year est.); Median household income: $69,038 (2006-2010 5-year est.); Average household income: $79,073 (2006-2010 5-year est.); Percent of households with income of $100,000 or more: 25.0% (2006-2010 5-year est.); Poverty rate: 0.0% (2006-2010 5-year est.).

Education: Percent of population age 25 and over with: High school diploma (including GED) or higher: 93.2% (2006-2010 5-year est.); Bachelor's degree or higher: 30.9% (2006-2010 5-year est.); Master's degree or higher: 14.8% (2006-2010 5-year est.).

Housing: Homeownership rate: 58.2% (2010); Median home value: $201,900 (2006-2010 5-year est.); Median contract rent: $642 per month (2006-2010 5-year est.); Median year structure built: before 1940 (2006-2010 5-year est.).

Transportation: Commute to work: 97.4% car, 0.0% public transportation, 1.3% walk, 1.3% work from home (2006-2010 5-year est.); Travel time to work: 26.0% less than 15 minutes, 8.4% 15 to 30 minutes, 26.0% 30 to 45 minutes, 15.6% 45 to 60 minutes, 24.0% 60 minutes or more (2006-2010 5-year est.).

RED LION (borough).

Aka Adamsville. Covers a land area of 1.311 square miles and a water area of 0 square miles. Located at 39.90° N. Lat; 76.61° W. Long. Elevation is 919 feet.

History: Incorporated 1880.

Population: 6,130 (1990); 6,149 (2000); 6,373 (2010); Density: 4,860.1 persons per square mile (2010); Race: 95.3% White, 1.7% Black, 0.5% Asian, 0.3% American Indian/Alaska Native, 0.0% Native Hawaiian/Other Pacific Islander, 2.2% Other, 2.3% Hispanic of any race (2010); Average household size: 2.45 (2010); Median age: 34.0 (2010); Males per 100 females: 95.9 (2010); Marriage status: 25.7% never married, 54.3% now married, 6.0% widowed, 14.0% divorced (2006-2010 5-year est.); Foreign born: 0.8% (2006-2010 5-year est.); Ancestry (includes multiple ancestries): 49.1% German, 15.5% Irish, 12.0% American, 6.7% Italian, 6.2% English (2006-2010 5-year est.).

Economy: Single-family building permits issued: 0 (2011); Multi-family building permits issued: 0 (2011); Employment by occupation: 5.3% management, 2.8% professional, 8.3% services, 16.0% sales, 0.8% farming, 14.9% construction, 11.9% production (2006-2010 5-year est.).

Income: Per capita income: $25,368 (2006-2010 5-year est.); Median household income: $46,875 (2006-2010 5-year est.); Average household income: $60,933 (2006-2010 5-year est.); Percent of households with

income of $100,000 or more: 13.5% (2006-2010 5-year est.); Poverty rate: 4.9% (2006-2010 5-year est.).

Education: Percent of population age 25 and over with: High school diploma (including GED) or higher: 91.2% (2006-2010 5-year est.); Bachelor's degree or higher: 16.7% (2006-2010 5-year est.); Master's degree or higher: 6.3% (2006-2010 5-year est.).

School District(s)

Red Lion Area SD (KG-12)

    2010-11 Enrollment: 5,537 . . . . (717) 244-4518

Housing: Homeownership rate: 57.9% (2010); Median home value: $139,900 (2006-2010 5-year est.); Median contract rent: $532 per month (2006-2010 5-year est.); Median year structure built: 1950 (2006-2010 5-year est.).

Transportation: Commute to work: 91.0% car, 1.6% public transportation, 2.9% walk, 2.0% work from home (2006-2010 5-year est.); Travel time to work: 25.9% less than 15 minutes, 38.1% 15 to 30 minutes, 22.2% 30 to 45 minutes, 6.4% 45 to 60 minutes, 7.4% 60 minutes or more (2006-2010 5-year est.)

Additional Information Contacts

Borough of Red Lion . . . . (717) 244-3475
  http://www.redlionpa.org

York County Chamber of Commerce . . . . (717) 848-4000
  http://www.yorkchamber.com

SEVEN VALLEYS (borough). Aka Smyser. Covers a land area of 1.089 square miles and a water area of 0 square miles. Located at 39.85° N. Lat; 76.77° W. Long. Elevation is 489 feet.

Population: 483 (1990); 492 (2000); 517 (2010); Density: 474.6 persons per square mile (2010); Race: 96.7% White, 0.6% Black, 0.4% Asian, 1.2% American Indian/Alaska Native, 0.0% Native Hawaiian/Other Pacific Islander, 1.1% Other, 0.8% Hispanic of any race (2010); Average household size: 2.69 (2010); Median age: 37.8 (2010); Males per 100 females: 103.5 (2010); Marriage status: 21.6% never married, 62.4% now married, 4.3% widowed, 11.8% divorced (2006-2010 5-year est.); Foreign born: 1.9% (2006-2010 5-year est.); Ancestry (includes multiple ancestries): 32.5% German, 20.0% Irish, 17.8% American, 9.1% English, 5.5% Italian (2006-2010 5-year est.).

Economy: Single-family building permits issued: 0 (2011); Multi-family building permits issued: 0 (2011); Employment by occupation: 11.3% management, 5.3% professional, 5.7% services, 15.8% sales, 2.3% farming, 12.8% construction, 14.3% production (2006-2010 5-year est.).

Income: Per capita income: $22,722 (2006-2010 5-year est.); Median household income: $53,000 (2006-2010 5-year est.); Average household income: $64,232 (2006-2010 5-year est.); Percent of households with income of $100,000 or more: 12.3% (2006-2010 5-year est.); Poverty rate: 21.7% (2006-2010 5-year est.).

Education: Percent of population age 25 and over with: High school diploma (including GED) or higher: 81.3% (2006-2010 5-year est.); Bachelor's degree or higher: 19.0% (2006-2010 5-year est.); Master's degree or higher: 3.4% (2006-2010 5-year est.).

Housing: Homeownership rate: 78.7% (2010); Median home value: $142,200 (2006-2010 5-year est.); Median contract rent: $558 per month (2006-2010 5-year est.); Median year structure built: before 1940 (2006-2010 5-year est.).

Transportation: Commute to work: 84.8% car, 0.0% public transportation, 8.4% walk, 5.6% work from home (2006-2010 5-year est.); Travel time to work: 17.8% less than 15 minutes, 43.6% 15 to 30 minutes, 20.8% 30 to 45 minutes, 8.1% 45 to 60 minutes, 9.7% 60 minutes or more (2006-2010 5-year est.)

SHILOH (CDP). Covers a land area of 4.216 square miles and a water area of 0 square miles. Located at 39.97° N. Lat; 76.79° W. Long. Elevation is 463 feet.

Population: 8,245 (1990); 10,192 (2000); 11,218 (2010); Density: 2,660.7 persons per square mile (2010); Race: 91.4% White, 4.5% Black, 1.4% Asian, 0.1% American Indian/Alaska Native, 0.0% Native Hawaiian/Other Pacific Islander, 2.6% Other, 3.1% Hispanic of any race (2010); Average household size: 2.35 (2010); Median age: 45.2 (2010); Males per 100 females: 91.2 (2010); Marriage status: 18.9% never married, 59.3% now married, 11.3% widowed, 10.5% divorced (2006-2010 5-year est.); Foreign born: 4.1% (2006-2010 5-year est.); Ancestry (includes multiple ancestries): 43.3% German, 12.7% Irish, 10.8% American, 9.0% English, 6.3% Italian (2006-2010 5-year est.).

Economy: Employment by occupation: 16.1% management, 4.3% professional, 5.7% services, 18.7% sales, 4.4% farming, 4.6% construction, 4.7% production (2006-2010 5-year est.).

Income: Per capita income: $29,555 (2006-2010 5-year est.); Median household income: $63,006 (2006-2010 5-year est.); Average household income: $71,213 (2006-2010 5-year est.); Percent of households with income of $100,000 or more: 21.4% (2006-2010 5-year est.); Poverty rate: 3.5% (2006-2010 5-year est.).

Education: Percent of population age 25 and over with: High school diploma (including GED) or higher: 89.4% (2006-2010 5-year est.); Bachelor's degree or higher: 25.8% (2006-2010 5-year est.); Master's degree or higher: 9.4% (2006-2010 5-year est.).

Housing: Homeownership rate: 76.7% (2010); Median home value: $173,300 (2006-2010 5-year est.); Median contract rent: $772 per month (2006-2010 5-year est.); Median year structure built: 1983 (2006-2010 5-year est.).

Transportation: Commute to work: 93.9% car, 0.6% public transportation, 0.8% walk, 3.6% work from home (2006-2010 5-year est.); Travel time to work: 30.4% less than 15 minutes, 46.6% 15 to 30 minutes, 9.4% 30 to 45 minutes, 5.4% 45 to 60 minutes, 8.2% 60 minutes or more (2006-2010 5-year est.)

Additional Information Contacts

York County Chamber of Commerce . . . . (717) 848-4000
  http://www.yorkchamber.com

SHREWSBURY (borough). Aka Hungerford. Covers a land area of 1.812 square miles and a water area of 0 square miles. Located at 39.77° N. Lat; 76.68° W. Long. Elevation is 984 feet.

Population: 2,672 (1990); 3,378 (2000); 3,823 (2010); Density: 2,110.0 persons per square mile (2010); Race: 93.5% White, 3.0% Black, 1.4% Asian, 0.2% American Indian/Alaska Native, 0.0% Native Hawaiian/Other Pacific Islander, 1.9% Other, 2.5% Hispanic of any race (2010); Average household size: 2.48 (2010); Median age: 45.3 (2010); Males per 100 females: 87.0 (2010); Marriage status: 19.5% never married, 66.0% now married, 6.0% widowed, 8.6% divorced (2006-2010 5-year est.); Foreign born: 2.4% (2006-2010 5-year est.); Ancestry (includes multiple ancestries): 43.3% German, 17.5% Irish, 14.2% English, 9.7% Italian, 7.6% French (2006-2010 5-year est.).

Economy: Single-family building permits issued: 1 (2011); Multi-family building permits issued: 0 (2011); Employment by occupation: 7.7% management, 8.6% professional, 10.8% services, 14.9% sales, 6.1% farming, 12.9% construction, 8.2% production (2006-2010 5-year est.).

Income: Per capita income: $27,352 (2006-2010 5-year est.); Median household income: $59,583 (2006-2010 5-year est.); Average household income: $70,116 (2006-2010 5-year est.); Percent of households with income of $100,000 or more: 30.1% (2006-2010 5-year est.); Poverty rate: 6.0% (2006-2010 5-year est.).

Education: Percent of population age 25 and over with: High school diploma (including GED) or higher: 93.7% (2006-2010 5-year est.); Bachelor's degree or higher: 32.4% (2006-2010 5-year est.); Master's degree or higher: 9.4% (2006-2010 5-year est.).

School District(s)

Southern York County SD (KG-12)

    2010-11 Enrollment: 3,176 . . . . (717) 235-4811

Housing: Homeownership rate: 76.1% (2010); Median home value: $233,200 (2006-2010 5-year est.); Median contract rent: $582 per month (2006-2010 5-year est.); Median year structure built: 1980 (2006-2010 5-year est.).

Transportation: Commute to work: 91.1% car, 0.0% public transportation, 4.3% walk, 4.6% work from home (2006-2010 5-year est.); Travel time to work: 27.6% less than 15 minutes, 15.1% 15 to 30 minutes, 17.1% 30 to 45 minutes, 19.7% 45 to 60 minutes, 20.5% 60 minutes or more (2006-2010 5-year est.)

Additional Information Contacts

York County Chamber of Commerce . . . . (717) 848-4000
  http://www.yorkchamber.com

SHREWSBURY (township). Aka Hungerford. Covers a land area of 29.062 square miles and a water area of 0.009 square miles. Located at 39.75° N. Lat; 76.72° W. Long. Elevation is 984 feet.

Population: 5,898 (1990); 5,947 (2000); 6,447 (2010); Density: 221.8 persons per square mile (2010); Race: 94.8% White, 3.0% Black, 1.1% Asian, 0.1% American Indian/Alaska Native, 0.0% Native Hawaiian/Other Pacific Islander, 1.0% Other, 1.0% Hispanic of any race (2010); Average household size: 2.54 (2010); Median age: 46.8 (2010); Males per 100

females: 98.7 (2010); Marriage status: 21.8% never married, 64.5% now married, 5.6% widowed, 8.1% divorced (2006-2010 5-year est.); Foreign born: 2.9% (2006-2010 5-year est.); Ancestry (includes multiple ancestries): 33.3% German, 19.3% Irish, 16.0% English, 9.0% Italian, 6.4% American (2006-2010 5-year est.).

Economy: Single-family building permits issued: 28 (2011); Multi-family building permits issued: 0 (2011); Employment by occupation: 11.5% management, 8.0% professional, 9.2% services, 17.7% sales, 3.6% farming, 11.8% construction, 8.2% production (2006-2010 5-year est.).

Income: Per capita income: $32,921 (2006-2010 5-year est.); Median household income: $77,024 (2006-2010 5-year est.); Average household income: $85,249 (2006-2010 5-year est.); Percent of households with income of $100,000 or more: 29.8% (2006-2010 5-year est.); Poverty rate: 3.2% (2006-2010 5-year est.).

Education: Percent of population age 25 and over with: High school diploma (including GED) or higher: 89.6% (2006-2010 5-year est.); Bachelor's degree or higher: 27.7% (2006-2010 5-year est.); Master's degree or higher: 10.4% (2006-2010 5-year est.).

Housing: Homeownership rate: 85.8% (2010); Median home value: $255,900 (2006-2010 5-year est.); Median contract rent: $638 per month (2006-2010 5-year est.); Median year structure built: 1979 (2006-2010 5-year est.).

Transportation: Commute to work: 95.5% car, 0.0% public transportation, 1.4% walk, 2.2% work from home (2006-2010 5-year est.); Travel time to work: 22.7% less than 15 minutes, 22.9% 15 to 30 minutes, 24.2% 30 to 45 minutes, 15.3% 45 to 60 minutes, 14.8% 60 minutes or more (2006-2010 5-year est.)

Additional Information Contacts

Shrewsbury Township...........................(717) 235-3011
   http://www.shrewsburytownship.org
York County Chamber of Commerce ....(717) 848-4000
   http://www.yorkchamber.com

SPRING GARDEN (township). Covers a land area of 6.763 square miles and a water area of 0.020 square miles. Located at 39.94° N. Lat; 76.72° W. Long.

Population: 11,189 (1990); 11,974 (2000); 12,578 (2010); Density: 1,859.9 persons per square mile (2010); Race: 91.8% White, 3.8% Black, 1.7% Asian, 0.2% American Indian/Alaska Native, 0.0% Native Hawaiian/Other Pacific Islander, 2.5% Other, 3.5% Hispanic of any race (2010); Average household size: 2.45 (2010); Median age: 38.8 (2010); Males per 100 females: 94.1 (2010); Marriage status: 28.5% never married, 57.2% now married, 7.3% widowed, 7.0% divorced (2006-2010 5-year est.); Foreign born: 2.8% (2006-2010 5-year est.); Ancestry (includes multiple ancestries): 44.2% German, 16.7% Irish, 7.7% Italian, 7.6% English, 7.0% American (2006-2010 5-year est.).

Economy: Single-family building permits issued: 15 (2011); Multi-family building permits issued: 0 (2011); Employment by occupation: 11.4% management, 4.6% professional, 8.2% services, 17.7% sales, 2.8% farming, 4.5% construction, 4.6% production (2006-2010 5-year est.).

Income: Per capita income: $33,662 (2006-2010 5-year est.); Median household income: $68,650 (2006-2010 5-year est.); Average household income: $92,857 (2006-2010 5-year est.); Percent of households with income of $100,000 or more: 30.1% (2006-2010 5-year est.); Poverty rate: 6.6% (2006-2010 5-year est.).

Education: Percent of population age 25 and over with: High school diploma (including GED) or higher: 93.4% (2006-2010 5-year est.); Bachelor's degree or higher: 42.2% (2006-2010 5-year est.); Master's degree or higher: 15.6% (2006-2010 5-year est.).

Housing: Homeownership rate: 87.9% (2010); Median home value: $164,500 (2006-2010 5-year est.); Median contract rent: $781 per month (2006-2010 5-year est.); Median year structure built: 1954 (2006-2010 5-year est.).

Safety: Violent crime rate: 29.3 per 10,000 population; Property crime rate: 363.0 per 10,000 population (2011).

Transportation: Commute to work: 92.2% car, 0.7% public transportation, 5.1% walk, 1.6% work from home (2006-2010 5-year est.); Travel time to work: 46.6% less than 15 minutes, 35.8% 15 to 30 minutes, 6.1% 30 to 45 minutes, 6.5% 45 to 60 minutes, 5.0% 60 minutes or more (2006-2010 5-year est.)

Additional Information Contacts

Spring Garden Township..........................(717) 848-2858
   http://www.springgardentwp.org
York County Chamber of Commerce ....(717) 848-4000
   http://www.yorkchamber.com

SPRING GROVE (borough). Aka Smiths Station. Covers a land area of 0.775 square miles and a water area of 0 square miles. Located at 39.88° N. Lat; 76.86° W. Long. Elevation is 476 feet.

History: Laid out 1747, incorporated 1882.

Population: 1,863 (1990); 2,050 (2000); 2,167 (2010); Density: 2,795.6 persons per square mile (2010); Race: 93.9% White, 0.7% Black, 0.5% Asian, 0.0% American Indian/Alaska Native, 0.0% Native Hawaiian/Other Pacific Islander, 4.9% Other, 6.1% Hispanic of any race (2010); Average household size: 2.51 (2010); Median age: 36.8 (2010); Males per 100 females: 101.8 (2010); Marriage status: 21.9% never married, 63.5% now married, 5.7% widowed, 8.9% divorced (2006-2010 5-year est.); Foreign born: 1.3% (2006-2010 5-year est.); Ancestry (includes multiple ancestries): 47.1% German, 9.6% Irish, 8.7% American, 5.0% English, 3.1% Italian (2006-2010 5-year est.).

Economy: Single-family building permits issued: 0 (2011); Multi-family building permits issued: 0 (2011); Employment by occupation: 5.7% management, 2.1% professional, 11.2% services, 12.8% sales, 3.1% farming, 12.8% construction, 13.6% production (2006-2010 5-year est.).

Income: Per capita income: $24,916 (2006-2010 5-year est.); Median household income: $53,915 (2006-2010 5-year est.); Average household income: $58,879 (2006-2010 5-year est.); Percent of households with income of $100,000 or more: 10.8% (2006-2010 5-year est.); Poverty rate: 4.4% (2006-2010 5-year est.).

Education: Percent of population age 25 and over with: High school diploma (including GED) or higher: 88.3% (2006-2010 5-year est.); Bachelor's degree or higher: 8.7% (2006-2010 5-year est.); Master's degree or higher: 3.8% (2006-2010 5-year est.).

School District(s)

Spring Grove Area SD (KG-12)
   2010-11 Enrollment: 3,827 ....(717) 225-4731

Housing: Homeownership rate: 65.5% (2010); Median home value: $156,200 (2006-2010 5-year est.); Median contract rent: $542 per month (2006-2010 5-year est.); Median year structure built: 1955 (2006-2010 5-year est.).

Transportation: Commute to work: 90.2% car, 0.0% public transportation, 5.3% walk, 2.8% work from home (2006-2010 5-year est.); Travel time to work: 28.0% less than 15 minutes, 48.9% 15 to 30 minutes, 12.7% 30 to 45 minutes, 3.5% 45 to 60 minutes, 6.9% 60 minutes or more (2006-2010 5-year est.)

Additional Information Contacts

Borough of Spring Grove..........................(717) 225-5791
   http://www.springgroveboro.com
York County Chamber of Commerce ....(717) 848-4000
   http://www.yorkchamber.com

SPRINGETTSBURY (township). Covers a land area of 16.376 square miles and a water area of 0.001 square miles. Located at 39.99° N. Lat; 76.68° W. Long.

Population: 21,369 (1990); 23,883 (2000); 26,668 (2010); Density: 1,628.5 persons per square mile (2010); Race: 82.9% White, 6.8% Black, 3.0% Asian, 0.2% American Indian/Alaska Native, 0.0% Native Hawaiian/Other Pacific Islander, 7.1% Other, 7.1% Hispanic of any race (2010); Average household size: 2.37 (2010); Median age: 42.1 (2010); Males per 100 females: 107.4 (2010); Marriage status: 27.6% never married, 54.8% now married, 8.1% widowed, 9.5% divorced (2006-2010 5-year est.); Foreign born: 7.7% (2006-2010 5-year est.); Ancestry (includes multiple ancestries): 42.5% German, 12.3% Irish, 10.3% English, 6.2% American, 6.2% Italian (2006-2010 5-year est.).

Economy: Unemployment rate: 8.2% (August 2012); Total civilian labor force: 13,005 (August 2012); Single-family building permits issued: 15 (2011); Multi-family building permits issued: 8 (2011); Employment by occupation: 16.6% management, 3.9% professional, 9.8% services, 16.2% sales, 3.3% farming, 5.7% construction, 5.7% production (2006-2010 5-year est.).

Income: Per capita income: $29,372 (2006-2010 5-year est.); Median household income: $62,224 (2006-2010 5-year est.); Average household income: $74,359 (2006-2010 5-year est.); Percent of households with income of $100,000 or more: 22.6% (2006-2010 5-year est.); Poverty rate: 5.9% (2006-2010 5-year est.).

Taxes: Total city taxes per capita: $347 (2009); City property taxes per capita: $71 (2009).

Education: Percent of population age 25 and over with: High school diploma (including GED) or higher: 86.5% (2006-2010 5-year est.); Bachelor's degree or higher: 28.6% (2006-2010 5-year est.); Master's degree or higher: 12.2% (2006-2010 5-year est.).

Housing: Homeownership rate: 72.3% (2010); Median home value: $181,300 (2006-2010 5-year est.); Median contract rent: $743 per month (2006-2010 5-year est.); Median year structure built: 1969 (2006-2010 5-year est.).

Safety: Violent crime rate: 16.8 per 10,000 population; Property crime rate: 356.2 per 10,000 population (2011).

Transportation: Commute to work: 93.0% car, 0.9% public transportation, 1.5% walk, 3.4% work from home (2006-2010 5-year est.); Travel time to work: 36.4% less than 15 minutes, 38.7% 15 to 30 minutes, 13.5% 30 to 45 minutes, 5.9% 45 to 60 minutes, 5.6% 60 minutes or more (2006-2010 5-year est.)

Additional Information Contacts

Springettsbury Township . . . . (717) 757-3521
  http://www.springettsbury.com
York County Chamber of Commerce . . . . (717) 848-4000
  http://www.yorkchamber.com

SPRINGFIELD (township). Covers a land area of 26.366 square miles and a water area of 0.299 square miles. Located at 39.83° N. Lat; 76.74° W. Long.

Population: 3,918 (1990); 3,889 (2000); 5,152 (2010); Density: 195.4 persons per square mile (2010); Race: 90.6% White, 6.0% Black, 1.4% Asian, 0.1% American Indian/Alaska Native, 0.0% Native Hawaiian/Other Pacific Islander, 1.9% Other, 1.6% Hispanic of any race (2010); Average household size: 2.65 (2010); Median age: 43.6 (2010); Males per 100 females: 101.0 (2010); Marriage status: 15.9% never married, 70.5% now married, 3.8% widowed, 9.9% divorced (2006-2010 5-year est.); Foreign born: 3.7% (2006-2010 5-year est.); Ancestry (includes multiple ancestries): 52.8% German, 18.6% Irish, 8.3% English, 7.4% American, 5.2% Polish (2006-2010 5-year est.).

Economy: Single-family building permits issued: 26 (2011); Multi-family building permits issued: 0 (2011); Employment by occupation: 13.9% management, 10.0% professional, 11.4% services, 13.4% sales, 1.4% farming, 10.3% construction, 4.7% production (2006-2010 5-year est.).

Income: Per capita income: $34,515 (2006-2010 5-year est.); Median household income: $72,139 (2006-2010 5-year est.); Average household income: $89,466 (2006-2010 5-year est.); Percent of households with income of $100,000 or more: 36.4% (2006-2010 5-year est.); Poverty rate: 0.8% (2006-2010 5-year est.).

Taxes: Total city taxes per capita: $175 (2009); City property taxes per capita: $25 (2009).

Education: Percent of population age 25 and over with: High school diploma (including GED) or higher: 91.3% (2006-2010 5-year est.); Bachelor's degree or higher: 31.0% (2006-2010 5-year est.); Master's degree or higher: 13.6% (2006-2010 5-year est.).

Housing: Homeownership rate: 86.0% (2010); Median home value: $235,100 (2006-2010 5-year est.); Median contract rent: $679 per month (2006-2010 5-year est.); Median year structure built: 1980 (2006-2010 5-year est.).

Transportation: Commute to work: 97.1% car, 0.0% public transportation, 0.0% walk, 2.0% work from home (2006-2010 5-year est.); Travel time to work: 16.8% less than 15 minutes, 41.2% 15 to 30 minutes, 15.4% 30 to 45 minutes, 13.2% 45 to 60 minutes, 13.4% 60 minutes or more (2006-2010 5-year est.)

Additional Information Contacts

Mercer Area Chamber of Commerce . . . . (724) 662-4185
  http://www.mercerareachamber.com

SPRY (CDP). Covers a land area of 2.586 square miles and a water area of 0 square miles. Located at 39.91° N. Lat; 76.69° W. Long. Elevation is 705 feet.

Population: 4,271 (1990); 4,903 (2000); 4,891 (2010); Density: 1,891.7 persons per square mile (2010); Race: 93.2% White, 2.7% Black, 1.6% Asian, 0.2% American Indian/Alaska Native, 0.0% Native Hawaiian/Other Pacific Islander, 2.3% Other, 2.9% Hispanic of any race (2010); Average household size: 2.34 (2010); Median age: 42.8 (2010); Males per 100 females: 90.5 (2010); Marriage status: 22.9% never married, 55.9% now married, 7.5% widowed, 13.8% divorced (2006-2010 5-year est.); Foreign born: 5.1% (2006-2010 5-year est.); Ancestry (includes multiple ancestries): 43.3% German, 12.9% Irish, 9.7% English, 6.4% Italian, 5.6% American (2006-2010 5-year est.).

Economy: Employment by occupation: 10.1% management, 4.9% professional, 7.4% services, 18.4% sales, 1.9% farming, 13.4% construction, 7.2% production (2006-2010 5-year est.).

Income: Per capita income: $29,507 (2006-2010 5-year est.); Median household income: $59,945 (2006-2010 5-year est.); Average household income: $66,535 (2006-2010 5-year est.); Percent of households with income of $100,000 or more: 21.7% (2006-2010 5-year est.); Poverty rate: 6.7% (2006-2010 5-year est.).

Education: Percent of population age 25 and over with: High school diploma (including GED) or higher: 91.9% (2006-2010 5-year est.); Bachelor's degree or higher: 29.2% (2006-2010 5-year est.); Master's degree or higher: 12.0% (2006-2010 5-year est.).

Housing: Homeownership rate: 65.7% (2010); Median home value: $169,700 (2006-2010 5-year est.); Median contract rent: $741 per month (2006-2010 5-year est.); Median year structure built: 1974 (2006-2010 5-year est.).

Transportation: Commute to work: 95.6% car, 0.6% public transportation, 2.0% walk, 1.9% work from home (2006-2010 5-year est.); Travel time to work: 30.0% less than 15 minutes, 41.4% 15 to 30 minutes, 12.3% 30 to 45 minutes, 9.4% 45 to 60 minutes, 6.8% 60 minutes or more (2006-2010 5-year est.)

Additional Information Contacts

York County Chamber of Commerce . . . . (717) 848-4000
  http://www.yorkchamber.com

STEWARTSTOWN (borough). Covers a land area of 0.843 square miles and a water area of 0 square miles. Located at 39.75° N. Lat; 76.59° W. Long. Elevation is 860 feet.

Population: 1,332 (1990); 1,752 (2000); 2,089 (2010); Density: 2,477.9 persons per square mile (2010); Race: 95.5% White, 1.9% Black, 0.7% Asian, 0.3% American Indian/Alaska Native, 0.0% Native Hawaiian/Other Pacific Islander, 1.6% Other, 1.5% Hispanic of any race (2010); Average household size: 2.57 (2010); Median age: 37.4 (2010); Males per 100 females: 97.4 (2010); Marriage status: 22.2% never married, 61.6% now married, 4.3% widowed, 11.9% divorced (2006-2010 5-year est.); Foreign born: 1.0% (2006-2010 5-year est.); Ancestry (includes multiple ancestries): 41.3% German, 18.3% Irish, 13.7% English, 9.6% Italian, 6.1% French (2006-2010 5-year est.).

Economy: Single-family building permits issued: 1 (2011); Multi-family building permits issued: 0 (2011); Employment by occupation: 12.8% management, 3.3% professional, 7.9% services, 21.6% sales, 7.1% farming, 11.9% construction, 6.4% production (2006-2010 5-year est.).

Income: Per capita income: $28,149 (2006-2010 5-year est.); Median household income: $67,031 (2006-2010 5-year est.); Average household income: $73,470 (2006-2010 5-year est.); Percent of households with income of $100,000 or more: 28.2% (2006-2010 5-year est.); Poverty rate: 9.3% (2006-2010 5-year est.).

Education: Percent of population age 25 and over with: High school diploma (including GED) or higher: 89.2% (2006-2010 5-year est.); Bachelor's degree or higher: 23.9% (2006-2010 5-year est.); Master's degree or higher: 8.4% (2006-2010 5-year est.).

School District(s)

South Eastern SD (PK-12)
  2010-11 Enrollment: 2,954 . . . . (717) 382-4843

Housing: Homeownership rate: 74.1% (2010); Median home value: $212,400 (2006-2010 5-year est.); Median contract rent: $768 per month (2006-2010 5-year est.); Median year structure built: 1961 (2006-2010 5-year est.).

Safety: Violent crime rate: 9.5 per 10,000 population; Property crime rate: 219.5 per 10,000 population (2011).

Transportation: Commute to work: 89.4% car, 0.3% public transportation, 1.8% walk, 6.4% work from home (2006-2010 5-year est.); Travel time to work: 19.6% less than 15 minutes, 14.9% 15 to 30 minutes, 21.6% 30 to 45 minutes, 21.2% 45 to 60 minutes, 22.7% 60 minutes or more (2006-2010 5-year est.)

Additional Information Contacts

York County Chamber of Commerce . . . . (717) 848-4000
  http://www.yorkchamber.com

STONYBROOK (CDP). Covers a land area of 1.608 square miles and a water area of 0 square miles. Located at 39.98° N. Lat; 76.63° W. Long. Elevation is 407 feet.

Population: n/a (1990); n/a (2000); 2,384 (2010); Density: 1,482.9 persons per square mile (2010); Race: 89.2% White, 4.5% Black, 3.5% Asian, 0.0% American Indian/Alaska Native, 0.0% Native Hawaiian/Other Pacific Islander, 2.8% Other, 2.6% Hispanic of any race (2010); Average household size: 2.67 (2010); Median age: 44.3 (2010); Males per 100 females: 100.7 (2010); Marriage status: 13.0% never married, 80.1% now

married, 5.4% widowed, 1.5% divorced (2006-2010 5-year est.); Foreign born: 10.0% (2006-2010 5-year est.); Ancestry (includes multiple ancestries): 37.5% German, 17.4% English, 15.9% Irish, 9.1% American, 4.3% French (2006-2010 5-year est.).

Economy: Employment by occupation: 14.7% management, 9.2% professional, 5.9% services, 12.3% sales, 3.0% farming, 2.9% construction, 7.9% production (2006-2010 5-year est.).

Income: Per capita income: $35,916 (2006-2010 5-year est.); Median household income: $78,125 (2006-2010 5-year est.); Average household income: $91,739 (2006-2010 5-year est.); Percent of households with income of $100,000 or more: 37.2% (2006-2010 5-year est.); Poverty rate: 2.3% (2006-2010 5-year est.).

Education: Percent of population age 25 and over with: High school diploma (including GED) or higher: 92.2% (2006-2010 5-year est.); Bachelor's degree or higher: 41.5% (2006-2010 5-year est.); Master's degree or higher: 18.5% (2006-2010 5-year est.).

Housing: Homeownership rate: 96.1% (2010); Median home value: $238,200 (2006-2010 5-year est.); Median contract rent: n/a per month (2006-2010 5-year est.); Median year structure built: 1977 (2006-2010 5-year est.).

Transportation: Commute to work: 94.3% car, 0.0% public transportation, 1.6% walk, 3.1% work from home (2006-2010 5-year est.); Travel time to work: 30.3% less than 15 minutes, 41.9% 15 to 30 minutes, 16.6% 30 to 45 minutes, 5.5% 45 to 60 minutes, 5.6% 60 minutes or more (2006-2010 5-year est.)

SUSQUEHANNA TRAILS (CDP).

Covers a land area of 3.130 square miles and a water area of 0 square miles. Located at 39.76° N. Lat; 76.37° W. Long. Elevation is 463 feet.

Population: 1,419 (1990); 2,134 (2000); 2,264 (2010); Density: 723.2 persons per square mile (2010); Race: 96.7% White, 0.9% Black, 0.2% Asian, 0.3% American Indian/Alaska Native, 0.0% Native Hawaiian/Other Pacific Islander, 1.9% Other, 1.2% Hispanic of any race (2010); Average household size: 2.77 (2010); Median age: 38.0 (2010); Males per 100 females: 103.0 (2010); Marriage status: 26.0% never married, 64.9% now married, 4.9% widowed, 4.3% divorced (2006-2010 5-year est.); Foreign born: 0.7% (2006-2010 5-year est.); Ancestry (includes multiple ancestries): 39.9% German, 13.2% Irish, 6.9% English, 6.2% Scottish, 6.1% Italian (2006-2010 5-year est.).

Economy: Employment by occupation: 2.9% management, 1.2% professional, 15.8% services, 21.9% sales, 2.0% farming, 20.0% construction, 16.6% production (2006-2010 5-year est.).

Income: Per capita income: $27,408 (2006-2010 5-year est.); Median household income: $65,669 (2006-2010 5-year est.); Average household income: $73,537 (2006-2010 5-year est.); Percent of households with income of $100,000 or more: 23.3% (2006-2010 5-year est.); Poverty rate: 5.6% (2006-2010 5-year est.).

Education: Percent of population age 25 and over with: High school diploma (including GED) or higher: 80.8% (2006-2010 5-year est.); Bachelor's degree or higher: 9.4% (2006-2010 5-year est.); Master's degree or higher: 4.0% (2006-2010 5-year est.).

Housing: Homeownership rate: 90.4% (2010); Median home value: $202,800 (2006-2010 5-year est.); Median contract rent: $817 per month (2006-2010 5-year est.); Median year structure built: 1985 (2006-2010 5-year est.).

Transportation: Commute to work: 98.9% car, 0.0% public transportation, 0.0% walk, 1.1% work from home (2006-2010 5-year est.); Travel time to work: 14.5% less than 15 minutes, 5.8% 15 to 30 minutes, 34.6% 30 to 45 minutes, 20.1% 45 to 60 minutes, 25.0% 60 minutes or more (2006-2010 5-year est.)

Additional Information Contacts
Lancaster Chamber of Commerce & Industry . . . . (717) 397-3531
  http://www.lancasterchamber.com

THOMASVILLE (unincorporated postal area)
Zip Code: 17364
  Covers a land area of 16.704 square miles and a water area of 0 square miles. Located at 39.92° N. Lat; 76.89° W. Long. Elevation is 482 feet.
  Population: 3,907 (2010); Density: 233.9 persons per square mile (2010); Race: 95.8% White, 0.8% Black, 0.4% Asian, 0.1% American Indian/Alaska Native, 0.1% Native Hawaiian/Other Pacific Islander, 2.8% Other, 3.3% Hispanic of any race (2010); Average household size: 2.68 (2010); Median age: 41.0 (2010); Males per 100 females: 105.3 (2010); Homeownership rate: 87.3% (2010)

TYLER RUN (CDP).

Covers a land area of 0.958 square miles and a water area of 0 square miles. Located at 39.93° N. Lat; 76.70° W. Long.

Population: n/a (1990); n/a (2000); 1,901 (2010); Density: 1,984.6 persons per square mile (2010); Race: 94.3% White, 3.4% Black, 1.2% Asian, 0.1% American Indian/Alaska Native, 0.1% Native Hawaiian/Other Pacific Islander, 0.9% Other, 1.3% Hispanic of any race (2010); Average household size: 1.97 (2010); Median age: 51.9 (2010); Males per 100 females: 79.2 (2010); Marriage status: 13.2% never married, 52.8% now married, 19.6% widowed, 14.4% divorced (2006-2010 5-year est.); Foreign born: 0.0% (2006-2010 5-year est.); Ancestry (includes multiple ancestries): 62.4% German, 18.3% Irish, 12.9% English, 7.2% American, 5.2% Italian (2006-2010 5-year est.).

Economy: Employment by occupation: 19.2% management, 4.0% professional, 4.2% services, 17.8% sales, 1.3% farming, 9.4% construction, 1.9% production (2006-2010 5-year est.).

Income: Per capita income: $32,562 (2006-2010 5-year est.); Median household income: $48,344 (2006-2010 5-year est.); Average household income: $59,936 (2006-2010 5-year est.); Percent of households with income of $100,000 or more: 17.1% (2006-2010 5-year est.); Poverty rate: 12.7% (2006-2010 5-year est.).

Education: Percent of population age 25 and over with: High school diploma (including GED) or higher: 92.0% (2006-2010 5-year est.); Bachelor's degree or higher: 33.8% (2006-2010 5-year est.); Master's degree or higher: 10.9% (2006-2010 5-year est.).

Housing: Homeownership rate: 67.1% (2010); Median home value: $179,200 (2006-2010 5-year est.); Median contract rent: $634 per month (2006-2010 5-year est.); Median year structure built: 1974 (2006-2010 5-year est.).

Transportation: Commute to work: 89.8% car, 2.7% public transportation, 0.0% walk, 7.5% work from home (2006-2010 5-year est.); Travel time to work: 31.8% less than 15 minutes, 38.0% 15 to 30 minutes, 13.5% 30 to 45 minutes, 2.9% 45 to 60 minutes, 13.8% 60 minutes or more (2006-2010 5-year est.)

VALLEY GREEN (CDP).

Covers a land area of 1.399 square miles and a water area of 0 square miles. Located at 40.16° N. Lat; 76.79° W. Long. Elevation is 367 feet.

Population: 3,017 (1990); 3,550 (2000); 3,429 (2010); Density: 2,450.5 persons per square mile (2010); Race: 93.8% White, 1.8% Black, 0.6% Asian, 0.3% American Indian/Alaska Native, 0.0% Native Hawaiian/Other Pacific Islander, 3.5% Other, 3.7% Hispanic of any race (2010); Average household size: 2.59 (2010); Median age: 35.9 (2010); Males per 100 females: 94.9 (2010); Marriage status: 22.1% never married, 58.3% now married, 3.0% widowed, 16.6% divorced (2006-2010 5-year est.); Foreign born: 1.7% (2006-2010 5-year est.); Ancestry (includes multiple ancestries): 49.2% German, 16.6% Irish, 9.1% Italian, 7.6% English, 6.2% American (2006-2010 5-year est.).

Economy: Employment by occupation: 8.9% management, 6.9% professional, 7.5% services, 19.6% sales, 13.2% farming, 6.0% construction, 7.8% production (2006-2010 5-year est.).

Income: Per capita income: $28,526 (2006-2010 5-year est.); Median household income: $60,761 (2006-2010 5-year est.); Average household income: $66,049 (2006-2010 5-year est.); Percent of households with income of $100,000 or more: 18.1% (2006-2010 5-year est.); Poverty rate: 10.0% (2006-2010 5-year est.).

Education: Percent of population age 25 and over with: High school diploma (including GED) or higher: 90.9% (2006-2010 5-year est.); Bachelor's degree or higher: 16.9% (2006-2010 5-year est.); Master's degree or higher: 2.9% (2006-2010 5-year est.).

Housing: Homeownership rate: 87.5% (2010); Median home value: $140,000 (2006-2010 5-year est.); Median contract rent: $309 per month (2006-2010 5-year est.); Median year structure built: 1983 (2006-2010 5-year est.).

Transportation: Commute to work: 99.3% car, 0.7% public transportation, 0.0% walk, 0.0% work from home (2006-2010 5-year est.); Travel time to work: 19.6% less than 15 minutes, 35.3% 15 to 30 minutes, 28.1% 30 to 45 minutes, 7.8% 45 to 60 minutes, 9.2% 60 minutes or more (2006-2010 5-year est.)

Additional Information Contacts
West Shore Chamber of Commerce . . . . (717) 761-0702
  http://www.wschamber.org

VALLEY VIEW (CDP). Covers a land area of 0.781 square miles and a water area of 0 square miles. Located at 39.95° N. Lat; 76.70° W. Long. Elevation is 617 feet.

Population: 2,911 (1990); 2,743 (2000); 2,817 (2010); Density: 3,607.5 persons per square mile (2010); Race: 91.8% White, 3.3% Black, 1.6% Asian, 0.4% American Indian/Alaska Native, 0.1% Native Hawaiian/Other Pacific Islander, 2.8% Other, 3.7% Hispanic of any race (2010); Average household size: 2.36 (2010); Median age: 41.4 (2010); Males per 100 females: 96.4 (2010); Marriage status: 20.3% never married, 62.6% now married, 9.0% widowed, 8.1% divorced (2006-2010 5-year est.); Foreign born: 3.9% (2006-2010 5-year est.); Ancestry (includes multiple ancestries): 43.6% German, 11.8% Irish, 6.9% American, 6.8% English, 5.4% Italian (2006-2010 5-year est.).

Economy: Employment by occupation: 9.6% management, 3.5% professional, 6.7% services, 13.7% sales, 2.3% farming, 7.8% construction, 10.4% production (2006-2010 5-year est.).

Income: Per capita income: $28,507 (2006-2010 5-year est.); Median household income: $62,050 (2006-2010 5-year est.); Average household income: $69,053 (2006-2010 5-year est.); Percent of households with income of $100,000 or more: 26.2% (2006-2010 5-year est.); Poverty rate: 10.9% (2006-2010 5-year est.).

Education: Percent of population age 25 and over with: High school diploma (including GED) or higher: 92.0% (2006-2010 5-year est.); Bachelor's degree or higher: 32.1% (2006-2010 5-year est.); Master's degree or higher: 14.4% (2006-2010 5-year est.).

Housing: Homeownership rate: 89.1% (2010); Median home value: $145,900 (2006-2010 5-year est.); Median contract rent: $795 per month (2006-2010 5-year est.); Median year structure built: 1953 (2006-2010 5-year est.).

Transportation: Commute to work: 94.2% car, 1.3% public transportation, 1.5% walk, 2.1% work from home (2006-2010 5-year est.); Travel time to work: 46.0% less than 15 minutes, 36.6% 15 to 30 minutes, 8.1% 30 to 45 minutes, 2.8% 45 to 60 minutes, 6.4% 60 minutes or more (2006-2010 5-year est.).

Additional Information Contacts
York County Chamber of Commerce . . . . (717) 848-4000
http://www.yorkchamber.com

WARRINGTON (township). Covers a land area of 35.296 square miles and a water area of 0.805 square miles. Located at 40.07° N. Lat; 76.92° W. Long.

Population: 4,275 (1990); 4,435 (2000); 4,532 (2010); Density: 128.4 persons per square mile (2010); Race: 97.8% White, 0.2% Black, 0.3% Asian, 0.1% American Indian/Alaska Native, 0.0% Native Hawaiian/Other Pacific Islander, 1.6% Other, 1.3% Hispanic of any race (2010); Average household size: 2.49 (2010); Median age: 45.8 (2010); Males per 100 females: 103.0 (2010); Marriage status: 23.3% never married, 65.2% now married, 4.5% widowed, 7.0% divorced (2006-2010 5-year est.); Foreign born: 4.4% (2006-2010 5-year est.); Ancestry (includes multiple ancestries): 36.7% German, 11.8% Irish, 8.6% English, 7.6% American, 4.6% Dutch (2006-2010 5-year est.).

Economy: Single-family building permits issued: 6 (2011); Multi-family building permits issued: 0 (2011); Employment by occupation: 12.9% management, 3.8% professional, 11.1% services, 15.9% sales, 5.0% farming, 14.6% construction, 6.2% production (2006-2010 5-year est.).

Income: Per capita income: $29,681 (2006-2010 5-year est.); Median household income: $58,592 (2006-2010 5-year est.); Average household income: $79,186 (2006-2010 5-year est.); Percent of households with income of $100,000 or more: 22.4% (2006-2010 5-year est.); Poverty rate: 5.3% (2006-2010 5-year est.).

Education: Percent of population age 25 and over with: High school diploma (including GED) or higher: 85.5% (2006-2010 5-year est.); Bachelor's degree or higher: 19.8% (2006-2010 5-year est.); Master's degree or higher: 5.0% (2006-2010 5-year est.).

Housing: Homeownership rate: 86.3% (2010); Median home value: $213,000 (2006-2010 5-year est.); Median contract rent: $499 per month (2006-2010 5-year est.); Median year structure built: 1975 (2006-2010 5-year est.).

Transportation: Commute to work: 92.6% car, 1.0% public transportation, 0.5% walk, 4.3% work from home (2006-2010 5-year est.); Travel time to work: 13.7% less than 15 minutes, 33.0% 15 to 30 minutes, 36.9% 30 to 45 minutes, 7.7% 45 to 60 minutes, 8.7% 60 minutes or more (2006-2010 5-year est.)

Additional Information Contacts
York County Chamber of Commerce . . . . (717) 848-4000
http://www.yorkchamber.com

WASHINGTON (township). Covers a land area of 28.042 square miles and a water area of 0.013 square miles. Located at 40.01° N. Lat; 76.99° W. Long.

Population: 2,291 (1990); 2,460 (2000); 2,673 (2010); Density: 95.3 persons per square mile (2010); Race: 98.7% White, 0.2% Black, 0.1% Asian, 0.1% American Indian/Alaska Native, 0.0% Native Hawaiian/Other Pacific Islander, 0.9% Other, 1.4% Hispanic of any race (2010); Average household size: 2.64 (2010); Median age: 44.3 (2010); Males per 100 females: 105.8 (2010); Marriage status: 21.3% never married, 66.5% now married, 4.6% widowed, 7.7% divorced (2006-2010 5-year est.); Foreign born: 0.3% (2006-2010 5-year est.); Ancestry (includes multiple ancestries): 56.4% German, 11.8% Irish, 11.7% English, 9.0% American, 3.5% Dutch (2006-2010 5-year est.).

Economy: Single-family building permits issued: 2 (2011); Multi-family building permits issued: 0 (2011); Employment by occupation: 8.5% management, 3.8% professional, 6.0% services, 18.7% sales, 1.0% farming, 23.1% construction, 16.2% production (2006-2010 5-year est.).

Income: Per capita income: $28,270 (2006-2010 5-year est.); Median household income: $61,726 (2006-2010 5-year est.); Average household income: $71,138 (2006-2010 5-year est.); Percent of households with income of $100,000 or more: 17.8% (2006-2010 5-year est.); Poverty rate: 1.9% (2006-2010 5-year est.).

Education: Percent of population age 25 and over with: High school diploma (including GED) or higher: 88.9% (2006-2010 5-year est.); Bachelor's degree or higher: 15.7% (2006-2010 5-year est.); Master's degree or higher: 2.7% (2006-2010 5-year est.).

Housing: Homeownership rate: 85.9% (2010); Median home value: $203,300 (2006-2010 5-year est.); Median contract rent: $510 per month (2006-2010 5-year est.); Median year structure built: 1976 (2006-2010 5-year est.).

Transportation: Commute to work: 92.1% car, 0.3% public transportation, 1.3% walk, 6.0% work from home (2006-2010 5-year est.); Travel time to work: 13.7% less than 15 minutes, 36.4% 15 to 30 minutes, 36.4% 30 to 45 minutes, 7.9% 45 to 60 minutes, 5.6% 60 minutes or more (2006-2010 5-year est.)

Additional Information Contacts
York County Chamber of Commerce . . . . (717) 848-4000
http://www.yorkchamber.com

WEIGELSTOWN (CDP). Covers a land area of 5.814 square miles and a water area of 0 square miles. Located at 39.98° N. Lat; 76.83° W. Long. Elevation is 515 feet.

Population: 9,048 (1990); 10,117 (2000); 12,875 (2010); Density: 2,214.3 persons per square mile (2010); Race: 90.9% White, 4.7% Black, 0.9% Asian, 0.2% American Indian/Alaska Native, 0.0% Native Hawaiian/Other Pacific Islander, 3.3% Other, 4.0% Hispanic of any race (2010); Average household size: 2.52 (2010); Median age: 38.9 (2010); Males per 100 females: 94.0 (2010); Marriage status: 21.6% never married, 60.6% now married, 7.0% widowed, 10.7% divorced (2006-2010 5-year est.); Foreign born: 1.4% (2006-2010 5-year est.); Ancestry (includes multiple ancestries): 46.0% German, 12.2% Irish, 7.4% American, 6.5% English, 3.9% Italian (2006-2010 5-year est.).

Economy: Employment by occupation: 7.5% management, 2.9% professional, 11.8% services, 21.4% sales, 6.8% farming, 10.5% construction, 12.0% production (2006-2010 5-year est.).

Income: Per capita income: $23,586 (2006-2010 5-year est.); Median household income: $51,982 (2006-2010 5-year est.); Average household income: $59,532 (2006-2010 5-year est.); Percent of households with income of $100,000 or more: 15.2% (2006-2010 5-year est.); Poverty rate: 6.0% (2006-2010 5-year est.).

Education: Percent of population age 25 and over with: High school diploma (including GED) or higher: 86.9% (2006-2010 5-year est.); Bachelor's degree or higher: 13.5% (2006-2010 5-year est.); Master's degree or higher: 4.0% (2006-2010 5-year est.).

Housing: Homeownership rate: 80.5% (2010); Median home value: $150,700 (2006-2010 5-year est.); Median contract rent: $626 per month (2006-2010 5-year est.); Median year structure built: 1982 (2006-2010 5-year est.).

Transportation: Commute to work: 95.1% car, 0.3% public transportation, 1.1% walk, 2.8% work from home (2006-2010 5-year est.); Travel time to work: 20.9% less than 15 minutes, 42.6% 15 to 30 minutes, 21.8% 30 to

45 minutes, 6.2% 45 to 60 minutes, 8.5% 60 minutes or more (2006-2010 5-year est.)

Additional Information Contacts
York County Chamber of Commerce . . . . (717) 848-4000
  http://www.yorkchamber.com

WELLSVILLE (borough). Covers a land area of 0.144 square miles and a water area of 0 square miles. Located at 40.05° N. Lat; 76.94° W. Long. Elevation is 522 feet.
Population: 304 (1990); 279 (2000); 242 (2010); Density: 1,676.1 persons per square mile (2010); Race: 97.1% White, 0.0% Black, 0.4% Asian, 0.8% American Indian/Alaska Native, 0.0% Native Hawaiian/Other Pacific Islander, 1.7% Other, 1.7% Hispanic of any race (2010); Average household size: 2.07 (2010); Median age: 42.0 (2010); Males per 100 females: 101.7 (2010); Marriage status: 17.3% never married, 56.5% now married, 14.9% widowed, 11.3% divorced (2006-2010 5-year est.); Foreign born: 3.4% (2006-2010 5-year est.); Ancestry (includes multiple ancestries): 60.4% German, 8.2% English, 5.8% Norwegian, 5.3% Irish, 4.8% Ukrainian (2006-2010 5-year est.).
Economy: Single-family building permits issued: 0 (2011); Multi-family building permits issued: 0 (2011); Employment by occupation: 5.0% management, 0.0% professional, 8.0% services, 22.0% sales, 14.0% farming, 22.0% construction, 14.0% production (2006-2010 5-year est.).
Income: Per capita income: $22,135 (2006-2010 5-year est.); Median household income: $43,333 (2006-2010 5-year est.); Average household income: $50,324 (2006-2010 5-year est.); Percent of households with income of $100,000 or more: 6.4% (2006-2010 5-year est.); Poverty rate: 15.8% (2006-2010 5-year est.).
Education: Percent of population age 25 and over with: High school diploma (including GED) or higher: 78.1% (2006-2010 5-year est.); Bachelor's degree or higher: 7.9% (2006-2010 5-year est.); Master's degree or higher: 3.3% (2006-2010 5-year est.).
School District(s)
Northern York County SD (KG-12)
  2010-11 Enrollment: 3,178 . . . . (717) 432-8691
Housing: Homeownership rate: 67.5% (2010); Median home value: $137,500 (2006-2010 5-year est.); Median contract rent: $445 per month (2006-2010 5-year est.); Median year structure built: before 1940 (2006-2010 5-year est.).
Transportation: Commute to work: 96.0% car, 0.0% public transportation, 2.0% walk, 2.0% work from home (2006-2010 5-year est.); Travel time to work: 12.2% less than 15 minutes, 42.9% 15 to 30 minutes, 27.6% 30 to 45 minutes, 11.2% 45 to 60 minutes, 6.1% 60 minutes or more (2006-2010 5-year est.)

WEST MANCHESTER (township). Covers a land area of 19.942 square miles and a water area of 0.077 square miles. Located at 39.95° N. Lat; 76.79° W. Long.
Population: 14,261 (1990); 17,035 (2000); 18,894 (2010); Density: 947.5 persons per square mile (2010); Race: 91.0% White, 4.9% Black, 1.2% Asian, 0.1% American Indian/Alaska Native, 0.1% Native Hawaiian/Other Pacific Islander, 2.7% Other, 3.0% Hispanic of any race (2010); Average household size: 2.33 (2010); Median age: 44.7 (2010); Males per 100 females: 93.2 (2010); Marriage status: 19.8% never married, 59.5% now married, 9.6% widowed, 11.0% divorced (2006-2010 5-year est.); Foreign born: 3.9% (2006-2010 5-year est.); Ancestry (includes multiple ancestries): 43.1% German, 12.7% Irish, 11.4% American, 7.2% English, 5.4% Italian (2006-2010 5-year est.).
Economy: Single-family building permits issued: 4 (2011); Multi-family building permits issued: 0 (2011); Employment by occupation: 13.2% management, 4.1% professional, 7.8% services, 17.0% sales, 3.6% farming, 7.6% construction, 6.6% production (2006-2010 5-year est.).
Income: Per capita income: $29,101 (2006-2010 5-year est.); Median household income: $60,051 (2006-2010 5-year est.); Average household income: $68,535 (2006-2010 5-year est.); Percent of households with income of $100,000 or more: 18.9% (2006-2010 5-year est.); Poverty rate: 4.9% (2006-2010 5-year est.).
Education: Percent of population age 25 and over with: High school diploma (including GED) or higher: 87.6% (2006-2010 5-year est.); Bachelor's degree or higher: 21.4% (2006-2010 5-year est.); Master's degree or higher: 8.1% (2006-2010 5-year est.).
Housing: Homeownership rate: 78.5% (2010); Median home value: $160,200 (2006-2010 5-year est.); Median contract rent: $676 per month (2006-2010 5-year est.); Median year structure built: 1975 (2006-2010 5-year est.).

Safety: Violent crime rate: 16.4 per 10,000 population; Property crime rate: 327.1 per 10,000 population (2011).
Transportation: Commute to work: 93.9% car, 0.7% public transportation, 1.4% walk, 3.2% work from home (2006-2010 5-year est.); Travel time to work: 31.2% less than 15 minutes, 45.4% 15 to 30 minutes, 10.9% 30 to 45 minutes, 5.2% 45 to 60 minutes, 7.4% 60 minutes or more (2006-2010 5-year est.)
Additional Information Contacts
West Manchester Township . . . . (717) 792-3505
  http://www.westmanchestertownship.com
York County Chamber of Commerce . . . . (717) 848-4000
  http://www.yorkchamber.com

WEST MANHEIM (township). Covers a land area of 19.439 square miles and a water area of 0.659 square miles. Located at 39.75° N. Lat; 76.94° W. Long. Elevation is 965 feet.
Population: 4,590 (1990); 4,865 (2000); 7,744 (2010); Density: 398.4 persons per square mile (2010); Race: 92.9% White, 3.9% Black, 1.2% Asian, 0.1% American Indian/Alaska Native, 0.0% Native Hawaiian/Other Pacific Islander, 1.9% Other, 1.6% Hispanic of any race (2010); Average household size: 2.68 (2010); Median age: 40.2 (2010); Males per 100 females: 99.2 (2010); Marriage status: 20.2% never married, 61.6% now married, 5.0% widowed, 13.2% divorced (2006-2010 5-year est.); Foreign born: 1.6% (2006-2010 5-year est.); Ancestry (includes multiple ancestries): 40.9% German, 15.6% Irish, 13.3% American, 10.3% English, 5.2% Italian (2006-2010 5-year est.).
Economy: Single-family building permits issued: 38 (2011); Multi-family building permits issued: 2 (2011); Employment by occupation: 10.4% management, 4.2% professional, 10.1% services, 18.1% sales, 4.2% farming, 11.8% construction, 5.8% production (2006-2010 5-year est.).
Income: Per capita income: $29,203 (2006-2010 5-year est.); Median household income: $79,154 (2006-2010 5-year est.); Average household income: $77,962 (2006-2010 5-year est.); Percent of households with income of $100,000 or more: 26.5% (2006-2010 5-year est.); Poverty rate: 4.3% (2006-2010 5-year est.).
Education: Percent of population age 25 and over with: High school diploma (including GED) or higher: 92.4% (2006-2010 5-year est.); Bachelor's degree or higher: 21.1% (2006-2010 5-year est.); Master's degree or higher: 6.1% (2006-2010 5-year est.).
Housing: Homeownership rate: 87.4% (2010); Median home value: $213,300 (2006-2010 5-year est.); Median contract rent: $764 per month (2006-2010 5-year est.); Median year structure built: 1986 (2006-2010 5-year est.).
Safety: Violent crime rate: 2.6 per 10,000 population; Property crime rate: 90.1 per 10,000 population (2011).
Transportation: Commute to work: 94.6% car, 0.0% public transportation, 0.9% walk, 4.1% work from home (2006-2010 5-year est.); Travel time to work: 22.1% less than 15 minutes, 31.3% 15 to 30 minutes, 22.8% 30 to 45 minutes, 7.4% 45 to 60 minutes, 16.3% 60 minutes or more (2006-2010 5-year est.)
Additional Information Contacts
Hanover Area Chamber of Commerce . . . . (717) 637-6130
  http://www.hanoverchamber.com

WEST YORK (borough). Covers a land area of 0.526 square miles and a water area of 0 square miles. Located at 39.95° N. Lat; 76.76° W. Long. Elevation is 387 feet.
History: Incorporated 1905.
Population: 4,283 (1990); 4,321 (2000); 4,617 (2010); Density: 8,785.7 persons per square mile (2010); Race: 82.1% White, 8.5% Black, 0.8% Asian, 0.5% American Indian/Alaska Native, 0.1% Native Hawaiian/Other Pacific Islander, 8.0% Other, 9.1% Hispanic of any race (2010); Average household size: 2.40 (2010); Median age: 33.3 (2010); Males per 100 females: 91.8 (2010); Marriage status: 38.3% never married, 38.1% now married, 7.1% widowed, 16.6% divorced (2006-2010 5-year est.); Foreign born: 1.0% (2006-2010 5-year est.); Ancestry (includes multiple ancestries): 44.7% German, 12.9% Irish, 6.7% English, 6.4% American, 3.4% Italian (2006-2010 5-year est.).
Economy: Single-family building permits issued: 0 (2011); Multi-family building permits issued: 0 (2011); Employment by occupation: 7.6% management, 2.4% professional, 6.7% services, 25.8% sales, 5.3% farming, 7.3% construction, 6.6% production (2006-2010 5-year est.).
Income: Per capita income: $22,338 (2006-2010 5-year est.); Median household income: $49,018 (2006-2010 5-year est.); Average household income: $49,376 (2006-2010 5-year est.); Percent of households with

income of $100,000 or more: 5.0% (2006-2010 5-year est.); Poverty rate: 12.1% (2006-2010 5-year est.).

Education: Percent of population age 25 and over with: High school diploma (including GED) or higher: 86.8% (2006-2010 5-year est.); Bachelor's degree or higher: 15.0% (2006-2010 5-year est.); Master's degree or higher: 3.1% (2006-2010 5-year est.).

Housing: Homeownership rate: 57.3% (2010); Median home value: $105,900 (2006-2010 5-year est.); Median contract rent: $520 per month (2006-2010 5-year est.); Median year structure built: before 1940 (2006-2010 5-year est.).

Safety: Violent crime rate: 30.2 per 10,000 population; Property crime rate: 153.3 per 10,000 population (2011).

Transportation: Commute to work: 90.9% car, 2.1% public transportation, 4.6% walk, 0.8% work from home (2006-2010 5-year est.); Travel time to work: 43.6% less than 15 minutes, 39.2% 15 to 30 minutes, 10.2% 30 to 45 minutes, 1.4% 45 to 60 minutes, 5.6% 60 minutes or more (2006-2010 5-year est.)

Additional Information Contacts
York County Chamber of Commerce . . . . (717) 848-4000
   http://www.yorkchamber.com

WINDSOR (borough). Covers a land area of 0.548 square miles and a water area of 0 square miles. Located at 39.92° N. Lat; 76.58° W. Long. Elevation is 682 feet.

Population: 1,355 (1990); 1,331 (2000); 1,319 (2010); Density: 2,405.3 persons per square mile (2010); Race: 96.1% White, 1.1% Black, 0.4% Asian, 0.1% American Indian/Alaska Native, 0.0% Native Hawaiian/Other Pacific Islander, 2.3% Other, 3.6% Hispanic of any race (2010); Average household size: 2.66 (2010); Median age: 31.5 (2010); Males per 100 females: 99.2 (2010); Marriage status: 34.8% never married, 47.3% now married, 1.3% widowed, 16.6% divorced (2006-2010 5-year est.); Foreign born: 0.0% (2006-2010 5-year est.); Ancestry (includes multiple ancestries): 39.2% German, 14.8% Irish, 9.5% Italian, 7.6% Dutch, 6.7% American (2006-2010 5-year est.).

Economy: Single-family building permits issued: 0 (2011); Multi-family building permits issued: 0 (2011); Employment by occupation: 5.5% management, 3.7% professional, 8.2% services, 20.8% sales, 4.7% farming, 14.9% construction, 13.0% production (2006-2010 5-year est.).

Income: Per capita income: $20,728 (2006-2010 5-year est.); Median household income: $53,043 (2006-2010 5-year est.); Average household income: $58,198 (2006-2010 5-year est.); Percent of households with income of $100,000 or more: 12.1% (2006-2010 5-year est.); Poverty rate: 13.8% (2006-2010 5-year est.).

Education: Percent of population age 25 and over with: High school diploma (including GED) or higher: 77.1% (2006-2010 5-year est.); Bachelor's degree or higher: 5.7% (2006-2010 5-year est.); Master's degree or higher: 1.6% (2006-2010 5-year est.).

School District(s)
Red Lion Area SD (KG-12)
   2010-11 Enrollment: 5,537 . . . . (717) 244-4518

Housing: Homeownership rate: 68.9% (2010); Median home value: $122,500 (2006-2010 5-year est.); Median contract rent: $586 per month (2006-2010 5-year est.); Median year structure built: before 1940 (2006-2010 5-year est.).

Transportation: Commute to work: 94.1% car, 1.6% public transportation, 1.3% walk, 1.6% work from home (2006-2010 5-year est.); Travel time to work: 20.4% less than 15 minutes, 49.4% 15 to 30 minutes, 10.9% 30 to 45 minutes, 6.8% 45 to 60 minutes, 12.4% 60 minutes or more (2006-2010 5-year est.)

Additional Information Contacts
York County Chamber of Commerce . . . . (717) 848-4000
   http://www.yorkchamber.com

WINDSOR (township). Covers a land area of 27.277 square miles and a water area of 0.015 square miles. Located at 39.95° N. Lat; 76.62° W. Long. Elevation is 682 feet.

History: Incorporated 1905.

Population: 9,520 (1990); 12,807 (2000); 17,504 (2010); Density: 641.7 persons per square mile (2010); Race: 92.0% White, 4.6% Black, 1.4% Asian, 0.1% American Indian/Alaska Native, 0.0% Native Hawaiian/Other Pacific Islander, 1.9% Other, 2.1% Hispanic of any race (2010); Average household size: 2.67 (2010); Median age: 40.6 (2010); Males per 100 females: 98.2 (2010); Marriage status: 22.6% never married, 65.8% now married, 4.7% widowed, 6.9% divorced (2006-2010 5-year est.); Foreign born: 2.5% (2006-2010 5-year est.); Ancestry (includes multiple

ancestries): 44.7% German, 14.0% Irish, 10.2% American, 9.8% English, 8.3% Italian (2006-2010 5-year est.).

Economy: Single-family building permits issued: 43 (2011); Multi-family building permits issued: 0 (2011); Employment by occupation: 11.0% management, 6.8% professional, 7.5% services, 13.3% sales, 3.0% farming, 10.9% construction, 8.6% production (2006-2010 5-year est.).

Income: Per capita income: $29,391 (2006-2010 5-year est.); Median household income: $68,349 (2006-2010 5-year est.); Average household income: $77,217 (2006-2010 5-year est.); Percent of households with income of $100,000 or more: 29.4% (2006-2010 5-year est.); Poverty rate: 4.9% (2006-2010 5-year est.).

Education: Percent of population age 25 and over with: High school diploma (including GED) or higher: 88.8% (2006-2010 5-year est.); Bachelor's degree or higher: 22.0% (2006-2010 5-year est.); Master's degree or higher: 7.4% (2006-2010 5-year est.).

Housing: Homeownership rate: 86.5% (2010); Median home value: $189,400 (2006-2010 5-year est.); Median contract rent: $734 per month (2006-2010 5-year est.); Median year structure built: 1991 (2006-2010 5-year est.).

Transportation: Commute to work: 94.2% car, 0.2% public transportation, 0.4% walk, 4.0% work from home (2006-2010 5-year est.); Travel time to work: 24.5% less than 15 minutes, 37.1% 15 to 30 minutes, 16.6% 30 to 45 minutes, 9.0% 45 to 60 minutes, 12.9% 60 minutes or more (2006-2010 5-year est.)

Additional Information Contacts
Windsor Township. . . . . (717) 244-3512
   http://www.windsortwp.com
York County Chamber of Commerce . . . . (717) 848-4000
   http://www.yorkchamber.com

WINTERSTOWN (borough). Covers a land area of 2.414 square miles and a water area of 0 square miles. Located at 39.84° N. Lat; 76.62° W. Long. Elevation is 856 feet.

Population: 581 (1990); 546 (2000); 632 (2010); Density: 261.8 persons per square mile (2010); Race: 98.9% White, 0.0% Black, 0.3% Asian, 0.0% American Indian/Alaska Native, 0.0% Native Hawaiian/Other Pacific Islander, 0.8% Other, 0.8% Hispanic of any race (2010); Average household size: 2.54 (2010); Median age: 45.2 (2010); Males per 100 females: 95.1 (2010); Marriage status: 24.5% never married, 55.5% now married, 9.3% widowed, 10.7% divorced (2006-2010 5-year est.); Foreign born: 2.2% (2006-2010 5-year est.); Ancestry (includes multiple ancestries): 52.5% German, 14.8% Irish, 13.3% American, 9.5% English, 6.6% Italian (2006-2010 5-year est.).

Economy: Single-family building permits issued: 0 (2011); Multi-family building permits issued: 0 (2011); Employment by occupation: 4.4% management, 4.4% professional, 10.4% services, 18.2% sales, 2.4% farming, 21.9% construction, 7.7% production (2006-2010 5-year est.).

Income: Per capita income: $27,308 (2006-2010 5-year est.); Median household income: $46,477 (2006-2010 5-year est.); Average household income: $58,606 (2006-2010 5-year est.); Percent of households with income of $100,000 or more: 17.3% (2006-2010 5-year est.); Poverty rate: 5.8% (2006-2010 5-year est.).

Education: Percent of population age 25 and over with: High school diploma (including GED) or higher: 82.2% (2006-2010 5-year est.); Bachelor's degree or higher: 15.4% (2006-2010 5-year est.); Master's degree or higher: 6.0% (2006-2010 5-year est.).

Housing: Homeownership rate: 79.1% (2010); Median home value: $162,500 (2006-2010 5-year est.); Median contract rent: $535 per month (2006-2010 5-year est.); Median year structure built: 1978 (2006-2010 5-year est.).

Transportation: Commute to work: 98.6% car, 0.0% public transportation, 0.0% walk, 1.4% work from home (2006-2010 5-year est.); Travel time to work: 19.7% less than 15 minutes, 30.0% 15 to 30 minutes, 19.7% 30 to 45 minutes, 16.6% 45 to 60 minutes, 14.1% 60 minutes or more (2006-2010 5-year est.)

WRIGHTSVILLE (borough). Covers a land area of 0.663 square miles and a water area of 0 square miles. Located at 40.02° N. Lat; 76.53° W. Long. Elevation is 289 feet.

History: Settled 1730, laid out 1811, incorporated 1834.

Population: 2,396 (1990); 2,223 (2000); 2,310 (2010); Density: 3,482.1 persons per square mile (2010); Race: 95.8% White, 0.7% Black, 0.3% Asian, 0.1% American Indian/Alaska Native, 0.0% Native Hawaiian/Other Pacific Islander, 3.1% Other, 2.8% Hispanic of any race (2010); Average household size: 2.46 (2010); Median age: 39.0 (2010); Males per 100

females: 96.9 (2010); Marriage status: 25.8% never married, 51.9% now married, 7.1% widowed, 15.3% divorced (2006-2010 5-year est.); Foreign born: 4.3% (2006-2010 5-year est.); Ancestry (includes multiple ancestries): 43.6% German, 18.9% Irish, 9.5% Italian, 5.9% American, 5.2% English (2006-2010 5-year est.).

Economy: Single-family building permits issued: 1 (2011); Multi-family building permits issued: 0 (2011); Employment by occupation: 6.4% management, 1.0% professional, 8.7% services, 15.4% sales, 3.0% farming, 12.2% construction, 14.3% production (2006-2010 5-year est.).

Income: Per capita income: $23,920 (2006-2010 5-year est.); Median household income: $48,413 (2006-2010 5-year est.); Average household income: $56,489 (2006-2010 5-year est.); Percent of households with income of $100,000 or more: 9.1% (2006-2010 5-year est.); Poverty rate: 8.8% (2006-2010 5-year est.).

Education: Percent of population age 25 and over with: High school diploma (including GED) or higher: 82.0% (2006-2010 5-year est.); Bachelor's degree or higher: 14.0% (2006-2010 5-year est.); Master's degree or higher: 4.1% (2006-2010 5-year est.).

School District(s)

Eastern York SD (KG-12)

   2010-11 Enrollment: 2,583 . . . . (717) 252-1555

Housing: Homeownership rate: 69.2% (2010); Median home value: $123,700 (2006-2010 5-year est.); Median contract rent: $547 per month (2006-2010 5-year est.); Median year structure built: before 1940 (2006-2010 5-year est.).

Safety: Violent crime rate: 73.4 per 10,000 population; Property crime rate: 185.6 per 10,000 population (2011).

Transportation: Commute to work: 89.9% car, 1.0% public transportation, 5.4% walk, 0.4% work from home (2006-2010 5-year est.); Travel time to work: 20.7% less than 15 minutes, 53.2% 15 to 30 minutes, 16.8% 30 to 45 minutes, 4.5% 45 to 60 minutes, 4.8% 60 minutes or more (2006-2010 5-year est.)

Additional Information Contacts

Susquehanna Valley Chamber of Commerce . . . . (717) 684-5249

   http://www.parivertowns.com

YOE (borough). Covers a land area of 0.238 square miles and a water area of 0 square miles. Located at 39.91° N. Lat; 76.64° W. Long. Elevation is 709 feet.

Population: 967 (1990); 1,022 (2000); 1,018 (2010); Density: 4,283.4 persons per square mile (2010); Race: 90.8% White, 4.2% Black, 0.3% Asian, 0.5% American Indian/Alaska Native, 0.0% Native Hawaiian/Other Pacific Islander, 4.2% Other, 4.3% Hispanic of any race (2010); Average household size: 2.36 (2010); Median age: 31.3 (2010); Males per 100 females: 101.2 (2010); Marriage status: 33.7% never married, 40.7% now married, 8.2% widowed, 17.4% divorced (2006-2010 5-year est.); Foreign born: 2.0% (2006-2010 5-year est.); Ancestry (includes multiple ancestries): 42.8% German, 13.1% Irish, 9.9% American, 6.9% English, 6.7% Polish (2006-2010 5-year est.).

Economy: Single-family building permits issued: 0 (2011); Multi-family building permits issued: 0 (2011); Employment by occupation: 7.1% management, 3.6% professional, 14.0% services, 16.8% sales, 6.7% farming, 8.8% construction, 15.1% production (2006-2010 5-year est.).

Income: Per capita income: $21,549 (2006-2010 5-year est.); Median household income: $37,115 (2006-2010 5-year est.); Average household income: $45,526 (2006-2010 5-year est.); Percent of households with income of $100,000 or more: 4.9% (2006-2010 5-year est.); Poverty rate: 14.2% (2006-2010 5-year est.).

Education: Percent of population age 25 and over with: High school diploma (including GED) or higher: 83.5% (2006-2010 5-year est.); Bachelor's degree or higher: 8.9% (2006-2010 5-year est.); Master's degree or higher: 3.7% (2006-2010 5-year est.).

Housing: Homeownership rate: 50.1% (2010); Median home value: $143,400 (2006-2010 5-year est.); Median contract rent: $533 per month (2006-2010 5-year est.); Median year structure built: 1956 (2006-2010 5-year est.).

Transportation: Commute to work: 92.7% car, 0.0% public transportation, 1.5% walk, 0.0% work from home (2006-2010 5-year est.); Travel time to work: 34.6% less than 15 minutes, 39.5% 15 to 30 minutes, 7.5% 30 to 45 minutes, 9.8% 45 to 60 minutes, 8.5% 60 minutes or more (2006-2010 5-year est.)

Additional Information Contacts

York County Chamber of Commerce . . . . (717) 848-4000

   http://www.yorkchamber.com

YORK (city). County seat. Covers a land area of 5.293 square miles and a water area of 0.049 square miles. Located at 39.96° N. Lat; 76.73° W. Long. Elevation is 387 feet.

History: In 1741, Richard, Thomas, and John Penn ordered Thomas Cookson, then deputy surveyor of Lancaster County, which then included York County, to lay off in lots a tract of land where the Monocacy Road crossed Codorus Creek. In 1749, the land west of the Susquehanna River was formed into a new county, with York as the seat. English and Scots-Irish had settled on the rich farmland, and were soon joined by many German immigrants. York became an industrial community, and was incorporated as a city in 1887.

Population: 42,200 (1990); 40,862 (2000); 43,718 (2010); Density: 8,260.3 persons per square mile (2010); Race: 51.2% White, 28.0% Black, 1.2% Asian, 0.6% American Indian/Alaska Native, 0.0% Native Hawaiian/Other Pacific Islander, 19.0% Other, 28.5% Hispanic of any race (2010); Average household size: 2.62 (2010); Median age: 30.1 (2010); Males per 100 females: 92.9 (2010); Marriage status: 46.3% never married, 35.6% now married, 5.9% widowed, 12.2% divorced (2006-2010 5-year est.); Foreign born: 8.3% (2006-2010 5-year est.); Ancestry (includes multiple ancestries): 19.6% German, 7.3% Irish, 5.0% Italian, 3.7% American, 3.5% English (2006-2010 5-year est.).

Economy: Unemployment rate: 13.3% (August 2012); Total civilian labor force: 20,808 (August 2012); Single-family building permits issued: 5 (2011); Multi-family building permits issued: 0 (2011); Employment by occupation: 5.3% management, 1.8% professional, 17.2% services, 15.2% sales, 5.0% farming, 6.3% construction, 9.0% production (2006-2010 5-year est.).

Income: Per capita income: $14,287 (2006-2010 5-year est.); Median household income: $28,583 (2006-2010 5-year est.); Average household income: $36,357 (2006-2010 5-year est.); Percent of households with income of $100,000 or more: 3.9% (2006-2010 5-year est.); Poverty rate: 36.6% (2006-2010 5-year est.).

Taxes: Total city taxes per capita: $544 (2009); City property taxes per capita: $357 (2009).

Education: Percent of population age 25 and over with: High school diploma (including GED) or higher: 73.7% (2006-2010 5-year est.); Bachelor's degree or higher: 10.2% (2006-2010 5-year est.); Master's degree or higher: 2.8% (2006-2010 5-year est.).

School District(s)

Central York SD (KG-12)

   2010-11 Enrollment: 5,667 . . . . (717) 846-6789

Crispus Attucks Youthbuild CS (12-12)

   2010-11 Enrollment: 109 . . . . (717) 848-3610

Dallastown Area SD (KG-12)

   2010-11 Enrollment: 6,050 . . . . (717) 244-4021

Helen Thackston Charter School (05-08)

   2010-11 Enrollment: 411 . . . . (717) 846-6160

Lincoln CS (KG-05)

   2010-11 Enrollment: 740 . . . . (717) 699-1573

New Hope Academy CS (06-12)

   2010-11 Enrollment: 522 . . . . (717) 845-4046

Northeastern York SD (KG-12)

   2010-11 Enrollment: 3,766 . . . . (717) 266-3667

Red Lion Area SD (KG-12)

   2010-11 Enrollment: 5,537 . . . . (717) 244-4518

Spring Grove Area SD (KG-12)

   2010-11 Enrollment: 3,827 . . . . (717) 225-4731

West York Area SD (PK-12)

   2010-11 Enrollment: 3,141 . . . . (717) 792-2796

York City SD (PK-12)

   2010-11 Enrollment: 5,724 . . . . (717) 845-3571

York Co School of Technology (09-12)

   2010-11 Enrollment: 1,576 . . . . (717) 741-0820

York County Hs (-)

   2010-11 Enrollment: n/a . . . . (717) 718-5836

York Suburban SD (KG-12)

   2010-11 Enrollment: 2,968 . . . . (717) 848-2814

Four-year College(s)

Pennsylvania State University-Penn State York (Public)

   Fall 2010 Enrollment: 1,224 . . . . (717) 771-4000

   2011-12 Tuition: In-state $12,966; Out-of-state $19,406

The Art Institutes of York-PA (Private, For-profit)

   Fall 2010 Enrollment: 660 . . . . (717) 757-1000

   2011-12 Tuition: In-state $17,544; Out-of-state $17,544

York College Pennsylvania (Private, Not-for-profit)
   Fall 2010 Enrollment: 5,279 . . . . (717) 846-7788
   2011-12 Tuition: In-state $15,880; Out-of-state $15,880
Two-year College(s)
Consolidated School of Business-York (Private, For-profit)
   Fall 2010 Enrollment: 187 . . . . (717) 764-9550
YTI Career Institute-York (Private, For-profit)
   Fall 2010 Enrollment: 3,744 . . . . (717) 757-1100
Yorktowne Business Institute (Private, For-profit)
   Fall 2010 Enrollment: 283 . . . . (717) 846-5000
   2011-12 Tuition: In-state $12,120; Out-of-state $12,120
Vocational/Technical School(s)
Baltimore School of Massage-York (Private, For-profit)
   Fall 2010 Enrollment: 200 . . . . (717) 268-1881
   2011-12 Tuition: $11,869
Empire Beauty School-York (Private, For-profit)
   Fall 2010 Enrollment: 301 . . . . (800) 223-3271
   2011-12 Tuition: $14,490
York County School of Technology Practical Nursing (Public)
   Fall 2010 Enrollment: 171 . . . . (717) 741-0820
   2011-12 Tuition: In-state $12,448; Out-of-state $14,223
Housing: Homeownership rate: 41.8% (2010); Median home value: $80,100 (2006-2010 5-year est.); Median contract rent: $492 per month (2006-2010 5-year est.); Median year structure built: 1940 (2006-2010 5-year est.).
Hospitals: HealthSouth Rehabilitation Hospital of York (102 beds); Memorial Hospital (100 beds); York Hospital (466 beds)
Safety: Violent crime rate: 164.4 per 10,000 population; Property crime rate: 394.7 per 10,000 population (2011).
Newspapers: Weekly Record (Community news; Circulation 51,000); York Daily Record (Local news; Circulation 79,674); The York Dispatch (Local news; Circulation 79,674); York Sunday News (Local news; Circulation 93,000)
Transportation: Commute to work: 80.9% car, 8.0% public transportation, 5.9% walk, 2.3% work from home (2006-2010 5-year est.); Travel time to work: 36.4% less than 15 minutes, 42.2% 15 to 30 minutes, 11.0% 30 to 45 minutes, 5.2% 45 to 60 minutes, 5.2% 60 minutes or more (2006-2010 5-year est.).
Airports: York (general aviation)
Additional Information Contacts
City of York . . . . (717) 849-2221
   http://www.yorkcity.org
York County Chamber of Commerce . . . . (717) 848-4000
   http://www.yorkchamber.com

YORK (township). Covers a land area of 25.238 square miles and a water area of 0.403 square miles. Located at 39.91° N. Lat; 76.67° W. Long. Elevation is 387 feet.
History: A meeting place (1777—1778) of the Continental Congress. During the Civil War, occupied briefly (1863) by Confederates. York University of Pennsylvania is here. Harley-Davidson Motorcycle Museum and plant tours, Fire Museum of York, Agriculture Museum of York, Industrial Museum of York County. Several colonial houses remain. Laid out 1741; Incorporated as a city 1887.
Population: 19,227 (1990); 23,637 (2000); 27,793 (2010); Density: 1,101.2 persons per square mile (2010); Race: 91.2% White, 3.7% Black, 2.3% Asian, 0.2% American Indian/Alaska Native, 0.0% Native Hawaiian/Other Pacific Islander, 2.6% Other, 3.3% Hispanic of any race (2010); Average household size: 2.34 (2010); Median age: 43.3 (2010); Males per 100 females: 90.8 (2010); Marriage status: 21.1% never married, 59.8% now married, 7.5% widowed, 11.6% divorced (2006-2010 5-year est.); Foreign born: 4.7% (2006-2010 5-year est.); Ancestry (includes multiple ancestries): 45.8% German, 12.3% Irish, 10.0% English, 6.3% American, 5.3% Italian (2006-2010 5-year est.).
Economy: Unemployment rate: 6.9% (August 2012); Total civilian labor force: 14,874 (August 2012); Single-family building permits issued: 32 (2011); Multi-family building permits issued: 21 (2011); Employment by occupation: 13.6% management, 5.8% professional, 8.6% services, 17.6% sales, 2.7% farming, 8.9% construction, 5.5% production (2006-2010 5-year est.).
Income: Per capita income: $32,778 (2006-2010 5-year est.); Median household income: $63,269 (2006-2010 5-year est.); Average household income: $77,612 (2006-2010 5-year est.); Percent of households with income of $100,000 or more: 25.5% (2006-2010 5-year est.); Poverty rate: 6.0% (2006-2010 5-year est.).

Taxes: Total city taxes per capita: $286 (2009); City property taxes per capita: $45 (2009).
Education: Percent of population age 25 and over with: High school diploma (including GED) or higher: 91.5% (2006-2010 5-year est.); Bachelor's degree or higher: 29.2% (2006-2010 5-year est.); Master's degree or higher: 11.3% (2006-2010 5-year est.).
Four-year College(s)
Pennsylvania State University-Penn State York (Public)
   Fall 2010 Enrollment: 1,224 . . . . (717) 771-4000
   2011-12 Tuition: In-state $12,966; Out-of-state $19,406
The Art Institutes of York-PA (Private, For-profit)
   Fall 2010 Enrollment: 660 . . . . (717) 757-1000
   2011-12 Tuition: In-state $17,544; Out-of-state $17,544
York College Pennsylvania (Private, Not-for-profit)
   Fall 2010 Enrollment: 5,279 . . . . (717) 846-7788
   2011-12 Tuition: In-state $15,880; Out-of-state $15,880
Two-year College(s)
Consolidated School of Business-York (Private, For-profit)
   Fall 2010 Enrollment: 187 . . . . (717) 764-9550
YTI Career Institute-York (Private, For-profit)
   Fall 2010 Enrollment: 3,744 . . . . (717) 757-1100
Yorktowne Business Institute (Private, For-profit)
   Fall 2010 Enrollment: 283 . . . . (717) 846-5000
   2011-12 Tuition: In-state $12,120; Out-of-state $12,120
Vocational/Technical School(s)
Baltimore School of Massage-York (Private, For-profit)
   Fall 2010 Enrollment: 200 . . . . (717) 268-1881
   2011-12 Tuition: $11,869
Empire Beauty School-York (Private, For-profit)
   Fall 2010 Enrollment: 301 . . . . (800) 223-3271
   2011-12 Tuition: $14,490
York County School of Technology Practical Nursing (Public)
   Fall 2010 Enrollment: 171 . . . . (717) 741-0820
   2011-12 Tuition: In-state $12,448; Out-of-state $14,223
Housing: Homeownership rate: 70.2% (2010); Median home value: $191,800 (2006-2010 5-year est.); Median contract rent: $732 per month (2006-2010 5-year est.); Median year structure built: 1982 (2006-2010 5-year est.).
Hospitals: HealthSouth Rehabilitation Hospital of York (102 beds); Memorial Hospital (100 beds); York Hospital (466 beds)
Newspapers: Weekly Record (Community news; Circulation 51,000); York Daily Record (Local news; Circulation 79,674); The York Dispatch (Local news; Circulation 79,674); York Sunday News (Local news; Circulation 93,000)
Transportation: Commute to work: 95.2% car, 0.2% public transportation, 1.1% walk, 3.3% work from home (2006-2010 5-year est.); Travel time to work: 30.5% less than 15 minutes, 39.0% 15 to 30 minutes, 12.6% 30 to 45 minutes, 8.4% 45 to 60 minutes, 9.4% 60 minutes or more (2006-2010 5-year est.)
Airports: York (general aviation)
Additional Information Contacts
York County Chamber of Commerce . . . . (717) 848-4000
   http://www.yorkchamber.com
York Township . . . . (717) 741-3861
   http://www.yorktownship.com

YORK HAVEN (borough). Covers a land area of 0.298 square miles and a water area of 0.027 square miles. Located at 40.11° N. Lat; 76.72° W. Long. Elevation is 384 feet.
Population: 758 (1990); 809 (2000); 709 (2010); Density: 2,381.5 persons per square mile (2010); Race: 91.4% White, 2.0% Black, 0.4% Asian, 1.1% American Indian/Alaska Native, 0.0% Native Hawaiian/Other Pacific Islander, 5.1% Other, 7.3% Hispanic of any race (2010); Average household size: 2.78 (2010); Median age: 29.7 (2010); Males per 100 females: 114.2 (2010); Marriage status: 34.2% never married, 49.0% now married, 5.6% widowed, 11.3% divorced (2006-2010 5-year est.); Foreign born: 3.1% (2006-2010 5-year est.); Ancestry (includes multiple ancestries): 48.6% German, 14.3% Irish, 10.0% English, 6.3% Italian, 6.0% American (2006-2010 5-year est.).
Economy: Single-family building permits issued: 0 (2011); Multi-family building permits issued: 0 (2011); Employment by occupation: 11.8% management, 4.2% professional, 20.2% services, 13.0% sales, 0.6% farming, 14.5% construction, 7.6% production (2006-2010 5-year est.).
Income: Per capita income: $17,564 (2006-2010 5-year est.); Median household income: $39,609 (2006-2010 5-year est.); Average household

income: $46,773 (2006-2010 5-year est.); Percent of households with income of $100,000 or more: 6.5% (2006-2010 5-year est.); Poverty rate: 18.6% (2006-2010 5-year est.).

Education: Percent of population age 25 and over with: High school diploma (including GED) or higher: 72.4% (2006-2010 5-year est.); Bachelor's degree or higher: 9.3% (2006-2010 5-year est.); Master's degree or higher: 0.5% (2006-2010 5-year est.).

School District(s)

Northeastern York SD (KG-12)

    2010-11 Enrollment: 3,766 . . . . (717) 266-3667

Housing: Homeownership rate: 45.9% (2010); Median home value: $83,600 (2006-2010 5-year est.); Median contract rent: $575 per month (2006-2010 5-year est.); Median year structure built: before 1940 (2006-2010 5-year est.).

Transportation: Commute to work: 90.3% car, 0.0% public transportation, 1.3% walk, 8.5% work from home (2006-2010 5-year est.); Travel time to work: 18.5% less than 15 minutes, 43.2% 15 to 30 minutes, 28.1% 30 to 45 minutes, 6.8% 45 to 60 minutes, 3.4% 60 minutes or more (2006-2010 5-year est.)

YORK NEW SALEM (unincorporated postal area)

Zip Code: 17371

    Covers a land area of 0.200 square miles and a water area of 0 square miles. Located at 39.90° N. Lat; 76.78° W. Long. Population: 257 (2010); Density: 1,281.3 persons per square mile (2010); Race: 97.7% White, 0.0% Black, 0.0% Asian, 0.0% American Indian/Alaska Native, 0.0% Native Hawaiian/Other Pacific Islander, 2.3% Other, 1.9% Hispanic of any race (2010); Average household size: 2.57 (2010); Median age: 40.1 (2010); Males per 100 females: 119.7 (2010); Homeownership rate: 77.0% (2010)

YORKANA (borough). Covers a land area of 0.171 square miles and a water area of 0 square miles. Located at 39.98° N. Lat; 76.58° W. Long. Elevation is 630 feet.

Population: 212 (1990); 239 (2000); 229 (2010); Density: 1,335.8 persons per square mile (2010); Race: 97.8% White, 0.9% Black, 0.0% Asian, 0.4% American Indian/Alaska Native, 0.0% Native Hawaiian/Other Pacific Islander, 0.9% Other, 3.9% Hispanic of any race (2010); Average household size: 2.39 (2010); Median age: 39.6 (2010); Males per 100 females: 104.5 (2010); Marriage status: 24.5% never married, 63.8% now married, 3.6% widowed, 8.2% divorced (2006-2010 5-year est.); Foreign born: 0.0% (2006-2010 5-year est.); Ancestry (includes multiple ancestries): 54.4% German, 12.4% English, 8.0% American, 7.1% Irish, 4.0% Scottish (2006-2010 5-year est.).

Economy: Single-family building permits issued: 0 (2011); Multi-family building permits issued: 0 (2011); Employment by occupation: 3.1% management, 0.0% professional, 10.9% services, 14.8% sales, 3.9% farming, 16.4% construction, 10.9% production (2006-2010 5-year est.).

Income: Per capita income: $22,846 (2006-2010 5-year est.); Median household income: $53,250 (2006-2010 5-year est.); Average household income: $54,763 (2006-2010 5-year est.); Percent of households with income of $100,000 or more: 9.7% (2006-2010 5-year est.); Poverty rate: 8.8% (2006-2010 5-year est.).

Education: Percent of population age 25 and over with: High school diploma (including GED) or higher: 80.8% (2006-2010 5-year est.); Bachelor's degree or higher: 11.0% (2006-2010 5-year est.); Master's degree or higher: 3.5% (2006-2010 5-year est.).

Housing: Homeownership rate: 69.8% (2010); Median home value: $155,200 (2006-2010 5-year est.); Median contract rent: $593 per month (2006-2010 5-year est.); Median year structure built: before 1940 (2006-2010 5-year est.).

Transportation: Commute to work: 96.7% car, 0.0% public transportation, 0.0% walk, 1.6% work from home (2006-2010 5-year est.); Travel time to work: 30.8% less than 15 minutes, 27.5% 15 to 30 minutes, 27.5% 30 to 45 minutes, 1.7% 45 to 60 minutes, 12.5% 60 minutes or more (2006-2010 5-year est.)

YORKLYN (CDP). Covers a land area of 0.454 square miles and a water area of 0 square miles. Located at 39.99° N. Lat; 76.64° W. Long. Elevation is 433 feet.

Population: n/a (1990); n/a (2000); 1,912 (2010); Density: 4,207.5 persons per square mile (2010); Race: 84.0% White, 7.1% Black, 2.4% Asian, 0.3% American Indian/Alaska Native, 0.1% Native Hawaiian/Other Pacific Islander, 6.1% Other, 6.9% Hispanic of any race (2010); Average household size: 2.57 (2010); Median age: 40.3 (2010); Males per 100

females: 95.5 (2010); Marriage status: 23.7% never married, 60.4% now married, 7.8% widowed, 8.1% divorced (2006-2010 5-year est.); Foreign born: 2.3% (2006-2010 5-year est.); Ancestry (includes multiple ancestries): 42.9% German, 9.8% English, 9.1% Irish, 7.4% American, 2.8% Finnish (2006-2010 5-year est.).

Economy: Employment by occupation: 8.6% management, 2.4% professional, 23.8% services, 16.9% sales, 1.3% farming, 2.9% construction, 2.6% production (2006-2010 5-year est.).

Income: Per capita income: $23,226 (2006-2010 5-year est.); Median household income: $51,195 (2006-2010 5-year est.); Average household income: $56,838 (2006-2010 5-year est.); Percent of households with income of $100,000 or more: 8.7% (2006-2010 5-year est.); Poverty rate: 5.4% (2006-2010 5-year est.).

Education: Percent of population age 25 and over with: High school diploma (including GED) or higher: 86.2% (2006-2010 5-year est.); Bachelor's degree or higher: 12.2% (2006-2010 5-year est.); Master's degree or higher: 2.9% (2006-2010 5-year est.).

Housing: Homeownership rate: 68.9% (2010); Median home value: $155,800 (2006-2010 5-year est.); Median contract rent: $684 per month (2006-2010 5-year est.); Median year structure built: 1962 (2006-2010 5-year est.).

Transportation: Commute to work: 90.3% car, 2.9% public transportation, 0.0% walk, 1.8% work from home (2006-2010 5-year est.); Travel time to work: 23.9% less than 15 minutes, 44.9% 15 to 30 minutes, 19.5% 30 to 45 minutes, 2.9% 45 to 60 minutes, 8.8% 60 minutes or more (2006-2010 5-year est.);

A

Aaronsburg CDP *Centre County*,237
Aaronsburg CDP *Washington County*,873
Abbott township *Potter County*,761
Abbottstown borough *Adams County*,1
Abington township *Lackawanna County*,514
Abington township *Montgomery County*,679
Ackermanville CDP *Northampton County*,713
Acme postal area *Westmoreland County*,911
Acosta postal area *Somerset County*,806
Adah postal area *Fayette County*,420
Adams County,1 - 13
Adams township *Butler County*,184
Adams township *Cambria County*,203
Adams township *Snyder County*,798
Adamsburg borough *Westmoreland County*,911
Adamstown borough *Lancaster County*,528
Adamsville CDP *Crawford County*,337
Addison borough *Somerset County*,806
Addison township *Somerset County*,806
Adrian postal area *Armstrong County*,59
Airville postal area *York County*,944
Akron borough *Lancaster County*,528
Alba borough *Bradford County*,146
Albany township *Berks County*,101
Albany township *Bradford County*,146
Albion borough *Erie County*,408
Albrightsville CDP *Carbon County*,229
Alburtis borough *Lehigh County*,579
Aldan borough *Delaware County*,383
Aleppo township *Allegheny County*,14
Aleppo township *Greene County*,458
Alexandria borough *Huntingdon County*,469
Alfarata CDP *Mifflin County*,659
Aliquippa city *Beaver County*,74
Allegany township *Potter County*,761
Allegheny County,14 - 58
Allegheny township *Blair County*,137
Allegheny township *Butler County*,184
Allegheny township *Cambria County*,204
Allegheny township *Somerset County*,806
Allegheny township *Venango County*,854
Allegheny township *Westmoreland County*,911
Alleghenyville CDP *Berks County*,102
Allen township *Northampton County*,713
Allenport borough *Washington County*,874
Allenport CDP *Huntingdon County*,469
Allensville CDP *Mifflin County*,659
Allentown city *Lehigh County*,580
Allenwood CDP *Union County*,848
Allison Park CDP *Allegheny County*,14
Allison CDP *Fayette County*,420
Allison township *Clinton County*,312
Allport CDP *Clearfield County*,294
Almedia CDP *Columbia County*,322
Alsace Manor CDP *Berks County*,102
Alsace township *Berks County*,102
Altamont CDP *Schuylkill County*,769
Altoona city *Blair County*,137
Alum Bank postal area *Bedford County*,89
Alverda postal area *Indiana County*,483
Alverton postal area *Westmoreland County*,911
Amberson postal area *Franklin County*,443

Ambler borough *Montgomery County*,679
Ambridge borough *Beaver County*,74
Amity Gardens CDP *Berks County*,103
Amity township *Berks County*,102
Amity township *Erie County*,408
Amwell township *Washington County*,874
Amwell township *Washington County*,874
Ancient Oaks CDP *Lehigh County*,580
Andreas postal area *Schuylkill County*,769
Anita postal area *Jefferson County*,497
Annin township *McKean County*,637
Annville CDP/twp *Lebanon County*,568
Anthony township *Lycoming County*,621
Anthony township *Montour County*,710
Antis township *Blair County*,137
Antrim township *Franklin County*,444
Apolacon township *Susquehanna County*,825
Apollo borough *Armstrong County*,59
Applewold borough *Armstrong County*,59
Ararat township *Susquehanna County*,826
Arcadia University CDP *Montgomery County*,680
Arcadia postal area *Indiana County*,483
Archbald borough *Lackawanna County*,514
Ardara postal area *Westmoreland County*,911
Ardmore CDP *Montgomery County*,680
Arendtsville borough *Adams County*,1
Aristes CDP *Columbia County*,322
Arlington Heights CDP *Monroe County*,669
Armagh borough *Indiana County*,483
Armagh township *Mifflin County*,659
Armbrust postal area *Westmoreland County*,911
Armenia township *Bradford County*,147
Armstrong County,59 - 72
Armstrong township *Indiana County*,483
Armstrong township *Lycoming County*,621
Arnold City CDP *Fayette County*,421
Arnold city *Westmoreland County*,911
Arnot CDP *Tioga County*,837
Arona borough *Westmoreland County*,912
Artemas postal area *Bedford County*,89
Ashfield postal area *Carbon County*,229
Ashland borough *Schuylkill County*,770
Ashland township *Clarion County*,283
Ashley borough *Luzerne County*,592
Ashville borough *Cambria County*,204
Aspers CDP *Adams County*,2
Aspinwall borough *Allegheny County*,15
Aston township *Delaware County*,383
Asylum township *Bradford County*,147
Atglen borough *Chester County*,256
Athens borough *Bradford County*,147
Athens township *Bradford County*,148
Athens township *Crawford County*,337
Atkinson Mills CDP *Mifflin County*,660
Atlantic CDP *Crawford County*,337
Atlas CDP *Northumberland County*,728
Atlasburg CDP *Washington County*,874
Atwood borough *Armstrong County*,60
Auburn borough *Schuylkill County*,770
Auburn township *Susquehanna County*,826
Audubon CDP *Montgomery County*,680
Aultman postal area *Indiana County*,484
Austin borough *Potter County*,761
Avalon borough *Allegheny County*,15
Avella CDP *Washington County*,874
Avis borough *Clinton County*,312

Avoca borough *Luzerne County*,592
Avon CDP *Lebanon County*,568
Avondale borough *Chester County*,256
Avonia CDP *Erie County*,408
Avonmore borough *Westmoreland County*,912
Ayr township *Fulton County*,453

B

Baden borough *Beaver County*,74
Baidland CDP *Washington County*,875
Baileyville CDP *Centre County*,237
Bainbridge CDP *Lancaster County*,529
Bairdford CDP *Allegheny County*,15
Bakerstown CDP *Allegheny County*,15
Bala Cynwyd postal area *Montgomery County*,681
Bald Eagle township *Clinton County*,312
Baldwin borough *Allegheny County*,16
Baldwin township *Allegheny County*,16
Bally borough *Berks County*,103
Bangor borough *Northampton County*,714
Banks township *Carbon County*,229
Banks township *Indiana County*,484
Barkeyville borough *Venango County*,854
Barnesville postal area *Schuylkill County*,770
Barnett township *Forest County*,440
Barnett township *Jefferson County*,497
Barr township *Cambria County*,204
Barree township *Huntingdon County*,470
Barrett township *Monroe County*,669
Barrville CDP *Mifflin County*,660
Barry township *Schuylkill County*,770
Bart township *Lancaster County*,529
Barto postal area *Berks County*,103
Bartonsville postal area *Monroe County*,669
Bastress township *Lycoming County*,622
Bath borough *Northampton County*,714
Baumstown CDP *Berks County*,103
Beach Lake postal area *Wayne County*,900
Beale township *Juniata County*,507
Beallsville borough *Washington County*,875
Bear Creek Village borough *Luzerne County*,593
Bear Creek township *Luzerne County*,592
Bear Lake borough *Warren County*,864
Bear Rocks CDP *Fayette County*,421
Beaver County,73 - 88
Beaver Falls city *Beaver County*,75
Beaver Meadows borough *Carbon County*,229
Beaver Springs CDP *Snyder County*,798
Beaver borough *Beaver County*,75
Beaver township *Clarion County*,283
Beaver township *Columbia County*,322
Beaver township *Crawford County*,337
Beaver township *Jefferson County*,498
Beaver township *Snyder County*,798
Beaverdale CDP *Cambria County*,204
Beavertown borough *Snyder County*,798
Beccaria township *Clearfield County*,294
Bechtelsville borough *Berks County*,104
Bedford County,89 - 100
Bedford borough *Bedford County*,89
Bedford township *Bedford County*,90
Bedminster township *Bucks County*,161

Beech Creek borough *Clinton County*,313
Beech Creek township *Clinton County*,313
Beech Mountain Lakes CDP *Luzerne County*,593
Belfast CDP *Northampton County*,714
Belfast township *Fulton County*,454
Bell Acres borough *Allegheny County*,16
Bell township *Clearfield County*,295
Bell township *Jefferson County*,498
Bell township *Westmoreland County*,912
Belle Vernon borough *Fayette County*,421
Bellefonte borough *Centre County*,238
Belleville CDP *Mifflin County*,660
Bellevue borough *Allegheny County*,17
Bellwood borough *Blair County*,138
Belmont CDP *Cambria County*,205
Belsano postal area *Cambria County*,205
Ben Avon Heights borough *Allegheny County*,17
Ben Avon borough *Allegheny County*,17
Bendersville borough *Adams County*,2
Benezett postal area *Elk County*,402
Benezette township *Elk County*,402
Benner township *Centre County*,238
Bensalem township *Bucks County*,161
Benson borough *Somerset County*,807
Bentleyville borough *Washington County*,875
Benton borough *Columbia County*,322
Benton township *Columbia County*,323
Benton township *Lackawanna County*,514
Berks County,101 - 135
Berlin borough *Somerset County*,807
Berlin township *Wayne County*,900
Bern township *Berks County*,104
Bernville borough *Berks County*,104
Berrysburg borough *Dauphin County*,367
Berwick borough *Columbia County*,323
Berwick township *Adams County*,2
Berwyn CDP *Chester County*,256
Bessemer borough *Lawrence County*,558
Bethany borough *Wayne County*,901
Bethel Park municipality *Allegheny County*,17
Bethel CDP *Berks County*,104
Bethel township *Armstrong County*,60
Bethel township *Berks County*,105
Bethel township *Delaware County*,384
Bethel township *Fulton County*,454
Bethel township *Lebanon County*,569
Bethlehem city *Northampton County*,715
Bethlehem township *Northampton County*,715
Beurys Lake CDP *Schuylkill County*,770
Beyer postal area *Indiana County*,484
Big Bass Lake CDP *Lackawanna County*,515
Big Beaver borough *Beaver County*,76
Big Cove Tannery postal area *Fulton County*,454
Big Run borough *Jefferson County*,498
Bigler CDP *Clearfield County*,295
Bigler township *Clearfield County*,295
Biglerville borough *Adams County*,2
Bingham township *Potter County*,761
Birchwood Lakes CDP *Pike County*,753
Bird-in-Hand CDP *Lancaster County*,529
Birdsboro borough *Berks County*,105
Birmingham borough *Huntingdon County*,470
Birmingham township *Chester County*,257

Black Creek township *Luzerne County*,593
Black Lick CDP *Indiana County*,484
Black Lick township *Indiana County*,484
Black township *Somerset County*,807
Blacklick township *Cambria County*,205
Blain borough *Perry County*,742
Blaine township *Washington County*,875
Blair County,136 - 145
Blair township *Blair County*,138
Blairs Mills postal area *Huntingdon County*,470
Blairsville borough *Indiana County*,484
Blakely borough *Lackawanna County*,515
Blakeslee postal area *Monroe County*,669
Blanchard CDP *Centre County*,238
Blandburg CDP *Cambria County*,205
Blandon CDP *Berks County*,105
Blawnox borough *Allegheny County*,18
Bloom township *Clearfield County*,295
Bloomfield borough *Perry County*,742
Bloomfield township *Bedford County*,90
Bloomfield township *Crawford County*,338
Blooming Grove township *Pike County*,753
Blooming Valley borough *Crawford County*,338
Bloomsburg town *Columbia County*,323
Bloss township *Tioga County*,837
Blossburg borough *Tioga County*,837
Blue Ball CDP *Lancaster County*,529
Blue Bell CDP *Montgomery County*,681
Blue Ridge Summit CDP *Franklin County*,444
Blythe township *Schuylkill County*,771
Boalsburg CDP *Centre County*,239
Bobtown CDP *Greene County*,458
Boggs township *Armstrong County*,60
Boggs township *Centre County*,239
Boggs township *Clearfield County*,296
Boiling Springs CDP *Cumberland County*,354
Bolivar borough *Westmoreland County*,912
Bonneauville borough *Adams County*,3
Boothwyn CDP *Delaware County*,384
Boston CDP *Allegheny County*,18
Boswell borough *Somerset County*,807
Bowers CDP *Berks County*,106
Bowmanstown borough *Carbon County*,230
Bowmansville CDP *Lancaster County*,530
Boyers postal area *Butler County*,184
Boyertown borough *Berks County*,106
Boynton postal area *Somerset County*,808
Brackenridge borough *Allegheny County*,18
Brackney postal area *Susquehanna County*,826
Braddock Hills borough *Allegheny County*,19
Braddock borough *Allegheny County*,19
Bradenville CDP *Westmoreland County*,913
Bradford County,146 - 160
Bradford Woods borough *Allegheny County*,19
Bradford city *McKean County*,637
Bradford township *Clearfield County*,296
Bradford township *McKean County*,638
Bradfordwoods postal area *Allegheny County*,19
Brady township *Butler County*,185
Brady township *Clarion County*,284

Brady township *Clearfield County*,296
Brady township *Huntingdon County*,470
Brady township *Lycoming County*,622
Bradys Bend township *Armstrong County*,60
Braintrim township *Wyoming County*,937
Branch township *Schuylkill County*,771
Branchdale CDP *Schuylkill County*,771
Brandamore postal area *Chester County*,257
Brandonville CDP *Schuylkill County*,771
Bratton township *Mifflin County*,660
Brave CDP *Greene County*,458
Brecknock township *Berks County*,106
Brecknock township *Lancaster County*,530
Breezewood postal area *Bedford County*,90
Breinigsville CDP *Lehigh County*,581
Brentwood borough *Allegheny County*,19
Bressler CDP *Dauphin County*,367
Briar Creek borough *Columbia County*,324
Briar Creek township *Columbia County*,324
Brickerville CDP *Lancaster County*,530
Bridgeport borough *Montgomery County*,681
Bridgeton township *Bucks County*,162
Bridgeville borough *Allegheny County*,20
Bridgewater borough *Beaver County*,76
Bridgewater township *Susquehanna County*,826
Brighton township *Beaver County*,76
Brisbin borough *Clearfield County*,296
Bristol borough *Bucks County*,162
Bristol township *Bucks County*,163
Brittany Farms-The Highlands CDP *Bucks County*,163
Broad Top City borough *Huntingdon County*,470
Broad Top township *Bedford County*,90
Brockport postal area *Elk County*,402
Brockton postal area *Schuylkill County*,772
Brockway borough *Jefferson County*,498
Brodheadsville CDP *Monroe County*,669
Brogue postal area *York County*,944
Brokenstraw township *Warren County*,865
Brookfield township *Tioga County*,837
Brookhaven borough *Delaware County*,384
Brooklyn township *Susquehanna County*,826
Brookville borough *Jefferson County*,499
Broomall CDP *Delaware County*,385
Brothersvalley township *Somerset County*,808
Brown township *Lycoming County*,622
Brown township *Mifflin County*,661
Brownstown borough *Cambria County*,206
Brownstown CDP *Lancaster County*,530
Brownsville borough *Fayette County*,421
Brownsville township *Fayette County*,422
Browntown CDP *Luzerne County*,593
Bruin borough *Butler County*,185
Brush Creek township *Fulton County*,454
Brush Valley township *Indiana County*,485
Bryn Athyn borough *Montgomery County*,681
Bryn Mawr CDP *Montgomery County*,682
Buck Hill Falls postal area *Monroe County*,670
Buck Run CDP *Schuylkill County*,772
Buck township *Luzerne County*,594
Buckhorn CDP *Columbia County*,324
Buckingham township *Bucks County*,163
Buckingham township *Wayne County*,901

CDP = Census Designated Place

CDP = Census Designated Place

CDP = Census Designated Place

CDP = Census Designated Place

CDP = Census Designated Place

CDP = Census Designated Place

CDP = Census Designated Place

CDP = Census Designated Place

CDP = Census Designated Place

Marienville CDP *Forest County*,442
Marietta borough *Lancaster County*,545
Marion Center borough *Indiana County*,492
Marion Heights borough *Northumberland County*,733
Marion CDP *Franklin County*,447
Marion township *Beaver County*,83
Marion township *Berks County*,118
Marion township *Butler County*,194
Marion township *Centre County*,245
Marklesburg borough *Huntingdon County*,475
Markleton postal area *Somerset County*,814
Markleysburg borough *Fayette County*,430
Marlborough township *Montgomery County*,694
Marlin CDP *Schuylkill County*,782
Marple township *Delaware County*,393
Mars borough *Butler County*,195
Marshall township *Allegheny County*,37
Marshalls Creek postal area *Monroe County*,673
Marshallton CDP *Northumberland County*,733
Marsteller postal area *Cambria County*,216
Martic township *Lancaster County*,545
Martin postal area *Fayette County*,430
Martins Creek CDP *Northampton County*,720
Martinsburg borough *Blair County*,142
Mary D postal area *Schuylkill County*,782
Marysville borough *Perry County*,745
Masontown borough *Fayette County*,430
Masthope CDP *Pike County*,756
Matamoras borough *Pike County*,757
Mather CDP *Greene County*,464
Mattawana CDP *Mifflin County*,665
Maxatawny township *Berks County*,119
Mayberry township *Montour County*,712
Mayfield borough *Lackawanna County*,521
Mayport postal area *Clarion County*,289
Maytown CDP *Lancaster County*,546
McAdoo borough *Schuylkill County*,782
McAlisterville CDP *Juniata County*,510
McCalmont township *Jefferson County*,501
McCandless township *Allegheny County*,37
McClellandtown postal area *Fayette County*,431
McClure borough *Snyder County*,801
McConnellsburg borough *Fulton County*,455
McConnellstown CDP *Huntingdon County*,476
McDonald borough *Washington County*,888
McElhattan CDP *Clinton County*,318
McEwensville borough *Northumberland County*,733
McGovern CDP *Washington County*,888
McGrann postal area *Armstrong County*,66
McHenry township *Lycoming County*,628
McIntyre township *Lycoming County*,628
McKean County,636 - 643
McKean borough *Erie County*,414
McKean township *Erie County*,414
McKeansburg CDP *Schuylkill County*,782
McKees Rocks borough *Allegheny County*,37
McKeesport city *Allegheny County*,37
McKnightstown CDP *Adams County*,10
McMurray CDP *Washington County*,888
McNett township *Lycoming County*,629

McSherrystown borough *Adams County*,10
McVeytown borough *Mifflin County*,665
Mead township *Warren County*,868
Meadowlands CDP *Washington County*,889
Meadowood CDP *Butler County*,195
Meadville city *Crawford County*,344
Mechanicsburg borough *Cumberland County*,359
Mechanicsville borough *Schuylkill County*,782
Media borough *Delaware County*,393
Mehoopany township *Wyoming County*,939
Melcroft postal area *Fayette County*,431
Menallen township *Adams County*,10
Menallen township *Fayette County*,431
Menno township *Mifflin County*,665
Mentcle postal area *Indiana County*,493
Mercer County,644 - 658
Mercer borough *Mercer County*,651
Mercer township *Butler County*,195
Mercersburg borough *Franklin County*,448
Meridian CDP *Butler County*,195
Merion Station postal area *Montgomery County*,694
Merrittstown postal area *Fayette County*,431
Mertztown CDP *Berks County*,119
Meshoppen borough *Wyoming County*,940
Meshoppen township *Wyoming County*,940
Messiah College CDP *Cumberland County*,359
Metal township *Franklin County*,448
Mexico CDP *Juniata County*,510
Meyersdale borough *Somerset County*,814
Middle Paxton township *Dauphin County*,375
Middle Smithfield township *Monroe County*,673
Middle Taylor township *Cambria County*,216
Middleburg borough *Snyder County*,801
Middlebury Center postal area *Tioga County*,843
Middlebury township *Tioga County*,843
Middlecreek township *Snyder County*,801
Middlecreek township *Somerset County*,814
Middleport borough *Schuylkill County*,783
Middlesex township *Butler County*,196
Middlesex township *Cumberland County*,359
Middletown borough *Dauphin County*,375
Middletown CDP *Northampton County*,721
Middletown township *Bucks County*,171
Middletown township *Delaware County*,393
Middletown township *Susquehanna County*,833
Midland borough *Beaver County*,83
Midway borough *Washington County*,889
Midway CDP *Adams County*,11
Mifflin County,659 - 667
Mifflin borough *Juniata County*,510
Mifflin township *Columbia County*,331
Mifflin township *Dauphin County*,375
Mifflin township *Lycoming County*,629
Mifflinburg borough *Union County*,851
Mifflintown borough *Juniata County*,510
Mifflinville CDP *Columbia County*,331
Milan postal area *Bradford County*,151
Milanville postal area *Wayne County*,905
Mildred postal area *Sullivan County*,824
Miles township *Centre County*,245

Milesburg borough *Centre County*,245
Milford Square CDP *Bucks County*,171
Milford borough *Pike County*,757
Milford township *Bucks County*,171
Milford township *Juniata County*,511
Milford township *Pike County*,757
Milford township *Somerset County*,815
Mill Creek borough *Huntingdon County*,476
Mill Creek township *Lycoming County*,629
Mill Creek township *Mercer County*,652
Mill Hall borough *Clinton County*,318
Mill Run postal area *Fayette County*,431
Mill Village borough *Erie County*,415
Millbourne borough *Delaware County*,394
Millcreek township *Clarion County*,289
Millcreek township *Erie County*,415
Millcreek township *Lebanon County*,573
Miller township *Huntingdon County*,476
Miller township *Perry County*,745
Millersburg borough *Dauphin County*,376
Millerstown borough *Perry County*,746
Millersville borough *Lancaster County*,546
Millerton CDP *Tioga County*,843
Millheim borough *Centre County*,246
Millmont postal area *Union County*,851
Millrift postal area *Pike County*,757
Mills postal area *Potter County*,764
Millsboro CDP *Washington County*,889
Millstone township *Elk County*,405
Millvale borough *Allegheny County*,38
Millville borough *Columbia County*,331
Millwood CDP *Westmoreland County*,924
Milnesville postal area *Luzerne County*,608
Milroy CDP *Mifflin County*,665
Milton borough *Northumberland County*,733
Mineral Point postal area *Cambria County*,216
Mineral Springs postal area *Clearfield County*,306
Mineral township *Venango County*,859
Minersville borough *Schuylkill County*,783
Mingoville CDP *Centre County*,246
Mocanaqua CDP *Luzerne County*,608
Modena borough *Chester County*,269
Mohnton borough *Berks County*,119
Mohrsville CDP *Berks County*,119
Monaca borough *Beaver County*,83
Monaghan township *York County*,955
Monessen city *Westmoreland County*,924
Monocacy Station postal area *Berks County*,120
Monongahela city *Washington County*,889
Monongahela township *Greene County*,464
Monroe County,668 - 677
Monroe borough *Bradford County*,151
Monroe township *Bedford County*,96
Monroe township *Bradford County*,151
Monroe township *Clarion County*,289
Monroe township *Cumberland County*,360
Monroe township *Juniata County*,511
Monroe township *Snyder County*,801
Monroe township *Wyoming County*,940
Monroeton postal area *Bradford County*,152
Monroeville municipality *Allegheny County*,38
Mont Alto borough *Franklin County*,448
Mont Clare postal area *Montgomery County*,694

Montandon CDP *Northumberland County*,734
Montgomery County,678 - 708
Montgomery borough *Lycoming County*,629
Montgomery township *Franklin County*,449
Montgomery township *Indiana County*,493
Montgomery township *Montgomery County*,694
Montgomeryville CDP *Montgomery County*,694
Montour County,709 - 712
Montour township *Columbia County*,331
Montoursville borough *Lycoming County*,630
Montrose Manor CDP *Berks County*,120
Montrose borough *Susquehanna County*,833
Monument CDP *Centre County*,246
Moon township *Allegheny County*,39
Moore township *Northampton County*,721
Moosic borough *Lackawanna County*,521
Moreland township *Lycoming County*,630
Morgan township *Greene County*,464
Morgantown CDP *Berks County*,120
Morris Run postal area *Tioga County*,843
Morris township *Clearfield County*,306
Morris township *Greene County*,464
Morris township *Huntingdon County*,476
Morris township *Tioga County*,843
Morris township *Washington County*,890
Morrisdale CDP *Clearfield County*,306
Morrisville borough *Bucks County*,171
Morrisville CDP *Greene County*,465
Morton borough *Delaware County*,394
Moscow borough *Lackawanna County*,522
Moshannon CDP *Centre County*,246
Mount Aetna CDP *Berks County*,120
Mount Bethel postal area *Northampton County*,721
Mount Carbon borough *Schuylkill County*,783
Mount Carmel borough *Northumberland County*,734
Mount Carmel township *Northumberland County*,734
Mount Cobb CDP *Lackawanna County*,522
Mount Eagle CDP *Centre County*,246
Mount Gretna Heights CDP *Lebanon County*,573
Mount Gretna borough *Lebanon County*,573
Mount Holly Springs borough *Cumberland County*,360
Mount Jewett borough *McKean County*,642
Mount Joy borough *Lancaster County*,546
Mount Joy township *Adams County*,11
Mount Joy township *Lancaster County*,547
Mount Lebanon township *Allegheny County*,39
Mount Morris CDP *Greene County*,465
Mount Oliver borough *Allegheny County*,39
Mount Penn borough *Berks County*,120
Mount Pleasant Mills CDP *Snyder County*,802
Mount Pleasant borough *Westmoreland County*,924
Mount Pleasant township *Adams County*,11
Mount Pleasant township *Columbia County*,332
Mount Pleasant township *Washington County*,890
Mount Pleasant township *Wayne County*,905

Mount Pleasant township *Westmoreland County*,925
Mount Pocono borough *Monroe County*,673
Mount Union borough *Huntingdon County*,477
Mount Wolf borough *York County*,955
Mountain Top CDP *Luzerne County*,608
Mountainhome CDP *Monroe County*,673
Mountville borough *Lancaster County*,547
Muddy Creek township *Butler County*,196
Muhlenberg Park CDP *Berks County*,121
Muhlenberg township *Berks County*,121
Muir CDP *Schuylkill County*,783
Muncy Creek township *Lycoming County*,631
Muncy Valley postal area *Sullivan County*,825
Muncy borough *Lycoming County*,630
Muncy township *Lycoming County*,630
Mundys Corner CDP *Cambria County*,216
Munhall borough *Allegheny County*,40
Munson postal area *Clearfield County*,306
Munster township *Cambria County*,217
Murrysville municipality *Westmoreland County*,925
Muse CDP *Washington County*,890
Myerstown borough *Lebanon County*,574

N

Nanticoke city *Luzerne County*,608
Nanty-Glo borough *Cambria County*,217
Naomi CDP *Fayette County*,431
Napier township *Bedford County*,96
Narberth borough *Montgomery County*,695
Narvon postal area *Lancaster County*,548
Natrona Heights postal area *Allegheny County*,40
Nazareth borough *Northampton County*,721
Needmore CDP *Fulton County*,456
Neelyton postal area *Huntingdon County*,477
Nelson township *Tioga County*,843
Nemacolin CDP *Greene County*,465
Nescopeck borough *Luzerne County*,609
Nescopeck township *Luzerne County*,609
Neshannock township *Lawrence County*,561
Nesquehoning borough *Carbon County*,233
Nether Providence township *Delaware County*,394
Neville township *Allegheny County*,40
New Albany borough *Bradford County*,152
New Alexandria borough *Westmoreland County*,925
New Baltimore borough *Somerset County*,815
New Beaver borough *Lawrence County*,561
New Bedford CDP *Lawrence County*,561
New Berlin borough *Union County*,852
New Berlinville CDP *Berks County*,121
New Bethlehem borough *Clarion County*,289
New Bloomfield postal area *Perry County*,746
New Brighton borough *Beaver County*,84
New Britain borough *Bucks County*,172
New Britain township *Bucks County*,172
New Buffalo borough *Perry County*,746
New Castle Northwest CDP *Lawrence County*,562
New Castle city *Lawrence County*,562
New Castle township *Schuylkill County*,784

New Centerville borough *Somerset County*,815
New Columbia CDP *Union County*,852
New Columbus borough *Luzerne County*,609
New Cumberland borough *Cumberland County*,360
New Derry postal area *Westmoreland County*,926
New Eagle borough *Washington County*,890
New Enterprise postal area *Bedford County*,97
New Florence borough *Westmoreland County*,926
New Freedom borough *York County*,956
New Freeport CDP *Greene County*,465
New Galilee borough *Beaver County*,84
New Garden township *Chester County*,269
New Geneva postal area *Fayette County*,432
New Germantown postal area *Perry County*,746
New Hanover township *Montgomery County*,695
New Holland borough *Lancaster County*,548
New Hope borough *Bucks County*,172
New Jerusalem CDP *Berks County*,121
New Kensington city *Westmoreland County*,926
New Kingstown CDP *Cumberland County*,360
New Lebanon borough *Mercer County*,652
New London township *Chester County*,269
New Market CDP *York County*,956
New Milford borough *Susquehanna County*,833
New Milford township *Susquehanna County*,833
New Millport postal area *Clearfield County*,306
New Morgan borough *Berks County*,122
New Oxford borough *Adams County*,11
New Paris borough *Bedford County*,97
New Park postal area *York County*,956
New Philadelphia borough *Schuylkill County*,784
New Providence postal area *Lancaster County*,548
New Ringgold borough *Schuylkill County*,784
New Salem borough *York County*,956
New Salem CDP *Fayette County*,432
New Schaefferstown CDP *Berks County*,122
New Sewickley township *Beaver County*,84
New Stanton borough *Westmoreland County*,926
New Tripoli CDP *Lehigh County*,587
New Vernon township *Mercer County*,652
New Washington borough *Clearfield County*,306
New Wilmington borough *Lawrence County*,562
Newberry township *York County*,956
Newburg borough *Clearfield County*,307
Newburg borough *Cumberland County*,361
Newell borough *Fayette County*,432
Newfoundland postal area *Wayne County*,905
Newlin township *Chester County*,270
Newmanstown CDP *Lebanon County*,574
Newport borough *Perry County*,746
Newport township *Luzerne County*,609

CDP = Census Designated Place

Newry borough *Blair County*,143
Newton Hamilton borough *Mifflin County*,666
Newton township *Lackawanna County*,522
Newtown Grant CDP *Bucks County*,173
Newtown Square postal area *Delaware County*,395
Newtown borough *Bucks County*,173
Newtown CDP *Schuylkill County*,784
Newtown township *Bucks County*,173
Newtown township *Delaware County*,395
Newville borough *Cumberland County*,361
Nicholson borough *Wyoming County*,940
Nicholson township *Fayette County*,432
Nicholson township *Wyoming County*,941
Nicktown postal area *Cambria County*,217
Nineveh postal area *Greene County*,465
Nippenose township *Lycoming County*,631
Nittany CDP *Centre County*,247
Nixon CDP *Butler County*,196
Noblestown CDP *Allegheny County*,40
Nockamixon township *Bucks County*,174
Normalville postal area *Fayette County*,432
Norristown borough *Montgomery County*,695
North Abington township *Lackawanna County*,523
North Annville township *Lebanon County*,574
North Apollo borough *Armstrong County*,67
North Beaver township *Lawrence County*,563
North Belle Vernon borough *Westmoreland County*,927
North Bend postal area *Clinton County*,318
North Bethlehem township *Washington County*,891
North Braddock borough *Allegheny County*,41
North Branch township *Wyoming County*,941
North Buffalo township *Armstrong County*,67
North Catasauqua borough *Northampton County*,722
North Centre township *Columbia County*,332
North Charleroi borough *Washington County*,891
North Codorus township *York County*,957
North Cornwall township *Lebanon County*,574
North Coventry township *Chester County*,270
North East borough *Erie County*,415
North East township *Erie County*,416
North Fayette township *Allegheny County*,41
North Franklin township *Washington County*,891
North Heidelberg township *Berks County*,122
North Hopewell township *York County*,957
North Huntingdon township *Westmoreland County*,927
North Irwin borough *Westmoreland County*,927
North Lebanon township *Lebanon County*,575
North Londonderry township *Lebanon County*,575
North Mahoning township *Indiana County*,493
North Manheim township *Schuylkill County*,785
North Middleton township *Cumberland County*,361

North Newton township *Cumberland County*,362
North Philipsburg CDP *Centre County*,247
North Sewickley township *Beaver County*,85
North Shenango township *Crawford County*,345
North Strabane township *Washington County*,892
North Towanda township *Bradford County*,152
North Union township *Fayette County*,432
North Union township *Schuylkill County*,785
North Vandergrift CDP *Armstrong County*,67
North Versailles township *Allegheny County*,41
North Wales borough *Montgomery County*,696
North Warren CDP *Warren County*,868
North Washington postal area *Butler County*,196
North Whitehall township *Lehigh County*,587
North Woodbury township *Blair County*,143
North York borough *York County*,957
Northampton County,713 - 726
Northampton borough *Northampton County*,722
Northampton township *Bucks County*,174
Northampton township *Somerset County*,815
Northeast Madison township *Perry County*,747
Northern Cambria borough *Cambria County*,217
Northmoreland township *Wyoming County*,941
Northumberland County,727 - 740
Northumberland borough *Northumberland County*,735
Northwest Harborcreek CDP *Erie County*,416
Northwood CDP *Blair County*,143
Norvelt CDP *Westmoreland County*,928
Norwegian township *Schuylkill County*,785
Norwich township *McKean County*,642
Norwood borough *Delaware County*,395
Nottingham township *Washington County*,892
Noxen CDP *Wyoming County*,941
Noxen township *Wyoming County*,942
Noyes township *Clinton County*,319
Nu Mine postal area *Armstrong County*,67
Nuangola borough *Luzerne County*,610
Numidia CDP *Columbia County*,332
Nuremberg CDP *Schuylkill County*,786

O

O'Hara township *Allegheny County*,42
Oak Hills CDP *Butler County*,197
Oak Ridge postal area *Armstrong County*,67
Oakdale borough *Allegheny County*,42
Oakland Mills postal area *Juniata County*,511
Oakland borough *Susquehanna County*,834
Oakland CDP *Cambria County*,218
Oakland CDP *Lawrence County*,563
Oakland township *Butler County*,197
Oakland township *Susquehanna County*,834
Oakland township *Venango County*,859
Oakmont borough *Allegheny County*,42

Oaks postal area *Montgomery County*,696
Oakwood CDP *Lawrence County*,563
Oberlin CDP *Dauphin County*,376
Ogle township *Somerset County*,816
Ohio township *Allegheny County*,43
Ohiopyle borough *Fayette County*,433
Ohioville borough *Beaver County*,85
Oil City city *Venango County*,859
Oil Creek township *Crawford County*,345
Oil Creek township *Venango County*,859
Oklahoma borough *Westmoreland County*,928
Oklahoma CDP *Clearfield County*,307
Olanta postal area *Clearfield County*,307
Old Forge borough *Lackawanna County*,523
Old Lycoming township *Lycoming County*,631
Old Orchard CDP *Northampton County*,722
Old Zionsville postal area *Lehigh County*,587
Oley CDP *Berks County*,122
Oley township *Berks County*,123
Oliveburg postal area *Jefferson County*,502
Oliver CDP *Fayette County*,433
Oliver township *Jefferson County*,502
Oliver township *Mifflin County*,666
Oliver township *Perry County*,747
Olyphant borough *Lackawanna County*,523
Oneida CDP *Schuylkill County*,786
Oneida township *Huntingdon County*,477
Ono postal area *Lebanon County*,575
Ontelaunee township *Berks County*,123
Orange township *Columbia County*,332
Orangeville borough *Columbia County*,333
Orbisonia borough *Huntingdon County*,477
Orchard Hills CDP *Armstrong County*,67
Orefield postal area *Lehigh County*,587
Oregon township *Wayne County*,905
Oreland CDP *Montgomery County*,696
Orrstown borough *Franklin County*,449
Orrtanna CDP *Adams County*,12
Orviston CDP *Centre County*,247
Orwell township *Bradford County*,152
Orwigsburg borough *Schuylkill County*,786
Orwin CDP *Schuylkill County*,786
Osceola Mills borough *Clearfield County*,307
Osceola township *Tioga County*,844
Osterburg postal area *Bedford County*,97
Oswayo borough *Potter County*,764
Oswayo township *Potter County*,765
Otter Creek township *Mercer County*,652
Otto township *McKean County*,643
Ottsville postal area *Bucks County*,174
Oval CDP *Lycoming County*,632
Overfield township *Wyoming County*,942
Overton township *Bradford County*,153
Oxford borough *Chester County*,270
Oxford township *Adams County*,12

P

Packer township *Carbon County*,234
Paint borough *Somerset County*,816
Paint township *Clarion County*,290
Paint township *Somerset County*,816
Palm postal area *Montgomery County*,696
Palmdale CDP *Dauphin County*,376

CDP = Census Designated Place

Palmer Heights CDP *Northampton County*,723

Palmer township *Northampton County*,722

Palmerton borough *Carbon County*,234

Palmyra borough *Lebanon County*,575

Palmyra township *Pike County*,757

Palmyra township *Wayne County*,906

Palo Alto borough *Schuylkill County*,787

Paoli CDP *Chester County*,271

Paradise CDP *Lancaster County*,548

Paradise township *Lancaster County*,548

Paradise township *Monroe County*,674

Paradise township *York County*,958

Pardeesville CDP *Luzerne County*,610

Paris CDP *Washington County*,892

Park Crest CDP *Schuylkill County*,787

Park Forest Village CDP *Centre County*,247

Parker Ford postal area *Chester County*,271

Parker city *Armstrong County*,68

Parker township *Butler County*,197

Parkesburg borough *Chester County*,271

Parkhill postal area *Cambria County*,218

Parks township *Armstrong County*,68

Parkside borough *Delaware County*,395

Parkville CDP *York County*,958

Parryville borough *Carbon County*,234

Patterson Heights borough *Beaver County*,86

Patterson township *Beaver County*,85

Patton borough *Cambria County*,218

Patton township *Centre County*,248

Paupack township *Wayne County*,906

Pavia township *Bedford County*,97

Paxinos postal area *Northumberland County*,735

Paxtang borough *Dauphin County*,376

Paxtonia CDP *Dauphin County*,377

Paxtonville CDP *Snyder County*,802

Peach Bottom township *York County*,958

Peckville postal area *Lackawanna County*,523

Pen Argyl borough *Northampton County*,723

Pen Mar CDP *Franklin County*,449

Penbrook borough *Dauphin County*,377

Penfield postal area *Clearfield County*,307

Penn Estates CDP *Monroe County*,674

Penn Forest township *Carbon County*,235

Penn Hills township *Allegheny County*,43

Penn Lake Park borough *Luzerne County*,610

Penn Run postal area *Indiana County*,493

Penn State Erie Behrend) CDP *Erie County*,416

Penn Wynne CDP *Montgomery County*,696

Penn borough *Westmoreland County*,928

Penn township *Berks County*,123

Penn township *Butler County*,197

Penn township *Centre County*,248

Penn township *Chester County*,271

Penn township *Clearfield County*,308

Penn township *Cumberland County*,362

Penn township *Huntingdon County*,477

Penn township *Lancaster County*,549

Penn township *Lycoming County*,632

Penn township *Perry County*,747

Penn township *Snyder County*,802

Penn township *Westmoreland County*,928

Penn township *York County*,958

Penndel borough *Bucks County*,174

Penns Creek CDP *Snyder County*,802

Pennsburg borough *Montgomery County*,697

Pennsbury Village borough *Allegheny County*,43

Pennsbury township *Chester County*,272

Pennside CDP *Berks County*,124

Pennsylvania Furnace postal area *Centre County*,248

Pennville CDP *York County*,959

Pennwyn CDP *Berks County*,124

Penryn CDP *Lancaster County*,549

Pequea township *Lancaster County*,549

Perkasie borough *Bucks County*,175

Perkiomen township *Montgomery County*,697

Perkiomenville postal area *Montgomery County*,697

Perry County,741 - 749

Perry township *Armstrong County*,68

Perry township *Berks County*,124

Perry township *Clarion County*,290

Perry township *Fayette County*,433

Perry township *Greene County*,466

Perry township *Jefferson County*,502

Perry township *Lawrence County*,563

Perry township *Mercer County*,653

Perry township *Snyder County*,803

Perryopolis borough *Fayette County*,433

Peters township *Franklin County*,449

Peters township *Washington County*,892

Petersburg borough *Huntingdon County*,478

Petrolia borough *Butler County*,198

Philadelphia County,750 - 752

Philipsburg borough *Centre County*,248

Phoenixville borough *Chester County*,272

Piatt township *Lycoming County*,632

Picture Rocks borough *Lycoming County*,632

Pike County,753 - 759

Pike township *Berks County*,124

Pike township *Bradford County*,153

Pike township *Clearfield County*,308

Pike township *Potter County*,765

Pikes Creek CDP *Luzerne County*,610

Pillow borough *Dauphin County*,377

Pine Creek township *Clinton County*,319

Pine Creek township *Jefferson County*,502

Pine Glen CDP *Centre County*,249

Pine Grove Mills CDP *Centre County*,249

Pine Grove borough *Schuylkill County*,787

Pine Grove township *Schuylkill County*,787

Pine Grove township *Warren County*,869

Pine Ridge CDP *Pike County*,758

Pine township *Allegheny County*,43

Pine township *Armstrong County*,68

Pine township *Clearfield County*,308

Pine township *Columbia County*,333

Pine township *Crawford County*,345

Pine township *Indiana County*,493

Pine township *Lycoming County*,633

Pine township *Mercer County*,653

Pinegrove township *Venango County*,860

Piney township *Clarion County*,290

Pipersville postal area *Bucks County*,175

Pitcairn borough *Allegheny County*,44

Pitman postal area *Schuylkill County*,788

Pittsburgh city *Allegheny County*,44

Pittsfield township *Warren County*,869

Pittston city *Luzerne County*,611

Pittston township *Luzerne County*,611

Plain Grove township *Lawrence County*,564

Plainfield CDP *Cumberland County*,362

Plainfield township *Northampton County*,723

Plains CDP *Luzerne County*,611

Plains township *Luzerne County*,611

Platea borough *Erie County*,416

Pleasant Gap CDP *Centre County*,249

Pleasant Hall postal area *Franklin County*,450

Pleasant Hill CDP *Lebanon County*,576

Pleasant Hills borough *Allegheny County*,46

Pleasant Mount postal area *Wayne County*,906

Pleasant Unity postal area *Westmoreland County*,929

Pleasant Valley township *Potter County*,765

Pleasant View CDP *Armstrong County*,69

Pleasant township *Warren County*,869

Pleasantville borough *Bedford County*,97

Pleasantville borough *Venango County*,860

Plum borough *Allegheny County*,46

Plum township *Venango County*,860

Plumcreek township *Armstrong County*,69

Plumstead township *Bucks County*,175

Plumsteadville CDP *Bucks County*,175

Plumville borough *Indiana County*,494

Plunketts Creek township *Lycoming County*,633

Plymouth Meeting CDP *Montgomery County*,698

Plymouth borough *Luzerne County*,612

Plymouth township *Luzerne County*,612

Plymouth township *Montgomery County*,697

Plymptonville CDP *Clearfield County*,308

Pocono Lake postal area *Monroe County*,674

Pocono Manor postal area *Monroe County*,675

Pocono Mountain Lake Estates CDP *Pike County*,758

Pocono Pines CDP *Monroe County*,675

Pocono Ranch Lands CDP *Pike County*,758

Pocono Springs CDP *Wayne County*,906

Pocono Summit postal area *Monroe County*,675

Pocono Woodland Lakes CDP *Pike County*,758

Pocono township *Monroe County*,674

Pocopson township *Chester County*,272

Point Marion borough *Fayette County*,434

Point Pleasant postal area *Bucks County*,176

Point township *Northumberland County*,735

Polk borough *Venango County*,860

Polk township *Jefferson County*,503

Polk township *Monroe County*,675

Pomeroy CDP *Chester County*,273

Port Allegany borough *McKean County*,643

Port Carbon borough *Schuylkill County*,788

Port Clinton borough *Schuylkill County*,788

Port Matilda borough *Centre County*,249

Port Royal borough *Juniata County*,511

Port Trevorton CDP *Snyder County*,803

Port Vue borough *Allegheny County*,46

Portage borough *Cambria County*,218

Portage township *Cambria County*,218

Portage township *Cameron County*,228

Portage township *Potter County*,765

CDP = Census Designated Place

Porter township *Clarion County*,290
Porter township *Clinton County*,319
Porter township *Huntingdon County*,478
Porter township *Jefferson County*,503
Porter township *Lycoming County*,633
Porter township *Pike County*,759
Porter township *Schuylkill County*,788
Portersville borough *Butler County*,198
Portland borough *Northampton County*,724
Potlicker Flats CDP *Mifflin County*,666
Potter County,760 - 768
Potter township *Beaver County*,86
Potter township *Centre County*,250
Pottersdale postal area *Clearfield County*,309
Potts Grove postal area *Northumberland County*,735
Pottsgrove CDP *Montgomery County*,698
Pottstown borough *Montgomery County*,698
Pottsville city *Schuylkill County*,788
Poyntelle postal area *Wayne County*,907
President township *Venango County*,861
Presto postal area *Allegheny County*,47
Preston Park postal area *Wayne County*,907
Preston township *Wayne County*,907
Price township *Monroe County*,675
Pricedale postal area *Westmoreland County*,929
Pringle borough *Luzerne County*,612
Progress CDP *Dauphin County*,377
Prompton borough *Wayne County*,907
Prospect Park borough *Delaware County*,396
Prospect Park CDP *Cameron County*,228
Prospect borough *Butler County*,198
Prosperity postal area *Washington County*,893
Providence township *Lancaster County*,549
Pulaski township *Beaver County*,86
Pulaski township *Lawrence County*,564
Punxsutawney borough *Jefferson County*,503
Putnam township *Tioga County*,844
Pymatuning Central CDP *Crawford County*,346
Pymatuning North CDP *Crawford County*,346
Pymatuning South CDP *Crawford County*,346
Pymatuning township *Mercer County*,653

Q

Quakake postal area *Schuylkill County*,789
Quakertown borough *Bucks County*,176
Quarryville borough *Lancaster County*,550
Quecreek postal area *Somerset County*,816
Queen postal area *Bedford County*,97
Queens Gate CDP *York County*,959
Quemahoning township *Somerset County*,817
Quentin CDP *Lebanon County*,576
Quincy township *Franklin County*,450

R

Raccoon township *Beaver County*,86
Radnor township *Delaware County*,396
Railroad borough *York County*,959
Rainsburg borough *Bedford County*,98

Ralpho township *Northumberland County*,735
Ralston postal area *Lycoming County*,633
Ramblewood CDP *Centre County*,250
Ramey borough *Clearfield County*,309
Randolph township *Crawford County*,346
Rankin borough *Allegheny County*,47
Ranshaw CDP *Northumberland County*,736
Ransom township *Lackawanna County*,523
Rapho township *Lancaster County*,550
Raubsville CDP *Northampton County*,724
Rauchtown CDP *Clinton County*,319
Ravine CDP *Schuylkill County*,789
Rayburn township *Armstrong County*,69
Rayne township *Indiana County*,494
Reade township *Cambria County*,219
Reading city *Berks County*,125
Reading township *Adams County*,12
Reamstown CDP *Lancaster County*,550
Rebersburg CDP *Centre County*,250
Rebuck postal area *Northumberland County*,736
Rector postal area *Westmoreland County*,929
Red Hill borough *Montgomery County*,699
Red Lion borough *York County*,959
Redbank township *Armstrong County*,69
Redbank township *Clarion County*,291
Redstone township *Fayette County*,434
Reed township *Dauphin County*,378
Reeders postal area *Monroe County*,676
Reedsville CDP *Mifflin County*,666
Refton CDP *Lancaster County*,551
Rehrersburg CDP *Berks County*,125
Reiffton CDP *Berks County*,125
Reilly township *Schuylkill County*,789
Reinerton CDP *Schuylkill County*,789
Reinholds CDP *Lancaster County*,551
Renfrew postal area *Butler County*,198
Rennerdale CDP *Allegheny County*,47
Renningers CDP *Schuylkill County*,790
Reno postal area *Venango County*,861
Renovo borough *Clinton County*,320
Republic CDP *Fayette County*,434
Reserve township *Allegheny County*,47
Revloc CDP *Cambria County*,219
Rew CDP *McKean County*,643
Reynolds Heights CDP *Mercer County*,653
Reynoldsville borough *Jefferson County*,503
Rheems CDP *Lancaster County*,551
Rice township *Luzerne County*,612
Rices Landing borough *Greene County*,466
Riceville CDP *Crawford County*,347
Richboro CDP *Bucks County*,176
Richeyville postal area *Washington County*,893
Richfield CDP *Juniata County*,512
Richhill township *Greene County*,466
Richland borough *Lebanon County*,576
Richland township *Allegheny County*,48
Richland township *Bucks County*,176
Richland township *Cambria County*,219
Richland township *Clarion County*,291
Richland township *Venango County*,861
Richlandtown borough *Bucks County*,177
Richmond township *Berks County*,126
Richmond township *Crawford County*,347
Richmond township *Tioga County*,844
Riddlesburg postal area *Bedford County*,98

Ridgebury township *Bradford County*,153
Ridgway borough *Elk County*,405
Ridgway township *Elk County*,406
Ridley Park borough *Delaware County*,397
Ridley township *Delaware County*,396
Riegelsville borough *Bucks County*,177
Rillton postal area *Westmoreland County*,929
Rimersburg borough *Clarion County*,291
Ringgold township *Jefferson County*,504
Ringtown borough *Schuylkill County*,790
Riverside borough *Northumberland County*,736
Riverside CDP *Cambria County*,220
Riverview Park CDP *Berks County*,126
Rixford postal area *McKean County*,643
Roaring Branch postal area *Tioga County*,844
Roaring Brook township *Lackawanna County*,524
Roaring Creek township *Columbia County*,333
Roaring Spring borough *Blair County*,143
Robertsdale postal area *Huntingdon County*,478
Robeson township *Berks County*,126
Robesonia borough *Berks County*,126
Robinson CDP *Indiana County*,494
Robinson township *Allegheny County*,48
Robinson township *Washington County*,893
Rochester Mills postal area *Indiana County*,494
Rochester borough *Beaver County*,87
Rochester township *Beaver County*,87
Rock Glen postal area *Luzerne County*,613
Rockdale township *Crawford County*,347
Rockefeller township *Northumberland County*,736
Rockhill Furnace postal area *Huntingdon County*,479
Rockhill borough *Huntingdon County*,478
Rockland township *Berks County*,127
Rockland township *Venango County*,861
Rockledge borough *Montgomery County*,699
Rockton postal area *Clearfield County*,309
Rockwood borough *Somerset County*,817
Rogersville CDP *Greene County*,466
Rohrsburg CDP *Columbia County*,333
Rome borough *Bradford County*,153
Rome township *Bradford County*,154
Rome township *Crawford County*,347
Ronco CDP *Fayette County*,435
Ronks CDP *Lancaster County*,551
Roscoe borough *Washington County*,893
Rose Valley borough *Delaware County*,397
Rose township *Jefferson County*,504
Roseto borough *Northampton County*,724
Roseville borough *Tioga County*,844
Ross township *Allegheny County*,48
Ross township *Luzerne County*,613
Ross township *Monroe County*,676
Rossiter CDP *Indiana County*,494
Rosslyn Farms borough *Allegheny County*,48
Rostraver township *Westmoreland County*,929
Rote CDP *Clinton County*,320
Rothsville CDP *Lancaster County*,552
Roulette CDP *Potter County*,766

CDP = Census Designated Place

Roulette township *Potter County*,766
Rouseville borough *Venango County*,862
Rouzerville CDP *Franklin County*,450
Rowes Run CDP *Fayette County*,435
Rowland postal area *Pike County*,759
Roxbury postal area *Franklin County*,450
Royalton borough *Dauphin County*,378
Royersford borough *Montgomery County*,699
Ruffs Dale postal area *Westmoreland County*,929
Rupert CDP *Columbia County*,334
Rural Ridge postal area *Allegheny County*,49
Rural Valley borough *Armstrong County*,70
Ruscombmanor township *Berks County*,127
Rush township *Centre County*,250
Rush township *Dauphin County*,378
Rush township *Northumberland County*,736
Rush township *Schuylkill County*,790
Rush township *Susquehanna County*,834
Russell CDP *Warren County*,869
Russellton CDP *Allegheny County*,49
Rutherford CDP *Dauphin County*,378
Rutland township *Tioga County*,845
Rutledge borough *Delaware County*,397
Ryan township *Schuylkill County*,790
Rye township *Perry County*,747

S

S.N.P.J. borough *Lawrence County*,564
Sabinsville postal area *Tioga County*,845
Sacramento postal area *Schuylkill County*,791
Sadsbury township *Chester County*,273
Sadsbury township *Crawford County*,348
Sadsbury township *Lancaster County*,552
Saegertown borough *Crawford County*,348
Sagamore postal area *Armstrong County*,70
Saint Benedict postal area *Cambria County*,220
Saint Clair borough *Schuylkill County*,791
Saint Clair township *Westmoreland County*,929
Saint Clairsville borough *Bedford County*,98
Saint Lawrence borough *Berks County*,127
Saint Marys city *Elk County*,406
Saint Michael CDP *Cambria County*,220
Saint Petersburg borough *Clarion County*,291
Saint Thomas township *Franklin County*,450
Saint Vincent College CDP *Westmoreland County*,930
Salem township *Clarion County*,292
Salem township *Luzerne County*,613
Salem township *Mercer County*,654
Salem township *Wayne County*,907
Salem township *Westmoreland County*,930
Salford township *Montgomery County*,700
Salina postal area *Westmoreland County*,930
Salisbury borough *Somerset County*,817
Salisbury township *Lancaster County*,552
Salisbury township *Lehigh County*,587
Salix CDP *Cambria County*,220
Salladasburg borough *Lycoming County*,633
Salona postal area *Clinton County*,320
Saltillo borough *Huntingdon County*,479
Saltlick township *Fayette County*,435

Saltsburg borough *Indiana County*,495
Salunga CDP *Lancaster County*,552
Sanatoga CDP *Montgomery County*,700
Sand Hill CDP *Lebanon County*,576
Sandy Creek township *Mercer County*,654
Sandy Lake borough *Mercer County*,654
Sandy Lake township *Mercer County*,654
Sandy Ridge CDP *Centre County*,251
Sandy CDP *Clearfield County*,309
Sandy township *Clearfield County*,309
Sandycreek township *Venango County*,862
Sankertown borough *Cambria County*,220
Sarver postal area *Butler County*,198
Sassamansville postal area *Montgomery County*,700
Saville township *Perry County*,748
Saw Creek CDP *Pike County*,759
Saxonburg borough *Butler County*,199
Saxton borough *Bedford County*,98
Saylorsburg CDP *Monroe County*,676
Sayre borough *Bradford County*,154
Scalp Level borough *Cambria County*,221
Scenery Hill postal area *Washington County*,893
Schaefferstown CDP *Lebanon County*,577
Schellsburg borough *Bedford County*,98
Schlusser CDP *Cumberland County*,362
Schnecksville CDP *Lehigh County*,588
Schoeneck CDP *Lancaster County*,553
Schubert CDP *Berks County*,127
Schuylkill County,769 - 796
Schuylkill Haven borough *Schuylkill County*,791
Schuylkill township *Chester County*,273
Schuylkill township *Schuylkill County*,791
Schwenksville borough *Montgomery County*,700
Sciota postal area *Monroe County*,676
Scotland CDP *Franklin County*,451
Scotrun postal area *Monroe County*,676
Scott township *Allegheny County*,49
Scott township *Columbia County*,334
Scott township *Lackawanna County*,524
Scott township *Lawrence County*,564
Scott township *Wayne County*,907
Scottdale borough *Westmoreland County*,930
Scranton city *Lackawanna County*,524
Scrubgrass township *Venango County*,862
Seanor postal area *Somerset County*,817
Selinsgrove borough *Snyder County*,803
Sellersville borough *Bucks County*,177
Seltzer CDP *Schuylkill County*,792
Seminole postal area *Armstrong County*,70
Seneca CDP *Venango County*,862
Sergeant township *McKean County*,643
Seven Fields borough *Butler County*,199
Seven Springs borough *Fayette County*,435 - 436
Seven Springs borough *Somerset County*,817
Seven Valleys borough *York County*,960
Seward borough *Westmoreland County*,930
Sewickley Heights borough *Allegheny County*,50
Sewickley Hills borough *Allegheny County*,50
Sewickley borough *Allegheny County*,49

Sewickley township *Westmoreland County*,931
Shade Gap borough *Huntingdon County*,479
Shade township *Somerset County*,818
Shady Grove postal area *Franklin County*,451
Shaler township *Allegheny County*,50
Shamokin Dam borough *Snyder County*,803
Shamokin city *Northumberland County*,737
Shamokin township *Northumberland County*,737
Shanksville borough *Somerset County*,818
Shanor-Northvue CDP *Butler County*,199
Sharon Hill borough *Delaware County*,397
Sharon city *Mercer County*,655
Sharon township *Potter County*,766
Sharpsburg borough *Allegheny County*,50
Sharpsville borough *Mercer County*,655
Shartlesville CDP *Berks County*,128
Shavertown CDP *Luzerne County*,613
Shawnee On Delaware postal area *Monroe County*,676
Sheakleyville borough *Mercer County*,655
Sheatown CDP *Luzerne County*,614
Sheffield CDP *Warren County*,870
Sheffield township *Warren County*,870
Shelocta borough *Indiana County*,495
Shenandoah Heights CDP *Schuylkill County*,792
Shenandoah borough *Schuylkill County*,792
Shenango township *Lawrence County*,565
Shenango township *Mercer County*,656
Sheppton CDP *Schuylkill County*,793
Shermans Dale postal area *Perry County*,748
Sheshequin township *Bradford County*,154
Shickshinny borough *Luzerne County*,614
Shillington borough *Berks County*,128
Shiloh CDP *York County*,960
Shinglehouse borough *Potter County*,766
Shippen township *Cameron County*,228
Shippen township *Tioga County*,845
Shippensburg University CDP *Cumberland County*,363
Shippensburg borough *Cumberland County*,363
Shippensburg township *Cumberland County*,363
Shippenville borough *Clarion County*,292
Shippingport borough *Beaver County*,87
Shiremanstown borough *Cumberland County*,363
Shirley township *Huntingdon County*,479
Shirleysburg borough *Huntingdon County*,479
Shoemakersville borough *Berks County*,128
Shohola township *Pike County*,759
Shrewsbury borough *York County*,960
Shrewsbury township *Lycoming County*,634
Shrewsbury township *Sullivan County*,825
Shrewsbury township *York County*,960
Shunk postal area *Sullivan County*,825
Sidman CDP *Cambria County*,221
Sierra View CDP *Monroe County*,676
Sigel postal area *Jefferson County*,504
Siglerville CDP *Mifflin County*,667
Silkworth CDP *Luzerne County*,614
Silver Lake township *Susquehanna County*,834

CDP = Census Designated Place

Silver Spring township *Cumberland County*,364

Silverdale borough *Bucks County*,177

Simpson CDP *Lackawanna County*,525

Sinking Spring borough *Berks County*,129

Sinnamahoning postal area *Cameron County*,228

Sipesville postal area *Somerset County*,818

Six Mile Run postal area *Bedford County*,99

Skippack CDP *Montgomery County*,700

Skippack township *Montgomery County*,701

Skyline View CDP *Dauphin County*,379

Skytop postal area *Monroe County*,677

Slabtown CDP *Columbia County*,334

Slatedale CDP *Lehigh County*,588

Slatington borough *Lehigh County*,588

Slickville CDP *Westmoreland County*,931

Sligo borough *Clarion County*,292

Slippery Rock University CDP *Butler County*,200

Slippery Rock borough *Butler County*,199

Slippery Rock township *Butler County*,200

Slippery Rock township *Lawrence County*,565

Slocum township *Luzerne County*,614

Slovan CDP *Washington County*,893

Smethport borough *McKean County*,644

Smicksburg borough *Indiana County*,495

Smith township *Washington County*,894

Smithfield borough *Fayette County*,436

Smithfield township *Bradford County*,154

Smithfield township *Huntingdon County*,480

Smithfield township *Monroe County*,677

Smithmill postal area *Clearfield County*,309

Smithton borough *Westmoreland County*,931

Smock CDP *Fayette County*,436

Smoketown CDP *Lancaster County*,553

Snake Spring township *Bedford County*,99

Snow Shoe borough *Centre County*,251

Snow Shoe township *Centre County*,251

Snyder County,797 - 804

Snyder township *Blair County*,144

Snyder township *Jefferson County*,504

Snydertown borough *Northumberland County*,737

Snydertown CDP *Centre County*,252

Solebury township *Bucks County*,178

Somerset County,805 - 820

Somerset borough *Somerset County*,818

Somerset township *Somerset County*,819

Somerset township *Washington County*,894

Soudersburg CDP *Lancaster County*,553

Souderton borough *Montgomery County*,701

South Abington township *Lackawanna County*,525

South Annville township *Lebanon County*,577

South Beaver township *Beaver County*,87

South Bend township *Armstrong County*,70

South Bethlehem borough *Armstrong County*,70

South Buffalo township *Armstrong County*,71

South Canaan township *Wayne County*,908

South Centre township *Columbia County*,334

South Coatesville borough *Chester County*,273

South Connellsville borough *Fayette County*,436

South Coventry township *Chester County*,274

South Creek township *Bradford County*,155

South Fayette township *Allegheny County*,51

South Fork borough *Cambria County*,221

South Franklin township *Washington County*,894

South Gibson postal area *Susquehanna County*,835

South Greensburg borough *Westmoreland County*,931

South Hanover township *Dauphin County*,379

South Heidelberg township *Berks County*,129

South Heights borough *Beaver County*,88

South Huntingdon township *Westmoreland County*,932

South Lebanon township *Lebanon County*,577

South Londonderry township *Lebanon County*,577

South Mahoning township *Indiana County*,495

South Manheim township *Schuylkill County*,793

South Middleton township *Cumberland County*,364

South Montrose postal area *Susquehanna County*,835

South Mountain postal area *Franklin County*,451

South New Castle borough *Lawrence County*,565

South Newton township *Cumberland County*,364

South Park Township CDP *Allegheny County*,51

South Park township *Allegheny County*,51

South Philipsburg CDP *Centre County*,252

South Pottstown CDP *Chester County*,274

South Pymatuning township *Mercer County*,656

South Renovo borough *Clinton County*,320

South Shenango township *Crawford County*,348

South Sterling postal area *Wayne County*,908

South Strabane township *Washington County*,894

South Temple CDP *Berks County*,129

South Union township *Fayette County*,437

South Uniontown CDP *Fayette County*,437

South Versailles township *Allegheny County*,52

South Waverly borough *Bradford County*,155

South Whitehall township *Lehigh County*,589

South Williamsport borough *Lycoming County*,634

South Woodbury township *Bedford County*,99

Southampton township *Bedford County*,99

Southampton township *Cumberland County*,365

Southampton township *Franklin County*,451

Southampton township *Somerset County*,819

Southmont borough *Cambria County*,221

Southview CDP *Washington County*,895

Southwest Greensburg borough *Westmoreland County*,932

Southwest Madison township *Perry County*,748

Southwest township *Warren County*,870

Spangler postal area *Cambria County*,222

Sparta township *Crawford County*,349

Spartansburg borough *Crawford County*,349

Speers borough *Washington County*,895

Spinnerstown CDP *Bucks County*,178

Spraggs postal area *Greene County*,467

Sprankle Mills postal area *Jefferson County*,505

Spring Brook township *Lackawanna County*,525

Spring Church postal area *Armstrong County*,71

Spring City borough *Chester County*,274

Spring Creek township *Elk County*,406

Spring Creek township *Warren County*,870

Spring Garden township *York County*,961

Spring Glen postal area *Schuylkill County*,793

Spring Grove borough *York County*,961

Spring Hill CDP *Cambria County*,222

Spring House CDP *Montgomery County*,701

Spring Mills CDP *Centre County*,252

Spring Mount CDP *Montgomery County*,702

Spring Ridge CDP *Berks County*,130

Spring Run postal area *Franklin County*,451

Spring township *Berks County*,129

Spring township *Centre County*,252

Spring township *Crawford County*,349

Spring township *Perry County*,748

Spring township *Snyder County*,804

Springboro borough *Crawford County*,349

Springdale borough *Allegheny County*,52

Springdale township *Allegheny County*,52

Springettsbury township *York County*,961

Springfield township *Bradford County*,155

Springfield township *Bucks County*,178

Springfield township *Delaware County*,398

Springfield township *Erie County*,417

Springfield township *Fayette County*,437

Springfield township *Huntingdon County*,480

Springfield township *Mercer County*,656

Springfield township *Montgomery County*,702

Springfield township *York County*,962

Springhill township *Fayette County*,437

Springhill township *Greene County*,467

Springmont CDP *Berks County*,130

Springs postal area *Somerset County*,819

Springtown postal area *Bucks County*,178

Springville township *Susquehanna County*,835

Sproul postal area *Blair County*,144

Spruce Creek township *Huntingdon County*,480

Spruce Hill township *Juniata County*,512

Spry CDP *York County*,962

Stahlstown postal area *Westmoreland County*,932

Standing Stone township *Bradford County*,155

Star Junction CDP *Fayette County*,438

Starbrick CDP *Warren County*,871

Starford postal area *Indiana County*,496

Starlight postal area *Wayne County*,908

Starrucca borough *Wayne County*,908

CDP = Census Designated Place

State College borough *Centre County*,253
State Line CDP *Franklin County*,451
Steelton borough *Dauphin County*,379
Sterling township *Wayne County*,908
Steuben township *Crawford County*,350
Stevens CDP *Lancaster County*,553
Stevens township *Bradford County*,156
Stevensville postal area *Bradford County*,156
Stewardson township *Potter County*,767
Stewart township *Fayette County*,438
Stewartstown borough *York County*,962
Stiles CDP *Lehigh County*,589
Stillwater borough *Columbia County*,335
Stockdale borough *Washington County*,895
Stockertown borough *Northampton County*,724
Stoneboro borough *Mercer County*,656
Stonerstown CDP *Bedford County*,100
Stony Creek Mills CDP *Berks County*,130
Stonybrook CDP *York County*,962
Stonycreek township *Cambria County*,222
Stonycreek township *Somerset County*,819
Stormstown CDP *Centre County*,253
Stouchsburg CDP *Berks County*,130
Stowe CDP *Montgomery County*,702
Stowe township *Allegheny County*,52
Stoystown borough *Somerset County*,820
Straban township *Adams County*,12
Strabane postal area *Washington County*,895
Strasburg borough *Lancaster County*,554
Strasburg township *Lancaster County*,554
Strattanville borough *Clarion County*,293
Strausstown borough *Berks County*,131
Strodes Mills CDP *Mifflin County*,667
Strong CDP *Northumberland County*,738
Strongstown postal area *Indiana County*,496
Stroud township *Monroe County*,677
Stroudsburg borough *Monroe County*,677
Stump Creek postal area *Jefferson County*,505
Sturgeon CDP *Allegheny County*,53
Sugar Grove borough *Warren County*,871
Sugar Grove township *Mercer County*,657
Sugar Grove township *Warren County*,871
Sugar Notch borough *Luzerne County*,615
Sugar Run postal area *Bradford County*,156
Sugarcreek borough *Venango County*,863
Sugarcreek township *Armstrong County*,71
Sugarloaf township *Columbia County*,335
Sugarloaf township *Luzerne County*,615
Sullivan County,821 - 824
Sullivan township *Tioga County*,845
Summerdale postal area *Cumberland County*,365
Summerhill borough *Cambria County*,222
Summerhill township *Cambria County*,222
Summerhill township *Crawford County*,350
Summerville borough *Jefferson County*,505
Summit Hill borough *Carbon County*,235
Summit Station CDP *Schuylkill County*,793
Summit township *Butler County*,200
Summit township *Crawford County*,350
Summit township *Erie County*,417
Summit township *Potter County*,767
Summit township *Somerset County*,820
Sun Valley CDP *Monroe County*,678
Sunbury city *Northumberland County*,738

Sunrise Lake CDP *Pike County*,759
Susquehanna County,825 - 835
Susquehanna Depot borough *Susquehanna County*,835
Susquehanna Trails CDP *York County*,963
Susquehanna township *Cambria County*,223
Susquehanna township *Dauphin County*,379
Susquehanna township *Juniata County*,512
Susquehanna township *Lycoming County*,634
Sutersville borough *Westmoreland County*,932
Swarthmore borough *Delaware County*,398
Swartzville CDP *Lancaster County*,554
Swatara township *Dauphin County*,380
Swatara township *Lebanon County*,578
Sweden Valley CDP *Potter County*,767
Sweden township *Potter County*,767
Sweet Valley postal area *Luzerne County*,615
Swengel postal area *Union County*,852
Swiftwater postal area *Monroe County*,678
Swissvale borough *Allegheny County*,53
Swoyersville borough *Luzerne County*,615
Sybertsville postal area *Luzerne County*,616
Sycamore postal area *Greene County*,467
Sykesville borough *Jefferson County*,505
Sylvania borough *Bradford County*,156
Sylvania township *Potter County*,768

T

Table Rock CDP *Adams County*,13
Tafton postal area *Pike County*,760
Tamaqua borough *Schuylkill County*,793
Tamiment postal area *Pike County*,760
Tannersville postal area *Monroe County*,678
Tarentum borough *Allegheny County*,53
Tarrs postal area *Westmoreland County*,933
Tatamy borough *Northampton County*,725
Taylor borough *Lackawanna County*,526
Taylor township *Blair County*,144
Taylor township *Centre County*,253
Taylor township *Fulton County*,456
Taylor township *Lawrence County*,566
Taylorstown CDP *Washington County*,896
Telford borough *Montgomery County*,702
Tell township *Huntingdon County*,480
Temple CDP *Berks County*,131
Templeton CDP *Armstrong County*,71
Terre Hill borough *Lancaster County*,554
Terry township *Bradford County*,156
Texas township *Wayne County*,909
Tharptown *Uniontown)* CDP *Northumberland County*,738
The Hideout CDP *Wayne County*,909
Thomasville postal area *York County*,963
Thompson borough *Susquehanna County*,835
Thompson township *Fulton County*,456
Thompson township *Susquehanna County*,836
Thompsontown borough *Juniata County*,512
Thompsonville CDP *Washington County*,896
Thornburg borough *Allegheny County*,53
Thornbury township *Chester County*,275
Thornbury township *Delaware County*,398
Thorndale CDP *Chester County*,275

Thornhurst township *Lackawanna County*,526
Thornton postal area *Delaware County*,399
Three Springs borough *Huntingdon County*,481
Throop borough *Lackawanna County*,526
Tidioute borough *Warren County*,871
Tilden township *Berks County*,131
Timber Hills CDP *Lebanon County*,578
Timblin borough *Jefferson County*,505
Tinicum township *Bucks County*,179
Tinicum township *Delaware County*,399
Tioga County,836 - 846
Tioga borough *Tioga County*,846
Tioga township *Tioga County*,846
Tiona postal area *Warren County*,872
Tionesta borough *Forest County*,442
Tionesta township *Forest County*,443
Tipton CDP *Blair County*,144
Titusville city *Crawford County*,350
Toboyne township *Perry County*,748
Toby township *Clarion County*,293
Tobyhanna township *Monroe County*,678
Todd township *Fulton County*,456
Todd township *Huntingdon County*,481
Toftrees CDP *Centre County*,254
Topton borough *Berks County*,131
Torrance postal area *Westmoreland County*,933
Toughkenamon CDP *Chester County*,275
Towamencin township *Montgomery County*,703
Towamensing Trails CDP *Carbon County*,235
Towamensing township *Carbon County*,235
Towanda borough *Bradford County*,157
Towanda township *Bradford County*,157
Tower City borough *Schuylkill County*,794
Townville borough *Crawford County*,351
Trafford borough *Westmoreland County*,933
Trainer borough *Delaware County*,399
Transfer postal area *Mercer County*,657
Trappe borough *Montgomery County*,703
Treasure Lake CDP *Clearfield County*,310
Tredyffrin township *Chester County*,275
Treichlers postal area *Northampton County*,725
Tremont borough *Schuylkill County*,794
Tremont township *Schuylkill County*,794
Tresckow CDP *Carbon County*,236
Trevorton CDP *Northumberland County*,738
Trevose CDP *Bucks County*,179
Trexlertown CDP *Lehigh County*,589
Triumph township *Warren County*,872
Trooper CDP *Montgomery County*,703
Trout Run postal area *Lycoming County*,634
Troutville borough *Clearfield County*,310
Troxelville CDP *Snyder County*,804
Troy borough *Bradford County*,157
Troy township *Bradford County*,158
Troy township *Crawford County*,351
Trucksville CDP *Luzerne County*,616
Trumbauersville borough *Bucks County*,179
Tullytown borough *Bucks County*,179
Tulpehocken township *Berks County*,132
Tunkhannock borough *Wyoming County*,942
Tunkhannock township *Monroe County*,678

CDP = Census Designated Place

Tunkhannock township *Wyoming County*,942
Tunnelhill borough *Cambria County*,223
Turbett township *Juniata County*,513
Turbot township *Northumberland County*,739
Turbotville borough *Northumberland County*,739
Turtle Creek borough *Allegheny County*,54
Turtlepoint postal area *McKean County*,644
Tuscarora CDP *Schuylkill County*,794
Tuscarora township *Bradford County*,158
Tuscarora township *Juniata County*,513
Tuscarora township *Perry County*,749
Twilight borough *Washington County*,896
Twin Rocks postal area *Cambria County*,223
Tyler Hill postal area *Wayne County*,909
Tyler Run CDP *York County*,963
Tylersburg CDP *Clarion County*,293
Tyrone borough *Blair County*,145
Tyrone township *Adams County*,13
Tyrone township *Blair County*,145
Tyrone township *Perry County*,749

U

Uledi postal area *Fayette County*,438
Ulster township *Bradford County*,158
Ulysses borough *Potter County*,768
Ulysses township *Potter County*,768
Union City borough *Erie County*,417
Union County,847 - 853
Union Dale borough *Susquehanna County*,836
Union Deposit CDP *Dauphin County*,380
Union township *Adams County*,13
Union township *Berks County*,132
Union township *Centre County*,254
Union township *Clearfield County*,310
Union township *Crawford County*,351
Union township *Erie County*,417
Union township *Fulton County*,457
Union township *Huntingdon County*,481
Union township *Jefferson County*,505
Union township *Lawrence County*,566
Union township *Lebanon County*,578
Union township *Luzerne County*,616
Union township *Mifflin County*,667
Union township *Schuylkill County*,795
Union township *Snyder County*,804
Union township *Tioga County*,846
Union township *Union County*,852
Union township *Washington County*,896
Uniontown city *Fayette County*,438
Unionville borough *Centre County*,254
Unionville CDP *Butler County*,201
United postal area *Westmoreland County*,933
Unity township *Westmoreland County*,933
Unityville postal area *Lycoming County*,634
University of Pittsburgh Johnstown CDP *Cambria County*,223
University Park postal area *Centre County*,254
Upland borough *Delaware County*,399
Upper Allen township *Cumberland County*,365
Upper Augusta township *Northumberland County*,739
Upper Bern township *Berks County*,132

Upper Black Eddy postal area *Bucks County*,180
Upper Burrell township *Westmoreland County*,933
Upper Chichester township *Delaware County*,400
Upper Darby township *Delaware County*,400
Upper Dublin township *Montgomery County*,704
Upper Exeter CDP *Luzerne County*,616
Upper Fairfield township *Lycoming County*,635
Upper Frankford township *Cumberland County*,365
Upper Frederick township *Montgomery County*,704
Upper Gwynedd township *Montgomery County*,704
Upper Hanover township *Montgomery County*,705
Upper Leacock township *Lancaster County*,555
Upper Macungie township *Lehigh County*,589
Upper Mahanoy township *Northumberland County*,739
Upper Mahantongo township *Schuylkill County*,795
Upper Makefield township *Bucks County*,180
Upper Merion township *Montgomery County*,705
Upper Mifflin township *Cumberland County*,366
Upper Milford township *Lehigh County*,590
Upper Moreland township *Montgomery County*,705
Upper Mount Bethel township *Northampton County*,725
Upper Nazareth township *Northampton County*,725
Upper Oxford township *Chester County*,276
Upper Paxton township *Dauphin County*,380
Upper Pottsgrove township *Montgomery County*,705
Upper Providence township *Delaware County*,400
Upper Providence township *Montgomery County*,706
Upper Saint Clair CDP/twp *Allegheny County*,54
Upper Salford township *Montgomery County*,706
Upper Saucon township *Lehigh County*,590
Upper Southampton township *Bucks County*,180
Upper Tulpehocken township *Berks County*,132
Upper Turkeyfoot township *Somerset County*,820
Upper Tyrone township *Fayette County*,439
Upper Uwchlan township *Chester County*,276
Upper Yoder township *Cambria County*,224
Upperstrasburg postal area *Franklin County*,452
Ursina borough *Somerset County*,820
Utica borough *Venango County*,863
Uwchlan township *Chester County*,276

V

Valencia borough *Butler County*,201

Valier postal area *Jefferson County*,506
Valley Green CDP *York County*,963
Valley View CDP *Schuylkill County*,795
Valley View CDP *York County*,964
Valley township *Armstrong County*,71
Valley township *Chester County*,277
Valley township *Montour County*,712
Valley-Hi borough *Fulton County*,457
Van Voorhis CDP *Washington County*,897
Vanderbilt borough *Fayette County*,439
Vandergrift borough *Westmoreland County*,934
Vandling borough *Lackawanna County*,527
Vanport township *Beaver County*,88
Venango County,854 - 863
Venango borough *Crawford County*,352
Venango township *Butler County*,201
Venango township *Crawford County*,352
Venango township *Erie County*,418
Venetia postal area *Washington County*,897
Venus postal area *Venango County*,863
Vernon township *Crawford County*,352
Verona borough *Allegheny County*,54
Versailles borough *Allegheny County*,55
Vestaburg postal area *Washington County*,897
Vicksburg CDP *Union County*,852
Victory township *Venango County*,863
Villa Maria postal area *Lawrence County*,566
Village Green-Green Ridge CDP *Delaware County*,401
Village Shires CDP *Bucks County*,180
Villanova postal area *Delaware County*,401
Vinco CDP *Cambria County*,224
Vintondale borough *Cambria County*,224
Virginville CDP *Berks County*,133
Volant borough *Lawrence County*,566
Vowinckel CDP *Clarion County*,293

W

Wagner CDP *Mifflin County*,667
Wakefield CDP *Lancaster County*,555
Walker township *Centre County*,254
Walker township *Huntingdon County*,481
Walker township *Juniata County*,513
Walker township *Schuylkill County*,795
Wall borough *Allegheny County*,55
Wallace township *Chester County*,277
Wallaceton borough *Clearfield County*,310
Wallenpaupack Lake Estates CDP *Wayne County*,909
Waller CDP *Columbia County*,335
Wallingford postal area *Delaware County*,401
Walnut Bottom postal area *Cumberland County*,366
Walnutport borough *Northampton County*,726
Walnuttown CDP *Berks County*,133
Walston postal area *Jefferson County*,506
Wampum borough *Lawrence County*,566
Wanamie CDP *Luzerne County*,616
Wapwallopen postal area *Luzerne County*,617
Ward township *Tioga County*,846
Warfordsburg postal area *Fulton County*,457
Warminster Heights CDP *Bucks County*,181
Warminster township *Bucks County*,181

CDP = Census Designated Place

Warren Center postal area *Bradford County*,159

Warren County,864 - 872

Warren city *Warren County*,872

Warren township *Bradford County*,158

Warren township *Franklin County*,452

Warrendale postal area *Allegheny County*,55

Warrington township *Bucks County*,181

Warrington township *York County*,964

Warrior Run borough *Luzerne County*,617

Warriors Mark township *Huntingdon County*,482

Warsaw township *Jefferson County*,506

Warwick township *Bucks County*,182

Warwick township *Chester County*,277

Warwick township *Lancaster County*,555

Washington Boro CDP *Lancaster County*,555

Washington County,873 - 899

Washington Crossing postal area *Bucks County*,182

Washington city *Washington County*,897

Washington township *Armstrong County*,72

Washington township *Berks County*,133

Washington township *Butler County*,201

Washington township *Cambria County*,224

Washington township *Clarion County*,294

Washington township *Dauphin County*,381

Washington township *Erie County*,418

Washington township *Fayette County*,439

Washington township *Franklin County*,452

Washington township *Greene County*,467

Washington township *Indiana County*,496

Washington township *Jefferson County*,506

Washington township *Lawrence County*,567

Washington township *Lehigh County*,590

Washington township *Lycoming County*,635

Washington township *Northampton County*,726

Washington township *Northumberland County*,740

Washington township *Schuylkill County*,796

Washington township *Snyder County*,805

Washington township *Westmoreland County*,934

Washington township *Wyoming County*,943

Washington township *York County*,964

Washingtonville borough *Montour County*,712

Waterfall postal area *Fulton County*,457

Waterford borough *Erie County*,418

Waterford township *Erie County*,419

Waterville postal area *Lycoming County*,635

Watson township *Lycoming County*,635

Watson township *Warren County*,872

Watsontown borough *Northumberland County*,740

Watts township *Perry County*,749

Wattsburg borough *Erie County*,419

Waverly CDP *Lackawanna County*,527

Waymart borough *Wayne County*,909

Wayne County,900 - 909

Wayne Heights CDP *Franklin County*,452

Wayne township *Armstrong County*,72

Wayne township *Clinton County*,320

Wayne township *Crawford County*,352

Wayne township *Dauphin County*,381

Wayne township *Erie County*,419

Wayne township *Greene County*,467

Wayne township *Lawrence County*,567

Wayne township *Mifflin County*,668

Wayne township *Schuylkill County*,796

Waynesboro borough *Franklin County*,452

Waynesburg borough *Greene County*,467

Weatherly borough *Carbon County*,236

Webster CDP *Westmoreland County*,934

Weedville CDP *Elk County*,407

Weigelstown CDP *York County*,964

Weikert postal area *Union County*,853

Weisenberg township *Lehigh County*,590

Weissport East CDP *Carbon County*,236

Weissport borough *Carbon County*,236

Wellersburg borough *Somerset County*,821

Wells Tannery postal area *Fulton County*,457

Wells township *Bradford County*,159

Wells township *Fulton County*,457

Wellsboro borough *Tioga County*,847

Wellsville borough *York County*,965

Wendel postal area *Westmoreland County*,935

Wernersville borough *Berks County*,133

Wescosville CDP *Lehigh County*,591

Wesleyville borough *Erie County*,419

West Abington township *Lackawanna County*,527

West Alexander CDP *Washington County*,897

West Beaver township *Snyder County*,805

West Bethlehem township *Washington County*,898

West Bradford township *Chester County*,277

West Branch township *Potter County*,768

West Brandywine township *Chester County*,278

West Brownsville borough *Washington County*,898

West Brunswick township *Schuylkill County*,796

West Buffalo township *Union County*,853

West Burlington township *Bradford County*,159

West Caln township *Chester County*,278

West Cameron township *Northumberland County*,740

West Carroll township *Cambria County*,225

West Chester borough *Chester County*,278

West Chillisquaque township *Northumberland County*,741

West Cocalico township *Lancaster County*,556

West Conshohocken borough *Montgomery County*,706

West Cornwall township *Lebanon County*,578

West Decatur CDP *Clearfield County*,311

West Deer township *Allegheny County*,55

West Donegal township *Lancaster County*,556

West Earl township *Lancaster County*,556

West Easton borough *Northampton County*,726

West Elizabeth borough *Allegheny County*,56

West Fairview CDP *Cumberland County*,366

West Fallowfield township *Chester County*,279

West Fallowfield township *Crawford County*,353

West Falls CDP *Wyoming County*,943

West Finley township *Washington County*,898

West Franklin township *Armstrong County*,72

West Goshen township *Chester County*,279

West Grove borough *Chester County*,279

West Hamburg CDP *Berks County*,134

West Hanover township *Dauphin County*,381

West Hazleton borough *Luzerne County*,617

West Hemlock township *Montour County*,712

West Hempfield township *Lancaster County*,557

West Hickory postal area *Forest County*,443

West Hills CDP *Armstrong County*,72

West Homestead borough *Allegheny County*,56

West Keating township *Clinton County*,321

West Kittanning borough *Armstrong County*,73

West Lampeter township *Lancaster County*,557

West Lawn CDP *Berks County*,134

West Lebanon township *Lebanon County*,579

West Leechburg borough *Westmoreland County*,935

West Leisenring postal area *Fayette County*,439

West Liberty borough *Butler County*,201

West Mahanoy township *Schuylkill County*,796

West Mahoning township *Indiana County*,496

West Manchester township *York County*,965

West Manheim township *York County*,965

West Marlborough township *Chester County*,280

West Mayfield borough *Beaver County*,88

West Mead township *Crawford County*,353

West Middlesex borough *Mercer County*,657

West Middletown borough *Washington County*,898

West Mifflin borough *Allegheny County*,56

West Milton CDP *Union County*,853

West Nanticoke CDP *Luzerne County*,617

West Nantmeal township *Chester County*,280

West Newton borough *Westmoreland County*,935

West Norriton township *Montgomery County*,707

West Nottingham township *Chester County*,280

West Penn township *Schuylkill County*,797

West Pennsboro township *Cumberland County*,366

West Perry township *Snyder County*,805

West Pike Run township *Washington County*,899

West Pikeland township *Chester County*,280

West Pittsburg CDP *Lawrence County*,567

West Pittston borough *Luzerne County*,617

West Pottsgrove township *Montgomery County*,707

West Providence township *Bedford County*,100

West Reading borough *Berks County*,134

West Rockhill township *Bucks County*,182

West Sadsbury township *Chester County*,281

CDP = Census Designated Place

West Saint Clair township *Bedford County*,100
West Salem township *Mercer County*,657
West Shenango township *Crawford County*,353
West Springfield postal area *Erie County*,420
West Sunbury borough *Butler County*,202
West Taylor township *Cambria County*,225
West View borough *Allegheny County*,56
West Vincent township *Chester County*,281
West Waynesburg CDP *Greene County*,468
West Wheatfield township *Indiana County*,496
West Whiteland township *Chester County*,281
West Wyoming borough *Luzerne County*,618
West Wyomissing CDP *Berks County*,135
West York borough *York County*,965
West township *Huntingdon County*,482
Westfall township *Pike County*,760
Westfield borough *Tioga County*,847
Westfield township *Tioga County*,847
Westland CDP *Washington County*,899
Westmont borough *Cambria County*,225
Westmoreland City postal area *Westmoreland County*,935
Westmoreland County,910 - 935
Weston CDP *Luzerne County*,618
Westover borough *Clearfield County*,311
Westport postal area *Clinton County*,321
Westtown township *Chester County*,282
Westwood CDP *Chester County*,282
Wetmore township *McKean County*,644
Wexford postal area *Allegheny County*,57
Wharton township *Fayette County*,439
Wharton township *Potter County*,769
Wheatfield township *Perry County*,749
Wheatland borough *Mercer County*,658
Whitaker borough *Allegheny County*,57
White Deer township *Union County*,853
White Haven borough *Luzerne County*,618
White Mills CDP *Wayne County*,910
White Oak borough *Allegheny County*,57
White township *Beaver County*,88
White township *Cambria County*,225
White township *Indiana County*,496
Whitehall borough *Allegheny County*,57
Whitehall township *Lehigh County*,591
Whiteley township *Greene County*,468
Whitemarsh township *Montgomery County*,707
Whitfield CDP *Berks County*,135
Whitney postal area *Westmoreland County*,935
Whitpain township *Montgomery County*,707
Wickerham Manor-Fisher CDP *Washington County*,899
Wickhaven postal area *Fayette County*,440
Wiconisco township *Dauphin County*,381
Wiconsico CDP *Dauphin County*,382
Wilburton Number One CDP *Columbia County*,336

Wilburton Number Two CDP *Columbia County*,336
Wilburton postal area *Columbia County*,335
Wilcox CDP *Elk County*,407
Wilkes-Barre city *Luzerne County*,619
Wilkes-Barre township *Luzerne County*,619
Wilkins township *Allegheny County*,58
Wilkinsburg borough *Allegheny County*,58
Williams township *Dauphin County*,382
Williams township *Northampton County*,726
Williamsburg borough *Blair County*,145
Williamson postal area *Franklin County*,453
Williamsport city *Lycoming County*,635
Williamstown borough *Dauphin County*,382
Willistown township *Chester County*,282
Willow Grove CDP *Montgomery County*,708
Willow Hill postal area *Franklin County*,453
Willow Street CDP *Lancaster County*,557
Wilmerding borough *Allegheny County*,58
Wilmington township *Lawrence County*,567
Wilmington township *Mercer County*,658
Wilmore borough *Cambria County*,226
Wilmot township *Bradford County*,159
Wilson borough *Northampton County*,727
Winburne postal area *Clearfield County*,311
Wind Gap borough *Northampton County*,727
Wind Ridge CDP *Greene County*,468
Windber borough *Somerset County*,821
Windham township *Bradford County*,160
Windham township *Wyoming County*,943
Windsor borough *York County*,966
Windsor township *Berks County*,135
Windsor township *York County*,966
Winfield CDP *Union County*,854
Winfield township *Butler County*,202
Winslow township *Jefferson County*,506
Winterstown borough *York County*,966
Witmer CDP *Lancaster County*,557
Wolf Creek township *Mercer County*,658
Wolf township *Lycoming County*,636
Wolfdale CDP *Washington County*,899
Womelsdorf borough *Berks County*,135
Wood township *Huntingdon County*,482
Woodbourne CDP *Bucks County*,182
Woodbury borough *Bedford County*,100
Woodbury township *Bedford County*,101
Woodbury township *Blair County*,145
Woodcock borough *Crawford County*,353
Woodcock township *Crawford County*,354
Woodland Heights CDP *Venango County*,864
Woodland postal area *Clearfield County*,311
Woodlyn CDP *Delaware County*,401
Woodside CDP *Bucks County*,182
Woodward CDP *Centre County*,255
Woodward township *Clearfield County*,311
Woodward township *Clinton County*,321
Woodward township *Lycoming County*,636
Woolrich postal area *Clinton County*,321
Worcester township *Montgomery County*,708

Wormleysburg borough *Cumberland County*,366
Worth township *Butler County*,202
Worth township *Centre County*,255
Worth township *Mercer County*,658
Worthington borough *Armstrong County*,73
Worthville borough *Jefferson County*,507
Woxhall CDP *Montgomery County*,709
Wright township *Luzerne County*,620
Wrightstown township *Bucks County*,183
Wrightsville borough *York County*,966
Wyalusing borough *Bradford County*,160
Wyalusing township *Bradford County*,160
Wyano CDP *Westmoreland County*,935
Wycombe postal area *Bucks County*,183
Wylandville CDP *Washington County*,900
Wyncote CDP *Montgomery County*,709
Wyndmoor CDP *Montgomery County*,709
Wynnewood postal area *Montgomery County*,709
Wyoming County,936 - 943
Wyoming borough *Luzerne County*,620
Wyomissing borough *Berks County*,136
Wysox township *Bradford County*,160

Y

Yardley borough *Bucks County*,183
Yatesboro postal area *Armstrong County*,73
Yatesville borough *Luzerne County*,620
Yeadon borough *Delaware County*,401
Yeagertown CDP *Mifflin County*,668
Yoe borough *York County*,967
York County,944 - 969
York Haven borough *York County*,968
York New Salem postal area *York County*,969
York Springs borough *Adams County*,13
York city *York County*,967
York township *York County*,968
Yorkana borough *York County*,969
Yorklyn CDP *York County*,969
Young township *Indiana County*,497
Young township *Jefferson County*,507
Youngstown borough *Westmoreland County*,936
Youngsville borough *Warren County*,873
Youngwood borough *Westmoreland County*,936
Yukon CDP *Westmoreland County*,936

Z

Zelienople borough *Butler County*,203
Zerbe township *Northumberland County*,741
Zieglerville postal area *Montgomery County*,709
Zion Grove postal area *Schuylkill County*,797
Zion CDP *Centre County*,255
Zionsville postal area *Lehigh County*,591
Zullinger postal area *Franklin County*,453

CDP = Census Designated Place

Comparative
Statistics

Population

Place	1990 Census	2000 Census	2010 Census
Abington township *Montgomery Co.*	56,322	56,103	55,310
Allentown city *Lehigh Co.*	105,066	106,632	118,032
Allison Park cdp *Allegheny Co.*	n/a	n/a	21,552
Altoona city *Blair Co.*	52,151	49,523	46,320
Baldwin borough *Allegheny Co.*	21,923	19,999	19,767
Bensalem township *Bucks Co.*	56,788	58,434	60,427
Bethel Park municipality *Allegheny Co.*	33,823	33,556	32,313
Bethlehem township *Northampton Co.*	16,425	21,171	23,730
Bethlehem city *Northampton Co.*	71,428	71,329	74,982
Bristol township *Bucks Co.*	57,129	55,521	54,582
Buckingham township *Bucks Co.*	9,364	16,442	20,075
Chambersburg borough *Franklin Co.*	16,251	17,862	20,268
Cheltenham township *Montgomery Co.*	34,923	36,875	36,793
Chester city *Delaware Co.*	42,042	36,854	33,972
Coolbaugh township *Monroe Co.*	6,764	15,205	20,564
Cranberry township *Butler Co.*	14,764	23,625	28,098
Derry township *Dauphin Co.*	18,408	21,273	24,679
Dover township *York Co.*	15,726	18,074	21,078
Drexel Hill cdp *Delaware Co.*	29,744	29,364	28,043
East Hempfield township *Lancaster Co.*	18,559	21,399	23,522
East Pennsboro township *Cumberland Co.*	16,588	18,254	20,228
Easton city *Northampton Co.*	26,276	26,263	26,800
Erie city *Erie Co.*	108,718	103,717	101,786
Exeter township *Berks Co.*	17,252	21,161	25,550
Falls township *Bucks Co.*	35,053	34,865	34,300
Hampden township *Cumberland Co.*	20,384	24,135	28,044
Harrisburg city *Dauphin Co.*	52,376	48,950	49,528
Haverford township *Delaware Co.*	49,848	48,498	48,491
Hazleton city *Luzerne Co.*	24,730	23,329	25,340
Hempfield township *Westmoreland Co.*	42,694	40,721	43,241
Horsham township *Montgomery Co.*	21,900	24,232	26,147
Johnstown city *Cambria Co.*	28,134	23,906	20,978
King of Prussia cdp *Montgomery Co.*	18,406	18,511	19,936
Lancaster city *Lancaster Co.*	56,188	56,348	59,322
Lebanon city *Lebanon Co.*	24,787	24,461	25,477
Levittown cdp *Bucks Co.*	55,427	53,966	52,983
Lower Macungie township *Lehigh Co.*	16,832	19,220	30,633
Lower Makefield township *Bucks Co.*	25,083	32,681	32,559
Lower Merion township *Montgomery Co.*	58,003	59,850	57,825
Lower Paxton township *Dauphin Co.*	39,128	44,424	47,360
Lower Providence township *Montgomery Co.*	19,351	22,390	25,436
Manheim township *Lancaster Co.*	28,823	33,697	38,133
Manor township *Lancaster Co.*	14,157	16,498	19,612
Marple township *Delaware Co.*	23,111	23,737	23,428
McCandless township *Allegheny Co.*	28,781	29,022	28,457
McKeesport city *Allegheny Co.*	26,016	24,040	19,731
Middletown township *Bucks Co.*	43,063	44,141	45,436
Millcreek township *Erie Co.*	46,820	52,129	53,515
Monroeville municipality *Allegheny Co.*	29,304	29,349	28,386
Montgomery township *Montgomery Co.*	12,175	22,025	24,790
Moon township *Allegheny Co.*	19,638	22,290	24,185

Place	1990 Census	2000 Census	2010 Census
Mount Lebanon township *Allegheny Co.*	33,655	33,017	33,137
Muhlenberg township *Berks Co.*	14,043	16,305	19,628
Murrysville municipality *Westmoreland Co.*	17,368	18,872	20,079
New Castle city *Lawrence Co.*	28,334	26,309	23,273
Newtown township *Bucks Co.*	13,907	18,206	19,299
Norristown borough *Montgomery Co.*	30,749	31,282	34,324
North Huntingdon township *Westmoreland Co.*	28,325	29,123	30,609
Northampton township *Bucks Co.*	35,406	39,384	39,726
Palmer township *Northampton Co.*	14,965	16,809	20,691
Penn township *Westmoreland Co.*	16,059	19,591	20,005
Penn Hills township *Allegheny Co.*	51,479	46,809	42,329
Peters township *Washington Co.*	14,542	17,566	21,213
Philadelphia city *Philadelphia Co.*	1,585,577	1,517,550	1,526,006
Pittsburgh city *Allegheny Co.*	369,785	334,563	305,704
Plum borough *Allegheny Co.*	25,609	26,940	27,126
Pottstown borough *Montgomery Co.*	21,831	21,859	22,377
Radnor township *Delaware Co.*	28,710	30,878	31,531
Reading city *Berks Co.*	78,441	81,207	88,082
Ridley township *Delaware Co.*	31,175	30,791	30,768
Ross township *Allegheny Co.*	33,496	32,551	31,105
Scranton city *Lackawanna Co.*	81,805	76,415	76,089
Shaler township *Allegheny Co.*	30,276	29,757	28,757
South Whitehall township *Lehigh Co.*	18,125	18,028	19,180
Spring township *Berks Co.*	18,840	21,805	27,119
Springettsbury township *York Co.*	21,369	23,883	26,668
Springfield township *Montgomery Co.*	19,612	19,533	19,418
Springfield township *Delaware Co.*	24,172	23,677	24,211
State College borough *Centre Co.*	38,933	38,420	42,034
Stroud township *Monroe Co.*	10,614	13,978	19,213
Susquehanna township *Dauphin Co.*	18,643	21,895	24,036
Swatara township *Dauphin Co.*	19,681	22,611	23,362
Tredyffrin township *Chester Co.*	28,021	29,062	29,332
Unity township *Westmoreland Co.*	19,973	21,137	22,607
Upper Darby township *Delaware Co.*	81,177	81,821	82,795
Upper Dublin township *Montgomery Co.*	24,028	25,878	25,569
Upper Macungie township *Lehigh Co.*	8,744	13,895	20,063
Upper Merion township *Montgomery Co.*	25,819	26,863	28,395
Upper Moreland township *Montgomery Co.*	25,252	24,993	24,015
Upper Providence township *Montgomery Co.*	9,722	15,398	21,219
Upper Saint Clair cdp/township *Allegheny Co.*	19,692	20,053	19,229
Warminster township *Bucks Co.*	32,846	31,383	32,682
Warrington township *Bucks Co.*	12,169	17,580	23,418
West Goshen township *Chester Co.*	18,110	20,495	21,866
West Mifflin borough *Allegheny Co.*	23,644	22,464	20,313
Whitehall township *Lehigh Co.*	22,794	24,896	26,738
Wilkes-Barre city *Luzerne Co.*	47,444	43,123	41,498
Williamsport city *Lycoming Co.*	31,933	30,706	29,381
York city *York Co.*	42,200	40,862	43,718
York township *York Co.*	19,227	23,637	27,793

Physical Characteristics

Place	Density (persons per square mile)	Land Area (square miles)	Water Area (square miles)	Elevation (feet)
Abington township *Montgomery Co.*	3,566.2	15.50	0.00	341
Allentown city *Lehigh Co.*	6,727.1	17.54	0.47	338
Allison Park cdp *Allegheny Co.*	1,557.4	13.83	0.00	860
Altoona city *Blair Co.*	4,675.3	9.90	0.00	1,165
Baldwin borough *Allegheny Co.*	3,418.1	5.78	0.10	1,145
Bensalem township *Bucks Co.*	3,046.1	19.83	1.09	98
Bethel Park municipality *Allegheny Co.*	2,768.7	11.67	0.00	1,198
Bethlehem township *Northampton Co.*	1,649.8	14.38	0.17	358
Bethlehem city *Northampton Co.*	3,925.4	19.10	0.35	358
Bristol township *Bucks Co.*	3,423.8	15.94	1.25	20
Buckingham township *Bucks Co.*	610.5	32.88	0.13	236
Chambersburg borough *Franklin Co.*	2,926.9	6.92	0.00	617
Cheltenham township *Montgomery Co.*	4,068.2	9.04	0.00	128
Chester city *Delaware Co.*	7,020.3	4.83	1.16	13
Coolbaugh township *Monroe Co.*	238.5	86.20	1.77	505
Cranberry township *Butler Co.*	1,231.1	22.82	0.00	n/a
Derry township *Dauphin Co.*	907.2	27.20	0.19	n/a
Dover township *York Co.*	507.2	41.55	0.23	446
Drexel Hill cdp *Delaware Co.*	8,779.4	3.19	0.00	246
East Hempfield township *Lancaster Co.*	1,116.4	21.06	0.09	n/a
East Pennsboro township *Cumberland Co.*	1,946.6	10.39	0.31	n/a
Easton city *Northampton Co.*	6,581.7	4.07	0.61	318
Erie city *Erie Co.*	5,334.5	19.08	0.19	653
Exeter township *Berks Co.*	1,054.4	24.23	0.34	n/a
Falls township *Bucks Co.*	1,613.7	21.25	5.31	n/a
Hampden township *Cumberland Co.*	1,617.1	17.34	0.52	n/a
Harrisburg city *Dauphin Co.*	6,092.1	8.12	3.73	335
Haverford township *Delaware Co.*	4,875.8	9.94	0.00	n/a
Hazleton city *Luzerne Co.*	4,215.4	6.01	0.00	1,657
Hempfield township *Westmoreland Co.*	563.6	76.72	0.14	n/a
Horsham township *Montgomery Co.*	1,509.5	17.32	0.00	249
Johnstown city *Cambria Co.*	3,559.8	5.89	0.19	1,168
King of Prussia cdp *Montgomery Co.*	2,349.2	8.48	0.15	200
Lancaster city *Lancaster Co.*	8,210.0	7.22	0.12	361
Lebanon city *Lebanon Co.*	6,113.5	4.16	0.00	469
Levittown cdp *Bucks Co.*	5,215.4	10.15	0.09	30
Lower Macungie township *Lehigh Co.*	1,370.6	22.34	0.11	n/a
Lower Makefield township *Bucks Co.*	1,821.9	17.87	0.41	n/a
Lower Merion township *Montgomery Co.*	2,442.9	23.67	0.16	n/a
Lower Paxton township *Dauphin Co.*	1,681.2	28.17	0.00	n/a
Lower Providence township *Montgomery Co.*	1,668.1	15.24	0.20	n/a
Manheim township *Lancaster Co.*	1,598.4	23.85	0.21	410
Manor township *Lancaster Co.*	511.6	38.33	10.28	n/a
Marple township *Delaware Co.*	2,296.4	10.20	0.31	410
McCandless township *Allegheny Co.*	1,724.8	16.49	0.10	n/a
McKeesport city *Allegheny Co.*	3,911.5	5.04	0.36	764
Middletown township *Bucks Co.*	2,404.2	18.89	0.42	n/a
Millcreek township *Erie Co.*	1,668.5	32.07	0.72	n/a
Monroeville municipality *Allegheny Co.*	1,438.1	19.73	0.00	1,230
Montgomery township *Montgomery Co.*	2,332.2	10.62	0.00	n/a

Place	Density (persons per square mile)	Land Area (square miles)	Water Area (square miles)	Elevation (feet)
Moon township *Allegheny Co.*	1,010.9	23.92	0.29	1,171
Mount Lebanon township *Allegheny Co.*	5,451.9	6.07	0.00	1,060
Muhlenberg township *Berks Co.*	1,666.9	11.77	0.22	331
Murrysville municipality *Westmoreland Co.*	545.1	36.83	0.00	899
New Castle city *Lawrence Co.*	2,801.5	8.30	0.22	853
Newtown township *Bucks Co.*	1,621.6	11.90	0.07	157
Norristown borough *Montgomery Co.*	9,752.9	3.51	0.08	157
North Huntingdon township *Westmoreland Co.*	1,123.0	27.25	0.05	n/a
Northampton township *Bucks Co.*	1,546.9	25.68	0.44	n/a
Palmer township *Northampton Co.*	1,923.9	10.75	0.09	n/a
Penn township *Westmoreland Co.*	650.3	30.76	0.00	984
Penn Hills township *Allegheny Co.*	2,214.1	19.11	0.23	942
Peters township *Washington Co.*	1,085.0	19.55	0.17	n/a
Philadelphia city *Philadelphia Co.*	11,379.5	134.10	8.60	39
Pittsburgh city *Allegheny Co.*	5,521.4	55.36	2.97	764
Plum borough *Allegheny Co.*	949.1	28.58	0.37	1,138
Pottstown borough *Montgomery Co.*	4,578.3	4.88	0.07	151
Radnor township *Delaware Co.*	2,288.8	13.77	0.01	433
Reading city *Berks Co.*	8,911.9	9.88	0.25	305
Ridley township *Delaware Co.*	6,010.9	5.11	0.19	n/a
Ross township *Allegheny Co.*	2,148.9	14.47	0.00	n/a
Scranton city *Lackawanna Co.*	3,006.4	25.30	0.22	755
Shaler township *Allegheny Co.*	2,596.5	11.07	0.09	n/a
South Whitehall township *Lehigh Co.*	1,123.0	17.07	0.17	n/a
Spring township *Berks Co.*	1,467.5	18.48	0.06	n/a
Springettsbury township *York Co.*	1,628.5	16.37	0.00	n/a
Springfield township *Montgomery Co.*	2,863.9	6.78	0.01	n/a
Springfield township *Delaware Co.*	3,830.5	6.32	0.01	249
State College borough *Centre Co.*	9,223.2	4.55	0.00	1,165
Stroud township *Monroe Co.*	618.7	31.05	0.26	n/a
Susquehanna township *Dauphin Co.*	1,802.0	13.33	1.93	n/a
Swatara township *Dauphin Co.*	1,790.1	13.05	2.48	417
Tredyffrin township *Chester Co.*	1,484.1	19.76	0.08	n/a
Unity township *Westmoreland Co.*	335.2	67.44	0.13	n/a
Upper Darby township *Delaware Co.*	10,580.3	7.82	0.00	66
Upper Dublin township *Montgomery Co.*	1,932.7	13.22	0.03	n/a
Upper Macungie township *Lehigh Co.*	769.6	26.06	0.19	n/a
Upper Merion township *Montgomery Co.*	1,674.7	16.95	0.31	n/a
Upper Moreland township *Montgomery Co.*	3,012.3	7.97	0.00	n/a
Upper Providence township *Montgomery Co.*	1,191.5	17.80	0.35	n/a
Upper Saint Clair cdp/township *Allegheny Co.*	1,958.5	9.81	0.00	1,099
Warminster township *Bucks Co.*	3,216.1	10.16	0.02	308
Warrington township *Bucks Co.*	1,709.8	13.69	0.09	394
West Goshen township *Chester Co.*	1,844.9	11.85	0.14	436
West Mifflin borough *Allegheny Co.*	1,429.1	14.21	0.29	1,096
Whitehall township *Lehigh Co.*	2,127.7	12.56	0.30	n/a
Wilkes-Barre city *Luzerne Co.*	5,945.0	6.98	0.32	535
Williamsport city *Lycoming Co.*	3,365.1	8.73	0.69	518
York city *York Co.*	8,260.3	5.29	0.04	387
York township *York Co.*	1,101.2	25.23	0.40	387

NOTE: Data as of 2010

Population by Race/Hispanic Origin

Place	White[1] (%)	Black[1] (%)	Asian[1] (%)	AIAN[1,2] (%)	NHOPI[1,3] (%)	Other (%)	Hispanic[4] (%)
Abington township *Montgomery Co.*	79.7	12.4	4.9	0.1	0.0	2.9	3.2
Allentown city *Lehigh Co.*	58.5	12.5	2.2	0.8	0.0	26.0	42.8
Allison Park cdp *Allegheny Co.*	94.4	1.5	3.1	0.1	0.0	0.9	0.9
Altoona city *Blair Co.*	93.8	3.3	0.4	0.1	0.0	2.4	1.3
Baldwin borough *Allegheny Co.*	91.6	5.3	1.2	0.1	0.0	1.8	1.1
Bensalem township *Bucks Co.*	75.6	7.3	10.2	0.5	0.0	6.4	8.4
Bethel Park municipality *Allegheny Co.*	96.1	1.3	1.4	0.1	0.0	1.1	1.0
Bethlehem township *Northampton Co.*	86.7	4.7	4.4	0.2	0.1	3.9	7.9
Bethlehem city *Northampton Co.*	76.4	6.9	2.9	0.3	0.0	13.5	24.4
Bristol township *Bucks Co.*	81.0	10.2	2.8	0.2	0.0	5.8	7.4
Buckingham township *Bucks Co.*	93.8	1.1	3.4	0.1	0.0	1.6	2.4
Chambersburg borough *Franklin Co.*	77.0	9.2	1.4	0.3	0.1	12.0	15.7
Cheltenham township *Montgomery Co.*	57.4	31.1	7.7	0.2	0.0	3.6	3.9
Chester city *Delaware Co.*	17.2	74.7	0.6	0.4	0.1	7.0	9.0
Coolbaugh township *Monroe Co.*	56.4	27.8	1.8	0.7	0.1	13.2	23.3
Cranberry township *Butler Co.*	94.4	1.2	2.8	0.1	0.0	1.5	1.6
Derry township *Dauphin Co.*	84.7	4.5	7.5	0.2	0.0	3.1	3.0
Dover township *York Co.*	93.1	3.3	0.7	0.3	0.0	2.6	3.2
Drexel Hill cdp *Delaware Co.*	85.5	7.7	4.3	0.1	0.0	2.4	2.6
East Hempfield township *Lancaster Co.*	88.8	2.8	3.5	0.1	0.0	4.8	6.9
East Pennsboro township *Cumberland Co.*	89.0	2.7	5.1	0.1	0.0	3.1	2.8
Easton city *Northampton Co.*	67.2	16.8	2.4	0.4	0.1	13.1	19.9
Erie city *Erie Co.*	75.0	16.8	1.5	0.3	0.1	6.3	6.9
Exeter township *Berks Co.*	91.9	3.3	1.9	0.1	0.0	2.8	3.6
Falls township *Bucks Co.*	86.5	5.8	4.2	0.2	0.0	3.3	4.4
Hampden township *Cumberland Co.*	88.9	1.7	7.1	0.1	0.0	2.2	2.0
Harrisburg city *Dauphin Co.*	30.7	52.4	3.5	0.5	0.1	12.8	18.0
Haverford township *Delaware Co.*	91.2	2.7	4.2	0.1	0.0	1.8	1.9
Hazleton city *Luzerne Co.*	69.4	4.0	0.8	0.4	0.0	25.4	37.3
Hempfield township *Westmoreland Co.*	95.5	2.4	0.9	0.1	0.0	1.1	0.9
Horsham township *Montgomery Co.*	86.0	4.3	7.2	0.1	0.0	2.4	2.9
Johnstown city *Cambria Co.*	80.0	14.6	0.2	0.2	0.0	5.0	3.1
King of Prussia cdp *Montgomery Co.*	71.8	5.7	18.6	0.3	0.0	3.6	4.2
Lancaster city *Lancaster Co.*	55.2	16.3	3.0	0.7	0.1	24.7	39.3
Lebanon city *Lebanon Co.*	74.1	5.9	1.1	0.5	0.0	18.4	32.1
Levittown cdp *Bucks Co.*	90.4	3.8	1.7	0.3	0.0	3.8	5.1
Lower Macungie township *Lehigh Co.*	87.4	3.3	6.0	0.1	0.0	3.2	5.0
Lower Makefield township *Bucks Co.*	89.6	2.3	6.3	0.1	0.0	1.7	2.4
Lower Merion township *Montgomery Co.*	85.7	5.6	6.0	0.1	0.0	2.6	3.0
Lower Paxton township *Dauphin Co.*	78.8	12.2	4.6	0.1	0.0	4.3	4.6
Lower Providence township *Montgomery Co.*	81.0	7.1	9.7	0.1	0.0	2.1	2.9
Manheim township *Lancaster Co.*	87.6	3.0	5.0	0.1	0.0	4.3	6.6
Manor township *Lancaster Co.*	91.8	2.6	1.7	0.2	0.0	3.7	6.3
Marple township *Delaware Co.*	89.6	2.1	7.0	0.1	0.0	1.2	1.3
McCandless township *Allegheny Co.*	91.9	1.7	5.0	0.1	0.0	1.3	1.1
McKeesport city *Allegheny Co.*	62.3	31.9	0.3	0.3	0.0	5.2	2.3
Middletown township *Bucks Co.*	90.1	3.2	3.9	0.2	0.0	2.6	3.1
Millcreek township *Erie Co.*	94.7	1.5	1.8	0.1	0.0	1.9	1.8
Monroeville municipality *Allegheny Co.*	79.5	11.7	5.9	0.2	0.0	2.7	1.5
Montgomery township *Montgomery Co.*	76.7	4.6	16.6	0.1	0.0	2.0	2.2

Place	White[1] (%)	Black[1] (%)	Asian[1] (%)	AIAN[1,2] (%)	NHOPI[1,3] (%)	Other (%)	Hispanic[4] (%)
Moon township *Allegheny Co.*	89.8	4.5	3.1	0.1	0.0	2.5	2.0
Mount Lebanon township *Allegheny Co.*	93.6	1.1	3.7	0.0	0.0	1.6	1.8
Muhlenberg township *Berks Co.*	85.9	4.3	1.5	0.3	0.0	8.0	13.8
Murrysville municipality *Westmoreland Co.*	93.7	0.8	4.4	0.1	0.0	1.0	1.0
New Castle city *Lawrence Co.*	83.2	12.2	0.4	0.1	0.0	4.1	1.6
Newtown township *Bucks Co.*	89.3	1.2	7.9	0.1	0.0	1.5	1.9
Norristown borough *Montgomery Co.*	40.9	35.9	2.1	0.4	0.1	20.6	28.3
North Huntingdon township *Westmoreland Co.*	97.8	0.7	0.6	0.1	0.0	0.8	0.6
Northampton township *Bucks Co.*	94.9	0.6	3.5	0.1	0.0	0.9	1.5
Palmer township *Northampton Co.*	86.5	5.3	4.1	0.2	0.0	3.9	6.1
Penn township *Westmoreland Co.*	98.2	0.5	0.5	0.1	0.0	0.7	0.7
Penn Hills township *Allegheny Co.*	61.4	34.6	0.8	0.2	0.0	3.0	1.4
Peters township *Washington Co.*	96.2	0.5	2.0	0.1	0.0	1.2	1.5
Philadelphia city *Philadelphia Co.*	41.0	43.4	6.3	0.5	0.0	8.8	12.3
Pittsburgh city *Allegheny Co.*	66.0	26.1	4.4	0.2	0.0	3.3	2.3
Plum borough *Allegheny Co.*	93.9	3.6	1.1	0.1	0.0	1.3	0.9
Pottstown borough *Montgomery Co.*	72.1	19.5	0.9	0.3	0.1	7.1	8.0
Radnor township *Delaware Co.*	85.8	3.9	7.9	0.1	0.0	2.3	3.0
Reading city *Berks Co.*	48.4	13.2	1.2	0.9	0.1	36.2	58.2
Ridley township *Delaware Co.*	90.0	5.7	2.2	0.1	0.0	2.0	1.9
Ross township *Allegheny Co.*	94.0	2.1	2.5	0.1	0.0	1.3	1.1
Scranton city *Lackawanna Co.*	84.1	5.5	3.0	0.2	0.0	7.2	9.9
Shaler township *Allegheny Co.*	97.4	0.7	0.9	0.1	0.0	0.9	0.8
South Whitehall township *Lehigh Co.*	89.8	2.8	4.7	0.1	0.0	2.6	4.7
Spring township *Berks Co.*	87.9	4.8	3.2	0.2	0.0	3.9	6.1
Springettsbury township *York Co.*	82.9	6.8	3.0	0.2	0.0	7.1	7.1
Springfield township *Montgomery Co.*	83.6	11.1	2.8	0.1	0.0	2.4	2.4
Springfield township *Delaware Co.*	93.4	1.7	3.8	0.1	0.0	1.0	1.1
State College borough *Centre Co.*	83.2	3.8	9.8	0.2	0.0	3.0	3.9
Stroud township *Monroe Co.*	70.8	16.4	3.6	0.3	0.0	8.9	15.2
Susquehanna township *Dauphin Co.*	67.3	23.6	3.6	0.1	0.0	5.4	4.9
Swatara township *Dauphin Co.*	71.0	18.4	3.4	0.1	0.1	7.0	8.3
Tredyffrin township *Chester Co.*	85.1	3.3	9.8	0.1	0.0	1.7	2.2
Unity township *Westmoreland Co.*	97.2	0.7	1.0	0.1	0.0	1.0	0.9
Upper Darby township *Delaware Co.*	56.6	27.5	11.1	0.2	0.0	4.6	4.5
Upper Dublin township *Montgomery Co.*	83.0	6.6	8.5	0.1	0.0	1.8	1.8
Upper Macungie township *Lehigh Co.*	85.0	2.7	9.0	0.1	0.0	3.2	4.9
Upper Merion township *Montgomery Co.*	76.0	5.5	14.7	0.2	0.0	3.6	3.9
Upper Moreland township *Montgomery Co.*	87.0	5.1	4.4	0.2	0.1	3.2	3.6
Upper Providence township *Montgomery Co.*	86.6	3.5	7.9	0.1	0.0	1.9	2.2
Upper Saint Clair cdp/township *Allegheny Co.*	92.1	0.8	5.7	0.0	0.0	1.4	1.3
Warminster township *Bucks Co.*	89.3	3.1	1.9	0.2	0.1	5.4	7.7
Warrington township *Bucks Co.*	88.5	2.1	6.1	0.2	0.0	3.1	4.2
West Goshen township *Chester Co.*	88.8	3.7	4.7	0.2	0.0	2.6	3.7
West Mifflin borough *Allegheny Co.*	86.5	11.0	0.4	0.1	0.0	2.0	1.2
Whitehall township *Lehigh Co.*	82.9	5.7	4.1	0.3	0.0	7.0	10.7
Wilkes-Barre city *Luzerne Co.*	79.2	10.9	1.4	0.3	0.0	8.2	11.3
Williamsport city *Lycoming Co.*	80.8	13.5	0.7	0.2	0.0	4.8	2.6
York city *York Co.*	51.2	28.0	1.2	0.6	0.0	19.0	28.5
York township *York Co.*	91.2	3.7	2.3	0.2	0.0	2.6	3.3

NOTE: Data as of 2010; (1) Exclude multiple race combinations; (2) American Indian/Alaska Native; (3) Native Hawaiian/Other Pacific Islander; (4) May be of any race

Avg. Household Size, Median Age, Male/Female Ratio & Foreign Born

Place	Average Household Size (persons)	Median Age (years)	Males per 100 Females	Foreign Born (%)
Abington township *Montgomery Co.*	2.55	42.8	90.5	8.3
Allentown city *Lehigh Co.*	2.64	32.7	93.0	14.0
Allison Park cdp *Allegheny Co.*	2.42	44.8	91.3	4.9
Altoona city *Blair Co.*	2.34	38.9	92.4	1.2
Baldwin borough *Allegheny Co.*	2.28	44.7	90.8	2.1
Bensalem township *Bucks Co.*	2.55	39.6	97.9	15.7
Bethel Park municipality *Allegheny Co.*	2.35	46.1	91.3	3.1
Bethlehem township *Northampton Co.*	2.64	43.9	94.0	12.0
Bethlehem city *Northampton Co.*	2.34	35.7	92.5	6.9
Bristol township *Bucks Co.*	2.73	38.8	98.8	7.8
Buckingham township *Bucks Co.*	2.86	43.2	96.3	7.0
Chambersburg borough *Franklin Co.*	2.33	37.1	87.3	10.8
Cheltenham township *Montgomery Co.*	2.44	40.0	83.4	12.4
Chester city *Delaware Co.*	2.64	29.9	89.5	2.8
Coolbaugh township *Monroe Co.*	2.95	37.4	95.6	10.9
Cranberry township *Butler Co.*	2.72	38.0	97.1	3.8
Derry township *Dauphin Co.*	2.33	38.3	90.5	9.2
Dover township *York Co.*	2.52	40.9	96.6	1.3
Drexel Hill cdp *Delaware Co.*	2.48	37.5	93.1	9.0
East Hempfield township *Lancaster Co.*	2.43	44.2	94.9	4.7
East Pennsboro township *Cumberland Co.*	2.35	40.5	92.3	7.4
Easton city *Northampton Co.*	2.55	31.9	101.5	9.1
Erie city *Erie Co.*	2.36	33.2	93.3	5.7
Exeter township *Berks Co.*	2.61	41.4	95.0	3.2
Falls township *Bucks Co.*	2.61	39.1	95.2	8.7
Hampden township *Cumberland Co.*	2.44	42.6	93.5	7.6
Harrisburg city *Dauphin Co.*	2.36	32.2	92.7	7.1
Haverford township *Delaware Co.*	2.63	40.5	90.8	7.1
Hazleton city *Luzerne Co.*	2.54	37.6	93.6	19.9
Hempfield township *Westmoreland Co.*	2.30	46.2	98.8	1.6
Horsham township *Montgomery Co.*	2.67	40.5	94.6	9.9
Johnstown city *Cambria Co.*	2.08	41.8	87.9	1.6
King of Prussia cdp *Montgomery Co.*	2.31	37.8	98.9	21.8
Lancaster city *Lancaster Co.*	2.58	30.5	98.7	9.8
Lebanon city *Lebanon Co.*	2.42	35.6	93.7	4.5
Levittown cdp *Bucks Co.*	2.85	39.4	98.0	4.5
Lower Macungie township *Lehigh Co.*	2.65	41.0	93.7	8.5
Lower Makefield township *Bucks Co.*	2.74	43.5	93.5	9.4
Lower Merion township *Montgomery Co.*	2.43	43.4	85.3	11.5
Lower Paxton township *Dauphin Co.*	2.34	41.2	92.0	7.4
Lower Providence township *Montgomery Co.*	2.66	40.8	108.6	10.9
Manheim township *Lancaster Co.*	2.44	44.0	89.1	7.8
Manor township *Lancaster Co.*	2.46	41.4	93.2	5.0
Marple township *Delaware Co.*	2.61	46.7	91.5	12.5
McCandless township *Allegheny Co.*	2.36	44.0	90.2	5.6
McKeesport city *Allegheny Co.*	2.25	41.5	86.7	1.8
Middletown township *Bucks Co.*	2.65	42.6	95.4	5.8
Millcreek township *Erie Co.*	2.32	42.8	92.8	4.9
Monroeville municipality *Allegheny Co.*	2.21	45.9	89.5	7.8
Montgomery township *Montgomery Co.*	2.68	41.3	92.5	14.0

Place	Average Household Size (persons)	Median Age (years)	Males per 100 Females	Foreign Born (%)
Moon township *Allegheny Co.*	2.37	39.0	99.0	5.3
Mount Lebanon township *Allegheny Co.*	2.30	43.8	87.7	6.7
Muhlenberg township *Berks Co.*	2.49	42.9	93.3	6.0
Murrysville municipality *Westmoreland Co.*	2.51	47.4	96.5	5.6
New Castle city *Lawrence Co.*	2.30	40.8	90.1	1.4
Newtown township *Bucks Co.*	2.59	42.1	91.5	10.1
Norristown borough *Montgomery Co.*	2.79	31.2	99.3	19.3
North Huntingdon township *Westmoreland Co.*	2.47	44.9	94.8	1.3
Northampton township *Bucks Co.*	2.84	44.4	94.6	10.5
Palmer township *Northampton Co.*	2.53	44.9	92.0	7.6
Penn township *Westmoreland Co.*	2.63	44.9	96.8	1.7
Penn Hills township *Allegheny Co.*	2.24	45.3	86.6	2.8
Peters township *Washington Co.*	2.88	43.0	96.8	3.4
Philadelphia city *Philadelphia Co.*	2.45	33.5	89.3	11.5
Pittsburgh city *Allegheny Co.*	2.07	33.2	94.0	6.9
Plum borough *Allegheny Co.*	2.48	42.6	95.3	3.2
Pottstown borough *Montgomery Co.*	2.36	36.1	92.1	2.4
Radnor township *Delaware Co.*	2.46	27.5	91.5	11.6
Reading city *Berks Co.*	2.85	28.9	94.3	17.4
Ridley township *Delaware Co.*	2.55	40.1	93.5	4.4
Ross township *Allegheny Co.*	2.15	45.4	88.5	3.8
Scranton city *Lackawanna Co.*	2.35	37.9	92.9	6.2
Shaler township *Allegheny Co.*	2.38	45.2	92.5	2.2
South Whitehall township *Lehigh Co.*	2.38	47.4	89.6	8.0
Spring township *Berks Co.*	2.46	41.4	94.3	7.7
Springettsbury township *York Co.*	2.37	42.1	107.4	7.7
Springfield township *Montgomery Co.*	2.45	45.3	86.5	5.1
Springfield township *Delaware Co.*	2.76	43.2	93.1	4.4
State College borough *Centre Co.*	2.30	21.5	117.2	9.8
Stroud township *Monroe Co.*	2.81	40.2	95.0	13.5
Susquehanna township *Dauphin Co.*	2.20	42.3	86.0	6.3
Swatara township *Dauphin Co.*	2.35	40.0	97.4	8.9
Tredyffrin township *Chester Co.*	2.42	42.9	89.5	10.1
Unity township *Westmoreland Co.*	2.40	44.1	98.6	1.7
Upper Darby township *Delaware Co.*	2.60	34.7	92.8	18.4
Upper Dublin township *Montgomery Co.*	2.69	43.9	94.6	9.6
Upper Macungie township *Lehigh Co.*	2.71	39.1	97.2	10.8
Upper Merion township *Montgomery Co.*	2.35	39.4	98.9	18.1
Upper Moreland township *Montgomery Co.*	2.39	41.2	94.9	6.4
Upper Providence township *Montgomery Co.*	2.82	38.7	93.9	7.6
Upper Saint Clair cdp/township *Allegheny Co.*	2.75	44.3	96.5	7.9
Warminster township *Bucks Co.*	2.51	44.6	94.0	9.1
Warrington township *Bucks Co.*	2.86	39.8	98.9	10.7
West Goshen township *Chester Co.*	2.70	38.7	95.8	7.2
West Mifflin borough *Allegheny Co.*	2.30	44.8	89.8	1.1
Whitehall township *Lehigh Co.*	2.40	41.6	90.6	13.3
Wilkes-Barre city *Luzerne Co.*	2.28	36.5	95.6	4.6
Williamsport city *Lycoming Co.*	2.27	29.7	104.4	1.3
York city *York Co.*	2.62	30.1	92.9	8.3
York township *York Co.*	2.34	43.3	90.8	4.7

NOTE: Average Household Size, Median Age, and Males per 100 Females as of 2010. Foreign Born figures are 2006-2010 5-year estimates.

Five Largest Ancestry Groups

Place	Group 1	Group 2	Group 3	Group 4	Group 5
Abington township *Montgomery Co.*	Irish (25.5%)	German (22.4%)	Italian (13.8%)	English (8.8%)	Polish (7.3%)
Allentown city *Lehigh Co.*	German (17.2%)	Irish (7.6%)	Italian (6.5%)	Penn German (3.7%)	English (3.6%)
Allison Park cdp *Allegheny Co.*	German (41.2%)	Irish (21.8%)	Italian (17.0%)	Polish (10.9%)	English (7.7%)
Altoona city *Blair Co.*	German (42.3%)	Irish (21.8%)	Italian (15.1%)	English (7.5%)	Polish (5.2%)
Baldwin borough *Allegheny Co.*	German (40.1%)	Irish (25.6%)	Italian (19.5%)	Polish (14.9%)	English (7.1%)
Bensalem township *Bucks Co.*	Irish (26.5%)	German (22.1%)	Italian (14.5%)	Polish (9.2%)	English (7.8%)
Bethel Park municipality *Allegheny Co.*	German (37.7%)	Irish (24.7%)	Italian (21.5%)	English (11.1%)	Polish (11.0%)
Bethlehem township *Northampton Co.*	German (25.3%)	Italian (19.5%)	Irish (15.1%)	Polish (6.3%)	English (5.9%)
Bethlehem city *Northampton Co.*	German (22.7%)	Irish (14.1%)	Italian (11.1%)	English (6.1%)	Polish (5.0%)
Bristol township *Bucks Co.*	Irish (29.6%)	German (25.4%)	Italian (14.4%)	English (10.0%)	Polish (9.6%)
Buckingham township *Bucks Co.*	Irish (28.5%)	Italian (22.8%)	German (20.7%)	English (12.8%)	Polish (8.0%)
Chambersburg borough *Franklin Co.*	German (30.9%)	Irish (13.0%)	English (6.8%)	American (6.1%)	Italian (3.2%)
Cheltenham township *Montgomery Co.*	Irish (14.9%)	German (12.0%)	Italian (8.0%)	Russian (6.7%)	English (6.4%)
Chester city *Delaware Co.*	Irish (2.9%)	German (2.3%)	Italian (1.9%)	English (1.4%)	Polish (1.1%)
Coolbaugh township *Monroe Co.*	Irish (11.9%)	Italian (11.5%)	German (11.5%)	Polish (6.3%)	English (4.0%)
Cranberry township *Butler Co.*	German (35.6%)	Irish (22.4%)	Italian (20.4%)	English (9.0%)	Polish (8.4%)
Derry township *Dauphin Co.*	German (35.6%)	Irish (17.7%)	Italian (14.5%)	English (12.0%)	Polish (3.7%)
Dover township *York Co.*	German (47.8%)	Irish (11.7%)	American (8.5%)	English (7.6%)	Italian (3.7%)
Drexel Hill cdp *Delaware Co.*	Irish (39.7%)	Italian (25.0%)	German (17.9%)	English (6.5%)	Polish (4.5%)
East Hempfield township *Lancaster Co.*	German (40.6%)	Irish (17.0%)	English (12.2%)	Italian (8.2%)	American (4.6%)
East Pennsboro township *Cumberland Co.*	German (39.8%)	Irish (17.9%)	Italian (9.7%)	English (7.7%)	American (5.5%)
Easton city *Northampton Co.*	German (21.7%)	Italian (13.6%)	Irish (12.8%)	English (5.6%)	American (5.3%)
Erie city *Erie Co.*	German (27.3%)	Irish (17.4%)	Italian (15.5%)	Polish (12.7%)	English (5.8%)
Exeter township *Berks Co.*	German (40.5%)	Irish (17.5%)	Italian (15.1%)	Polish (10.0%)	English (9.3%)
Falls township *Bucks Co.*	Irish (28.2%)	German (27.8%)	Italian (15.0%)	English (12.7%)	Polish (8.6%)
Hampden township *Cumberland Co.*	German (34.0%)	Irish (19.5%)	English (10.6%)	Italian (10.4%)	Polish (5.9%)
Harrisburg city *Dauphin Co.*	German (11.4%)	Irish (5.9%)	Italian (3.8%)	English (2.5%)	Polish (1.6%)
Haverford township *Delaware Co.*	Irish (38.1%)	German (20.1%)	Italian (20.0%)	English (10.2%)	Polish (4.6%)
Hazleton city *Luzerne Co.*	Italian (20.2%)	Polish (13.0%)	German (12.6%)	Irish (10.3%)	Slovak (8.2%)
Hempfield township *Westmoreland Co.*	German (37.5%)	Italian (21.1%)	Irish (16.6%)	English (11.0%)	Polish (10.7%)
Horsham township *Montgomery Co.*	Irish (28.6%)	German (28.5%)	Italian (16.5%)	English (12.2%)	Polish (8.0%)
Johnstown city *Cambria Co.*	German (24.2%)	Irish (15.7%)	Italian (12.7%)	Slovak (8.0%)	English (7.3%)
King of Prussia cdp *Montgomery Co.*	Irish (20.7%)	German (18.0%)	Italian (17.4%)	Polish (7.6%)	English (6.2%)
Lancaster city *Lancaster Co.*	German (20.1%)	Irish (8.3%)	English (5.1%)	Italian (4.2%)	American (2.4%)
Lebanon city *Lebanon Co.*	German (32.5%)	Irish (11.7%)	Italian (5.8%)	Penn German (4.0%)	American (3.8%)
Levittown cdp *Bucks Co.*	Irish (34.2%)	German (30.5%)	Italian (15.2%)	Polish (11.0%)	English (10.7%)
Lower Macungie township *Lehigh Co.*	German (32.6%)	Irish (17.4%)	Italian (14.8%)	English (8.0%)	Polish (5.3%)
Lower Makefield township *Bucks Co.*	Irish (24.8%)	German (22.0%)	Italian (16.3%)	English (12.4%)	Polish (8.1%)
Lower Merion township *Montgomery Co.*	Irish (15.4%)	German (13.9%)	Russian (10.8%)	English (9.5%)	Italian (9.4%)
Lower Paxton township *Dauphin Co.*	German (34.1%)	Irish (14.0%)	Italian (9.7%)	English (8.1%)	American (5.4%)
Lower Providence township *Montgomery Co.*	Italian (24.7%)	Irish (23.6%)	German (22.3%)	English (7.9%)	Polish (6.6%)
Manheim township *Lancaster Co.*	German (36.7%)	Irish (13.6%)	English (12.5%)	Italian (6.5%)	American (4.9%)
Manor township *Lancaster Co.*	German (45.9%)	Irish (12.9%)	English (10.5%)	Italian (8.3%)	American (7.7%)
Marple township *Delaware Co.*	Irish (27.2%)	Italian (26.0%)	German (16.2%)	English (9.4%)	Polish (4.2%)
McCandless township *Allegheny Co.*	German (39.0%)	Irish (22.8%)	Italian (16.1%)	Polish (10.0%)	English (7.9%)
McKeesport city *Allegheny Co.*	German (16.8%)	Irish (13.2%)	Italian (11.9%)	Polish (9.0%)	English (7.2%)
Middletown township *Bucks Co.*	Irish (29.2%)	German (28.3%)	Italian (16.4%)	English (10.6%)	Polish (9.4%)
Millcreek township *Erie Co.*	German (35.7%)	Irish (20.1%)	Italian (17.1%)	Polish (12.6%)	English (10.0%)
Monroeville municipality *Allegheny Co.*	German (24.2%)	Irish (19.8%)	Italian (15.0%)	Polish (7.3%)	English (7.1%)
Montgomery township *Montgomery Co.*	Irish (26.6%)	German (21.2%)	Italian (17.4%)	English (8.4%)	Polish (5.4%)

Place	Group 1	Group 2	Group 3	Group 4	Group 5
Moon township *Allegheny Co.*	German (32.3%)	Irish (22.7%)	Italian (21.2%)	Polish (11.9%)	English (10.4%)
Mount Lebanon township *Allegheny Co.*	German (30.2%)	Irish (24.8%)	Italian (19.8%)	English (12.4%)	Polish (8.5%)
Muhlenberg township *Berks Co.*	German (40.0%)	Italian (14.2%)	Irish (12.9%)	English (6.8%)	Penn German (6.0%)
Murrysville municipality *Westmoreland Co.*	German (34.8%)	Italian (22.0%)	Irish (18.5%)	English (14.7%)	Polish (7.9%)
New Castle city *Lawrence Co.*	Italian (31.2%)	German (20.7%)	Irish (15.8%)	Polish (8.2%)	English (7.1%)
Newtown township *Bucks Co.*	Irish (26.0%)	German (20.8%)	Italian (18.9%)	English (12.4%)	Polish (8.9%)
Norristown borough *Montgomery Co.*	Italian (13.5%)	Irish (11.7%)	German (9.1%)	American (4.2%)	Polish (3.6%)
North Huntingdon township *Westmoreland Co.*	German (33.7%)	Irish (21.8%)	Italian (17.6%)	English (11.2%)	Polish (10.9%)
Northampton township *Bucks Co.*	Irish (29.0%)	German (24.2%)	Italian (17.6%)	English (9.4%)	Polish (8.6%)
Palmer township *Northampton Co.*	German (26.5%)	Italian (21.6%)	Irish (16.0%)	English (9.4%)	Polish (6.5%)
Penn township *Westmoreland Co.*	German (34.7%)	Italian (22.8%)	Irish (19.7%)	English (12.9%)	Polish (8.9%)
Penn Hills township *Allegheny Co.*	German (20.0%)	Italian (16.8%)	Irish (15.1%)	English (6.6%)	Polish (5.9%)
Peters township *Washington Co.*	German (30.2%)	Irish (21.8%)	Italian (21.0%)	English (13.9%)	Polish (12.1%)
Philadelphia city *Philadelphia Co.*	Irish (13.0%)	Italian (8.3%)	German (8.2%)	Polish (3.9%)	English (3.1%)
Pittsburgh city *Allegheny Co.*	German (21.4%)	Irish (16.7%)	Italian (13.4%)	Polish (8.0%)	English (5.4%)
Plum borough *Allegheny Co.*	German (32.1%)	Italian (24.7%)	Irish (21.9%)	English (10.0%)	Polish (9.0%)
Pottstown borough *Montgomery Co.*	German (25.0%)	Irish (17.3%)	Italian (11.9%)	English (8.6%)	Polish (7.3%)
Radnor township *Delaware Co.*	Irish (25.6%)	German (15.4%)	Italian (14.1%)	English (13.5%)	Polish (5.0%)
Reading city *Berks Co.*	German (12.0%)	Irish (6.0%)	Italian (5.1%)	Polish (4.1%)	Penn German (2.4%)
Ridley township *Delaware Co.*	Irish (42.9%)	Italian (26.9%)	German (19.9%)	English (11.4%)	Polish (5.0%)
Ross township *Allegheny Co.*	German (40.1%)	Irish (24.8%)	Italian (16.5%)	Polish (10.1%)	English (8.8%)
Scranton city *Lackawanna Co.*	Irish (30.6%)	Italian (21.1%)	German (19.1%)	Polish (14.4%)	Welsh (6.0%)
Shaler township *Allegheny Co.*	German (44.8%)	Irish (22.7%)	Italian (20.5%)	Polish (17.0%)	English (7.8%)
South Whitehall township *Lehigh Co.*	German (28.9%)	Irish (15.4%)	Italian (12.7%)	English (5.9%)	Penn German (5.9%)
Spring township *Berks Co.*	German (40.1%)	Italian (15.1%)	Irish (14.7%)	Polish (8.7%)	English (7.8%)
Springettsbury township *York Co.*	German (42.5%)	Irish (12.3%)	English (10.3%)	American (6.2%)	Italian (6.2%)
Springfield township *Montgomery Co.*	Irish (31.2%)	German (21.2%)	Italian (16.6%)	English (11.9%)	Polish (5.1%)
Springfield township *Delaware Co.*	Irish (43.4%)	Italian (31.1%)	German (19.1%)	English (10.7%)	Polish (4.0%)
State College borough *Centre Co.*	German (21.3%)	Irish (14.7%)	Italian (10.0%)	Polish (6.3%)	English (5.5%)
Stroud township *Monroe Co.*	German (19.8%)	Italian (16.9%)	Irish (14.9%)	English (7.5%)	Polish (3.3%)
Susquehanna township *Dauphin Co.*	German (31.3%)	Irish (14.2%)	English (7.0%)	Italian (6.9%)	Polish (3.8%)
Swatara township *Dauphin Co.*	German (26.4%)	Irish (12.2%)	Italian (7.1%)	English (5.6%)	American (5.2%)
Tredyffrin township *Chester Co.*	Irish (24.9%)	German (23.9%)	English (16.4%)	Italian (14.8%)	Polish (4.6%)
Unity township *Westmoreland Co.*	German (31.0%)	Italian (23.8%)	Irish (17.9%)	English (11.4%)	Polish (10.8%)
Upper Darby township *Delaware Co.*	Irish (27.3%)	Italian (15.7%)	German (11.9%)	English (5.4%)	Polish (3.3%)
Upper Dublin township *Montgomery Co.*	German (21.0%)	Irish (20.7%)	Italian (14.4%)	English (10.6%)	Russian (8.3%)
Upper Macungie township *Lehigh Co.*	German (32.7%)	Irish (15.9%)	Italian (14.5%)	English (7.6%)	Polish (6.3%)
Upper Merion township *Montgomery Co.*	Irish (21.5%)	German (18.5%)	Italian (18.1%)	Polish (8.3%)	English (7.9%)
Upper Moreland township *Montgomery Co.*	Irish (30.9%)	German (28.1%)	Italian (15.8%)	English (12.5%)	Polish (5.5%)
Upper Providence township *Montgomery Co.*	German (28.2%)	Irish (25.4%)	Italian (21.3%)	English (10.5%)	Polish (8.9%)
Upper Saint Clair cdp/township *Allegheny Co.*	German (31.1%)	Irish (25.4%)	Italian (18.3%)	English (10.8%)	Polish (7.9%)
Warminster township *Bucks Co.*	Irish (27.7%)	German (27.2%)	Italian (16.6%)	English (10.6%)	Polish (8.1%)
Warrington township *Bucks Co.*	Irish (30.0%)	German (28.1%)	Italian (17.9%)	English (10.6%)	Polish (8.2%)
West Goshen township *Chester Co.*	Irish (29.4%)	German (24.1%)	Italian (19.1%)	English (16.3%)	Polish (4.5%)
West Mifflin borough *Allegheny Co.*	German (26.4%)	Irish (21.4%)	Slovak (14.3%)	Italian (13.3%)	Polish (10.6%)
Whitehall township *Lehigh Co.*	German (28.8%)	Irish (10.4%)	Italian (8.3%)	Polish (5.5%)	Slovak (4.5%)
Wilkes-Barre city *Luzerne Co.*	Irish (21.8%)	Polish (19.4%)	German (17.8%)	Italian (12.3%)	Welsh (5.6%)
Williamsport city *Lycoming Co.*	German (30.8%)	Irish (16.0%)	Italian (11.4%)	English (7.2%)	Polish (6.1%)
York city *York Co.*	German (19.6%)	Irish (7.3%)	Italian (5.0%)	American (3.7%)	English (3.5%)
York township *York Co.*	German (45.8%)	Irish (12.3%)	English (10.0%)	American (6.3%)	Italian (5.3%)

NOTE: Figures are 2006-2010 5-year estimates; "French" excludes Basque; Please refer to the Explanation of Data for more information.

Marriage Status

Place	Never Married (%)	Now Married (%)	Widowed (%)	Divorced (%)
Abington township *Montgomery Co.*	27.5	57.1	8.3	7.1
Allentown city *Lehigh Co.*	39.7	42.7	6.8	10.7
Allison Park cdp *Allegheny Co.*	28.2	59.4	8.1	4.3
Altoona city *Blair Co.*	32.8	47.7	8.7	10.8
Baldwin borough *Allegheny Co.*	25.4	57.5	9.6	7.5
Bensalem township *Bucks Co.*	30.9	53.0	6.9	9.3
Bethel Park municipality *Allegheny Co.*	23.3	61.1	8.0	7.5
Bethlehem township *Northampton Co.*	21.6	64.6	7.4	6.4
Bethlehem city *Northampton Co.*	41.0	41.5	7.4	10.1
Bristol township *Bucks Co.*	28.9	52.4	7.1	11.6
Buckingham township *Bucks Co.*	21.3	67.0	6.2	5.6
Chambersburg borough *Franklin Co.*	31.1	45.4	10.6	12.8
Cheltenham township *Montgomery Co.*	33.1	50.8	7.0	9.1
Chester city *Delaware Co.*	56.0	27.5	7.4	9.2
Coolbaugh township *Monroe Co.*	30.4	54.6	5.0	10.0
Cranberry township *Butler Co.*	20.0	68.8	4.8	6.4
Derry township *Dauphin Co.*	27.2	57.7	6.9	8.2
Dover township *York Co.*	21.4	60.9	6.2	11.5
Drexel Hill cdp *Delaware Co.*	32.7	52.0	6.7	8.5
East Hempfield township *Lancaster Co.*	23.0	64.4	6.0	6.6
East Pennsboro township *Cumberland Co.*	28.6	55.9	6.1	9.4
Easton city *Northampton Co.*	46.2	37.3	5.5	11.1
Erie city *Erie Co.*	41.2	39.9	7.7	11.2
Exeter township *Berks Co.*	21.7	63.4	5.5	9.4
Falls township *Bucks Co.*	29.6	52.5	7.6	10.3
Hampden township *Cumberland Co.*	21.8	64.8	6.3	7.2
Harrisburg city *Dauphin Co.*	49.5	30.8	7.2	12.5
Haverford township *Delaware Co.*	29.5	56.6	7.7	6.1
Hazleton city *Luzerne Co.*	33.5	46.1	9.3	11.1
Hempfield township *Westmoreland Co.*	25.1	57.8	8.0	9.1
Horsham township *Montgomery Co.*	29.3	57.8	4.6	8.3
Johnstown city *Cambria Co.*	34.3	41.1	10.8	13.8
King of Prussia cdp *Montgomery Co.*	31.6	54.3	6.6	7.5
Lancaster city *Lancaster Co.*	46.3	36.8	5.0	11.9
Lebanon city *Lebanon Co.*	37.0	39.2	8.6	15.2
Levittown cdp *Bucks Co.*	26.8	54.6	7.4	11.1
Lower Macungie township *Lehigh Co.*	19.2	67.2	6.3	7.3
Lower Makefield township *Bucks Co.*	22.8	66.1	4.3	6.8
Lower Merion township *Montgomery Co.*	28.7	58.6	5.9	6.8
Lower Paxton township *Dauphin Co.*	29.3	53.7	5.9	11.1
Lower Providence township *Montgomery Co.*	28.0	59.0	5.7	7.2
Manheim township *Lancaster Co.*	21.9	61.8	8.3	8.1
Manor township *Lancaster Co.*	25.2	60.8	5.4	8.7
Marple township *Delaware Co.*	27.1	57.4	9.1	6.4
McCandless township *Allegheny Co.*	27.3	59.2	6.9	6.7
McKeesport city *Allegheny Co.*	41.6	33.1	12.1	13.2
Middletown township *Bucks Co.*	32.4	51.8	7.9	7.9
Millcreek township *Erie Co.*	26.8	55.6	7.6	10.0
Monroeville municipality *Allegheny Co.*	29.0	55.9	8.3	6.7
Montgomery township *Montgomery Co.*	24.7	63.2	6.0	6.1

Place	Never Married (%)	Now Married (%)	Widowed (%)	Divorced (%)
Moon township *Allegheny Co.*	36.3	51.4	6.1	6.2
Mount Lebanon township *Allegheny Co.*	22.4	61.0	8.1	8.5
Muhlenberg township *Berks Co.*	26.5	53.6	9.1	10.7
Murrysville municipality *Westmoreland Co.*	21.2	66.7	5.5	6.6
New Castle city *Lawrence Co.*	30.0	48.6	9.9	11.5
Newtown township *Bucks Co.*	23.9	62.7	6.0	7.5
Norristown borough *Montgomery Co.*	45.3	39.7	6.3	8.7
North Huntingdon township *Westmoreland Co.*	21.1	65.7	7.5	5.8
Northampton township *Bucks Co.*	25.1	65.9	4.5	4.5
Palmer township *Northampton Co.*	18.9	63.0	8.1	9.9
Penn township *Westmoreland Co.*	22.6	64.1	6.3	6.9
Penn Hills township *Allegheny Co.*	30.1	50.9	9.8	9.2
Peters township *Washington Co.*	19.4	69.6	5.7	5.3
Philadelphia city *Philadelphia Co.*	49.2	34.3	7.7	8.7
Pittsburgh city *Allegheny Co.*	48.4	34.2	7.9	9.6
Plum borough *Allegheny Co.*	25.1	61.5	7.0	6.4
Pottstown borough *Montgomery Co.*	34.6	43.2	7.7	14.5
Radnor township *Delaware Co.*	46.2	43.8	4.7	5.4
Reading city *Berks Co.*	45.3	38.4	5.6	10.7
Ridley township *Delaware Co.*	32.6	50.4	8.2	8.8
Ross township *Allegheny Co.*	28.2	54.1	8.8	9.0
Scranton city *Lackawanna Co.*	39.0	41.6	9.7	9.8
Shaler township *Allegheny Co.*	25.1	60.6	7.3	7.0
South Whitehall township *Lehigh Co.*	21.1	58.3	10.2	10.4
Spring township *Berks Co.*	29.8	55.4	6.4	8.4
Springettsbury township *York Co.*	27.6	54.8	8.1	9.5
Springfield township *Montgomery Co.*	29.4	54.9	9.3	6.4
Springfield township *Delaware Co.*	25.5	58.9	9.1	6.5
State College borough *Centre Co.*	82.6	13.8	1.3	2.3
Stroud township *Monroe Co.*	22.6	61.2	7.5	8.7
Susquehanna township *Dauphin Co.*	28.6	50.2	8.3	12.9
Swatara township *Dauphin Co.*	35.8	47.2	6.8	10.2
Tredyffrin township *Chester Co.*	26.6	59.3	6.1	8.0
Unity township *Westmoreland Co.*	29.9	54.8	7.8	7.5
Upper Darby township *Delaware Co.*	37.6	48.6	5.7	8.1
Upper Dublin township *Montgomery Co.*	24.1	64.3	6.0	5.6
Upper Macungie township *Lehigh Co.*	20.5	67.3	5.6	6.6
Upper Merion township *Montgomery Co.*	29.6	56.3	6.4	7.7
Upper Moreland township *Montgomery Co.*	28.6	54.4	8.4	8.6
Upper Providence township *Montgomery Co.*	22.8	64.7	6.2	6.2
Upper Saint Clair cdp/township *Allegheny Co.*	21.1	68.0	6.2	4.7
Warminster township *Bucks Co.*	25.5	57.6	9.7	7.2
Warrington township *Bucks Co.*	23.3	65.7	5.0	6.0
West Goshen township *Chester Co.*	27.9	61.0	4.5	6.6
West Mifflin borough *Allegheny Co.*	30.1	52.4	9.7	7.8
Whitehall township *Lehigh Co.*	28.7	54.2	7.6	9.5
Wilkes-Barre city *Luzerne Co.*	44.5	36.5	9.3	9.6
Williamsport city *Lycoming Co.*	45.7	36.4	6.7	11.1
York city *York Co.*	46.3	35.6	5.9	12.2
York township *York Co.*	21.1	59.8	7.5	11.6

NOTE: Figures are 2006-2010 5-year estimates.

Employment and Building Permits Issued

Place	Unemployment Rate (%)	Total Civilian Labor Force	Single-Family Building Permits	Multi-Family Building Permits
Abington township *Montgomery Co.*	7.2	29,491	5	0
Allentown city *Lehigh Co.*	12.1	58,095	31	0
Allison Park cdp *Allegheny Co.*	n/a	n/a	n/a	n/a
Altoona city *Blair Co.*	8.8	23,367	4	0
Baldwin borough *Allegheny Co.*	n/a	n/a	13	0
Bensalem township *Bucks Co.*	8.5	34,836	31	0
Bethel Park municipality *Allegheny Co.*	5.9	18,269	8	0
Bethlehem township *Northampton Co.*	n/a	n/a	20	0
Bethlehem city *Northampton Co.*	9.6	36,696	18	2
Bristol township *Bucks Co.*	10.7	30,096	3	0
Buckingham township *Bucks Co.*	n/a	n/a	43	0
Chambersburg borough *Franklin Co.*	n/a	n/a	34	0
Cheltenham township *Montgomery Co.*	8.2	19,534	4	0
Chester city *Delaware Co.*	15.1	14,152	2	0
Coolbaugh township *Monroe Co.*	n/a	n/a	46	0
Cranberry township *Butler Co.*	4.7	16,787	127	64
Derry township *Dauphin Co.*	n/a	n/a	22	12
Dover township *York Co.*	n/a	n/a	41	0
Drexel Hill cdp *Delaware Co.*	n/a	n/a	n/a	n/a
East Hempfield township *Lancaster Co.*	n/a	n/a	70	0
East Pennsboro township *Cumberland Co.*	n/a	n/a	20	96
Easton city *Northampton Co.*	10.6	13,242	43	15
Erie city *Erie Co.*	8.9	50,362	6	9
Exeter township *Berks Co.*	6.9	13,873	16	4
Falls township *Bucks Co.*	8.5	18,900	7	0
Hampden township *Cumberland Co.*	5.3	15,498	103	0
Harrisburg city *Dauphin Co.*	11.0	23,784	12	0
Haverford township *Delaware Co.*	6.2	25,518	24	0
Hazleton city *Luzerne Co.*	14.7	12,697	0	0
Hempfield township *Westmoreland Co.*	7.0	23,752	47	0
Horsham township *Montgomery Co.*	6.7	14,942	7	2
Johnstown city *Cambria Co.*	11.1	9,198	0	0
King of Prussia cdp *Montgomery Co.*	n/a	n/a	n/a	n/a
Lancaster city *Lancaster Co.*	9.7	28,223	8	0
Lebanon city *Lebanon Co.*	9.4	13,151	1	0
Levittown cdp *Bucks Co.*	n/a	n/a	n/a	n/a
Lower Macungie township *Lehigh Co.*	5.6	16,950	52	0
Lower Makefield township *Bucks Co.*	5.8	17,657	25	0
Lower Merion township *Montgomery Co.*	5.6	28,833	28	0
Lower Paxton township *Dauphin Co.*	6.7	26,995	55	0
Lower Providence township *Montgomery Co.*	7.0	13,159	8	0
Manheim township *Lancaster Co.*	6.5	19,471	79	0
Manor township *Lancaster Co.*	n/a	n/a	34	28
Marple township *Delaware Co.*	n/a	n/a	17	0
McCandless township *Allegheny Co.*	5.4	16,302	27	0
McKeesport city *Allegheny Co.*	10.9	8,571	0	0
Middletown township *Bucks Co.*	7.8	24,970	10	0
Millcreek township *Erie Co.*	6.4	29,648	44	154
Monroeville municipality *Allegheny Co.*	7.3	16,295	8	0
Montgomery township *Montgomery Co.*	n/a	n/a	133	0

Place	Unemployment Rate (%)	Total Civilian Labor Force	Single-Family Building Permits	Multi-Family Building Permits
Moon township Allegheny Co.	n/a	n/a	66	0
Mount Lebanon township Allegheny Co.	4.9	18,152	6	0
Muhlenberg township Berks Co.	n/a	n/a	28	0
Murrysville municipality Westmoreland Co.	n/a	n/a	56	0
New Castle city Lawrence Co.	10.9	9,883	1	0
Newtown township Bucks Co.	n/a	n/a	24	5
Norristown borough Montgomery Co.	8.8	17,650	0	6
North Huntingdon township Westmoreland Co.	6.8	17,390	52	4
Northampton township Bucks Co.	7.3	21,924	7	0
Palmer township Northampton Co.	n/a	n/a	51	0
Penn township Westmoreland Co.	n/a	n/a	13	0
Penn Hills township Allegheny Co.	8.1	23,737	1	0
Peters township Washington Co.	n/a	n/a	85	0
Philadelphia city Philadelphia Co.	11.5	655,604	445	1,107
Pittsburgh city Allegheny Co.	8.2	157,701	284	0
Plum borough Allegheny Co.	6.7	15,726	40	0
Pottstown borough Montgomery Co.	n/a	n/a	2	0
Radnor township Delaware Co.	6.9	14,579	7	0
Reading city Berks Co.	11.5	36,976	0	0
Ridley township Delaware Co.	8.5	15,870	5	0
Ross township Allegheny Co.	6.1	18,414	3	0
Scranton city Lackawanna Co.	10.0	37,533	14	0
Shaler township Allegheny Co.	7.1	16,744	8	0
South Whitehall township Lehigh Co.	n/a	n/a	18	0
Spring township Berks Co.	6.7	14,500	31	0
Springettsbury township York Co.	8.2	13,005	15	8
Springfield township Montgomery Co.	n/a	n/a	2	0
Springfield township Delaware Co.	n/a	n/a	4	0
State College borough Centre Co.	7.2	18,853	0	0
Stroud township Monroe Co.	n/a	n/a	12	0
Susquehanna township Dauphin Co.	n/a	n/a	40	0
Swatara township Dauphin Co.	n/a	n/a	64	0
Tredyffrin township Chester Co.	5.9	15,887	4	0
Unity township Westmoreland Co.	n/a	n/a	43	0
Upper Darby township Delaware Co.	8.7	43,588	0	0
Upper Dublin township Montgomery Co.	6.0	13,224	6	16
Upper Macungie township Lehigh Co.	n/a	n/a	104	0
Upper Merion township Montgomery Co.	5.6	17,218	3	0
Upper Moreland township Montgomery Co.	7.2	13,324	3	0
Upper Providence township Montgomery Co.	n/a	n/a	36	0
Upper Saint Clair cdp/township Allegheny Co.	n/a	n/a	9	0
Warminster township Bucks Co.	8.3	17,514	43	0
Warrington township Bucks Co.	n/a	n/a	5	0
West Goshen township Chester Co.	n/a	n/a	34	7
West Mifflin borough Allegheny Co.	8.5	10,775	1	0
Whitehall township Lehigh Co.	8.3	14,908	25	0
Wilkes-Barre city Luzerne Co.	11.5	20,040	1	0
Williamsport city Lycoming Co.	9.3	15,089	0	10
York city York Co.	13.3	20,808	5	0
York township York Co.	6.9	14,874	32	21

NOTE: Unemployment Rate and Civilian Labor Force as of August 2012; Building permit data covers 2011; n/a not available.

Employment by Occupation

Place	Sales (%)	Profess. (%)	Mgmt (%)	Services (%)	Production (%)	Construct. (%)	Farming (%)
Abington township *Montgomery Co.*	17.7	5.1	13.7	6.3	4.0	7.7	4.6
Allentown city *Lehigh Co.*	17.9	3.4	6.4	12.5	8.3	8.1	4.9
Allison Park cdp *Allegheny Co.*	17.0	5.5	17.1	6.6	3.0	4.7	4.8
Altoona city *Blair Co.*	21.0	2.0	6.6	12.0	5.4	7.3	5.2
Baldwin borough *Allegheny Co.*	22.6	6.5	11.4	10.1	5.3	8.5	5.1
Bensalem township *Bucks Co.*	19.2	5.3	9.5	9.1	6.6	9.3	5.3
Bethel Park municipality *Allegheny Co.*	16.9	7.1	16.1	6.4	3.6	6.5	5.4
Bethlehem township *Northampton Co.*	16.8	6.5	13.6	7.7	5.9	6.3	2.9
Bethlehem city *Northampton Co.*	18.2	3.9	8.6	12.1	6.5	7.0	5.0
Bristol township *Bucks Co.*	21.0	2.9	7.1	9.2	9.1	11.1	3.4
Buckingham township *Bucks Co.*	13.4	4.9	23.8	4.0	1.6	7.2	2.6
Chambersburg borough *Franklin Co.*	17.7	4.0	8.8	8.8	7.5	9.0	3.5
Cheltenham township *Montgomery Co.*	16.6	6.4	17.7	6.9	2.7	4.1	3.0
Chester city *Delaware Co.*	18.7	2.2	4.5	17.9	7.4	5.9	2.0
Coolbaugh township *Monroe Co.*	20.7	2.9	6.9	16.6	6.8	9.5	6.8
Cranberry township *Butler Co.*	13.7	10.2	19.1	7.0	4.5	6.1	3.0
Derry township *Dauphin Co.*	13.5	6.6	14.3	8.7	4.7	4.0	2.3
Dover township *York Co.*	20.2	4.0	8.1	10.1	12.0	11.3	5.6
Drexel Hill cdp *Delaware Co.*	19.5	5.4	13.3	6.4	3.8	8.0	3.6
East Hempfield township *Lancaster Co.*	13.7	4.1	15.0	8.1	4.0	4.8	5.0
East Pennsboro township *Cumberland Co.*	23.8	8.1	12.5	10.2	4.2	6.4	5.2
Easton city *Northampton Co.*	15.8	2.1	7.1	15.0	8.5	9.3	4.2
Erie city *Erie Co.*	18.4	3.1	7.2	13.6	6.9	6.3	4.5
Exeter township *Berks Co.*	18.4	5.5	13.3	8.2	5.9	7.8	4.5
Falls township *Bucks Co.*	20.6	6.1	9.0	8.6	7.5	10.2	4.8
Hampden township *Cumberland Co.*	16.8	9.3	17.0	5.5	3.8	3.3	4.5
Harrisburg city *Dauphin Co.*	22.6	2.7	7.6	11.2	6.8	4.7	4.7
Haverford township *Delaware Co.*	13.7	5.8	18.2	5.4	2.6	5.9	3.3
Hazleton city *Luzerne Co.*	15.9	1.4	4.1	12.0	12.4	8.5	4.5
Hempfield township *Westmoreland Co.*	17.2	4.7	11.8	9.6	6.0	7.5	3.9
Horsham township *Montgomery Co.*	15.1	6.8	17.8	5.6	4.7	6.8	3.7
Johnstown city *Cambria Co.*	19.1	1.7	4.2	16.9	5.2	7.6	4.2
King of Prussia cdp *Montgomery Co.*	15.9	14.5	16.5	5.1	4.3	3.9	3.2
Lancaster city *Lancaster Co.*	17.0	1.3	6.1	13.0	9.2	8.5	5.6
Lebanon city *Lebanon Co.*	17.0	1.9	7.1	14.1	7.9	7.0	6.6
Levittown cdp *Bucks Co.*	20.3	3.5	8.7	9.3	7.8	10.9	4.7
Lower Macungie township *Lehigh Co.*	15.3	7.8	17.4	5.9	3.5	3.6	3.0
Lower Makefield township *Bucks Co.*	13.6	7.4	27.1	3.6	1.6	2.5	2.5
Lower Merion township *Montgomery Co.*	12.2	5.8	18.7	6.0	1.5	1.8	2.5
Lower Paxton township *Dauphin Co.*	19.5	7.0	15.6	7.3	4.1	5.2	4.9
Lower Providence township *Montgomery Co.*	16.9	12.5	17.3	6.2	3.8	5.4	2.9
Manheim township *Lancaster Co.*	15.5	4.9	15.4	7.1	4.8	7.4	3.4
Manor township *Lancaster Co.*	15.7	3.8	9.7	8.2	7.5	9.6	5.2
Marple township *Delaware Co.*	16.3	4.7	13.1	7.0	3.7	9.7	3.5
McCandless township *Allegheny Co.*	15.9	6.8	17.6	6.7	3.2	5.1	4.2
McKeesport city *Allegheny Co.*	19.1	1.1	7.6	14.2	5.2	8.0	6.1
Middletown township *Bucks Co.*	18.4	5.7	14.3	7.4	3.7	7.0	4.8
Millcreek township *Erie Co.*	17.6	4.8	11.7	7.1	4.6	6.0	3.5
Monroeville municipality *Allegheny Co.*	14.1	8.6	15.0	8.6	3.8	5.2	5.1
Montgomery township *Montgomery Co.*	15.3	7.5	19.2	4.9	3.3	3.7	3.5

Place	Sales (%)	Profess. (%)	Mgmt (%)	Services (%)	Production (%)	Construct. (%)	Farming (%)
Moon township *Allegheny Co.*	20.2	7.2	16.3	6.2	4.2	4.5	5.2
Mount Lebanon township *Allegheny Co.*	14.5	6.6	19.0	5.7	1.8	2.8	3.3
Muhlenberg township *Berks Co.*	19.3	1.8	9.3	9.5	6.8	8.3	5.0
Murrysville municipality *Westmoreland Co.*	14.8	7.6	18.3	4.9	4.4	6.0	1.7
New Castle city *Lawrence Co.*	21.1	2.4	6.7	13.3	5.6	5.8	6.1
Newtown township *Bucks Co.*	12.6	6.3	23.3	5.1	3.2	4.0	2.5
Norristown borough *Montgomery Co.*	16.2	2.5	8.2	11.8	5.5	10.5	5.1
North Huntingdon township *Westmoreland Co.*	16.7	6.6	11.8	8.8	6.8	9.0	3.5
Northampton township *Bucks Co.*	14.9	6.9	19.0	5.7	3.3	6.0	3.5
Palmer township *Northampton Co.*	17.2	5.4	10.5	7.8	5.5	7.0	3.6
Penn township *Westmoreland Co.*	14.5	8.3	15.8	8.5	5.9	8.9	3.5
Penn Hills township *Allegheny Co.*	17.5	3.9	9.7	11.4	6.8	8.3	5.3
Peters township *Washington Co.*	15.2	5.4	20.0	6.6	2.5	5.4	3.1
Philadelphia city *Philadelphia Co.*	17.9	3.4	8.6	12.4	5.2	6.2	5.1
Pittsburgh city *Allegheny Co.*	16.5	5.3	9.5	12.4	3.2	5.0	5.0
Plum borough *Allegheny Co.*	18.7	6.0	11.9	10.0	5.9	7.6	3.4
Pottstown borough *Montgomery Co.*	20.0	4.2	7.1	12.7	8.0	8.7	3.3
Radnor township *Delaware Co.*	16.3	5.6	19.2	7.5	1.7	2.6	3.9
Reading city *Berks Co.*	16.2	0.9	4.7	13.8	12.5	9.2	5.3
Ridley township *Delaware Co.*	19.5	4.5	11.3	9.2	6.8	11.7	5.3
Ross township *Allegheny Co.*	16.4	5.3	14.8	7.4	2.7	6.5	4.0
Scranton city *Lackawanna Co.*	19.5	2.0	7.5	13.5	6.7	7.9	4.4
Shaler township *Allegheny Co.*	20.2	4.2	14.2	8.7	3.6	6.8	3.3
South Whitehall township *Lehigh Co.*	18.2	6.8	13.6	6.6	5.3	5.9	2.2
Spring township *Berks Co.*	15.7	4.2	11.1	8.5	5.1	5.0	5.6
Springettsbury township *York Co.*	16.2	3.9	16.6	9.8	5.7	5.7	3.3
Springfield township *Montgomery Co.*	15.1	4.7	18.6	5.9	3.0	6.6	2.7
Springfield township *Delaware Co.*	18.3	5.8	15.5	5.6	4.4	8.0	3.6
State College borough *Centre Co.*	16.3	8.1	6.4	11.2	1.9	3.4	4.2
Stroud township *Monroe Co.*	19.0	4.1	12.4	10.0	4.2	5.8	4.1
Susquehanna township *Dauphin Co.*	21.0	6.3	13.6	5.5	4.2	5.7	5.6
Swatara township *Dauphin Co.*	17.3	4.8	10.6	8.1	8.9	6.6	6.8
Tredyffrin township *Chester Co.*	11.8	12.4	20.6	3.3	1.3	2.6	2.0
Unity township *Westmoreland Co.*	17.0	5.0	12.7	9.9	5.2	6.2	2.3
Upper Darby township *Delaware Co.*	19.6	4.2	10.6	10.8	4.4	6.7	4.4
Upper Dublin township *Montgomery Co.*	14.1	8.3	18.5	3.5	3.0	4.0	2.3
Upper Macungie township *Lehigh Co.*	13.8	10.0	17.9	2.6	3.4	4.5	3.6
Upper Merion township *Montgomery Co.*	15.6	12.6	17.4	5.1	3.9	4.4	3.1
Upper Moreland township *Montgomery Co.*	17.4	4.3	13.2	9.3	5.3	8.9	4.7
Upper Providence township *Montgomery Co.*	14.5	9.3	23.5	4.3	2.1	4.2	3.6
Upper Saint Clair cdp/township *Allegheny Co.*	15.9	7.3	22.2	3.7	2.2	3.2	2.4
Warminster township *Bucks Co.*	20.5	4.2	11.2	10.3	5.6	10.5	4.5
Warrington township *Bucks Co.*	19.0	8.6	16.8	4.2	5.0	7.2	2.8
West Goshen township *Chester Co.*	16.4	7.5	19.1	6.3	3.7	7.8	3.7
West Mifflin borough *Allegheny Co.*	21.5	3.8	8.4	10.1	5.6	10.2	4.3
Whitehall township *Lehigh Co.*	18.3	4.9	8.8	9.5	6.7	8.6	6.1
Wilkes-Barre city *Luzerne Co.*	20.6	1.9	7.2	14.5	6.8	5.6	5.6
Williamsport city *Lycoming Co.*	15.5	2.1	6.2	13.8	8.2	7.1	5.7
York city *York Co.*	15.2	1.8	5.3	17.2	9.0	6.3	5.0
York township *York Co.*	17.6	5.8	13.6	8.6	5.5	8.9	2.7

NOTE: Figures are 2006-2010 5-year estimates.

Educational Attainment

Place	Percent of Population 25 Years and Over with:		
	High School Diploma including Equivalency	Bachelor's Degree or Higher	Master's Degree or Higher
Abington township *Montgomery Co.*	93.1	42.1	17.7
Allentown city *Lehigh Co.*	76.2	16.6	6.1
Allison Park cdp *Allegheny Co.*	96.3	48.8	20.2
Altoona city *Blair Co.*	88.5	15.8	4.2
Baldwin borough *Allegheny Co.*	92.4	22.1	7.4
Bensalem township *Bucks Co.*	87.7	22.7	8.2
Bethel Park municipality *Allegheny Co.*	94.9	40.8	13.2
Bethlehem township *Northampton Co.*	91.1	35.9	13.0
Bethlehem city *Northampton Co.*	84.1	26.6	10.9
Bristol township *Bucks Co.*	87.4	13.0	3.7
Buckingham township *Bucks Co.*	96.1	54.5	24.9
Chambersburg borough *Franklin Co.*	78.8	20.9	8.3
Cheltenham township *Montgomery Co.*	94.5	52.6	26.0
Chester city *Delaware Co.*	76.9	8.7	3.1
Coolbaugh township *Monroe Co.*	88.1	20.0	5.1
Cranberry township *Butler Co.*	97.5	53.5	17.6
Derry township *Dauphin Co.*	95.2	51.4	25.0
Dover township *York Co.*	86.0	13.7	4.7
Drexel Hill cdp *Delaware Co.*	93.2	39.2	15.4
East Hempfield township *Lancaster Co.*	93.4	42.5	16.1
East Pennsboro township *Cumberland Co.*	89.1	28.8	10.0
Easton city *Northampton Co.*	77.3	16.8	6.0
Erie city *Erie Co.*	85.4	19.5	6.8
Exeter township *Berks Co.*	90.8	30.5	10.0
Falls township *Bucks Co.*	89.4	19.7	4.8
Hampden township *Cumberland Co.*	96.1	48.4	18.8
Harrisburg city *Dauphin Co.*	78.5	16.6	6.1
Haverford township *Delaware Co.*	95.6	53.4	24.8
Hazleton city *Luzerne Co.*	77.7	11.8	3.6
Hempfield township *Westmoreland Co.*	92.8	28.5	10.0
Horsham township *Montgomery Co.*	94.0	45.8	17.7
Johnstown city *Cambria Co.*	83.3	13.3	4.2
King of Prussia cdp *Montgomery Co.*	94.9	52.8	24.3
Lancaster city *Lancaster Co.*	73.7	16.4	5.4
Lebanon city *Lebanon Co.*	76.2	9.1	3.1
Levittown cdp *Bucks Co.*	90.8	15.6	4.3
Lower Macungie township *Lehigh Co.*	93.6	47.9	21.6
Lower Makefield township *Bucks Co.*	97.7	61.9	29.8
Lower Merion township *Montgomery Co.*	97.8	73.1	43.4
Lower Paxton township *Dauphin Co.*	94.4	34.9	12.2
Lower Providence township *Montgomery Co.*	91.4	43.3	18.2
Manheim township *Lancaster Co.*	92.0	42.7	15.8
Manor township *Lancaster Co.*	88.4	26.1	7.6
Marple township *Delaware Co.*	89.6	34.9	13.7
McCandless township *Allegheny Co.*	96.2	54.5	24.0
McKeesport city *Allegheny Co.*	82.7	9.6	3.5
Middletown township *Bucks Co.*	91.6	31.1	11.4
Millcreek township *Erie Co.*	93.9	33.6	13.4
Monroeville municipality *Allegheny Co.*	94.5	40.7	14.2
Montgomery township *Montgomery Co.*	95.5	55.1	22.8

Place	Percent of Population 25 Years and Over with:		
	High School Diploma including Equivalency	Bachelor's Degree or Higher	Master's Degree or Higher
Moon township *Allegheny Co.*	97.0	44.6	15.0
Mount Lebanon township *Allegheny Co.*	97.9	63.4	28.7
Muhlenberg township *Berks Co.*	84.4	17.1	7.0
Murrysville municipality *Westmoreland Co.*	96.3	49.0	19.4
New Castle city *Lawrence Co.*	80.5	13.8	4.4
Newtown township *Bucks Co.*	97.3	58.5	24.8
Norristown borough *Montgomery Co.*	77.2	16.2	5.7
North Huntingdon township *Westmoreland Co.*	94.6	27.1	9.7
Northampton township *Bucks Co.*	95.9	47.1	18.3
Palmer township *Northampton Co.*	91.1	29.7	10.2
Penn township *Westmoreland Co.*	94.3	36.0	12.4
Penn Hills township *Allegheny Co.*	91.2	22.6	7.6
Peters township *Washington Co.*	94.6	54.0	23.4
Philadelphia city *Philadelphia Co.*	79.4	22.2	9.3
Pittsburgh city *Allegheny Co.*	88.3	33.8	16.2
Plum borough *Allegheny Co.*	94.7	32.6	10.4
Pottstown borough *Montgomery Co.*	84.1	17.3	4.1
Radnor township *Delaware Co.*	96.4	71.3	36.0
Reading city *Berks Co.*	64.7	9.8	3.2
Ridley township *Delaware Co.*	88.6	21.5	7.6
Ross township *Allegheny Co.*	93.9	38.4	13.5
Scranton city *Lackawanna Co.*	83.1	18.6	6.6
Shaler township *Allegheny Co.*	91.7	32.8	10.7
South Whitehall township *Lehigh Co.*	91.2	38.7	16.9
Spring township *Berks Co.*	91.9	33.3	12.0
Springettsbury township *York Co.*	86.5	28.6	12.2
Springfield township *Montgomery Co.*	94.1	51.4	23.9
Springfield township *Delaware Co.*	94.1	40.4	13.1
State College borough *Centre Co.*	95.3	66.0	36.8
Stroud township *Monroe Co.*	89.3	28.2	10.3
Susquehanna township *Dauphin Co.*	92.0	36.8	12.8
Swatara township *Dauphin Co.*	87.6	22.6	6.7
Tredyffrin township *Chester Co.*	97.4	72.3	34.4
Unity township *Westmoreland Co.*	91.9	30.6	12.4
Upper Darby township *Delaware Co.*	87.8	29.7	11.1
Upper Dublin township *Montgomery Co.*	97.3	62.2	28.7
Upper Macungie township *Lehigh Co.*	92.8	43.8	19.9
Upper Merion township *Montgomery Co.*	95.0	54.5	25.2
Upper Moreland township *Montgomery Co.*	93.3	32.7	10.2
Upper Providence township *Montgomery Co.*	95.4	51.5	19.0
Upper Saint Clair cdp/township *Allegheny Co.*	98.3	66.9	28.5
Warminster township *Bucks Co.*	89.7	24.5	7.5
Warrington township *Bucks Co.*	95.8	46.7	17.8
West Goshen township *Chester Co.*	95.6	50.6	18.2
West Mifflin borough *Allegheny Co.*	92.5	17.7	5.8
Whitehall township *Lehigh Co.*	87.4	24.1	8.6
Wilkes-Barre city *Luzerne Co.*	83.5	14.5	4.7
Williamsport city *Lycoming Co.*	82.0	18.3	7.1
York city *York Co.*	73.7	10.2	2.8
York township *York Co.*	91.5	29.2	11.3

NOTE: Figures are 2006-2010 5-year estimates.

Income and Poverty

Place	Average Household Income ($)	Median Household Income ($)	Per Capita Income ($)	Households w/$100,000+ Income (%)	Poverty Rate (%)
Abington township *Montgomery Co.*	98,724	75,542	38,663	34.7	4.4
Allentown city *Lehigh Co.*	46,815	36,202	18,139	8.7	24.6
Allison Park cdp *Allegheny Co.*	95,529	74,034	37,297	30.7	7.4
Altoona city *Blair Co.*	46,245	35,629	19,245	7.6	17.8
Baldwin borough *Allegheny Co.*	56,590	48,514	24,917	12.9	10.5
Bensalem township *Bucks Co.*	70,002	59,668	27,707	21.4	6.4
Bethel Park municipality *Allegheny Co.*	77,084	61,074	31,642	25.5	3.2
Bethlehem township *Northampton Co.*	90,845	71,743	34,313	34.4	3.0
Bethlehem city *Northampton Co.*	56,206	44,310	23,042	13.1	16.8
Bristol township *Bucks Co.*	63,657	54,626	24,364	16.6	7.9
Buckingham township *Bucks Co.*	137,621	111,207	47,957	55.5	3.2
Chambersburg borough *Franklin Co.*	49,632	38,547	21,351	10.2	20.5
Cheltenham township *Montgomery Co.*	96,548	72,584	39,879	35.7	6.7
Chester city *Delaware Co.*	36,576	26,787	14,251	4.5	35.1
Coolbaugh township *Monroe Co.*	59,536	54,290	20,327	13.5	15.6
Cranberry township *Butler Co.*	101,589	88,791	37,726	43.3	2.8
Derry township *Dauphin Co.*	89,499	65,427	37,797	29.4	6.7
Dover township *York Co.*	61,529	52,247	25,202	15.0	6.1
Drexel Hill cdp *Delaware Co.*	78,116	66,287	31,575	29.3	4.7
East Hempfield township *Lancaster Co.*	90,494	69,265	37,294	30.3	5.9
East Pennsboro township *Cumberland Co.*	70,264	59,155	28,334	21.1	6.0
Easton city *Northampton Co.*	51,634	38,613	18,899	11.2	20.3
Erie city *Erie Co.*	43,955	32,218	18,242	6.8	25.0
Exeter township *Berks Co.*	83,896	69,093	32,883	28.1	4.5
Falls township *Bucks Co.*	69,635	62,799	27,054	21.2	6.4
Hampden township *Cumberland Co.*	102,762	82,674	42,904	39.0	3.7
Harrisburg city *Dauphin Co.*	40,740	31,525	18,009	6.6	30.2
Haverford township *Delaware Co.*	106,521	86,451	40,825	42.7	3.3
Hazleton city *Luzerne Co.*	43,556	32,169	18,215	6.1	20.1
Hempfield township *Westmoreland Co.*	72,079	55,416	29,213	21.4	5.8
Horsham township *Montgomery Co.*	109,401	81,888	41,429	37.6	4.6
Johnstown city *Cambria Co.*	32,931	24,819	16,383	3.2	30.7
King of Prussia cdp *Montgomery Co.*	85,694	72,357	38,780	32.6	4.1
Lancaster city *Lancaster Co.*	40,846	32,737	15,768	5.8	27.6
Lebanon city *Lebanon Co.*	42,408	33,840	18,539	5.6	22.9
Levittown cdp *Bucks Co.*	70,393	64,298	25,345	21.1	6.1
Lower Macungie township *Lehigh Co.*	100,009	80,344	38,688	40.0	4.5
Lower Makefield township *Bucks Co.*	146,839	121,260	52,988	61.7	1.6
Lower Merion township *Montgomery Co.*	184,975	111,165	73,031	54.6	5.4
Lower Paxton township *Dauphin Co.*	78,513	64,758	33,767	26.2	5.4
Lower Providence township *Montgomery Co.*	106,153	88,964	36,828	43.2	2.9
Manheim township *Lancaster Co.*	92,533	66,031	37,307	29.4	5.7
Manor township *Lancaster Co.*	69,363	58,607	28,179	17.9	4.0
Marple township *Delaware Co.*	93,928	76,723	34,639	36.9	4.4
McCandless township *Allegheny Co.*	95,623	75,132	38,491	34.6	5.4
McKeesport city *Allegheny Co.*	34,483	25,943	15,992	3.7	29.1
Middletown township *Bucks Co.*	93,940	78,861	33,377	35.7	5.7
Millcreek township *Erie Co.*	70,505	53,745	30,051	21.4	7.2
Monroeville municipality *Allegheny Co.*	69,255	57,254	30,813	19.6	6.3
Montgomery township *Montgomery Co.*	110,773	86,875	40,891	44.7	2.0

Place	Average Household Income ($)	Median Household Income ($)	Per Capita Income ($)	Households w/$100,000+ Income (%)	Poverty Rate (%)
Moon township *Allegheny Co.*	86,639	70,387	32,451	31.0	8.0
Mount Lebanon township *Allegheny Co.*	104,460	77,742	44,561	39.8	3.9
Muhlenberg township *Berks Co.*	65,834	55,132	26,635	16.3	9.1
Murrysville municipality *Westmoreland Co.*	104,408	81,883	41,817	38.1	2.4
New Castle city *Lawrence Co.*	39,791	30,690	16,756	4.0	21.2
Newtown township *Bucks Co.*	126,367	107,430	47,867	55.0	3.1
Norristown borough *Montgomery Co.*	52,464	43,551	20,123	10.8	18.0
North Huntingdon township *Westmoreland Co.*	71,358	64,282	28,035	22.6	4.2
Northampton township *Bucks Co.*	125,588	105,148	43,253	53.4	2.3
Palmer township *Northampton Co.*	77,899	67,545	31,652	27.2	2.9
Penn township *Westmoreland Co.*	80,107	67,720	30,345	31.0	6.0
Penn Hills township *Allegheny Co.*	55,370	45,893	24,336	10.8	9.2
Peters township *Washington Co.*	121,750	100,109	40,461	50.0	3.8
Philadelphia city *Philadelphia Co.*	51,060	36,251	21,117	11.9	25.1
Pittsburgh city *Allegheny Co.*	54,453	36,019	24,833	12.5	21.9
Plum borough *Allegheny Co.*	75,725	66,700	29,637	22.2	4.3
Pottstown borough *Montgomery Co.*	52,181	43,311	22,648	11.0	14.9
Radnor township *Delaware Co.*	146,789	85,942	49,482	43.9	6.8
Reading city *Berks Co.*	35,916	28,197	13,135	3.7	35.0
Ridley township *Delaware Co.*	66,920	57,558	26,847	21.2	7.3
Ross township *Allegheny Co.*	72,686	57,354	33,121	21.3	6.8
Scranton city *Lackawanna Co.*	46,619	35,606	19,068	9.1	18.8
Shaler township *Allegheny Co.*	70,371	62,416	29,576	19.4	3.8
South Whitehall township *Lehigh Co.*	88,208	64,854	36,274	27.5	3.8
Spring township *Berks Co.*	74,098	62,471	29,364	21.6	6.3
Springettsbury township *York Co.*	74,359	62,224	29,372	22.6	5.9
Springfield township *Montgomery Co.*	113,456	94,732	42,937	45.9	6.1
Springfield township *Delaware Co.*	102,141	88,613	36,391	45.3	3.8
State College borough *Centre Co.*	42,235	23,513	13,336	11.0	48.4
Stroud township *Monroe Co.*	80,401	65,747	30,256	27.8	3.7
Susquehanna township *Dauphin Co.*	74,265	60,758	33,889	23.0	5.4
Swatara township *Dauphin Co.*	62,289	53,673	24,981	15.1	9.8
Tredyffrin township *Chester Co.*	138,788	99,728	59,231	49.9	4.3
Unity township *Westmoreland Co.*	72,213	56,474	27,972	21.2	7.5
Upper Darby township *Delaware Co.*	65,355	52,572	25,278	20.0	11.5
Upper Dublin township *Montgomery Co.*	137,363	107,285	49,085	54.7	3.5
Upper Macungie township *Lehigh Co.*	100,480	90,188	36,465	44.0	3.5
Upper Merion township *Montgomery Co.*	100,157	77,955	44,063	38.2	4.6
Upper Moreland township *Montgomery Co.*	73,918	63,167	32,075	24.2	4.2
Upper Providence township *Montgomery Co.*	126,445	107,438	44,946	53.6	2.4
Upper Saint Clair cdp/township *Allegheny Co.*	143,037	112,828	51,589	55.1	2.2
Warminster township *Bucks Co.*	72,268	59,980	28,280	23.8	8.0
Warrington township *Bucks Co.*	105,949	93,386	36,805	45.5	1.3
West Goshen township *Chester Co.*	103,888	89,233	38,891	40.6	6.1
West Mifflin borough *Allegheny Co.*	53,099	44,190	23,201	11.0	11.3
Whitehall township *Lehigh Co.*	62,651	52,200	26,253	16.7	8.0
Wilkes-Barre city *Luzerne Co.*	39,379	29,518	16,712	6.0	25.4
Williamsport city *Lycoming Co.*	42,476	27,138	17,446	7.4	28.2
York city *York Co.*	36,357	28,583	14,287	3.9	36.6
York township *York Co.*	77,612	63,269	32,778	25.5	6.0

NOTE: Figures are 2006-2010 5-year estimates.

Taxes

Place	Total City Taxes Per Capita ($)	City Property Taxes Per Capita ($)
Abington township *Montgomery Co.*	538	220
Allentown city *Lehigh Co.*	466	275
Allison Park cdp *Allegheny Co.*	n/a	n/a
Altoona city *Blair Co.*	375	235
Baldwin borough *Allegheny Co.*	388	263
Bensalem township *Bucks Co.*	296	188
Bethel Park municipality *Allegheny Co.*	n/a	n/a
Bethlehem township *Northampton Co.*	n/a	n/a
Bethlehem city *Northampton Co.*	451	264
Bristol township *Bucks Co.*	360	177
Buckingham township *Bucks Co.*	335	25
Chambersburg borough *Franklin Co.*	389	199
Cheltenham township *Montgomery Co.*	596	362
Chester city *Delaware Co.*	513	189
Coolbaugh township *Monroe Co.*	n/a	n/a
Cranberry township *Butler Co.*	491	173
Derry township *Dauphin Co.*	460	92
Dover township *York Co.*	208	52
Drexel Hill cdp *Delaware Co.*	n/a	n/a
East Hempfield township *Lancaster Co.*	344	118
East Pennsboro township *Cumberland Co.*	259	77
Easton city *Northampton Co.*	475	334
Erie city *Erie Co.*	441	262
Exeter township *Berks Co.*	291	111
Falls township *Bucks Co.*	120	68
Hampden township *Cumberland Co.*	281	21
Harrisburg city *Dauphin Co.*	603	338
Haverford township *Delaware Co.*	437	352
Hazleton city *Luzerne Co.*	283	74
Hempfield township *Westmoreland Co.*	n/a	n/a
Horsham township *Montgomery Co.*	423	91
Johnstown city *Cambria Co.*	374	246
King of Prussia cdp *Montgomery Co.*	n/a	n/a
Lancaster city *Lancaster Co.*	485	319
Lebanon city *Lebanon Co.*	255	87
Levittown cdp *Bucks Co.*	n/a	n/a
Lower Macungie township *Lehigh Co.*	n/a	n/a
Lower Makefield township *Bucks Co.*	303	241
Lower Merion township *Montgomery Co.*	753	473
Lower Paxton township *Dauphin Co.*	265	56
Lower Providence township *Montgomery Co.*	311	93
Manheim township *Lancaster Co.*	n/a	n/a
Manor township *Lancaster Co.*	n/a	n/a
Marple township *Delaware Co.*	405	251
McCandless township *Allegheny Co.*	n/a	n/a
McKeesport city *Allegheny Co.*	274	101
Middletown township *Bucks Co.*	285	170
Millcreek township *Erie Co.*	306	145
Monroeville municipality *Allegheny Co.*	753	154
Montgomery township *Montgomery Co.*	n/a	n/a

Place	Total City Taxes Per Capita ($)	City Property Taxes Per Capita ($)
Moon township *Allegheny Co.*	n/a	n/a
Mount Lebanon township *Allegheny Co.*	747	357
Muhlenberg township *Berks Co.*	n/a	n/a
Murrysville municipality *Westmoreland Co.*	n/a	n/a
New Castle city *Lawrence Co.*	408	218
Newtown township *Bucks Co.*	n/a	n/a
Norristown borough *Montgomery Co.*	650	331
North Huntingdon township *Westmoreland Co.*	n/a	n/a
Northampton township *Bucks Co.*	326	133
Palmer township *Northampton Co.*	430	174
Penn township *Westmoreland Co.*	323	160
Penn Hills township *Allegheny Co.*	398	156
Peters township *Washington Co.*	n/a	n/a
Philadelphia city *Philadelphia Co.*	1,901	276
Pittsburgh city *Allegheny Co.*	1,116	413
Plum borough *Allegheny Co.*	346	192
Pottstown borough *Montgomery Co.*	n/a	n/a
Radnor township *Delaware Co.*	755	299
Reading city *Berks Co.*	469	190
Ridley township *Delaware Co.*	408	315
Ross township *Allegheny Co.*	n/a	n/a
Scranton city *Lackawanna Co.*	642	197
Shaler township *Allegheny Co.*	280	131
South Whitehall township *Lehigh Co.*	n/a	n/a
Spring township *Berks Co.*	n/a	n/a
Springettsbury township *York Co.*	347	71
Springfield township *Montgomery Co.*	462	225
Springfield township *Delaware Co.*	n/a	n/a
State College borough *Centre Co.*	262	112
Stroud township *Monroe Co.*	n/a	n/a
Susquehanna township *Dauphin Co.*	369	124
Swatara township *Dauphin Co.*	n/a	n/a
Tredyffrin township *Chester Co.*	434	265
Unity township *Westmoreland Co.*	n/a	n/a
Upper Darby township *Delaware Co.*	527	467
Upper Dublin township *Montgomery Co.*	701	371
Upper Macungie township *Lehigh Co.*	357	65
Upper Merion township *Montgomery Co.*	830	224
Upper Moreland township *Montgomery Co.*	n/a	n/a
Upper Providence township *Montgomery Co.*	468	3
Upper Saint Clair cdp/township *Allegheny Co.*	701	228
Warminster township *Bucks Co.*	n/a	n/a
Warrington township *Bucks Co.*	333	118
West Goshen township *Chester Co.*	n/a	n/a
West Mifflin borough *Allegheny Co.*	n/a	n/a
Whitehall township *Lehigh Co.*	n/a	n/a
Wilkes-Barre city *Luzerne Co.*	513	161
Williamsport city *Lycoming Co.*	n/a	n/a
York city *York Co.*	544	357
York township *York Co.*	286	45

NOTE: Data as of 2009.

Housing

Place	Homeownership Rate (%)	Median Home Value ($)	Median Year Structure Built	Median Rent ($/month)
Abington township *Montgomery Co.*	78.2	268,400	1955	903
Allentown city *Lehigh Co.*	48.5	143,500	1951	676
Allison Park cdp *Allegheny Co.*	77.7	181,300	1970	753
Altoona city *Blair Co.*	64.5	79,800	before 1940	405
Baldwin borough *Allegheny Co.*	76.3	106,900	1956	583
Bensalem township *Bucks Co.*	58.5	263,600	1973	913
Bethel Park municipality *Allegheny Co.*	79.2	147,100	1964	730
Bethlehem township *Northampton Co.*	86.3	267,100	1982	792
Bethlehem city *Northampton Co.*	53.6	175,900	1955	705
Bristol township *Bucks Co.*	74.3	223,100	1959	787
Buckingham township *Bucks Co.*	92.4	546,200	1991	1,166
Chambersburg borough *Franklin Co.*	48.5	152,700	1956	533
Cheltenham township *Montgomery Co.*	63.0	293,000	1951	889
Chester city *Delaware Co.*	38.5	66,900	1951	610
Coolbaugh township *Monroe Co.*	80.2	155,000	1986	737
Cranberry township *Butler Co.*	83.5	230,600	1990	828
Derry township *Dauphin Co.*	63.1	234,500	1975	751
Dover township *York Co.*	83.9	156,600	1981	640
Drexel Hill cdp *Delaware Co.*	67.6	204,400	1949	798
East Hempfield township *Lancaster Co.*	71.7	229,100	1978	801
East Pennsboro township *Cumberland Co.*	70.0	162,100	1972	634
Easton city *Northampton Co.*	46.5	139,200	before 1940	660
Erie city *Erie Co.*	52.3	82,400	1946	454
Exeter township *Berks Co.*	86.2	189,900	1981	787
Falls township *Bucks Co.*	71.7	240,100	1963	884
Hampden township *Cumberland Co.*	79.8	228,500	1983	719
Harrisburg city *Dauphin Co.*	38.8	79,200	before 1940	560
Haverford township *Delaware Co.*	85.2	309,400	1951	898
Hazleton city *Luzerne Co.*	53.4	93,300	1942	476
Hempfield township *Westmoreland Co.*	81.4	148,200	1971	481
Horsham township *Montgomery Co.*	75.3	330,600	1977	940
Johnstown city *Cambria Co.*	48.2	44,800	before 1940	316
King of Prussia cdp *Montgomery Co.*	59.0	310,100	1968	1,012
Lancaster city *Lancaster Co.*	43.9	94,900	before 1940	568
Lebanon city *Lebanon Co.*	45.7	86,300	1945	470
Levittown cdp *Bucks Co.*	83.8	235,800	1957	881
Lower Macungie township *Lehigh Co.*	88.2	280,000	1991	1,060
Lower Makefield township *Bucks Co.*	88.0	449,000	1982	1,504
Lower Merion township *Montgomery Co.*	76.3	551,100	1953	1,106
Lower Paxton township *Dauphin Co.*	67.1	177,900	1975	741
Lower Providence township *Montgomery Co.*	77.2	331,200	1974	1,030
Manheim township *Lancaster Co.*	71.7	222,700	1975	816
Manor township *Lancaster Co.*	76.0	172,600	1980	706
Marple township *Delaware Co.*	84.7	345,700	1959	846
McCandless township *Allegheny Co.*	76.5	187,700	1971	727
McKeesport city *Allegheny Co.*	53.7	47,100	1941	388
Middletown township *Bucks Co.*	75.6	316,700	1974	976
Millcreek township *Erie Co.*	69.9	142,500	1973	612
Monroeville municipality *Allegheny Co.*	67.4	122,200	1964	712
Montgomery township *Montgomery Co.*	90.8	332,800	1990	1,271

Place	Homeownership Rate (%)	Median Home Value ($)	Median Year Structure Built	Median Rent ($/month)
Moon township *Allegheny Co.*	71.6	169,800	1972	688
Mount Lebanon township *Allegheny Co.*	71.4	192,800	1950	661
Muhlenberg township *Berks Co.*	79.4	156,200	1964	598
Murrysville municipality *Westmoreland Co.*	89.0	207,700	1973	609
New Castle city *Lawrence Co.*	60.8	56,600	before 1940	410
Newtown township *Bucks Co.*	86.4	379,900	1987	1,341
Norristown borough *Montgomery Co.*	41.5	153,100	1944	789
North Huntingdon township *Westmoreland Co.*	87.1	147,500	1966	510
Northampton township *Bucks Co.*	91.8	415,500	1979	1,150
Palmer township *Northampton Co.*	86.7	239,800	1972	836
Penn township *Westmoreland Co.*	90.7	172,900	1975	439
Penn Hills township *Allegheny Co.*	76.8	86,200	1956	538
Peters township *Washington Co.*	94.2	286,600	1979	680
Philadelphia city *Philadelphia Co.*	54.1	135,200	1946	656
Pittsburgh city *Allegheny Co.*	47.6	85,200	before 1940	572
Plum borough *Allegheny Co.*	79.0	132,100	1970	638
Pottstown borough *Montgomery Co.*	55.3	142,100	1944	627
Radnor township *Delaware Co.*	65.1	609,600	1960	1,185
Reading city *Berks Co.*	42.4	65,500	before 1940	529
Ridley township *Delaware Co.*	75.2	199,500	1955	773
Ross township *Allegheny Co.*	74.7	139,300	1962	621
Scranton city *Lackawanna Co.*	51.3	106,300	before 1940	474
Shaler township *Allegheny Co.*	86.4	135,700	1959	571
South Whitehall township *Lehigh Co.*	81.3	234,400	1970	709
Spring township *Berks Co.*	78.3	185,400	1975	801
Springettsbury township *York Co.*	72.3	181,300	1969	743
Springfield township *Montgomery Co.*	80.1	327,100	1954	1,048
Springfield township *Delaware Co.*	91.1	298,600	1955	903
State College borough *Centre Co.*	20.3	237,900	1971	743
Stroud township *Monroe Co.*	81.0	229,600	1980	743
Susquehanna township *Dauphin Co.*	70.0	159,600	1972	761
Swatara township *Dauphin Co.*	70.1	149,700	1969	630
Tredyffrin township *Chester Co.*	78.5	447,700	1971	1,099
Unity township *Westmoreland Co.*	80.3	162,000	1969	503
Upper Darby township *Delaware Co.*	60.5	163,600	1948	753
Upper Dublin township *Montgomery Co.*	86.8	406,500	1971	1,201
Upper Macungie township *Lehigh Co.*	81.6	292,600	1992	1,048
Upper Merion township *Montgomery Co.*	67.2	324,200	1968	1,010
Upper Moreland township *Montgomery Co.*	62.4	264,800	1959	895
Upper Providence township *Montgomery Co.*	89.7	331,500	1990	910
Upper Saint Clair cdp/township *Allegheny Co.*	92.0	236,400	1969	1,394
Warminster township *Bucks Co.*	71.0	306,100	1967	880
Warrington township *Bucks Co.*	83.7	392,000	1989	950
West Goshen township *Chester Co.*	74.3	362,300	1974	1,025
West Mifflin borough *Allegheny Co.*	78.0	85,500	1955	380
Whitehall township *Lehigh Co.*	63.9	195,300	1968	794
Wilkes-Barre city *Luzerne Co.*	48.9	77,700	before 1940	444
Williamsport city *Lycoming Co.*	41.9	86,700	before 1940	463
York city *York Co.*	41.8	80,100	1940	492
York township *York Co.*	70.2	191,800	1982	732

NOTE: Homeownership Rate as of 2010; Median Rent, Median Home Value, and Median Age of Housing are 2006-2010 5-year estimates.

Commute to Work

Place	Automobile (%)	Public Transportation (%)	Walk (%)	Work from Home (%)
Abington township *Montgomery Co.*	87.7	7.1	1.9	3.0
Allentown city *Lehigh Co.*	86.3	4.9	5.4	2.3
Allison Park cdp *Allegheny Co.*	89.7	2.9	1.3	5.4
Altoona city *Blair Co.*	91.3	0.9	3.8	2.2
Baldwin borough *Allegheny Co.*	87.4	7.1	2.2	2.8
Bensalem township *Bucks Co.*	90.7	5.2	1.7	1.8
Bethel Park municipality *Allegheny Co.*	84.2	9.2	1.6	4.2
Bethlehem township *Northampton Co.*	93.4	1.6	0.7	3.5
Bethlehem city *Northampton Co.*	88.4	2.8	5.0	2.6
Bristol township *Bucks Co.*	94.4	3.1	0.6	1.3
Buckingham township *Bucks Co.*	87.7	1.3	1.9	8.0
Chambersburg borough *Franklin Co.*	92.1	0.2	4.5	2.2
Cheltenham township *Montgomery Co.*	80.9	10.5	4.0	3.7
Chester city *Delaware Co.*	74.1	15.0	6.6	3.1
Coolbaugh township *Monroe Co.*	88.2	7.1	0.2	3.1
Cranberry township *Butler Co.*	90.9	1.5	1.2	5.4
Derry township *Dauphin Co.*	87.5	0.5	7.4	3.6
Dover township *York Co.*	94.7	0.2	1.0	3.4
Drexel Hill cdp *Delaware Co.*	82.9	10.3	2.5	3.5
East Hempfield township *Lancaster Co.*	92.4	0.5	1.0	5.9
East Pennsboro township *Cumberland Co.*	91.2	1.5	4.0	2.7
Easton city *Northampton Co.*	86.4	3.8	4.3	4.6
Erie city *Erie Co.*	87.8	3.8	5.3	1.6
Exeter township *Berks Co.*	94.1	0.9	0.8	3.6
Falls township *Bucks Co.*	94.6	1.5	1.8	1.3
Hampden township *Cumberland Co.*	94.1	0.4	1.0	3.9
Harrisburg city *Dauphin Co.*	76.8	8.4	9.2	1.3
Haverford township *Delaware Co.*	85.1	6.8	3.0	4.1
Hazleton city *Luzerne Co.*	90.3	1.4	4.9	1.3
Hempfield township *Westmoreland Co.*	94.7	0.7	1.4	3.0
Horsham township *Montgomery Co.*	88.9	4.0	2.4	4.0
Johnstown city *Cambria Co.*	81.0	5.2	9.5	1.8
King of Prussia cdp *Montgomery Co.*	89.1	4.5	2.7	3.3
Lancaster city *Lancaster Co.*	76.8	6.2	11.4	3.3
Lebanon city *Lebanon Co.*	89.1	1.1	7.5	1.6
Levittown cdp *Bucks Co.*	95.2	2.0	0.6	1.6
Lower Macungie township *Lehigh Co.*	93.3	0.5	0.1	5.6
Lower Makefield township *Bucks Co.*	82.4	7.8	1.9	7.4
Lower Merion township *Montgomery Co.*	73.1	10.0	7.7	8.3
Lower Paxton township *Dauphin Co.*	94.2	1.1	1.8	2.1
Lower Providence township *Montgomery Co.*	90.0	3.2	1.7	4.1
Manheim township *Lancaster Co.*	92.2	1.1	0.9	4.6
Manor township *Lancaster Co.*	93.8	0.4	1.1	2.5
Marple township *Delaware Co.*	88.2	4.2	1.9	4.7
McCandless township *Allegheny Co.*	90.1	3.5	0.8	4.9
McKeesport city *Allegheny Co.*	81.4	8.1	7.0	3.0
Middletown township *Bucks Co.*	92.2	2.4	0.9	3.6
Millcreek township *Erie Co.*	94.8	0.2	1.8	2.2
Monroeville municipality *Allegheny Co.*	88.2	5.5	2.1	3.3
Montgomery township *Montgomery Co.*	90.0	3.9	1.6	3.7

Place	Automobile (%)	Public Transportation (%)	Walk (%)	Work from Home (%)
Moon township *Allegheny Co.*	88.5	2.5	4.1	2.9
Mount Lebanon township *Allegheny Co.*	79.2	12.0	2.9	5.1
Muhlenberg township *Berks Co.*	92.5	1.6	2.1	2.4
Murrysville municipality *Westmoreland Co.*	91.3	1.7	0.5	6.1
New Castle city *Lawrence Co.*	90.2	2.2	3.6	1.6
Newtown township *Bucks Co.*	90.7	2.4	1.6	5.4
Norristown borough *Montgomery Co.*	76.2	10.4	9.5	1.3
North Huntingdon township *Westmoreland Co.*	93.4	2.4	0.4	3.3
Northampton township *Bucks Co.*	89.8	3.4	1.0	5.4
Palmer township *Northampton Co.*	94.3	1.0	0.8	3.3
Penn township *Westmoreland Co.*	94.9	1.9	0.1	2.8
Penn Hills township *Allegheny Co.*	88.1	7.3	1.4	2.6
Peters township *Washington Co.*	85.6	3.9	1.7	7.6
Philadelphia city *Philadelphia Co.*	60.1	26.2	8.4	2.6
Pittsburgh city *Allegheny Co.*	63.8	19.5	11.8	3.1
Plum borough *Allegheny Co.*	92.0	3.8	0.9	2.5
Pottstown borough *Montgomery Co.*	87.9	2.3	5.5	2.4
Radnor township *Delaware Co.*	71.5	7.4	12.3	7.1
Reading city *Berks Co.*	78.6	7.3	8.4	3.0
Ridley township *Delaware Co.*	89.2	4.4	3.8	1.6
Ross township *Allegheny Co.*	90.3	4.1	2.0	3.3
Scranton city *Lackawanna Co.*	87.9	2.5	7.3	1.4
Shaler township *Allegheny Co.*	91.7	3.0	1.1	3.0
South Whitehall township *Lehigh Co.*	93.7	0.3	1.4	4.4
Spring township *Berks Co.*	92.4	0.8	2.6	3.1
Springettsbury township *York Co.*	93.0	0.9	1.5	3.4
Springfield township *Montgomery Co.*	81.6	7.7	2.2	7.6
Springfield township *Delaware Co.*	89.1	6.3	1.0	3.0
State College borough *Centre Co.*	46.5	6.1	39.4	4.0
Stroud township *Monroe Co.*	85.8	7.9	1.9	3.2
Susquehanna township *Dauphin Co.*	94.4	2.3	0.5	1.7
Swatara township *Dauphin Co.*	94.5	1.1	1.0	1.9
Tredyffrin township *Chester Co.*	82.5	7.7	1.8	6.8
Unity township *Westmoreland Co.*	90.0	0.8	3.9	5.3
Upper Darby township *Delaware Co.*	78.1	14.9	3.3	2.4
Upper Dublin township *Montgomery Co.*	86.1	7.8	0.9	4.8
Upper Macungie township *Lehigh Co.*	94.0	0.3	2.1	3.3
Upper Merion township *Montgomery Co.*	88.8	4.8	2.4	3.5
Upper Moreland township *Montgomery Co.*	89.2	3.7	3.0	3.1
Upper Providence township *Montgomery Co.*	91.6	1.2	1.9	4.4
Upper Saint Clair cdp/township *Allegheny Co.*	86.0	6.5	0.6	5.7
Warminster township *Bucks Co.*	92.2	3.3	1.2	2.8
Warrington township *Bucks Co.*	91.4	3.1	0.8	4.2
West Goshen township *Chester Co.*	92.0	1.2	1.0	5.2
West Mifflin borough *Allegheny Co.*	86.4	8.0	2.5	2.9
Whitehall township *Lehigh Co.*	92.3	2.9	2.3	2.1
Wilkes-Barre city *Luzerne Co.*	85.7	3.3	7.9	2.1
Williamsport city *Lycoming Co.*	80.0	4.7	10.8	2.8
York city *York Co.*	80.9	8.0	5.9	2.3
York township *York Co.*	95.2	0.2	1.1	3.3

NOTE: Figures are 2006-2010 5-year estimates.

Travel Time to Work

Place	Less than 15 Minutes (%)	15 to 30 Minutes (%)	30 to 45 Minutes (%)	45 to 60 Minutes (%)	60 Minutes or More (%)
Abington township *Montgomery Co.*	28.5	28.6	22.3	11.4	9.2
Allentown city *Lehigh Co.*	31.5	43.3	13.0	5.0	7.2
Allison Park cdp *Allegheny Co.*	21.2	34.4	28.4	10.4	5.6
Altoona city *Blair Co.*	54.7	30.3	7.6	3.5	4.0
Baldwin borough *Allegheny Co.*	21.1	34.1	25.5	11.2	8.0
Bensalem township *Bucks Co.*	23.9	39.1	20.3	8.9	7.7
Bethel Park municipality *Allegheny Co.*	25.2	25.6	26.0	15.4	7.7
Bethlehem township *Northampton Co.*	27.7	36.6	14.3	5.2	16.2
Bethlehem city *Northampton Co.*	39.6	36.7	11.7	3.8	8.2
Bristol township *Bucks Co.*	31.5	39.6	15.5	6.7	6.7
Buckingham township *Bucks Co.*	21.5	21.0	20.8	16.0	20.7
Chambersburg borough *Franklin Co.*	46.7	29.2	16.5	3.6	4.0
Cheltenham township *Montgomery Co.*	20.3	29.6	30.2	11.1	8.7
Chester city *Delaware Co.*	31.2	40.6	16.6	7.3	4.4
Coolbaugh township *Monroe Co.*	17.4	30.3	16.0	3.6	32.8
Cranberry township *Butler Co.*	27.2	20.8	33.1	13.4	5.5
Derry township *Dauphin Co.*	46.2	30.9	14.1	4.0	4.8
Dover township *York Co.*	20.9	44.3	21.3	6.5	6.9
Drexel Hill cdp *Delaware Co.*	20.8	25.5	28.1	15.7	9.9
East Hempfield township *Lancaster Co.*	35.9	42.8	13.3	4.4	3.6
East Pennsboro township *Cumberland Co.*	35.0	48.5	11.7	2.1	2.7
Easton city *Northampton Co.*	28.6	34.4	16.1	8.3	12.6
Erie city *Erie Co.*	45.1	40.4	10.3	1.9	2.2
Exeter township *Berks Co.*	26.1	41.1	14.0	8.6	10.2
Falls township *Bucks Co.*	29.1	43.4	14.7	5.7	7.1
Hampden township *Cumberland Co.*	28.8	53.6	11.5	3.4	2.7
Harrisburg city *Dauphin Co.*	38.6	44.1	11.1	3.0	3.2
Haverford township *Delaware Co.*	22.5	34.1	27.1	10.7	5.6
Hazleton city *Luzerne Co.*	42.3	38.9	10.2	3.0	5.5
Hempfield township *Westmoreland Co.*	36.9	34.7	12.0	7.5	8.9
Horsham township *Montgomery Co.*	25.3	32.3	23.4	9.8	9.2
Johnstown city *Cambria Co.*	41.7	40.1	9.0	5.1	4.1
King of Prussia cdp *Montgomery Co.*	31.4	34.1	19.3	7.5	7.7
Lancaster city *Lancaster Co.*	38.9	41.1	12.1	4.3	3.5
Lebanon city *Lebanon Co.*	41.0	31.9	14.5	7.8	4.9
Levittown cdp *Bucks Co.*	31.9	40.7	15.9	5.9	5.7
Lower Macungie township *Lehigh Co.*	32.7	37.2	15.0	4.9	10.1
Lower Makefield township *Bucks Co.*	21.9	32.8	17.1	10.8	17.3
Lower Merion township *Montgomery Co.*	26.0	33.6	26.6	9.1	4.8
Lower Paxton township *Dauphin Co.*	30.2	53.2	11.5	2.4	2.7
Lower Providence township *Montgomery Co.*	24.6	33.6	23.4	8.6	9.8
Manheim township *Lancaster Co.*	39.6	39.4	12.0	4.0	5.0
Manor township *Lancaster Co.*	31.6	44.4	14.9	3.6	5.4
Marple township *Delaware Co.*	22.6	36.2	27.0	8.3	5.8
McCandless township *Allegheny Co.*	20.7	34.7	31.5	10.2	2.9
McKeesport city *Allegheny Co.*	34.8	28.0	19.9	11.4	5.9
Middletown township *Bucks Co.*	28.3	39.0	17.5	7.7	7.6
Millcreek township *Erie Co.*	40.8	49.8	7.0	0.7	1.7
Monroeville municipality *Allegheny Co.*	27.9	31.1	23.4	11.9	5.7
Montgomery township *Montgomery Co.*	20.4	33.1	21.1	12.0	13.4

Place	Less than 15 Minutes (%)	15 to 30 Minutes (%)	30 to 45 Minutes (%)	45 to 60 Minutes (%)	60 Minutes or More (%)
Moon township *Allegheny Co.*	35.9	33.7	17.9	7.0	5.5
Mount Lebanon township *Allegheny Co.*	23.3	31.4	30.4	8.0	6.8
Muhlenberg township *Berks Co.*	39.9	45.4	7.1	2.5	5.1
Murrysville municipality *Westmoreland Co.*	24.4	28.7	22.7	14.7	9.6
New Castle city *Lawrence Co.*	51.4	26.8	10.8	5.1	5.9
Newtown township *Bucks Co.*	22.4	29.5	21.8	10.5	15.8
Norristown borough *Montgomery Co.*	27.4	40.4	20.5	5.8	5.9
North Huntingdon township *Westmoreland Co.*	25.4	32.4	20.4	11.4	10.4
Northampton township *Bucks Co.*	21.3	31.5	21.6	11.0	14.6
Palmer township *Northampton Co.*	32.0	32.6	14.6	4.7	16.1
Penn township *Westmoreland Co.*	21.5	35.0	19.4	9.6	14.5
Penn Hills township *Allegheny Co.*	21.9	34.3	26.1	9.6	8.0
Peters township *Washington Co.*	23.7	32.1	24.5	12.0	7.7
Philadelphia city *Philadelphia Co.*	16.1	32.7	26.9	11.8	12.5
Pittsburgh city *Allegheny Co.*	27.1	44.4	18.4	5.5	4.5
Plum borough *Allegheny Co.*	20.0	35.0	20.4	15.3	9.3
Pottstown borough *Montgomery Co.*	32.4	32.0	19.6	8.0	8.0
Radnor township *Delaware Co.*	35.9	29.6	19.9	9.0	5.5
Reading city *Berks Co.*	31.9	40.1	14.3	6.5	7.1
Ridley township *Delaware Co.*	31.1	32.0	22.2	10.4	4.3
Ross township *Allegheny Co.*	20.5	46.5	24.9	4.2	3.9
Scranton city *Lackawanna Co.*	49.2	34.7	9.9	2.6	3.6
Shaler township *Allegheny Co.*	18.6	45.0	25.3	6.8	4.4
South Whitehall township *Lehigh Co.*	36.1	45.5	7.0	3.3	8.1
Spring township *Berks Co.*	41.5	41.0	8.1	3.0	6.4
Springettsbury township *York Co.*	36.4	38.7	13.5	5.9	5.6
Springfield township *Montgomery Co.*	20.3	33.0	27.2	10.9	8.6
Springfield township *Delaware Co.*	18.5	31.4	28.4	14.0	7.6
State College borough *Centre Co.*	55.0	35.2	6.4	1.5	2.0
Stroud township *Monroe Co.*	35.3	23.8	8.6	5.6	26.7
Susquehanna township *Dauphin Co.*	36.5	49.8	8.3	2.9	2.6
Swatara township *Dauphin Co.*	35.5	50.3	9.7	2.3	2.2
Tredyffrin township *Chester Co.*	32.1	34.4	14.8	7.9	10.9
Unity township *Westmoreland Co.*	43.7	34.9	11.0	4.8	5.6
Upper Darby township *Delaware Co.*	17.3	27.6	29.7	14.9	10.5
Upper Dublin township *Montgomery Co.*	23.2	30.6	24.7	12.3	9.1
Upper Macungie township *Lehigh Co.*	35.9	40.6	11.3	2.9	9.4
Upper Merion township *Montgomery Co.*	30.2	35.0	19.1	8.5	7.2
Upper Moreland township *Montgomery Co.*	29.8	35.2	18.7	9.1	7.1
Upper Providence township *Montgomery Co.*	22.4	27.7	25.2	14.1	10.5
Upper Saint Clair cdp/township *Allegheny Co.*	21.3	31.6	24.7	12.5	9.9
Warminster township *Bucks Co.*	29.3	31.7	23.2	7.8	8.0
Warrington township *Bucks Co.*	24.0	34.4	18.9	11.2	11.5
West Goshen township *Chester Co.*	34.4	27.8	20.5	10.5	6.8
West Mifflin borough *Allegheny Co.*	26.9	35.6	22.8	8.4	6.3
Whitehall township *Lehigh Co.*	34.2	42.0	14.0	2.9	6.9
Wilkes-Barre city *Luzerne Co.*	51.2	32.9	8.9	2.8	4.3
Williamsport city *Lycoming Co.*	57.2	31.6	6.1	1.8	3.3
York city *York Co.*	36.4	42.2	11.0	5.2	5.2
York township *York Co.*	30.5	39.0	12.6	8.4	9.4

NOTE: Figures are 2006-2010 5-year estimates.

Crime

Place	Violent Crime Rate (crimes per 10,000 population)	Property Crime Rate (crimes per 10,000 population)
Abington township *Montgomery Co.*	15.1	213.4
Allentown city *Lehigh Co.*	54.6	386.4
Allison Park cdp *Allegheny Co.*	n/a	n/a
Altoona city *Blair Co.*	30.8	234.6
Baldwin borough *Allegheny Co.*	9.6	79.2
Bensalem township *Bucks Co.*	15.3	377.4
Bethel Park municipality *Allegheny Co.*	8.0	100.9
Bethlehem township *Northampton Co.*	5.0	171.8
Bethlehem city *Northampton Co.*	29.1	247.5
Bristol township *Bucks Co.*	23.0	329.6
Buckingham township *Bucks Co.*	4.5	61.6
Chambersburg borough *Franklin Co.*	34.9	336.9
Cheltenham township *Montgomery Co.*	20.6	278.0
Chester city *Delaware Co.*	n/a	387.9
Coolbaugh township *Monroe Co.*	n/a	n/a
Cranberry township *Butler Co.*	2.5	121.3
Derry township *Dauphin Co.*	15.8	214.9
Dover township *York Co.*	n/a	n/a
Drexel Hill cdp *Delaware Co.*	n/a	n/a
East Hempfield township *Lancaster Co.*	8.1	201.7
East Pennsboro township *Cumberland Co.*	6.4	171.0
Easton city *Northampton Co.*	35.7	309.5
Erie city *Erie Co.*	42.2	366.1
Exeter township *Berks Co.*	5.1	151.4
Falls township *Bucks Co.*	14.0	281.6
Hampden township *Cumberland Co.*	3.9	127.3
Harrisburg city *Dauphin Co.*	140.3	506.2
Haverford township *Delaware Co.*	6.8	134.4
Hazleton city *Luzerne Co.*	46.0	177.4
Hempfield township *Westmoreland Co.*	n/a	n/a
Horsham township *Montgomery Co.*	7.6	114.4
Johnstown city *Cambria Co.*	66.9	425.7
King of Prussia cdp *Montgomery Co.*	n/a	n/a
Lancaster city *Lancaster Co.*	84.7	506.5
Lebanon city *Lebanon Co.*	34.0	251.6
Levittown cdp *Bucks Co.*	n/a	n/a
Lower Macungie township *Lehigh Co.*	n/a	n/a
Lower Makefield township *Bucks Co.*	8.0	147.9
Lower Merion township *Montgomery Co.*	9.0	176.9
Lower Paxton township *Dauphin Co.*	25.0	256.4
Lower Providence township *Montgomery Co.*	16.5	105.0
Manheim township *Lancaster Co.*	8.6	228.5
Manor township *Lancaster Co.*	4.6	118.9
Marple township *Delaware Co.*	4.3	171.9
McCandless township *Allegheny Co.*	1.8	86.2
McKeesport city *Allegheny Co.*	169.7	385.5
Middletown township *Bucks Co.*	8.3	312.9
Millcreek township *Erie Co.*	8.6	204.7
Monroeville municipality *Allegheny Co.*	19.0	120.1
Montgomery township *Montgomery Co.*	2.4	206.7

Place	Violent Crime Rate (crimes per 10,000 population)	Property Crime Rate (crimes per 10,000 population)
Moon township *Allegheny Co.*	6.6	108.4
Mount Lebanon township *Allegheny Co.*	5.4	63.2
Muhlenberg township *Berks Co.*	14.2	379.9
Murrysville municipality *Westmoreland Co.*	3.0	46.7
New Castle city *Lawrence Co.*	n/a	n/a
Newtown township *Bucks Co.*	6.7	117.6
Norristown borough *Montgomery Co.*	106.6	289.5
North Huntingdon township *Westmoreland Co.*	4.2	109.4
Northampton township *Bucks Co.*	0.5	70.3
Palmer township *Northampton Co.*	5.8	193.2
Penn township *Westmoreland Co.*	7.0	60.8
Penn Hills township *Allegheny Co.*	33.2	200.2
Peters township *Washington Co.*	3.8	67.7
Philadelphia city *Philadelphia Co.*	119.3	389.4
Pittsburgh city *Allegheny Co.*	80.2	326.1
Plum borough *Allegheny Co.*	n/a	n/a
Pottstown borough *Montgomery Co.*	84.6	474.9
Radnor township *Delaware Co.*	4.7	119.8
Reading city *Berks Co.*	85.8	373.6
Ridley township *Delaware Co.*	17.2	180.3
Ross township *Allegheny Co.*	9.6	214.1
Scranton city *Lackawanna Co.*	29.6	334.9
Shaler township *Allegheny Co.*	4.5	112.0
South Whitehall township *Lehigh Co.*	10.4	399.1
Spring township *Berks Co.*	2.2	104.0
Springettsbury township *York Co.*	16.8	356.2
Springfield township *Montgomery Co.*	18.5	94.5
Springfield township *Delaware Co.*	6.2	320.7
State College borough *Centre Co.*	10.1	157.8
Stroud township *Monroe Co.*	n/a	n/a
Susquehanna township *Dauphin Co.*	18.7	177.5
Swatara township *Dauphin Co.*	68.3	339.6
Tredyffrin township *Chester Co.*	4.1	89.7
Unity township *Westmoreland Co.*	n/a	n/a
Upper Darby township *Delaware Co.*	50.9	268.8
Upper Dublin township *Montgomery Co.*	9.7	95.5
Upper Macungie township *Lehigh Co.*	n/a	n/a
Upper Merion township *Montgomery Co.*	8.4	498.8
Upper Moreland township *Montgomery Co.*	4.6	204.6
Upper Providence township *Montgomery Co.*	3.8	140.0
Upper Saint Clair cdp/township *Allegheny Co.*	2.1	49.2
Warminster township *Bucks Co.*	9.2	178.1
Warrington township *Bucks Co.*	10.6	94.9
West Goshen township *Chester Co.*	10.9	177.8
West Mifflin borough *Allegheny Co.*	22.1	294.9
Whitehall township *Lehigh Co.*	13.0	542.8
Wilkes-Barre city *Luzerne Co.*	51.2	356.2
Williamsport city *Lycoming Co.*	33.9	425.4
York city *York Co.*	164.4	394.7
York township *York Co.*	n/a	n/a

NOTE: Data as of 2011.

Education

Pennsylvania Public School Educational Profile

Category	Value	Category	Value
Schools *(2009-2010)*	3,245	**Diploma Recipients** *(2008-2009)*	130,658
Instructional Level		White, Non-Hispanic	103,712
Primary	1,848	Black, Non-Hispanic	16,424
Middle	557	Asian/Pacific Islander, Non-Hispanic	3,428
High	698	American Indian/Alaskan Native, Non-Hisp.	169
Other/Not Reported	142	Hispanic	6,509
Curriculum		**Staff** *(2009-2010)*	
Regular	3,133	Teachers (FTE)	130,988.4
Special Education	12	Salary[1] ($)	62,215
Vocational	87	Librarians/Media Specialists (FTE)	2,189.7
Alternative	13	Guidance Counselors (FTE)	4,711.1
Type		**Ratios** *(2009-2010)*	
Magnet	53	Number of Students per Teacher	13.5 to 1
Charter	135	Number of Students per Librarian	809.8 to 1
Title I Eligible	2,453	Number of Students per Guidance Counselor	376.4 to 1
School-wide Title I	1,335	**Finances** *(2007-2008)*	
Students *(2009-2010)*	1,773,141	Current Expenditures ($ per student)	
Gender (%)		Total	11,741
Male	51.3	Instruction	7,131
Female	48.7	Support Services	4,158
Race/Ethnicity (%)		Other	452
White, Non-Hispanic	72.5	General Revenue ($ per student)	
Black, Non-Hispanic	15.4	Total	13,859
Asian/Pacific Islander	3.1	From Federal Sources	996
American Indian/Alaskan Native	0.2	From State Sources	5,063
Hispanic	7.7	From Local Sources	7,800
Special Programs (%)		Long-Term Debt ($ per student)	
Individual Education Program (IEP)	16.6	At beginning of fiscal year	13,356
English Language Learner (ELL)	2.6	At end of fiscal year	13,884
Eligible for Free Lunch Program	31.1	**College Entrance Exam Scores**	
Eligible for Reduced-Price Lunch Program	6.5	SAT Reasoning Test[TM] *(2011)*	
Average Freshman Grad. Rate (%) *(2008-2009)*	80.5	Participation Rate (%)	73
White, Non-Hispanic	84.4	Mean Critical Reading Score	493
Black, Non-Hispanic	64.0	Mean Math Score	501
Asian/Pacific Islander, Non-Hispanic	99.3	Mean Writing Score	479
American Indian/Alaskan Native, Non-Hisp.	72.5	ACT *(2011)*	
Hispanic	65.3	Participation Rate (%)	17
High School Drop-out Rate (%) *(2008-2009)*	2.3	Mean Composite Score	22.3
White, Non-Hispanic	1.6	Mean English Score	21.9
Black, Non-Hispanic	4.6	Mean Math Score	22.6
Asian/Pacific Islander, Non-Hispanic	1.5	Mean Reading Score	22.6
American Indian/Alaskan Native, Non-Hisp.	3.4	Mean Science Score	21.8
Hispanic	5.9		

Note: *For an explanation of data, please refer to the User's Guide in the front of the book; (1) Average salary for classroom teachers in 2011-12*

Number of Schools

Rank	Number	District Name	City
1	273	Philadelphia City SD	Philadelphia
2	69	Pittsburgh SD	Pittsburgh
3	24	Reading SD	Reading
4	23	Central Bucks SD	Doylestown
4	23	Erie City SD	Erie
6	22	Allentown City SD	Allentown
6	22	Bethlehem Area SD	Bethlehem
8	20	Lancaster SD	Lancaster
9	19	Central Dauphin SD	Harrisburg
10	18	Scranton SD	Scranton
11	17	Chambersburg Area SD	Chambersburg
11	17	Harrisburg City SD	Harrisburg
11	17	North Penn SD	Lansdale
14	16	West Chester Area SD	West Chester
14	16	West Shore SD	New Cumberland
16	15	Council Rock SD	Newtown
16	15	Pennsbury SD	Fallsington
18	14	Butler Area SD	Butler
18	14	Downingtown Area SD	Downingtown
18	14	Upper Darby SD	Drexel Hill
21	13	Altoona Area SD	Altoona
21	13	Mifflin County SD	Lewistown
21	13	Millcreek Township SD	Erie
21	13	Pocono Mountain SD	Swiftwater
25	12	Bristol Township SD	Levittown
25	12	Juniata County SD	Mifflintown
25	12	Keystone Central SD	Lock Haven
25	12	Neshaminy SD	Langhorne
25	12	North Allegheny SD	Pittsburgh
25	12	Spring-Ford Area SD	Royersford
25	12	Warren County SD	North Warren
32	11	Armstrong SD	Ford City
32	11	Canon-Mcmillan SD	Canonsburg
32	11	Coatesville Area SD	Coatesville
32	11	Connellsville Area SD	Connellsville
32	11	Hempfield Area SD	Greensburg
32	11	Norristown Area SD	Norristown
32	11	Pennridge SD	Perkasie
32	11	Quakertown Community SD	Quakertown
32	11	State College Area SD	State College
32	11	William Penn SD	Lansdowne
42	10	Boyertown Area SD	Boyertown
42	10	Carlisle Area SD	Carlisle
42	10	Cumberland Valley SD	Mechanicsburg
42	10	Dubois Area SD	Du Bois
42	10	East Penn SD	Emmaus
42	10	E Stroudsburg Area SD	E Stroudsburg
42	10	Easton Area SD	Easton
42	10	Hazleton Area SD	Hazleton
42	10	Hempfield SD	Landisville
42	10	Lower Merion SD	Ardmore
42	10	Mount Lebanon SD	Pittsburgh
42	10	Parkland SD	Allentown
42	10	Penn Manor SD	Lancaster
42	10	Souderton Area SD	Souderton
42	10	Williamsport Area SD	Williamsport
42	10	Wilson SD	West Lawn
42	10	York City SD	York
59	9	Abington SD	Abington
59	9	Albert Gallatin Area SD	Uniontown
59	9	Bensalem Township SD	Bensalem
59	9	Centennial SD	Warminster
59	9	Chester-Upland SD	Chester
59	9	Crawford Central SD	Meadville
59	9	Kiski Area SD	Leechburg
59	9	Manheim Township SD	Lititz
59	9	Red Lion Area SD	Red Lion
59	9	Ridley SD	Folsom
59	9	Seneca Valley SD	Harmony
59	9	Stroudsburg Area SD	Stroudsburg
59	9	Uniontown Area SD	Uniontown
59	9	Wilkes-Barre Area SD	Wilkes Barre
59	9	Wyoming Valley West SD	Kingston
74	8	Bethel Park SD	Bethel Park
74	8	Franklin Area SD	Franklin
74	8	Gateway SD	Monroeville
74	8	Hatboro-Horsham SD	Horsham
74	8	Lower Dauphin SD	Hummelstown
74	8	Mechanicsburg Area SD	Mechanicsburg
74	8	North Hills SD	Pittsburgh
74	8	Northeastern York SD	Manchester
74	8	Penn-Trafford SD	Harrison City
74	8	Punxsutawney Area SD	Punxsutawney
74	8	Shaler Area SD	Glenshaw
74	8	Tredyffrin-Easttown SD	Wayne
74	8	Woodland Hills SD	Pittsburgh
87	7	Athens Area SD	Athens
87	7	Central York SD	York
87	7	Cheltenham Township SD	Elkins Park
87	7	Colonial SD	Plymth Meeting
87	7	Dallastown Area SD	Dallastown
87	7	Delaware Valley SD	Milford
87	7	Dover Area SD	Dover
87	7	Elizabethtown Area SD	Elizabethtown
87	7	Ephrata Area SD	Ephrata
87	7	Grove City Area SD	Grove City
87	7	Haverford Township SD	Havertown
87	7	Lebanon SD	Lebanon
87	7	Mckeesport Area SD	Mckeesport
87	7	Methacton SD	Norristown
87	7	Mifflinburg Area SD	Mifflinburg
87	7	Moon Area SD	Moon Township
87	7	New Castle Area SD	New Castle
87	7	Norwin SD	N Huntingdon
87	7	Owen J Roberts SD	Pottstown
87	7	Perkiomen Valley SD	Collegeville
87	7	Pleasant Valley SD	Brodheadsville
87	7	Plum Borough SD	Plum
87	7	Pottstown SD	Pottstown
87	7	Shikellamy SD	Sunbury
87	7	Solanco SD	Quarryville
87	7	West Mifflin Area SD	West Mifflin
87	7	Wissahickon SD	Ambler
114	6	Abington Heights SD	Clarks Summit
114	6	Bellefonte Area SD	Bellefonte
114	6	Berwick Area SD	Berwick
114	6	Big Spring SD	Newville
114	6	Chichester SD	Aston
114	6	Clearfield Area SD	Clearfield
114	6	Cocalico SD	Denver
114	6	Conestoga Valley SD	Lancaster
114	6	Conneaut SD	Linesville
114	6	Cornwall-Lebanon SD	Lebanon
114	6	Corry Area SD	Corry
114	6	Daniel Boone Area SD	Birdsboro
114	6	Danville Area SD	Danville
114	6	Donegal SD	Mount Joy
114	6	Eastern Lebanon County SD	Myerstown
114	6	Elizabeth Forward SD	Elizabeth
114	6	Exeter Township SD	Reading
114	6	Fox Chapel Area SD	Pittsburgh
114	6	Gettysburg Area SD	Gettysburg
114	6	Governor Mifflin SD	Shillington
114	6	Great Valley SD	Malvern
114	6	Highlands SD	Natrona Heights
114	6	Hollidaysburg Area SD	Hollidaysburg
114	6	Huntingdon Area SD	Huntingdon
114	6	Indiana Area SD	Indiana
114	6	Interboro SD	Prospect Park
114	6	Jersey Shore Area SD	Jersey Shore
114	6	Laurel Highlands SD	Uniontown
114	6	Lehighton Area SD	Lehighton
114	6	Marple Newtown SD	Newtown Square
114	6	Midd-West SD	Middleburg
114	6	Montour SD	Mckees Rocks
114	6	Mount Pleasant Area SD	Mount Pleasant
114	6	Nazareth Area SD	Nazareth
114	6	New Kensington-Arnold SD	New Kensington
114	6	North Pocono SD	Moscow
114	6	Northampton Area SD	Northampton
114	6	Northern Lebanon SD	Fredericksburg
114	6	Northern Tioga SD	Elkland
114	6	Northern York County SD	Dillsburg
114	6	Oil City Area SD	Oil City
114	6	Oxford Area SD	Oxford
114	6	Penn Hills SD	Pittsburgh
114	6	Penn-Delco SD	Aston
114	6	Penncrest SD	Saegertown
114	6	Phoenixville Area SD	Phoenixville
114	6	Pine-Richland SD	Gibsonia
114	6	Rose Tree Media SD	Media
114	6	Shippensburg Area SD	Shippensburg
114	6	Somerset Area SD	Somerset
114	6	South Eastern SD	Fawn Grove
114	6	South Western SD	Hanover
114	6	Southeast Delco SD	Folcroft
114	6	Southern Lehigh SD	Center Valley
114	6	Southern Tioga SD	Blossburg
114	6	Spring Grove Area SD	Spring Grove
114	6	Titusville Area SD	Titusville
114	6	Trinity Area SD	Washington
114	6	Tunkhannock Area SD	Tunkhannock
114	6	Tuscarora SD	Mercersburg
114	6	Unionville-Chadds Ford SD	Kennett Square
114	6	Upper Dublin SD	Maple Glen
114	6	Upper Merion Area SD	King of Prussia
114	6	Upper Saint Clair SD	Pittsburgh
114	6	Wallingford-Swarthmore SD	Wallingford
114	6	Warwick SD	Lititz
114	6	Wayne Highlands SD	Honesdale
114	6	Waynesboro Area SD	Waynesboro
114	6	West Perry SD	Elliottsburg
114	6	West York Area SD	York
184	5	Ambridge Area SD	Ambridge
184	5	Bald Eagle Area SD	Wingate
184	5	Baldwin-Whitehall SD	Pittsburgh
184	5	Bangor Area SD	Bangor
184	5	Bedford Area SD	Bedford
184	5	Belle Vernon Area SD	Belle Vernon
184	5	Blackhawk SD	Beaver Falls
184	5	Blairsville-Saltsburg SD	Blairsville
184	5	Bloomsburg Area SD	Bloomsburg
184	5	Blue Mountain SD	Orwigsburg
184	5	Brownsville Area SD	Brownsville
184	5	Central Valley SD	Monaca
184	5	Conewago Valley SD	New Oxford
184	5	Derry Area SD	Derry
184	5	Derry Township SD	Hershey
184	5	Eastern Lancaster County SD	New Holland
184	5	Eastern York SD	Wrightsville
184	5	Ellwood City Area SD	Ellwood City
184	5	Fleetwood Area SD	Fleetwood
184	5	Fort Leboeuf SD	Waterford
184	5	Franklin Regional SD	Murrysville
184	5	Freedom Area SD	Freedom
184	5	Freeport Area SD	Sarver
184	5	Garnet Valley SD	Glen Mills
184	5	Greater Latrobe SD	Latrobe
184	5	Greater Nanticoke Area SD	Nanticoke
184	5	Greensburg Salem SD	Greensburg
184	5	Hampton Township SD	Allison Park
184	5	Hanover Area SD	Hanover Twp
184	5	Hanover Public SD	Hanover
184	5	Harbor Creek SD	Harborcreek
184	5	Hermitage SD	Hermitage
184	5	Hopewell Area SD	Aliquippa
184	5	Kennett Consolidated SD	Kennett Square
184	5	Keystone Oaks SD	Pittsburgh
184	5	Kutztown Area SD	Kutztown
184	5	Lampeter-Strasburg SD	Lampeter
184	5	Ligonier Valley SD	Ligonier
184	5	Manheim Central SD	Manheim
184	5	Marion Center Area SD	Marion Center
184	5	Mars Area SD	Mars
184	5	Middletown Area SD	Middletown
184	5	Milton Area SD	Milton
184	5	Mount Union Area SD	Mount Union
184	5	Octorara Area SD	Atglen
184	5	Palisades SD	Kintnersville
184	5	Palmerton Area SD	Palmerton
184	5	Palmyra Area SD	Palmyra
184	5	Penn Cambria SD	Cresson
184	5	Peters Township SD	Mcmurray
184	5	Philipsburg-Osceola Area SD	Philipsburg
184	5	Pittston Area SD	Pittston
184	5	Pottsgrove SD	Pottstown
184	5	Radnor Township SD	Wayne
184	5	Ringgold SD	New Eagle
184	5	Saint Marys Area SD	Saint Marys
184	5	Selinsgrove Area SD	Selinsgrove
184	5	Sharon City SD	Sharon
184	5	Slippery Rock Area SD	Slippery Rock
184	5	Southern York County SD	Glen Rock
184	5	Steel Valley SD	Munhall
184	5	Susquehanna Township SD	Harrisburg
184	5	Tamaqua Area SD	Tamaqua
184	5	Troy Area SD	Troy
184	5	Twin Valley SD	Elverson
184	5	Upper Adams SD	Biglerville
184	5	Wallenpaupack Area SD	Hawley
184	5	West Allegheny SD	Oakdale
184	5	West Jefferson Hills SD	Jefferson Hills

Note: This section only includes districts with 1,500 or more students; All categories are ranked from high to low

184	5	Western Wayne SD	South Canaan
184	5	Whitehall-Coplay SD	Whitehall
184	5	Wilson Area SD	Easton
184	5	Wyoming Area SD	Exeter
184	5	York Suburban SD	York
184	5	Yough SD	Herminie
259	4	Annville-Cleona SD	Annville
259	4	Avon Grove SD	West Grove
259	4	Beaver Area SD	Beaver
259	4	Big Beaver Falls Area SD	Beaver Falls
259	4	Bradford Area SD	Bradford
259	4	Brandywine Heights Area SD	Topton
259	4	Brookville Area SD	Brookville
259	4	Burrell SD	Lower Burrell
259	4	Central Cambria SD	Ebensburg
259	4	Central Greene SD	Waynesburg
259	4	Chartiers Valley SD	Pittsburgh
259	4	Chestnut Ridge SD	Fishertown
259	4	Conrad Weiser Area SD	Robesonia
259	4	Crestwood SD	Mountain Top
259	4	Dallas SD	Dallas
259	4	Deer Lakes SD	Russellton
259	4	East Allegheny SD	N Versailles
259	4	East Lycoming SD	Hughesville
259	4	East Pennsboro Area SD	Enola
259	4	General Mclane SD	Edinboro
259	4	Greater Johnstown SD	Johnstown
259	4	Greencastle-Antrim SD	Greencastle
259	4	Hamburg Area SD	Hamburg
259	4	Karns City Area SD	Karns City
259	4	Lake-Lehman SD	Dallas
259	4	Lewisburg Area SD	Lewisburg
259	4	Littlestown Area SD	Littlestown
259	4	Mcguffey SD	Claysville
259	4	Montoursville Area SD	Montoursville
259	4	Muhlenberg SD	Reading
259	4	New Hope-Solebury SD	New Hope
259	4	North East SD	North East
259	4	Northern Lehigh SD	Slatington
259	4	Northwestern Lehigh SD	New Tripoli
259	4	Northwestern SD	Albion
259	4	Pequea Valley SD	Kinzers
259	4	Quaker Valley SD	Sewickley
259	4	Riverside Beaver County SD	Ellwood City
259	4	Salisbury Township SD	Allentown
259	4	South Butler County SD	Saxonburg
259	4	South Middleton SD	Boiling Springs
259	4	Southmoreland SD	Scottdale
259	4	Spring Cove SD	Roaring Spring
259	4	Springfield SD	Springfield
259	4	Springfield Township SD	Oreland
259	4	Upper Moreland Township SD	Willow Grove
259	4	Upper Perkiomen SD	Pennsburg
259	4	Valley View SD	Archbald
259	4	Warrior Run SD	Turbotville
259	4	Wellsboro Area SD	Wellsboro
309	3	Bermudian Springs SD	York Springs
309	3	Catasauqua Area SD	Catasauqua
309	3	Central Columbia SD	Bloomsburg
309	3	Charleroi SD	Charleroi
309	3	Dunmore SD	Dunmore
309	3	Fairview SD	Fairview
309	3	Forest Hills SD	Sidman
309	3	Girard SD	Girard
309	3	Jim Thorpe Area SD	Jim Thorpe
309	3	Lakeland SD	Jermyn
309	3	Lower Moreland Township SD	Huntingdon Vlly
309	3	Mid Valley SD	Throop
309	3	Montrose Area SD	Montrose
309	3	New Brighton Area SD	New Brighton
309	3	Oley Valley SD	Oley
309	3	Panther Valley SD	Lansford
309	3	Pen Argyl Area SD	Pen Argyl
309	3	Pine Grove Area SD	Pine Grove
309	3	Pottsville Area SD	Pottsville
309	3	Riverside SD	Taylor
309	3	Saucon Valley SD	Hellertown
309	3	Schuylkill Valley SD	Leesport
309	3	Shamokin Area SD	Coal Township
309	3	South Allegheny SD	Mckeesport
309	3	South Fayette Township SD	Mcdonald
309	3	South Park SD	South Park
309	3	Susquenita SD	Duncannon
309	3	Towanda Area SD	Towanda
309	3	Tulpehocken Area SD	Bethel
309	3	Tyrone Area SD	Tyrone
309	3	Washington SD	Washington
309	3	Wattsburg Area SD	Erie
309	3	Westmont Hilltop SD	Johnstown
309	3	Wyomissing Area SD	Wyomissing
343	2	Carbondale Area SD	Carbondale
343	2	Mohawk Area SD	Bessemer
343	2	Moniteau SD	West Sunbury
343	2	Mount Carmel Area SD	Mount Carmel
343	2	North Schuylkill SD	Ashland
343	2	Richland SD	Johnstown
349	1	Agora Cyber CS	Wayne
349	1	Chester Community CS	Chester
349	1	Commonwealth Connections Acade	Harrisburg
349	1	Lehigh Career & Technical Inst	Schnecksville
349	1	Pennsylvania Cyber CS	Midland
349	1	Pennsylvania Leadership Charter	West Chester
349	1	Pennsylvania Virtual CS	Norristown
349	1	York County School of Technology	York

Number of Teachers

Rank	Number	District Name	City
1	11,103.7	Philadelphia City SD	Philadelphia
2	2,228.9	Pittsburgh SD	Pittsburgh
3	1,201.9	Central Bucks SD	Doylestown
4	1,161.2	Allentown City SD	Allentown
5	1,149.3	Reading SD	Reading
6	995.9	Bethlehem Area SD	Bethlehem
7	975.0	Pocono Mountain SD	Swiftwater
8	971.0	Erie City SD	Erie
9	912.0	North Penn SD	Lansdale
10	854.3	Council Rock SD	Newtown
11	842.1	Lancaster SD	Lancaster
12	839.3	Upper Darby SD	Drexel Hill
13	835.0	Central Dauphin SD	Harrisburg
14	823.8	West Chester Area SD	West Chester
15	817.1	Downingtown Area SD	Downingtown
16	768.0	Pennsbury SD	Fallsington
17	709.5	Harrisburg City SD	Harrisburg
18	706.0	Scranton SD	Scranton
19	684.9	Easton Area SD	Easton
20	645.6	Hazleton Area SD	Hazleton
21	629.6	Lower Merion SD	Ardmore
22	617.0	E Stroudsburg Area SD	E Stroudsburg
23	598.5	West Shore SD	New Cumberland
24	589.9	Neshaminy SD	Langhorne
25	576.5	North Allegheny SD	Pittsburgh
26	566.1	Parkland SD	Allentown
27	555.3	Spring-Ford Area SD	Royersford
28	553.3	State College Area SD	State College
29	544.7	Chambersburg Area SD	Chambersburg
30	537.8	Coatesville Area SD	Coatesville
31	536.4	Seneca Valley SD	Harmony
32	534.7	Butler Area SD	Butler
33	528.0	Altoona Area SD	Altoona
34	526.4	Cumberland Valley SD	Mechanicsburg
35	523.9	Norristown Area SD	Norristown
36	520.5	Abington SD	Abington
37	493.4	Wilkes-Barre Area SD	Wilkes Barre
38	490.1	Bristol Township SD	Levittown
39	485.6	Souderton Area SD	Souderton
40	479.9	East Penn SD	Emmaus
41	466.4	Hempfield SD	Landisville
42	461.9	Pennridge SD	Perkasie
43	456.5	Pleasant Valley SD	Brodheadsville
44	454.4	Boyertown Area SD	Boyertown
45	451.1	Stroudsburg Area SD	Stroudsburg
46	445.7	Tredyffrin-Easttown SD	Wayne
47	441.0	York City SD	York
48	436.5	Mifflin County SD	Lewistown
49	427.3	Williamsport Area SD	Williamsport
50	424.9	Armstrong SD	Ford City
51	421.5	Bensalem Township SD	Bensalem
52	421.0	Hempfield Area SD	Greensburg
53	420.3	Ridley SD	Folsom
54	419.0	Warren County SD	North Warren
55	405.0	Centennial SD	Warminster
56	403.8	Fox Chapel Area SD	Pittsburgh
57	398.7	Dallastown Area SD	Dallastown
58	394.6	Mount Lebanon SD	Pittsburgh
59	392.4	Wilson SD	West Lawn
60	392.1	Manheim Township SD	Lititz
61	392.0	Methacton SD	Norristown
62	385.3	Hatboro-Horsham SD	Horsham
63	384.6	Shaler Area SD	Glenshaw
64	384.4	Garnet Valley SD	Glen Mills
65	383.6	Northampton Area SD	Northampton
66	381.0	Penn Hills SD	Pittsburgh
67	376.9	Delaware Valley SD	Milford
68	372.4	Red Lion Area SD	Red Lion
69	367.3	Bethel Park SD	Bethel Park
70	366.8	Colonial SD	Plymth Meeting
71	366.5	Perkiomen Valley SD	Collegeville
72	360.8	Owen J Roberts SD	Pottstown
73	359.3	Wissahickon SD	Ambler
74	359.0	Penn Manor SD	Lancaster
75	356.1	Millcreek Township SD	Erie
76	355.4	Cheltenham Township SD	Elkins Park
77	354.5	Central York SD	York
78	349.0	Woodland Hills SD	Pittsburgh
79	346.8	Quakertown Community SD	Quakertown
80	341.7	Carlisle Area SD	Carlisle
81	341.0	Connellsville Area SD	Connellsville
82	337.6	North Hills SD	Pittsburgh
83	337.2	William Penn SD	Lansdowne
84	333.0	Avon Grove SD	West Grove
85	329.0	Waynesboro Area SD	Waynesboro
86	328.5	Keystone Central SD	Lock Haven
87	328.0	Wyoming Valley West SD	Kingston
88	325.5	Upper Dublin SD	Maple Glen
89	317.7	Cornwall-Lebanon SD	Lebanon
90	316.9	Pine-Richland SD	Gibsonia
91	313.5	Nazareth Area SD	Nazareth
92	308.1	Norwin SD	N Huntingdon
93	305.9	Dubois Area SD	Du Bois
94	304.2	Mckeesport Area SD	Mckeesport
95	303.6	Haverford Township SD	Havertown
96	301.6	Rose Tree Media SD	Media
97	301.3	Crawford Central SD	Meadville
98	301.0	Gateway SD	Monroeville
99	300.8	Canon-Mcmillan SD	Canonsburg
100	297.5	Exeter Township SD	Reading
101	296.9	Unionville-Chadds Ford SD	Kennett Square
102	295.6	Warwick SD	Lititz
103	294.8	Lower Dauphin SD	Hummelstown
104	293.4	Great Valley SD	Malvern
105	293.2	Southeast Delco SD	Folcroft
106	291.0	Lebanon SD	Lebanon
107	290.9	Radnor Township SD	Wayne
108	284.3	Kennett Consolidated SD	Kennett Square
109	278.5	Upper Saint Clair SD	Pittsburgh
110	277.5	Governor Mifflin SD	Shillington
111	277.3	Chichester SD	Aston
112	276.8	Plum Borough SD	Plum
113	274.8	Moon Area SD	Moon Township
114	273.8	Mechanicsburg Area SD	Mechanicsburg
115	271.8	Northeastern York SD	Manchester
116	271.5	Wallingford-Swarthmore SD	Wallingford
117	269.8	Penncrest SD	Saegertown
118	269.7	Upper Merion Area SD	King of Prussia
119	269.5	Conestoga Valley SD	Lancaster
120	268.0	Chester-Upland SD	Chester
121	267.0	Spring Grove Area SD	Spring Grove
122	265.6	Interboro SD	Prospect Park
123	265.1	Peters Township SD	Mcmurray
124	264.9	South Western SD	Hanover
125	263.6	Marple Newtown SD	Newtown Square
126	263.0	Phoenixville Area SD	Phoenixville
127	262.9	Albert Gallatin Area SD	Uniontown
128	261.9	Elizabethtown Area SD	Elizabethtown
129	258.5	Baldwin-Whitehall SD	Pittsburgh
130	258.1	Hollidaysburg Area SD	Hollidaysburg
131	257.7	Whitehall-Coplay SD	Whitehall
132	255.3	Ephrata Area SD	Ephrata
133	252.0	Greater Latrobe SD	Latrobe
134	251.5	South Eastern SD	Fawn Grove
135	250.5	Abington Heights SD	Clarks Summit
136	249.2	Franklin Regional SD	Murrysville
137	247.7	Twin Valley SD	Elverson
138	246.8	Penn-Trafford SD	Harrison City
139	245.9	Derry Township SD	Hershey
140	245.0	Chartiers Valley SD	Pittsburgh
140	245.0	New Castle Area SD	New Castle
140	245.0	Pottstown SD	Pottstown
143	244.2	Daniel Boone Area SD	Birdsboro
144	243.4	Bangor Area SD	Bangor
145	242.6	Oxford Area SD	Oxford
146	242.0	Uniontown Area SD	Uniontown

Note: This section only includes districts with 1,500 or more students; All categories are ranked from high to low

147	240.0	West Mifflin Area SD	West Mifflin
148	239.8	Solanco SD	Quarryville
149	239.0	Trinity Area SD	Washington
150	238.0	Springfield SD	Springfield
151	237.8	Ringgold SD	New Eagle
152	236.8	Berwick Area SD	Berwick
153	236.5	Tunkhannock Area SD	Tunkhannock
154	236.4	Kiski Area SD	Leechburg
155	236.1	Big Spring SD	Newville
156	235.5	Cocalico SD	Denver
157	234.5	Dover Area SD	Dover
158	233.7	Conewago Valley SD	New Oxford
159	233.5	Muhlenberg SD	Reading
160	231.6	Laurel Highlands SD	Uniontown
161	231.3	West Allegheny SD	Oakdale
162	231.1	Pottsgrove SD	Pottstown
163	230.7	Indiana Area SD	Indiana
164	229.5	Wallenpaupack Area SD	Hawley
165	229.1	Gettysburg Area SD	Gettysburg
166	228.5	Montour SD	Mckees Rocks
167	227.5	Southern York County SD	Glen Rock
168	226.0	Northern York County SD	Dillsburg
169	225.0	Penn-Delco SD	Aston
170	224.6	Greater Johnstown SD	Johnstown
171	223.7	Susquehanna Township SD	Harrisburg
172	222.8	Bellefonte Area SD	Bellefonte
173	218.8	Wayne Highlands SD	Honesdale
174	217.7	Shippensburg Area SD	Shippensburg
175	217.6	Juniata County SD	Mifflintown
176	215.5	Highlands SD	Natrona Heights
177	214.8	West York Area SD	York
178	214.0	North Pocono SD	Moscow
179	213.8	Palmyra Area SD	Palmyra
180	213.5	Blue Mountain SD	Orwigsburg
181	213.0	Eastern Lancaster County SD	New Holland
182	212.2	East Pennsboro Area SD	Enola
183	210.5	Lampeter-Strasburg SD	Lampeter
183	210.5	Pittston Area SD	Pittston
185	210.3	York Suburban SD	York
186	210.2	Conrad Weiser Area SD	Robesonia
187	207.1	Upper Moreland Township SD	Willow Grove
188	207.0	Manheim Central SD	Manheim
189	205.0	Danville Area SD	Danville
190	204.7	Upper Perkiomen SD	Pennsburg
191	204.0	Bradford Area SD	Bradford
192	203.7	Southern Lehigh SD	Center Valley
193	201.2	Northern Tioga SD	Elkland
194	201.0	Jersey Shore Area SD	Jersey Shore
195	200.4	West Perry SD	Elliottsburg
196	199.4	Fleetwood Area SD	Fleetwood
197	198.0	Eastern York SD	Wrightsville
198	197.9	Elizabeth Forward SD	Elizabeth
199	197.0	Blackhawk SD	Beaver Falls
200	195.0	Agora Cyber CS	Wayne
201	194.0	Mars Area SD	Mars
202	193.5	Pottsville Area SD	Pottsville
203	192.1	Middletown Area SD	Middletown
204	190.2	Selinsgrove Area SD	Selinsgrove
205	188.0	Clearfield Area SD	Clearfield
206	187.5	Greensburg Salem SD	Greensburg
207	183.0	Lehighton Area SD	Lehighton
208	182.3	Corry Area SD	Corry
209	181.7	Grove City Area SD	Grove City
210	181.3	Punxsutawney Area SD	Punxsutawney
211	180.5	Somerset Area SD	Somerset
212	179.5	Milton Area SD	Milton
213	178.0	Huntingdon Area SD	Huntingdon
214	177.9	Conneaut SD	Linesville
215	176.5	Hamburg Area SD	Hamburg
215	176.5	Western Wayne SD	South Canaan
217	174.5	Midd-West SD	Middleburg
218	173.5	Central Greene SD	Waynesburg
219	173.4	Saucon Valley SD	Hellertown
220	172.3	Athens Area SD	Athens
221	172.0	South Middleton SD	Boiling Springs
222	170.6	Ambridge Area SD	Ambridge
223	170.0	Valley View SD	Archbald
224	169.9	Springfield Township SD	Oreland
225	169.8	Belle Vernon Area SD	Belle Vernon
226	169.6	Dallas SD	Dallas
227	169.3	Shikellamy SD	Sunbury
228	169.0	Tuscarora SD	Mercersburg
229	168.0	West Jefferson Hills SD	Jefferson Hills
230	167.5	Northern Lebanon SD	Fredericksburg
230	167.5	South Butler County SD	Saxonburg
232	167.3	Shamokin Area SD	Coal Township
233	167.0	Crestwood SD	Mountain Top
234	166.3	Mifflinburg Area SD	Mifflinburg
235	166.1	Northwestern Lehigh SD	New Tripoli
236	165.0	Lake-Lehman SD	Dallas
236	165.0	Southern Tioga SD	Blossburg
238	164.9	Derry Area SD	Derry
239	162.6	Wilson Area SD	Easton
240	161.9	Franklin Area SD	Franklin
241	160.1	Mount Pleasant Area SD	Mount Pleasant
242	159.5	Titusville Area SD	Titusville
243	159.0	Wyoming Area SD	Exeter
244	158.2	Hopewell Area SD	Aliquippa
245	158.0	Harbor Creek SD	Harborcreek
246	157.3	Eastern Lebanon County SD	Myerstown
247	157.0	Deer Lakes SD	Russellton
247	157.0	General Mclane SD	Edinboro
249	156.5	Keystone Oaks SD	Pittsburgh
250	155.5	Quaker Valley SD	Sewickley
251	155.1	Pennsylvania Cyber CS	Midland
252	154.0	Chester Community CS	Chester
252	154.0	Greencastle-Antrim SD	Greencastle
254	153.0	Fort Leboeuf SD	Waterford
254	153.0	Jim Thorpe Area SD	Jim Thorpe
256	152.8	Susquenita SD	Duncannon
257	152.5	Lower Moreland Township SD	Huntingdon Vlly
258	151.2	Littlestown Area SD	Littlestown
259	151.1	Donegal SD	Mount Joy
260	150.9	Oil City Area SD	Oil City
261	150.5	Mcguffey SD	Claysville
262	149.0	Philipsburg-Osceola Area SD	Philipsburg
262	149.0	Yough SD	Herminie
264	148.9	Bedford Area SD	Bedford
265	148.6	Saint Marys Area SD	Saint Marys
266	148.5	Sharon City SD	Sharon
267	148.4	Octorara Area SD	Atglen
268	147.5	Steel Valley SD	Munhall
269	146.8	Pequea Valley SD	Kinzers
269	146.8	Slippery Rock Area SD	Slippery Rock
271	146.7	Southmoreland SD	Scottdale
272	146.5	North Schuylkill SD	Ashland
273	146.0	Bald Eagle Area SD	Wingate
274	144.9	New Kensington-Arnold SD	New Kensington
275	143.9	Hampton Township SD	Allison Park
276	143.5	Lewisburg Area SD	Lewisburg
277	143.3	Palisades SD	Kintnersville
278	142.3	Oley Valley SD	Oley
279	142.0	Forest Hills SD	Sidman
279	142.0	Montoursville Area SD	Montoursville
281	141.9	Girard SD	Girard
282	140.8	Brandywine Heights Area SD	Topton
283	140.0	Central Columbia SD	Bloomsburg
284	139.5	Big Beaver Falls Area SD	Beaver Falls
285	139.1	Central Valley SD	Monaca
286	139.0	Ellwood City Area SD	Ellwood City
287	138.0	Washington SD	Washington
288	137.8	Hermitage SD	Hermitage
288	137.8	Northern Lehigh SD	Slatington
290	137.7	Schuylkill Valley SD	Leesport
291	137.5	Commonwealth Connections Acade	Harrisburg
291	137.5	Montrose Area SD	Montrose
293	137.0	Kutztown Area SD	Kutztown
294	135.6	Bermudian Springs SD	York Springs
295	135.5	Brownsville Area SD	Brownsville
295	135.5	Hanover Area SD	Hanover Twp
297	134.6	Pennsylvania Leadership Charter	West Chester
298	134.3	South Park SD	South Park
299	134.2	Bloomsburg Area SD	Bloomsburg
300	134.0	Pine Grove Area SD	Pine Grove
301	133.8	Tyrone Area SD	Tyrone
302	132.1	Blairsville-Saltsburg SD	Blairsville
302	132.1	Greater Nanticoke Area SD	Nanticoke
304	131.5	Warrior Run SD	Turbotville
305	131.2	Freeport Area SD	Sarver
306	130.0	Tulpehocken Area SD	Bethel
307	127.8	Penn Cambria SD	Cresson
308	126.0	Hanover Public SD	Hanover
309	125.8	Spring Cove SD	Roaring Spring
310	125.3	Salisbury Township SD	Allentown
311	124.8	Beaver Area SD	Beaver
312	124.6	Pen Argyl Area SD	Pen Argyl
313	124.0	Riverside SD	Taylor
314	123.5	East Allegheny SD	N Versailles
315	123.0	Catasauqua Area SD	Catasauqua
316	122.1	Burrell SD	Lower Burrell
317	121.7	Brookville Area SD	Brookville
318	121.2	Pennsylvania Virtual CS	Norristown
319	121.0	New Brighton Area SD	New Brighton
320	120.8	Central Cambria SD	Ebensburg
321	120.5	North East SD	North East
322	120.0	Mohawk Area SD	Bessemer
323	119.1	Palmerton Area SD	Palmerton
324	119.0	Wellsboro Area SD	Wellsboro
325	118.7	Charleroi SD	Charleroi
326	118.6	East Lycoming SD	Hughesville
327	118.5	Northwestern SD	Albion
328	118.1	Upper Adams SD	Biglerville
329	118.0	South Allegheny SD	Mckeesport
330	117.7	Chestnut Ridge SD	Fishertown
331	117.4	Mount Union Area SD	Mount Union
332	115.6	New Hope-Solebury SD	New Hope
333	115.0	Marion Center Area SD	Marion Center
333	115.0	Troy Area SD	Troy
335	114.5	Panther Valley SD	Lansford
336	112.5	Karns City Area SD	Karns City
337	112.0	Riverside Beaver County SD	Ellwood City
338	110.8	Wyomissing Area SD	Wyomissing
338	110.8	York County School of Technology	York
340	110.4	Tamaqua Area SD	Tamaqua
341	109.6	Towanda Area SD	Towanda
342	108.5	Westmont Hilltop SD	Johnstown
343	108.2	Carbondale Area SD	Carbondale
344	107.8	Wattsburg Area SD	Erie
345	107.0	Mount Carmel Area SD	Mount Carmel
346	106.2	South Fayette Township SD	Mcdonald
347	106.0	Freedom Area SD	Freedom
348	105.0	Lakeland SD	Jermyn
349	103.2	Dunmore SD	Dunmore
350	102.9	Ligonier Valley SD	Ligonier
351	102.5	Fairview SD	Fairview
352	102.1	Annville-Cleona SD	Annville
353	101.2	Moniteau SD	West Sunbury
354	98.0	Mid Valley SD	Throop
355	96.0	Lehigh Career & Technical Inst	Schnecksville
356	90.6	Richland SD	Johnstown

Number of Students

Rank	Number	District Name	City
1	165,694	Philadelphia City SD	Philadelphia
2	27,945	Pittsburgh SD	Pittsburgh
3	20,436	Central Bucks SD	Doylestown
4	17,869	Reading SD	Reading
5	17,465	Allentown City SD	Allentown
6	14,881	Bethlehem Area SD	Bethlehem
7	12,684	North Penn SD	Lansdale
8	12,423	Erie City SD	Erie
9	12,152	Council Rock SD	Newtown
10	11,823	Downingtown Area SD	Downingtown
11	11,821	Upper Darby SD	Drexel Hill
12	11,800	West Chester Area SD	West Chester
13	11,124	Lancaster SD	Lancaster
14	10,979	Pennsbury SD	Fallsington
15	10,929	Pocono Mountain SD	Swiftwater
16	10,900	Central Dauphin SD	Harrisburg
17	10,314	Hazleton Area SD	Hazleton
18	9,548	Scranton SD	Scranton
19	9,292	Parkland SD	Allentown
20	9,188	Easton Area SD	Easton
21	8,666	Neshaminy SD	Langhorne
22	8,539	Pennsylvania Cyber CS	Midland
23	8,485	Chambersburg Area SD	Chambersburg
24	8,112	Harrisburg City SD	Harrisburg
25	8,047	North Allegheny SD	Pittsburgh
26	8,016	E Stroudsburg Area SD	E Stroudsburg
27	7,998	East Penn SD	Emmaus
28	7,995	Altoona Area SD	Altoona
29	7,892	West Shore SD	New Cumberland
30	7,839	Butler Area SD	Butler
31	7,717	Cumberland Valley SD	Mechanicsburg
32	7,705	Spring-Ford Area SD	Royersford
33	7,423	Abington SD	Abington
34	7,349	Seneca Valley SD	Harmony
35	7,320	Millcreek Township SD	Erie
36	7,248	Pennridge SD	Perkasie
37	7,087	Hempfield SD	Landisville
38	7,022	State College Area SD	State College
39	7,009	Lower Merion SD	Ardmore
40	6,990	Boyertown Area SD	Boyertown

Note: This section only includes districts with 1,500 or more students; All categories are ranked from high to low

41	6,885	Coatesville Area SD	Coatesville
42	6,863	Souderton Area SD	Souderton
43	6,862	Wilkes-Barre Area SD	Wilkes Barre
44	6,717	Norristown Area SD	Norristown
45	6,288	Tredyffrin-Easttown SD	Wayne
46	6,253	Hempfield Area SD	Greensburg
47	6,213	Bristol Township SD	Levittown
48	6,064	Bensalem Township SD	Bensalem
49	5,979	Centennial SD	Warminster
50	5,950	Dallastown Area SD	Dallastown
51	5,885	Pleasant Valley SD	Brodheadsville
52	5,878	Perkiomen Valley SD	Collegeville
53	5,805	Wilson SD	West Lawn
54	5,802	York City SD	York
55	5,788	Manheim Township SD	Lititz
55	5,788	Ridley SD	Folsom
57	5,763	Stroudsburg Area SD	Stroudsburg
58	5,665	Red Lion Area SD	Red Lion
59	5,631	Armstrong SD	Ford City
60	5,599	Northampton Area SD	Northampton
61	5,587	Central York SD	York
62	5,564	Haverford Township SD	Havertown
63	5,540	Mifflin County SD	Lewistown
64	5,481	Williamsport Area SD	Williamsport
65	5,460	Delaware Valley SD	Milford
66	5,430	Avon Grove SD	West Grove
67	5,415	William Penn SD	Lansdowne
68	5,371	Quakertown Community SD	Quakertown
69	5,332	Methacton SD	Norristown
70	5,300	Mount Lebanon SD	Pittsburgh
71	5,235	Norwin SD	N Huntingdon
72	5,169	Penn Manor SD	Lancaster
73	5,136	Warren County SD	North Warren
74	5,119	Hatboro-Horsham SD	Horsham
75	4,968	Shaler Area SD	Glenshaw
76	4,954	Wyoming Valley West SD	Kingston
77	4,905	Owen J Roberts SD	Pottstown
78	4,896	Connellsville Area SD	Connellsville
79	4,838	Canon-Mcmillan SD	Canonsburg
80	4,782	Carlisle Area SD	Carlisle
81	4,764	Bethel Park SD	Bethel Park
82	4,743	Garnet Valley SD	Glen Mills
83	4,709	Nazareth Area SD	Nazareth
84	4,674	Cornwall-Lebanon SD	Lebanon
85	4,671	Colonial SD	Plymth Meeting
86	4,577	Penn Hills SD	Pittsburgh
87	4,550	Pine-Richland SD	Gibsonia
88	4,528	Warwick SD	Lititz
89	4,484	Agora Cyber CS	Wayne
90	4,481	Wissahickon SD	Ambler
91	4,449	Lebanon SD	Lebanon
91	4,449	Peters Township SD	Mcmurray
93	4,434	Keystone Central SD	Lock Haven
94	4,426	Chester-Upland SD	Chester
95	4,402	North Hills SD	Pittsburgh
96	4,395	Exeter Township SD	Reading
97	4,386	Cheltenham Township SD	Elkins Park
98	4,362	Fox Chapel Area SD	Pittsburgh
99	4,310	Woodland Hills SD	Pittsburgh
100	4,293	Penn-Trafford SD	Harrison City
101	4,285	Governor Mifflin SD	Shillington
102	4,266	Southeast Delco SD	Folcroft
103	4,240	Waynesboro Area SD	Waynesboro
104	4,220	Greater Latrobe SD	Latrobe
105	4,202	Kennett Consolidated SD	Kennett Square
106	4,198	Upper Dublin SD	Maple Glen
107	4,192	Whitehall-Coplay SD	Whitehall
108	4,191	Baldwin-Whitehall SD	Pittsburgh
109	4,166	Plum Borough SD	Plum
110	4,155	Unionville-Chadds Ford SD	Kennett Square
111	4,115	Dubois Area SD	Du Bois
112	4,098	Upper Saint Clair SD	Pittsburgh
113	4,074	Conestoga Valley SD	Lancaster
114	4,062	Ephrata Area SD	Ephrata
115	4,060	Crawford Central SD	Meadville
116	4,045	Great Valley SD	Malvern
116	4,045	South Western SD	Hanover
118	4,034	Conewago Valley SD	New Oxford
119	4,027	Kiski Area SD	Leechburg
120	4,021	Elizabethtown Area SD	Elizabethtown
121	3,978	Daniel Boone Area SD	Birdsboro
122	3,963	Mckeesport Area SD	Mckeesport
123	3,946	Gateway SD	Monroeville
124	3,863	Spring Grove Area SD	Spring Grove
125	3,861	Lower Dauphin SD	Hummelstown
126	3,788	Upper Merion Area SD	King of Prussia
127	3,779	Wallenpaupack Area SD	Hawley
128	3,745	Rose Tree Media SD	Media
129	3,741	Oxford Area SD	Oxford
130	3,735	Northeastern York SD	Manchester
131	3,729	Solanco SD	Quarryville
132	3,723	Moon Area SD	Moon Township
133	3,703	Mechanicsburg Area SD	Mechanicsburg
134	3,691	Pennsylvania Virtual CS	Norristown
135	3,690	Franklin Regional SD	Murrysville
136	3,682	Radnor Township SD	Wayne
137	3,680	Dover Area SD	Dover
138	3,677	Albert Gallatin Area SD	Uniontown
139	3,652	Commonwealth Connections Acade	Harrisburg
140	3,602	Interboro SD	Prospect Park
141	3,597	Penncrest SD	Saegertown
142	3,551	Derry Township SD	Hershey
143	3,539	Springfield SD	Springfield
144	3,527	Muhlenberg SD	Reading
145	3,511	Hollidaysburg Area SD	Hollidaysburg
146	3,504	Wallingford-Swarthmore SD	Wallingford
147	3,484	Marple Newtown SD	Newtown Square
147	3,484	Trinity Area SD	Washington
149	3,474	Abington Heights SD	Clarks Summit
150	3,411	Chartiers Valley SD	Pittsburgh
151	3,408	Twin Valley SD	Elverson
152	3,400	Shippensburg Area SD	Shippensburg
153	3,385	Penn-Delco SD	Aston
154	3,376	Laurel Highlands SD	Uniontown
155	3,370	Pittston Area SD	Pittston
156	3,364	Chichester SD	Aston
157	3,353	New Castle Area SD	New Castle
158	3,347	Bangor Area SD	Bangor
159	3,339	Cocalico SD	Denver
160	3,319	Phoenixville Area SD	Phoenixville
161	3,274	North Pocono SD	Moscow
162	3,267	Pottsgrove SD	Pottstown
163	3,248	Eastern Lancaster County SD	New Holland
164	3,246	West Allegheny SD	Oakdale
165	3,245	Palmyra Area SD	Palmyra
166	3,200	Lampeter-Strasburg SD	Lampeter
167	3,178	West Mifflin Area SD	West Mifflin
168	3,177	Greater Johnstown SD	Johnstown
168	3,177	Southern York County SD	Glen Rock
170	3,167	Northern York County SD	Dillsburg
171	3,166	Gettysburg Area SD	Gettysburg
172	3,153	Ringgold SD	New Eagle
173	3,110	Upper Perkiomen SD	Pennsburg
174	3,106	Hampton Township SD	Allison Park
175	3,084	Berwick Area SD	Berwick
176	3,083	Pottstown SD	Pottstown
177	3,069	Juniata County SD	Mifflintown
178	3,064	Uniontown Area SD	Uniontown
179	3,063	Southern Lehigh SD	Center Valley
180	3,059	Mars Area SD	Mars
181	3,053	South Eastern SD	Fawn Grove
182	3,048	Greencastle-Antrim SD	Greencastle
182	3,048	Upper Moreland Township SD	Willow Grove
184	3,036	Crestwood SD	Mountain Top
185	3,031	Pottsville Area SD	Pottsville
186	2,997	Wayne Highlands SD	Honesdale
187	2,988	Greensburg Salem SD	Greensburg
188	2,981	Susquehanna Township SD	Harrisburg
189	2,966	Montour SD	Mckees Rocks
190	2,945	Big Spring SD	Newville
191	2,943	West York Area SD	York
192	2,932	Blue Mountain SD	Orwigsburg
193	2,925	Conrad Weiser Area SD	Robesonia
194	2,898	Bellefonte Area SD	Bellefonte
195	2,882	West Jefferson Hills SD	Jefferson Hills
196	2,874	Manheim Central SD	Manheim
197	2,872	York Suburban SD	York
198	2,850	Shikellamy SD	Sunbury
199	2,839	Tunkhannock Area SD	Tunkhannock
200	2,836	Donegal SD	Mount Joy
200	2,836	East Pennsboro Area SD	Enola
202	2,831	Indiana Area SD	Indiana
203	2,806	Highlands SD	Natrona Heights
204	2,802	Ambridge Area SD	Ambridge
205	2,753	Belle Vernon Area SD	Belle Vernon
206	2,740	South Butler County SD	Saxonburg
207	2,739	Jersey Shore Area SD	Jersey Shore
208	2,729	Dallas SD	Dallas
209	2,714	Selinsgrove Area SD	Selinsgrove
210	2,708	Grove City Area SD	Grove City
211	2,686	Fleetwood Area SD	Fleetwood
212	2,681	Bradford Area SD	Bradford
213	2,670	West Perry SD	Elliottsburg
214	2,667	Lehigh Career & Technical Inst	Schnecksville
215	2,616	Octorara Area SD	Atglen
216	2,613	Valley View SD	Archbald
217	2,604	Elizabeth Forward SD	Elizabeth
218	2,573	Tuscarora SD	Mercersburg
219	2,557	Blackhawk SD	Beaver Falls
220	2,545	Conneaut SD	Linesville
221	2,540	Eastern York SD	Wrightsville
222	2,515	Wyoming Area SD	Exeter
223	2,514	Clearfield Area SD	Clearfield
224	2,499	Hamburg Area SD	Hamburg
225	2,484	Chester Community CS	Chester
226	2,458	Eastern Lebanon County SD	Myerstown
227	2,456	Lehighton Area SD	Lehighton
228	2,451	Hopewell Area SD	Aliquippa
229	2,445	Shamokin Area SD	Coal Township
230	2,431	Somerset Area SD	Somerset
231	2,428	Danville Area SD	Danville
232	2,425	Punxsutawney Area SD	Punxsutawney
233	2,411	Saucon Valley SD	Hellertown
234	2,400	Northern Lebanon SD	Fredericksburg
235	2,380	South Fayette Township SD	Mcdonald
236	2,366	Northwestern Lehigh SD	New Tripoli
237	2,335	Yough SD	Herminie
238	2,334	Derry Area SD	Derry
239	2,333	Central Valley SD	Monaca
240	2,332	Middletown Area SD	Middletown
241	2,330	Corry Area SD	Corry
242	2,308	Slippery Rock Area SD	Slippery Rock
243	2,300	Western Wayne SD	South Canaan
244	2,288	Saint Marys Area SD	Saint Marys
245	2,283	Milton Area SD	Milton
246	2,278	Athens Area SD	Athens
247	2,257	Bedford Area SD	Bedford
248	2,249	Greater Nanticoke Area SD	Nanticoke
249	2,245	Wilson Area SD	Easton
250	2,235	Oil City Area SD	Oil City
251	2,222	Mount Pleasant Area SD	Mount Pleasant
252	2,215	New Kensington-Arnold SD	New Kensington
253	2,206	South Middleton SD	Boiling Springs
254	2,205	Keystone Oaks SD	Pittsburgh
255	2,192	General Mclane SD	Edinboro
255	2,192	Mifflinburg Area SD	Mifflinburg
257	2,190	Fort Leboeuf SD	Waterford
257	2,190	Midd-West SD	Middleburg
259	2,187	Jim Thorpe Area SD	Jim Thorpe
260	2,184	Northern Tioga SD	Elkland
261	2,183	Littlestown Area SD	Littlestown
262	2,142	Titusville Area SD	Titusville
263	2,131	South Park SD	South Park
264	2,129	Sharon City SD	Sharon
265	2,125	Huntingdon Area SD	Huntingdon
266	2,098	Mcguffey SD	Claysville
267	2,097	Franklin Area SD	Franklin
267	2,097	Hermitage SD	Hermitage
269	2,089	Lake-Lehman SD	Dallas
270	2,086	Central Greene SD	Waynesburg
271	2,083	Tamaqua Area SD	Tamaqua
272	2,073	Lower Moreland Township SD	Huntingdon Vlly
273	2,071	Bermudian Springs SD	York Springs
273	2,071	Springfield Township SD	Oreland
275	2,067	Southern Tioga SD	Blossburg
276	2,042	Southmoreland SD	Scottdale
277	2,031	Forest Hills SD	Sidman
278	2,029	Quaker Valley SD	Sewickley
279	2,020	Pennsylvania Leadership Charter	West Chester
280	2,019	Girard SD	Girard
281	2,015	Hanover Area SD	Hanover Twp
282	2,009	Harbor Creek SD	Harborcreek
283	2,002	Schuylkill Valley SD	Leesport
284	1,991	Beaver Area SD	Beaver
285	1,986	Central Columbia SD	Bloomsburg
286	1,983	Philipsburg-Osceola Area SD	Philipsburg
287	1,980	Freeport Area SD	Sarver
288	1,969	Deer Lakes SD	Russellton
289	1,968	Ellwood City Area SD	Ellwood City
290	1,965	Tyrone Area SD	Tyrone
291	1,956	North Schuylkill SD	Ashland
292	1,949	Oley Valley SD	Oley
293	1,939	Northern Lehigh SD	Slatington
294	1,935	Palmerton Area SD	Palmerton
295	1,934	Brownsville Area SD	Brownsville

Note: This section only includes districts with 1,500 or more students; All categories are ranked from high to low

295	1,934	Susquenita SD	Duncannon
297	1,932	Montoursville Area SD	Montoursville
298	1,925	Burrell SD	Lower Burrell
299	1,905	Lewisburg Area SD	Lewisburg
300	1,901	East Allegheny SD	N Versailles
301	1,897	Palisades SD	Kintnersville
302	1,890	Blairsville-Saltsburg SD	Blairsville
303	1,875	Bald Eagle Area SD	Wingate
304	1,861	Ligonier Valley SD	Ligonier
305	1,858	Wyomissing Area SD	Wyomissing
306	1,851	Mid Valley SD	Throop
307	1,849	Pen Argyl Area SD	Pen Argyl
308	1,844	Spring Cove SD	Roaring Spring
309	1,839	Steel Valley SD	Munhall
310	1,800	Brandywine Heights Area SD	Topton
311	1,794	Central Cambria SD	Ebensburg
312	1,782	Pequea Valley SD	Kinzers
313	1,752	Big Beaver Falls Area SD	Beaver Falls
314	1,749	North East SD	North East
315	1,736	Westmont Hilltop SD	Johnstown
316	1,732	New Brighton Area SD	New Brighton
317	1,731	Upper Adams SD	Biglerville
318	1,727	Penn Cambria SD	Cresson
319	1,693	Montrose Area SD	Montrose
320	1,687	Bloomsburg Area SD	Bloomsburg
321	1,676	Chestnut Ridge SD	Fishertown
322	1,672	Warrior Run SD	Turbotville
323	1,669	Salisbury Township SD	Allentown
324	1,661	Panther Valley SD	Lansford
325	1,659	Towanda Area SD	Towanda
326	1,647	Pine Grove Area SD	Pine Grove
327	1,645	Hanover Public SD	Hanover
327	1,645	Karns City Area SD	Karns City
329	1,637	Northwestern SD	Albion
330	1,623	Dunmore SD	Dunmore
331	1,619	Fairview SD	Fairview
332	1,615	Catasauqua Area SD	Catasauqua
333	1,614	Wattsburg Area SD	Erie
334	1,609	Charleroi SD	Charleroi
335	1,608	Kutztown Area SD	Kutztown
335	1,608	Riverside Beaver County SD	Ellwood City
337	1,605	Brookville Area SD	Brookville
338	1,602	East Lycoming SD	Hughesville
339	1,598	Lakeland SD	Jermyn
340	1,594	Mohawk Area SD	Bessemer
340	1,594	South Allegheny SD	Mckeesport
342	1,588	Freedom Area SD	Freedom
342	1,588	Richland SD	Johnstown
344	1,585	Washington SD	Washington
345	1,583	Moniteau SD	West Sunbury
346	1,579	Troy Area SD	Troy
347	1,568	Mount Carmel Area SD	Mount Carmel
348	1,566	New Hope-Solebury SD	New Hope
349	1,565	Annville-Cleona SD	Annville
350	1,548	Carbondale Area SD	Carbondale
351	1,547	Tulpehocken Area SD	Bethel
352	1,529	Wellsboro Area SD	Wellsboro
353	1,525	York County School of Technology	York
354	1,508	Marion Center Area SD	Marion Center
354	1,508	Riverside SD	Taylor
356	1,506	Mount Union Area SD	Mount Union

Male Students

Rank	Percent	District Name	City
1	59.5	Lehigh Career & Technical Inst	Schnecksville
2	59.1	Grove City Area SD	Grove City
3	58.9	York County School of Technology	York
4	55.2	General Mclane SD	Edinboro
5	54.2	Pine Grove Area SD	Pine Grove
6	54.1	Mount Carmel Area SD	Mount Carmel
7	53.9	Mcguffey SD	Claysville
8	53.8	Centennial SD	Warminster
8	53.8	Upper Moreland Township SD	Willow Grove
10	53.5	Northern Lebanon SD	Fredericksburg
10	53.5	Sharon City SD	Sharon
12	53.4	Middletown Area SD	Middletown
13	53.3	Catasauqua Area SD	Catasauqua
13	53.3	Dallas SD	Dallas
13	53.3	Hamburg Area SD	Hamburg
16	53.2	Ambridge Area SD	Ambridge
16	53.2	North Pocono SD	Moscow
16	53.2	Slippery Rock Area SD	Slippery Rock
19	53.1	E Stroudsburg Area SD	E Stroudsburg
19	53.1	Marple Newtown SD	Newtown Square
19	53.1	New Brighton Area SD	New Brighton
22	53.0	Freeport Area SD	Sarver
23	52.9	Bedford Area SD	Bedford
23	52.9	Chestnut Ridge SD	Fishertown
23	52.9	Mckeesport Area SD	Mckeesport
26	52.8	Lehighton Area SD	Lehighton
26	52.8	Mifflinburg Area SD	Mifflinburg
26	52.8	Moniteau SD	West Sunbury
26	52.8	Somerset Area SD	Somerset
30	52.7	Beaver Area SD	Beaver
30	52.7	Butler Area SD	Butler
30	52.7	Clearfield Area SD	Clearfield
30	52.7	Fort Leboeuf SD	Waterford
30	52.7	Palmerton Area SD	Palmerton
30	52.7	Penn Cambria SD	Cresson
30	52.7	Penncrest SD	Saegertown
30	52.7	Salisbury Township SD	Allentown
30	52.7	South Butler County SD	Saxonburg
30	52.7	Southern Lehigh SD	Center Valley
40	52.6	Baldwin-Whitehall SD	Pittsburgh
40	52.6	Carbondale Area SD	Carbondale
42	52.5	Bethlehem Area SD	Bethlehem
42	52.5	Connellsville Area SD	Connellsville
42	52.5	Governor Mifflin SD	Shillington
42	52.5	Littlestown Area SD	Littlestown
42	52.5	Northampton Area SD	Northampton
42	52.5	Penn-Trafford SD	Harrison City
42	52.5	Pequea Valley SD	Kinzers
42	52.5	Upper Perkiomen SD	Pennsburg
50	52.4	Abington SD	Abington
50	52.4	Bensalem Township SD	Bensalem
50	52.4	Berwick Area SD	Berwick
50	52.4	East Lycoming SD	Hughesville
50	52.4	Lower Moreland Township SD	Huntingdon Vlly
50	52.4	North Schuylkill SD	Ashland
50	52.4	South Park SD	South Park
50	52.4	Towanda Area SD	Towanda
50	52.4	Warren County SD	North Warren
59	52.3	Annville-Cleona SD	Annville
59	52.3	Armstrong SD	Ford City
59	52.3	Big Beaver Falls Area SD	Beaver Falls
59	52.3	Derry Area SD	Derry
59	52.3	Keystone Oaks SD	Pittsburgh
59	52.3	Pocono Mountain SD	Swiftwater
59	52.3	South Western SD	Hanover
59	52.3	Wilson Area SD	Easton
67	52.2	Huntingdon Area SD	Huntingdon
67	52.2	Ligonier Valley SD	Ligonier
67	52.2	Mount Union Area SD	Mount Union
67	52.2	Penn Hills SD	Pittsburgh
67	52.2	Springfield SD	Springfield
67	52.2	Tunkhannock Area SD	Tunkhannock
67	52.2	Western Wayne SD	South Canaan
67	52.2	William Penn SD	Lansdowne
75	52.1	Abington Heights SD	Clarks Summit
75	52.1	Allentown City SD	Allentown
75	52.1	Belle Vernon Area SD	Belle Vernon
75	52.1	Daniel Boone Area SD	Birdsboro
75	52.1	Ephrata Area SD	Ephrata
75	52.1	Greensburg Salem SD	Greensburg
75	52.1	Hazleton Area SD	Hazleton
75	52.1	Hollidaysburg Area SD	Hollidaysburg
75	52.1	Lakeland SD	Jermyn
75	52.1	New Castle Area SD	New Castle
75	52.1	New Hope-Solebury SD	New Hope
75	52.1	Oley Valley SD	Oley
75	52.1	Palisades SD	Kintnersville
75	52.1	Pine-Richland SD	Gibsonia
75	52.1	Selinsgrove Area SD	Selinsgrove
75	52.1	Spring Grove Area SD	Spring Grove
75	52.1	Wilson SD	West Lawn
92	52.0	Albert Gallatin Area SD	Uniontown
92	52.0	Central Cambria SD	Ebensburg
92	52.0	Central Dauphin SD	Harrisburg
92	52.0	Manheim Central SD	Manheim
92	52.0	Mifflin County SD	Lewistown
92	52.0	North East SD	North East
92	52.0	Pennridge SD	Perkasie
92	52.0	Pottsgrove SD	Pottstown
92	52.0	Rose Tree Media SD	Media
92	52.0	South Eastern SD	Fawn Grove
92	52.0	Upper Darby SD	Drexel Hill
92	52.0	Warrior Run SD	Turbotville
104	51.9	Corry Area SD	Corry
104	51.9	Dover Area SD	Dover
104	51.9	Downingtown Area SD	Downingtown
104	51.9	Eastern York SD	Wrightsville
104	51.9	Forest Hills SD	Sidman
104	51.9	Franklin Regional SD	Murrysville
104	51.9	Freedom Area SD	Freedom
104	51.9	Girard SD	Girard
104	51.9	Juniata County SD	Mifflintown
104	51.9	Lancaster SD	Lancaster
104	51.9	Mohawk Area SD	Bessemer
104	51.9	North Hills SD	Pittsburgh
104	51.9	Northern York County SD	Dillsburg
104	51.9	Phoenixville Area SD	Phoenixville
104	51.9	Pleasant Valley SD	Brodheadsville
104	51.9	Shamokin Area SD	Coal Township
104	51.9	Southeast Delco SD	Folcroft
104	51.9	Upper Saint Clair SD	Pittsburgh
104	51.9	West Chester Area SD	West Chester
123	51.8	Avon Grove SD	West Grove
123	51.8	Crawford Central SD	Meadville
123	51.8	Erie City SD	Erie
123	51.8	Greater Nanticoke Area SD	Nanticoke
123	51.8	North Allegheny SD	Pittsburgh
123	51.8	Northern Lehigh SD	Slatington
123	51.8	Oxford Area SD	Oxford
123	51.8	Parkland SD	Allentown
123	51.8	Tamaqua Area SD	Tamaqua
123	51.8	Wyomissing Area SD	Wyomissing
123	51.8	York City SD	York
134	51.7	Delaware Valley SD	Milford
134	51.7	Donegal SD	Mount Joy
134	51.7	Laurel Highlands SD	Uniontown
134	51.7	Oil City Area SD	Oil City
134	51.7	Trinity Area SD	Washington
139	51.6	Bangor Area SD	Bangor
139	51.6	Bermudian Springs SD	York Springs
139	51.6	Blue Mountain SD	Orwigsburg
139	51.6	Bristol Township SD	Levittown
139	51.6	Central Greene SD	Waynesburg
139	51.6	Chartiers Valley SD	Pittsburgh
139	51.6	Deer Lakes SD	Russellton
139	51.6	Fleetwood Area SD	Fleetwood
139	51.6	Harbor Creek SD	Harborcreek
139	51.6	Jim Thorpe Area SD	Jim Thorpe
139	51.6	Kiski Area SD	Leechburg
139	51.6	Lampeter-Strasburg SD	Lampeter
139	51.6	Lower Dauphin SD	Hummelstown
139	51.6	Northwestern Lehigh SD	New Tripoli
139	51.6	Owen J Roberts SD	Pottstown
139	51.6	Plum Borough SD	Plum
139	51.6	Quakertown Community SD	Quakertown
139	51.6	Schuylkill Valley SD	Leesport
139	51.6	Spring-Ford Area SD	Royersford
139	51.6	Upper Adams SD	Biglerville
139	51.6	Wissahickon SD	Ambler
160	51.5	Charleroi SD	Charleroi
160	51.5	Coatesville Area SD	Coatesville
160	51.5	Colonial SD	Plymth Meeting
160	51.5	Danville Area SD	Danville
160	51.5	Jersey Shore Area SD	Jersey Shore
160	51.5	Lewisburg Area SD	Lewisburg
160	51.5	Millcreek Township SD	Erie
160	51.5	Milton Area SD	Milton
160	51.5	Montoursville Area SD	Montoursville
160	51.5	Northern Tioga SD	Elkland
160	51.5	Reading SD	Reading
160	51.5	Tulpehocken Area SD	Bethel
172	51.4	Altoona Area SD	Altoona
172	51.4	Great Valley SD	Malvern
172	51.4	Greater Johnstown SD	Johnstown
172	51.4	Haverford Township SD	Havertown
172	51.4	Nazareth Area SD	Nazareth
172	51.4	Penn-Delco SD	Aston
172	51.4	Perkiomen Valley SD	Collegeville
172	51.4	Richland SD	Johnstown
172	51.4	Ridley SD	Folsom
172	51.4	Shippensburg Area SD	Shippensburg
172	51.4	Tuscarora SD	Mercersburg
172	51.4	Upper Dublin SD	Maple Glen
172	51.4	Woodland Hills SD	Pittsburgh
185	51.3	Bald Eagle Area SD	Wingate
185	51.3	Bethel Park SD	Bethel Park
185	51.3	Blairsville-Saltsburg SD	Blairsville
185	51.3	Central Columbia SD	Bloomsburg
185	51.3	Cheltenham Township SD	Elkins Park

Note: This section only includes districts with 1,500 or more students; All categories are ranked from high to low

185	51.3	Conrad Weiser Area SD	Robesonia	269	50.7	Shikellamy SD	Sunbury	
185	51.3	Council Rock SD	Newtown	269	50.7	Steel Valley SD	Munhall	
185	51.3	Easton Area SD	Easton	269	50.7	Twin Valley SD	Elverson	
185	51.3	Fox Chapel Area SD	Pittsburgh	269	50.7	Upper Merion Area SD	King of Prussia	
185	51.3	Hampton Township SD	Allison Park	269	50.7	Wattsburg Area SD	Erie	
185	51.3	Hempfield Area SD	Greensburg	269	50.7	Wayne Highlands SD	Honesdale	
185	51.3	Mount Pleasant Area SD	Mount Pleasant	269	50.7	Yough SD	Herminie	
185	51.3	Muhlenberg SD	Reading	282	50.6	Athens Area SD	Athens	
185	51.3	Radnor Township SD	Wayne	282	50.6	Bloomsburg Area SD	Bloomsburg	
185	51.3	Red Lion Area SD	Red Lion	282	50.6	Cocalico SD	Denver	
185	51.3	Riverside Beaver County SD	Ellwood City	282	50.6	Eastern Lancaster County SD	New Holland	
185	51.3	Seneca Valley SD	Harmony	282	50.6	Ellwood City Area SD	Ellwood City	
202	51.2	Eastern Lebanon County SD	Myerstown	282	50.6	Hatboro-Horsham SD	Horsham	
202	51.2	Exeter Township SD	Reading	282	50.6	Mid Valley SD	Throop	
202	51.2	Lebanon SD	Lebanon	282	50.6	Norwin SD	N Huntingdon	
202	51.2	Mechanicsburg Area SD	Mechanicsburg	282	50.6	Penn Manor SD	Lancaster	
202	51.2	Montour SD	Mckees Rocks	282	50.6	Southern Tioga SD	Blossburg	
202	51.2	Montrose Area SD	Montrose	282	50.6	York Suburban SD	York	
202	51.2	Panther Valley SD	Lansford	293	50.5	Central York SD	York	
202	51.2	Pen Argyl Area SD	Pen Argyl	293	50.5	East Penn SD	Emmaus	
202	51.2	Washington SD	Washington	293	50.5	Garnet Valley SD	Glen Mills	
202	51.2	Williamsport Area SD	Williamsport	293	50.5	Interboro SD	Prospect Park	
212	51.1	Carlisle Area SD	Carlisle	293	50.5	Pittston Area SD	Pittston	
212	51.1	Conestoga Valley SD	Lancaster	293	50.5	Solanco SD	Quarryville	
212	51.1	Cumberland Valley SD	Mechanicsburg	293	50.5	South Middleton SD	Boiling Springs	
212	51.1	Elizabethtown Area SD	Elizabethtown	293	50.5	State College Area SD	State College	
212	51.1	Keystone Central SD	Lock Haven	293	50.5	Susquenita SD	Duncannon	
212	51.1	Manheim Township SD	Lititz	293	50.5	Troy Area SD	Troy	
212	51.1	Marion Center Area SD	Marion Center	293	50.5	Wallingford-Swarthmore SD	Wallingford	
212	51.1	Neshaminy SD	Langhorne	304	50.4	Chester Community CS	Chester	
212	51.1	New Kensington-Arnold SD	New Kensington	304	50.4	Derry Township SD	Hershey	
212	51.1	North Penn SD	Lansdale	304	50.4	Methacton SD	Norristown	
212	51.1	Peters Township SD	Mcmurray	304	50.4	Midd-West SD	Middleburg	
212	51.1	South Fayette Township SD	Mcdonald	304	50.4	Northeastern York SD	Manchester	
212	51.1	Unionville-Chadds Ford SD	Kennett Square	304	50.4	Pottsville Area SD	Pottsville	
212	51.1	West Allegheny SD	Oakdale	304	50.4	Southern York County SD	Glen Rock	
226	51.0	Boyertown Area SD	Boyertown	304	50.4	Susquehanna Township SD	Harrisburg	
226	51.0	Central Bucks SD	Doylestown	304	50.4	Warwick SD	Lititz	
226	51.0	Cornwall-Lebanon SD	Lebanon	304	50.4	Waynesboro Area SD	Waynesboro	
226	51.0	Crestwood SD	Mountain Top	314	50.3	East Allegheny SD	N Versailles	
226	51.0	Dallastown Area SD	Dallastown	314	50.3	Greencastle-Antrim SD	Greencastle	
226	51.0	Greater Latrobe SD	Latrobe	314	50.3	Lower Merion SD	Ardmore	
226	51.0	Hempfield SD	Landisville	314	50.3	Mount Lebanon SD	Pittsburgh	
226	51.0	Kennett Consolidated SD	Kennett Square	314	50.3	West Shore SD	New Cumberland	
226	51.0	Pottstown SD	Pottstown	314	50.3	Whitehall-Coplay SD	Whitehall	
226	51.0	Saint Marys Area SD	Saint Marys	320	50.2	Kutztown Area SD	Kutztown	
226	51.0	Shaler Area SD	Glenshaw	320	50.2	Moon Area SD	Moon Township	
226	51.0	Tyrone Area SD	Tyrone	320	50.2	Palmyra Area SD	Palmyra	
226	51.0	West Jefferson Hills SD	Jefferson Hills	323	50.1	Harrisburg City SD	Harrisburg	
226	51.0	Westmont Hilltop SD	Johnstown	323	50.1	Quaker Valley SD	Sewickley	
240	50.9	Canon-Mcmillan SD	Canonsburg	323	50.1	Wyoming Area SD	Exeter	
240	50.9	Chambersburg Area SD	Chambersburg	326	50.0	Big Spring SD	Newville	
240	50.9	Chichester SD	Aston	326	50.0	Conewago Valley SD	New Oxford	
240	50.9	Hanover Public SD	Hanover	326	50.0	Hanover Area SD	Hanover Twp	
240	50.9	Highlands SD	Natrona Heights	326	50.0	Hermitage SD	Hermitage	
240	50.9	Hopewell Area SD	Aliquippa	326	50.0	Mars Area SD	Mars	
240	50.9	Pennsbury SD	Fallsington	326	50.0	Octorara Area SD	Atglen	
240	50.9	Philipsburg-Osceola Area SD	Philipsburg	326	50.0	Punxsutawney Area SD	Punxsutawney	
240	50.9	Saucon Valley SD	Hellertown	326	50.0	Titusville Area SD	Titusville	
240	50.9	Souderton Area SD	Souderton	334	49.9	Valley View SD	Archbald	
240	50.9	Spring Cove SD	Roaring Spring	335	49.8	Burrell SD	Lower Burrell	
240	50.9	West Perry SD	Elliottsburg	335	49.8	Karns City Area SD	Karns City	
240	50.9	West York Area SD	York	335	49.8	Lake-Lehman SD	Dallas	
240	50.9	Wyoming Valley West SD	Kingston	335	49.8	Tredyffrin-Easttown SD	Wayne	
254	50.8	Bradford Area SD	Bradford	339	49.7	Franklin Area SD	Franklin	
254	50.8	Brookville Area SD	Brookville	339	49.7	Indiana Area SD	Indiana	
254	50.8	Central Valley SD	Monaca	339	49.7	Ringgold SD	New Eagle	
254	50.8	Conneaut SD	Linesville	339	49.7	Riverside SD	Taylor	
254	50.8	Dubois Area SD	Du Bois	339	49.7	Southmoreland SD	Scottdale	
254	50.8	East Pennsboro Area SD	Enola	344	49.6	Chester-Upland SD	Chester	
254	50.8	Norristown Area SD	Norristown	344	49.6	Uniontown Area SD	Uniontown	
254	50.8	Philadelphia City SD	Philadelphia	346	49.5	Bellefonte Area SD	Bellefonte	
254	50.8	Scranton SD	Scranton	346	49.5	Elizabeth Forward SD	Elizabeth	
254	50.8	South Allegheny SD	Mckeesport	348	49.4	Brandywine Heights Area SD	Topton	
254	50.8	Springfield Township SD	Oreland	348	49.4	Dunmore SD	Dunmore	
254	50.8	Stroudsburg Area SD	Stroudsburg	350	49.3	Pennsylvania Virtual CS	Norristown	
254	50.8	Wallenpaupack Area SD	Hawley	351	48.9	Fairview SD	Fairview	
254	50.8	West Mifflin Area SD	West Mifflin	352	48.6	Commonwealth Connections Acade	Harrisburg	
254	50.8	Wilkes-Barre Area SD	Wilkes Barre	352	48.6	Wellsboro Area SD	Wellsboro	
269	50.7	Blackhawk SD	Beaver Falls	354	47.6	Agora Cyber CS	Wayne	
269	50.7	Brownsville Area SD	Brownsville	355	45.4	Pennsylvania Cyber CS	Midland	
269	50.7	Gateway SD	Monroeville	356	45.6	Pennsylvania Leadership Charter	West Chester	
269	50.7	Gettysburg Area SD	Gettysburg					
269	50.7	Northwestern SD	Albion					
269	50.7	Pittsburgh SD	Pittsburgh					

Female Students

Rank	Percent	District Name	City
1	54.4	Pennsylvania Leadership Charter	West Chester
2	53.6	Pennsylvania Cyber CS	Midland
3	52.4	Agora Cyber CS	Wayne
4	51.4	Commonwealth Connections Acade	Harrisburg
4	51.4	Wellsboro Area SD	Wellsboro
6	51.1	Fairview SD	Fairview
7	50.7	Pennsylvania Virtual CS	Norristown
8	50.6	Brandywine Heights Area SD	Topton
8	50.6	Dunmore SD	Dunmore
10	50.5	Bellefonte Area SD	Bellefonte
10	50.5	Elizabeth Forward SD	Elizabeth
12	50.4	Chester-Upland SD	Chester
12	50.4	Uniontown Area SD	Uniontown
14	50.3	Franklin Area SD	Franklin
14	50.3	Indiana Area SD	Indiana
14	50.3	Ringgold SD	New Eagle
14	50.3	Riverside SD	Taylor
14	50.3	Southmoreland SD	Scottdale
19	50.2	Burrell SD	Lower Burrell
19	50.2	Karns City Area SD	Karns City
19	50.2	Lake-Lehman SD	Dallas
19	50.2	Tredyffrin-Easttown SD	Wayne
23	50.1	Valley View SD	Archbald
24	50.0	Big Spring SD	Newville
24	50.0	Conewago Valley SD	New Oxford
24	50.0	Hanover Area SD	Hanover Twp
24	50.0	Hermitage SD	Hermitage
24	50.0	Mars Area SD	Mars
24	50.0	Octorara Area SD	Atglen
24	50.0	Punxsutawney Area SD	Punxsutawney
24	50.0	Titusville Area SD	Titusville
32	49.9	Harrisburg City SD	Harrisburg
32	49.9	Quaker Valley SD	Sewickley
32	49.9	Wyoming Area SD	Exeter
35	49.8	Kutztown Area SD	Kutztown
35	49.8	Moon Area SD	Moon Township
35	49.8	Palmyra Area SD	Palmyra
38	49.7	East Allegheny SD	N Versailles
38	49.7	Greencastle-Antrim SD	Greencastle
38	49.7	Lower Merion SD	Ardmore
38	49.7	Mount Lebanon SD	Pittsburgh
38	49.7	West Shore SD	New Cumberland
38	49.7	Whitehall-Coplay SD	Whitehall
44	49.6	Chester Community CS	Chester
44	49.6	Derry Township SD	Hershey
44	49.6	Methacton SD	Norristown
44	49.6	Midd-West SD	Middleburg
44	49.6	Northeastern York SD	Manchester
44	49.6	Pottsville Area SD	Pottsville
44	49.6	Southern York County SD	Glen Rock
44	49.6	Susquehanna Township SD	Harrisburg
44	49.6	Warwick SD	Lititz
44	49.6	Waynesboro Area SD	Waynesboro
54	49.5	Central York SD	York
54	49.5	East Penn SD	Emmaus
54	49.5	Garnet Valley SD	Glen Mills
54	49.5	Interboro SD	Prospect Park
54	49.5	Pittston Area SD	Pittston
54	49.5	Solanco SD	Quarryville
54	49.5	South Middleton SD	Boiling Springs
54	49.5	State College Area SD	State College
54	49.5	Susquenita SD	Duncannon
54	49.5	Troy Area SD	Troy
54	49.5	Wallingford-Swarthmore SD	Wallingford
65	49.4	Athens Area SD	Athens
65	49.4	Bloomsburg Area SD	Bloomsburg
65	49.4	Cocalico SD	Denver
65	49.4	Eastern Lancaster County SD	New Holland
65	49.4	Ellwood City Area SD	Ellwood City
65	49.4	Hatboro-Horsham SD	Horsham
65	49.4	Mid Valley SD	Throop
65	49.4	Norwin SD	N Huntingdon
65	49.4	Penn Manor SD	Lancaster
65	49.4	Southern Tioga SD	Blossburg
65	49.4	York Suburban SD	York
76	49.3	Blackhawk SD	Beaver Falls
76	49.3	Brownsville Area SD	Brownsville
76	49.3	Gateway SD	Monroeville
76	49.3	Gettysburg Area SD	Gettysburg
76	49.3	Northwestern SD	Albion
76	49.3	Pittsburgh SD	Pittsburgh
76	49.3	Shikellamy SD	Sunbury

Note: This section only includes districts with 1,500 or more students; All categories are ranked from high to low

Rank	Score	District	City	Rank	Score	District	City	Rank	Score	District	City
76	49.3	Steel Valley SD	Munhall	156	48.7	Muhlenberg SD	Reading	235	48.1	West Chester Area SD	West Chester
76	49.3	Twin Valley SD	Elverson	156	48.7	Radnor Township SD	Wayne	254	48.0	Albert Gallatin Area SD	Uniontown
76	49.3	Upper Merion Area SD	King of Prussia	156	48.7	Red Lion Area SD	Red Lion	254	48.0	Central Cambria SD	Ebensburg
76	49.3	Wattsburg Area SD	Erie	156	48.7	Riverside Beaver County SD	Ellwood City	254	48.0	Central Dauphin SD	Harrisburg
76	49.3	Wayne Highlands SD	Honesdale	156	48.7	Seneca Valley SD	Harmony	254	48.0	Manheim Central SD	Manheim
76	49.3	Yough SD	Herminie	173	48.6	Altoona Area SD	Altoona	254	48.0	Mifflin County SD	Lewistown
89	49.2	Bradford Area SD	Bradford	173	48.6	Great Valley SD	Malvern	254	48.0	North East SD	North East
89	49.2	Brookville Area SD	Brookville	173	48.6	Greater Johnstown SD	Johnstown	254	48.0	Pennridge SD	Perkasie
89	49.2	Central Valley SD	Monaca	173	48.6	Haverford Township SD	Havertown	254	48.0	Pottsgrove SD	Pottstown
89	49.2	Conneaut SD	Linesville	173	48.6	Nazareth Area SD	Nazareth	254	48.0	Rose Tree Media SD	Media
89	49.2	Dubois Area SD	Du Bois	173	48.6	Penn-Delco SD	Aston	254	48.0	South Eastern SD	Fawn Grove
89	49.2	East Pennsboro Area SD	Enola	173	48.6	Perkiomen Valley SD	Collegeville	254	48.0	Upper Darby SD	Drexel Hill
89	49.2	Norristown Area SD	Norristown	173	48.6	Richland SD	Johnstown	254	48.0	Warrior Run SD	Turbotville
89	49.2	Philadelphia City SD	Philadelphia	173	48.6	Ridley SD	Folsom	266	47.9	Abington Heights SD	Clarks Summit
89	49.2	Scranton SD	Scranton	173	48.6	Shippensburg Area SD	Shippensburg	266	47.9	Allentown City SD	Allentown
89	49.2	South Allegheny SD	Mckeesport	173	48.6	Tuscarora SD	Mercersburg	266	47.9	Belle Vernon Area SD	Belle Vernon
89	49.2	Springfield Township SD	Oreland	173	48.6	Upper Dublin SD	Maple Glen	266	47.9	Daniel Boone Area SD	Birdsboro
89	49.2	Stroudsburg Area SD	Stroudsburg	173	48.6	Woodland Hills SD	Pittsburgh	266	47.9	Ephrata Area SD	Ephrata
89	49.2	Wallenpaupack Area SD	Hawley	186	48.5	Charleroi SD	Charleroi	266	47.9	Greensburg Salem SD	Greensburg
89	49.2	West Mifflin Area SD	West Mifflin	186	48.5	Coatesville Area SD	Coatesville	266	47.9	Hazleton Area SD	Hazleton
89	49.2	Wilkes-Barre Area SD	Wilkes Barre	186	48.5	Colonial SD	Plymth Meeting	266	47.9	Hollidaysburg Area SD	Hollidaysburg
104	49.1	Canon-Mcmillan SD	Canonsburg	186	48.5	Danville Area SD	Danville	266	47.9	Lakeland SD	Jermyn
104	49.1	Chambersburg Area SD	Chambersburg	186	48.5	Jersey Shore Area SD	Jersey Shore	266	47.9	New Castle Area SD	New Castle
104	49.1	Chichester SD	Aston	186	48.5	Lewisburg Area SD	Lewisburg	266	47.9	New Hope-Solebury SD	New Hope
104	49.1	Hanover Public SD	Hanover	186	48.5	Millcreek Township SD	Erie	266	47.9	Oley Valley SD	Oley
104	49.1	Highlands SD	Natrona Heights	186	48.5	Milton Area SD	Milton	266	47.9	Palisades SD	Kintnersville
104	49.1	Hopewell Area SD	Aliquippa	186	48.5	Montoursville Area SD	Montoursville	266	47.9	Pine-Richland SD	Gibsonia
104	49.1	Pennsbury SD	Fallsington	186	48.5	Northern Tioga SD	Elkland	266	47.9	Selinsgrove Area SD	Selinsgrove
104	49.1	Philipsburg-Osceola Area SD	Philipsburg	186	48.5	Reading SD	Reading	266	47.9	Spring Grove Area SD	Spring Grove
104	49.1	Saucon Valley SD	Hellertown	186	48.5	Tulpehocken Area SD	Bethel	266	47.9	Wilson SD	West Lawn
104	49.1	Souderton Area SD	Souderton	198	48.4	Bangor Area SD	Bangor	283	47.8	Huntingdon Area SD	Huntingdon
104	49.1	Spring Cove SD	Roaring Spring	198	48.4	Bermudian Springs SD	York Springs	283	47.8	Ligonier Valley SD	Ligonier
104	49.1	West Perry SD	Elliottsburg	198	48.4	Blue Mountain SD	Orwigsburg	283	47.8	Mount Union Area SD	Mount Union
104	49.1	West York Area SD	York	198	48.4	Bristol Township SD	Levittown	283	47.8	Penn Hills SD	Pittsburgh
104	49.1	Wyoming Valley West SD	Kingston	198	48.4	Central Greene SD	Waynesburg	283	47.8	Springfield SD	Springfield
118	49.0	Boyertown Area SD	Boyertown	198	48.4	Chartiers Valley SD	Pittsburgh	283	47.8	Tunkhannock Area SD	Tunkhannock
118	49.0	Central Bucks SD	Doylestown	198	48.4	Deer Lakes SD	Russellton	283	47.8	Western Wayne SD	South Canaan
118	49.0	Cornwall-Lebanon SD	Lebanon	198	48.4	Fleetwood Area SD	Fleetwood	283	47.8	William Penn SD	Lansdowne
118	49.0	Crestwood SD	Mountain Top	198	48.4	Harbor Creek SD	Harborcreek	291	47.7	Annville-Cleona SD	Annville
118	49.0	Dallastown Area SD	Dallastown	198	48.4	Jim Thorpe Area SD	Jim Thorpe	291	47.7	Armstrong SD	Ford City
118	49.0	Greater Latrobe SD	Latrobe	198	48.4	Kiski Area SD	Leechburg	291	47.7	Big Beaver Falls Area SD	Beaver Falls
118	49.0	Hempfield SD	Landisville	198	48.4	Lampeter-Strasburg SD	Lampeter	291	47.7	Derry Area SD	Derry
118	49.0	Kennett Consolidated SD	Kennett Square	198	48.4	Lower Dauphin SD	Hummelstown	291	47.7	Keystone Oaks SD	Pittsburgh
118	49.0	Pottstown SD	Pottstown	198	48.4	Northwestern Lehigh SD	New Tripoli	291	47.7	Pocono Mountain SD	Swiftwater
118	49.0	Saint Marys Area SD	Saint Marys	198	48.4	Owen J Roberts SD	Pottstown	291	47.7	South Western SD	Hanover
118	49.0	Shaler Area SD	Glenshaw	198	48.4	Plum Borough SD	Plum	291	47.7	Wilson Area SD	Easton
118	49.0	Tyrone Area SD	Tyrone	198	48.4	Quakertown Community SD	Quakertown	299	47.6	Abington SD	Abington
118	49.0	West Jefferson Hills SD	Jefferson Hills	198	48.4	Schuylkill Valley SD	Leesport	299	47.6	Bensalem Township SD	Bensalem
118	49.0	Westmont Hilltop SD	Johnstown	198	48.4	Spring-Ford Area SD	Royersford	299	47.6	Berwick Area SD	Berwick
132	48.9	Carlisle Area SD	Carlisle	198	48.4	Upper Adams SD	Biglerville	299	47.6	East Lycoming SD	Hughesville
132	48.9	Conestoga Valley SD	Lancaster	198	48.4	Wissahickon SD	Ambler	299	47.6	Lower Moreland Township SD	Huntingdon Vlly
132	48.9	Cumberland Valley SD	Mechanicsburg	219	48.3	Delaware Valley SD	Milford	299	47.6	North Schuylkill SD	Ashland
132	48.9	Elizabethtown Area SD	Elizabethtown	219	48.3	Donegal SD	Mount Joy	299	47.6	South Park SD	South Park
132	48.9	Exeter Township SD	Reading	219	48.3	Laurel Highlands SD	Uniontown	299	47.6	Towanda Area SD	Towanda
132	48.9	Keystone Central SD	Lock Haven	219	48.3	Oil City Area SD	Oil City	299	47.6	Warren County SD	North Warren
132	48.9	Manheim Township SD	Lititz	219	48.3	Trinity Area SD	Washington	308	47.5	Bethlehem Area SD	Bethlehem
132	48.9	Marion Center Area SD	Marion Center	224	48.2	Avon Grove SD	West Grove	308	47.5	Connellsville Area SD	Connellsville
132	48.9	Neshaminy SD	Langhorne	224	48.2	Crawford Central SD	Meadville	308	47.5	Governor Mifflin SD	Shillington
132	48.9	New Kensington-Arnold SD	New Kensington	224	48.2	Erie City SD	Erie	308	47.5	Littlestown Area SD	Littlestown
132	48.9	North Penn SD	Lansdale	224	48.2	Greater Nanticoke Area SD	Nanticoke	308	47.5	Northampton Area SD	Northampton
132	48.9	Peters Township SD	Mcmurray	224	48.2	North Allegheny SD	Pittsburgh	308	47.5	Penn-Trafford SD	Harrison City
132	48.9	South Fayette Township SD	Mcdonald	224	48.2	Northern Lehigh SD	Slatington	308	47.5	Pequea Valley SD	Kinzers
132	48.9	Unionville-Chadds Ford SD	Kennett Square	224	48.2	Oxford Area SD	Oxford	308	47.5	Upper Perkiomen SD	Pennsburg
132	48.9	West Allegheny SD	Oakdale	224	48.2	Parkland SD	Allentown	316	47.4	Baldwin-Whitehall SD	Pittsburgh
147	48.8	Eastern Lebanon County SD	Myerstown	224	48.2	Tamaqua Area SD	Tamaqua	316	47.4	Carbondale Area SD	Carbondale
147	48.8	Lebanon SD	Lebanon	224	48.2	Wyomissing Area SD	Wyomissing	318	47.3	Beaver Area SD	Beaver
147	48.8	Mechanicsburg Area SD	Mechanicsburg	224	48.2	York City SD	York	318	47.3	Butler Area SD	Butler
147	48.8	Montour SD	Mckees Rocks	235	48.1	Corry Area SD	Corry	318	47.3	Clearfield Area SD	Clearfield
147	48.8	Montrose Area SD	Montrose	235	48.1	Dover Area SD	Dover	318	47.3	Fort Leboeuf SD	Waterford
147	48.8	Panther Valley SD	Lansford	235	48.1	Downingtown Area SD	Downingtown	318	47.3	Palmerton Area SD	Palmerton
147	48.8	Pen Argyl Area SD	Pen Argyl	235	48.1	Eastern York SD	Wrightsville	318	47.3	Penn Cambria SD	Cresson
147	48.8	Washington SD	Washington	235	48.1	Forest Hills SD	Sidman	318	47.3	Penncrest SD	Saegertown
147	48.8	Williamsport Area SD	Williamsport	235	48.1	Franklin Regional SD	Murrysville	318	47.3	Salisbury Township SD	Allentown
156	48.7	Bald Eagle Area SD	Wingate	235	48.1	Freedom Area SD	Freedom	318	47.3	South Butler County SD	Saxonburg
156	48.7	Bethel Park SD	Bethel Park	235	48.1	Girard SD	Girard	318	47.3	Southern Lehigh SD	Center Valley
156	48.7	Blairsville-Saltsburg SD	Blairsville	235	48.1	Juniata County SD	Mifflintown	328	47.2	Lehighton Area SD	Lehighton
156	48.7	Central Columbia SD	Bloomsburg	235	48.1	Lancaster SD	Lancaster	328	47.2	Mifflinburg Area SD	Mifflinburg
156	48.7	Cheltenham Township SD	Elkins Park	235	48.1	Mohawk Area SD	Bessemer	328	47.2	Moniteau SD	West Sunbury
156	48.7	Conrad Weiser Area SD	Robesonia	235	48.1	North Hills SD	Pittsburgh	328	47.2	Somerset Area SD	Somerset
156	48.7	Council Rock SD	Newtown	235	48.1	Northern York County SD	Dillsburg	332	47.1	Bedford Area SD	Bedford
156	48.7	Easton Area SD	Easton	235	48.1	Phoenixville Area SD	Phoenixville	332	47.1	Chestnut Ridge SD	Fishertown
156	48.7	Fox Chapel Area SD	Pittsburgh	235	48.1	Pleasant Valley SD	Brodheadsville	332	47.1	Mckeesport Area SD	Mckeesport
156	48.7	Hampton Township SD	Allison Park	235	48.1	Shamokin Area SD	Coal Township	335	47.0	Freeport Area SD	Sarver
156	48.7	Hempfield Area SD	Greensburg	235	48.1	Southeast Delco SD	Folcroft	336	46.9	E Stroudsburg Area SD	E Stroudsburg
156	48.7	Mount Pleasant Area SD	Mount Pleasant	235	48.1	Upper Saint Clair SD	Pittsburgh	336	46.9	Marple Newtown SD	Newtown Square

Note: This section only includes districts with 1,500 or more students; All categories are ranked from high to low

Rank	Percent	District Name	City
336	46.9	New Brighton Area SD	New Brighton
339	46.8	Ambridge Area SD	Ambridge
339	46.8	North Pocono SD	Moscow
339	46.8	Slippery Rock Area SD	Slippery Rock
342	46.7	Catasauqua Area SD	Catasauqua
342	46.7	Dallas SD	Dallas
342	46.7	Hamburg Area SD	Hamburg
345	46.6	Middletown Area SD	Middletown
346	46.5	Northern Lebanon SD	Fredericksburg
346	46.5	Sharon City SD	Sharon
348	46.2	Centennial SD	Warminster
348	46.2	Upper Moreland Township SD	Willow Grove
350	46.1	Mcguffey SD	Claysville
351	45.9	Mount Carmel Area SD	Mount Carmel
352	45.8	Pine Grove Area SD	Pine Grove
353	44.8	General Mclane SD	Edinboro
354	41.1	York County School of Technology	York
355	40.9	Grove City Area SD	Grove City
356	40.5	Lehigh Career & Technical Inst	Schnecksville

Individual Education Program Students

Rank	Percent	District Name	City
1	29.9	Franklin Area SD	Franklin
2	26.8	Oil City Area SD	Oil City
3	26.2	York City SD	York
4	25.8	Chester Community CS	Chester
5	25.6	Corry Area SD	Corry
6	23.7	New Kensington-Arnold SD	New Kensington
7	23.0	Woodland Hills SD	Pittsburgh
8	22.7	Carbondale Area SD	Carbondale
9	22.5	Harrisburg City SD	Harrisburg
10	22.3	Bristol Township SD	Levittown
10	22.3	Ridley SD	Folsom
12	22.2	Kutztown Area SD	Kutztown
13	22.0	Phoenixville Area SD	Phoenixville
14	21.9	Haverford Township SD	Havertown
15	21.8	Altoona Area SD	Altoona
15	21.8	Norristown Area SD	Norristown
17	21.7	Bensalem Township SD	Bensalem
18	21.6	Brookville Area SD	Brookville
18	21.6	Central Greene SD	Waynesburg
18	21.6	Erie City SD	Erie
21	21.5	Neshaminy SD	Langhorne
21	21.5	Pittsburgh SD	Pittsburgh
21	21.5	Williamsport Area SD	Williamsport
24	21.3	Greater Johnstown SD	Johnstown
24	21.3	Northwestern SD	Albion
24	21.3	Washington SD	Washington
27	21.2	Highlands SD	Natrona Heights
28	21.1	Berwick Area SD	Berwick
28	21.1	Garnet Valley SD	Glen Mills
30	21.0	Penn Hills SD	Pittsburgh
30	21.0	Punxsutawney Area SD	Punxsutawney
32	20.9	Pottstown SD	Pottstown
32	20.9	Steel Valley SD	Munhall
34	20.8	Blairsville-Saltsburg SD	Blairsville
34	20.8	East Allegheny SD	N Versailles
34	20.8	Mount Union Area SD	Mount Union
34	20.8	Wyoming Valley West SD	Kingston
38	20.7	Interboro SD	Prospect Park
39	20.6	Big Spring SD	Newville
39	20.6	Coatesville Area SD	Coatesville
39	20.6	Hanover Area SD	Hanover Twp
39	20.6	Susquenita SD	Duncannon
43	20.5	Albert Gallatin Area SD	Uniontown
43	20.5	Lancaster SD	Lancaster
45	20.4	Chester-Upland SD	Chester
45	20.4	Shaler Area SD	Glenshaw
45	20.4	Tamaqua Area SD	Tamaqua
48	20.3	Clearfield Area SD	Clearfield
48	20.3	E Stroudsburg Area SD	E Stroudsburg
50	20.2	Sharon City SD	Sharon
50	20.2	Somerset Area SD	Somerset
52	20.0	Huntingdon Area SD	Huntingdon
52	20.0	Jim Thorpe Area SD	Jim Thorpe
52	20.0	Upper Perkiomen SD	Pennsburg
55	19.9	Connellsville Area SD	Connellsville
55	19.9	Salisbury Township SD	Allentown
57	19.8	Armstrong SD	Ford City
57	19.8	Chichester SD	Aston
57	19.8	Crawford Central SD	Meadville
57	19.8	Warren County SD	North Warren
61	19.7	Marple Newtown SD	Newtown Square
61	19.7	Titusville Area SD	Titusville
63	19.6	Wallingford-Swarthmore SD	Wallingford
64	19.5	Panther Valley SD	Lansford
65	19.4	Athens Area SD	Athens
65	19.4	Greater Nanticoke Area SD	Nanticoke
65	19.4	Montrose Area SD	Montrose
65	19.4	Scranton SD	Scranton
65	19.4	Southeast Delco SD	Folcroft
70	19.3	Charleroi SD	Charleroi
70	19.3	Owen J Roberts SD	Pottstown
70	19.3	Wattsburg Area SD	Erie
73	19.2	Centennial SD	Warminster
73	19.2	Conrad Weiser Area SD	Robesonia
73	19.2	New Castle Area SD	New Castle
76	19.1	Palisades SD	Kintnersville
77	19.0	Girard SD	Girard
77	19.0	Mckeesport Area SD	Mckeesport
77	19.0	Middletown Area SD	Middletown
77	19.0	Riverside SD	Taylor
81	18.9	Fort Leboeuf SD	Waterford
81	18.9	Reading SD	Reading
81	18.9	Saint Marys Area SD	Saint Marys
84	18.8	Brandywine Heights Area SD	Topton
84	18.8	Gateway SD	Monroeville
84	18.8	Wissahickon SD	Ambler
87	18.7	Bloomsburg Area SD	Bloomsburg
87	18.7	Lebanon SD	Lebanon
87	18.7	Pottsgrove SD	Pottstown
87	18.7	West Shore SD	New Cumberland
87	18.7	Wilson SD	West Lawn
92	18.6	Exeter Township SD	Reading
92	18.6	Mifflinburg Area SD	Mifflinburg
92	18.6	Penn-Delco SD	Aston
92	18.6	Pequea Valley SD	Kinzers
96	18.5	Northern Lehigh SD	Slatington
96	18.5	Oxford Area SD	Oxford
96	18.5	Southmoreland SD	Scottdale
99	18.4	North Schuylkill SD	Ashland
99	18.4	Philipsburg-Osceola Area SD	Philipsburg
99	18.4	Pocono Mountain SD	Swiftwater
99	18.4	Spring Cove SD	Roaring Spring
99	18.4	Wallenpaupack Area SD	Hawley
104	18.3	Ambridge Area SD	Ambridge
104	18.3	Deer Lakes SD	Russellton
104	18.3	West Perry SD	Elliottsburg
107	18.2	Jersey Shore Area SD	Jersey Shore
107	18.2	Spring-Ford Area SD	Royersford
109	18.1	Catasauqua Area SD	Catasauqua
109	18.1	Eastern York SD	Wrightsville
109	18.1	Lower Dauphin SD	Hummelstown
109	18.1	Northampton Area SD	Northampton
109	18.1	Troy Area SD	Troy
109	18.1	Tyrone Area SD	Tyrone
115	18.0	Blue Mountain SD	Orwigsburg
115	18.0	Colonial SD	Plymth Meeting
115	18.0	Marion Center Area SD	Marion Center
115	18.0	Octorara Area SD	Atglen
115	18.0	Penn Manor SD	Lancaster
115	18.0	Pennsbury SD	Fallsington
121	17.9	Keystone Central SD	Lock Haven
121	17.9	Midd-West SD	Middleburg
121	17.9	Pennridge SD	Perkasie
124	17.8	Boyertown Area SD	Boyertown
124	17.8	Dubois Area SD	Du Bois
124	17.8	Muhlenberg SD	Reading
124	17.8	Penn Cambria SD	Cresson
124	17.8	William Penn SD	Lansdowne
129	17.7	Agora Cyber CS	Wayne
129	17.7	Brownsville Area SD	Brownsville
129	17.7	Harbor Creek SD	Harborcreek
129	17.7	North Penn SD	Lansdale
129	17.7	Springfield Township SD	Oreland
134	17.6	Lakeland SD	Jermyn
134	17.6	Northeastern York SD	Manchester
134	17.6	Palmerton Area SD	Palmerton
137	17.5	Ringgold SD	New Eagle
137	17.5	Uniontown Area SD	Uniontown
139	17.4	Council Rock SD	Newtown
139	17.4	Pine Grove Area SD	Pine Grove
139	17.4	Pottsville Area SD	Pottsville
139	17.4	Shamokin Area SD	Coal Township
139	17.4	Shippensburg Area SD	Shippensburg
139	17.4	Susquehanna Township SD	Harrisburg
139	17.4	Tunkhannock Area SD	Tunkhannock
146	17.3	Bellefonte Area SD	Bellefonte
146	17.3	Central Cambria SD	Ebensburg
146	17.3	Donegal SD	Mount Joy
149	17.2	Hempfield SD	Landisville
149	17.2	Rose Tree Media SD	Media
151	17.1	Downingtown Area SD	Downingtown
151	17.1	Hanover Public SD	Hanover
151	17.1	Wellsboro Area SD	Wellsboro
154	17.0	Governor Mifflin SD	Shillington
154	17.0	Manheim Central SD	Manheim
154	17.0	New Hope-Solebury SD	New Hope
157	16.9	East Pennsboro Area SD	Enola
157	16.9	Tulpehocken Area SD	Bethel
157	16.9	Upper Darby SD	Drexel Hill
157	16.9	Wyomissing Area SD	Wyomissing
161	16.8	Lower Merion SD	Ardmore
161	16.8	Mount Pleasant Area SD	Mount Pleasant
161	16.8	South Allegheny SD	Mckeesport
164	16.7	Bethel Park SD	Bethel Park
164	16.7	Chambersburg Area SD	Chambersburg
164	16.7	Oley Valley SD	Oley
164	16.7	Shikellamy SD	Sunbury
164	16.7	South Middleton SD	Boiling Springs
164	16.7	Southern Tioga SD	Blossburg
164	16.7	Wilson Area SD	Easton
171	16.6	Bedford Area SD	Bedford
171	16.6	Milton Area SD	Milton
171	16.6	Parkland SD	Allentown
171	16.6	Wilkes-Barre Area SD	Wilkes Barre
175	16.5	Cocalico SD	Denver
175	16.5	Fleetwood Area SD	Fleetwood
175	16.5	Mifflin County SD	Lewistown
175	16.5	Upper Merion Area SD	King of Prussia
179	16.4	Great Valley SD	Malvern
179	16.4	West York Area SD	York
179	16.4	Whitehall-Coplay SD	Whitehall
182	16.3	Allentown City SD	Allentown
182	16.3	Conneaut SD	Linesville
182	16.3	Seneca Valley SD	Harmony
182	16.3	Southern York County SD	Glen Rock
182	16.3	Tredyffrin-Easttown SD	Wayne
182	16.3	Unionville-Chadds Ford SD	Kennett Square
188	16.2	Belle Vernon Area SD	Belle Vernon
188	16.2	Butler Area SD	Butler
188	16.2	Commonwealth Connections Acade	Harrisburg
188	16.2	Dover Area SD	Dover
188	16.2	Eastern Lebanon County SD	Myerstown
188	16.2	Methacton SD	Norristown
188	16.2	Radnor Township SD	Wayne
188	16.2	Springfield SD	Springfield
188	16.2	Tuscarora SD	Mercersburg
197	16.1	Bald Eagle Area SD	Wingate
197	16.1	Bethlehem Area SD	Bethlehem
197	16.1	Montour SD	Mckees Rocks
197	16.1	Northern Tioga SD	Elkland
197	16.1	Penncrest SD	Saegertown
202	16.0	Carlisle Area SD	Carlisle
202	16.0	Hopewell Area SD	Aliquippa
202	16.0	Kennett Consolidated SD	Kennett Square
202	16.0	Moniteau SD	West Sunbury
202	16.0	West Allegheny SD	Oakdale
207	15.9	South Eastern SD	Fawn Grove
207	15.9	Wayne Highlands SD	Honesdale
209	15.8	Chestnut Ridge SD	Fishertown
209	15.8	Ephrata Area SD	Ephrata
209	15.8	Lehighton Area SD	Lehighton
209	15.8	Philadelphia City SD	Philadelphia
209	15.8	Red Lion Area SD	Red Lion
214	15.7	Greensburg Salem SD	Greensburg
214	15.7	Hatboro-Horsham SD	Horsham
214	15.7	Lampeter-Strasburg SD	Lampeter
214	15.7	Schuylkill Valley SD	Leesport
214	15.7	Twin Valley SD	Elverson
214	15.7	Warwick SD	Lititz
220	15.6	Big Beaver Falls Area SD	Beaver Falls
220	15.6	Elizabeth Forward SD	Elizabeth
220	15.6	Fox Chapel Area SD	Pittsburgh
220	15.6	Indiana Area SD	Indiana
220	15.6	Lake-Lehman SD	Dallas
220	15.6	Mid Valley SD	Throop
220	15.6	West Mifflin Area SD	West Mifflin
220	15.6	Wyoming Area SD	Exeter
228	15.5	Freedom Area SD	Freedom
228	15.5	Northern Lebanon SD	Fredericksburg
228	15.5	Northwestern Lehigh SD	New Tripoli
231	15.4	Palmyra Area SD	Palmyra

Note: This section only includes districts with 1,500 or more students; All categories are ranked from high to low

Rank		District Name	City
232	15.3	Cheltenham Township SD	Elkins Park
232	15.3	Laurel Highlands SD	Uniontown
232	15.3	Mcguffey SD	Claysville
232	15.3	Yough SD	Herminie
236	15.2	Annville-Cleona SD	Annville
236	15.2	Valley View SD	Archbald
238	15.1	Cornwall-Lebanon SD	Lebanon
239	15.0	Canon-Mcmillan SD	Canonsburg
239	15.0	Central Columbia SD	Bloomsburg
239	15.0	Danville Area SD	Danville
239	15.0	Delaware Valley SD	Milford
239	15.0	Ellwood City Area SD	Ellwood City
239	15.0	Keystone Oaks SD	Pittsburgh
239	15.0	North Pocono SD	Moscow
239	15.0	Pleasant Valley SD	Brodheadsville
239	15.0	South Western SD	Hanover
239	15.0	Upper Moreland Township SD	Willow Grove
239	15.0	Western Wayne SD	South Canaan
250	14.9	Easton Area SD	Easton
250	14.9	North Hills SD	Pittsburgh
250	14.9	Pen Argyl Area SD	Pen Argyl
250	14.9	Warrior Run SD	Turbotville
250	14.9	West Chester Area SD	West Chester
255	14.8	Daniel Boone Area SD	Birdsboro
255	14.8	Souderton Area SD	Souderton
255	14.8	Upper Adams SD	Biglerville
258	14.7	Bradford Area SD	Bradford
258	14.7	Dallastown Area SD	Dallastown
258	14.7	Saucon Valley SD	Hellertown
261	14.6	Central Dauphin SD	Harrisburg
261	14.6	Upper Saint Clair SD	Pittsburgh
261	14.6	York Suburban SD	York
264	14.5	Moon Area SD	Moon Township
264	14.5	Quakertown Community SD	Quakertown
264	14.5	Stroudsburg Area SD	Stroudsburg
267	14.4	Bangor Area SD	Bangor
267	14.4	Burrell SD	Lower Burrell
267	14.4	Franklin Regional SD	Murrysville
267	14.4	Lower Moreland Township SD	Huntingdon Vlly
271	14.3	Avon Grove SD	West Grove
271	14.3	Conewago Valley SD	New Oxford
271	14.3	Riverside Beaver County SD	Ellwood City
274	14.2	Cumberland Valley SD	Mechanicsburg
274	14.2	Elizabethtown Area SD	Elizabethtown
274	14.2	Northern York County SD	Dillsburg
277	14.1	Hempfield Area SD	Greensburg
277	14.1	Spring Grove Area SD	Spring Grove
277	14.1	Towanda Area SD	Towanda
280	14.0	Mount Carmel Area SD	Mount Carmel
281	13.9	Conestoga Valley SD	Lancaster
281	13.9	Forest Hills SD	Sidman
281	13.9	Hamburg Area SD	Hamburg
284	13.8	East Penn SD	Emmaus
284	13.8	Hermitage SD	Hermitage
284	13.8	Mount Lebanon SD	Pittsburgh
284	13.8	Quaker Valley SD	Sewickley
284	13.8	Solanco SD	Quarryville
289	13.7	Millcreek Township SD	Erie
289	13.7	State College Area SD	State College
291	13.6	Beaver Area SD	Beaver
291	13.6	Gettysburg Area SD	Gettysburg
291	13.6	Hollidaysburg Area SD	Hollidaysburg
291	13.6	Kiski Area SD	Leechburg
291	13.6	Perkiomen Valley SD	Collegeville
291	13.6	Trinity Area SD	Washington
297	13.5	Abington Heights SD	Clarks Summit
297	13.5	Central Bucks SD	Doylestown
297	13.5	Central Valley SD	Monaca
297	13.5	Eastern Lancaster County SD	New Holland
301	13.3	General Mclane SD	Edinboro
301	13.3	Greencastle-Antrim SD	Greencastle
301	13.3	New Brighton Area SD	New Brighton
304	13.2	North East SD	North East
304	13.2	Pennsylvania Leadership Charter	West Chester
304	13.2	Pittston Area SD	Pittston
307	13.1	Dunmore SD	Dunmore
307	13.1	Hazleton Area SD	Hazleton
307	13.1	Littlestown Area SD	Littlestown
307	13.1	Southern Lehigh SD	Center Valley
311	13.0	Pine-Richland SD	Gibsonia
312	12.9	Mechanicsburg Area SD	Mechanicsburg
312	12.9	Upper Dublin SD	Maple Glen
314	12.8	Fairview SD	Fairview
314	12.8	Ligonier Valley SD	Ligonier
314	12.8	Manheim Township SD	Lititz
317	12.7	Derry Area SD	Derry
318	12.6	Greater Latrobe SD	Latrobe
318	12.6	Montoursville Area SD	Montoursville
320	12.5	Abington SD	Abington
320	12.5	Dallas SD	Dallas
320	12.5	Mohawk Area SD	Bessemer
323	12.4	Lewisburg Area SD	Lewisburg
323	12.4	Nazareth Area SD	Nazareth
323	12.4	Selinsgrove Area SD	Selinsgrove
323	12.4	Waynesboro Area SD	Waynesboro
327	12.3	Chartiers Valley SD	Pittsburgh
328	12.2	Baldwin-Whitehall SD	Pittsburgh
329	12.1	Derry Township SD	Hershey
329	12.1	Plum Borough SD	Plum
331	11.9	Norwin SD	N Huntingdon
332	11.8	South Park SD	South Park
333	11.7	Karns City Area SD	Karns City
333	11.7	Slippery Rock Area SD	Slippery Rock
336	11.6	South Butler County SD	Saxonburg
336	11.5	Blackhawk SD	Beaver Falls
336	11.5	Richland SD	Johnstown
338	11.4	West Jefferson Hills SD	Jefferson Hills
339	11.3	Hampton Township SD	Allison Park
340	11.1	Pennsylvania Virtual CS	Norristown
341	11.0	Central York SD	York
342	10.9	Freeport Area SD	Sarver
343	10.6	North Allegheny SD	Pittsburgh
343	10.6	Pennsylvania Cyber CS	Midland
345	10.5	Crestwood SD	Mountain Top
346	10.4	Westmont Hilltop SD	Johnstown
347	10.3	Juniata County SD	Mifflintown
348	9.7	Bermudian Springs SD	York Springs
349	9.6	Grove City Area SD	Grove City
350	9.2	Penn-Trafford SD	Harrison City
351	9.0	East Lycoming SD	Hughesville
352	8.9	South Fayette Township SD	Mcdonald
353	7.0	Peters Township SD	Mcmurray
354	6.1	Mars Area SD	Mars
355	0.0	Lehigh Career & Technical Inst	Schnecksville
355	0.0	York County School of Technology	York

English Language Learner Students

Rank	Percent	District Name	City
1	20.8	York City SD	York
2	19.7	Reading SD	Reading
3	18.0	Lancaster SD	Lancaster
4	13.5	Kennett Consolidated SD	Kennett Square
5	12.5	Lebanon SD	Lebanon
6	11.8	Allentown City SD	Allentown
7	10.5	Norristown Area SD	Norristown
8	9.8	Hazleton Area SD	Hazleton
9	8.9	Hanover Public SD	Hanover
10	8.4	Harrisburg City SD	Harrisburg
11	8.3	Oxford Area SD	Oxford
12	7.7	Bethlehem Area SD	Bethlehem
13	7.3	Philadelphia City SD	Philadelphia
14	6.8	Erie City SD	Erie
15	6.7	Avon Grove SD	West Grove
15	6.7	Scranton SD	Scranton
17	6.0	Upper Darby SD	Drexel Hill
18	5.9	Wilkes-Barre Area SD	Wilkes Barre
19	5.5	Upper Adams SD	Biglerville
20	5.3	Conestoga Valley SD	Lancaster
21	5.2	Lower Moreland Township SD	Huntingdon Vlly
22	5.0	Bensalem Township SD	Bensalem
23	4.7	Muhlenberg SD	Reading
24	4.3	Baldwin-Whitehall SD	Pittsburgh
24	4.3	Chambersburg Area SD	Chambersburg
24	4.3	Pocono Mountain SD	Swiftwater
24	4.3	Whitehall-Coplay SD	Whitehall
28	3.9	Bristol Township SD	Levittown
29	3.8	Manheim Township SD	Lititz
29	3.8	Salisbury Township SD	Allentown
29	3.8	Souderton Area SD	Souderton
32	3.7	Bermudian Springs SD	York Springs
32	3.7	Easton Area SD	Easton
32	3.7	Gettysburg Area SD	Gettysburg
32	3.7	North Penn SD	Lansdale
32	3.7	Tulpehocken Area SD	Bethel
37	3.6	Coatesville Area SD	Coatesville
37	3.6	Cornwall-Lebanon SD	Lebanon
37	3.6	Wissahickon SD	Ambler
40	3.5	Centennial SD	Warminster
40	3.5	Hempfield SD	Landisville
40	3.5	Milton Area SD	Milton
43	3.2	Central Dauphin SD	Harrisburg
43	3.2	West Chester Area SD	West Chester
43	3.2	York Suburban SD	York
46	3.1	York County School of Technology	York
47	3.0	William Penn SD	Lansdowne
48	2.8	Conewago Valley SD	New Oxford
48	2.8	Marple Newtown SD	Newtown Square
48	2.8	Upper Merion Area SD	King of Prussia
51	2.7	Southeast Delco SD	Folcroft
52	2.6	Radnor Township SD	Wayne
53	2.5	Chester Community CS	Chester
53	2.5	Eastern Lancaster County SD	New Holland
53	2.5	West Shore SD	New Cumberland
53	2.5	Wilson Area SD	Easton
57	2.4	Catasauqua Area SD	Catasauqua
58	2.3	Ephrata Area SD	Ephrata
58	2.3	Stroudsburg Area SD	Stroudsburg
60	2.2	Donegal SD	Mount Joy
61	2.1	Cheltenham Township SD	Elkins Park
61	2.1	Keystone Oaks SD	Pittsburgh
61	2.1	Lehigh Career & Technical Inst	Schnecksville
61	2.1	Mechanicsburg Area SD	Mechanicsburg
65	2.0	Abington SD	Abington
65	2.0	E Stroudsburg Area SD	E Stroudsburg
65	2.0	State College Area SD	State College
65	2.0	Upper Moreland Township SD	Willow Grove
65	2.0	Wilson SD	West Lawn
70	1.9	Chartiers Valley SD	Pittsburgh
70	1.9	East Pennsboro Area SD	Enola
70	1.9	Great Valley SD	Malvern
70	1.9	Methacton SD	Norristown
70	1.9	Phoenixville Area SD	Phoenixville
70	1.9	Pottstown SD	Pottstown
70	1.9	Selinsgrove Area SD	Selinsgrove
77	1.8	Carlisle Area SD	Carlisle
77	1.8	New Hope-Solebury SD	New Hope
79	1.7	Cocalico SD	Denver
79	1.7	Cumberland Valley SD	Mechanicsburg
79	1.7	East Penn SD	Emmaus
79	1.7	Fleetwood Area SD	Fleetwood
79	1.7	Northern Lebanon SD	Fredericksburg
79	1.7	Octorara Area SD	Atglen
79	1.7	Wyomissing Area SD	Wyomissing
86	1.6	Indiana Area SD	Indiana
86	1.6	Lewisburg Area SD	Lewisburg
86	1.6	Quakertown Community SD	Quakertown
86	1.6	Rose Tree Media SD	Media
86	1.6	Springfield Township SD	Oreland
91	1.5	Central York SD	York
91	1.5	Chichester SD	Aston
91	1.5	Council Rock SD	Newtown
91	1.5	Dallastown Area SD	Dallastown
91	1.5	Parkland SD	Allentown
91	1.5	Pennsbury SD	Fallsington
91	1.5	South Middleton SD	Boiling Springs
91	1.5	Tredyffrin-Easttown SD	Wayne
99	1.4	Berwick Area SD	Berwick
99	1.4	Grove City Area SD	Grove City
99	1.4	Lower Merion SD	Ardmore
99	1.4	Springfield SD	Springfield
103	1.3	Colonial SD	Plymth Meeting
103	1.3	Gateway SD	Monroeville
103	1.3	Lampeter-Strasburg SD	Lampeter
103	1.3	Mount Lebanon SD	Pittsburgh
103	1.3	Neshaminy SD	Langhorne
103	1.3	North Hills SD	Pittsburgh
103	1.3	Penn Manor SD	Lancaster
103	1.3	Pennridge SD	Perkasie
103	1.3	Pennsylvania Leadership Charter	West Chester
103	1.3	Pittsburgh SD	Pittsburgh
103	1.3	Warwick SD	Lititz
103	1.3	West York Area SD	York
115	1.2	Conrad Weiser Area SD	Robesonia
115	1.2	Governor Mifflin SD	Shillington
115	1.2	Juniata County SD	Mifflintown
115	1.2	Susquehanna Township SD	Harrisburg
115	1.2	Upper Dublin SD	Maple Glen
120	1.1	Annville-Cleona SD	Annville
120	1.1	Bellefonte Area SD	Bellefonte
120	1.1	Downingtown Area SD	Downingtown
120	1.1	Elizabethtown Area SD	Elizabethtown
120	1.1	Manheim Central SD	Manheim
120	1.1	Pottsgrove SD	Pottstown

Note: This section only includes districts with 1,500 or more students; All categories are ranked from high to low

120	1.1	Shikellamy SD	Sunbury
120	1.1	Upper Saint Clair SD	Pittsburgh
128	1.0	Bloomsburg Area SD	Bloomsburg
128	1.0	Crestwood SD	Mountain Top
128	1.0	Exeter Township SD	Reading
128	1.0	Greater Nanticoke Area SD	Nanticoke
128	1.0	Haverford Township SD	Havertown
128	1.0	Northern Lehigh SD	Slatington
128	1.0	Pen Argyl Area SD	Pen Argyl
128	1.0	Pleasant Valley SD	Brodheadsville
136	0.9	Derry Township SD	Hershey
136	0.9	Dover Area SD	Dover
136	0.9	Eastern Lebanon County SD	Myerstown
136	0.9	Fox Chapel Area SD	Pittsburgh
136	0.9	Hermitage SD	Hermitage
136	0.9	Millcreek Township SD	Erie
136	0.9	Northeastern York SD	Manchester
136	0.9	Schuylkill Valley SD	Leesport
136	0.9	Sharon City SD	Sharon
136	0.9	South Western SD	Hanover
136	0.9	Spring Grove Area SD	Spring Grove
136	0.9	Tuscarora SD	Mercersburg
136	0.9	Unionville-Chadds Ford SD	Kennett Square
136	0.9	Wallingford-Swarthmore SD	Wallingford
150	0.8	Mars Area SD	Mars
150	0.8	North Allegheny SD	Pittsburgh
150	0.8	Northampton Area SD	Northampton
150	0.8	Palmyra Area SD	Palmyra
150	0.8	Penn-Delco SD	Aston
150	0.8	Quaker Valley SD	Sewickley
150	0.8	Riverside SD	Taylor
150	0.8	Wyoming Valley West SD	Kingston
158	0.7	Dunmore SD	Dunmore
158	0.7	Fairview SD	Fairview
158	0.7	Garnet Valley SD	Glen Mills
158	0.7	Hamburg Area SD	Hamburg
158	0.7	Littlestown Area SD	Littlestown
158	0.7	Red Lion Area SD	Red Lion
158	0.7	Seneca Valley SD	Harmony
158	0.7	Somerset Area SD	Somerset
158	0.7	Southern Lehigh SD	Center Valley
158	0.7	Westmont Hilltop SD	Johnstown
168	0.6	Belle Vernon Area SD	Belle Vernon
168	0.6	Greater Johnstown SD	Johnstown
168	0.6	Hanover Area SD	Hanover Twp
168	0.6	Hatboro-Horsham SD	Horsham
168	0.6	Lehighton Area SD	Lehighton
168	0.6	Mid Valley SD	Throop
168	0.6	Middletown Area SD	Middletown
168	0.6	Montour SD	Mckees Rocks
168	0.6	Montrose Area SD	Montrose
168	0.6	Palmerton Area SD	Palmerton
168	0.6	Pequea Valley SD	Kinzers
168	0.6	Saucon Valley SD	Hellertown
168	0.6	Shamokin Area SD	Coal Township
168	0.6	Solanco SD	Quarryville
168	0.6	South Eastern SD	Fawn Grove
168	0.6	Spring-Ford Area SD	Royersford
168	0.6	Tamaqua Area SD	Tamaqua
168	0.6	Titusville Area SD	Titusville
168	0.6	Twin Valley SD	Elverson
168	0.6	Upper Perkiomen SD	Pennsburg
188	0.5	Abington Heights SD	Clarks Summit
188	0.5	Bangor Area SD	Bangor
188	0.5	Bethel Park SD	Bethel Park
188	0.5	Burrell SD	Lower Burrell
188	0.5	Central Bucks SD	Doylestown
188	0.5	Central Valley SD	Monaca
188	0.5	Crawford Central SD	Meadville
188	0.5	Danville Area SD	Danville
188	0.5	Greencastle-Antrim SD	Greencastle
188	0.5	Hollidaysburg Area SD	Hollidaysburg
188	0.5	Huntingdon Area SD	Huntingdon
188	0.5	Interboro SD	Prospect Park
188	0.5	Mount Carmel Area SD	Mount Carmel
188	0.5	Northern York County SD	Dillsburg
188	0.5	Panther Valley SD	Lansford
188	0.5	Pottsville Area SD	Pottsville
188	0.5	Ridley SD	Folsom
188	0.5	South Fayette Township SD	Mcdonald
188	0.5	Southern York County SD	Glen Rock
188	0.5	Steel Valley SD	Munhall
188	0.5	West Allegheny SD	Oakdale
188	0.5	West Jefferson Hills SD	Jefferson Hills
210	0.4	Canon-Mcmillan SD	Canonsburg
210	0.4	Charleroi SD	Charleroi
210	0.4	Clearfield Area SD	Clearfield
210	0.4	Commonwealth Connections Acade	Harrisburg
210	0.4	Franklin Area SD	Franklin
210	0.4	Franklin Regional SD	Murrysville
210	0.4	Hampton Township SD	Allison Park
210	0.4	Harbor Creek SD	Harborcreek
210	0.4	Mifflin County SD	Lewistown
210	0.4	Northwestern SD	Albion
210	0.4	Oley Valley SD	Oley
210	0.4	Owen J Roberts SD	Pottstown
210	0.4	Palisades SD	Kintnersville
210	0.4	Penn Hills SD	Pittsburgh
210	0.4	Shippensburg Area SD	Shippensburg
210	0.4	Slippery Rock Area SD	Slippery Rock
210	0.4	South Park SD	South Park
210	0.4	Southmoreland SD	Scottdale
210	0.4	Tunkhannock Area SD	Tunkhannock
210	0.4	Warrior Run SD	Turbotville
210	0.4	Wayne Highlands SD	Honesdale
210	0.4	Wyoming Area SD	Exeter
232	0.3	Blue Mountain SD	Orwigsburg
232	0.3	Central Columbia SD	Bloomsburg
232	0.3	Dallas SD	Dallas
232	0.3	Daniel Boone Area SD	Birdsboro
232	0.3	Deer Lakes SD	Russellton
232	0.3	Delaware Valley SD	Milford
232	0.3	East Allegheny SD	N Versailles
232	0.3	East Lycoming SD	Hughesville
232	0.3	Girard SD	Girard
232	0.3	Lower Dauphin SD	Hummelstown
232	0.3	Mifflinburg Area SD	Mifflinburg
232	0.3	Moon Area SD	Moon Township
232	0.3	Nazareth Area SD	Nazareth
232	0.3	New Kensington-Arnold SD	New Kensington
232	0.3	Northwestern Lehigh SD	New Tripoli
232	0.3	Richland SD	Johnstown
232	0.3	Riverside Beaver County SD	Ellwood City
232	0.3	Shaler Area SD	Glenshaw
232	0.3	Tyrone Area SD	Tyrone
232	0.3	Valley View SD	Archbald
232	0.3	Wallenpaupack Area SD	Hawley
232	0.3	Washington SD	Washington
232	0.3	Waynesboro Area SD	Waynesboro
232	0.3	Woodland Hills SD	Pittsburgh
256	0.2	Agora Cyber CS	Wayne
256	0.2	Big Beaver Falls Area SD	Beaver Falls
256	0.2	Big Spring SD	Newville
256	0.2	Blairsville-Saltsburg SD	Blairsville
256	0.2	Boyertown Area SD	Boyertown
256	0.2	Butler Area SD	Butler
256	0.2	Carbondale Area SD	Carbondale
256	0.2	Central Cambria SD	Ebensburg
256	0.2	Central Greene SD	Waynesburg
256	0.2	Chestnut Ridge SD	Fishertown
256	0.2	Eastern York SD	Wrightsville
256	0.2	Fort Leboeuf SD	Waterford
256	0.2	General Mclane SD	Edinboro
256	0.2	Greater Latrobe SD	Latrobe
256	0.2	Greensburg Salem SD	Greensburg
256	0.2	Highlands SD	Natrona Heights
256	0.2	Hopewell Area SD	Aliquippa
256	0.2	Jim Thorpe Area SD	Jim Thorpe
256	0.2	Kutztown Area SD	Kutztown
256	0.2	Ligonier Valley SD	Ligonier
256	0.2	Montoursville Area SD	Montoursville
256	0.2	New Castle Area SD	New Castle
256	0.2	North Pocono SD	Moscow
256	0.2	Penncrest SD	Saegertown
256	0.2	Peters Township SD	Mcmurray
256	0.2	Philipsburg-Osceola Area SD	Philipsburg
256	0.2	Pine Grove Area SD	Pine Grove
256	0.2	Pine-Richland SD	Gibsonia
256	0.2	Pittston Area SD	Pittston
256	0.2	Plum Borough SD	Plum
256	0.2	Southern Tioga SD	Blossburg
256	0.2	Spring Cove SD	Roaring Spring
256	0.2	Susquenita SD	Duncannon
256	0.2	Towanda Area SD	Towanda
256	0.2	Wellsboro Area SD	Wellsboro
256	0.2	Williamsport Area SD	Williamsport
292	0.1	Altoona Area SD	Altoona
292	0.1	Ambridge Area SD	Ambridge
292	0.1	Armstrong SD	Ford City
292	0.1	Athens Area SD	Athens
292	0.1	Beaver Area SD	Beaver
292	0.1	Bedford Area SD	Bedford
292	0.1	Blackhawk SD	Beaver Falls
292	0.1	Bradford Area SD	Bradford
292	0.1	Brandywine Heights Area SD	Topton
292	0.1	Conneaut SD	Linesville
292	0.1	Connellsville Area SD	Connellsville
292	0.1	Corry Area SD	Corry
292	0.1	Ellwood City Area SD	Ellwood City
292	0.1	Hempfield Area SD	Greensburg
292	0.1	Jersey Shore Area SD	Jersey Shore
292	0.1	Keystone Central SD	Lock Haven
292	0.1	Kiski Area SD	Leechburg
292	0.1	Lakeland SD	Jermyn
292	0.1	Laurel Highlands SD	Uniontown
292	0.1	Mckeesport Area SD	Mckeesport
292	0.1	Mount Union Area SD	Mount Union
292	0.1	New Brighton Area SD	New Brighton
292	0.1	North East SD	North East
292	0.1	North Schuylkill SD	Ashland
292	0.1	Norwin SD	N Huntingdon
292	0.1	Penn Cambria SD	Cresson
292	0.1	Penn-Trafford SD	Harrison City
292	0.1	Pennsylvania Virtual CS	Norristown
292	0.1	Perkiomen Valley SD	Collegeville
292	0.1	Punxsutawney Area SD	Punxsutawney
292	0.1	Ringgold SD	New Eagle
292	0.1	South Allegheny SD	Mckeesport
292	0.1	Trinity Area SD	Washington
292	0.1	Warren County SD	North Warren
292	0.1	Wattsburg Area SD	Erie
292	0.1	West Mifflin Area SD	West Mifflin
292	0.1	Western Wayne SD	South Canaan
329	0.0	Albert Gallatin Area SD	Uniontown
329	0.0	Bald Eagle Area SD	Wingate
329	0.0	Brookville Area SD	Brookville
329	0.0	Brownsville Area SD	Brownsville
329	0.0	Chester-Upland SD	Chester
329	0.0	Derry Area SD	Derry
329	0.0	Dubois Area SD	Du Bois
329	0.0	Elizabeth Forward SD	Elizabeth
329	0.0	Forest Hills SD	Sidman
329	0.0	Freedom Area SD	Freedom
329	0.0	Freeport Area SD	Sarver
329	0.0	Karns City Area SD	Karns City
329	0.0	Lake-Lehman SD	Dallas
329	0.0	Marion Center Area SD	Marion Center
329	0.0	Mcguffey SD	Claysville
329	0.0	Midd-West SD	Middleburg
329	0.0	Mohawk Area SD	Bessemer
329	0.0	Moniteau SD	West Sunbury
329	0.0	Mount Pleasant Area SD	Mount Pleasant
329	0.0	Northern Tioga SD	Elkland
329	0.0	Oil City Area SD	Oil City
329	0.0	Pennsylvania Cyber CS	Midland
329	0.0	Saint Marys Area SD	Saint Marys
329	0.0	South Butler County SD	Saxonburg
329	0.0	Troy Area SD	Troy
329	0.0	Uniontown Area SD	Uniontown
329	0.0	West Perry SD	Elliottsburg
329	0.0	Yough SD	Herminie

Students Eligible for Free Lunch

Rank	Percent	District Name	City
1	84.5	Reading SD	Reading
2	84.0	Chester Community CS	Chester
3	79.5	Philadelphia City SD	Philadelphia
4	78.5	Harrisburg City SD	Harrisburg
5	68.2	Lancaster SD	Lancaster
5	68.2	Pittsburgh SD	Pittsburgh
7	67.3	Chester-Upland SD	Chester
8	66.2	Allentown City SD	Allentown
9	65.6	Greater Johnstown SD	Johnstown
10	65.0	Erie City SD	Erie
11	64.9	Lebanon SD	Lebanon
12	63.2	William Penn SD	Lansdowne
13	59.4	Sharon City SD	Sharon
14	58.8	Mckeesport Area SD	Mckeesport
15	58.2	Washington SD	Washington
16	57.6	Woodland Hills SD	Pittsburgh
17	56.8	Big Beaver Falls Area SD	Beaver Falls
18	55.7	Wilkes-Barre Area SD	Wilkes Barre
19	55.1	New Castle Area SD	New Castle

Note: This section only includes districts with 1,500 or more students; All categories are ranked from high to low

20	54.9	Norristown Area SD	Norristown	105	30.2	Yough SD	Herminie	190	19.6	Slippery Rock Area SD	Slippery Rock
21	54.7	Southeast Delco SD	Folcroft	106	30.1	Girard SD	Girard	191	19.5	Delaware Valley SD	Milford
22	52.7	Panther Valley SD	Lansford	106	30.1	Tyrone Area SD	Tyrone	192	19.4	Ephrata Area SD	Ephrata
23	52.4	Pottstown SD	Pottstown	108	30.0	Marion Center Area SD	Marion Center	193	19.3	Dover Area SD	Dover
24	51.4	Hazleton Area SD	Hazleton	108	30.0	Moniteau SD	West Sunbury	193	19.3	Gateway SD	Monroeville
25	51.1	Albert Gallatin Area SD	Uniontown	110	29.4	Karns City Area SD	Karns City	193	19.3	Shaler Area SD	Glenshaw
26	51.0	Carbondale Area SD	Carbondale	111	29.2	Bloomsburg Area SD	Bloomsburg	196	19.2	Ridley SD	Folsom
27	49.3	Scranton SD	Scranton	111	29.2	Somerset Area SD	Somerset	197	19.1	Susquenita SD	Duncannon
28	48.7	Brownsville Area SD	Brownsville	113	29.1	Freedom Area SD	Freedom	198	19.0	Bermudian Springs SD	York Springs
29	47.7	New Kensington-Arnold SD	New Kensington	113	29.1	North East SD	North East	198	19.0	General Mclane SD	Edinboro
30	47.4	Williamsport Area SD	Williamsport	115	29.0	Jim Thorpe Area SD	Jim Thorpe	200	18.7	North Pocono SD	Moscow
31	47.2	Steel Valley SD	Munhall	116	28.9	Pittston Area SD	Pittston	200	18.7	Octorara Area SD	Atglen
31	47.2	Uniontown Area SD	Uniontown	117	28.7	Bedford Area SD	Bedford	202	18.6	Greater Latrobe SD	Latrobe
33	46.6	York City SD	York	117	28.7	Brookville Area SD	Brookville	202	18.6	Lake-Lehman SD	Dallas
34	46.0	Agora Cyber CS	Wayne	119	28.5	Bensalem Township SD	Bensalem	202	18.6	Lewisburg Area SD	Lewisburg
35	44.4	Connellsville Area SD	Connellsville	120	28.4	North Schuylkill SD	Ashland	202	18.6	Warrior Run SD	Turbotville
36	44.1	Altoona Area SD	Altoona	121	28.2	Chestnut Ridge SD	Fishertown	206	18.5	Centennial SD	Warminster
37	43.9	Mount Union Area SD	Mount Union	122	27.8	Midd-West SD	Middleburg	206	18.5	Danville Area SD	Danville
38	43.3	Oil City Area SD	Oil City	123	27.5	Kennett Consolidated SD	Kennett Square	208	18.4	Central Valley SD	Monaca
39	43.1	East Allegheny SD	N Versailles	123	27.5	Kiski Area SD	Leechburg	209	18.2	Palmerton Area SD	Palmerton
39	43.1	Titusville Area SD	Titusville	123	27.5	Tunkhannock Area SD	Tunkhannock	209	18.2	Pen Argyl Area SD	Pen Argyl
41	42.9	Corry Area SD	Corry	126	27.3	Wayne Highlands SD	Honesdale	209	18.2	West Shore SD	New Cumberland
42	42.8	Greater Nanticoke Area SD	Nanticoke	127	27.2	Mount Pleasant Area SD	Mount Pleasant	212	17.7	Dunmore SD	Dunmore
43	42.0	Clearfield Area SD	Clearfield	128	26.9	Forest Hills SD	Sidman	212	17.7	East Pennsboro Area SD	Enola
44	41.8	Wyoming Valley West SD	Kingston	128	26.9	Gettysburg Area SD	Gettysburg	214	17.6	Cornwall-Lebanon SD	Lebanon
45	41.7	Highlands SD	Natrona Heights	130	26.8	Lehighton Area SD	Lehighton	214	17.6	Hopewell Area SD	Aliquippa
46	41.6	New Brighton Area SD	New Brighton	131	26.7	Fort Leboeuf SD	Waterford	216	17.5	Conrad Weiser Area SD	Robesonia
47	41.4	Laurel Highlands SD	Uniontown	131	26.7	Mcguffey SD	Claysville	217	17.4	Spring Grove Area SD	Spring Grove
47	41.4	Penn Hills SD	Pittsburgh	133	26.6	Bangor Area SD	Bangor	218	17.3	Eastern Lancaster County SD	New Holland
47	41.4	Shamokin Area SD	Coal Township	134	26.4	Oxford Area SD	Oxford	219	17.2	Mechanicsburg Area SD	Mechanicsburg
50	40.9	Lehigh Career & Technical Inst	Schnecksville	135	26.3	Juniata County SD	Mifflintown	220	17.1	Burrell SD	Lower Burrell
51	40.5	Bristol Township SD	Levittown	136	26.2	Wellsboro Area SD	Wellsboro	221	17.0	Trinity Area SD	Washington
52	40.3	Pottsville Area SD	Pottsville	137	26.1	Muhlenberg SD	Reading	222	16.9	Blackhawk SD	Beaver Falls
53	40.2	Hanover Area SD	Hanover Twp	138	25.9	Northern Lehigh SD	Slatington	223	16.7	Manheim Central SD	Manheim
54	40.1	Pocono Mountain SD	Swiftwater	139	25.6	Tamaqua Area SD	Tamaqua	223	16.7	Wyomissing Area SD	Wyomissing
55	39.5	Chichester SD	Aston	140	25.5	Mohawk Area SD	Bessemer	225	16.5	Phoenixville Area SD	Phoenixville
56	38.9	Northwestern SD	Albion	141	25.4	Jersey Shore Area SD	Jersey Shore	226	16.4	Chartiers Valley SD	Pittsburgh
57	38.0	Conneaut SD	Linesville	141	25.4	Saint Marys Area SD	Saint Marys	227	16.3	Montoursville Area SD	Montoursville
57	38.0	Franklin Area SD	Franklin	143	25.3	Ligonier Valley SD	Ligonier	228	16.1	Central Columbia SD	Bloomsburg
59	36.6	Northern Tioga SD	Elkland	143	25.3	Pequea Valley SD	Kinzers	229	15.6	Canon-Mcmillan SD	Canonsburg
60	36.4	Milton Area SD	Milton	143	25.3	Wattsburg Area SD	Erie	229	15.6	Governor Mifflin SD	Shillington
61	36.2	Upper Darby SD	Drexel Hill	146	25.2	Penn Cambria SD	Cresson	229	15.6	Hempfield Area SD	Greensburg
62	36.0	Philipsburg-Osceola Area SD	Philipsburg	147	25.1	Catasauqua Area SD	Catasauqua	229	15.6	Penn Manor SD	Lancaster
63	35.6	Mount Carmel Area SD	Mount Carmel	147	25.1	Middletown Area SD	Middletown	233	15.5	Hermitage SD	Hermitage
64	35.5	Riverside SD	Taylor	149	24.6	West York Area SD	York	234	15.4	Big Spring SD	Newville
64	35.5	South Allegheny SD	Mckeesport	150	24.5	Pine Grove Area SD	Pine Grove	234	15.4	Central York SD	York
66	35.0	Bradford Area SD	Bradford	150	24.5	Spring Cove SD	Roaring Spring	234	15.4	Eastern Lebanon County SD	Myerstown
66	35.0	Crawford Central SD	Meadville	152	24.2	Pleasant Valley SD	Brodheadsville	237	15.3	Deer Lakes SD	Russellton
66	35.0	Greensburg Salem SD	Greensburg	153	24.1	Belle Vernon Area SD	Belle Vernon	237	15.3	West Allegheny SD	Oakdale
69	34.9	Berwick Area SD	Berwick	154	23.9	Central Cambria SD	Ebensburg	237	15.3	Westmont Hilltop SD	Johnstown
69	34.9	Commonwealth Connections Acade	Harrisburg	154	23.9	Conewago Valley SD	New Oxford	240	14.8	Bald Eagle Area SD	Wingate
69	34.9	E Stroudsburg Area SD	E Stroudsburg	156	23.6	Northeastern York SD	Manchester	241	14.7	York Suburban SD	York
72	34.8	Central Greene SD	Waynesburg	157	23.5	Wyoming Area SD	Exeter	242	14.4	South Western SD	Hanover
72	34.8	Keystone Central SD	Lock Haven	158	23.4	Selinsgrove Area SD	Selinsgrove	243	14.2	Pennsylvania Virtual CS	Norristown
74	34.6	Charleroi SD	Charleroi	159	23.2	Hamburg Area SD	Hamburg	244	14.1	Greencastle-Antrim SD	Greencastle
74	34.6	Southmoreland SD	Scottdale	160	23.1	Waynesboro Area SD	Waynesboro	244	14.1	Kutztown Area SD	Kutztown
76	34.4	West Mifflin Area SD	West Mifflin	161	23.0	Carlisle Area SD	Carlisle	244	14.1	Schuylkill Valley SD	Leesport
77	34.2	York County School of Technology	York	162	22.9	Stroudsburg Area SD	Stroudsburg	247	13.9	Southern York County SD	Glen Rock
78	34.1	Towanda Area SD	Towanda	163	22.8	Butler Area SD	Butler	248	13.8	Brandywine Heights Area SD	Topton
79	34.0	Wallenpaupack Area SD	Hawley	163	22.8	Indiana Area SD	Indiana	248	13.8	Crestwood SD	Mountain Top
80	33.6	Troy Area SD	Troy	165	22.4	Mifflinburg Area SD	Mifflinburg	250	13.7	Blue Mountain SD	Orwigsburg
81	33.4	Dubois Area SD	Du Bois	166	22.0	Riverside Beaver County SD	Ellwood City	250	13.7	Fox Chapel Area SD	Pittsburgh
81	33.4	Hanover Public SD	Hanover	167	21.9	Baldwin-Whitehall SD	Pittsburgh	252	13.6	Quakertown Community SD	Quakertown
83	33.3	Blairsville-Saltsburg SD	Blairsville	168	21.8	Whitehall-Coplay SD	Whitehall	252	13.6	Warwick SD	Lititz
84	32.9	Derry Area SD	Derry	169	21.7	Keystone Oaks SD	Pittsburgh	254	13.5	Norwin SD	N Huntingdon
85	32.8	Punxsutawney Area SD	Punxsutawney	170	21.6	West Perry SD	Elliottsburg	255	13.4	North Hills SD	Pittsburgh
86	32.3	Pennsylvania Leadership Charter	West Chester	171	21.5	Tuscarora SD	Mercersburg	256	13.3	South Butler County SD	Saxonburg
87	32.0	Athens Area SD	Athens	172	21.4	Interboro SD	Prospect Park	257	13.2	Manheim Township SD	Lititz
88	31.7	Ringgold SD	New Eagle	173	21.2	Central Dauphin SD	Harrisburg	258	13.0	Twin Valley SD	Elverson
89	31.6	Mifflin County SD	Lewistown	173	21.2	Hollidaysburg Area SD	Hollidaysburg	259	12.8	Dallastown Area SD	Dallastown
90	31.5	Coatesville Area SD	Coatesville	173	21.2	Solanco SD	Quarryville	259	12.8	South Park SD	South Park
91	31.4	Mid Valley SD	Throop	176	21.1	Valley View SD	Archbald	259	12.8	Upper Merion Area SD	King of Prussia
92	31.3	Grove City Area SD	Grove City	177	20.9	Pottsgrove SD	Pottstown	259	12.8	Upper Perkiomen SD	Pennsburg
92	31.3	Penncrest SD	Saegertown	178	20.7	Bellefonte Area SD	Bellefonte	259	12.8	Wilson SD	West Lawn
92	31.3	Warren County SD	North Warren	178	20.7	Wilson Area SD	Easton	264	12.7	Freeport Area SD	Sarver
95	31.2	Easton Area SD	Easton	180	20.6	Susquehanna Township SD	Harrisburg	265	12.6	Lower Dauphin SD	Hummelstown
96	31.0	Armstrong SD	Ford City	181	20.5	East Lycoming SD	Hughesville	266	12.5	Cocalico SD	Denver
96	31.0	Western Wayne SD	South Canaan	182	20.4	Lakeland SD	Jermyn	266	12.5	Dallas SD	Dallas
98	30.8	Chambersburg Area SD	Chambersburg	183	20.3	Elizabeth Forward SD	Elizabeth	266	12.5	Fairview SD	Fairview
98	30.8	Shikellamy SD	Sunbury	184	20.2	Eastern York SD	Wrightsville	266	12.5	Salisbury Township SD	Allentown
100	30.7	Ambridge Area SD	Ambridge	184	20.2	Tulpehocken Area SD	Bethel	270	12.4	Annville-Cleona SD	Annville
100	30.7	Ellwood City Area SD	Ellwood City	186	20.1	Littlestown Area SD	Littlestown	270	12.4	Fleetwood Area SD	Fleetwood
100	30.7	Upper Adams SD	Biglerville	187	19.9	Conestoga Valley SD	Lancaster	272	12.3	Northampton Area SD	Northampton
103	30.6	Huntingdon Area SD	Huntingdon	188	19.8	Millcreek Township SD	Erie	272	12.3	Richland SD	Johnstown
104	30.3	Southern Tioga SD	Blossburg	189	19.7	Donegal SD	Mount Joy	272	12.3	South Eastern SD	Fawn Grove

Note: This section only includes districts with 1,500 or more students; All categories are ranked from high to low

Rank	Percent	District Name	City
272	12.3	State College Area SD	State College
276	12.2	North Penn SD	Lansdale
277	12.1	Neshaminy SD	Langhorne
277	12.1	Northern Lebanon SD	Fredericksburg
279	11.9	Harbor Creek SD	Harborcreek
280	11.8	Colonial SD	Plymth Meeting
280	11.8	Daniel Boone Area SD	Birdsboro
282	11.7	Upper Moreland Township SD	Willow Grove
283	11.6	Abington SD	Abington
283	11.6	Exeter Township SD	Reading
283	11.6	Penn-Delco SD	Aston
283	11.6	Red Lion Area SD	Red Lion
287	11.4	Elizabethtown Area SD	Elizabethtown
288	11.2	Moon Area SD	Moon Township
289	10.9	Hempfield SD	Landisville
290	10.7	Plum Borough SD	Plum
291	10.6	Quaker Valley SD	Sewickley
292	10.5	Beaver Area SD	Beaver
292	10.5	Oley Valley SD	Oley
294	10.0	Wissahickon SD	Ambler
295	9.9	East Penn SD	Emmaus
296	9.8	Derry Township SD	Hershey
296	9.8	Montour SD	Mckees Rocks
296	9.8	Palmyra Area SD	Palmyra
296	9.8	South Fayette Township SD	Mcdonald
296	9.8	South Middleton SD	Boiling Springs
301	9.7	Avon Grove SD	West Grove
302	9.6	Cheltenham Township SD	Elkins Park
302	9.6	Northern York County SD	Dillsburg
304	9.5	Saucon Valley SD	Hellertown
305	9.4	Souderton Area SD	Souderton
306	8.8	West Jefferson Hills SD	Jefferson Hills
307	8.7	Boyertown Area SD	Boyertown
308	8.5	Palisades SD	Kintnersville
308	8.5	Parkland SD	Allentown
310	8.3	Penn-Trafford SD	Harrison City
310	8.3	Pennridge SD	Perkasie
312	8.0	Lampeter-Strasburg SD	Lampeter
312	8.0	Pennsbury SD	Fallsington
312	8.0	Seneca Valley SD	Harmony
315	7.8	Owen J Roberts SD	Pottstown
316	7.6	Perkiomen Valley SD	Collegeville
317	7.5	Cumberland Valley SD	Mechanicsburg
317	7.5	Nazareth Area SD	Nazareth
319	7.0	Franklin Regional SD	Murrysville
320	6.9	Springfield Township SD	Oreland
321	6.7	Haverford Township SD	Havertown
321	6.7	Rose Tree Media SD	Media
321	6.7	West Chester Area SD	West Chester
324	6.5	Springfield SD	Springfield
325	6.3	Southern Lehigh SD	Center Valley
326	6.1	Spring-Ford Area SD	Royersford
327	5.9	Abington Heights SD	Clarks Summit
327	5.9	Bethel Park SD	Bethel Park
327	5.9	Marple Newtown SD	Newtown Square
330	5.8	Northwestern Lehigh SD	New Tripoli
331	5.6	Upper Dublin SD	Maple Glen
332	5.4	Hatboro-Horsham SD	Horsham
333	5.3	Mars Area SD	Mars
334	5.2	Great Valley SD	Malvern
334	5.2	Wallingford-Swarthmore SD	Wallingford
336	4.9	Mount Lebanon SD	Pittsburgh
337	4.6	Lower Merion SD	Ardmore
338	4.2	Hampton Township SD	Allison Park
339	4.0	Central Bucks SD	Doylestown
340	3.8	Downingtown Area SD	Downingtown
340	3.8	Pine-Richland SD	Gibsonia
340	3.8	Radnor Township SD	Wayne
343	3.7	Methacton SD	Norristown
344	3.0	Garnet Valley SD	Glen Mills
345	2.9	Lower Moreland Township SD	Huntingdon Vlly
346	2.7	Upper Saint Clair SD	Pittsburgh
347	2.2	North Allegheny SD	Pittsburgh
347	2.2	Peters Township SD	Mcmurray
349	1.9	New Hope-Solebury SD	New Hope
350	1.7	Council Rock SD	Newtown
351	1.1	Bethlehem Area SD	Bethlehem
352	0.8	Unionville-Chadds Ford SD	Kennett Square
353	0.1	Montrose Area SD	Montrose
n/a	n/a	Pennsylvania Cyber CS	Midland
n/a	n/a	Shippensburg Area SD	Shippensburg
n/a	n/a	Tredyffrin-Easttown SD	Wayne

Students Eligible for Reduced-Price Lunch

Rank	Percent	District Name	City
1	16.9	Agora Cyber CS	Wayne
2	16.2	Pennsylvania Leadership Charter	West Chester
3	16.0	Highlands SD	Natrona Heights
4	15.1	Spring Cove SD	Roaring Spring
5	14.7	Northern Tioga SD	Elkland
6	14.4	Forest Hills SD	Sidman
7	14.3	Southern Tioga SD	Blossburg
8	14.1	Fort Leboeuf SD	Waterford
8	14.1	Pennsylvania Virtual CS	Norristown
10	14.0	Marion Center Area SD	Marion Center
11	13.7	Brookville Area SD	Brookville
11	13.7	Jim Thorpe Area SD	Jim Thorpe
13	13.3	Commonwealth Connections Acade	Harrisburg
13	13.3	Mount Carmel Area SD	Mount Carmel
15	13.0	Bloomsburg Area SD	Bloomsburg
16	12.8	Conneaut SD	Linesville
16	12.8	Midd-West SD	Middleburg
16	12.8	Western Wayne SD	South Canaan
19	12.5	North Schuylkill SD	Ashland
19	12.5	Upper Adams SD	Biglerville
21	12.4	Penn Hills SD	Pittsburgh
21	12.4	Wallenpaupack Area SD	Hawley
23	12.2	Bedford Area SD	Bedford
23	12.2	Chestnut Ridge SD	Fishertown
23	12.2	Juniata County SD	Mifflintown
23	12.2	Mcguffey SD	Claysville
27	12.1	Corry Area SD	Corry
28	12.0	Girard SD	Girard
29	11.9	Mifflin County SD	Lewistown
30	11.8	Jersey Shore Area SD	Jersey Shore
30	11.8	Penn Cambria SD	Cresson
32	11.6	Philipsburg-Osceola Area SD	Philipsburg
33	11.5	Hanover Area SD	Hanover Twp
34	11.4	Freeport Area SD	Sarver
34	11.4	Moniteau SD	West Sunbury
36	11.3	Catasauqua Area SD	Catasauqua
36	11.3	Milton Area SD	Milton
36	11.3	Troy Area SD	Troy
39	11.2	Ellwood City Area SD	Ellwood City
39	11.2	Northeastern York SD	Manchester
39	11.2	Southeast Delco SD	Folcroft
42	11.1	Armstrong SD	Ford City
42	11.1	Lakeland SD	Jermyn
42	11.1	Spring Grove Area SD	Spring Grove
42	11.1	Wellsboro Area SD	Wellsboro
42	11.1	Wyoming Valley West SD	Kingston
47	11.0	Shamokin Area SD	Coal Township
47	11.0	Slippery Rock Area SD	Slippery Rock
47	11.0	Tuscarora SD	Mercersburg
47	11.0	Williamsport Area SD	Williamsport
51	10.9	Altoona Area SD	Altoona
52	10.8	E Stroudsburg Area SD	E Stroudsburg
52	10.8	Huntingdon Area SD	Huntingdon
52	10.8	Ligonier Valley SD	Ligonier
55	10.7	Blairsville-Saltsburg SD	Blairsville
55	10.7	Bristol Township SD	Levittown
55	10.7	Muhlenberg SD	Reading
55	10.7	Punxsutawney Area SD	Punxsutawney
59	10.6	Albert Gallatin Area SD	Uniontown
59	10.6	West Perry SD	Elliottsburg
61	10.5	Dover Area SD	Dover
61	10.5	Karns City Area SD	Karns City
61	10.5	North East SD	North East
61	10.5	Southmoreland SD	Scottdale
61	10.5	Susquenita SD	Duncannon
66	10.4	Clearfield Area SD	Clearfield
66	10.4	Franklin Area SD	Franklin
66	10.4	Greater Nanticoke Area SD	Nanticoke
66	10.4	Waynesboro Area SD	Waynesboro
66	10.4	Yough SD	Herminie
71	10.3	Freedom Area SD	Freedom
71	10.3	Keystone Central SD	Lock Haven
71	10.3	Pottsville Area SD	Pottsville
71	10.3	Wayne Highlands SD	Honesdale
71	10.3	William Penn SD	Lansdowne
76	10.2	Pequea Valley SD	Kinzers
76	10.2	Towanda Area SD	Towanda
76	10.2	York County School of Technology	York
79	10.1	Big Beaver Falls Area SD	Beaver Falls
79	10.1	Ephrata Area SD	Ephrata
79	10.1	Pine Grove Area SD	Pine Grove

Rank	Percent	District Name	City
82	10.0	Athens Area SD	Athens
82	10.0	Dubois Area SD	Du Bois
82	10.0	Selinsgrove Area SD	Selinsgrove
82	10.0	Titusville Area SD	Titusville
86	9.9	Derry Area SD	Derry
86	9.9	Pottstown SD	Pottstown
86	9.9	Warrior Run SD	Turbotville
89	9.8	Donegal SD	Mount Joy
89	9.8	Lancaster SD	Lancaster
89	9.8	Saint Marys Area SD	Saint Marys
92	9.7	Mount Pleasant Area SD	Mount Pleasant
92	9.7	South Allegheny SD	Mckeesport
92	9.7	Warren County SD	North Warren
95	9.6	East Lycoming SD	Hughesville
95	9.6	New Brighton Area SD	New Brighton
97	9.5	Shikellamy SD	Sunbury
98	9.4	Hazleton Area SD	Hazleton
98	9.4	Lebanon SD	Lebanon
98	9.4	Mifflinburg Area SD	Mifflinburg
98	9.4	Mount Union Area SD	Mount Union
98	9.4	Riverside Beaver County SD	Ellwood City
98	9.4	Wattsburg Area SD	Erie
98	9.4	West York Area SD	York
105	9.3	Central Cambria SD	Ebensburg
105	9.3	Middletown Area SD	Middletown
107	9.2	Berwick Area SD	Berwick
107	9.2	Cocalico SD	Denver
107	9.2	Connellsville Area SD	Connellsville
107	9.2	Laurel Highlands SD	Uniontown
107	9.2	Millcreek Township SD	Erie
107	9.2	Wyoming Area SD	Exeter
113	9.1	Hollidaysburg Area SD	Hollidaysburg
113	9.1	Penncrest SD	Saegertown
115	9.0	Ambridge Area SD	Ambridge
115	9.0	Greater Johnstown SD	Johnstown
115	9.0	Northern Lehigh SD	Slatington
115	9.0	Oxford Area SD	Oxford
115	9.0	Penn Manor SD	Lancaster
115	9.0	Pocono Mountain SD	Swiftwater
121	8.9	Somerset Area SD	Somerset
121	8.9	Susquehanna Township SD	Harrisburg
123	8.8	Eastern York SD	Wrightsville
123	8.8	Lehigh Career & Technical Inst	Schnecksville
123	8.8	Pittston Area SD	Pittston
123	8.8	Woodland Hills SD	Pittsburgh
127	8.7	Allentown City SD	Allentown
127	8.7	Conestoga Valley SD	Lancaster
127	8.7	Washington SD	Washington
127	8.7	Whitehall-Coplay SD	Whitehall
131	8.6	Bellefonte Area SD	Bellefonte
131	8.6	Lake-Lehman SD	Dallas
133	8.5	Keystone Oaks SD	Pittsburgh
133	8.5	Solanco SD	Quarryville
135	8.4	Baldwin-Whitehall SD	Pittsburgh
135	8.4	Bensalem Township SD	Bensalem
135	8.4	Mckeesport Area SD	Mckeesport
135	8.4	Riverside SD	Taylor
139	8.3	Burrell SD	Lower Burrell
139	8.3	Conewago Valley SD	New Oxford
139	8.3	Hamburg Area SD	Hamburg
139	8.3	Tulpehocken Area SD	Bethel
143	8.2	Bangor Area SD	Bangor
143	8.2	Bradford Area SD	Bradford
143	8.2	Eastern Lancaster County SD	New Holland
143	8.2	Hopewell Area SD	Aliquippa
143	8.2	Interboro SD	Prospect Park
143	8.2	Littlestown Area SD	Littlestown
143	8.2	Wilkes-Barre Area SD	Wilkes Barre
150	8.1	Bald Eagle Area SD	Wingate
150	8.1	Brownsville Area SD	Brownsville
150	8.1	Manheim Central SD	Manheim
150	8.1	Oil City Area SD	Oil City
150	8.1	Pen Argyl Area SD	Pen Argyl
150	8.1	Wilson Area SD	Easton
156	8.0	Chichester SD	Aston
156	8.0	East Allegheny SD	N Versailles
156	8.0	Erie City SD	Erie
156	8.0	Upper Darby SD	Drexel Hill
160	7.9	Big Spring SD	Newville
160	7.9	Elizabeth Forward SD	Elizabeth
160	7.9	South Western SD	Hanover
160	7.9	Tyrone Area SD	Tyrone
164	7.8	Danville Area SD	Danville
164	7.8	Kiski Area SD	Leechburg
164	7.8	Norristown Area SD	Norristown

Note: This section only includes districts with 1,500 or more students; All categories are ranked from high to low

Rank	Number	District Name	City
167	7.7	Bermudian Springs SD	York Springs
167	7.7	North Hills SD	Pittsburgh
167	7.7	Uniontown Area SD	Uniontown
167	7.7	Upper Perkiomen SD	Pennsburg
167	7.7	West Mifflin Area SD	West Mifflin
172	7.6	Central Dauphin SD	Harrisburg
172	7.6	Northwestern SD	Albion
174	7.5	Chambersburg Area SD	Chambersburg
174	7.5	Charleroi SD	Charleroi
174	7.5	Deer Lakes SD	Russellton
174	7.5	General Mclane SD	Edinboro
174	7.5	Pleasant Valley SD	Brodheadsville
179	7.4	Lehighton Area SD	Lehighton
179	7.4	Steel Valley SD	Munhall
179	7.4	Tunkhannock Area SD	Tunkhannock
182	7.3	Indiana Area SD	Indiana
183	7.2	Carbondale Area SD	Carbondale
183	7.2	Palmerton Area SD	Palmerton
185	7.1	Reading SD	Reading
185	7.1	Ringgold SD	New Eagle
185	7.1	Twin Valley SD	Elverson
185	7.1	Westmont Hilltop SD	Johnstown
189	7.0	Conrad Weiser Area SD	Robesonia
189	7.0	Gettysburg Area SD	Gettysburg
189	7.0	Governor Mifflin SD	Shillington
189	7.0	Kennett Consolidated SD	Kennett Square
189	7.0	Sharon City SD	Sharon
194	6.9	East Pennsboro Area SD	Enola
194	6.9	Mohawk Area SD	Bessemer
196	6.7	Chartiers Valley SD	Pittsburgh
196	6.7	Coatesville Area SD	Coatesville
198	6.6	Harbor Creek SD	Harborcreek
198	6.6	Lampeter-Strasburg SD	Lampeter
198	6.6	Norwin SD	N Huntingdon
201	6.5	Crawford Central SD	Meadville
201	6.5	Easton Area SD	Easton
203	6.4	Annville-Cleona SD	Annville
203	6.4	Carlisle Area SD	Carlisle
203	6.4	New Kensington-Arnold SD	New Kensington
206	6.3	Beaver Area SD	Beaver
206	6.3	Grove City Area SD	Grove City
206	6.3	Scranton SD	Scranton
206	6.3	Shaler Area SD	Glenshaw
210	6.2	Central Greene SD	Waynesburg
210	6.2	Cornwall-Lebanon SD	Lebanon
210	6.2	Delaware Valley SD	Milford
210	6.2	Greater Latrobe SD	Latrobe
210	6.2	Kutztown Area SD	Kutztown
215	6.1	Belle Vernon Area SD	Belle Vernon
215	6.1	Eastern Lebanon County SD	Myerstown
215	6.1	Gateway SD	Monroeville
215	6.1	Plum Borough SD	Plum
215	6.1	Quakertown Community SD	Quakertown
215	6.1	Red Lion Area SD	Red Lion
221	6.0	Central Columbia SD	Bloomsburg
221	6.0	Hanover Public SD	Hanover
221	6.0	Northampton Area SD	Northampton
221	6.0	Tamaqua Area SD	Tamaqua
225	5.9	Blackhawk SD	Beaver Falls
225	5.9	Centennial SD	Warminster
225	5.9	Fairview SD	Fairview
225	5.9	Pittsburgh SD	Pittsburgh
225	5.9	Warwick SD	Lititz
230	5.8	Hempfield Area SD	Greensburg
230	5.8	Mid Valley SD	Throop
230	5.8	Octorara Area SD	Atglen
233	5.7	Stroudsburg Area SD	Stroudsburg
234	5.6	Hempfield SD	Landisville
234	5.6	South Butler County SD	Saxonburg
236	5.5	Central York SD	York
236	5.5	Exeter Township SD	Reading
236	5.5	Ridley SD	Folsom
236	5.5	South Park SD	South Park
236	5.5	West Allegheny SD	Oakdale
236	5.5	York Suburban SD	York
242	5.4	Canon-Mcmillan SD	Canonsburg
242	5.4	Elizabethtown Area SD	Elizabethtown
242	5.4	Greencastle-Antrim SD	Greencastle
242	5.4	Harrisburg City SD	Harrisburg
246	5.3	East Penn SD	Emmaus
246	5.3	Montoursville Area SD	Montoursville
246	5.3	Trinity Area SD	Washington
249	5.2	Dallastown Area SD	Dallastown
249	5.2	New Castle Area SD	New Castle
249	5.2	North Pocono SD	Moscow
249	5.2	Northern Lebanon SD	Fredericksburg
249	5.2	Oley Valley SD	Oley
249	5.2	Richland SD	Johnstown
249	5.2	South Eastern SD	Fawn Grove
256	5.1	Butler Area SD	Butler
256	5.1	Pottsgrove SD	Pottstown
258	5.0	Boyertown Area SD	Boyertown
258	5.0	Chester Community CS	Chester
258	5.0	Lower Dauphin SD	Hummelstown
258	5.0	Salisbury Township SD	Allentown
258	5.0	West Shore SD	New Cumberland
263	4.9	Cheltenham Township SD	Elkins Park
263	4.9	Mechanicsburg Area SD	Mechanicsburg
263	4.9	Wilson SD	West Lawn
266	4.8	Blue Mountain SD	Orwigsburg
266	4.8	Central Valley SD	Monaca
266	4.8	Hermitage SD	Hermitage
269	4.7	Palmyra Area SD	Palmyra
269	4.7	Pennridge SD	Perkasie
269	4.7	Upper Moreland Township SD	Willow Grove
272	4.6	Fleetwood Area SD	Fleetwood
272	4.6	Valley View SD	Archbald
274	4.5	Daniel Boone Area SD	Birdsboro
274	4.5	Montour SD	Mckees Rocks
274	4.5	Neshaminy SD	Langhorne
274	4.5	Upper Merion Area SD	King of Prussia
278	4.4	Manheim Township SD	Lititz
278	4.4	Saucon Valley SD	Hellertown
280	4.3	Schuylkill Valley SD	Leesport
281	4.2	Abington SD	Abington
281	4.2	Crestwood SD	Mountain Top
281	4.2	Dallas SD	Dallas
281	4.2	North Penn SD	Lansdale
281	4.2	Penn-Delco SD	Aston
281	4.2	Quaker Valley SD	Sewickley
287	4.1	Brandywine Heights Area SD	Topton
287	4.1	Greensburg Salem SD	Greensburg
287	4.1	Northern York County SD	Dillsburg
287	4.1	Parkland SD	Allentown
287	4.1	Southern York County SD	Glen Rock
292	3.9	Chester-Upland SD	Chester
292	3.9	Dunmore SD	Dunmore
292	3.9	Owen J Roberts SD	Pottstown
292	3.9	Souderton Area SD	Souderton
292	3.9	West Jefferson Hills SD	Jefferson Hills
297	3.8	Palisades SD	Kintnersville
297	3.8	Phoenixville Area SD	Phoenixville
299	3.7	Franklin Regional SD	Murrysville
300	3.6	Cumberland Valley SD	Mechanicsburg
300	3.6	Hampton Township SD	Allison Park
300	3.6	Lewisburg Area SD	Lewisburg
300	3.6	Penn-Trafford SD	Harrison City
300	3.6	State College Area SD	State College
300	3.6	Wyomissing Area SD	Wyomissing
306	3.5	Colonial SD	Plymth Meeting
306	3.5	Hatboro-Horsham SD	Horsham
306	3.5	Moon Area SD	Moon Township
309	3.4	Northwestern Lehigh SD	New Tripoli
309	3.4	Pennsbury SD	Fallsington
309	3.4	South Middleton SD	Boiling Springs
309	3.4	Southern Lehigh SD	Center Valley
313	3.3	Abington Heights SD	Clarks Summit
313	3.3	Seneca Valley SD	Harmony
315	3.2	Derry Township SD	Hershey
315	3.2	Marple Newtown SD	Newtown Square
315	3.2	Nazareth Area SD	Nazareth
315	3.2	York City SD	York
319	3.0	Springfield SD	Springfield
320	2.9	Fox Chapel Area SD	Pittsburgh
320	2.9	Mars Area SD	Mars
320	2.9	Rose Tree Media SD	Media
320	2.9	South Fayette Township SD	Mcdonald
324	2.7	Haverford Township SD	Havertown
325	2.6	Bethel Park SD	Bethel Park
325	2.6	Perkiomen Valley SD	Collegeville
325	2.6	Springfield Township SD	Oreland
328	2.5	Spring-Ford Area SD	Royersford
328	2.5	Wissahickon SD	Ambler
330	2.3	Lower Merion SD	Ardmore
331	2.1	Great Valley SD	Malvern
331	2.1	Philadelphia City SD	Philadelphia
333	2.0	Avon Grove SD	West Grove
333	2.0	Upper Dublin SD	Maple Glen
335	1.9	Central Bucks SD	Doylestown
335	1.9	Wallingford-Swarthmore SD	Wallingford
337	1.8	North Allegheny SD	Pittsburgh
337	1.8	West Chester Area SD	West Chester
339	1.7	Garnet Valley SD	Glen Mills
339	1.7	Lower Moreland Township SD	Huntingdon Vlly
339	1.7	Pine-Richland SD	Gibsonia
342	1.6	Mount Lebanon SD	Pittsburgh
343	1.5	Upper Saint Clair SD	Pittsburgh
344	1.1	Downingtown Area SD	Downingtown
345	1.0	Methacton SD	Norristown
346	0.9	Council Rock SD	Newtown
347	0.8	Radnor Township SD	Wayne
348	0.6	Peters Township SD	Mcmurray
348	0.6	Unionville-Chadds Ford SD	Kennett Square
350	0.2	New Hope-Solebury SD	New Hope
351	0.1	Bethlehem Area SD	Bethlehem
352	0.0	Montrose Area SD	Montrose
352	0.0	Panther Valley SD	Lansford
n/a	n/a	Pennsylvania Cyber CS	Midland
n/a	n/a	Shippensburg Area SD	Shippensburg
n/a	n/a	Tredyffrin-Easttown SD	Wayne

Student/Teacher Ratio

(number of students per teacher)

Rank	Number	District Name	City
1	10.8	Fox Chapel Area SD	Pittsburgh
2	10.9	Northern Tioga SD	Elkland
3	11.1	Lower Merion SD	Ardmore
4	11.2	Pocono Mountain SD	Swiftwater
5	11.4	Harrisburg City SD	Harrisburg
6	11.5	Washington SD	Washington
7	11.7	Kutztown Area SD	Kutztown
8	11.8	Danville Area SD	Danville
9	11.9	Huntingdon Area SD	Huntingdon
9	11.9	Tulpehocken Area SD	Bethel
11	12.0	Central Greene SD	Waynesburg
11	12.0	Penn Hills SD	Pittsburgh
11	12.0	Tunkhannock Area SD	Tunkhannock
14	12.1	Chichester SD	Aston
14	12.1	Middletown Area SD	Middletown
14	12.1	Pequea Valley SD	Kinzers
14	12.1	South Eastern SD	Fawn Grove
18	12.2	Riverside SD	Taylor
18	12.2	Springfield Township SD	Oreland
20	12.3	Cheltenham Township SD	Elkins Park
20	12.3	Garnet Valley SD	Glen Mills
20	12.3	Indiana Area SD	Indiana
20	12.3	Montrose Area SD	Montrose
20	12.3	Pine Grove Area SD	Pine Grove
20	12.3	Warren County SD	North Warren
20	12.3	Woodland Hills SD	Pittsburgh
27	12.4	Rose Tree Media SD	Media
28	12.5	Big Spring SD	Newville
28	12.5	Deer Lakes SD	Russellton
28	12.5	Pittsburgh SD	Pittsburgh
28	12.5	Southern Tioga SD	Blossburg
28	12.5	Steel Valley SD	Munhall
28	12.5	Wissahickon SD	Ambler
34	12.6	Big Beaver Falls Area SD	Beaver Falls
34	12.6	Bloomsburg Area SD	Bloomsburg
34	12.6	Midd-West SD	Middleburg
34	12.6	Phoenixville Area SD	Phoenixville
34	12.6	Pottstown SD	Pottstown
39	12.7	Bristol Township SD	Levittown
39	12.7	Colonial SD	Plymth Meeting
39	12.7	Harbor Creek SD	Harborcreek
39	12.7	Lake-Lehman SD	Dallas
39	12.7	Mifflin County SD	Lewistown
39	12.7	Milton Area SD	Milton
39	12.7	Radnor Township SD	Wayne
39	12.7	State College Area SD	State College
39	12.7	Susquenita SD	Duncannon
39	12.7	Uniontown Area SD	Uniontown
39	12.7	Warrior Run SD	Turbotville
50	12.8	Bald Eagle Area SD	Wingate
50	12.8	Brandywine Heights Area SD	Topton
50	12.8	Coatesville Area SD	Coatesville
50	12.8	Corry Area SD	Corry
50	12.8	Eastern York SD	Wrightsville
50	12.8	Erie City SD	Erie
50	12.8	Mount Union Area SD	Mount Union
50	12.8	Norristown Area SD	Norristown
50	12.8	South Middleton SD	Boiling Springs
50	12.8	Stroudsburg Area SD	Stroudsburg

Note: This section only includes districts with 1,500 or more students; All categories are ranked from high to low

50	12.8	Wellsboro Area SD	Wellsboro
50	12.8	Williamsport Area SD	Williamsport
62	12.9	Pleasant Valley SD	Brodheadsville
62	12.9	Shaler Area SD	Glenshaw
62	12.9	Upper Dublin SD	Maple Glen
62	12.9	Wallingford-Swarthmore SD	Wallingford
62	12.9	Waynesboro Area SD	Waynesboro
67	13.0	Bellefonte Area SD	Bellefonte
67	13.0	Berwick Area SD	Berwick
67	13.0	Bethel Park SD	Bethel Park
67	13.0	Blackhawk SD	Beaver Falls
67	13.0	E Stroudsburg Area SD	E Stroudsburg
67	13.0	Franklin Area SD	Franklin
67	13.0	Highlands SD	Natrona Heights
67	13.0	Mckeesport Area SD	Mckeesport
67	13.0	Montour SD	Mckees Rocks
67	13.0	North Hills SD	Pittsburgh
67	13.0	Quaker Valley SD	Sewickley
67	13.0	Western Wayne SD	South Canaan
79	13.1	Bradford Area SD	Bradford
79	13.1	Catasauqua Area SD	Catasauqua
79	13.1	Central Dauphin SD	Harrisburg
79	13.1	Gateway SD	Monroeville
79	13.1	Hanover Public SD	Hanover
79	13.1	Lower Dauphin SD	Hummelstown
79	13.1	Marion Center Area SD	Marion Center
86	13.2	Athens Area SD	Athens
86	13.2	Brookville Area SD	Brookville
86	13.2	Elizabeth Forward SD	Elizabeth
86	13.2	Lancaster SD	Lancaster
86	13.2	Marple Newtown SD	Newtown Square
86	13.2	Mifflinburg Area SD	Mifflinburg
86	13.2	Palisades SD	Kintnersville
86	13.2	West Mifflin Area SD	West Mifflin
86	13.2	West Shore SD	New Cumberland
86	13.2	York City SD	York
96	13.3	Armstrong SD	Ford City
96	13.3	Hatboro-Horsham SD	Horsham
96	13.3	Lewisburg Area SD	Lewisburg
96	13.3	Mohawk Area SD	Bessemer
96	13.3	Penncrest SD	Saegertown
96	13.3	Philipsburg-Osceola Area SD	Philipsburg
96	13.3	Ringgold SD	New Eagle
96	13.3	Salisbury Township SD	Allentown
96	13.3	Susquehanna Township SD	Harrisburg
96	13.3	West Perry SD	Elliottsburg
106	13.4	Clearfield Area SD	Clearfield
106	13.4	East Pennsboro Area SD	Enola
106	13.4	Easton Area SD	Easton
106	13.4	Lehighton Area SD	Lehighton
106	13.4	Mount Lebanon SD	Pittsburgh
106	13.4	North Schuylkill SD	Ashland
106	13.4	Punxsutawney Area SD	Punxsutawney
106	13.4	Titusville Area SD	Titusville
114	13.5	Crawford Central SD	Meadville
114	13.5	Dubois Area SD	Du Bois
114	13.5	East Lycoming SD	Hughesville
114	13.5	Fleetwood Area SD	Fleetwood
114	13.5	Keystone Central SD	Lock Haven
114	13.5	Mechanicsburg Area SD	Mechanicsburg
114	13.5	Moon Area SD	Moon Township
114	13.5	New Hope-Solebury SD	New Hope
114	13.5	Penn Cambria SD	Cresson
114	13.5	Scranton SD	Scranton
114	13.5	Somerset Area SD	Somerset
114	13.5	South Allegheny SD	Mckeesport
126	13.6	Charleroi SD	Charleroi
126	13.6	Hollidaysburg Area SD	Hollidaysburg
126	13.6	Interboro SD	Prospect Park
126	13.6	Jersey Shore Area SD	Jersey Shore
126	13.6	Lower Moreland Township SD	Huntingdon Vlly
126	13.6	Methacton SD	Norristown
126	13.6	Montoursville Area SD	Montoursville
126	13.6	Owen J Roberts SD	Pottstown
134	13.7	Blue Mountain SD	Orwigsburg
134	13.7	New Castle Area SD	New Castle
134	13.7	Northeastern York SD	Manchester
134	13.7	Oley Valley SD	Oley
134	13.7	Seneca Valley SD	Harmony
134	13.7	Troy Area SD	Troy
134	13.7	Wayne Highlands SD	Honesdale
134	13.7	West York Area SD	York
134	13.7	York Suburban SD	York
143	13.8	Bangor Area SD	Bangor
143	13.8	Gettysburg Area SD	Gettysburg
143	13.8	Great Valley SD	Malvern
143	13.8	Northwestern SD	Albion
143	13.8	Ridley SD	Folsom
143	13.8	Twin Valley SD	Elverson
143	13.8	Wilson Area SD	Easton
143	13.8	York County School of Technology	York
151	13.9	Abington Heights SD	Clarks Summit
151	13.9	Chartiers Valley SD	Pittsburgh
151	13.9	Conrad Weiser Area SD	Robesonia
151	13.9	Manheim Central SD	Manheim
151	13.9	Mcguffey SD	Claysville
151	13.9	Mount Pleasant Area SD	Mount Pleasant
151	13.9	North Penn SD	Lansdale
151	13.9	Saucon Valley SD	Hellertown
151	13.9	Southmoreland SD	Scottdale
151	13.9	Spring-Ford Area SD	Royersford
151	13.9	Wilkes-Barre Area SD	Wilkes Barre
162	14.0	Albert Gallatin Area SD	Uniontown
162	14.0	Carlisle Area SD	Carlisle
162	14.0	General Mclane SD	Edinboro
162	14.0	North Allegheny SD	Pittsburgh
162	14.0	Northern York County SD	Dillsburg
162	14.0	Southern York County SD	Glen Rock
162	14.0	Unionville-Chadds Ford SD	Kennett Square
162	14.0	Upper Merion Area SD	King of Prussia
162	14.0	West Allegheny SD	Oakdale
171	14.1	Greater Johnstown SD	Johnstown
171	14.1	Juniata County SD	Mifflintown
171	14.1	Keystone Oaks SD	Pittsburgh
171	14.1	Northern Lehigh SD	Slatington
171	14.1	Pottsgrove SD	Pottstown
171	14.1	Souderton Area SD	Souderton
171	14.1	Tredyffrin-Easttown SD	Wayne
171	14.1	Upper Darby SD	Drexel Hill
179	14.2	Central Columbia SD	Bloomsburg
179	14.2	Chestnut Ridge SD	Fishertown
179	14.2	Cocalico SD	Denver
179	14.2	Council Rock SD	Newtown
179	14.2	Derry Area SD	Derry
179	14.2	Ellwood City Area SD	Ellwood City
179	14.2	Girard SD	Girard
179	14.2	Hamburg Area SD	Hamburg
179	14.2	Northwestern Lehigh SD	New Tripoli
188	14.3	Abington SD	Abington
188	14.3	Blairsville-Saltsburg SD	Blairsville
188	14.3	Brownsville Area SD	Brownsville
188	14.3	Carbondale Area SD	Carbondale
188	14.3	Conneaut SD	Linesville
188	14.3	Forest Hills SD	Sidman
188	14.3	Fort Leboeuf SD	Waterford
188	14.3	Jim Thorpe Area SD	Jim Thorpe
188	14.3	New Brighton Area SD	New Brighton
188	14.3	Northern Lebanon SD	Fredericksburg
188	14.3	Pennsbury SD	Fallsington
188	14.3	Selinsgrove Area SD	Selinsgrove
188	14.3	Sharon City SD	Sharon
188	14.3	West Chester Area SD	West Chester
202	14.4	Bensalem Township SD	Bensalem
202	14.4	Connellsville Area SD	Connellsville
202	14.4	Derry Township SD	Hershey
202	14.4	Littlestown Area SD	Littlestown
202	14.4	Penn Manor SD	Lancaster
202	14.4	Pine-Richland SD	Gibsonia
202	14.4	Riverside Beaver County SD	Ellwood City
209	14.5	Delaware Valley SD	Milford
209	14.5	Downingtown Area SD	Downingtown
209	14.5	North East SD	North East
209	14.5	Panther Valley SD	Lansford
209	14.5	Schuylkill Valley SD	Leesport
209	14.5	Southeast Delco SD	Folcroft
209	14.5	Spring Grove Area SD	Spring Grove
216	14.6	Karns City Area SD	Karns City
216	14.6	Laurel Highlands SD	Uniontown
216	14.6	Northampton Area SD	Northampton
216	14.6	Shamokin Area SD	Coal Township
216	14.6	Trinity Area SD	Washington
221	14.7	Butler Area SD	Butler
221	14.7	Cornwall-Lebanon SD	Lebanon
221	14.7	Cumberland Valley SD	Mechanicsburg
221	14.7	Mount Carmel Area SD	Mount Carmel
221	14.7	Neshaminy SD	Langhorne
221	14.7	Spring Cove SD	Roaring Spring
221	14.7	Tyrone Area SD	Tyrone
221	14.7	Upper Adams SD	Biglerville
221	14.7	Upper Moreland Township SD	Willow Grove
221	14.7	Upper Saint Clair SD	Pittsburgh
231	14.8	Centennial SD	Warminster
231	14.8	Exeter Township SD	Reading
231	14.8	Franklin Regional SD	Murrysville
231	14.8	Kennett Consolidated SD	Kennett Square
231	14.8	Manheim Township SD	Lititz
231	14.8	Oil City Area SD	Oil City
231	14.8	Pen Argyl Area SD	Pen Argyl
231	14.8	Wilson SD	West Lawn
239	14.9	Bethlehem Area SD	Bethlehem
239	14.9	Central Cambria SD	Ebensburg
239	14.9	Dallastown Area SD	Dallastown
239	14.9	Grove City Area SD	Grove City
239	14.9	Hanover Area SD	Hanover Twp
239	14.9	Hempfield Area SD	Greensburg
239	14.9	Philadelphia City SD	Philadelphia
239	14.9	Springfield SD	Springfield
247	15.0	Allentown City SD	Allentown
247	15.0	Freedom Area SD	Freedom
247	15.0	Nazareth Area SD	Nazareth
247	15.0	Penn-Delco SD	Aston
247	15.0	Pennsylvania Leadership Charter	West Chester
247	15.0	Southern Lehigh SD	Center Valley
247	15.0	Wattsburg Area SD	Erie
254	15.1	Altoona Area SD	Altoona
254	15.1	Conestoga Valley SD	Lancaster
254	15.1	Freeport Area SD	Sarver
254	15.1	Muhlenberg SD	Reading
254	15.1	Plum Borough SD	Plum
254	15.1	Towanda Area SD	Towanda
254	15.1	Wyoming Valley West SD	Kingston
261	15.2	Bedford Area SD	Bedford
261	15.2	Eastern Lancaster County SD	New Holland
261	15.2	Hempfield SD	Landisville
261	15.2	Hermitage SD	Hermitage
261	15.2	Lakeland SD	Jermyn
261	15.2	Lampeter-Strasburg SD	Lampeter
261	15.2	Palmyra Area SD	Palmyra
261	15.2	Red Lion Area SD	Red Lion
261	15.2	Tuscarora SD	Mercersburg
261	15.2	Upper Perkiomen SD	Pennsburg
271	15.3	Annville-Cleona SD	Annville
271	15.3	Bermudian Springs SD	York Springs
271	15.3	Lebanon SD	Lebanon
271	15.3	New Kensington-Arnold SD	New Kensington
271	15.3	North Pocono SD	Moscow
271	15.3	South Western SD	Hanover
271	15.3	Warwick SD	Lititz
278	15.4	Boyertown Area SD	Boyertown
278	15.4	East Allegheny SD	N Versailles
278	15.4	Elizabethtown Area SD	Elizabethtown
278	15.4	Governor Mifflin SD	Shillington
278	15.4	Oxford Area SD	Oxford
278	15.4	Saint Marys Area SD	Saint Marys
278	15.4	Valley View SD	Archbald
285	15.5	Hopewell Area SD	Aliquippa
285	15.5	Quakertown Community SD	Quakertown
285	15.5	Reading SD	Reading
288	15.6	Chambersburg Area SD	Chambersburg
288	15.6	Eastern Lebanon County SD	Myerstown
288	15.6	Moniteau SD	West Sunbury
288	15.6	Shippensburg Area SD	Shippensburg
288	15.6	Solanco SD	Quarryville
293	15.7	Dover Area SD	Dover
293	15.7	Dunmore SD	Dunmore
293	15.7	Pennridge SD	Perkasie
293	15.7	Pottsville Area SD	Pottsville
293	15.7	Slippery Rock Area SD	Slippery Rock
293	15.7	Yough SD	Herminie
299	15.8	Burrell SD	Lower Burrell
299	15.8	Central York SD	York
299	15.8	Fairview SD	Fairview
299	15.8	Mars Area SD	Mars
299	15.8	Wyoming Area SD	Exeter
304	15.9	Ephrata Area SD	Ephrata
304	15.9	Greensburg Salem SD	Greensburg
304	15.9	South Park SD	South Park
307	16.0	Beaver Area SD	Beaver
307	16.0	Hazleton Area SD	Hazleton
307	16.0	Perkiomen Valley SD	Collegeville
307	16.0	Pittston Area SD	Pittston
307	16.0	Westmont Hilltop SD	Johnstown
312	16.1	Canon-Mcmillan SD	Canonsburg
312	16.1	Chester Community CS	Chester
312	16.1	Dallas SD	Dallas

Note: This section only includes districts with 1,500 or more students; All categories are ranked from high to low

312	16.1	William Penn SD	Lansdowne
316	16.2	Baldwin-Whitehall SD	Pittsburgh
316	16.2	Belle Vernon Area SD	Belle Vernon
316	16.2	Palmerton Area SD	Palmerton
319	16.3	Avon Grove SD	West Grove
319	16.3	Daniel Boone Area SD	Birdsboro
319	16.3	Whitehall-Coplay SD	Whitehall
322	16.4	Ambridge Area SD	Ambridge
322	16.4	Parkland SD	Allentown
322	16.4	South Butler County SD	Saxonburg
325	16.5	Chester-Upland SD	Chester
325	16.5	Wallenpaupack Area SD	Hawley
327	16.7	East Penn SD	Emmaus
327	16.7	Greater Latrobe SD	Latrobe
329	16.8	Central Valley SD	Monaca
329	16.8	Peters Township SD	Mcmurray
329	16.8	Shikellamy SD	Sunbury
329	16.8	Wyomissing Area SD	Wyomissing
333	17.0	Central Bucks SD	Doylestown
333	17.0	Greater Nanticoke Area SD	Nanticoke
333	17.0	Kiski Area SD	Leechburg
333	17.0	Norwin SD	N Huntingdon
337	17.2	West Jefferson Hills SD	Jefferson Hills
338	17.3	Conewago Valley SD	New Oxford
339	17.4	Penn-Trafford SD	Harrison City
340	17.5	Richland SD	Johnstown
341	17.6	Octorara Area SD	Atglen
342	18.1	Ligonier Valley SD	Ligonier
343	18.2	Crestwood SD	Mountain Top
344	18.3	Haverford Township SD	Havertown
345	18.8	Donegal SD	Mount Joy
346	18.9	Mid Valley SD	Throop
346	18.9	Tamaqua Area SD	Tamaqua
348	19.8	Greencastle-Antrim SD	Greencastle
349	20.6	Millcreek Township SD	Erie
350	21.6	Hampton Township SD	Allison Park
351	22.4	South Fayette Township SD	Mcdonald
352	23.0	Agora Cyber CS	Wayne
353	26.6	Commonwealth Connections Acade	Harrisburg
354	27.8	Lehigh Career & Technical Inst	Schnecksville
355	30.5	Pennsylvania Virtual CS	Norristown
356	55.1	Pennsylvania Cyber CS	Midland

Student/Librarian Ratio

(number of students per librarian)

Rank	Number	District Name	City
1	391.5	New Hope-Solebury SD	New Hope
2	402.0	Kutztown Area SD	Kutztown
3	414.2	Bristol Township SD	Levittown
4	417.3	Salisbury Township SD	Allentown
5	424.2	Conneaut SD	Linesville
6	438.0	Big Beaver Falls Area SD	Beaver Falls
7	455.6	Athens Area SD	Athens
8	459.8	Steel Valley SD	Munhall
9	465.3	Ligonier Valley SD	Ligonier
10	471.8	Indiana Area SD	Indiana
11	475.9	Middletown Area SD	Middletown
12	476.3	Lewisburg Area SD	Lewisburg
13	483.5	Brownsville Area SD	Brownsville
14	484.6	Blairsville-Saltsburg SD	Blairsville
15	495.8	Philipsburg-Osceola Area SD	Philipsburg
16	507.3	Quaker Valley SD	Sewickley
17	507.8	Ephrata Area SD	Ephrata
17	507.8	Forest Hills SD	Sidman
19	509.7	Wellsboro Area SD	Wellsboro
20	510.5	Southmoreland SD	Scottdale
21	513.6	Warren County SD	North Warren
22	515.7	Tulpehocken Area SD	Bethel
23	516.8	Southern Tioga SD	Blossburg
24	517.8	Springfield Township SD	Oreland
25	521.1	Freeport Area SD	Sarver
26	521.7	Annville-Cleona SD	Annville
27	526.3	Troy Area SD	Troy
28	529.3	Freedom Area SD	Freedom
29	530.0	Mount Lebanon SD	Pittsburgh
30	531.3	Huntingdon Area SD	Huntingdon
31	533.6	Northeastern York SD	Manchester
32	536.0	Riverside Beaver County SD	Ellwood City
33	538.0	Wattsburg Area SD	Erie
34	538.3	Catasauqua Area SD	Catasauqua
35	539.7	Fairview SD	Fairview
36	540.2	State College Area SD	State College
37	541.1	Upper Merion Area SD	King of Prussia
38	542.0	Palisades SD	Kintnersville
39	545.7	Northwestern SD	Albion
40	547.5	Midd-West SD	Middleburg
41	548.3	Hanover Public SD	Hanover
42	549.0	Pine Grove Area SD	Pine Grove
43	550.6	Belle Vernon Area SD	Belle Vernon
44	551.2	Manheim Township SD	Lititz
45	551.3	Keystone Oaks SD	Pittsburgh
46	551.5	South Middleton SD	Boiling Springs
47	553.0	Towanda Area SD	Towanda
48	553.7	Panther Valley SD	Lansford
49	556.2	Lancaster SD	Lancaster
50	557.3	Warrior Run SD	Turbotville
51	562.3	Bloomsburg Area SD	Bloomsburg
52	564.3	Bedford Area SD	Bedford
52	564.3	Montrose Area SD	Montrose
54	572.0	Saint Marys Area SD	Saint Marys
55	574.8	Manheim Central SD	Manheim
56	577.3	New Brighton Area SD	New Brighton
57	580.0	Crawford Central SD	Meadville
58	580.7	Marple Newtown SD	Newtown Square
59	581.0	Pittston Area SD	Pittston
60	583.0	North East SD	North East
61	583.1	North Allegheny SD	Pittsburgh
62	585.4	Upper Saint Clair SD	Pittsburgh
63	589.1	Abington SD	Abington
64	590.0	Palmyra Area SD	Palmyra
65	594.0	Pequea Valley SD	Kinzers
66	595.5	Bethel Park SD	Bethel Park
67	596.2	Susquehanna Township SD	Harrisburg
68	596.8	Quakertown Community SD	Quakertown
69	597.6	Greensburg Salem SD	Greensburg
70	599.4	Wayne Highlands SD	Honesdale
71	599.5	Penncrest SD	Saegertown
72	600.0	Brandywine Heights Area SD	Topton
73	601.0	Pittsburgh SD	Pittsburgh
74	607.1	Cocalico SD	Denver
75	610.6	South Eastern SD	Fawn Grove
76	612.6	Southern Lehigh SD	Center Valley
77	612.8	Albert Gallatin Area SD	Uniontown
77	612.8	Hopewell Area SD	Aliquippa
77	612.8	Uniontown Area SD	Uniontown
80	613.7	Radnor Township SD	Wayne
81	614.0	Lehighton Area SD	Lehighton
82	614.5	Eastern Lebanon County SD	Myerstown
83	616.3	Pen Argyl Area SD	Pen Argyl
84	621.0	Shaler Area SD	Glenshaw
85	621.5	Solanco SD	Quarryville
86	623.6	Wilson Area SD	Easton
87	624.8	Hamburg Area SD	Hamburg
88	625.9	Coatesville Area SD	Coatesville
89	626.6	Cheltenham Township SD	Elkins Park
90	633.2	Gettysburg Area SD	Gettysburg
91	635.6	West Mifflin Area SD	West Mifflin
92	639.6	Council Rock SD	Newtown
93	641.2	Central Dauphin SD	Harrisburg
94	641.5	Fox Chapel Area SD	Pittsburgh
95	643.8	Spring Grove Area SD	Spring Grove
96	644.0	Montoursville Area SD	Montoursville
97	644.6	Chestnut Ridge SD	Fishertown
98	644.7	Susquenita SD	Duncannon
99	645.0	Palmerton Area SD	Palmerton
100	646.3	Northern Lehigh SD	Slatington
101	646.9	Warwick SD	Lititz
102	647.1	Hampton Township SD	Allison Park
103	649.6	Eastern Lancaster County SD	New Holland
104	649.7	Oley Valley SD	Oley
105	652.7	Chambersburg Area SD	Chambersburg
106	653.4	Pottsgrove SD	Pottstown
107	653.9	Penn Hills SD	Pittsburgh
108	656.0	Pottstown SD	Pottstown
109	656.3	Deer Lakes SD	Russellton
110	662.5	Armstrong SD	Ford City
111	663.1	Woodland Hills SD	Pittsburgh
112	663.8	Burrell SD	Lower Burrell
112	663.8	Phoenixville Area SD	Phoenixville
114	664.3	Centennial SD	Warminster
115	667.3	Schuylkill Valley SD	Leesport
116	667.5	West Perry SD	Elliottsburg
117	667.6	North Penn SD	Lansdale
118	669.4	Bangor Area SD	Bangor
119	670.3	Bradford Area SD	Bradford
120	671.7	Hanover Area SD	Hanover Twp
121	673.8	Bensalem Township SD	Bensalem
122	674.2	Daniel Boone Area SD	Birdsboro
122	674.2	Great Valley SD	Malvern
124	674.5	West Shore SD	New Cumberland
125	675.0	Hempfield SD	Landisville
125	675.0	Wilson SD	West Lawn
127	676.3	West Allegheny SD	Oakdale
128	676.9	Moon Area SD	Moon Township
129	677.0	Colonial SD	Plymth Meeting
129	677.0	Grove City Area SD	Grove City
131	677.2	North Hills SD	Pittsburgh
132	678.5	Selinsgrove Area SD	Selinsgrove
133	678.6	Shikellamy SD	Sunbury
134	680.0	Shippensburg Area SD	Shippensburg
135	680.2	Oxford Area SD	Oxford
136	681.6	Twin Valley SD	Elverson
137	682.0	Scranton SD	Scranton
138	685.0	South Butler County SD	Saxonburg
139	686.3	Souderton Area SD	Souderton
140	688.1	Wyomissing Area SD	Wyomissing
141	689.2	Penn Manor SD	Lancaster
142	689.4	Wissahickon SD	Ambler
143	690.3	Bermudian Springs SD	York Springs
144	691.0	Lower Moreland Township SD	Huntingdon Vlly
145	694.8	Hempfield Area SD	Greensburg
146	695.3	Central Greene SD	Waynesburg
147	696.8	Trinity Area SD	Washington
148	697.5	Juniata County SD	Mifflintown
149	698.7	Tredyffrin-Easttown SD	Wayne
150	699.0	Hermitage SD	Hermitage
151	699.4	Connellsville Area SD	Connellsville
152	699.7	Upper Dublin SD	Maple Glen
153	700.5	Spring-Ford Area SD	Royersford
154	700.7	Owen J Roberts SD	Pottstown
155	700.8	Wallingford-Swarthmore SD	Wallingford
156	700.9	Lower Merion SD	Ardmore
157	706.0	Southern York County SD	Glen Rock
158	706.7	Waynesboro Area SD	Waynesboro
159	708.3	Pennsbury SD	Fallsington
160	709.0	East Pennsboro Area SD	Enola
161	709.8	Tunkhannock Area SD	Tunkhannock
162	710.2	Derry Township SD	Hershey
163	714.0	Titusville Area SD	Titusville
164	714.2	Governor Mifflin SD	Shillington
165	717.5	Gateway SD	Monroeville
166	718.0	York Suburban SD	York
167	720.5	West Jefferson Hills SD	Jefferson Hills
168	724.5	Bellefonte Area SD	Bellefonte
169	724.8	Pennridge SD	Perkasie
170	727.7	Littlestown Area SD	Littlestown
171	728.0	Northern Tioga SD	Elkland
172	729.0	Jim Thorpe Area SD	Jim Thorpe
173	730.0	Fort Leboeuf SD	Waterford
174	730.7	General Mclane SD	Edinboro
174	730.7	Mifflinburg Area SD	Mifflinburg
176	731.3	Conrad Weiser Area SD	Robesonia
177	732.5	Exeter Township SD	Reading
178	735.6	Pleasant Valley SD	Brodheadsville
179	735.8	Boyertown Area SD	Boyertown
179	735.8	West York Area SD	York
181	736.0	Dover Area SD	Dover
182	736.3	Big Spring SD	Newville
183	737.4	Ambridge Area SD	Ambridge
184	737.5	West Chester Area SD	West Chester
185	739.4	Northwestern Lehigh SD	New Tripoli
186	740.7	Mount Pleasant Area SD	Mount Pleasant
187	745.0	Oil City Area SD	Oil City
188	748.9	Franklin Area SD	Franklin
189	749.0	Rose Tree Media SD	Media
190	753.0	Mount Union Area SD	Mount Union
191	754.0	Marion Center Area SD	Marion Center
191	754.0	Riverside SD	Taylor
193	758.3	Pine-Richland SD	Gibsonia
194	760.4	East Allegheny SD	N Versailles
195	761.0	Milton Area SD	Milton
196	761.1	South Park SD	South Park
197	761.7	Methacton SD	Norristown
198	762.0	Upper Moreland Township SD	Willow Grove
199	762.4	Wilkes-Barre Area SD	Wilkes Barre
200	763.2	South Western SD	Hanover
201	764.0	Hatboro-Horsham SD	Horsham
202	766.7	Western Wayne SD	South Canaan
203	767.4	Fleetwood Area SD	Fleetwood
204	769.3	Slippery Rock Area SD	Slippery Rock
205	769.4	Unionville-Chadds Ford SD	Kennett Square
206	773.6	William Penn SD	Lansdowne
207	774.0	Carbondale Area SD	Carbondale

Note: This section only includes districts with 1,500 or more students; All categories are ranked from high to low

208	776.7	Corry Area SD	Corry
209	777.5	Upper Perkiomen SD	Pennsburg
210	779.0	Cornwall-Lebanon SD	Lebanon
211	780.0	Delaware Valley SD	Milford
212	784.0	Mount Carmel Area SD	Mount Carmel
213	788.3	Ringgold SD	New Eagle
214	791.4	Mifflin County SD	Lewistown
215	791.5	Moniteau SD	West Sunbury
216	791.8	Northern York County SD	Dillsburg
217	792.5	Washington SD	Washington
218	792.6	Mckeesport Area SD	Mckeesport
219	794.0	Richland SD	Johnstown
220	797.0	Mohawk Area SD	Bessemer
220	797.0	South Allegheny SD	Mckeesport
222	799.0	Lakeland SD	Jermyn
223	801.0	East Lycoming SD	Hughesville
224	802.2	Franklin Regional SD	Murrysville
225	802.5	Brookville Area SD	Brookville
226	803.7	Saucon Valley SD	Hellertown
227	804.2	Elizabethtown Area SD	Elizabethtown
228	804.5	Charleroi SD	Charleroi
229	806.3	Canon-Mcmillan SD	Canonsburg
230	806.8	Conewago Valley SD	New Oxford
231	808.3	Punxsutawney Area SD	Punxsutawney
232	809.3	Danville Area SD	Danville
233	811.2	Harrisburg City SD	Harrisburg
234	811.5	Dunmore SD	Dunmore
235	814.8	Conestoga Valley SD	Lancaster
236	818.6	Interboro SD	Prospect Park
237	821.0	Downingtown Area SD	Downingtown
238	822.5	Karns City Area SD	Karns City
239	825.7	Wyoming Valley West SD	Kingston
240	829.6	Parkland SD	Allentown
241	833.2	Tamaqua Area SD	Tamaqua
242	835.3	Easton Area SD	Easton
243	838.0	Clearfield Area SD	Clearfield
244	838.3	New Castle Area SD	New Castle
245	838.4	Whitehall-Coplay SD	Whitehall
246	839.2	Mcguffey SD	Claysville
247	839.6	Norristown Area SD	Norristown
248	839.7	Perkiomen Valley SD	Collegeville
249	840.4	Kennett Consolidated SD	Kennett Square
250	843.0	Haverford Township SD	Havertown
251	844.0	Greater Latrobe SD	Latrobe
251	844.0	Laurel Highlands SD	Uniontown
253	846.3	Penn-Delco SD	Aston
254	846.7	Eastern York SD	Wrightsville
255	852.3	Blackhawk SD	Beaver Falls
256	852.8	Chartiers Valley SD	Pittsburgh
257	853.2	Southeast Delco SD	Folcroft
258	858.7	Central Bucks SD	Doylestown
259	860.1	Stroudsburg Area SD	Stroudsburg
260	860.6	Pocono Mountain SD	Swiftwater
261	863.5	Penn Cambria SD	Cresson
262	865.5	Upper Adams SD	Biglerville
263	868.0	Elizabeth Forward SD	Elizabeth
263	868.0	Westmont Hilltop SD	Johnstown
265	868.5	Abington Heights SD	Clarks Summit
266	871.0	Valley View SD	Archbald
267	877.8	Hollidaysburg Area SD	Hollidaysburg
268	886.0	New Kensington-Arnold SD	New Kensington
269	886.3	Donegal SD	Mount Joy
270	886.4	Plum Borough SD	Plum
271	886.8	Keystone Central SD	Lock Haven
272	889.8	Peters Township SD	Mcmurray
273	890.7	E Stroudsburg Area SD	E Stroudsburg
274	897.0	Central Cambria SD	Ebensburg
275	897.7	Derry Area SD	Derry
276	909.3	Upper Darby SD	Drexel Hill
277	909.7	Dallas SD	Dallas
278	911.5	Butler Area SD	Butler
279	913.0	Jersey Shore Area SD	Jersey Shore
280	916.4	Reading SD	Reading
281	918.6	Seneca Valley SD	Harmony
282	925.8	Mechanicsburg Area SD	Mechanicsburg
283	930.0	East Penn SD	Emmaus
284	931.2	Central York SD	York
285	933.2	Northampton Area SD	Northampton
286	934.0	Yough SD	Herminie
287	934.3	Octorara Area SD	Atglen
288	934.4	Greater Johnstown SD	Johnstown
289	935.3	Highlands SD	Natrona Heights
290	937.5	Bald Eagle Area SD	Wingate
291	941.8	Bethlehem Area SD	Bethlehem
292	948.6	Garnet Valley SD	Glen Mills
293	952.5	Greencastle-Antrim SD	Greencastle
294	956.4	Carlisle Area SD	Carlisle
295	962.9	Neshaminy SD	Langhorne
296	965.3	Lower Dauphin SD	Hummelstown
297	967.0	York City SD	York
298	969.7	Lampeter-Strasburg SD	Lampeter
299	977.3	Blue Mountain SD	Orwigsburg
300	978.0	North Schuylkill SD	Ashland
301	982.5	Tyrone Area SD	Tyrone
302	984.0	Ellwood City Area SD	Ellwood City
303	988.7	Montour SD	Mckees Rocks
304	991.7	Dallastown Area SD	Dallastown
305	993.0	Central Columbia SD	Bloomsburg
306	994.5	Wallenpaupack Area SD	Hawley
307	995.5	Beaver Area SD	Beaver
308	1,004.5	Harbor Creek SD	Harborcreek
309	1,007.7	Muhlenberg SD	Reading
310	1,010.3	Pottsville Area SD	Pottsville
311	1,012.0	Crestwood SD	Mountain Top
312	1,019.7	Mars Area SD	Mars
313	1,028.0	Berwick Area SD	Berwick
314	1,028.8	Dubois Area SD	Du Bois
315	1,034.8	South Fayette Township SD	Mcdonald
316	1,044.5	Lake-Lehman SD	Dallas
317	1,047.0	Norwin SD	N Huntingdon
318	1,047.8	Baldwin-Whitehall SD	Pittsburgh
319	1,064.5	Sharon City SD	Sharon
320	1,084.7	Spring Cove SD	Roaring Spring
321	1,086.0	Avon Grove SD	West Grove
322	1,088.8	Mid Valley SD	Throop
323	1,091.3	North Pocono SD	Moscow
324	1,102.4	Cumberland Valley SD	Mechanicsburg
325	1,112.3	Lebanon SD	Lebanon
326	1,121.3	Chichester SD	Aston
327	1,124.5	Greater Nanticoke Area SD	Nanticoke
328	1,164.3	Allentown City SD	Allentown
329	1,200.0	Northern Lebanon SD	Fredericksburg
330	1,222.5	Shamokin Area SD	Coal Township
331	1,286.5	Tuscarora SD	Mercersburg
332	1,296.1	Central Valley SD	Monaca
333	1,370.3	Williamsport Area SD	Williamsport
334	1,388.6	Kiski Area SD	Leechburg
335	1,416.3	Red Lion Area SD	Red Lion
336	1,431.0	Penn-Trafford SD	Harrison City
337	1,525.0	York County School of Technology	York
338	1,552.9	Erie City SD	Erie
339	1,569.7	Nazareth Area SD	Nazareth
340	1,665.6	Altoona Area SD	Altoona
341	1,769.5	Springfield SD	Springfield
342	2,019.0	Girard SD	Girard
343	2,033.3	Millcreek Township SD	Erie
344	2,213.0	Chester-Upland SD	Chester
345	2,431.0	Somerset Area SD	Somerset
346	2,469.4	Philadelphia City SD	Philadelphia
347	2,578.5	Hazleton Area SD	Hazleton
348	2,894.0	Ridley SD	Folsom
n/a	n/a	Agora Cyber CS	Wayne
n/a	n/a	Chester Community CS	Chester
n/a	n/a	Commonwealth Connections Acade	Harrisburg
n/a	n/a	Lehigh Career & Technical Inst	Schnecksville
n/a	n/a	Pennsylvania Cyber CS	Midland
n/a	n/a	Pennsylvania Leadership Charter	West Chester
n/a	n/a	Pennsylvania Virtual CS	Norristown
n/a	n/a	Wyoming Area SD	Exeter

Student/Counselor Ratio

(number of students per counselor)

Rank	Number	District Name	City
1	232.3	Wyomissing Area SD	Wyomissing
2	232.5	Pocono Mountain SD	Swiftwater
3	255.6	Western Wayne SD	South Canaan
4	261.1	York Suburban SD	York
5	264.2	Mckeesport Area SD	Mckeesport
6	267.7	Phoenixville Area SD	Phoenixville
7	267.9	Bald Eagle Area SD	Wingate
8	269.0	Wattsburg Area SD	Erie
9	269.6	Lower Merion SD	Ardmore
10	274.1	Williamsport Area SD	Williamsport
11	275.4	Coatesville Area SD	Coatesville
12	276.4	Carlisle Area SD	Carlisle
13	277.5	South Eastern SD	Fawn Grove
14	277.8	Mount Pleasant Area SD	Mount Pleasant
15	278.4	Oley Valley SD	Oley
16	278.7	Warrior Run SD	Turbotville
17	280.3	Chichester SD	Aston
18	282.1	Penn-Delco SD	Aston
19	286.5	Tulpehocken Area SD	Bethel
20	287.8	Gettysburg Area SD	Gettysburg
20	287.8	West Chester Area SD	West Chester
22	288.1	Rose Tree Media SD	Media
23	289.8	Bellefonte Area SD	Bellefonte
24	290.3	Marple Newtown SD	Newtown Square
25	291.3	Corry Area SD	Corry
26	291.4	Upper Merion Area SD	King of Prussia
27	291.5	Middletown Area SD	Middletown
28	291.9	Colonial SD	Plymth Meeting
29	292.0	Big Beaver Falls Area SD	Beaver Falls
30	295.9	Springfield Township SD	Oreland
31	296.8	Unionville-Chadds Ford SD	Kennett Square
32	299.3	Wilson Area SD	Easton
33	299.4	Tredyffrin-Easttown SD	Wayne
34	300.0	Bethlehem Area SD	Bethlehem
34	300.0	Brandywine Heights Area SD	Topton
36	301.6	Marion Center Area SD	Marion Center
36	301.6	Riverside SD	Taylor
38	303.1	Punxsutawney Area SD	Punxsutawney
39	303.5	Danville Area SD	Danville
40	305.0	York County School of Technology	York
41	307.2	Wallenpaupack Area SD	Hawley
42	311.2	Great Valley SD	Malvern
43	312.1	Hatboro-Horsham SD	Horsham
44	312.9	Midd-West SD	Middleburg
45	313.1	West York Area SD	York
46	313.2	New Hope-Solebury SD	New Hope
47	314.6	Indiana Area SD	Indiana
48	315.0	Blairsville-Saltsburg SD	Blairsville
49	315.1	South Middleton SD	Boiling Springs
50	316.2	Palisades SD	Kintnersville
51	316.3	State College Area SD	State College
52	317.0	Washington SD	Washington
53	317.5	Eastern York SD	Wrightsville
53	317.5	Lewisburg Area SD	Lewisburg
55	317.8	Lancaster SD	Lancaster
56	318.5	Wallingford-Swarthmore SD	Wallingford
57	318.8	South Allegheny SD	Mckeesport
58	319.3	Manheim Central SD	Manheim
59	319.7	Crawford Central SD	Meadville
60	320.6	E Stroudsburg Area SD	E Stroudsburg
60	320.6	Muhlenberg SD	Reading
62	321.6	Kutztown Area SD	Kutztown
63	322.9	Upper Dublin SD	Maple Glen
64	323.0	Catasauqua Area SD	Catasauqua
65	323.2	Northern Lehigh SD	Slatington
66	323.6	South Western SD	Hanover
67	324.7	Wissahickon SD	Ambler
68	324.9	Cheltenham Township SD	Elkins Park
69	326.0	Annville-Cleona SD	Annville
70	326.1	Milton Area SD	Milton
71	327.8	Upper Saint Clair SD	Pittsburgh
72	328.6	North Penn SD	Lansdale
73	329.0	Hanover Public SD	Hanover
74	329.5	Neshaminy SD	Langhorne
75	329.6	Montour SD	Mckees Rocks
76	330.5	Philipsburg-Osceola Area SD	Philipsburg
77	331.5	Woodland Hills SD	Pittsburgh
78	333.0	Wayne Highlands SD	Honesdale
79	333.8	Salisbury Township SD	Allentown
79	333.8	West Perry SD	Elliottsburg
81	334.4	Brookville Area SD	Brookville
82	334.7	Bangor Area SD	Bangor
82	334.7	Radnor Township SD	Wayne
84	335.2	Clearfield Area SD	Clearfield
85	335.5	Fox Chapel Area SD	Pittsburgh
86	335.8	Fleetwood Area SD	Fleetwood
86	335.8	Hanover Area SD	Hanover Twp
88	335.9	Spring Grove Area SD	Spring Grove
89	336.6	Mechanicsburg Area SD	Mechanicsburg
90	336.7	Pennsylvania Leadership Charter	West Chester
91	336.9	Bensalem Township SD	Bensalem
92	337.2	General Mclane SD	Edinboro
93	337.4	Bloomsburg Area SD	Bloomsburg
94	338.0	Northwestern Lehigh SD	New Tripoli
95	338.2	Quaker Valley SD	Sewickley
96	338.6	Montrose Area SD	Montrose
97	339.3	Selinsgrove Area SD	Selinsgrove
98	340.3	Easton Area SD	Easton
99	340.8	Twin Valley SD	Elverson
100	341.9	Mount Lebanon SD	Pittsburgh

Note: This section only includes districts with 1,500 or more students; All categories are ranked from high to low

101	342.9	Dubois Area SD	Du Bois
102	343.1	West Shore SD	New Cumberland
103	344.4	Saucon Valley SD	Hellertown
104	344.5	Norristown Area SD	Norristown
104	344.5	Southern Tioga SD	Blossburg
106	344.9	Franklin Regional SD	Murrysville
106	344.9	Lebanon SD	Lebanon
108	345.5	Lower Moreland Township SD	Huntingdon Vlly
109	346.1	Gateway SD	Monroeville
110	346.2	Upper Adams SD	Biglerville
111	349.4	William Penn SD	Lansdowne
112	349.8	North East SD	North East
113	350.1	Hopewell Area SD	Aliquippa
114	350.4	Reading SD	Reading
115	350.8	Cumberland Valley SD	Mechanicsburg
116	351.0	Lower Dauphin SD	Hummelstown
117	351.1	Hollidaysburg Area SD	Hollidaysburg
118	351.3	Montoursville Area SD	Montoursville
119	351.7	Centennial SD	Warminster
120	352.2	North Hills SD	Pittsburgh
121	353.0	Southern York County SD	Glen Rock
122	353.5	Octorara Area SD	Atglen
123	353.9	Springfield SD	Springfield
124	354.1	Red Lion Area SD	Red Lion
125	354.5	East Pennsboro Area SD	Enola
126	354.9	Chester Community CS	Chester
127	355.5	Methacton SD	Norristown
128	356.4	Pequea Valley SD	Kinzers
129	356.5	Penn Manor SD	Lancaster
130	357.0	Hamburg Area SD	Hamburg
131	357.3	Tyrone Area SD	Tyrone
132	358.4	Spring-Ford Area SD	Royersford
133	360.0	Pennsbury SD	Fallsington
134	360.2	Stroudsburg Area SD	Stroudsburg
135	360.6	Palmyra Area SD	Palmyra
136	360.9	Eastern Lancaster County SD	New Holland
137	362.0	Avon Grove SD	West Grove
138	362.6	York City SD	York
139	363.0	Pottsgrove SD	Pottstown
140	363.5	East Penn SD	Emmaus
141	364.5	Jim Thorpe Area SD	Jim Thorpe
142	364.8	Garnet Valley SD	Glen Mills
143	365.0	Fort Leboeuf SD	Waterford
144	365.6	Conrad Weiser Area SD	Robesonia
145	365.7	Abington Heights SD	Clarks Summit
146	366.3	Exeter Township SD	Reading
147	366.9	Warren County SD	North Warren
148	367.4	South Park SD	South Park
149	367.5	Keystone Oaks SD	Pittsburgh
150	367.8	Pleasant Valley SD	Brodheadsville
150	367.8	Steel Valley SD	Munhall
152	368.0	Dover Area SD	Dover
153	368.1	Big Spring SD	Newville
154	368.9	Chambersburg Area SD	Chambersburg
155	369.5	Keystone Central SD	Lock Haven
156	369.8	Pen Argyl Area SD	Pen Argyl
157	371.7	Parkland SD	Allentown
158	371.9	Dallastown Area SD	Dallastown
159	372.5	Central York SD	York
160	372.6	Susquehanna Township SD	Harrisburg
161	373.3	Valley View SD	Archbald
162	373.5	Northeastern York SD	Manchester
163	374.1	Oxford Area SD	Oxford
164	376.1	Grove City Area SD	Grove City
165	377.3	Owen J Roberts SD	Pottstown
166	377.8	Shippensburg Area SD	Shippensburg
167	381.0	Upper Moreland Township SD	Willow Grove
168	381.1	Whitehall-Coplay SD	Whitehall
169	381.3	Saint Marys Area SD	Saint Marys
170	381.4	Downingtown Area SD	Downingtown
170	381.4	Penn Hills SD	Pittsburgh
172	382.0	Kennett Consolidated SD	Kennett Square
173	382.3	Wellsboro Area SD	Wellsboro
174	383.0	Bradford Area SD	Bradford
174	383.0	Uniontown Area SD	Uniontown
176	384.3	Conestoga Valley SD	Lancaster
177	384.7	Slippery Rock Area SD	Slippery Rock
178	385.5	Berwick Area SD	Berwick
179	385.9	Manheim Township SD	Lititz
180	386.8	Susquenita SD	Duncannon
181	387.0	Carbondale Area SD	Carbondale
181	387.0	Palmerton Area SD	Palmerton
181	387.0	Philadelphia City SD	Philadelphia
181	387.0	Wilson SD	West Lawn
185	389.2	Yough SD	Herminie
186	389.5	Governor Mifflin SD	Shillington
187	389.9	Dallas SD	Dallas
188	390.0	Delaware Valley SD	Milford
189	394.6	Derry Township SD	Hershey
190	394.8	Troy Area SD	Troy
191	394.9	Quakertown Community SD	Quakertown
192	397.2	Central Columbia SD	Bloomsburg
193	399.5	Lakeland SD	Jermyn
194	399.7	Penncrest SD	Saegertown
195	400.0	Northern Lebanon SD	Fredericksburg
196	400.2	Interboro SD	Prospect Park
197	400.3	North Allegheny SD	Pittsburgh
198	400.4	Schuylkill Valley SD	Leesport
199	401.8	Harbor Creek SD	Harborcreek
200	402.0	Riverside Beaver County SD	Ellwood City
201	402.1	Elizabethtown Area SD	Elizabethtown
202	402.3	Charleroi SD	Charleroi
203	402.4	Council Rock SD	Newtown
204	403.2	Canon-Mcmillan SD	Canonsburg
205	403.4	Hempfield Area SD	Greensburg
206	403.7	Central Dauphin SD	Harrisburg
207	404.8	Fairview SD	Fairview
208	405.0	Hempfield SD	Landisville
209	405.6	Harrisburg City SD	Harrisburg
209	405.6	Tunkhannock Area SD	Tunkhannock
211	405.8	Dunmore SD	Dunmore
212	405.9	Nazareth Area SD	Nazareth
213	406.2	Ephrata Area SD	Ephrata
213	406.2	Forest Hills SD	Sidman
215	408.4	Southmoreland SD	Scottdale
216	409.3	Lehighton Area SD	Lehighton
216	409.3	North Pocono SD	Moscow
216	409.3	Northwestern SD	Albion
219	411.3	Karns City Area SD	Karns City
220	411.8	Pine Grove Area SD	Pine Grove
221	413.6	Pine-Richland SD	Gibsonia
222	413.7	Moon Area SD	Moon Township
223	414.0	Shaler Area SD	Glenshaw
224	414.3	Solanco SD	Quarryville
225	414.8	Towanda Area SD	Towanda
226	415.2	South Butler County SD	Saxonburg
227	416.6	Plum Borough SD	Plum
228	417.2	Central Greene SD	Waynesburg
229	417.4	Cocalico SD	Denver
230	417.8	Lake-Lehman SD	Dallas
231	418.9	Blue Mountain SD	Orwigsburg
232	419.0	Chestnut Ridge SD	Fishertown
233	419.6	Mcguffey SD	Claysville
234	422.0	Laurel Highlands SD	Uniontown
235	423.0	Ligonier Valley SD	Ligonier
236	423.7	Peters Township SD	Mcmurray
237	424.2	Conneaut SD	Linesville
238	425.0	Huntingdon Area SD	Huntingdon
239	425.8	Sharon City SD	Sharon
240	426.2	Blackhawk SD	Beaver Falls
241	426.4	Chartiers Valley SD	Pittsburgh
241	426.4	Pennridge SD	Perkasie
243	426.9	Greensburg Salem SD	Greensburg
244	428.4	Titusville Area SD	Titusville
245	428.9	Souderton Area SD	Souderton
246	431.8	Penn Cambria SD	Cresson
247	433.0	New Brighton Area SD	New Brighton
248	433.7	Crestwood SD	Mountain Top
249	434.0	Westmont Hilltop SD	Johnstown
250	436.6	Abington SD	Abington
250	436.6	Littlestown Area SD	Littlestown
252	437.5	Burrell SD	Lower Burrell
253	438.2	Oil City Area SD	Oil City
254	438.4	Juniata County SD	Mifflintown
255	440.1	Seneca Valley SD	Harmony
256	442.0	Daniel Boone Area SD	Birdsboro
257	443.7	Hampton Township SD	Allison Park
258	443.8	Bristol Township SD	Levittown
259	444.2	Altoona Area SD	Altoona
260	444.3	Upper Perkiomen SD	Pennsburg
261	445.1	Connellsville Area SD	Connellsville
261	445.1	Haverford Township SD	Havertown
263	447.9	Northampton Area SD	Northampton
264	448.4	Agora Cyber CS	Wayne
265	448.5	Central Cambria SD	Ebensburg
266	450.2	Donegal SD	Mount Joy
267	450.4	Ringgold SD	New Eagle
268	451.0	Boyertown Area SD	Boyertown
269	451.4	Bedford Area SD	Bedford
270	452.2	Perkiomen Valley SD	Collegeville
271	452.4	Northern York County SD	Dillsburg
272	452.8	Tamaqua Area SD	Tamaqua
273	453.7	Freedom Area SD	Freedom
274	454.0	West Mifflin Area SD	West Mifflin
275	454.7	Scranton SD	Scranton
276	456.2	Central Bucks SD	Doylestown
277	457.1	Lampeter-Strasburg SD	Lampeter
278	458.8	Belle Vernon Area SD	Belle Vernon
279	459.6	Albert Gallatin Area SD	Uniontown
280	459.8	Lehigh Career & Technical Inst	Schnecksville
281	460.1	Erie City SD	Erie
282	461.0	Spring Cove SD	Roaring Spring
283	463.7	West Allegheny SD	Oakdale
284	466.8	Derry Area SD	Derry
285	468.9	Greater Latrobe SD	Latrobe
286	471.1	Waynesboro Area SD	Waynesboro
287	474.0	Southeast Delco SD	Folcroft
288	475.0	Shikellamy SD	Sunbury
289	475.3	East Allegheny SD	N Versailles
290	476.4	Bethel Park SD	Bethel Park
291	483.5	Brownsville Area SD	Brownsville
292	486.0	Pittsburgh SD	Pittsburgh
293	486.2	Somerset Area SD	Somerset
294	489.0	North Schuylkill SD	Ashland
294	489.0	Shamokin Area SD	Coal Township
296	491.6	Eastern Lebanon County SD	Myerstown
297	492.3	Deer Lakes SD	Russellton
298	495.0	Freeport Area SD	Sarver
299	495.4	Wyoming Valley West SD	Kingston
300	496.4	Northern Tioga SD	Elkland
301	497.7	Trinity Area SD	Washington
302	497.8	Beaver Area SD	Beaver
303	502.0	Mount Union Area SD	Mount Union
304	503.0	Wyoming Area SD	Exeter
305	503.1	Warwick SD	Lititz
306	503.4	Kiski Area SD	Leechburg
307	504.8	Girard SD	Girard
308	514.6	Tuscarora SD	Mercersburg
309	517.8	Bermudian Springs SD	York Springs
310	522.7	Mount Carmel Area SD	Mount Carmel
311	523.5	Norwin SD	N Huntingdon
312	524.3	Franklin Area SD	Franklin
312	524.3	Hermitage SD	Hermitage
314	526.2	Ridley SD	Folsom
315	527.7	Moniteau SD	West Sunbury
316	529.3	Richland SD	Johnstown
317	529.5	Greater Johnstown SD	Johnstown
318	531.3	Mohawk Area SD	Bessemer
319	540.6	Butler Area SD	Butler
320	547.8	Jersey Shore Area SD	Jersey Shore
321	548.0	Mifflinburg Area SD	Mifflinburg
322	553.5	South Fayette Township SD	Mcdonald
323	553.7	Panther Valley SD	Lansford
324	560.9	Mid Valley SD	Throop
325	561.2	Highlands SD	Natrona Heights
326	562.3	Greater Nanticoke Area SD	Nanticoke
327	562.9	Upper Darby SD	Drexel Hill
328	563.4	Allentown City SD	Allentown
329	569.5	Athens Area SD	Athens
330	571.8	Wilkes-Barre Area SD	Wilkes Barre
331	576.3	Conewago Valley SD	New Oxford
332	582.9	New Kensington-Arnold SD	New Kensington
333	609.6	Greencastle-Antrim SD	Greencastle
334	611.8	Mars Area SD	Mars
335	612.6	Southern Lehigh SD	Center Valley
336	616.6	Pottstown SD	Pottstown
337	651.0	Elizabeth Forward SD	Elizabeth
338	656.0	Ellwood City Area SD	Ellwood City
339	670.6	New Castle Area SD	New Castle
340	673.6	Pottsville Area SD	Pottsville
341	674.0	Pittston Area SD	Pittston
342	698.5	Baldwin-Whitehall SD	Pittsburgh
343	700.5	Ambridge Area SD	Ambridge
344	715.5	Penn-Trafford SD	Harrison City
345	720.5	West Jefferson Hills SD	Jefferson Hills
346	736.7	Hazleton Area SD	Hazleton
347	750.8	Armstrong SD	Ford City
348	791.4	Mifflin County SD	Lewistown
349	801.0	East Lycoming SD	Hughesville
350	922.8	Pennsylvania Virtual CS	Norristown
351	934.8	Cornwall-Lebanon SD	Lebanon
352	1,143.8	Millcreek Township SD	Erie
353	1,475.3	Chester-Upland SD	Chester
354	1,826.0	Commonwealth Connections Acade	Harrisburg
355	2,134.8	Pennsylvania Cyber CS	Midland

Note: This section only includes districts with 1,500 or more students; All categories are ranked from high to low

| n/a | n/a | Central Valley SD | Monaca |

Current Expenditures per Student

Rank	Dollars	District Name	City
1	20,123	Lower Merion SD	Ardmore
2	17,000	Cheltenham Township SD	Elkins Park
3	16,320	Upper Merion Area SD	King of Prussia
4	16,229	New Hope-Solebury SD	New Hope
5	15,933	Radnor Township SD	Wayne
6	15,790	Springfield Township SD	Oreland
7	15,497	Pittsburgh SD	Pittsburgh
8	15,283	Colonial SD	Plymth Meeting
9	15,181	Phoenixville Area SD	Phoenixville
10	15,158	Wissahickon SD	Ambler
11	14,824	Quaker Valley SD	Sewickley
12	14,589	Bristol Township SD	Levittown
13	14,581	Neshaminy SD	Langhorne
14	14,506	Great Valley SD	Malvern
15	14,297	Rose Tree Media SD	Media
16	14,214	Norristown Area SD	Norristown
17	14,165	Bensalem Township SD	Bensalem
18	14,033	Tredyffrin-Easttown SD	Wayne
19	14,028	Marple Newtown SD	Newtown Square
20	13,769	Coatesville Area SD	Coatesville
21	13,699	Palisades SD	Kintnersville
22	13,567	Abington SD	Abington
23	13,484	Kutztown Area SD	Kutztown
24	13,483	Fox Chapel Area SD	Pittsburgh
25	13,387	Pottstown SD	Pottstown
26	13,360	Wallingford-Swarthmore SD	Wallingford
27	13,268	Lower Moreland Township SD	Huntingdon Vlly
28	13,082	Council Rock SD	Newtown
29	13,072	Unionville-Chadds Ford SD	Kennett Square
30	13,049	Harrisburg City SD	Harrisburg
31	13,038	North Penn SD	Lansdale
32	12,961	Gateway SD	Monroeville
33	12,957	York City SD	York
34	12,930	Indiana Area SD	Indiana
35	12,886	E Stroudsburg Area SD	E Stroudsburg
36	12,855	West Chester Area SD	West Chester
37	12,827	Chester-Upland SD	Chester
38	12,802	Woodland Hills SD	Pittsburgh
39	12,801	William Penn SD	Lansdowne
40	12,735	Garnet Valley SD	Glen Mills
41	12,598	Pocono Mountain SD	Swiftwater
42	12,583	Upper Dublin SD	Maple Glen
43	12,577	Springfield SD	Springfield
44	12,566	Hatboro-Horsham SD	Horsham
45	12,546	Western Wayne SD	South Canaan
46	12,521	Pennsbury SD	Fallsington
47	12,445	Wyomissing Area SD	Wyomissing
48	12,443	Keystone Oaks SD	Pittsburgh
49	12,437	Penn Hills SD	Pittsburgh
50	12,390	Quakertown Community SD	Quakertown
51	12,389	State College Area SD	State College
52	12,373	Methacton SD	Norristown
53	12,356	Tulpehocken Area SD	Bethel
54	12,333	Spring-Ford Area SD	Royersford
55	12,261	Deer Lakes SD	Russellton
56	12,223	Saucon Valley SD	Hellertown
57	12,211	Wallenpaupack Area SD	Hawley
58	12,207	Montour SD	Mckees Rocks
59	12,157	Upper Moreland Township SD	Willow Grove
60	12,145	Schuylkill Valley SD	Leesport
61	12,135	Marion Center Area SD	Marion Center
62	12,129	Pottsgrove SD	Pottstown
63	12,080	Chichester SD	Aston
64	12,057	Armstrong SD	Ford City
65	12,042	Steel Valley SD	Munhall
66	12,006	Kennett Consolidated SD	Kennett Square
67	11,962	Moon Area SD	Moon Township
68	11,961	North Allegheny SD	Pittsburgh
69	11,959	Gettysburg Area SD	Gettysburg
70	11,940	Brandywine Heights Area SD	Topton
71	11,939	Salisbury Township SD	Allentown
72	11,913	Washington SD	Washington
73	11,842	Upper Saint Clair SD	Pittsburgh
74	11,822	Chester Community CS	Chester
75	11,789	York Suburban SD	York
76	11,784	North Hills SD	Pittsburgh
77	11,704	Riverside SD	Taylor
78	11,690	Centennial SD	Warminster
79	11,625	Hanover Public SD	Hanover
80	11,558	Octorara Area SD	Atglen
81	11,546	Ridley SD	Folsom
82	11,521	Owen J Roberts SD	Pottstown
83	11,520	Mount Lebanon SD	Pittsburgh
84	11,506	Keystone Central SD	Lock Haven
85	11,476	Tunkhannock Area SD	Tunkhannock
86	11,418	Haverford Township SD	Havertown
87	11,405	Catasauqua Area SD	Catasauqua
88	11,390	Montrose Area SD	Montrose
88	11,390	Perkiomen Valley SD	Collegeville
90	11,388	Upper Perkiomen SD	Pennsburg
91	11,345	Blairsville-Saltsburg SD	Blairsville
92	11,338	Elizabeth Forward SD	Elizabeth
93	11,313	Punxsutawney Area SD	Punxsutawney
94	11,303	Wellsboro Area SD	Wellsboro
95	11,290	Mckeesport Area SD	Mckeesport
96	11,275	Wayne Highlands SD	Honesdale
97	11,223	Shaler Area SD	Glenshaw
98	11,212	Oley Valley SD	Oley
99	11,200	Wilkes-Barre Area SD	Wilkes Barre
100	11,198	Bethel Park SD	Bethel Park
101	11,164	Interboro SD	Prospect Park
102	11,143	West Allegheny SD	Oakdale
103	11,132	Middletown Area SD	Middletown
104	11,102	Athens Area SD	Athens
105	11,077	Pequea Valley SD	Kinzers
106	11,059	Lancaster SD	Lancaster
107	11,034	Stroudsburg Area SD	Stroudsburg
108	11,030	Souderton Area SD	Souderton
109	11,024	Danville Area SD	Danville
110	11,022	Southern Lehigh SD	Center Valley
111	11,009	South Fayette Township SD	Mcdonald
112	10,992	Pennridge SD	Perkasie
113	10,986	Big Beaver Falls Area SD	Beaver Falls
114	10,985	Erie City SD	Erie
115	10,949	Warren County SD	North Warren
116	10,872	Southern Tioga SD	Blossburg
117	10,856	Hampton Township SD	Allison Park
118	10,825	Southeast Delco SD	Folcroft
119	10,820	Baldwin-Whitehall SD	Pittsburgh
120	10,810	Brownsville Area SD	Brownsville
121	10,808	Franklin Area SD	Franklin
122	10,789	Northwestern Lehigh SD	New Tripoli
123	10,781	Dallastown Area SD	Dallastown
124	10,766	Riverside Beaver County SD	Ellwood City
125	10,759	Williamsport Area SD	Williamsport
126	10,735	Bald Eagle Area SD	Wingate
127	10,682	Mcguffey SD	Claysville
128	10,659	Twin Valley SD	Elverson
129	10,652	Bellefonte Area SD	Bellefonte
130	10,649	Pennsylvania Leadership Charter	West Chester
131	10,624	Penn-Delco SD	Aston
132	10,613	Penncrest SD	Saegertown
133	10,610	Southern York County SD	Glen Rock
134	10,593	East Allegheny SD	N Versailles
135	10,557	Connellsville Area SD	Connellsville
136	10,543	Troy Area SD	Troy
137	10,527	Highlands SD	Natrona Heights
137	10,527	Ligonier Valley SD	Ligonier
139	10,518	Hempfield SD	Landisville
140	10,507	New Castle Area SD	New Castle
141	10,492	Central Greene SD	Waynesburg
141	10,492	West Mifflin Area SD	West Mifflin
143	10,486	Dubois Area SD	Du Bois
144	10,477	Central Dauphin SD	Harrisburg
145	10,464	Northern Tioga SD	Elkland
146	10,426	Greater Johnstown SD	Johnstown
147	10,420	Downingtown Area SD	Downingtown
148	10,413	Pleasant Valley SD	Brodheadsville
149	10,403	Derry Township SD	Hershey
150	10,394	Lewisburg Area SD	Lewisburg
151	10,378	Uniontown Area SD	Uniontown
152	10,370	Chartiers Valley SD	Pittsburgh
153	10,366	South Park SD	South Park
154	10,339	Central Bucks SD	Doylestown
155	10,338	Agora Cyber CS	Wayne
156	10,301	Titusville Area SD	Titusville
157	10,294	Jersey Shore Area SD	Jersey Shore
158	10,293	Northampton Area SD	Northampton
159	10,291	Big Spring SD	Newville
160	10,290	Brookville Area SD	Brookville
161	10,281	Bradford Area SD	Bradford
162	10,277	Eastern York SD	Wrightsville
163	10,197	Wilson SD	West Lawn
164	10,165	Bloomsburg Area SD	Bloomsburg
165	10,161	Lehighton Area SD	Lehighton
166	10,159	Governor Mifflin SD	Shillington
167	10,149	Lebanon SD	Lebanon
168	10,142	Berwick Area SD	Berwick
169	10,139	Carlisle Area SD	Carlisle
169	10,139	Hanover Area SD	Hanover Twp
171	10,115	Parkland SD	Allentown
172	10,096	Oil City Area SD	Oil City
173	10,095	Boyertown Area SD	Boyertown
174	10,089	Towanda Area SD	Towanda
175	10,074	Corry Area SD	Corry
176	10,054	Pine-Richland SD	Gibsonia
177	10,050	Harbor Creek SD	Harborcreek
178	10,039	Philipsburg-Osceola Area SD	Philipsburg
179	10,037	Ambridge Area SD	Ambridge
180	10,032	New Kensington-Arnold SD	New Kensington
181	10,023	Lake-Lehman SD	Dallas
182	10,011	Susquehanna Township SD	Harrisburg
183	10,005	Commonwealth Connections Acade	Harrisburg
184	9,986	Carbondale Area SD	Carbondale
184	9,986	Hempfield Area SD	Greensburg
186	9,974	Albert Gallatin Area SD	Uniontown
186	9,974	Manheim Central SD	Manheim
188	9,965	Selinsgrove Area SD	Selinsgrove
189	9,959	Wilson Area SD	Easton
190	9,956	Bethlehem Area SD	Bethlehem
191	9,950	Clearfield Area SD	Clearfield
192	9,949	Easton Area SD	Easton
193	9,934	Conrad Weiser Area SD	Robesonia
194	9,920	Panther Valley SD	Lansford
195	9,912	Lower Dauphin SD	Hummelstown
196	9,905	South Eastern SD	Fawn Grove
197	9,893	Ellwood City Area SD	Ellwood City
198	9,884	Midd-West SD	Middleburg
199	9,883	Upper Adams SD	Biglerville
200	9,878	Shamokin Area SD	Coal Township
201	9,874	Penn Cambria SD	Cresson
202	9,866	Seneca Valley SD	Harmony
203	9,852	Exeter Township SD	Reading
204	9,842	Hopewell Area SD	Aliquippa
205	9,840	Shikellamy SD	Sunbury
206	9,822	Conneaut SD	Linesville
207	9,814	Abington Heights SD	Clarks Summit
207	9,814	Mechanicsburg Area SD	Mechanicsburg
209	9,811	Hollidaysburg Area SD	Hollidaysburg
210	9,800	Crawford Central SD	Meadville
211	9,794	Freeport Area SD	Sarver
212	9,791	Blackhawk SD	Beaver Falls
213	9,790	North Pocono SD	Moscow
214	9,776	Annville-Cleona SD	Annville
215	9,759	Montoursville Area SD	Montoursville
215	9,759	Muhlenberg SD	Reading
217	9,758	Somerset Area SD	Somerset
218	9,756	New Brighton Area SD	New Brighton
219	9,750	Conestoga Valley SD	Lancaster
220	9,749	Lampeter-Strasburg SD	Lampeter
221	9,739	West Perry SD	Elliottsburg
222	9,735	Plum Borough SD	Plum
223	9,731	Scranton SD	Scranton
224	9,729	Pen Argyl Area SD	Pen Argyl
225	9,728	Hamburg Area SD	Hamburg
226	9,715	Tamaqua Area SD	Tamaqua
227	9,714	Delaware Valley SD	Milford
227	9,714	Northern Lehigh SD	Slatington
229	9,710	Eastern Lancaster County SD	New Holland
230	9,708	Moniteau SD	West Sunbury
231	9,705	Bangor Area SD	Bangor
232	9,695	Mount Union Area SD	Mount Union
233	9,690	East Penn SD	Emmaus
234	9,689	Dover Area SD	Dover
235	9,686	Susquenita SD	Duncannon
236	9,679	Northeastern York SD	Manchester
237	9,675	Ephrata Area SD	Ephrata
238	9,673	Fairview SD	Fairview
239	9,667	Wyoming Valley West SD	Kingston
240	9,651	Upper Darby SD	Drexel Hill
241	9,647	Freedom Area SD	Freedom
242	9,645	Derry Area SD	Derry
243	9,642	Eastern Lebanon County SD	Myerstown
244	9,638	Jim Thorpe Area SD	Jim Thorpe
245	9,637	South Middleton SD	Boiling Springs
246	9,600	Canon-Mcmillan SD	Canonsburg
247	9,595	Hermitage SD	Hermitage
248	9,589	Wattsburg Area SD	Erie
249	9,570	Fleetwood Area SD	Fleetwood

Note: This section only includes districts with 1,500 or more students; All categories are ranked from high to low

250	9,557	Milton Area SD	Milton
251	9,554	Karns City Area SD	Karns City
252	9,521	General Mclane SD	Edinboro
253	9,508	Pine Grove Area SD	Pine Grove
254	9,498	Cornwall-Lebanon SD	Lebanon
255	9,484	Cocalico SD	Denver
256	9,483	Chestnut Ridge SD	Fishertown
257	9,482	Manheim Township SD	Lititz
258	9,477	Mount Pleasant Area SD	Mount Pleasant
258	9,477	Warrior Run SD	Turbotville
260	9,474	Spring Grove Area SD	Spring Grove
261	9,471	Central Cambria SD	Ebensburg
262	9,468	Millcreek Township SD	Erie
263	9,456	Mifflin County SD	Lewistown
264	9,441	Daniel Boone Area SD	Birdsboro
265	9,426	Red Lion Area SD	Red Lion
266	9,419	Laurel Highlands SD	Uniontown
267	9,399	Philadelphia City SD	Philadelphia
268	9,364	Charleroi SD	Charleroi
269	9,355	South Allegheny SD	Mckeesport
270	9,310	Altoona Area SD	Altoona
270	9,310	Waynesboro Area SD	Waynesboro
272	9,304	Blue Mountain SD	Orwigsburg
273	9,298	Avon Grove SD	West Grove
274	9,295	Trinity Area SD	Washington
275	9,272	East Lycoming SD	Hughesville
275	9,272	West York Area SD	York
277	9,270	Southmoreland SD	Scottdale
278	9,264	Nazareth Area SD	Nazareth
279	9,263	Mohawk Area SD	Bessemer
280	9,251	West Jefferson Hills SD	Jefferson Hills
281	9,246	Sharon City SD	Sharon
282	9,241	Bedford Area SD	Bedford
283	9,231	Northern Lebanon SD	Fredericksburg
284	9,226	Beaver Area SD	Beaver
285	9,215	Northern York County SD	Dillsburg
286	9,214	Mid Valley SD	Throop
287	9,175	Penn Manor SD	Lancaster
288	9,174	Franklin Regional SD	Murrysville
289	9,167	Forest Hills SD	Sidman
290	9,164	Elizabethtown Area SD	Elizabethtown
291	9,163	Mifflinburg Area SD	Mifflinburg
292	9,141	South Western SD	Hanover
293	9,120	Butler Area SD	Butler
293	9,120	Tyrone Area SD	Tyrone
295	9,109	Greensburg Salem SD	Greensburg
296	9,097	Oxford Area SD	Oxford
297	9,080	Chambersburg Area SD	Chambersburg
298	9,075	Central York SD	York
298	9,075	West Shore SD	New Cumberland
300	9,062	Huntingdon Area SD	Huntingdon
301	9,055	Spring Cove SD	Roaring Spring
302	9,053	Donegal SD	Mount Joy
303	9,032	Cumberland Valley SD	Mechanicsburg
303	9,032	Wyoming Area SD	Exeter
305	9,022	Grove City Area SD	Grove City
306	8,993	Central Columbia SD	Bloomsburg
307	8,992	Westmont Hilltop SD	Johnstown
308	8,973	Reading SD	Reading
309	8,947	Pennsylvania Virtual CS	Norristown
310	8,946	Ringgold SD	New Eagle
311	8,937	Palmerton Area SD	Palmerton
312	8,931	Littlestown Area SD	Littlestown
313	8,914	Allentown City SD	Allentown
314	8,856	Warwick SD	Lititz
315	8,840	Dallas SD	Dallas
316	8,834	Burrell SD	Lower Burrell
317	8,829	Richland SD	Johnstown
318	8,825	Saint Marys Area SD	Saint Marys
319	8,810	Lakeland SD	Jermyn
320	8,809	Solanco SD	Quarryville
321	8,766	East Pennsboro Area SD	Enola
322	8,759	Girard SD	Girard
322	8,759	Pittston Area SD	Pittston
324	8,729	Slippery Rock Area SD	Slippery Rock
325	8,700	Belle Vernon Area SD	Belle Vernon
326	8,626	Crestwood SD	Mountain Top
327	8,611	Greencastle-Antrim SD	Greencastle
328	8,602	Penn-Trafford SD	Harrison City
329	8,601	Juniata County SD	Mifflintown
330	8,595	Shippensburg Area SD	Shippensburg
331	8,581	Yough SD	Herminie
332	8,579	North East SD	North East
332	8,579	North Schuylkill SD	Ashland
334	8,568	Greater Nanticoke Area SD	Nanticoke
335	8,550	Mars Area SD	Mars
336	8,454	Bermudian Springs SD	York Springs
337	8,453	Peters Township SD	Mcmurray
338	8,445	Tuscarora SD	Mercersburg
339	8,419	Kiski Area SD	Leechburg
340	8,409	Conewago Valley SD	New Oxford
341	8,388	Pottsville Area SD	Pottsville
342	8,383	Greater Latrobe SD	Latrobe
343	8,376	South Butler County SD	Saxonburg
344	8,300	Norwin SD	N Huntingdon
345	8,272	Dunmore SD	Dunmore
345	8,272	Palmyra Area SD	Palmyra
347	8,134	Hazleton Area SD	Hazleton
348	8,094	Whitehall-Coplay SD	Whitehall
349	8,068	Fort Leboeuf SD	Waterford
350	8,059	Northwestern SD	Albion
351	7,938	Valley View SD	Archbald
352	7,673	Mount Carmel Area SD	Mount Carmel
353	7,335	Pennsylvania Cyber CS	Midland
n/a	n/a	Central Valley SD	Monaca
n/a	n/a	Lehigh Career & Technical Inst	Schnecksville
n/a	n/a	York County School of Technology	York

Total General Revenue per Student

Rank	Dollars	District Name	City
1	25,279	Lower Merion SD	Ardmore
2	24,227	Pittsburgh SD	Pittsburgh
3	22,864	Chester-Upland SD	Chester
4	20,899	Phoenixville Area SD	Phoenixville
5	20,707	Springfield Township SD	Oreland
6	20,524	Cheltenham Township SD	Elkins Park
7	20,235	New Hope-Solebury SD	New Hope
8	19,522	Radnor Township SD	Wayne
9	19,359	Quaker Valley SD	Sewickley
10	19,295	Rose Tree Media SD	Media
11	19,235	Upper Merion Area SD	King of Prussia
12	19,109	York City SD	York
13	18,859	Wissahickon SD	Ambler
14	18,623	Bensalem Township SD	Bensalem
15	18,539	Coatesville Area SD	Coatesville
16	18,306	Bristol Township SD	Levittown
17	18,293	Great Valley SD	Malvern
18	18,123	Colonial SD	Plymth Meeting
19	17,227	Norristown Area SD	Norristown
20	17,182	Woodland Hills SD	Pittsburgh
21	17,146	Neshaminy SD	Langhorne
22	17,134	Montour SD	Mckees Rocks
23	17,061	Palisades SD	Kintnersville
24	16,987	Marple Newtown SD	Newtown Square
25	16,879	Pocono Mountain SD	Swiftwater
26	16,796	Wallingford-Swarthmore SD	Wallingford
27	16,756	Owen J Roberts SD	Pottstown
28	16,752	Pequea Valley SD	Kinzers
29	16,582	Fox Chapel Area SD	Pittsburgh
30	16,445	Abington SD	Abington
31	16,392	Harrisburg City SD	Harrisburg
32	16,279	Pennridge SD	Perkasie
33	16,202	Tredyffrin-Easttown SD	Wayne
34	16,147	Lower Moreland Township SD	Huntingdon Vlly
35	16,083	Hanover Public SD	Hanover
36	16,078	Saucon Valley SD	Hellertown
37	16,023	Chichester SD	Aston
38	15,999	Pottsgrove SD	Pottstown
39	15,989	Pottstown SD	Pottstown
40	15,823	Octorara Area SD	Atglen
41	15,758	Southern Lehigh SD	Center Valley
42	15,695	Kutztown Area SD	Kutztown
43	15,674	Garnet Valley SD	Glen Mills
44	15,671	West Chester Area SD	West Chester
45	15,633	Tulpehocken Area SD	Bethel
46	15,581	Kennett Consolidated SD	Kennett Square
47	15,547	Gateway SD	Monroeville
48	15,529	Salisbury Township SD	Allentown
49	15,528	Unionville-Chadds Ford SD	Kennett Square
50	15,473	Springfield SD	Springfield
51	15,316	Middletown Area SD	Middletown
52	15,304	Keystone Oaks SD	Pittsburgh
53	15,166	Catasauqua Area SD	Catasauqua
54	15,163	Council Rock SD	Newtown
55	15,112	Wyomissing Area SD	Wyomissing
56	15,099	Quakertown Community SD	Quakertown
57	15,086	Washington SD	Washington
58	15,074	Downingtown Area SD	Downingtown
59	15,069	Hatboro-Horsham SD	Horsham
60	15,042	Gettysburg Area SD	Gettysburg
61	15,032	York Suburban SD	York
62	15,018	Central Dauphin SD	Harrisburg
63	15,007	State College Area SD	State College
64	14,999	Spring-Ford Area SD	Royersford
65	14,988	Pennsbury SD	Fallsington
66	14,944	North Penn SD	Lansdale
67	14,927	Brandywine Heights Area SD	Topton
67	14,927	East Allegheny SD	N Versailles
69	14,922	Upper Dublin SD	Maple Glen
70	14,866	Philadelphia City SD	Philadelphia
71	14,855	Schuylkill Valley SD	Leesport
72	14,840	Deer Lakes SD	Russellton
73	14,829	Lancaster SD	Lancaster
74	14,808	Carlisle Area SD	Carlisle
75	14,765	Blairsville-Saltsburg SD	Blairsville
76	14,750	Methacton SD	Norristown
77	14,731	Wayne Highlands SD	Honesdale
78	14,719	Franklin Area SD	Franklin
79	14,612	Penn Hills SD	Pittsburgh
80	14,611	Indiana Area SD	Indiana
81	14,594	Chartiers Valley SD	Pittsburgh
82	14,569	Wallenpaupack Area SD	Hawley
83	14,566	Manheim Central SD	Manheim
84	14,542	West Allegheny SD	Oakdale
85	14,537	Derry Township SD	Hershey
86	14,535	Upper Moreland Township SD	Willow Grove
87	14,509	Moon Area SD	Moon Township
88	14,506	William Penn SD	Lansdowne
89	14,503	North Hills SD	Pittsburgh
90	14,477	E Stroudsburg Area SD	E Stroudsburg
91	14,473	Steel Valley SD	Munhall
92	14,471	Erie City SD	Erie
93	14,414	Baldwin-Whitehall SD	Pittsburgh
94	14,347	Perkiomen Valley SD	Collegeville
95	14,332	Armstrong SD	Ford City
96	14,308	Northwestern Lehigh SD	New Tripoli
97	14,281	Susquenita SD	Duncannon
98	14,271	Western Wayne SD	South Canaan
99	14,209	Mckeesport Area SD	Mckeesport
100	14,181	Jim Thorpe Area SD	Jim Thorpe
101	14,165	Haverford Township SD	Havertown
102	14,152	North Allegheny SD	Pittsburgh
103	14,132	Conrad Weiser Area SD	Robesonia
104	14,113	Oley Valley SD	Oley
105	14,110	Souderton Area SD	Souderton
106	14,090	Hempfield SD	Landisville
107	14,081	South Fayette Township SD	Mcdonald
108	14,052	Sharon City SD	Sharon
109	14,048	Marion Center Area SD	Marion Center
110	13,997	Punxsutawney Area SD	Punxsutawney
111	13,990	Cocalico SD	Denver
112	13,971	Penn-Delco SD	Aston
113	13,964	Dallastown Area SD	Dallastown
114	13,918	Centennial SD	Warminster
115	13,888	Riverside SD	Taylor
116	13,877	Wilkes-Barre Area SD	Wilkes Barre
117	13,834	Bethel Park SD	Bethel Park
118	13,828	Hamburg Area SD	Hamburg
119	13,808	Shaler Area SD	Glenshaw
120	13,794	Upper Saint Clair SD	Pittsburgh
121	13,773	Lampeter-Strasburg SD	Lampeter
122	13,756	West Mifflin Area SD	West Mifflin
123	13,750	Wellsboro Area SD	Wellsboro
124	13,747	Wilson Area SD	Easton
125	13,742	Ridley SD	Folsom
126	13,726	Mount Lebanon SD	Pittsburgh
127	13,721	Carbondale Area SD	Carbondale
128	13,711	New Kensington-Arnold SD	New Kensington
129	13,710	Keystone Central SD	Lock Haven
130	13,626	Central Greene SD	Waynesburg
131	13,618	Hampton Township SD	Allison Park
132	13,600	Oxford Area SD	Oxford
133	13,556	Montrose Area SD	Montrose
134	13,534	Interboro SD	Prospect Park
135	13,512	Southeast Delco SD	Folcroft
136	13,487	Upper Perkiomen SD	Pennsburg
137	13,471	Bethlehem Area SD	Bethlehem
138	13,458	Parkland SD	Allentown
139	13,457	Berwick Area SD	Berwick
140	13,437	Athens Area SD	Athens
141	13,419	Eastern York SD	Wrightsville
142	13,408	Greater Johnstown SD	Johnstown
143	13,402	Northampton Area SD	Northampton

Note: This section only includes districts with 1,500 or more students; All categories are ranked from high to low

144	13,385	Southern York County SD	Glen Rock
145	13,364	Stroudsburg Area SD	Stroudsburg
146	13,357	West York Area SD	York
147	13,348	Conestoga Valley SD	Lancaster
148	13,337	Spring Grove Area SD	Spring Grove
149	13,307	Chester Community CS	Chester
150	13,297	Harbor Creek SD	Harborcreek
151	13,290	Ephrata Area SD	Ephrata
152	13,267	Eastern Lancaster County SD	New Holland
153	13,261	Northern Lehigh SD	Slatington
154	13,247	Tunkhannock Area SD	Tunkhannock
155	13,235	New Castle Area SD	New Castle
156	13,217	Big Beaver Falls Area SD	Beaver Falls
157	13,203	Ligonier Valley SD	Ligonier
158	13,191	Mechanicsburg Area SD	Mechanicsburg
159	13,161	Northeastern York SD	Manchester
160	13,143	Danville Area SD	Danville
161	13,086	Philipsburg-Osceola Area SD	Philipsburg
162	13,084	Lower Dauphin SD	Hummelstown
163	13,076	Central York SD	York
164	13,069	Brookville Area SD	Brookville
165	13,066	Bloomsburg Area SD	Bloomsburg
165	13,066	Lewisburg Area SD	Lewisburg
167	13,050	Easton Area SD	Easton
168	13,049	Central Bucks SD	Doylestown
169	13,046	Trinity Area SD	Washington
170	13,031	Mcguffey SD	Claysville
171	13,022	Dover Area SD	Dover
172	13,015	South Eastern SD	Fawn Grove
173	13,010	Wilson SD	West Lawn
174	12,934	Somerset Area SD	Somerset
175	12,917	Avon Grove SD	West Grove
176	12,907	Hopewell Area SD	Aliquippa
177	12,890	Bald Eagle Area SD	Wingate
178	12,885	Exeter Township SD	Reading
179	12,875	Big Spring SD	Newville
180	12,863	Abington Heights SD	Clarks Summit
180	12,863	Muhlenberg SD	Reading
182	12,850	Riverside Beaver County SD	Ellwood City
183	12,839	Highlands SD	Natrona Heights
184	12,791	Corry Area SD	Corry
185	12,790	Bellefonte Area SD	Bellefonte
186	12,751	Williamsport Area SD	Williamsport
187	12,709	Warren County SD	North Warren
188	12,697	Pine-Richland SD	Gibsonia
189	12,676	West Perry SD	Elliottsburg
190	12,675	Fleetwood Area SD	Fleetwood
191	12,660	East Penn SD	Emmaus
192	12,658	South Middleton SD	Boiling Springs
193	12,654	Susquehanna Township SD	Harrisburg
194	12,641	West Jefferson Hills SD	Jefferson Hills
195	12,637	Lehighton Area SD	Lehighton
196	12,624	Twin Valley SD	Elverson
197	12,596	Penncrest SD	Saegertown
198	12,583	Upper Adams SD	Biglerville
199	12,578	Governor Mifflin SD	Shillington
200	12,574	Bradford Area SD	Bradford
201	12,570	Bangor Area SD	Bangor
202	12,556	Jersey Shore Area SD	Jersey Shore
203	12,554	Midd-West SD	Middleburg
204	12,546	Troy Area SD	Troy
205	12,538	Pleasant Valley SD	Brodheadsville
206	12,537	Chambersburg Area SD	Chambersburg
207	12,515	South Park SD	South Park
208	12,506	Ambridge Area SD	Ambridge
209	12,489	Titusville Area SD	Titusville
210	12,476	Clearfield Area SD	Clearfield
211	12,457	Nazareth Area SD	Nazareth
212	12,454	Northern Tioga SD	Elkland
213	12,452	Crawford Central SD	Meadville
213	12,452	Mount Pleasant Area SD	Mount Pleasant
215	12,448	Conneaut SD	Linesville
216	12,447	Connellsville Area SD	Connellsville
217	12,439	Fairview SD	Fairview
218	12,438	Greensburg Salem SD	Greensburg
219	12,433	South Allegheny SD	Mckeesport
220	12,396	Pine Grove Area SD	Pine Grove
221	12,387	General Mclane SD	Edinboro
222	12,383	Franklin Regional SD	Murrysville
223	12,382	Blue Mountain SD	Orwigsburg
224	12,373	Red Lion Area SD	Red Lion
225	12,341	Donegal SD	Mount Joy
226	12,325	Hermitage SD	Hermitage
227	12,293	Albert Gallatin Area SD	Uniontown
228	12,287	Hempfield Area SD	Greensburg
229	12,283	Elizabethtown Area SD	Elizabethtown
230	12,275	Lake-Lehman SD	Dallas
231	12,255	Butler Area SD	Butler
232	12,250	Mohawk Area SD	Bessemer
233	12,222	Southern Tioga SD	Blossburg
234	12,204	Brownsville Area SD	Brownsville
235	12,177	Towanda Area SD	Towanda
236	12,176	Pen Argyl Area SD	Pen Argyl
237	12,163	Richland SD	Johnstown
238	12,154	Tamaqua Area SD	Tamaqua
239	12,153	Penn Cambria SD	Cresson
240	12,147	Chestnut Ridge SD	Fishertown
241	12,129	Cornwall-Lebanon SD	Lebanon
242	12,125	Plum Borough SD	Plum
243	12,122	Daniel Boone Area SD	Birdsboro
244	12,111	Penn Manor SD	Lancaster
245	12,106	Lebanon SD	Lebanon
246	12,105	Manheim Township SD	Lititz
247	12,101	Southmoreland SD	Scottdale
248	12,072	Wattsburg Area SD	Erie
249	12,058	Burrell SD	Lower Burrell
250	12,050	Panther Valley SD	Lansford
251	12,035	Elizabeth Forward SD	Elizabeth
252	12,001	Boyertown Area SD	Boyertown
252	12,001	Solanco SD	Quarryville
254	11,983	Waynesboro Area SD	Waynesboro
255	11,968	Northwestern SD	Albion
256	11,964	Cumberland Valley SD	Mechanicsburg
257	11,962	Palmerton Area SD	Palmerton
258	11,952	Oil City Area SD	Oil City
259	11,946	Uniontown Area SD	Uniontown
260	11,939	Ringgold SD	New Eagle
261	11,933	Blackhawk SD	Beaver Falls
261	11,933	Selinsgrove Area SD	Selinsgrove
263	11,922	Eastern Lebanon County SD	Myerstown
263	11,922	Montoursville Area SD	Montoursville
265	11,908	Charleroi SD	Charleroi
266	11,901	Spring Cove SD	Roaring Spring
267	11,895	Warwick SD	Lititz
268	11,881	Canon-Mcmillan SD	Canonsburg
269	11,874	Shikellamy SD	Sunbury
270	11,858	Fort Leboeuf SD	Waterford
271	11,840	South Western SD	Hanover
272	11,832	Moniteau SD	West Sunbury
273	11,817	Freeport Area SD	Sarver
274	11,797	Karns City Area SD	Karns City
275	11,774	Annville-Cleona SD	Annville
276	11,754	Delaware Valley SD	Milford
277	11,728	Hollidaysburg Area SD	Hollidaysburg
278	11,723	New Brighton Area SD	New Brighton
279	11,718	North Pocono SD	Moscow
280	11,705	Ellwood City Area SD	Ellwood City
281	11,699	Dubois Area SD	Du Bois
282	11,666	East Lycoming SD	Hughesville
283	11,654	Laurel Highlands SD	Uniontown
284	11,651	Northern York County SD	Dillsburg
285	11,625	Freedom Area SD	Freedom
286	11,617	Littlestown Area SD	Littlestown
287	11,616	Tuscarora SD	Mercersburg
288	11,589	Derry Area SD	Derry
289	11,581	Seneca Valley SD	Harmony
290	11,569	Agora Cyber CS	Wayne
291	11,548	Dallas SD	Dallas
292	11,502	Beaver Area SD	Beaver
293	11,484	Mount Union Area SD	Mount Union
294	11,467	Shamokin Area SD	Coal Township
295	11,453	Central Cambria SD	Ebensburg
296	11,426	Kiski Area SD	Leechburg
297	11,408	Northern Lebanon SD	Fredericksburg
298	11,388	Tyrone Area SD	Tyrone
299	11,383	Upper Darby SD	Drexel Hill
300	11,360	Mars Area SD	Mars
301	11,343	Wyoming Valley West SD	Kingston
302	11,327	Forest Hills SD	Sidman
303	11,326	Central Columbia SD	Bloomsburg
304	11,308	East Pennsboro Area SD	Enola
305	11,297	Yough SD	Herminie
306	11,272	North East SD	North East
307	11,264	Greater Latrobe SD	Latrobe
308	11,221	Scranton SD	Scranton
309	11,201	Bedford Area SD	Bedford
310	11,116	Millcreek Township SD	Erie
311	11,098	Allentown City SD	Allentown
312	11,089	Belle Vernon Area SD	Belle Vernon
313	11,084	Hanover Area SD	Hanover Twp
314	11,073	Milton Area SD	Milton
315	11,053	Mid Valley SD	Throop
316	11,044	Palmyra Area SD	Palmyra
317	11,035	North Schuylkill SD	Ashland
318	11,009	Commonwealth Connections Acade	Harrisburg
319	11,007	Shippensburg Area SD	Shippensburg
320	10,970	Slippery Rock Area SD	Slippery Rock
321	10,961	Altoona Area SD	Altoona
322	10,939	Pottsville Area SD	Pottsville
323	10,929	Bermudian Springs SD	York Springs
324	10,919	Grove City Area SD	Grove City
325	10,871	West Shore SD	New Cumberland
326	10,808	Whitehall-Coplay SD	Whitehall
327	10,794	Reading SD	Reading
328	10,745	Pittston Area SD	Pittston
329	10,677	Mifflinburg Area SD	Mifflinburg
329	10,677	Warrior Run SD	Turbotville
331	10,668	Huntingdon Area SD	Huntingdon
332	10,627	Greater Nanticoke Area SD	Nanticoke
333	10,585	South Butler County SD	Saxonburg
334	10,534	Conewago Valley SD	New Oxford
335	10,530	Greencastle-Antrim SD	Greencastle
336	10,529	Westmont Hilltop SD	Johnstown
337	10,513	Norwin SD	N Huntingdon
338	10,492	Mifflin County SD	Lewistown
339	10,476	Lakeland SD	Jermyn
340	10,459	Girard SD	Girard
341	10,435	Dunmore SD	Dunmore
342	10,405	Pennsylvania Leadership Charter	West Chester
343	10,277	Peters Township SD	Mcmurray
344	10,228	Penn-Trafford SD	Harrison City
345	10,172	Saint Marys Area SD	Saint Marys
346	10,041	Wyoming Area SD	Exeter
347	9,712	Juniata County SD	Mifflintown
348	9,623	Hazleton Area SD	Hazleton
349	9,575	Mount Carmel Area SD	Mount Carmel
350	9,412	Crestwood SD	Mountain Top
351	9,234	Valley View SD	Archbald
352	9,218	Pennsylvania Virtual CS	Norristown
353	9,150	Pennsylvania Cyber CS	Midland
n/a	n/a	Central Valley SD	Monaca
n/a	n/a	Lehigh Career & Technical Inst	Schnecksville
n/a	n/a	York County School of Technology	York

Long-Term Debt per Student (end of FY)

Rank	Dollars	District Name	City
1	33,764	Lower Merion SD	Ardmore
2	32,406	Montour SD	Mckees Rocks
3	31,717	Radnor Township SD	Wayne
4	30,855	Richland SD	Johnstown
5	30,471	Quaker Valley SD	Sewickley
6	30,162	Springfield Township SD	Oreland
7	29,212	Ambridge Area SD	Ambridge
8	28,656	Southern Lehigh SD	Center Valley
9	28,573	Catasauqua Area SD	Catasauqua
10	27,684	Harrisburg City SD	Harrisburg
11	27,030	Garnet Valley SD	Glen Mills
12	26,406	Pine-Richland SD	Gibsonia
13	26,268	West Chester Area SD	West Chester
14	25,699	Upper Moreland Township SD	Willow Grove
15	25,647	Northwestern Lehigh SD	New Tripoli
16	25,592	Reading SD	Reading
17	25,360	Lower Moreland Township SD	Huntingdon Vlly
18	25,274	South Fayette Township SD	Mcdonald
19	25,264	West Allegheny SD	Oakdale
20	25,200	Mars Area SD	Mars
21	25,173	New Hope-Solebury SD	New Hope
22	24,708	Spring Grove Area SD	Spring Grove
23	24,625	Perkiomen Valley SD	Collegeville
24	24,445	Owen J Roberts SD	Pottstown
25	24,319	Northeastern York SD	Manchester
26	24,296	Moon Area SD	Moon Township
27	24,288	South Park SD	South Park
28	24,057	Coatesville Area SD	Coatesville
29	24,056	Oxford Area SD	Oxford
30	23,802	Spring-Ford Area SD	Royersford
31	23,320	Wallingford-Swarthmore SD	Wallingford
32	23,165	Jim Thorpe Area SD	Jim Thorpe
33	22,829	Daniel Boone Area SD	Birdsboro
34	22,714	Wellsboro Area SD	Wellsboro
35	22,654	Hampton Township SD	Allison Park
36	22,564	Great Valley SD	Malvern
37	22,549	Haverford Township SD	Havertown

Note: This section only includes districts with 1,500 or more students; All categories are ranked from high to low

38	22,303	Eastern York SD	Wrightsville
39	22,277	Mckeesport Area SD	Mckeesport
40	22,173	Twin Valley SD	Elverson
41	22,034	Upper Merion Area SD	King of Prussia
42	21,982	Pocono Mountain SD	Swiftwater
43	21,743	East Allegheny SD	N Versailles
44	21,625	Hanover Public SD	Hanover
45	21,621	Norwin SD	N Huntingdon
46	21,559	Conneaut SD	Linesville
47	21,476	Annville-Cleona SD	Annville
48	21,404	Keystone Oaks SD	Pittsburgh
49	21,360	Derry Township SD	Hershey
50	20,860	Uniontown Area SD	Uniontown
51	20,645	Baldwin-Whitehall SD	Pittsburgh
52	20,611	Chichester SD	Aston
53	20,604	Phoenixville Area SD	Phoenixville
54	20,393	Pennridge SD	Perkasie
55	20,360	Pequea Valley SD	Kinzers
56	20,357	Saucon Valley SD	Hellertown
57	20,329	Octorara Area SD	Atglen
58	20,318	Muhlenberg SD	Reading
59	20,154	Wilson SD	West Lawn
60	20,031	Athens Area SD	Athens
61	19,926	Chester-Upland SD	Chester
62	19,887	Troy Area SD	Troy
63	19,768	Lampeter-Strasburg SD	Lampeter
64	19,669	Blairsville-Saltsburg SD	Blairsville
65	19,641	Wattsburg Area SD	Erie
66	19,540	Rose Tree Media SD	Media
67	19,468	Middletown Area SD	Middletown
68	19,406	Beaver Area SD	Beaver
69	19,220	Somerset Area SD	Somerset
70	19,202	Canon-Mcmillan SD	Canonsburg
71	19,193	Bethlehem Area SD	Bethlehem
72	19,092	Burrell SD	Lower Burrell
73	19,021	North Pocono SD	Moscow
74	18,990	Mcguffey SD	Claysville
75	18,966	Philadelphia City SD	Philadelphia
76	18,897	Greater Johnstown SD	Johnstown
77	18,818	Oley Valley SD	Oley
78	18,756	Upper Dublin SD	Maple Glen
79	18,566	Manheim Township SD	Lititz
80	18,544	Warwick SD	Lititz
81	18,497	Shaler Area SD	Glenshaw
82	18,416	Springfield SD	Springfield
83	18,384	E Stroudsburg Area SD	E Stroudsburg
84	18,311	Nazareth Area SD	Nazareth
85	18,285	Brandywine Heights Area SD	Topton
86	18,234	Schuylkill Valley SD	Leesport
87	18,216	Quakertown Community SD	Quakertown
88	18,185	Central Dauphin SD	Harrisburg
89	18,175	Trinity Area SD	Washington
90	18,076	Yough SD	Herminie
91	18,016	East Penn SD	Emmaus
92	17,968	North Allegheny SD	Pittsburgh
93	17,928	Easton Area SD	Easton
93	17,928	Souderton Area SD	Souderton
95	17,816	Plum Borough SD	Plum
96	17,730	Dallas SD	Dallas
97	17,650	Palmyra Area SD	Palmyra
98	17,591	Palisades SD	Kintnersville
99	17,590	Kennett Consolidated SD	Kennett Square
100	17,506	Hermitage SD	Hermitage
101	17,445	Riverside SD	Taylor
102	17,443	Dallastown Area SD	Dallastown
103	17,382	Hopewell Area SD	Aliquippa
104	17,364	Ephrata Area SD	Ephrata
105	17,298	Manheim Central SD	Manheim
106	17,269	Southmoreland SD	Scottdale
107	17,221	York City SD	York
108	17,217	Pittsburgh SD	Pittsburgh
109	17,097	Downingtown Area SD	Downingtown
110	17,076	Governor Mifflin SD	Shillington
111	16,957	Hamburg Area SD	Hamburg
112	16,783	Central York SD	York
113	16,704	Exeter Township SD	Reading
114	16,646	Bellefonte Area SD	Bellefonte
115	16,548	Towanda Area SD	Towanda
116	16,460	Central Bucks SD	Doylestown
117	16,435	Abington SD	Abington
118	16,416	Hollidaysburg Area SD	Hollidaysburg
119	16,409	Fairview SD	Fairview
120	16,391	Brownsville Area SD	Brownsville
121	16,379	Northampton Area SD	Northampton
122	16,136	Susquenita SD	Duncannon

123	16,106	Upper Saint Clair SD	Pittsburgh
124	16,049	Kutztown Area SD	Kutztown
125	16,010	Mechanicsburg Area SD	Mechanicsburg
126	15,834	Red Lion Area SD	Red Lion
127	15,800	West Jefferson Hills SD	Jefferson Hills
128	15,465	Tulpehocken Area SD	Bethel
129	15,415	Central Greene SD	Waynesburg
130	15,375	Deer Lakes SD	Russellton
131	15,284	Methacton SD	Norristown
132	15,228	Stroudsburg Area SD	Stroudsburg
133	15,159	Pittston Area SD	Pittston
134	15,122	Penn-Delco SD	Aston
135	14,946	Eastern Lebanon County SD	Myerstown
136	14,878	Panther Valley SD	Lansford
137	14,856	Bangor Area SD	Bangor
138	14,852	Parkland SD	Allentown
139	14,809	Charleroi SD	Charleroi
140	14,616	Cumberland Valley SD	Mechanicsburg
141	14,565	Hempfield Area SD	Greensburg
142	14,476	Southern York County SD	Glen Rock
143	14,449	Pottsgrove SD	Pottstown
144	14,326	Big Beaver Falls Area SD	Beaver Falls
145	14,223	New Kensington-Arnold SD	New Kensington
146	14,217	Bermudian Springs SD	York Springs
147	14,121	Fleetwood Area SD	Fleetwood
148	14,104	Wallenpaupack Area SD	Hawley
149	13,948	Ligonier Valley SD	Ligonier
150	13,897	North Hills SD	Pittsburgh
151	13,856	Unionville-Chadds Ford SD	Kennett Square
152	13,810	Mount Lebanon SD	Pittsburgh
153	13,768	West Mifflin Area SD	West Mifflin
154	13,667	Gateway SD	Monroeville
155	13,618	Bloomsburg Area SD	Bloomsburg
156	13,531	Neshaminy SD	Langhorne
157	13,395	Big Spring SD	Newville
158	13,354	York Suburban SD	York
159	13,274	Upper Adams SD	Biglerville
160	13,269	Bensalem Township SD	Bensalem
161	13,246	Hempfield SD	Landisville
162	13,244	Council Rock SD	Newtown
163	13,124	Fort Leboeuf SD	Waterford
164	13,117	Jersey Shore Area SD	Jersey Shore
165	13,111	Chestnut Ridge SD	Fishertown
166	13,108	South Eastern SD	Fawn Grove
167	13,084	Wyomissing Area SD	Wyomissing
168	13,018	Northern York County SD	Dillsburg
169	12,901	Cheltenham Township SD	Elkins Park
170	12,753	Butler Area SD	Butler
171	12,695	Punxsutawney Area SD	Punxsutawney
171	12,695	Southern Tioga SD	Blossburg
173	12,630	South Middleton SD	Boiling Springs
174	12,586	Peters Township SD	Mcmurray
175	12,495	Seneca Valley SD	Harmony
176	12,485	Selinsgrove Area SD	Selinsgrove
177	12,454	Western Wayne SD	South Canaan
178	12,451	Hanover Area SD	Hanover Twp
179	12,395	Conestoga Valley SD	Lancaster
180	12,359	Greensburg Salem SD	Greensburg
181	12,350	Berwick Area SD	Berwick
182	12,274	Spring Cove SD	Roaring Spring
183	12,204	Ridley SD	Folsom
184	12,196	East Pennsboro Area SD	Enola
185	12,192	East Lycoming SD	Hughesville
186	12,057	Scranton SD	Scranton
187	12,036	Woodland Hills SD	Pittsburgh
188	12,021	Pleasant Valley SD	Brodheadsville
189	12,019	Tyrone Area SD	Tyrone
190	11,951	Brookville Area SD	Brookville
191	11,947	Blue Mountain SD	Orwigsburg
192	11,926	Harbor Creek SD	Harborcreek
193	11,871	Cornwall-Lebanon SD	Lebanon
194	11,827	Chambersburg Area SD	Chambersburg
195	11,728	Sharon City SD	Sharon
196	11,709	North East SD	North East
197	11,708	Mohawk Area SD	Bessemer
198	11,692	Colonial SD	Plymth Meeting
199	11,598	New Castle Area SD	New Castle
200	11,545	Whitehall-Coplay SD	Whitehall
201	11,460	Pottstown SD	Pottstown
202	11,377	Avon Grove SD	West Grove
203	11,362	Shippensburg Area SD	Shippensburg
204	11,353	Wayne Highlands SD	Honesdale
205	11,305	Wilson Area SD	Easton
206	11,302	Elizabeth Forward SD	Elizabeth
207	11,289	Pennsbury SD	Fallsington

208	11,242	Steel Valley SD	Munhall
209	11,160	Kiski Area SD	Leechburg
210	11,100	Conrad Weiser Area SD	Robesonia
211	11,056	Corry Area SD	Corry
212	11,005	Littlestown Area SD	Littlestown
213	10,965	Chartiers Valley SD	Pittsburgh
214	10,939	Lower Dauphin SD	Hummelstown
215	10,910	South Allegheny SD	Mckeesport
216	10,855	Franklin Regional SD	Murrysville
217	10,828	Philipsburg-Osceola Area SD	Philipsburg
218	10,713	Marple Newtown SD	Newtown Square
219	10,681	Wyoming Area SD	Exeter
220	10,671	General Mclane SD	Edinboro
221	10,669	Connellsville Area SD	Connellsville
222	10,626	Freeport Area SD	Sarver
223	10,594	Hazleton Area SD	Hazleton
223	10,594	Northern Tioga SD	Elkland
225	10,530	Gettysburg Area SD	Gettysburg
226	10,447	Indiana Area SD	Indiana
227	10,377	Central Columbia SD	Bloomsburg
228	10,368	Carlisle Area SD	Carlisle
229	10,257	Lewisburg Area SD	Lewisburg
230	10,252	Belle Vernon Area SD	Belle Vernon
231	10,226	Susquehanna Township SD	Harrisburg
232	10,204	Norristown Area SD	Norristown
233	10,180	South Butler County SD	Saxonburg
234	10,142	Girard SD	Girard
235	10,090	Albert Gallatin Area SD	Uniontown
236	10,024	West York Area SD	York
237	9,977	Cocalico SD	Denver
238	9,957	Penn Cambria SD	Cresson
239	9,937	Greater Latrobe SD	Latrobe
240	9,924	Crawford Central SD	Meadville
241	9,883	Highlands SD	Natrona Heights
242	9,870	Mount Pleasant Area SD	Mount Pleasant
243	9,829	West Perry SD	Elliottsburg
244	9,787	Tredyffrin-Easttown SD	Wayne
245	9,779	Salisbury Township SD	Allentown
246	9,757	Northern Lebanon SD	Fredericksburg
247	9,704	Laurel Highlands SD	Uniontown
248	9,611	Riverside Beaver County SD	Ellwood City
249	9,561	Interboro SD	Prospect Park
250	9,501	Tunkhannock Area SD	Tunkhannock
251	9,478	Erie City SD	Erie
252	9,450	Moniteau SD	West Sunbury
253	9,398	Penn Manor SD	Lancaster
254	9,294	Lancaster SD	Lancaster
255	9,291	Mifflin County SD	Lewistown
256	9,134	North Schuylkill SD	Ashland
257	9,106	Mount Carmel Area SD	Mount Carmel
258	9,079	Shikellamy SD	Sunbury
259	9,047	Upper Perkiomen SD	Pennsburg
260	9,026	Bedford Area SD	Bedford
261	8,802	Hatboro-Horsham SD	Horsham
262	8,732	Armstrong SD	Ford City
263	8,514	Valley View SD	Archbald
264	8,390	Waynesboro Area SD	Waynesboro
265	8,381	Greater Nanticoke Area SD	Nanticoke
266	8,379	Marion Center Area SD	Marion Center
267	8,349	Palmerton Area SD	Palmerton
268	8,304	State College Area SD	State College
269	8,288	Derry Area SD	Derry
270	8,269	North Penn SD	Lansdale
271	8,251	Boyertown Area SD	Boyertown
272	8,198	Keystone Central SD	Lock Haven
273	8,174	Lebanon SD	Lebanon
274	8,173	Titusville Area SD	Titusville
275	8,160	Ringgold SD	New Eagle
276	8,126	Dover Area SD	Dover
277	8,112	Mid Valley SD	Throop
278	8,102	Conewago Valley SD	New Oxford
279	8,098	New Brighton Area SD	New Brighton
280	8,034	Abington Heights SD	Clarks Summit
281	7,999	Huntingdon Area SD	Huntingdon
282	7,882	Tuscarora SD	Mercersburg
283	7,878	South Western SD	Hanover
284	7,824	Tamaqua Area SD	Tamaqua
285	7,811	Millcreek Township SD	Erie
286	7,803	Bradford Area SD	Bradford
287	7,694	Donegal SD	Mount Joy
288	7,627	Eastern Lancaster County SD	New Holland
289	7,573	Danville Area SD	Danville
290	7,465	Pine Grove Area SD	Pine Grove
291	7,403	Altoona Area SD	Altoona
292	7,187	Slippery Rock Area SD	Slippery Rock

Note: This section only includes districts with 1,500 or more students; All categories are ranked from high to low

293	6,999	Southeast Delco SD	Folcroft
294	6,989	Fox Chapel Area SD	Pittsburgh
295	6,936	Crestwood SD	Mountain Top
296	6,908	Dunmore SD	Dunmore
297	6,872	Wissahickon SD	Ambler
298	6,841	Northern Lehigh SD	Slatington
299	6,744	Elizabethtown Area SD	Elizabethtown
300	6,560	Wilkes-Barre Area SD	Wilkes Barre
301	6,460	Williamsport Area SD	Williamsport
302	6,184	Milton Area SD	Milton
303	6,021	Mount Union Area SD	Mount Union
304	5,902	Lake-Lehman SD	Dallas
305	5,877	Greencastle-Antrim SD	Greencastle
306	5,711	Washington SD	Washington
307	5,663	West Shore SD	New Cumberland
308	5,556	Lehighton Area SD	Lehighton
309	5,434	Midd-West SD	Middleburg
310	5,396	Dubois Area SD	Du Bois
311	5,305	Solanco SD	Quarryville
312	5,292	Central Cambria SD	Ebensburg
313	5,243	Carbondale Area SD	Carbondale
314	5,227	Montoursville Area SD	Montoursville
315	5,187	Northwestern SD	Albion
316	5,119	Forest Hills SD	Sidman
317	4,985	Ellwood City Area SD	Ellwood City
318	4,970	Warren County SD	North Warren
319	4,645	Freedom Area SD	Freedom
320	4,612	Karns City Area SD	Karns City
321	4,539	Allentown City SD	Allentown
322	4,454	Delaware Valley SD	Milford
323	4,431	Bald Eagle Area SD	Wingate
324	4,338	Blackhawk SD	Beaver Falls
325	4,317	Saint Marys Area SD	Saint Marys
326	4,291	Pen Argyl Area SD	Pen Argyl
327	4,267	Upper Darby SD	Drexel Hill
328	4,231	Penn-Trafford SD	Harrison City
329	4,135	Bristol Township SD	Levittown
330	4,121	William Penn SD	Lansdowne
331	4,010	Oil City Area SD	Oil City
332	3,722	Franklin Area SD	Franklin
333	3,636	Penncrest SD	Saegertown
334	3,339	Penn Hills SD	Pittsburgh
335	3,330	Westmont Hilltop SD	Johnstown
336	3,222	Mifflinburg Area SD	Mifflinburg
337	3,036	Montrose Area SD	Montrose
338	2,948	Clearfield Area SD	Clearfield
339	2,799	Pottsville Area SD	Pottsville
340	2,369	Centennial SD	Warminster
341	1,464	Juniata County SD	Mifflintown
342	1,250	Warrior Run SD	Turbotville
343	1,082	Bethel Park SD	Bethel Park
344	1,060	Wyoming Valley West SD	Kingston
345	931	Pennsylvania Leadership Charter	West Chester
346	666	Pennsylvania Cyber CS	Midland
347	513	Grove City Area SD	Grove City
348	31	Shamokin Area SD	Coal Township
349	0	Agora Cyber CS	Wayne
349	0	Chester Community CS	Chester
349	0	Commonwealth Connections Acade	Harrisburg
349	0	Lakeland SD	Jermyn
349	0	Pennsylvania Virtual CS	Norristown
n/a	n/a	Central Valley SD	Monaca
n/a	n/a	Lehigh Career & Technical Inst	Schnecksville
n/a	n/a	York County School of Technology	York

Number of Diploma Recipients

Rank	Number	District Name	City
1	8,377	Philadelphia City SD	Philadelphia
2	1,716	Pittsburgh SD	Pittsburgh
3	1,529	Central Bucks SD	Doylestown
4	1,142	Bethlehem Area SD	Bethlehem
5	1,086	Council Rock SD	Newtown
6	1,068	Allentown City SD	Allentown
7	1,037	North Penn SD	Lansdale
8	971	Pocono Mountain SD	Swiftwater
9	919	West Chester Area SD	West Chester
10	899	Downingtown Area SD	Downingtown
11	863	Pennsylvania Cyber CS	Midland
12	862	Central Dauphin SD	Harrisburg
13	858	Pennsbury SD	Fallsington
14	803	Upper Darby SD	Drexel Hill
15	777	Hazleton Area SD	Hazleton
16	773	Parkland SD	Allentown
17	767	Neshaminy SD	Langhorne
18	760	Reading SD	Reading
19	728	Erie City SD	Erie
20	690	North Allegheny SD	Pittsburgh
21	684	West Shore SD	New Cumberland
22	681	East Penn SD	Emmaus
23	679	Scranton SD	Scranton
24	652	E Stroudsburg Area SD	E Stroudsburg
25	637	Abington SD	Abington
26	634	Easton Area SD	Easton
27	596	State College Area SD	State College
28	591	Chambersburg Area SD	Chambersburg
29	589	Butler Area SD	Butler
30	588	Cumberland Valley SD	Mechanicsburg
31	581	Lancaster SD	Lancaster
31	581	Millcreek Township SD	Erie
33	580	Lower Merion SD	Ardmore
34	564	Hempfield SD	Landisville
35	551	Coatesville Area SD	Coatesville
35	551	Pennridge SD	Perkasie
37	537	Seneca Valley SD	Harmony
38	531	Boyertown Area SD	Boyertown
39	527	Ridley SD	Folsom
40	519	Altoona Area SD	Altoona
41	509	Souderton Area SD	Souderton
42	505	Spring-Ford Area SD	Royersford
43	503	Harrisburg City SD	Harrisburg
44	493	Wilkes-Barre Area SD	Wilkes Barre
45	490	Tredyffrin-Easttown SD	Wayne
46	480	Hempfield Area SD	Greensburg
47	479	Bensalem Township SD	Bensalem
48	477	Centennial SD	Warminster
48	477	Mount Lebanon SD	Pittsburgh
50	474	Penn Manor SD	Lancaster
51	467	Pleasant Valley SD	Brodheadsville
52	455	Northampton Area SD	Northampton
53	454	Wilson SD	West Lawn
54	450	Delaware Valley SD	Milford
55	445	Manheim Township SD	Lititz
55	445	Methacton SD	Norristown
57	444	Shaler Area SD	Glenshaw
58	441	Colonial SD	Plymth Meeting
59	438	Norristown Area SD	Norristown
60	433	Mifflin County SD	Lewistown
61	422	Bristol Township SD	Levittown
61	422	Haverford Township SD	Havertown
63	420	Warren County SD	North Warren
64	416	Norwin SD	N Huntingdon
65	414	Chester-Upland SD	Chester
66	412	Fox Chapel Area SD	Pittsburgh
67	409	Quakertown Community SD	Quakertown
68	407	Hatboro-Horsham SD	Horsham
68	407	Upper Dublin SD	Maple Glen
70	403	Cheltenham Township SD	Elkins Park
71	402	Penn Hills SD	Pittsburgh
72	392	North Hills SD	Pittsburgh
73	390	Penn-Trafford SD	Harrison City
74	386	Central York SD	York
75	383	Avon Grove SD	West Grove
75	383	Cornwall-Lebanon SD	Lebanon
77	381	Warwick SD	Lititz
78	380	Dallastown Area SD	Dallastown
79	379	William Penn SD	Lansdowne
80	377	Nazareth Area SD	Nazareth
81	375	Wissahickon SD	Ambler
82	371	Bethel Park SD	Bethel Park
83	364	Perkiomen Valley SD	Collegeville
84	362	Gateway SD	Monroeville
85	360	Red Lion Area SD	Red Lion
86	358	Stroudsburg Area SD	Stroudsburg
87	357	Williamsport Area SD	Williamsport
88	356	Peters Township SD	Mcmurray
89	355	Armstrong SD	Ford City
90	354	Baldwin-Whitehall SD	Pittsburgh
91	350	Keystone Central SD	Lock Haven
92	349	Rose Tree Media SD	Media
93	346	Whitehall-Coplay SD	Whitehall
94	345	Plum Borough SD	Plum
95	343	Unionville-Chadds Ford SD	Kennett Square
96	335	Garnet Valley SD	Glen Mills
97	332	Kiski Area SD	Leechburg
97	332	Pine-Richland SD	Gibsonia
99	330	Interboro SD	Prospect Park
99	330	Pennsylvania Leadership Charter	West Chester
99	330	Woodland Hills SD	Pittsburgh
102	328	Wyoming Valley West SD	Kingston
103	326	Greater Latrobe SD	Latrobe
103	326	Upper Saint Clair SD	Pittsburgh
105	324	Penncrest SD	Saegertown
106	322	Carlisle Area SD	Carlisle
106	322	Governor Mifflin SD	Shillington
108	318	Wallenpaupack Area SD	Hawley
109	314	Lower Dauphin SD	Hummelstown
110	313	Elizabethtown Area SD	Elizabethtown
111	311	Exeter Township SD	Reading
112	309	Connellsville Area SD	Connellsville
113	306	Canon-Mcmillan SD	Canonsburg
113	306	Great Valley SD	Malvern
113	306	Hollidaysburg Area SD	Hollidaysburg
116	305	Marple Newtown SD	Newtown Square
117	304	Albert Gallatin Area SD	Uniontown
118	301	Cocalico SD	Denver
118	301	Derry Township SD	Hershey
120	297	Abington Heights SD	Clarks Summit
120	297	Waynesboro Area SD	Waynesboro
122	295	Crawford Central SD	Meadville
123	292	Mckeesport Area SD	Mckeesport
123	292	Penn-Delco SD	Aston
125	291	Franklin Regional SD	Murrysville
126	289	Wallingford-Swarthmore SD	Wallingford
127	287	Ephrata Area SD	Ephrata
127	287	West Mifflin Area SD	West Mifflin
129	286	South Western SD	Hanover
130	285	Eastern Lancaster County SD	New Holland
130	285	Radnor Township SD	Wayne
132	284	Owen J Roberts SD	Pottstown
133	282	Moon Area SD	Moon Township
134	280	Trinity Area SD	Washington
134	280	Upper Moreland Township SD	Willow Grove
136	279	Solanco SD	Quarryville
137	277	Lampeter-Strasburg SD	Lampeter
138	276	Pittston Area SD	Pittston
138	276	Twin Valley SD	Elverson
138	276	York County School of Technology	York
141	274	Conewago Valley SD	New Oxford
141	274	Manheim Central SD	Manheim
143	272	Crestwood SD	Mountain Top
143	272	Pottsville Area SD	Pottsville
145	269	Oxford Area SD	Oxford
146	268	Dubois Area SD	Du Bois
147	266	Upper Merion Area SD	King of Prussia
148	265	Mechanicsburg Area SD	Mechanicsburg
149	263	Belle Vernon Area SD	Belle Vernon
149	263	Gettysburg Area SD	Gettysburg
151	262	Chartiers Valley SD	Pittsburgh
151	262	Daniel Boone Area SD	Birdsboro
151	262	York City SD	York
154	261	Chichester SD	Aston
154	261	Greensburg Salem SD	Greensburg
156	259	Muhlenberg SD	Reading
156	259	Southeast Delco SD	Folcroft
158	257	Bangor Area SD	Bangor
158	257	Spring Grove Area SD	Spring Grove
160	256	Shippensburg Area SD	Shippensburg
161	255	Springfield SD	Springfield
162	253	North Pocono SD	Moscow
163	252	Conestoga Valley SD	Lancaster
164	251	Conrad Weiser Area SD	Robesonia
165	250	West Allegheny SD	Oakdale
166	249	Big Spring SD	Newville
167	248	East Pennsboro Area SD	Enola
168	247	Southern York County SD	Glen Rock
169	246	Bellefonte Area SD	Bellefonte
169	246	Kennett Consolidated SD	Kennett Square
169	246	West Jefferson Hills SD	Jefferson Hills
172	245	Elizabeth Forward SD	Elizabeth
172	245	Hampton Township SD	Allison Park
172	245	Northern York County SD	Dillsburg
175	243	Bradford Area SD	Bradford
176	240	Indiana Area SD	Indiana
177	239	Juniata County SD	Mifflintown
178	236	Montour SD	Mckees Rocks
179	234	Hopewell Area SD	Aliquippa
180	233	Wayne Highlands SD	Honesdale
181	232	Ringgold SD	New Eagle
182	230	Northeastern York SD	Manchester
182	230	Upper Perkiomen SD	Pennsburg
184	227	Southern Lehigh SD	Center Valley
185	226	Blackhawk SD	Beaver Falls
185	226	Clearfield Area SD	Clearfield

Note: This section only includes districts with 1,500 or more students; All categories are ranked from high to low

187	225	Laurel Highlands SD	Uniontown
188	224	Blue Mountain SD	Orwigsburg
188	224	Susquehanna Township SD	Harrisburg
190	220	South Butler County SD	Saxonburg
191	219	Palmyra Area SD	Palmyra
191	219	Yough SD	Herminie
193	217	Dover Area SD	Dover
193	217	Mars Area SD	Mars
195	216	Greater Johnstown SD	Johnstown
196	215	Derry Area SD	Derry
197	214	Grove City Area SD	Grove City
197	214	Punxsutawney Area SD	Punxsutawney
197	214	Saint Marys Area SD	Saint Marys
197	214	Shikellamy SD	Sunbury
201	213	Dallas SD	Dallas
202	212	Berwick Area SD	Berwick
203	211	South Eastern SD	Fawn Grove
204	210	Valley View SD	Archbald
205	208	Somerset Area SD	Somerset
205	208	Tunkhannock Area SD	Tunkhannock
205	208	Uniontown Area SD	Uniontown
208	207	Northern Lebanon SD	Fredericksburg
209	206	West York Area SD	York
210	205	Conneaut SD	Linesville
210	205	Wyoming Area SD	Exeter
212	204	Fleetwood Area SD	Fleetwood
212	204	Greencastle-Antrim SD	Greencastle
212	204	Phoenixville Area SD	Phoenixville
215	203	Donegal SD	Mount Joy
215	203	York Suburban SD	York
217	202	Danville Area SD	Danville
217	202	New Castle Area SD	New Castle
219	201	Keystone Oaks SD	Pittsburgh
220	200	Octorara Area SD	Atglen
220	200	Oil City Area SD	Oil City
222	198	Saucon Valley SD	Hellertown
223	194	Lebanon SD	Lebanon
224	192	Eastern Lebanon County SD	Myerstown
225	191	Hermitage SD	Hermitage
226	190	Selinsgrove Area SD	Selinsgrove
227	189	Eastern York SD	Wrightsville
228	188	Ambridge Area SD	Ambridge
229	187	Corry Area SD	Corry
230	185	Tuscarora SD	Mercersburg
231	183	General Mclane SD	Edinboro
231	183	Pottsgrove SD	Pottstown
233	182	Jersey Shore Area SD	Jersey Shore
233	182	Mount Pleasant Area SD	Mount Pleasant
233	182	Northern Tioga SD	Elkland
236	181	Northwestern Lehigh SD	New Tripoli
237	180	Bedford Area SD	Bedford
237	180	Palisades SD	Kintnersville
239	179	Milton Area SD	Milton
239	179	Wilson Area SD	Easton
241	178	Forest Hills SD	Sidman
241	178	Montoursville Area SD	Montoursville
243	177	Southmoreland SD	Scottdale
244	176	West Perry SD	Elliottsburg
245	175	Lower Moreland Township SD	Huntingdon Vlly
245	175	Slippery Rock Area SD	Slippery Rock
247	174	Highlands SD	Natrona Heights
247	174	Midd-West SD	Middleburg
249	173	Athens Area SD	Athens
250	172	Franklin Area SD	Franklin
251	171	Littlestown Area SD	Littlestown
252	170	Greater Nanticoke Area SD	Nanticoke
253	169	Bald Eagle Area SD	Wingate
253	169	Beaver Area SD	Beaver
253	169	Lehighton Area SD	Lehighton
256	168	Huntingdon Area SD	Huntingdon
257	167	Hamburg Area SD	Hamburg
258	166	Shamokin Area SD	Coal Township
259	165	Brandywine Heights Area SD	Topton
259	165	Spring Cove SD	Roaring Spring
261	164	Central Cambria SD	Ebensburg
261	164	Oley Valley SD	Oley
261	164	Penn Cambria SD	Cresson
264	163	Fort Leboeuf SD	Waterford
264	163	South Middleton SD	Boiling Springs
266	162	Mifflinburg Area SD	Mifflinburg
267	161	Girard SD	Girard
268	160	Dunmore SD	Dunmore
269	159	Mcguffey SD	Claysville
269	159	North East SD	North East
269	159	Pen Argyl Area SD	Pen Argyl
272	158	South Fayette Township SD	Mcdonald
272	158	South Park SD	South Park
274	157	Central Columbia SD	Bloomsburg
274	157	Northern Lehigh SD	Slatington
274	157	Tamaqua Area SD	Tamaqua
277	156	Bermudian Springs SD	York Springs
277	156	Harbor Creek SD	Harborcreek
277	156	Westmont Hilltop SD	Johnstown
280	155	Blairsville-Saltsburg SD	Blairsville
280	155	Ligonier Valley SD	Ligonier
280	155	Springfield Township SD	Oreland
283	154	Central Greene SD	Waynesburg
283	154	Lakeland SD	Jermyn
283	154	Pequea Valley SD	Kinzers
283	154	Schuylkill Valley SD	Leesport
287	153	Deer Lakes SD	Russellton
287	153	Richland SD	Johnstown
289	152	Lake-Lehman SD	Dallas
289	152	Salisbury Township SD	Allentown
289	152	Southern Tioga SD	Blossburg
292	151	Freedom Area SD	Freedom
293	150	Susquenita SD	Duncannon
294	147	Riverside Beaver County SD	Ellwood City
294	147	Titusville Area SD	Titusville
296	146	Freeport Area SD	Sarver
296	146	Hanover Area SD	Hanover Twp
296	146	Pottstown SD	Pottstown
296	146	Towanda Area SD	Towanda
300	145	Middletown Area SD	Middletown
301	144	Agora Cyber CS	Wayne
301	144	Fairview SD	Fairview
301	144	Montrose Area SD	Montrose
301	144	Pine Grove Area SD	Pine Grove
301	144	Tulpehocken Area SD	Bethel
306	143	Mount Carmel Area SD	Mount Carmel
306	143	Steel Valley SD	Munhall
308	142	Burrell SD	Lower Burrell
308	142	Kutztown Area SD	Kutztown
310	141	South Allegheny SD	Mckeesport
310	141	Wyomissing Area SD	Wyomissing
312	139	Jim Thorpe Area SD	Jim Thorpe
312	139	North Schuylkill SD	Ashland
314	137	Sharon City SD	Sharon
315	136	Brookville Area SD	Brookville
315	136	Western Wayne SD	South Canaan
317	135	Northwestern SD	Albion
317	135	Upper Adams SD	Biglerville
319	132	East Allegheny SD	N Versailles
319	132	Moniteau SD	West Sunbury
321	131	Chestnut Ridge SD	Fishertown
321	131	Ellwood City Area SD	Ellwood City
321	131	Panther Valley SD	Lansford
321	131	Warrior Run SD	Turbotville
325	130	Mohawk Area SD	Bessemer
325	130	New Kensington-Arnold SD	New Kensington
327	129	Troy Area SD	Troy
327	129	Wattsburg Area SD	Erie
329	128	Big Beaver Falls Area SD	Beaver Falls
329	128	Brownsville Area SD	Brownsville
329	128	Lewisburg Area SD	Lewisburg
329	128	Philipsburg-Osceola Area SD	Philipsburg
333	126	Karns City Area SD	Karns City
334	125	Charleroi SD	Charleroi
334	125	Quaker Valley SD	Sewickley
336	123	East Lycoming SD	Hughesville
337	122	Mid Valley SD	Throop
337	122	Palmerton Area SD	Palmerton
339	121	New Brighton Area SD	New Brighton
340	120	Tyrone Area SD	Tyrone
341	115	New Hope-Solebury SD	New Hope
342	114	Wellsboro Area SD	Wellsboro
343	113	Annville-Cleona SD	Annville
344	112	Catasauqua Area SD	Catasauqua
344	112	Washington SD	Washington
346	111	Mount Union Area SD	Mount Union
347	108	Bloomsburg Area SD	Bloomsburg
348	107	Marion Center Area SD	Marion Center
349	102	Riverside SD	Taylor
350	98	Pennsylvania Virtual CS	Norristown
351	95	Carbondale Area SD	Carbondale
352	91	Commonwealth Connections Acade	Harrisburg
353	89	Hanover Public SD	Hanover
n/a	n/a	Central Valley SD	Monaca
n/a	n/a	Chester Community CS	Chester
n/a	n/a	Lehigh Career & Technical Inst	Schnecksville

High School Drop-out Rate

Rank	Percent	District Name	City
1	11.2	Chester-Upland SD	Chester
2	11.0	Agora Cyber CS	Wayne
3	10.0	Reading SD	Reading
4	9.1	Allentown City SD	Allentown
5	7.2	Pennsylvania Leadership Charter	West Chester
5	7.2	York City SD	York
7	7.0	Philadelphia City SD	Philadelphia
8	6.3	Harrisburg City SD	Harrisburg
9	5.6	Altoona Area SD	Altoona
9	5.6	Pittsburgh SD	Pittsburgh
11	5.2	Brownsville Area SD	Brownsville
12	4.9	Lancaster SD	Lancaster
13	4.8	Waynesboro Area SD	Waynesboro
14	4.6	Lebanon SD	Lebanon
14	4.6	Western Wayne SD	South Canaan
16	4.5	New Kensington-Arnold SD	New Kensington
16	4.5	Williamsport Area SD	Williamsport
18	4.4	Hazleton Area SD	Hazleton
19	4.3	Clearfield Area SD	Clearfield
20	4.2	Shikellamy SD	Sunbury
21	4.1	Greater Johnstown SD	Johnstown
22	4.0	Dubois Area SD	Du Bois
23	3.9	Albert Gallatin Area SD	Uniontown
23	3.9	Pottsville Area SD	Pottsville
23	3.9	Washington SD	Washington
26	3.7	Tamaqua Area SD	Tamaqua
26	3.7	Tyrone Area SD	Tyrone
28	3.6	Laurel Highlands SD	Uniontown
28	3.6	Mid Valley SD	Throop
28	3.6	Woodland Hills SD	Pittsburgh
31	3.5	Mckeesport Area SD	Mckeesport
31	3.5	Norristown Area SD	Norristown
33	3.4	Athens Area SD	Athens
33	3.4	Donegal SD	Mount Joy
35	3.2	Lehighton Area SD	Lehighton
35	3.2	Mount Pleasant Area SD	Mount Pleasant
35	3.2	North East SD	North East
35	3.2	Northern Tioga SD	Elkland
35	3.2	Philipsburg-Osceola Area SD	Philipsburg
35	3.2	Slippery Rock Area SD	Slippery Rock
35	3.2	Troy Area SD	Troy
35	3.2	Tuscarora SD	Mercersburg
43	3.1	Penn Hills SD	Pittsburgh
43	3.1	Punxsutawney Area SD	Punxsutawney
45	3.0	Hanover Public SD	Hanover
45	3.0	Jersey Shore Area SD	Jersey Shore
45	3.0	Kiski Area SD	Leechburg
45	3.0	Muhlenberg SD	Reading
45	3.0	Warren County SD	North Warren
50	2.9	Bethlehem Area SD	Bethlehem
50	2.9	Crawford Central SD	Meadville
50	2.9	Gettysburg Area SD	Gettysburg
50	2.9	North Schuylkill SD	Ashland
50	2.9	Pine Grove Area SD	Pine Grove
50	2.9	York County School of Technology	York
56	2.8	Bedford Area SD	Bedford
56	2.8	Berwick Area SD	Berwick
56	2.8	Manheim Central SD	Manheim
56	2.8	Pennsylvania Cyber CS	Midland
56	2.8	Southeast Delco SD	Folcroft
56	2.8	Towanda Area SD	Towanda
62	2.7	Chichester SD	Aston
63	2.6	Bristol Township SD	Levittown
63	2.6	Central Dauphin SD	Harrisburg
63	2.6	Eastern York SD	Wrightsville
63	2.6	Midd-West SD	Middleburg
63	2.6	Wellsboro Area SD	Wellsboro
63	2.6	West Perry SD	Elliottsburg
69	2.5	Big Spring SD	Newville
69	2.5	Southern Tioga SD	Blossburg
69	2.5	Upper Darby SD	Drexel Hill
72	2.4	Bensalem Township SD	Bensalem
72	2.4	Easton Area SD	Easton
72	2.4	Mcguffey SD	Claysville
72	2.4	Mifflin County SD	Lewistown
72	2.4	Pennsylvania Virtual CS	Norristown
72	2.4	Sharon City SD	Sharon
72	2.4	Southmoreland SD	Scottdale
79	2.3	Ambridge Area SD	Ambridge
79	2.3	Chambersburg Area SD	Chambersburg
79	2.3	Northern York County SD	Dillsburg
79	2.3	Panther Valley SD	Lansford

Note: This section only includes districts with 1,500 or more students; All categories are ranked from high to low

Rank		District	Location	Rank		District	Location	Rank		District	Location
79	2.3	Shamokin Area SD	Coal Township	161	1.4	Hempfield Area SD	Greensburg	249	0.8	Elizabeth Forward SD	Elizabeth
79	2.3	West Shore SD	New Cumberland	161	1.4	Hollidaysburg Area SD	Hollidaysburg	249	0.8	Fairview SD	Fairview
85	2.2	Keystone Oaks SD	Pittsburgh	161	1.4	Lake-Lehman SD	Dallas	249	0.8	Fleetwood Area SD	Fleetwood
85	2.2	Mechanicsburg Area SD	Mechanicsburg	161	1.4	Mohawk Area SD	Bessemer	249	0.8	Neshaminy SD	Langhorne
85	2.2	Northern Lebanon SD	Fredericksburg	161	1.4	Northern Lehigh SD	Slatington	249	0.8	Northwestern Lehigh SD	New Tripoli
85	2.2	Pen Argyl Area SD	Pen Argyl	161	1.4	Riverside Beaver County SD	Ellwood City	249	0.8	Penncrest SD	Saegertown
85	2.2	Wyoming Valley West SD	Kingston	161	1.4	Shaler Area SD	Glenshaw	249	0.8	Saucon Valley SD	Hellertown
90	2.1	Brookville Area SD	Brookville	161	1.4	Springfield SD	Springfield	249	0.8	Selinsgrove Area SD	Selinsgrove
90	2.1	Central Greene SD	Waynesburg	161	1.4	Susquenita SD	Duncannon	249	0.8	Seneca Valley SD	Harmony
90	2.1	Conneaut SD	Linesville	161	1.4	Upper Adams SD	Biglerville	249	0.8	Souderton Area SD	Souderton
90	2.1	Daniel Boone Area SD	Birdsboro	178	1.3	Belle Vernon Area SD	Belle Vernon	249	0.8	State College Area SD	State College
90	2.1	East Pennsboro Area SD	Enola	178	1.3	Bellefonte Area SD	Bellefonte	249	0.8	Trinity Area SD	Washington
90	2.1	Ellwood City Area SD	Ellwood City	178	1.3	Bradford Area SD	Bradford	249	0.8	Twin Valley SD	Elverson
90	2.1	Franklin Area SD	Franklin	178	1.3	Connellsville Area SD	Connellsville	249	0.8	Uniontown Area SD	Uniontown
90	2.1	Kennett Consolidated SD	Kennett Square	178	1.3	Conrad Weiser Area SD	Robesonia	249	0.8	West Chester Area SD	West Chester
90	2.1	New Castle Area SD	New Castle	178	1.3	General Mclane SD	Edinboro	268	0.7	Cheltenham Township SD	Elkins Park
90	2.1	Somerset Area SD	Somerset	178	1.3	Greater Latrobe SD	Latrobe	268	0.7	Fort Leboeuf SD	Waterford
100	2.0	Greensburg Salem SD	Greensburg	178	1.3	Hamburg Area SD	Hamburg	268	0.7	Freedom Area SD	Freedom
100	2.0	New Brighton Area SD	New Brighton	178	1.3	Milton Area SD	Milton	268	0.7	Governor Mifflin SD	Shillington
100	2.0	Northeastern York SD	Manchester	178	1.3	Oley Valley SD	Oley	268	0.7	Greater Nanticoke Area SD	Nanticoke
100	2.0	Pottstown SD	Pottstown	178	1.3	Shippensburg Area SD	Shippensburg	268	0.7	Nazareth Area SD	Nazareth
100	2.0	Ridley SD	Folsom	178	1.3	Wattsburg Area SD	Erie	268	0.7	Penn Manor SD	Lancaster
100	2.0	Scranton SD	Scranton	178	1.3	West Allegheny SD	Oakdale	268	0.7	Plum Borough SD	Plum
100	2.0	Solanco SD	Quarryville	191	1.2	East Penn SD	Emmaus	268	0.7	South Allegheny SD	Mckeesport
100	2.0	South Middleton SD	Boiling Springs	191	1.2	Interboro SD	Prospect Park	268	0.7	Warwick SD	Lititz
100	2.0	Titusville Area SD	Titusville	191	1.2	Kutztown Area SD	Kutztown	268	0.7	West Mifflin Area SD	West Mifflin
109	1.9	Big Beaver Falls Area SD	Beaver Falls	191	1.2	Palisades SD	Kintnersville	268	0.7	Wilson Area SD	Easton
109	1.9	Cumberland Valley SD	Mechanicsburg	191	1.2	Penn Cambria SD	Cresson	280	0.6	Beaver Area SD	Beaver
109	1.9	Derry Area SD	Derry	191	1.2	South Butler County SD	Saxonburg	280	0.6	Bethel Park SD	Bethel Park
109	1.9	Forest Hills SD	Sidman	191	1.2	Spring Cove SD	Roaring Spring	280	0.6	Central York SD	York
109	1.9	Hanover Area SD	Hanover Twp	191	1.2	Wallenpaupack Area SD	Hawley	280	0.6	Cocalico SD	Denver
109	1.9	Hermitage SD	Hermitage	199	1.1	Abington SD	Abington	280	0.6	Deer Lakes SD	Russellton
109	1.9	Montoursville Area SD	Montoursville	199	1.1	Boyertown Area SD	Boyertown	280	0.6	Freeport Area SD	Sarver
109	1.9	Mount Carmel Area SD	Mount Carmel	199	1.1	Burrell SD	Lower Burrell	280	0.6	Marple Newtown SD	Newtown Square
109	1.9	Oil City Area SD	Oil City	199	1.1	Centennial SD	Warminster	280	0.6	Parkland SD	Allentown
109	1.9	Palmyra Area SD	Palmyra	199	1.1	Charleroi SD	Charleroi	280	0.6	Southern Lehigh SD	Center Valley
109	1.9	Schuylkill Valley SD	Leesport	199	1.1	Dallas SD	Dallas	280	0.6	Upper Moreland Township SD	Willow Grove
120	1.8	Butler Area SD	Butler	199	1.1	Gateway SD	Monroeville	280	0.6	West Jefferson Hills SD	Jefferson Hills
120	1.8	Carbondale Area SD	Carbondale	199	1.1	Harbor Creek SD	Harborcreek	291	0.5	Avon Grove SD	West Grove
120	1.8	Conewago Valley SD	New Oxford	199	1.1	Huntingdon Area SD	Huntingdon	291	0.5	Chartiers Valley SD	Pittsburgh
120	1.8	Dunmore SD	Dunmore	199	1.1	Keystone Central SD	Lock Haven	291	0.5	Colonial SD	Plymth Meeting
120	1.8	Karns City Area SD	Karns City	199	1.1	Lampeter-Strasburg SD	Lampeter	291	0.5	Council Rock SD	Newtown
120	1.8	Northwestern SD	Albion	199	1.1	Mount Union Area SD	Mount Union	291	0.5	Downingtown Area SD	Downingtown
120	1.8	Red Lion Area SD	Red Lion	199	1.1	Penn-Delco SD	Aston	291	0.5	Fox Chapel Area SD	Pittsburgh
120	1.8	Saint Marys Area SD	Saint Marys	199	1.1	Perkiomen Valley SD	Collegeville	291	0.5	Haverford Township SD	Havertown
120	1.8	South Fayette Township SD	Mcdonald	199	1.1	Pleasant Valley SD	Brodheadsville	291	0.5	Hempfield SD	Landisville
120	1.8	Upper Perkiomen SD	Pennsburg	199	1.1	Pottsgrove SD	Pottstown	291	0.5	Lower Merion SD	Ardmore
130	1.7	Bloomsburg Area SD	Bloomsburg	199	1.1	Richland SD	Johnstown	291	0.5	Mars Area SD	Mars
130	1.7	Coatesville Area SD	Coatesville	199	1.1	Riverside SD	Taylor	291	0.5	Methacton SD	Norristown
130	1.7	Danville Area SD	Danville	199	1.1	Southern York County SD	Glen Rock	291	0.5	Moon Area SD	Moon Township
130	1.7	Ringgold SD	New Eagle	199	1.1	Tulpehocken Area SD	Bethel	291	0.5	Octorara Area SD	Atglen
130	1.7	Stroudsburg Area SD	Stroudsburg	219	1.0	Crestwood SD	Mountain Top	291	0.5	Pennridge SD	Perkasie
130	1.7	Tunkhannock Area SD	Tunkhannock	219	1.0	Highlands SD	Natrona Heights	291	0.5	Pennsbury SD	Fallsington
130	1.7	Wayne Highlands SD	Honesdale	219	1.0	Hopewell Area SD	Aliquippa	306	0.4	Central Bucks SD	Doylestown
137	1.6	Canon-Mcmillan SD	Canonsburg	219	1.0	Juniata County SD	Mifflintown	306	0.4	Dallastown Area SD	Dallastown
137	1.6	Carlisle Area SD	Carlisle	219	1.0	Marion Center Area SD	Marion Center	306	0.4	Derry Township SD	Hershey
137	1.6	East Lycoming SD	Hughesville	219	1.0	North Pocono SD	Moscow	306	0.4	Manheim Township SD	Lititz
137	1.6	Ephrata Area SD	Ephrata	219	1.0	Northampton Area SD	Northampton	306	0.4	North Hills SD	Pittsburgh
137	1.6	Erie City SD	Erie	219	1.0	Norwin SD	N Huntingdon	306	0.4	Radnor Township SD	Wayne
137	1.6	Indiana Area SD	Indiana	219	1.0	Oxford Area SD	Oxford	306	0.4	Rose Tree Media SD	Media
137	1.6	Middletown Area SD	Middletown	219	1.0	Spring Grove Area SD	Spring Grove	306	0.4	York Suburban SD	York
137	1.6	Moniteau SD	West Sunbury	219	1.0	Westmont Hilltop SD	Johnstown	314	0.3	North Allegheny SD	Pittsburgh
137	1.6	Pocono Mountain SD	Swiftwater	219	1.0	Whitehall-Coplay SD	Whitehall	314	0.3	Wallingford-Swarthmore SD	Wallingford
137	1.6	Warrior Run SD	Turbotville	219	1.0	William Penn SD	Lansdowne	314	0.3	Wissahickon SD	Ambler
137	1.6	Wilkes-Barre Area SD	Wilkes Barre	219	1.0	Wilson SD	West Lawn	317	0.2	Mount Lebanon SD	Pittsburgh
137	1.6	Wyomissing Area SD	Wyomissing	233	0.9	Annville-Cleona SD	Annville	n/a	n/a	Central Valley SD	Monaca
149	1.5	Armstrong SD	Ford City	233	0.9	Bangor Area SD	Bangor	n/a	n/a	Hampton Township SD	Allison Park
149	1.5	Chestnut Ridge SD	Fishertown	233	0.9	Blue Mountain SD	Orwigsburg	n/a	n/a	Jim Thorpe Area SD	Jim Thorpe
149	1.5	Cornwall-Lebanon SD	Lebanon	233	0.9	Conestoga Valley SD	Lancaster	n/a	n/a	Lewisburg Area SD	Lewisburg
149	1.5	Elizabethtown Area SD	Elizabethtown	233	0.9	E Stroudsburg Area SD	E Stroudsburg	n/a	n/a	Lower Moreland Township SD	Huntingdon Vlly
149	1.5	Exeter Township SD	Reading	233	0.9	Girard SD	Girard	n/a	n/a	Owen J Roberts SD	Pottstown
149	1.5	Littlestown Area SD	Littlestown	233	0.9	Hatboro-Horsham SD	Horsham	n/a	n/a	Pine-Richland SD	Gibsonia
149	1.5	Lower Dauphin SD	Hummelstown	233	0.9	Mifflinburg Area SD	Mifflinburg	n/a	n/a	Quaker Valley SD	Sewickley
149	1.5	Palmerton Area SD	Palmerton	233	0.9	Millcreek Township SD	Erie	n/a	n/a	Springfield Township SD	Oreland
149	1.5	South Western SD	Hanover	233	0.9	New Hope-Solebury SD	New Hope	n/a	n/a	Steel Valley SD	Munhall
149	1.5	Susquehanna Township SD	Harrisburg	233	0.9	North Penn SD	Lansdale	n/a	n/a	Tredyffrin-Easttown SD	Wayne
149	1.5	West York Area SD	York	233	0.9	Pequea Valley SD	Kinzers	n/a	n/a	Unionville-Chadds Ford SD	Kennett Square
149	1.5	Yough SD	Herminie	233	0.9	Phoenixville Area SD	Phoenixville	n/a	n/a	Upper Saint Clair SD	Pittsburgh
161	1.4	Brandywine Heights Area SD	Topton	233	0.9	Spring-Ford Area SD	Royersford	n/a	n/a	Valley View SD	Archbald
161	1.4	Central Columbia SD	Bloomsburg	233	0.9	Upper Merion Area SD	King of Prussia	n/a	n/a	Chester Community CS	Chester
161	1.4	Corry Area SD	Corry	233	0.9	Wyoming Area SD	Exeter	n/a	n/a	Lehigh Career & Technical Inst	Schnecksville
161	1.4	Delaware Valley SD	Milford	249	0.8	Baldwin-Whitehall SD	Pittsburgh	n/a	n/a	Abington Heights SD	Clarks Summit
161	1.4	Dover Area SD	Dover	249	0.8	Bermudian Springs SD	York Springs	n/a	n/a	Bald Eagle Area SD	Wingate
161	1.4	Eastern Lebanon County SD	Myerstown	249	0.8	Blairsville-Saltsburg SD	Blairsville	n/a	n/a	Blackhawk SD	Beaver Falls
161	1.4	Greencastle-Antrim SD	Greencastle	249	0.8	Eastern Lancaster County SD	New Holland	n/a	n/a	Catasauqua Area SD	Catasauqua

Note: This section only includes districts with 1,500 or more students; All categories are ranked from high to low

Rank	Percent	District Name	City
n/a	n/a	Central Cambria SD	Ebensburg
n/a	n/a	Commonwealth Connections Acade	Harrisburg
n/a	n/a	East Allegheny SD	N Versailles
n/a	n/a	Franklin Regional SD	Murrysville
n/a	n/a	Garnet Valley SD	Glen Mills
n/a	n/a	Great Valley SD	Malvern
n/a	n/a	Grove City Area SD	Grove City
n/a	n/a	Lakeland SD	Jermyn
n/a	n/a	Ligonier Valley SD	Ligonier
n/a	n/a	Montour SD	Mckees Rocks
n/a	n/a	Montrose Area SD	Montrose
n/a	n/a	Penn-Trafford SD	Harrison City
n/a	n/a	Peters Township SD	Mcmurray
n/a	n/a	Pittston Area SD	Pittston
n/a	n/a	Quakertown Community SD	Quakertown
n/a	n/a	Salisbury Township SD	Allentown
n/a	n/a	South Eastern SD	Fawn Grove
n/a	n/a	South Park SD	South Park
n/a	n/a	Upper Dublin SD	Maple Glen

Average Freshman Graduation Rate

Rank	Percent	District Name	City
1	100.0	Bald Eagle Area SD	Wingate
1	100.0	Colonial SD	Plymth Meeting
1	100.0	Commonwealth Connections Acade	Harrisburg
1	100.0	Council Rock SD	Newtown
1	100.0	Crestwood SD	Mountain Top
1	100.0	Deer Lakes SD	Russellton
1	100.0	Garnet Valley SD	Glen Mills
1	100.0	Hampton Township SD	Allison Park
1	100.0	Haverford Township SD	Havertown
1	100.0	Lower Merion SD	Ardmore
1	100.0	Lower Moreland Township SD	Huntingdon Vlly
1	100.0	Marple Newtown SD	Newtown Square
1	100.0	Mount Lebanon SD	Pittsburgh
1	100.0	Pennsylvania Cyber CS	Midland
1	100.0	Pennsylvania Leadership Charter	West Chester
1	100.0	Peters Township SD	Mcmurray
1	100.0	Richland SD	Johnstown
1	100.0	Rose Tree Media SD	Media
1	100.0	Spring Cove SD	Roaring Spring
1	100.0	Unionville-Chadds Ford SD	Kennett Square
1	100.0	West Jefferson Hills SD	Jefferson Hills
22	99.3	Radnor Township SD	Wayne
23	99.1	New Hope-Solebury SD	New Hope
23	99.1	North Allegheny SD	Pittsburgh
25	99.0	Tredyffrin-Easttown SD	Wayne
26	98.8	Central Cambria SD	Ebensburg
27	98.5	Upper Dublin SD	Maple Glen
27	98.5	Upper Saint Clair SD	Pittsburgh
29	98.3	Parkland SD	Allentown
30	97.9	Corry Area SD	Corry
31	97.6	Wallingford-Swarthmore SD	Wallingford
32	97.5	Springfield Township SD	Oreland
33	97.1	Downingtown Area SD	Downingtown
34	97.0	Belle Vernon Area SD	Belle Vernon
34	97.0	Norwin SD	N Huntingdon
34	97.0	Penn-Trafford SD	Harrison City
34	97.0	Shippensburg Area SD	Shippensburg
38	96.9	East Pennsboro Area SD	Enola
38	96.9	North Pocono SD	Moscow
40	96.7	Somerset Area SD	Somerset
40	96.7	Wyoming Area SD	Exeter
42	96.5	Cocalico SD	Denver
43	96.4	Dunmore SD	Dunmore
44	96.3	Valley View SD	Archbald
44	96.3	Wattsburg Area SD	Erie
44	96.3	Westmont Hilltop SD	Johnstown
47	96.2	Central Bucks SD	Doylestown
48	96.1	West Chester Area SD	West Chester
49	96.0	Fairview SD	Fairview
49	96.0	Franklin Regional SD	Murrysville
49	96.0	Penn Manor SD	Lancaster
49	96.0	Pine Grove Area SD	Pine Grove
53	95.9	Great Valley SD	Malvern
54	95.8	Wilson SD	West Lawn
55	95.7	Nazareth Area SD	Nazareth
55	95.7	Pine-Richland SD	Gibsonia
55	95.7	Schuylkill Valley SD	Leesport
58	95.6	Millcreek Township SD	Erie
59	95.5	Methacton SD	Norristown
60	95.1	Dallas SD	Dallas
60	95.1	Souderton Area SD	Souderton
62	95.0	Pennridge SD	Perkasie
63	94.9	Chartiers Valley SD	Pittsburgh
64	94.7	West Mifflin Area SD	West Mifflin
65	94.4	Eastern Lancaster County SD	New Holland
65	94.4	Fleetwood Area SD	Fleetwood
65	94.4	Springfield SD	Springfield
68	94.2	Penn-Delco SD	Aston
69	94.0	Owen J Roberts SD	Pottstown
69	94.0	South Fayette Township SD	Mcdonald
69	94.0	South Park SD	South Park
69	94.0	Spring-Ford Area SD	Royersford
69	94.0	State College Area SD	State College
74	93.9	Beaver Area SD	Beaver
74	93.9	Keystone Oaks SD	Pittsburgh
74	93.9	Mars Area SD	Mars
74	93.9	North Penn SD	Lansdale
78	93.8	Indiana Area SD	Indiana
79	93.7	East Penn SD	Emmaus
79	93.7	Tunkhannock Area SD	Tunkhannock
81	93.6	Fox Chapel Area SD	Pittsburgh
81	93.6	Perkiomen Valley SD	Collegeville
81	93.6	Ridley SD	Folsom
81	93.6	Riverside Beaver County SD	Ellwood City
85	93.5	Abington SD	Abington
85	93.5	Bellefonte Area SD	Bellefonte
85	93.5	Ephrata Area SD	Ephrata
85	93.5	Manheim Township SD	Lititz
89	93.4	General Mclane SD	Edinboro
90	93.3	Quaker Valley SD	Sewickley
91	93.2	Neshaminy SD	Langhorne
91	93.2	Yough SD	Herminie
93	93.1	North Hills SD	Pittsburgh
94	93.0	Hollidaysburg Area SD	Hollidaysburg
95	92.9	Coatesville Area SD	Coatesville
95	92.9	Derry Township SD	Hershey
95	92.9	Northern Lehigh SD	Slatington
95	92.9	Panther Valley SD	Lansford
95	92.9	Pittston Area SD	Pittston
95	92.9	Warwick SD	Lititz
101	92.8	Lakeland SD	Jermyn
101	92.8	Lewisburg Area SD	Lewisburg
101	92.8	South Allegheny SD	Mckeesport
104	92.7	Upper Moreland Township SD	Willow Grove
105	92.6	Freedom Area SD	Freedom
105	92.6	Lampeter-Strasburg SD	Lampeter
107	92.5	Bethel Park SD	Bethel Park
107	92.5	Governor Mifflin SD	Shillington
107	92.5	Hempfield Area SD	Greensburg
107	92.5	Saucon Valley SD	Hellertown
111	92.4	Baldwin-Whitehall SD	Pittsburgh
111	92.4	Oxford Area SD	Oxford
111	92.4	Upper Merion Area SD	King of Prussia
114	92.3	Manheim Central SD	Manheim
115	92.1	Northern York County SD	Dillsburg
115	92.1	Penn Cambria SD	Cresson
117	92.0	Northern Lebanon SD	Fredericksburg
117	92.0	Whitehall-Coplay SD	Whitehall
119	91.8	Cornwall-Lebanon SD	Lebanon
119	91.8	Palisades SD	Kintnersville
121	91.7	Abington Heights SD	Clarks Summit
121	91.7	Mid Valley SD	Throop
121	91.7	Shaler Area SD	Glenshaw
121	91.7	Wissahickon SD	Ambler
125	91.6	Butler Area SD	Butler
125	91.6	Conewago Valley SD	New Oxford
125	91.6	Delaware Valley SD	Milford
125	91.6	Tuscarora SD	Mercersburg
129	91.4	Cheltenham Township SD	Elkins Park
130	91.3	Hanover Area SD	Hanover Twp
131	91.1	Hopewell Area SD	Aliquippa
132	91.0	Girard SD	Girard
132	91.0	Hermitage SD	Hermitage
132	91.0	Wyomissing Area SD	Wyomissing
135	90.9	North East SD	North East
136	90.8	Forest Hills SD	Sidman
136	90.8	Montoursville Area SD	Montoursville
136	90.8	Scranton SD	Scranton
139	90.7	E Stroudsburg Area SD	E Stroudsburg
140	90.6	Muhlenberg SD	Reading
140	90.6	Trinity Area SD	Washington
140	90.6	Tulpehocken Area SD	Bethel
143	90.5	Mount Carmel Area SD	Mount Carmel
143	90.5	Salisbury Township SD	Allentown
145	90.4	Exeter Township SD	Reading
145	90.4	Kutztown Area SD	Kutztown
147	90.3	Canon-Mcmillan SD	Canonsburg
147	90.3	Chestnut Ridge SD	Fishertown
147	90.3	Gateway SD	Monroeville
150	90.2	Centennial SD	Warminster
151	90.1	Franklin Area SD	Franklin
151	90.1	Pennsbury SD	Fallsington
151	90.1	South Middleton SD	Boiling Springs
154	90.0	Boyertown Area SD	Boyertown
155	89.9	Twin Valley SD	Elverson
156	89.8	Palmyra Area SD	Palmyra
157	89.7	Avon Grove SD	West Grove
158	89.6	Bedford Area SD	Bedford
158	89.6	Northwestern Lehigh SD	New Tripoli
158	89.6	Seneca Valley SD	Harmony
161	89.5	Bensalem Township SD	Bensalem
161	89.5	Brookville Area SD	Brookville
161	89.5	Mount Union Area SD	Mount Union
164	89.3	Conrad Weiser Area SD	Robesonia
164	89.3	Eastern Lebanon County SD	Myerstown
166	89.2	Brandywine Heights Area SD	Topton
166	89.2	Derry Area SD	Derry
166	89.2	Pottsville Area SD	Pottsville
169	89.1	Bethlehem Area SD	Bethlehem
169	89.1	Hatboro-Horsham SD	Horsham
169	89.1	Montour SD	Mckees Rocks
169	89.1	Oley Valley SD	Oley
169	89.1	Wilson Area SD	Easton
174	89.0	Annville-Cleona SD	Annville
174	89.0	Southern Lehigh SD	Center Valley
174	89.0	Towanda Area SD	Towanda
174	89.0	William Penn SD	Lansdowne
178	88.8	Pen Argyl Area SD	Pen Argyl
178	88.8	Penncrest SD	Saegertown
178	88.8	Pocono Mountain SD	Swiftwater
181	88.7	West Allegheny SD	Oakdale
182	88.6	Bangor Area SD	Bangor
182	88.6	Blairsville-Saltsburg SD	Blairsville
184	88.5	Central York SD	York
184	88.5	Quakertown Community SD	Quakertown
186	88.4	Elizabethtown Area SD	Elizabethtown
187	88.3	Wallenpaupack Area SD	Hawley
188	88.1	Greater Latrobe SD	Latrobe
188	88.1	Saint Marys Area SD	Saint Marys
190	87.9	Greencastle-Antrim SD	Greencastle
190	87.9	Mount Pleasant Area SD	Mount Pleasant
192	87.8	Elizabeth Forward SD	Elizabeth
192	87.8	Interboro SD	Prospect Park
194	87.5	Susquehanna Township SD	Harrisburg
195	87.4	Cumberland Valley SD	Mechanicsburg
195	87.4	Hempfield SD	Landisville
195	87.4	Southern Tioga SD	Blossburg
198	87.3	Plum Borough SD	Plum
199	87.2	Chambersburg Area SD	Chambersburg
199	87.2	East Lycoming SD	Hughesville
201	87.1	Danville Area SD	Danville
201	87.1	York Suburban SD	York
203	87.0	Dallastown Area SD	Dallastown
203	87.0	Northampton Area SD	Northampton
203	87.0	Oil City Area SD	Oil City
203	87.0	South Butler County SD	Saxonburg
207	86.9	Karns City Area SD	Karns City
208	86.8	Blue Mountain SD	Orwigsburg
208	86.8	Southmoreland SD	Scottdale
208	86.8	Upper Perkiomen SD	Pennsburg
211	86.7	Mohawk Area SD	Bessemer
211	86.7	Montrose Area SD	Montrose
211	86.7	Southern York County SD	Glen Rock
214	86.6	Blackhawk SD	Beaver Falls
215	86.4	Freeport Area SD	Sarver
216	86.3	Easton Area SD	Easton
216	86.3	Lower Dauphin SD	Hummelstown
216	86.3	Marion Center Area SD	Marion Center
216	86.3	Punxsutawney Area SD	Punxsutawney
220	86.2	Huntingdon Area SD	Huntingdon
220	86.2	Moon Area SD	Moon Township
222	86.0	Kiski Area SD	Leechburg
223	85.8	Hazleton Area SD	Hazleton
224	85.6	Keystone Central SD	Lock Haven
225	85.4	Albert Gallatin Area SD	Uniontown
226	85.3	Wayne Highlands SD	Honesdale
227	85.2	Athens Area SD	Athens
228	85.1	Pequea Valley SD	Kinzers
229	85.0	Mcguffey SD	Claysville
230	84.9	West Shore SD	New Cumberland
231	84.8	Gettysburg Area SD	Gettysburg

Note: This section only includes districts with 1,500 or more students; All categories are ranked from high to low

231	84.8	Juniata County SD	Mifflintown
231	84.8	Mifflinburg Area SD	Mifflinburg
234	84.6	Greater Nanticoke Area SD	Nanticoke
235	84.5	Burrell SD	Lower Burrell
235	84.5	Daniel Boone Area SD	Birdsboro
235	84.5	Fort Leboeuf SD	Waterford
238	84.4	Big Spring SD	Newville
238	84.4	Milton Area SD	Milton
240	84.3	Bermudian Springs SD	York Springs
240	84.3	Crawford Central SD	Meadville
240	84.3	Solanco SD	Quarryville
243	84.2	Brownsville Area SD	Brownsville
244	84.1	Bradford Area SD	Bradford
245	84.0	Clearfield Area SD	Clearfield
246	83.8	Wilkes-Barre Area SD	Wilkes Barre
247	83.7	Central Greene SD	Waynesburg
248	83.5	Moniteau SD	West Sunbury
249	83.4	Central Dauphin SD	Harrisburg
250	83.2	Spring Grove Area SD	Spring Grove
251	83.1	Lake-Lehman SD	Dallas
252	82.7	Conneaut SD	Linesville
253	82.5	Mifflin County SD	Lewistown
253	82.5	Warren County SD	North Warren
255	82.4	Ligonier Valley SD	Ligonier
255	82.4	South Eastern SD	Fawn Grove
257	82.3	Mechanicsburg Area SD	Mechanicsburg
257	82.3	Northwestern SD	Albion
259	82.2	Jim Thorpe Area SD	Jim Thorpe
259	82.2	Slippery Rock Area SD	Slippery Rock
259	82.2	Tamaqua Area SD	Tamaqua
262	82.1	Greater Johnstown SD	Johnstown
262	82.1	Greensburg Salem SD	Greensburg
264	82.0	Lehighton Area SD	Lehighton
265	81.8	Central Columbia SD	Bloomsburg
266	81.5	East Allegheny SD	N Versailles
267	81.3	Northern Tioga SD	Elkland
268	81.1	Troy Area SD	Troy
269	80.8	Harbor Creek SD	Harborcreek
270	80.6	Donegal SD	Mount Joy
270	80.6	Phoenixville Area SD	Phoenixville
272	80.4	Wyoming Valley West SD	Kingston
273	80.0	Tyrone Area SD	Tyrone
274	79.9	North Schuylkill SD	Ashland
274	79.9	Penn Hills SD	Pittsburgh
274	79.9	Titusville Area SD	Titusville
277	79.6	Charleroi SD	Charleroi
277	79.6	Northeastern York SD	Manchester
279	79.4	Octorara Area SD	Atglen
280	79.2	Palmerton Area SD	Palmerton
281	79.0	Waynesboro Area SD	Waynesboro
282	78.9	Upper Adams SD	Biglerville
283	78.8	Eastern York SD	Wrightsville
284	78.6	New Brighton Area SD	New Brighton
284	78.6	Wellsboro Area SD	Wellsboro
286	78.4	Chichester SD	Aston
287	78.3	Bloomsburg Area SD	Bloomsburg
287	78.3	Kennett Consolidated SD	Kennett Square
289	78.2	Norristown Area SD	Norristown
290	78.0	Ambridge Area SD	Ambridge
290	78.0	Carlisle Area SD	Carlisle
290	78.0	Highlands SD	Natrona Heights
293	77.9	Riverside SD	Taylor
294	77.7	Pleasant Valley SD	Brodheadsville
295	77.6	Big Beaver Falls Area SD	Beaver Falls
296	77.5	Warrior Run SD	Turbotville
297	77.4	Bristol Township SD	Levittown
298	77.2	West Perry SD	Elliottsburg
299	77.1	Berwick Area SD	Berwick
299	77.1	Red Lion Area SD	Red Lion
299	77.1	South Western SD	Hanover
302	77.0	Shikellamy SD	Sunbury
303	76.7	Littlestown Area SD	Littlestown
303	76.7	Midd-West SD	Middleburg
305	76.3	Middletown Area SD	Middletown
306	76.1	Ringgold SD	New Eagle
307	75.8	Upper Darby SD	Drexel Hill
308	75.3	Dubois Area SD	Du Bois
308	75.3	Philipsburg-Osceola Area SD	Philipsburg
310	75.2	Catasauqua Area SD	Catasauqua
311	74.9	Hamburg Area SD	Hamburg
312	74.8	Carbondale Area SD	Carbondale
313	74.4	West York Area SD	York
314	74.3	Chester-Upland SD	Chester
314	74.3	Dover Area SD	Dover
316	74.1	Altoona Area SD	Altoona
317	73.5	Shamokin Area SD	Coal Township
318	73.2	Susquenita SD	Duncannon
319	73.1	Selinsgrove Area SD	Selinsgrove
320	72.9	Harrisburg City SD	Harrisburg
321	71.7	Laurel Highlands SD	Uniontown
322	71.1	Jersey Shore Area SD	Jersey Shore
323	71.0	Sharon City SD	Sharon
324	70.9	Pottsgrove SD	Pottstown
325	70.8	Ellwood City Area SD	Ellwood City
326	70.7	Williamsport Area SD	Williamsport
327	69.6	Uniontown Area SD	Uniontown
328	69.3	Grove City Area SD	Grove City
329	69.0	Conestoga Valley SD	Lancaster
330	67.9	Mckeesport Area SD	Mckeesport
331	67.7	Western Wayne SD	South Canaan
332	67.3	Allentown City SD	Allentown
333	67.2	Stroudsburg Area SD	Stroudsburg
334	67.1	Washington SD	Washington
335	66.4	Erie City SD	Erie
336	66.0	New Kensington-Arnold SD	New Kensington
337	64.8	Pittsburgh SD	Pittsburgh
338	64.4	Southeast Delco SD	Folcroft
339	64.3	Woodland Hills SD	Pittsburgh
340	63.3	New Castle Area SD	New Castle
341	62.2	Hanover Public SD	Hanover
342	60.2	Lancaster SD	Lancaster
343	59.3	Armstrong SD	Ford City
343	59.3	Pottstown SD	Pottstown
345	59.2	Connellsville Area SD	Connellsville
346	59.1	Steel Valley SD	Munhall
347	59.0	Lebanon SD	Lebanon
348	55.5	Reading SD	Reading
349	53.5	Philadelphia City SD	Philadelphia
350	46.9	York City SD	York
351	35.3	Pennsylvania Virtual CS	Norristown
n/a	n/a	Agora Cyber CS	Wayne
n/a	n/a	Central Valley SD	Monaca
n/a	n/a	Chester Community CS	Chester
n/a	n/a	Lehigh Career & Technical Inst	Schnecksville
n/a	n/a	York County School of Technology	York

Note: This section only includes districts with 1,500 or more students; All categories are ranked from high to low

The ★ Nation's Report Card | **Mathematics**
2011 State Snapshot Report

Overall Results

- In 2011, the average score of fourth-grade students in Pennsylvania was 246. This was higher than the average score of 240 for public school students in the nation.
- The average score for students in Pennsylvania in 2011 (246) was not significantly different from their average score in 2009 (244) and was higher than their average score in 1992 (224).
- In 2011, the score gap between students in Pennsylvania at the 75th percentile and students at the 25th percentile was 38 points. This performance gap was not significantly different from that of 1992 (42 points).
- The percentage of students in Pennsylvania who performed at or above the NAEP *Proficient* level was 48 percent in 2011. This percentage was not significantly different from that in 2009 (46 percent) and was greater than that in 1992 (22 percent).
- The percentage of students in Pennsylvania who performed at or above the NAEP *Basic* level was 87 percent in 2011. This percentage was not significantly different from that in 2009 (84 percent) and was greater than that in 1992 (65 percent).

Achievement-Level Percentages and Average Score Results

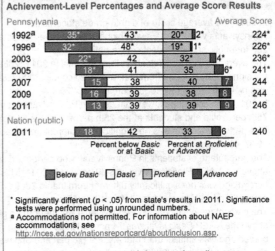

Pennsylvania

Year					Average Score
1992ᵃ	35*	43*	20*	2*	224*
1996ᵃ	32*	48*	19*	1*	226*
2003	22*	42	32*	4*	236*
2005	18*	41	35	6*	241*
2007	15	38	40	7	244
2009	16	39	38	8	244
2011	13	39	39	9	246

Nation (public)

Year					
2011	18	42	33	6	240

Percent below *Basic* or at *Basic*   Percent at *Proficient* or *Advanced*

■ Below *Basic*   □ *Basic*   ▨ *Proficient*   ■ *Advanced*

* Significantly different (*p* < .05) from state's results in 2011. Significance tests were performed using unrounded numbers.
ᵃ Accommodations not permitted. For information about NAEP accommodations, see http://nces.ed.gov/nationsreportcard/about/inclusion.asp.

NOTE: Detail may not sum to totals because of rounding.

Compare the Average Score in 2011 to Other States/Jurisdictions

■ District of Columbia
■ DoDEA¹

¹ Department of Defense Education Activity (overseas and domestic schools).

In 2011, the average score in Pennsylvania (246) was
- lower than those in 3 states/jurisdictions
- higher than those in 32 states/jurisdictions
- not significantly different from those in 16 states/jurisdictions

Average Scores for State/Jurisdiction and Nation (public)

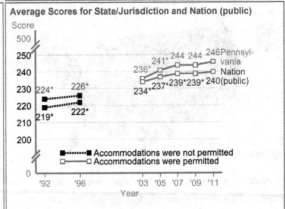

* Significantly different (*p* < .05) from 2011. Significance tests were performed using unrounded numbers.

NOTE: For information about NAEP accommodations, see http://nces.ed.gov/nationsreportcard/about/inclusion.asp.

Results for Student Groups in 2011

Reporting groups	Percent of students	Avg. score	Percentages at or above Basic	Percentages at or above Proficient	Percent at Advanced
Race/Ethnicity					
White	73	251	92	56	11
Black	13	224	67	17	1
Hispanic	9	226	69	20	2
Asian	3	265	96	75	26
American Indian/Alaska Native	#	‡	‡	‡	‡
Native Hawaiian/Pacific Islander	#	‡	‡	‡	‡
Two or more races	1	234	81	27	5
Gender					
Male	51	247	86	49	10
Female	49	245	87	46	8
National School Lunch Program					
Eligible	40	231	74	26	3
Not eligible	59	256	95	62	13

\# Rounds to zero.   ‡ Reporting standards not met.

NOTE: Detail may not sum to totals because of rounding, and because the "Information not available" category for the National School Lunch Program, which provides free/reduced-price lunches, is not displayed. Black includes African American and Hispanic includes Latino. Race categories exclude Hispanic origin.

Score Gaps for Student Groups

- In 2011, Black students had an average score that was 28 points lower than White students. This performance gap was narrower than that in 1992 (36 points).
- In 2011, Hispanic students had an average score that was 26 points lower than White students. This performance gap was not significantly different from that in 1992 (29 points).
- In 2011, male students in Pennsylvania had an average score that was not significantly different from female students.
- In 2011, students who were eligible for free/reduced-price school lunch, an indicator of low family income, had an average score that was 25 points lower than students who were not eligible for free/reduced-price school lunch. This performance gap was not significantly different from that in 1996 (24 points).

 NATIONAL CENTER FOR EDUCATION STATISTICS
Institute of Education Sciences

NOTE: Statistical comparisons are calculated on the basis of unrounded scale scores or percentages.
SOURCE: U.S. Department of Education, Institute of Education Sciences, National Center for Education Statistics, National Assessment of Educational Progress (NAEP), various years, 1992–2011 Mathematics Assessments.

The Nation's Report Card

Mathematics
2011 State Snapshot Report

Pennsylvania
Grade 8
Public Schools

Overall Results

- In 2011, the average score of eighth-grade students in Pennsylvania was 286. This was higher than the average score of 283 for public school students in the nation.
- The average score for students in Pennsylvania in 2011 (286) was not significantly different from their average score in 2009 (288) and was higher than their average score in 1990 (266).
- In 2011, the score gap between students in Pennsylvania at the 75th percentile and students at the 25th percentile was 51 points. This performance gap was not significantly different from that of 1990 (46 points).
- The percentage of students in Pennsylvania who performed at or above the NAEP *Proficient* level was 39 percent in 2011. This percentage was not significantly different from that in 2009 (40 percent) and was greater than that in 1990 (17 percent).
- The percentage of students in Pennsylvania who performed at or above the NAEP *Basic* level was 74 percent in 2011. This percentage was smaller than that in 2009 (78 percent) and was greater than that in 1990 (56 percent).

Achievement-Level Percentages and Average Score Results

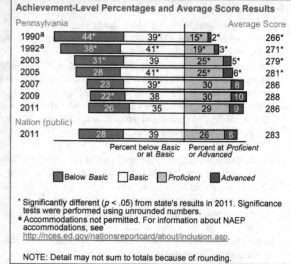

Pennsylvania

Year					Average Score
1990[a]	44*	39*	15*	2*	266*
1992[a]	38*	41*	19*	3*	271*
2003	31*	39	25*	5*	279*
2005	28	41*	25*	6*	281*
2007	23	39*	30	8	286
2009	22*	38	30	10	288
2011	26	35	29	9	286

Nation (public)

2011	28	39	26	8	283

Percent below *Basic* or at *Basic*   Percent at *Proficient* or *Advanced*

■ Below *Basic*   □ *Basic*   ▨ *Proficient*   ■ *Advanced*

* Significantly different (*p* < .05) from state's results in 2011. Significance tests were performed using unrounded numbers.
[a] Accommodations not permitted. For information about NAEP accommodations, see http://nces.ed.gov/nationsreportcard/about/inclusion.asp.

NOTE: Detail may not sum to totals because of rounding.

Compare the Average Score in 2011 to Other States/Jurisdictions

■ District of Columbia
▨ DoDEA[1]

[1] Department of Defense Education Activity (overseas and domestic schools).

In 2011, the average score in Pennsylvania (286) was
- lower than those in 11 states/jurisdictions
- higher than those in 23 states/jurisdictions
- not significantly different from those in 17 states/jurisdictions

Average Scores for State/Jurisdiction and Nation (public)

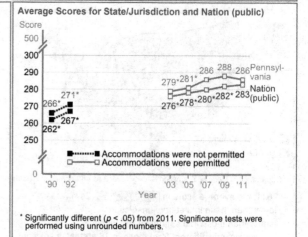

Accommodations were not permitted
Accommodations were permitted

* Significantly different (*p* < .05) from 2011. Significance tests were performed using unrounded numbers.

NOTE: For information about NAEP accommodations, see http://nces.ed.gov/nationsreportcard/about/inclusion.asp.

Results for Student Groups in 2011

Reporting groups	Percent of students	Avg. score	Percentages at or above Basic	Percentages at or above Proficient	Percent at Advanced
Race/Ethnicity					
White	70	294	83	47	11
Black	19	257	44	9	1
Hispanic	7	269	58	22	3
Asian	3	312	87	63	34
American Indian/Alaska Native	#	‡	‡	‡	‡
Native Hawaiian/Pacific Islander	#	‡	‡	‡	‡
Two or more races	1	‡	‡	‡	‡
Gender					
Male	51	287	74	40	10
Female	49	285	74	38	9
National School Lunch Program					
Eligible	40	268	57	20	2
Not eligible	59	298	85	52	14

Rounds to zero.   ‡ Reporting standards not met.

NOTE: Detail may not sum to totals because of rounding, and because the "Information not available" category for the National School Lunch Program, which provides free/reduced-price lunches, is not displayed. Black includes African American and Hispanic includes Latino. Race categories exclude Hispanic origin.

Score Gaps for Student Groups

- In 2011, Black students had an average score that was 37 points lower than White students. This performance gap was not significantly different from that in 1990 (36 points).
- In 2011, Hispanic students had an average score that was 25 points lower than White students. Data are not reported for Hispanic students in 1990, because reporting standards were not met.
- In 2011, male students in Pennsylvania had an average score that was not significantly different from female students.
- In 2011, students who were eligible for free/reduced-price school lunch, an indicator of low family income, had an average score that was 30 points lower than students who were not eligible for free/reduced-price school lunch. This performance gap was not significantly different from that in 2003 (31 points).

NOTE: Statistical comparisons are calculated on the basis of unrounded scale scores or percentages.
SOURCE: U.S. Department of Education, Institute of Education Sciences, National Center for Education Statistics, National Assessment of Educational Progress (NAEP), various years, 1990–2011 Mathematics Assessments.

The Nation's Report Card

Reading
2011 State Snapshot Report

Pennsylvania
Grade 4
Public Schools

Overall Results

- In 2011, the average score of fourth-grade students in Pennsylvania was 227. This was higher than the average score of 220 for public school students in the nation.
- The average score for students in Pennsylvania in 2011 (227) was not significantly different from their average score in 2009 (224) and was higher than their average score in 1992 (221).
- In 2011, the score gap between students in Pennsylvania at the 75th percentile and students at the 25th percentile was 46 points. This performance gap was not significantly different from that of 1992 (44 points).
- The percentage of students in Pennsylvania who performed at or above the NAEP *Proficient* level was 41 percent in 2011. This percentage was greater than that in 2009 (37 percent) and was greater than that in 1992 (32 percent).
- The percentage of students in Pennsylvania who performed at or above the NAEP *Basic* level was 74 percent in 2011. This percentage was greater than that in 2009 (70 percent) and was greater than that in 1992 (68 percent).

Achievement-Level Percentages and Average Score Results

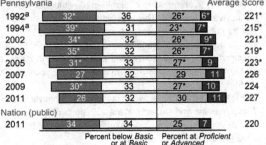

* Significantly different (*p* < .05) from state's results in 2011. Significance tests were performed using unrounded numbers.
a Accommodations not permitted. For information about NAEP accommodations, see http://nces.ed.gov/nationsreportcard/about/inclusion.asp.

NOTE: Detail may not sum to totals because of rounding.

Compare the Average Score in 2011 to Other States/Jurisdictions

- District of Columbia
- DoDEA[1]

[1] Department of Defense Education Activity (overseas and domestic schools).

In 2011, the average score in Pennsylvania (227) was
- lower than those in 4 states/jurisdictions
- higher than those in 38 states/jurisdictions
- not significantly different from those in 9 states/jurisdictions

Average Scores for State/Jurisdiction and Nation (public)

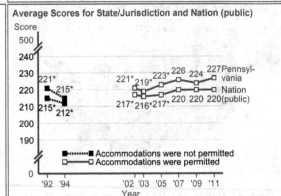

* Significantly different (*p* < .05) from 2011. Significance tests were performed using unrounded numbers.

NOTE: For information about NAEP accommodations, see http://nces.ed.gov/nationsreportcard/about/inclusion.asp.

Results for Student Groups in 2011

Reporting groups	Percent of students	Avg. score	Percentages at or above Basic	Percentages at or above Proficient	Percent at Advanced
Race/Ethnicity					
White	74	233	81	47	13
Black	13	204	48	19	3
Hispanic	8	202	48	17	3
Asian	3	244	84	62	26
American Indian/Alaska Native	#	‡	‡	‡	‡
Native Hawaiian/Pacific Islander	#	‡	‡	‡	‡
Two or more races	1	232	77	46	17
Gender					
Male	51	223	69	38	9
Female	49	232	78	45	13
National School Lunch Program					
Eligible	40	211	57	24	4
Not eligible	59	238	85	53	15

Rounds to zero.   ‡ Reporting standards not met.

NOTE: Detail may not sum to totals because of rounding, and because the "Information not available" category for the National School Lunch Program, which provides free/reduced-price lunches, is not displayed. Black includes African American and Hispanic includes Latino. Race categories exclude Hispanic origin.

Score Gaps for Student Groups

- In 2011, Black students had an average score that was 29 points lower than White students. This performance gap was narrower than that in 1992 (36 points).
- In 2011, Hispanic students had an average score that was 31 points lower than White students. This performance gap was not significantly different from that in 1992 (35 points).
- In 2011, female students in Pennsylvania had an average score that was higher than male students by 9 points.
- In 2011, students who were eligible for free/reduced-price school lunch, an indicator of low family income, had an average score that was 27 points lower than students who were not eligible for free/reduced-price school lunch. This performance gap was not significantly different from that in 2002 (32 points).

NOTE: Statistical comparisons are calculated on the basis of unrounded scale scores or percentages.
SOURCE: U.S. Department of Education, Institute of Education Sciences, National Center for Education Statistics, National Assessment of Educational Progress (NAEP), various years, 1992–2011 Reading Assessments.

NATIONAL CENTER FOR EDUCATION STATISTICS
Institute of Education Sciences

The Nation's Report Card — Reading 2011 State Snapshot Report

Pennsylvania
Grade 8
Public Schools

Overall Results

- In 2011, the average score of eighth-grade students in Pennsylvania was 268. This was higher than the average score of 264 for public school students in the nation.
- The average score for students in Pennsylvania in 2011 (268) was not significantly different from their average score in 2009 (271) and was not significantly different from their average score in 2002 (265).
- In 2011, the score gap between students in Pennsylvania at the 75th percentile and students at the 25th percentile was 46 points. This performance gap was not significantly different from that of 2002 (44 points).
- The percentage of students in Pennsylvania who performed at or above the NAEP *Proficient* level was 38 percent in 2011. This percentage was not significantly different from that in 2009 (40 percent) and was not significantly different from that in 2002 (35 percent).
- The percentage of students in Pennsylvania who performed at or above the NAEP *Basic* level was 77 percent in 2011. This percentage was smaller than that in 2009 (81 percent) and was not significantly different from that in 2002 (77 percent).

Achievement-Level Percentages and Average Score Results

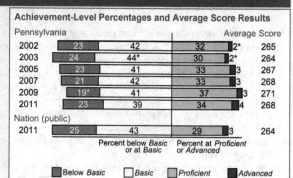

Pennsylvania				Average Score
2002	23	42	32	2*	265
2003	24	44*	30	2*	264
2005	23	41	33	3	267
2007	21	42	33	3	268
2009	19*	41	37	3	271
2011	23	39	34	4	268

Nation (public)
| 2011 | 25 | 43 | 29 | 3 | 264 |

Percent below *Basic* or at *Basic* — Percent at *Proficient* or *Advanced*

■ Below *Basic*   □ *Basic*   ▨ *Proficient*   ■ *Advanced*

* Significantly different (*p* < .05) from state's results in 2011. Significance tests were performed using unrounded numbers.

NOTE: Detail may not sum to totals because of rounding.

Compare the Average Score in 2011 to Other States/Jurisdictions

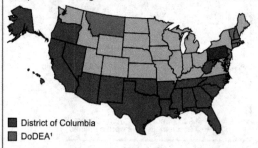

■ District of Columbia
■ DoDEA[1]

[1] Department of Defense Education Activity (overseas and domestic schools).

In 2011, the average score in Pennsylvania (268) was
- lower than those in 7 states/jurisdictions
- higher than those in 20 states/jurisdictions
- not significantly different from those in 24 states/jurisdictions

Average Scores for State/Jurisdiction and Nation (public)

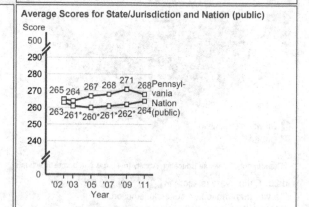

Score

Pennsylvania: 265 264 267 268 271 268
Nation (public): 263 261* 260* 261* 262* 264

Year: '02 '03 '05 '07 '09 '11

* Significantly different (*p* < .05) from 2011. Significance tests were performed using unrounded numbers.

Results for Student Groups in 2011

Reporting groups	Percent of students	Avg. score	Percentages at or above		Percent at Advanced
			Basic	*Proficient*	
Race/Ethnicity					
White	70	275	85	46	5
Black	19	244	54	13	#
Hispanic	6	250	60	16	1
Asian	3	285	85	62	13
American Indian/Alaska Native	#	‡	‡	‡	‡
Native Hawaiian/Pacific Islander	#	‡	‡	‡	‡
Two or more races	1	‡	‡	‡	‡
Gender					
Male	50	263	74	32	3
Female	50	272	81	44	6
National School Lunch Program					
Eligible	40	252	63	20	1
Not eligible	60	278	87	50	6

Rounds to zero.   ‡ Reporting standards not met.

NOTE: Detail may not sum to totals because of rounding, and because the "Information not available" category for the National School Lunch Program, which provides free/reduced-price lunches, is not displayed. Black includes African American and Hispanic includes Latino. Race categories exclude Hispanic origin.

Score Gaps for Student Groups

- In 2011, Black students had an average score that was 32 points lower than White students. This performance gap was not significantly different from that in 2002 (35 points).
- In 2011, Hispanic students had an average score that was 25 points lower than White students. This performance gap was not significantly different from that in 2002 (31 points).
- In 2011, female students in Pennsylvania had an average score that was higher than male students by 9 points.
- In 2011, students who were eligible for free/reduced-price school lunch, an indicator of low family income, had an average score that was 27 points lower than students who were not eligible for free/reduced-price school lunch. This performance gap was not significantly different from that in 2002 (28 points).

NOTE: Statistical comparisons are calculated on the basis of unrounded scale scores or percentages.
SOURCE: U.S. Department of Education, Institute of Education Sciences, National Center for Education Statistics, National Assessment of Educational Progress (NAEP), various years, 2002–2011 Reading Assessments.

Pennsylvania
Grade 4
Public Schools

The Nation's Report Card — Science 2009 — State Snapshot Report

2009 Science Assessment Content

Guided by a new framework, the NAEP science assessment was updated in 2009 to keep the content current with key developments in science, curriculum standards, assessments, and research. The 2009 framework organizes science content into three broad content areas.

Physical science includes concepts related to properties and changes of matter, forms of energy, energy transfer and conservation, position and motion of objects, and forces affecting motion.

Life science includes concepts related to organization and development, matter and energy transformations, interdependence, heredity and reproduction, and evolution and diversity.

Earth and space sciences includes concepts related to objects in the universe, the history of the Earth, properties of Earth materials, tectonics, energy in Earth systems, climate and weather, and biogeochemical cycles.

The 2009 science assessment was composed of 143 questions at grade 4, 162 at grade 8, and 179 at grade 12. Students responded to only a portion of the questions, which included both multiple-choice questions and questions that required a written response.

Compare the Average Score in 2009 to Other States/Jurisdictions

☐ District of Columbia
■ DoDEA[1]

[1] Department of Defense Education Activity (overseas and domestic schools).

In 2009, the average score in **Pennsylvania** was
- lower than those in 10 states/jurisdictions
- higher than those in 18 states/jurisdictions
- not significantly different from those in 18 states/jurisdictions
- 5 states/jurisdictions did not participate

Overall Results

- In 2009, the average score of fourth-grade students in Pennsylvania was 154. This was higher than the average score of 149 for public school students in the nation.
- The percentage of students in Pennsylvania who performed at or above the NAEP *Proficient* level was 38 percent in 2009. This percentage was greater than the nation (32 percent).
- The percentage of students in Pennsylvania who performed at or above the NAEP *Basic* level was 76 percent in 2009. This percentage was greater than the nation (71 percent).

Achievement-Level Percentages and Average Score Results

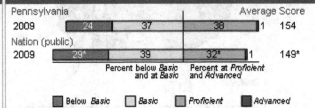

				Average Score
Pennsylvania 2009	24	37	38	1	154
Nation (public) 2009	29*	39	32*	1	149*

Percent below *Basic* and at *Basic* — Percent at *Proficient* and *Advanced*

■ Below *Basic*   ☐ *Basic*   ▨ *Proficient*   ■ *Advanced*

* Significantly different (*p* < .05) from Pennsylvania. Significance tests were performed using unrounded numbers.

NOTE: Detail may not sum to totals because of rounding.

Results for Student Groups in 2009

Reporting Groups	Percent of students	Avg. score	Percentages at or above Basic	Percentages at or above Proficient	Percent at Advanced
Gender					
Male	52	156	77	41	1
Female	48	151	74	36	#
Race/Ethnicity					
White	71	164	87	48	1
Black	15	121	39	7	#
Hispanic	9	125	46	12	#
Asian/Pacific Islander	4	166	84	53	2
American Indian/Alaska Native	#	‡	‡	‡	‡
National School Lunch Program					
Eligible	39	133	54	17	#
Not eligible	61	167	89	52	1

Rounds to zero.   ‡ Reporting standards not met.

NOTE: Detail may not sum to totals because of rounding, and because the "Information not available" category for the National School Lunch Program, which provides free/reduced-price lunches, and the "Unclassified" category for race/ethnicity are not displayed.

Score Gaps for Student Groups

- In 2009, male students in Pennsylvania had an average score that was higher than female students.
- In 2009, Black students had an average score that was 43 points lower than White students. This performance gap was wider than the nation (35 points).
- In 2009, Hispanic students had an average score that was 39 points lower than White students. This performance gap was not significantly different from the nation (32 points).
- In 2009, students who were eligible for free/reduced-price school lunch, an indicator of low family income, had an average score that was 34 points lower than students who were not eligible for free/reduced-price school lunch. This performance gap was wider than the nation (29 points).

NOTE: Statistical comparisons are calculated on the basis of unrounded scale scores or percentages.
SOURCE: U.S. Department of Education, Institute of Education Sciences, National Center for Education Statistics, National Assessment of Educational Progress (NAEP), 2009 Science Assessment.

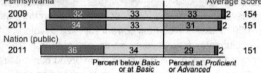

The Nation's Report Card Science **2011 State Snapshot Report**

Pennsylvania
Grade 8
Public Schools

Overall Results

- In 2011, the average score of eighth-grade students in Pennsylvania was 151. This was not significantly different from the average score of 151 for public school students in the nation.
- The average score for students in Pennsylvania in 2011 (151) was not significantly different from their average score in 2009 (154).
- In 2011, the score gap between students in Pennsylvania at the 75th percentile and students at the 25th percentile was 47 points. This performance gap was not significantly different from that of 2009 (45 points).
- The percentage of students in Pennsylvania who performed at or above the NAEP *Proficient* level was 33 percent in 2011. This percentage was not significantly different from that in 2009 (35 percent).
- The percentage of students in Pennsylvania who performed at or above the NAEP *Basic* level was 66 percent in 2011. This percentage was not significantly different from that in 2009 (68 percent).

Achievement-Level Percentages and Average Score Results

Pennsylvania					Average Score
2009	32	33	33	2	154
2011	34	33	31	2	151
Nation (public)					
2011	36	34	29	2	151

Percent below *Basic* or at *Basic*   Percent at *Proficient* or *Advanced*

■ Below *Basic*   □ *Basic*   ▨ *Proficient*   ■ *Advanced*

NOTE: Detail may not sum to totals because of rounding.

Compare the Average Score in 2011 to Other States/Jurisdictions

■ District of Columbia
▨ DoDEA[1]

[1] Department of Defense Education Activity (overseas and domestic schools).

In 2011, the average score in Pennsylvania (151) was
- lower than those in 24 states/jurisdictions
- higher than those in 12 states/jurisdictions
- not significantly different from those in 15 states/jurisdictions

Average Scores for State/Jurisdiction and Nation (public)

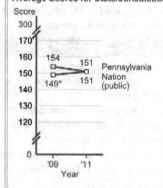

* Significantly different (*p* < .05) from 2011. Significance tests were performed using unrounded numbers.

Results for Student Groups in 2011

Reporting Groups	Percent of students	Avg. score	Percentages at or above		Percent at Advanced
			Basic	Proficient	
Race/Ethnicity					
White	70	163	80	43	2
Black	19	120	26	5	#
Hispanic	7	118	28	8	#
Asian	3	163	79	49	4
American Indian/Alaska Native	#	‡	‡	‡	‡
Native Hawaiian/Pacific Islander	#	‡	‡	‡	‡
Two or more races	1	‡	‡	‡	‡
Gender					
Male	51	155	70	38	2
Female	49	147	61	28	1
National School Lunch Program					
Eligible	40	132	43	14	#
Not eligible	59	165	82	46	3

Rounds to zero.   ‡ Reporting standards not met.

NOTE: Detail may not sum to totals because of rounding, and because the "Information not available" category for the National School Lunch Program, which provides free/reduced-price lunches, is not displayed. Black includes African American and Hispanic includes Latino. Race categories exclude Hispanic origin.

Score Gaps for Student Groups

- In 2011, Black students had an average score that was 43 points lower than White students. This performance gap was not significantly different from that in 2009 (38 points).
- In 2011, Hispanic students had an average score that was 45 points lower than White students. This performance gap was not significantly different from that in 2009 (41 points).
- In 2011, male students in Pennsylvania had an average score that was higher than female students by 8 points.
- In 2011, students who were eligible for free/reduced-price school lunch, an indicator of low family income, had an average score that was 33 points lower than students who were not eligible for free/reduced-price school lunch. This performance gap was not significantly different from that in 2009 (32 points).

NOTE: Statistical comparisons are calculated on the basis of unrounded scale scores or percentages.
SOURCE: U.S. Department of Education, Institute of Education Sciences, National Center for Education Statistics, National Assessment of Educational Progress (NAEP), 2009 and 2011 Science Assessments.

The writing assessment of the National Assessment of Educational Progress (NAEP) measures narrative, informative, and persuasive writing–three purposes identified in the NAEP framework. The NAEP writing scale ranges from 0 to 300.

Overall Writing Results for Pennsylvania

- The average scale score for fourth-grade students in Pennsylvania was 156.

- Pennsylvania's average score (156) was higher[1] than that of the nation's public schools (153).

- Students' average scale scores in Pennsylvania were higher than those in 26 jurisdictions[2], not significantly different from those in 16 jurisdictions, and lower than those in 5 jurisdictions.

- The percentage of students who performed at or above the NAEP *Proficient* level was 29 percent. The percentage of students who performed at or above the *Basic* level was 88 percent.

Student Percentage at Each Achievement Level

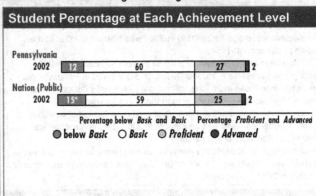

Percentage below *Basic* and *Basic*   Percentage *Proficient* and *Advanced*
● below *Basic*   ○ *Basic*   ○ *Proficient*   ● *Advanced*

Performance of NAEP Reporting Groups in Pennsylvania

Reporting groups	Percentage of students	Average Score	Percentage of students at			
			Below *Basic*	*Basic*	*Proficient*	*Advanced*
Male	51	148 ↑	16 ↓	64	19	1
Female	49	164	7 ↓	56	34	3
White	77	161	8 ↓	58	31	2
Black	17	135	25	66	9 ↓	#
Hispanic	4	136	28	63	8 ↓	1
Asian/Pacific Islander	2	---	---	---	---	---
American Indian/Alaska Native	#	---	---	---	---	---
Free/reduced-priced school lunch						
Eligible	34	137	22	67	10 ↓	#
Not eligible	63	166	6 ↓	56	36	3
Information not available	3	162	7	60	29	4

Average Score Gaps Between Selected Groups

- Female students in Pennsylvania had an average score that was higher than that of male students (16 points). This performance gap was not significantly different from that of the Nation (18 points).

- White students had an average score that was higher than that of Black students (26 points). This performance gap was not significantly different from that of the Nation (20 points).

- White students had an average score that was higher than that of Hispanic students (25 points). This performance gap was not significantly different from that of the Nation (19 points).

- Students who were not eligible for free/reduced-price school lunch had an average score that was higher than that of students who were eligible (28 points). This performance gap was wider than that of the Nation (22 points).

Writing Scale Scores at Selected Percentiles

Scale Score Distribution

	25th Percentile	50th Percentile	75th Percentile
Pennsylvania	*132* ↑	*156*	*180*
Nation (Public)	*128*	*153*	*178*

An examination of scores at different percentiles on the 0-300 NAEP writing scale at each grade indicates how well students at lower, middle, and higher levels of the distribution performed. For example, the data above shows that 75 percent of students in public schools nationally scored below *178*, while 75 percent of students in Pennsylvania scored below *180*.

Percentage rounds to zero.   --- Reporting standards not met; sample size insufficient to permit a reliable estimate.
* Significantly different from Pennsylvania.   ↑ Significantly higher than, ↓ lower than appropriate subgroup in the nation (public).
[1] Comparisons (higher/lower/not different) are based on statistical tests. The .05 level was used for testing statistical significance.
[2] "Jurisdictions" includes participating states and other jurisdictions (such as Guam or the District of Columbia).
NOTE: Detail may not sum to totals because of rounding. Score gaps are calculated based on differences between unrounded average scale scores.
Visit http://nces.ed.gov/nationsreportcard/states/ for additional results and detailed information.
SOURCE: U.S. Department of Education, Institute of Education Sciences, National Center for Education Statistics, National Assessment of Educational Progress (NAEP), 2002 Writing Assessment.

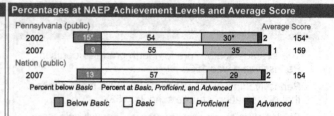

The National Assessment of Educational Progress (NAEP) assesses writing for three purposes identified in the NAEP framework: narrative, informative, and persuasive. The NAEP writing scale ranges from 0 to 300.

Overall Writing Results for Pennsylvania

- In 2007, the average scale score for eighth-grade students in Pennsylvania was 159. This was higher than their average score in 2002 (154).[1]
- Pennsylvania's average score (159) in 2007 was higher than that of the nation's public schools (154).
- Of the 45 states and one other jurisdiction that participated in the 2007 eighth-grade assessment, students' average scale score in Pennsylvania was higher than those in 26 jurisdictions, not significantly different from those in 15 jurisdictions, and lower than those in 4 jurisdictions.[2]
- The percentage of students in Pennsylvania who performed at or above the NAEP *Proficient* level was 36 percent in 2007. This percentage was greater than that in 2002 (32 percent).
- The percentage of students in Pennsylvania who performed at or above the NAEP *Basic* level was 91 percent in 2007. This percentage was greater than that in 2002 (85 percent).

Percentages at NAEP Achievement Levels and Average Score

Pennsylvania (public)   Average Score

Year				Avg
2002	15*	54	30*	2	154*
2007	9	55	35	1	159

Nation (public)

Year				Avg
2007	13	57	29	2	154

Percent below *Basic*   Percent at *Basic*, *Proficient*, and *Advanced*

■ Below *Basic*   □ *Basic*   ▨ *Proficient*   ■ *Advanced*

NOTE: The NAEP grade 8 writing achievement levels correspond to the following scale points: Below *Basic*, 113 or lower; *Basic*, 114–172; *Proficient*, 173–223; *Advanced*, 224 or above.

Performance of NAEP Reporting Groups in Pennsylvania: 2007

Reporting groups	Percent of students	Average score	Percent below *Basic*	Percent of students at or above *Basic*	*Proficient*	Percent *Advanced*
Male	51	151↑	13↓	87↑	26	1
Female	49	168	5	95	47	2
White	76	164↑	6↓	94↑	42	1
Black	15	138↑	21↓	79↑	13	#
Hispanic	6	145↑	17	83	20	1
Asian/Pacific Islander	3	170	4	96	50	2
American Indian/Alaska Native	#	‡	‡	‡	‡	‡
Eligible for National School Lunch Program	30	144↑	17↓	83↑	19	#
Not eligible for National School Lunch Program	70	166	5	95	44	2

Average Score Gaps Between Selected Groups

- In 2007, male students in Pennsylvania had an average score that was lower than that of female students by 17 points. This performance gap was not significantly different from that of 2002 (21 points).
- In 2007, Black students had an average score that was lower than that of White students by 26 points. This performance gap was narrower than that of 2002 (36 points).
- In 2007, Hispanic students had an average score that was lower than that of White students by 19 points. This performance gap was not significantly different from that of 2002 (27 points).
- In 2007, students who were eligible for free/reduced-price school lunch, an indicator of poverty, had an average score that was lower than that of students who were not eligible for free/reduced-price school lunch by 22 points. This performance gap was narrower than that of 2002 (33 points).
- In 2007, the score gap between students at the 75th percentile and students at the 25th percentile was 43 points. This performance gap was narrower than that of 2002 (50 points).

Writing Scores at Selected Percentiles in Pennsylvania

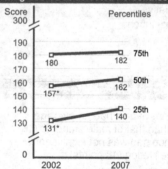

NOTE: Scores at selected percentiles on the NAEP writing scale indicate how well students at lower, middle, and higher levels performed.

Rounds to zero.   ‡ Reporting standards not met.
* Significantly different from 2007.   ↑ Significantly higher than 2002. ↓ Significantly lower than 2002.
[1] Comparisons (higher/lower/narrower/wider/not different) are based on statistical tests. The .05 level with appropriate adjustments for multiple comparisons was used for testing statistical significance. Statistical comparisons are calculated on the basis of unrounded scale scores or percentages. Comparisons across jurisdictions and comparisons with the nation or within a jurisdiction across years may be affected by differences in exclusion rates for students with disabilities (SD) and English language learners (ELL). The exclusion rates for SD and ELL in Pennsylvania were 3 percent and 1 percent in 2007, respectively. For more information on NAEP significance testing, see http://nces.ed.gov/nationsreportcard/writing/interpret-results.asp#statistical.
[2] "Jurisdiction" refers to states, the District of Columbia, and the Department of Defense Education Activity schools.
NOTE: Detail may not sum to totals because of rounding and because the "Information not available" category for the National School Lunch Program, which provides free and reduced-price lunches, and the "Unclassified" category for race/ethnicity are not displayed. Visit http://nces.ed.gov/nationsreportcard/states/ for additional results and detailed information.
SOURCE: U.S. Department of Education, Institute of Education Sciences, National Center for Education Statistics, National Assessment of Educational Progress (NAEP), 2002 and 2007 Writing Assessments.

State PSSA Results in Grade 3 Mathematics

Student Group[1]	Academic Year	Participation Rate	Percentage of students in each Performance Level				Percentage of students Proficient and above State
			Below Basic	Basic	Proficient	Advanced	0 20 40 60 80 100
All Students	2010–2011	100%	5%	12%	37%	46%	83%
	2009–2010	100%	4%	11%	41%	43%	84%
Male	2010–2011	100%	5%	11%	36%	47%	84%
	2009–2010	100%	5%	11%	41%	43%	84%
Female	2010–2011	100%	5%	12%	38%	44%	83%
	2009–2010	100%	4%	12%	41%	43%	84%
White	2010–2011	100%	3%	9%	37%	52%	88%
	2009–2010	100%	2%	8%	41%	49%	89%
Black	2010–2011	100%	13%	21%	41%	24%	65%
	2009–2010	100%	12%	22%	44%	22%	66%
Latino/Hispanic	2010–2011	100%	11%	20%	40%	29%	69%
	2009–2010	100%	10%	20%	44%	27%	71%
Asian	2010–2011	100%	3%	6%	27%	65%	91%
	2009–2010	100%	2%	6%	30%	62%	92%
Native American	2010–2011	100%	7%	10%	43%	39%	83%
	2009–2010	99%	7%	16%	44%	32%	76%
Multiracial	2010–2011	100%	7%	15%	40%	38%	78%
	2009–2010	100%	5%	15%	46%	34%	80%
IEP	2010–2011	100%	18%	23%	36%	23%	59%
	2009–2010	100%	16%	23%	39%	22%	61%
English Language Learners	2010–2011	100%	20%	27%	37%	16%	53%
	2009–2010	100%	16%	26%	40%	18%	58%
Migrant	2010–2011	98%	23%	21%	41%	14%	55%
	2009–2010	99%	14%	32%	42%	12%	54%
Economically Disadvantaged	2010–2011	100%	9%	18%	42%	31%	73%
	2009–2010	100%	8%	18%	45%	29%	74%

NOTE:
This is the first year the PSSA-M Reading and Science assessments were administered.
Percentages may not total 100 due to rounding.
This table reflects all students enrolled for any portion of the academic year, meaning that these numbers may not match the results reported for Accountability purposes.
— Indicates fewer than 10 students in a group. To provide meaningful results and to protect the privacy of individual students, data are printed only when the total number of students in a group is at least 10.
[1] There can be overlap among the groups since a student may belong to more than one of these groups.

State PSSA Results in Grade 3 Reading

Student Group[1]	Academic Year	Participation Rate	Percentage of students in each Performance Level				Percentage of students Proficient and above State					
			Below Basic	Basic	Proficient	Advanced	0	20	40	60	80	100
All Students	**2010–2011**	**100%**	**13%**	**10%**	**49%**	**28%**					77%	
	2009–2010	100%	13%	12%	48%	27%					75%	
Male	**2010–2011**	**100%**	**16%**	**10%**	**49%**	**25%**					74%	
	2009–2010	100%	15%	13%	47%	24%					72%	
Female	**2010–2011**	**100%**	**11%**	**9%**	**49%**	**31%**					80%	
	2009–2010	100%	11%	11%	48%	30%					78%	
White	**2010–2011**	**100%**	**9%**	**8%**	**50%**	**33%**					83%	
	2009–2010	100%	9%	10%	50%	32%					82%	
Black	**2010–2011**	**100%**	**27%**	**16%**	**46%**	**12%**				58%		
	2009–2010	99%	27%	20%	43%	10%				53%		
Latino/Hispanic	**2010–2011**	**99%**	**26%**	**14%**	**46%**	**14%**				60%		
	2009–2010	99%	26%	18%	43%	12%				55%		
Asian	**2010–2011**	**97%**	**9%**	**7%**	**44%**	**41%**					85%	
	2009–2010	98%	8%	8%	44%	40%					84%	
Native American	**2010–2011**	**100%**	**15%**	**11%**	**45%**	**29%**					73%	
	2009–2010	100%	19%	16%	45%	19%				64%		
Multiracial	**2010–2011**	**99%**	**17%**	**12%**	**49%**	**22%**					71%	
	2009–2010	99%	16%	15%	48%	21%				69%		
IEP	**2010–2011**	**99%**	**40%**	**14%**	**35%**	**11%**			46%			
	2009–2010	99%	39%	17%	33%	10%			44%			
English Language Learners	**2010–2011**	**93%**	**45%**	**18%**	**33%**	**4%**		37%				
	2009–2010	94%	43%	22%	32%	4%		36%				
Migrant	**2010–2011**	**93%**	**53%**	**9%**	**30%**	**8%**		38%				
	2009–2010	97%	48%	19%	28%	4%		33%				
Economically Disadvantaged	**2010–2011**	**99%**	**22%**	**14%**	**49%**	**16%**				64%		
	2009–2010	99%	22%	17%	47%	14%				61%		

NOTE:

This is the first year the PSSA-M Reading and Science assessments were administered.

Percentages may not total 100 due to rounding.

This table reflects all students enrolled for any portion of the academic year, meaning that these numbers may not match the results reported for Accountability purposes.

— Indicates fewer than 10 students in a group. To provide meaningful results and to protect the privacy of individual students, data are printed only when the total number of students in a group is at least 10.

[1] There can be overlap among the groups since a student may belong to more than one of these groups.

State PSSA Results in Grade 4 Mathematics

Student Group[1]	Academic Year	Participation Rate	Percentage of students in each Performance Level				Percentage of students Proficient and above State
			Below Basic	Basic	Proficient	Advanced	0　20　40　60　80　100
All Students	**2010–2011**	**100%**	**7%**	**8%**	**31%**	**54%**	85%
	2009–2010	100%	7%	8%	31%	54%	84%
Male	**2010–2011**	**100%**	**8%**	**7%**	**29%**	**56%**	85%
	2009–2010	100%	7%	8%	29%	56%	85%
Female	**2010–2011**	**100%**	**7%**	**8%**	**33%**	**52%**	85%
	2009–2010	100%	7%	9%	33%	51%	84%
White	**2010–2011**	**100%**	**4%**	**6%**	**30%**	**60%**	90%
	2009–2010	100%	4%	6%	29%	61%	90%
Black	**2010–2011**	**100%**	**18%**	**14%**	**37%**	**31%**	68%
	2009–2010	100%	19%	16%	37%	28%	65%
Latino/Hispanic	**2010–2011**	**100%**	**15%**	**13%**	**37%**	**36%**	72%
	2009–2010	100%	16%	14%	37%	33%	70%
Asian	**2010–2011**	**100%**	**4%**	**4%**	**19%**	**74%**	92%
	2009–2010	100%	3%	3%	19%	74%	94%
Native American	**2010–2011**	**100%**	**13%**	**7%**	**37%**	**43%**	80%
	2009–2010	100%	9%	10%	41%	41%	82%
Multiracial	**2010–2011**	**100%**	**9%**	**10%**	**34%**	**47%**	81%
	2009–2010	99%	11%	10%	35%	45%	80%
IEP	**2010–2011**	**100%**	**22%**	**14%**	**35%**	**29%**	64%
	2009–2010	99%	21%	14%	35%	30%	64%
English Language Learners	**2010–2011**	**100%**	**27%**	**18%**	**36%**	**20%**	55%
	2009–2010	100%	27%	18%	35%	20%	55%
Migrant	**2010–2011**	**98%**	**31%**	**6%**	**40%**	**23%**	63%
	2009–2010	100%	26%	16%	40%	18%	59%
Economically Disadvantaged	**2010–2011**	**100%**	**13%**	**12%**	**37%**	**38%**	75%
	2009–2010	100%	13%	13%	37%	37%	74%

NOTE:

This is the first year the PSSA-M Reading and Science assessments were administered.

Percentages may not total 100 due to rounding.

This table reflects all students enrolled for any portion of the academic year, meaning that these numbers may not match the results reported for Accountability purposes.

— Indicates fewer than 10 students in a group. To provide meaningful results and to protect the privacy of individual students, data are printed only when the total number of students in a group is at least 10.

[1] There can be overlap among the groups since a student may belong to more than one of these groups.

State PSSA Results in Grade 4 Reading

Student Group[1]	Academic Year	Participation Rate	Percentage of students in each Performance Level				Percentage of students Proficient and above
			Below Basic	Basic	Proficient	Advanced	State
All Students	**2010–2011**	**100%**	**12%**	**15%**	**38%**	**35%**	**73%**
	2009–2010	100%	13%	14%	36%	36%	73%
Male	**2010–2011**	**100%**	**14%**	**17%**	**38%**	**32%**	**70%**
	2009–2010	100%	15%	15%	36%	33%	69%
Female	**2010–2011**	**100%**	**9%**	**14%**	**38%**	**39%**	**76%**
	2009–2010	100%	11%	13%	36%	40%	76%
White	**2010–2011**	**100%**	**7%**	**13%**	**39%**	**40%**	**80%**
	2009–2010	100%	9%	12%	37%	42%	79%
Black	**2010–2011**	**99%**	**25%**	**24%**	**34%**	**17%**	**51%**
	2009–2010	99%	28%	23%	34%	16%	50%
Latino/Hispanic	**2010–2011**	**99%**	**23%**	**22%**	**36%**	**20%**	**55%**
	2009–2010	99%	26%	21%	34%	19%	53%
Asian	**2010–2011**	**97%**	**6%**	**9%**	**32%**	**53%**	**85%**
	2009–2010	98%	6%	9%	33%	52%	86%
Native American	**2010–2011**	**99%**	**17%**	**17%**	**36%**	**29%**	**66%**
	2009–2010	100%	17%	12%	42%	29%	70%
Multiracial	**2010–2011**	**100%**	**14%**	**20%**	**37%**	**29%**	**66%**
	2009–2010	99%	16%	17%	37%	30%	67%
IEP	**2010–2011**	**99%**	**34%**	**23%**	**29%**	**14%**	**44%**
	2009–2010	99%	39%	22%	26%	13%	40%
English Language Learners	**2010–2011**	**92%**	**44%**	**27%**	**23%**	**5%**	**28%**
	2009–2010	93%	43%	26%	25%	7%	31%
Migrant	**2010–2011**	**86%**	**40%**	**20%**	**27%**	**13%**	**40%**
	2009–2010	94%	46%	25%	23%	6%	29%
Economically Disadvantaged	**2010–2011**	**99%**	**20%**	**22%**	**38%**	**20%**	**58%**
	2009–2010	99%	22%	20%	37%	21%	58%

NOTE:
This is the first year the PSSA-M Reading and Science assessments were administered.
Percentages may not total 100 due to rounding.
This table reflects all students enrolled for any portion of the academic year, meaning that these numbers may not match the results reported for Accountability purposes.

— Indicates fewer than 10 students in a group. To provide meaningful results and to protect the privacy of individual students, data are printed only when the total number of students in a group is at least 10.

[1] There can be overlap among the groups since a student may belong to more than one of these groups.

State PSSA Results in Grade 4 Science

Student Group[1]	Academic Year	Participation Rate	Percentage of students in each Performance Level				Percentage of students Proficient and above State					
			Below Basic	Basic	Proficient	Advanced	0	20	40	60	80	100
All Students	**2010–2011**	**100%**	**6%**	**12%**	**38%**	**45%**					83%	
	2009–2010	100%	8%	11%	36%	46%					81%	
Male	**2010–2011**	**100%**	**6%**	**11%**	**36%**	**47%**					83%	
	2009–2010	100%	9%	10%	34%	47%					81%	
Female	**2010–2011**	**100%**	**5%**	**12%**	**40%**	**42%**					83%	
	2009–2010	100%	7%	11%	37%	44%					82%	
White	**2010–2011**	**100%**	**2%**	**8%**	**37%**	**53%**					90%	
	2009–2010	100%	4%	7%	35%	54%					89%	
Black	**2010–2011**	**99%**	**16%**	**25%**	**42%**	**17%**			59%			
	2009–2010	99%	22%	22%	38%	17%			56%			
Latino/Hispanic	**2010–2011**	**100%**	**13%**	**22%**	**44%**	**21%**			64%			
	2009–2010	100%	19%	21%	40%	20%			60%			
Asian	**2010–2011**	**100%**	**4%**	**8%**	**32%**	**56%**					88%	
	2009–2010	100%	4%	8%	31%	57%					88%	
Native American	**2010–2011**	**99%**	**10%**	**12%**	**38%**	**39%**				77%		
	2009–2010	100%	8%	12%	39%	41%				80%		
Multiracial	**2010–2011**	**99%**	**8%**	**16%**	**42%**	**34%**				77%		
	2009–2010	99%	11%	13%	40%	36%				76%		
IEP	**2010–2011**	**99%**	**15%**	**22%**	**40%**	**23%**			62%			
	2009–2010	99%	19%	19%	38%	24%			61%			
English Language Learners	**2010–2011**	**100%**	**26%**	**32%**	**34%**	**7%**		41%				
	2009–2010	100%	33%	27%	33%	8%		40%				
Migrant	**2010–2011**	**98%**	**31%**	**22%**	**32%**	**15%**		48%				
	2009–2010	98%	33%	29%	34%	4%		38%				
Economically Disadvantaged	**2010–2011**	**100%**	**11%**	**19%**	**44%**	**27%**				71%		
	2009–2010	100%	15%	18%	40%	28%				68%		

NOTE:
This is the first year the PSSA-M Reading and Science assessments were administered.
Percentages may not total 100 due to rounding.
This table reflects all students enrolled for any portion of the academic year, meaning that these numbers may not match the results reported for Accountability purposes.

— Indicates fewer than 10 students in a group. To provide meaningful results and to protect the privacy of individual students, data are printed only when the total number of students in a group is at least 10.

[1] There can be overlap among the groups since a student may belong to more than one of these groups.

State PSSA Results in Grade 5 Mathematics

Student Group[1]	Academic Year	Participation Rate	Percentage of students in each Performance Level				Percentage of students Proficient and above State
			Below Basic	Basic	Proficient	Advanced	0 20 40 60 80 100
All Students	2010–2011	100%	8%	16%	30%	46%	76%
	2009–2010	100%	9%	17%	27%	47%	74%
Male	2010–2011	100%	8%	16%	29%	47%	76%
	2009–2010	100%	9%	16%	26%	49%	74%
Female	2010–2011	100%	8%	17%	31%	44%	75%
	2009–2010	100%	9%	18%	28%	46%	74%
White	2010–2011	100%	5%	13%	30%	52%	82%
	2009–2010	100%	6%	14%	27%	54%	80%
Black	2010–2011	100%	19%	26%	32%	23%	54%
	2009–2010	100%	21%	27%	28%	24%	52%
Latino/Hispanic	2010–2011	100%	18%	24%	31%	27%	58%
	2009–2010	100%	19%	25%	27%	28%	56%
Asian	2010–2011	100%	4%	8%	20%	68%	88%
	2009–2010	100%	4%	9%	18%	69%	87%
Native American	2010–2011	99%	11%	24%	31%	34%	65%
	2009–2010	100%	8%	24%	32%	36%	68%
Multiracial	2010–2011	100%	10%	19%	32%	39%	71%
	2009–2010	99%	12%	20%	27%	41%	68%
IEP	2010–2011	99%	24%	27%	28%	21%	49%
	2009–2010	99%	29%	26%	24%	21%	45%
English Language Learners	2010–2011	100%	35%	30%	23%	12%	35%
	2009–2010	100%	35%	31%	21%	14%	34%
Migrant	2010–2011	100%	31%	24%	28%	17%	45%
	2009–2010	100%	30%	35%	23%	13%	36%
Economically Disadvantaged	2010–2011	100%	14%	23%	33%	30%	63%
	2009–2010	100%	16%	24%	29%	31%	60%

NOTE:
This is the first year the PSSA-M Reading and Science assessments were administered.
Percentages may not total 100 due to rounding.
This table reflects all students enrolled for any portion of the academic year, meaning that these numbers may not match the results reported for Accountability purposes.
— Indicates fewer than 10 students in a group. To provide meaningful results and to protect the privacy of individual students, data are printed only when the total number of students in a group is at least 10.
[1] There can be overlap among the groups since a student may belong to more than one of these groups.

State PSSA Results in Grade 5 Reading

Student Group[1]	Academic Year	Participation Rate	Percentage of students in each Performance Level				Percentage of students Proficient and above
			Below Basic	Basic	Proficient	Advanced	State
All Students	**2010–2011**	**100%**	**15%**	**18%**	**45%**	**22%**	67%
	2009–2010	100%	17%	19%	41%	23%	64%
Male	**2010–2011**	**100%**	**17%**	**19%**	**44%**	**19%**	63%
	2009–2010	100%	20%	20%	41%	19%	60%
Female	**2010–2011**	**100%**	**12%**	**17%**	**45%**	**26%**	71%
	2009–2010	100%	14%	18%	41%	26%	68%
White	**2010–2011**	**100%**	**10%**	**17%**	**48%**	**26%**	73%
	2009–2010	100%	12%	17%	44%	26%	71%
Black	**2010–2011**	**100%**	**30%**	**24%**	**37%**	**9%**	46%
	2009–2010	99%	34%	25%	32%	9%	41%
Latino/Hispanic	**2010–2011**	**99%**	**32%**	**23%**	**35%**	**10%**	46%
	2009–2010	99%	35%	23%	32%	11%	42%
Asian	**2010–2011**	**98%**	**9%**	**12%**	**42%**	**37%**	79%
	2009–2010	98%	10%	13%	37%	39%	77%
Native American	**2010–2011**	**99%**	**16%**	**21%**	**45%**	**18%**	63%
	2009–2010	100%	20%	22%	47%	11%	58%
Multiracial	**2010–2011**	**100%**	**16%**	**21%**	**44%**	**19%**	63%
	2009–2010	99%	19%	21%	41%	18%	59%
IEP	**2010–2011**	**99%**	**44%**	**23%**	**26%**	**7%**	33%
	2009–2010	99%	52%	22%	21%	6%	27%
English Language Learners	**2010–2011**	**92%**	**61%**	**22%**	**15%**	**2%**	16%
	2009–2010	93%	63%	22%	13%	3%	15%
Migrant	**2010–2011**	**96%**	**53%**	**26%**	**14%**	**8%**	22%
	2009–2010	99%	49%	27%	19%	5%	24%
Economically Disadvantaged	**2010–2011**	**99%**	**25%**	**24%**	**40%**	**11%**	51%
	2009–2010	99%	29%	24%	36%	12%	48%

NOTE:

This is the first year the PSSA-M Reading and Science assessments were administered.

Percentages may not total 100 due to rounding.

This table reflects all students enrolled for any portion of the academic year, meaning that these numbers may not match the results reported for Accountability purposes.

— Indicates fewer than 10 students in a group. To provide meaningful results and to protect the privacy of individual students, data are printed only when the total number of students in a group is at least 10.

[1] There can be overlap among the groups since a student may belong to more than one of these groups.

State PSSA Results in Grade 6 Mathematics

Student Group[1]	Academic Year	Participation Rate	Percentage of students in each Performance Level				Percentage of students Proficient and above State					
			Below Basic	Basic	Proficient	Advanced	0	20	40	60	80	100
All Students	**2010–2011**	100%	10%	11%	25%	53%	78%					
	2009–2010	100%	10%	13%	25%	53%	78%					
Male	**2010–2011**	100%	12%	11%	24%	53%	77%					
	2009–2010	100%	11%	12%	24%	53%	77%					
Female	**2010–2011**	100%	9%	11%	26%	54%	79%					
	2009–2010	100%	8%	13%	26%	53%	79%					
White	**2010–2011**	100%	7%	9%	24%	60%	84%					
	2009–2010	100%	6%	10%	24%	60%	84%					
Black	**2010–2011**	100%	22%	18%	29%	31%	59%					
	2009–2010	100%	22%	21%	28%	28%	57%					
Latino/Hispanic	**2010–2011**	100%	23%	17%	28%	32%	60%					
	2009–2010	100%	21%	21%	28%	31%	59%					
Asian	**2010–2011**	100%	4%	6%	14%	76%	90%					
	2009–2010	100%	4%	6%	15%	76%	90%					
Native American	**2010–2011**	99%	16%	16%	25%	43%	69%					
	2009–2010	99%	13%	16%	23%	47%	70%					
Multiracial	**2010–2011**	100%	15%	13%	26%	47%	72%					
	2009–2010	99%	14%	16%	28%	42%	70%					
IEP	**2010–2011**	99%	35%	20%	25%	20%	45%					
	2009–2010	99%	34%	23%	23%	20%	43%					
English Language Learners	**2010–2011**	100%	43%	22%	21%	14%	35%					
	2009–2010	100%	39%	25%	22%	14%	36%					
Migrant	**2010–2011**	100%	24%	13%	42%	22%	64%					
	2009–2010	99%	29%	15%	32%	25%	56%					
Economically Disadvantaged	**2010–2011**	100%	18%	16%	29%	36%	65%					
	2009–2010	100%	17%	19%	29%	35%	64%					

NOTE:

This is the first year the PSSA-M Reading and Science assessments were administered.

Percentages may not total 100 due to rounding.

This table reflects all students enrolled for any portion of the academic year, meaning that these numbers may not match the results reported for Accountability purposes.

— Indicates fewer than 10 students in a group. To provide meaningful results and to protect the privacy of individual students, data are printed only when the total number of students in a group is at least 10.

[1] There can be overlap among the groups since a student may belong to more than one of these groups.

State PSSA Results in Grade 6 Reading

Student Group[1]	Academic Year	Participation Rate	Percentage of students in each Performance Level				Percentage of students Proficient and above State
			Below Basic	Basic	Proficient	Advanced	0 20 40 60 80 100
All Students	**2010–2011**	**100%**	**13%**	**17%**	**30%**	**39%**	70%
	2009–2010	100%	15%	16%	31%	38%	68%
Male	**2010–2011**	**99%**	**16%**	**18%**	**31%**	**36%**	67%
	2009–2010	99%	18%	17%	31%	34%	65%
Female	**2010–2011**	**100%**	**11%**	**16%**	**30%**	**42%**	73%
	2009–2010	100%	12%	16%	31%	42%	72%
White	**2010–2011**	**100%**	**8%**	**14%**	**31%**	**46%**	77%
	2009–2010	100%	10%	14%	32%	44%	76%
Black	**2010–2011**	**99%**	**28%**	**27%**	**28%**	**17%**	46%
	2009–2010	99%	30%	25%	29%	17%	45%
Latino/Hispanic	**2010–2011**	**99%**	**31%**	**25%**	**27%**	**17%**	44%
	2009–2010	99%	32%	23%	28%	17%	45%
Asian	**2010–2011**	**98%**	**9%**	**12%**	**25%**	**54%**	79%
	2009–2010	97%	8%	11%	27%	55%	82%
Native American	**2010–2011**	**99%**	**17%**	**21%**	**33%**	**30%**	62%
	2009–2010	99%	21%	17%	33%	29%	62%
Multiracial	**2010–2011**	**99%**	**17%**	**19%**	**31%**	**32%**	63%
	2009–2010	99%	20%	19%	32%	29%	61%
IEP	**2010–2011**	**99%**	**44%**	**25%**	**20%**	**11%**	32%
	2009–2010	99%	50%	22%	18%	10%	27%
English Language Learners	**2010–2011**	**93%**	**64%**	**24%**	**11%**	**2%**	13%
	2009–2010	93%	61%	22%	13%	3%	16%
Migrant	**2010–2011**	**95%**	**45%**	**34%**	**9%**	**11%**	21%
	2009–2010	98%	54%	21%	20%	5%	24%
Economically Disadvantaged	**2010–2011**	**99%**	**24%**	**24%**	**30%**	**22%**	52%
	2009–2010	99%	26%	23%	31%	21%	51%

NOTE:
This is the first year the PSSA-M Reading and Science assessments were administered.
Percentages may not total 100 due to rounding.
This table reflects all students enrolled for any portion of the academic year, meaning that these numbers may not match the results reported for Accountability purposes.
— Indicates fewer than 10 students in a group. To provide meaningful results and to protect the privacy of individual students, data are printed only when the total number of students in a group is at least 10.
[1] There can be overlap among the groups since a student may belong to more than one of these groups.

State PSSA Results in Grade 7 Mathematics

Student Group[1]	Academic Year	Participation Rate	Percentage of students in each Performance Level				Percentage of students Proficient and above State					
			Below Basic	Basic	Proficient	Advanced	0	20	40	60	80	100
All Students	**2010–2011**	100%	11%	11%	25%	53%	78%					
	2009–2010	100%	12%	10%	24%	54%	78%					
Male	**2010–2011**	100%	12%	11%	24%	53%	77%					
	2009–2010	99%	13%	10%	23%	54%	77%					
Female	**2010–2011**	100%	10%	11%	26%	53%	79%					
	2009–2010	100%	11%	10%	25%	54%	79%					
White	**2010–2011**	100%	7%	9%	24%	60%	84%					
	2009–2010	100%	8%	9%	23%	61%	84%					
Black	**2010–2011**	99%	25%	17%	29%	29%	58%					
	2009–2010	99%	26%	17%	27%	30%	57%					
Latino/Hispanic	**2010–2011**	99%	24%	17%	28%	31%	59%					
	2009–2010	99%	26%	17%	27%	31%	58%					
Asian	**2010–2011**	100%	5%	5%	13%	77%	90%					
	2009–2010	100%	5%	5%	15%	76%	90%					
Native American	**2010–2011**	100%	21%	9%	24%	47%	70%					
	2009–2010	99%	15%	9%	21%	54%	75%					
Multiracial	**2010–2011**	100%	15%	13%	28%	44%	72%					
	2009–2010	99%	18%	13%	27%	43%	70%					
IEP	**2010–2011**	99%	38%	19%	24%	18%	42%					
	2009–2010	99%	40%	18%	23%	18%	41%					
English Language Learners	**2010–2011**	100%	46%	20%	21%	13%	34%					
	2009–2010	99%	43%	19%	22%	16%	38%					
Migrant	**2010–2011**	100%	38%	19%	21%	22%	43%					
	2009–2010	96%	42%	12%	24%	22%	46%					
Economically Disadvantaged	**2010–2011**	99%	20%	16%	29%	35%	65%					
	2009–2010	99%	21%	16%	28%	36%	64%					

NOTE:
This is the first year the PSSA-M Reading and Science assessments were administered.
Percentages may not total 100 due to rounding.
This table reflects all students enrolled for any portion of the academic year, meaning that these numbers may not match the results reported for Accountability purposes.

— Indicates fewer than 10 students in a group. To provide meaningful results and to protect the privacy of individual students, data are printed only when the total number of students in a group is at least 10.

[1] There can be overlap among the groups since a student may belong to more than one of these groups.

State PSSA Results in Grade 7 Reading

Student Group[1]	Academic Year	Participation Rate	Percentage of students in each Performance Level				Percentage of students Proficient and above State					
			Below Basic	Basic	Proficient	Advanced	0	20	40	60	80	100
All Students	**2010–2011**	**99%**	**10%**	**15%**	**33%**	**43%**					76%	
	2009–2010	99%	11%	15%	32%	42%				73%		
Male	**2010–2011**	**99%**	**12%**	**17%**	**33%**	**38%**					71%	
	2009–2010	99%	15%	17%	32%	37%				68%		
Female	**2010–2011**	**99%**	**6%**	**13%**	**32%**	**48%**					80%	
	2009–2010	99%	8%	14%	31%	47%					78%	
White	**2010–2011**	**100%**	**6%**	**12%**	**32%**	**49%**					82%	
	2009–2010	100%	8%	13%	31%	48%					79%	
Black	**2010–2011**	**99%**	**19%**	**25%**	**35%**	**21%**				56%		
	2009–2010	99%	22%	24%	34%	20%			54%			
Latino/Hispanic	**2010–2011**	**98%**	**22%**	**23%**	**34%**	**21%**				55%		
	2009–2010	98%	25%	25%	31%	19%			50%			
Asian	**2010–2011**	**98%**	**6%**	**9%**	**24%**	**61%**					86%	
	2009–2010	97%	6%	10%	25%	59%					84%	
Native American	**2010–2011**	**100%**	**14%**	**17%**	**31%**	**37%**					68%	
	2009–2010	99%	12%	15%	35%	39%				73%		
Multiracial	**2010–2011**	**99%**	**12%**	**18%**	**35%**	**34%**					70%	
	2009–2010	99%	14%	19%	35%	32%				66%		
IEP	**2010–2011**	**99%**	**36%**	**28%**	**25%**	**12%**		36%				
	2009–2010	99%	41%	27%	22%	10%		31%				
English Language Learners	**2010–2011**	**91%**	**49%**	**31%**	**16%**	**3%**	20%					
	2009–2010	91%	48%	32%	17%	3%	20%					
Migrant	**2010–2011**	**93%**	**40%**	**30%**	**22%**	**8%**	30%					
	2009–2010	95%	40%	27%	29%	4%	33%					
Economically Disadvantaged	**2010–2011**	**99%**	**17%**	**23%**	**35%**	**25%**				60%		
	2009–2010	99%	20%	22%	34%	24%				58%		

NOTE:
This is the first year the PSSA-M Reading and Science assessments were administered.
Percentages may not total 100 due to rounding.
This table reflects all students enrolled for any portion of the academic year, meaning that these numbers may not match the results
reported for Accountability purposes.
— Indicates fewer than 10 students in a group. To provide meaningful results and to protect
   the privacy of individual students, data are printed only when the total number of students
   in a group is at least 10.
[1] There can be overlap among the groups since a student may belong to more than one of these groups.

State PSSA Results in Grade 8 Mathematics

Student Group[1]	Academic Year	Participation Rate	Percentage of students in each Performance Level				Percentage of students Proficient and above State
			Below Basic	Basic	Proficient	Advanced	0 20 40 60 80 100
All Students	2010–2011	100%	12%	12%	27%	50%	76%
	2009–2010	99%	12%	13%	24%	51%	75%
Male	2010–2011	99%	13%	12%	26%	50%	76%
	2009–2010	99%	13%	13%	23%	51%	74%
Female	2010–2011	100%	11%	12%	28%	50%	77%
	2009–2010	100%	11%	13%	25%	51%	76%
White	2010–2011	100%	7%	10%	27%	56%	83%
	2009–2010	100%	8%	11%	24%	57%	81%
Black	2010–2011	99%	26%	19%	29%	26%	55%
	2009–2010	99%	27%	20%	26%	27%	53%
Latino/Hispanic	2010–2011	99%	26%	18%	28%	28%	56%
	2009–2010	99%	27%	18%	25%	29%	54%
Asian	2010–2011	100%	5%	6%	16%	73%	89%
	2009–2010	100%	6%	6%	15%	73%	88%
Native American	2010–2011	98%	18%	11%	20%	51%	71%
	2009–2010	99%	15%	13%	28%	44%	72%
Multiracial	2010–2011	100%	16%	15%	26%	43%	69%
	2009–2010	98%	20%	19%	24%	36%	60%
IEP	2010–2011	99%	40%	20%	24%	16%	40%
	2009–2010	98%	41%	21%	22%	16%	38%
English Language Learners	2010–2011	100%	46%	20%	20%	14%	34%
	2009–2010	99%	45%	21%	21%	13%	34%
Migrant	2010–2011	100%	39%	25%	16%	19%	36%
	2009–2010	100%	30%	17%	29%	24%	53%
Economically Disadvantaged	2010–2011	99%	21%	17%	30%	32%	61%
	2009–2010	99%	22%	19%	27%	33%	59%

NOTE:
This is the first year the PSSA-M Reading and Science assessments were administered.
Percentages may not total 100 due to rounding.
This table reflects all students enrolled for any portion of the academic year, meaning that these numbers may not match the results reported for Accountability purposes.
— Indicates fewer than 10 students in a group. To provide meaningful results and to protect the privacy of individual students, data are printed only when the total number of students in a group is at least 10.
[1] There can be overlap among the groups since a student may belong to more than one of these groups.

State PSSA Results in Grade 8 Reading

Student Group[1]	Academic Year	Participation Rate	Percentage of students in each Performance Level				Percentage of students Proficient and above
			Below Basic	Basic	Proficient	Advanced	State 0 20 40 60 80 100
All Students	2010–2011	99%	9%	9%	24%	57%	81%
	2009–2010	99%	9%	9%	29%	53%	81%
Male	2010–2011	99%	12%	11%	26%	51%	77%
	2009–2010	99%	12%	11%	30%	47%	77%
Female	2010–2011	99%	6%	8%	22%	63%	85%
	2009–2010	99%	6%	8%	27%	59%	86%
White	2010–2011	100%	6%	7%	22%	65%	87%
	2009–2010	100%	6%	8%	27%	59%	86%
Black	2010–2011	99%	19%	17%	31%	33%	64%
	2009–2010	99%	17%	16%	35%	32%	67%
Latino/Hispanic	2010–2011	98%	23%	17%	29%	31%	60%
	2009–2010	98%	21%	16%	32%	31%	63%
Asian	2010–2011	97%	7%	6%	16%	72%	88%
	2009–2010	97%	5%	5%	19%	71%	90%
Native American	2010–2011	98%	12%	11%	20%	57%	77%
	2009–2010	100%	11%	13%	24%	52%	77%
Multiracial	2010–2011	99%	11%	10%	29%	50%	79%
	2009–2010	98%	13%	12%	33%	41%	74%
IEP	2010–2011	98%	35%	20%	26%	18%	45%
	2009–2010	98%	36%	22%	28%	14%	42%
English Language Learners	2010–2011	91%	49%	23%	20%	7%	27%
	2009–2010	92%	41%	24%	26%	9%	35%
Migrant	2010–2011	94%	38%	21%	29%	12%	41%
	2009–2010	97%	35%	11%	39%	15%	54%
Economically Disadvantaged	2010–2011	99%	17%	16%	30%	37%	67%
	2009–2010	99%	16%	15%	35%	34%	69%

NOTE:
This is the first year the PSSA-M Reading and Science assessments were administered.
Percentages may not total 100 due to rounding.
This table reflects all students enrolled for any portion of the academic year, meaning that these numbers may not match the results reported for Accountability purposes.
— Indicates fewer than 10 students in a group. To provide meaningful results and to protect the privacy of individual students, data are printed only when the total number of students in a group is at least 10.
[1] There can be overlap among the groups since a student may belong to more than one of these groups.

State PSSA Results in Grade 8 Science

Student Group[1]	Academic Year	Participation Rate	Percentage of students in each Performance Level				Percentage of students Proficient and above State
			Below Basic	Basic	Proficient	Advanced	0 20 40 60 80 100
All Students	**2010–2011**	**99%**	**23%**	**19%**	**34%**	**24%**	58%
	2009–2010	99%	26%	17%	34%	23%	57%
Male	**2010–2011**	**99%**	**24%**	**17%**	**32%**	**26%**	59%
	2009–2010	99%	27%	16%	32%	25%	58%
Female	**2010–2011**	**99%**	**22%**	**20%**	**35%**	**22%**	57%
	2009–2010	99%	25%	19%	35%	21%	56%
White	**2010–2011**	**99%**	**15%**	**18%**	**38%**	**29%**	67%
	2009–2010	99%	18%	17%	38%	28%	66%
Black	**2010–2011**	**98%**	**50%**	**23%**	**21%**	**6%**	27%
	2009–2010	98%	54%	20%	20%	5%	25%
Latino/Hispanic	**2010–2011**	**98%**	**50%**	**22%**	**21%**	**7%**	28%
	2009–2010	98%	52%	20%	21%	7%	28%
Asian	**2010–2011**	**100%**	**15%**	**14%**	**31%**	**39%**	70%
	2009–2010	100%	17%	13%	33%	37%	70%
Native American	**2010–2011**	**98%**	**24%**	**19%**	**34%**	**23%**	57%
	2009–2010	99%	28%	19%	35%	18%	53%
Multiracial	**2010–2011**	**98%**	**27%**	**23%**	**30%**	**20%**	50%
	2009–2010	98%	38%	21%	28%	14%	42%
IEP	**2010–2011**	**98%**	**57%**	**20%**	**17%**	**6%**	23%
	2009–2010	98%	62%	18%	15%	5%	20%
English Language Learners	**2010–2011**	**98%**	**77%**	**16%**	**6%**	**1%**	7%
	2009–2010	99%	76%	15%	7%	1%	8%
Migrant	**2010–2011**	**100%**	**76%**	**10%**	**12%**	**1%**	13%
	2009–2010	100%	65%	18%	16%	1%	17%
Economically Disadvantaged	**2010–2011**	**99%**	**40%**	**23%**	**26%**	**10%**	36%
	2009–2010	98%	44%	21%	26%	10%	36%

NOTE:
This is the first year the PSSA-M Reading and Science assessments were administered.
Percentages may not total 100 due to rounding.
This table reflects all students enrolled for any portion of the academic year, meaning that these numbers may not match the results reported for Accountability purposes.

— Indicates fewer than 10 students in a group. To provide meaningful results and to protect the privacy of individual students, data are printed only when the total number of students in a group is at least 10.

[1] There can be overlap among the groups since a student may belong to more than one of these groups.

State PSSA Results in Grade 11 Mathematics

Student Group[1]	Academic Year	Participation Rate	Percentage of students in each Performance Level				Percentage of students Proficient and above State					
			Below Basic	Basic	Proficient	Advanced	0	20	40	60	80	100
All Students	**2010–2011**	**99%**	**22%**	**18%**	**31%**	**29%**				60%		
	2009–2010	99%	25%	16%	27%	32%				59%		
Male	**2010–2011**	**99%**	**23%**	**17%**	**30%**	**30%**				60%		
	2009–2010	99%	26%	15%	26%	33%				60%		
Female	**2010–2011**	**99%**	**21%**	**19%**	**32%**	**27%**				60%		
	2009–2010	99%	25%	16%	28%	31%				59%		
White	**2010–2011**	**99%**	**16%**	**17%**	**34%**	**33%**					66%	
	2009–2010	99%	19%	15%	29%	36%					65%	
Black	**2010–2011**	**98%**	**44%**	**22%**	**25%**	**10%**		34%				
	2009–2010	97%	50%	17%	21%	12%		33%				
Latino/Hispanic	**2010–2011**	**98%**	**43%**	**22%**	**24%**	**11%**		35%				
	2009–2010	98%	47%	19%	21%	13%		34%				
Asian	**2010–2011**	**100%**	**9%**	**10%**	**25%**	**56%**						81%
	2009–2010	100%	10%	8%	21%	61%						82%
Native American	**2010–2011**	**100%**	**30%**	**26%**	**29%**	**15%**			44%			
	2009–2010	99%	37%	15%	25%	23%			48%			
Multiracial	**2010–2011**	**98%**	**31%**	**21%**	**27%**	**20%**			48%			
	2009–2010	97%	41%	17%	22%	19%			41%			
IEP	**2010–2011**	**97%**	**63%**	**18%**	**14%**	**5%**	19%					
	2009–2010	96%	67%	14%	13%	6%	19%					
English Language Learners	**2010–2011**	**99%**	**60%**	**17%**	**14%**	**9%**		23%				
	2009–2010	99%	63%	13%	14%	10%		24%				
Migrant	**2010–2011**	**98%**	**68%**	**9%**	**11%**	**11%**		23%				
	2009–2010	98%	62%	22%	7%	9%	16%					
Economically Disadvantaged	**2010–2011**	**98%**	**37%**	**22%**	**27%**	**14%**			41%			
	2009–2010	98%	41%	18%	24%	16%			40%			

NOTE:

This is the first year the PSSA-M Reading and Science assessments were administered.

Percentages may not total 100 due to rounding.

This table reflects all students enrolled for any portion of the academic year, meaning that these numbers may not match the results reported for Accountability purposes.

— Indicates fewer than 10 students in a group. To provide meaningful results and to protect the privacy of individual students, data are printed only when the total number of students in a group is at least 10.

[1] There can be overlap among the groups since a student may belong to more than one of these groups.

State PSSA Results in Grade 11 Reading

Student Group[1]	Academic Year	Participation Rate	Percentage of students in each Performance Level				Percentage of students Proficient and above State					
			Below Basic	Basic	Proficient	Advanced	0	20	40	60	80	100
All Students	**2010–2011**	**99%**	**16%**	**15%**	**33%**	**36%**					69%	
	2009–2010	99%	18%	15%	33%	34%				67%		
Male	**2010–2011**	**99%**	**19%**	**16%**	**33%**	**32%**				65%		
	2009–2010	98%	22%	15%	33%	30%				63%		
Female	**2010–2011**	**99%**	**13%**	**14%**	**33%**	**39%**				73%		
	2009–2010	99%	15%	14%	33%	37%				71%		
White	**2010–2011**	**99%**	**11%**	**13%**	**34%**	**41%**				75%		
	2009–2010	99%	13%	13%	35%	39%				73%		
Black	**2010–2011**	**97%**	**34%**	**22%**	**30%**	**15%**			44%			
	2009–2010	97%	37%	21%	28%	14%			42%			
Latino/Hispanic	**2010–2011**	**98%**	**35%**	**20%**	**29%**	**16%**			45%			
	2009–2010	97%	36%	20%	29%	15%			44%			
Asian	**2010–2011**	**98%**	**13%**	**12%**	**27%**	**48%**				75%		
	2009–2010	98%	13%	12%	28%	47%				75%		
Native American	**2010–2011**	**99%**	**22%**	**17%**	**33%**	**27%**				60%		
	2009–2010	98%	21%	21%	28%	29%			57%			
Multiracial	**2010–2011**	**98%**	**19%**	**19%**	**32%**	**30%**				61%		
	2009–2010	97%	28%	18%	32%	22%			53%			
IEP	**2010–2011**	**97%**	**54%**	**20%**	**19%**	**7%**		26%				
	2009–2010	97%	58%	19%	17%	6%		23%				
English Language Learners	**2010–2011**	**93%**	**71%**	**17%**	**9%**	**3%**		12%				
	2009–2010	94%	71%	18%	10%	2%		11%				
Migrant	**2010–2011**	**96%**	**65%**	**12%**	**19%**	**5%**		23%				
	2009–2010	96%	67%	18%	7%	9%		16%				
Economically Disadvantaged	**2010–2011**	**98%**	**29%**	**20%**	**32%**	**19%**			51%			
	2009–2010	98%	32%	20%	31%	17%			48%			

NOTE:

This is the first year the PSSA-M Reading and Science assessments were administered.

Percentages may not total 100 due to rounding.

This table reflects all students enrolled for any portion of the academic year, meaning that these numbers may not match the results reported for Accountability purposes.

— Indicates fewer than 10 students in a group. To provide meaningful results and to protect the privacy of individual students, data are printed only when the total number of students in a group is at least 10.

[1] There can be overlap among the groups since a student may belong to more than one of these groups.

State PSSA Results in Grade 11 Science

Student Group[1]	Academic Year	Participation Rate	Percentage of students in each Performance Level				Percentage of students Proficient and above State
			Below Basic	Basic	Proficient	Advanced	0 20 40 60 80 100
All Students	**2010–2011**	**97%**	**19%**	**40%**	**26%**	**14%**	40%
	2009–2010	97%	19%	41%	25%	15%	39%
Male	**2010–2011**	**97%**	**19%**	**37%**	**27%**	**17%**	44%
	2009–2010	97%	20%	39%	25%	16%	41%
Female	**2010–2011**	**97%**	**19%**	**44%**	**26%**	**11%**	37%
	2009–2010	97%	19%	43%	25%	13%	38%
White	**2010–2011**	**98%**	**12%**	**41%**	**31%**	**17%**	47%
	2009–2010	98%	13%	42%	29%	17%	46%
Black	**2010–2011**	**92%**	**48%**	**40%**	**10%**	**2%**	12%
	2009–2010	91%	48%	40%	9%	3%	12%
Latino/Hispanic	**2010–2011**	**93%**	**45%**	**41%**	**11%**	**4%**	15%
	2009–2010	93%	43%	43%	11%	4%	14%
Asian	**2010–2011**	**98%**	**16%**	**33%**	**27%**	**24%**	51%
	2009–2010	97%	14%	34%	27%	25%	52%
Native American	**2010–2011**	**99%**	**27%**	**40%**	**23%**	**10%**	33%
	2009–2010	98%	21%	48%	20%	10%	31%
Multiracial	**2010–2011**	**95%**	**26%**	**44%**	**22%**	**8%**	30%
	2009–2010	95%	36%	42%	14%	8%	22%
IEP	**2010–2011**	**94%**	**52%**	**37%**	**8%**	**3%**	11%
	2009–2010	94%	55%	36%	6%	2%	9%
English Language Learners	**2010–2011**	**95%**	**74%**	**22%**	**3%**	**1%**	3%
	2009–2010	95%	72%	27%	2%	0%	2%
Migrant	**2010–2011**	**98%**	**62%**	**36%**	**0%**	**2%**	2%
	2009–2010	95%	60%	31%	10%	0%	10%
Economically Disadvantaged	**2010–2011**	**95%**	**35%**	**44%**	**16%**	**5%**	21%
	2009–2010	94%	35%	45%	15%	5%	20%

NOTE:
This is the first year the PSSA-M Reading and Science assessments were administered.
Percentages may not total 100 due to rounding.
This table reflects all students enrolled for any portion of the academic year, meaning that these numbers may not match the results reported for Accountability purposes.
— Indicates fewer than 10 students in a group. To provide meaningful results and to protect the privacy of individual students, data are printed only when the total number of students in a group is at least 10.
[1] There can be overlap among the groups since a student may belong to more than one of these groups.

Ancestry and Ethnicity

State Profile

Population: 12,702,379

Ancestry	Population	%
Afghan (704)	876	0.01
African, Sub-Saharan (69,793)	83,254	0.66
African (44,115)	53,706	0.43
Cape Verdean (199)	355	<0.01
Ethiopian (3,174)	3,372	0.03
Ghanaian (1,632)	1,774	0.01
Kenyan (1,115)	1,277	0.01
Liberian (6,971)	7,515	0.06
Nigerian (5,398)	6,451	0.05
Senegalese (396)	477	<0.01
Sierra Leonean (952)	1,036	0.01
Somalian (239)	250	<0.01
South African (850)	1,323	0.01
Sudanese (1,003)	1,027	0.01
Ugandan (192)	215	<0.01
Zimbabwean (201)	201	<0.01
Other Sub-Saharan African (3,356)	4,275	0.03
Albanian (6,778)	8,869	0.07
Alsatian (150)	599	<0.01
American (550,441)	550,441	4.36
Arab (35,720)	61,004	0.48
Arab (5,177)	6,995	0.06
Egyptian (5,649)	6,728	0.05
Iraqi (838)	955	0.01
Jordanian (1,528)	1,616	0.01
Lebanese (7,381)	19,891	0.16
Moroccan (2,390)	2,980	0.02
Palestinian (1,360)	1,727	0.01
Syrian (7,413)	14,843	0.12
Other Arab (3,984)	5,269	0.04
Armenian (5,101)	9,325	0.07
Assyrian/Chaldean/Syriac (267)	386	<0.01
Australian (1,239)	2,907	0.02
Austrian (14,151)	59,263	0.47
Basque (192)	521	<0.01
Belgian (2,483)	9,754	0.08
Brazilian (5,805)	7,831	0.06
British (18,564)	39,949	0.32
Bulgarian (1,970)	2,544	0.02
Cajun (153)	425	<0.01
Canadian (6,707)	14,976	0.12
Carpatho Rusyn (1,228)	2,480	0.02
Celtic (792)	1,798	0.01
Croatian (17,378)	50,995	0.40
Cypriot (343)	375	<0.01
Czech (12,702)	57,652	0.46
Czechoslovakian (10,228)	23,548	0.19
Danish (4,295)	19,001	0.15
Dutch (52,955)	268,376	2.13
Eastern European (20,336)	22,509	0.18
English (274,054)	1,052,986	8.35
Estonian (444)	1,136	0.01
European (73,687)	79,980	0.63
Finnish (2,224)	8,401	0.07
French, ex. Basque (34,470)	234,946	1.86
French Canadian (10,441)	30,828	0.24
German (1,302,473)	3,533,978	28.02
German Russian (178)	320	<0.01
Greek (30,129)	66,404	0.53
Guyanese (1,783)	2,750	0.02
Hungarian (39,070)	144,444	1.15
Icelander (248)	638	0.01
Iranian (3,731)	4,863	0.04
Irish (591,624)	2,251,268	17.85
Israeli (2,306)	3,461	0.03
Italian (608,889)	1,577,604	12.51
Latvian (1,817)	3,754	0.03
Lithuanian (24,057)	82,290	0.65
Luxemburger (110)	415	<0.01
Macedonian (463)	1,117	0.01
Maltese (203)	703	0.01
New Zealander (203)	346	<0.01
Northern European (4,286)	4,622	0.04

Ancestry	Population	%
Norwegian (11,722)	43,252	0.34
Pennsylvania German (116,138)	173,129	1.37
Polish (291,984)	880,890	6.98
Portuguese (8,178)	19,008	0.15
Romanian (8,849)	19,304	0.15
Russian (77,198)	202,430	1.60
Scandinavian (3,016)	7,796	0.06
Scotch-Irish (86,484)	251,093	1.99
Scottish (50,503)	210,517	1.67
Serbian (7,086)	19,549	0.15
Slavic (6,153)	17,175	0.14
Slovak (88,698)	244,706	1.94
Slovene (6,310)	16,861	0.13
Soviet Union (59)	59	<0.01
Swedish (26,095)	114,312	0.91
Swiss (17,438)	71,887	0.57
Turkish (4,739)	6,319	0.05
Ukrainian (49,800)	117,955	0.94
Welsh (31,875)	187,607	1.49
West Indian, ex. Hispanic (49,541)	63,964	0.51
Bahamian (383)	516	<0.01
Barbadian (1,533)	2,183	0.02
Belizean (566)	624	<0.01
Bermudan (292)	423	<0.01
British West Indian (1,114)	1,596	0.01
Dutch West Indian (156)	267	<0.01
Haitian (17,394)	19,433	0.15
Jamaican (19,465)	25,515	0.20
Trinidadian/Tobagonian (3,782)	5,362	0.04
U.S. Virgin Islander (784)	835	0.01
West Indian (4,023)	7,115	0.06
Other West Indian (49)	95	<0.01
Yugoslavian (6,768)	12,582	0.10

Hispanic Origin	Population	%
Hispanic or Latino (of any race)	719,660	5.67
Central American, ex. Mexican	35,453	0.28
Costa Rican	3,048	0.02
Guatemalan	11,462	0.09
Honduran	7,055	0.06
Nicaraguan	2,400	0.02
Panamanian	3,234	0.03
Salvadoran	7,952	0.06
Other Central American	302	<0.01
Cuban	17,930	0.14
Dominican Republic	62,348	0.49
Mexican	129,568	1.02
Puerto Rican	366,082	2.88
South American	48,126	0.38
Argentinean	4,269	0.03
Bolivian	895	0.01
Chilean	2,521	0.02
Colombian	16,525	0.13
Ecuadorian	10,680	0.08
Paraguayan	500	<0.01
Peruvian	7,783	0.06
Uruguayan	1,181	0.01
Venezuelan	3,243	0.03
Other South American	529	<0.01
Other Hispanic or Latino	60,153	0.47

Race*	Population	%
African-American/Black (1,377,689)	1,507,965	11.87
Not Hispanic (1,327,091)	1,432,537	11.28
Hispanic (50,598)	75,428	0.59
American Indian/Alaska Native (26,843)	81,092	0.64
Not Hispanic (16,909)	62,066	0.49
Hispanic (9,934)	19,026	0.15
Alaska Athabascan (Ala. Nat.) (58)	92	<0.01
Aleut (Alaska Native) (63)	108	<0.01
Apache (215)	911	0.01
Arapaho (7)	41	<0.01
Blackfeet (447)	3,347	0.03
Canadian/French Am. Ind. (118)	288	<0.01
Central American Ind. (280)	443	<0.01
Cherokee (2,612)	14,552	0.11

Race*	Population	%
Cheyenne (50)	185	<0.01
Chickasaw (50)	186	<0.01
Chippewa (348)	770	0.01
Choctaw (227)	787	0.01
Colville (4)	15	<0.01
Comanche (49)	133	<0.01
Cree (53)	217	<0.01
Creek (130)	393	<0.01
Crow (23)	150	<0.01
Delaware (407)	1,680	0.01
Hopi (30)	82	<0.01
Houma (18)	28	<0.01
Inupiat (Alaska Native) (43)	91	<0.01
Iroquois (942)	2,816	0.02
Kiowa (40)	98	<0.01
Lumbee (250)	505	<0.01
Menominee (9)	27	<0.01
Mexican American Ind. (1,048)	1,520	0.01
Navajo (252)	619	<0.01
Osage (18)	80	<0.01
Ottawa (11)	36	<0.01
Paiute (9)	36	<0.01
Pima (19)	36	<0.01
Potawatomi (85)	157	<0.01
Pueblo (92)	204	<0.01
Puget Sound Salish (29)	41	<0.01
Seminole (105)	660	0.01
Shoshone (36)	98	<0.01
Sioux (491)	1,695	0.01
South American Ind. (970)	2,122	0.02
Spanish American Ind. (253)	383	<0.01
Tlingit-Haida (Alaska Native) (48)	95	<0.01
Tohono O'Odham (34)	63	<0.01
Tsimshian (Alaska Native) (7)	13	<0.01
Ute (13)	33	<0.01
Yakama (5)	10	<0.01
Yaqui (29)	61	<0.01
Yuman (7)	18	<0.01
Yup'ik (Alaska Native) (13)	25	<0.01
Asian (349,088)	402,587	3.17
Not Hispanic (346,288)	394,941	3.11
Hispanic (2,800)	7,646	0.06
Bangladeshi (3,812)	4,262	0.03
Bhutanese (946)	1,198	0.01
Burmese (1,665)	1,822	0.01
Cambodian (12,042)	14,118	0.11
Chinese, ex. Taiwanese (81,419)	92,970	0.73
Filipino (21,948)	33,021	0.26
Hmong (945)	1,021	0.01
Indian (103,026)	113,389	0.89
Indonesian (3,165)	3,926	0.03
Japanese (6,492)	12,699	0.10
Korean (40,505)	47,429	0.37
Laotian (2,589)	3,280	0.03
Malaysian (543)	768	0.01
Nepalese (1,078)	1,429	0.01
Pakistani (9,252)	10,330	0.08
Sri Lankan (954)	1,100	0.01
Taiwanese (3,220)	3,830	0.03
Thai (2,721)	4,103	0.03
Vietnamese (39,008)	44,605	0.35
Hawaii Native/Pacific Islander (3,653)	12,424	0.10
Not Hispanic (2,715)	8,756	0.07
Hispanic (938)	3,668	0.03
Fijian (39)	92	<0.01
Guamanian/Chamorro (968)	1,605	0.01
Marshallese (19)	22	<0.01
Native Hawaiian (940)	3,043	0.02
Samoan (453)	1,118	0.01
Tongan (85)	137	<0.01
White (10,406,288)	10,604,187	83.48
Not Hispanic (10,094,652)	10,248,965	80.69
Hispanic (311,636)	355,222	2.80

*Notes: † The Census 2010 population figure is used to calculate the percentages in the Hispanic Origin and Race categories. Ancestry percentages are based on the 2006-2010 American Community Survey population (not shown); ‡ Numbers in parentheses indicate the number of people reporting a single ancestry; * Numbers in parentheses indicate the number of persons reporting this race alone, not in combination with any other race; Please refer to the Explanation of Data for more information.*

County Profiles

Adams County

Population: 101,407

Ancestry	Population	%
Afghan (0)	0	<0.01
African, Sub-Saharan (72)	112	0.11
African (61)	101	0.10
Cape Verdean (0)	0	<0.01
Ethiopian (0)	0	<0.01
Ghanaian (0)	0	<0.01
Kenyan (11)	11	0.01
Liberian (0)	0	<0.01
Nigerian (0)	0	<0.01
Senegalese (0)	0	<0.01
Sierra Leonean (0)	0	<0.01
Somalian (0)	0	<0.01
South African (0)	0	<0.01
Sudanese (0)	0	<0.01
Ugandan (0)	0	<0.01
Zimbabwean (0)	0	<0.01
Other Sub-Saharan African (0)	0	<0.01
Albanian (0)	0	<0.01
Alsatian (0)	8	0.01
American (9,961)	9,961	9.88
Arab (44)	110	0.11
Arab (0)	0	<0.01
Egyptian (0)	0	<0.01
Iraqi (0)	0	<0.01
Jordanian (0)	0	<0.01
Lebanese (3)	7	0.01
Moroccan (0)	0	<0.01
Palestinian (0)	16	0.02
Syrian (20)	52	0.05
Other Arab (21)	35	0.03
Armenian (0)	0	<0.01
Assyrian/Chaldean/Syriac (0)	0	<0.01
Australian (23)	53	0.05
Austrian (33)	161	0.16
Basque (0)	8	0.01
Belgian (53)	64	0.06
Brazilian (0)	0	<0.01
British (136)	319	0.32
Bulgarian (0)	0	<0.01
Cajun (7)	14	0.01
Canadian (70)	139	0.14
Carpatho Rusyn (0)	9	0.01
Celtic (0)	0	<0.01
Croatian (43)	141	0.14
Cypriot (0)	0	<0.01
Czech (63)	211	0.21
Czechoslovakian (43)	72	0.07
Danish (36)	212	0.21
Dutch (464)	2,205	2.19
Eastern European (66)	66	0.07
English (3,493)	9,964	9.88
Estonian (0)	0	<0.01
European (640)	652	0.65
Finnish (6)	67	0.07
French, ex. Basque (432)	2,560	2.54
French Canadian (97)	265	0.26
German (21,065)	39,841	39.51
German Russian (0)	0	<0.01
Greek (210)	520	0.52
Guyanese (0)	17	0.02
Hungarian (118)	422	0.42
Icelander (0)	0	<0.01
Iranian (0)	0	<0.01
Irish (3,800)	14,505	14.38
Israeli (9)	26	0.03
Italian (1,692)	4,817	4.78
Latvian (6)	6	0.01
Lithuanian (44)	151	0.15
Luxemburger (0)	6	0.01
Macedonian (0)	0	<0.01
Maltese (0)	0	<0.01
New Zealander (0)	0	<0.01

Ancestry	Population	%
Northern European (61)	61	0.06
Norwegian (120)	564	0.56
Pennsylvania German (1,180)	1,537	1.52
Polish (827)	3,093	3.07
Portuguese (53)	175	0.17
Romanian (5)	50	0.05
Russian (162)	587	0.58
Scandinavian (15)	78	0.08
Scotch-Irish (681)	1,937	1.92
Scottish (456)	2,079	2.06
Serbian (12)	67	0.07
Slavic (12)	65	0.06
Slovak (198)	428	0.42
Slovene (12)	27	0.03
Soviet Union (0)	0	<0.01
Swedish (135)	554	0.55
Swiss (57)	417	0.41
Turkish (9)	9	0.01
Ukrainian (74)	304	0.30
Welsh (190)	973	0.96
West Indian, ex. Hispanic (118)	178	0.18
Bahamian (0)	0	<0.01
Barbadian (18)	24	0.02
Belizean (0)	0	<0.01
Bermudan (0)	0	<0.01
British West Indian (0)	0	<0.01
Dutch West Indian (0)	0	<0.01
Haitian (0)	0	<0.01
Jamaican (72)	97	0.10
Trinidadian/Tobagonian (14)	31	0.03
U.S. Virgin Islander (0)	0	<0.01
West Indian (14)	26	0.03
Other West Indian (0)	0	<0.01
Yugoslavian (64)	101	0.10

Hispanic Origin	Population	%
Hispanic or Latino (of any race)	6,115	6.03
Central American, ex. Mexican	194	0.19
Costa Rican	12	0.01
Guatemalan	71	0.07
Honduran	37	0.04
Nicaraguan	13	0.01
Panamanian	11	0.01
Salvadoran	50	0.05
Other Central American	0	<0.01
Cuban	74	0.07
Dominican Republic	38	0.04
Mexican	4,570	4.51
Puerto Rican	832	0.82
South American	188	0.19
Argentinean	13	0.01
Bolivian	8	0.01
Chilean	15	0.01
Colombian	37	0.04
Ecuadorian	20	0.02
Paraguayan	0	<0.01
Peruvian	85	0.08
Uruguayan	1	<0.01
Venezuelan	9	0.01
Other South American	0	<0.01
Other Hispanic or Latino	219	0.22

Race*	Population	%
African-American/Black (1,561)	2,117	2.09
Not Hispanic (1,450)	1,947	1.92
Hispanic (111)	170	0.17
American Indian/Alaska Native (213)	617	0.61
Not Hispanic (146)	496	0.49
Hispanic (67)	121	0.12
Alaska Athabascan (Ala. Nat.) (1)	1	<0.01
Aleut (Alaska Native) (0)	0	<0.01
Apache (2)	10	0.01
Arapaho (0)	0	<0.01
Blackfeet (4)	27	0.03
Canadian/French Am. Ind. (0)	0	<0.01
Central American Ind. (1)	2	<0.01

	Population	%
Cherokee (35)	129	0.13
Cheyenne (0)	1	<0.01
Chickasaw (0)	0	<0.01
Chippewa (5)	10	0.01
Choctaw (2)	6	0.01
Colville (0)	0	<0.01
Comanche (0)	0	<0.01
Cree (1)	2	<0.01
Creek (6)	7	0.01
Crow (0)	0	<0.01
Delaware (0)	8	0.01
Hopi (3)	3	<0.01
Houma (0)	0	<0.01
Inupiat (Alaska Native) (0)	0	<0.01
Iroquois (4)	21	0.02
Kiowa (1)	1	<0.01
Lumbee (0)	2	<0.01
Menominee (0)	0	<0.01
Mexican American Ind. (16)	22	0.02
Navajo (7)	14	0.01
Osage (1)	1	<0.01
Ottawa (0)	0	<0.01
Paiute (0)	0	<0.01
Pima (0)	0	<0.01
Potawatomi (4)	4	<0.01
Pueblo (0)	1	<0.01
Puget Sound Salish (0)	0	<0.01
Seminole (0)	1	<0.01
Shoshone (0)	0	<0.01
Sioux (3)	6	0.01
South American Ind. (2)	5	<0.01
Spanish American Ind. (0)	2	<0.01
Tlingit-Haida (Alaska Native) (0)	1	<0.01
Tohono O'Odham (0)	0	<0.01
Tsimshian (Alaska Native) (0)	0	<0.01
Ute (0)	0	<0.01
Yakama (0)	0	<0.01
Yaqui (0)	1	<0.01
Yuman (0)	0	<0.01
Yup'ik (Alaska Native) (0)	2	<0.01
Asian (746)	1,016	1.00
Not Hispanic (737)	991	0.98
Hispanic (9)	25	0.02
Bangladeshi (5)	8	0.01
Bhutanese (0)	0	<0.01
Burmese (16)	17	0.02
Cambodian (6)	6	0.01
Chinese, ex. Taiwanese (133)	170	0.17
Filipino (127)	206	0.20
Hmong (0)	0	<0.01
Indian (113)	140	0.14
Indonesian (3)	4	<0.01
Japanese (40)	92	0.09
Korean (97)	132	0.13
Laotian (22)	32	0.03
Malaysian (0)	0	<0.01
Nepalese (9)	10	0.01
Pakistani (23)	23	0.02
Sri Lankan (4)	4	<0.01
Taiwanese (2)	5	<0.01
Thai (14)	29	0.03
Vietnamese (80)	90	0.09
Hawaii Native/Pacific Islander (20)	68	0.07
Not Hispanic (20)	56	0.06
Hispanic (0)	12	0.01
Fijian (1)	1	<0.01
Guamanian/Chamorro (0)	8	0.01
Marshallese (0)	0	<0.01
Native Hawaiian (10)	29	0.03
Samoan (3)	4	<0.01
Tongan (0)	0	<0.01
White (94,979)	96,214	94.88
Not Hispanic (91,830)	92,791	91.50
Hispanic (3,149)	3,423	3.38

Notes: † The Census 2010 population figure is used to calculate the percentages in the Hispanic Origin and Race categories. Ancestry percentages are based on the 2006-2010 American Community Survey population (not shown); ‡ Numbers in parentheses indicate the number of people reporting a single ancestry; * Numbers in parentheses indicate the number of persons reporting this race alone, not in combination with any other race; Please refer to the Explanation of Data for more information.

Allegheny County

Population: 1,223,348

Ancestry	Population	%
Afghan (62)	123	0.01
African, Sub-Saharan (8,256)	9,391	0.77
African (6,556)	7,407	0.61
Cape Verdean (6)	6	<0.01
Ethiopian (239)	239	0.02
Ghanaian (90)	90	0.01
Kenyan (47)	54	<0.01
Liberian (84)	84	0.01
Nigerian (560)	783	0.06
Senegalese (35)	36	<0.01
Sierra Leonean (76)	76	0.01
Somalian (57)	57	<0.01
South African (37)	65	0.01
Sudanese (38)	38	<0.01
Ugandan (80)	80	0.01
Zimbabwean (36)	36	<0.01
Other Sub-Saharan African (315)	340	0.03
Albanian (30)	184	0.02
Alsatian (17)	144	0.01
American (37,299)	37,299	3.05
Arab (4,012)	7,948	0.65
Arab (695)	785	0.06
Egyptian (378)	473	0.04
Iraqi (102)	117	0.01
Jordanian (13)	13	<0.01
Lebanese (1,201)	3,457	0.28
Moroccan (227)	342	0.03
Palestinian (102)	126	0.01
Syrian (807)	1,958	0.16
Other Arab (487)	677	0.06
Armenian (112)	291	0.02
Assyrian/Chaldean/Syriac (0)	3	<0.01
Australian (158)	322	0.03
Austrian (1,679)	7,102	0.58
Basque (54)	67	0.01
Belgian (399)	1,733	0.14
Brazilian (198)	297	0.02
British (1,960)	3,923	0.32
Bulgarian (385)	463	0.04
Cajun (24)	77	0.01
Canadian (638)	1,080	0.09
Carpatho Rusyn (388)	729	0.06
Celtic (72)	154	0.01
Croatian (5,874)	18,175	1.49
Cypriot (102)	102	0.01
Czech (1,993)	8,967	0.73
Czechoslovakian (1,622)	3,691	0.30
Danish (250)	1,367	0.11
Dutch (1,608)	10,424	0.85
Eastern European (2,345)	2,708	0.22
English (20,944)	99,246	8.11
Estonian (12)	42	<0.01
European (7,433)	8,138	0.67
Finnish (170)	686	0.06
French, ex. Basque (2,315)	21,703	1.77
French Canadian (754)	2,134	0.17
German (87,418)	348,979	28.53
German Russian (56)	79	0.01
Greek (4,339)	9,019	0.74
Guyanese (81)	227	0.02
Hungarian (6,707)	25,216	2.06
Icelander (23)	51	<0.01
Iranian (349)	483	0.04
Irish (54,671)	248,120	20.29
Israeli (163)	322	0.03
Italian (78,016)	204,500	16.72
Latvian (95)	309	0.03
Lithuanian (2,583)	8,754	0.72
Luxemburger (10)	68	0.01
Macedonian (104)	209	0.02
Maltese (11)	48	<0.01
New Zealander (24)	24	<0.01
Northern European (445)	461	0.04
Norwegian (794)	3,528	0.29
Pennsylvania German (659)	1,956	0.16

Ancestry	Population	%
Polish (36,220)	117,739	9.63
Portuguese (329)	919	0.08
Romanian (584)	1,858	0.15
Russian (7,511)	22,864	1.87
Scandinavian (533)	939	0.08
Scotch-Irish (9,023)	30,257	2.47
Scottish (4,972)	24,747	2.02
Serbian (1,930)	5,415	0.44
Slavic (1,150)	2,873	0.23
Slovak (17,810)	50,916	4.16
Slovene (1,716)	4,684	0.38
Soviet Union (0)	0	<0.01
Swedish (1,958)	10,590	0.87
Swiss (632)	4,366	0.36
Turkish (1,237)	1,449	0.12
Ukrainian (4,540)	13,303	1.09
Welsh (1,885)	15,698	1.28
West Indian, ex. Hispanic (1,977)	2,692	0.22
Bahamian (29)	44	<0.01
Barbadian (77)	140	0.01
Belizean (10)	10	<0.01
Bermudan (14)	40	<0.01
British West Indian (56)	56	<0.01
Dutch West Indian (0)	0	<0.01
Haitian (465)	522	0.04
Jamaican (820)	1,113	0.09
Trinidadian/Tobagonian (142)	142	0.01
U.S. Virgin Islander (11)	11	<0.01
West Indian (353)	614	0.05
Other West Indian (0)	0	<0.01
Yugoslavian (886)	1,664	0.14

Hispanic Origin	Population	%
Hispanic or Latino (of any race)	19,070	1.56
Central American, ex. Mexican	1,317	0.11
Costa Rican	120	0.01
Guatemalan	498	0.04
Honduran	173	0.01
Nicaraguan	98	0.01
Panamanian	215	0.02
Salvadoran	209	0.02
Other Central American	4	<0.01
Cuban	971	0.08
Dominican Republic	396	0.03
Mexican	6,892	0.56
Puerto Rican	3,880	0.32
South American	2,765	0.23
Argentinean	476	0.04
Bolivian	100	0.01
Chilean	277	0.02
Colombian	686	0.06
Ecuadorian	216	0.02
Paraguayan	47	<0.01
Peruvian	504	0.04
Uruguayan	56	<0.01
Venezuelan	372	0.03
Other South American	31	<0.01
Other Hispanic or Latino	2,849	0.23

Race*	Population	%
African-American/Black (161,861)	176,356	14.42
Not Hispanic (159,998)	173,398	14.17
Hispanic (1,863)	2,958	0.24
American Indian/Alaska Native (1,702)	7,150	0.58
Not Hispanic (1,426)	6,263	0.51
Hispanic (276)	887	0.07
Alaska Athabascan (Ala. Nat.) (7)	11	<0.01
Aleut (Alaska Native) (10)	17	<0.01
Apache (16)	90	0.01
Arapaho (1)	3	<0.01
Blackfeet (38)	443	0.04
Canadian/French Am. Ind. (17)	33	<0.01
Central American Ind. (13)	25	<0.01
Cherokee (223)	1,595	0.13
Cheyenne (6)	28	<0.01
Chickasaw (5)	35	<0.01
Chippewa (34)	84	0.01
Choctaw (16)	103	0.01
Colville (0)	0	<0.01

	Population	%
Comanche (3)	8	<0.01
Cree (7)	18	<0.01
Creek (15)	59	<0.01
Crow (1)	17	<0.01
Delaware (13)	44	<0.01
Hopi (2)	8	<0.01
Houma (4)	4	<0.01
Inupiat (Alaska Native) (2)	6	<0.01
Iroquois (60)	214	0.02
Kiowa (8)	11	<0.01
Lumbee (8)	20	<0.01
Menominee (0)	1	<0.01
Mexican American Ind. (61)	125	0.01
Navajo (18)	48	<0.01
Osage (3)	17	<0.01
Ottawa (1)	3	<0.01
Paiute (0)	7	<0.01
Pima (0)	1	<0.01
Potawatomi (8)	15	<0.01
Pueblo (5)	23	<0.01
Puget Sound Salish (2)	4	<0.01
Seminole (18)	100	0.01
Shoshone (1)	6	<0.01
Sioux (49)	190	0.02
South American Ind. (29)	73	0.01
Spanish American Ind. (7)	8	<0.01
Tlingit-Haida (Alaska Native) (2)	6	<0.01
Tohono O'Odham (0)	1	<0.01
Tsimshian (Alaska Native) (1)	1	<0.01
Ute (6)	9	<0.01
Yakama (0)	1	<0.01
Yaqui (3)	6	<0.01
Yuman (0)	1	<0.01
Yup'ik (Alaska Native) (0)	1	<0.01
Asian (34,090)	39,444	3.22
Not Hispanic (33,944)	39,046	3.19
Hispanic (146)	398	0.03
Bangladeshi (162)	178	0.01
Bhutanese (225)	285	0.02
Burmese (357)	376	0.03
Cambodian (80)	122	0.01
Chinese, ex. Taiwanese (9,086)	10,198	0.83
Filipino (1,497)	2,488	0.20
Hmong (6)	6	<0.01
Indian (12,576)	13,595	1.11
Indonesian (147)	214	0.02
Japanese (1,130)	1,873	0.15
Korean (3,318)	3,984	0.33
Laotian (29)	43	<0.01
Malaysian (76)	114	0.01
Nepalese (255)	332	0.03
Pakistani (897)	991	0.08
Sri Lankan (113)	129	0.01
Taiwanese (619)	723	0.06
Thai (406)	515	0.04
Vietnamese (1,946)	2,405	0.20
Hawaii Native/Pacific Islander (278)	861	0.07
Not Hispanic (251)	746	0.06
Hispanic (27)	115	0.01
Fijian (3)	7	<0.01
Guamanian/Chamorro (53)	111	0.01
Marshallese (0)	0	<0.01
Native Hawaiian (83)	234	0.02
Samoan (58)	130	0.01
Tongan (17)	27	<0.01
White (997,295)	1,016,627	83.10
Not Hispanic (986,212)	1,003,797	82.05
Hispanic (11,083)	12,830	1.05

*Notes: † The Census 2010 population figure is used to calculate the percentages in the Hispanic Origin and Race categories. Ancestry percentages are based on the 2006-2010 American Community Survey population (not shown); ‡ Numbers in parentheses indicate the number of people reporting a single ancestry; * Numbers in parentheses indicate the number of persons reporting this race alone, not in combination with any other race; Please refer to the Explanation of Data for more information.*

Armstrong County

Population: 68,941

Ancestry	Population	%
Afghan (0)	0	<0.01
African, Sub-Saharan (14)	17	0.02
African (14)	17	0.02
Cape Verdean (0)	0	<0.01
Ethiopian (0)	0	<0.01
Ghanaian (0)	0	<0.01
Kenyan (0)	0	<0.01
Liberian (0)	0	<0.01
Nigerian (0)	0	<0.01
Senegalese (0)	0	<0.01
Sierra Leonean (0)	0	<0.01
Somalian (0)	0	<0.01
South African (0)	0	<0.01
Sudanese (0)	0	<0.01
Ugandan (0)	0	<0.01
Zimbabwean (0)	0	<0.01
Other Sub-Saharan African (0)	0	<0.01
Albanian (0)	0	<0.01
Alsatian (0)	0	<0.01
American (3,583)	3,583	5.16
Arab (14)	91	0.13
Arab (0)	6	0.01
Egyptian (0)	0	<0.01
Iraqi (0)	0	<0.01
Jordanian (0)	0	<0.01
Lebanese (0)	8	0.01
Moroccan (0)	0	<0.01
Palestinian (0)	0	<0.01
Syrian (14)	77	0.11
Other Arab (0)	0	<0.01
Armenian (0)	3	<0.01
Assyrian/Chaldean/Syriac (0)	0	<0.01
Australian (0)	0	<0.01
Austrian (96)	258	0.37
Basque (0)	0	<0.01
Belgian (34)	228	0.33
Brazilian (0)	20	0.03
British (127)	247	0.36
Bulgarian (0)	0	<0.01
Cajun (0)	1	<0.01
Canadian (9)	38	0.05
Carpatho Rusyn (0)	0	<0.01
Celtic (3)	3	<0.01
Croatian (118)	241	0.35
Cypriot (0)	0	<0.01
Czech (200)	639	0.92
Czechoslovakian (35)	87	0.13
Danish (0)	23	0.03
Dutch (327)	2,665	3.84
Eastern European (56)	56	0.08
English (1,668)	6,243	8.98
Estonian (0)	0	<0.01
European (318)	360	0.52
Finnish (20)	50	0.07
French, ex. Basque (232)	1,198	1.72
French Canadian (26)	75	0.11
German (10,031)	28,881	41.56
German Russian (0)	0	<0.01
Greek (34)	90	0.13
Guyanese (0)	0	<0.01
Hungarian (164)	819	1.18
Icelander (0)	0	<0.01
Iranian (0)	0	<0.01
Irish (2,854)	13,475	19.39
Israeli (0)	0	<0.01
Italian (3,000)	7,417	10.67
Latvian (0)	0	<0.01
Lithuanian (41)	252	0.36
Luxemburger (15)	15	0.02
Macedonian (21)	21	0.03
Maltese (0)	0	<0.01
New Zealander (0)	0	<0.01
Northern European (0)	0	<0.01
Norwegian (44)	149	0.21
Pennsylvania German (485)	765	1.10

	Population	%
Polish (1,729)	4,958	7.13
Portuguese (7)	25	0.04
Romanian (40)	56	0.08
Russian (138)	465	0.67
Scandinavian (17)	20	0.03
Scotch-Irish (836)	2,483	3.57
Scottish (477)	1,413	2.03
Serbian (0)	18	0.03
Slavic (33)	74	0.11
Slovak (1,024)	3,077	4.43
Slovene (36)	87	0.13
Soviet Union (0)	0	<0.01
Swedish (37)	533	0.77
Swiss (47)	171	0.25
Turkish (14)	14	0.02
Ukrainian (211)	767	1.10
Welsh (88)	671	0.97
West Indian, ex. Hispanic (0)	0	<0.01
Bahamian (0)	0	<0.01
Barbadian (0)	0	<0.01
Belizean (0)	0	<0.01
Bermudan (0)	0	<0.01
British West Indian (0)	0	<0.01
Dutch West Indian (0)	0	<0.01
Haitian (0)	0	<0.01
Jamaican (0)	0	<0.01
Trinidadian/Tobagonian (0)	0	<0.01
U.S. Virgin Islander (0)	0	<0.01
West Indian (0)	0	<0.01
Other West Indian (0)	0	<0.01
Yugoslavian (18)	23	0.03

Hispanic Origin	Population	%
Hispanic or Latino (of any race)	366	0.53
Central American, ex. Mexican	24	0.03
Costa Rican	0	<0.01
Guatemalan	7	0.01
Honduran	5	0.01
Nicaraguan	0	<0.01
Panamanian	6	0.01
Salvadoran	6	0.01
Other Central American	0	<0.01
Cuban	4	0.01
Dominican Republic	4	0.01
Mexican	137	0.20
Puerto Rican	70	0.10
South American	18	0.03
Argentinean	2	<0.01
Bolivian	0	<0.01
Chilean	0	<0.01
Colombian	4	0.01
Ecuadorian	5	0.01
Paraguayan	0	<0.01
Peruvian	1	<0.01
Uruguayan	1	<0.01
Venezuelan	5	0.01
Other South American	0	<0.01
Other Hispanic or Latino	109	0.16

Race*	Population	%
African-American/Black (553)	806	1.17
Not Hispanic (540)	788	1.14
Hispanic (13)	18	0.03
American Indian/Alaska Native (45)	210	0.30
Not Hispanic (41)	199	0.29
Hispanic (4)	11	0.02
Alaska Athabascan (Ala. Nat.) (0)	0	<0.01
Aleut (Alaska Native) (0)	0	<0.01
Apache (1)	3	<0.01
Arapaho (0)	0	<0.01
Blackfeet (1)	14	0.02
Canadian/French Am. Ind. (0)	0	<0.01
Central American Ind. (2)	2	<0.01
Cherokee (14)	60	0.09
Cheyenne (0)	0	<0.01
Chickasaw (0)	2	<0.01
Chippewa (2)	2	<0.01
Choctaw (1)	3	<0.01
Colville (0)	0	<0.01

	Population	%
Comanche (0)	0	<0.01
Cree (0)	0	<0.01
Creek (0)	0	<0.01
Crow (0)	0	<0.01
Delaware (0)	3	<0.01
Hopi (0)	0	<0.01
Houma (0)	0	<0.01
Inupiat (Alaska Native) (0)	0	<0.01
Iroquois (0)	7	0.01
Kiowa (0)	0	<0.01
Lumbee (0)	0	<0.01
Menominee (0)	0	<0.01
Mexican American Ind. (2)	2	<0.01
Navajo (0)	0	<0.01
Osage (0)	1	<0.01
Ottawa (0)	0	<0.01
Paiute (0)	0	<0.01
Pima (0)	0	<0.01
Potawatomi (2)	2	<0.01
Pueblo (0)	0	<0.01
Puget Sound Salish (0)	0	<0.01
Seminole (0)	1	<0.01
Shoshone (0)	0	<0.01
Sioux (0)	9	0.01
South American Ind. (0)	0	<0.01
Spanish American Ind. (0)	0	<0.01
Tlingit-Haida (Alaska Native) (0)	0	<0.01
Tohono O'Odham (0)	0	<0.01
Tsimshian (Alaska Native) (0)	0	<0.01
Ute (0)	0	<0.01
Yakama (0)	0	<0.01
Yaqui (0)	0	<0.01
Yuman (0)	0	<0.01
Yup'ik (Alaska Native) (0)	0	<0.01
Asian (150)	238	0.35
Not Hispanic (147)	226	0.33
Hispanic (3)	12	0.02
Bangladeshi (0)	0	<0.01
Bhutanese (0)	0	<0.01
Burmese (0)	0	<0.01
Cambodian (0)	1	<0.01
Chinese, ex. Taiwanese (51)	57	0.08
Filipino (22)	40	0.06
Hmong (1)	1	<0.01
Indian (33)	61	0.09
Indonesian (3)	3	<0.01
Japanese (4)	10	0.01
Korean (17)	31	0.04
Laotian (0)	1	<0.01
Malaysian (0)	0	<0.01
Nepalese (0)	0	<0.01
Pakistani (1)	1	<0.01
Sri Lankan (0)	0	<0.01
Taiwanese (1)	2	<0.01
Thai (4)	4	0.01
Vietnamese (5)	10	0.01
Hawaii Native/Pacific Islander (9)	18	0.03
Not Hispanic (8)	17	0.02
Hispanic (1)	1	<0.01
Fijian (0)	0	<0.01
Guamanian/Chamorro (3)	3	<0.01
Marshallese (0)	0	<0.01
Native Hawaiian (4)	11	0.02
Samoan (1)	1	<0.01
Tongan (0)	0	<0.01
White (67,565)	68,082	98.75
Not Hispanic (67,326)	67,805	98.35
Hispanic (239)	277	0.40

*Notes: † The Census 2010 population figure is used to calculate the percentages in the Hispanic Origin and Race categories. Ancestry percentages are based on the 2006-2010 American Community Survey population (not shown); ‡ Numbers in parentheses indicate the number of people reporting a single ancestry; * Numbers in parentheses indicate the number of persons reporting this race alone, not in combination with any other race; Please refer to the Explanation of Data for more information.*

Beaver County

Population: 170,539

Ancestry	Population	%
Afghan (0)	0	<0.01
African, Sub-Saharan (163)	229	0.13
African (160)	203	0.12
Cape Verdean (0)	0	<0.01
Ethiopian (0)	0	<0.01
Ghanaian (0)	0	<0.01
Kenyan (0)	0	<0.01
Liberian (3)	9	0.01
Nigerian (0)	0	<0.01
Senegalese (0)	0	<0.01
Sierra Leonean (0)	0	<0.01
Somalian (0)	0	<0.01
South African (0)	17	0.01
Sudanese (0)	0	<0.01
Ugandan (0)	0	<0.01
Zimbabwean (0)	0	<0.01
Other Sub-Saharan African (0)	0	<0.01
Albanian (0)	9	0.01
Alsatian (0)	0	<0.01
American (6,565)	6,565	3.83
Arab (410)	1,151	0.67
Arab (21)	66	0.04
Egyptian (34)	34	0.02
Iraqi (0)	0	<0.01
Jordanian (10)	10	0.01
Lebanese (239)	730	0.43
Moroccan (0)	3	<0.01
Palestinian (0)	0	<0.01
Syrian (79)	272	0.16
Other Arab (27)	36	0.02
Armenian (0)	63	0.04
Assyrian/Chaldean/Syriac (0)	0	<0.01
Australian (0)	5	<0.01
Austrian (143)	852	0.50
Basque (0)	0	<0.01
Belgian (27)	207	0.12
Brazilian (19)	58	0.03
British (167)	386	0.22
Bulgarian (0)	33	0.02
Cajun (0)	0	<0.01
Canadian (203)	344	0.20
Carpatho Rusyn (30)	40	0.02
Celtic (6)	12	0.01
Croatian (1,509)	4,237	2.47
Cypriot (0)	0	<0.01
Czech (398)	1,395	0.81
Czechoslovakian (174)	524	0.31
Danish (23)	130	0.08
Dutch (313)	3,409	1.99
Eastern European (115)	153	0.09
English (3,673)	16,880	9.84
Estonian (0)	46	0.03
European (729)	810	0.47
Finnish (63)	174	0.10
French, ex. Basque (449)	3,652	2.13
French Canadian (194)	434	0.25
German (14,635)	54,071	31.52
German Russian (0)	4	<0.01
Greek (1,051)	1,691	0.99
Guyanese (0)	0	<0.01
Hungarian (748)	3,391	1.98
Icelander (0)	0	<0.01
Iranian (0)	0	<0.01
Irish (6,499)	32,702	19.06
Israeli (30)	30	0.02
Italian (12,291)	30,136	17.56
Latvian (0)	0	<0.01
Lithuanian (154)	528	0.31
Luxemburger (0)	0	<0.01
Macedonian (0)	0	<0.01
Maltese (0)	0	<0.01
New Zealander (0)	0	<0.01
Northern European (0)	0	<0.01
Norwegian (128)	426	0.25
Pennsylvania German (235)	508	0.30

Ancestry	Population	%
Polish (4,421)	13,251	7.72
Portuguese (11)	143	0.08
Romanian (36)	416	0.24
Russian (561)	2,071	1.21
Scandinavian (25)	25	0.01
Scotch-Irish (2,335)	6,654	3.88
Scottish (614)	3,144	1.83
Serbian (1,256)	2,792	1.63
Slavic (170)	517	0.30
Slovak (2,002)	5,863	3.42
Slovene (79)	332	0.19
Soviet Union (0)	0	<0.01
Swedish (215)	1,335	0.78
Swiss (67)	338	0.20
Turkish (19)	30	0.02
Ukrainian (934)	2,682	1.56
Welsh (265)	2,140	1.25
West Indian, ex. Hispanic (40)	236	0.14
Bahamian (0)	0	<0.01
Barbadian (0)	6	<0.01
Belizean (0)	0	<0.01
Bermudan (0)	0	<0.01
British West Indian (0)	0	<0.01
Dutch West Indian (0)	13	0.01
Haitian (23)	23	0.01
Jamaican (17)	22	0.01
Trinidadian/Tobagonian (0)	138	0.08
U.S. Virgin Islander (0)	0	<0.01
West Indian (0)	34	0.02
Other West Indian (0)	0	<0.01
Yugoslavian (153)	283	0.16

Hispanic Origin	Population	%
Hispanic or Latino (of any race)	1,998	1.17
Central American, ex. Mexican	142	0.08
Costa Rican	11	0.01
Guatemalan	25	0.01
Honduran	9	0.01
Nicaraguan	10	0.01
Panamanian	39	0.02
Salvadoran	47	0.03
Other Central American	1	<0.01
Cuban	51	0.03
Dominican Republic	38	0.02
Mexican	946	0.55
Puerto Rican	364	0.21
South American	116	0.07
Argentinean	22	0.01
Bolivian	2	<0.01
Chilean	12	0.01
Colombian	33	0.02
Ecuadorian	7	<0.01
Paraguayan	1	<0.01
Peruvian	21	0.01
Uruguayan	2	<0.01
Venezuelan	16	0.01
Other South American	0	<0.01
Other Hispanic or Latino	341	0.20

Race*	Population	%
African-American/Black (10,676)	12,703	7.45
Not Hispanic (10,586)	12,523	7.34
Hispanic (90)	180	0.11
American Indian/Alaska Native (181)	870	0.51
Not Hispanic (158)	789	0.46
Hispanic (23)	81	0.05
Alaska Athabascan (Ala. Nat.) (6)	6	<0.01
Aleut (Alaska Native) (0)	0	<0.01
Apache (3)	9	0.01
Arapaho (0)	0	<0.01
Blackfeet (4)	38	0.02
Canadian/French Am. Ind. (0)	0	<0.01
Central American Ind. (2)	3	<0.01
Cherokee (18)	219	0.13
Cheyenne (0)	1	<0.01
Chickasaw (0)	0	<0.01
Chippewa (7)	10	0.01
Choctaw (4)	13	0.01
Colville (0)	0	<0.01

Race*	Population	%
Comanche (1)	2	<0.01
Cree (0)	2	<0.01
Creek (0)	3	<0.01
Crow (0)	0	<0.01
Delaware (1)	9	0.01
Hopi (0)	1	<0.01
Houma (0)	0	<0.01
Inupiat (Alaska Native) (0)	0	<0.01
Iroquois (10)	36	0.02
Kiowa (0)	0	<0.01
Lumbee (6)	9	0.01
Menominee (0)	0	<0.01
Mexican American Ind. (0)	3	<0.01
Navajo (3)	7	<0.01
Osage (0)	2	<0.01
Ottawa (0)	0	<0.01
Paiute (0)	0	<0.01
Pima (0)	0	<0.01
Potawatomi (1)	2	<0.01
Pueblo (0)	0	<0.01
Puget Sound Salish (0)	0	<0.01
Seminole (2)	4	<0.01
Shoshone (0)	1	<0.01
Sioux (9)	43	0.03
South American Ind. (2)	3	<0.01
Spanish American Ind. (1)	2	<0.01
Tlingit-Haida (Alaska Native) (2)	2	<0.01
Tohono O'Odham (0)	0	<0.01
Tsimshian (Alaska Native) (0)	0	<0.01
Ute (0)	2	<0.01
Yakama (0)	0	<0.01
Yaqui (0)	3	<0.01
Yuman (0)	1	<0.01
Yup'ik (Alaska Native) (2)	2	<0.01
Asian (724)	1,077	0.63
Not Hispanic (717)	1,049	0.62
Hispanic (7)	28	0.02
Bangladeshi (1)	2	<0.01
Bhutanese (0)	0	<0.01
Burmese (0)	0	<0.01
Cambodian (3)	6	<0.01
Chinese, ex. Taiwanese (204)	248	0.15
Filipino (135)	239	0.14
Hmong (1)	1	<0.01
Indian (99)	134	0.08
Indonesian (6)	8	<0.01
Japanese (37)	96	0.06
Korean (81)	138	0.08
Laotian (1)	3	<0.01
Malaysian (1)	3	<0.01
Nepalese (1)	3	<0.01
Pakistani (19)	20	0.01
Sri Lankan (2)	3	<0.01
Taiwanese (9)	12	0.01
Thai (18)	25	0.01
Vietnamese (69)	85	0.05
Hawaii Native/Pacific Islander (40)	115	0.07
Not Hispanic (32)	99	0.06
Hispanic (8)	16	0.01
Fijian (0)	0	<0.01
Guamanian/Chamorro (10)	14	0.01
Marshallese (0)	0	<0.01
Native Hawaiian (11)	54	0.03
Samoan (3)	11	0.01
Tongan (0)	0	<0.01
White (155,561)	158,272	92.81
Not Hispanic (154,196)	156,711	91.89
Hispanic (1,365)	1,561	0.92

*Notes: † The Census 2010 population figure is used to calculate the percentages in the Hispanic Origin and Race categories. Ancestry percentages are based on the 2006-2010 American Community Survey population (not shown); ‡ Numbers in parentheses indicate the number of people reporting a single ancestry; * Numbers in parentheses indicate the number of persons reporting this race alone, not in combination with any other race; Please refer to the Explanation of Data for more information.*

Bedford County

Population: 49,762

Ancestry	Population	%
Afghan (0)	0	<0.01
African, Sub-Saharan (22)	22	0.04
African (19)	19	0.04
Cape Verdean (0)	0	<0.01
Ethiopian (3)	3	0.01
Ghanaian (0)	0	<0.01
Kenyan (0)	0	<0.01
Liberian (0)	0	<0.01
Nigerian (0)	0	<0.01
Senegalese (0)	0	<0.01
Sierra Leonean (0)	0	<0.01
Somalian (0)	0	<0.01
South African (0)	0	<0.01
Sudanese (0)	0	<0.01
Ugandan (0)	0	<0.01
Zimbabwean (0)	0	<0.01
Other Sub-Saharan African (0)	0	<0.01
Albanian (0)	0	<0.01
Alsatian (0)	0	<0.01
American (5,062)	5,062	10.15
Arab (4)	10	0.02
Arab (0)	0	<0.01
Egyptian (4)	4	0.01
Iraqi (0)	0	<0.01
Jordanian (0)	0	<0.01
Lebanese (0)	6	0.01
Moroccan (0)	0	<0.01
Palestinian (0)	0	<0.01
Syrian (0)	0	<0.01
Other Arab (0)	0	<0.01
Armenian (0)	0	<0.01
Assyrian/Chaldean/Syriac (0)	0	<0.01
Australian (0)	0	<0.01
Austrian (41)	194	0.39
Basque (0)	0	<0.01
Belgian (38)	65	0.13
Brazilian (0)	0	<0.01
British (27)	61	0.12
Bulgarian (9)	14	0.03
Cajun (0)	0	<0.01
Canadian (15)	22	0.04
Carpatho Rusyn (0)	3	0.01
Celtic (2)	2	<0.01
Croatian (19)	41	0.08
Cypriot (0)	0	<0.01
Czech (23)	143	0.29
Czechoslovakian (42)	50	0.10
Danish (17)	31	0.06
Dutch (375)	1,958	3.93
Eastern European (9)	9	0.02
English (1,441)	4,125	8.27
Estonian (0)	0	<0.01
European (141)	147	0.29
Finnish (8)	10	0.02
French, ex. Basque (244)	1,178	2.36
French Canadian (32)	87	0.17
German (11,131)	21,324	42.75
German Russian (0)	0	<0.01
Greek (28)	62	0.12
Guyanese (0)	0	<0.01
Hungarian (70)	444	0.89
Icelander (3)	3	0.01
Iranian (0)	0	<0.01
Irish (1,254)	5,919	11.87
Israeli (0)	0	<0.01
Italian (669)	1,748	3.50
Latvian (0)	3	0.01
Lithuanian (22)	77	0.15
Luxemburger (0)	0	<0.01
Macedonian (0)	17	0.03
Maltese (0)	0	<0.01
New Zealander (0)	0	<0.01
Northern European (11)	11	0.02
Norwegian (25)	112	0.22
Pennsylvania German (586)	656	1.32

Ancestry	Population	%
Polish (340)	964	1.93
Portuguese (9)	9	0.02
Romanian (0)	0	<0.01
Russian (55)	167	0.33
Scandinavian (0)	0	<0.01
Scotch-Irish (384)	918	1.84
Scottish (184)	738	1.48
Serbian (0)	3	0.01
Slavic (6)	18	0.04
Slovak (117)	339	0.68
Slovene (2)	2	<0.01
Soviet Union (0)	0	<0.01
Swedish (59)	220	0.44
Swiss (218)	451	0.90
Turkish (0)	0	<0.01
Ukrainian (26)	164	0.33
Welsh (149)	682	1.37
West Indian, ex. Hispanic (3)	15	0.03
Bahamian (0)	0	<0.01
Barbadian (0)	0	<0.01
Belizean (0)	0	<0.01
Bermudan (0)	0	<0.01
British West Indian (0)	0	<0.01
Dutch West Indian (3)	3	0.01
Haitian (0)	0	<0.01
Jamaican (0)	0	<0.01
Trinidadian/Tobagonian (0)	0	<0.01
U.S. Virgin Islander (0)	0	<0.01
West Indian (0)	12	0.02
Other West Indian (0)	0	<0.01
Yugoslavian (0)	50	0.10

Hispanic Origin	Population	%
Hispanic or Latino (of any race)	450	0.90
Central American, ex. Mexican	21	0.04
Costa Rican	0	<0.01
Guatemalan	4	0.01
Honduran	0	<0.01
Nicaraguan	0	<0.01
Panamanian	1	<0.01
Salvadoran	12	0.02
Other Central American	4	0.01
Cuban	19	0.04
Dominican Republic	19	0.04
Mexican	170	0.34
Puerto Rican	108	0.22
South American	13	0.03
Argentinean	0	<0.01
Bolivian	0	<0.01
Chilean	0	<0.01
Colombian	7	0.01
Ecuadorian	2	0.01
Paraguayan	0	<0.01
Peruvian	4	0.01
Uruguayan	0	<0.01
Venezuelan	0	<0.01
Other South American	0	<0.01
Other Hispanic or Latino	100	0.20

Race*	Population	%
African-American/Black (238)	395	0.79
Not Hispanic (236)	384	0.77
Hispanic (2)	11	0.02
American Indian/Alaska Native (75)	221	0.44
Not Hispanic (57)	188	0.38
Hispanic (18)	33	0.07
Alaska Athabascan (Ala. Nat.) (2)	9	0.02
Aleut (Alaska Native) (0)	2	<0.01
Apache (0)	5	0.01
Arapaho (0)	0	<0.01
Blackfeet (1)	10	0.02
Canadian/French Am. Ind. (0)	0	<0.01
Central American Ind. (0)	0	<0.01
Cherokee (21)	59	0.12
Cheyenne (0)	0	<0.01
Chickasaw (0)	0	<0.01
Chippewa (3)	6	0.01
Choctaw (1)	2	<0.01
Colville (0)	0	<0.01

Race*	Population	%
Comanche (0)	0	<0.01
Cree (0)	0	<0.01
Creek (0)	1	<0.01
Crow (0)	0	<0.01
Delaware (0)	4	0.01
Hopi (0)	0	<0.01
Houma (0)	0	<0.01
Inupiat (Alaska Native) (0)	0	<0.01
Iroquois (1)	8	0.02
Kiowa (0)	0	<0.01
Lumbee (0)	0	<0.01
Menominee (0)	0	<0.01
Mexican American Ind. (8)	10	0.02
Navajo (0)	1	<0.01
Osage (0)	0	<0.01
Ottawa (0)	0	<0.01
Paiute (0)	0	<0.01
Pima (0)	0	<0.01
Potawatomi (0)	1	<0.01
Pueblo (0)	0	<0.01
Puget Sound Salish (0)	0	<0.01
Seminole (0)	0	<0.01
Shoshone (0)	0	<0.01
Sioux (1)	5	0.01
South American Ind. (3)	3	0.01
Spanish American Ind. (1)	2	<0.01
Tlingit-Haida (Alaska Native) (0)	0	<0.01
Tohono O'Odham (0)	0	<0.01
Tsimshian (Alaska Native) (0)	0	<0.01
Ute (0)	0	<0.01
Yakama (0)	0	<0.01
Yaqui (0)	0	<0.01
Yuman (0)	0	<0.01
Yup'ik (Alaska Native) (1)	1	<0.01
Asian (101)	178	0.36
Not Hispanic (101)	171	0.34
Hispanic (0)	7	0.01
Bangladeshi (0)	0	<0.01
Bhutanese (0)	0	<0.01
Burmese (0)	0	<0.01
Cambodian (0)	0	<0.01
Chinese, ex. Taiwanese (17)	20	0.04
Filipino (22)	47	0.09
Hmong (0)	0	<0.01
Indian (21)	30	0.06
Indonesian (0)	0	<0.01
Japanese (10)	29	0.06
Korean (11)	20	0.04
Laotian (0)	0	<0.01
Malaysian (0)	0	<0.01
Nepalese (0)	0	<0.01
Pakistani (1)	1	<0.01
Sri Lankan (0)	0	<0.01
Taiwanese (2)	2	<0.01
Thai (3)	8	0.02
Vietnamese (5)	7	0.01
Hawaii Native/Pacific Islander (14)	24	0.05
Not Hispanic (5)	13	0.03
Hispanic (9)	11	0.02
Fijian (0)	0	<0.01
Guamanian/Chamorro (10)	13	0.03
Marshallese (0)	0	<0.01
Native Hawaiian (1)	6	0.01
Samoan (1)	1	<0.01
Tongan (0)	0	<0.01
White (48,782)	49,166	98.80
Not Hispanic (48,535)	48,883	98.23
Hispanic (247)	283	0.57

Notes: † The Census 2010 population figure is used to calculate the percentages in the Hispanic Origin and Race categories. Ancestry percentages are based on the 2006-2010 American Community Survey population (not shown); ‡ Numbers in parentheses indicate the number of people reporting a single ancestry; * Numbers in parentheses indicate the number of persons reporting this race alone, not in combination with any other race; Please refer to the Explanation of Data for more information.

Berks County

Population: 411,442

Ancestry	Population	%
Afghan (169)	169	0.04
African, Sub-Saharan (744)	1,176	0.29
African (486)	800	0.20
Cape Verdean (0)	19	<0.01
Ethiopian (84)	96	0.02
Ghanaian (0)	17	<0.01
Kenyan (64)	64	0.02
Liberian (36)	39	0.01
Nigerian (43)	89	0.02
Senegalese (0)	0	<0.01
Sierra Leonean (14)	14	<0.01
Somalian (0)	0	<0.01
South African (8)	8	<0.01
Sudanese (0)	0	<0.01
Ugandan (0)	0	<0.01
Zimbabwean (0)	0	<0.01
Other Sub-Saharan African (9)	30	0.01
Albanian (98)	121	0.03
Alsatian (0)	17	<0.01
American (18,889)	18,889	4.64
Arab (286)	628	0.15
Arab (53)	88	0.02
Egyptian (71)	75	0.02
Iraqi (0)	0	<0.01
Jordanian (0)	13	<0.01
Lebanese (85)	160	0.04
Moroccan (0)	21	0.01
Palestinian (2)	2	<0.01
Syrian (43)	192	0.05
Other Arab (32)	77	0.02
Armenian (10)	17	<0.01
Assyrian/Chaldean/Syriac (0)	0	<0.01
Australian (7)	70	0.02
Austrian (300)	1,777	0.44
Basque (16)	30	0.01
Belgian (41)	139	0.03
Brazilian (76)	103	0.03
British (530)	1,434	0.35
Bulgarian (5)	26	0.01
Cajun (32)	32	0.01
Canadian (214)	624	0.15
Carpatho Rusyn (0)	14	<0.01
Celtic (44)	54	0.01
Croatian (99)	347	0.09
Cypriot (0)	17	<0.01
Czech (261)	1,191	0.29
Czechoslovakian (283)	681	0.17
Danish (150)	438	0.11
Dutch (3,527)	13,547	3.33
Eastern European (110)	144	0.04
English (5,983)	26,110	6.41
Estonian (12)	27	0.01
European (1,290)	1,360	0.33
Finnish (15)	251	0.06
French, ex. Basque (889)	7,467	1.83
French Canadian (497)	1,380	0.34
German (74,549)	149,593	36.73
German Russian (0)	0	<0.01
Greek (943)	2,833	0.70
Guyanese (69)	110	0.03
Hungarian (750)	3,287	0.81
Icelander (0)	0	<0.01
Iranian (35)	35	0.01
Irish (10,441)	52,307	12.84
Israeli (9)	9	<0.01
Italian (12,494)	41,265	10.13
Latvian (70)	178	0.04
Lithuanian (557)	1,954	0.48
Luxemburger (0)	7	<0.01
Macedonian (0)	0	<0.01
Maltese (27)	27	0.01
New Zealander (0)	0	<0.01
Northern European (164)	169	0.04
Norwegian (332)	1,210	0.30
Pennsylvania German (14,018)	19,611	4.81

Ancestry	Population	%
Polish (8,328)	25,823	6.34
Portuguese (118)	382	0.09
Romanian (720)	998	0.25
Russian (885)	3,064	0.75
Scandinavian (110)	369	0.09
Scotch-Irish (1,142)	4,456	1.09
Scottish (962)	4,804	1.18
Serbian (14)	88	0.02
Slavic (106)	451	0.11
Slovak (1,326)	4,149	1.02
Slovene (73)	146	0.04
Soviet Union (0)	0	<0.01
Swedish (596)	2,589	0.64
Swiss (830)	3,038	0.75
Turkish (46)	46	0.01
Ukrainian (881)	3,003	0.74
Welsh (910)	6,071	1.49
West Indian, ex. Hispanic (2,926)	3,321	0.82
Bahamian (0)	0	<0.01
Barbadian (69)	85	0.02
Belizean (0)	0	<0.01
Bermudan (17)	31	0.01
British West Indian (0)	10	<0.01
Dutch West Indian (0)	0	<0.01
Haitian (1,523)	1,624	0.40
Jamaican (775)	919	0.23
Trinidadian/Tobagonian (162)	170	0.04
U.S. Virgin Islander (256)	289	0.07
West Indian (124)	193	0.05
Other West Indian (0)	0	<0.01
Yugoslavian (104)	248	0.06

Hispanic Origin	Population	%
Hispanic or Latino (of any race)	67,355	16.37
Central American, ex. Mexican	2,129	0.52
Costa Rican	61	0.01
Guatemalan	598	0.15
Honduran	401	0.10
Nicaraguan	108	0.03
Panamanian	130	0.03
Salvadoran	808	0.20
Other Central American	23	0.01
Cuban	772	0.19
Dominican Republic	10,545	2.56
Mexican	10,890	2.65
Puerto Rican	36,333	8.83
South American	2,374	0.58
Argentinean	82	0.02
Bolivian	23	0.01
Chilean	51	0.01
Colombian	1,111	0.27
Ecuadorian	705	0.17
Paraguayan	15	<0.01
Peruvian	229	0.06
Uruguayan	42	0.01
Venezuelan	85	0.02
Other South American	31	0.01
Other Hispanic or Latino	4,312	1.05

Race*	Population	%
African-American/Black (20,143)	25,062	6.09
Not Hispanic (16,517)	19,482	4.74
Hispanic (3,626)	5,580	1.36
American Indian/Alaska Native (1,285)	2,962	0.72
Not Hispanic (536)	1,647	0.40
Hispanic (749)	1,315	0.32
Alaska Athabascan (Ala. Nat.) (0)	0	<0.01
Aleut (Alaska Native) (0)	0	<0.01
Apache (4)	23	0.01
Arapaho (0)	1	<0.01
Blackfeet (21)	112	0.03
Canadian/French Am. Ind. (2)	7	<0.01
Central American Ind. (10)	18	<0.01
Cherokee (86)	371	0.09
Cheyenne (0)	2	<0.01
Chickasaw (4)	4	<0.01
Chippewa (22)	46	0.01
Choctaw (5)	18	<0.01
Colville (0)	0	<0.01

Race*	Population	%
Comanche (2)	7	<0.01
Cree (0)	7	<0.01
Creek (5)	10	<0.01
Crow (1)	4	<0.01
Delaware (13)	83	0.02
Hopi (0)	0	<0.01
Houma (0)	0	<0.01
Inupiat (Alaska Native) (3)	5	<0.01
Iroquois (29)	53	0.01
Kiowa (0)	1	<0.01
Lumbee (5)	12	<0.01
Menominee (1)	5	<0.01
Mexican American Ind. (48)	86	0.02
Navajo (5)	19	<0.01
Osage (0)	0	<0.01
Ottawa (0)	0	<0.01
Paiute (0)	1	<0.01
Pima (0)	0	<0.01
Potawatomi (10)	12	<0.01
Pueblo (21)	32	0.01
Puget Sound Salish (0)	0	<0.01
Seminole (6)	31	0.01
Shoshone (1)	1	<0.01
Sioux (16)	55	0.01
South American Ind. (47)	116	0.03
Spanish American Ind. (13)	18	<0.01
Tlingit-Haida (Alaska Native) (2)	3	<0.01
Tohono O'Odham (2)	2	<0.01
Tsimshian (Alaska Native) (1)	1	<0.01
Ute (0)	1	<0.01
Yakama (0)	0	<0.01
Yaqui (1)	1	<0.01
Yuman (0)	0	<0.01
Yup'ik (Alaska Native) (0)	0	<0.01
Asian (5,385)	6,861	1.67
Not Hispanic (5,244)	6,429	1.56
Hispanic (141)	432	0.10
Bangladeshi (26)	33	0.01
Bhutanese (0)	0	<0.01
Burmese (8)	9	<0.01
Cambodian (18)	24	0.01
Chinese, ex. Taiwanese (986)	1,189	0.29
Filipino (520)	825	0.20
Hmong (82)	85	0.02
Indian (1,373)	1,635	0.40
Indonesian (20)	31	0.01
Japanese (133)	311	0.08
Korean (402)	623	0.15
Laotian (85)	105	0.03
Malaysian (1)	5	<0.01
Nepalese (18)	21	0.01
Pakistani (144)	166	0.04
Sri Lankan (20)	38	0.01
Taiwanese (19)	30	0.01
Thai (53)	89	0.02
Vietnamese (1,247)	1,401	0.34
Hawaii Native/Pacific Islander (128)	607	0.15
Not Hispanic (58)	235	0.06
Hispanic (70)	372	0.09
Fijian (0)	7	<0.01
Guamanian/Chamorro (44)	87	0.02
Marshallese (0)	0	<0.01
Native Hawaiian (26)	96	0.02
Samoan (14)	36	0.01
Tongan (2)	2	<0.01
White (342,148)	350,598	85.21
Not Hispanic (316,406)	320,933	78.00
Hispanic (25,742)	29,665	7.21

*Notes: † The Census 2010 population figure is used to calculate the percentages in the Hispanic Origin and Race categories. Ancestry percentages are based on the 2006-2010 American Community Survey population (not shown); ‡ Numbers in parentheses indicate the number of people reporting a single ancestry; * Numbers in parentheses indicate the number of persons reporting this race alone, not in combination with any other race; Please refer to the Explanation of Data for more information.*

Blair County

Population: 127,089

Ancestry	Population	%
Afghan (0)	0	<0.01
African, Sub-Saharan (177)	202	0.16
African (99)	124	0.10
Cape Verdean (0)	0	<0.01
Ethiopian (13)	13	0.01
Ghanaian (65)	65	0.05
Kenyan (0)	0	<0.01
Liberian (0)	0	<0.01
Nigerian (0)	0	<0.01
Senegalese (0)	0	<0.01
Sierra Leonean (0)	0	<0.01
Somalian (0)	0	<0.01
South African (0)	0	<0.01
Sudanese (0)	0	<0.01
Ugandan (0)	0	<0.01
Zimbabwean (0)	0	<0.01
Other Sub-Saharan African (0)	0	<0.01
Albanian (14)	14	0.01
Alsatian (0)	0	<0.01
American (7,492)	7,492	5.90
Arab (95)	209	0.16
Arab (12)	20	0.02
Egyptian (0)	0	<0.01
Iraqi (0)	0	<0.01
Jordanian (0)	0	<0.01
Lebanese (35)	121	0.10
Moroccan (0)	0	<0.01
Palestinian (0)	0	<0.01
Syrian (9)	29	0.02
Other Arab (39)	39	0.03
Armenian (35)	139	0.11
Assyrian/Chaldean/Syriac (0)	0	<0.01
Australian (0)	2	<0.01
Austrian (65)	257	0.20
Basque (0)	0	<0.01
Belgian (0)	22	0.02
Brazilian (0)	39	0.03
British (77)	301	0.24
Bulgarian (0)	0	<0.01
Cajun (0)	17	0.01
Canadian (13)	51	0.04
Carpatho Rusyn (0)	0	<0.01
Celtic (0)	0	<0.01
Croatian (101)	301	0.24
Cypriot (15)	15	0.01
Czech (77)	252	0.20
Czechoslovakian (62)	166	0.13
Danish (45)	88	0.07
Dutch (417)	3,713	2.92
Eastern European (30)	30	0.02
English (3,786)	10,543	8.30
Estonian (0)	0	<0.01
European (590)	625	0.49
Finnish (17)	69	0.05
French, ex. Basque (463)	2,721	2.14
French Canadian (79)	291	0.23
German (22,066)	54,807	43.13
German Russian (0)	0	<0.01
Greek (206)	492	0.39
Guyanese (0)	0	<0.01
Hungarian (174)	733	0.58
Icelander (0)	0	<0.01
Iranian (0)	0	<0.01
Irish (5,451)	25,556	20.11
Israeli (0)	0	<0.01
Italian (5,644)	14,316	11.27
Latvian (0)	0	<0.01
Lithuanian (31)	119	0.09
Luxemburger (0)	0	<0.01
Macedonian (0)	8	0.01
Maltese (0)	0	<0.01
New Zealander (0)	0	<0.01
Northern European (52)	52	0.04
Norwegian (39)	163	0.13
Pennsylvania German (1,424)	2,096	1.65

Ancestry (cont.)	Population	%
Polish (1,486)	5,314	4.18
Portuguese (13)	98	0.08
Romanian (19)	39	0.03
Russian (135)	491	0.39
Scandinavian (3)	26	0.02
Scotch-Irish (1,110)	3,208	2.52
Scottish (541)	2,254	1.77
Serbian (0)	31	0.02
Slavic (59)	175	0.14
Slovak (417)	1,096	0.86
Slovene (10)	46	0.04
Soviet Union (0)	0	<0.01
Swedish (345)	1,110	0.87
Swiss (195)	564	0.44
Turkish (0)	0	<0.01
Ukrainian (150)	484	0.38
Welsh (220)	1,508	1.19
West Indian, ex. Hispanic (61)	138	0.11
Bahamian (0)	0	<0.01
Barbadian (0)	0	<0.01
Belizean (0)	0	<0.01
Bermudan (0)	0	<0.01
British West Indian (0)	0	<0.01
Dutch West Indian (0)	0	<0.01
Haitian (47)	124	0.10
Jamaican (0)	0	<0.01
Trinidadian/Tobagonian (14)	14	0.01
U.S. Virgin Islander (0)	0	<0.01
West Indian (0)	0	<0.01
Other West Indian (0)	0	<0.01
Yugoslavian (18)	106	0.08

Hispanic Origin	Population	%
Hispanic or Latino (of any race)	1,230	0.97
Central American, ex. Mexican	67	0.05
Costa Rican	14	0.01
Guatemalan	24	0.02
Honduran	4	<0.01
Nicaraguan	8	0.01
Panamanian	13	0.01
Salvadoran	4	<0.01
Other Central American	0	<0.01
Cuban	59	0.05
Dominican Republic	29	0.02
Mexican	468	0.37
Puerto Rican	314	0.25
South American	115	0.09
Argentinean	12	0.01
Bolivian	1	<0.01
Chilean	9	0.01
Colombian	27	0.02
Ecuadorian	14	0.01
Paraguayan	0	<0.01
Peruvian	40	0.03
Uruguayan	0	<0.01
Venezuelan	12	0.01
Other South American	0	<0.01
Other Hispanic or Latino	178	0.14

Race*	Population	%
African-American/Black (2,129)	3,034	2.39
Not Hispanic (2,051)	2,903	2.28
Hispanic (78)	131	0.10
American Indian/Alaska Native (143)	520	0.41
Not Hispanic (125)	473	0.37
Hispanic (18)	47	0.04
Alaska Athabascan (Ala. Nat.) (0)	0	<0.01
Aleut (Alaska Native) (0)	0	<0.01
Apache (0)	7	0.01
Arapaho (0)	0	<0.01
Blackfeet (3)	37	0.03
Canadian/French Am. Ind. (1)	1	<0.01
Central American Ind. (0)	0	<0.01
Cherokee (16)	94	0.07
Cheyenne (0)	2	<0.01
Chickasaw (0)	2	<0.01
Chippewa (3)	5	<0.01
Choctaw (0)	2	<0.01
Colville (0)	0	<0.01

Race* (cont.)	Population	%
Comanche (3)	5	<0.01
Cree (0)	2	<0.01
Creek (1)	6	<0.01
Crow (0)	1	<0.01
Delaware (8)	24	0.02
Hopi (3)	3	<0.01
Houma (0)	0	<0.01
Inupiat (Alaska Native) (0)	0	<0.01
Iroquois (7)	36	0.03
Kiowa (0)	0	<0.01
Lumbee (1)	3	<0.01
Menominee (0)	0	<0.01
Mexican American Ind. (1)	3	<0.01
Navajo (7)	7	0.01
Osage (0)	0	<0.01
Ottawa (0)	0	<0.01
Paiute (0)	0	<0.01
Pima (0)	0	<0.01
Potawatomi (1)	1	<0.01
Pueblo (0)	0	<0.01
Puget Sound Salish (0)	0	<0.01
Seminole (1)	2	<0.01
Shoshone (0)	1	<0.01
Sioux (2)	10	0.01
South American Ind. (1)	3	<0.01
Spanish American Ind. (0)	0	<0.01
Tlingit-Haida (Alaska Native) (0)	0	<0.01
Tohono O'Odham (0)	0	<0.01
Tsimshian (Alaska Native) (0)	0	<0.01
Ute (0)	0	<0.01
Yakama (0)	0	<0.01
Yaqui (2)	2	<0.01
Yuman (0)	0	<0.01
Yup'ik (Alaska Native) (0)	0	<0.01
Asian (706)	982	0.77
Not Hispanic (689)	946	0.74
Hispanic (17)	36	0.03
Bangladeshi (1)	2	<0.01
Bhutanese (0)	0	<0.01
Burmese (0)	0	<0.01
Cambodian (3)	3	<0.01
Chinese, ex. Taiwanese (165)	191	0.15
Filipino (83)	148	0.12
Hmong (0)	0	<0.01
Indian (179)	220	0.17
Indonesian (0)	2	<0.01
Japanese (35)	64	0.05
Korean (91)	142	0.11
Laotian (5)	5	<0.01
Malaysian (3)	4	<0.01
Nepalese (4)	4	<0.01
Pakistani (21)	23	0.02
Sri Lankan (18)	19	0.01
Taiwanese (7)	8	0.01
Thai (13)	24	0.02
Vietnamese (64)	99	0.08
Hawaii Native/Pacific Islander (29)	80	0.06
Not Hispanic (26)	74	0.06
Hispanic (3)	6	<0.01
Fijian (0)	0	<0.01
Guamanian/Chamorro (7)	12	0.01
Marshallese (0)	0	<0.01
Native Hawaiian (2)	18	0.01
Samoan (3)	7	0.01
Tongan (0)	0	<0.01
White (122,238)	123,692	97.33
Not Hispanic (121,495)	122,848	96.66
Hispanic (743)	844	0.66

Notes: † The Census 2010 population figure is used to calculate the percentages in the Hispanic Origin and Race categories. Ancestry percentages are based on the 2006-2010 American Community Survey population (not shown); ‡ Numbers in parentheses indicate the number of people reporting a single ancestry; * Numbers in parentheses indicate the number of persons reporting this race alone, not in combination with any other race; Please refer to the Explanation of Data for more information.

Bradford County

Population: 62,622

Ancestry	Population	%
Afghan (0)	0	<0.01
African, Sub-Saharan (39)	71	0.11
African (21)	53	0.08
Cape Verdean (0)	0	<0.01
Ethiopian (0)	0	<0.01
Ghanaian (0)	0	<0.01
Kenyan (0)	0	<0.01
Liberian (0)	0	<0.01
Nigerian (0)	0	<0.01
Senegalese (0)	0	<0.01
Sierra Leonean (0)	0	<0.01
Somalian (0)	0	<0.01
South African (0)	0	<0.01
Sudanese (0)	0	<0.01
Ugandan (0)	0	<0.01
Zimbabwean (18)	18	0.03
Other Sub-Saharan African (0)	0	<0.01
Albanian (0)	0	<0.01
Alsatian (2)	6	0.01
American (4,633)	4,633	7.42
Arab (24)	31	0.05
Arab (0)	0	<0.01
Egyptian (0)	0	<0.01
Iraqi (0)	0	<0.01
Jordanian (0)	0	<0.01
Lebanese (0)	0	<0.01
Moroccan (0)	0	<0.01
Palestinian (5)	5	0.01
Syrian (15)	22	0.04
Other Arab (4)	4	0.01
Armenian (4)	4	0.01
Assyrian/Chaldean/Syriac (0)	0	<0.01
Australian (0)	0	<0.01
Austrian (31)	141	0.23
Basque (0)	0	<0.01
Belgian (7)	27	0.04
Brazilian (0)	0	<0.01
British (94)	145	0.23
Bulgarian (0)	62	0.10
Cajun (0)	0	<0.01
Canadian (11)	66	0.11
Carpatho Rusyn (0)	0	<0.01
Celtic (0)	0	<0.01
Croatian (17)	20	0.03
Cypriot (0)	0	<0.01
Czech (33)	203	0.33
Czechoslovakian (15)	38	0.06
Danish (21)	83	0.13
Dutch (517)	2,903	4.65
Eastern European (36)	43	0.07
English (4,084)	9,769	15.65
Estonian (0)	6	0.01
European (251)	287	0.46
Finnish (4)	9	0.01
French, ex. Basque (297)	1,771	2.84
French Canadian (141)	290	0.46
German (4,989)	14,754	23.64
German Russian (0)	0	<0.01
Greek (82)	139	0.22
Guyanese (0)	0	<0.01
Hungarian (74)	202	0.32
Icelander (0)	0	<0.01
Iranian (11)	11	0.02
Irish (3,155)	10,296	16.50
Israeli (0)	0	<0.01
Italian (1,717)	4,621	7.40
Latvian (3)	3	<0.01
Lithuanian (75)	192	0.31
Luxemburger (0)	6	0.01
Macedonian (0)	0	<0.01
Maltese (0)	0	<0.01
New Zealander (0)	0	<0.01
Northern European (34)	34	0.05
Norwegian (99)	204	0.33
Pennsylvania German (823)	1,323	2.12

Ancestry (cont.)	Population	%
Polish (774)	2,533	4.06
Portuguese (14)	22	0.04
Romanian (5)	13	0.02
Russian (57)	186	0.30
Scandinavian (15)	52	0.08
Scotch-Irish (427)	1,078	1.73
Scottish (407)	1,324	2.12
Serbian (0)	0	<0.01
Slavic (14)	34	0.05
Slovak (123)	231	0.37
Slovene (11)	11	0.02
Soviet Union (0)	0	<0.01
Swedish (189)	802	1.28
Swiss (58)	254	0.41
Turkish (0)	9	0.01
Ukrainian (240)	524	0.84
Welsh (408)	1,552	2.49
West Indian, ex. Hispanic (42)	42	0.07
Bahamian (0)	0	<0.01
Barbadian (0)	0	<0.01
Belizean (0)	0	<0.01
Bermudan (0)	0	<0.01
British West Indian (7)	7	0.01
Dutch West Indian (3)	3	<0.01
Haitian (5)	5	0.01
Jamaican (13)	13	0.02
Trinidadian/Tobagonian (0)	0	<0.01
U.S. Virgin Islander (14)	14	0.02
West Indian (0)	0	<0.01
Other West Indian (0)	0	<0.01
Yugoslavian (7)	7	0.01

Hispanic Origin	Population	%
Hispanic or Latino (of any race)	702	1.12
Central American, ex. Mexican	54	0.09
Costa Rican	3	<0.01
Guatemalan	19	0.03
Honduran	10	0.02
Nicaraguan	2	<0.01
Panamanian	4	0.01
Salvadoran	16	0.03
Other Central American	0	<0.01
Cuban	22	0.04
Dominican Republic	23	0.04
Mexican	211	0.34
Puerto Rican	246	0.39
South American	59	0.09
Argentinean	5	0.01
Bolivian	0	<0.01
Chilean	4	0.01
Colombian	22	0.04
Ecuadorian	18	0.03
Paraguayan	0	<0.01
Peruvian	9	0.01
Uruguayan	0	<0.01
Venezuelan	1	<0.01
Other South American	0	<0.01
Other Hispanic or Latino	87	0.14

Race*	Population	%
African-American/Black (311)	502	0.80
Not Hispanic (269)	438	0.70
Hispanic (42)	64	0.10
American Indian/Alaska Native (154)	452	0.72
Not Hispanic (127)	417	0.67
Hispanic (27)	35	0.06
Alaska Athabascan (Ala. Nat.) (0)	0	<0.01
Aleut (Alaska Native) (0)	0	<0.01
Apache (2)	12	0.02
Arapaho (0)	0	<0.01
Blackfeet (1)	22	0.04
Canadian/French Am. Ind. (1)	1	<0.01
Central American Ind. (0)	0	<0.01
Cherokee (13)	64	0.10
Cheyenne (2)	2	<0.01
Chickasaw (3)	3	<0.01
Chippewa (1)	2	<0.01
Choctaw (2)	9	0.01
Colville (0)	1	<0.01

Race* (cont.)	Population	%
Comanche (0)	0	<0.01
Cree (0)	3	<0.01
Creek (0)	4	0.01
Crow (0)	0	<0.01
Delaware (4)	18	0.03
Hopi (1)	1	<0.01
Houma (1)	1	<0.01
Inupiat (Alaska Native) (0)	0	<0.01
Iroquois (19)	55	0.09
Kiowa (0)	0	<0.01
Lumbee (0)	0	<0.01
Menominee (0)	0	<0.01
Mexican American Ind. (6)	6	0.01
Navajo (3)	5	0.01
Osage (0)	0	<0.01
Ottawa (0)	0	<0.01
Paiute (0)	0	<0.01
Pima (0)	0	<0.01
Potawatomi (0)	2	<0.01
Pueblo (0)	1	<0.01
Puget Sound Salish (0)	0	<0.01
Seminole (2)	3	<0.01
Shoshone (0)	2	<0.01
Sioux (1)	4	0.01
South American Ind. (6)	6	0.01
Spanish American Ind. (0)	0	<0.01
Tlingit-Haida (Alaska Native) (0)	1	<0.01
Tohono O'Odham (0)	0	<0.01
Tsimshian (Alaska Native) (0)	0	<0.01
Ute (0)	0	<0.01
Yakama (0)	0	<0.01
Yaqui (1)	2	<0.01
Yuman (0)	0	<0.01
Yup'ik (Alaska Native) (1)	1	<0.01
Asian (339)	463	0.74
Not Hispanic (330)	449	0.72
Hispanic (9)	14	0.02
Bangladeshi (0)	0	<0.01
Bhutanese (0)	0	<0.01
Burmese (1)	1	<0.01
Cambodian (0)	0	<0.01
Chinese, ex. Taiwanese (84)	89	0.14
Filipino (49)	76	0.12
Hmong (0)	0	<0.01
Indian (99)	126	0.20
Indonesian (1)	1	<0.01
Japanese (13)	45	0.07
Korean (39)	49	0.08
Laotian (0)	0	<0.01
Malaysian (0)	0	<0.01
Nepalese (11)	11	0.02
Pakistani (11)	11	0.02
Sri Lankan (1)	2	<0.01
Taiwanese (2)	3	<0.01
Thai (11)	13	0.02
Vietnamese (10)	10	0.02
Hawaii Native/Pacific Islander (7)	25	0.04
Not Hispanic (5)	23	0.04
Hispanic (2)	2	<0.01
Fijian (0)	0	<0.01
Guamanian/Chamorro (3)	5	0.01
Marshallese (0)	0	<0.01
Native Hawaiian (2)	7	0.01
Samoan (1)	3	<0.01
Tongan (0)	0	<0.01
White (61,035)	61,650	98.45
Not Hispanic (60,584)	61,148	97.65
Hispanic (451)	502	0.80

Notes: † The Census 2010 population figure is used to calculate the percentages in the Hispanic Origin and Race categories. Ancestry percentages are based on the 2006-2010 American Community Survey population (not shown); ‡ Numbers in parentheses indicate the number of people reporting a single ancestry; * Numbers in parentheses indicate the number of persons reporting this race alone, not in combination with any other race; Please refer to the Explanation of Data for more information.

Bucks County

Population: 625,249

Ancestry	Population	%
Afghan (0)	0	<0.01
African, Sub-Saharan (2,785)	2,995	0.48
African (2,100)	2,256	0.36
Cape Verdean (0)	7	<0.01
Ethiopian (0)	0	<0.01
Ghanaian (91)	98	0.02
Kenyan (16)	33	0.01
Liberian (443)	459	0.07
Nigerian (83)	90	0.01
Senegalese (0)	0	<0.01
Sierra Leonean (0)	0	<0.01
Somalian (0)	0	<0.01
South African (52)	52	0.01
Sudanese (0)	0	<0.01
Ugandan (0)	0	<0.01
Zimbabwean (0)	0	<0.01
Other Sub-Saharan African (0)	0	<0.01
Albanian (409)	674	0.11
Alsatian (12)	19	<0.01
American (24,263)	24,263	3.90
Arab (1,368)	2,437	0.39
Arab (25)	153	0.02
Egyptian (252)	308	0.05
Iraqi (0)	0	<0.01
Jordanian (17)	17	<0.01
Lebanese (402)	855	0.14
Moroccan (341)	382	0.06
Palestinian (12)	29	<0.01
Syrian (58)	281	0.05
Other Arab (261)	412	0.07
Armenian (393)	857	0.14
Assyrian/Chaldean/Syriac (0)	16	<0.01
Australian (130)	220	0.04
Austrian (568)	3,222	0.52
Basque (10)	10	<0.01
Belgian (152)	430	0.07
Brazilian (461)	567	0.09
British (1,055)	2,385	0.38
Bulgarian (60)	80	0.01
Cajun (9)	49	0.01
Canadian (488)	1,281	0.21
Carpatho Rusyn (29)	29	<0.01
Celtic (48)	213	0.03
Croatian (201)	585	0.09
Cypriot (13)	13	<0.01
Czech (338)	2,165	0.35
Czechoslovakian (459)	1,030	0.17
Danish (359)	1,584	0.25
Dutch (1,794)	9,179	1.47
Eastern European (2,074)	2,232	0.36
English (15,861)	68,953	11.07
Estonian (62)	105	0.02
European (5,015)	5,429	0.87
Finnish (93)	403	0.06
French, ex. Basque (1,600)	13,734	2.20
French Canadian (741)	2,376	0.38
German (52,711)	173,833	27.91
German Russian (0)	0	<0.01
Greek (1,894)	4,212	0.68
Guyanese (186)	267	0.04
Hungarian (1,830)	7,867	1.26
Icelander (45)	60	0.01
Iranian (320)	351	0.06
Irish (49,726)	166,515	26.73
Israeli (213)	300	0.05
Italian (36,438)	98,471	15.81
Latvian (258)	486	0.08
Lithuanian (1,391)	4,786	0.77
Luxemburger (0)	8	<0.01
Macedonian (31)	79	0.01
Maltese (0)	38	0.01
New Zealander (0)	0	<0.01
Northern European (398)	427	0.07
Norwegian (825)	2,985	0.48
Pennsylvania German (3,506)	6,313	1.01

Ancestry	Population	%
Polish (15,787)	52,163	8.37
Portuguese (483)	1,523	0.24
Romanian (649)	1,627	0.26
Russian (9,579)	19,028	3.05
Scandinavian (167)	484	0.08
Scotch-Irish (3,734)	11,692	1.88
Scottish (3,049)	12,201	1.96
Serbian (50)	187	0.03
Slavic (222)	571	0.09
Slovak (1,799)	4,547	0.73
Slovene (63)	142	0.02
Soviet Union (27)	27	<0.01
Swedish (1,205)	5,930	0.95
Swiss (295)	2,128	0.34
Turkish (541)	652	0.10
Ukrainian (6,645)	11,001	1.77
Welsh (1,251)	8,429	1.35
West Indian, ex. Hispanic (1,022)	1,341	0.22
Bahamian (11)	11	<0.01
Barbadian (99)	107	0.02
Belizean (0)	0	<0.01
Bermudan (0)	9	<0.01
British West Indian (11)	11	<0.01
Dutch West Indian (0)	6	<0.01
Haitian (401)	415	0.07
Jamaican (252)	506	0.08
Trinidadian/Tobagonian (33)	50	0.01
U.S. Virgin Islander (17)	17	<0.01
West Indian (198)	209	0.03
Other West Indian (0)	0	<0.01
Yugoslavian (333)	683	0.11

Hispanic Origin	Population	%
Hispanic or Latino (of any race)	26,782	4.28
Central American, ex. Mexican	2,819	0.45
Costa Rican	481	0.08
Guatemalan	1,101	0.18
Honduran	324	0.05
Nicaraguan	113	0.02
Panamanian	108	0.02
Salvadoran	664	0.11
Other Central American	28	<0.01
Cuban	946	0.15
Dominican Republic	626	0.10
Mexican	6,867	1.10
Puerto Rican	10,397	1.66
South American	2,706	0.43
Argentinean	258	0.04
Bolivian	24	<0.01
Chilean	103	0.02
Colombian	784	0.13
Ecuadorian	806	0.13
Paraguayan	20	<0.01
Peruvian	450	0.07
Uruguayan	49	0.01
Venezuelan	181	0.03
Other South American	31	<0.01
Other Hispanic or Latino	2,421	0.39

Race*	Population	%
African-American/Black (22,376)	26,633	4.26
Not Hispanic (21,454)	25,063	4.01
Hispanic (922)	1,570	0.25
American Indian/Alaska Native (1,232)	3,470	0.55
Not Hispanic (750)	2,701	0.43
Hispanic (482)	769	0.12
Alaska Athabascan (Ala. Nat.) (1)	5	<0.01
Aleut (Alaska Native) (1)	1	<0.01
Apache (13)	50	0.01
Arapaho (0)	1	<0.01
Blackfeet (15)	149	0.02
Canadian/French Am. Ind. (2)	10	<0.01
Central American Ind. (11)	17	<0.01
Cherokee (86)	588	0.09
Cheyenne (4)	10	<0.01
Chickasaw (3)	15	<0.01
Chippewa (15)	38	0.01
Choctaw (8)	34	0.01
Colville (0)	0	<0.01

	Population	%
Comanche (8)	11	<0.01
Cree (1)	12	<0.01
Creek (9)	26	<0.01
Crow (0)	3	<0.01
Delaware (34)	144	0.02
Hopi (10)	10	<0.01
Houma (0)	0	<0.01
Inupiat (Alaska Native) (0)	1	<0.01
Iroquois (47)	131	0.02
Kiowa (4)	5	<0.01
Lumbee (15)	38	0.01
Menominee (2)	2	<0.01
Mexican American Ind. (170)	194	0.03
Navajo (5)	25	<0.01
Osage (4)	8	<0.01
Ottawa (0)	0	<0.01
Paiute (0)	0	<0.01
Pima (4)	5	<0.01
Potawatomi (1)	3	<0.01
Pueblo (2)	2	<0.01
Puget Sound Salish (2)	2	<0.01
Seminole (4)	26	<0.01
Shoshone (2)	6	<0.01
Sioux (28)	92	0.01
South American Ind. (54)	93	0.01
Spanish American Ind. (5)	7	<0.01
Tlingit-Haida (Alaska Native) (0)	0	<0.01
Tohono O'Odham (1)	1	<0.01
Tsimshian (Alaska Native) (0)	0	<0.01
Ute (0)	0	<0.01
Yakama (0)	0	<0.01
Yaqui (1)	4	<0.01
Yuman (0)	0	<0.01
Yup'ik (Alaska Native) (0)	0	<0.01
Asian (24,008)	27,501	4.40
Not Hispanic (23,893)	27,130	4.34
Hispanic (115)	371	0.06
Bangladeshi (145)	160	0.03
Bhutanese (0)	0	<0.01
Burmese (30)	34	0.01
Cambodian (208)	249	0.04
Chinese, ex. Taiwanese (3,998)	4,599	0.74
Filipino (1,701)	2,523	0.40
Hmong (1)	6	<0.01
Indian (11,501)	12,247	1.96
Indonesian (48)	78	0.01
Japanese (301)	691	0.11
Korean (2,952)	3,438	0.55
Laotian (44)	64	0.01
Malaysian (11)	20	<0.01
Nepalese (31)	34	0.01
Pakistani (691)	777	0.12
Sri Lankan (46)	52	0.01
Taiwanese (191)	221	0.04
Thai (129)	188	0.03
Vietnamese (1,324)	1,551	0.25
Hawaii Native/Pacific Islander (174)	544	0.09
Not Hispanic (138)	424	0.07
Hispanic (36)	120	0.02
Fijian (3)	5	<0.01
Guamanian/Chamorro (66)	88	0.01
Marshallese (2)	2	<0.01
Native Hawaiian (43)	155	0.02
Samoan (13)	29	<0.01
Tongan (8)	9	<0.01
White (557,647)	566,557	90.61
Not Hispanic (543,207)	550,321	88.02
Hispanic (14,440)	16,236	2.60

Notes: † The Census 2010 population figure is used to calculate the percentages in the Hispanic Origin and Race categories. Ancestry percentages are based on the 2006-2010 American Community Survey population (not shown); ‡ Numbers in parentheses indicate the number of people reporting a single ancestry; * Numbers in parentheses indicate the number of persons reporting this race alone, not in combination with any other race; Please refer to the Explanation of Data for more information.

Butler County

Population: 183,862

Ancestry	Population	%
Afghan (0)	0	<0.01
African, Sub-Saharan (312)	339	0.19
African (35)	55	0.03
Cape Verdean (0)	0	<0.01
Ethiopian (0)	0	<0.01
Ghanaian (0)	0	<0.01
Kenyan (0)	0	<0.01
Liberian (0)	0	<0.01
Nigerian (260)	260	0.14
Senegalese (0)	0	<0.01
Sierra Leonean (0)	0	<0.01
Somalian (0)	0	<0.01
South African (9)	16	0.01
Sudanese (0)	0	<0.01
Ugandan (8)	8	<0.01
Zimbabwean (0)	0	<0.01
Other Sub-Saharan African (0)	0	<0.01
Albanian (0)	17	0.01
Alsatian (8)	15	0.01
American (7,771)	7,771	4.26
Arab (174)	558	0.31
Arab (6)	15	0.01
Egyptian (8)	8	<0.01
Iraqi (0)	0	<0.01
Jordanian (33)	33	0.02
Lebanese (40)	228	0.12
Moroccan (4)	4	<0.01
Palestinian (29)	29	0.02
Syrian (54)	222	0.12
Other Arab (0)	19	0.01
Armenian (36)	41	0.02
Assyrian/Chaldean/Syriac (0)	0	<0.01
Australian (0)	0	<0.01
Austrian (231)	761	0.42
Basque (0)	0	<0.01
Belgian (65)	410	0.22
Brazilian (35)	70	0.04
British (179)	606	0.33
Bulgarian (15)	15	0.01
Cajun (0)	0	<0.01
Canadian (34)	183	0.10
Carpatho Rusyn (7)	14	0.01
Celtic (41)	41	0.02
Croatian (338)	1,302	0.71
Cypriot (0)	0	<0.01
Czech (211)	1,400	0.77
Czechoslovakian (302)	638	0.35
Danish (20)	171	0.09
Dutch (229)	3,383	1.85
Eastern European (169)	197	0.11
English (4,001)	18,018	9.87
Estonian (0)	0	<0.01
European (1,263)	1,287	0.70
Finnish (27)	198	0.11
French, ex. Basque (662)	5,597	3.07
French Canadian (198)	536	0.29
German (24,000)	78,956	43.25
German Russian (0)	0	<0.01
Greek (293)	760	0.42
Guyanese (0)	0	<0.01
Hungarian (674)	2,882	1.58
Icelander (0)	0	<0.01
Iranian (9)	125	0.07
Irish (6,837)	39,565	21.67
Israeli (28)	28	0.02
Italian (6,545)	24,335	13.33
Latvian (0)	14	0.01
Lithuanian (134)	811	0.44
Luxemburger (0)	0	<0.01
Macedonian (0)	0	<0.01
Maltese (0)	15	0.01
New Zealander (0)	0	<0.01
Northern European (7)	22	0.01
Norwegian (176)	504	0.28
Pennsylvania German (284)	680	0.37

Ancestry	Population	%
Polish (3,410)	12,875	7.05
Portuguese (14)	45	0.02
Romanian (45)	180	0.10
Russian (548)	2,491	1.36
Scandinavian (80)	216	0.12
Scotch-Irish (2,675)	8,629	4.73
Scottish (1,176)	4,940	2.71
Serbian (141)	720	0.39
Slavic (153)	311	0.17
Slovak (1,762)	5,770	3.16
Slovene (117)	434	0.24
Soviet Union (0)	0	<0.01
Swedish (284)	1,509	0.83
Swiss (86)	625	0.34
Turkish (0)	26	0.01
Ukrainian (805)	2,118	1.16
Welsh (339)	3,026	1.66
West Indian, ex. Hispanic (46)	46	0.03
Bahamian (3)	3	<0.01
Barbadian (0)	0	<0.01
Belizean (0)	0	<0.01
Bermudan (0)	0	<0.01
British West Indian (0)	0	<0.01
Dutch West Indian (0)	0	<0.01
Haitian (0)	0	<0.01
Jamaican (43)	43	0.02
Trinidadian/Tobagonian (0)	0	<0.01
U.S. Virgin Islander (0)	0	<0.01
West Indian (0)	0	<0.01
Other West Indian (0)	0	<0.01
Yugoslavian (69)	161	0.09

Hispanic Origin	Population	%
Hispanic or Latino (of any race)	1,941	1.06
Central American, ex. Mexican	134	0.07
Costa Rican	2	<0.01
Guatemalan	60	0.03
Honduran	21	0.01
Nicaraguan	7	<0.01
Panamanian	15	0.01
Salvadoran	29	0.02
Other Central American	0	<0.01
Cuban	68	0.04
Dominican Republic	57	0.03
Mexican	745	0.41
Puerto Rican	499	0.27
South American	179	0.10
Argentinean	29	0.02
Bolivian	2	<0.01
Chilean	6	<0.01
Colombian	54	0.03
Ecuadorian	24	0.01
Paraguayan	1	<0.01
Peruvian	22	0.01
Uruguayan	10	0.01
Venezuelan	28	0.02
Other South American	3	<0.01
Other Hispanic or Latino	259	0.14

Race*	Population	%
African-American/Black (2,021)	2,722	1.48
Not Hispanic (1,954)	2,626	1.43
Hispanic (67)	96	0.05
American Indian/Alaska Native (194)	712	0.39
Not Hispanic (166)	661	0.36
Hispanic (28)	51	0.03
Alaska Athabascan (Ala. Nat.) (0)	0	<0.01
Aleut (Alaska Native) (0)	0	<0.01
Apache (1)	8	<0.01
Arapaho (0)	0	<0.01
Blackfeet (2)	37	0.02
Canadian/French Am. Ind. (3)	3	<0.01
Central American Ind. (0)	0	<0.01
Cherokee (36)	176	0.10
Cheyenne (1)	6	<0.01
Chickasaw (0)	2	<0.01
Chippewa (3)	6	<0.01
Choctaw (4)	7	<0.01
Colville (0)	0	<0.01

	Population	%
Comanche (2)	2	<0.01
Cree (1)	4	<0.01
Creek (0)	5	<0.01
Crow (0)	2	<0.01
Delaware (3)	7	<0.01
Hopi (0)	0	<0.01
Houma (0)	0	<0.01
Inupiat (Alaska Native) (0)	0	<0.01
Iroquois (11)	32	0.02
Kiowa (4)	4	<0.01
Lumbee (5)	5	<0.01
Menominee (0)	0	<0.01
Mexican American Ind. (5)	6	<0.01
Navajo (6)	7	<0.01
Osage (0)	4	<0.01
Ottawa (0)	1	<0.01
Paiute (0)	0	<0.01
Pima (0)	0	<0.01
Potawatomi (0)	0	<0.01
Pueblo (3)	4	<0.01
Puget Sound Salish (1)	1	<0.01
Seminole (2)	15	0.01
Shoshone (0)	1	<0.01
Sioux (6)	29	0.02
South American Ind. (1)	1	<0.01
Spanish American Ind. (2)	2	<0.01
Tlingit-Haida (Alaska Native) (0)	1	<0.01
Tohono O'Odham (3)	4	<0.01
Tsimshian (Alaska Native) (4)	4	<0.01
Ute (0)	0	<0.01
Yakama (0)	0	<0.01
Yaqui (0)	1	<0.01
Yuman (0)	0	<0.01
Yup'ik (Alaska Native) (0)	0	<0.01
Asian (1,838)	2,322	1.26
Not Hispanic (1,826)	2,293	1.25
Hispanic (12)	29	0.02
Bangladeshi (1)	1	<0.01
Bhutanese (0)	0	<0.01
Burmese (10)	10	0.01
Cambodian (14)	14	0.01
Chinese, ex. Taiwanese (390)	480	0.26
Filipino (174)	284	0.15
Hmong (0)	0	<0.01
Indian (568)	632	0.34
Indonesian (12)	14	0.01
Japanese (103)	162	0.09
Korean (215)	311	0.17
Laotian (4)	6	<0.01
Malaysian (2)	6	<0.01
Nepalese (4)	6	<0.01
Pakistani (41)	45	0.02
Sri Lankan (33)	34	0.02
Taiwanese (21)	27	0.01
Thai (35)	42	0.02
Vietnamese (155)	181	0.10
Hawaii Native/Pacific Islander (50)	111	0.06
Not Hispanic (47)	101	0.05
Hispanic (3)	10	0.01
Fijian (0)	0	<0.01
Guamanian/Chamorro (9)	14	0.01
Marshallese (0)	0	<0.01
Native Hawaiian (13)	29	0.02
Samoan (15)	25	0.01
Tongan (1)	2	<0.01
White (177,605)	179,199	97.46
Not Hispanic (176,259)	177,736	96.67
Hispanic (1,346)	1,463	0.80

*Notes: † The Census 2010 population figure is used to calculate the percentages in the Hispanic Origin and Race categories. Ancestry percentages are based on the 2006-2010 American Community Survey population (not shown); ‡ Numbers in parentheses indicate the number of people reporting a single ancestry; * Numbers in parentheses indicate the number of persons reporting this race alone, not in combination with any other race; Please refer to the Explanation of Data for more information.*

Cambria County

Population: 143,679

Ancestry	Population	%
Afghan (0)	0	<0.01
African, Sub-Saharan (147)	211	0.15
African (130)	185	0.13
Cape Verdean (0)	0	<0.01
Ethiopian (0)	0	<0.01
Ghanaian (17)	17	0.01
Kenyan (0)	0	<0.01
Liberian (0)	0	<0.01
Nigerian (0)	0	<0.01
Senegalese (0)	0	<0.01
Sierra Leonean (0)	0	<0.01
Somalian (0)	0	<0.01
South African (0)	9	0.01
Sudanese (0)	0	<0.01
Ugandan (0)	0	<0.01
Zimbabwean (0)	0	<0.01
Other Sub-Saharan African (0)	0	<0.01
Albanian (4)	11	0.01
Alsatian (0)	0	<0.01
American (6,370)	6,370	4.40
Arab (320)	689	0.48
Arab (0)	0	<0.01
Egyptian (0)	0	<0.01
Iraqi (0)	0	<0.01
Jordanian (0)	0	<0.01
Lebanese (264)	539	0.37
Moroccan (0)	0	<0.01
Palestinian (0)	0	<0.01
Syrian (26)	59	0.04
Other Arab (30)	91	0.06
Armenian (13)	43	0.03
Assyrian/Chaldean/Syriac (0)	0	<0.01
Australian (12)	15	0.01
Austrian (186)	770	0.53
Basque (0)	0	<0.01
Belgian (42)	211	0.15
Brazilian (0)	0	<0.01
British (124)	288	0.20
Bulgarian (9)	16	0.01
Cajun (0)	27	0.02
Canadian (11)	120	0.08
Carpatho Rusyn (72)	194	0.13
Celtic (0)	0	<0.01
Croatian (564)	1,295	0.89
Cypriot (0)	0	<0.01
Czech (185)	1,233	0.85
Czechoslovakian (279)	567	0.39
Danish (20)	35	0.02
Dutch (626)	3,489	2.41
Eastern European (101)	121	0.08
English (2,613)	12,092	8.35
Estonian (0)	0	<0.01
European (555)	582	0.40
Finnish (31)	70	0.05
French, ex. Basque (498)	3,463	2.39
French Canadian (102)	213	0.15
German (15,833)	49,352	34.10
German Russian (0)	0	<0.01
Greek (128)	371	0.26
Guyanese (0)	0	<0.01
Hungarian (1,010)	3,848	2.66
Icelander (0)	0	<0.01
Iranian (59)	59	0.04
Irish (5,448)	26,736	18.47
Israeli (0)	3	<0.01
Italian (5,803)	16,778	11.59
Latvian (3)	9	0.01
Lithuanian (163)	625	0.43
Luxemburger (0)	3	<0.01
Macedonian (12)	12	0.01
Maltese (0)	0	<0.01
New Zealander (0)	0	<0.01
Northern European (0)	0	<0.01
Norwegian (48)	293	0.20
Pennsylvania German (889)	1,876	1.30

Ancestry	Population	%
Polish (5,226)	16,075	11.11
Portuguese (44)	58	0.04
Romanian (32)	161	0.11
Russian (629)	2,017	1.39
Scandinavian (22)	87	0.06
Scotch-Irish (1,088)	2,508	1.73
Scottish (563)	2,558	1.77
Serbian (310)	639	0.44
Slavic (297)	730	0.50
Slovak (4,770)	10,898	7.53
Slovene (393)	884	0.61
Soviet Union (0)	0	<0.01
Swedish (106)	706	0.49
Swiss (52)	418	0.29
Turkish (16)	61	0.04
Ukrainian (664)	1,441	1.00
Welsh (427)	2,700	1.87
West Indian, ex. Hispanic (102)	166	0.11
Bahamian (0)	0	<0.01
Barbadian (0)	3	<0.01
Belizean (0)	0	<0.01
Bermudan (0)	0	<0.01
British West Indian (0)	0	<0.01
Dutch West Indian (0)	0	<0.01
Haitian (18)	27	0.02
Jamaican (67)	76	0.05
Trinidadian/Tobagonian (17)	21	0.01
U.S. Virgin Islander (0)	0	<0.01
West Indian (0)	39	0.03
Other West Indian (0)	0	<0.01
Yugoslavian (94)	166	0.11

Hispanic Origin	Population	%
Hispanic or Latino (of any race)	2,006	1.40
Central American, ex. Mexican	71	0.05
Costa Rican	1	<0.01
Guatemalan	25	0.02
Honduran	9	0.01
Nicaraguan	3	<0.01
Panamanian	12	0.01
Salvadoran	20	0.01
Other Central American	1	<0.01
Cuban	106	0.07
Dominican Republic	51	0.04
Mexican	807	0.56
Puerto Rican	467	0.33
South American	98	0.07
Argentinean	2	<0.01
Bolivian	2	<0.01
Chilean	4	<0.01
Colombian	55	0.04
Ecuadorian	12	0.01
Paraguayan	2	<0.01
Peruvian	19	0.01
Uruguayan	0	<0.01
Venezuelan	2	<0.01
Other South American	0	<0.01
Other Hispanic or Latino	406	0.28

Race*	Population	%
African-American/Black (5,222)	6,406	4.46
Not Hispanic (5,073)	6,161	4.29
Hispanic (149)	245	0.17
American Indian/Alaska Native (147)	535	0.37
Not Hispanic (108)	466	0.32
Hispanic (39)	69	0.05
Alaska Athabascan (Ala. Nat.) (0)	0	<0.01
Aleut (Alaska Native) (0)	0	<0.01
Apache (2)	5	<0.01
Arapaho (0)	0	<0.01
Blackfeet (3)	23	0.02
Canadian/French Am. Ind. (0)	0	<0.01
Central American Ind. (0)	0	<0.01
Cherokee (23)	113	0.08
Cheyenne (0)	5	<0.01
Chickasaw (1)	1	<0.01
Chippewa (1)	2	<0.01
Choctaw (4)	6	<0.01
Colville (0)	0	<0.01

	Population	%
Comanche (0)	1	<0.01
Cree (0)	3	<0.01
Creek (1)	3	<0.01
Crow (0)	2	<0.01
Delaware (0)	5	<0.01
Hopi (0)	0	<0.01
Houma (0)	0	<0.01
Inupiat (Alaska Native) (1)	2	<0.01
Iroquois (12)	28	0.02
Kiowa (0)	0	<0.01
Lumbee (1)	2	<0.01
Menominee (0)	0	<0.01
Mexican American Ind. (8)	8	0.01
Navajo (3)	5	<0.01
Osage (0)	0	<0.01
Ottawa (0)	1	<0.01
Paiute (0)	0	<0.01
Pima (0)	0	<0.01
Potawatomi (0)	0	<0.01
Pueblo (0)	0	<0.01
Puget Sound Salish (2)	2	<0.01
Seminole (0)	2	<0.01
Shoshone (0)	0	<0.01
Sioux (3)	4	<0.01
South American Ind. (5)	6	<0.01
Spanish American Ind. (1)	1	<0.01
Tlingit-Haida (Alaska Native) (0)	0	<0.01
Tohono O'Odham (0)	0	<0.01
Tsimshian (Alaska Native) (0)	0	<0.01
Ute (0)	0	<0.01
Yakama (0)	0	<0.01
Yaqui (0)	0	<0.01
Yuman (0)	0	<0.01
Yup'ik (Alaska Native) (0)	0	<0.01
Asian (729)	962	0.67
Not Hispanic (720)	933	0.65
Hispanic (9)	29	0.02
Bangladeshi (10)	10	0.01
Bhutanese (0)	0	<0.01
Burmese (2)	2	<0.01
Cambodian (1)	1	<0.01
Chinese, ex. Taiwanese (145)	171	0.12
Filipino (101)	150	0.10
Hmong (0)	1	<0.01
Indian (264)	305	0.21
Indonesian (1)	1	<0.01
Japanese (28)	67	0.05
Korean (67)	118	0.08
Laotian (0)	3	<0.01
Malaysian (1)	1	<0.01
Nepalese (1)	1	<0.01
Pakistani (10)	12	0.01
Sri Lankan (1)	1	<0.01
Taiwanese (1)	2	<0.01
Thai (11)	16	0.01
Vietnamese (47)	56	0.04
Hawaii Native/Pacific Islander (29)	88	0.06
Not Hispanic (28)	80	0.06
Hispanic (1)	8	<0.01
Fijian (1)	1	<0.01
Guamanian/Chamorro (1)	6	<0.01
Marshallese (2)	2	<0.01
Native Hawaiian (11)	20	0.01
Samoan (5)	18	0.01
Tongan (0)	1	<0.01
White (135,206)	136,823	95.23
Not Hispanic (134,073)	135,533	94.33
Hispanic (1,133)	1,290	0.90

Notes: † The Census 2010 population figure is used to calculate the percentages in the Hispanic Origin and Race categories. Ancestry percentages are based on the 2006-2010 American Community Survey population (not shown); ‡ Numbers in parentheses indicate the number of people reporting a single ancestry; * Numbers in parentheses indicate the number of persons reporting this race alone, not in combination with any other race; Please refer to the Explanation of Data for more information.

Cameron County

Population: 5,085

Ancestry	Population	%
Afghan (0)	0	<0.01
African, Sub-Saharan (0)	0	<0.01
African (0)	0	<0.01
Cape Verdean (0)	0	<0.01
Ethiopian (0)	0	<0.01
Ghanaian (0)	0	<0.01
Kenyan (0)	0	<0.01
Liberian (0)	0	<0.01
Nigerian (0)	0	<0.01
Senegalese (0)	0	<0.01
Sierra Leonean (0)	0	<0.01
Somalian (0)	0	<0.01
South African (0)	0	<0.01
Sudanese (0)	0	<0.01
Ugandan (0)	0	<0.01
Zimbabwean (0)	0	<0.01
Other Sub-Saharan African (0)	0	<0.01
Albanian (0)	0	<0.01
Alsatian (0)	0	<0.01
American (584)	584	11.24
Arab (0)	0	<0.01
Arab (0)	0	<0.01
Egyptian (0)	0	<0.01
Iraqi (0)	0	<0.01
Jordanian (0)	0	<0.01
Lebanese (0)	0	<0.01
Moroccan (0)	0	<0.01
Palestinian (0)	0	<0.01
Syrian (0)	0	<0.01
Other Arab (0)	0	<0.01
Armenian (0)	0	<0.01
Assyrian/Chaldean/Syriac (0)	0	<0.01
Australian (0)	0	<0.01
Austrian (31)	78	1.50
Basque (0)	4	0.08
Belgian (0)	4	0.08
Brazilian (0)	0	<0.01
British (0)	0	<0.01
Bulgarian (0)	0	<0.01
Cajun (0)	0	<0.01
Canadian (11)	11	0.21
Carpatho Rusyn (0)	0	<0.01
Celtic (0)	0	<0.01
Croatian (2)	5	0.10
Cypriot (0)	0	<0.01
Czech (15)	37	0.71
Czechoslovakian (7)	11	0.21
Danish (0)	0	<0.01
Dutch (27)	102	1.96
Eastern European (0)	0	<0.01
English (203)	620	11.93
Estonian (0)	0	<0.01
European (32)	32	0.62
Finnish (2)	2	0.04
French, ex. Basque (10)	132	2.54
French Canadian (0)	0	<0.01
German (612)	1,797	34.58
German Russian (0)	0	<0.01
Greek (0)	39	0.75
Guyanese (0)	0	<0.01
Hungarian (0)	37	0.71
Icelander (0)	0	<0.01
Iranian (0)	0	<0.01
Irish (143)	748	14.39
Israeli (0)	0	<0.01
Italian (274)	685	13.18
Latvian (0)	0	<0.01
Lithuanian (8)	49	0.94
Luxemburger (0)	0	<0.01
Macedonian (0)	0	<0.01
Maltese (0)	0	<0.01
New Zealander (0)	0	<0.01
Northern European (0)	0	<0.01
Norwegian (4)	14	0.27
Pennsylvania German (38)	92	1.77

Ancestry	Population	%
Polish (86)	258	4.96
Portuguese (11)	11	0.21
Romanian (2)	5	0.10
Russian (0)	18	0.35
Scandinavian (0)	0	<0.01
Scotch-Irish (61)	120	2.31
Scottish (18)	121	2.33
Serbian (0)	0	<0.01
Slavic (0)	0	<0.01
Slovak (15)	57	1.10
Slovene (8)	10	0.19
Soviet Union (0)	0	<0.01
Swedish (68)	284	5.46
Swiss (3)	25	0.48
Turkish (0)	0	<0.01
Ukrainian (0)	2	0.04
Welsh (22)	73	1.40
West Indian, ex. Hispanic (0)	0	<0.01
Bahamian (0)	0	<0.01
Barbadian (0)	0	<0.01
Belizean (0)	0	<0.01
Bermudan (0)	0	<0.01
British West Indian (0)	0	<0.01
Dutch West Indian (0)	0	<0.01
Haitian (0)	0	<0.01
Jamaican (0)	0	<0.01
Trinidadian/Tobagonian (0)	0	<0.01
U.S. Virgin Islander (0)	0	<0.01
West Indian (0)	0	<0.01
Other West Indian (0)	0	<0.01
Yugoslavian (0)	3	0.06

Hispanic Origin	Population	%
Hispanic or Latino (of any race)	19	0.37
Central American, ex. Mexican	1	0.02
Costa Rican	0	<0.01
Guatemalan	0	<0.01
Honduran	0	<0.01
Nicaraguan	0	<0.01
Panamanian	1	0.02
Salvadoran	0	<0.01
Other Central American	0	<0.01
Cuban	0	<0.01
Dominican Republic	0	<0.01
Mexican	13	0.26
Puerto Rican	5	0.10
South American	0	<0.01
Argentinean	0	<0.01
Bolivian	0	<0.01
Chilean	0	<0.01
Colombian	0	<0.01
Ecuadorian	0	<0.01
Paraguayan	0	<0.01
Peruvian	0	<0.01
Uruguayan	0	<0.01
Venezuelan	0	<0.01
Other South American	0	<0.01
Other Hispanic or Latino	0	<0.01

Race*	Population	%
African-American/Black (13)	28	0.55
Not Hispanic (12)	27	0.53
Hispanic (1)	1	0.02
American Indian/Alaska Native (13)	33	0.65
Not Hispanic (13)	33	0.65
Hispanic (0)	0	<0.01
Alaska Athabascan (Ala. Nat.) (0)	0	<0.01
Aleut (Alaska Native) (0)	0	<0.01
Apache (0)	0	<0.01
Arapaho (0)	0	<0.01
Blackfeet (0)	0	<0.01
Canadian/French Am. Ind. (0)	0	<0.01
Central American Ind. (0)	0	<0.01
Cherokee (0)	4	0.08
Cheyenne (0)	0	<0.01
Chickasaw (0)	0	<0.01
Chippewa (0)	2	0.04
Choctaw (1)	2	0.04
Colville (0)	0	<0.01

Race*	Population	%
Comanche (0)	0	<0.01
Cree (0)	1	0.02
Creek (0)	0	<0.01
Crow (0)	0	<0.01
Delaware (0)	2	0.04
Hopi (0)	0	<0.01
Houma (0)	0	<0.01
Inupiat (Alaska Native) (0)	0	<0.01
Iroquois (2)	4	0.08
Kiowa (0)	0	<0.01
Lumbee (0)	0	<0.01
Menominee (0)	0	<0.01
Mexican American Ind. (0)	0	<0.01
Navajo (0)	0	<0.01
Osage (0)	0	<0.01
Ottawa (0)	0	<0.01
Paiute (0)	0	<0.01
Pima (0)	0	<0.01
Potawatomi (0)	0	<0.01
Pueblo (0)	0	<0.01
Puget Sound Salish (0)	0	<0.01
Seminole (0)	0	<0.01
Shoshone (0)	0	<0.01
Sioux (1)	2	0.04
South American Ind. (0)	0	<0.01
Spanish American Ind. (0)	0	<0.01
Tlingit-Haida (Alaska Native) (0)	0	<0.01
Tohono O'Odham (0)	0	<0.01
Tsimshian (Alaska Native) (0)	0	<0.01
Ute (0)	0	<0.01
Yakama (0)	0	<0.01
Yaqui (0)	0	<0.01
Yuman (0)	0	<0.01
Yup'ik (Alaska Native) (0)	0	<0.01
Asian (14)	19	0.37
Not Hispanic (14)	19	0.37
Hispanic (0)	0	<0.01
Bangladeshi (0)	0	<0.01
Bhutanese (0)	0	<0.01
Burmese (0)	0	<0.01
Cambodian (0)	0	<0.01
Chinese, ex. Taiwanese (6)	6	0.12
Filipino (5)	7	0.14
Hmong (0)	0	<0.01
Indian (1)	2	0.04
Indonesian (0)	0	<0.01
Japanese (1)	2	0.04
Korean (0)	0	<0.01
Laotian (0)	0	<0.01
Malaysian (0)	0	<0.01
Nepalese (0)	0	<0.01
Pakistani (0)	0	<0.01
Sri Lankan (0)	0	<0.01
Taiwanese (0)	0	<0.01
Thai (0)	0	<0.01
Vietnamese (1)	1	0.02
Hawaii Native/Pacific Islander (0)	1	0.02
Not Hispanic (0)	1	0.02
Hispanic (0)	0	<0.01
Fijian (0)	0	<0.01
Guamanian/Chamorro (0)	0	<0.01
Marshallese (0)	0	<0.01
Native Hawaiian (0)	1	0.02
Samoan (0)	0	<0.01
Tongan (0)	0	<0.01
White (5,000)	5,042	99.15
Not Hispanic (4,985)	5,027	98.86
Hispanic (15)	15	0.29

*Notes: † The Census 2010 population figure is used to calculate the percentages in the Hispanic Origin and Race categories. Ancestry percentages are based on the 2006-2010 American Community Survey population (not shown); ‡ Numbers in parentheses indicate the number of people reporting a single ancestry; * Numbers in parentheses indicate the number of persons reporting this race alone, not in combination with any other race; Please refer to the Explanation of Data for more information.*

Carbon County

Population: 65,249

Ancestry	Population	%
Afghan (0)	0	<0.01
African, Sub-Saharan (16)	162	0.25
African (14)	47	0.07
Cape Verdean (0)	0	<0.01
Ethiopian (0)	0	<0.01
Ghanaian (0)	0	<0.01
Kenyan (0)	0	<0.01
Liberian (0)	0	<0.01
Nigerian (0)	0	<0.01
Senegalese (0)	0	<0.01
Sierra Leonean (0)	0	<0.01
Somalian (0)	0	<0.01
South African (2)	115	0.18
Sudanese (0)	0	<0.01
Ugandan (0)	0	<0.01
Zimbabwean (0)	0	<0.01
Other Sub-Saharan African (0)	0	<0.01
Albanian (0)	13	0.02
Alsatian (0)	0	<0.01
American (4,299)	4,299	6.66
Arab (0)	20	0.03
Arab (0)	0	<0.01
Egyptian (0)	0	<0.01
Iraqi (0)	0	<0.01
Jordanian (0)	0	<0.01
Lebanese (0)	2	<0.01
Moroccan (0)	0	<0.01
Palestinian (0)	0	<0.01
Syrian (0)	18	0.03
Other Arab (0)	0	<0.01
Armenian (2)	4	0.01
Assyrian/Chaldean/Syriac (0)	0	<0.01
Australian (0)	5	0.01
Austrian (61)	262	0.41
Basque (0)	0	<0.01
Belgian (0)	0	<0.01
Brazilian (0)	0	<0.01
British (87)	124	0.19
Bulgarian (12)	28	0.04
Cajun (0)	0	<0.01
Canadian (5)	18	0.03
Carpatho Rusyn (10)	10	0.02
Celtic (0)	4	0.01
Croatian (34)	96	0.15
Cypriot (0)	0	<0.01
Czech (156)	453	0.70
Czechoslovakian (86)	192	0.30
Danish (30)	47	0.07
Dutch (917)	3,139	4.86
Eastern European (103)	103	0.16
English (1,040)	3,551	5.50
Estonian (0)	15	0.02
European (514)	641	0.99
Finnish (0)	74	0.11
French, ex. Basque (64)	743	1.15
French Canadian (109)	321	0.50
German (11,504)	22,141	34.29
German Russian (0)	0	<0.01
Greek (186)	481	0.75
Guyanese (0)	0	<0.01
Hungarian (264)	911	1.41
Icelander (0)	0	<0.01
Iranian (0)	0	<0.01
Irish (2,675)	10,600	16.42
Israeli (0)	0	<0.01
Italian (2,289)	6,865	10.63
Latvian (0)	0	<0.01
Lithuanian (189)	609	0.94
Luxemburger (0)	0	<0.01
Macedonian (10)	10	0.02
Maltese (0)	0	<0.01
New Zealander (0)	0	<0.01
Northern European (42)	42	0.07
Norwegian (95)	143	0.22
Pennsylvania German (3,456)	4,909	7.60

Ancestry	Population	%
Polish (1,656)	4,374	6.77
Portuguese (129)	207	0.32
Romanian (5)	33	0.05
Russian (283)	1,075	1.67
Scandinavian (34)	150	0.23
Scotch-Irish (133)	569	0.88
Scottish (112)	604	0.94
Serbian (0)	0	<0.01
Slavic (53)	139	0.22
Slovak (2,064)	4,301	6.66
Slovene (37)	60	0.09
Soviet Union (0)	0	<0.01
Swedish (122)	491	0.76
Swiss (3)	71	0.11
Turkish (0)	0	<0.01
Ukrainian (414)	843	1.31
Welsh (292)	1,447	2.24
West Indian, ex. Hispanic (143)	217	0.34
Bahamian (0)	0	<0.01
Barbadian (0)	0	<0.01
Belizean (0)	0	<0.01
Bermudan (0)	0	<0.01
British West Indian (0)	12	0.02
Dutch West Indian (0)	0	<0.01
Haitian (0)	0	<0.01
Jamaican (104)	104	0.16
Trinidadian/Tobagonian (0)	0	<0.01
U.S. Virgin Islander (0)	0	<0.01
West Indian (39)	101	0.16
Other West Indian (0)	0	<0.01
Yugoslavian (16)	30	0.05

Hispanic Origin	Population	%
Hispanic or Latino (of any race)	2,145	3.29
Central American, ex. Mexican	112	0.17
Costa Rican	14	0.02
Guatemalan	31	0.05
Honduran	29	0.04
Nicaraguan	1	<0.01
Panamanian	7	0.01
Salvadoran	30	0.05
Other Central American	0	<0.01
Cuban	84	0.13
Dominican Republic	112	0.17
Mexican	346	0.53
Puerto Rican	1,207	1.85
South American	104	0.16
Argentinean	8	0.01
Bolivian	1	<0.01
Chilean	11	0.02
Colombian	21	0.03
Ecuadorian	16	0.02
Paraguayan	1	<0.01
Peruvian	32	0.05
Uruguayan	7	0.01
Venezuelan	6	0.01
Other South American	1	<0.01
Other Hispanic or Latino	180	0.28

Race*	Population	%
African-American/Black (976)	1,270	1.95
Not Hispanic (888)	1,132	1.73
Hispanic (88)	138	0.21
American Indian/Alaska Native (123)	402	0.62
Not Hispanic (100)	333	0.51
Hispanic (23)	69	0.11
Alaska Athabascan (Ala. Nat.) (0)	0	<0.01
Aleut (Alaska Native) (0)	0	<0.01
Apache (0)	5	0.01
Arapaho (0)	0	<0.01
Blackfeet (1)	14	0.02
Canadian/French Am. Ind. (0)	0	<0.01
Central American Ind. (0)	0	<0.01
Cherokee (10)	51	0.08
Cheyenne (0)	0	<0.01
Chickasaw (0)	0	<0.01
Chippewa (1)	2	<0.01
Choctaw (5)	6	0.01
Colville (0)	0	<0.01

Race*	Population	%
Comanche (0)	2	<0.01
Cree (0)	1	<0.01
Creek (0)	0	<0.01
Crow (0)	0	<0.01
Delaware (17)	41	0.06
Hopi (0)	0	<0.01
Houma (0)	2	<0.01
Inupiat (Alaska Native) (0)	0	<0.01
Iroquois (4)	12	0.02
Kiowa (0)	0	<0.01
Lumbee (3)	4	0.01
Menominee (0)	0	<0.01
Mexican American Ind. (3)	6	0.01
Navajo (1)	2	<0.01
Osage (0)	0	<0.01
Ottawa (0)	0	<0.01
Paiute (0)	0	<0.01
Pima (0)	0	<0.01
Potawatomi (0)	0	<0.01
Pueblo (0)	2	<0.01
Puget Sound Salish (0)	0	<0.01
Seminole (2)	7	0.01
Shoshone (0)	0	<0.01
Sioux (6)	14	0.02
South American Ind. (3)	14	0.02
Spanish American Ind. (0)	0	<0.01
Tlingit-Haida (Alaska Native) (0)	0	<0.01
Tohono O'Odham (2)	6	0.01
Tsimshian (Alaska Native) (0)	0	<0.01
Ute (0)	0	<0.01
Yakama (0)	0	<0.01
Yaqui (1)	1	<0.01
Yuman (0)	0	<0.01
Yup'ik (Alaska Native) (0)	3	<0.01
Asian (311)	464	0.71
Not Hispanic (304)	433	0.66
Hispanic (7)	31	0.05
Bangladeshi (0)	0	<0.01
Bhutanese (0)	0	<0.01
Burmese (0)	0	<0.01
Cambodian (5)	5	0.01
Chinese, ex. Taiwanese (75)	106	0.16
Filipino (60)	109	0.17
Hmong (0)	0	<0.01
Indian (57)	90	0.14
Indonesian (0)	6	0.01
Japanese (12)	25	0.04
Korean (45)	60	0.09
Laotian (0)	0	<0.01
Malaysian (0)	0	<0.01
Nepalese (0)	0	<0.01
Pakistani (11)	18	0.03
Sri Lankan (7)	12	0.02
Taiwanese (0)	0	<0.01
Thai (3)	7	0.01
Vietnamese (15)	21	0.03
Hawaii Native/Pacific Islander (27)	50	0.08
Not Hispanic (24)	41	0.06
Hispanic (3)	9	0.01
Fijian (0)	0	<0.01
Guamanian/Chamorro (4)	6	0.01
Marshallese (0)	0	<0.01
Native Hawaiian (14)	29	0.04
Samoan (0)	9	0.01
Tongan (0)	0	<0.01
White (62,519)	63,227	96.90
Not Hispanic (61,168)	61,703	94.57
Hispanic (1,351)	1,524	2.34

Notes: † The Census 2010 population figure is used to calculate the percentages in the Hispanic Origin and Race categories. Ancestry percentages are based on the 2006-2010 American Community Survey population (not shown); ‡ Numbers in parentheses indicate the number of people reporting a single ancestry; * Numbers in parentheses indicate the number of persons reporting this race alone, not in combination with any other race; Please refer to the Explanation of Data for more information.

Centre County
Population: 153,990

Ancestry	Population	%
Afghan (0)	0	<0.01
African, Sub-Saharan (467)	576	0.38
African (170)	261	0.17
Cape Verdean (0)	0	<0.01
Ethiopian (56)	56	0.04
Ghanaian (0)	0	<0.01
Kenyan (0)	0	<0.01
Liberian (42)	42	0.03
Nigerian (156)	156	0.10
Senegalese (0)	0	<0.01
Sierra Leonean (15)	33	0.02
Somalian (0)	0	<0.01
South African (10)	10	0.01
Sudanese (18)	18	0.01
Ugandan (0)	0	<0.01
Zimbabwean (0)	0	<0.01
Other Sub-Saharan African (0)	0	<0.01
Albanian (9)	9	0.01
Alsatian (0)	0	<0.01
American (8,599)	8,599	5.68
Arab (464)	786	0.52
Arab (7)	7	<0.01
Egyptian (17)	48	0.03
Iraqi (0)	0	<0.01
Jordanian (0)	16	0.01
Lebanese (68)	278	0.18
Moroccan (80)	80	0.05
Palestinian (72)	72	0.05
Syrian (27)	76	0.05
Other Arab (193)	209	0.14
Armenian (57)	109	0.07
Assyrian/Chaldean/Syriac (0)	9	0.01
Australian (12)	12	0.01
Austrian (139)	592	0.39
Basque (0)	0	<0.01
Belgian (0)	58	0.04
Brazilian (140)	179	0.12
British (449)	949	0.63
Bulgarian (34)	34	0.02
Cajun (0)	0	<0.01
Canadian (93)	183	0.12
Carpatho Rusyn (0)	28	0.02
Celtic (38)	51	0.03
Croatian (92)	361	0.24
Cypriot (0)	0	<0.01
Czech (197)	943	0.62
Czechoslovakian (140)	377	0.25
Danish (105)	505	0.33
Dutch (1,071)	4,290	2.83
Eastern European (263)	263	0.17
English (3,305)	13,021	8.60
Estonian (0)	18	0.01
European (1,936)	2,042	1.35
Finnish (9)	144	0.10
French, ex. Basque (566)	3,291	2.17
French Canadian (144)	438	0.29
German (15,656)	42,216	27.88
German Russian (0)	0	<0.01
Greek (138)	622	0.41
Guyanese (61)	79	0.05
Hungarian (476)	1,331	0.88
Icelander (40)	53	0.04
Iranian (82)	82	0.05
Irish (4,707)	20,295	13.40
Israeli (30)	60	0.04
Italian (3,535)	11,643	7.69
Latvian (22)	40	0.03
Lithuanian (199)	737	0.49
Luxemburger (0)	18	0.01
Macedonian (26)	43	0.03
Maltese (0)	0	<0.01
New Zealander (0)	0	<0.01
Northern European (115)	115	0.08
Norwegian (218)	819	0.54
Pennsylvania German (963)	1,730	1.14

Ancestry (cont.)	Population	%
Polish (2,078)	7,677	5.07
Portuguese (87)	235	0.16
Romanian (106)	232	0.15
Russian (1,342)	2,849	1.88
Scandinavian (82)	180	0.12
Scotch-Irish (1,106)	3,115	2.06
Scottish (753)	3,697	2.44
Serbian (60)	199	0.13
Slavic (137)	297	0.20
Slovak (1,016)	2,805	1.85
Slovene (105)	174	0.11
Soviet Union (0)	0	<0.01
Swedish (538)	2,028	1.34
Swiss (308)	1,011	0.67
Turkish (173)	200	0.13
Ukrainian (392)	1,345	0.89
Welsh (584)	2,210	1.46
West Indian, ex. Hispanic (234)	315	0.21
Bahamian (0)	0	<0.01
Barbadian (0)	0	<0.01
Belizean (11)	11	0.01
Bermudan (0)	0	<0.01
British West Indian (0)	0	<0.01
Dutch West Indian (0)	56	0.04
Haitian (86)	86	0.06
Jamaican (121)	139	0.09
Trinidadian/Tobagonian (16)	16	0.01
U.S. Virgin Islander (0)	0	<0.01
West Indian (0)	7	<0.01
Other West Indian (0)	0	<0.01
Yugoslavian (10)	77	0.05

Hispanic Origin	Population	%
Hispanic or Latino (of any race)	3,690	2.40
Central American, ex. Mexican	302	0.20
Costa Rican	35	0.02
Guatemalan	93	0.06
Honduran	32	0.02
Nicaraguan	36	0.02
Panamanian	51	0.03
Salvadoran	55	0.04
Other Central American	0	<0.01
Cuban	220	0.14
Dominican Republic	146	0.09
Mexican	785	0.51
Puerto Rican	953	0.62
South American	651	0.42
Argentinean	72	0.05
Bolivian	21	0.01
Chilean	58	0.04
Colombian	198	0.13
Ecuadorian	77	0.05
Paraguayan	2	<0.01
Peruvian	118	0.08
Uruguayan	13	0.01
Venezuelan	87	0.06
Other South American	5	<0.01
Other Hispanic or Latino	633	0.41

Race*	Population	%
African-American/Black (4,638)	5,491	3.57
Not Hispanic (4,456)	5,213	3.39
Hispanic (182)	278	0.18
American Indian/Alaska Native (191)	727	0.47
Not Hispanic (153)	609	0.40
Hispanic (38)	118	0.08
Alaska Athabascan (Ala. Nat.) (0)	0	<0.01
Aleut (Alaska Native) (0)	1	<0.01
Apache (1)	9	0.01
Arapaho (0)	0	<0.01
Blackfeet (5)	19	0.01
Canadian/French Am. Ind. (3)	3	<0.01
Central American Ind. (1)	2	<0.01
Cherokee (18)	109	0.07
Cheyenne (1)	1	<0.01
Chickasaw (3)	6	<0.01
Chippewa (5)	10	0.01
Choctaw (3)	10	0.01
Colville (0)	0	<0.01

Race* (cont.)	Population	%
Comanche (2)	4	<0.01
Cree (1)	1	<0.01
Creek (3)	7	<0.01
Crow (1)	3	<0.01
Delaware (4)	13	0.01
Hopi (0)	0	<0.01
Houma (0)	0	<0.01
Inupiat (Alaska Native) (3)	5	<0.01
Iroquois (5)	26	0.02
Kiowa (6)	7	<0.01
Lumbee (3)	8	0.01
Menominee (0)	0	<0.01
Mexican American Ind. (11)	12	0.01
Navajo (8)	10	0.01
Osage (0)	0	<0.01
Ottawa (0)	0	<0.01
Paiute (0)	0	<0.01
Pima (0)	0	<0.01
Potawatomi (0)	2	<0.01
Pueblo (2)	5	<0.01
Puget Sound Salish (0)	0	<0.01
Seminole (2)	2	<0.01
Shoshone (0)	1	<0.01
Sioux (6)	21	0.01
South American Ind. (8)	17	0.01
Spanish American Ind. (0)	2	<0.01
Tlingit-Haida (Alaska Native) (0)	0	<0.01
Tohono O'Odham (0)	5	<0.01
Tsimshian (Alaska Native) (0)	0	<0.01
Ute (0)	0	<0.01
Yakama (0)	0	<0.01
Yaqui (0)	1	<0.01
Yuman (0)	0	<0.01
Yup'ik (Alaska Native) (0)	0	<0.01
Asian (7,986)	9,030	5.86
Not Hispanic (7,934)	8,934	5.80
Hispanic (52)	96	0.06
Bangladeshi (48)	54	0.04
Bhutanese (0)	0	<0.01
Burmese (15)	20	0.01
Cambodian (24)	32	0.02
Chinese, ex. Taiwanese (3,113)	3,360	2.18
Filipino (224)	403	0.26
Hmong (3)	3	<0.01
Indian (1,726)	1,884	1.22
Indonesian (32)	49	0.03
Japanese (211)	376	0.24
Korean (1,481)	1,602	1.04
Laotian (2)	6	<0.01
Malaysian (151)	166	0.11
Nepalese (18)	19	0.01
Pakistani (113)	127	0.08
Sri Lankan (39)	44	0.03
Taiwanese (292)	313	0.20
Thai (88)	117	0.08
Vietnamese (161)	218	0.14
Hawaii Native/Pacific Islander (48)	137	0.09
Not Hispanic (42)	117	0.08
Hispanic (6)	20	0.01
Fijian (0)	0	<0.01
Guamanian/Chamorro (19)	24	0.02
Marshallese (0)	0	<0.01
Native Hawaiian (8)	34	0.02
Samoan (10)	18	0.01
Tongan (1)	1	<0.01
White (137,625)	139,757	90.76
Not Hispanic (135,427)	137,329	89.18
Hispanic (2,198)	2,428	1.58

*Notes: † The Census 2010 population figure is used to calculate the percentages in the Hispanic Origin and Race categories. Ancestry percentages are based on the 2006-2010 American Community Survey population (not shown); ‡ Numbers in parentheses indicate the number of people reporting a single ancestry; * Numbers in parentheses indicate the number of persons reporting this race alone, not in combination with any other race; Please refer to the Explanation of Data for more information.*

Chester County

Population: 498,886

Ancestry	Population	%
Afghan (0)	0	<0.01
African, Sub-Saharan (1,533)	1,763	0.36
African (743)	934	0.19
Cape Verdean (10)	10	<0.01
Ethiopian (0)	23	0.01
Ghanaian (9)	9	<0.01
Kenyan (73)	73	0.01
Liberian (30)	34	0.01
Nigerian (414)	426	0.09
Senegalese (0)	0	<0.01
Sierra Leonean (14)	14	<0.01
Somalian (0)	0	<0.01
South African (47)	47	0.01
Sudanese (47)	47	0.01
Ugandan (23)	23	<0.01
Zimbabwean (0)	0	<0.01
Other Sub-Saharan African (123)	123	0.03
Albanian (311)	495	0.10
Alsatian (7)	28	0.01
American (22,106)	22,106	4.51
Arab (1,066)	1,791	0.37
Arab (56)	86	0.02
Egyptian (260)	333	0.07
Iraqi (0)	0	<0.01
Jordanian (96)	96	0.02
Lebanese (282)	631	0.13
Moroccan (44)	84	0.02
Palestinian (34)	65	0.01
Syrian (19)	192	0.04
Other Arab (275)	304	0.06
Armenian (376)	811	0.17
Assyrian/Chaldean/Syriac (74)	100	0.02
Australian (94)	135	0.03
Austrian (471)	2,620	0.53
Basque (27)	63	0.01
Belgian (82)	376	0.08
Brazilian (303)	425	0.09
British (2,017)	3,658	0.75
Bulgarian (80)	80	0.02
Cajun (0)	0	<0.01
Canadian (509)	1,038	0.21
Carpatho Rusyn (0)	59	0.01
Celtic (42)	122	0.02
Croatian (366)	839	0.17
Cypriot (9)	9	<0.01
Czech (268)	2,013	0.41
Czechoslovakian (223)	666	0.14
Danish (228)	1,228	0.25
Dutch (1,811)	9,185	1.87
Eastern European (964)	1,147	0.23
English (16,263)	67,172	13.69
Estonian (8)	39	0.01
European (4,678)	5,079	1.04
Finnish (178)	490	0.10
French, ex. Basque (1,752)	12,757	2.60
French Canadian (552)	1,886	0.38
German (28,701)	115,452	23.53
German Russian (0)	33	0.01
Greek (1,727)	3,768	0.77
Guyanese (51)	66	0.01
Hungarian (1,202)	4,146	0.85
Icelander (0)	37	0.01
Iranian (322)	373	0.08
Irish (35,155)	119,155	24.29
Israeli (75)	99	0.02
Italian (27,501)	76,659	15.63
Latvian (182)	374	0.08
Lithuanian (696)	2,943	0.60
Luxemburger (0)	21	<0.01
Macedonian (65)	75	0.02
Maltese (31)	117	0.02
New Zealander (14)	22	<0.01
Northern European (295)	361	0.07
Norwegian (746)	3,474	0.71
Pennsylvania German (2,568)	4,489	0.92

Ancestry	Population	%
Polish (6,425)	26,173	5.34
Portuguese (250)	751	0.15
Romanian (361)	836	0.17
Russian (2,434)	8,193	1.67
Scandinavian (166)	455	0.09
Scotch-Irish (4,624)	12,559	2.56
Scottish (3,376)	13,498	2.75
Serbian (229)	458	0.09
Slavic (131)	516	0.11
Slovak (1,306)	4,513	0.92
Slovene (65)	241	0.05
Soviet Union (0)	0	<0.01
Swedish (1,217)	5,046	1.03
Swiss (540)	2,750	0.56
Turkish (272)	299	0.06
Ukrainian (1,580)	4,651	0.95
Welsh (1,420)	8,539	1.74
West Indian, ex. Hispanic (723)	1,177	0.24
Bahamian (0)	0	<0.01
Barbadian (3)	34	0.01
Belizean (12)	12	<0.01
Bermudan (42)	42	0.01
British West Indian (59)	109	0.02
Dutch West Indian (6)	6	<0.01
Haitian (165)	199	0.04
Jamaican (343)	565	0.12
Trinidadian/Tobagonian (73)	113	0.02
U.S. Virgin Islander (0)	0	<0.01
West Indian (11)	88	0.02
Other West Indian (9)	9	<0.01
Yugoslavian (173)	433	0.09

Hispanic Origin	Population	%
Hispanic or Latino (of any race)	32,503	6.52
Central American, ex. Mexican	1,414	0.28
Costa Rican	69	0.01
Guatemalan	714	0.14
Honduran	218	0.04
Nicaraguan	42	0.01
Panamanian	126	0.03
Salvadoran	238	0.05
Other Central American	7	<0.01
Cuban	720	0.14
Dominican Republic	311	0.06
Mexican	18,860	3.78
Puerto Rican	7,225	1.45
South American	2,294	0.46
Argentinean	305	0.06
Bolivian	81	0.02
Chilean	156	0.03
Colombian	662	0.13
Ecuadorian	548	0.11
Paraguayan	25	0.01
Peruvian	248	0.05
Uruguayan	34	0.01
Venezuelan	226	0.05
Other South American	9	<0.01
Other Hispanic or Latino	1,679	0.34

Race*	Population	%
African-American/Black (30,623)	34,958	7.01
Not Hispanic (29,388)	33,044	6.62
Hispanic (1,235)	1,914	0.38
American Indian/Alaska Native (862)	2,767	0.55
Not Hispanic (535)	2,128	0.43
Hispanic (327)	639	0.13
Alaska Athabascan (Ala. Nat.) (0)	0	<0.01
Aleut (Alaska Native) (3)	3	<0.01
Apache (0)	22	<0.01
Arapaho (0)	2	<0.01
Blackfeet (14)	102	0.02
Canadian/French Am. Ind. (5)	11	<0.01
Central American Ind. (4)	4	<0.01
Cherokee (85)	606	0.12
Cheyenne (0)	3	<0.01
Chickasaw (1)	9	<0.01
Chippewa (12)	37	0.01
Choctaw (11)	34	0.01
Colville (0)	0	<0.01

	Population	%
Comanche (2)	4	<0.01
Cree (0)	1	<0.01
Creek (4)	13	<0.01
Crow (1)	3	<0.01
Delaware (14)	83	0.02
Hopi (0)	3	<0.01
Houma (0)	0	<0.01
Inupiat (Alaska Native) (1)	6	<0.01
Iroquois (24)	63	0.01
Kiowa (1)	3	<0.01
Lumbee (10)	26	0.01
Menominee (0)	0	<0.01
Mexican American Ind. (128)	164	0.03
Navajo (4)	28	0.01
Osage (2)	3	<0.01
Ottawa (0)	1	<0.01
Paiute (0)	0	<0.01
Pima (1)	2	<0.01
Potawatomi (1)	7	<0.01
Pueblo (0)	0	<0.01
Puget Sound Salish (0)	0	<0.01
Seminole (1)	25	0.01
Shoshone (4)	7	<0.01
Sioux (17)	58	0.01
South American Ind. (18)	43	0.01
Spanish American Ind. (7)	13	<0.01
Tlingit-Haida (Alaska Native) (4)	5	<0.01
Tohono O'Odham (0)	0	<0.01
Tsimshian (Alaska Native) (0)	0	<0.01
Ute (3)	3	<0.01
Yakama (0)	0	<0.01
Yaqui (1)	1	<0.01
Yuman (0)	0	<0.01
Yup'ik (Alaska Native) (0)	1	<0.01
Asian (19,296)	21,917	4.39
Not Hispanic (19,216)	21,643	4.34
Hispanic (80)	274	0.05
Bangladeshi (82)	95	0.02
Bhutanese (0)	0	<0.01
Burmese (22)	27	0.01
Cambodian (93)	137	0.03
Chinese, ex. Taiwanese (4,851)	5,476	1.10
Filipino (1,112)	1,653	0.33
Hmong (6)	8	<0.01
Indian (8,480)	9,013	1.81
Indonesian (39)	67	0.01
Japanese (308)	634	0.13
Korean (1,689)	2,040	0.41
Laotian (91)	122	0.02
Malaysian (17)	30	0.01
Nepalese (23)	25	0.01
Pakistani (363)	391	0.08
Sri Lankan (77)	81	0.02
Taiwanese (256)	292	0.06
Thai (124)	201	0.04
Vietnamese (1,196)	1,430	0.29
Hawaii Native/Pacific Islander (161)	417	0.08
Not Hispanic (117)	314	0.06
Hispanic (44)	103	0.02
Fijian (3)	11	<0.01
Guamanian/Chamorro (56)	66	0.01
Marshallese (1)	1	<0.01
Native Hawaiian (35)	122	0.02
Samoan (10)	35	0.01
Tongan (11)	18	<0.01
White (426,707)	434,580	87.11
Not Hispanic (409,561)	415,735	83.33
Hispanic (17,146)	18,845	3.78

*Notes: † The Census 2010 population figure is used to calculate the percentages in the Hispanic Origin and Race categories. Ancestry percentages are based on the 2006-2010 American Community Survey population (not shown); ‡ Numbers in parentheses indicate the number of people reporting a single ancestry; * Numbers in parentheses indicate the number of persons reporting this race alone, not in combination with any other race; Please refer to the Explanation of Data for more information.*

Clarion County

Population: 39,988

Ancestry	Population	%
Afghan (0)	0	<0.01
African, Sub-Saharan (4)	26	0.06
African (0)	19	0.05
Cape Verdean (0)	0	<0.01
Ethiopian (0)	0	<0.01
Ghanaian (0)	0	<0.01
Kenyan (0)	0	<0.01
Liberian (0)	0	<0.01
Nigerian (0)	0	<0.01
Senegalese (0)	0	<0.01
Sierra Leonean (0)	0	<0.01
Somalian (0)	0	<0.01
South African (0)	0	<0.01
Sudanese (0)	0	<0.01
Ugandan (0)	0	<0.01
Zimbabwean (0)	0	<0.01
Other Sub-Saharan African (4)	7	0.02
Albanian (0)	0	<0.01
Alsatian (0)	0	<0.01
American (2,225)	2,225	5.52
Arab (0)	67	0.17
Arab (0)	38	0.09
Egyptian (0)	29	0.07
Iraqi (0)	0	<0.01
Jordanian (0)	0	<0.01
Lebanese (0)	0	<0.01
Moroccan (0)	0	<0.01
Palestinian (0)	0	<0.01
Syrian (0)	0	<0.01
Other Arab (0)	0	<0.01
Armenian (0)	0	<0.01
Assyrian/Chaldean/Syriac (0)	0	<0.01
Australian (8)	8	0.02
Austrian (30)	78	0.19
Basque (0)	0	<0.01
Belgian (8)	59	0.15
Brazilian (0)	0	<0.01
British (53)	142	0.35
Bulgarian (0)	3	0.01
Cajun (0)	0	<0.01
Canadian (0)	34	0.08
Carpatho Rusyn (0)	0	<0.01
Celtic (2)	5	0.01
Croatian (13)	84	0.21
Cypriot (0)	0	<0.01
Czech (74)	125	0.31
Czechoslovakian (0)	39	0.10
Danish (16)	41	0.10
Dutch (295)	1,909	4.74
Eastern European (11)	14	0.03
English (823)	2,881	7.15
Estonian (3)	3	0.01
European (133)	139	0.34
Finnish (4)	4	0.01
French, ex. Basque (175)	875	2.17
French Canadian (31)	136	0.34
German (8,378)	17,785	44.14
German Russian (0)	0	<0.01
Greek (3)	13	0.03
Guyanese (0)	0	<0.01
Hungarian (32)	202	0.50
Icelander (0)	0	<0.01
Iranian (0)	0	<0.01
Irish (1,399)	6,529	16.21
Israeli (0)	0	<0.01
Italian (855)	2,591	6.43
Latvian (0)	3	0.01
Lithuanian (28)	105	0.26
Luxemburger (0)	0	<0.01
Macedonian (0)	0	<0.01
Maltese (0)	0	<0.01
New Zealander (0)	0	<0.01
Northern European (3)	3	0.01
Norwegian (14)	65	0.16
Pennsylvania German (458)	570	1.41

Ancestry	Population	%
Polish (463)	1,344	3.34
Portuguese (13)	40	0.10
Romanian (0)	0	<0.01
Russian (86)	242	0.60
Scandinavian (0)	4	0.01
Scotch-Irish (563)	1,380	3.43
Scottish (272)	1,045	2.59
Serbian (8)	20	0.05
Slavic (9)	17	0.04
Slovak (77)	154	0.38
Slovene (0)	9	0.02
Soviet Union (0)	0	<0.01
Swedish (138)	599	1.49
Swiss (45)	105	0.26
Turkish (0)	9	0.02
Ukrainian (13)	88	0.22
Welsh (86)	346	0.86
West Indian, ex. Hispanic (16)	16	0.04
Bahamian (0)	0	<0.01
Barbadian (0)	0	<0.01
Belizean (0)	0	<0.01
Bermudan (0)	0	<0.01
British West Indian (0)	0	<0.01
Dutch West Indian (0)	0	<0.01
Haitian (0)	0	<0.01
Jamaican (16)	16	0.04
Trinidadian/Tobagonian (0)	0	<0.01
U.S. Virgin Islander (0)	0	<0.01
West Indian (0)	0	<0.01
Other West Indian (0)	0	<0.01
Yugoslavian (0)	0	<0.01

Hispanic Origin	Population	%
Hispanic or Latino (of any race)	245	0.61
Central American, ex. Mexican	22	0.06
Costa Rican	7	0.02
Guatemalan	9	0.02
Honduran	0	<0.01
Nicaraguan	5	0.01
Panamanian	1	<0.01
Salvadoran	0	<0.01
Other Central American	0	<0.01
Cuban	16	0.04
Dominican Republic	6	0.02
Mexican	109	0.27
Puerto Rican	56	0.14
South American	14	0.04
Argentinean	3	0.01
Bolivian	0	<0.01
Chilean	5	0.01
Colombian	3	0.01
Ecuadorian	1	<0.01
Paraguayan	0	<0.01
Peruvian	1	<0.01
Uruguayan	0	<0.01
Venezuelan	1	<0.01
Other South American	0	<0.01
Other Hispanic or Latino	22	0.06

Race*	Population	%
African-American/Black (484)	619	1.55
Not Hispanic (468)	600	1.50
Hispanic (16)	19	0.05
American Indian/Alaska Native (58)	187	0.47
Not Hispanic (45)	159	0.40
Hispanic (13)	28	0.07
Alaska Athabascan (Ala. Nat.) (0)	0	<0.01
Aleut (Alaska Native) (0)	0	<0.01
Apache (0)	3	0.01
Arapaho (0)	0	<0.01
Blackfeet (0)	1	<0.01
Canadian/French Am. Ind. (2)	4	0.01
Central American Ind. (0)	0	<0.01
Cherokee (9)	33	0.08
Cheyenne (0)	2	0.01
Chickasaw (0)	0	<0.01
Chippewa (1)	1	<0.01
Choctaw (2)	2	0.01
Colville (0)	0	<0.01

Race*	Population	%
Comanche (0)	0	<0.01
Cree (1)	1	<0.01
Creek (1)	4	0.01
Crow (0)	0	<0.01
Delaware (1)	3	0.01
Hopi (0)	0	<0.01
Houma (0)	0	<0.01
Inupiat (Alaska Native) (0)	0	<0.01
Iroquois (9)	27	0.07
Kiowa (0)	0	<0.01
Lumbee (0)	0	<0.01
Menominee (0)	0	<0.01
Mexican American Ind. (0)	0	<0.01
Navajo (2)	4	0.01
Osage (0)	0	<0.01
Ottawa (0)	0	<0.01
Paiute (0)	0	<0.01
Pima (0)	0	<0.01
Potawatomi (0)	0	<0.01
Pueblo (0)	0	<0.01
Puget Sound Salish (0)	0	<0.01
Seminole (0)	1	<0.01
Shoshone (0)	0	<0.01
Sioux (1)	3	0.01
South American Ind. (0)	0	<0.01
Spanish American Ind. (0)	0	<0.01
Tlingit-Haida (Alaska Native) (1)	1	<0.01
Tohono O'Odham (0)	0	<0.01
Tsimshian (Alaska Native) (0)	0	<0.01
Ute (0)	0	<0.01
Yakama (0)	0	<0.01
Yaqui (0)	0	<0.01
Yuman (0)	0	<0.01
Yup'ik (Alaska Native) (1)	1	<0.01
Asian (191)	258	0.65
Not Hispanic (191)	257	0.64
Hispanic (0)	1	<0.01
Bangladeshi (0)	0	<0.01
Bhutanese (0)	0	<0.01
Burmese (0)	0	<0.01
Cambodian (1)	1	<0.01
Chinese, ex. Taiwanese (52)	62	0.16
Filipino (19)	37	0.09
Hmong (0)	0	<0.01
Indian (41)	48	0.12
Indonesian (0)	0	<0.01
Japanese (5)	11	0.03
Korean (33)	49	0.12
Laotian (0)	0	<0.01
Malaysian (0)	0	<0.01
Nepalese (0)	0	<0.01
Pakistani (1)	1	<0.01
Sri Lankan (0)	0	<0.01
Taiwanese (1)	2	0.01
Thai (6)	7	0.02
Vietnamese (17)	18	0.05
Hawaii Native/Pacific Islander (8)	15	0.04
Not Hispanic (5)	12	0.03
Hispanic (3)	3	0.01
Fijian (0)	0	<0.01
Guamanian/Chamorro (4)	4	0.01
Marshallese (0)	0	<0.01
Native Hawaiian (0)	6	0.02
Samoan (1)	1	<0.01
Tongan (0)	0	<0.01
White (38,873)	39,164	97.94
Not Hispanic (38,724)	38,989	97.50
Hispanic (149)	175	0.44

Notes: † The Census 2010 population figure is used to calculate the percentages in the Hispanic Origin and Race categories. Ancestry percentages are based on the 2006-2010 American Community Survey population (not shown); ‡ Numbers in parentheses indicate the number of people reporting a single ancestry; * Numbers in parentheses indicate the number of persons reporting this race alone, not in combination with any other race; Please refer to the Explanation of Data for more information.

Clearfield County

Population: 81,642

Ancestry	Population	%
Afghan (0)	0	<0.01
African, Sub-Saharan (27)	27	0.03
African (23)	23	0.03
Cape Verdean (0)	0	<0.01
Ethiopian (0)	0	<0.01
Ghanaian (0)	0	<0.01
Kenyan (0)	0	<0.01
Liberian (0)	0	<0.01
Nigerian (0)	0	<0.01
Senegalese (0)	0	<0.01
Sierra Leonean (4)	4	<0.01
Somalian (0)	0	<0.01
South African (0)	0	<0.01
Sudanese (0)	0	<0.01
Ugandan (0)	0	<0.01
Zimbabwean (0)	0	<0.01
Other Sub-Saharan African (0)	0	<0.01
Albanian (0)	0	<0.01
Alsatian (0)	0	<0.01
American (12,533)	12,533	15.26
Arab (113)	167	0.20
Arab (0)	0	<0.01
Egyptian (0)	0	<0.01
Iraqi (0)	0	<0.01
Jordanian (0)	0	<0.01
Lebanese (76)	125	0.15
Moroccan (0)	0	<0.01
Palestinian (0)	0	<0.01
Syrian (37)	42	0.05
Other Arab (0)	0	<0.01
Armenian (0)	0	<0.01
Assyrian/Chaldean/Syriac (0)	0	<0.01
Australian (15)	15	0.02
Austrian (110)	340	0.41
Basque (0)	0	<0.01
Belgian (47)	115	0.14
Brazilian (10)	10	0.01
British (57)	134	0.16
Bulgarian (0)	0	<0.01
Cajun (0)	0	<0.01
Canadian (69)	161	0.20
Carpatho Rusyn (0)	18	0.02
Celtic (4)	18	0.02
Croatian (13)	64	0.08
Cypriot (0)	0	<0.01
Czech (121)	516	0.63
Czechoslovakian (143)	248	0.30
Danish (21)	82	0.10
Dutch (316)	3,102	3.78
Eastern European (25)	35	0.04
English (3,281)	9,475	11.54
Estonian (0)	0	<0.01
European (194)	216	0.26
Finnish (6)	16	0.02
French, ex. Basque (795)	3,021	3.68
French Canadian (28)	164	0.20
German (6,780)	20,538	25.01
German Russian (0)	0	<0.01
Greek (40)	190	0.23
Guyanese (0)	0	<0.01
Hungarian (211)	434	0.53
Icelander (0)	0	<0.01
Iranian (0)	11	0.01
Irish (3,025)	10,388	12.65
Israeli (0)	0	<0.01
Italian (2,796)	6,716	8.18
Latvian (0)	0	<0.01
Lithuanian (220)	592	0.72
Luxemburger (0)	0	<0.01
Macedonian (0)	0	<0.01
Maltese (0)	0	<0.01
New Zealander (0)	0	<0.01
Northern European (22)	22	0.03
Norwegian (137)	304	0.37
Pennsylvania German (477)	847	1.03

Ancestry (cont.)	Population	%
Polish (1,950)	5,216	6.35
Portuguese (0)	23	0.03
Romanian (0)	18	0.02
Russian (174)	481	0.59
Scandinavian (15)	20	0.02
Scotch-Irish (668)	1,581	1.92
Scottish (680)	2,187	2.66
Serbian (57)	69	0.08
Slavic (50)	214	0.26
Slovak (1,421)	2,799	3.41
Slovene (32)	75	0.09
Soviet Union (0)	0	<0.01
Swedish (601)	2,310	2.81
Swiss (19)	229	0.28
Turkish (3)	3	<0.01
Ukrainian (258)	596	0.73
Welsh (161)	1,022	1.24
West Indian, ex. Hispanic (29)	29	0.04
Bahamian (0)	0	<0.01
Barbadian (0)	0	<0.01
Belizean (0)	0	<0.01
Bermudan (0)	0	<0.01
British West Indian (0)	0	<0.01
Dutch West Indian (10)	10	0.01
Haitian (0)	0	<0.01
Jamaican (11)	11	0.01
Trinidadian/Tobagonian (0)	0	<0.01
U.S. Virgin Islander (0)	0	<0.01
West Indian (8)	8	0.01
Other West Indian (0)	0	<0.01
Yugoslavian (0)	15	0.02

Hispanic Origin	Population	%
Hispanic or Latino (of any race)	1,907	2.34
Central American, ex. Mexican	91	0.11
Costa Rican	2	<0.01
Guatemalan	42	0.05
Honduran	19	0.02
Nicaraguan	4	<0.01
Panamanian	7	0.01
Salvadoran	17	0.02
Other Central American	0	<0.01
Cuban	74	0.09
Dominican Republic	357	0.44
Mexican	599	0.73
Puerto Rican	145	0.18
South American	232	0.28
Argentinean	0	<0.01
Bolivian	2	<0.01
Chilean	3	<0.01
Colombian	180	0.22
Ecuadorian	20	0.02
Paraguayan	1	<0.01
Peruvian	13	0.02
Uruguayan	2	<0.01
Venezuelan	11	0.01
Other South American	0	<0.01
Other Hispanic or Latino	409	0.50

Race*	Population	%
African-American/Black (1,862)	2,107	2.58
Not Hispanic (1,697)	1,887	2.31
Hispanic (165)	220	0.27
American Indian/Alaska Native (86)	313	0.38
Not Hispanic (51)	254	0.31
Hispanic (35)	59	0.07
Alaska Athabascan (Ala. Nat.) (0)	0	<0.01
Aleut (Alaska Native) (0)	0	<0.01
Apache (0)	10	0.01
Arapaho (0)	0	<0.01
Blackfeet (5)	16	0.02
Canadian/French Am. Ind. (0)	0	<0.01
Central American Ind. (0)	1	<0.01
Cherokee (5)	53	0.06
Cheyenne (0)	3	<0.01
Chickasaw (0)	0	<0.01
Chippewa (4)	4	<0.01
Choctaw (1)	2	<0.01
Colville (0)	0	<0.01

Race* (cont.)	Population	%
Comanche (0)	0	<0.01
Cree (0)	1	<0.01
Creek (0)	0	<0.01
Crow (0)	0	<0.01
Delaware (4)	6	0.01
Hopi (0)	1	<0.01
Houma (0)	0	<0.01
Inupiat (Alaska Native) (0)	0	<0.01
Iroquois (1)	21	0.03
Kiowa (1)	1	<0.01
Lumbee (0)	0	<0.01
Menominee (0)	0	<0.01
Mexican American Ind. (7)	11	0.01
Navajo (0)	1	<0.01
Osage (0)	0	<0.01
Ottawa (0)	2	<0.01
Paiute (0)	0	<0.01
Pima (0)	0	<0.01
Potawatomi (0)	0	<0.01
Pueblo (1)	1	<0.01
Puget Sound Salish (0)	0	<0.01
Seminole (0)	7	0.01
Shoshone (0)	0	<0.01
Sioux (0)	4	<0.01
South American Ind. (0)	1	<0.01
Spanish American Ind. (0)	3	<0.01
Tlingit-Haida (Alaska Native) (0)	0	<0.01
Tohono O'Odham (0)	0	<0.01
Tsimshian (Alaska Native) (0)	0	<0.01
Ute (0)	3	<0.01
Yakama (0)	0	<0.01
Yaqui (0)	0	<0.01
Yuman (0)	0	<0.01
Yup'ik (Alaska Native) (0)	0	<0.01
Asian (389)	559	0.68
Not Hispanic (384)	547	0.67
Hispanic (5)	12	0.01
Bangladeshi (2)	3	<0.01
Bhutanese (0)	0	<0.01
Burmese (2)	2	<0.01
Cambodian (6)	7	0.01
Chinese, ex. Taiwanese (78)	92	0.11
Filipino (50)	82	0.10
Hmong (0)	0	<0.01
Indian (110)	139	0.17
Indonesian (0)	1	<0.01
Japanese (13)	44	0.05
Korean (48)	77	0.09
Laotian (7)	7	<0.01
Malaysian (1)	1	<0.01
Nepalese (0)	1	<0.01
Pakistani (17)	19	0.02
Sri Lankan (0)	1	<0.01
Taiwanese (2)	3	<0.01
Thai (3)	12	0.01
Vietnamese (36)	44	0.05
Hawaii Native/Pacific Islander (16)	35	0.04
Not Hispanic (15)	33	0.04
Hispanic (1)	2	<0.01
Fijian (0)	0	<0.01
Guamanian/Chamorro (3)	7	0.01
Marshallese (0)	0	<0.01
Native Hawaiian (8)	13	0.02
Samoan (0)	1	<0.01
Tongan (0)	0	<0.01
White (77,912)	78,557	96.22
Not Hispanic (77,031)	77,532	94.97
Hispanic (881)	1,025	1.26

*Notes: † The Census 2010 population figure is used to calculate the percentages in the Hispanic Origin and Race categories. Ancestry percentages are based on the 2006-2010 American Community Survey population (not shown); ‡ Numbers in parentheses indicate the number of people reporting a single ancestry; * Numbers in parentheses indicate the number of persons reporting this race alone, not in combination with any other race; Please refer to the Explanation of Data for more information.*

Clinton County

Population: 39,238

Ancestry	Population	%
Afghan (0)	0	<0.01
African, Sub-Saharan (50)	55	0.14
African (3)	8	0.02
Cape Verdean (0)	0	<0.01
Ethiopian (0)	0	<0.01
Ghanaian (0)	0	<0.01
Kenyan (0)	0	<0.01
Liberian (0)	0	<0.01
Nigerian (0)	0	<0.01
Senegalese (8)	8	0.02
Sierra Leonean (0)	0	<0.01
Somalian (0)	0	<0.01
South African (0)	0	<0.01
Sudanese (0)	0	<0.01
Ugandan (0)	0	<0.01
Zimbabwean (8)	8	0.02
Other Sub-Saharan African (31)	31	0.08
Albanian (0)	0	<0.01
Alsatian (0)	41	0.11
American (2,376)	2,376	6.10
Arab (35)	35	0.09
Arab (0)	0	<0.01
Egyptian (5)	5	0.01
Iraqi (0)	0	<0.01
Jordanian (0)	0	<0.01
Lebanese (0)	0	<0.01
Moroccan (0)	0	<0.01
Palestinian (0)	0	<0.01
Syrian (0)	0	<0.01
Other Arab (30)	30	0.08
Armenian (0)	0	<0.01
Assyrian/Chaldean/Syriac (0)	0	<0.01
Australian (0)	0	<0.01
Austrian (25)	146	0.37
Basque (0)	0	<0.01
Belgian (8)	30	0.08
Brazilian (5)	5	0.01
British (65)	124	0.32
Bulgarian (0)	0	<0.01
Cajun (0)	15	0.04
Canadian (7)	27	0.07
Carpatho Rusyn (0)	0	<0.01
Celtic (0)	0	<0.01
Croatian (3)	27	0.07
Cypriot (0)	0	<0.01
Czech (63)	131	0.34
Czechoslovakian (6)	16	0.04
Danish (0)	115	0.30
Dutch (315)	1,517	3.89
Eastern European (33)	33	0.08
English (985)	3,037	7.79
Estonian (0)	0	<0.01
European (272)	289	0.74
Finnish (14)	41	0.11
French, ex. Basque (263)	872	2.24
French Canadian (22)	93	0.24
German (7,043)	14,612	37.50
German Russian (0)	0	<0.01
Greek (21)	52	0.13
Guyanese (0)	0	<0.01
Hungarian (26)	134	0.34
Icelander (3)	3	0.01
Iranian (0)	0	<0.01
Irish (1,762)	5,794	14.87
Israeli (0)	0	<0.01
Italian (1,279)	3,448	8.85
Latvian (5)	5	0.01
Lithuanian (75)	240	0.62
Luxemburger (0)	0	<0.01
Macedonian (0)	0	<0.01
Maltese (0)	0	<0.01
New Zealander (0)	0	<0.01
Northern European (28)	44	0.11
Norwegian (46)	127	0.33
Pennsylvania German (830)	1,064	2.73

Ancestry	Population	%
Polish (413)	1,230	3.16
Portuguese (5)	19	0.05
Romanian (26)	39	0.10
Russian (56)	181	0.46
Scandinavian (6)	6	0.02
Scotch-Irish (279)	755	1.94
Scottish (143)	547	1.40
Serbian (0)	0	<0.01
Slavic (3)	15	0.04
Slovak (141)	330	0.85
Slovene (18)	18	0.05
Soviet Union (0)	0	<0.01
Swedish (184)	652	1.67
Swiss (122)	296	0.76
Turkish (0)	0	<0.01
Ukrainian (27)	77	0.20
Welsh (96)	375	0.96
West Indian, ex. Hispanic (57)	57	0.15
Bahamian (0)	0	<0.01
Barbadian (0)	0	<0.01
Belizean (0)	0	<0.01
Bermudan (0)	0	<0.01
British West Indian (0)	0	<0.01
Dutch West Indian (0)	0	<0.01
Haitian (0)	0	<0.01
Jamaican (34)	34	0.09
Trinidadian/Tobagonian (23)	23	0.06
U.S. Virgin Islander (0)	0	<0.01
West Indian (0)	0	<0.01
Other West Indian (0)	0	<0.01
Yugoslavian (0)	0	<0.01

Hispanic Origin	Population	%
Hispanic or Latino (of any race)	437	1.11
Central American, ex. Mexican	29	0.07
Costa Rican	1	<0.01
Guatemalan	10	0.03
Honduran	9	0.02
Nicaraguan	0	<0.01
Panamanian	1	<0.01
Salvadoran	8	0.02
Other Central American	0	<0.01
Cuban	19	0.05
Dominican Republic	22	0.06
Mexican	147	0.37
Puerto Rican	132	0.34
South American	15	0.04
Argentinean	2	0.01
Bolivian	1	<0.01
Chilean	0	<0.01
Colombian	6	0.02
Ecuadorian	2	0.01
Paraguayan	0	<0.01
Peruvian	2	0.01
Uruguayan	1	<0.01
Venezuelan	1	<0.01
Other South American	0	<0.01
Other Hispanic or Latino	73	0.19

Race*	Population	%
African-American/Black (625)	753	1.92
Not Hispanic (612)	732	1.87
Hispanic (13)	21	0.05
American Indian/Alaska Native (34)	149	0.38
Not Hispanic (29)	143	0.36
Hispanic (5)	6	0.02
Alaska Athabascan (Ala. Nat.) (0)	0	<0.01
Aleut (Alaska Native) (0)	0	<0.01
Apache (0)	4	0.01
Arapaho (0)	0	<0.01
Blackfeet (1)	8	0.02
Canadian/French Am. Ind. (0)	1	<0.01
Central American Ind. (0)	0	<0.01
Cherokee (8)	38	0.10
Cheyenne (0)	0	<0.01
Chickasaw (0)	0	<0.01
Chippewa (1)	1	<0.01
Choctaw (1)	1	<0.01
Colville (0)	0	<0.01

Race* (cont.)	Population	%
Comanche (0)	0	<0.01
Cree (0)	1	<0.01
Creek (1)	2	0.01
Crow (2)	4	0.01
Delaware (1)	7	0.02
Hopi (0)	0	<0.01
Houma (0)	0	<0.01
Inupiat (Alaska Native) (2)	3	0.01
Iroquois (2)	10	0.03
Kiowa (0)	4	0.01
Lumbee (0)	0	<0.01
Menominee (0)	0	<0.01
Mexican American Ind. (0)	0	<0.01
Navajo (0)	0	<0.01
Osage (0)	0	<0.01
Ottawa (0)	0	<0.01
Paiute (0)	0	<0.01
Pima (0)	0	<0.01
Potawatomi (0)	0	<0.01
Pueblo (0)	0	<0.01
Puget Sound Salish (0)	0	<0.01
Seminole (0)	0	<0.01
Shoshone (0)	0	<0.01
Sioux (1)	2	0.01
South American Ind. (2)	2	0.01
Spanish American Ind. (0)	0	<0.01
Tlingit-Haida (Alaska Native) (0)	0	<0.01
Tohono O'Odham (0)	0	<0.01
Tsimshian (Alaska Native) (0)	0	<0.01
Ute (0)	0	<0.01
Yakama (0)	0	<0.01
Yaqui (0)	0	<0.01
Yuman (0)	0	<0.01
Yup'ik (Alaska Native) (0)	0	<0.01
Asian (200)	269	0.69
Not Hispanic (199)	268	0.68
Hispanic (1)	1	<0.01
Bangladeshi (3)	3	0.01
Bhutanese (0)	0	<0.01
Burmese (0)	0	<0.01
Cambodian (0)	0	<0.01
Chinese, ex. Taiwanese (39)	50	0.13
Filipino (22)	36	0.09
Hmong (0)	0	<0.01
Indian (61)	69	0.18
Indonesian (1)	2	0.01
Japanese (7)	22	0.06
Korean (27)	41	0.10
Laotian (0)	0	<0.01
Malaysian (0)	0	<0.01
Nepalese (0)	0	<0.01
Pakistani (4)	4	0.01
Sri Lankan (6)	6	0.02
Taiwanese (5)	6	0.02
Thai (11)	18	0.05
Vietnamese (10)	10	0.03
Hawaii Native/Pacific Islander (15)	23	0.06
Not Hispanic (15)	22	0.06
Hispanic (0)	1	<0.01
Fijian (0)	0	<0.01
Guamanian/Chamorro (2)	4	0.01
Marshallese (0)	0	<0.01
Native Hawaiian (11)	12	0.03
Samoan (0)	0	<0.01
Tongan (0)	0	<0.01
White (37,860)	38,187	97.32
Not Hispanic (37,618)	37,923	96.65
Hispanic (242)	264	0.67

*Notes: † The Census 2010 population figure is used to calculate the percentages in the Hispanic Origin and Race categories. Ancestry percentages are based on the 2006-2010 American Community Survey population (not shown); ‡ Numbers in parentheses indicate the number of people reporting a single ancestry; * Numbers in parentheses indicate the number of persons reporting this race alone, not in combination with any other race; Please refer to the Explanation of Data for more information.*

Columbia County

Population: 67,295

Ancestry	Population	%
Afghan (0)	0	<0.01
African, Sub-Saharan (45)	45	0.07
African (31)	31	0.05
Cape Verdean (0)	0	<0.01
Ethiopian (13)	13	0.02
Ghanaian (1)	1	<0.01
Kenyan (0)	0	<0.01
Liberian (0)	0	<0.01
Nigerian (0)	0	<0.01
Senegalese (0)	0	<0.01
Sierra Leonean (0)	0	<0.01
Somalian (0)	0	<0.01
South African (0)	0	<0.01
Sudanese (0)	0	<0.01
Ugandan (0)	0	<0.01
Zimbabwean (0)	0	<0.01
Other Sub-Saharan African (0)	0	<0.01
Albanian (0)	13	0.02
Alsatian (0)	0	<0.01
American (3,145)	3,145	4.72
Arab (28)	28	0.04
Arab (0)	0	<0.01
Egyptian (0)	0	<0.01
Iraqi (0)	0	<0.01
Jordanian (0)	0	<0.01
Lebanese (13)	13	0.02
Moroccan (0)	0	<0.01
Palestinian (0)	0	<0.01
Syrian (0)	0	<0.01
Other Arab (15)	15	0.02
Armenian (2)	40	0.06
Assyrian/Chaldean/Syriac (0)	3	<0.01
Australian (0)	19	0.03
Austrian (91)	326	0.49
Basque (0)	17	0.03
Belgian (16)	16	0.02
Brazilian (0)	0	<0.01
British (152)	304	0.46
Bulgarian (0)	0	<0.01
Cajun (0)	0	<0.01
Canadian (39)	64	0.10
Carpatho Rusyn (11)	25	0.04
Celtic (0)	0	<0.01
Croatian (20)	38	0.06
Cypriot (0)	0	<0.01
Czech (226)	338	0.51
Czechoslovakian (26)	139	0.21
Danish (43)	94	0.14
Dutch (1,724)	4,780	7.17
Eastern European (24)	46	0.07
English (2,708)	6,242	9.37
Estonian (0)	0	<0.01
European (308)	315	0.47
Finnish (14)	27	0.04
French, ex. Basque (433)	1,532	2.30
French Canadian (21)	130	0.20
German (12,213)	24,552	36.84
German Russian (0)	0	<0.01
Greek (135)	319	0.48
Guyanese (0)	0	<0.01
Hungarian (237)	805	1.21
Icelander (0)	0	<0.01
Iranian (16)	16	0.02
Irish (2,888)	8,986	13.48
Israeli (0)	0	<0.01
Italian (2,388)	5,565	8.35
Latvian (0)	0	<0.01
Lithuanian (129)	599	0.90
Luxemburger (0)	0	<0.01
Macedonian (0)	0	<0.01
Maltese (0)	0	<0.01
New Zealander (0)	0	<0.01
Northern European (3)	9	0.01
Norwegian (97)	238	0.36
Pennsylvania German (1,810)	2,834	4.25

Ancestry	Population	%
Polish (1,722)	4,593	6.89
Portuguese (72)	75	0.11
Romanian (23)	32	0.05
Russian (241)	579	0.87
Scandinavian (59)	76	0.11
Scotch-Irish (324)	660	0.99
Scottish (286)	1,019	1.53
Serbian (27)	60	0.09
Slavic (19)	58	0.09
Slovak (264)	838	1.26
Slovene (0)	14	0.02
Soviet Union (0)	0	<0.01
Swedish (140)	427	0.64
Swiss (26)	145	0.22
Turkish (0)	16	0.02
Ukrainian (450)	923	1.39
Welsh (606)	1,868	2.80
West Indian, ex. Hispanic (25)	26	0.04
Bahamian (0)	0	<0.01
Barbadian (0)	0	<0.01
Belizean (0)	0	<0.01
Bermudan (0)	0	<0.01
British West Indian (0)	0	<0.01
Dutch West Indian (0)	0	<0.01
Haitian (0)	0	<0.01
Jamaican (25)	26	0.04
Trinidadian/Tobagonian (0)	0	<0.01
U.S. Virgin Islander (0)	0	<0.01
West Indian (0)	0	<0.01
Other West Indian (0)	0	<0.01
Yugoslavian (13)	16	0.02

Hispanic Origin	Population	%
Hispanic or Latino (of any race)	1,349	2.00
Central American, ex. Mexican	219	0.33
Costa Rican	11	0.02
Guatemalan	35	0.05
Honduran	9	0.01
Nicaraguan	12	0.02
Panamanian	5	0.01
Salvadoran	142	0.21
Other Central American	5	0.01
Cuban	54	0.08
Dominican Republic	54	0.08
Mexican	265	0.39
Puerto Rican	533	0.79
South American	96	0.14
Argentinean	4	0.01
Bolivian	4	0.01
Chilean	10	0.01
Colombian	31	0.05
Ecuadorian	17	0.03
Paraguayan	0	<0.01
Peruvian	29	0.04
Uruguayan	1	<0.01
Venezuelan	0	<0.01
Other South American	0	<0.01
Other Hispanic or Latino	128	0.19

Race*	Population	%
African-American/Black (1,246)	1,514	2.25
Not Hispanic (1,190)	1,434	2.13
Hispanic (56)	80	0.12
American Indian/Alaska Native (87)	334	0.50
Not Hispanic (57)	288	0.43
Hispanic (30)	46	0.07
Alaska Athabascan (Ala. Nat.) (0)	0	<0.01
Aleut (Alaska Native) (1)	1	<0.01
Apache (1)	15	0.02
Arapaho (0)	0	<0.01
Blackfeet (1)	24	0.04
Canadian/French Am. Ind. (0)	2	<0.01
Central American Ind. (6)	6	0.01
Cherokee (9)	46	0.07
Cheyenne (0)	1	<0.01
Chickasaw (0)	0	<0.01
Chippewa (0)	0	<0.01
Choctaw (0)	3	<0.01
Colville (0)	0	<0.01

	Population	%
Comanche (0)	1	<0.01
Cree (0)	0	<0.01
Creek (0)	2	<0.01
Crow (1)	1	<0.01
Delaware (0)	18	0.03
Hopi (0)	0	<0.01
Houma (0)	0	<0.01
Inupiat (Alaska Native) (0)	0	<0.01
Iroquois (5)	23	0.03
Kiowa (0)	0	<0.01
Lumbee (3)	7	0.01
Menominee (0)	0	<0.01
Mexican American Ind. (3)	5	<0.01
Navajo (0)	0	<0.01
Osage (0)	0	<0.01
Ottawa (0)	0	<0.01
Paiute (0)	0	<0.01
Pima (0)	0	<0.01
Potawatomi (0)	0	<0.01
Pueblo (0)	0	<0.01
Puget Sound Salish (0)	1	<0.01
Seminole (1)	4	0.01
Shoshone (1)	1	<0.01
Sioux (4)	11	0.02
South American Ind. (0)	2	<0.01
Spanish American Ind. (0)	0	<0.01
Tlingit-Haida (Alaska Native) (0)	0	<0.01
Tohono O'Odham (0)	0	<0.01
Tsimshian (Alaska Native) (0)	0	<0.01
Ute (0)	0	<0.01
Yakama (0)	0	<0.01
Yaqui (0)	0	<0.01
Yuman (0)	0	<0.01
Yup'ik (Alaska Native) (0)	0	<0.01
Asian (563)	713	1.06
Not Hispanic (547)	686	1.02
Hispanic (16)	27	0.04
Bangladeshi (5)	22	0.03
Bhutanese (0)	0	<0.01
Burmese (0)	3	<0.01
Cambodian (2)	3	<0.01
Chinese, ex. Taiwanese (131)	150	0.22
Filipino (46)	79	0.12
Hmong (1)	1	<0.01
Indian (176)	203	0.30
Indonesian (11)	12	0.02
Japanese (14)	41	0.06
Korean (60)	76	0.11
Laotian (0)	1	<0.01
Malaysian (1)	1	<0.01
Nepalese (13)	15	0.02
Pakistani (8)	14	0.02
Sri Lankan (3)	3	<0.01
Taiwanese (2)	2	<0.01
Thai (10)	13	0.02
Vietnamese (57)	60	0.09
Hawaii Native/Pacific Islander (15)	31	0.05
Not Hispanic (14)	28	0.04
Hispanic (1)	3	<0.01
Fijian (0)	0	<0.01
Guamanian/Chamorro (12)	16	0.02
Marshallese (0)	0	<0.01
Native Hawaiian (1)	3	<0.01
Samoan (1)	3	<0.01
Tongan (0)	0	<0.01
White (64,227)	64,882	96.41
Not Hispanic (63,500)	64,063	95.20
Hispanic (727)	819	1.22

*Notes: † The Census 2010 population figure is used to calculate the percentages in the Hispanic Origin and Race categories. Ancestry percentages are based on the 2006-2010 American Community Survey population (not shown); ‡ Numbers in parentheses indicate the number of people reporting a single ancestry; * Numbers in parentheses indicate the number of persons reporting this race alone, not in combination with any other race; Please refer to the Explanation of Data for more information.*

Crawford County

Population: 88,765

Ancestry	Population	%
Afghan (0)	3	<0.01
African, Sub-Saharan (9)	41	0.05
African (0)	7	0.01
Cape Verdean (0)	0	<0.01
Ethiopian (0)	0	<0.01
Ghanaian (0)	0	<0.01
Kenyan (0)	0	<0.01
Liberian (0)	0	<0.01
Nigerian (0)	0	<0.01
Senegalese (0)	0	<0.01
Sierra Leonean (0)	0	<0.01
Somalian (0)	0	<0.01
South African (9)	31	0.03
Sudanese (0)	0	<0.01
Ugandan (0)	0	<0.01
Zimbabwean (0)	0	<0.01
Other Sub-Saharan African (0)	3	<0.01
Albanian (11)	11	0.01
Alsatian (0)	0	<0.01
American (4,719)	4,719	5.29
Arab (171)	324	0.36
Arab (3)	3	<0.01
Egyptian (0)	0	<0.01
Iraqi (3)	3	<0.01
Jordanian (8)	8	0.01
Lebanese (50)	184	0.21
Moroccan (0)	0	<0.01
Palestinian (0)	0	<0.01
Syrian (30)	49	0.05
Other Arab (77)	77	0.09
Armenian (0)	0	<0.01
Assyrian/Chaldean/Syriac (2)	8	0.01
Australian (4)	24	0.03
Austrian (81)	185	0.21
Basque (0)	0	<0.01
Belgian (6)	32	0.04
Brazilian (0)	0	<0.01
British (90)	208	0.23
Bulgarian (3)	19	0.02
Cajun (0)	0	<0.01
Canadian (47)	87	0.10
Carpatho Rusyn (7)	7	0.01
Celtic (17)	17	0.02
Croatian (69)	318	0.36
Cypriot (0)	0	<0.01
Czech (160)	618	0.69
Czechoslovakian (38)	116	0.13
Danish (18)	154	0.17
Dutch (437)	2,751	3.09
Eastern European (18)	18	0.02
English (2,952)	10,719	12.02
Estonian (0)	3	<0.01
European (536)	566	0.63
Finnish (30)	118	0.13
French, ex. Basque (422)	3,118	3.50
French Canadian (73)	394	0.44
German (10,871)	30,749	34.49
German Russian (0)	0	<0.01
Greek (113)	323	0.36
Guyanese (0)	0	<0.01
Hungarian (306)	972	1.09
Icelander (0)	12	0.01
Iranian (0)	0	<0.01
Irish (3,557)	16,052	18.01
Israeli (0)	0	<0.01
Italian (2,951)	7,453	8.36
Latvian (10)	10	0.01
Lithuanian (138)	278	0.31
Luxemburger (0)	0	<0.01
Macedonian (0)	0	<0.01
Maltese (0)	0	<0.01
New Zealander (0)	0	<0.01
Northern European (41)	41	0.05
Norwegian (78)	519	0.58
Pennsylvania German (807)	1,191	1.34

Ancestry	Population	%
Polish (1,886)	5,688	6.38
Portuguese (27)	91	0.10
Romanian (17)	52	0.06
Russian (156)	798	0.90
Scandinavian (7)	37	0.04
Scotch-Irish (1,140)	3,334	3.74
Scottish (545)	2,133	2.39
Serbian (23)	121	0.14
Slavic (146)	208	0.23
Slovak (468)	1,149	1.29
Slovene (5)	96	0.11
Soviet Union (0)	0	<0.01
Swedish (456)	1,904	2.14
Swiss (314)	778	0.87
Turkish (40)	40	0.04
Ukrainian (252)	593	0.67
Welsh (176)	1,334	1.50
West Indian, ex. Hispanic (53)	76	0.09
Bahamian (0)	0	<0.01
Barbadian (0)	0	<0.01
Belizean (0)	0	<0.01
Bermudan (0)	0	<0.01
British West Indian (0)	0	<0.01
Dutch West Indian (0)	0	<0.01
Haitian (29)	29	0.03
Jamaican (24)	47	0.05
Trinidadian/Tobagonian (0)	0	<0.01
U.S. Virgin Islander (0)	0	<0.01
West Indian (0)	0	<0.01
Other West Indian (0)	0	<0.01
Yugoslavian (16)	109	0.12

Hispanic Origin	Population	%
Hispanic or Latino (of any race)	823	0.93
Central American, ex. Mexican	25	0.03
Costa Rican	4	<0.01
Guatemalan	9	0.01
Honduran	3	<0.01
Nicaraguan	1	<0.01
Panamanian	5	0.01
Salvadoran	3	<0.01
Other Central American	0	<0.01
Cuban	20	0.02
Dominican Republic	6	0.01
Mexican	313	0.35
Puerto Rican	241	0.27
South American	40	0.05
Argentinean	1	<0.01
Bolivian	2	<0.01
Chilean	2	<0.01
Colombian	15	0.02
Ecuadorian	4	<0.01
Paraguayan	0	<0.01
Peruvian	14	0.02
Uruguayan	0	<0.01
Venezuelan	2	<0.01
Other South American	0	<0.01
Other Hispanic or Latino	178	0.20

Race*	Population	%
African-American/Black (1,547)	2,064	2.33
Not Hispanic (1,503)	1,982	2.23
Hispanic (44)	82	0.09
American Indian/Alaska Native (162)	486	0.55
Not Hispanic (150)	456	0.51
Hispanic (12)	30	0.03
Alaska Athabascan (Ala. Nat.) (0)	0	<0.01
Aleut (Alaska Native) (0)	0	<0.01
Apache (1)	9	0.01
Arapaho (0)	0	<0.01
Blackfeet (8)	35	0.04
Canadian/French Am. Ind. (1)	2	<0.01
Central American Ind. (0)	0	<0.01
Cherokee (34)	91	0.10
Cheyenne (0)	0	<0.01
Chickasaw (0)	0	<0.01
Chippewa (1)	3	<0.01
Choctaw (1)	10	0.01
Colville (0)	0	<0.01

	Population	%
Comanche (0)	1	<0.01
Cree (0)	0	<0.01
Creek (1)	3	<0.01
Crow (0)	0	<0.01
Delaware (2)	5	0.01
Hopi (0)	0	<0.01
Houma (0)	0	<0.01
Inupiat (Alaska Native) (0)	1	<0.01
Iroquois (6)	41	0.05
Kiowa (0)	1	<0.01
Lumbee (0)	0	<0.01
Menominee (0)	0	<0.01
Mexican American Ind. (5)	5	0.01
Navajo (1)	3	<0.01
Osage (0)	0	<0.01
Ottawa (0)	0	<0.01
Paiute (0)	0	<0.01
Pima (0)	0	<0.01
Potawatomi (3)	3	<0.01
Pueblo (0)	2	<0.01
Puget Sound Salish (1)	1	<0.01
Seminole (3)	4	<0.01
Shoshone (0)	0	<0.01
Sioux (3)	19	0.02
South American Ind. (1)	1	<0.01
Spanish American Ind. (0)	0	<0.01
Tlingit-Haida (Alaska Native) (3)	3	<0.01
Tohono O'Odham (0)	0	<0.01
Tsimshian (Alaska Native) (0)	0	<0.01
Ute (0)	0	<0.01
Yakama (0)	0	<0.01
Yaqui (0)	1	<0.01
Yuman (1)	1	<0.01
Yup'ik (Alaska Native) (0)	0	<0.01
Asian (403)	558	0.63
Not Hispanic (397)	548	0.62
Hispanic (6)	10	0.01
Bangladeshi (0)	0	<0.01
Bhutanese (0)	0	<0.01
Burmese (0)	0	<0.01
Cambodian (5)	8	0.01
Chinese, ex. Taiwanese (121)	144	0.16
Filipino (89)	137	0.15
Hmong (0)	0	<0.01
Indian (81)	100	0.11
Indonesian (0)	0	<0.01
Japanese (32)	59	0.07
Korean (29)	54	0.06
Laotian (0)	1	<0.01
Malaysian (0)	0	<0.01
Nepalese (0)	0	<0.01
Pakistani (0)	0	<0.01
Sri Lankan (4)	4	<0.01
Taiwanese (5)	7	0.01
Thai (3)	8	0.01
Vietnamese (14)	18	0.02
Hawaii Native/Pacific Islander (19)	36	0.04
Not Hispanic (13)	30	0.03
Hispanic (6)	6	0.01
Fijian (0)	2	<0.01
Guamanian/Chamorro (9)	9	0.01
Marshallese (0)	0	<0.01
Native Hawaiian (6)	17	0.02
Samoan (2)	12	0.01
Tongan (0)	0	<0.01
White (85,448)	86,435	97.38
Not Hispanic (84,930)	85,829	96.69
Hispanic (518)	606	0.68

Cumberland County

Population: 235,406

Ancestry	Population	%
Afghan (50)	50	0.02
African, Sub-Saharan (413)	849	0.37
African (146)	467	0.20
Cape Verdean (0)	0	<0.01
Ethiopian (52)	52	0.02
Ghanaian (12)	12	0.01
Kenyan (47)	47	0.02
Liberian (62)	62	0.03
Nigerian (8)	36	0.02
Senegalese (0)	0	<0.01
Sierra Leonean (0)	0	<0.01
Somalian (54)	54	0.02
South African (0)	15	0.01
Sudanese (0)	0	<0.01
Ugandan (0)	0	<0.01
Zimbabwean (0)	0	<0.01
Other Sub-Saharan African (32)	104	0.04
Albanian (99)	99	0.04
Alsatian (0)	0	<0.01
American (14,331)	14,331	6.19
Arab (1,534)	2,065	0.89
Arab (47)	101	0.04
Egyptian (861)	888	0.38
Iraqi (33)	33	0.01
Jordanian (0)	0	<0.01
Lebanese (125)	308	0.13
Moroccan (255)	266	0.11
Palestinian (73)	138	0.06
Syrian (97)	288	0.12
Other Arab (43)	43	0.02
Armenian (95)	324	0.14
Assyrian/Chaldean/Syriac (0)	15	0.01
Australian (18)	37	0.02
Austrian (259)	1,082	0.47
Basque (0)	0	<0.01
Belgian (47)	158	0.07
Brazilian (98)	198	0.09
British (350)	1,096	0.47
Bulgarian (52)	77	0.03
Cajun (0)	0	<0.01
Canadian (202)	537	0.23
Carpatho Rusyn (13)	13	0.01
Celtic (18)	66	0.03
Croatian (267)	926	0.40
Cypriot (0)	0	<0.01
Czech (205)	883	0.38
Czechoslovakian (153)	370	0.16
Danish (128)	664	0.29
Dutch (1,165)	5,062	2.19
Eastern European (238)	254	0.11
English (5,936)	21,184	9.16
Estonian (33)	33	0.01
European (2,607)	2,766	1.20
Finnish (92)	242	0.10
French, ex. Basque (1,214)	6,300	2.72
French Canadian (326)	664	0.29
German (38,727)	86,984	37.60
German Russian (0)	0	<0.01
Greek (793)	1,403	0.61
Guyanese (28)	35	0.02
Hungarian (431)	1,638	0.71
Icelander (0)	0	<0.01
Iranian (0)	25	0.01
Irish (9,034)	36,543	15.80
Israeli (15)	15	0.01
Italian (6,062)	18,553	8.02
Latvian (18)	18	0.01
Lithuanian (351)	1,277	0.55
Luxemburger (0)	0	<0.01
Macedonian (26)	41	0.02
Maltese (46)	69	0.03
New Zealander (8)	8	<0.01
Northern European (152)	152	0.07
Norwegian (402)	1,278	0.55
Pennsylvania German (1,892)	2,909	1.26

Ancestry	Population	%
Polish (2,982)	9,979	4.31
Portuguese (92)	298	0.13
Romanian (69)	185	0.08
Russian (503)	1,598	0.69
Scandinavian (61)	183	0.08
Scotch-Irish (2,238)	6,611	2.86
Scottish (1,284)	5,414	2.34
Serbian (118)	246	0.11
Slavic (45)	215	0.09
Slovak (588)	1,907	0.82
Slovene (83)	278	0.12
Soviet Union (0)	0	<0.01
Swedish (415)	2,243	0.97
Swiss (834)	2,112	0.91
Turkish (24)	64	0.03
Ukrainian (391)	988	0.43
Welsh (852)	4,197	1.81
West Indian, ex. Hispanic (403)	586	0.25
Bahamian (0)	0	<0.01
Barbadian (21)	21	0.01
Belizean (0)	0	<0.01
Bermudan (0)	0	<0.01
British West Indian (23)	23	0.01
Dutch West Indian (0)	0	<0.01
Haitian (81)	95	0.04
Jamaican (224)	317	0.14
Trinidadian/Tobagonian (0)	0	<0.01
U.S. Virgin Islander (0)	0	<0.01
West Indian (54)	130	0.06
Other West Indian (0)	0	<0.01
Yugoslavian (967)	1,330	0.57

Hispanic Origin	Population	%
Hispanic or Latino (of any race)	6,448	2.74
Central American, ex. Mexican	542	0.23
Costa Rican	14	0.01
Guatemalan	180	0.08
Honduran	114	0.05
Nicaraguan	22	0.01
Panamanian	94	0.04
Salvadoran	115	0.05
Other Central American	3	<0.01
Cuban	224	0.10
Dominican Republic	192	0.08
Mexican	1,550	0.66
Puerto Rican	2,364	1.00
South American	554	0.24
Argentinean	60	0.03
Bolivian	19	0.01
Chilean	37	0.02
Colombian	119	0.05
Ecuadorian	124	0.05
Paraguayan	16	0.01
Peruvian	130	0.06
Uruguayan	18	0.01
Venezuelan	25	0.01
Other South American	6	<0.01
Other Hispanic or Latino	1,022	0.43

Race*	Population	%
African-American/Black (7,527)	9,604	4.08
Not Hispanic (7,237)	9,087	3.86
Hispanic (290)	517	0.22
American Indian/Alaska Native (363)	1,208	0.51
Not Hispanic (293)	1,043	0.44
Hispanic (70)	165	0.07
Alaska Athabascan (Ala. Nat.) (3)	3	<0.01
Aleut (Alaska Native) (1)	3	<0.01
Apache (5)	13	0.01
Arapaho (1)	4	<0.01
Blackfeet (7)	54	0.02
Canadian/French Am. Ind. (3)	5	<0.01
Central American Ind. (1)	7	<0.01
Cherokee (57)	299	0.13
Cheyenne (1)	4	<0.01
Chickasaw (0)	8	<0.01
Chippewa (14)	20	0.01
Choctaw (7)	15	0.01
Colville (0)	0	<0.01

	Population	%
Comanche (2)	5	<0.01
Cree (6)	12	0.01
Creek (2)	6	<0.01
Crow (1)	4	<0.01
Delaware (5)	14	0.01
Hopi (0)	3	<0.01
Houma (0)	0	<0.01
Inupiat (Alaska Native) (0)	2	<0.01
Iroquois (27)	41	0.02
Kiowa (0)	4	<0.01
Lumbee (3)	3	<0.01
Menominee (0)	1	<0.01
Mexican American Ind. (21)	31	0.01
Navajo (5)	12	0.01
Osage (2)	6	<0.01
Ottawa (0)	0	<0.01
Paiute (1)	1	<0.01
Pima (0)	3	<0.01
Potawatomi (3)	5	<0.01
Pueblo (2)	6	<0.01
Puget Sound Salish (1)	2	<0.01
Seminole (3)	8	<0.01
Shoshone (0)	0	<0.01
Sioux (16)	42	0.02
South American Ind. (14)	20	0.01
Spanish American Ind. (0)	1	<0.01
Tlingit-Haida (Alaska Native) (0)	2	<0.01
Tohono O'Odham (0)	0	<0.01
Tsimshian (Alaska Native) (0)	0	<0.01
Ute (0)	0	<0.01
Yakama (0)	1	<0.01
Yaqui (0)	1	<0.01
Yuman (0)	0	<0.01
Yup'ik (Alaska Native) (2)	2	<0.01
Asian (7,072)	8,393	3.57
Not Hispanic (7,028)	8,259	3.51
Hispanic (44)	134	0.06
Bangladeshi (29)	33	0.01
Bhutanese (0)	0	<0.01
Burmese (68)	68	0.03
Cambodian (54)	82	0.03
Chinese, ex. Taiwanese (752)	951	0.40
Filipino (459)	744	0.32
Hmong (2)	10	<0.01
Indian (3,097)	3,268	1.39
Indonesian (11)	28	0.01
Japanese (124)	286	0.12
Korean (875)	1,135	0.48
Laotian (45)	63	0.03
Malaysian (4)	8	<0.01
Nepalese (12)	14	0.01
Pakistani (180)	194	0.08
Sri Lankan (37)	45	0.02
Taiwanese (46)	58	0.02
Thai (59)	106	0.05
Vietnamese (965)	1,104	0.47
Hawaii Native/Pacific Islander (65)	223	0.09
Not Hispanic (60)	192	0.08
Hispanic (5)	31	0.01
Fijian (0)	2	<0.01
Guamanian/Chamorro (22)	47	0.02
Marshallese (1)	1	<0.01
Native Hawaiian (15)	70	0.03
Samoan (10)	15	0.01
Tongan (1)	1	<0.01
White (213,934)	217,802	92.52
Not Hispanic (210,514)	213,852	90.84
Hispanic (3,420)	3,950	1.68

*Notes: † The Census 2010 population figure is used to calculate the percentages in the Hispanic Origin and Race categories. Ancestry percentages are based on the 2006-2010 American Community Survey population (not shown); ‡ Numbers in parentheses indicate the number of people reporting a single ancestry; * Numbers in parentheses indicate the number of persons reporting this race alone, not in combination with any other race; Please refer to the Explanation of Data for more information.*

Dauphin County

Population: 268,100

Ancestry	Population	%
Afghan (0)	0	<0.01
African, Sub-Saharan (2,011)	2,380	0.90
African (1,362)	1,646	0.62
Cape Verdean (15)	23	0.01
Ethiopian (68)	68	0.03
Ghanaian (12)	12	<0.01
Kenyan (0)	0	<0.01
Liberian (0)	0	<0.01
Nigerian (61)	81	0.03
Senegalese (18)	18	0.01
Sierra Leonean (0)	0	<0.01
Somalian (0)	0	<0.01
South African (50)	107	0.04
Sudanese (273)	273	0.10
Ugandan (21)	21	0.01
Zimbabwean (0)	0	<0.01
Other Sub-Saharan African (131)	131	0.05
Albanian (0)	0	<0.01
Alsatian (0)	9	<0.01
American (11,654)	11,654	4.40
Arab (807)	1,210	0.46
Arab (73)	286	0.11
Egyptian (430)	430	0.16
Iraqi (0)	26	0.01
Jordanian (0)	0	<0.01
Lebanese (16)	88	0.03
Moroccan (115)	127	0.05
Palestinian (95)	95	0.04
Syrian (15)	52	0.02
Other Arab (63)	106	0.04
Armenian (85)	113	0.04
Assyrian/Chaldean/Syriac (0)	17	0.01
Australian (15)	63	0.02
Austrian (270)	1,095	0.41
Basque (0)	14	0.01
Belgian (49)	128	0.05
Brazilian (17)	38	0.01
British (282)	864	0.33
Bulgarian (29)	43	0.02
Cajun (3)	30	0.01
Canadian (96)	265	0.10
Carpatho Rusyn (0)	30	0.01
Celtic (4)	77	0.03
Croatian (1,029)	2,566	0.97
Cypriot (0)	0	<0.01
Czech (274)	1,436	0.54
Czechoslovakian (144)	370	0.14
Danish (80)	243	0.09
Dutch (1,417)	6,684	2.52
Eastern European (375)	383	0.14
English (4,204)	17,906	6.76
Estonian (0)	13	<0.01
European (1,880)	2,023	0.76
Finnish (22)	93	0.04
French, ex. Basque (544)	4,886	1.85
French Canadian (192)	611	0.23
German (38,467)	85,784	32.39
German Russian (44)	44	0.02
Greek (352)	705	0.27
Guyanese (0)	0	<0.01
Hungarian (724)	2,558	0.97
Icelander (0)	0	<0.01
Iranian (68)	94	0.04
Irish (6,802)	32,428	12.25
Israeli (147)	147	0.06
Italian (7,281)	21,540	8.13
Latvian (10)	10	<0.01
Lithuanian (457)	1,429	0.54
Luxemburger (0)	0	<0.01
Macedonian (26)	112	0.04
Maltese (0)	0	<0.01
New Zealander (23)	23	0.01
Northern European (139)	161	0.06
Norwegian (219)	822	0.31
Pennsylvania German (2,971)	4,170	1.57

Ancestry	Population	%
Polish (2,514)	9,205	3.48
Portuguese (57)	264	0.10
Romanian (201)	314	0.12
Russian (886)	2,799	1.06
Scandinavian (31)	147	0.06
Scotch-Irish (1,471)	5,353	2.02
Scottish (783)	3,502	1.32
Serbian (304)	801	0.30
Slavic (148)	634	0.24
Slovak (648)	2,279	0.86
Slovene (175)	376	0.14
Soviet Union (0)	0	<0.01
Swedish (365)	1,866	0.70
Swiss (295)	1,473	0.56
Turkish (134)	180	0.07
Ukrainian (548)	1,440	0.54
Welsh (809)	4,136	1.56
West Indian, ex. Hispanic (1,008)	1,469	0.55
Bahamian (0)	8	<0.01
Barbadian (18)	89	0.03
Belizean (0)	0	<0.01
Bermudan (165)	165	0.06
British West Indian (44)	44	0.02
Dutch West Indian (0)	0	<0.01
Haitian (138)	169	0.06
Jamaican (220)	459	0.17
Trinidadian/Tobagonian (155)	175	0.07
U.S. Virgin Islander (0)	0	<0.01
West Indian (268)	360	0.14
Other West Indian (0)	0	<0.01
Yugoslavian (393)	595	0.22

Hispanic Origin	Population	%
Hispanic or Latino (of any race)	18,795	7.01
Central American, ex. Mexican	574	0.21
Costa Rican	21	0.01
Guatemalan	190	0.07
Honduran	134	0.05
Nicaraguan	16	0.01
Panamanian	97	0.04
Salvadoran	110	0.04
Other Central American	6	<0.01
Cuban	554	0.21
Dominican Republic	1,169	0.44
Mexican	3,464	1.29
Puerto Rican	10,754	4.01
South American	1,079	0.40
Argentinean	62	0.02
Bolivian	18	0.01
Chilean	44	0.02
Colombian	214	0.08
Ecuadorian	354	0.13
Paraguayan	10	<0.01
Peruvian	309	0.12
Uruguayan	9	<0.01
Venezuelan	53	0.02
Other South American	6	<0.01
Other Hispanic or Latino	1,201	0.45

Race*	Population	%
African-American/Black (48,386)	54,153	20.20
Not Hispanic (46,320)	50,931	19.00
Hispanic (2,066)	3,222	1.20
American Indian/Alaska Native (578)	2,037	0.76
Not Hispanic (396)	1,590	0.59
Hispanic (182)	447	0.17
Alaska Athabascan (Ala. Nat.) (0)	0	<0.01
Aleut (Alaska Native) (0)	4	<0.01
Apache (5)	19	0.01
Arapaho (0)	5	<0.01
Blackfeet (13)	83	0.03
Canadian/French Am. Ind. (9)	13	<0.01
Central American Ind. (2)	5	<0.01
Cherokee (67)	425	0.16
Cheyenne (0)	4	<0.01
Chickasaw (5)	10	<0.01
Chippewa (17)	28	0.01
Choctaw (9)	19	0.01
Colville (0)	0	<0.01

Race* (cont.)	Population	%
Comanche (0)	1	<0.01
Cree (0)	6	<0.01
Creek (3)	4	<0.01
Crow (0)	4	<0.01
Delaware (2)	19	0.01
Hopi (0)	1	<0.01
Houma (1)	1	<0.01
Inupiat (Alaska Native) (1)	5	<0.01
Iroquois (19)	51	0.02
Kiowa (8)	10	<0.01
Lumbee (8)	12	<0.01
Menominee (1)	1	<0.01
Mexican American Ind. (7)	15	0.01
Navajo (6)	12	<0.01
Osage (0)	3	<0.01
Ottawa (0)	0	<0.01
Paiute (1)	2	<0.01
Pima (0)	1	<0.01
Potawatomi (1)	3	<0.01
Pueblo (0)	5	<0.01
Puget Sound Salish (0)	1	<0.01
Seminole (2)	25	0.01
Shoshone (1)	1	<0.01
Sioux (10)	39	0.01
South American Ind. (17)	46	0.02
Spanish American Ind. (10)	12	<0.01
Tlingit-Haida (Alaska Native) (1)	1	<0.01
Tohono O'Odham (1)	4	<0.01
Tsimshian (Alaska Native) (0)	0	<0.01
Ute (0)	0	<0.01
Yakama (0)	2	<0.01
Yaqui (0)	2	<0.01
Yuman (0)	0	<0.01
Yup'ik (Alaska Native) (2)	2	<0.01
Asian (8,580)	9,957	3.71
Not Hispanic (8,507)	9,749	3.64
Hispanic (73)	208	0.08
Bangladeshi (17)	21	0.01
Bhutanese (99)	138	0.05
Burmese (70)	78	0.03
Cambodian (267)	313	0.12
Chinese, ex. Taiwanese (1,439)	1,637	0.61
Filipino (436)	680	0.25
Hmong (0)	0	<0.01
Indian (2,525)	2,809	1.05
Indonesian (159)	168	0.06
Japanese (117)	276	0.10
Korean (408)	582	0.22
Laotian (42)	54	0.02
Malaysian (3)	3	<0.01
Nepalese (53)	72	0.03
Pakistani (349)	397	0.15
Sri Lankan (22)	25	0.01
Taiwanese (57)	75	0.03
Thai (170)	206	0.08
Vietnamese (2,038)	2,247	0.84
Hawaii Native/Pacific Islander (78)	355	0.13
Not Hispanic (44)	223	0.08
Hispanic (34)	132	0.05
Fijian (0)	0	<0.01
Guamanian/Chamorro (20)	33	0.01
Marshallese (0)	0	<0.01
Native Hawaiian (19)	102	0.04
Samoan (4)	31	0.01
Tongan (0)	0	<0.01
White (194,910)	201,869	75.30
Not Hispanic (187,402)	192,934	71.96
Hispanic (7,508)	8,935	3.33

*Notes: † The Census 2010 population figure is used to calculate the percentages in the Hispanic Origin and Race categories. Ancestry percentages are based on the 2006-2010 American Community Survey population (not shown); ‡ Numbers in parentheses indicate the number of people reporting a single ancestry; * Numbers in parentheses indicate the number of persons reporting this race alone, not in combination with any other race; Please refer to the Explanation of Data for more information.*

Delaware County
Population: 558,979

Ancestry	Population	%
Afghan (197)	197	0.04
African, Sub-Saharan (10,112)	11,150	2.00
African (3,617)	4,097	0.74
Cape Verdean (0)	11	<0.01
Ethiopian (534)	534	0.10
Ghanaian (331)	395	0.07
Kenyan (107)	118	0.02
Liberian (3,264)	3,349	0.60
Nigerian (823)	913	0.16
Senegalese (191)	201	0.04
Sierra Leonean (681)	729	0.13
Somalian (21)	21	<0.01
South African (130)	130	0.02
Sudanese (91)	95	0.02
Ugandan (0)	15	<0.01
Zimbabwean (21)	21	<0.01
Other Sub-Saharan African (301)	521	0.09
Albanian (664)	917	0.16
Alsatian (10)	50	0.01
American (12,133)	12,133	2.18
Arab (1,746)	2,698	0.48
Arab (189)	262	0.05
Egyptian (373)	416	0.07
Iraqi (25)	38	0.01
Jordanian (0)	0	<0.01
Lebanese (309)	885	0.16
Moroccan (208)	208	0.04
Palestinian (0)	59	0.01
Syrian (306)	420	0.08
Other Arab (336)	410	0.07
Armenian (1,309)	2,077	0.37
Assyrian/Chaldean/Syriac (98)	98	0.02
Australian (58)	183	0.03
Austrian (194)	1,475	0.27
Basque (0)	48	0.01
Belgian (70)	339	0.06
Brazilian (107)	215	0.04
British (1,148)	2,267	0.41
Bulgarian (171)	191	0.03
Cajun (23)	32	0.01
Canadian (233)	856	0.15
Carpatho Rusyn (0)	12	<0.01
Celtic (175)	207	0.04
Croatian (186)	477	0.09
Cypriot (0)	0	<0.01
Czech (184)	1,410	0.25
Czechoslovakian (191)	530	0.10
Danish (179)	1,216	0.22
Dutch (801)	6,075	1.09
Eastern European (1,068)	1,127	0.20
English (10,564)	51,960	9.34
Estonian (25)	73	0.01
European (3,634)	3,823	0.69
Finnish (157)	696	0.13
French, ex. Basque (1,033)	9,103	1.64
French Canadian (477)	1,284	0.23
German (16,851)	88,639	15.93
German Russian (0)	0	<0.01
Greek (3,328)	5,183	0.93
Guyanese (10)	10	<0.01
Hungarian (685)	2,967	0.53
Icelander (10)	61	0.01
Iranian (684)	704	0.13
Irish (58,167)	159,534	28.67
Israeli (171)	259	0.05
Italian (42,361)	100,921	18.14
Latvian (59)	197	0.04
Lithuanian (963)	3,867	0.69
Luxemburger (18)	42	0.01
Macedonian (0)	9	<0.01
Maltese (0)	22	<0.01
New Zealander (4)	4	<0.01
Northern European (181)	181	0.03
Norwegian (542)	2,708	0.49
Pennsylvania German (901)	1,798	0.32

Ancestry (cont.)	Population	%
Polish (7,366)	26,263	4.72
Portuguese (189)	675	0.12
Romanian (310)	879	0.16
Russian (3,333)	7,938	1.43
Scandinavian (177)	418	0.08
Scotch-Irish (4,195)	9,926	1.78
Scottish (2,315)	9,160	1.65
Serbian (206)	295	0.05
Slavic (108)	252	0.05
Slovak (679)	2,264	0.41
Slovene (28)	114	0.02
Soviet Union (0)	0	<0.01
Swedish (719)	4,038	0.73
Swiss (212)	1,291	0.23
Turkish (163)	210	0.04
Ukrainian (1,568)	4,664	0.84
Welsh (894)	6,317	1.14
West Indian, ex. Hispanic (4,881)	5,974	1.07
Bahamian (16)	51	0.01
Barbadian (203)	235	0.04
Belizean (13)	13	<0.01
Bermudan (7)	12	<0.01
British West Indian (77)	123	0.02
Dutch West Indian (0)	0	<0.01
Haitian (1,627)	1,908	0.34
Jamaican (2,169)	2,623	0.47
Trinidadian/Tobagonian (481)	548	0.10
U.S. Virgin Islander (118)	118	0.02
West Indian (170)	343	0.06
Other West Indian (0)	0	<0.01
Yugoslavian (73)	216	0.04

Hispanic Origin	Population	%
Hispanic or Latino (of any race)	16,537	2.96
Central American, ex. Mexican	1,383	0.25
Costa Rican	171	0.03
Guatemalan	484	0.09
Honduran	241	0.04
Nicaraguan	95	0.02
Panamanian	116	0.02
Salvadoran	251	0.04
Other Central American	25	<0.01
Cuban	834	0.15
Dominican Republic	470	0.08
Mexican	2,879	0.52
Puerto Rican	6,327	1.13
South American	2,601	0.47
Argentinean	290	0.05
Bolivian	44	0.01
Chilean	97	0.02
Colombian	513	0.09
Ecuadorian	1,089	0.19
Paraguayan	67	0.01
Peruvian	303	0.05
Uruguayan	35	0.01
Venezuelan	153	0.03
Other South American	10	<0.01
Other Hispanic or Latino	2,043	0.37

Race*	Population	%
African-American/Black (110,260)	116,695	20.88
Not Hispanic (108,231)	113,671	20.34
Hispanic (2,029)	3,024	0.54
American Indian/Alaska Native (874)	3,602	0.64
Not Hispanic (674)	2,996	0.54
Hispanic (200)	606	0.11
Alaska Athabascan (Ala. Nat.) (0)	0	<0.01
Aleut (Alaska Native) (2)	6	<0.01
Apache (10)	27	<0.01
Arapaho (0)	6	<0.01
Blackfeet (12)	147	0.03
Canadian/French Am. Ind. (2)	15	<0.01
Central American Ind. (8)	12	<0.01
Cherokee (84)	681	0.12
Cheyenne (5)	11	<0.01
Chickasaw (7)	12	<0.01
Chippewa (15)	24	<0.01
Choctaw (7)	42	0.01
Colville (1)	5	<0.01

Race* (cont.)	Population	%
Comanche (1)	1	<0.01
Cree (0)	7	<0.01
Creek (1)	13	<0.01
Crow (1)	8	<0.01
Delaware (13)	93	0.02
Hopi (1)	1	<0.01
Houma (0)	2	<0.01
Inupiat (Alaska Native) (1)	2	<0.01
Iroquois (24)	86	0.02
Kiowa (0)	6	<0.01
Lumbee (12)	33	0.01
Menominee (0)	1	<0.01
Mexican American Ind. (26)	54	0.01
Navajo (9)	35	0.01
Osage (0)	4	<0.01
Ottawa (2)	5	<0.01
Paiute (1)	1	<0.01
Pima (0)	0	<0.01
Potawatomi (7)	12	<0.01
Pueblo (4)	10	<0.01
Puget Sound Salish (0)	0	<0.01
Seminole (3)	38	0.01
Shoshone (1)	5	<0.01
Sioux (16)	62	0.01
South American Ind. (23)	92	0.02
Spanish American Ind. (11)	18	<0.01
Tlingit-Haida (Alaska Native) (1)	1	<0.01
Tohono O'Odham (3)	3	<0.01
Tsimshian (Alaska Native) (0)	0	<0.01
Ute (0)	3	<0.01
Yakama (0)	0	<0.01
Yaqui (0)	0	<0.01
Yuman (1)	2	<0.01
Yup'ik (Alaska Native) (0)	0	<0.01
Asian (26,277)	29,523	5.28
Not Hispanic (26,144)	29,190	5.22
Hispanic (133)	333	0.06
Bangladeshi (880)	988	0.18
Bhutanese (0)	0	<0.01
Burmese (58)	65	0.01
Cambodian (533)	693	0.12
Chinese, ex. Taiwanese (5,669)	6,630	1.19
Filipino (1,501)	2,231	0.40
Hmong (72)	79	0.01
Indian (7,319)	8,120	1.45
Indonesian (82)	127	0.02
Japanese (477)	807	0.14
Korean (3,466)	3,845	0.69
Laotian (280)	343	0.06
Malaysian (51)	59	0.01
Nepalese (53)	55	0.01
Pakistani (1,101)	1,213	0.22
Sri Lankan (66)	77	0.01
Taiwanese (167)	214	0.04
Thai (237)	323	0.06
Vietnamese (3,136)	3,543	0.63
Hawaii Native/Pacific Islander (145)	555	0.10
Not Hispanic (114)	458	0.08
Hispanic (31)	97	0.02
Fijian (4)	11	<0.01
Guamanian/Chamorro (37)	76	0.01
Marshallese (0)	3	<0.01
Native Hawaiian (32)	149	0.03
Samoan (5)	39	0.01
Tongan (3)	4	<0.01
White (405,233)	413,730	74.02
Not Hispanic (397,424)	404,650	72.39
Hispanic (7,809)	9,080	1.62

Notes: † The Census 2010 population figure is used to calculate the percentages in the Hispanic Origin and Race categories. Ancestry percentages are based on the 2006-2010 American Community Survey population (not shown); ‡ Numbers in parentheses indicate the number of people reporting a single ancestry; * Numbers in parentheses indicate the number of persons reporting this race alone, not in combination with any other race; Please refer to the Explanation of Data for more information.

Elk County

Population: 31,946

Ancestry	Population	%
Afghan (0)	0	<0.01
African, Sub-Saharan (0)	0	<0.01
African (0)	0	<0.01
Cape Verdean (0)	0	<0.01
Ethiopian (0)	0	<0.01
Ghanaian (0)	0	<0.01
Kenyan (0)	0	<0.01
Liberian (0)	0	<0.01
Nigerian (0)	0	<0.01
Senegalese (0)	0	<0.01
Sierra Leonean (0)	0	<0.01
Somalian (0)	0	<0.01
South African (0)	0	<0.01
Sudanese (0)	0	<0.01
Ugandan (0)	0	<0.01
Zimbabwean (0)	0	<0.01
Other Sub-Saharan African (0)	0	<0.01
Albanian (0)	0	<0.01
Alsatian (0)	0	<0.01
American (1,842)	1,842	5.67
Arab (14)	42	0.13
Arab (14)	14	0.04
Egyptian (0)	0	<0.01
Iraqi (0)	0	<0.01
Jordanian (0)	0	<0.01
Lebanese (0)	20	0.06
Moroccan (0)	0	<0.01
Palestinian (0)	0	<0.01
Syrian (0)	8	0.02
Other Arab (0)	0	<0.01
Armenian (0)	0	<0.01
Assyrian/Chaldean/Syriac (0)	0	<0.01
Australian (0)	0	<0.01
Austrian (54)	173	0.53
Basque (0)	0	<0.01
Belgian (3)	31	0.10
Brazilian (0)	0	<0.01
British (32)	46	0.14
Bulgarian (0)	0	<0.01
Cajun (0)	0	<0.01
Canadian (0)	0	<0.01
Carpatho Rusyn (0)	0	<0.01
Celtic (0)	0	<0.01
Croatian (65)	211	0.65
Cypriot (0)	0	<0.01
Czech (6)	77	0.24
Czechoslovakian (13)	13	0.04
Danish (0)	23	0.07
Dutch (62)	724	2.23
Eastern European (0)	0	<0.01
English (490)	2,198	6.77
Estonian (0)	0	<0.01
European (42)	42	0.13
Finnish (0)	0	<0.01
French, ex. Basque (77)	997	3.07
French Canadian (56)	155	0.48
German (6,408)	15,316	47.16
German Russian (0)	0	<0.01
Greek (0)	34	0.10
Guyanese (0)	0	<0.01
Hungarian (94)	151	0.46
Icelander (0)	0	<0.01
Iranian (0)	0	<0.01
Irish (849)	5,027	15.48
Israeli (0)	0	<0.01
Italian (2,498)	6,804	20.95
Latvian (0)	0	<0.01
Lithuanian (46)	163	0.50
Luxemburger (0)	0	<0.01
Macedonian (0)	0	<0.01
Maltese (0)	0	<0.01
New Zealander (0)	0	<0.01
Northern European (2)	2	0.01
Norwegian (15)	71	0.22
Pennsylvania German (104)	253	0.78

Ancestry (cont.)	Population	%
Polish (827)	2,638	8.12
Portuguese (39)	73	0.22
Romanian (0)	0	<0.01
Russian (11)	93	0.29
Scandinavian (17)	42	0.13
Scotch-Irish (138)	505	1.55
Scottish (45)	213	0.66
Serbian (12)	26	0.08
Slavic (37)	154	0.47
Slovak (116)	255	0.79
Slovene (12)	102	0.31
Soviet Union (0)	0	<0.01
Swedish (414)	2,422	7.46
Swiss (39)	523	1.61
Turkish (0)	0	<0.01
Ukrainian (5)	79	0.24
Welsh (8)	151	0.46
West Indian, ex. Hispanic (5)	10	0.03
Bahamian (0)	0	<0.01
Barbadian (0)	0	<0.01
Belizean (0)	0	<0.01
Bermudan (0)	0	<0.01
British West Indian (0)	0	<0.01
Dutch West Indian (0)	0	<0.01
Haitian (0)	0	<0.01
Jamaican (0)	5	0.02
Trinidadian/Tobagonian (0)	0	<0.01
U.S. Virgin Islander (0)	0	<0.01
West Indian (5)	5	0.02
Other West Indian (0)	0	<0.01
Yugoslavian (86)	168	0.52

Hispanic Origin	Population	%
Hispanic or Latino (of any race)	183	0.57
Central American, ex. Mexican	12	0.04
Costa Rican	0	<0.01
Guatemalan	8	0.03
Honduran	0	<0.01
Nicaraguan	0	<0.01
Panamanian	0	<0.01
Salvadoran	4	0.01
Other Central American	0	<0.01
Cuban	2	0.01
Dominican Republic	3	0.01
Mexican	91	0.28
Puerto Rican	36	0.11
South American	13	0.04
Argentinean	0	<0.01
Bolivian	0	<0.01
Chilean	0	<0.01
Colombian	2	0.01
Ecuadorian	0	<0.01
Paraguayan	0	<0.01
Peruvian	10	0.03
Uruguayan	1	<0.01
Venezuelan	0	<0.01
Other South American	0	<0.01
Other Hispanic or Latino	26	0.08

Race*	Population	%
African-American/Black (89)	157	0.49
Not Hispanic (85)	148	0.46
Hispanic (4)	9	0.03
American Indian/Alaska Native (34)	112	0.35
Not Hispanic (32)	107	0.33
Hispanic (2)	5	0.02
Alaska Athabascan (Ala. Nat.) (0)	0	<0.01
Aleut (Alaska Native) (2)	3	0.01
Apache (1)	3	0.01
Arapaho (0)	0	<0.01
Blackfeet (0)	3	0.01
Canadian/French Am. Ind. (0)	0	<0.01
Central American Ind. (0)	0	<0.01
Cherokee (10)	31	0.10
Cheyenne (0)	0	<0.01
Chickasaw (0)	2	0.01
Chippewa (0)	0	<0.01
Choctaw (1)	1	<0.01
Colville (0)	0	<0.01

Race* (cont.)	Population	%
Comanche (0)	0	<0.01
Cree (0)	1	<0.01
Creek (0)	0	<0.01
Crow (0)	0	<0.01
Delaware (1)	1	<0.01
Hopi (0)	0	<0.01
Houma (0)	0	<0.01
Inupiat (Alaska Native) (0)	0	<0.01
Iroquois (1)	10	0.03
Kiowa (0)	0	<0.01
Lumbee (0)	0	<0.01
Menominee (0)	0	<0.01
Mexican American Ind. (0)	1	<0.01
Navajo (0)	1	<0.01
Osage (2)	2	0.01
Ottawa (0)	0	<0.01
Paiute (0)	0	<0.01
Pima (0)	0	<0.01
Potawatomi (0)	0	<0.01
Pueblo (1)	1	<0.01
Puget Sound Salish (0)	0	<0.01
Seminole (0)	0	<0.01
Shoshone (0)	0	<0.01
Sioux (0)	3	0.01
South American Ind. (0)	1	<0.01
Spanish American Ind. (0)	0	<0.01
Tlingit-Haida (Alaska Native) (0)	0	<0.01
Tohono O'Odham (0)	0	<0.01
Tsimshian (Alaska Native) (0)	0	<0.01
Ute (0)	0	<0.01
Yakama (0)	0	<0.01
Yaqui (0)	0	<0.01
Yuman (0)	0	<0.01
Yup'ik (Alaska Native) (0)	0	<0.01
Asian (96)	147	0.46
Not Hispanic (95)	145	0.45
Hispanic (1)	2	0.01
Bangladeshi (0)	0	<0.01
Bhutanese (0)	0	<0.01
Burmese (0)	0	<0.01
Cambodian (0)	2	0.01
Chinese, ex. Taiwanese (24)	27	0.08
Filipino (32)	47	0.15
Hmong (0)	0	<0.01
Indian (19)	23	0.07
Indonesian (0)	0	<0.01
Japanese (6)	15	0.05
Korean (4)	11	0.03
Laotian (0)	0	<0.01
Malaysian (0)	0	<0.01
Nepalese (0)	0	<0.01
Pakistani (0)	0	<0.01
Sri Lankan (0)	0	<0.01
Taiwanese (0)	2	0.01
Thai (1)	8	0.03
Vietnamese (8)	11	0.03
Hawaii Native/Pacific Islander (6)	22	0.07
Not Hispanic (5)	21	0.07
Hispanic (1)	1	<0.01
Fijian (0)	0	<0.01
Guamanian/Chamorro (0)	1	<0.01
Marshallese (0)	0	<0.01
Native Hawaiian (2)	9	0.03
Samoan (2)	3	0.01
Tongan (2)	5	0.02
White (31,469)	31,663	99.11
Not Hispanic (31,345)	31,516	98.65
Hispanic (124)	147	0.46

*Notes: † The Census 2010 population figure is used to calculate the percentages in the Hispanic Origin and Race categories. Ancestry percentages are based on the 2006-2010 American Community Survey population (not shown); ‡ Numbers in parentheses indicate the number of people reporting a single ancestry; * Numbers in parentheses indicate the number of persons reporting this race alone, not in combination with any other race; Please refer to the Explanation of Data for more information.*

Erie County

Population: 280,566

Ancestry	Population	%
Afghan (85)	85	0.03
African, Sub-Saharan (3,143)	4,363	1.56
African (2,539)	3,745	1.34
Cape Verdean (0)	0	<0.01
Ethiopian (0)	0	<0.01
Ghanaian (0)	0	<0.01
Kenyan (17)	17	0.01
Liberian (0)	0	<0.01
Nigerian (31)	31	0.01
Senegalese (0)	0	<0.01
Sierra Leonean (0)	0	<0.01
Somalian (96)	96	0.03
South African (27)	27	0.01
Sudanese (221)	221	0.08
Ugandan (0)	0	<0.01
Zimbabwean (0)	0	<0.01
Other Sub-Saharan African (212)	226	0.08
Albanian (201)	201	0.07
Alsatian (0)	7	<0.01
American (11,324)	11,324	4.06
Arab (519)	976	0.35
Arab (206)	327	0.12
Egyptian (13)	13	<0.01
Iraqi (186)	228	0.08
Jordanian (0)	0	<0.01
Lebanese (51)	147	0.05
Moroccan (6)	14	0.01
Palestinian (15)	31	0.01
Syrian (18)	156	0.06
Other Arab (24)	60	0.02
Armenian (156)	221	0.08
Assyrian/Chaldean/Syriac (0)	0	<0.01
Australian (0)	37	0.01
Austrian (304)	980	0.35
Basque (29)	38	0.01
Belgian (14)	155	0.06
Brazilian (106)	162	0.06
British (359)	815	0.29
Bulgarian (12)	28	0.01
Cajun (0)	0	<0.01
Canadian (222)	378	0.14
Carpatho Rusyn (23)	88	0.03
Celtic (18)	80	0.03
Croatian (313)	796	0.29
Cypriot (0)	0	<0.01
Czech (475)	1,754	0.63
Czechoslovakian (523)	904	0.32
Danish (249)	1,241	0.44
Dutch (705)	5,127	1.84
Eastern European (68)	79	0.03
English (6,280)	25,398	9.10
Estonian (67)	100	0.04
European (1,494)	1,580	0.57
Finnish (128)	483	0.17
French, ex. Basque (561)	5,880	2.11
French Canadian (292)	797	0.29
German (24,072)	89,220	31.95
German Russian (2)	2	<0.01
Greek (369)	976	0.35
Guyanese (0)	7	<0.01
Hungarian (811)	2,931	1.05
Icelander (0)	30	0.01
Iranian (46)	107	0.04
Irish (10,195)	50,289	18.01
Israeli (6)	6	<0.01
Italian (13,856)	39,040	13.98
Latvian (32)	52	0.02
Lithuanian (273)	949	0.34
Luxemburger (17)	40	0.01
Macedonian (10)	29	0.01
Maltese (12)	12	<0.01
New Zealander (0)	0	<0.01
Northern European (45)	55	0.02
Norwegian (198)	777	0.28
Pennsylvania German (358)	837	0.30

Ancestry	Population	%
Polish (13,159)	35,681	12.78
Portuguese (181)	925	0.33
Romanian (265)	583	0.21
Russian (1,558)	4,301	1.54
Scandinavian (46)	127	0.05
Scotch-Irish (2,128)	6,961	2.49
Scottish (1,299)	4,843	1.73
Serbian (47)	160	0.06
Slavic (209)	654	0.23
Slovak (1,981)	5,402	1.93
Slovene (157)	323	0.12
Soviet Union (0)	0	<0.01
Swedish (1,544)	7,103	2.54
Swiss (106)	778	0.28
Turkish (65)	158	0.06
Ukrainian (1,272)	2,421	0.87
Welsh (316)	2,455	0.88
West Indian, ex. Hispanic (479)	547	0.20
Bahamian (0)	0	<0.01
Barbadian (0)	0	<0.01
Belizean (0)	0	<0.01
Bermudan (0)	0	<0.01
British West Indian (20)	20	0.01
Dutch West Indian (0)	0	<0.01
Haitian (251)	282	0.10
Jamaican (150)	171	0.06
Trinidadian/Tobagonian (23)	39	0.01
U.S. Virgin Islander (0)	0	<0.01
West Indian (35)	35	0.01
Other West Indian (0)	0	<0.01
Yugoslavian (798)	921	0.33

Hispanic Origin	Population	%
Hispanic or Latino (of any race)	9,518	3.39
Central American, ex. Mexican	333	0.12
Costa Rican	52	0.02
Guatemalan	55	0.02
Honduran	51	0.02
Nicaraguan	24	0.01
Panamanian	40	0.01
Salvadoran	111	0.04
Other Central American	0	<0.01
Cuban	168	0.06
Dominican Republic	155	0.06
Mexican	2,032	0.72
Puerto Rican	5,725	2.04
South American	277	0.10
Argentinean	13	<0.01
Bolivian	4	<0.01
Chilean	18	0.01
Colombian	132	0.05
Ecuadorian	27	0.01
Paraguayan	0	<0.01
Peruvian	41	0.01
Uruguayan	1	<0.01
Venezuelan	41	0.01
Other South American	0	<0.01
Other Hispanic or Latino	828	0.30

Race*	Population	%
African-American/Black (20,155)	23,932	8.53
Not Hispanic (19,485)	22,803	8.13
Hispanic (670)	1,129	0.40
American Indian/Alaska Native (566)	1,721	0.61
Not Hispanic (447)	1,471	0.52
Hispanic (119)	250	0.09
Alaska Athabascan (Ala. Nat.) (0)	0	<0.01
Aleut (Alaska Native) (1)	2	<0.01
Apache (3)	13	<0.01
Arapaho (0)	0	<0.01
Blackfeet (16)	93	0.03
Canadian/French Am. Ind. (7)	11	<0.01
Central American Ind. (2)	6	<0.01
Cherokee (62)	282	0.10
Cheyenne (0)	1	<0.01
Chickasaw (0)	4	<0.01
Chippewa (17)	32	0.01
Choctaw (6)	21	0.01
Colville (0)	0	<0.01

Race*	Population	%
Comanche (1)	1	<0.01
Cree (3)	7	<0.01
Creek (4)	13	<0.01
Crow (0)	5	<0.01
Delaware (2)	7	<0.01
Hopi (1)	3	<0.01
Houma (0)	0	<0.01
Inupiat (Alaska Native) (0)	0	<0.01
Iroquois (84)	203	0.07
Kiowa (0)	0	<0.01
Lumbee (2)	3	<0.01
Menominee (0)	0	<0.01
Mexican American Ind. (13)	27	0.01
Navajo (4)	10	<0.01
Osage (0)	0	<0.01
Ottawa (0)	0	<0.01
Paiute (0)	0	<0.01
Pima (0)	0	<0.01
Potawatomi (1)	1	<0.01
Pueblo (2)	3	<0.01
Puget Sound Salish (1)	1	<0.01
Seminole (1)	8	<0.01
Shoshone (4)	5	<0.01
Sioux (15)	62	0.02
South American Ind. (4)	17	0.01
Spanish American Ind. (1)	1	<0.01
Tlingit-Haida (Alaska Native) (5)	8	<0.01
Tohono O'Odham (0)	4	<0.01
Tsimshian (Alaska Native) (0)	0	<0.01
Ute (2)	3	<0.01
Yakama (0)	0	<0.01
Yaqui (0)	0	<0.01
Yuman (2)	2	<0.01
Yup'ik (Alaska Native) (0)	1	<0.01
Asian (3,077)	3,992	1.42
Not Hispanic (3,036)	3,901	1.39
Hispanic (41)	91	0.03
Bangladeshi (17)	20	0.01
Bhutanese (332)	395	0.14
Burmese (118)	130	0.05
Cambodian (6)	8	<0.01
Chinese, ex. Taiwanese (534)	632	0.23
Filipino (265)	453	0.16
Hmong (5)	5	<0.01
Indian (703)	817	0.29
Indonesian (9)	11	<0.01
Japanese (64)	174	0.06
Korean (226)	361	0.13
Laotian (18)	18	0.01
Malaysian (4)	5	<0.01
Nepalese (69)	139	0.05
Pakistani (56)	62	0.02
Sri Lankan (10)	10	<0.01
Taiwanese (23)	30	0.01
Thai (36)	64	0.02
Vietnamese (404)	474	0.17
Hawaii Native/Pacific Islander (90)	251	0.09
Not Hispanic (72)	209	0.07
Hispanic (18)	42	0.01
Fijian (0)	1	<0.01
Guamanian/Chamorro (25)	49	0.02
Marshallese (1)	1	<0.01
Native Hawaiian (24)	64	0.02
Samoan (5)	15	0.01
Tongan (0)	0	<0.01
White (247,569)	252,928	90.15
Not Hispanic (242,787)	247,371	88.17
Hispanic (4,782)	5,557	1.98

Notes: † The Census 2010 population figure is used to calculate the percentages in the Hispanic Origin and Race categories. Ancestry percentages are based on the 2006-2010 American Community Survey population (not shown); ‡ Numbers in parentheses indicate the number of people reporting a single ancestry; * Numbers in parentheses indicate the number of persons reporting this race alone, not in combination with any other race; Please refer to the Explanation of Data for more information.

Fayette County
Population: 136,606

Ancestry	Population	%
Afghan (0)	0	<0.01
African, Sub-Saharan (523)	649	0.47
African (506)	632	0.46
Cape Verdean (0)	0	<0.01
Ethiopian (8)	8	0.01
Ghanaian (0)	0	<0.01
Kenyan (0)	0	<0.01
Liberian (0)	0	<0.01
Nigerian (0)	0	<0.01
Senegalese (0)	0	<0.01
Sierra Leonean (0)	0	<0.01
Somalian (0)	0	<0.01
South African (0)	0	<0.01
Sudanese (0)	0	<0.01
Ugandan (9)	9	0.01
Zimbabwean (0)	0	<0.01
Other Sub-Saharan African (0)	0	<0.01
Albanian (9)	16	0.01
Alsatian (0)	0	<0.01
American (6,718)	6,718	4.84
Arab (453)	1,211	0.87
Arab (0)	0	<0.01
Egyptian (0)	0	<0.01
Iraqi (0)	0	<0.01
Jordanian (0)	0	<0.01
Lebanese (373)	1,005	0.72
Moroccan (0)	0	<0.01
Palestinian (0)	0	<0.01
Syrian (80)	206	0.15
Other Arab (0)	0	<0.01
Armenian (16)	48	0.03
Assyrian/Chaldean/Syriac (0)	0	<0.01
Australian (0)	9	0.01
Austrian (129)	770	0.55
Basque (0)	0	<0.01
Belgian (36)	155	0.11
Brazilian (0)	0	<0.01
British (162)	301	0.22
Bulgarian (0)	0	<0.01
Cajun (0)	0	<0.01
Canadian (36)	83	0.06
Carpatho Rusyn (78)	88	0.06
Celtic (0)	3	<0.01
Croatian (477)	1,467	1.06
Cypriot (0)	0	<0.01
Czech (386)	1,240	0.89
Czechoslovakian (294)	477	0.34
Danish (14)	24	0.02
Dutch (619)	6,579	4.74
Eastern European (61)	61	0.04
English (3,555)	13,612	9.81
Estonian (6)	6	<0.01
European (498)	524	0.38
Finnish (40)	71	0.05
French, ex. Basque (361)	2,350	1.69
French Canadian (37)	80	0.06
German (9,618)	34,868	25.12
German Russian (0)	0	<0.01
Greek (178)	383	0.28
Guyanese (0)	0	<0.01
Hungarian (957)	2,993	2.16
Icelander (0)	0	<0.01
Iranian (3)	3	<0.01
Irish (5,035)	23,818	17.16
Israeli (0)	9	0.01
Italian (7,718)	19,402	13.98
Latvian (0)	0	<0.01
Lithuanian (24)	258	0.19
Luxemburger (0)	33	0.02
Macedonian (0)	0	<0.01
Maltese (0)	0	<0.01
New Zealander (0)	0	<0.01
Northern European (58)	58	0.04
Norwegian (88)	283	0.20
Pennsylvania German (527)	1,006	0.72

Ancestry	Population	%
Polish (5,249)	13,263	9.55
Portuguese (34)	110	0.08
Romanian (64)	241	0.17
Russian (610)	2,376	1.71
Scandinavian (11)	36	0.03
Scotch-Irish (832)	2,709	1.95
Scottish (492)	1,967	1.42
Serbian (87)	384	0.28
Slavic (114)	235	0.17
Slovak (3,935)	9,498	6.84
Slovene (263)	444	0.32
Soviet Union (0)	0	<0.01
Swedish (88)	550	0.40
Swiss (84)	380	0.27
Turkish (0)	0	<0.01
Ukrainian (312)	539	0.39
Welsh (317)	1,565	1.13
West Indian, ex. Hispanic (110)	149	0.11
Bahamian (31)	31	0.02
Barbadian (0)	0	<0.01
Belizean (0)	0	<0.01
Bermudan (0)	0	<0.01
British West Indian (0)	0	<0.01
Dutch West Indian (0)	0	<0.01
Haitian (0)	0	<0.01
Jamaican (79)	118	0.09
Trinidadian/Tobagonian (0)	0	<0.01
U.S. Virgin Islander (0)	0	<0.01
West Indian (0)	0	<0.01
Other West Indian (0)	0	<0.01
Yugoslavian (24)	67	0.05

Hispanic Origin	Population	%
Hispanic or Latino (of any race)	1,049	0.77
Central American, ex. Mexican	52	0.04
Costa Rican	1	<0.01
Guatemalan	20	0.01
Honduran	1	<0.01
Nicaraguan	5	<0.01
Panamanian	12	0.01
Salvadoran	13	0.01
Other Central American	0	<0.01
Cuban	24	0.02
Dominican Republic	4	<0.01
Mexican	354	0.26
Puerto Rican	168	0.12
South American	45	0.03
Argentinean	10	0.01
Bolivian	0	<0.01
Chilean	0	<0.01
Colombian	15	0.01
Ecuadorian	6	<0.01
Paraguayan	1	<0.01
Peruvian	5	<0.01
Uruguayan	1	<0.01
Venezuelan	7	0.01
Other South American	0	<0.01
Other Hispanic or Latino	402	0.29

Race*	Population	%
African-American/Black (6,325)	7,580	5.55
Not Hispanic (6,270)	7,469	5.47
Hispanic (55)	111	0.08
American Indian/Alaska Native (184)	685	0.50
Not Hispanic (161)	625	0.46
Hispanic (23)	60	0.04
Alaska Athabascan (Ala. Nat.) (0)	4	<0.01
Aleut (Alaska Native) (0)	0	<0.01
Apache (1)	7	0.01
Arapaho (0)	0	<0.01
Blackfeet (3)	27	0.02
Canadian/French Am. Ind. (2)	3	<0.01
Central American Ind. (2)	3	<0.01
Cherokee (42)	179	0.13
Cheyenne (4)	6	<0.01
Chickasaw (2)	2	<0.01
Chippewa (4)	8	0.01
Choctaw (1)	7	0.01
Colville (0)	0	<0.01

	Population	%
Comanche (2)	2	<0.01
Cree (0)	2	<0.01
Creek (0)	0	<0.01
Crow (0)	0	<0.01
Delaware (0)	6	<0.01
Hopi (0)	0	<0.01
Houma (0)	0	<0.01
Inupiat (Alaska Native) (0)	0	<0.01
Iroquois (5)	30	0.02
Kiowa (0)	0	<0.01
Lumbee (1)	2	<0.01
Menominee (0)	0	<0.01
Mexican American Ind. (5)	5	<0.01
Navajo (7)	15	0.01
Osage (0)	2	<0.01
Ottawa (0)	0	<0.01
Paiute (0)	0	<0.01
Pima (1)	4	<0.01
Potawatomi (1)	1	<0.01
Pueblo (0)	0	<0.01
Puget Sound Salish (0)	0	<0.01
Seminole (1)	3	<0.01
Shoshone (0)	0	<0.01
Sioux (0)	14	0.01
South American Ind. (1)	1	<0.01
Spanish American Ind. (0)	0	<0.01
Tlingit-Haida (Alaska Native) (1)	1	<0.01
Tohono O'Odham (0)	0	<0.01
Tsimshian (Alaska Native) (0)	0	<0.01
Ute (0)	0	<0.01
Yakama (0)	0	<0.01
Yaqui (0)	0	<0.01
Yuman (0)	0	<0.01
Yup'ik (Alaska Native) (0)	0	<0.01
Asian (405)	589	0.43
Not Hispanic (397)	561	0.41
Hispanic (8)	28	0.02
Bangladeshi (0)	0	<0.01
Bhutanese (0)	0	<0.01
Burmese (0)	0	<0.01
Cambodian (1)	4	<0.01
Chinese, ex. Taiwanese (66)	81	0.06
Filipino (58)	111	0.08
Hmong (3)	3	<0.01
Indian (107)	140	0.10
Indonesian (9)	11	0.01
Japanese (24)	46	0.03
Korean (66)	94	0.07
Laotian (0)	0	<0.01
Malaysian (0)	0	<0.01
Nepalese (0)	0	<0.01
Pakistani (6)	11	0.01
Sri Lankan (0)	0	<0.01
Taiwanese (4)	5	<0.01
Thai (11)	18	0.01
Vietnamese (34)	49	0.04
Hawaii Native/Pacific Islander (24)	48	0.04
Not Hispanic (23)	39	0.03
Hispanic (1)	9	0.01
Fijian (0)	0	<0.01
Guamanian/Chamorro (2)	5	<0.01
Marshallese (0)	0	<0.01
Native Hawaiian (3)	11	0.01
Samoan (11)	13	0.01
Tongan (0)	0	<0.01
White (127,418)	129,173	94.56
Not Hispanic (126,888)	128,550	94.10
Hispanic (530)	623	0.46

*Notes: † The Census 2010 population figure is used to calculate the percentages in the Hispanic Origin and Race categories. Ancestry percentages are based on the 2006-2010 American Community Survey population (not shown); ‡ Numbers in parentheses indicate the number of people reporting a single ancestry; * Numbers in parentheses indicate the number of persons reporting this race alone, not in combination with any other race; Please refer to the Explanation of Data for more information.*

Forest County

Population: 7,716

Ancestry	Population	%
Afghan (0)	0	<0.01
African, Sub-Saharan (0)	0	<0.01
African (0)	0	<0.01
Cape Verdean (0)	0	<0.01
Ethiopian (0)	0	<0.01
Ghanaian (0)	0	<0.01
Kenyan (0)	0	<0.01
Liberian (0)	0	<0.01
Nigerian (0)	0	<0.01
Senegalese (0)	0	<0.01
Sierra Leonean (0)	0	<0.01
Somalian (0)	0	<0.01
South African (0)	0	<0.01
Sudanese (0)	0	<0.01
Ugandan (0)	0	<0.01
Zimbabwean (0)	0	<0.01
Other Sub-Saharan African (0)	0	<0.01
Albanian (0)	0	<0.01
Alsatian (0)	0	<0.01
American (252)	252	3.32
Arab (0)	0	<0.01
Arab (0)	0	<0.01
Egyptian (0)	0	<0.01
Iraqi (0)	0	<0.01
Jordanian (0)	0	<0.01
Lebanese (0)	0	<0.01
Moroccan (0)	0	<0.01
Palestinian (0)	0	<0.01
Syrian (0)	0	<0.01
Other Arab (0)	0	<0.01
Armenian (0)	0	<0.01
Assyrian/Chaldean/Syriac (0)	0	<0.01
Australian (0)	0	<0.01
Austrian (6)	13	0.17
Basque (0)	0	<0.01
Belgian (0)	0	<0.01
Brazilian (0)	0	<0.01
British (0)	2	0.03
Bulgarian (0)	0	<0.01
Cajun (0)	0	<0.01
Canadian (0)	0	<0.01
Carpatho Rusyn (0)	0	<0.01
Celtic (0)	0	<0.01
Croatian (11)	17	0.22
Cypriot (0)	0	<0.01
Czech (8)	51	0.67
Czechoslovakian (2)	4	0.05
Danish (2)	2	0.03
Dutch (22)	339	4.47
Eastern European (0)	0	<0.01
English (140)	664	8.75
Estonian (0)	0	<0.01
European (24)	26	0.34
Finnish (0)	2	0.03
French, ex. Basque (84)	189	2.49
French Canadian (18)	68	0.90
German (852)	2,472	32.59
German Russian (0)	0	<0.01
Greek (13)	21	0.28
Guyanese (0)	0	<0.01
Hungarian (10)	27	0.36
Icelander (0)	0	<0.01
Iranian (0)	0	<0.01
Irish (232)	997	13.14
Israeli (0)	0	<0.01
Italian (92)	321	4.23
Latvian (0)	0	<0.01
Lithuanian (2)	15	0.20
Luxemburger (0)	0	<0.01
Macedonian (0)	0	<0.01
Maltese (0)	0	<0.01
New Zealander (0)	0	<0.01
Northern European (0)	0	<0.01
Norwegian (2)	18	0.24
Pennsylvania German (49)	52	0.69

	Population	%
Polish (91)	266	3.51
Portuguese (0)	0	<0.01
Romanian (0)	4	0.05
Russian (9)	91	1.20
Scandinavian (14)	14	0.18
Scotch-Irish (69)	225	2.97
Scottish (29)	67	0.88
Serbian (0)	0	<0.01
Slavic (0)	0	<0.01
Slovak (49)	133	1.75
Slovene (21)	44	0.58
Soviet Union (0)	0	<0.01
Swedish (32)	157	2.07
Swiss (5)	8	0.11
Turkish (0)	0	<0.01
Ukrainian (1)	31	0.41
Welsh (0)	32	0.42
West Indian, ex. Hispanic (0)	0	<0.01
Bahamian (0)	0	<0.01
Barbadian (0)	0	<0.01
Belizean (0)	0	<0.01
Bermudan (0)	0	<0.01
British West Indian (0)	0	<0.01
Dutch West Indian (0)	0	<0.01
Haitian (0)	0	<0.01
Jamaican (0)	0	<0.01
Trinidadian/Tobagonian (0)	0	<0.01
U.S. Virgin Islander (0)	0	<0.01
West Indian (0)	0	<0.01
Other West Indian (0)	0	<0.01
Yugoslavian (0)	5	0.07

Hispanic Origin	Population	%
Hispanic or Latino (of any race)	418	5.42
Central American, ex. Mexican	2	0.03
Costa Rican	0	<0.01
Guatemalan	1	0.01
Honduran	1	0.01
Nicaraguan	0	<0.01
Panamanian	0	<0.01
Salvadoran	0	<0.01
Other Central American	0	<0.01
Cuban	1	0.01
Dominican Republic	1	0.01
Mexican	26	0.34
Puerto Rican	85	1.10
South American	1	0.01
Argentinean	0	<0.01
Bolivian	0	<0.01
Chilean	0	<0.01
Colombian	1	0.01
Ecuadorian	0	<0.01
Paraguayan	0	<0.01
Peruvian	0	<0.01
Uruguayan	0	<0.01
Venezuelan	0	<0.01
Other South American	0	<0.01
Other Hispanic or Latino	302	3.91

Race*	Population	%
African-American/Black (1,389)	1,405	18.21
Not Hispanic (1,374)	1,389	18.00
Hispanic (15)	16	0.21
American Indian/Alaska Native (13)	40	0.52
Not Hispanic (11)	38	0.49
Hispanic (2)	2	0.03
Alaska Athabascan (Ala. Nat.) (0)	0	<0.01
Aleut (Alaska Native) (0)	0	<0.01
Apache (0)	0	<0.01
Arapaho (0)	0	<0.01
Blackfeet (0)	1	0.01
Canadian/French Am. Ind. (0)	0	<0.01
Central American Ind. (1)	1	0.01
Cherokee (1)	8	0.10
Cheyenne (1)	1	0.01
Chickasaw (0)	0	<0.01
Chippewa (0)	0	<0.01
Choctaw (0)	0	<0.01
Colville (0)	0	<0.01

	Population	%
Comanche (0)	0	<0.01
Cree (0)	0	<0.01
Creek (0)	0	<0.01
Crow (0)	0	<0.01
Delaware (0)	0	<0.01
Hopi (0)	0	<0.01
Houma (0)	0	<0.01
Inupiat (Alaska Native) (0)	0	<0.01
Iroquois (5)	5	0.06
Kiowa (0)	0	<0.01
Lumbee (0)	2	0.03
Menominee (0)	0	<0.01
Mexican American Ind. (1)	1	0.01
Navajo (0)	0	<0.01
Osage (0)	0	<0.01
Ottawa (0)	0	<0.01
Paiute (0)	0	<0.01
Pima (0)	0	<0.01
Potawatomi (1)	1	0.01
Pueblo (0)	0	<0.01
Puget Sound Salish (0)	0	<0.01
Seminole (0)	0	<0.01
Shoshone (0)	0	<0.01
Sioux (0)	0	<0.01
South American Ind. (0)	0	<0.01
Spanish American Ind. (0)	0	<0.01
Tlingit-Haida (Alaska Native) (0)	0	<0.01
Tohono O'Odham (0)	0	<0.01
Tsimshian (Alaska Native) (0)	0	<0.01
Ute (0)	0	<0.01
Yakama (0)	0	<0.01
Yaqui (0)	0	<0.01
Yuman (0)	0	<0.01
Yup'ik (Alaska Native) (0)	0	<0.01
Asian (12)	16	0.21
Not Hispanic (12)	16	0.21
Hispanic (0)	0	<0.01
Bangladeshi (0)	0	<0.01
Bhutanese (0)	0	<0.01
Burmese (0)	0	<0.01
Cambodian (0)	0	<0.01
Chinese, ex. Taiwanese (0)	0	<0.01
Filipino (3)	5	0.06
Hmong (0)	0	<0.01
Indian (1)	2	0.03
Indonesian (0)	0	<0.01
Japanese (1)	2	0.03
Korean (0)	0	<0.01
Laotian (0)	0	<0.01
Malaysian (0)	0	<0.01
Nepalese (0)	0	<0.01
Pakistani (0)	0	<0.01
Sri Lankan (0)	0	<0.01
Taiwanese (0)	0	<0.01
Thai (0)	0	<0.01
Vietnamese (1)	1	0.01
Hawaii Native/Pacific Islander (1)	3	0.04
Not Hispanic (1)	3	0.04
Hispanic (0)	0	<0.01
Fijian (0)	0	<0.01
Guamanian/Chamorro (0)	0	<0.01
Marshallese (0)	0	<0.01
Native Hawaiian (1)	1	0.01
Samoan (0)	2	0.03
Tongan (0)	0	<0.01
White (5,937)	5,980	77.50
Not Hispanic (5,850)	5,892	76.36
Hispanic (87)	88	1.14

Notes: † The Census 2010 population figure is used to calculate the percentages in the Hispanic Origin and Race categories. Ancestry percentages are based on the 2006-2010 American Community Survey population (not shown); ‡ Numbers in parentheses indicate the number of people reporting a single ancestry; * Numbers in parentheses indicate the number of persons reporting this race alone, not in combination with any other race; Please refer to the Explanation of Data for more information.

Franklin County

Population: 149,618

Ancestry	Population	%
Afghan (0)	0	<0.01
African, Sub-Saharan (163)	377	0.26
African (88)	153	0.10
Cape Verdean (0)	0	<0.01
Ethiopian (36)	95	0.06
Ghanaian (0)	0	<0.01
Kenyan (0)	0	<0.01
Liberian (3)	3	<0.01
Nigerian (36)	110	0.08
Senegalese (0)	0	<0.01
Sierra Leonean (0)	0	<0.01
Somalian (0)	0	<0.01
South African (0)	0	<0.01
Sudanese (0)	0	<0.01
Ugandan (0)	0	<0.01
Zimbabwean (0)	0	<0.01
Other Sub-Saharan African (0)	16	0.01
Albanian (0)	0	<0.01
Alsatian (2)	2	<0.01
American (14,803)	14,803	10.10
Arab (390)	465	0.32
Arab (0)	0	<0.01
Egyptian (35)	35	0.02
Iraqi (0)	0	<0.01
Jordanian (0)	0	<0.01
Lebanese (11)	29	0.02
Moroccan (231)	231	0.16
Palestinian (21)	44	0.03
Syrian (61)	95	0.06
Other Arab (31)	31	0.02
Armenian (13)	13	0.01
Assyrian/Chaldean/Syriac (0)	0	<0.01
Australian (0)	0	<0.01
Austrian (87)	488	0.33
Basque (0)	0	<0.01
Belgian (86)	170	0.12
Brazilian (69)	69	0.05
British (176)	620	0.42
Bulgarian (4)	4	<0.01
Cajun (0)	6	<0.01
Canadian (140)	206	0.14
Carpatho Rusyn (0)	0	<0.01
Celtic (0)	0	<0.01
Croatian (6)	118	0.08
Cypriot (0)	0	<0.01
Czech (57)	255	0.17
Czechoslovakian (101)	117	0.08
Danish (50)	194	0.13
Dutch (430)	2,642	1.80
Eastern European (47)	47	0.03
English (4,383)	11,632	7.94
Estonian (19)	30	0.02
European (1,710)	1,776	1.21
Finnish (16)	97	0.07
French, ex. Basque (539)	2,826	1.93
French Canadian (164)	579	0.40
German (30,699)	57,992	39.57
German Russian (0)	0	<0.01
Greek (300)	590	0.40
Guyanese (0)	0	<0.01
Hungarian (260)	595	0.41
Icelander (0)	17	0.01
Iranian (0)	0	<0.01
Irish (4,435)	18,736	12.78
Israeli (38)	38	0.03
Italian (2,237)	6,394	4.36
Latvian (4)	14	0.01
Lithuanian (77)	254	0.17
Luxemburger (16)	46	0.03
Macedonian (0)	0	<0.01
Maltese (0)	0	<0.01
New Zealander (13)	13	0.01
Northern European (71)	81	0.06
Norwegian (134)	304	0.21
Pennsylvania German (1,315)	1,506	1.03

Ancestry (cont.)	Population	%
Polish (1,126)	3,449	2.35
Portuguese (40)	109	0.07
Romanian (33)	60	0.04
Russian (139)	434	0.30
Scandinavian (51)	141	0.10
Scotch-Irish (1,629)	4,214	2.88
Scottish (833)	3,127	2.13
Serbian (73)	142	0.10
Slavic (0)	10	0.01
Slovak (185)	507	0.35
Slovene (39)	72	0.05
Soviet Union (0)	0	<0.01
Swedish (331)	1,238	0.84
Swiss (685)	2,005	1.37
Turkish (12)	12	0.01
Ukrainian (94)	277	0.19
Welsh (220)	1,318	0.90
West Indian, ex. Hispanic (148)	240	0.16
Bahamian (0)	0	<0.01
Barbadian (0)	0	<0.01
Belizean (0)	0	<0.01
Bermudan (0)	0	<0.01
British West Indian (0)	0	<0.01
Dutch West Indian (0)	0	<0.01
Haitian (27)	27	0.02
Jamaican (121)	180	0.12
Trinidadian/Tobagonian (0)	16	0.01
U.S. Virgin Islander (0)	0	<0.01
West Indian (0)	17	0.01
Other West Indian (0)	0	<0.01
Yugoslavian (23)	58	0.04

Hispanic Origin	Population	%
Hispanic or Latino (of any race)	6,438	4.30
Central American, ex. Mexican	1,246	0.83
Costa Rican	26	0.02
Guatemalan	842	0.56
Honduran	107	0.07
Nicaraguan	8	0.01
Panamanian	44	0.03
Salvadoran	210	0.14
Other Central American	9	0.01
Cuban	109	0.07
Dominican Republic	268	0.18
Mexican	2,634	1.76
Puerto Rican	1,354	0.90
South American	214	0.14
Argentinean	7	<0.01
Bolivian	33	0.02
Chilean	36	0.02
Colombian	42	0.03
Ecuadorian	13	0.01
Paraguayan	8	0.01
Peruvian	55	0.04
Uruguayan	1	<0.01
Venezuelan	19	0.01
Other South American	0	<0.01
Other Hispanic or Latino	613	0.41

Race*	Population	%
African-American/Black (4,700)	6,257	4.18
Not Hispanic (4,348)	5,677	3.79
Hispanic (352)	580	0.39
American Indian/Alaska Native (302)	953	0.64
Not Hispanic (230)	803	0.54
Hispanic (72)	150	0.10
Alaska Athabascan (Ala. Nat.) (1)	4	<0.01
Aleut (Alaska Native) (0)	0	<0.01
Apache (8)	20	0.01
Arapaho (0)	1	<0.01
Blackfeet (5)	41	0.03
Canadian/French Am. Ind. (0)	1	<0.01
Central American Ind. (0)	1	<0.01
Cherokee (41)	193	0.13
Cheyenne (0)	4	<0.01
Chickasaw (1)	1	<0.01
Chippewa (3)	8	0.01
Choctaw (3)	12	0.01
Colville (0)	0	<0.01

Race* (cont.)	Population	%
Comanche (0)	2	<0.01
Cree (1)	8	0.01
Creek (1)	2	<0.01
Crow (2)	3	<0.01
Delaware (4)	9	0.01
Hopi (0)	0	<0.01
Houma (0)	0	<0.01
Inupiat (Alaska Native) (0)	1	<0.01
Iroquois (9)	28	0.02
Kiowa (0)	0	<0.01
Lumbee (9)	14	0.01
Menominee (0)	0	<0.01
Mexican American Ind. (14)	21	0.01
Navajo (15)	20	0.01
Osage (0)	0	<0.01
Ottawa (0)	0	<0.01
Paiute (0)	0	<0.01
Pima (0)	0	<0.01
Potawatomi (6)	13	0.01
Pueblo (0)	1	<0.01
Puget Sound Salish (0)	0	<0.01
Seminole (3)	7	<0.01
Shoshone (5)	6	<0.01
Sioux (11)	31	0.02
South American Ind. (2)	7	<0.01
Spanish American Ind. (0)	1	<0.01
Tlingit-Haida (Alaska Native) (1)	2	<0.01
Tohono O'Odham (1)	5	<0.01
Tsimshian (Alaska Native) (0)	1	<0.01
Ute (0)	0	<0.01
Yakama (0)	0	<0.01
Yaqui (0)	0	<0.01
Yuman (0)	0	<0.01
Yup'ik (Alaska Native) (0)	0	<0.01
Asian (1,310)	1,781	1.19
Not Hispanic (1,294)	1,710	1.14
Hispanic (16)	71	0.05
Bangladeshi (7)	7	<0.01
Bhutanese (0)	0	<0.01
Burmese (4)	4	<0.01
Cambodian (8)	8	0.01
Chinese, ex. Taiwanese (226)	281	0.19
Filipino (190)	318	0.21
Hmong (1)	1	<0.01
Indian (243)	297	0.20
Indonesian (53)	56	0.04
Japanese (42)	96	0.06
Korean (203)	306	0.20
Laotian (3)	9	0.01
Malaysian (3)	7	<0.01
Nepalese (13)	14	0.01
Pakistani (69)	75	0.05
Sri Lankan (1)	1	<0.01
Taiwanese (11)	12	0.01
Thai (38)	65	0.04
Vietnamese (118)	151	0.10
Hawaii Native/Pacific Islander (29)	104	0.07
Not Hispanic (17)	70	0.05
Hispanic (12)	34	0.02
Fijian (2)	2	<0.01
Guamanian/Chamorro (15)	25	0.02
Marshallese (0)	0	<0.01
Native Hawaiian (8)	30	0.02
Samoan (0)	0	<0.01
Tongan (1)	2	<0.01
White (137,674)	140,182	93.69
Not Hispanic (135,004)	137,007	91.57
Hispanic (2,670)	3,175	2.12

*Notes: † The Census 2010 population figure is used to calculate the percentages in the Hispanic Origin and Race categories. Ancestry percentages are based on the 2006-2010 American Community Survey population (not shown); ‡ Numbers in parentheses indicate the number of people reporting a single ancestry; * Numbers in parentheses indicate the number of persons reporting this race alone, not in combination with any other race; Please refer to the Explanation of Data for more information.*

Fulton County

Population: 14,845

Ancestry	Population	%
Afghan (0)	0	<0.01
African, Sub-Saharan (0)	9	0.06
African (0)	9	0.06
Cape Verdean (0)	0	<0.01
Ethiopian (0)	0	<0.01
Ghanaian (0)	0	<0.01
Kenyan (0)	0	<0.01
Liberian (0)	0	<0.01
Nigerian (0)	0	<0.01
Senegalese (0)	0	<0.01
Sierra Leonean (0)	0	<0.01
Somalian (0)	0	<0.01
South African (0)	0	<0.01
Sudanese (0)	0	<0.01
Ugandan (0)	0	<0.01
Zimbabwean (0)	0	<0.01
Other Sub-Saharan African (0)	0	<0.01
Albanian (0)	0	<0.01
Alsatian (0)	0	<0.01
American (1,861)	1,861	12.54
Arab (13)	45	0.30
Arab (0)	0	<0.01
Egyptian (0)	0	<0.01
Iraqi (0)	0	<0.01
Jordanian (0)	0	<0.01
Lebanese (0)	16	0.11
Moroccan (0)	0	<0.01
Palestinian (0)	0	<0.01
Syrian (13)	29	0.20
Other Arab (0)	0	<0.01
Armenian (0)	0	<0.01
Assyrian/Chaldean/Syriac (0)	0	<0.01
Australian (0)	0	<0.01
Austrian (3)	12	0.08
Basque (0)	0	<0.01
Belgian (0)	3	0.02
Brazilian (0)	0	<0.01
British (0)	4	0.03
Bulgarian (22)	22	0.15
Cajun (0)	0	<0.01
Canadian (3)	6	0.04
Carpatho Rusyn (0)	0	<0.01
Celtic (0)	0	<0.01
Croatian (3)	3	0.02
Cypriot (0)	0	<0.01
Czech (3)	26	0.18
Czechoslovakian (4)	4	0.03
Danish (6)	9	0.06
Dutch (43)	376	2.53
Eastern European (3)	3	0.02
English (469)	1,071	7.22
Estonian (0)	0	<0.01
European (62)	72	0.49
Finnish (2)	2	0.01
French, ex. Basque (229)	688	4.64
French Canadian (17)	17	0.11
German (2,952)	5,644	38.03
German Russian (0)	0	<0.01
Greek (0)	3	0.02
Guyanese (0)	0	<0.01
Hungarian (0)	32	0.22
Icelander (0)	0	<0.01
Iranian (0)	0	<0.01
Irish (492)	2,067	13.93
Israeli (0)	0	<0.01
Italian (172)	399	2.69
Latvian (0)	3	0.02
Lithuanian (0)	11	0.07
Luxemburger (0)	0	<0.01
Macedonian (0)	0	<0.01
Maltese (0)	0	<0.01
New Zealander (0)	0	<0.01
Northern European (0)	0	<0.01
Norwegian (20)	57	0.38
Pennsylvania German (32)	51	0.34

Ancestry	Population	%
Polish (86)	245	1.65
Portuguese (9)	25	0.17
Romanian (0)	0	<0.01
Russian (0)	11	0.07
Scandinavian (0)	7	0.05
Scotch-Irish (166)	267	1.80
Scottish (60)	164	1.11
Serbian (0)	0	<0.01
Slavic (0)	16	0.11
Slovak (6)	16	0.11
Slovene (0)	0	<0.01
Soviet Union (0)	0	<0.01
Swedish (13)	73	0.49
Swiss (4)	19	0.13
Turkish (0)	0	<0.01
Ukrainian (3)	29	0.20
Welsh (25)	85	0.57
West Indian, ex. Hispanic (0)	3	0.02
Bahamian (0)	0	<0.01
Barbadian (0)	0	<0.01
Belizean (0)	0	<0.01
Bermudan (0)	0	<0.01
British West Indian (0)	0	<0.01
Dutch West Indian (0)	0	<0.01
Haitian (0)	0	<0.01
Jamaican (0)	0	<0.01
Trinidadian/Tobagonian (0)	0	<0.01
U.S. Virgin Islander (0)	0	<0.01
West Indian (0)	3	0.02
Other West Indian (0)	0	<0.01
Yugoslavian (0)	0	<0.01

Hispanic Origin	Population	%
Hispanic or Latino (of any race)	123	0.83
Central American, ex. Mexican	18	0.12
Costa Rican	0	<0.01
Guatemalan	18	0.12
Honduran	0	<0.01
Nicaraguan	0	<0.01
Panamanian	0	<0.01
Salvadoran	0	<0.01
Other Central American	0	<0.01
Cuban	1	0.01
Dominican Republic	3	0.02
Mexican	56	0.38
Puerto Rican	18	0.12
South American	0	<0.01
Argentinean	0	<0.01
Bolivian	0	<0.01
Chilean	0	<0.01
Colombian	0	<0.01
Ecuadorian	0	<0.01
Paraguayan	0	<0.01
Peruvian	0	<0.01
Uruguayan	0	<0.01
Venezuelan	0	<0.01
Other South American	0	<0.01
Other Hispanic or Latino	27	0.18

Race*	Population	%
African-American/Black (151)	225	1.52
Not Hispanic (144)	211	1.42
Hispanic (7)	14	0.09
American Indian/Alaska Native (28)	95	0.64
Not Hispanic (26)	88	0.59
Hispanic (2)	7	0.05
Alaska Athabascan (Ala. Nat.) (0)	0	<0.01
Aleut (Alaska Native) (0)	0	<0.01
Apache (0)	1	0.01
Arapaho (0)	0	<0.01
Blackfeet (0)	4	0.03
Canadian/French Am. Ind. (0)	1	0.01
Central American Ind. (0)	0	<0.01
Cherokee (6)	21	0.14
Cheyenne (0)	0	<0.01
Chickasaw (0)	0	<0.01
Chippewa (0)	0	<0.01
Choctaw (1)	1	0.01
Colville (0)	0	<0.01

	Population	%
Comanche (0)	0	<0.01
Cree (0)	0	<0.01
Creek (0)	0	<0.01
Crow (0)	0	<0.01
Delaware (0)	5	0.03
Hopi (0)	0	<0.01
Houma (0)	0	<0.01
Inupiat (Alaska Native) (0)	0	<0.01
Iroquois (0)	2	0.01
Kiowa (0)	0	<0.01
Lumbee (0)	0	<0.01
Menominee (1)	1	0.01
Mexican American Ind. (1)	1	0.01
Navajo (0)	0	<0.01
Osage (0)	0	<0.01
Ottawa (0)	0	<0.01
Paiute (0)	0	<0.01
Pima (0)	0	<0.01
Potawatomi (0)	0	<0.01
Pueblo (0)	0	<0.01
Puget Sound Salish (0)	0	<0.01
Seminole (0)	1	0.01
Shoshone (0)	0	<0.01
Sioux (0)	0	<0.01
South American Ind. (0)	0	<0.01
Spanish American Ind. (1)	1	0.01
Tlingit-Haida (Alaska Native) (0)	0	<0.01
Tohono O'Odham (0)	1	0.01
Tsimshian (Alaska Native) (0)	1	0.01
Ute (0)	0	<0.01
Yakama (0)	0	<0.01
Yaqui (0)	0	<0.01
Yuman (0)	0	<0.01
Yup'ik (Alaska Native) (0)	0	<0.01
Asian (19)	36	0.24
Not Hispanic (19)	32	0.22
Hispanic (0)	4	0.03
Bangladeshi (0)	0	<0.01
Bhutanese (0)	0	<0.01
Burmese (0)	0	<0.01
Cambodian (0)	0	<0.01
Chinese, ex. Taiwanese (8)	8	0.05
Filipino (2)	12	0.08
Hmong (0)	0	<0.01
Indian (1)	1	0.01
Indonesian (0)	0	<0.01
Japanese (1)	3	0.02
Korean (5)	8	0.05
Laotian (0)	0	<0.01
Malaysian (0)	0	<0.01
Nepalese (0)	0	<0.01
Pakistani (0)	0	<0.01
Sri Lankan (0)	0	<0.01
Taiwanese (0)	0	<0.01
Thai (2)	2	0.01
Vietnamese (0)	2	0.01
Hawaii Native/Pacific Islander (1)	6	0.04
Not Hispanic (1)	5	0.03
Hispanic (0)	1	0.01
Fijian (0)	0	<0.01
Guamanian/Chamorro (0)	0	<0.01
Marshallese (0)	0	<0.01
Native Hawaiian (1)	5	0.03
Samoan (0)	0	<0.01
Tongan (0)	0	<0.01
White (14,450)	14,600	98.35
Not Hispanic (14,387)	14,525	97.84
Hispanic (63)	75	0.51

Notes: † The Census 2010 population figure is used to calculate the percentages in the Hispanic Origin and Race categories. Ancestry percentages are based on the 2006-2010 American Community Survey population (not shown); ‡ Numbers in parentheses indicate the number of people reporting a single ancestry; * Numbers in parentheses indicate the number of persons reporting this race alone, not in combination with any other race; Please refer to the Explanation of Data for more information.

Greene County
Population: 38,686

Ancestry	Population	%
Afghan (0)	0	<0.01
African, Sub-Saharan (29)	38	0.10
African (29)	29	0.07
Cape Verdean (0)	0	<0.01
Ethiopian (0)	9	0.02
Ghanaian (0)	0	<0.01
Kenyan (0)	0	<0.01
Liberian (0)	0	<0.01
Nigerian (0)	0	<0.01
Senegalese (0)	0	<0.01
Sierra Leonean (0)	0	<0.01
Somalian (0)	0	<0.01
South African (0)	0	<0.01
Sudanese (0)	0	<0.01
Ugandan (0)	0	<0.01
Zimbabwean (0)	0	<0.01
Other Sub-Saharan African (0)	0	<0.01
Albanian (0)	0	<0.01
Alsatian (0)	0	<0.01
American (2,796)	2,796	7.17
Arab (36)	188	0.48
Arab (0)	0	<0.01
Egyptian (0)	0	<0.01
Iraqi (0)	0	<0.01
Jordanian (0)	0	<0.01
Lebanese (11)	151	0.39
Moroccan (0)	0	<0.01
Palestinian (0)	0	<0.01
Syrian (25)	25	0.06
Other Arab (0)	12	0.03
Armenian (5)	5	0.01
Assyrian/Chaldean/Syriac (0)	0	<0.01
Australian (0)	0	<0.01
Austrian (13)	101	0.26
Basque (0)	0	<0.01
Belgian (4)	28	0.07
Brazilian (0)	0	<0.01
British (17)	52	0.13
Bulgarian (0)	0	<0.01
Cajun (0)	0	<0.01
Canadian (32)	32	0.08
Carpatho Rusyn (0)	0	<0.01
Celtic (0)	5	0.01
Croatian (120)	311	0.80
Cypriot (0)	0	<0.01
Czech (43)	381	0.98
Czechoslovakian (21)	117	0.30
Danish (0)	23	0.06
Dutch (169)	1,678	4.30
Eastern European (17)	17	0.04
English (1,271)	4,406	11.30
Estonian (0)	0	<0.01
European (115)	131	0.34
Finnish (3)	16	0.04
French, ex. Basque (106)	485	1.24
French Canadian (48)	115	0.29
German (2,582)	10,372	26.59
German Russian (0)	0	<0.01
Greek (55)	94	0.24
Guyanese (0)	0	<0.01
Hungarian (193)	825	2.12
Icelander (0)	0	<0.01
Iranian (0)	0	<0.01
Irish (1,669)	7,445	19.09
Israeli (0)	5	0.01
Italian (953)	3,559	9.12
Latvian (0)	0	<0.01
Lithuanian (28)	71	0.18
Luxemburger (0)	0	<0.01
Macedonian (0)	6	0.02
Maltese (0)	0	<0.01
New Zealander (0)	0	<0.01
Northern European (7)	7	0.02
Norwegian (31)	73	0.19
Pennsylvania German (93)	162	0.42

Ancestry	Population	%
Polish (718)	2,291	5.87
Portuguese (10)	26	0.07
Romanian (0)	4	0.01
Russian (97)	727	1.86
Scandinavian (13)	13	0.03
Scotch-Irish (956)	1,906	4.89
Scottish (248)	835	2.14
Serbian (6)	44	0.11
Slavic (41)	57	0.15
Slovak (394)	1,261	3.23
Slovene (34)	97	0.25
Soviet Union (0)	0	<0.01
Swedish (32)	211	0.54
Swiss (0)	136	0.35
Turkish (0)	7	0.02
Ukrainian (16)	84	0.22
Welsh (26)	311	0.80
West Indian, ex. Hispanic (0)	9	0.02
Bahamian (0)	0	<0.01
Barbadian (0)	0	<0.01
Belizean (0)	0	<0.01
Bermudan (0)	0	<0.01
British West Indian (0)	0	<0.01
Dutch West Indian (0)	0	<0.01
Haitian (0)	0	<0.01
Jamaican (0)	9	0.02
Trinidadian/Tobagonian (0)	0	<0.01
U.S. Virgin Islander (0)	0	<0.01
West Indian (0)	0	<0.01
Other West Indian (0)	0	<0.01
Yugoslavian (16)	41	0.11

Hispanic Origin	Population	%
Hispanic or Latino (of any race)	465	1.20
Central American, ex. Mexican	5	0.01
Costa Rican	0	<0.01
Guatemalan	5	0.01
Honduran	0	<0.01
Nicaraguan	0	<0.01
Panamanian	0	<0.01
Salvadoran	0	<0.01
Other Central American	0	<0.01
Cuban	10	0.03
Dominican Republic	5	0.01
Mexican	130	0.34
Puerto Rican	53	0.14
South American	8	0.02
Argentinean	2	0.01
Bolivian	2	0.01
Chilean	0	<0.01
Colombian	1	<0.01
Ecuadorian	2	0.01
Paraguayan	0	<0.01
Peruvian	1	<0.01
Uruguayan	0	<0.01
Venezuelan	0	<0.01
Other South American	0	<0.01
Other Hispanic or Latino	254	0.66

Race*	Population	%
African-American/Black (1,282)	1,398	3.61
Not Hispanic (1,272)	1,377	3.56
Hispanic (10)	21	0.05
American Indian/Alaska Native (67)	260	0.67
Not Hispanic (59)	247	0.64
Hispanic (8)	13	0.03
Alaska Athabascan (Ala. Nat.) (0)	1	<0.01
Aleut (Alaska Native) (0)	0	<0.01
Apache (0)	6	0.02
Arapaho (0)	0	<0.01
Blackfeet (6)	14	0.04
Canadian/French Am. Ind. (0)	0	<0.01
Central American Ind. (0)	0	<0.01
Cherokee (16)	85	0.22
Cheyenne (0)	1	<0.01
Chickasaw (0)	0	<0.01
Chippewa (0)	0	<0.01
Choctaw (3)	12	0.03
Colville (0)	0	<0.01

	Population	%
Comanche (0)	0	<0.01
Cree (0)	0	<0.01
Creek (0)	0	<0.01
Crow (0)	1	<0.01
Delaware (2)	2	0.01
Hopi (0)	0	<0.01
Houma (0)	0	<0.01
Inupiat (Alaska Native) (0)	0	<0.01
Iroquois (2)	7	0.02
Kiowa (0)	0	<0.01
Lumbee (0)	0	<0.01
Menominee (0)	0	<0.01
Mexican American Ind. (2)	2	0.01
Navajo (1)	1	<0.01
Osage (0)	2	0.01
Ottawa (0)	0	<0.01
Paiute (0)	3	0.01
Pima (0)	0	<0.01
Potawatomi (0)	0	<0.01
Pueblo (0)	0	<0.01
Puget Sound Salish (0)	0	<0.01
Seminole (0)	0	<0.01
Shoshone (0)	0	<0.01
Sioux (0)	2	0.01
South American Ind. (0)	0	<0.01
Spanish American Ind. (0)	0	<0.01
Tlingit-Haida (Alaska Native) (0)	0	<0.01
Tohono O'Odham (0)	0	<0.01
Tsimshian (Alaska Native) (0)	0	<0.01
Ute (0)	0	<0.01
Yakama (0)	0	<0.01
Yaqui (0)	0	<0.01
Yuman (0)	0	<0.01
Yup'ik (Alaska Native) (0)	0	<0.01
Asian (113)	174	0.45
Not Hispanic (113)	170	0.44
Hispanic (0)	4	0.01
Bangladeshi (0)	0	<0.01
Bhutanese (0)	0	<0.01
Burmese (0)	0	<0.01
Cambodian (0)	0	<0.01
Chinese, ex. Taiwanese (29)	34	0.09
Filipino (13)	35	0.09
Hmong (0)	0	<0.01
Indian (19)	24	0.06
Indonesian (0)	1	<0.01
Japanese (10)	16	0.04
Korean (7)	17	0.04
Laotian (0)	0	<0.01
Malaysian (0)	0	<0.01
Nepalese (0)	0	<0.01
Pakistani (0)	0	<0.01
Sri Lankan (2)	3	0.01
Taiwanese (2)	2	0.01
Thai (1)	3	0.01
Vietnamese (7)	11	0.03
Hawaii Native/Pacific Islander (7)	24	0.06
Not Hispanic (6)	22	0.06
Hispanic (1)	2	0.01
Fijian (0)	0	<0.01
Guamanian/Chamorro (1)	2	0.01
Marshallese (0)	0	<0.01
Native Hawaiian (2)	12	0.03
Samoan (2)	3	0.01
Tongan (0)	0	<0.01
White (36,584)	36,949	95.51
Not Hispanic (36,409)	36,755	95.01
Hispanic (175)	194	0.50

*Notes: † The Census 2010 population figure is used to calculate the percentages in the Hispanic Origin and Race categories. Ancestry percentages are based on the 2006-2010 American Community Survey population (not shown); ‡ Numbers in parentheses indicate the number of people reporting a single ancestry; * Numbers in parentheses indicate the number of persons reporting this race alone, not in combination with any other race; Please refer to the Explanation of Data for more information.*

Huntingdon County

Population: 45,913

Ancestry	Population	%
Afghan (0)	0	<0.01
African, Sub-Saharan (19)	27	0.06
African (19)	27	0.06
Cape Verdean (0)	0	<0.01
Ethiopian (0)	0	<0.01
Ghanaian (0)	0	<0.01
Kenyan (0)	0	<0.01
Liberian (0)	0	<0.01
Nigerian (0)	0	<0.01
Senegalese (0)	0	<0.01
Sierra Leonean (0)	0	<0.01
Somalian (0)	0	<0.01
South African (0)	0	<0.01
Sudanese (0)	0	<0.01
Ugandan (0)	0	<0.01
Zimbabwean (0)	0	<0.01
Other Sub-Saharan African (0)	0	<0.01
Albanian (43)	43	0.09
Alsatian (1)	1	<0.01
American (2,675)	2,675	5.84
Arab (14)	51	0.11
Arab (0)	0	<0.01
Egyptian (7)	22	0.05
Iraqi (0)	0	<0.01
Jordanian (0)	0	<0.01
Lebanese (0)	15	0.03
Moroccan (7)	7	0.02
Palestinian (0)	0	<0.01
Syrian (0)	7	0.02
Other Arab (0)	0	<0.01
Armenian (0)	0	<0.01
Assyrian/Chaldean/Syriac (0)	0	<0.01
Australian (0)	25	0.05
Austrian (21)	96	0.21
Basque (0)	0	<0.01
Belgian (27)	68	0.15
Brazilian (0)	0	<0.01
British (36)	57	0.12
Bulgarian (0)	8	0.02
Cajun (0)	3	0.01
Canadian (0)	0	<0.01
Carpatho Rusyn (0)	0	<0.01
Celtic (3)	3	0.01
Croatian (23)	44	0.10
Cypriot (0)	0	<0.01
Czech (3)	110	0.24
Czechoslovakian (31)	111	0.24
Danish (23)	53	0.12
Dutch (300)	1,856	4.05
Eastern European (7)	41	0.09
English (1,349)	3,877	8.46
Estonian (0)	0	<0.01
European (75)	78	0.17
Finnish (0)	0	<0.01
French, ex. Basque (84)	656	1.43
French Canadian (30)	53	0.12
German (7,937)	17,537	38.27
German Russian (0)	0	<0.01
Greek (13)	45	0.10
Guyanese (0)	0	<0.01
Hungarian (28)	105	0.23
Icelander (0)	0	<0.01
Iranian (0)	0	<0.01
Irish (1,989)	7,686	16.77
Israeli (0)	0	<0.01
Italian (576)	2,091	4.56
Latvian (0)	0	<0.01
Lithuanian (22)	40	0.09
Luxemburger (0)	0	<0.01
Macedonian (18)	26	0.06
Maltese (0)	0	<0.01
New Zealander (0)	0	<0.01
Northern European (6)	6	0.01
Norwegian (23)	110	0.24
Pennsylvania German (672)	988	2.16

Ancestry	Population	%
Polish (406)	997	2.18
Portuguese (9)	39	0.09
Romanian (7)	23	0.05
Russian (84)	337	0.74
Scandinavian (4)	10	0.02
Scotch-Irish (539)	1,289	2.81
Scottish (165)	795	1.73
Serbian (0)	19	0.04
Slavic (36)	47	0.10
Slovak (32)	275	0.60
Slovene (35)	49	0.11
Soviet Union (0)	0	<0.01
Swedish (90)	294	0.64
Swiss (29)	178	0.39
Turkish (0)	0	<0.01
Ukrainian (57)	156	0.34
Welsh (116)	657	1.43
West Indian, ex. Hispanic (17)	86	0.19
Bahamian (0)	0	<0.01
Barbadian (0)	0	<0.01
Belizean (0)	0	<0.01
Bermudan (0)	0	<0.01
British West Indian (0)	0	<0.01
Dutch West Indian (0)	0	<0.01
Haitian (0)	0	<0.01
Jamaican (17)	17	0.04
Trinidadian/Tobagonian (0)	0	<0.01
U.S. Virgin Islander (0)	0	<0.01
West Indian (0)	69	0.15
Other West Indian (0)	0	<0.01
Yugoslavian (0)	2	<0.01

Hispanic Origin	Population	%
Hispanic or Latino (of any race)	727	1.58
Central American, ex. Mexican	30	0.07
Costa Rican	0	<0.01
Guatemalan	12	0.03
Honduran	5	0.01
Nicaraguan	6	0.01
Panamanian	4	0.01
Salvadoran	3	0.01
Other Central American	0	<0.01
Cuban	10	0.02
Dominican Republic	16	0.03
Mexican	150	0.33
Puerto Rican	91	0.20
South American	30	0.07
Argentinean	1	<0.01
Bolivian	1	<0.01
Chilean	7	0.02
Colombian	6	0.01
Ecuadorian	5	0.01
Paraguayan	1	<0.01
Peruvian	7	0.02
Uruguayan	1	<0.01
Venezuelan	1	<0.01
Other South American	0	<0.01
Other Hispanic or Latino	400	0.87

Race*	Population	%
African-American/Black (2,392)	2,610	5.68
Not Hispanic (2,369)	2,569	5.60
Hispanic (23)	41	0.09
American Indian/Alaska Native (41)	173	0.38
Not Hispanic (36)	162	0.35
Hispanic (5)	11	0.02
Alaska Athabascan (Ala. Nat.) (0)	0	<0.01
Aleut (Alaska Native) (0)	0	<0.01
Apache (2)	4	0.01
Arapaho (0)	0	<0.01
Blackfeet (2)	7	0.02
Canadian/French Am. Ind. (0)	0	<0.01
Central American Ind. (0)	0	<0.01
Cherokee (6)	31	0.07
Cheyenne (0)	0	<0.01
Chickasaw (0)	0	<0.01
Chippewa (1)	1	<0.01
Choctaw (3)	5	0.01
Colville (0)	0	<0.01

	Population	%
Comanche (0)	0	<0.01
Cree (1)	4	0.01
Creek (0)	0	<0.01
Crow (0)	0	<0.01
Delaware (0)	3	0.01
Hopi (0)	0	<0.01
Houma (0)	0	<0.01
Inupiat (Alaska Native) (0)	0	<0.01
Iroquois (2)	10	0.02
Kiowa (0)	0	<0.01
Lumbee (0)	0	<0.01
Menominee (0)	0	<0.01
Mexican American Ind. (0)	4	0.01
Navajo (0)	0	<0.01
Osage (0)	0	<0.01
Ottawa (0)	0	<0.01
Paiute (0)	0	<0.01
Pima (0)	0	<0.01
Potawatomi (0)	0	<0.01
Pueblo (0)	0	<0.01
Puget Sound Salish (0)	0	<0.01
Seminole (0)	0	<0.01
Shoshone (0)	0	<0.01
Sioux (0)	1	<0.01
South American Ind. (0)	1	<0.01
Spanish American Ind. (0)	0	<0.01
Tlingit-Haida (Alaska Native) (0)	0	<0.01
Tohono O'Odham (4)	4	0.01
Tsimshian (Alaska Native) (0)	0	<0.01
Ute (0)	0	<0.01
Yakama (0)	0	<0.01
Yaqui (0)	0	<0.01
Yuman (0)	0	<0.01
Yup'ik (Alaska Native) (0)	0	<0.01
Asian (184)	256	0.56
Not Hispanic (181)	244	0.53
Hispanic (3)	12	0.03
Bangladeshi (0)	0	<0.01
Bhutanese (0)	0	<0.01
Burmese (0)	0	<0.01
Cambodian (0)	0	<0.01
Chinese, ex. Taiwanese (72)	89	0.19
Filipino (25)	35	0.08
Hmong (0)	0	<0.01
Indian (16)	22	0.05
Indonesian (0)	0	<0.01
Japanese (16)	32	0.07
Korean (17)	24	0.05
Laotian (0)	1	<0.01
Malaysian (0)	0	<0.01
Nepalese (0)	0	<0.01
Pakistani (0)	0	<0.01
Sri Lankan (0)	0	<0.01
Taiwanese (2)	2	<0.01
Thai (1)	3	0.01
Vietnamese (16)	16	0.03
Hawaii Native/Pacific Islander (2)	15	0.03
Not Hispanic (0)	8	0.02
Hispanic (2)	7	0.02
Fijian (0)	0	<0.01
Guamanian/Chamorro (2)	2	<0.01
Marshallese (0)	0	<0.01
Native Hawaiian (0)	3	<0.01
Samoan (0)	2	<0.01
Tongan (0)	0	<0.01
White (42,470)	42,884	93.40
Not Hispanic (42,197)	42,571	92.72
Hispanic (273)	313	0.68

Notes: † The Census 2010 population figure is used to calculate the percentages in the Hispanic Origin and Race categories. Ancestry percentages are based on the 2006-2010 American Community Survey population (not shown); ‡ Numbers in parentheses indicate the number of people reporting a single ancestry; * Numbers in parentheses indicate the number of persons reporting this race alone, not in combination with any other race; Please refer to the Explanation of Data for more information.

Indiana County

Population: 88,880

Ancestry	Population	%
Afghan (0)	0	<0.01
African, Sub-Saharan (103)	124	0.14
African (71)	87	0.10
Cape Verdean (0)	0	<0.01
Ethiopian (0)	5	0.01
Ghanaian (0)	0	<0.01
Kenyan (0)	0	<0.01
Liberian (7)	7	0.01
Nigerian (25)	25	0.03
Senegalese (0)	0	<0.01
Sierra Leonean (0)	0	<0.01
Somalian (0)	0	<0.01
South African (0)	0	<0.01
Sudanese (0)	0	<0.01
Ugandan (0)	0	<0.01
Zimbabwean (0)	0	<0.01
Other Sub-Saharan African (0)	0	<0.01
Albanian (6)	6	0.01
Alsatian (0)	0	<0.01
American (3,944)	3,944	4.44
Arab (149)	241	0.27
Arab (61)	61	0.07
Egyptian (15)	15	0.02
Iraqi (0)	0	<0.01
Jordanian (0)	0	<0.01
Lebanese (28)	51	0.06
Moroccan (0)	0	<0.01
Palestinian (0)	0	<0.01
Syrian (13)	82	0.09
Other Arab (32)	32	0.04
Armenian (0)	0	<0.01
Assyrian/Chaldean/Syriac (0)	0	<0.01
Australian (0)	9	0.01
Austrian (29)	245	0.28
Basque (0)	0	<0.01
Belgian (12)	49	0.06
Brazilian (0)	0	<0.01
British (56)	150	0.17
Bulgarian (0)	11	0.01
Cajun (0)	0	<0.01
Canadian (33)	99	0.11
Carpatho Rusyn (18)	28	0.03
Celtic (0)	0	<0.01
Croatian (260)	508	0.57
Cypriot (0)	0	<0.01
Czech (249)	830	0.94
Czechoslovakian (201)	349	0.39
Danish (0)	27	0.03
Dutch (281)	3,393	3.82
Eastern European (102)	102	0.11
English (2,126)	7,898	8.90
Estonian (0)	0	<0.01
European (302)	338	0.38
Finnish (10)	34	0.04
French, ex. Basque (242)	1,456	1.64
French Canadian (28)	71	0.08
German (9,026)	28,666	32.30
German Russian (0)	0	<0.01
Greek (196)	290	0.33
Guyanese (0)	0	<0.01
Hungarian (581)	1,887	2.13
Icelander (0)	7	0.01
Iranian (0)	0	<0.01
Irish (4,455)	17,956	20.23
Israeli (0)	0	<0.01
Italian (3,946)	10,241	11.54
Latvian (0)	0	<0.01
Lithuanian (72)	179	0.20
Luxemburger (0)	0	<0.01
Macedonian (0)	12	0.01
Maltese (0)	0	<0.01
New Zealander (0)	0	<0.01
Northern European (10)	10	0.01
Norwegian (106)	360	0.41
Pennsylvania German (1,168)	1,584	1.78

Ancestry (cont.)	Population	%
Polish (2,434)	6,446	7.26
Portuguese (32)	59	0.07
Romanian (8)	53	0.06
Russian (210)	871	0.98
Scandinavian (3)	17	0.02
Scotch-Irish (1,537)	3,673	4.14
Scottish (650)	2,210	2.49
Serbian (87)	237	0.27
Slavic (19)	75	0.08
Slovak (1,571)	4,100	4.62
Slovene (57)	180	0.20
Soviet Union (0)	0	<0.01
Swedish (212)	1,063	1.20
Swiss (51)	259	0.29
Turkish (0)	0	<0.01
Ukrainian (284)	918	1.03
Welsh (219)	1,457	1.64
West Indian, ex. Hispanic (44)	75	0.08
Bahamian (0)	0	<0.01
Barbadian (0)	0	<0.01
Belizean (0)	0	<0.01
Bermudan (0)	0	<0.01
British West Indian (0)	0	<0.01
Dutch West Indian (0)	0	<0.01
Haitian (30)	30	0.03
Jamaican (0)	31	0.03
Trinidadian/Tobagonian (14)	14	0.02
U.S. Virgin Islander (0)	0	<0.01
West Indian (0)	0	<0.01
Other West Indian (0)	0	<0.01
Yugoslavian (45)	155	0.17

Hispanic Origin	Population	%
Hispanic or Latino (of any race)	947	1.07
Central American, ex. Mexican	77	0.09
Costa Rican	2	<0.01
Guatemalan	33	0.04
Honduran	20	0.02
Nicaraguan	4	<0.01
Panamanian	6	0.01
Salvadoran	11	0.01
Other Central American	1	<0.01
Cuban	40	0.05
Dominican Republic	43	0.05
Mexican	289	0.33
Puerto Rican	211	0.24
South American	69	0.08
Argentinean	11	0.01
Bolivian	0	<0.01
Chilean	0	<0.01
Colombian	20	0.02
Ecuadorian	7	0.01
Paraguayan	0	<0.01
Peruvian	16	0.02
Uruguayan	5	0.01
Venezuelan	10	0.01
Other South American	0	<0.01
Other Hispanic or Latino	218	0.25

Race*	Population	%
African-American/Black (2,434)	2,826	3.18
Not Hispanic (2,374)	2,733	3.07
Hispanic (60)	93	0.10
American Indian/Alaska Native (124)	417	0.47
Not Hispanic (103)	383	0.43
Hispanic (21)	34	0.04
Alaska Athabascan (Ala. Nat.) (0)	0	<0.01
Aleut (Alaska Native) (0)	0	<0.01
Apache (5)	7	0.01
Arapaho (0)	2	<0.01
Blackfeet (1)	21	0.02
Canadian/French Am. Ind. (0)	2	<0.01
Central American Ind. (0)	0	<0.01
Cherokee (23)	69	0.08
Cheyenne (0)	3	<0.01
Chickasaw (0)	1	<0.01
Chippewa (5)	9	0.01
Choctaw (4)	4	<0.01
Colville (0)	0	<0.01

Race* (cont.)	Population	%
Comanche (0)	2	<0.01
Cree (0)	0	<0.01
Creek (1)	1	<0.01
Crow (0)	6	0.01
Delaware (4)	9	0.01
Hopi (0)	0	<0.01
Houma (0)	0	<0.01
Inupiat (Alaska Native) (0)	0	<0.01
Iroquois (8)	41	0.05
Kiowa (0)	0	<0.01
Lumbee (0)	2	<0.01
Menominee (0)	0	<0.01
Mexican American Ind. (6)	9	0.01
Navajo (1)	1	<0.01
Osage (0)	0	<0.01
Ottawa (0)	0	<0.01
Paiute (0)	0	<0.01
Pima (0)	0	<0.01
Potawatomi (0)	1	<0.01
Pueblo (0)	0	<0.01
Puget Sound Salish (0)	0	<0.01
Seminole (0)	0	<0.01
Shoshone (1)	4	<0.01
Sioux (6)	11	0.01
South American Ind. (1)	2	<0.01
Spanish American Ind. (0)	0	<0.01
Tlingit-Haida (Alaska Native) (1)	1	<0.01
Tohono O'Odham (0)	0	<0.01
Tsimshian (Alaska Native) (0)	0	<0.01
Ute (0)	0	<0.01
Yakama (0)	0	<0.01
Yaqui (0)	0	<0.01
Yuman (0)	0	<0.01
Yup'ik (Alaska Native) (0)	0	<0.01
Asian (774)	949	1.07
Not Hispanic (768)	932	1.05
Hispanic (6)	17	0.02
Bangladeshi (7)	11	0.01
Bhutanese (0)	0	<0.01
Burmese (0)	0	<0.01
Cambodian (0)	9	0.01
Chinese, ex. Taiwanese (219)	253	0.28
Filipino (43)	78	0.09
Hmong (0)	0	<0.01
Indian (140)	171	0.19
Indonesian (10)	11	0.01
Japanese (24)	48	0.05
Korean (124)	154	0.17
Laotian (0)	0	<0.01
Malaysian (11)	11	0.01
Nepalese (3)	4	<0.01
Pakistani (42)	46	0.05
Sri Lankan (4)	4	<0.01
Taiwanese (56)	57	0.06
Thai (13)	15	0.02
Vietnamese (38)	56	0.06
Hawaii Native/Pacific Islander (10)	39	0.04
Not Hispanic (9)	34	0.04
Hispanic (1)	5	0.01
Fijian (0)	0	<0.01
Guamanian/Chamorro (4)	6	0.01
Marshallese (0)	0	<0.01
Native Hawaiian (1)	17	0.02
Samoan (1)	4	<0.01
Tongan (0)	0	<0.01
White (84,360)	85,135	95.79
Not Hispanic (83,864)	84,583	95.17
Hispanic (496)	552	0.62

*Notes: † The Census 2010 population figure is used to calculate the percentages in the Hispanic Origin and Race categories. Ancestry percentages are based on the 2006-2010 American Community Survey population (not shown); ‡ Numbers in parentheses indicate the number of people reporting a single ancestry; * Numbers in parentheses indicate the number of persons reporting this race alone, not in combination with any other race; Please refer to the Explanation of Data for more information.*

Jefferson County

Population: 45,200

Ancestry	Population	%
Afghan (0)	0	<0.01
African, Sub-Saharan (0)	34	0.08
African (0)	29	0.06
Cape Verdean (0)	0	<0.01
Ethiopian (0)	0	<0.01
Ghanaian (0)	0	<0.01
Kenyan (0)	0	<0.01
Liberian (0)	0	<0.01
Nigerian (0)	0	<0.01
Senegalese (0)	0	<0.01
Sierra Leonean (0)	0	<0.01
Somalian (0)	0	<0.01
South African (0)	0	<0.01
Sudanese (0)	5	0.01
Ugandan (0)	0	<0.01
Zimbabwean (0)	0	<0.01
Other Sub-Saharan African (0)	0	<0.01
Albanian (0)	0	<0.01
Alsatian (0)	0	<0.01
American (3,037)	3,037	6.71
Arab (37)	41	0.09
Arab (27)	27	0.06
Egyptian (0)	0	<0.01
Iraqi (0)	0	<0.01
Jordanian (0)	0	<0.01
Lebanese (10)	14	0.03
Moroccan (0)	0	<0.01
Palestinian (0)	0	<0.01
Syrian (0)	0	<0.01
Other Arab (0)	0	<0.01
Armenian (0)	0	<0.01
Assyrian/Chaldean/Syriac (0)	0	<0.01
Australian (0)	0	<0.01
Austrian (24)	97	0.21
Basque (0)	10	0.02
Belgian (3)	8	0.02
Brazilian (0)	0	<0.01
British (29)	98	0.22
Bulgarian (0)	0	<0.01
Cajun (0)	0	<0.01
Canadian (11)	33	0.07
Carpatho Rusyn (0)	0	<0.01
Celtic (0)	0	<0.01
Croatian (11)	59	0.13
Cypriot (0)	0	<0.01
Czech (30)	161	0.36
Czechoslovakian (27)	78	0.17
Danish (2)	54	0.12
Dutch (381)	2,756	6.09
Eastern European (0)	7	0.02
English (1,284)	4,299	9.50
Estonian (0)	0	<0.01
European (185)	185	0.41
Finnish (6)	19	0.04
French, ex. Basque (156)	878	1.94
French Canadian (12)	33	0.07
German (6,025)	15,883	35.11
German Russian (0)	0	<0.01
Greek (22)	45	0.10
Guyanese (0)	0	<0.01
Hungarian (85)	349	0.77
Icelander (0)	0	<0.01
Iranian (0)	0	<0.01
Irish (1,505)	6,630	14.65
Israeli (0)	0	<0.01
Italian (2,149)	5,142	11.37
Latvian (0)	0	<0.01
Lithuanian (69)	255	0.56
Luxemburger (0)	0	<0.01
Macedonian (0)	0	<0.01
Maltese (0)	0	<0.01
New Zealander (0)	0	<0.01
Northern European (3)	3	0.01
Norwegian (5)	40	0.09
Pennsylvania German (463)	635	1.40

Ancestry	Population	%
Polish (720)	2,058	4.55
Portuguese (6)	15	0.03
Romanian (4)	4	0.01
Russian (46)	234	0.52
Scandinavian (4)	16	0.04
Scotch-Irish (586)	1,348	2.98
Scottish (225)	1,148	2.54
Serbian (0)	7	0.02
Slavic (98)	258	0.57
Slovak (415)	710	1.57
Slovene (8)	8	0.02
Soviet Union (0)	0	<0.01
Swedish (302)	1,178	2.60
Swiss (50)	158	0.35
Turkish (10)	30	0.07
Ukrainian (52)	98	0.22
Welsh (104)	594	1.31
West Indian, ex. Hispanic (7)	38	0.08
Bahamian (0)	0	<0.01
Barbadian (0)	0	<0.01
Belizean (0)	0	<0.01
Bermudan (0)	0	<0.01
British West Indian (0)	0	<0.01
Dutch West Indian (0)	0	<0.01
Haitian (0)	0	<0.01
Jamaican (7)	7	0.02
Trinidadian/Tobagonian (0)	0	<0.01
U.S. Virgin Islander (0)	0	<0.01
West Indian (0)	31	0.07
Other West Indian (0)	0	<0.01
Yugoslavian (6)	6	0.01

Hispanic Origin	Population	%
Hispanic or Latino (of any race)	275	0.61
Central American, ex. Mexican	7	0.02
Costa Rican	0	<0.01
Guatemalan	5	0.01
Honduran	1	<0.01
Nicaraguan	0	<0.01
Panamanian	1	<0.01
Salvadoran	0	<0.01
Other Central American	0	<0.01
Cuban	9	0.02
Dominican Republic	8	0.02
Mexican	109	0.24
Puerto Rican	64	0.14
South American	12	0.03
Argentinean	2	<0.01
Bolivian	0	<0.01
Chilean	1	<0.01
Colombian	0	<0.01
Ecuadorian	4	0.01
Paraguayan	0	<0.01
Peruvian	3	0.01
Uruguayan	0	<0.01
Venezuelan	2	<0.01
Other South American	0	<0.01
Other Hispanic or Latino	66	0.15

Race*	Population	%
African-American/Black (157)	275	0.61
Not Hispanic (147)	258	0.57
Hispanic (10)	17	0.04
American Indian/Alaska Native (86)	264	0.58
Not Hispanic (72)	247	0.55
Hispanic (14)	17	0.04
Alaska Athabascan (Ala. Nat.) (0)	0	<0.01
Aleut (Alaska Native) (0)	0	<0.01
Apache (5)	10	0.02
Arapaho (0)	0	<0.01
Blackfeet (2)	16	0.04
Canadian/French Am. Ind. (0)	0	<0.01
Central American Ind. (0)	0	<0.01
Cherokee (12)	33	0.07
Cheyenne (0)	0	<0.01
Chickasaw (0)	0	<0.01
Chippewa (2)	2	<0.01
Choctaw (0)	1	<0.01
Colville (0)	0	<0.01

	Population	%
Comanche (0)	5	0.01
Cree (0)	0	<0.01
Creek (0)	1	<0.01
Crow (0)	0	<0.01
Delaware (0)	2	<0.01
Hopi (0)	1	<0.01
Houma (0)	0	<0.01
Inupiat (Alaska Native) (1)	1	<0.01
Iroquois (13)	27	0.06
Kiowa (0)	0	<0.01
Lumbee (0)	0	<0.01
Menominee (0)	0	<0.01
Mexican American Ind. (0)	0	<0.01
Navajo (0)	0	<0.01
Osage (0)	0	<0.01
Ottawa (0)	0	<0.01
Paiute (0)	0	<0.01
Pima (0)	0	<0.01
Potawatomi (0)	0	<0.01
Pueblo (0)	0	<0.01
Puget Sound Salish (0)	0	<0.01
Seminole (0)	1	<0.01
Shoshone (0)	1	<0.01
Sioux (5)	12	0.03
South American Ind. (0)	0	<0.01
Spanish American Ind. (0)	0	<0.01
Tlingit-Haida (Alaska Native) (0)	0	<0.01
Tohono O'Odham (0)	0	<0.01
Tsimshian (Alaska Native) (0)	0	<0.01
Ute (0)	0	<0.01
Yakama (0)	0	<0.01
Yaqui (0)	0	<0.01
Yuman (0)	1	<0.01
Yup'ik (Alaska Native) (0)	0	<0.01
Asian (92)	154	0.34
Not Hispanic (91)	149	0.33
Hispanic (1)	5	0.01
Bangladeshi (0)	0	<0.01
Bhutanese (0)	0	<0.01
Burmese (0)	0	<0.01
Cambodian (0)	0	<0.01
Chinese, ex. Taiwanese (24)	32	0.07
Filipino (15)	39	0.09
Hmong (0)	0	<0.01
Indian (17)	23	0.05
Indonesian (1)	2	<0.01
Japanese (9)	13	0.03
Korean (14)	24	0.05
Laotian (0)	0	<0.01
Malaysian (0)	0	<0.01
Nepalese (0)	0	<0.01
Pakistani (0)	1	<0.01
Sri Lankan (0)	0	<0.01
Taiwanese (0)	0	<0.01
Thai (1)	2	<0.01
Vietnamese (9)	10	0.02
Hawaii Native/Pacific Islander (3)	15	0.03
Not Hispanic (3)	15	0.03
Hispanic (0)	0	<0.01
Fijian (0)	0	<0.01
Guamanian/Chamorro (1)	2	<0.01
Marshallese (0)	0	<0.01
Native Hawaiian (2)	3	0.01
Samoan (0)	0	<0.01
Tongan (0)	0	<0.01
White (44,446)	44,800	99.12
Not Hispanic (44,264)	44,599	98.67
Hispanic (182)	201	0.44

Notes: † The Census 2010 population figure is used to calculate the percentages in the Hispanic Origin and Race categories. Ancestry percentages are based on the 2006-2010 American Community Survey population (not shown); ‡ Numbers in parentheses indicate the number of people reporting a single ancestry; * Numbers in parentheses indicate the number of persons reporting this race alone, not in combination with any other race; Please refer to the Explanation of Data for more information.

Juniata County

Population: 24,636

Ancestry	Population	%
Afghan (0)	0	<0.01
African, Sub-Saharan (11)	15	0.06
African (11)	13	0.05
Cape Verdean (0)	0	<0.01
Ethiopian (0)	0	<0.01
Ghanaian (0)	0	<0.01
Kenyan (0)	0	<0.01
Liberian (0)	2	0.01
Nigerian (0)	0	<0.01
Senegalese (0)	0	<0.01
Sierra Leonean (0)	0	<0.01
Somalian (0)	0	<0.01
South African (0)	0	<0.01
Sudanese (0)	0	<0.01
Ugandan (0)	0	<0.01
Zimbabwean (0)	0	<0.01
Other Sub-Saharan African (0)	0	<0.01
Albanian (46)	46	0.19
Alsatian (0)	0	<0.01
American (1,992)	1,992	8.17
Arab (6)	6	0.02
Arab (0)	0	<0.01
Egyptian (0)	0	<0.01
Iraqi (0)	0	<0.01
Jordanian (0)	0	<0.01
Lebanese (0)	0	<0.01
Moroccan (0)	0	<0.01
Palestinian (0)	0	<0.01
Syrian (6)	6	0.02
Other Arab (0)	0	<0.01
Armenian (4)	4	0.02
Assyrian/Chaldean/Syriac (0)	0	<0.01
Australian (0)	6	0.02
Austrian (27)	47	0.19
Basque (0)	0	<0.01
Belgian (0)	14	0.06
Brazilian (0)	0	<0.01
British (0)	21	0.09
Bulgarian (0)	0	<0.01
Cajun (0)	0	<0.01
Canadian (10)	14	0.06
Carpatho Rusyn (0)	7	0.03
Celtic (0)	0	<0.01
Croatian (0)	0	<0.01
Cypriot (0)	0	<0.01
Czech (0)	21	0.09
Czechoslovakian (4)	4	0.02
Danish (0)	10	0.04
Dutch (166)	803	3.29
Eastern European (10)	14	0.06
English (514)	1,683	6.90
Estonian (0)	0	<0.01
European (166)	226	0.93
Finnish (0)	0	<0.01
French, ex. Basque (71)	365	1.50
French Canadian (16)	70	0.29
German (6,776)	11,827	48.50
German Russian (0)	0	<0.01
Greek (0)	22	0.09
Guyanese (0)	0	<0.01
Hungarian (0)	127	0.52
Icelander (0)	0	<0.01
Iranian (0)	0	<0.01
Irish (675)	3,059	12.54
Israeli (0)	0	<0.01
Italian (287)	807	3.31
Latvian (0)	0	<0.01
Lithuanian (13)	113	0.46
Luxemburger (0)	0	<0.01
Macedonian (0)	0	<0.01
Maltese (0)	0	<0.01
New Zealander (0)	0	<0.01
Northern European (0)	0	<0.01
Norwegian (20)	23	0.09
Pennsylvania German (535)	610	2.50

Ancestry	Population	%
Polish (110)	486	1.99
Portuguese (5)	11	0.05
Romanian (6)	12	0.05
Russian (0)	196	0.80
Scandinavian (0)	0	<0.01
Scotch-Irish (280)	590	2.42
Scottish (98)	356	1.46
Serbian (7)	7	0.03
Slavic (0)	0	<0.01
Slovak (15)	132	0.54
Slovene (0)	0	<0.01
Soviet Union (0)	0	<0.01
Swedish (36)	184	0.75
Swiss (153)	612	2.51
Turkish (0)	0	<0.01
Ukrainian (8)	43	0.18
Welsh (33)	197	0.81
West Indian, ex. Hispanic (29)	29	0.12
Bahamian (0)	0	<0.01
Barbadian (0)	0	<0.01
Belizean (29)	29	0.12
Bermudan (0)	0	<0.01
British West Indian (0)	0	<0.01
Dutch West Indian (0)	0	<0.01
Haitian (0)	0	<0.01
Jamaican (0)	0	<0.01
Trinidadian/Tobagonian (0)	0	<0.01
U.S. Virgin Islander (0)	0	<0.01
West Indian (0)	0	<0.01
Other West Indian (0)	0	<0.01
Yugoslavian (14)	14	0.06

Hispanic Origin	Population	%
Hispanic or Latino (of any race)	623	2.53
Central American, ex. Mexican	151	0.61
Costa Rican	0	<0.01
Guatemalan	12	0.05
Honduran	45	0.18
Nicaraguan	1	<0.01
Panamanian	0	<0.01
Salvadoran	93	0.38
Other Central American	0	<0.01
Cuban	2	0.01
Dominican Republic	19	0.08
Mexican	77	0.31
Puerto Rican	195	0.79
South American	47	0.19
Argentinean	0	<0.01
Bolivian	0	<0.01
Chilean	23	0.09
Colombian	19	0.08
Ecuadorian	2	0.01
Paraguayan	0	<0.01
Peruvian	3	0.01
Uruguayan	0	<0.01
Venezuelan	0	<0.01
Other South American	0	<0.01
Other Hispanic or Latino	132	0.54

Race*	Population	%
African-American/Black (151)	233	0.95
Not Hispanic (134)	205	0.83
Hispanic (17)	28	0.11
American Indian/Alaska Native (31)	120	0.49
Not Hispanic (24)	99	0.40
Hispanic (7)	21	0.09
Alaska Athabascan (Ala. Nat.) (0)	2	0.01
Aleut (Alaska Native) (1)	3	0.01
Apache (0)	0	<0.01
Arapaho (0)	0	<0.01
Blackfeet (0)	1	<0.01
Canadian/French Am. Ind. (0)	0	<0.01
Central American Ind. (0)	0	<0.01
Cherokee (1)	26	0.11
Cheyenne (0)	0	<0.01
Chickasaw (0)	0	<0.01
Chippewa (0)	0	<0.01
Choctaw (0)	0	<0.01
Colville (0)	0	<0.01

Race* (cont.)	Population	%
Comanche (0)	0	<0.01
Cree (5)	20	0.08
Creek (0)	0	<0.01
Crow (0)	0	<0.01
Delaware (0)	0	<0.01
Hopi (0)	0	<0.01
Houma (0)	0	<0.01
Inupiat (Alaska Native) (0)	0	<0.01
Iroquois (3)	7	0.03
Kiowa (0)	0	<0.01
Lumbee (0)	0	<0.01
Menominee (0)	0	<0.01
Mexican American Ind. (1)	1	<0.01
Navajo (1)	1	<0.01
Osage (1)	1	<0.01
Ottawa (0)	0	<0.01
Paiute (0)	0	<0.01
Pima (0)	0	<0.01
Potawatomi (0)	0	<0.01
Pueblo (1)	1	<0.01
Puget Sound Salish (0)	0	<0.01
Seminole (0)	1	<0.01
Shoshone (0)	0	<0.01
Sioux (0)	0	<0.01
South American Ind. (0)	0	<0.01
Spanish American Ind. (2)	3	0.01
Tlingit-Haida (Alaska Native) (3)	3	0.01
Tohono O'Odham (0)	0	<0.01
Tsimshian (Alaska Native) (0)	0	<0.01
Ute (0)	0	<0.01
Yakama (0)	0	<0.01
Yaqui (0)	0	<0.01
Yuman (0)	0	<0.01
Yup'ik (Alaska Native) (0)	0	<0.01
Asian (85)	123	0.50
Not Hispanic (85)	120	0.49
Hispanic (0)	3	0.01
Bangladeshi (0)	0	<0.01
Bhutanese (0)	0	<0.01
Burmese (0)	0	<0.01
Cambodian (7)	10	0.04
Chinese, ex. Taiwanese (25)	26	0.11
Filipino (8)	19	0.08
Hmong (0)	0	<0.01
Indian (15)	25	0.10
Indonesian (0)	0	<0.01
Japanese (0)	2	0.01
Korean (15)	20	0.08
Laotian (4)	6	0.02
Malaysian (0)	0	<0.01
Nepalese (0)	0	<0.01
Pakistani (4)	4	0.02
Sri Lankan (0)	0	<0.01
Taiwanese (0)	0	<0.01
Thai (0)	3	0.01
Vietnamese (5)	5	0.02
Hawaii Native/Pacific Islander (3)	12	0.05
Not Hispanic (1)	10	0.04
Hispanic (2)	2	0.01
Fijian (0)	0	<0.01
Guamanian/Chamorro (0)	1	<0.01
Marshallese (0)	0	<0.01
Native Hawaiian (0)	6	0.02
Samoan (1)	3	0.01
Tongan (0)	0	<0.01
White (23,845)	24,072	97.71
Not Hispanic (23,584)	23,758	96.44
Hispanic (261)	314	1.27

*Notes: † The Census 2010 population figure is used to calculate the percentages in the Hispanic Origin and Race categories. Ancestry percentages are based on the 2006-2010 American Community Survey population (not shown); ‡ Numbers in parentheses indicate the number of people reporting a single ancestry; * Numbers in parentheses indicate the number of persons reporting this race alone, not in combination with any other race; Please refer to the Explanation of Data for more information.*

Lackawanna County

Population: 214,437

Ancestry	Population	%
Afghan (11)	23	0.01
African, Sub-Saharan (80)	221	0.10
African (72)	133	0.06
Cape Verdean (0)	0	<0.01
Ethiopian (0)	0	<0.01
Ghanaian (0)	7	<0.01
Kenyan (0)	11	0.01
Liberian (0)	48	0.02
Nigerian (8)	22	0.01
Senegalese (0)	0	<0.01
Sierra Leonean (0)	0	<0.01
Somalian (0)	0	<0.01
South African (0)	0	<0.01
Sudanese (0)	0	<0.01
Ugandan (0)	0	<0.01
Zimbabwean (0)	0	<0.01
Other Sub-Saharan African (0)	0	<0.01
Albanian (14)	27	0.01
Alsatian (0)	0	<0.01
American (5,212)	5,212	2.44
Arab (612)	1,522	0.71
Arab (157)	209	0.10
Egyptian (188)	198	0.09
Iraqi (0)	0	<0.01
Jordanian (0)	0	<0.01
Lebanese (197)	1,003	0.47
Moroccan (5)	5	<0.01
Palestinian (0)	0	<0.01
Syrian (10)	52	0.02
Other Arab (55)	55	0.03
Armenian (0)	65	0.03
Assyrian/Chaldean/Syriac (11)	11	0.01
Australian (39)	113	0.05
Austrian (220)	1,108	0.52
Basque (0)	0	<0.01
Belgian (38)	50	0.02
Brazilian (324)	346	0.16
British (121)	235	0.11
Bulgarian (89)	89	0.04
Cajun (0)	0	<0.01
Canadian (29)	123	0.06
Carpatho Rusyn (154)	235	0.11
Celtic (0)	3	<0.01
Croatian (38)	112	0.05
Cypriot (0)	0	<0.01
Czech (151)	770	0.36
Czechoslovakian (178)	452	0.21
Danish (69)	354	0.17
Dutch (244)	2,513	1.18
Eastern European (143)	165	0.08
English (3,526)	16,426	7.69
Estonian (0)	0	<0.01
European (801)	867	0.41
Finnish (31)	126	0.06
French, ex. Basque (331)	2,439	1.14
French Canadian (129)	476	0.22
German (8,719)	39,808	18.63
German Russian (0)	0	<0.01
Greek (285)	685	0.32
Guyanese (0)	0	<0.01
Hungarian (322)	1,633	0.76
Icelander (0)	8	<0.01
Iranian (59)	82	0.04
Irish (19,307)	58,615	27.42
Israeli (32)	46	0.02
Italian (20,320)	51,871	24.27
Latvian (14)	26	0.01
Lithuanian (1,151)	4,352	2.04
Luxemburger (0)	0	<0.01
Macedonian (0)	13	0.01
Maltese (0)	0	<0.01
New Zealander (0)	10	<0.01
Northern European (3)	3	<0.01
Norwegian (86)	397	0.19
Pennsylvania German (347)	871	0.41

Ancestry	Population	%
Polish (13,828)	38,958	18.23
Portuguese (344)	436	0.20
Romanian (81)	195	0.09
Russian (2,521)	9,536	4.46
Scandinavian (32)	96	0.04
Scotch-Irish (707)	1,944	0.91
Scottish (629)	2,748	1.29
Serbian (28)	117	0.05
Slavic (133)	250	0.12
Slovak (2,501)	7,181	3.36
Slovene (100)	223	0.10
Soviet Union (0)	0	<0.01
Swedish (168)	1,046	0.49
Swiss (52)	496	0.23
Turkish (172)	177	0.08
Ukrainian (1,709)	3,802	1.78
Welsh (2,317)	13,476	6.31
West Indian, ex. Hispanic (109)	230	0.11
Bahamian (0)	0	<0.01
Barbadian (0)	14	0.01
Belizean (0)	0	<0.01
Bermudan (0)	0	<0.01
British West Indian (0)	0	<0.01
Dutch West Indian (0)	0	<0.01
Haitian (14)	54	0.03
Jamaican (49)	81	0.04
Trinidadian/Tobagonian (26)	26	0.01
U.S. Virgin Islander (0)	0	<0.01
West Indian (20)	55	0.03
Other West Indian (0)	0	<0.01
Yugoslavian (17)	41	0.02

Hispanic Origin	Population	%
Hispanic or Latino (of any race)	10,682	4.98
Central American, ex. Mexican	649	0.30
Costa Rican	20	0.01
Guatemalan	65	0.03
Honduran	321	0.15
Nicaraguan	30	0.01
Panamanian	22	0.01
Salvadoran	175	0.08
Other Central American	16	0.01
Cuban	222	0.10
Dominican Republic	765	0.36
Mexican	2,463	1.15
Puerto Rican	4,656	2.17
South American	832	0.39
Argentinean	71	0.03
Bolivian	21	0.01
Chilean	26	0.01
Colombian	199	0.09
Ecuadorian	162	0.08
Paraguayan	12	0.01
Peruvian	172	0.08
Uruguayan	135	0.06
Venezuelan	27	0.01
Other South American	7	<0.01
Other Hispanic or Latino	1,095	0.51

Race*	Population	%
African-American/Black (5,423)	7,125	3.32
Not Hispanic (4,794)	6,196	2.89
Hispanic (629)	929	0.43
American Indian/Alaska Native (330)	932	0.43
Not Hispanic (220)	770	0.36
Hispanic (110)	162	0.08
Alaska Athabascan (Ala. Nat.) (0)	0	<0.01
Aleut (Alaska Native) (0)	2	<0.01
Apache (7)	11	0.01
Arapaho (0)	0	<0.01
Blackfeet (4)	31	0.01
Canadian/French Am. Ind. (1)	4	<0.01
Central American Ind. (0)	2	<0.01
Cherokee (25)	139	0.06
Cheyenne (1)	2	<0.01
Chickasaw (0)	0	<0.01
Chippewa (1)	8	<0.01
Choctaw (0)	2	<0.01
Colville (0)	0	<0.01

Race*	Population	%
Comanche (0)	1	<0.01
Cree (0)	1	<0.01
Creek (5)	6	<0.01
Crow (1)	3	<0.01
Delaware (5)	18	0.01
Hopi (0)	0	<0.01
Houma (0)	0	<0.01
Inupiat (Alaska Native) (0)	0	<0.01
Iroquois (26)	52	0.02
Kiowa (0)	0	<0.01
Lumbee (0)	0	<0.01
Menominee (0)	0	<0.01
Mexican American Ind. (12)	15	0.01
Navajo (3)	3	<0.01
Osage (0)	0	<0.01
Ottawa (0)	0	<0.01
Paiute (1)	1	<0.01
Pima (0)	0	<0.01
Potawatomi (0)	0	<0.01
Pueblo (9)	10	<0.01
Puget Sound Salish (0)	0	<0.01
Seminole (3)	4	<0.01
Shoshone (0)	0	<0.01
Sioux (5)	32	0.01
South American Ind. (3)	7	<0.01
Spanish American Ind. (3)	5	<0.01
Tlingit-Haida (Alaska Native) (0)	1	<0.01
Tohono O'Odham (2)	2	<0.01
Tsimshian (Alaska Native) (0)	0	<0.01
Ute (0)	0	<0.01
Yakama (0)	0	<0.01
Yaqui (2)	2	<0.01
Yuman (0)	0	<0.01
Yup'ik (Alaska Native) (0)	0	<0.01
Asian (3,644)	4,378	2.04
Not Hispanic (3,601)	4,278	1.99
Hispanic (43)	100	0.05
Bangladeshi (27)	29	0.01
Bhutanese (54)	101	0.05
Burmese (4)	8	<0.01
Cambodian (4)	8	<0.01
Chinese, ex. Taiwanese (401)	488	0.23
Filipino (268)	389	0.18
Hmong (0)	0	<0.01
Indian (1,672)	1,858	0.87
Indonesian (261)	291	0.14
Japanese (43)	112	0.05
Korean (165)	247	0.12
Laotian (160)	188	0.09
Malaysian (7)	8	<0.01
Nepalese (37)	84	0.04
Pakistani (93)	108	0.05
Sri Lankan (7)	7	<0.01
Taiwanese (19)	21	0.01
Thai (36)	63	0.03
Vietnamese (209)	243	0.11
Hawaii Native/Pacific Islander (55)	136	0.06
Not Hispanic (41)	101	0.05
Hispanic (14)	35	0.02
Fijian (1)	1	<0.01
Guamanian/Chamorro (15)	22	0.01
Marshallese (0)	0	<0.01
Native Hawaiian (10)	27	0.01
Samoan (1)	14	0.01
Tongan (0)	0	<0.01
White (197,296)	200,261	93.39
Not Hispanic (192,250)	194,587	90.74
Hispanic (5,046)	5,674	2.65

Notes: † The Census 2010 population figure is used to calculate the percentages in the Hispanic Origin and Race categories. Ancestry percentages are based on the 2006-2010 American Community Survey population (not shown); ‡ Numbers in parentheses indicate the number of people reporting a single ancestry; * Numbers in parentheses indicate the number of persons reporting this race alone, not in combination with any other race; Please refer to the Explanation of Data for more information.

Lancaster County
Population: 519,445

Ancestry	Population	%
Afghan (0)	0	<0.01
African, Sub-Saharan (1,604)	1,889	0.37
African (1,042)	1,285	0.25
Cape Verdean (14)	14	<0.01
Ethiopian (239)	244	0.05
Ghanaian (21)	21	<0.01
Kenyan (112)	122	0.02
Liberian (47)	47	0.01
Nigerian (0)	0	<0.01
Senegalese (0)	0	<0.01
Sierra Leonean (0)	0	<0.01
Somalian (0)	0	<0.01
South African (40)	53	0.01
Sudanese (23)	23	<0.01
Ugandan (0)	0	<0.01
Zimbabwean (12)	12	<0.01
Other Sub-Saharan African (54)	68	0.01
Albanian (60)	84	0.02
Alsatian (4)	15	<0.01
American (38,840)	38,840	7.60
Arab (492)	1,035	0.20
Arab (78)	86	0.02
Egyptian (159)	159	0.03
Iraqi (16)	16	<0.01
Jordanian (15)	15	<0.01
Lebanese (109)	465	0.09
Moroccan (17)	71	0.01
Palestinian (0)	0	<0.01
Syrian (21)	112	0.02
Other Arab (77)	111	0.02
Armenian (143)	200	0.04
Assyrian/Chaldean/Syriac (0)	0	<0.01
Australian (43)	176	0.03
Austrian (427)	1,684	0.33
Basque (0)	10	<0.01
Belgian (121)	240	0.05
Brazilian (32)	44	0.01
British (1,166)	2,017	0.39
Bulgarian (32)	32	0.01
Cajun (0)	0	<0.01
Canadian (211)	569	0.11
Carpatho Rusyn (15)	27	0.01
Celtic (40)	60	0.01
Croatian (77)	405	0.08
Cypriot (13)	13	<0.01
Czech (456)	1,436	0.28
Czechoslovakian (127)	563	0.11
Danish (290)	788	0.15
Dutch (2,644)	8,724	1.71
Eastern European (319)	363	0.07
English (14,460)	41,461	8.11
Estonian (33)	63	0.01
European (5,065)	5,489	1.07
Finnish (85)	333	0.07
French, ex. Basque (2,091)	9,761	1.91
French Canadian (569)	1,722	0.34
German (109,069)	199,974	39.11
German Russian (0)	0	<0.01
Greek (1,168)	2,357	0.46
Guyanese (3)	3	<0.01
Hungarian (461)	1,613	0.32
Icelander (0)	27	0.01
Iranian (11)	24	<0.01
Irish (13,052)	58,264	11.40
Israeli (0)	13	<0.01
Italian (10,785)	29,172	5.71
Latvian (46)	125	0.02
Lithuanian (323)	1,288	0.25
Luxemburger (0)	0	<0.01
Macedonian (10)	32	0.01
Maltese (0)	22	<0.01
New Zealander (0)	4	<0.01
Northern European (275)	275	0.05
Norwegian (608)	1,942	0.38
Pennsylvania German (10,177)	11,182	2.19

Ancestry	Population	%
Polish (4,322)	14,399	2.82
Portuguese (126)	360	0.07
Romanian (246)	468	0.09
Russian (1,739)	3,855	0.75
Scandinavian (59)	154	0.03
Scotch-Irish (3,521)	9,923	1.94
Scottish (1,991)	7,438	1.45
Serbian (77)	146	0.03
Slavic (68)	227	0.04
Slovak (795)	2,057	0.40
Slovene (84)	233	0.05
Soviet Union (0)	0	<0.01
Swedish (1,276)	4,508	0.88
Swiss (5,102)	18,762	3.67
Turkish (300)	348	0.07
Ukrainian (1,106)	2,243	0.44
Welsh (894)	5,976	1.17
West Indian, ex. Hispanic (965)	1,337	0.26
Bahamian (0)	0	<0.01
Barbadian (36)	36	0.01
Belizean (32)	32	0.01
Bermudan (0)	0	<0.01
British West Indian (37)	37	0.01
Dutch West Indian (0)	0	<0.01
Haitian (570)	673	0.13
Jamaican (172)	402	0.08
Trinidadian/Tobagonian (12)	40	0.01
U.S. Virgin Islander (0)	0	<0.01
West Indian (106)	117	0.02
Other West Indian (0)	0	<0.01
Yugoslavian (342)	553	0.11

Hispanic Origin	Population	%
Hispanic or Latino (of any race)	44,930	8.65
Central American, ex. Mexican	1,319	0.25
Costa Rican	111	0.02
Guatemalan	497	0.10
Honduran	231	0.04
Nicaraguan	49	0.01
Panamanian	74	0.01
Salvadoran	349	0.07
Other Central American	8	<0.01
Cuban	1,713	0.33
Dominican Republic	3,024	0.58
Mexican	3,803	0.73
Puerto Rican	30,403	5.85
South American	2,126	0.41
Argentinean	114	0.02
Bolivian	33	0.01
Chilean	81	0.02
Colombian	1,024	0.20
Ecuadorian	361	0.07
Paraguayan	26	0.01
Peruvian	315	0.06
Uruguayan	43	0.01
Venezuelan	97	0.02
Other South American	32	0.01
Other Hispanic or Latino	2,542	0.49

Race*	Population	%
African-American/Black (19,035)	24,600	4.74
Not Hispanic (16,087)	20,026	3.86
Hispanic (2,948)	4,574	0.88
American Indian/Alaska Native (1,195)	3,056	0.59
Not Hispanic (658)	2,082	0.40
Hispanic (537)	974	0.19
Alaska Athabascan (Ala. Nat.) (5)	5	<0.01
Aleut (Alaska Native) (1)	1	<0.01
Apache (12)	38	0.01
Arapaho (0)	0	<0.01
Blackfeet (10)	93	0.02
Canadian/French Am. Ind. (6)	20	<0.01
Central American Ind. (26)	31	0.01
Cherokee (118)	509	0.10
Cheyenne (3)	7	<0.01
Chickasaw (5)	7	<0.01
Chippewa (10)	34	0.01
Choctaw (9)	27	0.01
Colville (0)	0	<0.01

Race*	Population	%
Comanche (2)	15	<0.01
Cree (7)	13	<0.01
Creek (6)	12	<0.01
Crow (0)	3	<0.01
Delaware (11)	44	0.01
Hopi (0)	2	<0.01
Houma (0)	0	<0.01
Inupiat (Alaska Native) (5)	8	<0.01
Iroquois (42)	102	0.02
Kiowa (1)	2	<0.01
Lumbee (7)	12	<0.01
Menominee (0)	0	<0.01
Mexican American Ind. (33)	44	0.01
Navajo (14)	32	0.01
Osage (1)	7	<0.01
Ottawa (0)	1	<0.01
Paiute (1)	1	<0.01
Pima (1)	2	<0.01
Potawatomi (8)	10	<0.01
Pueblo (0)	2	<0.01
Puget Sound Salish (1)	1	<0.01
Seminole (1)	12	<0.01
Shoshone (5)	7	<0.01
Sioux (22)	67	0.01
South American Ind. (90)	161	0.03
Spanish American Ind. (12)	16	<0.01
Tlingit-Haida (Alaska Native) (2)	2	<0.01
Tohono O'Odham (1)	2	<0.01
Tsimshian (Alaska Native) (0)	0	<0.01
Ute (0)	0	<0.01
Yakama (1)	1	<0.01
Yaqui (2)	3	<0.01
Yuman (0)	0	<0.01
Yup'ik (Alaska Native) (0)	0	<0.01
Asian (9,860)	11,613	2.24
Not Hispanic (9,726)	11,269	2.17
Hispanic (134)	344	0.07
Bangladeshi (33)	39	0.01
Bhutanese (191)	223	0.04
Burmese (194)	204	0.04
Cambodian (631)	720	0.14
Chinese, ex. Taiwanese (1,528)	1,876	0.36
Filipino (575)	886	0.17
Hmong (630)	668	0.13
Indian (1,504)	1,746	0.34
Indonesian (31)	43	0.01
Japanese (202)	411	0.08
Korean (690)	917	0.18
Laotian (257)	311	0.06
Malaysian (16)	30	0.01
Nepalese (91)	140	0.03
Pakistani (123)	143	0.03
Sri Lankan (19)	21	<0.01
Taiwanese (25)	36	0.01
Thai (90)	148	0.03
Vietnamese (2,534)	2,855	0.55
Hawaii Native/Pacific Islander (164)	491	0.09
Not Hispanic (108)	283	0.05
Hispanic (56)	208	0.04
Fijian (0)	1	<0.01
Guamanian/Chamorro (58)	87	0.02
Marshallese (1)	1	<0.01
Native Hawaiian (40)	118	0.02
Samoan (17)	36	0.01
Tongan (0)	0	<0.01
White (460,171)	468,961	90.28
Not Hispanic (440,969)	447,018	86.06
Hispanic (19,202)	21,943	4.22

*Notes: † The Census 2010 population figure is used to calculate the percentages in the Hispanic Origin and Race categories. Ancestry percentages are based on the 2006-2010 American Community Survey population (not shown); ‡ Numbers in parentheses indicate the number of people reporting a single ancestry; * Numbers in parentheses indicate the number of persons reporting this race alone, not in combination with any other race; Please refer to the Explanation of Data for more information.*

Lawrence County

Population: 91,108

Ancestry	Population	%
Afghan (0)	0	<0.01
African, Sub-Saharan (122)	135	0.15
African (104)	117	0.13
Cape Verdean (0)	0	<0.01
Ethiopian (0)	0	<0.01
Ghanaian (0)	0	<0.01
Kenyan (0)	0	<0.01
Liberian (18)	18	0.02
Nigerian (0)	0	<0.01
Senegalese (0)	0	<0.01
Sierra Leonean (0)	0	<0.01
Somalian (0)	0	<0.01
South African (0)	0	<0.01
Sudanese (0)	0	<0.01
Ugandan (0)	0	<0.01
Zimbabwean (0)	0	<0.01
Other Sub-Saharan African (0)	0	<0.01
Albanian (0)	14	0.02
Alsatian (0)	0	<0.01
American (3,529)	3,529	3.85
Arab (380)	1,078	1.18
Arab (54)	146	0.16
Egyptian (0)	59	0.06
Iraqi (0)	0	<0.01
Jordanian (0)	0	<0.01
Lebanese (119)	383	0.42
Moroccan (0)	0	<0.01
Palestinian (0)	0	<0.01
Syrian (207)	490	0.53
Other Arab (0)	0	<0.01
Armenian (0)	27	0.03
Assyrian/Chaldean/Syriac (0)	0	<0.01
Australian (0)	0	<0.01
Austrian (44)	234	0.26
Basque (0)	0	<0.01
Belgian (5)	29	0.03
Brazilian (0)	0	<0.01
British (35)	184	0.20
Bulgarian (6)	6	0.01
Cajun (0)	0	<0.01
Canadian (12)	39	0.04
Carpatho Rusyn (0)	0	<0.01
Celtic (0)	0	<0.01
Croatian (238)	1,013	1.10
Cypriot (0)	0	<0.01
Czech (138)	438	0.48
Czechoslovakian (0)	62	0.07
Danish (48)	112	0.12
Dutch (221)	1,662	1.81
Eastern European (36)	52	0.06
English (2,758)	8,641	9.42
Estonian (0)	2	<0.01
European (359)	386	0.42
Finnish (142)	305	0.33
French, ex. Basque (215)	1,797	1.96
French Canadian (58)	167	0.18
German (6,846)	25,993	28.35
German Russian (0)	0	<0.01
Greek (198)	718	0.78
Guyanese (0)	0	<0.01
Hungarian (304)	1,138	1.24
Icelander (0)	3	<0.01
Iranian (0)	0	<0.01
Irish (3,179)	15,887	17.33
Israeli (0)	30	0.03
Italian (12,221)	24,437	26.65
Latvian (0)	0	<0.01
Lithuanian (49)	107	0.12
Luxemburger (0)	0	<0.01
Macedonian (0)	52	0.06
Maltese (0)	0	<0.01
New Zealander (0)	0	<0.01
Northern European (19)	29	0.03
Norwegian (5)	93	0.10
Pennsylvania German (256)	325	0.35

Ancestry	Population	%
Polish (2,422)	7,922	8.64
Portuguese (15)	20	0.02
Romanian (177)	409	0.45
Russian (227)	807	0.88
Scandinavian (8)	22	0.02
Scotch-Irish (1,846)	5,256	5.73
Scottish (618)	2,030	2.21
Serbian (8)	116	0.13
Slavic (37)	234	0.26
Slovak (590)	1,886	2.06
Slovene (70)	210	0.23
Soviet Union (0)	0	<0.01
Swedish (178)	746	0.81
Swiss (93)	245	0.27
Turkish (2)	8	0.01
Ukrainian (121)	303	0.33
Welsh (365)	2,056	2.24
West Indian, ex. Hispanic (22)	33	0.04
Bahamian (0)	0	<0.01
Barbadian (0)	0	<0.01
Belizean (0)	0	<0.01
Bermudan (13)	13	0.01
British West Indian (0)	0	<0.01
Dutch West Indian (0)	0	<0.01
Haitian (0)	0	<0.01
Jamaican (3)	14	0.02
Trinidadian/Tobagonian (0)	0	<0.01
U.S. Virgin Islander (6)	6	0.01
West Indian (0)	0	<0.01
Other West Indian (0)	0	<0.01
Yugoslavian (40)	68	0.07

Hispanic Origin	Population	%
Hispanic or Latino (of any race)	931	1.02
Central American, ex. Mexican	44	0.05
Costa Rican	4	<0.01
Guatemalan	16	0.02
Honduran	3	<0.01
Nicaraguan	10	0.01
Panamanian	4	<0.01
Salvadoran	7	0.01
Other Central American	0	<0.01
Cuban	39	0.04
Dominican Republic	34	0.04
Mexican	352	0.39
Puerto Rican	290	0.32
South American	56	0.06
Argentinean	7	0.01
Bolivian	0	<0.01
Chilean	3	<0.01
Colombian	14	0.02
Ecuadorian	13	0.01
Paraguayan	2	<0.01
Peruvian	12	0.01
Uruguayan	0	<0.01
Venezuelan	5	0.01
Other South American	0	<0.01
Other Hispanic or Latino	116	0.13

Race*	Population	%
African-American/Black (3,501)	4,514	4.95
Not Hispanic (3,448)	4,413	4.84
Hispanic (53)	101	0.11
American Indian/Alaska Native (74)	402	0.44
Not Hispanic (54)	361	0.40
Hispanic (20)	41	0.05
Alaska Athabascan (Ala. Nat.) (0)	0	<0.01
Aleut (Alaska Native) (0)	1	<0.01
Apache (0)	6	0.01
Arapaho (0)	0	<0.01
Blackfeet (2)	18	0.02
Canadian/French Am. Ind. (0)	0	<0.01
Central American Ind. (0)	1	<0.01
Cherokee (17)	105	0.12
Cheyenne (0)	0	<0.01
Chickasaw (0)	0	<0.01
Chippewa (0)	5	0.01
Choctaw (4)	6	0.01
Colville (0)	0	<0.01

Race*	Population	%
Comanche (0)	0	<0.01
Cree (0)	0	<0.01
Creek (0)	0	<0.01
Crow (0)	1	<0.01
Delaware (1)	7	0.01
Hopi (0)	0	<0.01
Houma (0)	0	<0.01
Inupiat (Alaska Native) (0)	1	<0.01
Iroquois (4)	12	0.01
Kiowa (0)	0	<0.01
Lumbee (0)	0	<0.01
Menominee (0)	0	<0.01
Mexican American Ind. (2)	3	<0.01
Navajo (0)	2	<0.01
Osage (0)	0	<0.01
Ottawa (0)	0	<0.01
Paiute (0)	0	<0.01
Pima (0)	0	<0.01
Potawatomi (0)	0	<0.01
Pueblo (0)	0	<0.01
Puget Sound Salish (0)	0	<0.01
Seminole (0)	2	<0.01
Shoshone (0)	0	<0.01
Sioux (1)	6	0.01
South American Ind. (1)	6	0.01
Spanish American Ind. (0)	0	<0.01
Tlingit-Haida (Alaska Native) (0)	0	<0.01
Tohono O'Odham (0)	0	<0.01
Tsimshian (Alaska Native) (0)	0	<0.01
Ute (0)	0	<0.01
Yakama (0)	0	<0.01
Yaqui (0)	0	<0.01
Yuman (0)	0	<0.01
Yup'ik (Alaska Native) (0)	0	<0.01
Asian (370)	549	0.60
Not Hispanic (365)	524	0.58
Hispanic (5)	25	0.03
Bangladeshi (0)	0	<0.01
Bhutanese (0)	0	<0.01
Burmese (0)	0	<0.01
Cambodian (10)	10	0.01
Chinese, ex. Taiwanese (69)	90	0.10
Filipino (81)	125	0.14
Hmong (10)	10	0.01
Indian (42)	61	0.07
Indonesian (1)	1	<0.01
Japanese (13)	32	0.04
Korean (61)	94	0.10
Laotian (0)	0	<0.01
Malaysian (0)	1	<0.01
Nepalese (3)	3	<0.01
Pakistani (11)	16	0.02
Sri Lankan (3)	3	<0.01
Taiwanese (2)	2	<0.01
Thai (9)	12	0.01
Vietnamese (34)	50	0.05
Hawaii Native/Pacific Islander (10)	32	0.04
Not Hispanic (9)	30	0.03
Hispanic (1)	2	<0.01
Fijian (0)	0	<0.01
Guamanian/Chamorro (2)	2	<0.01
Marshallese (0)	0	<0.01
Native Hawaiian (1)	8	0.01
Samoan (5)	9	0.01
Tongan (0)	0	<0.01
White (85,484)	86,862	95.34
Not Hispanic (84,872)	86,162	94.57
Hispanic (612)	700	0.77

*Notes: † The Census 2010 population figure is used to calculate the percentages in the Hispanic Origin and Race categories. Ancestry percentages are based on the 2006-2010 American Community Survey population (not shown); ‡ Numbers in parentheses indicate the number of people reporting a single ancestry; * Numbers in parentheses indicate the number of persons reporting this race alone, not in combination with any other race; Please refer to the Explanation of Data for more information.*

Lebanon County

Population: 133,568

Ancestry	Population	%
Afghan (0)	0	<0.01
African, Sub-Saharan (229)	314	0.24
African (87)	172	0.13
Cape Verdean (0)	0	<0.01
Ethiopian (35)	35	0.03
Ghanaian (0)	0	<0.01
Kenyan (95)	95	0.07
Liberian (0)	0	<0.01
Nigerian (12)	12	0.01
Senegalese (0)	0	<0.01
Sierra Leonean (0)	0	<0.01
Somalian (0)	0	<0.01
South African (0)	0	<0.01
Sudanese (0)	0	<0.01
Ugandan (0)	0	<0.01
Zimbabwean (0)	0	<0.01
Other Sub-Saharan African (0)	0	<0.01
Albanian (4)	45	0.03
Alsatian (0)	0	<0.01
American (8,307)	8,307	6.32
Arab (63)	262	0.20
Arab (25)	25	0.02
Egyptian (19)	32	0.02
Iraqi (0)	0	<0.01
Jordanian (0)	0	<0.01
Lebanese (19)	184	0.14
Moroccan (0)	0	<0.01
Palestinian (0)	0	<0.01
Syrian (0)	21	0.02
Other Arab (0)	0	<0.01
Armenian (35)	48	0.04
Assyrian/Chaldean/Syriac (0)	0	<0.01
Australian (17)	43	0.03
Austrian (79)	283	0.22
Basque (0)	0	<0.01
Belgian (9)	18	0.01
Brazilian (0)	30	0.02
British (102)	329	0.25
Bulgarian (13)	38	0.03
Cajun (0)	0	<0.01
Canadian (18)	207	0.16
Carpatho Rusyn (0)	0	<0.01
Celtic (13)	28	0.02
Croatian (82)	175	0.13
Cypriot (0)	0	<0.01
Czech (126)	492	0.37
Czechoslovakian (122)	234	0.18
Danish (24)	204	0.16
Dutch (1,065)	3,285	2.50
Eastern European (34)	39	0.03
English (2,451)	8,091	6.16
Estonian (0)	0	<0.01
European (1,262)	1,294	0.99
Finnish (26)	59	0.04
French, ex. Basque (527)	2,385	1.82
French Canadian (174)	259	0.20
German (31,447)	57,199	43.55
German Russian (21)	21	0.02
Greek (135)	462	0.35
Guyanese (0)	0	<0.01
Hungarian (191)	1,268	0.97
Icelander (0)	0	<0.01
Iranian (0)	8	0.01
Irish (2,714)	15,221	11.59
Israeli (0)	0	<0.01
Italian (2,666)	8,486	6.46
Latvian (22)	35	0.03
Lithuanian (117)	443	0.34
Luxemburger (0)	0	<0.01
Macedonian (8)	8	0.01
Maltese (0)	6	<0.01
New Zealander (0)	0	<0.01
Northern European (31)	31	0.02
Norwegian (178)	465	0.35
Pennsylvania German (3,477)	4,652	3.54

Ancestry	Population	%
Polish (1,191)	3,643	2.77
Portuguese (14)	134	0.10
Romanian (143)	195	0.15
Russian (143)	633	0.48
Scandinavian (0)	14	0.01
Scotch-Irish (577)	1,986	1.51
Scottish (401)	1,584	1.21
Serbian (70)	132	0.10
Slavic (101)	167	0.13
Slovak (408)	1,629	1.24
Slovene (14)	28	0.02
Soviet Union (0)	0	<0.01
Swedish (141)	891	0.68
Swiss (624)	2,622	2.00
Turkish (0)	7	0.01
Ukrainian (218)	514	0.39
Welsh (266)	1,069	0.81
West Indian, ex. Hispanic (59)	247	0.19
Bahamian (0)	0	<0.01
Barbadian (0)	0	<0.01
Belizean (0)	0	<0.01
Bermudan (0)	0	<0.01
British West Indian (0)	0	<0.01
Dutch West Indian (0)	0	<0.01
Haitian (45)	45	0.03
Jamaican (0)	19	0.01
Trinidadian/Tobagonian (14)	73	0.06
U.S. Virgin Islander (0)	0	<0.01
West Indian (0)	110	0.08
Other West Indian (0)	0	<0.01
Yugoslavian (89)	178	0.14

Hispanic Origin	Population	%
Hispanic or Latino (of any race)	12,410	9.29
Central American, ex. Mexican	299	0.22
Costa Rican	10	0.01
Guatemalan	46	0.03
Honduran	83	0.06
Nicaraguan	38	0.03
Panamanian	31	0.02
Salvadoran	88	0.07
Other Central American	3	<0.01
Cuban	254	0.19
Dominican Republic	975	0.73
Mexican	1,067	0.80
Puerto Rican	8,898	6.66
South American	381	0.29
Argentinean	21	0.02
Bolivian	5	<0.01
Chilean	49	0.04
Colombian	132	0.10
Ecuadorian	36	0.03
Paraguayan	1	<0.01
Peruvian	106	0.08
Uruguayan	2	<0.01
Venezuelan	25	0.02
Other South American	4	<0.01
Other Hispanic or Latino	536	0.40

Race*	Population	%
African-American/Black (2,885)	3,885	2.91
Not Hispanic (2,134)	2,763	2.07
Hispanic (751)	1,122	0.84
American Indian/Alaska Native (250)	655	0.49
Not Hispanic (133)	440	0.33
Hispanic (117)	215	0.16
Alaska Athabascan (Ala. Nat.) (1)	1	<0.01
Aleut (Alaska Native) (0)	2	<0.01
Apache (3)	8	0.01
Arapaho (0)	0	<0.01
Blackfeet (5)	14	0.01
Canadian/French Am. Ind. (1)	2	<0.01
Central American Ind. (1)	2	<0.01
Cherokee (14)	93	0.07
Cheyenne (3)	4	<0.01
Chickasaw (0)	1	<0.01
Chippewa (5)	9	0.01
Choctaw (0)	6	<0.01
Colville (0)	0	<0.01

Race*	Population	%
Comanche (0)	0	<0.01
Cree (1)	3	<0.01
Creek (6)	9	0.01
Crow (1)	1	<0.01
Delaware (6)	16	0.01
Hopi (0)	0	<0.01
Houma (0)	0	<0.01
Inupiat (Alaska Native) (1)	1	<0.01
Iroquois (7)	17	0.01
Kiowa (2)	2	<0.01
Lumbee (1)	2	<0.01
Menominee (0)	0	<0.01
Mexican American Ind. (4)	7	0.01
Navajo (2)	6	<0.01
Osage (0)	0	<0.01
Ottawa (0)	0	<0.01
Paiute (0)	0	<0.01
Pima (0)	0	<0.01
Potawatomi (1)	1	<0.01
Pueblo (0)	1	<0.01
Puget Sound Salish (0)	0	<0.01
Seminole (1)	1	<0.01
Shoshone (0)	0	<0.01
Sioux (4)	9	0.01
South American Ind. (19)	39	0.03
Spanish American Ind. (3)	3	<0.01
Tlingit-Haida (Alaska Native) (0)	0	<0.01
Tohono O'Odham (0)	0	<0.01
Tsimshian (Alaska Native) (0)	0	<0.01
Ute (0)	1	<0.01
Yakama (0)	0	<0.01
Yaqui (1)	1	<0.01
Yuman (0)	0	<0.01
Yup'ik (Alaska Native) (0)	0	<0.01
Asian (1,533)	1,887	1.41
Not Hispanic (1,504)	1,824	1.37
Hispanic (29)	63	0.05
Bangladeshi (10)	10	0.01
Bhutanese (0)	0	<0.01
Burmese (11)	11	0.01
Cambodian (230)	287	0.21
Chinese, ex. Taiwanese (210)	238	0.18
Filipino (167)	237	0.18
Hmong (1)	3	<0.01
Indian (303)	358	0.27
Indonesian (8)	11	0.01
Japanese (33)	70	0.05
Korean (130)	192	0.14
Laotian (8)	11	0.01
Malaysian (0)	0	<0.01
Nepalese (5)	5	<0.01
Pakistani (43)	51	0.04
Sri Lankan (0)	0	<0.01
Taiwanese (6)	6	<0.01
Thai (11)	24	0.02
Vietnamese (248)	290	0.22
Hawaii Native/Pacific Islander (36)	111	0.08
Not Hispanic (30)	84	0.06
Hispanic (6)	27	0.02
Fijian (0)	0	<0.01
Guamanian/Chamorro (11)	32	0.02
Marshallese (1)	1	<0.01
Native Hawaiian (8)	27	0.02
Samoan (1)	3	<0.01
Tongan (0)	0	<0.01
White (121,566)	123,454	92.43
Not Hispanic (116,010)	117,170	87.72
Hispanic (5,556)	6,284	4.70

*Notes: † The Census 2010 population figure is used to calculate the percentages in the Hispanic Origin and Race categories. Ancestry percentages are based on the 2006-2010 American Community Survey population (not shown); ‡ Numbers in parentheses indicate the number of people reporting a single ancestry; * Numbers in parentheses indicate the number of persons reporting this race alone, not in combination with any other race; Please refer to the Explanation of Data for more information.*

Lehigh County

Population: 349,497

Ancestry	Population	%
Afghan (13)	101	0.03
African, Sub-Saharan (1,110)	1,294	0.38
African (753)	913	0.27
Cape Verdean (16)	16	<0.01
Ethiopian (24)	24	0.01
Ghanaian (0)	0	<0.01
Kenyan (39)	39	0.01
Liberian (0)	7	<0.01
Nigerian (93)	93	0.03
Senegalese (0)	0	<0.01
Sierra Leonean (0)	0	<0.01
Somalian (0)	0	<0.01
South African (12)	12	<0.01
Sudanese (0)	0	<0.01
Ugandan (0)	0	<0.01
Zimbabwean (0)	0	<0.01
Other Sub-Saharan African (173)	190	0.06
Albanian (377)	635	0.18
Alsatian (0)	9	<0.01
American (11,536)	11,536	3.35
Arab (4,829)	6,398	1.86
Arab (537)	613	0.18
Egyptian (338)	399	0.12
Iraqi (0)	0	<0.01
Jordanian (13)	13	<0.01
Lebanese (446)	795	0.23
Moroccan (27)	40	0.01
Palestinian (46)	56	0.02
Syrian (3,074)	4,051	1.18
Other Arab (348)	431	0.13
Armenian (91)	120	0.03
Assyrian/Chaldean/Syriac (9)	20	0.01
Australian (10)	129	0.04
Austrian (2,116)	6,636	1.93
Basque (12)	12	<0.01
Belgian (44)	137	0.04
Brazilian (88)	110	0.03
British (403)	954	0.28
Bulgarian (112)	127	0.04
Cajun (7)	7	<0.01
Canadian (149)	261	0.08
Carpatho Rusyn (8)	19	0.01
Celtic (36)	181	0.05
Croatian (81)	274	0.08
Cypriot (0)	0	<0.01
Czech (208)	1,630	0.47
Czechoslovakian (462)	970	0.28
Danish (116)	360	0.10
Dutch (2,666)	9,647	2.80
Eastern European (524)	604	0.18
English (4,507)	19,363	5.63
Estonian (0)	0	<0.01
European (1,585)	1,723	0.50
Finnish (34)	210	0.06
French, ex. Basque (955)	5,856	1.70
French Canadian (338)	1,015	0.30
German (41,984)	97,248	28.27
German Russian (9)	42	0.01
Greek (787)	2,125	0.62
Guyanese (102)	174	0.05
Hungarian (2,239)	8,939	2.60
Icelander (0)	19	0.01
Iranian (87)	115	0.03
Irish (9,655)	42,698	12.41
Israeli (169)	186	0.05
Italian (10,981)	34,032	9.89
Latvian (23)	101	0.03
Lithuanian (427)	1,380	0.40
Luxemburger (0)	11	<0.01
Macedonian (0)	35	0.01
Maltese (28)	78	0.02
New Zealander (0)	0	<0.01
Northern European (163)	175	0.05
Norwegian (236)	1,056	0.31
Pennsylvania German (13,175)	18,943	5.51

Ancestry (cont.)	Population	%
Polish (5,405)	17,019	4.95
Portuguese (290)	932	0.27
Romanian (289)	625	0.18
Russian (1,240)	4,482	1.30
Scandinavian (68)	256	0.07
Scotch-Irish (994)	3,516	1.02
Scottish (1,051)	4,397	1.28
Serbian (55)	151	0.04
Slavic (20)	150	0.04
Slovak (3,592)	9,428	2.74
Slovene (140)	300	0.09
Soviet Union (10)	10	<0.01
Swedish (428)	2,610	0.76
Swiss (199)	1,395	0.41
Turkish (78)	110	0.03
Ukrainian (1,918)	5,199	1.51
Welsh (1,506)	6,897	2.01
West Indian, ex. Hispanic (1,684)	2,356	0.68
Bahamian (32)	32	0.01
Barbadian (44)	60	0.02
Belizean (0)	0	<0.01
Bermudan (0)	0	<0.01
British West Indian (47)	63	0.02
Dutch West Indian (0)	0	<0.01
Haitian (381)	490	0.14
Jamaican (912)	1,099	0.32
Trinidadian/Tobagonian (81)	103	0.03
U.S. Virgin Islander (0)	0	<0.01
West Indian (187)	509	0.15
Other West Indian (0)	0	<0.01
Yugoslavian (297)	637	0.19

Hispanic Origin	Population	%
Hispanic or Latino (of any race)	65,615	18.77
Central American, ex. Mexican	2,642	0.76
Costa Rican	119	0.03
Guatemalan	598	0.17
Honduran	902	0.26
Nicaraguan	149	0.04
Panamanian	204	0.06
Salvadoran	650	0.19
Other Central American	20	0.01
Cuban	859	0.25
Dominican Republic	10,912	3.12
Mexican	3,829	1.10
Puerto Rican	37,980	10.87
South American	4,677	1.34
Argentinean	145	0.04
Bolivian	57	0.02
Chilean	371	0.11
Colombian	1,268	0.36
Ecuadorian	1,659	0.47
Paraguayan	6	<0.01
Peruvian	856	0.24
Uruguayan	88	0.03
Venezuelan	174	0.05
Other South American	53	0.02
Other Hispanic or Latino	4,716	1.35

Race*	Population	%
African-American/Black (21,440)	26,269	7.52
Not Hispanic (17,230)	20,150	5.77
Hispanic (4,210)	6,119	1.75
American Indian/Alaska Native (1,279)	2,902	0.83
Not Hispanic (442)	1,461	0.42
Hispanic (837)	1,441	0.41
Alaska Athabascan (Ala. Nat.) (4)	4	<0.01
Aleut (Alaska Native) (13)	13	<0.01
Apache (3)	24	<0.01
Arapaho (0)	3	<0.01
Blackfeet (11)	73	0.02
Canadian/French Am. Ind. (1)	1	<0.01
Central American Ind. (34)	48	0.01
Cherokee (76)	371	0.11
Cheyenne (3)	3	<0.01
Chickasaw (1)	2	<0.01
Chippewa (16)	37	0.01
Choctaw (8)	24	0.01
Colville (0)	0	<0.01

Race* (cont.)	Population	%
Comanche (4)	7	<0.01
Cree (5)	5	<0.01
Creek (0)	4	<0.01
Crow (0)	7	<0.01
Delaware (13)	83	0.02
Hopi (0)	6	<0.01
Houma (0)	0	<0.01
Inupiat (Alaska Native) (0)	0	<0.01
Iroquois (19)	33	0.01
Kiowa (0)	0	<0.01
Lumbee (2)	10	<0.01
Menominee (0)	0	<0.01
Mexican American Ind. (51)	64	0.02
Navajo (7)	15	<0.01
Osage (0)	0	<0.01
Ottawa (2)	7	<0.01
Paiute (0)	0	<0.01
Pima (2)	2	<0.01
Potawatomi (1)	1	<0.01
Pueblo (3)	5	<0.01
Puget Sound Salish (5)	6	<0.01
Seminole (3)	14	<0.01
Shoshone (2)	5	<0.01
Sioux (17)	30	0.01
South American Ind. (89)	183	0.05
Spanish American Ind. (24)	28	0.01
Tlingit-Haida (Alaska Native) (1)	1	<0.01
Tohono O'Odham (4)	4	<0.01
Tsimshian (Alaska Native) (0)	0	<0.01
Ute (0)	0	<0.01
Yakama (0)	0	<0.01
Yaqui (1)	1	<0.01
Yuman (0)	0	<0.01
Yup'ik (Alaska Native) (0)	1	<0.01
Asian (10,247)	12,223	3.50
Not Hispanic (10,090)	11,770	3.37
Hispanic (157)	453	0.13
Bangladeshi (80)	98	0.03
Bhutanese (0)	0	<0.01
Burmese (140)	155	0.04
Cambodian (78)	100	0.03
Chinese, ex. Taiwanese (1,869)	2,207	0.63
Filipino (749)	1,113	0.32
Hmong (16)	16	<0.01
Indian (3,773)	4,171	1.19
Indonesian (31)	48	0.01
Japanese (223)	403	0.12
Korean (801)	961	0.27
Laotian (17)	30	0.01
Malaysian (15)	32	0.01
Nepalese (10)	11	<0.01
Pakistani (369)	416	0.12
Sri Lankan (39)	40	0.01
Taiwanese (90)	112	0.03
Thai (73)	100	0.03
Vietnamese (1,512)	1,759	0.50
Hawaii Native/Pacific Islander (126)	533	0.15
Not Hispanic (65)	246	0.07
Hispanic (61)	287	0.08
Fijian (2)	3	<0.01
Guamanian/Chamorro (23)	37	0.01
Marshallese (0)	0	<0.01
Native Hawaiian (24)	101	0.03
Samoan (15)	46	0.01
Tongan (8)	9	<0.01
White (276,286)	284,459	81.39
Not Hispanic (250,245)	254,911	72.94
Hispanic (26,041)	29,548	8.45

Notes: † The Census 2010 population figure is used to calculate the percentages in the Hispanic Origin and Race categories. Ancestry percentages are based on the 2006-2010 American Community Survey population (not shown); ‡ Numbers in parentheses indicate the number of people reporting a single ancestry; * Numbers in parentheses indicate the number of persons reporting this race alone, not in combination with any other race; Please refer to the Explanation of Data for more information.

Luzerne County

Population: 320,918

Ancestry	Population	%
Afghan (0)	0	<0.01
African, Sub-Saharan (402)	526	0.16
African (308)	404	0.13
Cape Verdean (0)	17	0.01
Ethiopian (0)	0	<0.01
Ghanaian (7)	7	<0.01
Kenyan (0)	0	<0.01
Liberian (0)	0	<0.01
Nigerian (80)	80	0.03
Senegalese (0)	0	<0.01
Sierra Leonean (0)	0	<0.01
Somalian (0)	0	<0.01
South African (0)	3	<0.01
Sudanese (0)	8	<0.01
Ugandan (0)	0	<0.01
Zimbabwean (0)	0	<0.01
Other Sub-Saharan African (7)	7	<0.01
Albanian (348)	348	0.11
Alsatian (0)	0	<0.01
American (10,544)	10,544	3.30
Arab (1,007)	2,578	0.81
Arab (121)	169	0.05
Egyptian (68)	85	0.03
Iraqi (0)	0	<0.01
Jordanian (76)	76	0.02
Lebanese (424)	1,356	0.42
Moroccan (0)	0	<0.01
Palestinian (0)	14	<0.01
Syrian (289)	849	0.27
Other Arab (29)	29	0.01
Armenian (17)	17	0.01
Assyrian/Chaldean/Syriac (17)	17	0.01
Australian (0)	54	0.02
Austrian (748)	2,631	0.82
Basque (11)	11	<0.01
Belgian (0)	38	0.01
Brazilian (41)	41	0.01
British (336)	642	0.20
Bulgarian (39)	39	0.01
Cajun (0)	0	<0.01
Canadian (27)	98	0.03
Carpatho Rusyn (56)	61	0.02
Celtic (3)	3	<0.01
Croatian (36)	192	0.06
Cypriot (0)	0	<0.01
Czech (362)	1,604	0.50
Czechoslovakian (438)	723	0.23
Danish (65)	196	0.06
Dutch (1,400)	9,176	2.88
Eastern European (571)	608	0.19
English (5,125)	21,969	6.88
Estonian (0)	0	<0.01
European (986)	1,045	0.33
Finnish (32)	82	0.03
French, ex. Basque (562)	4,336	1.36
French Canadian (102)	432	0.14
German (14,031)	59,643	18.69
German Russian (0)	32	0.01
Greek (537)	2,157	0.68
Guyanese (0)	46	0.01
Hungarian (639)	2,520	0.79
Icelander (0)	0	<0.01
Iranian (0)	19	0.01
Irish (16,910)	63,846	20.01
Israeli (12)	12	<0.01
Italian (20,235)	54,739	17.15
Latvian (35)	35	0.01
Lithuanian (3,491)	11,004	3.45
Luxemburger (0)	0	<0.01
Macedonian (0)	24	0.01
Maltese (0)	8	<0.01
New Zealander (0)	0	<0.01
Northern European (19)	19	0.01
Norwegian (183)	662	0.21
Pennsylvania German (2,032)	3,917	1.23

Ancestry	Population	%
Polish (31,108)	75,045	23.52
Portuguese (118)	286	0.09
Romanian (519)	611	0.19
Russian (2,254)	9,976	3.13
Scandinavian (62)	183	0.06
Scotch-Irish (800)	2,447	0.77
Scottish (857)	3,318	1.04
Serbian (74)	91	0.03
Slavic (386)	864	0.27
Slovak (6,611)	18,516	5.80
Slovene (80)	142	0.04
Soviet Union (0)	0	<0.01
Swedish (233)	1,445	0.45
Swiss (125)	558	0.17
Turkish (45)	106	0.03
Ukrainian (1,544)	3,745	1.17
Welsh (3,233)	15,996	5.01
West Indian, ex. Hispanic (645)	785	0.25
Bahamian (0)	0	<0.01
Barbadian (0)	0	<0.01
Belizean (0)	0	<0.01
Bermudan (0)	0	<0.01
British West Indian (45)	45	0.01
Dutch West Indian (84)	84	0.03
Haitian (422)	472	0.15
Jamaican (82)	143	0.04
Trinidadian/Tobagonian (0)	15	<0.01
U.S. Virgin Islander (0)	0	<0.01
West Indian (12)	26	0.01
Other West Indian (0)	0	<0.01
Yugoslavian (168)	260	0.08

Hispanic Origin	Population	%
Hispanic or Latino (of any race)	21,491	6.70
Central American, ex. Mexican	713	0.22
Costa Rican	53	0.02
Guatemalan	157	0.05
Honduran	182	0.06
Nicaraguan	48	0.01
Panamanian	56	0.02
Salvadoran	217	0.07
Other Central American	0	<0.01
Cuban	314	0.10
Dominican Republic	7,714	2.40
Mexican	3,933	1.23
Puerto Rican	5,443	1.70
South American	1,031	0.32
Argentinean	89	0.03
Bolivian	18	0.01
Chilean	23	0.01
Colombian	210	0.07
Ecuadorian	280	0.09
Paraguayan	0	<0.01
Peruvian	243	0.08
Uruguayan	89	0.03
Venezuelan	57	0.02
Other South American	22	0.01
Other Hispanic or Latino	2,343	0.73

Race*	Population	%
African-American/Black (10,767)	13,250	4.13
Not Hispanic (9,539)	11,318	3.53
Hispanic (1,228)	1,932	0.60
American Indian/Alaska Native (558)	1,631	0.51
Not Hispanic (280)	1,094	0.34
Hispanic (278)	537	0.17
Alaska Athabascan (Ala. Nat.) (0)	1	<0.01
Aleut (Alaska Native) (1)	2	<0.01
Apache (2)	19	0.01
Arapaho (0)	0	<0.01
Blackfeet (12)	50	0.02
Canadian/French Am. Ind. (3)	16	<0.01
Central American Ind. (14)	18	0.01
Cherokee (40)	221	0.07
Cheyenne (1)	3	<0.01
Chickasaw (0)	0	<0.01
Chippewa (10)	19	0.01
Choctaw (3)	11	<0.01
Colville (0)	2	<0.01

	Population	%
Comanche (1)	1	<0.01
Cree (1)	3	<0.01
Creek (2)	9	<0.01
Crow (0)	5	<0.01
Delaware (2)	23	0.01
Hopi (0)	0	<0.01
Houma (3)	7	<0.01
Inupiat (Alaska Native) (1)	2	<0.01
Iroquois (14)	50	0.02
Kiowa (1)	6	<0.01
Lumbee (5)	6	<0.01
Menominee (0)	0	<0.01
Mexican American Ind. (30)	44	0.01
Navajo (6)	11	<0.01
Osage (0)	0	<0.01
Ottawa (0)	0	<0.01
Paiute (0)	0	<0.01
Pima (0)	0	<0.01
Potawatomi (0)	0	<0.01
Pueblo (7)	7	<0.01
Puget Sound Salish (3)	3	<0.01
Seminole (1)	10	<0.01
Shoshone (0)	3	<0.01
Sioux (11)	40	0.01
South American Ind. (15)	48	0.01
Spanish American Ind. (11)	18	0.01
Tlingit-Haida (Alaska Native) (0)	0	<0.01
Tohono O'Odham (1)	1	<0.01
Tsimshian (Alaska Native) (0)	0	<0.01
Ute (0)	0	<0.01
Yakama (0)	0	<0.01
Yaqui (1)	1	<0.01
Yuman (0)	0	<0.01
Yup'ik (Alaska Native) (0)	0	<0.01
Asian (3,135)	3,988	1.24
Not Hispanic (3,079)	3,845	1.20
Hispanic (56)	143	0.04
Bangladeshi (34)	39	0.01
Bhutanese (1)	1	<0.01
Burmese (5)	5	<0.01
Cambodian (9)	14	<0.01
Chinese, ex. Taiwanese (550)	655	0.20
Filipino (348)	561	0.17
Hmong (5)	5	<0.01
Indian (1,164)	1,277	0.40
Indonesian (24)	37	0.01
Japanese (81)	188	0.06
Korean (250)	369	0.11
Laotian (14)	20	0.01
Malaysian (2)	2	<0.01
Nepalese (1)	1	<0.01
Pakistani (88)	111	0.03
Sri Lankan (2)	2	<0.01
Taiwanese (30)	34	0.01
Thai (25)	63	0.02
Vietnamese (370)	410	0.13
Hawaii Native/Pacific Islander (57)	272	0.08
Not Hispanic (41)	141	0.04
Hispanic (16)	131	0.04
Fijian (3)	3	<0.01
Guamanian/Chamorro (19)	39	0.01
Marshallese (0)	0	<0.01
Native Hawaiian (19)	69	0.02
Samoan (5)	17	0.01
Tongan (0)	0	<0.01
White (290,943)	295,183	91.98
Not Hispanic (283,058)	286,016	89.12
Hispanic (7,885)	9,167	2.86

*Notes: † The Census 2010 population figure is used to calculate the percentages in the Hispanic Origin and Race categories. Ancestry percentages are based on the 2006-2010 American Community Survey population (not shown); ‡ Numbers in parentheses indicate the number of people reporting a single ancestry; * Numbers in parentheses indicate the number of persons reporting this race alone, not in combination with any other race; Please refer to the Explanation of Data for more information.*

Lycoming County

Population: 116,111

Ancestry	Population	%
Afghan (0)	0	<0.01
African, Sub-Saharan (169)	176	0.15
African (126)	133	0.11
Cape Verdean (0)	0	<0.01
Ethiopian (0)	0	<0.01
Ghanaian (0)	0	<0.01
Kenyan (43)	43	0.04
Liberian (0)	0	<0.01
Nigerian (0)	0	<0.01
Senegalese (0)	0	<0.01
Sierra Leonean (0)	0	<0.01
Somalian (0)	0	<0.01
South African (0)	0	<0.01
Sudanese (0)	0	<0.01
Ugandan (0)	0	<0.01
Zimbabwean (0)	0	<0.01
Other Sub-Saharan African (0)	0	<0.01
Albanian (0)	0	<0.01
Alsatian (11)	11	0.01
American (7,829)	7,829	6.73
Arab (125)	252	0.22
Arab (23)	23	0.02
Egyptian (0)	0	<0.01
Iraqi (0)	0	<0.01
Jordanian (0)	0	<0.01
Lebanese (54)	135	0.12
Moroccan (0)	0	<0.01
Palestinian (0)	0	<0.01
Syrian (33)	68	0.06
Other Arab (15)	26	0.02
Armenian (13)	30	0.03
Assyrian/Chaldean/Syriac (0)	0	<0.01
Australian (9)	17	0.01
Austrian (87)	318	0.27
Basque (0)	0	<0.01
Belgian (6)	40	0.03
Brazilian (3)	7	0.01
British (201)	420	0.36
Bulgarian (4)	9	0.01
Cajun (0)	31	0.03
Canadian (83)	166	0.14
Carpatho Rusyn (0)	0	<0.01
Celtic (18)	84	0.07
Croatian (0)	23	0.02
Cypriot (0)	0	<0.01
Czech (40)	260	0.22
Czechoslovakian (55)	111	0.10
Danish (25)	154	0.13
Dutch (816)	4,368	3.75
Eastern European (63)	63	0.05
English (3,469)	10,037	8.62
Estonian (0)	0	<0.01
European (652)	698	0.60
Finnish (7)	27	0.02
French, ex. Basque (412)	2,317	1.99
French Canadian (68)	290	0.25
German (23,028)	48,019	41.26
German Russian (0)	0	<0.01
Greek (86)	152	0.13
Guyanese (4)	4	<0.01
Hungarian (136)	449	0.39
Icelander (0)	0	<0.01
Iranian (0)	0	<0.01
Irish (3,688)	17,178	14.76
Israeli (0)	0	<0.01
Italian (4,199)	10,619	9.12
Latvian (12)	17	0.01
Lithuanian (46)	169	0.15
Luxemburger (0)	0	<0.01
Macedonian (0)	0	<0.01
Maltese (3)	3	<0.01
New Zealander (0)	0	<0.01
Northern European (39)	39	0.03
Norwegian (145)	418	0.36
Pennsylvania German (1,664)	2,486	2.14

	Population	%
Polish (1,726)	5,546	4.77
Portuguese (27)	48	0.04
Romanian (19)	181	0.16
Russian (87)	562	0.48
Scandinavian (8)	184	0.16
Scotch-Irish (659)	1,719	1.48
Scottish (572)	2,082	1.79
Serbian (0)	3	<0.01
Slavic (87)	143	0.12
Slovak (155)	432	0.37
Slovene (0)	36	0.03
Soviet Union (0)	0	<0.01
Swedish (336)	1,297	1.11
Swiss (131)	389	0.33
Turkish (13)	46	0.04
Ukrainian (118)	427	0.37
Welsh (352)	1,624	1.40
West Indian, ex. Hispanic (98)	158	0.14
Bahamian (0)	0	<0.01
Barbadian (0)	0	<0.01
Belizean (18)	18	0.02
Bermudan (0)	0	<0.01
British West Indian (3)	3	<0.01
Dutch West Indian (0)	0	<0.01
Haitian (27)	60	0.05
Jamaican (18)	22	0.02
Trinidadian/Tobagonian (4)	4	<0.01
U.S. Virgin Islander (4)	4	<0.01
West Indian (24)	47	0.04
Other West Indian (0)	0	<0.01
Yugoslavian (24)	31	0.03

Hispanic Origin	Population	%
Hispanic or Latino (of any race)	1,559	1.34
Central American, ex. Mexican	84	0.07
Costa Rican	8	0.01
Guatemalan	27	0.02
Honduran	13	0.01
Nicaraguan	5	<0.01
Panamanian	15	0.01
Salvadoran	14	0.01
Other Central American	2	<0.01
Cuban	57	0.05
Dominican Republic	54	0.05
Mexican	475	0.41
Puerto Rican	580	0.50
South American	84	0.07
Argentinean	7	0.01
Bolivian	2	<0.01
Chilean	4	<0.01
Colombian	18	0.02
Ecuadorian	19	0.02
Paraguayan	3	<0.01
Peruvian	13	0.01
Uruguayan	2	<0.01
Venezuelan	13	0.01
Other South American	3	<0.01
Other Hispanic or Latino	225	0.19

Race*	Population	%
African-American/Black (5,203)	6,541	5.63
Not Hispanic (5,060)	6,310	5.43
Hispanic (143)	231	0.20
American Indian/Alaska Native (217)	727	0.63
Not Hispanic (191)	651	0.56
Hispanic (26)	76	0.07
Alaska Athabascan (Ala. Nat.) (0)	0	<0.01
Aleut (Alaska Native) (2)	2	<0.01
Apache (7)	19	0.02
Arapaho (0)	0	<0.01
Blackfeet (4)	40	0.03
Canadian/French Am. Ind. (2)	5	<0.01
Central American Ind. (0)	0	<0.01
Cherokee (16)	136	0.12
Cheyenne (1)	1	<0.01
Chickasaw (1)	4	<0.01
Chippewa (11)	16	0.01
Choctaw (1)	5	<0.01
Colville (0)	0	<0.01

	Population	%
Comanche (3)	3	<0.01
Cree (0)	2	<0.01
Creek (0)	0	<0.01
Crow (0)	0	<0.01
Delaware (10)	25	0.02
Hopi (0)	0	<0.01
Houma (0)	0	<0.01
Inupiat (Alaska Native) (1)	1	<0.01
Iroquois (8)	38	0.03
Kiowa (0)	0	<0.01
Lumbee (7)	9	0.01
Menominee (0)	0	<0.01
Mexican American Ind. (3)	4	<0.01
Navajo (11)	14	0.01
Osage (0)	0	<0.01
Ottawa (0)	0	<0.01
Paiute (0)	0	<0.01
Pima (0)	0	<0.01
Potawatomi (2)	3	<0.01
Pueblo (0)	0	<0.01
Puget Sound Salish (0)	0	<0.01
Seminole (0)	2	<0.01
Shoshone (0)	0	<0.01
Sioux (2)	13	0.01
South American Ind. (2)	4	<0.01
Spanish American Ind. (1)	1	<0.01
Tlingit-Haida (Alaska Native) (0)	0	<0.01
Tohono O'Odham (0)	0	<0.01
Tsimshian (Alaska Native) (0)	0	<0.01
Ute (0)	0	<0.01
Yakama (0)	0	<0.01
Yaqui (1)	1	<0.01
Yuman (0)	0	<0.01
Yup'ik (Alaska Native) (1)	1	<0.01
Asian (671)	900	0.78
Not Hispanic (663)	872	0.75
Hispanic (8)	28	0.02
Bangladeshi (6)	6	<0.01
Bhutanese (0)	0	<0.01
Burmese (3)	3	<0.01
Cambodian (2)	3	<0.01
Chinese, ex. Taiwanese (145)	176	0.15
Filipino (110)	185	0.16
Hmong (0)	0	<0.01
Indian (125)	165	0.14
Indonesian (6)	10	0.01
Japanese (2)	52	0.04
Korean (118)	163	0.14
Laotian (5)	6	<0.01
Malaysian (0)	0	<0.01
Nepalese (0)	0	<0.01
Pakistani (25)	27	0.02
Sri Lankan (5)	5	<0.01
Taiwanese (5)	6	0.01
Thai (6)	11	0.01
Vietnamese (48)	59	0.05
Hawaii Native/Pacific Islander (25)	76	0.07
Not Hispanic (24)	59	0.05
Hispanic (1)	17	0.01
Fijian (0)	0	<0.01
Guamanian/Chamorro (4)	7	0.01
Marshallese (0)	0	<0.01
Native Hawaiian (7)	30	0.03
Samoan (3)	23	0.02
Tongan (0)	0	<0.01
White (107,573)	109,447	94.26
Not Hispanic (106,710)	108,427	93.38
Hispanic (863)	1,020	0.88

*Notes: † The Census 2010 population figure is used to calculate the percentages in the Hispanic Origin and Race categories. Ancestry percentages are based on the 2006-2010 American Community Survey population (not shown); ‡ Numbers in parentheses indicate the number of people reporting a single ancestry; * Numbers in parentheses indicate the number of persons reporting this race alone, not in combination with any other race; Please refer to the Explanation of Data for more information.*

McKean County

Population: 43,450

Ancestry	Population	%
Afghan (15)	15	0.03
African, Sub-Saharan (24)	52	0.12
African (24)	52	0.12
Cape Verdean (0)	0	<0.01
Ethiopian (0)	0	<0.01
Ghanaian (0)	0	<0.01
Kenyan (0)	0	<0.01
Liberian (0)	0	<0.01
Nigerian (0)	0	<0.01
Senegalese (0)	0	<0.01
Sierra Leonean (0)	0	<0.01
Somalian (0)	0	<0.01
South African (0)	0	<0.01
Sudanese (0)	0	<0.01
Ugandan (0)	0	<0.01
Zimbabwean (0)	0	<0.01
Other Sub-Saharan African (0)	0	<0.01
Albanian (0)	0	<0.01
Alsatian (0)	0	<0.01
American (2,758)	2,758	6.29
Arab (87)	144	0.33
Arab (13)	13	0.03
Egyptian (0)	0	<0.01
Iraqi (0)	0	<0.01
Jordanian (7)	7	0.02
Lebanese (10)	67	0.15
Moroccan (40)	40	0.09
Palestinian (14)	14	0.03
Syrian (3)	3	0.01
Other Arab (0)	0	<0.01
Armenian (34)	34	0.08
Assyrian/Chaldean/Syriac (0)	0	<0.01
Australian (2)	2	<0.01
Austrian (83)	197	0.45
Basque (0)	0	<0.01
Belgian (3)	66	0.15
Brazilian (9)	9	0.02
British (4)	63	0.14
Bulgarian (0)	0	<0.01
Cajun (0)	0	<0.01
Canadian (49)	61	0.14
Carpatho Rusyn (0)	0	<0.01
Celtic (0)	0	<0.01
Croatian (8)	64	0.15
Cypriot (0)	0	<0.01
Czech (115)	308	0.70
Czechoslovakian (46)	46	0.10
Danish (15)	52	0.12
Dutch (96)	1,012	2.31
Eastern European (0)	3	0.01
English (1,734)	4,740	10.81
Estonian (0)	11	0.03
European (290)	315	0.72
Finnish (0)	0	<0.01
French, ex. Basque (271)	1,320	3.01
French Canadian (65)	243	0.55
German (4,236)	13,282	30.29
German Russian (0)	0	<0.01
Greek (40)	129	0.29
Guyanese (0)	0	<0.01
Hungarian (42)	153	0.35
Icelander (0)	0	<0.01
Iranian (0)	0	<0.01
Irish (1,950)	7,566	17.25
Israeli (0)	0	<0.01
Italian (2,210)	5,605	12.78
Latvian (11)	21	0.05
Lithuanian (14)	45	0.10
Luxemburger (0)	0	<0.01
Macedonian (0)	0	<0.01
Maltese (0)	0	<0.01
New Zealander (0)	0	<0.01
Northern European (12)	12	0.03
Norwegian (28)	103	0.23
Pennsylvania German (219)	587	1.34

Ancestry	Population	%
Polish (697)	2,273	5.18
Portuguese (4)	13	0.03
Romanian (6)	32	0.07
Russian (53)	143	0.33
Scandinavian (17)	28	0.06
Scotch-Irish (329)	844	1.92
Scottish (179)	895	2.04
Serbian (0)	14	0.03
Slavic (49)	120	0.27
Slovak (145)	264	0.60
Slovene (56)	107	0.24
Soviet Union (0)	0	<0.01
Swedish (1,443)	3,826	8.72
Swiss (91)	261	0.60
Turkish (0)	0	<0.01
Ukrainian (50)	107	0.24
Welsh (96)	417	0.95
West Indian, ex. Hispanic (28)	74	0.17
Bahamian (0)	0	<0.01
Barbadian (0)	0	<0.01
Belizean (0)	0	<0.01
Bermudan (0)	0	<0.01
British West Indian (0)	0	<0.01
Dutch West Indian (0)	0	<0.01
Haitian (15)	29	0.07
Jamaican (13)	25	0.06
Trinidadian/Tobagonian (0)	0	<0.01
U.S. Virgin Islander (0)	0	<0.01
West Indian (0)	20	0.05
Other West Indian (0)	0	<0.01
Yugoslavian (0)	5	0.01

Hispanic Origin	Population	%
Hispanic or Latino (of any race)	757	1.74
Central American, ex. Mexican	22	0.05
Costa Rican	0	<0.01
Guatemalan	6	0.01
Honduran	3	0.01
Nicaraguan	3	0.01
Panamanian	5	0.01
Salvadoran	5	0.01
Other Central American	0	<0.01
Cuban	10	0.02
Dominican Republic	14	0.03
Mexican	436	1.00
Puerto Rican	180	0.41
South American	15	0.03
Argentinean	2	<0.01
Bolivian	0	<0.01
Chilean	1	<0.01
Colombian	7	0.02
Ecuadorian	2	<0.01
Paraguayan	0	<0.01
Peruvian	3	0.01
Uruguayan	0	<0.01
Venezuelan	0	<0.01
Other South American	0	<0.01
Other Hispanic or Latino	80	0.18

Race*	Population	%
African-American/Black (1,046)	1,185	2.73
Not Hispanic (1,008)	1,138	2.62
Hispanic (38)	47	0.11
American Indian/Alaska Native (100)	269	0.62
Not Hispanic (83)	242	0.56
Hispanic (17)	27	0.06
Alaska Athabascan (Ala. Nat.) (0)	0	<0.01
Aleut (Alaska Native) (1)	1	<0.01
Apache (3)	6	0.01
Arapaho (0)	0	<0.01
Blackfeet (1)	14	0.03
Canadian/French Am. Ind. (0)	0	<0.01
Central American Ind. (0)	0	<0.01
Cherokee (9)	40	0.09
Cheyenne (0)	0	<0.01
Chickasaw (0)	0	<0.01
Chippewa (3)	4	0.01
Choctaw (0)	5	0.01
Colville (0)	0	<0.01

Race*	Population	%
Comanche (0)	3	0.01
Cree (0)	0	<0.01
Creek (0)	0	<0.01
Crow (0)	0	<0.01
Delaware (0)	0	<0.01
Hopi (0)	0	<0.01
Houma (0)	0	<0.01
Inupiat (Alaska Native) (0)	0	<0.01
Iroquois (33)	67	0.15
Kiowa (0)	0	<0.01
Lumbee (0)	1	<0.01
Menominee (0)	0	<0.01
Mexican American Ind. (0)	1	<0.01
Navajo (1)	1	<0.01
Osage (0)	0	<0.01
Ottawa (0)	0	<0.01
Paiute (0)	0	<0.01
Pima (0)	0	<0.01
Potawatomi (0)	0	<0.01
Pueblo (0)	0	<0.01
Puget Sound Salish (0)	0	<0.01
Seminole (0)	0	<0.01
Shoshone (0)	0	<0.01
Sioux (1)	3	0.01
South American Ind. (5)	5	0.01
Spanish American Ind. (0)	0	<0.01
Tlingit-Haida (Alaska Native) (0)	0	<0.01
Tohono O'Odham (0)	0	<0.01
Tsimshian (Alaska Native) (0)	0	<0.01
Ute (0)	0	<0.01
Yakama (0)	0	<0.01
Yaqui (0)	0	<0.01
Yuman (0)	0	<0.01
Yup'ik (Alaska Native) (0)	0	<0.01
Asian (193)	273	0.63
Not Hispanic (191)	268	0.62
Hispanic (2)	5	0.01
Bangladeshi (5)	5	0.01
Bhutanese (0)	0	<0.01
Burmese (0)	0	<0.01
Cambodian (0)	0	<0.01
Chinese, ex. Taiwanese (45)	55	0.13
Filipino (47)	71	0.16
Hmong (0)	0	<0.01
Indian (40)	49	0.11
Indonesian (0)	0	<0.01
Japanese (11)	22	0.05
Korean (20)	38	0.09
Laotian (0)	0	<0.01
Malaysian (0)	0	<0.01
Nepalese (0)	0	<0.01
Pakistani (8)	8	0.02
Sri Lankan (1)	1	<0.01
Taiwanese (3)	7	0.02
Thai (0)	0	<0.01
Vietnamese (8)	9	0.02
Hawaii Native/Pacific Islander (3)	16	0.04
Not Hispanic (3)	15	0.03
Hispanic (0)	1	<0.01
Fijian (0)	0	<0.01
Guamanian/Chamorro (0)	0	<0.01
Marshallese (0)	0	<0.01
Native Hawaiian (0)	4	0.01
Samoan (0)	1	<0.01
Tongan (0)	0	<0.01
White (41,661)	42,028	96.73
Not Hispanic (41,039)	41,377	95.23
Hispanic (622)	651	1.50

Notes: † The Census 2010 population figure is used to calculate the percentages in the Hispanic Origin and Race categories. Ancestry percentages are based on the 2006-2010 American Community Survey population (not shown); ‡ Numbers in parentheses indicate the number of people reporting a single ancestry; * Numbers in parentheses indicate the number of persons reporting this race alone, not in combination with any other race; Please refer to the Explanation of Data for more information.

Mercer County

Population: 116,638

Ancestry	Population	%
Afghan (0)	0	<0.01
African, Sub-Saharan (346)	436	0.37
African (346)	352	0.30
Cape Verdean (0)	0	<0.01
Ethiopian (0)	0	<0.01
Ghanaian (0)	0	<0.01
Kenyan (0)	53	0.05
Liberian (0)	0	<0.01
Nigerian (0)	31	0.03
Senegalese (0)	0	<0.01
Sierra Leonean (0)	0	<0.01
Somalian (0)	0	<0.01
South African (0)	0	<0.01
Sudanese (0)	0	<0.01
Ugandan (0)	0	<0.01
Zimbabwe (0)	0	<0.01
Other Sub-Saharan African (0)	0	<0.01
Albanian (0)	0	<0.01
Alsatian (0)	0	<0.01
American (5,924)	5,924	5.05
Arab (86)	196	0.17
Arab (0)	0	<0.01
Egyptian (21)	31	0.03
Iraqi (0)	0	<0.01
Jordanian (0)	0	<0.01
Lebanese (36)	51	0.04
Moroccan (0)	0	<0.01
Palestinian (16)	16	0.01
Syrian (13)	93	0.08
Other Arab (0)	5	<0.01
Armenian (0)	0	<0.01
Assyrian/Chaldean/Syriac (0)	0	<0.01
Australian (8)	8	0.01
Austrian (90)	354	0.30
Basque (0)	3	<0.01
Belgian (18)	69	0.06
Brazilian (0)	0	<0.01
British (180)	360	0.31
Bulgarian (0)	0	<0.01
Cajun (0)	0	<0.01
Canadian (39)	68	0.06
Carpatho Rusyn (19)	86	0.07
Celtic (13)	37	0.03
Croatian (476)	1,395	1.19
Cypriot (0)	0	<0.01
Czech (151)	1,019	0.87
Czechoslovakian (117)	272	0.23
Danish (40)	113	0.10
Dutch (434)	3,686	3.14
Eastern European (44)	44	0.04
English (3,398)	12,767	10.88
Estonian (0)	0	<0.01
European (709)	760	0.65
Finnish (29)	98	0.08
French, ex. Basque (297)	2,127	1.81
French Canadian (131)	478	0.41
German (10,478)	36,620	31.22
German Russian (0)	0	<0.01
Greek (256)	619	0.53
Guyanese (28)	28	0.02
Hungarian (786)	2,628	2.24
Icelander (0)	0	<0.01
Iranian (6)	6	0.01
Irish (4,425)	19,763	16.85
Israeli (0)	0	<0.01
Italian (5,757)	14,996	12.78
Latvian (24)	38	0.03
Lithuanian (96)	277	0.24
Luxemburger (0)	0	<0.01
Macedonian (34)	55	0.05
Maltese (2)	2	<0.01
New Zealander (0)	0	<0.01
Northern European (63)	63	0.05
Norwegian (128)	549	0.47
Pennsylvania German (1,410)	1,871	1.60

Ancestry	Population	%
Polish (2,112)	6,511	5.55
Portuguese (7)	73	0.06
Romanian (171)	412	0.35
Russian (175)	1,043	0.89
Scandinavian (12)	92	0.08
Scotch-Irish (1,769)	5,108	4.35
Scottish (787)	2,880	2.46
Serbian (190)	578	0.49
Slavic (76)	190	0.16
Slovak (1,638)	4,757	4.06
Slovene (72)	303	0.26
Soviet Union (0)	0	<0.01
Swedish (237)	1,476	1.26
Swiss (182)	480	0.41
Turkish (0)	0	<0.01
Ukrainian (174)	463	0.39
Welsh (247)	1,958	1.67
West Indian, ex. Hispanic (185)	215	0.18
Bahamian (0)	0	<0.01
Barbadian (0)	0	<0.01
Belizean (99)	99	0.08
Bermudan (0)	0	<0.01
British West Indian (0)	0	<0.01
Dutch West Indian (0)	8	0.01
Haitian (15)	15	0.01
Jamaican (71)	79	0.07
Trinidadian/Tobagonian (0)	14	0.01
U.S. Virgin Islander (0)	0	<0.01
West Indian (0)	0	<0.01
Other West Indian (0)	0	<0.01
Yugoslavian (43)	128	0.11

Hispanic Origin	Population	%
Hispanic or Latino (of any race)	1,248	1.07
Central American, ex. Mexican	37	0.03
Costa Rican	1	<0.01
Guatemalan	16	0.01
Honduran	4	<0.01
Nicaraguan	4	<0.01
Panamanian	6	0.01
Salvadoran	6	0.01
Other Central American	0	<0.01
Cuban	43	0.04
Dominican Republic	29	0.02
Mexican	452	0.39
Puerto Rican	288	0.25
South American	64	0.05
Argentinean	11	0.01
Bolivian	0	<0.01
Chilean	6	0.01
Colombian	29	0.02
Ecuadorian	3	<0.01
Paraguayan	0	<0.01
Peruvian	7	0.01
Uruguayan	0	<0.01
Venezuelan	6	0.01
Other South American	2	<0.01
Other Hispanic or Latino	335	0.29

Race*	Population	%
African-American/Black (6,726)	7,811	6.70
Not Hispanic (6,620)	7,649	6.56
Hispanic (106)	162	0.14
American Indian/Alaska Native (156)	605	0.52
Not Hispanic (132)	549	0.47
Hispanic (24)	56	0.05
Alaska Athabascan (Ala. Nat.) (1)	1	<0.01
Aleut (Alaska Native) (0)	0	<0.01
Apache (0)	2	<0.01
Arapaho (0)	0	<0.01
Blackfeet (5)	28	0.02
Canadian/French Am. Ind. (2)	5	<0.01
Central American Ind. (3)	3	<0.01
Cherokee (28)	151	0.13
Cheyenne (0)	8	0.01
Chickasaw (0)	0	<0.01
Chippewa (5)	9	0.01
Choctaw (0)	1	<0.01
Colville (0)	0	<0.01

	Population	%
Comanche (0)	0	<0.01
Cree (0)	2	<0.01
Creek (0)	1	<0.01
Crow (0)	0	<0.01
Delaware (9)	20	0.02
Hopi (0)	0	<0.01
Houma (0)	1	<0.01
Inupiat (Alaska Native) (0)	3	<0.01
Iroquois (14)	44	0.04
Kiowa (0)	0	<0.01
Lumbee (0)	0	<0.01
Menominee (0)	0	<0.01
Mexican American Ind. (5)	5	<0.01
Navajo (1)	7	0.01
Osage (0)	0	<0.01
Ottawa (0)	0	<0.01
Paiute (0)	0	<0.01
Pima (0)	0	<0.01
Potawatomi (0)	0	<0.01
Pueblo (0)	0	<0.01
Puget Sound Salish (0)	0	<0.01
Seminole (0)	0	<0.01
Shoshone (0)	2	<0.01
Sioux (8)	20	0.02
South American Ind. (1)	1	<0.01
Spanish American Ind. (1)	2	<0.01
Tlingit-Haida (Alaska Native) (0)	0	<0.01
Tohono O'Odham (0)	0	<0.01
Tsimshian (Alaska Native) (0)	0	<0.01
Ute (0)	0	<0.01
Yakama (0)	0	<0.01
Yaqui (0)	0	<0.01
Yuman (0)	0	<0.01
Yup'ik (Alaska Native) (0)	0	<0.01
Asian (728)	968	0.83
Not Hispanic (726)	958	0.82
Hispanic (2)	10	0.01
Bangladeshi (0)	0	<0.01
Bhutanese (0)	0	<0.01
Burmese (2)	2	<0.01
Cambodian (2)	2	<0.01
Chinese, ex. Taiwanese (167)	199	0.17
Filipino (72)	115	0.10
Hmong (0)	0	<0.01
Indian (132)	160	0.14
Indonesian (1)	1	<0.01
Japanese (54)	81	0.07
Korean (119)	195	0.17
Laotian (3)	3	<0.01
Malaysian (0)	1	<0.01
Nepalese (0)	0	<0.01
Pakistani (24)	25	0.02
Sri Lankan (0)	0	<0.01
Taiwanese (9)	10	0.01
Thai (5)	5	<0.01
Vietnamese (69)	84	0.07
Hawaii Native/Pacific Islander (16)	74	0.06
Not Hispanic (15)	71	0.06
Hispanic (1)	3	<0.01
Fijian (0)	0	<0.01
Guamanian/Chamorro (3)	6	0.01
Marshallese (0)	0	<0.01
Native Hawaiian (4)	36	0.03
Samoan (4)	12	0.01
Tongan (0)	1	<0.01
White (106,890)	108,560	93.07
Not Hispanic (106,176)	107,725	92.36
Hispanic (714)	835	0.72

Notes: † The Census 2010 population figure is used to calculate the percentages in the Hispanic Origin and Race categories. Ancestry percentages are based on the 2006-2010 American Community Survey population (not shown); ‡ Numbers in parentheses indicate the number of people reporting a single ancestry; * Numbers in parentheses indicate the number of persons reporting this race alone, not in combination with any other race; Please refer to the Explanation of Data for more information.

Mifflin County

Population: 46,682

Ancestry	Population	%
Afghan (0)	0	<0.01
African, Sub-Saharan (9)	9	0.02
African (0)	0	<0.01
Cape Verdean (0)	0	<0.01
Ethiopian (9)	9	0.02
Ghanaian (0)	0	<0.01
Kenyan (0)	0	<0.01
Liberian (0)	0	<0.01
Nigerian (0)	0	<0.01
Senegalese (0)	0	<0.01
Sierra Leonean (0)	0	<0.01
Somalian (0)	0	<0.01
South African (0)	0	<0.01
Sudanese (0)	0	<0.01
Ugandan (0)	0	<0.01
Zimbabwean (0)	0	<0.01
Other Sub-Saharan African (0)	0	<0.01
Albanian (0)	0	<0.01
Alsatian (0)	0	<0.01
American (4,863)	4,863	10.44
Arab (32)	33	0.07
Arab (0)	0	<0.01
Egyptian (0)	0	<0.01
Iraqi (0)	0	<0.01
Jordanian (0)	0	<0.01
Lebanese (8)	9	0.02
Moroccan (0)	0	<0.01
Palestinian (0)	0	<0.01
Syrian (24)	24	0.05
Other Arab (0)	0	<0.01
Armenian (0)	0	<0.01
Assyrian/Chaldean/Syriac (0)	0	<0.01
Australian (0)	0	<0.01
Austrian (14)	84	0.18
Basque (0)	0	<0.01
Belgian (0)	0	<0.01
Brazilian (0)	0	<0.01
British (18)	100	0.21
Bulgarian (0)	0	<0.01
Cajun (0)	0	<0.01
Canadian (0)	0	<0.01
Carpatho Rusyn (0)	0	<0.01
Celtic (5)	17	0.04
Croatian (0)	30	0.06
Cypriot (0)	0	<0.01
Czech (6)	13	0.03
Czechoslovakian (30)	30	0.06
Danish (0)	0	<0.01
Dutch (400)	2,113	4.54
Eastern European (0)	0	<0.01
English (1,285)	3,463	7.43
Estonian (0)	0	<0.01
European (231)	231	0.50
Finnish (0)	0	<0.01
French, ex. Basque (125)	703	1.51
French Canadian (12)	69	0.15
German (9,358)	18,439	39.58
German Russian (0)	0	<0.01
Greek (0)	18	0.04
Guyanese (0)	0	<0.01
Hungarian (16)	114	0.24
Icelander (0)	0	<0.01
Iranian (8)	8	0.02
Irish (1,710)	6,023	12.93
Israeli (0)	0	<0.01
Italian (657)	1,603	3.44
Latvian (0)	0	<0.01
Lithuanian (28)	123	0.26
Luxemburger (0)	0	<0.01
Macedonian (0)	8	0.02
Maltese (0)	0	<0.01
New Zealander (0)	0	<0.01
Northern European (0)	0	<0.01
Norwegian (27)	309	0.66
Pennsylvania German (1,181)	1,345	2.89
Polish (254)	790	1.70
Portuguese (8)	8	0.02
Romanian (24)	29	0.06
Russian (94)	203	0.44
Scandinavian (0)	0	<0.01
Scotch-Irish (513)	1,285	2.76
Scottish (212)	780	1.67
Serbian (0)	31	0.07
Slavic (0)	0	<0.01
Slovak (35)	111	0.24
Slovene (0)	0	<0.01
Soviet Union (0)	0	<0.01
Swedish (26)	185	0.40
Swiss (213)	692	1.49
Turkish (6)	6	0.01
Ukrainian (83)	209	0.45
Welsh (159)	477	1.02
West Indian, ex. Hispanic (12)	12	0.03
Bahamian (0)	0	<0.01
Barbadian (0)	0	<0.01
Belizean (0)	0	<0.01
Bermudan (0)	0	<0.01
British West Indian (0)	0	<0.01
Dutch West Indian (0)	0	<0.01
Haitian (10)	10	0.02
Jamaican (2)	2	<0.01
Trinidadian/Tobagonian (0)	0	<0.01
U.S. Virgin Islander (0)	0	<0.01
West Indian (0)	0	<0.01
Other West Indian (0)	0	<0.01
Yugoslavian (34)	34	0.07

Hispanic Origin	Population	%
Hispanic or Latino (of any race)	534	1.14
Central American, ex. Mexican	41	0.09
Costa Rican	0	<0.01
Guatemalan	13	0.03
Honduran	14	0.03
Nicaraguan	1	<0.01
Panamanian	10	0.02
Salvadoran	3	0.01
Other Central American	0	<0.01
Cuban	3	0.01
Dominican Republic	16	0.03
Mexican	131	0.28
Puerto Rican	281	0.60
South American	13	0.03
Argentinean	0	<0.01
Bolivian	0	<0.01
Chilean	2	<0.01
Colombian	4	0.01
Ecuadorian	1	<0.01
Paraguayan	0	<0.01
Peruvian	1	<0.01
Uruguayan	1	<0.01
Venezuelan	4	0.01
Other South American	0	<0.01
Other Hispanic or Latino	49	0.10

Race*	Population	%
African-American/Black (300)	518	1.11
Not Hispanic (282)	480	1.03
Hispanic (18)	38	0.08
American Indian/Alaska Native (52)	164	0.35
Not Hispanic (52)	161	0.34
Hispanic (0)	3	0.01
Alaska Athabascan (Ala. Nat.) (0)	0	<0.01
Aleut (Alaska Native) (7)	11	0.02
Apache (0)	1	<0.01
Arapaho (0)	1	<0.01
Blackfeet (0)	2	<0.01
Canadian/French Am. Ind. (0)	0	<0.01
Central American Ind. (0)	0	<0.01
Cherokee (7)	28	0.06
Cheyenne (0)	0	<0.01
Chickasaw (0)	3	0.01
Chippewa (1)	1	<0.01
Choctaw (0)	1	<0.01
Colville (0)	0	<0.01
Comanche (0)	0	<0.01
Cree (2)	2	<0.01
Creek (0)	0	<0.01
Crow (0)	0	<0.01
Delaware (0)	5	0.01
Hopi (0)	0	<0.01
Houma (0)	0	<0.01
Inupiat (Alaska Native) (0)	0	<0.01
Iroquois (3)	10	0.02
Kiowa (0)	0	<0.01
Lumbee (0)	0	<0.01
Menominee (0)	0	<0.01
Mexican American Ind. (0)	0	<0.01
Navajo (0)	0	<0.01
Osage (0)	1	<0.01
Ottawa (0)	0	<0.01
Paiute (0)	0	<0.01
Pima (0)	0	<0.01
Potawatomi (0)	0	<0.01
Pueblo (0)	0	<0.01
Puget Sound Salish (0)	0	<0.01
Seminole (0)	0	<0.01
Shoshone (0)	0	<0.01
Sioux (0)	13	0.03
South American Ind. (0)	0	<0.01
Spanish American Ind. (0)	0	<0.01
Tlingit-Haida (Alaska Native) (3)	3	0.01
Tohono O'Odham (0)	0	<0.01
Tsimshian (Alaska Native) (1)	1	<0.01
Ute (0)	0	<0.01
Yakama (0)	0	<0.01
Yaqui (1)	1	<0.01
Yuman (0)	0	<0.01
Yup'ik (Alaska Native) (0)	0	<0.01
Asian (168)	279	0.60
Not Hispanic (167)	274	0.59
Hispanic (1)	5	0.01
Bangladeshi (0)	0	<0.01
Bhutanese (0)	0	<0.01
Burmese (0)	0	<0.01
Cambodian (0)	0	<0.01
Chinese, ex. Taiwanese (31)	33	0.07
Filipino (20)	41	0.09
Hmong (0)	0	<0.01
Indian (54)	71	0.15
Indonesian (0)	0	<0.01
Japanese (9)	36	0.08
Korean (30)	59	0.13
Laotian (6)	15	0.03
Malaysian (0)	0	<0.01
Nepalese (0)	0	<0.01
Pakistani (0)	0	<0.01
Sri Lankan (0)	0	<0.01
Taiwanese (0)	1	<0.01
Thai (4)	6	0.01
Vietnamese (9)	11	0.02
Hawaii Native/Pacific Islander (7)	21	0.04
Not Hispanic (6)	18	0.04
Hispanic (1)	3	0.01
Fijian (0)	0	<0.01
Guamanian/Chamorro (1)	3	0.01
Marshallese (0)	0	<0.01
Native Hawaiian (4)	12	0.03
Samoan (0)	2	<0.01
Tongan (0)	0	<0.01
White (45,531)	45,992	98.52
Not Hispanic (45,199)	45,603	97.69
Hispanic (332)	389	0.83

Notes: † The Census 2010 population figure is used to calculate the percentages in the Hispanic Origin and Race categories. Ancestry percentages are based on the 2006-2010 American Community Survey population (not shown); ‡ Numbers in parentheses indicate the number of people reporting a single ancestry; * Numbers in parentheses indicate the number of persons reporting this race alone, not in combination with any other race; Please refer to the Explanation of Data for more information.

Monroe County

Population: 169,842

Ancestry	Population	%
Afghan (0)	0	<0.01
African, Sub-Saharan (1,119)	1,258	0.75
African (669)	793	0.47
Cape Verdean (0)	0	<0.01
Ethiopian (0)	0	<0.01
Ghanaian (109)	109	0.06
Kenyan (53)	53	0.03
Liberian (0)	15	0.01
Nigerian (80)	80	0.05
Senegalese (0)	0	<0.01
Sierra Leonean (0)	0	<0.01
Somalian (0)	0	<0.01
South African (0)	0	<0.01
Sudanese (0)	0	<0.01
Ugandan (0)	0	<0.01
Zimbabwean (0)	0	<0.01
Other Sub-Saharan African (208)	208	0.12
Albanian (58)	70	0.04
Alsatian (0)	0	<0.01
American (4,823)	4,823	2.87
Arab (1,008)	1,433	0.85
Arab (195)	240	0.14
Egyptian (140)	152	0.09
Iraqi (0)	0	<0.01
Jordanian (175)	175	0.10
Lebanese (65)	296	0.18
Moroccan (122)	122	0.07
Palestinian (133)	133	0.08
Syrian (102)	227	0.14
Other Arab (76)	88	0.05
Armenian (37)	103	0.06
Assyrian/Chaldean/Syriac (0)	0	<0.01
Australian (109)	115	0.07
Austrian (294)	793	0.47
Basque (0)	0	<0.01
Belgian (32)	107	0.06
Brazilian (272)	321	0.19
British (98)	352	0.21
Bulgarian (251)	283	0.17
Cajun (0)	10	0.01
Canadian (62)	136	0.08
Carpatho Rusyn (11)	11	0.01
Celtic (0)	0	<0.01
Croatian (209)	309	0.18
Cypriot (39)	39	0.02
Czech (234)	813	0.48
Czechoslovakian (87)	303	0.18
Danish (200)	497	0.30
Dutch (1,271)	4,340	2.58
Eastern European (279)	279	0.17
English (3,218)	12,086	7.19
Estonian (0)	17	0.01
European (626)	736	0.44
Finnish (87)	254	0.15
French, ex. Basque (443)	3,233	1.92
French Canadian (98)	384	0.23
German (14,975)	39,099	23.26
German Russian (0)	0	<0.01
Greek (764)	1,352	0.80
Guyanese (220)	409	0.24
Hungarian (403)	1,532	0.91
Icelander (0)	0	<0.01
Iranian (94)	101	0.06
Irish (8,523)	28,641	17.04
Israeli (0)	46	0.03
Italian (12,795)	28,348	16.87
Latvian (12)	49	0.03
Lithuanian (145)	777	0.46
Luxemburger (0)	0	<0.01
Macedonian (0)	0	<0.01
Maltese (26)	42	0.02
New Zealander (0)	0	<0.01
Northern European (0)	0	<0.01
Norwegian (236)	1,121	0.67
Pennsylvania German (2,010)	2,778	1.65

Ancestry	Population	%
Polish (4,705)	11,419	6.79
Portuguese (286)	685	0.41
Romanian (453)	587	0.35
Russian (723)	2,390	1.42
Scandinavian (36)	161	0.10
Scotch-Irish (886)	2,055	1.22
Scottish (602)	2,353	1.40
Serbian (0)	0	<0.01
Slavic (128)	160	0.10
Slovak (597)	1,285	0.76
Slovene (18)	51	0.03
Soviet Union (0)	0	<0.01
Swedish (664)	1,621	0.96
Swiss (103)	433	0.26
Turkish (14)	29	0.02
Ukrainian (540)	1,145	0.68
Welsh (628)	2,386	1.42
West Indian, ex. Hispanic (2,488)	3,476	2.07
Bahamian (20)	20	0.01
Barbadian (108)	185	0.11
Belizean (175)	175	0.10
Bermudan (0)	0	<0.01
British West Indian (66)	141	0.08
Dutch West Indian (0)	0	<0.01
Haitian (549)	636	0.38
Jamaican (828)	1,364	0.81
Trinidadian/Tobagonian (89)	238	0.14
U.S. Virgin Islander (239)	239	0.14
West Indian (414)	478	0.28
Other West Indian (0)	0	<0.01
Yugoslavian (67)	145	0.09

Hispanic Origin	Population	%
Hispanic or Latino (of any race)	22,288	13.12
Central American, ex. Mexican	1,242	0.73
Costa Rican	97	0.06
Guatemalan	254	0.15
Honduran	245	0.14
Nicaraguan	83	0.05
Panamanian	232	0.14
Salvadoran	319	0.19
Other Central American	12	0.01
Cuban	764	0.45
Dominican Republic	2,154	1.27
Mexican	1,082	0.64
Puerto Rican	12,536	7.38
South American	2,814	1.66
Argentinean	154	0.09
Bolivian	46	0.03
Chilean	84	0.05
Colombian	888	0.52
Ecuadorian	815	0.48
Paraguayan	14	0.01
Peruvian	585	0.34
Uruguayan	82	0.05
Venezuelan	94	0.06
Other South American	52	0.03
Other Hispanic or Latino	1,696	1.00

Race*	Population	%
African-American/Black (22,348)	25,002	14.72
Not Hispanic (20,461)	22,258	13.11
Hispanic (1,887)	2,744	1.62
American Indian/Alaska Native (572)	1,681	0.99
Not Hispanic (358)	1,232	0.73
Hispanic (214)	449	0.26
Alaska Athabascan (Ala. Nat.) (0)	0	<0.01
Aleut (Alaska Native) (2)	2	<0.01
Apache (2)	22	0.01
Arapaho (0)	0	<0.01
Blackfeet (23)	72	0.04
Canadian/French Am. Ind. (0)	1	<0.01
Central American Ind. (25)	28	0.02
Cherokee (62)	293	0.17
Cheyenne (1)	2	<0.01
Chickasaw (0)	1	<0.01
Chippewa (2)	14	0.01
Choctaw (1)	22	0.01
Colville (1)	1	<0.01

Race*	Population	%
Comanche (2)	3	<0.01
Cree (0)	2	<0.01
Creek (1)	2	<0.01
Crow (0)	3	<0.01
Delaware (21)	70	0.04
Hopi (0)	1	<0.01
Houma (0)	0	<0.01
Inupiat (Alaska Native) (0)	0	<0.01
Iroquois (20)	83	0.05
Kiowa (0)	4	<0.01
Lumbee (2)	6	<0.01
Menominee (0)	0	<0.01
Mexican American Ind. (17)	31	0.02
Navajo (0)	2	<0.01
Osage (0)	0	<0.01
Ottawa (0)	0	<0.01
Paiute (0)	1	<0.01
Pima (1)	5	<0.01
Potawatomi (3)	6	<0.01
Pueblo (0)	1	<0.01
Puget Sound Salish (4)	4	<0.01
Seminole (2)	14	0.01
Shoshone (1)	5	<0.01
Sioux (8)	27	0.02
South American Ind. (62)	101	0.06
Spanish American Ind. (5)	7	<0.01
Tlingit-Haida (Alaska Native) (0)	0	<0.01
Tohono O'Odham (3)	4	<0.01
Tsimshian (Alaska Native) (0)	0	<0.01
Ute (0)	0	<0.01
Yakama (0)	0	<0.01
Yaqui (1)	1	<0.01
Yuman (0)	0	<0.01
Yup'ik (Alaska Native) (0)	0	<0.01
Asian (3,484)	4,458	2.62
Not Hispanic (3,395)	4,223	2.49
Hispanic (89)	235	0.14
Bangladeshi (16)	16	0.01
Bhutanese (0)	0	<0.01
Burmese (2)	4	<0.01
Cambodian (25)	31	0.02
Chinese, ex. Taiwanese (581)	821	0.48
Filipino (768)	994	0.59
Hmong (2)	2	<0.01
Indian (1,126)	1,353	0.80
Indonesian (19)	27	0.02
Japanese (70)	142	0.08
Korean (319)	396	0.23
Laotian (6)	13	0.01
Malaysian (11)	15	0.01
Nepalese (5)	5	<0.01
Pakistani (175)	214	0.13
Sri Lankan (9)	11	0.01
Taiwanese (32)	35	0.02
Thai (60)	70	0.04
Vietnamese (132)	148	0.09
Hawaii Native/Pacific Islander (79)	270	0.16
Not Hispanic (60)	183	0.11
Hispanic (19)	87	0.05
Fijian (2)	2	<0.01
Guamanian/Chamorro (12)	21	0.01
Marshallese (0)	0	<0.01
Native Hawaiian (17)	45	0.03
Samoan (16)	24	0.01
Tongan (1)	1	<0.01
White (131,162)	134,953	79.46
Not Hispanic (119,741)	122,223	71.96
Hispanic (11,421)	12,730	7.50

Notes: † The Census 2010 population figure is used to calculate the percentages in the Hispanic Origin and Race categories. Ancestry percentages are based on the 2006-2010 American Community Survey population (not shown); ‡ Numbers in parentheses indicate the number of people reporting a single ancestry; * Numbers in parentheses indicate the number of persons reporting this race alone, not in combination with any other race; Please refer to the Explanation of Data for more information.

Montgomery County
Population: 799,874

Ancestry	Population	%
Afghan (9)	9	<0.01
African, Sub-Saharan (3,400)	4,068	0.51
African (2,062)	2,480	0.31
Cape Verdean (69)	96	0.01
Ethiopian (107)	121	0.02
Ghanaian (177)	177	0.02
Kenyan (187)	187	0.02
Liberian (31)	58	0.01
Nigerian (344)	359	0.05
Senegalese (10)	32	<0.01
Sierra Leonean (0)	10	<0.01
Somalian (0)	0	<0.01
South African (157)	227	0.03
Sudanese (105)	105	0.01
Ugandan (51)	51	0.01
Zimbabwean (55)	55	0.01
Other Sub-Saharan African (45)	110	0.01
Albanian (284)	519	0.07
Alsatian (36)	124	0.02
American (28,494)	28,494	3.60
Arab (2,463)	3,762	0.48
Arab (405)	621	0.08
Egyptian (925)	1,051	0.13
Iraqi (219)	219	0.03
Jordanian (92)	111	0.01
Lebanese (397)	961	0.12
Moroccan (11)	63	0.01
Palestinian (47)	106	0.01
Syrian (82)	187	0.02
Other Arab (285)	443	0.06
Armenian (822)	1,507	0.19
Assyrian/Chaldean/Syriac (0)	8	<0.01
Australian (101)	333	0.04
Austrian (861)	4,440	0.56
Basque (0)	0	<0.01
Belgian (195)	497	0.06
Brazilian (323)	624	0.08
British (1,999)	3,805	0.48
Bulgarian (103)	131	0.02
Cajun (0)	0	<0.01
Canadian (677)	1,210	0.15
Carpatho Rusyn (0)	7	<0.01
Celtic (71)	122	0.02
Croatian (302)	863	0.11
Cypriot (66)	75	0.01
Czech (597)	3,333	0.42
Czechoslovakian (502)	1,232	0.16
Danish (172)	1,426	0.18
Dutch (2,352)	12,229	1.55
Eastern European (4,761)	5,147	0.65
English (16,398)	74,751	9.46
Estonian (56)	195	0.02
European (6,654)	7,507	0.95
Finnish (120)	488	0.06
French, ex. Basque (1,967)	14,086	1.78
French Canadian (736)	2,248	0.28
German (55,748)	190,480	24.10
German Russian (4)	15	<0.01
Greek (1,861)	4,143	0.52
Guyanese (112)	160	0.02
Hungarian (2,167)	8,581	1.09
Icelander (34)	88	0.01
Iranian (670)	1,054	0.13
Irish (52,106)	178,537	22.59
Israeli (554)	796	0.10
Italian (50,176)	124,058	15.69
Latvian (381)	636	0.08
Lithuanian (1,419)	5,188	0.66
Luxemburger (16)	48	0.01
Macedonian (18)	64	0.01
Maltese (10)	118	0.01
New Zealander (37)	50	0.01
Northern European (457)	504	0.06
Norwegian (1,013)	3,383	0.43
Pennsylvania German (5,852)	9,680	1.22

Ancestry	Population	%
Polish (16,916)	55,685	7.04
Portuguese (693)	1,604	0.20
Romanian (1,023)	2,498	0.32
Russian (13,994)	27,696	3.50
Scandinavian (158)	509	0.06
Scotch-Irish (5,220)	14,136	1.79
Scottish (3,320)	14,132	1.79
Serbian (115)	424	0.05
Slavic (224)	759	0.10
Slovak (1,849)	6,201	0.78
Slovene (88)	219	0.03
Soviet Union (22)	22	<0.01
Swedish (1,229)	6,244	0.79
Swiss (744)	3,643	0.46
Turkish (199)	510	0.06
Ukrainian (4,000)	9,507	1.20
Welsh (1,039)	9,701	1.23
West Indian, ex. Hispanic (4,068)	5,504	0.70
Bahamian (119)	140	0.02
Barbadian (209)	349	0.04
Belizean (134)	145	0.02
Bermudan (22)	22	<0.01
British West Indian (93)	156	0.02
Dutch West Indian (0)	0	<0.01
Haitian (893)	1,042	0.13
Jamaican (1,993)	2,685	0.34
Trinidadian/Tobagonian (279)	401	0.05
U.S. Virgin Islander (0)	18	<0.01
West Indian (322)	505	0.06
Other West Indian (26)	41	0.01
Yugoslavian (158)	529	0.07

Hispanic Origin	Population	%
Hispanic or Latino (of any race)	34,233	4.28
Central American, ex. Mexican	2,894	0.36
Costa Rican	276	0.03
Guatemalan	927	0.12
Honduran	652	0.08
Nicaraguan	153	0.02
Panamanian	222	0.03
Salvadoran	634	0.08
Other Central American	30	<0.01
Cuban	1,338	0.17
Dominican Republic	789	0.10
Mexican	13,386	1.67
Puerto Rican	9,356	1.17
South American	3,486	0.44
Argentinean	477	0.06
Bolivian	94	0.01
Chilean	198	0.02
Colombian	1,041	0.13
Ecuadorian	548	0.07
Paraguayan	78	0.01
Peruvian	605	0.08
Uruguayan	85	0.01
Venezuelan	323	0.04
Other South American	37	<0.01
Other Hispanic or Latino	2,984	0.37

Race*	Population	%
African-American/Black (69,351)	77,347	9.67
Not Hispanic (67,582)	74,415	9.30
Hispanic (1,769)	2,932	0.37
American Indian/Alaska Native (1,174)	4,225	0.53
Not Hispanic (791)	3,343	0.42
Hispanic (383)	882	0.11
Alaska Athabascan (Ala. Nat.) (8)	12	<0.01
Aleut (Alaska Native) (2)	3	<0.01
Apache (7)	29	<0.01
Arapaho (0)	2	<0.01
Blackfeet (10)	132	0.02
Canadian/French Am. Ind. (12)	23	<0.01
Central American Ind. (10)	22	<0.01
Cherokee (116)	788	0.10
Cheyenne (3)	12	<0.01
Chickasaw (0)	2	<0.01
Chippewa (12)	19	<0.01
Choctaw (12)	47	0.01
Colville (0)	0	<0.01

	Population	%
Comanche (1)	5	<0.01
Cree (2)	6	<0.01
Creek (2)	24	<0.01
Crow (0)	7	<0.01
Delaware (13)	116	0.01
Hopi (3)	13	<0.01
Houma (0)	0	<0.01
Inupiat (Alaska Native) (0)	4	<0.01
Iroquois (26)	86	0.01
Kiowa (3)	3	<0.01
Lumbee (29)	51	0.01
Menominee (1)	2	<0.01
Mexican American Ind. (73)	102	0.01
Navajo (6)	25	<0.01
Osage (0)	3	<0.01
Ottawa (0)	4	<0.01
Paiute (0)	2	<0.01
Pima (0)	0	<0.01
Potawatomi (3)	5	<0.01
Pueblo (3)	9	<0.01
Puget Sound Salish (1)	3	<0.01
Seminole (7)	40	0.01
Shoshone (0)	0	<0.01
Sioux (24)	89	0.01
South American Ind. (30)	73	0.01
Spanish American Ind. (21)	26	<0.01
Tlingit-Haida (Alaska Native) (1)	11	<0.01
Tohono O'Odham (1)	2	<0.01
Tsimshian (Alaska Native) (0)	3	<0.01
Ute (2)	2	<0.01
Yakama (0)	0	<0.01
Yaqui (1)	4	<0.01
Yuman (1)	2	<0.01
Yup'ik (Alaska Native) (0)	0	<0.01
Asian (51,565)	56,841	7.11
Not Hispanic (51,354)	56,285	7.04
Hispanic (211)	556	0.07
Bangladeshi (1,116)	1,222	0.15
Bhutanese (0)	0	<0.01
Burmese (133)	145	0.02
Cambodian (646)	847	0.11
Chinese, ex. Taiwanese (9,219)	10,555	1.32
Filipino (2,366)	3,360	0.42
Hmong (7)	10	<0.01
Indian (16,767)	17,963	2.25
Indonesian (103)	139	0.02
Japanese (706)	1,294	0.16
Korean (13,417)	14,282	1.79
Laotian (229)	280	0.04
Malaysian (34)	60	0.01
Nepalese (104)	120	0.02
Pakistani (884)	981	0.12
Sri Lankan (120)	145	0.02
Taiwanese (394)	511	0.06
Thai (244)	388	0.05
Vietnamese (3,719)	4,178	0.52
Hawaii Native/Pacific Islander (296)	775	0.10
Not Hispanic (221)	620	0.08
Hispanic (75)	155	0.02
Fijian (6)	13	<0.01
Guamanian/Chamorro (85)	123	0.02
Marshallese (2)	2	<0.01
Native Hawaiian (49)	176	0.02
Samoan (62)	121	0.02
Tongan (17)	30	<0.01
White (649,021)	661,998	82.76
Not Hispanic (631,784)	642,545	80.33
Hispanic (17,237)	19,453	2.43

Notes: † *The Census 2010 population figure is used to calculate the percentages in the Hispanic Origin and Race categories. Ancestry percentages are based on the 2006-2010 American Community Survey population (not shown); ‡ Numbers in parentheses indicate the number of people reporting a single ancestry; * Numbers in parentheses indicate the number of persons reporting this race alone, not in combination with any other race; Please refer to the Explanation of Data for more information.*

Montour County

Population: 18,267

Ancestry	Population	%
Afghan (0)	0	<0.01
African, Sub-Saharan (27)	27	0.15
African (0)	0	<0.01
Cape Verdean (0)	0	<0.01
Ethiopian (0)	0	<0.01
Ghanaian (0)	0	<0.01
Kenyan (0)	0	<0.01
Liberian (0)	0	<0.01
Nigerian (0)	0	<0.01
Senegalese (0)	0	<0.01
Sierra Leonean (0)	0	<0.01
Somalian (0)	0	<0.01
South African (0)	0	<0.01
Sudanese (27)	27	0.15
Ugandan (0)	0	<0.01
Zimbabwean (0)	0	<0.01
Other Sub-Saharan African (0)	0	<0.01
Albanian (0)	0	<0.01
Alsatian (0)	0	<0.01
American (1,195)	1,195	6.58
Arab (29)	59	0.33
Arab (0)	0	<0.01
Egyptian (29)	29	0.16
Iraqi (0)	0	<0.01
Jordanian (0)	0	<0.01
Lebanese (0)	30	0.17
Moroccan (0)	0	<0.01
Palestinian (0)	0	<0.01
Syrian (0)	0	<0.01
Other Arab (0)	0	<0.01
Armenian (0)	0	<0.01
Assyrian/Chaldean/Syriac (0)	0	<0.01
Australian (0)	0	<0.01
Austrian (50)	91	0.50
Basque (8)	8	0.04
Belgian (0)	0	<0.01
Brazilian (14)	40	0.22
British (33)	37	0.20
Bulgarian (104)	104	0.57
Cajun (0)	0	<0.01
Canadian (0)	0	<0.01
Carpatho Rusyn (0)	0	<0.01
Celtic (0)	0	<0.01
Croatian (0)	7	0.04
Cypriot (0)	0	<0.01
Czech (0)	22	0.12
Czechoslovakian (0)	5	0.03
Danish (26)	143	0.79
Dutch (300)	941	5.18
Eastern European (54)	54	0.30
English (793)	1,993	10.98
Estonian (0)	0	<0.01
European (126)	136	0.75
Finnish (0)	0	<0.01
French, ex. Basque (42)	485	2.67
French Canadian (18)	24	0.13
German (3,249)	6,566	36.17
German Russian (0)	0	<0.01
Greek (10)	38	0.21
Guyanese (0)	0	<0.01
Hungarian (10)	72	0.40
Icelander (0)	10	0.06
Iranian (0)	0	<0.01
Irish (690)	2,062	11.36
Israeli (0)	0	<0.01
Italian (350)	1,040	5.73
Latvian (0)	0	<0.01
Lithuanian (88)	157	0.86
Luxemburger (0)	0	<0.01
Macedonian (0)	0	<0.01
Maltese (0)	0	<0.01
New Zealander (0)	0	<0.01
Northern European (7)	7	0.04
Norwegian (9)	35	0.19
Pennsylvania German (586)	766	4.22

Ancestry (cont.)	Population	%
Polish (254)	828	4.56
Portuguese (28)	31	0.17
Romanian (3)	3	0.02
Russian (36)	67	0.37
Scandinavian (7)	19	0.10
Scotch-Irish (58)	229	1.26
Scottish (73)	358	1.97
Serbian (0)	9	0.05
Slavic (0)	5	0.03
Slovak (124)	247	1.36
Slovene (0)	9	0.05
Soviet Union (0)	0	<0.01
Swedish (6)	124	0.68
Swiss (36)	129	0.71
Turkish (0)	0	<0.01
Ukrainian (57)	143	0.79
Welsh (111)	528	2.91
West Indian, ex. Hispanic (0)	0	<0.01
Bahamian (0)	0	<0.01
Barbadian (0)	0	<0.01
Belizean (0)	0	<0.01
Bermudan (0)	0	<0.01
British West Indian (0)	0	<0.01
Dutch West Indian (0)	0	<0.01
Haitian (0)	0	<0.01
Jamaican (0)	0	<0.01
Trinidadian/Tobagonian (0)	0	<0.01
U.S. Virgin Islander (0)	0	<0.01
West Indian (0)	0	<0.01
Other West Indian (0)	0	<0.01
Yugoslavian (0)	0	<0.01

Hispanic Origin	Population	%
Hispanic or Latino (of any race)	324	1.77
Central American, ex. Mexican	19	0.10
Costa Rican	0	<0.01
Guatemalan	6	0.03
Honduran	2	0.01
Nicaraguan	3	0.02
Panamanian	4	0.02
Salvadoran	4	0.02
Other Central American	0	<0.01
Cuban	27	0.15
Dominican Republic	11	0.06
Mexican	74	0.41
Puerto Rican	108	0.59
South American	64	0.35
Argentinean	0	<0.01
Bolivian	5	0.03
Chilean	1	0.01
Colombian	45	0.25
Ecuadorian	3	0.02
Paraguayan	0	<0.01
Peruvian	10	0.05
Uruguayan	0	<0.01
Venezuelan	0	<0.01
Other South American	0	<0.01
Other Hispanic or Latino	21	0.11

Race*	Population	%
African-American/Black (256)	336	1.84
Not Hispanic (237)	309	1.69
Hispanic (19)	27	0.15
American Indian/Alaska Native (16)	73	0.40
Not Hispanic (12)	63	0.34
Hispanic (4)	10	0.05
Alaska Athabascan (Ala. Nat.) (1)	1	0.01
Aleut (Alaska Native) (0)	0	<0.01
Apache (0)	0	<0.01
Arapaho (0)	0	<0.01
Blackfeet (0)	3	0.02
Canadian/French Am. Ind. (0)	0	<0.01
Central American Ind. (0)	0	<0.01
Cherokee (0)	10	0.05
Cheyenne (0)	0	<0.01
Chickasaw (0)	0	<0.01
Chippewa (0)	0	<0.01
Choctaw (0)	0	<0.01
Colville (0)	0	<0.01

Race* (cont.)	Population	%
Comanche (0)	0	<0.01
Cree (0)	0	<0.01
Creek (0)	1	0.01
Crow (0)	0	<0.01
Delaware (0)	1	0.01
Hopi (0)	0	<0.01
Houma (0)	0	<0.01
Inupiat (Alaska Native) (0)	0	<0.01
Iroquois (1)	7	0.04
Kiowa (0)	0	<0.01
Lumbee (0)	0	<0.01
Menominee (0)	0	<0.01
Mexican American Ind. (1)	3	0.02
Navajo (2)	2	0.01
Osage (0)	0	<0.01
Ottawa (0)	0	<0.01
Paiute (0)	0	<0.01
Pima (0)	0	<0.01
Potawatomi (0)	0	<0.01
Pueblo (0)	0	<0.01
Puget Sound Salish (0)	0	<0.01
Seminole (0)	0	<0.01
Shoshone (0)	1	0.01
Sioux (0)	0	<0.01
South American Ind. (0)	0	<0.01
Spanish American Ind. (0)	0	<0.01
Tlingit-Haida (Alaska Native) (0)	0	<0.01
Tohono O'Odham (0)	0	<0.01
Tsimshian (Alaska Native) (0)	0	<0.01
Ute (0)	0	<0.01
Yakama (0)	0	<0.01
Yaqui (0)	0	<0.01
Yuman (0)	0	<0.01
Yup'ik (Alaska Native) (0)	0	<0.01
Asian (326)	369	2.02
Not Hispanic (323)	364	1.99
Hispanic (3)	5	0.03
Bangladeshi (2)	2	0.01
Bhutanese (0)	0	<0.01
Burmese (0)	0	<0.01
Cambodian (0)	0	<0.01
Chinese, ex. Taiwanese (71)	75	0.41
Filipino (18)	24	0.13
Hmong (0)	0	<0.01
Indian (159)	177	0.97
Indonesian (0)	0	<0.01
Japanese (7)	10	0.05
Korean (21)	26	0.14
Laotian (0)	0	<0.01
Malaysian (1)	1	0.01
Nepalese (3)	5	0.03
Pakistani (26)	29	0.16
Sri Lankan (0)	0	<0.01
Taiwanese (0)	0	<0.01
Thai (1)	1	0.01
Vietnamese (14)	18	0.10
Hawaii Native/Pacific Islander (2)	3	0.02
Not Hispanic (2)	3	0.02
Hispanic (0)	0	<0.01
Fijian (0)	0	<0.01
Guamanian/Chamorro (1)	1	0.01
Marshallese (0)	0	<0.01
Native Hawaiian (1)	2	0.01
Samoan (0)	0	<0.01
Tongan (0)	0	<0.01
White (17,408)	17,572	96.20
Not Hispanic (17,206)	17,350	94.98
Hispanic (202)	222	1.22

Notes: † The Census 2010 population figure is used to calculate the percentages in the Hispanic Origin and Race categories. Ancestry percentages are based on the 2006-2010 American Community Survey population (not shown); ‡ Numbers in parentheses indicate the number of people reporting a single ancestry; * Numbers in parentheses indicate the number of persons reporting this race alone, not in combination with any other race; Please refer to the Explanation of Data for more information.

Northampton County

Population: 297,735

Ancestry	Population	%
Afghan (40)	48	0.02
African, Sub-Saharan (921)	1,061	0.36
African (289)	348	0.12
Cape Verdean (0)	5	<0.01
Ethiopian (20)	61	0.02
Ghanaian (50)	50	0.02
Kenyan (81)	81	0.03
Liberian (24)	24	0.01
Nigerian (349)	384	0.13
Senegalese (43)	43	0.01
Sierra Leonean (12)	12	<0.01
Somalian (0)	0	<0.01
South African (45)	45	0.02
Sudanese (0)	0	<0.01
Ugandan (0)	0	<0.01
Zimbabwean (0)	0	<0.01
Other Sub-Saharan African (8)	8	<0.01
Albanian (91)	108	0.04
Alsatian (0)	0	<0.01
American (13,101)	13,101	4.45
Arab (1,564)	2,587	0.88
Arab (252)	282	0.10
Egyptian (222)	389	0.13
Iraqi (0)	0	<0.01
Jordanian (45)	74	0.03
Lebanese (495)	904	0.31
Moroccan (0)	0	<0.01
Palestinian (0)	0	<0.01
Syrian (505)	788	0.27
Other Arab (45)	150	0.05
Armenian (76)	151	0.05
Assyrian/Chaldean/Syriac (31)	31	0.01
Australian (66)	82	0.03
Austrian (1,057)	3,315	1.13
Basque (0)	59	0.02
Belgian (54)	176	0.06
Brazilian (288)	337	0.11
British (537)	1,247	0.42
Bulgarian (103)	103	0.03
Cajun (0)	0	<0.01
Canadian (250)	527	0.18
Carpatho Rusyn (30)	30	0.01
Celtic (0)	0	<0.01
Croatian (137)	370	0.13
Cypriot (11)	11	<0.01
Czech (190)	1,619	0.55
Czechoslovakian (222)	683	0.23
Danish (123)	471	0.16
Dutch (2,529)	10,052	3.41
Eastern European (368)	440	0.15
English (5,707)	23,279	7.90
Estonian (23)	105	0.04
European (1,675)	1,869	0.63
Finnish (44)	142	0.05
French, ex. Basque (744)	5,181	1.76
French Canadian (199)	683	0.23
German (31,639)	87,044	29.55
German Russian (12)	12	<0.01
Greek (1,084)	2,427	0.82
Guyanese (116)	260	0.09
Hungarian (3,648)	11,314	3.84
Icelander (0)	0	<0.01
Iranian (127)	127	0.04
Irish (8,456)	43,124	14.64
Israeli (9)	59	0.02
Italian (17,698)	45,234	15.36
Latvian (34)	102	0.03
Lithuanian (306)	1,185	0.40
Luxemburger (0)	0	<0.01
Macedonian (16)	16	0.01
Maltese (0)	0	<0.01
New Zealander (14)	30	0.01
Northern European (50)	76	0.03
Norwegian (523)	1,482	0.50
Pennsylvania German (9,258)	14,088	4.78

	Population	%
Polish (5,000)	17,349	5.89
Portuguese (1,209)	1,877	0.64
Romanian (212)	338	0.11
Russian (1,155)	3,387	1.15
Scandinavian (72)	166	0.06
Scotch-Irish (901)	3,388	1.15
Scottish (860)	4,300	1.46
Serbian (43)	152	0.05
Slavic (100)	411	0.14
Slovak (2,226)	7,016	2.38
Slovene (250)	425	0.14
Soviet Union (0)	0	<0.01
Swedish (267)	1,823	0.62
Swiss (159)	1,304	0.44
Turkish (422)	460	0.16
Ukrainian (1,531)	4,375	1.49
Welsh (963)	6,030	2.05
West Indian, ex. Hispanic (1,172)	1,567	0.53
Bahamian (28)	28	0.01
Barbadian (0)	22	0.01
Belizean (26)	26	0.01
Bermudan (0)	0	<0.01
British West Indian (32)	40	0.01
Dutch West Indian (8)	20	0.01
Haitian (346)	419	0.14
Jamaican (354)	510	0.17
Trinidadian/Tobagonian (268)	315	0.11
U.S. Virgin Islander (3)	3	<0.01
West Indian (107)	184	0.06
Other West Indian (0)	0	<0.01
Yugoslavian (140)	206	0.07

Hispanic Origin	Population	%
Hispanic or Latino (of any race)	31,179	10.47
Central American, ex. Mexican	1,912	0.64
Costa Rican	166	0.06
Guatemalan	667	0.22
Honduran	304	0.10
Nicaraguan	161	0.05
Panamanian	121	0.04
Salvadoran	476	0.16
Other Central American	17	0.01
Cuban	647	0.22
Dominican Republic	1,754	0.59
Mexican	3,197	1.07
Puerto Rican	18,805	6.32
South American	2,779	0.93
Argentinean	168	0.06
Bolivian	32	0.01
Chilean	148	0.05
Colombian	1,115	0.37
Ecuadorian	530	0.18
Paraguayan	12	<0.01
Peruvian	541	0.18
Uruguayan	78	0.03
Venezuelan	130	0.04
Other South American	25	0.01
Other Hispanic or Latino	2,085	0.70

Race*	Population	%
African-American/Black (14,986)	18,278	6.14
Not Hispanic (13,207)	15,485	5.20
Hispanic (1,779)	2,793	0.94
American Indian/Alaska Native (609)	1,800	0.60
Not Hispanic (329)	1,274	0.43
Hispanic (280)	526	0.18
Alaska Athabascan (Ala. Nat.) (0)	1	<0.01
Aleut (Alaska Native) (0)	2	<0.01
Apache (2)	13	<0.01
Arapaho (0)	0	<0.01
Blackfeet (8)	64	0.02
Canadian/French Am. Ind. (0)	3	<0.01
Central American Ind. (6)	11	<0.01
Cherokee (50)	315	0.11
Cheyenne (0)	1	<0.01
Chickasaw (1)	1	<0.01
Chippewa (5)	20	0.01
Choctaw (2)	13	<0.01
Colville (0)	0	<0.01

	Population	%
Comanche (0)	3	<0.01
Cree (1)	1	<0.01
Creek (2)	7	<0.01
Crow (0)	1	<0.01
Delaware (17)	98	0.03
Hopi (0)	1	<0.01
Houma (0)	0	<0.01
Inupiat (Alaska Native) (0)	0	<0.01
Iroquois (23)	48	0.02
Kiowa (0)	0	<0.01
Lumbee (2)	4	<0.01
Menominee (0)	2	<0.01
Mexican American Ind. (15)	29	0.01
Navajo (8)	23	0.01
Osage (0)	0	<0.01
Ottawa (3)	6	<0.01
Paiute (1)	2	<0.01
Pima (0)	0	<0.01
Potawatomi (0)	2	<0.01
Pueblo (5)	5	<0.01
Puget Sound Salish (0)	0	<0.01
Seminole (3)	12	<0.01
Shoshone (0)	2	<0.01
Sioux (10)	29	0.01
South American Ind. (68)	118	0.04
Spanish American Ind. (5)	5	<0.01
Tlingit-Haida (Alaska Native) (1)	5	<0.01
Tohono O'Odham (0)	0	<0.01
Tsimshian (Alaska Native) (0)	0	<0.01
Ute (0)	0	<0.01
Yakama (0)	1	<0.01
Yaqui (0)	0	<0.01
Yuman (0)	0	<0.01
Yup'ik (Alaska Native) (0)	0	<0.01
Asian (7,203)	8,602	2.89
Not Hispanic (7,131)	8,362	2.81
Hispanic (72)	240	0.08
Bangladeshi (46)	49	0.02
Bhutanese (0)	0	<0.01
Burmese (19)	20	0.01
Cambodian (21)	30	0.01
Chinese, ex. Taiwanese (1,400)	1,632	0.55
Filipino (750)	1,033	0.35
Hmong (0)	0	<0.01
Indian (2,674)	2,943	0.99
Indonesian (30)	54	0.02
Japanese (134)	307	0.10
Korean (558)	710	0.24
Laotian (4)	7	<0.01
Malaysian (13)	20	0.01
Nepalese (18)	26	0.01
Pakistani (329)	359	0.12
Sri Lankan (37)	37	0.01
Taiwanese (83)	97	0.03
Thai (91)	129	0.04
Vietnamese (791)	898	0.30
Hawaii Native/Pacific Islander (98)	327	0.11
Not Hispanic (74)	219	0.07
Hispanic (24)	108	0.04
Fijian (1)	1	<0.01
Guamanian/Chamorro (42)	56	0.02
Marshallese (0)	0	<0.01
Native Hawaiian (22)	75	0.03
Samoan (7)	22	0.01
Tongan (5)	6	<0.01
White (256,895)	262,572	88.19
Not Hispanic (241,163)	244,941	82.27
Hispanic (15,732)	17,631	5.92

*Notes: † The Census 2010 population figure is used to calculate the percentages in the Hispanic Origin and Race categories. Ancestry percentages are based on the 2006-2010 American Community Survey population (not shown); ‡ Numbers in parentheses indicate the number of people reporting a single ancestry; * Numbers in parentheses indicate the number of persons reporting this race alone, not in combination with any other race; Please refer to the Explanation of Data for more information.*

Northumberland County

Population: 94,528

Ancestry	Population	%
Afghan (0)	0	<0.01
African, Sub-Saharan (0)	9	0.01
African (0)	9	0.01
Cape Verdean (0)	0	<0.01
Ethiopian (0)	0	<0.01
Ghanaian (0)	0	<0.01
Kenyan (0)	0	<0.01
Liberian (0)	0	<0.01
Nigerian (0)	0	<0.01
Senegalese (0)	0	<0.01
Sierra Leonean (0)	0	<0.01
Somalian (0)	0	<0.01
South African (0)	0	<0.01
Sudanese (0)	0	<0.01
Ugandan (0)	0	<0.01
Zimbabwean (0)	0	<0.01
Other Sub-Saharan African (0)	0	<0.01
Albanian (0)	0	<0.01
Alsatian (0)	0	<0.01
American (6,456)	6,456	6.86
Arab (39)	60	0.06
Arab (0)	0	<0.01
Egyptian (12)	12	0.01
Iraqi (0)	0	<0.01
Jordanian (0)	0	<0.01
Lebanese (12)	20	0.02
Moroccan (0)	0	<0.01
Palestinian (0)	0	<0.01
Syrian (15)	26	0.03
Other Arab (0)	2	<0.01
Armenian (4)	4	<0.01
Assyrian/Chaldean/Syriac (0)	0	<0.01
Australian (10)	20	0.02
Austrian (199)	642	0.68
Basque (0)	0	<0.01
Belgian (13)	21	0.02
Brazilian (0)	0	<0.01
British (52)	114	0.12
Bulgarian (8)	8	0.01
Cajun (0)	0	<0.01
Canadian (38)	89	0.09
Carpatho Rusyn (0)	0	<0.01
Celtic (0)	0	<0.01
Croatian (4)	15	0.02
Cypriot (0)	0	<0.01
Czech (28)	203	0.22
Czechoslovakian (33)	99	0.11
Danish (22)	148	0.16
Dutch (1,707)	6,468	6.87
Eastern European (0)	0	<0.01
English (2,030)	5,413	5.75
Estonian (0)	0	<0.01
European (203)	210	0.22
Finnish (12)	30	0.03
French, ex. Basque (336)	1,599	1.70
French Canadian (23)	123	0.13
German (19,311)	35,020	37.22
German Russian (0)	0	<0.01
Greek (49)	122	0.13
Guyanese (0)	0	<0.01
Hungarian (253)	644	0.68
Icelander (0)	0	<0.01
Iranian (0)	0	<0.01
Irish (2,821)	10,837	11.52
Israeli (0)	0	<0.01
Italian (3,278)	7,931	8.43
Latvian (15)	15	0.02
Lithuanian (351)	919	0.98
Luxemburger (0)	0	<0.01
Macedonian (0)	0	<0.01
Maltese (0)	3	<0.01
New Zealander (0)	0	<0.01
Northern European (43)	43	0.05
Norwegian (36)	121	0.13
Pennsylvania German (1,817)	2,434	2.59

Ancestry	Population	%
Polish (4,785)	10,994	11.68
Portuguese (56)	88	0.09
Romanian (28)	53	0.06
Russian (301)	830	0.88
Scandinavian (0)	16	0.02
Scotch-Irish (365)	986	1.05
Scottish (417)	1,281	1.36
Serbian (5)	5	0.01
Slavic (47)	72	0.08
Slovak (538)	1,148	1.22
Slovene (0)	0	<0.01
Soviet Union (0)	0	<0.01
Swedish (104)	543	0.58
Swiss (167)	471	0.50
Turkish (0)	12	0.01
Ukrainian (704)	1,678	1.78
Welsh (363)	1,738	1.85
West Indian, ex. Hispanic (9)	26	0.03
Bahamian (0)	0	<0.01
Barbadian (0)	0	<0.01
Belizean (0)	0	<0.01
Bermudan (0)	0	<0.01
British West Indian (0)	0	<0.01
Dutch West Indian (0)	0	<0.01
Haitian (0)	0	<0.01
Jamaican (9)	26	0.03
Trinidadian/Tobagonian (0)	0	<0.01
U.S. Virgin Islander (0)	0	<0.01
West Indian (0)	0	<0.01
Other West Indian (0)	0	<0.01
Yugoslavian (0)	23	0.02

Hispanic Origin	Population	%
Hispanic or Latino (of any race)	2,253	2.38
Central American, ex. Mexican	101	0.11
Costa Rican	4	<0.01
Guatemalan	35	0.04
Honduran	47	0.05
Nicaraguan	3	<0.01
Panamanian	9	0.01
Salvadoran	3	<0.01
Other Central American	0	<0.01
Cuban	36	0.04
Dominican Republic	101	0.11
Mexican	401	0.42
Puerto Rican	1,169	1.24
South American	105	0.11
Argentinean	6	0.01
Bolivian	3	<0.01
Chilean	5	0.01
Colombian	13	0.01
Ecuadorian	24	0.03
Paraguayan	0	<0.01
Peruvian	45	0.05
Uruguayan	0	<0.01
Venezuelan	9	0.01
Other South American	0	<0.01
Other Hispanic or Latino	340	0.36

Race*	Population	%
African-American/Black (1,921)	2,392	2.53
Not Hispanic (1,814)	2,212	2.34
Hispanic (107)	180	0.19
American Indian/Alaska Native (146)	462	0.49
Not Hispanic (115)	405	0.43
Hispanic (31)	57	0.06
Alaska Athabascan (Ala. Nat.) (0)	0	<0.01
Aleut (Alaska Native) (0)	0	<0.01
Apache (3)	14	0.01
Arapaho (0)	0	<0.01
Blackfeet (1)	17	0.02
Canadian/French Am. Ind. (4)	5	0.01
Central American Ind. (0)	0	<0.01
Cherokee (14)	92	0.10
Cheyenne (2)	2	<0.01
Chickasaw (0)	0	<0.01
Chippewa (0)	2	<0.01
Choctaw (5)	5	0.01
Colville (0)	0	<0.01

	Population	%
Comanche (0)	2	<0.01
Cree (1)	2	<0.01
Creek (2)	5	0.01
Crow (0)	1	<0.01
Delaware (7)	13	0.01
Hopi (0)	2	<0.01
Houma (0)	0	<0.01
Inupiat (Alaska Native) (0)	0	<0.01
Iroquois (3)	9	0.01
Kiowa (0)	0	<0.01
Lumbee (3)	3	<0.01
Menominee (0)	0	<0.01
Mexican American Ind. (5)	5	0.01
Navajo (1)	1	<0.01
Osage (0)	0	<0.01
Ottawa (0)	0	<0.01
Paiute (1)	1	<0.01
Pima (6)	6	0.01
Potawatomi (1)	1	<0.01
Pueblo (1)	6	0.01
Puget Sound Salish (0)	0	<0.01
Seminole (0)	0	<0.01
Shoshone (0)	1	<0.01
Sioux (2)	9	0.01
South American Ind. (5)	8	0.01
Spanish American Ind. (3)	10	0.01
Tlingit-Haida (Alaska Native) (1)	1	<0.01
Tohono O'Odham (0)	0	<0.01
Tsimshian (Alaska Native) (0)	0	<0.01
Ute (0)	2	<0.01
Yakama (0)	0	<0.01
Yaqui (0)	0	<0.01
Yuman (0)	0	<0.01
Yup'ik (Alaska Native) (0)	0	<0.01
Asian (332)	459	0.49
Not Hispanic (325)	449	0.47
Hispanic (7)	10	0.01
Bangladeshi (0)	0	<0.01
Bhutanese (0)	0	<0.01
Burmese (1)	2	<0.01
Cambodian (2)	7	0.01
Chinese, ex. Taiwanese (66)	79	0.08
Filipino (69)	110	0.12
Hmong (0)	0	<0.01
Indian (43)	56	0.06
Indonesian (11)	11	0.01
Japanese (31)	48	0.05
Korean (38)	65	0.07
Laotian (1)	1	<0.01
Malaysian (0)	0	<0.01
Nepalese (3)	3	<0.01
Pakistani (11)	11	0.01
Sri Lankan (0)	0	<0.01
Taiwanese (0)	0	<0.01
Thai (10)	10	0.01
Vietnamese (29)	39	0.04
Hawaii Native/Pacific Islander (13)	42	0.04
Not Hispanic (10)	32	0.03
Hispanic (3)	10	0.01
Fijian (0)	0	<0.01
Guamanian/Chamorro (5)	6	0.01
Marshallese (0)	0	<0.01
Native Hawaiian (6)	19	0.02
Samoan (2)	4	<0.01
Tongan (0)	0	<0.01
White (90,156)	91,095	96.37
Not Hispanic (89,166)	89,907	95.11
Hispanic (990)	1,188	1.26

Notes: † The Census 2010 population figure is used to calculate the percentages in the Hispanic Origin and Race categories. Ancestry percentages are based on the 2006-2010 American Community Survey population (not shown); ‡ Numbers in parentheses indicate the number of people reporting a single ancestry; * Numbers in parentheses indicate the number of persons reporting this race alone, not in combination with any other race; Please refer to the Explanation of Data for more information.

Perry County

Population: 45,969

Ancestry	Population	%
Afghan (0)	0	<0.01
African, Sub-Saharan (34)	34	0.07
African (34)	34	0.07
Cape Verdean (0)	0	<0.01
Ethiopian (0)	0	<0.01
Ghanaian (0)	0	<0.01
Kenyan (0)	0	<0.01
Liberian (0)	0	<0.01
Nigerian (0)	0	<0.01
Senegalese (0)	0	<0.01
Sierra Leonean (0)	0	<0.01
Somalian (0)	0	<0.01
South African (0)	0	<0.01
Sudanese (0)	0	<0.01
Ugandan (0)	0	<0.01
Zimbabwean (0)	0	<0.01
Other Sub-Saharan African (0)	0	<0.01
Albanian (0)	0	<0.01
Alsatian (0)	0	<0.01
American (3,907)	3,907	8.57
Arab (51)	107	0.23
Arab (0)	0	<0.01
Egyptian (12)	12	0.03
Iraqi (0)	0	<0.01
Jordanian (0)	0	<0.01
Lebanese (17)	73	0.16
Moroccan (0)	0	<0.01
Palestinian (0)	0	<0.01
Syrian (22)	22	0.05
Other Arab (0)	0	<0.01
Armenian (0)	0	<0.01
Assyrian/Chaldean/Syriac (0)	0	<0.01
Australian (0)	5	0.01
Austrian (58)	95	0.21
Basque (0)	0	<0.01
Belgian (8)	8	0.02
Brazilian (0)	0	<0.01
British (54)	146	0.32
Bulgarian (0)	0	<0.01
Cajun (0)	0	<0.01
Canadian (7)	23	0.05
Carpatho Rusyn (0)	0	<0.01
Celtic (0)	5	0.01
Croatian (23)	115	0.25
Cypriot (0)	0	<0.01
Czech (15)	104	0.23
Czechoslovakian (11)	55	0.12
Danish (17)	59	0.13
Dutch (202)	1,333	2.92
Eastern European (10)	10	0.02
English (829)	2,877	6.31
Estonian (0)	0	<0.01
European (257)	257	0.56
Finnish (0)	8	0.02
French, ex. Basque (101)	736	1.61
French Canadian (85)	115	0.25
German (11,408)	21,332	46.78
German Russian (0)	0	<0.01
Greek (140)	243	0.53
Guyanese (5)	5	0.01
Hungarian (29)	127	0.28
Icelander (0)	0	<0.01
Iranian (0)	0	<0.01
Irish (1,388)	6,747	14.80
Israeli (0)	0	<0.01
Italian (508)	2,124	4.66
Latvian (4)	8	0.02
Lithuanian (49)	166	0.36
Luxemburger (0)	0	<0.01
Macedonian (0)	10	0.02
Maltese (0)	0	<0.01
New Zealander (0)	0	<0.01
Northern European (18)	18	0.04
Norwegian (39)	133	0.29
Pennsylvania German (719)	901	1.98

Ancestry	Population	%
Polish (439)	1,146	2.51
Portuguese (7)	24	0.05
Romanian (0)	6	0.01
Russian (66)	225	0.49
Scandinavian (9)	41	0.09
Scotch-Irish (368)	1,120	2.46
Scottish (201)	801	1.76
Serbian (6)	6	0.01
Slavic (5)	17	0.04
Slovak (76)	246	0.54
Slovene (0)	18	0.04
Soviet Union (0)	0	<0.01
Swedish (59)	288	0.63
Swiss (102)	263	0.58
Turkish (0)	0	<0.01
Ukrainian (33)	135	0.30
Welsh (139)	604	1.32
West Indian, ex. Hispanic (0)	3	0.01
Bahamian (0)	3	0.01
Barbadian (0)	0	<0.01
Belizean (0)	0	<0.01
Bermudan (0)	0	<0.01
British West Indian (0)	0	<0.01
Dutch West Indian (0)	0	<0.01
Haitian (0)	0	<0.01
Jamaican (0)	0	<0.01
Trinidadian/Tobagonian (0)	0	<0.01
U.S. Virgin Islander (0)	0	<0.01
West Indian (0)	0	<0.01
Other West Indian (0)	0	<0.01
Yugoslavian (27)	85	0.19

Hispanic Origin	Population	%
Hispanic or Latino (of any race)	588	1.28
Central American, ex. Mexican	29	0.06
Costa Rican	1	<0.01
Guatemalan	15	0.03
Honduran	9	0.02
Nicaraguan	0	<0.01
Panamanian	1	<0.01
Salvadoran	2	<0.01
Other Central American	1	<0.01
Cuban	24	0.05
Dominican Republic	6	0.01
Mexican	162	0.35
Puerto Rican	269	0.59
South American	16	0.03
Argentinean	1	<0.01
Bolivian	0	<0.01
Chilean	1	<0.01
Colombian	4	0.01
Ecuadorian	1	<0.01
Paraguayan	0	<0.01
Peruvian	4	0.01
Uruguayan	0	<0.01
Venezuelan	5	0.01
Other South American	0	<0.01
Other Hispanic or Latino	82	0.18

Race*	Population	%
African-American/Black (296)	485	1.06
Not Hispanic (284)	458	1.00
Hispanic (12)	27	0.06
American Indian/Alaska Native (72)	267	0.58
Not Hispanic (58)	240	0.52
Hispanic (14)	27	0.06
Alaska Athabascan (Ala. Nat.) (0)	0	<0.01
Aleut (Alaska Native) (1)	1	<0.01
Apache (2)	8	0.02
Arapaho (0)	0	<0.01
Blackfeet (5)	11	0.02
Canadian/French Am. Ind. (0)	0	<0.01
Central American Ind. (0)	3	0.01
Cherokee (11)	51	0.11
Cheyenne (0)	0	<0.01
Chickasaw (0)	0	<0.01
Chippewa (0)	5	0.01
Choctaw (2)	3	0.01
Colville (1)	4	0.01

Race (continued)	Population	%
Comanche (0)	0	<0.01
Cree (0)	2	<0.01
Creek (0)	0	<0.01
Crow (0)	0	<0.01
Delaware (1)	2	<0.01
Hopi (0)	0	<0.01
Houma (0)	0	<0.01
Inupiat (Alaska Native) (0)	0	<0.01
Iroquois (3)	12	0.03
Kiowa (0)	0	<0.01
Lumbee (2)	4	0.01
Menominee (0)	0	<0.01
Mexican American Ind. (4)	4	0.01
Navajo (1)	6	0.01
Osage (0)	0	<0.01
Ottawa (0)	0	<0.01
Paiute (0)	0	<0.01
Pima (0)	0	<0.01
Potawatomi (0)	0	<0.01
Pueblo (0)	0	<0.01
Puget Sound Salish (0)	0	<0.01
Seminole (0)	3	0.01
Shoshone (0)	1	<0.01
Sioux (1)	4	0.01
South American Ind. (0)	0	<0.01
Spanish American Ind. (0)	0	<0.01
Tlingit-Haida (Alaska Native) (0)	0	<0.01
Tohono O'Odham (0)	0	<0.01
Tsimshian (Alaska Native) (0)	0	<0.01
Ute (0)	0	<0.01
Yakama (0)	0	<0.01
Yaqui (0)	0	<0.01
Yuman (0)	0	<0.01
Yup'ik (Alaska Native) (0)	0	<0.01
Asian (164)	239	0.52
Not Hispanic (163)	232	0.50
Hispanic (1)	7	0.02
Bangladeshi (0)	0	<0.01
Bhutanese (0)	0	<0.01
Burmese (2)	2	<0.01
Cambodian (23)	24	0.05
Chinese, ex. Taiwanese (18)	32	0.07
Filipino (21)	46	0.10
Hmong (0)	0	<0.01
Indian (16)	26	0.06
Indonesian (1)	1	<0.01
Japanese (12)	21	0.05
Korean (27)	40	0.09
Laotian (2)	2	<0.01
Malaysian (0)	0	<0.01
Nepalese (1)	1	<0.01
Pakistani (7)	7	0.02
Sri Lankan (0)	0	<0.01
Taiwanese (0)	0	<0.01
Thai (7)	8	0.02
Vietnamese (12)	17	0.04
Hawaii Native/Pacific Islander (19)	33	0.07
Not Hispanic (14)	26	0.06
Hispanic (5)	7	0.02
Fijian (0)	0	<0.01
Guamanian/Chamorro (7)	7	0.02
Marshallese (0)	0	<0.01
Native Hawaiian (3)	12	0.03
Samoan (0)	0	<0.01
Tongan (0)	0	<0.01
White (44,779)	45,221	98.37
Not Hispanic (44,427)	44,815	97.49
Hispanic (352)	406	0.88

*Notes: † The Census 2010 population figure is used to calculate the percentages in the Hispanic Origin and Race categories. Ancestry percentages are based on the 2006-2010 American Community Survey population (not shown); ‡ Numbers in parentheses indicate the number of people reporting a single ancestry; * Numbers in parentheses indicate the number of persons reporting this race alone, not in combination with any other race; Please refer to the Explanation of Data for more information.*

Philadelphia County

Population: 1,526,006

Ancestry	Population	%
Afghan (52)	52	<0.01
African, Sub-Saharan (24,827)	29,046	1.93
African (15,876)	18,871	1.25
Cape Verdean (69)	129	0.01
Ethiopian (1,542)	1,572	0.10
Ghanaian (584)	584	0.04
Kenyan (94)	147	0.01
Liberian (2,867)	3,198	0.21
Nigerian (1,648)	1,877	0.12
Senegalese (91)	139	0.01
Sierra Leonean (136)	144	0.01
Somalian (11)	22	<0.01
South African (164)	235	0.02
Sudanese (160)	167	0.01
Ugandan (0)	8	<0.01
Zimbabwean (51)	51	<0.01
Other Sub-Saharan African (1,534)	1,902	0.13
Albanian (3,540)	3,892	0.26
Alsatian (13)	54	<0.01
American (20,637)	20,637	1.37
Arab (6,122)	7,763	0.52
Arab (1,709)	2,081	0.14
Egyptian (491)	580	0.04
Iraqi (211)	218	0.01
Jordanian (928)	939	0.06
Lebanese (507)	991	0.07
Moroccan (516)	684	0.05
Palestinian (607)	621	0.04
Syrian (294)	637	0.04
Other Arab (859)	1,012	0.07
Armenian (949)	1,315	0.09
Assyrian/Chaldean/Syriac (8)	8	<0.01
Australian (194)	243	0.02
Austrian (476)	2,580	0.17
Basque (0)	59	<0.01
Belgian (63)	214	0.01
Brazilian (2,390)	2,622	0.17
British (1,248)	2,578	0.17
Bulgarian (103)	150	0.01
Cajun (17)	38	<0.01
Canadian (534)	1,094	0.07
Carpatho Rusyn (33)	46	<0.01
Celtic (41)	41	<0.01
Croatian (382)	916	0.06
Cypriot (75)	75	<0.01
Czech (545)	2,209	0.15
Czechoslovakian (389)	721	0.05
Danish (181)	830	0.06
Dutch (1,200)	5,855	0.39
Eastern European (3,053)	3,363	0.22
English (10,881)	47,303	3.14
Estonian (55)	147	0.01
European (4,424)	4,939	0.33
Finnish (108)	326	0.02
French, ex. Basque (2,120)	12,027	0.80
French Canadian (497)	1,636	0.11
German (28,175)	122,783	8.16
German Russian (0)	0	<0.01
Greek (2,136)	4,288	0.28
Guyanese (545)	638	0.04
Hungarian (1,262)	5,463	0.36
Icelander (58)	86	0.01
Iranian (550)	665	0.04
Irish (68,684)	195,849	13.01
Israeli (567)	861	0.06
Italian (60,356)	125,080	8.31
Latvian (250)	570	0.04
Lithuanian (1,629)	5,334	0.35
Luxemburger (15)	29	<0.01
Macedonian (10)	10	<0.01
Maltese (0)	0	<0.01
New Zealander (38)	52	<0.01
Northern European (315)	361	0.02
Norwegian (599)	2,417	0.16
Pennsylvania German (853)	1,967	0.13

Ancestry	Population	%
Polish (21,876)	58,395	3.88
Portuguese (2,044)	3,158	0.21
Romanian (980)	2,101	0.14
Russian (13,897)	25,520	1.70
Scandinavian (251)	504	0.03
Scotch-Irish (3,872)	9,813	0.65
Scottish (1,963)	8,768	0.58
Serbian (286)	493	0.03
Slavic (153)	498	0.03
Slovak (750)	2,480	0.16
Slovene (186)	273	0.02
Soviet Union (0)	0	<0.01
Swedish (852)	3,719	0.25
Swiss (267)	1,886	0.13
Turkish (609)	786	0.05
Ukrainian (7,300)	13,262	0.88
Welsh (629)	4,345	0.29
West Indian, ex. Hispanic (21,124)	25,436	1.69
Bahamian (59)	104	0.01
Barbadian (607)	635	0.04
Belizean (0)	31	<0.01
Bermudan (29)	29	<0.01
British West Indian (458)	541	0.04
Dutch West Indian (0)	0	<0.01
Haitian (8,400)	9,026	0.60
Jamaican (8,311)	10,082	0.67
Trinidadian/Tobagonian (1,700)	2,407	0.16
U.S. Virgin Islander (100)	100	0.01
West Indian (1,446)	2,445	0.16
Other West Indian (14)	36	<0.01
Yugoslavian (239)	406	0.03

Hispanic Origin	Population	%
Hispanic or Latino (of any race)	187,611	12.29
Central American, ex. Mexican	7,511	0.49
Costa Rican	903	0.06
Guatemalan	2,262	0.15
Honduran	1,642	0.11
Nicaraguan	874	0.06
Panamanian	737	0.05
Salvadoran	1,049	0.07
Other Central American	44	<0.01
Cuban	3,930	0.26
Dominican Republic	15,963	1.05
Mexican	15,531	1.02
Puerto Rican	121,643	7.97
South American	9,969	0.65
Argentinean	1,006	0.07
Bolivian	112	0.01
Chilean	357	0.02
Colombian	4,675	0.31
Ecuadorian	1,542	0.10
Paraguayan	74	<0.01
Peruvian	1,085	0.07
Uruguayan	234	0.02
Venezuelan	773	0.05
Other South American	111	0.01
Other Hispanic or Latino	13,064	0.86

Race*	Population	%
African-American/Black (661,839)	686,870	45.01
Not Hispanic (644,287)	662,568	43.42
Hispanic (17,552)	24,302	1.59
American Indian/Alaska Native (6,996)	17,495	1.15
Not Hispanic (3,498)	11,409	0.75
Hispanic (3,498)	6,086	0.40
Alaska Athabascan (Ala. Nat.) (5)	6	<0.01
Aleut (Alaska Native) (4)	8	<0.01
Apache (31)	118	0.01
Arapaho (4)	7	<0.01
Blackfeet (105)	679	0.04
Canadian/French Am. Ind. (8)	34	<0.01
Central American Ind. (65)	111	0.01
Cherokee (463)	2,484	0.16
Cheyenne (5)	12	<0.01
Chickasaw (5)	28	<0.01
Chippewa (17)	63	<0.01
Choctaw (25)	92	0.01
Colville (0)	0	<0.01

	Population	%
Comanche (3)	9	<0.01
Cree (3)	25	<0.01
Creek (16)	59	<0.01
Crow (2)	15	<0.01
Delaware (71)	239	0.02
Hopi (5)	7	<0.01
Houma (1)	2	<0.01
Inupiat (Alaska Native) (1)	3	<0.01
Iroquois (72)	216	0.01
Kiowa (0)	9	<0.01
Lumbee (51)	121	0.01
Menominee (1)	6	<0.01
Mexican American Ind. (126)	185	0.01
Navajo (35)	99	0.01
Osage (5)	5	<0.01
Ottawa (1)	2	<0.01
Paiute (2)	4	<0.01
Pima (1)	2	<0.01
Potawatomi (4)	14	<0.01
Pueblo (13)	42	<0.01
Puget Sound Salish (3)	5	<0.01
Seminole (21)	189	0.01
Shoshone (4)	11	<0.01
Sioux (55)	199	0.01
South American Ind. (273)	657	0.04
Spanish American Ind. (98)	156	0.01
Tlingit-Haida (Alaska Native) (3)	18	<0.01
Tohono O'Odham (2)	3	<0.01
Tsimshian (Alaska Native) (0)	1	<0.01
Ute (0)	0	<0.01
Yakama (2)	2	<0.01
Yaqui (5)	10	<0.01
Yuman (2)	8	<0.01
Yup'ik (Alaska Native) (2)	5	<0.01
Asian (96,405)	106,720	6.99
Not Hispanic (95,521)	104,551	6.85
Hispanic (884)	2,169	0.14
Bangladeshi (883)	978	0.06
Bhutanese (43)	51	<0.01
Burmese (341)	388	0.03
Cambodian (8,707)	9,912	0.65
Chinese, ex. Taiwanese (29,396)	32,773	2.15
Filipino (4,978)	6,849	0.45
Hmong (77)	83	0.01
Indian (18,520)	20,809	1.36
Indonesian (1,921)	2,222	0.15
Japanese (1,034)	1,956	0.13
Korean (6,217)	7,074	0.46
Laotian (1,084)	1,350	0.09
Malaysian (88)	130	0.01
Nepalese (181)	220	0.01
Pakistani (2,423)	2,683	0.18
Sri Lankan (148)	172	0.01
Taiwanese (639)	736	0.05
Thai (386)	627	0.04
Vietnamese (14,431)	16,268	1.07
Hawaii Native/Pacific Islander (744)	3,125	0.20
Not Hispanic (457)	1,938	0.13
Hispanic (287)	1,187	0.08
Fijian (7)	14	<0.01
Guamanian/Chamorro (186)	272	0.02
Marshallese (0)	0	<0.01
Native Hawaiian (203)	538	0.04
Samoan (84)	198	0.01
Tongan (7)	9	<0.01
White (626,221)	655,021	42.92
Not Hispanic (562,585)	581,693	38.12
Hispanic (63,636)	73,328	4.81

Notes: † The Census 2010 population figure is used to calculate the percentages in the Hispanic Origin and Race categories. Ancestry percentages are based on the 2006-2010 American Community Survey population (not shown); ‡ Numbers in parentheses indicate the number of people reporting a single ancestry; * Numbers in parentheses indicate the number of persons reporting this race alone, not in combination with any other race; Please refer to the Explanation of Data for more information.

Pike County

Population: 57,369

Ancestry	Population	%
Afghan (0)	0	<0.01
African, Sub-Saharan (319)	334	0.59
African (293)	308	0.54
Cape Verdean (0)	0	<0.01
Ethiopian (0)	0	<0.01
Ghanaian (0)	0	<0.01
Kenyan (0)	0	<0.01
Liberian (10)	10	0.02
Nigerian (0)	0	<0.01
Senegalese (0)	0	<0.01
Sierra Leonean (0)	0	<0.01
Somalian (0)	0	<0.01
South African (7)	7	0.01
Sudanese (0)	0	<0.01
Ugandan (0)	0	<0.01
Zimbabwean (0)	0	<0.01
Other Sub-Saharan African (9)	9	0.02
Albanian (0)	0	<0.01
Alsatian (0)	0	<0.01
American (1,701)	1,701	2.98
Arab (16)	81	0.14
Arab (6)	19	0.03
Egyptian (10)	10	0.02
Iraqi (0)	0	<0.01
Jordanian (0)	0	<0.01
Lebanese (0)	18	0.03
Moroccan (0)	0	<0.01
Palestinian (0)	0	<0.01
Syrian (0)	34	0.06
Other Arab (0)	0	<0.01
Armenian (13)	18	0.03
Assyrian/Chaldean/Syriac (10)	10	0.02
Australian (0)	0	<0.01
Austrian (71)	242	0.42
Basque (0)	0	<0.01
Belgian (23)	153	0.27
Brazilian (192)	224	0.39
British (117)	181	0.32
Bulgarian (10)	10	0.02
Cajun (0)	0	<0.01
Canadian (50)	124	0.22
Carpatho Rusyn (0)	0	<0.01
Celtic (0)	0	<0.01
Croatian (26)	54	0.09
Cypriot (0)	0	<0.01
Czech (0)	332	0.58
Czechoslovakian (28)	67	0.12
Danish (105)	332	0.58
Dutch (301)	1,947	3.42
Eastern European (32)	32	0.06
English (1,484)	5,577	9.79
Estonian (0)	0	<0.01
European (273)	311	0.55
Finnish (14)	97	0.17
French, ex. Basque (242)	1,720	3.02
French Canadian (60)	325	0.57
German (4,395)	14,387	25.24
German Russian (0)	0	<0.01
Greek (263)	476	0.84
Guyanese (33)	33	0.06
Hungarian (468)	905	1.59
Icelander (0)	0	<0.01
Iranian (15)	15	0.03
Irish (3,276)	12,772	22.41
Israeli (0)	0	<0.01
Italian (6,046)	12,814	22.48
Latvian (16)	16	0.03
Lithuanian (63)	268	0.47
Luxemburger (0)	0	<0.01
Macedonian (0)	0	<0.01
Maltese (0)	0	<0.01
New Zealander (17)	55	0.10
Northern European (0)	0	<0.01
Norwegian (149)	576	1.01
Pennsylvania German (57)	300	0.53

Ancestry	Population	%
Polish (1,449)	4,523	7.94
Portuguese (59)	244	0.43
Romanian (129)	161	0.28
Russian (502)	1,301	2.28
Scandinavian (99)	108	0.19
Scotch-Irish (139)	596	1.05
Scottish (238)	1,289	2.26
Serbian (6)	6	0.01
Slavic (0)	9	0.02
Slovak (245)	339	0.59
Slovene (10)	16	0.03
Soviet Union (0)	0	<0.01
Swedish (159)	457	0.80
Swiss (67)	248	0.44
Turkish (34)	34	0.06
Ukrainian (295)	798	1.40
Welsh (126)	711	1.25
West Indian, ex. Hispanic (347)	467	0.82
Bahamian (0)	0	<0.01
Barbadian (0)	33	0.06
Belizean (7)	7	0.01
Bermudan (0)	4	0.01
British West Indian (9)	9	0.02
Dutch West Indian (0)	0	<0.01
Haitian (33)	82	0.14
Jamaican (245)	251	0.44
Trinidadian/Tobagonian (53)	63	0.11
U.S. Virgin Islander (0)	0	<0.01
West Indian (0)	18	0.03
Other West Indian (0)	0	<0.01
Yugoslavian (40)	40	0.07

Hispanic Origin	Population	%
Hispanic or Latino (of any race)	5,173	9.02
Central American, ex. Mexican	241	0.42
Costa Rican	18	0.03
Guatemalan	51	0.09
Honduran	47	0.08
Nicaraguan	22	0.04
Panamanian	44	0.08
Salvadoran	53	0.09
Other Central American	6	0.01
Cuban	251	0.44
Dominican Republic	350	0.61
Mexican	277	0.48
Puerto Rican	2,918	5.09
South American	601	1.05
Argentinean	43	0.07
Bolivian	5	0.01
Chilean	25	0.04
Colombian	214	0.37
Ecuadorian	166	0.29
Paraguayan	9	0.02
Peruvian	96	0.17
Uruguayan	15	0.03
Venezuelan	13	0.02
Other South American	15	0.03
Other Hispanic or Latino	535	0.93

Race*	Population	%
African-American/Black (3,322)	3,875	6.75
Not Hispanic (3,050)	3,434	5.99
Hispanic (272)	441	0.77
American Indian/Alaska Native (176)	602	1.05
Not Hispanic (127)	459	0.80
Hispanic (49)	143	0.25
Alaska Athabascan (Ala. Nat.) (0)	0	<0.01
Aleut (Alaska Native) (0)	0	<0.01
Apache (0)	2	<0.01
Arapaho (0)	0	<0.01
Blackfeet (3)	27	0.05
Canadian/French Am. Ind. (3)	10	0.02
Central American Ind. (2)	4	0.01
Cherokee (26)	111	0.19
Cheyenne (0)	0	<0.01
Chickasaw (1)	1	<0.01
Chippewa (6)	9	0.02
Choctaw (3)	10	0.02
Colville (0)	0	<0.01

	Population	%
Comanche (0)	0	<0.01
Cree (0)	4	0.01
Creek (1)	2	<0.01
Crow (0)	0	<0.01
Delaware (9)	50	0.09
Hopi (0)	6	0.01
Houma (0)	0	<0.01
Inupiat (Alaska Native) (1)	1	<0.01
Iroquois (10)	31	0.05
Kiowa (0)	0	<0.01
Lumbee (0)	0	<0.01
Menominee (0)	0	<0.01
Mexican American Ind. (2)	4	0.01
Navajo (2)	3	0.01
Osage (0)	0	<0.01
Ottawa (0)	0	<0.01
Paiute (0)	0	<0.01
Pima (0)	0	<0.01
Potawatomi (0)	0	<0.01
Pueblo (0)	0	<0.01
Puget Sound Salish (0)	0	<0.01
Seminole (0)	1	<0.01
Shoshone (0)	0	<0.01
Sioux (2)	9	0.02
South American Ind. (15)	45	0.08
Spanish American Ind. (0)	0	<0.01
Tlingit-Haida (Alaska Native) (0)	0	<0.01
Tohono O'Odham (0)	0	<0.01
Tsimshian (Alaska Native) (0)	0	<0.01
Ute (0)	1	<0.01
Yakama (0)	0	<0.01
Yaqui (0)	0	<0.01
Yuman (0)	0	<0.01
Yup'ik (Alaska Native) (0)	0	<0.01
Asian (597)	798	1.39
Not Hispanic (583)	755	1.32
Hispanic (14)	43	0.07
Bangladeshi (9)	9	0.02
Bhutanese (0)	0	<0.01
Burmese (8)	8	0.01
Cambodian (26)	26	0.05
Chinese, ex. Taiwanese (119)	153	0.27
Filipino (134)	184	0.32
Hmong (0)	0	<0.01
Indian (148)	205	0.36
Indonesian (0)	2	<0.01
Japanese (21)	49	0.09
Korean (61)	85	0.15
Laotian (0)	0	<0.01
Malaysian (0)	0	<0.01
Nepalese (0)	0	<0.01
Pakistani (5)	5	0.01
Sri Lankan (5)	5	0.01
Taiwanese (2)	3	0.01
Thai (5)	9	0.02
Vietnamese (25)	31	0.05
Hawaii Native/Pacific Islander (16)	32	0.06
Not Hispanic (13)	27	0.05
Hispanic (3)	5	<0.01
Fijian (0)	0	<0.01
Guamanian/Chamorro (2)	2	<0.01
Marshallese (0)	0	<0.01
Native Hawaiian (3)	9	0.02
Samoan (0)	2	<0.01
Tongan (0)	0	<0.01
White (50,856)	51,913	90.49
Not Hispanic (47,549)	48,270	84.14
Hispanic (3,307)	3,643	6.35

*Notes: † The Census 2010 population figure is used to calculate the percentages in the Hispanic Origin and Race categories. Ancestry percentages are based on the 2006-2010 American Community Survey population (not shown); ‡ Numbers in parentheses indicate the number of people reporting a single ancestry; * Numbers in parentheses indicate the number of persons reporting this race alone, not in combination with any other race; Please refer to the Explanation of Data for more information.*

Potter County

Population: 17,457

Ancestry	Population	%
Afghan (0)	0	<0.01
African, Sub-Saharan (0)	14	0.08
African (0)	0	<0.01
Cape Verdean (0)	2	0.01
Ethiopian (0)	0	<0.01
Ghanaian (0)	0	<0.01
Kenyan (0)	0	<0.01
Liberian (0)	0	<0.01
Nigerian (0)	0	<0.01
Senegalese (0)	0	<0.01
Sierra Leonean (0)	0	<0.01
Somalian (0)	0	<0.01
South African (0)	0	<0.01
Sudanese (0)	0	<0.01
Ugandan (0)	0	<0.01
Zimbabwean (0)	0	<0.01
Other Sub-Saharan African (0)	12	0.07
Albanian (0)	0	<0.01
Alsatian (0)	0	<0.01
American (1,254)	1,254	7.13
Arab (7)	7	0.04
Arab (0)	0	<0.01
Egyptian (0)	0	<0.01
Iraqi (0)	0	<0.01
Jordanian (0)	0	<0.01
Lebanese (0)	0	<0.01
Moroccan (0)	0	<0.01
Palestinian (0)	0	<0.01
Syrian (7)	7	0.04
Other Arab (0)	0	<0.01
Armenian (0)	0	<0.01
Assyrian/Chaldean/Syriac (0)	0	<0.01
Australian (0)	0	<0.01
Austrian (15)	91	0.52
Basque (0)	0	<0.01
Belgian (0)	0	<0.01
Brazilian (0)	0	<0.01
British (36)	68	0.39
Bulgarian (0)	0	<0.01
Cajun (0)	5	0.03
Canadian (3)	15	0.09
Carpatho Rusyn (0)	0	<0.01
Celtic (0)	0	<0.01
Croatian (8)	14	0.08
Cypriot (0)	0	<0.01
Czech (9)	52	0.30
Czechoslovakian (2)	10	0.06
Danish (9)	76	0.43
Dutch (94)	399	2.27
Eastern European (0)	0	<0.01
English (1,032)	2,402	13.66
Estonian (0)	0	<0.01
European (77)	92	0.52
Finnish (0)	11	0.06
French, ex. Basque (60)	496	2.82
French Canadian (29)	128	0.73
German (2,344)	5,365	30.51
German Russian (0)	0	<0.01
Greek (20)	38	0.22
Guyanese (0)	0	<0.01
Hungarian (33)	81	0.46
Icelander (3)	3	0.02
Iranian (0)	0	<0.01
Irish (800)	2,624	14.92
Israeli (0)	0	<0.01
Italian (355)	1,002	5.70
Latvian (0)	0	<0.01
Lithuanian (18)	45	0.26
Luxemburger (0)	4	0.02
Macedonian (0)	4	0.02
Maltese (0)	0	<0.01
New Zealander (0)	0	<0.01
Northern European (6)	6	0.03
Norwegian (8)	41	0.23
Pennsylvania German (128)	221	1.26

Ancestry	Population	%
Polish (335)	838	4.77
Portuguese (0)	16	0.09
Romanian (34)	51	0.29
Russian (9)	60	0.34
Scandinavian (7)	15	0.09
Scotch-Irish (90)	298	1.69
Scottish (124)	381	2.17
Serbian (0)	4	0.02
Slavic (8)	30	0.17
Slovak (38)	121	0.69
Slovene (4)	25	0.14
Soviet Union (0)	0	<0.01
Swedish (160)	405	2.30
Swiss (134)	204	1.16
Turkish (0)	0	<0.01
Ukrainian (46)	78	0.44
Welsh (62)	210	1.19
West Indian, ex. Hispanic (0)	0	<0.01
Bahamian (0)	0	<0.01
Barbadian (0)	0	<0.01
Belizean (0)	0	<0.01
Bermudan (0)	0	<0.01
British West Indian (0)	0	<0.01
Dutch West Indian (0)	0	<0.01
Haitian (0)	0	<0.01
Jamaican (0)	0	<0.01
Trinidadian/Tobagonian (0)	0	<0.01
U.S. Virgin Islander (0)	0	<0.01
West Indian (0)	0	<0.01
Other West Indian (0)	0	<0.01
Yugoslavian (10)	17	0.10

Hispanic Origin	Population	%
Hispanic or Latino (of any race)	181	1.04
Central American, ex. Mexican	13	0.07
Costa Rican	7	0.04
Guatemalan	4	0.02
Honduran	1	0.01
Nicaraguan	0	<0.01
Panamanian	0	<0.01
Salvadoran	1	0.01
Other Central American	0	<0.01
Cuban	4	0.02
Dominican Republic	2	0.01
Mexican	63	0.36
Puerto Rican	66	0.38
South American	14	0.08
Argentinean	2	0.01
Bolivian	0	<0.01
Chilean	0	<0.01
Colombian	5	0.03
Ecuadorian	0	<0.01
Paraguayan	0	<0.01
Peruvian	3	0.02
Uruguayan	0	<0.01
Venezuelan	4	0.02
Other South American	0	<0.01
Other Hispanic or Latino	19	0.11

Race*	Population	%
African-American/Black (67)	92	0.53
Not Hispanic (61)	84	0.48
Hispanic (6)	8	0.05
American Indian/Alaska Native (45)	122	0.70
Not Hispanic (32)	109	0.62
Hispanic (13)	13	0.07
Alaska Athabascan (Ala. Nat.) (0)	0	<0.01
Aleut (Alaska Native) (0)	0	<0.01
Apache (3)	5	0.03
Arapaho (0)	0	<0.01
Blackfeet (0)	2	0.01
Canadian/French Am. Ind. (0)	3	0.02
Central American Ind. (0)	0	<0.01
Cherokee (7)	17	0.10
Cheyenne (0)	0	<0.01
Chickasaw (0)	0	<0.01
Chippewa (4)	4	0.02
Choctaw (0)	1	0.01
Colville (0)	0	<0.01

Race*	Population	%
Comanche (0)	0	<0.01
Cree (0)	0	<0.01
Creek (0)	0	<0.01
Crow (0)	0	<0.01
Delaware (2)	6	0.03
Hopi (0)	0	<0.01
Houma (0)	0	<0.01
Inupiat (Alaska Native) (2)	2	0.01
Iroquois (4)	12	0.07
Kiowa (0)	0	<0.01
Lumbee (0)	0	<0.01
Menominee (0)	1	0.01
Mexican American Ind. (1)	1	0.01
Navajo (0)	0	<0.01
Osage (0)	0	<0.01
Ottawa (0)	0	<0.01
Paiute (0)	0	<0.01
Pima (0)	0	<0.01
Potawatomi (0)	0	<0.01
Pueblo (0)	0	<0.01
Puget Sound Salish (0)	0	<0.01
Seminole (0)	0	<0.01
Shoshone (0)	0	<0.01
Sioux (1)	4	0.02
South American Ind. (0)	0	<0.01
Spanish American Ind. (0)	0	<0.01
Tlingit-Haida (Alaska Native) (0)	0	<0.01
Tohono O'Odham (0)	0	<0.01
Tsimshian (Alaska Native) (0)	0	<0.01
Ute (0)	0	<0.01
Yakama (0)	0	<0.01
Yaqui (0)	0	<0.01
Yuman (0)	0	<0.01
Yup'ik (Alaska Native) (0)	0	<0.01
Asian (45)	80	0.46
Not Hispanic (45)	80	0.46
Hispanic (0)	0	<0.01
Bangladeshi (0)	0	<0.01
Bhutanese (0)	0	<0.01
Burmese (0)	0	<0.01
Cambodian (3)	4	0.02
Chinese, ex. Taiwanese (11)	22	0.13
Filipino (12)	23	0.13
Hmong (0)	0	<0.01
Indian (11)	16	0.09
Indonesian (0)	0	<0.01
Japanese (2)	6	0.03
Korean (3)	8	0.05
Laotian (0)	0	<0.01
Malaysian (0)	0	<0.01
Nepalese (0)	0	<0.01
Pakistani (0)	0	<0.01
Sri Lankan (0)	0	<0.01
Taiwanese (0)	0	<0.01
Thai (0)	0	<0.01
Vietnamese (1)	1	0.01
Hawaii Native/Pacific Islander (1)	8	0.05
Not Hispanic (1)	8	0.05
Hispanic (0)	0	<0.01
Fijian (0)	0	<0.01
Guamanian/Chamorro (0)	2	0.01
Marshallese (0)	0	<0.01
Native Hawaiian (0)	0	<0.01
Samoan (0)	0	<0.01
Tongan (0)	0	<0.01
White (17,128)	17,265	98.90
Not Hispanic (17,000)	17,133	98.14
Hispanic (128)	132	0.76

Notes: † The Census 2010 population figure is used to calculate the percentages in the Hispanic Origin and Race categories. Ancestry percentages are based on the 2006-2010 American Community Survey population (not shown); ‡ Numbers in parentheses indicate the number of people reporting a single ancestry; * Numbers in parentheses indicate the number of persons reporting this race alone, not in combination with any other race; Please refer to the Explanation of Data for more information.

Schuylkill County

Population: 148,289

Ancestry	Population	%
Afghan (0)	0	<0.01
African, Sub-Saharan (110)	178	0.12
African (97)	157	0.11
Cape Verdean (0)	0	<0.01
Ethiopian (0)	0	<0.01
Ghanaian (0)	0	<0.01
Kenyan (0)	0	<0.01
Liberian (0)	0	<0.01
Nigerian (0)	8	0.01
Senegalese (0)	0	<0.01
Sierra Leonean (0)	0	<0.01
Somalian (0)	0	<0.01
South African (13)	13	0.01
Sudanese (0)	0	<0.01
Ugandan (0)	0	<0.01
Zimbabwean (0)	0	<0.01
Other Sub-Saharan African (0)	0	<0.01
Albanian (12)	43	0.03
Alsatian (3)	3	<0.01
American (5,727)	5,727	3.86
Arab (274)	764	0.52
Arab (0)	0	<0.01
Egyptian (12)	12	0.01
Iraqi (29)	29	0.02
Jordanian (0)	0	<0.01
Lebanese (124)	555	0.37
Moroccan (25)	34	0.02
Palestinian (0)	0	<0.01
Syrian (27)	77	0.05
Other Arab (57)	57	0.04
Armenian (0)	6	<0.01
Assyrian/Chaldean/Syriac (0)	0	<0.01
Australian (6)	14	0.01
Austrian (212)	1,142	0.77
Basque (7)	15	0.01
Belgian (9)	50	0.03
Brazilian (0)	0	<0.01
British (74)	196	0.13
Bulgarian (6)	6	<0.01
Cajun (0)	0	<0.01
Canadian (39)	205	0.14
Carpatho Rusyn (9)	9	0.01
Celtic (0)	10	0.01
Croatian (27)	129	0.09
Cypriot (0)	0	<0.01
Czech (123)	701	0.47
Czechoslovakian (272)	808	0.54
Danish (14)	59	0.04
Dutch (3,028)	12,265	8.27
Eastern European (335)	385	0.26
English (1,446)	7,607	5.13
Estonian (0)	0	<0.01
European (322)	348	0.23
Finnish (29)	57	0.04
French, ex. Basque (271)	2,241	1.51
French Canadian (136)	315	0.21
German (20,702)	49,274	33.23
German Russian (0)	0	<0.01
Greek (354)	1,464	0.99
Guyanese (0)	0	<0.01
Hungarian (180)	1,144	0.77
Icelander (0)	0	<0.01
Iranian (0)	0	<0.01
Irish (7,760)	28,998	19.56
Israeli (4)	4	<0.01
Italian (4,300)	14,691	9.91
Latvian (12)	25	0.02
Lithuanian (2,471)	8,080	5.45
Luxemburger (0)	0	<0.01
Macedonian (7)	7	<0.01
Maltese (0)	0	<0.01
New Zealander (0)	0	<0.01
Northern European (69)	69	0.05
Norwegian (107)	445	0.30
Pennsylvania German (4,394)	7,342	4.95

Ancestry	Population	%
Polish (6,002)	17,006	11.47
Portuguese (105)	224	0.15
Romanian (43)	63	0.04
Russian (486)	1,849	1.25
Scandinavian (10)	14	0.01
Scotch-Irish (222)	690	0.47
Scottish (160)	991	0.67
Serbian (18)	38	0.03
Slavic (102)	230	0.16
Slovak (1,892)	5,222	3.52
Slovene (45)	82	0.06
Soviet Union (0)	0	<0.01
Swedish (170)	692	0.47
Swiss (211)	831	0.56
Turkish (3)	26	0.02
Ukrainian (1,963)	4,451	3.00
Welsh (738)	4,540	3.06
West Indian, ex. Hispanic (167)	260	0.18
Bahamian (35)	41	0.03
Barbadian (0)	0	<0.01
Belizean (0)	0	<0.01
Bermudan (0)	0	<0.01
British West Indian (0)	11	0.01
Dutch West Indian (0)	0	<0.01
Haitian (15)	15	0.01
Jamaican (92)	122	0.08
Trinidadian/Tobagonian (0)	9	0.01
U.S. Virgin Islander (0)	0	<0.01
West Indian (25)	62	0.04
Other West Indian (0)	0	<0.01
Yugoslavian (20)	40	0.03

Hispanic Origin	Population	%
Hispanic or Latino (of any race)	4,080	2.75
Central American, ex. Mexican	154	0.10
Costa Rican	13	0.01
Guatemalan	46	0.03
Honduran	29	0.02
Nicaraguan	2	<0.01
Panamanian	13	0.01
Salvadoran	48	0.03
Other Central American	3	<0.01
Cuban	83	0.06
Dominican Republic	317	0.21
Mexican	1,071	0.72
Puerto Rican	1,329	0.90
South American	143	0.10
Argentinean	16	0.01
Bolivian	1	<0.01
Chilean	6	<0.01
Colombian	40	0.03
Ecuadorian	31	0.02
Paraguayan	1	<0.01
Peruvian	28	0.02
Uruguayan	1	<0.01
Venezuelan	19	0.01
Other South American	0	<0.01
Other Hispanic or Latino	983	0.66

Race*	Population	%
African-American/Black (3,967)	4,652	3.14
Not Hispanic (3,841)	4,436	2.99
Hispanic (126)	216	0.15
American Indian/Alaska Native (212)	614	0.41
Not Hispanic (162)	515	0.35
Hispanic (50)	99	0.07
Alaska Athabascan (Ala. Nat.) (0)	0	<0.01
Aleut (Alaska Native) (0)	0	<0.01
Apache (2)	7	<0.01
Arapaho (0)	0	<0.01
Blackfeet (1)	12	0.01
Canadian/French Am. Ind. (1)	2	<0.01
Central American Ind. (0)	0	<0.01
Cherokee (25)	101	0.07
Cheyenne (0)	1	<0.01
Chickasaw (0)	0	<0.01
Chippewa (5)	7	<0.01
Choctaw (4)	16	0.01
Colville (1)	2	<0.01

Race*	Population	%
Comanche (0)	2	<0.01
Cree (0)	0	<0.01
Creek (0)	4	<0.01
Crow (0)	5	<0.01
Delaware (9)	20	0.01
Hopi (0)	1	<0.01
Houma (0)	0	<0.01
Inupiat (Alaska Native) (0)	0	<0.01
Iroquois (18)	51	0.03
Kiowa (1)	7	<0.01
Lumbee (1)	2	<0.01
Menominee (2)	2	<0.01
Mexican American Ind. (9)	9	0.01
Navajo (1)	4	<0.01
Osage (0)	0	<0.01
Ottawa (0)	0	<0.01
Paiute (0)	1	<0.01
Pima (0)	0	<0.01
Potawatomi (0)	0	<0.01
Pueblo (0)	0	<0.01
Puget Sound Salish (0)	0	<0.01
Seminole (0)	6	<0.01
Shoshone (0)	1	<0.01
Sioux (11)	20	0.01
South American Ind. (2)	11	0.01
Spanish American Ind. (0)	0	<0.01
Tlingit-Haida (Alaska Native) (0)	0	<0.01
Tohono O'Odham (0)	0	<0.01
Tsimshian (Alaska Native) (0)	0	<0.01
Ute (0)	0	<0.01
Yakama (0)	0	<0.01
Yaqui (0)	0	<0.01
Yuman (0)	0	<0.01
Yup'ik (Alaska Native) (0)	0	<0.01
Asian (710)	970	0.65
Not Hispanic (703)	939	0.63
Hispanic (7)	31	0.02
Bangladeshi (0)	0	<0.01
Bhutanese (0)	0	<0.01
Burmese (1)	1	<0.01
Cambodian (2)	2	<0.01
Chinese, ex. Taiwanese (131)	160	0.11
Filipino (91)	167	0.11
Hmong (0)	0	<0.01
Indian (200)	237	0.16
Indonesian (2)	3	<0.01
Japanese (22)	52	0.04
Korean (85)	143	0.10
Laotian (0)	0	<0.01
Malaysian (2)	3	<0.01
Nepalese (1)	1	<0.01
Pakistani (67)	68	0.05
Sri Lankan (0)	0	<0.01
Taiwanese (0)	0	<0.01
Thai (10)	18	0.01
Vietnamese (70)	85	0.06
Hawaii Native/Pacific Islander (26)	91	0.06
Not Hispanic (24)	70	0.05
Hispanic (2)	21	0.01
Fijian (0)	0	<0.01
Guamanian/Chamorro (4)	13	0.01
Marshallese (1)	1	<0.01
Native Hawaiian (11)	34	0.02
Samoan (1)	6	<0.01
Tongan (0)	4	<0.01
White (140,013)	141,383	95.34
Not Hispanic (138,248)	139,358	93.98
Hispanic (1,765)	2,025	1.37

*Notes: † The Census 2010 population figure is used to calculate the percentages in the Hispanic Origin and Race categories. Ancestry percentages are based on the 2006-2010 American Community Survey population (not shown); ‡ Numbers in parentheses indicate the number of people reporting a single ancestry; * Numbers in parentheses indicate the number of persons reporting this race alone, not in combination with any other race; Please refer to the Explanation of Data for more information.*

Snyder County

Population: 39,702

Ancestry	Population	%
Afghan (0)	0	<0.01
African, Sub-Saharan (27)	27	0.07
African (27)	27	0.07
Cape Verdean (0)	0	<0.01
Ethiopian (0)	0	<0.01
Ghanaian (0)	0	<0.01
Kenyan (0)	0	<0.01
Liberian (0)	0	<0.01
Nigerian (0)	0	<0.01
Senegalese (0)	0	<0.01
Sierra Leonean (0)	0	<0.01
Somalian (0)	0	<0.01
South African (0)	0	<0.01
Sudanese (0)	0	<0.01
Ugandan (0)	0	<0.01
Zimbabwean (0)	0	<0.01
Other Sub-Saharan African (0)	0	<0.01
Albanian (0)	0	<0.01
Alsatian (0)	0	<0.01
American (3,022)	3,022	7.67
Arab (14)	93	0.24
Arab (14)	14	0.04
Egyptian (0)	79	0.20
Iraqi (0)	0	<0.01
Jordanian (0)	0	<0.01
Lebanese (0)	0	<0.01
Moroccan (0)	0	<0.01
Palestinian (0)	0	<0.01
Syrian (0)	0	<0.01
Other Arab (0)	0	<0.01
Armenian (0)	0	<0.01
Assyrian/Chaldean/Syriac (0)	0	<0.01
Australian (0)	0	<0.01
Austrian (33)	107	0.27
Basque (0)	0	<0.01
Belgian (0)	0	<0.01
Brazilian (0)	0	<0.01
British (27)	69	0.18
Bulgarian (0)	0	<0.01
Cajun (0)	0	<0.01
Canadian (38)	66	0.17
Carpatho Rusyn (0)	0	<0.01
Celtic (0)	10	0.03
Croatian (2)	2	0.01
Cypriot (0)	0	<0.01
Czech (43)	129	0.33
Czechoslovakian (14)	33	0.08
Danish (4)	33	0.08
Dutch (517)	1,544	3.92
Eastern European (23)	23	0.06
English (764)	2,553	6.48
Estonian (0)	0	<0.01
European (208)	224	0.57
Finnish (0)	16	0.04
French, ex. Basque (108)	770	1.95
French Canadian (17)	105	0.27
German (12,705)	19,369	49.16
German Russian (0)	0	<0.01
Greek (26)	32	0.08
Guyanese (15)	15	0.04
Hungarian (24)	188	0.48
Icelander (0)	0	<0.01
Iranian (0)	0	<0.01
Irish (763)	3,652	9.27
Israeli (0)	0	<0.01
Italian (753)	2,088	5.30
Latvian (0)	0	<0.01
Lithuanian (115)	192	0.49
Luxemburger (0)	0	<0.01
Macedonian (0)	0	<0.01
Maltese (0)	3	0.01
New Zealander (0)	27	0.07
Northern European (6)	6	0.02
Norwegian (24)	112	0.28
Pennsylvania German (910)	1,137	2.89

Ancestry	Population	%
Polish (344)	1,115	2.83
Portuguese (11)	34	0.09
Romanian (28)	54	0.14
Russian (40)	257	0.65
Scandinavian (0)	15	0.04
Scotch-Irish (133)	345	0.88
Scottish (174)	511	1.30
Serbian (3)	3	0.01
Slavic (21)	39	0.10
Slovak (16)	129	0.33
Slovene (0)	0	<0.01
Soviet Union (0)	0	<0.01
Swedish (54)	200	0.51
Swiss (179)	835	2.12
Turkish (13)	13	0.03
Ukrainian (33)	112	0.28
Welsh (87)	508	1.29
West Indian, ex. Hispanic (17)	18	0.05
Bahamian (0)	0	<0.01
Barbadian (0)	1	<0.01
Belizean (0)	0	<0.01
Bermudan (0)	0	<0.01
British West Indian (0)	0	<0.01
Dutch West Indian (0)	0	<0.01
Haitian (2)	2	0.01
Jamaican (15)	15	0.04
Trinidadian/Tobagonian (0)	0	<0.01
U.S. Virgin Islander (0)	0	<0.01
West Indian (0)	0	<0.01
Other West Indian (0)	0	<0.01
Yugoslavian (11)	11	0.03

Hispanic Origin	Population	%
Hispanic or Latino (of any race)	657	1.65
Central American, ex. Mexican	41	0.10
Costa Rican	1	<0.01
Guatemalan	17	0.04
Honduran	11	0.03
Nicaraguan	2	0.01
Panamanian	0	<0.01
Salvadoran	10	0.03
Other Central American	0	<0.01
Cuban	13	0.03
Dominican Republic	19	0.05
Mexican	77	0.19
Puerto Rican	388	0.98
South American	53	0.13
Argentinean	4	0.01
Bolivian	0	<0.01
Chilean	8	0.02
Colombian	15	0.04
Ecuadorian	4	0.01
Paraguayan	6	0.02
Peruvian	13	0.03
Uruguayan	0	<0.01
Venezuelan	3	0.01
Other South American	0	<0.01
Other Hispanic or Latino	66	0.17

Race*	Population	%
African-American/Black (428)	550	1.39
Not Hispanic (375)	489	1.23
Hispanic (53)	61	0.15
American Indian/Alaska Native (53)	178	0.45
Not Hispanic (43)	151	0.38
Hispanic (10)	27	0.07
Alaska Athabascan (Ala. Nat.) (0)	0	<0.01
Aleut (Alaska Native) (0)	0	<0.01
Apache (0)	5	0.01
Arapaho (0)	0	<0.01
Blackfeet (2)	7	0.02
Canadian/French Am. Ind. (6)	6	0.02
Central American Ind. (2)	2	0.01
Cherokee (3)	28	0.07
Cheyenne (0)	0	<0.01
Chickasaw (0)	0	<0.01
Chippewa (3)	4	0.01
Choctaw (4)	6	0.02
Colville (0)	0	<0.01

	Population	%
Comanche (0)	0	<0.01
Cree (0)	0	<0.01
Creek (0)	0	<0.01
Crow (0)	1	<0.01
Delaware (0)	5	0.01
Hopi (0)	0	<0.01
Houma (0)	0	<0.01
Inupiat (Alaska Native) (0)	0	<0.01
Iroquois (2)	6	0.02
Kiowa (0)	0	<0.01
Lumbee (0)	0	<0.01
Menominee (0)	0	<0.01
Mexican American Ind. (1)	6	0.02
Navajo (0)	3	0.01
Osage (0)	0	<0.01
Ottawa (0)	0	<0.01
Paiute (0)	3	0.01
Pima (0)	0	<0.01
Potawatomi (0)	0	<0.01
Pueblo (0)	0	<0.01
Puget Sound Salish (0)	0	<0.01
Seminole (0)	0	<0.01
Shoshone (0)	0	<0.01
Sioux (2)	8	0.02
South American Ind. (1)	5	0.01
Spanish American Ind. (0)	0	<0.01
Tlingit-Haida (Alaska Native) (0)	0	<0.01
Tohono O'Odham (0)	0	<0.01
Tsimshian (Alaska Native) (0)	0	<0.01
Ute (0)	0	<0.01
Yakama (0)	0	<0.01
Yaqui (0)	0	<0.01
Yuman (0)	0	<0.01
Yup'ik (Alaska Native) (0)	0	<0.01
Asian (214)	269	0.68
Not Hispanic (211)	261	0.66
Hispanic (3)	8	0.02
Bangladeshi (0)	0	<0.01
Bhutanese (0)	0	<0.01
Burmese (1)	1	<0.01
Cambodian (0)	0	<0.01
Chinese, ex. Taiwanese (77)	83	0.21
Filipino (12)	23	0.06
Hmong (0)	0	<0.01
Indian (40)	48	0.12
Indonesian (3)	6	0.02
Japanese (8)	15	0.04
Korean (25)	42	0.11
Laotian (0)	0	<0.01
Malaysian (0)	0	<0.01
Nepalese (1)	1	<0.01
Pakistani (15)	16	0.04
Sri Lankan (4)	4	0.01
Taiwanese (0)	0	<0.01
Thai (5)	5	0.01
Vietnamese (19)	23	0.06
Hawaii Native/Pacific Islander (6)	17	0.04
Not Hispanic (5)	14	0.04
Hispanic (1)	3	0.01
Fijian (0)	0	<0.01
Guamanian/Chamorro (1)	1	<0.01
Marshallese (0)	0	<0.01
Native Hawaiian (0)	1	<0.01
Samoan (0)	0	<0.01
Tongan (0)	0	<0.01
White (38,476)	38,783	97.69
Not Hispanic (38,127)	38,389	96.69
Hispanic (349)	394	0.99

*Notes: † The Census 2010 population figure is used to calculate the percentages in the Hispanic Origin and Race categories. Ancestry percentages are based on the 2006-2010 American Community Survey population (not shown); ‡ Numbers in parentheses indicate the number of people reporting a single ancestry; * Numbers in parentheses indicate the number of persons reporting this race alone, not in combination with any other race; Please refer to the Explanation of Data for more information.*

Somerset County

Population: 77,742

Ancestry	Population	%
Afghan (0)	0	<0.01
African, Sub-Saharan (63)	91	0.12
African (63)	91	0.12
Cape Verdean (0)	0	<0.01
Ethiopian (0)	0	<0.01
Ghanaian (0)	0	<0.01
Kenyan (0)	0	<0.01
Liberian (0)	0	<0.01
Nigerian (0)	0	<0.01
Senegalese (0)	0	<0.01
Sierra Leonean (0)	0	<0.01
Somalian (0)	0	<0.01
South African (0)	0	<0.01
Sudanese (0)	0	<0.01
Ugandan (0)	0	<0.01
Zimbabwean (0)	0	<0.01
Other Sub-Saharan African (0)	0	<0.01
Albanian (0)	0	<0.01
Alsatian (0)	0	<0.01
American (5,137)	5,137	6.57
Arab (21)	49	0.06
Arab (0)	0	<0.01
Egyptian (0)	16	0.02
Iraqi (0)	0	<0.01
Jordanian (0)	0	<0.01
Lebanese (21)	26	0.03
Moroccan (0)	0	<0.01
Palestinian (0)	0	<0.01
Syrian (0)	7	0.01
Other Arab (0)	0	<0.01
Armenian (0)	0	<0.01
Assyrian/Chaldean/Syriac (0)	5	0.01
Australian (0)	0	<0.01
Austrian (103)	357	0.46
Basque (0)	0	<0.01
Belgian (2)	61	0.08
Brazilian (0)	0	<0.01
British (44)	170	0.22
Bulgarian (0)	0	<0.01
Cajun (0)	0	<0.01
Canadian (47)	69	0.09
Carpatho Rusyn (49)	120	0.15
Celtic (1)	1	<0.01
Croatian (86)	291	0.37
Cypriot (0)	0	<0.01
Czech (209)	462	0.59
Czechoslovakian (22)	117	0.15
Danish (0)	19	0.02
Dutch (439)	2,674	3.42
Eastern European (37)	37	0.05
English (2,152)	6,593	8.43
Estonian (0)	0	<0.01
European (373)	373	0.48
Finnish (0)	8	0.01
French, ex. Basque (145)	1,403	1.79
French Canadian (48)	62	0.08
German (16,399)	32,998	42.19
German Russian (0)	0	<0.01
Greek (31)	69	0.09
Guyanese (0)	0	<0.01
Hungarian (581)	1,617	2.07
Icelander (0)	0	<0.01
Iranian (0)	0	<0.01
Irish (1,621)	9,494	12.14
Israeli (0)	0	<0.01
Italian (2,449)	5,830	7.45
Latvian (0)	0	<0.01
Lithuanian (52)	73	0.09
Luxemburger (0)	0	<0.01
Macedonian (0)	0	<0.01
Maltese (0)	0	<0.01
New Zealander (0)	0	<0.01
Northern European (32)	32	0.04
Norwegian (33)	102	0.13
Pennsylvania German (1,313)	1,984	2.54

Ancestry (cont.)	Population	%
Polish (1,678)	4,808	6.15
Portuguese (23)	45	0.06
Romanian (8)	53	0.07
Russian (199)	845	1.08
Scandinavian (30)	50	0.06
Scotch-Irish (383)	1,248	1.60
Scottish (259)	1,309	1.67
Serbian (37)	151	0.19
Slavic (23)	94	0.12
Slovak (856)	1,988	2.54
Slovene (83)	195	0.25
Soviet Union (0)	0	<0.01
Swedish (114)	321	0.41
Swiss (228)	843	1.08
Turkish (0)	0	<0.01
Ukrainian (154)	410	0.52
Welsh (212)	1,154	1.48
West Indian, ex. Hispanic (0)	22	0.03
Bahamian (0)	0	<0.01
Barbadian (0)	0	<0.01
Belizean (0)	0	<0.01
Bermudan (0)	0	<0.01
British West Indian (0)	0	<0.01
Dutch West Indian (0)	0	<0.01
Haitian (0)	0	<0.01
Jamaican (0)	0	<0.01
Trinidadian/Tobagonian (0)	0	<0.01
U.S. Virgin Islander (0)	0	<0.01
West Indian (0)	22	0.03
Other West Indian (0)	0	<0.01
Yugoslavian (11)	24	0.03

Hispanic Origin	Population	%
Hispanic or Latino (of any race)	840	1.08
Central American, ex. Mexican	30	0.04
Costa Rican	1	<0.01
Guatemalan	8	0.01
Honduran	4	0.01
Nicaraguan	1	<0.01
Panamanian	1	<0.01
Salvadoran	15	0.02
Other Central American	0	<0.01
Cuban	14	0.02
Dominican Republic	0	<0.01
Mexican	292	0.38
Puerto Rican	81	0.10
South American	22	0.03
Argentinean	2	<0.01
Bolivian	0	<0.01
Chilean	1	<0.01
Colombian	4	0.01
Ecuadorian	1	<0.01
Paraguayan	1	<0.01
Peruvian	9	0.01
Uruguayan	0	<0.01
Venezuelan	4	0.01
Other South American	0	<0.01
Other Hispanic or Latino	401	0.52

Race*	Population	%
African-American/Black (1,863)	2,008	2.58
Not Hispanic (1,856)	1,996	2.57
Hispanic (7)	12	0.02
American Indian/Alaska Native (86)	282	0.36
Not Hispanic (76)	266	0.34
Hispanic (10)	16	0.02
Alaska Athabascan (Ala. Nat.) (0)	0	<0.01
Aleut (Alaska Native) (6)	6	0.01
Apache (1)	4	0.01
Arapaho (0)	0	<0.01
Blackfeet (1)	10	0.01
Canadian/French Am. Ind. (0)	0	<0.01
Central American Ind. (0)	0	<0.01
Cherokee (11)	70	0.09
Cheyenne (0)	2	<0.01
Chickasaw (0)	0	<0.01
Chippewa (4)	7	0.01
Choctaw (0)	1	<0.01
Colville (0)	0	<0.01

Race* (cont.)	Population	%
Comanche (0)	0	<0.01
Cree (0)	1	<0.01
Creek (0)	0	<0.01
Crow (0)	0	<0.01
Delaware (4)	8	0.01
Hopi (0)	0	<0.01
Houma (0)	0	<0.01
Inupiat (Alaska Native) (1)	1	<0.01
Iroquois (6)	10	0.01
Kiowa (0)	0	<0.01
Lumbee (0)	0	<0.01
Menominee (0)	0	<0.01
Mexican American Ind. (5)	5	0.01
Navajo (3)	4	0.01
Osage (0)	0	<0.01
Ottawa (0)	0	<0.01
Paiute (0)	0	<0.01
Pima (0)	0	<0.01
Potawatomi (0)	0	<0.01
Pueblo (0)	0	<0.01
Puget Sound Salish (0)	0	<0.01
Seminole (1)	1	<0.01
Shoshone (0)	0	<0.01
Sioux (2)	10	0.01
South American Ind. (1)	1	<0.01
Spanish American Ind. (0)	0	<0.01
Tlingit-Haida (Alaska Native) (1)	1	<0.01
Tohono O'Odham (0)	0	<0.01
Tsimshian (Alaska Native) (0)	0	<0.01
Ute (0)	0	<0.01
Yakama (0)	0	<0.01
Yaqui (0)	0	<0.01
Yuman (0)	0	<0.01
Yup'ik (Alaska Native) (0)	0	<0.01
Asian (239)	338	0.43
Not Hispanic (238)	334	0.43
Hispanic (1)	4	0.01
Bangladeshi (0)	0	<0.01
Bhutanese (0)	0	<0.01
Burmese (1)	1	<0.01
Cambodian (2)	3	<0.01
Chinese, ex. Taiwanese (39)	47	0.06
Filipino (38)	56	0.07
Hmong (0)	0	<0.01
Indian (52)	66	0.08
Indonesian (0)	0	<0.01
Japanese (9)	19	0.02
Korean (31)	44	0.06
Laotian (0)	0	<0.01
Malaysian (0)	0	<0.01
Nepalese (2)	2	<0.01
Pakistani (7)	7	0.01
Sri Lankan (0)	0	<0.01
Taiwanese (0)	0	<0.01
Thai (3)	12	0.02
Vietnamese (24)	31	0.04
Hawaii Native/Pacific Islander (17)	45	0.06
Not Hispanic (16)	44	0.06
Hispanic (1)	1	<0.01
Fijian (0)	0	<0.01
Guamanian/Chamorro (1)	7	0.01
Marshallese (3)	3	<0.01
Native Hawaiian (5)	14	0.02
Samoan (3)	8	0.01
Tongan (0)	0	<0.01
White (74,603)	75,054	96.54
Not Hispanic (74,265)	74,691	96.08
Hispanic (338)	363	0.47

*Notes: † The Census 2010 population figure is used to calculate the percentages in the Hispanic Origin and Race categories. Ancestry percentages are based on the 2006-2010 American Community Survey population (not shown); ‡ Numbers in parentheses indicate the number of people reporting a single ancestry; * Numbers in parentheses indicate the number of persons reporting this race alone, not in combination with any other race; Please refer to the Explanation of Data for more information.*

Sullivan County

Population: 6,428

Ancestry	Population	%
Afghan (0)	0	<0.01
African, Sub-Saharan (0)	0	<0.01
African (0)	0	<0.01
Cape Verdean (0)	0	<0.01
Ethiopian (0)	0	<0.01
Ghanaian (0)	0	<0.01
Kenyan (0)	0	<0.01
Liberian (0)	0	<0.01
Nigerian (0)	0	<0.01
Senegalese (0)	0	<0.01
Sierra Leonean (0)	0	<0.01
Somalian (0)	0	<0.01
South African (0)	0	<0.01
Sudanese (0)	0	<0.01
Ugandan (0)	0	<0.01
Zimbabwean (0)	0	<0.01
Other Sub-Saharan African (0)	0	<0.01
Albanian (0)	0	<0.01
Alsatian (0)	0	<0.01
American (250)	250	3.87
Arab (3)	3	0.05
Arab (0)	0	<0.01
Egyptian (3)	3	0.05
Iraqi (0)	0	<0.01
Jordanian (0)	0	<0.01
Lebanese (0)	0	<0.01
Moroccan (0)	0	<0.01
Palestinian (0)	0	<0.01
Syrian (0)	0	<0.01
Other Arab (0)	0	<0.01
Armenian (0)	8	0.12
Assyrian/Chaldean/Syriac (0)	0	<0.01
Australian (0)	0	<0.01
Austrian (17)	61	0.94
Basque (0)	0	<0.01
Belgian (0)	4	0.06
Brazilian (0)	0	<0.01
British (0)	2	0.03
Bulgarian (0)	0	<0.01
Cajun (0)	0	<0.01
Canadian (0)	0	<0.01
Carpatho Rusyn (0)	4	0.06
Celtic (0)	0	<0.01
Croatian (0)	0	<0.01
Cypriot (0)	0	<0.01
Czech (5)	21	0.32
Czechoslovakian (0)	0	<0.01
Danish (0)	3	0.05
Dutch (67)	258	3.99
Eastern European (0)	0	<0.01
English (297)	888	13.73
Estonian (0)	0	<0.01
European (2)	2	0.03
Finnish (0)	0	<0.01
French, ex. Basque (28)	208	3.22
French Canadian (5)	5	0.08
German (1,105)	2,342	36.21
German Russian (0)	0	<0.01
Greek (26)	26	0.40
Guyanese (0)	0	<0.01
Hungarian (4)	24	0.37
Icelander (0)	0	<0.01
Iranian (0)	0	<0.01
Irish (396)	1,332	20.60
Israeli (0)	0	<0.01
Italian (274)	516	7.98
Latvian (0)	0	<0.01
Lithuanian (20)	43	0.66
Luxemburger (0)	0	<0.01
Macedonian (0)	0	<0.01
Maltese (0)	0	<0.01
New Zealander (0)	0	<0.01
Northern European (0)	0	<0.01
Norwegian (12)	21	0.32
Pennsylvania German (109)	162	2.51

Polish (155)	424	6.56
Portuguese (9)	16	0.25
Romanian (0)	0	<0.01
Russian (16)	134	2.07
Scandinavian (0)	0	<0.01
Scotch-Irish (63)	148	2.29
Scottish (18)	120	1.86
Serbian (0)	0	<0.01
Slavic (4)	4	0.06
Slovak (27)	47	0.73
Slovene (0)	0	<0.01
Soviet Union (0)	0	<0.01
Swedish (43)	75	1.16
Swiss (2)	46	0.71
Turkish (0)	0	<0.01
Ukrainian (3)	20	0.31
Welsh (34)	90	1.39
West Indian, ex. Hispanic (0)	0	<0.01
Bahamian (0)	0	<0.01
Barbadian (0)	0	<0.01
Belizean (0)	0	<0.01
Bermudan (0)	0	<0.01
British West Indian (0)	0	<0.01
Dutch West Indian (0)	0	<0.01
Haitian (0)	0	<0.01
Jamaican (0)	0	<0.01
Trinidadian/Tobagonian (0)	0	<0.01
U.S. Virgin Islander (0)	0	<0.01
West Indian (0)	0	<0.01
Other West Indian (0)	0	<0.01
Yugoslavian (0)	0	<0.01

Hispanic Origin	Population	%
Hispanic or Latino (of any race)	92	1.43
Central American, ex. Mexican	7	0.11
Costa Rican	4	0.06
Guatemalan	1	0.02
Honduran	0	<0.01
Nicaraguan	0	<0.01
Panamanian	2	0.03
Salvadoran	0	<0.01
Other Central American	0	<0.01
Cuban	4	0.06
Dominican Republic	3	0.05
Mexican	20	0.31
Puerto Rican	13	0.20
South American	6	0.09
Argentinean	0	<0.01
Bolivian	0	<0.01
Chilean	2	0.03
Colombian	0	<0.01
Ecuadorian	1	0.02
Paraguayan	0	<0.01
Peruvian	2	0.03
Uruguayan	0	<0.01
Venezuelan	1	0.02
Other South American	0	<0.01
Other Hispanic or Latino	39	0.61

Race*	Population	%
African-American/Black (168)	174	2.71
Not Hispanic (163)	169	2.63
Hispanic (5)	5	0.08
American Indian/Alaska Native (26)	57	0.89
Not Hispanic (26)	53	0.82
Hispanic (0)	4	0.06
Alaska Athabascan (Ala. Nat.) (0)	0	<0.01
Aleut (Alaska Native) (0)	0	<0.01
Apache (1)	1	0.02
Arapaho (0)	0	<0.01
Blackfeet (0)	0	<0.01
Canadian/French Am. Ind. (0)	0	<0.01
Central American Ind. (0)	0	<0.01
Cherokee (4)	10	0.16
Cheyenne (0)	0	<0.01
Chickasaw (0)	0	<0.01
Chippewa (0)	0	<0.01
Choctaw (0)	1	0.02
Colville (0)	0	<0.01

Comanche (0)	0	<0.01
Cree (0)	0	<0.01
Creek (0)	0	<0.01
Crow (0)	0	<0.01
Delaware (3)	8	0.12
Hopi (0)	0	<0.01
Houma (0)	0	<0.01
Inupiat (Alaska Native) (0)	0	<0.01
Iroquois (3)	3	0.05
Kiowa (0)	0	<0.01
Lumbee (0)	0	<0.01
Menominee (0)	0	<0.01
Mexican American Ind. (0)	0	<0.01
Navajo (0)	0	<0.01
Osage (0)	0	<0.01
Ottawa (0)	0	<0.01
Paiute (0)	0	<0.01
Pima (0)	0	<0.01
Potawatomi (0)	0	<0.01
Pueblo (0)	0	<0.01
Puget Sound Salish (0)	0	<0.01
Seminole (0)	0	<0.01
Shoshone (0)	0	<0.01
Sioux (1)	2	0.03
South American Ind. (0)	0	<0.01
Spanish American Ind. (0)	0	<0.01
Tlingit-Haida (Alaska Native) (0)	0	<0.01
Tohono O'Odham (0)	0	<0.01
Tsimshian (Alaska Native) (0)	0	<0.01
Ute (0)	0	<0.01
Yakama (0)	0	<0.01
Yaqui (0)	0	<0.01
Yuman (0)	0	<0.01
Yup'ik (Alaska Native) (0)	0	<0.01
Asian (20)	22	0.34
Not Hispanic (19)	21	0.33
Hispanic (1)	1	0.02
Bangladeshi (0)	0	<0.01
Bhutanese (0)	0	<0.01
Burmese (0)	0	<0.01
Cambodian (0)	0	<0.01
Chinese, ex. Taiwanese (1)	1	0.02
Filipino (2)	2	0.03
Hmong (0)	0	<0.01
Indian (6)	6	0.09
Indonesian (0)	0	<0.01
Japanese (0)	0	<0.01
Korean (8)	8	0.12
Laotian (0)	0	<0.01
Malaysian (0)	0	<0.01
Nepalese (0)	0	<0.01
Pakistani (0)	0	<0.01
Sri Lankan (1)	1	0.02
Taiwanese (0)	0	<0.01
Thai (0)	0	<0.01
Vietnamese (0)	2	0.03
Hawaii Native/Pacific Islander (0)	4	0.06
Not Hispanic (0)	4	0.06
Hispanic (0)	0	<0.01
Fijian (0)	0	<0.01
Guamanian/Chamorro (0)	2	0.03
Marshallese (0)	0	<0.01
Native Hawaiian (0)	1	0.02
Samoan (0)	0	<0.01
Tongan (0)	0	<0.01
White (6,163)	6,206	96.55
Not Hispanic (6,089)	6,128	95.33
Hispanic (74)	78	1.21

*Notes: † The Census 2010 population figure is used to calculate the percentages in the Hispanic Origin and Race categories. Ancestry percentages are based on the 2006-2010 American Community Survey population (not shown); ‡ Numbers in parentheses indicate the number of people reporting a single ancestry; * Numbers in parentheses indicate the number of persons reporting this race alone, not in combination with any other race; Please refer to the Explanation of Data for more information.*

Susquehanna County

Population: 43,356

Ancestry	Population	%
Afghan (0)	0	<0.01
African, Sub-Saharan (20)	23	0.05
African (20)	23	0.05
Cape Verdean (0)	0	<0.01
Ethiopian (0)	0	<0.01
Ghanaian (0)	0	<0.01
Kenyan (0)	0	<0.01
Liberian (0)	0	<0.01
Nigerian (0)	0	<0.01
Senegalese (0)	0	<0.01
Sierra Leonean (0)	0	<0.01
Somalian (0)	0	<0.01
South African (0)	0	<0.01
Sudanese (0)	0	<0.01
Ugandan (0)	0	<0.01
Zimbabwean (0)	0	<0.01
Other Sub-Saharan African (0)	0	<0.01
Albanian (0)	0	<0.01
Alsatian (0)	0	<0.01
American (1,612)	1,612	3.72
Arab (40)	53	0.12
Arab (3)	3	0.01
Egyptian (0)	0	<0.01
Iraqi (0)	0	<0.01
Jordanian (0)	0	<0.01
Lebanese (6)	19	0.04
Moroccan (0)	0	<0.01
Palestinian (0)	0	<0.01
Syrian (31)	31	0.07
Other Arab (0)	0	<0.01
Armenian (16)	19	0.04
Assyrian/Chaldean/Syriac (0)	0	<0.01
Australian (3)	55	0.13
Austrian (50)	142	0.33
Basque (0)	0	<0.01
Belgian (0)	9	0.02
Brazilian (2)	2	<0.01
British (43)	132	0.30
Bulgarian (0)	0	<0.01
Cajun (0)	0	<0.01
Canadian (53)	70	0.16
Carpatho Rusyn (7)	17	0.04
Celtic (0)	0	<0.01
Croatian (55)	60	0.14
Cypriot (0)	0	<0.01
Czech (19)	131	0.30
Czechoslovakian (33)	88	0.20
Danish (14)	95	0.22
Dutch (212)	1,691	3.90
Eastern European (35)	38	0.09
English (2,900)	9,012	20.79
Estonian (0)	0	<0.01
European (277)	299	0.69
Finnish (0)	19	0.04
French, ex. Basque (265)	1,577	3.64
French Canadian (111)	180	0.42
German (2,692)	10,970	25.31
German Russian (0)	0	<0.01
Greek (80)	139	0.32
Guyanese (0)	0	<0.01
Hungarian (52)	248	0.57
Icelander (0)	0	<0.01
Iranian (0)	12	0.03
Irish (2,245)	9,267	21.38
Israeli (0)	3	0.01
Italian (1,588)	4,570	10.54
Latvian (0)	0	<0.01
Lithuanian (206)	536	1.24
Luxemburger (0)	0	<0.01
Macedonian (0)	0	<0.01
Maltese (0)	0	<0.01
New Zealander (0)	0	<0.01
Northern European (20)	20	0.05
Norwegian (41)	136	0.31
Pennsylvania German (273)	464	1.07
Polish (1,148)	4,095	9.45
Portuguese (59)	177	0.41
Romanian (4)	4	0.01
Russian (310)	880	2.03
Scandinavian (9)	39	0.09
Scotch-Irish (231)	791	1.82
Scottish (249)	1,058	2.44
Serbian (21)	58	0.13
Slavic (7)	67	0.15
Slovak (301)	964	2.22
Slovene (72)	189	0.44
Soviet Union (0)	0	<0.01
Swedish (90)	462	1.07
Swiss (50)	247	0.57
Turkish (14)	14	0.03
Ukrainian (96)	287	0.66
Welsh (449)	2,333	5.38
West Indian, ex. Hispanic (25)	42	0.10
Bahamian (0)	0	<0.01
Barbadian (0)	0	<0.01
Belizean (0)	0	<0.01
Bermudan (0)	0	<0.01
British West Indian (13)	30	0.07
Dutch West Indian (0)	0	<0.01
Haitian (5)	5	0.01
Jamaican (4)	4	0.01
Trinidadian/Tobagonian (0)	0	<0.01
U.S. Virgin Islander (3)	3	0.01
West Indian (0)	0	<0.01
Other West Indian (0)	0	<0.01
Yugoslavian (9)	59	0.14

Hispanic Origin	Population	%
Hispanic or Latino (of any race)	564	1.30
Central American, ex. Mexican	37	0.09
Costa Rican	3	0.01
Guatemalan	11	0.03
Honduran	3	0.01
Nicaraguan	0	<0.01
Panamanian	8	0.02
Salvadoran	12	0.03
Other Central American	0	<0.01
Cuban	32	0.07
Dominican Republic	8	0.02
Mexican	167	0.39
Puerto Rican	208	0.48
South American	48	0.11
Argentinean	4	0.01
Bolivian	0	<0.01
Chilean	5	0.01
Colombian	9	0.02
Ecuadorian	20	0.05
Paraguayan	0	<0.01
Peruvian	2	<0.01
Uruguayan	6	0.01
Venezuelan	2	<0.01
Other South American	0	<0.01
Other Hispanic or Latino	64	0.15

Race*	Population	%
African-American/Black (156)	256	0.59
Not Hispanic (150)	241	0.56
Hispanic (6)	15	0.03
American Indian/Alaska Native (57)	201	0.46
Not Hispanic (52)	192	0.44
Hispanic (5)	9	0.02
Alaska Athabascan (Ala. Nat.) (2)	2	<0.01
Aleut (Alaska Native) (0)	0	<0.01
Apache (0)	2	<0.01
Arapaho (0)	0	<0.01
Blackfeet (3)	12	0.03
Canadian/French Am. Ind. (0)	0	<0.01
Central American Ind. (2)	2	<0.01
Cherokee (8)	24	0.06
Cheyenne (0)	0	<0.01
Chickasaw (0)	1	<0.01
Chippewa (1)	1	<0.01
Choctaw (0)	2	<0.01
Colville (0)	0	<0.01

	Population	%
Comanche (0)	0	<0.01
Cree (0)	0	<0.01
Creek (0)	0	<0.01
Crow (0)	0	<0.01
Delaware (1)	8	0.02
Hopi (0)	0	<0.01
Houma (0)	0	<0.01
Inupiat (Alaska Native) (0)	0	<0.01
Iroquois (2)	11	0.03
Kiowa (0)	0	<0.01
Lumbee (0)	0	<0.01
Menominee (0)	0	<0.01
Mexican American Ind. (0)	0	<0.01
Navajo (0)	0	<0.01
Osage (0)	0	<0.01
Ottawa (0)	0	<0.01
Paiute (0)	0	<0.01
Pima (0)	0	<0.01
Potawatomi (0)	0	<0.01
Pueblo (0)	0	<0.01
Puget Sound Salish (0)	0	<0.01
Seminole (0)	0	<0.01
Shoshone (0)	0	<0.01
Sioux (7)	12	0.03
South American Ind. (0)	3	0.01
Spanish American Ind. (0)	0	<0.01
Tlingit-Haida (Alaska Native) (0)	0	<0.01
Tohono O'Odham (3)	3	0.01
Tsimshian (Alaska Native) (0)	0	<0.01
Ute (0)	1	<0.01
Yakama (0)	0	<0.01
Yaqui (0)	0	<0.01
Yuman (0)	0	<0.01
Yup'ik (Alaska Native) (0)	0	<0.01
Asian (123)	212	0.49
Not Hispanic (121)	208	0.48
Hispanic (2)	4	0.01
Bangladeshi (0)	0	<0.01
Bhutanese (0)	0	<0.01
Burmese (0)	0	<0.01
Cambodian (1)	3	0.01
Chinese, ex. Taiwanese (41)	52	0.12
Filipino (26)	57	0.13
Hmong (0)	0	<0.01
Indian (20)	28	0.06
Indonesian (0)	0	<0.01
Japanese (5)	15	0.03
Korean (20)	37	0.09
Laotian (0)	2	<0.01
Malaysian (0)	0	<0.01
Nepalese (0)	0	<0.01
Pakistani (1)	2	<0.01
Sri Lankan (0)	0	<0.01
Taiwanese (0)	0	<0.01
Thai (3)	10	0.02
Vietnamese (3)	3	0.01
Hawaii Native/Pacific Islander (12)	40	0.09
Not Hispanic (9)	28	0.06
Hispanic (3)	12	0.03
Fijian (0)	0	<0.01
Guamanian/Chamorro (0)	6	0.01
Marshallese (1)	1	<0.01
Native Hawaiian (5)	9	0.02
Samoan (2)	8	0.02
Tongan (0)	0	<0.01
White (42,510)	42,845	98.82
Not Hispanic (42,117)	42,429	97.86
Hispanic (393)	416	0.96

Notes: † The Census 2010 population figure is used to calculate the percentages in the Hispanic Origin and Race categories. Ancestry percentages are based on the 2006-2010 American Community Survey population (not shown); ‡ Numbers in parentheses indicate the number of people reporting a single ancestry; * Numbers in parentheses indicate the number of persons reporting this race alone, not in combination with any other race; Please refer to the Explanation of Data for more information.

Tioga County

Population: 41,981

Ancestry	Population	%
Afghan (0)	0	<0.01
African, Sub-Saharan (64)	68	0.16
African (64)	68	0.16
Cape Verdean (0)	0	<0.01
Ethiopian (0)	0	<0.01
Ghanaian (0)	0	<0.01
Kenyan (0)	0	<0.01
Liberian (0)	0	<0.01
Nigerian (0)	0	<0.01
Senegalese (0)	0	<0.01
Sierra Leonean (0)	0	<0.01
Somalian (0)	0	<0.01
South African (0)	0	<0.01
Sudanese (0)	0	<0.01
Ugandan (0)	0	<0.01
Zimbabwean (0)	0	<0.01
Other Sub-Saharan African (0)	0	<0.01
Albanian (4)	11	0.03
Alsatian (0)	0	<0.01
American (3,598)	3,598	8.64
Arab (58)	68	0.16
Arab (0)	0	<0.01
Egyptian (28)	28	0.07
Iraqi (0)	0	<0.01
Jordanian (0)	0	<0.01
Lebanese (19)	25	0.06
Moroccan (0)	0	<0.01
Palestinian (0)	0	<0.01
Syrian (11)	15	0.04
Other Arab (0)	0	<0.01
Armenian (0)	0	<0.01
Assyrian/Chaldean/Syriac (0)	0	<0.01
Australian (0)	0	<0.01
Austrian (7)	65	0.16
Basque (0)	0	<0.01
Belgian (8)	26	0.06
Brazilian (0)	0	<0.01
British (65)	185	0.44
Bulgarian (0)	0	<0.01
Cajun (0)	0	<0.01
Canadian (8)	19	0.05
Carpatho Rusyn (0)	0	<0.01
Celtic (3)	3	0.01
Croatian (6)	18	0.04
Cypriot (0)	0	<0.01
Czech (42)	131	0.31
Czechoslovakian (35)	49	0.12
Danish (9)	74	0.18
Dutch (225)	1,223	2.94
Eastern European (3)	3	0.01
English (3,197)	7,348	17.65
Estonian (0)	0	<0.01
European (263)	279	0.67
Finnish (2)	39	0.09
French, ex. Basque (138)	1,055	2.53
French Canadian (70)	125	0.30
German (4,923)	11,799	28.34
German Russian (0)	0	<0.01
Greek (19)	87	0.21
Guyanese (6)	9	0.02
Hungarian (35)	163	0.39
Icelander (7)	7	0.02
Iranian (0)	0	<0.01
Irish (1,396)	5,701	13.69
Israeli (0)	0	<0.01
Italian (839)	2,382	5.72
Latvian (3)	9	0.02
Lithuanian (36)	74	0.18
Luxemburger (0)	0	<0.01
Macedonian (0)	0	<0.01
Maltese (0)	0	<0.01
New Zealander (8)	8	0.02
Northern European (49)	49	0.12
Norwegian (69)	134	0.32
Pennsylvania German (357)	542	1.30

Ancestry	Population	%
Polish (984)	2,186	5.25
Portuguese (36)	111	0.27
Romanian (4)	16	0.04
Russian (33)	145	0.35
Scandinavian (6)	65	0.16
Scotch-Irish (308)	844	2.03
Scottish (328)	1,071	2.57
Serbian (0)	0	<0.01
Slavic (3)	77	0.18
Slovak (48)	105	0.25
Slovene (4)	4	0.01
Soviet Union (0)	0	<0.01
Swedish (246)	935	2.25
Swiss (71)	253	0.61
Turkish (0)	0	<0.01
Ukrainian (45)	143	0.34
Welsh (285)	1,054	2.53
West Indian, ex. Hispanic (70)	89	0.21
Bahamian (0)	0	<0.01
Barbadian (0)	9	0.02
Belizean (0)	0	<0.01
Bermudan (0)	0	<0.01
British West Indian (0)	0	<0.01
Dutch West Indian (9)	9	0.02
Haitian (7)	7	0.02
Jamaican (49)	59	0.14
Trinidadian/Tobagonian (0)	0	<0.01
U.S. Virgin Islander (0)	0	<0.01
West Indian (5)	5	0.01
Other West Indian (0)	0	<0.01
Yugoslavian (3)	34	0.08

Hispanic Origin	Population	%
Hispanic or Latino (of any race)	437	1.04
Central American, ex. Mexican	22	0.05
Costa Rican	4	0.01
Guatemalan	5	0.01
Honduran	7	0.02
Nicaraguan	0	<0.01
Panamanian	1	<0.01
Salvadoran	5	0.01
Other Central American	0	<0.01
Cuban	22	0.05
Dominican Republic	10	0.02
Mexican	111	0.26
Puerto Rican	171	0.41
South American	39	0.09
Argentinean	5	0.01
Bolivian	2	<0.01
Chilean	3	0.01
Colombian	3	0.01
Ecuadorian	2	<0.01
Paraguayan	15	0.04
Peruvian	6	0.01
Uruguayan	0	<0.01
Venezuelan	3	0.01
Other South American	0	<0.01
Other Hispanic or Latino	62	0.15

Race*	Population	%
African-American/Black (333)	491	1.17
Not Hispanic (322)	466	1.11
Hispanic (11)	25	0.06
American Indian/Alaska Native (91)	293	0.70
Not Hispanic (81)	269	0.64
Hispanic (10)	24	0.06
Alaska Athabascan (Ala. Nat.) (1)	1	<0.01
Aleut (Alaska Native) (1)	1	<0.01
Apache (0)	2	<0.01
Arapaho (0)	0	<0.01
Blackfeet (4)	19	0.05
Canadian/French Am. Ind. (0)	0	<0.01
Central American Ind. (0)	1	<0.01
Cherokee (17)	66	0.16
Cheyenne (1)	2	<0.01
Chickasaw (0)	0	<0.01
Chippewa (1)	5	0.01
Choctaw (2)	6	0.01
Colville (0)	0	<0.01

Race*	Population	%
Comanche (0)	0	<0.01
Cree (0)	0	<0.01
Creek (2)	4	0.01
Crow (1)	2	<0.01
Delaware (3)	9	0.02
Hopi (1)	1	<0.01
Houma (0)	0	<0.01
Inupiat (Alaska Native) (0)	0	<0.01
Iroquois (7)	34	0.08
Kiowa (0)	0	<0.01
Lumbee (0)	0	<0.01
Menominee (0)	0	<0.01
Mexican American Ind. (0)	0	<0.01
Navajo (0)	2	<0.01
Osage (0)	0	<0.01
Ottawa (0)	0	<0.01
Paiute (0)	1	<0.01
Pima (0)	0	<0.01
Potawatomi (1)	1	<0.01
Pueblo (0)	2	<0.01
Puget Sound Salish (0)	2	<0.01
Seminole (0)	1	<0.01
Shoshone (0)	0	<0.01
Sioux (2)	5	0.01
South American Ind. (2)	2	<0.01
Spanish American Ind. (0)	1	<0.01
Tlingit-Haida (Alaska Native) (0)	0	<0.01
Tohono O'Odham (0)	0	<0.01
Tsimshian (Alaska Native) (0)	0	<0.01
Ute (0)	0	<0.01
Yakama (2)	2	<0.01
Yaqui (0)	0	<0.01
Yuman (0)	0	<0.01
Yup'ik (Alaska Native) (0)	0	<0.01
Asian (183)	261	0.62
Not Hispanic (181)	251	0.60
Hispanic (2)	10	0.02
Bangladeshi (0)	0	<0.01
Bhutanese (0)	0	<0.01
Burmese (0)	0	<0.01
Cambodian (1)	2	<0.01
Chinese, ex. Taiwanese (59)	77	0.18
Filipino (50)	68	0.16
Hmong (0)	0	<0.01
Indian (22)	35	0.08
Indonesian (0)	2	<0.01
Japanese (14)	22	0.05
Korean (24)	36	0.09
Laotian (0)	0	<0.01
Malaysian (0)	0	<0.01
Nepalese (0)	0	<0.01
Pakistani (3)	7	0.02
Sri Lankan (0)	0	<0.01
Taiwanese (1)	1	<0.01
Thai (5)	9	0.02
Vietnamese (1)	1	<0.01
Hawaii Native/Pacific Islander (4)	19	0.05
Not Hispanic (4)	19	0.05
Hispanic (0)	0	<0.01
Fijian (0)	0	<0.01
Guamanian/Chamorro (0)	0	<0.01
Marshallese (0)	0	<0.01
Native Hawaiian (2)	10	0.02
Samoan (1)	3	<0.01
Tongan (0)	0	<0.01
White (40,852)	41,271	98.31
Not Hispanic (40,560)	40,934	97.51
Hispanic (292)	337	0.80

*Notes: † The Census 2010 population figure is used to calculate the percentages in the Hispanic Origin and Race categories. Ancestry percentages are based on the 2006-2010 American Community Survey population (not shown); ‡ Numbers in parentheses indicate the number of people reporting a single ancestry; * Numbers in parentheses indicate the number of persons reporting this race alone, not in combination with any other race; Please refer to the Explanation of Data for more information.*

Union County

Population: 44,947

Ancestry	Population	%
Afghan (0)	0	<0.01
African, Sub-Saharan (193)	240	0.53
African (156)	195	0.43
Cape Verdean (0)	0	<0.01
Ethiopian (8)	8	0.02
Ghanaian (0)	0	<0.01
Kenyan (0)	0	<0.01
Liberian (0)	0	<0.01
Nigerian (29)	29	0.06
Senegalese (0)	0	<0.01
Sierra Leonean (0)	0	<0.01
Somalian (0)	0	<0.01
South African (0)	0	<0.01
Sudanese (0)	0	<0.01
Ugandan (0)	0	<0.01
Zimbabwean (0)	0	<0.01
Other Sub-Saharan African (0)	8	0.02
Albanian (0)	0	<0.01
Alsatian (0)	0	<0.01
American (2,703)	2,703	6.02
Arab (114)	158	0.35
Arab (0)	5	0.01
Egyptian (0)	0	<0.01
Iraqi (14)	14	0.03
Jordanian (0)	0	<0.01
Lebanese (15)	22	0.05
Moroccan (69)	69	0.15
Palestinian (0)	0	<0.01
Syrian (0)	32	0.07
Other Arab (16)	16	0.04
Armenian (15)	30	0.07
Assyrian/Chaldean/Syriac (0)	0	<0.01
Australian (0)	4	0.01
Austrian (24)	178	0.40
Basque (0)	0	<0.01
Belgian (34)	69	0.15
Brazilian (0)	32	0.07
British (110)	263	0.59
Bulgarian (0)	0	<0.01
Cajun (0)	0	<0.01
Canadian (52)	120	0.27
Carpatho Rusyn (0)	0	<0.01
Celtic (0)	10	0.02
Croatian (0)	4	0.01
Cypriot (0)	0	<0.01
Czech (43)	100	0.22
Czechoslovakian (45)	45	0.10
Danish (7)	47	0.10
Dutch (395)	1,512	3.37
Eastern European (107)	107	0.24
English (1,313)	4,005	8.93
Estonian (0)	0	<0.01
European (249)	255	0.57
Finnish (0)	17	0.04
French, ex. Basque (99)	1,067	2.38
French Canadian (129)	275	0.61
German (8,862)	17,126	38.17
German Russian (0)	0	<0.01
Greek (59)	98	0.22
Guyanese (40)	40	0.09
Hungarian (28)	124	0.28
Icelander (0)	0	<0.01
Iranian (0)	0	<0.01
Irish (1,014)	4,834	10.77
Israeli (0)	0	<0.01
Italian (895)	3,129	6.97
Latvian (24)	24	0.05
Lithuanian (75)	261	0.58
Luxemburger (0)	0	<0.01
Macedonian (0)	0	<0.01
Maltese (0)	0	<0.01
New Zealander (0)	0	<0.01
Northern European (0)	0	<0.01
Norwegian (53)	149	0.33
Pennsylvania German (922)	1,069	2.38

Ancestry (cont.)	Population	%
Polish (480)	1,778	3.96
Portuguese (0)	39	0.09
Romanian (0)	47	0.10
Russian (130)	640	1.43
Scandinavian (0)	40	0.09
Scotch-Irish (204)	594	1.32
Scottish (184)	695	1.55
Serbian (0)	4	0.01
Slavic (0)	38	0.08
Slovak (36)	121	0.27
Slovene (6)	6	0.01
Soviet Union (0)	0	<0.01
Swedish (304)	625	1.39
Swiss (719)	1,071	2.39
Turkish (24)	24	0.05
Ukrainian (57)	292	0.65
Welsh (93)	709	1.58
West Indian, ex. Hispanic (227)	303	0.68
Bahamian (0)	0	<0.01
Barbadian (0)	0	<0.01
Belizean (0)	0	<0.01
Bermudan (0)	0	<0.01
British West Indian (14)	14	0.03
Dutch West Indian (0)	0	<0.01
Haitian (79)	79	0.18
Jamaican (94)	139	0.31
Trinidadian/Tobagonian (13)	37	0.08
U.S. Virgin Islander (13)	13	0.03
West Indian (14)	21	0.05
Other West Indian (0)	0	<0.01
Yugoslavian (3)	3	0.01

Hispanic Origin	Population	%
Hispanic or Latino (of any race)	2,346	5.22
Central American, ex. Mexican	150	0.33
Costa Rican	2	<0.01
Guatemalan	30	0.07
Honduran	37	0.08
Nicaraguan	6	0.01
Panamanian	29	0.06
Salvadoran	35	0.08
Other Central American	11	0.02
Cuban	76	0.17
Dominican Republic	223	0.50
Mexican	841	1.87
Puerto Rican	745	1.66
South American	143	0.32
Argentinean	10	0.02
Bolivian	8	0.02
Chilean	4	0.01
Colombian	71	0.16
Ecuadorian	8	0.02
Paraguayan	0	<0.01
Peruvian	14	0.03
Uruguayan	0	<0.01
Venezuelan	7	0.02
Other South American	21	0.05
Other Hispanic or Latino	168	0.37

Race*	Population	%
African-American/Black (3,324)	3,633	8.08
Not Hispanic (3,048)	3,298	7.34
Hispanic (276)	335	0.75
American Indian/Alaska Native (159)	341	0.76
Not Hispanic (125)	275	0.61
Hispanic (34)	66	0.15
Alaska Athabascan (Ala. Nat.) (0)	0	<0.01
Aleut (Alaska Native) (0)	0	<0.01
Apache (3)	9	0.02
Arapaho (0)	0	<0.01
Blackfeet (4)	13	0.03
Canadian/French Am. Ind. (1)	2	<0.01
Central American Ind. (0)	1	<0.01
Cherokee (7)	43	0.10
Cheyenne (0)	1	<0.01
Chickasaw (0)	1	<0.01
Chippewa (2)	2	<0.01
Choctaw (0)	0	<0.01
Colville (0)	0	<0.01

Race* (cont.)	Population	%
Comanche (0)	0	<0.01
Cree (0)	0	<0.01
Creek (4)	6	0.01
Crow (0)	0	<0.01
Delaware (4)	9	0.02
Hopi (0)	0	<0.01
Houma (0)	0	<0.01
Inupiat (Alaska Native) (1)	1	<0.01
Iroquois (2)	11	0.02
Kiowa (1)	1	<0.01
Lumbee (0)	0	<0.01
Menominee (0)	0	<0.01
Mexican American Ind. (5)	7	0.02
Navajo (4)	6	0.01
Osage (0)	1	<0.01
Ottawa (0)	0	<0.01
Paiute (0)	0	<0.01
Pima (0)	1	<0.01
Potawatomi (0)	2	<0.01
Pueblo (0)	0	<0.01
Puget Sound Salish (0)	0	<0.01
Seminole (0)	0	<0.01
Shoshone (1)	3	0.01
Sioux (5)	9	0.02
South American Ind. (7)	11	0.02
Spanish American Ind. (0)	1	<0.01
Tlingit-Haida (Alaska Native) (0)	0	<0.01
Tohono O'Odham (0)	0	<0.01
Tsimshian (Alaska Native) (0)	0	<0.01
Ute (0)	0	<0.01
Yakama (0)	0	<0.01
Yaqui (0)	1	<0.01
Yuman (0)	0	<0.01
Yup'ik (Alaska Native) (1)	1	<0.01
Asian (522)	695	1.55
Not Hispanic (520)	681	1.52
Hispanic (2)	14	0.03
Bangladeshi (2)	2	<0.01
Bhutanese (0)	0	<0.01
Burmese (0)	0	<0.01
Cambodian (2)	3	0.01
Chinese, ex. Taiwanese (139)	171	0.38
Filipino (52)	88	0.20
Hmong (2)	2	<0.01
Indian (75)	101	0.22
Indonesian (2)	2	<0.01
Japanese (27)	47	0.10
Korean (76)	99	0.22
Laotian (6)	10	0.02
Malaysian (0)	4	<0.01
Nepalese (1)	1	<0.01
Pakistani (13)	15	0.03
Sri Lankan (0)	0	<0.01
Taiwanese (4)	6	0.01
Thai (1)	10	0.02
Vietnamese (50)	61	0.14
Hawaii Native/Pacific Islander (24)	77	0.17
Not Hispanic (21)	67	0.15
Hispanic (3)	10	0.02
Fijian (0)	0	<0.01
Guamanian/Chamorro (5)	9	0.02
Marshallese (0)	0	<0.01
Native Hawaiian (5)	21	0.05
Samoan (0)	2	<0.01
Tongan (0)	0	<0.01
White (39,414)	39,982	88.95
Not Hispanic (38,311)	38,742	86.19
Hispanic (1,103)	1,240	2.76

Notes: † The Census 2010 population figure is used to calculate the percentages in the Hispanic Origin and Race categories. Ancestry percentages are based on the 2006-2010 American Community Survey population (not shown); ‡ Numbers in parentheses indicate the number of people reporting a single ancestry; * Numbers in parentheses indicate the number of persons reporting this race alone, not in combination with any other race; Please refer to the Explanation of Data for more information.

Venango County

Population: 54,984

Ancestry	Population	%
Afghan (0)	0	<0.01
African, Sub-Saharan (48)	70	0.13
African (38)	47	0.08
Cape Verdean (0)	0	<0.01
Ethiopian (0)	0	<0.01
Ghanaian (0)	0	<0.01
Kenyan (0)	0	<0.01
Liberian (0)	0	<0.01
Nigerian (0)	0	<0.01
Senegalese (0)	0	<0.01
Sierra Leonean (0)	0	<0.01
Somalian (0)	0	<0.01
South African (10)	23	0.04
Sudanese (0)	0	<0.01
Ugandan (0)	0	<0.01
Zimbabwean (0)	0	<0.01
Other Sub-Saharan African (0)	0	<0.01
Albanian (0)	0	<0.01
Alsatian (2)	2	<0.01
American (3,350)	3,350	6.06
Arab (32)	52	0.09
Arab (0)	0	<0.01
Egyptian (18)	18	0.03
Iraqi (0)	0	<0.01
Jordanian (0)	0	<0.01
Lebanese (14)	34	0.06
Moroccan (0)	0	<0.01
Palestinian (0)	0	<0.01
Syrian (0)	0	<0.01
Other Arab (0)	0	<0.01
Armenian (0)	0	<0.01
Assyrian/Chaldean/Syriac (3)	3	0.01
Australian (0)	11	0.02
Austrian (10)	102	0.18
Basque (18)	35	0.06
Belgian (9)	120	0.22
Brazilian (0)	0	<0.01
British (18)	71	0.13
Bulgarian (0)	0	<0.01
Cajun (0)	0	<0.01
Canadian (35)	43	0.08
Carpatho Rusyn (0)	0	<0.01
Celtic (0)	0	<0.01
Croatian (63)	170	0.31
Cypriot (0)	0	<0.01
Czech (53)	207	0.37
Czechoslovakian (20)	111	0.20
Danish (0)	44	0.08
Dutch (160)	1,871	3.38
Eastern European (7)	7	0.01
English (2,150)	6,103	11.03
Estonian (0)	0	<0.01
European (338)	357	0.65
Finnish (9)	18	0.03
French, ex. Basque (301)	1,583	2.86
French Canadian (57)	226	0.41
German (7,570)	21,028	38.01
German Russian (0)	0	<0.01
Greek (40)	114	0.21
Guyanese (0)	0	<0.01
Hungarian (102)	452	0.82
Icelander (2)	2	<0.01
Iranian (0)	0	<0.01
Irish (2,048)	9,899	17.89
Israeli (0)	0	<0.01
Italian (1,427)	3,807	6.88
Latvian (0)	6	0.01
Lithuanian (22)	138	0.25
Luxemburger (0)	7	0.01
Macedonian (0)	0	<0.01
Maltese (0)	0	<0.01
New Zealander (0)	0	<0.01
Northern European (0)	0	<0.01
Norwegian (17)	46	0.08
Pennsylvania German (129)	400	0.72

Ancestry	Population	%
Polish (1,130)	2,762	4.99
Portuguese (0)	26	0.05
Romanian (18)	54	0.10
Russian (40)	249	0.45
Scandinavian (13)	46	0.08
Scotch-Irish (859)	2,422	4.38
Scottish (415)	1,517	2.74
Serbian (5)	7	0.01
Slavic (29)	86	0.16
Slovak (169)	425	0.77
Slovene (16)	24	0.04
Soviet Union (0)	0	<0.01
Swedish (287)	857	1.55
Swiss (38)	196	0.35
Turkish (8)	16	0.03
Ukrainian (76)	310	0.56
Welsh (120)	792	1.43
West Indian, ex. Hispanic (26)	26	0.05
Bahamian (0)	0	<0.01
Barbadian (0)	0	<0.01
Belizean (0)	0	<0.01
Bermudan (0)	0	<0.01
British West Indian (0)	0	<0.01
Dutch West Indian (26)	26	0.05
Haitian (0)	0	<0.01
Jamaican (0)	0	<0.01
Trinidadian/Tobagonian (0)	0	<0.01
U.S. Virgin Islander (0)	0	<0.01
West Indian (0)	0	<0.01
Other West Indian (0)	0	<0.01
Yugoslavian (0)	21	0.04

Hispanic Origin	Population	%
Hispanic or Latino (of any race)	478	0.87
Central American, ex. Mexican	30	0.05
Costa Rican	8	0.01
Guatemalan	12	0.02
Honduran	9	0.02
Nicaraguan	0	<0.01
Panamanian	1	<0.01
Salvadoran	0	<0.01
Other Central American	0	<0.01
Cuban	32	0.06
Dominican Republic	7	0.01
Mexican	173	0.31
Puerto Rican	130	0.24
South American	32	0.06
Argentinean	0	<0.01
Bolivian	1	<0.01
Chilean	1	<0.01
Colombian	9	0.02
Ecuadorian	7	0.01
Paraguayan	2	<0.01
Peruvian	7	0.01
Uruguayan	0	<0.01
Venezuelan	5	0.01
Other South American	0	<0.01
Other Hispanic or Latino	74	0.13

Race*	Population	%
African-American/Black (571)	896	1.63
Not Hispanic (567)	882	1.60
Hispanic (4)	14	0.03
American Indian/Alaska Native (85)	298	0.54
Not Hispanic (81)	284	0.52
Hispanic (4)	14	0.03
Alaska Athabascan (Ala. Nat.) (2)	2	<0.01
Aleut (Alaska Native) (0)	1	<0.01
Apache (1)	7	0.01
Arapaho (0)	0	<0.01
Blackfeet (4)	15	0.03
Canadian/French Am. Ind. (0)	0	<0.01
Central American Ind. (0)	0	<0.01
Cherokee (10)	63	0.11
Cheyenne (1)	1	<0.01
Chickasaw (0)	0	<0.01
Chippewa (6)	11	0.02
Choctaw (4)	6	0.01
Colville (0)	0	<0.01

	Population	%
Comanche (1)	2	<0.01
Cree (0)	0	<0.01
Creek (0)	0	<0.01
Crow (0)	0	<0.01
Delaware (2)	2	<0.01
Hopi (0)	0	<0.01
Houma (0)	0	<0.01
Inupiat (Alaska Native) (0)	1	<0.01
Iroquois (17)	45	0.08
Kiowa (0)	0	<0.01
Lumbee (0)	0	<0.01
Menominee (0)	0	<0.01
Mexican American Ind. (0)	2	<0.01
Navajo (2)	2	<0.01
Osage (0)	0	<0.01
Ottawa (0)	0	<0.01
Paiute (0)	0	<0.01
Pima (0)	0	<0.01
Potawatomi (0)	0	<0.01
Pueblo (2)	2	<0.01
Puget Sound Salish (0)	0	<0.01
Seminole (1)	1	<0.01
Shoshone (0)	0	<0.01
Sioux (2)	14	0.03
South American Ind. (1)	3	0.01
Spanish American Ind. (0)	0	<0.01
Tlingit-Haida (Alaska Native) (1)	1	<0.01
Tohono O'Odham (0)	0	<0.01
Tsimshian (Alaska Native) (0)	0	<0.01
Ute (0)	0	<0.01
Yakama (0)	0	<0.01
Yaqui (0)	1	<0.01
Yuman (0)	0	<0.01
Yup'ik (Alaska Native) (0)	0	<0.01
Asian (197)	287	0.52
Not Hispanic (196)	279	0.51
Hispanic (1)	8	0.01
Bangladeshi (0)	0	<0.01
Bhutanese (0)	0	<0.01
Burmese (0)	0	<0.01
Cambodian (2)	2	<0.01
Chinese, ex. Taiwanese (44)	57	0.10
Filipino (29)	51	0.09
Hmong (0)	0	<0.01
Indian (43)	52	0.09
Indonesian (1)	1	<0.01
Japanese (19)	33	0.06
Korean (26)	44	0.08
Laotian (1)	3	0.01
Malaysian (0)	0	<0.01
Nepalese (0)	0	<0.01
Pakistani (0)	0	<0.01
Sri Lankan (0)	0	<0.01
Taiwanese (1)	1	<0.01
Thai (6)	9	0.02
Vietnamese (12)	14	0.03
Hawaii Native/Pacific Islander (11)	36	0.07
Not Hispanic (10)	31	0.06
Hispanic (1)	5	0.01
Fijian (0)	0	<0.01
Guamanian/Chamorro (4)	7	0.01
Marshallese (0)	0	<0.01
Native Hawaiian (4)	18	0.03
Samoan (2)	3	0.01
Tongan (0)	0	<0.01
White (53,390)	53,979	98.17
Not Hispanic (53,052)	53,609	97.50
Hispanic (338)	370	0.67

Notes: † The Census 2010 population figure is used to calculate the percentages in the Hispanic Origin and Race categories. Ancestry percentages are based on the 2006-2010 American Community Survey population (not shown); ‡ Numbers in parentheses indicate the number of people reporting a single ancestry; * Numbers in parentheses indicate the number of persons reporting this race alone, not in combination with any other race; Please refer to the Explanation of Data for more information.

Warren County

Population: 41,815

Ancestry	Population	%
Afghan (0)	0	<0.01
African, Sub-Saharan (0)	0	<0.01
African (0)	0	<0.01
Cape Verdean (0)	0	<0.01
Ethiopian (0)	0	<0.01
Ghanaian (0)	0	<0.01
Kenyan (0)	0	<0.01
Liberian (0)	0	<0.01
Nigerian (0)	0	<0.01
Senegalese (0)	0	<0.01
Sierra Leonean (0)	0	<0.01
Somalian (0)	0	<0.01
South African (0)	0	<0.01
Sudanese (0)	0	<0.01
Ugandan (0)	0	<0.01
Zimbabwean (0)	0	<0.01
Other Sub-Saharan African (0)	0	<0.01
Albanian (0)	24	0.06
Alsatian (12)	12	0.03
American (2,020)	2,020	4.82
Arab (38)	63	0.15
Arab (0)	4	0.01
Egyptian (6)	6	0.01
Iraqi (0)	0	<0.01
Jordanian (0)	0	<0.01
Lebanese (26)	37	0.09
Moroccan (0)	0	<0.01
Palestinian (0)	0	<0.01
Syrian (0)	10	0.02
Other Arab (6)	6	0.01
Armenian (0)	0	<0.01
Assyrian/Chaldean/Syriac (0)	0	<0.01
Australian (0)	0	<0.01
Austrian (48)	97	0.23
Basque (0)	0	<0.01
Belgian (3)	20	0.05
Brazilian (9)	9	0.02
British (58)	102	0.24
Bulgarian (0)	0	<0.01
Cajun (0)	0	<0.01
Canadian (31)	63	0.15
Carpatho Rusyn (0)	2	<0.01
Celtic (0)	0	<0.01
Croatian (18)	80	0.19
Cypriot (0)	0	<0.01
Czech (152)	294	0.70
Czechoslovakian (21)	49	0.12
Danish (189)	438	1.05
Dutch (235)	1,364	3.26
Eastern European (30)	35	0.08
English (2,339)	6,778	16.19
Estonian (0)	0	<0.01
European (190)	221	0.53
Finnish (0)	0	<0.01
French, ex. Basque (113)	988	2.36
French Canadian (77)	251	0.60
German (4,844)	12,840	30.66
German Russian (0)	0	<0.01
Greek (36)	79	0.19
Guyanese (0)	0	<0.01
Hungarian (75)	327	0.78
Icelander (0)	0	<0.01
Iranian (10)	10	0.02
Irish (1,446)	6,004	14.34
Israeli (0)	15	0.04
Italian (1,439)	3,981	9.51
Latvian (0)	0	<0.01
Lithuanian (4)	69	0.16
Luxemburger (0)	0	<0.01
Macedonian (0)	0	<0.01
Maltese (0)	0	<0.01
New Zealander (3)	11	0.03
Northern European (36)	36	0.09
Norwegian (116)	199	0.48
Pennsylvania German (263)	510	1.22

Ancestry	Population	%
Polish (1,167)	2,760	6.59
Portuguese (10)	21	0.05
Romanian (3)	3	0.01
Russian (57)	293	0.70
Scandinavian (30)	39	0.09
Scotch-Irish (418)	1,261	3.01
Scottish (299)	881	2.10
Serbian (3)	8	0.02
Slavic (28)	55	0.13
Slovak (194)	439	1.05
Slovene (13)	57	0.14
Soviet Union (0)	0	<0.01
Swedish (1,806)	5,469	13.06
Swiss (96)	454	1.08
Turkish (0)	0	<0.01
Ukrainian (40)	148	0.35
Welsh (67)	464	1.11
West Indian, ex. Hispanic (0)	2	<0.01
Bahamian (0)	0	<0.01
Barbadian (0)	0	<0.01
Belizean (0)	0	<0.01
Bermudan (0)	0	<0.01
British West Indian (0)	0	<0.01
Dutch West Indian (0)	2	<0.01
Haitian (0)	0	<0.01
Jamaican (0)	0	<0.01
Trinidadian/Tobagonian (0)	0	<0.01
U.S. Virgin Islander (0)	0	<0.01
West Indian (0)	0	<0.01
Other West Indian (0)	0	<0.01
Yugoslavian (21)	81	0.19

Hispanic Origin	Population	%
Hispanic or Latino (of any race)	305	0.73
Central American, ex. Mexican	14	0.03
Costa Rican	0	<0.01
Guatemalan	9	0.02
Honduran	2	<0.01
Nicaraguan	0	<0.01
Panamanian	2	<0.01
Salvadoran	0	<0.01
Other Central American	1	<0.01
Cuban	15	0.04
Dominican Republic	5	0.01
Mexican	125	0.30
Puerto Rican	75	0.18
South American	23	0.06
Argentinean	5	0.01
Bolivian	0	<0.01
Chilean	5	0.01
Colombian	10	0.02
Ecuadorian	0	<0.01
Paraguayan	1	<0.01
Peruvian	1	<0.01
Uruguayan	0	<0.01
Venezuelan	1	<0.01
Other South American	0	<0.01
Other Hispanic or Latino	48	0.11

Race*	Population	%
African-American/Black (149)	241	0.58
Not Hispanic (136)	221	0.53
Hispanic (13)	20	0.05
American Indian/Alaska Native (80)	222	0.53
Not Hispanic (71)	207	0.50
Hispanic (9)	15	0.04
Alaska Athabascan (Ala. Nat.) (0)	0	<0.01
Aleut (Alaska Native) (0)	0	<0.01
Apache (1)	2	<0.01
Arapaho (0)	0	<0.01
Blackfeet (0)	13	0.03
Canadian/French Am. Ind. (0)	0	<0.01
Central American Ind. (0)	0	<0.01
Cherokee (5)	28	0.07
Cheyenne (0)	0	<0.01
Chickasaw (0)	2	<0.01
Chippewa (3)	3	0.01
Choctaw (3)	3	0.01
Colville (0)	0	<0.01

Race*	Population	%
Comanche (0)	0	<0.01
Cree (0)	0	<0.01
Creek (0)	0	<0.01
Crow (0)	0	<0.01
Delaware (1)	2	<0.01
Hopi (0)	0	<0.01
Houma (0)	0	<0.01
Inupiat (Alaska Native) (0)	0	<0.01
Iroquois (25)	59	0.14
Kiowa (0)	0	<0.01
Lumbee (0)	0	<0.01
Menominee (0)	0	<0.01
Mexican American Ind. (6)	7	0.02
Navajo (0)	0	<0.01
Osage (0)	0	<0.01
Ottawa (0)	0	<0.01
Paiute (0)	0	<0.01
Pima (1)	1	<0.01
Potawatomi (0)	0	<0.01
Pueblo (0)	0	<0.01
Puget Sound Salish (0)	0	<0.01
Seminole (1)	1	<0.01
Shoshone (0)	0	<0.01
Sioux (0)	5	0.01
South American Ind. (0)	1	<0.01
Spanish American Ind. (0)	0	<0.01
Tlingit-Haida (Alaska Native) (0)	0	<0.01
Tohono O'Odham (0)	0	<0.01
Tsimshian (Alaska Native) (0)	0	<0.01
Ute (0)	0	<0.01
Yakama (0)	0	<0.01
Yaqui (0)	0	<0.01
Yuman (0)	0	<0.01
Yup'ik (Alaska Native) (0)	0	<0.01
Asian (157)	231	0.55
Not Hispanic (156)	230	0.55
Hispanic (1)	1	<0.01
Bangladeshi (0)	0	<0.01
Bhutanese (0)	0	<0.01
Burmese (0)	0	<0.01
Cambodian (0)	0	<0.01
Chinese, ex. Taiwanese (34)	36	0.09
Filipino (20)	47	0.11
Hmong (0)	0	<0.01
Indian (45)	60	0.14
Indonesian (0)	0	<0.01
Japanese (14)	23	0.06
Korean (21)	35	0.08
Laotian (0)	0	<0.01
Malaysian (1)	1	<0.01
Nepalese (0)	0	<0.01
Pakistani (6)	7	0.02
Sri Lankan (0)	0	<0.01
Taiwanese (2)	2	<0.01
Thai (0)	0	<0.01
Vietnamese (6)	13	0.03
Hawaii Native/Pacific Islander (12)	33	0.08
Not Hispanic (12)	29	0.07
Hispanic (0)	4	0.01
Fijian (0)	0	<0.01
Guamanian/Chamorro (5)	6	0.01
Marshallese (0)	0	<0.01
Native Hawaiian (5)	10	0.02
Samoan (1)	1	<0.01
Tongan (0)	0	<0.01
White (41,031)	41,352	98.89
Not Hispanic (40,827)	41,125	98.35
Hispanic (204)	227	0.54

Notes: † The Census 2010 population figure is used to calculate the percentages in the Hispanic Origin and Race categories. Ancestry percentages are based on the 2006-2010 American Community Survey population (not shown); ‡ Numbers in parentheses indicate the number of people reporting a single ancestry; * Numbers in parentheses indicate the number of persons reporting this race alone, not in combination with any other race; Please refer to the Explanation of Data for more information.

Washington County

Population: 207,820

Ancestry	Population	%
Afghan (0)	0	<0.01
African, Sub-Saharan (263)	374	0.18
African (263)	374	0.18
Cape Verdean (0)	0	<0.01
Ethiopian (0)	0	<0.01
Ghanaian (0)	0	<0.01
Kenyan (0)	0	<0.01
Liberian (0)	0	<0.01
Nigerian (0)	0	<0.01
Senegalese (0)	0	<0.01
Sierra Leonean (0)	0	<0.01
Somalian (0)	0	<0.01
South African (0)	0	<0.01
Sudanese (0)	0	<0.01
Ugandan (0)	0	<0.01
Zimbabwean (0)	0	<0.01
Other Sub-Saharan African (0)	0	<0.01
Albanian (2)	18	0.01
Alsatian (0)	12	0.01
American (6,888)	6,888	3.33
Arab (400)	1,011	0.49
Arab (21)	21	0.01
Egyptian (25)	31	0.01
Iraqi (0)	0	<0.01
Jordanian (0)	0	<0.01
Lebanese (163)	408	0.20
Moroccan (0)	0	<0.01
Palestinian (0)	0	<0.01
Syrian (191)	538	0.26
Other Arab (0)	13	0.01
Armenian (0)	0	<0.01
Assyrian/Chaldean/Syriac (0)	0	<0.01
Australian (20)	55	0.03
Austrian (237)	1,205	0.58
Basque (0)	0	<0.01
Belgian (255)	1,192	0.58
Brazilian (28)	44	0.02
British (208)	402	0.19
Bulgarian (44)	85	0.04
Cajun (0)	0	<0.01
Canadian (74)	162	0.08
Carpatho Rusyn (41)	161	0.08
Celtic (0)	11	0.01
Croatian (796)	2,617	1.26
Cypriot (0)	0	<0.01
Czech (379)	1,818	0.88
Czechoslovakian (457)	957	0.46
Danish (62)	186	0.09
Dutch (343)	3,182	1.54
Eastern European (208)	249	0.12
English (6,352)	25,465	12.30
Estonian (0)	0	<0.01
European (1,181)	1,237	0.60
Finnish (46)	266	0.13
French, ex. Basque (862)	6,110	2.95
French Canadian (111)	274	0.13
German (12,080)	55,462	26.79
German Russian (0)	0	<0.01
Greek (647)	1,749	0.84
Guyanese (0)	0	<0.01
Hungarian (1,833)	5,712	2.76
Icelander (0)	0	<0.01
Iranian (0)	0	<0.01
Irish (8,233)	39,239	18.96
Israeli (0)	0	<0.01
Italian (14,445)	39,407	19.04
Latvian (13)	44	0.02
Lithuanian (383)	1,529	0.74
Luxemburger (3)	3	<0.01
Macedonian (0)	45	0.02
Maltese (0)	0	<0.01
New Zealander (0)	0	<0.01
Northern European (63)	63	0.03
Norwegian (116)	462	0.22
Pennsylvania German (245)	530	0.26

	Population	%
Polish (6,873)	22,604	10.92
Portuguese (70)	214	0.10
Romanian (63)	88	0.04
Russian (1,152)	4,772	2.31
Scandinavian (29)	29	0.01
Scotch-Irish (3,898)	11,333	5.48
Scottish (967)	4,446	2.15
Serbian (220)	967	0.47
Slavic (245)	596	0.29
Slovak (3,378)	9,186	4.44
Slovene (584)	1,911	0.92
Soviet Union (0)	0	<0.01
Swedish (254)	1,239	0.60
Swiss (144)	633	0.31
Turkish (0)	25	0.01
Ukrainian (604)	1,738	0.84
Welsh (455)	2,485	1.20
West Indian, ex. Hispanic (7)	67	0.03
Bahamian (0)	0	<0.01
Barbadian (0)	31	0.01
Belizean (0)	0	<0.01
Bermudan (0)	0	<0.01
British West Indian (0)	0	<0.01
Dutch West Indian (7)	7	<0.01
Haitian (0)	8	<0.01
Jamaican (0)	21	0.01
Trinidadian/Tobagonian (0)	0	<0.01
U.S. Virgin Islander (0)	0	<0.01
West Indian (0)	0	<0.01
Other West Indian (0)	0	<0.01
Yugoslavian (130)	283	0.14

Hispanic Origin	Population	%
Hispanic or Latino (of any race)	2,366	1.14
Central American, ex. Mexican	108	0.05
Costa Rican	4	<0.01
Guatemalan	43	0.02
Honduran	20	0.01
Nicaraguan	10	<0.01
Panamanian	20	0.01
Salvadoran	11	0.01
Other Central American	0	<0.01
Cuban	78	0.04
Dominican Republic	24	0.01
Mexican	943	0.45
Puerto Rican	417	0.20
South American	132	0.06
Argentinean	20	0.01
Bolivian	4	<0.01
Chilean	17	0.01
Colombian	34	0.02
Ecuadorian	20	0.01
Paraguayan	0	<0.01
Peruvian	22	0.01
Uruguayan	2	<0.01
Venezuelan	13	0.01
Other South American	0	<0.01
Other Hispanic or Latino	664	0.32

Race*	Population	%
African-American/Black (6,757)	8,767	4.22
Not Hispanic (6,650)	8,556	4.12
Hispanic (107)	211	0.10
American Indian/Alaska Native (251)	1,036	0.50
Not Hispanic (214)	952	0.46
Hispanic (37)	84	0.04
Alaska Athabascan (Ala. Nat.) (2)	4	<0.01
Aleut (Alaska Native) (0)	1	<0.01
Apache (5)	15	0.01
Arapaho (0)	0	<0.01
Blackfeet (1)	51	0.02
Canadian/French Am. Ind. (0)	0	<0.01
Central American Ind. (0)	0	<0.01
Cherokee (52)	291	0.14
Cheyenne (0)	4	<0.01
Chickasaw (1)	1	<0.01
Chippewa (4)	11	0.01
Choctaw (2)	10	<0.01
Colville (0)	0	<0.01

	Population	%
Comanche (0)	0	<0.01
Cree (0)	2	<0.01
Creek (4)	7	<0.01
Crow (1)	11	0.01
Delaware (3)	11	0.01
Hopi (0)	0	<0.01
Houma (1)	1	<0.01
Inupiat (Alaska Native) (5)	5	<0.01
Iroquois (7)	39	0.02
Kiowa (0)	0	<0.01
Lumbee (2)	2	<0.01
Menominee (0)	0	<0.01
Mexican American Ind. (10)	15	0.01
Navajo (2)	11	0.01
Osage (0)	1	<0.01
Ottawa (0)	0	<0.01
Paiute (0)	0	<0.01
Pima (0)	0	<0.01
Potawatomi (5)	5	<0.01
Pueblo (1)	1	<0.01
Puget Sound Salish (0)	0	<0.01
Seminole (0)	0	<0.01
Shoshone (0)	0	<0.01
Sioux (9)	23	0.01
South American Ind. (4)	4	<0.01
Spanish American Ind. (0)	0	<0.01
Tlingit-Haida (Alaska Native) (0)	0	<0.01
Tohono O'Odham (0)	0	<0.01
Tsimshian (Alaska Native) (0)	0	<0.01
Ute (0)	0	<0.01
Yakama (0)	0	<0.01
Yaqui (0)	4	<0.01
Yuman (0)	0	<0.01
Yup'ik (Alaska Native) (0)	0	<0.01
Asian (1,327)	1,784	0.86
Not Hispanic (1,313)	1,725	0.83
Hispanic (14)	59	0.03
Bangladeshi (4)	7	<0.01
Bhutanese (0)	0	<0.01
Burmese (4)	4	<0.01
Cambodian (3)	3	<0.01
Chinese, ex. Taiwanese (319)	388	0.19
Filipino (161)	303	0.15
Hmong (0)	0	<0.01
Indian (447)	512	0.25
Indonesian (19)	30	0.01
Japanese (60)	128	0.06
Korean (115)	164	0.08
Laotian (7)	8	<0.01
Malaysian (2)	3	<0.01
Nepalese (0)	0	<0.01
Pakistani (29)	32	0.02
Sri Lankan (2)	4	<0.01
Taiwanese (8)	10	<0.01
Thai (22)	46	0.02
Vietnamese (86)	106	0.05
Hawaii Native/Pacific Islander (31)	105	0.05
Not Hispanic (28)	94	0.05
Hispanic (3)	11	0.01
Fijian (0)	0	<0.01
Guamanian/Chamorro (5)	16	0.01
Marshallese (0)	0	<0.01
Native Hawaiian (12)	38	0.02
Samoan (5)	16	0.01
Tongan (0)	1	<0.01
White (195,657)	198,640	95.58
Not Hispanic (194,171)	196,925	94.76
Hispanic (1,486)	1,715	0.83

*Notes: † The Census 2010 population figure is used to calculate the percentages in the Hispanic Origin and Race categories. Ancestry percentages are based on the 2006-2010 American Community Survey population (not shown); ‡ Numbers in parentheses indicate the number of people reporting a single ancestry; * Numbers in parentheses indicate the number of persons reporting this race alone, not in combination with any other race; Please refer to the Explanation of Data for more information.*

Wayne County

Population: 52,822

Ancestry	Population	%
Afghan (1)	1	<0.01
African, Sub-Saharan (73)	140	0.27
African (53)	120	0.23
Cape Verdean (0)	0	<0.01
Ethiopian (0)	0	<0.01
Ghanaian (0)	0	<0.01
Kenyan (0)	0	<0.01
Liberian (0)	0	<0.01
Nigerian (20)	20	0.04
Senegalese (0)	0	<0.01
Sierra Leonean (0)	0	<0.01
Somalian (0)	0	<0.01
South African (0)	0	<0.01
Sudanese (0)	0	<0.01
Ugandan (0)	0	<0.01
Zimbabwean (0)	0	<0.01
Other Sub-Saharan African (0)	0	<0.01
Albanian (0)	4	0.01
Alsatian (0)	0	<0.01
American (3,153)	3,153	6.03
Arab (105)	222	0.42
Arab (10)	10	0.02
Egyptian (3)	3	0.01
Iraqi (0)	0	<0.01
Jordanian (0)	0	<0.01
Lebanese (7)	61	0.12
Moroccan (0)	0	<0.01
Palestinian (28)	31	0.06
Syrian (57)	117	0.22
Other Arab (0)	0	<0.01
Armenian (3)	33	0.06
Assyrian/Chaldean/Syriac (4)	4	0.01
Australian (8)	8	0.02
Austrian (108)	356	0.68
Basque (0)	0	<0.01
Belgian (0)	33	0.06
Brazilian (35)	35	0.07
British (38)	126	0.24
Bulgarian (6)	6	0.01
Cajun (0)	0	<0.01
Canadian (29)	62	0.12
Carpatho Rusyn (10)	10	0.02
Celtic (0)	7	0.01
Croatian (10)	48	0.09
Cypriot (0)	0	<0.01
Czech (74)	221	0.42
Czechoslovakian (40)	66	0.13
Danish (10)	240	0.46
Dutch (185)	1,322	2.53
Eastern European (7)	7	0.01
English (1,501)	7,105	13.58
Estonian (30)	37	0.07
European (69)	86	0.16
Finnish (23)	44	0.08
French, ex. Basque (179)	1,378	2.63
French Canadian (22)	104	0.20
German (4,999)	17,212	32.91
German Russian (0)	0	<0.01
Greek (156)	419	0.80
Guyanese (0)	0	<0.01
Hungarian (126)	443	0.85
Icelander (0)	0	<0.01
Iranian (9)	12	0.02
Irish (3,331)	12,685	24.25
Israeli (5)	5	0.01
Italian (2,654)	6,430	12.29
Latvian (7)	21	0.04
Lithuanian (146)	460	0.88
Luxemburger (0)	0	<0.01
Macedonian (0)	0	<0.01
Maltese (0)	0	<0.01
New Zealander (0)	0	<0.01
Northern European (2)	2	<0.01
Norwegian (191)	511	0.98
Pennsylvania German (161)	253	0.48

Ancestry	Population	%
Polish (1,717)	5,447	10.41
Portuguese (23)	101	0.19
Romanian (69)	118	0.23
Russian (304)	1,143	2.19
Scandinavian (30)	77	0.15
Scotch-Irish (216)	632	1.21
Scottish (261)	910	1.74
Serbian (10)	10	0.02
Slavic (21)	46	0.09
Slovak (233)	812	1.55
Slovene (94)	202	0.39
Soviet Union (0)	0	<0.01
Swedish (64)	306	0.59
Swiss (13)	190	0.36
Turkish (0)	0	<0.01
Ukrainian (136)	303	0.58
Welsh (296)	1,375	2.63
West Indian, ex. Hispanic (41)	136	0.26
Bahamian (0)	0	<0.01
Barbadian (0)	0	<0.01
Belizean (0)	0	<0.01
Bermudan (0)	47	0.09
British West Indian (0)	0	<0.01
Dutch West Indian (0)	0	<0.01
Haitian (12)	36	0.07
Jamaican (18)	35	0.07
Trinidadian/Tobagonian (0)	7	0.01
U.S. Virgin Islander (0)	0	<0.01
West Indian (11)	11	0.02
Other West Indian (0)	0	<0.01
Yugoslavian (16)	45	0.09

Hispanic Origin	Population	%
Hispanic or Latino (of any race)	1,816	3.44
Central American, ex. Mexican	56	0.11
Costa Rican	6	0.01
Guatemalan	7	0.01
Honduran	13	0.02
Nicaraguan	3	0.01
Panamanian	12	0.02
Salvadoran	15	0.03
Other Central American	0	<0.01
Cuban	86	0.16
Dominican Republic	68	0.13
Mexican	352	0.67
Puerto Rican	821	1.55
South American	135	0.26
Argentinean	18	0.03
Bolivian	3	0.01
Chilean	17	0.03
Colombian	40	0.08
Ecuadorian	34	0.06
Paraguayan	1	<0.01
Peruvian	15	0.03
Uruguayan	1	<0.01
Venezuelan	4	0.01
Other South American	2	<0.01
Other Hispanic or Latino	298	0.56

Race*	Population	%
African-American/Black (1,644)	1,881	3.56
Not Hispanic (1,563)	1,768	3.35
Hispanic (81)	113	0.21
American Indian/Alaska Native (101)	286	0.54
Not Hispanic (85)	250	0.47
Hispanic (16)	36	0.07
Alaska Athabascan (Ala. Nat.) (0)	0	<0.01
Aleut (Alaska Native) (0)	0	<0.01
Apache (3)	3	0.01
Arapaho (0)	0	<0.01
Blackfeet (3)	8	0.02
Canadian/French Am. Ind. (0)	0	<0.01
Central American Ind. (0)	0	<0.01
Cherokee (14)	48	0.09
Cheyenne (1)	1	<0.01
Chickasaw (0)	0	<0.01
Chippewa (1)	7	0.01
Choctaw (0)	1	<0.01
Colville (0)	0	<0.01

Race*	Population	%
Comanche (0)	0	<0.01
Cree (0)	1	<0.01
Creek (1)	2	<0.01
Crow (2)	2	<0.01
Delaware (4)	14	0.03
Hopi (0)	0	<0.01
Houma (0)	0	<0.01
Inupiat (Alaska Native) (0)	0	<0.01
Iroquois (4)	21	0.04
Kiowa (0)	0	<0.01
Lumbee (12)	12	0.02
Menominee (0)	0	<0.01
Mexican American Ind. (1)	3	0.01
Navajo (0)	4	0.01
Osage (0)	0	<0.01
Ottawa (1)	1	<0.01
Paiute (0)	0	<0.01
Pima (0)	0	<0.01
Potawatomi (0)	2	<0.01
Pueblo (0)	0	<0.01
Puget Sound Salish (0)	0	<0.01
Seminole (0)	0	<0.01
Shoshone (1)	2	<0.01
Sioux (0)	1	<0.01
South American Ind. (5)	9	0.02
Spanish American Ind. (0)	0	<0.01
Tlingit-Haida (Alaska Native) (0)	0	<0.01
Tohono O'Odham (0)	0	<0.01
Tsimshian (Alaska Native) (0)	0	<0.01
Ute (0)	0	<0.01
Yakama (0)	0	<0.01
Yaqui (0)	0	<0.01
Yuman (0)	0	<0.01
Yup'ik (Alaska Native) (0)	0	<0.01
Asian (255)	385	0.73
Not Hispanic (252)	371	0.70
Hispanic (3)	14	0.03
Bangladeshi (4)	4	0.01
Bhutanese (1)	4	0.01
Burmese (0)	0	<0.01
Cambodian (1)	1	<0.01
Chinese, ex. Taiwanese (60)	71	0.13
Filipino (36)	66	0.12
Hmong (1)	1	<0.01
Indian (49)	66	0.12
Indonesian (3)	8	0.02
Japanese (17)	34	0.06
Korean (42)	63	0.12
Laotian (4)	4	0.01
Malaysian (1)	1	<0.01
Nepalese (0)	0	<0.01
Pakistani (4)	5	0.01
Sri Lankan (0)	0	<0.01
Taiwanese (4)	4	0.01
Thai (4)	4	0.01
Vietnamese (13)	18	0.03
Hawaii Native/Pacific Islander (4)	24	0.05
Not Hispanic (3)	21	0.04
Hispanic (1)	3	0.01
Fijian (0)	0	<0.01
Guamanian/Chamorro (2)	2	<0.01
Marshallese (0)	0	<0.01
Native Hawaiian (2)	7	0.01
Samoan (0)	1	<0.01
Tongan (0)	0	<0.01
White (49,759)	50,301	95.23
Not Hispanic (48,590)	49,038	92.84
Hispanic (1,169)	1,263	2.39

*Notes: † The Census 2010 population figure is used to calculate the percentages in the Hispanic Origin and Race categories. Ancestry percentages are based on the 2006-2010 American Community Survey population (not shown); ‡ Numbers in parentheses indicate the number of people reporting a single ancestry; * Numbers in parentheses indicate the number of persons reporting this race alone, not in combination with any other race; Please refer to the Explanation of Data for more information.*

Westmoreland County

Population: 365,169

Ancestry	Population	%
Afghan (0)	0	<0.01
African, Sub-Saharan (1,274)	1,539	0.42
African (1,214)	1,431	0.39
Cape Verdean (0)	0	<0.01
Ethiopian (0)	0	<0.01
Ghanaian (0)	0	<0.01
Kenyan (8)	8	<0.01
Liberian (0)	0	<0.01
Nigerian (43)	56	0.02
Senegalese (0)	0	<0.01
Sierra Leonean (0)	0	<0.01
Somalian (0)	0	<0.01
South African (9)	44	0.01
Sudanese (0)	0	<0.01
Ugandan (0)	0	<0.01
Zimbabwean (0)	0	<0.01
Other Sub-Saharan African (0)	0	<0.01
Albanian (15)	78	0.02
Alsatian (10)	10	<0.01
American (14,148)	14,148	3.87
Arab (893)	2,171	0.59
Arab (5)	12	<0.01
Egyptian (30)	43	0.01
Iraqi (0)	0	<0.01
Jordanian (0)	0	<0.01
Lebanese (244)	592	0.16
Moroccan (12)	55	0.02
Palestinian (9)	25	0.01
Syrian (497)	1,348	0.37
Other Arab (96)	96	0.03
Armenian (4)	111	0.03
Assyrian/Chaldean/Syriac (0)	0	<0.01
Australian (0)	36	0.01
Austrian (358)	1,741	0.48
Basque (0)	0	<0.01
Belgian (88)	610	0.17
Brazilian (0)	107	0.03
British (340)	664	0.18
Bulgarian (0)	0	<0.01
Cajun (0)	0	<0.01
Canadian (202)	562	0.15
Carpatho Rusyn (85)	159	0.04
Celtic (0)	14	<0.01
Croatian (1,627)	4,476	1.22
Cypriot (0)	0	<0.01
Czech (952)	3,606	0.99
Czechoslovakian (535)	1,343	0.37
Danish (186)	405	0.11
Dutch (792)	7,323	2.00
Eastern European (549)	614	0.17
English (8,388)	39,365	10.76
Estonian (0)	0	<0.01
European (1,666)	1,827	0.50
Finnish (82)	335	0.09
French, ex. Basque (542)	6,100	1.67
French Canadian (135)	477	0.13
German (32,728)	121,549	33.22
German Russian (0)	0	<0.01
Greek (788)	1,989	0.54
Guyanese (0)	0	<0.01
Hungarian (2,237)	7,839	2.14
Icelander (23)	51	0.01
Iranian (26)	26	0.01
Irish (12,796)	66,002	18.04
Israeli (0)	0	<0.01
Italian (28,336)	73,381	20.06
Latvian (56)	66	0.02
Lithuanian (832)	2,312	0.63
Luxemburger (0)	0	<0.01
Macedonian (11)	22	0.01
Maltese (10)	23	0.01
New Zealander (0)	0	<0.01
Northern European (39)	39	0.01
Norwegian (220)	815	0.22
Pennsylvania German (1,670)	3,075	0.84

Ancestry	Population	%
Polish (12,851)	39,939	10.92
Portuguese (18)	111	0.03
Romanian (217)	404	0.11
Russian (1,686)	5,734	1.57
Scandinavian (104)	151	0.04
Scotch-Irish (3,606)	11,476	3.14
Scottish (2,086)	8,599	2.35
Serbian (637)	2,351	0.64
Slavic (372)	1,307	0.36
Slovak (9,154)	24,541	6.71
Slovene (499)	1,753	0.48
Soviet Union (0)	0	<0.01
Swedish (798)	4,220	1.15
Swiss (111)	863	0.24
Turkish (0)	0	<0.01
Ukrainian (1,150)	3,303	0.90
Welsh (811)	4,853	1.33
West Indian, ex. Hispanic (84)	270	0.07
Bahamian (0)	0	<0.01
Barbadian (0)	43	0.01
Belizean (0)	0	<0.01
Bermudan (0)	0	<0.01
British West Indian (0)	91	0.02
Dutch West Indian (0)	0	<0.01
Haitian (38)	43	0.01
Jamaican (33)	65	0.02
Trinidadian/Tobagonian (4)	4	<0.01
U.S. Virgin Islander (0)	0	<0.01
West Indian (9)	24	0.01
Other West Indian (0)	0	<0.01
Yugoslavian (214)	525	0.14

Hispanic Origin	Population	%
Hispanic or Latino (of any race)	3,179	0.87
Central American, ex. Mexican	193	0.05
Costa Rican	10	<0.01
Guatemalan	96	0.03
Honduran	23	0.01
Nicaraguan	7	<0.01
Panamanian	27	0.01
Salvadoran	30	0.01
Other Central American	0	<0.01
Cuban	170	0.05
Dominican Republic	61	0.02
Mexican	1,194	0.33
Puerto Rican	742	0.20
South American	223	0.06
Argentinean	34	0.01
Bolivian	15	<0.01
Chilean	23	0.01
Colombian	60	0.02
Ecuadorian	30	0.01
Paraguayan	4	<0.01
Peruvian	26	0.01
Uruguayan	2	<0.01
Venezuelan	28	0.01
Other South American	1	<0.01
Other Hispanic or Latino	596	0.16

Race*	Population	%
African-American/Black (8,562)	11,473	3.14
Not Hispanic (8,425)	11,179	3.06
Hispanic (137)	294	0.08
American Indian/Alaska Native (351)	1,417	0.39
Not Hispanic (305)	1,292	0.35
Hispanic (46)	125	0.03
Alaska Athabascan (Ala. Nat.) (4)	4	<0.01
Aleut (Alaska Native) (0)	2	<0.01
Apache (3)	25	0.01
Arapaho (0)	1	<0.01
Blackfeet (5)	60	0.02
Canadian/French Am. Ind. (2)	4	<0.01
Central American Ind. (5)	5	<0.01
Cherokee (58)	335	0.09
Cheyenne (0)	4	<0.01
Chickasaw (0)	12	<0.01
Chippewa (3)	7	<0.01
Choctaw (3)	17	<0.01
Colville (0)	0	<0.01

Race*	Population	%
Comanche (2)	5	<0.01
Cree (0)	2	<0.01
Creek (9)	20	0.01
Crow (3)	5	<0.01
Delaware (10)	23	0.01
Hopi (0)	0	<0.01
Houma (1)	1	<0.01
Inupiat (Alaska Native) (3)	4	<0.01
Iroquois (20)	77	0.02
Kiowa (1)	1	<0.01
Lumbee (3)	4	<0.01
Menominee (0)	0	<0.01
Mexican American Ind. (8)	13	<0.01
Navajo (8)	21	0.01
Osage (0)	3	<0.01
Ottawa (0)	1	<0.01
Paiute (0)	0	<0.01
Pima (1)	1	<0.01
Potawatomi (1)	4	<0.01
Pueblo (1)	1	<0.01
Puget Sound Salish (2)	2	<0.01
Seminole (0)	10	<0.01
Shoshone (1)	2	<0.01
Sioux (9)	43	0.01
South American Ind. (3)	6	<0.01
Spanish American Ind. (0)	1	<0.01
Tlingit-Haida (Alaska Native) (1)	1	<0.01
Tohono O'Odham (0)	0	<0.01
Tsimshian (Alaska Native) (0)	0	<0.01
Ute (0)	0	<0.01
Yakama (0)	0	<0.01
Yaqui (0)	0	<0.01
Yuman (0)	0	<0.01
Yup'ik (Alaska Native) (0)	0	<0.01
Asian (2,704)	3,444	0.94
Not Hispanic (2,692)	3,392	0.93
Hispanic (12)	52	0.01
Bangladeshi (13)	16	<0.01
Bhutanese (0)	0	<0.01
Burmese (6)	6	<0.01
Cambodian (8)	16	<0.01
Chinese, ex. Taiwanese (805)	932	0.26
Filipino (228)	422	0.12
Hmong (0)	1	<0.01
Indian (738)	834	0.23
Indonesian (7)	20	0.01
Japanese (92)	210	0.06
Korean (247)	348	0.10
Laotian (8)	19	0.01
Malaysian (3)	3	<0.01
Nepalese (0)	0	<0.01
Pakistani (97)	104	0.03
Sri Lankan (14)	16	<0.01
Taiwanese (37)	47	0.01
Thai (40)	65	0.02
Vietnamese (253)	310	0.08
Hawaii Native/Pacific Islander (62)	182	0.05
Not Hispanic (59)	162	0.04
Hispanic (3)	20	0.01
Fijian (0)	0	<0.01
Guamanian/Chamorro (6)	20	0.01
Marshallese (1)	1	<0.01
Native Hawaiian (17)	54	0.01
Samoan (17)	32	0.01
Tongan (0)	0	<0.01
White (348,182)	352,403	96.50
Not Hispanic (346,111)	350,052	95.86
Hispanic (2,071)	2,351	0.64

Notes: † The Census 2010 population figure is used to calculate the percentages in the Hispanic Origin and Race categories. Ancestry percentages are based on the 2006-2010 American Community Survey population (not shown); ‡ Numbers in parentheses indicate the number of people reporting a single ancestry; * Numbers in parentheses indicate the number of persons reporting this race alone, not in combination with any other race; Please refer to the Explanation of Data for more information.

Wyoming County

Population: 28,276

Ancestry	Population	%
Afghan (0)	0	<0.01
African, Sub-Saharan (48)	48	0.17
African (48)	48	0.17
Cape Verdean (0)	0	<0.01
Ethiopian (0)	0	<0.01
Ghanaian (0)	0	<0.01
Kenyan (0)	0	<0.01
Liberian (0)	0	<0.01
Nigerian (0)	0	<0.01
Senegalese (0)	0	<0.01
Sierra Leonean (0)	0	<0.01
Somalian (0)	0	<0.01
South African (0)	0	<0.01
Sudanese (0)	0	<0.01
Ugandan (0)	0	<0.01
Zimbabwean (0)	0	<0.01
Other Sub-Saharan African (0)	0	<0.01
Albanian (0)	0	<0.01
Alsatian (0)	0	<0.01
American (1,732)	1,732	6.13
Arab (19)	57	0.20
Arab (0)	0	<0.01
Egyptian (0)	0	<0.01
Iraqi (0)	0	<0.01
Jordanian (0)	0	<0.01
Lebanese (12)	39	0.14
Moroccan (0)	0	<0.01
Palestinian (0)	0	<0.01
Syrian (7)	18	0.06
Other Arab (0)	0	<0.01
Armenian (0)	18	0.06
Assyrian/Chaldean/Syriac (0)	0	<0.01
Australian (10)	10	0.04
Austrian (28)	102	0.36
Basque (0)	0	<0.01
Belgian (7)	12	0.04
Brazilian (12)	12	0.04
British (25)	73	0.26
Bulgarian (0)	0	<0.01
Cajun (0)	0	<0.01
Canadian (20)	34	0.12
Carpatho Rusyn (0)	0	<0.01
Celtic (0)	0	<0.01
Croatian (7)	14	0.05
Cypriot (0)	0	<0.01
Czech (29)	99	0.35
Czechoslovakian (9)	84	0.30
Danish (6)	65	0.23
Dutch (254)	1,100	3.89
Eastern European (7)	10	0.04
English (1,359)	4,134	14.63
Estonian (0)	0	<0.01
European (134)	145	0.51
Finnish (0)	7	0.02
French, ex. Basque (86)	725	2.57
French Canadian (16)	70	0.25
German (2,072)	7,351	26.01
German Russian (0)	6	0.02
Greek (11)	100	0.35
Guyanese (0)	12	0.04
Hungarian (44)	150	0.53
Icelander (0)	0	<0.01
Iranian (0)	0	<0.01
Irish (1,433)	5,605	19.83
Israeli (3)	3	0.01
Italian (870)	3,316	11.73
Latvian (0)	0	<0.01
Lithuanian (214)	842	2.98
Luxemburger (0)	0	<0.01
Macedonian (0)	0	<0.01
Maltese (0)	0	<0.01
New Zealander (0)	5	0.02
Northern European (2)	2	0.01
Norwegian (23)	79	0.28
Pennsylvania German (334)	674	2.38

Ancestry	Population	%
Polish (1,376)	3,861	13.66
Portuguese (0)	7	0.02
Romanian (0)	5	0.02
Russian (131)	489	1.73
Scandinavian (0)	11	0.04
Scotch-Irish (131)	370	1.31
Scottish (86)	489	1.73
Serbian (4)	4	0.01
Slavic (24)	49	0.17
Slovak (150)	696	2.46
Slovene (0)	2	0.01
Soviet Union (0)	0	<0.01
Swedish (35)	256	0.91
Swiss (4)	82	0.29
Turkish (0)	0	<0.01
Ukrainian (38)	117	0.41
Welsh (415)	1,758	6.22
West Indian, ex. Hispanic (0)	32	0.11
Bahamian (0)	0	<0.01
Barbadian (0)	0	<0.01
Belizean (0)	0	<0.01
Bermudan (0)	0	<0.01
British West Indian (0)	0	<0.01
Dutch West Indian (0)	0	<0.01
Haitian (0)	20	0.07
Jamaican (0)	0	<0.01
Trinidadian/Tobagonian (0)	0	<0.01
U.S. Virgin Islander (0)	0	<0.01
West Indian (0)	12	0.04
Other West Indian (0)	0	<0.01
Yugoslavian (5)	5	0.02

Hispanic Origin	Population	%
Hispanic or Latino (of any race)	437	1.55
Central American, ex. Mexican	50	0.18
Costa Rican	1	<0.01
Guatemalan	5	0.02
Honduran	12	0.04
Nicaraguan	0	<0.01
Panamanian	7	0.02
Salvadoran	25	0.09
Other Central American	0	<0.01
Cuban	16	0.06
Dominican Republic	7	0.02
Mexican	133	0.47
Puerto Rican	148	0.52
South American	42	0.15
Argentinean	1	<0.01
Bolivian	1	<0.01
Chilean	5	0.02
Colombian	1	<0.01
Ecuadorian	16	0.06
Paraguayan	3	0.01
Peruvian	10	0.04
Uruguayan	3	0.01
Venezuelan	2	0.01
Other South American	0	<0.01
Other Hispanic or Latino	41	0.14

Race*	Population	%
African-American/Black (208)	307	1.09
Not Hispanic (185)	282	1.00
Hispanic (23)	25	0.09
American Indian/Alaska Native (54)	161	0.57
Not Hispanic (51)	153	0.54
Hispanic (3)	8	0.03
Alaska Athabascan (Ala. Nat.) (0)	0	<0.01
Aleut (Alaska Native) (0)	0	<0.01
Apache (2)	4	0.01
Arapaho (0)	0	<0.01
Blackfeet (0)	4	0.01
Canadian/French Am. Ind. (0)	0	<0.01
Central American Ind. (0)	1	<0.01
Cherokee (4)	21	0.07
Cheyenne (0)	1	<0.01
Chickasaw (0)	0	<0.01
Chippewa (2)	2	0.01
Choctaw (1)	1	<0.01
Colville (0)	0	<0.01

Race* (cont.)	Population	%
Comanche (0)	0	<0.01
Cree (0)	0	<0.01
Creek (0)	0	<0.01
Crow (0)	1	<0.01
Delaware (9)	13	0.05
Hopi (0)	0	<0.01
Houma (0)	0	<0.01
Inupiat (Alaska Native) (0)	0	<0.01
Iroquois (9)	30	0.11
Kiowa (0)	0	<0.01
Lumbee (0)	0	<0.01
Menominee (0)	0	<0.01
Mexican American Ind. (0)	0	<0.01
Navajo (0)	0	<0.01
Osage (0)	0	<0.01
Ottawa (0)	0	<0.01
Paiute (0)	0	<0.01
Pima (0)	0	<0.01
Potawatomi (0)	0	<0.01
Pueblo (0)	0	<0.01
Puget Sound Salish (0)	0	<0.01
Seminole (4)	4	0.01
Shoshone (0)	0	<0.01
Sioux (1)	1	<0.01
South American Ind. (1)	2	0.01
Spanish American Ind. (0)	0	<0.01
Tlingit-Haida (Alaska Native) (0)	1	<0.01
Tohono O'Odham (0)	0	<0.01
Tsimshian (Alaska Native) (0)	0	<0.01
Ute (0)	0	<0.01
Yakama (0)	0	<0.01
Yaqui (0)	0	<0.01
Yuman (0)	0	<0.01
Yup'ik (Alaska Native) (0)	0	<0.01
Asian (95)	139	0.49
Not Hispanic (94)	138	0.49
Hispanic (1)	1	<0.01
Bangladeshi (0)	0	<0.01
Bhutanese (0)	0	<0.01
Burmese (0)	0	<0.01
Cambodian (0)	0	<0.01
Chinese, ex. Taiwanese (18)	23	0.08
Filipino (17)	31	0.11
Hmong (0)	0	<0.01
Indian (29)	41	0.14
Indonesian (0)	0	<0.01
Japanese (9)	16	0.06
Korean (7)	12	0.04
Laotian (5)	5	0.02
Malaysian (0)	0	<0.01
Nepalese (2)	2	0.01
Pakistani (0)	0	<0.01
Sri Lankan (0)	0	<0.01
Taiwanese (0)	1	<0.01
Thai (2)	3	0.01
Vietnamese (1)	2	0.01
Hawaii Native/Pacific Islander (3)	12	0.04
Not Hispanic (3)	10	0.04
Hispanic (0)	2	0.01
Fijian (0)	0	<0.01
Guamanian/Chamorro (2)	4	0.01
Marshallese (0)	0	<0.01
Native Hawaiian (0)	4	0.01
Samoan (0)	0	<0.01
Tongan (0)	0	<0.01
White (27,545)	27,792	98.29
Not Hispanic (27,270)	27,491	97.22
Hispanic (275)	301	1.06

Notes: † The Census 2010 population figure is used to calculate the percentages in the Hispanic Origin and Race categories. Ancestry percentages are based on the 2006-2010 American Community Survey population (not shown); ‡ Numbers in parentheses indicate the number of people reporting a single ancestry; * Numbers in parentheses indicate the number of persons reporting this race alone, not in combination with any other race; Please refer to the Explanation of Data for more information.

York County

Population: 434,972

Ancestry	Population	%
Afghan (0)	0	<0.01
African, Sub-Saharan (1,459)	2,078	0.49
African (934)	1,237	0.29
Cape Verdean (0)	0	<0.01
Ethiopian (84)	84	0.02
Ghanaian (56)	103	0.02
Kenyan (21)	21	<0.01
Liberian (0)	0	<0.01
Nigerian (192)	400	0.09
Senegalese (0)	0	<0.01
Sierra Leonean (0)	0	<0.01
Somalian (0)	0	<0.01
South African (12)	12	<0.01
Sudanese (0)	0	<0.01
Ugandan (0)	0	<0.01
Zimbabwean (0)	0	<0.01
Other Sub-Saharan African (160)	221	0.05
Albanian (15)	50	0.01
Alsatian (0)	0	<0.01
American (34,355)	34,355	8.02
Arab (351)	564	0.13
Arab (54)	54	0.01
Egyptian (127)	155	0.04
Iraqi (0)	14	<0.01
Jordanian (0)	0	<0.01
Lebanese (123)	259	0.06
Moroccan (28)	28	0.01
Palestinian (0)	0	<0.01
Syrian (19)	44	0.01
Other Arab (0)	10	<0.01
Armenian (106)	234	0.05
Assyrian/Chaldean/Syriac (0)	0	<0.01
Australian (30)	100	0.02
Austrian (95)	994	0.23
Basque (0)	0	<0.01
Belgian (60)	153	0.04
Brazilian (99)	380	0.09
British (681)	1,531	0.36
Bulgarian (35)	61	0.01
Cajun (31)	31	0.01
Canadian (337)	611	0.14
Carpatho Rusyn (15)	31	0.01
Celtic (11)	14	<0.01
Croatian (291)	720	0.17
Cypriot (0)	6	<0.01
Czech (223)	1,467	0.34
Czechoslovakian (182)	364	0.09
Danish (112)	767	0.18
Dutch (2,490)	9,553	2.23
Eastern European (149)	175	0.04
English (13,139)	36,942	8.63
Estonian (0)	0	<0.01
European (2,538)	2,876	0.67
Finnish (75)	321	0.07
French, ex. Basque (1,630)	8,693	2.03
French Canadian (562)	1,302	0.30
German (99,174)	180,920	42.25
German Russian (30)	30	0.01
Greek (847)	1,700	0.40
Guyanese (68)	96	0.02
Hungarian (408)	1,571	0.37
Icelander (0)	0	<0.01
Iranian (55)	100	0.02
Irish (12,827)	55,844	13.04
Israeli (17)	26	0.01
Italian (8,662)	25,642	5.99
Latvian (31)	31	0.01
Lithuanian (397)	1,172	0.27
Luxemburger (0)	0	<0.01
Macedonian (0)	3	<0.01
Maltese (0)	47	0.01
New Zealander (0)	0	<0.01
Northern European (53)	53	0.01
Norwegian (594)	1,973	0.46
Pennsylvania German (3,264)	4,065	0.95

Ancestry	Population	%
Polish (4,240)	14,214	3.32
Portuguese (87)	365	0.09
Romanian (213)	433	0.10
Russian (880)	2,431	0.57
Scandinavian (62)	257	0.06
Scotch-Irish (3,101)	8,820	2.06
Scottish (1,810)	7,251	1.69
Serbian (101)	215	0.05
Slavic (27)	291	0.07
Slovak (597)	1,688	0.39
Slovene (46)	239	0.06
Soviet Union (0)	0	<0.01
Swedish (678)	3,162	0.74
Swiss (517)	2,750	0.64
Turkish (22)	38	0.01
Ukrainian (691)	1,512	0.35
Welsh (804)	5,157	1.20
West Indian, ex. Hispanic (1,114)	1,468	0.34
Bahamian (0)	0	<0.01
Barbadian (21)	21	0.01
Belizean (0)	16	<0.01
Bermudan (5)	9	<0.01
British West Indian (0)	0	<0.01
Dutch West Indian (0)	14	<0.01
Haitian (600)	600	0.14
Jamaican (374)	583	0.14
Trinidadian/Tobagonian (72)	96	0.02
U.S. Virgin Islander (0)	0	<0.01
West Indian (42)	120	0.03
Other West Indian (0)	9	<0.01
Yugoslavian (171)	312	0.07

Hispanic Origin	Population	%
Hispanic or Latino (of any race)	24,397	5.61
Central American, ex. Mexican	1,130	0.26
Costa Rican	58	0.01
Guatemalan	270	0.06
Honduran	148	0.03
Nicaraguan	89	0.02
Panamanian	142	0.03
Salvadoran	412	0.09
Other Central American	11	<0.01
Cuban	467	0.11
Dominican Republic	1,733	0.40
Mexican	4,974	1.14
Puerto Rican	13,493	3.10
South American	931	0.21
Argentinean	72	0.02
Bolivian	32	0.01
Chilean	50	0.01
Colombian	304	0.07
Ecuadorian	194	0.04
Paraguayan	11	<0.01
Peruvian	202	0.05
Uruguayan	21	<0.01
Venezuelan	36	0.01
Other South American	9	<0.01
Other Hispanic or Latino	1,669	0.38

Race*	Population	%
African-American/Black (24,344)	29,371	6.75
Not Hispanic (22,493)	26,596	6.11
Hispanic (1,851)	2,775	0.64
American Indian/Alaska Native (942)	2,832	0.65
Not Hispanic (635)	2,260	0.52
Hispanic (307)	572	0.13
Alaska Athabascan (Ala. Nat.) (1)	1	<0.01
Aleut (Alaska Native) (0)	0	<0.01
Apache (11)	51	<0.01
Arapaho (1)	2	<0.01
Blackfeet (15)	110	0.03
Canadian/French Am. Ind. (5)	13	<0.01
Central American Ind. (19)	32	0.01
Cherokee (118)	608	0.14
Cheyenne (4)	9	<0.01
Chickasaw (0)	0	<0.01
Chippewa (6)	22	0.01
Choctaw (12)	23	0.01
Colville (0)	0	<0.01

Race*	Population	%
Comanche (1)	5	<0.01
Cree (2)	11	<0.01
Creek (8)	14	<0.01
Crow (1)	5	<0.01
Delaware (4)	15	<0.01
Hopi (0)	3	<0.01
Houma (6)	6	<0.01
Inupiat (Alaska Native) (6)	13	<0.01
Iroquois (28)	94	0.02
Kiowa (0)	5	<0.01
Lumbee (26)	49	0.01
Menominee (0)	2	<0.01
Mexican American Ind. (40)	62	0.01
Navajo (10)	16	<0.01
Osage (0)	3	<0.01
Ottawa (1)	1	<0.01
Paiute (0)	4	<0.01
Pima (0)	0	<0.01
Potawatomi (4)	9	<0.01
Pueblo (2)	10	<0.01
Puget Sound Salish (0)	0	<0.01
Seminole (2)	5	<0.01
Shoshone (0)	3	<0.01
Sioux (30)	79	0.02
South American Ind. (21)	32	0.01
Spanish American Ind. (5)	6	<0.01
Tlingit-Haida (Alaska Native) (6)	7	<0.01
Tohono O'Odham (0)	2	<0.01
Tsimshian (Alaska Native) (0)	0	<0.01
Ute (2)	2	<0.01
Yakama (0)	0	<0.01
Yaqui (3)	3	<0.01
Yuman (0)	0	<0.01
Yup'ik (Alaska Native) (0)	0	<0.01
Asian (5,407)	7,005	1.61
Not Hispanic (5,336)	6,752	1.55
Hispanic (71)	253	0.06
Bangladeshi (74)	80	0.02
Bhutanese (0)	0	<0.01
Burmese (6)	6	<0.01
Cambodian (256)	310	0.07
Chinese, ex. Taiwanese (944)	1,174	0.27
Filipino (525)	918	0.21
Hmong (10)	10	<0.01
Indian (1,206)	1,424	0.33
Indonesian (22)	48	0.01
Japanese (134)	375	0.09
Korean (601)	867	0.20
Laotian (84)	99	0.02
Malaysian (6)	9	<0.01
Nepalese (18)	18	<0.01
Pakistani (183)	226	0.05
Sri Lankan (22)	28	0.01
Taiwanese (19)	24	0.01
Thai (42)	84	0.02
Vietnamese (1,037)	1,173	0.27
Hawaii Native/Pacific Islander (123)	404	0.09
Not Hispanic (108)	284	0.07
Hispanic (15)	120	0.03
Fijian (2)	4	<0.01
Guamanian/Chamorro (13)	41	0.01
Marshallese (2)	2	<0.01
Native Hawaiian (52)	136	0.03
Samoan (17)	30	0.01
Tongan (0)	4	<0.01
White (385,135)	392,901	90.33
Not Hispanic (374,779)	380,982	87.59
Hispanic (10,356)	11,919	2.74

Notes: † The Census 2010 population figure is used to calculate the percentages in the Hispanic Origin and Race categories. Ancestry percentages are based on the 2006-2010 American Community Survey population (not shown); ‡ Numbers in parentheses indicate the number of people reporting a single ancestry; * Numbers in parentheses indicate the number of persons reporting this race alone, not in combination with any other race; Please refer to the Explanation of Data for more information.

Place Profiles

Abington

Place Type: Township
County: Montgomery
Population: 55,310

Ancestry	Population	%
Afghan (0)	0	<0.01
African, Sub-Saharan (183)	240	0.43
African (150)	164	0.30
Cape Verdean (0)	0	<0.01
Ethiopian (0)	0	<0.01
Ghanaian (0)	0	<0.01
Kenyan (0)	0	<0.01
Liberian (0)	0	<0.01
Nigerian (14)	14	0.03
Senegalese (0)	0	<0.01
Sierra Leonean (0)	10	0.02
Somalian (0)	0	<0.01
South African (0)	0	<0.01
Sudanese (0)	0	<0.01
Ugandan (0)	0	<0.01
Zimbabwean (0)	0	<0.01
Other Sub-Saharan African (19)	52	0.09
Albanian (82)	121	0.22
Alsatian (0)	0	<0.01
American (2,004)	2,004	3.62
Arab (38)	159	0.29
Arab (0)	0	<0.01
Egyptian (23)	23	0.04
Iraqi (0)	0	<0.01
Jordanian (0)	0	<0.01
Lebanese (0)	94	0.17
Moroccan (0)	0	<0.01
Palestinian (0)	11	0.02
Syrian (0)	16	0.03
Other Arab (15)	15	0.03
Armenian (10)	10	0.02
Assyrian/Chaldean/Syriac (0)	0	<0.01
Australian (27)	37	0.07
Austrian (94)	410	0.74
Basque (0)	0	<0.01
Belgian (23)	75	0.14
Brazilian (10)	32	0.06
British (81)	298	0.54
Bulgarian (26)	26	0.05
Cajun (0)	0	<0.01
Canadian (11)	56	0.10
Carpatho Rusyn (0)	0	<0.01
Celtic (0)	0	<0.01
Croatian (33)	33	0.06
Cypriot (0)	0	<0.01
Czech (92)	173	0.31
Czechoslovakian (40)	73	0.13
Danish (9)	41	0.07
Dutch (60)	322	0.58
Eastern European (282)	337	0.61
English (792)	4,855	8.76
Estonian (11)	11	0.02
European (516)	590	1.06
Finnish (0)	20	0.04
French, ex. Basque (100)	1,102	1.99
French Canadian (49)	101	0.18
German (3,011)	12,435	22.44
German Russian (0)	0	<0.01
Greek (132)	337	0.61
Guyanese (74)	74	0.13
Hungarian (104)	458	0.83
Icelander (0)	0	<0.01
Iranian (56)	65	0.12
Irish (4,660)	14,146	25.53
Israeli (20)	79	0.14
Italian (2,864)	7,624	13.76
Latvian (57)	70	0.13
Lithuanian (92)	330	0.60
Luxemburger (0)	0	<0.01
Macedonian (0)	0	<0.01
Maltese (0)	14	0.03
New Zealander (0)	0	<0.01
Northern European (63)	63	0.11
Norwegian (31)	115	0.21
Pennsylvania German (121)	336	0.61
Polish (975)	4,038	7.29
Portuguese (141)	240	0.43
Romanian (95)	279	0.50
Russian (1,139)	2,330	4.20
Scandinavian (0)	5	0.01
Scotch-Irish (375)	1,152	2.08
Scottish (270)	1,043	1.88
Serbian (0)	0	<0.01
Slavic (0)	22	0.04
Slovak (102)	282	0.51
Slovene (28)	28	0.05
Soviet Union (0)	0	<0.01
Swedish (34)	470	0.85
Swiss (6)	162	0.29
Turkish (0)	17	0.03
Ukrainian (471)	885	1.60
Welsh (29)	562	1.01
West Indian, ex. Hispanic (529)	672	1.21
Bahamian (0)	0	<0.01
Barbadian (50)	60	0.11
Belizean (0)	0	<0.01
Bermudan (0)	0	<0.01
British West Indian (11)	11	0.02
Dutch West Indian (0)	0	<0.01
Haitian (87)	119	0.21
Jamaican (222)	264	0.48
Trinidadian/Tobagonian (15)	74	0.13
U.S. Virgin Islander (0)	0	<0.01
West Indian (144)	144	0.26
Other West Indian (0)	0	<0.01
Yugoslavian (22)	32	0.06

Hispanic Origin	Population	%
Hispanic or Latino (of any race)	1,771	3.20
Central American, ex. Mexican	187	0.34
Costa Rican	21	0.04
Guatemalan	62	0.11
Honduran	15	0.03
Nicaraguan	17	0.03
Panamanian	18	0.03
Salvadoran	43	0.08
Other Central American	11	0.02
Cuban	111	0.20
Dominican Republic	27	0.05
Mexican	261	0.47
Puerto Rican	683	1.23
South American	294	0.53
Argentinean	42	0.08
Bolivian	4	0.01
Chilean	11	0.02
Colombian	100	0.18
Ecuadorian	28	0.05
Paraguayan	1	<0.01
Peruvian	69	0.12
Uruguayan	10	0.02
Venezuelan	29	0.05
Other South American	0	<0.01
Other Hispanic or Latino	208	0.38

Race*	Population	%
African-American/Black (6,850)	7,513	13.58
Not Hispanic (6,711)	7,266	13.14
Hispanic (139)	247	0.45
American Indian/Alaska Native (57)	296	0.54
Not Hispanic (40)	231	0.42
Hispanic (17)	65	0.12
Alaska Athabascan (Ala. Nat.) (1)	1	<0.01
Aleut (Alaska Native) (0)	0	<0.01
Apache (0)	6	0.01
Arapaho (0)	0	<0.01
Blackfeet (1)	9	0.02
Canadian/French Am. Ind. (0)	1	<0.01
Central American Ind. (0)	0	<0.01
Cherokee (15)	91	0.16
Cheyenne (0)	0	<0.01
Chickasaw (0)	0	<0.01
Chippewa (0)	0	<0.01
Choctaw (0)	1	<0.01
Colville (0)	0	<0.01
Comanche (0)	0	<0.01
Cree (1)	3	0.01
Creek (0)	0	<0.01
Crow (0)	0	<0.01
Delaware (1)	5	0.01
Hopi (0)	0	<0.01
Houma (0)	0	<0.01
Inupiat (Alaska Native) (0)	3	0.01
Iroquois (0)	2	<0.01
Kiowa (0)	0	<0.01
Lumbee (3)	10	0.02
Menominee (0)	0	<0.01
Mexican American Ind. (3)	3	0.01
Navajo (0)	4	0.01
Osage (0)	0	<0.01
Ottawa (0)	0	<0.01
Paiute (0)	0	<0.01
Pima (0)	0	<0.01
Potawatomi (0)	0	<0.01
Pueblo (0)	0	<0.01
Puget Sound Salish (0)	0	<0.01
Seminole (0)	0	<0.01
Shoshone (0)	0	<0.01
Sioux (1)	3	0.01
South American Ind. (4)	8	0.01
Spanish American Ind. (0)	0	<0.01
Tlingit-Haida (Alaska Native) (0)	0	<0.01
Tohono O'Odham (0)	0	<0.01
Tsimshian (Alaska Native) (0)	0	<0.01
Ute (0)	0	<0.01
Yakama (0)	0	<0.01
Yaqui (0)	0	<0.01
Yuman (0)	0	<0.01
Yup'ik (Alaska Native) (0)	0	<0.01
Asian (2,686)	3,030	5.48
Not Hispanic (2,673)	2,985	5.40
Hispanic (13)	45	0.08
Bangladeshi (19)	19	0.03
Bhutanese (0)	0	<0.01
Burmese (10)	10	0.02
Cambodian (37)	46	0.08
Chinese, ex. Taiwanese (346)	424	0.77
Filipino (130)	212	0.38
Hmong (2)	2	<0.01
Indian (401)	455	0.82
Indonesian (8)	10	0.02
Japanese (45)	92	0.17
Korean (1,337)	1,396	2.52
Laotian (28)	37	0.07
Malaysian (1)	1	<0.01
Nepalese (7)	7	0.01
Pakistani (51)	55	0.10
Sri Lankan (4)	4	0.01
Taiwanese (21)	31	0.06
Thai (21)	29	0.05
Vietnamese (155)	186	0.34
Hawaii Native/Pacific Islander (8)	53	0.10
Not Hispanic (7)	48	0.09
Hispanic (1)	5	0.01
Fijian (0)	0	<0.01
Guamanian/Chamorro (0)	3	0.01
Marshallese (0)	0	<0.01
Native Hawaiian (1)	6	0.01
Samoan (2)	3	0.01
Tongan (0)	0	<0.01
White (44,083)	45,025	81.40
Not Hispanic (43,122)	43,861	79.30
Hispanic (961)	1,164	2.10

Notes: † The Census 2010 population figure is used to calculate the percentages in the Hispanic Origin and Race categories. Ancestry percentages are based on the 2006-2010 American Community Survey population (not shown); ‡ Numbers in parentheses indicate the number of people reporting a single ancestry; * Numbers in parentheses indicate the number of persons reporting this race alone, not in combination with any other race; Please refer to the Explanation of Data for more information.

Allentown

Place Type: City
County: Lehigh
Population: 118,032

Ancestry	Population	%
Afghan (0)	0	<0.01
African, Sub-Saharan (526)	562	0.48
African (423)	459	0.39
Cape Verdean (16)	16	0.01
Ethiopian (24)	24	0.02
Ghanaian (0)	0	<0.01
Kenyan (31)	31	0.03
Liberian (0)	0	<0.01
Nigerian (32)	32	0.03
Senegalese (0)	0	<0.01
Sierra Leonean (0)	0	<0.01
Somalian (0)	0	<0.01
South African (0)	0	<0.01
Sudanese (0)	0	<0.01
Ugandan (0)	0	<0.01
Zimbabwean (0)	0	<0.01
Other Sub-Saharan African (0)	0	<0.01
Albanian (111)	126	0.11
Alsatian (0)	9	0.01
American (3,325)	3,325	2.86
Arab (2,632)	3,112	2.67
Arab (335)	360	0.31
Egyptian (166)	166	0.14
Iraqi (0)	0	<0.01
Jordanian (0)	0	<0.01
Lebanese (66)	113	0.10
Moroccan (13)	13	0.01
Palestinian (46)	46	0.04
Syrian (1,751)	2,119	1.82
Other Arab (255)	295	0.25
Armenian (15)	15	0.01
Assyrian/Chaldean/Syriac (9)	20	0.02
Australian (10)	120	0.10
Austrian (610)	1,440	1.24
Basque (0)	0	<0.01
Belgian (20)	20	0.02
Brazilian (29)	43	0.04
British (84)	217	0.19
Bulgarian (47)	47	0.04
Cajun (0)	0	<0.01
Canadian (51)	64	0.05
Carpatho Rusyn (0)	0	<0.01
Celtic (0)	0	<0.01
Croatian (24)	24	0.02
Cypriot (0)	0	<0.01
Czech (62)	163	0.14
Czechoslovakian (180)	338	0.29
Danish (0)	57	0.05
Dutch (665)	2,721	2.34
Eastern European (110)	110	0.09
English (982)	4,215	3.62
Estonian (0)	0	<0.01
European (213)	264	0.23
Finnish (0)	15	0.01
French, ex. Basque (288)	1,293	1.11
French Canadian (45)	185	0.16
German (8,060)	20,043	17.22
German Russian (0)	0	<0.01
Greek (214)	573	0.49
Guyanese (79)	79	0.07
Hungarian (468)	1,829	1.57
Icelander (0)	0	<0.01
Iranian (43)	56	0.05
Irish (2,162)	8,860	7.61
Israeli (0)	0	<0.01
Italian (2,866)	7,606	6.53
Latvian (0)	0	<0.01
Lithuanian (76)	232	0.20
Luxemburger (0)	11	0.01
Macedonian (0)	19	0.02
Maltese (0)	0	<0.01
New Zealander (0)	0	<0.01
Northern European (38)	38	0.03

Ancestry	Population	%
Norwegian (37)	141	0.12
Pennsylvania German (2,851)	4,292	3.69
Polish (1,174)	3,566	3.06
Portuguese (51)	136	0.12
Romanian (103)	147	0.13
Russian (248)	919	0.79
Scandinavian (0)	1	<0.01
Scotch-Irish (200)	913	0.78
Scottish (257)	970	0.83
Serbian (13)	24	0.02
Slavic (0)	13	0.01
Slovak (648)	1,543	1.33
Slovene (73)	73	0.06
Soviet Union (10)	10	0.01
Swedish (125)	502	0.43
Swiss (42)	242	0.21
Turkish (41)	53	0.05
Ukrainian (418)	1,122	0.96
Welsh (208)	1,050	0.90
West Indian, ex. Hispanic (1,069)	1,351	1.16
Bahamian (32)	32	0.03
Barbadian (23)	23	0.02
Belizean (0)	0	<0.01
Bermudan (0)	0	<0.01
British West Indian (47)	63	0.05
Dutch West Indian (0)	0	<0.01
Haitian (265)	265	0.23
Jamaican (590)	724	0.62
Trinidadian/Tobagonian (51)	67	0.06
U.S. Virgin Islander (0)	0	<0.01
West Indian (61)	177	0.15
Other West Indian (0)	0	<0.01
Yugoslavian (25)	25	0.02

Hispanic Origin	Population	%
Hispanic or Latino (of any race)	50,461	42.75
Central American, ex. Mexican	1,911	1.62
Costa Rican	65	0.06
Guatemalan	420	0.36
Honduran	749	0.63
Nicaraguan	89	0.08
Panamanian	143	0.12
Salvadoran	440	0.37
Other Central American	5	<0.01
Cuban	458	0.39
Dominican Republic	9,340	7.91
Mexican	2,448	2.07
Puerto Rican	29,640	25.11
South American	3,048	2.58
Argentinean	49	0.04
Bolivian	20	0.02
Chilean	259	0.22
Colombian	755	0.64
Ecuadorian	1,241	1.05
Paraguayan	3	<0.01
Peruvian	565	0.48
Uruguayan	61	0.05
Venezuelan	75	0.06
Other South American	20	0.02
Other Hispanic or Latino	3,616	3.06

Race*	Population	%
African-American/Black (14,812)	17,916	15.18
Not Hispanic (11,336)	12,976	10.99
Hispanic (3,476)	4,940	4.19
American Indian/Alaska Native (893)	1,792	1.52
Not Hispanic (200)	645	0.55
Hispanic (693)	1,147	0.97
Alaska Athabascan (Ala. Nat.) (0)	0	<0.01
Aleut (Alaska Native) (2)	2	<0.01
Apache (0)	8	0.01
Arapaho (0)	0	<0.01
Blackfeet (4)	33	0.03
Canadian/French Am. Ind. (1)	1	<0.01
Central American Ind. (27)	40	0.03
Cherokee (41)	170	0.14
Cheyenne (1)	1	<0.01
Chickasaw (1)	1	<0.01
Chippewa (6)	12	0.01

Race*	Population	%
Choctaw (1)	13	0.01
Colville (0)	0	<0.01
Comanche (3)	4	<0.01
Cree (5)	5	<0.01
Creek (2)	2	<0.01
Crow (0)	5	<0.01
Delaware (7)	21	0.02
Hopi (0)	3	<0.01
Houma (0)	0	<0.01
Inupiat (Alaska Native) (0)	0	<0.01
Iroquois (13)	19	0.02
Kiowa (0)	0	<0.01
Lumbee (0)	4	<0.01
Menominee (0)	0	<0.01
Mexican American Ind. (43)	51	0.04
Navajo (3)	4	<0.01
Osage (0)	0	<0.01
Ottawa (0)	0	<0.01
Paiute (0)	0	<0.01
Pima (0)	0	<0.01
Potawatomi (0)	0	<0.01
Pueblo (0)	1	<0.01
Puget Sound Salish (0)	1	<0.01
Seminole (1)	5	<0.01
Shoshone (2)	5	<0.01
Sioux (7)	18	0.02
South American Ind. (69)	135	0.11
Spanish American Ind. (23)	27	0.02
Tlingit-Haida (Alaska Native) (0)	0	<0.01
Tohono O'Odham (3)	3	<0.01
Tsimshian (Alaska Native) (0)	0	<0.01
Ute (0)	0	<0.01
Yakama (0)	0	<0.01
Yaqui (1)	1	<0.01
Yuman (0)	0	<0.01
Yup'ik (Alaska Native) (0)	1	<0.01
Asian (2,542)	3,274	2.77
Not Hispanic (2,452)	2,981	2.53
Hispanic (90)	293	0.25
Bangladeshi (15)	18	0.02
Bhutanese (0)	0	<0.01
Burmese (108)	121	0.10
Cambodian (64)	80	0.07
Chinese, ex. Taiwanese (390)	502	0.43
Filipino (220)	324	0.27
Hmong (0)	0	<0.01
Indian (542)	688	0.58
Indonesian (5)	7	0.01
Japanese (40)	93	0.08
Korean (168)	192	0.16
Laotian (10)	20	0.02
Malaysian (2)	7	0.01
Nepalese (5)	5	<0.01
Pakistani (68)	76	0.06
Sri Lankan (11)	12	0.01
Taiwanese (13)	15	0.01
Thai (25)	35	0.03
Vietnamese (736)	853	0.72
Hawaii Native/Pacific Islander (55)	307	0.26
Not Hispanic (11)	83	0.07
Hispanic (44)	224	0.19
Fijian (0)	0	<0.01
Guamanian/Chamorro (8)	11	0.01
Marshallese (0)	0	<0.01
Native Hawaiian (10)	43	0.04
Samoan (10)	23	0.02
Tongan (0)	1	<0.01
White (69,061)	73,671	62.42
Not Hispanic (50,964)	53,079	44.97
Hispanic (18,097)	20,592	17.45

Notes: † The Census 2010 population figure is used to calculate the percentages in the Hispanic Origin and Race categories. Ancestry percentages are based on the 2006-2010 American Community Survey population (not shown); ‡ Numbers in parentheses indicate the number of people reporting a single ancestry; * Numbers in parentheses indicate the number of persons reporting this race alone, not in combination with any other race; Please refer to the Explanation of Data for more information.

Bensalem

Place Type: Township
County: Bucks
Population: 60,427

Ancestry	Population	%
Afghan (0)	0	<0.01
African, Sub-Saharan (283)	356	0.59
African (262)	319	0.53
Cape Verdean (0)	0	<0.01
Ethiopian (0)	0	<0.01
Ghanaian (0)	0	<0.01
Kenyan (0)	0	<0.01
Liberian (11)	27	0.04
Nigerian (10)	10	0.02
Senegalese (0)	0	<0.01
Sierra Leonean (0)	0	<0.01
Somalian (0)	0	<0.01
South African (0)	0	<0.01
Sudanese (0)	0	<0.01
Ugandan (0)	0	<0.01
Zimbabwean (0)	0	<0.01
Other Sub-Saharan African (0)	0	<0.01
Albanian (16)	51	0.08
Alsatian (0)	0	<0.01
American (1,276)	1,276	2.12
Arab (51)	103	0.17
Arab (0)	0	<0.01
Egyptian (13)	13	0.02
Iraqi (0)	0	<0.01
Jordanian (0)	0	<0.01
Lebanese (8)	26	0.04
Moroccan (0)	0	<0.01
Palestinian (0)	0	<0.01
Syrian (0)	16	0.03
Other Arab (30)	48	0.08
Armenian (40)	40	0.07
Assyrian/Chaldean/Syriac (0)	0	<0.01
Australian (0)	0	<0.01
Austrian (27)	236	0.39
Basque (0)	0	<0.01
Belgian (0)	14	0.02
Brazilian (79)	100	0.17
British (34)	57	0.09
Bulgarian (0)	0	<0.01
Cajun (0)	0	<0.01
Canadian (20)	26	0.04
Carpatho Rusyn (0)	0	<0.01
Celtic (26)	26	0.04
Croatian (0)	24	0.04
Cypriot (0)	0	<0.01
Czech (16)	112	0.19
Czechoslovakian (8)	8	0.01
Danish (8)	58	0.10
Dutch (44)	301	0.50
Eastern European (94)	94	0.16
English (1,113)	4,695	7.79
Estonian (0)	0	<0.01
European (282)	306	0.51
Finnish (15)	22	0.04
French, ex. Basque (355)	1,378	2.29
French Canadian (7)	96	0.16
German (3,900)	13,336	22.13
German Russian (0)	0	<0.01
Greek (147)	270	0.45
Guyanese (0)	81	0.13
Hungarian (161)	453	0.75
Icelander (0)	0	<0.01
Iranian (0)	0	<0.01
Irish (5,404)	15,954	26.47
Israeli (23)	23	0.04
Italian (3,471)	8,721	14.47
Latvian (0)	16	0.03
Lithuanian (125)	370	0.61
Luxemburger (0)	0	<0.01
Macedonian (17)	52	0.09
Maltese (0)	0	<0.01
New Zealander (0)	0	<0.01
Northern European (24)	24	0.04

Ancestry (cont.)	Population	%
Norwegian (21)	183	0.30
Pennsylvania German (71)	219	0.36
Polish (1,888)	5,563	9.23
Portuguese (38)	67	0.11
Romanian (30)	106	0.18
Russian (758)	1,323	2.19
Scandinavian (0)	0	<0.01
Scotch-Irish (383)	962	1.60
Scottish (165)	579	0.96
Serbian (0)	0	<0.01
Slavic (0)	0	<0.01
Slovak (132)	265	0.44
Slovene (0)	11	0.02
Soviet Union (10)	10	0.02
Swedish (36)	276	0.46
Swiss (16)	57	0.09
Turkish (107)	107	0.18
Ukrainian (950)	1,352	2.24
Welsh (49)	420	0.70
West Indian, ex. Hispanic (167)	179	0.30
Bahamian (11)	11	0.02
Barbadian (99)	99	0.16
Belizean (0)	0	<0.01
Bermudan (0)	0	<0.01
British West Indian (0)	0	<0.01
Dutch West Indian (0)	0	<0.01
Haitian (0)	0	<0.01
Jamaican (26)	38	0.06
Trinidadian/Tobagonian (14)	14	0.02
U.S. Virgin Islander (17)	17	0.03
West Indian (0)	0	<0.01
Other West Indian (0)	0	<0.01
Yugoslavian (38)	71	0.12

Hispanic Origin	Population	%
Hispanic or Latino (of any race)	5,091	8.43
Central American, ex. Mexican	539	0.89
Costa Rican	74	0.12
Guatemalan	272	0.45
Honduran	77	0.13
Nicaraguan	22	0.04
Panamanian	15	0.02
Salvadoran	79	0.13
Other Central American	0	<0.01
Cuban	92	0.15
Dominican Republic	75	0.12
Mexican	1,879	3.11
Puerto Rican	1,452	2.40
South American	689	1.14
Argentinean	26	0.04
Bolivian	2	<0.01
Chilean	11	0.02
Colombian	121	0.20
Ecuadorian	416	0.69
Paraguayan	0	<0.01
Peruvian	80	0.13
Uruguayan	7	0.01
Venezuelan	20	0.03
Other South American	6	0.01
Other Hispanic or Latino	365	0.60

Race*	Population	%
African-American/Black (4,419)	5,040	8.34
Not Hispanic (4,240)	4,750	7.86
Hispanic (179)	290	0.48
American Indian/Alaska Native (296)	638	1.06
Not Hispanic (108)	409	0.68
Hispanic (188)	229	0.38
Alaska Athabascan (Ala. Nat.) (0)	1	<0.01
Aleut (Alaska Native) (0)	0	<0.01
Apache (4)	13	0.02
Arapaho (0)	0	<0.01
Blackfeet (2)	24	0.04
Canadian/French Am. Ind. (0)	2	<0.01
Central American Ind. (2)	2	<0.01
Cherokee (10)	74	0.12
Cheyenne (0)	0	<0.01
Chickasaw (0)	0	<0.01
Chippewa (1)	2	<0.01

Race* (cont.)	Population	%
Choctaw (0)	1	<0.01
Colville (0)	0	<0.01
Comanche (0)	1	<0.01
Cree (0)	0	<0.01
Creek (3)	5	0.01
Crow (0)	0	<0.01
Delaware (4)	13	0.02
Hopi (0)	0	<0.01
Houma (0)	0	<0.01
Inupiat (Alaska Native) (0)	0	<0.01
Iroquois (5)	21	0.03
Kiowa (0)	0	<0.01
Lumbee (0)	5	0.01
Menominee (1)	1	<0.01
Mexican American Ind. (112)	113	0.19
Navajo (1)	6	0.01
Osage (0)	0	<0.01
Ottawa (0)	0	<0.01
Paiute (0)	0	<0.01
Pima (2)	3	<0.01
Potawatomi (0)	1	<0.01
Pueblo (2)	2	<0.01
Puget Sound Salish (0)	0	<0.01
Seminole (0)	4	0.01
Shoshone (0)	0	<0.01
Sioux (3)	11	0.02
South American Ind. (6)	14	0.02
Spanish American Ind. (4)	5	0.01
Tlingit-Haida (Alaska Native) (0)	0	<0.01
Tohono O'Odham (0)	0	<0.01
Tsimshian (Alaska Native) (0)	0	<0.01
Ute (0)	0	<0.01
Yakama (0)	0	<0.01
Yaqui (0)	0	<0.01
Yuman (0)	0	<0.01
Yup'ik (Alaska Native) (0)	0	<0.01
Asian (6,163)	6,706	11.10
Not Hispanic (6,150)	6,653	11.01
Hispanic (13)	53	0.09
Bangladeshi (57)	67	0.11
Bhutanese (0)	0	<0.01
Burmese (0)	0	<0.01
Cambodian (23)	32	0.05
Chinese, ex. Taiwanese (467)	537	0.89
Filipino (338)	423	0.70
Hmong (0)	0	<0.01
Indian (4,272)	4,480	7.41
Indonesian (8)	8	0.01
Japanese (40)	81	0.13
Korean (268)	312	0.52
Laotian (7)	12	0.02
Malaysian (3)	5	0.01
Nepalese (13)	16	0.03
Pakistani (260)	284	0.47
Sri Lankan (6)	6	0.01
Taiwanese (12)	19	0.03
Thai (15)	23	0.04
Vietnamese (219)	251	0.42
Hawaii Native/Pacific Islander (23)	81	0.13
Not Hispanic (8)	53	0.09
Hispanic (15)	28	0.05
Fijian (0)	0	<0.01
Guamanian/Chamorro (17)	19	0.03
Marshallese (0)	0	<0.01
Native Hawaiian (4)	16	0.03
Samoan (0)	0	<0.01
Tongan (0)	0	<0.01
White (45,712)	46,896	77.61
Not Hispanic (43,561)	44,411	73.50
Hispanic (2,151)	2,485	4.11

*Notes: † The Census 2010 population figure is used to calculate the percentages in the Hispanic Origin and Race categories. Ancestry percentages are based on the 2006-2010 American Community Survey population (not shown); ‡ Numbers in parentheses indicate the number of people reporting a single ancestry; * Numbers in parentheses indicate the number of persons reporting this race alone, not in combination with any other race; Please refer to the Explanation of Data for more information.*

Bethlehem

Place Type: City
County: Northampton
Population: 55,639

Ancestry	Population	%
Afghan (40)	40	0.07
African, Sub-Saharan (231)	249	0.45
African (103)	121	0.22
Cape Verdean (0)	0	<0.01
Ethiopian (20)	20	0.04
Ghanaian (0)	0	<0.01
Kenyan (35)	35	0.06
Liberian (0)	0	<0.01
Nigerian (30)	30	0.05
Senegalese (43)	43	0.08
Sierra Leonean (0)	0	<0.01
Somalian (0)	0	<0.01
South African (0)	0	<0.01
Sudanese (0)	0	<0.01
Ugandan (0)	0	<0.01
Zimbabwean (0)	0	<0.01
Other Sub-Saharan African (0)	0	<0.01
Albanian (0)	0	<0.01
Alsatian (0)	0	<0.01
American (1,272)	1,272	2.29
Arab (306)	384	0.69
Arab (225)	225	0.41
Egyptian (16)	16	0.03
Iraqi (0)	0	<0.01
Jordanian (0)	0	<0.01
Lebanese (14)	47	0.08
Moroccan (0)	0	<0.01
Palestinian (0)	0	<0.01
Syrian (39)	84	0.15
Other Arab (12)	12	0.02
Armenian (21)	21	0.04
Assyrian/Chaldean/Syriac (8)	8	0.01
Australian (0)	0	<0.01
Austrian (135)	544	0.98
Basque (0)	12	0.02
Belgian (0)	14	0.03
Brazilian (22)	22	0.04
British (97)	342	0.62
Bulgarian (10)	10	0.02
Cajun (0)	0	<0.01
Canadian (53)	117	0.21
Carpatho Rusyn (13)	13	0.02
Celtic (0)	0	<0.01
Croatian (11)	54	0.10
Cypriot (0)	0	<0.01
Czech (27)	344	0.62
Czechoslovakian (23)	91	0.16
Danish (26)	64	0.12
Dutch (220)	1,021	1.84
Eastern European (73)	93	0.17
English (696)	3,258	5.88
Estonian (0)	0	<0.01
European (314)	329	0.59
Finnish (29)	29	0.05
French, ex. Basque (142)	1,049	1.89
French Canadian (37)	67	0.12
German (3,712)	12,068	21.77
German Russian (0)	0	<0.01
Greek (241)	553	1.00
Guyanese (12)	133	0.24
Hungarian (830)	2,523	4.55
Icelander (0)	0	<0.01
Iranian (64)	64	0.12
Irish (1,337)	7,207	13.00
Israeli (0)	0	<0.01
Italian (2,062)	6,357	11.47
Latvian (0)	0	<0.01
Lithuanian (154)	308	0.56
Luxemburger (0)	0	<0.01
Macedonian (16)	16	0.03
Maltese (0)	0	<0.01
New Zealander (14)	14	0.03
Northern European (0)	0	<0.01

Ancestry	Population	%
Norwegian (58)	178	0.32
Pennsylvania German (952)	1,688	3.04
Polish (768)	2,523	4.55
Portuguese (413)	587	1.06
Romanian (26)	54	0.10
Russian (205)	717	1.29
Scandinavian (12)	22	0.04
Scotch-Irish (169)	630	1.14
Scottish (229)	864	1.56
Serbian (0)	11	0.02
Slavic (12)	63	0.11
Slovak (681)	1,659	2.99
Slovene (173)	231	0.42
Soviet Union (0)	0	<0.01
Swedish (35)	376	0.68
Swiss (19)	228	0.41
Turkish (142)	169	0.30
Ukrainian (295)	724	1.31
Welsh (78)	931	1.68
West Indian, ex. Hispanic (239)	366	0.66
Bahamian (0)	0	<0.01
Barbadian (0)	12	0.02
Belizean (0)	0	<0.01
Bermudan (0)	0	<0.01
British West Indian (0)	0	<0.01
Dutch West Indian (0)	12	0.02
Haitian (134)	134	0.24
Jamaican (78)	142	0.26
Trinidadian/Tobagonian (9)	19	0.03
U.S. Virgin Islander (3)	3	0.01
West Indian (15)	44	0.08
Other West Indian (0)	0	<0.01
Yugoslavian (45)	55	0.10

Hispanic Origin	Population	%
Hispanic or Latino (of any race)	15,296	27.49
Central American, ex. Mexican	534	0.96
Costa Rican	18	0.03
Guatemalan	240	0.43
Honduran	75	0.13
Nicaraguan	72	0.13
Panamanian	42	0.08
Salvadoran	84	0.15
Other Central American	3	0.01
Cuban	163	0.29
Dominican Republic	783	1.41
Mexican	863	1.55
Puerto Rican	11,715	21.06
South American	628	1.13
Argentinean	32	0.06
Bolivian	16	0.03
Chilean	68	0.12
Colombian	198	0.36
Ecuadorian	144	0.26
Paraguayan	2	<0.01
Peruvian	113	0.20
Uruguayan	12	0.02
Venezuelan	42	0.08
Other South American	1	<0.01
Other Hispanic or Latino	610	1.10

Race*	Population	%
African-American/Black (4,205)	5,221	9.38
Not Hispanic (3,244)	3,772	6.78
Hispanic (961)	1,449	2.60
American Indian/Alaska Native (204)	465	0.84
Not Hispanic (58)	231	0.42
Hispanic (146)	234	0.42
Alaska Athabascan (Ala. Nat.) (0)	0	<0.01
Aleut (Alaska Native) (0)	0	<0.01
Apache (0)	1	<0.01
Arapaho (0)	0	<0.01
Blackfeet (3)	17	0.03
Canadian/French Am. Ind. (0)	0	<0.01
Central American Ind. (4)	7	0.01
Cherokee (6)	55	0.10
Cheyenne (0)	0	<0.01
Chickasaw (0)	0	<0.01
Chippewa (0)	0	<0.01

Race*	Population	%
Choctaw (1)	2	<0.01
Colville (0)	0	<0.01
Comanche (0)	1	<0.01
Cree (0)	0	<0.01
Creek (0)	0	<0.01
Crow (0)	0	<0.01
Delaware (2)	15	0.03
Hopi (0)	0	<0.01
Houma (0)	0	<0.01
Inupiat (Alaska Native) (0)	0	<0.01
Iroquois (4)	13	0.02
Kiowa (0)	0	<0.01
Lumbee (1)	2	<0.01
Menominee (0)	0	<0.01
Mexican American Ind. (1)	5	0.01
Navajo (2)	5	0.01
Osage (0)	0	<0.01
Ottawa (3)	3	0.01
Paiute (0)	1	<0.01
Pima (0)	0	<0.01
Potawatomi (0)	0	<0.01
Pueblo (5)	5	0.01
Puget Sound Salish (0)	0	<0.01
Seminole (1)	6	0.01
Shoshone (0)	0	<0.01
Sioux (0)	5	0.01
South American Ind. (39)	54	0.10
Spanish American Ind. (1)	1	<0.01
Tlingit-Haida (Alaska Native) (0)	0	<0.01
Tohono O'Odham (0)	0	<0.01
Tsimshian (Alaska Native) (0)	0	<0.01
Ute (0)	0	<0.01
Yakama (0)	0	<0.01
Yaqui (0)	0	<0.01
Yuman (0)	0	<0.01
Yup'ik (Alaska Native) (0)	0	<0.01
Asian (1,704)	2,012	3.62
Not Hispanic (1,666)	1,915	3.44
Hispanic (38)	97	0.17
Bangladeshi (2)	3	0.01
Bhutanese (0)	0	<0.01
Burmese (13)	14	0.03
Cambodian (4)	5	0.01
Chinese, ex. Taiwanese (537)	601	1.08
Filipino (95)	144	0.26
Hmong (0)	0	<0.01
Indian (436)	478	0.86
Indonesian (9)	13	0.02
Japanese (44)	80	0.14
Korean (183)	221	0.40
Laotian (1)	2	<0.01
Malaysian (9)	12	0.02
Nepalese (3)	6	0.01
Pakistani (69)	70	0.13
Sri Lankan (12)	12	0.02
Taiwanese (32)	35	0.06
Thai (51)	57	0.10
Vietnamese (134)	159	0.29
Hawaii Native/Pacific Islander (24)	92	0.17
Not Hispanic (16)	45	0.08
Hispanic (8)	47	0.08
Fijian (0)	0	<0.01
Guamanian/Chamorro (4)	7	0.01
Marshallese (0)	0	<0.01
Native Hawaiian (7)	24	0.04
Samoan (0)	0	<0.01
Tongan (5)	5	0.01
White (41,293)	42,972	77.23
Not Hispanic (34,329)	35,169	63.21
Hispanic (6,964)	7,803	14.02

Notes: † The Census 2010 population figure is used to calculate the percentages in the Hispanic Origin and Race categories. Ancestry percentages are based on the 2006-2010 American Community Survey population (not shown); ‡ Numbers in parentheses indicate the number of people reporting a single ancestry; * Numbers in parentheses indicate the number of persons reporting this race alone, not in combination with any other race; Please refer to the Explanation of Data for more information.

Bethlehem

Place Type: City
County: Northampton
Population: 74,982

Ancestry	Population	%
Afghan (40)	103	0.14
African, Sub-Saharan (325)	413	0.55
African (197)	285	0.38
Cape Verdean (0)	0	<0.01
Ethiopian (20)	20	0.03
Ghanaian (0)	0	<0.01
Kenyan (35)	35	0.05
Liberian (0)	0	<0.01
Nigerian (30)	30	0.04
Senegalese (43)	43	0.06
Sierra Leonean (0)	0	<0.01
Somalian (0)	0	<0.01
South African (0)	0	<0.01
Sudanese (0)	0	<0.01
Ugandan (0)	0	<0.01
Zimbabwean (0)	0	<0.01
Other Sub-Saharan African (0)	0	<0.01
Albanian (0)	0	<0.01
Alsatian (0)	0	<0.01
American (1,759)	1,759	2.35
Arab (413)	564	0.75
Arab (225)	225	0.30
Egyptian (16)	16	0.02
Iraqi (0)	0	<0.01
Jordanian (5)	5	0.01
Lebanese (27)	60	0.08
Moroccan (0)	0	<0.01
Palestinian (0)	0	<0.01
Syrian (128)	224	0.30
Other Arab (12)	34	0.05
Armenian (0)	21	0.03
Assyrian/Chaldean/Syriac (8)	8	0.01
Australian (0)	9	0.01
Austrian (166)	783	1.05
Basque (0)	12	0.02
Belgian (0)	14	0.02
Brazilian (39)	39	0.05
British (127)	446	0.60
Bulgarian (10)	10	0.01
Cajun (0)	0	<0.01
Canadian (53)	147	0.20
Carpatho Rusyn (13)	13	0.02
Celtic (0)	11	0.01
Croatian (21)	75	0.10
Cypriot (0)	0	<0.01
Czech (27)	415	0.56
Czechoslovakian (40)	166	0.22
Danish (34)	97	0.13
Dutch (380)	1,828	2.45
Eastern European (73)	103	0.14
English (1,030)	4,577	6.12
Estonian (0)	0	<0.01
European (472)	487	0.65
Finnish (29)	29	0.04
French, ex. Basque (167)	1,480	1.98
French Canadian (56)	86	0.12
German (5,259)	16,986	22.72
German Russian (0)	0	<0.01
Greek (280)	657	0.88
Guyanese (12)	173	0.23
Hungarian (1,019)	3,458	4.63
Icelander (0)	0	<0.01
Iranian (64)	64	0.09
Irish (2,138)	10,563	14.13
Israeli (0)	0	<0.01
Italian (2,593)	8,299	11.10
Latvian (0)	8	0.01
Lithuanian (180)	430	0.58
Luxemburger (0)	0	<0.01
Macedonian (16)	16	0.02
Maltese (0)	0	<0.01
New Zealander (14)	14	0.02
Northern European (0)	0	<0.01

Ancestry	Population	%
Norwegian (71)	232	0.31
Pennsylvania German (1,594)	2,599	3.48
Polish (1,041)	3,725	4.98
Portuguese (433)	625	0.84
Romanian (48)	76	0.10
Russian (286)	1,042	1.39
Scandinavian (12)	22	0.03
Scotch-Irish (256)	935	1.25
Scottish (280)	1,079	1.44
Serbian (24)	43	0.06
Slavic (12)	80	0.11
Slovak (973)	2,574	3.44
Slovene (203)	316	0.42
Soviet Union (0)	0	<0.01
Swedish (43)	556	0.74
Swiss (42)	285	0.38
Turkish (157)	184	0.25
Ukrainian (335)	864	1.16
Welsh (264)	1,433	1.92
West Indian, ex. Hispanic (261)	428	0.57
Bahamian (0)	0	<0.01
Barbadian (0)	12	0.02
Belizean (0)	0	<0.01
Bermudan (0)	0	<0.01
British West Indian (0)	0	<0.01
Dutch West Indian (0)	12	0.02
Haitian (134)	134	0.18
Jamaican (90)	154	0.21
Trinidadian/Tobagonian (19)	29	0.04
U.S. Virgin Islander (3)	3	<0.01
West Indian (15)	84	0.11
Other West Indian (0)	0	<0.01
Yugoslavian (53)	63	0.08

Hispanic Origin	Population	%
Hispanic or Latino (of any race)	18,268	24.36
Central American, ex. Mexican	643	0.86
Costa Rican	27	0.04
Guatemalan	275	0.37
Honduran	90	0.12
Nicaraguan	86	0.11
Panamanian	46	0.06
Salvadoran	116	0.15
Other Central American	3	<0.01
Cuban	196	0.26
Dominican Republic	1,010	1.35
Mexican	1,085	1.45
Puerto Rican	13,722	18.30
South American	804	1.07
Argentinean	37	0.05
Bolivian	17	0.02
Chilean	79	0.11
Colombian	240	0.32
Ecuadorian	200	0.27
Paraguayan	3	<0.01
Peruvian	155	0.21
Uruguayan	22	0.03
Venezuelan	50	0.07
Other South American	1	<0.01
Other Hispanic or Latino	808	1.08

Race*	Population	%
African-American/Black (5,199)	6,519	8.69
Not Hispanic (4,087)	4,815	6.42
Hispanic (1,112)	1,704	2.27
American Indian/Alaska Native (259)	608	0.81
Not Hispanic (83)	307	0.41
Hispanic (176)	301	0.40
Alaska Athabascan (Ala. Nat.) (0)	0	<0.01
Aleut (Alaska Native) (0)	0	<0.01
Apache (0)	2	<0.01
Arapaho (0)	0	<0.01
Blackfeet (3)	22	0.03
Canadian/French Am. Ind. (0)	0	<0.01
Central American Ind. (6)	10	0.01
Cherokee (10)	79	0.11
Cheyenne (0)	0	<0.01
Chickasaw (0)	0	<0.01
Chippewa (0)	0	<0.01

Race*	Population	%
Choctaw (1)	3	<0.01
Colville (0)	0	<0.01
Comanche (0)	1	<0.01
Cree (0)	0	<0.01
Creek (0)	0	<0.01
Crow (0)	0	<0.01
Delaware (3)	22	0.03
Hopi (0)	0	<0.01
Houma (0)	0	<0.01
Inupiat (Alaska Native) (0)	0	<0.01
Iroquois (4)	13	0.02
Kiowa (0)	0	<0.01
Lumbee (1)	2	<0.01
Menominee (0)	0	<0.01
Mexican American Ind. (1)	5	0.01
Navajo (4)	7	0.01
Osage (0)	0	<0.01
Ottawa (4)	5	0.01
Paiute (0)	1	<0.01
Pima (0)	0	<0.01
Potawatomi (0)	0	<0.01
Pueblo (5)	6	0.01
Puget Sound Salish (1)	1	<0.01
Seminole (1)	7	0.01
Shoshone (0)	0	<0.01
Sioux (2)	8	0.01
South American Ind. (47)	73	0.10
Spanish American Ind. (1)	1	<0.01
Tlingit-Haida (Alaska Native) (0)	0	<0.01
Tohono O'Odham (0)	0	<0.01
Tsimshian (Alaska Native) (0)	0	<0.01
Ute (0)	0	<0.01
Yakama (0)	0	<0.01
Yaqui (0)	0	<0.01
Yuman (0)	0	<0.01
Yup'ik (Alaska Native) (0)	0	<0.01
Asian (2,143)	2,530	3.37
Not Hispanic (2,103)	2,418	3.22
Hispanic (40)	112	0.15
Bangladeshi (2)	3	<0.01
Bhutanese (0)	0	<0.01
Burmese (22)	23	0.03
Cambodian (9)	12	0.02
Chinese, ex. Taiwanese (614)	693	0.92
Filipino (150)	221	0.29
Hmong (0)	0	<0.01
Indian (588)	633	0.84
Indonesian (12)	18	0.02
Japanese (48)	95	0.13
Korean (240)	283	0.38
Laotian (1)	2	<0.01
Malaysian (11)	14	0.02
Nepalese (3)	6	0.01
Pakistani (77)	83	0.11
Sri Lankan (15)	15	0.02
Taiwanese (32)	35	0.05
Thai (55)	62	0.08
Vietnamese (190)	217	0.29
Hawaii Native/Pacific Islander (31)	121	0.16
Not Hispanic (22)	69	0.09
Hispanic (9)	52	0.07
Fijian (0)	0	<0.01
Guamanian/Chamorro (5)	10	0.01
Marshallese (0)	0	<0.01
Native Hawaiian (10)	36	0.05
Samoan (1)	1	<0.01
Tongan (5)	5	0.01
White (57,305)	59,451	79.29
Not Hispanic (49,032)	50,150	66.88
Hispanic (8,273)	9,301	12.40

*Notes: † The Census 2010 population figure is used to calculate the percentages in the Hispanic Origin and Race categories. Ancestry percentages are based on the 2006-2010 American Community Survey population (not shown); ‡ Numbers in parentheses indicate the number of people reporting a single ancestry; * Numbers in parentheses indicate the number of persons reporting this race alone, not in combination with any other race; Please refer to the Explanation of Data for more information.*

Bristol

Place Type: Township
County: Bucks
Population: 54,582

Ancestry	Population	%
Afghan (0)	0	<0.01
African, Sub-Saharan (1,318)	1,378	2.51
African (1,011)	1,057	1.92
Cape Verdean (0)	0	<0.01
Ethiopian (0)	0	<0.01
Ghanaian (55)	62	0.11
Kenyan (0)	0	<0.01
Liberian (243)	243	0.44
Nigerian (9)	16	0.03
Senegalese (0)	0	<0.01
Sierra Leonean (0)	0	<0.01
Somalian (0)	0	<0.01
South African (0)	0	<0.01
Sudanese (0)	0	<0.01
Ugandan (0)	0	<0.01
Zimbabwean (0)	0	<0.01
Other Sub-Saharan African (0)	0	<0.01
Albanian (27)	27	0.05
Alsatian (12)	12	0.02
American (1,396)	1,396	2.54
Arab (182)	245	0.45
Arab (0)	0	<0.01
Egyptian (97)	97	0.18
Iraqi (0)	0	<0.01
Jordanian (0)	0	<0.01
Lebanese (18)	42	0.08
Moroccan (0)	0	<0.01
Palestinian (0)	0	<0.01
Syrian (35)	74	0.13
Other Arab (32)	32	0.06
Armenian (13)	13	0.02
Assyrian/Chaldean/Syriac (0)	0	<0.01
Australian (0)	0	<0.01
Austrian (26)	85	0.15
Basque (0)	0	<0.01
Belgian (19)	118	0.21
Brazilian (0)	0	<0.01
British (77)	120	0.22
Bulgarian (0)	13	0.02
Cajun (0)	0	<0.01
Canadian (0)	18	0.03
Carpatho Rusyn (19)	19	0.03
Celtic (0)	0	<0.01
Croatian (0)	0	<0.01
Cypriot (0)	0	<0.01
Czech (12)	72	0.13
Czechoslovakian (25)	88	0.16
Danish (30)	75	0.14
Dutch (142)	942	1.71
Eastern European (17)	24	0.04
English (1,398)	5,476	9.96
Estonian (0)	0	<0.01
European (84)	101	0.18
Finnish (0)	60	0.11
French, ex. Basque (88)	927	1.69
French Canadian (85)	233	0.42
German (4,960)	13,990	25.43
German Russian (0)	0	<0.01
Greek (131)	307	0.56
Guyanese (53)	53	0.10
Hungarian (156)	648	1.18
Icelander (0)	0	<0.01
Iranian (0)	10	0.02
Irish (5,896)	16,287	29.61
Israeli (0)	0	<0.01
Italian (2,898)	7,904	14.37
Latvian (0)	0	<0.01
Lithuanian (118)	379	0.69
Luxemburger (0)	0	<0.01
Macedonian (14)	14	0.03
Maltese (0)	0	<0.01
New Zealander (0)	0	<0.01
Northern European (40)	40	0.07

Ancestry	Population	%
Norwegian (31)	88	0.16
Pennsylvania German (68)	196	0.36
Polish (1,630)	5,282	9.60
Portuguese (14)	73	0.13
Romanian (12)	37	0.07
Russian (194)	478	0.87
Scandinavian (10)	65	0.12
Scotch-Irish (412)	1,261	2.29
Scottish (252)	809	1.47
Serbian (15)	15	0.03
Slavic (29)	96	0.17
Slovak (317)	558	1.01
Slovene (0)	13	0.02
Soviet Union (0)	0	<0.01
Swedish (46)	295	0.54
Swiss (0)	72	0.13
Turkish (167)	201	0.37
Ukrainian (433)	704	1.28
Welsh (120)	715	1.30
West Indian, ex. Hispanic (239)	264	0.48
Bahamian (0)	0	<0.01
Barbadian (0)	0	<0.01
Belizean (0)	0	<0.01
Bermudan (0)	0	<0.01
British West Indian (0)	0	<0.01
Dutch West Indian (0)	0	<0.01
Haitian (199)	206	0.37
Jamaican (40)	58	0.11
Trinidadian/Tobagonian (0)	0	<0.01
U.S. Virgin Islander (0)	0	<0.01
West Indian (0)	0	<0.01
Other West Indian (0)	0	<0.01
Yugoslavian (0)	14	0.03

Hispanic Origin	Population	%
Hispanic or Latino (of any race)	4,040	7.40
Central American, ex. Mexican	335	0.61
Costa Rican	113	0.21
Guatemalan	108	0.20
Honduran	20	0.04
Nicaraguan	20	0.04
Panamanian	10	0.02
Salvadoran	59	0.11
Other Central American	5	0.01
Cuban	65	0.12
Dominican Republic	121	0.22
Mexican	1,100	2.02
Puerto Rican	1,873	3.43
South American	260	0.48
Argentinean	19	0.03
Bolivian	0	<0.01
Chilean	13	0.02
Colombian	93	0.17
Ecuadorian	69	0.13
Paraguayan	1	<0.01
Peruvian	32	0.06
Uruguayan	6	0.01
Venezuelan	20	0.04
Other South American	7	0.01
Other Hispanic or Latino	286	0.52

Race*	Population	%
African-American/Black (5,576)	6,353	11.64
Not Hispanic (5,425)	6,069	11.12
Hispanic (151)	284	0.52
American Indian/Alaska Native (136)	473	0.87
Not Hispanic (92)	381	0.70
Hispanic (44)	92	0.17
Alaska Athabascan (Ala. Nat.) (0)	3	0.01
Aleut (Alaska Native) (0)	0	<0.01
Apache (0)	8	0.01
Arapaho (0)	1	<0.01
Blackfeet (1)	27	0.05
Canadian/French Am. Ind. (0)	0	<0.01
Central American Ind. (4)	9	0.02
Cherokee (8)	73	0.13
Cheyenne (0)	0	<0.01
Chickasaw (0)	0	<0.01
Chippewa (0)	3	0.01

Race*	Population	%
Choctaw (3)	3	0.01
Colville (0)	0	<0.01
Comanche (0)	0	<0.01
Cree (0)	3	0.01
Creek (0)	0	<0.01
Crow (0)	0	<0.01
Delaware (3)	13	0.02
Hopi (0)	0	<0.01
Houma (0)	0	<0.01
Inupiat (Alaska Native) (0)	0	<0.01
Iroquois (7)	22	0.04
Kiowa (0)	1	<0.01
Lumbee (2)	4	0.01
Menominee (0)	0	<0.01
Mexican American Ind. (12)	17	0.03
Navajo (0)	2	<0.01
Osage (0)	0	<0.01
Ottawa (0)	0	<0.01
Paiute (0)	0	<0.01
Pima (0)	0	<0.01
Potawatomi (0)	0	<0.01
Pueblo (0)	0	<0.01
Puget Sound Salish (0)	0	<0.01
Seminole (0)	6	0.01
Shoshone (0)	0	<0.01
Sioux (3)	16	0.03
South American Ind. (7)	11	0.02
Spanish American Ind. (0)	0	<0.01
Tlingit-Haida (Alaska Native) (0)	0	<0.01
Tohono O'Odham (0)	0	<0.01
Tsimshian (Alaska Native) (0)	0	<0.01
Ute (0)	0	<0.01
Yakama (0)	0	<0.01
Yaqui (0)	0	<0.01
Yuman (0)	0	<0.01
Yup'ik (Alaska Native) (0)	0	<0.01
Asian (1,546)	1,896	3.47
Not Hispanic (1,527)	1,840	3.37
Hispanic (19)	56	0.10
Bangladeshi (10)	11	0.02
Bhutanese (0)	0	<0.01
Burmese (2)	2	<0.01
Cambodian (62)	72	0.13
Chinese, ex. Taiwanese (123)	162	0.30
Filipino (231)	319	0.58
Hmong (0)	0	<0.01
Indian (810)	899	1.65
Indonesian (3)	4	0.01
Japanese (15)	44	0.08
Korean (95)	135	0.25
Laotian (1)	1	<0.01
Malaysian (0)	0	<0.01
Nepalese (4)	4	0.01
Pakistani (35)	59	0.11
Sri Lankan (5)	9	0.02
Taiwanese (1)	1	<0.01
Thai (12)	18	0.03
Vietnamese (95)	110	0.20
Hawaii Native/Pacific Islander (18)	73	0.13
Not Hispanic (18)	65	0.12
Hispanic (0)	8	0.01
Fijian (0)	0	<0.01
Guamanian/Chamorro (14)	19	0.03
Marshallese (0)	0	<0.01
Native Hawaiian (0)	9	0.02
Samoan (0)	2	<0.01
Tongan (0)	0	<0.01
White (44,190)	45,446	83.26
Not Hispanic (42,197)	43,161	79.08
Hispanic (1,993)	2,285	4.19

Notes: † The Census 2010 population figure is used to calculate the percentages in the Hispanic Origin and Race categories. Ancestry percentages are based on the 2006-2010 American Community Survey population (not shown); ‡ Numbers in parentheses indicate the number of people reporting a single ancestry; * Numbers in parentheses indicate the number of persons reporting this race alone, not in combination with any other race; Please refer to the Explanation of Data for more information.

Erie

Place Type: City
County: Erie
Population: 101,786

Ancestry	Population	%
Afghan (85)	85	0.08
African, Sub-Saharan (3,074)	4,228	4.16
African (2,494)	3,634	3.58
Cape Verdean (0)	0	<0.01
Ethiopian (0)	0	<0.01
Ghanaian (0)	0	<0.01
Kenyan (17)	17	0.02
Liberian (0)	0	<0.01
Nigerian (7)	7	0.01
Senegalese (0)	0	<0.01
Sierra Leonean (0)	0	<0.01
Somalian (96)	96	0.09
South African (27)	27	0.03
Sudanese (221)	221	0.22
Ugandan (0)	0	<0.01
Zimbabwean (0)	0	<0.01
Other Sub-Saharan African (212)	226	0.22
Albanian (136)	136	0.13
Alsatian (0)	7	0.01
American (2,350)	2,350	2.31
Arab (262)	532	0.52
Arab (46)	152	0.15
Egyptian (8)	8	0.01
Iraqi (166)	208	0.20
Jordanian (0)	0	<0.01
Lebanese (36)	98	0.10
Moroccan (6)	6	0.01
Palestinian (0)	0	<0.01
Syrian (0)	37	0.04
Other Arab (0)	23	0.02
Armenian (153)	183	0.18
Assyrian/Chaldean/Syriac (0)	0	<0.01
Australian (0)	22	0.02
Austrian (45)	350	0.34
Basque (0)	0	<0.01
Belgian (14)	89	0.09
Brazilian (53)	107	0.11
British (98)	151	0.15
Bulgarian (12)	12	0.01
Cajun (0)	0	<0.01
Canadian (79)	88	0.09
Carpatho Rusyn (17)	37	0.04
Celtic (0)	15	0.01
Croatian (123)	352	0.35
Cypriot (0)	0	<0.01
Czech (134)	626	0.62
Czechoslovakian (114)	187	0.18
Danish (40)	310	0.31
Dutch (169)	1,425	1.40
Eastern European (19)	19	0.02
English (1,236)	5,870	5.78
Estonian (0)	12	0.01
European (424)	436	0.43
Finnish (0)	182	0.18
French, ex. Basque (80)	1,680	1.65
French Canadian (105)	199	0.20
German (6,379)	27,772	27.33
German Russian (2)	2	<0.01
Greek (173)	350	0.34
Guyanese (0)	7	0.01
Hungarian (225)	1,120	1.10
Icelander (0)	0	<0.01
Iranian (11)	20	0.02
Irish (3,859)	17,685	17.40
Israeli (6)	6	0.01
Italian (5,781)	15,798	15.54
Latvian (0)	20	0.02
Lithuanian (92)	349	0.34
Luxemburger (0)	10	0.01
Macedonian (10)	10	0.01
Maltese (0)	0	<0.01
New Zealander (0)	0	<0.01
Northern European (0)	0	<0.01

Ancestry	Population	%
Norwegian (51)	188	0.18
Pennsylvania German (101)	329	0.32
Polish (5,072)	12,920	12.71
Portuguese (80)	415	0.41
Romanian (52)	174	0.17
Russian (554)	1,342	1.32
Scandinavian (0)	0	<0.01
Scotch-Irish (667)	2,432	2.39
Scottish (278)	984	0.97
Serbian (32)	69	0.07
Slavic (22)	127	0.12
Slovak (383)	1,499	1.47
Slovene (22)	61	0.06
Soviet Union (0)	0	<0.01
Swedish (214)	1,830	1.80
Swiss (20)	167	0.16
Turkish (11)	69	0.07
Ukrainian (637)	864	0.85
Welsh (39)	743	0.73
West Indian, ex. Hispanic (345)	353	0.35
Bahamian (0)	0	<0.01
Barbadian (0)	0	<0.01
Belizean (0)	0	<0.01
Bermudan (0)	0	<0.01
British West Indian (20)	20	0.02
Dutch West Indian (0)	0	<0.01
Haitian (211)	211	0.21
Jamaican (79)	87	0.09
Trinidadian/Tobagonian (0)	0	<0.01
U.S. Virgin Islander (0)	0	<0.01
West Indian (35)	35	0.03
Other West Indian (0)	0	<0.01
Yugoslavian (684)	697	0.69

Hispanic Origin	Population	%
Hispanic or Latino (of any race)	7,005	6.88
Central American, ex. Mexican	188	0.18
Costa Rican	29	0.03
Guatemalan	22	0.02
Honduran	23	0.02
Nicaraguan	18	0.02
Panamanian	14	0.01
Salvadoran	82	0.08
Other Central American	0	<0.01
Cuban	98	0.10
Dominican Republic	110	0.11
Mexican	1,271	1.25
Puerto Rican	4,752	4.67
South American	132	0.13
Argentinean	7	0.01
Bolivian	0	<0.01
Chilean	6	0.01
Colombian	74	0.07
Ecuadorian	8	0.01
Paraguayan	0	<0.01
Peruvian	19	0.02
Uruguayan	1	<0.01
Venezuelan	17	0.02
Other South American	0	<0.01
Other Hispanic or Latino	454	0.45

Race*	Population	%
African-American/Black (17,141)	20,022	19.67
Not Hispanic (16,535)	19,010	18.68
Hispanic (606)	1,012	0.99
American Indian/Alaska Native (291)	909	0.89
Not Hispanic (210)	743	0.73
Hispanic (81)	166	0.16
Alaska Athabascan (Ala. Nat.) (0)	0	<0.01
Aleut (Alaska Native) (1)	1	<0.01
Apache (2)	9	0.01
Arapaho (0)	0	<0.01
Blackfeet (6)	48	0.05
Canadian/French Am. Ind. (1)	4	<0.01
Central American Ind. (1)	4	<0.01
Cherokee (22)	135	0.13
Cheyenne (0)	0	<0.01
Chickasaw (0)	4	<0.01
Chippewa (3)	7	0.01

Race*	Population	%
Choctaw (2)	10	0.01
Colville (0)	0	<0.01
Comanche (1)	1	<0.01
Cree (0)	2	<0.01
Creek (4)	7	<0.01
Crow (0)	3	<0.01
Delaware (1)	1	<0.01
Hopi (1)	1	<0.01
Houma (0)	0	<0.01
Inupiat (Alaska Native) (0)	0	<0.01
Iroquois (50)	105	0.10
Kiowa (0)	0	<0.01
Lumbee (0)	0	<0.01
Menominee (0)	0	<0.01
Mexican American Ind. (7)	17	0.02
Navajo (3)	7	0.01
Osage (0)	0	<0.01
Ottawa (0)	0	<0.01
Paiute (0)	0	<0.01
Pima (0)	0	<0.01
Potawatomi (0)	0	<0.01
Pueblo (1)	1	<0.01
Puget Sound Salish (0)	0	<0.01
Seminole (0)	5	<0.01
Shoshone (1)	2	<0.01
Sioux (6)	33	0.03
South American Ind. (0)	7	0.01
Spanish American Ind. (0)	0	<0.01
Tlingit-Haida (Alaska Native) (2)	5	<0.01
Tohono O'Odham (0)	0	<0.01
Tsimshian (Alaska Native) (0)	0	<0.01
Ute (0)	1	<0.01
Yakama (0)	0	<0.01
Yaqui (0)	0	<0.01
Yuman (2)	2	<0.01
Yup'ik (Alaska Native) (0)	0	<0.01
Asian (1,515)	1,997	1.96
Not Hispanic (1,498)	1,951	1.92
Hispanic (17)	46	0.05
Bangladeshi (2)	2	<0.01
Bhutanese (332)	395	0.39
Burmese (110)	121	0.12
Cambodian (1)	2	<0.01
Chinese, ex. Taiwanese (145)	182	0.18
Filipino (102)	185	0.18
Hmong (0)	0	<0.01
Indian (230)	294	0.29
Indonesian (4)	4	<0.01
Japanese (21)	72	0.07
Korean (47)	100	0.10
Laotian (7)	7	0.01
Malaysian (2)	3	<0.01
Nepalese (68)	138	0.14
Pakistani (9)	9	0.01
Sri Lankan (0)	0	<0.01
Taiwanese (2)	2	<0.01
Thai (18)	32	0.03
Vietnamese (288)	326	0.32
Hawaii Native/Pacific Islander (53)	154	0.15
Not Hispanic (43)	135	0.13
Hispanic (10)	19	0.02
Fijian (0)	1	<0.01
Guamanian/Chamorro (12)	31	0.03
Marshallese (0)	0	<0.01
Native Hawaiian (8)	29	0.03
Samoan (3)	6	0.01
Tongan (0)	0	<0.01
White (76,327)	79,875	78.47
Not Hispanic (73,073)	76,023	74.69
Hispanic (3,254)	3,852	3.78

*Notes: † The Census 2010 population figure is used to calculate the percentages in the Hispanic Origin and Race categories. Ancestry percentages are based on the 2006-2010 American Community Survey population (not shown); ‡ Numbers in parentheses indicate the number of people reporting a single ancestry; * Numbers in parentheses indicate the number of persons reporting this race alone, not in combination with any other race; Please refer to the Explanation of Data for more information.*

Lancaster

Place Type: City
County: Lancaster
Population: 59,322

Ancestry	Population	%
Afghan (0)	0	<0.01
African, Sub-Saharan (764)	820	1.39
African (618)	659	1.12
Cape Verdean (14)	14	0.02
Ethiopian (82)	87	0.15
Ghanaian (0)	0	<0.01
Kenyan (0)	10	0.02
Liberian (0)	0	<0.01
Nigerian (0)	0	<0.01
Senegalese (0)	0	<0.01
Sierra Leonean (0)	0	<0.01
Somalian (0)	0	<0.01
South African (27)	27	0.05
Sudanese (23)	23	0.04
Ugandan (0)	0	<0.01
Zimbabwean (0)	0	<0.01
Other Sub-Saharan African (0)	0	<0.01
Albanian (0)	0	<0.01
Alsatian (4)	4	0.01
American (1,406)	1,406	2.39
Arab (0)	30	0.05
Arab (0)	0	<0.01
Egyptian (0)	0	<0.01
Iraqi (0)	0	<0.01
Jordanian (0)	0	<0.01
Lebanese (0)	15	0.03
Moroccan (0)	0	<0.01
Palestinian (0)	0	<0.01
Syrian (0)	15	0.03
Other Arab (0)	0	<0.01
Armenian (52)	52	0.09
Assyrian/Chaldean/Syriac (0)	0	<0.01
Australian (0)	0	<0.01
Austrian (0)	93	0.16
Basque (0)	0	<0.01
Belgian (0)	16	0.03
Brazilian (5)	17	0.03
British (34)	188	0.32
Bulgarian (0)	0	<0.01
Cajun (0)	0	<0.01
Canadian (0)	34	0.06
Carpatho Rusyn (0)	0	<0.01
Celtic (18)	18	0.03
Croatian (0)	8	0.01
Cypriot (0)	0	<0.01
Czech (30)	72	0.12
Czechoslovakian (0)	0	<0.01
Danish (8)	73	0.12
Dutch (55)	396	0.67
Eastern European (41)	41	0.07
English (1,035)	3,009	5.12
Estonian (0)	0	<0.01
European (197)	197	0.33
Finnish (0)	56	0.10
French, ex. Basque (111)	704	1.20
French Canadian (18)	63	0.11
German (5,665)	11,795	20.05
German Russian (0)	0	<0.01
Greek (81)	178	0.30
Guyanese (0)	0	<0.01
Hungarian (61)	221	0.38
Icelander (0)	0	<0.01
Iranian (0)	0	<0.01
Irish (1,084)	4,900	8.33
Israeli (0)	13	0.02
Italian (935)	2,451	4.17
Latvian (8)	8	0.01
Lithuanian (0)	68	0.12
Luxemburger (0)	0	<0.01
Macedonian (0)	0	<0.01
Maltese (0)	0	<0.01
New Zealander (0)	0	<0.01
Northern European (0)	0	<0.01

Ancestry	Population	%
Norwegian (76)	166	0.28
Pennsylvania German (75)	143	0.24
Polish (381)	1,142	1.94
Portuguese (0)	20	0.03
Romanian (33)	50	0.09
Russian (109)	381	0.65
Scandinavian (16)	38	0.06
Scotch-Irish (282)	842	1.43
Scottish (35)	452	0.77
Serbian (0)	0	<0.01
Slavic (10)	10	0.02
Slovak (21)	54	0.09
Slovene (0)	0	<0.01
Soviet Union (0)	0	<0.01
Swedish (29)	237	0.40
Swiss (115)	714	1.21
Turkish (174)	174	0.30
Ukrainian (4)	76	0.13
Welsh (16)	328	0.56
West Indian, ex. Hispanic (289)	367	0.62
Bahamian (0)	0	<0.01
Barbadian (36)	36	0.06
Belizean (32)	32	0.05
Bermudan (0)	0	<0.01
British West Indian (10)	10	0.02
Dutch West Indian (0)	0	<0.01
Haitian (143)	187	0.32
Jamaican (55)	78	0.13
Trinidadian/Tobagonian (0)	0	<0.01
U.S. Virgin Islander (0)	0	<0.01
West Indian (13)	24	0.04
Other West Indian (0)	0	<0.01
Yugoslavian (44)	70	0.12

Hispanic Origin	Population	%
Hispanic or Latino (of any race)	23,329	39.33
Central American, ex. Mexican	405	0.68
Costa Rican	20	0.03
Guatemalan	103	0.17
Honduran	94	0.16
Nicaraguan	15	0.03
Panamanian	25	0.04
Salvadoran	143	0.24
Other Central American	5	0.01
Cuban	994	1.68
Dominican Republic	1,905	3.21
Mexican	1,046	1.76
Puerto Rican	17,341	29.23
South American	571	0.96
Argentinean	34	0.06
Bolivian	1	<0.01
Chilean	14	0.02
Colombian	208	0.35
Ecuadorian	157	0.26
Paraguayan	5	0.01
Peruvian	108	0.18
Uruguayan	15	0.03
Venezuelan	26	0.04
Other South American	3	0.01
Other Hispanic or Latino	1,067	1.80

Race*	Population	%
African-American/Black (9,683)	11,899	20.06
Not Hispanic (7,869)	9,178	15.47
Hispanic (1,814)	2,721	4.59
American Indian/Alaska Native (433)	900	1.52
Not Hispanic (172)	445	0.75
Hispanic (261)	455	0.77
Alaska Athabascan (Ala. Nat.) (2)	2	<0.01
Aleut (Alaska Native) (1)	1	<0.01
Apache (1)	7	0.01
Arapaho (0)	0	<0.01
Blackfeet (5)	28	0.05
Canadian/French Am. Ind. (3)	4	0.01
Central American Ind. (18)	19	0.03
Cherokee (27)	112	0.19
Cheyenne (0)	0	<0.01
Chickasaw (0)	0	<0.01
Chippewa (3)	6	0.01

Race*	Population	%
Choctaw (0)	3	0.01
Colville (0)	0	<0.01
Comanche (0)	3	0.01
Cree (2)	4	0.01
Creek (0)	4	0.01
Crow (0)	0	<0.01
Delaware (1)	5	0.01
Hopi (0)	2	<0.01
Houma (0)	0	<0.01
Inupiat (Alaska Native) (0)	2	<0.01
Iroquois (9)	25	0.04
Kiowa (0)	0	<0.01
Lumbee (0)	0	<0.01
Menominee (0)	0	<0.01
Mexican American Ind. (6)	10	0.02
Navajo (1)	2	<0.01
Osage (0)	0	<0.01
Ottawa (0)	0	<0.01
Paiute (1)	1	<0.01
Pima (1)	1	<0.01
Potawatomi (1)	1	<0.01
Pueblo (0)	1	<0.01
Puget Sound Salish (1)	1	<0.01
Seminole (0)	4	0.01
Shoshone (0)	0	<0.01
Sioux (6)	22	0.04
South American Ind. (41)	77	0.13
Spanish American Ind. (8)	11	0.02
Tlingit-Haida (Alaska Native) (0)	0	<0.01
Tohono O'Odham (0)	0	<0.01
Tsimshian (Alaska Native) (0)	0	<0.01
Ute (0)	0	<0.01
Yakama (1)	1	<0.01
Yaqui (2)	3	0.01
Yuman (0)	0	<0.01
Yup'ik (Alaska Native) (0)	0	<0.01
Asian (1,773)	2,087	3.52
Not Hispanic (1,729)	1,965	3.31
Hispanic (44)	122	0.21
Bangladeshi (3)	8	0.01
Bhutanese (177)	209	0.35
Burmese (128)	135	0.23
Cambodian (200)	230	0.39
Chinese, ex. Taiwanese (158)	208	0.35
Filipino (80)	129	0.22
Hmong (19)	19	0.03
Indian (172)	230	0.39
Indonesian (4)	8	0.01
Japanese (28)	50	0.08
Korean (68)	94	0.16
Laotian (10)	14	0.02
Malaysian (6)	8	0.01
Nepalese (40)	87	0.15
Pakistani (10)	12	0.02
Sri Lankan (5)	6	0.01
Taiwanese (1)	1	<0.01
Thai (10)	14	0.02
Vietnamese (531)	594	1.00
Hawaii Native/Pacific Islander (43)	191	0.32
Not Hispanic (17)	56	0.09
Hispanic (26)	135	0.23
Fijian (0)	0	<0.01
Guamanian/Chamorro (12)	27	0.05
Marshallese (0)	0	<0.01
Native Hawaiian (10)	30	0.05
Samoan (5)	8	0.01
Tongan (0)	0	<0.01
White (32,729)	35,384	59.65
Not Hispanic (24,501)	25,936	43.72
Hispanic (8,228)	9,448	15.93

Notes: † The Census 2010 population figure is used to calculate the percentages in the Hispanic Origin and Race categories. Ancestry percentages are based on the 2006-2010 American Community Survey population (not shown); ‡ Numbers in parentheses indicate the number of people reporting a single ancestry; * Numbers in parentheses indicate the number of persons reporting this race alone, not in combination with any other race; Please refer to the Explanation of Data for more information.

Levittown

Place Type: CDP
County: Bucks
Population: 52,983

Ancestry	Population	%
Afghan (0)	0	<0.01
African, Sub-Saharan (254)	292	0.56
African (213)	244	0.47
Cape Verdean (0)	0	<0.01
Ethiopian (0)	0	<0.01
Ghanaian (6)	13	0.03
Kenyan (0)	0	<0.01
Liberian (35)	35	0.07
Nigerian (0)	0	<0.01
Senegalese (0)	0	<0.01
Sierra Leonean (0)	0	<0.01
Somalian (0)	0	<0.01
South African (0)	0	<0.01
Sudanese (0)	0	<0.01
Ugandan (0)	0	<0.01
Zimbabwean (0)	0	<0.01
Other Sub-Saharan African (0)	0	<0.01
Albanian (0)	0	<0.01
Alsatian (12)	12	0.02
American (1,650)	1,650	3.17
Arab (46)	68	0.13
Arab (0)	0	<0.01
Egyptian (21)	21	0.04
Iraqi (0)	0	<0.01
Jordanian (0)	0	<0.01
Lebanese (25)	25	0.05
Moroccan (0)	0	<0.01
Palestinian (0)	0	<0.01
Syrian (0)	22	0.04
Other Arab (0)	0	<0.01
Armenian (30)	43	0.08
Assyrian/Chaldean/Syriac (0)	0	<0.01
Australian (0)	0	<0.01
Austrian (34)	92	0.18
Basque (10)	10	0.02
Belgian (0)	99	0.19
Brazilian (0)	4	0.01
British (70)	87	0.17
Bulgarian (0)	13	0.03
Cajun (0)	0	<0.01
Canadian (39)	86	0.17
Carpatho Rusyn (0)	0	<0.01
Celtic (0)	0	<0.01
Croatian (0)	0	<0.01
Cypriot (0)	0	<0.01
Czech (25)	152	0.29
Czechoslovakian (55)	105	0.20
Danish (17)	60	0.12
Dutch (157)	828	1.59
Eastern European (39)	46	0.09
English (1,401)	5,585	10.74
Estonian (0)	0	<0.01
European (190)	225	0.43
Finnish (0)	48	0.09
French, ex. Basque (76)	1,085	2.09
French Canadian (52)	344	0.66
German (5,088)	15,853	30.49
German Russian (0)	0	<0.01
Greek (100)	302	0.58
Guyanese (70)	70	0.13
Hungarian (154)	498	0.96
Icelander (0)	0	<0.01
Iranian (0)	0	<0.01
Irish (6,062)	17,768	34.18
Israeli (0)	0	<0.01
Italian (2,596)	7,926	15.25
Latvian (12)	12	0.02
Lithuanian (136)	469	0.90
Luxemburger (0)	0	<0.01
Macedonian (0)	13	0.03
Maltese (0)	9	0.02
New Zealander (0)	0	<0.01
Northern European (30)	30	0.06

Ancestry (cont.)	Population	%
Norwegian (31)	137	0.26
Pennsylvania German (68)	182	0.35
Polish (1,692)	5,707	10.98
Portuguese (0)	32	0.06
Romanian (37)	129	0.25
Russian (208)	600	1.15
Scandinavian (0)	55	0.11
Scotch-Irish (408)	1,218	2.34
Scottish (321)	822	1.58
Serbian (0)	26	0.05
Slavic (28)	103	0.20
Slovak (283)	621	1.19
Slovene (0)	0	<0.01
Soviet Union (0)	0	<0.01
Swedish (37)	334	0.64
Swiss (0)	43	0.08
Turkish (175)	209	0.40
Ukrainian (361)	752	1.45
Welsh (138)	825	1.59
West Indian, ex. Hispanic (123)	130	0.25
Bahamian (0)	0	<0.01
Barbadian (0)	0	<0.01
Belizean (0)	0	<0.01
Bermudan (0)	0	<0.01
British West Indian (0)	0	<0.01
Dutch West Indian (0)	0	<0.01
Haitian (96)	103	0.20
Jamaican (19)	19	0.04
Trinidadian/Tobagonian (8)	8	0.02
U.S. Virgin Islander (0)	0	<0.01
West Indian (0)	0	<0.01
Other West Indian (0)	0	<0.01
Yugoslavian (0)	40	0.08

Hispanic Origin	Population	%
Hispanic or Latino (of any race)	2,685	5.07
Central American, ex. Mexican	220	0.42
Costa Rican	70	0.13
Guatemalan	82	0.15
Honduran	24	0.05
Nicaraguan	1	<0.01
Panamanian	7	0.01
Salvadoran	36	0.07
Other Central American	0	<0.01
Cuban	84	0.16
Dominican Republic	88	0.17
Mexican	589	1.11
Puerto Rican	1,293	2.44
South American	198	0.37
Argentinean	18	0.03
Bolivian	2	<0.01
Chilean	12	0.02
Colombian	86	0.16
Ecuadorian	30	0.06
Paraguayan	0	<0.01
Peruvian	22	0.04
Uruguayan	5	0.01
Venezuelan	18	0.03
Other South American	5	0.01
Other Hispanic or Latino	213	0.40

Race*	Population	%
African-American/Black (2,000)	2,461	4.64
Not Hispanic (1,904)	2,274	4.29
Hispanic (96)	187	0.35
American Indian/Alaska Native (154)	392	0.74
Not Hispanic (81)	282	0.53
Hispanic (73)	110	0.21
Alaska Athabascan (Ala. Nat.) (0)	3	0.01
Aleut (Alaska Native) (0)	0	<0.01
Apache (0)	8	0.02
Arapaho (0)	1	<0.01
Blackfeet (1)	26	0.05
Canadian/French Am. Ind. (0)	0	<0.01
Central American Ind. (4)	8	0.02
Cherokee (13)	61	0.12
Cheyenne (3)	3	0.01
Chickasaw (0)	0	<0.01
Chippewa (0)	2	<0.01

Race* (cont.)	Population	%
Choctaw (0)	0	<0.01
Colville (0)	0	<0.01
Comanche (0)	0	<0.01
Cree (0)	4	0.01
Creek (0)	3	0.01
Crow (0)	0	<0.01
Delaware (8)	15	0.03
Hopi (0)	0	<0.01
Houma (0)	0	<0.01
Inupiat (Alaska Native) (0)	0	<0.01
Iroquois (6)	22	0.04
Kiowa (0)	0	<0.01
Lumbee (2)	4	0.01
Menominee (0)	0	<0.01
Mexican American Ind. (8)	11	0.02
Navajo (0)	1	<0.01
Osage (0)	0	<0.01
Ottawa (0)	0	<0.01
Paiute (0)	0	<0.01
Pima (0)	0	<0.01
Potawatomi (0)	0	<0.01
Pueblo (0)	0	<0.01
Puget Sound Salish (0)	0	<0.01
Seminole (1)	2	<0.01
Shoshone (0)	0	<0.01
Sioux (6)	15	0.03
South American Ind. (13)	20	0.04
Spanish American Ind. (0)	0	<0.01
Tlingit-Haida (Alaska Native) (0)	0	<0.01
Tohono O'Odham (0)	0	<0.01
Tsimshian (Alaska Native) (0)	0	<0.01
Ute (0)	0	<0.01
Yakama (0)	0	<0.01
Yaqui (0)	0	<0.01
Yuman (0)	0	<0.01
Yup'ik (Alaska Native) (0)	0	<0.01
Asian (926)	1,231	2.32
Not Hispanic (917)	1,196	2.26
Hispanic (9)	35	0.07
Bangladeshi (0)	0	<0.01
Bhutanese (0)	0	<0.01
Burmese (2)	2	<0.01
Cambodian (40)	49	0.09
Chinese, ex. Taiwanese (129)	166	0.31
Filipino (165)	242	0.46
Hmong (0)	1	<0.01
Indian (272)	304	0.57
Indonesian (1)	8	0.02
Japanese (20)	52	0.10
Korean (160)	215	0.41
Laotian (1)	1	<0.01
Malaysian (0)	0	<0.01
Nepalese (0)	0	<0.01
Pakistani (20)	34	0.06
Sri Lankan (6)	10	0.02
Taiwanese (11)	11	0.02
Thai (13)	20	0.04
Vietnamese (71)	97	0.18
Hawaii Native/Pacific Islander (16)	64	0.12
Not Hispanic (16)	48	0.09
Hispanic (0)	16	0.03
Fijian (0)	1	<0.01
Guamanian/Chamorro (9)	11	0.02
Marshallese (0)	0	<0.01
Native Hawaiian (0)	11	0.02
Samoan (4)	6	0.01
Tongan (0)	0	<0.01
White (47,900)	48,870	92.24
Not Hispanic (46,421)	47,173	89.03
Hispanic (1,479)	1,697	3.20

*Notes: † The Census 2010 population figure is used to calculate the percentages in the Hispanic Origin and Race categories. Ancestry percentages are based on the 2006-2010 American Community Survey population (not shown); ‡ Numbers in parentheses indicate the number of people reporting a single ancestry; * Numbers in parentheses indicate the number of persons reporting this race alone, not in combination with any other race; Please refer to the Explanation of Data for more information.*

Lower Merion

Place Type: Township
County: Montgomery
Population: 57,825

Ancestry	Population	%
Afghan (0)	0	<0.01
African, Sub-Saharan (375)	416	0.72
African (140)	152	0.26
Cape Verdean (0)	0	<0.01
Ethiopian (0)	14	0.02
Ghanaian (0)	0	<0.01
Kenyan (70)	70	0.12
Liberian (0)	0	<0.01
Nigerian (20)	35	0.06
Senegalese (0)	0	<0.01
Sierra Leonean (0)	0	<0.01
Somalian (0)	0	<0.01
South African (137)	137	0.24
Sudanese (0)	0	<0.01
Ugandan (0)	0	<0.01
Zimbabwean (0)	0	<0.01
Other Sub-Saharan African (8)	8	0.01
Albanian (18)	70	0.12
Alsatian (0)	4	0.01
American (2,084)	2,084	3.59
Arab (83)	195	0.34
Arab (0)	15	0.03
Egyptian (0)	0	<0.01
Iraqi (21)	21	0.04
Jordanian (0)	0	<0.01
Lebanese (62)	105	0.18
Moroccan (0)	28	0.05
Palestinian (0)	26	0.04
Syrian (0)	0	<0.01
Other Arab (0)	0	<0.01
Armenian (11)	110	0.19
Assyrian/Chaldean/Syriac (0)	0	<0.01
Australian (8)	8	0.01
Austrian (126)	648	1.12
Basque (0)	0	<0.01
Belgian (69)	120	0.21
Brazilian (37)	37	0.06
British (336)	509	0.88
Bulgarian (0)	6	0.01
Cajun (0)	0	<0.01
Canadian (134)	241	0.42
Carpatho Rusyn (0)	0	<0.01
Celtic (10)	10	0.02
Croatian (15)	96	0.17
Cypriot (66)	66	0.11
Czech (40)	154	0.27
Czechoslovakian (12)	44	0.08
Danish (0)	66	0.11
Dutch (70)	480	0.83
Eastern European (1,966)	1,986	3.42
English (1,445)	5,531	9.53
Estonian (0)	28	0.05
European (1,083)	1,134	1.95
Finnish (9)	22	0.04
French, ex. Basque (260)	1,058	1.82
French Canadian (76)	142	0.24
German (1,920)	8,094	13.95
German Russian (0)	0	<0.01
Greek (285)	649	1.12
Guyanese (0)	0	<0.01
Hungarian (188)	635	1.09
Icelander (0)	32	0.06
Iranian (197)	362	0.62
Irish (3,344)	8,965	15.45
Israeli (243)	377	0.65
Italian (2,512)	5,480	9.44
Latvian (49)	151	0.26
Lithuanian (107)	514	0.89
Luxemburger (0)	0	<0.01
Macedonian (18)	54	0.09
Maltese (0)	0	<0.01
New Zealander (0)	0	<0.01
Northern European (98)	98	0.17

Ancestry	Population	%
Norwegian (89)	260	0.45
Pennsylvania German (48)	99	0.17
Polish (1,199)	3,877	6.68
Portuguese (14)	86	0.15
Romanian (150)	478	0.82
Russian (3,632)	6,253	10.77
Scandinavian (0)	54	0.09
Scotch-Irish (419)	1,085	1.87
Scottish (403)	1,205	2.08
Serbian (33)	95	0.16
Slavic (41)	76	0.13
Slovak (25)	125	0.22
Slovene (0)	10	0.02
Soviet Union (22)	22	0.04
Swedish (195)	520	0.90
Swiss (28)	192	0.33
Turkish (5)	59	0.10
Ukrainian (394)	703	1.21
Welsh (42)	406	0.70
West Indian, ex. Hispanic (257)	378	0.65
Bahamian (0)	0	<0.01
Barbadian (21)	21	0.04
Belizean (0)	0	<0.01
Bermudan (0)	0	<0.01
British West Indian (0)	0	<0.01
Dutch West Indian (0)	0	<0.01
Haitian (125)	146	0.25
Jamaican (103)	154	0.27
Trinidadian/Tobagonian (0)	39	0.07
U.S. Virgin Islander (0)	0	<0.01
West Indian (8)	18	0.03
Other West Indian (0)	0	<0.01
Yugoslavian (27)	67	0.12

Hispanic Origin	Population	%
Hispanic or Latino (of any race)	1,718	2.97
Central American, ex. Mexican	193	0.33
Costa Rican	10	0.02
Guatemalan	62	0.11
Honduran	30	0.05
Nicaraguan	26	0.04
Panamanian	34	0.06
Salvadoran	29	0.05
Other Central American	2	<0.01
Cuban	156	0.27
Dominican Republic	55	0.10
Mexican	343	0.59
Puerto Rican	319	0.55
South American	446	0.77
Argentinean	79	0.14
Bolivian	10	0.02
Chilean	37	0.06
Colombian	116	0.20
Ecuadorian	34	0.06
Paraguayan	12	0.02
Peruvian	76	0.13
Uruguayan	16	0.03
Venezuelan	60	0.10
Other South American	6	0.01
Other Hispanic or Latino	206	0.36

Race*	Population	%
African-American/Black (3,246)	3,608	6.24
Not Hispanic (3,165)	3,484	6.03
Hispanic (81)	124	0.21
American Indian/Alaska Native (39)	218	0.38
Not Hispanic (27)	168	0.29
Hispanic (12)	50	0.09
Alaska Athabascan (Ala. Nat.) (0)	0	<0.01
Aleut (Alaska Native) (0)	0	<0.01
Apache (0)	1	<0.01
Arapaho (0)	1	<0.01
Blackfeet (0)	2	<0.01
Canadian/French Am. Ind. (0)	1	<0.01
Central American Ind. (0)	0	<0.01
Cherokee (6)	33	0.06
Cheyenne (0)	1	<0.01
Chickasaw (0)	0	<0.01
Chippewa (0)	0	<0.01

Race (continued)	Population	%
Choctaw (0)	6	0.01
Colville (0)	0	<0.01
Comanche (0)	0	<0.01
Cree (0)	0	<0.01
Creek (0)	2	<0.01
Crow (0)	0	<0.01
Delaware (0)	0	<0.01
Hopi (0)	2	<0.01
Houma (0)	0	<0.01
Inupiat (Alaska Native) (0)	0	<0.01
Iroquois (1)	4	0.01
Kiowa (0)	2	<0.01
Lumbee (0)	3	0.01
Menominee (0)	0	<0.01
Mexican American Ind. (4)	7	0.01
Navajo (1)	3	0.01
Osage (0)	0	<0.01
Ottawa (0)	2	<0.01
Paiute (0)	0	<0.01
Pima (0)	0	<0.01
Potawatomi (0)	0	<0.01
Pueblo (0)	0	<0.01
Puget Sound Salish (0)	0	<0.01
Seminole (0)	4	0.01
Shoshone (0)	0	<0.01
Sioux (0)	1	<0.01
South American Ind. (3)	7	0.01
Spanish American Ind. (0)	0	<0.01
Tlingit-Haida (Alaska Native) (0)	4	0.01
Tohono O'Odham (0)	1	<0.01
Tsimshian (Alaska Native) (0)	3	0.01
Ute (0)	0	<0.01
Yakama (0)	0	<0.01
Yaqui (0)	0	<0.01
Yuman (0)	0	<0.01
Yup'ik (Alaska Native) (0)	0	<0.01
Asian (3,488)	4,085	7.06
Not Hispanic (3,469)	4,024	6.96
Hispanic (19)	61	0.11
Bangladeshi (8)	9	0.02
Bhutanese (0)	0	<0.01
Burmese (7)	8	0.01
Cambodian (11)	11	0.02
Chinese, ex. Taiwanese (1,301)	1,477	2.55
Filipino (197)	291	0.50
Hmong (0)	0	<0.01
Indian (783)	906	1.57
Indonesian (5)	6	0.01
Japanese (134)	221	0.38
Korean (556)	651	1.13
Laotian (5)	10	0.02
Malaysian (9)	18	0.03
Nepalese (12)	12	0.02
Pakistani (77)	95	0.16
Sri Lankan (20)	28	0.05
Taiwanese (57)	70	0.12
Thai (33)	44	0.08
Vietnamese (155)	185	0.32
Hawaii Native/Pacific Islander (19)	61	0.11
Not Hispanic (17)	56	0.10
Hispanic (2)	5	0.01
Fijian (2)	5	0.01
Guamanian/Chamorro (3)	4	0.01
Marshallese (0)	0	<0.01
Native Hawaiian (4)	12	0.02
Samoan (1)	5	0.01
Tongan (7)	18	0.03
White (49,563)	50,501	87.33
Not Hispanic (48,375)	49,193	85.07
Hispanic (1,188)	1,308	2.26

Notes: † The Census 2010 population figure is used to calculate the percentages in the Hispanic Origin and Race categories. Ancestry percentages are based on the 2006-2010 American Community Survey population (not shown); ‡ Numbers in parentheses indicate the number of people reporting a single ancestry; * Numbers in parentheses indicate the number of persons reporting this race alone, not in combination with any other race; Please refer to the Explanation of Data for more information.

Millcreek

Place Type: Township
County: Erie
Population: 53,515

Ancestry	Population	%
Afghan (0)	0	<0.01
African, Sub-Saharan (15)	15	0.03
African (15)	15	0.03
Cape Verdean (0)	0	<0.01
Ethiopian (0)	0	<0.01
Ghanaian (0)	0	<0.01
Kenyan (0)	0	<0.01
Liberian (0)	0	<0.01
Nigerian (0)	0	<0.01
Senegalese (0)	0	<0.01
Sierra Leonean (0)	0	<0.01
Somalian (0)	0	<0.01
South African (0)	0	<0.01
Sudanese (0)	0	<0.01
Ugandan (0)	0	<0.01
Zimbabwean (0)	0	<0.01
Other Sub-Saharan African (0)	0	<0.01
Albanian (0)	0	<0.01
Alsatian (0)	0	<0.01
American (1,872)	1,872	3.53
Arab (193)	276	0.52
Arab (136)	151	0.29
Egyptian (5)	5	0.01
Iraqi (0)	0	<0.01
Jordanian (0)	0	<0.01
Lebanese (0)	8	0.02
Moroccan (0)	0	<0.01
Palestinian (15)	31	0.06
Syrian (13)	44	0.08
Other Arab (24)	37	0.07
Armenian (0)	24	0.05
Assyrian/Chaldean/Syriac (0)	0	<0.01
Australian (0)	0	<0.01
Austrian (113)	273	0.52
Basque (0)	9	0.02
Belgian (0)	33	0.06
Brazilian (13)	13	0.02
British (54)	209	0.39
Bulgarian (0)	16	0.03
Cajun (0)	0	<0.01
Canadian (84)	145	0.27
Carpatho Rusyn (0)	36	0.07
Celtic (0)	0	<0.01
Croatian (87)	201	0.38
Cypriot (0)	0	<0.01
Czech (50)	218	0.41
Czechoslovakian (143)	250	0.47
Danish (68)	179	0.34
Dutch (75)	681	1.29
Eastern European (32)	43	0.08
English (885)	5,292	9.99
Estonian (11)	19	0.04
European (89)	121	0.23
Finnish (30)	82	0.15
French, ex. Basque (136)	1,061	2.00
French Canadian (125)	199	0.38
German (5,615)	18,920	35.73
German Russian (0)	0	<0.01
Greek (79)	226	0.43
Guyanese (0)	0	<0.01
Hungarian (208)	861	1.63
Icelander (0)	0	<0.01
Iranian (27)	35	0.07
Iraqi (2,029)	10,633	20.08
Israeli (0)	0	<0.01
Italian (3,442)	9,038	17.07
Latvian (14)	14	0.03
Lithuanian (123)	265	0.50
Luxemburger (0)	10	0.02
Macedonian (0)	0	<0.01
Maltese (0)	0	<0.01
New Zealander (0)	0	<0.01
Northern European (39)	49	0.09

	Population	%
Norwegian (72)	231	0.44
Pennsylvania German (121)	191	0.36
Polish (2,232)	6,656	12.57
Portuguese (47)	247	0.47
Romanian (165)	203	0.38
Russian (508)	1,163	2.20
Scandinavian (17)	82	0.15
Scotch-Irish (349)	1,130	2.13
Scottish (299)	929	1.75
Serbian (9)	39	0.07
Slavic (21)	145	0.27
Slovak (213)	886	1.67
Slovene (14)	37	0.07
Soviet Union (0)	0	<0.01
Swedish (465)	1,705	3.22
Swiss (45)	203	0.38
Turkish (54)	80	0.15
Ukrainian (316)	658	1.24
Welsh (43)	450	0.85
West Indian, ex. Hispanic (64)	80	0.15
Bahamian (0)	0	<0.01
Barbadian (0)	0	<0.01
Belizean (0)	0	<0.01
Bermudan (0)	0	<0.01
British West Indian (0)	0	<0.01
Dutch West Indian (0)	0	<0.01
Haitian (15)	15	0.03
Jamaican (26)	26	0.05
Trinidadian/Tobagonian (23)	39	0.07
U.S. Virgin Islander (0)	0	<0.01
West Indian (0)	0	<0.01
Other West Indian (0)	0	<0.01
Yugoslavian (98)	140	0.26

Hispanic Origin	Population	%
Hispanic or Latino (of any race)	983	1.84
Central American, ex. Mexican	75	0.14
Costa Rican	14	0.03
Guatemalan	17	0.03
Honduran	14	0.03
Nicaraguan	4	0.01
Panamanian	11	0.02
Salvadoran	15	0.03
Other Central American	0	<0.01
Cuban	32	0.06
Dominican Republic	18	0.03
Mexican	305	0.57
Puerto Rican	340	0.64
South American	101	0.19
Argentinean	2	<0.01
Bolivian	1	<0.01
Chilean	4	0.01
Colombian	51	0.10
Ecuadorian	10	0.02
Paraguayan	0	<0.01
Peruvian	18	0.03
Uruguayan	0	<0.01
Venezuelan	15	0.03
Other South American	0	<0.01
Other Hispanic or Latino	112	0.21

Race*	Population	%
African-American/Black (793)	1,160	2.17
Not Hispanic (758)	1,100	2.06
Hispanic (35)	60	0.11
American Indian/Alaska Native (67)	229	0.43
Not Hispanic (61)	207	0.39
Hispanic (6)	22	0.04
Alaska Athabascan (Ala. Nat.) (0)	0	<0.01
Aleut (Alaska Native) (0)	1	<0.01
Apache (1)	1	<0.01
Arapaho (0)	0	<0.01
Blackfeet (1)	11	0.02
Canadian/French Am. Ind. (0)	0	<0.01
Central American Ind. (0)	0	<0.01
Cherokee (6)	32	0.06
Cheyenne (0)	0	<0.01
Chickasaw (0)	0	<0.01
Chippewa (1)	9	0.02

	Population	%
Choctaw (4)	6	0.01
Colville (0)	0	<0.01
Comanche (0)	0	<0.01
Cree (0)	2	<0.01
Creek (0)	1	<0.01
Crow (0)	1	<0.01
Delaware (0)	0	<0.01
Hopi (0)	0	<0.01
Houma (0)	0	<0.01
Inupiat (Alaska Native) (0)	0	<0.01
Iroquois (6)	28	0.05
Kiowa (0)	0	<0.01
Lumbee (1)	1	<0.01
Menominee (0)	0	<0.01
Mexican American Ind. (2)	3	0.01
Navajo (0)	1	<0.01
Osage (0)	0	<0.01
Ottawa (0)	0	<0.01
Paiute (0)	0	<0.01
Pima (0)	0	<0.01
Potawatomi (0)	0	<0.01
Pueblo (0)	0	<0.01
Puget Sound Salish (0)	0	<0.01
Seminole (1)	1	<0.01
Shoshone (3)	3	0.01
Sioux (4)	6	0.01
South American Ind. (2)	5	0.01
Spanish American Ind. (0)	0	<0.01
Tlingit-Haida (Alaska Native) (2)	2	<0.01
Tohono O'Odham (0)	4	0.01
Tsimshian (Alaska Native) (0)	0	<0.01
Ute (1)	1	<0.01
Yakama (0)	0	<0.01
Yaqui (0)	0	<0.01
Yuman (0)	0	<0.01
Yup'ik (Alaska Native) (0)	0	<0.01
Asian (977)	1,180	2.20
Not Hispanic (962)	1,154	2.16
Hispanic (15)	26	0.05
Bangladeshi (13)	13	0.02
Bhutanese (0)	0	<0.01
Burmese (8)	9	0.02
Cambodian (1)	2	<0.01
Chinese, ex. Taiwanese (235)	271	0.51
Filipino (69)	122	0.23
Hmong (1)	1	<0.01
Indian (356)	377	0.70
Indonesian (5)	7	0.01
Japanese (20)	54	0.10
Korean (91)	116	0.22
Laotian (2)	2	<0.01
Malaysian (1)	1	<0.01
Nepalese (0)	0	<0.01
Pakistani (43)	45	0.08
Sri Lankan (10)	10	0.02
Taiwanese (12)	13	0.02
Thai (9)	18	0.03
Vietnamese (75)	89	0.17
Hawaii Native/Pacific Islander (9)	26	0.05
Not Hispanic (9)	24	0.04
Hispanic (0)	2	<0.01
Fijian (0)	0	<0.01
Guamanian/Chamorro (2)	4	0.01
Marshallese (0)	0	<0.01
Native Hawaiian (3)	8	0.01
Samoan (1)	4	0.01
Tongan (0)	0	<0.01
White (50,677)	51,334	95.92
Not Hispanic (50,073)	50,664	94.67
Hispanic (604)	670	1.25

*Notes: † The Census 2010 population figure is used to calculate the percentages in the Hispanic Origin and Race categories. Ancestry percentages are based on the 2006-2010 American Community Survey population (not shown); ‡ Numbers in parentheses indicate the number of people reporting a single ancestry; * Numbers in parentheses indicate the number of persons reporting this race alone, not in combination with any other race; Please refer to the Explanation of Data for more information.*

Philadelphia

Place Type: City
County: Philadelphia
Population: 1,526,006

Ancestry	Population	%
Afghan (52)	52	<0.01
African, Sub-Saharan (24,827)	29,046	1.93
African (15,876)	18,871	1.25
Cape Verdean (69)	129	0.01
Ethiopian (1,542)	1,572	0.10
Ghanaian (584)	584	0.04
Kenyan (94)	147	0.01
Liberian (2,867)	3,198	0.21
Nigerian (1,648)	1,877	0.12
Senegalese (91)	139	0.01
Sierra Leonean (136)	144	0.01
Somalian (11)	22	<0.01
South African (164)	235	0.02
Sudanese (160)	167	0.01
Ugandan (0)	8	<0.01
Zimbabwean (51)	51	<0.01
Other Sub-Saharan African (1,534)	1,902	0.13
Albanian (3,540)	3,892	0.26
Alsatian (13)	54	<0.01
American (20,637)	20,637	1.37
Arab (6,122)	7,763	0.52
Arab (1,709)	2,081	0.14
Egyptian (491)	580	0.04
Iraqi (211)	218	0.01
Jordanian (928)	939	0.06
Lebanese (507)	991	0.07
Moroccan (516)	684	0.05
Palestinian (607)	621	0.04
Syrian (294)	637	0.04
Other Arab (859)	1,012	0.07
Armenian (949)	1,315	0.09
Assyrian/Chaldean/Syriac (8)	8	<0.01
Australian (194)	243	0.02
Austrian (476)	2,580	0.17
Basque (0)	59	<0.01
Belgian (63)	214	0.01
Brazilian (2,390)	2,622	0.17
British (1,248)	2,578	0.17
Bulgarian (103)	150	0.01
Cajun (17)	38	<0.01
Canadian (534)	1,094	0.07
Carpatho Rusyn (33)	46	<0.01
Celtic (41)	41	<0.01
Croatian (382)	916	0.06
Cypriot (75)	75	<0.01
Czech (545)	2,209	0.15
Czechoslovakian (389)	721	0.05
Danish (181)	830	0.06
Dutch (1,200)	5,855	0.39
Eastern European (3,053)	3,363	0.22
English (10,881)	47,303	3.14
Estonian (55)	147	0.01
European (4,424)	4,939	0.33
Finnish (108)	326	0.02
French, ex. Basque (2,120)	12,027	0.80
French Canadian (497)	1,636	0.11
German (28,175)	122,783	8.16
German Russian (0)	0	<0.01
Greek (2,136)	4,288	0.28
Guyanese (545)	638	0.04
Hungarian (1,262)	5,463	0.36
Icelander (58)	86	0.01
Iranian (550)	665	0.04
Irish (68,684)	195,849	13.01
Israeli (567)	861	0.06
Italian (60,356)	125,080	8.31
Latvian (250)	570	0.04
Lithuanian (1,629)	5,334	0.35
Luxemburger (15)	29	<0.01
Macedonian (10)	10	<0.01
Maltese (0)	0	<0.01
New Zealander (38)	52	<0.01
Northern European (315)	361	0.02

Ancestry	Population	%
Norwegian (599)	2,417	0.16
Pennsylvania German (853)	1,967	0.13
Polish (21,876)	58,395	3.88
Portuguese (2,044)	3,158	0.21
Romanian (980)	2,101	0.14
Russian (13,897)	25,520	1.70
Scandinavian (251)	504	0.03
Scotch-Irish (3,872)	9,813	0.65
Scottish (1,963)	8,768	0.58
Serbian (286)	493	0.03
Slavic (153)	498	0.03
Slovak (750)	2,480	0.16
Slovene (186)	273	0.02
Soviet Union (0)	0	<0.01
Swedish (852)	3,719	0.25
Swiss (267)	1,886	0.13
Turkish (609)	786	0.05
Ukrainian (7,300)	13,262	0.88
Welsh (629)	4,345	0.29
West Indian, ex. Hispanic (21,124)	25,436	1.69
Bahamian (59)	104	0.01
Barbadian (607)	635	0.04
Belizean (0)	31	<0.01
Bermudan (29)	29	<0.01
British West Indian (458)	541	0.04
Dutch West Indian (0)	0	<0.01
Haitian (8,400)	9,026	0.60
Jamaican (8,311)	10,082	0.67
Trinidadian/Tobagonian (1,700)	2,407	0.16
U.S. Virgin Islander (100)	100	0.01
West Indian (1,446)	2,445	0.16
Other West Indian (14)	36	<0.01
Yugoslavian (239)	406	0.03

Hispanic Origin	Population	%
Hispanic or Latino (of any race)	187,611	12.29
Central American, ex. Mexican	7,511	0.49
Costa Rican	903	0.06
Guatemalan	2,262	0.15
Honduran	1,642	0.11
Nicaraguan	874	0.06
Panamanian	737	0.05
Salvadoran	1,049	0.07
Other Central American	44	<0.01
Cuban	3,930	0.26
Dominican Republic	15,963	1.05
Mexican	15,531	1.02
Puerto Rican	121,643	7.97
South American	9,969	0.65
Argentinean	1,006	0.07
Bolivian	112	0.01
Chilean	357	0.02
Colombian	4,675	0.31
Ecuadorian	1,542	0.10
Paraguayan	74	<0.01
Peruvian	1,085	0.07
Uruguayan	234	0.02
Venezuelan	773	0.05
Other South American	111	0.01
Other Hispanic or Latino	13,064	0.86

Race*	Population	%
African-American/Black (661,839)	686,870	45.01
Not Hispanic (644,287)	662,568	43.42
Hispanic (17,552)	24,302	1.59
American Indian/Alaska Native (6,996)	17,495	1.15
Not Hispanic (3,498)	11,409	0.75
Hispanic (3,498)	6,086	0.40
Alaska Athabascan (Ala. Nat.) (5)	6	<0.01
Aleut (Alaska Native) (4)	8	<0.01
Apache (31)	118	0.01
Arapaho (4)	7	<0.01
Blackfeet (105)	679	0.04
Canadian/French Am. Ind. (8)	34	<0.01
Central American Ind. (65)	111	0.01
Cherokee (463)	2,484	0.16
Cheyenne (0)	12	<0.01
Chickasaw (5)	28	<0.01
Chippewa (17)	63	<0.01

Race*	Population	%
Choctaw (25)	92	0.01
Colville (0)	0	<0.01
Comanche (3)	9	<0.01
Cree (3)	25	<0.01
Creek (16)	59	<0.01
Crow (2)	15	<0.01
Delaware (71)	239	0.02
Hopi (5)	7	<0.01
Houma (1)	2	<0.01
Inupiat (Alaska Native) (1)	3	<0.01
Iroquois (72)	216	0.01
Kiowa (0)	9	<0.01
Lumbee (51)	121	0.01
Menominee (1)	6	<0.01
Mexican American Ind. (126)	185	0.01
Navajo (35)	99	0.01
Osage (1)	5	<0.01
Ottawa (1)	2	<0.01
Paiute (2)	4	<0.01
Pima (1)	2	<0.01
Potawatomi (4)	14	<0.01
Pueblo (13)	42	<0.01
Puget Sound Salish (3)	5	<0.01
Seminole (21)	189	0.01
Shoshone (4)	11	<0.01
Sioux (55)	199	0.01
South American Ind. (273)	657	0.04
Spanish American Ind. (98)	156	0.01
Tlingit-Haida (Alaska Native) (3)	18	<0.01
Tohono O'Odham (2)	3	<0.01
Tsimshian (Alaska Native) (0)	1	<0.01
Ute (0)	0	<0.01
Yakama (2)	2	<0.01
Yaqui (5)	10	<0.01
Yuman (2)	8	<0.01
Yup'ik (Alaska Native) (2)	5	<0.01
Asian (96,405)	106,720	6.99
Not Hispanic (95,521)	104,551	6.85
Hispanic (884)	2,169	0.14
Bangladeshi (883)	978	0.06
Bhutanese (43)	51	<0.01
Burmese (341)	388	0.03
Cambodian (8,707)	9,912	0.65
Chinese, ex. Taiwanese (29,396)	32,773	2.15
Filipino (4,978)	6,849	0.45
Hmong (77)	83	0.01
Indian (18,520)	20,809	1.36
Indonesian (1,921)	2,222	0.15
Japanese (1,034)	1,956	0.13
Korean (6,217)	7,074	0.46
Laotian (1,084)	1,350	0.09
Malaysian (88)	130	0.01
Nepalese (181)	220	0.01
Pakistani (2,423)	2,683	0.18
Sri Lankan (148)	172	0.01
Taiwanese (639)	736	0.05
Thai (386)	627	0.04
Vietnamese (14,431)	16,268	1.07
Hawaii Native/Pacific Islander (744)	3,125	0.20
Not Hispanic (457)	1,938	0.13
Hispanic (287)	1,187	0.08
Fijian (7)	14	<0.01
Guamanian/Chamorro (186)	272	0.02
Marshallese (0)	0	<0.01
Native Hawaiian (203)	538	0.04
Samoan (84)	198	0.01
Tongan (7)	9	<0.01
White (626,221)	655,021	42.92
Not Hispanic (562,585)	581,693	38.12
Hispanic (63,636)	73,328	4.81

Notes: † The Census 2010 population figure is used to calculate the percentages in the Hispanic Origin and Race categories. Ancestry percentages are based on the 2006-2010 American Community Survey population (not shown); ‡ Numbers in parentheses indicate the number of people reporting a single ancestry; * Numbers in parentheses indicate the number of persons reporting this race alone, not in combination with any other race; Please refer to the Explanation of Data for more information.

Pittsburgh

Place Type: City
County: Allegheny
Population: 305,704

Ancestry	Population	%
Afghan (0)	0	<0.01
African, Sub-Saharan (4,056)	4,577	1.49
African (3,209)	3,558	1.16
Cape Verdean (6)	6	<0.01
Ethiopian (112)	112	0.04
Ghanaian (45)	45	0.01
Kenyan (14)	21	0.01
Liberian (71)	71	0.02
Nigerian (267)	391	0.13
Senegalese (35)	36	0.01
Sierra Leonean (55)	55	0.02
Somalian (57)	57	0.02
South African (0)	15	<0.01
Sudanese (38)	38	0.01
Ugandan (0)	0	<0.01
Zimbabwean (36)	36	0.01
Other Sub-Saharan African (111)	136	0.04
Albanian (11)	85	0.03
Alsatian (17)	91	0.03
American (7,699)	7,699	2.50
Arab (1,839)	2,859	0.93
Arab (388)	388	0.13
Egyptian (108)	152	0.05
Iraqi (91)	104	0.03
Jordanian (0)	0	<0.01
Lebanese (395)	934	0.30
Moroccan (197)	312	0.10
Palestinian (25)	25	0.01
Syrian (275)	499	0.16
Other Arab (360)	445	0.14
Armenian (31)	77	0.02
Assyrian/Chaldean/Syriac (0)	0	<0.01
Australian (38)	38	0.01
Austrian (218)	1,622	0.53
Basque (0)	0	<0.01
Belgian (19)	171	0.06
Brazilian (69)	106	0.03
British (546)	1,143	0.37
Bulgarian (113)	127	0.04
Cajun (24)	77	0.02
Canadian (201)	308	0.10
Carpatho Rusyn (20)	116	0.04
Celtic (14)	38	0.01
Croatian (771)	2,304	0.75
Cypriot (102)	102	0.03
Czech (297)	1,676	0.54
Czechoslovakian (325)	773	0.25
Danish (26)	299	0.10
Dutch (519)	2,016	0.65
Eastern European (1,035)	1,195	0.39
English (3,539)	16,692	5.42
Estonian (0)	13	<0.01
European (2,043)	2,300	0.75
Finnish (32)	181	0.06
French, ex. Basque (452)	4,106	1.33
French Canadian (278)	499	0.16
German (16,287)	66,031	21.44
German Russian (0)	0	<0.01
Greek (979)	2,108	0.68
Guyanese (8)	57	0.02
Hungarian (1,381)	4,477	1.45
Icelander (0)	0	<0.01
Iranian (116)	187	0.06
Irish (12,283)	51,563	16.74
Israeli (109)	210	0.07
Italian (16,620)	41,352	13.43
Latvian (68)	138	0.04
Lithuanian (729)	2,260	0.73
Luxemburger (0)	22	0.01
Macedonian (30)	44	0.01
Maltese (11)	11	<0.01
New Zealander (21)	21	0.01
Northern European (192)	192	0.06

Ancestry	Population	%
Norwegian (150)	682	0.22
Pennsylvania German (133)	385	0.12
Polish (7,981)	24,743	8.03
Portuguese (93)	276	0.09
Romanian (155)	559	0.18
Russian (2,580)	6,191	2.01
Scandinavian (213)	337	0.11
Scotch-Irish (1,600)	5,558	1.80
Scottish (936)	4,798	1.56
Serbian (361)	993	0.32
Slavic (180)	428	0.14
Slovak (2,134)	5,935	1.93
Slovene (144)	739	0.24
Soviet Union (0)	0	<0.01
Swedish (316)	2,007	0.65
Swiss (156)	838	0.27
Turkish (422)	485	0.16
Ukrainian (1,046)	2,972	0.96
Welsh (290)	2,729	0.89
West Indian, ex. Hispanic (925)	1,313	0.43
Bahamian (29)	44	0.01
Barbadian (22)	77	0.02
Belizean (10)	10	<0.01
Bermudan (14)	37	0.01
British West Indian (9)	9	<0.01
Dutch West Indian (0)	0	<0.01
Haitian (252)	285	0.09
Jamaican (336)	480	0.16
Trinidadian/Tobagonian (123)	123	0.04
U.S. Virgin Islander (0)	0	<0.01
West Indian (130)	248	0.08
Other West Indian (0)	0	<0.01
Yugoslavian (86)	141	0.05

Hispanic Origin	Population	%
Hispanic or Latino (of any race)	6,964	2.28
Central American, ex. Mexican	500	0.16
Costa Rican	47	0.02
Guatemalan	186	0.06
Honduran	56	0.02
Nicaraguan	36	0.01
Panamanian	81	0.03
Salvadoran	93	0.03
Other Central American	1	<0.01
Cuban	397	0.13
Dominican Republic	157	0.05
Mexican	2,292	0.75
Puerto Rican	1,336	0.44
South American	1,162	0.38
Argentinean	244	0.08
Bolivian	29	0.01
Chilean	139	0.05
Colombian	263	0.09
Ecuadorian	75	0.02
Paraguayan	20	0.01
Peruvian	211	0.07
Uruguayan	23	0.01
Venezuelan	142	0.05
Other South American	16	0.01
Other Hispanic or Latino	1,120	0.37

Race*	Population	%
African-American/Black (79,710)	84,819	27.75
Not Hispanic (78,847)	83,539	27.33
Hispanic (863)	1,280	0.42
American Indian/Alaska Native (584)	2,540	0.83
Not Hispanic (505)	2,253	0.74
Hispanic (79)	287	0.09
Alaska Athabascan (Ala. Nat.) (2)	5	<0.01
Aleut (Alaska Native) (1)	1	<0.01
Apache (8)	36	0.01
Arapaho (0)	0	<0.01
Blackfeet (6)	199	0.07
Canadian/French Am. Ind. (5)	15	<0.01
Central American Ind. (3)	10	<0.01
Cherokee (72)	533	0.17
Cheyenne (5)	11	<0.01
Chickasaw (2)	13	<0.01
Chippewa (12)	30	0.01

Race*	Population	%
Choctaw (3)	22	0.01
Colville (0)	0	<0.01
Comanche (0)	2	<0.01
Cree (1)	6	<0.01
Creek (7)	20	0.01
Crow (0)	8	<0.01
Delaware (3)	13	<0.01
Hopi (0)	4	<0.01
Houma (0)	0	<0.01
Inupiat (Alaska Native) (1)	2	<0.01
Iroquois (10)	50	0.02
Kiowa (3)	4	<0.01
Lumbee (5)	12	<0.01
Menominee (0)	0	<0.01
Mexican American Ind. (19)	36	0.01
Navajo (1)	16	0.01
Osage (0)	3	<0.01
Ottawa (0)	0	<0.01
Paiute (0)	0	<0.01
Pima (0)	0	<0.01
Potawatomi (0)	2	<0.01
Pueblo (0)	8	<0.01
Puget Sound Salish (0)	0	<0.01
Seminole (8)	31	0.01
Shoshone (0)	1	<0.01
Sioux (18)	70	0.02
South American Ind. (9)	26	0.01
Spanish American Ind. (6)	7	<0.01
Tlingit-Haida (Alaska Native) (1)	3	<0.01
Tohono O'Odham (0)	0	<0.01
Tsimshian (Alaska Native) (1)	1	<0.01
Ute (1)	1	<0.01
Yakama (0)	0	<0.01
Yaqui (0)	1	<0.01
Yuman (0)	0	<0.01
Yup'ik (Alaska Native) (0)	0	<0.01
Asian (13,465)	15,412	5.04
Not Hispanic (13,393)	15,233	4.98
Hispanic (72)	179	0.06
Bangladeshi (47)	57	0.02
Bhutanese (53)	56	0.02
Burmese (141)	145	0.05
Cambodian (36)	48	0.02
Chinese, ex. Taiwanese (4,405)	4,872	1.59
Filipino (505)	807	0.26
Hmong (3)	3	<0.01
Indian (3,657)	4,025	1.32
Indonesian (54)	72	0.02
Japanese (641)	938	0.31
Korean (1,768)	2,002	0.65
Laotian (9)	17	0.01
Malaysian (49)	69	0.02
Nepalese (95)	111	0.04
Pakistani (187)	217	0.07
Sri Lankan (37)	46	0.02
Taiwanese (416)	461	0.15
Thai (207)	245	0.08
Vietnamese (693)	826	0.27
Hawaii Native/Pacific Islander (86)	286	0.09
Not Hispanic (76)	236	0.08
Hispanic (10)	50	0.02
Fijian (0)	4	<0.01
Guamanian/Chamorro (14)	29	0.01
Marshallese (0)	0	<0.01
Native Hawaiian (31)	74	0.02
Samoan (26)	72	0.02
Tongan (6)	7	<0.01
White (201,766)	208,065	68.06
Not Hispanic (198,186)	203,879	66.69
Hispanic (3,580)	4,186	1.37

*Notes: † The Census 2010 population figure is used to calculate the percentages in the Hispanic Origin and Race categories. Ancestry percentages are based on the 2006-2010 American Community Survey population (not shown); ‡ Numbers in parentheses indicate the number of people reporting a single ancestry; * Numbers in parentheses indicate the number of persons reporting this race alone, not in combination with any other race; Please refer to the Explanation of Data for more information.*

Reading

Place Type: City
County: Berks
Population: 88,082

Ancestry	Population	%
Afghan (0)	0	<0.01
African, Sub-Saharan (150)	306	0.35
African (88)	212	0.24
Cape Verdean (0)	0	<0.01
Ethiopian (18)	18	0.02
Ghanaian (0)	14	0.02
Kenyan (13)	13	0.01
Liberian (31)	31	0.04
Nigerian (0)	0	<0.01
Senegalese (0)	0	<0.01
Sierra Leonean (0)	0	<0.01
Somalian (0)	0	<0.01
South African (0)	0	<0.01
Sudanese (0)	0	<0.01
Ugandan (0)	0	<0.01
Zimbabwean (0)	0	<0.01
Other Sub-Saharan African (0)	18	0.02
Albanian (96)	96	0.11
Alsatian (0)	0	<0.01
American (1,395)	1,395	1.60
Arab (49)	83	0.09
Arab (26)	48	0.05
Egyptian (0)	0	<0.01
Iraqi (0)	0	<0.01
Jordanian (0)	0	<0.01
Lebanese (12)	12	<0.01
Moroccan (0)	0	<0.01
Palestinian (0)	0	<0.01
Syrian (11)	23	0.03
Other Arab (0)	0	<0.01
Armenian (0)	0	<0.01
Assyrian/Chaldean/Syriac (0)	0	<0.01
Australian (0)	0	<0.01
Austrian (10)	132	0.15
Basque (0)	0	<0.01
Belgian (0)	31	0.04
Brazilian (0)	16	0.02
British (20)	103	0.12
Bulgarian (0)	0	<0.01
Cajun (0)	0	<0.01
Canadian (38)	215	0.25
Carpatho Rusyn (0)	0	<0.01
Celtic (0)	0	<0.01
Croatian (0)	76	0.09
Cypriot (0)	0	<0.01
Czech (18)	173	0.20
Czechoslovakian (17)	29	0.03
Danish (0)	14	0.02
Dutch (363)	1,551	1.77
Eastern European (13)	26	0.03
English (519)	1,859	2.13
Estonian (0)	0	<0.01
European (148)	148	0.17
Finnish (0)	18	0.02
French, ex. Basque (94)	630	0.72
French Canadian (24)	62	0.07
German (4,070)	10,470	11.98
German Russian (0)	0	<0.01
Greek (127)	197	0.23
Guyanese (0)	0	<0.01
Hungarian (79)	221	0.25
Icelander (0)	0	<0.01
Iranian (0)	0	<0.01
Irish (1,096)	5,261	6.02
Israeli (9)	9	0.01
Italian (1,314)	4,489	5.14
Latvian (21)	73	0.08
Lithuanian (103)	267	0.31
Luxemburger (0)	0	<0.01
Macedonian (0)	0	<0.01
Maltese (0)	0	<0.01
New Zealander (0)	0	<0.01
Northern European (13)	13	0.01

Ancestry	Population	%
Norwegian (80)	183	0.21
Pennsylvania German (1,369)	2,056	2.35
Polish (1,623)	3,558	4.07
Portuguese (34)	38	0.04
Romanian (331)	436	0.50
Russian (47)	178	0.20
Scandinavian (11)	11	0.01
Scotch-Irish (56)	357	0.41
Scottish (43)	345	0.39
Serbian (8)	8	0.01
Slavic (19)	68	0.08
Slovak (109)	353	0.40
Slovene (20)	20	0.02
Soviet Union (0)	0	<0.01
Swedish (10)	88	0.10
Swiss (24)	164	0.19
Turkish (46)	46	0.05
Ukrainian (61)	340	0.39
Welsh (99)	531	0.61
West Indian, ex. Hispanic (1,259)	1,590	1.82
Bahamian (0)	0	<0.01
Barbadian (57)	68	0.08
Belizean (0)	0	<0.01
Bermudan (0)	0	<0.01
British West Indian (0)	0	<0.01
Dutch West Indian (0)	0	<0.01
Haitian (365)	451	0.52
Jamaican (443)	575	0.66
Trinidadian/Tobagonian (121)	129	0.15
U.S. Virgin Islander (256)	289	0.33
West Indian (17)	78	0.09
Other West Indian (0)	0	<0.01
Yugoslavian (60)	68	0.08

Hispanic Origin	Population	%
Hispanic or Latino (of any race)	51,230	58.16
Central American, ex. Mexican	1,436	1.63
Costa Rican	17	0.02
Guatemalan	402	0.46
Honduran	270	0.31
Nicaraguan	62	0.07
Panamanian	40	0.05
Salvadoran	637	0.72
Other Central American	8	0.01
Cuban	360	0.41
Dominican Republic	8,716	9.90
Mexican	8,602	9.77
Puerto Rican	28,160	31.97
South American	1,240	1.41
Argentinean	33	0.04
Bolivian	7	0.01
Chilean	19	0.02
Colombian	612	0.69
Ecuadorian	409	0.46
Paraguayan	6	0.01
Peruvian	93	0.11
Uruguayan	19	0.02
Venezuelan	31	0.04
Other South American	11	0.01
Other Hispanic or Latino	2,716	3.08

Race*	Population	%
African-American/Black (11,624)	14,345	16.29
Not Hispanic (8,774)	10,042	11.40
Hispanic (2,850)	4,303	4.89
American Indian/Alaska Native (794)	1,430	1.62
Not Hispanic (183)	434	0.49
Hispanic (611)	996	1.13
Alaska Athabascan (Ala. Nat.) (0)	0	<0.01
Aleut (Alaska Native) (0)	0	<0.01
Apache (2)	4	<0.01
Arapaho (0)	0	<0.01
Blackfeet (17)	49	0.06
Canadian/French Am. Ind. (1)	1	<0.01
Central American Ind. (7)	14	0.02
Cherokee (29)	120	0.14
Cheyenne (0)	0	<0.01
Chickasaw (0)	0	<0.01
Chippewa (9)	19	0.02

Race*	Population	%
Choctaw (1)	7	0.01
Colville (0)	0	<0.01
Comanche (0)	1	<0.01
Cree (0)	5	0.01
Creek (0)	1	<0.01
Crow (0)	0	<0.01
Delaware (3)	15	0.02
Hopi (0)	0	<0.01
Houma (0)	0	<0.01
Inupiat (Alaska Native) (3)	3	<0.01
Iroquois (8)	14	0.02
Kiowa (0)	0	<0.01
Lumbee (3)	5	0.01
Menominee (1)	1	<0.01
Mexican American Ind. (35)	59	0.07
Navajo (1)	1	<0.01
Osage (0)	0	<0.01
Ottawa (0)	0	<0.01
Paiute (0)	1	<0.01
Pima (0)	0	<0.01
Potawatomi (3)	3	<0.01
Pueblo (17)	26	0.03
Puget Sound Salish (0)	0	<0.01
Seminole (3)	4	<0.01
Shoshone (0)	0	<0.01
Sioux (4)	12	0.01
South American Ind. (32)	74	0.08
Spanish American Ind. (12)	17	0.02
Tlingit-Haida (Alaska Native) (1)	1	<0.01
Tohono O'Odham (2)	2	<0.01
Tsimshian (Alaska Native) (0)	0	<0.01
Ute (0)	0	<0.01
Yakama (0)	0	<0.01
Yaqui (0)	0	<0.01
Yuman (0)	0	<0.01
Yup'ik (Alaska Native) (0)	0	<0.01
Asian (1,039)	1,323	1.50
Not Hispanic (958)	1,097	1.25
Hispanic (81)	226	0.26
Bangladeshi (1)	1	<0.01
Bhutanese (0)	0	<0.01
Burmese (4)	4	<0.01
Cambodian (3)	5	0.01
Chinese, ex. Taiwanese (169)	192	0.22
Filipino (49)	79	0.09
Hmong (3)	3	<0.01
Indian (125)	176	0.20
Indonesian (10)	13	0.01
Japanese (33)	63	0.07
Korean (47)	83	0.09
Laotian (36)	39	0.04
Malaysian (0)	0	<0.01
Nepalese (0)	0	<0.01
Pakistani (13)	18	0.02
Sri Lankan (0)	0	<0.01
Taiwanese (0)	0	<0.01
Thai (8)	14	0.02
Vietnamese (493)	538	0.61
Hawaii Native/Pacific Islander (72)	351	0.40
Not Hispanic (20)	59	0.07
Hispanic (52)	292	0.33
Fijian (0)	0	<0.01
Guamanian/Chamorro (24)	38	0.04
Marshallese (0)	0	<0.01
Native Hawaiian (13)	49	0.06
Samoan (6)	15	0.02
Tongan (1)	1	<0.01
White (42,617)	46,727	53.05
Not Hispanic (25,258)	26,621	30.22
Hispanic (17,359)	20,106	22.83

Notes: † The Census 2010 population figure is used to calculate the percentages in the Hispanic Origin and Race categories. Ancestry percentages are based on the 2006-2010 American Community Survey population (not shown); ‡ Numbers in parentheses indicate the number of people reporting a single ancestry; * Numbers in parentheses indicate the number of persons reporting this race alone, not in combination with any other race; Please refer to the Explanation of Data for more information.

Scranton

Place Type: City
County: Lackawanna
Population: 76,089

Ancestry	Population	%
Afghan (0)	0	<0.01
African, Sub-Saharan (55)	93	0.12
African (47)	85	0.11
Cape Verdean (0)	0	<0.01
Ethiopian (0)	0	<0.01
Ghanaian (0)	0	<0.01
Kenyan (0)	0	<0.01
Liberian (0)	0	<0.01
Nigerian (8)	8	0.01
Senegalese (0)	0	<0.01
Sierra Leonean (0)	0	<0.01
Somalian (0)	0	<0.01
South African (0)	0	<0.01
Sudanese (0)	0	<0.01
Ugandan (0)	0	<0.01
Zimbabwean (0)	0	<0.01
Other Sub-Saharan African (0)	0	<0.01
Albanian (0)	0	<0.01
Alsatian (0)	0	<0.01
American (1,834)	1,834	2.41
Arab (225)	541	0.71
Arab (36)	86	0.11
Egyptian (45)	45	0.06
Iraqi (0)	0	<0.01
Jordanian (0)	0	<0.01
Lebanese (117)	383	0.50
Moroccan (5)	5	<0.01
Palestinian (0)	0	<0.01
Syrian (0)	0	<0.01
Other Arab (22)	22	0.03
Armenian (0)	41	0.05
Assyrian/Chaldean/Syriac (0)	0	<0.01
Australian (0)	10	0.01
Austrian (68)	301	0.40
Basque (0)	0	<0.01
Belgian (20)	20	0.03
Brazilian (283)	305	0.40
British (56)	88	0.12
Bulgarian (55)	55	0.07
Cajun (0)	0	<0.01
Canadian (20)	71	0.09
Carpatho Rusyn (26)	35	0.05
Celtic (0)	3	<0.01
Croatian (0)	29	0.04
Cypriot (0)	0	<0.01
Czech (11)	209	0.27
Czechoslovakian (16)	78	0.10
Danish (48)	103	0.14
Dutch (55)	707	0.93
Eastern European (7)	7	0.01
English (936)	4,507	5.93
Estonian (0)	0	<0.01
European (441)	457	0.60
Finnish (26)	51	0.07
French, ex. Basque (115)	787	1.03
French Canadian (63)	190	0.25
German (3,405)	14,561	19.14
German Russian (0)	0	<0.01
Greek (59)	203	0.27
Guyanese (0)	0	<0.01
Hungarian (112)	512	0.67
Icelander (0)	8	0.01
Iranian (56)	56	0.07
Irish (8,546)	23,274	30.60
Israeli (22)	22	0.03
Italian (6,015)	16,031	21.08
Latvian (14)	26	0.03
Lithuanian (486)	1,584	2.08
Luxemburger (0)	0	<0.01
Macedonian (0)	0	<0.01
Maltese (0)	0	<0.01
New Zealander (0)	10	0.01
Northern European (0)	0	<0.01

Ancestry	Population	%
Norwegian (15)	53	0.07
Pennsylvania German (111)	330	0.43
Polish (3,557)	10,984	14.44
Portuguese (153)	165	0.22
Romanian (28)	83	0.11
Russian (583)	2,676	3.52
Scandinavian (0)	0	<0.01
Scotch-Irish (292)	608	0.80
Scottish (153)	479	0.63
Serbian (0)	33	0.04
Slavic (40)	64	0.08
Slovak (361)	1,344	1.77
Slovene (41)	49	0.06
Soviet Union (0)	0	<0.01
Swedish (78)	327	0.43
Swiss (17)	169	0.22
Turkish (172)	172	0.23
Ukrainian (535)	1,060	1.39
Welsh (829)	4,539	5.97
West Indian, ex. Hispanic (87)	161	0.21
Bahamian (0)	0	<0.01
Barbadian (0)	0	<0.01
Belizean (0)	0	<0.01
Bermudan (0)	0	<0.01
British West Indian (0)	0	<0.01
Dutch West Indian (0)	0	<0.01
Haitian (14)	47	0.06
Jamaican (27)	44	0.06
Trinidadian/Tobagonian (26)	26	0.03
U.S. Virgin Islander (0)	0	<0.01
West Indian (20)	44	0.06
Other West Indian (0)	0	<0.01
Yugoslavian (0)	0	<0.01

Hispanic Origin	Population	%
Hispanic or Latino (of any race)	7,531	9.90
Central American, ex. Mexican	448	0.59
Costa Rican	11	0.01
Guatemalan	34	0.04
Honduran	268	0.35
Nicaraguan	18	0.02
Panamanian	12	0.02
Salvadoran	100	0.13
Other Central American	5	0.01
Cuban	125	0.16
Dominican Republic	605	0.80
Mexican	1,945	2.56
Puerto Rican	3,172	4.17
South American	466	0.61
Argentinean	39	0.05
Bolivian	8	0.01
Chilean	11	0.01
Colombian	96	0.13
Ecuadorian	125	0.16
Paraguayan	4	0.01
Peruvian	98	0.13
Uruguayan	69	0.09
Venezuelan	16	0.02
Other South American	0	<0.01
Other Hispanic or Latino	770	1.01

Race*	Population	%
African-American/Black (4,150)	5,226	6.87
Not Hispanic (3,657)	4,513	5.93
Hispanic (493)	713	0.94
American Indian/Alaska Native (178)	462	0.61
Not Hispanic (100)	353	0.46
Hispanic (78)	109	0.14
Alaska Athabascan *(Ala. Nat.)* (0)	0	<0.01
Aleut *(Alaska Native)* (0)	0	<0.01
Apache (3)	5	<0.01
Arapaho (0)	0	<0.01
Blackfeet (2)	14	0.02
Canadian/French Am. Ind. (0)	0	<0.01
Central American Ind. (0)	2	<0.01
Cherokee (20)	61	0.08
Cheyenne (0)	0	<0.01
Chickasaw (0)	0	<0.01
Chippewa (1)	4	0.01

Race*	Population	%
Choctaw (0)	1	<0.01
Colville (0)	0	<0.01
Comanche (0)	1	<0.01
Cree (0)	0	<0.01
Creek (5)	6	0.01
Crow (0)	0	<0.01
Delaware (0)	4	0.01
Hopi (0)	0	<0.01
Houma (0)	0	<0.01
Inupiat *(Alaska Native)* (0)	0	<0.01
Iroquois (14)	14	0.02
Kiowa (0)	0	<0.01
Lumbee (0)	0	<0.01
Menominee (0)	0	<0.01
Mexican American Ind. (7)	7	0.01
Navajo (2)	2	<0.01
Osage (0)	0	<0.01
Ottawa (0)	0	<0.01
Paiute (0)	0	<0.01
Pima (0)	0	<0.01
Potawatomi (0)	0	<0.01
Pueblo (3)	3	<0.01
Puget Sound Salish (0)	0	<0.01
Seminole (1)	1	<0.01
Shoshone (0)	0	<0.01
Sioux (0)	16	0.02
South American Ind. (2)	6	0.01
Spanish American Ind. (0)	2	<0.01
Tlingit-Haida *(Alaska Native)* (0)	0	<0.01
Tohono O'Odham (0)	0	<0.01
Tsimshian *(Alaska Native)* (0)	0	<0.01
Ute (0)	0	<0.01
Yakama (0)	0	<0.01
Yaqui (0)	0	<0.01
Yuman (0)	0	<0.01
Yup'ik *(Alaska Native)* (0)	0	<0.01
Asian (2,269)	2,642	3.47
Not Hispanic (2,240)	2,577	3.39
Hispanic (29)	65	0.09
Bangladeshi (3)	3	<0.01
Bhutanese (54)	101	0.13
Burmese (0)	4	0.01
Cambodian (4)	7	0.01
Chinese, ex. Taiwanese (142)	186	0.24
Filipino (126)	173	0.23
Hmong (0)	0	<0.01
Indian (1,147)	1,247	1.64
Indonesian (238)	260	0.34
Japanese (15)	42	0.06
Korean (56)	82	0.11
Laotian (112)	133	0.17
Malaysian (7)	7	0.01
Nepalese (33)	80	0.11
Pakistani (50)	54	0.07
Sri Lankan (1)	1	<0.01
Taiwanese (1)	1	<0.01
Thai (18)	33	0.04
Vietnamese (142)	159	0.21
Hawaii Native/Pacific Islander (32)	83	0.11
Not Hispanic (21)	55	0.07
Hispanic (11)	28	0.04
Fijian (0)	0	<0.01
Guamanian/Chamorro (7)	11	0.01
Marshallese (0)	0	<0.01
Native Hawaiian (4)	12	0.02
Samoan (0)	5	0.01
Tongan (0)	0	<0.01
White (64,001)	65,659	86.29
Not Hispanic (60,954)	62,216	81.77
Hispanic (3,047)	3,443	4.52

*Notes: † The Census 2010 population figure is used to calculate the percentages in the Hispanic Origin and Race categories. Ancestry percentages are based on the 2006-2010 American Community Survey population (not shown); ‡ Numbers in parentheses indicate the number of people reporting a single ancestry; * Numbers in parentheses indicate the number of persons reporting this race alone, not in combination with any other race; Please refer to the Explanation of Data for more information.*

Upper Darby

Place Type: Township
County: Delaware
Population: 82,795

Ancestry	Population	%
Afghan (115)	115	0.14
African, Sub-Saharan (3,941)	4,163	5.05
African (1,129)	1,251	1.52
Cape Verdean (0)	0	<0.01
Ethiopian (442)	442	0.54
Ghanaian (126)	134	0.16
Kenyan (0)	0	<0.01
Liberian (1,465)	1,530	1.86
Nigerian (284)	300	0.36
Senegalese (191)	191	0.23
Sierra Leonean (116)	116	0.14
Somalian (0)	0	<0.01
South African (0)	0	<0.01
Sudanese (7)	7	0.01
Ugandan (0)	0	<0.01
Zimbabwean (0)	0	<0.01
Other Sub-Saharan African (181)	192	0.23
Albanian (228)	278	0.34
Alsatian (0)	0	<0.01
American (1,141)	1,141	1.39
Arab (552)	719	0.87
Arab (79)	104	0.13
Egyptian (178)	207	0.25
Iraqi (0)	0	<0.01
Jordanian (0)	0	<0.01
Lebanese (56)	144	0.17
Moroccan (9)	9	0.01
Palestinian (0)	0	<0.01
Syrian (213)	213	0.26
Other Arab (17)	42	0.05
Armenian (188)	423	0.51
Assyrian/Chaldean/Syriac (0)	0	<0.01
Australian (21)	21	0.03
Austrian (0)	93	0.11
Basque (0)	33	0.04
Belgian (19)	39	0.05
Brazilian (0)	0	<0.01
British (65)	196	0.24
Bulgarian (0)	0	<0.01
Cajun (0)	0	<0.01
Canadian (0)	41	0.05
Carpatho Rusyn (0)	0	<0.01
Celtic (33)	33	0.04
Croatian (25)	25	0.03
Cypriot (0)	0	<0.01
Czech (0)	116	0.14
Czechoslovakian (42)	63	0.08
Danish (0)	211	0.26
Dutch (179)	748	0.91
Eastern European (0)	0	<0.01
English (837)	4,439	5.39
Estonian (0)	0	<0.01
European (373)	383	0.46
Finnish (24)	64	0.08
French, ex. Basque (118)	1,276	1.55
French Canadian (31)	133	0.16
German (1,472)	9,780	11.87
German Russian (0)	0	<0.01
Greek (1,046)	1,276	1.55
Guyanese (10)	10	0.01
Hungarian (78)	208	0.25
Icelander (0)	51	0.06
Iranian (8)	8	0.01
Irish (9,453)	22,488	27.30
Israeli (0)	0	<0.01
Italian (5,974)	12,902	15.66
Latvian (0)	17	0.02
Lithuanian (38)	308	0.37
Luxemburger (0)	0	<0.01
Macedonian (0)	9	0.01
Maltese (0)	0	<0.01
New Zealander (0)	0	<0.01
Northern European (37)	37	0.04

Ancestry	Population	%
Norwegian (19)	157	0.19
Pennsylvania German (120)	269	0.33
Polish (725)	2,753	3.34
Portuguese (28)	52	0.06
Romanian (40)	143	0.17
Russian (212)	482	0.59
Scandinavian (0)	0	<0.01
Scotch-Irish (365)	808	0.98
Scottish (303)	1,018	1.24
Serbian (63)	63	0.08
Slavic (0)	0	<0.01
Slovak (32)	214	0.26
Slovene (0)	0	<0.01
Soviet Union (0)	0	<0.01
Swedish (82)	505	0.61
Swiss (23)	70	0.08
Turkish (53)	53	0.06
Ukrainian (43)	364	0.44
Welsh (125)	619	0.75
West Indian, ex. Hispanic (2,017)	2,118	2.57
Bahamian (9)	9	0.01
Barbadian (85)	85	0.10
Belizean (0)	0	<0.01
Bermudan (0)	0	<0.01
British West Indian (44)	75	0.09
Dutch West Indian (0)	0	<0.01
Haitian (698)	698	0.85
Jamaican (692)	762	0.93
Trinidadian/Tobagonian (411)	411	0.50
U.S. Virgin Islander (59)	59	0.07
West Indian (19)	19	0.02
Other West Indian (0)	0	<0.01
Yugoslavian (24)	55	0.07

Hispanic Origin	Population	%
Hispanic or Latino (of any race)	3,755	4.54
Central American, ex. Mexican	502	0.61
Costa Rican	33	0.04
Guatemalan	220	0.27
Honduran	143	0.17
Nicaraguan	11	0.01
Panamanian	20	0.02
Salvadoran	53	0.06
Other Central American	22	0.03
Cuban	110	0.13
Dominican Republic	133	0.16
Mexican	715	0.86
Puerto Rican	821	0.99
South American	1,080	1.30
Argentinean	32	0.04
Bolivian	7	0.01
Chilean	6	0.01
Colombian	99	0.12
Ecuadorian	783	0.95
Paraguayan	20	0.02
Peruvian	76	0.09
Uruguayan	9	0.01
Venezuelan	46	0.06
Other South American	2	<0.01
Other Hispanic or Latino	394	0.48

Race*	Population	%
African-American/Black (22,731)	24,093	29.10
Not Hispanic (22,341)	23,509	28.39
Hispanic (390)	584	0.71
American Indian/Alaska Native (165)	669	0.81
Not Hispanic (119)	555	0.67
Hispanic (46)	114	0.14
Alaska Athabascan (Ala. Nat.) (0)	0	<0.01
Aleut (Alaska Native) (0)	1	<0.01
Apache (4)	10	<0.01
Arapaho (0)	0	<0.01
Blackfeet (1)	33	0.04
Canadian/French Am. Ind. (2)	2	<0.01
Central American Ind. (0)	0	<0.01
Cherokee (15)	92	0.11
Cheyenne (0)	2	<0.01
Chickasaw (3)	3	<0.01
Chippewa (1)	5	0.01

Race*	Population	%
Choctaw (3)	20	0.02
Colville (0)	0	<0.01
Comanche (0)	0	<0.01
Cree (0)	2	<0.01
Creek (0)	3	<0.01
Crow (0)	0	<0.01
Delaware (6)	22	0.03
Hopi (0)	0	<0.01
Houma (0)	0	<0.01
Inupiat (Alaska Native) (0)	1	<0.01
Iroquois (3)	10	0.01
Kiowa (0)	0	<0.01
Lumbee (2)	3	<0.01
Menominee (0)	0	<0.01
Mexican American Ind. (6)	12	0.01
Navajo (0)	3	<0.01
Osage (0)	0	<0.01
Ottawa (2)	2	<0.01
Paiute (0)	0	<0.01
Pima (0)	0	<0.01
Potawatomi (0)	0	<0.01
Pueblo (0)	0	<0.01
Puget Sound Salish (0)	0	<0.01
Seminole (0)	2	<0.01
Shoshone (0)	0	<0.01
Sioux (2)	7	0.01
South American Ind. (2)	8	0.01
Spanish American Ind. (0)	3	<0.01
Tlingit-Haida (Alaska Native) (1)	1	<0.01
Tohono O'Odham (0)	0	<0.01
Tsimshian (Alaska Native) (0)	0	<0.01
Ute (0)	3	<0.01
Yakama (0)	0	<0.01
Yaqui (0)	0	<0.01
Yuman (0)	0	<0.01
Yup'ik (Alaska Native) (0)	0	<0.01
Asian (9,218)	9,903	11.96
Not Hispanic (9,182)	9,825	11.87
Hispanic (36)	78	0.09
Bangladeshi (542)	605	0.73
Bhutanese (0)	0	<0.01
Burmese (15)	15	0.02
Cambodian (211)	294	0.36
Chinese, ex. Taiwanese (1,398)	1,655	2.00
Filipino (433)	565	0.68
Hmong (57)	58	0.07
Indian (2,906)	3,208	3.87
Indonesian (29)	40	0.05
Japanese (69)	111	0.13
Korean (465)	526	0.64
Laotian (152)	172	0.21
Malaysian (11)	11	0.01
Nepalese (32)	34	0.04
Pakistani (626)	693	0.84
Sri Lankan (8)	9	0.01
Taiwanese (9)	14	0.02
Thai (86)	103	0.12
Vietnamese (1,702)	1,849	2.23
Hawaii Native/Pacific Islander (36)	151	0.18
Not Hispanic (29)	129	0.16
Hispanic (7)	22	0.03
Fijian (0)	0	<0.01
Guamanian/Chamorro (7)	19	0.02
Marshallese (0)	0	<0.01
Native Hawaiian (11)	31	0.04
Samoan (2)	5	0.01
Tongan (1)	1	<0.01
White (46,835)	48,402	58.46
Not Hispanic (45,341)	46,606	56.29
Hispanic (1,494)	1,796	2.17

Notes: † The Census 2010 population figure is used to calculate the percentages in the Hispanic Origin and Race categories. Ancestry percentages are based on the 2006-2010 American Community Survey population (not shown); ‡ Numbers in parentheses indicate the number of people reporting a single ancestry; * Numbers in parentheses indicate the number of persons reporting this race alone, not in combination with any other race; Please refer to the Explanation of Data for more information.

Ancestry Group Rankings

Afghan

Top 10 Places Sorted by Population
Based on all places, regardless of total population

Place	Population	%
Muhlenberg (township) Berks County	169	0.88
Hyde Park (cdp) Berks County	120	4.54
Upper Darby (township) Delaware County	115	0.14
Bethlehem (city) Northampton County	103	0.14
Erie (city) Erie County	85	0.08
Bethlehem (city) Lehigh County	63	0.33
Philadelphia (city) Philadelphia County	52	<0.01
Upper Allen (township) Cumberland County	50	0.29
Fox Chapel (borough) Allegheny County	49	0.91
Haverford (township) Delaware County	48	0.10

Top 10 Places Sorted by Percent of Total Population
Based on all places, regardless of total population

Place	Population	%
Hyde Park (cdp) Berks County	120	4.54
Fox Chapel (borough) Allegheny County	49	0.91
Muhlenberg (township) Berks County	169	0.88
Indiana (township) Allegheny County	47	0.66
Abington (township) Lackawanna County	11	0.64
Lafayette (township) McKean County	15	0.60
Bethlehem (city) Lehigh County	63	0.33
Upper Allen (township) Cumberland County	50	0.29
Richland (township) Allegheny County	27	0.25
Upper Macungie (township) Lehigh County	38	0.20

Top 10 Places Sorted by Percent of Total Population
Based on places with total population of 50,000 or more

Place	Population	%
Upper Darby (township) Delaware County	115	0.14
Bethlehem (city) Northampton County	103	0.14
Erie (city) Erie County	85	0.08
Bethlehem (city) Northampton County	40	0.07
Philadelphia (city) Philadelphia County	52	<0.01
Abington (township) Montgomery County	0	0.00
Allentown (city) Lehigh County	0	0.00
Bensalem (township) Bucks County	0	0.00
Bristol (township) Bucks County	0	0.00
Lancaster (city) Lancaster County	0	0.00

African, Sub-Saharan

Top 10 Places Sorted by Population
Based on all places, regardless of total population

Place	Population	%
Philadelphia (city) Philadelphia County	29,046	1.93
Pittsburgh (city) Allegheny County	4,577	1.49
Erie (city) Erie County	4,228	4.16
Upper Darby (township) Delaware County	4,163	5.05
Darby (borough) Delaware County	1,568	14.79
Yeadon (borough) Delaware County	1,504	13.11
Bristol (township) Bucks County	1,378	2.51
Harrisburg (city) Dauphin County	848	1.72
Lancaster (city) Lancaster County	820	1.39
Norristown (borough) Montgomery County	807	2.39

Top 10 Places Sorted by Percent of Total Population
Based on all places, regardless of total population

Place	Population	%
Slickville (cdp) Westmoreland County	168	43.30
Colwyn (borough) Delaware County	659	26.22
Southview (cdp) Washington County	24	16.00
Darby (borough) Delaware County	1,568	14.79
Allison (cdp) Fayette County	68	13.26
Yeadon (borough) Delaware County	1,504	13.11
Duquesne (city) Allegheny County	696	11.95
Rankin (borough) Allegheny County	185	9.09
Lincoln University (cdp) Chester County	164	8.48
Pine Ridge (cdp) Pike County	170	7.88

Top 10 Places Sorted by Percent of Total Population
Based on places with total population of 50,000 or more

Place	Population	%
Upper Darby (township) Delaware County	4,163	5.05
Erie (city) Erie County	4,228	4.16
Bristol (township) Bucks County	1,378	2.51
Philadelphia (city) Philadelphia County	29,046	1.93
Pittsburgh (city) Allegheny County	4,577	1.49
Lancaster (city) Lancaster County	820	1.39
Lower Merion (township) Montgomery County	416	0.72
Bensalem (township) Bucks County	356	0.59
Levittown (cdp) Bucks County	292	0.56
Bethlehem (city) Northampton County	413	0.55

African, Sub-Saharan: African

Top 10 Places Sorted by Population
Based on all places, regardless of total population

Place	Population	%
Philadelphia (city) Philadelphia County	18,871	1.25
Erie (city) Erie County	3,634	3.58
Pittsburgh (city) Allegheny County	3,558	1.16
Upper Darby (township) Delaware County	1,251	1.52
Bristol (township) Bucks County	1,057	1.92
Darby (borough) Delaware County	777	7.33
Harrisburg (city) Dauphin County	743	1.51
Duquesne (city) Allegheny County	696	11.95
Lancaster (city) Lancaster County	659	1.12
Wilkinsburg (borough) Allegheny County	655	4.01

Top 10 Places Sorted by Percent of Total Population
Based on all places, regardless of total population

Place	Population	%
Slickville (cdp) Westmoreland County	168	43.30
Southview (cdp) Washington County	24	16.00
Allison (cdp) Fayette County	68	13.26
Duquesne (city) Allegheny County	696	11.95
Colwyn (borough) Delaware County	243	9.67
Rankin (borough) Allegheny County	185	9.09
Pine Ridge (cdp) Pike County	170	7.88
Darby (borough) Delaware County	777	7.33
Bressler (cdp) Dauphin County	89	6.12
Republic (cdp) Fayette County	84	5.65

Top 10 Places Sorted by Percent of Total Population
Based on places with total population of 50,000 or more

Place	Population	%
Erie (city) Erie County	3,634	3.58
Bristol (township) Bucks County	1,057	1.92
Upper Darby (township) Delaware County	1,251	1.52
Philadelphia (city) Philadelphia County	18,871	1.25
Pittsburgh (city) Allegheny County	3,558	1.16
Lancaster (city) Lancaster County	659	1.12
Bensalem (township) Bucks County	319	0.53
Levittown (cdp) Bucks County	244	0.47
Allentown (city) Lehigh County	459	0.39
Bethlehem (city) Northampton County	285	0.38

African, Sub-Saharan: Cape Verdean

Top 10 Places Sorted by Population
Based on all places, regardless of total population

Place	Population	%
Philadelphia (city) Philadelphia County	129	0.01
Cheltenham (township) Montgomery County	96	0.26
Wyomissing (borough) Berks County	19	0.18
Wilkes-Barre (city) Luzerne County	17	0.04
Allentown (city) Lehigh County	16	0.01
Colonial Park (cdp) Dauphin County	15	0.11
Lower Paxton (township) Dauphin County	15	0.03
Lancaster (city) Lancaster County	14	0.02
Upper Chichester (township) Delaware County	11	0.07
West Whiteland (township) Chester County	10	0.06

Top 10 Places Sorted by Percent of Total Population
Based on all places, regardless of total population

Place	Population	%
Cheltenham (township) Montgomery County	96	0.2
Sweden (township) Potter County	2	0.2
Wyomissing (borough) Berks County	19	0.18
Colonial Park (cdp) Dauphin County	15	0.1
Richboro (cdp) Bucks County	7	0.1
Middletown (borough) Dauphin County	8	0.0
Upper Chichester (township) Delaware County	11	0.07
West Whiteland (township) Chester County	10	0.06
Northampton (borough) Northampton County	5	0.0
Wilkes-Barre (city) Luzerne County	17	0.04

Top 10 Places Sorted by Percent of Total Population
Based on places with total population of 50,000 or more

Place	Population	%
Lancaster (city) Lancaster County	14	0.02
Philadelphia (city) Philadelphia County	129	0.0
Allentown (city) Lehigh County	16	0.0
Pittsburgh (city) Allegheny County	6	<0.0
Abington (township) Montgomery County	0	0.00
Bensalem (township) Bucks County	0	0.00
Bethlehem (city) Northampton County	0	0.00
Bethlehem (city) Northampton County	0	0.00
Bristol (township) Bucks County	0	0.00
Erie (city) Erie County	0	0.00

African, Sub-Saharan: Ethiopian

Top 10 Places Sorted by Population
Based on all places, regardless of total population

Place	Population	%
Philadelphia (city) Philadelphia County	1,572	0.10
Upper Darby (township) Delaware County	442	0.54
Pittsburgh (city) Allegheny County	112	0.04
Lancaster (city) Lancaster County	87	0.15
Wilkinsburg (borough) Allegheny County	83	0.51
Greencastle (borough) Franklin County	82	2.07
Yeadon (borough) Delaware County	71	0.62
East Lampeter (township) Lancaster County	70	0.44
State College (borough) Centre County	56	0.13
West Hempfield (township) Lancaster County	53	0.33

Top 10 Places Sorted by Percent of Total Population
Based on all places, regardless of total population

Place	Population	%
Lincoln Park (cdp) Berks County	48	3.43
Greencastle (borough) Franklin County	82	2.07
Wormleysburg (borough) Cumberland County	52	1.74
Campbelltown (cdp) Lebanon County	35	0.97
Morgantown (cdp) Berks County	8	0.90
Penbrook (borough) Dauphin County	21	0.70
Belle Vernon (borough) Fayette County	8	0.70
Yeadon (borough) Delaware County	71	0.62
Upper Darby (township) Delaware County	442	0.54
South Londonderry (township) Lebanon County	35	0.52

Top 10 Places Sorted by Percent of Total Population
Based on places with total population of 50,000 or more

Place	Population	%
Upper Darby (township) Delaware County	442	0.54
Lancaster (city) Lancaster County	87	0.15
Philadelphia (city) Philadelphia County	1,572	0.10
Pittsburgh (city) Allegheny County	112	0.04
Bethlehem (city) Northampton County	20	0.04
Bethlehem (city) Northampton County	20	0.03
Allentown (city) Lehigh County	24	0.02
Reading (city) Berks County	18	0.02
Lower Merion (township) Montgomery County	14	0.02
Abington (township) Montgomery County	0	0.00

African, Sub-Saharan: Ghanaian

Top 10 Places Sorted by Population
Based on all places, regardless of total population

Place	Population	%
Philadelphia (city) Philadelphia County	584	0.04
Upper Darby (township) Delaware County	134	0.16
Sanatoga (cdp) Montgomery County	124	1.50
Lower Pottsgrove (township) Montgomery County	124	1.04
Chester (township) Delaware County	109	2.68
Middle Smithfield (township) Monroe County	109	0.70
Yeadon (borough) Delaware County	99	0.86
Springfield (township) York County	62	1.25
Bristol (township) Bucks County	62	0.11
Cheltenham (township) Montgomery County	53	0.14

Top 10 Places Sorted by Percent of Total Population
Based on all places, regardless of total population

Place	Population	%
Chester (township) Delaware County	109	2.68
Sanatoga (cdp) Montgomery County	124	1.50
Springfield (township) York County	62	1.25
Lower Pottsgrove (township) Montgomery County	124	1.04
Yeadon (borough) Delaware County	99	0.86
Freemansburg (borough) Northampton County	22	0.86
Middle Smithfield (township) Monroe County	109	0.70
Allegheny (township) Cambria County	17	0.61
Antis (township) Blair County	37	0.57
Glenburn (township) Lackawanna County	7	0.54

Top 10 Places Sorted by Percent of Total Population
Based on places with total population of 50,000 or more

Place	Population	%
Upper Darby (township) Delaware County	134	0.16
Bristol (township) Bucks County	62	0.11
Philadelphia (city) Philadelphia County	584	0.04
Levittown (cdp) Bucks County	13	0.03
Reading (city) Berks County	14	0.02
Pittsburgh (city) Allegheny County	45	0.01
Abington (township) Montgomery County	0	0.00
Allentown (city) Lehigh County	0	0.00
Bensalem (township) Bucks County	0	0.00
Bethlehem (city) Northampton County	0	0.00

African, Sub-Saharan: Kenyan

Top 10 Places Sorted by Population
Based on all places, regardless of total population

Place	Population	%
Philadelphia (city) Philadelphia County	147	0.01
Lebanon (city) Lebanon County	86	0.34
Bryn Mawr (cdp) Montgomery County	70	1.99
Lower Merion (township) Montgomery County	70	0.12
Pine (township) Mercer County	53	1.05
Coolbaugh (township) Monroe County	53	0.26
Paoli (cdp) Chester County	52	0.99
Clifton Heights (borough) Delaware County	51	0.77
Nether Providence (township) Delaware County	50	0.37
Easton (city) Northampton County	46	0.17

Top 10 Places Sorted by Percent of Total Population
Based on all places, regardless of total population

Place	Population	%
Bryn Mawr (cdp) Montgomery County	70	1.99
Quentin (cdp) Lebanon County	9	1.86
Plumsteadville (cdp) Bucks County	33	1.26
Pine (township) Mercer County	53	1.05
Biglerville (borough) Adams County	11	1.05
East Petersburg (borough) Lancaster County	45	1.00
Paoli (cdp) Chester County	52	0.99
Clifton Heights (borough) Delaware County	51	0.77
South Williamsport (borough) Lycoming County	43	0.68
Messiah College (cdp) Cumberland County	14	0.57

Top 10 Places Sorted by Percent of Total Population
Based on places with total population of 50,000 or more

Place	Population	%
Lower Merion (township) Montgomery County	70	0.12
Bethlehem (city) Northampton County	35	0.06
Bethlehem (city) Northampton County	35	0.05
Allentown (city) Lehigh County	31	0.03

Place	Population	%
Erie (city) Erie County	17	0.02
Lancaster (city) Lancaster County	10	0.02
Philadelphia (city) Philadelphia County	147	0.01
Pittsburgh (city) Allegheny County	21	0.01
Reading (city) Berks County	13	0.01
Abington (township) Montgomery County	0	0.00

African, Sub-Saharan: Liberian

Top 10 Places Sorted by Population
Based on all places, regardless of total population

Place	Population	%
Philadelphia (city) Philadelphia County	3,198	0.21
Upper Darby (township) Delaware County	1,530	1.86
Yeadon (borough) Delaware County	612	5.33
Darby (borough) Delaware County	566	5.34
Bristol (township) Bucks County	243	0.44
Collingdale (borough) Delaware County	203	2.32
Falls (township) Bucks County	158	0.46
Ridley (township) Delaware County	118	0.38
Colwyn (borough) Delaware County	101	4.02
Fairless Hills (cdp) Bucks County	79	0.90

Top 10 Places Sorted by Percent of Total Population
Based on all places, regardless of total population

Place	Population	%
Shelocta (borough) Indiana County	7	5.93
Darby (borough) Delaware County	566	5.34
Yeadon (borough) Delaware County	612	5.33
Colwyn (borough) Delaware County	101	4.02
Collingdale (borough) Delaware County	203	2.32
Toftrees (cdp) Centre County	42	1.92
Upper Darby (township) Delaware County	1,530	1.86
Upland (borough) Delaware County	56	1.76
Enola (cdp) Cumberland County	62	0.94
Fairless Hills (cdp) Bucks County	79	0.90

Top 10 Places Sorted by Percent of Total Population
Based on places with total population of 50,000 or more

Place	Population	%
Upper Darby (township) Delaware County	1,530	1.86
Bristol (township) Bucks County	243	0.44
Philadelphia (city) Philadelphia County	3,198	0.21
Levittown (cdp) Bucks County	35	0.07
Reading (city) Berks County	31	0.04
Bensalem (township) Bucks County	27	0.04
Pittsburgh (city) Allegheny County	71	0.02
Abington (township) Montgomery County	0	0.00
Allentown (city) Lehigh County	0	0.00
Bethlehem (city) Northampton County	0	0.00

African, Sub-Saharan: Nigerian

Top 10 Places Sorted by Population
Based on all places, regardless of total population

Place	Population	%
Philadelphia (city) Philadelphia County	1,877	0.12
Pittsburgh (city) Allegheny County	391	0.13
Upper Darby (township) Delaware County	300	0.36
Jackson (township) Butler County	251	6.83
Aldan (borough) Delaware County	241	5.77
Norristown (borough) Montgomery County	216	0.64
Palmer (township) Northampton County	159	0.79
West Manchester (township) York County	150	0.80
Swissvale (borough) Allegheny County	127	1.40
Yeadon (borough) Delaware County	109	0.95

Top 10 Places Sorted by Percent of Total Population
Based on all places, regardless of total population

Place	Population	%
Jackson (township) Butler County	251	6.83
Aldan (borough) Delaware County	241	5.77
Lincoln University (cdp) Chester County	94	4.86
Leesport (borough) Berks County	72	3.53
Greencastle (borough) Franklin County	80	2.02
Lemont (cdp) Centre County	47	1.96
Lower Oxford (township) Chester County	94	1.86
Haverford College (cdp) Delaware County	18	1.56
Swissvale (borough) Allegheny County	127	1.40
Conewago (township) York County	100	1.40

African, Sub-Saharan: Senegalese

Top 10 Places Sorted by Percent of Total Population
Based on places with total population of 50,000 or more

Place	Population	%
Upper Darby (township) Delaware County	300	0.36
Pittsburgh (city) Allegheny County	391	0.13
Philadelphia (city) Philadelphia County	1,877	0.12
Lower Merion (township) Montgomery County	35	0.06
Bethlehem (city) Northampton County	30	0.05
Bethlehem (city) Northampton County	30	0.04
Allentown (city) Lehigh County	32	0.03
Bristol (township) Bucks County	16	0.03
Abington (township) Montgomery County	14	0.03
Bensalem (township) Bucks County	10	0.02

African, Sub-Saharan: Senegalese

Top 10 Places Sorted by Population
Based on all places, regardless of total population

Place	Population	%
Upper Darby (township) Delaware County	191	0.23
Philadelphia (city) Philadelphia County	139	0.01
Bethlehem (city) Northampton County	43	0.08
Bethlehem (city) Northampton County	43	0.06
Pittsburgh (city) Allegheny County	36	0.01
Wyncote (cdp) Montgomery County	20	0.63
Cheltenham (township) Montgomery County	20	0.05
Swatara (township) Dauphin County	18	0.08
Norristown (borough) Montgomery County	12	0.04
Middletown (township) Delaware County	10	0.06

Top 10 Places Sorted by Percent of Total Population
Based on all places, regardless of total population

Place	Population	%
Wyncote (cdp) Montgomery County	20	0.63
Wayne (township) Clinton County	8	0.47
Upper Darby (township) Delaware County	191	0.23
Bethlehem (city) Northampton County	43	0.08
Swatara (township) Dauphin County	18	0.08
Bethlehem (city) Northampton County	43	0.06
Middletown (township) Delaware County	10	0.06
Cheltenham (township) Montgomery County	20	0.05
Norristown (borough) Montgomery County	12	0.04
Philadelphia (city) Philadelphia County	139	0.01

Top 10 Places Sorted by Percent of Total Population
Based on places with total population of 50,000 or more

Place	Population	%
Upper Darby (township) Delaware County	191	0.23
Bethlehem (city) Northampton County	43	0.08
Bethlehem (city) Northampton County	43	0.06
Philadelphia (city) Philadelphia County	139	0.01
Pittsburgh (city) Allegheny County	36	0.01
Abington (township) Montgomery County	0	0.00
Allentown (city) Lehigh County	0	0.00
Bensalem (township) Bucks County	0	0.00
Bristol (township) Bucks County	0	0.00
Erie (city) Erie County	0	0.00

African, Sub-Saharan: Sierra Leonean

Top 10 Places Sorted by Population
Based on all places, regardless of total population

Place	Population	%
Colwyn (borough) Delaware County	231	9.19
Yeadon (borough) Delaware County	197	1.72
Darby (borough) Delaware County	156	1.47
Philadelphia (city) Philadelphia County	144	0.01
Upper Darby (township) Delaware County	116	0.14
Pittsburgh (city) Allegheny County	55	0.02
State College (borough) Centre County	33	0.08
East Lansdowne (borough) Delaware County	21	0.79
Monroeville (municipality) Allegheny County	21	0.07
Kutztown University (cdp) Berks County	14	0.56

Top 10 Places Sorted by Percent of Total Population
Based on all places, regardless of total population

Place	Population	%
Colwyn (borough) Delaware County	231	9.19
Yeadon (borough) Delaware County	197	1.72
Darby (borough) Delaware County	156	1.47

Place	Population	%
East Lansdowne (borough) Delaware County	21	0.79
Kutztown University (cdp) Berks County	14	0.56
Maxatawny (township) Berks County	14	0.18
Upper Darby (township) Delaware County	116	0.14
Folcroft (borough) Delaware County	8	0.12
Coatesville (city) Chester County	14	0.11
State College (borough) Centre County	33	0.08

Top 10 Places Sorted by Percent of Total Population
Based on places with total population of 50,000 or more

Place	Population	%
Upper Darby (township) Delaware County	116	0.14
Pittsburgh (city) Allegheny County	55	0.02
Abington (township) Montgomery County	10	0.02
Philadelphia (city) Philadelphia County	144	0.01
Allentown (city) Lehigh County	0	0.00
Bensalem (township) Bucks County	0	0.00
Bethlehem (city) Northampton County	0	0.00
Bethlehem (city) Northampton County	0	0.00
Bristol (township) Bucks County	0	0.00
Erie (city) Erie County	0	0.00

African, Sub-Saharan: Somalian

Top 10 Places Sorted by Population
Based on all places, regardless of total population

Place	Population	%
Erie (city) Erie County	96	0.09
Pittsburgh (city) Allegheny County	57	0.02
Lower Allen (township) Cumberland County	54	0.30
Philadelphia (city) Philadelphia County	22	<0.01
East Lansdowne (borough) Delaware County	21	0.79
Aaronsburg (cdp) Centre County	0	0.00
Aaronsburg (cdp) Washington County	0	0.00
Abbott (township) Potter County	0	0.00
Abbottstown (borough) Adams County	0	0.00
Abington (township) Lackawanna County	0	0.00

Top 10 Places Sorted by Percent of Total Population
Based on all places, regardless of total population

Place	Population	%
East Lansdowne (borough) Delaware County	21	0.79
Lower Allen (township) Cumberland County	54	0.30
Erie (city) Erie County	96	0.09
Pittsburgh (city) Allegheny County	57	0.02
Philadelphia (city) Philadelphia County	22	<0.01
Aaronsburg (cdp) Centre County	0	0.00
Aaronsburg (cdp) Washington County	0	0.00
Abbott (township) Potter County	0	0.00
Abbottstown (borough) Adams County	0	0.00
Abington (township) Lackawanna County	0	0.00

Top 10 Places Sorted by Percent of Total Population
Based on places with total population of 50,000 or more

Place	Population	%
Erie (city) Erie County	96	0.09
Pittsburgh (city) Allegheny County	57	0.02
Philadelphia (city) Philadelphia County	22	<0.01
Abington (township) Montgomery County	0	0.00
Allentown (city) Lehigh County	0	0.00
Bensalem (township) Bucks County	0	0.00
Bethlehem (city) Northampton County	0	0.00
Bethlehem (city) Northampton County	0	0.00
Bristol (township) Bucks County	0	0.00
Lancaster (city) Lancaster County	0	0.00

African, Sub-Saharan: South African

Top 10 Places Sorted by Population
Based on all places, regardless of total population

Place	Population	%
Philadelphia (city) Philadelphia County	235	0.02
Lower Merion (township) Montgomery County	137	0.24
Penn Forest (township) Carbon County	102	1.15
Derry (township) Dauphin County	86	0.36
Lansdowne (borough) Delaware County	51	0.48
Middletown (township) Bucks County	49	0.11
Collegeville (borough) Montgomery County	38	0.74
Upper Providence (township) Delaware County	38	0.37
Lehigh (township) Northampton County	33	0.32
North Huntingdon (township) Westmoreland County	33	0.11

Top 10 Places Sorted by Percent of Total Population
Based on all places, regardless of total population

Place	Population	%
Penn Forest (township) Carbon County	102	1.15
Cherrytree (township) Venango County	16	1.10
Buck (township) Luzerne County	3	0.99
Collegeville (borough) Montgomery County	38	0.74
Milford (borough) Pike County	7	0.66
Lansdowne (borough) Delaware County	51	0.48
Weatherly (borough) Carbon County	11	0.43
Lehigh (township) Carbon County	2	0.41
Upper Providence (township) Delaware County	38	0.37
Derry (township) Dauphin County	86	0.36

Top 10 Places Sorted by Percent of Total Population
Based on places with total population of 50,000 or more

Place	Population	%
Lower Merion (township) Montgomery County	137	0.24
Lancaster (city) Lancaster County	27	0.05
Erie (city) Erie County	27	0.03
Philadelphia (city) Philadelphia County	235	0.02
Pittsburgh (city) Allegheny County	15	<0.01
Abington (township) Montgomery County	0	0.00
Allentown (city) Lehigh County	0	0.00
Bensalem (township) Bucks County	0	0.00
Bethlehem (city) Northampton County	0	0.00
Bethlehem (city) Northampton County	0	0.00

African, Sub-Saharan: Sudanese

Top 10 Places Sorted by Population
Based on all places, regardless of total population

Place	Population	%
Erie (city) Erie County	221	0.22
Swatara (township) Dauphin County	217	0.94
Philadelphia (city) Philadelphia County	167	0.01
Lansdale (borough) Montgomery County	79	0.49
Tredyffrin (township) Chester County	47	0.16
Millbourne (borough) Delaware County	44	4.18
Colonial Park (cdp) Dauphin County	42	0.32
Lower Paxton (township) Dauphin County	42	0.09
Pittsburgh (city) Allegheny County	38	0.01
Mahoning (township) Montour County	27	0.65

Top 10 Places Sorted by Percent of Total Population
Based on all places, regardless of total population

Place	Population	%
Millbourne (borough) Delaware County	44	4.18
Swatara (township) Dauphin County	217	0.94
Mahoning (township) Montour County	27	0.65
Lansdale (borough) Montgomery County	79	0.49
Colonial Park (cdp) Dauphin County	42	0.32
Brockway (borough) Jefferson County	5	0.24
Erie (city) Erie County	221	0.22
Yeadon (borough) Delaware County	22	0.19
Tredyffrin (township) Chester County	47	0.16
Newport (township) Luzerne County	8	0.15

Top 10 Places Sorted by Percent of Total Population
Based on places with total population of 50,000 or more

Place	Population	%
Erie (city) Erie County	221	0.22
Lancaster (city) Lancaster County	23	0.04
Philadelphia (city) Philadelphia County	167	0.01
Pittsburgh (city) Allegheny County	38	0.01
Upper Darby (township) Delaware County	7	0.01
Abington (township) Montgomery County	0	0.00
Allentown (city) Lehigh County	0	0.00
Bensalem (township) Bucks County	0	0.00
Bethlehem (city) Northampton County	0	0.00
Bethlehem (city) Northampton County	0	0.00

African, Sub-Saharan: Ugandan

Top 10 Places Sorted by Population
Based on all places, regardless of total population

Place	Population	%
Braddock Hills (borough) Allegheny County	60	3.22
Horsham (township) Montgomery County	51	0.20
East Whiteland (township) Chester County	23	0.22

Place	Population	%
Lower Paxton (township) Dauphin County	21	0.04
Moon (township) Allegheny County	20	0.08
Swarthmore (borough) Delaware County	15	0.24
North Union (township) Fayette County	9	0.07
Harrisville (borough) Butler County	8	0.87
Philadelphia (city) Philadelphia County	8	<0.01
Aaronsburg (cdp) Centre County	0	0.00

Top 10 Places Sorted by Percent of Total Population
Based on all places, regardless of total population

Place	Population	%
Braddock Hills (borough) Allegheny County	60	3.22
Harrisville (borough) Butler County	8	0.87
Swarthmore (borough) Delaware County	15	0.24
East Whiteland (township) Chester County	23	0.22
Horsham (township) Montgomery County	51	0.20
Moon (township) Allegheny County	20	0.08
North Union (township) Fayette County	9	0.07
Lower Paxton (township) Dauphin County	21	0.04
Philadelphia (city) Philadelphia County	8	<0.01
Aaronsburg (cdp) Centre County	0	0.00

Top 10 Places Sorted by Percent of Total Population
Based on places with total population of 50,000 or more

Place	Population	%
Philadelphia (city) Philadelphia County	8	<0.01
Abington (township) Montgomery County	0	0.00
Allentown (city) Lehigh County	0	0.00
Bensalem (township) Bucks County	0	0.00
Bethlehem (city) Northampton County	0	0.00
Bethlehem (city) Northampton County	0	0.00
Bristol (township) Bucks County	0	0.00
Erie (city) Erie County	0	0.00
Lancaster (city) Lancaster County	0	0.00
Levittown (cdp) Bucks County	0	0.00

African, Sub-Saharan: Zimbabwean

Top 10 Places Sorted by Population
Based on all places, regardless of total population

Place	Population	%
Limerick (township) Montgomery County	55	0.32
Philadelphia (city) Philadelphia County	51	<0.01
Pittsburgh (city) Allegheny County	36	0.01
East Lansdowne (borough) Delaware County	21	0.79
Athens (township) Bradford County	18	0.35
Manheim (township) Lancaster County	12	0.03
Wayne (township) Clinton County	8	0.47
Aaronsburg (cdp) Centre County	0	0.00
Aaronsburg (cdp) Washington County	0	0.00
Abbott (township) Potter County	0	0.00

Top 10 Places Sorted by Percent of Total Population
Based on all places, regardless of total population

Place	Population	%
East Lansdowne (borough) Delaware County	21	0.79
Wayne (township) Clinton County	8	0.47
Athens (township) Bradford County	18	0.35
Limerick (township) Montgomery County	55	0.32
Manheim (township) Lancaster County	12	0.03
Pittsburgh (city) Allegheny County	36	0.01
Philadelphia (city) Philadelphia County	51	<0.01
Aaronsburg (cdp) Centre County	0	0.00
Aaronsburg (cdp) Washington County	0	0.00
Abbott (township) Potter County	0	0.00

Top 10 Places Sorted by Percent of Total Population
Based on places with total population of 50,000 or more

Place	Population	%
Pittsburgh (city) Allegheny County	36	0.01
Philadelphia (city) Philadelphia County	51	<0.01
Abington (township) Montgomery County	0	0.00
Allentown (city) Lehigh County	0	0.00
Bensalem (township) Bucks County	0	0.00
Bethlehem (city) Northampton County	0	0.00
Bethlehem (city) Northampton County	0	0.00
Bristol (township) Bucks County	0	0.00
Erie (city) Erie County	0	0.00
Lancaster (city) Lancaster County	0	0.00

African, Sub-Saharan: Other

Top 10 Places Sorted by Population
Based on all places, regardless of total population

Place	Population	%
Philadelphia (city) Philadelphia County	1,902	0.13
Erie (city) Erie County	226	0.22
Sharon Hill (borough) Delaware County	198	3.51
Upper Darby (township) Delaware County	192	0.23
Price (township) Monroe County	184	5.29
Pittsburgh (city) Allegheny County	136	0.04
Fullerton (cdp) Lehigh County	101	0.67
Whitehall (township) Lehigh County	101	0.38
Shiloh (cdp) York County	97	0.85
West Manchester (township) York County	97	0.52

Top 10 Places Sorted by Percent of Total Population
Based on all places, regardless of total population

Place	Population	%
Price (township) Monroe County	184	5.29
Sharon Hill (borough) Delaware County	198	3.51
West Branch (township) Potter County	12	2.90
Colwyn (borough) Delaware County	53	2.11
Millbourne (borough) Delaware County	20	1.90
Highland (township) Clarion County	7	1.11
Wayne (township) Clinton County	16	0.94
Brentwood (borough) Allegheny County	90	0.93
Shiloh (cdp) York County	97	0.85
Emmaus (borough) Lehigh County	89	0.79

Top 10 Places Sorted by Percent of Total Population
Based on places with total population of 50,000 or more

Place	Population	%
Upper Darby (township) Delaware County	192	0.23
Erie (city) Erie County	226	0.22
Philadelphia (city) Philadelphia County	1,902	0.13
Abington (township) Montgomery County	52	0.09
Pittsburgh (city) Allegheny County	136	0.04
Reading (city) Berks County	18	0.02
Lower Merion (township) Montgomery County	8	0.01
Allentown (city) Lehigh County	0	0.00
Bensalem (township) Bucks County	0	0.00
Bethlehem (city) Northampton County	0	0.00

Albanian

Top 10 Places Sorted by Population
Based on all places, regardless of total population

Place	Population	%
Philadelphia (city) Philadelphia County	3,892	0.26
Upper Darby (township) Delaware County	278	0.34
South Whitehall (township) Lehigh County	267	1.40
Emmaus (borough) Lehigh County	223	1.98
Lehman (township) Luzerne County	204	5.88
Drexel Hill (cdp) Delaware County	158	0.55
Erie (city) Erie County	136	0.13
Solebury (township) Bucks County	129	1.51
Allentown (city) Lehigh County	126	0.11
Abington (township) Montgomery County	121	0.22

Top 10 Places Sorted by Percent of Total Population
Based on all places, regardless of total population

Place	Population	%
Albrightsville (cdp) Carbon County	13	6.67
Lehman (township) Luzerne County	204	5.88
Port Royal (borough) Juniata County	46	3.88
Brodheadsville (cdp) Monroe County	58	3.36
Lattimer (cdp) Luzerne County	13	3.25
Wind Gap (borough) Northampton County	87	3.17
West Hazleton (borough) Luzerne County	120	2.72
Porter (township) Huntingdon County	43	2.14
Emmaus (borough) Lehigh County	223	1.98
Solebury (township) Bucks County	129	1.51

Top 10 Places Sorted by Percent of Total Population
Based on places with total population of 50,000 or more

Place	Population	%
Upper Darby (township) Delaware County	278	0.34
Philadelphia (city) Philadelphia County	3,892	0.26
Abington (township) Montgomery County	121	0.22
Erie (city) Erie County	136	0.13

Lower Merion (township) Montgomery County	70	0.12
Allentown (city) Lehigh County	126	0.11
Reading (city) Berks County	96	0.11
Bensalem (township) Bucks County	51	0.08
Bristol (township) Bucks County	27	0.05
Pittsburgh (city) Allegheny County	85	0.03

Alsatian

Top 10 Places Sorted by Population
Based on all places, regardless of total population

Place	Population	%
Pittsburgh (city) Allegheny County	91	0.03
Philadelphia (city) Philadelphia County	54	<0.01
Lamar (township) Clinton County	41	1.64
Worcester (township) Montgomery County	31	0.33
Monroeville (municipality) Allegheny County	27	0.10
Upper Moreland (township) Montgomery County	25	0.10
Springfield (township) Montgomery County	22	0.11
New London (township) Chester County	21	0.38
Middletown (township) Delaware County	21	0.13
Marple (township) Delaware County	21	0.09

Top 10 Places Sorted by Percent of Total Population
Based on all places, regardless of total population

Place	Population	%
Lamar (township) Clinton County	41	1.64
East Butler (borough) Butler County	8	1.13
Middleport (borough) Schuylkill County	3	0.71
Warren (township) Franklin County	2	0.56
Burlington (township) Bradford County	4	0.51
Stevens (township) Bradford County	2	0.47
Muse (cdp) Washington County	12	0.45
Riverview Park (cdp) Berks County	14	0.41
New London (township) Chester County	21	0.38
Wyncote (cdp) Montgomery County	12	0.38

Top 10 Places Sorted by Percent of Total Population
Based on places with total population of 50,000 or more

Place	Population	%
Pittsburgh (city) Allegheny County	91	0.03
Bristol (township) Bucks County	12	0.02
Levittown (cdp) Bucks County	12	0.02
Allentown (city) Lehigh County	9	0.01
Erie (city) Erie County	7	0.01
Lancaster (city) Lancaster County	4	0.01
Lower Merion (township) Montgomery County	4	0.01
Philadelphia (city) Philadelphia County	54	<0.01
Abington (township) Montgomery County	0	0.00
Bensalem (township) Bucks County	0	0.00

American

Top 10 Places Sorted by Population
Based on all places, regardless of total population

Place	Population	%
Philadelphia (city) Philadelphia County	20,637	1.37
Pittsburgh (city) Allegheny County	7,699	2.50
Allentown (city) Lehigh County	3,325	2.86
Sandy (township) Clearfield County	3,282	30.33
Lower Paxton (township) Dauphin County	2,524	5.39
Erie (city) Erie County	2,350	2.31
Altoona (city) Blair County	2,185	4.66
West Manchester (township) York County	2,136	11.44
Lower Merion (township) Montgomery County	2,084	3.59
Northampton (township) Bucks County	2,076	5.21

Top 10 Places Sorted by Percent of Total Population
Based on all places, regardless of total population

Place	Population	%
Trafford (borough) Allegheny County	30	78.95
Wallaceton (borough) Clearfield County	139	47.93
Oklahoma (cdp) Clearfield County	319	39.09
Troutville (borough) Clearfield County	105	37.50
Treasure Lake (cdp) Clearfield County	1,542	35.89
Stevens (cdp) Lancaster County	305	35.67
Orviston (cdp) Centre County	22	35.48
Bradford (township) Clearfield County	1,051	34.15
Huston (township) Clearfield County	461	33.95
Nittany (cdp) Centre County	279	32.03

Top 10 Places Sorted by Percent of Total Population
Based on places with total population of 50,000 or more

Place	Population	%
Abington (township) Montgomery County	2,004	3.62
Lower Merion (township) Montgomery County	2,084	3.59
Millcreek (township) Erie County	1,872	3.53
Levittown (cdp) Bucks County	1,650	3.17
Allentown (city) Lehigh County	3,325	2.86
Bristol (township) Bucks County	1,396	2.54
Pittsburgh (city) Allegheny County	7,699	2.50
Scranton (city) Lackawanna County	1,834	2.41
Lancaster (city) Lancaster County	1,406	2.39
Bethlehem (city) Northampton County	1,759	2.35

Arab: Total

Top 10 Places Sorted by Population
Based on all places, regardless of total population

Place	Population	%
Philadelphia (city) Philadelphia County	7,763	0.52
Allentown (city) Lehigh County	3,112	2.67
Pittsburgh (city) Allegheny County	2,859	0.93
Whitehall (township) Lehigh County	1,261	4.76
Hampden (township) Cumberland County	946	3.45
Fullerton (cdp) Lehigh County	854	5.67
Upper Darby (township) Delaware County	719	0.87
Wilkes-Barre (city) Luzerne County	618	1.49
Bethlehem (city) Northampton County	564	0.75
Scranton (city) Lackawanna County	541	0.71

Top 10 Places Sorted by Percent of Total Population
Based on all places, regardless of total population

Place	Population	%
Utica (borough) Venango County	18	11.32
Highland (township) Clarion County	58	9.16
Bulger (cdp) Washington County	41	8.42
Glenfield (borough) Allegheny County	13	7.43
Sun Valley (cdp) Monroe County	175	7.16
Fayetteville (cdp) Franklin County	217	6.90
Hostetter (cdp) Westmoreland County	50	6.83
Paxtang (borough) Dauphin County	98	6.53
Georgetown (cdp) Luzerne County	116	6.49
Palo Alto (borough) Schuylkill County	65	6.26

Top 10 Places Sorted by Percent of Total Population
Based on places with total population of 50,000 or more

Place	Population	%
Allentown (city) Lehigh County	3,112	2.67
Pittsburgh (city) Allegheny County	2,859	0.93
Upper Darby (township) Delaware County	719	0.87
Bethlehem (city) Northampton County	564	0.75
Scranton (city) Lackawanna County	541	0.71
Bethlehem (city) Northampton County	384	0.69
Philadelphia (city) Philadelphia County	7,763	0.52
Erie (city) Erie County	532	0.52
Millcreek (township) Erie County	276	0.52
Bristol (township) Bucks County	245	0.45

Arab: Arab

Top 10 Places Sorted by Population
Based on all places, regardless of total population

Place	Population	%
Philadelphia (city) Philadelphia County	2,081	0.14
Pittsburgh (city) Allegheny County	388	0.13
Allentown (city) Lehigh County	360	0.31
Lower Paxton (township) Dauphin County	245	0.52
Bethlehem (city) Northampton County	225	0.41
Bethlehem (city) Northampton County	225	0.30
Upper Gwynedd (township) Montgomery County	158	1.03
Erie (city) Erie County	152	0.15
Millcreek (township) Erie County	151	0.29
Stroudsburg (borough) Monroe County	140	2.44

Top 10 Places Sorted by Percent of Total Population
Based on all places, regardless of total population

Place	Population	%
Highland (township) Clarion County	29	4.58
Green Lane (borough) Montgomery County	18	4.06
West Pittsburg (cdp) Lawrence County	23	3.42

Place		Population	%
Wattsburg (borough) Erie County		11	2.93
Taylor (township) Lawrence County		23	2.54
Stroudsburg (borough) Monroe County		140	2.44
Strattanville (borough) Clarion County		9	1.42
Haverford College (cdp) Delaware County		16	1.39
Young (township) Jefferson County		24	1.31
Hughestown (borough) Luzerne County		15	1.13

Top 10 Places Sorted by Percent of Total Population
Based on places with total population of 50,000 or more

Place	Population	%
Bethlehem (city) Northampton County	225	0.41
Allentown (city) Lehigh County	360	0.31
Bethlehem (city) Northampton County	225	0.30
Millcreek (township) Erie County	151	0.29
Erie (city) Erie County	152	0.15
Philadelphia (city) Philadelphia County	2,081	0.14
Pittsburgh (city) Allegheny County	388	0.13
Upper Darby (township) Delaware County	104	0.13
Scranton (city) Lackawanna County	86	0.11
Reading (city) Berks County	48	0.05

Arab: Egyptian

Top 10 Places Sorted by Population
Based on all places, regardless of total population

Place	Population	%
Hampden (township) Cumberland County	600	2.19
Philadelphia (city) Philadelphia County	580	0.04
Lansdale (borough) Montgomery County	324	2.00
Bethlehem (township) Northampton County	230	0.98
Lower Paxton (township) Dauphin County	224	0.48
Upper Darby (township) Delaware County	207	0.25
Allentown (city) Lehigh County	166	0.14
Pittsburgh (city) Allegheny County	152	0.05
Montgomery (township) Montgomery County	145	0.60
Upper Macungie (township) Lehigh County	141	0.74

Top 10 Places Sorted by Percent of Total Population
Based on all places, regardless of total population

Place	Population	%
Utica (borough) Venango County	18	11.32
Paxtang (borough) Dauphin County	81	5.40
Highland (township) Clarion County	29	4.58
Wrightsville (borough) York County	89	3.87
Wormleysburg (borough) Cumberland County	112	3.75
Hatfield (borough) Montgomery County	106	3.34
Leetsdale (borough) Allegheny County	38	3.25
Tullytown (borough) Bucks County	56	2.99
Shiremanstown (borough) Cumberland County	43	2.86
Hampden (township) Cumberland County	600	2.19

Top 10 Places Sorted by Percent of Total Population
Based on places with total population of 50,000 or more

Place	Population	%
Upper Darby (township) Delaware County	207	0.25
Bristol (township) Bucks County	97	0.18
Allentown (city) Lehigh County	166	0.14
Scranton (city) Lackawanna County	45	0.06
Pittsburgh (city) Allegheny County	152	0.05
Philadelphia (city) Philadelphia County	580	0.04
Abington (township) Montgomery County	23	0.04
Levittown (cdp) Bucks County	21	0.04
Bethlehem (city) Northampton County	16	0.03
Bethlehem (city) Northampton County	16	0.02

Arab: Iraqi

Top 10 Places Sorted by Population
Based on all places, regardless of total population

Place	Population	%
Philadelphia (city) Philadelphia County	218	0.01
Erie (city) Erie County	208	0.20
Lower Moreland (township) Montgomery County	177	1.40
Pittsburgh (city) Allegheny County	104	0.03
Lower Allen (township) Cumberland County	33	0.18
Washington (township) Schuylkill County	29	0.98
Derry (township) Dauphin County	26	0.11
Haverford (township) Delaware County	25	0.05
Lower Merion (township) Montgomery County	21	0.04
Manheim (township) Lancaster County	16	0.04

Top 10 Places Sorted by Percent of Total Population
Based on all places, regardless of total population

Place	Population	%
Lower Moreland (township) Montgomery County	177	1.40
Washington (township) Schuylkill County	29	0.98
Rutledge (borough) Delaware County	4	0.42
Rosslyn Farms (borough) Allegheny County	2	0.40
Kelly (township) Union County	14	0.26
North Shenango (township) Crawford County	3	0.22
Edinboro (borough) Erie County	14	0.21
Erie (city) Erie County	208	0.20
Lower Allen (township) Cumberland County	33	0.18
Conneaut (township) Erie County	6	0.14

Top 10 Places Sorted by Percent of Total Population
Based on places with total population of 50,000 or more

Place	Population	%
Erie (city) Erie County	208	0.20
Lower Merion (township) Montgomery County	21	0.04
Pittsburgh (city) Allegheny County	104	0.03
Philadelphia (city) Philadelphia County	218	0.01
Abington (township) Montgomery County	0	0.00
Allentown (city) Lehigh County	0	0.00
Bensalem (township) Bucks County	0	0.00
Bethlehem (city) Northampton County	0	0.00
Bethlehem (city) Northampton County	0	0.00
Bristol (township) Bucks County	0	0.00

Arab: Jordanian

Top 10 Places Sorted by Population
Based on all places, regardless of total population

Place	Population	%
Philadelphia (city) Philadelphia County	939	0.06
Sun Valley (cdp) Monroe County	175	7.16
Chestnuthill (township) Monroe County	175	1.03
Hanover (township) Northampton County	59	0.55
West Caln (township) Chester County	58	0.66
Upper Dublin (township) Montgomery County	40	0.16
Kingston (borough) Luzerne County	39	0.29
Coatesville (city) Chester County	38	0.30
Plains (cdp) Luzerne County	37	0.93
Plains (township) Luzerne County	37	0.37

Top 10 Places Sorted by Percent of Total Population
Based on all places, regardless of total population

Place	Population	%
Sun Valley (cdp) Monroe County	175	7.16
Chestnuthill (township) Monroe County	175	1.03
Plains (cdp) Luzerne County	37	0.93
West Caln (township) Chester County	58	0.66
Hanover (township) Northampton County	59	0.55
Big Beaver (borough) Beaver County	10	0.52
Plains (township) Luzerne County	37	0.37
Walnutport (borough) Northampton County	7	0.33
Fleetwood (borough) Berks County	13	0.31
Cambridge Springs (borough) Crawford County	8	0.31

Top 10 Places Sorted by Percent of Total Population
Based on places with total population of 50,000 or more

Place	Population	%
Philadelphia (city) Philadelphia County	939	0.06
Bethlehem (city) Northampton County	5	0.01
Abington (township) Montgomery County	0	0.00
Allentown (city) Lehigh County	0	0.00
Bensalem (township) Bucks County	0	0.00
Bethlehem (city) Northampton County	0	0.00
Bristol (township) Bucks County	0	0.00
Erie (city) Erie County	0	0.00
Lancaster (city) Lancaster County	0	0.00
Levittown (cdp) Bucks County	0	0.00

Arab: Lebanese

Top 10 Places Sorted by Population
Based on all places, regardless of total population

Place	Population	%
Philadelphia (city) Philadelphia County	991	0.07
Pittsburgh (city) Allegheny County	934	0.30
Scranton (city) Lackawanna County	383	0.50

Place		Population	%
Uniontown (city) Fayette County		374	3.49
North Union (township) Fayette County		332	2.55
Wilkes-Barre (city) Luzerne County		320	0.77
Whitehall (township) Lehigh County		309	1.17
Fullerton (cdp) Lehigh County		283	1.88
Mount Lebanon (township) Allegheny County		248	0.76
Hopewell (township) Beaver County		234	1.85

Top 10 Places Sorted by Percent of Total Population
Based on all places, regardless of total population

Place	Population	%
Glenfield (borough) Allegheny County	13	7.43
Palo Alto (borough) Schuylkill County	65	6.26
Upper Exeter (cdp) Luzerne County	46	5.84
Langeloth (cdp) Washington County	22	5.02
Oliver (cdp) Fayette County	97	4.48
East Uniontown (cdp) Fayette County	92	3.72
Gordon (borough) Schuylkill County	28	3.68
Abington (township) Lackawanna County	61	3.57
Uniontown (city) Fayette County	374	3.49
Patterson Heights (borough) Beaver County	24	3.38

Top 10 Places Sorted by Percent of Total Population
Based on places with total population of 50,000 or more

Place	Population	%
Scranton (city) Lackawanna County	383	0.50
Pittsburgh (city) Allegheny County	934	0.30
Lower Merion (township) Montgomery County	105	0.18
Upper Darby (township) Delaware County	144	0.17
Abington (township) Montgomery County	94	0.17
Allentown (city) Lehigh County	113	0.10
Erie (city) Erie County	98	0.10
Bethlehem (city) Northampton County	60	0.08
Bethlehem (city) Northampton County	47	0.08
Bristol (township) Bucks County	42	0.08

Arab: Moroccan

Top 10 Places Sorted by Population
Based on all places, regardless of total population

Place	Population	%
Philadelphia (city) Philadelphia County	684	0.05
Pittsburgh (city) Allegheny County	312	0.10
Fayetteville (cdp) Franklin County	217	6.90
Greene (township) Franklin County	217	1.36
Feasterville (cdp) Bucks County	176	5.84
Lower Southampton (township) Bucks County	176	0.92
Lemoyne (borough) Cumberland County	116	2.60
Radnor (township) Delaware County	79	0.25
Swatara (township) Dauphin County	77	0.33
Middletown (township) Bucks County	69	0.15

Top 10 Places Sorted by Percent of Total Population
Based on all places, regardless of total population

Place	Population	%
Fayetteville (cdp) Franklin County	217	6.90
Feasterville (cdp) Bucks County	176	5.84
Lemoyne (borough) Cumberland County	116	2.60
Devon (cdp) Chester County	34	2.20
Mammoth (cdp) Westmoreland County	10	1.73
Greene (township) Franklin County	217	1.36
Mount Holly Springs (borough) Cumberland County	23	1.17
Hamlin (township) McKean County	6	1.00
Lower Southampton (township) Bucks County	176	0.92
Mount Joy (borough) Lancaster County	57	0.78

Top 10 Places Sorted by Percent of Total Population
Based on places with total population of 50,000 or more

Place	Population	%
Pittsburgh (city) Allegheny County	312	0.10
Philadelphia (city) Philadelphia County	684	0.05
Lower Merion (township) Montgomery County	28	0.05
Allentown (city) Lehigh County	13	0.01
Upper Darby (township) Delaware County	9	0.01
Erie (city) Erie County	6	0.01
Scranton (city) Lackawanna County	5	0.01
Abington (township) Montgomery County	0	0.00
Bensalem (township) Bucks County	0	0.00
Bethlehem (city) Northampton County	0	0.00

Arab: Palestinian

Top 10 Places Sorted by Population
Based on all places, regardless of total population

Place	Population	%
Philadelphia (city) Philadelphia County	621	0.04
Hampden (township) Cumberland County	106	0.39
Susquehanna (township) Dauphin County	95	0.40
Arlington Heights (cdp) Monroe County	76	1.19
Stroud (township) Monroe County	76	0.41
Hamilton (township) Monroe County	57	0.62
Miles (township) Centre County	56	3.66
Allentown (city) Lehigh County	46	0.04
Bethel Park (municipality) Allegheny County	45	0.14
Hamilton (township) Franklin County	44	0.42

Top 10 Places Sorted by Percent of Total Population
Based on all places, regardless of total population

Place	Population	%
Miles (township) Centre County	56	3.66
South Canaan (township) Wayne County	28	1.58
Haverford College (cdp) Delaware County	16	1.39
Sandy Lake (township) Mercer County	16	1.20
Arlington Heights (cdp) Monroe County	76	1.19
Fox Run (cdp) Butler County	29	0.84
Hamilton (township) Monroe County	57	0.62
Lafayette (township) McKean County	14	0.56
Clifton Heights (borough) Delaware County	36	0.54
Cetronia (cdp) Lehigh County	10	0.51

Top 10 Places Sorted by Percent of Total Population
Based on places with total population of 50,000 or more

Place	Population	%
Millcreek (township) Erie County	31	0.06
Philadelphia (city) Philadelphia County	621	0.04
Allentown (city) Lehigh County	46	0.04
Lower Merion (township) Montgomery County	26	0.04
Abington (township) Montgomery County	11	0.02
Pittsburgh (city) Allegheny County	25	0.01
Bensalem (township) Bucks County	0	0.00
Bethlehem (city) Northampton County	0	0.00
Bethlehem (city) Northampton County	0	0.00
Bristol (township) Bucks County	0	0.00

Arab: Syrian

Top 10 Places Sorted by Population
Based on all places, regardless of total population

Place	Population	%
Allentown (city) Lehigh County	2,119	1.82
Whitehall (township) Lehigh County	717	2.71
Philadelphia (city) Philadelphia County	637	0.04
Pittsburgh (city) Allegheny County	499	0.16
Fullerton (cdp) Lehigh County	371	2.46
South Whitehall (township) Lehigh County	309	1.62
Bethlehem (city) Northampton County	224	0.30
Upper Darby (township) Delaware County	213	0.26
Northampton (borough) Northampton County	198	2.00
Salisbury (township) Lehigh County	197	1.45

Top 10 Places Sorted by Percent of Total Population
Based on all places, regardless of total population

Place	Population	%
Hostetter (cdp) Westmoreland County	50	6.83
Georgetown (cdp) Luzerne County	116	6.49
Bulger (cdp) Washington County	29	5.95
Stiles (cdp) Lehigh County	51	5.23
Oakwood (cdp) Lawrence County	109	5.20
Lanesboro (borough) Susquehanna County	27	5.01
McDonald (borough) Allegheny County	19	5.00
Dorneyville (cdp) Lehigh County	193	4.30
Wilkes-Barre (township) Luzerne County	116	3.86
Shavertown (cdp) Luzerne County	64	3.22

Top 10 Places Sorted by Percent of Total Population
Based on places with total population of 50,000 or more

Place	Population	%
Allentown (city) Lehigh County	2,119	1.82
Bethlehem (city) Northampton County	224	0.30
Upper Darby (township) Delaware County	213	0.26
Pittsburgh (city) Allegheny County	499	0.16

Place	Population	%
Bethlehem (city) Northampton County	84	0.15
Bristol (township) Bucks County	74	0.13
Millcreek (township) Erie County	44	0.08
Philadelphia (city) Philadelphia County	637	0.04
Erie (city) Erie County	37	0.04
Levittown (cdp) Bucks County	22	0.04

Arab: Other

Top 10 Places Sorted by Population
Based on all places, regardless of total population

Place	Population	%
Philadelphia (city) Philadelphia County	1,012	0.07
Pittsburgh (city) Allegheny County	445	0.14
Allentown (city) Lehigh County	295	0.25
Tredyffrin (township) Chester County	269	0.91
Patton (township) Centre County	179	1.22
Haverford (township) Delaware County	176	0.36
King of Prussia (cdp) Montgomery County	134	0.68
Upper Merion (township) Montgomery County	134	0.48
Chesterbrook (cdp) Chester County	126	2.84
Park Forest Village (cdp) Centre County	104	1.03

Top 10 Places Sorted by Percent of Total Population
Based on all places, regardless of total population

Place	Population	%
Salladasburg (borough) Lycoming County	12	5.06
Logan (township) Clinton County	30	4.44
Lyons (borough) Berks County	19	4.19
South Shenango (township) Crawford County	77	4.03
Pymatuning Central (cdp) Crawford County	77	3.25
Allenwood (cdp) Union County	16	3.06
Chesterbrook (cdp) Chester County	126	2.84
New Galilee (borough) Beaver County	9	2.12
Pulaski (township) Beaver County	27	1.84
Flourtown (cdp) Montgomery County	81	1.79

Top 10 Places Sorted by Percent of Total Population
Based on places with total population of 50,000 or more

Place	Population	%
Allentown (city) Lehigh County	295	0.25
Pittsburgh (city) Allegheny County	445	0.14
Bensalem (township) Bucks County	48	0.08
Philadelphia (city) Philadelphia County	1,012	0.07
Millcreek (township) Erie County	37	0.07
Bristol (township) Bucks County	32	0.06
Upper Darby (township) Delaware County	42	0.05
Bethlehem (city) Northampton County	34	0.05
Scranton (city) Lackawanna County	22	0.03
Abington (township) Montgomery County	15	0.03

Armenian

Top 10 Places Sorted by Population
Based on all places, regardless of total population

Place	Population	%
Philadelphia (city) Philadelphia County	1,315	0.09
Upper Darby (township) Delaware County	423	0.51
Marple (township) Delaware County	421	1.80
Drexel Hill (cdp) Delaware County	265	0.92
Horsham (cdp) Montgomery County	261	1.81
Horsham (township) Montgomery County	261	1.01
Haverford (township) Delaware County	246	0.51
Erie (city) Erie County	183	0.18
Concord (township) Delaware County	160	0.99
East Goshen (township) Chester County	148	0.82

Top 10 Places Sorted by Percent of Total Population
Based on all places, regardless of total population

Place	Population	%
Freeport (township) Greene County	5	2.01
Wormleysburg (borough) Cumberland County	57	1.91
Effort (cdp) Monroe County	32	1.84
Horsham (cdp) Montgomery County	261	1.81
Marple (township) Delaware County	421	1.80
Forks (township) Sullivan County	8	1.75
Haycock (township) Bucks County	39	1.68
Montrose Manor (cdp) Berks County	7	1.52
Gamble (township) Lycoming County	13	1.50
Spring House (cdp) Montgomery County	56	1.48

Top 10 Places Sorted by Percent of Total Population
Based on places with total population of 50,000 or more

Place	Population	%
Upper Darby (township) Delaware County	423	0.51
Lower Merion (township) Montgomery County	110	0.19
Erie (city) Erie County	183	0.18
Philadelphia (city) Philadelphia County	1,315	0.09
Lancaster (city) Lancaster County	52	0.09
Levittown (cdp) Bucks County	43	0.08
Bensalem (township) Bucks County	40	0.07
Scranton (city) Lackawanna County	41	0.05
Millcreek (township) Erie County	24	0.05
Bethlehem (city) Northampton County	21	0.04

Assyrian/Chaldean/Syriac

Top 10 Places Sorted by Population
Based on all places, regardless of total population

Place	Population	%
Haverford (township) Delaware County	75	0.15
Downingtown (borough) Chester County	57	0.72
Bethlehem (township) Northampton County	23	0.10
Allentown (city) Lehigh County	20	0.02
West Brandywine (township) Chester County	18	0.24
Dallas (township) Luzerne County	17	0.19
Lower Paxton (township) Dauphin County	17	0.04
Newtown (township) Bucks County	16	0.08
Rose Valley (borough) Delaware County	15	1.55
Messiah College (cdp) Cumberland County	15	0.61

Top 10 Places Sorted by Percent of Total Population
Based on all places, regardless of total population

Place	Population	%
Rose Valley (borough) Delaware County	15	1.55
Atglen (borough) Chester County	12	0.93
Downingtown (borough) Chester County	57	0.72
Saegertown (borough) Crawford County	8	0.70
Messiah College (cdp) Cumberland County	15	0.61
Mineral (township) Venango County	3	0.58
Middlecreek (township) Somerset County	5	0.50
Gold Key Lake (cdp) Pike County	10	0.47
Dreher (township) Wayne County	4	0.35
Pine (township) Columbia County	3	0.31

Top 10 Places Sorted by Percent of Total Population
Based on places with total population of 50,000 or more

Place	Population	%
Allentown (city) Lehigh County	20	0.02
Bethlehem (city) Northampton County	8	0.01
Bethlehem (city) Northampton County	8	0.01
Philadelphia (city) Philadelphia County	8	<0.01
Abington (township) Montgomery County	0	0.00
Bensalem (township) Bucks County	0	0.00
Bristol (township) Bucks County	0	0.00
Erie (city) Erie County	0	0.00
Lancaster (city) Lancaster County	0	0.00
Levittown (cdp) Bucks County	0	0.00

Australian

Top 10 Places Sorted by Population
Based on all places, regardless of total population

Place	Population	%
Philadelphia (city) Philadelphia County	243	0.02
Allentown (city) Lehigh County	120	0.10
Middle Smithfield (township) Monroe County	109	0.70
Haverford (township) Delaware County	85	0.18
Norristown (borough) Montgomery County	79	0.23
Northampton (borough) Northampton County	65	0.66
West Hempfield (township) Lancaster County	65	0.41
Moosic (borough) Lackawanna County	64	1.14
Upper Uwchlan (township) Chester County	64	0.61
Franklin Park (borough) Allegheny County	50	0.39

Top 10 Places Sorted by Percent of Total Population
Based on all places, regardless of total population

Place	Population	%
Mount Gretna (borough) Lebanon County	7	4.61
Allenport (cdp) Huntingdon County	22	4.55
Great Bend (borough) Susquehanna County	39	3.96

Place	Population	%
Fredericksburg (cdp) Crawford County	20	3.24
Friendsville (borough) Susquehanna County	4	3.20
Haverford College (cdp) Delaware County	34	2.95
Bryn Athyn (borough) Montgomery County	27	2.30
Upper Exeter (cdp) Luzerne County	18	2.29
Fredericktown (cdp) Washington County	5	1.26
Moosic (borough) Lackawanna County	64	1.14

Top 10 Places Sorted by Percent of Total Population
Based on places with total population of 50,000 or more

Place	Population	%
Allentown (city) Lehigh County	120	0.10
Abington (township) Montgomery County	37	0.07
Upper Darby (township) Delaware County	21	0.03
Philadelphia (city) Philadelphia County	243	0.02
Erie (city) Erie County	22	0.02
Pittsburgh (city) Allegheny County	38	0.01
Scranton (city) Lackawanna County	10	0.01
Bethlehem (city) Northampton County	9	0.01
Lower Merion (township) Montgomery County	8	0.01
Bensalem (township) Bucks County	0	0.00

Austrian

Top 10 Places Sorted by Population
Based on all places, regardless of total population

Place	Population	%
Philadelphia (city) Philadelphia County	2,580	0.17
Pittsburgh (city) Allegheny County	1,622	0.53
Allentown (city) Lehigh County	1,440	1.24
Whitehall (township) Lehigh County	902	3.40
Bethlehem (city) Northampton County	783	1.05
Lower Merion (township) Montgomery County	648	1.12
Lower Macungie (township) Lehigh County	559	1.95
Bethlehem (city) Northampton County	544	0.98
North Whitehall (township) Lehigh County	481	3.08
Salisbury (township) Lehigh County	433	3.20

Top 10 Places Sorted by Percent of Total Population
Based on all places, regardless of total population

Place	Population	%
Vicksburg (cdp) Union County	48	21.24
Jamison City (cdp) Columbia County	14	13.33
Lenhartsville (borough) Berks County	22	12.43
Coplay (borough) Lehigh County	286	8.82
Oneida (cdp) Schuylkill County	16	8.70
Haverford College (cdp) Delaware County	95	8.24
Deer Lake (borough) Schuylkill County	53	7.35
Nuremberg (cdp) Schuylkill County	27	7.24
New Tripoli (cdp) Lehigh County	58	7.09
Stiles (cdp) Lehigh County	68	6.97

Top 10 Places Sorted by Percent of Total Population
Based on places with total population of 50,000 or more

Place	Population	%
Allentown (city) Lehigh County	1,440	1.24
Lower Merion (township) Montgomery County	648	1.12
Bethlehem (city) Northampton County	783	1.05
Bethlehem (city) Northampton County	544	0.98
Abington (township) Montgomery County	410	0.74
Pittsburgh (city) Allegheny County	1,622	0.53
Millcreek (township) Erie County	273	0.52
Scranton (city) Lackawanna County	301	0.40
Bensalem (township) Bucks County	236	0.39
Erie (city) Erie County	350	0.34

Basque

Top 10 Places Sorted by Population
Based on all places, regardless of total population

Place	Population	%
Upper St. Clair (cdp/township) Allegheny County	67	0.35
Philadelphia (city) Philadelphia County	59	<0.01
Middletown (cdp) Northampton County	38	0.53
Bethlehem (township) Northampton County	38	0.16
East Whiteland (township) Chester County	36	0.34
Sugarcreek (borough) Venango County	35	0.66
Drexel Hill (cdp) Delaware County	33	0.12
Upper Darby (township) Delaware County	33	0.04
Birdsboro (borough) Berks County	30	0.58
Corry (city) Erie County	21	0.32

Top 10 Places Sorted by Percent of Total Population
Based on all places, regardless of total population

Place	Population	%
Mayberry (township) Montour County	8	2.63
Lumber (township) Cameron County	4	1.94
Sugarcreek (borough) Venango County	35	0.66
Birdsboro (borough) Berks County	30	0.58
Middletown (cdp) Northampton County	38	0.53
East Berlin (borough) Adams County	8	0.48
Upper St. Clair (cdp/township) Allegheny County	67	0.35
East Whiteland (township) Chester County	36	0.34
Corry (city) Erie County	21	0.32
Stoneboro (borough) Mercer County	3	0.29

Top 10 Places Sorted by Percent of Total Population
Based on places with total population of 50,000 or more

Place	Population	%
Upper Darby (township) Delaware County	33	0.04
Bethlehem (city) Northampton County	12	0.02
Bethlehem (city) Northampton County	12	0.02
Levittown (cdp) Bucks County	10	0.02
Millcreek (township) Erie County	9	0.02
Philadelphia (city) Philadelphia County	59	<0.01
Abington (township) Montgomery County	0	0.00
Allentown (city) Lehigh County	0	0.00
Bensalem (township) Bucks County	0	0.00
Bristol (township) Bucks County	0	0.00

Belgian

Top 10 Places Sorted by Population
Based on all places, regardless of total population

Place	Population	%
Philadelphia (city) Philadelphia County	214	0.01
Harrison (township) Allegheny County	174	1.66
Pittsburgh (city) Allegheny County	171	0.06
Rostraver (township) Westmoreland County	133	1.16
South Fayette (township) Allegheny County	132	0.95
McDonald (borough) Washington County	128	5.41
Smith (township) Washington County	125	2.79
Lower Merion (township) Montgomery County	120	0.21
Cecil (township) Washington County	118	1.07
Bristol (township) Bucks County	118	0.21

Top 10 Places Sorted by Percent of Total Population
Based on all places, regardless of total population

Place	Population	%
McDonald (borough) Allegheny County	48	12.63
Bulger (cdp) Washington County	58	11.91
Joffre (cdp) Washington County	46	7.31
Midway (borough) Washington County	55	6.24
Ward (township) Tioga County	8	5.80
Point Marion (borough) Fayette County	59	5.45
McDonald (borough) Washington County	128	5.41
Allenport (borough) Washington County	23	5.28
Dunlo (cdp) Cambria County	11	5.02
Ford Cliff (borough) Armstrong County	20	4.35

Top 10 Places Sorted by Percent of Total Population
Based on places with total population of 50,000 or more

Place	Population	%
Lower Merion (township) Montgomery County	120	0.21
Bristol (township) Bucks County	118	0.21
Levittown (cdp) Bucks County	99	0.19
Abington (township) Montgomery County	75	0.14
Erie (city) Erie County	89	0.09
Pittsburgh (city) Allegheny County	171	0.06
Millcreek (township) Erie County	33	0.06
Upper Darby (township) Delaware County	39	0.05
Reading (city) Berks County	31	0.04
Scranton (city) Lackawanna County	20	0.03

Brazilian

Top 10 Places Sorted by Population
Based on all places, regardless of total population

Place	Population	%
Philadelphia (city) Philadelphia County	2,622	0.17
Scranton (city) Lackawanna County	305	0.40
Richland (township) Bucks County	267	2.14

Place	Population	%
Bethlehem (township) Northampton County	266	1.1
Springettsbury (township) York County	250	0.9
Norristown (borough) Montgomery County	235	0.7
East York (cdp) York County	205	2.2
Lehman (township) Pike County	183	1.7
State College (borough) Centre County	158	0.3
Saw Creek (cdp) Pike County	141	2.7

Top 10 Places Sorted by Percent of Total Population
Based on all places, regardless of total population

Place	Population	%
Durham (township) Bucks County	35	2.8
Mount Pocono (borough) Monroe County	89	2.8
Saw Creek (cdp) Pike County	141	2.7
East York (cdp) York County	205	2.2
Richland (township) Bucks County	267	2.14
Washingtonville (borough) Montour County	4	1.7
Lehman (township) Pike County	183	1.76
Beech Mountain Lakes (cdp) Luzerne County	33	1.7
Monroe (township) Cumberland County	77	1.33
Milford (township) Pike County	24	1.30

Top 10 Places Sorted by Percent of Total Population
Based on places with total population of 50,000 or more

Place	Population	%
Scranton (city) Lackawanna County	305	0.40
Philadelphia (city) Philadelphia County	2,622	0.17
Bensalem (township) Bucks County	100	0.17
Erie (city) Erie County	107	0.11
Lower Merion (township) Montgomery County	37	0.06
Abington (township) Montgomery County	32	0.06
Bethlehem (city) Northampton County	39	0.05
Allentown (city) Lehigh County	43	0.04
Bethlehem (city) Northampton County	22	0.04
Pittsburgh (city) Allegheny County	106	0.03

British

Top 10 Places Sorted by Population
Based on all places, regardless of total population

Place	Population	%
Philadelphia (city) Philadelphia County	2,578	0.17
Pittsburgh (city) Allegheny County	1,143	0.37
Lower Merion (township) Montgomery County	509	0.88
Bethlehem (city) Northampton County	446	0.60
Haverford (township) Delaware County	388	0.80
Radnor (township) Delaware County	351	1.12
Bethlehem (city) Northampton County	342	0.62
Mount Lebanon (township) Allegheny County	306	0.93
Abington (township) Montgomery County	298	0.54
Manheim (township) Lancaster County	283	0.76

Top 10 Places Sorted by Percent of Total Population
Based on all places, regardless of total population

Place	Population	%
Farmington (cdp) Fayette County	80	11.38
Gouglersville (cdp) Berks County	22	8.66
Noblestown (cdp) Allegheny County	25	8.12
Mingoville (cdp) Centre County	28	7.63
Heath (township) Jefferson County	7	5.26
Lincoln Park (cdp) Berks County	73	5.21
Watson (township) Lycoming County	27	4.99
Orrtanna (cdp) Adams County	8	4.94
Hopwood (cdp) Fayette County	83	4.42
Cooke (township) Cumberland County	9	4.41

Top 10 Places Sorted by Percent of Total Population
Based on places with total population of 50,000 or more

Place	Population	%
Lower Merion (township) Montgomery County	509	0.88
Bethlehem (city) Northampton County	342	0.62
Bethlehem (city) Northampton County	446	0.60
Abington (township) Montgomery County	298	0.54
Millcreek (township) Erie County	209	0.39
Pittsburgh (city) Allegheny County	1,143	0.37
Lancaster (city) Lancaster County	188	0.32
Upper Darby (township) Delaware County	196	0.24
Bristol (township) Bucks County	120	0.22
Allentown (city) Lehigh County	217	0.19

Bulgarian

Top 10 Places Sorted by Population
Based on all places, regardless of total population

Place	Population	%
Philadelphia (city) Philadelphia County	150	0.01
Pittsburgh (city) Allegheny County	127	0.04
Danville (borough) Montour County	104	2.21
East Stroudsburg (borough) Monroe County	104	1.04
Ross (township) Monroe County	97	1.62
Wind Gap (borough) Northampton County	93	3.38
Pine (township) Allegheny County	88	0.82
California (borough) Washington County	81	1.23
Monroe (township) Bradford County	62	4.94
Scranton (city) Lackawanna County	55	0.07

Top 10 Places Sorted by Percent of Total Population
Based on all places, regardless of total population

Place	Population	%
Monroe (township) Bradford County	62	4.94
Wind Gap (borough) Northampton County	93	3.38
Danville (borough) Montour County	104	2.21
Alleghenyville (cdp) Berks County	18	2.17
Effort (cdp) Monroe County	32	1.84
McConnellsburg (borough) Fulton County	22	1.80
Penndel (borough) Bucks County	42	1.79
Blue Ball (cdp) Lancaster County	14	1.78
Ross (township) Monroe County	97	1.62
Trappe (borough) Montgomery County	43	1.25

Top 10 Places Sorted by Percent of Total Population
Based on places with total population of 50,000 or more

Place	Population	%
Scranton (city) Lackawanna County	55	0.07
Abington (township) Montgomery County	26	0.05
Pittsburgh (city) Allegheny County	127	0.04
Allentown (city) Lehigh County	47	0.04
Millcreek (township) Erie County	16	0.03
Levittown (cdp) Bucks County	13	0.03
Bristol (township) Bucks County	13	0.02
Bethlehem (city) Northampton County	10	0.02
Philadelphia (city) Philadelphia County	150	0.01
Erie (city) Erie County	12	0.01

Cajun

Top 10 Places Sorted by Population
Based on all places, regardless of total population

Place	Population	%
Pittsburgh (city) Allegheny County	77	0.02
Philadelphia (city) Philadelphia County	38	<0.01
Faxon (cdp) Lycoming County	31	2.08
Susquehanna Trails (cdp) York County	31	1.21
Peach Bottom (township) York County	31	0.65
Loyalsock (township) Lycoming County	31	0.28
Johnstown (city) Cambria County	27	0.13
Warminster (township) Bucks County	24	0.07
Harrisburg (city) Dauphin County	24	0.05
Concord (township) Delaware County	23	0.14

Top 10 Places Sorted by Percent of Total Population
Based on all places, regardless of total population

Place	Population	%
Sylvania (township) Potter County	2	2.30
Faxon (cdp) Lycoming County	31	2.08
Susquehanna Trails (cdp) York County	31	1.21
Dauphin (borough) Dauphin County	6	0.80
Carbon (township) Huntingdon County	3	0.73
Peach Bottom (township) York County	31	0.65
Woodbourne (cdp) Bucks County	18	0.51
Hanover (township) Lehigh County	7	0.44
Reiffton (cdp) Berks County	16	0.39
Applewold (borough) Armstrong County	1	0.33

Top 10 Places Sorted by Percent of Total Population
Based on places with total population of 50,000 or more

Place	Population	%
Pittsburgh (city) Allegheny County	77	0.02
Philadelphia (city) Philadelphia County	38	<0.01
Abington (township) Montgomery County	0	0.00
Allentown (city) Lehigh County	0	0.00

Bensalem (township) Bucks County	0	0.00
Bethlehem (city) Northampton County	0	0.00
Bethlehem (city) Northampton County	0	0.00
Bristol (township) Bucks County	0	0.00
Erie (city) Erie County	0	0.00
Lancaster (city) Lancaster County	0	0.00

Canadian

Top 10 Places Sorted by Population
Based on all places, regardless of total population

Place	Population	%
Philadelphia (city) Philadelphia County	1,094	0.07
Pittsburgh (city) Allegheny County	308	0.10
Northampton (township) Bucks County	256	0.64
Radnor (township) Delaware County	253	0.81
Lower Merion (township) Montgomery County	241	0.42
Reading (city) Berks County	215	0.25
Murrysville (municipality) Westmoreland County	147	0.74
Bethlehem (city) Northampton County	147	0.20
Haverford (township) Delaware County	146	0.30
Millcreek (township) Erie County	145	0.27

Top 10 Places Sorted by Percent of Total Population
Based on all places, regardless of total population

Place	Population	%
Coral (cdp) Indiana County	29	9.32
Farmington (cdp) Fayette County	56	7.97
Eagleville (cdp) Centre County	16	6.72
Masthope (cdp) Pike County	30	5.94
Silverdale (borough) Bucks County	37	4.60
Glasgow (borough) Beaver County	2	3.85
Sewickley Heights (borough) Allegheny County	29	3.81
Salix (cdp) Cambria County	46	3.50
New Baltimore (borough) Somerset County	7	3.37
Klingerstown (cdp) Schuylkill County	3	2.83

Top 10 Places Sorted by Percent of Total Population
Based on places with total population of 50,000 or more

Place	Population	%
Lower Merion (township) Montgomery County	241	0.42
Millcreek (township) Erie County	145	0.27
Reading (city) Berks County	215	0.25
Bethlehem (city) Northampton County	117	0.21
Bethlehem (city) Northampton County	147	0.20
Levittown (cdp) Bucks County	86	0.17
Pittsburgh (city) Allegheny County	308	0.10
Abington (township) Montgomery County	56	0.10
Erie (city) Erie County	88	0.09
Scranton (city) Lackawanna County	71	0.09

Carpatho Rusyn

Top 10 Places Sorted by Population
Based on all places, regardless of total population

Place	Population	%
Pittsburgh (city) Allegheny County	116	0.04
Windber (borough) Somerset County	88	2.10
Dunmore (borough) Lackawanna County	69	0.49
Hermitage (city) Mercer County	64	0.40
Elizabeth (township) Allegheny County	52	0.39
Donora (borough) Washington County	51	1.03
Plains (cdp) Luzerne County	49	1.23
Glassport (borough) Allegheny County	49	1.08
Plains (township) Luzerne County	49	0.49
Philadelphia (city) Philadelphia County	46	<0.01

Top 10 Places Sorted by Percent of Total Population
Based on all places, regardless of total population

Place	Population	%
Arnold City (cdp) Fayette County	25	2.98
Greenock (cdp) Allegheny County	44	2.33
Deer Lake (cdp) Fayette County	14	2.11
Windber (borough) Somerset County	88	2.10
Elco (borough) Washington County	5	1.78
North Belle Vernon (borough) Westmoreland County	26	1.37
Enlow (cdp) Allegheny County	10	1.32
Plains (cdp) Luzerne County	49	1.23
Paint (borough) Somerset County	11	1.16
Southmont (borough) Cambria County	26	1.10

Top 10 Places Sorted by Percent of Total Population
Based on places with total population of 50,000 or more

Place	Population	%
Millcreek (township) Erie County	36	0.07
Scranton (city) Lackawanna County	35	0.05
Pittsburgh (city) Allegheny County	116	0.04
Erie (city) Erie County	37	0.04
Bristol (township) Bucks County	19	0.03
Bethlehem (city) Northampton County	13	0.02
Bethlehem (city) Northampton County	13	0.02
Philadelphia (city) Philadelphia County	46	<0.01
Abington (township) Montgomery County	0	0.00
Allentown (city) Lehigh County	0	0.00

Celtic

Top 10 Places Sorted by Population
Based on all places, regardless of total population

Place	Population	%
Whitehall (township) Lehigh County	91	0.34
Springfield (township) Delaware County	83	0.35
Hershey (cdp) Dauphin County	70	0.54
Derry (township) Dauphin County	70	0.29
Bristol (borough) Bucks County	67	0.68
Lower Southampton (township) Bucks County	57	0.30
Williamsport (city) Lycoming County	48	0.16
Fullerton (cdp) Lehigh County	46	0.31
Mount Penn (borough) Berks County	44	1.41
Philadelphia (city) Philadelphia County	41	<0.01

Top 10 Places Sorted by Percent of Total Population
Based on all places, regardless of total population

Place	Population	%
Mount Gretna (borough) Lebanon County	4	2.63
Mount Penn (borough) Berks County	44	1.41
Newville (borough) Cumberland County	18	1.39
East Side (borough) Carbon County	4	1.06
New Britain (borough) Bucks County	32	1.02
Spring Ridge (cdp) Berks County	10	0.95
Graham (township) Clearfield County	15	0.92
Oliver (township) Mifflin County	17	0.89
Manns Choice (borough) Bedford County	2	0.85
Connoquenessing (township) Butler County	31	0.76

Top 10 Places Sorted by Percent of Total Population
Based on places with total population of 50,000 or more

Place	Population	%
Upper Darby (township) Delaware County	33	0.04
Bensalem (township) Bucks County	26	0.04
Lancaster (city) Lancaster County	18	0.03
Lower Merion (township) Montgomery County	10	0.02
Pittsburgh (city) Allegheny County	38	0.01
Erie (city) Erie County	15	0.01
Bethlehem (city) Northampton County	11	0.01
Philadelphia (city) Philadelphia County	41	<0.01
Scranton (city) Lackawanna County	3	<0.01
Abington (township) Montgomery County	0	0.00

Croatian

Top 10 Places Sorted by Population
Based on all places, regardless of total population

Place	Population	%
Pittsburgh (city) Allegheny County	2,304	0.75
Philadelphia (city) Philadelphia County	916	0.06
North Huntingdon (township) Westmoreland County	911	3.01
Shaler (township) Allegheny County	834	2.91
McCandless (township) Allegheny County	725	2.56
Swatara (township) Dauphin County	692	2.99
Ross (township) Allegheny County	678	2.18
Allison Park (cdp) Allegheny County	668	3.00
Lower Paxton (township) Dauphin County	668	1.43
Monroeville (municipality) Allegheny County	578	2.04

Top 10 Places Sorted by Percent of Total Population
Based on all places, regardless of total population

Place	Population	%
Hendersonville (cdp) Washington County	72	36.73
Crown (cdp) Clarion County	26	22.03

Place	Population	%
Enhaut (cdp) Dauphin County	148	16.39
Harrison City (cdp) Westmoreland County	16	14.16
Bressler (cdp) Dauphin County	189	13.00
West Sunbury (borough) Butler County	23	12.23
Russellton (cdp) Allegheny County	146	10.47
Naomi (cdp) Fayette County	11	9.65
Bairdford (cdp) Allegheny County	65	9.64
Bulger (cdp) Washington County	44	9.03

Top 10 Places Sorted by Percent of Total Population
Based on places with total population of 50,000 or more

Place	Population	%
Pittsburgh (city) Allegheny County	2,304	0.75
Millcreek (township) Erie County	201	0.38
Erie (city) Erie County	352	0.35
Lower Merion (township) Montgomery County	96	0.17
Bethlehem (city) Northampton County	75	0.10
Bethlehem (city) Northampton County	54	0.10
Reading (city) Berks County	76	0.09
Philadelphia (city) Philadelphia County	916	0.06
Abington (township) Montgomery County	33	0.06
Scranton (city) Lackawanna County	29	0.04

Cypriot

Top 10 Places Sorted by Population
Based on all places, regardless of total population

Place	Population	%
Pittsburgh (city) Allegheny County	102	0.03
Philadelphia (city) Philadelphia County	75	<0.01
Lower Merion (township) Montgomery County	66	0.11
Arlington Heights (cdp) Monroe County	24	0.38
Stroud (township) Monroe County	24	0.13
Bryn Mawr (cdp) Montgomery County	17	0.48
Centre (township) Berks County	17	0.43
Antis (township) Blair County	15	0.23
Middle Smithfield (township) Monroe County	15	0.10
Lancaster (township) Lancaster County	13	0.08

Top 10 Places Sorted by Percent of Total Population
Based on all places, regardless of total population

Place	Population	%
Bryn Mawr (cdp) Montgomery County	17	0.48
Centre (township) Berks County	17	0.43
Arlington Heights (cdp) Monroe County	24	0.38
Stewartstown (borough) York County	6	0.27
Parkesburg (borough) Chester County	9	0.25
Antis (township) Blair County	15	0.23
Stroud (township) Monroe County	24	0.13
Lower Merion (township) Montgomery County	66	0.11
Middle Smithfield (township) Monroe County	15	0.10
Hanover (township) Northampton County	11	0.10

Top 10 Places Sorted by Percent of Total Population
Based on places with total population of 50,000 or more

Place	Population	%
Lower Merion (township) Montgomery County	66	0.11
Pittsburgh (city) Allegheny County	102	0.03
Philadelphia (city) Philadelphia County	75	<0.01
Abington (township) Montgomery County	0	0.00
Allentown (city) Lehigh County	0	0.00
Bensalem (township) Bucks County	0	0.00
Bethlehem (city) Northampton County	0	0.00
Bethlehem (city) Northampton County	0	0.00
Bristol (township) Bucks County	0	0.00
Erie (city) Erie County	0	0.00

Czech

Top 10 Places Sorted by Population
Based on all places, regardless of total population

Place	Population	%
Philadelphia (city) Philadelphia County	2,209	0.15
Pittsburgh (city) Allegheny County	1,676	0.54
Erie (city) Erie County	626	0.62
Lower Paxton (township) Dauphin County	453	0.97
Windsor (township) York County	447	2.67
North Huntingdon (township) Westmoreland County	430	1.42
Bethlehem (city) Northampton County	415	0.56
Moon (township) Allegheny County	370	1.57

Place	Population	%
Shaler (township) Allegheny County	364	1.27
State College (borough) Centre County	357	0.85

Top 10 Places Sorted by Percent of Total Population
Based on all places, regardless of total population

Place	Population	%
Harrison City (cdp) Westmoreland County	15	13.27
Atlasburg (cdp) Washington County	24	10.48
Lenhartsville (borough) Berks County	17	9.60
Cairnbrook (cdp) Somerset County	43	9.51
New Washington (borough) Clearfield County	9	9.18
Fairview (township) Mercer County	85	8.45
Clinton (cdp) Allegheny County	34	7.34
DeSales University (cdp) Lehigh County	121	7.21
Falls Creek (borough) Clearfield County	3	6.82
New Columbus (borough) Luzerne County	15	6.67

Top 10 Places Sorted by Percent of Total Population
Based on places with total population of 50,000 or more

Place	Population	%
Erie (city) Erie County	626	0.62
Bethlehem (city) Northampton County	344	0.62
Bethlehem (city) Northampton County	415	0.56
Pittsburgh (city) Allegheny County	1,676	0.54
Millcreek (township) Erie County	218	0.41
Abington (township) Montgomery County	173	0.31
Levittown (cdp) Bucks County	152	0.29
Scranton (city) Lackawanna County	209	0.27
Lower Merion (township) Montgomery County	154	0.27
Reading (city) Berks County	173	0.20

Czechoslovakian

Top 10 Places Sorted by Population
Based on all places, regardless of total population

Place	Population	%
Pittsburgh (city) Allegheny County	773	0.25
Philadelphia (city) Philadelphia County	721	0.05
Allentown (city) Lehigh County	338	0.29
Millcreek (township) Erie County	250	0.47
Hempfield (township) Westmoreland County	207	0.48
North Huntingdon (township) Westmoreland County	197	0.65
Erie (city) Erie County	187	0.18
Pottsville (city) Schuylkill County	166	1.14
Bethlehem (city) Northampton County	166	0.22
McKeesport (city) Allegheny County	165	0.81

Top 10 Places Sorted by Percent of Total Population
Based on all places, regardless of total population

Place	Population	%
East Keating (township) Clinton County	3	17.65
Harrison City (cdp) Westmoreland County	15	13.27
Englewood (cdp) Schuylkill County	51	10.49
Hometown (cdp) Schuylkill County	118	8.08
Allport (cdp) Clearfield County	15	6.15
Elk (township) Tioga County	2	6.06
Beurys Lake (cdp) Schuylkill County	9	5.00
New Salem (cdp) Fayette County	32	4.89
Branchdale (cdp) Schuylkill County	12	4.58
Hegins (cdp) Schuylkill County	29	3.74

Top 10 Places Sorted by Percent of Total Population
Based on places with total population of 50,000 or more

Place	Population	%
Millcreek (township) Erie County	250	0.47
Allentown (city) Lehigh County	338	0.29
Pittsburgh (city) Allegheny County	773	0.25
Bethlehem (city) Northampton County	166	0.22
Levittown (cdp) Bucks County	105	0.20
Erie (city) Erie County	187	0.18
Bethlehem (city) Northampton County	91	0.16
Bristol (township) Bucks County	88	0.16
Abington (township) Montgomery County	73	0.13
Scranton (city) Lackawanna County	78	0.10

Danish

Top 10 Places Sorted by Population
Based on all places, regardless of total population

Place	Population	%
Philadelphia (city) Philadelphia County	830	0.06
Erie (city) Erie County	310	0.31
Pittsburgh (city) Allegheny County	299	0.10
Northampton (township) Bucks County	272	0.68
Middletown (township) Bucks County	271	0.64
Radnor (township) Delaware County	212	0.68
Upper Darby (township) Delaware County	211	0.26
Richboro (cdp) Bucks County	199	3.06
Haverford (township) Delaware County	181	0.37
Millcreek (township) Erie County	179	0.34

Top 10 Places Sorted by Percent of Total Population
Based on all places, regardless of total population

Place	Population	%
Timber Hills (cdp) Lebanon County	35	10.51
Waverly (cdp) Lackawanna County	35	6.69
Pocono Woodland Lakes (cdp) Pike County	167	5.87
Goodville (cdp) Lancaster County	15	5.84
Spring Creek (township) Warren County	38	4.57
Hereford (cdp) Berks County	46	4.55
Sheffield (cdp) Warren County	49	4.40
Columbus (cdp) Warren County	29	4.10
Cherry Grove (township) Warren County	9	3.72
Glen Osborne (borough) Allegheny County	16	3.48

Top 10 Places Sorted by Percent of Total Population
Based on places with total population of 50,000 or more

Place	Population	%
Millcreek (township) Erie County	179	0.34
Erie (city) Erie County	310	0.31
Upper Darby (township) Delaware County	211	0.26
Scranton (city) Lackawanna County	103	0.14
Bristol (township) Bucks County	75	0.14
Bethlehem (city) Northampton County	97	0.13
Lancaster (city) Lancaster County	73	0.12
Bethlehem (city) Northampton County	64	0.12
Levittown (cdp) Bucks County	60	0.12
Lower Merion (township) Montgomery County	66	0.11

Dutch

Top 10 Places Sorted by Population
Based on all places, regardless of total population

Place	Population	%
Philadelphia (city) Philadelphia County	5,855	0.39
Allentown (city) Lehigh County	2,721	2.34
Pittsburgh (city) Allegheny County	2,016	0.65
Bethlehem (city) Northampton County	1,828	2.45
Reading (city) Berks County	1,551	1.77
Pottsville (city) Schuylkill County	1,491	10.27
Erie (city) Erie County	1,425	1.40
Lower Paxton (township) Dauphin County	1,222	2.61
Bethlehem (city) Northampton County	1,021	1.84
Bristol (township) Bucks County	942	1.71

Top 10 Places Sorted by Percent of Total Population
Based on all places, regardless of total population

Place	Population	%
Foundryville (cdp) Columbia County	89	45.41
Mount Carbon (borough) Schuylkill County	43	43.00
Tipton (cdp) Blair County	440	40.89
Bird-in-Hand (cdp) Lancaster County	121	39.54
Siglerville (cdp) Mifflin County	30	35.29
Barrville (cdp) Mifflin County	37	28.68
Slatedale (cdp) Lehigh County	130	28.51
Allport (cdp) Clearfield County	67	27.46
Hegins (cdp) Schuylkill County	208	26.80
Starrucca (borough) Wayne County	53	26.24

Top 10 Places Sorted by Percent of Total Population
Based on places with total population of 50,000 or more

Place	Population	%
Bethlehem (city) Northampton County	1,828	2.45
Allentown (city) Lehigh County	2,721	2.34
Bethlehem (city) Northampton County	1,021	1.84
Reading (city) Berks County	1,551	1.77

Place	Population	%
Bristol (township) Bucks County	942	1.71
Levittown (cdp) Bucks County	828	1.59
Erie (city) Erie County	1,425	1.40
Millcreek (township) Erie County	681	1.29
Scranton (city) Lackawanna County	707	0.93
Upper Darby (township) Delaware County	748	0.91

Eastern European

Top 10 Places Sorted by Population
Based on all places, regardless of total population

Place	Population	%
Philadelphia (city) Philadelphia County	3,363	0.22
Lower Merion (township) Montgomery County	1,986	3.42
Pittsburgh (city) Allegheny County	1,195	0.39
Northampton (township) Bucks County	591	1.48
Cheltenham (township) Montgomery County	566	1.54
Upper Dublin (township) Montgomery County	546	2.13
Abington (township) Montgomery County	337	0.61
Haverford (township) Delaware County	289	0.60
Radnor (township) Delaware County	282	0.90
Lower Makefield (township) Bucks County	275	0.84

Top 10 Places Sorted by Percent of Total Population
Based on all places, regardless of total population

Place	Population	%
Wilmore (borough) Cambria County	10	7.58
Eyers Grove (cdp) Columbia County	6	6.00
Devon (cdp) Chester County	79	5.12
Penn Wynne (cdp) Montgomery County	235	4.04
Salem (township) Westmoreland County	258	3.88
Kelayres (cdp) Schuylkill County	21	3.79
Landisville (cdp) Lancaster County	69	3.61
Waverly (cdp) Lackawanna County	18	3.44
Lower Merion (township) Montgomery County	1,986	3.42
Roscoe (borough) Washington County	22	3.34

Top 10 Places Sorted by Percent of Total Population
Based on places with total population of 50,000 or more

Place	Population	%
Lower Merion (township) Montgomery County	1,986	3.42
Abington (township) Montgomery County	337	0.61
Pittsburgh (city) Allegheny County	1,195	0.39
Philadelphia (city) Philadelphia County	3,363	0.22
Bethlehem (city) Northampton County	93	0.17
Bensalem (township) Bucks County	94	0.16
Bethlehem (city) Northampton County	103	0.14
Allentown (city) Lehigh County	110	0.09
Levittown (cdp) Bucks County	46	0.09
Millcreek (township) Erie County	43	0.08

English

Top 10 Places Sorted by Population
Based on all places, regardless of total population

Place	Population	%
Philadelphia (city) Philadelphia County	47,303	3.14
Pittsburgh (city) Allegheny County	16,692	5.42
Erie (city) Erie County	5,870	5.78
Levittown (cdp) Bucks County	5,585	10.74
Lower Merion (township) Montgomery County	5,531	9.53
Bristol (township) Bucks County	5,476	9.96
Millcreek (township) Erie County	5,292	9.99
Haverford (township) Delaware County	4,959	10.22
Abington (township) Montgomery County	4,855	8.76
Tredyffrin (township) Chester County	4,846	16.44

Top 10 Places Sorted by Percent of Total Population
Based on all places, regardless of total population

Place	Population	%
Graceton (cdp) Indiana County	263	72.85
Adamsville (cdp) Crawford County	46	48.94
Green Hills (borough) Washington County	6	42.86
Marion (cdp) Franklin County	232	41.06
Wyalusing (borough) Bradford County	190	39.18
Slovan (cdp) Washington County	152	37.72
Seven Springs (borough) Somerset County	15	37.50
Little Britain (cdp) Lancaster County	81	36.99
Alfarata (cdp) Mifflin County	98	35.90
Nelson (township) Tioga County	206	35.76

Top 10 Places Sorted by Percent of Total Population
Based on places with total population of 50,000 or more

Place	Population	%
Levittown (cdp) Bucks County	5,585	10.74
Millcreek (township) Erie County	5,292	9.99
Bristol (township) Bucks County	5,476	9.96
Lower Merion (township) Montgomery County	5,531	9.53
Abington (township) Montgomery County	4,855	8.76
Bensalem (township) Bucks County	4,695	7.79
Bethlehem (city) Northampton County	4,577	6.12
Scranton (city) Lackawanna County	4,507	5.93
Bethlehem (city) Northampton County	3,258	5.88
Erie (city) Erie County	5,870	5.78

Estonian

Top 10 Places Sorted by Population
Based on all places, regardless of total population

Place	Population	%
Philadelphia (city) Philadelphia County	147	0.01
Lower Saucon (township) Northampton County	82	0.76
Aliquippa (city) Beaver County	46	0.47
Solebury (township) Bucks County	45	0.53
Cheltenham (township) Montgomery County	44	0.12
Horsham (township) Montgomery County	39	0.15
Edgmont (township) Delaware County	37	0.93
Mount Joy (township) Lancaster County	35	0.37
Carlisle (borough) Cumberland County	33	0.18
Bryn Athyn (borough) Montgomery County	32	2.73

Top 10 Places Sorted by Percent of Total Population
Based on all places, regardless of total population

Place	Population	%
Bryn Athyn (borough) Montgomery County	32	2.73
Preston (township) Wayne County	16	1.72
Woodcock (borough) Crawford County	3	1.30
Albany (township) Berks County	15	0.97
Edgmont (township) Delaware County	37	0.93
Saylorsburg (cdp) Monroe County	17	0.80
Lower Saucon (township) Northampton County	82	0.76
Oakdale (borough) Allegheny County	9	0.68
Brownstown (cdp) Lancaster County	12	0.57
Solebury (township) Bucks County	45	0.53

Top 10 Places Sorted by Percent of Total Population
Based on places with total population of 50,000 or more

Place	Population	%
Lower Merion (township) Montgomery County	28	0.05
Millcreek (township) Erie County	19	0.04
Abington (township) Montgomery County	11	0.02
Philadelphia (city) Philadelphia County	147	0.01
Erie (city) Erie County	12	0.01
Pittsburgh (city) Allegheny County	13	<0.01
Allentown (city) Lehigh County	0	0.00
Bensalem (township) Bucks County	0	0.00
Bethlehem (city) Northampton County	0	0.00
Bethlehem (city) Northampton County	0	0.00

European

Top 10 Places Sorted by Population
Based on all places, regardless of total population

Place	Population	%
Philadelphia (city) Philadelphia County	4,939	0.33
Pittsburgh (city) Allegheny County	2,300	0.75
Lower Merion (township) Montgomery County	1,134	1.95
Abington (township) Montgomery County	590	1.06
Manheim (township) Lancaster County	586	1.57
Haverford (township) Delaware County	530	1.09
Lower Makefield (township) Bucks County	528	1.61
Radnor (township) Delaware County	527	1.68
State College (borough) Centre County	523	1.25
Lower Paxton (township) Dauphin County	495	1.06

Top 10 Places Sorted by Percent of Total Population
Based on all places, regardless of total population

Place	Population	%
East Earl (cdp) Lancaster County	194	12.52
Mingoville (cdp) Centre County	42	11.44
Hickory Hills (cdp) Luzerne County	58	11.24

Place	Population	%
Orrtanna (cdp) Adams County	17	10.49
Ronks (cdp) Lancaster County	27	10.15
Seven Springs (borough) Somerset County	4	10.00
Fannett (township) Franklin County	233	9.24
Kempton (cdp) Berks County	14	9.21
Seven Springs (borough) Fayette County	4	9.09
Rowes Run (cdp) Fayette County	79	8.98

Top 10 Places Sorted by Percent of Total Population
Based on places with total population of 50,000 or more

Place	Population	%
Lower Merion (township) Montgomery County	1,134	1.95
Abington (township) Montgomery County	590	1.06
Pittsburgh (city) Allegheny County	2,300	0.75
Bethlehem (city) Northampton County	487	0.65
Scranton (city) Lackawanna County	457	0.60
Bethlehem (city) Northampton County	329	0.59
Bensalem (township) Bucks County	306	0.51
Upper Darby (township) Delaware County	383	0.46
Erie (city) Erie County	436	0.43
Levittown (cdp) Bucks County	225	0.43

Finnish

Top 10 Places Sorted by Population
Based on all places, regardless of total population

Place	Population	%
Philadelphia (city) Philadelphia County	326	0.02
Erie (city) Erie County	182	0.18
Pittsburgh (city) Allegheny County	181	0.06
Ridley (township) Delaware County	142	0.46
Woodlyn (cdp) Delaware County	130	1.43
Hamilton (township) Monroe County	111	1.22
Lower Burrell (city) Westmoreland County	110	0.92
Lower Makefield (township) Bucks County	100	0.31
New Castle (city) Lawrence County	97	0.41
Hempfield (township) Westmoreland County	87	0.20

Top 10 Places Sorted by Percent of Total Population
Based on all places, regardless of total population

Place	Population	%
Colebrook (township) Clinton County	15	4.97
Bernville (borough) Berks County	46	4.82
Fayette City (borough) Fayette County	14	3.49
Kilbuck (township) Allegheny County	23	3.33
Soudersburg (cdp) Lancaster County	16	3.04
Fawn Lake Forest (cdp) Pike County	28	2.96
Klingerstown (cdp) Schuylkill County	3	2.83
Yorklyn (cdp) York County	51	2.79
Marlin (cdp) Schuylkill County	16	2.45
Wolfdale (cdp) Washington County	69	2.37

Top 10 Places Sorted by Percent of Total Population
Based on places with total population of 50,000 or more

Place	Population	%
Erie (city) Erie County	182	0.18
Millcreek (township) Erie County	82	0.15
Bristol (township) Bucks County	60	0.11
Lancaster (city) Lancaster County	56	0.10
Levittown (cdp) Bucks County	48	0.09
Upper Darby (township) Delaware County	64	0.08
Scranton (city) Lackawanna County	51	0.07
Pittsburgh (city) Allegheny County	181	0.06
Bethlehem (city) Northampton County	29	0.05
Bethlehem (city) Northampton County	29	0.04

French, except Basque

Top 10 Places Sorted by Population
Based on all places, regardless of total population

Place	Population	%
Philadelphia (city) Philadelphia County	12,027	0.80
Pittsburgh (city) Allegheny County	4,106	1.33
Erie (city) Erie County	1,680	1.65
Bethlehem (city) Northampton County	1,480	1.98
Bensalem (township) Bucks County	1,378	2.29
Allentown (city) Lehigh County	1,293	1.11
Upper Darby (township) Delaware County	1,276	1.55
Manheim (township) Lancaster County	1,188	3.18
Abington (township) Montgomery County	1,102	1.99
Levittown (cdp) Bucks County	1,085	2.09

Top 10 Places Sorted by Percent of Total Population
Based on all places, regardless of total population

Place	Population	%
New Kingstown (cdp) Cumberland County	219	32.78
Cross Creek (cdp) Washington County	30	21.74
Eagles Mere (borough) Sullivan County	10	19.61
Bigler (cdp) Clearfield County	34	19.43
East Freedom (cdp) Blair County	118	18.38
Stewardson (township) Potter County	6	18.18
Covington (township) Clearfield County	92	17.29
Geneva (cdp) Crawford County	21	17.07
Callimont (borough) Somerset County	7	17.07
Potlicker Flats (cdp) Mifflin County	48	16.96

Top 10 Places Sorted by Percent of Total Population
Based on places with total population of 50,000 or more

Place	Population	%
Bensalem (township) Bucks County	1,378	2.29
Levittown (cdp) Bucks County	1,085	2.09
Millcreek (township) Erie County	1,061	2.00
Abington (township) Montgomery County	1,102	1.99
Bethlehem (city) Northampton County	1,480	1.98
Bethlehem (city) Northampton County	1,049	1.89
Lower Merion (township) Montgomery County	1,058	1.82
Bristol (township) Bucks County	927	1.69
Erie (city) Erie County	1,680	1.65
Upper Darby (township) Delaware County	1,276	1.55

French Canadian

Top 10 Places Sorted by Population
Based on all places, regardless of total population

Place	Population	%
Philadelphia (city) Philadelphia County	1,636	0.11
Pittsburgh (city) Allegheny County	499	0.16
Levittown (cdp) Bucks County	344	0.66
Lower Providence (township) Montgomery County	279	1.12
Manheim (township) Lancaster County	250	0.67
Lower Macungie (township) Lehigh County	249	0.87
Falls (township) Bucks County	244	0.71
Lower Paxton (township) Dauphin County	243	0.52
Bristol (township) Bucks County	233	0.42
Exeter (township) Berks County	222	0.89

Top 10 Places Sorted by Percent of Total Population
Based on all places, regardless of total population

Place	Population	%
Liberty (borough) Tioga County	20	6.99
Hereford (cdp) Berks County	65	6.44
Kennerdell (cdp) Venango County	12	6.38
Columbus (cdp) Warren County	41	5.79
Chapman (township) Snyder County	89	5.19
Barnett (township) Forest County	24	5.17
Hendersonville (cdp) Washington County	10	5.10
Nicholson (borough) Wyoming County	41	4.96
Smock (cdp) Fayette County	29	4.44
Baumstown (cdp) Berks County	20	4.35

Top 10 Places Sorted by Percent of Total Population
Based on places with total population of 50,000 or more

Place	Population	%
Levittown (cdp) Bucks County	344	0.66
Bristol (township) Bucks County	233	0.42
Millcreek (township) Erie County	199	0.38
Scranton (city) Lackawanna County	190	0.25
Lower Merion (township) Montgomery County	142	0.24
Erie (city) Erie County	199	0.20
Abington (township) Montgomery County	101	0.18
Pittsburgh (city) Allegheny County	499	0.16
Allentown (city) Lehigh County	185	0.16
Upper Darby (township) Delaware County	133	0.16

German

Top 10 Places Sorted by Population
Based on all places, regardless of total population

Place	Population	%
Philadelphia (city) Philadelphia County	122,783	8.16
Pittsburgh (city) Allegheny County	66,031	21.44
Erie (city) Erie County	27,772	27.33

Allentown (city) Lehigh County	20,043	17.22
Altoona (city) Blair County	19,843	42.32
Millcreek (township) Erie County	18,920	35.73
Bethlehem (city) Northampton County	16,986	22.72
Hempfield (township) Westmoreland County	16,121	37.52
Lower Paxton (township) Dauphin County	15,978	34.14
Levittown (cdp) Bucks County	15,853	30.49

Top 10 Places Sorted by Percent of Total Population
Based on all places, regardless of total population

Place	Population	%
Emlenton (borough) Clarion County	10	100.00
Cold Spring (township) Lebanon County	9	100.00
Seven Springs (borough) Fayette County	4	100.00
Valley-Hi (borough) Fulton County	3	100.00
Frystown (cdp) Berks County	468	86.51
Dalmatia (cdp) Northumberland County	507	81.91
Leeper (cdp) Clarion County	127	79.87
Table Rock (cdp) Adams County	25	78.13
Summit Station (cdp) Schuylkill County	96	77.42
Lower Mahanoy (township) Northumberland County	1,467	77.37

Top 10 Places Sorted by Percent of Total Population
Based on places with total population of 50,000 or more

Place	Population	%
Millcreek (township) Erie County	18,920	35.73
Levittown (cdp) Bucks County	15,853	30.49
Erie (city) Erie County	27,772	27.33
Bristol (township) Bucks County	13,990	25.43
Bethlehem (city) Northampton County	16,986	22.72
Abington (township) Montgomery County	12,435	22.44
Bensalem (township) Bucks County	13,336	22.13
Bethlehem (city) Northampton County	12,068	21.77
Pittsburgh (city) Allegheny County	66,031	21.44
Lancaster (city) Lancaster County	11,795	20.05

German Russian

Top 10 Places Sorted by Population
Based on all places, regardless of total population

Place	Population	%
McKees Rocks (borough) Allegheny County	48	0.78
Lower Macungie (township) Lehigh County	42	0.15
East Nottingham (township) Chester County	33	0.40
Hilldale (cdp) Luzerne County	26	1.81
Plains (township) Luzerne County	26	0.26
Coraopolis (borough) Allegheny County	23	0.40
Lower Paxton (township) Dauphin County	22	0.05
Lebanon (city) Lebanon County	21	0.08
Springfield (township) York County	20	0.40
Wilson (borough) Northampton County	12	0.15

Top 10 Places Sorted by Percent of Total Population
Based on all places, regardless of total population

Place	Population	%
Hilldale (cdp) Luzerne County	26	1.81
McKees Rocks (borough) Allegheny County	48	0.78
Jacobus (borough) York County	10	0.56
Patterson Heights (borough) Beaver County	4	0.56
East Nottingham (township) Chester County	33	0.40
Coraopolis (borough) Allegheny County	23	0.40
Springfield (township) York County	20	0.40
Tunkhannock (borough) Wyoming County	6	0.32
Plains (township) Luzerne County	26	0.26
Harveys Lake (borough) Luzerne County	6	0.22

Top 10 Places Sorted by Percent of Total Population
Based on places with total population of 50,000 or more

Place	Population	%
Erie (city) Erie County	2	<0.01
Abington (township) Montgomery County	0	0.00
Allentown (city) Lehigh County	0	0.00
Bensalem (township) Bucks County	0	0.00
Bethlehem (city) Northampton County	0	0.00
Bethlehem (city) Northampton County	0	0.00
Bristol (township) Bucks County	0	0.00
Lancaster (city) Lancaster County	0	0.00
Levittown (cdp) Bucks County	0	0.00
Lower Merion (township) Montgomery County	0	0.00

Greek

Top 10 Places Sorted by Population
Based on all places, regardless of total population

Place	Population	%
Philadelphia (city) Philadelphia County	4,288	0.28
Pittsburgh (city) Allegheny County	2,108	0.68
Upper Darby (township) Delaware County	1,276	1.55
Bethlehem (city) Northampton County	657	0.88
Lower Merion (township) Montgomery County	649	1.12
Marple (township) Delaware County	632	2.70
Hazleton (city) Luzerne County	616	2.48
Allentown (city) Lehigh County	573	0.49
Manheim (township) Lancaster County	569	1.52
Bethlehem (city) Northampton County	553	1.00

Top 10 Places Sorted by Percent of Total Population
Based on all places, regardless of total population

Place	Population	%
Martins Creek (cdp) Northampton County	110	17.83
Rennerdale (cdp) Allegheny County	170	11.96
Deer Lake (cdp) Fayette County	78	11.78
Venango (borough) Crawford County	19	9.36
Foster (township) Luzerne County	316	9.23
Aristes (cdp) Columbia County	25	8.62
Cumbola (cdp) Schuylkill County	32	8.12
Langeloth (cdp) Washington County	33	7.53
New Salem (cdp) Fayette County	42	6.41
Brodheadsville (cdp) Monroe County	105	6.08

Top 10 Places Sorted by Percent of Total Population
Based on places with total population of 50,000 or more

Place	Population	%
Upper Darby (township) Delaware County	1,276	1.55
Lower Merion (township) Montgomery County	649	1.12
Bethlehem (city) Northampton County	553	1.00
Bethlehem (city) Northampton County	657	0.88
Pittsburgh (city) Allegheny County	2,108	0.68
Abington (township) Montgomery County	337	0.61
Levittown (cdp) Bucks County	302	0.58
Bristol (township) Bucks County	307	0.56
Allentown (city) Lehigh County	573	0.49
Bensalem (township) Bucks County	270	0.45

Guyanese

Top 10 Places Sorted by Population
Based on all places, regardless of total population

Place	Population	%
Philadelphia (city) Philadelphia County	638	0.04
Stroud (township) Monroe County	186	0.99
Bethlehem (city) Northampton County	173	0.23
Arlington Heights (cdp) Monroe County	164	2.56
Bethlehem (city) Northampton County	133	0.24
Bensalem (township) Bucks County	81	0.13
Allentown (city) Lehigh County	79	0.07
Abington (township) Montgomery County	74	0.13
Falls (township) Bucks County	70	0.20
Levittown (cdp) Bucks County	70	0.13

Top 10 Places Sorted by Percent of Total Population
Based on all places, regardless of total population

Place	Population	%
Arlington Heights (cdp) Monroe County	164	2.56
Lincoln University (cdp) Chester County	44	2.28
Yoe (borough) York County	16	1.80
Factoryville (borough) Wyoming County	12	1.05
Flying Hills (cdp) Berks County	25	1.01
Stroud (township) Monroe County	186	0.99
Hokendauqua (cdp) Lehigh County	32	0.89
Lower Oxford (township) Chester County	44	0.87
Jackson (township) Monroe County	60	0.86
Spry (cdp) York County	41	0.84

Top 10 Places Sorted by Percent of Total Population
Based on places with total population of 50,000 or more

Place	Population	%
Bethlehem (city) Northampton County	133	0.24
Bethlehem (city) Northampton County	173	0.23
Bensalem (township) Bucks County	81	0.13
Abington (township) Montgomery County	74	0.13

Place	Population	%
Levittown (cdp) Bucks County	70	0.13
Bristol (township) Bucks County	53	0.10
Allentown (city) Lehigh County	79	0.07
Philadelphia (city) Philadelphia County	638	0.04
Pittsburgh (city) Allegheny County	57	0.02
Upper Darby (township) Delaware County	10	0.01

Hungarian

Top 10 Places Sorted by Population
Based on all places, regardless of total population

Place	Population	%
Philadelphia (city) Philadelphia County	5,463	0.36
Pittsburgh (city) Allegheny County	4,477	1.45
Bethlehem (city) Northampton County	3,458	4.63
Bethlehem (city) Northampton County	2,523	4.55
Allentown (city) Lehigh County	1,829	1.57
North Huntingdon (township) Westmoreland County	1,284	4.24
Bethlehem (township) Northampton County	1,213	5.17
Erie (city) Erie County	1,120	1.10
Munhall (borough) Allegheny County	1,051	9.17
Whitehall (township) Lehigh County	993	3.75

Top 10 Places Sorted by Percent of Total Population
Based on all places, regardless of total population

Place	Population	%
Martins Creek (cdp) Northampton County	173	28.04
Hostetter (cdp) Westmoreland County	140	19.13
Hiller (cdp) Fayette County	235	18.08
Rush (township) Dauphin County	40	17.02
Slatedale (cdp) Lehigh County	76	16.67
Centerville (borough) Washington County	520	15.87
New Schaefferstown (cdp) Berks County	23	15.65
Van Voorhis (cdp) Washington County	64	15.24
Fairhope (cdp) Fayette County	136	14.29
Allison (cdp) Fayette County	68	13.26

Top 10 Places Sorted by Percent of Total Population
Based on places with total population of 50,000 or more

Place	Population	%
Bethlehem (city) Northampton County	3,458	4.63
Bethlehem (city) Northampton County	2,523	4.55
Millcreek (township) Erie County	861	1.63
Allentown (city) Lehigh County	1,829	1.57
Pittsburgh (city) Allegheny County	4,477	1.45
Bristol (township) Bucks County	648	1.18
Erie (city) Erie County	1,120	1.10
Lower Merion (township) Montgomery County	635	1.09
Levittown (cdp) Bucks County	498	0.96
Abington (township) Montgomery County	458	0.83

Icelander

Top 10 Places Sorted by Population
Based on all places, regardless of total population

Place	Population	%
Philadelphia (city) Philadelphia County	86	0.01
Upper Darby (township) Delaware County	51	0.06
State College (borough) Centre County	47	0.11
Salem (township) Westmoreland County	46	0.69
Drexel Hill (cdp) Delaware County	41	0.14
West Goshen (township) Chester County	37	0.17
Ardmore (cdp) Montgomery County	32	0.26
Lower Merion (township) Montgomery County	32	0.06
Sellersville (borough) Bucks County	26	0.60
Cheltenham (township) Montgomery County	25	0.07

Top 10 Places Sorted by Percent of Total Population
Based on all places, regardless of total population

Place	Population	%
Grugan (township) Clinton County	3	4.48
Portage (township) Potter County	3	1.42
Heilwood (cdp) Indiana County	7	0.90
Venango (township) Erie County	19	0.78
Salem (township) Westmoreland County	46	0.69
Sellersville (borough) Bucks County	26	0.60
Allegheny (township) Venango County	2	0.50
Green Lane (borough) Montgomery County	2	0.45
Salunga (cdp) Lancaster County	11	0.38
Pine (township) Indiana County	7	0.34

Top 10 Places Sorted by Percent of Total Population
Based on places with total population of 50,000 or more

Place	Population	%
Upper Darby (township) Delaware County	51	0.06
Lower Merion (township) Montgomery County	32	0.06
Philadelphia (city) Philadelphia County	86	0.01
Scranton (city) Lackawanna County	8	0.01
Abington (township) Montgomery County	0	0.00
Allentown (city) Lehigh County	0	0.00
Bensalem (township) Bucks County	0	0.00
Bethlehem (city) Northampton County	0	0.00
Bethlehem (city) Northampton County	0	0.00
Bristol (township) Bucks County	0	0.00

Iranian

Top 10 Places Sorted by Population
Based on all places, regardless of total population

Place	Population	%
Philadelphia (city) Philadelphia County	665	0.04
Lower Merion (township) Montgomery County	362	0.62
Marple (township) Delaware County	245	1.05
Broomall (cdp) Delaware County	216	1.92
Radnor (township) Delaware County	209	0.67
Pittsburgh (city) Allegheny County	187	0.06
Northampton (township) Bucks County	186	0.47
Upper Merion (township) Montgomery County	158	0.56
Springfield (township) Montgomery County	157	0.81
Glenolden (borough) Delaware County	145	2.02

Top 10 Places Sorted by Percent of Total Population
Based on all places, regardless of total population

Place	Population	%
Oakland (cdp) Cambria County	37	2.34
Modena (borough) Chester County	10	2.15
Glenolden (borough) Delaware County	145	2.02
Broomall (cdp) Delaware County	216	1.92
Sewickley Heights (borough) Allegheny County	13	1.71
Spring House (cdp) Montgomery County	57	1.51
Lightstreet (cdp) Columbia County	16	1.50
Flourtown (cdp) Montgomery County	67	1.48
Slippery Rock (township) Butler County	79	1.46
East Greenville (borough) Montgomery County	43	1.44

Top 10 Places Sorted by Percent of Total Population
Based on places with total population of 50,000 or more

Place	Population	%
Lower Merion (township) Montgomery County	362	0.62
Abington (township) Montgomery County	65	0.12
Bethlehem (city) Northampton County	64	0.12
Bethlehem (city) Northampton County	64	0.09
Scranton (city) Lackawanna County	56	0.07
Millcreek (township) Erie County	35	0.07
Pittsburgh (city) Allegheny County	187	0.06
Allentown (city) Lehigh County	56	0.05
Philadelphia (city) Philadelphia County	665	0.04
Erie (city) Erie County	20	0.02

Irish

Top 10 Places Sorted by Population
Based on all places, regardless of total population

Place	Population	%
Philadelphia (city) Philadelphia County	195,849	13.01
Pittsburgh (city) Allegheny County	51,563	16.74
Scranton (city) Lackawanna County	23,274	30.60
Upper Darby (township) Delaware County	22,488	27.30
Haverford (township) Delaware County	18,506	38.12
Levittown (cdp) Bucks County	17,768	34.18
Erie (city) Erie County	17,685	17.40
Bristol (township) Bucks County	16,287	29.61
Bensalem (township) Bucks County	15,954	26.47
Abington (township) Montgomery County	14,146	25.53

Top 10 Places Sorted by Percent of Total Population
Based on all places, regardless of total population

Place	Population	%
Cold Spring (township) Lebanon County	9	100.00
Edenborn (cdp) Fayette County	81	79.41
Van Voorhis (cdp) Washington County	312	74.29

Place	Population	%
Grugan (township) Clinton County	48	71.64
Gibraltar (cdp) Berks County	351	59.29
Hublersburg (cdp) Centre County	27	54.00
Eddystone (borough) Delaware County	1,301	52.67
St. Michael (cdp) Cambria County	146	52.14
Heckscherville (cdp) Schuylkill County	150	51.90
Revloc (cdp) Cambria County	392	51.58

Top 10 Places Sorted by Percent of Total Population
Based on places with total population of 50,000 or more

Place	Population	%
Levittown (cdp) Bucks County	17,768	34.18
Scranton (city) Lackawanna County	23,274	30.60
Bristol (township) Bucks County	16,287	29.61
Upper Darby (township) Delaware County	22,488	27.30
Bensalem (township) Bucks County	15,954	26.47
Abington (township) Montgomery County	14,146	25.53
Millcreek (township) Erie County	10,633	20.08
Erie (city) Erie County	17,685	17.40
Pittsburgh (city) Allegheny County	51,563	16.74
Lower Merion (township) Montgomery County	8,965	15.45

Israeli

Top 10 Places Sorted by Population
Based on all places, regardless of total population

Place	Population	%
Philadelphia (city) Philadelphia County	861	0.06
Lower Merion (township) Montgomery County	377	0.65
Pittsburgh (city) Allegheny County	210	0.07
Collingdale (borough) Delaware County	143	1.63
Newtown (borough) Bucks County	135	5.99
Schnecksville (cdp) Lehigh County	118	4.25
North Whitehall (township) Lehigh County	118	0.76
Harrisburg (city) Dauphin County	104	0.21
Haverford (township) Delaware County	79	0.16
Abington (township) Montgomery County	79	0.14

Top 10 Places Sorted by Percent of Total Population
Based on all places, regardless of total population

Place	Population	%
Newtown (borough) Bucks County	135	5.99
Schnecksville (cdp) Lehigh County	118	4.25
Eagleville (cdp) Centre County	10	4.20
Trexlertown (cdp) Lehigh County	68	3.66
Haverford College (cdp) Delaware County	39	3.38
Abbottstown (borough) Adams County	26	2.73
Collingdale (borough) Delaware County	143	1.63
Narberth (borough) Montgomery County	50	1.17
Carmichaels (borough) Greene County	5	1.08
Thorndale (cdp) Chester County	31	0.92

Top 10 Places Sorted by Percent of Total Population
Based on places with total population of 50,000 or more

Place	Population	%
Lower Merion (township) Montgomery County	377	0.65
Abington (township) Montgomery County	79	0.14
Pittsburgh (city) Allegheny County	210	0.07
Philadelphia (city) Philadelphia County	861	0.06
Bensalem (township) Bucks County	23	0.04
Scranton (city) Lackawanna County	22	0.03
Lancaster (city) Lancaster County	13	0.02
Reading (city) Berks County	9	0.01
Erie (city) Erie County	6	0.01
Allentown (city) Lehigh County	0	0.00

Italian

Top 10 Places Sorted by Population
Based on all places, regardless of total population

Place	Population	%
Philadelphia (city) Philadelphia County	125,080	8.31
Pittsburgh (city) Allegheny County	41,352	13.43
Scranton (city) Lackawanna County	16,031	21.08
Erie (city) Erie County	15,798	15.54
Upper Darby (township) Delaware County	12,902	15.66
Haverford (township) Delaware County	9,724	20.03
Hempfield (township) Westmoreland County	9,075	21.12
Millcreek (township) Erie County	9,038	17.07
Bensalem (township) Bucks County	8,721	14.47
Bethlehem (city) Northampton County	8,299	11.10

Top 10 Places Sorted by Percent of Total Population
Based on all places, regardless of total population

Place	Population	%
Westland (cdp) Washington County	71	70.30
Emlenton (borough) Clarion County	7	70.00
Atlasburg (cdp) Washington County	144	62.88
Yatesville (borough) Luzerne County	360	51.87
Meadowlands (cdp) Washington County	208	51.36
Baidland (cdp) Washington County	1,092	47.27
Masthope (cdp) Pike County	235	46.53
Hublersburg (cdp) Centre County	23	46.00
Browntown (cdp) Luzerne County	689	45.87
Baileyville (cdp) Centre County	97	43.89

Top 10 Places Sorted by Percent of Total Population
Based on places with total population of 50,000 or more

Place	Population	%
Scranton (city) Lackawanna County	16,031	21.08
Millcreek (township) Erie County	9,038	17.07
Upper Darby (township) Delaware County	12,902	15.66
Erie (city) Erie County	15,798	15.54
Levittown (cdp) Bucks County	7,926	15.25
Bensalem (township) Bucks County	8,721	14.47
Bristol (township) Bucks County	7,904	14.37
Abington (township) Montgomery County	7,624	13.76
Pittsburgh (city) Allegheny County	41,352	13.43
Bethlehem (city) Northampton County	6,357	11.47

Latvian

Top 10 Places Sorted by Population
Based on all places, regardless of total population

Place	Population	%
Philadelphia (city) Philadelphia County	570	0.04
Lower Merion (township) Montgomery County	151	0.26
Middletown (township) Bucks County	149	0.33
Pittsburgh (city) Allegheny County	138	0.04
Tredyffrin (township) Chester County	108	0.37
Reading (city) Berks County	73	0.08
Upper Providence (township) Montgomery County	70	0.35
Abington (township) Montgomery County	70	0.13
Northampton (township) Bucks County	61	0.15
Washington (township) Berks County	52	1.39

Top 10 Places Sorted by Percent of Total Population
Based on all places, regardless of total population

Place	Population	%
Durham (township) Bucks County	38	3.14
Daisytown (borough) Cambria County	9	3.03
Washington (township) Berks County	52	1.39
Liberty (borough) Tioga County	3	1.05
Ben Avon Heights (borough) Allegheny County	4	1.01
Freemansburg (borough) Northampton County	24	0.94
Edgmont (township) Delaware County	37	0.93
Trappe (borough) Montgomery County	27	0.78
Yardley (borough) Bucks County	18	0.78
Chapman (township) Clinton County	5	0.72

Top 10 Places Sorted by Percent of Total Population
Based on places with total population of 50,000 or more

Place	Population	%
Lower Merion (township) Montgomery County	151	0.26
Abington (township) Montgomery County	70	0.13
Reading (city) Berks County	73	0.08
Philadelphia (city) Philadelphia County	570	0.04
Pittsburgh (city) Allegheny County	138	0.04
Scranton (city) Lackawanna County	26	0.03
Bensalem (township) Bucks County	16	0.03
Millcreek (township) Erie County	14	0.03
Erie (city) Erie County	20	0.02
Upper Darby (township) Delaware County	17	0.02

Lithuanian

Top 10 Places Sorted by Population
Based on all places, regardless of total population

Place	Population	%
Philadelphia (city) Philadelphia County	5,334	0.35
Pittsburgh (city) Allegheny County	2,260	0.73
Scranton (city) Lackawanna County	1,584	2.08
Wilkes-Barre (city) Luzerne County	1,109	2.67
Pottsville (city) Schuylkill County	715	4.92
Hanover (township) Luzerne County	693	6.24
West Mahanoy (township) Schuylkill County	636	21.94
Kingston (borough) Luzerne County	625	4.72
Mount Lebanon (township) Allegheny County	583	1.78
Kingston (township) Luzerne County	575	8.22

Top 10 Places Sorted by Percent of Total Population
Based on all places, regardless of total population

Place	Population	%
Seven Springs (borough) Fayette County	4	100.00
Force (cdp) Elk County	65	33.16
Altamont (cdp) Schuylkill County	239	32.34
Seltzer (cdp) Schuylkill County	95	32.09
New Philadelphia (borough) Schuylkill County	306	27.06
Brandonville (cdp) Schuylkill County	40	23.26
West Mahanoy (township) Schuylkill County	636	21.94
Cumbola (cdp) Schuylkill County	69	17.51
Shenandoah Heights (cdp) Schuylkill County	212	16.71
Middleport (borough) Schuylkill County	58	13.78

Top 10 Places Sorted by Percent of Total Population
Based on places with total population of 50,000 or more

Place	Population	%
Scranton (city) Lackawanna County	1,584	2.08
Levittown (cdp) Bucks County	469	0.90
Lower Merion (township) Montgomery County	514	0.89
Pittsburgh (city) Allegheny County	2,260	0.73
Bristol (township) Bucks County	379	0.69
Bensalem (township) Bucks County	370	0.61
Abington (township) Montgomery County	330	0.60
Bethlehem (city) Northampton County	430	0.58
Bethlehem (city) Northampton County	308	0.56
Millcreek (township) Erie County	265	0.50

Luxemburger

Top 10 Places Sorted by Population
Based on all places, regardless of total population

Place	Population	%
Springhill (township) Fayette County	33	1.13
Plymouth (township) Montgomery County	32	0.19
Hamilton (township) Franklin County	31	0.30
South Fayette (township) Allegheny County	30	0.22
Philadelphia (city) Philadelphia County	29	<0.01
Nether Providence (township) Delaware County	24	0.18
Pittsburgh (city) Allegheny County	22	0.01
State College (borough) Centre County	18	0.04
Edinboro (borough) Erie County	17	0.26
Pennsburg (borough) Montgomery County	16	0.44

Top 10 Places Sorted by Percent of Total Population
Based on all places, regardless of total population

Place	Population	%
Stevens (township) Bradford County	6	1.40
Springhill (township) Fayette County	33	1.13
Leechburg (borough) Armstrong County	15	0.68
Hebron (township) Potter County	4	0.56
Warren (township) Franklin County	2	0.56
Hasson Heights (cdp) Venango County	7	0.55
Pennsburg (borough) Montgomery County	16	0.44
Middle Taylor (township) Cambria County	3	0.44
Atglen (borough) Chester County	4	0.31
Hamilton (township) Franklin County	31	0.30

Top 10 Places Sorted by Percent of Total Population
Based on places with total population of 50,000 or more

Place	Population	%
Millcreek (township) Erie County	10	0.02
Pittsburgh (city) Allegheny County	22	0.01
Allentown (city) Lehigh County	11	0.01
Erie (city) Erie County	10	0.01
Philadelphia (city) Philadelphia County	29	<0.01
Abington (township) Montgomery County	0	0.00
Bensalem (township) Bucks County	0	0.00
Bethlehem (city) Northampton County	0	0.00
Bethlehem (city) Northampton County	0	0.00
Bristol (township) Bucks County	0	0.00

Macedonian

Top 10 Places Sorted by Population
Based on all places, regardless of total population

Place	Population	%
Hampton (township) Allegheny County	54	0.3
Allison Park (cdp) Allegheny County	54	0.2
Lower Merion (township) Montgomery County	54	0.0
Bensalem (township) Bucks County	52	0.09
Ellwood City (borough) Lawrence County	46	0.62
Ellwood City (borough) Lawrence County	46	0.5
North Strabane (township) Washington County	45	0.35
Pittsburgh (city) Allegheny County	44	0.0
State College (borough) Centre County	43	0.10
Easttown (township) Chester County	35	0.33

Top 10 Places Sorted by Percent of Total Population
Based on all places, regardless of total population

Place	Population	%
Kistler (borough) Mifflin County	8	2.1
Juniata (township) Huntingdon County	10	1.9
Towamensing Trails (cdp) Carbon County	10	1.56
Orbisonia (borough) Huntingdon County	8	1.02
Black Lick (township) Indiana County	12	1.01
West Middlesex (borough) Mercer County	7	0.85
Shenango (township) Mercer County	33	0.84
Ford City (borough) Armstrong County	21	0.69
Greene (township) Mercer County	8	0.64
Ellwood City (borough) Lawrence County	46	0.62

Top 10 Places Sorted by Percent of Total Population
Based on places with total population of 50,000 or more

Place	Population	%
Lower Merion (township) Montgomery County	54	0.09
Bensalem (township) Bucks County	52	0.09
Bethlehem (city) Northampton County	16	0.03
Bristol (township) Bucks County	14	0.03
Levittown (cdp) Bucks County	13	0.03
Allentown (city) Lehigh County	19	0.02
Bethlehem (city) Northampton County	16	0.02
Pittsburgh (city) Allegheny County	44	0.01
Erie (city) Erie County	10	0.01
Upper Darby (township) Delaware County	9	0.01

Maltese

Top 10 Places Sorted by Population
Based on all places, regardless of total population

Place	Population	%
Montgomery (township) Montgomery County	78	0.32
Upper Saucon (township) Lehigh County	52	0.36
Springettsbury (township) York County	47	0.18
Shaler (township) Allegheny County	37	0.13
Carlisle (borough) Cumberland County	35	0.19
Penn (township) Chester County	32	0.65
Pocono (township) Monroe County	31	0.28
Solebury (township) Bucks County	29	0.34
Pocopson (township) Chester County	28	0.63
Laureldale (borough) Berks County	27	0.69

Top 10 Places Sorted by Percent of Total Population
Based on all places, regardless of total population

Place	Population	%
Quentin (cdp) Lebanon County	6	1.24
Shickshinny (borough) Luzerne County	8	0.92
Trexlertown (cdp) Lehigh County	15	0.81
Laureldale (borough) Berks County	27	0.69
Penn (township) Chester County	32	0.65
Pocopson (township) Chester County	28	0.63
Fox Run (cdp) Butler County	15	0.43
Beaver Springs (cdp) Snyder County	3	0.43
West Grove (borough) Chester County	11	0.39
Upper Saucon (township) Lehigh County	52	0.36

Top 10 Places Sorted by Percent of Total Population
Based on places with total population of 50,000 or more

Place	Population	%
Abington (township) Montgomery County	14	0.03
Levittown (cdp) Bucks County	9	0.02
Pittsburgh (city) Allegheny County	11	<0.01
Allentown (city) Lehigh County	0	0.00

Place	Population	%
Bensalem (township) Bucks County	0	0.00
Bethlehem (city) Northampton County	0	0.00
Bethlehem (city) Northampton County	0	0.00
Bristol (township) Bucks County	0	0.00
Erie (city) Erie County	0	0.00
Lancaster (city) Lancaster County	0	0.00

New Zealander

Top 10 Places Sorted by Population
Based on all places, regardless of total population

Place	Population	%
Palmyra (township) Pike County	55	1.63
Philadelphia (city) Philadelphia County	52	<0.01
Shamokin Dam (borough) Snyder County	27	1.40
Londonderry (township) Dauphin County	23	0.44
Pittsburgh (city) Allegheny County	21	0.01
Lower Saucon (township) Northampton County	16	0.15
West Chester (borough) Chester County	14	0.08
Bethlehem (city) Northampton County	14	0.03
Bethlehem (city) Northampton County	14	0.02
Royersford (borough) Montgomery County	13	0.28

Top 10 Places Sorted by Percent of Total Population
Based on all places, regardless of total population

Place	Population	%
Palmyra (township) Pike County	55	1.63
Shamokin Dam (borough) Snyder County	27	1.40
Spring Creek (township) Warren County	8	0.96
Londonderry (township) Dauphin County	23	0.44
Jackson (township) Tioga County	8	0.44
Overfield (township) Wyoming County	5	0.37
Chalfant (borough) Allegheny County	3	0.32
Royersford (borough) Montgomery County	13	0.28
Schwenksville (borough) Montgomery County	4	0.28
West Pikeland (township) Chester County	8	0.20

Top 10 Places Sorted by Percent of Total Population
Based on places with total population of 50,000 or more

Place	Population	%
Bethlehem (city) Northampton County	14	0.03
Bethlehem (city) Northampton County	14	0.02
Pittsburgh (city) Allegheny County	21	0.01
Scranton (city) Lackawanna County	10	0.01
Philadelphia (city) Philadelphia County	52	<0.01
Abington (township) Montgomery County	0	0.00
Allentown (city) Lehigh County	0	0.00
Bensalem (township) Bucks County	0	0.00
Bristol (township) Bucks County	0	0.00
Erie (city) Erie County	0	0.00

Northern European

Top 10 Places Sorted by Population
Based on all places, regardless of total population

Place	Population	%
Philadelphia (city) Philadelphia County	361	0.02
Pittsburgh (city) Allegheny County	192	0.06
East Hempfield (township) Lancaster County	139	0.60
Lower Merion (township) Montgomery County	98	0.17
Northampton (township) Bucks County	92	0.23
Warwick (township) Bucks County	85	0.60
Whitehall (township) Lehigh County	83	0.31
Fullerton (cdp) Lehigh County	70	0.47
Royersford (borough) Montgomery County	69	1.48
Newtown (township) Bucks County	69	0.36

Top 10 Places Sorted by Percent of Total Population
Based on all places, regardless of total population

Place	Population	%
Monument (cdp) Centre County	13	9.35
Eyers Grove (cdp) Columbia County	9	9.00
Bechtelsville (borough) Berks County	50	6.32
Deerfield (township) Tioga County	25	3.28
Old Orchard (cdp) Northampton County	59	2.34
Conewago (township) Dauphin County	66	2.22
Unionville (borough) Centre County	6	2.05
Morris (township) Tioga County	10	1.91
Hector (township) Potter County	6	1.81
Sandy Lake (borough) Mercer County	10	1.70

Top 10 Places Sorted by Percent of Total Population
Based on places with total population of 50,000 or more

Place	Population	%
Lower Merion (township) Montgomery County	98	0.17
Abington (township) Montgomery County	63	0.11
Millcreek (township) Erie County	49	0.09
Bristol (township) Bucks County	40	0.07
Pittsburgh (city) Allegheny County	192	0.06
Levittown (cdp) Bucks County	30	0.06
Upper Darby (township) Delaware County	37	0.04
Bensalem (township) Bucks County	24	0.04
Allentown (city) Lehigh County	38	0.03
Philadelphia (city) Philadelphia County	361	0.02

Norwegian

Top 10 Places Sorted by Population
Based on all places, regardless of total population

Place	Population	%
Philadelphia (city) Philadelphia County	2,417	0.16
Pittsburgh (city) Allegheny County	682	0.22
Tredyffrin (township) Chester County	528	1.79
Haverford (township) Delaware County	354	0.73
Derry (township) Dauphin County	328	1.36
Mount Lebanon (township) Allegheny County	328	1.00
State College (borough) Centre County	309	0.74
Hampden (township) Cumberland County	300	1.10
Lower Merion (township) Montgomery County	260	0.45
Ferguson (township) Centre County	258	1.51

Top 10 Places Sorted by Percent of Total Population
Based on all places, regardless of total population

Place	Population	%
Summit Station (cdp) Schuylkill County	58	46.77
Foundryville (cdp) Columbia County	24	12.24
Grindstone (cdp) Fayette County	56	7.52
New Buffalo (borough) Perry County	9	7.38
Upper Oxford (township) Chester County	177	6.84
Oley (cdp) Berks County	99	6.74
Beech Mountain Lakes (cdp) Luzerne County	127	6.56
Wellsville (borough) York County	12	5.80
Victory (township) Venango County	23	5.71
Nicholson (borough) Wyoming County	45	5.44

Top 10 Places Sorted by Percent of Total Population
Based on places with total population of 50,000 or more

Place	Population	%
Lower Merion (township) Montgomery County	260	0.45
Millcreek (township) Erie County	231	0.44
Bethlehem (city) Northampton County	178	0.32
Bethlehem (city) Northampton County	232	0.31
Bensalem (township) Bucks County	183	0.30
Lancaster (city) Lancaster County	166	0.28
Levittown (cdp) Bucks County	137	0.26
Pittsburgh (city) Allegheny County	682	0.22
Reading (city) Berks County	183	0.21
Abington (township) Montgomery County	115	0.21

Pennsylvania German

Top 10 Places Sorted by Population
Based on all places, regardless of total population

Place	Population	%
Allentown (city) Lehigh County	4,292	3.69
Bethlehem (city) Northampton County	2,599	3.48
Reading (city) Berks County	2,056	2.35
Philadelphia (city) Philadelphia County	1,967	0.13
Bethlehem (city) Northampton County	1,688	3.04
Lehigh (township) Northampton County	1,634	15.60
North Whitehall (township) Lehigh County	1,556	9.97
Salisbury (township) Lancaster County	1,526	14.01
Washington (township) Lehigh County	1,238	18.66
Muhlenberg (township) Berks County	1,161	6.04

Top 10 Places Sorted by Percent of Total Population
Based on all places, regardless of total population

Place	Population	%
Hublersburg (cdp) Centre County	50	100.00
Kirkwood (cdp) Lancaster County	164	49.25
Sidman (cdp) Cambria County	102	39.23
Slatedale (cdp) Lehigh County	175	38.38
Ronks (cdp) Lancaster County	99	37.22
West Mahoning (township) Indiana County	486	34.01
Farmersville (cdp) Lancaster County	514	31.08
Atlantic (cdp) Crawford County	13	26.00
Fort Indiantown Gap (cdp) Lebanon County	31	25.83
Wilburton Number Two (cdp) Columbia County	20	24.10

Top 10 Places Sorted by Percent of Total Population
Based on places with total population of 50,000 or more

Place	Population	%
Allentown (city) Lehigh County	4,292	3.69
Bethlehem (city) Northampton County	2,599	3.48
Bethlehem (city) Northampton County	1,688	3.04
Reading (city) Berks County	2,056	2.35
Abington (township) Montgomery County	336	0.61
Scranton (city) Lackawanna County	330	0.43
Bensalem (township) Bucks County	219	0.36
Bristol (township) Bucks County	196	0.36
Millcreek (township) Erie County	191	0.36
Levittown (cdp) Bucks County	182	0.35

Polish

Top 10 Places Sorted by Population
Based on all places, regardless of total population

Place	Population	%
Philadelphia (city) Philadelphia County	58,395	3.88
Pittsburgh (city) Allegheny County	24,743	8.03
Erie (city) Erie County	12,920	12.71
Scranton (city) Lackawanna County	10,984	14.44
Wilkes-Barre (city) Luzerne County	8,088	19.44
Millcreek (township) Erie County	6,656	12.57
Levittown (cdp) Bucks County	5,707	10.98
Bensalem (township) Bucks County	5,563	9.23
Bristol (township) Bucks County	5,282	9.60
Shaler (township) Allegheny County	4,867	16.96

Top 10 Places Sorted by Percent of Total Population
Based on all places, regardless of total population

Place	Population	%
Eagle Lake (cdp) Lackawanna County	20	100.00
Grier City (cdp) Schuylkill County	59	51.75
Dupont (borough) Luzerne County	1,319	48.78
Marshallton (cdp) Northumberland County	772	46.12
Summit Station (cdp) Schuylkill County	56	45.16
Sheatown (cdp) Luzerne County	215	43.43
West Nanticoke (cdp) Luzerne County	229	42.10
Nanticoke (city) Luzerne County	4,390	41.84
Georgetown (cdp) Luzerne County	745	41.67
Duryea (borough) Luzerne County	2,010	41.49

Top 10 Places Sorted by Percent of Total Population
Based on places with total population of 50,000 or more

Place	Population	%
Scranton (city) Lackawanna County	10,984	14.44
Erie (city) Erie County	12,920	12.71
Millcreek (township) Erie County	6,656	12.57
Levittown (cdp) Bucks County	5,707	10.98
Bristol (township) Bucks County	5,282	9.60
Bensalem (township) Bucks County	5,563	9.23
Pittsburgh (city) Allegheny County	24,743	8.03
Abington (township) Montgomery County	4,038	7.29
Lower Merion (township) Montgomery County	3,877	6.68
Bethlehem (city) Northampton County	3,725	4.98

Portuguese

Top 10 Places Sorted by Population
Based on all places, regardless of total population

Place	Population	%
Philadelphia (city) Philadelphia County	3,158	0.21
Bethlehem (city) Northampton County	625	0.84
Bethlehem (city) Northampton County	587	1.06
Erie (city) Erie County	415	0.41
Bethlehem (city) Northampton County	318	1.36
Pittsburgh (city) Allegheny County	276	0.09
Whitehall (township) Lehigh County	249	0.94
Millcreek (township) Erie County	247	0.47
Abington (township) Montgomery County	240	0.43
Stroud (township) Monroe County	212	1.13

Top 10 Places Sorted by Percent of Total Population
Based on all places, regardless of total population

Place	Population	%
New Morgan (borough) Berks County	2	11.76
Benson (borough) Somerset County	19	10.80
Fredericktown (cdp) Washington County	28	7.07
Roseto (borough) Northampton County	87	5.77
Strattanville (borough) Clarion County	35	5.54
Sullivan (township) Tioga County	72	4.93
Fountain Springs (cdp) Schuylkill County	16	4.52
Toughkenamon (cdp) Chester County	58	4.08
Hawley (borough) Wayne County	45	4.03
Goldsboro (borough) York County	35	3.98

Top 10 Places Sorted by Percent of Total Population
Based on places with total population of 50,000 or more

Place	Population	%
Bethlehem (city) Northampton County	587	1.06
Bethlehem (city) Northampton County	625	0.84
Millcreek (township) Erie County	247	0.47
Abington (township) Montgomery County	240	0.43
Erie (city) Erie County	415	0.41
Scranton (city) Lackawanna County	165	0.22
Philadelphia (city) Philadelphia County	3,158	0.21
Lower Merion (township) Montgomery County	86	0.15
Bristol (township) Bucks County	73	0.13
Allentown (city) Lehigh County	136	0.12

Romanian

Top 10 Places Sorted by Population
Based on all places, regardless of total population

Place	Population	%
Philadelphia (city) Philadelphia County	2,101	0.14
Pittsburgh (city) Allegheny County	559	0.18
Lower Merion (township) Montgomery County	478	0.82
Reading (city) Berks County	436	0.50
Northampton (township) Bucks County	297	0.75
Abington (township) Montgomery County	279	0.50
Spring (township) Berks County	243	0.91
Millcreek (township) Erie County	203	0.38
Ross (township) Allegheny County	199	0.64
Lower Southampton (township) Bucks County	187	0.98

Top 10 Places Sorted by Percent of Total Population
Based on all places, regardless of total population

Place	Population	%
Pocono Springs (cdp) Wayne County	71	8.03
Smoketown (cdp) Lancaster County	27	7.16
West Milton (cdp) Union County	36	5.56
Penns Creek (cdp) Snyder County	28	5.47
Deer Lake (cdp) Fayette County	36	5.44
Ward (township) Tioga County	6	4.35
Pardeesville (cdp) Luzerne County	31	4.32
Conashaugh Lakes (cdp) Pike County	29	4.30
Gamble (township) Lycoming County	37	4.28
Lehigh (township) Wayne County	71	3.71

Top 10 Places Sorted by Percent of Total Population
Based on places with total population of 50,000 or more

Place	Population	%
Lower Merion (township) Montgomery County	478	0.82
Reading (city) Berks County	436	0.50
Abington (township) Montgomery County	279	0.50
Millcreek (township) Erie County	203	0.38
Levittown (cdp) Bucks County	129	0.25
Pittsburgh (city) Allegheny County	559	0.18
Bensalem (township) Bucks County	106	0.18
Erie (city) Erie County	174	0.17
Upper Darby (township) Delaware County	143	0.17
Philadelphia (city) Philadelphia County	2,101	0.14

Russian

Top 10 Places Sorted by Population
Based on all places, regardless of total population

Place	Population	%
Philadelphia (city) Philadelphia County	25,520	1.70
Lower Merion (township) Montgomery County	6,253	10.77
Pittsburgh (city) Allegheny County	6,191	2.01

Place	Population	%
Scranton (city) Lackawanna County	2,676	3.52
Northampton (township) Bucks County	2,533	6.36
Cheltenham (township) Montgomery County	2,477	6.73
Abington (township) Montgomery County	2,330	4.20
Upper Dublin (township) Montgomery County	2,127	8.31
Haverford (township) Delaware County	2,125	4.38
Lower Makefield (township) Bucks County	1,661	5.08

Top 10 Places Sorted by Percent of Total Population
Based on all places, regardless of total population

Place	Population	%
Hendersonville (cdp) Washington County	82	41.84
Sandy Ridge (cdp) Centre County	50	22.62
Buffington (cdp) Fayette County	31	19.50
Hookstown (borough) Beaver County	37	18.88
Mount Gretna Heights (cdp) Lebanon County	28	17.07
Grindstone (cdp) Fayette County	121	16.24
Coal Center (borough) Washington County	41	14.70
Green Hills (borough) Washington County	2	14.29
Wyncote (cdp) Montgomery County	452	14.28
Mayfield (borough) Lackawanna County	249	13.41

Top 10 Places Sorted by Percent of Total Population
Based on places with total population of 50,000 or more

Place	Population	%
Lower Merion (township) Montgomery County	6,253	10.77
Abington (township) Montgomery County	2,330	4.20
Scranton (city) Lackawanna County	2,676	3.52
Millcreek (township) Erie County	1,163	2.20
Bensalem (township) Bucks County	1,323	2.19
Pittsburgh (city) Allegheny County	6,191	2.01
Philadelphia (city) Philadelphia County	25,520	1.70
Bethlehem (city) Northampton County	1,042	1.39
Erie (city) Erie County	1,342	1.32
Bethlehem (city) Northampton County	717	1.29

Scandinavian

Top 10 Places Sorted by Population
Based on all places, regardless of total population

Place	Population	%
Philadelphia (city) Philadelphia County	504	0.03
Pittsburgh (city) Allegheny County	337	0.11
Radnor (township) Delaware County	152	0.48
Upper Macungie (township) Lehigh County	134	0.70
Williamsport (city) Lycoming County	131	0.44
Warminster (township) Bucks County	117	0.36
State College (borough) Centre County	105	0.25
Penn Forest (township) Carbon County	84	0.94
Millcreek (township) Erie County	82	0.15
Southampton (township) Franklin County	70	0.91

Top 10 Places Sorted by Percent of Total Population
Based on all places, regardless of total population

Place	Population	%
New Buffalo (borough) Perry County	6	4.92
McKnightstown (cdp) Adams County	12	4.65
Sylvania (township) Potter County	4	4.60
Slippery Rock University (cdp) Butler County	15	4.57
Harleigh (cdp) Luzerne County	37	3.43
Packer (township) Carbon County	27	2.76
Hovey (township) Armstrong County	3	2.75
Tionesta (borough) Forest County	14	2.68
Jackson (township) Mercer County	34	2.59
Alba (borough) Bradford County	4	2.34

Top 10 Places Sorted by Percent of Total Population
Based on places with total population of 50,000 or more

Place	Population	%
Millcreek (township) Erie County	82	0.15
Bristol (township) Bucks County	65	0.12
Pittsburgh (city) Allegheny County	337	0.11
Levittown (cdp) Bucks County	55	0.11
Lower Merion (township) Montgomery County	54	0.09
Lancaster (city) Lancaster County	38	0.06
Bethlehem (city) Northampton County	22	0.04
Philadelphia (city) Philadelphia County	504	0.03
Bethlehem (city) Northampton County	22	0.03
Reading (city) Berks County	11	0.01

Scotch-Irish

Top 10 Places Sorted by Population
Based on all places, regardless of total population

Place	Population	%
Philadelphia (city) Philadelphia County	9,813	0.65
Pittsburgh (city) Allegheny County	5,558	1.80
Erie (city) Erie County	2,432	2.39
Hempfield (township) Westmoreland County	1,444	3.36
Bristol (township) Bucks County	1,261	2.29
Levittown (cdp) Bucks County	1,218	2.34
Abington (township) Montgomery County	1,152	2.08
Millcreek (township) Erie County	1,130	2.13
Altoona (city) Blair County	1,085	2.31
Lower Merion (township) Montgomery County	1,085	1.87

Top 10 Places Sorted by Percent of Total Population
Based on all places, regardless of total population

Place	Population	%
West Alexander (cdp) Washington County	248	30.05
Smoketown (cdp) Lancaster County	86	22.81
Birmingham (borough) Huntingdon County	22	21.57
Donegal (township) Washington County	580	21.19
Cross Creek (cdp) Washington County	27	19.57
Buffalo (township) Washington County	384	17.42
Allenport (cdp) Huntingdon County	83	17.18
Eau Claire (borough) Butler County	39	16.53
Lumber City (borough) Clearfield County	11	16.18
Hickory (cdp) Washington County	141	15.81

Top 10 Places Sorted by Percent of Total Population
Based on places with total population of 50,000 or more

Place	Population	%
Erie (city) Erie County	2,432	2.39
Levittown (cdp) Bucks County	1,218	2.34
Bristol (township) Bucks County	1,261	2.29
Millcreek (township) Erie County	1,130	2.13
Abington (township) Montgomery County	1,152	2.08
Lower Merion (township) Montgomery County	1,085	1.87
Pittsburgh (city) Allegheny County	5,558	1.80
Bensalem (township) Bucks County	962	1.60
Lancaster (city) Lancaster County	842	1.43
Bethlehem (city) Northampton County	935	1.25

Scottish

Top 10 Places Sorted by Population
Based on all places, regardless of total population

Place	Population	%
Philadelphia (city) Philadelphia County	8,768	0.58
Pittsburgh (city) Allegheny County	4,798	1.56
Haverford (township) Delaware County	1,239	2.55
Lower Merion (township) Montgomery County	1,205	2.08
Mount Lebanon (township) Allegheny County	1,079	3.29
Bethlehem (city) Northampton County	1,079	1.44
Abington (township) Montgomery County	1,043	1.88
Lower Makefield (township) Bucks County	1,032	3.15
Hempfield (township) Westmoreland County	1,021	2.38
Upper Darby (township) Delaware County	1,018	1.24

Top 10 Places Sorted by Percent of Total Population
Based on all places, regardless of total population

Place	Population	%
Dunlo (cdp) Cambria County	45	20.55
Noblestown (cdp) Allegheny County	57	18.51
Lumber City (cdp) Mifflin County	42	18.50
Mount Gretna Heights (cdp) Lebanon County	29	17.68
Baileyville (cdp) Centre County	36	16.29
Fort Loudon (cdp) Franklin County	170	15.65
Cashtown (cdp) Adams County	140	15.23
Slatedale (cdp) Lehigh County	69	15.13
Sheppton (cdp) Schuylkill County	32	14.41
Springmont (cdp) Berks County	68	13.88

Top 10 Places Sorted by Percent of Total Population
Based on places with total population of 50,000 or more

Place	Population	%
Lower Merion (township) Montgomery County	1,205	2.08
Abington (township) Montgomery County	1,043	1.88
Millcreek (township) Erie County	929	1.75
Levittown (cdp) Bucks County	822	1.58

Place	Population	%
Pittsburgh (city) Allegheny County	4,798	1.56
Bethlehem (city) Northampton County	864	1.56
Bristol (township) Bucks County	809	1.47
Bethlehem (city) Northampton County	1,079	1.44
Upper Darby (township) Delaware County	1,018	1.24
Erie (city) Erie County	984	0.97

Serbian

Top 10 Places Sorted by Population
Based on all places, regardless of total population

Place	Population	%
Pittsburgh (city) Allegheny County	993	0.32
Philadelphia (city) Philadelphia County	493	0.03
North Huntingdon (township) Westmoreland County	453	1.49
Hopewell (township) Beaver County	423	3.34
Hempfield (township) Westmoreland County	360	0.84
Hermitage (city) Mercer County	317	1.96
Penn (township) Westmoreland County	302	1.52
Center (township) Beaver County	296	2.53
Cranberry (township) Butler County	283	1.03
Baldwin (borough) Allegheny County	271	1.38

Top 10 Places Sorted by Percent of Total Population
Based on all places, regardless of total population

Place	Population	%
Glasgow (borough) Beaver County	8	15.38
Slovan (cdp) Washington County	43	10.67
Midland (borough) Beaver County	241	8.91
Wall (borough) Allegheny County	41	7.51
Homewood (borough) Beaver County	8	6.40
Newburg (borough) Cumberland County	19	5.65
Ohioville (borough) Beaver County	200	5.61
Riverside (cdp) Cambria County	20	4.50
Export (borough) Westmoreland County	40	4.40
Ellwood City (borough) Beaver County	33	4.10

Top 10 Places Sorted by Percent of Total Population
Based on places with total population of 50,000 or more

Place	Population	%
Pittsburgh (city) Allegheny County	993	0.32
Lower Merion (township) Montgomery County	95	0.16
Upper Darby (township) Delaware County	63	0.08
Erie (city) Erie County	69	0.07
Millcreek (township) Erie County	39	0.07
Bethlehem (city) Northampton County	43	0.06
Levittown (cdp) Bucks County	26	0.05
Scranton (city) Lackawanna County	33	0.04
Philadelphia (city) Philadelphia County	493	0.03
Bristol (township) Bucks County	15	0.03

Slavic

Top 10 Places Sorted by Population
Based on all places, regardless of total population

Place	Population	%
Philadelphia (city) Philadelphia County	498	0.03
Pittsburgh (city) Allegheny County	428	0.14
Lower Paxton (township) Dauphin County	232	0.50
Derry (township) Dauphin County	198	0.82
Hempfield (township) Westmoreland County	183	0.43
Millcreek (township) Erie County	145	0.27
Shaler (township) Allegheny County	141	0.49
North Braddock (borough) Allegheny County	138	2.72
Hopewell (township) Beaver County	135	1.07
New Castle (city) Lawrence County	135	0.57

Top 10 Places Sorted by Percent of Total Population
Based on all places, regardless of total population

Place	Population	%
Kerrtown (cdp) Crawford County	38	11.55
Southview (cdp) Washington County	10	6.67
Seltzer (cdp) Schuylkill County	19	6.42
Calumet (cdp) Westmoreland County	61	5.99
Palmdale (cdp) Dauphin County	107	5.17
Sullivan (township) Tioga County	74	5.07
Dunlo (cdp) Cambria County	11	5.02
Exeter (township) Luzerne County	102	4.57
Blaine (township) Washington County	22	4.47
Spring Hill (cdp) Cambria County	41	3.96

Top 10 Places Sorted by Percent of Total Population
Based on places with total population of 50,000 or more

Place	Population	%
Millcreek (township) Erie County	145	0.27
Levittown (cdp) Bucks County	103	0.20
Bristol (township) Bucks County	96	0.17
Pittsburgh (city) Allegheny County	428	0.14
Lower Merion (township) Montgomery County	76	0.13
Erie (city) Erie County	127	0.12
Bethlehem (city) Northampton County	80	0.11
Bethlehem (city) Northampton County	63	0.11
Reading (city) Berks County	68	0.08
Scranton (city) Lackawanna County	64	0.08

Slovak

Top 10 Places Sorted by Population
Based on all places, regardless of total population

Place	Population	%
Pittsburgh (city) Allegheny County	5,935	1.93
North Huntingdon (township) Westmoreland County	3,038	10.02
West Mifflin (borough) Allegheny County	2,921	14.25
Hempfield (township) Westmoreland County	2,694	6.27
Bethlehem (city) Northampton County	2,574	3.44
Philadelphia (city) Philadelphia County	2,480	0.16
Hazleton (city) Luzerne County	2,045	8.22
Johnstown (city) Cambria County	1,712	7.98
Unity (township) Westmoreland County	1,706	7.63
Munhall (borough) Allegheny County	1,676	14.63

Top 10 Places Sorted by Percent of Total Population
Based on all places, regardless of total population

Place	Population	%
Jeddo (borough) Luzerne County	44	40.74
Mammoth (cdp) Westmoreland County	234	40.55
Dicksonville (cdp) Indiana County	167	35.68
Tresckow (cdp) Carbon County	258	30.32
Norvelt (cdp) Westmoreland County	275	29.19
Hawk Run (cdp) Clearfield County	84	27.01
Lattimer (cdp) Luzerne County	103	25.75
Sutersville (borough) Westmoreland County	156	24.61
Banks (township) Carbon County	304	24.34
Beaver Meadows (borough) Carbon County	195	24.10

Top 10 Places Sorted by Percent of Total Population
Based on places with total population of 50,000 or more

Place	Population	%
Bethlehem (city) Northampton County	2,574	3.44
Bethlehem (city) Northampton County	1,659	2.99
Pittsburgh (city) Allegheny County	5,935	1.93
Scranton (city) Lackawanna County	1,344	1.77
Millcreek (township) Erie County	886	1.67
Erie (city) Erie County	1,499	1.47
Allentown (city) Lehigh County	1,543	1.33
Levittown (cdp) Bucks County	621	1.19
Bristol (township) Bucks County	558	1.01
Abington (township) Montgomery County	282	0.51

Slovene

Top 10 Places Sorted by Population
Based on all places, regardless of total population

Place	Population	%
Pittsburgh (city) Allegheny County	739	0.24
Hempfield (township) Westmoreland County	328	0.76
Bethlehem (city) Northampton County	316	0.42
Philadelphia (city) Philadelphia County	273	0.02
North Strabane (township) Washington County	265	2.07
Peters (township) Washington County	264	1.29
North Fayette (township) Allegheny County	246	1.82
Bethlehem (city) Northampton County	231	0.42
Cecil (township) Washington County	225	2.05
Penn (township) Westmoreland County	224	1.12

Top 10 Places Sorted by Percent of Total Population
Based on all places, regardless of total population

Place	Population	%
Southview (cdp) Washington County	17	11.33
Vandling (borough) Lackawanna County	49	8.48

Place	Population	%
Yukon (cdp) Westmoreland County	40	7.52
Dunlo (cdp) Cambria County	16	7.31
Rowes Run (cdp) Fayette County	63	7.16
Forest City (borough) Susquehanna County	121	6.93
Clinton (township) Wayne County	116	6.56
Hickory (township) Forest County	34	5.29
Imperial (cdp) Allegheny County	120	5.16
Riverside (cdp) Cambria County	22	4.95

Top 10 Places Sorted by Percent of Total Population
Based on places with total population of 50,000 or more

Place	Population	%
Bethlehem (city) Northampton County	316	0.42
Bethlehem (city) Northampton County	231	0.42
Pittsburgh (city) Allegheny County	739	0.24
Millcreek (township) Erie County	37	0.07
Allentown (city) Lehigh County	73	0.06
Erie (city) Erie County	61	0.06
Scranton (city) Lackawanna County	49	0.06
Abington (township) Montgomery County	28	0.05
Philadelphia (city) Philadelphia County	273	0.02
Reading (city) Berks County	20	0.02

Soviet Union

Top 10 Places Sorted by Population
Based on all places, regardless of total population

Place	Population	%
Lower Merion (township) Montgomery County	22	0.04
Northampton (township) Bucks County	17	0.04
Bryn Mawr (cdp) Montgomery County	11	0.31
Bensalem (township) Bucks County	10	0.02
Allentown (city) Lehigh County	10	0.01
Aaronsburg (cdp) Centre County	0	0.00
Aaronsburg (cdp) Washington County	0	0.00
Abbott (township) Potter County	0	0.00
Abbottstown (borough) Adams County	0	0.00
Abington (township) Lackawanna County	0	0.00

Top 10 Places Sorted by Percent of Total Population
Based on all places, regardless of total population

Place	Population	%
Bryn Mawr (cdp) Montgomery County	11	0.31
Lower Merion (township) Montgomery County	22	0.04
Northampton (township) Bucks County	17	0.04
Bensalem (township) Bucks County	10	0.02
Allentown (city) Lehigh County	10	0.01
Aaronsburg (cdp) Centre County	0	0.00
Aaronsburg (cdp) Washington County	0	0.00
Abbott (township) Potter County	0	0.00
Abbottstown (borough) Adams County	0	0.00
Abington (township) Lackawanna County	0	0.00

Top 10 Places Sorted by Percent of Total Population
Based on places with total population of 50,000 or more

Place	Population	%
Lower Merion (township) Montgomery County	22	0.04
Bensalem (township) Bucks County	10	0.02
Allentown (city) Lehigh County	10	0.01
Abington (township) Montgomery County	0	0.00
Bethlehem (city) Northampton County	0	0.00
Bethlehem (city) Northampton County	0	0.00
Bristol (township) Bucks County	0	0.00
Erie (city) Erie County	0	0.00
Lancaster (city) Lancaster County	0	0.00
Levittown (cdp) Bucks County	0	0.00

Swedish

Top 10 Places Sorted by Population
Based on all places, regardless of total population

Place	Population	%
Philadelphia (city) Philadelphia County	3,719	0.25
Pittsburgh (city) Allegheny County	2,007	0.65
Erie (city) Erie County	1,830	1.80
Millcreek (township) Erie County	1,705	3.22
Warren (city) Warren County	1,264	12.93
Hempfield (township) Westmoreland County	725	1.69
Bethlehem (city) Northampton County	556	0.74
Kane (borough) McKean County	547	14.43
Haverford (township) Delaware County	542	1.12

Conewango (township) Warren County	532	14.83

Top 10 Places Sorted by Percent of Total Population
Based on all places, regardless of total population

Place	Population	%
Edenborn (cdp) Fayette County	62	60.78
Cherry Grove (township) Warren County	89	36.78
Wetmore (township) McKean County	481	28.31
Landingville (borough) Schuylkill County	55	28.21
Sergeant (township) McKean County	45	26.95
Kersey (cdp) Elk County	251	26.01
Elk (township) Warren County	116	23.43
Grier City (cdp) Schuylkill County	26	22.81
Farmington (township) Warren County	325	21.72
Gordonville (cdp) Lancaster County	149	21.35

Top 10 Places Sorted by Percent of Total Population
Based on places with total population of 50,000 or more

Place	Population	%
Millcreek (township) Erie County	1,705	3.22
Erie (city) Erie County	1,830	1.80
Lower Merion (township) Montgomery County	520	0.90
Abington (township) Montgomery County	470	0.85
Bethlehem (city) Northampton County	556	0.74
Bethlehem (city) Northampton County	376	0.68
Pittsburgh (city) Allegheny County	2,007	0.65
Levittown (cdp) Bucks County	334	0.64
Upper Darby (township) Delaware County	505	0.61
Bristol (township) Bucks County	295	0.54

Swiss

Top 10 Places Sorted by Population
Based on all places, regardless of total population

Place	Population	%
Philadelphia (city) Philadelphia County	1,886	0.13
Brecknock (township) Lancaster County	1,027	14.39
East Earl (township) Lancaster County	838	13.17
Pittsburgh (city) Allegheny County	838	0.27
Ephrata (township) Lancaster County	785	8.54
East Lampeter (township) Lancaster County	756	4.75
Lancaster (city) Lancaster County	714	1.21
Ephrata (borough) Lancaster County	673	5.03
West Lampeter (township) Lancaster County	647	4.36
Warwick (township) Lancaster County	628	3.60

Top 10 Places Sorted by Percent of Total Population
Based on all places, regardless of total population

Place	Population	%
Goodville (cdp) Lancaster County	78	30.35
Laurel Mountain (borough) Westmoreland County	48	20.51
Allensville (cdp) Mifflin County	80	18.74
Blue Ball (cdp) Lancaster County	146	18.58
Bingham (township) Potter County	121	17.36
Guys Mills (cdp) Crawford County	26	16.46
Farmington (township) Fayette County	110	15.65
Beaver (township) Crawford County	118	15.28
Millerton (cdp) Tioga County	47	15.26
Soudersburg (cdp) Lancaster County	79	14.99

Top 10 Places Sorted by Percent of Total Population
Based on places with total population of 50,000 or more

Place	Population	%
Lancaster (city) Lancaster County	714	1.21
Bethlehem (city) Northampton County	228	0.41
Bethlehem (city) Northampton County	285	0.38
Millcreek (township) Erie County	203	0.38
Lower Merion (township) Montgomery County	192	0.33
Abington (township) Montgomery County	162	0.29
Pittsburgh (city) Allegheny County	838	0.27
Scranton (city) Lackawanna County	169	0.22
Allentown (city) Lehigh County	242	0.21
Reading (city) Berks County	164	0.19

Turkish

Top 10 Places Sorted by Population
Based on all places, regardless of total population

Place	Population	%
Philadelphia (city) Philadelphia County	786	0.05

Pittsburgh (city) Allegheny County	485	0.16
Whitehall (borough) Allegheny County	223	1.60
Levittown (cdp) Bucks County	209	0.40
Bristol (township) Bucks County	201	0.37
Birmingham (township) Chester County	198	4.67
Bethlehem (city) Northampton County	184	0.25
Lancaster (city) Lancaster County	174	0.30
Scranton (city) Lackawanna County	172	0.23
State College (borough) Centre County	171	0.41

Top 10 Places Sorted by Percent of Total Population
Based on all places, regardless of total population

Place	Population	%
Birmingham (township) Chester County	198	4.67
Hilldale (cdp) Luzerne County	45	3.14
Freemansburg (borough) Northampton County	76	2.98
Allegheny (township) Venango County	11	2.72
Herrick (township) Susquehanna County	14	1.74
Whitehall (borough) Allegheny County	223	1.60
Avalon (borough) Allegheny County	72	1.51
Pennsbury Village (borough) Allegheny County	10	1.49
Strattanville (borough) Clarion County	9	1.42
Hepburn (township) Lycoming County	37	1.34

Top 10 Places Sorted by Percent of Total Population
Based on places with total population of 50,000 or more

Place	Population	%
Levittown (cdp) Bucks County	209	0.40
Bristol (township) Bucks County	201	0.37
Lancaster (city) Lancaster County	174	0.30
Bethlehem (city) Northampton County	169	0.30
Bethlehem (city) Northampton County	184	0.25
Scranton (city) Lackawanna County	172	0.23
Bensalem (township) Bucks County	107	0.18
Pittsburgh (city) Allegheny County	485	0.16
Millcreek (township) Erie County	80	0.15
Lower Merion (township) Montgomery County	59	0.10

Ukrainian

Top 10 Places Sorted by Population
Based on all places, regardless of total population

Place	Population	%
Philadelphia (city) Philadelphia County	13,262	0.88
Pittsburgh (city) Allegheny County	2,972	0.96
Bensalem (township) Bucks County	1,352	2.24
Northampton (township) Bucks County	1,274	3.20
Allentown (city) Lehigh County	1,122	0.96
Scranton (city) Lackawanna County	1,060	1.39
Abington (township) Montgomery County	885	1.60
Bethlehem (city) Northampton County	864	1.16
Erie (city) Erie County	864	0.85
Lower Southampton (township) Bucks County	827	4.34

Top 10 Places Sorted by Percent of Total Population
Based on all places, regardless of total population

Place	Population	%
Forestville (cdp) Schuylkill County	176	47.70
Seltzer (cdp) Schuylkill County	72	24.32
Cairnbrook (cdp) Somerset County	106	23.45
Cass (township) Schuylkill County	387	19.48
New Schaefferstown (cdp) Berks County	23	15.65
Altamont (cdp) Schuylkill County	112	15.16
Gilberton (borough) Schuylkill County	112	13.45
Slickville (cdp) Westmoreland County	52	13.40
Heckscherville (cdp) Schuylkill County	36	12.46
Potlicker Flats (cdp) Mifflin County	34	12.01

Top 10 Places Sorted by Percent of Total Population
Based on places with total population of 50,000 or more

Place	Population	%
Bensalem (township) Bucks County	1,352	2.24
Abington (township) Montgomery County	885	1.60
Levittown (cdp) Bucks County	752	1.45
Scranton (city) Lackawanna County	1,060	1.39
Bethlehem (city) Northampton County	724	1.31
Bristol (township) Bucks County	704	1.28
Millcreek (township) Erie County	658	1.24
Lower Merion (township) Montgomery County	703	1.21
Bethlehem (city) Northampton County	864	1.16
Pittsburgh (city) Allegheny County	2,972	0.96

Welsh

Top 10 Places Sorted by Population
Based on all places, regardless of total population

Place	Population	%
Scranton (city) Lackawanna County	4,539	5.97
Philadelphia (city) Philadelphia County	4,345	0.29
Pittsburgh (city) Allegheny County	2,729	0.89
Wilkes-Barre (city) Luzerne County	2,318	5.57
Bethlehem (city) Northampton County	1,433	1.92
Allentown (city) Lehigh County	1,050	0.90
Bethlehem (city) Northampton County	931	1.68
Lower Paxton (township) Dauphin County	895	1.91
Hanover (township) Luzerne County	890	8.05
Kingston (borough) Luzerne County	841	6.35

Top 10 Places Sorted by Percent of Total Population
Based on all places, regardless of total population

Place	Population	%
Valley-Hi (borough) Fulton County	3	100.00
Jacksonville (cdp) Centre County	25	24.75
Jamison City (cdp) Columbia County	20	19.05
Dunlo (cdp) Cambria County	38	17.35
Timber Hills (cdp) Lebanon County	55	16.52
Vicksburg (cdp) Union County	37	16.37
Waverly (cdp) Lackawanna County	76	14.53
Green Hills (borough) Washington County	2	14.29
Newton (township) Lackawanna County	395	14.09
Grier City (cdp) Schuylkill County	16	14.04

Top 10 Places Sorted by Percent of Total Population
Based on places with total population of 50,000 or more

Place	Population	%
Scranton (city) Lackawanna County	4,539	5.97
Bethlehem (city) Northampton County	1,433	1.92
Bethlehem (city) Northampton County	931	1.68
Levittown (cdp) Bucks County	825	1.59
Bristol (township) Bucks County	715	1.30
Abington (township) Montgomery County	562	1.01
Allentown (city) Lehigh County	1,050	0.90
Pittsburgh (city) Allegheny County	2,729	0.89
Millcreek (township) Erie County	450	0.85
Upper Darby (township) Delaware County	619	0.75

West Indian, excluding Hispanic

Top 10 Places Sorted by Population
Based on all places, regardless of total population

Place	Population	%
Philadelphia (city) Philadelphia County	25,436	1.69
Upper Darby (township) Delaware County	2,118	2.57
Reading (city) Berks County	1,590	1.82
Allentown (city) Lehigh County	1,351	1.16
Cheltenham (township) Montgomery County	1,325	3.60
Pittsburgh (city) Allegheny County	1,313	0.43
York (city) York County	949	2.18
Yeadon (borough) Delaware County	770	6.71
Harrisburg (city) Dauphin County	752	1.52
Abington (township) Montgomery County	672	1.21

Top 10 Places Sorted by Percent of Total Population
Based on all places, regardless of total population

Place	Population	%
Slickville (cdp) Westmoreland County	134	34.54
Albrightsville (cdp) Carbon County	54	27.69
East Lansdowne (borough) Delaware County	365	13.80
Curtin (township) Centre County	56	8.95
Lincoln University (cdp) Chester County	166	8.58
Colwyn (borough) Delaware County	188	7.48
Yatesville (borough) Luzerne County	48	6.92
Yeadon (borough) Delaware County	770	6.71
New Holland (borough) Lancaster County	343	6.42
Orrtanna (cdp) Adams County	10	6.19

Top 10 Places Sorted by Percent of Total Population
Based on places with total population of 50,000 or more

Place	Population	%
Upper Darby (township) Delaware County	2,118	2.57
Reading (city) Berks County	1,590	1.82
Philadelphia (city) Philadelphia County	25,436	1.69
Abington (township) Montgomery County	672	1.21

Place	Population	%
Allentown (city) Lehigh County	1,351	1.16
Bethlehem (city) Northampton County	366	0.66
Lower Merion (township) Montgomery County	378	0.65
Lancaster (city) Lancaster County	367	0.62
Bethlehem (city) Northampton County	428	0.57
Bristol (township) Bucks County	264	0.48

West Indian: Bahamian, excluding Hispanic

Top 10 Places Sorted by Population
Based on all places, regardless of total population

Place	Population	%
Philadelphia (city) Philadelphia County	104	0.01
Whitpain (township) Montgomery County	90	0.48
Pittsburgh (city) Allegheny County	44	0.01
Port Carbon (borough) Schuylkill County	41	2.21
Wyndmoor (cdp) Montgomery County	39	0.66
Springfield (township) Montgomery County	39	0.20
Concord (township) Delaware County	35	0.22
Allentown (city) Lehigh County	32	0.03
Uniontown (city) Fayette County	31	0.29
Hellertown (borough) Northampton County	28	0.48

Top 10 Places Sorted by Percent of Total Population
Based on all places, regardless of total population

Place	Population	%
Port Carbon (borough) Schuylkill County	41	2.21
Cornwells Heights (cdp) Bucks County	11	0.79
Wyndmoor (cdp) Montgomery County	39	0.66
Whitpain (township) Montgomery County	90	0.48
Hellertown (borough) Northampton County	28	0.48
East Butler (borough) Butler County	3	0.43
Uniontown (city) Fayette County	31	0.29
Concord (township) Delaware County	35	0.22
Duncannon (borough) Perry County	3	0.21
Springfield (township) Montgomery County	39	0.20

Top 10 Places Sorted by Percent of Total Population
Based on places with total population of 50,000 or more

Place	Population	%
Allentown (city) Lehigh County	32	0.03
Bensalem (township) Bucks County	11	0.02
Philadelphia (city) Philadelphia County	104	0.01
Pittsburgh (city) Allegheny County	44	0.01
Upper Darby (township) Delaware County	9	0.01
Abington (township) Montgomery County	0	0.00
Bethlehem (city) Northampton County	0	0.00
Bethlehem (city) Northampton County	0	0.00
Bristol (township) Bucks County	0	0.00
Erie (city) Erie County	0	0.00

West Indian: Barbadian, excluding Hispanic

Top 10 Places Sorted by Population
Based on all places, regardless of total population

Place	Population	%
Philadelphia (city) Philadelphia County	635	0.04
Bensalem (township) Bucks County	99	0.16
Upper Darby (township) Delaware County	85	0.10
Whitemarsh (township) Montgomery County	79	0.46
Pittsburgh (city) Allegheny County	77	0.02
Colwyn (borough) Delaware County	75	2.98
Linglestown (cdp) Dauphin County	71	1.04
Lower Paxton (township) Dauphin County	71	0.15
Reading (city) Berks County	68	0.08
Stroudsburg (borough) Monroe County	62	1.08

Top 10 Places Sorted by Percent of Total Population
Based on all places, regardless of total population

Place	Population	%
Slickville (cdp) Westmoreland County	43	11.08
Orrtanna (cdp) Adams County	10	6.17
Homewood (borough) Beaver County	6	4.80
Colwyn (borough) Delaware County	75	2.98
Highland (township) Adams County	10	1.15
Stroudsburg (borough) Monroe County	62	1.08
Linglestown (cdp) Dauphin County	71	1.04
Sierra View (cdp) Monroe County	50	0.88
Lincoln University (cdp) Chester County	15	0.78

Place	Population	%
Pocono Woodland Lakes (cdp) Pike County	21	0.74

Top 10 Places Sorted by Percent of Total Population
Based on places with total population of 50,000 or more

Place	Population	%
Bensalem (township) Bucks County	99	0.16
Abington (township) Montgomery County	60	0.11
Upper Darby (township) Delaware County	85	0.10
Reading (city) Berks County	68	0.08
Lancaster (city) Lancaster County	36	0.06
Philadelphia (city) Philadelphia County	635	0.04
Lower Merion (township) Montgomery County	21	0.04
Pittsburgh (city) Allegheny County	77	0.02
Allentown (city) Lehigh County	23	0.02
Bethlehem (city) Northampton County	12	0.02

West Indian: Belizean, excluding Hispanic

Top 10 Places Sorted by Population
Based on all places, regardless of total population

Place	Population	%
Sierra View (cdp) Monroe County	175	3.09
Chestnuthill (township) Monroe County	175	1.03
Cheltenham (township) Montgomery County	117	0.32
Hempfield (township) Mercer County	99	2.62
Lancaster (city) Lancaster County	32	0.05
Philadelphia (city) Philadelphia County	31	<0.01
Turbett (township) Juniata County	29	3.82
Williamsport (city) Lycoming County	18	0.06
Perkiomen (township) Montgomery County	17	0.19
Shiloh (cdp) York County	16	0.14

Top 10 Places Sorted by Percent of Total Population
Based on all places, regardless of total population

Place	Population	%
Turbett (township) Juniata County	29	3.82
Sierra View (cdp) Monroe County	175	3.09
Hempfield (township) Mercer County	99	2.62
Chestnuthill (township) Monroe County	175	1.03
Cheltenham (township) Montgomery County	117	0.32
Shohola (township) Pike County	7	0.26
Perkiomen (township) Montgomery County	17	0.19
Middletown (cdp) Northampton County	12	0.17
Shiloh (cdp) York County	16	0.14
Harleysville (cdp) Montgomery County	11	0.12

Top 10 Places Sorted by Percent of Total Population
Based on places with total population of 50,000 or more

Place	Population	%
Lancaster (city) Lancaster County	32	0.05
Philadelphia (city) Philadelphia County	31	<0.01
Pittsburgh (city) Allegheny County	10	<0.01
Abington (township) Montgomery County	0	0.00
Allentown (city) Lehigh County	0	0.00
Bensalem (township) Bucks County	0	0.00
Bethlehem (city) Northampton County	0	0.00
Bethlehem (city) Northampton County	0	0.00
Bristol (township) Bucks County	0	0.00
Erie (city) Erie County	0	0.00

West Indian: Bermudan, excluding Hispanic

Top 10 Places Sorted by Population
Based on all places, regardless of total population

Place	Population	%
Progress (cdp) Dauphin County	165	1.72
Susquehanna (township) Dauphin County	165	0.70
Salem (township) Wayne County	47	1.12
Exton (cdp) Chester County	42	0.92
West Whiteland (township) Chester County	42	0.23
Pittsburgh (city) Allegheny County	37	0.01
Philadelphia (city) Philadelphia County	29	<0.01
Cumru (township) Berks County	17	0.11
Maxatawny (township) Berks County	14	0.18
King of Prussia (cdp) Montgomery County	13	0.07

Top 10 Places Sorted by Percent of Total Population
Based on all places, regardless of total population

Place	Population	%
Montrose Manor (cdp) Berks County	8	1.74
Progress (cdp) Dauphin County	165	1.72
Salem (township) Wayne County	47	1.12
Exton (cdp) Chester County	42	0.92
Susquehanna (township) Dauphin County	165	0.70
Monaghan (township) York County	9	0.35
West Whiteland (township) Chester County	42	0.23
Colwyn (borough) Delaware County	5	0.20
Maxatawny (township) Berks County	14	0.18
Cumru (township) Berks County	17	0.11

Top 10 Places Sorted by Percent of Total Population
Based on places with total population of 50,000 or more

Place	Population	%
Pittsburgh (city) Allegheny County	37	0.01
Philadelphia (city) Philadelphia County	29	<0.01
Abington (township) Montgomery County	0	0.00
Allentown (city) Lehigh County	0	0.00
Bensalem (township) Bucks County	0	0.00
Bethlehem (city) Northampton County	0	0.00
Bethlehem (city) Northampton County	0	0.00
Bristol (township) Bucks County	0	0.00
Erie (city) Erie County	0	0.00
Lancaster (city) Lancaster County	0	0.00

West Indian: British West Indian, excluding Hispanic

Top 10 Places Sorted by Population
Based on all places, regardless of total population

Place	Population	%
Philadelphia (city) Philadelphia County	541	0.04
Slickville (cdp) Westmoreland County	91	23.45
Salem (township) Westmoreland County	91	1.37
Price (township) Monroe County	75	2.15
Upper Darby (township) Delaware County	75	0.09
Allentown (city) Lehigh County	63	0.05
Downingtown (borough) Chester County	52	0.66
Perkiomen (township) Montgomery County	46	0.52
Hazleton (city) Luzerne County	45	0.18
Chestnuthill (township) Monroe County	38	0.22

Top 10 Places Sorted by Percent of Total Population
Based on all places, regardless of total population

Place	Population	%
Slickville (cdp) Westmoreland County	91	23.45
Thompson (township) Susquehanna County	26	5.18
Price (township) Monroe County	75	2.15
Salem (township) Westmoreland County	91	1.37
Packer (township) Carbon County	12	1.23
Palo Alto (borough) Schuylkill County	11	1.06
Downingtown (borough) Chester County	52	0.66
Indian Mountain Lake (cdp) Monroe County	32	0.63
Perkiomen (township) Montgomery County	46	0.52
Stroudsburg (borough) Monroe County	28	0.49

Top 10 Places Sorted by Percent of Total Population
Based on places with total population of 50,000 or more

Place	Population	%
Upper Darby (township) Delaware County	75	0.09
Allentown (city) Lehigh County	63	0.05
Philadelphia (city) Philadelphia County	541	0.04
Erie (city) Erie County	20	0.02
Abington (township) Montgomery County	11	0.02
Lancaster (city) Lancaster County	10	0.02
Pittsburgh (city) Allegheny County	9	<0.01
Bensalem (township) Bucks County	0	0.00
Bethlehem (city) Northampton County	0	0.00
Bethlehem (city) Northampton County	0	0.00

West Indian: Dutch West Indian, excluding Hispanic

Top 10 Places Sorted by Population
Based on all places, regardless of total population

Place	Population	%
Nanticoke (city) Luzerne County	84	0.80

Curtin (township) Centre County	56	8.95
Franklin (city) Venango County	26	0.39
Manchester (borough) York County	14	0.52
New Brighton (borough) Beaver County	13	0.21
Bethlehem (city) Northampton County	12	0.02
Bethlehem (city) Northampton County	12	0.02
DuBois (city) Clearfield County	10	0.13
Putnam (township) Tioga County	9	1.69
Greenville (borough) Mercer County	8	0.13

Top 10 Places Sorted by Percent of Total Population
Based on all places, regardless of total population

Place	Population	%
Curtin (township) Centre County	56	8.95
Putnam (township) Tioga County	9	1.69
Nanticoke (city) Luzerne County	84	0.80
Triumph (township) Warren County	2	0.68
Manchester (borough) York County	14	0.52
Avondale (borough) Chester County	6	0.42
Franklin (city) Venango County	26	0.39
Harrison (township) Bedford County	3	0.35
Terry (township) Bradford County	3	0.34
New Brighton (borough) Beaver County	13	0.21

Top 10 Places Sorted by Percent of Total Population
Based on places with total population of 50,000 or more

Place	Population	%
Bethlehem (city) Northampton County	12	0.02
Bethlehem (city) Northampton County	12	0.02
Abington (township) Montgomery County	0	0.00
Allentown (city) Lehigh County	0	0.00
Bensalem (township) Bucks County	0	0.00
Bristol (township) Bucks County	0	0.00
Erie (city) Erie County	0	0.00
Lancaster (city) Lancaster County	0	0.00
Levittown (cdp) Bucks County	0	0.00
Lower Merion (township) Montgomery County	0	0.00

West Indian: Haitian, excluding Hispanic

Top 10 Places Sorted by Population
Based on all places, regardless of total population

Place	Population	%
Philadelphia (city) Philadelphia County	9,026	0.60
Upper Darby (township) Delaware County	698	0.85
York (city) York County	560	1.28
Reading (city) Berks County	451	0.52
Lansdowne (borough) Delaware County	402	3.77
Spring (township) Berks County	356	1.33
New Holland (borough) Lancaster County	343	6.42
Middle Smithfield (township) Monroe County	335	2.15
Wilkes-Barre (city) Luzerne County	335	0.81
Pittsburgh (city) Allegheny County	285	0.09

Top 10 Places Sorted by Percent of Total Population
Based on all places, regardless of total population

Place	Population	%
Yatesville (borough) Luzerne County	48	6.92
East Lansdowne (borough) Delaware County	170	6.43
New Holland (borough) Lancaster County	343	6.42
Reiffton (cdp) Berks County	211	5.20
Jefferson (township) Berks County	100	4.95
Arcadia University (cdp) Montgomery County	29	3.81
Lansdowne (borough) Delaware County	402	3.77
Lincoln University (cdp) Chester County	68	3.52
Millbourne (borough) Delaware County	37	3.52
Womelsdorf (borough) Berks County	97	3.47

Top 10 Places Sorted by Percent of Total Population
Based on places with total population of 50,000 or more

Place	Population	%
Upper Darby (township) Delaware County	698	0.85
Philadelphia (city) Philadelphia County	9,026	0.60
Reading (city) Berks County	451	0.52
Bristol (township) Bucks County	206	0.37
Lancaster (city) Lancaster County	187	0.32
Lower Merion (township) Montgomery County	146	0.25
Bethlehem (city) Northampton County	134	0.24
Allentown (city) Lehigh County	265	0.23
Erie (city) Erie County	211	0.21
Abington (township) Montgomery County	119	0.21

West Indian: Jamaican, excluding Hispanic

Top 10 Places Sorted by Population
Based on all places, regardless of total population

Place	Population	%
Philadelphia (city) Philadelphia County	10,082	0.67
Upper Darby (township) Delaware County	762	0.93
Allentown (city) Lehigh County	724	0.62
Cheltenham (township) Montgomery County	713	1.94
Reading (city) Berks County	575	0.66
Yeadon (borough) Delaware County	571	4.98
Pittsburgh (city) Allegheny County	480	0.16
Norristown (borough) Montgomery County	442	1.31
Stroud (township) Monroe County	418	2.23
Harrisburg (city) Dauphin County	321	0.65

Top 10 Places Sorted by Percent of Total Population
Based on all places, regardless of total population

Place	Population	%
Albrightsville (cdp) Carbon County	54	27.69
East Lansdowne (borough) Delaware County	146	5.52
Yeadon (borough) Delaware County	571	4.98
Penn Estates (cdp) Monroe County	165	3.93
Kidder (township) Carbon County	65	3.56
Mount Penn (borough) Berks County	90	2.89
Clifton Heights (borough) Delaware County	192	2.88
Mount Pocono (borough) Monroe County	83	2.62
Gregg (township) Union County	117	2.29
Shrewsbury (township) York County	143	2.24

Top 10 Places Sorted by Percent of Total Population
Based on places with total population of 50,000 or more

Place	Population	%
Upper Darby (township) Delaware County	762	0.93
Philadelphia (city) Philadelphia County	10,082	0.67
Reading (city) Berks County	575	0.66
Allentown (city) Lehigh County	724	0.62
Abington (township) Montgomery County	264	0.48
Lower Merion (township) Montgomery County	154	0.27
Bethlehem (city) Northampton County	142	0.26
Bethlehem (city) Northampton County	154	0.21
Pittsburgh (city) Allegheny County	480	0.16
Lancaster (city) Lancaster County	78	0.13

West Indian: Trinidadian and Tobagonian, excluding Hispanic

Top 10 Places Sorted by Population
Based on all places, regardless of total population

Place	Population	%
Philadelphia (city) Philadelphia County	2,407	0.16
Upper Darby (township) Delaware County	411	0.50
Easton (city) Northampton County	237	0.88
Monaca (borough) Beaver County	130	2.24
Reading (city) Berks County	129	0.15
Pittsburgh (city) Allegheny County	123	0.04
Hamilton (township) Monroe County	110	1.20
Skippack (township) Montgomery County	96	0.74
Linglestown (cdp) Dauphin County	91	1.33
Lower Paxton (township) Dauphin County	91	0.19

Top 10 Places Sorted by Percent of Total Population
Based on all places, regardless of total population

Place	Population	%
Monaca (borough) Beaver County	130	2.24
Old Orchard (cdp) Northampton County	48	1.91
Linglestown (cdp) Dauphin County	91	1.33
Hamilton (township) Monroe County	110	1.20
Dean (township) Cambria County	4	1.15
Marcus Hook (borough) Delaware County	26	1.13
Wayne (township) Clinton County	17	1.00
Colwyn (borough) Delaware County	23	0.92
Easton (city) Northampton County	237	0.88
Lincoln University (cdp) Chester County	17	0.88

Top 10 Places Sorted by Percent of Total Population
Based on places with total population of 50,000 or more

Place	Population	%
Upper Darby (township) Delaware County	411	0.50

Philadelphia (city) Philadelphia County	2,407	0.16
Reading (city) Berks County	129	0.15
Abington (township) Montgomery County	74	0.13
Lower Merion (township) Montgomery County	39	0.07
Millcreek (township) Erie County	39	0.07
Allentown (city) Lehigh County	67	0.06
Pittsburgh (city) Allegheny County	123	0.04
Bethlehem (city) Northampton County	29	0.04
Scranton (city) Lackawanna County	26	0.03

West Indian: U.S. Virgin Islander, excluding Hispanic

Top 10 Places Sorted by Population
Based on all places, regardless of total population

Place	Population	%
Reading (city) Berks County	289	0.33
Polk (township) Monroe County	225	2.86
Philadelphia (city) Philadelphia County	100	0.01
Upper Darby (township) Delaware County	59	0.07
East Lansdowne (borough) Delaware County	41	1.55
Glenolden (borough) Delaware County	18	0.25
Horsham (cdp) Montgomery County	18	0.12
Horsham (township) Montgomery County	18	0.07
Bensalem (township) Bucks County	17	0.03
Wysox (township) Bradford County	14	0.80

Top 10 Places Sorted by Percent of Total Population
Based on all places, regardless of total population

Place	Population	%
Polk (township) Monroe County	225	2.86
East Lansdowne (borough) Delaware County	41	1.55
Wysox (township) Bradford County	14	0.80
Bessemer (borough) Lawrence County	6	0.51
Reading (city) Berks County	289	0.33
Glenolden (borough) Delaware County	18	0.25
Gregg (township) Union County	13	0.25
Stroudsburg (borough) Monroe County	14	0.24
Montrose (borough) Susquehanna County	3	0.13
Horsham (cdp) Montgomery County	18	0.12

Top 10 Places Sorted by Percent of Total Population
Based on places with total population of 50,000 or more

Place	Population	%
Reading (city) Berks County	289	0.33
Upper Darby (township) Delaware County	59	0.07
Bensalem (township) Bucks County	17	0.03
Philadelphia (city) Philadelphia County	100	0.01
Bethlehem (city) Northampton County	3	0.01
Bethlehem (city) Northampton County	3	<0.01
Abington (township) Montgomery County	0	0.00
Allentown (city) Lehigh County	0	0.00
Bristol (township) Bucks County	0	0.00
Erie (city) Erie County	0	0.00

West Indian: West Indian, excluding Hispanic

Top 10 Places Sorted by Population
Based on all places, regardless of total population

Place	Population	%
Philadelphia (city) Philadelphia County	2,445	0.16
Pittsburgh (city) Allegheny County	248	0.08
Allentown (city) Lehigh County	177	0.15
Coolbaugh (township) Monroe County	173	0.86
Abington (township) Montgomery County	144	0.26
Pocono (township) Monroe County	141	1.27
Whitehall (township) Lehigh County	137	0.52
Lower Paxton (township) Dauphin County	125	0.27
Buckingham (township) Bucks County	122	0.63
Harrisburg (city) Dauphin County	122	0.25

Top 10 Places Sorted by Percent of Total Population
Based on all places, regardless of total population

Place	Population	%
Crenshaw (cdp) Jefferson County	29	4.90
Fredericksburg (cdp) Lebanon County	62	4.87
Macungie (borough) Lehigh County	104	3.37
Cogan House (township) Lycoming County	23	2.29
Hokendauqua (cdp) Lehigh County	71	1.98
Hallam (borough) York County	42	1.69

Place	Population	%
North Annville (township) Lebanon County	40	1.55
Womelsdorf (borough) Berks County	38	1.36
Gibraltar (cdp) Berks County	8	1.35
Stowe (township) Allegheny County	85	1.33

Top 10 Places Sorted by Percent of Total Population
Based on places with total population of 50,000 or more

Place	Population	%
Abington (township) Montgomery County	144	0.26
Philadelphia (city) Philadelphia County	2,445	0.16
Allentown (city) Lehigh County	177	0.15
Bethlehem (city) Northampton County	84	0.11
Reading (city) Berks County	78	0.09
Pittsburgh (city) Allegheny County	248	0.08
Bethlehem (city) Northampton County	44	0.08
Scranton (city) Lackawanna County	44	0.06
Lancaster (city) Lancaster County	24	0.04
Erie (city) Erie County	35	0.03

West Indian: Other, excluding Hispanic

Top 10 Places Sorted by Population
Based on all places, regardless of total population

Place	Population	%
Philadelphia (city) Philadelphia County	36	<0.01
Cheltenham (township) Montgomery County	26	0.07
Upper Merion (township) Montgomery County	15	0.05
Phoenixville (borough) Chester County	9	0.06
Springettsbury (township) York County	9	0.03
Aaronsburg (cdp) Centre County	0	0.00
Aaronsburg (cdp) Washington County	0	0.00
Abbott (township) Potter County	0	0.00
Abbottstown (borough) Adams County	0	0.00
Abington (township) Lackawanna County	0	0.00

Top 10 Places Sorted by Percent of Total Population
Based on all places, regardless of total population

Place	Population	%
Cheltenham (township) Montgomery County	26	0.07
Phoenixville (borough) Chester County	9	0.06
Upper Merion (township) Montgomery County	15	0.05
Springettsbury (township) York County	9	0.03
Philadelphia (city) Philadelphia County	36	<0.01
Aaronsburg (cdp) Centre County	0	0.00
Aaronsburg (cdp) Washington County	0	0.00
Abbott (township) Potter County	0	0.00
Abbottstown (borough) Adams County	0	0.00
Abington (township) Lackawanna County	0	0.00

Top 10 Places Sorted by Percent of Total Population
Based on places with total population of 50,000 or more

Place	Population	%
Philadelphia (city) Philadelphia County	36	<0.01
Abington (township) Montgomery County	0	0.00
Allentown (city) Lehigh County	0	0.00
Bensalem (township) Bucks County	0	0.00
Bethlehem (city) Northampton County	0	0.00
Bethlehem (city) Northampton County	0	0.00
Bristol (township) Bucks County	0	0.00
Erie (city) Erie County	0	0.00
Lancaster (city) Lancaster County	0	0.00
Levittown (cdp) Bucks County	0	0.00

Yugoslavian

Top 10 Places Sorted by Population
Based on all places, regardless of total population

Place	Population	%
Erie (city) Erie County	697	0.69
Philadelphia (city) Philadelphia County	406	0.03
Emmaus (borough) Lehigh County	384	3.41
Lower Paxton (township) Dauphin County	371	0.79
Whitehall (borough) Allegheny County	272	1.95
North Middleton (township) Cumberland County	237	2.17
Schlusser (cdp) Cumberland County	205	3.93
East Pennsboro (township) Cumberland County	201	1.01
Lower Allen (township) Cumberland County	174	0.97
Carlisle (borough) Cumberland County	162	0.87

Top 10 Places Sorted by Percent of Total Population
Based on all places, regardless of total population

Place	Population	%
Commodore (cdp) Indiana County	56	31.64
Eagleville (cdp) Centre County	31	13.03
Mapletown (cdp) Greene County	10	8.62
West Middletown (borough) Washington County	6	4.84
Haysville (borough) Allegheny County	3	4.00
Schlusser (cdp) Cumberland County	205	3.93
Spring Creek (township) Elk County	4	3.42
Emmaus (borough) Lehigh County	384	3.41
Arnot (cdp) Tioga County	11	3.38
Bulger (cdp) Washington County	15	3.08

Top 10 Places Sorted by Percent of Total Population
Based on places with total population of 50,000 or more

Place	Population	%
Erie (city) Erie County	697	0.69
Millcreek (township) Erie County	140	0.26
Bensalem (township) Bucks County	71	0.12
Lancaster (city) Lancaster County	70	0.12
Lower Merion (township) Montgomery County	67	0.12
Bethlehem (city) Northampton County	55	0.10
Reading (city) Berks County	68	0.08
Bethlehem (city) Northampton County	63	0.08
Levittown (cdp) Bucks County	40	0.08
Upper Darby (township) Delaware County	55	0.07

Hispanic Origin Rankings

Hispanic or Latino (of any race)

Top 10 Places Sorted by Population
Based on all places, regardless of total population

Place	Population	%
Philadelphia (city) Philadelphia County	187,611	12.29
Reading (city) Berks County	51,230	58.16
Allentown (city) Lehigh County	50,461	42.75
Lancaster (city) Lancaster County	23,329	39.33
Bethlehem (city) Northampton County	18,268	24.36
Bethlehem (city) Northampton County	15,296	27.49
York (city) York County	12,458	28.50
Norristown (borough) Montgomery County	9,714	28.30
Hazleton (city) Luzerne County	9,454	37.31
Harrisburg (city) Dauphin County	8,939	18.05

Top 10 Places Sorted by Percent of Total Population
Based on all places, regardless of total population

Place	Population	%
Avondale (borough) Chester County	746	58.97
Reading (city) Berks County	51,230	58.16
Toughkenamon (cdp) Chester County	865	57.98
Kennett Square (borough) Chester County	2,963	48.80
York Springs (borough) Adams County	384	46.10
Allentown (city) Lehigh County	50,461	42.75
Lancaster (city) Lancaster County	23,329	39.33
Hazleton (city) Luzerne County	9,454	37.31
West Hazleton (borough) Luzerne County	1,624	35.35
West Grove (borough) Chester County	1,005	35.21

Top 10 Places Sorted by Percent of Total Population
Based on places with total population of 50,000 or more

Place	Population	%
Reading (city) Berks County	51,230	58.16
Allentown (city) Lehigh County	50,461	42.75
Lancaster (city) Lancaster County	23,329	39.33
Bethlehem (city) Northampton County	15,296	27.49
Bethlehem (city) Northampton County	18,268	24.36
Philadelphia (city) Philadelphia County	187,611	12.29
Scranton (city) Lackawanna County	7,531	9.90
Bensalem (township) Bucks County	5,091	8.43
Bristol (township) Bucks County	4,040	7.40
Erie (city) Erie County	7,005	6.88

Central American, excluding Mexican

Top 10 Places Sorted by Population
Based on all places, regardless of total population

Place	Population	%
Philadelphia (city) Philadelphia County	7,511	0.49
Allentown (city) Lehigh County	1,911	1.62
Reading (city) Berks County	1,436	1.63
Chambersburg (borough) Franklin County	821	4.05
Bethlehem (city) Northampton County	643	0.86
Easton (city) Northampton County	562	2.10
Bensalem (township) Bucks County	539	0.89
Bethlehem (city) Northampton County	534	0.96
Upper Darby (township) Delaware County	502	0.61
Pittsburgh (city) Allegheny County	500	0.16

Top 10 Places Sorted by Percent of Total Population
Based on all places, regardless of total population

Place	Population	%
Warminster Heights (cdp) Bucks County	263	6.38
Mifflintown (borough) Juniata County	56	5.98
Souderton (borough) Montgomery County	303	4.58
Laceyville (borough) Wyoming County	16	4.22
Chambersburg (borough) Franklin County	821	4.05
Telford (borough) Montgomery County	85	3.19
Haysville (borough) Allegheny County	2	2.86
Dublin (borough) Bucks County	59	2.73
Phoenixville (borough) Chester County	425	2.59
Mifflin (borough) Juniata County	16	2.49

Top 10 Places Sorted by Percent of Total Population
Based on places with total population of 50,000 or more

Place	Population	%
Reading (city) Berks County	1,436	1.63
Allentown (city) Lehigh County	1,911	1.62
Bethlehem (city) Northampton County	534	0.96
Bensalem (township) Bucks County	539	0.89
Bethlehem (city) Northampton County	643	0.86
Lancaster (city) Lancaster County	405	0.68
Upper Darby (township) Delaware County	502	0.61
Bristol (township) Bucks County	335	0.61
Scranton (city) Lackawanna County	448	0.59
Philadelphia (city) Philadelphia County	7,511	0.49

Central American: Costa Rican

Top 10 Places Sorted by Population
Based on all places, regardless of total population

Place	Population	%
Philadelphia (city) Philadelphia County	903	0.06
Bristol (township) Bucks County	113	0.21
Morrisville (borough) Bucks County	92	1.05
Bensalem (township) Bucks County	74	0.12
Levittown (cdp) Bucks County	70	0.13
Allentown (city) Lehigh County	65	0.06
Falls (township) Bucks County	52	0.15
Pittsburgh (city) Allegheny County	47	0.02
Easton (city) Northampton County	40	0.15
Upper Darby (township) Delaware County	33	0.04

Top 10 Places Sorted by Percent of Total Population
Based on all places, regardless of total population

Place	Population	%
Sweden Valley (cdp) Potter County	3	1.35
Morrisville (borough) Bucks County	92	1.05
Chewton (cdp) Lawrence County	4	0.82
Sweden (township) Potter County	7	0.80
Bird-in-Hand (cdp) Lancaster County	3	0.75
Thornburg (borough) Allegheny County	3	0.66
Shrewsbury (township) Sullivan County	2	0.63
Cross Roads (borough) York County	3	0.59
Forks (township) Sullivan County	2	0.53
Utica (borough) Venango County	1	0.53

Top 10 Places Sorted by Percent of Total Population
Based on places with total population of 50,000 or more

Place	Population	%
Bristol (township) Bucks County	113	0.21
Levittown (cdp) Bucks County	70	0.13
Bensalem (township) Bucks County	74	0.12
Philadelphia (city) Philadelphia County	903	0.06
Allentown (city) Lehigh County	65	0.06
Upper Darby (township) Delaware County	33	0.04
Bethlehem (city) Northampton County	27	0.04
Abington (township) Montgomery County	21	0.04
Erie (city) Erie County	29	0.03
Lancaster (city) Lancaster County	20	0.03

Central American: Guatemalan

Top 10 Places Sorted by Population
Based on all places, regardless of total population

Place	Population	%
Philadelphia (city) Philadelphia County	2,262	0.15
Chambersburg (borough) Franklin County	621	3.06
Allentown (city) Lehigh County	420	0.36
Reading (city) Berks County	402	0.46
Phoenixville (borough) Chester County	355	2.16
Bethlehem (city) Northampton County	275	0.37
Bensalem (township) Bucks County	272	0.45
Bethlehem (city) Northampton County	240	0.43
Upper Darby (township) Delaware County	220	0.27
Pittsburgh (city) Allegheny County	186	0.06

Top 10 Places Sorted by Percent of Total Population
Based on all places, regardless of total population

Place	Population	%
Chambersburg (borough) Franklin County	621	3.06
Phoenixville (borough) Chester County	355	2.16
Table Rock (cdp) Adams County	1	1.60
Millbourne (borough) Delaware County	18	1.55
Warminster Heights (cdp) Bucks County	54	1.31
Gratz (borough) Dauphin County	9	1.18
Dublin (borough) Bucks County	25	1.10
Birmingham (borough) Huntingdon County	1	1.11
Avondale (borough) Chester County	12	0.98
Marion (cdp) Franklin County	8	0.84

Top 10 Places Sorted by Percent of Total Population
Based on places with total population of 50,000 or more

Place	Population	%
Reading (city) Berks County	402	0.46
Bensalem (township) Bucks County	272	0.45
Bethlehem (city) Northampton County	240	0.43
Bethlehem (city) Northampton County	275	0.37
Allentown (city) Lehigh County	420	0.36
Upper Darby (township) Delaware County	220	0.27
Bristol (township) Bucks County	108	0.20
Lancaster (city) Lancaster County	103	0.17
Philadelphia (city) Philadelphia County	2,262	0.15
Levittown (cdp) Bucks County	82	0.15

Central American: Honduran

Top 10 Places Sorted by Population
Based on all places, regardless of total population

Place	Population	%
Philadelphia (city) Philadelphia County	1,642	0.11
Allentown (city) Lehigh County	749	0.63
Reading (city) Berks County	270	0.31
Scranton (city) Lackawanna County	268	0.35
Upper Darby (township) Delaware County	143	0.17
Norristown (borough) Montgomery County	126	0.37
Souderton (borough) Montgomery County	123	1.86
Easton (city) Northampton County	104	0.39
Lancaster (city) Lancaster County	94	0.16
Bethlehem (city) Northampton County	90	0.12

Top 10 Places Sorted by Percent of Total Population
Based on all places, regardless of total population

Place	Population	%
Laceyville (borough) Wyoming County	11	2.90
Souderton (borough) Montgomery County	123	1.86
Telford (borough) Montgomery County	42	1.58
Mifflin (borough) Juniata County	9	1.40
Weissport (borough) Carbon County	5	1.21
McVeytown (borough) Mifflin County	4	1.17
Telford (borough) Montgomery County	54	1.11
York Springs (borough) Adams County	8	0.96
Dublin (borough) Bucks County	20	0.93
Yorkana (borough) York County	2	0.87

Top 10 Places Sorted by Percent of Total Population
Based on places with total population of 50,000 or more

Place	Population	%
Allentown (city) Lehigh County	749	0.63
Scranton (city) Lackawanna County	268	0.35
Reading (city) Berks County	270	0.31
Upper Darby (township) Delaware County	143	0.17
Lancaster (city) Lancaster County	94	0.16
Bensalem (township) Bucks County	77	0.13
Bethlehem (city) Northampton County	75	0.13
Bethlehem (city) Northampton County	90	0.12
Philadelphia (city) Philadelphia County	1,642	0.11
Lower Merion (township) Montgomery County	30	0.05

Please refer to the Explanation of Data in the front of the book for more detailed information.

Central American: Nicaraguan

Top 10 Places Sorted by Population
Based on all places, regardless of total population

Place	Population	%
Philadelphia (city) Philadelphia County	874	0.06
Allentown (city) Lehigh County	89	0.08
Bethlehem (city) Northampton County	86	0.11
Bethlehem (city) Northampton County	72	0.13
Reading (city) Berks County	62	0.07
Easton (city) Northampton County	38	0.14
Pittsburgh (city) Allegheny County	36	0.01
Coolbaugh (township) Monroe County	28	0.14
Lower Merion (township) Montgomery County	26	0.04
Lebanon (city) Lebanon County	25	0.10

Top 10 Places Sorted by Percent of Total Population
Based on all places, regardless of total population

Place	Population	%
Birmingham (borough) Huntingdon County	1	1.11
Patterson Heights (borough) Beaver County	6	0.94
Pennwyn (cdp) Berks County	3	0.38
West Lebanon (township) Lebanon County	3	0.38
Eldred (borough) McKean County	3	0.36
Freemansburg (borough) Northampton County	9	0.34
Leetsdale (borough) Allegheny County	4	0.33
Abington (township) Lackawanna County	5	0.29
Morrisdale (cdp) Clearfield County	2	0.27
Pocono Woodland Lakes (cdp) Pike County	8	0.25

Top 10 Places Sorted by Percent of Total Population
Based on places with total population of 50,000 or more

Place	Population	%
Bethlehem (city) Northampton County	72	0.13
Bethlehem (city) Northampton County	86	0.11
Allentown (city) Lehigh County	89	0.08
Reading (city) Berks County	62	0.07
Philadelphia (city) Philadelphia County	874	0.06
Lower Merion (township) Montgomery County	26	0.04
Bensalem (township) Bucks County	22	0.04
Bristol (township) Bucks County	20	0.04
Abington (township) Montgomery County	17	0.03
Lancaster (city) Lancaster County	15	0.03

Central American: Panamanian

Top 10 Places Sorted by Population
Based on all places, regardless of total population

Place	Population	%
Philadelphia (city) Philadelphia County	737	0.05
Allentown (city) Lehigh County	143	0.12
Pittsburgh (city) Allegheny County	81	0.03
Coolbaugh (township) Monroe County	75	0.36
Stroud (township) Monroe County	48	0.25
Bethlehem (city) Northampton County	46	0.06
Bethlehem (city) Northampton County	42	0.08
Reading (city) Berks County	40	0.05
Lehman (township) Pike County	37	0.35
York (city) York County	37	0.08

Top 10 Places Sorted by Percent of Total Population
Based on all places, regardless of total population

Place	Population	%
Haysville (borough) Allegheny County	2	2.86
Newton Hamilton (borough) Mifflin County	3	1.46
Cedar Crest (cdp) Mifflin County	2	1.03
Seltzer (cdp) Schuylkill County	3	0.86
Reed (township) Dauphin County	2	0.84
Strong (cdp) Northumberland County	1	0.68
Saw Creek (cdp) Pike County	23	0.57
Courtdale (borough) Luzerne County	4	0.55
West Sunbury (borough) Butler County	1	0.52
Penn Estates (cdp) Monroe County	23	0.51

Top 10 Places Sorted by Percent of Total Population
Based on places with total population of 50,000 or more

Place	Population	%
Allentown (city) Lehigh County	143	0.12
Bethlehem (city) Northampton County	42	0.08
Bethlehem (city) Northampton County	46	0.06
Lower Merion (township) Montgomery County	34	0.06

Place	Population	%
Philadelphia (city) Philadelphia County	737	0.05
Reading (city) Berks County	40	0.05
Lancaster (city) Lancaster County	25	0.04
Pittsburgh (city) Allegheny County	81	0.03
Abington (township) Montgomery County	18	0.03
Upper Darby (township) Delaware County	20	0.02

Central American: Salvadoran

Top 10 Places Sorted by Population
Based on all places, regardless of total population

Place	Population	%
Philadelphia (city) Philadelphia County	1,049	0.07
Reading (city) Berks County	637	0.72
Allentown (city) Lehigh County	440	0.37
Warminster (township) Bucks County	218	0.67
Easton (city) Northampton County	177	0.66
Warminster Heights (cdp) Bucks County	166	4.03
Lancaster (city) Lancaster County	143	0.24
York (city) York County	131	0.30
Chambersburg (borough) Franklin County	126	0.62
Souderton (borough) Montgomery County	122	1.84

Top 10 Places Sorted by Percent of Total Population
Based on all places, regardless of total population

Place	Population	%
Mifflintown (borough) Juniata County	52	5.56
Warminster Heights (cdp) Bucks County	166	4.03
Meshoppen (borough) Wyoming County	12	2.13
Souderton (borough) Montgomery County	122	1.84
Buckhorn (cdp) Columbia County	5	1.57
Witmer (cdp) Lancaster County	7	1.42
Laceyville (borough) Wyoming County	5	1.32
Telford (borough) Montgomery County	31	1.16
South Temple (cdp) Berks County	16	1.12
Goldsboro (borough) York County	10	1.05

Top 10 Places Sorted by Percent of Total Population
Based on places with total population of 50,000 or more

Place	Population	%
Reading (city) Berks County	637	0.72
Allentown (city) Lehigh County	440	0.37
Lancaster (city) Lancaster County	143	0.24
Bethlehem (city) Northampton County	116	0.15
Bethlehem (city) Northampton County	84	0.15
Scranton (city) Lackawanna County	100	0.13
Bensalem (township) Bucks County	79	0.13
Bristol (township) Bucks County	59	0.11
Erie (city) Erie County	82	0.08
Abington (township) Montgomery County	43	0.08

Central American: Other Central American

Top 10 Places Sorted by Population
Based on all places, regardless of total population

Place	Population	%
Philadelphia (city) Philadelphia County	44	<0.01
Upper Darby (township) Delaware County	22	0.03
Fullerton (cdp) Lehigh County	12	0.08
Whitehall (township) Lehigh County	12	0.04
Abington (township) Montgomery County	11	0.02
Spring (township) Berks County	9	0.03
York (city) York County	9	0.02
Coolbaugh (township) Monroe County	8	0.04
Reading (city) Berks County	8	0.01
Dublin (borough) Bucks County	7	0.32

Top 10 Places Sorted by Percent of Total Population
Based on all places, regardless of total population

Place	Population	%
Stonerstown (cdp) Bedford County	4	1.06
North Abington (township) Lackawanna County	3	0.43
Dublin (borough) Bucks County	7	0.32
Liberty (township) Bedford County	4	0.29
Pocono Ranch Lands (cdp) Pike County	3	0.28
Spring Brook (township) Lackawanna County	6	0.22
Port Carbon (borough) Schuylkill County	3	0.16
Telford (borough) Bucks County	3	0.14
Milford (township) Pike County	2	0.13
Lewisburg (borough) Union County	7	0.12

Top 10 Places Sorted by Percent of Total Population
Based on places with total population of 50,000 or more

Place	Population	%
Upper Darby (township) Delaware County	22	0.03
Abington (township) Montgomery County	11	0.02
Reading (city) Berks County	8	0.01
Bristol (township) Bucks County	5	0.01
Lancaster (city) Lancaster County	5	0.01
Scranton (city) Lackawanna County	5	0.01
Bethlehem (city) Northampton County	3	0.01
Philadelphia (city) Philadelphia County	44	<0.01
Allentown (city) Lehigh County	5	<0.01
Bethlehem (city) Northampton County	3	<0.01

Cuban

Top 10 Places Sorted by Population
Based on all places, regardless of total population

Place	Population	%
Philadelphia (city) Philadelphia County	3,930	0.26
Lancaster (city) Lancaster County	994	1.68
Allentown (city) Lehigh County	458	0.39
Pittsburgh (city) Allegheny County	397	0.13
Reading (city) Berks County	360	0.41
Harrisburg (city) Dauphin County	219	0.44
Bethlehem (city) Northampton County	196	0.26
York (city) York County	178	0.41
Bethlehem (city) Northampton County	163	0.29
Lower Merion (township) Montgomery County	156	0.27

Top 10 Places Sorted by Percent of Total Population
Based on all places, regardless of total population

Place	Population	%
Lancaster (city) Lancaster County	994	1.68
Conashaugh Lakes (cdp) Pike County	20	1.55
McKnightstown (cdp) Adams County	3	1.33
Decatur (township) Clearfield County	55	1.21
Schellsburg (borough) Bedford County	4	1.18
Oakland (borough) Susquehanna County	7	1.14
Pocono Mountain Lake Estates (cdp) Pike County	9	1.07
Brooklyn (township) Susquehanna County	10	1.04
Lehman (township) Pike County	110	1.03
Pine Ridge (cdp) Pike County	28	1.03

Top 10 Places Sorted by Percent of Total Population
Based on places with total population of 50,000 or more

Place	Population	%
Lancaster (city) Lancaster County	994	1.68
Reading (city) Berks County	360	0.41
Allentown (city) Lehigh County	458	0.39
Bethlehem (city) Northampton County	163	0.29
Lower Merion (township) Montgomery County	156	0.27
Philadelphia (city) Philadelphia County	3,930	0.26
Bethlehem (city) Northampton County	196	0.26
Abington (township) Montgomery County	111	0.20
Scranton (city) Lackawanna County	125	0.16
Levittown (cdp) Bucks County	84	0.16

Dominican Republic

Top 10 Places Sorted by Population
Based on all places, regardless of total population

Place	Population	%
Philadelphia (city) Philadelphia County	15,963	1.05
Allentown (city) Lehigh County	9,340	7.91
Reading (city) Berks County	8,716	9.90
Hazleton (city) Luzerne County	5,327	21.02
Lancaster (city) Lancaster County	1,905	3.21
York (city) York County	1,212	2.77
Bethlehem (city) Northampton County	1,010	1.35
West Hazleton (borough) Luzerne County	939	20.44
Bethlehem (city) Northampton County	783	1.41
Lebanon (city) Lebanon County	778	3.05

Top 10 Places Sorted by Percent of Total Population
Based on all places, regardless of total population

Place	Population	%
Hazleton (city) Luzerne County	5,327	21.02
West Hazleton (borough) Luzerne County	939	20.44
Reading (city) Berks County	8,716	9.90

Place	Population	%
Allentown (city) Lehigh County	9,340	7.91
Decatur (township) Clearfield County	354	7.78
Hazle (township) Luzerne County	430	4.50
Hyde Park (cdp) Berks County	90	3.56
Lancaster (city) Lancaster County	1,905	3.21
Lebanon (city) Lebanon County	778	3.05
Fullerton (cdp) Lehigh County	441	2.95

Top 10 Places Sorted by Percent of Total Population
Based on places with total population of 50,000 or more

Place	Population	%
Reading (city) Berks County	8,716	9.90
Allentown (city) Lehigh County	9,340	7.91
Lancaster (city) Lancaster County	1,905	3.21
Bethlehem (city) Northampton County	783	1.41
Bethlehem (city) Northampton County	1,010	1.35
Philadelphia (city) Philadelphia County	15,963	1.05
Scranton (city) Lackawanna County	605	0.80
Bristol (township) Bucks County	121	0.22
Levittown (cdp) Bucks County	88	0.17
Upper Darby (township) Delaware County	133	0.16

Mexican

Top 10 Places Sorted by Population
Based on all places, regardless of total population

Place	Population	%
Philadelphia (city) Philadelphia County	15,531	1.02
Reading (city) Berks County	8,602	9.77
Norristown (borough) Montgomery County	7,578	22.08
New Garden (township) Chester County	2,791	23.29
Kennett Square (borough) Chester County	2,634	43.38
Allentown (city) Lehigh County	2,448	2.07
Pittsburgh (city) Allegheny County	2,292	0.75
Wilkes-Barre (city) Luzerne County	1,995	4.81
Scranton (city) Lackawanna County	1,945	2.56
Bensalem (township) Bucks County	1,879	3.11

Top 10 Places Sorted by Percent of Total Population
Based on all places, regardless of total population

Place	Population	%
Toughkenamon (cdp) Chester County	796	53.35
Avondale (borough) Chester County	674	53.28
Kennett Square (borough) Chester County	2,634	43.38
York Springs (borough) Adams County	341	40.94
West Grove (borough) Chester County	900	31.53
New Garden (township) Chester County	2,791	23.29
Norristown (borough) Montgomery County	7,578	22.08
Oxford (borough) Chester County	1,039	20.46
Aspers (cdp) Adams County	67	19.14
Flora Dale (cdp) Adams County	7	18.42

Top 10 Places Sorted by Percent of Total Population
Based on places with total population of 50,000 or more

Place	Population	%
Reading (city) Berks County	8,602	9.77
Bensalem (township) Bucks County	1,879	3.11
Scranton (city) Lackawanna County	1,945	2.56
Allentown (city) Lehigh County	2,448	2.07
Bristol (township) Bucks County	1,100	2.02
Lancaster (city) Lancaster County	1,046	1.76
Bethlehem (city) Northampton County	863	1.55
Bethlehem (city) Northampton County	1,085	1.45
Erie (city) Erie County	1,271	1.25
Levittown (cdp) Bucks County	589	1.11

Puerto Rican

Top 10 Places Sorted by Population
Based on all places, regardless of total population

Place	Population	%
Philadelphia (city) Philadelphia County	121,643	7.97
Allentown (city) Lehigh County	29,640	25.11
Reading (city) Berks County	28,160	31.97
Lancaster (city) Lancaster County	17,341	29.23
Bethlehem (city) Northampton County	13,722	18.30
Bethlehem (city) Northampton County	11,715	21.06
York (city) York County	8,440	19.31
Lebanon (city) Lebanon County	6,081	23.87
Harrisburg (city) Dauphin County	5,685	11.48
Erie (city) Erie County	4,752	4.67

Top 10 Places Sorted by Percent of Total Population
Based on all places, regardless of total population

Place	Population	%
Reading (city) Berks County	28,160	31.97
Lancaster (city) Lancaster County	17,341	29.23
Allentown (city) Lehigh County	29,640	25.11
Lebanon (city) Lebanon County	6,081	23.87
Bethlehem (city) Northampton County	11,715	21.06
York (city) York County	8,440	19.31
Bethlehem (city) Northampton County	13,722	18.30
Fountain Hill (borough) Lehigh County	739	16.08
Penn Estates (cdp) Monroe County	715	15.91
Freemansburg (borough) Northampton County	413	15.67

Top 10 Places Sorted by Percent of Total Population
Based on places with total population of 50,000 or more

Place	Population	%
Reading (city) Berks County	28,160	31.97
Lancaster (city) Lancaster County	17,341	29.23
Allentown (city) Lehigh County	29,640	25.11
Bethlehem (city) Northampton County	11,715	21.06
Bethlehem (city) Northampton County	13,722	18.30
Philadelphia (city) Philadelphia County	121,643	7.97
Erie (city) Erie County	4,752	4.67
Scranton (city) Lackawanna County	3,172	4.17
Bristol (township) Bucks County	1,873	3.43
Levittown (cdp) Bucks County	1,293	2.44

South American

Top 10 Places Sorted by Population
Based on all places, regardless of total population

Place	Population	%
Philadelphia (city) Philadelphia County	9,969	0.65
Allentown (city) Lehigh County	3,048	2.58
Reading (city) Berks County	1,240	1.41
Pittsburgh (city) Allegheny County	1,162	0.38
Upper Darby (township) Delaware County	1,080	1.30
Bethlehem (city) Northampton County	804	1.07
Bensalem (township) Bucks County	689	1.14
Bethlehem (city) Northampton County	628	1.13
Easton (city) Northampton County	575	2.15
Lancaster (city) Lancaster County	571	0.96

Top 10 Places Sorted by Percent of Total Population
Based on all places, regardless of total population

Place	Population	%
Decatur (township) Clearfield County	197	4.33
Penn Estates (cdp) Monroe County	169	3.76
Millbourne (borough) Delaware County	43	3.71
Freemansburg (borough) Northampton County	96	3.64
Saw Creek (cdp) Pike County	135	3.36
Emerald Lakes (cdp) Monroe County	82	2.84
Lehman (township) Pike County	296	2.78
Pine Ridge (cdp) Pike County	72	2.66
Allentown (city) Lehigh County	3,048	2.58
Albrightsville (cdp) Carbon County	5	2.48

Top 10 Places Sorted by Percent of Total Population
Based on places with total population of 50,000 or more

Place	Population	%
Allentown (city) Lehigh County	3,048	2.58
Reading (city) Berks County	1,240	1.41
Upper Darby (township) Delaware County	1,080	1.30
Bensalem (township) Bucks County	689	1.14
Bethlehem (city) Northampton County	628	1.13
Bethlehem (city) Northampton County	804	1.07
Lancaster (city) Lancaster County	571	0.96
Lower Merion (township) Montgomery County	446	0.77
Philadelphia (city) Philadelphia County	9,969	0.65
Scranton (city) Lackawanna County	466	0.61

South American: Argentinean

Top 10 Places Sorted by Population
Based on all places, regardless of total population

Place	Population	%
Philadelphia (city) Philadelphia County	1,006	0.07
Pittsburgh (city) Allegheny County	244	0.08
Lower Merion (township) Montgomery County	79	0.14
Allentown (city) Lehigh County	49	0.04
State College (borough) Centre County	47	0.11
Haverford (township) Delaware County	46	0.09
Abington (township) Montgomery County	42	0.08
Cheltenham (township) Montgomery County	39	0.11
Scranton (city) Lackawanna County	39	0.05
Bethlehem (city) Northampton County	37	0.05

Top 10 Places Sorted by Percent of Total Population
Based on all places, regardless of total population

Place	Population	%
Shiremanstown (borough) Cumberland County	14	0.89
Lemont Furnace (cdp) Fayette County	7	0.85
Wanamie (cdp) Luzerne County	5	0.82
Pocono Mountain Lake Estates (cdp) Pike County	6	0.71
Hyde Park (borough) Westmoreland County	3	0.60
Wiconisco (cdp) Dauphin County	5	0.54
Freemansburg (borough) Northampton County	14	0.53
Summit (township) Potter County	1	0.53
Plainfield (cdp) Cumberland County	2	0.50
Pomeroy (cdp) Chester County	2	0.50

Top 10 Places Sorted by Percent of Total Population
Based on places with total population of 50,000 or more

Place	Population	%
Lower Merion (township) Montgomery County	79	0.14
Pittsburgh (city) Allegheny County	244	0.08
Abington (township) Montgomery County	42	0.08
Philadelphia (city) Philadelphia County	1,006	0.07
Lancaster (city) Lancaster County	34	0.06
Bethlehem (city) Northampton County	32	0.06
Scranton (city) Lackawanna County	39	0.05
Bethlehem (city) Northampton County	37	0.05
Allentown (city) Lehigh County	49	0.04
Reading (city) Berks County	33	0.04

South American: Bolivian

Top 10 Places Sorted by Population
Based on all places, regardless of total population

Place	Population	%
Philadelphia (city) Philadelphia County	112	0.01
Pittsburgh (city) Allegheny County	29	0.01
Allentown (city) Lehigh County	20	0.02
Chambersburg (borough) Franklin County	17	0.08
Bethlehem (city) Northampton County	17	0.02
Bethlehem (city) Northampton County	16	0.03
East Fallowfield (township) Chester County	11	0.15
Haverford (township) Delaware County	11	0.02
Coolbaugh (township) Monroe County	10	0.05
Springettsbury (township) York County	10	0.04

Top 10 Places Sorted by Percent of Total Population
Based on all places, regardless of total population

Place	Population	%
Haverford College (cdp) Delaware County	8	0.60
Biglerville (borough) Adams County	4	0.33
Fayetteville (cdp) Franklin County	8	0.26
Bowmansville (cdp) Lancaster County	5	0.24
South Coatesville (borough) Chester County	3	0.23
Fawn Grove (borough) York County	1	0.22
Coalport (borough) Clearfield County	1	0.19
Quentin (cdp) Lebanon County	1	0.17
Waverly (cdp) Lackawanna County	1	0.17
Mohnton (borough) Berks County	5	0.16

Top 10 Places Sorted by Percent of Total Population
Based on places with total population of 50,000 or more

Place	Population	%
Bethlehem (city) Northampton County	16	0.03
Allentown (city) Lehigh County	20	0.02
Bethlehem (city) Northampton County	17	0.02
Lower Merion (township) Montgomery County	10	0.02
Philadelphia (city) Philadelphia County	112	0.01
Pittsburgh (city) Allegheny County	29	0.01
Scranton (city) Lackawanna County	8	0.01
Reading (city) Berks County	7	0.01
Upper Darby (township) Delaware County	7	0.01
Abington (township) Montgomery County	4	0.01

South American: Chilean

Top 10 Places Sorted by Population
Based on all places, regardless of total population

Place	Population	%
Philadelphia (city) Philadelphia County	357	0.02
Allentown (city) Lehigh County	259	0.22
Pittsburgh (city) Allegheny County	139	0.05
Bethlehem (city) Northampton County	79	0.11
Bethlehem (city) Northampton County	68	0.12
Lower Merion (township) Montgomery County	37	0.06
State College (borough) Centre County	35	0.08
Whitehall (township) Lehigh County	29	0.11
Tredyffrin (township) Chester County	25	0.09
Radnor (township) Delaware County	23	0.07

Top 10 Places Sorted by Percent of Total Population
Based on all places, regardless of total population

Place	Population	%
Baileyville (cdp) Centre County	3	1.49
Mifflintown (borough) Juniata County	8	0.85
Iola (cdp) Columbia County	1	0.69
Hopewell (township) Huntingdon County	4	0.68
Laurel Mountain (borough) Westmoreland County	1	0.60
Richfield (cdp) Juniata County	3	0.55
Cochranville (cdp) Chester County	3	0.45
Marianne (cdp) Clarion County	5	0.43
Port Royal (borough) Juniata County	4	0.43
Dreher (township) Wayne County	6	0.42

Top 10 Places Sorted by Percent of Total Population
Based on places with total population of 50,000 or more

Place	Population	%
Allentown (city) Lehigh County	259	0.22
Bethlehem (city) Northampton County	68	0.12
Bethlehem (city) Northampton County	79	0.11
Lower Merion (township) Montgomery County	37	0.06
Pittsburgh (city) Allegheny County	139	0.05
Philadelphia (city) Philadelphia County	357	0.02
Reading (city) Berks County	19	0.02
Lancaster (city) Lancaster County	14	0.02
Bristol (township) Bucks County	13	0.02
Levittown (cdp) Bucks County	12	0.02

South American: Colombian

Top 10 Places Sorted by Population
Based on all places, regardless of total population

Place	Population	%
Philadelphia (city) Philadelphia County	4,675	0.31
Allentown (city) Lehigh County	755	0.64
Reading (city) Berks County	612	0.69
Pittsburgh (city) Allegheny County	263	0.09
Easton (city) Northampton County	248	0.93
Bethlehem (city) Northampton County	240	0.32
Lancaster (city) Lancaster County	208	0.35
Bethlehem (city) Northampton County	198	0.36
Decatur (township) Clearfield County	166	3.65
Coolbaugh (township) Monroe County	151	0.73

Top 10 Places Sorted by Percent of Total Population
Based on all places, regardless of total population

Place	Population	%
Decatur (township) Clearfield County	166	3.65
Freemansburg (borough) Northampton County	40	1.52
Frystown (cdp) Berks County	5	1.32
Pine Ridge (cdp) Pike County	32	1.18
New Holland (borough) Lancaster County	63	1.17
Penn Estates (cdp) Monroe County	52	1.16
Wheatland (borough) Mercer County	7	1.11
Palmer Heights (cdp) Northampton County	41	1.09
Jeddo (borough) Luzerne County	1	1.02
Emerald Lakes (cdp) Monroe County	28	0.97

Top 10 Places Sorted by Percent of Total Population
Based on places with total population of 50,000 or more

Place	Population	%
Reading (city) Berks County	612	0.69
Allentown (city) Lehigh County	755	0.64
Bethlehem (city) Northampton County	198	0.36
Lancaster (city) Lancaster County	208	0.35

Bethlehem (city) Northampton County	240	0.32
Philadelphia (city) Philadelphia County	4,675	0.31
Bensalem (township) Bucks County	121	0.20
Lower Merion (township) Montgomery County	116	0.20
Abington (township) Montgomery County	100	0.18
Bristol (township) Bucks County	93	0.17

South American: Ecuadorian

Top 10 Places Sorted by Population
Based on all places, regardless of total population

Place	Population	%
Philadelphia (city) Philadelphia County	1,542	0.10
Allentown (city) Lehigh County	1,241	1.05
Upper Darby (township) Delaware County	783	0.95
Bensalem (township) Bucks County	416	0.69
Reading (city) Berks County	409	0.46
Bethlehem (city) Northampton County	200	0.27
Lancaster (city) Lancaster County	157	0.26
East Whiteland (township) Chester County	152	1.43
Stroud (township) Monroe County	145	0.75
Harrisburg (city) Dauphin County	144	0.29

Top 10 Places Sorted by Percent of Total Population
Based on all places, regardless of total population

Place	Population	%
Millbourne (borough) Delaware County	43	3.71
Cross Creek (cdp) Washington County	3	2.19
Schubert (cdp) Berks County	4	1.61
East Whiteland (township) Chester County	152	1.43
Penn Estates (cdp) Monroe County	64	1.42
Saw Creek (cdp) Pike County	56	1.39
Meshoppen (borough) Wyoming County	7	1.24
East Lansdowne (borough) Delaware County	32	1.20
Harleigh (cdp) Luzerne County	12	1.09
Allentown (city) Lehigh County	1,241	1.05

Top 10 Places Sorted by Percent of Total Population
Based on places with total population of 50,000 or more

Place	Population	%
Allentown (city) Lehigh County	1,241	1.05
Upper Darby (township) Delaware County	783	0.95
Bensalem (township) Bucks County	416	0.69
Reading (city) Berks County	409	0.46
Bethlehem (city) Northampton County	200	0.27
Lancaster (city) Lancaster County	157	0.26
Bethlehem (city) Northampton County	144	0.26
Scranton (city) Lackawanna County	125	0.16
Bristol (township) Bucks County	69	0.13
Philadelphia (city) Philadelphia County	1,542	0.10

South American: Paraguayan

Top 10 Places Sorted by Population
Based on all places, regardless of total population

Place	Population	%
Philadelphia (city) Philadelphia County	74	<0.01
Haverford (township) Delaware County	24	0.05
Upper Darby (township) Delaware County	20	0.02
Pittsburgh (city) Allegheny County	20	0.01
Lower Merion (township) Montgomery County	12	0.02
Perkiomen (township) Montgomery County	11	0.12
Delmar (township) Tioga County	10	0.35
Marple (township) Delaware County	9	0.04
Whitpain (township) Montgomery County	8	0.04
Hamilton (township) Franklin County	7	0.06

Top 10 Places Sorted by Percent of Total Population
Based on all places, regardless of total population

Place	Population	%
Morris (township) Tioga County	4	0.66
Bethany (borough) Wayne County	1	0.41
Delmar (township) Tioga County	10	0.35
Port Clinton (borough) Schuylkill County	1	0.31
North Abington (township) Lackawanna County	2	0.28
Arcadia University (cdp) Montgomery County	1	0.17
Matamoras (borough) Pike County	4	0.16
Windsor (township) Berks County	3	0.13
Chapman (township) Snyder County	2	0.13
Perkiomen (township) Montgomery County	11	0.12

Top 10 Places Sorted by Percent of Total Population
Based on places with total population of 50,000 or more

Place	Population	%
Upper Darby (township) Delaware County	20	0.02
Lower Merion (township) Montgomery County	12	0.02
Pittsburgh (city) Allegheny County	20	0.01
Reading (city) Berks County	6	0.01
Lancaster (city) Lancaster County	5	0.01
Scranton (city) Lackawanna County	4	0.01
Philadelphia (city) Philadelphia County	74	<0.01
Allentown (city) Lehigh County	3	<0.01
Bethlehem (city) Northampton County	3	<0.01
Bethlehem (city) Northampton County	2	<0.01

South American: Peruvian

Top 10 Places Sorted by Population
Based on all places, regardless of total population

Place	Population	%
Philadelphia (city) Philadelphia County	1,085	0.07
Allentown (city) Lehigh County	565	0.48
Pittsburgh (city) Allegheny County	211	0.07
Bethlehem (city) Northampton County	155	0.21
Easton (city) Northampton County	149	0.56
Coolbaugh (township) Monroe County	139	0.68
Bethlehem (city) Northampton County	113	0.20
Lancaster (city) Lancaster County	108	0.18
Scranton (city) Lackawanna County	98	0.13
Reading (city) Berks County	93	0.11

Top 10 Places Sorted by Percent of Total Population
Based on all places, regardless of total population

Place	Population	%
Bowers (cdp) Berks County	3	0.92
Sweden Valley (cdp) Potter County	2	0.90
Freemansburg (borough) Northampton County	19	0.72
Conashaugh Lakes (cdp) Pike County	9	0.70
Abbottstown (borough) Adams County	7	0.69
Coolbaugh (township) Monroe County	139	0.68
Penn Estates (cdp) Monroe County	30	0.67
Price (township) Monroe County	24	0.67
Saw Creek (cdp) Pike County	26	0.65
Pleasant Hill (cdp) Lebanon County	16	0.61

Top 10 Places Sorted by Percent of Total Population
Based on places with total population of 50,000 or more

Place	Population	%
Allentown (city) Lehigh County	565	0.48
Bethlehem (city) Northampton County	155	0.21
Bethlehem (city) Northampton County	113	0.20
Lancaster (city) Lancaster County	108	0.18
Scranton (city) Lackawanna County	98	0.13
Bensalem (township) Bucks County	80	0.13
Lower Merion (township) Montgomery County	76	0.13
Abington (township) Montgomery County	69	0.12
Reading (city) Berks County	93	0.11
Upper Darby (township) Delaware County	76	0.09

South American: Uruguayan

Top 10 Places Sorted by Population
Based on all places, regardless of total population

Place	Population	%
Philadelphia (city) Philadelphia County	234	0.02
Scranton (city) Lackawanna County	69	0.09
Allentown (city) Lehigh County	61	0.05
Old Forge (borough) Lackawanna County	43	0.52
Wilkes-Barre (city) Luzerne County	33	0.08
Hazleton (city) Luzerne County	24	0.09
Pittsburgh (city) Allegheny County	23	0.01
Bethlehem (city) Northampton County	22	0.03
Duryea (borough) Luzerne County	21	0.43
Easton (city) Northampton County	21	0.08

Top 10 Places Sorted by Percent of Total Population
Based on all places, regardless of total population

Place	Population	%
Albrightsville (cdp) Carbon County	5	2.48
Woxhall (cdp) Montgomery County	7	0.53
Old Forge (borough) Lackawanna County	43	0.52

Place	Population	%
Glenfield (borough) Allegheny County	1	0.49
Duryea (borough) Luzerne County	21	0.43
Emerald Lakes (cdp) Monroe County	10	0.35
Penn Estates (cdp) Monroe County	15	0.33
Muhlenberg Park (cdp) Berks County	4	0.28
Great Bend (township) Susquehanna County	5	0.26
Kidder (township) Carbon County	5	0.26

Top 10 Places Sorted by Percent of Total Population
Based on places with total population of 50,000 or more

Place	Population	%
Scranton (city) Lackawanna County	69	0.09
Allentown (city) Lehigh County	61	0.05
Bethlehem (city) Northampton County	22	0.03
Lower Merion (township) Montgomery County	16	0.03
Lancaster (city) Lancaster County	15	0.03
Philadelphia (city) Philadelphia County	234	0.02
Reading (city) Berks County	19	0.02
Bethlehem (city) Northampton County	12	0.02
Abington (township) Montgomery County	10	0.02
Pittsburgh (city) Allegheny County	23	0.01

South American: Venezuelan

Top 10 Places Sorted by Population
Based on all places, regardless of total population

Place	Population	%
Philadelphia (city) Philadelphia County	773	0.05
Pittsburgh (city) Allegheny County	142	0.05
Allentown (city) Lehigh County	75	0.06
Lower Merion (township) Montgomery County	60	0.10
Bethlehem (city) Northampton County	50	0.07
Upper Darby (township) Delaware County	46	0.06
Bethlehem (city) Northampton County	42	0.08
State College (borough) Centre County	40	0.10
Reading (city) Berks County	31	0.04
Coolbaugh (township) Monroe County	30	0.15

Top 10 Places Sorted by Percent of Total Population
Based on all places, regardless of total population

Place	Population	%
Brisbin (borough) Clearfield County	4	0.97
Wampum (borough) Lawrence County	5	0.70
Hickory Hills (cdp) Luzerne County	2	0.36
Shinglehouse (borough) Potter County	4	0.35
Tatamy (borough) Northampton County	4	0.33
Plumville (borough) Indiana County	1	0.33
Sierra View (cdp) Monroe County	15	0.31
Rehrersburg (cdp) Berks County	1	0.31
Beech Mountain Lakes (cdp) Luzerne County	6	0.30
Saw Creek (cdp) Pike County	11	0.27

Top 10 Places Sorted by Percent of Total Population
Based on places with total population of 50,000 or more

Place	Population	%
Lower Merion (township) Montgomery County	60	0.10
Bethlehem (city) Northampton County	42	0.08
Bethlehem (city) Northampton County	50	0.07
Allentown (city) Lehigh County	75	0.06
Upper Darby (township) Delaware County	46	0.06
Philadelphia (city) Philadelphia County	773	0.05
Pittsburgh (city) Allegheny County	142	0.05
Abington (township) Montgomery County	29	0.05
Reading (city) Berks County	31	0.04
Lancaster (city) Lancaster County	26	0.04

South American: Other South American

Top 10 Places Sorted by Population
Based on all places, regardless of total population

Place	Population	%
Philadelphia (city) Philadelphia County	111	0.01
Allentown (city) Lehigh County	20	0.02
Pittsburgh (city) Allegheny County	16	0.01
Lewisburg (borough) Union County	12	0.21
Coolbaugh (township) Monroe County	11	0.05
Reading (city) Berks County	11	0.01
Spring (township) Berks County	10	0.04
Whitehall (township) Lehigh County	10	0.04
Chestnuthill (township) Monroe County	9	0.05
Stroud (township) Monroe County	9	0.05

Top 10 Places Sorted by Percent of Total Population
Based on all places, regardless of total population

Place	Population	%
Lincoln Park (cdp) Berks County	8	0.50
Pocono Ranch Lands (cdp) Pike County	5	0.47
Hanover (township) Lehigh County	4	0.25
Marietta (borough) Lancaster County	6	0.23
Lewisburg (borough) Union County	12	0.21
Hokendauqua (cdp) Lehigh County	6	0.18
Covington (township) Lackawanna County	4	0.18
Hickory Hills (cdp) Luzerne County	1	0.18
Clark (borough) Mercer County	1	0.16
Caernarvon (township) Lancaster County	5	0.11

Top 10 Places Sorted by Percent of Total Population
Based on places with total population of 50,000 or more

Place	Population	%
Allentown (city) Lehigh County	20	0.02
Philadelphia (city) Philadelphia County	111	0.01
Pittsburgh (city) Allegheny County	16	0.01
Reading (city) Berks County	11	0.01
Bristol (township) Bucks County	7	0.01
Bensalem (township) Bucks County	6	0.01
Lower Merion (township) Montgomery County	6	0.01
Levittown (cdp) Bucks County	5	0.01
Lancaster (city) Lancaster County	3	0.01
Upper Darby (township) Delaware County	2	<0.01

Other Hispanic or Latino

Top 10 Places Sorted by Population
Based on all places, regardless of total population

Place	Population	%
Philadelphia (city) Philadelphia County	13,064	0.86
Allentown (city) Lehigh County	3,616	3.06
Reading (city) Berks County	2,716	3.08
Pittsburgh (city) Allegheny County	1,120	0.37
Lancaster (city) Lancaster County	1,067	1.80
Hazleton (city) Luzerne County	931	3.67
Bethlehem (city) Northampton County	808	1.08
Scranton (city) Lackawanna County	770	1.01
York (city) York County	729	1.67
Bethlehem (city) Northampton County	610	1.10

Top 10 Places Sorted by Percent of Total Population
Based on all places, regardless of total population

Place	Population	%
Marienville (cdp) Forest County	301	9.60
Mifflin (borough) Juniata County	55	8.57
Jenks (township) Forest County	302	8.32
Smithfield (township) Huntingdon County	338	7.70
Karthaus (township) Clearfield County	58	7.15
Mahanoy (township) Schuylkill County	224	7.11
Bern (township) Berks County	405	5.96
Ryan (township) Schuylkill County	139	5.65
Butler (township) Schuylkill County	281	5.38
Woodward (township) Clearfield County	214	5.36

Top 10 Places Sorted by Percent of Total Population
Based on places with total population of 50,000 or more

Place	Population	%
Reading (city) Berks County	2,716	3.08
Allentown (city) Lehigh County	3,616	3.06
Lancaster (city) Lancaster County	1,067	1.80
Bethlehem (city) Northampton County	610	1.10
Bethlehem (city) Northampton County	808	1.08
Scranton (city) Lackawanna County	770	1.01
Philadelphia (city) Philadelphia County	13,064	0.86
Bensalem (township) Bucks County	365	0.60
Bristol (township) Bucks County	286	0.52
Upper Darby (township) Delaware County	394	0.48

Racial Group Rankings

African-American/Black

Top 10 Places Sorted by Population
Based on all places, regardless of total population

Place	Population	%
Philadelphia (city) Philadelphia County	686,870	45.01
Pittsburgh (city) Allegheny County	84,819	27.75
Harrisburg (city) Dauphin County	27,947	56.43
Chester (city) Delaware County	26,257	77.29
Upper Darby (township) Delaware County	24,093	29.10
Erie (city) Erie County	20,022	19.67
Allentown (city) Lehigh County	17,916	15.18
Penn Hills (township) Allegheny County	15,514	36.65
Reading (city) Berks County	14,345	16.29
York (city) York County	14,290	32.69

Top 10 Places Sorted by Percent of Total Population
Based on all places, regardless of total population

Place	Population	%
Lincoln University (cdp) Chester County	1,693	98.09
Cheyney University (cdp) Delaware County	940	95.14
Yeadon (borough) Delaware County	10,367	90.60
Colwyn (borough) Delaware County	2,102	82.56
Darby (borough) Delaware County	8,751	81.88
Chester (township) Delaware County	3,183	80.79
Rankin (borough) Allegheny County	1,706	80.40
Chester (city) Delaware County	26,257	77.29
Braddock (borough) Allegheny County	1,618	74.94
Wilkinsburg (borough) Allegheny County	11,047	69.35

Top 10 Places Sorted by Percent of Total Population
Based on places with total population of 50,000 or more

Place	Population	%
Philadelphia (city) Philadelphia County	686,870	45.01
Upper Darby (township) Delaware County	24,093	29.10
Pittsburgh (city) Allegheny County	84,819	27.75
Lancaster (city) Lancaster County	11,899	20.06
Erie (city) Erie County	20,022	19.67
Reading (city) Berks County	14,345	16.29
Allentown (city) Lehigh County	17,916	15.18
Abington (township) Montgomery County	7,513	13.58
Bristol (township) Bucks County	6,353	11.64
Bethlehem (city) Northampton County	5,221	9.38

African-American/Black: Not Hispanic

Top 10 Places Sorted by Population
Based on all places, regardless of total population

Place	Population	%
Philadelphia (city) Philadelphia County	662,568	43.42
Pittsburgh (city) Allegheny County	83,539	27.33
Harrisburg (city) Dauphin County	26,151	52.80
Chester (city) Delaware County	25,408	74.79
Upper Darby (township) Delaware County	23,509	28.39
Erie (city) Erie County	19,010	18.68
Penn Hills (township) Allegheny County	15,331	36.22
Allentown (city) Lehigh County	12,976	10.99
Norristown (borough) Montgomery County	12,756	37.16
York (city) York County	12,458	28.50

Top 10 Places Sorted by Percent of Total Population
Based on all places, regardless of total population

Place	Population	%
Lincoln University (cdp) Chester County	1,631	94.50
Cheyney University (cdp) Delaware County	915	92.61
Yeadon (borough) Delaware County	10,244	89.52
Colwyn (borough) Delaware County	2,080	81.70
Darby (borough) Delaware County	8,616	80.62
Rankin (borough) Allegheny County	1,690	79.64
Chester (township) Delaware County	3,120	79.19
Chester (city) Delaware County	25,408	74.79
Braddock (borough) Allegheny County	1,601	74.15
Wilkinsburg (borough) Allegheny County	10,901	68.43

Top 10 Places Sorted by Percent of Total Population
Based on places with total population of 50,000 or more

Place	Population	%
Philadelphia (city) Philadelphia County	662,568	43.42
Upper Darby (township) Delaware County	23,509	28.39
Pittsburgh (city) Allegheny County	83,539	27.33
Erie (city) Erie County	19,010	18.68
Lancaster (city) Lancaster County	9,178	15.47
Abington (township) Montgomery County	7,266	13.14
Reading (city) Berks County	10,042	11.40
Bristol (township) Bucks County	6,069	11.12
Allentown (city) Lehigh County	12,976	10.99
Bensalem (township) Bucks County	4,750	7.86

African-American/Black: Hispanic

Top 10 Places Sorted by Population
Based on all places, regardless of total population

Place	Population	%
Philadelphia (city) Philadelphia County	24,302	1.59
Allentown (city) Lehigh County	4,940	4.19
Reading (city) Berks County	4,303	4.89
Lancaster (city) Lancaster County	2,721	4.59
York (city) York County	1,832	4.19
Harrisburg (city) Dauphin County	1,796	3.63
Bethlehem (city) Northampton County	1,704	2.27
Bethlehem (city) Northampton County	1,449	2.60
Pittsburgh (city) Allegheny County	1,280	0.42
Erie (city) Erie County	1,012	0.99

Top 10 Places Sorted by Percent of Total Population
Based on all places, regardless of total population

Place	Population	%
Reading (city) Berks County	4,303	4.89
Lancaster (city) Lancaster County	2,721	4.59
Decatur (township) Clearfield County	194	4.27
Allentown (city) Lehigh County	4,940	4.19
York (city) York County	1,832	4.19
Gregg (township) Union County	204	4.09
Penn Estates (cdp) Monroe County	181	4.03
Saw Creek (cdp) Pike County	162	4.03
Pleasant Hill (cdp) Lebanon County	105	3.97
Harrisburg (city) Dauphin County	1,796	3.63

Top 10 Places Sorted by Percent of Total Population
Based on places with total population of 50,000 or more

Place	Population	%
Reading (city) Berks County	4,303	4.89
Lancaster (city) Lancaster County	2,721	4.59
Allentown (city) Lehigh County	4,940	4.19
Bethlehem (city) Northampton County	1,449	2.60
Bethlehem (city) Northampton County	1,704	2.27
Philadelphia (city) Philadelphia County	24,302	1.59
Erie (city) Erie County	1,012	0.99
Scranton (city) Lackawanna County	713	0.94
Upper Darby (township) Delaware County	584	0.71
Bristol (township) Bucks County	284	0.52

American Indian/Alaska Native

Top 10 Places Sorted by Population
Based on all places, regardless of total population

Place	Population	%
Philadelphia (city) Philadelphia County	17,495	1.15
Pittsburgh (city) Allegheny County	2,540	0.83
Allentown (city) Lehigh County	1,792	1.52
Reading (city) Berks County	1,430	1.62
Erie (city) Erie County	909	0.89
Lancaster (city) Lancaster County	900	1.52
Harrisburg (city) Dauphin County	726	1.47
York (city) York County	686	1.57
Upper Darby (township) Delaware County	669	0.81
Bensalem (township) Bucks County	638	1.06

Top 10 Places Sorted by Percent of Total Population
Based on all places, regardless of total population

Place	Population	%
Aaronsburg (cdp) Washington County	14	5.41
Grugan (township) Clinton County	2	3.92
Spring Creek (township) Elk County	9	3.86
Forksville (borough) Sullivan County	5	3.45
West Liberty (borough) Butler County	10	2.92
Shippingport (borough) Beaver County	6	2.80
McHenry (township) Lycoming County	4	2.80
Sylvania (borough) Bradford County	6	2.74
Greensboro (borough) Greene County	7	2.69
Shirleysburg (borough) Huntingdon County	4	2.67

Top 10 Places Sorted by Percent of Total Population
Based on places with total population of 50,000 or more

Place	Population	%
Reading (city) Berks County	1,430	1.62
Allentown (city) Lehigh County	1,792	1.52
Lancaster (city) Lancaster County	900	1.52
Philadelphia (city) Philadelphia County	17,495	1.15
Bensalem (township) Bucks County	638	1.06
Erie (city) Erie County	909	0.89
Bristol (township) Bucks County	473	0.87
Bethlehem (city) Northampton County	465	0.84
Pittsburgh (city) Allegheny County	2,540	0.83
Upper Darby (township) Delaware County	669	0.81

American Indian/Alaska Native: Not Hispanic

Top 10 Places Sorted by Population
Based on all places, regardless of total population

Place	Population	%
Philadelphia (city) Philadelphia County	11,409	0.75
Pittsburgh (city) Allegheny County	2,253	0.74
Erie (city) Erie County	743	0.73
Allentown (city) Lehigh County	645	0.55
Upper Darby (township) Delaware County	555	0.67
Harrisburg (city) Dauphin County	511	1.03
Lancaster (city) Lancaster County	445	0.75
Reading (city) Berks County	434	0.49
York (city) York County	417	0.95
Bensalem (township) Bucks County	409	0.68

Top 10 Places Sorted by Percent of Total Population
Based on all places, regardless of total population

Place	Population	%
Aaronsburg (cdp) Washington County	14	5.41
Grugan (township) Clinton County	2	3.92
Spring Creek (township) Elk County	9	3.86
Forksville (borough) Sullivan County	5	3.45
West Liberty (borough) Butler County	10	2.92
Shippingport (borough) Beaver County	6	2.80
McHenry (township) Lycoming County	4	2.80
Sylvania (borough) Bradford County	6	2.74
Greensboro (borough) Greene County	7	2.69
Shirleysburg (borough) Huntingdon County	4	2.67

Top 10 Places Sorted by Percent of Total Population
Based on places with total population of 50,000 or more

Place	Population	%
Philadelphia (city) Philadelphia County	11,409	0.75
Lancaster (city) Lancaster County	445	0.75
Pittsburgh (city) Allegheny County	2,253	0.74
Erie (city) Erie County	743	0.73
Bristol (township) Bucks County	381	0.70
Bensalem (township) Bucks County	409	0.68
Upper Darby (township) Delaware County	555	0.67
Allentown (city) Lehigh County	645	0.55
Levittown (cdp) Bucks County	282	0.53
Reading (city) Berks County	434	0.49

Please refer to the Explanation of Data in the front of the book for more detailed information.

American Indian/Alaska Native: Hispanic

Top 10 Places Sorted by Population
Based on all places, regardless of total population

Place	Population	%
Philadelphia (city) Philadelphia County	6,086	0.40
Allentown (city) Lehigh County	1,147	0.97
Reading (city) Berks County	996	1.13
Lancaster (city) Lancaster County	455	0.77
Bethlehem (city) Northampton County	301	0.40
Pittsburgh (city) Allegheny County	287	0.09
York (city) York County	269	0.62
Bethlehem (city) Northampton County	234	0.42
Bensalem (township) Bucks County	229	0.38
Harrisburg (city) Dauphin County	215	0.43

Top 10 Places Sorted by Percent of Total Population
Based on all places, regardless of total population

Place	Population	%
Foxburg (borough) Clarion County	3	1.64
Mayberry (township) Montour County	4	1.60
Albrightsville (cdp) Carbon County	3	1.49
Sweden Valley (cdp) Potter County	3	1.35
Avondale (borough) Chester County	16	1.26
Fredonia (borough) Mercer County	6	1.20
Chest (township) Cambria County	4	1.15
Aspers (cdp) Adams County	4	1.14
Reading (city) Berks County	996	1.13
Orviston (cdp) Centre County	1	1.05

Top 10 Places Sorted by Percent of Total Population
Based on places with total population of 50,000 or more

Place	Population	%
Reading (city) Berks County	996	1.13
Allentown (city) Lehigh County	1,147	0.97
Lancaster (city) Lancaster County	455	0.77
Bethlehem (city) Northampton County	234	0.42
Philadelphia (city) Philadelphia County	6,086	0.40
Bethlehem (city) Northampton County	301	0.40
Bensalem (township) Bucks County	229	0.38
Levittown (cdp) Bucks County	110	0.21
Bristol (township) Bucks County	92	0.17
Erie (city) Erie County	166	0.16

Alaska Native: Alaska Athabascan

Top 10 Places Sorted by Population
Based on all places, regardless of total population

Place	Population	%
Independence (township) Beaver County	6	0.24
Philadelphia (city) Philadelphia County	6	<0.01
Cumberland Valley (township) Bedford County	5	0.31
Pittsburgh (city) Allegheny County	5	<0.01
Arnold City (cdp) Fayette County	4	0.80
Washington (township) Fayette County	4	0.10
St. Clair (township) Westmoreland County	3	0.20
Fort Washington (cdp) Montgomery County	3	0.06
Wescosville (cdp) Lehigh County	3	0.05
Bristol (township) Bucks County	3	0.01

Top 10 Places Sorted by Percent of Total Population
Based on all places, regardless of total population

Place	Population	%
Arnold City (cdp) Fayette County	4	0.80
Woodbury (borough) Bedford County	2	0.70
Cumberland Valley (township) Bedford County	5	0.31
Independence (township) Beaver County	6	0.24
Hyndman (borough) Bedford County	2	0.22
St. Clair (township) Westmoreland County	3	0.20
Apolacon (township) Susquehanna County	1	0.20
Mather (cdp) Greene County	1	0.14
Washington (township) Fayette County	4	0.10
Milford (township) Juniata County	2	0.10

Top 10 Places Sorted by Percent of Total Population
Based on places with total population of 50,000 or more

Place	Population	%
Bristol (township) Bucks County	3	0.01
Levittown (cdp) Bucks County	3	0.01
Philadelphia (city) Philadelphia County	6	<0.01
Pittsburgh (city) Allegheny County	5	<0.01

Lancaster (city) Lancaster County	2	<0.01
Abington (township) Montgomery County	1	<0.01
Bensalem (township) Bucks County	1	<0.01
Allentown (city) Lehigh County	0	0.00
Bethlehem (city) Northampton County	0	0.00
Bethlehem (city) Northampton County	0	0.00

Alaska Native: Aleut

Top 10 Places Sorted by Population
Based on all places, regardless of total population

Place	Population	%
Philadelphia (city) Philadelphia County	8	<0.01
Quemahoning (township) Somerset County	6	0.30
Slatington (borough) Lehigh County	5	0.12
Granville (township) Mifflin County	5	0.10
Lewistown (borough) Mifflin County	5	0.06
Lincoln (borough) Allegheny County	4	0.37
Washington (township) Lehigh County	4	0.06
Leet (township) Allegheny County	3	0.18
Fox (township) Elk County	3	0.08
Allison Park (cdp) Allegheny County	3	0.01

Top 10 Places Sorted by Percent of Total Population
Based on all places, regardless of total population

Place	Population	%
Lincoln (borough) Allegheny County	4	0.37
Quemahoning (township) Somerset County	6	0.30
Beale (township) Juniata County	2	0.24
Seward (borough) Westmoreland County	1	0.20
Leet (township) Allegheny County	3	0.18
Cherryville (cdp) Northampton County	2	0.13
Richland (township) Venango County	1	0.13
Slatington (borough) Lehigh County	5	0.12
Everett (borough) Bedford County	2	0.11
Port Royal (borough) Juniata County	1	0.11

Top 10 Places Sorted by Percent of Total Population
Based on places with total population of 50,000 or more

Place	Population	%
Philadelphia (city) Philadelphia County	8	<0.01
Allentown (city) Lehigh County	2	<0.01
Erie (city) Erie County	1	<0.01
Lancaster (city) Lancaster County	1	<0.01
Millcreek (township) Erie County	1	<0.01
Pittsburgh (city) Allegheny County	1	<0.01
Upper Darby (township) Delaware County	1	<0.01
Abington (township) Montgomery County	0	0.00
Bensalem (township) Bucks County	0	0.00
Bethlehem (city) Northampton County	0	0.00

American Indian: Apache

Top 10 Places Sorted by Population
Based on all places, regardless of total population

Place	Population	%
Philadelphia (city) Philadelphia County	118	0.01
Pittsburgh (city) Allegheny County	36	0.01
York (city) York County	13	0.03
Bensalem (township) Bucks County	13	0.02
McKeesport (city) Allegheny County	11	0.06
Waynesboro (borough) Franklin County	10	0.09
Upper Darby (township) Delaware County	10	0.01
Harrisburg (city) Dauphin County	9	0.02
Erie (city) Erie County	9	0.01
Berwick (borough) Columbia County	8	0.08

Top 10 Places Sorted by Percent of Total Population
Based on all places, regardless of total population

Place	Population	%
Frizzleburg (cdp) Lawrence County	4	0.66
Weston (cdp) Luzerne County	2	0.62
Hawk Run (cdp) Clearfield County	3	0.56
Chalfant (borough) Allegheny County	4	0.50
Glendon (borough) Northampton County	2	0.45
Spring Creek (township) Elk County	1	0.43
Mountainhome (cdp) Monroe County	5	0.42
Roulette (cdp) Potter County	3	0.39
Polk (township) Jefferson County	1	0.38
Cummings (township) Lycoming County	1	0.37

Top 10 Places Sorted by Percent of Total Population
Based on places with total population of 50,000 or more

Place	Population	%
Bensalem (township) Bucks County	13	0.02
Levittown (cdp) Bucks County	8	0.02
Philadelphia (city) Philadelphia County	118	0.01
Pittsburgh (city) Allegheny County	36	0.01
Upper Darby (township) Delaware County	10	0.01
Erie (city) Erie County	9	0.01
Allentown (city) Lehigh County	8	0.01
Bristol (township) Bucks County	8	0.01
Lancaster (city) Lancaster County	7	0.01
Abington (township) Montgomery County	6	0.01

American Indian: Arapaho

Top 10 Places Sorted by Population
Based on all places, regardless of total population

Place	Population	%
Philadelphia (city) Philadelphia County	7	<0.01
Clifton Heights (borough) Delaware County	5	0.08
Derry (township) Dauphin County	4	0.02
Heidelberg (township) Lehigh County	3	0.09
Buffington (township) Indiana County	2	0.15
Hopewell (township) Cumberland County	2	0.09
Windsor (township) York County	2	0.01
Blawnox (borough) Allegheny County	1	0.07
Oliver (township) Mifflin County	1	0.05
Amity Gardens (cdp) Berks County	1	0.03

Top 10 Places Sorted by Percent of Total Population
Based on all places, regardless of total population

Place	Population	%
Buffington (township) Indiana County	2	0.15
Heidelberg (township) Lehigh County	3	0.09
Hopewell (township) Cumberland County	2	0.09
Clifton Heights (borough) Delaware County	5	0.08
Blawnox (borough) Allegheny County	1	0.07
Oliver (township) Mifflin County	1	0.05
Amity Gardens (cdp) Berks County	1	0.03
Fayetteville (cdp) Franklin County	1	0.03
Derry (township) Dauphin County	4	0.02
Forest Hills (borough) Allegheny County	1	0.02

Top 10 Places Sorted by Percent of Total Population
Based on places with total population of 50,000 or more

Place	Population	%
Philadelphia (city) Philadelphia County	7	<0.01
Bristol (township) Bucks County	1	<0.01
Levittown (cdp) Bucks County	1	<0.01
Lower Merion (township) Montgomery County	1	<0.01
Abington (township) Montgomery County	0	0.00
Allentown (city) Lehigh County	0	0.00
Bensalem (township) Bucks County	0	0.00
Bethlehem (city) Northampton County	0	0.00
Bethlehem (city) Northampton County	0	0.00
Erie (city) Erie County	0	0.00

American Indian: Blackfeet

Top 10 Places Sorted by Population
Based on all places, regardless of total population

Place	Population	%
Philadelphia (city) Philadelphia County	679	0.04
Pittsburgh (city) Allegheny County	199	0.07
Reading (city) Berks County	49	0.06
Erie (city) Erie County	48	0.05
Penn Hills (township) Allegheny County	34	0.08
York (city) York County	33	0.08
Upper Darby (township) Delaware County	33	0.04
Allentown (city) Lehigh County	33	0.03
Lancaster (city) Lancaster County	28	0.05
Bristol (township) Bucks County	27	0.05

Top 10 Places Sorted by Percent of Total Population
Based on all places, regardless of total population

Place	Population	%
Aaronsburg (cdp) Washington County	4	1.54
Gray (township) Greene County	3	1.37
Harmonsburg (cdp) Crawford County	3	0.75

Place	Population	%
Newry (borough) Blair County	2	0.74
Morrisdale (cdp) Clearfield County	5	0.66
Pymatuning North (cdp) Crawford County	2	0.64
Starbrick (cdp) Warren County	3	0.57
Jerseytown (cdp) Columbia County	1	0.54
Bobtown (cdp) Greene County	4	0.53
McKean (borough) Erie County	2	0.52

Top 10 Places Sorted by Percent of Total Population
Based on places with total population of 50,000 or more

Place	Population	%
Pittsburgh (city) Allegheny County	199	0.07
Reading (city) Berks County	49	0.06
Erie (city) Erie County	48	0.05
Lancaster (city) Lancaster County	28	0.05
Bristol (township) Bucks County	27	0.05
Levittown (cdp) Bucks County	26	0.05
Philadelphia (city) Philadelphia County	679	0.04
Upper Darby (township) Delaware County	33	0.04
Bensalem (township) Bucks County	24	0.04
Allentown (city) Lehigh County	33	0.03

American Indian: Canadian/French American Indian

Top 10 Places Sorted by Population
Based on all places, regardless of total population

Place	Population	%
Philadelphia (city) Philadelphia County	34	<0.01
Pittsburgh (city) Allegheny County	15	<0.01
Avalon (borough) Allegheny County	12	0.26
Towamencin (township) Montgomery County	7	0.04
Londonderry (township) Chester County	6	0.28
Yeadon (borough) Delaware County	6	0.05
West Perry (township) Snyder County	5	0.47
Harrisburg (city) Dauphin County	5	0.01
Porter (township) Pike County	4	0.82
Lampeter (cdp) Lancaster County	4	0.24

Top 10 Places Sorted by Percent of Total Population
Based on all places, regardless of total population

Place	Population	%
Porter (township) Pike County	4	0.82
West Perry (township) Snyder County	5	0.47
Londonderry (township) Chester County	6	0.28
Avalon (borough) Allegheny County	12	0.26
Lampeter (cdp) Lancaster County	4	0.24
Stevens (township) Bradford County	1	0.23
Loganton (borough) Clinton County	1	0.21
Ashland (cdp) Clarion County	2	0.18
Marianne (cdp) Clarion County	2	0.17
Sandy Lake (township) Mercer County	2	0.16

Top 10 Places Sorted by Percent of Total Population
Based on places with total population of 50,000 or more

Place	Population	%
Lancaster (city) Lancaster County	4	0.01
Philadelphia (city) Philadelphia County	34	<0.01
Pittsburgh (city) Allegheny County	15	<0.01
Erie (city) Erie County	4	<0.01
Bensalem (township) Bucks County	2	<0.01
Upper Darby (township) Delaware County	2	<0.01
Abington (township) Montgomery County	1	<0.01
Allentown (city) Lehigh County	1	<0.01
Lower Merion (township) Montgomery County	1	<0.01
Reading (city) Berks County	1	<0.01

American Indian: Central American Indian

Top 10 Places Sorted by Population
Based on all places, regardless of total population

Place	Population	%
Philadelphia (city) Philadelphia County	111	0.01
Allentown (city) Lehigh County	40	0.03
Lancaster (city) Lancaster County	19	0.03
Reading (city) Berks County	14	0.02
York (city) York County	11	0.03
Bethlehem (city) Northampton County	10	0.01
Pittsburgh (city) Allegheny County	10	<0.01
Bristol (township) Bucks County	9	0.02
Trooper (cdp) Montgomery County	8	0.14

Place	Population	%
Lower Providence (township) Montgomery County	8	0.03

Top 10 Places Sorted by Percent of Total Population
Based on all places, regardless of total population

Place	Population	%
Beaver (township) Columbia County	6	0.65
Hunterstown (cdp) Adams County	2	0.37
Rural Valley (borough) Armstrong County	2	0.23
Glendon (borough) Northampton County	1	0.23
Farmersville (cdp) Lancaster County	2	0.20
Dupont (borough) Luzerne County	5	0.18
Trooper (cdp) Montgomery County	8	0.14
Spring (township) Perry County	3	0.14
Hughestown (borough) Luzerne County	2	0.14
Shamokin Dam (borough) Snyder County	2	0.12

Top 10 Places Sorted by Percent of Total Population
Based on places with total population of 50,000 or more

Place	Population	%
Allentown (city) Lehigh County	40	0.03
Lancaster (city) Lancaster County	19	0.03
Reading (city) Berks County	14	0.02
Bristol (township) Bucks County	9	0.02
Levittown (cdp) Bucks County	8	0.02
Philadelphia (city) Philadelphia County	111	0.01
Bethlehem (city) Northampton County	10	0.01
Bethlehem (city) Northampton County	7	0.01
Pittsburgh (city) Allegheny County	10	<0.01
Erie (city) Erie County	4	<0.01

American Indian: Cherokee

Top 10 Places Sorted by Population
Based on all places, regardless of total population

Place	Population	%
Philadelphia (city) Philadelphia County	2,484	0.16
Pittsburgh (city) Allegheny County	533	0.17
Allentown (city) Lehigh County	170	0.14
Harrisburg (city) Dauphin County	143	0.29
Erie (city) Erie County	135	0.13
Reading (city) Berks County	120	0.14
York (city) York County	114	0.26
Lancaster (city) Lancaster County	112	0.19
Penn Hills (township) Allegheny County	98	0.23
Upper Darby (township) Delaware County	92	0.11

Top 10 Places Sorted by Percent of Total Population
Based on all places, regardless of total population

Place	Population	%
Aaronsburg (cdp) Washington County	10	3.86
Spring Creek (township) Elk County	6	2.58
West Liberty (borough) Butler County	8	2.33
New Paris (borough) Bedford County	4	2.15
Roseville (borough) Tioga County	4	2.12
Greensboro (borough) Greene County	5	1.92
Shanksville (borough) Somerset County	4	1.69
Fredonia (borough) Mercer County	8	1.59
Branchdale (cdp) Schuylkill County	5	1.29
Confluence (borough) Somerset County	10	1.28

Top 10 Places Sorted by Percent of Total Population
Based on places with total population of 50,000 or more

Place	Population	%
Lancaster (city) Lancaster County	112	0.19
Pittsburgh (city) Allegheny County	533	0.17
Philadelphia (city) Philadelphia County	2,484	0.16
Abington (township) Montgomery County	91	0.16
Allentown (city) Lehigh County	170	0.14
Reading (city) Berks County	120	0.14
Erie (city) Erie County	135	0.13
Bristol (township) Bucks County	73	0.13
Bensalem (township) Bucks County	74	0.12
Levittown (cdp) Bucks County	61	0.12

American Indian: Cheyenne

Top 10 Places Sorted by Population
Based on all places, regardless of total population

Place	Population	%
Philadelphia (city) Philadelphia County	12	<0.01

Place	Population	%
Pittsburgh (city) Allegheny County	11	<0.01
Sharon (city) Mercer County	5	0.04
Penn Hills (township) Allegheny County	5	0.01
Clearfield (township) Butler County	4	0.15
Hanover (township) Washington County	4	0.15
Swarthmore (borough) Delaware County	4	0.06
Uniontown (city) Fayette County	4	0.04
Middletown (township) Bucks County	4	0.01
Lawson Heights (cdp) Westmoreland County	3	0.14

Top 10 Places Sorted by Percent of Total Population
Based on all places, regardless of total population

Place	Population	%
Glenfield (borough) Allegheny County	1	0.49
White (township) Cambria County	2	0.24
East Freedom (cdp) Blair County	2	0.21
Chatham (township) Tioga County	1	0.17
Port Matilda (borough) Centre County	1	0.17
Smock (cdp) Fayette County	1	0.17
Wyalusing (borough) Bradford County	1	0.17
Clearfield (township) Butler County	4	0.15
Hanover (township) Washington County	4	0.15
Mocanaqua (cdp) Luzerne County	1	0.15

Top 10 Places Sorted by Percent of Total Population
Based on places with total population of 50,000 or more

Place	Population	%
Levittown (cdp) Bucks County	3	0.01
Philadelphia (city) Philadelphia County	12	<0.01
Pittsburgh (city) Allegheny County	11	<0.01
Upper Darby (township) Delaware County	2	<0.01
Allentown (city) Lehigh County	1	<0.01
Lower Merion (township) Montgomery County	1	<0.01
Abington (township) Montgomery County	0	0.00
Bensalem (township) Bucks County	0	0.00
Bethlehem (city) Northampton County	0	0.00
Bethlehem (city) Northampton County	0	0.00

American Indian: Chickasaw

Top 10 Places Sorted by Population
Based on all places, regardless of total population

Place	Population	%
Philadelphia (city) Philadelphia County	28	<0.01
Pittsburgh (city) Allegheny County	13	<0.01
Hampden (township) Cumberland County	6	0.02
Warminster (township) Bucks County	6	0.02
Middletown (township) Delaware County	5	0.03
Lower Paxton (township) Dauphin County	5	0.01
Jeannette (city) Westmoreland County	4	0.04
Ephrata (borough) Lancaster County	4	0.03
Monroeville (municipality) Allegheny County	4	0.01
Shaler (township) Allegheny County	4	0.01

Top 10 Places Sorted by Percent of Total Population
Based on all places, regardless of total population

Place	Population	%
Highland (township) Elk County	2	0.41
Plunketts Creek (township) Lycoming County	2	0.29
West Hills (cdp) Armstrong County	2	0.16
Mars (borough) Butler County	2	0.12
North Warren (cdp) Warren County	2	0.10
Newtown (borough) Bucks County	2	0.09
South Coatesville (borough) Chester County	1	0.08
North Mahoning (township) Indiana County	1	0.07
Arnold (city) Westmoreland County	3	0.06
Granville (township) Mifflin County	3	0.06

Top 10 Places Sorted by Percent of Total Population
Based on places with total population of 50,000 or more

Place	Population	%
Philadelphia (city) Philadelphia County	28	<0.01
Pittsburgh (city) Allegheny County	13	<0.01
Erie (city) Erie County	4	<0.01
Upper Darby (township) Delaware County	3	<0.01
Allentown (city) Lehigh County	1	<0.01
Abington (township) Montgomery County	0	0.00
Bensalem (township) Bucks County	0	0.00
Bethlehem (city) Northampton County	0	0.00
Bethlehem (city) Northampton County	0	0.00
Bristol (township) Bucks County	0	0.00

American Indian: Chippewa

Top 10 Places Sorted by Population
Based on all places, regardless of total population

Place	Population	%
Philadelphia (city) Philadelphia County	63	<0.01
Pittsburgh (city) Allegheny County	30	0.01
Reading (city) Berks County	19	0.02
Allentown (city) Lehigh County	12	0.01
Easton (city) Northampton County	10	0.04
Millcreek (township) Erie County	9	0.02
McKeesport (city) Allegheny County	8	0.04
Oil City (city) Venango County	7	0.07
Amity (township) Berks County	7	0.06
Erie (city) Erie County	7	0.01

Top 10 Places Sorted by Percent of Total Population
Based on all places, regardless of total population

Place	Population	%
Oswayo (borough) Potter County	1	0.72
Rowes Run (cdp) Fayette County	3	0.53
Palmdale (cdp) Dauphin County	5	0.38
Lower Turkeyfoot (township) Somerset County	2	0.33
Richlandtown (borough) Bucks County	4	0.30
Mahaffey (borough) Clearfield County	1	0.27
Richland (township) Venango County	2	0.26
McDonald (borough) Allegheny County	1	0.26
Hawley (borough) Wayne County	3	0.25
Lincoln (township) Bedford County	1	0.24

Top 10 Places Sorted by Percent of Total Population
Based on places with total population of 50,000 or more

Place	Population	%
Reading (city) Berks County	19	0.02
Millcreek (township) Erie County	9	0.02
Pittsburgh (city) Allegheny County	30	0.01
Allentown (city) Lehigh County	12	0.01
Erie (city) Erie County	7	0.01
Lancaster (city) Lancaster County	6	0.01
Upper Darby (township) Delaware County	5	0.01
Scranton (city) Lackawanna County	4	0.01
Bristol (township) Bucks County	3	0.01
Philadelphia (city) Philadelphia County	63	<0.01

American Indian: Choctaw

Top 10 Places Sorted by Population
Based on all places, regardless of total population

Place	Population	%
Philadelphia (city) Philadelphia County	92	0.01
Pittsburgh (city) Allegheny County	22	0.01
Upper Darby (township) Delaware County	20	0.02
Allentown (city) Lehigh County	13	0.01
Shaler (township) Allegheny County	12	0.04
Harrisburg (city) Dauphin County	11	0.02
Erie (city) Erie County	10	0.01
Perkasie (borough) Bucks County	7	0.08
Douglass (township) Montgomery County	7	0.07
Chambersburg (borough) Franklin County	7	0.03

Top 10 Places Sorted by Percent of Total Population
Based on all places, regardless of total population

Place	Population	%
Grugan (township) Clinton County	1	1.96
Gray (township) Greene County	3	1.37
Forksville (borough) Sullivan County	1	0.69
Richhill (township) Greene County	6	0.67
Aleppo (township) Greene County	3	0.60
Coburn (cdp) Centre County	1	0.42
Leetsdale (borough) Allegheny County	5	0.41
Liberty (township) Tioga County	4	0.38
Pinegrove (township) Venango County	5	0.37
New Ringgold (borough) Schuylkill County	1	0.36

Top 10 Places Sorted by Percent of Total Population
Based on places with total population of 50,000 or more

Place	Population	%
Upper Darby (township) Delaware County	20	0.02
Philadelphia (city) Philadelphia County	92	0.01
Pittsburgh (city) Allegheny County	22	0.01
Allentown (city) Lehigh County	13	0.01

Erie (city) Erie County	10	0.01
Reading (city) Berks County	7	0.01
Lower Merion (township) Montgomery County	6	0.01
Millcreek (township) Erie County	6	0.01
Bristol (township) Bucks County	3	0.01
Lancaster (city) Lancaster County	3	0.01

American Indian: Colville

Top 10 Places Sorted by Population
Based on all places, regardless of total population

Place	Population	%
Parkside (borough) Delaware County	5	0.21
Tyrone (township) Perry County	4	0.19
Mahanoy City (borough) Schuylkill County	2	0.05
Swoyersville (borough) Luzerne County	2	0.04
Mount Pocono (borough) Monroe County	1	0.03
Towanda (borough) Bradford County	1	0.03
Aaronsburg (cdp) Centre County	0	0.00
Aaronsburg (cdp) Washington County	0	0.00
Abbott (township) Potter County	0	0.00
Abbottstown (borough) Adams County	0	0.00

Top 10 Places Sorted by Percent of Total Population
Based on all places, regardless of total population

Place	Population	%
Parkside (borough) Delaware County	5	0.21
Tyrone (township) Perry County	4	0.19
Mahanoy City (borough) Schuylkill County	2	0.05
Swoyersville (borough) Luzerne County	2	0.04
Mount Pocono (borough) Monroe County	1	0.03
Towanda (borough) Bradford County	1	0.03
Aaronsburg (cdp) Centre County	0	0.00
Aaronsburg (cdp) Washington County	0	0.00
Abbott (township) Potter County	0	0.00
Abbottstown (borough) Adams County	0	0.00

Top 10 Places Sorted by Percent of Total Population
Based on places with total population of 50,000 or more

Place	Population	%
Abington (township) Montgomery County	0	0.00
Allentown (city) Lehigh County	0	0.00
Bensalem (township) Bucks County	0	0.00
Bethlehem (city) Northampton County	0	0.00
Bethlehem (city) Northampton County	0	0.00
Bristol (township) Bucks County	0	0.00
Erie (city) Erie County	0	0.00
Lancaster (city) Lancaster County	0	0.00
Levittown (cdp) Bucks County	0	0.00
Lower Merion (township) Montgomery County	0	0.00

American Indian: Comanche

Top 10 Places Sorted by Population
Based on all places, regardless of total population

Place	Population	%
Philadelphia (city) Philadelphia County	9	<0.01
East Lampeter (township) Lancaster County	6	0.04
Rose (township) Jefferson County	5	0.40
Milford (township) Bucks County	4	0.04
Allentown (city) Lehigh County	4	<0.01
Hepburn (township) Lycoming County	3	0.11
North Woodbury (township) Blair County	3	0.11
Lower Chanceford (township) York County	3	0.10
Bradford (city) McKean County	3	0.03
Lansdale (borough) Montgomery County	3	0.02

Top 10 Places Sorted by Percent of Total Population
Based on all places, regardless of total population

Place	Population	%
Rose (township) Jefferson County	5	0.40
New Market (cdp) York County	1	0.12
Hepburn (township) Lycoming County	3	0.11
North Woodbury (township) Blair County	3	0.11
Lower Chanceford (township) York County	3	0.10
Lewis (township) Northumberland County	2	0.10
Linesville (borough) Crawford County	1	0.10
East Uniontown (cdp) Fayette County	2	0.08
Williamsburg (borough) Blair County	1	0.08
East Deer (township) Allegheny County	1	0.07

American Indian: Cree

Top 10 Places Sorted by Percent of Total Population
Based on places with total population of 50,000 or more

Place	Population	%
Lancaster (city) Lancaster County	3	0.01
Philadelphia (city) Philadelphia County	9	<0.01
Allentown (city) Lehigh County	4	<0.01
Pittsburgh (city) Allegheny County	2	<0.01
Bensalem (township) Bucks County	1	<0.01
Bethlehem (city) Northampton County	1	<0.01
Bethlehem (city) Northampton County	1	<0.01
Erie (city) Erie County	1	<0.01
Reading (city) Berks County	1	<0.01
Scranton (city) Lackawanna County	1	<0.01

American Indian: Cree

Top 10 Places Sorted by Population
Based on all places, regardless of total population

Place	Population	%
Philadelphia (city) Philadelphia County	25	<0.01
Fayette (township) Juniata County	14	0.40
York (city) York County	6	0.01
Pittsburgh (city) Allegheny County	6	<0.01
Walker (township) Juniata County	5	0.18
Reading (city) Berks County	5	0.01
Allentown (city) Lehigh County	5	<0.01
Greene (township) Pike County	4	0.10
Lancaster (city) Lancaster County	4	0.01
Levittown (cdp) Bucks County	4	0.01

Top 10 Places Sorted by Percent of Total Population
Based on all places, regardless of total population

Place	Population	%
Fayette (township) Juniata County	14	0.40
Finleyville (borough) Washington County	1	0.22
Walker (township) Juniata County	5	0.18
Warriors Mark (township) Huntingdon County	3	0.17
Braddock (borough) Allegheny County	3	0.14
Troy (township) Bradford County	2	0.12
Carrolltown (borough) Cambria County	1	0.12
Windham (township) Bradford County	1	0.11
Greene (township) Pike County	4	0.10
Brownstown (cdp) Lancaster County	2	0.07

Top 10 Places Sorted by Percent of Total Population
Based on places with total population of 50,000 or more

Place	Population	%
Reading (city) Berks County	5	0.01
Lancaster (city) Lancaster County	4	0.01
Levittown (cdp) Bucks County	4	0.01
Abington (township) Montgomery County	3	0.01
Bristol (township) Bucks County	3	0.01
Philadelphia (city) Philadelphia County	25	<0.01
Pittsburgh (city) Allegheny County	6	<0.01
Allentown (city) Lehigh County	5	<0.01
Erie (city) Erie County	2	<0.01
Millcreek (township) Erie County	2	<0.01

American Indian: Creek

Top 10 Places Sorted by Population
Based on all places, regardless of total population

Place	Population	%
Philadelphia (city) Philadelphia County	59	<0.01
Pittsburgh (city) Allegheny County	20	0.01
Wilkinsburg (borough) Allegheny County	13	0.08
Murrysville (municipality) Westmoreland County	7	0.03
McCandless (township) Allegheny County	7	0.02
Norristown (borough) Montgomery County	7	0.02
Erie (city) Erie County	7	0.01
Chester (city) Delaware County	6	0.02
Scranton (city) Lackawanna County	6	0.01
Carroll Valley (borough) Adams County	5	0.13

Top 10 Places Sorted by Percent of Total Population
Based on all places, regardless of total population

Place	Population	%
Rome (borough) Bradford County	3	0.68
Overton (township) Bradford County	1	0.40
Lake Arthur Estates (cdp) Butler County	2	0.34

Place	Population	%
Rimersburg (borough) Clarion County	3	0.32
Portland (borough) Northampton County	1	0.19
McElhattan (cdp) Clinton County	1	0.17
Masthope (cdp) Pike County	1	0.15
South Greensburg (borough) Westmoreland County	3	0.14
Carroll Valley (borough) Adams County	5	0.13
East Cameron (township) Northumberland County	1	0.13

Top 10 Places Sorted by Percent of Total Population
Based on places with total population of 50,000 or more

Place	Population	%
Pittsburgh (city) Allegheny County	20	0.01
Erie (city) Erie County	7	0.01
Scranton (city) Lackawanna County	6	0.01
Bensalem (township) Bucks County	5	0.01
Lancaster (city) Lancaster County	4	0.01
Levittown (cdp) Bucks County	3	0.01
Philadelphia (city) Philadelphia County	59	<0.01
Upper Darby (township) Delaware County	3	<0.01
Allentown (city) Lehigh County	2	<0.01
Lower Merion (township) Montgomery County	2	<0.01

American Indian: Crow

Top 10 Places Sorted by Population
Based on all places, regardless of total population

Place	Population	%
Philadelphia (city) Philadelphia County	15	<0.01
Pittsburgh (city) Allegheny County	8	<0.01
Pottstown (borough) Montgomery County	6	0.03
Armstrong (township) Indiana County	5	0.17
Washington (township) Schuylkill County	5	0.16
Allentown (city) Lehigh County	5	<0.01
Burgettstown (borough) Washington County	3	0.22
Gibsonia (cdp) Allegheny County	3	0.11
Nockamixon (township) Bucks County	3	0.09
Salem (township) Luzerne County	3	0.07

Top 10 Places Sorted by Percent of Total Population
Based on all places, regardless of total population

Place	Population	%
Roseville (borough) Tioga County	1	0.53
Fredericktown (cdp) Washington County	2	0.50
Burgettstown (borough) Washington County	3	0.22
Carmichaels (borough) Greene County	1	0.21
Armstrong (township) Indiana County	5	0.17
Washington (township) Schuylkill County	5	0.16
Windham (township) Wyoming County	1	0.12
Gibsonia (cdp) Allegheny County	3	0.11
Bald Eagle (township) Clinton County	2	0.10
Nockamixon (township) Bucks County	3	0.09

Top 10 Places Sorted by Percent of Total Population
Based on places with total population of 50,000 or more

Place	Population	%
Philadelphia (city) Philadelphia County	15	<0.01
Pittsburgh (city) Allegheny County	8	<0.01
Allentown (city) Lehigh County	5	<0.01
Erie (city) Erie County	3	<0.01
Millcreek (township) Erie County	1	<0.01
Abington (township) Montgomery County	0	0.00
Bensalem (township) Bucks County	0	0.00
Bethlehem (city) Northampton County	0	0.00
Bethlehem (city) Northampton County	0	0.00
Bristol (township) Bucks County	0	0.00

American Indian: Delaware

Top 10 Places Sorted by Population
Based on all places, regardless of total population

Place	Population	%
Philadelphia (city) Philadelphia County	239	0.02
Dingman (township) Pike County	22	0.18
Bethlehem (city) Northampton County	22	0.03
Upper Darby (township) Delaware County	22	0.03
Allentown (city) Lehigh County	21	0.02
Chestnuthill (township) Monroe County	16	0.09
Bethlehem (city) Northampton County	15	0.03
Levittown (cdp) Bucks County	15	0.03
Reading (city) Berks County	15	0.02
Coolbaugh (township) Monroe County	14	0.07

Top 10 Places Sorted by Percent of Total Population
Based on all places, regardless of total population

Place	Population	%
Guys Mills (cdp) Crawford County	3	2.42
Foundryville (cdp) Columbia County	4	1.56
North Branch (township) Wyoming County	2	0.97
Abbott (township) Potter County	2	0.83
Ogle (township) Somerset County	4	0.80
Monroe (borough) Bradford County	3	0.54
Meshoppen (borough) Wyoming County	3	0.53
Sun Valley (cdp) Monroe County	12	0.50
La Plume (township) Lackawanna County	3	0.50
Forkston (township) Wyoming County	2	0.50

Top 10 Places Sorted by Percent of Total Population
Based on places with total population of 50,000 or more

Place	Population	%
Bethlehem (city) Northampton County	22	0.03
Upper Darby (township) Delaware County	22	0.03
Bethlehem (city) Northampton County	15	0.03
Levittown (cdp) Bucks County	15	0.03
Philadelphia (city) Philadelphia County	239	0.02
Allentown (city) Lehigh County	21	0.02
Reading (city) Berks County	15	0.02
Bensalem (township) Bucks County	13	0.02
Bristol (township) Bucks County	13	0.02
Abington (township) Montgomery County	5	0.01

American Indian: Hopi

Top 10 Places Sorted by Population
Based on all places, regardless of total population

Place	Population	%
Philadelphia (city) Philadelphia County	7	<0.01
Greene (township) Pike County	5	0.13
Doylestown (borough) Bucks County	5	0.06
Buckingham (township) Bucks County	5	0.02
Pottstown (borough) Montgomery County	5	0.02
Pittsburgh (city) Allegheny County	4	<0.01
Northwood (cdp) Blair County	3	1.01
Snyder (township) Blair County	3	0.09
Catasauqua (borough) Lehigh County	3	0.05
Gettysburg (borough) Adams County	3	0.04

Top 10 Places Sorted by Percent of Total Population
Based on all places, regardless of total population

Place	Population	%
Northwood (cdp) Blair County	3	1.01
Greene (township) Pike County	5	0.13
Snyder (township) Blair County	3	0.09
Milford (township) Pike County	1	0.07
Waterford (borough) Erie County	1	0.07
Doylestown (borough) Bucks County	5	0.06
Cheswick (borough) Allegheny County	1	0.06
Catasauqua (borough) Lehigh County	3	0.05
Gettysburg (borough) Adams County	3	0.04
Delmar (township) Tioga County	1	0.04

Top 10 Places Sorted by Percent of Total Population
Based on places with total population of 50,000 or more

Place	Population	%
Philadelphia (city) Philadelphia County	7	<0.01
Pittsburgh (city) Allegheny County	4	<0.01
Allentown (city) Lehigh County	3	<0.01
Lancaster (city) Lancaster County	2	<0.01
Lower Merion (township) Montgomery County	2	<0.01
Erie (city) Erie County	1	<0.01
Abington (township) Montgomery County	0	0.00
Bensalem (township) Bucks County	0	0.00
Bethlehem (city) Northampton County	0	0.00
Bethlehem (city) Northampton County	0	0.00

American Indian: Houma

Top 10 Places Sorted by Population
Based on all places, regardless of total population

Place	Population	%
Salem (township) Luzerne County	7	0.16
East York (cdp) York County	4	0.05
Springettsbury (township) York County	4	0.01

Place	Population	%
Brentwood (borough) Allegheny County	3	0.03
Lansdowne (borough) Delaware County	2	0.02
Penn Forest (township) Carbon County	2	0.02
Philadelphia (city) Philadelphia County	2	<0.01
Long Branch (borough) Washington County	1	0.22
Canton (borough) Bradford County	1	0.05
Lawnton (cdp) Dauphin County	1	0.03

Top 10 Places Sorted by Percent of Total Population
Based on all places, regardless of total population

Place	Population	%
Long Branch (borough) Washington County	1	0.22
Salem (township) Luzerne County	7	0.16
East York (cdp) York County	4	0.05
Canton (borough) Bradford County	1	0.05
Brentwood (borough) Allegheny County	3	0.03
Lawnton (cdp) Dauphin County	1	0.03
Manheim (township) York County	1	0.03
Lansdowne (borough) Delaware County	2	0.02
Penn Forest (township) Carbon County	2	0.02
Springettsbury (township) York County	4	0.01

Top 10 Places Sorted by Percent of Total Population
Based on places with total population of 50,000 or more

Place	Population	%
Philadelphia (city) Philadelphia County	2	<0.01
Abington (township) Montgomery County	0	0.00
Allentown (city) Lehigh County	0	0.00
Bensalem (township) Bucks County	0	0.00
Bethlehem (city) Northampton County	0	0.00
Bethlehem (city) Northampton County	0	0.00
Bristol (township) Bucks County	0	0.00
Erie (city) Erie County	0	0.00
Lancaster (city) Lancaster County	0	0.00
Levittown (cdp) Bucks County	0	0.00

Alaska Native: Inupiat (Eskimo)

Top 10 Places Sorted by Population
Based on all places, regardless of total population

Place	Population	%
Churchtown (cdp) Lancaster County	5	1.06
Caernarvon (township) Lancaster County	5	0.11
Shrewsbury (township) York County	4	0.06
West Brownsville (borough) Washington County	3	0.30
Hanover (borough) York County	3	0.02
Sharon (city) Mercer County	3	0.02
Abington (township) Montgomery County	3	0.01
North Huntingdon (township) Westmoreland County	3	<0.01
Philadelphia (city) Philadelphia County	3	<0.01
Reading (city) Berks County	3	<0.01

Top 10 Places Sorted by Percent of Total Population
Based on all places, regardless of total population

Place	Population	%
Churchtown (cdp) Lancaster County	5	1.06
Colebrook (township) Clinton County	2	1.01
Hebron (township) Potter County	2	0.34
West Brownsville (borough) Washington County	3	0.30
Loganton (borough) Clinton County	1	0.21
Carrolltown (borough) Cambria County	1	0.12
Caernarvon (township) Lancaster County	5	0.11
Royalton (borough) Dauphin County	1	0.11
Pleasant Gap (cdp) Centre County	2	0.07
Greenwood (township) Crawford County	1	0.07

Top 10 Places Sorted by Percent of Total Population
Based on places with total population of 50,000 or more

Place	Population	%
Abington (township) Montgomery County	3	0.01
Philadelphia (city) Philadelphia County	3	<0.01
Reading (city) Berks County	3	<0.01
Lancaster (city) Lancaster County	2	<0.01
Pittsburgh (city) Allegheny County	2	<0.01
Upper Darby (township) Delaware County	1	<0.01
Allentown (city) Lehigh County	0	0.00
Bensalem (township) Bucks County	0	0.00
Bethlehem (city) Northampton County	0	0.00
Bethlehem (city) Northampton County	0	0.00

American Indian: Iroquois

Top 10 Places Sorted by Population
Based on all places, regardless of total population

Place	Population	%
Philadelphia (city) Philadelphia County	216	0.01
Erie (city) Erie County	105	0.10
Pittsburgh (city) Allegheny County	50	0.02
Millcreek (township) Erie County	28	0.05
Lancaster (city) Lancaster County	25	0.04
Bristol (township) Bucks County	22	0.04
Levittown (cdp) Bucks County	22	0.04
Bensalem (township) Bucks County	21	0.03
Allentown (city) Lehigh County	19	0.02
Bradford (city) McKean County	18	0.21

Top 10 Places Sorted by Percent of Total Population
Based on all places, regardless of total population

Place	Population	%
Falls Creek (borough) Clearfield County	1	2.08
Harmonsburg (cdp) Crawford County	8	2.00
Grugan (township) Clinton County	1	1.96
Overton (township) Bradford County	4	1.62
Nicholson (borough) Wyoming County	11	1.43
Hannasville (cdp) Venango County	2	1.14
Lumber (township) Cameron County	2	1.03
Starbrick (cdp) Warren County	5	0.96
Girard (township) Clearfield County	5	0.94
Sylvania (borough) Bradford County	2	0.91

Top 10 Places Sorted by Percent of Total Population
Based on places with total population of 50,000 or more

Place	Population	%
Erie (city) Erie County	105	0.10
Millcreek (township) Erie County	28	0.05
Lancaster (city) Lancaster County	25	0.04
Bristol (township) Bucks County	22	0.04
Levittown (cdp) Bucks County	22	0.04
Bensalem (township) Bucks County	21	0.03
Pittsburgh (city) Allegheny County	50	0.02
Allentown (city) Lehigh County	19	0.02
Reading (city) Berks County	14	0.02
Scranton (city) Lackawanna County	14	0.02

American Indian: Kiowa

Top 10 Places Sorted by Population
Based on all places, regardless of total population

Place	Population	%
Philadelphia (city) Philadelphia County	9	<0.01
Walker (township) Schuylkill County	6	0.57
Lansdowne (borough) Delaware County	6	0.06
State College (borough) Centre County	6	0.01
McCandless (township) Allegheny County	5	0.02
Mill Hall (borough) Clinton County	4	0.25
Clay (township) Butler County	4	0.15
Mount Pocono (borough) Monroe County	4	0.13
West Hanover (township) Dauphin County	4	0.04
Pittsburgh (city) Allegheny County	4	<0.01

Top 10 Places Sorted by Percent of Total Population
Based on all places, regardless of total population

Place	Population	%
Walker (township) Schuylkill County	6	0.57
Mill Hall (borough) Clinton County	4	0.25
Clay (township) Butler County	4	0.15
Mount Pocono (borough) Monroe County	4	0.13
Rice (township) Luzerne County	3	0.09
Highspire (borough) Dauphin County	2	0.08
Emigsville (cdp) York County	2	0.07
Lansdowne (borough) Delaware County	6	0.06
Shippensburg (borough) Cumberland County	2	0.05
West Hanover (township) Dauphin County	4	0.04

Top 10 Places Sorted by Percent of Total Population
Based on places with total population of 50,000 or more

Place	Population	%
Philadelphia (city) Philadelphia County	9	<0.01
Pittsburgh (city) Allegheny County	4	<0.01
Lower Merion (township) Montgomery County	2	<0.01
Bristol (township) Bucks County	1	<0.01

Abington (township) Montgomery County	0	0.00
Allentown (city) Lehigh County	0	0.00
Bensalem (township) Bucks County	0	0.00
Bethlehem (city) Northampton County	0	0.00
Bethlehem (city) Northampton County	0	0.00
Erie (city) Erie County	0	0.00

American Indian: Lumbee

Top 10 Places Sorted by Population
Based on all places, regardless of total population

Place	Population	%
Philadelphia (city) Philadelphia County	121	0.01
Pittsburgh (city) Allegheny County	12	<0.01
Middletown (township) Bucks County	11	0.02
Abington (township) Montgomery County	10	0.02
Canaan (township) Wayne County	9	0.23
Penn (township) York County	8	0.05
Cheltenham (township) Montgomery County	7	0.02
Spry (cdp) York County	6	0.12
Chanceford (township) York County	6	0.10
York (township) York County	6	0.02

Top 10 Places Sorted by Percent of Total Population
Based on all places, regardless of total population

Place	Population	%
Hickory (township) Forest County	2	0.36
Penn (township) Centre County	4	0.34
Deemston (borough) Washington County	2	0.28
Oval (cdp) Lycoming County	1	0.28
Catawissa (borough) Columbia County	4	0.26
McKean (borough) Erie County	1	0.26
Canaan (township) Wayne County	9	0.23
Franklin (township) Luzerne County	4	0.23
North York (borough) York County	4	0.21
Dalmatia (cdp) Northumberland County	1	0.20

Top 10 Places Sorted by Percent of Total Population
Based on places with total population of 50,000 or more

Place	Population	%
Abington (township) Montgomery County	10	0.02
Philadelphia (city) Philadelphia County	121	0.01
Bensalem (township) Bucks County	5	0.01
Reading (city) Berks County	5	0.01
Bristol (township) Bucks County	4	0.01
Levittown (cdp) Bucks County	4	0.01
Lower Merion (township) Montgomery County	3	0.01
Pittsburgh (city) Allegheny County	12	<0.01
Allentown (city) Lehigh County	4	<0.01
Upper Darby (township) Delaware County	3	<0.01

American Indian: Menominee

Top 10 Places Sorted by Population
Based on all places, regardless of total population

Place	Population	%
Philadelphia (city) Philadelphia County	6	<0.01
Alsace (township) Berks County	4	0.11
North Codorus (township) York County	2	0.02
West Branch (township) Potter County	1	0.25
Gordon (borough) Schuylkill County	1	0.13
Enhaut (cdp) Dauphin County	1	0.10
West Easton (borough) Northampton County	1	0.08
Bethel (township) Fulton County	1	0.07
Eagleville (cdp) Montgomery County	1	0.02
Royersford (borough) Montgomery County	1	0.02

Top 10 Places Sorted by Percent of Total Population
Based on all places, regardless of total population

Place	Population	%
West Branch (township) Potter County	1	0.25
Gordon (borough) Schuylkill County	1	0.13
Alsace (township) Berks County	4	0.11
Enhaut (cdp) Dauphin County	1	0.10
West Easton (borough) Northampton County	1	0.08
Bethel (township) Fulton County	1	0.07
North Codorus (township) York County	2	0.02
Eagleville (cdp) Montgomery County	1	0.02
Royersford (borough) Montgomery County	1	0.02
Schlusser (cdp) Cumberland County	1	0.02

Top 10 Places Sorted by Percent of Total Population
Based on places with total population of 50,000 or more

Place	Population	%
Philadelphia (city) Philadelphia County	6	<0.01
Bensalem (township) Bucks County	1	<0.01
Reading (city) Berks County	1	<0.01
Abington (township) Montgomery County	0	0.00
Allentown (city) Lehigh County	0	0.00
Bethlehem (city) Northampton County	0	0.00
Bethlehem (city) Northampton County	0	0.00
Bristol (township) Bucks County	0	0.00
Erie (city) Erie County	0	0.00
Lancaster (city) Lancaster County	0	0.00

American Indian: Mexican American Indian

Top 10 Places Sorted by Population
Based on all places, regardless of total population

Place	Population	%
Philadelphia (city) Philadelphia County	185	0.01
Bensalem (township) Bucks County	113	0.19
Reading (city) Berks County	59	0.07
Allentown (city) Lehigh County	51	0.04
New Garden (township) Chester County	44	0.37
Pittsburgh (city) Allegheny County	36	0.01
Kennett (township) Chester County	18	0.24
Bristol (township) Bucks County	17	0.03
Erie (city) Erie County	17	0.02
Kennett Square (borough) Chester County	16	0.26

Top 10 Places Sorted by Percent of Total Population
Based on all places, regardless of total population

Place	Population	%
Armagh (borough) Indiana County	1	0.82
Toughkenamon (cdp) Chester County	11	0.74
Avondale (borough) Chester County	9	0.71
Wyalusing (borough) Bradford County	4	0.67
East Salem (cdp) Juniata County	1	0.54
West St. Clair (township) Bedford County	8	0.46
North Abington (township) Lackawanna County	3	0.43
Highland (township) Adams County	4	0.42
New Garden (township) Chester County	44	0.37
Bechtelsville (borough) Berks County	3	0.32

Top 10 Places Sorted by Percent of Total Population
Based on places with total population of 50,000 or more

Place	Population	%
Bensalem (township) Bucks County	113	0.19
Reading (city) Berks County	59	0.07
Allentown (city) Lehigh County	51	0.04
Bristol (township) Bucks County	17	0.03
Erie (city) Erie County	17	0.02
Levittown (cdp) Bucks County	11	0.02
Lancaster (city) Lancaster County	10	0.02
Philadelphia (city) Philadelphia County	185	0.01
Pittsburgh (city) Allegheny County	36	0.01
Upper Darby (township) Delaware County	12	0.01

American Indian: Navajo

Top 10 Places Sorted by Population
Based on all places, regardless of total population

Place	Population	%
Philadelphia (city) Philadelphia County	99	0.01
Pittsburgh (city) Allegheny County	16	0.01
Easton (city) Northampton County	9	0.03
Radnor (township) Delaware County	7	0.02
Bethlehem (city) Northampton County	7	0.01
Erie (city) Erie County	7	0.01
Menallen (township) Adams County	6	0.17
West Reading (borough) Berks County	6	0.14
Kelly (township) Union County	6	0.11
Dunbar (township) Fayette County	6	0.08

Top 10 Places Sorted by Percent of Total Population
Based on all places, regardless of total population

Place	Population	%
Frankfort Springs (borough) Beaver County	1	0.77
Wells (township) Bradford County	4	0.49

Place	Population	%
Mocanaqua (cdp) Luzerne County	3	0.46
French Creek (township) Mercer County	3	0.39
Picture Rocks (borough) Lycoming County	2	0.29
Neville (township) Allegheny County	3	0.28
Mount Aetna (cdp) Berks County	1	0.28
Point Marion (borough) Fayette County	3	0.26
Paint (township) Clarion County	4	0.24
Dale (borough) Cambria County	3	0.24

Top 10 Places Sorted by Percent of Total Population
Based on places with total population of 50,000 or more

Place	Population	%
Philadelphia (city) Philadelphia County	99	0.01
Pittsburgh (city) Allegheny County	16	0.01
Bethlehem (city) Northampton County	7	0.01
Erie (city) Erie County	7	0.01
Bensalem (township) Bucks County	6	0.01
Bethlehem (city) Northampton County	5	0.01
Abington (township) Montgomery County	4	0.01
Lower Merion (township) Montgomery County	3	0.01
Allentown (city) Lehigh County	4	<0.01
Upper Darby (township) Delaware County	3	<0.01

American Indian: Osage

Top 10 Places Sorted by Population
Based on all places, regardless of total population

Place	Population	%
Philadelphia (city) Philadelphia County	5	<0.01
Gordonville (cdp) Lancaster County	4	0.79
Clinton (township) Butler County	4	0.14
Leacock (township) Lancaster County	4	0.08
Camp Hill (borough) Cumberland County	3	0.04
Mount Lebanon (township) Allegheny County	3	0.01
Pittsburgh (city) Allegheny County	3	<0.01
Johnsonburg (borough) Elk County	2	0.08
Tinicum (township) Bucks County	2	0.05
Coraopolis (borough) Allegheny County	2	0.04

Top 10 Places Sorted by Percent of Total Population
Based on all places, regardless of total population

Place	Population	%
Gordonville (cdp) Lancaster County	4	0.79
Gardners (cdp) Adams County	1	0.67
Greenwood (township) Juniata County	1	0.16
Clinton (township) Butler County	4	0.14
Leacock (township) Lancaster County	4	0.08
Johnsonburg (borough) Elk County	2	0.08
Morrisville (cdp) Greene County	1	0.08
Bressler (cdp) Dauphin County	1	0.07
Milroy (cdp) Mifflin County	1	0.07
Monongahela (township) Greene County	1	0.06

Top 10 Places Sorted by Percent of Total Population
Based on places with total population of 50,000 or more

Place	Population	%
Philadelphia (city) Philadelphia County	5	<0.01
Pittsburgh (city) Allegheny County	3	<0.01
Abington (township) Montgomery County	0	0.00
Allentown (city) Lehigh County	0	0.00
Bensalem (township) Bucks County	0	0.00
Bethlehem (city) Northampton County	0	0.00
Bethlehem (city) Northampton County	0	0.00
Bristol (township) Bucks County	0	0.00
Erie (city) Erie County	0	0.00
Lancaster (city) Lancaster County	0	0.00

American Indian: Ottawa

Top 10 Places Sorted by Population
Based on all places, regardless of total population

Place	Population	%
Bethlehem (city) Northampton County	5	0.01
Hanover (township) Lehigh County	3	0.19
Bethlehem (city) Northampton County	3	0.01
Curwensville (borough) Clearfield County	2	0.08
Breinigsville (cdp) Lehigh County	2	0.05
Bethlehem (city) Lehigh County	2	0.01
Palmer (township) Northampton County	2	0.01
Upper Macungie (township) Lehigh County	2	0.01
Haverford (township) Delaware County	2	<0.01

Place	Population	%
Lower Merion (township) Montgomery County	2	<0.01

Top 10 Places Sorted by Percent of Total Population
Based on all places, regardless of total population

Place	Population	%
Hanover (township) Lehigh County	3	0.19
Wall (borough) Allegheny County	1	0.17
Curwensville (borough) Clearfield County	2	0.08
Breinigsville (cdp) Lehigh County	2	0.05
Cherry Ridge (township) Wayne County	1	0.05
Palmer Heights (cdp) Northampton County	1	0.03
Parkesburg (borough) Chester County	1	0.03
Port Vue (borough) Allegheny County	1	0.03
Narberth (borough) Montgomery County	1	0.02
Bethlehem (city) Northampton County	5	0.01

Top 10 Places Sorted by Percent of Total Population
Based on places with total population of 50,000 or more

Place	Population	%
Bethlehem (city) Northampton County	5	0.01
Bethlehem (city) Northampton County	3	0.01
Lower Merion (township) Montgomery County	2	<0.01
Philadelphia (city) Philadelphia County	2	<0.01
Upper Darby (township) Delaware County	2	<0.01
Abington (township) Montgomery County	0	0.00
Allentown (city) Lehigh County	0	0.00
Bensalem (township) Bucks County	0	0.00
Bristol (township) Bucks County	0	0.00
Erie (city) Erie County	0	0.00

American Indian: Paiute

Top 10 Places Sorted by Population
Based on all places, regardless of total population

Place	Population	%
Kennedy (township) Allegheny County	4	0.05
Philadelphia (city) Philadelphia County	4	<0.01
Dravosburg (borough) Allegheny County	3	0.17
Jefferson (township) Greene County	3	0.13
Monroe (township) Snyder County	3	0.08
Halfway House (cdp) Montgomery County	2	0.07
Franklin (township) York County	2	0.04
Upper Pottsgrove (township) Montgomery County	2	0.04
Trevorton (cdp) Northumberland County	1	0.05
Zerbe (township) Northumberland County	1	0.05

Top 10 Places Sorted by Percent of Total Population
Based on all places, regardless of total population

Place	Population	%
Dravosburg (borough) Allegheny County	3	0.17
Jefferson (township) Greene County	3	0.13
Monroe (township) Snyder County	3	0.08
Halfway House (cdp) Montgomery County	2	0.07
Kennedy (township) Allegheny County	4	0.05
Trevorton (cdp) Northumberland County	1	0.05
Zerbe (township) Northumberland County	1	0.05
Franklin (township) York County	2	0.04
Upper Pottsgrove (township) Montgomery County	2	0.04
Charleston (township) Tioga County	1	0.03

Top 10 Places Sorted by Percent of Total Population
Based on places with total population of 50,000 or more

Place	Population	%
Philadelphia (city) Philadelphia County	4	<0.01
Bethlehem (city) Northampton County	1	<0.01
Bethlehem (city) Northampton County	1	<0.01
Lancaster (city) Lancaster County	1	<0.01
Reading (city) Berks County	1	<0.01
Abington (township) Montgomery County	0	0.00
Allentown (city) Lehigh County	0	0.00
Bensalem (township) Bucks County	0	0.00
Bristol (township) Bucks County	0	0.00
Erie (city) Erie County	0	0.00

American Indian: Pima

Top 10 Places Sorted by Population
Based on all places, regardless of total population

Place	Population	%
Northumberland (borough) Northumberland County	4	0.11

Place	Population	%
Masontown (borough) Fayette County	3	0.09
Ross (township) Monroe County	3	0.05
New Cumberland (borough) Cumberland County	3	0.04
Bensalem (township) Bucks County	3	<0.01
Fountain Hill (borough) Lehigh County	2	0.04
Coolbaugh (township) Monroe County	2	0.01
Philadelphia (city) Philadelphia County	2	<0.01
Millersburg (borough) Dauphin County	1	0.04
Point (township) Northumberland County	1	0.03

Top 10 Places Sorted by Percent of Total Population
Based on all places, regardless of total population

Place	Population	%
Northumberland (borough) Northumberland County	4	0.11
Masontown (borough) Fayette County	3	0.09
Ross (township) Monroe County	3	0.05
New Cumberland (borough) Cumberland County	3	0.04
Fountain Hill (borough) Lehigh County	2	0.04
Millersburg (borough) Dauphin County	1	0.04
Point (township) Northumberland County	1	0.03
Kelly (township) Union County	1	0.02
Lionville (cdp) Chester County	1	0.02
West Rockhill (township) Bucks County	1	0.02

Top 10 Places Sorted by Percent of Total Population
Based on places with total population of 50,000 or more

Place	Population	%
Bensalem (township) Bucks County	3	<0.01
Philadelphia (city) Philadelphia County	2	<0.01
Lancaster (city) Lancaster County	1	<0.01
Abington (township) Montgomery County	0	0.00
Allentown (city) Lehigh County	0	0.00
Bethlehem (city) Northampton County	0	0.00
Bethlehem (city) Northampton County	0	0.00
Bristol (township) Bucks County	0	0.00
Erie (city) Erie County	0	0.00
Levittown (cdp) Bucks County	0	0.00

American Indian: Potawatomi

Top 10 Places Sorted by Population
Based on all places, regardless of total population

Place	Population	%
Philadelphia (city) Philadelphia County	14	<0.01
East Whiteland (township) Chester County	5	0.05
Greene (township) Franklin County	5	0.03
Manor (township) Lancaster County	5	0.03
Waynesboro (borough) Franklin County	4	0.04
Cumru (township) Berks County	4	0.03
York (city) York County	4	0.01
Hamiltonban (township) Adams County	3	0.13
Gibsonia (cdp) Allegheny County	3	0.11
Penn Estates (cdp) Monroe County	3	0.07

Top 10 Places Sorted by Percent of Total Population
Based on all places, regardless of total population

Place	Population	%
Burlington (township) Bradford County	2	0.25
Green (township) Forest County	1	0.19
Stouchsburg (cdp) Berks County	1	0.17
Hamiltonban (township) Adams County	3	0.13
Manchester (township) Wayne County	1	0.12
Gibsonia (cdp) Allegheny County	3	0.11
Moreland (township) Lycoming County	1	0.11
Liberty (township) Adams County	1	0.08
West Easton (borough) Northampton County	1	0.08
Penn Estates (cdp) Monroe County	3	0.07

Top 10 Places Sorted by Percent of Total Population
Based on places with total population of 50,000 or more

Place	Population	%
Philadelphia (city) Philadelphia County	14	<0.01
Reading (city) Berks County	3	<0.01
Pittsburgh (city) Allegheny County	2	<0.01
Bensalem (township) Bucks County	1	<0.01
Lancaster (city) Lancaster County	1	<0.01
Abington (township) Montgomery County	0	0.00
Allentown (city) Lehigh County	0	0.00
Bethlehem (city) Northampton County	0	0.00
Bethlehem (city) Northampton County	0	0.00
Bristol (township) Bucks County	0	0.00

American Indian: Pueblo

Top 10 Places Sorted by Population
Based on all places, regardless of total population

Place	Population	%
Philadelphia (city) Philadelphia County	42	<0.01
Reading (city) Berks County	26	0.03
Pittsburgh (city) Allegheny County	8	<0.01
Monroeville (municipality) Allegheny County	7	0.02
Hazleton (city) Luzerne County	6	0.02
Bethlehem (city) Northampton County	6	0.01
Milton (borough) Northumberland County	5	0.07
Carbondale (city) Lackawanna County	5	0.06
Bethlehem (city) Northampton County	5	0.01
Swarthmore (borough) Delaware County	4	0.06

Top 10 Places Sorted by Percent of Total Population
Based on all places, regardless of total population

Place	Population	%
Ben Avon Heights (borough) Allegheny County	3	0.81
Richfield (cdp) Juniata County	1	0.18
East Chillisquaque (township) Northumberland County	1	0.15
Knox (township) Clearfield County	1	0.15
Kilbuck (township) Allegheny County	1	0.14
Hyde Park (cdp) Berks County	3	0.12
Glen Rock (borough) York County	2	0.10
Conneaut Lakeshore (cdp) Crawford County	2	0.08
Forward (township) Butler County	2	0.08
Milton (borough) Northumberland County	5	0.07

Top 10 Places Sorted by Percent of Total Population
Based on places with total population of 50,000 or more

Place	Population	%
Reading (city) Berks County	26	0.03
Bethlehem (city) Northampton County	6	0.01
Bethlehem (city) Northampton County	5	0.01
Philadelphia (city) Philadelphia County	42	<0.01
Pittsburgh (city) Allegheny County	8	<0.01
Scranton (city) Lackawanna County	3	<0.01
Bensalem (township) Bucks County	2	<0.01
Allentown (city) Lehigh County	1	<0.01
Erie (city) Erie County	1	<0.01
Lancaster (city) Lancaster County	1	<0.01

American Indian: Puget Sound Salish

Top 10 Places Sorted by Population
Based on all places, regardless of total population

Place	Population	%
Philadelphia (city) Philadelphia County	5	<0.01
Tobyhanna (township) Monroe County	4	0.05
Upper Saucon (township) Lehigh County	3	0.02
Osceola (township) Tioga County	2	0.30
Barr (township) Cambria County	2	0.10
Luzerne (borough) Luzerne County	2	0.07
Camp Hill (borough) Cumberland County	2	0.03
Whitehall (borough) Allegheny County	2	0.01
Riegelsville (borough) Bucks County	1	0.12
Bear Creek (township) Luzerne County	1	0.04

Top 10 Places Sorted by Percent of Total Population
Based on all places, regardless of total population

Place	Population	%
Osceola (township) Tioga County	2	0.30
Riegelsville (borough) Bucks County	1	0.12
Barr (township) Cambria County	2	0.10
Luzerne (borough) Luzerne County	2	0.07
Tobyhanna (township) Monroe County	4	0.05
Bear Creek (township) Luzerne County	1	0.04
Hemlock (township) Columbia County	1	0.04
Muddy Creek (township) Butler County	1	0.04
Camp Hill (borough) Cumberland County	2	0.03
Forward (township) Allegheny County	1	0.03

Top 10 Places Sorted by Percent of Total Population
Based on places with total population of 50,000 or more

Place	Population	%
Philadelphia (city) Philadelphia County	5	<0.01
Allentown (city) Lehigh County	1	<0.01
Bethlehem (city) Northampton County	1	<0.01

Place	Population	%
Lancaster (city) Lancaster County	1	<0.01
Abington (township) Montgomery County	0	0.00
Bensalem (township) Bucks County	0	0.00
Bethlehem (city) Northampton County	0	0.00
Bristol (township) Bucks County	0	0.00
Erie (city) Erie County	0	0.00
Levittown (cdp) Bucks County	0	0.00

American Indian: Seminole

Top 10 Places Sorted by Population
Based on all places, regardless of total population

Place	Population	%
Philadelphia (city) Philadelphia County	189	0.01
Pittsburgh (city) Allegheny County	31	0.01
McKeesport (city) Allegheny County	13	0.07
Harrisburg (city) Dauphin County	13	0.03
Monroeville (municipality) Allegheny County	10	0.04
Tunkhannock (township) Monroe County	7	0.10
Bethlehem (city) Northampton County	7	0.01
Sierra View (cdp) Monroe County	6	0.12
Wilkinsburg (borough) Allegheny County	6	0.04
Bethlehem (city) Northampton County	6	0.01

Top 10 Places Sorted by Percent of Total Population
Based on all places, regardless of total population

Place	Population	%
Oklahoma (cdp) Clearfield County	4	0.51
Bloom (township) Clearfield County	2	0.48
Washington (township) Wyoming County	4	0.28
East Pittsburgh (borough) Allegheny County	4	0.22
Montour (township) Columbia County	3	0.22
Perry (township) Berks County	5	0.21
Ackermanville (cdp) Northampton County	1	0.16
Baldwin (township) Allegheny County	3	0.15
Bell (township) Westmoreland County	3	0.13
Eldred (township) Schuylkill County	1	0.13

Top 10 Places Sorted by Percent of Total Population
Based on places with total population of 50,000 or more

Place	Population	%
Philadelphia (city) Philadelphia County	189	0.01
Pittsburgh (city) Allegheny County	31	0.01
Bethlehem (city) Northampton County	7	0.01
Bethlehem (city) Northampton County	6	0.01
Bristol (township) Bucks County	6	0.01
Bensalem (township) Bucks County	4	0.01
Lancaster (city) Lancaster County	4	0.01
Lower Merion (township) Montgomery County	4	0.01
Allentown (city) Lehigh County	5	<0.01
Erie (city) Erie County	5	<0.01

American Indian: Shoshone

Top 10 Places Sorted by Population
Based on all places, regardless of total population

Place	Population	%
Philadelphia (city) Philadelphia County	11	<0.01
Wayne Heights (cdp) Franklin County	5	0.20
Columbia (borough) Lancaster County	5	0.05
Washington (township) Franklin County	5	0.04
Allentown (city) Lehigh County	5	<0.01
Tredyffrin (township) Chester County	4	0.01
Buffington (township) Indiana County	3	0.23
Oakdale (borough) Allegheny County	3	0.21
Lower Chanceford (township) York County	3	0.10
Chester (city) Delaware County	3	0.01

Top 10 Places Sorted by Percent of Total Population
Based on all places, regardless of total population

Place	Population	%
Buffington (township) Indiana County	3	0.23
Greens Landing (cdp) Bradford County	2	0.22
Oakdale (borough) Allegheny County	3	0.21
Wayne Heights (cdp) Franklin County	5	0.20
Lower Chanceford (township) York County	3	0.10
Derry (township) Montour County	1	0.09
Saylorsburg (cdp) Monroe County	1	0.09
Drumore (township) Lancaster County	2	0.08
Mountainhome (cdp) Monroe County	1	0.08
Linntown (cdp) Union County	1	0.07

Top 10 Places Sorted by Percent of Total Population
Based on places with total population of 50,000 or more

Place	Population	%
Millcreek (township) Erie County	3	0.01
Philadelphia (city) Philadelphia County	11	<0.01
Allentown (city) Lehigh County	5	<0.01
Erie (city) Erie County	2	<0.01
Pittsburgh (city) Allegheny County	1	<0.01
Abington (township) Montgomery County	0	0.00
Bensalem (township) Bucks County	0	0.00
Bethlehem (city) Northampton County	0	0.00
Bethlehem (city) Northampton County	0	0.00
Bristol (township) Bucks County	0	0.00

American Indian: Sioux

Top 10 Places Sorted by Population
Based on all places, regardless of total population

Place	Population	%
Philadelphia (city) Philadelphia County	199	0.01
Pittsburgh (city) Allegheny County	70	0.02
Erie (city) Erie County	33	0.03
Lancaster (city) Lancaster County	22	0.04
Allentown (city) Lehigh County	18	0.02
Bristol (township) Bucks County	16	0.03
Scranton (city) Lackawanna County	16	0.02
Ambler (borough) Montgomery County	15	0.23
Levittown (cdp) Bucks County	15	0.03
Penn Hills (township) Allegheny County	12	0.03

Top 10 Places Sorted by Percent of Total Population
Based on all places, regardless of total population

Place	Population	%
Shippingport (borough) Beaver County	4	1.87
Seven Valleys (borough) York County	7	1.35
Callery (borough) Butler County	4	1.02
Wharton (township) Potter County	1	1.01
Ravine (cdp) Schuylkill County	5	0.76
Polk (township) Jefferson County	2	0.75
Slovan (cdp) Washington County	3	0.54
Briar Creek (borough) Columbia County	3	0.45
Mountainhome (cdp) Monroe County	5	0.42
Lehigh (township) Carbon County	2	0.42

Top 10 Places Sorted by Percent of Total Population
Based on places with total population of 50,000 or more

Place	Population	%
Lancaster (city) Lancaster County	22	0.04
Erie (city) Erie County	33	0.03
Bristol (township) Bucks County	16	0.03
Levittown (cdp) Bucks County	15	0.03
Pittsburgh (city) Allegheny County	70	0.02
Allentown (city) Lehigh County	18	0.02
Scranton (city) Lackawanna County	16	0.02
Bensalem (township) Bucks County	11	0.02
Philadelphia (city) Philadelphia County	199	0.01
Reading (city) Berks County	12	0.01

American Indian: South American Indian

Top 10 Places Sorted by Population
Based on all places, regardless of total population

Place	Population	%
Philadelphia (city) Philadelphia County	657	0.04
Allentown (city) Lehigh County	135	0.11
Lancaster (city) Lancaster County	77	0.13
Reading (city) Berks County	74	0.08
Bethlehem (city) Northampton County	73	0.10
Bethlehem (city) Northampton County	54	0.10
Lehman (township) Pike County	34	0.32
Coolbaugh (township) Monroe County	28	0.14
Pittsburgh (city) Allegheny County	26	0.01
Lebanon (city) Lebanon County	25	0.10

Top 10 Places Sorted by Percent of Total Population
Based on all places, regardless of total population

Place	Population	%
Saw Creek (cdp) Pike County	21	0.52
South Waverly (borough) Bradford County	5	0.49
Ackermanville (cdp) Northampton County	3	0.49

Place	Population	%
Hopewell (borough) Bedford County	1	0.43
Bethany (borough) Wayne County	1	0.41
Pocono Ranch Lands (cdp) Pike County	4	0.38
Adamstown (borough) Lancaster County	6	0.34
Adamstown (borough) Lancaster County	6	0.34
Mill Creek (township) Lycoming County	2	0.33
Lehman (township) Pike County	34	0.32

Top 10 Places Sorted by Percent of Total Population
Based on places with total population of 50,000 or more

Place	Population	%
Lancaster (city) Lancaster County	77	0.13
Allentown (city) Lehigh County	135	0.11
Bethlehem (city) Northampton County	73	0.10
Bethlehem (city) Northampton County	54	0.10
Reading (city) Berks County	74	0.08
Philadelphia (city) Philadelphia County	657	0.04
Levittown (cdp) Bucks County	20	0.04
Bensalem (township) Bucks County	14	0.02
Bristol (township) Bucks County	11	0.02
Pittsburgh (city) Allegheny County	26	0.01

American Indian: Spanish American Indian

Top 10 Places Sorted by Population
Based on all places, regardless of total population

Place	Population	%
Philadelphia (city) Philadelphia County	156	0.01
Allentown (city) Lehigh County	27	0.02
Norristown (borough) Montgomery County	17	0.05
Reading (city) Berks County	17	0.02
Lancaster (city) Lancaster County	11	0.02
Hazleton (city) Luzerne County	8	0.03
West Goshen (township) Chester County	7	0.03
Chester (city) Delaware County	7	0.02
Harrisburg (city) Dauphin County	7	0.01
Pittsburgh (city) Allegheny County	7	<0.01

Top 10 Places Sorted by Percent of Total Population
Based on all places, regardless of total population

Place	Population	%
Pomeroy (cdp) Chester County	4	1.00
Vandling (borough) Lackawanna County	3	0.40
Hughestown (borough) Luzerne County	5	0.36
Oberlin (cdp) Dauphin County	2	0.34
Lebanon South (cdp) Lebanon County	3	0.13
West St. Clair (township) Bedford County	2	0.12
Sadsbury (township) Chester County	4	0.11
Fayette (township) Juniata County	3	0.09
Thompson (township) Fulton County	1	0.09
Terre Hill (borough) Lancaster County	1	0.08

Top 10 Places Sorted by Percent of Total Population
Based on places with total population of 50,000 or more

Place	Population	%
Allentown (city) Lehigh County	27	0.02
Reading (city) Berks County	17	0.02
Lancaster (city) Lancaster County	11	0.02
Philadelphia (city) Philadelphia County	156	0.01
Bensalem (township) Bucks County	5	0.01
Pittsburgh (city) Allegheny County	7	<0.01
Upper Darby (township) Delaware County	3	<0.01
Scranton (city) Lackawanna County	2	<0.01
Bethlehem (city) Northampton County	1	<0.01
Bethlehem (city) Northampton County	1	<0.01

Alaska Native: Tlingit-Haida

Top 10 Places Sorted by Population
Based on all places, regardless of total population

Place	Population	%
Philadelphia (city) Philadelphia County	18	<0.01
Erie (city) Erie County	5	<0.01
Carroll (township) York County	4	0.07
Franconia (township) Montgomery County	4	0.03
Lower Merion (township) Montgomery County	4	0.01
Port Royal (borough) Juniata County	3	0.32
Cambridge (township) Crawford County	3	0.19
Walnutport (borough) Northampton County	3	0.14
Pittsburgh (city) Allegheny County	3	<0.01

Place	Population	%
Juniata Terrace (borough) Mifflin County	2	0.37

Top 10 Places Sorted by Percent of Total Population
Based on all places, regardless of total population

Place	Population	%
Juniata Terrace (borough) Mifflin County	2	0.37
Port Royal (borough) Juniata County	3	0.32
Cooperstown (borough) Venango County	1	0.22
Cambridge (township) Crawford County	3	0.19
Walnutport (borough) Northampton County	3	0.14
Exeter (township) Wyoming County	1	0.14
Cherryville (cdp) Northampton County	2	0.13
Glenburn (cdp) Lackawanna County	1	0.10
Yoe (borough) York County	1	0.10
Ashland (township) Clarion County	1	0.09

Top 10 Places Sorted by Percent of Total Population
Based on places with total population of 50,000 or more

Place	Population	%
Lower Merion (township) Montgomery County	4	0.01
Philadelphia (city) Philadelphia County	18	<0.01
Erie (city) Erie County	5	<0.01
Pittsburgh (city) Allegheny County	3	<0.01
Millcreek (township) Erie County	2	<0.01
Reading (city) Berks County	1	<0.01
Upper Darby (township) Delaware County	1	<0.01
Abington (township) Montgomery County	0	0.00
Allentown (city) Lehigh County	0	0.00
Bensalem (township) Bucks County	0	0.00

American Indian: Tohono O'Odham

Top 10 Places Sorted by Population
Based on all places, regardless of total population

Place	Population	%
Shirley (township) Huntingdon County	4	0.16
Jim Thorpe (borough) Carbon County	4	0.08
College (township) Centre County	4	0.04
Millcreek (township) Erie County	4	0.01
Hallstead (borough) Susquehanna County	3	0.23
Metal (township) Franklin County	3	0.16
Stroud (township) Monroe County	3	0.02
Chester (city) Delaware County	3	0.01
Allentown (city) Lehigh County	3	<0.01
Philadelphia (city) Philadelphia County	3	<0.01

Top 10 Places Sorted by Percent of Total Population
Based on all places, regardless of total population

Place	Population	%
Hallstead (borough) Susquehanna County	3	0.23
Shirley (township) Huntingdon County	4	0.16
Metal (township) Franklin County	3	0.16
Trumbauersville (borough) Bucks County	1	0.10
Taylor (township) Fulton County	1	0.09
Jim Thorpe (borough) Carbon County	4	0.08
Penbrook (borough) Dauphin County	2	0.07
College (township) Centre County	4	0.04
Lehighton (borough) Carbon County	2	0.04
Center (township) Butler County	2	0.03

Top 10 Places Sorted by Percent of Total Population
Based on places with total population of 50,000 or more

Place	Population	%
Millcreek (township) Erie County	4	0.01
Allentown (city) Lehigh County	3	<0.01
Philadelphia (city) Philadelphia County	3	<0.01
Reading (city) Berks County	2	<0.01
Lower Merion (township) Montgomery County	1	<0.01
Abington (township) Montgomery County	0	0.00
Bensalem (township) Bucks County	0	0.00
Bethlehem (city) Northampton County	0	0.00
Bethlehem (city) Northampton County	0	0.00
Bristol (township) Bucks County	0	0.00

Alaska Native: Tsimshian

Top 10 Places Sorted by Population
Based on all places, regardless of total population

Place	Population	%
Oakland (township) Butler County	4	0.13

Place	Population	%
Lower Merion (township) Montgomery County	3	0.01
Todd (township) Fulton County	1	0.07
Leesport (borough) Berks County	1	0.05
Greencastle (borough) Franklin County	1	0.03
Derry (township) Mifflin County	1	0.01
Philadelphia (city) Philadelphia County	1	<0.01
Pittsburgh (city) Allegheny County	1	<0.01
Aaronsburg (cdp) Centre County	0	0.00
Aaronsburg (cdp) Washington County	0	0.00

Top 10 Places Sorted by Percent of Total Population
Based on all places, regardless of total population

Place	Population	%
Oakland (township) Butler County	4	0.13
Todd (township) Fulton County	1	0.07
Leesport (borough) Berks County	1	0.05
Greencastle (borough) Franklin County	1	0.03
Lower Merion (township) Montgomery County	3	0.01
Derry (township) Mifflin County	1	0.01
Philadelphia (city) Philadelphia County	1	<0.01
Pittsburgh (city) Allegheny County	1	<0.01
Aaronsburg (cdp) Centre County	0	0.00
Aaronsburg (cdp) Washington County	0	0.00

Top 10 Places Sorted by Percent of Total Population
Based on places with total population of 50,000 or more

Place	Population	%
Lower Merion (township) Montgomery County	3	0.01
Philadelphia (city) Philadelphia County	1	<0.01
Pittsburgh (city) Allegheny County	1	<0.01
Abington (township) Montgomery County	0	0.00
Allentown (city) Lehigh County	0	0.00
Bensalem (township) Bucks County	0	0.00
Bethlehem (city) Northampton County	0	0.00
Bethlehem (city) Northampton County	0	0.00
Bristol (township) Bucks County	0	0.00
Erie (city) Erie County	0	0.00

American Indian: Ute

Top 10 Places Sorted by Population
Based on all places, regardless of total population

Place	Population	%
Hawk Run (cdp) Clearfield County	3	0.56
Morris (township) Clearfield County	3	0.10
Upper Darby (township) Delaware County	3	<0.01
Mount Oliver (borough) Allegheny County	2	0.06
Mount Carmel (borough) Northumberland County	2	0.03
Hopewell (township) Beaver County	2	0.02
Swissvale (borough) Allegheny County	2	0.02
Upper Uwchlan (township) Chester County	2	0.02
York (city) York County	2	<0.01
New Milford (borough) Susquehanna County	1	0.12

Top 10 Places Sorted by Percent of Total Population
Based on all places, regardless of total population

Place	Population	%
Hawk Run (cdp) Clearfield County	3	0.56
New Milford (borough) Susquehanna County	1	0.12
Morris (township) Clearfield County	3	0.10
Mount Oliver (borough) Allegheny County	2	0.06
Rockledge (borough) Montgomery County	1	0.04
Mount Carmel (borough) Northumberland County	2	0.03
Greene (township) Pike County	1	0.03
Laureldale (borough) Berks County	1	0.03
Waterford (township) Erie County	1	0.03
Hopewell (township) Beaver County	2	0.02

Top 10 Places Sorted by Percent of Total Population
Based on places with total population of 50,000 or more

Place	Population	%
Upper Darby (township) Delaware County	3	<0.01
Erie (city) Erie County	1	<0.01
Millcreek (township) Erie County	1	<0.01
Pittsburgh (city) Allegheny County	1	<0.01
Abington (township) Montgomery County	0	0.00
Allentown (city) Lehigh County	0	0.00
Bensalem (township) Bucks County	0	0.00
Bethlehem (city) Northampton County	0	0.00
Bethlehem (city) Northampton County	0	0.00
Bristol (township) Bucks County	0	0.00

American Indian: Yakama

Top 10 Places Sorted by Population
Based on all places, regardless of total population

Place	Population	%
Colonial Park (cdp) Dauphin County	2	0.02
Lower Paxton (township) Dauphin County	2	<0.01
Philadelphia (city) Philadelphia County	2	<0.01
Tioga (borough) Tioga County	1	0.15
Elkland (borough) Tioga County	1	0.05
McKeesport (city) Allegheny County	1	0.01
Silver Spring (township) Cumberland County	1	0.01
Easton (city) Northampton County	1	<0.01
Lancaster (city) Lancaster County	1	<0.01
Aaronsburg (cdp) Centre County	0	0.00

Top 10 Places Sorted by Percent of Total Population
Based on all places, regardless of total population

Place	Population	%
Tioga (borough) Tioga County	1	0.15
Elkland (borough) Tioga County	1	0.05
Colonial Park (cdp) Dauphin County	2	0.02
McKeesport (city) Allegheny County	1	0.01
Silver Spring (township) Cumberland County	1	0.01
Lower Paxton (township) Dauphin County	2	<0.01
Philadelphia (city) Philadelphia County	2	<0.01
Easton (city) Northampton County	1	<0.01
Lancaster (city) Lancaster County	1	<0.01
Aaronsburg (cdp) Centre County	0	0.00

Top 10 Places Sorted by Percent of Total Population
Based on places with total population of 50,000 or more

Place	Population	%
Philadelphia (city) Philadelphia County	2	<0.01
Lancaster (city) Lancaster County	1	<0.01
Abington (township) Montgomery County	0	0.00
Allentown (city) Lehigh County	0	0.00
Bensalem (township) Bucks County	0	0.00
Bethlehem (city) Northampton County	0	0.00
Bethlehem (city) Northampton County	0	0.00
Bristol (township) Bucks County	0	0.00
Erie (city) Erie County	0	0.00
Levittown (cdp) Bucks County	0	0.00

American Indian: Yaqui

Top 10 Places Sorted by Population
Based on all places, regardless of total population

Place	Population	%
Philadelphia (city) Philadelphia County	10	<0.01
Peters (township) Washington County	4	0.02
East Greenville (borough) Montgomery County	3	0.10
West Deer (township) Allegheny County	3	0.03
Lancaster (city) Lancaster County	3	0.01
Sheshequin (township) Bradford County	2	0.15
Scott (township) Lackawanna County	2	0.04
New Brighton (borough) Beaver County	2	0.03
Plumstead (township) Bucks County	2	0.02
Derry (township) Dauphin County	2	0.01

Top 10 Places Sorted by Percent of Total Population
Based on all places, regardless of total population

Place	Population	%
Schubert (cdp) Berks County	1	0.40
Weissport (borough) Carbon County	1	0.24
Sheshequin (township) Bradford County	2	0.15
East Greenville (borough) Montgomery County	3	0.10
Hughesville (borough) Lycoming County	1	0.05
Scott (township) Lackawanna County	2	0.04
Sandycreek (township) Venango County	1	0.04
West Deer (township) Allegheny County	3	0.03
New Brighton (borough) Beaver County	2	0.03
Codorus (township) York County	1	0.03

Top 10 Places Sorted by Percent of Total Population
Based on places with total population of 50,000 or more

Place	Population	%
Lancaster (city) Lancaster County	3	0.01
Philadelphia (city) Philadelphia County	10	<0.01
Allentown (city) Lehigh County	1	<0.01
Pittsburgh (city) Allegheny County	1	<0.01

Place	Population	%
Abington (township) Montgomery County	0	0.00
Bensalem (township) Bucks County	0	0.00
Bethlehem (city) Northampton County	0	0.00
Bethlehem (city) Northampton County	0	0.00
Bristol (township) Bucks County	0	0.00
Erie (city) Erie County	0	0.00

American Indian: Yuman

Top 10 Places Sorted by Population
Based on all places, regardless of total population

Place	Population	%
Philadelphia (city) Philadelphia County	8	<0.01
Thornbury (township) Delaware County	2	0.02
Erie (city) Erie County	2	<0.01
Pine Creek (township) Jefferson County	1	0.07
Midland (borough) Beaver County	1	0.04
Titusville (city) Crawford County	1	0.02
Bellevue (borough) Allegheny County	1	0.01
East Norriton (township) Montgomery County	1	0.01
Hatboro (borough) Montgomery County	1	0.01
Aaronsburg (cdp) Centre County	0	0.00

Top 10 Places Sorted by Percent of Total Population
Based on all places, regardless of total population

Place	Population	%
Pine Creek (township) Jefferson County	1	0.07
Midland (borough) Beaver County	1	0.04
Thornbury (township) Delaware County	2	0.02
Titusville (city) Crawford County	1	0.02
Bellevue (borough) Allegheny County	1	0.01
East Norriton (township) Montgomery County	1	0.01
Hatboro (borough) Montgomery County	1	0.01
Philadelphia (city) Philadelphia County	8	<0.01
Erie (city) Erie County	2	<0.01
Aaronsburg (cdp) Centre County	0	0.00

Top 10 Places Sorted by Percent of Total Population
Based on places with total population of 50,000 or more

Place	Population	%
Philadelphia (city) Philadelphia County	8	<0.01
Erie (city) Erie County	2	<0.01
Abington (township) Montgomery County	0	0.00
Allentown (city) Lehigh County	0	0.00
Bensalem (township) Bucks County	0	0.00
Bethlehem (city) Northampton County	0	0.00
Bethlehem (city) Northampton County	0	0.00
Bristol (township) Bucks County	0	0.00
Lancaster (city) Lancaster County	0	0.00
Levittown (cdp) Bucks County	0	0.00

Alaska Native: Yup'ik

Top 10 Places Sorted by Population
Based on all places, regardless of total population

Place	Population	%
Philadelphia (city) Philadelphia County	5	<0.01
Lower Towamensing (township) Carbon County	3	0.09
Arendtsville (borough) Adams County	2	0.21
Penbrook (borough) Dauphin County	2	0.07
Ohioville (borough) Beaver County	2	0.06
Plunketts Creek (township) Lycoming County	1	0.15
East Brady (borough) Clarion County	1	0.11
Linntown (cdp) Union County	1	0.07
Broad Top (township) Bedford County	1	0.06
Wysox (township) Bradford County	1	0.06

Top 10 Places Sorted by Percent of Total Population
Based on all places, regardless of total population

Place	Population	%
Arendtsville (borough) Adams County	2	0.21
Plunketts Creek (township) Lycoming County	1	0.15
East Brady (borough) Clarion County	1	0.11
Lower Towamensing (township) Carbon County	3	0.09
Penbrook (borough) Dauphin County	2	0.07
Linntown (cdp) Union County	1	0.07
Ohioville (borough) Beaver County	2	0.06
Broad Top (township) Bedford County	1	0.06
Wysox (township) Bradford County	1	0.06
Corry (city) Erie County	1	0.02

Top 10 Places Sorted by Percent of Total Population
Based on places with total population of 50,000 or more

Place	Population	%
Philadelphia (city) Philadelphia County	5	<0.01
Allentown (city) Lehigh County	1	<0.01
Abington (township) Montgomery County	0	0.00
Bensalem (township) Bucks County	0	0.00
Bethlehem (city) Northampton County	0	0.00
Bethlehem (city) Northampton County	0	0.00
Bristol (township) Bucks County	0	0.00
Erie (city) Erie County	0	0.00
Lancaster (city) Lancaster County	0	0.00
Levittown (cdp) Bucks County	0	0.00

Asian

Top 10 Places Sorted by Population
Based on all places, regardless of total population

Place	Population	%
Philadelphia (city) Philadelphia County	106,720	6.99
Pittsburgh (city) Allegheny County	15,412	5.04
Upper Darby (township) Delaware County	9,903	11.96
Bensalem (township) Bucks County	6,706	11.10
State College (borough) Centre County	4,583	10.90
Upper Merion (township) Montgomery County	4,511	15.89
Montgomery (township) Montgomery County	4,351	17.55
Lower Merion (township) Montgomery County	4,085	7.06
King of Prussia (cdp) Montgomery County	3,952	19.82
Allentown (city) Lehigh County	3,274	2.77

Top 10 Places Sorted by Percent of Total Population
Based on all places, regardless of total population

Place	Population	%
Millbourne (borough) Delaware County	687	59.28
Hatfield (borough) Montgomery County	818	24.86
King of Prussia (cdp) Montgomery County	3,952	19.82
Exton (cdp) Chester County	887	18.32
East Caln (township) Chester County	858	17.73
Montgomery (township) Montgomery County	4,351	17.55
Hatfield (township) Montgomery County	2,964	17.18
Chesterbrook (cdp) Chester County	749	16.32
Upper Merion (township) Montgomery County	4,511	15.89
Montgomeryville (cdp) Montgomery County	1,942	15.38

Top 10 Places Sorted by Percent of Total Population
Based on places with total population of 50,000 or more

Place	Population	%
Upper Darby (township) Delaware County	9,903	11.96
Bensalem (township) Bucks County	6,706	11.10
Lower Merion (township) Montgomery County	4,085	7.06
Philadelphia (city) Philadelphia County	106,720	6.99
Abington (township) Montgomery County	3,030	5.48
Pittsburgh (city) Allegheny County	15,412	5.04
Bethlehem (city) Northampton County	2,012	3.62
Lancaster (city) Lancaster County	2,087	3.52
Scranton (city) Lackawanna County	2,642	3.47
Bristol (township) Bucks County	1,896	3.47

Asian: Not Hispanic

Top 10 Places Sorted by Population
Based on all places, regardless of total population

Place	Population	%
Philadelphia (city) Philadelphia County	104,551	6.85
Pittsburgh (city) Allegheny County	15,233	4.98
Upper Darby (township) Delaware County	9,825	11.87
Bensalem (township) Bucks County	6,653	11.01
State College (borough) Centre County	4,534	10.79
Upper Merion (township) Montgomery County	4,473	15.75
Montgomery (township) Montgomery County	4,336	17.49
Lower Merion (township) Montgomery County	4,024	6.96
King of Prussia (cdp) Montgomery County	3,919	19.66
Cheltenham (township) Montgomery County	3,092	8.40

Top 10 Places Sorted by Percent of Total Population
Based on all places, regardless of total population

Place	Population	%
Millbourne (borough) Delaware County	682	58.84
Hatfield (borough) Montgomery County	812	24.68
King of Prussia (cdp) Montgomery County	3,919	19.66

Exton (cdp) Chester County		887	18.32
East Caln (township) Chester County		856	17.69
Montgomery (township) Montgomery County		4,336	17.49
Hatfield (township) Montgomery County		2,949	17.10
Chesterbrook (cdp) Chester County		749	16.32
Upper Merion (township) Montgomery County		4,473	15.75
Montgomeryville (cdp) Montgomery County		1,930	15.29

Top 10 Places Sorted by Percent of Total Population
Based on places with total population of 50,000 or more

Place	Population	%
Upper Darby (township) Delaware County	9,825	11.87
Bensalem (township) Bucks County	6,653	11.01
Lower Merion (township) Montgomery County	4,024	6.96
Philadelphia (city) Philadelphia County	104,551	6.85
Abington (township) Montgomery County	2,985	5.40
Pittsburgh (city) Allegheny County	15,233	4.98
Bethlehem (city) Northampton County	1,915	3.44
Scranton (city) Lackawanna County	2,577	3.39
Bristol (township) Bucks County	1,840	3.37
Lancaster (city) Lancaster County	1,965	3.31

Asian: Hispanic

Top 10 Places Sorted by Population
Based on all places, regardless of total population

Place	Population	%
Philadelphia (city) Philadelphia County	2,169	0.14
Allentown (city) Lehigh County	293	0.25
Reading (city) Berks County	226	0.26
Pittsburgh (city) Allegheny County	179	0.06
Lancaster (city) Lancaster County	122	0.21
Bethlehem (city) Northampton County	112	0.15
York (city) York County	102	0.23
Bethlehem (city) Northampton County	97	0.17
Upper Darby (township) Delaware County	78	0.09
Harrisburg (city) Dauphin County	70	0.14

Top 10 Places Sorted by Percent of Total Population
Based on all places, regardless of total population

Place	Population	%
Wellsville (borough) York County	4	1.65
Lenhartsville (borough) Berks County	2	1.21
Holiday Pocono (cdp) Carbon County	4	0.84
Terry (township) Bradford County	8	0.81
Stockdale (borough) Washington County	4	0.80
Bird-in-Hand (cdp) Lancaster County	3	0.75
Hop Bottom (borough) Susquehanna County	2	0.59
Needmore (cdp) Fulton County	1	0.59
Pennwyn (cdp) Berks County	4	0.51
Warminster Heights (cdp) Bucks County	20	0.48

Top 10 Places Sorted by Percent of Total Population
Based on places with total population of 50,000 or more

Place	Population	%
Reading (city) Berks County	226	0.26
Allentown (city) Lehigh County	293	0.25
Lancaster (city) Lancaster County	122	0.21
Bethlehem (city) Northampton County	97	0.17
Bethlehem (city) Northampton County	112	0.15
Philadelphia (city) Philadelphia County	2,169	0.14
Lower Merion (township) Montgomery County	61	0.11
Bristol (township) Bucks County	56	0.10
Upper Darby (township) Delaware County	78	0.09
Scranton (city) Lackawanna County	65	0.09

Asian: Bangladeshi

Top 10 Places Sorted by Population
Based on all places, regardless of total population

Place	Population	%
Philadelphia (city) Philadelphia County	978	0.06
Upper Darby (township) Delaware County	605	0.73
Lansdale (borough) Montgomery County	564	3.47
Hatfield (borough) Montgomery County	219	6.66
Hatfield (township) Montgomery County	192	1.11
Millbourne (borough) Delaware County	171	14.75
Bensalem (township) Bucks County	67	0.11
Pittsburgh (city) Allegheny County	57	0.02
Upper Macungie (township) Lehigh County	47	0.23
Towamencin (township) Montgomery County	36	0.20

Top 10 Places Sorted by Percent of Total Population
Based on all places, regardless of total population

Place	Population	%
Millbourne (borough) Delaware County	171	14.75
Hatfield (borough) Montgomery County	219	6.66
Lansdale (borough) Montgomery County	564	3.47
Douglassville (cdp) Berks County	6	1.34
East Lansdowne (borough) Delaware County	35	1.31
Hatfield (township) Montgomery County	192	1.11
Lime Ridge (cdp) Columbia County	7	0.79
Upper Darby (township) Delaware County	605	0.73
Rose Valley (borough) Delaware County	5	0.55
Breinigsville (cdp) Lehigh County	21	0.51

Top 10 Places Sorted by Percent of Total Population
Based on places with total population of 50,000 or more

Place	Population	%
Upper Darby (township) Delaware County	605	0.73
Bensalem (township) Bucks County	67	0.11
Philadelphia (city) Philadelphia County	978	0.06
Abington (township) Montgomery County	19	0.03
Pittsburgh (city) Allegheny County	57	0.02
Allentown (city) Lehigh County	18	0.02
Millcreek (township) Erie County	13	0.02
Bristol (township) Bucks County	11	0.02
Lower Merion (township) Montgomery County	9	0.02
Lancaster (city) Lancaster County	8	0.01

Asian: Bhutanese

Top 10 Places Sorted by Population
Based on all places, regardless of total population

Place	Population	%
Erie (city) Erie County	395	0.39
Lancaster (city) Lancaster County	209	0.35
Whitehall (borough) Allegheny County	105	0.75
Harrisburg (city) Dauphin County	101	0.20
Scranton (city) Lackawanna County	101	0.13
Pittsburgh (city) Allegheny County	56	0.02
Castle Shannon (borough) Allegheny County	51	0.61
Philadelphia (city) Philadelphia County	51	<0.01
Lower Paxton (township) Dauphin County	34	0.07
Penn Hills (township) Allegheny County	20	0.05

Top 10 Places Sorted by Percent of Total Population
Based on all places, regardless of total population

Place	Population	%
Whitehall (borough) Allegheny County	105	0.75
Blue Ball (cdp) Lancaster County	7	0.68
Castle Shannon (borough) Allegheny County	51	0.61
Erie (city) Erie County	395	0.39
Lancaster (city) Lancaster County	209	0.35
Leetsdale (borough) Allegheny County	4	0.33
Mount Oliver (borough) Allegheny County	11	0.32
Harrisburg (city) Dauphin County	101	0.20
Akron (borough) Lancaster County	7	0.18
Emsworth (borough) Allegheny County	4	0.16

Top 10 Places Sorted by Percent of Total Population
Based on places with total population of 50,000 or more

Place	Population	%
Erie (city) Erie County	395	0.39
Lancaster (city) Lancaster County	209	0.35
Scranton (city) Lackawanna County	101	0.13
Pittsburgh (city) Allegheny County	56	0.02
Philadelphia (city) Philadelphia County	51	<0.01
Abington (township) Montgomery County	0	0.00
Allentown (city) Lehigh County	0	0.00
Bensalem (township) Bucks County	0	0.00
Bethlehem (city) Northampton County	0	0.00
Bethlehem (city) Northampton County	0	0.00

Asian: Burmese

Top 10 Places Sorted by Population
Based on all places, regardless of total population

Place	Population	%
Philadelphia (city) Philadelphia County	388	0.03
Whitehall (borough) Allegheny County	151	1.08
Pittsburgh (city) Allegheny County	145	0.05

Lancaster (city) Lancaster County		135	0.23
Erie (city) Erie County		121	0.12
Allentown (city) Lehigh County		121	0.10
Harrisburg (city) Dauphin County		61	0.12
Cheltenham (township) Montgomery County		32	0.09
Lititz (borough) Lancaster County		30	0.32
Castle Shannon (borough) Allegheny County		25	0.30

Top 10 Places Sorted by Percent of Total Population
Based on all places, regardless of total population

Place	Population	%
Whitehall (borough) Allegheny County	151	1.08
Wormleysburg (borough) Cumberland County	18	0.59
Lititz (borough) Lancaster County	30	0.32
Jamestown (borough) Mercer County	2	0.32
Castle Shannon (borough) Allegheny County	25	0.30
Lima (cdp) Delaware County	8	0.29
Lancaster (city) Lancaster County	135	0.23
Palmdale (cdp) Dauphin County	3	0.23
Riegelsville (borough) Bucks County	2	0.23
Reinholds (cdp) Lancaster County	4	0.22

Top 10 Places Sorted by Percent of Total Population
Based on places with total population of 50,000 or more

Place	Population	%
Lancaster (city) Lancaster County	135	0.23
Erie (city) Erie County	121	0.12
Allentown (city) Lehigh County	121	0.10
Pittsburgh (city) Allegheny County	145	0.05
Philadelphia (city) Philadelphia County	388	0.03
Bethlehem (city) Northampton County	23	0.03
Bethlehem (city) Northampton County	14	0.03
Upper Darby (township) Delaware County	15	0.02
Abington (township) Montgomery County	10	0.02
Millcreek (township) Erie County	9	0.02

Asian: Cambodian

Top 10 Places Sorted by Population
Based on all places, regardless of total population

Place	Population	%
Philadelphia (city) Philadelphia County	9,912	0.65
Upper Darby (township) Delaware County	294	0.36
Lancaster (city) Lancaster County	230	0.39
Manheim (township) Lancaster County	140	0.37
York (city) York County	138	0.32
Cheltenham (township) Montgomery County	133	0.36
Lansdale (borough) Montgomery County	125	0.77
Upper Merion (township) Montgomery County	93	0.33
King of Prussia (cdp) Montgomery County	92	0.46
Harrisburg (city) Dauphin County	89	0.18

Top 10 Places Sorted by Percent of Total Population
Based on all places, regardless of total population

Place	Population	%
Soudersburg (cdp) Lancaster County	14	2.59
East Lansdowne (borough) Delaware County	28	1.05
Millbourne (borough) Delaware County	10	0.86
Lansdale (borough) Montgomery County	125	0.77
Cleona (borough) Lebanon County	14	0.67
Philadelphia (city) Philadelphia County	9,912	0.65
Pine Ridge (cdp) Pike County	17	0.63
Campbelltown (cdp) Lebanon County	21	0.58
Smoketown (cdp) Lancaster County	2	0.56
East Hanover (township) Lebanon County	15	0.54

Top 10 Places Sorted by Percent of Total Population
Based on places with total population of 50,000 or more

Place	Population	%
Philadelphia (city) Philadelphia County	9,912	0.65
Lancaster (city) Lancaster County	230	0.39
Upper Darby (township) Delaware County	294	0.36
Bristol (township) Bucks County	72	0.13
Levittown (cdp) Bucks County	49	0.09
Abington (township) Montgomery County	46	0.08
Allentown (city) Lehigh County	80	0.07
Bensalem (township) Bucks County	32	0.05
Pittsburgh (city) Allegheny County	48	0.02
Bethlehem (city) Northampton County	12	0.02

Asian: Chinese, except Taiwanese

Top 10 Places Sorted by Population
Based on all places, regardless of total population

Place	Population	%
Philadelphia (city) Philadelphia County	32,773	2.15
Pittsburgh (city) Allegheny County	4,872	1.59
Upper Darby (township) Delaware County	1,655	2.00
State College (borough) Centre County	1,618	3.85
Lower Merion (township) Montgomery County	1,477	2.55
Tredyffrin (township) Chester County	1,130	3.85
Ferguson (township) Centre County	1,030	5.82
Radnor (township) Delaware County	800	2.54
Lower Providence (township) Montgomery County	766	3.01
Upper Merion (township) Montgomery County	759	2.67

Top 10 Places Sorted by Percent of Total Population
Based on all places, regardless of total population

Place	Population	%
Chesterbrook (cdp) Chester County	309	6.73
Ferguson (township) Centre County	1,030	5.82
Park Forest Village (cdp) Centre County	547	5.66
Colony Park (cdp) Berks County	60	5.58
Penn Wynne (cdp) Montgomery County	295	5.18
Swarthmore (borough) Delaware County	284	4.59
Franklin Park (borough) Allegheny County	569	4.22
Millbourne (borough) Delaware County	46	3.97
Audubon (cdp) Montgomery County	328	3.89
State College (borough) Centre County	1,618	3.85

Top 10 Places Sorted by Percent of Total Population
Based on places with total population of 50,000 or more

Place	Population	%
Lower Merion (township) Montgomery County	1,477	2.55
Philadelphia (city) Philadelphia County	32,773	2.15
Upper Darby (township) Delaware County	1,655	2.00
Pittsburgh (city) Allegheny County	4,872	1.59
Bethlehem (city) Northampton County	601	1.08
Bethlehem (city) Northampton County	693	0.92
Bensalem (township) Bucks County	537	0.89
Abington (township) Montgomery County	424	0.77
Millcreek (township) Erie County	271	0.51
Allentown (city) Lehigh County	502	0.43

Asian: Filipino

Top 10 Places Sorted by Population
Based on all places, regardless of total population

Place	Population	%
Philadelphia (city) Philadelphia County	6,849	0.45
Pittsburgh (city) Allegheny County	807	0.26
Upper Darby (township) Delaware County	565	0.68
Bensalem (township) Bucks County	423	0.70
Allentown (city) Lehigh County	324	0.27
Bristol (township) Bucks County	319	0.58
Lower Merion (township) Montgomery County	291	0.50
Upper Merion (township) Montgomery County	264	0.93
Levittown (cdp) Bucks County	242	0.46
Cheltenham (township) Montgomery County	228	0.62

Top 10 Places Sorted by Percent of Total Population
Based on all places, regardless of total population

Place	Population	%
Millbourne (borough) Delaware County	28	2.42
Smicksburg (borough) Indiana County	1	2.17
Kerrtown (cdp) Crawford County	6	1.97
Starrucca (borough) Wayne County	3	1.73
Penn Estates (cdp) Monroe County	72	1.60
Triumph (township) Warren County	5	1.58
Saw Creek (cdp) Pike County	60	1.49
Sugar Grove (borough) Warren County	9	1.47
Mill Village (borough) Erie County	6	1.46
Coal Center (borough) Washington County	2	1.44

Top 10 Places Sorted by Percent of Total Population
Based on places with total population of 50,000 or more

Place	Population	%
Bensalem (township) Bucks County	423	0.70
Upper Darby (township) Delaware County	565	0.68
Bristol (township) Bucks County	319	0.58
Lower Merion (township) Montgomery County	291	0.50

Place	Population	%
Levittown (cdp) Bucks County	242	0.46
Philadelphia (city) Philadelphia County	6,849	0.45
Abington (township) Montgomery County	212	0.38
Bethlehem (city) Northampton County	221	0.29
Allentown (city) Lehigh County	324	0.27
Pittsburgh (city) Allegheny County	807	0.26

Asian: Hmong

Top 10 Places Sorted by Population
Based on all places, regardless of total population

Place	Population	%
East Cocalico (township) Lancaster County	120	1.16
Philadelphia (city) Philadelphia County	83	0.01
Leola (cdp) Lancaster County	70	0.97
Ephrata (township) Lancaster County	65	0.69
Swartzville (cdp) Lancaster County	64	2.80
Upper Leacock (township) Lancaster County	59	0.68
Upper Darby (township) Delaware County	58	0.07
Brecknock (township) Berks County	57	1.24
West Earl (township) Lancaster County	55	0.70
Clay (township) Lancaster County	50	0.79

Top 10 Places Sorted by Percent of Total Population
Based on all places, regardless of total population

Place	Population	%
Swartzville (cdp) Lancaster County	64	2.80
Adamstown (borough) Lancaster County	46	2.60
Adamstown (borough) Lancaster County	46	2.57
Stevens (cdp) Lancaster County	11	1.80
Blue Ball (cdp) Lancaster County	18	1.75
Brecknock (township) Berks County	57	1.24
Hopeland (cdp) Lancaster County	9	1.22
East Cocalico (township) Lancaster County	120	1.16
Fivepointville (cdp) Lancaster County	13	1.12
Leola (cdp) Lancaster County	70	0.97

Top 10 Places Sorted by Percent of Total Population
Based on places with total population of 50,000 or more

Place	Population	%
Upper Darby (township) Delaware County	58	0.07
Lancaster (city) Lancaster County	19	0.03
Philadelphia (city) Philadelphia County	83	0.01
Pittsburgh (city) Allegheny County	3	<0.01
Reading (city) Berks County	3	<0.01
Abington (township) Montgomery County	2	<0.01
Levittown (cdp) Bucks County	1	<0.01
Millcreek (township) Erie County	1	<0.01
Allentown (city) Lehigh County	0	0.00
Bensalem (township) Bucks County	0	0.00

Asian: Indian

Top 10 Places Sorted by Population
Based on all places, regardless of total population

Place	Population	%
Philadelphia (city) Philadelphia County	20,809	1.36
Bensalem (township) Bucks County	4,480	7.41
Pittsburgh (city) Allegheny County	4,025	1.32
Upper Darby (township) Delaware County	3,208	3.87
Upper Merion (township) Montgomery County	2,352	8.28
King of Prussia (cdp) Montgomery County	2,198	11.03
Scott (township) Allegheny County	1,620	9.52
Hatfield (township) Montgomery County	1,619	9.39
Lower Providence (township) Montgomery County	1,268	4.99
Montgomery (township) Montgomery County	1,261	5.09

Top 10 Places Sorted by Percent of Total Population
Based on all places, regardless of total population

Place	Population	%
Millbourne (borough) Delaware County	398	34.34
Hatfield (borough) Montgomery County	430	13.07
Exton (cdp) Chester County	592	12.23
East Caln (township) Chester County	565	11.68
King of Prussia (cdp) Montgomery County	2,198	11.03
Wormleysburg (borough) Cumberland County	305	9.93
Scott (township) Allegheny County	1,620	9.52
Hatfield (township) Montgomery County	1,619	9.39
Upper Uwchlan (township) Chester County	1,020	9.09
Upper Merion (township) Montgomery County	2,352	8.28

Top 10 Places Sorted by Percent of Total Population
Based on places with total population of 50,000 or more

Place	Population	%
Bensalem (township) Bucks County	4,480	7.41
Upper Darby (township) Delaware County	3,208	3.87
Bristol (township) Bucks County	899	1.61
Scranton (city) Lackawanna County	1,247	1.64
Lower Merion (township) Montgomery County	906	1.57
Philadelphia (city) Philadelphia County	20,809	1.36
Pittsburgh (city) Allegheny County	4,025	1.32
Bethlehem (city) Northampton County	478	0.86
Bethlehem (city) Northampton County	633	0.84
Abington (township) Montgomery County	455	0.82

Asian: Indonesian

Top 10 Places Sorted by Population
Based on all places, regardless of total population

Place	Population	%
Philadelphia (city) Philadelphia County	2,222	0.15
Scranton (city) Lackawanna County	260	0.34
Pittsburgh (city) Allegheny County	72	0.02
Harrisburg (city) Dauphin County	49	0.10
Swatara (township) Dauphin County	47	0.20
Chambersburg (borough) Franklin County	46	0.23
Upper Darby (township) Delaware County	40	0.05
Lower Paxton (township) Dauphin County	35	0.07
Monroeville (municipality) Allegheny County	29	0.10
State College (borough) Centre County	23	0.05

Top 10 Places Sorted by Percent of Total Population
Based on all places, regardless of total population

Place	Population	%
Adamsburg (borough) Westmoreland County	2	1.16
Brady (township) Lycoming County	3	0.58
Ford Cliff (borough) Armstrong County	2	0.54
Haverford College (cdp) Delaware County	7	0.53
Millbourne (borough) Delaware County	6	0.52
Union Deposit (cdp) Dauphin County	2	0.49
Rutherford (cdp) Dauphin County	18	0.42
Kennerdell (cdp) Venango County	1	0.40
Henry Clay (township) Fayette County	8	0.39
Ranshaw (cdp) Northumberland County	2	0.39

Top 10 Places Sorted by Percent of Total Population
Based on places with total population of 50,000 or more

Place	Population	%
Scranton (city) Lackawanna County	260	0.34
Philadelphia (city) Philadelphia County	2,222	0.15
Upper Darby (township) Delaware County	40	0.05
Pittsburgh (city) Allegheny County	72	0.02
Bethlehem (city) Northampton County	18	0.02
Bethlehem (city) Northampton County	13	0.02
Abington (township) Montgomery County	10	0.02
Levittown (cdp) Bucks County	8	0.02
Reading (city) Berks County	13	0.01
Bensalem (township) Bucks County	8	0.01

Asian: Japanese

Top 10 Places Sorted by Population
Based on all places, regardless of total population

Place	Population	%
Philadelphia (city) Philadelphia County	1,956	0.13
Pittsburgh (city) Allegheny County	938	0.31
Lower Merion (township) Montgomery County	221	0.38
Radnor (township) Delaware County	189	0.60
State College (borough) Centre County	163	0.39
Haverford (township) Delaware County	111	0.23
Upper Darby (township) Delaware County	111	0.13
Bethlehem (city) Northampton County	95	0.13
Tredyffrin (township) Chester County	94	0.32
Allentown (city) Lehigh County	93	0.08

Top 10 Places Sorted by Percent of Total Population
Based on all places, regardless of total population

Place	Population	%
Baileyville (cdp) Centre County	3	1.49
Mertztown (cdp) Berks County	8	1.20
Toftrees (cdp) Centre County	24	1.17

Place	Population	%
Pine (township) Lycoming County	3	1.02
Haverford College (cdp) Delaware County	13	0.98
Benezette (township) Elk County	2	0.97
Byrnedale (cdp) Elk County	4	0.94
Bryn Mawr (cdp) Montgomery County	35	0.93
Laurelton (cdp) Union County	2	0.90
Swarthmore (borough) Delaware County	53	0.86

Top 10 Places Sorted by Percent of Total Population
Based on places with total population of 50,000 or more

Place	Population	%
Lower Merion (township) Montgomery County	221	0.38
Pittsburgh (city) Allegheny County	938	0.31
Abington (township) Montgomery County	92	0.17
Bethlehem (city) Northampton County	80	0.14
Philadelphia (city) Philadelphia County	1,956	0.13
Upper Darby (township) Delaware County	111	0.13
Bethlehem (city) Northampton County	95	0.13
Bensalem (township) Bucks County	81	0.13
Millcreek (township) Erie County	54	0.10
Levittown (cdp) Bucks County	52	0.10

Asian: Korean

Top 10 Places Sorted by Population
Based on all places, regardless of total population

Place	Population	%
Philadelphia (city) Philadelphia County	7,074	0.46
Pittsburgh (city) Allegheny County	2,002	0.65
Montgomery (township) Montgomery County	1,765	7.12
Abington (township) Montgomery County	1,396	2.52
Cheltenham (township) Montgomery County	1,066	2.90
Whitpain (township) Montgomery County	1,056	5.59
Upper Dublin (township) Montgomery County	1,047	4.09
State College (borough) Centre County	841	2.00
Montgomeryville (cdp) Montgomery County	792	6.27
Horsham (township) Montgomery County	760	2.91

Top 10 Places Sorted by Percent of Total Population
Based on all places, regardless of total population

Place	Population	%
Montgomery (township) Montgomery County	1,765	7.12
Montgomeryville (cdp) Montgomery County	792	6.27
Whitpain (township) Montgomery County	1,056	5.59
Siglerville (cdp) Mifflin County	5	4.72
Blue Bell (cdp) Montgomery County	279	4.60
Upper Dublin (township) Montgomery County	1,047	4.09
Maple Glen (cdp) Montgomery County	267	3.96
Worcester (township) Montgomery County	376	3.86
Spring House (cdp) Montgomery County	137	3.60
Lower Moreland (township) Montgomery County	462	3.56

Top 10 Places Sorted by Percent of Total Population
Based on places with total population of 50,000 or more

Place	Population	%
Abington (township) Montgomery County	1,396	2.52
Lower Merion (township) Montgomery County	651	1.13
Pittsburgh (city) Allegheny County	2,002	0.65
Upper Darby (township) Delaware County	526	0.64
Bensalem (township) Bucks County	312	0.52
Philadelphia (city) Philadelphia County	7,074	0.46
Levittown (cdp) Bucks County	215	0.41
Bethlehem (city) Northampton County	221	0.40
Bethlehem (city) Northampton County	283	0.38
Bristol (township) Bucks County	135	0.25

Asian: Laotian

Top 10 Places Sorted by Population
Based on all places, regardless of total population

Place	Population	%
Philadelphia (city) Philadelphia County	1,350	0.09
Upper Darby (township) Delaware County	172	0.21
Scranton (city) Lackawanna County	133	0.17
Collingdale (borough) Delaware County	48	0.55
Rapho (township) Lancaster County	42	0.40
Reading (city) Berks County	39	0.04
Abington (township) Montgomery County	37	0.07
King of Prussia (cdp) Montgomery County	36	0.18
Upper Merion (township) Montgomery County	36	0.13
Ephrata (township) Lancaster County	29	0.31

Top 10 Places Sorted by Percent of Total Population
Based on all places, regardless of total population

Place	Population	%
New Kingstown (cdp) Cumberland County	5	1.01
Brownstown (cdp) Lancaster County	24	0.85
Montrose Manor (cdp) Berks County	5	0.83
Bear Creek Village (borough) Luzerne County	2	0.78
Collingdale (borough) Delaware County	48	0.55
Huntington (township) Adams County	13	0.55
Manheim (borough) Lancaster County	25	0.51
Stevens (cdp) Lancaster County	3	0.49
Mifflintown (borough) Juniata County	4	0.43
Rapho (township) Lancaster County	42	0.40

Top 10 Places Sorted by Percent of Total Population
Based on places with total population of 50,000 or more

Place	Population	%
Upper Darby (township) Delaware County	172	0.21
Scranton (city) Lackawanna County	133	0.17
Philadelphia (city) Philadelphia County	1,350	0.09
Abington (township) Montgomery County	37	0.07
Reading (city) Berks County	39	0.04
Allentown (city) Lehigh County	20	0.02
Lancaster (city) Lancaster County	14	0.02
Bensalem (township) Bucks County	12	0.02
Lower Merion (township) Montgomery County	10	0.02
Pittsburgh (city) Allegheny County	17	0.01

Asian: Malaysian

Top 10 Places Sorted by Population
Based on all places, regardless of total population

Place	Population	%
State College (borough) Centre County	145	0.34
Philadelphia (city) Philadelphia County	130	0.01
Pittsburgh (city) Allegheny County	69	0.02
Millbourne (borough) Delaware County	21	1.81
Lower Merion (township) Montgomery County	18	0.03
Bethlehem (city) Northampton County	14	0.02
King of Prussia (cdp) Montgomery County	12	0.06
Upper Merion (township) Montgomery County	12	0.04
Bethlehem (city) Northampton County	12	0.02
Upper Darby (township) Delaware County	11	0.01

Top 10 Places Sorted by Percent of Total Population
Based on all places, regardless of total population

Place	Population	%
Millbourne (borough) Delaware County	21	1.81
West Sunbury (borough) Butler County	1	0.52
State College (borough) Centre County	145	0.34
Milesburg (borough) Centre County	3	0.27
Jordan (township) Clearfield County	1	0.22
Harmar (township) Allegheny County	6	0.21
Versailles (borough) Allegheny County	3	0.20
Adamstown (borough) Lancaster County	3	0.17
Adamstown (borough) Lancaster County	3	0.17
Kilbuck (township) Allegheny County	1	0.14

Top 10 Places Sorted by Percent of Total Population
Based on places with total population of 50,000 or more

Place	Population	%
Lower Merion (township) Montgomery County	18	0.03
Pittsburgh (city) Allegheny County	69	0.02
Bethlehem (city) Northampton County	14	0.02
Bethlehem (city) Northampton County	12	0.02
Philadelphia (city) Philadelphia County	130	0.01
Upper Darby (township) Delaware County	11	0.01
Lancaster (city) Lancaster County	8	0.01
Allentown (city) Lehigh County	7	0.01
Scranton (city) Lackawanna County	7	0.01
Bensalem (township) Bucks County	5	0.01

Asian: Nepalese

Top 10 Places Sorted by Population
Based on all places, regardless of total population

Place	Population	%
Philadelphia (city) Philadelphia County	220	0.01
Erie (city) Erie County	138	0.14
Pittsburgh (city) Allegheny County	111	0.04

Place	Population	%
Lancaster (city) Lancaster County	87	0.15
Scranton (city) Lackawanna County	80	0.11
Whitehall (borough) Allegheny County	55	0.39
Castle Shannon (borough) Allegheny County	36	0.43
Upper Darby (township) Delaware County	34	0.04
Harrisburg (city) Dauphin County	27	0.05
Lower Paxton (township) Dauphin County	26	0.05

Top 10 Places Sorted by Percent of Total Population
Based on all places, regardless of total population

Place	Population	%
Millbourne (borough) Delaware County	6	0.52
Castle Shannon (borough) Allegheny County	36	0.43
Whitehall (borough) Allegheny County	55	0.39
Blue Ridge Summit (cdp) Franklin County	3	0.34
Sewickley (borough) Allegheny County	10	0.26
Bryn Athyn (borough) Montgomery County	3	0.22
Akron (borough) Lancaster County	8	0.21
Sayre (borough) Bradford County	11	0.20
Wyomissing (borough) Berks County	18	0.17
Exton (cdp) Chester County	8	0.17

Top 10 Places Sorted by Percent of Total Population
Based on places with total population of 50,000 or more

Place	Population	%
Lancaster (city) Lancaster County	87	0.15
Erie (city) Erie County	138	0.14
Scranton (city) Lackawanna County	80	0.11
Pittsburgh (city) Allegheny County	111	0.04
Upper Darby (township) Delaware County	34	0.04
Bensalem (township) Bucks County	16	0.03
Lower Merion (township) Montgomery County	12	0.02
Philadelphia (city) Philadelphia County	220	0.01
Abington (township) Montgomery County	7	0.01
Bethlehem (city) Northampton County	6	0.01

Asian: Pakistani

Top 10 Places Sorted by Population
Based on all places, regardless of total population

Place	Population	%
Philadelphia (city) Philadelphia County	2,683	0.18
Upper Darby (township) Delaware County	693	0.84
Bensalem (township) Bucks County	284	0.47
Pittsburgh (city) Allegheny County	217	0.07
Monroeville (municipality) Allegheny County	169	0.60
Upper Merion (township) Montgomery County	139	0.49
Lower Paxton (township) Dauphin County	121	0.26
King of Prussia (cdp) Montgomery County	111	0.56
Lower Makefield (township) Bucks County	95	0.29
Lower Merion (township) Montgomery County	95	0.16

Top 10 Places Sorted by Percent of Total Population
Based on all places, regardless of total population

Place	Population	%
Morton (borough) Delaware County	42	1.57
Millbourne (borough) Delaware County	14	1.21
Deerfield (township) Tioga County	7	1.06
Nuangola (borough) Luzerne County	6	0.88
Upper Darby (township) Delaware County	693	0.84
Glen Campbell (borough) Indiana County	2	0.82
Bryn Mawr (cdp) Montgomery County	29	0.77
Liverpool (borough) Perry County	7	0.73
Breinigsville (cdp) Lehigh County	29	0.70
Rice (township) Luzerne County	21	0.63

Top 10 Places Sorted by Percent of Total Population
Based on places with total population of 50,000 or more

Place	Population	%
Upper Darby (township) Delaware County	693	0.84
Bensalem (township) Bucks County	284	0.47
Philadelphia (city) Philadelphia County	2,683	0.18
Lower Merion (township) Montgomery County	95	0.16
Bethlehem (city) Northampton County	70	0.13
Bethlehem (city) Northampton County	83	0.11
Bristol (township) Bucks County	59	0.11
Abington (township) Montgomery County	55	0.10
Millcreek (township) Erie County	45	0.08
Pittsburgh (city) Allegheny County	217	0.07

Asian: Sri Lankan

Top 10 Places Sorted by Population
Based on all places, regardless of total population

Place	Population	%
Philadelphia (city) Philadelphia County	172	0.01
Pittsburgh (city) Allegheny County	46	0.02
Lower Merion (township) Montgomery County	28	0.05
West Whiteland (township) Chester County	25	0.14
Haverford (township) Delaware County	23	0.05
State College (borough) Centre County	22	0.05
Exton (cdp) Chester County	19	0.39
Lower Macungie (township) Lehigh County	18	0.06
McCandless (township) Allegheny County	18	0.06
Bethlehem (city) Northampton County	15	0.02

Top 10 Places Sorted by Percent of Total Population
Based on all places, regardless of total population

Place	Population	%
Exton (cdp) Chester County	19	0.39
Slippery Rock (borough) Butler County	12	0.33
Perry (township) Berks County	7	0.29
Fox (township) Sullivan County	1	0.28
Towamensing Trails (cdp) Carbon County	6	0.26
Haverford College (cdp) Delaware County	3	0.23
Westwood (cdp) Chester County	2	0.21
Ancient Oaks (cdp) Lehigh County	13	0.20
Bald Eagle (township) Clinton County	4	0.19
Castanea (cdp) Clinton County	2	0.18

Top 10 Places Sorted by Percent of Total Population
Based on places with total population of 50,000 or more

Place	Population	%
Lower Merion (township) Montgomery County	28	0.05
Pittsburgh (city) Allegheny County	46	0.02
Bethlehem (city) Northampton County	15	0.02
Bethlehem (city) Northampton County	12	0.02
Levittown (cdp) Bucks County	10	0.02
Millcreek (township) Erie County	10	0.02
Bristol (township) Bucks County	9	0.02
Philadelphia (city) Philadelphia County	172	0.01
Allentown (city) Lehigh County	12	0.01
Upper Darby (township) Delaware County	9	0.01

Asian: Taiwanese

Top 10 Places Sorted by Population
Based on all places, regardless of total population

Place	Population	%
Philadelphia (city) Philadelphia County	736	0.05
Pittsburgh (city) Allegheny County	461	0.15
State College (borough) Centre County	169	0.40
Ferguson (township) Centre County	92	0.52
Lower Merion (township) Montgomery County	70	0.12
Tredyffrin (township) Chester County	69	0.24
Park Forest Village (cdp) Centre County	59	0.61
Lower Macungie (township) Lehigh County	56	0.18
Montgomery (township) Montgomery County	55	0.22
Upper Dublin (township) Montgomery County	43	0.17

Top 10 Places Sorted by Percent of Total Population
Based on all places, regardless of total population

Place	Population	%
Thornburg (borough) Allegheny County	4	0.88
Lewis Run (borough) McKean County	4	0.65
Park Forest Village (cdp) Centre County	59	0.61
Spring Ridge (cdp) Berks County	6	0.60
Ferguson (township) Centre County	92	0.52
Gallagher (township) Clinton County	2	0.52
State College (borough) Centre County	169	0.40
Haverford College (cdp) Delaware County	5	0.38
Hydetown (borough) Crawford County	2	0.38
Chesterbrook (cdp) Chester County	17	0.37

Top 10 Places Sorted by Percent of Total Population
Based on places with total population of 50,000 or more

Place	Population	%
Pittsburgh (city) Allegheny County	461	0.15
Lower Merion (township) Montgomery County	70	0.12
Bethlehem (city) Northampton County	35	0.06
Abington (township) Montgomery County	31	0.06

Place	Population	%
Philadelphia (city) Philadelphia County	736	0.05
Bethlehem (city) Northampton County	35	0.05
Bensalem (township) Bucks County	19	0.03
Upper Darby (township) Delaware County	14	0.02
Millcreek (township) Erie County	13	0.02
Levittown (cdp) Bucks County	11	0.02

Asian: Thai

Top 10 Places Sorted by Population
Based on all places, regardless of total population

Place	Population	%
Philadelphia (city) Philadelphia County	627	0.04
Pittsburgh (city) Allegheny County	245	0.08
Upper Darby (township) Delaware County	103	0.12
Derry (township) Dauphin County	89	0.36
Hershey (cdp) Dauphin County	78	0.55
Harrisburg (city) Dauphin County	66	0.13
Bethlehem (city) Northampton County	62	0.08
Bethlehem (city) Northampton County	57	0.10
State College (borough) Centre County	55	0.13
Lower Merion (township) Montgomery County	44	0.08

Top 10 Places Sorted by Percent of Total Population
Based on all places, regardless of total population

Place	Population	%
Wilcox (cdp) Elk County	3	0.78
Iola (cdp) Columbia County	1	0.69
Freeport (township) Greene County	2	0.65
Bethel (cdp) Berks County	3	0.60
Ogle (township) Somerset County	3	0.60
Lathrop (township) Susquehanna County	5	0.59
Idaville (cdp) Adams County	1	0.56
Hershey (cdp) Dauphin County	78	0.55
Revloc (cdp) Cambria County	3	0.53
Houtzdale (borough) Clearfield County	4	0.50

Top 10 Places Sorted by Percent of Total Population
Based on places with total population of 50,000 or more

Place	Population	%
Upper Darby (township) Delaware County	103	0.12
Bethlehem (city) Northampton County	57	0.10
Pittsburgh (city) Allegheny County	245	0.08
Bethlehem (city) Northampton County	62	0.08
Lower Merion (township) Montgomery County	44	0.08
Abington (township) Montgomery County	29	0.05
Philadelphia (city) Philadelphia County	627	0.04
Scranton (city) Lackawanna County	33	0.04
Bensalem (township) Bucks County	23	0.04
Levittown (cdp) Bucks County	20	0.04

Asian: Vietnamese

Top 10 Places Sorted by Population
Based on all places, regardless of total population

Place	Population	%
Philadelphia (city) Philadelphia County	16,268	1.07
Upper Darby (township) Delaware County	1,849	2.23
Allentown (city) Lehigh County	853	0.72
Pittsburgh (city) Allegheny County	826	0.27
Harrisburg (city) Dauphin County	786	1.59
Manheim (township) Lancaster County	760	1.99
Lancaster (city) Lancaster County	594	1.00
Reading (city) Berks County	538	0.61
Lower Paxton (township) Dauphin County	464	0.98
Susquehanna (township) Dauphin County	375	1.56

Top 10 Places Sorted by Percent of Total Population
Based on all places, regardless of total population

Place	Population	%
Telford (borough) Montgomery County	111	4.17
Telford (borough) Montgomery County	187	3.84
Telford (borough) Bucks County	76	3.44
Souderton (borough) Montgomery County	227	3.43
East Lansdowne (borough) Delaware County	74	2.77
Homestead (borough) Allegheny County	81	2.56
Webster (cdp) Westmoreland County	6	2.35
Upper Darby (township) Delaware County	1,849	2.23
Progress (cdp) Dauphin County	213	2.18
Riverview Park (cdp) Berks County	72	2.13

Top 10 Places Sorted by Percent of Total Population
Based on places with total population of 50,000 or more

Place	Population	%
Upper Darby (township) Delaware County	1,849	2.23
Philadelphia (city) Philadelphia County	16,268	1.07
Lancaster (city) Lancaster County	594	1.00
Allentown (city) Lehigh County	853	0.72
Reading (city) Berks County	538	0.61
Bensalem (township) Bucks County	251	0.42
Abington (township) Montgomery County	186	0.34
Erie (city) Erie County	326	0.32
Lower Merion (township) Montgomery County	185	0.32
Bethlehem (city) Northampton County	217	0.29

Hawaii Native/Pacific Islander

Top 10 Places Sorted by Population
Based on all places, regardless of total population

Place	Population	%
Philadelphia (city) Philadelphia County	3,125	0.20
Reading (city) Berks County	351	0.40
Allentown (city) Lehigh County	307	0.26
Pittsburgh (city) Allegheny County	286	0.09
Lancaster (city) Lancaster County	191	0.32
Erie (city) Erie County	154	0.15
Upper Darby (township) Delaware County	151	0.18
Harrisburg (city) Dauphin County	127	0.26
Bethlehem (city) Northampton County	121	0.16
Bethlehem (city) Northampton County	92	0.17

Top 10 Places Sorted by Percent of Total Population
Based on all places, regardless of total population

Place	Population	%
Naomi (cdp) Fayette County	5	7.25
Callimont (borough) Somerset County	1	2.44
Atkinson Mills (cdp) Mifflin County	3	1.72
Oswayo (borough) Potter County	2	1.44
Wellsville (borough) York County	3	1.24
McKeansburg (cdp) Schuylkill County	2	1.23
Millbourne (borough) Delaware County	14	1.21
Colebrook (township) Clinton County	2	1.01
Crucible (cdp) Greene County	7	0.97
Benezette (township) Elk County	2	0.97

Top 10 Places Sorted by Percent of Total Population
Based on places with total population of 50,000 or more

Place	Population	%
Reading (city) Berks County	351	0.40
Lancaster (city) Lancaster County	191	0.32
Allentown (city) Lehigh County	307	0.26
Philadelphia (city) Philadelphia County	3,125	0.20
Upper Darby (township) Delaware County	151	0.18
Bethlehem (city) Northampton County	92	0.17
Bethlehem (city) Northampton County	121	0.16
Erie (city) Erie County	154	0.15
Bensalem (township) Bucks County	81	0.13
Bristol (township) Bucks County	73	0.13

Hawaii Native/Pacific Islander: Not Hispanic

Top 10 Places Sorted by Population
Based on all places, regardless of total population

Place	Population	%
Philadelphia (city) Philadelphia County	1,938	0.13
Pittsburgh (city) Allegheny County	236	0.08
Erie (city) Erie County	135	0.13
Upper Darby (township) Delaware County	129	0.16
Allentown (city) Lehigh County	83	0.07
Bethlehem (city) Northampton County	69	0.09
Bristol (township) Bucks County	65	0.12
Reading (city) Berks County	59	0.07
Lower Merion (township) Montgomery County	56	0.10
Lancaster (city) Lancaster County	56	0.09

Top 10 Places Sorted by Percent of Total Population
Based on all places, regardless of total population

Place	Population	%
Naomi (cdp) Fayette County	5	7.25
Callimont (borough) Somerset County	1	2.44

Place	Population	%
Atkinson Mills (cdp) Mifflin County	3	1.72
Oswayo (borough) Potter County	2	1.44
McKeansburg (cdp) Schuylkill County	2	1.23
Colebrook (township) Clinton County	2	1.01
Benezette (township) Elk County	2	0.97
Millbourne (borough) Delaware County	11	0.95
Crucible (cdp) Greene County	6	0.83
East Butler (borough) Butler County	6	0.82

Top 10 Places Sorted by Percent of Total Population
Based on places with total population of 50,000 or more

Place	Population	%
Upper Darby (township) Delaware County	129	0.16
Philadelphia (city) Philadelphia County	1,938	0.13
Erie (city) Erie County	135	0.13
Bristol (township) Bucks County	65	0.12
Lower Merion (township) Montgomery County	56	0.10
Bethlehem (city) Northampton County	69	0.09
Lancaster (city) Lancaster County	56	0.09
Bensalem (township) Bucks County	53	0.09
Abington (township) Montgomery County	48	0.09
Levittown (cdp) Bucks County	48	0.09

Hawaii Native/Pacific Islander: Hispanic

Top 10 Places Sorted by Population
Based on all places, regardless of total population

Place	Population	%
Philadelphia (city) Philadelphia County	1,187	0.08
Reading (city) Berks County	292	0.33
Allentown (city) Lehigh County	224	0.19
Lancaster (city) Lancaster County	135	0.23
Harrisburg (city) Dauphin County	78	0.16
York (city) York County	61	0.14
Hazleton (city) Luzerne County	59	0.23
Bethlehem (city) Northampton County	52	0.07
Pittsburgh (city) Allegheny County	50	0.02
Norristown (borough) Montgomery County	48	0.14

Top 10 Places Sorted by Percent of Total Population
Based on all places, regardless of total population

Place	Population	%
Wellsville (borough) York County	3	1.24
Spruce Creek (township) Huntingdon County	2	0.83
Harrison (township) Bedford County	8	0.82
Jackson (township) Perry County	4	0.73
McHenry (township) Lycoming County	1	0.70
Great Bend (borough) Susquehanna County	5	0.68
Montrose Manor (cdp) Berks County	4	0.66
Fort Loudon (cdp) Franklin County	5	0.56
Wakefield (cdp) Lancaster County	3	0.49
East Vandergrift (borough) Westmoreland County	3	0.45

Top 10 Places Sorted by Percent of Total Population
Based on places with total population of 50,000 or more

Place	Population	%
Reading (city) Berks County	292	0.33
Lancaster (city) Lancaster County	135	0.23
Allentown (city) Lehigh County	224	0.19
Philadelphia (city) Philadelphia County	1,187	0.08
Bethlehem (city) Northampton County	47	0.08
Bethlehem (city) Northampton County	52	0.07
Bensalem (township) Bucks County	28	0.05
Scranton (city) Lackawanna County	28	0.04
Upper Darby (township) Delaware County	22	0.03
Levittown (cdp) Bucks County	16	0.03

Hawaii Native/Pacific Islander: Fijian

Top 10 Places Sorted by Population
Based on all places, regardless of total population

Place	Population	%
Philadelphia (city) Philadelphia County	14	<0.01
Cain (township) Chester County	5	0.04
Coatesville (city) Chester County	5	0.04
Haverford (township) Delaware County	5	0.01
Lower Merion (township) Montgomery County	5	0.01
Reiffton (cdp) Berks County	4	0.10
Aston (township) Delaware County	4	0.02
Exeter (township) Berks County	4	0.02
Pittsburgh (city) Allegheny County	4	<0.01

Place	Population	%
Heidelberg (township) Lehigh County	3	0.09

Top 10 Places Sorted by Percent of Total Population
Based on all places, regardless of total population

Place	Population	%
Spring (township) Crawford County	2	0.13
Reiffton (cdp) Berks County	4	0.10
Elder (township) Cambria County	1	0.10
Heidelberg (township) Lehigh County	3	0.09
West Reading (borough) Berks County	2	0.05
Cain (township) Chester County	5	0.04
Coatesville (city) Chester County	5	0.04
Telford (borough) Montgomery County	1	0.04
Pennsburg (borough) Montgomery County	1	0.03
Aston (township) Delaware County	4	0.02

Top 10 Places Sorted by Percent of Total Population
Based on places with total population of 50,000 or more

Place	Population	%
Lower Merion (township) Montgomery County	5	0.01
Philadelphia (city) Philadelphia County	14	<0.01
Pittsburgh (city) Allegheny County	4	<0.01
Erie (city) Erie County	1	<0.01
Levittown (cdp) Bucks County	1	<0.01
Abington (township) Montgomery County	0	0.00
Allentown (city) Lehigh County	0	0.00
Bensalem (township) Bucks County	0	0.00
Bethlehem (city) Northampton County	0	0.00
Bethlehem (city) Northampton County	0	0.00

Hawaii Native/Pacific Islander: Guamanian or Chamorro

Top 10 Places Sorted by Population
Based on all places, regardless of total population

Place	Population	%
Philadelphia (city) Philadelphia County	272	0.02
Reading (city) Berks County	38	0.04
Erie (city) Erie County	31	0.03
Norristown (borough) Montgomery County	29	0.08
Pittsburgh (city) Allegheny County	29	0.01
Lancaster (city) Lancaster County	27	0.05
Phoenixville (borough) Chester County	26	0.16
Bethlehem (township) Northampton County	22	0.09
Bensalem (township) Bucks County	19	0.03
Bristol (township) Bucks County	19	0.03

Top 10 Places Sorted by Percent of Total Population
Based on all places, regardless of total population

Place	Population	%
Colebrook (township) Clinton County	2	1.01
Spruce Creek (township) Huntingdon County	2	0.83
Harrison (township) Bedford County	8	0.82
Greenwood (township) Clearfield County	3	0.81
Pomeroy (cdp) Chester County	3	0.75
Jackson (township) Perry County	4	0.73
Idaville (cdp) Adams County	1	0.56
Parker (township) Butler County	3	0.47
Sandy Lake (borough) Mercer County	3	0.46
Catawissa (borough) Columbia County	7	0.45

Top 10 Places Sorted by Percent of Total Population
Based on places with total population of 50,000 or more

Place	Population	%
Lancaster (city) Lancaster County	27	0.05
Reading (city) Berks County	38	0.04
Erie (city) Erie County	31	0.03
Bensalem (township) Bucks County	19	0.03
Bristol (township) Bucks County	19	0.03
Philadelphia (city) Philadelphia County	272	0.02
Upper Darby (township) Delaware County	19	0.02
Levittown (cdp) Bucks County	11	0.02
Pittsburgh (city) Allegheny County	29	0.01
Allentown (city) Lehigh County	11	0.01

Hawaii Native/Pacific Islander: Marshallese

Top 10 Places Sorted by Population
Based on all places, regardless of total population

Place	Population	%
Meyersdale (borough) Somerset County	3	0.14
Manchester (borough) York County	2	0.07
East Rockhill (township) Bucks County	2	0.04
Johnstown (city) Cambria County	2	0.01
Nether Providence (township) Delaware County	2	0.01
Middletown (township) Susquehanna County	1	0.26
Campbelltown (cdp) Lebanon County	1	0.03
West Brunswick (township) Schuylkill County	1	0.03
Greene (township) Erie County	1	0.02
East Whiteland (township) Chester County	1	0.01

Top 10 Places Sorted by Percent of Total Population
Based on all places, regardless of total population

Place	Population	%
Middletown (township) Susquehanna County	1	0.26
Meyersdale (borough) Somerset County	3	0.14
Manchester (borough) York County	2	0.07
East Rockhill (township) Bucks County	2	0.04
Campbelltown (cdp) Lebanon County	1	0.03
West Brunswick (township) Schuylkill County	1	0.03
Greene (township) Erie County	1	0.02
Johnstown (city) Cambria County	2	0.01
Nether Providence (township) Delaware County	2	0.01
East Whiteland (township) Chester County	1	0.01

Top 10 Places Sorted by Percent of Total Population
Based on places with total population of 50,000 or more

Place	Population	%
Abington (township) Montgomery County	0	0.00
Allentown (city) Lehigh County	0	0.00
Bensalem (township) Bucks County	0	0.00
Bethlehem (city) Northampton County	0	0.00
Bethlehem (city) Northampton County	0	0.00
Bristol (township) Bucks County	0	0.00
Erie (city) Erie County	0	0.00
Lancaster (city) Lancaster County	0	0.00
Levittown (cdp) Bucks County	0	0.00
Lower Merion (township) Montgomery County	0	0.00

Hawaii Native/Pacific Islander: Native Hawaiian

Top 10 Places Sorted by Population
Based on all places, regardless of total population

Place	Population	%
Philadelphia (city) Philadelphia County	538	0.04
Pittsburgh (city) Allegheny County	74	0.02
Reading (city) Berks County	49	0.06
Allentown (city) Lehigh County	43	0.04
Bethlehem (city) Northampton County	36	0.05
Upper Darby (township) Delaware County	31	0.04
Lancaster (city) Lancaster County	30	0.05
Erie (city) Erie County	29	0.03
Bethlehem (city) Northampton County	24	0.04
Harrisburg (city) Dauphin County	21	0.04

Top 10 Places Sorted by Percent of Total Population
Based on all places, regardless of total population

Place	Population	%
Atkinson Mills (cdp) Mifflin County	3	1.72
Wellsville (borough) York County	3	1.24
McKeansburg (cdp) Schuylkill County	2	1.23
Crucible (cdp) Greene County	7	0.97
Benezette (township) Elk County	2	0.97
Prompton (borough) Wayne County	2	0.80
Bigler (township) Clearfield County	3	0.75
Landingville (borough) Schuylkill County	1	0.63
Gratz (borough) Dauphin County	4	0.52
Benson (borough) Somerset County	1	0.52

Top 10 Places Sorted by Percent of Total Population
Based on places with total population of 50,000 or more

Place	Population	%
Reading (city) Berks County	49	0.06

Bethlehem (city) Northampton County	36	0.05
Lancaster (city) Lancaster County	30	0.05
Philadelphia (city) Philadelphia County	538	0.04
Allentown (city) Lehigh County	43	0.04
Upper Darby (township) Delaware County	31	0.04
Bethlehem (city) Northampton County	24	0.04
Erie (city) Erie County	29	0.03
Bensalem (township) Bucks County	16	0.03
Pittsburgh (city) Allegheny County	74	0.02

Hawaii Native/Pacific Islander: Samoan

Top 10 Places Sorted by Population
Based on all places, regardless of total population

Place	Population	%
Philadelphia (city) Philadelphia County	198	0.01
Pittsburgh (city) Allegheny County	72	0.02
Allentown (city) Lehigh County	23	0.02
Lansdale (borough) Montgomery County	19	0.12
Hatfield (township) Montgomery County	17	0.10
Norristown (borough) Montgomery County	16	0.05
Reading (city) Berks County	15	0.02
Pocono (township) Monroe County	11	0.10
Kenmar (cdp) Lycoming County	10	0.24
Connellsville (city) Fayette County	10	0.13

Top 10 Places Sorted by Percent of Total Population
Based on all places, regardless of total population

Place	Population	%
Newry (borough) Blair County	2	0.74
McEwensville (borough) Northumberland County	2	0.72
Great Bend (borough) Susquehanna County	5	0.68
Washington (township) Butler County	5	0.38
Dale (borough) Cambria County	4	0.32
Jamestown (borough) Mercer County	2	0.32
Enlow (cdp) Allegheny County	3	0.30
Fredericksburg (cdp) Crawford County	2	0.27
Millbourne (borough) Delaware County	3	0.26
Gamble (township) Lycoming County	2	0.26

Top 10 Places Sorted by Percent of Total Population
Based on places with total population of 50,000 or more

Place	Population	%
Pittsburgh (city) Allegheny County	72	0.02
Allentown (city) Lehigh County	23	0.02
Reading (city) Berks County	15	0.02
Philadelphia (city) Philadelphia County	198	0.01
Lancaster (city) Lancaster County	8	0.01
Erie (city) Erie County	6	0.01
Levittown (cdp) Bucks County	6	0.01
Lower Merion (township) Montgomery County	5	0.01
Scranton (city) Lackawanna County	5	0.01
Upper Darby (township) Delaware County	5	0.01

Hawaii Native/Pacific Islander: Tongan

Top 10 Places Sorted by Population
Based on all places, regardless of total population

Place	Population	%
Lower Merion (township) Montgomery County	18	0.03
Ardmore (cdp) Montgomery County	13	0.10
West Norriton (township) Montgomery County	9	0.06
Philadelphia (city) Philadelphia County	9	<0.01
Upper Saucon (township) Lehigh County	8	0.05
Coatesville (city) Chester County	7	0.05
Pittsburgh (city) Allegheny County	7	<0.01
Franklin Park (borough) Allegheny County	5	0.04
Warminster (township) Bucks County	5	0.02
Bethlehem (city) Northampton County	5	0.01

Top 10 Places Sorted by Percent of Total Population
Based on all places, regardless of total population

Place	Population	%
Westwood (cdp) Chester County	3	0.32
Tremont (borough) Schuylkill County	3	0.17
Ardmore (cdp) Montgomery County	13	0.10
West Norriton (township) Montgomery County	9	0.06
Lincoln Park (cdp) Berks County	1	0.06
Upper Saucon (township) Lehigh County	8	0.05
Coatesville (city) Chester County	7	0.05
Jay (township) Elk County	1	0.05

Franklin Park (borough) Allegheny County	5	0.04
Valley (township) Chester County	3	0.04

Top 10 Places Sorted by Percent of Total Population
Based on places with total population of 50,000 or more

Place	Population	%
Lower Merion (township) Montgomery County	18	0.03
Bethlehem (city) Northampton County	5	0.01
Bethlehem (city) Northampton County	5	0.01
Philadelphia (city) Philadelphia County	9	<0.01
Pittsburgh (city) Allegheny County	7	<0.01
Allentown (city) Lehigh County	1	<0.01
Reading (city) Berks County	1	<0.01
Upper Darby (township) Delaware County	1	<0.01
Abington (township) Montgomery County	0	0.00
Bensalem (township) Bucks County	0	0.00

White

Top 10 Places Sorted by Population
Based on all places, regardless of total population

Place	Population	%
Philadelphia (city) Philadelphia County	655,021	42.92
Pittsburgh (city) Allegheny County	208,065	68.06
Erie (city) Erie County	79,875	78.47
Allentown (city) Lehigh County	73,671	62.42
Scranton (city) Lackawanna County	65,659	86.29
Bethlehem (city) Northampton County	59,451	79.29
Millcreek (township) Erie County	51,334	95.92
Lower Merion (township) Montgomery County	50,501	87.33
Levittown (cdp) Bucks County	48,870	92.24
Upper Darby (township) Delaware County	48,402	58.46

Top 10 Places Sorted by Percent of Total Population
Based on all places, regardless of total population

Place	Population	%
Lilly (borough) Cambria County	968	100.00
Chapman (township) Clinton County	848	100.00
Washington (township) Lawrence County	799	100.00
Houtzdale (borough) Clearfield County	797	100.00
Greenville (township) Somerset County	668	100.00
Eldred (township) Warren County	650	100.00
Noxen (cdp) Wyoming County	633	100.00
Southampton (township) Somerset County	630	100.00
Sutersville (borough) Westmoreland County	605	100.00
Franklin (township) Columbia County	595	100.00

Top 10 Places Sorted by Percent of Total Population
Based on places with total population of 50,000 or more

Place	Population	%
Millcreek (township) Erie County	51,334	95.92
Levittown (cdp) Bucks County	48,870	92.24
Lower Merion (township) Montgomery County	50,501	87.33
Scranton (city) Lackawanna County	65,659	86.29
Bristol (township) Bucks County	45,446	83.26
Abington (township) Montgomery County	45,025	81.40
Bethlehem (city) Northampton County	59,451	79.29
Erie (city) Erie County	79,875	78.47
Bensalem (township) Bucks County	46,896	77.61
Bethlehem (city) Northampton County	42,972	77.23

White: Not Hispanic

Top 10 Places Sorted by Population
Based on all places, regardless of total population

Place	Population	%
Philadelphia (city) Philadelphia County	581,693	38.12
Pittsburgh (city) Allegheny County	203,879	66.69
Erie (city) Erie County	76,023	74.69
Scranton (city) Lackawanna County	62,216	81.77
Allentown (city) Lehigh County	53,079	44.97
Millcreek (township) Erie County	50,664	94.67
Bethlehem (city) Northampton County	50,150	66.88
Lower Merion (township) Montgomery County	49,193	85.07
Levittown (cdp) Bucks County	47,173	89.03
Upper Darby (township) Delaware County	46,606	56.29

Top 10 Places Sorted by Percent of Total Population
Based on all places, regardless of total population

Place	Population	%
Eldred (township) Warren County	650	100.00
Sutersville (borough) Westmoreland County	605	100.00
Austin (borough) Potter County	562	100.00
Hawthorn (borough) Clarion County	494	100.00
Highland (township) Elk County	492	100.00
Carbon (township) Huntingdon County	375	100.00
Arona (borough) Westmoreland County	370	100.00
Berrysburg (borough) Dauphin County	368	100.00
Noyes (township) Clinton County	357	100.00
Stoystown (borough) Somerset County	355	100.00

Top 10 Places Sorted by Percent of Total Population
Based on places with total population of 50,000 or more

Place	Population	%
Millcreek (township) Erie County	50,664	94.67
Levittown (cdp) Bucks County	47,173	89.03
Lower Merion (township) Montgomery County	49,193	85.07
Scranton (city) Lackawanna County	62,216	81.77
Abington (township) Montgomery County	43,861	79.30
Bristol (township) Bucks County	43,161	79.08
Erie (city) Erie County	76,023	74.69
Bensalem (township) Bucks County	44,411	73.50
Bethlehem (city) Northampton County	50,150	66.88
Pittsburgh (city) Allegheny County	203,879	66.69

White: Hispanic

Top 10 Places Sorted by Population
Based on all places, regardless of total population

Place	Population	%
Philadelphia (city) Philadelphia County	73,328	4.81
Allentown (city) Lehigh County	20,592	17.45
Reading (city) Berks County	20,106	22.83
Lancaster (city) Lancaster County	9,448	15.93
Bethlehem (city) Northampton County	9,301	12.40
Bethlehem (city) Northampton County	7,803	14.02
York (city) York County	5,207	11.91
Pittsburgh (city) Allegheny County	4,186	1.37
Erie (city) Erie County	3,852	3.78
Norristown (borough) Montgomery County	3,669	10.69

Top 10 Places Sorted by Percent of Total Population
Based on all places, regardless of total population

Place	Population	%
Avondale (borough) Chester County	362	28.62
Toughkenamon (cdp) Chester County	398	26.68
Kennett Square (borough) Chester County	1,527	25.15
Reading (city) Berks County	20,106	22.83
West Grove (borough) Chester County	557	19.52
York Springs (borough) Adams County	162	19.45
Allentown (city) Lehigh County	20,592	17.45
Lancaster (city) Lancaster County	9,448	15.93
Flora Dale (cdp) Adams County	6	15.79
Lafayette (township) McKean County	368	15.66

Top 10 Places Sorted by Percent of Total Population
Based on places with total population of 50,000 or more

Place	Population	%
Reading (city) Berks County	20,106	22.83
Allentown (city) Lehigh County	20,592	17.45
Lancaster (city) Lancaster County	9,448	15.93
Bethlehem (city) Northampton County	7,803	14.02
Bethlehem (city) Northampton County	9,301	12.40
Philadelphia (city) Philadelphia County	73,328	4.81
Scranton (city) Lackawanna County	3,443	4.52
Bristol (township) Bucks County	2,285	4.19
Bensalem (township) Bucks County	2,485	4.11
Erie (city) Erie County	3,852	3.78

Climate

Pennsylvania Physical Features and Climate Narrative

PHYSICAL FEATURES. The erratic course of the Delaware River is the only natural boundary of Pennsylvania. All others are arbitrary boundaries that do not conform to physical features. Notable contrasts in topography, climate, and soils exist. Within this 45,126-square-mile area lies a great variety of physical land forms of which the most notable is the Appalachian Mountain system composed of two ranges, the Blue Ridge and the Allegheny. These mountains divide the Commonwealth into three major topographical sections. In addition, two plain areas of relatively small size also exist, one in the southeast and the other in the northwest.

In the extreme southeast is the Coastal Plain situated along the Delaware River and covering an area 50 miles long and 10 miles wide. The land is low, flat, and poorly drained. Bordering the Coastal Plain and extending 60 to 80 miles northwest to the Blue Ridge is the Piedmont Plateau, with elevations ranging from 100 to 500 feet and including rolling or undulating uplands, low hills, fertile valleys, and well-drained soils. Just northwest of the Piedmont and between the Blue Ridge and Allegheny Mountains is the Ridge and Valley Region, 80 to 100 miles wide and characterized by parallel ridges and valleys oriented northeast-southwest. The mountain ridges vary from 1,300 to 1,600 feet above sea level. North and west of the Ridge and Valley Region and extending to the New York and Ohio borders is the area known as the Allegheny Plateau. This is the largest natural division of the State and occupies more than half its area. It is crossed by many deep narrow valleys and drained by the Delaware, Susquehanna, Allegheny, and Monongahela River systems. Elevations are generally 1,000 to 2,000 feet above sea level. Bordering Lake Erie is a narrow 40-mile strip of flat, rich land three to four miles wide called the Lake Erie Plain.

GENERAL CLIMATE. Pennsylvania is generally considered to have a humid continental type of climate, but the varied physiographic features have a marked effect on the weather and climate of the various sections within the State. The prevailing westerly winds carry most of the weather disturbances that affect Pennsylvania from the interior of the continent, so that the Atlantic Ocean has only limited influence upon the climate of the State.

TEMPERATURE. Throughout the State temperatures generally remain between 0 and 100°F. and average from near 47°F. annually in the north-central mountains to 57°F. annually in the extreme southeast. Summers are generally warm, averaging about 68°F. along Lake Erie to 74°F. in southeastern counties. High temperatures, 90°F. or above, occur on the average of 10 to 20 days per year in most sections. During the coldest months temperatures average near the freezing point with daily minimum readings sometimes near 0°F. or below. Freezing temperatures occur on the average of 100 or more days annually with the greatest number of occurrences in mountainous regions.

PRECIPITATION. Precipitation is fairly evenly distributed throughout the year. Annual amounts generally range between 34 to 52 inches, while the majority of places receive 38 to 46 inches. Greatest amounts usually occur in spring and summer months, while February is the driest month. Precipitation tends to be somewhat greater in eastern sections due primarily to coastal storms which occasionally frequent the area. During the warm season these storms bring heavy rain, while in winter heavy snow or a mixture of rain and snow may be produced. Thunderstorms, which average between 30 and 35 per year, are concentrated in the warm months and are responsible for most of the summertime rainfall. Winter precipitation is usually three to four inches less than summer rainfall and is produced most frequently from northeastward-moving storms. When temperatures are low enough these storms sometimes cause heavy snow which may accumulate to 20 inches or more. Annual snowfall ranges between wide limits from year to year and place to place. Some years are quite lean as snowfall may total less than 10 inches while other years may produce upwards to 100 inches mostly in northern and mountainous areas. Measurable snow generally occurs between November 20 and March 15 although snow has been observed as early as the beginning of October and as late as May, especially in northern counties. Greatest monthly amounts usually fall in December and January, however, greatest amounts from individual storms generally occur in March as the moisture supply increases with the annual march of temperature.

STORMS. Hurricanes or low pressure systems with a tropical origin seldom affect the State. However, tornadoes do occur in Pennsylvania. At least one tornado has been noted in almost all counties. On the average, five or six tornadoes are observed annually in Pennsylvania, and the State ranks 27th nationally. June is the month of highest frequency, followed closely by July and August. Principal areas of tornado concentration are in the extreme northwest, the Southwest Plateau, and the Southeastern Piedmont.

CLIMATIC AREAS. The topographic features of Pennsylvania divide the State into four rather distinct climatic areas: (1) the Southeastern Coastal Plain and Piedmont Plateau; (2) the Ridge and Valley Province; (3) the Allegheny Plateau; and (4) the Lake Erie Plain.

In the Southeastern Coastal Plain and Piedmont Plateau summers are long and at times uncomfortably hot. Daily temperatures reach 90°F. or above on the average of 25 days during the summer season. From about July 1 to the middle of September this area occasionally experiences uncomfortably warm periods, four to five days to a week in length, during which light wind movement and high relative humidity make conditions oppressive. In general, the winters are comparatively mild, with an average of less than 100 days with minimum temperatures below the freezing point. Average annual precipitation in the area ranges from about 30 inches in the lower Susquehanna Valley to about 46 in Chester County. Under the influence of an occasional severe coastal storm, a normal month's rainfall, or more, may occur within a period of 48 hours. The average seasonal snowfall is about 30 inches, and fields are ordinarily snow covered about one-third of the time during the winter season.

The Ridge and Valley Province is not rugged enough for a true mountain type of climate, but it does have many of the characteristics of such a climate. The mountain-and-valley influence on the air movements causes somewhat greater temperature extremes than are experienced in the southeastern part of the State where the modifying coastal and Chesapeake Bay influence hold them relatively constant, and the daily range of temperature increases somewhat under the valley influences. The effects of nocturnal radiation in the valleys and the tendency for cool airmasses to flow down them at night result in a shortening of the growing season by causing freezes later in spring and earlier in fall than would otherwise occur. The annual precipitation in this area has a mean value of three or four inches more than in the southeastern part of the State, but its geographic distribution is less uniform. The mountain ridges are high enough to have some deflecting influence on general storm winds, while summer showers and thunderstorms are often shunted up the valleys. Seasonal snowfall of the Ridge and Valley Province varies considerably within short distances.

The Allegheny Plateau is fairly typical of a continental type of climate, with changeable temperatures and more frequent precipitation than other parts of the State. In the more northerly sections the influence of latitude, together with higher elevation and radiation conditions, serve to make this the coldest area in the State. Occasionally, winter minimum temperatures are severe. The daily temperature range is fairly large. Annual precipitation has a mean of about 41 inches, ranging from less than 35 inches to more than 45 inches. The seasonal snowfall averages 54 inches in northern areas, while southern sections receive several inches less. Fields are normally snow covered three-fourths of the time during the winter season. Although average annual precipitation is about equal to that for the State as a whole, it usually occurs in smaller amounts at more frequent intervals.

Although the Lake Erie Plain is of relatively small size, it has a unique and agriculturally advantageous climate typical of the coastal areas surrounding much of the Great Lakes. Both in spring and autumn the lake water exerts a retarding influence on the temperature regime and the freeze-free season is extended about 45 days. In the autumn this prevents early freezing temperatures. Annual precipitation totals about 34.5 inches, which is fairly evenly distributed throughout the year. Snowfall exceeds 54 inches per year, with heavy snows sometimes experienced late in April.

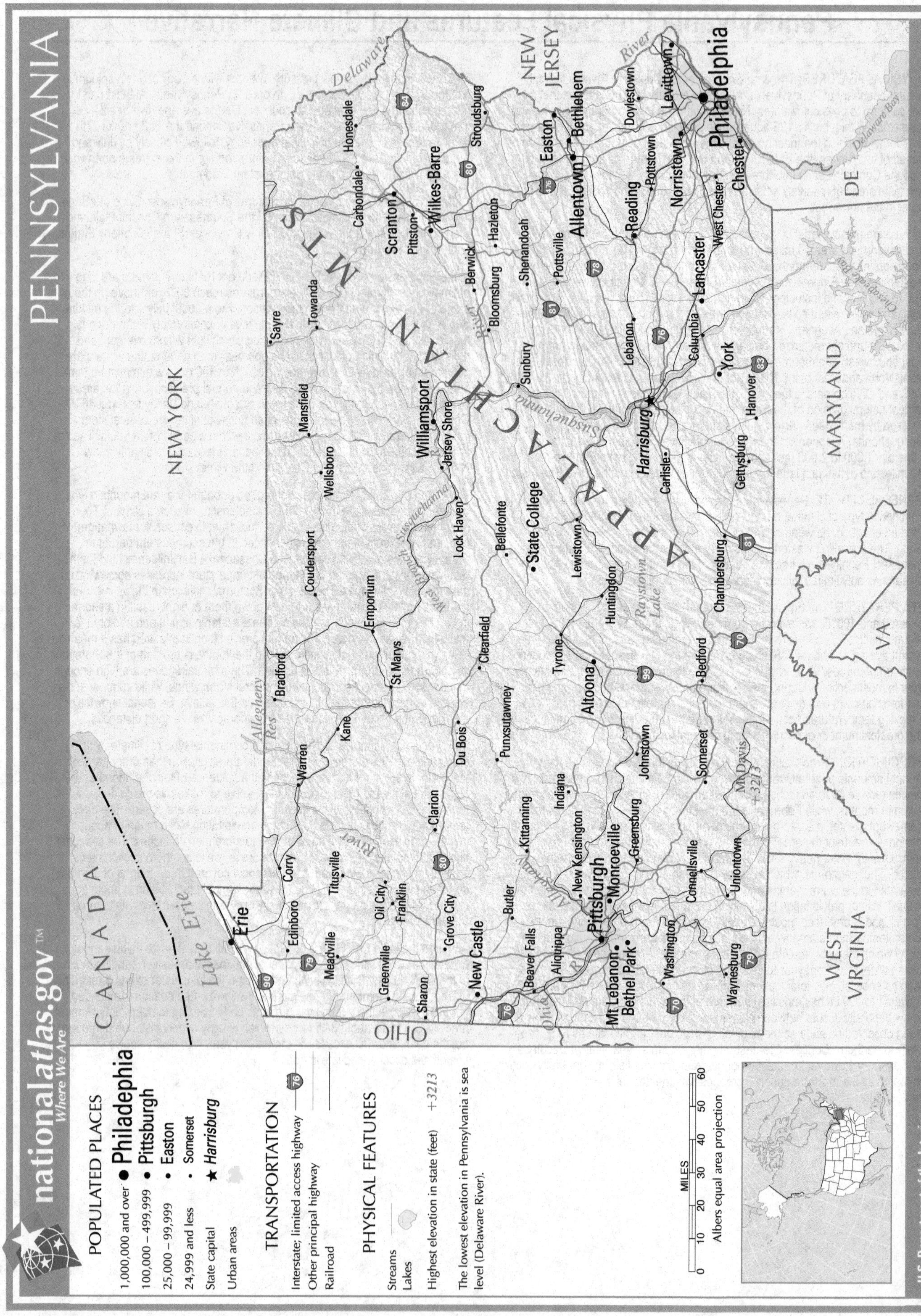

PENNSYLVANIA

nationalatlas.gov ™
Where We Are

POPULATED PLACES

1,000,000 and over • Philadephia
100,000 – 499,999 • Pittsburgh
25,000 – 99,999 • Easton
24,999 and less • Somerset
State capital ★ Harrisburg
Urban areas

TRANSPORTATION

Interstate; limited access highway
Other principal highway
Railroad

PHYSICAL FEATURES

Streams
Lakes
Highest elevation in state (feet) +3213

The lowest elevation in Pennsylvania is sea level (Delaware River).

MILES
0 10 20 30 40 50 60
Albers equal area projection

U.S. Department of the Interior
U.S. Geological Survey

The National Atlas of the United States of America®

CANADA

Lake Erie

NEW YORK

OHIO

WEST VIRGINIA

MARYLAND

VA

DE

NEW JERSEY

Delaware

Chesapeake Bay

Delaware Bay

Erie
Edinboro
Corry
Titusville
Oil City
Franklin
Meadville
Greenville
Sharon
New Castle
Grove City
Butler
Beaver Falls
Aliquippa
Pittsburgh
Monroeville
New Kensington
Kittanning
Indiana
Greensburg
Johnstown
Somerset
Mt Davis +3213
Connellsville
Uniontown
Waynesburg
Washington
Mt Lebanon
Bethel Park
Clarion
Kane
Warren
Bradford
St Marys
Du Bois
Punxsutawney
Clearfield
Tyrone
Altoona
Bedford
Chambersburg
Huntingdon
Raystown Lake
Lewistown
State College
Bellefonte
Lock Haven
Jersey Shore
Williamsport
Emporium
Coudersport
Wellsboro
Mansfield
Sayre
Towanda
Sunbury
Harrisburg
Carlisle
Gettysburg
Hanover
York
Columbia
Lancaster
Lebanon
Reading
Pottsville
Shenandoah
Hazleton
Bloomsburg
Berwick
Pittston
Scranton
Carbondale
Honesdale
Wilkes-Barre
Stroudsburg
Easton
Bethlehem
Allentown
Pottstown
Norristown
Doylestown
Levittown
Philadelphia
Chester
West Chester

APPALACHIAN MTS

Susquehanna
West Branch Susquehanna
Allegheny Res
Allegheny River
Ohio
Delaware River

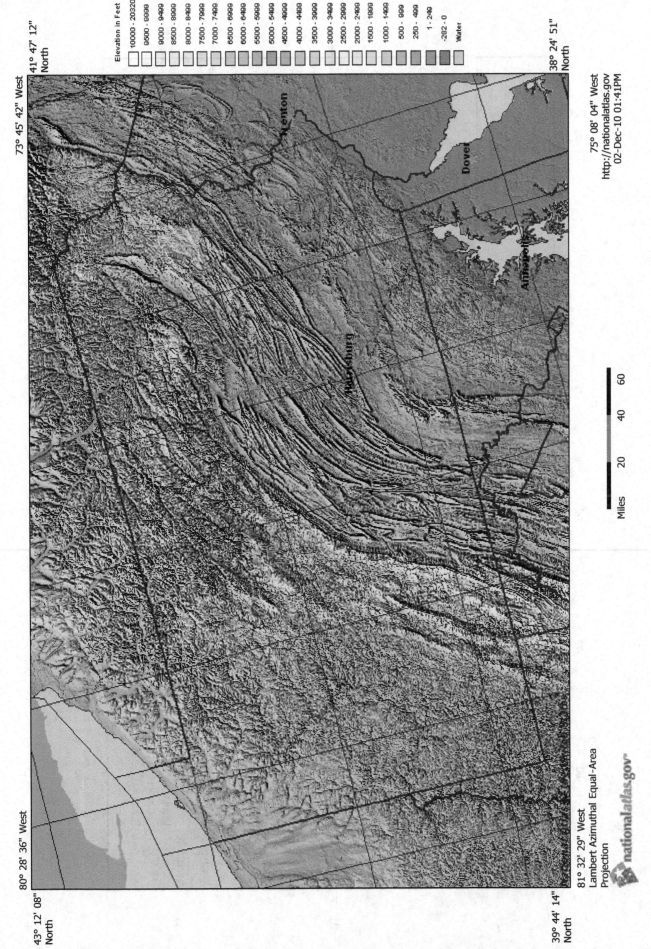

Elevation in Feet

10000 - 20320
9500 - 9999
9000 - 9499
8500 - 8999
8000 - 8499
7500 - 7999
7000 - 7499
6500 - 6999
6000 - 6499
5500 - 5999
5000 - 5499
4500 - 4999
4000 - 4499
3500 - 3999
3000 - 3499
2500 - 2999
2000 - 2499
1500 - 1999
1000 - 1499
500 - 999
250 - 499
1 - 249
-282 - 0
Water

41° 47' 12"
North

73° 45' 42" West

43° 12' 08"
North

80° 28' 36" West

38° 24' 51"
North

75° 08' 04" West
http://nationalatlas.gov
02-Dec-10 01:41PM

39° 44' 14"
North

81° 32' 29" West
Lambert Azimuthal Equal-Area
Projection

Miles   20   40   60

nationalatlas.gov

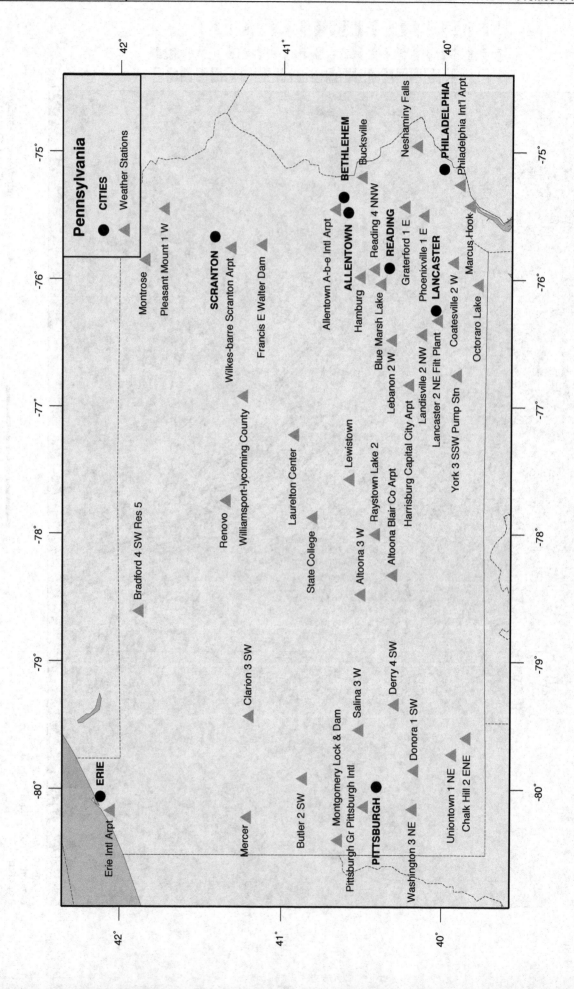

Pennsylvania Weather Stations by County

County	Station Name
Allegheny	Pittsburgh Intl Arpt
Beaver	Montgomery Lock & Dam
Berks	Blue Marsh Lake
	Hamburg
	Reading 4 NNW
Blair	Altoona 3 W
	Altoona Blair Co Arpt
Bucks	Bucksville
	Neshaminy Falls
Butler	Butler 2 SW
Centre	State College
Chester	Coatesville 2 W
	Phoenixville 1 E
Clarion	Clarion 3 SW
Clinton	Renovo
Delaware	Marcus Hook
Erie	Erie Intl Arpt
Fayette	Chalk Hill 2 ENE
	Uniontown 1 NE
Huntingdon	Raystown Lake 2
Lancaster	Lancaster 2 NE Filt Plant
	Landisville 2 NW
	Octoraro Lake
Lebanon	Lebanon 2 W
Lehigh	Allentown A-B-E Intl Arpt
Luzerne	Francis E Walter Dam
	Wilkes-Barre Scranton Arpt
Lycoming	Williamsport-Lycoming County
Mckean	Bradford 4 SW Res 5
Mercer	Mercer
Mifflin	Lewistown
Montgomery	Graterford 1 E
Philadelphia	Philadelphia Int'l Arpt
Susquehanna	Montrose
Union	Laurelton Center
Washington	Donora 1 SW
	Washington 3 NE

County	Station Name
Wayne	Pleasant Mount 1 W
Westmoreland	Derry 4 SW
	Salina 3 W
York	Harrisburg Capital City Arpt
	York 3 SSW Pump Stn

See User Guide for station inclusion criteria.

Pennsylvania Weather Stations by City

City	Station Name	Miles
Abington Twp	Moorestown, NJ	13.2
	Graterford 1 E	18.2
	Neshaminy Falls	9.6
	Philadelphia Int'l Arpt	18.0
	Phoenixville 1 E	19.8
Allentown	Allentown A-B-E Intl Arpt	3.7
	Bucksville	16.0
Altoona	Altoona Blair Co Arpt	15.3
	Altoona 3 W	3.6
	Raystown Lake 2	21.7
Bensalem Twp	Hightstown 2 W, NJ	22.4
	Indian Mills 2 W, NJ	23.2
	Moorestown, NJ	10.2
	Neshaminy Falls	2.6
	Philadelphia Int'l Arpt	23.0
Bethel Park	Donora 1 SW	14.1
	Pittsburgh Intl Arpt	15.9
	Washington 3 NE	12.3
Bethlehem	Belvidere Bridge, NJ	20.9
	Allentown A-B-E Intl Arpt	4.2
	Bucksville	12.8
Bristol Twp	Hightstown 2 W, NJ	18.3
	Indian Mills 2 W, NJ	23.2
	Moorestown, NJ	12.5
	Neshaminy Falls	4.7
Cheltenham Twp	Moorestown, NJ	11.8
	Graterford 1 E	19.0
	Marcus Hook	23.3
	Neshaminy Falls	11.1
	Philadelphia Int'l Arpt	15.4
	Phoenixville 1 E	19.4
Chester	Newark University Farm, DE	23.0
	Wilm. New Castle Co. Arpt, DE	17.6
	Wilmington Porter Rsvr, DE	10.4
	Moorestown, NJ	22.9
	Marcus Hook	3.4
	Philadelphia Int'l Arpt	7.4
	Phoenixville 1 E	19.5
Erie	Erie Intl Arpt	6.0
Falls Twp	Hightstown 2 W, NJ	15.0
	Moorestown, NJ	16.4
	Neshaminy Falls	6.8
Harrisburg	Harrisburg Capital City Arpt	3.8
	Lebanon 2 W	21.9
Haverford Twp	Wilmington Porter Rsvr, DE	19.0
	Moorestown, NJ	18.3
	Graterford 1 E	18.5
	Marcus Hook	12.8
	Neshaminy Falls	22.3
	Philadelphia Int'l Arpt	9.0
	Phoenixville 1 E	13.6

City	Station Name	Miles
Hempfield Twp	Derry 4 SW	12.7
	Donora 1 SW	17.7
	Salina 3 W	15.6
Lancaster	Coatesville 2 W	23.5
	Lancaster 2 NE Filt Plant	1.4
	Landisville 2 NW	8.7
	Lebanon 2 W	22.1
	Octoraro Lake	21.3
Levittown	Hightstown 2 W, NJ	16.9
	Indian Mills 2 W, NJ	24.7
	Moorestown, NJ	14.3
	Neshaminy Falls	5.2
Lower Macungie Twp	Allentown A-B-E Intl Arpt	9.4
	Bucksville	19.2
	Graterford 1 E	22.5
	Hamburg	22.2
	Reading 4 NNW	21.4
Lower Makefield Twp	Flemington 5 NNW, NJ	23.7
	Hightstown 2 W, NJ	15.3
	Moorestown, NJ	18.8
	Neshaminy Falls	7.4
Lower Merion Twp	Wilmington Porter Rsvr, DE	21.9
	Moorestown, NJ	16.8
	Graterford 1 E	17.2
	Marcus Hook	15.6
	Neshaminy Falls	19.6
	Philadelphia Int'l Arpt	10.5
	Phoenixville 1 E	13.7
Lower Paxton Twp	Harrisburg Capital City Arpt	7.0
	Landisville 2 NW	23.6
	Lebanon 2 W	17.7
Manheim Twp	Blue Marsh Lake	25.0
	Coatesville 2 W	24.0
	Lancaster 2 NE Filt Plant	2.6
	Landisville 2 NW	7.4
	Lebanon 2 W	19.3
	Octoraro Lake	23.7
Middletown Twp	Hightstown 2 W, NJ	18.9
	Moorestown, NJ	14.5
	Neshaminy Falls	2.9
Millcreek Twp	Erie Intl Arpt	3.1
Mount Lebanon	Donora 1 SW	17.4
	Pittsburgh Intl Arpt	12.9
	Washington 3 NE	15.1
Norristown	Moorestown, NJ	22.5
	Graterford 1 E	9.1
	Marcus Hook	21.4
	Neshaminy Falls	20.8
	Philadelphia Int'l Arpt	18.5
	Phoenixville 1 E	8.4
Northampton Twp	Hightstown 2 W, NJ	22.8
	Moorestown, NJ	16.5
	Bucksville	23.2

City	Station Name	Miles
Northampton Twp (cont.)	Graterford 1 E	23.4
	Neshaminy Falls	4.4
Penn Hills	Donora 1 SW	21.3
	Pittsburgh Intl Arpt	21.4
	Salina 3 W	14.9
Philadelphia	Indian Mills 2 W, NJ	23.7
	Moorestown, NJ	9.6
	Graterford 1 E	22.1
	Marcus Hook	19.6
	Neshaminy Falls	14.2
	Philadelphia Int'l Arpt	10.7
	Phoenixville 1 E	20.5
Pittsburgh	Donora 1 SW	19.8
	Pittsburgh Intl Arpt	14.3
	Salina 3 W	22.7
	Washington 3 NE	21.1
Radnor Twp	Wilmington Porter Rsvr, DE	20.5
	Moorestown, NJ	21.5
	Graterford 1 E	14.4
	Marcus Hook	15.2
	Neshaminy Falls	23.3
	Philadelphia Int'l Arpt	13.4
	Phoenixville 1 E	9.3
Reading	Blue Marsh Lake	6.4
	Coatesville 2 W	24.9
	Hamburg	14.7
	Reading 4 NNW	5.2
Ross Twp	Butler 2 SW	22.9
	Montgomery Lock & Dam	20.7
	Pittsburgh Intl Arpt	11.2
	Salina 3 W	24.9
Scranton	Francis E Walter Dam	20.8
	Pleasant Mount 1 W	24.8
	Wilkes-Barre Scranton Arpt	6.6
State College	Lewistown	21.1
	State College	0.6
Upper Darby Twp	Wilmington Porter Rsvr, DE	18.3
	Moorestown, NJ	16.9
	Graterford 1 E	21.1
	Marcus Hook	11.6
	Neshaminy Falls	22.4
	Philadelphia Int'l Arpt	6.4
	Phoenixville 1 E	16.2
Warminster Twp	Moorestown, NJ	17.7
	Bucksville	21.2
	Graterford 1 E	18.1
	Neshaminy Falls	8.4
	Philadelphia Int'l Arpt	24.4
	Phoenixville 1 E	22.3
Wilkes-Barre	Francis E Walter Dam	11.6
	Wilkes-Barre Scranton Arpt	9.9
York	Harrisburg Capital City Arpt	18.7

City	Station Name	Miles
York (cont.)	Lancaster 2 NE Filt Plant	24.4
	Landisville 2 NW	19.0
	York 3 SSW Pump Stn	3.3

Note: Miles is the distance between the geographic center of the city and the weather station.

Pennsylvania Weather Stations by Elevation

Feet	Station Name
1,979	Chalk Hill 2 ENE
1,798	Pleasant Mount 1 W
1,691	Bradford 4 SW Res 5
1,507	Francis E Walter Dam
1,479	Altoona Blair Co Arpt
1,419	Montrose
1,319	Altoona 3 W
1,299	Washington 3 NE
1,220	Mercer
1,169	State College
1,149	Pittsburgh Intl Arpt
1,108	Salina 3 W
1,060	Derry 4 SW
1,040	Clarion 3 SW
1,000	Butler 2 SW
956	Uniontown 1 NE
930	Wilkes-Barre Scranton Arpt
839	Raystown Lake 2
799	Laurelton Center
762	Donora 1 SW
729	Erie Intl Arpt
689	Montgomery Lock & Dam
660	Renovo
640	Coatesville 2 W
520	Williamsport-Lycoming County
459	Bucksville
459	Lewistown
450	Lebanon 2 W
390	Allentown A-B-E Intl Arpt
390	York 3 SSW Pump Stn
359	Landisville 2 NW
359	Reading 4 NNW
350	Blue Marsh Lake
350	Hamburg
339	Harrisburg Capital City Arpt
270	Lancaster 2 NE Filt Plant
259	Octoraro Lake
240	Graterford 1 E
104	Phoenixville 1 E
60	Neshaminy Falls
9	Marcus Hook
4	Philadelphia Int'l Arpt

See User Guide for station inclusion criteria.

Allentown A-B-E Int'l Airport

Allentown is located in the east central section of the state and in the Lehigh River valley. Twelve miles to the north is Blue Mountain, a ridge from 1,000 to 1,800 feet in height. The South Mountain, 500 to 1,000 feet high, fringes the southern edge of the city. Otherwise the country is generally rolling with numerous small streams. A modified climate prevails. Temperatures are usually moderate and precipitation generally ample with the largest amounts occurring during the summer months when precipitation is generally showery. General climatological features of the area are slightly modified by the mountain ranges so that at times during the winter there is a temperature difference of 10 to 15 degrees between Allentown and Philadelphia, only 50 miles to the south.

The growing season averages 177 days, and generally ranges from 170 to 185 days. It begins late in April and ends late in October. The average occurrence of the last temperature of 32 degrees in the spring is late April, and the average first fall minimum of 32 degrees is mid-October.

Maximum temperatures during most years are not excessively high and temperatures above 100 degrees are seldom recorded. However, the average humidity in the valley is quite high, and combined with the normal summer temperatures, causes periods of discomfort.

Winters in the valley are comparatively mild. Minimum temperatures during December, January, and February are usually below freezing, but below zero temperatures are seldom recorded.

Seasonal snowfall is quite variable. Freezing rain is a common problem throughout the Lehigh Valley. Snowstorms producing 10 inches or more occur an average of once in two years. The accumulation of snowfall over the drainage area of the Lehigh River to the north of Allentown, combined with spring rains, frequently presents a flood threat to the city and surrounding area. The valley is also subject to torrential rains that cause quick rises in the river and feeder creeks.

The area is seldom subject to destructive storms of large extent. Heavy thunderstorms and tornadoes occasionally cause damage over limited areas. An exception to the usual weather was the storm that battered the east coast on November 25, 1950, when gusts of 88 mph were observed at the station.

Allentown A-B-E Int'l Airport *Lehigh County*   Elevation: 390 ft.   Latitude: 40° 39' N   Longitude: 75° 27' W

	JAN	FEB	MAR	APR	MAY	JUN	JUL	AUG	SEP	OCT	NOV	DEC	YEAR
Mean Maximum Temp. (°F)	36.4	40.1	49.4	61.5	71.8	80.3	84.5	82.9	75.4	63.9	52.6	40.9	61.6
Mean Temp. (°F)	28.6	31.4	39.6	50.6	60.6	69.7	74.2	72.5	64.7	53.2	43.3	32.9	51.8
Mean Minimum Temp. (°F)	20.7	22.6	29.7	39.6	49.4	59.1	63.7	62.1	54.0	42.5	34.0	24.9	41.8
Extreme Maximum Temp. (°F)	70	76	87	92	94	97	101	99	99	90	79	72	101
Extreme Minimum Temp. (°F)	-15	-8	4	16	29	40	46	41	32	21	15	-5	-15
Days Maximum Temp. ≥ 90°F	0	0	0	0	1	3	7	4	1	0	0	0	16
Days Maximum Temp. ≤ 32°F	11	6	1	0	0	0	0	0	0	0	0	6	24
Days Minimum Temp. ≤ 32°F	27	24	19	6	0	0	0	0	0	4	14	25	119
Days Minimum Temp. ≤ 0°F	1	0	0	0	0	0	0	0	0	0	0	0	1
Heating Degree Days (base 65°F)	1,122	944	781	432	175	24	2	7	87	368	644	987	5,573
Cooling Degree Days (base 65°F)	0	0	1	6	46	171	293	247	85	9	0	0	858
Mean Precipitation (in.)	2.97	2.59	3.38	3.59	4.12	4.36	4.71	3.66	4.43	3.82	3.50	3.51	44.64
Maximum Precipitation (in.)*	8.4	5.4	7.2	10.1	10.6	8.6	10.4	12.1	8.9	7.5	9.7	7.9	67.7
Minimum Precipitation (in.)*	0.7	0.9	1.0	0.6	0.1	0.3	0.4	0.8	0.9	0.1	0.7	0.4	29.8
Extreme Maximum Daily Precip. (in.)	1.93	2.94	2.72	3.46	2.90	2.66	3.37	4.19	6.37	8.71	2.66	2.16	8.71
Days With ≥ 0.1" Precipitation	6	5	7	7	8	8	7	6	6	6	6	6	78
Days With ≥ 0.5" Precipitation	2	2	2	2	3	3	3	2	3	2	2	3	29
Days With ≥ 1.0" Precipitation	1	0	1	1	1	1	1	1	1	1	1	1	11
Mean Snowfall (in.)	10.0	10.0	5.5	1.0	trace	trace	0.0	0.0	0.0	trace	0.8	5.4	32.7
Maximum Snowfall (in.)*	34	30	31	13	trace	0	0	0	0	1	8	28	74
Maximum 24-hr. Snowfall (in.)*	12	24	17	11	trace	0	0	0	0	1	6	13	24
Maximum Snow Depth (in.)	na	na	na	na	na	na	na	na	na	na	na	na	na
Days With ≥ 1.0" Snow Depth	na	na	na	na	na	na	na	na	na	na	na	na	na
Thunderstorm Days*	< 1	< 1	1	2	4	6	7	6	3	1	1	< 1	31
Foggy Days*	14	12	13	12	16	16	18	20	19	17	15	14	186
Predominant Sky Cover*	OVR	OVR	OVR	OVR	OVR	OVR	OVR	OVR	OVR	OVR	OVR	OVR	OVR
Mean Relative Humidity 7am (%)*	77	76	76	75	78	79	82	86	88	87	82	79	80
Mean Relative Humidity 4pm (%)*	62	57	52	48	51	52	52	55	57	55	60	64	55
Mean Dewpoint (°F)*	19	20	26	36	48	57	62	62	55	44	33	23	41
Prevailing Wind Direction*	W	W	WNW	WSW	WSW	WSW	WSW	WSW	WSW	WSW	W	W	WSW
Prevailing Wind Speed (mph)*	14	15	16	10	9	9	8	8	8	9	13	13	12
Maximum Wind Gust (mph)*	68	64	60	68	54	77	66	92	60	63	78	62	92

Note: (*) Period of record is 1948-1995

Erie Int'l Airport

Erie is located on the southeast shore of Lake Erie and observations are made at Erie International Airport, which is six miles southwest of the center of the city and about one mile from the lake shore. The terrain rises gradually in a series of ridges paralleling the shoreline to 500 feet above the lake level three to four miles inland and to 1,000 feet about 15 miles inland. Snowfall from instability showers moving southward off the lake usually increases due to the upslope terrain. Snowfall is somewhat higher south of the city than along the lake shore.

During the winter months, the many cold air masses moving south from Canada are modified by the relatively warm waters of Lake Erie. However, the temperature difference between air and water produces an excess of cloudiness and frequent snow from November through March.

Spring weather is quite variable in Erie, but generally cloudy and cool. Proximity to the lake frequently prevents killing frosts that occur inland. This has led to the establishment of numerous vineyards and orchards in a narrow belt along the shore. Summer heat waves are tempered by cool lake breezes that may reach several miles inland, and days with temperatures above 90 degrees are infrequent. Summer thunderstorms are usually less destructive in Erie than inland areas because of the stabilizing effects of Lake Erie.

Autumn, with long dry periods and an abundance of sunshine, is usually the most pleasant period of the year in Erie. The growing season is extended by the influence of the warmer waters of the lake. Precipitation is well distributed throughout the year, although the number of days with measurable amounts varies considerably from a low average of about one day in three for the period June through September to about one-half of the days from November through March, when snow flurries and squalls move in from the lake.

Erie Int'l Airport *Erie County*   Elevation: 729 ft.   Latitude: 42° 05' N   Longitude: 80° 11' W

	JAN	FEB	MAR	APR	MAY	JUN	JUL	AUG	SEP	OCT	NOV	DEC	YEAR
Mean Maximum Temp. (°F)	33.8	35.5	43.5	55.7	66.5	75.6	79.8	78.6	72.0	60.6	49.7	38.3	57.5
Mean Temp. (°F)	27.4	28.4	35.5	46.9	57.4	67.0	71.7	70.7	64.0	53.0	43.3	32.6	49.8
Mean Minimum Temp. (°F)	21.1	21.2	27.5	38.1	48.2	58.3	63.5	62.7	55.9	45.3	36.8	26.7	42.1
Extreme Maximum Temp. (°F)	70	75	82	89	90	100	99	94	93	87	78	75	100
Extreme Minimum Temp. (°F)	-18	-11	-9	12	30	38	48	37	37	25	17	-6	-18
Days Maximum Temp. ≥ 90°F	0	0	0	0	0	1	1	1	0	0	0	0	3
Days Maximum Temp. ≤ 32°F	15	12	6	0	0	0	0	0	0	0	1	9	43
Days Minimum Temp. ≤ 32°F	26	24	22	9	0	0	0	0	0	1	9	23	114
Days Minimum Temp. ≤ 0°F	2	1	0	0	0	0	0	0	0	0	0	0	3
Heating Degree Days (base 65°F)	1,157	1,029	908	543	264	60	6	10	99	375	646	999	6,096
Cooling Degree Days (base 65°F)	0	0	2	7	34	126	220	193	75	10	0	0	667
Mean Precipitation (in.)	2.90	2.35	3.04	3.37	3.38	3.79	3.54	3.63	4.65	4.07	3.89	3.84	42.45
Maximum Precipitation (in.)*	5.5	5.7	6.8	7.1	7.8	7.7	7.7	11.1	10.6	9.9	10.4	6.9	61.7
Minimum Precipitation (in.)*	0.9	0.6	0.6	1.6	1.0	0.8	0.6	1.0	1.3	0.4	1.5	1.4	28.1
Extreme Maximum Daily Precip. (in.)	1.51	2.11	1.56	1.54	1.86	4.61	2.01	3.29	3.91	2.76	2.47	1.48	4.61
Days With ≥ 0.1" Precipitation	8	7	8	9	8	7	7	6	8	9	9	11	97
Days With ≥ 0.5" Precipitation	1	1	1	2	2	2	2	2	3	3	2	2	23
Days With ≥ 1.0" Precipitation	0	0	0	0	0	0	1	1	1	1	0	0	5
Mean Snowfall (in.)	29.0	17.3	14.0	3.3	trace	trace	trace	trace	trace	0.2	7.9	27.9	99.6
Maximum Snowfall (in.)*	62	32	27	10	trace	0	0	0	0	4	36	67	147
Maximum 24-hr. Snowfall (in.)*	13	12	12	7	trace	0	0	0	0	3	17	14	17
Maximum Snow Depth (in.)	na	na	na	na	na	na	na	na	na	na	na	na	na
Days With ≥ 1.0" Snow Depth	na	17	na	1	na	na	na	na	na	na	na	13	na
Thunderstorm Days*	< 1	< 1	2	3	4	6	7	7	4	2	1	< 1	36
Foggy Days*	12	12	14	12	12	11	10	11	11	10	12	13	140
Predominant Sky Cover*	OVR	OVR	OVR	OVR	OVR	OVR	SCT	OVR	OVR	OVR	OVR	OVR	OVR
Mean Relative Humidity 7am (%)*	78	79	78	75	75	78	79	82	81	77	76	77	78
Mean Relative Humidity 4pm (%)*	73	72	67	60	58	60	61	62	63	64	69	73	65
Mean Dewpoint (°F)*	19	20	26	35	45	56	61	60	54	43	33	24	40
Prevailing Wind Direction*	SSW	WSW	WSW	WSW	S	S	S	S	S	S	S	SSW	S
Prevailing Wind Speed (mph)*	14	14	14	14	9	9	8	8	9	10	13	14	12
Maximum Wind Gust (mph)*	78	74	67	71	54	62	69	54	69	62	69	60	78

Note: (*) Period of record is 1948-1995

Harrisburg Capital City Airport

Harrisburg, the capital of Pennsylvania, is situated on the east bank of the Susquehanna River. It is in the Great Valley formed by the eastern foothills of the Appalachian Chain, and about 60 miles southeast of the Commonwealths geographic center. It is nestled in a saucer-like bowl, 10 miles south of Blue Mountain, which serves as a barrier to the severe winter climate experienced 50 to 100 miles to the north and west. Although the severity of the winter climate is lessened, the city lies a little too far inland to derive the full benefits of the coastal climate.

Air masses change with some regularity, and any one condition does not persist for many days in succession. The mountain barrier occasionally prevents cold waves from reaching the Great Valley. The city is favorably located to receive precipitation produced when warm, maritime air from the Atlantic Ocean is forced upslope to cross the Blue Ridge Mountains.

The growing season in the Harrisburg area is about 192 days. Prolonged dry spells occur on occasion. Flood stage on the Susquehanna River occurs on the average of about every three years in Harrisburg, but serious flooding is much less frequent. About one-third of all floods have occurred during the month of March. Tropical hurricanes rarely reach Harrisburg with destructive winds, but have produced rainfalls in excess of 15 inches.

Harrisburg Capital City Airport *York County*   Elevation: 339 ft.   Latitude: 40° 13' N   Longitude: 76° 51' W

	JAN	FEB	MAR	APR	MAY	JUN	JUL	AUG	SEP	OCT	NOV	DEC	YEAR
Mean Maximum Temp. (°F)	na	na	na	na	na	na	na	na	na	na	na	na	na
Mean Temp. (°F)	na	na	na	na	na	na	na	na	na	na	na	na	na
Mean Minimum Temp. (°F)	na	na	na	na	na	na	na	na	na	na	na	na	na
Extreme Maximum Temp. (°F)	na	na	na	na	na	na	na	na	na	na	na	na	na
Extreme Minimum Temp. (°F)	na	na	na	na	na	na	na	na	na	na	na	na	na
Days Maximum Temp. ≥ 90°F	na	na	na	na	na	na	na	na	na	na	na	na	na
Days Maximum Temp. ≤ 32°F	na	na	na	na	na	na	na	na	na	na	na	na	na
Days Minimum Temp. ≤ 32°F	na	na	na	na	na	na	na	na	na	na	na	na	na
Days Minimum Temp. ≤ 0°F	na	na	na	na	na	na	na	na	na	na	na	na	na
Heating Degree Days (base 65°F)	na	na	na	na	na	na	na	na	na	na	na	na	na
Cooling Degree Days (base 65°F)	na	na	na	na	na	na	na	na	na	na	na	na	na
Mean Precipitation (in.)	na	na	na	na	na	na	na	na	na	na	na	na	na
Maximum Precipitation (in.)*	8.0	5.9	6.1	8.0	9.7	18.5	9.7	9.1	15.0	9.9	7.2	7.6	59.3
Minimum Precipitation (in.)*	0.4	0.2	1.0	0.4	0.5	0.1	0.8	0.9	0.6	trace	0.8	0.2	29.0
Extreme Maximum Daily Precip. (in.)	na	na	na	na	na	na	na	na	na	na	na	na	na
Days With ≥ 0.1" Precipitation	na	na	na	na	na	na	na	na	na	na	na	na	na
Days With ≥ 0.5" Precipitation	na	na	na	na	na	na	na	na	na	na	na	na	na
Days With ≥ 1.0" Precipitation	na	na	na	na	na	na	na	na	na	na	na	na	na
Mean Snowfall (in.)	na	na	na	na	na	na	na	na	na	na	na	na	na
Maximum Snowfall (in.)*	34	30	23	10	trace	0	0	0	0	1	15	28	82
Maximum 24-hr. Snowfall (in.)*	14	24	11	6	trace	0	0	0	0	1	9	10	24
Maximum Snow Depth (in.)	na	na	na	na	na	na	na	na	na	na	na	na	na
Days With ≥ 1.0" Snow Depth	na	na	na	na	na	na	na	na	na	na	na	na	na
Thunderstorm Days*	< 1	< 1	1	2	5	6	7	5	3	1	1	< 1	31
Foggy Days*	12	11	11	10	13	12	13	16	15	15	13	12	153
Predominant Sky Cover*	OVR	OVR	OVR	OVR	OVR	OVR	OVR	OVR	OVR	OVR	OVR	OVR	OVR
Mean Relative Humidity 7am (%)*	71	71	70	71	75	77	79	83	85	82	77	72	76
Mean Relative Humidity 4pm (%)*	56	53	49	47	51	51	52	54	55	53	56	58	53
Mean Dewpoint (°F)*	18	20	26	36	48	58	63	62	56	44	33	23	41
Prevailing Wind Direction*	WNW	WNW	WNW	WNW	W	W	W	W	W	W	WNW	WNW	WNW
Prevailing Wind Speed (mph)*	13	14	14	13	8	8	7	7	7	8	13	13	10
Maximum Wind Gust (mph)*	na	na	na	na	na	na	na	na	na	30	na	na	30

Note: (*) Period of record is 1948-1991

Philadelphia Int'l Airport

The Appalachian Mountains to the west and the Atlantic Ocean to the east have a moderating effect on climate. Periods of very high or very low temperatures seldom last for more than three or four days. Temperatures below zero or above 100 degrees are a rarity. On occasion, the area becomes engulfed with maritime air during the summer months, and high humidity adds to the discomfort of seasonably warm temperatures.

Precipitation is fairly evenly distributed throughout the year with maximum amounts during the late summer months. Much of the summer rainfall is from local thunderstorms and amounts vary in different areas of the city. This is due, in part, to the higher elevations to the west and north. Snowfall amounts are often considerably larger in the northern suburbs than in the central and southern parts of the city. In many cases, the precipitation will change from snow to rain within the city. Single storms of 10 inches or more occur about every five years.

The prevailing wind direction for the summer months is from the southwest, while northwesterly winds prevail during the winter. The annual prevailing direction is from the west-southwest. Destructive velocities are comparatively rare and occur mostly in gustiness during summer thunderstorms. High winds occurring in the winter months, as a rule, come with the advance of cold air after the passage of a deep low pressure system. Only rarely have hurricanes in the vicinity caused widespread damage, primarily because of flooding.

Flood stages in the Schuylkill River normally occur about twice a year. Flood stages seldom last over 12 hours and usually occur after excessive thunderstorms. Flooding rarely occurs on the Delaware River.

Philadelphia Int'l Airport *Philadelphia County*   Elevation: 4 ft.   Latitude: 39° 52' N   Longitude: 75° 14' W

	JAN	FEB	MAR	APR	MAY	JUN	JUL	AUG	SEP	OCT	NOV	DEC	YEAR
Mean Maximum Temp. (°F)	40.2	43.7	52.3	63.8	73.8	82.5	87.0	85.3	78.0	66.5	55.8	44.8	64.5
Mean Temp. (°F)	32.9	35.6	43.2	53.9	63.8	73.0	78.0	76.6	69.1	57.4	47.5	37.4	55.7
Mean Minimum Temp. (°F)	25.5	27.4	34.1	43.9	53.8	63.4	68.9	67.9	60.2	48.3	39.0	30.0	46.9
Extreme Maximum Temp. (°F)	73	74	86	95	97	100	103	101	98	89	81	73	103
Extreme Minimum Temp. (°F)	-7	3	7	19	35	44	52	44	40	28	19	1	-7
Days Maximum Temp. ≥ 90°F	0	0	0	0	1	5	11	7	2	0	0	0	26
Days Maximum Temp. ≤ 32°F	7	4	1	0	0	0	0	0	0	0	0	3	15
Days Minimum Temp. ≤ 32°F	24	21	13	1	0	0	0	0	0	0	6	19	84
Days Minimum Temp. ≤ 0°F	0	0	0	0	0	0	0	0	0	0	0	0	0
Heating Degree Days (base 65°F)	989	824	668	339	107	9	0	1	33	253	520	848	4,591
Cooling Degree Days (base 65°F)	0	0	1	12	77	255	409	368	163	25	1	0	1,311
Mean Precipitation (in.)	3.03	2.48	3.77	3.63	3.73	3.42	4.36	3.45	3.75	3.18	3.02	3.47	41.29
Maximum Precipitation (in.)*	8.9	6.4	7.0	8.1	7.4	7.9	10.4	9.7	8.8	6.0	9.1	7.4	54.4
Minimum Precipitation (in.)*	0.4	0.7	0.7	0.5	0.5	0.1	0.6	0.5	0.4	0.1	0.3	0.3	29.3
Extreme Maximum Daily Precip. (in.)	2.32	1.90	2.24	4.19	2.49	2.48	4.68	4.40	6.63	5.53	2.07	2.72	6.63
Days With ≥ 0.1" Precipitation	6	5	7	7	7	6	6	5	5	5	6	6	71
Days With ≥ 0.5" Precipitation	2	2	3	2	3	2	3	2	2	2	2	2	27
Days With ≥ 1.0" Precipitation	1	0	1	1	1	1	1	1	1	1	1	1	11
Mean Snowfall (in.)	5.4	6.6	3.0	0.5	trace	trace	trace	0.0	0.0	trace	0.3	3.0	18.8
Maximum Snowfall (in.)*	23	28	13	4	trace	0	0	0	0	2	9	19	57
Maximum 24-hr. Snowfall (in.)*	9	21	12	4	trace	0	0	0	0	2	5	12	21
Maximum Snow Depth (in.)	12	23	12	3	trace	trace	trace	0	0	trace	5	21	23
Days With ≥ 1.0" Snow Depth	6	5	2	0	0	0	0	0	0	0	0	2	15
Thunderstorm Days*	< 1	< 1	1	2	4	5	6	5	2	1	1	< 1	27
Foggy Days*	13	11	12	11	14	15	16	16	15	15	13	13	164
Predominant Sky Cover*	OVR	OVR	OVR	OVR	OVR	OVR	OVR	OVR	OVR	OVR	OVR	OVR	OVR
Mean Relative Humidity 7am (%)*	74	73	73	72	75	77	79	82	83	83	79	75	77
Mean Relative Humidity 4pm (%)*	59	55	51	48	51	52	54	55	55	54	57	60	54
Mean Dewpoint (°F)*	22	22	29	38	50	59	65	64	57	46	36	26	43
Prevailing Wind Direction*	WNW	WNW	WNW	WNW	SW	SW	SW	SW	SW	WSW	WNW	WNW	SW
Prevailing Wind Speed (mph)*	13	14	14	13	10	9	9	8	9	8	12	13	12
Maximum Wind Gust (mph)*	59	60	69	64	67	54	61	56	53	63	61	63	69

Note: (*) Period of record is 1948-1995

Pittsburgh Int'l Airport

Pittsburgh lies at the foothills of the Allegheny Mountains at the confluence of the Allegheny and Monongahela Rivers which form the Ohio. The city is a little over 100 miles southeast of Lake Erie. It has a humid continental type of climate modified only slightly by its nearness to the Atlantic Seaboard and the Great Lakes.

The predominant winter air masses influencing the climate of Pittsburgh have a polar continental source in Canada and move in from the Hudson Bay region or the Canadian Rockies. During the summer, frequent invasions of air from the Gulf of Mexico bring warm humid weather. Occasionally, Gulf air reaches as far north as Pittsburgh during the winter and produces intermittent periods of thawing. The last spring temperature of 32 degrees usually occurs in late April and the first in late October. The average growing season is about 180 days. There is a wide variation in the time of the first and last frosts over a radius of 25 miles from the center of Pittsburgh due to terrain differences.

Precipitation is distributed well throughout the year. During the winter months about a fourth of the precipitation occurs as snow and there is about a 50 percent chance of measurable precipitation on any day. Thunderstorms occur normally during all months, except midwinter, and have a maximum frequency in midsummer. The first appreciable snowfall generally occurs in late November and usually the last occurs early in April. Snow lies on the ground in the suburbs on an average of about 33 days during the year.

Seven months of the year, April through October, have sunshine more than 50 percent of the possible time. During the remaining five months cloudiness is heavier because the track of migratory storms from west to east is closer to the area and because of the frequent periods of cloudy, showery weather associated with north-west winds from across the Great Lakes. Cold air drainage induced by the many hills leads to the frequent formation of early morning fog which may be quite persis-tent in the river valleys during the colder months.

The Allegheny River flowing south and the Monongahela River flowing north meet to form the Ohio River at Pittsburgh. Heavier rainfall and steeper topography cause the Monongahela River to flood more frequently than the Allegheny River.

Both rivers combine to cause the Ohio River at Pittsburgh to reach the 25 foot flood stage approximately once every four years. The serious flood level of 30 feet is reached much less frequently.

Pittsburgh Int'l Airport *Allegheny County*   Elevation: 1,149 ft.   Latitude: 40° 30' N   Longitude: 80° 14' W

	JAN	FEB	MAR	APR	MAY	JUN	JUL	AUG	SEP	OCT	NOV	DEC	YEAR
Mean Maximum Temp. (°F)	36.1	39.6	49.2	61.7	71.0	79.3	82.8	81.7	74.6	62.7	51.3	39.9	60.8
Mean Temp. (°F)	28.6	31.3	39.5	50.9	60.2	68.7	72.8	71.6	64.4	52.8	43.0	32.6	51.4
Mean Minimum Temp. (°F)	21.1	22.9	29.8	40.0	49.2	58.1	62.8	61.6	54.0	42.8	34.7	25.3	41.9
Extreme Maximum Temp. (°F)	72	76	82	89	91	98	103	100	93	87	79	74	103
Extreme Minimum Temp. (°F)	-22	-7	-1	14	28	36	45	39	34	23	10	-12	-22
Days Maximum Temp. ≥ 90°F	0	0	0	0	0	2	4	3	0	0	0	0	9
Days Maximum Temp. ≤ 32°F	12	9	3	0	0	0	0	0	0	0	1	9	34
Days Minimum Temp. ≤ 32°F	26	23	20	7	1	0	0	0	0	4	13	24	118
Days Minimum Temp. ≤ 0°F	1	1	0	0	0	0	0	0	0	0	0	1	3
Heating Degree Days (base 65°F)	1,121	947	784	427	188	35	4	8	94	381	655	997	5,641
Cooling Degree Days (base 65°F)	0	0	2	10	45	154	252	221	81	9	0	0	774
Mean Precipitation (in.)	2.65	2.33	3.06	3.15	3.91	4.27	3.96	3.59	3.04	2.30	3.11	2.84	38.21
Maximum Precipitation (in.)*	6.3	6.0	6.1	7.6	6.6	10.3	8.7	7.9	6.0	8.2	11.0	8.5	52.2
Minimum Precipitation (in.)*	0.8	0.5	1.1	0.5	1.2	0.6	1.6	0.5	0.3	0.2	0.9	0.4	26.8
Extreme Maximum Daily Precip. (in.)	1.82	1.19	1.61	1.50	2.48	3.11	3.48	2.30	5.95	1.66	1.86	2.76	5.95
Days With ≥ 0.1" Precipitation	7	6	8	8	8	8	7	6	6	6	7	7	84
Days With ≥ 0.5" Precipitation	1	2	2	2	3	3	3	3	2	1	2	2	26
Days With ≥ 1.0" Precipitation	0	0	0	0	1	1	1	1	0	0	0	0	4
Mean Snowfall (in.)	11.4	8.8	7.8	1.5	trace	trace	trace	trace	trace	0.4	2.4	8.1	40.4
Maximum Snowfall (in.)*	40	24	34	8	3	0	0	0	0	9	30	21	77
Maximum 24-hr. Snowfall (in.)*	12	10	24	5	3	0	0	0	0	7	12	9	24
Maximum Snow Depth (in.)	15	12	25	7	trace	trace	trace	trace	trace	1	7	8	25
Days With ≥ 1.0" Snow Depth	13	10	5	1	0	0	0	0	0	0	1	8	38
Thunderstorm Days*	< 1	< 1	2	3	5	7	7	6	3	1	1	< 1	35
Foggy Days*	14	12	13	11	15	16	18	21	18	15	13	14	180
Predominant Sky Cover*	OVR	OVR	OVR	OVR	OVR	OVR	OVR	OVR	OVR	OVR	OVR	OVR	OVR
Mean Relative Humidity 7am (%)*	76	75	76	73	76	79	82	85	85	81	78	77	79
Mean Relative Humidity 4pm (%)*	64	60	54	49	50	51	53	54	54	53	60	65	55
Mean Dewpoint (°F)*	18	20	27	36	46	56	60	60	53	41	32	23	40
Prevailing Wind Direction*	WSW	WSW	WSW	WSW	WSW	WSW	WSW	WSW	WSW	WSW	WSW	WSW	WSW
Prevailing Wind Speed (mph)*	14	13	14	14	12	10	9	9	10	12	13	14	12
Maximum Wind Gust (mph)*	68	78	76	74	61	71	83	89	62	77	71	62	89

Note: (*) Period of record is 1948-1995

Wilkes-Barre Scranton Airport

The Wilkes-Barre Scranton National Weather Service Office is located about midway between the two cities, at the southwest end of the crescent-shaped Lackawanna River Valley. The river flows through this valley and empties into the Susquehanna River and the Wyoming Valley a few miles west of the airport. The surrounding mountains protect both cities and the airport from high winds. They influence the temperature and precipitation during both summer and winter, causing wide departures in both within a few miles of the station. Because of the proximity of the mountains, the climate is relatively cool in summer with frequent shower and thunderstorm activity, usually of brief duration. The winter temperatures in the valley are not severe.

Although severe snowstorms are infrequent, when they do occur they approach blizzard conditions.

While the incidence of tornadoes is very low, Wilkes-Barre has occasionally been hit with these storms which caused loss of life and great property damage.

The area has felt the effects of tropical storms. Considerable wind damage has occasionally occurred, but the most devastating damage has come from flooding caused by the large amounts of precipitation deposited by the storms.

Wilkes-Barre Scranton Airport *Luzerne County*   Elevation: 930 ft.   Latitude: 41° 20' N   Longitude: 75° 44' W

	JAN	FEB	MAR	APR	MAY	JUN	JUL	AUG	SEP	OCT	NOV	DEC	YEAR
Mean Maximum Temp. (°F)	33.7	37.1	46.3	59.2	70.1	77.9	82.1	80.5	72.6	61.0	49.6	37.9	59.0
Mean Temp. (°F)	26.4	29.2	37.2	49.0	59.1	67.5	71.9	70.4	62.7	51.4	41.7	31.1	49.8
Mean Minimum Temp. (°F)	19.2	21.2	28.1	38.7	48.2	56.9	61.5	60.3	52.7	41.7	33.8	24.3	40.5
Extreme Maximum Temp. (°F)	67	71	85	93	93	95	101	98	95	87	80	71	101
Extreme Minimum Temp. (°F)	-21	-6	-3	14	29	35	44	38	29	22	9	-9	-21
Days Maximum Temp. ≥ 90°F	0	0	0	0	0	2	4	3	1	0	0	0	10
Days Maximum Temp. ≤ 32°F	14	10	3	0	0	0	0	0	0	0	1	9	37
Days Minimum Temp. ≤ 32°F	27	24	21	7	1	0	0	0	0	4	14	25	123
Days Minimum Temp. ≤ 0°F	2	0	0	0	0	0	0	0	0	0	0	1	3
Heating Degree Days (base 65°F)	1,188	1,007	855	481	210	47	7	15	123	420	692	1,044	6,089
Cooling Degree Days (base 65°F)	0	0	1	6	35	127	226	189	60	6	0	0	650
Mean Precipitation (in.)	2.33	2.05	2.56	3.32	3.53	4.06	3.83	3.41	3.97	3.25	3.15	2.59	38.05
Maximum Precipitation (in.)*	6.5	8.1	4.8	9.6	8.0	7.6	7.3	11.8	8.1	8.1	7.7	6.6	50.8
Minimum Precipitation (in.)*	0.4	0.2	0.5	1.0	0.8	0.3	1.0	0.7	0.8	trace	0.8	0.3	26.2
Extreme Maximum Daily Precip. (in.)	2.06	2.86	2.22	2.83	1.92	2.85	2.82	3.69	5.98	4.01	3.37	2.16	5.98
Days With ≥ 0.1" Precipitation	5	5	7	7	8	8	7	7	6	5	6	6	77
Days With ≥ 0.5" Precipitation	1	1	2	2	2	2	3	2	2	2	2	2	23
Days With ≥ 1.0" Precipitation	0	0	0	1	1	1	1	1	1	1	1	0	8
Mean Snowfall (in.)	na	na	na	na	na	na	na	na	na	na	na	na	na
Maximum Snowfall (in.)*	42	22	32	27	2	0	0	0	trace	4	23	34	82
Maximum 24-hr. Snowfall (in.)*	18	13	19	9	2	0	0	0	trace	4	19	12	19
Maximum Snow Depth (in.)	na	na	na	na	na	na	na	na	na	na	na	na	na
Days With ≥ 1.0" Snow Depth	na	na	na	na	na	na	na	na	na	na	na	na	na
Thunderstorm Days*	< 1	< 1	1	2	4	6	7	5	3	1	< 1	< 1	29
Foggy Days*	12	9	11	9	11	12	14	15	15	12	11	12	143
Predominant Sky Cover*	OVR	OVR	OVR	OVR	OVR	OVR	OVR	OVR	OVR	OVR	OVR	OVR	OVR
Mean Relative Humidity 7am (%)*	76	75	74	72	76	81	83	86	87	84	79	78	79
Mean Relative Humidity 4pm (%)*	64	60	55	50	50	53	54	56	58	56	63	66	57
Mean Dewpoint (°F)*	17	18	25	34	45	56	60	60	53	42	32	22	39
Prevailing Wind Direction*	SW	SW	NW	SW	SW	SW	SW	SW	SW	SW	SW	SW	SW
Prevailing Wind Speed (mph)*	10	10	12	10	10	9	9	8	9	9	9	9	9
Maximum Wind Gust (mph)*	74	59	56	64	64	58	58	51	52	58	61	64	74

Note: (*) Period of record is 1949-1995

Williamsport Airport

The climate of the Lycoming valley is favorably influenced by the lower elevation of the area compared to the surrounding terrain. Since the prevailing winds reach the area from the southwest to the north, there is a slight moderating effect on winter extremes of cold. Radiation cooling on clear nights is somewhat more frequent than in adjacent areas. Deep valley fogs occasionally persist until nearly midday. Cold air drainage from the surrounding hills is experienced during several nights but the cool temperatures are often modified by the proximity of the river and adjacent damp areas. The winters are milder than those experienced to the west and cold spells are frequently interrupted by incursions of warmer coastal weather. In summer the air frequently becomes trapped in the valley and higher temperatures and humidities result, generally benefitting the local agriculture.

The long irregular range south of the river forms an effective barrier to free air movement. Moderate or strong south to southwest winds are deflected to southeast or south winds in crossing the range and the air becomes quite turbulent with distinct wave effects. Banner clouds with one to three rolls are frequently observed with low overcasts.

An average growing season of 168 days extends from April 29 to October 14. Snowfall in the valley is generally uniform but varies considerably with the rise in terrain. Snow depth on the ridge two miles south of the observation point is frequently double the amount at the station.

Williamsport Airport *Lycoming County*   Elevation: 520 ft.   Latitude: 41° 15' N   Longitude: 76° 55' W

	JAN	FEB	MAR	APR	MAY	JUN	JUL	AUG	SEP	OCT	NOV	DEC	YEAR
Mean Maximum Temp. (°F)	34.7	38.6	48.2	61.3	72.1	80.1	84.2	82.4	74.1	62.4	50.3	38.7	60.6
Mean Temp. (°F)	27.0	30.0	38.3	50.1	60.0	68.8	73.0	71.6	63.7	52.0	41.8	31.4	50.6
Mean Minimum Temp. (°F)	19.3	21.2	28.3	38.9	47.8	57.3	61.9	60.7	53.1	41.5	33.2	24.1	40.6
Extreme Maximum Temp. (°F)	65	71	87	94	96	97	103	99	96	90	81	70	103
Extreme Minimum Temp. (°F)	-20	-8	-2	15	28	36	46	39	32	21	13	-13	-20
Days Maximum Temp. ≥ 90°F	0	0	0	0	1	3	6	4	1	0	0	0	15
Days Maximum Temp. ≤ 32°F	12	7	2	0	0	0	0	0	0	0	0	8	29
Days Minimum Temp. ≤ 32°F	28	24	21	7	1	0	0	0	0	4	14	25	124
Days Minimum Temp. ≤ 0°F	2	1	0	0	0	0	0	0	0	0	0	1	4
Heating Degree Days (base 65°F)	1,170	985	821	445	190	33	3	10	102	402	690	1,034	5,885
Cooling Degree Days (base 65°F)	0	0	0	6	42	152	259	221	69	6	0	0	755
Mean Precipitation (in.)	2.58	2.32	3.08	3.39	3.62	3.92	4.26	3.79	4.03	3.40	3.68	2.84	40.91
Maximum Precipitation (in.)*	8.3	8.4	6.0	7.5	7.3	16.8	9.6	7.7	10.0	9.6	8.1	7.4	61.3
Minimum Precipitation (in.)*	0.5	0.3	0.8	0.7	0.8	0.7	1.0	0.9	0.5	0.2	0.8	0.7	31.1
Extreme Maximum Daily Precip. (in.)	2.62	2.21	1.93	2.36	1.81	2.75	3.29	4.32	6.29	2.95	3.68	3.29	6.29
Days With ≥ 0.1" Precipitation	5	5	7	7	8	8	7	6	6	6	6	6	77
Days With ≥ 0.5" Precipitation	2	2	2	2	3	3	3	3	2	2	2	2	28
Days With ≥ 1.0" Precipitation	0	0	1	1	1	1	1	1	1	1	1	1	10
Mean Snowfall (in.)	11.1	8.1	7.1	1.1	trace	trace	trace	trace	0.0	0.1	2.1	7.0	36.6
Maximum Snowfall (in.)*	40	34	30	14	trace	0	0	0	0	1	14	36	77
Maximum 24-hr. Snowfall (in.)*	20	20	15	9	trace	0	0	0	0	1	11	15	20
Maximum Snow Depth (in.)	*26*	*16*	na	na	na	na	na	*trace*	na	na	na	na	na
Days With ≥ 1.0" Snow Depth	*13*	*11*	na	na	na	na	na	*0*	na	na	na	na	na
Thunderstorm Days*	< 1	< 1	1	2	5	7	8	6	3	1	1	< 1	34
Foggy Days*	14	12	14	13	16	19	21	24	23	20	16	15	207
Predominant Sky Cover*	OVR	OVR	OVR	OVR	OVR	OVR	OVR	OVR	OVR	OVR	OVR	OVR	OVR
Mean Relative Humidity 7am (%)*	76	76	76	75	80	84	87	90	92	88	81	78	82
Mean Relative Humidity 4pm (%)*	60	56	51	47	49	52	53	55	57	55	61	63	55
Mean Dewpoint (°F)*	18	19	25	35	47	57	62	61	55	43	33	22	40
Prevailing Wind Direction*	W	WNW	WNW	W	W	W	W	W	W	W	W	W	W
Prevailing Wind Speed (mph)*	13	13	13	12	9	9	8	8	8	9	12	12	10
Maximum Wind Gust (mph)*	59	55	60	60	55	79	58	61	54	47	63	64	79

Note: (*) Period of record is 1948-1995

Altoona 3 W *Blair County*   Elevation: 1,319 ft.   Latitude: 40° 30' N   Longitude: 78° 28' W

	JAN	FEB	MAR	APR	MAY	JUN	JUL	AUG	SEP	OCT	NOV	DEC	YEAR
Mean Maximum Temp. (°F)	33.0	36.4	45.2	58.4	68.3	76.8	80.7	79.6	72.0	60.6	49.0	37.2	58.1
Mean Temp. (°F)	25.6	28.2	36.1	48.3	57.9	66.5	70.6	69.4	62.2	50.7	41.0	30.2	48.9
Mean Minimum Temp. (°F)	18.1	19.9	27.1	38.1	47.4	56.1	60.5	59.2	52.3	40.8	32.9	23.0	39.6
Extreme Maximum Temp. (°F)	67	71	83	89	90	92	99	98	92	85	80	72	99
Extreme Minimum Temp. (°F)	-20	-8	-3	11	30	34	44	34	33	20	11	-11	-20
Days Maximum Temp. ≥ 90°F	0	0	0	0	0	1	2	2	0	0	0	0	5
Days Maximum Temp. ≤ 32°F	15	10	4	0	0	0	0	0	0	0	1	10	40
Days Minimum Temp. ≤ 32°F	28	25	22	8	1	0	0	0	0	5	15	27	131
Days Minimum Temp. ≤ 0°F	2	1	0	0	0	0	0	0	0	0	0	1	4
Heating Degree Days (base 65°F)	1,215	1,033	888	500	242	56	10	20	127	440	714	1,073	6,318
Cooling Degree Days (base 65°F)	0	0	1	6	28	107	191	166	50	5	0	0	554
Mean Precipitation (in.)	2.61	2.47	3.56	3.60	4.46	4.04	3.86	3.58	3.79	3.49	4.01	3.06	42.53
Extreme Maximum Daily Precip. (in.)	2.35	1.58	2.46	1.61	2.78	3.27	3.00	2.80	3.83	3.32	4.49	2.04	4.49
Days With ≥ 0.1" Precipitation	6	6	8	8	9	8	7	6	6	6	7	7	84
Days With ≥ 0.5" Precipitation	2	2	2	3	3	3	3	3	2	2	2	2	29
Days With ≥ 1.0" Precipitation	0	0	1	1	1	1	1	1	1	1	1	0	9
Mean Snowfall (in.)	10.6	8.3	6.9	0.9	trace	0.0	0.0	0.0	0.0	trace	1.4	6.9	35.0
Maximum Snow Depth (in.)	22	16	30	6	trace	0	0	0	0	0	14	13	30
Days With ≥ 1.0" Snow Depth	13	11	7	1	0	0	0	0	0	0	1	8	41

Altoona Blair Co Arpt *Blair County*   Elevation: 1,479 ft.   Latitude: 40° 18' N   Longitude: 78° 19' W

	JAN	FEB	MAR	APR	MAY	JUN	JUL	AUG	SEP	OCT	NOV	DEC	YEAR
Mean Maximum Temp. (°F)	34.3	38.2	46.5	59.7	69.3	77.7	81.8	80.2	72.8	61.4	49.9	38.1	59.2
Mean Temp. (°F)	27.5	30.4	37.7	49.4	58.7	67.4	71.5	69.9	62.6	51.7	42.0	31.3	50.0
Mean Minimum Temp. (°F)	20.6	22.6	28.8	39.0	48.2	57.2	61.2	59.5	52.3	41.9	34.0	24.4	40.8
Extreme Maximum Temp. (°F)	68	74	85	88	92	94	100	96	94	82	77	74	100
Extreme Minimum Temp. (°F)	-25	-9	1	12	27	35	44	36	31	21	11	-11	-25
Days Maximum Temp. ≥ 90°F	0	0	0	0	0	1	4	2	0	0	0	0	7
Days Maximum Temp. ≤ 32°F	14	9	4	0	0	0	0	0	0	0	1	10	38
Days Minimum Temp. ≤ 32°F	27	24	20	7	1	0	0	0	0	4	13	25	121
Days Minimum Temp. ≤ 0°F	1	0	0	0	0	0	0	0	0	0	0	0	1
Heating Degree Days (base 65°F)	1,154	972	843	467	220	49	6	19	127	412	683	1,039	5,991
Cooling Degree Days (base 65°F)	0	0	2	6	32	129	216	178	61	7	0	0	631
Mean Precipitation (in.)	2.19	2.09	3.11	3.28	3.67	3.35	3.33	2.91	3.42	2.49	3.31	2.16	35.31
Extreme Maximum Daily Precip. (in.)	1.94	2.34	1.64	2.56	2.37	2.10	2.66	2.19	5.55	2.08	5.03	1.65	5.55
Days With ≥ 0.1" Precipitation	5	5	7	7	8	7	7	6	6	5	6	5	74
Days With ≥ 0.5" Precipitation	1	1	2	2	2	2	2	2	2	2	2	1	21
Days With ≥ 1.0" Precipitation	0	0	1	1	1	1	1	1	1	1	1	0	9
Mean Snowfall (in.)	na	na	na	na	na	na	na	na	na	na	na	na	na
Maximum Snow Depth (in.)	na	na	na	na	na	na	na	na	na	na	na	na	na
Days With ≥ 1.0" Snow Depth	na	na	na	na	na	na	na	na	na	na	na	na	na

Blue Marsh Lake *Berks County*   Elevation: 350 ft.   Latitude: 40° 23' N   Longitude: 76° 02' W

	JAN	FEB	MAR	APR	MAY	JUN	JUL	AUG	SEP	OCT	NOV	DEC	YEAR
Mean Maximum Temp. (°F)	*36.0*	39.4	47.7	60.4	70.6	79.8	84.4	82.9	75.4	63.8	*52.0*	*40.9*	*61.1*
Mean Temp. (°F)	*27.8*	30.1	38.2	49.5	59.5	68.8	73.7	72.2	64.2	*52.4*	*42.7*	*32.9*	*51.0*
Mean Minimum Temp. (°F)	*19.4*	20.7	28.6	38.4	48.4	57.7	62.8	61.5	53.0	*41.3*	*33.3*	24.7	40.8
Extreme Maximum Temp. (°F)	70	74	85	90	95	97	102	101	97	91	79	73	102
Extreme Minimum Temp. (°F)	-17	-12	0	15	29	35	46	40	30	21	14	-2	-17
Days Maximum Temp. ≥ 90°F	0	0	0	0	0	3	6	4	1	0	0	0	14
Days Maximum Temp. ≤ 32°F	11	7	2	0	0	0	0	0	0	0	0	6	26
Days Minimum Temp. ≤ 32°F	26	23	20	7	1	0	0	0	0	5	14	24	120
Days Minimum Temp. ≤ 0°F	1	0	0	0	0	0	0	0	0	0	0	0	1
Heating Degree Days (base 65°F)	*1,147*	981	829	463	201	36	4	9	99	*392*	*664*	*987*	*5,812*
Cooling Degree Days (base 65°F)	*0*	0	0	5	39	157	279	241	82	*8*	*0*	*0*	*811*
Mean Precipitation (in.)	3.03	2.50	3.62	3.91	4.09	4.52	4.45	3.79	4.39	3.66	3.73	3.68	45.37
Extreme Maximum Daily Precip. (in.)	na	na	na	na	na	*3.63*	na	*4.00*	*4.69*	na	na	na	na
Days With ≥ 0.1" Precipitation	4	4	5	5	6	6	6	5	5	4	4	5	59
Days With ≥ 0.5" Precipitation	2	1	2	2	2	3	3	2	2	1	2	2	24
Days With ≥ 1.0" Precipitation	0	0	1	1	1	1	1	1	1	1	1	1	10
Mean Snowfall (in.)	7.0	6.2	3.6	0.5	0.0	0.0	0.0	0.0	0.0	0.0	0.5	3.3	21.1
Maximum Snow Depth (in.)	38	25	17	5	0	0	0	0	0	0	4	11	38
Days With ≥ 1.0" Snow Depth	8	7	3	0	0	0	0	0	0	0	0	3	21

Bradford 4 SW Res 5 *Mckean County*   Elevation: 1,691 ft.   Latitude: 41° 54' N   Longitude: 78° 43' W

	JAN	FEB	MAR	APR	MAY	JUN	JUL	AUG	SEP	OCT	NOV	DEC	YEAR
Mean Maximum Temp. (°F)	30.3	33.1	41.9	55.6	67.0	75.0	78.6	77.1	70.1	58.2	46.2	34.3	55.6
Mean Temp. (°F)	21.2	23.0	31.2	43.8	54.0	62.6	66.4	65.1	58.1	46.8	37.3	26.2	44.6
Mean Minimum Temp. (°F)	12.1	12.8	20.5	32.0	41.0	50.2	54.1	53.1	46.0	35.3	28.3	18.0	33.6
Extreme Maximum Temp. (°F)	64	66	83	87	90	91	98	93	91	83	75	68	98
Extreme Minimum Temp. (°F)	-26	-18	-22	8	21	28	35	28	28	14	1	-22	-26
Days Maximum Temp. ≥ 90°F	0	0	0	0	0	0	1	0	0	0	0	0	1
Days Maximum Temp. ≤ 32°F	18	14	8	1	0	0	0	0	0	0	3	14	58
Days Minimum Temp. ≤ 32°F	29	27	27	17	6	0	0	0	2	13	22	29	172
Days Minimum Temp. ≤ 0°F	6	5	2	0	0	0	0	0	0	0	0	3	16
Heating Degree Days (base 65°F)	1,352	1,182	1,040	631	346	121	48	65	220	559	825	1,197	7,586
Cooling Degree Days (base 65°F)	0	0	0	0	2	12	56	97	75	19	1	0	262
Mean Precipitation (in.)	3.14	2.51	3.42	3.76	4.32	5.29	4.94	4.58	4.38	4.04	4.04	3.71	48.13
Extreme Maximum Daily Precip. (in.)	1.66	1.78	2.00	1.63	2.60	3.20	3.12	4.18	4.02	2.50	2.20	1.56	4.18
Days With ≥ 0.1" Precipitation	9	7	8	9	9	9	9	8	8	9	10	11	106
Days With ≥ 0.5" Precipitation	2	1	2	2	3	4	4	3	3	3	2	2	31
Days With ≥ 1.0" Precipitation	0	0	0	0	1	1	1	1	1	1	1	0	7
Mean Snowfall (in.)	18.0	13.5	10.8	2.2	0.1	0.0	0.0	0.0	0.0	0.5	7.5	19.5	72.1
Maximum Snow Depth (in.)	23	31	25	6	1	0	0	0	0	4	20	35	35
Days With ≥ 1.0" Snow Depth	25	23	16	2	0	0	0	0	0	0	5	19	90

The period of record for all cooperative weather station data is 1980 – 2009. See User Guide for detailed explanation of data.

Bucksville *Bucks County*   Elevation: 459 ft.   Latitude: 40° 30' N   Longitude: 75° 12' W

	JAN	FEB	MAR	APR	MAY	JUN	JUL	AUG	SEP	OCT	NOV	DEC	YEAR
Mean Maximum Temp. (°F)	37.5	40.9	49.5	62.4	72.0	80.0	84.2	82.1	75.2	64.3	53.5	42.3	62.0
Mean Temp. (°F)	28.3	30.9	38.6	50.2	59.9	68.7	73.2	71.5	64.1	52.6	43.0	33.2	51.2
Mean Minimum Temp. (°F)	19.0	20.9	27.6	38.0	47.8	57.4	62.1	60.7	52.9	41.0	32.5	24.0	40.3
Extreme Maximum Temp. (°F)	69	74	88	94	94	96	100	100	98	87	80	75	100
Extreme Minimum Temp. (°F)	-23	-19	-3	15	27	36	44	39	31	21	11	-9	-23
Days Maximum Temp. ≥ 90°F	0	0	0	0	1	3	6	4	1	0	0	0	15
Days Maximum Temp. ≤ 32°F	10	6	1	0	0	0	0	0	0	0	0	4	21
Days Minimum Temp. ≤ 32°F	28	24	22	8	1	0	0	0	0	6	16	25	130
Days Minimum Temp. ≤ 0°F	2	1	0	0	0	0	0	0	0	0	0	0	3
Heating Degree Days (base 65°F)	1,131	958	814	442	193	34	3	10	96	383	653	980	5,697
Cooling Degree Days (base 65°F)	0	0	0	6	42	151	262	217	76	8	0	0	762
Mean Precipitation (in.)	3.52	2.86	3.96	4.42	4.19	4.34	5.27	4.04	4.65	4.35	3.83	4.29	49.72
Extreme Maximum Daily Precip. (in.)	2.63	3.15	2.30	4.73	3.21	3.88	3.44	4.63	5.55	na	3.61	4.38	na
Days With ≥ 0.1" Precipitation	6	5	6	6	7	7	7	5	5	5	5	6	70
Days With ≥ 0.5" Precipitation	3	2	3	3	3	3	4	3	3	2	3	3	35
Days With ≥ 1.0" Precipitation	1	1	1	1	1	1	2	1	1	1	1	1	13
Mean Snowfall (in.)	7.7	7.1	4.8	1.5	0.0	trace	0.0	0.0	0.0	trace	0.6	3.3	25.0
Maximum Snow Depth (in.)	26	24	18	10	0	trace	0	0	0	trace	5	14	26
Days With ≥ 1.0" Snow Depth	10	10	4	0	0	0	0	0	0	0	0	5	29

Butler 2 SW *Butler County*   Elevation: 1,000 ft.   Latitude: 40° 51' N   Longitude: 79° 55' W

	JAN	FEB	MAR	APR	MAY	JUN	JUL	AUG	SEP	OCT	NOV	DEC	YEAR
Mean Maximum Temp. (°F)	35.3	38.4	47.2	60.6	70.4	78.8	82.5	81.7	74.6	62.5	50.9	39.2	60.2
Mean Temp. (°F)	26.8	29.0	36.6	48.1	57.5	66.4	70.5	69.6	62.3	50.8	41.3	31.1	49.2
Mean Minimum Temp. (°F)	18.4	19.4	26.0	35.5	44.7	54.0	58.4	57.5	50.0	39.0	31.7	23.0	38.1
Extreme Maximum Temp. (°F)	69	75	84	90	91	97	102	100	94	87	79	74	102
Extreme Minimum Temp. (°F)	-20	-14	-7	9	25	33	39	32	31	17	10	-14	-20
Days Maximum Temp. ≥ 90°F	0	0	0	0	0	2	4	3	1	0	0	0	10
Days Maximum Temp. ≤ 32°F	13	9	4	0	0	0	0	0	0	0	1	8	35
Days Minimum Temp. ≤ 32°F	27	25	23	12	2	0	0	0	0	7	17	26	139
Days Minimum Temp. ≤ 0°F	3	2	0	0	0	0	0	0	0	0	0	1	6
Heating Degree Days (base 65°F)	1,176	1,013	873	505	249	61	12	19	128	438	704	1,044	6,222
Cooling Degree Days (base 65°F)	0	0	0	4	25	111	188	170	54	4	0	0	556
Mean Precipitation (in.)	2.83	2.44	3.25	3.41	4.11	3.96	4.41	3.84	3.74	2.77	3.50	3.11	41.37
Extreme Maximum Daily Precip. (in.)	1.83	1.67	1.98	1.80	3.32	2.30	2.94	3.95	4.72	2.73	2.02	1.93	4.72
Days With ≥ 0.1" Precipitation	7	6	8	8	9	8	8	7	7	7	8	7	90
Days With ≥ 0.5" Precipitation	1	1	2	2	3	3	3	3	2	2	2	2	26
Days With ≥ 1.0" Precipitation	0	0	0	1	1	1	1	1	1	0	1	0	7
Mean Snowfall (in.)	11.7	8.0	5.4	0.8	trace	0.0	0.0	0.0	0.0	0.1	1.1	7.0	34.1
Maximum Snow Depth (in.)	22	17	15	5	trace	0	0	0	0	1	5	12	22
Days With ≥ 1.0" Snow Depth	16	13	6	1	0	0	0	0	0	0	2	10	48

Chalk Hill 2 ENE *Fayette County*   Elevation: 1,979 ft.   Latitude: 39° 51' N   Longitude: 79° 35' W

	JAN	FEB	MAR	APR	MAY	JUN	JUL	AUG	SEP	OCT	NOV	DEC	YEAR
Mean Maximum Temp. (°F)	34.8	38.7	47.8	60.7	68.8	75.1	78.0	76.7	70.2	60.4	49.5	38.5	58.3
Mean Temp. (°F)	27.0	29.7	37.7	48.9	57.4	65.0	68.6	67.4	60.7	50.2	40.7	30.8	48.7
Mean Minimum Temp. (°F)	19.2	20.7	27.6	37.1	45.9	54.8	59.2	58.1	51.1	40.0	31.8	23.1	39.1
Extreme Maximum Temp. (°F)	70	72	83	87	89	88	94	91	87	80	77	73	94
Extreme Minimum Temp. (°F)	-27	-15	-12	7	25	31	37	32	29	18	2	-17	-27
Days Maximum Temp. ≥ 90°F	0	0	0	0	0	0	0	0	0	0	0	0	0
Days Maximum Temp. ≤ 32°F	14	9	4	0	0	0	0	0	0	0	2	10	39
Days Minimum Temp. ≤ 32°F	27	24	21	11	2	0	0	0	0	7	16	25	133
Days Minimum Temp. ≤ 0°F	3	2	0	0	0	0	0	0	0	0	0	1	6
Heating Degree Days (base 65°F)	1,170	991	840	480	246	69	20	32	155	453	723	1,052	6,231
Cooling Degree Days (base 65°F)	0	0	0	3	16	74	139	113	32	2	0	0	380
Mean Precipitation (in.)	4.21	3.66	4.75	4.95	5.36	5.06	5.35	4.30	4.38	3.60	4.44	4.18	54.24
Extreme Maximum Daily Precip. (in.)	2.24	2.08	2.19	2.10	2.08	2.36	3.19	4.64	2.88	2.35	2.90	2.08	4.64
Days With ≥ 0.1" Precipitation	10	9	10	11	11	10	9	8	8	7	9	10	112
Days With ≥ 0.5" Precipitation	3	2	3	3	4	3	4	3	3	3	3	3	37
Days With ≥ 1.0" Precipitation	1	1	1	1	1	1	1	1	1	1	1	1	12
Mean Snowfall (in.)	26.0	18.1	14.8	5.0	0.1	0.0	0.0	0.0	0.0	0.7	6.4	16.6	87.7
Maximum Snow Depth (in.)	28	38	29	12	trace	0	0	0	0	5	22	24	38
Days With ≥ 1.0" Snow Depth	22	20	11	2	0	0	0	0	0	0	5	16	76

Clarion 3 SW *Clarion County*   Elevation: 1,040 ft.   Latitude: 41° 12' N   Longitude: 79° 26' W

	JAN	FEB	MAR	APR	MAY	JUN	JUL	AUG	SEP	OCT	NOV	DEC	YEAR
Mean Maximum Temp. (°F)	33.7	37.0	47.0	60.7	71.5	79.4	82.9	81.7	74.2	61.8	48.9	36.9	59.6
Mean Temp. (°F)	25.3	27.2	35.5	47.4	57.7	66.1	70.1	69.1	61.9	50.1	39.8	29.3	48.3
Mean Minimum Temp. (°F)	16.9	17.4	23.9	34.1	43.8	52.7	57.2	56.4	49.5	38.4	30.6	21.6	36.9
Extreme Maximum Temp. (°F)	69	72	84	90	93	99	100	98	93	86	78	70	100
Extreme Minimum Temp. (°F)	-23	-16	-12	10	21	27	37	31	26	19	9	-14	-23
Days Maximum Temp. ≥ 90°F	0	0	0	0	1	2	4	3	0	0	0	0	10
Days Maximum Temp. ≤ 32°F	14	10	4	0	0	0	0	0	0	0	2	10	40
Days Minimum Temp. ≤ 32°F	28	26	25	14	3	0	0	0	1	9	18	27	151
Days Minimum Temp. ≤ 0°F	3	2	1	0	0	0	0	0	0	0	0	1	7
Heating Degree Days (base 65°F)	1,225	1,062	910	524	247	66	15	21	135	459	750	1,100	6,514
Cooling Degree Days (base 65°F)	0	0	0	2	26	104	178	153	48	3	0	0	514
Mean Precipitation (in.)	3.02	2.50	3.16	3.69	4.16	4.99	5.01	4.53	4.54	3.29	4.04	3.38	46.31
Extreme Maximum Daily Precip. (in.)	1.60	1.60	2.26	2.60	2.15	2.52	4.95	2.39	4.10	2.18	2.17	1.69	4.95
Days With ≥ 0.1" Precipitation	8	7	8	9	9	9	8	8	7	8	8	8	97
Days With ≥ 0.5" Precipitation	2	1	2	2	3	4	4	3	3	2	3	2	31
Days With ≥ 1.0" Precipitation	0	0	0	1	1	1	2	1	1	0	1	0	8
Mean Snowfall (in.)	10.2	7.5	5.1	0.8	0.0	0.0	0.0	0.0	0.0	trace	1.5	7.3	32.4
Maximum Snow Depth (in.)	21	15	12	4	0	0	0	0	0	0	6	16	21
Days With ≥ 1.0" Snow Depth	18	16	8	1	0	0	0	0	0	0	2	11	56

The period of record for all cooperative weather station data is 1980 – 2009. See User Guide for detailed explanation of data.

Coatesville 2 W *Chester County* Elevation: 640 ft. Latitude: 39° 59' N Longitude: 75° 52' W

	JAN	FEB	MAR	APR	MAY	JUN	JUL	AUG	SEP	OCT	NOV	DEC	YEAR
Mean Maximum Temp. (°F)	38.2	41.0	50.2	61.8	71.9	80.6	84.7	83.2	75.3	64.6	53.5	42.1	62.2
Mean Temp. (°F)	29.9	31.9	40.0	50.5	60.4	69.4	74.0	72.7	64.5	53.7	43.6	33.7	52.0
Mean Minimum Temp. (°F)	21.5	22.7	29.7	39.2	48.9	58.2	63.3	62.1	53.7	42.6	33.7	25.2	41.7
Extreme Maximum Temp. (°F)	71	74	88	92	94	96	100	100	96	89	80	75	100
Extreme Minimum Temp. (°F)	-14	-5	-4	21	29	36	45	39	34	21	10	-3	-14
Days Maximum Temp. ≥ 90°F	0	0	0	0	1	3	7	4	1	0	0	0	16
Days Maximum Temp. ≤ 32°F	9	6	1	0	0	0	0	0	0	0	0	5	21
Days Minimum Temp. ≤ 32°F	27	24	20	6	0	0	0	0	0	4	15	25	121
Days Minimum Temp. ≤ 0°F	1	0	0	0	0	0	0	0	0	0	0	0	1
Heating Degree Days (base 65°F)	1,083	930	770	434	182	27	2	7	92	357	635	963	5,482
Cooling Degree Days (base 65°F)	0	0	1	7	46	168	288	252	84	12	0	0	858
Mean Precipitation (in.)	4.12	3.19	4.71	4.14	4.44	3.93	4.75	4.00	5.07	4.24	4.21	4.07	50.87
Extreme Maximum Daily Precip. (in.)	2.41	1.82	3.60	3.19	3.05	3.12	2.77	3.58	7.85	6.62	2.84	3.27	7.85
Days With ≥ 0.1" Precipitation	7	6	7	7	8	7	7	6	6	6	7	7	81
Days With ≥ 0.5" Precipitation	3	2	3	3	3	3	3	3	3	3	3	3	35
Days With ≥ 1.0" Precipitation	1	1	1	1	1	1	1	1	2	1	1	1	13
Mean Snowfall (in.)	10.8	10.2	5.2	1.4	0.0	trace	0.0	0.0	0.0	trace	1.0	4.3	32.9
Maximum Snow Depth (in.)	29	21	15	5	0	trace	0	0	0	trace	4	12	29
Days With ≥ 1.0" Snow Depth	12	11	4	0	0	0	0	0	0	0	1	6	34

Derry 4 SW *Westmoreland County* Elevation: 1,060 ft. Latitude: 40° 18' N Longitude: 79° 20' W

	JAN	FEB	MAR	APR	MAY	JUN	JUL	AUG	SEP	OCT	NOV	DEC	YEAR
Mean Maximum Temp. (°F)	37.2	40.1	49.1	61.6	71.4	79.5	83.4	82.1	75.4	64.0	52.2	40.6	61.4
Mean Temp. (°F)	28.5	30.7	38.2	49.2	58.9	67.6	71.8	70.6	63.6	52.3	42.4	32.4	50.5
Mean Minimum Temp. (°F)	19.8	21.3	27.2	36.7	46.4	55.7	60.1	59.1	51.8	40.5	32.6	24.1	39.6
Extreme Maximum Temp. (°F)	72	76	84	90	93	96	102	98	93	88	83	76	102
Extreme Minimum Temp. (°F)	-29	-18	-10	6	21	32	36	32	24	17	7	-14	-29
Days Maximum Temp. ≥ 90°F	0	0	0	0	0	2	5	3	1	0	0	0	11
Days Maximum Temp. ≤ 32°F	11	7	3	0	0	0	0	0	0	0	1	8	30
Days Minimum Temp. ≤ 32°F	26	24	21	11	2	0	0	0	1	6	15	24	130
Days Minimum Temp. ≤ 0°F	3	1	0	0	0	0	0	0	0	0	0	1	5
Heating Degree Days (base 65°F)	1,124	965	827	474	220	49	7	15	109	396	671	1,005	5,862
Cooling Degree Days (base 65°F)	0	0	2	6	36	135	230	197	74	8	0	0	688
Mean Precipitation (in.)	3.62	3.05	4.09	4.32	4.83	4.76	4.99	4.29	4.39	3.06	4.36	3.57	49.33
Extreme Maximum Daily Precip. (in.)	2.34	2.10	2.10	2.04	2.00	2.30	4.15	3.58	5.51	2.07	2.15	2.10	5.51
Days With ≥ 0.1" Precipitation	10	9	11	11	11	10	9	8	8	8	10	10	115
Days With ≥ 0.5" Precipitation	2	1	3	3	4	3	3	3	3	2	3	2	32
Days With ≥ 1.0" Precipitation	0	0	1	1	1	1	1	1	1	0	1	0	8
Mean Snowfall (in.)	14.4	9.7	7.9	1.2	trace	0.0	0.0	0.0	0.0	0.2	2.1	9.3	44.8
Maximum Snow Depth (in.)	21	20	19	3	trace	0	0	0	0	2	12	26	26
Days With ≥ 1.0" Snow Depth	14	11	5	1	0	0	0	0	0	0	2	9	42

Donora 1 SW *Washington County* Elevation: 762 ft. Latitude: 40° 10' N Longitude: 79° 52' W

	JAN	FEB	MAR	APR	MAY	JUN	JUL	AUG	SEP	OCT	NOV	DEC	YEAR
Mean Maximum Temp. (°F)	39.6	43.2	52.4	64.7	74.0	81.8	85.1	84.3	78.0	66.7	54.9	43.3	64.0
Mean Temp. (°F)	30.9	33.5	41.3	52.3	61.5	70.0	74.0	73.1	66.4	54.8	44.8	34.6	53.1
Mean Minimum Temp. (°F)	22.1	23.6	30.2	39.6	49.0	58.1	62.8	61.8	54.7	42.9	34.6	25.8	42.1
Extreme Maximum Temp. (°F)	74	78	85	92	93	99	102	98	95	89	82	77	102
Extreme Minimum Temp. (°F)	-19	-5	0	12	26	37	40	41	34	21	12	-11	-19
Days Maximum Temp. ≥ 90°F	0	0	0	0	1	3	6	5	1	0	0	0	16
Days Maximum Temp. ≤ 32°F	9	5	1	0	0	0	0	0	0	0	0	6	21
Days Minimum Temp. ≤ 32°F	26	23	19	7	1	0	0	0	0	3	13	24	116
Days Minimum Temp. ≤ 0°F	1	0	0	0	0	0	0	0	0	0	0	0	1
Heating Degree Days (base 65°F)	1,051	886	728	384	157	24	1	4	63	323	601	936	5,158
Cooling Degree Days (base 65°F)	0	0	1	10	55	180	287	261	112	14	0	0	920
Mean Precipitation (in.)	2.52	2.16	3.21	3.20	4.06	3.89	3.89	3.45	2.91	2.50	3.14	2.65	37.58
Extreme Maximum Daily Precip. (in.)	2.00	1.55	1.80	1.94	2.10	1.92	3.45	3.72	4.36	1.52	1.95	2.00	4.36
Days With ≥ 0.1" Precipitation	6	5	8	8	9	8	8	6	6	6	7	7	84
Days With ≥ 0.5" Precipitation	1	1	2	2	3	3	3	2	2	2	2	1	24
Days With ≥ 1.0" Precipitation	0	0	1	0	1	1	1	1	1	0	1	0	7
Mean Snowfall (in.)	6.1	3.1	3.4	0.2	0.0	0.0	0.0	0.0	0.0	trace	0.6	3.6	17.0
Maximum Snow Depth (in.)	24	14	20	1	0	0	0	0	0	0	3	10	24
Days With ≥ 1.0" Snow Depth	8	4	2	0	0	0	0	0	0	0	1	5	20

Francis E Walter Dam *Luzerne County* Elevation: 1,507 ft. Latitude: 41° 07' N Longitude: 75° 44' W

	JAN	FEB	MAR	APR	MAY	JUN	JUL	AUG	SEP	OCT	NOV	DEC	YEAR
Mean Maximum Temp. (°F)	na	35.2	43.5	56.4	67.7	75.5	79.3	78.7	70.3	59.1	na	na	na
Mean Temp. (°F)	na	24.8	32.6	44.3	55.1	63.3	67.3	66.3	58.1	47.0	na	na	na
Mean Minimum Temp. (°F)	na	14.5	21.7	32.2	42.5	51.0	55.1	54.0	45.8	34.9	na	na	na
Extreme Maximum Temp. (°F)	67	69	84	90	91	95	95	98	91	86	77	66	98
Extreme Minimum Temp. (°F)	-26	-15	-8	5	24	29	35	32	23	12	4	-22	-26
Days Maximum Temp. ≥ 90°F	0	0	0	0	0	1	1	1	0	0	0	0	3
Days Maximum Temp. ≤ 32°F	13	10	5	0	0	0	0	0	0	0	2	10	40
Days Minimum Temp. ≤ 32°F	25	23	24	15	4	0	0	0	2	13	18	24	148
Days Minimum Temp. ≤ 0°F	4	3	1	0	0	0	0	0	0	0	0	2	10
Heating Degree Days (base 65°F)	na	1,130	995	617	312	110	39	54	222	550	na	na	na
Cooling Degree Days (base 65°F)	na	0	0	2	13	65	116	99	21	0	na	na	na
Mean Precipitation (in.)	2.89	2.44	3.14	4.02	4.34	5.02	4.68	4.37	4.67	4.08	3.88	3.32	46.85
Extreme Maximum Daily Precip. (in.)	na	2.16	na	na	3.16	3.35	2.89	3.00	5.44	2.55	na	na	na
Days With ≥ 0.1" Precipitation	4	5	6	7	7	8	7	7	6	6	5	5	73
Days With ≥ 0.5" Precipitation	1	1	2	2	3	3	3	3	3	2	2	2	27
Days With ≥ 1.0" Precipitation	0	0	0	1	1	1	1	1	1	1	1	1	9
Mean Snowfall (in.)	12.9	9.3	8.9	3.6	0.0	0.0	0.0	0.0	0.0	0.4	2.1	7.9	45.1
Maximum Snow Depth (in.)	33	28	50	15	0	0	0	0	0	5	7	14	50
Days With ≥ 1.0" Snow Depth	18	16	10	2	0	0	0	0	0	0	2	10	58

The period of record for all cooperative weather station data is 1980 – 2009. See User Guide for detailed explanation of data.

Graterford 1 E *Montgomery County*   Elevation: 240 ft.   Latitude: 40° 14' N   Longitude: 75° 26' W

	JAN	FEB	MAR	APR	MAY	JUN	JUL	AUG	SEP	OCT	NOV	DEC	YEAR
Mean Maximum Temp. (°F)	38.2	41.3	49.5	61.4	71.2	80.5	85.2	83.5	76.7	65.8	54.7	43.3	62.6
Mean Temp. (°F)	28.5	31.2	38.6	49.5	59.2	68.8	73.6	71.3	63.8	52.2	43.7	32.9	51.1
Mean Minimum Temp. (°F)	19.0	21.1	28.2	37.6	47.1	57.1	61.8	59.0	50.8	38.7	32.3	22.6	39.6
Extreme Maximum Temp. (°F)	72	71	87	93	94	99	103	101	99	91	82	75	103
Extreme Minimum Temp. (°F)	-17	-9	2	13	21	28	41	28	22	10	8	-3	-17
Days Maximum Temp. ≥ 90°F	0	0	0	0	1	4	8	5	1	0	0	0	19
Days Maximum Temp. ≤ 32°F	9	5	1	0	0	0	0	0	0	0	0	4	19
Days Minimum Temp. ≤ 32°F	29	24	22	8	1	0	0	0	1	9	16	26	136
Days Minimum Temp. ≤ 0°F	1	0	0	0	0	0	0	0	0	0	0	0	1
Heating Degree Days (base 65°F)	1,123	947	812	465	210	42	4	17	108	401	633	987	5,749
Cooling Degree Days (base 65°F)	0	0	1	6	37	163	276	217	77	11	1	0	789
Mean Precipitation (in.)	3.01	2.13	3.49	3.97	4.08	3.93	4.38	4.19	4.52	3.81	3.72	3.55	44.78
Extreme Maximum Daily Precip. (in.)	2.14	2.29	3.23	4.00	3.64	3.59	3.19	4.09	5.90	3.40	2.50	3.05	5.90
Days With ≥ 0.1" Precipitation	5	4	6	7	7	7	7	7	5	6	6	6	73
Days With ≥ 0.5" Precipitation	2	1	2	3	3	3	3	3	3	3	3	3	32
Days With ≥ 1.0" Precipitation	1	0	1	1	1	1	1	1	1	1	1	1	11
Mean Snowfall (in.)	2.9	4.3	0.9	0.3	0.0	0.0	0.0	0.0	0.0	0.0	0.2	1.9	10.5
Maximum Snow Depth (in.)	9	25	8	3	0	0	0	0	0	0	5	8	25
Days With ≥ 1.0" Snow Depth	1	0	0	0	0	0	0	0	0	0	0	0	1

Hamburg *Berks County*   Elevation: 350 ft.   Latitude: 40° 33' N   Longitude: 75° 59' W

	JAN	FEB	MAR	APR	MAY	JUN	JUL	AUG	SEP	OCT	NOV	DEC	YEAR
Mean Maximum Temp. (°F)	36.7	40.4	49.3	61.8	72.1	80.6	84.7	83.1	75.3	64.0	52.5	40.6	61.8
Mean Temp. (°F)	28.1	31.1	39.5	50.7	60.8	69.7	74.1	72.6	64.6	52.6	43.1	32.3	51.6
Mean Minimum Temp. (°F)	19.5	21.8	29.6	39.6	49.3	58.8	63.4	62.0	53.8	41.1	33.6	23.9	41.4
Extreme Maximum Temp. (°F)	69	75	88	95	96	97	103	100	96	89	80	75	103
Extreme Minimum Temp. (°F)	-19	-4	3	15	31	39	41	41	34	22	14	-6	-19
Days Maximum Temp. ≥ 90°F	0	0	0	0	1	3	7	5	1	0	0	0	17
Days Maximum Temp. ≤ 32°F	10	6	1	0	0	0	0	0	0	0	0	6	23
Days Minimum Temp. ≤ 32°F	28	25	19	5	0	0	0	0	0	4	15	27	123
Days Minimum Temp. ≤ 0°F	1	0	0	0	0	0	0	0	0	0	0	0	1
Heating Degree Days (base 65°F)	1,136	952	785	428	172	26	2	6	87	385	651	1,006	5,636
Cooling Degree Days (base 65°F)	0	0	0	7	47	174	290	249	81	8	0	0	857
Mean Precipitation (in.)	2.97	2.61	3.47	3.66	4.38	4.84	4.51	3.95	4.50	3.76	3.83	3.60	46.08
Extreme Maximum Daily Precip. (in.)	1.80	1.92	2.88	3.87	4.21	3.69	3.02	4.00	3.73	3.11	3.67	3.14	4.21
Days With ≥ 0.1" Precipitation	6	5	7	7	8	8	7	7	6	6	6	6	79
Days With ≥ 0.5" Precipitation	2	2	2	2	3	3	3	2	3	2	3	2	29
Days With ≥ 1.0" Precipitation	1	1	1	1	1	1	1	1	1	1	1	1	12
Mean Snowfall (in.)	6.6	5.7	3.1	0.5	0.0	0.0	0.0	0.0	0.0	0.0	0.4	3.0	19.3
Maximum Snow Depth (in.)	24	19	16	4	0	0	0	0	0	0	2	9	24
Days With ≥ 1.0" Snow Depth	10	7	3	0	0	0	0	0	0	0	0	5	25

Lancaster 2 NE Filt Plant *Lancaster County*   Elevation: 270 ft.   Latitude: 40° 03' N   Longitude: 76° 17' W

	JAN	FEB	MAR	APR	MAY	JUN	JUL	AUG	SEP	OCT	NOV	DEC	YEAR
Mean Maximum Temp. (°F)	38.4	41.8	50.8	62.9	72.9	81.2	85.3	83.9	76.5	65.1	53.9	42.6	63.0
Mean Temp. (°F)	30.4	33.0	40.9	51.9	61.5	70.4	74.9	73.4	65.9	54.3	44.4	34.6	53.0
Mean Minimum Temp. (°F)	22.3	24.1	31.0	40.7	50.1	59.6	64.3	62.9	55.2	43.4	34.8	26.5	42.9
Extreme Maximum Temp. (°F)	70	76	88	93	94	96	102	101	99	91	82	76	102
Extreme Minimum Temp. (°F)	-16	-7	-2	16	32	36	46	37	34	23	12	-3	-16
Days Maximum Temp. ≥ 90°F	0	0	0	0	1	4	7	5	1	0	0	0	18
Days Maximum Temp. ≤ 32°F	9	5	1	0	0	0	0	0	0	0	0	5	20
Days Minimum Temp. ≤ 32°F	27	23	18	5	0	0	0	0	0	3	13	24	113
Days Minimum Temp. ≤ 0°F	1	0	0	0	0	0	0	0	0	0	0	0	1
Heating Degree Days (base 65°F)	1,067	899	740	395	153	21	1	5	69	339	612	936	5,237
Cooling Degree Days (base 65°F)	0	0	1	8	53	190	314	272	102	12	0	0	952
Mean Precipitation (in.)	2.87	2.40	3.38	3.42	3.93	4.09	4.35	3.20	4.42	3.90	3.55	3.20	42.71
Extreme Maximum Daily Precip. (in.)	1.80	1.88	3.24	2.45	2.80	2.74	4.54	2.24	6.11	5.60	2.75	2.60	6.11
Days With ≥ 0.1" Precipitation	6	6	7	7	8	7	7	6	6	6	6	6	78
Days With ≥ 0.5" Precipitation	2	1	2	2	3	3	3	2	3	2	3	2	28
Days With ≥ 1.0" Precipitation	0	0	1	1	1	1	1	1	1	1	1	1	10
Mean Snowfall (in.)	6.5	6.1	2.1	0.4	0.0	0.0	0.0	0.0	0.0	0.0	0.4	2.9	18.4
Maximum Snow Depth (in.)	26	24	13	2	0	0	0	0	0	0	3	14	26
Days With ≥ 1.0" Snow Depth	6	6	2	0	0	0	0	0	0	0	0	3	17

Landisville 2 NW *Lancaster County*   Elevation: 359 ft.   Latitude: 40° 07' N   Longitude: 76° 26' W

	JAN	FEB	MAR	APR	MAY	JUN	JUL	AUG	SEP	OCT	NOV	DEC	YEAR
Mean Maximum Temp. (°F)	38.6	42.4	51.8	64.3	74.3	82.5	86.1	84.9	77.8	66.4	54.5	42.6	63.9
Mean Temp. (°F)	29.9	32.7	40.8	51.8	61.9	70.6	74.3	72.9	65.4	54.2	44.3	34.0	52.7
Mean Minimum Temp. (°F)	21.1	22.9	29.8	39.3	49.4	58.8	62.3	60.8	53.1	41.8	34.1	25.4	41.6
Extreme Maximum Temp. (°F)	69	77	86	91	94	98	102	102	97	91	81	76	102
Extreme Minimum Temp. (°F)	-24	-16	-4	18	30	34	42	35	31	21	11	-8	-24
Days Maximum Temp. ≥ 90°F	0	0	0	0	1	4	8	6	2	0	0	0	21
Days Maximum Temp. ≤ 32°F	8	4	1	0	0	0	0	0	0	0	0	5	18
Days Minimum Temp. ≤ 32°F	26	23	19	7	0	0	0	0	0	6	14	24	119
Days Minimum Temp. ≤ 0°F	1	1	0	0	0	0	0	0	0	0	0	0	2
Heating Degree Days (base 65°F)	1,082	907	742	397	147	18	2	7	77	343	613	953	5,288
Cooling Degree Days (base 65°F)	0	0	1	8	56	194	296	258	97	14	0	0	924
Mean Precipitation (in.)	2.77	2.38	3.36	3.52	4.08	4.10	4.55	3.59	4.17	3.60	3.68	3.06	42.86
Extreme Maximum Daily Precip. (in.)	1.80	2.60	1.75	2.15	3.10	3.04	4.37	3.38	4.64	4.10	3.00	1.86	4.64
Days With ≥ 0.1" Precipitation	6	5	7	7	8	7	7	6	6	6	6	6	77
Days With ≥ 0.5" Precipitation	2	2	3	3	3	3	3	2	3	2	3	2	31
Days With ≥ 1.0" Precipitation	1	0	1	1	1	1	1	1	1	1	1	1	11
Mean Snowfall (in.)	8.0	7.5	3.8	0.5	0.0	0.0	0.0	0.0	0.0	0.0	0.6	3.9	24.3
Maximum Snow Depth (in.)	27	21	16	4	0	0	0	0	0	0	4	9	27
Days With ≥ 1.0" Snow Depth	9	8	3	0	0	0	0	0	0	0	0	5	25

The period of record for all cooperative weather station data is 1980 – 2009. See User Guide for detailed explanation of data.

Laurelton Center *Union County*   Elevation: 799 ft.   Latitude: 40° 54' N   Longitude: 77° 13' W

	JAN	FEB	MAR	APR	MAY	JUN	JUL	AUG	SEP	OCT	NOV	DEC	YEAR
Mean Maximum Temp. (°F)	36.9	41.8	51.2	65.4	75.5	82.7	86.5	84.8	76.5	65.4	52.7	40.1	63.3
Mean Temp. (°F)	27.7	31.3	39.0	51.2	61.1	69.1	73.4	71.9	64.1	52.7	42.3	31.4	51.3
Mean Minimum Temp. (°F)	18.4	20.8	26.7	36.9	46.6	55.4	60.2	58.9	51.6	40.1	31.7	22.6	39.2
Extreme Maximum Temp. (°F)	67	76	89	94	98	100	105	99	97	87	81	74	105
Extreme Minimum Temp. (°F)	-22	-6	-8	15	26	33	42	33	30	20	12	-11	-22
Days Maximum Temp. ≥ 90°F	0	0	0	0	2	5	10	6	1	0	0	0	24
Days Maximum Temp. ≤ 32°F	10	4	1	0	0	0	0	0	0	0	0	6	21
Days Minimum Temp. ≤ 32°F	29	25	23	10	2	0	0	0	0	7	17	26	139
Days Minimum Temp. ≤ 0°F	2	1	0	0	0	0	0	0	0	0	0	1	4
Heating Degree Days (base 65°F)	1,150	947	801	416	166	28	3	8	97	380	676	1,035	5,707
Cooling Degree Days (base 65°F)	0	0	1	8	51	157	268	229	75	7	0	0	796
Mean Precipitation (in.)	2.81	2.46	3.43	3.85	3.98	4.39	4.14	3.99	4.49	3.41	3.90	2.72	43.57
Extreme Maximum Daily Precip. (in.)	2.82	3.39	2.10	2.15	2.53	2.75	4.40	4.30	5.11	4.13	3.26	1.76	5.11
Days With ≥ 0.1" Precipitation	6	5	7	8	8	8	7	7	7	6	7	6	82
Days With ≥ 0.5" Precipitation	2	2	2	3	3	3	3	3	3	2	3	2	31
Days With ≥ 1.0" Precipitation	1	0	1	1	1	1	1	1	1	1	1	1	11
Mean Snowfall (in.)	9.4	na	4.2	0.9	0.0	0.0	0.0	0.0	0.0	0.1	0.8	na	na
Maximum Snow Depth (in.)	52	24	26	5	0	0	0	0	0	2	6	11	52
Days With ≥ 1.0" Snow Depth	10	7	4	0	0	0	0	0	0	0	1	7	29

Lebanon 2 W *Lebanon County*   Elevation: 450 ft.   Latitude: 40° 20' N   Longitude: 76° 28' W

	JAN	FEB	MAR	APR	MAY	JUN	JUL	AUG	SEP	OCT	NOV	DEC	YEAR
Mean Maximum Temp. (°F)	37.0	40.6	49.6	61.8	71.8	80.2	84.2	82.7	75.3	64.2	52.9	41.3	61.8
Mean Temp. (°F)	28.9	31.7	39.5	50.5	60.2	69.0	73.3	71.7	64.3	53.1	43.2	33.2	51.6
Mean Minimum Temp. (°F)	20.8	22.8	29.4	39.0	48.5	57.8	62.4	60.9	53.3	41.9	33.4	25.0	41.3
Extreme Maximum Temp. (°F)	67	75	84	91	93	96	102	98	98	89	82	75	102
Extreme Minimum Temp. (°F)	-22	-10	-4	18	30	37	44	38	33	21	12	-2	-22
Days Maximum Temp. ≥ 90°F	0	0	0	0	0	3	6	4	1	0	0	0	14
Days Maximum Temp. ≤ 32°F	10	6	1	0	0	0	0	0	0	0	0	6	23
Days Minimum Temp. ≤ 32°F	27	24	20	7	0	0	0	0	0	4	14	25	121
Days Minimum Temp. ≤ 0°F	1	0	0	0	0	0	0	0	0	0	0	0	1
Heating Degree Days (base 65°F)	1,110	935	783	434	183	29	2	9	92	371	647	979	5,574
Cooling Degree Days (base 65°F)	0	0	0	5	40	157	267	225	77	9	0	0	780
Mean Precipitation (in.)	2.73	2.42	3.18	3.74	4.10	4.19	4.51	3.59	3.80	3.45	3.49	3.23	42.43
Extreme Maximum Daily Precip. (in.)	2.00	2.04	2.70	2.10	2.60	4.27	3.33	2.70	5.16	3.68	2.75	2.56	5.16
Days With ≥ 0.1" Precipitation	6	5	6	7	8	7	7	6	6	6	6	6	76
Days With ≥ 0.5" Precipitation	2	2	2	3	3	3	3	2	3	2	2	2	29
Days With ≥ 1.0" Precipitation	1	0	1	1	1	1	1	1	1	1	1	1	11
Mean Snowfall (in.)	7.6	6.3	3.2	0.2	0.0	0.0	0.0	0.0	0.0	trace	0.6	4.0	21.9
Maximum Snow Depth (in.)	30	na	14	3	0	0	0	0	0	trace	1	na	na
Days With ≥ 1.0" Snow Depth	7	6	2	0	0	0	0	0	0	0	0	4	19

Lewistown *Mifflin County*   Elevation: 459 ft.   Latitude: 40° 35' N   Longitude: 77° 34' W

	JAN	FEB	MAR	APR	MAY	JUN	JUL	AUG	SEP	OCT	NOV	DEC	YEAR
Mean Maximum Temp. (°F)	36.5	40.0	49.0	61.9	72.2	80.2	84.4	83.4	75.5	63.9	52.1	40.3	61.6
Mean Temp. (°F)	28.3	30.9	38.7	50.2	60.0	68.6	72.9	71.8	64.2	52.3	42.6	32.4	51.1
Mean Minimum Temp. (°F)	20.1	21.8	28.3	38.5	47.7	56.8	61.4	60.2	52.5	40.7	33.1	24.6	40.5
Extreme Maximum Temp. (°F)	71	76	87	94	96	95	102	98	98	89	80	75	102
Extreme Minimum Temp. (°F)	-17	-6	3	15	28	38	41	35	30	21	11	-6	-17
Days Maximum Temp. ≥ 90°F	0	0	0	0	1	3	6	5	1	0	0	0	16
Days Maximum Temp. ≤ 32°F	10	6	2	0	0	0	0	0	0	0	0	6	24
Days Minimum Temp. ≤ 32°F	28	25	21	7	1	0	0	0	0	5	15	25	127
Days Minimum Temp. ≤ 0°F	1	0	0	0	0	0	0	0	0	0	0	0	1
Heating Degree Days (base 65°F)	1,130	957	810	443	189	33	3	8	92	393	665	1,002	5,725
Cooling Degree Days (base 65°F)	0	0	0	6	40	147	256	227	74	8	0	0	759
Mean Precipitation (in.)	2.59	2.29	3.44	3.44	4.20	4.18	3.96	3.43	3.84	3.29	3.53	2.90	41.09
Extreme Maximum Daily Precip. (in.)	1.60	2.85	3.27	2.35	2.74	2.53	2.65	2.71	5.40	3.70	3.54	1.99	5.40
Days With ≥ 0.1" Precipitation	6	5	7	8	9	8	7	6	6	6	7	6	81
Days With ≥ 0.5" Precipitation	2	2	2	3	3	3	3	2	2	2	2	2	28
Days With ≥ 1.0" Precipitation	0	0	1	1	1	1	1	1	1	1	1	0	8
Mean Snowfall (in.)	9.0	6.3	5.4	0.3	0.0	0.0	0.0	0.0	0.0	trace	0.5	4.6	26.1
Maximum Snow Depth (in.)	33	19	22	2	0	0	0	0	0	1	4	12	33
Days With ≥ 1.0" Snow Depth	11	8	4	0	0	0	0	0	0	0	1	6	30

Marcus Hook *Delaware County*   Elevation: 9 ft.   Latitude: 39° 49' N   Longitude: 75° 25' W

	JAN	FEB	MAR	APR	MAY	JUN	JUL	AUG	SEP	OCT	NOV	DEC	YEAR
Mean Maximum Temp. (°F)	39.9	44.0	51.5	63.7	73.5	82.5	87.1	85.1	77.5	65.4	55.0	44.3	64.1
Mean Temp. (°F)	34.1	37.2	43.9	55.0	64.6	73.8	78.7	77.0	69.6	57.8	48.3	38.4	56.5
Mean Minimum Temp. (°F)	28.2	30.4	36.3	46.3	55.5	65.0	70.2	68.8	61.8	50.2	41.5	32.5	48.9
Extreme Maximum Temp. (°F)	67	71	83	95	97	100	103	100	100	87	77	74	103
Extreme Minimum Temp. (°F)	-4	6	10	20	40	50	58	50	43	34	20	3	-4
Days Maximum Temp. ≥ 90°F	0	0	0	0	1	5	12	7	2	0	0	0	27
Days Maximum Temp. ≤ 32°F	7	3	1	0	0	0	0	0	0	0	0	3	14
Days Minimum Temp. ≤ 32°F	20	17	9	1	0	0	0	0	0	0	4	15	66
Days Minimum Temp. ≤ 0°F	0	0	0	0	0	0	0	0	0	0	0	0	0
Heating Degree Days (base 65°F)	953	779	648	308	97	8	0	1	30	239	496	818	4,377
Cooling Degree Days (base 65°F)	0	0	1	14	90	276	431	379	175	23	1	0	1,390
Mean Precipitation (in.)	2.42	2.26	3.24	3.22	3.66	2.95	4.14	2.81	4.25	3.01	3.09	2.86	37.91
Extreme Maximum Daily Precip. (in.)	1.95	2.63	2.40	2.00	2.50	3.41	7.50	2.78	11.68	4.64	2.68	1.97	11.68
Days With ≥ 0.1" Precipitation	5	4	5	6	6	6	5	4	5	5	6	5	62
Days With ≥ 0.5" Precipitation	2	2	2	2	3	2	2	2	3	2	2	2	26
Days With ≥ 1.0" Precipitation	1	1	1	1	1	1	1	1	1	1	1	1	12
Mean Snowfall (in.)	na	2.7	na	trace	0.0	0.0	0.0	0.0	0.0	0.0	trace	na	na
Maximum Snow Depth (in.)	na	na	na	na	na	na	na	na	na	na	na	na	na
Days With ≥ 1.0" Snow Depth	na	0	na	0	0	0	0	0	0	0	0	0	na

The period of record for all cooperative weather station data is 1980 – 2009. See User Guide for detailed explanation of data.

Mercer *Mercer County* Elevation: 1,220 ft. Latitude: 41° 13' N Longitude: 80° 14' W

	JAN	FEB	MAR	APR	MAY	JUN	JUL	AUG	SEP	OCT	NOV	DEC	YEAR
Mean Maximum Temp. (°F)	34.7	38.4	47.9	60.8	70.3	77.7	81.6	80.5	74.1	62.4	49.9	39.1	59.8
Mean Temp. (°F)	25.6	28.3	36.4	47.9	57.5	65.4	69.4	67.9	61.5	50.3	40.4	30.5	48.4
Mean Minimum Temp. (°F)	16.4	18.0	24.9	34.9	44.6	53.0	57.1	55.6	48.8	38.1	30.7	21.5	37.0
Extreme Maximum Temp. (°F)	68	74	82	88	90	94	99	96	93	88	78	73	99
Extreme Minimum Temp. (°F)	-32	-16	-13	11	21	29	36	31	25	17	7	-18	-32
Days Maximum Temp. ≥ 90°F	0	0	0	0	0	1	3	2	0	0	0	0	6
Days Maximum Temp. ≤ 32°F	13	9	3	0	0	0	0	0	0	0	1	8	34
Days Minimum Temp. ≤ 32°F	28	25	24	13	3	0	0	0	1	9	18	25	146
Days Minimum Temp. ≤ 0°F	4	2	1	0	0	0	0	0	0	0	0	1	8
Heating Degree Days (base 65°F)	1,215	1,032	881	511	249	75	21	32	147	452	731	1,062	6,408
Cooling Degree Days (base 65°F)	0	0	1	4	24	93	165	129	48	4	0	0	468
Mean Precipitation (in.)	2.89	2.46	3.18	3.63	3.82	4.51	4.67	3.86	4.01	2.92	3.53	3.27	42.75
Extreme Maximum Daily Precip. (in.)	1.90	1.44	1.98	1.58	2.12	3.29	3.42	2.84	4.47	2.03	2.77	1.77	4.47
Days With ≥ 0.1" Precipitation	7	6	8	8	8	8	7	6	7	6	7	8	86
Days With ≥ 0.5" Precipitation	1	1	2	2	3	3	3	3	2	2	2	2	26
Days With ≥ 1.0" Precipitation	1	0	1	1	1	1	1	1	1	0	0	0	7
Mean Snowfall (in.)	13.3	9.6	7.9	2.3	trace	0.0	0.0	0.0	0.0	0.2	3.6	9.8	46.7
Maximum Snow Depth (in.)	15	12	9	6	trace	0	0	0	0	2	6	14	15
Days With ≥ 1.0" Snow Depth	19	15	8	1	0	0	0	0	0	0	3	11	57

Montgomery Lock & Dam *Beaver County* Elevation: 689 ft. Latitude: 40° 39' N Longitude: 80° 23' W

	JAN	FEB	MAR	APR	MAY	JUN	JUL	AUG	SEP	OCT	NOV	DEC	YEAR
Mean Maximum Temp. (°F)	37.1	40.9	50.2	63.6	72.5	80.4	83.6	82.3	75.8	64.2	52.5	40.8	62.0
Mean Temp. (°F)	29.8	32.3	40.1	51.6	60.8	69.3	73.3	72.1	65.5	54.2	44.0	33.7	52.2
Mean Minimum Temp. (°F)	22.5	23.8	30.0	39.6	49.1	58.0	62.9	61.8	55.2	44.2	35.5	26.5	42.4
Extreme Maximum Temp. (°F)	71	76	82	89	89	98	105	100	93	86	82	74	105
Extreme Minimum Temp. (°F)	-18	-4	-4	14	26	37	45	39	35	25	8	-9	-18
Days Maximum Temp. ≥ 90°F	0	0	0	0	0	2	4	3	0	0	0	0	9
Days Maximum Temp. ≤ 32°F	11	7	2	0	0	0	0	0	0	0	0	6	26
Days Minimum Temp. ≤ 32°F	25	22	19	7	1	0	0	0	0	2	11	22	109
Days Minimum Temp. ≤ 0°F	1	0	0	0	0	0	0	0	0	0	0	0	1
Heating Degree Days (base 65°F)	1,084	917	766	402	165	28	2	6	74	336	623	964	5,367
Cooling Degree Days (base 65°F)	0	0	0	7	43	162	266	232	96	10	0	0	816
Mean Precipitation (in.)	2.53	2.10	2.93	3.24	3.84	3.72	4.38	3.37	3.62	2.36	3.06	2.71	37.86
Extreme Maximum Daily Precip. (in.)	1.96	1.34	1.60	1.78	1.94	2.40	4.99	3.27	8.74	2.00	1.93	2.72	8.74
Days With ≥ 0.1" Precipitation	6	6	7	8	8	8	8	6	6	6	7	7	83
Days With ≥ 0.5" Precipitation	1	1	2	2	3	3	3	2	2	1	2	1	23
Days With ≥ 1.0" Precipitation	0	0	0	0	1	1	1	1	1	0	0	0	5
Mean Snowfall (in.)	4.0	2.9	2.4	0.2	0.0	0.0	0.0	0.0	0.0	trace	0.2	2.4	12.1
Maximum Snow Depth (in.)	13	12	19	4	0	0	0	0	0	0	5	7	19
Days With ≥ 1.0" Snow Depth	9	7	3	0	0	0	0	0	0	0	0	5	24

Montrose *Susquehanna County* Elevation: 1,419 ft. Latitude: 41° 52' N Longitude: 75° 51' W

	JAN	FEB	MAR	APR	MAY	JUN	JUL	AUG	SEP	OCT	NOV	DEC	YEAR
Mean Maximum Temp. (°F)	30.4	33.6	41.9	54.8	66.4	74.9	79.2	77.8	70.4	58.5	46.1	34.7	55.7
Mean Temp. (°F)	21.5	23.8	31.8	43.8	54.6	63.7	67.9	66.4	58.9	47.4	37.3	26.6	45.3
Mean Minimum Temp. (°F)	12.6	14.0	21.7	32.8	42.8	52.4	56.5	55.0	47.3	36.3	28.4	18.5	34.9
Extreme Maximum Temp. (°F)	62	65	83	90	89	95	97	94	92	83	78	66	97
Extreme Minimum Temp. (°F)	-22	-18	-17	7	20	30	38	35	23	17	3	-17	-22
Days Maximum Temp. ≥ 90°F	0	0	0	0	0	0	1	1	0	0	0	0	2
Days Maximum Temp. ≤ 32°F	18	13	6	1	0	0	0	0	0	0	2	13	53
Days Minimum Temp. ≤ 32°F	29	27	26	15	4	0	0	0	1	11	21	29	163
Days Minimum Temp. ≤ 0°F	6	4	1	0	0	0	0	0	0	0	0	2	13
Heating Degree Days (base 65°F)	1,344	1,160	1,025	634	331	103	32	50	206	541	828	1,186	7,440
Cooling Degree Days (base 65°F)	0	0	0	3	13	68	126	99	27	1	0	0	337
Mean Precipitation (in.)	3.10	2.73	3.44	4.11	3.99	4.52	4.27	3.49	3.95	3.92	3.76	3.30	44.58
Extreme Maximum Daily Precip. (in.)	1.69	1.67	2.38	3.85	3.18	6.63	2.10	2.57	5.40	3.58	2.77	2.52	6.63
Days With ≥ 0.1" Precipitation	8	7	8	8	8	9	8	7	6	7	8	8	92
Days With ≥ 0.5" Precipitation	2	2	2	3	3	3	3	2	2	3	2	2	29
Days With ≥ 1.0" Precipitation	0	0	1	1	1	1	1	1	1	1	1	1	10
Mean Snowfall (in.)	21.5	15.5	15.9	5.6	0.1	0.0	0.0	0.0	trace	0.7	7.0	15.5	81.8
Maximum Snow Depth (in.)	40	31	28	13	2	0	0	0	trace	5	21	18	40
Days With ≥ 1.0" Snow Depth	23	22	15	2	0	0	0	0	0	0	4	16	82

Neshaminy Falls *Bucks County* Elevation: 60 ft. Latitude: 40° 09' N Longitude: 74° 57' W

	JAN	FEB	MAR	APR	MAY	JUN	JUL	AUG	SEP	OCT	NOV	DEC	YEAR
Mean Maximum Temp. (°F)	42.0	45.0	52.8	64.2	74.1	83.0	87.2	85.9	79.0	67.4	56.8	45.4	65.2
Mean Temp. (°F)	31.7	33.8	41.0	51.5	61.3	70.8	75.4	74.0	66.8	54.7	45.2	35.1	53.4
Mean Minimum Temp. (°F)	21.2	22.6	29.4	38.9	48.5	58.4	63.5	62.0	54.3	42.0	33.4	24.9	41.6
Extreme Maximum Temp. (°F)	73	73	88	95	96	100	102	102	98	88	82	76	102
Extreme Minimum Temp. (°F)	-11	-3	-1	16	32	34	45	37	30	20	11	-10	-11
Days Maximum Temp. ≥ 90°F	0	0	0	0	2	6	11	9	2	0	0	0	30
Days Maximum Temp. ≤ 32°F	6	3	1	0	0	0	0	0	0	0	0	3	13
Days Minimum Temp. ≤ 32°F	27	24	20	7	0	0	0	0	0	4	15	25	122
Days Minimum Temp. ≤ 0°F	1	0	0	0	0	0	0	0	0	0	0	0	1
Heating Degree Days (base 65°F)	1,026	877	736	407	160	20	1	3	57	324	589	921	5,121
Cooling Degree Days (base 65°F)	0	0	0	8	51	201	330	290	117	12	1	0	1,010
Mean Precipitation (in.)	3.48	2.68	4.27	4.20	4.32	4.51	5.16	4.14	4.53	3.75	3.73	3.87	48.64
Extreme Maximum Daily Precip. (in.)	2.55	1.96	2.27	4.95	2.72	3.94	4.18	3.85	5.83	5.63	2.96	4.20	5.83
Days With ≥ 0.1" Precipitation	7	6	8	7	7	7	7	6	6	6	6	7	80
Days With ≥ 0.5" Precipitation	2	2	3	3	3	3	3	3	3	3	3	3	34
Days With ≥ 1.0" Precipitation	1	1	1	1	1	1	2	1	1	1	1	1	13
Mean Snowfall (in.)	3.7	3.4	2.1	0.3	0.0	0.0	0.0	0.0	0.0	trace	trace	2.4	11.9
Maximum Snow Depth (in.)	23	17	9	9	0	0	0	0	0	0	0	4	14	23
Days With ≥ 1.0" Snow Depth	6	5	2	0	0	0	0	0	0	0	0	2	15

The period of record for all cooperative weather station data is 1980 – 2009. See User Guide for detailed explanation of data.

Octoraro Lake Lancaster County　Elevation: 259 ft.　Latitude: 39° 48' N　Longitude: 76° 03' W

	JAN	FEB	MAR	APR	MAY	JUN	JUL	AUG	SEP	OCT	NOV	DEC	YEAR
Mean Maximum Temp. (°F)	40.1	44.1	52.8	65.3	75.1	83.3	87.1	85.6	78.1	66.9	55.2	44.1	64.8
Mean Temp. (°F)	30.2	33.1	41.1	51.6	61.6	70.3	74.6	73.1	65.5	54.2	43.9	34.2	52.8
Mean Minimum Temp. (°F)	20.4	22.1	29.2	38.0	47.9	57.1	61.9	60.5	52.8	41.2	32.5	24.3	40.7
Extreme Maximum Temp. (°F)	72	75	91	95	95	99	103	104	97	88	80	75	104
Extreme Minimum Temp. (°F)	-19	-17	-4	18	24	34	42	36	31	12	11	-4	-19
Days Maximum Temp. ≥ 90°F	0	0	0	0	2	6	11	8	2	0	0	0	29
Days Maximum Temp. ≤ 32°F	7	3	1	0	0	0	0	0	0	0	0	4	15
Days Minimum Temp. ≤ 32°F	27	25	20	9	1	0	0	0	0	6	16	25	129
Days Minimum Temp. ≤ 0°F	1	0	0	0	0	0	0	0	0	0	0	0	1
Heating Degree Days (base 65°F)	1,072	893	734	403	149	21	1	5	74	339	625	946	5,262
Cooling Degree Days (base 65°F)	0	0	0	7	52	187	304	263	96	12	0	0	921
Mean Precipitation (in.)	3.34	2.74	3.94	3.78	4.09	3.87	4.12	3.93	4.76	3.71	3.67	3.65	45.60
Extreme Maximum Daily Precip. (in.)	2.20	2.70	3.95	2.52	2.50	3.80	2.55	3.70	6.82	5.24	3.16	3.49	6.82
Days With ≥ 0.1" Precipitation	7	5	7	7	8	6	7	6	6	5	6	7	77
Days With ≥ 0.5" Precipitation	2	2	3	3	3	3	3	3	3	2	3	3	33
Days With ≥ 1.0" Precipitation	1	1	1	1	1	1	1	1	1	1	1	1	12
Mean Snowfall (in.)	4.1	6.2	1.2	0.2	0.0	0.0	0.0	0.0	0.0	0.0	0.3	2.5	14.5
Maximum Snow Depth (in.)	na	na	na	5	0	0	0	0	0	0	1	na	na
Days With ≥ 1.0" Snow Depth	na	na	1	0	0	0	0	0	0	0	0	2	na

Phoenixville 1 E Chester County　Elevation: 104 ft.　Latitude: 40° 07' N　Longitude: 75° 30' W

	JAN	FEB	MAR	APR	MAY	JUN	JUL	AUG	SEP	OCT	NOV	DEC	YEAR
Mean Maximum Temp. (°F)	40.7	43.5	51.9	63.9	74.0	82.4	86.1	84.8	77.8	66.5	55.4	43.7	64.2
Mean Temp. (°F)	31.2	33.4	40.9	51.9	61.6	70.5	74.8	73.4	65.9	54.4	44.3	34.2	53.1
Mean Minimum Temp. (°F)	21.7	23.2	29.9	39.9	49.2	58.6	63.5	61.9	54.0	42.3	33.1	24.7	41.8
Extreme Maximum Temp. (°F)	71	75	84	94	96	100	103	103	98	91	83	77	103
Extreme Minimum Temp. (°F)	-13	1	5	19	30	33	42	34	32	21	8	-4	-13
Days Maximum Temp. ≥ 90°F	0	0	0	0	1	5	9	6	2	0	0	0	23
Days Maximum Temp. ≤ 32°F	6	3	1	0	0	0	0	0	0	0	0	4	14
Days Minimum Temp. ≤ 32°F	27	24	19	6	0	0	0	0	0	5	15	26	122
Days Minimum Temp. ≤ 0°F	1	0	0	0	0	0	0	0	0	0	0	0	1
Heating Degree Days (base 65°F)	1,039	886	739	396	156	19	1	6	71	336	616	949	5,214
Cooling Degree Days (base 65°F)	0	0	0	10	57	192	314	275	106	15	1	0	970
Mean Precipitation (in.)	2.97	2.46	3.47	3.66	3.54	3.67	4.08	3.38	4.09	3.39	3.60	3.71	42.02
Extreme Maximum Daily Precip. (in.)	1.80	2.63	2.63	3.98	3.25	2.57	2.91	2.33	5.13	4.20	2.05	2.47	5.13
Days With ≥ 0.1" Precipitation	6	6	7	6	7	6	7	6	5	6	6	6	74
Days With ≥ 0.5" Precipitation	2	2	3	3	2	2	3	2	3	2	3	3	30
Days With ≥ 1.0" Precipitation	1	0	1	1	1	1	1	1	1	1	1	1	11
Mean Snowfall (in.)	na	na	na	0.0	0.0	0.0	0.0	0.0	0.0	0.0	0.0	trace	na
Maximum Snow Depth (in.)	na	na	na	0	0	na	0	0	0	0	na	na	na
Days With ≥ 1.0" Snow Depth	na	na	na	0	0	0	0	0	0	0	0	0	na

Pleasant Mount 1 W Wayne County　Elevation: 1,798 ft.　Latitude: 41° 44' N　Longitude: 75° 27' W

	JAN	FEB	MAR	APR	MAY	JUN	JUL	AUG	SEP	OCT	NOV	DEC	YEAR
Mean Maximum Temp. (°F)	28.8	32.1	39.7	52.9	64.3	72.3	76.6	75.5	68.0	56.6	44.8	33.2	53.7
Mean Temp. (°F)	20.2	22.5	29.9	42.4	53.2	61.9	66.1	65.0	57.3	46.1	36.3	25.4	43.9
Mean Minimum Temp. (°F)	11.5	12.9	20.1	31.8	42.1	51.5	55.6	54.4	46.7	35.6	27.8	17.5	34.0
Extreme Maximum Temp. (°F)	61	67	79	86	89	90	95	92	88	82	75	65	95
Extreme Minimum Temp. (°F)	-25	-16	-14	4	19	30	39	33	25	15	3	-24	-25
Days Maximum Temp. ≥ 90°F	0	0	0	0	0	0	0	0	0	0	0	0	0
Days Maximum Temp. ≤ 32°F	20	15	9	1	0	0	0	0	0	0	3	15	63
Days Minimum Temp. ≤ 32°F	30	27	28	17	4	0	0	0	1	13	22	29	171
Days Minimum Temp. ≤ 0°F	6	4	1	0	0	0	0	0	0	0	0	3	14
Heating Degree Days (base 65°F)	1,384	1,194	1,081	672	366	132	48	67	240	579	854	1,223	7,840
Cooling Degree Days (base 65°F)	0	0	0	1	8	47	89	74	17	1	0	0	237
Mean Precipitation (in.)	3.20	2.66	3.35	4.21	4.66	4.98	4.55	4.05	4.77	4.54	4.11	3.62	48.70
Extreme Maximum Daily Precip. (in.)	2.01	1.82	1.88	3.72	2.73	5.22	2.98	2.50	4.75	3.31	3.20	3.53	5.22
Days With ≥ 0.1" Precipitation	7	6	7	9	9	9	8	8	7	7	7	7	91
Days With ≥ 0.5" Precipitation	2	2	2	3	3	3	3	3	3	3	3	2	32
Days With ≥ 1.0" Precipitation	0	0	1	1	1	1	1	1	1	1	1	1	10
Mean Snowfall (in.)	18.9	13.6	11.7	3.3	trace	0.0	0.0	0.0	0.0	0.3	4.5	13.4	65.7
Maximum Snow Depth (in.)	51	39	40	12	trace	0	0	0	0	6	18	24	51
Days With ≥ 1.0" Snow Depth	25	24	18	3	0	0	0	0	0	0	4	17	91

Raystown Lake 2 Huntingdon County　Elevation: 839 ft.　Latitude: 40° 26' N　Longitude: 78° 00' W

	JAN	FEB	MAR	APR	MAY	JUN	JUL	AUG	SEP	OCT	NOV	DEC	YEAR
Mean Maximum Temp. (°F)	36.3	39.5	48.0	60.8	70.8	79.5	83.8	82.7	75.2	63.4	51.7	40.5	61.0
Mean Temp. (°F)	28.1	30.2	37.6	49.4	59.0	67.9	72.5	71.3	63.9	52.4	42.5	32.7	50.6
Mean Minimum Temp. (°F)	19.9	20.9	27.3	38.0	47.2	56.2	61.2	59.8	52.6	41.3	33.2	24.9	40.2
Extreme Maximum Temp. (°F)	70	79	84	91	93	97	104	99	96	89	82	74	104
Extreme Minimum Temp. (°F)	-15	-3	1	15	29	36	42	37	29	20	14	-7	-15
Days Maximum Temp. ≥ 90°F	0	0	0	0	0	2	6	4	1	0	0	0	13
Days Maximum Temp. ≤ 32°F	11	7	3	0	0	0	0	0	0	0	1	7	29
Days Minimum Temp. ≤ 32°F	27	24	22	8	1	0	0	0	0	5	14	25	126
Days Minimum Temp. ≤ 0°F	1	0	0	0	0	0	0	0	0	0	0	0	1
Heating Degree Days (base 65°F)	1,137	978	842	468	212	43	4	10	99	392	669	994	5,848
Cooling Degree Days (base 65°F)	0	0	1	6	33	134	242	212	73	9	0	0	710
Mean Precipitation (in.)	2.46	2.10	3.11	3.48	3.99	3.72	3.38	3.34	3.31	3.13	3.35	2.66	38.03
Extreme Maximum Daily Precip. (in.)	2.73	1.96	2.06	1.76	3.02	2.27	2.58	3.17	4.55	3.72	3.42	2.62	4.55
Days With ≥ 0.1" Precipitation	5	5	6	7	8	8	6	6	6	5	6	5	73
Days With ≥ 0.5" Precipitation	1	1	2	2	3	2	2	2	2	2	2	2	23
Days With ≥ 1.0" Precipitation	0	0	0	0	1	1	1	1	1	1	1	0	7
Mean Snowfall (in.)	6.3	6.7	3.5	0.6	0.0	0.0	0.0	0.0	0.0	trace	0.9	3.7	21.7
Maximum Snow Depth (in.)	20	na	15	2	0	0	0	0	0	0	5	na	na
Days With ≥ 1.0" Snow Depth	6	na	2	0	0	0	0	0	0	0	0	4	na

Reading 4 NNW *Berks County*   Elevation: 359 ft.   Latitude: 40° 25' N   Longitude: 75° 56' W

	JAN	FEB	MAR	APR	MAY	JUN	JUL	AUG	SEP	OCT	NOV	DEC	YEAR
Mean Maximum Temp. (°F)	37.8	41.2	50.0	62.0	72.8	81.0	85.4	84.0	76.7	65.5	53.9	42.2	62.7
Mean Temp. (°F)	29.4	32.2	40.2	51.1	61.6	70.3	75.0	73.5	65.8	54.3	44.6	34.1	52.7
Mean Minimum Temp. (°F)	21.1	23.1	30.3	40.1	50.4	59.6	64.5	63.0	54.8	43.0	35.1	25.9	42.6
Extreme Maximum Temp. (°F)	71	77	88	93	96	97	102	102	100	92	82	77	102
Extreme Minimum Temp. (°F)	-20	-5	-2	16	30	39	46	42	34	23	16	-4	-20
Days Maximum Temp. ≥ 90°F	0	0	0	0	1	4	9	6	1	0	0	0	21
Days Maximum Temp. ≤ 32°F	9	5	1	0	0	0	0	0	0	0	0	5	20
Days Minimum Temp. ≤ 32°F	26	23	19	5	0	0	0	0	0	3	12	23	111
Days Minimum Temp. ≤ 0°F	1	0	0	0	0	0	0	0	0	0	0	0	1
Heating Degree Days (base 65°F)	1,096	923	764	418	156	25	2	7	76	342	607	951	5,367
Cooling Degree Days (base 65°F)	0	0	1	8	59	192	318	277	105	16	1	0	977
Mean Precipitation (in.)	2.95	2.66	3.44	3.65	4.04	4.29	4.53	3.54	4.36	3.64	3.52	3.14	43.76
Extreme Maximum Daily Precip. (in.)	3.00	2.55	2.79	2.25	3.77	3.68	4.35	4.08	6.25	4.65	2.85	3.22	6.25
Days With ≥ 0.1" Precipitation	6	5	7	7	8	8	7	6	6	5	6	6	77
Days With ≥ 0.5" Precipitation	2	2	2	2	2	3	3	2	3	3	3	2	29
Days With ≥ 1.0" Precipitation	1	1	1	1	1	1	1	1	1	1	1	1	12
Mean Snowfall (in.)	na	6.8	3.6	0.2	0.0	0.0	0.0	0.0	0.0	0.0	0.6	3.8	na
Maximum Snow Depth (in.)	na	na	18	trace	0	0	0	0	0	0	3	na	na
Days With ≥ 1.0" Snow Depth	na	3	1	0	0	0	0	0	0	0	0	2	na

Renovo *Clinton County*   Elevation: 660 ft.   Latitude: 41° 20' N   Longitude: 77° 44' W

	JAN	FEB	MAR	APR	MAY	JUN	JUL	AUG	SEP	OCT	NOV	DEC	YEAR
Mean Maximum Temp. (°F)	34.7	38.5	47.4	60.9	72.0	79.8	83.6	82.4	74.4	62.7	50.3	38.6	60.4
Mean Temp. (°F)	26.5	28.9	36.7	48.5	58.4	67.1	71.3	70.3	62.7	51.2	41.1	31.0	49.5
Mean Minimum Temp. (°F)	18.2	19.3	25.9	36.0	44.8	54.4	59.0	58.2	51.0	39.7	31.7	23.4	38.5
Extreme Maximum Temp. (°F)	68	72	86	92	96	96	103	98	96	88	81	73	103
Extreme Minimum Temp. (°F)	-16	-5	-2	15	25	36	42	40	32	20	11	-9	-16
Days Maximum Temp. ≥ 90°F	0	0	0	0	1	3	6	4	1	0	0	0	15
Days Maximum Temp. ≤ 32°F	12	7	2	0	0	0	0	0	0	0	1	7	29
Days Minimum Temp. ≤ 32°F	28	25	23	11	2	0	0	0	0	6	17	26	138
Days Minimum Temp. ≤ 0°F	3	1	0	0	0	0	0	0	0	0	0	1	5
Heating Degree Days (base 65°F)	1,188	1,014	870	493	226	50	7	12	118	424	712	1,046	6,160
Cooling Degree Days (base 65°F)	0	0	0	5	28	120	210	183	57	5	0	0	608
Mean Precipitation (in.)	2.37	2.25	3.11	3.34	3.42	4.30	3.74	3.76	3.80	3.05	3.49	2.72	39.35
Extreme Maximum Daily Precip. (in.)	1.73	2.42	2.12	1.84	2.25	3.30	2.30	3.48	4.57	2.85	3.28	1.87	4.57
Days With ≥ 0.1" Precipitation	6	6	7	8	9	9	7	7	7	6	7	6	85
Days With ≥ 0.5" Precipitation	1	1	2	2	2	3	3	3	3	2	2	2	26
Days With ≥ 1.0" Precipitation	0	0	1	0	0	1	1	1	1	1	1	0	7
Mean Snowfall (in.)	9.7	7.2	5.7	0.5	0.0	0.0	0.0	0.0	0.0	0.1	1.2	6.1	30.5
Maximum Snow Depth (in.)	18	17	24	4	0	0	0	0	0	trace	6	13	24
Days With ≥ 1.0" Snow Depth	16	12	6	0	0	0	0	0	0	0	1	8	43

Salina 3 W *Westmoreland County*   Elevation: 1,108 ft.   Latitude: 40° 31' N   Longitude: 79° 33' W

	JAN	FEB	MAR	APR	MAY	JUN	JUL	AUG	SEP	OCT	NOV	DEC	YEAR
Mean Maximum Temp. (°F)	36.9	40.1	49.1	62.0	71.4	79.7	83.2	82.3	75.7	63.8	52.3	40.8	61.5
Mean Temp. (°F)	27.2	29.5	37.2	48.7	57.8	66.4	70.3	69.1	62.4	51.1	41.7	31.4	49.4
Mean Minimum Temp. (°F)	17.5	18.8	25.4	35.3	44.4	53.0	57.5	56.1	49.3	38.4	31.1	21.9	37.4
Extreme Maximum Temp. (°F)	71	76	83	90	92	96	101	100	95	88	80	74	101
Extreme Minimum Temp. (°F)	-30	-16	-9	12	21	29	36	32	29	17	8	-20	-30
Days Maximum Temp. ≥ 90°F	0	0	0	0	0	2	4	4	1	0	0	0	11
Days Maximum Temp. ≤ 32°F	12	8	3	0	0	0	0	0	0	0	1	7	31
Days Minimum Temp. ≤ 32°F	28	25	24	13	3	0	0	0	1	9	17	26	146
Days Minimum Temp. ≤ 0°F	3	2	0	0	0	0	0	0	0	0	0	1	6
Heating Degree Days (base 65°F)	1,164	999	856	486	243	62	13	22	128	431	691	1,035	6,130
Cooling Degree Days (base 65°F)	0	0	0	5	27	110	184	155	57	6	0	0	544
Mean Precipitation (in.)	2.88	2.41	3.34	3.53	4.16	4.28	4.66	4.04	3.54	2.64	3.67	3.06	42.21
Extreme Maximum Daily Precip. (in.)	2.51	2.22	1.80	1.80	2.02	1.95	4.09	2.25	5.99	2.00	2.07	2.43	5.99
Days With ≥ 0.1" Precipitation	8	6	8	9	9	8	8	7	7	6	8	8	92
Days With ≥ 0.5" Precipitation	1	1	2	2	3	3	3	3	2	2	2	2	26
Days With ≥ 1.0" Precipitation	0	0	1	1	1	1	1	1	1	0	1	0	8
Mean Snowfall (in.)	9.8	6.6	4.6	0.6	0.0	0.0	0.0	0.0	0.0	trace	1.4	5.2	28.2
Maximum Snow Depth (in.)	27	18	16	3	0	0	0	0	0	trace	7	23	27
Days With ≥ 1.0" Snow Depth	13	11	5	0	0	0	0	0	0	0	1	7	37

State College *Centre County*   Elevation: 1,169 ft.   Latitude: 40° 48' N   Longitude: 77° 52' W

	JAN	FEB	MAR	APR	MAY	JUN	JUL	AUG	SEP	OCT	NOV	DEC	YEAR
Mean Maximum Temp. (°F)	34.2	37.5	46.1	59.5	69.7	77.8	81.5	80.2	72.4	60.9	49.7	38.2	59.0
Mean Temp. (°F)	26.7	29.1	36.5	48.9	58.9	67.6	71.5	70.1	62.4	50.9	41.2	31.0	49.6
Mean Minimum Temp. (°F)	19.1	20.6	26.8	38.1	48.0	57.3	61.4	60.0	52.4	40.9	32.8	23.8	40.1
Extreme Maximum Temp. (°F)	67	73	84	90	93	94	102	97	93	86	80	71	102
Extreme Minimum Temp. (°F)	-18	-4	-1	11	29	35	44	36	33	16	10	-11	-18
Days Maximum Temp. ≥ 90°F	0	0	0	0	0	1	3	2	0	0	0	0	6
Days Maximum Temp. ≤ 32°F	13	9	3	0	0	0	0	0	0	0	1	9	35
Days Minimum Temp. ≤ 32°F	27	25	22	8	0	0	0	0	0	5	16	26	129
Days Minimum Temp. ≤ 0°F	2	1	0	0	0	0	0	0	0	0	0	0	3
Heating Degree Days (base 65°F)	1,181	1,008	878	484	219	48	7	17	127	436	706	1,047	6,158
Cooling Degree Days (base 65°F)	0	0	1	7	37	132	216	182	56	6	0	0	637
Mean Precipitation (in.)	2.68	2.49	3.42	3.32	3.42	4.09	3.46	3.84	3.61	3.03	3.37	2.79	39.52
Extreme Maximum Daily Precip. (in.)	1.78	2.38	2.90	2.07	1.64	2.59	1.63	3.66	5.05	3.65	3.25	2.05	5.05
Days With ≥ 0.1" Precipitation	6	6	7	8	8	8	8	6	6	6	6	6	81
Days With ≥ 0.5" Precipitation	1	2	2	2	2	3	2	3	2	2	2	2	25
Days With ≥ 1.0" Precipitation	0	0	1	0	1	1	1	1	1	1	1	0	8
Mean Snowfall (in.)	12.5	10.4	10.2	1.4	trace	0.0	0.0	0.0	0.0	0.4	2.6	7.8	45.3
Maximum Snow Depth (in.)	22	20	31	4	trace	0	0	0	0	3	13	12	31
Days With ≥ 1.0" Snow Depth	15	13	7	0	0	0	0	0	0	0	2	9	46

The period of record for all cooperative weather station data is 1980 – 2009. See User Guide for detailed explanation of data.

Uniontown 1 NE *Fayette County*   Elevation: 956 ft.   Latitude: 39° 55' N   Longitude: 79° 43' W

	JAN	FEB	MAR	APR	MAY	JUN	JUL	AUG	SEP	OCT	NOV	DEC	YEAR
Mean Maximum Temp. (°F)	39.4	42.3	51.1	63.0	72.4	80.4	83.9	82.9	76.6	64.9	53.9	42.8	62.8
Mean Temp. (°F)	30.2	32.1	39.3	49.9	59.4	67.9	72.0	70.9	63.9	52.3	42.9	33.6	51.2
Mean Minimum Temp. (°F)	21.0	21.9	27.4	36.8	46.4	55.4	60.2	58.8	51.3	39.6	31.8	24.3	39.6
Extreme Maximum Temp. (°F)	73	77	84	93	92	96	102	99	94	88	81	77	102
Extreme Minimum Temp. (°F)	-22	-15	-3	15	26	34	37	34	29	16	9	-14	-22
Days Maximum Temp. ≥ 90°F	0	0	0	0	0	2	5	4	1	0	0	0	12
Days Maximum Temp. ≤ 32°F	10	6	2	0	0	0	0	0	0	0	1	7	26
Days Minimum Temp. ≤ 32°F	26	24	21	11	2	0	0	0	0	8	17	24	133
Days Minimum Temp. ≤ 0°F	2	1	0	0	0	0	0	0	0	0	0	1	4
Heating Degree Days (base 65°F)	1,071	924	792	453	204	44	6	13	102	396	658	967	5,630
Cooling Degree Days (base 65°F)	0	0	1	7	38	138	232	203	76	8	0	0	703
Mean Precipitation (in.)	3.04	2.73	3.74	3.65	4.50	4.34	4.68	3.73	3.42	2.95	3.67	3.05	43.50
Extreme Maximum Daily Precip. (in.)	1.77	1.68	2.75	2.04	2.65	2.75	3.82	2.70	2.38	1.82	3.23	1.64	3.82
Days With ≥ 0.1" Precipitation	8	7	8	9	10	9	8	7	7	7	8	8	96
Days With ≥ 0.5" Precipitation	2	2	2	2	3	3	3	3	2	2	2	2	28
Days With ≥ 1.0" Precipitation	0	0	1	0	1	1	1	1	1	1	1	0	8
Mean Snowfall (in.)	*8.9*	*5.3*	4.7	0.4	trace	0.0	0.0	0.0	0.0	trace	0.9	4.3	*24.5*
Maximum Snow Depth (in.)	*20*	*15*	*19*	*1*	trace	*0*	0	0	*0*	*1*	*6*	*16*	*20*
Days With ≥ 1.0" Snow Depth	*9*	5	*3*	0	0	0	0	0	0	0	1	*6*	*24*

Washington 3 NE *Washington County*   Elevation: 1,299 ft.   Latitude: 40° 11' N   Longitude: 80° 11' W

	JAN	FEB	MAR	APR	MAY	JUN	JUL	AUG	SEP	OCT	NOV	DEC	YEAR
Mean Maximum Temp. (°F)	36.3	39.1	48.7	60.8	69.8	78.1	81.8	81.1	74.1	62.4	51.3	39.6	60.3
Mean Temp. (°F)	28.2	30.3	38.5	49.8	58.8	67.3	71.3	70.3	63.2	51.9	42.6	31.9	50.3
Mean Minimum Temp. (°F)	20.1	21.6	28.5	38.7	47.8	56.5	60.9	59.4	52.2	41.3	33.8	24.2	40.4
Extreme Maximum Temp. (°F)	70	75	82	87	90	*93*	100	*99*	95	87	80	82	*100*
Extreme Minimum Temp. (°F)	-25	-8	0	10	20	*34*	40	*29*	30	20	10	-16	*-25*
Days Maximum Temp. ≥ 90°F	0	0	0	0	0	1	3	3	0	0	0	0	7
Days Maximum Temp. ≤ 32°F	13	9	4	0	0	0	0	0	0	0	2	9	37
Days Minimum Temp. ≤ 32°F	27	24	20	9	1	0	0	0	0	5	15	25	126
Days Minimum Temp. ≤ 0°F	2	1	0	0	0	0	0	0	0	0	0	1	4
Heating Degree Days (base 65°F)	1,133	973	817	461	223	52	8	16	113	410	668	1,019	5,893
Cooling Degree Days (base 65°F)	0	0	2	10	38	129	213	186	65	10	0	0	653
Mean Precipitation (in.)	3.00	2.31	3.31	3.03	4.25	3.94	3.89	3.18	3.35	2.40	3.49	2.95	39.10
Extreme Maximum Daily Precip. (in.)	1.92	1.86	1.60	1.35	2.14	*2.20*	3.93	*2.60*	5.18	*1.24*	2.11	2.30	*5.18*
Days With ≥ 0.1" Precipitation	7	6	7	8	9	8	7	6	6	6	8	7	85
Days With ≥ 0.5" Precipitation	2	1	2	2	3	2	3	2	2	1	2	2	24
Days With ≥ 1.0" Precipitation	1	0	1	1	1	1	1	1	1	0	1	0	8
Mean Snowfall (in.)	8.5	5.4	4.8	0.9	trace	0.0	0.0	0.0	0.0	trace	1.4	5.1	26.1
Maximum Snow Depth (in.)	20	*16*	26	9	trace	0	0	*0*	0	*trace*	7	10	*26*
Days With ≥ 1.0" Snow Depth	12	10	5	1	0	0	0	0	0	0	1	8	37

York 3 SSW Pump Stn *York County*   Elevation: 390 ft.   Latitude: 39° 55' N   Longitude: 76° 45' W

	JAN	FEB	MAR	APR	MAY	JUN	JUL	AUG	SEP	OCT	NOV	DEC	YEAR
Mean Maximum Temp. (°F)	40.5	44.7	54.1	66.2	75.8	83.6	87.3	85.7	78.7	67.8	55.6	44.0	65.3
Mean Temp. (°F)	31.1	34.2	42.2	52.9	62.4	71.0	75.2	73.6	66.5	55.2	44.9	34.9	53.7
Mean Minimum Temp. (°F)	21.7	23.7	30.4	39.6	49.0	58.4	62.9	61.5	54.2	42.5	34.1	25.8	42.0
Extreme Maximum Temp. (°F)	73	78	88	93	98	98	102	101	98	92	85	77	102
Extreme Minimum Temp. (°F)	-21	-14	-3	17	29	35	43	35	33	19	12	-3	-21
Days Maximum Temp. ≥ 90°F	0	0	0	0	2	6	11	7	2	0	0	0	28
Days Maximum Temp. ≤ 32°F	7	3	1	0	0	0	0	0	0	0	0	4	15
Days Minimum Temp. ≤ 32°F	27	23	19	7	1	0	0	0	0	5	15	24	121
Days Minimum Temp. ≤ 0°F	1	0	0	0	0	0	0	0	0	0	0	0	1
Heating Degree Days (base 65°F)	1,043	864	700	365	137	18	1	5	66	316	598	926	5,039
Cooling Degree Days (base 65°F)	0	0	0	10	63	206	323	279	117	19	0	0	1,018
Mean Precipitation (in.)	3.01	2.84	3.77	3.59	4.23	3.73	3.91	3.41	4.14	3.26	3.60	3.22	42.71
Extreme Maximum Daily Precip. (in.)	2.52	3.39	2.03	2.17	3.04	3.00	3.68	2.20	5.19	2.82	3.58	3.14	5.19
Days With ≥ 0.1" Precipitation	6	6	7	7	8	7	7	6	6	5	6	6	77
Days With ≥ 0.5" Precipitation	2	2	3	3	3	2	3	2	2	2	2	2	28
Days With ≥ 1.0" Precipitation	1	1	1	1	1	1	1	1	1	1	1	1	12
Mean Snowfall (in.)	8.5	7.7	3.5	0.5	0.0	0.0	0.0	0.0	0.0	0.0	0.7	3.2	24.1
Maximum Snow Depth (in.)	33	*24*	*8*	*1*	0	0	0	0	*0*	*0*	*3*	9	*33*
Days With ≥ 1.0" Snow Depth	8	*7*	1	0	0	0	0	0	0	0	0	4	*20*

The period of record for all cooperative weather station data is 1980 – 2009. See User Guide for detailed explanation of data.

Pennsylvania Weather Station Rankings

Annual Extreme Maximum Temperature

	Highest			Lowest	
Rank	Station Name	°F	Rank	Station Name	°F
1	Laurelton Center	**105**	1	Chalk Hill 2 ENE	94
1	Montgomery Lock & Dam	105	2	Pleasant Mount 1 W	95
3	Octoraro Lake	104	3	Montrose	97
3	Raystown Lake 2	104	4	Bradford 4 SW Res 5	98
5	Graterford 1 E	**103**	4	Francis E Walter Dam	98
5	Hamburg	103	6	Altoona 3 W	99
5	Marcus Hook	**103**	6	Mercer	99
5	Philadelphia Int'l Arpt	103	8	Altoona Blair Co Arpt	100
5	Phoenixville 1 E	**103**	8	Bucksville	**100**
5	Pittsburgh Intl Arpt	103	8	Clarion 3 SW	100
5	Renovo	103	8	Coatesville 2 W	**100**
5	Williamsport-Lycoming County	103	8	Erie Intl Arpt	100
13	Blue Marsh Lake	102	8	Washington 3 NE	**100**
13	Butler 2 SW	102	14	Allentown A-B-E Intl Arpt	101
13	Derry 4 SW	102	14	Salina 3 W	101
13	Donora 1 SW	102	14	Wilkes-Barre Scranton Arpt	101
13	Lancaster 2 NE Filt Plant	102	17	Blue Marsh Lake	102
13	Landisville 2 NW	102	17	Butler 2 SW	102
13	Lebanon 2 W	102	17	Derry 4 SW	102
13	Lewistown	102	17	Donora 1 SW	102
13	Neshaminy Falls	102	17	Lancaster 2 NE Filt Plant	102
13	Reading 4 NNW	102	17	Landisville 2 NW	102
13	State College	102	17	Lebanon 2 W	102
13	Uniontown 1 NE	102	17	Lewistown	102
13	York 3 SSW Pump Stn	102	17	Neshaminy Falls	102

Annual Mean Maximum Temperature

	Highest			Lowest	
Rank	Station Name	°F	Rank	Station Name	°F
1	York 3 SSW Pump Stn	65.3	1	Pleasant Mount 1 W	53.7
2	Neshaminy Falls	65.2	2	Bradford 4 SW Res 5	55.6
3	Octoraro Lake	64.8	3	Montrose	55.7
4	Philadelphia Int'l Arpt	64.5	4	Erie Intl Arpt	57.5
5	Phoenixville 1 E	**64.2**	5	Altoona 3 W	58.1
6	Marcus Hook	**64.1**	6	Chalk Hill 2 ENE	58.3
7	Donora 1 SW	64.0	7	State College	59.0
8	Landisville 2 NW	63.9	7	Wilkes-Barre Scranton Arpt	59.0
9	Laurelton Center	**63.3**	9	Altoona Blair Co Arpt	59.2
10	Lancaster 2 NE Filt Plant	63.0	10	Clarion 3 SW	59.6
11	Uniontown 1 NE	62.8	11	Mercer	59.8
12	Reading 4 NNW	62.7	12	Butler 2 SW	60.2
13	Graterford 1 E	**62.6**	13	Washington 3 NE	60.3
14	Coatesville 2 W	**62.3**	14	Renovo	60.4
15	Bucksville	**62.0**	15	Williamsport-Lycoming County	60.6
15	Montgomery Lock & Dam	62.0	16	Pittsburgh Intl Arpt	60.8
17	Hamburg	61.8	17	Raystown Lake 2	61.0
17	Lebanon 2 W	61.8	18	Blue Marsh Lake	**61.1**
19	Allentown A-B-E Intl Arpt	61.6	19	Derry 4 SW	61.4
19	Lewistown	61.6	20	Salina 3 W	61.5
21	Salina 3 W	61.5	21	Allentown A-B-E Intl Arpt	61.6
22	Derry 4 SW	61.4	21	Lewistown	61.6
23	Blue Marsh Lake	**61.1**	23	Hamburg	61.8
24	Raystown Lake 2	61.0	23	Lebanon 2 W	61.8
25	Pittsburgh Intl Arpt	60.8	25	Bucksville	**62.0**

Rankings include 25 highest/lowest stations. If state has less than 25 stations, all stations are included. The period of record is 1980–2009. See User Guide for detailed explanation of data.

Annual Mean Temperature

	Highest				Lowest	
Rank	Station Name	°F		Rank	Station Name	°F
1	Marcus Hook	**56.5**		1	Pleasant Mount 1 W	43.9
2	Philadelphia Int'l Arpt	55.7		2	Bradford 4 SW Res 5	44.6
3	York 3 SSW Pump Stn	53.7		3	Montrose	45.3
4	Neshaminy Falls	53.4		4	Clarion 3 SW	48.3
5	Donora 1 SW	53.1		5	Mercer	**48.4**
5	Phoenixville 1 E	**53.1**		6	Chalk Hill 2 ENE	48.7
7	Lancaster 2 NE Filt Plant	53.0		7	Altoona 3 W	48.9
8	Octoraro Lake	52.8		8	Butler 2 SW	49.2
9	Landisville 2 NW	52.7		9	Salina 3 W	49.4
9	Reading 4 NNW	52.7		10	Renovo	49.5
11	Montgomery Lock & Dam	52.2		11	State College	49.6
12	Coatesville 2 W	**52.0**		12	Erie Intl Arpt	49.8
13	Allentown A-B-E Intl Arpt	51.8		12	Wilkes-Barre Scranton Arpt	49.8
14	Hamburg	51.6		14	Altoona Blair Co Arpt	50.0
14	Lebanon 2 W	51.6		15	Washington 3 NE	50.4
16	Pittsburgh Intl Arpt	51.4		16	Derry 4 SW	50.5
17	Laurelton Center	**51.3**		17	Raystown Lake 2	50.6
18	Bucksville	**51.2**		17	Williamsport-Lycoming County	50.6
18	Uniontown 1 NE	51.2		19	Blue Marsh Lake	**51.0**
20	Graterford 1 E	**51.1**		20	Graterford 1 E	**51.1**
20	Lewistown	51.1		20	Lewistown	51.1
22	Blue Marsh Lake	**51.0**		22	Bucksville	**51.2**
23	Raystown Lake 2	50.6		22	Uniontown 1 NE	51.2
23	Williamsport-Lycoming County	50.6		24	Laurelton Center	**51.3**
25	Derry 4 SW	50.5		25	Pittsburgh Intl Arpt	51.4

Annual Mean Minimum Temperature

	Highest				Lowest	
Rank	Station Name	°F		Rank	Station Name	°F
1	Marcus Hook	**48.9**		1	Bradford 4 SW Res 5	33.6
2	Philadelphia Int'l Arpt	46.9		2	Pleasant Mount 1 W	34.0
3	Lancaster 2 NE Filt Plant	42.9		3	Montrose	34.9
4	Reading 4 NNW	42.6		4	Clarion 3 SW	36.9
5	Montgomery Lock & Dam	42.4		5	Mercer	**37.0**
6	Donora 1 SW	42.1		6	Salina 3 W	37.4
6	Erie Intl Arpt	42.1		7	Butler 2 SW	38.1
8	York 3 SSW Pump Stn	42.0		8	Renovo	38.5
9	Allentown A-B-E Intl Arpt	41.9		9	Chalk Hill 2 ENE	39.1
9	Pittsburgh Intl Arpt	41.9		10	Laurelton Center	**39.2**
11	Phoenixville 1 E	**41.8**		11	Altoona 3 W	39.6
12	Coatesville 2 W	**41.7**		11	Derry 4 SW	39.6
13	Landisville 2 NW	41.6		11	Graterford 1 E	**39.6**
13	Neshaminy Falls	41.6		11	Uniontown 1 NE	39.6
15	Hamburg	41.4		15	State College	40.1
16	Lebanon 2 W	41.3		16	Raystown Lake 2	40.2
17	Altoona Blair Co Arpt	40.8		17	Bucksville	**40.3**
17	Blue Marsh Lake	**40.8**		18	Washington 3 NE	40.4
19	Octoraro Lake	40.7		19	Lewistown	40.5
20	Wilkes-Barre Scranton Arpt	40.6		20	Wilkes-Barre Scranton Arpt	40.6
20	Williamsport-Lycoming County	40.6		20	Williamsport-Lycoming County	40.6
22	Lewistown	40.5		22	Octoraro Lake	40.7
23	Washington 3 NE	40.4		23	Altoona Blair Co Arpt	40.8
24	Bucksville	**40.3**		23	Blue Marsh Lake	**40.8**
25	Raystown Lake 2	40.2		25	Lebanon 2 W	41.3

Rankings include 25 highest/lowest stations. If state has less than 25 stations, all stations are included. The period of record is 1980–2009. See User Guide for detailed explanation of data.

Annual Extreme Minimum Temperature

	Highest				Lowest	
Rank	Station Name	°F		Rank	Station Name	°F
1	Marcus Hook	*-4*		1	Mercer	-32
2	Philadelphia Int'l Arpt	-7		2	Salina 3 W	-30
3	Neshaminy Falls	-11		3	Derry 4 SW	-29
4	Phoenixville 1 E	*-13*		4	Chalk Hill 2 ENE	-27
5	Coatesville 2 W	*-14*		5	Bradford 4 SW Res 5	-26
6	Allentown A-B-E Intl Arpt	-15		5	Francis E Walter Dam	-26
6	Raystown Lake 2	-15		7	Altoona Blair Co Arpt	-25
8	Lancaster 2 NE Filt Plant	-16		7	Pleasant Mount 1 W	-25
8	Renovo	-16		7	Washington 3 NE	*-25*
10	Blue Marsh Lake	-17		10	Landisville 2 NW	-24
10	Graterford 1 E	*-17*		11	Bucksville	*-23*
10	Lewistown	-17		11	Clarion 3 SW	-23
13	Erie Intl Arpt	-18		13	Laurelton Center	*-22*
13	Montgomery Lock & Dam	-18		13	Lebanon 2 W	-22
13	State College	-18		13	Montrose	-22
16	Donora 1 SW	-19		13	Pittsburgh Intl Arpt	-22
16	Hamburg	-19		13	Uniontown 1 NE	-22
16	Octoraro Lake	-19		18	Wilkes-Barre Scranton Arpt	-21
19	Altoona 3 W	-20		18	York 3 SSW Pump Stn	-21
19	Butler 2 SW	-20		20	Altoona 3 W	-20
19	Reading 4 NNW	-20		20	Butler 2 SW	-20
19	Williamsport-Lycoming County	-20		20	Reading 4 NNW	-20
23	Wilkes-Barre Scranton Arpt	-21		20	Williamsport-Lycoming County	-20
23	York 3 SSW Pump Stn	-21		24	Donora 1 SW	-19
25	Laurelton Center	*-22*		24	Hamburg	-19

July Mean Maximum Temperature

	Highest				Lowest	
Rank	Station Name	°F		Rank	Station Name	°F
1	York 3 SSW Pump Stn	87.3		1	Pleasant Mount 1 W	76.6
2	Neshaminy Falls	87.2		2	Chalk Hill 2 ENE	78.0
3	Marcus Hook	*87.1*		3	Bradford 4 SW Res 5	78.6
3	Octoraro Lake	87.1		4	Montrose	79.2
5	Philadelphia Int'l Arpt	87.0		5	Francis E Walter Dam	79.3
6	Laurelton Center	*86.5*		6	Erie Intl Arpt	79.8
7	Landisville 2 NW	86.1		7	Altoona 3 W	80.7
7	Phoenixville 1 E	86.1		8	State College	81.5
9	Reading 4 NNW	85.4		9	Mercer	81.6
10	Lancaster 2 NE Filt Plant	85.3		10	Altoona Blair Co Arpt	81.8
11	Graterford 1 E	85.2		10	Washington 3 NE	81.8
12	Donora 1 SW	85.1		12	Wilkes-Barre Scranton Arpt	82.1
13	Coatesville 2 W	*84.7*		13	Butler 2 SW	82.5
13	Hamburg	84.7		14	Pittsburgh Intl Arpt	82.8
15	Allentown A-B-E Intl Arpt	84.6		15	Clarion 3 SW	82.9
16	Blue Marsh Lake	84.4		16	Salina 3 W	83.2
16	Lewistown	84.4		17	Derry 4 SW	83.4
18	Bucksville	84.2		18	Renovo	83.6
18	Lebanon 2 W	84.2		19	Montgomery Lock & Dam	83.7
18	Williamsport-Lycoming County	84.2		20	Raystown Lake 2	83.8
21	Uniontown 1 NE	83.9		21	Uniontown 1 NE	83.9
22	Raystown Lake 2	83.8		22	Bucksville	84.2
23	Montgomery Lock & Dam	83.7		22	Lebanon 2 W	84.2
24	Renovo	83.6		22	Williamsport-Lycoming County	84.2
25	Derry 4 SW	83.4		25	Blue Marsh Lake	84.4

Rankings include 25 highest/lowest stations. If state has less than 25 stations, all stations are included. The period of record is 1980–2009. See User Guide for detailed explanation of data.

January Mean Minimum Temperature

Highest			Lowest		
Rank	**Station Name**	**°F**	**Rank**	**Station Name**	**°F**
1	Marcus Hook	28.2	1	Pleasant Mount 1 W	11.5
2	Philadelphia Int'l Arpt	25.5	2	Bradford 4 SW Res 5	12.1
3	Montgomery Lock & Dam	22.5	3	Montrose	12.6
4	Lancaster 2 NE Filt Plant	22.3	4	Mercer	16.4
5	Donora 1 SW	22.1	5	Clarion 3 SW	16.9
6	Phoenixville 1 E	*21.8*	6	Salina 3 W	17.5
7	York 3 SSW Pump Stn	21.7	7	Altoona 3 W	18.1
8	Coatesville 2 W	*21.5*	8	Renovo	18.2
9	Neshaminy Falls	21.2	9	Butler 2 SW	18.4
10	Erie Intl Arpt	21.1	9	Laurelton Center	18.4
10	Landisville 2 NW	21.1	11	Bucksville	19.0
10	Pittsburgh Intl Arpt	21.1	11	Graterford 1 E	19.0
10	Reading 4 NNW	21.1	13	State College	19.1
14	Uniontown 1 NE	21.0	14	Wilkes-Barre Scranton Arpt	19.2
15	Lebanon 2 W	20.8	15	Chalk Hill 2 ENE	19.3
16	Allentown A-B-E Intl Arpt	20.7	15	Williamsport-Lycoming County	19.3
17	Altoona Blair Co Arpt	20.6	17	Blue Marsh Lake	*19.5*
18	Octoraro Lake	20.4	17	Hamburg	19.5
19	Lewistown	20.1	19	Derry 4 SW	19.8
19	Washington 3 NE	20.1	20	Raystown Lake 2	19.9
21	Raystown Lake 2	19.9	21	Lewistown	20.1
22	Derry 4 SW	19.8	21	Washington 3 NE	20.1
23	Blue Marsh Lake	*19.5*	23	Octoraro Lake	20.4
23	Hamburg	19.5	24	Altoona Blair Co Arpt	20.6
25	Chalk Hill 2 ENE	19.3	25	Allentown A-B-E Intl Arpt	20.7

Number of Days Annually Maximum Temperature ≥ 90°F

Highest			Lowest		
Rank	**Station Name**	**Days**	**Rank**	**Station Name**	**Days**
1	Neshaminy Falls	30	1	Chalk Hill 2 ENE	0
2	Octoraro Lake	29	1	Pleasant Mount 1 W	0
3	York 3 SSW Pump Stn	28	3	Bradford 4 SW Res 5	1
4	Marcus Hook	*27*	4	Montrose	2
5	Philadelphia Int'l Arpt	26	5	Erie Intl Arpt	3
6	Laurelton Center	*24*	5	Francis E Walter Dam	3
7	Phoenixville 1 E	*23*	7	Altoona 3 W	5
8	Landisville 2 NW	21	8	Mercer	6
8	Reading 4 NNW	21	8	State College	6
10	Graterford 1 E	*19*	10	Altoona Blair Co Arpt	7
11	Lancaster 2 NE Filt Plant	18	10	Washington 3 NE	7
12	Hamburg	17	12	Montgomery Lock & Dam	9
13	Allentown A-B-E Intl Arpt	16	12	Pittsburgh Intl Arpt	9
13	Coatesville 2 W	*16*	14	Butler 2 SW	10
13	Donora 1 SW	16	14	Clarion 3 SW	10
13	Lewistown	16	14	Wilkes-Barre Scranton Arpt	10
17	Bucksville	*15*	17	Derry 4 SW	11
17	Renovo	15	17	Salina 3 W	11
17	Williamsport-Lycoming County	15	19	Uniontown 1 NE	12
20	Blue Marsh Lake	14	20	Raystown Lake 2	13
20	Lebanon 2 W	14	21	Blue Marsh Lake	14
22	Raystown Lake 2	13	21	Lebanon 2 W	14
23	Uniontown 1 NE	12	23	Bucksville	*15*
24	Derry 4 SW	11	23	Renovo	15
24	Salina 3 W	11	23	Williamsport-Lycoming County	15

Rankings include 25 highest/lowest stations. If state has less than 25 stations, all stations are included. The period of record is 1980–2009. See User Guide for detailed explanation of data.

Number of Days Annually Maximum Temperature ≤ 32°F

	Highest			Lowest	
Rank	Station Name	Days	Rank	Station Name	Days
1	Pleasant Mount 1 W	63	1	Neshaminy Falls	13
2	Bradford 4 SW Res 5	58	2	Marcus Hook	*14*
3	Montrose	53	2	Phoenixville 1 E	*14*
4	Erie Intl Arpt	43	4	Octoraro Lake	15
5	Altoona 3 W	40	4	Philadelphia Int'l Arpt	15
5	Clarion 3 SW	40	4	York 3 SSW Pump Stn	15
5	Francis E Walter Dam	40	7	Landisville 2 NW	18
8	Chalk Hill 2 ENE	39	8	Graterford 1 E	19
9	Altoona Blair Co Arpt	38	9	Lancaster 2 NE Filt Plant	20
10	Washington 3 NE	37	9	Reading 4 NNW	20
10	Wilkes-Barre Scranton Arpt	37	11	Bucksville	*21*
12	Butler 2 SW	35	11	Coatesville 2 W	*21*
12	State College	35	11	Donora 1 SW	21
14	Mercer	34	11	Laurelton Center	*21*
14	Pittsburgh Intl Arpt	34	15	Hamburg	23
16	Salina 3 W	31	15	Lebanon 2 W	23
17	Derry 4 SW	30	17	Allentown A-B-E Intl Arpt	24
18	Raystown Lake 2	29	17	Lewistown	24
18	Renovo	29	19	Blue Marsh Lake	26
18	Williamsport-Lycoming County	29	19	Montgomery Lock & Dam	26
21	Blue Marsh Lake	26	19	Uniontown 1 NE	26
21	Montgomery Lock & Dam	26	22	Raystown Lake 2	29
21	Uniontown 1 NE	26	22	Renovo	29
24	Allentown A-B-E Intl Arpt	24	22	Williamsport-Lycoming County	29
24	Lewistown	24	25	Derry 4 SW	30

Number of Days Annually Minimum Temperature ≤ 32°F

	Highest			Lowest	
Rank	Station Name	Days	Rank	Station Name	Days
1	Bradford 4 SW Res 5	172	1	Marcus Hook	*66*
2	Pleasant Mount 1 W	171	2	Philadelphia Int'l Arpt	84
3	Montrose	163	3	Montgomery Lock & Dam	109
4	Clarion 3 SW	151	4	Reading 4 NNW	111
5	Francis E Walter Dam	148	5	Lancaster 2 NE Filt Plant	113
6	Mercer	146	6	Erie Intl Arpt	114
6	Salina 3 W	146	7	Donora 1 SW	116
8	Butler 2 SW	139	8	Pittsburgh Intl Arpt	118
8	Laurelton Center	*139*	9	Allentown A-B-E Intl Arpt	119
10	Renovo	138	9	Landisville 2 NW	119
11	Graterford 1 E	*136*	11	Blue Marsh Lake	120
12	Chalk Hill 2 ENE	133	12	Altoona Blair Co Arpt	121
12	Uniontown 1 NE	133	12	Coatesville 2 W	*121*
14	Altoona 3 W	131	12	Lebanon 2 W	121
15	Bucksville	*130*	12	York 3 SSW Pump Stn	121
15	Derry 4 SW	130	16	Neshaminy Falls	122
17	Octoraro Lake	129	16	Phoenixville 1 E	*122*
17	State College	129	18	Hamburg	123
19	Lewistown	127	18	Wilkes-Barre Scranton Arpt	123
20	Raystown Lake 2	126	20	Williamsport-Lycoming County	124
20	Washington 3 NE	126	21	Raystown Lake 2	126
22	Williamsport-Lycoming County	124	21	Washington 3 NE	126
23	Hamburg	123	23	Lewistown	127
23	Wilkes-Barre Scranton Arpt	123	24	Octoraro Lake	129
25	Neshaminy Falls	122	24	State College	129

Rankings include 25 highest/lowest stations. If state has less than 25 stations, all stations are included. The period of record is 1980–2009. See User Guide for detailed explanation of data.

Number of Days Annually Minimum Temperature ≤ 0°F

	Highest			Lowest	
Rank	Station Name	Days	Rank	Station Name	Days
1	Bradford 4 SW Res 5	16	1	Marcus Hook	0
2	Pleasant Mount 1 W	14	1	Philadelphia Int'l Arpt	0
3	Montrose	13	3	Allentown A-B-E Intl Arpt	1
4	Francis E Walter Dam	10	3	Altoona Blair Co Arpt	1
5	Mercer	8	3	Blue Marsh Lake	1
6	Clarion 3 SW	7	3	Coatesville 2 W	1
7	Butler 2 SW	6	3	Donora 1 SW	1
7	Chalk Hill 2 ENE	6	3	Graterford 1 E	1
7	Salina 3 W	6	3	Hamburg	1
10	Derry 4 SW	5	3	Lancaster 2 NE Filt Plant	1
10	Renovo	5	3	Lebanon 2 W	1
12	Altoona 3 W	4	3	Lewistown	1
12	Laurelton Center	4	3	Montgomery Lock & Dam	1
12	Uniontown 1 NE	4	3	Neshaminy Falls	1
12	Washington 3 NE	4	3	Octoraro Lake	1
12	Williamsport-Lycoming County	4	3	Phoenixville 1 E	1
17	Bucksville	3	3	Raystown Lake 2	1
17	Erie Intl Arpt	3	3	Reading 4 NNW	1
17	Pittsburgh Intl Arpt	3	3	York 3 SSW Pump Stn	1
17	State College	3	20	Landisville 2 NW	2
17	Wilkes-Barre Scranton Arpt	3	21	Bucksville	3
22	Landisville 2 NW	2	21	Erie Intl Arpt	3
23	Allentown A-B-E Intl Arpt	1	21	Pittsburgh Intl Arpt	3
23	Altoona Blair Co Arpt	1	21	State College	3
23	Blue Marsh Lake	1	21	Wilkes-Barre Scranton Arpt	3

Number of Annual Heating Degree Days

	Highest			Lowest	
Rank	Station Name	Num.	Rank	Station Name	Num.
1	Pleasant Mount 1 W	7,840	1	Marcus Hook	4,377
2	Bradford 4 SW Res 5	7,586	2	Philadelphia Int'l Arpt	4,591
3	Montrose	7,440	3	York 3 SSW Pump Stn	5,039
4	Clarion 3 SW	6,514	4	Neshaminy Falls	5,121
5	Mercer	6,408	5	Donora 1 SW	5,158
6	Altoona 3 W	6,318	6	Phoenixville 1 E	5,214
7	Chalk Hill 2 ENE	6,231	7	Lancaster 2 NE Filt Plant	5,237
8	Butler 2 SW	6,222	8	Octoraro Lake	5,262
9	Renovo	6,160	9	Landisville 2 NW	5,288
10	State College	6,158	10	Montgomery Lock & Dam	5,367
11	Salina 3 W	6,130	10	Reading 4 NNW	5,367
12	Erie Intl Arpt	6,096	12	Coatesville 2 W	5,482
13	Wilkes-Barre Scranton Arpt	6,089	13	Allentown A-B-E Intl Arpt	5,573
14	Altoona Blair Co Arpt	5,991	14	Lebanon 2 W	5,574
15	Washington 3 NE	5,893	15	Uniontown 1 NE	5,630
16	Williamsport-Lycoming County	5,885	16	Hamburg	5,636
17	Derry 4 SW	5,862	17	Pittsburgh Intl Arpt	5,641
18	Raystown Lake 2	5,848	18	Bucksville	5,697
19	Blue Marsh Lake	5,812	19	Laurelton Center	5,707
20	Graterford 1 E	5,749	20	Lewistown	5,725
21	Lewistown	5,725	21	Graterford 1 E	5,749
22	Laurelton Center	5,707	22	Blue Marsh Lake	5,812
23	Bucksville	5,697	23	Raystown Lake 2	5,848
24	Pittsburgh Intl Arpt	5,641	24	Derry 4 SW	5,862
25	Hamburg	5,636	25	Williamsport-Lycoming County	5,885

Rankings include 25 highest/lowest stations. If state has less than 25 stations, all stations are included. The period of record is 1980–2009. See User Guide for detailed explanation of data.

Number of Annual Cooling Degree Days

	Highest			Lowest	
Rank	Station Name	Num.	Rank	Station Name	Num.
1	Marcus Hook	*1,390*	1	Pleasant Mount 1 W	237
2	Philadelphia Int'l Arpt	1,311	2	Bradford 4 SW Res 5	262
3	York 3 SSW Pump Stn	1,018	3	Montrose	337
4	Neshaminy Falls	1,010	4	Chalk Hill 2 ENE	380
5	Reading 4 NNW	977	5	Mercer	*468*
6	Phoenixville 1 E	*970*	6	Clarion 3 SW	514
7	Lancaster 2 NE Filt Plant	952	7	Salina 3 W	544
8	Landisville 2 NW	924	8	Altoona 3 W	554
9	Octoraro Lake	921	9	Butler 2 SW	556
10	Donora 1 SW	920	10	Renovo	608
11	Allentown A-B-E Intl Arpt	858	11	Altoona Blair Co Arpt	631
11	Coatesville 2 W	*858*	12	State College	637
13	Hamburg	857	13	Wilkes-Barre Scranton Arpt	650
14	Montgomery Lock & Dam	816	14	Washington 3 NE	653
15	Blue Marsh Lake	*811*	15	Erie Intl Arpt	667
16	Laurelton Center	*796*	16	Derry 4 SW	*688*
17	Graterford 1 E	*789*	17	Uniontown 1 NE	703
18	Lebanon 2 W	780	18	Raystown Lake 2	710
19	Pittsburgh Intl Arpt	774	19	Williamsport-Lycoming County	755
20	Bucksville	*762*	20	Lewistown	759
21	Lewistown	759	21	Bucksville	*762*
22	Williamsport-Lycoming County	755	22	Pittsburgh Intl Arpt	774
23	Raystown Lake 2	710	23	Lebanon 2 W	780
24	Uniontown 1 NE	703	24	Graterford 1 E	*789*
25	Derry 4 SW	*688*	25	Laurelton Center	*796*

Annual Precipitation

	Highest			Lowest	
Rank	Station Name	Inches	Rank	Station Name	Inches
1	Chalk Hill 2 ENE	54.24	1	Altoona Blair Co Arpt	35.31
2	Coatesville 2 W	*50.87*	2	Donora 1 SW	37.58
3	Bucksville	*49.72*	3	Montgomery Lock & Dam	37.86
4	Derry 4 SW	49.33	4	Marcus Hook	*37.91*
5	Pleasant Mount 1 W	48.70	5	Raystown Lake 2	38.03
6	Neshaminy Falls	48.64	6	Wilkes-Barre Scranton Arpt	38.05
7	Bradford 4 SW Res 5	48.13	7	Pittsburgh Intl Arpt	38.21
8	Francis E Walter Dam	46.85	8	Washington 3 NE	39.10
9	Clarion 3 SW	46.31	9	Renovo	39.35
10	Hamburg	46.08	10	State College	39.52
11	Octoraro Lake	45.60	11	Williamsport-Lycoming County	40.91
12	Blue Marsh Lake	45.37	12	Lewistown	41.09
13	Graterford 1 E	44.78	13	Philadelphia Int'l Arpt	41.29
14	Allentown A-B-E Intl Arpt	44.64	14	Butler 2 SW	41.37
15	Montrose	44.58	15	Phoenixville 1 E	*42.02*
16	Reading 4 NNW	43.76	16	Salina 3 W	42.21
17	Laurelton Center	*43.57*	17	Lebanon 2 W	42.43
18	Uniontown 1 NE	43.50	18	Erie Intl Arpt	42.45
19	Landisville 2 NW	42.86	19	Altoona 3 W	42.53
20	Mercer	42.75	20	Lancaster 2 NE Filt Plant	42.71
21	Lancaster 2 NE Filt Plant	42.71	20	York 3 SSW Pump Stn	42.71
21	York 3 SSW Pump Stn	42.71	22	Mercer	42.75
23	Altoona 3 W	42.53	23	Landisville 2 NW	42.86
24	Erie Intl Arpt	42.45	24	Uniontown 1 NE	43.50
25	Lebanon 2 W	42.43	25	Laurelton Center	*43.57*

Rankings include 25 highest/lowest stations. If state has less than 25 stations, all stations are included. The period of record is 1980–2009. See User Guide for detailed explanation of data.

Annual Extreme Maximum Daily Precipitation

	Highest				Lowest	
Rank	Station Name	Inches		Rank	Station Name	Inches
1	Marcus Hook	**11.68**		1	Uniontown 1 NE	3.82
2	Montgomery Lock & Dam	8.74		2	Bradford 4 SW Res 5	4.18
3	Allentown A-B-E Intl Arpt	8.71		3	Hamburg	4.21
4	Coatesville 2 W	**7.85**		4	Donora 1 SW	4.36
5	Octoraro Lake	6.82		5	Mercer	**4.47**
6	Montrose	6.63		6	Altoona 3 W	4.49
6	Philadelphia Int'l Arpt	6.63		7	Raystown Lake 2	4.55
8	Williamsport-Lycoming County	6.29		8	Renovo	4.57
9	Reading 4 NNW	6.25		9	Erie Intl Arpt	4.61
10	Lancaster 2 NE Filt Plant	6.11		10	Chalk Hill 2 ENE	4.64
11	Salina 3 W	5.99		10	Landisville 2 NW	4.64
12	Wilkes-Barre Scranton Arpt	5.98		12	Butler 2 SW	4.72
13	Pittsburgh Intl Arpt	5.95		13	Clarion 3 SW	4.95
14	Graterford 1 E	**5.90**		14	State College	5.05
15	Neshaminy Falls	5.83		15	Laurelton Center	**5.11**
16	Altoona Blair Co Arpt	5.55		16	Phoenixville 1 E	**5.13**
17	Derry 4 SW	5.51		17	Lebanon 2 W	5.16
18	Lewistown	5.40		18	Washington 3 NE	**5.18**
19	Pleasant Mount 1 W	5.22		19	York 3 SSW Pump Stn	5.19
20	York 3 SSW Pump Stn	5.19		20	Pleasant Mount 1 W	5.22
21	Washington 3 NE	**5.18**		21	Lewistown	5.40
22	Lebanon 2 W	5.16		22	Derry 4 SW	5.51
23	Phoenixville 1 E	**5.13**		23	Altoona Blair Co Arpt	5.55
24	Laurelton Center	**5.11**		24	Neshaminy Falls	5.83
25	State College	5.05		25	Graterford 1 E	**5.90**

Number of Days Annually With ≥ 0.1 Inches of Precipitation

	Highest				Lowest	
Rank	Station Name	Days		Rank	Station Name	Days
1	Derry 4 SW	115		1	Blue Marsh Lake	59
2	Chalk Hill 2 ENE	112		2	Marcus Hook	**62**
3	Bradford 4 SW Res 5	106		3	Bucksville	**70**
4	Clarion 3 SW	97		4	Philadelphia Int'l Arpt	71
4	Erie Intl Arpt	97		5	Francis E Walter Dam	73
6	Uniontown 1 NE	96		5	Graterford 1 E	**73**
7	Montrose	92		5	Raystown Lake 2	73
7	Salina 3 W	92		8	Altoona Blair Co Arpt	74
9	Pleasant Mount 1 W	91		8	Phoenixville 1 E	**74**
10	Butler 2 SW	90		10	Lebanon 2 W	76
11	Mercer	86		11	Landisville 2 NW	77
12	Renovo	85		11	Octoraro Lake	77
12	Washington 3 NE	85		11	Reading 4 NNW	77
14	Altoona 3 W	84		11	Wilkes-Barre Scranton Arpt	77
14	Donora 1 SW	84		11	Williamsport-Lycoming County	77
14	Pittsburgh Intl Arpt	84		11	York 3 SSW Pump Stn	77
17	Montgomery Lock & Dam	83		17	Allentown A-B-E Intl Arpt	78
18	Laurelton Center	**82**		17	Lancaster 2 NE Filt Plant	78
19	Coatesville 2 W	**81**		19	Hamburg	79
19	Lewistown	81		20	Neshaminy Falls	80
19	State College	81		21	Coatesville 2 W	**81**
22	Neshaminy Falls	80		21	Lewistown	81
23	Hamburg	79		21	State College	81
24	Allentown A-B-E Intl Arpt	78		24	Laurelton Center	**82**
24	Lancaster 2 NE Filt Plant	78		25	Montgomery Lock & Dam	83

Rankings include 25 highest/lowest stations. If state has less than 25 stations, all stations are included. The period of record is 1980–2009. See User Guide for detailed explanation of data.

Number of Days Annually With ≥ 0.5 Inches of Precipitation

Highest			Lowest		
Rank	Station Name	Days	Rank	Station Name	Days
1	Chalk Hill 2 ENE	37	1	Altoona Blair Co Arpt	21
2	Bucksville	35	2	Erie Intl Arpt	23
2	Coatesville 2 W	35	2	Montgomery Lock & Dam	23
4	Neshaminy Falls	34	2	Raystown Lake 2	23
5	Octoraro Lake	33	2	Wilkes-Barre Scranton Arpt	23
6	Bradford 4 SW Res 5	32	6	Blue Marsh Lake	24
6	Derry 4 SW	32	6	Donora 1 SW	24
6	Graterford 1 E	32	6	Washington 3 NE	24
6	Pleasant Mount 1 W	32	9	State College	25
10	Clarion 3 SW	31	10	Butler 2 SW	26
10	Landisville 2 NW	31	10	Marcus Hook	26
10	Laurelton Center	31	10	Mercer	26
13	Phoenixville 1 E	30	10	Pittsburgh Intl Arpt	26
14	Allentown A-B-E Intl Arpt	29	10	Renovo	26
14	Altoona 3 W	29	10	Salina 3 W	26
14	Hamburg	29	16	Francis E Walter Dam	27
14	Lebanon 2 W	29	16	Philadelphia Int'l Arpt	27
14	Montrose	29	18	Lancaster 2 NE Filt Plant	28
14	Reading 4 NNW	29	18	Lewistown	28
20	Lancaster 2 NE Filt Plant	28	18	Uniontown 1 NE	28
20	Lewistown	28	18	Williamsport-Lycoming County	28
20	Uniontown 1 NE	28	18	York 3 SSW Pump Stn	28
20	Williamsport-Lycoming County	28	23	Allentown A-B-E Intl Arpt	29
20	York 3 SSW Pump Stn	28	23	Altoona 3 W	29
25	Francis E Walter Dam	27	23	Hamburg	29

Number of Days Annually With ≥ 1.0 Inches of Precipitation

Highest			Lowest		
Rank	Station Name	Days	Rank	Station Name	Days
1	Bucksville	13	1	Pittsburgh Intl Arpt	4
1	Coatesville 2 W	13	2	Erie Intl Arpt	5
1	Neshaminy Falls	13	2	Montgomery Lock & Dam	5
4	Chalk Hill 2 ENE	12	4	Bradford 4 SW Res 5	7
4	Hamburg	12	4	Butler 2 SW	7
4	Marcus Hook	12	4	Donora 1 SW	7
4	Octoraro Lake	12	4	Mercer	7
4	Reading 4 NNW	12	4	Raystown Lake 2	7
4	York 3 SSW Pump Stn	12	4	Renovo	7
10	Allentown A-B-E Intl Arpt	11	10	Clarion 3 SW	8
10	Graterford 1 E	11	10	Derry 4 SW	8
10	Landisville 2 NW	11	10	Lewistown	8
10	Laurelton Center	11	10	Salina 3 W	8
10	Lebanon 2 W	11	10	State College	8
10	Philadelphia Int'l Arpt	11	10	Uniontown 1 NE	8
10	Phoenixville 1 E	11	10	Washington 3 NE	8
17	Blue Marsh Lake	10	10	Wilkes-Barre Scranton Arpt	8
17	Lancaster 2 NE Filt Plant	10	18	Altoona 3 W	9
17	Montrose	10	18	Altoona Blair Co Arpt	9
17	Pleasant Mount 1 W	10	18	Francis E Walter Dam	9
17	Williamsport-Lycoming County	10	21	Blue Marsh Lake	10
22	Altoona 3 W	9	21	Lancaster 2 NE Filt Plant	10
22	Altoona Blair Co Arpt	9	21	Montrose	10
22	Francis E Walter Dam	9	21	Pleasant Mount 1 W	10
25	Clarion 3 SW	8	21	Williamsport-Lycoming County	10

Annual Snowfall

	Highest			Lowest	
Rank	Station Name	Inches	Rank	Station Name	Inches
1	Erie Intl Arpt	99.6	1	Graterford 1 E	*10.5*
2	Chalk Hill 2 ENE	87.7	2	Neshaminy Falls	*11.9*
3	Montrose	81.8	3	Montgomery Lock & Dam	*12.1*
4	Bradford 4 SW Res 5	72.1	4	Octoraro Lake	*14.5*
5	Pleasant Mount 1 W	65.7	5	Donora 1 SW	17.0
6	Mercer	46.7	6	Lancaster 2 NE Filt Plant	18.4
7	State College	45.3	7	Philadelphia Int'l Arpt	18.8
8	Francis E Walter Dam	45.1	8	Hamburg	19.3
9	Derry 4 SW	44.8	9	Blue Marsh Lake	21.1
10	Pittsburgh Intl Arpt	40.4	10	Raystown Lake 2	*21.7*
11	Williamsport-Lycoming County	36.6	11	Lebanon 2 W	*21.9*
12	Altoona 3 W	35.0	12	York 3 SSW Pump Stn	24.1
13	Butler 2 SW	34.1	13	Landisville 2 NW	24.3
14	Coatesville 2 W	*32.9*	14	Uniontown 1 NE	*24.5*
15	Allentown A-B-E Intl Arpt	*32.7*	15	Bucksville	*25.0*
16	Clarion 3 SW	32.4	16	Lewistown	26.1
17	Renovo	30.5	16	Washington 3 NE	26.1
18	Salina 3 W	28.2	18	Salina 3 W	28.2
19	Lewistown	26.1	19	Renovo	30.5
19	Washington 3 NE	26.1	20	Clarion 3 SW	32.4
21	Bucksville	*25.0*	21	Allentown A-B-E Intl Arpt	*32.7*
22	Uniontown 1 NE	*24.5*	22	Coatesville 2 W	*32.9*
23	Landisville 2 NW	24.3	23	Butler 2 SW	34.1
24	York 3 SSW Pump Stn	24.1	24	Altoona 3 W	35.0
25	Lebanon 2 W	*21.9*	25	Williamsport-Lycoming County	36.6

Annual Maximum Snow Depth

	Highest			Lowest	
Rank	Station Name	Inches	Rank	Station Name	Inches
1	Laurelton Center	*52*	1	Mercer	15
2	Pleasant Mount 1 W	51	2	Montgomery Lock & Dam	19
3	Francis E Walter Dam	50	3	Uniontown 1 NE	*20*
4	Montrose	40	4	Clarion 3 SW	21
5	Blue Marsh Lake	38	5	Butler 2 SW	22
5	Chalk Hill 2 ENE	38	6	Neshaminy Falls	*23*
7	Bradford 4 SW Res 5	35	6	Philadelphia Int'l Arpt	23
8	Lewistown	33	8	Donora 1 SW	24
8	York 3 SSW Pump Stn	*33*	8	Hamburg	24
10	State College	31	8	Renovo	24
11	Altoona 3 W	30	11	Graterford 1 E	*25*
12	Coatesville 2 W	*29*	11	Pittsburgh Intl Arpt	25
13	Landisville 2 NW	27	13	Bucksville	*26*
13	Salina 3 W	27	13	Derry 4 SW	*26*
15	Bucksville	*26*	13	Lancaster 2 NE Filt Plant	26
15	Derry 4 SW	*26*	13	Washington 3 NE	*26*
15	Lancaster 2 NE Filt Plant	26	17	Landisville 2 NW	27
15	Washington 3 NE	*26*	17	Salina 3 W	27
19	Graterford 1 E	*25*	19	Coatesville 2 W	*29*
19	Pittsburgh Intl Arpt	25	20	Altoona 3 W	30
21	Donora 1 SW	24	21	State College	31
21	Hamburg	24	22	Lewistown	33
21	Renovo	24	22	York 3 SSW Pump Stn	*33*
24	Neshaminy Falls	*23*	24	Bradford 4 SW Res 5	35
24	Philadelphia Int'l Arpt	23	25	Blue Marsh Lake	38

Rankings include 25 highest/lowest stations. If state has less than 25 stations, all stations are included. The period of record is 1980–2009. See User Guide for detailed explanation of data.

Number of Days Annually With ≥ 1.0 Inch Snow Depth

	Highest			Lowest	
Rank	Station Name	Days	Rank	Station Name	Days
1	Pleasant Mount 1 W	91	1	Graterford 1 E	1
2	Bradford 4 SW Res 5	90	2	Neshaminy Falls	15
3	Montrose	82	2	Philadelphia Int'l Arpt	15
4	Chalk Hill 2 ENE	76	4	Lancaster 2 NE Filt Plant	17
5	Francis E Walter Dam	58	5	Lebanon 2 W	19
6	Mercer	57	6	Donora 1 SW	20
7	Clarion 3 SW	56	6	York 3 SSW Pump Stn	20
8	Butler 2 SW	48	8	Blue Marsh Lake	21
9	State College	46	9	Montgomery Lock & Dam	24
10	Renovo	43	9	Uniontown 1 NE	24
11	Derry 4 SW	42	11	Hamburg	25
12	Altoona 3 W	41	11	Landisville 2 NW	25
13	Pittsburgh Intl Arpt	38	13	Bucksville	29
14	Salina 3 W	37	13	Laurelton Center	29
14	Washington 3 NE	37	15	Lewistown	30
16	Coatesville 2 W	34	16	Coatesville 2 W	34
17	Lewistown	30	17	Salina 3 W	37
18	Bucksville	29	17	Washington 3 NE	37
18	Laurelton Center	29	19	Pittsburgh Intl Arpt	38
20	Hamburg	25	20	Altoona 3 W	41
20	Landisville 2 NW	25	21	Derry 4 SW	42
22	Montgomery Lock & Dam	24	22	Renovo	43
22	Uniontown 1 NE	24	23	State College	46
24	Blue Marsh Lake	21	24	Butler 2 SW	48
25	Donora 1 SW	20	25	Clarion 3 SW	56

Rankings include 25 highest/lowest stations. If state has less than 25 stations, all stations are included. The period of record is 1980–2009. See User Guide for detailed explanation of data.

Significant Storm Events in Pennsylvania: 2000 – 2009

Location or County	Date	Type	Mag.	Deaths	Injuries	Property Damage ($mil.)	Crop Damage ($mil.)
Chester and Philadelphia Counties	05/06/00	Excessive Heat	na	7	0	0.0	0.0
Philadelphia County	08/07/00	Excessive Heat	na	5	0	0.0	0.0
Montgomery	06/16/01	Flood	na	1	0	33.5	0.0
Southeast Pennsylvania	08/06/01	Excessive Heat	na	22	0	0.0	0.0
Allegheny	05/31/02	Thunderstorm Wind	105 mph	1	54	10.0	0.0
Southeast Pennsylvania	07/01/02	Excessive Heat	na	15	0	0.0	0.0
Southeast Pennsylvania	08/01/02	Excessive Heat	na	9	0	0.0	0.0
Southeast Pennsylvania	08/11/02	Excessive Heat	na	8	0	0.0	0.0
Mercer	11/10/02	Tornado	F2	1	19	1.0	0.0
Mckean	07/21/03	Tornado	F1	0	0	45.7	0.0
Crawford	07/21/03	Flash Flood	na	1	0	30.0	0.0
Southeast Pennsylvania	09/18/03	High Wind	60 mph	0	0	32.2	0.0
Centre and Clinton Counties	01/06/04	Winter Weather/Mix	na	6	12	1.5	0.0
Central Pennsylvania	09/17/04	Flood	na	2	0	50.0	0.0
Allegheny Co.	09/17/04	Flood	na	1	92	26.0	0.0
Bradford	09/17/04	Flash Flood	na	0	0	20.0	0.0
Luzerne	09/18/04	Flash Flood	na	0	0	100.0	0.0
Bucks County	09/18/04	Flood	na	0	0	24.0	0.0
Northhampton Co.	04/02/05	Flood	na	0	0	40.0	0.0
Monroe Co.	04/02/05	Flood	na	0	0	40.0	0.0
Bucks Co.	04/03/05	Flood	na	0	0	40.0	0.0
Bucks, Chester, Delaware, Montgomery, and Philadelphia Counties	07/18/05	Excessive Heat	na	6	0	0.0	0.0
Southeast Pennsylvania	07/25/05	Excessive Heat	na	7	0	0.0	0.0
Southeast Pennsylvania	08/02/05	Excessive Heat	na	5	0	0.0	0.0
Luzerne	06/27/06	Flash Flood	na	3	0	100.0	0.0
Susquehanna	06/27/06	Flash Flood	na	1	0	100.0	0.0
Wyoming	06/27/06	Flash Flood	na	0	0	60.0	0.0
Wayne	06/27/06	Flash Flood	na	1	0	50.0	0.0
Lackawanna	06/27/06	Flash Flood	na	0	0	50.0	0.0
Bradford	06/27/06	Flash Flood	na	0	0	25.0	0.0
Montgomery	06/27/06	Flood	na	0	0	22.0	0.0
Bucks	06/28/06	Flood	na	0	0	30.0	0.0
Southeast Pennsylvania	08/01/06	Excessive Heat	na	24	40	0.0	0.0

Note: Deaths, injuries, and damages are date and location specific.

2013 Title List

Visit **www.greyhouse.com** for Product Information, Table of Contents and Sample Pages

General Reference

America's College Museums
American Environmental Leaders: From Colonial Times to the Present
An African Biographical Dictionary
An Encyclopedia of Human Rights in the United States
Constitutional Amendments
Encyclopedia of African-American Writing
Encyclopedia of the Continental Congress
Encyclopedia of Gun Control & Gun Rights
Encyclopedia of Invasions & Conquests
Encyclopedia of Prisoners of War & Internment
Encyclopedia of Religion & Law in America
Encyclopedia of Rural America
Encyclopedia of the United States Cabinet, 1789-2010
Encyclopedia of War Journalism
Encyclopedia of Warrior Peoples & Fighting Groups
From Suffrage to the Senate: America's Political Women
Nations of the World
Political Corruption in America
Speakers of the House of Representatives, 1789-2009
The Environmental Debate: A Documentary History
The Evolution Wars: A Guide to the Debates
The Religious Right: A Reference Handbook
The Value of a Dollar: 1860-2009
The Value of a Dollar: Colonial Era
This is Who We Were: A Companion to the 1940 Census
This is Who We Were: The 1910s
This is Who We Were: The 1950s
US Land & Natural Resource Policy
Weather America
Working Americans 1770-1869 Vol. IX: Revol. War to the Civil War
Working Americans 1880-1999 Vol. I: The Working Class
Working Americans 1880-1999 Vol. II: The Middle Class
Working Americans 1880-1999 Vol. III: The Upper Class
Working Americans 1880-1999 Vol. IV: Their Children
Working Americans 1880-2003 Vol. V: At War
Working Americans 1880-2005 Vol. VI: Women at Work
Working Americans 1880-2006 Vol. VII: Social Movements
Working Americans 1880-2007 Vol. VIII: Immigrants
Working Americans 1880-2009 Vol. X: Sports & Recreation
Working Americans 1880-2010 Vol. XI: Inventors & Entrepreneurs
Working Americans 1880-2011 Vol. XII: Our History through Music
Working Americans 1880-2012 Vol. XIII: Education & Educators
World Cultural Leaders of the 20th & 21st Centuries

Business Information

Complete Television, Radio & Cable Industry Directory
Directory of Business Information Resources
Directory of Mail Order Catalogs
Directory of Venture Capital & Private Equity Firms
Environmental Resource Handbook
Food & Beverage Market Place
Grey House Homeland Security Directory
Grey House Performing Arts Directory
Hudson's Washington News Media Contacts Directory
New York State Directory
Sports Market Place Directory
The Rauch Guides – Industry Market Research Reports
Sweets Directory by McGraw Hill Construction

Health Information

Comparative Guide to American Hospitals
Complete Directory for Pediatric Disorders
Complete Directory for People with Chronic Illness
Complete Directory for People with Disabilities
Complete Mental Health Directory

Diabetes in America: A Geographic & Demographic Analysis
Directory of Health Care Group Purchasing Organizations
Directory of Hospital Personnel
HMO/PPO Directory
Medical Device Register
Obesity in America: A Geographic & Demographic Analysis
Older Americans Information Directory
Pharmaceutical Industry Directory

Statistics & Demographics

America's Top-Rated Cities
America's Top-Rated Small Towns & Cities
America's Top-Rated Smaller Cities
American Tally
Ancestry & Ethnicity in America
Comparative Guide to American Hospitals
Comparative Guide to American Suburbs
Profiles of America
Profiles of... Series – State Handbooks
The Hispanic Databook

Education Information

Charter School Movement
Comparative Guide to American Elementary & Secondary Schools
Complete Learning Disabilities Directory
Educators Resource Directory
Special Education

Financial Ratings Series

TheStreet.com Ratings Guide to Bond & Money Market Mutual Funds
TheStreet.com Ratings Guide to Common Stocks
TheStreet.com Ratings Guide to Exchange-Traded Funds
TheStreet.com Ratings Guide to Stock Mutual Funds
TheStreet.com Ratings Ultimate Guided Tour of Stock Investing
Weiss Ratings Consumer Box Set
Weiss Ratings Guide to Banks & Thrifts
Weiss Ratings Guide to Credit Unions
Weiss Ratings Guide to Health Insurers
Weiss Ratings Guide to Life & Annuity Insurers
Weiss Ratings Guide to Property & Casualty Insurers

Bowker's Books In Print®Titles

Books In Print®
Books In Print® Supplement
American Book Publishing Record® Annual
American Book Publishing Record® Monthly
Books Out Loud™
Bowker's Complete Video Directory™
Children's Books In Print®
Complete Directory of Large Print Books & Serials™
El-Hi Textbooks & Serials In Print®
Forthcoming Books®
Law Books & Serials In Print™
Medical & Health Care Books In Print™
Publishers, Distributors & Wholesalers of the US™
Subject Guide to Books In Print®
Subject Guide to Children's Books In Print®

Canadian General Reference

Associations Canada
Canadian Almanac & Directory
Canadian Environmental Resource Guide
Canadian Parliamentary Guide
Financial Services Canada
Governments Canada
Libraries Canada
The History of Canada

Grey House Publishing
4919 Route 22, PO Box 56, Amenia NY 12501-0056 | (800) 562-2139 | www.greyhouse.com | books@greyhouse.com